THE UNIVERSAL REFERENCE SYSTEM

Law, Jurisprudence,
and
Judicial Process

Volume VII of the

POLITICAL SCIENCE, GOVERNMENT, AND

PUBLIC POLICY SERIES

Included in this series:

POLITICAL SCIENCE, GOVERNMENT, & PUBLIC POLICY SERIES

Volume VII

Law, Jurisprudence,
and
Judicial Process

An annotated and intensively indexed compilation of significant
books, pamphlets, and articles, selected and processed by
The UNIVERSAL REFERENCE SYSTEM—a computerized
information retrieval service in the social and behavioral sciences.

Prepared under the direction of

ALFRED DE GRAZIA, GENERAL EDITOR
Professor of Social Theory in Government, New York University,
and Founder, *The American Behavioral Scientist*

CARL E. MARTINSON, MANAGING EDITOR

and

JOHN B. SIMEONE, CONSULTANT

Published by
PRINCETON RESEARCH PUBLISHING COMPANY
Princeton, New Jersey

For information, address:

UNIVERSAL REFERENCE SYSTEM
32 Nassau Street, Princeton, N.J. 08540

. . . and see the subscription information contained
on the last page of this volume.

Standard Book No. 87635-007-4
Library of Congress Catalog Card No. 68-57823

Printed and Bound in the U.S.A. by
KINGSPORT PRESS, INC., KINGSPORT, TENN.

Contents

Introduction to the CODEX of Law, Jurisprudence, and Judicial Process

Under *Law, Jurisprudence, and Judicial Process,* the UNIVERSAL REFERENCE SYSTEM deals with documents concerning the adjudication and enforcement of policies. The problems of analyzing prescribed behaviors and the deviations therefrom, together with the kinds and incidence of sanctions for deviance, are treated. Principles of the sociology of law, of the theory of law, of comparative legal systems, and of the nature of developing legal systems, such as international law, are represented. Judicial logic, behavior, and procedures are followed through the literature. Individual cases before the courts come into the listings only when analyzed by approaches that point up legal and judicial practices in a large sense, not so as to provide the usual material of a legal brief. It is "scholar's law" rather than "practitioner's law" that is covered in greater part. Again the science of the study of law, with its progressing methodology, is more the center of concern than the description of what procedures attorneys must or should follow.

Approximately 2,160 documents and 25,350 index entries are processed in CODEX VII on law. The frequency list of index terms shows fourteen terms that contain over 300 documents each, as for example Court Systems (CT/SYS–616), Constitutions (CONSTN–622), and Judicial and Adjudicative Process (ADJUD–762). These are useful listings for general studies or syllabi on major aspects of law, but are not recommended for special searches where specific sets of ideas or terms are involved.

The last few years have seen an increase in quantitative studies of judicial decisions and traits of judges. The term used increasingly to refer to this field is "jurimetrics." The field of law in general has experienced the same growth of professional journals as other fields, but the increase has been largely the output of law schools, where now even the most humble school is likely to boast a law review. The contents of prestigious journals such as those produced by the Law Schools of Yale University and the University of Chicago have been moving toward public policy concerns. The journals of political science, such as the *American Political Science Review,* have contained more of the jurimetric approach. There have been few new journals of the type of *Mull,* published informally out of the Yale University Law School, or *Law and Society,* published alongside the *American Behavioral Scientist* by Sage Publications.

How To Use This CODEX
(*Hypothetical Example is Used*)

1. Frame your need as specifically as possible. (Example: "I want articles written in 1968 that deal with the activities of labor leaders and small business owners in city politics in America.")
2. Scan the Dictionary of Descriptors in this Volume, page xv and following, for URS terms that match your subject. (Example: for cities you find MUNIC and LOC/G; for labor, LABOR; for small companies, SML/CO.) Find the number of titles each Descriptor carries. For rapidity select terms having few entries; for comprehensiveness, select terms having many entries.
3. Having identified terms that match your subject, enter the Index at one of them, say SML/CO, which heads a list of works on small business. For rapid identification of highly relevant titles, search the narrow right-hand column, which contains the Critical Descriptors; these index the primary facets of a work. Even if you read every title under a Descriptor, the critical column will help you identify works of high probable value. Titles are arranged by year of publication and within each year by format: books (B), long articles (L), short articles (S), and chapters (C). The designation "N" covers serials and titles lacking dates or published over several years. The Index entry carries author, title, secondary Descriptors (which index secondary facets of the work), page of the Catalog containing full citation and annotation, and Catalog accession number. Secondary Descriptors are always arranged in the order of the Topical and Methodological Index.
4. Listings of the document would be found in fourteen

SAMPLE CATALOG LISTING

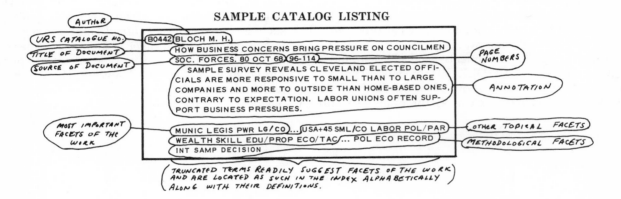

places in the Index, that is, under each of its numerous significant facets. One of them could be located in a search of "the small company in politics" as follows:

SAMPLE INDEX LISTING

5. Jot down the page numbers and the accession numbers of items that interest you and look them up in the Catalog. There you will find the full citation and a brief annotation of each work.
6. You may locate information on methods authors employ, as well as topics they discuss. Survey the methodological Descriptors in the Grazian Index, pp. xiii-xiv, and locate the relevant Descriptors in the Index of Documents. (Example: if you wished to discover whether any studies of urban business politics had employed recorded interviews, you would look up the term INT [interviews]).
7. Read the Topical and Methodological classification of terms (Grazian Index System) once or twice to grasp the ways in which ideas and groups of related ideas are compressed. The truncated Descriptors, though obvious, are defined in the dictionary of the Index.
8. Although the Catalog is arranged alphabetically by author (except for Volumes II and III), accession numbers have been retained. The major exception to alphabetical arrangement is the group of journals and unsigned articles that begin the Catalog.
9. The Catalogs of Volumes I, IV, V, VI, VII, VIII, IX, and X do not carry Descriptors.
10. The Directory of Publishers pertains to all ten CODEXes.

Concerning the
UNIVERSAL REFERENCE SYSTEM
in General

The UNIVERSAL REFERENCE SYSTEM is a computerized documentation and information retrieval system employing citations of material above a modest level of quality, appearing in all social and behavioral sciences, annotated. It is indexed by author and employs a set of Standard Descriptors that are arranged according to a master system of topics and methodological techniques, plus various Unique Descriptors.

The flow chart on page x, entitled "The Universal Reference System," shows the numerous steps taken to process documents which come from the intellectual community until they cycle back into the same community as delivered instruments of improved scholarship.

Background of the Work

The many fields of social sciences have suffered for a long time from inadequate searching systems and information storage. The rate of development of periodical and book literature is well known to be far beyond the capacities of the existing book-form document retrieval services. Thousands of new books appear each year, dealing with society and man. Thousands of journals pour forth articles. Hundreds of periodicals are founded each year.

Countries outside of the United States have gone into the social sciences, so that the need for making available foreign publications in intelligible form is ever greater. If there is a light year's distance between present capabilities and the best available service in the social sciences, there is an even greater distance to be traversed in bringing into use the material being published in languages other than English.

A vicious economic cycle is at work in the matter of information retrieval, too: Scholars and students give up research because there are no tools to search with, and therefore their demand for searching tools decreases because they have learned to get along without the materials. Thus, the standards of all the social sciences are lowered because of an anticipated lack of success in handling the problem of information retrieval. The economic risk, therefore, of an information retrieval service has to be taken into account: Many professionals are like the Bengal peasant who cannot aid in his own economic development because he cannot conceive of the nature of the problem and has learned to live as a victim outside of it.

A study in the June, 1964, issue of *The American Behavioral Scientist* magazine showed what the need is today, even before the full capabilities of new systems are appreciated. One-half of a sample of social and behavioral scientists reported that, due to inadequate bibliographic aids, they had discovered significant information on some research too late to use it, and that this information would have significantly affected the scope and nature of their research. In a number of cases, the problem of the researcher was reported to be inadequate access to pre-existing materials, and in other cases was said to be insufficient means of addressing oneself to current material.

So the current ways of information retrieval, or lack thereof, are deficient with respect both to retrospective searching and to current material, not to mention the alarming problem of access to prospective material, in the form of current research project activities and current news of scientific development in relevant categories.

The international scholarly associations centered mainly in Paris have endeavored, with help of UNESCO and other sources of aid, to bring out bibliographies and abstracting services. These services are not fully used, because of their format, their incompleteness, their lack of selectivity, their formulation in traditional and conventional terms of the social sciences (slighting the so-called inter-disciplinary subject matters in methodology), and the simple indexing that they employ. Continuous efforts are being made to solve such problems. Lately, such solutions have been sought via computerized systems. The American Council of Learned Societies, for example, has funded projects at New York University to which the computer is integral.

The Universal Reference System is endeavoring to take an immediately practical view of the literature-access problem, while designing the system so that it will remain open to advances and permit a number of alterations. One must contemplate projects leading to automatic reading and indexing; retrieval of information in the form of propositions, historical dates, and other factual materials; encyclopedic information-providing services; movement into other scientific fields joining social and natural science materials; automatized printing and reproduction of a large variety of materials in quantities ranging from individual to thousands of copies, and provision for televised or other rapid-fire communication services from information retrieval centers.

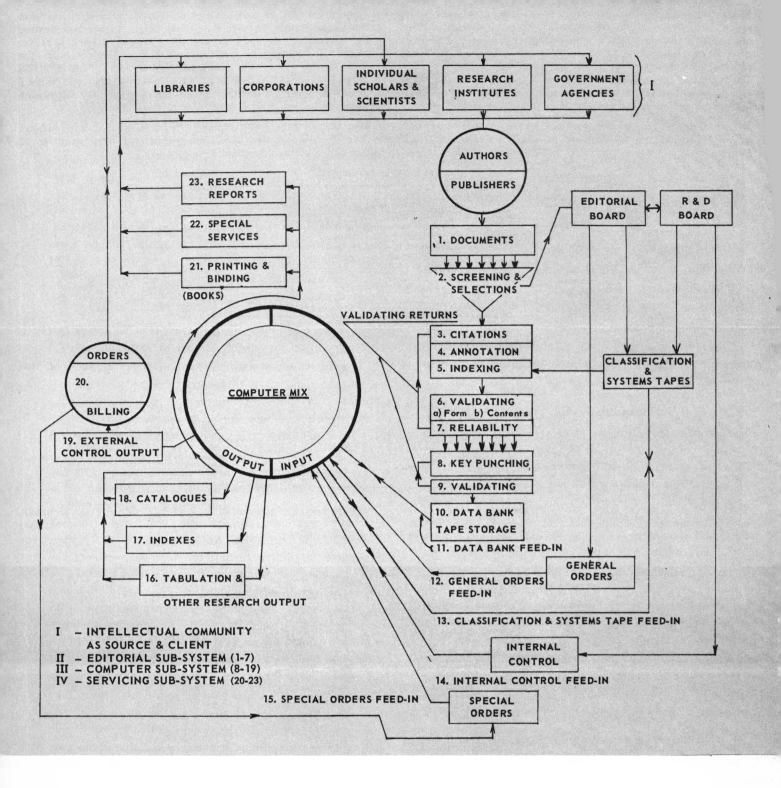

UNIVERSAL REFERENCE SYSTEM

A diagrammatic representation of the numerous steps taken to process documents which come from the intellectual community until they cycle back to the same community as pinpointed sources of information.

The Grazian Classification and Indexing System

The theory behind the URS Classification System is operational. It asks the question: *"Who says, 'Who does what with whom, where and when, by what means, why' and how does he know so?"* This question leads to the general categories and subcategories of the system, which is presented in its logical form on pages **xii-xiv**, along with the truncated terms used in the computerized Index of Documents. The advantage of reading the logical classification is that one will learn in a few minutes the general meaning of the truncated terms and can usually go directly and rapidly to the proper terms in the Index.

The Grazian classification cuts across various disciplines of social science to call attention to the methodological aspects of works which would appear to be important to scholars in the behavioral, instrumental, positivistic tradition of philosophy and science.

The constant recourse to method also serves as a screening device for eliminating numerous documents that are purely evaluative, journalistic, nonempirical, or of an intuitive type. The Grazian index contains some 351 Standard Descriptor categories at the present time. To them are added Unique Descriptors as they occur. Some additional categories logically subtending from the existing ones will be added as time goes on. These will be expanded as part of the original coding as the need is shown. (Several categories may be altered, too, on the same grounds.) From two to four of the Standard and Unique Descriptors are selected as most important facets of the work and are indicated as Critical Descriptors. These are printed apart in the Index of Documents.

The possibilities of utilizing cross-categories are immediate. Cross-categories can be used (both by the searcher and by the creator of the index) to provide a more specialized bibliography. This Cross-Faceting can permit adjusting to changes in the interests of scientists. An almost infinite number of cross-categories is possible, of course. The user of the system will find it set up beyond any existing system to facilitate this. In the future, and upon request, complicated cross-category or multi-faceted searches will be performed by the Universal Reference System's machinery. The ultimate instrumental goal is Controlled Faceting—contractible or expansible according to need and logic.

In practice, the Standard Descriptors, the Unique Descriptors, the Critical Descriptors, the Multiple Faceting, and the Cross-Faceting are interlaced in the operations of documentary analysis and control. Thus, to allow for gaps in the system, to go along with conventional practice, to employ more specialized terms, and to carry important proper nouns, the indexing rules permit the documentary analyst to add Unique Descriptors to the Standard Descriptors already taken from the master list. There are 63 of these in the *Codex of Legislative Process, Representation, and Decision-Making*. The total number of descriptors finally averaged 13 per item.

Some persons have inquired whether it might be useful to print out the whole descriptor rather than a truncated term. Several reasons arbitrate against this procedure, at least for the present. In most cases there is really no single term for which the printed-out truncated descriptor is the symbol. Most Standard Descriptors stand for several synonymous words and related ideas. Printing out the full descriptor *word* would be deluding in many cases, leading searchers to believe a word has only its face meaning.

Moreover, if all truncated descriptors were spelled out, the search time (after the first few searches) would be extended greatly since the eye would have to cover much more lettering and space. Furthermore, the size of the CODEX would be at least tripled, for the space provided for permuting would have to be open enough to carry the longest, not the average, words. There are other technical difficulties.

The repetition of numerous descriptors following each entry in the Index of Documents serves the purpose of targeting the search precisely. The richness of descriptors also postpones the moment of returning to the catalogue and thus enlarges the marginal utility of the first resort to the catalogue.

The intensive indexing of each document, which ranges from 10 to 20 entries, serves a purpose. Intensive indexing permits a document to exhibit all of its important facets to the searcher. The ratio of index carriage to title carriage is here termed the "carriage ratio." The carriage ratio of the URS is much higher than that of most bibliographies. The magnitude of the difference shows the meaning of high intensity indexing. Under other systems, unlike the URS CODEX, a topic is understated in the index. And, less obviously, topics other than the one carried as a flag in the title are sunk into oblivion; thus "Relations Between France and Indochina," which may be a valuable work on questions of economic development, would probably not be indexed on that question at all.

To sum up, the URS, when used as in this CODEX, thoroughly exposes the facets of a listed document. It makes the document thoroughly *retrievable*.

Also under consideration are suggestions to eliminate (or suppress) more of the descriptors. What is the optimal number? It is difficult to say, *a priori*. Experience and experiment will tell, over time. Meanwhile, the Critical Descriptors offer a researcher the "fast search," if he pleases. The more numerous group of descriptors in the final column offers a more complete faceting.

The search time of a researcher should be an important concern of a bibliographer. Search time begins to run, of course, with the knowledge of and access to a work that probably covers a searcher's need. It runs, too, with the ingenuity of the searcher's phrasing of his need. Then it runs with the presence of the works needed in the list searched; a missing document can be translated into lost time. An index saves time, too, when the term searched is the term under which a document is indexed; the need to compromise between detailed vocabularies and generalized ones is evident: it can reasonably be argued that more time is lost in research in social science in getting on the same semantic beam than in solving substantive problems of the "real world." Finally, the structure of an index should lessen search time while permitting a rich search.

Research and experimentation are in order, and it is hoped that a by-product of the initial publications of the Universal Reference System will be an increased stimulation of research into research procedures with respect to the URS' problems and to those of other reference systems.

Topical and Methodological Index (Grazian Index System)

The truncated descriptors (left of each column) and their expanded definitions (right of each column) that follow were employed in systematically computerizing the topics and methods of the Social and Behavioral Sciences. Truncated descriptors that are underscored in the listing that follows have not been carried in the left-hand index entry column of this CODEX; several others (denoted by a double underscore) have been entirely eliminated from this CODEX. Fuller definitions are included in the Index of Documents. So are proper names, place names, organization names, and incidents.

I. TOPICS

1. TIME—SPACE—CULTURE INDEX: Cultural-temporal location of subject.
   Centuries covered (e.g., -4; 14-19; 20)

PREHIST	Prehistoric.
MEDIT-7	Mediterranean and Near East, pre-Islamic.
PRE/AMER	Pre-European Americas.
CHRIST-17C	Christendom to 1700.
AFR	Sub-Sahara Africa.
ASIA	China, Japan, Korea.
S/ASIA	India, Southeast Asia, Oceania, except European settlements.
ISLAM	Islamic world.
MOD/EUR	Europe, 1700 to 1918, including European settlements.
USA-45	USA, 1700 to 1945.
WOR-45	Worldwide to 1945.
L/A+17C	Latin America since 1700.
EUR+WWI	Europe, 1918 to present, including colonies, but excluding Communist countries.
COM	Communist countries.
USA+45	USA since 1945.
WOR+45	Worldwide since 1945.
FUT	Future.
SPACE	Outer space.
UNIV	Free of historical position.
SEA	Locale of activity is aquatic.
AIR	Locale of activity is aerial.

   (Nations are readily identifiable.)

2. INSTITUTIONAL INDEX: (or subject treated).
   A. General

SOCIETY	Society as a whole.
CULTURE	Cultural patterns.
STRUCT	Social structure.
CONSTN	Constitution. Basic group structure.
LAW	Sanctioned practices, enforced ethics in a community.
ELITES	A power-holding group.
INTELL	Intelligentsia.
SOC/INTEG	Social Integration.
STRATA	Social strata.
CLIENT	Clients.

   B. Economic type

ECO/UNDEV	Developing countries.
ECO/DEV	Developed countries.

   C. Economic function

AGRI	Agriculture, including hunting.
R+D	Research and development organization.
FINAN	Financial services.
INDUS	All or most industry.
COM/IND	Communications industry.
CONSTRUC	Construction and building.
DIST/IND	Distributive system: Includes transportation, warehousing.
EXTR/IND	Extractive industry.
MARKET	Marketing system.
PROC/MFG	Processing or manufacturing.
SERV/IND	Service industry.

   D. Organizations

SML/CO	Small company: 50 employees or less.
LG/CO	Company of more than 50 employees.
LABOR	Labor unions.
PROF/ORG	Professional organizations, including guilds.
PUB/INST	Habitational institutions: hospitals, prisons, sanitariums, etc.
POL/PAR	Political party.
SCHOOL	School (except University).
ACADEM	Higher learning.
PERF/ART	Performing arts groupings.

SECT	Church, sect, religious group.
FAM	Family.
KIN	Kinship groups.
NEIGH	Neighborhood.
LOC/G	Local governments.
MUNIC	Cities, villages, towns.
PROVS	State or province.
NAT/G	National governments.
FACE/GP	Acquaintance group: face-to-face association.
VOL/ASSN	Voluntary association.
INT/ORG	International organizations.

3. ORGANIC OR INTERNAL STRUCTURE INDEX: Sub-groupings or substructures treated.

CONSULT	Consultants.
FORCES	Armed forces and police.
DELIB/GP	Conferences, committees, boards, cabinets.
LEGIS	Legislatures.
CT/SYS	Court systems.
EX/STRUC	Formal executive establishment.
TOP/EX	Individuals holding executive positions.
CHIEF	Chief officer of a government.
WORKER	Workers and work conditions.

4. PROCESSES AND PRACTICES: Procedures or tactics used by subject or discussed as subject.
   A. Creating and Sciencing

CREATE	Creative and innovative processes.
ACT/RES	Combined research and social action.
COMPUTER	Computer techniques.
INSPECT	Inspecting quality, output, legality.
OP/RES	Operations research.
PLAN	Planning.
PROB/SOLV	Problem-solving and decision-making.
TEC/DEV	Development and change of technology.

   B. Economizing

ACCT	Accounting, bookkeeping.
BAL/PWR	Balance of power.
BARGAIN	Bargaining, trade.
BUDGET	Budgeting, fiscal planning.
CAP/ISM	Enterprise, entrepreneurship.
DIPLOM	Diplomacy.
ECO/TAC	Economic measures or tactics.
FOR/AID	Foreign aid.
INT/TRADE	International trade.
RATION	Rationing, official control of goods or costs.
RENT	Renting.
TARIFFS	Tariffs.
TAX	Taxation.

   C. Awarding

GIVE	Giving, philanthropy.
LICENSE	Legal permit.
PAY	Paying.
RECEIVE	Receiving of welfare.
REPAR	Reparations.
TRIBUTE	Payments to dominant by minor power, racketeering.
WORSHIP	Worship, ritual.

   D. Symbolizing

DOMIN	Domination.
EDU/PROP	Education or propaganda.
LEGIT	Legitimacy.
PRESS	Printed media.
RUMOR	Rumor, gossip.
TV	Television.
WRITING	Writing.

   E. Evaluating

CONFER	Group consultation.
DEBATE	Organized collective arguments.

ETIQUET	Etiquette, fashion, manners.	
PRICE	Pricing.	
SENIOR	Seniority.	

F. Determining

ADJUD	Judicial behavior and personality.
ADMIN	Behavior of non-top executive personnel (except armed forces).
AGREE	Agreements, treaties, compacts.
AUTOMAT	Automation.
COLONIAL	Colonialism.
CONTROL	Specific ability of power to determine achievement.
EXEC	Executive, regularized management.
FEEDBACK	Feedback phenomena.
GAMBLE	Speculative activity.
LEAD	Leading.
LOBBY	Lobbying.
NEUTRAL	Neutralism, neutrality.
PARL/PROC	Parliamentary procedures (legislative).
PARTIC	Participation: civic apathy or activity.
REGION	Regionalism.
RISK	Risk, uncertainty, certainty.
ROUTINE	Procedural and work systems.
SANCTION	Sanctions of law and social law.
TASK	A specific operation within a work setting.
TIME	Timing, time-factor.

G. Forcing

ARMS/CONT	Arms control and disarmament.
COERCE	Force and violence.
CRIME	Criminal behavior.
CROWD	Mass behavior.
DEATH	Death-related behavior.
DETER	Military deterrence.
GUERRILLA	Guerrilla warfare.
MURDER	Murder, assassination.
NUC/PWR	All uses of nuclear energy.
REV	Revolution.
SUICIDE	Suicide.
WAR	War.
WEAPON	Conventional military weapons.

H. Choosing

APPORT	Apportionment of assemblies.
CHOOSE	Choice, election.
REPRESENT	Representation.
SUFF	Suffrage.

I. Consuming

DREAM	Dreaming.
LEISURE	Unobligated time expenditures.
SLEEP	Sleep-related behavior.
EATING	Eating, cuisine.

5. RELATIONS INDEX: Relationship of individuals and/or group under discussion.

CIVMIL/REL	Civil-military relation.
GOV/REL	Relations between local or state governments and governmental agencies.
GP/REL	Relations among groups, except nations.
INT/REL	Relations among sovereign states.
INGP/REL	Relations within groups.
PERS/REL	Relations between persons; interpersonal communication.
RACE/REL	Race relations.

6. CONDITIONS AND MEASURES (of activities being discussed).

ADJUST	Social adjustment, socialization.
BAL/PAY	Balance of payments.
CENTRAL	Centralization.
CONSEN	Consensus.
COST	Costs.
DEMAND	In economic sense, a demand.
DISCRIM	Social differentiation in support of inequalities.
EFFICIENCY	Effectiveness, measures.
EQUILIB	Equilibrium (technical).
FEDERAL	Federalism.
HAPPINESS	Satisfaction and unhappiness.
ILLEGIT	Bastardy.
INCOME	Income distribution, shares, earnings.
ISOLAT	Isolation and community.
LITERACY	Ability to read and write.
MAJORITY	Behavior of major parts of grouping.
MARRIAGE	Legal wedlock.

NAT/LISM	Nationalism.
OPTIMAL	Optimality in its economic usages.
OWN	Ownership.
PEACE	Freedom from conflict or termination of hostilities.
PRIVIL	Privilege, parliamentary.
PRODUC	Productivity.
PROFIT	Profit in economic sense.
RATIONAL	Instrumental rationality.
STRANGE	Estrangement or outsiders.
TOTALISM	Totalitarianism.
UTIL	Utility as in economics.
UTOPIA	Envisioned general social conditions.

7. PERSONALITY INDEX: Behavior of actors to their actions.

HABITAT	Ecology.
HEREDITY	Genetic influences on personality.
DRIVE	Drive, morale, or antithesis.
PERCEPT	Perception.
PERSON	Personality and human nature.
ROLE	Role, reference group feelings, cross-pressures.
AGE	Age factors in general.
AGE/C	Infants and children.
AGE/Y	Youth, adolescence.
AGE/A	Adults.
AGE/O	Old.
SEX	Sexual behavior.
SUPEGO	Conscience, superego, and responsibility.
RIGID/FLEX	Rigidity/flexibility; exclusive/inclusive.
ATTIT	Attitudes, opinions, ideology.
DISPL	Displacement and projection.
AUTHORIT	Authoritarianism, as personal behavior.
BIO/SOC	Bio-social processes: drugs, psychosomatic phenomena, etc.
ANOMIE	Alienation, anomie, generalized personal anxiety.

8. VALUES INDEX: Basically desired (or nondesired) conditions held or believed in by subjects.

HEALTH	Well-being, bodily and psychic integrity (sickness).
KNOWL	Enlightenment (ignorance).
LOVE	Affection, friendship (hatred).
MORAL	Rectitude, morality (immorality), goodness.
PWR	Power, participation in decision-making (impotence).
RESPECT	Respect, social class attitudes (contempt, disrespect).
SKILL	Skill, practical competence (incompetence).
WEALTH	Wealth, access to goods and services (poverty).
ALL/VALS	All, or six or more of above.
ORD/FREE	Security, order, restraint (change, experience, freedom).
SOVEREIGN	Sovereignty; home-rule.

9. IDEOLOGICAL TOPIC: Ideology discussed in work.

CATHISM	Roman Catholicism.
CONSERVE	Traditionalism.
FASCISM	Fascism.
LAISSEZ	Laissez-faire-ism (old liberal).
MARXISM	Marxism.
MYSTISM	Mysticism.
NEW/LIB	New Liberalism (welfare state).
OBJECTIVE	Value-free thought.
PACIFISM	Pacifism.
PLURISM	Socio-political order of autonomous groups.
POPULISM	Majoritarianism.
RELATISM	Relativism.
SOCISM	Socialism.
TECHRACY	Socio-political order dominated by technicians.
ALL/IDEOS	Three or more of above.

II. METHODOLOGY (What techniques are dealt with by the author and what techniques the document employs or describes).

10. ETHICAL STANDARDS APPLIED BY AUTHOR

ETHIC	Personal ethics (private and professional).
LAW/ETHIC	Ethics of laws and court processes.

POLICY	Treats ethics of public policies.	

11. IDEOLOGY OF AUTHOR (where clear).

ANARCH	Anarchism.
CATH	Roman Catholic.
CONVNTL	Conventional: unsystematic acceptance of values in common currency.
FASCIST	Totalitarian with nonworker, upper class, or leader cult.
MAJORIT	Majoritarian, consensual.
MARXIST	Marxist Communist in viewpoint.
MYSTIC	Otherworldly, mystical.
OLD/LIB	Old liberal, laissez-faire.
PACIFIST	Pacifist.
PLURIST	Pluralist.
REALPOL	Realpolitik, Machiavellism.
RELATIV	Relativist.
SOCIALIST	Socialist (except Communist).
TECHNIC	Technocratic.
TRADIT	Traditional or aristocratic.
WELF/ST	Welfare state advocate.

12. FIELD INDEX: Fields, discipline, or methodological approach of document.

ART/METH	Fine Arts, Graphics, Performing Arts, Aesthetics.
CRIMLGY	Criminology.
DECISION	Decision-making and gaming (game theory).
ECO	Economics and economic enterprise.
ECOMETRIC	Econometrics, mathematical economics.
EPIST	Epistemology, sociology of knowledge.
GEOG	Demography and geography.
HEAL	Health sciences.
HIST	History (including current events).
HUM	Methods of the "Humanities." Literary analysis.
INT/LAW	International law. Uses legal approach.
JURID	Uses legal approach. Concerns largely the laws.
MGT	Administrative management.
PHIL/SCI	Scientific method and Philosophy of Science.
POL	Deals with political and power process.
PSY	Psychology.
SOC	Sociology.
SOC/WK	Social services.

13. CONCEPTS: Document is noteworthy for systematic and/or basic treatment of:

CONCPT	Subject-matter abstract concepts.
METH/CNCPT	Methodological concepts.
MYTH	Treats assumptions unconsciously accepted, fictions.
NEW/IDEA	Word inventions, new concepts and ideas.

14. LOGIC, MATHEMATICS, AND LANGUAGE

LOG	Logic: syntax, semantics, pragmatics.
MATH	Mathematics.
STAT	Statistics.
AVERAGE	Mean, average behaviors.
PROBABIL	Probability, chance.
MODAL	Modal types, fashions.
CORREL	Correlations (statistical).
REGRESS	Regression analysis.
QUANT	Nature and limits of quantification.
CLASSIF	Classification, typology, set theory.
INDICATOR	Numerical indicator, index weights.
LING	Linguistics.
STYLE	The styles and terminology of scientific communications.

15. DIRECT OBSERVATION

OBS	Trained or participant observation.
SELF/OBS	Self-observation, psycho-drama.
OBS/ENVIR	Social milieu of and resistances to observation.
CONT/OBS	Controlled direct observation.
RECORD	Recording direct observations. (But not content analysis, q.v.)

16. INTERVIEWS

INT	Interviews, short or long, in general.
STAND/INT	Standardized interviews.
DEEP/INT	Depth interviews.
UNPLAN/INT	Impromptu interview.
RESIST/INT	Social resistance to interviewing.
REC/INT	Recording, systematizing, and analyzing of interviews.

17. QUESTIONNAIRES

QU	Questionnaires in general, short or long.
DEEP/QU	Depth questionnaires, including projective or probing.
QU/SEMANT	Semantic and social problems of questionnaires.
SYS/QU	Systematizing and analyzing questionnaires.

18. TESTS AND SCALES

TESTS	Theory and uses of tests and scales.
APT/TEST	Aptitude tests.
KNO/TEST	Tests for factual knowledge, beliefs, or abilities.
PERS/TEST	Personality tests.
PROJ/TEST	Projective tests.

19. UNIVERSES AND SAMPLING

CENSUS	Census.
SAMP	Sample survey in general.
SAMP/SIZ	Sizes and techniques of sampling.
NET/THEORY	Systematic group-member connections analysis.

20. ANALYSIS OF TEMPORAL SEQUENCES

BIOG	Biography, personality development, and psychoanalysis.
HIST/WRIT	Historiography.
TIME/SEQ	Chronology and genetic series of men, institutions, processes, etc.
TREND	Projection of trends, individual and social.
PREDICT	Prediction of future events.

21. COMMUNICATION CONTENT ANALYSIS

CON/ANAL	Quantitative content analysis.
DOC/ANAL	Conventional analysis of records or documents.

22. INFORMATION STORAGE AND RETRIEVAL

OLD/STOR	Conventional libraries, books, records, tape, film.
THING/STOR	Artifacts and material evidence.
COMPUT/IR	Mechanical and electronic information retrieval.

23. GRAPHICS AND AUDIO-VISUAL TECHNIQUES: Used in the research and/or in the presentation.

AUD/VIS	Film and sound, photographs.
CHARTS	Graphs, charts, diagrams, maps.
EXHIBIT	Exhibits.
PROG/TEAC	Programmed instruction.

24. COMPARATIVE ANALYSIS INDEX

METH/COMP	Of methods, approaches, styles.
IDEA/COMP	Of ideas, methods, ideologies.
PERS/COMP	Of persons.
GP/COMP	Of groups.
GOV/COMP	Of governments.
NAT/COMP	Of nations.

25. EXPERIMENTATION

LAB/EXP	Laboratory or strictly controlled groups.
SOC/EXP	"Social" experimentation.
HYPO/EXP	Hypothetical, intellectual constructs.

26. MODELS: Intellectual representations of objects or processes.

SIMUL	Scientific models.
ORG/CHARTS	Blueprints and organization charts.
STERTYP	Stereotypes, ideologies, utopias.
GAME	Game or Decision Theory models.

27. GENERAL THEORY

GEN/LAWS	Systems based on substantive relations, such as idealism, economic determinism.
GEN/METH	Systems based on methodology, such as cycles, pragmatism, sociometry.

28. SPECIAL FORMATS

ANTHOL	Anthology, symposium, collection.
BIBLIOG	Bibliography over fifty items, or of rare utility.
BIBLIOG/A	Contains bibliography over fifty items or of rare utility, annotated.
DICTIONARY	Dictionary.
INDEX	List of names or subjects.
METH	Document heavily emphasizes methodology (Part II) rather than topics (Part I).
T	Textbook.

Dictionary of Descriptors in this Volume

(Incorporating List of Frequency of Descriptors in Index)

This Dictionary contains all Descriptors employed in this volume, and thus enables you to identify in a few minutes every Descriptor that may pertain to your subject. The frequency list calls your attention to the number of works carried under each Descriptor and assists you in determining the term at which you may most advantageously begin your search in the Index. A modest system of cross-references may be found in the Dictionary that appears in the Index.

0001 AMERICAN JOURNAL OF INTERNATIONAL LAW.
CHICAGO: AM SOC INTERNAT LAW.
QUARTERLY FIRST PUBLISHED IN 1907 WHICH HAS BOOK REVIEW SECTION AND LIST OF BOOKS AND ARTICLES CURRENTLY PUBLISHED. TREATS CONTEMPORARY INTERNATIONAL LAW AND RELATIONS. INCLUDES SOURCES IN ENGLISH, FRENCH, AND GERMAN.

0002 AMERICAN POLITICAL SCIENCE REVIEW.
WASHINGTON: AMER POL SCI ASSOC.
QUARTERLY JOURNAL SINCE 1906 WHICH DEALS WITH GOVERNMENT, POLITICS, LAW, AND INTERNATIONAL RELATIONS. CONTAINS EXTENSIVE BOOK REVIEW SECTION AND BIBLIOGRAPHIES OF BOOKS, SERIALS, GOVERNMENT DOCUMENTS, PAMPHLETS, AND DOCTORAL DISSERTATIONS. CLASSIFIED IN FIVE CATEGORIES: POLITICAL THEORY, AMERICAN POLITICS, COMPARATIVE PUBLIC ADMINISTRATION, COMPARATIVE GOVERNMENT, AND INTERNATIONAL POLITICS.

0003 ANNALS OF THE AMERICAN ACADEMY OF POLITICAL AND SOCIAL SCIENCE.
PHILA: AMER ACAD POL & SOC SCI.
ISSUED BIMONTHLY. INCLUDES BOOK DEPARTMENT WITH CRITICAL REVIEWS OF LATEST WORKS IN AMERICAN HISTORY AND GOVERNMENT, EUROPEAN HISTORY AND GOVERNMENT, ASIA AND AFRICA, ECONOMICS, SOCIOLOGY AND ANTHROPOLOGY. INCLUDES UNANNOTATED BIBLIOGRAPHY OF RECENT WORKS IN SOCIAL SCIENCES, LISTED ALPHABETICALLY. FIRST PUBLISHED IN 1890.

0004 INTL. STUD. Q; JOURNAL OF INTERNATIONAL STUDIES ASSOCIATION.
LOS ANGELES: U OF S CAL INTL REL.
PUBLICATION, BEGUN IN 1962, WHICH ISSUES ANNUAL BIBLIOGRAPHY OF ABOUT 1,170 ITEMS. PUBLISHED CURRENTLY IN FIELD OF INTERNATIONAL RELATIONS. BIBLIOGRAPHY ORGANIZED TOPICALLY AND IS LIMITED TO ENGLISH-LANGUAGE PUBLICATIONS. INCLUDES SECTIONS ON POLITICAL, ECONOMIC, AND SOCIAL COMMUNITY FORMATION AND FACTORS AND RELATIONSHIPS OF PERSONALITY, CULTURE, NATIONALISM AND RACE IN ATTITUDES AND IDEOLOGIES.

0005 CANADIAN GOVERNMENT PUBLICATIONS (1955-)
OTTAWA: QUEEN'S PRINTER.
ANNUAL CATALOGUE INCORPORATING "DAILY CHECKLIST" AND "MONTHLY CATALOGUE OF GOVERNMENT PUBLICATIONS." ENTRIES SUBDIVIDED UNDER GENERAL TOPICS, PARLIAMENTARY PUBLICATIONS AND DEPARTMENTAL PUBLICATIONS. FIRST PART OF BOOK IN ENGLISH, SECOND IN FRENCH. INCLUDES SECTION OF INTERNATIONAL PUBLICATIONS.

0006 INDEX TO LEGAL PERIODICALS.
NEW YORK: H W WILSON.
PUBLISHED MONTHLY SINCE 1909. CITES ARTICLES ON SPECIFIC SUBJECTS FROM JOURNALS PUBLISHED IN US, CANADA, GREAT BRITAIN, NEW ZEALAND, AND AUSTRALIA. ARTICLES INDEXED ALPHABETICALLY UNDER SUBJECT. INDEXES ARTICLES OF FIVE PAGES, BOOK REVIEWS OF AT LEAST TWO PAGES, AND CASE NOTES. ANNUAL CUMULATION.

0007 INTERNATIONAL AFFAIRS.
LONDON: OXFORD U PR.
QUARTERLY WITH SECTION WHICH REVIEWS BOOKS, ARRANGED BY SUBJECT HEADINGS AND GEOGRAPHICAL AREAS. ALSO CONTAINS LIST OF CURRENT PUBLICATIONS NOT REVIEWED. CONCERNED WITH INTERNATIONAL RELATIONS, LAW, AND ECONOMICS. FIRST PUBLISHED 1922.

0008 INTERNATIONAL BOOK NEWS, 1928-1934.
BOSTON: WORLD PEACE FOUNDATION.
AN IRREGULARLY ISSUED BIBLIOGRAPHY, COVERING THE PERIOD FROM JANUARY, 1928 THROUGH MAY, 1934, PUBLISHED BY THE WORLD PEACE FOUNDATION. CATALOGS A GREAT VARIETY OF MATERIAL AVAILABLE FROM OFFICIAL AND SEMI-OFFICIAL INTERNATIONAL COOPERATIVE AGENCIES, AS WELL AS THE WORLD PEACE FOUNDATION ITSELF. DESCRIPTIVELY ANNOTATED LISTINGS ARE TOPICALLY ARRANGED AND DOCUMENT MATERIAL PUBLISHED FROM 1914 TO 1934.

0009 INTERNATIONAL STUDIES.
NEW YORK: ASIA PUBL HOUSE, 1941.
QUARTERLY PUBLICATION BEGUN IN 1941. CONTAINS BOOK REVIEWS WHICH DEAL WITH INTERNATIONAL POLITICS, LAW, AND ECONOMICS. TREATS WORLD BUT FOCUSES ON ASIA. PROVIDES SURVEY OF SOURCE MATERIAL AND RECENT RESEARCH. ANNUAL BIBLIOGRAPHY.

0010 JOURNAL OF INTERNATIONAL AFFAIRS.
NEW YORK: COLUMBIA U SCH INT AFF.
QUARTERLY PUBLICATION, BEGUN IN 1947, CONCERNED WITH CONTEMPORARY INTERNATIONAL RELATIONS. HAS BOOK REVIEW SECTION AND LIST OF BOOKS RECEIVED.

0011 JOURNAL OF POLITICS.
NEW YORK: SOUTHERN POL SCI ASSN.
QUARTERLY PUBLICATION, BEGUN IN 1939, WHICH DEALS WITH POLITICS, GOVERNMENT, AND LAW PRIMARILY IN US. INCLUDES FOREIGN COUNTRIES. CONTAINS BOOK REVIEW SECTION.

0012 MIDWEST JOURNAL OF POLITICAL SCIENCE.
DETROIT: WAYNE STATE U PR.
QUARTERLY PUBLICATION, BEGUN IN 1957, WITH BOOK REVIEW SECTION AND BIBLIOGRAPHICAL LISTING. TREATS VARIOUS ASPECTS OF POLITICAL SCIENCE, INTERNATIONAL RELATIONS, AND FOREIGN AFFAIRS. CONCERNED WITH US PRIMARILY, SOME FOREIGN.

0013 POLITICAL SCIENCE QUARTERLY.
NEW YORK: COLUMBIA U PRESS.
QUARTERLY PERIODICAL, BEGUN IN 1886, WHICH CONTAINS EXTENSIVE BOOK REVIEW SECTION AND BOOK NOTES. MAJORITY OF PUBLICATIONS REVIEWED ARE AMERICAN. JOURNAL TREATS ALL ASPECTS OF POLITICAL SCIENCE - NATIONAL GOVERNMENTS, THEORY, LABOR DISPUTES AND CONTROL, INTERNATIONAL RELATIONS, PROBLEMS OF MODERN WARFARE, ETC.

0014 TEXTBOOKS IN PRINT.
NEW YORK: RR BOWKER.
ANNUAL GUIDE TO TEXTBOOKS FOR ALL GRADES ISSUED BY MAJOR PUBLISHERS. ARRANGED BY SUBJECT AND BY GRADE LEVEL. TITLE AND SUBJECT INDEX. FIRST ISSUED IN 1872.

0015 ADVANCED MANAGEMENT.
NEW YORK: SOC ADVANCEMT MANAGEMT.
A MONTHLY PUBLICATION OF THE SOCIETY FOR THE ADVANCEMENT OF MANAGEMENT FIRST ISSUED IN 1934. ATTEMPTS TO PROMOTE DISCUSSION AND RESEARCH IN THE SCIENTIFIC STUDY OF THE PRINCIPLES GOVERNING ORGANIZED EFFORT IN INDUSTRIAL AND ECONOMIC LIFE. EARLIER ISSUES CONTAIN LENGTHY SECTION OF BIBLIOGRAPHIES AND SHORT BOOK REVIEWS.

0016 ARBITRATION JOURNAL.
NEW YORK: AMER ARBITRATION ASSN.
QUARTERLY PUBLICATION OF THE AMERICAN ARBITRATION ASSOC., WHICH REVIEWS AND ANALYZES CASES, PROBLEMS, AND LEGAL PROCEDURES OF DOMESTIC AND INTERNATIONAL COMMERCIAL ARBITRATION. MOST ISSUES INCLUDE A BRIEF CRITICALLY ANNOTATED LIST OF READINGS IN ARBITRATION AND AN UNANNOTATED LIST OF NOTES AND ARTICLES ON FOREIGN TRADE ARBITRATION. ALL ISSUES CONTAIN A REVIEW OF COURT DECISIONS IN ALL TYPES OF ARBITRATION CASES.

0017 AUSTRALIAN PUBLIC AFFAIRS INFORMATION SERVICE.
PARIS: EDITIONS DE L'EPARGNE.
ISSUED MONTHLY BY NATIONAL LIBRARY OF AUSTRALIA. GUIDE TO MATERIAL ON AUSTRALIAN POLITICAL, ECONOMIC, SOCIAL, AND CULTURAL AFFAIRS. INDEXES BOOKS AND ARTICLES, BOTH DOMESTIC AND FOREIGN, DURING CURRENT OR TWO PRECEDING YEARS. INCLUDES SELECTED LIST OF AUSTRALIAN PERIODICALS. ARRANGEMENT IS ALPHABETICAL BY SUBJECT. FIRST PUBLISHED JULY, 1945.

0018 BIBLIOGRAPHIE DE LA PHILOSOPHIE.
PARIS: INST INTL COLLAB DE PHIL.
FIRST PUBLISHED IN 1937, ONLY JOURNAL OF ITS KIND IN THE WORLD DEVOTED EXCLUSIVELY TO PROVIDING UP-TO-DATE INFORMATION AND ABSTRACTS OF BOOKS PUBLISHED IN PHILOSOPHY AND RELATED FIELDS. SINCE 1954, THE ENGLISH-FRENCH JOURNAL HAS BEEN ISSUED AS A QUARTERLY BULLETIN. BOOKS CLASSIFIED BY SUBJECT; CONSECUTIVELY NUMBERED OVER EACH ANNUM; INDEXES APPEAR IN FOURTH ISSUE OF EACH YEAR.

0019 BIBLIOGRAPHIE DER SOZIALWISSENSCHAFTEN.
DRESDEN: KRAUS, LTD, 1905.
COLLECTION OF PERIODICALS LISTING PUBLICATIONS IN THE SOCIAL SCIENCES. ARRANGED BY SUBJECT. IT COVERS ITEMS PUBLISHED IN ENCYCLOPEDIAS, BIBLIOGRAPHIES, AND COMPENDS THROUGHOUT THE WORLD ON THEORY OF POLITICAL AND SOCIAL ECONOMY, SOCIAL POLITICS, DEMOGRAPHY, LAW, ETHNOGRAPHY, ETC. CONTAINS AUTHOR, SUBJECT, AND TITLE INDEXES. PUBLISHED ANNUALLY SINCE 1905.

0020 DEUTSCHE BIBLIOGRAPHIE, HALBJAHRESVERZEICHNIS.
FRANKFURT: BUCHHANDLER VEREIN.
SEMIANNUAL COMPILATION OF "DEUTSCHE BIBLIOGRAPHIE" IN ALPHABETICAL LISTING BY AUTHOR AND SUBJECT. PUBLISHED SINCE 1951.

0021 FOREIGN AFFAIRS.
NEW YORK: COUNCIL ON FOREIGN REL.
QUARTERLY, FIRST PUBLISHED 1922, CONTAINING BOOK REVIEW SECTION AND LISTS OF DOCUMENTS AND PAMPHLETS PUBLISHED BY US AND BRITISH GOVERNMENTS AND BY INTERNATIONAL ORGANIZATIONS. DEALS WITH INTERNATIONAL RELATIONS SINCE WWI. INCLUDES TITLES IN ENGLISH, GERMAN, AND FRENCH.

0022 HANDBOOK OF LATIN AMERICAN STUDIES.
GAINESVILLE: U OF FLA PR.
ANNOTATED ANNUAL GUIDE LISTING ABOUT 4,000 BOOKS AND ARTICLES ON ALL SUBJECTS. ITEMS ARRANGED BY SUBJECT AND BY COUNTRY. FIRST PUBLISHED 1935.

0023 INTERNATIONAL BIBLIOGRAPHY ON CRIME AND DELINQUENCY.
NEW YORK: NATL COUNCIL ON CRIME.
PUBLISHED BY NATIONAL RESEARCH AND INFORMATION CENTER ON CRIME AND DELINQUENCY. APPEARS THREE TIMES A YEAR BEGINNING 1963. ENTRIES COVER PUBLICATIONS RECEIVED FROM US AND EUROPE NO EARLIER THAN 1959. AUTHOR INDEX LISTS ALPHABETICALLY EACH AUTHOR'S NAME AND SUBJECT HEADINGS UNDER WHICH WORK CAN BE FOUND. INCLUDES SPECIAL ANNOTATED NATIONAL BIBLIOGRAPHY SECTIONS.

0024 LATIN AMERICA IN PERIODICAL LITERATURE.
LOS ANGELES: U CAL LAT AMER STUD.
SUMMARIES INCLUDING BIBLIOGRAPHICAL INFORMATION OF
PERIODICALS ARTICLES PUBLISHED WITHIN AND OUTSIDE US. AB-
STRACTIONS ARRANGED TOPICALLY: SOCIAL SCIENCES; HUMANITIES;
SCIENCE AND TECHNOLOGY; MISCELLANEOUS. JOURNAL PUBLISHED
ON MONTHLY BASIS SINCE 1962. PERIODICALS ABSTRACTED
ARE THOSE RECEIVED AT UCLA LIBRARY IN THAT PERIOD. EACH
ISSUE CONTAINS ABOUT 130 ITEMS.

0025 PUBLISHERS' CIRCULAR, THE OFFICIAL ORGAN OF THE PUBLISHERS'
ASSOCIATION OF GREAT BRITAIN AND IRELAND.
SURREY: PUBL CIRCULAR LTD.
WEEKLY LISTING OF BRITISH PUBLICATIONS INCLUDING PAMPH-
LETS AND GOVERNMENT PUBLICATIONS. CHANGED IN 1959 TO "BRIT-
ISH BOOKS" AND ISSUED MONTHLY. FIRST PUBLISHED 1873.

0026 CANON LAW ABSTRACTS.
DRYGRANGE, SCOTLAND: ST ANDREWS COLLEGE.
A BIYEARLY REVIEW OF PERIODICAL LITERATURE IN CANON LAW
PUBLISHED BY THE CANON LAW SOCIETY OF GREAT BRITAIN.
FIRST APPEARED IN GESTETNERED FORM IN 1959 AND IN PRINTED
FORM IN JANUARY 1961. NOS 1-4 (FROM 1959-60) HAVE BEEN
REPRINTED IN AN OMNIBUS EDITION. ARRANGED UNDER SINGLE LIST
OF APPROPRIATE CANONS OF THE CODE. 600 ARTICLES SELECTED
FROM 35-40 PERIODICALS SUMMARIZED AND ANNOTATED EACH ISSUE.

0027 THE JAPAN SCIENCE REVIEW: LAW AND POLITICS: LIST OF BOOKS
AND ARTICLES ON LAW AND POLITICS.
TOKYO: UNION JAP SOC LAWS + POL.
DESIGNED TO INTRODUCE FOREIGN SCHOLARS TO CURRENT WORKS
IN JAPANESE LAW AND POLITICS. FIRST PUBLISHED IN 1956 AND
PUBLISHED ANNUALLY THROUGH 1960. SECTIONS ON LEGAL HISTORY
AND PHILOSOPHY; COMPARATIVE LAW; CONSTITUTION; ADMINISTRA-
TIVE AND INTERNATIONAL LAW; CIVIL LAW; COMMERCIAL AND CRIM-
INAL LAW; POLITICS AND INTERNATIONAL POLITICS; SOCIOLOGY
OF LAW.

0028 NEUE POLITISCHE LITERATUR; BERICHTE UBER DAS INTERNATIONALE
SCHRIFTTUM ZUR POLITIK.
FRANKFURT: EUROPAISCHE VERLAGS, 1956.
MONTHLY GERMAN PERIODICAL TREATING ALL ASPECTS OF NATION-
AL AND INTERNATIONAL POLITICS. CONTAINS EXTENSIVE BOOK RE-
VIEW SECTION OF LATEST BOOKS PUBLISHED IN WESTERN WORLD.

0029 PERSONNEL.
NEW YORK: AMER MANAGEMENT ASSN.
BIMONTHLY PERIODICAL CONCERNED WITH MANAGEMENT OF PEOPLE
AT WORK. INCLUDES BOOK REVIEW SECTION OF CURRENT PUBLI-
CATIONS.

0030 IN THE SHADOW OF FEAR; AMERICAN CIVIL LIBERTIES, 1948-49
(PAMPHLET)
NEW YORK: AMER CIVIL LIB UNION, 1949, 88 PP.
ANNUAL REPORT OF AMERICAN CIVIL LIBERTIES UNION CON-
TAINING SUMMARY OF EVENTS REFLECTING UPON CONDITION OF CIVIL
LIBERTIES THROUGHOUT THE COUNTRY. CHARACTERIZES DOMINANT
SPIRIT OF NATION IN 1949 AS BESET BY FEAR OF WAR, COMMUNIST
EXPANSION, AND ESPIONAGE. CONTENDS THIS NERVOUS CONSERVATISM
WAS RESPONSIBLE FOR FAILURE OF CONGRESS TO ENACT CIVIL
RIGHTS MEASURES AND REVOKE UNFAIR LEGISLATION.

0031 THE REGIONAL DIRECTOR AND THE PRESS (PAMPHLET)
INDIANAPOLIS: BOBBS-MERRILL, 1952, 7 PP.
RELATES 1939 REGIONAL DIRECTOR OF NATIONAL LABOR
RELATIONS BOARD'S EFFORTS TO STOP CINCINNATI NEWSPAPERS
FROM PRINTING SUPPOSEDLY FALSE STATEMENTS ABOUT NLRB.

0032 FOREIGN AFFAIRS BIBLIOGRAPHY: A SELECTED AND ANNOTATED LIST
OF BOOKS ON INTERNATIONAL RELATIONS 1919-1962 (4 VOLS.)
NEW YORK: FOREIGN AFFAIRS BIBL, 1933.
EACH VOLUME INCLUDES 19,000 ANNOTATED REFERENCES TO
BOOKS ON INTERNATIONAL AFFAIRS. LISTS ITEMS IN ALL IMPORTANT
LANGUAGES OF WORLD, INCLUDING PRINCIPAL ASIATIC LANGUAGES.
CONTAINS REFERENCES TO WORKS ON POLITICAL, SOCIAL, CULTURAL
AND RELIGIOUS FACTORS IN INTERNATIONAL RELATIONS; INTERNA-
TIONAL LAW, ORGANIZATION AND GOVERNMENT; THE TWO WORLD WARS;
AND PARTICULAR ISSUES OF GEOGRAPHIC REGIONS. 1ST VOL. 1933.

0033 BIBLIOGRAPHY ON THE COMMUNIST PROBLEM IN THE UNITED STATES.
NEW YORK: FUND FOR THE REPUBLIC, 1955, 474 PP.
BIBLIOGRAPHY DEVOTED TO LITERATURE RELATED TO COMMUNISM
IN THE US SINCE 1919. MAIN BIBLIOGRAPHY SUPPORTED BY FIVE
APPENDEXES: SHORT SELECTED BIBLIOGRAPHY DEALING WITH NA-
TIVE AMERICAN RADICALISM AND ANTECEDENTS OF ORGANIZED
COMMUNISM; BIBLIOGRAPHY OF IDEOLOGY OF COMMUNISM OUTSIDE
US; LIST OF COMMUNIST AND LEFT-WING PERIODICALS; LIST OF
READING MATERIALS; COLLECTION OF TRIALS ON MICROFILM.

0034 "AMERICAN BEHAVIORAL SCIENTIST."
AMER. BEHAVIORAL SCIENTIST, 5 (APR. 62), 1-39.
ENTIRE ISSUE DEVOTED TO SOCIAL RESEARCH AND AFRICAN
STUDIES. SPECIAL ARTICLES DEVOTED TO POLITICAL RESEARCH IN
NEW AFRICAN NATIONS; LEGAL STUDIES IN AFRICA; CENTERS OF
AFRICAN RESEARCH; SOVIET RESEARCH ON AFRICA; AND UN
SOURCE MATERIALS ON AFRICA.

0035 MISSISSIPPI BLACK PAPER: (FIFTY-SEVEN NEGRO AND WHITE
CITIZENS' TESTIMONY OF POLICE BRUTALITY...)
NEW YORK: RANDOM HOUSE, INC, 1965, 92 PP., LC#65-18103.
COLLECTED AFFIDAVITS AND STATEMENTS EXPOSING CORRUPTION
AND BRUTALITY IN A CONFEDERATE CLOSED SOCIETY.

0036 "FOCUS ON WORLD LAW."
INTERCOM, 9 (MAY-JUNE 67), 26-71.
INTRODUCTION TO INTERNATIONAL LAW, DEFINING ITS BOUNDS
AND INDICATING POTENTIAL USES. COVERS MAJOR PUBLIC AND
PRIVATE GROUPS CONCERNED WITH FIELD (ESPECIALLY UN BODIES),
US CONCERN, AND SOURCES OF FURTHER INFORMATION.

0037 "A PROPOS DES INCITATIONS FINANCIERES AUX GROUPEMENTS DES
COMMUNES: ESSAI D'INTERPRETATION."
REV. DROIT PUBLIC ET SCI. POL., (MAR.-APR. 67), 245-287.
ANALYZES NEW LEGISLATION IN FRANCE WHICH TENDED TO
FINANCIALLY ENCOURAGE THE REGROUPING OF TRADITIONAL LOCAL
POLITICAL SUBDIVISIONS. INTERPRETS THE MOTIVES, FORCES, AND
RESULTS OF THIS LEGISLATION.

0038 "THE STATE OF ZONING ADMINISTRATION IN ILLINOIS: PROCEDURAL
REQUIREMENTS OF JUDICIAL INTERVENTION."
NORTHWESTERN U. TRI-Q., 62 (JULY-AUG. 67), 462-491.
DISCUSSES CONFLICT INHERENT IN GOVERNMENT REGULATION
BETWEEN PRIVATE RIGHTS AND PUBLIC WELFARE IN FIELD OF ZONING
ADMINISTRATION. SHOWS HEADWAY ILLINOIS JUDICIARY HAS MADE
IN CLARIFYING ITS ROLE IN SETTLING DISPUTES. SUGGESTS FUR-
THER MEANS TOWARD EQUITABLE ADMINISTRATION OF STATE AND
LOCAL ZONING.

0039 "THE FEDERAL AGRICULTURAL STABILIZATION PROGRAM AND THE
NEGRO."
COLUMBIA LAW REV., 67 (JUNE 67), 1121-1136.
DISCUSSES INJUSTICE OF EXCLUDING NEGROES FROM PROGRAM
WHICH DETERMINES NUMBER OF ACRES OF BASIC COMMODITIES THAT
EVERY FARMER CAN PLANT OR SELL. PRLGRAM IS AGRICULTURAL
STABILIZATION AND CONSERVATION SERVICE AND IS CONTROLLED BY
PREJUDICED SOUTHERN WHITES WHO DISCOUNT ALL NEGRO FARMERS,
AND DO NOT ALLOW NEGRO REPRESENTATIVES TO THE SERVICE.
BELIEVES CONGRESS SHOULD CHANGE SYSTEM VIA COURTS.

0040 JUNZ A.J. ED.
PRESENT TRENDS IN AMERICAN NATIONAL GOVERNMENT.
LONDON: HANSARD SOCIETY, 1960, 232 PP.
STUDIES BY AMERICAN SCHOLARS ON DEVELOPMENTS IN AMERICAN
GOVERNMENT IN THE FIFTIES. ESSAYS OF AMERICAN POLITICAL
THOUGHT, ELECTION AND PARTY TRENDS, THE SUPREME COURT,
CIVIL LIBERTIES, CONGRESS AND THE PRESIDENCY INCLUDED.

0041 NJ LAW AND LEGISLATIVE BUREAU
NEW JERSEY LEGISLAVTIVE REAPPORTIONMENT (PAMPHLET)
TRENTON: N J ST DEPT OF EDUC, 1957, 52 PP.
SUMMARY OF LEGISLATIVE PROPOSALS TO REAPPORTION SEATS OF
GENERAL ASSEMBLY OF NEW JERSEY 1951-57. DESIGNED TO HELP
VOTERS AND LEGISLATORS DECIDE THE UNRESOLVED ISSUE OF
REAPPORTIONMENT.

0042 AARON T.J.
THE CONTROL OF POLICE DISCRETION: THE DANISH EXPERIENCE.
SPRINGFIELD: THOMAS, 1966, 107 PP., LC#66-24622.
DISCUSSES INSTITUTION OF DANISH OMBUDSMAN AS REPRESENTA-
TIVE OF PEOPLE TO PRESENT THEIR COMPLAINTS, IN THIS CASE,
ABOUT POLICE BEHAVIOR. CONSIDERS APPLICABILITY TO AMERICAN
POLICE SYSTEM.

0043 ABELS J.
THE TRUMAN SCANDALS.
CHICAGO: HENRY REGNERY CO, 1956, 329 PP., LC#56-8261.
ASSERTS THAT TRUMAN ADMINISTRATION WAS THE MOST
CORRUPT IN AMERICAN HISTORY. REPORTS ON RECORDS OF COURTS
AND CONGRESSIONAL INVESTIGATIONS. DISCUSSES TAX FIXING
IN EXCHANGE FOR CAMPAIGN CONTRIBUTIONS, AND BILLIONS IN
GOVERNMENT CONTRACTS AND SURPLUS PROPERTY LADLED OUT TO
POLITICAL FRIENDS AND HACKS.

0044 ABLARD C.D.
"EX PARTE CONTACTS WITH FEDERAL ADMINISTRATIVE AGENCIES."
AMER BAR ASSN., 47 (MAY 61), 473-476.
REPORT ON THE STATUS OF LEGISLATION PROPOSED BY THE ABA
TO RESTRICT "EX PARTE" COMMUNICATIONS IN ADMINISTRATIVE
ADJUDICATORY PROCEEDINGS. HOLDS THAT SUCH COMMUNICATIONS
HINDER DEMOCRATIC, REPRESENTATIVE PROCESSES BY GIVING UNFAIR
ADVANTAGE TO THOSE GROUPS INDULGING IN SUCH PRACTICES.

0045 ABRAHAM H.J.
COURTS AND JUDGES: AN INTRODUCTION TO THE JUDICIAL PROCESS.
NEW YORK: OXFORD U PR, 1959, 58 PP.
DISCUSSES NATURE OF LAW, ORGANIZATION AND PROCEDURE OF
US COURTS, ROLE OF JUDGES, AND POWER OF JUDICIAL REVIEW.
INCLUDES APPENDIX ON JURISDICTION OF NATIONAL JUDICIARY AND
US SUPREME COURT REVIEW.

0046 ABRAHAM H.J.
"THE JUDICIAL PROCESS."
NEW YORK: OXFORD U PR, 1962.

APPROXIMATELY 1200 UNANNOTATED ITEMS ARRANGED BY AUTHOR
WITHIN THE FOLLOWING HEADINGS: GENERAL WORKS, COMPARATIVE
CONSTITUTIONAL AND ADMINISTRATIVE LAW, CIVIL RIGHTS AND
LIBERTIES, BIOGRAPHIES OF JUSTICES OF THE SUPREME COURT.
ITEMS EXPLORE ENGLISH AND FRENCH LEGAL SYSTEMS AS WELL AS
AMERICAN.

0047 ADAMS B.
THE THEORY OF SOCIAL REVOLUTIONS.
NEW YORK: MACMILLAN, 1913, 235 PP.
RELATION BETWEEN COURTS AND POLITICS IS A FUNDAMENTAL
ISSUE WHICH MUST BE RESOLVED BEFORE SOCIAL STABILITY CAN BE
ATTAINED. AUTHOR OFFERS EVIDENCE THAT WITHOUT COURT REFORM,
SOCIETY WILL DEGENERATE. DISCUSSES PROPER LIMITATIONS OF
JUDICIAL FUNCTION, AND DESCRIBES FORESEEABLE DECLINE AND
FALL OF CAPITALISM.

0048 ADAMS J.
A DEFENSE OF THE CONSTITUTIONS OF GOVERNMENT OF THE UNITED
STATES OF AMERICA.
ORIGINAL PUBLISHER NOT AVAILABLE, 1787, 390 PP.
DEMOCRACY CAN BE PRESERVED ONLY THROUGH A PROPER BALANCE
OF POWERS. ENGLISH GOVERNMENT HAS LASTED FOR THIS REASON,
WHILE GERMAN AND OTHER MONARCHICAL GOVERNMENTS FAILED
THROUGH CONFUSION AS TO WHO HELD AUTHORITY. STRESSES IMPOR-
TANCE OF US GOVERNMENT BEGINNING WELL. ALL NATIONS MUST HAVE
POLITICAL PARTIES BUT CONTROL MUST BE THROUGH EITHER A
MONARCHY AND STANDING ARMY, OR A BALANCE IN CONSTITUTION.

0049 ADLER M.J.
HOW TO THINK ABOUT WAR AND PEACE.
NEW YORK: SIMON SCHUSTER, 1944, 308 PP.
PRESENTS WAYS OF STIMULATING CITIZENS INTO THINKING ABOUT
INTERNATIONAL PEACE-MAKING MEANS AND METHODS. ASSERTING THAT
PEACE IS POSSIBLE, SUGGESTS MEANS TO SECURE PEACE. PREDICTS
FUTURE TRENDS, AND CITES NEED FOR ESTABLISHMENT OF A WORLD
ORGANIZATION TO PROMOTE WORLD PEACE.

0050 ADOKO A.
"THE CONSTITUTION OF UGANDA."
TRANSITION, 7 (OCT. 67), 10-12.
ANALYZES AND REJECTS MOST CRITICISM OF UGANDAN CONSTITU-
TION, POINTING OUT MERITS OF IT. AUTHOR BELIEVES THAT NEW
CONSTITUTION WILL INSPIRE NATIONAL UNITY. DISCUSSES ABOLI-
TION OF KINGSHIP, METHODS FOR PRESIDENTIAL REMOVAL, EXECU-
TIVE CONTROL OVER THE ARMY, AND THE JUDICIAL PROCESS.

0051 ADRIAN C.R.
STATE AND LOCAL GOVERNMENTS: A STUDY IN THE POLITICAL
PROCESS.
NEW YORK: MCGRAW HILL, 1960, 531 PP., LC#59-15042.
RELATES STATE AND LOCAL GOVERNMENTS TO TOTAL POLITICAL
PROCESS. EXAMINES SOCIAL AND ECONOMIC ENVIRONMENT IN WHICH
IT EXISTS. PROVIDES NECESSARY BASIC INSIGHTS INTO
AMERICAN GOVERNMENT.

0052 ADRIAN C.R.
GOVERNING OVER FIFTY STATES AND THEIR COMMUNITIES.
NEW YORK: MCGRAW HILL, 1963, 130 PP., LC#63-13132.
DISCUSSION OF STATE AND LOCAL GOVERNMENT, RELATIONS TO
FEDERAL GOVERNMENT AND COMPARISON OF SYSTEMS INCLUDING
FUNCTIONS AND STRUCTURE OF COURTS, POLITICS, LEGISLATURES,
AND EXECUTIVES.

0053 AFRICAN BIBLIOGRAPHIC CENTER
A CURRENT BIBLIOGRAPHY ON AFRICAN AFFAIRS.
WASHINGTON: AFRICAN BIBLIOG CTR.
BIMONTHLY EVALUATION AND REVIEWS OF CURRENT PUBLICATIONS
FROM FOREIGN AND DOMESTIC PUBLISHING HOUSES. ALSO INCLUDES
JOURNAL ARTICLES. ITEMS ARRANGED BY GENERAL SUBJECT AND BY
GEOGRAPHICAL SUBJECT SECTION. AUTHOR INDEX. INCLUDES TOPICS
SUCH AS AFRICAN STUDIES, BIBLIOGRAPHY, CIVILIZATION, COM-
MERCE, FOREIGN ECONOMIC ASSISTANCE, POLITICS AND GOVERNMENT,
AND TECHNICAL ASSISTANCE.

0054 AGNEW P.C., HSU F.L.K.
"INTRODUCING CHANGE IN A MENTAL HOSPITAL."
HUMAN ORGANIZATION, 19 (WINTER 61), 195-199.
RESISTANCE IS TO BE EXPECTED BY VARIOUS SUBGROUPS TO
CHANGE PROPOSED FOR AN ORGANIZATION, BUT IT CAN BE REDUCED
IF A BALANCE IS ACHIEVED BETWEEN SELF-RELIANCE AND
SELF-RESPECT ON ONE HAND AND THE NEED FOR ENFORCING POLICY
AND AUTHORITY ON THE OTHER. A PAPER BY A WELL-KNOWN ANTHRO-
POLOGIST AND THE CHIEF OF A PSYCHIATRY SERVICE.

0055 AHLUWALIA K.
THE LEGAL STATUS, PRIVILEGES AND IMMUNITIES OF SPECIALIZED
AGENCIES OF UN AND CERTAIN OTHER INTERNATIONAL ORGANIZATIONS
THE HAGUE: MARTINUS NIJHOFF, 1964, 230 PP.
FACTUAL STUDY OF PRIVILEGES AND IMMUNITIES IN INTERNA-
TIONAL LAW. DISCUSSES LEGAL STATUS OF ARMED FORCES IN FOR-
EIGN COUNTRIES, PUBLIC VESSELS, AND DIPLOMATIC AGENTS. IN-
CLUDES UN ORGANIZATIONS, OFFICIALS AND REPRESENTATIVES OF
MEMBER STATES, AND RIGHTS OF HOST STATES TO EXPEL VISITING
EXPERTS.

0056 AIR UNIVERSITY LIBRARY
INDEX TO MILITARY PERIODICALS.
MONTGOMERY: MAXWELL AFB.
QUARTERLY SINCE 1949, SUPERSEDED BY ANNUAL AND TRIENNIAL
CUMULATIVE ISSUES. INDEXES SIGNIFICANT ARTICLES, NEWS ITEMS,
AND EDITORIALS APPEARING IN 70 MILITARY AND AERONAUTICAL
PERIODICALS. ALL ENTRIES IN ENGLISH. ITEMS ARRANGED BY SUB-
JECT AND BY COUNTRY.

0057 ALBI F.
TRATADO DE LOS MODOS DE GESTION DE LAS CORPORACIONES LOCALES
MADRID: AGUILAR, 1960, 771 PP.
EXAMINES MUNICIPAL PUBLIC ADMINISTRATION IN SPAIN IN ITS
LEGAL AND FUNCTIONAL ASPECTS. DISCUSSES RESPONSIBILITIES OF
MUNICIPAL GOVERNMENT AS OPPOSED TO NATIONAL GOVERNMENT,
EXPLAINING FINANCIAL AND POLITICAL OBLIGATION OF URBAN
GOVERNMENT TO MEET NEEDS OF LOCAL POPULATION. COVERS PROCESS
OF INCORPORATION AND MANAGEMENT.

0058 ALDRICH W.A.
"THE SUEZ CRISIS."
FOREIGN AFFAIRS, 45 (APR. 67), 541-552.
DESCRIBES THE SUEZ CRISIS FROM POINT OF VIEW OF AMERICAN
AMBASSADOR TO LONDON IN 1956. DISCUSSION OF BRITISH FEEL-
INGS OF AMERICAN ANTAGONISM TOWARD BRITISH MEASURES. BASIC
CONFLICT AROSE BETWEEN BRITISH FEELINGS OF JUSTIFICATION IN
USING MILITARY TACTICS TO ENFORCE INTERNATIONAL TREATY VIO-
LATED BY NASSER, AND AMERICAN FEELINGS THAT BRITISH INVASION
WAS A BETRAYAL OF US AND AN EXAMPLE OF COLONIALISM.

0059 ALEXANDER B.
"GIBRALTAR"
QUARTERLY REV., (JAN. 67), 1-11.
DISCUSSES REASONS FOR GIBRALTAR'S BEING BRITISH-ORIENTED,
GIBRALTARIANS' MOVE TOWARD SELF-GOVERNMENT, REASONS FOR
THE SPANISH BLOCKADE, AND THE STRATEGIC IMPORTANCE OF
GIBRALTAR.

0060 ALEXANDER F., STAUB H.
THE CRIMINAL, THE JUDGE, AND THE PUBLIC.
NEW YORK: FREE PRESS OF GLENCOE, 1956, 239 PP., LC#56-6879.
PSYCHOLOGICAL ANALYSIS OF CRIMINOLOGY AND PUNISHMENT
CONTENDS THAT THE CONTEMPORARY MANNER OF DEALING WITH CRIM-
INALS - THE IMPOSING OF PUNISHMENT - IS IN NEED OF CRITICAL
REVISION. DISCUSSES SOCIAL SIGNIFICANCE OF THE PUBLIC'S
"SENSE OF JUSTICE"; DEFINES THE CRIMINAL AND WHAT CONSTI-
TUTES AN ACT OF CRIMINALITY; PROPOSES NEW METHODS FOR DEAL-
ING WITH THE CRIMINAL. PRESENTS SEVERAL EXAMPLE CASES.

0061 ALEXANDER L.
"WAR CRIMES, THEIR SOCIAL-PSYCHOLOGICAL ASPECTS."
AMER. J. PSYCHIAT., 105 (SEPT. 48), 170-77.
DISCUSSES THE WAR CRIME OF THE SUBMISSION OF MEMBERS OF
THE MEDICAL PROFESSION IN NAZI GERMANY TO 'GROUP PRESSURE
ALTHOUGH NO OVERT COERCION WAS BROUGHT TO BEAR'.

0062 ALEXANDROWICZ C.H. ED.
A BIBLIOGRAPHY OF INDIAN LAW.
LONDON: OXFORD U PR, 1958, 69 PP.
ARRANGED BY TYPE OF SOURCE AND TYPE OF LAW WITH AN AN-
NOTATED INTRODUCTION DESCRIBING GENERAL MATERIALS AND
SECONDARY SOURCES. INDEX TO AUTHORS AND DIRECTORY OF PUB-
LISHERS CONCLUDE BOOK. MANY ITEMS IN ENGLISH.

0063 ALEXANDROWICZ C.H.
WORLD ECONOMIC AGENCIES: LAW AND PRACTICE.
LONDON: STEVENS, 1962, 310 PP.
DISCUSSES FORMATION AND OPERATION OF WORLD ECONOMIC AGEN-
CIES AS THEY INFLUENCE INTERNATIONAL LAW. EMPHASIZES INTER-
NAL STRUCTURE OF ORGANIZATIONS, DISTRIBUTION OF POWER, CON-
SEQUENCES OF UNIVERSAL MEMBERSHIP, LAW-PROMOTING FUNCTIONS,
AND SIGNIFICANCE OF ADMINISTRATIVE PROCEDURES AND JUSTICE.

0064 ALFRED H. ED.
PUBLIC OWNERSHIP IN THE USA: GOALS AND PRIORITIES.
NEW YORK: PEACE PUBL, 1961, 238 PP., LC#61-14075.
ANALYZES DEVELOPMENT AND EFFECTIVENESS OF PUBLICLY OWNED
PROJECTS IN US. ASSERTS PRIMACY OF SOCIAL SERVICES (THROUGH
PUBLIC OWNERSHIP WHEN DESIRED BY VOTERS) AS GOAL OF
CAPITALISTIC SYSTEM. CONSTITUTION SAID TO PROVIDE FOR
NATIONAL PLANNING.

0065 ALGER C.F.
"NON-RESOLUTION CONSEQUENCES OF THE UNITED NATIONS AND
THEIR EFFECT ON INTERNATIONAL CONFLICT."
J. CONFL. RESOLUT., 5 (JUNE 61), 128-46.
ANALYZES CHARACTERISTICS OF GENERAL ASSEMBLY. AIMS TO
PROVIDE DIRECTION FOR RESEARCH ON THE EFFECT OF THE UN
AND OTHER INTERNATIONAL ORGANIZATIONS ON INTERNATIONAL
RELATIONS.

0066 ALGER C.F.
"HYPOTHESES ON RELATIONSHIPS BETWEEN THE ORGANIZATION OF
INTERNATIONAL SOCIETY AND INTERNATIONAL ORDER."
PROC. AMER. SOC. INT. LAW, (1963), 36-46.
ATTEMPTS TO COMBINE PERSPECTIVES AND HYPOTHESES OF INTER-

NATIONAL LAW AND OF SOCIAL SCIENCE IN SEARCH OF THE ORIGINS
AND DYNAMICS OF THE RULE OF LAW.

0067 ALIGHIERI D.
ON WORLD GOVERNMENT.
INDIANAPOLIS: BOBBS-MERRILL, 1957, 80 PP.
SETS FORTH DOCTRINE OF WORLD POLITICS AND GOVERNMENT CON-
SISTING OF THREE FUNDAMENTAL THESES: FIRST, CONCEPT OF WORLD
UNITY ADVOCATING POLITICAL SUBORDINATION OF ALL KINGDOMS
AND REPUBLICS TO ONE SOVEREIGN RULE; SECOND, INDEPEN-
DENCE OF HEAD OF STATE FROM CONTROL OF RELIGIOUS AUTHORITY;
AND THIRD, ESSENTIAL ROMAN NATURE OF UNIVERSAL STATE BASED
ON ROMAN CORPUS JURIS.

0068 ALLEN C.K.
ASPECTS OF JUSTICE.
LONDON: STEVENS, 1958, 310 PP.
EXAMINES ETHICAL ASPECTS OF JUSTICE, RELATING IT TO LAW,
EXPEDIENCY, AND LIBERTY. DISCUSSES CRUELTY TO ANIMALS
AND CHILDREN, AND CRUELTY IN MATRIMONY. DISCUSSION CENTERS
ON PROVISIONS IN ENGLISH LAW.

0069 ALLEN C.K.
LAW IN THE MAKING.
LONDON: OXFORD U PR, 1958, 383 PP.
DISCUSSES CHIEF MATERIALS AND PROCESSES IN SOCIETY WHICH
MAKE UP GENERAL BODY OF LAW, FOCUSING ON ENGLISH LAW. SHOWS
HOW CUSTOM, PRECEDENT, AND IDEAS OF EQUITY OPERATE TO FORM
LAW. DESCRIBES FORMS AND FORCE OF LEGISLATION, BOTH
SUBORDINATE AND AUTONOMIC. EXAMINES CURRENT THEORIES OF
AUTONOMY, DEVOLUTION, AND CONSTITUTION.

0070 ALLOTT A.N. ED.
JUDICIAL AND LEGAL SYSTEMS IN AFRICA.
LONDON, WASH, DC: BUTTERWORTHS, 1962, 226 PP.
SUMMARIES OF LEGAL AND JUDICIAL SYSTEMS IN AFRICAN TERRI-
TORIES WHICH HAVE COMMON LAW AS THEIR BASIS OR WHICH HAVE
BEEN STRONGLY INFLUENCED BY IT. MAJOR SUBJECTS DISCUSSED IN-
CLUDE STRUCTURE OF COURTS, JURISDICTIONS, AND CHANNELS OF
APPEAL.

0071 AMDS W.E. ED., WELLFORD C.F. ED.
DELINQUENCY PREVENTION: THEORY AND PRACTICE.
ENGLEWOOD CLIFFS: PRENTICE HALL, 1967, 254 PP., LC#67-12188.
SURVEYS DEVELOPMENTS IN PREVENTION AND TREATMENT OF
DELINQUENCY, AND PROPOSES PROGRAM TO CONTROL JUVENILE
DELINQUENCY BEFORE IT OCCURS. INCLUDES PREDICTION OF
GROWTH OF PROBLEM THROUGH USE OF CONFIGURATION ANALYSIS,
EXAMINATION OF RELIGIOUS AND JUDICIAL INSTITUTIONS, AND
EVALUATION OF ROLES OF SCHOOL AND FAMILY.

0072 AMERICAN COUNCIL LEARNED SOC
THE ACLS CONSTITUENT SOCIETY JOURNAL PROJECT.
NEW YORK: AMER COUN LEARNED SOC.
AMERICAN COUNCIL OF LEARNED SOCIETIES IS ESTABLISHING A
BIBLIOGRAPHICAL DATA PROCESSING CENTER IN CONJUNCTION WITH
NYU'S INSTITUTE FOR COMPUTER RESEARCH IN THE HUMANITIES.
ONE OF FIRST PROJECTS IS COMPILATION OF ABSTRACTS FROM LEAD-
ING JOURNALS IN THE SOCIAL SCIENCES AND HUMANITIES. DATA
WILL BE PROCESSED TO PRODUCE ANNUAL INDEX OF CONSTITUENT SO-
CIETY JOURNALS AND SPECIALIZED INDEXES.

0073 AMER SOCIETY POL & LEGAL PHIL
THE PUBLIC INTEREST: NOMOS V.
GENEVA: MARTINUS NIJHOFF, 1962, LC#62-19400.
CHOSEN BY AMERICAN SOCIETY FOR POLITICAL AND LEGAL
PHILOSOPHY, ARTICLES RANGE FROM DISCUSSION OF ETHICAL
FOUNDATIONS TO THE "PUBLIC INTEREST IN THE IDEOLOGIES OF
NATIONAL DEVELOPMENT," "A LAWMAN'S VIEW OF THE PUBLIC
INTEREST," ETC. CONSISTS LARGELY OF THEORETICAL OR POLEMIC
ARTICLES.

0074 AMERICAN ASSEMBLY COLUMBIA U
THE COURTS, THE PUBLIC, AND THE LAW EXPLOSION.
ENGLEWOOD CLIFFS: PRENTICE HALL, 1965, 177 PP., LC#65-23292.
COLLECTION OF ESSAYS ON TRIAL COURTS AND JUDGES, THE FED-
ERAL AND STATE COURT SYSTEMS, AND PROBLEM OF COURT CONGES-
TION. EXAMINES QUALIFICATIONS OF JUDGES, THEIR ELECTION OR
APPOINTMENT, AND ADMINISTRATION OF CRIMINAL JUSTICE.

0075 AMERICAN ASSOCIATION LAW LIB
INDEX TO FOREIGN LEGAL PERIODICALS.
LONDON: U LON, INST ADVAN LEG ST, 1960.
MAKES AVAILABLE CONTENTS OF MAIN LEGAL PERIODICALS DEAL-
ING WITH INTERNATIONAL LAW, COMPARATIVE, AND MUNICIPAL
LAW OF ALL COUNTRIES EXCLUDING US AND UK. THREE QUARTERLY
PARTS WERE ISSUED DURING 1960, FOLLOWED BY ANNUAL BOUND
VOLUME. LEGAL ARTICLES ARE INDEXED IF AT LEAST FOUR
PAGES IN LENGTH. LISTS 253 REVIEWS. INCLUDES 51
COUNTRIES.

0076 AMERICAN CIVIL LIBERTIES UNION
"WE HOLD THESE TRUTHS" FREEDOM, JUSTICE, EQUALITY: REPORT ON
CIVIL LIBERTIES (A PERIODICAL PAMPHLET COVERING 1951-53)
NEW YORK: AMER CIVIL LIB UNION, 1953, 160 PP.
REPORT TO MEMBERS OF ACLU ON STATE OF CIVIL LIBERTIES IN

US FOR 1951-53. COVERS CENSORSHIP, ACADEMIC FREEDOM, RELIG-
IOUS FREEDOM, CIVIL RIGHTS, SELF-GOVERNMENT, PRIVACY, WITH
A REPORT ON COURT DECISIONS FOR PERIOD THAT AFFECT CIVIL
LIBERTIES.

0077 AMERICAN DOCUMENTATION INST
CATALOGUE OF AUXILIARY PUBLICATIONS IN MICROFILMS AND PHOTO-
PRINTS.
WASHINGTON: AMER DOCUMENT INST, 1946, 51 PP.
AN UNANNOTATED LISTING OF DOCUMENTS DEPOSITED WITH THE
AMERICAN DOCUMENTATION INSTITUTE UNDER ITS AUXILIARY PUBLI-
CATION PROGRAM. COVERS PUBLICATIONS ISSUED OR TRANSLATED IN
ENGLISH ON A WIDE RANGE OF SUBJECTS. ARTICLES LISTED ARE
SCIENTIFIC OR SCHOLARLY PAPERS TOO LONG TO BE PUBLISHED IN
JOURNALS; CHARTS, DIAGRAMS, OR ILLUSTRATIONS INCLUDED WITH
THE ARTICLE ON MICROFILM. TOPICALLY CLASSIFIED LISTINGS.

0078 AMERICAN FOREIGN LAW ASSN
BIOGRAPHICAL NOTES ON THE LAWS AND LEGAL LITERATURE OF
URUGUAY AND CURACAO.
CHICAGO: AMER FOREIGN LAW ASSOC, 1933, 42 PP.
SELECTED BIBLIOGRAPHY OF DOCUMENTS, MOST IN SPANISH.
ARRANGED BY TYPE OF LAW: CIVIL, COMMERCE, CRIMINAL, ETC.

0079 AMERICAN JEWISH COMMITTEE
GROUP RELATIONS IN THE UNITED STATES: PROBLEMS AND PERSPEC-
TIVES: A SELECTED, ANNOTATED BIBLIOGRAPHY (PAMPHLET)
NY: AM JEW COMM INST HUM REL, 1966, 17 PP.
ANNOTATED COMPILATION OF BOOKS AND PERIODICAL ARTICLES
DEALING WITH THE PROBLEMS OF CIVIL RIGHTS, RACE, AND MINOR-
ITY GROUPS IN THE US. ENTRIES DIVIDED INTO ELEVEN TOPICS.
INCLUDES SPECIFIC ETHNIC GROUPS, LEGAL, CONSTITUTIONAL, AND
RELIGIOUS ISSUES IN INTERGROUP RELATIONS, AND THE PROBLEMS
OF HOUSING, COLOR, AND INTEGRATION OF SCHOOLS. APPROXIMATELY
200 ENTRIES.

0080 AMERICAN JEWISH COMMITTEE
THE TYRANNY OF POVERTY (PAMPHLET)
NY: AM JEW COMM INST HUM REL, 1966, 18 PP.
A SELECTED BIBLIOGRAPHY OF BOOKS, PAMPHLETS, ARTICLES,
AND MEMORANDA ON GOVERNMENT AND COMMUNITY ACTION, EMPLOY-
MENT, EDUCATION, LEGAL AND SOCIAL SERVICES, ECONOMIC AND SO-
CIAL PROBLEMS. BRIEFLY ANNOTATED. CONTAINS 122 ITEMS. ALL
ENTRIES (EXCEPT ONE) ARE PUBLICATIONS OF THE 1960'S.

0081 AMERICAN JOURNAL COMP LAW
THE AMERICAN JOURNAL OF COMPARATIVE LAW READER.
NEW YORK: OCEANA PUBLISHING, 1966, 493 PP., LC#66-11925.
PRESENTS IN ECONOMIC FORMAT CONTRIBUTIONS THAT HAVE
APPEARED IN AMERICAN JOURNAL OF COMPARATIVE LAW. GROUPED IN
THREE PARTS: FIRST INCLUDES MAGISTRAL REVIEW OF COMPLEX OF
INSTITUTIONS CREATED TO COORDINATE NATIONAL LEGAL SYSTEMS;
SECOND INCLUDES REMEDIES PROVIDED TO REVIEW REGULATIONS
AND DECISIONS OF COMMUNITY INSTITUTIONS; THIRD DEALS
WITH INTERNATIONAL LAW, EUROPEAN COURT OF JUSTICE, ETC.

0082 AMERICAN LAW INSTITUTE
FOREIGN RELATIONS LAW OF THE UNITED STATES: RESTATEMENT,
SECOND.
NEW YORK: AMERICAN LAW INSTITUTE, 1962, 679 PP.
OFFICIAL DRAFT OF RESTATEMENT OF US FOREIGN RELATIONS
PROMULGATED BY AMERICAN LAW INSTITUTE IN 1962. INCLUDES
LAWS DERIVED FROM LEGISLATIVE AND EXECUTIVE ACTION,
INTERNATIONAL AGREEMENTS AND TRIBUNALS. COURTS AND PRECEDENT
DECISIONS BOTH ABROAD AND IN US. DRAWS UPON INTERNATIONAL
AND DOMESTIC LAW TO CLARIFY. DRAWS OPINIONS FROM GROUP
ACTION IN CONSIDERING LAWS.

0083 AMERICAN SOCIETY PUBLIC ADMIN
STRENGTHENING MANAGEMENT FOR DEMOCRATIC GOVERNMENT.
WASHINGTON: AM SOC PUBLIC ADMIN, 1958, 159 PP., LC#59-11123.
PRESENTS REPORTS ON DISCUSSIONS AT AMERICAN SOCIETY FOR
PUBLIC ADMINISTRATION'S 1958 CONFERENCE. FOCUSES ON
EXECUTIVE PROCESSES, SUCH AS PROGRAM PLANNING, STAFF
DELEGATION, AND PERFORMANCE MEASUREMENT AND ON LARGE-SCALE
ADMINISTRATIVE STRATEGY AND ORGANIZATION OF SEVERAL
SYSTEMS, SUCH AS COURTS.

0084 AMERICAN UNIVERSITY IN CAIRO
GUIDE TO UAR GOVERNMENT PUBLICATIONS AT THE AUC LIBRARY
(PAMPHLET)
CAIRO: AMERICAN UNIV. IN CAIRO LIB, 1965, 20 PP.
GUIDE COMPRISES GOVERNMENT AND ARAB LEAGUE PUBLICATIONS
AT AUC LIBRARY. MATERIAL IS ARRANGED ALPHABETICALLY ACCORD-
ING TO VARIOUS TITLES OF PUBLISHING DEPARTMENTS AND INSTI-
TUTES. INCLUDES TEXTS OF LAWS, RECENT STATISTICS, AND OFFI-
CAL REPORTS WHICH THROW LIGHT ON VARIOUS POLITICAL, ECONO-
MIC, AND SOCIAL ASPECTS OF UAR.

0085 AMRAM P.W.
"REPORT ON THE TENTH SESSION OF THE HAGUE CONFERENCE
ON PRIVATE INTERNATIONAL LAW."
AMER. J. INT. LAW, 59 (JAN. 65), 87-93.
FIRST U.S. PARTICIPATION AS FULL MEMBER OF CONFERENCE.
DISCUSSES CONVENTION ON INTERNATIONAL ADOPTION OF CHILDREN,
SERVICE ABROAD OF JUDICIAL-AND EXTRA-JUDICIAL DOCUMENTS IN

CIVIL AND COMMERCIAL MATTERS, AND 'CHOICE OF COURT.'

0086 ANAND R.P.
COMPULSORY JURISDICTION OF INTERNATIONAL COURT OF JUSTICE.
LONDON: ASIA PUBL., 1961, 342 PP.
PRESENTS HISTORICAL BACKGROUND OF INTERNATIONAL LAW, AND
POINTING TO ITS INHERENT WEAKNESSES ATTEMPTS TO OUTLINE A
PROGRAM FOR CREATING A MORE EFFICIENT WORLD JUDICIAL BODY.
CITES PAST EXAMPLES AND TECHNIQUES CONCERNED WITH ENFORCE-
MENT OF JURIDICAL DECREES, AND CALLS FOR MORE POWERS FOR
THE WORLD COURT.

0087 ANAND R.P.
"ATTITUDE OF THE ASIAN-AFRICAN STATES TOWARD CERTAIN
PROBLEMS OF INTERNATIONAL LAW."
INT. AND COMP. LAW Q., 15 (JAN. 66), 55-75.
AUTHOR DEEMS IT NECESSARY THAT AFRICA PLAY ROLE
IN FORMATION OF INTERNATIONAL LAW. MOST UNDERDEVELOPED NAT-
IONS HAVE EXPRESSED DISSATISFACTION, AT BANDUNG IN 1955, AND
THROUGH CALVO, DRAGO DOCTRINES, WITH PRESENT BODY OF INTER-
NATIONAL LAW. THESE STATES WANT A LAW OF PROTECTION, REPRE-
SENTATION ON I.C.J., AND A BODY OF LAW TO HELP THEM RAISE
THEIR STANDARD OF LIVING.

0088 ANASTAPLO G.
NOTES ON THE FIRST AMENDMENT TO THE CONSTITUTION OF THE
UNITED STATES (PART TWO)
CHICAGO: UNIV OF CHICAGO, 1964, 268 PP.
EXAMINES "REPUBLICAN BASIS" OF AMERICAN FREEDOM THROUGH
DETAILED ANALYSIS OF CONSTITUTIONAL PROVISIONS AND APPEALS
TO HISTORY. DISCUSSES ATTITUDE OF CONGRESS, SUPREME COURT,
AND STATE GOVERNMENTS TOWARD FREEDOM OF EXPRESSION THROUGH-
OUT COURSE OF US HISTORY.

0089 ANDERSON J.N.D.
ISLAMIC LAW IN THE MODERN WORLD.
NEW YORK: N.Y.U. PR., 1959, 106 PP.
EXAMINES NATURE OF ISLAMIC LAW. CONTRASTS ISLAMIC AND
WESTERN THEORIES OF LAW. SUMMARIZES HOW ISLAMIC LAW HAS BEEN
DISPLACED OR MODERNIZED. SURVEYS CONTEMPORARY LEGAL TRENDS
IN MUSLIM WORLD.

0090 ANDERSON J.W.
EISENHOWER, BROWNELL, AND THE CONGRESS - THE TANGLED
ORIGINS OF THE CIVIL RIGHTS BILL OF 1956-1957.
UNIVERSITY: U ALABAMA PR, 1964, 138 PP.
TREATS TORTUOUS PATH OF FIRST CIVIL RIGHTS LEGISLATION
PASSED BY CONGRESS IN 20TH CENTURY, DURING EISENHOWER
ADMINISTRATION. REVEALS FORCES THAT AFFECT CREATION OF
LEGISLATION AND INFLUENCE CONGRESSIONAL POLICY-MAKING.

0091 ANDERSON R.B.
SUPPLEMENT TO BEALE'S BIBLIOGRAPHY OF EARLY ENGLISH LAW
BOOKS.
CAMBRIDGE: HARVARD U PR, 1943, 50 PP.
UPDATES AND CORRECTS BEALE'S EARLIER CHECKLIST. SURVEYS,
DESCRIBES, AND ARRANGES HOLDINGS IN THE HARVARD LAW SCHOOL
LIBRARY AND, IF SUFFICIENT DESCRIPTIVE INFORMATION EXISTS,
IN OTHER COLLECTIONS AS WELL.

0092 ANDERSON S.V.
CANADIAN OMBUDSMAN PROPOSALS.
BERKELEY: U CAL, INST GOVT STUD, 1966, 168 PP.
REVIEW OF PROPOSALS SINCE 1960 FOR CREATION OF
PARLIAMENTARY GRIEVANCE COMMISSIONERS MODELED ON
SCANDINAVIAN OMBUDSMAN. PROPOSALS HAVE BEEN PUT FORWARD BY
MINORITY PARTIES, THEN PLACED IN LIMBO BY MAJORITY. PRESENTS
CHRONOLOGY OF EVENTS AND DEBATE, ANALYZES PROPOSALS, AND
APPRAISES CANADA'S NEED FOR AN OMBUDSMAN.

0093 ANDERSON W.
FUNDAMENTALS OF AMERICAN GOVERNMENT.
NEW YORK: HENRY HOLT & CO, 1940, 630 PP.
DISCUSSION OF FUNDAMENTALS OF AMERICAN POLITICAL INSTI-
TUTIONS, PROCESSES, AND FUNCTIONS. AMERICAN SYSTEM OF
GOVERNMENT CONSIDERED AS ONE INTEGRATED, ARTICULATED ENTITY;
MAIN STRUCTURAL FEATURES AND UNITS PRESENTED IN BEGINNING OF
TREATISE AND THEN GENERAL PRINCIPLES OF PUBLIC LAW AND PO-
LITICAL ORGANIZATION ARE OUTLINED. CONSIDERS PROCESSES OF
GOVERNMENT - POPULAR CONTROL, LEGISLATION, ADMINISTRATION.

0094 ANDERSON W., WEIDNER E.W.
STATE AND LOCAL GOVERNMENT IN THE UNITED STATES.
NEW YORK: HOLT RINEHART WINSTON, 1951, 744 PP.
TEXTBOOK ON STATE AND LOCAL GOVERNMENT FROM STRUCTURAL
AND FUNCTIONAL APPROACH COVERING RELATIONS AMONG LEVELS OF
GOVERNMENT, STATE, LOCAL, AND URBAN GOVERNMENTAL ORGANIZA-
TIONS, PUBLIC SERVICES, PERSONNEL AND FINANCE, AND VOTERS'
PLACE IN SYSTEM.

0095 ANDERSON W.
"THE PERILS OF 'SHARING'."
NATIONAL CIVIC REV., 56 (JUNE 67), 329-334.
REJECTS TAX-SHARING FUND PROPOSAL. ARGUES THAT IT WOULD
GIVE SOME STATES LESS THAN THEIR TAXPAYERS PAID AND OTHER
STATES, MORE. REJECTS THREE MYTHS THAT LIE BEHIND BILL: THAT

FEDERAL GOVERNMENT IS ROLLING IN UNNEEDED WEALTH, THAT BILL
WILL PUMP NEW PUBLIC FUNDS INTO STATE AND NATIONAL ECONOMY,
THAT STATES ARE INCAPABLE OF RAISING MONEY FOR SUPPORT OF
THEIR SERVICES.

0096 ANDREWS F.E.
CORPORATION GIVING.
NEW YORK: RUSSELL SAGE FDN, 1952, 361 PP.
A BOOK DETAILING THE GROWTH AND HISTORY, POLICIES, BUDG-
ETS, ADMINISTRATION OF CORPORATE GIVING AND THE USE OF
FOUNDATIONS. THE BENEFICIARIES AND THE LEGAL AND TAX FACTORS
ARE ALSO DISCUSSED IN DETAIL. DEALS WITH SPECIFIC PROBLEMS
SUCH AS PREVENTION OF PROFIT DISCLOSURE BY GIVING FORMULAS
AND THE STAKE OF BUSINESS IN EDUCATION.

0097 ANDRUS H.L.
LIBERALISM, CONSERVATISM, MORMONISM.
SALT LAKE CITY: DESERET BOOK CO, 1965, 100 PP., LC#65-27489.
UNIQUE ARTICLES REVEALING "TRUE PLAN FOR ACHIEVING
SOCIAL JUSTICE WITHOUT IMPINGING ON MAN'S FREEDOM AND
DIGNITY." PLAN GIVEN TO LATTER-DAY SAINTS THROUGH PROPHET
JOSEPH SMITH. LIBERALISM FAILS TO PRESERVE FREEDOM OF
MAN IN WELFARE STATE WHILE MODERN CONSERVATISM FAILS TO
ACHIEVE SOCIAL UNITY AND JUSTICE. TRUE PLAN PROVIDES BOTH.

0098 ANGELL R.C.
"THE SOCIAL INTEGRATION OF AMERICAN CITIES OF MORE THAN
1000,000 POPULATION" (BMR)
AMER. SOCIOLOGICAL REV., 12 (JUNE 47), 335-342.
STUDIES COMMON ELEMENTS OF SOCIAL INTEGRATION IN A
REPRESENTATIVE SAMPLING OF LARGE AMERICAN CITIES. USES CRIME
INDEX IN RELATION TO SIZE, BUT FINDS SIZE TO BE INVALID AS A
CAUSAL FACTOR IN INTEGRATION. USES OTHER INDEXES, SUCH AS
WEALTH, TO DETERMINE CAUSAL FACTORS. EXAMINES RELATIONSHIP
BETWEEN MOBILITY AND POPULATION COMPOSITION.

0099 ANTIEU C.J., CARROLL P.M., BURKE T.C.
RELIGION UNDER THE STATE CONSTITUTIONS.
BROOKLYN: CENTRAL BOOK CO, 1965, 277 PP., LC#65-27219.
OUTLINES PRESENT STATUS OF LAWS IN CHURCH-STATE RELATIONS
BELOW THE NATIONAL LEVEL. IN SOME CASES IMPORTANT STATE DE-
CISIONS THAT HAVE BEEN OVERTURNED BY SUPREME COURT RULINGS
ARE REPORTED, BUT CONCENTRATION IS ON STATE-BY-STATE
DESCRIPTIONS OF LEGAL DECISIONS.

0100 APPADORAI A.
THE SUBSTANCE OF POLITICS (6TH ED.)
MADRAS: OXFORD U PRESS, 1952, 524 PP.
TREATS ESSENTIAL PRINCIPLES OF POLITICAL THEORY AND
ORGANIZATION. PART ONE DISCUSSES THEORY; PART TWO TREATS
SPECIFIC POLITIES FROM THE GREEK CITY-STATES TO MAJOR MODERN
EUROPEAN STATES AND INDIA, AND CONSIDERS VARIOUS ASPECTS
OF POLITIES SUCH AS LEGISLATURES, JUDICIARY, AND EXECUTIVE.
INTENDED AS TEXTBOOK. BIBLIOGRAPHIES AT END OF EACH CHAPTER.

0101 APPLEBY P.H.
POLICY AND ADMINISTRATION.
UNIVERSITY: U ALABAMA PR, 1949, 173 PP.
SERIES OF LECTURES ON THE THEME THAT THE ADMINISTRATIVE
BRANCH OF GOVERNMENT MAKES POLICY AS WELL AS CARRIES OUT
POLICY. HOLDS THAT ADMINISTRATIVE AGENCIES, ESPECIALLY THOSE
WITH NARROW RANGE OF FUNCTIONS, TEND TO REPRESENT THEIR
SPECIFIC CLIENTELE, OFTEN TO THE DETRIMENT OF THE PUBLIC
INTEREST.

0102 APPLEBY P.H.
MORALITY AND ADMINISTRATION IN DEMOCRATIC GOVERNMENT.
BATON ROUGE: LOUISIANA ST U PR, 1952, 261 PP.
GENERAL DESCRIPTION OF FUNCTIONS OF BUREAUCRACY, WHOM IT
REPRESENTS AND HOW. CONSIDERS IMPACT OF PRESSURE GROUPS,
PUBLIC OPINION, THE COURTS, AND CONGRESS ON THE PRESIDENT,
EXECUTIVE DEPARTMENTS, AND REGULATORY AGENCIES.

0103 ARCHER P.
FREEDOM AT STAKE.
LONDON: THE BODLEY HEAD, 1966, 111 PP.
DISCUSSES GOVERNMENT REPRESSION OF HUMAN RIGHTS IN
ENGLAND. USES CASE STUDIES TO ILLUSTRATE NECESSITY OF LAWS
TO PROTECT CITIZENS FROM ADMINISTRATIVE INJUSTICE. TREATS
VIEWS AND POLICIES ON HUMAN RIGHTS IN SEVERAL COUNTRIES OUT-
SIDE ENGLAND.

0104 ARNOW K.
SELF-INSURANCE IN THE TREASURY (PAMPHLET)
INDIANAPOLIS: BOBBS-MERRILL, 1952, 52 PP.
CASE STUDY OF TWO "LOW TENSION" ADMINISTRATIVE PROBLEMS
IN THE US TREASURY DEPARTMENT. COMPARES TWO INSTANCES OF
ADMINISTERING TRANSFER OF SHIPPING METHODS TO A SELF-
INSURANCE BASIS. ILLUMINATES NEED FOR REFORM IN BUREAUCRATIC
PROCEDURE.

0105 ASAMOAH O.Y.
THE LEGAL SIGNIFICANCE OF THE DECLARATIONS OF THE GENERAL
ASSEMBLY OF THE UNITED NATIONS.
THE HAGUE: MARTINUS NIJHOFF, 1966, 274 PP.
EXPLAINS DIFFERENT TYPES OF DECLARATIONS OF UN GENERAL

ASSEMBLY RELATING TO DEVELOPMENT OF INTERNATIONAL LAW.
STATES EXISTING INTERNATIONAL LAWS AND NEW LAWS. EXAMINES
PROMOTION OF CHARTER PROGRAMS, AND INVESTIGATES SIGNIFI-
CANCE OF DECLARATIONS FOR GOVERNMENT OF US AND MEMBER
STATES.

0106 ASCH S.H.
POLICE AUTHORITY AND THE RIGHTS OF THE INDIVIDUAL.
NEW YORK: ARCO PUBL CO, 1967, 126 PP., LC#67-10090.
ROLE OF POLICE IN DEMOCRATIC SOCIETY. POLICE AUTHORITY
IN UPHOLDING LAW VERSUS HUMAN RIGHTS AND PRESERVATION OF
PERSONAL FREEDOM.

0107 ASIA FOUNDATION
LIBRARY NOTES.
SAN FRANCISCO: ASIA FOUNDATION.
BIMONTHLY PUBLICATION SINCE 1951 LISTING MATERIALS PRI-
MARILY ON ASIA. INCLUDES BOOKS, UN DOCUMENTS AND REPORTS,
SERIAL PUBLICATION, PAMPHLETS, FOREIGN AND DOMESTIC GOVERN-
MENT DOCUMENTS, AND ELUSIVE MATERIALS, CATEGORIZED BY COUN-
TRY AND SUBJECT. ALSO CONTAINS ABSTRACTS OF PERIODICAL ARTI-
CLES. ANNUAL INDEX. MATERIALS IN ENGLISH.

0108 ASSOCIATION BAR OF NYC
REPORT ON ADMISSION PROCEDURES TO NEW YORK STATE MENTAL
HOSPITALS.
ITHACA: CORNELL U PRESS, 1962, 303 PP., LC#62-18213.
REPORT ON ADMISSION PROCEDURES TO NEW YORK STATE MENTAL
HOSPITALS. DESCRIBES SHIFT FROM CUSTODY TO THERAPY TO MEET
MEDICAL NEEDS AND PROTECT CIVIL RIGHTS OF MENTALLY ILL.
THE USE OF VOLUNTARY AND INFORMAL ADMISSIONS AS ALLEVIATING
THE NEGATIVE EFFECTS OF JOINING THE HOSPITAL COMMUNITY ARE
DISCUSSED. PARTLY BASED ON FIELD INVESTIGATIONS.

0109 ASSOCIATION BAR OF NYC
RADIO, TELEVISION, AND THE ADMINISTRATION OF JUSTICE: A
DOCUMENTED SURVEY OF MATERIALS.
NEW YORK: COLUMBIA U PRESS, 1965, 321 PP., LC#65-28182.
EXAMINES INFLUENCE OF RADIO AND TELEVISION ON ADMINISTRA-
TION OF CIVIL AND CRIMINAL JUSTICE, INCLUDING NEWS
PERSONNEL, TECHNICAL APPARATUS, SPECIAL PROGRAMS, AND THE
WARREN COMMISSION REPORT.

0110 ATLANTIC INSTITUTE
ATLANTIC STUDIES.
BOULOGNE S. SEINE: ATLANTIC INSTITUTE.
PERIODICAL, APPEARING SINCE 1964, COVERS CURRENT POLITI-
CAL, ECONOMIC, MILITARY, SOCIAL, JUDICIAL, AND CULTURAL
STUDIES AMONG ATLANTIC COUNTRIES. ONLY STUDIES PLANNED OR
IN PROGRESS ARE REPORTED, NONE OF WHICH HAVE BEEN PUBLISHED
PRIOR TO INCLUSION. SPECIAL SECTION INCLUDES PUBLISHED RE-
SEARCH PREVIOUSLY ANNOTATED AS IN PROGRESS. ENGLISH AND
EUROPEAN LANGUAGES. ARRANGED BY SUBJECT.

0111 ATOMIC INDUSTRIAL FORUM
COMMENTARY ON LEGISLATION TO PERMIT PRIVATE OWNERSHIP OF
SPECIAL NUCLEAR MATERIAL (PAMPHLET)
NEW YORK: ATOMIC INDUS FORUM, 1963, 63 PP.
DISCUSSES ATOMIC ENERGY COMMISSION'S BILL TO PERMIT
PRIVATE OWNERSHIP OF SPECIAL NUCLEAR MATERIAL AND TO REVISE
ATOMIC ENERGY ACT OF 1954 TO AUTHORIZE TRANSACTIONS BY AEC
WITH PRIVATE PERSONS. PRESENTS ATOMIC ENERGY ACT AND TEXT
OF BILL AND ANALYZES ADVISABILITY OF CHANGES. BASICALLY
SUPPORTS BILL.

0112 ATOMIC INDUSTRIAL FORUM
MANAGEMENT AND ATOMIC ENERGY.
NEW YORK: ATOMIC INDUS FORUM, 1958, 460 PP.
PROCEEDINGS OF ATOMIC ENERGY MANAGEMENT CONFERENCE ON
STATUS AND GROWTH OF ATOMIC INDUSTRY. CONSIDERS POLICY,
HEALTH AND SAFETY, ASSESSMENT OF US POWER REACTOR PROGRAM,
FEASIBILITY OF SMALL REACTORS, SALE OF NUCLEAR PRODUCTS
OUTSIDE US, AMENDMENTS TO ATOMIC ENERGY ACT, NUCLEAR SHIPS,
REDUCTION OF COST, INTERNATIONAL ACTIVITIES, PEACEFUL USES,
INDEMNIFICATION LAW, AND RESEARCH DEVELOPMENTS.

0113 ATOMIC INDUSTRIAL FORUM
ATOMS FOR INDUSTRY: WORLD FORUM.
NEW YORK: ATOMIC INDUS FORUM, 1960, 160 PP.
DESCRIBES GROWTH OF INDUSTRIAL USES OF ATOMIC ENERGY, AND
PROCEDURES. IDENTIFIES UNPRECEDENTED PROBLEMS OF
USING ATOMS FOR SOCIAL PURPOSES, SUCH AS COST, SAFETY,
FINANCES, LEGAL CONTROL, AND PUBLIC INTEREST.

0114 ATTIA G.E.D.
LES FORCES ARMEES DES NATIONS UNIES EN COREE ET AU MOYEN-
ORIENT.
GENEVA: LIBRAIRIE DROZ, 1963, 467 PP.
FULLY DOCUMENTED LEGAL STUDY OF UN EFFORTS TO "MAINTAIN
THE PEACE" THROUGH THE SENDING OF INTERNATIONAL FORCES INTO
THE CONFLICT AREA. THE ROLES OF THE MAJOR POWERS, THE SECUR-
ITY COUNCIL, THE GENERAL ASSEMBLY AND PARTICIPANTS (BOTH
MEMBER AND NON-MEMBER STATES OF THE UN) ARE ANALYZED IN THE
KOREAN AND SUEZ CRISES.

0115 ATTIA G.E.O.

"LES FORCES ARMEES DES NATIONS UNIES EN COREE ET AU MOYEN-
ORIENT."
GENEVA: LIBRAIRIE DROZ, 1963.
LEGAL STUDY OF UN EFFORTS TO "MAINTAIN THE PEACE" BY
SENDING INTERNATIONAL FORCES INTO THE CONFLICT AREA. THE
BIBLIOGRAPHY OF OVER 600 ITEMS INCLUDES UN AND INDIVIDUAL
STATE DOCUMENTS AND BOOKS AND ARTICLES, IN FRENCH AND
ENGLISH, FROM 1921 TO 1958. DOCUMENTS ARRANGED BY SOURCE
AND DATE, OTHER ITEMS ALPHABETICALLY BY AUTHOR.

0116 AUERBACH C.A., GARRISON L.K. ET AL.
THE LEGAL PROCESS.
SAN FRANCISCO: CHANDLER, 1961, 915 PP., LC#61-12972.
DISCUSSES METHODS AND PROCESSES OF LEGAL DECISION-MAKING
BY JUDICIAL, LEGISLATIVE, EXECUTIVE, AND ADMINISTRATIVE
AGENCIES. EXAMINES LAW-MAKING FUNCTION OF JUDGE AND REVIEW
OF LEGISLATION AND ADMINISTRATIVE DECISIONS. STUDIES IN DE-
TAIL LEGISLATIVE PROCESS.

0117 AUERBACH J.S.
LABOR AND LIBERTY; THE LA FOLLETTE COMMITTEE AND THE NEW
DEAL.
INDIANAPOLIS: BOBBS-MERRILL, 1966, 246 PP., LC#66-28233.
DESCRIBES LA FOLLETTE'S CIVIL LIBERTIES COMMITTEE AND ITS
INVESTIGATION OF RELATIONSHIP BETWEEN LABOR ORGANIZATIONS
AND CIVIL LIBERTIES DURING DECADE OF NEW DEAL. EXAMINES
FUNCTIONS OF SUCH COMMITTEES; ROLE OF CHAIRMAN; SENSITIVITY
OF NEW DEAL TO BILL OF RIGHTS AND MEANING OF CIVIL LIBERTY;
AND LABOR ORGANIZATIONS DURING NEW DEAL.

0118 AUMANN F.R.
"THE INSTRUMENTALITIES OF JUSTICE: THEIR FORMS, FUNCTIONS,
AND LIMITATIONS."
COLUMBUS: OHIO STATE U PR, 1956.
EXAMINATION OF PROBLEMS OF LEGAL ADMINISTRATION FROM A
POLITICAL SCIENCE VIEWPOINT. ANALYZES PROBLEM OF SYSTEMATIZ-
ING JUSTICE THROUGH LAW WITH ATTENTION DIRECTED TO THE
EMERGENCE OF LAW FROM THE INFLUENCES OF ENGLISH COMMON LAW
AND ROMAN CIVIL LAW. DISCUSSES MACHINERY OF JUSTICE AND SOME
POPULAR ATTITUDES ON JUSTICE AND LAW. UNANNOTATED BIBLIOGRA-
PHY OF WORKS IN ENGLISH, TOPICALLY ARRANGED.

0119 AUSTIN J.
THE PROVINCE OF JURISPRUDENCE DETERMINED AND THE USES OF THE
STUDY OF JURISPRUDENCE.
LONDON: WEIDENFIELD & NICOLSON, 1954, 396 PP.
BELIEVES THAT THERE ARE CERTAIN PRINCIPLES AND
DISTINCTIONS THAT ARE NECESSARILY PART OF EVERY SYSTEM OF
LAW. IDENTIFIES CHARACTERISTICS OF POSITIVE LAW - COMMAND
AND HABIT OF OBEDIENCE - TO DISTINGUISH IT FROM MORALITY.
ANALYZES VOCABULARY OF LAW AND CLASSIFIES TERMS TO INCREASE
CLARITY.

0120 AUSTIN J., CAMPBELL R. ED.
LECTURES ON JURISPRUDENCE OR THE PHILOSOPHY OF POSITIVE LAW
(VOL. II) (4TH ED., REV.)
LONDON: JOHN MURRAY, 1873, 641 PP.
CONSIDERS LAW IN RELATION TO ITS SOURCES: WRITTEN AND
UNWRITTEN LAW, ROMAN ORIGINS, "NATURAL LAW," EQUITY, CODE
AND PANDECTS, ETC. DEFINES THE PURPOSES AND SUBJECTS OF LAW:
DISTINCTIONS BETWEEN RIGHTS AND DUTIES AND BETWEEN THINGS
AND PERSONS, THE IDEA OF STATUS, PROPERTY, PRINCIPAL AND
ACCESSORY, ETC. ALSO CONTAINS SPECIAL NOTES ON CRIMINAL LAW,
CODIFICATION, AND LAW REFORM.

0121 AVERY M.W.
GOVERNMENT OF WASHINGTON STATE.
SEATTLE: U OF WASHINGTON PR, 1961, 320 PP., LC#61-8211.
PRESENTS ACCOUNT OF PRESENT STRUCTURE OF STATE AND LOCAL
GOVERNMENT IN WASHINGTON. SHOWS POWERS AND DUTIES OF EACH
OFFICE AND ITS RELATIONS WITH OTHER AGENCIES. TRACES EVOLU-
TION OF OFFICES AND OFFERS SUGGESTIONS FOR GREATER EFFICIEN-
CY IN THEIR OPERATION. STATES MAIN PROBLEMS CONFRONTING LEG-
ISLATURE AND COURTS. STRESSES ROLE OF CITIZEN IN WORKING EF-
FECTIVELY FOR GOOD GOVERNMENT.

0122 AYLMER G.
THE KING'S SERVANTS.
NEW YORK: COLUMBIA U PRESS, 1961, 488 PP.
DESCRIBES ADMINISTRATIVE PROCEDURES, OFFICES, AND STRUC-
TURES UNDER CHARLES I, 1625-42. RELATES TYPE OF BUREAUCRACY
TO OVERTHROW BY CROMWELL, NOTING TYPES OF CHANGES AND
INNOVATIONS.

0123 AYMARD A., AUBOYER J., CROUZET M.
HISTOIRE GENERALE DES CIVILISATIONS (7 VOLS.)
PARIS: PR UNIV DE FRANCE, 1953.
EACH VOLUME DESCRIBES AND ANALYZES CIVILIZATIONS FROM A
HISTORICAL, ECONOMIC, INTELLECTUAL, AND SOCIOLOGICAL POINT
OF VIEW. INCLUDES ANCIENT GREECE, EGYPT, ROME, RENAISSANCE
ITALY, ETC., FOR EACH OF WHICH BIBLIOGRAPHIC INFORMATION IS
SUPPLIED FOR BOTH THE NONSPECIALIZED AND SCHOLARLY READER.
INCLUDES DOCUMENTS AS WELL AS ANALYSES.

0124 BAADE H. ED.
THE SOVIET IMPACT ON INTERNATIONAL LAW.

NEW YORK: OCEANA PUBLISHING, 1965, 174 PP., LC#65-22170.
12 SCHOLARS OF SOVIET STUDIES, INTERNATIONAL LAW AND INT-
ERNATIONAL ECONOMICS COMMENT ON SOVIET LEGAL DOCTRINE AND
PRACTICE CONCERNING TREATIES, INTERNATIONAL ORGANIZATION,
COLONIALISM, DISARMAMENT, PEACEFUL COEXISTENCE AND WARS OF
NATIONAL LIBERATION. ALSO DISCUSS SOVIET TRADE AND AID POL-
ICIES, AND THE LEGALITY OF US COUNTRIES PROHIBITING TRADE.

0125 BAADE H.W.
"THE ACQUIRED RIGHTS OF INTERNATIONAL PUBLIC SERVANTS; A
CASE STUDY IN RECEPTION OF PUBLIC LAW."
AMER. J. OF COMPARATIVE LAW, 15 (JAN. 67), 251-300.
STUDIES 275 DECISIONS BY INTERNATIONAL ADMINISTRATIVE
TRIBUNALS TO DETERMINE EXTENT OF PROTECTION TRIBUNALS OFFER
TO STAFF MEMBERS OF INTERNATIONAL ORGANIZATIONS AGAINST AD-
VERSE ADMINISTRATIVE ACTIONS. GIVES LIMITS OF TRIBUNALS'
POWER TO CHANGE DECISION. SUGGESTS THAT INTERNATIONAL PUBLIC
SERVANTS' ACQUIRED RIGHTS BE PROTECTED WHEN IT IS IMPORTANT
TO PUBLIC INTERESTS.

0126 BACHELDER G.L. ED., SHAW P.C. ED.
THE LITERATURE OF FEDERALISM: A SELECTED BIBLIOGRAPHY (REV
ED) (A PAMPHLET)
E LANSING: MSU COMM DEV & SERV, 1966, 18 PP.
BIBLIOGRAPHICAL LISTING OF 192 SOURCES PERTAINING TO
FEDERALISM. ENTRIES DIVIDED INTO: AMERICAN FEDERALISM,
GENERAL WORKS, FEDERALISM IN OTHER NATIONS, AND GOVERNMENTAL
UBLICATIONS. ITEMS CITED INCLUDE ENGLISH-LANGUAGE PERIODICAL
ARTICLES AND BOOKS PUBLISHED 1863 THROUGH 1965.

0127 BACKUS R.C., EDER P.J.
A GUIDE TO THE LAW AND LEGAL LITERATURE OF COLOMBIA.
WASHINGTON: US GOVERNMENT, 1943, 222 PP.
HISTORICAL SURVEY AND ACCOUNT OF CONSTITUTIONAL DEVELOP-
MENT AND CIVIL AND COMMERCIAL LAW. CHAPTERS ON LEGAL PERIOD-
ICALS, BIBLIOGRAPHY, GENERAL WORKS, INTERNATIONAL LAW AND
COLONIAL LAW. APPENDIX CONTAINS TABLE OF CITED LAWS AND
DECREES IN CHRONOLOGICAL ORDER.

0128 BACON F.
"OF JUDICATURE" (1612) IN F. BACON, ESSAYS."
NEW YORK: EP DUTTON, 1962.
WARNS JUDGES AGAINST OVERSTEPPING THEIR POWER TO INTER-
PRET LAW BY ATTEMPTS TO MAKE NEW LAWS. DEFENDS TRADITION AND
PRECEDENT AGAINST ATTEMPTS AT MODIFICATION. CAUTIONS JUDGES
ALSO AGAINST EXCESSIVE USE OF HARSH PENALTIES LEST THEY
LOSE THE TERROR ASSOCIATED WITH THEM AND BECOME COMMON IN
THE MINDS OF POPULACE. RECOMMENDS THAT LAWYERS REFRAIN FROM
THEATRICS AND TRICKS WHEN DEALING WITH CASES IN COURT.

0129 BACON F.
"OF THE TRUE GREATNESS OF KINGDOMS AND ESTATES" (1612) IN
F. BACON, ESSAYS."
NEW YORK: EP DUTTON, 1962.
PROPOSES THAT GREATNESS IN A NATION IS RESULT OF PROFES-
SING ARMS AS ITS PRINCIPAL HONOR, STUDY, AND OCCUPATION.
SUGGESTS THAT TO INSURE GREATNESS, NATIONS HAVE LAWS WHICH
PROMOTE WAGING OF JUST WARS. COMMENTS, "LET NO NATION SIT
TOO LONG UPON A PROVOCATION." URGES THAT KEEPING TREATIES
IS VITAL. COMMENDS WAR AS NECESSARY EXERCISE FOR HEALTHY
STATES, BUT WARNS AGAINST CIVIL STRIFE.

0130 BADEN A.L.
IMMIGRATION AND ITS RESTRICTION IN THE US (PAMPHLET)
WASHINGTON: LIBRARY OF CONGRESS, 1937, 86 PP.
SELECTED BIBLIOGRAPHY INDEXED BY AUTHOR AND SUBJECT.
INCLUDES BOOKS, PAMPHLETS, AND SPEECHED FROM "CONGRESSIONAL
RECORD" FROM 1930 TO 1937. CONTAINS 803 ITEMS, MIMEOGRAPHED.

0131 BADI J.
THE GOVERNMENT OF THE STATE OF ISRAEL: A CRITICAL ACCOUNT OF
ITS PARLIAMENT, EXECUTIVE, AND JUDICIARY.
NEW YORK: TWAYNE, 1963, 307 PP., LC#63-17404.
STUDIES DEVELOPMENT OF ISRAEL'S GOVERNMENTAL STRUCTURE,
DELINEATING NATURE AND FUNCTION OF BODIES OF GOVERNMENT AND
POLITICAL PARTIES. ANALYZES VARIOUS ASSEMBLIES AND CABINETS
THAT HAVE DIRECTED POLICY SINCE INDEPENDENCE. STATES THAT
ISRAEL'S FUTURE DEPENDS ON HER ABILITY TO SOLVE THREE PROB-
LEMS: ACHIEVEMENT OF ECONOMIC INDEPENDENCE, INTEGRATION OF
IMMIGRANTS, AND PEACE WITH ARABS.

0132 BAER E.
"THE GENERAL ACCOUNTING OFFICE: THE FEDERAL GOVERNMENT'S
AUDITOR."
AMER BAR ASSN., 47 (APR. 61), 359-362.
SHORT HISTORY AND DESCRIPTION OF THE FUNCTIONS OF THE GAO
IN REVIEWING ADMINISTRATIVE AGENCY ACTIVITIES AND
ADJUDICATORY DECISIONS.

0133 BAHRO H.
DAS KINDSCHAFTSRECHT IN DER UNION DER SOZIALISTITSCHEN
SOWJETREPUBLIKEN.
ALFRED METZNER VERLAG, 1966, 339 PP.
DISCUSSES SOURCES, DEVELOPMENT, AND NATURE OF SOVIET
CHILD LAW. EXAMINES PARENTS' RIGHTS IN RELATION TO CHILD'S
EDUCATION, RELIGION, AND PLACE OF DOMICILE, AS WELL AS ROLE

AND LEGAL STATUS OF GUARDIAN. CONCLUDES WITH DISCUSSION OF
CHILD WELFARE ADMINISTRATION IN USSR.

0134 BAILEY N.A.
LATIN AMERICA IN WORLD POLITICS.
NEW YORK: WALKER, 1967, 250 PP., LC#67-13242.
ANALYSIS OF LATIN AMERICA'S ROLE IN INTERNATIONAL AFFAIRS
WITH AN ATTEMPT TO CREATE AN ANALYTICAL FRAMEWORK WITH PRE-
DICTIVE VALIDITY. STRESSES WORLD VIEW RATHER THAN STRICTLY
INTER-AMERICAN RELATIONS AND DISCUSSES EFFECT OF COLD WAR
ON LATIN AMERICA. CONCLUDES THAT CLIENT STATUS OF REGION IS
PIVOTAL AND SEMI-PERMANENT. QUESTION FOR FUTURE IS: WHOSE
CLIENTS WILL LATIN AMERICA BE?

0135 BAILEY S.D.
VETO IN THE SECURITY COUNCIL (PAMPHLET)
NEW YORK: CARNEGIE ENDOWMENT, 1968, 66 PP.
REVIEWS USE OF THE VETO IN THE UN SECURITY COUNCIL
FROM 1946-67. DISCUSSES DIFFERENT TYPES OF CASES TO WHICH
THE VETO HAS BEEN APPLIED AND EFFORTS MADE TO CURB ITS USE.
STRESSES IMPORTANCE OF PRELIMINARY CONSULTATION TO AVOID
UNNECESSARY USE OF THE VETO.

0136 BAILEY S.K.
CONGRESS MAKES A LAW.
NEW YORK: COLUMBIA U PRESS, 1950, 282 PP.
ANALYZES LEGISLATIVE PROCESS INVOLVED IN US EMPLOYMENT
ACT OF 1946 IN ORDER TO GENERALIZE ABOUT CONGRESSIONAL
DECISION-MAKING PROCESS USED IN FORMULATING SOCIO-ECONOMIC
LEGISLATION. COMPLEXITY OF PROCEDURE LIES IN POWER STRUGGLES
OF PRIVATE, ADMINISTRATIVE, AND POLITICAL GROUPS. NOTES
NEED FOR INCREASED CONGRESSIONAL RESPONSIBILITY.

0137 BAINS J.S. ED.
STUDIES IN POLITICAL SCIENCE.
NEW YORK: ASIA PUBL HOUSE, 1961, 450 PP.
DEALS WITH INTERNATIONAL LAW AND RELATIONS INCLUDING JUR-
ISDICTION AND THEORY; POLITICAL RESEARCH AND THEORY; AND
PUBLIC ADMINISTRATION. CONCENTRATES ON WORK IN INDIA AND BY
INDIANS, BUT TOPICS ARE WORLD-WIDE.

0138 BAKER G.E.
STATE CONSTITUTIONS - REAPPORTIONMENT.
NEW YORK: NATL MUNICIPAL LEAGUE, 1960, 70 PP.
DISCUSSES PRESENT CONSTITUTIONAL PROVISIONS ON REPRESEN-
TATION AND LEADING PROPOSALS TO CHANGE THESE PROVISIONS.
EXAMINES METHODS OF REFORM AS COURT ACTION, INITIATIVE, AND
LEGISLATIVE INTERVENTION.

0139 BAKER G.E.
THE POLITICS OF REAPPORTIONMENT IN WASHINGTON STATE.
NEW YORK: NATL MUNICIPAL LEAGUE, 1960, 19 PP., LC#61-14639.
CASE STUDY OF LEAGUE OF WOMEN VOTERS' NEARLY SUCCESSFUL
INITIATIVE TO REAPPORTION WASHINGTON STATE LEGISLATURE.
ANALYZES STRATEGIES OF PROPONENTS AND OPPONENTS AND CAUSES
OF INITIATIVE'S DEFEAT, NOTABLY LACK OF SUFFICIENT, BROAD-
SCALE POLITICAL ADVICE.

0140 BAKER G.E.
THE REAPPORTIONMENT REVOLUTION; REPRESENTATION, POLITICAL
POWER, AND THE SUPREME COURT.
NEW YORK: RANDOM HOUSE, INC, 1966, 209 PP., LC#65-13758.
STUDIES LEGISLATIVE REAPPORTIONMENT IN HISTORICAL AND
POLITICAL PERSPECTIVE. DISCUSSES AMERICAN CONCEPT OF
EQUALITY, REPRESENTATION AT BOTH STATE AND NATIONAL LEVELS,
AND EFFECT OF URBANIZATION FOR RURAL-URBAN CONFLICT.
DESCRIBES COURT DECISIONS OF 1962-64, EMPHASIZING BAKER V.
CARR DECISION. CONSIDERS ONE MAN, ONE VOTE PRINCIPLE.
BELIEVES THAT REAPPORTIONMENT HAS IMPROVED REPRESENTATION.

0141 BAKER H.R.
"INMATE SELF-GOVERNMENT."
J. CRIM. LAW CRIM. POLICE SCI., 55 (MAR. 64), 39-47.
URGES A NEW LOOK AT THE MODERN COUNTERPART OF SELF-
GOVERNMENT - THE INMATE ADVISORY COUNCIL. IT SHOULD BE
CONSIDERED AS PART OF INMATE SOCIAL LIFE, A MORALE RAISING
DEVICE, AND A TWO-WAY COMMUNICATION CHANNEL BETWEEN STAFF
AND INMATES. WRITTEN BY A LEADING FIGURE IN THE US BUREAU
OF PRISONS, NOW AT TERRE HAUTE, INDIANA.

0142 BAKER L.
BACK TO BACK: THE DUEL BETWEEN FDR AND THE SUPREME COURT.
NEW YORK: MACMILLAN, 1967, 311 PP., LC#67-21244.
DISCUSSES THE EVENTS AND PERSONALITIES SURROUNDING FDR'S
ATTEMPT TO PACK THE SUPREME COURT. EXAMINES THE PERSONAL
POLITICS THAT DEFEATED THE PRESIDENT IN THE SENATE AND
ANALYZES THE COURT'S CHANGE OF ATTITUDE AFTER FEBRUARY,
1937.

0143 BAKKE E.W., KERR C., ANROD C.W.
UNIONS, MANAGEMENT AND THE PUBLIC* READINGS AND TEXT.
NEW YORK: HARCOURT BRACE, 1967, 750 PP.
AN INTRODUCTORY TEXT, WITH EXTENSIVE SUPPORTING READINGS
FROM MANY SOURCES, IN INDUSTRIAL RELATIONS. COVERS THE PAR-
TICIPANTS IN LABOR RELATIONS, THEIR PREMISES, THE PUBLIC AND
PRIVATE EFFECTS OF LABOR RELATIONS, AND THE POLICY FRAMEWORK

NEGOTIATORS WORK IN. INCLUDES STUDY AND DISCUSSION QUESTIONS FOR THE READER. SOURCE READINGS ARE BOTH HISTORICAL, LIKE BLACKSTONE AND MARX, AND CONTEMPORARY, LIKE GOLDBERG.

0144 BALDWIN G.B.
"THE DEPENDENCE OF SCIENCE ON LAW AND GOVERNMENT--THE INTERNATIONAL GEOPHYSICAL YEAR--A CASE STUDY."
WIS. LAW REV., (JAN. 64), 78-118.
    DEMONSTRATES THE NECESSARY INTERRELATIONSHIPS BETWEEN THE LEGAL SYSTEM, GOVERNMENT, AND INTERNATIONAL SCIENTIFIC INVESTIGATIONS '... IT SHOULD BE RECOGNIZED POLICY OF SOCIETY TO ENCOURAGE INTERNATIONAL SCIENCE NOT ONLY FOR THE ENHANCEMENT OF SCIENCE, BUT FOR THE GENERAL HEALTH OF SOCIETY AS WELL.'

0145 BALDWIN L.D.
WHISKEY REBELS; THE STORY OF A FRONTIER UPRISING.
PITTSBURGH: U OF PITTSBURGH PR, 1939, 326 PP.
    DISCUSSES SETTLEMENT OF WESTERN PENNSYLVANIA BY FRONTIERSMEN AND THEIR REACTION TO WHISKEY EXCISE LAW OF 1780. NARRATES EVENTS LEADING TO WHISKEY UPRISING, DESCRIBING BATTLE OF BOWER HILL IN 1793, OTHER BATTLES, AND PEACEFUL ATTEMPTS AT SETTLING UPRISING THAT WAS BECOMING REVOLUTION AGAINST FRONTIER AUTHORITIES. STATES THAT UPRISING HELPED STRENGTHEN FEDERALISTS' POWER.

0146 BAR ASSOCIATION OF ST LOUIS
CONSTITUTIONAL FREEDOM AND THE LAW.
NEW YORK: MCGRAW HILL, 1965, 232 PP.
    COLLECTION OF LECTURES ON PROTECTION OF CIVIL RIGHTS AND ENJOYMENT OF EQUAL RIGHTS IN EDUCATION, HOUSING, EMPLOYMENT, AND PUBLIC ACCOMMODATIONS. ALSO DISCUSSES THEORETICAL ASPECT OF FREEDOM UNDER GOVERNMENT. INCLUDES SENATOR DIRKSEN'S AND SENATOR HUMPHREY'S STATEMENTS ON CIVIL RIGHTS ACT OF 1964.

0147 BARBASH J.
LABOR'S GRASS ROOTS.
NEW YORK: HARPER & ROW, 1961, 250 PP., LC#61-14839.
    FOCUSES ON INTERNAL GOVERNMENT OF LOCAL UNIONS, INCLUDING THE FUNCTION OF LOCAL UNIONS, THEIR RELATIONS TO THE INTERNATIONAL UNION, THEIR REGULATION BY COURTS AND LAW, INCLUDING UNION ASSOCIATIONAL "LAW." INTERESTING INSIGHTS ON CONFLICT, CONTROVERSY, FACTIONS, AND THE OPERATION OF DEMOCRACY WITHIN LOCAL UNIONS.

0148 BARKER L.J., BARKER T.W.
FREEDOM, COURTS, POLITICS: STUDIES IN CIVIL LIBERTIES.
LONDON: PRENTICE HALL INTL, 1965, 324 PP., LC#65-23066.
    PLACES CIVIL LIBERTY PROBLEMS, INCLUDING THEIR MORAL AS-PECTS, IN PRACTICAL POLITICAL CONTEXT IN WHICH THEY MUST BE SOLVED; THE DYNAMICS OF SUCH PROBLEMS AND SUBTLE BEHIND-THE-NEWS ASPECTS; THE ROLE OF ORGANIZED INTEREST GROUPS AND COMMUNITY ATTITUDES.

0149 BARKUN M.
"CONFLICT RESOLUTION THROUGH IMPLICIT MEDIATION."
J. OF CONFLICT RESOLUTION, 8 (JUNE 64), 121-130.
    SUGGESTS THAT SOCIETIES USING MEDIATION PROCESS OF CONFLICT RESOLUTION HAVE LEGAL SYSTEM EVEN THOUGH THEY LACK CENTRALIZED SOVEREIGN POWER. MEDIATION REQUIRES CONSENSUS AND OBEDIENCE TO BE SUCCESSFUL. MAINTAINS THAT INTERNATIONAL GOVERNMENT IS IMPROBABLE BECAUSE OF UNWILLINGNESS OF NATIONS TO BE SUBORDINATED TO CENTRAL POWER AND BECAUSE OF LACK OF CONSENSUS AND OBEDIENCE.

0150 BARLOW R.B.
CITIZENSHIP AND CONSCIENCE: STUDIES IN THEORY AND PRACTICE OF RELIGIOUS TOLERATION IN ENGLAND DURING EIGHTEENTH CENTURY
PHILA: U OF PENN PR, 1962, 348 PP., LC#62-7197.
    ARGUES AGAINST HISTORIANS' OPINION THAT QUESTION OF RELI-GIOUS TOLERATION WAS PARTIALLY SETTLED BY 1660; SHOWS THAT THEORETICAL AND CONSTITUTIONAL POSITION ON THE ISSUE WAS "BY NO MEANS" CLEAR UNTIL MUCH LATER. STUDIES NUMEROUS DISSENT-ING GROUPS. INCLUDES 40-PAGE BIBLIOGRAPHY OF 18TH-CENTURY BOOKS AND PAPERS, AS WELL AS 20TH-CENTURY SECONDARY MATERI-ALS.

0151 BARNES H.E.
"SOCIOLOGY AND POLITICAL THEORY: A CONSIDERATION OF THE SOCIOLOGICAL BASIS OF POLITICS."
NEW YORK: ALFRED KNOPF, 1924.
    INTRODUCTION TO SIGNIFICANT AND REPRESENTATIVE TYPES OF SOCIOLOGICAL DOCTRINES RELATING TO MAJOR PROBLEMS OF POL-ITICAL SCIENCE. AMPLE FOOTNOTE REFERENCES INDICATE HOW ANY SUGGESTIVE INTERPRETATION MAY BE INVESTIGATED. BRIEF SUR-VEY OF SOCIOLOGICAL THOUGHT INTERPRETED FROM TOPICAL RATHER THAN PERSONAL POINT OF VIEW. LONG BIBLIOGRAPHY LISTS IMPORTANT BOOKS ON POLITICAL AND SOCIOLOGICAL THEORY.

0152 BARRON J.A.
"ACCESS TO THE PRESS."
HARVARD LAW REV., 80 (JUNE 67), 1641-1678.
    STATES THAT 18TH-CENTURY VIEW OF FIRST AMENDMENT AS ENCOURAGEMENT TO "FULL AND FREE DISCUSSION" IN PRESS IS NO LONGER WORKING. EXAMINES NEW TECHNOLOGY OF COMMUNICATIONS INDUSTRY, WHICH LIMITS ACCESS TO MEDIA AND TYPES OF NEWS

COVERED. EXAMINES SEVERAL COURT CASES AND URGES PASSAGE OF LAW THAT WOULD GUARANTEE FREE ACCESS TO ALL MEDIA FOR ALL POINTS OF VIEW.

0153 BARTLETT J.L.
"AMERICAN BOND ISSUES IN THE EUROPEAN ECONOMIC COMMUNITY."
STANFORD LAW REV., 19 (JUNE 67), 1337-1357.
    DISCUSSES RESULTS OF VOLUNTARY INVESTMENT GUIDELINES OF 1965 THAT FORCED AMERICAN BUSINESS TO SEEK FOREIGN SOURCES OF INVESTMENT CAPITAL FOR OVERSEAS OPERATIONS IN ORDER TO IMPROVE US BALANCE OF PAYMENTS. MAINTAINS THAT EUROPEAN CAPITAL MARKETS CAN MEET DEMAND AND SUGGESTS ESTABLISHMENT OF FINANCING SUBSIDIARIES IN US OR LUXEMBOURG TO OBTAIN FAVORABLE TAX TREATMENT FOR BOND FINANCING.

0154 BATTEN T.R.
PROBLEMS OF AFRICAN DEVELOPMENT (2ND ED.)
LONDON: OXFORD U PR, 1954, 358 PP.
    SURVEY OF EMERGING AFRICA. FIRST PART DEALS WITH PROB-LEMS OF ECONOMIC DEVELOPMENT, INCLUDING NATURAL RESOURCES, AGRICULTURE, INVESTMENT; SECOND PART DEALS WITH POLITICAL DEVELOPMENT, INCLUDING HEALTH, EDUCATION, TAXATION, LOCAL GOVERNMENT, AND LAW.

0155 BATY T.
INTERNATIONAL LAW IN SOUTH AFRICA.
LONDON: STEVENS AND HAYES, 1900, 127 PP.
    LECTURES ON LEGAL MATTERS AS THEY APPLY TO SOUTH AFRICA, INCLUDING PROBLEMS OF CONTRABAND, SOVEREIGNTY, CONDUCT OF WARFARE, ANNEXATION, AND SUMMARY OF TRANSVAAL CONVENTIONS OF 1881 AND 1884.

0156 BAXTER M.G.
DANIEL WEBSTER & THE SUPREME COURT.
AMHERST: U OF MASS PRESS, 1966, 265 PP., LC#66-28116.
    EXAMINES CONTRIBUTION OF WEBSTER AS LAWYER TO DEVELOPMENT OF AMERICAN CONSTITUTIONAL SYSTEM. COMPARES HIS ARGUMENTS AT BAR WITH COURT'S OPINIONS; REVEALS MUCH ABOUT EVOLUTION OF LEGAL RULES AND CONSTITUTIONAL DOCTRINES. ORGANIZED TOPICALLY, EACH CHAPTER CONCERNS A CLASS OF WEBSTER'S CASES ON A GIVEN SUBJECT OR CONSTITUTIONAL CLAUSE.

0157 BAYITCH S.A.
A GUIDE TO INTERAMERICAN LEGAL STUDIES: A SELECTIVE BIBLIOG-RAPHY OF WORKS IN ENGLISH.
CORAL GABLES: U OF MIAMI LAW LIB, 1957, 297 PP.
    ITEMS ARRANGED BY SUBJECT AND BY COUNTRY IN TWO SEPARATE BIBLIOGRAPHIES. EXHAUSTIVE LISTING.

0158 BAYITCH S.A.
LATIN AMERICA: A BIBLIOGRAPHICAL GUIDE.
CORAL GABLES: U OF MIAMI PR, 1961.
    UNANNOTATED LISTING OF BOOKS AND ARTICLES IN ENGLISH. MAJOR EMPHASIS ON LAW.

0159 BAYLEY D.H.
VIOLENT AGITATION AND THE DEMOCRATIC PROCESS IN INDIA.
PRINCETON: PRIN U, DEPT OF POL, 1960, 385 PP.
    STUDIES PROBLEM FOR DEMOCRACY CAUSED BY VIOLENT PUBLIC PROTEST AND AGITATION IN INDIA FROM 1950-60, INCLUDING NATURE OF PROTEST, GOVERNMENT'S REACTION TO IT, AND EFFECT OF TOTAL EVENT ON POLITICAL SYSTEM.

0160 BEAL E.F., WICKERSHAM E.D.
THE PRACTICE OF COLLECTIVE BARGAINING (3RD ED.)
HOMEWOOD: RICHARD IRWIN, 1967, 809 PP., LC#67-14355.
    COVERS THEORETICAL AND PRACTICAL PROBLEMS AND TREATS PROFESSIONAL ASSOCIATIONS, MANAGEMENT ORGANIZATIONS, ACTIVITIES IN LABOR RELATIONS, ROLE OF GOVERNMENT, UNION SECURITY, AND RIGHTS OF INDIVIDUAL. PRESENTS MAJOR STATUTORY LAWS AND SPECIFIC CASE STUDIES ILLUSTRATING THE PRINCIPLES AND PRACTICE OF COLLECTIVE BARGAINING. EMPHASIZES US, BUT INCLUDES CHAPTER ON FOREIGN COUNTRIES.

0161 BEALE J.H.
A BIBLIOGRAPHY OF EARLY ENGLISH LAW BOOKS.
CAMBRIDGE: HARVARD U PR, 1926, 304 PP.
    PROVIDES A CHECKLIST OF 1,299 ITEMS: STATUTES, ABRIDG-MENTS, SESSION LAWS; DECISIONS, YEARBOOKS, REPORTS; TREAT-IES, COLLECTED EDITIONS, AND VARIOUS OTHER ITEMS IN ENGLISH AND FRENCH; WITH AN APPENDIX DESCRIBING PRINTERS AND THEIR TECHNIQUES. ALSO INCLUDES TABLES AND ILLUSTRATIONS OF FRONTISPIECES AND TITLE PAGES. ONLY HARVARD LAW SCHOOL LIBRARY WAS SEARCHED.

0162 BEANEY W.B.
"CIVIL LIBERTIES AND STATUTORY CONSTRUCTION"(BMR)"
JOURNAL OF PUBLIC LAW, 8 (SPRING 59), 67-80.
    EMPHASIZES IMPORTANCE OF SUPREME COURT IN GUARDING IN-DIVIDUAL LIBERTY AGAINST OPPRESSIVE LEGISLATION. SINCE COURT IS A N INSTITUTION OF BASICALLY NEGATIVE POWER, IT PLAYS LARGE ROLE IN LIMITING OTHER BRANCHES.

0163 BEANEY W.M.
THE RIGHT TO COUNSEL IN AMERICAN COURTS.
ANN ARBOR: U OF MICH PR, 1955, 268 PP.

SKETCHES HISTORICAL BACKGROUND OF RIGHT TO COUNSEL IN ENGLISH AND EARLY AMERICAN LAW. EXAMINES PROCESS BY WHICH SIXTH AMENDMENT COUNSEL PROVISION HAS BEEN APPLIED IN FEDERAL COURTS. SURVEYS STATE CONSTITUTIONAL AND STATUTORY PROVISIONS AND CASES IN WHICH THEY HAVE BEEN APPLIED. INCLUDES INTERPRETATION OF US SUPREME COURT OF DUE-PROCESS CLAUSE OF FOURTEENTH AMENDMENT AS LIMITATION ON PROCEDURE.

0164 BEARD C.A.
THE SUPREME COURT AND THE CONSTITUTION.
ENGLEWOOD CLIFFS: PRENTICE HALL, 1912, 127 PP.
THOSE WHO ATTACK JUDICIAL CONTROL OVER LEGISLATURE FROM VIEWPOINT OF FRAMERS OF CONSTITUTION LACK HISTORICAL EVIDENCE. REVIEWS OPINIONS OF IMPORTANT MEMBERS OF CONSTITUTIONAL CONVENTION, CONCLUDING THAT THEY WERE NOT UNAWARE OF PROBABILITY OF JUDICIAL CONTROL. FRAMERS ESTABLISHED CHECKS AND BALANCES TO PROTECT MINORITY, TO KEEP POPULAR GOVERNMENT FROM TOO MUCH CONTROL, AND TO PROTECT PROPERTY RIGHTS.

0165 BEARD C.A.
AMERICAN GOVERNMENT AND POLITICS (REV. ED.)
NEW YORK: MACMILLAN, 1944, 872 PP.
REVISED VERSION OF 1910 EDITION. TEXTBOOK OF FEDERAL, STATE, AND LOCAL GOVERNMENTAL FUNCTIONS AND ORGANIZATION. UNANNOTATED BIBLIOGRAPHIES OF REFERENCES INCLUDED AT END OF EACH OF THE TWENTY-THREE CHAPTERS.

0166 BEARDSLEY A.R.
LEGAL BIBLIOGRAPHY AND THE USE OF LAW BOOKS.
CHICAGO: FOUNDATION PRESS, INC, 1937, 514 PP.
PRACTICAL TEXT ON LEGAL RESEARCH. EMPHASIZES DETAILS OF RESEARCH: COMPLETE DECISIONS, DATES OF DECISIONS, DIGEST AND INDEX HEADINGS. CHAPTERS ON BOOKS OF REFERENCE, SEARCH FOR AUTHORITIES, LAW AND LAW BOOKS, CONSTITUTIONS AND STATUTES. BIBLIOGRAPHY INCLUDED IN APPENDIX. TEXT INCLUDES PROBLEMS FOR "LABORATORY WORK."

0167 BEASLEY K.E.
STATE SUPERVISION OF MUNICIPAL DEBT IN KANSAS - A CASE STUDY
LAWRENCE: U KANSAS, GOV RES CTR, 1961, 220 PP.
TRACES DEVELOPMENT OF REGULATION OF MUNICIPAL DEBT IN KANSAS. FOCUSES ON LEGISLATIVE JUDICIAL, AND ADMINISTRATIVE SUPERVISION. INCLUDES STATISTICAL DATA AND TABLE OF CASES.

0168 BEBR G.
JUDICIAL CONTROL OF THE EUROPEAN COMMUNITIES.
NEW YORK: PRAEGER, 1962, 268 PP.
SYSTEMATIC LEGAL CASE-STUDY ANALYSIS OF STRUCTURE AND FUNCTIONS OF COURT OF JUSTICE AS IT IS RELATED TO EUROPEAN ECONOMIC COMMUNITY, COAL AND STEEL COMMUNITY, ATOMIC ENERGY COMMUNITY, AND THE NATIONAL INSTITUTIONS OF THE SIX-MEMBER NATIONS. CITIES THE LEGAL INNOVATIONS DEVELOPED BY THE COURT TO ENFORCE THE SUPRA-NATIONAL AUTHORITY GRANTED TO THE COMMUNITY.

0169 BECHHOEFER B.G.
"UNITED NATIONS PROCEDURES IN CASE OF VIOLATIONS OF DISARMAMENT AGREEMENTS."
J. ARMS CONTR., 1 (JULY 63), 191-202.
DISCUSSES UN'S STRUCTURE AND PAST HISTORY IN ORDER TO ASSESS UN'S EFFECTIVENESS AND AVAILIBILITY IN MATTERS CONCERNING DISARMAMENT VIOLATIONS. UN MILITARY FORCE AND INTERNATIONAL COURT OF JUSTICE ARE REJECTED AS POTENTIAL ORGANS OF CONTROL. RECOMMENDS SECURITY COUNCIL AND GENERAL ASSEMBLY AS POTENTIAL VEHICLES FOR EFFECTING SANCTIONS.

0170 BECK C.
CONTEMPT OF CONGRESS: A STUDY OF THE PROSECUTIONS INITIATED BY THE COMMITTEE ON UN-AMERICAN ACTIVITIES.
NEW ORLEANS: HOUSER PRESS, 1959, 263 PP.
STUDIES CONGRESSIONAL EXERCISE OF POWER TO PROSECUTE WITNESSES FOR REFUSING TO COMPLY WITH INVESTIGATING COMMITTEE DEMANDS, FOCUSING ON THE HOUSE UN-AMERICAN ACTIVITIES COMMITTEE. AN APPENDIX TABULATES THE CONTEMPT ACTIONS FOR ALL COMMITTEES OF CONGRESS SINCE 1944.

0171 BECKER O.
MASTER RESEARCH GUIDE.
INDIANAPOLIS: BOBBS-MERRILL, 1951, 531 PP., LC#51-4258.
A DESK BOOK COLLATING ALL THE LAW TITLES, AND THE SUBJECTS INCLUDED THEREIN, OF THE MAJOR LAW DIGESTS, ENCYCLOPEDIAS, AND SIMILAR PUBLICATIONS, TOGETHER WITH OTHER PERTINENT INFORMATION. PRESENTED IN A SINGLE ALPHABETICAL SERIES.

0172 BECKER T.L.
POLITICAL BEHAVIORALISM AND MODERN JURISPRUDENCE* A WORKING THEORY AND STUDY IN JUDICIAL DECISION-MAKING.
NEW YORK: RAND MCNALLY & CO, 1964, 177 PP., LC#65-18587.
PRIMARY AIM IS TO WED THE NEW POLITICAL SCIENCE JUDICIAL BEHAVIORAL ORIENTATION TO LEGAL REALISM. REVIEWS AND ANALYZES A WIDE RANGE OF PERTINENT LITERATURE. SETS UP THEORY AND EXPERIMENTS WHICH CONFIRM THE HYPOTHESIS THAT ONCE A LEGAL PRECEDENT IS CONTROLLING IN A DISPUTE IN APPELLATE LITIGATION, IT WILL INHIBIT A SUBSTANTIVE VALUE PREFERENCE OF THE

DECISION-MAKER WHO ASSUMES THE JUDICIAL ROLE.

0173 BECKER T.L.
"POLITICAL BEHAVIORALISM AND MODERN JURISPRUDENCE."
NEW YORK: RAND MCNALLY & CO, 1964.
A STUDY IN JUDICIAL DECISION-MAKING. ATTEMPTS TO ESTABLISH A WORKING THEORY OF APPELLATE JUDICIAL OPERATION. DETAILED REVIEW OF THE LITERATURE OF POLITICAL BEHAVIORALISTS AND JURISPRUDENTS. UNANNOTATED BIBLIOGRAPHY OF BOOKS, ARTICLES, AND CASES. ARRANGED ALPHABETICALLY BY AUTHOR.

0174 BEDFORD S.
THE FACES OF JUSTICE: A TRAVELLER'S REPORT.
NEW YORK: SIMON AND SCHUSTER, 1961, 316 PP., LC#61-9595.
ANALYSIS OF JUSTICE, HUMANITY, AND INDIVIDUAL AS SEEN IN COURTS AT ALL LEVELS IN ENGLAND, GERMANY, AUSTRIA, SWITZERLAND, AND FRANCE. CASE STUDIES OF EACH NATION BASED ON ASSUMPTION THAT "JUSTICE TO INDIVIDUAL IS HEART OF EVERY CIVILIZATION."

0175 BEDI A.S.
FREEDOM OF EXPRESSION AND SECURITY: COMPARATIVE STUDY OF FUNCTIONS OF SUPREME COURTS IN UNITED STATES AND INDIA.
NEW YORK: ASIA PUBL HOUSE, 1966, 483 PP.
COMPARES STANDS TAKEN BY SUPREME COURTS IN US AND INDIA ON PROBLEM OF RECONCILING INTERESTS OF FREEDOM AND DEMANDS OF SECURITY OF ONE ANTI-SEDITION LAW ALLEGED TO VIOLATE RIGHT OF FREE SPEECH. EXAMINES COMMON HERITAGE OF ENGLISH COMMON LAW AND ITS EFFECT ON PRESENT LEGAL SYSTEMS. STUDIES METHODOLOGY OF INTERPRETATION, JUDICAL TECHNIQUES, AND APPROACHES TO PROBLEM IN TWO SUPREME COURTS.

0176 BEELEY A.L.
THE BAIL SYSTEM IN CHICAGO.
CHICAGO: U OF CHICAGO PRESS, 1966, 189 PP.
DETAILED STUDY OF LEGAL AND ADMINISTRATIVE ASPECTS OF CHICAGO'S BAIL SYSTEM, WITH EMPHASIS ON POLICY AND PROCEDURE OF CONDITIONAL RELEASE SYSTEM. ALSO INCLUDES SEPARATE STATISTICAL STUDY OF UNSENTENCED JAIL PRISONERS IN CHICAGO.

0177 BEEM H.D.
AN INTRODUCTION TO LEGAL BIBLIOGRAPHY FOT THE NON-PROFESSIONAL STUDENT.
CARBONDALE: SOUTHERN ILL U PR, 1960, 110 PP.
INTRODUCES RESEARCH METHODS FOR STUDENTS NOT IN LAW, BUT REQUIRING SOME CONTACT WITH MATERIALS OF FIELD. DISCUSSES BASIC LEGAL THEORY, STATUTE INTERPRETATION, MAJOR REFERENCE BOOKS, OTHER FORMS OF REFERENCE MATERIALS, AND CITATION FORMS. DISCUSSES 50 IMPORTANT REFERENCE WORKS.

0178 BEER U.
FRUCHTBARKEITSREGELUNG ALS KONSEQUENZ VERANTWORTLICHER ELTERNSCHAFT.
TUBINGEN: KATZMANN VERLAG, 1966, 168 PP.
EXAMINES QUESTION OF STERILIZATION OF MALE AS EFFECTIVE BIRTH CONTROL MEASURE. DISCUSSES POPULATION INCREASE, LEGAL SITUATION IN GERMANY, CATHOLIC AND PROTESTANT POSITION, AND PRACTICES IN OTHER COUNTRIES.

0179 BEGGS D.W. ED., MCQUIGG R.B. ED.
AMERICA'S SCHOOLS AND CHURCHES: PARTNERS IN CONFLICT.
BLOOMINGTON: INDIANA U PR, 1965, 241 PP., LC#65-12279.
ESSAYS COMPASS HIGHLIGHTS OF LEGAL AND HISTORICAL BACKGROUND OF CURRENT CHURCH-STATE-SCHOOL ISSUES. OFFER DIFFERING VIEWPOINTS AND SOME PRACTICAL SUGGESTIONS: SOME LAUD DECISION UPHOLDING SEPARATION OF CHURCH AND STATE, OTHERS FEAR WEAKENING OF RELIGION, WHILE STILL OTHERS DEBATE WHETHER IT IS POSSIBLE TO TEACH ABOUT RELIGION WITHOUT FALLING INTO TRAP OF SECTARIAN PREJUDICE.

0180 BEISEL A.R.
CONTROL OVER ILLEGAL ENFORCEMENT OF THE CRIMINAL LAW: ROLE OF THE SUPREME COURT.
BOSTON: BOSTON U PR, 1955, 112 PP., LC#55-9910.
STUDY OF PROBLEMS ARISING WHEN ILLEGAL METHODS ARE USED BY POLICE TO ENFORCE CRIMINAL LAW AND ROLE OF SUPREME COURT IN DEALING WITH AND CONTROLLING THESE OCCURRENCES. CONSIDERS STANDARDS OF LEGALITY FOR SEARCHES AND SEIZURES, WIRE TAPPING, INVASIONS OF PRIVACY AND OTHER PREVALENT EXAMPLES OF ABUSE OF GOVERNMENTAL POWER BY POLICE. STRESSES NECESSITY OF LAWS TO PROTECT INDIVIDUAL PRIVACY.

0181 BEISER E.N.
THE TREATMENT OF LEGISLATIVE APPORTIONMENT BY THE STATE AND FEDERAL COURTS (DISSERTATION)
PRINCETON: PRIN U, DEPT OF POL, 1966, 300 PP.
COMPARATIVE ANALYSIS OF JUDICIAL PROCESS, STUDYING COURTS AND APPORTIONMENT, IMPACT OF SUPREME COURT RULING, AND DECISIONS OF STATE AND FEDERAL COURTS IN TEST CASES.

0182 BELL D.
"THE RACKET RIDDEN LONGSHOREMEN" (BMR)"
DISSENT, 6 (FALL 59), 417-429.
DISCUSSES RACKETEERING IN WATERFRONT WORKERS ON NEW YORK CITY AND ITS EFFECT ON LABOR UNIONS, COMMERCE, AND INDIVIDUAL WORKERS. PROPOSES THAT CRIME IS FUNCTIONAL IN MANY

RESPECTS, SIGNIFICANTLY IN THAT IT ESTABLISHED ORDER WHERE
NONE HAS PREVIOUSLY EXISTED.

0183 BELL J.
THE JOHNSON TREATMENT: HOW LYNDON JOHNSON TOOK OVER THE
PRESIDENCY AND MADE IT HIS OWN.
NEW YORK: HARPER & ROW, 1965, 305 PP., LC#64-25107.
   DETAILED ACCOUNT OF HOW "LBJ PICKED UP REINS OF
GOVERNMENT AND IN A YEAR PLACED HIS STAMP ON
ADMINISTRATION." THROUGH INTERVIEWS ANALYZES RELATIONS
WITH CONGRESS, DEPARTMENTS, OTHER NATIONS, AND ACTIONS
IN WORLD CRISES, CONSIDERING EFFECTS OF LBJ'S PERSONALITY.

0184 BEMIS S.F., GRIFFIN G.G.
GUIDE TO THE DIPLOMATIC HISTORY OF THE UNITED STATES, 1775-
1921.
NEW YORK: HOLT RINEHART WINSTON, 1935, 979 PP., LC#35-26001.
   AN EXTREMELY COMPLETE BIBLIOGRAPHIC GUIDE TO PRINTED
MATERIALS AND MANUSCRIPT SOURCES. DIVIDED INTO TWO MAIN
PARTS: PART 1, BIBLIOGRAPHY, LISTING 5,318 ANNOTATED ITEMS;
PART 2, REMARKS ON THE SOURCES, INCLUDING MANUSCRIPT
SOURCES. INDEXES OF COLLECTIONS OF PERSONAL PAPERS AND
AUTHORS.

0185 BEMIS S.F.
THE LATIN AMERICAN POLICY OF THE UNITED STATES: AN
HISTORICAL INTERPRETATION.
NEW YORK: HARCOURT BRACE, 1943, 470 PP.
   EXAMINES US POLICY IN LATIN AMERICA AS INFLUENCED BY
BELIEF IN SOVEREIGNTY OF NATIONS. BEGINS WITH TERRITORIAL
PROBLEMS OF NORTH AMERICA IN 1776. STUDIES MONROE DOCTRINE,
MANIFEST DESTINY, DOLLAR DIPLOMACY, WOODROW WILSON AND
MEXICO, DOCTRINE OF NONINTERVENTION, GOOD NEIGHBOR POLICY,
AND DIPLOMATIC RELATIONS THROUGH 1942. MAINTAINS THAT US
POLICY IS BASED ON INTERESTS OF NATIONAL SECURITY.

0186 BENES E.
INTERNATIONAL SECURITY.
CHICAGO: U. CHI. PR., 1939, 153 PP.
   DISCUSSES SECURITY ASPECTS OF NEGOTIATION OF TREATIES OF
MUTUAL ASSISTANCE. EXAMINES POLICY CONSISTENCIES AND INCON-
SISTENCIES OF GREAT POWERS. STRESSES ARBITRATION, DISARMA-
MENT AND SECURITY. APPRAISES ROLES OF ENGLAND AND GERMANY IN
POST-WORLD WAR ONE EUROPEAN DIPLOMACY.

0187 BENNETT G., ROSBERG C.G.
THE KENYATTA ELECTION: KENYA 1960-1961.
LONDON: OXFORD U PR, 1961, 230 PP.
   ANALYSIS OF AFRICAN POLITICS IN CASE OF KENYA ELECTIONS
OF 1960-61. EXAMINES LEGAL STRUCTURE, POLITICAL PARTIES,
CAMPAIGN, CANDIDATES, AND RESULTS OF ELECTION.

0188 BENNETT H.A.
THE COMMISSION AND THE COMMON LAW: A STUDY IN
ADMINISTRATIVE ADJUDICATION.
NEW YORK: EXPOSITION PRESS, 1964, 127 PP., LC#64-25097.
   A STUDY OF PROBLEMS IN ADMINISTRATIVE ADJUDICATION,
CARRIED ON THROUGH STUDYING ICC DECISIONS ON FREIGHT
FORWARDING. IS PARTICULARLY CONCERNED WITH UNNECESSARY
DEPARTURES FROM PRINCIPLES OF COMMON LAW. CONCLUDES THAT
ICC RECORD IS ONE OF "EXPEDIENCY AND MANIPULATION," THAT
CORRECT DECISIONS HAVE OFTEN BEEN INCORRECTLY REACHED, AND
THAT ICC ERRORS HAVE HAD TO BE - AND ARE - REDRESSED.

0189 BENTHAM A.
HANDBOOK OF POLITICAL FALLACIES.
BALTIMORE: JOHNS HOPKINS PR., 1952, 269 PP.
   PRESENTS A HANDBOOK ON THE ART OF VERBAL WARFARE IN
POLITICS. INTENDED FOR THE LOGICAL DISSECTION OF LEGISLATIVE
DEBATES AND A POSSIBLE WEAPON FOR PARLIAMENTARY REFORM. CON-
CENTRATION OF THE USE OF LOGIC IN THE SEEMINGLY AMBIGUOUS
VERBAL GAME OF POLITICS.

0190 BENTHAM J.
AN INTRODUCTION TO THE PRINCIPLES OF MORALS AND
LEGISLATION.
LONDON: CLARENDON PR., 1907, 378 PP.
   THEORY OF PLEASURE/PAIN AND UTILITY ANALYZING EFFICACY OF
JURISPRUDENCE.

0191 BENTHAM J., EVERETT C.W. ED.
A COMMENT OF THE COMMENTARIES (1765-69)
LONDON: OXFORD U PR, 1928, 253 PP.
   CRITICISM OF BLACKSTONE'S "THE NATURE OF LAWS IN GENERAL"
AND "OF THE LAWS OF ENGLAND" IN THE "COMMENTARIES." ATTEMPTS
TO SHOW THAT BLACKSTONE'S PHILOSOPHICAL IDEAS ARE VAGUE AND
THAT HIS SATISFACTION WITH EXISTING CONDITIONS RESULTS FROM
PERSONAL AND PROFESSIONAL PREJUDICES RATHER THAN RATIONAL
JUDGMENTS. OBJECTS TO UNWRITTEN LAW AS WILL OF JUDGES.
BELIEVES RIGHT AND WRONG ARE MEASURED BY HAPPINESS OF MOST.

0192 BENTHAM J.
THE RATIONALE OF PUNISHMENT.
ORIGINAL PUBLISHER NOT AVAILABLE, 1830, 439 PP.
   STATES THAT PUNISHMENT IS A NECESSARY EVIL IN RESPONSE
TO CRIME. DISCUSSES ITS USE AND ABUSE BY GOVERNMENTS, ASKING

FOR LEGISLATIVE CONTROL OF IT AND WARNING THAT ABUSES MAY
LEAD TO LOSS OF EFFECTIVENESS. CALLS FOR REFORMS IN JURIDI-
CAL SYSTEM OF ENGLAND, WHICH HE CALIMS IS OFTEN UNNECESSARI-
LY AND CAPRICIOUSLY HARSH. DISCUSSES NATURE AND TYPES OF
PUNISHMENT THEN IN USE.

0193 BENTHAM J.
"ON THE LIBERTY OF THE PRESS, AND PUBLIC DISCUSSION" IN J.
BOWRING, ED., THE WORKS OF JEREMY BENTHAM."
ORIGINAL PUBLISHER NOT AVAILABLE, 1843.
   SERIES OF FOUR LETTERS INTENDED FOR PUBLICATION IN SPAIN,
PROTESTING RESTRICTIONS ON THE PRESS AND A PROPOSED LAW
ABOLISHING THE RIGHT TO HOLD POLITICAL MEETINGS. MAINTAINS
THAT IT IS DESPOTISM TO ABOLISH THESE INDIVIDUAL LIBERTIES
FOR ANY REASON. ALSO ATTACKS THE CORTES, SPANISH LEGISLATIVE
BODY, BECAUSE IT IS AN ARISTOCRATIC BODY AND REPRESENTS ITS
OWN INTERESTS RATHER THAN THOSE OF THE PEOPLE.

0194 BENTHAM J.
"PRINCIPLES OF INTERNATIONAL LAW" IN J. BOWRING, ED., THE
WORKS OF JEREMY BENTHAM."
ORIGINAL PUBLISHER NOT AVAILABLE, 1843.
   FOUR ESSAYS CONSIDERING OBJECTS OF INTERNATIONAL LAW,
JURISDICTION, WAR, AND PEACE. AUTHOR BELIEVES THAT OBJECTS
OF INTERNATIONAL LAW INCLUDE DOING NO INJURY TO OTHER
NATIONS AND DOING GREATEST POSSIBLE GOOD TO OTHER NATIONS,
WHILE PROTECTING WELFARE OF ONE'S OWN NATION. CONSIDERS
POTENTIAL AND ACTUAL JURISDICTION, AND RIGHTFUL OR MORAL
JURISDICTION. DISCUSSES CAUSES OF WAR AND PLAN FOR PEACE.

0195 BENTHAM J.
"THE RATIONALE OF REWARD" IN J. BOWRING, ED., THE WORKS OF
JEREMY BENTHAM (VOL. 2)"
ORIGINAL PUBLISHER NOT AVAILABLE, 1843.
   DISCUSSES SOURCES OF REWARD, SUCH AS POWER, MONEY, AND
HONOR, AND CONSIDERS ADVANTAGES OF COMBINING USE OF POWER
AND REWARD. SUGGESTS ESTABLISHMENT OF LAWS THAT WILL BE
"SELF-EXECUTING" IN THAT INTEREST WILL BE COMBINED WITH
DUTY. BELIEVES REWARD SHOULD BE USED FRUGALLY AND AS AN
INSTRUMENT OF POWER. DISCUSSES SYSTEM OF REMUNERATION:
SALARIES, AND REWARD TO ENCOURAGE PRODUCTION.

0196 BENTHAM J.
THE THEORY OF LEGISLATION.
ORIGINAL PUBLISHER NOT AVAILABLE, 1876, 472 PP.
   SEEKS TO DETERMINE PRINCIPLES OF LEGISLATION; DEFENDS
PRINCIPLE OF UTILITY AS THAT WHICH BRINGS PLEASURE AND
AVOIDS PAIN. EXAMINES PRINCIPLES OF THE CIVIL CODE, ITS
MOTIVES, AND SOURCES OF LAW IN RIGHTS AND OBLIGATIONS;
DISCUSSES FAULTS AND CURES OF PENAL CODE. LEGISLATION
SHOULD MAKE POSSIBLE "GREATEST HAPPINESS OF GREATEST NUMBER"
AND PUNISHMENT SHOULD BE AVOIDED EXCEPT FOR GREATER GOOD.

0197 BENTHAM J.
DEFENCE OF USURY (1787)
ORIGINAL PUBLISHER NOT AVAILABLE, 1788, 232 PP.
   DENOUNCES PROHIBITORY USURY LAWS CONTROLLING RATE OF
INTEREST ON LENDING MONEY; FEELS THAT IT BENEFITS PUBLIC TO
HAVE UNLIMITED RATES. DISCIPLE OF ADAM SMITH INSISTS ON
EXTREME LOGICAL APPLICATION OF PRINCIPLES AND ARGUES AGAINST
SMITH'S APPROVAL OF FIVE-PER-CENT LIMITATION. ARGUES THAT
LOANS ON SECURITY WOULD HELP TECHNOLOGICAL PROGRESS EVEN IF
PROJECTS FAILED.

0198 BENTHAM J., MONTAGUE F.C. ED.
A FRAGMENT ON GOVERNMENT (1776)
LONDON: OXFORD U PR, 1891, 241 PP.
   REFUTATION OF SECOND PART OF BLACKSTONE'S INTRODUCTION TO
HIS "COMMENTARIES," CONCERNING NATURE OF LAW IN GENERAL.
PRIMARILY CONCERNS NATURE OF SOVEREIGNTY. BELIEVES THAT
SOVEREIGNTY REPRESENTS UNLIMITED AUTHORITY OVER PEOPLE, AND
THAT IT IS NOT SUBJECT TO LAW. RESISTANCE TO SOVEREIGN MAY
BE MORAL WHEN IT IS A QUESTION OF UTILITY, I.E., PRESERVING
HAPPINESS OF GREATEST NUMBER OF PEOPLE.

0200 BENTLEY A.F.
INQUIRY INTO INQUIRIES: ESSAYS IN SOCIAL THEORY.
BOSTON: BEACON PRESS, 1954, 365 PP., LC#54-6165.
   EXAMINES BASIC PROBLEMS IN NATURAL AND SOCIAL SCI-
ENCES, AND IN THE THEORY OF KNOWING AND THE KNOWN. CONTAINS
ESSAYS BY BENTLEY, 1910-54. THEME IS THAT REAL BASIS OF
GOVERNMENT IS FOUND WITHIN LEGISLATIVE-ADMINISTRATIVE-
ADJUDICATIVE ACTIVITIES OF NATION AND CURRENTS OF ACTIVITY
THAT GATHER AMONG PEOPLE WITHIN THESE SPHERES.

0201 BENTON W.E. ED.,
NUREMBERG: GERMAN VIEWS OF THE WAR TRIALS.
DALLAS: SOUTHERN METHODIST U PR, 1955, 232 PP., LC#55-5739.
   ESSAYS BY GERMAN PROFESSORS AND LAWYERS EXPRESSING LEARN-
ED OPINIONS ON COURSE AND RESULTS OF TRIALS, MANY IN DEFENSE
OF VERDICT. ALL ESSAYS WERE WRITTEN WITHIN A FEW YEARS AFTER
TRIALS AND SEEM TO CONFESS GERMAN GUILT.

0202 BERKELEY G., FRASER A.C. ED.
"DISCOURSE ON PASSIVE OBEDIENCE" (1712) THE WORKS... (VOL.
IV)"

LONDON: CLARENDON PRESS, 1901.
ESSAY ON MAN'S NECESSARY SUBMISSION TO THE PENALTIES
ASSIGNED BY CIVIL AUTHORITY FOR TRANSGRESSION OF ITS LAWS.
ARGUES THAT SINCE MAN IS INCAPABLE OF CALCULATING THE FULL
CONSEQUENCES OF HIS EVERY ACTION, HE MUST CONFORM TO UNI-
VERSAL RULES. BASED ON THE SUPPOSITION THAT CIVIL LAW IS A
REFLECTION OF DIVINE LAW, LOYALTY TO AUTHORITY IS SEEN AS
A MORAL DUTY AND REBELLION A SIN AGAINST GOD'S ETERNAL LAWS.

0203 BERKOWITZ M. ED., BOCK P.G. ED.
AMERICAN NATIONAL SECURITY: A READER IN THEORY AND POLICY.
NEW YORK: FREE PRESS OF GLENCOE, 1965, 448 PP., LC#64-23085.
DEALS WITH PROTECTION AND DEVELOPMENT OF UNITED STATES
NATIONAL INTERESTS (INTRODUCTION SUBSTITUTES "NATIONAL
SECURITY" AS MORE ACCURATE TERM). BIBLIOGRAPHY OF
APPROXIMATELY 650 ENGLISH BOOKS, DOCUMENTARY COLLECTIONS,
AND ARTICLES IS ARRANGED ALPHABETICALLY BY AUTHOR UNDER
GENERAL TOPICS FROM 1941 THROUGH 1962.

0204 BERKS R.N.
"THE US AND WEAPONS CONTROL."
CURRENT HIST., 47 (AUG. 64), 65-116.
EIGHT ARTICLES EXPLORING UNITED STATES VIEWS ON WEAPONS
CONTROL, DISARMAMENT, AND ALTERNATE PATHS TOWARD PEACE AND
MILITARY SECURITY.

0205 BERLE A.A. JR.
ECONOMIC POWER AND FREE SOCIETY (PAMPHLET)
NEW YORK: FUND FOR THE REPUBLIC, 1957, 20 PP.
BECAUSE OF WIDESPREAD OWNERSHIP OF STOCK, THE CORPORATE
HOLDING OF PROPERTY HAS BEEN SPLIT INTO MANAGING AND
CREATIVE FUNCTION AND PASSIVE RECEPTIVE FUNCTION. TREATS OF
HISTORICAL LIMITS ON CORPORATION, THE THEORETICAL DEMOCRACY
IN CORPORATIONS, AUTONOMY OF DIRECTORS, AND CHANGING
CONCEPTS OF POSSESSORY PRIVATE PROPERTY. MENTIONS POSSIBLE
CONSTITUTIONAL ARGUMENTS TO RESTRICT CORPORATION POWERS.

0206 BERMAN D.M.
A BILL BECOMES A LAW: THE CIVIL RIGHTS ACT OF 1960.
NEW YORK: MACMILLAN, 1962, 143 PP., LC#62-14953.
DESCRIPTION OF WAY BILL BECOMES LAW IN US, DISCUSSING
1960 CIVIL RIGHTS ACT BECAUSE OF ALL DEVICES UTILIZED TO
GET IT PASSED AND/OR TO STOP IT. DISCUSSES CONSERVATIVE BIAS
IN CONGRESS AND INCLUDES FULL TEXT OF ACT.

0207 BERMAN H.J.
JUSTICE IN RUSSIA; AN INTERPRETATION OF SOVIET LAW.
CAMBRIDGE: HARVARD U PR, 1950, 322 PP.
EXAMINES SOVIET LEGAL SYSTEM IN TERMS OF ASSUMPTIONS OF
SOVIET SOCIAL ORDER. MAINTAINS THAT SYSTEM DOES NOT DEPEND
SOLELY ON TERROR BUT HAS DEFINITE LEGAL PRINCIPLES AS WELL.
STUDIES SOCIALIST AND RUSSIAN LAW AND THEIR DEVELOPMENT AND
RELATIONSHIP. LOOKS AT LAWS' PARENTAL FUNCTIONS AS THEY
AFFECT EDUCATION, FAMILY LIFE, DISPUTES, LABOR, AND
PSYCHIATRY.

0208 BERMAN H.J.
"THE DILEMMA OF SOVIET LAW REFORM."
HARVARD LAW REV., 76 (MARCH 63), 929-51.
DESCRIBES THE CONFLICT BETWEEN RATIONAL AND HUMANE
REFORMS OF THE LAST DECADE AND THE ROLE OF SOVIET LAW AS A
MEANS TO ACHIEVE ENDS DETERMINED BY A PARTY HIERARCHY NOT
ITSELF SUBJECT TO LEGAL CONTROLS.

0209 BERNARD M.
FOUR LECTURES ON SUBJECTS CONNECTED WITH DIPLOMACY.
LONDON: MACMILLAN, 1868, 205 PP.
MAINTAINS THAT OBSERVANCE OF TREATIES IS MATTER OF MORAL
OBLIGATION WHICH IS RECOGNIZED IN THE SYSTEM OF POSITIVE
RULES DESIGNATED INTERNATIONAL LAW BUT IS NOT ASSISTED BY
IT. RECOMMENDS AUTHORITY ANALOGOUS TO LEGISLATORS AND JUDGES
TO EXERCISE CONTROL OVER CONTRACTS BETWEEN NATIONS.

0210 BERNHARD R.C.
"COMPETITION IN LAW AND ECONOMICS."
ANTI-TRUST BULLETIN, 7 (WINTER 67), 1099-1165.
EXAMINES NOTION OF COMPETITION IN ECONOMIC AND LEGAL
THEORY AND DECISION-MAKING, COMPARING DIFFERENCES AND SIMI-
LARITIES IN ITS USE. DISCUSSES EFFECT OF AMBIGUITY ON VIEWS
HELD BY COURTS, AND LEGAL AND POLICY RESULTS OF LACK OF
CONCISENESS IN TERMS DEFINING COMPETITION.

0211 BERNS W.
FREEDOM, VIRTUE AND THE FIRST AMENDMENT.
BATON ROUGE: LOUISIANA ST U PR, 1957, 264 PP., LC#57-11545.
QUESTIONS WHETHER THE LAW CAN REASONABLY LOOK UPON THE
FREEDOMS OF THE FIRST AMENDMENT AS RIGHTS; SEES FREEDOM IN
A LARGER CONTEXT THAN IS USUALLY DONE; ARGUES THAT JURISTS
MUST DISCARD LIBERAL THEORY OF LAW IN ORDER TO UNDERSTAND
PARTICULAR PROBLEMS RAISED IN PARTICULAR CASES.

0212 BERNS W.
FREEDOM, VIRTUE, AND THE FIRST AMENDMENT.
BATON ROUGE: LOUISIANA ST U PR, 1957, 264 PP., LC#57-11545.
AUTHOR RECOGNIZES FREEDOM AS MAJOR JUDICIAL AND LEGAL
PROBLEM. HE EXPLORES TENSION OF FREEDOM, ESPECIALLY FREEDOMS
OF FIRST AMENDMENT, AND LIBERAL LEGAL INTERPRETATIONS.
INDIVIDUAL CASES AND SUPREME COURT DECISIONS ARE CRITICALLY
DISCUSSED WITH REFERENCE TO FIRST AMENDMENT.

0213 BERNSTEIN H.
A BOOKSHELF ON BRAZIL.
ALBANY: U ST OF NY, ST EDUC DEPT, 1964, 23 PP.
ANNOTATED BIBLIOGRAPHY ON BRAZIL. COVERS THE SOCIAL
SCIENCES AND HUMANITIES; INCLUDES SECTIONS ON PERIODICLAS
AND BIBLIOGRAPHIES.

0214 BERNSTEIN M.H.
REGULATING BUSINESS BY INDEPENDENT COMMISSION.
PRINCETON: PRINCETON U PRESS, 1955, 306 PP., LC#55-5001.
CRITICALLY EVALUATES SEVEN INDEPENDENT REGULATORY
COMMISSIONS. EXAMINES ENVIRONMENT IN WHICH THEY DEVELOPED
AND THEIR OBJECTIVES. ANALYZES RISE AND DECLINE OF
COMMISSIONS AND APPRAISES COMMISSIONS' FUNCTIONS. FOCUSES ON
RELATIONSHIP OF COMMISSIONS TO PRESIDENT AND CONGRESS AND
OUTLINES PROBLEMS FACING COMMISSIONS IN DEVELOPING PUBLIC
SUPPORT FOR THEIR PROGRAMS.

0215 BERNSTEIN S.
ALTERNATIVES TO VIOLENCE: ALIENATED YOUTH AND RIOTS, RACE
AND POVERTY.
NEW YORK: ASSOCIATION PRESS, 1967, 192 PP., LC#67-14579.
INTERPRETS RIOTS IN MAJOR US CITIES, INCORPORATING RE-
SULTS OF INTERVIEWS WITH POLICE, EDUCATION, HEALTH, AND SO-
CIAL-WORK OFFICIALS. EXAMINES TYPES OF RIOTS, RIOT BEHAVIOR
AND TARGETS, YOUTH PARTICIPATION, ADULT INFLUENCE, AGENCY
ROLES, RACE AND NATIONALITY FACTORS. CONSIDERS YOUTH REAC-
TION AND INVOLVEMENT IN CIVIL RIGHTS ACTION AND ANTI-POVERTY
PROGRAMS. ANALYZES STRATEGIES FOR CHANGE.

0216 BERRODIN E.F.
"AT THE BARGAINING TABLE."
NATIONAL CIVIC REV., 56 (JULY 67), 392-397.
EXAMINES 1965 MICHIGAN LAW GIVING PUBLIC EMPLOYEES RIGHT
TO BARGAIN AND TO STRIKE. COMPARES IT WITH LAWS IN OTHER
STATES AND DESCRIBES REACTIONS OF EMPLOYERS TO IT. PROVIDES
SUGGESTIONS FOR MORE EFFECTIVE COLLECTIVE BARGAINING.

0217 BERTHOLD O.
KAISER, VOLK UND AVIGNON.
MUNICH: RUTTEN & LOENING VERLAG, 1960, 392 PP.
DOCUMENTARY ANALYSIS OF RELATIONSHIP BETWEEN PAPACY AND
EMPEROR IN 14TH-CENTURY GERMANY. EXAMINES POLICIES OF POPE
JOHN XXII AND EFFORTS OF LUDWIG THE BAVARIAN TO ESTABLISH
IMPERIAL POWER INDEPENDENT OF ROME.

0218 BERWANGER E.H.
WESTERN ANTI-NEGRO SENTIMENT AND LAWS 1846-60: A FACTOR IN
THE SLAVERY EXTENSION CONTROVERSY (PAPER)
CHAMPAIGN: U OF ILLINOIS, UNPUBL, 1964, 310 PP.
FOCUSES ON RACIAL ANTIPATHY TOWARD NEGRO AND ITS INFLU-
ENCE IN PREVENTING THE EXTENSION OF SLAVERY THROUGHOUT THE
COUNTRY. MAKES USE OF RECORDS OF CONSTITUTIONAL DEBATES,
LEGISLATIVE LAWS AND REPORTS, AND NEWSPAPER
CORRESPONDENCE AND EDITORIALS.

0219 BESTERMAN T.
A WORLD BIBLIOGRAPHY OF BIBLIOGRAPHIES (4TH ED.)
LAUSANNE: SOCIETAS BIBLIOGRAPH, 1966, 8425 PP.
AN ANNOTATED BIBLIOGRAPHY ARRANGED ALPHABETICALLY BY
SUBJECT. UNDER EACH HEADING THE ORDER OF ENTRIES IS ARRANGED
CHRONOLOGICALLY BY DATE OF PUBLICATION. SPECIAL POINTS CLAR-
IFIED IN TEXT BY CROSS-REFERENCES TO HEADINGS. FIRST EDITION
CARRIED SYSTEMATICALLY FROM 1470 TO 1935: THE FOURTH EDITION
IS CARRIED THROUGH 1963, WITH MANY LATER ENTRIES. ESTIMATES
ITEMS COVERED IN PUBLICATIONS LISTED. AUTHOR INDEX INCLUDED.

0220 BETH L.P.
"THE CASE FOR JUDICIAL PROTECTION OF CIVIL LIBERTIES" (BMR)"
J. OF POLITICS, 17 (FEB. 55), 100-112.
DISCUSSES SUPREME COURT'S ABDICATION OF SOCIAL AND
ECONOMIC POLICY TO LEGISLATIVE MAJORITIES, AND HOW IT HAS
HANDICAPPED RETENTION OF DECISIVE JUDICIAL CONTROL IN
FIELD OF CIVIL LIBERTY.

0221 BEVAN W., ALBERT R.S. ET AL.
"JURY BEHAVIOR AS A FUNCTION OF THE PRESTIGE OF THE FOREMAN
AND THE NATURE OF HIS LEADERSHIP" (BMR)"
JOURNAL OF PUBLIC LAW, 7 (1958), 419-449.
DESCRIBES RESULTS OF TWO EXPERIMENTS ON BEHAVIOR OF
JURIES CONDUCTED BY TEAM OF PSYCHOLOGISTS AND A LAWYER.
CHIEF INQUIRY IS ON EXTENT TO WHICH PERSONALITY OF FOREMAN
INFLUENCED DECISIONS OF INDIVIDUAL JURY MEMBERS.

0222 BEVANS C.I.
"GHANA AND UNITED STATES - UNITED KINGDOM AGREEMENTS."
AMER. J. INT. LAW, 59 (JAN. 65), 93-97.
'IN PRACTICE USA GOVERNMENT ENDEAVORS TO NEGOTIATE NEW
AGREEMENTS, AS APPROPRIATE, WITH A NEWLY INDEPENDENT STATE
AS SOON AS POSSIBLE - IN INTERIM, ARRIVES AT MUTUAL
UNDERSTANDING WITH THE NEW STATE SPECIFYING WHICH BILATERAL
AGREEMENTS BETWEEN USA AND FORMER PARENT STATE SHALL BE

CONSIDERED AS CONTINUING TO APPLY.'

0223 BEVERIDGE W.
THE PRICE OF PEACE.
NEW YORK: NORTON, 1945, 160 PP.
IMPUTES FORGING OF WAR TO INTERNATIONAL ANARCHY. RELATION OF WW I TO WW 2 AND CAUSES OF BOTH ARE EXAMINED. ANALYZES FAILURES OF VERSAILLES TREATY AND LEAGUE OF NATIONS. PRICE OF PEACE IS ACCEPTANCE AND ENFORCEMENT OF IMPARTIAL ARBITRATION IN ALL DISPUTES BETWEEN NATIONS. APPENDIX INCLUDES TEXTS OF PERTINENT CHARTERS, TREATIES SUCH AS FOURTEEN POINTS, CRIMEA CONFERENCE ET AL.

0224 BIBBY J., DAVIDSON R.
ON CAPITOL HILL.
NEW YORK: HOLT RINEHART WINSTON, 1967, 280 PP., LC#67-11299.
NINE CASE STUDIES OF US GOVERNMENT COMMITTEE WORK AND POLICY-MAKING PRESENT UNIQUE FACTORS FROM WHICH AN ATTEMPT IS MADE TO DESCRIBE PATTERNS OF BEHAVIOR IN THE POLITICAL SYSTEM. IDENTIFIES RELEVANT VARIABLES. CONSCIOUSLY COMBINES METHODS OF QUANTIFICATION AND QUALIFICATION. BIBLIOGRAPHY ON BILLS, LAWS, PARTY POLITICS, INTEREST GROUPS, COMMITTEES, CAMPAIGNS AND ELECTIONS.

0225 BIBLIOTHEQUE PALAIS DE LA PAIX
CATALOGUE OF THE PEACE PALACE LIBRARY, SUPPLEMENT 1937-1952 (7 VOLS.)
GENEVA: LEAGUE OF NATIONS, 1962.
SUPPLEMENTARY LISTING OF MATERIALS IN PEACE PALACE LIBRARY CONTAINED IN SEVEN VOLUMES. LISTS BIBLIOGRAPHIES, PERIODICALS, SERIAL WORKS, AND OTHER WORKS IN CHRONOLOGI- CAL ORDER. LIBRARY IS DEVOTED TO INTERNATIONAL LAW: PRIVATE, PUBLIC, AND COMMERCIAL.

0226 BICKEL A.
THE LEAST DANGEROUS BRANCH.
INDIANAPOLIS: BOBBS-MERRILL, 1962, 303 PP., LC#62-20685.
DISCUSSES THE FUNCTIONS OF THE US SUPREME COURT. RELATES THE PRACTICE OF JUDICIAL REVIEW FROM ITS CONCEPTION TO THE PRESENT DAY. CONCERNED WITH THE BASES AND LEGALITY OF VARI- OUS FUNCTIONS OF THE SUPREME COURT. ANALYZES COURT'S DECI- SIONS IN SEGREGATION, FREEDOM OF PRESS AND SPEECH, DRED SCOTT CASE, AND BIRTH-CONTROL CASES.

0227 BIDDLE F.
THE FEAR OF FREEDOM.
GARDEN CITY: DOUBLEDAY, 1951, 263 PP.
DISCUSSION OF CONTEMPORARY OBSESSION OF ANXIETY AND FEAR IN US; ITS HISTORICAL BACKGROUND AND PRESENT EXPRESSION; AND ITS EFFECT ON NATIONAL SECURITY AND ON FREE AMERICAN INSTITUTIONS.

0228 BIERZANECK R.
"LA NON-RECONAISSANCE ET LE DROIT INTERNATIONAL CONTEMPORAIN."
ANNU. FRANC. DR. INTER., 8 (1962), 117-37.
SURVEYS PATTERNS OF DIPLOMACY IN INTERNATIONAL RELATIONS. STUDIES INTERNATIONAL LAW AND NON-RECOGNITION OF NATIONS. EXAMINES ESTABLISHMENT AND SEVERING OF DIPLOMATIC RELATIONS. RELATES INTERNATIONAL LAW TO NATIONAL SECURITY PROBLEMS.

0229 BINANI G.D., RAMA RAO T.V.
INDIA AT A GLANCE (REV. ED.)
BOMBAY: ORIENT LONGMANS, 1954, 1756 PP.
A COMPREHENSIVE REFERENCE MANUAL ON INDIA THAT PROVIDES A CLASSIFIED SYSTEM OF INFORMATION ON 25 TOPICS OF GENERAL AND SPECIALIZED INTEREST. COORDINATES INFORMATION ON THE NATIONAL GOVERNMENT, FOREIGN POLICY, NATIONAL ECONOMY, COMMUNICATIONS, INDUSTRIAL FINANCE, PRODUCTION TRENDS, THE JUDICIAL SYSTEM, ETC. INCLUDES A GENERAL INDEX AND DETAILED TABLE OF CONTENTS.

0230 BIRD F.L., RYAN F.M.
THE RECALL OF PUBLIC OFFICERS; A STUDY OF THE OPERATION OF RECALL IN CALIFORNIA.
LONDON: MACMILLAN, 1930, 403 PP.
EXPLORES MANNER OF RECALL PROCEDURE IN CALIFORNIA AND EXTENT OF ITS USE. EXAMINES CAUSES OF RECALL MOVEMENTS AND WAYS IN WHICH ELECTORATES RESPOND TO POLITICAL EMERGENCIES EVOKED BY RECALL CAMPAIGNS. STUDIES ADOPTION OF LAW AND CONTENT OF LAW. COMPARES PROCESS IN SMALL, MEDIUM, AND LARGE CITIES AND IN STATE AND COUNTIES.

0231 BIRDSALL P.
VERSAILLES TWENTY YEARS AFTER.
LONDON: ALLEN & UNWIN, 1941, 350 PP.
ANALYSIS OF DIPLOMATIC FORCES WHICH SHAPED THE TREATY: PERSONAL AND POLITICAL FORCES PULLING BETWEEN WILSONIAN PRINCIPLES OF A NEW WORLD ORDER AND PRINCIPLES OF REACTION- ARY NATIONALISM. BIBLIOGRAPHY: 50 LISTINGS OF RECORDS AND PUBLISHED WORKS IN ENGLISH LISTED ALPHABETICALLY BY AUTHOR; 1920-38 PUBLICATIONS.

0232 BISHOP H.M. ED., HENDEL S. ED.
BASIC ISSUES OF AMERICAN DEMOCRACY.
NEW YORK: APPLETON, 1948, 323 PP.

READINGS ON A VARIETY OF TOPICS INCLUDING DEMOCRACY IN A CHANGING WORLD, CONSTITUTIONAL PRINCIPLES, POLITICAL POWER, AND FOREIGN POLICY. FIFTY-TWO SELECTIONS. BIBLIOGRAPHY OF 50 ENTRIES, IN ENGLISH, BOOKS AND ARTICLES, LISTED ALPHABETI- CALLY BY AUTHOR.

0233 BISHOP W.W. JR.
INTERNATIONAL LAW: CASES AND MATERIALS.
BOSTON: LITTLE BROWN, 1962, 964 PP., LC#61-10755.
COMPARES INTERNATIONAL LAW TO COMMON LAW. TREATS MAKING, EFFECT, INTERPRETATION, AND TERMINATION OF TREATIES, AND CONSIDERS LEGAL CONCEPTS NECESSARY TO INTERNATIONAL LAW. FOCUSES ON PROBLEMS INVOLVING STATE RESPONSIBILITY TO ALIENS AND RESULTANT CLAIMS, AND ON PROBLEMS OF WAR AND USE OF FORCE.

0234 BISSAINTHE M.
DICTIONNAIRE DE BIBLIOGRAPHIE HAITIENNE.
WASH D.C.: SCARECROW PRESS, 1951, 1052 PP., LC# 51-12164
EXTENSIVE BIBLIOGRAPHY OF BOOKS AND PAMPHLETS PUBLISHED IN HAITI OR ABROAD BY HAITIANS 1804-1949. LISTS JOURNALISTS WITH A KEY TO THEIR NEWSPAPERS. INCLUDES LIST OF PERIODICALS PUBLISHED BETWEEN 1764-1949. ITEMS IN ENGLISH, SPANISH, AND FRENCH ARRANGED ALPHABETICALLY BY AUTHOR, INCLUDING SUBJECT AND TITLE INDEXES.

0235 BLACHLY F.F., OATMAN M.E.
"THE GOVERNMENT AND ADMINISTRATION OF GERMANY."
BALTIMORE: JOHNS HOPKINS PRESS, 1920.
FIRST OF SERIES OF VOLUMES PUBLISHED BY THE INSTITUTE FOR GOVERNMENT RESEARCH CONCERNING ADMINISTRATIVE SYSTEMS OF CHIEF EUROPEAN NATIONS. EMPHASIS ON ADMINISTRATIVE AND GOV- ERNMENTAL SYSTEMS. UNDERLYING SOCIAL AND POLITICAL PHILOS- OPHY, CONSTITUTIONAL STRUCTURE, AND POLITICAL ACTION. COVERS CENTRAL GOVERNMENT AS WELL AS SUBORDINATE UNITS. EXTENSIVE, PARTIALLY ANNOTATED, BIBLIOGRAPHY.

0236 BLACK C.L. JR.
THE OCCASIONS OF JUSTICE: ESSAYS MOSTLY ON LAW.
NEW YORK: MACMILLAN, 1963, 213 PP., LC#63-11762.
ESSAYS BY JUSTICE BLACK CONCERNED WITH MANY ASPECTS OF THE LAW. INCLUDES VIEWS ON LAW IN COURTS; FREEDOM THROUGH LAW; EQUALITY UNDER LAW; CIVIL RIGHTS IN THE US; AND MATTERS OUTSIDE THE LEGAL CIRCLE.

0237 BLACK H.
"THE BILL OF RIGHTS" (BMR)"
NYU LAW REV., 35 (APR. 60), 865-881.
DISCUSSES BILL OF RIGHTS AS IT BEARS ON POWERS OF FEDERAL GOVERNMENT. DEALS SPECIFICALLY WITH THOSE CLAUSES WHICH SAFEGUARD RIGHT OF HABEAS CORPUS, FORBID BILLS OF ATTAINDER AND EX POST FACTO LAWS, GUARANTEE TRIAL BY JURY, AND DEFINE TREASON AND LIMIT WAY IT CAN BE TRIED AND PUNISHED. EXAMINES EACH AMENDMENT AND MAINTAINS THAT THEY INCLUDE ABSOLUTE GUARANTEES OF INDIVIDUAL RIGHTS.

0238 BLACKSTONE W.
COMMENTARIES ON THE LAWS OF ENGLAND (4 VOLS.) (4TH ED.)
LONDON: OXFORD U PR, 1770, 1896 PP.
COMMENTS ON NATURE AND EXTENT OF ENGLISH LAW. EXAMINES LAWS DEFINING RIGHTS OF PERSONS, RULERS, AND GROUPS, SUCH AS KING, CABINET, CLERGY, AND SERVANTS. DISCUSSES RIGHTS OF PROPERTY AND INHERITANCE. STUDIES COURT SYSTEM AND SETTLEMENT OF DISPUTES AND "PRIVATE WRONGS." EXPLORES LAWS RELATING TO PUBLIC WRONGS AND CRIMES, AND SYSTEMS OF PUNISHMENTS.

0239 BLAISDELL D.C.
"INTERNATIONAL ORGANIZATION."
NEW YORK: RONALD PRESS, 1966.
SELECTED BIBLIOGRAPHY OF BOOKS, PERIODICALS, DOCUMENTS, AND JOURNALS DEALING WITH ORGANIZATION OF THE NATION- STATES, PARTICULARLY THE UN AND ITS SPECIALIZED AGENCIES. SOURCES CATEGORIZED BY INDIVIDUAL CHAPTER. APPROXIMATELY 275 ENTRIES.

0240 BLAKEY G.R.
"ORGANIZED CRIME IN THE UNITED STATES."
CURRENT HISTORY, 52 (JUNE 67), 327-333.
TRACING THE DEVELOPMENT OF ORGANIZED CRIME FROM THE REVO- LUTIONARY PERIOD OF US HISTORY TO THE PRESENT, BLAKEY REVIEWS THE "FAMILY" STRUCTURE OF ORGANIZED CRIME AND ITS SUCCESSFUL OPERATION WITHIN A POLITICALLY DEMOCRATIC GOVERNMENTAL SYSTEM.

0241 BLANCHARD L.R.
MARTINIQUE: A SELECTED LIST OF REFERENCES (PAMPHLET)
WASHINGTON: LIBRARY OF CONGRESS, 1942, 57 PP.
SOME 250 MANUSCRIPTS, BIBLIOGRAPHIES, ALMANACS, MAPS, CHARTS, PERIODICALS, NEWSPAPER ARTICLES, AND BOOKS ARRANGED TOPICALLY WITH CONCLUDING SUBJECT INDEX. ITEMS ARE ALL AN- NOTATED AND FROM 1890-1942 WITH EMPHASIS ON POST-1923 PUBLICATIONS. SOME ARE IN ENGLISH, BUT MANY IN FRENCH. SOME US GOVERNMENT DOCUMENTS.

0242 BLANSHARD P.

GOD AND MAN IN WASHINGTON.
BOSTON: BEACON PRESS, 1960, 250 PP., LC#60-05815.
     DESCRIBES INTERACTION OF POLITICS AND RELIGION IN US NA-
TIONAL GOVERNMENT, AND ITS EFFECTS ON SUPREME COURT, CON-
GRESS, AND PRESIDENCY. STUDIES DEEP INFLUENCE OF RELIGION ON
POLICY AND PUBLIC OPINION, AND POSSIBILITY OF PLURALISM IN
SUCH A SOCIETY.

0244 BLAUSTEIN A.P.
MANUAL ON FOREIGN LEGAL PERIODICALS AND THEIR INDEX.
NEW YORK: OCEANA PUBLISHING, 1962, 137 PP., LC#62-11757.
     GUIDE TO 253 PERIODICALS LISTED IN "INDEX TO FOREIGN LE-
GAL PERIODICALS" DURING ITS FIRST YEAR OF PUBLICATION. PRO-
VIDES DATA ON TOPICS COVERED BY PERIODICALS AND LANGUAGES
IN WHICH PUBLISHED. ALSO INCLUDES BIBLIOGRAPHICAL DATA ON
TITLES LISTED.

0245 BLITZ L.F.
THE POLITICS AND ADMINISTRATION OF NIGERIAN GOVERNMENT.
NEW YORK: FREDERICK PRAEGER, 1965, 281 PP., LC#65-25824.
     INTRODUCTORY DISCUSSIONS OF NIGERIAN GOVERNMENT WHICH
PROVIDE DESCRIPTION OF HISTORICAL BACKGROUND OF NIGERIAN
NATION AND MAJOR GOVERNMENT INSTITUTIONS. DISCUSSES VARIOUS
LEVELS OF GOVERNMENT, POLITICAL PARTIES, COURT SYSTEMS, AND
FOREIGN RELATIONS. INTENDED AS INTRODUCTORY WORK FOR
NIGERIAN STUDENTS.

0246 BLOCH J.
STATES' RIGHTS: THE LAW OF THE LAND.
ATLANTA: HARRISON CO, 1958.
     TRACES HISTORY OF STATES' RIGHTS FROM COLONIAL PERIOD TO
PRESENT DAY SHOWING IMPORTANCE OF CONCEPT OF DUAL GOVERNMENT
AND DANGERS INHERENT IN TODAY'S SUBVERSION OF BASIC CONSTI-
TUTIONAL RIGHTS OF STATES BY SUPREME COURT RULINGS.

0247 BLOCK E.B.
THE VINDICATORS.
NEW YORK: POCKET BOOKS, 1963, 272 PP., LC#63-18203.
     STORIES OF PERSONS UNJUSTLY ACCUSED OF CRIMES, AND OF
COURAGEOUS POLICE OFFICERS, LAWYERS, AND CRIMINOLOGISTS
WHO SET THEM FREE.

0248 BLODGETT R.H.
"COMPARATIVE ECONOMIC SYSTEMS (REV. ED.)"
NEW YORK: MACMILLAN, 1949.
     TEXTBOOK TO STUDY OF COMPARATIVE ECONOMIC SYSTEMS
ORGANIZED BY ECONOMIC TOPIC: ECONOMIC PRINCIPLES; INSTITU-
TIONS; GOVERNMENT; DECISION-MAKING; ORGANIZATION OF PRODUC-
TION; AGRICULTURE, MARKETING; PRICE CONTROL; LABOR; INTER-
NATIONAL TRADE; PUBLIC FINANCE. LENGTHY DISCUSSION OF
MARXIAN SOCIALISM. SHORT BIBLIOGRAPHY.

0249 BLOOM G.F., NORTHRUP H.R.
ECONOMICS OF LABOR RELATIONS.
HOMEWOOD: RICHARD IRWIN, 1955, 784 PP.
     SURVEY OF DEVELOPMENT OF LABOR UNIONS, THEIR RELATIONS
WITH GOVERNMENT, KEY LABOR PROBLEMS IN CAPITALISTIC ECONOMY,
AND CONFLICTING VIEWS CONCERNING SOLUTIONS. COVERS ALL
POSSIBLE ASPECTS OF LABOR MOVEMENT ARRANGED FOR CLASSROOM
STUDY AND DISCUSSION. ANALYZES TAFT-HARTLEY ACT IN DETAIL.

0250 BLOOMFIELD L.M.
EGYPT, ISRAEL AND THE GULF OF AQABA: IN INTERNATIONAL LAW.
TORONTO: CARSWELL, 1957, 240 PP.
     CITES HISTORICAL, GEOGRAPHICAL AND LEGAL BACKGROUND OF
ARAB-ISRAELI DISPUTE OVER TRAVEL RIGHTS. LIST RESOLUTIONS
AND CITES SPECIFIC SETTLEMENTS AND ACTS OF AGGRESSION RE-
SULTING FROM BORDER DISPUTES, AND RELATES INVOLVEMENT OF
OTHER NATIONAL AND INTERNATIONAL ORGANIZATIONS IN ISSUES.

0251 BLOUSTEIN E.J. ED.
NUCLEAR ENERGY, PUBLIC POLICY, AND THE LAW.
NEW YORK: OCEANA PUBLISHING, 1964, 113 PP., LC#64-22787.
     CONSIDERS PROBLEMS OF NUCLEAR POWER FOR PEACEFUL USAGE:
HOW TO CAUSE LEAST RESENTMENT IN ESTABLISHING IT, ROLE OF
GOVERNMENT IN PROMOTING IT, SAFETY MEASURES, AND ECONOMIC
AND MORAL RESPONSIBILITY FOR ITS USE.

0252 BLUMBERG A.S.
"THE PRACTICE OF LAW AS CONFIDENCE GAME; ORGANIZATIONAL
COOPTATION OF A PROFESSION."
LAW AND SOCIETY REVIEW, 1 (JUNE 67), 15-39.
     DISCUSSES IMPACT OF THREE RECENT LANDMARK DECISIONS OF
US SUPREME COURT AFFECTING FUTURE OF CRIMINAL LAW
ADMINISTRATION AND ENFORCEMENT. QUESTIONS COMPATIBILITY OF
COURT'S CONCEPTION OF ROLE OF COUNSEL WITH SOCIAL REALITY.
ASSERTS THAT COURT DECISIONS OVERLOOK FORMAL ORGANIZATION OF
COURTS, RELATION BETWEEN LAWYER AND COURT, AND RELATION
BETWEEN LAWYER AND CLIENT.

0253 BLUMSTEIN A.
"POLICE TECHNOLOGY."
SCIENCE AND TECHNOLOGY, (DEC. 67), 42-50.
     DESCRIBES SUGGESTIONS MADE BY PRESIDENT'S COMMISSION ON
LAW ENFORCEMENT AND ADMINISTRATION OF JUSTICE'S TASK FORCE
ON SCIENCE AND TECHNOLOGY ON MODERNIZATION OF POLICE

TECHNOLOGY. PRESENTS EACH NEW DEVICE'S CONTRIBUTION TO
APPREHENSION OF CRIMINALS IN ORDER TO ENABLE INDIVIDUAL
FORCES TO CHOOSE METHOD THEY NEED MOST. URGES REVISION OF
CRIMINAL JUSTICE SYSTEM. ADVOCATES USE OF COMPUTERS.

0254 BOCHENSKI J.M., NIEMEYER G.
HANDBOOK ON COMMUNISM.
NEW YORK: FREDERICK PRAEGER, 1962, 686 PP., LC#62-17483.
     DISCUSSIONS OF MAIN ASPECTS OF COMMUNISM AND OF PAST 40
YEARS OF SOVIET POLICY AND PRACTICE. TOPICS ARE GENERAL AND
DISCUSSIONS STRESS BASIC CONCEPTS WHILE PROVIDING COMPLETE
HISTORICAL BACKGROUND OF EACH TOPIC. EMPHASIS IS ON PRINCI-
PLES AND POLICIES BASED ON THEM. INTENDED AS GUIDE FOR AVER-
AGE READER.

0255 BOCK E. ED.
GOVERNMENT REGULATION OF BUSINESS.
ENGLEWOOD CLIFFS: PRENTICE HALL, 1965, 448 PP., LC#65-16944.
     SEVEN CASE STUDIES DESCRIBE EVENTS AND FORCES AT WORK
WHEN GOVERNMENTAL AGENCIES INITIATE REGULATORY ACTIONS
IN BUSINESS. ANALYZES STRATEGY OF ONE OF THE MAJOR
PARTICIPANTS INVOLVED IN EACH OF THE CASES.

0256 BOCK E.A. ED., CAMPBELL A.K. ED.
CASE STUDIES IN AMERICAN GOVERNMENT.
ENGLEWOOD CLIFFS: PRENTICE HALL, 1962, 368 PP., LC#62-12624.
     COLLECTION OF CASE STUDIES TO BE USED AS TEXTBOOK SUPPLE-
MENT IN UNDERGRADUATE CLASSES IN POLITICAL SCIENCE. MAIN
TOPIC HEADINGS INCLUDE: CONSTITUTION, COURTS AND CIVIL
RIGHTS, POLITICS, LEGISLATIVE PROCESS, PRESIDENCY, GOVERN-
MENT, SCIENCE, AND THE ECONOMY. BOOK IS PART OF INTER-UNI-
VERSITY CASE PROGRAM.

0257 BOGEN J.I. ED., SHIPMAN S.S. ED.
FINANCIAL HANDBOOK (4TH ED.)
NEW YORK: RONALD PRESS, 1964, 1500 PP.
     HANDBOOK OF LEADING PRINCIPLES AND PRACTICES IN FIELD OF
FINANCE. EMPHASIZES EFFECTS OF CHANGES IN TAXATION, REGULA-
TIONS, AND LAW, BUT COVERS ALL ASPECTS OF FINANCE.

0258 BOHANNAN P., HUCKLEBERRY K.
"INSTITUTIONS OF DIVORCE, FAMILY, AND THE LAW."
LAW AND SOCIETY REVIEW, 1 (JUNE 67), 81-102.
     SEES FAMILY AS "BACK-UP INSTITUTION" THAT TAKES OVER
FUNCTIONS OTHER INSTITUTIONS FAIL TO PROVIDE. EXPLORES
EFFECT ON LEGAL INSTITUTIONS OF FAILURE OF SOCIETY TO
ACCEPT DIVORCE AS "BACKUP" FOR FAMILY AND TO INTEGRATE IT
INTO SOCIAL STRUCTURE. STUDIES COMPLETE SYSTEM FOR RECEIVING
AID IN FAMILY PROBLEMS AND FOR OBTAINING DIVORCES.

0259 BOHANNAN P. ED.
LAW AND WARFARE.
GARDEN CITY: NATURAL HISTORY PR, 1967, 441 PP., LC#67-10386.
     EXAMINES RESOLUTION OF CONFLICT FROM ANTHROPOLOGICAL
POINT OF VIEW. DISCUSSES TWO FORMS OF RESOLUTION: FIGHTING
AND ADMINISTERING OF RULES. EXPLORES NATURE OF LEGAL
PHENOMENA, INSTITUTIONS AND MEANS OF PEACEFUL SETTLEMENTS,
AND TYPES OF WARS AND VIOLENCE. COMPARES ETHNIC GROUPS'
JUDICIAL PROCESSES AND WARFARE.

0260 BOHATTA H., HODES F.
INTERNATIONALE BIBLIOGRAPHIE.
FRANKFURT: V KLOSTERMANN, 1950, 652 PP.
     A BIBLIOGRAPHY OF BIBLIOGRAPHIES LISTING NATIONAL AND
INTERNATIONAL BIBLIOGRAPHICAL PUBLICATIONS ON CULTURAL AS
WELL AS EXACT SCIENCES. INCLUDES BIBLIOGRAPHIES ON NEWS-
PAPERS, PRINTING, BOOK TRADE, ETC. IT IS ARRANGED BY SUBJECT
AND COUNTRY AND PURPORTS TO LIST ALL BIBLIOGRAPHIES PUB-
LISHED, EXCLUDING ONLY BIBLIOGRAPHIES OF PERSONS.

0261 BOHMER A., JAROSLAV J. ET AL.
LEGAL SOURCES AND BIBLIOGRAPHY OF CZECHOSLOVAKIA.
NEW YORK: FREDERICK PRAEGER, 1959, 180 PP., LC#58-9696.
     MATERIALS ARRANGED BY TYPE OF SOURCE, WITH MOST EMPHASIS
DISARMAMENT - THE DECADE UNDER KHRUSHCHEV, 1954-1964." THIS
COLLECTIONS OF LAWS, PARLIAMENTARY RECORDS, COURT REPORTS,
AND DEPARTMENTAL BULLETINS. MOST ITEMS ARE NOT IN ENGLISH.
SUBJECT INDEX IS PROVIDED.

0262 BOHN L.
"WHOSE NUCLEAR TEST: NON-PHYSICAL INSPECTION AND TEST BAN."
J. CONFL. RESOLUT., 7 (SEPT. 63), 379-393.
     SPECULATES ON ADVANTAGES OFFERED BY CONCEALED NUCLEAR-
TESTING WITH REGARD TO WEAPONS DEVELOPMENT AND THE
N-TH NATION PROBLEM. INABILITY OF PHYSICAL METHODS TO DETECT
MID-OCEAN OR SPACE EXPLOSIONS HAS NECESSITATED EMPLOYMENT
OF NON-PHYSICAL TECHNIQUES ANALOGOUS TO CRIMINAL INVESTIGAT-
ION AND COURT SYSTEMS.

0263 BOLES D.E.
THE TWO SWORDS.
AMES: IOWA STATE U PR, 1967, 407 PP., LC#67-12132.
     PRESENTS THE MOST IMPORTANT US SUPREME COURT AND STATE
COURT CASES INVOLVING THE CHURCH-STATE-SCHOOL ISSUE.
FOLLOWING A BRIEF HISTORICAL SKETCH, SALIENT PARTS OF EACH
DECISION ARE PRESENTED FROM COURT RECORDS, FOLLOWED BY

SUBSEQUENT PUBLIC REACTION IN NEWSPAPERS AND JOURNALS. OB-
JECTIVE ANALYSIS.

0264 BOLGAR V.
"THE PUBLIC INTEREST: A JURISPRUDENTIAL AND COMPARATIVE
OVERVIEW OF SYMPOSIUM ON FUNDAMENTAL CONCEPTS OF PUBLIC LAW"
JOURNAL OF PUBLIC LAW, 12 (JAN. 63), 13-52.
     SURVEYS THEORIES THAT ARE SOURCES OF DELIMITATION OF
PRIVATE RIGHTS FROM PUBLIC INTERESTS AND DEMONSTRATES
EVOLUTION OF CONCEPT OF PUBLIC INTEREST. COMPARES ISSUES
INVOLVING LEGAL REGULATION, ESPECIALLY THOSE IN FIELD OF
ADMINISTRATIVE CONTRACTS, IN FRANCE, SWITZERLAND, GERMANY,
AND COMMUNIST COUNTRIES.

0265 BONGER W.A.
CRIMINALITY AND ECONOMIC CONDITIONS.
NEW YORK: AGATHON PRESS, 1967, 706 PP., LC#67-20715.
     PUBLISHED ORIGINALLY IN 1916, EXAMINES EUROPEAN
SCHOOL OF THOUGHT ON CRIME AT THE BEGINNING OF MODERN
CRIMINAL SCIENCE. BELIEVES SOCIAL CONDITIONS TO BE MAJOR
CAUSE OF CRIME. ATTACKS CURRENT ECONOMIC SYSTEM OF LABOR
EXPLOITATION AND ADVOCATES PENOLOGICAL REFORM FOR BETTER
TREATMENT OF PRISONERS AND REDUCTION OF CAPITAL CRIMES.

0266 BORCHARD E.H., STUMBERG G.W.
GUIDE TO THE LAW AND LEGAL LITERATURE OF FRANCE.
WASHINGTON: LIBRARY OF CONGRESS, 1931, 242 PP., LC#30-26002.
     BIBLIOGRAPHICAL ESSAY AND GUIDE DESIGNED TO FURNISH
PRACTICAL INFORMATION ON THE LEGAL INSTITUTIONS OF FRANCE;
METHODS BY WHICH IT HAS SOLVED ECONOMIC AND SOCIAL PROBLEMS
FACING IT IN AN INDUSTRIAL AGE; LEGAL METHOD, DOCTRINE, AND
PHILOSOPHY OF SCIENTIFIC INVESTIGATION UNDERLYING CONSTITU-
TIONAL INSTITUTIONS.

0267 BORCHARD E.M.
BIBLIOGRAPHY OF INTERNATIONAL LAW AND CONTINENTAL LAW.
WASHINGTON: LIBRARY OF CONGRESS, 1913, 93 PP.
     DISCUSSES VARIOUS BOOKS DEALING WITH INTERNATIONAL AND
CONTINENTAL LAW. INCLUDES AN INTRODUCTION AND SECTIONS
DEVOTED TO SPECIFIC COUNTRIES, GENERAL AREAS SUCH AS
COMMERCIAL LAW, PUBLIC LAW (CONSTITUTIONAL, COLONIAL, AND
ADMINISTRATIVE), CRIMINAL LAW, CANON LAW. CONTAINS AN
INDEX, COMMENTS ON EACH WORK, FOOTNOTES, ETC.

0268 BORGATTA E.F. ED., FANSHEL D. ED., MEYER H.J. ED.
SOCIAL WORKERS' PERCEPTIONS OF CLIENTS.
NEW YORK: RUSSELL SAGE FDN, 1960, 92 PP., LC#60-10275.
     EXAMINES CHARACTERISTICS OF CASEWORK CLIENTS AS PERCEIVED
BY CASEWORKERS OF LARGE SOCIAL AGENCY. DISCUSSES THREE
CLIENT GROUPS: FEMALE CLIENTS, UNWED MOTHERS, AND MALE
CLIENTS. STUDIES PEOPLE WHO NEED HELP, WHAT CASEWORKERS
DO, AND WHAT IS ACCOMPLISHED.

0269 BORGESE G. ED.
COMMON CAUSE.
NEW YORK: COMM. FRAME WORLD CONST., 1947-51, 4 VOLS.
     REPORT PUBLISHED TO CLARIFY THE ISSUES SURROUNDING THE
QUESTION OF WORLD GOVERNMENT BY CONTRIBUTORS FROM THE
SPECIALIZED-STUDY FIELDS OF PSYCHOLOGY, SOCIOLOGY,
ECONOMICS, POLITICS AND PHILOSOPHY.

0270 BORGESE G.A.
GOLIATH: THE MARCH OF FASCISM.
NEW YORK: VIKING PRESS, 1937, 483 PP.
     DESCRIBES ORIGINS AND RISE OF FASCISM IN EUROPE, FOCUSING
ON ITALY. TRACES ITALIAN ROOTS BACK TO DANTE, MYTHS OF ROME,
AND MACHIAVELLI. DISCUSSES EARLY CAREER OF MUSSOLINI AND
HIS SUBSEQUENT ROLE IN FASCIST RISE. EXAMINES FASCIST
POLICIES TOWARD CHURCH, POLITICAL PARTIES, AND LAW. FEELS
EXPANSION OF ITALY IS DANGEROUS AND IMPLORES WORLD TO ACT
DECISIVELY.

0271 BORKIN J.
THE CORRUPT JUDGE.
NEW YORK: CLARKSON N POTTER, 1962, 310 PP., LC#62-19290.
     AN INQUIRY INTO BRIBERY AND OTHER SERIOUS CRIMES IN THE
FEDERAL COURTS. EXAMINES SEVERAL CASES IN WHICH JUDGES HAVE
BEEN ACCUSED OF CORRUPTION, AMONG THEM MARTIN MANTON, WARREN
DAVIS, AND ALBERT JOHNSON.

0272 BOTERO G.
THE REASON OF STATE AND THE GREATNESS OF CITIES.
LONDON: ROUTLEDGE & KEGAN PAUL, 1956, 298 PP.
     IN ENGLISH TRANSLATION OF TWO SEPARATE WORKS, BOTERO
SHOWS HIMSELF AS A REPRESENTATIVE POLITICAL THINKER OF
COUNTER-REFORMATION. HIS OWN PREFACE STATES THAT THE WORK
IS A REACTION AGAINST MACHIAVELLIANISM, AN ATTEMPT TO
RESTORE ETHICS AND CONSCIENCE TO THEIR RIGHTFUL PLACE IN
SCIENCES OF POLITICS, THOUGH HE RECOMMENDS, FOR EXAMPLE,
OBSERVANCE OF TREATIES ON GROUNDS OF EXPEDIENCY.

0273 BOULTON D.
OBJECTION OVERRULED.
LONDON: MACGIBBON AND KEE, LTD, 1967, 319 PP.
     STORY OF 16,000 MEN WHO REFUSED TO FIGHT FOR BRITAIN IN
WWI BECAUSE OF RELIGION, BELIEF IN SOCIALISM, OR BOTH.

TREATS POLITICAL TRADITION OF SOCIALSIM THAT PRODUCED THEIR
OBJECTION TO WAR AND EVENTS THAT LED TO THEIR CONSCRIPTION.
WITH NUMEROUS DIRECT QUOTATIONS FROM MEN, DESCRIBES THEIR
RESISTANCE TO CONSCRIPTION, TYPES OF SERVICE OBJECTED TO,
AND PUNISHMENTS.

0274 BOUVIER-AJAM M.
MANUEL TECHNIQUE ET PRATIQUE DU MAIRE ET DES ELUS ET AGENTS
COMMUNAUX.
PARIS: EDITIONS SOCIALES, 1964, 254 PP.
     GENERAL TEXT ON MUNICIPAL ORGANIZATION IN FRANCE, DUTIES
OF ELECTED OFFICIALS, AND MEANS FOR CARRYING OUT DUTIES.
RETRACES HISTORY OF "COMMUNAL" MOVEMENT IN FRANCE, SITUATES
"COMMUNE" IN ITS SOCIAL, JUDICIAL, AND POLITICAL FRAMEWORK,
DISCUSSES LAWS CONCERNING ELECTED OFFICIALS, ETC. INCLUDES
BIBLIOGRAPHY OF APPROXIMATELY 100 ITEMS LISTED BY SUBJECT.

0275 BOVY L.
LE MOUVEMENT SYNDICAL OUEST AFRICAIN D'EXPRESSION FRANCAISE.
BRUSSELS: CEN DOC ECO ET SOC AFR, 1965, 113 PP.
     ANNOTATED BIBLIOGRAPHY OF 518 BOOKS AND ARTICLES PUB-
LISHED IN WESTERN LANGUAGES (PRIMARILY FRENCH) SINCE 1943.
ANNOTATIONS PROVIDE COMPLETE BIBLIOGRAPHICAL INFORMATION
PLUS A CRITICAL AND DESCRIPTIVE SUMMARY. COVERS HISTORICAL,
JUDICIAL, IDEOLOGICAL, ECONOMIC, SOCIAL, AND RELIGIOUS AS-
PECTS OF THE ISSUE. ARRANGED IN ONE COMPREHENSIVE ALPHABET-
ICAL LISTING.

0276 BOWETT D.W.
SELF-DEFENSE IN INTERNATIONAL LAW.
MANCHESTER: U. PR., 1958, 294 PP.
     APPLYING LEGAL STANDARDS, AUTHOR ANALYZES THE RIGHT OF
SELF-DEFENSE, PAYING PARTICULAR ATTENTION TO THE PROVISIONS
AND EXPERIENCES UNDER THE U.N. CHARTER. DICHOTOMIZES WORK
INTO TWO TECHNICAL CATEGORIES: THE SUBSTANTIVE RIGHTS FOR
WHICH SELF-DEFENSE IS A PERMISSIBLE MEANS OF PROTECTION AND
THE ANTITHESIS OF THE RIGHTS OF SELF-DEFENSE AND 'JUST WAR'.

0277 BOWETT D.W.
THE LAW OF INTERNATIONAL INSTITUTIONS.
NEW YORK: PRAEGER, 1965, 347 PP.
     PRESENTS A DETAILED DESCRIPTION OF INTERNATIONAL INSTI-
TUTIONS ARISING IN THE WAKE OF TWO WORLD WARS. BESIDES OUT-
LINING INSTITUTIONAL STRUCTURES, E.G. THE UNITED NATIONS OR
THE WARSAW TREATY ORGANIZATION, FOCUSES ATTENTION ON GENERAL
PROBLEMS OF INTERNATIONAL ORGANIZATIONS.

0278 BOWETT D.W.
UNITED NATIONS FORCES* A LEGAL STUDY.
NEW YORK: FREDERICK PRAEGER, 1964, 579 PP., LC#64-22489.
     HISTORY OF INTERNATIONAL PEACE-KEEPING EXPORTS, ESPECIAL-
LY UN EFFORTS IN KOREA, SUEZ AND THE CONGO. LEGAL, ADMINIS-
TRATIVE AND FINANCIAL PROBLEMS OF SUCH EFFORTS ARE ANALYZED
SUGGESTIONS FOR RELATING THIS EFFORT TO GENERAL DISARMAMENT
AND THE OUTLINE FOR A PERMANENT UN MILITARY STAFF ARE MADE.
EXTENSIVE UN DOCUMENTATION.

0279 BOWIE R.R. ED., FRIEDRICH C.J. ED.
"STUDIES IN FEDERALISM."
BOSTON: LITTLE BROWN, 1954.
     REPRODUCTION OF STUDIES BY EUROPEAN FEDERAL MOVEMENT ON
THE FEDERAL LEGISLATURE, EXECUTIVE, JUDICIARY, DEFENSE,
FOREIGN AFFAIRS QUESTIONS. CONTAINS ALSO CONTRIBUTIONS IN
FIELDS OF COMMERCE, TRANSPORTATION, AND CUSTOMS, PUBLIC
FINANCE, AGRICULTURE, LABOR AND SOCIAL SECURITY, CITIZENSHIP
RIGHTS, APPENDEXES CONTAINING DRAFT RESOLUTIONS AND TREA-
TIES OF EUROPEAN COMMUNITY. EXTENSIVE BIBLIOGRAPHY.

0280 BOWIE R.R., ROSTOW E.V., BORK R.H.
GOVERNMENT REGULATION OF BUSINESS: CASES FROM THE NATIONAL
REPORTER SYSTEM.
BROOKLYN: FOUNDATION PRESS, 1963, 1770 PP.
     COLLECTION OF COURT CASES FROM 1897-1963 OF US SUPREME
COURT AND FEDERAL COURTS ON GOVERNMENT REGULATION OF
BUSINESS PROCEDURES. INCLUDES CASES INVOLVING ORDERS OF
FEDERAL TRADE COMMISSION, MONOPOLY AND ANTITRUST LAWS,
AND FAIR LABOR STANDARDS ACT.

0281 BOYD A.M., RIPS R.E.
UNITED STATES GOVERNMENT PUBLICATIONS (3RD ED.)
NEW YORK: H W WILSON, 1949, 627 PP.
     EXTENSIVE, COMPREHENSIVE, AND WELL-INDEXED GUIDE TO US
GOVERNMENT PUBLICATIONS WITH DETAILED ANNOTATION AND INTRO-
DUCTORY MATERIAL DEALING WITH THE NATURE, HISTORY, PRINTING,
DISTRIBUTION, AND AVAILABILITY OF VARIOUS GOVERNMENT PUBLI-
CATIONS. LISTED BY AGENCY WITH APPENDIXES, INDEXES, AND A
KEY TO CHARTS, ILLUSTRATIVE MATERIALS, ETC.

0282 BOYD W.J.
PATTERNS OF APPORTIONMENT (PAMPHLET)
NEW YORK: NATL MUNICIPAL LEAGUE, 1962, 24 PP.
     DISCUSSES MAJOR APPORTIONMENT PLANS SUCH AS THE FEDERAL
SYSTEM, AND LOWER AND UPPER HOUSE PLANS BASED ON POPULATION,
GEOGRAPHICAL AREAS, POLITICAL SUBDIVISIONS AND SINGLE AND
MULTI-MEMBER DISTRICTS.

0283 BRADEN G.D.
"THE SEARCH FOR OBJECTIVITY IN CONSTITUTIONAL LAW" (BMR)"
YALE LAW J., 57 (FEB. 48), 571-594.
EXAMINES VARIOUS SUPREME COURT JUSTICES' VIEWS AND
THEORIES OF CONSTITUTIONAL INTERPRETATION OF GOVERNMENTAL
LIMITATIONS DESIGNED TO CONTROL THEMSELVES AND THEIR
ASSOCIATES. MAINTAINS ALL THEORIES COLLAPSE BECAUSE THERE
IS NO OBJECTIVITY IN CONSTITUTIONAL LAW SINCE THERE ARE NO
ABSOLUTES.

0284 BRADLEY A.W.
"CONSTITUTION-MAKING IN UGANDA."
TRANSITION, 7 (AUG. 67), 25-31.
ANALYZES UGANDA GOVERNMENT'S PROPOSALS FOR A NEW CONSTI-
TUTION. DISCUSSES FEATURES OF THE PROPOSED CONSTITUTION:
UGANDA IS TO BE A UNITARY REPUBLIC; THE KINGDOMS AND DIS-
TRICTS ARE TO DISAPPEAR AS CONSTITUTIONAL UNITS OF GOVERN-
MENT; CABINET GOVERNMENT WILL CHANGE TO PRESIDENTIAL EXECU-
TIVE FORM; AND GREATER POWERS WILL BE GIVEN THE GOVERNMENT.
DISCUSSES CABINET, PRESIDENT, AND NATIONAL ASSEMBLY.

0285 BRAGER G.A. ED., PURCELL F.P. ED.
COMMUNITY ACTION AGAINST POVERTY.
NEW HAVEN: COLLEGE AND U PR, 1967, 349 PP., LC#67-17938.
REPORTS OF OBSERVATIONS AND EXPERIENCES BY KEY STAFF MEM-
BERS OF MOBILIZATION FOR YOUTH. CONTAINS ARTICLES ON POVERTY
ND SOCIAL WELFARE; DEMONSTRATION PROJECTS AND SOCIAL CHANGE;
MOBILIZING THE POOR FOR SOCIAL ACTION; NEW ROLES FOR THE
SOCIAL WORKER; THE LAW AND SOCIAL ACTION.

0286 BRAIBANTI R.J.D.
RESEARCH ON THE BUREAUCRACY OF PAKISTAN.
DURHAM: DUKE U PR, 1966, 565 PP., LC#66-14888.
NARRATES PROBLEMS OF PAKISTANI GOVERNMENT IN 1947-65 SO
AS TO SET TO ORDER THE PUBLIC RECORD AND IDENTIFY, CLASSIFY,
AND EVALUATE SOURCE MATERIALS FOR STUDY OF PAKISTANI BUREAU-
CRACY. DEALS WITH HISTORY AND ORGANIZATION OF BUREAUCRACY
AT LOCAL AND NATIONAL LEVELS. NOTES EFFECTS OF NATIONAL
ENVIRONMENT ON GOVERNMENT OPERATION. TRACES REFORM EFFORTS.

0287 BRANDT R.B. ED.
SOCIAL JUSTICE.
ENGLEWOOD CLIFFS: PRENTICE HALL, 1962, 171 PP., LC#62-16891.
FIVE ESSAYS ON THE ETHICS OF GOVERNMENT, ITS FOUNDATIONS
IN PHILOSOPHY, ECONOMICS, AND SOCIOLOGY. IN-DEPTH ANALYSIS
OF JUSTICE, INJUSTICE AND ITS RELATION TO LAW, EQUALITY, AND
SOCIAL DYNAMICS.

0288 BRAUN K.
LABOR DISPUTES AND THEIR SETTLEMENT.
BALTIMORE: JOHNS HOPKINS PRESS, 1955, 393 PP., LC#55-8425.
TRACES HISTORY OF LABOR MANAGEMENT DISPUTES AND PRINCI-
PLES OF CURRENT SETTLEMENT PRACTICES. THESE PRACTICES ARE
CONCILIATION, ARBITRATION, AND LITIGATION. EACH IS ANALYZED
ACCORDING TO PURPOSE AND SUCCESS UNDER SPECIFIC CIRCUM-
STANCES. OPINIONS FOR AND AGAINST EACH ARE DISCUSSED, THOUGH
NO ATTEMPT IS MADE TO GIVE RECOMMENDATIONS FOR OR AGAINST
ANY SPECIFIC METHOD OF LABOR SETTLEMENT.

0289 BRAUSCH G.E.
"AFRICAN ETHNOCRACIES: SOME SOCIOLOGICAL IMPLICATIONS OF
CONSTITUTIONAL CHANGE IN EMERGENT TERRITORIES OF AFRICA."
CIVILIZATIONS, 13 (NOS.1-2, 63), 82-97.
BASED ON THE SUPPOSITION THAT LEGISLATORS AND LAWYERS
ARE WILLING TO CONSIDER SOCIOLOGICAL AND ANTHROPOLOGICAL
FINDINGS AND TO CAST IN JURIDICAL TERMS SOME AFRICAN
ETHNOCRATIC PRINCIPLES OF PUBLIC LAW WHICH ARE STILL
PRACTICED.

0290 BREITEL C.D.
THE LAWMAKERS.
NEW YORK: ASSN OF BAR CITY OF NY, 1965, 50 PP.
DISCUSSES NATURE AND FUNCTION OF LAW AND EXAMINES LAW-
MAKING ROLE OF EXECUTIVE, LEGISLATURE, AND JUDICIARY.
ANALYZES IN DETAIL NATURE OF JUDICIAL PROCESS.

0291 BRENNAN D.G. ED.
ARMS CONTROL, DISARMAMENT, AND NATIONAL SECURITY.
NEW YORK: GEORGE BRAZILLER, 1961, 475 PP., LC#61-12952.
EXPLORES POTENTIAL ROUTES AND OBSTACLES TO ARMS CONTROL;
ILLUSTRATES MAJOR CONSIDERATIONS BEARING ON DECISIONS OF
NATIONAL POLICY. BEGINS WITH GOALS AND REQUIREMENTS OF ARMS
CONTROL; DISCUSSES POLICY ISSUES AND PROBLEMS, LIMITED WAR,
AND ECONOMIC IMPLICATIONS. SUBSTANCE OF ARMS CONTROL,
PARTICIPATION, AND TECHNIQUES ARE COVERED. ENDS WITH US
POLICY AND ARMS CONTROL THROUGH WORLD LAW.

0292 BRENNAN J.T.
THE COST OF THE AMERICAN JUDICIAL SYSTEM.
WESTHAVEN, CONN: PROF LIBRARY PRESS, 1966, 150 PP.
DISCUSSES COST OF COURT TRIALS, COST REDUCTION PROPOSALS,
JURY TRIAL PROCEDURES, WORKMEN'S COMPENSATION, TRIAL BY TV
TAPE, APPEALS, AND MOTIONS. INCLUDES MANY CONCRETE EXAMPLES.

0293 BRENNAN W.J. JR.
THE BILL OF RIGHTS AND THE STATES (PAMPHLET)
SANTA BARBARA: CTR DEMO INST, 1961, 24 PP.
DISCUSSES HISTORY OF BILL OF RIGHTS IN RELATION TO
FEDERAL-STATES RELATIONS AND INDIVIDUAL RIGHTS, ARGUING
THAT TOO FEW STATES HAVE ADOPTED THEIR OWN BILLS OF RIGHTS.

0294 BRETTON H.L.
STRESEMANN AND THE REVISION OF VERSAILLES: A FIGHT FOR
REASON.
STANFORD: STANFORD U PRESS, 1953, 199 PP., LC#53-6446.
STUDIES POLITICAL AND DIPLOMATIC PHASES OF PROCESS OF
REVISIONISM THROUGH WHICH TREATY OF VERSAILLES PASSED.
CONCENTRATES ON PERIOD 1918-30. EXAMINES ROLE OF GUSTAV
STRESEMANN IN MAKING AND CONDUCTING A REVISIONIST FOREIGN
POLICY. ATTEMPTS TO DISCOVER SEQUENCE OF ATTACKS ON TREATY,
AND INTERNATIONAL AND GERMAN BACKGROUND OF STRESEMANN'S
STRATEGY.

0295 BREUER E.H.
LEARNED HAND, JANUARY 27, 1872-AUGUST 18, 1961 (PAMPHLET)
ALBANY: U STATE NY FOR AREA STUD, 1964, 18 PP.
A PARTIALLY ANNOTATED BIBLIOGRAPHY OF THE WRITINGS, AD-
DRESSES, BIOGRAPHIES, AND OBITUARIES OF LEARNED HAND. HIS
WRITINGS ARE ARRANGED CHRONOLOGICALLY BY DATE OF PUBLICATION
FROM 1897 TO 1963. BIOGRAPHY OF HIS ACHIEVEMENTS AND DIS-
TINCTIONS SERVES AS AN INTRODUCTION.

0296 BREWER D.J.
THE MOVEMENT OF COERCION (PAMPHLET)
CHICAGO: BUILDING CON COUN, 1893, 15 PP.
SUPREME COURT JUSTICE'S VIEWS ON ROLE OF LAW IN LABOR-
MANAGEMENT DISPUTES, PROPERTY OWNERSHIP, AND PRIVATE
INDUSTRY.

0297 BRIERLY J.L.
THE LAW OF NATIONS (2ND ED.)
LONDON: OXFORD U PR, 1936, 271 PP.
MAINTAINS THAT LAW OF NATIONS IS NEITHER A CHIMERA NOR
A PANACEA, BUT AN INSTITUTION FOR BUILDING SANER
INTERNATIONAL ORDER. EXAMINES ORIGIN AND CHARACTER OF
INTERNATIONAL LAW, LEGAL ORGANIZATION, DISPUTES BETWEEN
STATES, TREATIES, FORCE, WAR, ETC.

0298 BRIERLY J.L.
THE OUTLOOK FOR INTERNATIONAL LAW.
OXFORD: CLARENDON, 1961, 1944, 142 PP.
FOCUSES ON SYSTEM OF INTERNATIONAL LAW, ITS SCOPE,
FUNCTIONS AND SHORTCOMINGS, AND PRESENTS HISTORY OF ITS ROLE
IN FOSTERING ORDERLINESS AMONG NATIONS. SUGGESTS WIDER
SUPPORT FOR ITS PRINCIPLES BY INDIVIDUAL STATES TO MAKE IT
MORE EFFECTIVE IN THE SETTLEMENT OF DISPUTES.

0299 BRIERLY J.L.
THE BASIS OF OBLIGATION IN INTERNATIONAL LAW, AND OTHER
PAPERS.
LONDON: OXFORD U PR, 1958, 387 PP.
COLLECTION OF JL BRIERLY'S WRITINGS ON INTERNATIONAL LAW.
SELECTIONS INCLUDED ILLUSTRATE THE PROGRESSIVENESS OF HIS
CONCEPTION OF LAW. TREAT MATTERS OF DOMESTIC JURISDICTION,
THEORY OF IMPLIED STATE COMPLICITY IN INTERNATIONAL CLAIMS,
NATURE OF DISPUTES, AND LEGISLATIVE FUNCTION IN
INTERNATIONAL RELATIONS.

0300 BRIGGS A.
CHARTIST STUDIES.
NEW YORK: ST MARTIN'S PRESS, 1959, 424 PP., LC#59-65123.
PRESENTS RESULTS OF RECENT STUDIES OF THE CHARTIST
MOVEMENT AND DEALS WITH CHARTISTS IN ASSORTED ENGLISH
CITIES. INCLUDES PROGRAMS, SUCH AS THE LAND PLAN AND THE
ANTI-CORN LAW LEAGUE.

0301 BRIGGS H.W. ED.
THE LAW OF NATIONS (2ND ED.)
NEW YORK: APPLETON, 1952, 1108 PP.
COMBINED TREATISE AND DOCUMENTARY SOURCE BOOK ON
INTERNATIONAL LAW. INCLUDES JURIDICAL ANALYSIS OF DOCUMENTS
SUCH AS TREATIES, DIPLOMATIC PAPERS, NATIONAL LEGISLATION,
ETC. DOCUMENTS GROUPED ACCORDING TO TOPICS AND DATE FROM
EARLY 20TH CENTURY.

0302 BRIGGS H.W.
THE INTERNATIONAL LAW COMMISSION.
ITHACA: CORNELL U PRESS, 1965, LC#65-11870.
ARTICLE-BY-ARTICLE ANALYSIS OF THE DRAFTING OF THE UN'S
INTERNATIONAL LAW COMMISSION CHAPTER. BASED ON EXTENSIVE
UN DOCUMENTATION. BRIGGS THEN FOLLOWS THE PROCEDURES OF THE
COMMISSION IN ACTION TO ILLUSTRATE THE PROCESS AND PROBLEMS
OF CODIFYING INTERNATIONAL LAW.

0303 BRODEN T.F.
"CONGRESSIONAL COMMITTEE REPORTS: THEIR ROLE AND HISTORY"
NOTRE DAME LAWYER, 33 (MAR. 58), 209-238.
TRACES THE HISTORY OF COMMITTEE REPORTS CONCERNING PRO-
POSED LEGISLATION. THE WRITTEN REPORT BECAME MANDATORY IN
THE HOUSE IN 1880 BUT NOT IN THE SENATE UNTIL AFTER WORLD
WAR II. CLAIMS THAT THESE REPORTS MAKE POSSIBLE MORE INTEL-
LIGENT LEGISLATIVE DEBATE. THE REPORTS SHOULD BE USED BY

LAWYERS IN INTERPRETING STATUTES.

0304 BROGAN D.W.
POLITICS IN AMERICA.
NEW YORK: HARPER & ROW, 1954, 467 PP., LC#54-12171.
STUDIES AMERICAN POLITICAL SYSTEM AT FEDERAL LEVEL.
EXAMINES CHARACTER OF AMERICAN POLITY, PARTY SYSTEM, EFFECT
OF RACE ON POLITICS, AND PARTY MACHINES. DISCUSSES POLITICS
AND MORALS. DESCRIBES CONVENTIONS, CAMPAIGNS, AND ELECTIONS.
EXPLORES RELATIONSHIP OF PRESIDENT AND CONGRESS AND OF
POLITICS TO LAW. MAINTAINS THAT SYSTEM HAS OWN LOGIC AND IS
SUCCESSFUL.

0305 BROMBERG W.
CRIME AND THE MIND.
NEW YORK: MACMILLAN, 1965, 431 PP., LC#65-20199.
PSYCHIATRIC ANALYSIS OF CRIME AND PUNISHMENT. FOCUS ON
BOTH THE CRIMINAL AND THE MEANING OF CRIME AND PUNISHMENT TO
SOCIETY. DISCUSSES TYPES OF PUNISHMENT AND REASONS FOR PUN-
ISHMENT, CRIME AND THE LAW, CRIMES OF AGGRESSION, JUVENILE
CRIME, CRIMES AGAINST PROPERTY, MEDICAL AND PSYCHIATRIC AP-
PLICATIONS TO CRIMINOLOGY, BUSINESS CRIMES, AND SEXUAL AND
DRUG CRIMES.

0306 BROMWICH L.
UNION CONSTITUTIONS.
NEW YORK: FUND FOR THE REPUBLIC, 1959, 43 PP.
ANALYSIS OF PROCEDURAL INADEQUACIES IN SUCH AREAS OF
UNION LIFE AS APPRENTICESHIP, RACIAL DISCRIMINATION,
UNION CONVENTIONS, THE CONSTITUTION AMENDING PROCESS,
CONCENTRATION OF POWER, NOMINATION OF OFFICERS, RECALL,
UNION DUE PROCESS IN SOME CASES, SUSPENSION OF MEMBERS AND
UNIONS, UNION PRESS AND DISCIPLINE. BASED ON SEVENTY UNIONS
WITH MEMBERSHIP OF ALMOST 16 MILLION.

0307 BROOKES E.H.
THE COMMONWEALTH TODAY.
PIETERMARITZBURG: U NATAL PR, 1959, 70 PP.
DISCUSSES NATURE OF BRITISH COMMONWEALTH AS SPIRITUAL,
LEGAL, AND ECONOMIC ENTITY. EXAMINES ITS OPERATION IN
AFRICA AND ITS RELATIONSHIP WITH US. DRAWS UPON EXAMPLES
FROM ROMAN EMPIRE AND SPECULATES UPON EXISTENCE OF WORLD-
STATE BY DRAWING UPON EXPERIENCE OF BRITISH EMPIRE.

0308 BROOKES E.H.
POWER, LAW, RIGHT, AND LOVE: A STUDY IN POLITICAL VALUES.
DURHAM: DUKE U PR, 1963, 84 PP., LC#63-18576.
DISCUSSES INTERRELATIONSHIP BETWEEN POLITICAL ACTION AND
RELIGIOUS FAITH. EXAMINES CONCEPT OF POWER AS LEGITIMATE
INSTRUMENT OF STATE AND DISCUSSES POSSIBILITIES OF CONTROL.
FREQUENT REFERENCE TO AFRICAN POLITICS.

0309 BROOKS S., ENGELENBURG F.V.
BRITAIN AND THE BOERS.
NEW YORK: N AMER REVIEW PUB CO, 1899, 48 PP.
A PRESENTATION OF VARIOUS VIEWS RELATED TO THE QUESTION
OF LEGITIMACY AND INTERNATIONAL LAW IN THE BRITAIN-BOER
WAR. DISCUSSES SOME OF THE HISTORICAL CIRCUMSTANCES THAT
PRODUCED THE WAR.

0310 BROOKS T.R.
TOIL AND TROUBLE, A HISTORY OF AMERICAN LABOR.
NEW YORK: DIAL, 1964, 301 PP., LC#63-17222.
DESCRIBES EVOLUTION OF LABOR IN AMERICA, ITS RELATION TO
RISE OF BIG BUSINESS, AND RISE OF LABOR UNIONS. ALSO DIS-
CUSSES ROLE OF GOVERNMENT REGULATION AND EFFECTS OF NEGRO
LABOR AND AUTOMATION.

0311 BROWN A.D., HELLMAN F.S.
COMPULSORY MILITARY TRAINING: SELECT LIST OF REFERENCES
(PAMPHLET)
WASHINGTON: LIBRARY OF CONGRESS, 1940, 25 PP.
218 ITEMS ANNOTATED. ARRANGED ALPHABETICALLY BY AUTHOR;
INDEXED BY AUTHOR AND SUBJECT. ENGLISH-LANGUAGE SOURCES,
1920-1940. IN 1941 A SUPPLEMENT WAS ISSUED CONTAINING 25
PAGES. 366 ITEMS WITH SAME FORMAT. BOOKS, ARTICLES, PAM-
PHLETS ON VARIOUS ATTITUDES TOWARDS CONSCRIPTION, ITS NEED,
CONSTITUTIONALITY, VALUE, ETC. ALL ARE COVERED.

0312 BROWN D.M.
"RECENT JAPANESE POLITICAL AND HISTORICAL MATERIALS."
AM. POL. SCI. REV., 43 (OCT. 49), 1010-1017.
UNANNOTATED BIBLIOGRAPHY OF DOCUMENTS FROM JAPAN CAPTURED
AT CLOSE OF WAR. THE ARTICLE SURVEYS THE NATURE AND SCOPE OF
THE DOCUMENTS OF THE INTERNATIONAL MILITARY TRIBUNAL FOR THE
FAR EAST. MATERIAL COVERS A RANGE FROM 1928 TO 1945.

0313 BROWN E.S.
MANUAL OF GOVERNMENT PUBLICATIONS.
NEW YORK: APPLETON, 1950, 121 PP.
ANNOTATED LISTING OF APPROXIMATELY 1,000 BOOKS, PERIODI-
CALS, ARTICLES, AND PAMPHLETS PUBLISHED BY US GOVERNMENT,
STATES, AND FOREIGN GOVERNMENTS. INCLUDES LAWS, CONSTITU-
TIONS, MUNICIPAL AND LOCAL GOVERNMENT, RECORDS OF LEGISLA-
TURES, AND INTERNATIONAL ORGANIZATIONS.

0314 BROWN L.N., GARNER J.F.
FRENCH ADMINISTRATIVE LAW.
LONDON, WASH, DC: BUTTERWORTHS, 1967, 160 PP.
COMPARE FRENCH LAW WITH ANGLO-SAXON. EXPLAIN THE LEGAL
INSTITUTIONS OF FRANCE AND BRITAIN THAT EXERCISE CONTROL
OVER ACTS OF THE ADMINISTRATION. DELINEATE BASIC LEGAL
STRUCTURE OF BOTH NATIONS, AND DISCUSS MERITS AND DEFECTS
OF THE FRENCH SYSTEM. GIVE MANY SPECIFIC CASES.

0315 BROWN R.M.
THE SOUTH CAROLINA REGULATORS.
CAMBRIDGE: HARVARD U PR, 1963, 230 PP., LC#63-07589.
STUDY OF GROUP IN BACK COUNTRY OF COLONIAL CAROLINA, WHO,
OUTSIDE EFFECTIVE LAW AND ORDER OF CHARLESTON, TOOK POWER
INTO OWN HANDS, LEARNING TO CLOTHE IT IN FORMS OF LEGITIMATE
AUTHORITY. WITH LEGAL DOCUMENTS.

0316 BROWNE D.G.
THE RISE OF SCOTLAND YARD: A HISTORY OF THE METROPOLITAN PO-
LICE.
LONDON: GEORGE HARRAP & CO, 1956, 392 PP.
HISTORY OF SCOTLAND YARD, SHOWING HOW IT IS BOUND UP WITH
ATIONAL AND POLITICAL BACKGROWUND OF OVER 120 YEARS, AND HOW
IT IS CREATION AND SERVANT OF PARLIAMENT; EXAMINES CONSEQU-
ENCES OF SUCH CLOSE CONTROL.

0317 BROWNLIE I.
"SOME LEGAL ASPECTS OF THE USE OF NUCLEAR WEAPONS."
INT. AND COMP. LAW Q., 14 (APR. 65), 437-451.
DEMONSTRATES THAT ANY CONCEIVABLE MILITARY USE OF NUCLEAR
WEAPONS IS IN FACT A VIOLATION OF EXISTING CUSTOM OR TREATY
LAW. PRIMARILY IN THAT THEY DO NOT DISCRIMINATE BETWEEN CIV-
ILIAN AND MILITARY TARGETS, OR RESPECT RIGHTS OF NEUTRALS.
DETERRENCE STRATEGY IS DECLARED ILLEGAL ON THE ABOVE GROUNDS
AND BECAUSE RESPONSE IS NOT PROPORTIONAL TO ATTACK.

0318 BROWNLIE I.
"NUCLEAR PROLIFERATION* SOME PROBLEMS OF CONTROL."
INTER-AM. ECO. AFFAIRS, 42 (OCT. 66), 600-608.
COMPARES SOVIET AND AMERICAN DRAFT TREATIES, POSSIBILITY
OF REGIONAL TREATIES, DISTRUST OF NON-NUCLEAR STATES IN MON-
OPOLY OF OTHERS, PROBLEMS OF "PEACEFUL USE" CONVERSIONS, EX-
PERIENCE WITH TEST BAN TREATY, AND FEARS OF ALLIANCE SHAR-
ING. CONCLUDES WITH 5 CONDITIONS FOR MAKING NON-PROLIFERA-
TION A PRACTICAL PROPOSAL.

0319 BROWNLIE I.
PRINCIPLES OF PUBLIC INTERNATIONAL LAW.
NEW YORK: OXFORD U PR, 1966, 646 PP.
EMPHASIZES TECHNICAL ASPECTS OF INTERNATIONAL LAW. COVERS
TOPICS OF SOVEREIGNTY, SOURCES OF INTERNATIONAL LAW, RECOG-
NITION, TREATIES, JUDICIAL SETTLEMENT OF INTERNATIONAL
PUTES, ETC. COMPREHENSIVE IN SCOPE. DESIGNED AS A REFERENCE
FOR UNDERGRADUATE AND GRADUATE STUDENTS. EXTENSIVELY FOOT-
NOTED WITH CITATION TO INTERNATIONAL AND DOMESTIC CASES.

0320 BRUCKER H.
FREEDOM OF INFORMATION.
NEW YORK: MACMILLAN, 1949, 300 PP.
CALLS INFORMATION SYSTEM "FOURTH BRANCH" OF GOVERNMENT.
DISCUSSES CONTROL OF PRESS AS A POLITICAL WEAPON AND PRESS
FREEDOM AS A FACTOR IN SUCCESSFUL DEMOCRACY. DISCUSSES
GOVERNMENT CONTROLS ON NEWS AND SELF-REGULATION BY NEWS
MEDIA. NOTES TENDENCY TOWARD CONCENTRATION OF REGULATORY
POWER IN CERTAIN GOVERNMENT AGENCIES. TRACES TRENDS IN NEWS-
PAPER OWNERSHIP AND SUGGESTS SYSTEMS FOR NEWS IMPROVEMENT.

0321 BRYCE J.
STUDIES IN HISTORY AND JURISPRUDENCE (2 VOLS.)
LONDON: CLARENDON PRESS, 1901, 1100 PP.
COMPARES HISTORY AND LAW OF ROME TO THOSE OF ENGLAND.
EXAMINES POLITICAL CONSTITUTIONS AND PROBLEMS OF
JURISPRUDENCE. SKETCHES HISTORY AND PECULIAR CONSTITUTION OF
ICELANDIC REPUBLIC. DISCUSSES CONSTITUTIONS OF US, TWO
DUTCH REPUBLICS IN SOUTH AFRICA, AND AUSTRALIA. STUDIES
NATURE OF OBEDIENCE AND SOVEREIGNTY, LAW OF NATURE, AND
METHODS OF LEGAL SCIENCE.

0322 BRYCE J.
MODERN DEMOCRACIES.
NEW YORK: MACMILLAN, 1921, 676 PP.
DESCRIBES WORKINGS OF MODERN DEMOCRACIES. DISCUSSES NORTH
AMERICAN MODEL AND ITS INFLUENCE ON AUSTRALIA AND NEW
ZEALAND. EXAMINES TRENDS IN DEMOCRATIC STATES, SUCH AS DE-
CLINE IN ROLE OF LEGISLATURES AND CHANGES IN JUDICIARY.

0323 BRYCE J.
INTERNATIONAL RELATIONS.
NEW YORK: MACMILLAN, 1922, 275 PP.
ANALYZES FORCES IN THE MIDDLE AGES, POLITICAL AND
NONPOLITICAL FORCES LEADING DIRECTLY TO WORLD WAR ONE: PROB-
LEMS OF DIPLOMACY, RELATION OF FOREIGN POLICY TO CITIZENS,
ADVANTAGES OF A CONCILIATION METHOD FOR SETTLING DISPUTES
AND THE POSSIBILITY OF CREATING A WORLD STATE. THE RESPONSI-
BILITY FOR PEACE IS IN THE ABILITY OF PEOPLE TO USE DEMO-
CRACY.

0324 BUCK A.E.
"PUBLIC BUDGETING."
NEW YORK: HARPER & ROW, 1929.
    DISCUSSION OF MODERN AMERICAN BUDGETARY PRACTICES ON NA-
TIONAL, STATE AND LOCAL LEVELS. RELATES BUDGET TO DEMOCRATIC
FORM OF GOVERNMENT AND TO LEGISLATIVE, ADMINISTRATIVE PROB-
LEMS ARISING FROM IT. HISTORY AND MANUAL OF BUDGETARY PRAC-
TICE. EVALUATES AND PREDICTS POSSIBLE BUDGETARY TRENDS.
INCLUDES SHORT SELECTED AND ANNOTATED BIBLIOGRAPHY.

0325 BUCKLAND W.W., MCNAIR A.D.
ROMAN LAW AND COMMON LAW; A COMPARISON IN OUTLINE (2ND REV.
ED.)
NEW YORK: CAMBRIDGE U PRESS, 1952, 439 PP., LC#52-13959.
    COMPARES IMPORTANT RULES AND INSTITUTIONS UNDER ROMAN
LAW AND ENGLISH COMMON LAW. FINDS DIFFERENCES INCLUDE
DIFFERENT CONCEPTS OF FAMILY, OWNERSHIP, INHERITANCE, AND
CONTRACT LEGALITY. EXAMINES EVOLUTION OF LAWS; LAWS OF
PERSONS, PROPERTY, SUCCESSION AND OBLIGATION; DELICTS AND
TORTS; AND LAWS OF PROCEDURE.

0326 BUELL R.
INTERNATIONAL RELATIONS.
NEW YORK: HOLT, 1929, 758 PP.
    A TEXTBOOK CASE STYLE STUDY, WELL-DOCUMENTED, OF THE
PROBLEMS ARISING HISTORICALLY AMONG STATES. ANALYSES ARE
MADE OF THE SOCIO-ECONOMIC BASES OF THESE DISPUTES AND THE
SETTLEMENTS ATTEMPTED OR ATTAINED IN THE PAST.

0327 BUGEDA LANZAS J.
A STATEMENT OF THE LAWS OF CUBA IN MATTERS AFFECTING
BUSINESS (2ND ED. REV., ENLARGED)
WASHINGTON: PAN AMERICAN UNION, 1958, 333 PP.
    SUMMARIZES BASIC CONSTITUTIONAL, STATUTORY, AND REGULA-
TORY PROVISIONS OF CUBA UP TO 1958, CONCERNING BUSINESS MAT-
TERS AND PERSONS INVOLVED IN THEM. EMPHASIZES COMMERCIAL,
INDUSTRIAL, AND LABOR LAW, AND RELATED MATTERS. BASED
UPON INFORMATION SUPPLIED BY PRACTICING CUBAN LAWYERS.
ONE OF A SERIES.

0328 BURCHFIELD L.
STUDENT'S GUIDE TO MATERIALS IN POLITICAL SCIENCE.
NEW YORK: HENRY HOLT & CO, 1935, 426 PP.
    DESIGNED TO INTRODUCE POLITICAL SCIENCE STUDENTS TO MORE
IMPORTANT SOURCE MATERIALS, FINDING DEVICES, BIBLIOGRAPHIES,
AND GENERAL REFERENCE WORKS WHICH WILL BE OF MAJOR ASSIS-
TANCE IN RESEARCH. CAREFULLY OUTLINED AND MANY
SECTIONS ARE CROSS-REFERENCED.

0329 BURDETTE F.L.
LOBBYISTS IN ACTION (PAMPHLET)
MANASSAS: NATL CAPITOL PUBL, 1950, 61 PP.
    STUDIES NATURE OF LOBBYING IN REGARD TO US DEMOCRATIC
SYSTEM AS APPLIED TO CONGRESS, METHODS USED TO ATTAIN GOALS
OF LOBBYING GROUPS AND REGULATION APPLIED TO THESE
GROUPS TO AVOID EXCESSIVE INFLUENCE ON FORMATION OF PUBLIC
POLICY. AUTHOR DISCUSSES CONTRIBUTIONS AND ABUSES OF SYSTEM
THAT AFFECT PUBLIC.

0330 BURDETTE F.L., WILLMORE J.N., WITHERSPOON J.V.
POLITICAL SCIENCE: A SELECTED BIBLIOGRAPHY OF BOOKS IN
PRINT, WITH ANNOTATIONS (PAMPHLET)
COLLEGE PARK: U MD, BUR PUB ADM, 1961, 97 PP., LC#61-64130.
    CONTAINS APPROXIMATELY 250 TITLES WITH EXTENSIVE THOUGH
NONCRITICAL ANNOTATIONS IN ALL FIELDS OF POLITICAL
SCIENCE: AMERICAN NATIONAL GOVERNMENT, COMPARATIVE GOVERN-
MENT, INTERNATIONAL POLITICS, POLITICAL PARTIES, PUBLIC
OPINION AND ELECTORAL PROCESS, POLITICAL THEORY, PUBLIC
ADMINISTRATION, PUBLIC LAW, AND LOCAL AND STATE GOVERNMENT.
DESIGNED FOR REFERENCE USERS.

0331 BURDETTE F.L.
"SELECTED ARTICLES AND DOCUMENTS ON AMERICAN GOVERNMENT AND
POLITICS."
AM. POL. SCI. REV., 60 (SEPT. 66), 728-737.
    AN UNANNOTATED BIBLIOGRAPHY ON AMERICAN GOVERNMENT AND
POLITICS. ENGLISH-LANGUAGE MATERIALS, PUBLISHED IN 1966;
390 ENTRIES. TOPICAL HEADINGS: MILITARY, HEALTH, EDUCATION,
WELFARE, BUSINESS, LABOR, AGRICULTURE, NATIONAL ECONOMY,
POLITICS, PUBLIC ADMINISTRATION, CONSTITUTIONAL LAW, NATION-
AL, STATE, AND LOCAL GOVERNMENTS, AND INTERGOVERNMENTAL
RELATIONS.

0332 BUREAU GOVERNMENT RES AND SERV
COUNTY GOVERNMENT REORGANIZATION - A SELECTED ANNOTATED BIB-
LIOGRAPHY (PAPER)
SEATTLE: U OF WASH, BUR GOVT RES, 1967, 10 PP.
    ANNOTATED COMPILATION OF 60 SOURCES ON COUNTY GOVERNMENT
STRUCTURE AND URBAN PROBLEMS IN THE US. INCLUDES BOOKS AND
GOVERNMENT PUBLICATIONS FROM 1948 THROUGH 1966. FIRST PART
CONSISTS OF GENERAL SOURCES; SECOND PART ON COUNTY CHARTER;
AND THIRD SECTION IS DIVIDED INTO STUDIES BY STATES.

0333 BUREAU OF NAT'L AFFAIRS
THE CIVIL RIGHTS ACT OF 1964.
WASHINGTON: BUREAU NATL AFFAIRS, 1964, 424 PP., LC#64-25380.

DISCUSSES LEGISLATIVE HISTORY AND EXAMINES CENTRAL PRO-
VISIONS OF CIVIL RIGHTS ACT OF 1964. INCLUDES APPENDIX GIV-
ING TEXT OF BILL, TEXT OF HOUSE JUDICIARY COMMITTEE REPORT,
PORTIONS OF SENATE AND HOUSE DEBATE, STATE ANTI-DISCRIMINA-
TION LAWS, AND US GOVERNMENT CONTRACTS.

0334 BUREAU OF NAT'L AFFAIRS INC.
A CURRENT LOOK AT: (1) THE NEGRO AND TITLE VII, (2) SEX AND
TITLE VII (PAMPHLET)
WASHINGTON: BUREAU NATL AFFAIRS, 1967, 23 PP.
    DISCUSSES CONSEQUENCES OF TITLE VII OF THE CIVIL RIGHTS
ACT OF 1964 WHICH MAKES DISCRIMINATION IN EMPLOYMENT ILLE-
GAL. SAMPLES BOTH LARGE AND SMALL COMPANIES TO ASCERTAIN
BOTH NEGRO AND FEMALE MEMBERSHIP IN WORK FORCE, ANALYZING
REASONS FOR THEIR INCREASE. DISCUSSES TYPES OF JOBS MOST
COMMONLY HELD BY NEGROES AND WOMEN.

0335 BUREAU OF NATIONAL AFFAIRS
LABOR RELATIONS REFERENCE MANUAL VOL 1, 1935-1937.
WASHINGTON: BUREAU NATL AFFAIRS, 1937, 979 PP.
    LISTS STATUTES ON LABOR RELATIONS, OPINIONS OF COURTS,
AND DECISIONS OF NATIONAL LABOR RELATIONS BOARD DURING FIRST
TWO YEARS.

0336 BUREAU OF NATIONAL AFFAIRS
THE MCCLELLAN COMMITTEE HEARINGS - 1957.
WASHINGTON: BUREAU NATL AFFAIRS, 1958, 508 PP.
    DAY-BY-DAY ACCOUNT OF MCCLELLAN COMMITTEE HEARINGS,
INCLUDING LIST OF WITNESSES AND ANALYSIS OF WHAT THE
RECORD DISCLOSED. CONTAINS TABLE LISTING 173 ACTS OF UNION
VIOLENCE IN A FIVE-STATE AREA INVOLVING BOTH TEAMSTERS AND
BARBERS. EVALUATES EVIDENCE OF LABOR-MANAGEMENT COLLUSION,
UNDEMOCRATIC PROCESSES IN UNIONS, POLITICAL ACTIVITIES OF
UNIONS, ETC.

0337 BUREAU OF NATIONAL AFFAIRS
FEDERAL-STATE REGULATION OF WELFARE FUNDS (REV. ED.)
WASHINGTON: BUREAU NATL AFFAIRS, 1962, 265 PP., LC#62-16834.
    EXAMINATION OF ORIGINAL WELFARE AND PENSION PLANS
DISCLOSURE ACT OF 1958 AND CHANGES MADE BY 1962 AMENDMENTS.
PROVIDES EDITORIAL ANALYSIS OF AMENDED ACT, INCLUDING
CHECKLISTS FOR PLAN DESCRIPTIONS AND ANNUAL REPORTS. CON-
TAINS TEXT OF FEDERAL ACT AS AMENDED, LEGISLATIVE RE-
PORTS ON ORIGINAL ACT AND AMENDMENTS, AND EXCERPTS FROM
CONGRESSIONAL DEBATES ON SUBJECT.

0338 BUREAU OF NATIONAL AFFAIRS
STATE FAIR EMPLOYMENT LAWS AND THEIR ADMINISTRATION.
WASHINGTON: BUREAU NATL AFFAIRS, 1964, 285 PP., LC#64-8502.
    MANUAL FOR CONDUCT OF EMPLOYER-EMPLOYEE RELATIONS DEAL-
ING WITH STATE FAIR EMPLOYMENT LAWS IN CONJUNCTION WITH THE
CIVIL RIGHTS ACT OF 1964. DISCUSSES FORMS OF STATE LAWS
AGAINST DISCRIMINATION IN EMPLOYMENT AND LISTS MAJOR POINTS
OF EXISTING STATE LAWS.

0339 BURGESS J.W.
"VON HOLST'S PUBLIC LAW OF THE UNITED STATES"
POLIT. SCI. QUART., 1 (DEC. 1886), 612-635.
    SECTION OF SURVEY OF PUBLIC LAW OF CIVILIZED WORLD.
CROSS-EXAMINES SECTION ON US TO GET BENEFIT OF FOREIGN
OPINION ON US LAW. COVERS CONSTITUTION'S GENESIS AND
OPERATION IN DETAIL. COMPARES IT TO CONSTITUTIONAL LAW OF
OTHER NATIONS.

0340 BURGESS J.W.
POLITICAL SCIENCE AND COMPARATIVE CONSTITUTIONAL LAW.
BOSTON: HOUGHTON MIFFLIN, 1890, 337 PP.
    FIRST PART ANALYZES VARIOUS CONCEPTS OF NATION AND STATE
AND DISCUSSES FORMATION OF AMERICAN, BRITISH, FRENCH, AND
GERMAN CONSTITUTIONS. SECOND PART COMPRISED OF COMPARATIVE
STUDY OF CONSTITUTIONAL LAW SYSTEMS OF THESE FOUR
COUNTRIES WITH EMPHASIS ON CONCEPT OF INDIVIDUAL FREEDOM.

0341 BURKE E.
A LETTER TO THE SHERIFFS OF BRISTOL (1777)
NEW YORK: HINDS, NOBLE, ELDRIDGE, 1904, 85 PP.
    STATES BURKE'S OPPOSITION TO THE PROPOSED SUSPENSION OF
"HABEAS CORPUS." ARGUES THAT THE PROPOSED LAW WOULD REQUIRE
REBELS CAUGHT IN AMERICA OR ON THE SEA TO BE BROUGHT TO
ENGLAND, WHERE WITHOUT WITNESSES THEY COULD NOT SECURE
JUSTICE. EXPLAINS THAT BURKE AVOIDS DEBATE ON THIS LAW
LEST COMMONS PASS AN EVEN HARSHER LAW.

0342 BURLAMAQUI J.J.
PRINCIPLES OF NATURAL AND POLITIC LAW (2 VOLS.) (1747-51)
ORIGINAL PUBLISHER NOT AVAILABLE, 1830, 466 PP.
    AUTHOR DOES NOT BELIEVE MEN ARE BORN KNOWING NATURAL LAW
BUT RATHER THAT THEY SO INTUITIVELY GRASP THE RIGHTNESS OR
WRONGNESS OF AN OBJECT THAT THIS KNOWLEDGE SEEMS TO BE
INNATE. AUTHOR SAYS THIS SHOULD BE THE BASIS OF ALL GOVERN-
MENT. THE CHIEF IDEA BINDING STATES TOGETHER, AND BY WHICH
THEIR LAWS ARE MADE, IS THE CONTRACT BETWEEN THE STATE AND
THE CITIZEN, WHICH IS BASED ON NATURAL LAW.

0343 BURNS A.C. ED.
PARLIAMENT AS AN EXPORT.

NEW YORK: BARNES AND NOBLE, 1966, 271 PP.
STUDIES ADOPTION OF PARLIAMENTARY SYSTEM BY FOREIGN COUN-
TRIES, PARTICULARLY MEMBERS OF COMMONWEALTH. EXAMINES OR-
GANIZATION AND PROCEDURES OF COMMONWEALTH PARLIAMENTS COVER-
ING POLITICAL PARTIES, ROLE OF MP, SECOND CHAMBER, AND
RELATIONSHIP TO EXECUTIVE, CIVIL SERVICE, AND COURTS.

0344 BURNS C.D.
POLITICAL IDEALS.
LONDON: OXFORD U. PR., 1929, 198 PP.
CONCERNED WITH MAN'S CONCEPTION OF HIS PRESENT STATE AND
HIS FUTURE ASPIRATIONS IN TERMS OF POLITICAL IDEALS. THE
CONCEPTS OF IMPERIALISM, INDIVIDUALISM, SOCIALISM,
DEMOCRACY, ETC. ARE DISCUSSED IN AN HISTORICAL RELATIONSHIP.

0345 BURR R.N. ED., HUSSEY R.D. ED.
DOCUMENTS ON INTER-AMERICAN COOPERATION: VOL. I, 1810-1881;
VOL. II, 1881-1948.
PHILADELPHIA: U OF PA PRESS, 1955, 214 PP.,LC#55-9972.
TWO-VOLUME WORK OF OFFICIAL AND PRIVATE DOCUMENTS RELATED
TO EFFORTS UNITING SPANISH AMERICAN COUNTRIES POLITICALLY OR
TEMPORARILY FOR CERTAIN GOALS AMONG THESE COUNTRIES THEM-
SELVES. VOLUME II DEALS WITH ORGANIZATION ON MORE FORMAL
LEVELS, INCLUDING NON-SPANISH AMERICAN COUNTRIES, LEADING TO
FORMATION OF PAN AMERICAN UNION AND OAS.

0346 BURRUS B.R.
INVESTIGATION AND DISCOVERY IN STATE ANTITRUST (PAMPHLET)
ANN ARBOR: U OF MICH LAW SCHOOL, 1967, 95 PP.
BEGINS WITH BACKGROUND INFORMATION ON ANTITRUST LAWS;
EXAMINES ENFORCEMENT PROCEDURES AND INVESTIGATIONS, STATE
PRETRIAL PROCEDURES, STATE PRECOMPLAINT INVESTIGATIVE
POWERS, AND CURRENT STATUS OF STATE. INCLUDES RIGHTS OF
DEFENDANTS, JUDICIAL VS. ADMINISTRATIVE PROCESS, STATE AND
FEDERAL LAWS, AND CRIMINAL AND CIVIL CASES. CONCLUDES WITH
BALANCING INTERESTS AND JUDICIAL SUPERINTENDENCE.

0347 BURRUS B.R.
ADMINSTRATIVE LAW AND LOCAL GOVERNMENT.
ANN ARBOR: U OF MICH LAW SCHOOL, 1963, 139 PP.
DISCUSSES CONSTITUTIONAL CONCEPTS OF LIMITATION, JUDICIAL
REVIEW, AND STATE ADMINISTRATIVE PROCEDURES. EMPHASIZES AD-
MINISTRATIVE FUNCTIONS ON LOCAL LEVELS, SUCH AS GRANTING OF
PERMITS, LICENSES, AND CERTIFICATES.

0348 BUTLER D.E.
THE ELECTORAL SYSTEM IN BRITAIN, 1918-1951.
LONDON: OXFORD U PR, 1953, 222 PP.
SYSTEMATIC ANALYSIS OF THE EVOLUTION OF BRITISH
ELECTORAL SYSTEM; PRESENTS DETAILED DESCRIPTION OF ITS
WORKING. ATTENTION CONFINED TO DESCRIPTION OF ACTUAL OR
ATTEMPTED LEGISLATIVE CHANGES IN THE PARLIAMENTARY ELECTORAL
SYSTEM AND TO AN ANALYSIS OF STATISTICS AVAILABLE
ON ITS WORKING.

0349 BUTLER G., MACOBY S.
THE DEVELOPMENT OF INTERNATIONAL LAW.
LONDON: LONGMANS/GREEN, 1928, 566 PP.
PRESENTS HISTORY OF INTERNATIONAL DIPLOMACY. ANALYZES
CHANGES IN INTERNATIONAL LAW AS FUNCTION OF 'CHANGES IN
THE STATE SYSTEM AND IN THE PRACTICE OF NATIONS'. DIVIDES
ANALYSIS INTO THREE PERIODS: 'THE PRINCE,' 'THE JUDGE,' AND
'THE CONCERT.'

0350 BUTLER N.M.
THE INTERNATIONAL MIND.
NEW YORK: SCRIBNER, 1913, 114 PP.
URGES SETTING UP OF INDEPENDENT JUDICIARY FOR SETTLE-
MENT OF INTERNATIONAL DISPUTES. BELIEVES IT WILL OFFER BEST
SOLUTION FOR SETTLING BUSINESS AND INTERNATIONAL RIVALRIES,
AND MAY PREVENT WAR BY REMOVING CAUSAL FACTORS. POINTS OUT
THAT COURT MUST HAVE FULL SUPPORT OF GOVERNMENTS INVOLVED,
PUBLIC OPINION, STATESMEN, AND JOURNALISTS TO BE EFFECTIVE.

0351 BUTTERFIELD H. ED., WIGHT M. ED.
DIPLOMATIC INVESTIGATIONS* ESSAYS IN THE THEORY OF INTER-
NATIONAL POLITICS.
CAMBRIDGE: HARVARD U PR, 1966, 227 PP.
12 PAPERS RESULTING FROM ROCKEFELLER FOUNDATION SPONSORED
COMMITTEE OF BRITISH SCHOLARS ON INTERNATIONAL POLITICAL
THEORY. THEY RECOGNIZE THAT THEIR APPROACH WITH ITS STRESS
ON THE HISTORICAL, THE NORMATIVE, THE PHILSOPHICAL, PRINCI-
PLES AND THE DIPLOMATIC COMMUNITY IS THE ANTITHESIS OF "MOD-
ERN" AMERICAN THINKING, BUT FEEL LESSONS CONCERNING INTERNA-
TIONAL COHESION DRAWN FROM CLASSICAL SOURCES ARE VALID.

0352 BYNKERSHOEK C., TENNEY F. ED.
QUAESTIONUM JURIS PUBLICI LIBRI DUO.
OXFORD: CLARENDON PR., 1930, 284 PP.
A CARNEGIE ENDOWMENT TRANSLATION OF THIS GREAT
EIGHTEENTH CENTURY CLASSIC ON THE NATURE, RULES, AND EFFECTS
OF WAR AND ON VARIOUS RIGHTS OF SOVEREIGN STATES.

0353 BYRD E.M. JR.
TREATIES AND EXECUTIVE AGREEMENTS IN THE UNITED STATES:
THEIR SEPARATE ROLES AND LIMITATIONS.

LONDON: HEINEMANN, 1960, 276 PP.
HISTORICAL AND ANALYTICAL TREATMENT OF UNITED STATES'
SHIFT FROM USE OF TREATIES TO USE OF EXECUTIVE AGREEMENTS.
COVERS THE FOUNDING FATHERS' WRITINGS ON FOREIGN AFFAIRS
AND TREATIES THEY MADE, THE SUPREME COURT'S VIEW, TREATY
POWER, JOINT CONGRESSIONAL-EXECUTIVE ACTIONS, PRESIDENTIAL
ACTIONS, AND FOREIGN AFFAIRS IN A FEDERAL SYSTEM.

0354 BYRNES R.F.
BIBLIOGRAPHY OF AMERICAN PUBLICATIONS ON EAST CENTRAL EUR-
OPE, 1945-1957 (VOL. XXII)
BLOOMINGTON: INDIANA U PR, 1957, 213 PP.
COMPILES, ANNOTATES, AND INDEXES 2,810 ITEMS PUBLISHED IN
US CONCERNING EAST CENTRAL EUROPE. ARRANGED BY COUNTRY
AND SUBDIVIDED TOPICALLY. DEALS WITH AREA STUDIES, HISTORY,
POLITICS, LAW, AND OTHER GENERAL SUBJECTS. INCLUDES A LONG
LIST OF JOURNALS SEARCHED FOR COMPILATION.

0355 CABLE G.W.
THE NEGRO QUESTION: A SELECTION OF WRITINGS ON CIVIL RIGHTS
IN THE SOUTH.
GARDEN CITY: DOUBLEDAY, 1958, 286 PP., LC#58-7796.
COLLECTED ESSAYS, ADDRESSES, AND LETTERS PROMOTING
UNLIMITED CIVIL RIGHTS, WITH EMPHASIS ON LITERATURE,
COLOR LINE, AND CONGREGATIONAL UNITY. INCLUDES FREEDMEN
AND THE CONVICT LEASE SYSTEM.

0356 CADWALDER J.L.
DIGEST OF THE PUBLISHED OPINIONS OF THE ATTORNEYS-GENERAL,
AND OF THE LEADING DECISIONS OF THE FEDERAL COURTS (REV ED)
WASHINGTON: US GOVERNMENT, 1877, 290 PP.
REFERENCES TO ALL PUBLISHED OPINIONS OF ATTORNEYS-GENERAL
UPON INTERNATIONAL LAW, PUBLIC TREATIES, QUESTIONS OF SIMI-
LAR NATURE ARISING BEFORE DEPARTMENT OF STATE, AND TO
LEADING DECISIONS OF FEDERAL COURT ON SAME SUBJECTS.
ARRANGEMENT IS BY SUBJECT. CONTAINS TABLE OF CASES.

0357 CAHIER P.
"LE DROIT INTERNE DES ORGANISATIONS INTERNATIONALES."
REV. GEN. DR. INT. PUB., 34 (NO.3, 63), 563-602.
BRIEF HISTORY OF INTERNAL LAW OF INTERNATIONAL ORGANIZA-
TIONS. SEEKS TO CLARIFY WHETHER INTERNATIONAL LAW APPLICABLE
TO MEMBER STATES OF SUPRA-NATIONAL ORGANIZATIONS. EXPLAINS
RELATIONS BETWEEN INTERNATIONAL ORGANIZATIONS AND NATIONAL
GOVERNMENTS.

0358 CAHIER P.
LE DROIT DIPLOMATIQUE CONTEMPORAIN.
GENEVA: LIBRAIRIE DROZ, 1967, 521 PP.
STUDY OF INTERNATIONAL LAW. CONSIDERS TRADITIONAL DIPLO-
MACY (FUNCTIONING OF EMBASSIES, ETC.), DIPLOMACY BETWEEN
CHIEFS AND MINISTERS OF STATE, "AD HOC" DIPLOMACY, AND
DIPLOMACY THROUGH INTERNATIONAL CONFERENCES AND
ORGANIZATIONS.

0359 CAHILL F.V.
JUDICIAL LEGISLATION: A STUDY IN AMERICAN LEGAL THEORY.
NEW YORK: RONALD PRESS, 1952, 165 PP.
DISCUSSES PHASES OF 20TH-CENTURY REASSESSMENT OF
PHILOSOPHY OF LAW, ESPECIALLY LEGISLATIVE FUNCTION OF THE
JUDICIARY. STATES THAT DISPUTE OVER JUDICIAL FUNCTION HAS
BEEN BASICALLY A POLITICAL ISSUE INVOLVING POPULAR CONTROL
OF LEGISLATIVE PROCESS. EXAMINES ROLE OF O.W. HOLMES, AND
IMPORTANCE OF SOCIOLOGICAL JURISPRUDENCE AND LEGAL REALISM.

0360 CAHN E.
"A DANGEROUS MYTH IN THE SCHOOL SEGREGATION CASES" (BMR)"
NYU LAW REV., 30 (JAN. 55), 150-169.
COMMENTS ON 1954 SUPREME COURT DECISIONS IN SCHOOL
SEGREGATION. DISCUSSES HISTORICAL FICTIONS CONCERNING
1896 PLESSY V. FERGUSON, AND BROWN AND BOLLING CASES.
EXAMINES COURT'S MODE OF INTERPRETING 14TH AMENDMENT IN
SEGREGATION CASES. MAINTAINS THAT PRINCIPLE OF EQUALITY NOW
IS FIRMLY ESTABLISHED IN US AND AMERICAN PEOPLE ALONE HAVE
POWER TO INSURE THAT PRINCIPLE BECOMES LIVING REALITY.

0361 CAHN E.
THE GREAT RIGHTS.
NEW YORK: MACMILLAN, 1963, 242 PP., LC#63-14939.
LECTURES BY JUSTICES HUGO L. BLACK, WILLIAM J. BRENNAN,
JR., WILLIAM O. DOUGLAS, AND CHIEF JUSTICE EARL WARREN
PRESENTING GENERAL PHILOSOPHY OF CIVIL LIBERTIES. TOPICS
INCLUDE RELATION OF BILL OF RIGHTS TO FEDERAL AND STATE
GOVERNMENT AND MILITARY, AND FURTHER EXTENSIONS OF BILL OF
RIGHTS. INCLUDES CHAPTER ON HERITAGE FROM MADISON AND TEXT
OF US CONSTITUTION.

0362 CAHN E.
CONFRONTING INJUSTICE.
BOSTON: LITTLE BROWN, 1966, 428 PP., LC#66-16560.
ESSAYS EMPHASIZING THE BILL OF RIGHTS AND THE JUDGES,
FACT-SKEPTICISM, AND SOCIAL PSYCHOLOGY. INCLUDE CONSUMERS,
THE LEGAL PROFESSION, AND MEANING OF JUSTICE.

0364 CALDWELL L.K.
RESEARCH METHODS IN PUBLIC ADMINISTRATION; AN OUTLINE OF

TOPICS AND READINGS (PAMPHLET)
ALBANY: STATE U OF NY AT ALBANY, 1953, 35 PP.
A DESCRIPTIVELY ANNOTATED BIBLIOGRAPHY DESIGNED TO ASSIST
THE EFFECTIVE APPLICATION OF TOOLS AND TECHNIQUES OF SOCIAL
RESEARCH TO ADMINISTRATIVE PROBLEMS OF THE PUBLIC SERVICE.
ATTENTION GIVEN TO INTERPRETATION OF STATISTICS, PUNCH-CARD
METHODS OF PROCESSING DATA, BIBLIOGRAPHICAL RESEARCH, AND
THE DOCUMENTATION OF RESEARCH PAPERS. ENTRIES LISTED ALPHA-
BETICALLY BY AUTHOR WITHIN EACH TOPICAL DIVISION.

0365 CALDWELL L.K.
"THE GOVERNMENT AND ADMINISTRATION OF NEW YORK."
NEW YORK: THOMAS Y CROWELL, 1954.
DESCRIPTIVE STUDY OF GOVERNMENT AND PUBLIC ADMINISTRA-
TION IN NEW YORK STATE. SELECTED, PARTIALLY-ANNOTATED BIBLI-
OGRAPHY OF PUBLIC RECORDS AND DOCUMENTARY MATERIALS RELATING
TO NY STATE GOVERNMENT; LIMITED TO ESSENTIAL OFFICIAL AND
SEMI-OFFICIAL SOURCES AND TO THE MORE COMPREHENSIVE GENERAL
WORKS. MOST ENTRIES CONSIST OF ANNUAL PUBLICATIONS OR POST-
1949 WORKS.

0366 CALIFORNIA LEGISLATURE
COMMITTEE ON ELECTIONS AND REAPPORTIONMENT, FINAL REPORT.
SACRAMENTO: ASSEM STATE OF CALIF, 1965, 320 PP.
EVALUATES EFFECTIVENESS OF NEW VOTING MACHINES USED IN
1964, AND ELECTRONIC DATA PROCESSING IN VARIOUS DEPARTMENTS.
ALSO STUDIES SIX CASES ON REAPPORTIONMENT AND PRESENTS
LEGISLATIVE COUNSEL'S OPINION OF IT.

0367 CALIFORNIA STATE LIBRARY
REAPPORTIONMENT, A SELECTIVE BIBLIOGRAPHY.
SACRAMENTO: CALIF STATE LIBRARY, 1966, 22 PP.
OVER 150 ENTRIES COVERING 1956-66 OF PUBLICATIONS IN ENG-
LISH ON REAPPORTIONMENT AVAILABLE TO CALIFORNIA LAW
LIBRARIES FROM CALIFORNIA STATE LIBRARY, LAW LIBRARY.

0368 CALLISON I.P.
COURTS OF INJUSTICE.
NEW YORK: TWAYNE, 1956, 775 PP.
MAINTAINS THAT US JUDICIAL SYSTEM "AS FASHIONED AND OPER-
ATED TODAY CONSTITUTES THE MOST DEVASTATING FAILURE OF MOD-
ERN TIMES." ARGUES THAT BASIC CAUSE OF FAILURE HAS BEEN
DEBASEMENT OF AMERICAN JUDGE AND RISE TO POWER OF INCOMPE-
TENT LAWYERS. INCLUDES EXTENSIVE DISCUSSION OF JUDICIAL SYS-
TEM AND PROCESS.

0369 CAM H.M., TURBERVILLE A.S.
BIBLIOGRAPHY OF ENGLISH CONSTITUTIONAL HISTORY (PAMPHLET)
LONDON: G BELL & SONS, 1929, 32 PP.
AN ANNOTATED BIBLIOGRAPHY OF BOOKS AND ARTICLES DEALING
WITH ENGLISH CONSTITUTIONAL HISTORY. CONTENTS ORGANIZED TOP-
ICALLY INTO 17 CATEGORIES COVERING GENERAL WORKS, CHRONO-
LOGICAL PERIODS, STRUCTURE OF GOVERNMENT, CONSTITUTIONAL
THEORY AND LAW, AND POLITICAL PARTIES. SOURCES COVER PERIOD
THROUGH 1928. ANNOTATIONS ARE CRITICAL AS WELL AS DESCRIP-
TIVE AND LIST CROSS REFERENCES.

0370 CAMPBELL E.
PARLIAMENTARY PRIVILEGE IN AUSTRALIA.
MELBOURNE: MELBOURNE UNIV PRESS, 1966, 218 PP., LC#66-22149.
DISCUSSES PRIVILEGES OF INDIVIDUALS AND PARLIAMENT AS A
WHOLE. NOTES EVOLUTION OF PARLIAMENTARY PRIVILEGE IN BRITAIN
AND DESCRIBES ITS DIRECT INFLUENCE ON AUSTRALIAN LAWS.
CONSIDERS THE FOLLOWING AREAS: MEMBERSHIP; REGULATION OF
INTERNAL PROCEEDINGS; POLITICAL PRACTICES; INVESTIGATIONS;
IMMUNITY TO LEGAL PROCESS; FREEDOM OF SPEECH AND DEBATE;
REPORTS OF PROCEEDINGS; AND LIBELS ON THE ASSEMBLY.

0371 CAMPBELL E.H., SMITH G.D.
UNITED STATES CITIZENSHIP AND QUALIFICATIONS FOR VOTING IN
WASHINGTON.
SEATTLE: U OF WASHINGTON PR, 1951, 94 PP.
MANUAL FOR PERSONS CONCERNED WITH DETERMINING QUESTIONS
OF US CITIZENSHIP, WITH SPECIAL REFERENCE TO APPLICABLE
PROVISIONS OF THE CONSTITUTION AND LAWS OF THE STATE OF
WASHINGTON RELATING TO VOTING QUALIFICATIONS. SUMMARIZES
SALIENT PROVISIONS OF FEDERAL STATUTES CURRENTLY IN EFFECT
AND ALSO THOSE WHICH HAVE BEEN RECENTLY REPEALED.

0372 CAMPBELL E.H., VOGEL J.H.
SURVEYS, SUBDIVISIONS AND PLATTING, AND BOUNDARIES:
WASHINGTON STATE LAW AND JUDICIAL DECISIONS.
SEATTLE: U OF WASH, BUR GOVT RES, 1965, 215 PP.
WORKING MANUAL FOR THOSE DEALING WITH PROBLEMS OF
SUBDIVIDING, PLATTING, AND BOUNDARIES. REVIEWS JUDICIAL
DECISIONS THROUGH 1904. ANALYSIS OF CONSTITUTIONAL
PROVISIONS, LAWS, AND JUDICIAL DECISIONS. INCLUDES DATA
RELATED TO PROBLEMS OF LOCATION OF LAND WITH REGARD TO
WATER RIGHTS, RULES FOR ESTABLISHING RIGHTS OF WAY, AND
ASPECTS OF LAND BOUNDARIES AND MONUMENTS.

0373 CANFIELD L.H.
THE PRESIDENCY OF WOODROW WILSON: PRELUDE TO A WORLD IN
CRISIS.
RUTHERFORD: FAIRLEIGH DICKEN PR, 1966, 299 PP., LC#66-24796.
ANALYSIS OF ALL ASPECTS OF WILSON'S PRESIDENTIAL

ADMINISTRATION. PORTRAYS HIS TERM AS TRAGEDY, HIS RISE TO
FAME IN HIS FIGHT FOR PEACE AND NEUTRALITY, AND HIS PHYSICAL
AND MENTAL DETERIORATION AFTER HIS PEOPLE REJECTED THE
LEAGUE OF NATIONS.

0374 CANTWELL F.V. HAWVER C. ET AL.
"PUBLIC OPINION AND THE LEGISLATIVE PROCESS"
AM. POL. SCI. REV., 40 (OCT. 46), 924-935.
TRACES THE INTERACTION OF PUBLIC OPINION AND THE EXECU-
TIVE AND LEGISLATIVE BRANCHES OF GOVERNMENT AS REFLECTED IN
ROOSEVELT'S PLAN TO REORGANIZE THE SUPREME COURT IN 1937.
TRIES TO MEASURE THE NATURE, EFFECT, AND COUNTER-EFFECT OF
PUBLIC OPINION. CONCLUDES THAT IT IS FALLACIOUS FOR LEGISLA-
TORS TO WAIT ON PUBLIC OPINION TO TELL THEM WHAT TO DO BE-
CAUSE PUBLIC OPINION DEPENDS ON LEADERSHIP FOR SUGGESTIONS.

0375 CAPLOW T.
THE SOCIOLOGY OF WORK.
MINNEAPOLIS: U OF MINN PR, 1954, 330 PP., LC#54-8208.
SOCIOLOGICAL DESCRIPTION OF OCCUPATIONAL INSTITUTIONS
WHICH HEAVILY EMPHASIZES THE DIVISION OF LABOR. SOCIOLOGY
OF WORK IS TREATED PRIMARILY AS THE STUDY OF THOSE SOCIAL
ROLES WHICH ARISE FROM CLASSIFICATION OF MEN BY WORK THEY
DO. DISCUSSION OF LABOR MARKET, VERTICAL MOBILITY, OCCUPA-
TIONAL STATUS, AND VOCATIONAL CHOICE. EXTENSIVE UNANNOTATED
BIBLIOGRAPHY CONTAINS RECENT TITLES IN ENGLISH.

0376 CARDOZO B.
THE GROWTH OF THE LAW.
NEW HAVEN: YALE U PR, 1924, 145 PP.
DESCRIBES THE PROBLEM OF JUDGE-MADE LAW AS THE TENSION
BETWEEN A NEED FOR CERTAINTY AND ORDER AND THE NECESSITY OF
GROWTH TO MEET NEW SITUATIONS, WITH DECISIONS RESULTING FROM
CONSIDERATION OF BOTH FACTORS. LOOKS TO AMERICAN LAW INSTI-
TUTE'S RESTATEMENTS AND UNIVERSITY LAW REVIEWS TO ANSWER
NEED FOR CERTAINTY. ARGUES THAT LEGAL GROWTH MUST BE GUIDED
BY A PHILOSOPHY OF LAW, BUT DOES NOT OFFER ONE.

0377 CARDOZO B.N.
THE NATURE OF THE JUDICIAL PROCESS.
NEW HAVEN: YALE U PR, 1921, 180 PP.
STUDY OF PHILOSOPHY AND METHOD OF JUDICIAL PROCESS IN US.
DISCUSSES VALUE AND INFLUENCE OF HISTORY, TRADITION, AND
SOCIOLOGY ON DECISIONS OF JUDGE. EXPLAINS POSITION OF JUDGE
AS LEGISLATOR.

0378 CARLIN J.E.
LAWYER'S ETHICS.
NEW YORK: RUSSELL SAGE FDN, 1966, 267 PP., LC#66-14516.
EXAMINES SOCIAL CONDITIONS OF MORAL INTEGRITY IN LEGAL
PROFESSION. BASED ON INFORMATION OBTAINED IN INTERVIEWS WITH
LAWYERS IN PRIVATE PRACTICE IN NEW YORK CITY. CENTERS ATTEN-
TION ON HOW SOCIAL ORGANIZATION OF LEGAL PROFESSION AFFECTS
ETHICAL BEHAVIOR OF LAWYERS. CONCERNED WITH INFLUENCES ARIS-
ING FROM CHARACTERISTICS OF LAWYER'S CLIENTELE, COURTS, COL-
LEAGUE GROUP, AND SOCIAL STRATIFICATION IN BAR.

0379 CARLSTON K.S.
LAW AND STRUCTURES OF SOCIAL ACTION.
NEW YORK: COLUMBIA U PRESS, 1956, 288 PP.
STUDY OF LAW IN ALL ASPECTS OF HUMAN SOCIETY; DEALS WITH
INTERPERSONAL AND INTERGROUP RELATIONS FROM PRIMITIVE
SOCIETY TO DIPLOMACY. EXAMINES CONCEPT OF STATE, ECONOMIC
CONTROL, INTERNATIONAL LAW, AND POSITION OF INDIVIDUAL
WITHIN ORGANIZATIONAL STRUCTURE.

0380 CARLSTON K.S.
"NATIONALIZATION: AN ANALYTIC APPROACH."
NORTHWEST. UNIV. LAW REV., 54 (1959), 405-33.
CONSIDERS THE DISPERSION OF POLITICAL SOVEREIGNTY
THROUGHOUT THE GLOBE, AND THE JARRING EFFECTS OF THE MULTI-
TUDE OF IDEOLOGIES AND ATTITUDES TOWARD PLANNING AND SOCIAL
ORGANIZATION WHICH HAVE COME INTO CONFLICT WITH THE INCREAS-
ING CENTRALIZATION OF THE INTERNATIONAL ECONOMIC SYSTEM.
THESE SAME FACTS HAVE ALSO MADE INTERNATIONAL LAW MORE
DIFFICULT TO DETERMINE AND TO APPLY.

0381 CARLSTON K.S.
LAW AND ORGANIZATION IN WORLD SOCIETY.
URBANA: U. ILL. PR., 1962, 356 PP., $6.50.
A BLEND OF LEGAL DOCTRINE AND ORGANIZATION THEORY
LEADING TOWARD A THEORY OF LAW AND ORDER IN WORLD SOCIETY.
THEORY IS BASED ON THE SUBJECT OF NATIONALIZATION OF CON-
CESSION AGREEMENTS WITH FOREIGN INVESTORS.

0382 CARLYLE A.J.
BIBLIOGRAPHY OF POLITICAL THEORY (PAMPHLET)
LONDON: G BELL & SONS, 1916, 8 PP.
AN ANNOTATED BIBLIOGRAPHY OF WORKS OF POLITICAL THEORY
COVERING THE MIDDLE AGES THROUGH THE 19TH CENTURY IN ENG-
LAND, FRANCE, AMERICA, AND GERMANY. WORKS LISTED ARE GENER-
ALLY SECONDARY SOURCES. CONTENTS ORGANIZED GEOGRAPHICALLY
WITHIN EACH CHRONOLOGICAL PERIOD. BRIEF CRITICAL
ANNOTATIONS.

0383 CARMEN I.H.

MOVIES, CENSORSHIP, AND THE LAW.
ANN ARBOR: U OF MICH PR, 1966, 339 PP., LC#66-14983.
EXAMINES METHODS OF MOTION PICTURE CENSORS IN THE US.
PRESENTS LEGAL GUIDELINES WHICH CONSTITUTION IMPOSES
ON THEIR PREROGATIVES, TOGETHER WITH STATE AND LOCAL
INTERPRETATIONS OF CENSORSHIP PRACTICE. CONTAINS SEVEN IN-
TERVIEWS WITH CENSORS REPRESENTING NATIONWIDE GEOGRAPHICAL
AREAS.

0384 CARMICHAEL D.M.
"FORTY YEARS OF WATER POLLUTION CONTROL IN WISCONSIN: A CASE
STUDY."
WISC. LAW REV., 67 (SPRING 67), 350-419.
HISTORY OF POLLUTION CONTROL EMPHASIZING PRESENT POLICY
AND ENFORCEMENT AND OF DEPARTMENT OF RESOURCE DEVELOPMENT
AND DRAINAGE BASIN HEARINGS.

0385 CARNEGIE ENDOWMENT INTL. PEACE
"HUMAN RIGHTS (ISSUES BEFORE THE NINETEENTH GENERAL
ASSEMBLY)."
INT. CONCIL., 550 (NOV. 64), 88-117.
DISCUSSES ISSUE OF RACIAL DISCRIMINATION AND PROBLEM OF
REFUGEES WHICH WERE RAISED DURING THE NINETEENTH SESSION.

0386 CARNEGIE ENDOWMENT INTL. PEACE
"LEGAL QUESTIONS (ISSUES BEFORE THE NINETEENTH GENERAL
ASSEMBLY)."
INT. CONCIL., 550 (NOV. 64), 187-97.
DISCUSSES ISSUES OF INTERNATIONAL LAW WHICH WERE RAISED
DURING NINETEENTH SESSION, INCLUDING CODIFICATION, DEVELOP-
MENT AND TREATIES.

0387 CARNELL F. ED.
THE POLITICS OF THE NEW STATES: A SELECT ANNOTATED BIBLIOG-
RAPHY WITH SPECIAL REFERENCE TO THE COMMONWEALTH.
LONDON: OXFORD U PR, 1961, 171 PP.
PARTIALLY ANNOTATED BIBLIOGRAPHY OF 1599 TITLES ON THE
NEW STATES OF AFRICA AND ASIA IN FRENCH AND ENGLISH. ITEMS
ARE ARRANGED BY TOPIC, CROSS-REFERENCED AND INDEXED BY
AUTHOR AND GEOGRAPHICAL LOCATION. SECTION ON APPROACHES TO
THE STUDY OF POLITICS INCLUDES WORKS ON WESTERN STATES.
COVERS GENERAL HISTORICAL BACKGROUND ON COLONIALISM AND
STUDIES OF PROBLEMS IN COLONIALISM.

0388 CARPENTER W.S.
FOUNDATIONS OF MODERN JURISPRUDENCE.
NEW YORK: APPLETON, 1958, 230 PP., LC#58-05314.
DESIGNED FOR THE UNDERGRADUATE, DEALS WITH THE HISTORY OF
LEGAL THEORIES AND SYSTEMS, TRIAL METHODS, AND LAW IN THE
MODERN WORLD.

0389 CARPER E.T.
LOBBYING AND THE NATURAL GAS BILL (PAMPHLET)
INDIANAPOLIS: BOBBS-MERRILL, 1962, 39 PP.
STUDIES PRESSURES FROM CONFLICTING INTEREST GROUPS OF
PRODUCERS AND CONSUMERS OVER PROPOSED AMENDMENTS TO NATURAL
GAS ACT, 1955-56. "ARROGANT LOBBYING" COUPLED WITH
DISCLOSURE OF BRIBERY PRECIPITATED EXECUTIVE VETO.

0390 CARPER E.T.
THE DEFENSE APPROPRIATIONS RIDER (PAMPHLET)
UNIVERSITY: U ALABAMA PR, 1960, 28 PP.
CASE STUDY OF 1955 RIDER TO DEFENSE BUDGET BILL, WHICH
GAVE CONGRESSIONAL COMMITTEES RIGHT TO DISAPPROVE SHUTDOWN
BY DEFENSE DEPARTMENT OF CERTAIN LOCAL INSTALLATIONS.
CONGRESS FELT IT ILLEGAL, YET PRESIDENT COULD NOT VETO BILL.
STUDY SHOWS FIGHT BETWEEN LEGISLATURE AND EXECUTIVE.
ANALYZES LOCAL PRESSURE IN NATIONAL POLICY-MAKING, USING
BOSTON NAVAL INSTALLATION AS EXAMPLE.

0391 CARPER E.T.
ILLINOIS GOES TO CONGRESS FOR ARMY LAND.
INDIANAPOLIS: BOBBS-MERRILL, 1962, 332 PP.
DESCRIBES SENATORS DOUGLAS'S AND DIRKSEN'S 2-YEAR
OCCUPATION WITH REQUESTS FROM SPORTSMEN AND A BUSINESS
SYNDICATE, EACH SEEKING SAME PIECE OF SURPLUS ARMY LAND.
CONGRESSIONAL LEGISLATION ULTIMATELY TRANSFERRED THE LAND,
IN LIEU OF FEDERAL AGENCY RESPONSIBLE, THE GENERAL
SERVICE ADMINISTRATION.

0392 CARR C.
"LEGISLATIVE CONTROL OF ADMINISTRATIVE RULES AND
REGULATIONS: PARLIAMENTARY SUPERVISION IN BRITAIN."
NYU LAW REV., 30 (MAY 55), 1045-1056.
DESCRIPTION OF DEVELOPMENT AND PRACTICE OF PARLIAMENTARY
REVIEW OF ADMINISTRATIVE RULES. PARLIAMENT HAS A STANDING
SCRUTINY COMMITTEE TO REVIEW ALL ADMINISTRATIVE RULES AND
DECIDE UPON WHICH SHOULD BE DISCUSSED BY PARLIAMENT BEFORE
BEING ALLOWED TO BECOME OPERATIVE.

0393 CARR E.H.
THE TWENTY YEARS' CRISIS 1919-1939.
LONDON: MACMILLAN, 1940, 307 PP.
DISCUSSES TRENDS OF INTERNATIONAL POLITICS 1919-1939.
EXPLAINS ORIGINS OF INTERNATIONAL SCIENCE. SHOWS CONFLICT
OF UTOPIAN AND REALISTIC IDEAS. TRACES PARTS PLAYED BY

POWER, LAW, MORALITY IN POLICY FORMULATION. HOPES MORALITY
WILL GUIDE NEW INTERNATIONAL ORDER.

0394 CARR R.K.
THE SUPREME COURT AND JUDICIAL REVIEW.
NEW YORK: FARRAR STRAUSS, 1942, 304 PP.
ANALYSIS AND APPRAISAL OF WAYS IN WHICH JUDICIAL REVIEW
HAS BEEN EXERCISED BY SUPREME COURT IN MOLDING PUBLIC
POLICY. FEELS COURT IS BEST UNDERSTOOD AS A POLITICAL AGENCY
SHARING THE POWER TO GOVERN WITH PRESIDENT AND CONGRESS.
DISCUSSES NATURE OF JUDICIAL POWER, WHY SUCH POWER WAS
GRANTED TO COURT, AND HOW IT HAS BEEN EXERCISED. STUDIES
INFLUENCES THAT HAVE SHAPED COURT'S DECISIONS.

0395 CARRINGTON P.D.
"POLITICAL QUESTIONS: THE JUDICIAL CHECK ON THE EXECUTIVE."
VIRGINIA LAW REV., 42 (FEB. 56), 175-201.
THE PRIME RESPONSIBILITY FOR REGULATING THE EXECUTIVE
BRANCH RESTS WITH THE CONGRESS AND THE PUBLIC. THE COURTS
SERVE ONLY AS A LIMITED CHECK, AND CAN ONLY ACT WHERE THE
CONSTITUTION OR CONGRESS EXPRESSLY CALLS FOR JUDICIAL
ACTION.

0396 CARROTHERS A.W.R.
LABOR ARBITRATION IN CANADA.
TORONTO: BUTTERWORTHS, 1961, 190 PP.
EVALUATES ARBITRATION AS METHOD OF SETTLING GRIEVANCES IN
LABOR DISPUTES. CONSIDERS RELEVANT SECTIONS OF ALL COLLEC-
TIVE BARGAINING STATUTES IN CANADA AND ARBITRATION STATUTES
OF COMMON LAW PROVINCES, WITH ILLUSTRATIVE CASE STUDIES IN
BASIC AREAS.

0397 CARSON P.
MATERIALS FOR WEST AFRICAN HISTORY IN THE ARCHIVES OF BEL-
GIUM AND HOLLAND.
LONDON: ATHLONE PRESS, 1962, 86 PP.
FIRST IN A SERIES OF VOLUMES COVERING EUROPEAN AR-
CHIVES, THIS BOOKS ARRANGES MATERIAL ACCORDING TO CITY AND
INSTITUTION WHERE FOUND; CATALOGUES LETTERS, RECEIPTS, MAPS,
CHARTS, SHIPS' RECORDS, AND MANY OTHER ITEMS. DOES NOT COVER
DIPLOMATIC RELATIONS AMONG EUROPEAN POWERS. 1,250 ENTRIES.

0398 CARTER G.M. ED.
FIVE AFRICAN STATES: RESPONSES TO DIVERSITY.
ITHACA: CORNELL U. PR., 1963, 643 PP., $10.00.
FIVE POLITICAL SCIENTISTS DESCRIBE THE CONGO, DAHOMEY,
CAMEROUN, RHODESIA AND NYASALAND, AND SOUTH AFRICA, RESPEC-
TIVELY, USING A COMMON OUTLINE WHOSE MAJOR HEADINGS ARE
HISTORICAL BACKGROUND, CONTEMPORARY SETTING, POLITICAL
PROCESS, CONTEMPORARY ISSUES, EXTERNAL RELATIONS.

0399 CARTER G.M. ED., WESTIN A.F. ED.
POLITICS IN EUROPE.
NEW YORK: HARCOURT BRACE, 1965, 205 PP., LC#65-17351.
CASE STUDIES ON GREAT BRITAIN, FRANCE, GERMANY, THE
COMMON MARKET, AND THE SOVIET UNION. THE FOUR COUNTIRES
DISCUSSED REPRESENT TYPES OF POLITICAL SYSTEMS; THE
COMMON MARKET, THE MOST SUCCESSFUL EUROPEAN SUPRANATIONAL
ORGANIZATION. EACH CASE CONCENTRATES ON A DEFFERENT
ASPECT OF POLITICAL SOCIETY: THE PRESS, THE LAW, CONSTITU-
TIONALISM, PRESSURE GROUPS, AND EUROPEAN INTEGRATION.

0400 CARTER P.G. ED.
STATISTICAL BULLETINS: AN ANNOTATED BIBLIOGRAPHY OF THE GEN-
ERAL STATISTICAL BULLETINS AND MAJOR POL SUBDIV OF WORLD.
WASHINGTON: LIBRARY OF CONGRESS, 1054, 93 PP., LC#54-60010.
AN ANNOTATED BIBLIOGRAPHY OF GENERAL STATISTICAL BULLE-
TINS ISSUED BY COUNTRY, COLONY, OR TERRITORY. PUBLISHED
AS A COMPANION TO THE BIBLIOGRAPHY ON NATIONAL STATISTICAL
YEARBOOKS. PROVIDES SUMMARY OF ALL IMPORTANT AVAILABLE
RECENT STATISTICS FOR REFERENCE IN ECONOMIC AND SOCIAL
RESEARCH, NOTES ON AGENCY SOURCES, AND BIBLIOGRAPHIES
FURNISH LEADS TO MORE DETAILED AND SPECIALIZED PUBLICATIONS.

0401 CARTER R.F., SUTTHOFF J.
COMMUNITIES AND THEIR SCHOOLS.
STANFORD: STAN U INST COMM RES, 1960, 228 PP.
RESEARCH REPORT INVESTIGATES SCHOOL-COMMUNITY RELATIONS,
HOW THEY CAN BE IMPROVED, HOW LEGAL PROVISIONS AFFECT
THEM, AND HOW VOTER TURNOUT AFFECTS SCHOOL BOND ISSUES.

0402 CARTER R.L., KENYON D. ET AL.
EQUALITY.
NEW YORK: PANTHEON BOOKS, 1965, 191 PP., LC#65-10210.
ESSAYS DISCUSSING "COMPENSATORY TREATMENT" IN EDUCATION,
HOUSING, AND EMPLOYMENT FOR NEGROES. GENERALLY FAVORS SUCH
TREATMENT AND ARGUES THAT FREQUENT OBJECTIONS TO "DIS-
CRIMINATION IN REVERSE" MISS THE REAL POINT, OR ARE
IRRELEVANT IN VIEW OF THE MANIFEST CONSEQUENCES OF PREVIOUS
DISCRIMINATION.

0403 CARTER R.M., WILKINS L.T.
"SOME FACTORS IN SENTENCING POLICY."
J. CRIM. LAW, CRIM., POLICE SCI., 58 (DEC. 67), 503-514.
DETERMINES THAT THE RELATIONSHIPS BETWEEN RECOMMENDA-
TIONS FOR PROBATION BY PROBATION OFFICERS AND THE DISPOSI-

TIONS BY THE COURT FOR PROBATION ARE HIGH. DATA REVEAL
THAT LENGTH OF SERVICE OF PROBATION OFFICER IS DIRECTLY RE-
LATED TO CONSERVATIVE VIEWS ON USE OF PROBATION. EMPLOYS
QUANTITATIVE AND QUALITATIVE EXAMINATIONS OF RELATION-
SHIP BETWEEN PROBATION RECOMMENDATIONS AND SENTENCING.

0404 CASSINELLI C.W.
THE POLITICS OF FREEDOM.
SEATTLE: U OF WASHINGTON PR, 1961, 214 PP., LC#61-11580.
ANALYZES MODERN DEMOCRATIC STATE, INCLUDING ITS INSTITU-
TIONS, PARTIES, POLICIES, CIVIL LIBERTIES, CONSENSUS,
FOUNDATIONS, AND PROSPECTS, AS WELL AS POLITICAL MYTHS OF
DEMOCRATIC STATE.

0405 CASTANEDA J.
"THE UNDERDEVELOPED NATIONS AND THE DEVELOPMENT OF INTERNA-
TIONAL LAW."
INT. ORGAN., 15 (WINTER 61), 38-48.
CLARIFIES POSSIBILITIES AND LIMITATIONS OF PURELY DECLAR-
ATIVE CODES OF CUSTOMARY RULES ADOPTED BY GENERAL ASSEMBLY
AS MEANS OF DISCHARGING THAT ORGAN'S RESPONSIBILITIES. CON-
CLUDES WITH EXAMINATION OF SOME OF UNDERLYING POLITICAL AS-
SUMPTIONS THAT FORM FOUNDATION OF THIS APPROACH.

0406 CASTBERG F.
FREEDOM OF SPEECH IN THE WEST.
NEW YORK: OCEANA PUBLISHING, 1960, 475 PP.
STUDY OF POLITICAL FREEDOM OF SPEECH IN FRANCE, WEST
GERMANY, AND US. GIVES ACCOUNT OF WHERE COURTS HAVE STOOD.
PROVIDES CASES TO ILLUSTRATE NATIONS' LAWS IN RESPECT TO
FREEDOM OF SPEECH. INCLUDES BACKGROUND TO HISTORICAL
DEVELOPMENT OF LEGAL CONCEPTS.

0407 CATHERINE R. ED., THUILLIER G. ED.
LA REVUE ADMINISTRATIVE.
PARIS: REVUE ADMINISTRATIVE.
A BIMONTHLY REVIEW OF MODERN ADMINISTRATION FIRST ISSUED
IN 1948. EACH ISSUE CONTAINS ARTICLES CONCERNING THE BUSI-
NESS AND FINANCE WORLD AS WELL AS MATERIAL ON JUDICIAL AND
GOVERNMENTAL FUNCTIONING. ANNOTATED BIBLIOGRAPHY OF TRADE
LITERATURE AND SEVERAL BOOK REVIEWS APPEAR IN EACH ISSUE.

0408 CAUGHEY J.W.
IN CLEAR AND PRESENT DANGER.
CHICAGO: U OF CHICAGO PRESS, 1958, 208 PP., LC#58-10815.
STUDIES PRESENT STATUS OF INDIVIDUAL LIBERTIES IN US IN
COLD WAR. DISCUSSES TO WHAT EXTENT OUR RIGHTS HAVE BEEN LIM-
ITED AS RESULT OF POSTWAR CONFLICT WITH SOVIET UNION. DEALS
WITH MCCARTHY INFLUENCE ON REDUCTION OF INDIVIDUAL FREEDOM.

0409 CAVAN R.S.
CRIMINOLOGY (2ND ED.)
NEW YORK: THOMAS Y CROWELL, 1955, 718 PP., LC#55-7304.
PRESENTS SOCIOLOGICAL ANALYSIS OF CRIMINAL AND HIS BEHAV-
IOR. PROVIDES DETAILED DESCRIPTION AND CRITICAL EVAL-
UATION OF LAW-ENFORCEMENT AGENCIES AND THEIR METHODS. APPEN-
DIXES INCLUDE HISTORICAL SURVEY OF THEORIES OF CRIMINALITY
AND DEFINITIONS OF CRIMES USED BY FBI.

0410 CAVERS D.F.
"ADMINISTRATIVE DECISION-MAKING IN NUCLEAR FACILITIES
LICENSING."
U. PENN. LAW REV., 110 (JAN. 62), 330-370.
AEC IS CHARGED WITH UPHOLDING PUBLIC INTEREST IN AREAS
OF SAFETY, EFFICIENCY, ETC., BUT HAS NOT DONE SO, SINCE MOST
OF ITS LICENSING ACTIONS ARE UNCONTESTED. IT OFTEN SERVES
MERELY AS A RUBBER STAMP FOR THE PLANS OF PRIVATE POWER
CORPORATIONS.

0411 CAVERS D.F.
THE CHOICE-OF-LAW PROCESS.
ANN ARBOR: U OF MICH PR, 1965, 336 PP., LC#65-21050.
PROVIDES ANALYTICAL FRAMEWORK FOR DISCUSSING THE JUDICIAL
CHOICE BETWEEN CONFLICTING LAWS WHICH MAY BE DETERMINATIVE
OF A PARTICULAR CONTROVERSY. SUMMARIZES COMPETING VIEWS OF
CHOICE-OF-LAW METHODOLOGY AND SUGGESTS REFORMS IN DOCTRINE
AND APPROACH.

0412 CAVES R.
AMERICAN INDUSTRY: STRUCTURE, CONDUCT, PERFORMANCE (2ND ED.)
ENGLEWOOD CLIFFS: PRENTICE HALL, 1967, 120 PP., LC#67-13124.
EXAMINES US ECONOMY REGARDING ORGANIZATION AND FUNCTION
OF MARKET SYSTEM. ANALYZES FORM OF COMPETITION, MONOPOLY,
AND PUBLIC POLICY PROTECTING AND RESTRICTING MARKET PERFOR-
MANCE.

0413 CHAFEE Z. JR.
FREE SPEECH IN THE UNITED STATES.
CAMBRIDGE: HARVARD U PR, 1941, 635 PP.
OUTLINES MAJOR ISSUES AND COURT CASES INVOLVING FREEDOM
OF SPEECH IN US SINCE 1915. STUDIES CONSTITUTIONAL BASES
AND WWI SEDITION CASES. DISCUSSES SUPREME COURT DECISIONS,
1930-40, AND HISTORY OF LAW OF SEDITION. DESCRIBES METHODS
OF CONTROLLING DANGEROUS DISCUSSIONS IN PEACETIME, AND
EXAMINES STATE OF FREE SPEECH IN 1941.

0414 CHAMBERLAIN J.P.
LEGISLATIVE PROCESS: NATION AND STATE.
NEW YORK: APPLETON, 1936, 369 PP.
DEPICTS EVOLUTION OF FORMAL PROCESS OF THE LAW-MAKING
FUNCTION OF THE NATIONAL AND STATE LEGISLATURES. ANALYZES
BOTH ORGANIZATIONAL AND PROCEDURAL ELEMENTS OF LEGISLATIVE
BODIES.

0415 CHAMBERLAIN N.W.
"STRIKES IN CONTEMPORARY CONTEXT."
INDUST. LABOR REL. REV., 20 (JULY 67), 602-617.
EXAMINES ACTUAL NECESSITY FOR WORK STOPPAGES IN FUNCTION-
ING OF COLLECTIVE BARGAINING. DEFINES EMERGENCY CONDITIONS
UNDER WHICH GOVERNMENT INTERVENTION SHOULD OCCUR. EXPLAINS
"ARSENAL-OF-WEAPONS" LEGISLATIVE APPROACH, BENEFITS OF
COMPULSORY ARBITRATION, AND "NON-STOPPAGE STRIKE" OR
"STRIKE-WORK AGREEMENT" WHICH IMPOSES FINES ON BOTH WORKERS
AND MANAGEMENT DURING NEGOTIATIONS, WHILE WORK CONTINUES.

0416 CHAMBERLIN E.H., BRADLEY P.H. ET AL.
LABOR UNIONS AND PUBLIC POLICY.
WASHINGTON: AMER ENTERPRISE INST, 1958, 177 PP., LC#58-10096
A NONPARTISAN RESEARCH ORGANIZATION'S STUDY, INCLUDING
THE ECONOMIC POWER OF LABOR, COLLECTIVE BARGAINING,
FREEDOM TO ORGANIZE AND INVOLUNTARY PARTICIPATION IN UNIONS,
STATE REGULATION, AND A SECTION ON LABOR UNION IMMUNITIES
BY DEAN ROSCOE POUND.

0417 CHAMBLISS W.J.
"TYPES OF DEVIANCE AND THE EFFECTIVENESS OF LEGAL SANCTIONS"
WISC. LAW REV., 67 (SUMMER 67), 703-719.
QUESTIONS EFFECTIVENESS OF LEGAL SANCTIONS IN CRIME
DETERRENCE. ASKS IF CRIMINAL SANCTIONS ARE SO STRUCTURED
THAT THEY MAXIMIZE WHATEVER DETERRENT EFFECT THEY MAY HAVE.
CONCLUDES THAT LEGAL SYSTEM PUNISHES MOST SEVERELY THOSE
PERSONS AND CRIMES THAT ARE LEAST DETERRABLE, AND PUNISHES
LEAST SEVERELY THOSE THAT ARE MOST DETERRABLE.

0418 CHANNING W.E.
DISCOURSES ON WAR (1820-1840)
BOSTON: GINN AND CO, 1903, 229 PP.
COLLECTION OF ESSAYS AND SPEECHES AGAINST WAR. WAR IS
WASTEFUL OF HUMAN RESOURCES AND ENERGY. BECAUSE OF THE
KILLING INVOLVED ANY WAR IS A CRIME AGAINST HUMANITY AND
ITS BENEFITS ACCRUE TO ONLY A VERY FEW. CHANNING FEELS
THAT IF ALL MEN WOULD LIVE BY CHRISTIAN PRINCIPLES OF LOVE
AND BROTHERHOOD, WAR WOULD CEASE BECAUSE EACH NATION WOULD
ACT JUSTLY AND NONE WOULD FIGHT.

0419 CHAPIN B.
THE AMERICAN LAW OF TREASON.
SEATTLE: U OF WASHINGTON PR, 1964, 172 PP., LC#64-11053.
REVOLUTIONARY AND EARLY NATIONAL ORIGINS OF AMERICAN
TREASON LAW; INCLUDES ENGLISH AND COLONIAL BACKGROUND,
LAW IN ACTION, AND CONSTITUTIONAL DEFINITION AND FIRST
APPLICATIONS.

0420 CHAPIN F.S. JR.
SELECTED REFERENCES ON URBAN PLANNING METHODS AND TECHNIQUES
CHAPEL HILL: U OF NC, CITY PLAN, 1967, 77 PP.
UNANNOTATED LISTING OF APPROXIMATELY 800 BOOKS AND PER-
IODICAL ARTICLES COMPILED FOR THE DEPARTMENT OF CITY AND
REGIONAL PLANNING AT THE UNIVERSITY OF NORTH CAROLINA. IN-
CLUDES SECTIONS ON PLANNING FOR INDUSTRIAL, COMMERCIAL, RES-
IDENTIAL, AND RECREATION AREAS, SCHOOL AND TRANSPORTATION
PLANNING, LAND USE, ECONOMY, POPULATION STUDIES, AND HUMAN
INTERACTION IN URBAN AREAS.

0421 CHAPMAN B.
"THE FRENCH CONSEIL D'ETAT."
PARLIAMENTARY AFFAIRS, 12 (SPRING 59), 164-173.
EXAMINES JURISDICTION, ADMINISTRATIVE OPERATIONS, AND
ADVISORY POWERS OF THE "CONSEIL D'ETAT" UNDER THE FIFTH
REPUBLIC. CRITICIZES THE GREAT DELAY BETWEEN COMMENCEMENT
OF A CASE AND THE FINAL VERDICT; CONTENDS THAT AN INCREASE
IN COUNCILLORS, ALTHOUGH AGAINST LAW, IS CHIEF SOLUTION TO
THIS DILEMMA. OBSERVES THAT CONTACT WITH PUBLIC SERVICES
GUARANTEES ADMINISTRATIVE ETHIC IN THE COURT.

0422 CHARLES R.
LA JUSTICE EN FRANCE.
PARIS: PR UNIV DE FRANCE, 1958, 127 PP.
DISCUSSES LEGAL STRUCTURE, BOTH CIVIL AND CRIMINAL, AS
WELL AS POLITICAL AND ADMINISTRATIVE JUSTICE IN MODERN
FRANCE. EXAMINES PROCEDURAL RULES AND SUBSTANTIVE CONTENT
OF FRENCH LEGAL SYSTEM.

0423 CHARLTON K.
EDUCATION IN RENAISSANCE ENGLAND.
TORONTO: TORONTO UNIV PRESS, 1965, 317 PP.
BRIEFLY SURVEYS MEDIEVAL PATTERN OF EDUCATION AND THE
EDUCATIONAL IDEAS OF ITALIAN HUMANISM. TRACES THEIR
RECEPTION AND MODIFICATION IN 16TH-CENTURY ENGLAND,
CONCLUDING WITH THEIR INFLUENCE ON COLONIAL AMERICA.
EVALUATES THE INFLUENCE OF EDUCATION ON PARLIAMENTARY
GOVERNMENT, BOTH ON THE LOCAL AND NATIONAL LEVELS.

0424 CHARMATZ J.P. ED., DAGGETT H.S.
COMPARATIVE STUDIES IN COMMUNITY PROPERTY LAW.
BATON ROUGE: LOUISIANA ST U PR, 1955, 190 PP., LC#55-11817.
STUDIES OF DEVELOPMENT AND PRINCIPLES OF COMMUNITY
PROPERTY LAW IN ARIZONA, CALIFORNIA, IDAHO, LOUISIANA,
NEVADA, NEW MEXICO, TEXAS, AND WASHINGTON. EXAMINES
THE LEGAL MARITAL PROPERTY REGIME ACCORDING TO THE
PROJECT OF THE FRENCH COMMISSION FOR REVISION OF THE
CIVIL CODE.

0425 CHARNAY J.P.
LE SUFFRAGE POLITIQUE EN FRANCE; ELECTIONS PARLEMENTAIRES,
ELECTION PRESIDENTIELLE, REFERENDUMS.
HAGUE: MOUTON & CO, 1965, 832 PP.
EXTENSIVE SURVEY OF PARLIAMENTARY AND PRESIDENTIAL
ELECTIONS, THEIR LEGAL ORGANIZATION, ADMINISTRATION, MANAGE-
MENT, AND SOCIOLOGICAL STRUCTURE. EMPHASIZES THE CANDIDATE
AND ELECTORAL PROCESS AND ITS EVOLUTION.

0426 CHEIN I., ET AL.
THE ROAD TO H; NARCOTICS, DELINQUENCY, AND SOCIAL POLICY.
NEW YORK: BASIC BOOKS, 1964, 482 PP., LC#63-17342.
STUDY OF JUVENILE DRUG ADDICTION IN NYC AND ITS RELATION
TO PERSONALITY AND GROUP MEMBERSHIP. EXAMINES DELINQUENCY
FACTOR AND EXISTING AND PROPOSED PUBLIC PROGRAMS FOR RE-
HABILITATION OF USER AND CONTROL OF DRUG ADDICTION.

0427 CHENERY W.L.
FREEDOM OF THE PRESS.
NEW YORK: HARCOURT BRACE, 1955, 256 PP., LC#55-7421.
TRACES FREEDOM OF PRESS IN COLONIAL AMERICA, NOTING CON-
TRIBUTION OF JEFFERSON AND PROSECUTION OF PETER ZENGER BY
BRITISH AS ESPECIALLY SIGNIFICANT. DISCUSSES IMPORTANT ECO-
NOMIC, POLITICAL, AND SOCIAL FACTORS AFFECTING DEVELOPMENT
OF JOURNALISTIC POLICIES AMONG US NEWSPAPERS. CONTENDS THAT
COMPETITION COMPELS PRESS TO REPORT NEWS COMPETENTLY. DIS-
CUSSES GOVERNMENT CONTROLS OF PRESS AND BROADCASTING.

0428 CHENEY F.
CARTELS, COMBINES, AND TRUSTS: A SELECTED LIST OF REFERENCES
WASHINGTON: LIBRARY OF CONGRESS, 1944, 123 PP.
AN ANNOTATED BIBLIOGRAPHY OF 847 BIBLIOGRAPHIES, BOOKS,
PERIODICALS CONCERNED WITH HISTORY AND DEVELOPMENT OF CAR-
TELS AND RELATED FORMS OF ORGANIZATION IN THE US AND FOREIGN
COUNTRIES. EMPHASIS GIVEN TO LEGAL AND POLITICAL ASPECTS AND
PROPOSALS MADE FOR THEIR POSTWAR CONTROL. ENTRIES ARRANGED
ALPHABETICALLY BY AUTHOR UNDER EACH TOPIC. COVERS
PERIOD FROM 1920 TO SEPTEMBER, 1944. MANY GERMAN SOURCES.

0429 CHICAGO U LAW SCHOOL
CONFERENCE ON JUDICIAL ADMINISTRATION.
CHICAGO: U OF CHICAGO LAW SCHOOL, 1957.
ESSAYS DISCUSSING ADMINISTRATION OF COURT SYSTEMS, ROLE
OF APPELLATE COURTS IN JUDICIAL ADMINISTRATION, AND OTHER
PROBLEMS OF JUDICIAL ADMINISTRATION ON FEDERAL, STATE, AND
MUNICIPAL LEVELS.

0430 CHILDS M.W.
THE EROSION OF INDIVIDUAL LIBERTIES.
ST LOUIS: ST LOUIS POST-DISPATCH, 1961, 32 PP.
ARTICLES ON THREAT TO INDIVIDUAL LIBERTIES POSED BY LEG-
ISLATIVE AND JUDICIAL INTERPRETATIONS OF FIRST AMENDMENT.
DISCUSS SOME IMPORTANT RECENT SUPREME COURT DECISIONS.

0431 CHIU H.
"COMMUNIST CHINA'S ATTITUDE TOWARD INTERNATIONAL LAW"
AMER. J. OF INT. LAW, 60 (JAN. 66), 245-267.
EXAMINES ATTITUDE OF COMMUNIST CHINA TOWARD BASIC
PROBLEMS OF INTERNATIONAL LAW SUCH AS ROLE, DEFINITION, AND
NATURE. DISCUSSES SYSTEMS AND SOURCES OF SUCH LAW, SCIENCE
OF INTERNATIONAL LAW IN COMMUNIST CHINA, AND RELATION
BETWEEN INTERNATIONAL AND MUNICIPAL LAW. MAINTAINS THAT
CHINESE VIEW OF INTERNATIONAL LAW IS MORE MARXIST-LENINIST
AND MORE PRIMITIVE THAN SOVIET VIEW.

0432 CHIU H., EDWARDS R.R.
"COMMUNIST CHINA'S ATTITUDE TOWARD THE UNITED NATIONS: A
LEGAL ANALYSIS."
AMER. J. OF INT. LAW, 62 (JAN. 68), 20-50.
TRACES HISTORY OF COMMUNIST CHINA'S ATTITUDE TOWARD UN.
FINDS HER SUPPORTING IT IN PRINCIPLE AND HOPEFUL FOR ITS
FUTURE IN ITS EARLY YEARS. UNTIL 1965 SHE WAS WILLIN TO BE
INVITED TO AND PARTICIPATE IN AD HOC UN DISCUSSIONS, AND TO
BE "REINSTATED." BUT SINCE 1965 CHINA HAS CONSIDERED UN A
US TOOL AND A PLACE FOR US-USSR BARGAINING, AND HAS LITTLE
HOPE OF A "RETURN TO CHARTER" OR WISH FOR ADMISSION.

0433 CHOJNACKI S. ED., PANKHURST R. ED., SHACK W.A. ED.
REGISTER ON CURRENT RESEARCH ON ETHIOPIA AND THE HORN
OF AFRICA.
ADDIS ABABA: INST ETHIOPIAN STUD, 1963, 44 PP.
AN UNANNOTATED BIBLIOGRAPHY LISTING 341 PROJECTS OF CUR-
RENT RESEARCH ON ETHIOPIA BEING CONDUCTED BOTH IN ETHIOPIA
AND ABROAD. PROVIDES INFORMATION ON THE STATE OF RESEARCH
AS OF 1963: STARTING DATE, DATE OF COMPLETION, PUBLICATIONS,
SCHOLARSHIPS INVOLVED, AND NAMES OF SUPERVISORS AND ASSIS-
TANTS. CLASSIFIED INTO 23 SUBJECT CATEGORIES.

0434 CHOWDHURI R.N.
INTERNATIONAL MANDATES AND TRUSTEESHIP SYSTEMS.
GENEVA: NIJHOFF, 1955, 328 PP.
DISCUSSES HISTORY, OPERATION, AND FUNCTION OF INTER-
NATIONAL MANDATE SYSTEM, TRUSTEESHIP SYSTEM, AND OF AGENCIES
ADMINISTERING THEM. PROVIDES EXAMPLES OF PROBLEMS FACING
TRUSTEESHIP COUNCIL AND SOLUTIONS REACHED.

0435 CHRIMES S.B.
ENGLISH CONSTITUTIONAL HISTORY (3RD ED.)
LONDON: OXFORD U PR, 1965, 202 PP.
OUTLINE OF PRESENT ENGLISH CONSTITUTION AND ITS
DELEGATION OF POWERS TO KING, CABINET, PARLIAMENT, JUDGES,
AND SUBJECTS. TRACES DEVELOPMENT OF CONSTITUTION FROM
MEDIEVAL FOUNDATIONS THROUGH 16TH AND 17TH CENTURIES,
THEORY OF COMPROMISE TO 19TH CENTURY, AND SEPARATION OF
POWERS AND RISE OF CABINET GOVERNMENT. BELIEVES THAT ENGLISH
CONSTITUTION OFFERS BEST SOLUTIONS TO PERENNIAL PROBLEMS.

0436 CHRISTMAN H.M. ED.
THE PUBLIC PAPERS OF CHIEF JUSTICE EARL WARREN.
NEW YORK: SIMON AND SCHUSTER, 1959, 237 PP., LC#59-9504.
COLLECTION INCLUDES SPEECHES GIVEN WHEN WARREN WAS
GOVERNOR OF CALIFORNIA ON CONSTITUTIONAL REFORM AND STATE
GOVERNMENT, EDUCATION, PENAL REFORM, PUBLIC HEALTH, ETC.
ALSO INCLUDES SPEECHES AFTER HE BECAME CHIEF JUSTICE ON LIB-
ERTY AND THE LAW, SUPREME COURT DECISIONS, AND AN ARTICLE ON
THE FUTURE OF LAW.

0437 CHROUST A.H.
THE RISE OF THE LEGAL PROFESSION IN AMERICA (3 VOLS.)
NORMAN: U OF OKLAHOMA PR, 1965, 652 PP., LC#65-11230.
VOLUME I TREATS THE COLONIAL PERIOD BY REGIONS. VOLUME II
TREATS THE REVOLUTION AND POST-REVOLUTIONARY ERA. THOUGH
LAWYERS PLAYED PROMINENT ROLE IN REVOLUTION, IT HURT THE
PROFESSION BY DRIVING OUT TORY LAWYERS AND ABSORBING OTHERS
INTO POLITICS.

0438 CICOUREL A.V.
"KINSHIP, MARRIAGE, AND DIVORCE IN COMPARATIVE FAMILY LAW."
LAW AND SOCIETY REVIEW, 1 (JUNE 67), 103-129.
TREATS FIELD OF COMPARATIVE FAMILY, MARRIAGE, AND DIVORCE
STUDIES, SUGGESTING THAT FOCUS SHOULD BE ON MEMBERS'
SOLUTIONS TO SOCIAL PROBLEMS AND ON INTERACTION BETWEEN
STATED NORMS AND ACTUAL PRACTICES. STUDIES SOURCES OF DATA,
MEANS OF MEASUREMENT, AND WAYS TO IMPROVE METHODS OF
COMPARATIVE STUDIES.

0439 CLAGETT H.L.
A GUIDE TO THE LAW AND LEGAL LITERATURE OF PARAGUAY.
WASHINGTON: LIBRARY OF CONGRESS, 1943, 59 PP.
SURVEY CONDUCTED UNDER AUSPICES OF LATIN AMERICAN SECTION
OF THE LAW LIBRARY OF CONGRESS. REVIEW OF IMPORTANT DEVELOP-
MENTS IN BIBLIOGRAPHICAL WORK, COLLECTIONS AND PERIODICALS.
CHAPTERS ON CRIMINAL, CONSTITUTIONAL, ADMINISTRATIVE, AND
INTERNATIONAL LAW. SECTIONS ON HISTORY AND PHILOSOPHY OF
LAW, COMMERCIAL AND INDUSTRIAL LEGISLATION, CIVIL AND
CRIMINAL CODES. INCLUDES NAME INDEX.

0440 CLAGETT H.L.
A GUIDE TO THE LAW AND LEGAL LITERATURE OF THE MEXICAN
STATES.
WASHINGTON: LIBRARY OF CONGRESS, 1945, 269 PP.
SURVEY OF IMPORTANT DEVELOPMENTS IN EVOLUTION OF MEXICAN
LAW. INFORMATION ON HISTORICAL BACKGROUND, LITERATURE,
CONSTITUTIONS, LAWS, AND CODES LISTED ACCORDING TO STATES.
INCLUDES NAMES INDEX. COMPILED FOR LIBRARY OF CONGRESS.

0441 CLAGETT H.L.
A GUIDE TO THE LAW AND LEGAL LITERATURE OF BOLIVIA.
WASHINGTON: LIBRARY OF CONGRESS, 1947, 110 PP.
ONE OF A SERIES OF ANNOTATED GUIDES PREPARED FOR INCLU-
SION IN THE "HANDBOOK OF LATIN AMERICAN STUDIES." A HEAVILY
DOCUMENTED DESCRIPTION OF THE LAW AND LEGAL LITERATURE IN
THIRTEEN CATEGORIES, RANGING FROM COMMERCIAL LAW TO THE
PHILOSOPHY OF LAW. SOURCES ARE IN SPANISH AND ENGLISH, AND
COVER FOUNDING OF BOLIVIA IN 1559 THROUGH LEGAL DOCUMENTS
OF 1945. MOST SOURCES PUBLISHED BETWEEN 1890-1930.

0442 CLAGETT H.L.
A GUIDE TO THE LAW AND LEGAL LITERATURE OF CHILE, 1917-1946.
WASHINGTON: LIBRARY OF CONGRESS, 1947, 103 PP.
ONE OF SERIES OF REPORTS ON THE LAW AND LEGAL LITERATURE
OF LATIN AMERICA PUBLISHED BY THE LAW LIBRARY DIVISION OF
THE LIBRARY OF CONGRESS. A HEAVILY DOCUMENTED REVIEW OF
GENERAL LEGISLATION, LEGAL HISTORY, JUDICIAL ORGANIZATION,
AND CIVIL PROCEDURE IN CHILE. REFERENCES PRIMARILY FROM
SPANISH AND SOME ENGLISH SOURCES.

0443 CLAGETT H.L.
A GUIDE TO THE LAW AND LEGAL LITERATURE OF ECUADOR.
WASHINGTON: LIBRARY OF CONGRESS, 1947, 100 PP.
ONE IN A SERIES OF REPORTS ON LAW AND LEGAL LITERATURE OF
LATIN AMERICA PUBLISHED BY THE LAW LIBRARY DIVISION OF THE

LIBRARY OF CONGRESS. A HEAVILY DOCUMENTED REVIEW OF INTER-
NATIONAL, MILITARY, AND CONSTITUTIONAL LAW, THE JUDICIAL
SYSTEM, AND CIVIL PROCEDURE. INCLUDES LEGAL PERIODICALS,
BIBLIOGRAPHIES, AND COLLECTIONS OF LAWS FROM PRIMARILY
SPANISH, BUT SOME FRENCH AND AMERICAN SOURCES.

0444 CLAGETT H.L.
A GUIDE TO THE LAW AND LEGAL LITERATURE OF PERU.
WASHINGTON: LIBRARY OF CONGRESS, 1947, 188 PP.
PREPARED UNDER AUSPICES OF LATIN AMERICAN SECTION OF THE
LAW LIBRARY OF CONGRESS. DOCUMENTATION OF GROWTH OF LEGAL
LITERATURE: PERIODICALS, COLLECTIONS, BIBLIOGRAPHIES, WORKS
IN PHILOSOPHY OF LAW, CIVIL CODES, COMMERCIAL LAW, JUDICIAL
SYSTEM, COURT REPORTS AND DIGESTS, CIVIL PROCEDURE, CRIMINAL
CODE, CRIMINAL PROCEDURE, CONSTITUTIONAL LAW, ADMINISTRATIVE
LAW, LABOR LEGISLATION, INTERNATIONAL LAW.

0445 CLAGETT H.L.
A GUIDE TO THE LAW AND LEGAL LITERATURE OF URUGUAY.
WASHINGTON: LIBRARY OF CONGRESS, 1947, 123 PP.
VOLUME IN SERIES OF WORKS SPONSORED BY LATIN AMERICAN
SECTION OF THE LAW LIBRARY OF CONGRESS. SURVEY OF HISTORICAL
LITERATURE IN JUDICIAL SYSTEM, CRIMINAL CODE, CRIMINAL PRO-
CEDURE, CONSTITUTIONAL LAW, CIVIL PROCEDURE. SECTIONS ON
HISTORY AND PHILOSOPHY OF LAW, BIBLIOGRAPHIES, COLLECTIONS,
AND LEGAL PERIODICALS. INDEX OF NAMES INCLUDED.

0446 CLAGETT H.L.
A GUIDE TO THE LAW AND LEGAL LITERATURE OF VENEZUELA.
WASHINGTON: LIBRARY OF CONGRESS, 1947, 128 PP.
ONE OF A SERIES ON THE LAW AND LEGAL LITERATURE OF LATIN
AMERICA PUBLISHED BY THE LAW LIBRARY OF THE LIBRARY OF
CONGRESS. HEAVILY DOCUMENTED REVIEW OF COLLECTIONS OF
CONSTITUTIONAL, COMMERCIAL, AND ADMINISTRATIVE LAW WITH
HISTORY AND TEXTS OF CIVIL AND CRIMINAL CODES AND PROCEDURE.
CONTAINS BIBLIOGRAPHIES, PERIODICALS, INDEXES, ETC., IN
SPANISH AND ENGLISH.

0447 CLAGETT H.L.
A GUIDE TO THE LAW AND LEGAL LITERATURE OF ARGENTINA,
1917-1946.
WASHINGTON: LIBRARY OF CONGRESS, 1948, 180 PP.
ONE IN A SERIES ON THE LAW AND LEGAL LITERATURE OF LATIN
AMERICA PUBLISHED BY THE LAW LIBRARY DIVISION OF THE
LIBRARY OF CONGRESS. HEAVILY DOCUMENTED SURVEY OF GENERAL
JURISPRUDENCE, CIVIL AND COMMERCIAL CODES, CONSTITUTIONAL,
ADMINISTRATIVE, AND INTERNATIONAL LAW. REFERENCES FROM
FRENCH, ENGLISH, AND SPANISH SOURCES. INTENDED AS
A SUPPLEMENT TO BORCHARD'S VOLUME.

0448 CLAGETT H.L.
"THE ADMINISTRATION OF JUSTICE IN LATIN AMERICA."
NEW YORK: OCEANA PUBLISHING, 1952.
SURVEY OF RELATIONS BETWEEN JUDICIAL POWERS AND OTHER
BRANCHES OF GOVERNMENT AS CONSTITUTIONALLY ARRANGED. GENERAL
DESCRIPTION OF VARIOUS CENTRALIZED AND FEDERAL SYSTEMS;
COMPARISON OF SUPREME COURT SYSTEMS; DISCUSSION OF SPECIAL
COURTS AND JURISDICTIONS. BIBLIOGRAPHY CONTAINS CITATIONS OF
LATEST BASIC LEGISLATION IN PRINT, WITH AT LEAST ONE WORK
DEALING WITH EACH TYPE OF COURT IN EACH COUNTRY.

0449 CLARK G., SOHN L.B.
WORLD PEACE THROUGH WORLD LAW.
CAMBRIDGE: HARVARD U. PR., 1960, 387 PP.
DEVELOPS A DETAILED PLAN FOR THE MAINTENANCE OF WORLD
PEACE BY MEANS OF AN EXTENSIVE REVISION OF THE UNITED
NATIONS CHARTER. PROPOSES THE ESTABLISHMENT OF A PERMANENT
WORLD POLICE FORCE AND THE COMPLETE DISARMAMENT OF ALL
NATIONS.

0450 CLARK G., SOHN L.B.
WORLD PEACE THROUGH WORLD LAW; TWO ALTERNATIVE PLANS.
CAMBRIDGE: HARVARD U PR, 1966, 535 PP., LC#66-21198.
PRESENTS PLAN FOR MAINTENANCE OF WORLD PEACE IN FORM OF
REVISED UN CHARTER. MAINTAINS THAT WORLD PEACE CANNOT EXIST
WITHOUT ENFORCEABLE WORLD LAW FOR PREVENTION OF WAR.
REVISES MEMBERSHIP, GENERAL ASSEMBLY, EXECUTIVE COUNCIL,
ECONOMIC AND SOCIAL AND TRUSTEESHIP COUNCILS, DISARMAMENT
PROCESS, WORLD POLICY FORCE, JUDICIAL AND REVENUE SYSTEMS,
PENALTIES, PRIVILEGES, AND RATIFICATION AND AMENDMENT PLANS.

0451 CLARK J.P.
THE RISE OF A NEW FEDERALISM.
NEW YORK: COLUMBIA U PRESS, 1938, 347 PP.
GENERAL SURVEY OF FEDERAL-STATE COOPERATION IN THE US.
EXPLORES DEVICES OF FEDERAL-STATE COOPERATION AND OPERA-
TION IN DEALING WITH ECONOMIC AND SOCIAL PROBLEMS.
SELECTED UNANNOTATED BIBLIOGRAPHY APPENDED TO TEXT. EACH
CHAPTER SUPPLEMENTED BY BIBLIOGRAPHY ARRANGED ACCORDING TO
FORMAT: LEGAL CASES, MANUSCRIPTS, AND PUBLISHED SOURCES.

0452 CLEMMER D.
"LEADERSHIP PHENOMENA IN A PRISON COMMUNITY."
J. CRIM. LAW CRIM. POLICE SCI., 28 (MAR.-APR. 38), 861-872.
STUDY BASED ON AN ILLINOIS STATE PENITENTIARY, OF A
DIFFICULT, GREATLY REGULATED, AND CHANGING INMATE POPULA-

TION. LEADER PERSONALITY TRAITS, METHODS OF GAINING LEADER
STATUS, TENURE OF LEADERS, AND EFFECT OF ABOVE ON PRISON
COMMUNITY ARE DISCUSSED.

0453 CLEMMER D.
THE PRISON COMMUNITY.
NEW YORK: RINEHART, 1958, 341 PP.
THIS FAMOUS STUDY IS A COMPREHENSIVE TREATMENT ON THE
SOCIAL PROCESSES OF AN ILLINOIS STATE PRISON. CONTAINS
A DISCUSSION OF SOCIAL GROUPS IN THE PRISON COMMUNITY,
LEADERSHIP PHENOMENA, AND SOCIAL CONTROLS BY THE DOMINANT
GROUP SET AGAINST THE PECULIAR PRISON CULTURE MILIEU.

0454 CLEVELAND H.
"CRISIS DIPLOMACY."
FOREIGN AFFAIRS, 41 (JULY 63), 638-649.
DISCUSSES MANAGEMENT OF A FOREIGN POLICY CRISIS. SUGGESTS
FIVE "LESSONS" FOR SUCH DECISION-MAKING: KEEPING OBJECTIVES
LIMITED, DECIDING LIMITS OF ACTION, SELECTING THE GENTLEST
FORM OF FORCE NECESSARY, WIDENING THE COMMUNITY OF THE
CONCERNED, RECOGNIZING THAT DECISION-MAKERS MUST ABIDE BY
THE LAWS, AND TAKING NOTICE OF PRECEDENTS MADE.

0455 CLINARD M.B.
SOCIOLOGY OF DEVIANT BEHAVIOR.
NEW YORK: RINEHART, 1957, 599 PP., LC#57-6449.
TEXTBOOK ON CAUSES, NATURE, AND FORMS OF DEVIANT
BEHAVIOR. COMPARES DEVIANT BEHAVIOR IN RURAL AND URBAN
AREAS, SUGGESTS ECONOMIC AND TECHNOLOGICAL FACTORS, AND
EXAMINES SEX CRIME, "CAREER CRIMINALS," DRUG ADDICTION,
ALCOHOLISM, MENTAL DISORDERS, SUICIDE, DISCRIMINATION,
ETC. DISCUSSES FORMS OF SOCIAL CONTROL OF DEVIANT BEHAVIOR.

0456 CLINARD M.B. ED.
ANOMIE AND DEVIANT BEHAVIOR: A DISCUSSION AND CRITIQUE.
NEW YORK: FREE PRESS OF GLENCOE, 1964, 324 PP., LC#64-20314.
ANOMIE AS A THEORETICAL TOOL FOR ANALYZING SOCIAL
DEVIATION IS EXAMINED, IN PART AGAINST EMPIRICAL RESULTS.
THE VIEWS OF DURKHEIM AND MERTON ARE APPRAISED, AND MERTON
ANSWERS HIS CRITICS. ANOMIE IS ANALYZED WITH RESPECT TO GANG
DELIQUENCY, MENTAL DISORDER, DRUG ADDICTION, AND
ALCOHOLISM. THERE IS AN EXTENSIVE BIBLIOGRAPHY.

0457 CLINARD M.B., QUINNEY R.
CRIMINAL BEHAVIOR SYSTEMS: A TYPOLOGY.
NEW YORK: HOLT RINEHART WINSTON, 1967, 498 PP., LC#67-18876.
STUDIES EIGHT TYPES OF CRIME AND DISCUSSES CONSTRUCTION,
FORMULATION AND UTILIZATION OF A TYPOLOGY OF CRIME, AND
RESEARCH ON TYPES OF CRIME. SELECTED BIBLIOGRAPHIES FOLLOW
DISCUSSION ON EACH TYPE OF CRIME. INCLUDES ARTICLES AND
BOOKS PUBLISHED 1940-65.

0458 CLOGGER T.J.
"THE BIG EAR."
QUARTERLY REV., 305 (OCT. 67), 420-428.
DISCUSSES ELECTRONIC EAVESDROPPING IN US AND ENGLAND.
DESCRIBES VARIOUS INTRICATE DEVICES USED, AND GIVES CASES,
SUCH AS THE RUSSIAN "BUGGING" OF THE AMERICAN EMBASSY IN
1960, WHERE SPYING DEVICES HAVE BEEN USED. NOTES SEVERAL
NEW COUNTER MEASURES THAT ARE BEING EMPLOYED.

0459 CLOWARD R.A.
"ILLEGITIMATE MEANS, ANOMIE, AND DEVIANT BEHAVIOR"
AMER. SOCIOLOGICAL REV., (APR. 59), 164-176.
THE THEORY OF ANOMIE HAS UNDERGONE TWO MAJOR PHASES OF
DEVELOPMENT, AS EXEMPLIFIED BY WORK OF DURKHEIM AND MERTON.
IN THIS PAPER A THIRD PHASE IS OUTLINED. THEORY FOCUSES
ON PRESSURES TOWARD DEVIANT BEHAVIOR ARISING FROM
DISCREPANCIES BETWEEN CULTURAL GOALS AND APPROVED MODES OF
ACCESS TO THEM. FOCUSES PRIMARILY UPON VARIATIONS IN
THE AVAILABILITY OF LEGITIMATE MEANS.

0460 CLYDE W.M.
THE STRUGGLE FOR THE FREEDOM OF THE PRESS FROM CAXTON TO
CROMWELL.
LONDON: OXFORD U PR, 1934, 360 PP.
SURVEY OF CENSORSHIP CONFLICT FROM ROYAL PREROGATIVE TO
TACTICS OF THE PROTECTORATE. CONSIDERS PRINTING AND
NEWSPAPERS.

0461 COHEN A. ED., LINDESMITH A. ED., SCHUESSLER K. ED.
THE SUTHERLAND PAPERS.
BLOOMINGTON: INDIANA U PR, 1956, 330 PP.
SELECTED PAPERS OF EDWIN SUTHERLAND, INFLUENTIAL
CRIMINOLOGIST, COVERING HIS THEORIES AND RESEARCH ON
CRIME CAUSATION, CONTROL, AND PREVENTION. WITH BIBLIOGRAPHY
OF SUTHERLAND'S WRITINGS.

0463 COHEN M.
"BASIC PRINCIPLES OF INTERNATIONAL LAW."
CAN. BAR REV., 42 (SEPT. 64), 449-62.
REASSESSES CLASSICAL PRINCIPLES OF INTERNATIONAL LAW,
PLACING SPECIAL EMPHASIS ON TRADITIONAL RELATIONS OF STATES.
ANALYZES DISILLUSIONMENT WITH INTERNATIONAL LAW AFTER BOTH
WORLD WARS AND PRESENTS NEW PERSPECTIVES ON NATURE OF LAW
AND LEGAL SYSTEMS IN GENERAL.

0464 COHEN M. ED.
LAW AND POLITICS IN SPACE: SPECIFIC AND URGENT PROBLEMS IN
THE LAW OF OUTER SPACE.
MONTREAL: MCGILL U. PR., 1964, 221 PP.
     CONFERENCE PAPERS PERTAIN TO INTERNATIONAL ARRANGEMENTS
FOR SATELLITE COMMUNICATIONS, POLLUTION AND CONTAMINATION IN
SPACE, ARMS CONTROL, DISARMAMENT AND OBSERVATION IN SPACE,
PROSPECTS FOR AN OUTER SPACE REGIME. FIND THAT MAJOR POWERS
USE LAW TO SERVE NATIONAL INTERESTS.

0465 COHEN M.B., COHEN R.A.
"PERSONALITY AS A FACTOR IN ADMINISTRATIVE DECISIONS."
PSYCHOANALYTIC QUART., 14 (FEB. 51), 47-53.
     FOUR CASE-STUDIES SHOWING HOW PERSONALITY STRUCTURE
AFFECTS ADMINISTRATION AND THE RANGE OF REPRESENTATION.
DISCUSSES DISTORTIONS BY LESS RATIONAL EMPLOYEES AND USE OF
DEFENSE MECHANISMS, BUT SHOWS, ALSO, THAT CERTAIN FEARS CAN
BE TURNED INTO AN EMPATHY USEFUL IN SOLVING COMMUNITY
PROJECT CONFLICT.

0466 COHEN M.L.
SELECTED BIBLIOGRAPHY OF FOREIGN AND INTERNATIONAL LAW.
PHILADELPHIA: VILLANOVA LAW SCH, 1964, 6 PP.
     ANNOTATED BIBLIOGRAPHY OF REFERENCE BOOKS FOR SMALL
AND MEDIUM-SIZE LIBRARIES. CONTAINS LISTINGS OF PUBLI-
CATION SERIES OR SURVEYS IN ENGLISH ON THE LAW OF
FOREIGN COUNTRIES AND SELECTED NON-DOCUMENTARY
SOURCES FOR INTERNATIONAL LAW REFERENCE WORK.

0467 COHEN M.R.
LAW AND THE SOCIAL ORDER: ESSAYS IN LEGAL PHILOSOPHY.
HAMDEN, CONN: ARCHON BOOKS, 1967, 403 PP., LC#67-28552.
     ORIGINALLY PUBLISHED IN 1933, THIS BOOK IS A RESULT OF
THE DEPRESSION. ATTACKS ATTITUDE OF FEDERAL COURTS TOWARD
LABOR LEGISLATION. FAVORS A "NEW DEAL" GOVERNMENT. SURVEYS
LEGAL ATTITUDE TOWARD SOCIAL WELFARE AND CURRENT INSTITU-
TIONS THAT BLOCK PROGRESS. IN DISCUSSING LEADING EUROPEAN
AND AMERICAN JURISTS, AUTHOR SIDES WITH THOSE WHO SUPPORT
SOCIAL WELFARE MEASURES.

0468 COHN H.J.
THE GOVERNMENT OF THE RHINE PALATINATE IN THE FIFTEENTH
CENTURY.
LONDON: OXFORD U PR, 1965, 289 PP.
     TRACES HISTORY OF RHINE PALATINATE FROM ISSUANCE OF
GOLDEN BULL IN 1356 TO END OF 15TH CENTURY. EXAMINES TERRI-
TORIAL EXPANSION, RIGHTS OF TERRITORIAL PRINCE, RELATIONS
WITH ROMAN CHURCH, AND ADMINISTRATIVE ASPECTS SUCH AS COURT
SYSTEM, FINANCIAL ADMINISTRATION, AND WORK OF COUNCILS AND
LOCAL ADMINISTRATIONS.

0469 COHN K.
"CRIMES AGAINST HUMANITY."
GERMAN FOREIGN POLICY, 6 (FEB. 67), 160-169.
     COMMENTARY ON 21ST SESSION OF COMMISSION FOR HUMAN RIGHTS
WHOSE ASSEMBLY, ACCORDING TO AUTHOR, WAS NECESSITATED BY
WEST GERMAN APPLICATION OF STATUTE OF LIMITATIONS TO CRIMES
AGAINST HUMANITY. DISCUSSION OF PROSECUTION OF WAR CRIMES
IN BOTH GERMANIES IN POST-WAR PERIOD WITH CONDEMNATION
OF CURRENT WEST GERMAN ATTITUDE TO WAR CRIMINALS AND NAZI
REGIME.

0470 COHN M.M.
AN INTRODUCTION TO THE STUDY OF THE CONSTITUTION.
BALTIMORE: JOHNS HOPKINS PRESS, 1892, 235 PP.
     ARGUES THAT GOVERNMENTAL STRUCTURES, AND IN PARTICULAR
THE US CONSTITUTION, ARE RESULT OF SOCIAL AND PHYSICAL
FACTORS, AND CANNOT BE CONSIDERED AS PRODUCTS OF
DISINTERESTED OR ABSTRACT INTELLIGENCE OR RESPONSES TO
THEORIES. SUCH STRUCTURES ARISE FROM HISTORY, AND ALTER
SLOWLY AND WITH COURSE OF EVENTS. A CONSERVATIVE READING OF
THE NATURE OF LAW, GOVERNMENT, AND CONSTITUTIONS.

0471 COKE E.
INSTITUTES OF THE LAWS OF ENGLAND (1628-1658)
ORIGINAL PUBLISHER NOT AVAILABLE, 1853, LC#22-20083.
     TECHNICAL RESTATEMENT OF ALL ENGLISH LAW, IN FOUR PARTS.
FIRST INSTITUTE (1628) IS A COMMENTARY UPON LITTLETON'S
"TENURES," COVERING LAW OF REAL PROPERTY (ESTATES, TENURE,
AND CO-OWNERSHIP). SECOND INSTITUTE (1642) IS A COMMENTARY
UPON THE PRINCIPAL STATUTES. THIRD INSTITUTE (1644) IS A
TREATISE ON CRIMINAL LAW. FOURTH INSTITUTE (1658) DESCRIBES
JURISDICTION AND HISTORY OF THE COURTS.

0472 COLEMAN J.W. JR.
DEATH AT THE COURT-HOUSE.
LEXINGTON: WINBURN PRESS, 1952, 28 PP.
     STUDY OF MOB ACTION IN LEXINGTON, KENTUCKY, REGARDING
MURDER SUSPECT. EXAMINES BACKGROUND LEADING TO MOB VIOLENCE
AND MEASURES TAKEN BY AUTHORITIES TO CONTROL SITUATION.

0473 COLEMAN-NORTON P.R.
ROMAN STATE AND CHRISTIAN CHURCH: A COLLECTION OF LEGAL
DOCUMENTS TO A.D. 535 (3 VOLS.)
LONDON:SOC PROM CHRIST KNOWLEDGE, 1966, 1358 PP.
     COLLECTION OF LEGAL DOCUMENTS AFFECTING CHRISTIAN CHURCH

DURING ROMAN EMPIRE FROM BEGINNING OF CHURCH TO CODE OF
JUSTINIAN I IN 534 A.D.

0474 COIGNE A.B.
STATUTE MAKING (2ND ED.)
CHICAGO: COMMERCE CLEARING HOUSE, 1965, 293 PP., LC#64-83
     TREATISE ON MEANS AND METHODS FOR ENACTMENT OF STATUTE
LAW IN US. EXPLAINS INSTRUMENTS AVAILABLE FOR ENACTMENT OF
STATUTE LAW, ORGANIZATION OF STATE AND FEDERAL LEGISLATURES.
REVIEWS PARLIAMENTARY PROCEDURE AND METHODS OF INTRODUCTING
AND PASSING BILLS. DISCUSSES PROCEDURES IN MASSACHUSETTS,
MAINE, AND NEBRASKA IN DETAIL. ALSO OUTLINES METHODS OF
AMENDING CONSTITUTION AND RATIFYING TREATIES.

0475 COLLINS I.
"THE GOVERNMENT AND THE NEWSPAPER PRESS IN FRANCE, 1814-1881
LONDON: OXFORD U PR, 1959.
     EXAMINES CONFLICTS BETWEEN GOVERNMENTAL REGULATIONS AND
JOURNALISTIC FREEDOMS IN FRANCE IN 19TH CENTURY. ANALYZES
CONTENT OF EACH OF THE PRESS LAWS OF PERIOD AND DISCUSSES
INTENTIONS WHICH LAY BEHIND THEIR PASSAGE. BIBLIOGRAPHY OF
SOURCES AND CONTEMPORARY WORKS APPENDED TO TEXT. INCLUDES
UNPUBLISHED DOCUMENTS FOUND IN THE ARCHIVES NATIONALE, PUB-
LISHED DOCUMENTS, JOURNALS, MEMOIRS, ETC.

0476 COLOMBOS C.J. ED.
THE INTERNATIONAL LAW OF THE SEA.
LONDON: LONGMANS, GREEN & CO, 1962, 754 PP.
     COMPILATION OF PRESENTLY ACCEPTED INTERNATIONAL MARITIME
LAW, COVERING SOURCES AND DEVELOPMENTS, TRADE, BODIES OF
WATER, FISHING, NAVIGATION, WARSHIPS AND CHANGES RESULTING
FROM WAR.

0477 COLORADO CIVIL SERVICE COMN
SECOND BIENNIAL REPORT TO THE GOVERNOR, 1909-1910.
DENVER: SMITH-BROOK PRINTING CO, 1910, 83 PP.
     RECORDS CIVIL SERVICE ACT, ITS RULES AND REGULATIONS.
REPORTS ON ACTIVITIES OF COMMISSION FOR TWO-YEAR PERIOD.

0478 COLUMBIA UNIVERSITY
A BIBLIOGRAPHY OF THE FACULTY OF POLITICAL SCIENCE OF
COLUMBIA UNIVERSITY, 1880-1930.
NEW YORK: COLUMBIA U PRESS, 1931, 366 PP.
     LIST OF TITLES OF BOOKS, ARTICLES, AND PAMPHLETS BY MEM-
BERS OF DEPARTMENT OF POLITICAL SCIENCE AT COLUMBIA. NAMES
ARRANGED IN CHRONOLOGY OF APPOINTMENT TO FACULTY AND PUBLI-
CATIONS LISTED SEPARATELY IN CHRONOLOGY OF PUBLICATION.
INCLUDES LIST OF DOCTORAL DISSERTATIONS WRITTEN UNDER THEIR
GUIDANCE.

0479 COMM. STUDY ORGAN. PEACE
"ORGANIZATION OF PEACE."
INT. CONCIL., 369 (APR. 41), 368-527.
     COLLECTION OF FIFTEEN BRIEF ESSAYS ON SOCIAL JUSTICE,
ECONOMIC ORGANIZATION OF PEACE, AND INTERNATIONAL POLITICAL
ORGANIZATION.

0480 COMM. STUDY ORGAN. PEACE
"A TEN YEAR RECORD, 1939-1949."
NEW YORK: AMER. ASS. UN, 1949, 48 PP.
     REVEALS ACTIVITIES OF COMMISSION FROM OUTBREAK OF WW 2 TO
1949 AND INCORPORATES PROSPECTS FOR UN CHARTER. EXAMINES
SPECIFIC PROBLEMS OF UN AND SEEKS MEANS OF STRENGTHENING
CHARTER.

0481 COMM. STUDY ORGAN. PEACE
REPORTS.
NEW YORK: 1940-55., 5VOLS.
     SERIES OF PAMPHLETS REPRESENTS A COMPREHENSIVE STUDY OF
THE ORGANIZATIONS NECESSARY FOR WORLD PEACE. REPORTS COVER
DISARMAMENT, ECONOMIC WELFARE, SELF-DEFENSE AND HUMAN RIGHTS
ON AN INTERNATIONAL LEVEL. DETAILED ANALYSIS OF COLLECTIVE
SECURITY UNDER THE UNITED NATIONS.

0482 COMM. STUDY ORGAN. PEACE
STRENGTHENING THE UNITED NATIONS.
NEW YORK: HARPER, 1957, 276 PP.
     RECOMMENDS CHANGES IN CHARTER, PRACTICES AND POLICIES
OF U.N. AS WELL AS MODIFICATION IN USA POLICY TOWARDS THE
WORLD-STRUCTURE. PROPOSES RESTRICTION OF VETO POWER,
GREATER USE OF WORLD COURT, EXPANSION OF TECHNICAL
ASSISTANCE AND PERMANENT POLICE-FORCE.

0483 COMM. STUDY ORGAN. PEACE
ORGANIZING PEACE IN THE NUCLEAR AGE.
NEW YORK: N.Y.U. PR., 1959, 245 PP.
     PRESENTS SPECIFIC METHODS BY WHICH THE UN CAN BE
STRENGTHENED SO THAT IT WILL BE ABLE TO AID MANKIND MORE
FULLY. THROUGH A SYSTEM OF INTERNATIONAL LAW RATHER THAN
THROUGH POLITICALLY ORIENTED ACTION FROM INDIVIDUAL MEMBERS,
IT IS HOPED THAT UN WILL SUCCEED WHERE THE NATIONS HAVE
FAILED.

0484 CONANT M.
ANTITRUST IN THE MOTION PICTURE INDUSTRY: ECONOMIC AND LEGAL
ANALYSIS.

BERKELEY: U OF CALIF PR, 1960, 240 PP., LC#60-7084.
ANALYZES AND EVALUATES IMPACT OF ANTITRUST ACTIONS ON
STRUCTURE, BEHAVIOR, AND PERFORMANCE OF THE FILM INDUSTRY.
EXAMINES DEVELOPMENT OF ANTITRUST LAW WITHIN THE
INDUSTRY. VIEWS GOVERNMENT PROSECUTIONS AS AN IMPETUS TO
PRIVATE TREBLE-DAMAGE ACTIONS. ECONOMIC ANALYSIS CENTERS
ON ALTERNATIVE PUBLIC POLICIES TOWARD PRICE DISCRIMINATION.
PRESENTS DATA ON MARKET SHARES AND TRADE PRACTICES.

0485 CONFERENCE ATLANTIC COMMUNITY
AN INTRODUCTORY BIBLIOGRAPHY.
LEYDEN: SYTHOFF, 1961, 900 PP.
ANNOTATED BIBLIOGRAPHY LIMITED TO BOOKS AND ARTICLES PUB-
LISHED SINCE 1945 IN UK, US, FRANCE, GERMANY, AUSTRIA, AND
ITALY. BASIC READING LIST FOR STUDY OF PROBLEMS OF ATLANTIC
COMMUNITY. WRITINGS ORGANIZED ACCORDING TO HISTORY AND
PROBLEMS OF COMMUNITY, ORGANIZATIONAL STRUCTURE OF PROGRESS,
RELATIONS OF COMMUNITY TO COMMUNIST WORLD. SUBJECT INDEX
AND CROSS-REFERENCING. EXTENSIVE CONTENT ANALYSIS.

0486 CONGRESSIONAL QUARTERLY SERV
REPRESENTATION AND APPORTIONMENT.
WASHINGTON: CONG QUARTERLY SERV, 1966, 96 PP., LC#66-28559.
TRACES EVOLUTION OF APPORTIONMENT THEORIES, 1776-1966,
USING SUPREME COURT DECISIONS TO INDICATE CHANGES IN POLICY.
EMPHASIZES IMPORTANCE OF BAKER V. CARR AS FIRST CASE OF
COURT-UPHELD RULING FOR ONE-MAN, ONE-VOTE. CHANGES IN
GOVERNMENT THEORY OF REPRESENTATION ALSO DISCUSSED.

0487 CONGRESSIONAL QUARTERLY SERV
FEDERAL ROLE IN EDUCATION (PAMPHLET)
WASHINGTON: US GOVERNMENT, 1965, 66 PP.
HISTORY OF EDUCATION ACT OF 1965, GOVERNMENT DESEGREGA-
TION POLICIES, AID TO EDUCATION PROGRAMS, GRANTS-IN-AID.

0488 CONGRESSIONAL QUARTERLY SERV
REVOLUTION IN CIVIL RIGHTS.
WASHINGTON: CONG QUARTERLY SERV, 1965, 94 PP., LC#65-20505.
SURVEY OF POSTWAR DEVELOPMENTS IN FIELD OF CIVIL RIGHTS.
EXAMINES LEGISLATION BEFORE 1964 ACT. DISCUSSES LOBBY
ACTIVITY, PROVISIONS OF CIVIL RIGHTS ACT OF 1964, ENFORCE-
MENT OF CIVIL RIGHTS LEGISLATION, AND 1965 VOTING RIGHTS
CRISIS.

0489 CONGRESSIONAL QUARTERLY SERV
POLITICS IN AMERICA, 1945-1964: THE POLITICS AND ISSUES OF
THE POSTWAR YEARS.
WASHINGTON: CONG QUARTERLY SERV, 1969, 124 PP., LC#65-29160.
DISCUSSION OF POSTWAR POLITICAL ISSUES, THE RESULTS IN
LECTIONS.ANALYSIS OF ELECTIONS RELATED IS MAJOR NATIONAL AND
INTERNATIONAL EVENTS. CONTAINS CHARTS ON ELECTION RESULTS
AND TRENDS IN PARTY STRENGTH. EXAMINES ELECTORAL COLLEGE,
APPORTIONMENT, VOTING LAWS, POLITICAL FINANCES, AND "EQUAL
TIME."

0490 CONGRESSIONAL QUARTERLY SERV
HOUSING A NATION (PAMPHLET)
WASHINGTON: CONG QUARTERLY SERV, 1966, 94 PP., LC#66-19946.
DISCUSSES GOVERNMENT PROGRAM FOR HOUSING. GIVES OBJEC-
TIVES AND METHODS OF PROGRAM AND DESCRIBES AGENCIES THAT
ADMINISTER IT. EXAMINES CONTROVERSY OVER PUBLIC HOUSING AND
URBAN RENEWAL, AND TRACES DEVELOPMENT OF PROGRAM. COVERS
MASS TRANSIT AID, HOUSING ACT OF 1965, AND ESTABLISHMENT
OF HOUSING DEPARTMENT.

0491 CONOVER H.F.
OFFICIAL PUBLICATIONS OF BRITISH EAST AFRICA (PAMPHLET)
WASHINGTON: LIBRARY OF CONGRESS, 1960, 67 PP., LC#61-60009.
A GUIDE TO THE PUBLICATIONS OF THE EAST AFRICA HIGH COM-
MISSION AND TO DOCUMENTS CONCERNING EAST AFRICA IN GENERAL.
FIRST PART OF A FOUR-VOLUME BIBLIOGRAPHY OF OFFICIAL BRITISH
EAST AFRICAN PUBLICATIONS. ANNOTATES 336 DEBATES, PROCEED-
INGS, REPORTS, GAZETTES, AND BIBLIOGRAPHIES. DOCUMENTS COVER
PERIOD FROM ABOUT 1930 THROUGH 1959.

0492 CONOVER H.F. ED.
FOREIGN RELATIONS OF THE UNITED STATES: A LIST OF RECENT
BOOKS (PAMPHLET)
WASHINGTON: LIBRARY OF CONGRESS, 1940, 55 PP.
A PARTIALLY ANNOTATED BIBLIOGRAPHY OF 388 BOOKS, PERIOD-
ICALS, AND PAMPHLETS IN ENGLISH AND FRENCH. SUPPLE-
MENT TO MIMEOGRAPHED LISTS RELEASED IN 1929 AND 1935. AR-
RANGED BY FORMAT AND SUBDIVIDED BY REGION. CONTAINS GUIDES
TO BIBLIOGRAPHIES, GENERAL WORKS, HISTORIES AND PE-
RIODICALS. INDEXED PRIMARILY BY AUTHOR AND BROAD SUBJECT
CLASSES. CONCENTRATES ON AMERICAN FOREIGN POLICY.

0493 CONOVER H.F. ED.
THE BALKANS: A SELECTED LIST OF REFERENCES.
WASHINGTON: LIBRARY OF CONGRESS, 1943, 264 PP.
A SERIES OF UNANNOTATED BIBLIOGRAPHIES ON THE BALKAN NA-
TIONS:ALBANIA, BULGARIA, RUMANIA, AND YUGOSLAVIA. RESTRICTED
IN MOST PART TO WORKS PUBLISHED SINCE TREATY OF VERSAILLES,
AND TO WRITINGS PUBLISHED IN WEST EUROPEAN LANGUAGES. WITHIN
EACH NATION, IS TOPICALLY ARRANGED AND INDEXED BOTH BY AU-
THOR AND SUBJECT. LISTS 2438 BOOKS, PERIODICALS, ARTICLES,

AND PAMPHLETS. COMPILED FOR LIBRARY OF CONGRESS.

0494 CONOVER H.F. ED.
THE GOVERNMENTS OF THE MAJOR FOREIGN POWERS: A BIBLIOGRAPHY.
WASHINGTON: LIBRARY OF CONGRESS, 1945, 45 PP.
LISTINGS OF 428 ENGLISH WORKS AS SUPPLEMENT TO TEXTBOOK
ON FOREIGN GOVERNMENTS PUBLISHED BY US MILITARY ACADEMY AT
WEST POINT. CLASSIFICATIONS FOLLOW CHAPTER HEADINGS OF THAT
WORK. INCLUDES ASPECTS OF POLITICAL AND MILITARY ORGANIZA-
TION OF FRANCE, GREAT BRITAIN, ITALY, GERMANY, USSR, AND
JAPAN. AUTHOR INDEX. COMPILED FOR LIBRARY OF CONGRESS.

0495 CONOVER H.F. ED.
THE NAZI STATE: WAR CRIMES AND WAR CRIMINALS.
WASHINGTON: LIBRARY OF CONGRESS, 1945, 131 PP.
BIBLIOGRAPHY COMPILED FOR US CHIEF OF COUNSEL FOR THE
PERSECUTION OF AXIS CRIMINALITY. MAIN EMPHASIS ON GERMAN
SOURCES BUT INCLUDES SOME FRENCH AND ENGLISH. BASIC
CLASSIFICATIONS: THEORY OF WAR CRIMES; THE NATIONALIST-SO-
CIALIST STATE; WAR ATROCITIES. THE LAST PART IS SUBDIVIDED
BY SUBJECT AND COUNTRY. INCLUDES 1,084 LISTINGS AND INDEX
WITH SOME CROSS-REFERENCING.

0496 CONOVER H.F. ED.
NORTH AND NORTHEAST AFRICA; A SELECTED ANNOTATED LIST OF
WRITINGS.
NEW YORK: NY PUBLIC LIBRARY, 1957, 182 PP., LC#57-60062.
AN ANNOTATED BIBLIOGRAPHY OF 343 BOOKS, PERIODICALS, AND
PAMPHLETS REVIEWING SOCIAL, ECONOMIC, AND POLITICAL ASPECTS
OF MAJOR ISSUES IN EACH COUNTRY UNDER CONSIDERATION. CONTENT
ARRANGED GEOGRAPHICALLY: ALGERIA, MOROCCO, TUNISIA, SAHARA,
LIBYA, SPANISH AFRICA, EGYPT, THE SUDAN, ETHIOPIA, AND THE
SOMALILANDS. SOURCES IN ENGLISH, FRENCH, ITALIAN, AND
SPANISH. MAIN CONCERN IS WITH CURRENT AFFAIRS.

0497 CONRING E.
KIRCHE UND STAAT NACH DER LEHRE DER NIEDERLANDISCHEN
CALVINISTEN IN DER ERSTEN HALFTE DES 17. JAHRHUNDERTS.
NEUKIRCHEN: NEUK VERL ERZIEHUNGS, 1965, 197 PP.
EXAMINES THEORIES OF CHURCH LAW, POSITION OF CHURCH IN
RELATION TO SECULAR AUTHORITY, AND RIGHT OF RESISTANCE TO
TYRANNY IN 17TH-CENTURY NETHERLANDS. DISCUSSES IN DETAIL
CHURCH GOVERNMENT AND AUTHORITY IN COMMUNITY.

0498 CONWELL-EVANS T.P.
THE LEAGUE COUNCIL IN ACTION.
LONDON: OXFORD U. PR., 1929, 291 PP.
A STUDY OF THE COUNCIL OF THE LEAGUE OF NATIONS AND ITS
PEACE FUNCTIONS. STUDIES THE COUNCIL AS A REPRESENTATIVE
WORLD BODY IN WHICH A JURISPRUDENCE DEVELOPS BASED ON NEW
PRINCIPLES IN INTERNATIONAL LAW.

0499 COOKE C.A.
CORPORATION TRUST AND COMPANY: AN ESSAY IN LEGAL HISTORY.
CAMBRIDGE: HARVARD U PR, 1951, 195 PP.
TRACES MINGLING OF LEGAL IDEAS AND ECONOMIC PURPOSES
WHICH PRODUCED THE MODERN JOINT STOCK COMPANY IN ENGLAND,
I.E., THE COMPANY WITH LIMITED LIABILITY AND TRANSFERABLE
SHARES. ATTEMPTS TO SHOW THERE HAS BEEN NO NECESSARY
CONNECTION BETWEEN CORPORATE FORM AND JOINT STOCK FUND.
SHOWS HOW THESE TWO CONCEPTS COALESCED IN MID-19TH CENTURY.
DISCUSSES COMPANIES ACT OF 1862.

0500 COOPER F.E.
THE LAWYER AND ADMINISTRATIVE AGENCIES.
ENGLEWOOD CLIFFS: PRENTICE HALL, 1957, 331 PP., LC#57-10617.
CONSIDERS PROBLEMS ATTORNEYS FACE IN REPRESENTING CLIENTS
BEFORE ADMINISTRATIVE TRIBUNALS. POINTS OUT SIGNIFICANT DIF-
FERENCES BETWEEN ADMINISTRATIVE AND JUDICIAL ADJUDICATION,
AND ROLE OF DISCRETIONARY POWER. TRACES PROCESSES IN DEALING
WITH CLIENT, PREPARING PLEADINGS, AND INTRODUCING EVIDENCE.
OUTLINES PROCEDURES TO BE FOLLOWED AT HEARINGS.

0501 COOPER F.E.
STATE ADMINISTRATIVE LAW (2 VOLS.)
INDIANAPOLIS: BOBBS-MERRILL, 1965, 951 PP., LC#65-20272.
EXAMINES STATUTORY AND CASE LAW OF STATES OF THE UNION
IN RELATION TO ADMINISTRATIVE PROCEDURE. DISCUSSES
PRINCIPLES OF DELEGATION, RULE-MAKING PROCEDURES,
CONCEPTS OF "RES JUDICATA" AND "STARE DECISIS," AND
JUDICIAL REVIEW OF ADMINISTRATIVE ACTION.

0502 COOPER L.
"ADMINISTRATIVE JUSTICE."
PUBLIC ADMINISTRATION, 32 (SUMMER 54), 165-171.
EXECUTIVE DECISIONS ARE ACTUALLY MADE WITHOUT REAL
CONTROL BY EITHER THE MINISTER OF PARLIAMENT, AND WITHOUT
DIRECT REFERENCE TO PUBLIC INTEREST. SUGGESTS COURTS BE
GIVEN ROLE OF MORE DIRECT INTERVENTION IN ADMINISTRATIVE
PROCEEDINGS.

0503 COPLIN W.D.
THE FUNCTIONS OF INTERNATIONAL LAW.
SKOKIE: RAND MCNALLY & CO, 1966, 294 PP., LC#66-19440.
ATTEMPTS TO DEVELOP GENERAL THEORY OF ROLE OF LAW AND
LEGISLATION IN INTERNATIONAL ENVIRONMENT; COVERS VARIOUS

ASPECTS OF THE LAW. INCLUDES A NUMBER OF INTERNATIONAL
TREATIES AS EXAMPLES. DISCUSSES SUBSTANTIVE LAW, LAW AS A
MEANS OF PREVENTING VIOLENCE, LAW TO PROMOTE WELFARE, AND
ATTEMPTS OF INTERNATIONAL ORGANIZATIONS TO ENFORCE IT.

0504 CORBETT P.E., SMITH A.A.
CANADA AND WORLD POLITICS.
LONDON: FABER/GWYER, 1928, 244 PP.
USING CANADA AS THE FOCAL POINT, ATTEMPTS TO EXAMINE THE
GENERAL POLICIES AND PROBLEMS OF THE DOMINIONS. PROBES INTO
PAST CONSTITUTIONS AND CONVENTIONS DEFINING AUTHORITY WITH-
IN AND AMONG THE DOMINIONS, AND SHOWS RELATIONSHIP WITH
OTHER NATIONS AND INTERNATIONAL ORGANIZATIONS, I.E. LEAGUE
OF NATIONS. PROPOSES IDEA OF 'PERSONAL UNION' AS BEST METHOD
OF PRESERVING THE BRITISH EMPIRE'S CONSTITUTIONAL UNITY.

0505 CORBETT P.E.
LAW AND SOCIETY IN THE RELATIONS OF STATES.
NEW YORK: HARCOURT BRACE, 1951, 337 PP.
BEGINS WITH STUDY OF WAY IN WHICH PRINCIPAL THEORIES OF
INTERNATIONAL LAW ORIGINATED. PROCEEDS WITH INQUIRY INTO
SOME FAMILIAR PATTERNS OF INTERNATIONAL PRACTICE, SHOWING
EXTENT TO WHICH THEY HAVE BEEN SHAPED BY LEGAL REASONING.
CONCLUDES THAT FUTURE OF INTERNATIONAL LAW IS ONE WITH
THE FUTURE OF INTERNATIONAL ORGANIZATION.

0506 CORBETT P.E.
MORALS LAW, AND POWER IN INTERNATIONAL RELATIONS.
LOS ANGELES: HAYNES FOUND., 1956, 51 PP.
URGES THAT MORALITY PLAY A PART IN POLICY-MAKING AND
ADVOCATES AN ENFORCEABLE, SUPRA-NATIONAL LAW. DEMANDS
NATIONS TO CURB THEIR POWERS IN ORDER TO PERMIT INTER-
NATIONAL COHESION.

0507 CORBETT P.E.
LAW IN DIPLOMACY.
PRINCETON: U. PR., 1959, 290 PP.
PROPOSES TO STUDY AND, IN SOME DEGREE, MEASURE THE INFLU-
ENCE OF LEGAL NOTIONS ON FOREIGN POLICY WITHOUT ASSUMING OR
ELABORATING UPON A SYSTEM OF INTERNATIONAL LAW. FOCUSES
ATTENTION UPON THE USE OF LEGAL LANGUAGE, CATEGORIES, AND
PROCEDURES IN BRITISH, AMERICAN AND SOVIET DIPOLMACY.

0508 CORET A.
"L'INDEPENDANCE DU SAMOA OCCIDENTAL."
REV. JURID. POLIT. OUTREMER, 16 (JAN.-MARCH 62), 135-172.
DISCUSSES HISTORICAL AND GEOGRAPHIC FACTORS WHICH LED TO
SAMOAN NATIONAL INDEPENDENCE. OUTLINES PROBLEMS ENCOUNTERED
AT CONSTITUTIONAL CONVENTION IN 1954 HELD TO CREATE POLITI-
CAL STRUCTURE. FOCUSES ON RELATION OF JUDICIAL ORGANIZATION
TO INTERNATIONAL LAW.

0509 CORLEY R.N., BLACK R.L.
THE LEGAL ENVIRONMENT OF BUSINESS.
NEW YORK: MCGRAW HILL, 1963, 378 PP., LC#63-15890.
TREATS LEGAL ENVIRONMENT IN WHICH BUSINESS DECISIONS OF
TODAY ARE MADE. DISCUSSES GENERAL MEANING AND NATURE OF LAW
AND THE ENVIRONMENT OF BUSINESS AS IT RESULTS FROM LAW.
REVEALS ATTITUDE OF GOVERNMENT TOWARD BUSINESS AND PRESENTS
TODAY'S MAJOR ISSUES IN LAW AND BUSINESS.

0510 CORNELL UNIVERSITY LIBRARY
SOUTHEAST ASIA ACCESSIONS LIST.
ITHACA: CORNELL U. DEPT ASIAN ST.
MONTHLY LISTING OF BOOKS, SERIALS, MONOGRAPHS, CONFER-
ENCES, GOVERNMENT DOCUMENTS. ITEMS ARE ARRANGED BY COUNTRY.
INCLUDES MATERIAL IN VARIOUS LANGUAGES FOR CAMBODIA, INDO-
NESIA, MALAYSIA, PHILIPPINES, THAILAND, AND VIETNAM. GIVES
FULL BIBLIOGRAPHIC INFORMATION.

0511 CORRY J.A.
DEMOCRATIC GOVERNMENT AND POLITICS.
TORONTO: TORONTO UNIV PRESS, 1946, 468 PP.
GENERAL INTRODUCTION TO POLITICAL PROCESS IN MODERN
DEMOCRATIC SOCIETIES. DISCUSSES CENTRAL ORGANS AS JUDICIARY,
PARTIES, PRESSURE GROUPS, ETC., WITHIN FRAMEWORK OF CON-
TINUOUSLY EXPANDING RESPONSIBILITIES. CONCLUDES WITH A COM-
PARISON OF DEMOCRACY AND DICTATORSHIP.

0512 CORWIN E.S.
"THE CONSTITUTION AS INSTRUMENT AND AS SYMBOL."
AM. POL. SCI. REV., 30 (DEC. 36), 1071-1085.
ANALYZES TWO FUNCTIONS OF US CONSTITUTION: FIRST, AS
INSTRUMENT OF POPULAR POWER FOR ACHIEVEMENT OF PROGRESS;
SECOND, AS SYMBOL PROTECTING PRIVATE INTEREST OR ADVANTAGE
AGAINST PUBLIC POWER. EXAMINES INTERRELATIONSHIPS OF THESE
CONCEPTS. ADVISES REVISION OF SYMBOL TO BRING IT INTO CON-
FORMITY WITH CONSTITUTIONAL INSTRUMENT FOR GOVERNMENT OF
THE PEOPLE, RATHER THAN BIG BUSINESS.

0513 CORWIN E.S.
LIBERTY AGAINST GOVERNMENT.
BATON ROUGE: LOUISIANA ST U PR, 1948, 210 PP.
DISCUSSES LIBERTY IN RELATION TO GOVERNMENT; INCLUDES
DEFINITION OF JUDICIAL LIBERTY, ITS ROMAN AND ENGLISH
ORIGINS, PROPERTY BEFORE CIVIL WAR, AND LIBERTY IN FOUR-

TEENTH AMENDMENT.

0514 CORWIN E.S.
LIBERTY AGAINST GOVERNMENT: THE RISE, FLOWERING AND DECLINE
OF A FAMOUS JURIDICAL CONCEPT.
BATON ROUGE: LOUISIANA ST U PR, 1948, 210 PP.
TREATMENT OF "LIBERTY" AS A JURIDICAL CONCEPT IMPLYING
CONSTITUTIONAL LIMITATIONS ON LEGISLATURES AND EXECUTIVES.
STUDIES BACKGROUND OF CONCEPT IN ROMAN AND ENGLISH LAW AND
TRACES SHIFTS IN CONCEPT IN AMERICAN LAW. PARTICULARLY
CONCERNED THAT 20TH-CENTURY DECISIONS WILL EQUATE EQUALITY,
A SOCIAL CONCEPT, WITH JURIDICAL CONCEPT OF LIBERTY, SO THAT
PROTECTION OF INDIVIDUALS FROM GOVERNMENT WILL FADE.

0515 CORWIN E.S.
"AMERICAN CONSTITUTIONAL HISTORY."
NEW YORK: HARPER & ROW, 1964.
COLLECTION OF TWELVE ESSAYS ON THEORY AND PRACTICE OF
JUDICIAL REVIEW. ESSAYS ARRANGED IN ACCORDANCE WITH THE
LOGIC OF SUBJECT MATTER RATHER THAN ORDER OF PUBLICATION
DATE. ANALYZES PROGRESS OF CONSTITUTIONAL THEORY BEFORE
PHILADELPHIA CONVENTION, SOCIAL PLANNING UNDER THE CONSTITU-
TION, AND STATESMANSHIP OF SUPREME COURT. BIBLIOG-
RAPHY OF HIS BOOKS, ARTICLES, AND REVIEWS APPENDED TO TEXT.

0516 CORY R.H. JR.
"INTERNATIONAL INSPECTION FROM PROPOSALS TO REALIZATION."
INT. ORG., 13 (AUTUMN 59), 495-504.
SURVEYS ADMINISTRATIVE, BUDGETARY, ORGANIZATIONAL, LEGAL,
AND POLITICAL PROBLEMS BARRING ESTABLISHMENT OF EFFECTIVE
INSPECTORATE CHECKING DEVELOPMENT AND SPREAD OF WEAPONS.
DISCUSSES RELATIONSHIPS OF INSPECTORATE WITH OTHER PARALLEL
INTERNATIONAL ORGANIZATIONS.

0517 COSSIO C.
LA POLITICA COMO CONCIENCIA; MEDITACION SOBRE LA ARGENTINA
DE 1955.
BUENOS AIRES: ABELEDO-PERROT, 1957, 305 PP.
ANALYSIS OF CONTEMPORARY ARGENTINE POLITICS EXAMINES
POLITICAL PARTIES AND REVOLUTION OF 1955. DESCRIBES PROBLEMS
OF POST-REVOLUTIONARY PERIOD REGARDING PERONISM, LEGISLA-
TIVE POWER, POWER OF CATHOLIC CHURCH, AND RIGHTS OF PEOPLE.
EXPLAINS PUBLIC OPINION AND ITS INFLUENCE ON NATIONAL POLICY
AND GOVERNMENT.

0518 COSTA RICA UNIVERSIDAD BIBL
LISTA DE TESIS DE GRADO DE LA UNIVERSIDAD DE COSTA RICA.
SAN JOSE: CIUDAD U, 1962, 131 PP.
BIBLIOGRAPHICAL LISTING OF THESES ACCEPTED AT THE UNIVER-
SITY OF COSTA RICA IN 1961. EACH ITEM INCLUDES AN ABSTRACT.
ENTRIES ARRANGED BY DEPARTMENT.

0519 COUNCIL BRITISH NATIONAL BIB
BRITISH NATIONAL BIBLIOGRAPHY.
LONDON: COUN BRIT NATL BIBLIOG, 1950, 700 PP.
A SUBJECT LIST OF BRITISH BOOKS PUBLISHED FROM 1950-67
BASED UPON BOOKS DEPOSITED AT THE CLASSIFIED OFFICE OF THE
BRITISH MUSEUM. OVER 20,000 ENTRIES IN EACH VOLUME.

0520 COUNCIL OF EUROPE
EUROPEAN CONVENTION ON HUMAN RIGHTS - COLLECTED TEXTS
(5TH ED.)
STRASBOURG: COUNCIL OF EUROPE, 1966, 125 PP.
COLLECTION OF DOCUMENTS ON RULES OF PROCEDURE, RATIFICA-
TIONS, MEMBERS, PROTOCOLS, DECLARATIONS, AND RESERVATIONS
OF EUROPEAN COMMISSION OF HUMAN RIGHTS. PRINTED IN ENGLISH
AND FRENCH.

0521 COUNCIL OF STATE GOVERNMENTS
STATE GOVERNMENT: AN ANNOTATED BIBLIOGRAPHY (PAMPHLET)
CHICAGO: COUNCIL OF STATE GOVTS, 1959, 46 PP.
ANNOTATED TOPICAL LISTING OF PERIODICALLY REVISED SOURCES
OF COMPARATIVE DATA ON STATE GOVERNMENT. SOME 450 PERIODICAL
INDEXES AND DIGESTS, REPORTING SERVICES, DIRECTORIES, BOOKS,
PERIODICAL ARTICLES, PAMPHLETS, AND REPORTS OF SPECIFIC
STATE LEGAL PROVISIONS. EMPHASIS IS ON STATE LAWS, ADMIN-
ISTRATIVE REGULATIONS, CHARACTERISTICS OF STATE OPERATIONS,
AND ADMINISTRATIVE ORGANIZATION. PUBLICATIONS ARE CURRENT.

0522 COUNCIL OF STATE GOVERNMENTS
INCREASED RIGHTS FOR DEFENDANTS IN STATE CRIMINAL
PROSECUTIONS.
CHICAGO: COUNCIL OF STATE GOVTS, 1963, 40 PP.
DISCUSSES SIX CRIMINAL CASES DECIDED BY US SUPREME COURT
IN 1963 AND THEIR IMPLICATION FOR ADMINISTRATION OF JUSTICE
IN STATE COURTS.

0523 COUNCIL OF STATE GOVERNMENTS
LEGISLATIVE APPORTIONMENT: A SUMMARY OF STATE ACTION.
CHICAGO: COUNCIL OF STATE GOVTS, 1964, 92 PP.
SUMMARIZES SIGNIFICANT ACTION TAKEN ON REAPPORTIONMENT BY
GOVERNORS, LEGISLATURES, STATE AND FEDERAL COURTS, AND
VOTERS 1960-64, FROM BAKER V. CARR TO WESBURY V. SANDERS.
INCLUDES TABLES LISTING STATES ORDERED TO REAPPORTION AND
STATES HAVING DONE SO AS OF APRIL, 1965.

0524 COUNCIL OF STATE GOVERNMENTS
THE HANDBOOK ON INTERSTATE CRIME CONTROL.
CHICAGO: COUNCIL OF STATE GOVTS, 1966, 179 PP., LC#66-28390.
CONTAINS COPIES OF UNIFORM LAWS DRAFTED AND RECOMMENDED
BY INTERSTATE COMMISSION ON CRIME, REGULATIONS CALLED FOR
THEREIN, AND LEGAL FORMS FOR THEIR PROPER ENFORCEMENT.
INCLUDES INFORMATION ON INTERSTATE COMPACT FOR SUPERVISION
OF PAROLEES AND PROBATIONERS; OUT-OF-STATE CONFINEMENT
ARRANGEMENTS; INTERSTATE CONPACT ON JUVENILES, EXTRADITION,
AND PURSUIT OF CRIMINALS ACROSS GOVERNMENTAL LINES.

0525 COUNCIL OF STATE GOVERNMENTS
AMERICAN LEGISLATURES: STRUCTURE AND PROCEDURES. SUMMARY
AND TABULATIONS OF A 1959 SURVEY.
CHICAGO: COUNCIL OF STATE GOVTS, 1959, 62 PP.
COMPARATIVE SURVEY OF VARIETY OF LEGISLATIVE STRUCTURAL
PROVISIONS AND PRACTICES AMONG 50 STATES, PUERTO RICO, GUAM,
AND VIRGIN ISLANDS. DISCUSSES PROPOSALS INVOLVING LEGISLA-
TIVE TERMS, SESSIONS, AND DELEGATES' COMPENSATIONS. ALSO
COVERS RECENT ACTION ON REAPPORTIONMENT AND STANDING
COMMITTEES.

0526 COUNCIL OF STATE GOVERNMENTS
OCCUPATIONAL LICENSING IN THE STATES.
CHICAGO: COUNCIL OF STATE GOVTS, 1952, 106 PP.
REPORT OF A QUESTIONNAIRE SURVEY OF ALL STATE GERNMENTS
ON OCCUPATIONAL LICENSING PRACTICES, PROCEDURES, LAWS,
OCCUPATIONS CORED, REPRESENTATION IN LICENSING ACTIVITIES,
AND SOCIAL AND ECONOMIC IMPLICATIONS OF LICENSING.

0527 COUTROT A.
THE FIGHT OVER THE 1959 PRIVATE EDUCATION LAW IN FRANCE
(PAMPHLET)
INDIANAPOLIS: BOBBS-MERRILL, 1966, 48 PP.
DESCRIBES EXECUTIVE AND PARLIAMENTARY HISTORY OF 1959
FRENCH LEGISLATION PROVIDING STATE AID TO CATHOLIC SCHOOLS.
ILLUMINATES FRENCH GOVERNMENT POLICY PROCESS. ANALYZES
SOCIAL CLEAVAGE IN FRENCH PUBLIC OPINION.

0528 COWAN T.A. ED.
"A SYMPOSIUM ON GROUP INTERESTS AND THE LAW"
RUTGERS LAW REV., 13 (SPRING 59), 429-602.
COLLECTION OF ARTICLES ON ALTERATIONS NECESSARY TO
ACCOMMODATE LAW TO GROWTH OF GROUP INTERESTS IN SOCIETY.

0529 COWEN D.V.
THE FOUNDATIONS OF FREEDOM.
LONDON: OXFORD U PR, 1961, 258 PP.
ANALYSIS OF LEGAL, ETHICAL, SOCIAL, AND PHILOSOPHICAL DI-
MENSIONS OF APARTHEID POLICIES IN SOUTH AFRICA. RAISES SUB-
STANTIVE QUESTION OF WHETHER WHITE'S ULTIMATELY DENY THEM-
SELVES FREEDOM AND DEMOCRACY WHEN THEY LIMIT AFRICAN FREE-
DOM AND OPPORTUNITY. SUGGESTS A RETURN TO CONSTITUTIONAL
GOVERNMENT FOR BENEFIT OF ALL SOUTH AFRICANS.

0530 COWEN Z.
THE BRITISH COMMONWEALTH OF NATIONS IN A CHANGING WORLD.
EVANSTON: NORTHWESTERN U PRESS, 1965, 117 PP., LC#65-12096.
TRACES DEVELOPMENT OF BRITISH COMMONWEALTH AND ITS INSTI-
TUTIONS, PARTICULARLY IN LEGAL AND STRUCTURAL PERSPECTIVE.
EXAMINES RECENT CHANGES AND INQUIRES INTO POLITICS AND
PROSPECTS OF CONTEMPORARY COMMONWEALTH.

0531 COWLING M.
1867 DISRAELI, GLADSTONE, AND REVOLUTION; THE PASSING OF THE
SECOND REFORM BILL.
CAMBRIDGE: UNIVERSITY PRESS, 1967, 451 PP., LC#67-13801.
EXAMINES MID-VICTORIAN POLITICAL SYSTEM ATTACKED BY JOHN
STUART MILL. DISCUSSES DECISION-MAKING PROCESS OF
GOVERNMENT OF PERIOD AND EXPLAINS HOW DECISION FOR REFORM
BILL OF 1867 WAS MADE NOT BY RADICAL LEADERS BUT BY HOUSE
OF COMMONS. STUDIES FACTORS RELATED TO PASSAGE OF BILL:
PARLIAMENTARY MANIPULATION AND CONSCIOUSNESS OF POPULAR
PRESSURES AND TENSION BETWEEN, ACROSS, AND WITHIN PARTIES.

0532 COX A.
"THE ROLE OF LAW IN PRESERVING UNION DEMOCRACY."
HARVARD LAW REV., 72 (1959), 609-644.
CONTENDS THAT LEGISLATION TO MAINTAIN DEMOCRATIC
PROCESSES WITHIN UNIONS IS NECESSARY, AND THAT SUCH LAWS
WOULD ALTER EXISTING UNION STRENGTH AND INDEPENDENCE.
SUGGESTS NEW REGULATIONS FOR ADMISSION AND EXPULSION OF
MEMBERS, UNION ELECTIONS, AND UNION TRUSTEESHIPS.

0533 COX A., HOWE M., WIGGINS J.R.
CIVIL RIGHTS, THE CONSTITUTION, AND THE COURTS.
CAMBRIDGE: HARVARD U PR, 1967, 72 PP.
THREE ADDRESSES ON CIVIL RIGHTS. CONCEPT OF "FEDERALISM"
HAS ADVERSELY AFFECTED NATIONAL CONSCIENCE ABOUT CIVIL
RIGHTS. CIVIL DISOBEDIENCE ANALYZED FOR VALIDITY AND IMPLI-
CATIONS FROM LEGAL POINT OF VIEW. SUCCESSES AND FAILURES OF
THE PRESS IN GIVING PROPER SCRUTINY OF ADMINISTRATION OF
JUSTICE INCLUDED.

0534 COX G.C.
THE PUBLIC CONSCIENCE: A CASEBOOK IN ETHICS.

NEW YORK: HOLT RINEHART WINSTON, 1922, 483 PP.
USES CASE METHOD AS BASIS OF SCIENTIFIC STUDY OF ETHICS
IN JUDGMENTS MADE IN STATUTE AND COMMON LAW. ANALYZES PROB-
LEM OF ESTABLISHING SOUND FOUNDATION FOR MORAL CONCEPTS.
DEMONSTRATES VALUE OF DEALING WITH CONCRETE EXPERIENCE AS
OPPOSED TO ABSTRACT, IMAGINARY SITUATIONS INVOLVING ETHICAL
QUESTIONS.

0535 COX H.
ECONOMIC LIBERTY.
LONDON: LONGMANS, GREEN & CO, 1920, 263 PP.
ESSAYS DEFEND FREEDOM OF INDIVIDUAL FROM ECONOMIC CON-
TROL BY STATE OR OTHER BODY. FREE ENTERPRISE MUST EXIST FOR
SOCIETY TO RUN SMOOTHLY; WHAT FEW GOVERNMENT CONTROLS SHOULD
EXIST MUST MERELY PROTECT INDIVIDUALS FROM IMPINGING UPON
EACH OTHER'S LIBERTY.

0536 CRAIG A.
ABOVE ALL LIBERTIES.
LONDON: ALLEN & UNWIN, 1942, 205 PP.
TRACES HISTORY OF CENSORSHIP IN ENGLAND FROM 1700'S END-
ING IN PRESENT OBSCENE LIBEL LAW. INVESTIGATES CHURCH IN-
FLUENCE IN MORAL DETERMINATION AND ARGUES AGAINST ANY CEN-
SORSHIP FROM STANDPOINT OF MAN'S RIGHT TO INTELLECTUAL FREE-
DOM AND SONAL ORAL DETERMINATION. DESCRIBES SEVERAL
CASES OF GOVERNMENT CENSORSHIP IN ENGLAND, FRANCE, AND THE
US. EXAMINES PROBLEM OF PORNOGRAPHY IN FREE LITERARY STATE.

0537 CRAIG A.
"ABOVE ALL LIBERTIES."
NEW YORK: W W NORTON, 1942.
CHAPTER-BY-CHAPTER BREAKDOWN OF BOOKS AND ARTICLES. THOSE
LISTED COVER WIDER GROUND THAN CHAPTERS INDICATE. AUTHOR HAS
NOT REPEATED ITEMS CONTAINED IN BIBLIOGRAPHY TO HIS BOOK
"THE BANNED BOOKS OF ENGLAND."

0538 CRAIG A.
SUPPRESSED BOOKS: A HISTORY OF THE CONCEPTION OF LITERARY
OBSCENITY.
CLEVELAND: WORLD, 1963, 285 PP., LC#63-14785.
NEGATING CAUSAL RELATIONSHIP BETWEEN READING AND BEHAV-
IOR, AUTHOR CATALOGUES MAN'S ATTEMPTED SUPRESSIONS OF SEX-
UAL MATERIAL IN LITERATURE; HOPES TO INFLUENCE PUBLIC AND
COURTS TO "TIDY UP" LAWS OF CENSORSHIP.

0539 CRAIG J.
ELEMENTS OF POLITICAL SCIENCE (3 VOLS.)
EDINBURGH: WILLIAM BLACKWOOD, 1814, 1186 PP.
EARLY ATTEMPT AT A GENERAL OVERVIEW OF SCIENCE OF
GOVERNMENT. BOOK ONE DEALS WITH THE NATURE OF GOVERNMENT:
ITS RIGHTS, RIGHTS OF THE INDIVIDUAL AND OF SOCIETY, AND
THE DISTRIBUTION OF POLITICAL POWER. BOOK TWO CONCERNS
DUTIES OF GOVERNMENT: ADMINISTRATION OF LAW, NATIONAL
DEFENSE, ECONOMIC REGULATION, PROPER DISTRIBUTION OR WEALTH.
BOOK THREE DISCUSSES REVENUE AND TAXATION.

0540 CRAIG J. ED.
BIBLIOGRAPHY OF PUBLIC ADMINISTRATION IN AUSTRALIA.
SYDNEY: U SYDNEY, GOVT & PUB ADM, 1955, 183 PP.
CLASSIFICATION BY SUBJECT OF RELEVANT DOCUMENTS FOUND IN
PAPERS OF NEW SOUTH WALES PARLIAMENT FOR YEARS 1856-1947 AND
OF COMMONWEALTH OF AUSTRALIA PARLIAMENT, 1901-1947. RELEVANT
GENERAL PERIODICALS LISTED. ARRANGEMENT WITHIN SUBJECT CLAS-
SIFICATION IS ALPHABETICAL. SECTIONS ON ADMINISTRATIVE
MACHINERY OF GOVERNMENT DOMINATE CONTENT OF WORK.

0541 CRANDALL S.B.
TREATIES: THEIR MAKING AND ENFORCEMENT.
NEW YORK: COLUMB. U. PR., 1904, 255 PP.
STUDIES TREATY MAKING WITH FOREIGN STATES FROM COLONIAL
DAYS TO PRESENT. DETAILED COVERAGE OF SCOPE AND TYPES OF
TREATIES.

0542 CRANE R.D.
"LAW AND STRATEGY IN SPACE."
ORBIS, 6 (SUMMER 62), 281-300.
USA MUST TAKE INITIATIVE IN FORMULATING SPACE LAWS WHICH
WOULD SERVE TO PROMOTE SCIENTIFIC RESEARCH AND ECONOMIC
PROGRESS. IN ORDER TO FACILITATE GROWTH OF A FREE AND
PEACEFUL WORLD ORDER, IT'S NECESSARY TO IMPLEMENT ON A
HIGHER MORAL LEVEL USA MILITARY AND POLITICAL STRATEGIES.

0543 CRANE R.D.
"SOVIET ATTITUDE TOWARD INTERNATIONAL SPACE LAW."
AMER. J. INT. LAW, 56 (JULY 62), 685-723.
SOVIET UNION FAVORS OFFENSIVE STRATEGY IN INTERNATIONAL
SPACE LAW. EMPLOY DOUBLE STANDARD, PROMOTING LAWS THAT FUR-
THER THEIR INTERESTS. URGES USA TO TAKE INITIATIVE IN DE-
VELOPING INTERNATIONAL SPACE COOPERATION.

0544 CRANE R.D.
"BASIC PRINCIPLES IN SOVIET SPACE LAW."
LAW CONTEMP. PROBL., 29 (AUTUMN 64), 943-55.
CONSIDERS THE THREE PRINCIPLES OF SOVIET SPACE LAW:
PEACEFUL COEXISTENCE, PEACEFUL COOPERATION, AND DISARMAMENT.
SUGGESTS THAT SOVIET MANIPULATION OF THEM BE UNDERSTOOD NOT

AS A MEANS OF RESOLVING CONFLICT BUT RATHER AS A METHOD OF DIRECTING CONFLICT TOWARDS THE ACHIEVEMENT OF COMMUNIST WORLD DOMINATION.

0545 CRANSTON M.
WHAT ARE HUMAN RIGHTS?
NEW YORK: BASIC BOOKS, 1962, 105 PP., LC#63-12842.
STUDY OF UNIVERSAL DECLARATION OF HUMAN RIGHTS, GIVING COGENT ANALYSIS OF DIFFERENCE BETWEEN UNIVERSAL "RIGHTS" AND "RIGHTS" BESTOWED BY "POSITIVE LAW." ASSERTS THERE IS NO NEED TO FLEE TO CLASSICAL NATURAL LAW THEORIES IN ORDER TO REFUTE LEGAL POSITIVISM.

0546 CRESSEY D.R.
"ACHIEVEMENT OF AN UNSTATED ORGANIZATIONAL GOAL: AN OBSERVATION ON PRISONS."
PACIFIC SOCIOLOGICAL REV., 1 (FALL 58), 43-49.
GOALS OF PRISONS FROM THE VIEWPOINT OF THE CRIMINAL, ESPECIALLY THAT OF PROTECTION OF INMATES FROM COMMUNITY REACTION AND FROM OTHER INMATES AND STAFF MEMBERS. TWO INSTITUTIONS OBSERVED ALLOWED THE ACTUALIZATION OF THE GOAL OF PROTECTION.

0547 CREYKE G. JR.
"THE PAYMENT GAP IN FEDERAL CONSTRUCTION CONTRACTS."
G. WASH. LAW REV., 35 (JUNE 67), 944-961.
REVIEWS POSSIBILITIES BY WHICH A GOVERNMENT CONTRACTOR FACED WITH A "PAYMENT GAP" MAY EITHER PROTECT HIMSELF OF OBTAIN RECOURSE. FOCUSES ON SERIOUS CONSEQUENCES WHICH CAN RESULT AND INDICATES STEPS HE SHOULD TAKE. FINDS THAT IMPROVED CONTRACT ADJUSTMENT AND APPEAL PROCEDURES MAY BRING DECLINE IN NUMBER OF PAYMENT CRISES.

0548 CROWE S.E.
THE BERLIN WEST AFRICA CONFERENCE, 1884-85.
LONDON: LONGMANS, GREEN & CO, 1942, 249 PP.
STUDIES 19TH-CENTURY EUROPEAN DIPLOMACY LEADING TO PARTITIONING OF AFRICA. TREATS EUROPEAN BALANCE OF POWER AND ITS INFLUENCE ON CONFERENCE, WHICH HAD BEEN CALLED TO CREATE FREEDOM OF TRADE IN CONGO BASIN. RELATES THIS CONFERENCE TO FREE TRADE AREAS AND SPHERES OF INFLUENCE FOR EUROPEAN POWERS.

0549 CULVER D.C.
BIBLIOGRAPHY OF CRIME AND CRIMINAL JUSTICE, 1927-1931.
NEW YORK: H W WILSON, 1934, 413 PP.
A PARTIALLY ANNOTATED BIBLIOGRAPHY OF 13,292 MATERIALS PUBLISHED OR IN MANUSCRIPT DURING THE FIVE-YEAR PERIOD, 1927-1931. VOLUME IS INTERNATIONAL IN SCOPE AND COVERS LAW ENFORCEMENT, CLASSES OF OFFENDERS, CRIMINAL LAW AND PROCEDURE, PUNISHMENT, PROBATION, AND PREVENTION. ANNOTATIONS ARE INFORMATIVE AND DESCRIPTIVE RATHER THAN CRITICAL. DETAILED SUBJECT INDEX.

0550 CULVER D.C.
METHODOLOGY OF SOCIAL SCIENCE RESEARCH: A BIBLIOGRAPHY.
BERKELEY: U OF CALIF PR, 1936, 159 PP.
A SELECTED AND ANNOTATED GUIDE TO MATERIALS ON THE TYPES OF METHODS AND TECHNIQUES WHICH HAVE BEEN USED IN RESEARCH IN THE SOCIAL SCIENCES. LIMITED TO STUDIES, RATHER THAN EXAMPLES, OF METHOD. SELECTION MADE FROM MATERIALS PUBLISHED IN ENGLISH SINCE 1920, EXCLUDING FIELDS OF PSYCHOLOGY AND EDUCATION. CONTAINS 1,509 ENTRIES ARRANGED IN A LOGICAL MANNER, ACCORDING TO ORDER OF STEPS IN A RESEARCH PROBLEM.

0551 CULVER D.C.
BIBLIOGRAPHY OF CRIME AND CRIMINAL JUSTICE, 1932-1937.
NEW YORK: H W WILSON, 1939, 391 PP.
A PARTIALLY ANNOTATED BIBLIOGRAPHY OF 9,314 MATERIALS IN ENGLISH PUBLISHED OR IN MANUSCRIPT DURING 1932-1937. DESIGNED AS A SUPPLEMENT TO THE 1927-1931 EDITION. VOLUME IS INTERNATIONAL IN SCOPE AND COVERS PSYCHOLOGICAL, SOCIOLOGICAL, LEGAL, PREVENTATIVE, PUNITIVE, AND ADMINISTRATIVE FACTORS OF CRIMINOLOGY. ANNOTATIONS ARE INFORMATIVE AND DESCRIPTIVE RATHER THAN CRITICAL.

0552 CUMMING J.
A CONTRIBUTION TOWARD A BIBLIOGRAPHY DEALING WITH CRIME AND COGNATE SUBJECTS (3RD ED.)
LONDON:MET POLICE DIST SCOTLAND YARD 1935, 107 PP.
UNANNOTATED BIBLIOGRAPHY OF BOOKS AND PERIODICALS COVERING CRIMINOLOGY THROUGH 1934. CHRONOLOGICALLY CLASSIFIES 1900 TITLES WITHIN 200 SUBJECT HEADINGS. TWO INDEXES: A COMBINED SUBJECT AND GEOGRAPHICAL INDEX, AND INDEX OF AUTHORS. FURNISHES MATERIAL FOR COMPARATIVE STUDY OF FACTS AND OPINIONS RELATING TO DIFFERENT PERIODS AND DIFFERENT COUNTRIES. SOURCES PRIMARILY ENGLISH; SOME FRENCH, SOME ITALIAN.

0553 CUMMINGS H.
LIBERTY UNDER LAW AND ADMINISTRATION.
NEW YORK: CHAS SCRIBNER'S SONS, 1934, 136 PP.
ESSAY BY FORMER US ATTORNEY GENERAL TREATS PROBLEM OF LIBERTY AND ITS RELATION TO LAW AND GOVERNMENT. INCLUDES SECTION ON LIBERTY IN HISTORY, LIBERTY IN LEGAL TERMS, AND LIBERTY UNDER ADMINISTRATION.

0554 CUMMINS L.
"THE FORMULATION OF THE "PLATT" AMENDMENT."
THE AMERICAS, 23 (APR. 67), 370-389.
STUDIES QUESTION OF AUTHORSHIP AND INTENT OF "PLATT" AMENDMENT TO DETERMINE OBJECTIVE OF US POLICY IN LATIN AMERICA. EXAMINES VARIOUS PRIMARY AND SECONDARY SOURCES AND CONCLUDES THAT "ITS SOLE PURPOSE WAS STRATEGIC."

0555 CUNNINGHAM W.B.
COMPULSORY CONCILIATION AND COLLECTIVE BARGAINING.
MONTREAL: MCGILL U PR, 1958, 123 PP.
EVALUATES COMPULSORY CONCILIATION IN PROVINCE OF NEW BRUNSWICK AS TO WHETHER IT EMASCULATES COLLECTIVE BARGAINING BY STUDYING CASES OF GOVERNMENT INTERVENTION, 1947-1956. DISCUSSES WHETHER ILLEGALIZING WORK STOPPAGES UNTIL CONCILIATION IS REQUESTED POSES MAJOR DIFFICULTY TO BARGAINING.

0556 CURRIE D.P. ED.
FEDERALISM AND THE NEW NATIONS OF AFRICA.
CHICAGO: U OF CHICAGO PRESS, 1964, 440 PP., LC#64-23421.
STUDIES AFRICAN PROBLEMS IN DIFFERENT REGIONS AND SYSTEM OF FEDERALISM IN AFRICA AS REGARDS ECONOMIC GROWTH, UNITY, AND TAXATION. RELATIONS OF INDIVIDUALS AND MINORITY GROUPS TO GOVERNMENT AND INTERNATIONAL LEGAL ASPECTS OF FEDERAL SYSTEM ARE EXAMINED IN COMPARISON WITH US AND CANADIAN FEDERALISM.

0557 CURRIER T.F.
A BIBLIOGRAPHY OF OLIVER WENDELL HOLMES.
NEW YORK: NEW YORK U PR, 1953, 707 PP.
AN EXTENSIVELY ANNOTATED BIBLIOGRAPHY OF THE EDITIONS, LEAFLETS, POEMS, AND PROSE OF OLIVER WENDELL HOLMES. WORKS ARRANGED CHRONOLOGICALLY WITHIN EACH OF THE FOUR CATEGORIES. APPENDIXES CONTAIN POPULAR LECTURES, PRINTED LETTERS, ENGLISH REPRINTS AND FOREIGN EDITIONS, BIOGRAPHY, AND CRITICISM. INDEXED BY BOTH AUTHOR AND TITLE.

0558 CURRY J.E., KING G.D.
RACE TENSIONS AND THE POLICE.
SPRINGFIELD: THOMAS, 1962, 137 PP., LC#61-17010.
STUDY OF COMMUNITY RACE RELATIONS IN REGARD TO ROLE OF POLICE. DEALS WITH SOCIOLOGICAL ASPECTS OF GROUP AND RACE RELATIONS, MEASURES TO PREVENT RACIAL VIOLENCE, AND POLICE TACTICS TO CONTROL UNRULY CROWD.

0559 CUSHMAN R.E.
LEADING CONSTITUTIONAL DECISIONS.
NEW YORK: APPLETON, 1955, 453 PP., LC#54-11851.
COLLECTION OF SUPREME COURT CASES FOR STUDENT OF AMERICAN GOVERNMENT WITH HISTORICAL INTRODUCTORY NOTES. INCLUDES SECTIONS ON AMENDMENTS, FEDERAL AND STATES RIGHTS, EXECUTIVE, JUDICIAL, AND LEGISLATIVE POWER, COMMERCE, AND TAXATION.

0561 DAHL R.A.
"DECISION-MAKING IN A DEMOCRACY: THE SUPREME COURT AS A NATIONAL POLICY-MAKER" (BMR)"
JOURNAL OF PUBLIC LAW, 6 (1958), 279-295.
CONSIDERS SUPREME COURT AS A POLITICAL INSTITUTION RATHER THAN LEGAL INSTITUTION. SEES COURT AS PART OF DOMINATING, COHESIVE ALLIANCES WHICH CONSTITUTE US POLITICS. SUPREME COURT ACTS AS SUPPORTING AGENT OF ALLIANCE AND POSSESSES POWER OF UNIQUE LEGITIMACY OF ITS INTERPRETATIONS OF CONSTITUTION.

0562 DALFEN C.M.
"THE WORLD COURT IN IDLE SPLENDOUR: THE BASIS OF STATES' ATTITUDES."
INT. J., 23 (WINTER 67), 124-139.
POINTS UP "FAILINGS" IN WORLD COURT AS STRUCTURALLY INHERENT. BECAUSE PARTICIPATION IS VOLUNTARY, COURT COULD NEVER BE SUCCESSFUL IN SETTLING MAJOR DISPUTES. ALSO, CRITICIZES FACT THAT SETTLEMENTS ARE MORE INCLINED TO BE POLITICAL THAN LEGAL.

0563 DALLIN A. ED., WESTIN A.F. ED.
POLITICS IN THE SOVIET UNION: 7 CASES.
NEW YORK: HARCOURT BRACE, 1966, 282 PP., LC#66-17594.
CASE STUDIES OF POLITICAL INTERACTION IN USSR: DESTALINIZATION AND HERITAGE OF TERROR; TWENTY-SECOND PARTY CONGRESS, 1961; KHRUSHCHEV AND PARTY-STATE CONTROL; FREEDOM AND CONTROL IN LITERATURE, 1962-63; SOCIAL CONTROL THROUGH LAW; KHRUSHCHEV AND THE MILITARY.

0564 DANELSKI D.J.
A SUPREME COURT JUSTICE IS APPOINTED.
NEW YORK: RANDOM HOUSE, INC, 1964, 202 PP., LC#64-22706.
HISTORY OF HARDING'S APPOINTMENT OF PIERCE BUTLER TO SUPREME COURT. EXAMINATION OF PERSONS INVOLVED, PERSONALITIES, AND ISSUES AT STAKE. ANALYZES PRESIDENTIAL APPOINTMENTS. CONSIDERS UTILITY OF CONCEPTS SUCH AS TRANSACTION, INFLUENCE, AND PERSONALITY.

0565 DANGERFIELD R.
IN DEFENSE OF THE SENATE.
NORMAN: U. OKLAHOMA PR., 1933.
EFFECT OF SENATE PARTICIPATION IN TREATY-RATIFICATION

SYSTEMATICALLY ANALYZED. FACTORS INFLUENCING SENATE ACTION, INCLUDING ORGANIZATIONS, INSTITUTIONS, AND PERSONALITIES, ARE EXAMINED. CONCLUDES THAT SENATE APPROVED MOST TREATIES EXPEDIENTLY AND RECOMMENDS FORMATION OF DELIBERATIVE ORGANS, E.G., A LEGISLATIVE-EXECUTIVE CABINET AND/OR THE LIKE, TO ENSURE EFFECTIVE FOREIGN POLICY.

0566 DANIEL C.
"FREEDOM, EQUITY, AND THE WAR ON POVERTY."
AMER. J. OF ECO. AND SOC., 26 (OCT. 67), 367-375.
STATES THAT IN ORDER FOR FREEDOM TO EXIST, MARKET COMPETITION AND POLITICAL SYSTEMS MUST BE FREE. DISCUSSES WAR ON POVERTY AS A MEANS WHEREBY EQUALITY OF OPPORTUNITY WILL BE PARTLY ATTAINED. MAINTAINS THAT THIS WAR REQUIRES A REDISTRIBUTION OF INCOME TO BRING ABOUT DISTRIBUTIVE JUSTICE.

0567 DARBY W.E.
INTERNATIONAL TRIBUNALS.
LONDON: PEACE SOCIETY, 1897, 168 PP.
VARIOUS SCHEMES OF INTERNATIONAL TRIBUNALS ARE PRESENTED: FROM THE AMPHICTYONIC COUNCIL OF ANCIENT GREECE TO ANGLO-AMERICAN ARBITRATION TREATY OF 1897 AS WELL AS PROPOSALS BY BENTHAM AND KANT. AUTHOR LISTS 140 INSTANCES OF INTER-NATIONAL ARBITRATION SINCE 1815 AS CONCLUSIVE PROOF OF PRACTICABILITY OF ARBITRATION AS CHIEF MEANS OF SETTLING INTERNATIONAL DISPUTES.

0568 DARWIN L.
"WHAT IS EUGENICS."
NEW YORK: GALTON, 1929, 88 PP.
ANALYZES EFFECT OF OVERPOPULATION ON DOMESTIC AND INTER-NATIONAL AFFAIRS. PROPOSES POPULATION CONTROL FOR IMPROVE-MENT OF HUMAN RACE BIOLOGICALLY AND SOCIALLY. RECOMMENDS SELECTIVE FAMILY LIMITATION AND ELIMINATION OF UNFIT MEM-BERS. CALLS FOR GOVERNMENT REGULATION OF BIRTH RATE.

0569 DASH S., SCHWARTZ R.F., KNOWLTON R.E.
THE EAVESDROPPERS.
NEW BRUNSWICK: RUTGERS U PR, 1959, 484 PP., LC#59-7511.
RESULTS OF STUDY BY PENNSYLVANIA BAR ASSOCIATION ON WIRE-TAPPING: WHERE PRACTICED; DEVICES USED, HOW THEY WORK AND HOW TO DETECT THEM; AND LAWS REGULATING IT.

0570 DAVIS A.
"CASTE, ECONOMY, AND VIOLENCE" (BMR)"
AMER. J. OF SOCIOLOGY, 51 (JULY 45), 7-15.
DISCUSSES CASTE IN SOUTH AS IT INTEGRATES INTO ONE SYSTEM ALL ASPECTS OF WHITE-NEGRO BEHAVIOR: SOCIAL, SEXUAL, ECONOMIC, ETC. MAINTAINS ECONOMIC INSTITUTION IS ONLY ONE NOT COMPLETELY ORGANIZED ON CASTE LINES. WHEN NEGROES AS GROUP ACHIEVE ECONOMIC MOBILITY, THEY MEET CONFLICT AND VIOLENCE FROM WHITES. EXAMINES SOCIAL CLASS, LEGAL SANCTIONS OF CASTE, CASTE DOGMAS, AND COMMUNITY STRUCTURE.

0571 DAVIS B.F., HIRSHBERG A.
THE DESPERATE AND THE DAMNED.
NEW YORK: THOMAS Y CROWELL, 1961, 229 PP., LC#61-7615.
STORY OF BERNICE DAVIS' ASSIGNMENTS AS NEWSPAPERWOMAN AT SAN QUENTIN PRISON, THE PRISONERS SHE KNEW, AND EXPERIENCES SHE HAD. QUESTIONS ADVISABILITY OF CAPITAL PUNISHMENT AND LAWS DEFINING CRIMINAL INSANITY.

0572 DAVIS F.J., FOSTER H.H. ET AL.
SOCIETY AND THE LAW.
NEW YORK: FREE PRESS OF GLENCOE, 1962, 488 PP., LC#62-11847.
EXPLORES RELATIONSHIP BETWEEN LAW AND SOCIOLOGY IN TERMS OF AMERICAN SOCIOLOGICAL THEORY AND METHOD. EMPHASIZES ANGLO-AMERICAN LAW. DISCUSSES LAW AND SOCIAL ORGANIZATION, LAW AND SOCIAL CHANGE, AND LAWYERS AS A PROFESSIONAL GROUP.

0573 DAVIS K., BLOMSTROM R.L.
BUSINESS AND ITS ENVIRONMENT.
NEW YORK: MCGRAW HILL, 1966, 403 PP., LC#65-28234.
BUSINESS CULTURE AS A DYNAMIC SOCIAL SYSTEM. INTEGRATION OF ALL POINTS OF VIEW FROM MANY DISCIPLINES TO GIVE OVER-ALL PICTURE. PRO-BUSINESS, BUT RETAINS ACADEMIC INTEGRITY. HISTORICAL BACKGROUND SUPPLEMENTED BY DISCUSSIONS OF CURRENT ISSUES, RELATIONSHIPS TO OTHER SUBGROUPS OF SOCIETY, AND ACTUAL CASES OF BUSINESS PRACTICE. WRITTEN AS A TEXTBOOK FOR STUDENTS.

0574 DAVIS K.C.
ADMINISTRATIVE LAW.
MINNEAPOLIS: WEST PUBL CO, 1951, 1024 PP.
DISCUSSES BASIC ADMINISTRATIVE PROCESSES AND REQUIREMENTS OF HEARING, NOTICE, AND OTHER SAFEGUARDS. EXAMINES PRINCI-PLES OF DELEGATION AND SEPARATION OF POWERS, AND PRESENTS NATURE OF JUDICIAL REVIEW OF ADMINISTRATIVE ACTION.

0575 DAVIS K.C.
ADMINISTRATIVE LAW TREATISE (VOLS. I AND IV)
MINNEAPOLIS: WEST PUBL CO, 1958, 1310 PP.
VOL. I DISCUSSES NATURE AND PROCESS OF ADMINISTRATIVE LAW. EXAMINES CONCEPT OF DELEGATION OF POWER, RULE-MAKING FUNCTION OF ADMINISTRATIVE AGENCIES, ADJUDICATIVE PROCEDURE,

AND SUBDELEGATION OF POWER. VOL. IV DISCUSSES NATURE OF UN-REVIEWABLE ADMINISTRATIVE ACTION, SCOPE OF REVIEWABLE EVI-DENCE, AND SCOPE OF REVIEW OF LEGAL CONCEPTS AS APPLIED TO FACTS.

0576 DAVIS K.C.
ADMINISTRATIVE LAW: CASES, TEXT, PROBLEMS.
ST PAUL, MINN: WEST PUBL CO, 1958.
TREATISE ON LAW SEEKS TO PRESENT SYSTEMATIC TREATMENT OF ADMINISTRATIVE LAW IN 1958. CRITICIZES SUPREME COURT FOR A NUMBER OF ITS RECENT DECISIONS. LAW IS SURVEYED WITH PERTINENT COMMENTS ON ARTICLES WHICH AUTHOR FEELS NEED EXPLANATION. A FOUR-VOLUME SET.

0577 DAVIS K.C.
ADMINISTRATIVE LAW TEXT.
MINNEAPOLIS: WEST PUBL CO, 1959, 617 PP.
DISCUSSES ADMINISTRATIVE PROCESSES IN US. EXAMINES RULE-MAKING POWER, ADJUDICATION PROCEDURES, INSTITUTIONAL DECI-SIONS, AND JURISDICTION OF ADMINISTRATIVE AGENCIES. ANALYZES IN DETAIL PROCEEDINGS FOR REVIEW OF ADMINISTRATIVE ACTION BY FEDERAL COURTS. TEXT INTENDED FOR LAW STUDENTS.

0578 DAVIS K.C.
ADMINISTRATIVE LAW AND GOVERNMENT.
MINNEAPOLIS: WEST PUBL CO, 1960, 547 PP.
DISCUSSES FUNDAMENTAL PROBLEMS OF ADMINISTRATIVE PROCESS IN US. EXAMINES CONCEPTS OF DELEGATION OF POWER, RULE-MAK-ING, RES JUDICATA AND STARE DECISIS, AND REVIEW OF ADMINIS-TRATIVE ACTION BY COURTS. EACH CHAPTER CONTAINS PROBLEM SECTION.

0579 DAY R.E.
CIVIL RIGHTS USA: PUBLIC SCHOOLS, SOUTHERN STATES - NORTH CAROLINA, 1963.
WASHINGTON: US GOVERNMENT, 1963, 60 PP.
EXAMINES PROGRESS OF DESEGREGATION IN NORTH CAROLINA COMMUNITIES, EMPHASIZING PROCRASTINATION AND SCHOOL BOARD ATTEMPTS TO EVADE COMPLIANCE WITH STATE-WIDE INTEGRATION. INCLUDES TOKEN DESGREGATION AND "VOLUNTARY" SEGREGATION.

0580 DE ARAGAO J.G.
LA JURIDICTION ADMINISTRATIVE AU BRESIL.
RIO DE JAN: DEP DE IMPR NACIONAL, 1955, 255 PP.
REVIEWS DUAL ADMINISTRATIVE JURISDICTION, 1824-89, AND SUBSEQUENT UNITY OF JURISDICTION, 1889-PRESENT. DUALITY WAS DUE TO FACT THAT "CONSEIL D'ETAT" HAD DE JURE AUTHORITY, BUT WAS A CONSULTATIVE BODY, WITH REAL AUTHORITY EXERCISED BY OTHERS. IN 1889, REVOLUTION ESTABLISHED REPUBLICAN FEDERATIVE GOVERNMENT WITH CLEAR DIVISION OF AUTHORITY.

0581 DE GRAZIA A.
POLITICAL ORGANIZATION.
NEW YORK: CROWELL COLLIER, 1952, 306 PP., LC#62-19200.
SURVEYS LAWS, CONSTITUTIONS, LEGISLATURES, EXECUTIVES, ADMINISTRATIVE AGENCIES, AND COURTS. EXPLAINS OPERATION OF POLITICAL BEHAVIOR WITHIN THESE INSTITUTIONS. ASSAYS RECENT DEVELOPMENTS IN POLITICAL SCIENCE.

0582 DE GRAZIA A.
"GENERAL THEORY OF APPORTIONMENT" (BMR)"
LAW AND CONTEMPORARY PROBLEMS, 17 (SPRING 52), 256-267.
DISCUSSES APPORTIONMENT AS DIVISION OF POPULATION INTO CONSTITUENCIES WHOSE ELECTORS SELECT PUBLIC OFFICERS. EXAMINES CRITERIA BY WHICH CONSTITUENCIES ARE DIVIDED AND BASIC CHANGES IN CRITERIA WHICH ARE PART OF HISTORICAL REVOLUTIONS.

0583 DE GRAZIA A.
APPORTIONMENT AND REPRESENTATIVE GOVERNMENT.
WASHINGTON: AMER ENTERPRISE INST, 1963, LC#63-12709.
EXAMINES FUNDAMENTALS OF APPORTIONMENT IN RELATION TO REPRESENTATIVE GOVERNMENT. CONSIDERS LIMITS OF FEDERAL JUDICIAL CONTROL OVER STATE GOVERNMENTAL ORGANIZATION, NATURE OF APPORTIONMENT, ITS EFFECTS ON SOCIETY AND HOW IT SHOULD BE ARRANGED.

0584 DE HUSZAR G.B. ED.
NEW PERSPECTIVES ON PEACE.
CHICAGO: U. CHI. PR., 1944, 261 PP.
CRITICIZES THREE MISCONCEPTIONS CONCERNING SUBJECT OF PEACE: THAT IT IS ABSENCE OF WAR, THAT IT IS A STATIC EVENT, THAT IT CAN BE ATTAINED SOLELY BY GOOD WILL. PRESENTS ESSAYS OUTLINING PROBLEMS OF PEACE IN TERMS OF: GEOGRAPHY, HISTORY, ETHNOLOGY, ECONOMICS, SOCIOLOGY, LAW, EDUCATION, PSYCHOLOGY, RELIGION AND PHILOSOPHY, RATHER THAN RESORTING TO A SINGLE DISCIPLINE FOR SOLUTIONS.

0585 DE HUSZAR G.B.
EQUALITY IN AMERICA: THE ISSUE OF MINORITY RIGHTS.
NEW YORK: H W WILSON, 1949, 259 PP.
ARTICLES, MOST FROM RECENT PERIODICALS, ON PROBLEM OF EQUALITY: VARIOUS FORMS OF DISCRIMINATION IN CHURCHES, ARMED FORCES, HOUSING, ELECTIONS, AND EDUCATION; AND VARIOUS RECOMMENDED REMEDIES THROUGH COMMUNITY ACTION, SCHOOLS, AND/OR LEGISLATION.

0586 DE LAVALLE H.
A STATEMENT OF THE LAWS OF PERU IN MATTERS AFFECTING BUSI-
NESS (3RD ED.)
WASHINGTON: PAN AMERICAN UNION, 1962, 234 PP.
SURVEY OF BASIC PERUVIAN LAW EMPHASIZING COMMERCIAL, IN-
DUSTRIAL, AND LABOR LAW. EXAMINES STATUS OF FOREIGNERS AND
THEIR INVESTMENTS AND NATURE OF CONTRACTS.

0587 DE MARTENS G.F.
RECUEIL GENERALE DE TRAITES ET AUTRES ACTES RELATIFS AUX
RAPPORTS DE DROIT INTERNATIONAL (41 VOLS.)
GREISWALD: LIBRAIRIE JULIUS ABEL.
LENGTHY SERIES FIRST BEGUN BY GEORGE MARTENS AND CON-
TINUED IN THE 20TH CENTURY BY HEINRICH TRIEPEL. COVERS
TREATIES AND AGREEMENTS OF EUROPEAN COUNTRIES FOR PERIOD
1760-1944. ALTHOUGH PRIMARILY CONCERNED WITH EUROPEAN EVENTS
RELATED TREATIES IN OTHER COUNTRIES ARE INCLUDED. IN FRENCH,
ARRANGED ALPHABETICALLY AND CHRONOLOGICALLY.

0588 DE MONTESQUIEU C.
THE SPIRIT OF LAWS (2 VOLS.) (TRANS. BY THOMAS NUGENT)
ORIGINAL PUBLISHER NOT AVAILABLE, 1823, 697 PP.
PRESENTS BASIC PRINCIPLES OF LAW AND FINDS THAT HISTORY
IS CONSEQUENCE OF LAW AND THAT EACH LAW IS CONNECTED TO
ANOTHER LAW. MAINTAINS THAT STRONGEST POLITICAL VIRTUE IS
LOVE OF COUNTRY. DISCUSSES MANY DIFFERENT RELATIONS OF LAWS
TO OTHER LAWS AND TO CLIMATE, RELIGION, REVOLUTIONS, AND
MONEY. TRACES ORIGINS OF FRENCH CIVIL LAWS. INCLUDES
ANALYSIS OF WORK BY D'ALEMBERT.

0589 DE NOIA J.
GUIDE TO OFFICIAL PUBLICATIONS OF OTHER AMERICAN REPUBLICS:
ECUADOR (VOL. IX)
WASHINGTON: LIBRARY OF CONGRESS, 1947, 56 PP.
CHECKLIST AND ANNOTATED BIBLIOGRAPHY OF OFFICIAL STATE
PUBLICATIONS ISSUED BY THE REPUBLIC OF ECUADOR SINCE 1822.
INDEXED BY TITLE AND ARRANGED BY AGENCY OR DEPARTMENT OF
PUBLICATION. PROVIDES A CHECKLIST FOR ALL HOLDINGS LISTED IN
THE LIBRARY OF CONGRESS CATALOG. PROJECT SPONSORED BY THE
STATE DEPARTMENT WITH THE COOPERATION OF THE DIRECTOR OF
THE HISPANIC FOUNDATION.

0590 DE NOIA J., CHILDS J.B., MCGEORGE H.
GUIDE TO OFFICIAL PUBLICATIONS OF THE OTHER AMERICAN RE-
PUBLICS: EL SALVADOR.
WASHINGTON: LIBRARY OF CONGRESS, 1947, 64 PP.
ANNOTATED BIBLIOGRAPHY AND GUIDE TO GOVERNMENT PUBLICA-
TIONS IN EL SALVADOR; ARRANGED BY AGENCY OR DEPARTMENT OF
ORIGIN AND INDEXED ALPHABETICALLY BY TITLE. ALSO INCLUDES
PREFATORY NOTE AND AN INTRODUCTION EXPLAINING GENERAL FACETS
OF STATE STRUCTURE TO FACILITATE THE USE OF GUIDE. COMPILED
FOR LIBRARY OF CONGRESS.

0591 DE NOIA J.
GUIDE TO OFFICIAL PUBLICATIONS OF THE OTHER AMERICAN REPUB-
LICS: NICARAGUA (VOL. XIV)
WASHINGTON: LIBRARY OF CONGRESS, 1947, 33 PP.
ANNOTATED AND INDEXED BIBLIOGRAPHY AND GUIDE TO THE HOLD-
INGS IN THE LIBRARY OF CONGRESS OF SERIES, SERIALS, MONO-
GRAPHS, AND OTHER STATE PUBLICATIONS ISSUED BY NICARAGUAN
REPUBLIC. ARRANGED BY DEPARTMENT OR AGENCY OF ISSUANCE.
INCLUDES GENERAL PUBLICATIONS AND OFFICIAL GAZETTES.
LISTS ALL MATERIAL SINCE 1821.

0592 DE NOIA J.
GUIDE TO OFFICIAL PUBLICATIONS OF THE OTHER AMERICAN REPUB-
LICS: PANAMA (VOL. XV)
WASHINGTON: LIBRARY OF CONGRESS, 1947, 34 PP.
INDEXED AND ANNOTATED BIBLIOGRAPHY AND GUIDE TO OFFICIAL
GOVERNMENT PUBLICATIONS AND DOCUMENTS OF PANAMA ARRANGED
BY AGENCY OR DEPARTMENT OF ISSUANCE. PART OF A LIBRARY OF
CONGRESS PROJECT BEGUN IN 1941 UNDER THE AEGIS OF THE
STATE DEPARTMENT'S INTERDEPARTMENTAL COMMITTEE ON SCIENTIFIC
AND CULTURAL COOPERATION. INCLUDES SERIALS, SERIES, AND
MONOGRAPHS PUBLISHED SINCE 1903.

0593 DE NOIA J.
GUIDE TO OFFICIAL PUBLICATIONS OF OTHER AMERICAN REPUBLICS:
PERU (VOL. XVII)
WASHINGTON: LIBRARY OF CONGRESS, 1948, 90 PP.
ANNOTATED CHECKLIST OF ALL OFFICIAL STATE PUBLICATIONS
ISSUED SINCE INDEPENDENCE IN 1826 BY THE PERUVIAN GOVERN-
MENT AND AVAILABLE IN THE LIBRARY OF CONGRESS. PART OF STATE
DEPARTMENT PROJECT. INCLUDES A SUBJECT-TITLE INDEX. DOCU-
MENTS ARE ARRANGED UNDER THE DEPARTMENT OR AGENCY OF
ISSUANCE.

0594 DE TOCQUEVILLE A.
DEMOCRACY IN AMERICA (VOLUME ONE).
CAMBRIDGE: SEVER, 1862, 254 PP.
EXAMINES AMERICAN POLITICAL PROCESS, INCLUDING THE GOV-
ERNMENT, PARTIES, THE CONSTITUTION, POPULAR SOVEREIGNTY AND
THE PRESS, AND ITS INTER-RELATIONSHIP WITH SOCIAL AND ECO-
NOMIC CONDITIONS. CONCLUDES REPUBLIC'S GREATEST DANGER TO BE
MAJORITY TYRANNY, AND ITS GREATEST SUPPORT TO BE CUSTOM AND
LAW. PREDICTS THAT AMERICA, LIKE RUSSIA, AS A GREAT POWER,

WILL CONTROL HALF THE WORLD.

0595 DE TOCQUEVILLE A.
DEMOCRACY IN AMERICA (4 VOLS.) (TRANS. BY HENRY REEVE)
LONDON: SAUNDERS & OTTEY, 1835, 1493 PP.
DEPICTS INFLUENCE OF DEMOCRATIC EQUALITY ON AMERICAN
GOVERNMENT. STUDIES ORIGINS AND SOCIAL CONDITIONS OF
AMERICA. EXAMINES CONSTITUTION, STATE AND LOCAL GOVERNMENT,
JUDICIAL POWER, POLITICAL PARTIES, FREEDOMS. DISCUSSES
EFFECT OF EQUALITY ON SOCIAL STRUCTURE AND METHODS USED TO
MAINTAIN EQUALITY. PRESENTS IMPACT OF DEMOCRACY ON OPINIONS,
FEELINGS, AND MANNERS OF AMERICANS.

0596 DE TOCQUEVILLE A.
DEMOCRACY IN AMERICA (1834-1840) (2 VOLS. IN I; TRANS. BY
G. LAWRENCE)
NEW YORK: HARPER & ROW, 1966, 784 PP.
DETAILED EXAMINATION OF AMERICA IN 1800'S BY FRENCH DEMO-
CRAT. DISCUSSES GOVERNMENT, CULTURE, AND LAW IN AMERICAN
SOCIETY, WHICH IS VIEWED AS A PORTENT OF THE FUTURE. CON-
SIDERS SOCIAL EQUALITY TO BE MOST OVERWHELMING FEATURE OF
AMERICAN SOCIETY, AND RELATES THIS TO SYSTEM OF GOVERNMENT,
TRACING ITS ROOTS IN HISTORY AND SPECIAL ENVIRONMENTAL CON-
DITIONS OF US. COMPARES US FAVORABLY WITH FRANCE.

0597 DE VATTEL E.
THE LAW OF NATIONS.
ORIGINAL PUBLISHER NOT AVAILABLE, 1796, 563 PP.
LAW OF NATIONS IS A SCIENCE, "CONSISTING IN A JUST AND
RATIONAL APPLICATION OF THE LAW OF NATURE" TO THE AFFAIRS OF
MAN AND PRINCES. STUDY BASED ON CHRISTIAN WOLFF'S WORK ON
SAME SUBJECT. DISAGREES WITH WOLFF THAT ESTABLISHMENT OF
LAW IS VOLUNTARY. BELIEVES MEN RESORT TO LAW ONLY TO PROTECT
THEMSELVES AGAINST "DEPRAVITY OF THE MULTITUDE." THERE ARE
VOLUNTARY LAWS, BUT NECESSARY ONES COME FROM LAW OF NATURE.

0598 DE VICTORIA F., SCOTT G.B. ED.
DE INDIS ET DE JURE BELLI (1557) IN F. DE VICTORIA, DE INDIS
ET DE JURE BELLI REFLECTIONES.
WASHINGTON: CARNEGIE ENDOWMENT, 1917, 475 PP.
WORK BY SPANISH THEOLOGIAN CONSISTS OF LECTURES ON THE
RIGHTS OF THE INDIANS AND THE RIGHTS OF WAR. BELIEVES THAT
CHRISTIANS MAY SERVE IN AND MAKE WAR. A WRONG COMMITTED IS
THE ONLY JUST REASON FOR MAKING WAR. DISCUSSES PUNISHMENT
OF WRONG-DOER. SUBJECTS DO NOT HAVE TO PARTICIPATE IF THEY
BELIEVE WAR UNJUST. DISCUSSES LAWFULNESS OF KILLING, SEI-
ZURE, ETC. RIGHTS OF INDIANS CONCERN RIGHTS TO PROPERTY.

0599 DE VISSCHER C.
THEORY AND REALITY IN PUBLIC INTERNATIONAL LAW.
PRINCETON: U. PR., 1957, 381 PP.
EXAMINES CONTENTS OF INTERNATIONAL LAW AND STUDIES POLIT-
ICAL SYSTEMS, POWER, POWER RELATIONSHIPS, IDEOLOGIES AND
INTERNATIONAL INSTITUTIONS. CONCLUDES THAT DESPITE LIMITA-
TIONS, INTERNATIONAL LAW CAN GENERATE PRINCIPLES TO GUIDE
SOVEREIGNTIES TOWARDS SUPPORTING HUMAN VALUES.

0600 DEAN A.W.
"SECOND GENEVA CONFERENCE OF THE LAW OF THE SEA: THE FIGHT
FOR FREEDOM OF THE SEAS."
AMER. J. INT. LAW, 54-55 (OCT.60 - JULY 61), 751-89, 675-80.
ATTEMPTS TO SETTLE CONTROVERSIES OVER WIDTH OF TERRITOR-
IAL SEA. SHOWS DANGERS TO FREEDOM OF NAVIGATION, FREE COM-
MERCE, AND COMMUNICATION INHERENT IN ANY EXTENSION. STUDIES
COMPROMISE BETWEEN USA PROPOSED SIX MILE LIMIT AND USSR PLAN
FOR TWELVE MILE EXTENSION OF RIGHTS. ALSO RECOUNTS PREVIOUS
AGREEMENTS OVER AIR SPACE AND RELATED ISSUES.

0601 DEBOLD R.C. ED., LEAF R.C. ED.
LSD, MAN AND SOCIETY.
MIDDLETON: WESLEYAN U PR, 1967, 219 PP., LC#67-24111.
BEGINS WITH LSD IN RELATION TO INDIVIDUAL - MOTIVATIONS,
ABUSES, CONSEQUENCES, AND THERAPEUTIC POTENTIAL. CONTINUES
WITH DISCUSSION OF IMPACT OF LSD ON SOCIETY IN AREAS OF LAW,
MEDICINE, AND RELIGION. CONCLUDING SECTION TREATS SUBSTANCE
ITSELF, PHARMACOLOGICAL PROPERTIES, AND NEUROLOGICAL AND
BEHAVIORAL EFFECTS.

0602 DECOTTIGNIES R., BIEVILLE MARC D.E.
LES NATIONALITES AFRICAINES.
PARIS: EDITIONS A PEDONE, 1963, 419 PP.
CONCERNS LAW IN AFRICAN STATES WHICH WERE FORMER FRENCH
COLONIES. ATTEMPTS TO DISTINGUISH COMMON MANIFESTATIONS OF
LAW IN STATES. STUDIES SPECIFIC LAW IN 14 STATES AND REPRO-
DUCES ACTUAL CODES.

0603 DEENER D.R. ED.
CANADA - UNITED STATES TREATY RELATIONS.
DURHAM: DUKE U PR, 1963, 250 PP., LC#63-13312.
GENERAL AND SPECIFIC TREATMENT OF CANADA'S TREATY
RELATIONS WITH US SINCE 1782. POLITICS, STRATEGY,
PROBLEMS, AND CASE STUDIES ARE INCLUDED.

0604 DELANY V.T.H.
THE ADMINISTRATION OF JUSTICE IN IRELAND.
DUBLIN: INST PUBLIC ADMIN, 1962, 91 PP.

HISTORY OF IRISH JUDICIARY SINCE 1800 INCLUDING SOURCES OF IRISH LAW, COURT SYSTEMS, CRIMINAL AND CIVIL JURISDICTION, COURT PERSONNEL, AND LEGAL FINANCES.

0605 DELEGACION NACIONAL DE PRENSA
FALANGE ESPANOL TRADICIONALISTA Y DE LAS JUNTAS OFENSIVAS NACIONALES SINDICALISTAS. IX CONSEJO NACIONAL (PAMPHLET) BURGOS,SPAIN: EDICIONES DEL MOVIMIENTO, 1961, 46 PP.
THREE DOCUMENTS FROM 1961 NINTH NATIONAL COUNCIL OF FALANGIST MOVEMENT INCLUDING CONSTITUTION OF MOVEMENT, SPEECH OF SECRETARY GENERAL OF MOVEMENT, AND SPEECH BY GENERALISSIMO FRANCO.

0606 DENNING A.
FREEDOM UNDER THE LAW.
TORONTO: CARSWELL, 1949, 126 PP.
SUMMARIZES DEVELOPMENT OF ENGLISH LAW, DETAILING ITS PROVISIONS ON PERSONAL FREEDOM, FREEDOM OF MIND AND CONSCIENCE, JUSTICE BETWEEN MAN AND STATE, AND POWERS OF EXECUTIVE.

0607 DERGE D.R.
"THE LAWYER AS DECISION-MAKER IN THE AMERICAN STATE LEGISLATURE."
J. OF POLITICS, 21 (AUG. 59), 408-33.
EXAMINES CHARACTERISTICS, ROLE AND BEHAVIOR OF LAWYERS AS DECISION-MAKERS IN STATE LEGISLATURES. DATA DRAWN FROM LOWER CHAMBERS OF MISSOURI AND ILLINOIS.

0608 DERWINSKI E.J.
"THE COST OF THE INTERNATIONAL COFFEE AGREEMENT."
INTER. AMER. ECON. AFF., 18 (AUTUMN 64), 93-96.
CONGRESSMAN DERWINSKI ACCUSES STATE DEPARTMENT OF MANIPULATING EXPORT-QUOTAS OF THE COFFEE AGREEMENT IN ORDER TO PROVIDE IMMENSE EXPANSION IN FOREIGN AID DONATIONS. DEPARTMENT IS CRITICIZED FOR FAILURE TO FULFILL ITS PLEDGE TO CONGRESS.

0609 DESMITH S.A.
JUDICIAL REVIEW OF ADMINISTRATIVE ACTION.
NEW YORK: OCEANA PUBLISHING, 1959, 486 PP., LC#59-12294.
DISCUSSES ROLE OF ENGLISH COURTS IN REVIEWING ACTS, ORDERS, AND DECISIONS OF MINISTERS, LOCAL AUTHORITIES, PUBLIC CORPORATIONS AND OFFICIALS, AND ADMINISTRATIVE TRIBUNALS. EXAMINES SCOPE OF JUDICIAL REMEDIES, CIRCUMSTANCES FOR RECOURSE TO COURTS, LEGAL STANDARDS TO WHICH EXERCISE OF DISCRETIONARY POWERS MUST CONFORM, AND TIMES WHEN ADMINISTRATION MUST EXPLAIN DECISIONS.

0610 DETTER I.
"THE PROBLEM OF UNEQUAL TREATIES."
INT. AND COMP. LAW Q., 15 (OCT. 66), 1069-1089.
THE PROLIFERATION OF NEW STATES IN THE UN AND THEIR DEMANDS TO BE TREATED AS SOVEREIGN EQUALS HAS HEATED CONTROVERSIAL NATURE OF "INEQUAL TREATIES, REBUS SIC STANTIBUS, AND PACTA SUNT SERVANDA." ASSESSES INTERNATIONAL VALIDITY OF TREATIES LIKE "CHINESE CAPITULATION TREATIES," SUGGESTS UN GENERAL ASSEMBLY AS CONTROL ORGAN.

0611 DEUTSCH E.P.
"A JUDICIAL PATH TO WORLD PEACE."
AMER BAR ASSN., 53 (DEC. 67), 1115-1120.
TRACES POLITICAL HISTORY OF THEORY OF, AND ATTEMPTS AT, INTERNATIONAL LAW ORGANIZATIONS. DISCUSSES THE PRESENT-DAY INTERNATIONAL COURT OF JUSTICE. FEELS ITS GREATEST DRAWBACK IS DISTRUST OF JUDGES' INDEPENDENCE; RECOMMENDS LIFETIME TENURE AND INTERNATIONAL SELECTION OF JUDGES. PROPOSES ASSURANCE TO STATES THAT COURT WILL NOT INTERFERE IN DOMESTIC AFFAIRS. HOPES FOR EXPANDED USE OF COURT.

0612 DEUTSCHE BIBLIOTH FRANKF A M
DEUTSCHE BIBLIOGRAPHIE.
FRANKFURT: DEUT BIBLIOG FRANKFE.
WEEKLY REGISTER (JAN 1965-JULY 1967) LISTING BOOKS PUBLISHED IN THE PRECEDING YEARS (1965 AND 1966). ARRANGED BY SUBJECT AND HAS SUCH CLASSIFICATIONS AS PHILOSOPHY, LAW, AND ADMINISTRATION, SOCIAL SCIENCES, POLITICS, DEFENSE, FINE ARTS, ETC. HAS A SUBJECT-AUTHOR INDEX. FOREIGN PUBLICATIONS INCLUDED.

0613 DEUTSCHE BUCHEREI
JAHRESVERZEICHNIS DER DEUTSCHEN HOCHSCHULSCHRIFTEN.
LEIPZIG: VEB VERL FUR BUCH-BIBL.
ANNUAL BIBLIOGRAPHY OF DISSERTATIONS AND ACADEMIC WRITINGS WITH APPROXIMATELY 10,000 LISTINGS PER YEAR. ORGANIZED BY ACADEMIC INSTITUTION, FACULTY, AND PLACE OF PUBLICATION. INDEXED BY SUBJECT AND AUTHOR WITH CROSS-REFERENCES UNDER MAIN TOPIC. VOLUME 80 (1964) WAS FIRST ISSUE TO APPEAR IN PAPERBACK.

0614 DEUTSCHE BUCHEREI
JAHRESVERZEICHNIS DES DEUTSCHEN SCHRIFTUMS.
LEIPZIG: VEB VERL FUR BUCH-BIBL.
ANNUAL BIBLIOGRAPHY OF BOOKS IN GERMAN PUBLISHED DURING THE PERIOD UNDER CONSIDERATION IN GERMANY, AUSTRIA, SWITZERLAND, AND OTHER COUNTRIES. EACH VOLUME DIVIDED INTO TWO

SECTIONS: WORKS ORGANIZED BY AUTHOR; WORKS INDEXED UNDER SUBJECT.

0615 DEUTSCHE BUCHEREI
DEUTSCHES BUCHERVERZEICHNIS.
LEIPZIG: VEB VERL FUR BUCH-BIBL.
ANNUAL LISTING OF PRIMARY PUBLICATIONS IN BOTH EAST AND WEST GERMANY. ENTRIES ARRANGE ALPHABETICALLY BY AUTHOR WITH A SUBJECT INDEX. FIRST PUBLISHED 1911.

0616 DEUTSCHE GESELLS. VOELKERRECHT
DIE VOLKERRECHTLICHEN DISSERTATIONEN AN DEN WESTDEUTSCHEN UNIVERSITATEN. 1945-1957.
KARLSRUHE: DEUTSCHE GESELLS. VOELKERRECHT,1958, 52 PP.
BIBLIOGRAPHY OF WEST GERMAN DISSERTATIONS ON INTERNATIONAL LAW.

0617 DEVLIN P.
THE CRIMINAL PROSECUTION IN ENGLAND.
NEW HAVEN: YALE U PR, 1958, 150 PP., LC#58-11251.
STUDY OF GENERAL LEGAL PRINCIPLES AND PROCEDURES INVOLVED IN ENGLISH SYSTEM OF PROSECUTION FOR CRIME. TRACES PROCESS FROM TIME OF ARREST THROUGH TIME OF ARRAIGNMENT. DISCUSSES RIGHTS AND DUTIES OF GOVERNMENT AND OF ACCUSED WHILE CASE IS BEING PREPARED FOR TRIAL.

0618 DEWEY J.
"ETHICS AND INTERNATIONAL RELATIONS."
FOR. AFF., 1 (MAR. 23), 85-95.
EXAMINES DEMISE OF NATURAL LAW AS APPLICABLE TO INTERNATIONAL RELATIONS. POSITS FAILURE OF BOTH HEGELIAN AND UTILITARIAN ETHICAL POSITIONS. ADVOCATES WORLD-WIDE AGREEMENT TO OUTLAW WAR AS FIRST STEP TOWARD A MODERN INTERNATIONAL ETHICS.

0619 DIAS R.W.M.
A BIBLIOGRAPHY OF JURISPRUDENCE (2ND ED.)
LONDON: BUTTERWORTHS, 1964, 234 PP.
AN ANNOTATED BIBLIOGRAPHY OF LEGAL BOOKS AND PERIODICALS, DESIGNED TO ACCOMPANY THE SECOND EDITION OF THE TEXTBOOK ENTITLED "JURISPRUDENCE." ENTRIES ORGANIZED INTO 20 CATEGORIES OF LEGAL, SOCIOLOGICAL, AND ECONOMIC DISCIPLINE AND SPECIALTY. COVERS WORKS PUBLISHED THROUGH 1962, BUT MOST BOOKS LISTED WERE ISSUED BETWEEN 1900-1950. ANNOTATIONS CRITICAL AS WELL AS DESCRIPTIVE. SOURCES IN ENGLISH.

0620 DICEY A.
LAW AND PUBLIC OPINION IN ENGLAND.
LONDON: MACMILLAN, 1905, 503 PP.
RELATES PROCESS OF ENGLISH LAW TO CURRENTS OF ENGLISH PUBLIC OPINION AND ESTABLISHES THEIR INTERDEPENDENCE.

0621 DICEY A.V.
LECTURES ON THE RELATION BETWEEN LAW AND PUBLIC OPINION IN ENGLAND DURING THE NINETEENTH CENTURY.
NEW YORK: MACMILLAN, 1905, 503 PP.
STUDIES RELATION BETWEEN CENTURY OF ENGLISH LEGISLATION AND SUCCESSIVE CURRENTS OF PUBLIC OPINION. MAINTAINS THAT LAWS ARE DEPENDENT ON SUPPORT OF PUBLIC. DESCRIBES CHARACTERISTICS OF LEGISLATIVE OPINION AND THREE MAIN CURRENTS OF PUBLIC OPINION: TORYISM, BENTHAMISM, AND COLLECTIVISM. EXAMINES CROSS-CURRENTS OF OPINION AND SPECIAL RELATION OF JUDICIAL LEGISLATION AND OPINION.

0622 DICKINSON E.
THE EQUALITY OF STATES IN INTERNATIONAL LAW.
CAMBRIDGE: HARVARD U. PR., 1920, 424 PP.
DISCUSSES SOURCES OF PRINCIPLE OF EQUALITY OF STATES FROM ANTIQUITY TO MODERN TIMES. EXAMINES INTERNAL AND EXTERNAL LIMITATIONS ON EQUALITY OF STATES. CONCLUDES THAT PRINCIPLE CANNOT BE APPLIED TO INTERNATIONAL ORGANIZATION AND THAT IT WAS NOT APPLIED TO THE LEAGUE OF NATIONS.

0623 DICKINSON J.
ADMINISTRATIVE JUSTICE AND THE SUPREMACY OF LAW IN THE UNITED STATES.
CAMBRIDGE: HARVARD U PR, 1927, 403 PP., LC#27-14657.
EXAMINES RELATIONSHIP OF FEDERAL REGULATORY AGENCIES AND LEGISLATED LAW IN HANDLING PROBLEMS OF GOVERNMENTAL REGULATION. NECESSITY FOR WIDE APPLICABILITY OF LAW MEANS THAT INTERPRETATION BECOMES NECESSARY. EVALUATES ADMINISTRATORS VS. JUDGES AS POLICY-MAKERS IN ECONOMIC REGULATION. ALSO CONSIDERS PROBLEM OF EDUCATING JUDGES TO BE CAPABLE OF DEALING WITH THESE PROBLEMS.

0624 DIEGUES M. ED., WOOD B. ED.
SOCIAL SCIENCE IN LATIN AMERICA.
NEW YORK: COLUMBIA U PRESS, 1967, 335 PP., LC#67-15255.
ANTHOLOGY OF PAPERS PRESENTED AT CONFERENCE ON LATIN AMERICAN STUDIES, MARCH, 1965. EXAMINES STATE OF SOCIAL SCIENCE RESEARCH AND INSTRUCTION IN ECONOMICS, HISTORY, POLITICAL SCIENCE, SOCIOLOGY, ANTHROPOLOGY, AND LAW IN LATIN AMERICA.

0625 DIESING P.
REASON IN SOCIETY; FIVE TYPES OF DECISIONS AND THEIR SOCIAL

CONDITIONS.
URBANA: U OF ILLINOIS PR, 1962, 262 PP., LC#62-7118.
EXPLORES FIVE KINDS OF RATIONALITY - TECHNICAL, ECONOMIC,
SOCIAL, LEGAL, AND POLITICAL. CONSIDERS CIRCUMSTANCES IN
WHICH EACH IS APPROPRIATE. DISCUSSES MORE SPECIFIC KINDS OF
ACTION, SUCH AS PSYCHOTHERAPY, LABOR ARBITRATION, JUDICIAL
DECISIONS, INTERGRATIVE DECISIONS, AND SOCIAL ROLES. STUDIES
NATURE OF REASON, TREATING IT AS CREATIVITY.

0626 DIETZE G. ED.
ESSAYS ON THE AMERICAN CONSTITUTION: A COMMEMORATIVE
VOLUME IN HONOR OF ALPHEUS T. MASON.
ENGLEWOOD CLIFFS: PRENTICE HALL, 1964, 245 PP., LC#64-19435.
ANTHOLOGY OF ESSAYS ON THE FOUNDING FATHERS: FREE GOVERN-
MENT; FEDERALISM; FOREIGN POLICY; CONSTITUTION ABROAD;
JUSTICE AND SCHOLARS; THE SUPREME COURT, BIOGRAPHY, AND THE
STUDY OF PUBLIC LAW.

0627 DILEY A.V.
INTRODUCTION TO THE STUDY OF THE LAW OF THE CONSTITUTION.
LONDON: MACMILLAN, 1960, 535 PP.
TREATS GUIDING PRINCIPLES OF ENGLISH CONSTITUTIONAL LAW.
COMPARES ENGLISH CONSTITUTIONALISM WITH THAT OF US AND
FRENCH REPUBLIC. DISCUSSES SOVEREIGNTY OF PARLIAMENT AND
ITS RELATION TO FEDERALISM. STUDIES NATURE OF RULE OF LAW,
RIGHTS TO PERSONAL FREEDOMS, MARTIAL LAW, ARMY, TAXES, AND
RESPONSIBILITIES OF MINISTERS. EXAMINES CONNECTION BETWEEN
LAW AND CONVENTIONS OF CONSTITUTION.

0628 DILLIARD I. ED.
ONE MAN'S STAND FOR FREEDOM: MR. JUSTICE BLACK AND THE BILL
OF RIGHTS.
NEW YORK: ALFRED KNOPF, 1963, 504 PP., LC#62-8691.
SELECTION OF SUPREME COURT DECISIONS FROM 1937-61,
WHICH INCLUDE CIVIL RIGHTS, JAPANESE-AMERICAN WARTIME
RELOCATION, THE HOUSE ON UN-AMERICAN ACTIVITIES COMMITTEE,
OATHS, AND THE COMMUNIST PARTY.

0629 DILLON D.R.
LATIN AMERICA, 1935-1949; A SELECTED BIBLIOGRAPHY.
NEW YORK: UNITED NATIONS, 1952.
COMPILATION OF IMPORTANT MATERIALS ON THE LAW, HISTORY,
INTERNATIONAL RELATIONS, ECONOMICS, SOCIOLOGY, AND EDUCATION
OF LATIN AMERICA IN GENERAL AND INDIVIDUAL NATIONS.

0630 DIVINE R.A.
AMERICAN IMMIGRATION POLICY, 1924-52.
NEW HAVEN: YALE U PR, 1957, 220 PP., LC#57-6336.
TRACES COURSE OF RESTRICTIVE IMMIGRATION POLICY, FOCUSING
ON CONTROVERSY BETWEEN SUPPORTERS AND OPPONENTS OF RESTRIC-
TION, AND EMPHASIZING EVOLUTION OF A GOVERNMENTAL PROGRAM
DESIGNED TO CONTROL QUANTITY AND QUALITY OF ALIENS. INCLUDES
DISCUSSION OF PROBLEMS OF 1930'S (DEPRESSION, REFUGEES, AND
SUBVERSIVES). ENACTMENT OF DISPLACED PERSONS LEGISLATION,
AND THE MCCARRAN ACT.

0631 DIXON R.G.
"NEW CONSTITUTIONAL FORMS FOR METROPOLIS: REAPPORTIONED
COUNTY BOARDS; LOCAL COUNCILS OF GOVERNMENT."
LAW AND CONTEMPORARY PROB., 30 (WINTER 65), 57-75.
THE AUTHOR SEES REAPPORTIONED COUNTY BOARDS AND COUNCILS
OF GOVERNMENT AS HOLDING "MUCH PROMISE" IN THE REORGANIZA-
TION OF METROPOLITAN AREAS.

0632 DIZARD W.P.
TELEVISION* A WORLD VIEW.
SYRACUSE: SYRACUSE U PRESS, 1966, 349 PP., LC#66-10323.
CAREFUL DOCUMENTATION OF ECONOMIC AND POLITICAL IMPACT OF
TELEVISION IN THE DIFFERENT GEO-POLITICAL AREAS; COMMUNIST
PRACTICES, CHARISMA, GLOBAL AND EDUCATIONAL NETWORKS, WEST-
ERN EXPERIENCES, AND TV IN THE POOR LANDS. WORLD TELEVISION
STATISTICS AND BIBLIOGRAPHY ARE INCLUDED.

0633 DOLE C.F.
THE AMERICAN CITIZEN.
BOSTON: D C HEATH, 1891, 315 PP.
DISCUSSION OF BASIC PRINCIPLES OF CITIZENSHIP AND
POLITICAL HABITS OF AMERICAN CITIZEN. BASIC OBJECT IS
TO "ILLUSTRATE THE MORAL PRINCIPLES WHICH UNDERLIE THE LIFE
OF CIVILIZED MEN." DISCUSSION RANGES FROM STRICTLY
PERSONAL POLITICAL HABITS TO FUNDAMENTAL PRINCIPLES OF
INTERNATIONAL LAW.

0634 DOMKE M.
"THE SETTLEMENT OF DISPUTES IN INTERNATIONAL TRADE."
UNIV. ILL. LAW FORUM (SPRING 59), 402-415.
TRADE ARBITRATIONS SHOULD BE BASED ON COOPERATION IN
ORDER TO PRESERVE COMMERCIAL BUSINESS RELATIONS. ONLY
EXPERIENCED ARBITERS SHOULD UNDERTAKE THIS TASK. CONTRACTS
SHOULD INCLUDE A CLAUSE NAMING ARBITERS TO MEET THE
EVENTUALITY OF A DISPUTE.

0635 DONALDSON A.G.
SOME COMPARATIVE ASPECTS OF IRISH LAW.
DURHAM: DUKE U PR, 1957, 293 PP., LC#57-8815.
STUDIES LEGAL AND CONSTITUTIONAL HISTORY OF IRISH LAW.
DISCUSSES IRELAND IN TERMS OF INTERNATIONAL LAW AND
DEVELOPMENT OF BRITISH COMMONWEALTH. COMPARISONS AND
CONTRASTS DRAWN WITH OTHER COMMONWEALTH COUNTRIES TO
ILLUMINATE IRELAND'S CONTRIBUTIONS. COVERS BOTH NORTHERN
IRELAND AND REPUBLIC OF IRELAND, AND CONTRASTS THEIR
ATTITUDES.

0636 DONNELLY R.C., GOLDSTEIN J., SCHWARTZ R.D.
CRIMINAL LAW: PROBLEMS FOR DECISION IN THE PROMULGATION,
INVOCATION AND ADMINISTRATION OF A LAW OF CRIMES.
NEW YORK: FREE PRESS OF GLENCOE, 1962, 1169 PP., LC#62-11759
EXAMINES PROBLEMS IN "PROMULGATION, INVOCATION, AND
ADMINISTRATION" OF CRIMINAL LAW. INCLUDES PROBLEMS OF
INSANITY, MITIGATING CIRCUMSTANCES, HOMOSEXUALITY, AND
PAROLE. EXPLAINS DIFFERENCES BETWEEN CIVIL AND CRIMINAL
LAW, PURPOSES OF SANCTIONS, REQUISITES OF CRIME, AND BASIS
OF LIABILITY.

0637 DOOLIN D.J.
COMMUNIST CHINA: THE POLITICS OF STUDENT OPPOSITION.
STANFORD: HOOVER INSTITUTE, 1964, 70 PP., LC#64-16879.
COLLECTION OF SPEECHES AND PAPERS BY COMMUNIST CHINESE
STUDENTS, OFFERED DURING THE 1957 PARTY THAW, ON ALLOWING
INTELLECTUAL CRITICISM OF PARTY POLICIES. ORIGINAL OF THIS
EDITION SMUGGLED INTO HONG KONG. ESPECIALLY CRITICAL OF
PARTY POLICY TOWARD HU FENG, OF STALIN, OF JUDICIAL SYSTEM,
AND OF QUESTIONABLE USE OF CHARGE "COUNTERREVOLUTIONARY."
DISCUSSES "RANK" IN CLASSLESS SOCIETY, AND PARTY LEADERSHIP.

0638 DORMAN M.
WE SHALL OVERCOME.
NEW YORK: DELACORTE PRESS, 1964, 340 PP., LC#64-11906.
ACCOUNT BY JOURNALIST OF CIVIL RIGHTS EVENTS IN 1962-63.
COVERS BOTH OUTBREAKS OF VIOLENCE, LIKE THAT AT THE
UNIVERSITY OF MISSISSIPPI AND THE MURDERS OF MEDGAR EVERS
AND WILLIAM MOORE, AND SUCH PEACEFUL EVENTS AS INTEGRATION
OF CLEMSON COLLEGE. ATTEMPTS TO SUGGEST SOME FACTORS THAT
DETERMINE WHETHER VIOLENCE OR ORDER PREVAILS IN SUCH CRISES.

0639 DOROSH J.T. ED.
GUIDE TO SOVIET BIBLIOGRAPHIES.
WASHINGTON: LIBRARY OF CONGRESS, 1950, 158 PP.
BIBLIOGRAPHY OF SEPARATELY PUBLISHED BIBLIOGRAPHIES IS-
SUED IN RUSSIAN OR RELATING TO RUSSIA, AVAILABLE IN LIBRARY
OF CONGRESS. ONLY BIBLIOGRAPHIES ISSUED SINCE 1917 INCLUDED.
CONTAINS SECTIONS ON THEORY, HISTORY, AND USE OF BIBLIOGRA-
PHY. TOPICAL ARRANGEMENT AND SUBJECT AND AUTHOR INDEXES.
CONTAINS 747 ITEMS.

0640 DOUGLAS W.O.
WE THE JUDGES.
GARDEN CITY: DOUBLEDAY, 1956, 475 PP., LC#56-05439.
FOLLOWS GROWTH OF AMERICAN CONSTITUTIONAL LAW FROM MAR-
SHALL TO WARREN, 1801-1953. DISCUSSES CHANGES IN JUDICIAL
POWER, COURT-SYSTEM, LEGISLATIVE PREROGATIVES, FEDERAL VS.
STATE POWER, FAIR TRIAL, AND EQUAL PROTECTION. COMPARES US
EVOLUTION TO INDIAN, WHICH, WHILE RECENT, WAS MUCH MORE
RAPID IN TEMPO.

0641 DOUGLAS W.O.
THE RIGHT OF THE PEOPLE.
GARDEN CITY: DOUBLEDAY, 1958, 238 PP., LC#58-5571.
TREATS "PHILOSOPHY OF FIRST AMENDMENT, CONFLICT OF FREE
EXPRESSION AND OTHER VALUES, AND CENSORSHIP AND RESTRAINT."
INCLUDES ANALYSIS OF CITIZENS PRIVATE RIGHTS IN RELIGION,
INVESTIGATION ETC., AND "ENCROACHMENT OF MILITARY IN
CIVIL LIFE." USES EXAMPLES OF SPECIFIC COURT CASES.

0642 DOUGLAS W.O.
DEMOCRACY'S MANIFESTO.
GARDEN CITY: DOUBLEDAY, 1962, 48 PP., LC#62-10468.
CALL BY JUSTICE DOUGLAS FOR IDEOLOGICAL COUNTER-OFFENSIVE
IN WORLD AFFAIRS WARNING THAT OUR POLICIES IN RESPONSE TO
COMMUNIST CHALLENGE HAVE BEEN NEGATIVE TO DATE, CITING
ALLIANCE FOR PROGRESS AS APPROPRIATE EXAMPLE.

0643 DOUGLAS W.O.
THE ANATOMY OF LIBERTY: THE RIGHTS OF MAN WITHOUT FORCE.
NEW YORK: TRIDENT PR, 1963, 194 PP., LC#63-12572.
STUDIES IN WORLD JURISPRUDENCE, LEADING TO CONCLUSION
THAT MEN MUST STRIVE FOR PERSONAL LIBERTY WITHIN RULE OF
LAW, SEEK TO SPREAD THIS OVER WORLD BY EDUCATION, AND NOT BY
FORCE, PROVIDE WELFARE FOR ALL, AND URGE MUTUAL UNDER-
STANDING LEADING TO PEACEFUL EXISTENCE.

0644 DOUGLAS W.O.
THE BIBLE AND THE SCHOOLS.
BOSTON: LITTLE BROWN, 1966, 65 PP., LC#66-10975.
SHORT STORY OF HISTORY OF RELATIONSHIP BETWEEN SECTARIAN
BELIEFS AND PUBLIC SCHOOLS. DOUGLAS IS IN FAVOR OF REMOVING
ALL SECTARIAN INFLUENCES FROM SCHOOLS SO THAT EDUCATION
MAY BE INSTILLING OF KNOWLEDGE ALL HAVE IN COMMON. FEELS
CHRISTIANITY HAS SUFFICIENT INNER STRENGTH TO SURVIVE AND
DOES NOT NEED STATE SUPPORT, PRIVILEGES, OR PRESTIGE TO DO
SO.

0645 DOUMA J. ED.
BIBLIOGRAPHY ON THE INTERNATIONAL COURT INCLUDING THE
PERMANENT COURT, 1918-1964.
NEW YORK: HUMANITIES PRESS, 1966, 387 PP., LC#52-4918.
ANNOTATED BIBLIOGRAPHY COVERING 1918-64, PUBLISHED AS
SUPPLEMENT TO SERIES BY HAMBRO. TWO PARTS: FIRST DEALS WITH
PERMANENT COURT OF INTERNATIONAL JUSTICE; SECOND CONCERNS
PRESENT COURT INSTITUTED BY UN. CONTAINS 3,572 ENTRIES IN
SEVERAL LANGUAGES. INCLUDES INDEXES OF SUBJECTS AND AUTHORS.

0646 PEPPER H.W.T.
"TAXATION OF BETTERMENT AND CAPITAL GAINS WITH SPECIAL
REFERENCE TO DEVELOPING COUNTRIES."
BUL. INTL FISCAL DOCUMENTS, 21 (APR. 67), 151-172.
QUESTIONS THE ECONOMIC VALIDITY OF CAPITAL GAINS TAXATION
IN COUNTRIES WHERE CAPITAL RISK IS HIGHER AND INCENTIVES TO
INVESTMENT MUST BE CORRESPONDINGLY HIGH. DISCUSSES "BETTER-
MENT" TAXES, STAMP DUTIES, AND CAPITAL GAINS TAXES, GIFTS,
ETC. AS ALTERNATIVE OR COMPLEMENTARY METHODS. CONCLUDES WITH
A LIST OF SUGGESTED FEATURES DESIRABLE IN INITIAL CAPITAL
GAINS TAX IN DEVELOPING COUNTRIES.

0647 DOYLE S.E.
"COMMUNICATION SATELLITES* INTERNAL ORGANIZATION FOR
DEVELOPMENT AND CONTROL."
CALIF. LAW REV., 55 (MAY 67), 431-448.
ARGUES THAT PROBLEM POSED BY COMMUNICATION SATELLITES IS
ORGANIZATION OF INTERNATIONAL COOPERATIVE TO DEVELOP AND
EXPLOIT SYSTEM. EXAMINES COMMUNICATIONS SATELLITE COOPERA-
TION AND INTELSAT AND EXPLORES POLICY PROBLEMS THAT BECOME
DIFFICULT AS SATELLITE TECHNOLOGY ADVANCES INCLUDING
QUESTIONS OF PRIVATE OWNERSHIP AND DIRECT BROADCASTING.

0648 DRESSLER D. ED.
READINGS IN CRIMINOLOGY AND PENOLOGY.
NEW YORK: COLUMBIA U PRESS, 1964, 698 PP., LC#64-14240.
STUDY OF TYPES OF CRIME; SOCIAL BACKGROUND OF CRIMINALS;
EXPLANATIONS OF CRIMINAL BEHAVIOR; ADMINISTRATION OF JUSTICE
BY COURTS AND POLICE; CORRECTIONAL PROCEDURES AND TREATMENT
PROGRAMS; AND STUDIES ON CRIME PREVENTION.

0649 DRINAN R.F.
RELIGION, THE COURTS, AND PUBLIC POLICY.
NEW YORK: MCGRAW HILL, 1963, 251 PP., LC#63-16195.
DISCUSSING CHURCH-STATE RELATIONSHIPS, FUNDAMENTAL PROB-
LEM COVERED IS COOPERATION, RATHER THAN SEPARATION,
SPECIFICALLY IN EDUCATION. CONSIDERS AID TO VARIOUS TYPES
OF SCHOOLS, PUBLIC, CHURCH-RELATED, PRIVATE, AND MEANS OF
CONTRIBUTING TO THEIR SUPPORT WITHOUT SUPPORTING RELIGION.

0650 DU BOIS W.E.B.
IN BATTLE FOR PEACE.
NEW YORK: MAINSTREAM, 1952, 192 PP.
STORY OF DU BOIS FOREIGN-AGENT TRIAL AND ACQUITTAL; HIS
WORK FOR PEACE; AND HIS LIFE-LONG CRUSADE FOR NEGRO
FREEDOM AND COLONIAL LIBERATION.

0651 DUBISSON M.
LA COUR INTERNATIONALE DE JUSTICE.
PARIS: LIB GEN DROIT ET JURIS, 1964, 470 PP.
HISTORY OF THE DEVELOPMENT, COMPETENCE, PERSONNEL, CHAR-
ACTERISTICS, RULINGS, CONSULTATIONS, EFFECTS AND ACCEPTANCE
OF THE RULINGS BY NATIONAL GOVERNMENTS, OF THE INTERNATIONAL
COURT OF JUSTICE. CASE AND CHARTER DATA APPENDED.

0652 DUBOIS J.
DANGER OVER PANAMA.
INDIANAPOLIS: BOBBS-MERRILL, 1964, 409 PP., LC#64-23196.
EXAMINES US RELATIONS WITH PANAMA SINCE 1846,
CONCENTRATING ON PERIOD SINCE WWII. DISCUSSES POLITICAL
HISTORY OF PANAMA, TREATIES WITH US ABOUT CANAL, FLAG WAR,
TREATY WAR, AND COMMUNIST ROLE IN THESE REVOLTS. LOOKS AT
PRESENT RELATIONS BETWEEN US AND PANAMA, AND FUTURE OF
POLICY ON CANAL. SUGGESTS SUBSIDIES TO CANAL ZONE SCHOOLS
TO EDUCATE PANAMANIANS AS PARTIAL SOLUTION.

0653 DUCLOUX L.
FROM BLACKMAIL TO TREASON.
LONDON: ANDRE DEUTSCH, 1958, 240 PP.
STUDIES POLITICAL CRIME AND CORRUPTION IN FRANCE,
1920-40. REFUTES BELIEF, ALLEGEDLY CIRCULATED BY ROYALIST
PROPAGANDISTS, THAT SURETE NATIONALE WAS INSTRUMENT OF PO-
LITICAL COERCION AND FOREIGN POWERS BETWEEN WORLD WARS.

0654 DUGARD J.
"THE REVOCATION OF THE MANDATE FOR SOUTH WEST AFRICA."
AMER. J. OF INT. LAW, 62 (JAN. 68), 78-97.
EXAMINES THE LEGALITY AND LEGAL EFFECT OF UN GENERAL AS-
SEMBLY'S DECISION TO TERMINATE S. AFRICA'S MANDATE FOR S.W.
AFRICA CONFERRED BY LEAGUE OF NATIONS. STUDIES ASSEMBLY'S
RIGHT TO DECLARE APARTHEID INCOMPATIBLE WITH MANDATE PRO-
VISIONS, RIGHT OF LEAGUE TO TERMINATE MANDATE UNILATER-
ALLY, AND WHETHER SUCH RIGHT SUCCEEDS TO UN. DECIDES EACH
IN AFFIRMATIVE, BUT ADVISES IMPLEMENTATION BY COUNCIL.

0655 DUGUIT L.

LAW IN THE MODERN STATE (TRANS. BY FRIDA AND HAROLD LASKI)
NEW YORK: B W HUEBSCH, INC, 1919, 248 PP.
RELATES HIS THEORY OF SOCIOLOGICAL INTERPRETATION OF
STATE TO MODERN PUBLIC LAW, MAINTAINING THAT LAW IS SUM
OF PRINCIPLES OF MORAL CODE NECESSARY TO ACHIEVEMENT OF
SOCIAL PURPOSE. DISCUSSES DISINTEGRATION OF THEORY OF
SOVEREIGN STATE AND RISE OF THEORY THAT STATE'S DUTY IS TO
PROVIDE PUBLIC SERVICE. DESCRIBES RELATION OF STATUTES AND
ADMINISTRATIVE LAWS TO THIS THEORY.

0656 DUMBAULD E.
THE BILL OF RIGHTS AND WHAT IT MEANS TODAY.
NORMAN: U OF OKLAHOMA PR, 1957, 242 PP., LC#57-5954.
NARRATES EVENTS LEADING UP TO ADOPTION OF BILL OF RIGHTS
AND ORIGINS OF EACH AMENDMENT. PROVIDES CURRENT JUDICIAL
INTERPRETATION OF EACH AMENDMENT AND DEFINITIONS OF
UNREASONABLE SEARCHES AND SEIZURES, DOUBLE JEOPARDY, DUE
PROCESS OF LAW, SELF-INCRIMINATION, JUST COMPENSATION, AND
CLEAR AND PRESENT DANGER. URGES PRESERVATION OF BILL OF
RIGHTS.

0657 DUMON F.
LA COMMUNAUTE FRANCO-AFRO-MALGACHE: SES ORIGINES, SES
INSTITUTIONS, SON EVOLUTION.
BRUSSELS: U LIBRE DE BRUXELLES, 1960, 294 PP.
CONSIDERS EVOLUTION AND NATURE OF FRENCH "COMMUNAUTE" IN
AFRICA. CONCERNS POLITICAL PARTIES, CONSTITUTIONAL
REVISIONS, AND MOVEMENTS FOR CONFEDERATION AND FEDERATION
BETWEEN AFRICAN COUNTRIES AND BETWEEN AFRICAN COUNTRIES AND
FRANCE. HALF OF BOOK CONTAINS REPRODUCTIONS OF
CONSTITUTIONS.

0658 DUMON F.
LE BRESIL; SES INSTITUTIONS POLITIQUES ET JUDICIARIES.
BRUSSELS: U LIBRE DE BRUXELLES, 1964, 291 PP.
STUDY OF BRAZILIAN POLITICAL AND JUDICIAL DEVELOPMENT TO
PRESENT REPUBLICAN SYSTEM. EXAMINES EXECUTIVE OFFICE,
CONSTITUTIONS, PUBLIC LAW, INSTITUTIONS, COURT JURISDICTION,
AND INTERPRETATION AND APPLICATION OF LAWS.

0659 DUNHAM A. ED., KURLAND P.B. ED.
MR. JUSTICE.
CHICAGO: U OF CHICAGO PRESS, 1963, 241 PP., LC#56-10080.
SHORT BIOGRAPHIES OF SUPREME COURT JUSTICES MARSHALL,
TANEY, HUGHES, STONE, BRADLEY, HOLMES, BRANDEIS,
SUTHERLAND, AND RUTLEDGE. BIOGRAPHIES WRITTEN BY OTHER
JUSTICES OR WELL-KNOWN LEGAL FIGURES WHO ARE AUTHORITIES
ON MEN ABOUT WHOM THEY WRITE. AUTHORS INCLUDE BIDDLE,
FREUND, AND STEVENS.

0660 DUNN F.S. ED.
CURRENT RESEARCH IN INTERNATIONAL AFFAIRS.
NEW YORK: CARNEGIE ENDOWMENT, 1952, 193 PP.
SURVEY OF RESEARCH CARRIED ON BY PRIVATE RESEARCH
AGENCIES AND SPECIAL RESEARCH INSTITUTES OF UNIVERSITIES IN
US AND UK. ARRANGED BY ORGANIZATIONS. CONTAINS 981 ITEMS ON
FOREIGN POLICY, INTERNATIONAL RELATIONS, AND INTERNATIONAL
LAW. ANNOTATED.

0661 DUNN F.S.
PEACE-MAKING AND THE SETTLEMENT WITH JAPAN.
PRINCETON: PRINCETON U PRESS, 1963, 204 PP., LC#63-07155.
STUDIES AMERICAN POLICY IN FAR EAST, ESPECIALLY WITH
JAPAN, IN DECADE AFTER PEARL HARBOR. DISCUSSES WAR-TIME
PEACE PLANS, PEACE-MAKING AND COLD WAR, SAN FRANCISCO CON-
FERENCE OF 1951, AND EFFECT OF TREATY ON WESTERN SECURITY
IN PACIFIC.

0662 DUNNILL F.
THE CIVIL SERVICE.
NEW YORK: MACMILLAN, 1956, 226 PP.
STUDY OF CIVIL SERVANTS AS INDIVIDUALS, THEIR LIVES,
INFLUENCES, AND THE PRESSURES THEY FACE. CONSIDERED ARE
RECRUITMENT, DEPLOYMENT, CONDITIONING, METHODS, PERSONALITY,
RELATIONS WITH PARLIAMENT AND LAW.

0663 DUNNING W.A.
"HISTORY OF POLITICAL THEORIES FROM LUTHER TO MONTESQUIEU."
LONDON: MACMILLAN, 1905.
SECOND VOLUME OF "HISTORY OF POLITICAL THEORIES," COV-
ERING THE 16TH CENTURY THROUGH THE MIDDLE OF THE 18TH CEN-
TURY. TWELVE CHAPTERS REVIEW POLITICAL PHILOSOPHY OF REF-
FORMATION, ANTI-MONARCHISTS, BODIN, GROTIUS, PURITAN REV-
OLUTION, HOBBES, SPINOZA, BOSSUET, LOCKE, HUME, AND MONTES-
QUIEU. BIBLIOGRAPHY OF ORIGINAL SOURCES, HISTORICAL, CRITI-
CAL, AND DESCRIPTIVE WORKS. EUROPEAN SOURCES.

0664 DUNNING W.A.
"A HISTORY OF POLITICAL THINKERS FROM ROUSSEAU TO SPENCER."
LONDON: MACMILLAN, 1920.
CONCLUDING VOLUME OF "HISTORY OF POLITICAL THEORIES,"
DESIGNED TO CARRY SUBJECT THROUGH 1880. TEN CHAPTERS COV-
ER ROUSSEAU, THE RISE OF ECONOMIC SCIENCE, AMERICAN AND
FRENCH REVOLUTIONS, GERMAN IDEALISTS, THEORIES OF CONSERVA-
TISM, ENGLISH UTILITARIANS, AND THE THEORIES OF CONSTITU-
TIONAL GOVERNMENT, NATIONALISM, AND SOCIALISM. BIBLIOGRAPHY

OF ORIGINAL SOURCES, HISTORICAL, AND CRITICAL WORKS.

0665 DUPRE J.S. LAKOU S.A.
SCIENCE AND THE NATION: POLICY AND POLITICS.
ENGLEWOOD CLIFFS: PRENTICE HALL, 1962, 181 PP., LC#62-9307.
APPRAISAL OF HOW GOVERNMENT CONTRACTS FOR RESEARCH HAVE
ALTERED SEPARATION OF PUBLIC AND PRIVATE SPHERES; HOW
INDUSTRY, GOVERNMENT, AND UNIVERSITIES HAVE FORMED A NEW
PARTNERSHIP; THE ROLE PLAYED BY SCIENTISTS IN SHAPING US
MILITARY AND FOREIGN POLICY; AND SCIENCE ADVISORY
COMMISSION.

0666 DUPRE L., DUPRE C.
"TILL DEATH DO US PART?"
AMERICA, 118 (1968), 224-228.
DISCUSS CATHOLIC LEGAL GROUNDS FOR THE TERMINATION OF
MARRIAGE. RELATE BIBLE'S AND CHURCH'S POSITIONS ON ADULTERY
AND DIVORCE. BELIEVE THAT MARRIAGE LAWS INVOLVE BOTH
COMMUNITY AND INDIVIDUAL INTERESTS AND RIGIDITY OF MAR-
RIAGE LAWS OFTEN RESULTS IN MARITAL INSTABILITY. DEAL
LARGELY WITH CONFLICT BETWEEN CANON AND CIVIL LAWS OVER
INDISSOLUBILITY OF MARRIAGE.

0667 DUROSELLE J.B.
HISTOIRE DIPLOMATIQUE DE 1919 A NOS JOURS (3RD ED.)
PARIS: LIBRARIE DALLOZ, 1962, 780 PP.
COMPACT AND COMPREHENSIVE DIPLOMATIC HISTORY FROM 1919-
1957. INTERESTING FOR FRENCH VIEWPOINT ON HISTORICAL ISSUES.
PARTIALLY ANNOTATED BIBLIOGRAPHY OF ABOUT 240 ITEMS ARRANGED
BY SUBJECT.

0668 DWYER R.J.
"THE ADMINISTRATIVE ROLE IN DESEGREGATION."
SOCIOLOGY AND SOCIAL RESEARCH, 43 (JAN. 59), 183-188.
DESCRIBES PATTERNS OF ADMINISTRATIVE POLICY AND ROLE OF
ADMINISTRATOR IN PUBLIC SCHOOL DESEGREGATION IN MISSOURI
FROM 1955-56. DIRECTION OF DESEGREGATION WAS DETERMINED BY
EXTENT AND NATURE OF OPPOSITION AND TENDED TOWARD SEGMENTAL,
GRADUAL DESEGREGATION. DISCUSSES STATUS OF NEGRO STUDENTS
AND ATTITUDES OF ADMINISTRATORS TO INTEGRATION. MAINTAINS
THAT STRONG LEADERSHIP IS NECESSARY FOR SUCCESS.

0669 DYCK H.L.
WEIMAR GERMANY AND SOVIET RUSSIA 1926-1933.
NEW YORK: COLUMBIA U PRESS, 1966, 279 PP., LC#66-14594.
STUDIES INSTABILITY OF DIPLOMATIC RELATIONS BETWEEN
GERMANY AND SOVIET RUSSIA FROM 1926-1933. DISCUSSES
NEUTRALITY OF TREATY OF BERLIN, INFLUENCE OF ANGLO-SOVIET
BREAK ON GERMAN-SOVIET RELATIONS, AND METHODS OF POLICY
FORMATION BY BOTH PARTIES.

0670 EAGLETON C.
INTERNATIONAL GOVERNMENT.
NEW YORK: RONALD, 1932, 672 PP.
OUTLINES THE PRINCIPLES OF INTERNATIONAL LAW AND THE
INSTITUTIONS, ORGANIZATIONS AND PROBLEMS OF INTERNATIONAL
SOCIETY. INTRODUCTORY SURVEY OF INTERNATIONAL RELATIONSHIPS
STRESSING GOVERNMENTAL ASPECT.

0671 EASTON D.
"POLITICAL ANTHROPOLOGY" IN BIENNIAL REVIEW OF ANTHROPOLOGY"
STANFORD: STANFORD U PRESS, 1959.
COVERS RECENT LITERATURE DEALING WITH POLITICAL ANTHRO-
POLOGY. DISCUSSES CENTRAL THEMES LIKE NATURE AND FUNCTION OF
LAW, IMPACT OF CIVILIZED UPON PRIMITIVE SOCIETIES, TRANS-
FORMATIONS OF POLITICAL ELITES, APPLICATION OF DATA TO
SOLUTION OF CURRENT POLITICAL ISSUES, AND INTRODUCTION OF
ANTHROPOLOGICAL CONCEPTS AND METHODS INTO STUDY OF MODERN
HIGHLY COMPLEX SOCIETIES.

0672 ECOLE NATIONALE D'ADMIN
BIBLIOGRAPHIE SELECTIVE D'OUVRAGES DE LANGUE FRANCAISE TRAI-
TANT DES PROBLEMES GOUVERNEMENTAUX ET ADMINISTRATIFS.
PARIS: ECOLE NATIONALE D'ADMIN, 1963.
FRENCH-LANGUAGE BIBLIOGRAPHY OF 540 ITEMS DESIGNED FOR
INSTITUTIONS IN FRENCH-SPEAKING AFRICA RESPONSIBLE FOR THE
TRAINING OF ADMINISTRATORS. PREPARED UNDER AUSPICES OF
DEVELOPMENT RESEARCH CENTER OF BOSTON UNIVERSITY.
INCLUDES INDEX AND ADDRESSES OF PUBLISHING HOUSES CITED.
BIBLIOGRAPHY GEARED TO TEACHING. INCLUDES TEXTBOOKS AND
WORKS PUBLISHED AFTER WWII.

0673 ECONOMIDES C.P.
LE POUVOIR DE DECISION DES ORGANISATIONS INTERNATIONALES
EUROPEENNES.
LEYDEN: AW SIJTHOFF, 1964, 167 PP., LC#64-7605.
COMPARATIVE STUDY OF POWER OF DECISION. CONSIDERS
EUROPEAN INTERNATIONAL AND INTERGOVERNMENTAL ORGANIZA-
TIONS SUCH AS NATO, COUNCIL OF EUROPE, AND OEEC; AND
SUPRANATIONAL ORGANIZATIONS SUCH AS EURATOM AND EEC. STUDIES
POWER OF DECISION IN REFERENCE TO MEMBER STATES AND TO
INTERNAL ORDER OF ORGANIZATIONS THEMSELVES.

0674 EDDY J.P.
JUSTICE OF THE PEACE.
LONDON: CASSELL & CO LTD, 1963, 195 PP.

TRACES DEVELOPMENT OF OFFICE OF JUSTICE OF PEACE 1361-
1962 WITH CONSTITUTIONAL IMPLICATIONS AND DIRECT RELATION TO
EVOLVING COURT SYSTEM BASED ON COMMON LAW. CONSIDERS PRESENT
ROLE OF JP IN ENGLISH JURISPRUDENCE AND STUDIES SOME BASIC
PROBLEMS FACED.

0675 EDGEWORTH A.B. JR.
"CIVIL RIGHTS PLUS THREE YEARS: BANKS AND THE ANTI-DISCRIMI-
NATION LAW"
BANKER'S MAGAZINE, 150 (SUMMER 67), 23-30.
EXAMINES EFFECTS OF 1964 CIVIL RIGHTS ACT ON EMPLOYMENT
PRACTICES OF FINANCIAL INSTITUTIONS. INCLUDES REVIEW OF PRO-
VISIONS OF ACT AND ENFORCEMENT PROCEDURES. DISCUSSES FUNC-
TION OF FEDERAL EQUAL EMPLOYMENT OPPORTUNITY COMMISSION.
MAINTAINS THAT EQUAL EMPLOYMENT POLICIES IN FINANCIAL INSTI-
TUTIONS WILL FURTHER EFFICIENCY AND HELP REDUCE SOCIAL
TENSIONS WHICH IS ADVANTAGEOUS TO SUCH INSTITUTIONS.

0676 EDWARDS C.D.
TRADE REGULATIONS OVERSEAS.
NEW YORK: OCEANA PUBLISHING, 1966, 752 PP., LC#64-23357.
DISCUSSES POLICIES OF COMMON MARKET COUNTRIES, IRELAND,
SOUTH AFRICA, NEW ZEALAND, AND JAPAN TOWARD MONOPOLIES, RE-
STRICTIVE AGREEMENTS, AND RESTRICTIVE BUSINESS PRACTICES.

0677 EHLE J.
THE FREE MEN.
NEW YORK: HARPER & ROW, 1965, 340 PP., LC#64-07829.
DESCRIBES INTEGRATION IN ONE TOWN FROM POINT OF VIEW
OF BOTH PROPONENT AND OPPONENT. DEVOTES MAJOR PORTION OF
WORK TO COURT TREATMENTS, POLICE BRUTALITY, AND LACK OF
JUSTICE FOR NEGROES.

0678 EHRLICH E.
FUNDAMENTAL PRINCIPLES OF THE SOCIOLOGY OF LAW (TRANS. BY
WALTER L. MOLL)
CAMBRIDGE: HARVARD U PR, 1936, 541 PP.
BASIC PRINCIPLES OF LAW ARE EXAMINED IN THE CONTEXT OF
SOCIAL ORDER. VARIETY OF CONCEPTS ARE RELATED TO GENERAL
THESIS THAT MAIN INSTITUTIONS ARE IDENTICAL IN CIVILIZED
SOCIETIES. EMPHASIS IS ON LEGAL HISTORY AND JURISTIC SCIENCE
AND ON LAW AS A RULE OF CONDUCT RATHER THAN AS APPLIED
BY THE COURTS.

0679 ELDRIDGE W.B.
NARCOTICS AND THE LAW: A CRITIQUE OF THE AMERICAN EXPERIMENT
IN NARCOTIC DRUG CONTROL.
NEW YORK: NEW YORK U PR, 1967, 246 PP., LC#67-25528.
STUDY IS LIMITED TO USE OF OPIATES AND THEIR SYNTHETICS.
INCLUDES TEXT OF THE UNIFORM NARCOTIC DRUG ACT AND SUMMARY
OF STATE PENALTIES FOR NARCOTIC VIOLATIONS. DEVELOPMENT OF
PROBLEM AND SOCIAL ATTITUDES TOWARD IT ARE DISCUSSED.
EVALUATES RESEARCH DONE TO DATE, AND APPROACHES TO CONTROL.
FINAL CHAPTER STRESSES URGENCY FOR UNDERSTANDING AND ACTION,
ENUMERATING AREAS WHERE MORE INFORMATION IS NEEDED.

0680 ELIAS T.O.
GROUNDWORK OF NIGERIAN LAW.
LONDON: ROUTLEDGE & KEGAN PAUL, 1954, 374 PP.
SURVEYS NIGERIAN LEGAL SYSTEM, COVERING CHRONOLOGICAL
DEVELOPMENT OF COURTS AND BASIC PRINCIPLES OF VARIOUS FIELDS
OF LAW. EXPLAINS SOURCES OF NIGERIAN LAW AND POSITION OF
LEGAL PROFESSION TODAY IN NIGERIAN SOCIETY.

0681 ELIAS T.O.
GOVERNMENT AND POLITICS IN AFRICA.
NEW YORK: ASIA PUBL HOUSE, 1963, 288 PP.
WRITTEN VERSION OF SERIES OF LECTURES DELIVERED IN INDIA
ON CONTEMPORARY PROBLEMS OF GOVERNMENT AND POLITICS IN AFRI-
CA. MATERIAL TOPICALLY AND CHRONOLOGICALLY ARRANGED. COVERS
PERIOD FROM ANCIENT AFRICAN CIVILIZATIONS THROUGH MOVE-
MENTS FOR REFORM IN CONTEMPORARY AFRICA. ORGANIZES
MATERIAL GEOGRAPHICALLY WITHIN EACH CHAPTER. BRIEF LISTS OF
BRITISH AND INDIAN SOURCES AT END OF EACH TOPIC.

0682 ELIAS T.O.
THE NIGERIAN LEGAL SYSTEM.
NEW YORK: HUMANITIES PRESS, 1963, 386 PP.
HISTORICAL STUDY OF IMPACT OF BRITISH COMMON LAW ON
NIGERIAN LEGAL SYSTEM. STUDIES LEGAL PROFESSION, AND COURT
SYSTEMS AND PROCEDURES OF TODAY.

0683 ELLERT R.B.
NATO 'FAIR TRIAL' SAFEGUARDS: PRECURSOR TO AN INTERNATIONAL
BILL OF PROCEDURAL RIGHTS.
THE HAGUE: MARTINUS NIJHOFF, 1963, 89 PP.
STUDY OF NATO AGREEMENT REGARDING CRIMINAL JURISDICTION
OVER MEMBERS OF NATO MILITARY FORCES STATIONED IN MEMBER
COUNTRIES. GRANTS JURISDICTION TO NATION IN WHICH LOCATED AT
TIME OF ALLEGED CRIME AND LEGAL GUARANTEES OF FAIR TRIAL.

0684 ELLIOTT S.D.
IMPROVING OUR COURTS.
NEW YORK: OCEANA PUBLISHING, 1959, 190 PP., LC#59-14271.
DISCUSSIONS OF JUDICIAL ADMINISTRATION AND OPERATION OF
US COURT SYSTEMS WHICH STRESS NEED FOR COORDINATION AND

UNIFICATION OF LEGAL SYSTEM. DISCUSSES GENERAL IMPROVEMENTS
MADE IN JUDICIAL ADMINISTRATION IN US 1906-56 AND PROVIDES
DETAILED DISCUSSIONS OF IMPROVEMENTS MADE 1952-58.

0685 ELLMAKER E.G.
"REVELATION OF RIGHTS."
PITTSBURGH: PHILLIP SWARTZWELDER, 1847, 151 PP.
ENDEAVORS TO REMOVE GREAT IMPEDIMENTS THAT HAVE LONG
BLOCKED TRUTH IN SCIENCE OF GOVERNMENT. GOVERNMENTS
IMMORAL IN NATURE AND UNCHRISTIAN IN ADMINISTRATION, WHICH
CONTRADICT CHARACTER OF GOD, OUGHT NOT BE BINDING UPON MAN.
DISCUSSES MAN'S NATURAL RIGHTS, GOVERNMENT IN GENERAL,
POLITICAL AND CIVIL LIBERTY, GOVERNMENT ADMINISTRATION,
CRIMINAL LAW, SLAVERY, AND ALTERATION OF US GOVERNMENT.

0686 EMBREE J.F., DOTSON L.O.
BIBLIOGRAPHY OF THE PEOPLES AND CULTURES OF MAINLAND SOUTH-
EAST ASIA.
NEW HAVEN: YALE U PR, 1950, 833 PP.
THOROUGH AND EXTENSIVE BIBLIOGRAPHY OF REFERENCES DEALING
WITH MAINLAND SOUTHEAST ASIA AND WRITTEN IN EUROPEAN
LANGUAGES. INCLUDES MAPS, LISTS OF BIBLIOGRAPHIES, AND
PERIODICALS. DIVIDED INTO SECTIONS BY COUNTRY, THEN SUB-
DIVIDED BY TOPICS SUCH AS ANTHROPOLOGY, ARCHEOLOGY,
ETHNOLOGY, HISTORY, LANGUAGE, FOLKLORE, ETC.

0687 EMDEN C.S.
THE PEOPLE AND THE CONSTITUTION (2ND ED.)
LONDON: OXFORD U PR, 1956, 339 PP.
DEVELOPMENT OF PEOPLE'S PART IN ENGLISH GOVERNMENT. CON-
STITUTIONAL HISTORY OF THE PEOPLE.

0688 ENDACOTT G.B.
GOVERNMENT AND PEOPLE IN HONG KONG 1841-1962: A CONSTITU-
TIONAL HISTORY.
HONG KONG: HONG KONG UNIV PRESS, 1964, 263 PP.
HISTORY OF HONG KONG'S CONSTITUTIONAL GOVERNMENT. POINTS
OUT CITY'S DISTINCTIVENESS AMONG BRITISH COLONIES.
SHOWS APPLICATION OF BRITISH IDEAS OF GOVERNMENT TO AN OVER-
WHELMING CHINESE COMMUNITY, AND ATTEMPT TO ADAPT COLONIAL
INSTITUTIONS SET UP IN HONG KONG TO ADMINISTRATIVE
NEEDS OF BRITISH COMMUNITIES LIVING IN THE TREATY PORTS.

0689 ENGEL J.
THE SECURITY OF THE FREE WORLD.
NEW YORK: WILSON, 1960, 211 PP., $3.00.
SERIES OF READINGS ON INTERNATIONAL RESPONSES TO THE COM-
MUNIST CHALLENGE. INCLUDES DISCUSSION OF NATURE OF SOVIET
AIMS, POSSIBILITIES AND PROBLEMS OF THE UN, NATO'S RECORD
AND ITS FUTURE, RELATIONS AMONG WESTERN NATIONS, ARMS CON-
TROL DISPUTES AND APPROACHES TO UNDERDEVELOPED WORLD.

0690 ENGEL S. ED.
LAW, STATE, AND INTERNATIONAL LEGAL ORDER.
KNOXVILLE: U OF TENN PR, 1964, 365 PP., LC#64-16881.
COLLECTION OF ESSAYS IN HONOR OF HANS KELSEN. EXAMINES
KELSEN'S PURE THEORY OF LAW AND HIS INFLUENCE ON LEGAL
THOUGHT. INCLUDES SOME ESSAYS ON LAW IN ATOMIC AGE AND
INTERNATIONAL LAW.

0691 ENKE S., SALERA V.
INTERNATIONAL ECONOMICS.
ENGLEWOOD CLIFFS: PRENTICE HALL, 1947, 731 PP.
DISCUSSES PRINCIPLES OF INTERNATIONAL TRADE AND FINANCE.
EXAMINES CLASSICAL THEORIES, TRADE CONTROL, CARTELS, COMMER-
CIAL TREATIES, TRADE POLICIES OF USSR, US, AND UK, MONETARY
AND FINANCIAL POLICIES, ETC.

0692 ENSOR R.C.K.
COURTS AND JUDGES IN FRANCE, GERMANY, AND ENGLAND.
LONDON: OXFORD U PR, 1933, 144 PP.
A SHORT STUDY OF LEGAL ADMINISTRATION IN FRANCE AND
GERMANY AND A COMPARATIVE ANALYSIS OF BRITISH PRACTICE.
OUTLINES THE COMPOSITION OF THE TWO CONTINENTAL COURT
SYSTEMS. COMPARES METHODS OF FILLING JUDICIAL POSTS, COURT
PROCEDURES IN CRIMINAL AND CIVIL CASES, METHODS OF APPEAL,
AND ULTIMATE JUDICIAL AUTHORITY IN THE THREE COUNTRIES.

0693 EPSTEIN F.T.
EAST GERMANY: A SELECTED BIBLIOGRAPHY (PAMPHLET)
WASHINGTON: LIBRARY OF CONGRESS, 1959, 55 PP., LC#59-60084.
SOME 350 ANNOTATED US GOVERNMENT DOCUMENTS, BIBLIOGRA-
PHIES, STATISTICAL HANDBOOKS, WEST GERMAN DOCUMENTS, PER-
IODICALS, LEGISLATION, MONOGRAPHS, AND BOOKS ON EAST GERMANY
PUBLISHED 1947-58. ARRANGED TOPICALLY AND BY TYPE
OF SOURCE, WITH MOST IN GERMAN. SUBJECT INDEX.

0694 EPSTEIN F.T. ED., WHITTAKER C.H. ED.
THE AMERICAN BIBLIOGRAPHY OF RUSSIAN AND EAST EUROPEAN
STUDIES FOR 1964.
BLOOMINGTON: INDIANA U PR, 1966, 119 PP., LC#58-63499.
BIBLIOGRAPHICAL LISTING OF BOOKS AND ARTICLES PUBLISHED
IN ENGLISH IN THE US IN 1964. ALSO INCLUDES BOOKS PUBLISHED
IN ENGLISH THROUGHOUT THE WORLD WITH THE EXCEPTION OF RUSSIA
AND EAST EUROPE. TRANSLATIONS NOT INCLUDED. ITEMS GROUPED
BY SUBJECT AND COUNTRY. CONTAINS AUTHOR INDEX. 2,260 EN-

TRIES.

0695 ERDMANN H.H. ED.
"ADMINISTRATIVE LAW AND FARM ECONOMICS."
JOURNAL OF FARM ECONOMICS, 44 (DEC. 62), 1627-1658.
ANTHOLOGY OF REPORTS AND DISCUSSIONS ON ADMINISTRATIVE
PROCESSES ON NATIONAL AND LOCAL LEVEL AND ROLE OF JUDICIAL
REVIEW IN ADMINISTRATIVE PROCESS. ALL REPORTS ARE RELATED TO
IMPACT ON AGRICULTURAL INDUSTRY.

0696 ERNST M.L.
"THE FIRST FREEDOM."
NEW YORK: MACMILLAN, 1946.
INCLUDES PARTIAL BIBLIOGRAPHY OF US GOVERNMENT PUBLICA-
TIONS, BOOKS, AND PERIODICALS. REFERENCE TO LEGAL MATERIAL,
SPEECHES, AND ARTICLES ALSO.

0697 ESMEIN A.
ELEMENTS DE DROIT CONSTITUTIONNEL.
PARIS: LIB SOC DU RECEUIL SIREY, 1896, 841 PP.
ELEMENTS OF CONSTITUTIONAL LAW. PART I EXAMINES MODERN
CONCEPT OF LIBERTY, AS IT DEVELOPED UNDER THE INSTITUTIONS
ESTABLISHED BY ENGLISH LAW AND THE PRINCIPLES PROCLAIMED BY
THE FRENCH REVOLUTION. PART II DEALS WITH CONSTITUTIONAL LAW
OF THE FRENCH REPUBLIC AND DISCUSSES THE PRECEDENTS OF THE
CONSTITUTION OF 1875, EXECUTIVE POWER, LEGISLATIVE POWER,
THE HIGH COURT, AND CONSTITUTIONAL REVISION.

0698 ESTEP R.
AN AIR POWER BIBLIOGRAPHY.
MONTGOMERY: AIR U, 1956, 199 PP.
COVERS PUBLICATIONS 1950-56 ON AIR POWER, EQUIPMENT,
PERFORMANCE, LAW, PUBLIC RELATIONS, BUDGETING AND
AREAS RELATED TO USAF; 3,250 ENTRIES.

0699 ESTEY M.
THE UNIONS: STRUCTURE, DEVELOPMENT, AND MANAGEMENT.
NEW YORK: HARCOURT BRACE, 1967, 125 PP., LC#67-14629.
INTRODUCTORY ANALYSIS OF WHAT UNIONS ARE, WHY THEY BEHAVE
AS THEY DO, AND RULES THAT GOVERN THEM. COVERS PATTERNS OF
UNION GROWTH IN RESPONSE TO CHANGING NEEDS, BUSINESS VS.
DEMOCRATIC FUNCTIONS OF UNIONS, AND DECISION-MAKING PROCESS.
EMPHASIZES NATURE OF UNIONS AS ORGANIZATIONS, AND
DIFFERENCES BETWEEN UNIONS AND BUSINESSES THEY DEAL WITH.

0700 ETTINGHAUSEN R. ED.
SELECTED AND ANNOTATED BIBLIOGRAPHY OF BOOKS AND PERIODICALS
IN WESTERN LANGUAGES DEALING WITH NEAR AND MIDDLE EAST.
WASHINGTON: MIDDLE EAST INST, 1952, 111 PP.
LISTS, ANNOTATES, AND INDEXES BY AUTHOR 1,719 ITEMS
COVERING THE NEAR AND MIDDLE EAST FROM ANCIENT TO PRESENT
TIMES. INCLUDES MAPS, CHARTS, GUIDE BOOKS, AS WELL AS
BIBLIOGRAPHIES, PERIODICALS, ETC. DEALING WITH ART, ARCHI-
TECTURE, ARCHEOLOGY, CULTURE, HISTORY, RELIGION, LITERATURE,
AND LAW IN EACH COUNTRY AND AREA. STRESSES MEDIEVAL PERIOD
AND AFTER.

0701 EULAU H., SPRAGUE J.D.
LAWYERS IN POLITICS: A STUDY IN PROFESSIONAL CONVERGENCE.
INDIANAPOLIS: BOBBS-MERRILL, 1964, 164 PP., LC#64-16712.
STUDY OF INFLUENCE OF LEGAL PROFESSION ON FUNCTIONING OF
LEGISLATURE. COMPARES LAWYER AND NON-LAWYER LEGISLATORS AND
CONCLUDES THAT LAWYER-POLITICIAN DOES NOT DIFFER APPRECIABLY
FROM OTHER POLITICIANS. EXPLAINS LACK OF DIFFERENCE IN TERMS
OF HIGH DEGREE OF CONVERGENCE BETWEEN LAW AND POLITICS.

0702 EUSDEN J.D.
PURITANS, LAWYERS, AND POLITICS IN EARLY SEVENTEENTH-CENTURY
ENGLAND.
NEW HAVEN: YALE U PR, 1958, 238 PP., LC#58-5457.
DISCUSSES PURITANISM AND COMMON LAW AND FINDS THEM
ADVOCATING PARALLEL IDEOLOGIES; BOTH INSISTED ON REASON
FOR UNDERSTANDING AND INSTITUTIONAL INDEPENDENCE, BOTH WERE
NARROW, INTOLERANT, AND EXAGGERATED; BOTH BELIEVED IN LAW
ALTHOUGH ONE WAS DIVINE AND OTHER FUNDAMENTAL. INCLUDES
HISTORICAL STUDY OF CONFLICTS AND RELATIONS OF TWO GROUPS.

0703 EVAN W.M. ED.
LAW AND SOCIOLOGY: EXPLORATORY ESSAYS.
NEW YORK: FREE PRESS OF GLENCOE, 1962, 235 PP., LC#62-11848.
VOLUME OF ESSAYS RESULTING FROM AN ORGANIZED SEMINAR OF
THE RUTGERS UNIVERSITY LAW SCHOOL IN 1956 SEEKING WAYS OF
BRIDGING THE CHASM BETWEEN LAW AND SOCIAL SCIENCE,
PARTICULARLY SOCIOLOGY. EIGHT ESSAYS IN ALL, PRESENTED
ACCORDING TO INDIVIDUAL TOPIC AREA. INCLUDES SUBJECT
INDEX.

0704 EVANS C. ED.
AMERICAN BIBLIOGRAPHY... (12 VOLUMES)
NEW YORK: PETERSMITH, 1941.
A CHRONOLOGICAL DICTIONARY OF ALL BOOKS, PAMPHLETS,
AND PERIODICAL PUBLICATIONS PRINTED IN THE UNITED STATES OF
AMERICA FROM GENESIS OF PRINTING IN 1639 DOWN TO AND
INCLUDING THE YEAR 1820.

0705 EVANS I.L.

NATIVE POLICY IN SOUTHERN AFRICA.
CAMBRIDGE: CAMBRIDGE UNIV PRESS, 1934, 177 PP.
ANALYSIS OF STATUS OF NATIVE AFRICAN POPULATION IN AREAS OF SOUTHERN AFRICA ADMINISTERED BY BRITISH IN UNION OF SOUTH AFRICA, SOUTHERN RHODESIA, SOUTH WEST AFRICA, AND HIGH COMMISSION TERRITORIES. EXPLAINS LEGAL POSITION OF NATIVE AFRICANS AND ACTUAL TREATMENT UNDER EUROPEAN RULE.

0706 EWALD R.F.
"ONE OF MANY POSSIBLE GAMES."
BACKGROUND, 9 (FEB. 66), 275-282.
AUTHOR EXPLAINS HOW CLARK AND SOHN'S MODEL OF THE DIS-ARMED FUTURE WORLD LENDS ITSELF THROUGH GAMING AS A SOUND TEACHING DEVICE IN INTERNATIONAL LAW AND ORGANIZATION.

0707 EYBERS G.W. ED.
SELECT CONSTITUTIONAL DOCUMENTS ILLUSTRATING SOUTH AFRICAN HISTORY 1795-1910.
NEW YORK: EP DUTTON, 1918, 582 PP., LC#18-17656.
COLLECTION OF DOCUMENTS OF THE FOUR TERRITORIES THAT WERE AMALGAMATED IN 1909 INTO THE UNION OF SOUTH AFRICA. ARRANGED BY TERRITORY, AND BY GENERAL AREA OF REFERENCE (CENTRAL GOVERNMENT, LOCAL GOVERNMENT, JUSTICE) FOR CAPE OF GOOD HOPE AND NATAL, CHRONOLOGICALLY FOR ORANGE FREE STATE AND SOUTH AFRICAN REPUBLIC. EXTENSIVE INTRODUCTION ON CONSTITUTIONAL HISTORY OF SOUTH AFRICA.

0708 EYRAUD M.
"LA FRANCE FACE A UN EVENTUEL TRAITE DE NON DISSEMINATION DES ARMES NUCLEAIRES."
POLITIQUE ETRANGERE, 32 (1967), 441-452, 4-5.
ANALYZES ECONOMIC CONSEQUENCES FOR FRANCE OF REJECTION OF NUCLEAR DISARMAMENT TREATY, ESPECIALLY IF A LARGE NUMBER OF NATIONS SIGN IT. ANALYZES AMERICAN INDUSTRIAL PRODUCTION DEPENDENT UPON NUCLEAR ENERGY, AND NOTES THAT THE US HAS THE GREATEST STOCKPILE OF NUCLEAR MATERIAL. BELIEVES THAT IF AFRICAN COUNTRIES GRANTING FRANCE MINING CONCESSIONS SIGN TREATY, FRENCH INDUSTRY WILL BE SERIOUSLY ENDANGERED.

0709 FABREGA J.
"ANTECEDENTES EXTRANJEROS EN LA CONSTITUCION PANAMENA."
CENTRO, 3 (FEB. 67), 25-29.
EXAMINES PANAMANIAN CONSTITUTION OF 1946 AND FOREIGN INFLUENCES UPON ITS FINAL FORM. STUDIES COLOMBIAN CONSTITUTION OF 1886, SOCIAL ASPECTS OF MEXICAN CONSTITUTION OF 1917, AND CONSTITUTIONS OF CUBA AND URUGUAY IN 1940.

0710 FACTS ON FILE, INC.
CIVIL RIGHTS 1960-63: THE NEGRO CAMPAIGN TO WIN EQUAL RIGHTS AND OPPORTUNITIES IN THE UNITED STATES.
NEW YORK: FACTS ON FILE, INC, 1964, 152 PP., LC#64-16075.
JOURNALISTIC RECAPITULATION OF EVENTS IN THE FIELD OF CIVIL RIGHTS DURING PERIOD INDICATED, COMPILED AS AN "INTERIM HISTORY" TO BRIDGE GAP BETWEEN DAY-TO-DAY NEWS COVERAGE AND LATER HISTORICAL TREATMENTS. COVERS BOTH MAJOR EVENTS, SUCH AS FREEDOM RIDES, SIT-INS, AND THE MEREDITH-UNIVERSITY OF MISSISSIPPI CRISIS, AND LARGER DEVELOPMENTS LIKE LEGISLATION, EMPLOYMENT, AND SCHOOL DESEGREGATION.

0711 FAGUET E.
LE LIBERALISME.
PARIS: SOCIETE FRANCAISE IMPRIM, 1903, 337 PP.
SYSTEMATICALLY TREATS STATE'S RIGHTS AND INDIVIDUAL LIBERTIES. INCLUDES EQUALITY AND FREEDOM OF THOUGHT AND ASSOCIATION. CONSIDERS ARISTOCRACY AND NATIONAL SOVEREIGNTY AS AGAINST LIBERTY.

0712 FAIRCHILD H.P.
THE ANATOMY OF FREEDOM.
NEW YORK: PHILOSOPHICAL LIB, 1957, 103 PP., LC#57-2561.
SHORT ANALYSIS OF BASIC CIVIL LIBERTIES IN US, HOW THEY WORK, AND HOW THEY ARE VIOLATED BY GOVERNMENT. EMPHASIS ON "NATIONAL SECURITY DRIVE" OF 1950'S. ALSO DISCUSSES EXTENSION OF DEMOCRACY TO ECONOMICS AND RELATION TO SOCIALISM.

0713 FAIRLIE J.A., KNEIER C.M.
COUNTY GOVERNMENT AND ADMINISTRATION.
NEW YORK: CENTURY CO, 1930, 585 PP., LC#30-1116.
EXPANSION OF AN EARLIER WORK ON SAME TOPIC. REVIEWS IN-CREASING IMPORTANCE OF COUNTY GOVERNMENT, BOTH IN SCOPE OF OLDER FUNCTIONS AND IN EXPANSION OF ACTIVITIES IN NEW DIREC-TIONS. REVIEWS RELFECTION OF THIS DEVELOPMENT IN GREATER VOLUME OF STATUTORY LEGISLATON AND INCREASING NUMBER OF JU-DICIAL OPINIONS BROUGHT BEFORE COURTS. ATTENTION GIVEN TO ADMINISTRATION AND OPERATION OF GOVERNMENTAL ACTIVITIES.

0714 FALK R.A.
"THE REALITY OF INTERNATIONAL LAW."
WORLD POLIT., 14 (JAN. 62), 353-63.
REVIEWS TWO BOOKS CONCERNED WITH THE POLITICAL SIGNIFI-CANCE OF INTERNATIONAL LAW AND THE RELATIONSHIPS BETWEEN LAW AND THE USE OF VIOLENCE. BOTH WORKS CONSIDER RELATIONS OF LEGAL ORDER AND NUCLEAR WAR AND THE EFFECT OF NATIONAL INTEREST UPON INTERNATIONAL LEGAL ORDER.

0715 FALK R.A.
LAW, MORALITY, AND WAR IN THE CONTEMPORARY WORLD.
NEW YORK: PRAEGER, 1963, 120 PP.
ASSERTS THAT INTERNATIONAL LAW PLACED ON THE BASIS OF A UTILITARIAN ETHICS WILL BEST SERVE THE SURVIVAL OF MANKIND IN THE NUCLEAR AGE. PROPOSES TO INTERRELATE NATIONAL INTEREST TO INTERNATIONAL COOPERATION. THE UPHOLDING OF STABILITY SHOULD BE A PRIMARY OBJECTIVE. THE MORAL USE OF FORCES PRESUPPOSES BENEFICIAL EFFECTS FOR ALL HUMANITY.

0716 FALK R.A.
THE ROLE OF DOMESTIC COURTS IN THE INTERNATIONAL LEGAL ORDER.
SYRACUSE: U. PR, 1964, 184 PP., $6.50.
CENTRAL THESIS IS THAT 'RULES OF DEFERENCE APPLIED BY DOMESTIC COURTS ADVANCE THE DEVELOPMENT OF INTERNATIONAL LAW FASTER THAN DOES AN INDISCRIMINATE INSISTANCE UPON APPLYING CHALLENGED SUBSTANTIVE NORMS IN ORDER TO DETERMINE THE VALIDITY OF THE OFFICIAL ACTS OF FOREIGN STATES.'

0717 FALK R.A.
"INTERNATIONAL LEGAL ORDER."
AMER. J. INT. LAW, 59 (JAN. 65), 66-71.
CONSTRUCTIVE CRITICISM OF THE 'SPECIFIC APPROACH' TO INTERNATIONAL LAW. DAMAGE INFLICTED UPON INTERNATIONAL LEGAL ORDER BY ALLOWING NEWLY INDEPENDENT STATES OF ASIA AND AFRICA TO PARTICIPATE AS FULL-FLEDGED MEMBERS. ASSERTS THAT CERTAIN DISTINGUISHED AMERICAN JURISTS ARE 'LENDING GOOD NAMES TO AN IMAGE OF WORLD COMMUNITY THAT APPEARS TO REFLECT SOCIALIST RATHER THAN WESTERN VALUES.

0718 FALK R.A.
THE AFTERMATH OF SABBATINO: BACKGROUND PAPERS AND PROCEEDINGS OF SEVENTH HAMMARSKJOLD FORUM.
NEW YORK: OCEANA PUBLISHING, 1965, 228 PP., LC#65-19486.
DISCUSSES PROBLEMS UNDERLYING AN ASSESSMENT OF THE APPROPRIATE ROLE FOR DOMESTIC COURTS IN CASES SIMILAR TO SABBATINO CASE. CASE WAS A DISAGREEMENT ABOUT DEGREE TO WHICH US COURTS CAN AND SHOULD EXAMINE MERITS OF AN ALLEGATION THAT FOREIGN EXPROPRIATION OF ALIEN PROPERTY VIOLATES RULES OF CUSTOMARY INTERNATIONAL LAW. AUTHOR AGREES WITH JUSTICE HARLAN'S MAJORITY OPINION.

0719 FALK R.A. ED., MENDLOVITZ P. ED.
THE STRATEGY OF WORLD ORDER* 4 VOLUMES.
NEW YORK: WORLD LAW FUND, 1966, 2296 PP., LC#66-14524.
ORDERED ANTHOLOGIES AIMED AT CREATING AN ACADEMIC DISCI-PLINE OF WORLD ORDER. READINGS ORGANIZED ABOUT PROBLEMS OF WAR PREVENTION AND TRANSFORMATION OF THE INTERNATIONAL SYS-TEM INTO ONE WHICH BETTER SERVES HUMAN VALUES. EDITORS ANA-LYZE AND QUESTION SELECTIONS IN TERMS OF CLARK AND SOHN'S MODEL. VOLUMES ENTITLED: TOWARD A THEORY OF WAR PREVENTION, INTERNATIONAL LAW, THE UN, DISARMAMENT AND ECON. DEV'MENT.

0720 FALL B.B.
"THE VIET-MINH REGIME."
ITHACA: CORNELL U, DEPT ASIAN ST, 1956.
STUDY OF VIET-MINH REGIME IN ORGANIZATIONAL AND ADMIN-ISTRATIVE ASPECTS. INSTITUTIONAL ANALYSIS SUPPORTED BY CULTURAL RESEARCH. AUTHOR DISCUSSES PERSONALITY AND CHARAC-TER OF LEADERS, PARTICULARLY HO CHI MINH, IDEOLOGICAL FOUN-DATIONS OF RULING PARTY, ECONOMIC DEVELOPMENT, ORGANIZATION OF ARMY. SELECTED BIBLIOGRAPHY CONFINED TO WORKS SPECIALIZ-ING ON VIETMINH REGIME IN FRENCH, ENGLISH, AND RUSSIAN.

0721 FARRAND M.
THE FRAMING OF THE CONSTITUTION OF THE UNITED STATES (1913)
NEW HAVEN: YALE U PR, 1922, 281 PP.
TRACES HISTORY OF THE CONSTITUTIONAL CONVENTION THROUGH LETTERS, DIARIES, AND PUBLIC ACCOUNTS. AUTHOR FINDS THAT THE CONVENTION WAS CALLED TO REMEDY CERTAIN DEFICIENCIES OF THE CONFEDERATION IN AS PRACTICAL A MANNER AS POSSIBLE. THROUGH COMPROMISE THE FRAMERS WERE ABLE TO WRITE A CONSTITUTION TO WHICH ALL COULD SUBSCRIBE IN PART. AUTHOR CALLS IT THE PRODUCT OF PLAIN MEN WORKING HONESTLY.

0722 FATOUROS A.A.
GOVERNMENT GUARANTEES TO FOREIGN INVESTORS.
NEW YORK: COLUMBIA U PRESS, 1962, 411 PP., LC#62-12873.
ANALYZES VARIOUS FORMS AND MODALITIES BY WHICH STATES EN-TER INTO ARRANGEMENTS WITH FOREIGN INVESTORS. ALSO STUDIES ASPECTS SUCH AS EXCHANGE RESTRICTIONS, EMPLOYMENT OF FOREIGN PERSONNEL, LEGAL EFFECTS OF TREATY PROMISES, AND STATE CONTRACTS.

0723 FAWCETT J.E.S.
THE BRITISH COMMONWEALTH IN INTERNATIONAL LAW.
LONDON: OXFORD U PR, 1963, 243 PP.
A STUDY OF THE MAKE-UP, LEGAL STATUS, TYPES OF INTERNA-TIONAL LAW ADHERED TO, PATTERNS OF INTERNAL LEGAL RELATIONS, AND LEGAL RELATIONSHIP TO CO-OPERATIVE INTERNATIONAL BODIES FOUND IN THE BRITISH COMMONWEALTH OF NATIONS AS OF 1962. ALL RELEVANT CASES, LEGISLATION, TREATIES, AND AGREEMENTS ARE CITED.

0724 FEERICK J.D.

FROM FAILING HANDS: THE STUDY OF PRESIDENTIAL SUCCESSION.
NEW YORK: FORDHAM U PR, 1965, 368 PP., LC#65-14917.
DISCUSSION OF HISTORY OF PRESIDENTIAL SUCCESSION FROM
COLONIAL GOVERNMENT TO PRESENT INCLUDING OCCASIONS WHEN
SUCCESSION TOOK OR SHOULD HAVE TAKEN PLACE. OPENS WITH DIS-
CUSSION OF KENNEDY'S ASSASSINATION AND JOHNSON'S SUCCESSION.
LAST PORTION DEALS WITH SUGGESTED IMPROVEMENTS OF SYSTEM AND
DEVELOPMENT OF OFFICE OF VICE-PRESIDENT.

0725 FEIFER G.
JUSTICE IN MOSCOW.
NEW YORK: SIMON AND SCHUSTER, 1964, 253 PP., LC#64-11199.
INVESTIGATES JUSTICE FOR COMMON MAN IN MOSCOW. THROUGH
PERSONAL OBSERVATIONS OF COURT PROCEEDINGS. INCLUDES ACTIONS
OF PEOPLE'S COURTS AND OF MOSCOW'S CITY COURTS ON CASES OF
DIVORCE, MURDER, CONSPIRACY, AND APPEALS AMONG OTHERS.

0726 FEILCHENFELD E.H.
THE INTERNATIONAL ECONOMIC LAW OF BELLIGERENT OCCUPATION.
WASHINGTON: CARNEGIE ENDOWMENT, 1942, 181 PP.
CITES HAGUE REGULATIONS OF 1907 REFERRING TO SECTION
PERTAINING TO MILITARY AUTHORITY OVER THE TERRITORY OF THE
HOSTILE STATE. BRINGS TOGETHER HISTORICAL INTERPRETATIONS
AND CURRENT PRACTICES RELATING TO THE ECONOMICS OF
BELLIGERENT OCCUPATION. OFFERS THESE AS AIDS TO THOSE
FORMULATING USA POLICY IN WW 2 MILITARY GOVERNMENT.

0727 FEINE H.E.
DIE BESETZUNG DER REICHSBISTUMER VOM WESTFALISCHEN FRIEDEN
BIS ZUR SAKULARISATION.
AMSTERDAM: VERLAG P SCHIPPERS, 1964, 444 PP.
DISCUSSES PROCESSES OF NOMINATION AND ELECTION, REQUIRE-
MENTS FOR OFFICE, IMPERIAL CAPITULATION, AND RIGHTS OF
SUCCESSION IN IMPERIAL DIOCESES OF GERMANY BETWEEN 1648 AND
1803.

0728 FEINE H.E.
REICH UND KIRCHE.
AALEN: SCIENTIA VERLAG, 1966, 322 PP.
EXAMINES RELATIONSHIP BETWEEN CHURCH AND STATE FROM END
OF MIDDLE AGES TO 1806. DISCUSSES SURVIVAL OF ROMAN LAW IN
CHURCH LAW, WORK OF PROMINENT HISTORIANS, AND SOURCES OF
CHURCH LAW AND PRACTICES.

0729 FEIS H.
"RESEARCH ACTIVITIES OF THE LEAGUE OF NATIONS."
OLD LYME: OLD LYME PR., 1929, 26 PP.
QUESTIONS CONCEPTIONS USES IN RESEARCH STUDIES AS TO
THEIR NATURE AND PURPOSE. NATURE OF WORK IS MAINLY IN ANA-
LYZING INTERNATIONAL PROPOSALS AND PRESENTING DATA.

0730 FELLMAN D.
THE DEFENDANT'S RIGHTS.
NEW YORK: RINEHART, 1958, 356 PP., LC#57-12386.
EXPLAINS RIGHTS OF THE ACCUSED, ILLUSTRATED WITH SUPREME
COURT DECISIONS. EMPHASIZES FEDERAL LAWS. TREATS PRELIMINARY
ACTIONS; RIGHTS TO NOTICE, FAIR HEARING, TRIAL BY JURY, AND
COUNSEL; WRIT OF HABEAS CORPUS; SEARCH AND SEIZURE; SELF-
INCRIMINATION; DOUPLE JEOPARDY; AND CRUEL PUNISHMENTS.
EXAMINES DEFICIENCIES IN LAWS DEALING WITH PERSONS ACCUSED
OF DISLOYALTY IN CIVIL SERVICE.

0731 FELLMAN D. ED.
THE SUPREME COURT AND EDUCATION.
NY: COLUMBIA U TEACHERS COLLEGE, 1960, 120 PP., LC#60-8488.
ANALYSIS OF 29 SELECTED SUPREME COURT DECISIONS PERTINENT
TO EDUCATION AS IT HAS RELATED TO RELIGION, RACIAL
INTEGRATION, AND ACADEMIC FREEDOM. INCLUDES BACKGROUND OF
EACH CASE AND ITS PARTICULAR EFFECT ON STATE AND LOCAL
EDUCATIONAL POLICY.

0732 FELLMAN D.
"ACADEMIC FREEDOM IN AMERICAN LAW."
WISC. LAW REV., (JAN. 61), 3-46.
AMERICAN DECISIONAL LAW REGARDING ACADEMIC FREEDOM AND
TENURE IN COLLEGES AND UNIVERSITIES IS FORMLESS AND ALMOST
RUDIMENTARY. AND MOST RELATED LEGISLATION ASSUMES THE RIGHT
OF THE STATE TO REGULATE TEACHERS AND TEACHING CONTENT AT
ALL LEVELS. YET THE RIGHT OF TEACHERS AND STUDENTS TO
ACADEMIC FREEDOM IS A FUNDAMENTAL LEGAL RIGHT ENTITLED TO
JUDICIAL PROTECTION.

0733 FELLMAN D.
RELIGION IN AMERICAN PUBLIC LAW.
BOSTON: BOSTON U PR, 1965, 115 PP., LC#65-17006.
TRACES DEVELOPMENT OF CHURCH-STATE RELATIONS IN LAW FROM
REVOLUTIONARY TIMES ON BOTH NATIONAL AND LOCAL LEVELS, OUT-
LINING MAJOR TRENDS AND GIVING RESULTS OF IMPORTANT JUDICIAL
DECISIONS RELATED TO RELIGION.

0734 FELLMAN D.
THE LIMITS OF FREEDOM.
NEW BRUNSWICK: RUTGERS U PR, 1959, 144 PP., LC#59-14425.
DISCUSSES BALANCE BETWEEN FREEDOM AND LICENSE IN THE
FRAMEWORK OF AMERICAN CONSTITUTIONAL LAW. BASIC SUBJECTS
ARE RELIGIOUS FREEDOM, THE RIGHT OF COMMUNICATION, AND THE
"RIGHT TO TALK POLITICS."

0735 FELSHER H., ROSEN M.
JUSTICE USA?
NEW YORK: MACMILLAN, 1966, 207 PP., LC#67-16687.
EXAMINES INFLUENCE AMERICAN PRESS HAS ON A SUSPECT'S
TRIAL BEFORE GRAND JURY VOTES AND INCLUDES SPECIFIC CASES.
AUTHORS ADMONISH THAT THE PRESS WILL HAVE TO RESTRAIN ITSELF
IF DEMOCRACY IS NOT TO BE WEAKENED AS ITS INFLUENCE IS SO
STRONG THAT IT HAS RUINED THE CHANCE FOR RIGHT TO FAIR TRIAL
IN MANY OUTSTANDING CASES.

0736 FENN DH J.R., GRUNEWALD D., KATZ R.N.
BUSINESS DECISION MAKING AND GOVERNMENT POLICY.
ENGLEWOOD CLIFFS: PRENTICE HALL, 1966, 386 PP.
CASEBOOK DEALS WITH AREAS OF COOPERATION BETWEEN CORPOR-
ATE GIANTS AND FEDERAL AGENCIES AND THE INDIVIDUAL AND HIS
LOCAL PLANNING BOARD. ANALYZES CASES INVOLVING GOVERNMENTAL
GRANTING OF LICENSES AND PROVISION OF SERVICES. DISCUSSES
PROBLEMS OF ACCESS TO VARIOUS DIVISIONS AND LEVELS OF GOV-
ERNMENT. CONTENDS THAT PARTICIPATION OF GOVERNMENT IN
BUSINESS AFFAIRS IS EXPANDING.

0737 FENWICK C.G.
INTERNATIONAL LAW.
NEW YORK: APPLETON, 1948, 623 PP.
DISCUSSES NATURE, SCOPE, AND STRUCTURE OF SUBJECT. RE-
LATES INTERNATIONAL LAW TO MUNICIPAL LAW. EXAMINES ORGANIZA-
TION OF INTERNATIONAL COMMUNITY, FOCUSING ON UN AND REGIONAL
PLANS. ANALYZES CONFLICT SETTLEMENT PROCEDURES.

0738 FENWICK C.G.
"ISSUES AT PUNTA DEL ESTE: NON-INTERVENTION VS COLLECTIVE
SECURITY."
AMER. J. INT. LAW, 56 (APR. 62), 469-74.
REVIEWS QUESTIONS IN INTERNATIONAL LAW RAISED AT MEETING
ON INTERPRETATION OF RIO TREATY (1947) AND ITS RELATION TO
CUBAN QUESTION. SUMMARIZES ACTIONS TAKEN AT PUNTA DEL ESTE.

0739 FERNEUIL T.
LES PRINCIPES DE 1789 ET LA SCIENCE SOCIALE.
PARIS: LIB HACHETTE ET CIE, 1889, 359 PP.
EXAMINES HISTORICAL PRECURSORS, SOCIAL FORCES, AND
IDEOLOGICAL TRENDS OF THE FRENCH REVOLUTION IN TERMS OF
SOCIOLOGY AND POLITICAL SCIENCE. DEALS WITH CONSTITUTIONAL
STRUCTURE, CONCEPTS OF INDIVIDUALISM AND COLLECTIVISM, AND
THE ROLE OF THE STATE AND ITS VARIOUS FUNCTIONS. STRESSES
GENERAL CONCEPTS SUCH AS NATURAL RIGHTS AND LEGITIMACY
RATHER THAN EMPIRICAL DATA.

0740 FERRELL J.S. ED.
CASES AND MATERIALS ON LOCAL APPORTIONMENT.
CHAPEL HILL: U OF N CAR PR, 1965, 260 PP.
THIS WORK CONTAINS SELECTED STATEMENTS OF THE US
SUPREME COURT IN STATE LEGISLATIVE APPORTIONMENT CASES,
COURT DECISIONS ON LOCAL GOVERNMENT REAPPORTIONMENT, STATE
STATUTES IN RESPONSE TO LOCAL REAPPORTIONMENT, ARTICLES
AND OTHER COMMENTARIES ON LOCAL LEGISLATIVE APPORTIONMENT,
AND MATERIALS RELATING TO LOCAL APPORTIONMENT IN NORTH
CAROLINA.

0741 FERRELL R.H.
PEACE IN THEIR TIME.
NEW HAVEN: YALE U PR, 1952, 286 PP., LC#52-5361.
DISCUSSES THE ORIGIN OF THE KELLOGG-BRIAND PACT OF 1928,
WHICH OUTLAWED WAR. ANALYZES INTERNATIONAL ATTEMPTS TO SE-
CURE A PERMANENT PEACE AFTER WWI. EMPHASIZES ARISTIDE BRI-
AND'S STRUGGLES IN THE NEGOTIATIONS. INCLUDES LEAGUE OF NA-
TIONS'S ROLE IN POST-WWI DIPLOMACY.

0742 FERRY W.H.
THE CORPORATION AND THE ECONOMY.
SANTA BARBARA: CTR DEMO INST, 1959, 122 PP.
NOTES ON THE PRESENT AND PAST USES OF CORPORATE POWER,
WITH PROPOSALS FOR FUTURE CONTROL. FOLLOWED BY A TRANSCRIPT
OF A DISCUSSION OF THE NOTES BY E. GOLDMAN, R. NIEBUHR,
R. HUTCHINS, AND OTHERS. HOLDS THAT THE PRIVATE
ORGANIZATION OF ECONOMIC ENTERPRISE, INVOLVING IMPORTANT
PUBLIC INTEREST, MUST CONFORM TO JUSTICE AND FREEDOM, AS
LABOR UNIONS SHOULD. DISCUSSES PLANNING IN MODERN SOCIETY.

0743 FESLER J.W. ED.
THE FIFTY STATES AND THEIR LOCAL GOVERNMENTS.
NEW YORK: ALFRED KNOPF, 1967, 603 PP., LC#66-12816.
ESSAYS ON VARIOUS ASPECTS OF STATE GOVERNMENT, INCLUDING
A BRIEF HISTORY OF STATE GOVERNMENT TO 1950, FUNCTIONS OF
STATE AND LOCAL GOVERNMENTS, INTERGOVERNMENTAL RELATIONS,
ELECTIONS, POLICY-MAKING, COURT SYSTEMS, AND ADMINISTRATIVE
ORGANIZATION. EMPHASIZE THE FUNCTIONS AND RELATIONSHIPS OF
STATE AND LOCAL GOVERNMENTS. CONCLUDE WITH DISCUSSION OF
FUTURE CHARACTER OF FEDERALISM.

0744 FICHTE J.G.
THE SCIENCE OF RIGHTS (TRANS. BY A.E. KROEGER)
LONDON: TRUEBNER AND CO, 1889, 505 PP.
STATES FICHTE'S PHILOSOPHY OF FREE WILL. ORGANIZED AROUND

THE DEDUCTION OF, APPLICABILITY OF, AND APPLICATION OF THE "CONCEPTION OF RIGHTS." TREATS STATE ORGANIZATION AND CONSTITUTION; MUNICIPAL AND PENAL LAW; AND "POLICE LAW." ALSO APPLIES FREE WILL PHILOSOPHY TO THE RIGHTS OF FAMILY, LAW OF MARRIAGE, PARENTS AND CHILDREN, AND LEGAL RELATIONSHIPS BETWEEN THE SEXES.

0745 FIELD G.C.
POLITICAL THEORY.
LONDON: METHUEN, 1956, 297 PP.
DISCUSSES VARIOUS ASPECTS OF POLITICAL THEORY AS CONCEPT OF SOVEREIGNTY, STATE, INDIVIDUAL LIBERTY, ETC. EXAMINES IN DETAIL MACHINERY OF DEMOCRACY AND RELATIONS BETWEEN STATES. CONCLUDES WITH ESSAY ON RELATION BETWEEN POLITICS, ECONOMICS, AND ETHICS.

0746 FIELD G.L.
THE SYNDICAL AND CORPORATIVE INSTITUTIONS OF ITALIAN FASCISM
NEW YORK: COLUMBIA U PRESS, 1938, 209 PP.
EXAMINES FASCISM IN ITALY BY CONSIDERING ITS THREE MAJOR INSTITUTIONS: DICTATORSHIP, SYNDICATE, AND CORPORATION. THE FIRST HAD THOROUGH LEGAL CONTROL, THE SECOND PROVIDED STATE CONTROL OF CAPITAL AND LABOR, AND THE THIRD HAD CONTROL OF VARIOUS ECONOMIC ACTIVITIES. WRITTEN AT PEAK OF FASCISM'S POPULARITY, WORK ATTEMPTS TO BE ANALYTIC.

0747 FIELD G.L.
"LAW AS AN OBJECTIVE POLITICAL CONCEPT" (BMR)"
AM. POL. SCI. REV., 43 (APR. 49), 229-249.
STATES THAT LAW, WHEN USED IN FACTUAL SENSE DENOTING AN OBSERVABLE SOCIAL PHENOMENON, REFERS TO A SYSTEM OF AUTHORITATIVE NORMS ASSOCIATED WITH A STATE. BELIEVES THAT LAW DOES NOT NORMALLY DETERMINE ADMINISTRATIVE OR JUDICIAL CONDUCT, BUT RESTRICTS THE RANGE OF CONDUCT. A SYSTEM OF LAW IS MANIFESTED IN FORMALIZATION OF ARGUMENTS USED IN EVALUATING CONDUCT WITHIN LEGALLY REGULATED AREAS.

0748 FIGGIS J.N.
CHURCHES IN THE MODERN STATE (2ND ED.)
LONDON: LONGMANS, GREEN & CO, 1914, 271 PP.
FOUR LECTURES ON CHURCH-STATE RELATIONS. DISCUSSES RIGHTS OF FREE CHURCHES IN A FREE STATE AND DIVISION OF POWERS BETWEEN THEM. SHOWS DEVELOPMENT OF LAWYERS' PREJUDICE AGAINST GIVING FREEDOM TO CHURCHES, AND URGES A MORE REALISTIC AND MORE USEFUL VIEW. COMPARES PAPACY'S POWER TO THAT OF A NATIONAL STATE.

0749 FINCHER F.
THE GOVERNMENT OF THE UNITED STATES.
ENGLEWOOD CLIFFS: PRENTICE HALL, 1967, 310 PP., LC#67-10169.
DISCUSSES FRAMEWORK AND FUNCTION OF US GOVERNMENT. INCLUDES BASIC LEGISLATIVE AND POLITICAL PROCESSES, COURTS, LOBBYING, AND PRESSURE GROUPS. EXAMINES GOVERNMENTAL ACTIVITY IN VARIOUS CONTEXTS, INCLUDING CIVIL RIGHTS AND LIBERTIES, BUSINESS-LABOR RELATIONS, PEACE AND NATIONAL SECURITY, AND HEALTH, EDUCATION, AND WELFARE. EMPHASIZES CONTEMPORARY PROBLEMS AND POLITICAL PHILOSOPHIES.

0750 FINE R.I.
"PEACE-KEEPING COSTS AND ARTICLE 19 OF THE UN CHARTER* AN INVITATION TO RESPONSIBILITY."
INT. AND COMP. LAW Q., 15 (APR. 66), 529-539.
A CRITIQUE OF SUGGESTIONS FOR AVOIDING ARTICLE 19 DILEMMAS THROUGH CONSENSUS AND NON-VOTING, VOLUNTARY FUND, TOKEN PAYMENTS, AND BINDING SUBMISSION TO THE ICJ. ADVOCATES INSTEAD THAT THE MIDDLE POWERS WHO BENEFIT MOST FROM COLLECTIVE SECURITY ACCEPT RESPONSIBILITY FOR IT BY INCREASING THE BINDING ASSESSMENTS ON THEMSELVES RETROACTIVELY AND NOW ON.

0751 FINK M.
A SELECTIVE BIBLIOGRAPHY ON STATE CONSTITUTIONAL REVISION (PAMPHLET)
ALBUQUERQUE: U NEW MEX LAW SCH, 1966, 26 PP.
LIST OF SELECTED MATERIALS PUBLISHED SINCE JANUARY 1, 1963, DEALING WITH STATE CONSTITUTIONAL REVISION AND SUBSTANTIVE AREAS OF THE CONSTITUTIONAL SYSTEM. INDEX OF AUTHORS AND EDITORS. ABOUT 400 BOOKS, PERIODICAL ARTICLES, AND GOVERNMENT DOCUMENTS.

0752 FINKELSTEIN L.S.
"THE UNITED NATIONS AND ORGANIZATIONS FOR CONTROL OF ARMAMENT."
INT. ORGAN., 16 (WINTER 62', 1-19.
DISCUSSES INDEPENDENT ROLE OF DISARMAMENT NEGOTIATIONS UNDER UN GUIDANCE. SUGGESTS THAT SUBORDINATING ARMS CONTROL TO UN MAKES TASK HARDER BECAUSE INTERESTED POWERS FAVOR AUTONOMOUS HANDLING OF PROBLEM. SUGGESTS ARMS CONTROL MIGHT BENEFIT IF THERE WERE A LIASON BETWEEN UN AND AGENCIES AND IF THE AGENCIES COULD REFER FOR SETTLEMENT BY UN CERTAIN POLITICAL QUESTIONS.

0753 FISCHER F.C.
THE GOVERNMENT OF MICHIGAN.
NEW YORK: ALLYN AND BACON, 1965, 230 PP.
STUDY OF MICHIGAN STATE LEGISLATURE AND LAW-MAKING, ADMINISTRATIVE DEPARTMENTS, COURT STRUCTURE, LOCAL GOVERN-MENT, AND STATE EDUCATION. DISCUSSES POLITICAL PARTIES, FINANCE OF GOVERNMENT, AND STATE INSTITUTIONS.

0754 FISCHER H. ED.
EINER IM VORDERGRUND: TARAS BORODAJKEWYCZ.
ZURICH: EUROPA VERLAG, 1966, 305 PP.
COLLECTION OF DOCUMENTS ON PROSECUTION OF FORMER NAZI AND UNIVERSITY PROFESSOR SINCE WWII, TARAS BORODAJKEWYCZ. INCLUDES ALL COURT RECORDS AND MANY NEWSPAPER ARTICLES.

0755 FISCHER L.
THE SOVIETS IN WORLD AFFAIRS.
NEW YORK: ALFRED KNOPF, 1960, 616 PP.
HISTORY OF SOVIET FOREIGN RELATIONS, 1917-29, INCLUDING VERSAILLES, BOLSHEVIK ATTITUDES TOWARD POLAND, UK, JAPAN, CHINESE REVOLUTION, DISARMAMENT, AND PARTICIPATION IN INTERNATIONAL CONFERENCES.

0756 FISCHER-GALATI S.A.
RUMANIA; A BIBLIOGRAPHIC GUIDE (PAMPHLET)
WASHINGTON: LIBRARY OF CONGRESS, 1963, 75 PP., LC#63-60076.
CRITICALLY ANNOTATED BIBLIOGRAPHY OF ESSENTIAL PUBLICATIONS, PRIMARILY MONOGRAPHS AND PERIODICALS, IN BOTH RUMANIAN AND WESTERN LANGUAGES. GUIDE CONSISTS OF TWO PARTS: A CONCISE BIBLIOGRAPHIC SURVEY COVERING IN ELEVEN SECTIONS MAJOR CATEGORIES OF KNOWLEDGE EXCLUSIVE OF MEDICINE AND NATURAL SCIENCE; DETAILED LISTING, ALPHABETICALLY ARRANGED AND CONSECUTIVELY NUMBERED, OF 748 ENTRIES DISCUSSED IN SURVEY.

0757 FISHER F.M.
"THE MATHEMATICAL ANALYSIS OF SUPREME COURT DECISIONS: THE USE AND ABUSE OF QUANTITATIVE METHODS."
AM. POL. SCI. REV., 52 (JUNE 58), 321-338.
EXPLORATION WITH STATEMENT OF AUTHOR'S CONCEPT OF LIMITATIONS OF MATHEMATICAL INTERPRETATIONS.

0758 FISK W.M.
ADMINISTRATIVE PROCEDURE IN A REGULATORY AGENCY: THE CAB AND THE NEW YORK-CHICAGO CASE (PAMPHLET)
INDIANAPOLIS: BOBBS-MERRILL, 1964.
STUDIES ECONOMIC REGULATION EXERCISED BY CIVIL AERONAUTICS BOARD OVER US AIR TRANSPORT INDUSTRY. EXAMINES CAB'S POWER IN DETERMINING AIR ROUTES, SERVICE POINTS, AND NATURE OF SERVICE. EMPHASIZES PROCEDURAL ASPECTS OF NEW YORK-CHICAGO CASE OF 1953 WHICH LED TO OVERHAUL OF STRUCTURE OF AIR ROUTES.

0759 FITCH R.E.
THE LIMITS OF LIBERTY.
MTN VIEW: PACIFIC PHIL INST ASSN, 1951, 116 PP.
SYSTEMATIC INQUIRY INTO NATURE OF LIBERTY FROM A METAPHYSICAL POINT OF VIEW. ATTEMPTS TO DEFINE LIMITS OF LIBERTY BY EXAMINING RELATIONSHIP BETWEEN LIBERTY AND LAW, AND MANNER IN WHICH THEY "MUTUALLY LIMIT AND ELUCIDATE ONE ANOTHER."

0760 FLECHTHEIM O.K. ED.
FUNDAMENTALS OF POLITICAL SCIENCE.
NEW YORK: RONALD PRESS, 1952, 587 PP. LC#52-7604.
INTRODUCTORY TEXT DEFINES FUNDAMENTAL PRINCIPLES GOVERNING POLITICAL RELATIONSHIPS; EMPHASIZES PRINCIPLES AND PROBLEMS RATHER THAN LAWS AND INSTITUTIONS. SURVEYS AND EVALUATES FORMS OF GOVERNMENT AND POLITICAL BEHAVIOR IN POLITICAL SYSTEMS THROUGHOUT WORLD. INCLUDES GROWTH OF POLITICAL IDEAS, ELEMENTS OF NATION STATE, CONSTITUTIONAL CONCEPT, PUBLIC OPINION, POLITICAL PARTIES, ETC.

0761 FLECHTHEIM O.K.
"BLOC FORMATION VS. DIALOGUE."
COEXISTENCE, 4 (JAN. 67), 39-48.
NEITHER THE POLITICAL NOR THE ECONOMIC STRUCTURES OF THE TWO NATION-BLOCS ARE AS OPPOSED AS THEY ARE MADE OUT TO BE, NOR ARE THEIR DIFFERENCES AS SIGNIFICANT AS THE TWO SIDES MAINTAIN. POWER CONSIDERATIONS ARE MORE IMPORTANT THAN EITHER. SOME FORM OF HONEST DIALOGUE, LOOKING TOWARD THE FUTURE WITHOUT IDEOLOGICAL OR UTOPIAN COLORING, IS VITALLY NECESSARY. THIS OUTLOOK COULD BE CALLED "FUTUROLOGY."

0762 FLEISCHER B.M.
THE ECONOMICS OF DELINQUENCY.
CHICAGO: QUADRANGLE BOOKS, INC, 1966, 127 PP., LC#66-11864.
APPLIES ECONOMIC THEORY AND ANALYSIS TO THE STUDY OF JUVENILE DELINQUENCY. INVESTIGATES EFFECTS OF ECONOMIC CHANGES, SUCH AS INCOME AND EMPLOYMENT, ON LEVELS OF JUVENILE DELINQUENCY. DEMONSTRATES THAT CHANGE IN ECONOMIC POSITION IS A CORE ELEMENT IN THE SOCIAL CONTROL OF DEVIANT BEHAVIOR.

0763 FLEMING R.W.
THE LABOR ARBITRATION PROCESS.
URBANA: U OF ILLINOIS PR, 1965, 227 PP., LC#65-19569.
DISCUSSES LABOR ARBITRATION, ITS PAST AND DEVELOPMENT; PROBLEMS OF COST, TIME-LAG AND FORMALITY, INDIVIDUAL RIGHTS, PROCEDURAL REGULARITY, EVIDENCE; AND STUDIES OF PREDICTABILITY IN ARBITRATION.

0764 FLEMMING D.
THE UNITED STATES AND THE LEAGUE OF NATIONS, 1918-1920.
NEW YORK: PUTNAM, 1932, 559 PP.
   TRACES IDEATIONAL ORIGINS OF LEAGUE, FRAMING OF TREATY
AND FATE OF TREATY IN SENATE. FOLLOWS COURSE OF DEBATE,
AMENDMENTS, COMPROMISES, AND COMMITTEE WORK. REJECTION OF
TREATY SEEN AS CONTINUANCE OF PREVIOUS ANTI-PEACE TREATY
POLICY. COOPERATION OF SOVEREIGN STATES ESSENTIAL TO LEAGUE.
ITS ECONOMIC INTERESTS DEMAND USA MEMBERSHIP.

0765 FLIESS P.J.
FREEDOM OF THE PRESS IN THE GERMAN REPUBLIC, 1918-1933.
BATON ROUGE: LOUISIANA ST U PR, 1955, 147 PP., LC#55-8960.
   CONCERNS THE WEIMAR REPUBLIC'S CONFLICT WITH THE PRESS
AND ITS SUPPRESSION OF RESPONSIBLE JOURNALISM. CONTAINS A
BIBLIOGRAPHY OF APPROXIMATELY 300 GERMAN, FRENCH, AND
ENGLISH BOOKS, NEWSPAPERS, PERIODICALS, AND PAMPHLETS FROM
1788 THROUGH 1946, ARRANGED ALPHABETICALLY BY AUTHOR
UNDER GENERAL TOPICS.

0766 FLINN M.W.
AN ECONOMIC AND SOCIAL HISTORY OF BRITAIN, 1066-1939.
NEW YORK: ST MARTIN'S PRESS, 1961, 388 PP.
   DISCUSSES BROAD SOCIETAL AND ECONOMIC SITUATION DURING
THE VARIOUS STAGES OF DEVELOPMENT. INCLUDES MEDIEVAL ERA,
RISE OF INDUSTRIALISM, REFORM PERIOD AND AFTER.

0767 FLORES R.H.
CATALOGO DE TESIS DOCTORALES DE LAS FACULTADES DE LA
UNIVERSIDAD DE EL SALVADOR.
EL SALVADOR: U DE EL SALVADOR, 1960, 620 PP.
   CATALOG OF DOCTORAL THESES PRESENTED FROM 1878 TO 1960
AT UNIVERSITY OF EL SALVADOR. ENTRIES ARRANGED BY FACULTY
AND CLASSIFIED BY DEWEY CLASSIFICATION SYSTEM.

0768 FLORIN J., HERZ J.H.
"BOLSHEVIST AND NATIONAL SOCIALIST DOCTRINES OF INTER-
NATIONAL LAW."
SOC. RES., 7 (FEB. 40), 1-31.
   CASE STUDY OF FUNCTION OF SOCIAL SCIENCE IN TOTALITARIAN
DICTATORSHIP. ADVANCES NEW FOUNDATION OF INTERNATIONAL LAW
BASED ON TOTALITARIAN IDEOLOGY. CONTENDS INTERNATIONAL LAW
REFLECTS NATIONS' ATTITUDES TOWARDS INTERNATIONAL RELATIONS.

0769 FORBES A.H. ED.
CURRENT RESEARCH IN BRITISH STUDIES.
MARQUETTE: NORTHERN MICH U PR, 1964, 88 PP.
   LIST OF 700 US AND CANADIAN SCHOLARS ENGAGED IN RESEARCH
IN BRITISH AND IMPERIAL HISTORY. SCHOLARS TOGETHER WITH RE-
SEARCH INTERESTS ARE LISTED BY MAJOR HISTORICAL PERIODS AND
BY SUBJECT. INCLUDES BIOGRAPHICAL STUDIES; PARLIAMENTARY
GOVERNMENT; ADMINISTRATION;CONSTITUTIONAL AND LEGAL HISTORY;
CULTURAL, LITERARY, AND RELIGIOUS HISTORY; AND EXTERNAL
AFFAIRS.

0770 FORGAC A.A.
NEW DIPLOMACY AND THE UNITED NATIONS.
NEW YORK: PAGEANT PR, 1965, 173 PP., LC#65-24549.
   TRACES EVOLUTION OF DIPLOMACY AND EXAMINES FUNCTIONS OF
DIPLOMATS AND FOREIGN OFFICE. DESCRIBES CEREMONIALS, TITLES
AND PRECEDENTS, AND ANALYZES DIPLOMATIC PRACTICES OF UK,
GERMANY, USSR, AND FRANCE. EXAMINES IMPACT OF UN ON MODERN
DIPLOMACY.

0771 FORSTER A., EPSTEIN B.
THE TROUBLE MAKERS.
GARDEN CITY: DOUBLEDAY, 1952, 317 PP., LC#52-7114.
   ANALYSIS OF RACIAL AND RELIGIOUS PREJUDICE IN US, WHICH
FOCUSES ON ACTIVITIES OF EXTREMIST INDIVIDUALS AND ORGANIZA-
TIONS. DISCUSSES USE OF VIOLENCE AND COERCIVE TACTICS AS
MEANS OF SUPRESSING MINORITY AND ETHNIC GROUPS. CONDEMNS
BIGOTRY AND PREJUDICE AS PRACTICED BY EXTREMIST ELEMENTS FOR
PREVENTING REALIZATION OF AMERICAN DEMOCRATIC IDEALS.

0772 FORTE W.E.
"THE FOOD AND DRUG ADMINISTRATION, THE FEDERAL TRADE COMMIS-
SION AND THE DECEPTIVE PACKAGING."
NYU LAW REV., 40 (NOV. 65), 860-904.
   CASE STUDIES OF ACTIONS TAKEN AGAINST MANUFACTURERS BY
FOOD AND DRUG ADMINISTRATION COMPARED WITH FTC ACTION
ON SIMILAR MATTERS EMPHASIZING PROCEDURE AND EFFECTIVENESS.

0773 FORTES A.B., WAGNER J.B.
HISTORIA ADMINISTRATIVA, JUDICIARIA E ECLESIASTICA DO RIO
GRANDE DO SUL.
PORTO ALEGRE: EDITORA GLOBO, 1963, 496 PP.
   ANALYZES ADMINISTRATIVE, JUDICIAL, AND ECCLESIASTICAL
DEVELOPMENT OF IMPORTANT BRAZILIAN STATE OF RIO GRANDE DO
SUL. DISCUSSES MUNICIPAL AND PROVINCIAL ADMINISTRATION OF
STATE IN COLONIAL TIMES AND SINCE INDEPENDENCE. EXAMINES
FORMATION AND ACTION OF JUDICIARY IN POLITICAL PROCESS.
COVERS CATHOLIC CHURCH'S HIERARCHY AND STRUCTURE IN STATE
DURING SAME PERIOD.

0774 FORTESCU J.
IN PRAISE OF ENGLISH LAW (1464) (TRANS. BY S.B. CHRIMES)
NEW YORK: CAMBRIDGE U PRESS, 1942, 235 PP.
   PRAISES CONSTITUTIONALISM IN MONARCHICAL STATES AS JUST
AND EFFICIENT MEANS OF PROVIDING ORDER AND AUTHORITY. CLAIMS
THAT KINGS DO NOT HAVE RIGHT TO CHANGE LAWS MADE BY PARLIA-
MENT AND TRADITION SINCE THERE IS A DIFFERENCE BETWEEN REGAL
AND POLITICAL GOVERNMENT SIMILAR TO MODERN DISTINCTION
BETWEEN EXECUTIVE AND LEGISLATIVE BRANCHES OF GOVERNMENT.
DEALS WITH BOTH CIVIL AND CRIMINAL LAWS.

0775 FORTESCUE G.K. ED.
SUBJECT INDEX OF THE MODERN WORKS ADDED TO THE LIBRARY OF
THE BRITISH MUSEUM IN THE YEARS 1881-1900 (3 VOLS.)
LONDON: W CLOWES & SONS, LTD. 1903.
   CONTAINS ABOUT 155,000 ENTRIES REFERRING TO BOOKS FIRST
PUBLISHED OR REISSUED BETWEEN JANUARY, 1881, AND DECEMBER,
1900. UNDER EACH COUNTRY ARE FOUND WORKS ON ANTIQUI-
TIES, ARMY, COLONIES, CONSTITUTION AND GOVERNMENT, HISTORY,
LAW, NAVY, POLITICS, SOCIAL LIFE, TOPOGRAPHY, TRADE, AND
FINANCE.

0776 FORTESCUE J., PLUMMER C. ED.
THE GOVERNANCE OF ENGLAND (1471-76)
LONDON: OXFORD U PR, 1926, 387 PP.
   EARLIEST CONSTITUTIONAL TREATISE WRITTEN IN ENGLISH.
EXAMINES GOVERNMENTAL EVILS OF HIS TIME, AND PROPOSES REME-
DIES. PROPOSES REORGANIZATION OF PRIVY COUNCIL, STRENGTHEN-
ING OF CROWN, AND REDUCTION OF POWER OF NOBLES. URGES KING
TO AVOID WEAKNESSES OF LANCASTRIAN RULE, ITS UNSOUND
FINANCE, AND ITS LACK OF GOVERNANCE AND JUSTICE.

0777 FOSTER J.W.
THE PRACTICE OF DIPLOMACY AS ILLUSTRATED IN THE FOREIGN RE-
LATIONS OF THE UNITED STATES.
BOSTON: HOUGHTON MIFFLIN, 1906, 401 PP.
   ILLUSTRATES ROLE OF DIPLOMAT IN FIELD OF INTERNATIONAL
RELATIONS. DESCRIBES RULES AND PROCEDURE OF DIPLOMATIC IN-
TERCOURSE. RECORDS FAILURES AND SUCCESSES OF AMERICAN DIPLO-
MACY ABROAD. INCLUDES SHORT BIBLIOGRAPHY, MOSTLY RECOLLEC-
TIONS, MEMOIRS, BIOGRAPHIES WITH SOME BOOKS ON INTERNATIONAL
LAW AND FOREIGN RELATIONS.

0778 FOUAD M.
LE REGIME DE LA PRESSE EN EGYPTE: THESE POUR LE DOCTORAT.
PARIS: LIB SOC DU RECEUIL SIREY, 1912, 120 PP.
   STUDY OF PRESS CENSORSHIP BY STATE. INCLUDES PRINTING,
ADVERTISING, AND LEGAL DISPOSITIONS.

0779 FOX A.B.
"NATO AND CONGRESS."
POLIT. SCI. QUART., 80 (SEPT. 65), 395-414.
   ANALYSIS OF RELATIONS BETWEEN THE EXECUTIVE BRANCH AND
PERTINENT CONGRESSIONAL COMMITTEES VIS-A-VIS NATO POLICY.
THE DISPERSION OF CONGRESSIONAL CONTROL BECAUSE OF A PLETH-
ORA OF COMPETING COMMITTEES IS CONTRASTED TO POWER OF THE
JOINT COMMITTEE ON ATOMIC ENERGY.

0780 FOX W.T.R.
UNITED STATES POLICY IN A TWO POWER WORLD.
NEW HAVEN: YALE U PR, 1947, 17 PP.
   DISCUSSES US-SOVIET RELATIONS, DECLARING NEED FOR US TO
SUPPORT NATIONS OF WESTERN EUROPE SO THAT THEY MAY FUNCTION
AS BUFFER STATES. ENCOURAGES FOREIGN AID TO NEUTRALS AS
SOUND ACTION, SINCE US DOES NOT NEED TO DOMINATE EUROPE TO
PREVENT SOVIETS FROM DOMINATING IT. MAJOR UNCERTAINTY
REVEALED IS EFFECT OF NUCLEAR WEAPONS IN INTERNATIONAL
AFFAIRS.

0781 FRAENKEL O.K.
OUR CIVIL LIBERTIES.
NEW YORK: VIKING PRESS, 1944, 277 PP.
   DISCUSSION OF FIRST TEN AMENDMENTS TO CONSTITUTION AND
SECTIONS THEREIN THAT DEAL WITH PERSONAL LIBERTIES UNDER
LAW. DATED.

0782 FRAENKEL O.K.
THE SUPREME COURT AND CIVIL LIBERTIES: HOW THE COURT HAS
PROTECTED THE BILL OF RIGHTS.
NEW YORK: OCEANA PUBLISHING, 1963, 189 PP., LC#62-21673.
   ANALYSIS OF COURT'S DEFENSE OF CIVIL LIBERTIES, GROUPED
BY TOPICS SUCH AS "LABOR RELATIONS" AND "RIGHT TO TRAVEL."
INCLUDES DESCRIPTION OF RELEVANT CASES.

0783 FRAGA IRIBARNE M.
RAZAS Y RACISMO IN NORTEAMERICA.
MADRID: ED CULTURA HISPANICA, 1950, 98 PP.
   ANALYZES US RACIAL COMPOSITION AND RACE RELATIONS.
EXAMINES LEGAL GUARANTEES AND RESTRICTIONS CONCERNING RACE
IN FEDERAL AND STATE LAW. ALSO DISCUSSES WORLDWIDE CONCEPTS
OF RACIAL EQUALITY AND INFERIORITY.

0784 FRANCIS R.G., STONE R.C.
SERVICE AND PROCEDURE IN BUREAUCRACY.
MINNEAPOLIS: U OF MINN PR, 1956, 201 PP., LC#56-9876.
   CASE STUDY OF A LOCAL OFFICE OF THE LOUISIANA DIVISION OF
THE FEDERAL EMPLOYMENT SECURITY SYSTEM. STUDIES CONTENT OF
OFFICIAL DOCUMENTS, RELATIONS BETWEEN MEMBERS OF THE

ORGANIZATION, AND ATTITUDES TOWARD CLIENTELE.

0785 FRANCK T.M.
EAST AFRICAN UNITY THROUGH LAW.
NEW HAVEN: YALE U PR, 1964, 184 PP., LC#64-20916.
ANALYSIS OF THE "CONSOCIATIONAL" APPROACH TO UNITY IN
EAST AFRICA AS A FUNCTIONALIST PATTERN APPLICABLE TO TOTAL
UNIFICATION OF AFRICA AS WELL AS REGIONAL UNION. THE METHODS
OF BUILDING UNITY THROUGH THE CREATION OF "LEGAL-CONSTITU-
TIONAL TECHNIQUES" AND INSTITUTION BUILDING ARE REVIEWED.

0786 FRANCK T.M.
"SOME PSYCHOLOGICAL FACTORS IN INTERNATIONAL THIRD-PARTY
DECISION-MAKING."
STANFORD LAW REV., 19 (JUNE 67), 1217-1247.
STUDIES PROBLEM OF PERSONAL BIAS OF THIRD PARTY IN INTER-
NATIONAL DECISION-MAKING. ENVIRONMENT AND SOCIETY INFLUENCE
EACH MAN. THEREFORE, IMPARTIAL DECISION-MAKER SHOULD BE
CONDITIONED BY BALANCE OF INFLUENCES STRUCTURED TO MAKE
HIM RESPONSIVE TO ALL SIDES. THIRD-PARTY DECISION-MAKING
SERVICES MUST DEVELOP OWN COMMUNITY NORMS, ROLES, & SYMBOLS
TO GENERATE INTERNATIONAL LOYALTY AND IDENTIFICATION.

0787 FRANK J.
LAW AND THE MODERN MIND.
NEW YORK: COWARD MCCANN, 1949, 368 PP.
PROPOSES THAT WIDESPREAD NOTION THAT LAW IS OR CAN BE
MADE APPROXIMATELY STATIONARY AND CERTAIN IS IRRATIONAL.
FINDS THAT BOTH THE GENERAL PUBLIC AND GREAT LAWYERS HAVE
TRIED TO SEARCH FOR LEGAL CERTAINTY. EXAMINES THESE ATTEMPTS
BY JURIES, JUDGES, AND ADVOCATES. STATES THAT JUSTICE O.W.
HOLMES ATTAINED SCIENTIFIC VIEW FREE OF MYTH OF FIXED
AUTHORITARIAN LAW.

0788 FRANK J.
COURTS ON TRIAL: MYTH AND REALITY IN AMERICAN JUSTICE.
PRINCETON: PRINCETON U PRESS, 1950, 441 PP.
EXAMINES WHAT TRIAL COURTS DO, WHAT THEY ARE SUPPOSED TO
DO, WHETHER OR NOT THEY DO WHAT THEY ARE SUPPOSED TO DO, AND
WHETHER THEY SHOULD DO IT. URGES REFORM OF COURT SYSTEM,
LAW STRUCTURE, LEGAL EDUCATION, AND JUDICIAL THEORY.
MAINTAINS THAT PRESENT SECRECY AND COMPLICATIONS OF LAW DO
NOT BENEFIT JUSTICE.

0789 FRANKFURTER F., LANDIS J.M.
THE BUSINESS OF THE SUPREME COURT; A STUDY IN THE FEDERAL
JUDICIAL SYSTEM.
CAMBRIDGE: HARVARD LAW REV ASSN, 1928, 349 PP.
CONCERNED WITH POLITICAL SIGNIFICANCE OF SUPREME COURT'S
JURISDICTION. SEEKS TO UNCOVER POLITICAL AND ECONOMIC POWER
UNDER CONSTITUTIONAL TECHNICALITIES AND TO FIT MEANING OF
SUCCESSIVE ACTS OF JUDICIARY INTO US HISTORY. INCLUDES ITS
RELATIONS WITH LOWER COURTS. SKETCHES NATURE OF COURTS
ESTABLISHED BY CONGRESS, VESTED POWERS, AND REVIEW OVER
THEM. REVIEWING POWER AND PROBLEMS OF SUPREME COURT STUDIED.

0790 FRANKFURTER F.
MR. JUSTICE HOLMES AND THE SUPREME COURT.
CAMBRIDGE: HARVARD U PR, 1938, 139 PP.
DISCUSSES ROLE OF SUPREME COURT, WHILE UNDER JUSTICE
HOLMES'S JURISDICTION, IN SHAPING SOCIAL AND ECONOMIC FORCES.
EXAMINES DECISIONS AFFECTING PROPERTY AND SOCIETY, CIVIL
LIBERTIES AND THE INDIVIDUAL, AND FREEDOM OF SPEECH.
INCLUDES HOLMES'S INTERPRETATION OF CONSTITUTIONAL POWERS OF
SUPREME COURT, OPINIONS ON FEDERAL STRUCTURE OF GOVERNMENT,
AND HIS ROLE AS MAKER OF LAW.

0791 FRANKFURTER F.
"SOME REFLECTIONS ON THE READING OF STATUTES"
RECORD OF ASSN. OF BAR OF NYC, 2 (JUNE 47), 213-237.
DISCUSSES INTRINSIC DIFFICULTIES OF LANGUAGE AND
CONSTRUCTION OF STATUTES. DESCRIBES DIFFICULT TASK OF JUDGE,
WHO MUST BE ACQUAINTED WITH LARGE NUMBER OF STATUTES.
STUDIES SCOPE OF JUDICIAL FUNCTION AND STATES THAT COURTS
HAVE LITTLE LAWMAKING FUNCTION TODAY. DISCUSSES PROBLEM OF
PURPOSE AND CONTENT OF STATUTES. PROPOSES SEVERAL "CANONS OF
CONSTRUCTION."

0792 FRANKFURTER F.
"THE SUPREME COURT IN THE MIRROR OF JUSTICES" (BMR)"
U. PENN. LAW REV., 105 (APR. 57), 781-796.
DISCUSSES WHETHER SUPREME COURT JUSTICES OUGHT TO
HAVE PRIOR JUDICIAL SERVICE. ANALYZES PERFORMANCE OF PAST
JUSTICES WITH AND WITHOUT JUDICAL EXPERIENCE. POINTS OUT
THAT MANY OF THE COURT'S FINEST JUSTICES HAD LITTLE
"TRAINING." STATES THAT INTELLECTUAL AND MORAL QUALITY
IS A MORE RELEVANT REQUIREMENT THAN PRIOR EXPERIENCE ON
THE BENCH.

0793 FREISEN J.
STAAT UND KATHOLISCHE KIRCHE IN DEN DEUTSCHEN BUNDESSTAATEN
(2 VOLS.)
AMSTERDAM: VERLAG P SCHIPPERS, 1964, 910 PP.
DISCUSSES ROLE OF CATHOLIC CHURCH IN RELATION TO MARRIAGE
LAWS, ADMINISTRATION OF INHERITANCE LAWS, EDUCATION, ETC.,
IN GERMAN STATES OF LIPPE, WALDECK-PYRMONT, ANHALT, SCHWARZ-
BURG-RUDOLSTADT, SCHWARZBURG-SONDERSHAUSEN, REUSS-GREIZ,
REUSS-SCHLEIZ, SACHSEN-ALTENBURG, SACHSEN-COBURG, AND
SACHSEN-GOTHA FROM 1800 TO PRESENT.

0794 FREUD A.
OF HUMAN SOVEREIGNTY.
NEW YORK: PHILOSOPHICAL LIB, 1964, 341 PP., LC#65-10993.
EXAMINES NATIONALISM AS CAUSE OF INTERNATIONAL UNREST,
THE ARMS RACE, NATIONAL BELLIGERENCE, AND WAR. SUGGESTS
INTEGRATION AND SUPRA-NATIONAL BLOCS AS REMEDIAL TACTICS.

0795 FREUND E.
THE POLICE POWER; PUBLIC POLICY AND CONSTITUTIONAL RIGHTS.
CHICAGO: U OF CHICAGO PRESS, 1904, 819 PP.
DEFINES POLICE POWER AS POWER OF PROMOTING PUBLIC WELFARE
BY RESTRAINING AND REGULATING USE OF LIBERTY AND PROPERTY.
BEGINS WITH NATURE AND METHODS OF POLICE POWER AND RELATION
TO DIVISIONS OF GOVERNMENT. DISCUSSES PRIMARY SOCIAL AND
ECONOMIC INTERESTS LAW MUST PROTECT. FINAL SECTION DEVOTED
TO FUNDAMENTAL RIGHTS UNDER POLICE POWER - LIBERTY,
PROPERTY, AND EQUALITY.

0796 FREUND G.
UNHOLY ALLIANCE.
NEW YORK: HARCOURT BRACE, 1957, 283 PP.
ILLUMINATES PREVIOUSLY OBSCURE ASPECTS OF GERMAN-SOVIET
COLLABORATION IN POST-WWI PERIOD FROM EXTENSIVE RESEARCH
INTO DOCUMENTARY MATERIAL ONLY RECENTLY AVAILABLE. COVERS
RELATIONS BETWEEN TWO COUNTRIES FROM BREST-LITOVSK TO 1927.
TOPICS COVERED RANGE FROM ANTI-WESTERN POLITICAL ALIGNMENT
TO LITTLE-KNOWN FACETS OF MILITARY COOPERATION.

0797 FREUND P.A.
THE SUPREME COURT OF THE UNITED STATES: ITS BUSINESS, PUR-
POSES, AND PERFORMANCE.
NEW YORK: MERIDIAN BOOKS, 1961, 224 PP., LC#61-15601.
INTERPRETATION OF COURT'S ROLE, PROBLEMS, AND ACHIEVE-
MENTS. DISCUSSES BUSINESS OF COURT, ITS CLEAVAGES, AND THE
MEANING OF LIBERALISM ON THE BENCH. SPECIAL ATTENTION GIVEN
TO ISSUES OF FEDERALISM AND CIVIL LIBERTIES AS PRESENTED FOR
RESOLUTION; DISCUSSES ROLE OF COUNSEL IN CONSTITUTIONAL
LITIGATION.

0798 FRIED R.C.
COMPARATIVE POLITICAL INSTITUTIONS.
NEW YORK: MACMILLAN, 1966, 152 PP., LC#66-17389.
VOLUME ONE IN SERIES "GOVERNMENT IN THE MODERN WORLD."
ANALYZES EXECUTIVES, LEGISLATURES, COURTS, BUREAUCRA-
CIES, ARMED FORCES, POLITICAL PARTIES, AND ELECTORATES.
EACH CHAPTER CONSIDERS POTENTIAL SOURCES OF POWER AND WEAK-
NESS, TREATED UNDER UNIFORM SET OF 12 CATEGORIES.

0799 FRIEDHEIM R.
"THE 'SATISFIED' AND 'DISSATISFIED' STATES NEGOTIATE
INTERNATIONAL LAW* A CASE STUDY."
WORLD POLITICS, 18 (OCT. 65).
UN CONFERENCES ON THE LAW OF THE SEA, 1958-1960, EXAM-
INED TO ILLUSTRATE DIFFICULTIES IN CREATING A LAW OF COMMON
CONSENT, AND IN EMPLOYING LAW AS ROAD TO PEACE. CONFERENCE
DEBATES ANALYZED TO EMPHASIZE IMPORTANT DIFFERENCES IN
ATTITUDES TOWARDS SUBSTANTIVE CONTENT OF THE LAW, TOWARDS
THE NATURE OF THE INTERNATIONAL SYSTEM, AND ON PROPER MEANS
OF NEGOTIATING LAW IN UN-SPONSORED CONFERENCE.

0800 FRIEDMAN L. ED.
SOUTHERN JUSTICE.
NEW YORK: PANTHEON BOOKS, 1965, 306 PP., LC#65-14581.
ANTHOLOGY OF ARTICLES BY LAWYERS INVOLVED IN CIVIL
RIGHTS CASES IN THE SOUTH. ARTICLES DEAL WITH SPECIFIC
PHASE OF ADMINISTRATION OF JUSTICE IN SOUTH: HOW LEGAL
INSTITUTIONS HAVE BEEN USED AGAINST NEGRO STRUGGLE FOR
CIVIL RIGHTS AND WHAT HAS BEEN DONE TO END THIS LEGAL
ABUSE.

0801 FRIEDMAN W. ED.
THE PUBLIC CORPORATION: A COMPARATIVE SYMPOSIUM (UNIVERSITY
OF TORONTO SCHOOL OF LAW COMPARATIVE LAW SERIES, VOL. I)
TORONTO: CARSWELL, 1954, 612 PP.
CONCERNS LEGAL STATUS AND ORGANIZATION OF THE PUBLIC
CORPORATION. INCLUDES 14 ESSAYS ON THE PUBLIC CORPORATION
IN AUSTRALIA, CANADA, FRANCE, GERMANY, ENGLAND, INDIA,
ISRAEL, ITALY, NEW ZEALAND, SOUTH AFRICA, SWEDEN, US, USSR;
STUDIES OF LEGAL RELATIONS OF A NATIONALIZED INDUSTRY
(BRITAIN'S NATIONAL COAL BOARD) AND AN INTERNATIONAL PUBLIC
CORPORATION; AND A FINAL COMPARATIVE ANALYSIS.

0802 FRIEDMANN W.
LAW AND SOCIAL CHANGE IN CONTEMPORARY BRITAIN.
LONDON: STEVENS, 1951, 322 PP.
SHOWS PATTERN OF LEGAL DEVELOPMENT AS INFLUENCED BY
SOCIAL BACKGROUND. FOCUSES ON LEGAL AND SOCIAL DEVELOPMENTS
IN UK, WITH COMPARATIVE REFERENCES TO OTHER COMMON LAW
SYSTEMS. BEGINS WITH COMMON LAW IN CHANGING SOCIETY, THEN
DISCUSSES PLACE OF PUBLIC LAW IN CONTEMPORARY ENGLISH
JURISPRUDENCE. COVERS STATUTE LAW AND WELFARE STATE.
CONCLUDES WITH WELFARE STATE AND RULE OF LAW.

0803 FRIEDMANN W.G.
LAW IN A CHANGING SOCIETY.
LONDON: STEVENS, 1959, 522 PP.
    ASSUMES THAT LAW MUST RESPOND TO SOCIAL CHANGE TO FULFILL
FUNCTION AS PARAMOUNT INSTRUMENT OF SOCIAL ORDER. DISCUSSES
THE INTERRELATION OF LEGAL AND SOCIAL CHANGE. ANALYZES THE
IMPACT OF SOCIAL CHANGE ON THE PRINCIPLE LEGAL INSTITUTIONS:
PROPERTY, CONTRACT, TORT, CRIMINAL LAW AND FAMILY LAW. ALSO
TRACES IMPACT ON LEGAL IDEOLOGIES, ON INTERNATIONAL INSTITU-
TIONS AND RELATIONS.

0804 FRIEDMANN W.G.
"THE USES OF 'GENERAL PRINCIPLES' IN THE DEVELOPMENT
OF INTERNATIONAL LAW."
AMER. J. INT. LAW, 57 (APRIL 63), 279-299.
    DISCUSSES THE CHANGING TRENDS IN INTERNATIONAL LAW. SINCE
THERE IS GENERAL DISAGREEMENT ON MANIFEST CONTENT OF NATURAL
LAW, THE 'GENERAL PRINCIPLES OF LAW RECOGNIZED BY CIVILIZED
NATIONS' PLAY AN INCREASING ROLE IN INTERNATIONAL CONDUCT.
PURPOSE IS TO REAFFIRM THE USE OF 'PRINCIPLES' ON A
PRAGMATIC BASIS.

0805 FRIEDMANN W.G.
THE CHANGING STRUCTURE OF INTERNATIONAL LAW.
NEW YORK: COLUMB. PR., 1964, 410 PP., $8.75.
    ANALYZES CHANGES IN STRUCTURE OF INTERNATIONAL RELATIONS
THAT, IN TURN, HAVE AFFECTED INTERNATIONAL LAW. STRESSES
DISTINCTION BETWEEN LAW OF COEXISTENCE AND LAW OF COOPERA-
TION. DEFINES PRINCIPLES AND PROCESSES OF LEGAL CHANGE IN
FIELD AND POINTS TO MANY FIELDS PREVIOUSLY CONCERN OF MUNI-
CIPAL LAW, NOW CONCERN OF INTERNATIONAL LAW.

0806 FRIEDMANN W.G., KALMANOFF G., MEAGHER R.F.
INTERNATIONAL FINANCIAL AID.
NEW YORK: COLUMBIA U PRESS, 1966, 498 PP., LC#66-20494.
    DESCRIBES MAGNITUDE AND CHARACTERISTICS OF INTERNATIONAL
FINANCIAL AID: METHODS AND POLICIES OF DONOR COUNTRIES AND
INTERNATIONAL INSTITUTIONS, CASE STUDIES OF RECIPIENT COUN-
TRIES AND MULTI-NATIONAL PROJECTS. POLICY ISSUES OF PLANNING
REQUIREMENTS, LOANS VERSUS GRANTS, AND TIED AID, DISCUSSED.
STATISTICS PRESENTED AND TRENDS PREDICTED.

0807 FRIEDRICH C.J.
"AUTHORITY, REASON AND DISCRETION" IN C. FRIEDRICH'S
AUTHORITY (BMR)"
CAMBRIDGE: HARVARD U PR, 1958.
    DISCUSSES PHENOMENA WHICH HELP EXPLAIN WHY AUTHORITY IS
NECESSARY PART OF ALL HUMAN RELATIONSHIPS AND COMMUNITIES.
ANALYZES REASONS WHY DISCRETION IS INDISPENSABLE IN ALL
POLITICAL AND LEGAL SYSTEMS. EXAMINES RELATION OF DISCRETION
TO THE RATIONAL ASPECT OF AUTHORITY.

0808 FRIEDRICH C.J. ED.
NOMOS V: THE PUBLIC INTEREST.
NEW YORK: ATHERTON PRESS, 1962, 256 PP., LC#62-19400.
    ESSAYS TREAT VARIOUS ASPECTS AND APPROACH SUBJECT FROM
DIVERSE VIEWS, INCLUDING PHILOSOPHICAL. MAJORITY OF ARTICLES
DEFINE TERM AND REFUTE CONTEMPORARY EXPLANATIONS.

0809 FRIEDRICH C.J. ED., CHAPMAN J.W. ED.
JUSTICE: NOMOS VI.
NEW YORK: LIBERAL ARTS PR, 1963, 325 PP., LC#63-19057.
    NATURE OF JUSTICE AND HOW IT HAS RELATED TO OTHER
CONCEPTS, SUCH AS LIBERTY AND LAW, AND TO OTHER PHILOSO-
PHIES, SUCH AS MARXISM AND UTILITARIANISM, IS DISCUSSED.

0810 FRIEDRICH C.J.
MAN AND HIS GOVERNMENT: AN EMPIRICAL THEORY OF POLITICS.
NEW YORK: MCGRAW HILL, 1963, 737 PP., LC#63-15892.
    LOOKS AT POLITICAL EXPERIENCE OF MANKIND IN ORDER TO SEE
WHAT CONTRIBUTES TO POLITICAL ORDER AND THE GOOD LIFE AND
WHAT DETRACTS. CONSIDERS POLITICAL PERSON AND POLITICAL ACT;
DIMENSIONS OF POWER; JUSTICE; EQUALITY; FREEDOM;
GOVERNING PROCESSES; MODES OF OPERATION; AND RANGE AND
LEVELS OF GOVERNMENT.

0811 FRIENDLY A., GOLDFARB R.L.
CRIME AND PUBLICITY.
NEW YORK: TWENTIETH CENT FUND, 1967, 335 PP., LC#67-15891.
    CONSIDERS ISSUES OF FREE PRESS AND FAIR TRIAL IN THE US.
FEELS CURBS SHOULD NOT BE IMPOSED ON PRESS TO PREVENT PUBLI-
CATION OF MATERIAL PREJUDICIAL TO DEFENDANT. MORE PROMISING
IS AVENUE OF SELF-RESTRAINT ON PART OF COURTS AND LAW-EN-
FORCEMENT MACHINERY IN NOT GIVING OUT PREJUDICIAL INFORMA-
TION. STRESSES ROLE OF PRESS AS "PUBLIC WATCHDOG."

0812 FROEBEL J.
THEORIE DER POLITIK, ALS ERGEBNIS EINER ERNEUERTEN PRUEFUNG
DEMOKRATISCHER LEHRMEINUNGEN.
VIENNA: DRUCK UND VERLAG, 1861, 334 PP.
    PRESENTS A THEORY OF POLITICS UNDERSTOOD AS RECIPROCAL
ACTION BETWEEN FACTS AND THE DEMANDS OF JUSTICE AND FREEDOM.
THE FIRST OF TWO PROJECTED VOLUMES, IT FOCUSES ON THE CLAIMS
OF JUSTICE AND FREEDOM, CONSIDERING POLITICS IN ITS RELATION
TO NATURAL, ETHICAL, AND RELIGIOUS VIEWS OF THE WORLD;
TREATS JUSTICE AND FREEDOM IN VARIOUS RELATIONSHIPS SUCH

AS LAW, THE STATE, SOVEREIGNTY, CHURCH, PEOPLE, PARTIES.

0813 FROMAN L.A. JR.
PEOPLE AND POLITICS: AN ANALYSIS OF THE AMERICAN POLITICAL
SYSTEM.
ENGLEWOOD CLIFFS: PRENTICE HALL, 1962, LC#62-19420.
    THEORIZES ON POLITICS. EXPLAINS AMERICAN POLITICS AS THE
DISTRIBUTION OF ADVANTAGES AND DISADVANTAGES AMONG PEOPLE
ON BASIS OF DIFFERENCES IN PEOPLE AND THEIR RESOURCES AND
DIFFERENCES IN DECISION-MAKING PROCESSES. DISCUSSES POLITICS
IN ITS RELATION TO THE INDIVIDUAL, TO GROUP, TO DECISION-
MAKING, TO CONGRESS, PRESIDENT, ELECTIONS, SUPREME COURT,
POLITICAL PARTIES, INTEREST GROUPS, AND PAYOFF DISTRIBUTION.

0814 FRYDENSBERG P. ED.
PEACE-KEEPING: EXPERIENCE AND EVALUATION: THE OSLO
PAPERS.
OSLO: NORWEGIAN INST OF INT AFF, 1964, 339 PP.
    CONTAINS REPORT OF STUDY COMMISSION SET UP BY NORWE-
GIAN INSTITUTE OF INTERNATIONAL AFFAIRS AND ITS STRATEGIC
STUDY GROUP IN 1961. VOLUME CONTAINS SECTIONS ON POLITI-
CAL AND PHILOSOPHICAL PROBLEMS; CENTRAL PLANNING OF
OPERATIONS; REGIONAL COMMAND, EARMARKING AND TRAINING;
AND LEGAL QUESTIONS INVOLVED IN UN CONFLICT MANAGEMENT.

0815 FRYE R.J.
HOUSING AND URBAN RENEWAL IN ALABAMA.
UNIVERSITY: U ALA, BUR PUBL ADM, 1965, 103 PP.
    DISCUSSES RELATIONSHIPS BETWEEN FEDERAL AND CITY GOVERN-
MENTS IN SPHERE OF URBAN RENEWAL, EMPHASIZING HISTORICAL AND
LEGAL FRAMEWORK OF PROGRAM, ORGANIZATIONAL ARRANGEMENTS AT
BOTH LEVELS FOR IMPLEMENTATION OF PROGRAMS, PROGRAM CONTENT,
AND PROCESSES THROUGH WHICH INTERGOVERNMENTAL ASPECTS OF THE
PROGRAMS MANIFEST THEMSELVES.

0816 FUCHS R.F.
"FAIRNESS AND EFFECTIVENESS IN ADMINISTRATIVE AGENCY
ORGANIZATION AND PROCEDURES."
INDIANA LAW J., 36 (FALL 60), 1-50.
    REFORM OF ORGANIZATION AND PROCEDURES SHOULD BE MADE TO
FURTHER PROTECT INDIVIDUAL RIGHTS AND THE PUBLIC INTEREST
AND TO INCREASE EFFICIENCY. ON THE WHOLE, ADMINISTRATIVE
AGENCIES HAVE GREATLY IMPROVED IN THESE AREAS IN RECENT
YEARS.

0817 FUCHS W.P. ED.
STAAT UND KIRCHE IM WANDEL DER JAHRHUNDERTE.
STUTTGART: KOHLHAMMER VERLAG, 1966, 219 PP.
    ESSAYS ON CHURCH-STATE RELATION IN CONTINENTAL EUROPE
AND ENGLAND FROM AGE OF CONSTANTINE TO PRESENT. EXAM-
INES RISE OF POLITICAL FREEDOM, NONCONFORMISM IN ENGLAND,
CHRISTIAN CHURCH AND MODERN DEMOCRACY, ETC.

0818 FULBRIGHT J.W.
OLD MYTHS AND NEW REALITIES.
NEW YORK: RANDOM HOUSE, INC, 1964, 147 PP., LC#64-22439.
    ESSAYS BASED ON SPEECHES MADE BY THE SENATOR IN 1963 ON
CHANGES IN NATURE OF COLD WAR, NATIONAL SECURITY, ATLANTIC
PARTNERSHIP, AND US PUBLIC OPINION ON INTERNATIONAL ISSUES.

0819 FULLER G.A. ED.
DEMOBILIZATION: A SELECTED LIST OF REFERENCES.
WASHINGTON: LIBRARY OF CONGRESS, 1945, 193 PP.
    COMPILES A LIST OF SELECTED REFERENCES ON DEMOBILIZATION
FROM BOOKS, PAMPHLETS, AND ARTICLES WRITTEN 1943-45.
MATERIAL IS ARRANGED IN FIVE AREAS: GENERAL TREATISES, DE-
MOBILIZATION OF ARMED FORCES, INDUSTRIAL DEMOBILIZATION, DE-
MOBILIZATION OF ECONOMIC CONTROLS, AND AGRICULTURE IN THE
TRANSITIONAL PERIOD. 1,222 ENTRIES.

0820 FULLER G.H. ED.
A SELECTED LIST OF RECENT REFERENCES ON THE CONSTITUTION OF
THE UNITED STATES (PAMPHLET)
WASHINGTON: LIBRARY OF CONGRESS, 1940, 50 PP.
    CONTAINS 434 ENTRIES, MOST WRITTEN 1930-40, OF ARTICLES,
BOOKS, AND BIBLIOGRAPHIES RELATING TO THE PHILOSOPHICAL
BASIS AND HISTORICAL DEVELOPMENT OF THE US CONSTITUTION.
COMPILED FOR LIBRARY OF CONGRESS.

0821 FULLER G.H. ED.
DEFENSE FINANCING: A SUPPLEMENTARY LIST OF REFERENCES
(PAMPHLET)
WASHINGTON: LIBRARY OF CONGRESS, 1942, 45 PP.
    CONTAINS 451 LISTINGS OF BOOKS AND ARTICLES SUPPLEMENTING
1941 BIBLIOGRAPHY "DEFENSE FINANCING." HAS SEPARATE CLASSI-
FICATIONS FOR US, UK, CANADA, AUSTRALIA, AND MISCELLANEOUS.
MANY LISTINGS ARE CONGRESSIONAL DISCUSSIONS AND REPORTS.

0822 FULLER G.H. ED.
MILITARY GOVERNMENT: A LIST OF REFERENCES (A PAMPHLET)
WASHINGTON: LIBRARY OF CONGRESS, 1944, 14 PP.
    CONTAINS 122 ENTRIES OF ARTICLES IN FRENCH, GERMAN, AND
ENGLISH CONCERNING LEGAL, ADMINISTRATIVE, AND SOCIOLOGICAL
PROBLEMS INVOLVED IN MILITARY JURISDICTION IN OCCUPIED
COUNTRIES. COMPILED FOR LIBRARY OF CONGRESS.

0823 FULLER G.H. ED.
RENEGOTIATION OF WAR CONTRACTS: A SELECTED LIST OF
REFERENCES (PAMPHLET)
WASHINGTON: LIBRARY OF CONGRESS, 1944, 18 PP.
LISTS 176 ARTICLES DEALING WITH LEGAL AND ECONOMIC AS-
PECTS OF RENEGOTIATING WAR CONTRACTS AFTER WORLD WAR II.
MOST ARTICLES FROM LEGAL REVIEWS AND CONGRESSIONAL RECORDS.

0824 FULLER G.H. ED.
TURKEY: A SELECTED LIST OF REFERENCES.
WASHINGTON: LIBRARY OF CONGRESS, 1944, 114 PP.
CONTAINS 916 LISTINGS OF BOOKS AND ARTICLES, MOST PUB-
LISHED 1930-44, DEALING WITH MANY ASPECTS OF MODERN AND
HISTORICAL TURKEY, INCLUDING GEOGRAPHY, GEOLOGY, POLITICAL
HISTORY, ECONOMIC AND SOCIAL CONDITIONS, ART AND LETTERS.
INCLUDES LISTING OF MAPS AND OTHER BIBLIOGRAPHIES. MANY
ENTRIES IN FRENCH AND GERMAN.

0825 GABRIEL P.P.
THE INTERNATIONAL TRANSFER OF CORPORATE SKILLS: MANAGEMENT
CONTRACTS IN LESS DEVELOPED COUNTRIES.
CAMBRIDGE: HARVARD BUS SCHOOL, 1967, 230 PP., LC#66-28809.
AUTHOR ARGUES THAT SKILLS UNDERDEVELOPED NATIONS NEED
TO IMPORT FROM THE ADVANCED ECONOMIES CANNOT BE DETACHED
FROM THE FIRMS POSSESSING THEM, AND THAT FIRMS IN DEVELOPED
AREAS SHOULD BE CONTRACTED TO MANAGE NEWLY ESTABLISHED
FOREIGN INDUSTRIES. DISCUSSES DEPENDENCE OF UNDERDEVELOPED
NATIONS ON THE WEST'S SKILLS WITHIN THE CONTEXT OF CON-
TRACTING MANAGEMENT TO SUPERVISE FOREIGN INDUSTRY.

0826 GAJENDRAGADKAR P.B.
LAW, LIBERTY AND SOCIAL JUSTICE.
NEW YORK: ASIA PUBL HOUSE, 1965, 159 PP.
DISCUSSES HINDU RELATION TO MODERN LAW AND NOTIONS OF
FREEDOM IN INDIA. STUDIES PROSPECT OF SOCIO-ECONOMIC PLAN-
NING'S INTERFERING WITH PERSONAL LIBERTY, AND MEANS OF HARM-
ONIOUS ADJUSTMENT.

0827 GALENSON W. ED.
TRADE UNIONS MONOGRAPH SERIES (A SERIES OF NINE TEXTS)
NEW YORK: JOHN WILEY, 1962.
SERIES FOCUSING ON ASPECTS OF DEMOCRATIC GOVERNMENT
WITHIN MAJOR LABOR UNIONS. EXAMINATION OF CONSTITUTIONS,
VOTING PROCEDURES, CONVENTIONS, AND LEADERSHIP. SO FAR, NINE
MONOGRAPHS, BY THE CENTER FOR THE STUDY OF DEMOCRATIC
INSTITUTIONS.

0828 GALLAGHER J.F.
SUPERVISORIAL DISTRICTING IN CALIFORNIA COUNTIES: 1960-1963
(PAMPHLET)
BERKELEY: U CAL, INST GOVT STUD, 1963, 48 PP.
EXAMINES EFFORTS OF CALIFORNIA CITIZENS AND PUBLIC OFFI-
CIALS TO BRING ABOUT REAPPORTIONMENT OF COUNTY SUPERVISORIAL
DISTRICTS. FOCUSES ON A 1963 OPINION BY CALIFORNIA SUPREME
COURT DIRECTING BOARD OF SUPERVISORS FROM MONTEREY COUNTY TO
REDRAW SUPERVISORIAL DISTRICTS TOWARD EQUALITY OF POPULAR
REPRESENTATION.

0829 GALLOWAY E. ED.
ABSTRACTS OF POSTWAR LITERATURE (VOL. IV) JAN.-JULY, 1945
NOS. 901-1074.
WASHINGTON: LIBRARY OF CONGRESS, 1945.
LAST VOLUME IN SERIES ENTITLED POSTWAR ABSTRACTS. CON-
TAINS ABSTRACTS OF 174 SELECTED BOOKS, PAMPHLETS, AND PE-
RIODICALS DEALING WITH A VARIETY OF POSTWAR PROBLEMS, NA-
TIONAL AND INTERNATIONAL.

0830 GANDOLFI A.
"REFLEXIONS SUR L'IMPOT DE CAPITATION EN AFRIQUE NOIRE."
REV. JURID. POLIT. OUTREMER, 16 (APR.-JUNE 62), 235-252.
STUDIES THE POLL-TAX: GOALS TO BE ACHIEVED THROUGH ITS
USE AND METHODS OF INSTITUTING IT. RELATES GOALS TO ECONOMIC
AND POLITICAL PROBLEMS OF DEVELOPING AFRICAN COUNTRIES, FO-
CUSING ON SENEGAL AND GHANA. STUDIES STRUCTURE OF LOCAL
ADMINISTRATIVE BOARDS.

0831 GANJI M.
INTERNATIONAL PROTECTION OF HUMAN RIGHTS.
GENEVA: LIBRAIRIE DROZ, 1962, 310 PP.
COMPARATIVE STUDY EMPHASIZES HUMANITARIAN INTERVENTION,
SLAVERY, AND EUROPEAN CONVENTION ON HUMAN RIGHTS. INCLUDES
UNIVERSAL RIGHTS DECLARATION, DRAFTING OF COVENANTS, AND
IMPLEMENTATION MEASURES.

0832 GANZ G.
"THE CONTROL OF INDUSTRY BY ADMINISTRATIVE PROCESS."
PUBLIC LAW, (SUMMER 67), 93-106.
ASSESSES SUITABILITY OF INDUSTRIAL DEVELOPMENT ACT OF
1966 AND LOCAL EMPLOYMENT ACT OF 1960 AND ADMINISTRATIVE
MACHINERY THEY PROVIDE FOR IMPLEMENTING GOVERNMENT POLICY IN
RELATION TO INDUSTRY. EXAMINES EXTENT OF PROTECTION OF
INDIVIDUALS UNDER TWO LAWS. SHOWS MOVEMENT AWAY FROM LEGAL
CONTROL OVER INDUSTRY TO ADMINISTRATIVE CONTROL.

0833 GARCIA ROBLES A.
THE DENUCLEARIZATION OF LATIN AMERICA (TRANS. BY MARJORIE

URQUIDI)
NEW YORK: TAPLINGER PUBL CO, 1967, 167 PP.
COLLECTION OF SPEECHES BY AUTHOR AND OF INTERNATIONAL
DOCUMENTS TREATING ORIGINS, SCOPE, AND OBJECTIVES OF
DENUCLEARIZATION PLANS IN LATIN AMERICA. MOST IMPORTANT
EVENTS LEADING TO WORLD-WIDE TREATY ARE JOINT DECLARATION OF
1963, UN RESOLUTION 1911, FORMATION OF PREPARATORY
COMMISSION OF DENUCLEARIZATION IN LATIN AMERICA AND ITS
FIRST THREE SESSIONS.

0834 GARCON M.
LETTRE OUVERTE A LA JUSTICE.
PARIS: MICHEL, EDITIONS ALBIN, 1966, 142 PP.
FIRST OF SERIES OF "LETTERS," WRITTEN BY NOTABLE FRENCH
LITERARY FIGURES, ATTACKING DIFFERENT EVILS IN SOCIETY.
WRITTEN AS GROUP OF FIVE LETTERS TO "JUSTICE." ATTACKS
SLOWNESS OF JUDICIAL PROCESS; GOVERNMENT FOR NOT UPHOLDING
JUSTICE; SUGGESTIONS THAT JUDICIARY MAKE USE OF SCIENTIFIC
PROCEDURES AND DEVICES; AND LAWYERS FOR VARIOUS PRACTICES,
SUCH AS WAY IN WHICH THEY OFTEN EXACT PAYMENT.

0835 GARDINER H.C.
CATHOLIC VIEWPOINT ON CENSORSHIP.
NEW YORK: HANOVER HOUSE, 1958, 192 PP., LC#58-6641.
EXPLANATION OF ROMAN CATHOLIC CHURCH ATTITUDE ON QUESTION
OF CENSORSHIP. DISCUSSES CONCEPT OF FREEDOM AND LEGAL RIGHTS
AS WELL AS AUTHORITY AND COERCION IN CONCEPT OF CENSORSHIP.
STUDIES US CENSORSHIP CONTROVERSY IN LEGAL ASPECTS AND IN
ACTIVITIES OF PRESSURE GROUPS TO RESOLVE QUESTION.

0836 GARDNER L.C.
ECONOMIC ASPECTS OF NEW DEAL DIPLOMACY.
MADISON: U. WISC. PR., 1964, 409 PP., $7.50.
INDICATES THAT THE NEW DEAL'S APPROACH TO FOREIGN
POLICY WAS AS MUCH SHAPED BY OLDER PRINCIPLES AND TRADI-
TIONS AS BY ANY INITIATED BY FDR. DISCUSSES THE ECONOMIC
ORIENTATION OF THE GOOD NEIGHBOR POLICY, THE ROLE OF
CORDELL HULL, AND THE INFLUENCE OF SUCH FINANCIERS AS
THOMAS LAMONT, NORMAN H. DAVIS, AND WILL CLAYTON.

0837 GARDNER R.N.
"COOPERATION IN OUTER SPACE."
FOR. AFF., 41 (JAN. 63), 344-59.
DEALS WITH COOPERATION IN OUTER SPACE AFFAIRS ON A BI-
LATERAL AND WORLD-WIDE BASIS FOR ULTIMATE ATTAINMENT OF
WORLD PEACE. PRESENT UN ACTIVITIES REVEAL MULTITUDE OF CO-
OPERATIVE PROJECTS DESPITE WHAT IS FELT TO BE OBSTRUCTIVE
EFFORTS BY USSR.

0838 GARDNER R.N.
"THE SOVIET UNION AND THE UNITED NATIONS."
LAW CONTEMP. PROBL., 29 (AUTUMN 64), 845-57.
DELINEATES BASIC INCOMPATIBILITIES BETWEEN COMMUNIST DOC-
TRINES AND PRINCIPLES OF THE UNITED NATIONS' CHARTER AS WELL
AS THE ACTUAL DISAGREEMENTS BETWEEN THE SOVIET UNION AND THE
WORLD ORGANIZATION.

0839 GARDNER R.N.
IN PURSUIT OF WORLD ORDER* US FOREIGN POLICY AND INTER-
NATIONAL ORGANIZATIONS.
NEW YORK: FREDERICK PRAEGER, 1964, 263 PP., LC#64-25587.
A HISTORY OF POSTWAR SUCCESS AT INTERNATIONAL COOPERA-
TION IN THE UN'S POLITICAL BODIES AND SPECIALIZED AGENCIES.
THE GOALS AND ALTERNATIVES FOR AMERICAN POLICY IN INTER-
NATIONAL PEACEKEEPING AND THE MULITLATERAL PROVISION OF
WORLD WELFARE HERE DISCUSSED WERE OFTEN THE PRODUCT OF THE
AUTHOR'S EFFORTS IN THE DEPARTMENT OF STATE.

0840 GARNER U.F.
ADMINISTRATIVE LAW.
LONDON, WASH, DC: BUTTERWORTHS, 1963, 408 PP.
DISCUSSES PROBLEMS FO LAW IN RELATION TO ADMINISTRATION,
INCLUDING POWERS OF CENTRAL GOVERNMENT, LEGISLATURE, REDRESS
OF GRIEVANCES, PUBLIC CORPORATIONS AND LOCAL AUTHORITIES.
BASED ON ENGLISH LAW.

0841 GASS O.
"THE LITERATURE OF AMERICAN GOVERNMENT."
COMMENTARY, 41 (JUNE 66), 67-72.
AUTHOR SEES BEST AND MOST ILLUMINATING BOOKS ON AMERICAN
GOVERNMENT AS PROFESSEDLY FRAGMENTARY ONES. HE CITES KEY'S
"THE RESPONSIBLE ELECTORATE," B. SCHWARTZ'S, "THE RIGHTS OF
PROPERTY," G.MCCONNELL'S, "PRIVATE POWER AND AMERICAN
DEMOCRACY," C.A. BEARD'S, "AN ECONOMIC INTERPRETATION OF THE
CONSTITUTION OF THE UNITED STATES," AND A.S. LINK'S
MULTI-VOLUMED WORK ON WILSON'S PRESIDENCY.

0842 GEERTZ C. ED.
OLD SOCIETIES AND NEW STATES: THE QUEST FOR MODERNITY IN
ASIA AND AFRICA.
NEW YORK: FREE PRESS OF GLENCOE, 1963, 310 PP., LC#63-8416.
STUDIES POLITICAL DEVELOPMENT IN STATES WHICH HAVE
ACHIEVED INDEPENDENCE SINCE 1945. INCLUDES COMPARATIVE
STUDIES OF NEW STATES; CULTURAL POLICY; POLITICAL RELIGION;
THE INTEGRATIVE REVOLUTION; EQUALITY, MODERNITY
AND CIVIL POLITICS; PROBLEMS OF LAW IN AFRICA; ROLE OF

EDUCATION DEVELOPMENT; AND POLITICAL SOCIALIZATION AND CULTURE CHANGE.

0843 GELLER M.A.
ADVERTISING AT THE CROSSROADS: FEDERAL REGULATION VS. VOLUNTARY CONTROLS.
NEW YORK: RONALD PRESS, 1952, 335 PP., LC#52-9274.
DISCUSSES MEDIA OF ADVERTISING AND QUESTION OF FEDERAL REGULATION VS. VOLUNTARY CONTROLS IN THIS FIELD REGARDING POSTAL SERVICE, NETWORK, AND FALSE ADVERTISING. INCLUDES EXAMPLE OF FTC STIPULATION AND KEY EXCERPTS FROM TV CODE OF NATIONAL BROADCASTERS AND BRITISH VOLUNTARY LIMITATION OF ADVERTISING. BIBLIOGRAPHY OF BOOKS AND PERIODICALS IN FIELD OF CONTROLS.

0844 GELLHORN W.
FEDERAL ADMINISTRATIVE PROCEEDINGS.
BALTIMORE: JOHNS HOPKINS PRESS, 1941, 150 PP.
HOLDS THAT ADMINISTRATIVE ADJUDICATIVE PROCEDURES ARE DEMOCRATIC, EFFICIENT, AND GENERALLY REPRESENT THE PUBLIC INTEREST. INTEREST GROUPS ARE STRONGLY REPRESENTED IN ADMINISTRATIVE PROCEEDINGS THROUGH INFORMAL RELATIONS BETWEEN ADMINISTRATIVE OFFICERS AND INTEREST GROUP REPRESENTATIVES.

0845 GELLHORN W. ED.
THE STATES AND SUBVERSION.
ITHACA: CORNELL U. PR., 1952, 454 PP.
STUDY OF GOVERNMENTAL PROGRAMS IN CALIFORNIA, ILLINOIS, CATES DISTRUST OF COMMUNITY FREEDOM. DESCRIBES STATUTES RELATED TO SUBVERSIVE ACTIVITY.

0846 GELLHORN W.
AMERICAN RIGHTS: THE CONSTITUTION IN ACTION.
NEW YORK: MACMILLAN, 1960, 232 PP., LC#60-5408.
DISCUSSES APPLICATION OF CONSTITUTION BY SUPREME COURT IN CASES RELATING TO FREE SPEECH, FREEDOM OF MOVEMENT, AND DESEGREGATION OF PUBLIC SCHOOLS. CENTERS ON GOVERNMENTAL INVASIONS OF FREE SPEECH AND ACTION.

0847 GELLHORN W.
OMBUDSMEN AND OTHERS: CITIZENS' PROTECTORS IN NINE COUNTRIES
CAMBRIDGE: HARVARD U PR, 1967, 448 PP., LC#66-23465.
STUDIES INSTITUTION OF OMBUDSMAN, REPRESENTATIVE OF PEOPLE IN CASES OF GOVERNMENTAL INJUSTICE. INCLUDES COUNTRIES OF DENMARK, FINLAND, NEW ZEALAND, NORWAY, SWEDEN, YUGOSLAVIA, POLAND, USSR, AND JAPAN. APPLIES FINDINGS TO DEVELOPMENT OF SUCH AN INSTITUTION IN US.

0848 GENTILI A.
DE LEGATIONIBUS.
NEW YORK: OXFORD U. PR., 1924, 198 PP.
SIXTEENTH CENTURY EMBRYONIC STUDY IN INTERNATIONAL LAW QUESTIONING THE RIGHT OF LEGATION FOR EXCOMMUNICATED PERSONS. DEFINES RELIGION AS AN EXCLUSIVE PERSONAL RELATIONSHIP TO GOD AND CONCLUDES THAT THE RIGHT OF LEGATION THUS REMAINS INTACT DESPITE RELIGIOUS DIFFERENCES.

0849 GENTILI A., SCOTT J.B. ED.
DE JURE BELLI, LIBRI TRES (1612) (VOL. 2)
LONDON: OXFORD U PR, 1933, 479 PP.
DISCUSSES WAR IN GENERAL, WHO MAY MAKE IT, AND WHAT CAUSES JUSTIFY IT. TREATS LAWFUL WAY OF CONDUCTING WAR; DECLARATIONS OF WAR; ACTS FORBIDDEN AND PERMITTED; TREATMENT OF ENEMY, PRISONERS, AND HOSTAGES; AND CONCLUSION OF TRUCES. DISCUSSES CONCLUSION OF WAR, RIGHTS OF OCCUPATION, AND ESTABLISHMENT OF PEACE. ATTEMPTS TO ESTABLISH BASIS FOR LAWS ON FACT RATHER THAN ABSTRACT OR THEOLOGICAL IDEAS.

0850 GERHARD H.
"COMMODITY TRADE STABILIZATION THROUGH INTERNATIONAL AGREEMENTS."
LAW CONTEMP. PROBL., 28 (SPRING 63), 276-293.
ADVOCATES A STRONGER SYSTEM OF INTERNATIONAL AGREEMENTS TO STABILIZE COMMODITY TRADING SUGGESTING THE MULTILATERAL USE OF GOVERNMENT ACTION IN FORM OF BUFFER-STOCK SCHEMES AND LONG-RUN PURCHASE CONTRACTS. ALSO CONCERNED WITH PRICE STABILIZATION AND THE MEANS BY WHICH IT CAN BE ATTAINED.

0851 GERTH H.
"THE NAZI PARTY: ITS LEADERSHIP AND COMPOSITION" (BMR)"
AMER. J. OF SOCIOLOGY, 45 (JAN. 40), 517-541.
EXPLAINS NAZI PARTY AS A FUSION OF TWO TYPES OF DOMINATION: CHARISMATIC AND BUREAUCRATIC. STATES THAT THERE IS NO PARTY DEMOCRACY BECAUSE ALL AUTHORITY EMANATES FROM THE LEADER. FINDS GREAT PERCENTAGE OF MEMBERS ARE MIDDLE CLASS AND/OR YOUNG. SHOWS THAT NEW BUREAUCRACY IS LESS RIGID THAN OLD PRUSSIAN SYSTEM BECAUSE OF ARBITRARY CONDUCT OF THE POLICE, JUDICIAL, AND ECONOMIC DEPARTMENTS.

0852 GERWIG R.
"PUBLIC AUTHORITIES IN THE UNITED STATES."
LAW AND CONTEMPORARY PROB., 26 (FALL 61), 591-618.
DISCUSSES THE DEFINITION OF PUBLIC AUTHORITIES, THEIR HISTORICAL DEVELOPMENT, THEIR STRUCTURE, SOME LEGAL ASPECTS, THE FUNDING, BOND ISSUING AND TAXING POWERS OF AUTHORITIES, AND THEIR SOVEREIGN IMMUNITY AND TORT LIABILITY.

0853 GESELLSCHAFT RECHTSVERGLEICH
BIBLIOGRAPHIE DES DEUTSCHEN RECHTS (BIBLIOGRAPHY OF GERMAN LAW, TRANS. BY COURTLAND PETERSON)
KARLSRVHE: VERLAG CF MULLER, 1964, 584 PP.
ANALYTIC AND THOROUGHLY CATEGORIZED BIBLIOGRAPHY OF WORKS, DOCUMENTS, STUDIES, TEXTS, ETC., INVOLVING GERMAN LAW. INCLUDES A LENGTHY INTRODUCTION BY PROFESSOR FRITZ BAUR ELUCIDATING GERMAN LAW AND LEGAL PROCEDURES SINCE 1949. BILINGUAL EDITION WITH ENGLISH AND GERMAN ANNOTATION.

0854 GHOSH P.K.
THE CONSTITUTION OF INDIA: HOW IT HAS BEEN FRAMED.
CALCUTTA: WORLD PRESS LTD, 1966, 427 PP.
PRESENTS HISTORICAL BACKGROUND OF INDIAN CONSTITUTION. NARRATES CONTEMPORARY POLITICAL EVENTS, SHOWING HOW THEY INFLUENCED DELIBERATIONS OF INDIAN CONSTITUENT ASSEMBLY. DISCUSSES SEVERAL SUPREME AND HIGH COURT DECISIONS THAT AMENDED CONSTITUTION, AND ANALYZES REGIONAL FORCES MAKING AMENDMENTS NECESSARY.

0855 GIANNELLA D.A. ED.
RELIGION AND THE PUBLIC ORDER: AN ANNUAL REVIEW OF CHURCH AND STATE, AND OF RELIGION, LAW, AND SOCIETY.
CHICAGO: U OF CHICAGO PRESS, 1964, 367 PP., LC#64-17164.
COLLECTS RECENT ESSAYS ON CHURCH-STATE RELATIONS, POLITICAL AFFAIRS, AND BIRTH CONTROL. DISCUSSES MAXIMUM AND MINIMUM THEORIES OF NATURAL LAW. INCLUDES SURVEY OF NEW BOOKS ON RELIGION, LAW, AND SOCIETY.

0856 GIBB A.D.
JUDICIAL CORRUPTION IN THE UNITED KINGDOM (PAMPHLET)
EDINBURGH: W GREEN & SON, 1957, 75 PP.
EXAMINES FOUR INDIVIDUAL CASES OF JUDICIAL CORRUPTION IN UK AS WELL AS GENERAL ASPECTS OF JUDICIAL MISRULE AND LACK OF INTEGRITY IN SCOTLAND.

0857 GIBBS C.R.
CONSTITUTIONAL AND STATUTORY PROVISIONS OF THE STATES (VOL. IX)
CHICAGO: COUNCIL OF STATE GOVTS, 1951, 86 PP.
LISTS AND SUMMARIZES STATE PROVISIONS AND STATUTES LIMITING, CONTROLLING, AND DEFINING LOBBIES AND THEIR PRACTICES. ALSO INCLUDES A CUMULATIVE INDEX TO OTHER VOLUMES IN THE SERIES.

0858 GIBNEY F.
THE OPERATORS.
NEW YORK: HARPER & ROW, 1960, 280 PP., LC#59-06307.
NON-TECHNICAL TREATMENT OF CULTURAL AMORALITY, "WHITE COLLAR CRIME", INSTITUTIONALIZING OF AMBIVALENT ATTITUDES TOWARD CRIME, AND FAILURE OF AMERICAN CULTURE TO COPE WITH BREAKDOWN OF MORES.

0859 GIBSON G.H.
"LABOR PIRACY ON THE BRANDYWINE."
LABOR HISTORY, 8 (SPRING 67),173-182.
DESCRIBES INCIDENTS OF LABOR PIRACY IN DELAWARE DURING FIRST DECADES OF 19TH CENTURY. SHOWS HOW RIVALS TRIED TO ENTICE WORKERS TO DIVULGE ADVANCED TECHNIQUES OF EMPLOYERS AND HOW BRANDYWINE MANUFACTURERS BANDED TOGETHER TO SECURE PROTECTIVE LEGISLATION. SUGGESTS MEANS OF SCREENING EMPLOYEES AND MAINTAINING THEM IN SENSITIVE POSITIONS. SUPPOSES THAT FINAL ANSWER MAY HAVE PSYCHOLOGICAL UNDERTONES.

0860 GILL N.N.
"PERMANENT ADVISORY COMMISSIONS IN THE FEDERAL GOVERNMENT."
J. OF POLITICS, 2 (NOV. 40), 411-435.
SOME 82 ADVISORY COMMITTEES WERE LOCATED IN THE COURSE OF THIS STUDY; THEIR INCREASE IS DUE TO THE EXPANSION OF GOVERNMENTAL ACTIVITIES. NOTES THREE CLASSES OF MEMBERS IN SUCH COMMITTEES, THE LATTER'S PROCEDURES AND PRIMARY FUNCTIONS, AS WELL AS FINANCIAL DETAILS, WITH A COMPREHENSIVE TABULAR ANALYSIS.

0861 GILLETTE J.M., REINHARDT J.M.
CURRENT SOCIAL PROBLEMS.
NEW YORK: AMERICAN BOOK, 1933.
DISCUSSES PROBLEMS OF POPULATION GROWTH, PSYCHO-PHYSICAL DEFECTS, RACE, FAMILY AND CHILD WELFARE, AND CONCLUDES WITH EXAMINING MEASURES INTENDED TO CONTROL CRIME, ALCOHOLISM, AND RELATED SOCIAL PROBLEMS.

0862 GILLETTE J.M., REINHARDT J.M.
PROBLEMS OF A CHANGING SOCIAL ORDER.
NEW YORK: AMERICAN BOOK, 1942, 824 PP.
DISCUSSES PROBLEMS OF SOCIAL ADJUSTMENT TO NATURE, POPULATION, AND WEALTH CONDITIONS. EXAMINES RACIAL ATTITUDES, FAMILY LIFE, CARE OF PHYSICALLY AND MENTALLY DEFICIENT, AND CONCLUDES WITH ANALYZING METHODS OF SOCIAL CONTROL OF CRIME, ALCOHOLISM, ETC.

0863 GILLETTE W.
THE RIGHT TO VOTE: POLITICS AND THE PASSAGE OF THE FIFTEENTH
AMENDMENT.
BALTIMORE: JOHNS HOPKINS PRESS, 1965, 181 PP., LC#65-17074.
THESIS IS THAT FRAMERS AND SUPPORTERS OF THE "RIGHT TO
VOTE" AMENDMENT WERE POLITICAL AND CONSTITUTIONAL MODERATES
WHO WANTED THE VOTE TO GO TO NORTHERN NEGROES.

0864 GILLIN J.L.
SOCIAL PATHOLOGY.
NEW YORK: APPLETON, 1946, 645 PP.
STUDIES ORIGINS AND CAUSES OF PERSONAL AND SOCIAL
MALADJUSTMENTS. DISCUSSES DISORDERS ARISING FROM POVERTY,
UNEMPLOYMENT, CRIME, RELIGION, CIVIL LIBERTIES, ETC. A GEN-
ERAL STUDY OF INCIDENCES OF UNSUCCESSFUL ADAPTATION TO THE
PHYSICAL AND CULTURAL ENVIRONMENT.

0865 GILLMOR D.M.
FREE PRESS AND FAIR TRIAL.
WASHINGTON: PUBLIC AFFAIRS PRESS, 1966, 254 PP., LC#66-28084.
EXAMINATION OF CONFLICT BETWEEN FREEDOM OF PRESS AND
PROTECTION OF INDIVIDUAL RIGHTS. INCLUDES TRIAL BY
PUBLICITY, TELEVISED COURT PROCEEDINGS, AND THE OSWALD AND
SHEPPARD CASE.

0866 GILMORE M.P.
ARGUMENT FROM ROMAN LAW IN POLITICAL THOUGHT, 1200-1600.
CAMBRIDGE: HARVARD U PR, 1941, 148 PP., LC#41-35035.
ESSAY ILLUSTRATING TWO GENERAL PROBLEMS: THE EXISTENCE OF
AN AUTHORITATIVE TRADITION, AND RELATION OF INDIVIDUALS TO
THAT TRADITION. ANALYZES EXAMPLES OF WAY IN WHICH POLITICAL
THEORISTS ADAPT DISTINCTIONS TAKEN FROM JUSTINIAN COMPILA-
TION OF ROMAN LAW AND MODIFY THEM TO OWN USES. EXAMPLES
CHOSEN FROM 1200-1600, DURING EMERGENCE OF NATIONAL STATE IN
EUROPE. BIBLIOGRAPHY OF SOURCES AND MODERN WORKS.

0867 GINSBERG M.
ON JUSTICE IN SOCIETY.
ITHACA: CORNELL U PRESS, 1965, 248 PP.
EXPLORES PROBLEMS OF RELATION OF JUSTICE TO EQUALITY AND
DIFFERENCES THAT NEED DIFFERENTIAL TREATMENT. SHOWS BEARING
OF JUSTICE ON MODERN SOCIAL PROBLEMS; DISCUSSES ETHICAL
BASIS OF PUNISHMENT AND SOCIETY'S ATTEMPT TO AVOID BOTH
FUSION AND SEPARATION OF MORALITY AND LAW. PHILOSOPHY
BASED ON RATIONALIST TRADITION.

0868 GINSBERG M. ED.
LAW AND OPINION IN ENGLAND.
BERKELEY: U OF CALIF PR, 1959, 405 PP.
RELATION OF DEVELOPMENTS IN ENGLISH LAW TO PUBLIC OPINION
DISCUSSED IN 17 LECTURES DELIVERED AT LONDON SCHOOL OF ECO-
NOMIC AND POLITICAL SCIENCE, 1957-58. COVERS PROPERTY, LA-
BOR, CRIME, ADMINISTRATION, AND HEALTH.

0869 GINSBURGS G.
"WARS OF NATIONAL LIBERATION - THE SOVIET THESIS."
LAW CONTEMP. PROBL., 29 (AUTUMN 64), 910-42.
SURVEYS AND REFUTES SOVIET LEGAL ARGUMENTS WHICH SUGGEST
THAT PRINCIPLES OF INTERNATIONAL LAW EXIST WHICH STATE THAT
ARMED HOSTILITIES IN COLONIAL AND DEPENDENT TERRITORIES ARE
CLASSIFIED AS INTERNATIONAL WARS.

0870 GINZBERG E.
DEMOCRATIC VALUES AND THE RIGHTS OF MANAGEMENT.
NEW YORK: COLUMBIA U PRESS, 1963, 217 PP., LC#63-20227.
THIS WORK PROVIDES A HISTORICAL, ECONOMIC, VALUE-
ORIENTED, AND LEGAL BACKGROUND FOR A RELATIVELY NEW APPROACH
TO UNION-MANAGEMENT ADJUSTMENT, THST IS, ARBITRATION. THE
ROLE AND DEMOCRATIC RESPONSIBILITIES OF THE ARBITRATOR IN
BALANCING THE EQUITIES AND RIGHTS OF BOTH SIDES ARE
DISCUSSED.

0871 GINZBURG B.
REDEDICATION TO FREEDOM.
NEW YORK: SIMON AND SCHUSTER, 1959, 177 PP., LC#59-7265.
DISCUSSES INVASIONS OF CONSTITUTIONAL RIGHTS BY US COURTS
AND LEGISLATURE. MAINTAINS THAT US GOVERNMENT HAS USED
COMMUNIST SCARE AS VEHICLE FOR IMPAIRMENT OF TRADITIONAL
RIGHTS OF FREE SPEECH. INDICTMENT OF HOUSE UN-AMERICAN AC-
TIVITIES COMMITTEE AND FBI.

0872 GIRAUD E.
"L'INTERDICTION DU RECOURS A LA FORCE, LA THEORIE ET LA
PRATIQUE DES NATIONS UNIES."
REV. GEN. DR. INT. PUB., 34 (NO.3, 63), 501-44.
SEVERAL PAPERS DEFINE AGGRESSION ACCORDING TO INTERNA-
TIONAL LAW AND UN CHARTER. ANALYZE UN IMPLEMENTATION OF
ARTICLE 2 OF CHARTER DURING MOST FAMOUS CRISES: ALGERIA,
HUNGARY, CONGO, CUBA.

0873 GJUPANOVIC H., ADAMOVITCH A.
LEGAL SOURCES AND BIBLIOGRAPHY OF YUGOSLAVIA.
NEW YORK: FREDERICK PRAEGER, 1964, 353 PP., LC#64-15520.
TOPICALLY ARRANGES, ANNOTATES, AND THOROUGHLY INDEXES BY
SUBJECT AND AUTHOR 2,467 ITEMS IN EUROPEAN LANGUAGES
RELATING TO THE DEVELOPMENT AND SUBSTANCE OF YUGOSLAVIAN

LAW. COVERS THE FORMATION OF YUGOSLAVIA, THE KINGDOM, WORLD
WAR II, AND THE PRESENT POLITICAL AND LEGAL ORDER. MATERIALS
ARE VERY DIVERSIFIED: DOCUMENTS, SERIALS, MONOGRAPHS, REC-
ORDS, COURT DECISIONS, TREATIES, PERIODICALS, ETC.

0874 GLASER D.
"NATIONAL GOALS AND INDICATORS FOR THE REDUCTION OF CRIME
AND DELINQUENCY."
ANN. ACAD. POL. SOC. SCI., (MAY 67),104-126.
STUDY OF FORMULATION OF CRIME-REDUCTION GOALS AND
ASSESSMENT OF PROGRESS TOWARD ACHIEVING THEM. SOME ANALYTIC
DISTINCTIONS ARE SUGGESTED TO PERMIT SEPARATE CONSIDERATION
OF GROUPS OF OFFENSES WHICH SHARE HIGHLY UNIQUE MEASUREMENT
AND GOAL-FORMULATION PROBLEMS. EFFECTIVENESS OF CORRECTIONAL
AGENCY PROGRAMS REQUIRES LONG-TERM DATA STUDIES. CREATION OF
NATIONAL AGENCY ADVISED TO CARRY PRIMARY RESPONSIBILITY.

0875 GLUECK S. ED.
ROSCOE POUND AND CRIMINAL JUSTICE.
NEW YORK: OCEANA PUBLISHING, 1965, 262 PP., LC#65-18283.
WORKS OF POUND ON "CRIMINAL JUSTICE, PROBATION, AND COURT
ORGANIZATION BOTH JUVENILE AND FAMILY." ANALYZES BASIC
THEMES IN POUND'S WORKS AND GIVES IMPRESSIONS OF THE MAN AND
HIS WORK.

0876 GODET M. ED.
INDEX BIBLIOGRAPHICUS: INTERNATIONAL CATALOGUE OF SOURCES OF
CURRENT BIBLIOGRAPHIC INFORMATION.
BOSTON: WORLD PEACE FOUNDATION, 1925, 233 PP.
SELECTED BIBLIOGRAPHY ARRANGED BY SUBJECT; PERIODICALS
AND INSTITUTIONAL PUBLICATIONS. MOST EUROPEAN LANGUAGES IN-
CLUDED. PUBLICATIONS DATE LARGELY FROM 1900-1925. COVERS
PHILOSOPHY, RELIGION, SOCIAL SCIENCES, LAW, PHILOLOGY, NATU-
RAL SCIENCES, MATHEMATICS. 1,000 ENTRIES.

0877 GODWIN W.
POLITICAL JUSTICE.
LONDON: SWAN SONNENSCHEIN, 1890, 155 PP.
PRESENTATION OF PHILOSOPHICAL ARGUMENTS ADVANCING THE
CAUSE OF "MORAL PROGRESS AND INTELLECTUAL ENLIGHTENMENT."
SHARP CRITICISM OF MONARCHY AND ARISTOCRACY AND A PLEA FOR
"REORGANIZATION OF SOCIETY ON A SIMPLER BASIS." ARGUES
FOR EQUALITY OF ALL MEN THROUGH EQUAL DISTRIBUTION OF
PROPERTY.

0879 GOLDSEN J.M. ED.
INTERNATIONAL POLITICAL IMPLICATIONS OF ACTIVITIES IN OUT-
ER SPACE.
SANTA MONICA: RAND, 1960.
TRANSCRIPT OF OCT. 59 CONFERENCE. INCLUDES PAPERS ON
'PUBLIC OPINION AND THE DEVELOPMENT OF SPACE TECHNOLOGY' BY
G. A. ALMOND, ON 'INTERNATIONAL IMPLICATIONS OF OUTER SPACE
ACTIVITIES' BY K. KNORR, AND ON 'OUTER SPACE AND INTERNA-
TIONAL POLITICS' BY K. W. DEUTSCH.

0880 GOLDWIN R.A. ED.
APPORTIONMENT AND REPRESENTATION.
CHICAGO: U OF CHICAGO PRESS, 1966, 150 PP.
PROBLEMS OF MALAPPORTIONMENT EXPLAINED AND CONFLICT BE-
TWEEN EQUAL PROTECTION AND EQUAL RIGHTS TO REPRESENTATION
DISCUSSED. FAVOR IMPARTIAL RATHER THAN EQUAL REPRESENTATION.

0881 GOMEZ ROBLES J.
A STATEMENT OF THE LAWS OF GUATEMALA IN MATTERS AFFECTING
BUSINESS (2ND ED. REV., ENLARGED)
WASHINGTON: PAN AMERICAN UNION, 1959, 323 PP.
SUMMARY OF BASIC CONSTITUTIONAL, STATUTORY, AND
REGULATORY PROVISIONS OF GUATEMALA UP TO 1959, AS THEY CON-
CERN COMMERCIAL MATTERS AND THE PERSONS WHO TRANSACT THEM.
ONE OF A SERIES, BASED UPON INFORMATION SUPPLIED BY
PRACTICING GUATEMALAN LAWYERS. INCLUDES TREATIES.

0882 GONNER R., SESTER J.
DAS KIRCHENPATRONATRECHT IM GROSSHERZOGTUM BADEN.
AMSTERDAM: VERLAG P SCHIPPERS, 1962, 318 PP.
DISCUSSES CHURCH PATRONAGE LAW IN DUCHY OF BADEN, GERMANY
FROM LATE MIDDLE AGES TO 19TH CENTURY. EXAMINES CATHOLIC AS
WELL AS PROTESTANT DEVELOPMENTS AND DISPUTES WITH SECULAR
AUTHORITIES.

0883 GONZALEZ NAVARRO M.
LA COLONIZACION EN MEXICO, 1877-1910.
MEXICO C: TALLERES DE IMPRESION, 1960, 160 PP.
EXAMINES PROGRAMS OF MEXICAN GOVERNMENT TO PROMOTE
IMMIGRATION AND COLONIZATION OF LAND. DISCUSSES ATTEMPTS TO
OFFER HOMESTEADING OPPORTUNITIES TO FOREIGNERS IN ORDER TO
IMPROVE AGRICULTURE AND INCREASE POPULATION. EXPLAINS THE
PROBLEMS IN PROGRAM AND THE ENDING OF OFFICIAL METHOD, WHICH
ADOPTED PRIVATE ACTIVITIES BY INDIVIDUALS WILLING TO HANDLE
THEIR OWN AFFAIRS DESPITE TROUBLES OF CLIMATE AND LOW PAY.

0884 GONZALEZ PALENCIA A
ESTUDIO HISTORICO SOBRE LA CENSURA GUBERNATIVA EN ESPANA
1800-1833.
MADRID: TIPOGRAFIA DE ARCHIVOS, 1934, 292 PP.
STUDY OF GOVERNMENTAL CENSORSHIP IN SPAIN FROM 1800-1833.

EXAMINES LAWS OF PRESS AND HOW APPLIED TO PUBLICATIONS
IN PERIOD. LISTS BOOKS CENSORED BY GOVERNMENT AND POLICIES
RELATED TO IMPORT AND EXPORT OF BOOKS.

0885 GOOCH G.P.
ENGLISH DEMOCRATIC IDEAS IN THE SEVENTEENTH CENTURY
(2ND ED.)
NEW YORK: CAMBRIDGE U PRESS, 1927, 315 PP.
   CONCERNED WITH DEMOCRATIC FEATURES OF ENGLISH MONARCHICAL
GOVERNMENT. BEGINS WITH ORIGIN AND GROWTH OF DEMOCRATIC
IDEAS. DISCUSSES ORIGIN OF REPUBLICANISM AND FOUNDATION OF
REPUBLIC; PRESENTS VIEW OF ANTAGONISTS OF OLIGARCHY AND
INCLUDES POLITICAL IDEAS OF THE ARMY, RISE OF INFLUENTIAL
RELIGIOUS BODIES, AND REVOLUTION OF 1688. RELATIONS WITH US
AND COMMONWEALTH AND MOVEMENT FOR LAW REFORM ARE STUDIED.

0886 GOODE W.J.
"COMMUNITY WITHIN A COMMUNITY: THE PROFESSIONS."
AMER. SOCIOLOGICAL REV., 22 (APR. 57), 194-200.
   EXPLORES "STRUCTURAL STRAINS AND SUPPORTS BETWEEN A
CONTAINED COMMUNITY AND THE LARGER SOCIETY, OF WHICH IT IS
A PART," AND ATTEMPTS TO APPLY TO FORMER THEORIES RELEVANT
TO THE LATTER. TWO LINKS (SOCIALIZATION AND CLIENT CHOICE)
ARE EXPLORED.

0887 GOODNOW F.J.
THE PRINCIPLES OF THE ADMINISTRATIVE LAW OF THE UNITED
STATES.
NEW YORK: G P PUTNAM'S SONS, 1905, 479 PP.
   STUDIES THEORY AND APPLICATION OF SEPARATION OF POWERS IN
US GOVERNMENT. TREATS POWERS AND STRUCTURE OF CHIEF
EXECUTIVE AUTHORITY IN STATE AND NATION. DISCUSSES STRUCTURE
OF LOCAL RURAL AND MUNICIPAL ADMINISTRATION, AND OF CIVIL
SERVICE. DESCRIBES METHODS AND FORMS OF ADMINISTRATIVE
ACTION. ANALYZES JUDICIAL AND LEGISLATIVE CONTROL OVER
ADMINISTRATIVE OFFICES.

0888 GOODNOW F.J.
"AN EXECUTIVE AND THE COURTS: JUDICIAL REMEDIES AGAINST
ADMINISTRATIVE ACTION"
POLIT. SCI. QUART., 1 (DEC. 86), 533-559.
   DEFINES PUBLIC LAW AS ONE PART CONSTITUTIONAL LAW AND ONE
PART ADMINISTRATIVE LAW. SPELLS OUT RULES GOVERNING RELATION
BETWEEN GOVERNMENT AND INDIVIDUAL CITIZEN OR ADMINISTRATIVE
LAW. ANALYZES ACCORDING TO KIND OF ADMINISTRATIVE ACTION
NECESSARY, THUS REMEDY GIVEN PERSON TO PROTECT HIS RIGHTS.
CITES SPECIFIC CASES IN US, FRANCE, AND ENGLAND.

0889 GOODNOW H.F.
THE CIVIL SERVICE OF PAKISTAN: BUREAUCRACY IN A NEW NATION.
NEW HAVEN: YALE U PR, 1964, 328 PP., LC#64-20918.
   COVERS CONDITIONS PRIOR TO 1958 UNDER INDIAN CIVIL SER-
VICE OF ENGLAND. AFTER 1958 PERIOD OF MILITARY RULE LED TO
INDEPENDENT CIVIL SERVICE. DONE AS CASE STUDY OF BUREAUCRACY
IN UNDEVELOPED NATIONS. ANALYZES POLITICAL ORGANIZATION IN
ALL NEW STATES. APPENDIX OF FISCAL REPORTS AND GOVERNMENT
JOB TITLES. EXTENSIVE BIBLIOGRAPHY OF BOOKS AND ARTICLES ON
INDIA AND BUREAUCRACY DEVELOPMENT.

0890 GOODRICH L.M., HAMBRO E.
"CHARTER OF THE UNITED NATIONS: COMMENTARY AND DOCUMENTS."
BOSTON: WORLD PEACE FOUNDATION, 1946.
   COMMENTARY ON CONSTITUTION INCLUDES DISCUSSION OF ITS
HISTORY AND ORIGINS, ORGANIZATION OF ORIGINATING CONFERENCE,
CONTENT OF CHARTER, ITS IMPLEMENTATION. HAS COMMENTARY ON
ARTICLES, LIST OF DOCUMENTS AND EXTENSIVE BIBLIOGRAPHY WHICH
CONTAINS REFERENCES TO MANY ORIGINAL SOURCES.

0891 GORDON D.L., DANGERFIELD R.
THE HIDDEN WEAPON: THE STORY OF ECONOMIC WARFARE.
NEW YORK: HARPER, 1947, 238 PP.
   DESCRIBES BRITISH AND AMERICAN DEVICES OF ECONOMIC WAR-
FARE DURING WW 2, DIRECTED TOWARDS CUTTING OF AXIS POWERS
FROM FOREIGN SUPPLIES OF STRATEGIC MATERIALS. CONSIDERS
NEUTRALITY AND INTERNATIONAL LAW GOVERNING RELATIONS OF NON-
BELLIGERENTS AND BELLIGERENTS TO BE NOW EXTINCT DUE TO NA-
TURE OF MODERN WAR. SEES NEED FOR ENFORCEABLE LAWS WHICH
WILL ELIMINATE WAR.

0892 GOSSETT W.T.
"ELECTING THE PRESIDENT: NEW HOPE FOR AN OLD IDEAL."
AMER BAR ASSN., 53 (DEC. 67), 1103-1106.
   DISCUSSES ELECTORAL COLLEGE SYSTEM AND WHY IT SHOULD BE
ABOLISHED. CONSIDERS IT ARCHAIC, AND UNDESIRABLE EVEN WHEN
FIRST ESTABLISHED. OBJECTS TO CHANCE THAT HOUSE MAY DECIDE
ELECTION, ELECTORS MAY NOT REPRESENT VOTERS, AND WILL OF
NATIONAL MAJORITY MAY BE THWARTED. SUPPORTS SYSTEM IN WHICH
ELECTION IS DECIDED BY MAJORITY, 40 PERCENT PLURALITY, OR
RUNOFF OF NATIONAL VOTE, WITH HOUSE PROCEDURAL POWERS.

0893 GOTLIEB A.
DISARMAMENT AND INTERNATIONAL LAW* A STUDY OF THE ROLE OF
LAW IN THE DISARMAMENT PROCESS.
TORONTO: CAN INST OF INTL AFF, 1965, 232 PP.
   AUTHOR IS PROFESSOR OF INTERNATIONAL LAW, DEPUTY LEGAL
HEAD OF CANADIAN DEPARTMENT OF EXTERNAL AFFAIRS, AND WAS ONE

OF HER DELEGATES TO GENEVA DISARMAMENT CONFERENCES. DISCUS-
SES LEGAL PROBLEMS FOUND IN SOVIET AND AMERICAN PROPOSALS.
APPENDICES HAVE SOVIET AND AMERICAN OUTLINES AND REVISIONS
TRANSPOSED.

0894 GOURNAY B.
PUBLIC ADMINISTRATION.
NEW YORK: CULTURAL CTR FRENCH EM, 1963, 207 PP.
   ANNOTATED TOPICAL LISTING OF 1,000 BOOKS, COURSES, MAN-
UALS, ANTHOLOGIES, MAGAZINE ARTICLES, THESES, REPORTS OF
STUDY GROUPS, AND DOCUMENTS EMANATING FROM CENTRAL FRENCH
ADMINISTRATIONS. ALL ITEMS DEAL WITH PUBLIC ADMINISTRATIONS
IN METROPOLITAN FRANCE; ALL WERE PUBLISHED 1944-58 AND
MOST ARE IN FRENCH. CONCLUDING AUTHOR AND PUBLISHER INDEX.
TITLES AND ANNOTATIONS GIVEN IN ENGLISH.

0895 GRACIA-MORA M.R.
"INTERNATIONAL RESPONSIBILITY FOR SUBVERSIVE ACTIVITIES
AND HOSTILE PROPAGANDA BY PRIVATE PERSONS AGAINST."
FOREIGN STATES.
   INDIANA LAW J., 35 (SPRING 60), 306-35.
   CHRONOLOGICAL SURVEY OF INTERNATIONAL LAW ON SUBJECT.
ANALYSIS OF MANNER IN WHICH USA AND BRITAIN, EUROPE,
SOUTH AMERICA, AND USSR PREVENT PRIVATE HOSTILE
ACTIVITY CONSTITUTING DANGER TO FOREIGN NATIONS.

0896 GRAHAM H.D.
CRISIS IN PRINT: DESEGREGATION AND THE PRESS IN TENNESSEE.
NASHVILLE: VANDERBILT U PR, 1967, 338 PP., LC#67-21654.
   EXAMINES SOUTH'S NATURE AT PRESENT AND ITS ADJUSTMENT TO
1954 SUPREME COURT DESEGREGATION RULING. STUDIES EDITORIALS
IN A VARIED SOUTHERN STATE, TENNESSEE. BELIEVES CITIZENS'
ATTITUDES ARE BETTER REFLECTED BY PRESS THAN BY POLITICAL
STRUCTURES OF MOST US STATES. FINDS TENNESSEE PRESS PLURAL-
ISTIC, FOSTERING ADJUSTMENT AND EXCHANGE OF IDEAS. ANNO-
TATES ABOUT 150 BOOKS AND ARTICLES, 1928-67.

0897 GRANT D.R., NIXON H.C.
STATE AND LOCAL GOVERNMENT IN AMERICA.
NEW YORK: ALLYN AND BACON, 1963, 439 PP., LC#63-14890.
   DISCUSSES ROLE AND FUNCTION OF STATE AND LOCAL
GOVERNMENTS IN US. EXAMINES POLICE POWER, CONSTITUTIONS,
VOTING, PARTY ORGANIZATION AND ELECTIONS, PUBLIC OPINION,
LEGISLATIVE PROCESSES, JUDICIARY, COUNTRY ADMINISTRATIONS,
URBAN AREAS, EDUCATION, AND PUBLIC WELFARE.

0898 GRASMUCK E.L.
COERCITIO STAAT UND KIRCHE IM DONATISTENSTREIT.
BONN: LUDWIG ROHRSCHEID VERLAG, 1964, 272 PP.
   DISCUSSES DISPUTE BETWEEN CHURCH AND STATE OVER DONATIST
CONTROVERSY IN FOURTH-CENTURY ROME. EXAMINES AUGUSTINE'S
CONCEPT OF STATE AND CHURCH AS WELL AS RELEVANT PORTIONS OF
ROMAN LAW.

0899 GRAVEN J.
"LE MOUVEAU DROIT PENAL INTERNATIONAL."
REV. DR. INT., 40 (NO. 4, 62, 330-48.
   ANALYZES DRAFTS OF INTERNATIONAL PENAL LAW MADE BY
SEVERAL COUNTRIES. EXAMINES CAPABILITIES OF COURT OF GENEVA.
POINTS OUT PROCEDURES AVAILABLE TO DEFENDENTS. BASES
ANALYSIS ON RECENT COURT DECISIONS.

0900 GRAVES W.B.
AMERICAN STATE GOVERNMENT.
BOSTON: D C HEATH, 1936, 829 PP.
   PROVIDES A BASIS FOR ASSESSING THE STRUCTURE, POLITICS,
LEGISLATURE, ADMINISTRATION, FINANCE, AND CONSTITUTION OF
STATE GOVERNMENTS. DESCRIBES INTERGOVERNMENTAL RELATIONS,
PROJECTS THE HISTORICAL TRENDS OF STATE GOVERNMENT, AND
PREDICTS FUTURE. INTENDED TO SUPPLEMENT AND UPDATE
OTHER TEXTS IN THIS FIELD. REGARDS STATE GOVERNMENTS AS
"GOING CONCERNS" RATHER THAN STATIC INSTITUTIONS.

0901 GRAVES W.B.
PUBLIC ADMINISTRATION: A COMPREHENSIVE BIBLIOGRAPHY ON
PUBLIC ADMINISTRATION IN THE UNITED STATES (PAMPHLET)
WASHINGTON: LIBRARY OF CONGRESS, 1950, 388 PP.
   SOME 5,500 UNANNOTATED BOOKS, ARTICLES, MONOGRAPHS, PUB-
LIC DOCUMENTS, AND BIBLIOGRAPHIES PUBLISHED 1924-49
AND ARRANGED TOPICALLY. TOPICS INCLUDE ADMINISTRATIVE STRUC-
TURE, PERSONNEL MANAGEMENT, FISCAL MANAGEMENT, INTERNAL AND
EXTERNAL MANAGEMENT.

0902 GREAT BRIT COMM MINISTERS PWR
REPORT.
LONDON: GT BR COMM ON MIN POWERS, 1932, 138 PP.
   CONSIDERS POWERS EXERCISED BY OR UNDER DIRECTION OF
MINISTERS OF THE CROWN BY WAY OF DELEGATED LEGISLATION AND
JUDICIAL DECISION. SUGGESTS SAFEGUARDS NECESSARY TO SECURE
CONSTITUTIONAL PRINCIPLES OF PARLIAMENTARY SOVEREIGNTY AND
SUPREMACY OF THE LAW.

0904 GREELY A.W.
PUBLIC DOCUMENTS OF THE FIRST FOURTEEN CONGRESSES, 1789-1817
WASHINGTON: GOVT PR OFFICE, 1900, 903 PP.
   ANNOTATED BIBLIOGRAPHY OF THE OFFICIAL JOURNALS, DOCU-

MENTS, AND REPORTS LISTING LIBRARIES IN WHICH LOCATED. AR-
RANGED CHRONOLOGICALLY WITH INDEX BY NAMES AT END.

0905 GREEN F.M.
CONSTITUTIONAL DEVELOPMENT IN THE SOUTH ATLANTIC STATES,
1776-1860; A STUDY IN THE EVOLUTION OF DEMOCRACY.
CHAPEL HILL: U OF N CAR PR, 1930, 328 PP.
ANALYZES SOCIAL, POLITICAL, AND ECONOMIC FACTORS INVOLVED
IN FORMATION OF CONSTITUTIONS OF FIVE OLDEST SOUTHERN
STATES. TRACES DEVELOPMENT, INFLUENCES LEADING TO REVISION
AND AMENDMENT, AND DEMOCRATIC ELEMENTS; INCLUDES ROLE OF
ELITE ARISTOCRATIC PLANTERS. DISCUSSES LEGISLATIVE,
EXECUTIVE, AND JUDICIAL STRUCTURES; SOCIAL AND ECONOMIC
SECTIONALISM; AND PARTY REPRESENTATION.

0906 GREEN L.C.
"POLITICAL OFFENSES, WAR CRIMES AND EXTRADITION."
INT. COMP. LAW QUART., 11 (APRIL 62), 329-54.
DEFINES ROLE OF INTERPOL IN APPREHENSION OF WAR CRIMI-
NALS. DISTINGUISHES BETWEEN POLITICAL OFFENSES AND WAR
CRIMES. SUGGESTS THAT LATTER TRANSGRESS AGAINST LAWS OF
WAR AND THAT WAR CRIMINALS SHOULD BE EXTRADITED.

0907 GREEN L.C.
"RHODESIAN OIL: BOOTLEGGERS OR PIRATES?"
INT. J., 21 (SUMMER 66), 350-353.
ANALYZES LEGAL ASPECTS OF SANCTIONS AGAINST RHODESIA, IN-
CLUDING LEGITIMACY OF BRITISH STAND, DEFINITION OF ILLEGAL
TRADE WITH RHODESIA, AND ATTITUDES IN UN AND OAU.

0908 GREENBERG S.
"JUDAISM AND WORLD JUSTICE."
WORLD JUSTICE, 5 (MAR. 64), 315-21.
ASSERTS CONCEPT OF JUSTICE IN THE JUDIAC TRADITION HOLDS
THAT LOVE FOR GOD IS BEST REFLECTED AND MOST FULLY REALIZED
IN ACTS OF LOVE AND CHARITY TOWARDS FELLOW MAN. HENCE A WAR-
LESS WORLD MAKES POSSIBLE MANKIND'S NOBLEST SELF-FULFILL-
MENT.

0909 GREENE L.E., AVERY R.S.
GOVERNMENT IN TENNESSEE (2ND ED.)
KNOXVILLE: U OF TENN PR, 1966, 371 PP., LC#66-21194.
CONTAINS MATERIAL ON STRUCTURE, FUNCTION, AND ADMINISTRA-
TION OF TENNESSEE STATE GOVERNMENT. INCLUDES COPY OF STATE
CONSTITUTION; DEALS WITH STATE POLITICS AND COURTS; COUNTY
GOVERNMENT; BUSINESS AND INDUSTRY; PUBLIC HEALTH, EDUCA-
TION, AND WELFARE; TRANSPORT FACILITIES, STATE REVENUES, AND
STATE AND LOCAL PLANNING.

0910 GREENE L.S., PARTHEMOS G.S.
AMERICAN GOVERNMENT POLICIES AND FUNCTIONS.
NEW YORK: CHAS SCRIBNER'S SONS, 1967, 450 PP., LC#67-10455.
ANALYZES FUNCTIONS AND POLICIES OF US GOVERNMENT AND
PROCEDURES THROUGH WHICH DECISIONS ARE MADE REGARDING PUBLIC
POLICY. STUDIES THEORIES DEFINING PUBLIC POLICIES, POLITICAL
ADMINISTRATIVE PROCESS, CONTENT OF MAJOR POLICIES, AND
POLICY PROBLEMS.

0911 GREENSPAN M.
THE MODERN LAW OF LAND WARFARE.
BERKELEY: U. CALIF. PR., 1959, 724 PP.
COMPREHENSIVE EXAMINATION OF PRECEDENTS AND PRACTICES OF
WAR LAWS. INSPECTING PREVIOUS SANCTIONS AND ENFORCEMENT
PROCEDURES, AUTHOR PRESENTS ABSTRACT MODEL OF METHODS AND
INSTRUMENTS OF WARFARE.

0912 GREENSPAN M.
"INTERNATIONAL LAW AND ITS PROTECTION FOR PARTICIPANTS IN
UNCONVENTIONAL WARFARE."
ANN. AMER. ACAD. POLIT. SOC. SCI., 341 (MAY 62), 30-41.
GENEVA CONVENTIONS APPLY TO PARTICIPANTS IN GUERRILLA
WARFARE SO LONG AS SATISFY FOLLOWING REQUIREMENTS: BELONG TO
ORGANIZED MOVEMENT IN CONFLICT, HAVE COMMANDERS BEARING RE-
SPONSIBILITY FOR SUBORDINATES, WEAR DISTINCTIVE INSIGNIA,
CARRY ARMS OPENLY, AND OBEY LAWS AND CUSTOMS OF WAR.

0913 GREGG R.W. ED.
INTERNATIONAL ORGANIZATION IN THE WESTERN HEMISPHERE.
SYRACUSE: SYRACUSE U PRESS, 1968, 262 PP., LC#68-15908.
EXAMINES RELATIONS AMONG NATIONS IN WESTERN HEMISPHERE
AND US DOMINANCE OF THESE RELATIONS. IDENTIFIES AND AN-
ALYZES THE POLITICAL, CULTURAL, AND PHYSICAL CHARACTERISTICS
OF LATIN AMERICA THAT HAVE SHAPED PRESENT INTER-AMERICAN
RELATIONS. ANALYZES AND DISCUSSES THE DEVELOPMENT AND FUNC-
TIONS OF THE OAS IN THE AREAS OF SECURITY, PEACEFUL SETTLE-
MENT OF DISPUTES, AND ECONOMIC AND SOCIAL DEVELOPMENT.

0914 GREGORY W.
LIST OF THE SERIAL PUBLICATIONS OF FOREIGN GOVERNMENTS,
1815-1931.
WASH, DC: AMER COUNC LEARNED SOC, 1932, 720 PP.
LISTS BY COUNTRY GOVERNMENT SERIAL PUBLICATIONS. INCLUDES
LAW REPORTS, DIGESTS, STATUTES, AND OFFICIAL GAZETTES.

0915 GREIG D.W.
"THE ADVISORY JURISDICTION OF THE INTERNATIONAL COURT AND

THE SETTLEMENT OF DISPUTES BETWEEN STATES."
INT. AND COMP. LAW, 15 (APR. 66), 325-368.
THE COURT SHOULD AVOID INVOLVING ITSELF IN BASICALLY POL-
ITICAL DISPUTES, FOR ITS WORK MAY BECOME COMPLETELY INSIG-
NIFICANT. STUDIES CUSTOM, UNION, AND EXPENSE CASES TO ILLUS-
TRATE HOW POLITICAL ISSUES ARE INVOLVED IN TREATY PROVISIONS
AND HOW DANGEROUS IT IS FOR THE COURT TO ENTER INTO POLIT-
ICAL CONTROVERSIES.

0916 GREY D.L.
"INTERVIEWING AT THE COURT."
PUBLIC OPINION QUART., 31 (1967), 285-289.
DISCUSSES PROBLEMS ENCOUNTERED IN INTERVIEWING FEDERAL
APPELLATE JUDGES AND SUPREME COURT JUSTICES. STUDY CENTERED
ON NEWS MEDIA COVERAGE OF SUPREME COURT.

0917 GRIFFIN A.P.C. ED.
LIST OF BOOKS RELATING TO THE THEORY OF COLONIZATION, GOV-
ERNMENT OF DEPENDENCIES, PROTECTORATES, AND RELATED TOPICS.
WASHINGTON: LIBRARY OF CONGRESS, 1900, 156 PP.
CONTAINS 2,000 LISTINGS OF BOOKS AND ARTICLES ON MANY
ASPECTS OF COLONIALISM. DIVIDED INTO 27 SEPARATE HEADINGS;
THE LISTINGS REFER TO WORKS ON THE THEORY OF COLONIALIZATION
AS WELL AS SPECIFIC REFERENCES TO THE POLICIES AND COLONIAL
HISTORIES OF THE US, UK, FRANCE, GERMANY, ITALY, SPAIN, THE
NETHERLANDS, AND PORTUGAL. MANY ENTRIES IN FRENCH, GERMAN,
AND SPANISH. MOST ARTICLES LISTED WERE PUBLISHED 1897-1900.

0918 GRIFFIN A.P.C. ED.
LIST OF BOOKS ON SAMOA (PAMPHLET)
WASHINGTON: LIBRARY OF CONGRESS, 1901, 54 PP.
CONTAINS ABOUT 500 LISTINGS OF BOOKS AND ARTICLES ON GUAM
AND SAMOA, MOST PUBLISHED IN LATE 19TH CENTURY. INCLUDES
MANY GOVERNMENTAL RECORDS OF US, UK, AND GERMAN DEALINGS
IN SAMOA. SOME ARTICLES IN GERMAN. COMPILED FOR LIBRARY OF
CONGRESS.

0919 GRIFFIN A.P.C. ED.
A LIST OF BOOKS RELATING TO TRUSTS (2ND REV. ED.) (PAMPHLET)
WASHINGTON: LIBRARY OF CONGRESS, 1902, 36 PP.
CONTAINS APPROXIMATELY 550 LISTINGS OF BOOKS AND ARTICLES
PUBLISHED 1885-1900 ON TRUSTS IN THE US AND EUROPE. LISTED
WORKS DEAL WITH POLITICAL, LEGAL, ECONOMIC, AND ETHICAL
ISSUES AND CONTAIN MANY DISCUSSIONS OF LEGISLATIVE INVES-
TIGATIONS. THIS BIBLIOGRAPHY IS DESIGNED AS A GENERAL INTRO-
DUCTION RATHER THAN A SPECIALIZED DIRECTORY. COMPILED FOR
LIBRARY OF CONGRESS.

0920 GRIFFIN A.P.C. ED.
LIST OF BOOKS ON THE CONSTITUTION OF THE UNITED STATES
(PAMPHLET)
WASHINGTON: LIBRARY OF CONGRESS, 1903, 14 PP.
ANNOTATED, UNINDEXED. ARRANGED ALPHABETICALLY BY AUTHOR.
INCLUDES US CONSTITUTION, LAW, INTERPRETATIONS, SUPREME
COURT, ETC. ABOUT 75 ITEMS, CHIEFLY BOOKS, ALL AMERICAN
PUBLICATIONS. COMPILED FOR LIBRARY OF CONGRESS.

0921 GRIFFIN A.P.C. ED.
LIST OF REFERENCES ON INDUSTRIAL ARBITRATION (PAMPHLET)
WASHINGTON: LIBRARY OF CONGRESS, 1903, 15 PP.
ANNOTATIONS OF ABOUT 130 ITEMS ARRANGED ALPHABETICALLY
BY AUTHOR. ABOUT 30 BOOKS FROM THE 1880'S; PERIODICALS LIST-
ED CHRONOLOGICALLY FROM 1886. LISTS FOREIGN DOCUMENTS FROM
FRANCE, CANADA, UK, NEW ZEALAND, AND OTHER COUNTRIES ON
BUSINESS-LABOR RELATIONS AND THE VALUE OF COLLECTIVE
BARGAINING, ARBITRATION, ETC. COMPILED FOR LIBRARY OF CONG-
RESS.

0922 GRIFFIN A.P.C. ED.
LISTS PUBLISHED 1902-03: GOVERNMENT OWNERSHIP OF RAILROADS
(PAMPHLET)
WASHINGTON: LIBRARY OF CONGRESS, 1903, 14 PP.
ABOUT 90 ENTRIES OF BOOKS, PUBLICATIONS, AND ARTICLES IN
PERIODICALS ON LEGALITY AND POSSIBILITY OF US GOVERNMENT'S
OWNING RR. SOME ENTRIES ARE IN FRENCH AND GERMAN AND PUBLI-
CATION RANGES FROM 1870-1903. ENTRIES ARE ALPHABETICAL BY
AUTHOR, EXCEPT ARTICLES WHICH ARE CHRONOLOGICAL FROM 1871-
1903.

0923 GRIFFIN A.P.C. ED.
LISTS PUBLISHED 1902-03: LABOR PARTICULARLY RELATING TO
STRIKES (PAMPHLET)
WASHINGTON: LIBRARY OF CONGRESS, 1903, 65 PP.
ABOUT 600 ENTRIES OF BOOKS, REPORTS AND ARTICLES IN PERI-
ODICALS ON STRIKES IN US AND ENGLAND. DEALS WITH MOTIVES FOR
STRIKES, DEMANDS, LEGISLATIVE ACTION, AND EFFECTS ON LA-
BOR. ARTICLES ARE IN FRENCH AND GERMAN AND PUBLICATION RAN-
GES FROM 1850-1903. ENTRIES ARE ALPHABETICAL BY AUTHOR, EX-
CEPT ARTICLES WHICH ARE CHRONOLOGICAL FROM 1859-1903.

0924 GRIFFIN A.P.C.
SELECT LIST OF BOOKS ON LABOR PARTICULARLY RELATING TO
STRIKES.
WASHINGTON: LIBRARY OF CONGRESS, 1903, 65 PP.
ANNOTATED LISTING OF APPROXIMATELY 500 BOOKS AND ARTICLES
WRITTEN IN ENGLISH, FRENCH, AND GERMAN PERTINENT TO ORGAN-

IZED LABOR, ESPECIALLY EMPHASIZING STRIKES. ENTRIES WRITTEN
FROM 1880 THROUGH 1902. INCLUDES RECORDS OF STRIKES, LOCK-
OUTS, AND ARBITRATION.

0925 GRIFFIN A.P.C. ED.
A LIST OF BOOKS RELATING TO RAILROADS IN THEIR RELATION TO
THE GOVERNMENT AND THE PUBLIC (PAMPHLET)
WASHINGTON: LIBRARY OF CONGRESS, 1904, 72 PP.
    CONTAINS APPROXIMATELY 700 LISTINGS OF BOOKS AND ARTICLES
CONCERNING HISTORY OF RAILROAD DEVELOPMENT, TRUSTS AND POOL-
ING, GOVERNMENTAL INVESTIGATIONS, SPEECHES IN CONGRESS, AND
JUDICIAL DECISIONS. CONTAINS AN APPENDIX DEALING SPECIFI-
CALLY WITH THE NORTHERN SECURITIES CASE. LISTINGS PUBLISHED
FROM 1875-1904. A FEW LISTINGS REFER TO FOREIGN RAILROADS,
BUT MOST DEAL WITH US RAIL SYSTEM.

0926 GRIFFIN A.P.C. ED.
REFERENCES ON CHINESE IMMIGRATIONS (PAMPHLET)
WASHINGTON: LIBRARY OF CONGRESS, 1904, 31 PP.
    ANNOTATED. ABOUT 60 BOOKS ARRANGED ALPHABETICALLY BY
AUTHOR; ALSO INCLUDES REPORTS OF DEBATES IN "CONGRESSIONAL
RECORD" AND ANNOTATES AROUND 150 GOVERNMENT DOCUMENTS
PERTINENT TO CHINESE IMMIGRATION; ABOUT 100 ARTICLES
LISTED CHRONOLOGICALLY FROM 1852. ENGLISH, GERMAN, AND
FRENCH SOURCES. COMPILED FOR LIBRARY OF CONGRESS.

0927 GRIFFIN A.P.C. ED.
LIST OF BOOKS ON RAILROADS IN FOREIGN COUNTRIES.
WASHINGTON: LIBRARY OF CONGRESS, 1905, 70 PP.
    ANNOTATED, LISTED BY COUNTRY, INDEXED BY AUTHOR AND SUB-
JECT. GERMAN, FRENCH, ENGLISH, AND ITALIAN SOURCES FROM
1890'S - 1905. INCLUDES PRINTED STATISTICS, ABSTRACTS, RAIL-
ROAD PERIODICALS, REPORTS, ETC. PURPORTS "TO PROVIDE MEANS
OF ASCERTAINING THE MAIN PROVISIONS OF RAILROAD ADMINISTRA-
TION IN THE SEVERAL COUNTRIES OF EUROPE." OVER 300 ITEMS.
COMPILED FOR LIBRARY OF CONGRESS.

0928 GRIFFIN A.P.C. ED.
LIST OF REFERENCES ON PRIMARY ELECTIONS (PAMPHLET)
WASHINGTON: LIBRARY OF CONGRESS, 1905, 24 PP.
    CONTAINS ABOUT 200 ENTRIES RELATED TO DISCUSSION AND EX-
POSITION OF PRIMARY ELECTION SYSTEMS IN THE US UP TO 1902.
DRAWS HEAVILY ON MYER'S "NOMINATING SYSTEMS: DIRECT PRIMA-
RIES VS CONVENTIONS IN THE US" FOR HISTORICAL SOURCES AND A
SUMMARY OF VARIOUS STATE LEGISLATION. COMPILED FOR LIBRARY
OF CONGRESS.

0929 GRIFFIN A.P.C. ED.
LIST OF BOOKS RELATING TO CHILD LABOR (PAMPHLET)
WASHINGTON: LIBRARY OF CONGRESS, 1906, 66 PP.
    LISTS APPROXIMATELY 330 TITLES OF BOOKS AND RELATED
ARTICLES DEALING WITH PROBLEMS OF CHILD LABOR, ESPECIALLY IN
LEGAL ASPECTS. MANY ENTRIES ANNOTATED; SOME LISTINGS OF PUB-
LICATIONS IN FRENCH AND GERMAN. MOST WORKS LISTED PUBLISHED
IN LATE 19TH- EARLY 20TH CENTURIES. COMPILED FOR LIBRARY OF
CONGRESS.

0930 GRIFFIN A.P.C. ED.
SELECT LIST OF REFERENCES ON THE NEGRO QUESTION (REV. ED.)
WASHINGTON: LIBRARY OF CONGRESS, 1906, 61 PP.
    OVER 200 BOOKS ARRANGED ALPHABETICALLY BY AUTHOR. ABOUT
350 ARTICLES LISTED CHRONOLOGICALLY FROM 1879 THROUGH 1906.
INDEXED BY AUTHOR. ENTRIES IN FRENCH AND GERMAN, BUT CHIEF-
LY ENGLISH ON VARIOUS RAMIFICATIONS OF THE "NEGRO QUES-
TION": CONSTITUTIONAL, RACIAL, SOCIAL, ECONOMIC. RECON-
STRUCTION, RACISM, KU KLUX KLAN, ETC. ARE ALSO INCLUDED.
LIBRARY OF CONGRESS COMPILATION.

0931 GRIFFIN A.P.C. ED.
LIST OF MORE RECENT WORKS ON FEDERAL CONTROL OF COMMERCE AND
CORPORATIONS (PAMPHLET)
WASHINGTON: LIBRARY OF CONGRESS, 1907, 50 PP.
    LISTS ABOUT 175 BOOKS AND ARTICLES PUBLISHED 1900-07
FROM CONGRESSIONAL RECORDS AND GENERAL PERIODICALS. WORKS
LISTED DISCUSS EXTENT AND VALIDITY OF FEDERAL CONTROL OVER
PRIVATE BUSINESS, ESPECIALLY IN ANTITRUST LEGISLATION.
LIBRARY OF CONGRESS COMPILATION.

0932 GRIFFIN A.P.C. ED.
LIST OF REFERENCES ON INTERNATIONAL ARBITRATION.
WASHINGTON: LIBRARY OF CONGRESS, 1908, 151 PP.
    LISTS APPROXIMATELY 900 ARTICLES, MANY ANNOTATED, CON-
CERNING INTERNATIONAL ARBITRATION; PRIMARILY CONCERNED WITH
THE 1907 HAGUE CONFERENCE. ALSO CONTAINS RELATED SECTIONS ON
ARMS LIMITATIONS AND FOREIGN DEBT COLLECTION, AS WELL AS
DISCUSSIONS OF FRENCH OCCUPATION OF MEXICO AND COLONIAL
QUESTIONS IN VENEZUELA AND SANTO DOMINGO. MANY ARTICLES IN
FRENCH AND GERMAN, AND ARE DATED FROM 1886 TO 1907.

0933 GRIFFIN A.P.C. ED.
LIST OF WORKS RELATING TO GOVERNMENT REGULATION OF INSURANCE
UNITED STATES AND FOREIGN COUNTRIES (2ND. ED.) (PAMPHLET)
WASHINGTON: LIBRARY OF CONGRESS, 1908, 67 PP.
    A GENERAL INTRODUCTORY LISTING OF ABOUT 500 REPORTS ON
FEDERAL SUPERVISION OF INSURANCE, PRIMARILY IN THE US. MOST
ENTRIES 1900-07; MANY IN FRENCH AND GERMAN. REFERS TO BOTH

LEGAL RECORDS IN CONGRESSIONAL PROCEEDINGS AND POPULAR
ARTICLES DEFENDING INSURANCE COMPANY POLICIES. COMPILED FOR
LIBRARY OF CONGRESS.

0934 GRIFFIN A.P.C. ED.
REFERENCES ON CORRUPT PRACTICES IN ELECTIONS (PAMPHLET)
WASHINGTON: LIBRARY OF CONGRESS, 1908, 12 PP.
    ANNOTATED BOOKS, ARTICLES, PAMPHLETS, ETC.; AROUND 100
ITEMS. ARRANGED ALPHABETICALLY BY AUTHOR, DATED FROM THE
TURN OF THE CENTURY THROUGH 1908 ON GERRYMANDERING, PAYOFFS,
BRIBERY, ETC. RECORDED AND DISCUSSED BY MISCELLANEOUS
SOURCES. CONTAINS A SELECTED LIST; UNINDEXED. COMPILED
FOR LIBRARY OF CONGRESS.

0935 GRIFFIN A.P.C. ED., MEYER H.H.B. ED.
SELECT LIST OF REFERENCES ON IMPEACHMENT (REV. ED.)
(PAMPHLET)
WASHINGTON: LIBRARY OF CONGRESS, 1912, 38 PP.
    FULLY ANNOTATED. ARRANGED BY SUBJECT AND INDEXED BY
AUTHOR. LISTS 183 ENGLISH AND FRENCH BOOKS, ARTICLES, AND
PAMPHLETS. PUBLICATIONS DATE FROM 18TH CENTURY. TREATS THE
CASES OF BLOUNT, PICKERING, CHASE, HUMPHREYS, JOHNSON, BEL-
KAP, SWAYNE, ARCHBALD, AND OTHERS FROM THE STATE LEGIS-
LATURES, THE UK, AND FRANCE. SUPPLEMENT PRINTED IN 1931
BY FLORENCE HELLMAN CONTAINS 45 MORE ENTRIES.

0936 GRIFFIN G.G. ED.
A GUIDE TO MANUSCRIPTS RELATING TO AMERICAN HISTORY IN
BRITISH DEPOSITORIES.
WASHINGTON: LIBRARY OF CONGRESS, 1946, 313 PP.
    NOT A COMPLETE LISTING OF DOCUMENTS RELATING TO US HIS-
TORY IN BRITISH DEPOSITORIES, BUT A GUIDE TO FACSIMILE
REPRODUCTIONS OF MANUSCRIPTS AVAILABLE IN THE LIBRARY OF
CONGRESS. SOURCES INCLUDE OFFICIAL ARCHIVES OF BRITAIN,
CANADA, SCOTLAND, WALES, IRELAND, AND VARIOUS PRIVATE
COLLECTIONS. MANUSCRIPTS ARE MOSTLY 18TH-CENTURY RECORDS
COVERING MANY DIVERSE TOPICS.

0937 GRIFFIN H.C.
"PREJUDICIAL PUBLICITY: SEARCH FOR A CIVIL REMEDY."
NOTRE DAME LAWYER, 42 (1967), 943-956.
    INVESTIGATES POSSIBILITY OF FINDING RELIEF FOR VICTIM OF
PREJUDICIAL PUBLICITY IN ONE OF CIVIL REMEDIES. EXPLORES
NEED FOR SYSTEM AND PRESENTS STATUATE TO MEET NEED BY MAKING
PRESS LIABLE FOR COSTS OF NEW TRIAL OR OTHER CHANGES, THERE-
BY REDUCING PREJUDICIAL PUBLICITY.

0938 GRIFFITH E.S.
"THE CHANGING PATTERN OF PUBLIC POLICY FORMATION."
AM. POL. SCI. REV., 38 (JUNE 44), 445-459.
    CONSIDERS CHANGES IN OVER-ALL CULTURE OF WHICH PUBLIC
POLICY FORMATION IS A PART AND MORE PRECISE CHANGES IN
POLICY FORMATION.

0939 GRIFFITH E.S. ED.
RESEARCH IN POLITICAL SCIENCE: THE WORK OF PANELS OF RE-
SEARCH COMMITTEE, APSA.
PRINCETON* UNIV. REF. SYSTEM, 1948, 238 PP., LC#49-63042.
    ARTICLES, MANY BY LEADING MEN IN THE FIELD, DISCUSSING
PROBLEMS OF POLITICAL SCIENCE RESEARCH. IN ADDITION TO
STANDARD DIVISIONS, STUDY OF WAR, MILITARY OCCUPATION,
AND POLITICAL COMMUNICATIONS ARE INCLUDED. EDITOR
CLOSES WITH CHAPTERS ON METHOD AND PROSPECTS. INCLUDES
LIST OF SOURCES.

0940 GRIFFITH J.A.G., STREET H.
PRINCIPLES OF ADMINISTRATIVE LAW (3RD ED.)
NEW YORK: PITMAN PUBLISHING, 1963, 339 PP., LC#63-24929.
    DISCUSSES PROBLEMS OF LAW IN ITS RELATION TO ADMINISTRA-
TION, INCLUDING LEGISLATIVE POWERS OF ADMINISTRATION AND
THEIR CONTROL, ADMINISTRATIVE AND JUDICIAL POWERS AND
CONTROL, AND PUBLIC CORPORATIONS.

0941 GRIFFITH W.E.
THE SINO-SOVIET RIFT.
CAMBRIDGE: M.I.T. PR., 1964, 508 PP.,
    CHRONOLOGICAL ACCOUNT, COMPREHENSIVELY DOCUMENTED, OF
SINO-SOVIET CONTROVERSY, NOTING REACTIONS TO SOVIET-YUGOSLAV
RAPPROCHEMENT, CUBAN CRISIS AND ITS AFTERMATH. PARTY CON-
RESSES, AND TEST BAN TREATY. COVERS PERIOD: FEB. 62-JAN. 63.

0942 GRINDEL C.W.
CONCEPT OF FREEDOM.
CHICAGO: HENRY REGNERY CO, 1955, 512 PP., LC#55-10062.
    DEALS WITH APPLICATION OF CONCEPT OF FREEDOM TO THEOLOGY,
ECONOMICS, LAW, INTERNATIONAL RELATIONS, EDUCATION, LABOR,
AND GOVERNMENT.

0943 GRISWOLD A.W.
THE FAR EASTERN POLICY OF THE UNITED STATES.
NEW YORK: HARCOURT BRACE, 1938, 530 PP.
    TRACES FAR EASTERN POLICY OF US FROM 1898-1938.
EMPHASIZES COMMERCIAL AIMS OF DIPLOMACY AND OPEN DOOR
POLICY. DISCUSSES ANNEXATION OF PHILIPPINES, THEODORE
ROOSEVELT'S POLICY, WWI, WILSON AND JAPAN, TREATIES AFTER
WWI, IMMIGRATION, LEAGUE OF NATIONS, CHINESE NATIONALISM

JAPAN'S MOVEMENT INTO MANCHURIA, AND FDR'S POLICY.

0944 GROB F.
THE RELATIVITY OF WAR AND PEACE: A STUDY IN LAW, HISTORY,
AND POLITICS.
TORONTO: RYERSON PRESS, 1949, 402 PP.
DISCUSSES DEFINITIONS OF PEACE AND WAR FROM POINT OF
VIEW OF INTERNATIONAL AND MUNICIPAL LAW, HISTORY, AND
POLITICS. REVIEWS TERMINOLOGY. TREATS CASES IN WHICH LEGAL
STANDING OF WAR OR PEACE HAS NEVER BEEN DECIDED AND BATTLES
FOUGHT IN PEACE TIME. STUDIES LEGAL DEBATES. MAINTAINS THAT
DEFINITIONS ARE RELATIVE TO SITUATION.

0945 GROGAN V.
ADMINISTRATIVE TRIBUNALS IN THE PUBLIC SERVICE.
DUBLIN: INST PUBLIC ADMIN, 1962, 76 PP.
STUDIES GROUPS WHOSE FUNCTION IS TO JUDGE ISSUES ARISING
IN ADMINISTRATION OF JUDICIAL CONTROL OVER TRIBUNALS AND
ADMINISTRATIVE LAW. COMPARES IRISH AND ENGLISH ADMINISTRA-
TIVE SYSTEMS.

0946 GRONING J.
BIBLIOTHECA JURIS GENTIUM COMMUNIS, QUA PRAECIPUORUM, ASIAE,
AFRICAE, ET AMERICAE, POPULORUM DE JURIS NATURAE...
HAMBURG: J GRONING, 1701, 150 PP.
BIBLIOGRAPHY OF LAWS COMMON TO NATIONS, DEALING WITH THE
PRINCIPAL PEOPLES OF AFRICA, ASIA, AND AMERICA.

0947 GRONING J.
BIBLIOTHECA JURIS GENTIUM EXOTICA.
HAMBURG: J GRONING, 1703, 150 PP.
BIBLIOGRAPHY OF LAW OF FOREIGN NATIONS INCLUDING AFRICA,
ASIA, AND AMERICA.

0948 GROSS B.M.
THE LEGISLATIVE STRUGGLE: A STUDY IN SOCIAL COMBAT.
NEW YORK: MCGRAW HILL, 1953, 459 PP., LC#52-11509.
ATTEMPTS TO DEVELOP A SYSTEMATIC METHOD OF DEALING WITH
LEGISLATION. EMPHASIZES PEOPLE IN ACTION AS ESSENCE OF
LEGISLATIVE ACTIVITY.

0949 GROSS L.
"THE PEACE OF WESTPHALIA, 1648-1948."
AMER. J. OF INT. LAW, 42 (JAN. 48), 20-41.
DISCUSSES BACKGROUND AND CHARACTER OF PEACE OF WESTPHALIA
AS FIRST ATTEMPT AT WORLD UNITY. IMPLICATIONS OF CHARTER
INCLUDE IMPETUS TO SYSTEM OF INTERNATIONAL LAW, STIMULUS TO
THEORY AND PRACTICE OF BALANCE OF POWER, AND DEVELOPMENT OF
WORLD-WIDE POLITICAL SYSTEM. CHARTER ENCOURAGED
INDIVIDUALISM OF NATIONAL STATES, AN UNDESIRABLE TRAIT STILL
EXTANT IN INTERNATIONAL AFFAIRS.

0950 GROSS L.
"IMMUNITIES AND PRIVILEGES OF DELIGATIONS TO THE UNITED
NATIONS."
INT. ORGAN., 16 (SUMMER 62), 483-520.
PRESENTS PROVISIONS ON STATUS OF DELEGATIONS. SHOWS PROB-
LEMS ARISING DURING STAY IN USA. SUGGESTS USA, AS HOST COUN-
TRY, RE-EVALUATE POSITION ON PROVISIONS OF GENERAL CONVEN-
TION AND ON CRITERIA FOR ACCREDITATION.

0951 GROSS L.
"PROBLEMS OF INTERNATIONAL ADJUDICATION AND COMPLIANCE
WITH INTERNATIONAL LAW: SOME SIMPLE SOLUTIONS."
AMER. J. INT. LAW, 59 (JAN. 65), 48-59.
'MORE AND SPEEDIER PROGRESS COULD BE MADE BY REDUCING THE
QUANTITY OF LAW - LESS LAW, LESS VIOLATION OF LAW, MORE
COMPLIANCE' AS USEFUL BASIS FOR LEGAL PRECEPTS. AUTHOR
APPLIES 'POSITIVE PLAIN-MEANING' AND 'SURVIVAL' PRINCIPLE.

0952 GROTIUS H.
DE JURE BELLI AC PACIS.
LONDON: BASSET, 1682, 571 PP.
EXAMINES NATURE OF INTERNATIONAL LAW. QUESTIONS WHETHER
ANY WAR CAN BE JUST. ANALYZES JUST AND UNJUST CAUSES OF WAR.
REASONS WHAT IN CONDUCT OF WAR IS LAWFUL, WHAT IS UNLAWFUL.

0953 GROVES H.E.
THE CONSTITUTION OF MALAYSIA.
SINGAPORE: MALAYSIA PUBL LTD, 1964, 239 PP.
DISCUSSES GENERAL CHARACTERISTICS OF MALAYSIAN
CONSTITUTION AND ARRANGES ARTICLES AROUND INSTITUTIONS AND
CONCEPTS WITH WHICH DOCUMENT IS CONCERNED. SHOWS HOW
CONSTITUTION HAS BEEN INTERPRETED BY COURTS AND BY
LEGISLATURE. AREAS COVERED ARE SELECTION OF RULER, CABINET,
CONFERENCE OF RULERS, PARLIAMENT, ELECTIONS, JUDICIARY,
FEDERALISM, CITIZENSHIP, LIBERTIES, AND AGENCIES.

0954 GRUNEWALD D., BASS H.L.
PUBLIC POLICY AND THE MODERN COOPERATION: SELECTED
READINGS.
NEW YORK: APPLETON, 1966, 380 PP., LC#66-10939.
STUDIES IN PUBLIC POLICY AND MODES OF COOPERATION. VIEWS
ISSUE OF LARGENESS IN BUSINESS COOPERATIONS AS
ECONOMICALLY, SOCIALLY, AND POLITICALLY SIGNIFICANT.
DISCUSSES ANTITRUST LAW AND POLICY; PUBLIC POLICY

TOWARD REGULATED SECTOR; TARIFFS, CARTELS, AND BUSINESS
ABROAD; AND SOCIAL SIGNIFICANCE OF THE MODERN COOPERATION.

0955 GRZYBOWSKI K.
SOVIET LEGAL INSTITUTIONS.
ANN ARBOR: U OF MICH PR, 1962, 284 PP., LC#62-12163.
DESCRIBES SOVIET JUDICIAL PROCESS, EMPHASIZING ATTEMPT
OF FRAMERS TO RESHAPE IDEAS AND ATTITUDES OF SOVIET CITIZENS
THROUGH EDUCATION. ROLE OF COURTS AS AN EDUCATIONAL FORCE
AND POWER THEY POSSESS TO ENFORCE THEIR DICTATES ARE DIS-
CUSSED. COMPARISONS ARE MADE TO US SYSTEM REGARDING CRIMES,
PUNISHMENT, PROCESSES, AND INSTITUTIONS.

0956 GRZYBOWSKI K.
THE SOCIALIST COMMONWEALTH OF NATIONS: ORGANIZATIONS AND
INSTITUTIONS.
NEW HAVEN: YALE U PR, 1964, 265 PP., LC#64-20919.
ANALYSIS OF LEGAL BASES AND PRACTICES OF THE SEVERAL
REGIONAL ORGANIZATIONS IN EASTERN EUROPE.

0957 GSOVSKI V. ED., KLESMENT J. ET AL.
LEGAL SOURCES AND BIBLIOGRAPHY OF THE BALTIC STATES
(ESTONIA, LATVIA, LITHUANIA)
NEW YORK: FREDERICK PRAEGER, 1963, 197 PP., LC#63-15981.
MATERIALS ORGANIZED BY SUBJECT AND COUNTRY FROM 1913 TO
1963. SOURCES OF ALL TYPES AND OFTEN IN BALTIC LANGUAGES.
AUTHOR, TITLE, AND SUBJECT INDEXES. CONTAINS 1,200 ITEMS.

0958 GSOVSKI V. ED., GRZYBOWSKI K. ED.
GOVERNMENT, LAW, AND COURTS IN THE SOVIET UNION AND EASTERN
EUROPE (2 VOLS.)
NEW YORK: FREDERICK PRAEGER, 1959, 2067 PP.
DEALS WITH ORIGIN AND SPECIFIC FEATURES OF SOVIET REGIME
IN EACH COUNTRY (USSR, AND EASTERN EUROPE), ADMINISTRATION
OF JUSTICE, JUDICIAL PROCEDURE, SUBSTANTIVE CRIMINAL LAW.
ANALYZES SOVIETIZATION OF CIVIL LAW, INCLUDING LAWS DEALING
WITH WORKER AND FACTORY, LAND AND PEASANT. ELUCIDATES RIGHTS
OF INDIVIDUALS AND THEIR PROTECTION WITHIN SOVIET ORBIT.

0959 GUAITA A.
BIBLIOGRAFIA ESPANOLA DE DERECHO ADMINISTRATIVO (PAMPHLET)
BARCELONA: INST DERECHO COMPAREDO, 1955, 113 PP.
BIBLIOGRAPHY OF ADMINISTRATIVE LAW WITH 80 PAGES OF EN-
TRIES, IN SPANISH, 1882-1953, LISTED TOPICALLY.

0960 GUINS G.C.
"SOVIET LAW AND SOVIET SOCIETY."
THE HAGUE: MARTINUS NIJHOFF, 1954.
DISCUSSION AND LENGTHY NOTES AND BIBLIOGRAPHY ON
VARIOUS ASPECTS OF SOVIET LAW AND SOCIETY: ETHICAL FOUNDA-
TIONS OF THE SOVIET STRUCTURE; MACHANISM OF THE PLANNED
SOCIETY; DUTIES AND RIGHTS OF PEASANTS AND WORKERS;
RULERS AND TOILERS; THE FAMILY AND THE STATE; SOVIET
JUSTICE; NATIONAL MINORITIES AND THEIR AUTONOMY; PEO-
PLE'S DEMOCRACIES AND SOVIET PATTERN FOR A UNITED WORLD.

0961 GUIZOT F.P.G.
HISTORY OF THE ORIGIN OF REPRESENTATIVE GOVERNMENT IN
EUROPE.
LONDON: HG BOHN, 1861, 520 PP.
TRACES DEVELOPMENT OF REPRESENTATION IN FRANCE, SPAIN,
AND ENGLAND 350-1850. CHAPTERS DEAL WITH PRIMITIVE
INSTITUTIONS, EFFECT OF MILITARY SERVICE, AND CONSTITUTIONAL
DEVELOPMENT. SECOND PART OF BOOK DEALS WITH TRANSFORMATION
OF ENGLAND FROM ABSOLUTE TO CONSTITUTIONAL MONARCHY AND
WITH RISE OF PARLIAMENT.

0962 GUMPLOWICZ L.
RECHTSSTAAT UND SOZIALISMUS.
OSNABRUCK: OTTO ZELLER, 1964, 548 PP.
DISCUSSES TRADITIONAL CONCEPTS OF THEORY OF STATE AS
PUBLIC AND PRIVATE LAW, ROLE OF JURISPRUDENCE, AND EXAMINES
CONCEPT OF PEOPLE AND STATE IN KANT, SAVIGNY, GROTIUS,
HOBBES, AND MANY OTHERS. DISCUSSES PRINCIPLES OF COMMUNISM
AND SOCIALISM.

0963 GURVITCH G.
"MAJOR PROBLEMS OF THE SOCIOLOGY OF LAW."
J. SOCIAL PHILOSOPHY, 6 (APR. 40), 197-215.
DISCUSSES THE INTER-RELATEDNESS OF SOCIOLOGY, MORALITY,
RELIGION, LAW, AND PHILOSOPHY. IS CONCERNED WITH GENERAL
PHILOSOPHIC APPROACH TO THE SOCIOLOGY OF LAW RATHER THAN
SOCIOLOGICAL JURISPRUDENCE. THESIS CONCERNS IMPORTANCE OF
MORAL AND RELIGIOUS BASES IN STUDY OF THE SOCIOLOGY OF LAW.

0964 GURVITCH G.
SOCIOLOGY OF LAW.
NEW YORK: PHILOSOPHICAL LIB, 1942, 309 PP.
DISCUSSES THEORY OF THE SOCIOLOGY OF LAW. SOCIOLOGY OF
LAW IS VIEWED AS A SCIENCE OF SOCIAL ENGINEERING, EMPLOYING
THOSE TECHNIQUES OF SOCIAL ENGINEERING BEST SUITED TO A
GIVEN INTERPRETATION OF THE NEEDS OF VARIOUS SOCIETIES AND
SYSTEMS OF LAW. ANALYZES WAY IN WHICH LAW REFLECTS THE
SOCIETY OF WHICH IT IS A PART.

0965 GUTTMANN A. ED., ZIEGLER B.M. ED.

COMMUNISM, THE COURTS, AND THE CONSTITUTION.
BOSTON: D C HEATH, 1964, 132 PP.
   DISCUSSES COMMUNIST PARTY IN US AND ITS MEMBERS' CIVIL
RIGHTS. PRESENTS ESSAYS BY AMERICAN COMMUNISTS ON THEIR
POLICIES. SMITH AND MCCARRAN ACTS AND COURT CASES RELATED
TO THEM. COMMENTS ON CONTROVERSY OVER COMMUNISTS' CIVIL
RIGHTS.

0966 GYORGY A. ED., GIBBS H.P. ED.
PROBLEMS IN INTERNATIONAL RELATIONS.
ENGLEWOOD CLIFFS: PRENTICE HALL, 1962, 330 PP., LC#55-6993.
   ESSAYS FOCUSING ON CASE STUDIES TOPICALLY GROUPED UNDER
COMMUNIST CHALLENGE AND WESTERN RESPONSE. ROLE
OF LESSER POWERS, IDEOLOGY, UN, AND INTERNATIONAL LAW.

0967 HAAR C.M.
LAW AND LAND: ANGLO-AMERICAN PLANNING PRACTICE.
CAMBRIDGE: HARVARD U PR, 1964, 290 PP., LC#64-11129.
   EXAMINES CITY PLANNING IN CONTEXT OF US AND BRITISH LEGAL
SYSTEMS. HOPES TO INDICATE HOW INSTITUTIONS OF LAW AND
PROPERTY CAN BE MOLDED INTO A MORE RATIONAL AND EFFECTIVE
MEANS OF ORGANIZING LAND USE. TREATS THEORY AND FRAMEWORK
OF PLANNING, FORMULATION OF PLANS, THE INDIVIDUAL'S RELATION
TO MACHINERY OF PLANNING, AND FINANCIAL BASES OF PLANNING.

0968 HABERLER G.
A SURVEY OF INTERNATIONAL TRADE THEORY.
LONDON: WM HODGE AND CO LTD, 1965, 386 PP.
   ATTEMPTING SYSTEMATIC TREATMENT OF PROBLEMS OF FOREIGN
TRADE, ADVOCATES FREE TRADE AS GENERAL POLICY. USES
STATISTICAL AND HISTORICAL ANALYSIS TO CONSIDER MONETARY
PROBLEMS, TARIFFS, MONOPOLY, AND TREATY EFFECTS IN SELECT
CASES: FRANCE, 1871; CANADA, 1900-14; AND GERMANY, 1918-32.

0969 HABERMAS J.
THEORIE UND PRAXIS.
BERLIN: H LUCHTERHAND VERL, 1963, 378 PP.
   CRITICAL ESSAYS ON NATURAL LAW, REVOLUTION, HEGEL'S CRI-
TIQUE OF FRENCH REVOLUTION, DIALECTICAL IDEALISM, DOGMA-
TISM, REASON, AND DECISION. INCLUDES APPENDIX OF THESES ON
MARXISM, BLOCH'S SPECULATIVE MATERIALISM, AND LOWITH'S RE-
TREAT FROM HISTORICAL CONSCIOUSNESS.

0970 HACKER A.
CONGRESSIONAL DISTRICTING: THE ISSUE OF EQUAL REPRESENTATION
WASHINGTON: BROOKINGS INST, 1963, 132 PP.
   ARGUES STRONGLY FOR EQUAL POPULATION DISTRICTS. BELIEVES
THAT CORRECTIVE ACTION WILL COME PRIMARILY FROM THE COURTS,
RATHER THAN THE STATES OR CONGRESS. DISCUSSES THE HISTORICAL
AND LEGAL BACKGROUND OF PRESENT APPORTIONMENT SYSTEMS AND
THEIR EFFECTS ON THE POLITICAL SYSTEM AND THE LIKELIHOOD OF
CHANGE IN THE FUTURE.

0971 HADDOW A.
"POLITICAL SCIENCE IN AMERICAN COLLEGES AND UNIVERSITIES
1636-1900."
NEW YORK: APPLETON, 1939.
   SURVEY OF COLLEGE AND UNIVERSITY INSTRUCTION IN POLITICAL
SCIENCE FROM THE COLONIAL PERIOD THROUGH THE 20TH CENTURY.
EXAMINES BEGINNINGS AND DEVELOPMENT OF POLITICAL SCIENCE
AS AN ACADEMIC DISCIPLINE IN THE US. UNANNOTATED BIBLIOGRA-
PHY OF 358 WORKS IN POLITICAL ECONOMY, POLITICAL PHILOSOPHY,
INTERNATIONAL LAW, CONSTITUTION, AND GOVERNMENT PRACTI-
CES; PRINTED LECTURES IN MORAL PHILOSOPHY AND LAW.

0972 HADWEN J.G., KAUFMANN J.
HOW UNITED NATIONS DECISIONS ARE MADE.
LEYDEN: SYTHOFF, 1962, 179 PP., $3.75.
   DESCRIBES MACHINERY OF UN FOR CONSIDERING ECONOMIC QUES-
TIONS AND INDICATES DETERMINANT FORCES AND PROCEDURES.
USE PERSONAL UN EXPERIENCE AS REFERENCE. ELUCIDATES UNWRIT-
TEN PROCEDURES OF NATIONAL DELEGATIONS.

0973 HAEFELE E.T., STEINBERG E.B.
GOVERNMENT CONTROLS ON TRANSPORT.
WASHINGTON: BROOKINGS INST, 1965, 102 PP., LC#65-28379.
   STUDIES NEED FOR TRANSPORT INVESTMENT IN EMERGING NATIONS
OF AFRICA AND UTILIZATION OF EXISTING FACILITIES. PROBLEM
OF CONTROL IS INTENSIFIED WHERE TWO NATIONS SHARE FACILITIES
AS THEY DO ON MUCH OF CONTINENT. EXAMINES INSTITUTIONS,
POLICIES, AND CONTROLS THAT DETERMINE TRANSPORT PATTERNS.

0974 HAENSCH G. ED.
PAN-AFRICANISM IN ACTION: AN ACCOUNT OF THE UAM
TIC AND ALPHABETICAL IN GERMAN, ENGLISH, FRENCH AND SPANISH.
LONDON: AM. ELSEVIER, 1965, 638 PP., LC#64-8710.
   TERMS USED IN INTERNATIONAL RELATIONS AND POLITICS ARE
FROM FEDERALISM TO MERE COOPERATION AMONG SOVEREIGNS. PRAC-
FOLLOWING SEQUENCE: NAMES OF STATES, DOMESTIC POLITICS, IN-
IENCES AND SECRETARY GENERAL OF THE NOW-DISSOLVED UNION AF-
TION, NEGOTIATION, TREATIES, ORGANIZATIONS, COURTS, WAR,
DISARMAMENT, AND NEUTRALITY), AND POLITICAL AND DIPLOMATIC
HISTORY. ALSO INDIVIDUAL ALPHABETIZED LANGUAGE INDEXES.

0975 HAGEN A.
STAAT UND KATHOLISCHE KIRCHE IN WURTTEMBERG IN DEN JAHREN

1848-1862 (2 VOLS.)
AMSTERDAM: VERLAG P SCHIPPERS, 1961, 606 PP.
   EXAMINES LEGAL POSITION OF CATHOLIC CHURCH IN WURTTEM-
BERG, GERMANY BETWEEN 1848 AND 1862. DISCUSSES STRUGGLES FOR
INSTITUTIONAL INDEPENDENCE AND NEGOTIATIONS WITH STATE TO
ACHIEVE INFLUENCE IN EDUCATION, MARRIAGE LAWS, AND POLITICS.

0976 HAGUE PERMANENT CT INTL JUSTIC
WORLD COURT REPORTS: COLLECTION OF THE JUDGEMENTS ORDERS AND
OPINIONS VOLUME 3 1932-35.
WASHINGTON: CARNEGIE ENDOWMENT, 1938, 549 PP., LC#34-42544.
   ACTUAL COURT CASES PRESENTED JUST PRIOR TO AMENDMENTS IN
STATUTE AND RULES. INCLUDES REQUESTS FOR ADVICE, CASES TER-
MINATED WITHOUT JUDGMENT, AND FULL CASES IN OFFICIAL ENG-
LISH VERSIONS OR TRANSLATIONS.

0977 HAGUE PERMANENT CT INTL JUSTIC
WORLD COURT REPORTS: COLLECTION OF THE JUDGEMENTS ORDERS AND
OPINIONS VOLUME 4 1936-42.
NEW YORK: COLUMBIA U PRESS, 1943, 513 PP.
   COURT'S JURISPRUDENCE JUST AFTER AMENDED STATUTES AND
RULES AND PRIOR TO GAP DURING WWI. INCLUDES TEN CASES, ONLY
EIGHT OF WHICH WERE DISPOSED OF BEFORE WAR. TEXT IN OFFICIAL
ENGLISH AND INCLUDES AMENDED STATUTES.

0978 HALDEMAN E., BASSET E.
"SERIALS OF AN INTERNATIONAL CHARACTER."
INSTITUTE OF INTERNAT. EDUCATION, 2 (MAY-JULY 21), 1-61.
   AN UNANNOTATED BIBLIOGRAPHY OF PERIODICALS AND SERIALS OF
AN INTERNATIONAL CHARACTER. ENGLISH-LANGUAGE AND FRENCH,
GERMAN, ITALIAN, AND SPANISH MATERIALS. RANGES FROM 1815
TO 1921. SUBJECT MATTER OF BIBLIOGRAPHY IS NONSPECIFIC AND
RANGES OVER MANY CATEGORIES OF KNOWLEDGE. 840 ENTRIES.

0979 HALEY A.G. ED., HEINRICH W. ED.
FIRST COLLOQUIUM ON THE LAW OF OUTER SPACE.
VIENNA: SPRINGER VERLAG, 1959.
   RECORD OF PROCEEDINGS OF SPACE LAW CONFERENCE, DISCUSSING
LEGAL BOUNDARIES, SCIENTIFIC SPACE STRATEGY, PROBLEMS OF
SOVEREIGNTY, AND INTERNATIONALIZATION OF OUTER SPACE.

0980 HALEY A.G.
SPACE LAW AND GOVERNMENT.
NEW YORK: APPLETON, 1963, 584 PP., $15.00.
   RANGES FROM THE TRADITIONAL BASES OF INTERNATIONAL LAW
AND PROBLEMS OF NATIONAL SOVEREIGNTY, ACROSS TECHNOLOGICAL
CAPABILITIES AND QUESTIONS OF LIABILITY AND REGULATION, TO
THE ROLE OF INTERGOVERNMENTAL AND NONGOVERNMENTAL AGENCIES
IN FOCUSING ATTENTION ON SCIENTIFIC AND LEGAL ASPECTS OF
SPACE EXPLORATION. A COMPREHENSIVE, DEFINITIVE STUDY OF
LEGAL AND SOCIOLOGICAL ISSUES OF SPACE FLIGHT.

0981 HALL A.B.
"DETERMINATION OF METHODS FOR ASCERTAINING THE FACTORS THAT
INFLUENCE JUDICIAL DECISIONS IN CASES INVOLVING DUE PROCESS"
AM. POL. SCI. REV., 20 (FEB. 26), 127-134.
   PROPOSES TO EVOLVE METHOD FOR SECURING BEHAVIOR PATTERN
OF JUDICIAL PROCESS. PROVIDES OBJECTIVE BASIS FOR CON-
STRUCTIVE CRITICISM OF WORK OF INDIVIDUAL JUDGE. AT-
TEMPTS TO INCREASE SCIENTIFIC AND INTELLIGIBLE STAND-
ARDS IN JUDICIAL DECISIONS AND REDUCE RHETORIC AND VERBIAGE.

0982 HALL J.
THEFT, LAW, AND SOCIETY.
BOSTON: LITTLE BROWN, 1935, 360 PP.
   DISCUSSES GROWTH OF LAW OF THEFT IN 18TH CENTURY AND
INAPPLICABILITY OF LAWS RELATING TO LARCENY. ADVOCATES
DIVISION OF LAW TO DEAL WITH DIFFERENT BEHAVIORS AND
DIFFERENT KINDS OF PEOPLE. ANALYZES SPECIFIC AREAS OF LEGAL
PROBLEMS: RECEIVING STOLEN PROPERTY AND AUTOMOBILE THEFT.
URGES TREATMENT OF THEFT AS SOCIAL PROBLEM.

0983 HALL J.
STUDIES IN JURISPRUDENCE AND CRIMINAL THEORY.
NEW YORK: OCEANA PUBLISHING, 1958, 300 PP., LC#58-9195.
   DISCUSSES ASPECTS OF LEGAL THEORY AND JURISPRUDENCE.
EXAMINES PLATO'S LEGAL PHILOSOPHY, RELATION BETWEEN CULTURE
AND JURISPRUDENCE, EVOLUTION OF US JURISPRUDENCE, CRIME AND
FEDERAL CRIMINAL PROCEDURE, CRIMINAL RESPONSIBILITY, AND
REFORMS IN CRIMINAL LAW.

0984 HALL J.
COMPARATIVE LAW AND SOCIAL THEORY.
BATON ROUGE: LOUISIANA STATE U. PR., 1963, 167 PP., $5.00.
   HOLDS THAT COMPARATIVE LAW IS A DISCIPLINE WHICH MIGHT
BE CALLED THE 'HUMANISTIC SOCIOLOGY OF LAW.' INCLUDES SUCH
ELEMENTS AS CULTURAL LEGAL HISTORY, SOCIO-LEGAL STUDIES
USING THE CASE HISTORY METHOD, WORLD UNIFICATION OF LAW,
AND THE BASIC COMPARISON OF POSITIVE LAW. POINTS OUT THE
IMPORTANCE OF A LEGAL ORIENTATION FOR ALL SOCIAL SCIENCE.

0985 HALL W.E.
A TREATISE ON INTERNATIONAL LAW.
OXFORD: CLARENDON PR., 1924, 952 PP.
   EXAMINES CHANGES IN INTERNATIONAL LAW RESULTING FROM
LEAGUE OF NATIONS AND PEACE TREATIES. ATTACKS OUTMODED BASES

OF LAW. VIEWS IT AS BASIS FOR SOLVING DIFFERENCES BETWEEN NATIONS. URGES EXTENSION OF LAW TO GRAPPLE WITH FUNDAMENTAL RELATIONSHIPS OF STATES.

0986 HALLER W.
DER SCHWEDISCHE JUSTITIEOMBUDSMAN.
ZURICH: POLYGRAPHISCHER VERLAG, 1964, 320 PP.
DISCUSSES BASIC FOUNDATIONS OF SWEDISH LAW, HISTORY OF OFFICE OF PARLIAMENTARY COMMISSIONER FOR JUDICIAL AND CIVIL-ADMINISTRATION, AND FUNCTIONS AND RESPONSIBILITIES OF COMMISSIONER (JUSTITIEOMBUDSMAN). COMPARES HIS FUNCTION TO SIMILAR PRACTICES IN OTHER COUNTRIES.

0987 HAMBRO C.J.
HOW TO WIN THE PEACE.
PHILADELPHIA: LIPPINCOTT, 1942, 384 PP.
INDICATES FRAMEWORK OF FUTURE UNIVERSAL FEDERATION OF STATES: INTERNATIONAL LAW COURTS AND LAW ENFORCEMENT, SANCTION SYSTEMS, ETC. FEELS INTERNATIONALISM IS KEY TO FUTURE.

0988 HAMILTON H.D. ED.
LEGISLATIVE APPORTIONMENT; KEY TO POWER.
NEW YORK: HARPER & ROW, 1964, 181 PP., LC#64-7649.
COLLECTION ON REQUIREMENTS FOR REAPPORTIONMENT OF STATE LEGISLATURES AND CONGRESSIONAL DISTRICTS AS RESULT OF FEDERAL SUPREME COURT DECISIONS. SIGNIFICANCE FOR FUTURE POLITICAL SYSTEM OF ELECTORAL CHANGES.

0989 HAMILTON H.D. ED.
REAPPORTIONING LEGISLATURES.
COLUMBUS: CHARLES MERRILL, 1966, 154 PP., LC#66-28769.
COLLECTION OF PAPERS DISCUSSING THEORY AND PRACTICE OF REPRESENTATION, INCLUDING FAIR APPORTIONMENT, CRITERIA OF RECENT COURT DECISIONS, COMPUTER DISTRICTING, AND RELATION TO ELECTION AND PARTY SYSTEMS.

0990 HAMILTON H.D.
"LEGISLATIVE CONSTITUENCIES: SINGLE-MEMBER DISTRICTS, MULTI-MEMBER DISTRICTS, AND FLOTERAL DISTRICTS."
WESTERN POLIT. QUART., 20 (JUNE 67), 321-340
ANALYZES AND COMPARES CHARACTERISTICS, CONSEQUENCES, AND MERITS OF SMD VS. MMD PATTERN OF REPRESENTATION IN US. CHALLENGES COURT RULING IN 1962 CASE BECAUSE COURT ONLY CONSIDERED THESE TWO TYPES OF DISTRICTS AS PRESENT IN US. FEELS THERE ARE MORE TYPES AND DISCUSSES AND DESCRIBES THEM IN THEIR FUNCTIONS, WARNING THAT ALL DISTRICTING SHOULD BE USED CAUTIOUSLY.

0991 HAMILTON W.H., ADAIR D.
THE POWER TO GOVERN.
NEW YORK: W W NORTON, 1937, 249 PP.
DISCUSSES CHARACTER, PARTICULARS, AND EFFECT ON COMMERCE OF THE CONSTITUTION WITH RESPECT TO PUBLIC OPINION, ECONOMY, PROBLEMS IN 1937, AND THE DOCUMENT ITSELF. EXAMINES ASPECTS OF SPECIFIC WARTIME POWERS, TREATIES, TAXES, TARIFFS, AND OTHER MEANS OF ENFORCEMENT. USES HISTORICAL LINGUISTICS TO DETERMINE WHAT CONSTITUTION'S FRAMERS INTENDED BY THEIR PHRASING.

0992 HAMSON C.J.
EXECUTIVE DISCRETION AND JUDICIAL CONTROL; AN ASPECT OF THE FRENCH CONSEIL D'ETAT.
LONDON: STEVENS, 1954, 222 PP.
STUDIES THE FRENCH POLITICAL INSTITUTION, DISCUSSING THE PROCEDURES AND RESPONSIBILITY OF THE CONSEIL. PRESENTS THE HISTORICAL DEVELOPMENTS AND EXAMINES THE PRINCIPLES UPON WHICH THE CONSEIL D'ETAT WORKS AS THE HIGHEST COURT IN FRANCE. CONCLUDES WITH A COMPARISON OF THE ENGLISH AND THE FRENCH JUDICIAL SYSTEM AT THIS HIGH LEVEL.

0993 HANBURY H.G.
ENGLISH COURTS OF LAW.
LONDON: OXFORD U PR, 1960, 196 PP.
DISCUSSES HISTORY OF ENGLISH JUDICIAL SYSTEM FROM REIGN OF HENRY II TO 20TH CENTURY. DISCUSSES ESTABLISHMENT AND EVOLUTION OF COURTS OF COMMON LAW AND CHANCERY. EXAMINES JUDICIAL SYSTEM IN RELATION TO OTHER BRANCHES OF GOVERNMENT AND CONSIDERS ROLES OF JUDGES, BARRISTERS, AND SOLICITORS IN CONSTITUTIONAL SYSTEM.

0994 HAND L.
THE BILL OF RIGHTS.
CAMBRIDGE: HARVARD U PR, 1958, 82 PP., LC#58-08248.
DESCRIBES FUNCTION OF US COURTS, ESPECIALLY THE SUPREME COURT, OF DECLARING STATUTES OF CONGRESS OR OF STATES INVALID, OR ACTS OF THE PRESIDENT, BECAUSE IN CONFLICT WITH THE BILL OF RIGHTS. CONSIDERS WHEN A COURT SHOULD INTERVENE, AND DISCUSSES THE FIFTH AND FOURTEENTH AMENDMENTS.

0995 HANNA W.J., HANNA J.L.
POLITICS IN BLACK AFRICA: A SELECTIVE BIBLIOGRAPHY OF RELEVANT PERIODICAL LITERATURE.
EAST LANSING: MICHIGAN STATE U, 1964, 139 PP., LC#64-64995.
LIST OF PERIODICAL ARTICLES SPECIFICALLY DESIGNED FOR SOCIAL SCIENTIST SPECIALIZING IN AFRICAN AFFAIRS. LISTS 1,283 ITEMS IN FRENCH AND ENGLISH ON TRADITION AND CHANGE,

COMMUNICATION, URBANIZATION, ECONOMY, COLONIALISM, NATIONALISM, LOCAL AND NATIONAL GOVERNMENT, LAW, INFLUENTIALS, POLITICAL PARTIES AND SELECTIONS, RACE RELATIONS, LABOR, AND INTERNATIONAL AFFAIRS.

0996 HANSON L.
GOVERNMENT AND THE PRESS 1695-1763.
LONDON: OXFORD U PR, 1936, 149 PP.
DESCRIBES RELATIONSHIP AND CONFLICT BETWEEN THE STATE AND THE PRESS, INCLUDING ADMINISTRATION OF CENSORSHIP LAWS, THE GOVERNMENT PRESS, AND DANIEL DEFOE. BIBLIOGRAPHY OF ABOUT 160 ENGLISH BOOKS, NEWSPAPERS, AND PERIODICALS FROM 1712 THROUGH 1934, ARRANGED ALPHABETICALLY BY AUTHOR AND TITLE.

0997 HANSON R.
FAIR REPRESENTATION COMES TO MARYLAND (PAMPHLET)
NEW YORK: MCGRAW HILL, 1964, 31 PP.
ANALYSIS OF REAPPORTIONMENT IN MARYLAND AS CAUSED BY SUPREME COURT DECISION ON EQUAL REPRESENTATION OF STATE LEGISLATURES IN CASE OF BAKER V. CARR.

0998 HANSON R.
THE POLITICAL THICKET.
ENGLEWOOD CLIFFS: PRENTICE HALL, 1966, 143 PP., LC#66-14700.
AN ANALYSIS OF HOW THE ISSUE OF REAPPORTIONMENT HAS BEEN DEALT WITH IN THE AMERICAN SYSTEM OF CONSTITUTIONAL DEMOCRACY. NOT CONCERNED WITH THE TECHNICAL ASPECTS OF REAPPORTIONMENT, BUT WITH THE INFLUENCE AND SIGNIFICANCE OF VALUES, CONSTITUTIONAL LAW, AND POLITICAL PRACTICE. AUTHOR RELATES THESE THREE VARIABLES TO DECISION-MAKING PROCESS, USING REAPPORTIONMENT ISSUE AS A MEANS OF ILLUSTRATION.

0999 HARGRETT L.
A BIBLIOGRAPHY OF THE CONSTITUTIONS AND LAWS OF THE AMERICAN INDIANS.
CAMBRIDGE: HARVARD U PR, 1947, 124 PP.
LIST OF CONSTITUTIONS AND LAWS WITH REFERENCE TO LOCATION IN LIBRARIES, ETC., PERTAINING TO SELF-GOVERNING TRIBES OF INDIAN TERRITORY. DOES NOT CONTINUE BEYOND DISSOLUTION OF INDIAN TERRITORY IN 1905. INCLUDES COMMENTS ON TRIBAL HISTORY AND GOVERNMENT.

1000 HARNETTY P.
"CANADA, SOUTH AFRICA AND THE COMMONWEALTH."
J. COMMONWEALTH POLIT. STUD., 2 (NOV. 63), 33-44.
EXAMINES CANADA'S ROLE IN THE WITHDRAWAL OF SOUTH AFRICA FROM THE COMMONWEALTH IN 1961. REGARDS CANADA'S CHANGE FROM A MODERATE POSITION TO A FIRM STAND AGAINST APARTHEID IN MAY 1960 AS ACTING IN ACCORDANCE WITH THE OTHER COMMONWEALTH NATIONS.

1001 HARPER S.N.
THE GOVERNMENT OF THE SOVIET UNION.
PRINCETON: VAN NOSTRAND, 1938, 204 PP.
DISCUSSES SOVIET INSTITUTIONS, GOVERNMENTAL STRUCTURES, AND METHODS OF GOVERNING IMMEDIATELY PRECEDING AND AFTER BOLSHEVIK RISE TO POWER. INCLUDES ECONOMIC STRUCTURES AND PLANS, PARTY POLICY, LAW-MAKING, PUBLIC ADMINISTRATION, AND PUBLIC SERVICES. ALSO TREATS ROLE OF INDIVIDUAL IN A COLLECTIVIZED STATE, INTERNATIONAL RELATIONSHIPS, GOAL OF WORLD REVOLUTION, AND 1937-38 TREASON TRIALS.

1002 HART J.
AN INTRODUCTION TO ADMINISTRATIVE LAW, WITH SELECTED CASES.
NEW YORK: F S CROFTS & CO, 1940, 621 PP.
GENERAL INTRODUCTION TO US ADMINISTRATIVE LAW. DEFINES ADMINISTRATIVE LAW, THEN DISCUSSES PUBLIC OFFICE AND OFFICERS. CONSIDERS POWERS OF ADMINISTRATIVE AUTHORITIES AND SCOPE AND LIMITS OF ADMINISTRATIVE POWERS. ENFORCEMENT OF ADMINISTRATIVE DECISIONS AND REMEDIES AGAINST ADMINISTRATIVE ACTION ARE TREATED. INCLUDES CRIMINAL, CONTRACTUAL, AND TORT LIABILITIES OF PUBLIC ADMINISTRATIVE OFFICERS.

1003 HART J.
"ADMINISTRATION AND THE COURTS."
ANN. ACAD. POL. SOC. SCI., 292 (MAR. 54), 88-94.
COURTS HAVE A TRADITIONAL CONSTITUTIONAL ROLE TO CONTROL AND CHECK ADMINISTRATION. BEST POSSIBLE POSITION OF COURTS IS THAT TAKEN SO FAR: NEITHER TRYING TO RUN ADMINISTRATIVE PROCESS NOR IGNORING IT.

1004 HARTUNG F.E.
CRIME, LAW, AND SOCIETY.
DETROIT: WAYNE STATE U PR, 1965, 320 PP., LC#65-13410.
THESIS IS THAT SOCIOCULTURAL LEARNING IS CRUCIAL IN DEVELOPMENT OF CRIMINALITY. FIRST EXPLAINS GENERAL THEORY OF CRIMINALITY AND SECOND EVALUATES TRENDS IN HANDLING OFFENDERS AND NONOFFENDERS. THEORY IS SOCIOLOGICAL AND IN ACCORD WITH CONCEPTION OF CRIME AS DELIBERATE AND INTENTIONAL.

1005 HARVARD LAW SCHOOL LIBRARY
ANNUAL LEGAL BIBLIOGRAPHY.
CAMBRIDGE: HARVARD LAW SCHOOL.
ANNUAL CUMULATION OF ARTICLES AND MONOGRAPHS RECEIVED BY HARVARD LAW SCHOOL LIBRARY INCLUDING ENTRIES IN "CURRENT

LEGAL BIBLIOGRAPHY." FIRST PUBLISHED 1961.

1006 HARVARD LAW SCHOOL LIBRARY
CURRENT LEGAL BIBLIOGRAPHY.
CAMBRIDGE: HARVARD LAW SCHOOL, 1960.
BIBLIOGRAPHY OF MATERIAL RECEIVED BY HARVARD'S LAW SCHOOL
LIBRARY PUBLISHED NINE TIMES A YEAR. INCLUDED IN "ANNUAL
LEGAL BIBLIOGRAPHY."

1007 HARVARD UNIVERSITY LAW LIBRARY
CATALOG OF INTERNATIONAL LAW AND RELATIONS.
NEW YORK: OCEANA PUBLISHING.
ANNUAL LISTING OF BOOKS, MONOGRAPHIC SERIES, SERIAL PUB-
LICATIONS, AND DOCUMENTS OF WORLD AUTHORS FROM ALL COUNTRIES
ON TOPICS OF INTERNATIONAL LAW. CATALOG BASED ON COLLECTION
OF SPANISH DIPLOMAT, MARQUIS DE OLIVAT. FIRST PUBLISHED
1965.

1008 HARVARD UNIVERSITY LAW LIBRARY
CATALOGUE OF THE LIBRARY OF THE LAW SCHOOL OF HARVARD
UNIVERSITY (3 VOLS.)
CAMBRIDGE: HARVARD U PR, 1909, 2462 PP.
CATALOGUE OF BOOKS ON AMERICAN AND ENGLISH COMMON LAW
CONTAINED IN THE HARVARD LAW LIBRARY. PUBLICATIONS AND CODES
COVER LEGAL HISTORY SINCE THE 14TH CENTURY. WORKS ENTERED
UNDER AUTHOR'S NAME ONLY.

1009 HARVARD UNIVERSITY LAW SCHOOL
INTERNATIONAL PROBLEMS OF FINANCIAL PROTECTION AGAINST
NUCLEAR RISK.
NEW YORK: ATOMIC INDUS FORUM, 1959, 96 PP.
STUDIES PROBLEMS DERIVING FROM POSSIBILITY OF SERIOUS
NUCLEAR INDUSTRIAL ACCIDENT AS TO LIABILITY LIMITATIONS,
INSURANCE, PROCESSING OF CLAIMS, COMPUTING PREMIUMS, AND
ROLE OF GOVERNMENT. ALSO CONCERNED WITH PROBLEMS OF
INTERNATIONAL COOPERATION IN THESE LAWSUITS.

1010 HARVEY W.B.
"THE RULE OF LAW IN HISTORICAL PERSPECTIVE."
MICHIGAN LAW REV., 59 (1961), 487-500.
RE-EXAMINES THE BASIC PROBLEM OF GOVERNMENT AND LAW.
DEMONSTRATES THAT EMERGING SOCIETIES AND OLDER ONES AS
WELL CHALLENGE TRADITIONAL CONCEPTS OF GOVERNMENT AND LAW
WITH INSISTENT DEMANDS FOR POSITIVE ACTION ON BROADER FRONTS
TO PROVIDE A BETTER LIFE FOR THE PEOPLE.

1011 HARVEY W.B.
LAW AND SOCIAL CHANGE IN GHANA.
PRINCETON: PRINCETON U PRESS, 1966, 453 PP., LC#65-17139.
STUDY OF LEGAL DEVELOPMENT IN GHANA AND IMPACT OF LAW ON
CHANGE IN LIFE AND POLITICS. DISCUSSES CONSTITUTION, POLITI-
CAL STRUCTURE, LEGAL RIGHT, AND POSITION OF LAWYER IN GHAN-
AIAN SOCIETY.

1012 HAUSMAN W.H. ED.
MANAGING ECONOMIC DEVELOPMENT IN AFRICA.
CAMBRIDGE: M I T PRESS, 1963, 253 PP., LC#63-16233.
ANTHOLOGY OF PAPERS ON MANAGEMENT OF AFRICAN ECONOMIC DE-
VELOPMENT COVERING PLANNING, MANPOWER, TECHNICAL ASSISTANCE,
CAPITAL, FOREIGN AID, LEGAL ASPECTS, AND US ROLE.

1013 HAUSNER G.
JUSTICE IN JERUSALEM.
NEW YORK: HARPER & ROW, 1966, 528 PP., LC#63-20290.
CHIEF PROSECUTOR AT TRIAL OF ADOLF EICHMANN REVIEWS HIS
ROLE IN TRIAL, PRESENTS HISTORY OF NAZI PERSECUTIONS AS
IT EMERGED IN PRETRIAL RESEARCH AND COURTROOM PROCEEDINGS,
AND DESCRIBES PRESSURES OF PUBLIC OPINION. RECOUNTS
TRIAL IN DETAIL.

1014 HAY P.
FEDERALISM AND SUPRANATIONAL ORGANIZATIONS: PATTERNS FOR
NEW LEGAL STRUCTURES.
URBANA: U OF ILLINOIS PR, 1966, 335 PP.
EXAMINES NATURE OF SUPRANATIONAL EEC LAW AND ITS
RELATION TO THE DOMESTIC LAW OF MEMBER STATES. DISCUSSES
PROVISIONS OF THE TREATY ESTABLISHING THE EUROPEAN ECONOMIC
COMMUNITY, AND POINTS OUT "FEDERAL" CHARACTER OF EEC AND
ITS LAW. REJECTS TRADITIONAL NOTION THAT SOVEREIGNTY IS AN
INALIENABLE ATTRIBUTE OF STATEHOOD, AND FINDS THAT MEMBERS
OF EEC HAVE ACTUALLY TRANSFERRED THEIR SOVEREIGN POWERS.

1015 HAYS B.
A SOUTHERN MODERATE SPEAKS.
CHAPEL HILL: U OF N CAR PR, 1959, 231 PP., LC#59-9064.
ADVOCATES MODERATE STAND ON DESEGREGATION ISSUE, TO BE
MANIFESTED BY A PROGRAM FOR PUBLIC EDUCATION, INCREASED ROLE
OF CHURCHES, AND WIDE ELASTICITY IN LOCAL APPLICATION OF
SUPREME COURT DECISIONS. AUTHOR HAS BEEN SOUTHERN POLITICIAN
AND HIS CAREER IS REVIEWED.

1016 HAYS P.R.
LABOR ARBITRATION: A DISSENTING VIEW.
NEW HAVEN: YALE U PR, 1966, 125 PP., LC#66-12501.
DISCUSSES LAWS RELATING TO AND PRACTICE OF LABOR
ARBITRATION. INCLUDES CHAPTER ON FUTURE OF SYSTEM AND

AUTHOR'S SUGGESTION THAT ALL DECISIONS BE HANDLED IN
REGULAR COURT SYSTEM IF COURTS ARE TO ENFORCE DECISIONS.

1017 HAZARD J.N.
"SETTLING DISPUTES IN SOVIET SOCIETY: THE FORMATIVE YEARS OF
LEGAL INSTITUTIONS."
NEW YORK: COLUMBIA U PRESS, 1960.
PROPOSES TO TEST WITH SOVIET DATA THE THESIS THAT MODERN
MAN CAN SETTLE HIS DISPUTES WITHOUT ELABORATELY ORGANIZED
TRIBUNALS, LEGAL REPRESENTATION, COMPLICATED LAWS, RULES OF
PROCEDURE, AND EVIDENCE. TRACES EVOLUTION OF CRIMINAL LAW
AND PROCEDURE ALONGSIDE CIVIL JURISDICTION AND PROCEDURE.
INCLUDES BIBLIOGRAPHY OF BOOKS, ARTICLES, SERIAL PUBLICA-
TIONS, COLLECTIONS OF STATUTORY MATERIAL, ETC. IN RUSSIAN.

1018 HAZARD J.N.
"CO-EXISTENCE LAW BOWS OUT."
AMER. J. INT. LAW, 59 (JAN. 65), 59-66.
INTERNATIONAL LAW ASSOCIATION, FOLLOWING LEAD OF UNITED
NATIONS, HAS REVISED ITS THINKING IN REGARD TO PEACEFUL CO-
EXISTENCE. FINDING CONCEPT OBSCURE AND IDEOLOGICALLY CON-
FUSING, ASSOCIATION IS NOW DEFINING ITS RESEARCH IN TERMS OF
INTERNATIONAL SECURITY AND COOPERATION.

1019 HEADICAR B.M. ED.
CATALOGUE OF THE BOOKS, PAMPHLETS, AND OTHER DOCUMENTS IN
THE EDWARD FRY LIBRARY OF INTERNATIONAL LAW...
LONDON: ST CLEMENT'S PRESS, 1923, 174 PP.
CATALOGUE ARRANGED IN TWO PARTS: FIRST PART ENTRIES ARE
PRINTED ACCORDING TO LOCATION IN HISTORY LIBRARY OF LONDON
SCHOOL OF ECONOMICS; IN SECOND PART CATALOGUE IS AN ALPHA-
BETICAL INDEX TO AUTHORS, SUBJECTS AND TITLES. VERY LITTLE
DESCRIPTION OF CONTENTS.

1020 HEAP D.
AN OUTLINE OF PLANNING LAW (3RD ED.)
LONDON: SWEET & MAXWELL, 1960, 213 PP.
OUTLINES LEGAL FRAMEWORK OF TOWN PLANNING, ESPECIALLY
TOWN AND COUNTRY PLANNING ACTS OF 1947-59, AND EXAMINES EF-
FECT OF LAWS ON CENTRAL AND LOCAL ADMINISTRATION. STUDIES
PLANS FOR DEVELOPMENT, CONTROL OF DEVELOPMENT AND ADVERTISE-
MENTS, PRESERVATION OF BUILDINGS AND LAND, ENFORCEMENT OF
CONTROL, AND DEVELOPMENT OF NEW TOWNS.

1021 HECTOR L.J.
"GOVERNMENT BY ANONYMITY: WHO WRITES OUR REGULATORY
OPINIONS?"
AMER BAR ASSN., 45 (DEC. 59).
COMMISSIONERS IN MOST FEDERAL AGENCIES DO NOT WRITE THEIR
OWN OPINIONS. SINCE KNOWING WHO MAKES DECISIONS IS ESSENTIAL
FOR THE PRESERVATION OF DEMOCRACY, COMMISSIONERS SHOULD BE
REQUIRED TO WRITE THEIR OWN OPINIONS.

1022 HEGEL G.W.F.
HEGEL'S POLITICAL WRITINGS (TRANS. BY T.M. KNOX)
LONDON: CLARENDON PRESS, 1964, 335 PP.
CONTAINS HEGEL'S POLITICAL WRITINGS ON GERMAN
CONSTITUTION, DOMESTIC AFFAIRS OF WURTTEMBERG, AND
PROCEEDINGS OF ESTATES ASSEMBLY OF WURTTEMBERG. INCLUDES
HEGEL'S THOUGHTS ON ENGLISH REFORM BILL.

1023 HEGEL G.W.F.
PHILOSOPHY OF RIGHT.
LONDON: OXFORD U PR, 1942, 382 PP.
ATTEMPTS TO PORTRAY THE STATE AS INHERENTLY RATIONAL.
BELIEVES THAT IT IS THE HARDEST THING FOR MAN TO BE ALIEN-
ATED FROM REASON AND SPIRIT UNDERLYING LAWS AND FROM KNOWL-
EDGE OF THE RIGHTS AND DUTIES OF BOTH MAN AND THE STATE.
SEES STATE AS EMBODIMENT OF ETHICS, AND ARGUES PHILOSOPHI-
CALLY FOR GOVERNMENT OF LAWS. DISCUSSES ROLE OF CHURCH AND
CITES WAR AS HAVING AN ETHICAL ASPECT.

1024 HEKHUIS D.J. ED., MCCLINTOCK C.G. ED., BURNS A.L. ED.
INTERNATIONAL STABILITY: MILITARY, ECONOMIC AND POLITICAL
DIMENSIONS.
NEW YORK: WILEY, 1964, 296 PP., $6.00.
ESSAYS DEFINE STABILITY, ANALYZE THREATS TO STABILITY,
AND STUDY MEANS FOR ALLEVIATING INSTABILITY. STUDY MUTUAL
DETERRENCE, REGIONAL DEFENSE, DISARMAMENT, ARMS CONTROL.

1025 HELLMAN F.S. ED.
SELECTED LIST OF REFERENCES ON THE CONSTITUTIONAL POWERS OF
THE PRESIDENT INCLUDING POWERS RECENTLY DELEGATED.
WASHINGTON: LIBRARY OF CONGRESS, 1933, 30 PP.
336 ITEMS, ANNOTATED. FROM THE TURN OF THE CENTURY TO
1933. BOOKS, ARTICLES, PAMPHLETS, ETC. INCLUDES BIBLIOG-
RAPHIES; NO INDEX. COMPILED FOR LIBRARY OF CONGRESS.

1026 HELLMAN F.S. ED.
THE SUPREME COURT ISSUE: SELECTED LIST OF REFERENCES.
WASHINGTON: LIBRARY OF CONGRESS, 1938, 42 PP.
AMPLY ANNOTATED, 490 ITEMS, INDEXED BY AUTHOR AND SOURCE.
BOOKS,PAMPHLETS, AND ARTICLES ON FDR'S ATTEMPT TO PACK
THE SUPREME COURT. ALSO TREATS PUBLIC AND LEGAL OPINIONS EX-
PRESSED IN 1937 AND 1938. COMPILED FOR LIBRARY OF CONGRESS.

1027
COUNTY GOVERNMENT IN THE UNITED STATES: A LIST OF RECENT
REFERENCES (PAMPHLET)
WASHINGTON: LIBRARY OF CONGRESS, 1940, 13 PP.
146-ITEM BIBLIOGRAPHY INCLUDES SUMMARY ANNOTATIONS ON
BOOKS, ARTICLES, PAMPHLETS, ETC. PRINTED AFTER 1938. NO
INDEX. LISTS THREE OTHER REFERENCE BIBLIOGRAPHIES ON SAME
SUBJECT. COMPILED FOR LIBRARY OF CONGRESS.

1028 HENDERSON D.F.
CONCILIATION AND JAPANESE LAW (VOL. II)
SEATTLE: U OF WASHINGTON PR, 1964, 237 PP., LC#64-18425.
STUDY OF MEDIATION IN JAPANESE LAW, INCLUDING MODERN ANA-
LOGIES TO TOKUGAWA CONCILIATION, MODERN STATUTORY CONCILIA-
TION, AND A PERSPECTIVE AND APPRAISAL.

1029 HENDERSON D.F.
CONCILIATION AND JAPANESE LAW (VOL. I)
SEATTLE: U OF WASHINGTON PR, 1964, 182 PP., LC#64-18425.
DISCUSSES TOKUGAWA PERIOD, 1603-1864. INCLUDES CONCEPT OF
CONCILIATION, ROLE OF LAW, COURT SYSTEM, CIVIL TRIALS, AND
CRITIQUE OF TOKUGAWA POLICY OF ENCOURAGING CONCILIATION.

1030 HENDERSON W.O.
THE GENESIS OF THE COMMON MARKET.
CHICAGO: QUADRANGLE BOOKS, INC, 1962, 201 PP., LC#62-20924.
STUDIES EVOLUTION OF EUROPEAN ECONOMIC COOPERATION FROM
ANGLO-FRENCH COMMERCIAL TREATY OF 1786 TO CREATION OF EEC
AFTER WWII. DISCUSSES SUCH MATTERS AS THE SLAVE TRADE,
FISHERIES, AND COMMUNICATIONS.

1031 HENKE W.
DAS RECHT DER POLITISCHEN PARTEIEN.
GOTTINGEN: OTTO SCHWARTZ & CO, 1964, 237 PP.
DISCUSSES LEGAL RIGHTS OF POLITICAL PARTIES AND RELATION
OF PARTIES TO THE ORGANS OF THE STATE. ALSO INQUIRES INTO
THEIR CONSTITUTIONAL RIGHTS AND DUTIES AS WELL AS THEIR LE-
GAL POSITION IN THE JUDICIAL PROCESS.

1032 HENKIN L.
ARMS CONTROL AND INSPECTION IN AMERICAN LAW.
NEW YORK: COLUMB. U. PR., 1958, 289 PP.
STUDIED FROM POINT OF VIEW OF LEGAL AND ADMINISTRATIVE
PROBLEMS INVOLVED IN ENFORCING AN INSPECTION SYSTEM IN USA.
WRITTEN PRIMARILY FOR THOSE INTERESTED IN DEVELOPMENT OF
INTERNATIONAL INSTITUTIONS. CONTENDS THAT THE PROVISIONS
OUTLINED MAKE NO OR FEW INROADS INTO ACCEPTED CONSTITU-
TIONAL LIMITATIONS.

1033 HERRING E.P.
PUBLIC ADMINISTRATION AND THE PUBLIC INTEREST.
NEW YORK: MCGRAW HILL, 1936, 416 PP.
A STUDY OF THE FEDERAL ADMINISTRATIVE MACHINERY SHOWING
THE DIFFICULTIES OF FEDERAL OFFICIALS IN DEALING WITH
POLITICIANS AND SPECIAL INTEREST ORGANIZATIONS AND ANALYZING
THE RELATIONS BETWEEN PRESSURE GROUPS AND OFFICIALS AND
THE VARIOUS EFFORTS BEING MADE TO ADJUST THE BUREAUCRACY TO
ITS HEAVY RESPONSIBILITIES.

1034 HERRMANN K.
DAS STAATSDENKEN BEI LEIBNIZ.
BONN: H BOUVIER & CO, VERLAG, 1958, 124 PP.
DISCUSSES LEIBNITZ'S CONCEPTIONS OF NATURE AND FUNCTION
OF STATE, LAW, EDUCATION, AND RELATIONS BETWEEN CHURCH AND
STATE. INCLUDES BRIEF DISCUSSION OF POLITICAL THOUGHT DURING
LEIBNITZ'S LIFETIME.

1035 HEWITT W.H. ED.
ADMINISTRATION OF CRIMINAL JUSTICE IN NEW YORK.
ROCHESTER: AQUEDUCT BOOKS, 1967, 397 PP., LC#67-20710.
MANUAL FOR LAW ENFORCEMENT OFFICERS THAT DESCRIBES, BY
WAY OF TEXT AND ILLUSTRATION, ADMINISTRATION OF JUSTICE
IN NEW YORK STATE AS IT AFFECTS POLICE IN PARTICULAR.
DEALS ONLY WITH THE CONVENTIONAL AREA OF CRIMINAL
PROSECUTION.

1036 HEYDECKER J.J., LEEB J.
THE NUREMBERG TRIAL: HISTORY OF NAZI GERMANY AS REVEALED
THROUGH THE TESTIMONY AT NUREMBERG.
CLEVELAND: WORLD, 1962, 398 PP., LC#62-9054.
RECREATES ATMOSPHERE OF POSTWAR GERMANY AND PRESENTS
HISTORY OF TRIAL IN ALL ASPECTS. BASED ON DOCUMENTS, FACTS,
AND RECORDS; VERY LITTLE SPECULATION AND EVALUATION.

1037 HEYSE T.
PROBLEMS FONCIERS ET REGIME DES TERRES (ASPECTS ECONO-
MIQUES, JURIDIQUES ET SOCIAUX)
BRUSSELS: CEDESA, 1960, 163 PP.
BIBLIOGRAPHY OF 875 ITEMS COVERING PUBLISHED LITERATURE
ON ECONOMIC, JUDICIAL, AND SOCIAL IMPLICATIONS OF TENURE OF
LAND IN THE BELGIAN CONGO AND RUANDI-URANDI FOR PERIOD 1948-
1959. EMPHASIZES PROBLEMS OF WATER AND HUNTING AND FISHING
RIGHTS FOR ECONOMICALLY UNDERDEVELOPED COUNTRIES AND ROLE
OF INTERNATIONAL ORGANIZATIONS IN SOLVING TERRITORIAL DIS-
PUTES. INCLUDES AUTHOR AND SUBJECT INDEXES.

1038 HIBBS A.R.
"SPACE TECHNOLOGY* THE THREAT AND THE PROMISE."
DISSERTATION ABSTRACTS, 3 (SPRING 65), 63-74.
AT PRESENT, SPACE WEAPONS SYSTEMS CANNOT COMPETE ON A
COST EFFECTIVENESS BASIS WITH EARTH-BASED MILITARY SYSTEMS.
THUS, IT IS A PROPITIOUS TIME FOR COMBINING A BAN ON WEAPONS
DEVELOPMENT WITH ARRANGEMENTS FOR COOPERATION IN SCIENTIFIC
SPACE RESEARCH

1039 HICKEY D.
"THE PHILOSOPHICAL ARGUMENT FOR WORLD GOVERNMENT."
WORLD JUSTICE, 6 (DEC. 64).
CITING PAST THEORIES AND DOCUMENTS, DISCUSSES THE MEANING
AND POSSIBILITY OF A WORLD GOVERNMENT CONCLUDING THAT 'FOR
THE SAKE OF PEACE AND PROSPERITY, FOR THE SAKE OF ORDER, SE-
CURITY AND THE FREE PURSUIT OF ART, CULTURE AND EDUCATION
A WORLD GOVERNMENT RULING A WORLD STATE IS A HUMAN NECES-
SITY.'

1040 HIDAYATULLAH M.
DEMOCRACY IN INDIA AND THE JUDICIAL PROCESS.
NEW YORK: ASIA PUBL HOUSE, 1966, 89 PP.
DISCUSSES FUNDAMENTAL PRINCIPLES OF DEMOCRACY AND EVOLU-
TION OF DEMOCRATIC GOVERNMENT IN INDIA. APPRAISES CAPACITY
OF DEMOCRACY IN INDIA TO WITHSTAND LOSS OF NEHRU. EXAMINES
INDIAN JUDICIAL PROCESS AND ITS RELATION TO PRESERVATION OF
DEMOCRATIC VALUES OF INDIAN PEOPLE.

1041 HIGGINS R.
THE DEVELOPMENT OF INTERNATIONAL LAW THROUGH THE POLITICAL
ORGANS OF THE UNITED NATIONS.
LONDON: OXFORD U PR, 1963, 402 PP.
EXAMINES LEGAL CONCEPTS OF STATEHOOD, DOMESTIC JURISDIC-
TION, RECOGNITION, USE OF FORCE, AND TREATIES. DISCUSSES UN
CHARTER PROVISIONS, INTERNATIONAL CUSTOM, AND MEANS BY WHICH
UN HAS SHAPED INTERNATIONAL LAW.

1042 HIGGINS R.
CONFLICT OF INTERESTS* INTERNATIONAL LAW IN A DIVIDED WORLD.
CHESTER SPRINGS: DUFOUR, 1965, 170 PP., LC#65-18353.
LEGAL PROBLEMS OF POLITICAL "PEACEFUL CO-EXISTENCE" COM-
PARED WITH HISTORICAL EXPERIENCES OF RELIGIOUS AND ECONOMIC
CO-EXISTENCE (THE RELATIONS OF RICH AND POOR NATIONS). AU-
THOR CONCLUDES THAT LEGAL GROWTH OCCURS WHERE SHARED EXPER-
IENCES ALLOW FOR DEVELOPMENT OF COMMON LAW NOT THROUGH
EXPLICIT ATTEMPTS AT CODIFICATION.

1043 HIGGINS R.
"THE INTERNATIONAL COURT AND SOUTH WEST AFRICA* SOME IMPLI-
CATIONS OF THE JUDGMENT."
INTER-AM. ECO. AFFAIRS, 42 (OCT. 66), 573-599.
AFTER A HISTORICAL AND LEGAL SUMMARY OF THE SOUTH WEST
AFRICAN MANDATE THE AUTHOR PRESENTS THE LEGAL AND POLITICAL
PROBLEMS INHERENT IN THE ICJ'S JUDGMENT OF JULY 18, 1966.
QUESTIONS WHETHER THE COURT HAD REVERSED EARLIER DECISIONS?
WHO IS ENTITLED TO BRING THIS TYPE OF CASE BEFORE THE COURT?
WHAT WAS THE EFFECT OF THE MAKE-UP OF THE COURT? AND DID THE
COURT EVADE DECISION FROM FEAR OF POLITICAL EMBROILMENT?

1044 HIGHSAW R.B.,
CONFLICT AND CHANGE IN LOCAL GOVERNMENT.
UNIVERSITY: U ALABAMA PR, 1965, 164 PP.
DISCUSSES PATTERNS OF LOCAL INTERGOVERNMENTAL
COOPERATION IN ALABAMA RELATING FOUR SPECIFIC CASE STUDIES.
STUDIES SETTING IN WHICH LOCAL COOPERATION FUNCTIONS AND
EFFECT OF JOINT EFFORT ON PUBLIC POLICY.

1045 HILL D.G., POLLOCK E.M.
"HUMAN RIGHTS LEGISLATION IN ONTARIO."
RACE, 9 (OCT. 67), 193-203.
TRACES BACKGROUND OF HUMAN RIGHTS LEGISLATION UP TO THE
ONTARIO HUMAN RIGHTS CODE OF 1962. EXAMINES FUNCTIONING OF
HUMAN RIGHTS COMMISSION, WHICH ATTEMPTS TO CONCILIATE DIS-
PUTES AND PLACES STRONG RELIANCE ON PERSONAL CONTACT. IF
NO SETTLEMENT IS REACHED, COMMISSION MAY RECOMMEND APPOINT-
MENT OF BOARD OF INQUIRY. EXAMINES CONPLAINTS, COMMISSION'S
EDUCATIONAL PROGRAM, AND COMMISSION-SPONSORED RESEARCH.

1046 HILL M.
IMMUNITIES AND PRIVILEGES OF INTERNATIONAL OFFICIALS.
WASHINGTON: CARNEGIE ENDOWMENT, 1947, 281 PP.
DESCRIBES EXPERIENCE OF LEAGUE OF NATIONS' OFFICIALS
IN SWITZERLAND, NETHERLANDS, CANADA, ET. AL. DOCUMENTS
IMMUNITIES AND PRIVILEGES OF LEAGUE OF NATIONS AND UN
OFFICIALS.

1047 HILL N.
CLAIMS TO TERRITORY IN INTERNATIONAL LAW AND RELATIONS.
NEW YORK: OXFORD U. PR., 1945, 248 PP.
ANALYZES TERRITORIAL DISPUTES, IN VIEW OF THEIR NATURE
AND PROCEDURES AVAILABLE FOR SOLUTION. DISCUSSES BOTH LEGAL
AND NON-LEGAL CLAIMS, PARTICULARLY THOSE IN EUROPE AND THE
WESTERN HEMISPHERE. CATEGORIZES CLAIMS INTO STRATEGIC, GEO-
GRAPHIC, ECONOMIC, HISTORIC, AND ETHNIC AND DISCUSSES EACH
GROUPING SEPARATELY.

1048 HILLS R.J.
"THE REPRESENTATIVE FUNCTION: NEGLECTED DIMENSION OF
LEADERSHIP BEHAVIOR"
ADMINISTRATIVE SCI. Q., 8 (JUNE 63), 83-101.
RESULTS OF EMPIRICAL TEST OF THESIS THAT CONCEPT OF LEAD-
ERSHIP INCLUDES LEADER'S REPRESENTATION OF GROUP TO THOSE IN
HIGHER AUTHORITY AND TO CLIENTELE. "LEADER BEHAVIOR DES-
CRIPTION" QUESTIONNAIRE DEVELOPED AND GIVEN TO ELEMENTARY
SCHOOL TEACHERS TO DESCRIBE LEADERSHIP OF PRINCIPALS.
HYPOTHESIS SUPPORTED.

1049 HINDERLING A.
DIE REFORMATORISCHE VERWALTUNGSGERICHTSBARKEIT.
WINTERTHUR: VERL H SCHELLENBERG, 1957, 101 PP.
EXAMINES CONCEPTS OF JURIDICAL AND ADMINISTRATIVE ADJUDI-
CATION. DISCUSSES IN DETAIL NATURE AND EXTENT OF JUDICIAL
REVIEW OF ADMINISTRATIVE DECREES. STUDIES VARIOUS TYPES
OF REVIEW COURTS AND INQUIRES INTO PROBLEM OF SEPARATION OF
POWERS.

1050 HIRSCH W.Z., SHAPIRO D.L.
"SOME ECONOMIC IMPLICATIONS OF CITY PLANNING."
UCLA LAW REV., 14 (AUG. 67), 1312-1327
DISCUSSES THESIS THAT LIMITATIONS ON CITY PLANNERS SHOULD
BE BASED ON ECONOMIC FUNCTIONS OF PLANNING, ESPECIALLY
ATTAINMENT OF ECONOMIC EFFICIENCY. ADVOCATES BENEFIT-COST
ANALYSIS, METHOD OF APPRAISING DESIRABILITY OF INTRUSION BY
PUBLIC OFFICIAL INTO ALLOCATIVE PROCESS, AND COMBINATION
OF ECONOMICS AND JURISPRUDENCE TO SOLVE PROBLEMS OF CITY
PLANNING.

1051 HIRSCHFIELD R.S.
THE CONSTITUTION AND THE COURT.
NEW YORK: MCGRAW HILL, 1962, 257 PP., LC#62-10672.
DEALS WITH ESSENTIAL ELEMENT IN DYNAMISM OF AMERICAN
GOVERNMENT: PROCESS OF CONSTITUTIONAL DEVELOPMENT THROUGH
JUDICIAL INTERPRETATION OF LAW. STUDIES SUPREME COURT
ACTION IN FOUR AREAS: ECONOMIC REGULATION, RACIAL EQUALITY,
CIVIL LIBERTY, AND WARTIME GOVERNMENT.

1052 HIRSHBERG H.S., MELINAT C.H.
SUBJECT GUIDE TO UNITED STATES GOVERNMENT PUBLICATIONS.
CHICAGO: AMER LIB ASSN, 1947, 228 PP.
COMPILATION OF BOOKS, PAMPHLETS, SERIALS, DIRECTORIES,
BIBLIOGRAPHIES, AND HANDBOOKS.

1053 HISS A.
IN THE COURT OF PUBLIC OPINION.
NEW YORK: ALFRED KNOPF, 1957, 434 PP., LC#57-7546.
ALGER HISS TELLS STORY OF HIS APPEARANCES BEFORE HOUSE
COMMITTEE ON UN-AMERICAN ACTIVITIES IN AUGUST, 1948.
DESCRIBES HIS BELATED CONFRONTATION WITH WHITTAKER CHAMBERS,
AND EVENTS LEADING TO HIS INDICTMENT AND TRIALS FOR PERJURY.
DISCUSSES CLIMATE OF OPINION AT THE TIME. TELLS OF THE
LEGAL STEPS TAKEN AFTER HIS CONVICTION, CULMINATING IN A
MOTION FOR RETRIAL ON GROUNDS OF NEW EVIDENCE OF FRAUD.

1054 HISTORICUS
"LETTERS AND SOME QUESTIONS OF INTERNATIONAL LAW."
LONDON: MACMILLAN, 1863, 44 PP.
AMERICAN CIVIL WAR POSED INTERNATIONAL LAW PROBLEMS FOR
BELLIGERENT AND NEUTRAL NATIONS. FOCUSES ON RIGHTS OF CAP-
TURE ON THE HIGH SEAS AND BLOCKADE-RUNNING. DEFINES NATURE
OF CONTRABAND CARGO.

1055 HITCHMAN J.M.
"THE PLATT AMENDMENT REVISITED: A BIBLIOGRAPHICAL SURVEY."
THE AMERICAS, 23 (APR. 67), 343-369.
DISCUSSES ORIGIN AND FORMULATION OF PLATT AMENDMENT AND
DEFINES VIEWS OF CUBAN AND AMERICAN SCHOLARS ON ITS PURPOSE
AND IMPACT.

1056 HOBBES T., TONNIES F. ED.
THE ELEMENTS OF LAW, NATURAL AND POLITIC (1650)
LONDON: CAMBRIDGE UNIV PRESS, 1928, 195 PP.
WORK IS DIVIDED INTO TWO PARTS, "HUMAN NATURE" AND "ELE-
MENTS OF LAW," AND CONSIDERS POWERS AND RIGHTS OF SOVER-
EIGNTY. MAN'S NATURE IS MADE UP OF REASON AND PASSION. CON-
CORD IS IMPOSSIBLE WITHOUT GOVERNMENT. PEOPLE GIVE RIGHTS TO
SOVEREIGN, AND PARTICULAR RIGHTS AND DEMANDS CEASE TO EXIST.
DEFINES MASTER AND SERVANT AND DISCUSSES SUCCESSION.
BELIEVES MONARCHY IS GOVERNMENT LEAST SUBJECT TO PASSION.

1057 HOBBES T.
A DIALOGUE BETWEEN A PHILOSOPHER AND A STUDENT OF THE COMMON
LAWS OF ENGLAND (1667?)
ORIGINAL PUBLISHER NOT AVAILABLE, 1840, 161 PP.
CRITICIZES ENGLISH LEGAL SYSTEM WITH RESPECT TO METHOD
OF LAW-MAKING, COURT SYSTEMS, AND TYPES OF PUNISHMENT. GIVES
SUMMARY OF HIS RATIONALE FOR LEGAL DECISIONS, AND STATEMENT
OF UTILITARIAN ETHICS WHICH ARE APPLIED TO EVALUATE ENGLISH
JURISPRUDENCE. EXAMINES CONCEPT OF SOVEREIGNTY AND ITS
MEANING IN SYSTEMS OF LAW, DENYING THE INDIVIDUAL ANY RIGHTS
OUTSIDE THE SYSTEM OF THE STATE.

1058 HOBSBAWM E.J.
PRIMITIVE REBELS; STUDIES IN ARCHAIC FORMS OF SOCIAL
MOVEMENT IN THE 19TH AND 20TH CENTURIES.
MANCHESTER: MANCHESTER UNIV PR, 1959, 208 PP.
ANALYZES REBELLIOUS SOCIAL MOVEMENTS AS PRIMITIVE FORM OF
ORGANIZED SOCIAL PROTEST. EXAMINES THE SOCIAL BANDIT IN GEN-
ERAL TERMS, AND IN THE MAFIA, THE CITY MOB, AND THE LABOR
SECTS. INCLUDES THE MILLENARIANISM OF THE LAZZARETTI, THE
ANDALUSIAN ANARCHISTS, THE SICILIAN FASCI, AND PEASANT
COMMUNISM, ALL OF WHICH HOPE FOR COMPLETE AND RADICAL CHANGE
IN THE WORLD. ENDS WITH STUDY OF RITUAL IN PROTEST GROUPS.

1059 HOBSON J.A.
TOWARDS INTERNATIONAL GOVERNMENT.
LONDON: ALLEN UNWIN, 1915 216 PP.
OUTLINES SKETCH FOR COUNCIL OF NATIONS WITH STRONG EXEC-
UTIVE POWER TO SECURE PEACEFUL CIVILIZATION. CLAIMS THAT
SOVEREIGNTY IS OBSOLETE AND NEW ERA OF INTERNATIONALISM
CALLS FOR INTERNATIONAL GOVERNMENT, COUNCILS, COURTS, ETC.

1060 HOCKING W.E.
PRESENT STATUS OF THE PHILOSOPHY OF LAW AND OF RIGHTS.
NEW HAVEN: YALE U PR, 1926, 97 PP.
DISCUSSES PHILOSOPHY OF LAW AND RIGHTS, PARTICULARLY AS
GUIDE TO LAWMAKERS. USES APPROACHES OF STAMMLER AND KOHLER
TO DELINEATE QUESTION OF WHETHER LAW SERVES ONLY "RIGHT" OR
ALSO CULTURE. DISCUSSES FUNCTION OF LAW IN SEEKING TO EFFECT
CERTAIN CONDITIONS, LIKE EQUALITY, BY PRESUMING THEM. SEES
RIGHT OF INDIVIDUAL TO SELF-DEVELOPMENT AS THE ONLY NATURAL
RIGHT. SUGGESTS WAYS LAW MAY ENCOURAGE IT WITHIN SOCIETY.

1061 HOCKING W.E.
FREEDOM OF THE PRESS: A FRAMEWORK OF PRINCIPLE.
CHICAGO: U OF CHICAGO PRESS, 1947, 243 PP.
EXAMINES LIMITS AND IMPEDIMENTS OF FREEDOM OF THE PRESS.
RELATES FREEDOM OF THE PRESS TO FREEDOM OF SPEECH. DISCUSSES
THE LIMITING OF THE FIRST AMENDMENT IN CASES OF MAINTAINING
SOCIAL ORDER. CONSIDERS THE INFLUENCE OF LOBBY AND POLITICAL
PRESSURES ON THE NEWSPAPERS.

1062 HODGKINSON R.G.
THE ORIGINS OF THE NATIONAL HEALTH SERVICE: THE MEDICAL
SERVICES OF THE NEW POOR LAW, 1834-1871.
BERKELEY: U OF CALIF PR, 1967, 725 PP.
STUDIES GROWTH OF BRITISH STATE MEDICAL SERVICES FROM
POOR LAW OF 1834 TO 20TH-CENTURY WELFARE STATE.
EXAMINES INADEQUACIES OF THIS LAW WHICH DETHRONED WEALTHY
RISTOCRATS BUT OFFERED LITTLE MEDICAL RELIEF FOR POOR IN NEW
RBAN SLUMS. REVIEWS LATER NATIONAL HEALTH SERVICE WHICH GREW
OUT OF OMISSIONS OF POOR LAW AND GAVE RISE TO A NEW POLITICS
OF POVERTY. DISCUSSES PRESENT FAILURES AND WEAKNESSES.

1063 HOEBEL E.A.
THE LAW OF PRIMITIVE MAN: A STUDY IN COMPARATIVE LEGAL
DYNAMICS.
CAMBRIDGE: HARVARD U PR, 1954, 357 PP., LC#54-9331.
DEVELOPS A GROUND OF IDEAS AND METHODS FOR STUDY OF
LAW IN PRIMITIVE SOCIETY. ANALYZES SEVEN PRIMITIVE CULTURES
WITH REFERENCE TO THEIR UNDERLYING JURAL POSTULATES AND TO
WAYS THESE ARE TRANSLATED INTO LEGAL FORMS AND ACTION.
THESE ANALYSES EXEMPLIFY OPERATION OF LAW IN TOTAL CULTURAL
SETTINGS ON PRIMITIVE LEVEL FROM MOST SIMPLE TO MOST
COMPLEX.

1064 HOEVELER H.J. ED.
INTERNATIONALE BEKAMPFUNG DES VERBRECHENS.
HAMBURG: VERLAG DEUTSCHE POLIZEI, 1966, 264 PP.
TRACES DEVELOPMENT OF INTERNATIONAL CRIMINOLOGY WITH REF-
ERENCE TO DRUG ADDICTION, MAFIA, PROSTITUTION, ETC. DIS-
CUSSES RISE OF EUROPEAN INTERNATIONAL LEGAL ORDER WITH EM-
PHASIS ON EXTRADITION AGREEMENTS. EXAMINES BRIEFLY POLICE
METHODS IN SWITZERLAND, AUSTRIA, ENGLAND (SCOTLAND YARD),
AND US (FBI).

1065 HOGAN J.D., IANNI F.A.
AMERICAN SOCIAL LEGISLATION.
NEW YORK: HARPER & ROW, 1956, 713 PP., LC#56-8845.
EXAMINES SOCIAL LEGISLATION IN FAMILY RELATIONS,
LABOR, SOCIAL SECURITY, ETC. ANALYZES US SOCIAL STRUCTURE
AND POINTS TO CONSIDERATIONS FOR FUTURE LEGISLATION.

1066 HOGAN W.N.
INTERNATIONAL CONFLICT AND COLLECTIVE SECURITY: THE
PRINCIPLE OF CONCERN IN INTERNATIONAL ORGANIZATION.
LEXINGTON: U OF KY PR, 1955, 202 PP., LC#55-7000.
DISCUSSES COLLECTIVE SECURITY THROUGH INTERNATIONAL
ORGANIZATION BASED ON THE PRINCIPLE THAT UNILATERAL VIOLENCE
AGAINST ANY MEMBER CONSTITUTES AN OFFENSE AGAINST ALL
MEMBERS. ANALYZES RELEVANT TRENDS SINCE WORLD WAR I FROM
VIEWPOINT OF STRUCTURE AND FUNCTION, ESPECIALLY AS APPLIED
TO THE LEAGUE OF NATIONS AND THE UN.

1067 HOGARTY R.A.
NEW JERSEY FARMERS AND MIGRANT HOUSING RULES (PAMPHLET)
INDIANAPOLIS: BOBBS-MERRILL, 1966, 19 PP.
DESCRIBES ATTEMPTS OF UNORGANIZED MIGRANT FARM LABOR
GROUP TO OVERCOME RESISTANCE OF WELL-ORGANIZED, HIGHLY

REPRESENTED NEW JERSEY GROWERS. ISSUE WAS TO CARRY OUT STATE REGULATION REQUIRING GROWERS TO PROVIDE HOT WATER IN MIGRANT HOUSING.

1068 HOGUE A.R.
ORIGINS OF THE COMMON LAW.
BLOOMINGTON: INDIANA U PR, 1966, 276 PP., LC#66-12767.
ELUCIDATES NATURE AND DEVELOPMENT OF ENGLISH COMMON LAW. STUDIES ITS STRUCTURE BETWEEN 1154 AND 1307, WHEN IT WAS A RELATIVELY SIMPLE BODY OF RULES ENFORCED IN ENGLISH ROYAL COURTS. SHOWS RELATION BETWEEN EARLY RULES OF COMMON LAW AND SOCIAL ORDER THEY SERVED. DESCRIBES MEDIEVAL FEUDAL AND AGRICULTURAL SOCIETY. POINTS UP LEGAL AND POLITICAL INSTITUTIONS WHICH FLOURISHED IN LATER YEARS.

1069 HOHFELD W.N.
FUNDAMENTAL LEGAL CONCEPTIONS.
NEW HAVEN: YALE U PR, 1964, 113 PP., LC#64-3677.
PRESENTS A SYSTEM OF ANALYSIS FOR LEGAL MATTERS ON AN ABSTRACT, CONCEPTUAL PLANE. APPROACHING LINGUISTICS, THIS WORK IS SEMANTIC ATTEMPT TO ESTABLISH CLEAR NOMENCLATURE IN FIELD OF JURISPRUDENCE. WHEN PUBLISHED IN 1919, WORK WAS REGARDED AS OF LITTLE VALUE. SINCE THAT TIME HOHFELD HAS BECOME OF INCREASING IMPORTANCE IN LEGAL THEORY.

1070 HOLCOMBE A.N.
"OUR MORE PERFECT UNION."
CAMBRIDGE: HARVARD U PR, 1950.
CRITICAL ESSAY ON US CONSTITUTION EMBODIES THESIS THAT CONSTITUTION MUST BE REGARDED AS AN UNFINISHED EXPERIMENT IN GOVERNMENT AND THAT FURTHER EXTENSION OF ITS PRINCIPLES IS ESSENTIAL FOR MAINTENANCE OF SATISFACTORY POSITION OF AMERI-CAN PEOPLE IN MODERN WORLD. ARGUES THAT CONSTITUTION HAS NOT BEEN ADJUSTED TO REFLECT TREND OF GREATER DEMANDS ON THE NA-TIONAL GOVERNMENT BY CITIZENS. NOTES CONTAIN BIBLIOGRAPHY.

1071 HOLCOMBE A.N.
HUMAN RIGHTS IN THE MODERN WORLD.
NEW YORK: NEW YORK U PR, 1948, 162 PP.
SERIES OF LECTURES CONCERNING CIVIL LIBERTIES IN THE CONTEXT OF A PROPOSED INTERNATIONAL BILL OF RIGHTS. THE AMERICAN BILL OF RIGHTS, CONSTITUTIONAL PRIVILEGES AND IMMUNITIES OF AMERICANS AND CITIZENS OF UN, THE PROBLEM OF ENFORCEMENT, HUMAN RIGHTS, AND RIGHTS OF NATIONS UNDER UN CHARTER ARE SUBJECTS INCLUDED.

1072 HOLCOMBE A.N.
A STRATEGY OF PEACE IN A CHANGING WORLD.
CAMBRIDGE: HARVARD U PR, 1967, 352 PP.
ON PROBLEMS OF PEACE, WORLD ORDER, AND WORLD LAW. PROB-LEMS AND POSSIBILITIES OF UN STUDIED, AND SUGGESTIONS MADE FOR CHANGES IN UN WHICH WOULD ENABLE IT TO SERVE AS A WORLD GOVERNMENTAL BODY TO END COLD WAR AND KEEP PEACE.

1073 HOLDSWORTH W.S.
A HISTORY OF ENGLISH LAW; THE COMMON LAW AND ITS RIVALS (VOL. V)
LONDON: METHUEN, 1924, 529 PP.
CONCERNED WITH ENGLISH LAW IN 16TH AND EARLY 17TH CENTURIES. BEGINS WITH DEVELOPMENTS OUTSIDE SPHERE OF COMMON LAW AND INCLUDES MARITIME, INTERNATIONAL, AND COMMERCIAL LAW. COVERS LAW ADMINISTERED BY STAR CHAMBER AND CHANCERY. CONCLUDES WITH DEVELOPMENT OF COMMON LAW PROPER AND STUDIES INFLUENCES ON ITS GROWTH SUCH AS CHANGING ROLE OF JUDGES, POLITICAL AND RELIGIOUS CHANGES, AND IMPORTANT LITERATURE.

1074 HOLDSWORTH W.S.
A HISTORY OF ENGLISH LAW; THE COMMON LAW AND ITS RIVALS (VOL. VI)
LONDON: METHUEN, 1924, 763 PP.
CONCERNED WITH PUBLIC AND ENACTED LAW OF 17TH CENTURY. BEGINS WITH LAW UNDER STUART KINGS AND DISCUSSES PERIOD OF CIVIL WAR AND COMMONWEALTH. INCLUDES POLITICAL THEORIES, PRINCIPLES OF PUBLIC LAW, ROYAL PROCLAMATIONS, AND LAWS ON COMMERCE AND INDUSTRY, AGRICULTURE, PRESS, AND FRAUDS. ENDS WITH PROFESSIONAL DEVELOPMENT OF LAW - GROWTH OF LEGAL PROFESSION, LAWYERS, DIVISIONS, AND LITERATURE.

1075 HOLDSWORTH W.S.
A HISTORY OF ENGLISH LAW; THE COMMON LAW AND ITS RIVALS (VOL. IV)
LONDON: METHUEN, 1924, 600 PP.
CONCERNED WITH DEVELOPMENT OF MODERN ENGLISH LAW AND INFLUENCES SHAPING LEGAL STRUCTURE. BEGINS WITH PUBLIC LAW OF 16TH CENTURY AND CLOSES WITH ENACTED LAW OF 16TH AND EARLY 17TH CENTURIES. INCLUDES CRIMINAL LAW AND PROCEDURE, LAND LAW AND ECCLESIASTICAL LAW, CIVIL PROCEDURE, USE OF COMMON LAW, PROCLAMATIONS AND STATUTES, COMMERCIAL AND AGRICULTURAL POLICIES, AND LAW IN EUROPEAN COURTS.

1076 HOLDSWORTH W.S.
THE HISTORIANS OF ANGLO-AMERICAN LAW.
NEW YORK: COLUMBIA U PRESS, 1928, 175 PP.
SURVEYS WORK OF SOME ENGLISH AND AMERICAN LAWYERS IN FIELD OF ANGLO-AMERICAN LEGAL HISTORY: 17TH AND 18TH CENTURY HISTORIANS, LATE 19TH CENTURY OXFORD LAWYERS, MAITLAND, AND

OTHERS. SUGGESTS THAT STUDY OF LEGAL HISTORY CAN TEACH LEGISLATURES HOW TO MAKE LAWS THAT WILL COMMAND RESPECT, AND TEACH CITIZENS HOW TO RESPECT LAW.

1077 HOLDSWORTH W.S.
A HISTORY OF ENGLISH LAW; THE CENTURIES OF SETTLEMENT AND REFORM (VOL. X)
LONDON: METHUEN, 1938, 600 PP.
HISTORY OF PUBLIC LAW AND OF SOURCES AND DEVELOPMENTS WHICH SHAPED 18TH-CENTURY ENGLISH LAW. EMPHASIZES POLITICAL BACKGROUND, PARLIAMENTARY SYSTEM, BEGINNING OF CABINET FORM OF GOVERNMENT AND OF COLONIAL CONSTITUTIONAL LAW. DISCUSSES DEVELOPMENTS IN SPHERE OF LOCAL GOVERNMENT SUCH AS STATUTES RELATING TO COMMERCE AND INDUSTRY. INCLUDES LOCAL LAW BODIES AND ROYAL PREROGATIVE, AND EXECUTIVE AND LEGISLATIVE POWER.

1078 HOLDSWORTH W.S.
A HISTORY OF ENGLISH LAW; THE CENTURIES OF SETTLEMENT AND REFORM (VOL. XII)
LONDON: METHUEN, 1938, 784 PP.
CONCERNED WITH PROFESSIONAL DEVELOPMENT OF LAW IN 18TH CENTURY. BEGINS WITH STUDY OF RANKS AND ORGANIZATIONS AND EDUCATION OF LAWYERS. DISCUSSES CHARACTER OF LEGAL REPORTS AND PUBLICATIONS; COVERS DEVELOPMENT OF EQUITY, LITERATURE OF COMMON LAW, RELATIONS BETWEEN LAW AND EQUITY, AND SPHERE OF CIVILIANS' PRACTICE. CLOSES WITH BLACKSTONE'S "COMMENTARIES." LEGAL BIOGRAPHIES STRESSED THROUGHOUT.

1079 HOLDSWORTH W.S.
A HISTORY OF ENGLISH LAW; THE CENTURIES OF SETTLEMENT AND REFORM (VOL. XI)
LONDON: METHUEN, 1938, 658 PP.
CONCERNS PUBLIC AND ENACTED LAW OF 18TH CENTURY. BEGINS WITH RELATIONS OF GREAT BRITAIN TO IRELAND, COLONIES, AND INDIA. DISCUSSES MERITS AND DEFECTS OF 18TH-CENTURY CONSTI-TUTION, FORMALITIES OF LEGISLATION, AND CONTRIBUTION OF 18TH-CENTURY STATUTES TO LEGAL DEVELOPMENT. INCLUDES CRIM-INAL LAW, LAND LAW, CONTRACT AND TORT, AND CIVIL PROCEDURE. ENDS WITH PRIVATE BILL LEGISLATION.

1080 HOLDSWORTH W.S.
A HISTORY OF ENGLISH LAW; THE CENTURIES OF SETTLEMENT AND REFORM, 1701-1875 (VOL. XIII)
LONDON: METHUEN, 1952, 803 PP.
CONCERNED WITH SOURCES AND GENERAL DEVELOPMENT OF LAW FROM 1793 TO REFORM ACT OF 1832. BEGINS WITH IDEAS OF PRE-EMINENT POLITICAL THINKERS, THEN STUDIES POLITICAL AND CONSTITUTIONAL BACKGROUND. INCLUDES REFORMS IN DIFFERENT BRANCHES OF THE LAW; CONCLUDES WITH STUDY OF PROFESSIONAL DEVELOPMENT OF LAW, EQUITY, AND SUBJECTS OF CIVILIANS' PRACTICE. DEPENDS THROUGHOUT ON LEGAL BIOGRAPHY.

1081 HOLDSWORTH W.S.
A HISTORY OF ENGLISH LAW; THE CENTURIES OF DEVELOPMENT AND REFORM (VOL. XIV)
LONDON: METHUEN, 1964, 403 PP.
CONCERNED WITH LEGAL DEVELOPMENTS IN PERIOD FROM REFORM ACT OF 1832 TO JUDICATURE ACTS OF 1873-75. BEGINS WITH DIVISIONS IN TORY AND WHIG PARTIES. DISCUSSES PUBLIC LEADERS AND RELATION OF ENGLISH LAW TO INTERNATIONAL LAW; INCLUDES PUBLIC LAW, CENTRAL GOVERNMENT AND EXECUTIVE STRUCTURE, LAW-MAKING POWERS OF BRANCHES OF GOVERNMENT, AND LOCAL GOVERNMENT. ENDS WITH REVIEW OF EMPIRE.

1082 HOLDSWORTH W.S., GOODHART A.L. ED., HANBURY H.G. ED.
A HISTORY OF ENGLISH LAW; THE CENTURIES OF SETTLEMENT AND REFORM (VOL. XV)
LONDON: METHUEN, 1965, 577 PP.
CONCERNED WITH REFORMS OF 1833-1875. BEGINS WITH ENACTED LAW PERTAINING TO COMMERCE AND INDUSTRY. DISCUSSES CIVIL PROCEDURE AND PLEADING, EVIDENCE, CRIMINAL AND LAND LAW, EQUITY, AND ECCLESIASTICAL LAW. STUDIES DEVELOPMENT OF LEGAL PROFESSION; SURVEYS LEGAL LITERATURE AND REPORTS. CLOSES WITH COMMON LAW AND LAWYERS AND APPRAISES CAREERS OF CHIEF JUSTICES, BARONS, JUDGES, AND PROMINENT LAWYERS.

1083 HOLDSWORTH W.S., GOODHART A.L. ED., HANBURY H.G. ED.
A HISTORY OF ENGLISH LAW; THE CENTURIES OF SETTLEMENT AND REFORM (VOL. XVI)
LONDON: METHUEN, 1966, 196 PP.
CONCERNED WITH CHANCELLORS, MASTERS OF THE ROLLS, LORDS JUSTICES IN CHANCERY, VICE-CHANCELLORS, AND CIVILIAN JUDGES IN PERIOD OF REFORM, 1833-75. DISCUSSES CAREER, WRITINGS, AND MAJOR CASES OF PROMINENT LEGAL FIGURES. DISCUSSES JUDICIAL COMMITTEE OF THE PRIVY COUNCIL, ITS MEMBERS, DECISIONS, AND ACHIEVEMENTS. CLOSES WITH EFFECT OF MODERN CODES OF LAW AND NEED FOR COMPARATIVE LAW STUDIES.

1084 HOLLAND T.E. ED.
STUDIES IN INTERNATIONAL LAW.
LONDON: OXFORD U. PR., 1898, 314 PP.
ESSAYS AND LECTURES ON THE LAW OF WAR WITH PARTICULAR EMPHASIS ON GENTILI'S IMPACT ON INTERNATIONAL LAW. TOPICS DISCUSSED INCLUDE: RELATION OF INTERNATIONAL LAW AND ACTS OF PARLIAMENT, TREATY RELATIONS BETWEEN RUSSIA AND TURKEY, AND THE INTERNATIONAL POSITION OF THE SUEZ CANAL.

1085 HOLLAND T.E.
LETTERS UPON WAR AND NEUTRALITY.
NEW YORK: LONGMANS, 1909, 166 PP.
COLLECTION OF LETTERS, PUBLISHED IN 'THE TIMES', ON IN-
TERNATIONAL LAW. DEALS WITH NON-MILITARY MEASURES FOR
SETTLING DISPUTES, CODIFICATION OF WAR LAWS, WAR CONDUCT,
RIGHTS AND DUTIES OF NEUTRALS, AND USES OF INTERNATIONAL
COURTS FOR ADJUDICATION.

1086 HOLLERAN M.P.
CHURCH AND STATE IN GUATEMALA.
NEW YORK: COLUMBIA U PRESS, 1949, 359 PP.
DESCRIBES INTIMATE RELATION BETWEEN DEVELOPMENT OF
CULTURE AND GOVERNMENT, AND PRESENCE OF CATHOLIC CHURCH,
BEGINNING WITH EARLY MISSIONARIES. DISCUSSES CHURCH AS
STRONG SOCIALIZING AGENT AND OFFERS REASONS FOR ITS SUCCESS.

1087 HOLMES O.W. JR.
THE COMMON LAW.
BOSTON: LITTLE BROWN, 1923, 422 PP., $5.00.
DEALS WITH COMMON LAW AS COMPRISING THE FUNDAMENTAL IDEAS
AND PHILOSOPHY OF LAW. PRESENTS A GENERAL VIEW OF THE COMMON
LAW, WHICH IS VIEWED AS COMPENDIUM OF CODES, ACTS AND LAWS
TO WHICH EACH GENERATION MAKES A CONTRIBUTION. USES HISTORY
OF THE LAW WHEN NECESSARY TO EXPLAIN A CONCEPTION OR INTER-
PRETATION OF A RULE. FREQUENTLY REFERS TO LEGAL CASES.

1088 HOLMES O.W.
JUSTICE HOLMES, EX CATHEDRA.
CHARLOTTESVILLE: MICHIE CO, 1966, 381 PP.
PRESENTS SELECTIONS FROM JUSTICE HOLMES' GENERAL
PROPOSITIONS, LEGAL DEFINITIONS, WISDOM, HUMOR, AND
ERUDITION. REVEALS SUBTLE INFLUENCE OF HOLMES ON TODAY'S
COURT. INCLUDES NUMEROUS ANECDOTES.

1089 HOLSTI K.J.
"RESOLVING INTERNATIONAL CONFLICTS* A TAXONOMY OF BEHAVIOR
AND SOME FIGURES ON PROCEDURES."
J. OF CONFLICT RESOLUTION, 10 (SEPT. 66), 272-296.
CONFLICTS ARE DEFINED AS INVOLVING PLANNED DEMAND-ACTIONS
BY STATES. FOLLOWING RESOLUTION MEANS ARE CATEGORIZED AND
DEFINED: "AVOIDANCE, CONQUEST, SUBMISSION-WITHDRAWAL, COM-
PROMISE, AWARD, PASSIVE SETTLEMENT." DATA ARE PRESENTED AND
GENERALIZATIONS DRAWN FROM 39 POST-1918 CONFLICTS.

1090 HOLSTI K.J.
INTERNATIONAL POLITICS* A FRAMEWORK FOR ANALYSIS.
ENGLEWOOD CLIFFS: PRENTICE HALL, 1967, 505 PP., LC#67-19787.
PRESENTS AN INTEGRATED FRAMEWORK FOR ANALYZING THE BEHAV-
IOR OF STATES WITH EMPAHSIS ON THE SYSTEMATIC AND DOMESTIC
SOURCES OF EXTERNAL POLITICAL GOALS, BARGAINING METHODS USED
TO ACHIEVE AND DEFEND OBJECTIVES AND INTERESTS, RESTRAINTS
ON POLICIES, AND BEHAVIOR AND PROCEDURES CONDUCIVE TO RESO-
LUTION OF INTERNATIONAL CONFLICTS. GOOD BIBLIOGRAPHIES AT
CHAPTER ENDS.

1091 HOLT S.
THE DICTIONARY OF AMERICAN GOVERNMENT.
NEW YORK: MCFADDEN BARTWELL, 1964, 284 PP.
ALPHABETICAL LISTING OF STATUTES, LAWS, ACTS, AGENCIES,
OFFICES, AND OTHER DATA ON FEDERAL, STATE, AND LOCAL GOVERN-
MENT.

1092 HOLTZMAN A.
INTEREST GROUPS AND LOBBYING.
NEW YORK: MACMILLAN, 1966, 154 PP., LC#66-14204.
ANALYSIS OF LOBBYING AS PART OF US DEMOCRATIC SYSTEM.
ALLOWS GROUPS TO EXPRESS INTEREST IN AND HAVE INFLUENCE ON
NATIONAL POLICY BY PERSUADING OFFICIALS IN ANY BRANCH OF
GOVERNMENT AND BY DIRECTLY INFLUENCING PUBLIC BY INITIATING
REFERENDUMS.

1093 HOOD W.C.
FINANCING OF ECONOMIC ACTIVITY IN CANADA.
OTTAWA: ROYAL COMN CANADA'S ECO, 1958, 700 PP.
STUDIES FLOW OF FUNDS TO AND FROM MAJOR SECTORS AND FI-
NANCIAL INSTITUTIONS OF CANADIAN ECONOMY CONTROLS EXER-
CISED OVER THESE FLOWS BY PRICES OF REAL AND FINANCIAL AS-
SETS, LAWS AND GOVERNMENT POLICY, AND PRIVATE PRACTICES AND
TRADITIONS. SHOWS RESPECTS IN WHICH SYSTEM WORKS WELL AND
THOSE IN WHICH ITS FUNCTIONING MIGHT BE IMPROVED.

1094 HOOK S.
POLITICAL POWER AND PERSONAL FREEDOM: CRITICAL STUDIES IN
DEMOCRACY, COMMUNISM AND CIVIL RIGHTS.
NEW YORK: CRITERION, 1959, 462 PP., LC#59-6126.
EXPLORES CONCEPTS OF DEMOCRACY, COEXISTENCE, TOLERANCE,
AND SOCIALISM. DISCUSSES PHILOSOPHICAL HERITAGE OF ATLANTIC
DEMOCRACIES, TYPES OF DEMOCRACY, AND DEMOCRACY AS A
PHILOSOPHY OF HISTORY. STUDIES CONFLICT BETWEEN COMMUNIST
AND DEMOCRATIC PHILOSOPHIES, THE INDIVIDUAL IN TOTALITARIAN
SOCIETY, AND SCIENCE AND DIALECTICAL MATERIALISM. PROPOSES
A SOCIALISTIC STATE WITHOUT UTOPIA.

1095 HOOK S.
THE PARADOXES OF FREEDOM.

BERKELEY: U OF CALIF PR, 1962, 152 PP., LC#62-16335.
DISCUSSES AND EXAMINES DEMOCRATIC VALUES SUCH AS HUMAN
RIGHTS, RATIONALISM, REPRESENTATION, JUDICIAL REVIEW,
CONSCIENCE, AND THE RIGHT TO REVOLUTION.

1096 HOPKINS J.F.K. ED.
ARABIC PERIODICAL LITERATURE, 1961.
CAMBRIDGE: HEFFER & SONS, LTD, 1966, 104 PP.
ANNOTATED BIBLIOGRAPHICAL GUIDE TO 23 ARABIC PERIOD-
ICALS PUBLISHED IN 1961, BOTH WITHIN AND OUTSIDE ARABIC-
SPEAKING AREAS. LIST WAS COMPILED UNDER AUSPICES OF THE
MIDDLE EAST CENTRE OF CAMBRIDGE UNIVERSITY. ARTICLES ARE
CLASSIFIED IN 18 TOPICAL CATEGORIES COVERING CURRENT AF-
FAIRS, SOCIAL SCIENCES, SCIENCE AND TECHNOLOGY, AND POLITI-
CAL QUESTIONS. ALL ARABIC NAMES AND TITLES TRANSLITERATED.

1097 HOPKINSON T.
SOUTH AFRICA.
NEW YORK: TIME, INC, 1964, 160 PP., LC#64-23718.
FROM "LIFE'S" WORLD LIBRARY - SURVEYS SOUTH AFRICA, ITS
HISTORY AND MODERN LIFE, EMPHASIZING PROBLEMS OF APARTHEID.

1098 HORRELL M.
LEGISLATION AND RACE RELATIONS (PAMPHLET)
JOHANNESBURG: S AFR INST RACE, 1963, 68 PP.
SUMMARY OF MAJOR LAWS ON RACE RELATIONS IN SOUTH AFRICA
FROM 1909-48. DISCUSSES IN DETAIL DEFINED LEGAL SITUA
TION SINCE 1948 OF APARTHEID POLICY.

1099 HORVATH B.
"COMPARATIVE CONFLICTS LAW AND THE CONCEPT OF CHANGING LAW."
AMER. J. OF COMPARATIVE LAW, 15 (JAN. 67), 136-158.
STUDIES PROFESSOR HESSEL E. YNTEMA'S VIEWS ON COMPARATIVE
CONFLICTS LAW IN GREAT DETAIL. EXAMINES APPLICATION OF
HIS THEORIES TO PROBLEMS OF LEGAL CHANGE, JUSTICE, AND LAW.

1100 HOWARD A.E.D.
"MR. JUSTICE BLACK: THE NEGRO PROTEST MOVEMENT AND THE RULE
OF LAW."
VIRGINIA LAW REV., 53 (JUNE 67), 1030-1090.
TRIBUTE TO SUPREME COURT JUSTICE BLACK EXAMINES MANNER
IN WHICH NEGRO PROTESTS HAVE POSED ISSUE OF CIVIL DISOBEDI-
ENCE AND COURT'S HANDLING OF CONSTITUTIONAL QUESTIONS IN
"DIRECT ACTION" CASES OF 1960'S. SUGGESTS THEORY OF JUSTICE
BLACK'S "RULE OF LAW" AS IT APPLIES TO THOSE UNDER LAW AND
LAWMAKERS.

1101 HOWARD C.G., SUMMERS R.S.
LAW: ITS NATURE, FUNCTIONS, AND LIMITS.
ENGLEWOOD CLIFFS: PRENTICE HALL, 1965, 466 PP., LC#65-16943.
DISCUSSES NATURE AND BASIC FUNCTIONS OF LAW, PARTICULAR
RELATIONSHIPS BETWEEN LAW AND SOCIAL CHANGE, AND LIMITS OF
EFFECTIVE LEGAL ACTION. USES PRIMARY SOURCE MATERIALS TO
EXPLAIN HOW LAW IS MAN'S CHIEF MEANS OF POLITICAL AND SOCIAL
CONTROL. INCLUDES COMPLETE ANALYSIS OF ONE EXEMPLARY COURT
CASE, AND COPY OF US CONSTITUTION.

1102 HOWARD W.S.
AMERICAN SLAVERS AND THE FEDERAL LAW: 1837-1862.
BERKELEY: U OF CALIF PR, 1963, 336 PP., LC#63-09800.
STUDY OF INEFFECTIVENESS OF US GOVERNMENT IN CRUSHING
SLAVE TRADE. CONSIDERATION OF REASONS FOR THIS IMPOTENCE.
DESCRIPTION OF SLAVE TRADE OPERATIONS AND TECHNIQUES.
PUBLISHED WORKS LISTED TOPICALLY, AND DOCUMENTS FOLLOWING;
50 ENTRIES, IN ENGLISH, 1841-1941.

1103 HOWE M.D.W.
THE GARDEN AND THE WILDERNESS.
CHICAGO: U OF CHICAGO PRESS, 1965, 179 PP., LC#65-24977.
LEGAL VIEW OF CHURCH-STATE RELATIONS PRESENTED WITH
DISCUSSION OF FEDERAL AID TO EDUCATION, INTERACTION BETWEEN
POLITICAL AND RELIGIOUS LIBERTY, CONFLICT OF NATIONALISM
WITH RELIGION AND EQUALITY VS. NEUTRALITY IN LAWS RELATING
TO THIS TOPIC.

1104 HOWE R.
THE STORY OF SCOTLAND YARD: A HISTORY OF THE CID FROM THE
EARLIEST TIMES TO THE PRESENT DAY.
NEW YORK: HORIZON PRESS, 1965, 176 PP., LC#66-16299.
HISTORY OF SCOTLAND YARD BY FORMER HEAD OF CRIMINAL
INVESTIGATION DEPARTMENT, DWELLING UPON CID AND ITS
DEVELOPMENT FROM FIRST DETECTIVES OF 1830'S TO TODAY'S
ELEVEN DEPARTMENTS OF SCIENTIFIC CRIMINAL INVESTIGATION.

1105 HOYT E.C.
NATIONAL POLICY AND INTERNATIONAL LAW* CASE STUDIES FROM
AMERICAN CANAL POLICY* MONOGRAPH NO. 1 -- 1966-1967.
DENVER: U OF DENVER, 1966, 80 PP.
ANALYSIS CONSIDERS HYPOTHESES ON THE INFLUENCE OF INTER-
NATIONAL LAW ON FOREIGN POLICY MAKING. ASSUMES IMPORTANCE OF
ISSUES, POWER OF PARTICIPANTS, AND LEGAL BACKGROUNDS OF DE-
CISION-MAKERS ARE IMPORTANT VARIABLES. CALLS FOR BUILDING
DATA BANK FROM CASE STUDIES SUCH AS HIS OF AMERICAN EFFORTS
TO BUILD PANAMA CANAL IN ACCORDANCE WITH TREATIES.

1106 HSUEH S.-.S.

GOVERNMENT AND ADMINISTRATION OF HONG KONG.
HONG KONG: U BOOK STORE, 1962, 99 PP.
    SHORT, NON-TECHNICAL STUDY OF STRUCTURE AND FUNCTION OF
GOVERNMENT OF HONG KONG. DESCRIBES IMPORTANT FUNCTION OF
COLONIAL OFFICE, AND ANALYZES STRUCTURES OF OFFICE OF GOVER-
NOR, EXECUTIVE COUNCIL, LEGISLATIVE COUNCIL, URBAN COUNCIL,
GOVERNMENT DEPARTMENTS, THE PUBLIC SERVICE, JUDICIARY, AND
ADMINISTRATION OF NEW TERRITORIES.

1107 HUBERT C.J.
"PLANNED UNIT DEVELOPMENT"
NEW JERSEY PLANS, 16 (SPRING 67), 34-37.
    ANALYZES POSITIVE ASPECTS OF ZONING IN COMMUNITY AS BASIS
FOR PRESENTING IDEA OF TOTALLY PLANNED COMMUNITIES: PUD.
FEELS PUD IS NOT SPREADING FAST ENOUGH BECAUSE COURTS AND
ADMINISTRATORS DO NOT UNDERSTAND IT. PRESENTS METHOD FOR
DEALING WITH PUD IN LEGISLATURES, EMPHASIZING NEED TO TREAT
ALL LAWS ON LAND USE CONTROL AS ONE UNIT OF PROCEDURE.

1108 HUDSON M.
"THE PERMANENT COURT OF INTERNATIONAL JUSTICE AND THE QUES-
TION OF AMERICAN PARTICIPATION."
CAMBRIDGE: HARVARD U. PR., 1925, 389 PP.
    A COLLECTION OF PAPERS ON ESTABLISHMENT OF THE COURT, AN-
NUAL REPORTS OF ACTIVITY AND THE QUESTION OF AMERICA'S RE-
LATION TO COURT. CONTAINS APPENDIX OF PERTINENT DOCUMENTS.
COURT AIDS PEACE BY SETTLING DISPUTES AND BY BUILDING UP
BODY OF INTERNATIONAL CASE LAW.

1109 HUDSON M.
"THE TEACHING OF INTERNATIONAL LAW IN AMERICA."
PROC. CONF. TEACHERS INT. LAW, 3 (1928), 68-90 AND 178-189.
    TRACES DEVELOPMENT OF INTERNATIONAL-LAW INSTRUCTION
THROUGH FIVE PERIODS: USA INDEPENDENCE, RISE OF LAW SCHOOLS
IN 1820'S, INTRODUCTION OF INTERNATIONAL-LAW LITERATURE,
CASE-SYSTEM ERA (1870-1920), AND THE INCEPTION OF INTERNAT-
IONAL ORGANIZATIONS AFTER WW 1. DEFINES ROLE OF LAW SCHOOLS
AND COLLEGES. 'FLOOR-DISCUSSION' OF AUTHOR'S PAPER EVALUATES
CURRENT TEACHING-METHODS AND CURRICULUM.

1110 HUDSON M.
BY PACIFIC MEANS.
NEW HAVEN: YALE U. PR., 1935, 200 PP.
    DESCRIBES AND ENUMERATES THE PACIFIC MEANS AVAILABLE TO
PARTIES IN DISPUTES: THE LEAGUE, THE PERMANENT COURT OF
INTERNATIONAL JUSTICE AND TREATIES ON PACIFIC SETTLEMENT
PRIOR TO AND SINCE 1920. EXPLORES IMPLEMENTATIONS OF
BRIAND-KELLOGG PACT.

1111 HUDSON M.
INTERNATIONAL TRIBUNALS PAST AND FUTURE.
WASHINGTON: CARNEGIE ENDOWMENT, 1944, 287 PP.
    SKETCHES EVOLUTION OF INTERNATIONAL TRIBUNALS FROM 1794
TO PRESENT AND DEALS EXTENSIVELY WITH GENERAL PROBLEMS OF
INTERNATIONAL TRIBUNALS CONCERNING STRUCTURE AND SCOPE OF
ACTION. ALSO PRESENTS SUGGESTIONS FOR FUTURE TREATMENT OF
PRESENT PROBLEMS OF ADJUDICATION. THESIS IS THAT ADMINISTRA-
TION OF INTERNATIONAL LAW MUST BE FRAMEWORK OF INTERNATIONAL
RELATIONS.

1112 HUDSON M.O. ED.
INTERNATIONAL LEGISLATION: 1929-1931.
WASHINGTON: CARNEGIE ENDOWMENT, 1936, 1180 PP.
    SUBTITLED "A COLLECTION OF THE TEXTS OF MULTIPARTITE
INTERNATIONAL INSTRUMENTS OF GENERAL INTEREST." UNIFORM
PRESENTATION OF LEGISLATIVE INSTRUMENTS NEEDED IN
INTERNATIONAL LAW; FOCUSES ON LEGISLATIVE PROCESS AS ONE OF
CHIEF METHODS IN 20TH-CENTURY INTERNATIONAL LAW. INCLUDES
INTERNATIONAL LABOR CONVENTIONS, PAYMENT OF REPARATIONS,
MARITIME LAW, WAR, ARBITRATION, AND CONCILIATION.

1113 HULL R.H., NOVOGROD J.C.
LAW AND VIETNAM.
NEW YORK: OCEANA PUBLISHING, 1968, 211 PP., LC#68-12440.
    OFFERS POTENTIALLY RELEVANT FACTS AND INTERNATIONAL LEGAL
POLICIES ON VIETNAM. AUTHORS BELIEVE THAT THE EVENTS OF
VIETNAM MUST BE APPRAISED FROM THE PERSPECTIVES OF A CITI-
ZEN OF THE LARGER COMMUNITY OF MANKIND AND IN TERMS OF THE
BASIC POLICIES OF MINIMUM WORLD PUBLIC ORDER PRESENTED BY
THE UN CHARTER.

1114 HUNT B.I.
BIPARTISANSHIP: A CASE STUDY OF THE FOREIGN ASSISTANCE
PROGRAM, 1947-56 (DOCTORAL THESIS)
AUSTIN: U OF TEXAS PR, 1958, 455 PP.
    STUDY OF PERIOD IN WHICH FOREIGN ASSISTANCE POLICIES WERE
FORMULATED AND CARRIED OUT ON BIPARTISAN BASIS. PARTICULAR
ATTENTION GIVEN TO PROGRAMS OF AID TO GREECE AND TURKEY, THE
MARSHALL PLAN, NATO, MUTUAL DEFENSE ASSISTANCE ACT OF 1951,
AND MUTUAL SECURITY ACT.

1115 HURST J.W.
THE GROWTH OF AMERICAN LAW; THE LAW MAKERS.
BOSTON: LITTLE BROWN, 1950, 502 PP.
    OUTLINES PRINCIPAL AGENCIES OF LAW IN US, 1790-1940.
EMPHASIZES FUNCTIONS PERFORMED BY LEGAL AGENCIES RATHER THAN

THEIR FORMAL STRUCTURE. LEGAL AGENCIES DISCUSSED INCLUDE
LEGISLATURES (STATE AND CONGRESS), COURTS, CONSTITUTION, THE
BAR, AND THE EXECUTIVE BRANCH. INCLUDES SELECTION AND TENURE
OF JUDGES, SOCIAL AND PHYSICAL SETTING OF LAW IN US, TYPES
OF LAW PRACTICE, AND ECONOMICS OF LEGAL PROFESSION.

1116 HURST J.W. ED.
LAW AND THE CONDITIONS OF FREEDOM IN THE NINETEENTH CENTURY
UNITED STATES.
MADISON: U OF WISCONSIN PR, 1956, 139 PP., LC#56-9304.
    SERIES OF LECTURES CONCERNING 19TH-CENTURY PRINCIPLES OF
LAW, LEGAL POLICY, AND POWER AND ORGANIZATION OF FEDERAL
GOVERNMENT. DISCUSSES GROUP-ORGANIZED SOCIETY AND DIFFICULTY
IN FULFILLING INDIVIDUAL FREEDOM, AND CONSIDERS POLICY OF
CONTROLLING ENVIRONMENT TO ENLARGE MEN'S PRACTICAL FREEDOM.

1117 HURST W.H.
JUSTICE HOLMES ON LEGAL HISTORY.
NEW YORK: MACMILLAN, 1964, 171 PP., LC#64-11763.
    DETAILED ANALYSIS OF OLIVER WENDELL HOLMES'S IDEAS AND
PHILOSOPHY ON ANGLO-AMERICAN LEGAL HISTORY, BASED LARGELY ON
HIS WORK AS JUDGE AND ALSO ON FRAGMENTARY WRITINGS. ATTEMPTS
TO DEFINE COMPLETE CONCEPTUAL SCHEME OF LEGAL HISTORY AS IT
PERTAINS TO AMERICAN SOCIETY, BASED ON HOLMES' WORK AND
WRITINGS.

1118 HUXLEY J.
FREEDOM AND CULTURE.
NEW YORK: COLUMBIA U PRESS, 1951, 270 PP.
    SIX ARTICLES ON FREEDOM IN MODERN WORLD, INCLUDING
FREEDOMS OF EDUCATION, INFORMATION, SCIENCE, AND RIGHTS OF
CREATIVE ARTIST.

1119 HYDE C.C.
INTERNATIONAL LAW, CHIEFLY AS INTERPRETED AND APPLIED BY THE
UNITED STATES (3 VOLS., 2ND REV. ED.)
BOSTON: LITTLE BROWN, 1947, 2489 PP.
    PORTRAYS US VIEWS ON INTERNATIONAL LAW UP UNTIL 1941.
OBSERVES HOW STATES ACT AND MAY BE EXPECTED TO ACT UNDER
CERTAIN CONDITIONS. DISCUSSES CERTAIN ASPECTS OF
INTERNATIONAL LAW, CLASSIFICATION OF STATES, NORMAL RIGHTS
AND DUTIES, NATIONALITY, DIPLOMATIC INTERCOURSE, WAR, ETC.

1120 HYNEMAN C.S.
THE SUPREME COURT ON TRIAL.
NEW YORK: ATHERTON PRESS, 1963, 308 PP., LC#63-11717.
    STUDIES SUPREME COURT IN THE AMERICAN POLITICAL SYSTEM,
INQUIRING INTO INFLUENCE OF COURT UPON MAKING OF PUBLIC
POLICY. ALSO DISCUSSES CONFLICT BETWEEN JUDICIAL POWER
AND DEMOCRATIC ASPIRATIONS.

1121 IANNIELLO L. ED.
MILESTONES ALONG THE MARCH: TWELVE HISTORIC CIVIL RIGHTS
DOCUMENTS--FROM WORLD WAR II TO SELMA.
NEW YORK: FREDERICK PRAEGER, 1965, 124 PP., LC#65-24709.
    TWELVE DOCUMENTS ON CIVIL RIGHTS, INCLUDING SUPREME
COURT DECISIONS ON RESTRICTIVE COVENANTS, SEGREGATION IN
WASHINGTON, D.C. AND SEGREGATED SCHOOLS, TEXTS OR SUMMAR-
IES OF 1957 AND 1964 CIVIL RIGHTS ACTS, RELEVANT EXEC-
UTIVE ORDERS OF PRESIDENTS ROOSEVELT AND TRUMAN, AND
SPEECHES OR PAPERS OF PRESIDENTS KENNEDY AND JOHNSON, HUBERT
HUMPHREY, AND MARTIN LUTHER KING.

1122 IKLE F.C.
HOW NATIONS NEGOTIATE.
NEW YORK: HARPER ROW, 1964, 272 PP., $5.95.
    RELATES THE PROCESS OF INTERNATIONAL NEGOTIATION TO ITS
POSSIBLE OUTCOMES. DESCRIBES HOW NATIONS NEGOTIATE FOR SIDE
EFFECTS, HOW THEY ARE CONTROLLED BY THEIR REPUTATIONS AS
BARGAINERS, HOW THEY ARE STEERED BY PRESSURE GROUPS WITHIN
THEIR OWN COUNTRIES, AND HOW NEGOTIATION IS EFFECTED BY
DIFFERENT PERSONALITY TYPES.

1123 INST INTL DES CIVILISATION DIF
THE CONSTITUTIONS AND ADMINISTRATIVE INSTITUTIONS OF THE
NEW STATES.
BRUSSELS: INTL INST DIFF CIVILIZ, 1965, 886 PP.
    EXAMINES LEGAL, ECONOMIC, POLITICAL, AND SOCIAL ASPECTS
OF CONSTITUTIONS IN NEW STATES AND ADMINISTRATIVE ASPECTS OF
THEM. ATTEMPTS DETERMINATION OF EFFECTIVENESS IN VARIOUS
COUNTRIES.

1124 INSTITUT DE DROIT INTL
TABLEAU GENERAL DES RESOLUTIONS (1873-1956)
PARIS: INST DE DROIT INTERNAT, 1957, 404 PP.
    COMPILATION OF PUBLIC LAWS AND PRIVATE RIGHTS, ESPECIALLY
THOSE OF FOREIGNERS. INCLUDES TERRITORIAL JURISDICTION,
ARBITRATION, COMMERCE AND CONTRACTS.

1125 INSTITUT INTERMEDIAIRE INTL
REPERTOIRE GENERAL DES TRAITES ET AUTRES ACTES DIPLOMATIQUES
CONCLUS DEPUIS 1895 JUSQU'EN 1920.
HAARLEM, NETH.: H.D. TJEENK WILLINK, 1926, 516 PP.
    A CHRONOLOGICALLY ARRANGED, UNANNOTATED BIBLIOGRAPHY OF
4,412 TREATIES AND DIPLOMATIC ARRANGEMENTS CONCLUDED BETWEEN
1895-1920, PRIMARILY AMONG WESTERN POWERS. PROVIDES ALPHA-

BERICAL TABLES OF TREATIES AND LISTING OF NATIONAL COLLEC-
TIONS OF DIPLOMATIC HISTORY. SEPARATE DIVISIONS OF BILATER-
AL AND MULTILATERAL TREATIES.

1126 INSTITUTE COMP STUDY POL SYS
DOMINICAN REPUBLIC ELECTION FACT BOOK.
WASHINGTON: INST COMP STUDY POL, 1966, 55 PP., LC#66-23504.
DISCUSSES POLITICAL HISTORY, POLITICAL PARTIES, ELECTION
ISSUES, LAWS, AND STRUCTURE OF GOVERNMENT OF DOMINICAN
REPUBLIC. ANALYZES 1962 ELECTION. TABLES ON ELECTORATE,
PRESIDENTIAL ELECTION RETURNS, AND DISTRIBUTION OF SEATS IN
SENATE AND CHAMBER OF DEPUTIES IN 1962.

1127 INSTITUTE DES RELATIONS INTL
LES ASPECTS ECONOMIQUES DU REARMEMENT (ETUDE DE L'INSTITUT
DES RELATIONS INTERNATIONALES A BRUXELLES)
BRUSSELS: INST REL INTERNAT, 1951, 236 PP.
EXAMINES COMPARATIVE ECONOMY OF REARMAMENT, EMPHASIZING
PRODUCTION, INVESTMENT, RAW MATERIALS, AND INTERNATIONAL
EXCHANGE.

1128 INSTITUTE JUDICIAL ADMIN
JUDGES: THEIR TEMPORARY APPOINTMENT, ASSIGNMENT AND TRANS-
FER: SURVEY OF FED AND STATE CONSTN'S STATUTES, ROLES OF CT.
NEW YORK: INST OF JUDICIAL ADMIN, 1962, 116 PP.
STUDY OF JUDGES, CONCENTRATING ON PERSON OR COURT HAVING
POWER OF APPOINTMENT OF JUDGES AND GIVING SPECIFIC POLICY
OF EACH STATE; ARRANGED BY STATE.

1129 INT. SOC. SCI. BULL.
"TECHNIQUES OF MEDIATION AND CONCILIATION."
INT. SOC. SCI. BULL., 10 (NO.1, 58), 507-628.
COMPILATION OF ARTICLES CONCERNING TECHNIQUES OF
MEDIATION AND CONCILIATION IN FIELDS OF INTERNATIONAL LAW
AND COLLECTIVE INDUSTRIAL DISPUTES. DISCUSSES THE FUNCTION
OF CONCILIATION IN CIVIL PROCEDURES OF MANY EUROPEAN NATIONS
AND OF USA.

1130 INTERNAT CONGRESS OF JURISTS
EXECUTIVE ACTION AND THE RULE OF RULE: REPORTION PROCEEDINGS
OF INT'T CONGRESS OF JURISTS,-RIO DE JANEIRO, BRAZIL.
RIO DE JANEIR: INTL CONG JURISTS, 1962, 187 PP.
CONGRESS RECOGNIZES ONE GREAT MODERN DILEMMA IS POWER OF
EXECUTIVE VS RIGHTS OF INDIVIDUAL. EXAMINES ROLE OF
JUDGES, LAWYERS, AND TEACHERS OF LAW IN STRIKING BALANCE BE-
TWEEN THE TWO, THUS ADJUSTING RULE OF LAW TO NEEDS OF
SOCIAL AND ECONOMIC DEVELOPMENT.

1131 INTERNATIONAL COMN JURISTS
AFRICAN CONFERENCE ON THE RULE OF LAW.
GENEVA: INTL COMN OF JURISTS, 1961, 181 PP.
PROCEEDINGS OF CONFERENCE OF INTERNATIONAL COMMISSION OF
JURISTS HELD IN LAGOS, NIGERIA IN JANUARY, 1961. PURPOSE OF
CONFERENCE WAS TO ASSESS LEGAL SYSTEMS AND POLITICAL SITUA-
TIONS IN NEWLY INDEPENDENT SUB-SAHARA STATES. REVIEWS DECI-
SIONS AND POLICIES ADOPTED BY CONFERENCE BASED ON CONCEPT OF
RULE OF LAW AS DEFINED AT 1955 ATHENS CONFERENCE.

1132 INTERNATIONAL CONCILIATION
ISSUES BEFORE THE 22ND GENERAL ASSEMBLY.
NEW YORK: CARNEGIE ENDOWMENT, 1967, 206 PP.
ANALYZES AND EVALUATES KEY INTERNATIONAL PROBLEMS OF UN.
POLICIES ARE DISCUSSED UNDER TOPICAL HEADINGS. INCLUDES
DECISIONS MADE. FEELS UN SHOULD BE MORE THAN PLACE TO BRING
PROBLEMS THAT INDIVIDUAL NATIONS CANNOT SOLVE ALONE. ONLY
IF ALL POLICIES ARE E MADE HERE CAN THERE BE WORLD PEACE.

1133 INTERNATIONAL COURT OF JUSTICE
CHARTER OF THE UNITED NATIONS, STATUTE AND RULES OF COURT
AND OTHER CONSTITUTIONAL DOCUMENTS.
THE HAGUE: INTL COURT OF JUSTICE, 1947, 141 PP.
CONTAINS UN CHARTER, STATUTE AND RULES OF THE ICJ, TO-
GETHER WITH FIVE UN RESOLUTIONS OF 1946 AS TO PRIVILEGES AND
IMMUNITIES OF COURT MEMBERS, THEIR PENSIONS, ADMINISTRATION
OF THE COURT, CONDITIONS UNDER WHICH THE IJC SHALL BE OPEN
TO STATES NOT PARTIES TO THE STATUTE, AND CONDITIONS UNDER
WHICH SWITZERLAND MAY BECOME A PARTY. IN FRENCH AND ENGLISH.

1134 INTERNATIONAL LAW ASSOCIATION
A FORTY YEARS' CATALOGUE OF THE BOOKS, PAMPHLETS AND PA-
PERS IN THE LIBRARY OF THE INTERNATIONAL LAW ASSOCIATION.
LONDON: R FLINT & CO, 1915, 70 PP.
BIBLIOGRAPHICAL INDEX TO 1,500 ITEMS IN ASSOCIATION'S
LIBRARY, TOPICALLY CLASSIFIED INTO FIVE MAIN CATEGORIES
COVERING: INTERNATIONAL LAW, POLITICS, COMPARATIVE LAW, CON-
STITUTIONAL LAW, AND MUNICIPAL LAW. MOST PUBLICATIONS DATE
FROM 1875.

1135 INTL ATOMIC ENERGY AGENCY
INTERNATIONAL CONVENTIONS ON CIVIL LIABILITY FOR NUCLEAR
DAMAGE.
VIENNA: INTL ATOMIC ENERGY COMN, 1966.
COMPILES FOUR INTERNATIONAL CONVENTIONS ON CIVIL LIABIL-
ITY FOR NUCLEAR DAMAGE. CONVENTIONS CHANNEL EXCLUSIVE LIA-
BILITY TO OPERATOR OF NUCLEAR INSTALLATION AND HOLD HIM
ABSOLUTELY LIABLE UPON PROOF OF CAUSATION. CONVENTIONS IN-

CLUDE PROVISIONS CONCERNING RIGHTS OF RECOURSE, ENFORCEMENT
OF FOREIGN JUDGMENTS, AND LIMITS OF LIABILITY.

1136 INTNTL COTTON ADVISORY COMMITT
GOVERNMENT REGULATIONS ON COTTON, 1962 (PAMPHLET)
WASHINGTON: INTL COTTON ADV COMM, 1962, 31 PP.
COLLECTION OF LAWS REGULATING COTTON INDUSTRY IN COUN-
TRIES THAT PRODUCE COTTON. INCLUDES CHANGES IN LAWS SINCE
1961 REGULATING PRODUCTION, EXPORTS, IMPORTS, CONSUMPTION,
AND PRICES.

1137 IRION F.C.
APPORTIONMENT OF THE NEW MEXICO LEGISLATURE.
ALBUQUERQUE: U N MEX, DEPT GOVT, 1964, 245 PP.
REPORTS BASIC FACTS ABOUT APPORTIONMENT OF NEW MEXICO
LEGISLATURE FROM 1880-1964 FOR USE OF PEOPLE CONCERNED WITH
REAPPORTIONING STATE AND AS SUMMARY TO GUIDE OTHER STATES.
BESIDES COMPENDIUM, AUTHOR COMMENTS ON ATTITUDES AND
IMPLICATIONS.

1138 ISORNI J.
LES CAS DE CONSCIENCE DE L'AVOCAT.
PARIS: LIB ACADEMIQUE PERRIN, 1965, 313 PP.
CONCERNS ROLE AND MORAL OBLIGATIONS OF A LAWYER. LAWYER
HAS RESPONSIBILITY NEVER TO COMPROMISE HIMSELF OR HIS OF-
FICE. CONSIDERS POLITICAL AND NONPOLITICAL CASES THAT
AUTHOR FEELS WERE CASES OF CONSCIENCE (DREYFUS, MARECHAL
NEY).

1139 JACKSON E.
MEETING OF THE MINDS: A WAY TO PEACE THROUGH MEDIATION.
NEW YORK: MCGRAW HILL, 1952, 200 PP.
STUDY IN PRACTICES AND TECHNIQUES OF MEDIATION IN BOTH
LABOR AND INTERNATIONAL DISPUTES. EXPLORES PARALLELS WITHIN
AREAS AND DISCUSSES PROBLEMS OF SECURING AGREEMENTS. VIEWS
THE RELATIONSHIP BETWEEN MEDIATION AND THE INSTITUTION AND
POWER SETTING IN WHICH IT TAKES PLACE. VIEWS MEDIATION AS
ART AND EMPHASIZES PERSONAL QUALITIES OF MEDIATOR. BELIEVES
EXPERIENCES IN TWO FIELDS ARE SIMILAR SO THAT UNITED NATIONS
MAY PROFIT FROM MEDIATION PROCEEDINGS.

1140 JACKSON E.
"THE FUTURE DEVELOPMENT OF THE UNITED NATIONS: SOME SUG-
GESTIONS FOR RESEARCH."
J. CONFL. RESOLUT., 5 (JUNE 61), 119-27.
SEES FUTURE OF UN CHARACTERIZED BY STRUGGLE FOR CON-
TROL OF THE ORGANIZATION. MAKES TWELVE PROPOSALS FOR
RESEARCH ON THE SECURITY COUNCIL, FINANCIAL MANAGEMENT, AND
INTERNATIONAL LAW.

1141 JACKSON R.H.
INTERNATIONAL CONFERENCE ON MILITARY TRIALS.
WASHINGTON: US GOVERNMENT, 1949, 441 PP.
A DOCUMENTARY RECORD OF NEGOTIATIONS OF THE REPRESENTA-
TIVES OF THE US, THE PROVISIONAL GOVERNMENT OF FRANCE, GREAT
BRITAIN, AND THE USSR AT THE LONDON CONFERENCE, JUNE 26-
AUGUST 8, 1945. CONTAINS FORMAL STATEMENTS ON PRINCIPLES
OF SUBSTANTIVE LAW AND METHODS OF PROCEDURE FOR THE PROSE-
CUTION AND TRIAL OF MAJOR EUROPEAN WAR CRIMINALS. CULMINATES
IN THE CHARTER OF THE INTERNATIONAL MILITARY TRIBUNAL.

1142 JACKSON R.M.
THE MACHINERY OF JUSTICE IN ENGLAND.
NEW YORK: CAMBRIDGE U PRESS, 1964, 455 PP.
DISCUSSES ENGLISH SYSTEM OF LAW AND COURTS AND ADMINI-
STRATIVE DETAILS LIKE PERSONNEL AND COSTS. GIVES HISTORICAL
INTRODUCTION AND EXAMINES CIVIL AND CRIMINAL JURISDICTION.

1143 JACOBINI H.B.
INTERNATIONAL LAW: A TEXT.
HOMEWOOD: DORSEY, 1962, 324 PP., LC#62-16518.
INTRODUCTION TO FIELD, PRIMARILY FOR STUDENTS IN LIBERAL
ARTS COURSES AND FOR GENERAL READERS. INCLUDES LAWS OF WAR
AND NEUTRALITY. THEORETICAL FRAMEWORK OF BOOK IS "A
POLITICAL CONCEPTION OF LAW," RATHER THAN A MORAL ONE.

1144 JACOBS C.E.
JUSTICE FRANKFURTER AND CIVIL LIBERTIES.
BERKELEY: U OF CALIF PR, 1961, 265 PP.
DISCUSSES JUSTICE FRANKFURTER'S CONCERN WITH CIVIL LIBER-
TIES ON SUPREME COURT, INCLUDING RELIGION, SPEECH, PRESS,
AND ASSEMBLY CLAUSES OF FIRST AMENDMENT, LIBERTY AND NA-
TIONAL SECURITY, AND FEDERAL PROCEDURAL RIGHTS.

1145 JACOBS P.
STATE OF UNIONS.
NEW YORK: ATHENEUM PUBLISHERS, 1963, 303 PP., LC#63-17853.
STUDY OF PRESENT SITUATION OF LABOR UNIONS IN US ECONOMY.
DEALS WITH JIMMY HOFFA AND OTHER LEADERS, CONGRESSIONAL
INVESTIGATION, INTERNAL PROCESSES, STATUS OF NEGRO, AND CON-
DITION OF COLLECTIVE BARGAINING.

1146 JACOBSON H.K., STEIN E.
DIPLOMATS, SCIENTISTS, AND POLITICIANS* THE UNITED STATES
AND THE NUCLEAR TEST BAN NEGOTIATIONS.
ANN ARBOR: U OF MICH PR, 1966, 538 PP., LC#66-11622.

DETAILED ANALYSIS OF THE NEGOTIATIONS, AND RELATED POLITICAL AND SCIENTIFIC EVENTS, CULMINATING IN THE MOSCOW TREATY BANNING NUCLEAR TESTING--FIRST FORMAL ARMS CONTROL AGREEMENT OF THE COLD WAR. RESULT OF ATTEMPT TO ASSESS THE IMPACT OF SCIENCE AND MODERN TECHNOLOGY ON THE PROCESS OF NEGOTIATION AND ON STRUCTURE AND FUNCTIONS OF INTERNATIONAL ORGANIZATION.

1147 JAMES L.F.
THE SUPREME COURT IN AMERICAN LIFE.
GLENVIEW, ILL: SCOTT, FORESMAN, 1954, 159 PP., LC#64-25409.
ANALYZES SUPREME COURT DECISIONS WHICH HAVE HELPED SHAPE AMERICAN HISTORY. PRESENTS CASES ON SLAVERY QUESTION, REGULATION OF BUSINESS, DEPRESSION CRISIS, INDIVIDUAL FREEDOM PROBLEMS, AND SEPARATION OF CHURCH AND STATE. SHOWS HOW JUDGES HAVE BOTH INFLUENCED AND BEEN INFLUENCED BY THEIR TIMES.

1148 JANOWITZ M.
SOCIAL CONTROL OF ESCALATED RIOTS (PAMPHLET)
CHICAGO: U CHI, CTR POLICY STUDY, 1968, 44 PP.
REVIEWS HISTORY OF URBAN VIOLENCE IN US AND ANALYZES PRESENT SITUATION IN ATTEMPT TO DETERMINE MEASURES TO AVERT SUCH VIOLENCE. EXAMINES LAW ENFORCEMENT AGENCIES, IMPACT OF MASS MEDIA, AND CONCEPT OF CONSTABULARY. BELIEVES SOCIAL TENSIONS TO BE PARTIAL EXPLANATION OF RIOTING; ORGANIZATIONAL WEAKNESSES OF LAW ENFORCEMENT AGENCIES AND MORAL AND SOCIAL CLIMATE ENCOURAGE VIOLENCE.

1149 JAPAN MINISTRY OF JUSTICE
CRIMINAL JUSTICE IN JAPAN.
TOKYO: JAPAN MINISTRY OF JUSTICE, 1958, 37 PP.
ATTEMPTS TO PRESENT CONCISE PICTURE OF ADMINISTRATION OF CRIMINAL JUSTICE IN POSTWAR JAPAN. DISCUSSES POLICE ACTIVITIES AND ORGANIZATION, CRIMINAL PROCEDURE, CONSTITUTIONAL GUARANTEES, CORRECTIONAL SERVICES AND REHABILITATION OF OFFENDERS. BRIEFLY EXAMINES JAPANESE LAWYERS.

1150 JAPAN MOMBUSHO DAIGAKU GAKIYUT
BIBLIOGRAPHY OF THE STUDIES ON LAW AND POLITICS (PAMPHLET)
TOKYO: JAPAN MINISTRY EDUCATION, 1955, 83 PP.
UNANNOTATED BIBLIOGRAPHY OF 918 WORKS IN FIELDS OF LAW AND POLITICS THAT APPEARED IN VARIOUS JAPANESE SCHOLARLY BOOKS, JOURNALS, BULLETINS, ETC., IN 1952. AUTHOR, TITLE, AND JOURNAL GIVEN IN BOTH ROMAN SCRIPT AND CHARACTERS. WORKS ARRANGED ALPHABETICALLY BY AUTHOR WITHIN 16 SUBJECT CLASSIFICATIONS, AND INDEXED BY AUTHOR. LIST OF ALL PERIODICALS MENTIONED IS APPENDED TO TEXT.

1151 JEFFERSON T.
"DEMOCRACY" (1816) IN BASIC WRITINGS."
NEW YORK: JOHN WILEY, 1944.
PROPOSES METHOD OF REPRESENTATIVE GOVERNMENT BASED ON GENERAL SUFFRAGE, EQUAL REPRESENTATION IN LEGISLATURE, DIRECT ELECTION OF THE EXECUTIVE, ELECTIVE JUDGES AND SHERIFFS, AND PERIODICAL AMENDMENTS TO THE CONSTITUTION. DISAGREES WITH IDEA THAT CONSTITUTIONS ARE TOO SACRED TO BE TOUCHED AND WITH NOTION THAT LAWS MADE IN PAST MAY NOT BE CHANGED TO SUIT PRESENT.

1152 JENKINS W.S.
A GUIDE TO THE MICROFILM COLLECTION OF EARLY STATE RECORDS.
WASHINGTON: LIBRARY OF CONGRESS, 1950, 761 PP., LC#50-62956.
A COMPREHENSIVE GUIDE TO 160,000 FEET OF FILM REPRESENTING 2,500,000 PAGES OF PRIMARY SOURCE MATERIAL. CLASSIFICATION ARRANGED BY STATE, SUBJECT, AND CHRONOLOGY, RESPECTIVELY. DESIGNED TO SERVE DUAL PURPOSE OF SUPPLYING USER WITH INFORMATION ON THE LOCATION OF BOTH THE ORIGINAL AND FILM OF EACH DOCUMENT, AND PROVIDING CATALOG FROM WHICH ORDERS FOR REPRODUCTIONS MAY BE FILLED. A MECHANIZED BIBLIOGRAPHY.

1153 JENKS C.W.
THE INTERNATIONAL PROTECTION OF TRADE UNION FREEDOM.
NEW YORK: PRAEGER, 1957, 592 PP.
STUDIES GROWTH, DEVELOPMENT AND EFFECTIVENESS OF CURRENT INTERNATIONAL LAWS GUARANTEEING FREEDOM OF ASSOCIATION TO THE WORLD'S TRADE UNIONS AND THE PROCEDURAL ARRANGEMENTS CONCERNED WITH THE LAWS. SPECULATES AS TO FUTURE EFFECTIVENESS OF LAWS IN CONNECTION WITH THE UNIONS'RIGHTS.

1154 JENKS C.W.
THE COMMON LAW OF MANKIND.
NEW YORK: PRAEGER, 1958, 456 PP.
DEALS WITH DEVELOPMENT OF LAW AFTER WW 2. GENERAL CONCEPTION THAT CONTEMPORARY INTERNATIONAL LAW CAN NO LONGER BE PRESENTED WITHIN ITS CLASSICAL FRAMEWORK. SUGGESTS THAT IT MUST BE REGARDED AS THE COMMON LAW OF MANKIND 'IN AN EARLY STAGE OF ITS DEVELOPMENT.'

1155 JENKS C.W.
"THE CHALLENGE OF UNIVERSALITY."
PROC. AMER. SOC. INT. LAW, (1959), 85-98.
A GREATER UNDERSTANDING OF THE VARIOUS LAW SYSTEMS FOUND THROUGHOUT THE WORLD WILL LEAD TO A SYSTEM OF INTERNATIONAL LAW THAT WILL BENEFIT ALL MANKIND BY ENSURING MAN'S RIGHTS AND FREEDOM.

1156 JENKS C.W.
HUMAN RIGHTS AND INTERNATIONAL LABOR STANDARDS.
NEW YORK: PRAEGER, 1960, 159 PP.
WITH REFERENCE TO FORCED LABOR, FREEDOM OF ASSOCIATION, DISCRIMINATION, SOCIAL SECURITY AND EMPLOYMENT SERVICES, EVALUATES THE PROMOTION AND PROTECTION OF HUMAN RIGHTS AS PROCLAIMED BY UNIVERSAL DECLARATION. OUTLINES CONTRIBUTIONS OF ILO TO THE FORMULATION OF LABOR STANDARDS.

1157 JENKS C.W.
INTERNATIONAL IMMUNITIES.
NEW YORK: OCEANA, 1961, 178 PP., $6.00.
DISCUSSES HISTORICAL DEVELOPMENT OF PRINCIPLE OF INTERNATIONAL IMMUNITY. ATTEMPTS TO POINT OUT FUTURE COURSE. CITES EXAMPLES OF BEHAVIOR OF INTERNATIONAL ORGANIZATIONS IN CONNECTION WITH IMPORTANT CASES.

1158 JENKS C.W.
THE PROPER LAW OF INTERNATIONAL ORGANISATIONS.
NEW YORK: OCEANA PUBLISHING, 1962, 282 PP., LC#62-12026.
A STUDY OF THE IMPACT OF CONTEMPORARY DEVELOPMENTS IN INTERNATIONAL ORGANIZATION ON PUBLIC AND PRIVATE INTERNATIONAL LAW AND ADMINISTRATIVE LAW. PRESENTS A RE-EVALUATION OF ACCEPTED CONCEPTS IN RELATION TO THE LEGAL STATUS AND TRANSACTIONS OF EMERGING INTERNATIONAL BODIES. NUMEROUS CASES CITED.

1159 JENKS C.W.
LAW, FREEDOM, AND WELFARE.
NEW YORK: OCEANA PUBLISHING, 1963, 162 PP.
EXAMINES INTERRELATIONSHIP OF LAW, FREEDOM, AND WELFARE IN ACTION FOR PEACE. STUDIES NEED FOR INTERNATIONAL LAW TO CONCERN ITSELF WITH SCIENTIFIC EFFORTS WHICH MIGHT CHANGE ENVIRONMENT ON EARTH. DISCUSSES AREAS WHERE LAW CAN CONTRIBUTE TO INTERNATIONAL PROBLEMS IN TIMES OF STRESS AND TENSION. ANALYZES EMERGENCE OF INTERDEPENDENCE RATHER THAN INDEPENDENCE OF STATES AS BASIS OF CONTEMPORARY LAW.

1160 JENKS C.W.
THE PROSPECTS OF INTERNATIONAL ADJUDICATION.
NEW YORK: OCEANA PUBLISHING, 1964, 805 PP., LC#63-15142.
EXPLORES PROSPECTS FOR DEEPENING RULE OF LAW IN WORLD AFFAIRS. FROM STANDPOINT OF MAKING INTERNATIONAL COURT OF JUSTICE A MORE EFFECTIVE INSTRUMENT, DISCUSSES POSSIBLE DEVELOPMENTS IN ITS JURISDICTION, JURISPRUDENCE, AND PROCEDURE. INCLUDES COMPULSORY JURISDICTION, GENERAL PRINCIPLES OF LAW, INTERNATIONAL PUBLIC POLICY, EQUITY, APPLICATION OF MUNICIPAL LAW, AND SECURING COMPLIANCE.

1161 JENKS C.W.
SPACE LAW.
NEW YORK: FREDERICK PRAEGER, 1965, 476 PP., LC#65-17859.
ANALYSIS OF DEVELOPMENT AND STATUS OF SPACE LAW. EXAMINES LAW AND CONCEPTS OF JURISDICTION EXISTING TODAY. UN ACTION ON ISSUE OF OUTER SPACE ACTIVITIES AND RIGHTS, AND LEGAL LITERATURE AVAILABLE.

1162 JENKS E.J.
LAW AND POLITICS IN THE MIDDLE AGES.
NEW YORK: HENRY HOLT & CO, 1897, 352 PP.
ATTEMPTS TO SELECT FROM MEDIEVAL HISTORY THOSE IDEAS AND INSTITUTIONS THAT INFLUENCED AND AFFECTED LATER CIVILIZATION. DESCRIBES SOCIAL FORCES THAT WORKED ON RUDIMENTARY NOTIONS OF LAW, FUSING ITS HISTORY WITH THAT OF SOCIETY. NOTES DEVELOPMENT OF BASIC TYPICAL SOCIETIES: CLAN, STATE, AND PARTNERSHIP. BELIEVES STATE-CLAN STRUGGLE HOLDS KEY TO INTERNAL POLITICS OF MIDDLE AGES.

1163 JENNINGS I.
PARLIAMENT.
WORCESTER: CLARK U PRESS, 1957, 574 PP., LC#57-14459.
ANALYZES THE BRITISH PARLIAMENT. TREATS THE MEMBERS, THE POLITICAL PARTIES AND THE OFFICIALS, THE ART OF MANAGEMENT, THE TECHNIQUE OF OPPOSITION, WHO MAKES THE LAWS, THE PROCESS OF LEGISLATION, FINANCIAL CONTROL, NATIONALIZED INDUSTRIES, HOUSE OF LORDS, PRIVATE BILL LEGISLATION, DELEGATED LEGISLATION AND PARLIAMENTARY DEMOCRACY.

1164 JENNINGS R.
PROGRESS OF INTERNATIONAL LAW.
NEW YORK: CAMBRIDGE, 1960, 223 PP.
TRACES EVOLUTION AND HISTORY OF CONTEMPORARY CONCEPT OF INTERNATIONAL LAW AND EXAMINES THE POSSIBILITIES FOR ITS FUTURE DEVELOPMENT.

1165 JENNINGS W.I., YOUNG C.M.
CONSTITUTIONAL LAWS OF THE COMMONWEALTH.
LONDON: OXFORD U PR, 1952, 515 PP.
COMPILES SIGNIFICANT CASES IN BRITISH CONSTITUTIONAL LAW, 1702-1947, REGARDING RELATION OF COLONIES TO ENGLAND. LAND OWNERSHIP, INDUSTRIAL DEVELOPMENT, AND CIVIL LAW. ALSO GIVES SUMMARY OF CONSTITUTIONS OF CANADA, IRELAND, NEW ZEALAND, AND AUSTRALIA.

1166 JESSUP P.C.
A MODERN LAW OF NATIONS.

NEW YORK: MACMILLAN, 1948, 236 PP.
EXPLORES SOME UNDERLYING BASES FOR A MODERN LAW OF
NATIONS. DISCUSSES PAST ATTEMPTS AT INTERGOVERNMENTAL RELA-
TIONSHIPS. STRESSES THAT INTERNATIONAL LAW MUST BE DIRECTLY
APPLICABLE TO THE INDIVIDUAL, AND THAT THERE MUST BE DEFI-
NITE COMMITMENT TO OBSERVANCE BY INTERNATIONAL SOCIETY.

1167 JESSUP P.C.
TRANSNATIONAL LAW.
NEW HAVEN: YALE U. PR., 1956, 113 PP.
THREE LECTURES ON THE LAW WHICH 'REGULATES ACTIONS OR
EVENTS THAT TRANSCEND NATIONAL FRONTIERS', CIVIL, CRIMINAL,
PUBLIC, AND PRIVATE. DEFINES THE TERMS AND DISCUSSES THE
PROBLEMS OF SEEKING PROPER JURISDICTION AND CHOOSING THE
CORRECT LAW.

1168 JIMENEZ E.
VOTING AND HANDLING OF DISPUTES IN THE SECURITY COUNCIL.
NEW YORK: CARNEGIE ENDOWMENT, 1950, 189 PP.
DESCRIBES EVOLUTION, LEGALITY, AND FUNCTION OF SECURITY
COUNCIL VOTING PROCEDURES, SUBMISSION OF DISPUTES, METHODS
OF SETTLEMENT, RESOLUTIONS, ETC. STRESSES GROWTH OF POWERS.

1169 JOHN OF SALISBURY
THE STATESMAN'S BOOK (1159) (TRANS. BY J. DICKINSON)
NEW YORK: ALFRED KNOPF, 1927, 410 PP.
COMMONWEALTH EXISTS THROUGH DIVINE FAVOR, WITH PRINCE AS
ITS HEAD. RIGHT OF PRINCE TO GOVERN IS DIVINE, AND RELATION-
SHIP TO PEOPLE IS PATERNAL. "HIGHER LAW" IS SUPREME OVER ALL
GOVERNMENTS. BELIEVES IN PAPAL SUPREMACY; CHURCH, LIKE GOV-
ERNMENT, IS INSTRUMENT OF APPLYING HIGHER LAW. TYRANNICIDE
IS JUSTIFIABLE BY "HIGHER LAW." MEN, IF GOOD AND FREE FROM
SIN, CAN LIVE WITHOUT GOVERNMENT AND BY LAW ALONE.

1170 JOHNSON O.H.
"THE ENGLISH TRADITION IN INTERNATIONAL LAW."
INT. COMP. LAW QUART., 11 (APR. 62), 416-45.
TRACES EXISTENCE AND COMPREHENSION OF INTERNATIONAL LAW
TO MIDDLE AGES. AREA NEGLECTED SINCE END OF PRIZE COURTS.
PROPOSES BROADER STUDY IN UNIVERSITIES. URGES OFFICIALS IN
PERTINENT POSITIONS TO GAIN FAMILARITY WITH SUBJECT.

1171 JOHNSTON D.M.
THE INTERNATIONAL LAW OF FISHERIES: A FRAMEWORK FOR POLICY-
ORIENTED INQUIRIES.
NEW HAVEN: YALE U PR, 1965, 554 PP., LC#65-22325.
SHOWS INABILITY OF CLASSIC LEGAL CONCEPTS, DOMINATED BY
IDEA OF TERRITORIAL SOVEREIGNTY, TO SATISFY CONTEMPORARY
NEEDS AND DEMANDS RELATING TO EXPLOITATION OF FISHERIES.
CONCLUDES THAT DEVELOPMENT OF LAW DEPENDS ON FUNCTIONAL
REASSESSMENT OF EXISTING LAW.

1172 JONES C.O.
EVERY SECOND YEAR: CONGRESSIONAL BEHAVIOR AND THE
TWO-YEAR TERM.
WASHINGTON: BROOKINGS INST, 1967, 118 PP., LC#67-30596.
QUESTIONING DESIRABILITY OF TWO-YEAR TERM FOR CON-
GRESSMEN. IS CONCERNED WITH WHETHER SHORT PRESENT TERM
OBLIGES CONGRESSMAN TO YIELD TOO MUCH TO CONSTITUENCY
PRESSURE, TO THE DETRIMENT OF THE LAW-MAKING FUNCTION.
SAYS CLOSE AND CONTINUING ASSOCIATION WITH THE PEOPLE IS
THE HEART OF A TRULY REPRESENTATIVE LEGISLATIVE SYSTEM.

1173 JORDAN E.
THEORY OF LEGISLATION: AN ESSAY ON THE DYNAMICS OF PUBLIC
MIND.
INDIANAPOLIS: PROGRESS PUBL CO, 1930, 486 PP.
A SPECULATIVE INQUIRY INTO THE NATURE OF THE "CORPORATE
WILL" AND ITS EXPRESSION THROUGH THE LEGISLATIVE PROCESS. A
STUDY OF THE TRANSFORMATION OF THE CORPORATE WILL INTO LAW.
INCLUDES A DISCUSSION OF THE JUDICIAL PROCESS.

1174 JOSEPH H.
IF THIS BE TREASON.
SKOKIE: RAND MCNALLY & CO, 1963, 192 PP.
DISCUSSES TREASON TRIAL OF SOUTH AFRICA. INCLUDES ORIGINS
OF TRIAL AND RESULTS. FOCUSES ON LAST YEAR OF TRIAL, MARCH
29, 1960 - MARCH 29, 1961. AUTHOR WAS ONE OF ACCUSED.

1175 JOUGHIN L.
"ACADEMIC DUE PROCESS."
LAW AND CONTEMPORARY PROB., 28 (SUMMER 63), 573-595.
EXPLORES RECENT POLICY STATEMENTS IN THE AREA OF DUE
PROCESS IN UNIVERSITIES, AND SEARCHES FOR THE BEST WAYS OF
HANDLING PERSONNEL DECISIONS AND SAFEGUARDING INDIVIDUAL
INTEGRITY, INCLUDING CONFRONTATION, NOTICE, RIGHT TO
COUNSEL, CLEAR CHARGES, RULES OF EVIDENCE AND APPELLATE
PROCEDURE.

1176 JUSTICE (SOCIETY)
THE CITIZEN AND THE ADMINISTRATION: THE REDRESS OF
GRIEVANCES (PAMPHLET)
LONDON: STEVENS, 1961, 104 PP.
REPORT BY BRITISH SECTION OF THE INTERNATIONAL COMMISSION
OF JURISTS ON METHODS OF REDRESS OPEN TO CITIZENS MALTREATED
BY THOSE IN AUTHORITY. CONCLUDES THAT SYSTEM OF APPEALS IS

DESIRABLE AND SUGGESTS APPOINTMENT OF "THE PARLIAMENTARY
COMMISSIONER," AN OFFICIAL LIKE SWEDISH OMBUDSMAN TO REP-
RESENT PEOPLE'S APPEALS.

1177 JUSTINIAN
THE DIGEST (DIGESTA CORPUS JURIS CIVILIS) (2 VOLS.)
(TRANS. BY C. H. MONRO)
NEW YORK: CAMBRIDGE U PRESS, 1909, 800 PP.
THE DIGEST OF JUSTINIAN'S CODIFICATION OF CIVIL LAW.
DEALS WITH LAWS OF DIVORCE, ADOPTION, SLAVERY, AND SO ON.
PRECEDING THE DIGEST IS THE EXPLANATION OF JUSTINIAN'S
REASON FOR THE WORK, WHICH WAS THE DESIRE TO CONSOLIDATE
THE EXISTING LEGAL STRUCTURE OF THE ROMAN EMPIRE.

1178 KAAS L.
DIE GEISTLICHE GERICHTSBARKEIT DER KATHOLISCHEN KIRCHE IN
PREUSSEN (2 VOLS.)
AMSTERDAM: VERLAG P SCHIPPERS, 1965, 962 PP.
EXAMINES JURISDICTION OF CATHOLIC CHURCH IN PRUSSIA FROM
REFORMATION TO PRESENT. DISCUSSES DISPUTES WITH STATE AS
WELL AS STRUCTURE AND PROCESSES OF ECCLESIASTICAL COURTS.

1179 KAFKA G.
FREIHEIT UND ANARCHIE.
MUNICH: E REINHARDT VERLAG, 1949, 115 PP.
DEALS WITH THE FOUR FREEDOMS (FREEDOM FROM WANT,
FREEDOM OF RELIGIOUS EXPRESSION, FREEDOM OF OPINION, AND
FREEDOM FROM FEAR) AS EXPRESSED IN THE ATLANTIC CHARTER.

1180 KAHNG T.J.
LAW, POLITICS, AND THE SECURITY COUNCIL* AN INQUIRY INTO THE
HANDLING OF LEGAL QUESTIONS.
LONDON: LONGMANS, GREEN & CO, 1964, 252 PP.
ANALYSIS OF PATTERN OF SECURITY COUNCIL'S HANDLING OF LE-
GAL QUESTIONS BY COMPARING ITS BEHAVIOR IN A WEALTH OF CASES
AGAINST BEHAVIOR PRESCRIBED BY CHARTER. QUESTIONS OF COMPE-
TENCE, PROCEDURES, AND NATIONAL RIGHTS AND DUTIES TREATED.
FINDS THAT COUNCIL IS CONCERNED WITH LEGALITY BUT PREFERS TO
DECIDE FOR ITSELF AND NOT SUBMIT QUESTIONS TO CHARTER-AU-
THORIZED BODIES.

1181 KALNOKI BEDO A., TORZSAY-BIBER G. ET AL.
LEGAL SOURCES AND BIBLIOGRAPHY OF HUNGARY.
NEW YORK: FREDERICK PRAEGER, 1956, 157 PP., LC#56-13220.
MATERIALS ORGANIZED BY TYPE OF SOURCE WITH GREATEST
EMPHASIS ON TREATISES. MOST OF THE 1000 ITEMS IN LANGUAGES
OTHER THAN ENGLISH. COLLECTIONS OF LAWS, COURT REPORTS, AND
TRANSLATION OF LAWS INCLUDED. SUBJECT INDEX. MID-EUROPEAN
LAW PROJECT.

1182 KAMISAR Y., INBAU F.E., ARNOLD T.
CRIMINAL JUSTICE IN OUR TIME.
CHARLOTTESVILLE: U PR OF VA, 1965, 161 PP., LC#65-26873.
ESSAYS EMPHASIZING AMERICAN CRIMINAL PROCEDURE, LAW EN-
FORCEMENT, INDIVIDUAL CIVIL RIGHTS, AND THE CRIMINAL TRIAL.
INCLUDES DISCUSSION OF INTERROGATION AND WIRETAPPING.

1183 KAPLAN H.E.
THE LAW OF CIVIL SERVICE.
ALBANY & NY: MATTHEW BENDER & CO, 1958, 440 PP.
SURVEYS FIELD OF CIVIL SERVICE LITIGATION DISCUSSING CON-
STITUTIONALITY OF CIVIL SERVICE LAW, ITS ADOPTION AND SCOPE,
MEANS OF HANDLING CASES, PUNISHMENTS, JUDICIAL REVIEW,
VETEREN PREFERENCES, AND LIMITATIONS ON EMPLOYEES POLITICAL
ACTIVITIES.

1184 KAPLAN M.A., KATZENBACH N.
THE POLITICAL FOUNDATIONS OF INTERNATIONAL LAW.
NEW YORK: WILEY, 1961 372 PP.
TRADITIONAL TOPICS ASSOCIATED WITH PATTERNS OF INTERNA-
TIONAL POLICY. ANALYZES AND EVALUATES FRAMEWORK OF VARYING
ORGANIZATIONAL DOCTRINES.

1185 KARIS T.
THE TREASON TRIAL IN SOUTH AFRICA: A GUIDE TO THE MICROFILM
RECORD OF THE TRIAL.
STANFORD: HOOVER INSTITUTE, 1965, 124 PP.
PROVIDES A GUIDE TO THE SOUTH AFRICAN TREASON TRIAL OF
1956-1961. ARRANGED TOPICALLY AND WITH EXTENSIVE RUNNING
COMMENTARY. SURVEYS THE TRIAL AND ITS POLITICAL MEANING.
A CHRONOLOGICAL GUIDE TO THE MICROFILM RECORD; CHARTS,
SELECTED DOCUMENTS, AND VERY THOROUGH INDEXES. INCLUDES A
BIBLIOGRAPHY OF BOOKS, ARTICLES, PAMPHLETS, ETC.

1186 KARPOV P.V.
"PEACEFUL COEXISTENCE AND INTERNATIONAL LAW."
LAW CONTEMP. PROBL., 29 (AUTUMN 64), 865-70.
ADVOCATES NECESSITY OF COEXISTANCE BETWEEN SOCIALISM AND
CAPITALISM AND OUTLINES BASIC PRINCIPLES OF THE DOCTRINE AS
THEY SHOULD BE APPLIED TO INTERNATIONAL LAW.

1187 KAUPER P.G.
"CHURCH AND STATE: COOPERATIVE SEPARATISM."
MICH. LAW REV., 60 (NOV. 61), 1-40.
A MIDDLE VIEW, EXTRACTED IN THE LEGALISTIC MANNER, AND
DEFENDED COMPETENTLY, BETWEEN STRICT SEPARATISM AND

CHURCH-STATE INTEGRATION. THE PERPLEXITY OF THE PROBLEM IS
SEEN IN THE INTERMINGLING OF FUNCTIONS IN THE CONTEXT OF
A SOCIAL COMMUNITY WHERE BOTH THE SECULAR AND RELIGIOUS
SOCIETIES INVOLVE THE SAME HUMAN RESOURCES. DISCUSSES
PROBLEMS OF EDUCATION AND TAXATION.

1188 KAUPER P.G.
CIVIL LIBERTIES AND THE CONSTITUTION.
ANN ARBOR: U OF MICH PR, 1962, 237 PP., LC#62-7723.
    REVIEWS AND ANALYZES RECENT MAJOR DECISIONS BY US SUPREME
COURT. ARGUES THAT GREATER PART OF CONSTITUTIONAL LITIGATION
TURNS ON QUESTIONS RELATED TO PROTECTION OF CIVIL LIBERTIES.
DISCUSSES DECISIONS ON CHURCH AND STATE; OBSCENITY AND
CENSORSHIP; FREEDOM OF ASSOCIATION AND FREEDOM FROM
DISCLOSURE.

1189 KAUPER P.G.
RELIGION AND THE CONSTITUTION.
BATON ROUGE: LOUISIANA ST U PR, 1964, 137 PP., LC#64-07898.
    DISCUSSES RELIGION IN RELATION TO CONSTITUTIONAL ORDER,
PROBLEM OF INTERPRETING FIRST AMENDMENT, CHURCHES AND GOV-
MENT FUNDS, CHURCHES AND SCHOOLS, AND INTERPRETATION OF
RELIGIOUS LIBERTY.

1190 KEAY E.A., RICHARDSON S.S.
THE NATIVE AND CUSTOMARY COURTS OF NIGERIA.
LONDON: SWEET AND MAXWELL, LTD, 1966, 381 PP.
    LEGAL ANTHROPOLOGICAL STUDY EXAMINES THE SPECIFIED NIGE-
RIAN COURTS, DISCUSSING ORIGINS, JURISTICION, STAFF, AND
LAWS TO BE ADMINISTERED. THE SYSTEM OF CONTROL AND
APPEAL, AS WELL AS POWER OF REVIEW IS STUDIED. ALSO INCLUDES
THE GENERAL PROCEDURE FOR BOTH CRIMINAL AND CIVIL MATTERS
THE VARIATIONS FOR REGIONS WITHIN NIGERIA ARE PRESENTED, AS
ARE MOSLEM AND CHRISTIAN INFLUENCES ON THE LEGAL SYSTEM.

1191 KEEFE W.J., OGUL M.S.
THE AMERICAN LEGISLATIVE PROCESS: CONGRESS AND THE STATES.
ENGLEWOOD CLIFFS: PRENTICE HALL, 1964, 498 PP., LC#64-15466.
    DESCRIBES AND ANALYZES THE AMERICAN LEGISLATIVE PROCESS.
MAINTAINS THAT LEGISLATIVE INSTITUTIONS MUST BE VIEWED IN
RELATION TO LARGER ENVIRONMENTS AND INCLUSIVE POLITICAL
SYSTEMS. HENCE, GIVES AS MUCH ATTENTION TO THE "OUTSIDERS"
SUCH AS PARTIES, INTEREST GROUPS, EXECUTIVES, AND COURTS, AS
TO THE LEGISLATURES THEMSELVES. DEALS BOTH WITH CONGRESS AND
WITH STATE LEGISLATURES.

1192 KEEFE W.J., OGDAL M.S.
THE AMERICAN LEGISLATIVE PROCESS.
ENGLEWOOD CLIFFS: PRENTICE HALL, 1965, 478 PP., LC#64-15466.
    DISCUSSES ROLE OF CONGRESS IN AMERICAN GOVERNMENT. SEES
IT AS PRESERVING PLURALISM, COMBATING GROWING STRENGTH OF
THE EXECUTIVE, AND REPRESENTING BROAD SPECTRUM OF OPINION.
ALSO DEALS WITH ITS RELATION TO COURT SYSTEMS AND SPECIAL
PROBLEMS AND PROCESSES OF THE LEGISLATURE IN DETERMINING
OPINION AND INTEREST IN ISSUES.

1193 KEETON G.W., SCHWARZENBERGER G.
MAKING INTERNATIONAL LAW WORK.
LONDON: STEVENS, 1946, 266 PP.
    NOTHING LESS THAN WORLD GOVERNMENT CAN PROVIDE SECURE
BASIS FOR INTERNATIONAL LAW. IN ABSENCE OF WORLD FEDERATION,
POWERS MAY MAINTAIN AN UNEASY EQUILIBRIUM BUT THAT RULE OF
LAW BETWEEN NATIONS WILL REMAIN AS PRECARIOUS AS IN THE
PAST. DISCUSSES DEVELOPMENT OF INTERNATIONAL LAW AND SURVEYS
EXISTING PROBLEMS.

1194 KEFAUVER E.
CRIME IN AMERICA.
GARDEN CITY: DOUBLEDAY, 1951, 333 PP.
    STUDIES SPECIFIC AREAS OF CRIME CONCENTRATION IN US, SUCH
AS MIAMI, CHICAGO, AND DETROIT. CONCENTRATES ON THE MAFIA
AND AL CAPONE, AND THE NATIONAL CRIME SYNDICATE. INCLUDES
ILLUSTRATIONS.

1195 KEIR D.L., LAWSON F.H.
CASES IN CONSTITUTIONAL LAW.
LONDON: OXFORD U PR, 1948, 530 PP.
    COVERS 1606-1931, INCLUDING ALL IMPORTANT CASES DEALING
WITH PREROGATIVE, PARLIAMENTARY PRIVILEGE, TAXATION, THE
CROWN, PUBLIC AUTHORITIES, MARTIAL LAW, AND COLONIES. BRIEF
INTRODUCTION RELATES EACH SECTION TO DEVELOPMENT OF BRITISH
LEGAL SYSTEM.

1196 KEITT L.
AN ANNOTATED BIBLIOGRAPHY OF BIBLIOGRAPHIES OF STATUTORY MA-
TERIALS OF THE UNITED STATES.
CAMBRIDGE: HARVARD U PR, 1934, 191 PP.
    COMPRISES BIBLIOGRAPHIES OF STATUTE LAW, SESSION LAWS,
CODES AND INDEXES. MATERIAL RELATING TO CONSTITUTIONS, AND
LEGISLATIVE JOURNALS FROM COLONIES TO DATE IN 479 TITLES.
MOST PUBLISHED CIRCA 1875-1930. ARRANGEMENT IS FIRST BY TYPE
OF BIBLIOGRAPHY (GENERAL AND JURISDICTIONAL, LAW LIBRARY
CATALOGUES) AND THEN BY VARYING SYSTEMS.

1197 KELSEN H.
LAW AND PEACE IN INTERNATIONAL RELATIONS.

CAMBRIDGE: HARVARD U. PR, 1942, 181 PP.
    DEFINES LAW AS AN ORDER FOR THE PROMOTION OF PEACE.
ANALYZES STRUCTURE OF PREVAILING SYSTEM OF NORMS LABELED
INTERNATIONAL LAW TO SEE IF IT CONFORMS TO HIS CONCEPT.
ADVOCATES ESTABLISHMENT OF INTERNATIONAL COURT WITH
COMPULSORY JURISDICTION AS FIRST STEP IN REFORMING INTER-
NATIONAL RELATIONS.

1198 KELSEN H.
THE LAW OF THE UNITED NATIONS.
NEW YORK: PRAEGER, 1951, 994 PP.
    A JURISTIC APPROACH TO PROBLEMS FACED BY UN. THESIS IS
THAT WORDING OF LAWS PERMITS VARYING INTERPRETATIONS THAT
ALLOW AFFECTED ORGANS TO DEVELOP AND EXPAND. PRESENTS ALL
POSSIBLE INTERPRETATIONS OF BASIC PROBLEMS OF UN.

1199 KELSEN H.
"RECENT TRENDS IN THE LAW OF THE UNITED NATIONS."
LONDON: STEVENS, 1951, 991-94.
    SUPPLEMENT TO BOOK 'THE LAW OF THE UNITED NATIONS.' VIEWS
RECENT EVENTS SUCH AS NATO AND THE KOREAN WAR AS RELEVANT
LEGAL PROBLEMS. REFLECTS ON GENERAL ASSEMBLY MOTION 'UNITING
FOR PEACE.' THESIS IS THAT WORDING OF LAWS PERMITS VARYING
INTERPRETATIONS. LAW ADAPTED TO CHANGING CIRCUMSTANCES.

1200 KELSEN H.
PRINCIPLES OF INTERNATIONAL LAW.
NEW YORK: RINEHART, 1952, 461 PP.
    EXAMINATION OF NATURE OF INTERNATIONAL LAW WITH REFERENCE
TO SPHERES OF VALIDITY, ESSENTIAL FUNCTIONS AND APPLICATION.

1201 KELSEN H.
WHAT IS JUSTICE.
BERKELEY: U OF CALIF PR, 1957, 397 PP., LC#56-8474.
    COLLECTION OF ESSAYS ON PROBLEMS OF JUSTICE IN RELATION
TO LAW, PHILOSOPHY, AND SCIENCE. DISCUSSES CONCEPTS OF JUS-
TICE IN BIBLE, AMONG GREEKS; EXAMINES THEORETICAL QUESTIONS
SUCH AS CAUSALITY AND RETRIBUTION, SCIENCE AND POLITICS,
AND VALUE JUDGMENTS IN SCIENCE OF LAW.

1202 KENNEDY R.F.
"TOWARD A NATION WHERE THE LAW IS KING."
CURRENT, (MAR. 67), 9-14.
    SEES BASIC NEED FOR CRIME REDUCTION TO BE BUILDING OF
SOCIETY, BUT AS TEMPORARY MEASURE ADVOCATES IMPROVEMENT IN
LAW ENFORCEMENT. CRITICIZES CURRENT POLICE ADMINISTRATION,
POLICE RECRUITING, AND PENOLOGY. PROBATION AND JAIL REFORMS
ARE URGED.

1203 KENNEDY W.P.
THE LAW AND CUSTOM OF THE SOUTH AFRICAN CONSTITUTION.
LONDON: OXFORD U PR, 1935, 640 PP.
    STUDIES DEVELOPMENT AND NATURE OF SOUTH AFRICAN CONSTITU-
TION AND DISCUSSES ITS OPERATION THROUGH EXECUTIVE BRANCH
AND PARLIAMENT. INCLUDES DISCUSSION OF ORGANS OF PROVINCIAL
GOVERNMENTS, THE ADMINISTRATION OF JUSTICE, AND FOREIGN
RELATIONS.

1204 KERR M.H.
ISLAMIC REFORM: THE POLITICAL AND LEGAL THEORIES OF
MUHAMMAD 'ABDUH AND RASHID RIDA.
BERKELEY: U OF CALIF PR, 1966, 249 PP., LC#65-24177.
    STUDY OF CERTAIN ISLAMIC THEORIES OF RELIGIOUS BASIS OF
LAW AND GOVERNMENT. INTERPRETATION OF CLASSIC JURISTIC
TRADITION OF THOUGHT, WITH PARTICULAR EMPHASIS ON ELEMENTS
CRUCIAL TO MODERN REFORMATION POLICIES. ANALYZES EFFORTS OF
TWO LEADING MODERNISTS TO DEVELOP CONCEPTS OF NATURAL
LAW, POPULAR SOVEREIGNTY, AND UTILITARIAN JURISPRUDENCE.
SELECT BIBLIOGRAPHY.

1205 KERREMANS-RAMIOULL
LE PROBLEME DE LA DELINQUENCE JUVENILE (2ND ED.)
BRUSSELS: CEN DOC ECO ET SOC AFR, 1959, 64 PP.
    UNANNOTATED BIBLIOGRAPHY OF 1,027 BOOKS AND ARTICLES
PUBLISHED IN WESTERN AND SLAVIC LANGUAGES SINCE 1925. ORGAN-
IZED IN ONE COMPREHENSIVE ALPHABETICAL LISTING AND INDEXED
BY AUTHOR. EMPHASIS ON POST-1946 PUBLICATIONS.

1207 KETCHAM E.H.
PRELIMINARY SELECT BIBLIOGRAPHY OF INTERNATIONAL LAW (PAM-
PHLET)
SYRACUSE: SYRACUSE U PRESS, 1937, 69 PP.
    UNANNOTATED MATERIALS ARRANGED BY SUBJECT IN ENGLISH AND
FRENCH. PRIMARILY DEVOTED TO PERIODICALS IN THE DISCIPLINE.
APPROXIMATELY 1400 ITEMS.

1208 KETCHAM O.W.
"GUIDELINES FROM GAULT: REVOLUTIONARY REQUIREMENTS AND
REAPPRAISAL."
VIRGINIA LAW REV., 53 (DEC. 67), 1700-1718.
    DISCUSSES THE IMPLICATIONS OF THE SUPREME COURT CASE "IN
RE GAULT" IN WHICH THE SUPREME COURT EMPHASIZED THE NECES-
SITY OF FORMAL DUE PROCESS OF LAW IN JUVENILE COURT CASES.
STATES THAT INSTEAD OF DEVOTING MUCH OF ITS TIME TO THE
PREVENTION OF DELINQUENCY, THE JUVENILE COURT WILL BE EX-
PECTED TO CONCENTRATE UPON ADJUDICATION AND ORDERED

CORRECTION.

1209 KHADDURI M.
WAR AND PEACE IN THE LAW OF ISLAM.
BALTIMORE: JOHNS HOPKINS PR., 1955, 321 PP., $5.50.
AIMS TO RECONSTRUCT THE CLASSICAL LEGAL THEORY OF ISLAM,
AS WELL AS PRINCIPLES AND RULES GOVERNING ISLAM'S RELA-
TIONS WITH NON-MUSLIM COUNTRIES. ALSO DISCUSSES THE EFFORTS
IN RECENT TIMES AIMED AT ADAPTING ISLAM TO THE PRINCIPLES
AND PURPOSES OF THE MODERN COMMUNITY OF NATIONS. DIVIDED
INTO: FUNDAMENTAL CONCEPTS OF MUSLIM LAW, THE LAW OF WAR:
THE JIHAD: THE LAW OF PEACE.

1210 KHADDURI M., LIEBESNY H.J.
LAW IN THE MIDDLE EAST.
WASHINGTON: MIDDLE EAST INST, 1955, 393 PP.
COMPARES ISLAMIC AND WESTERN LAW, WITH SPECIAL EMPHASIS
ON THE DIFFERENCES IN SPIRITUAL BELIEFS WHICH UNDERLIE SIG-
NIFICANT DISSIMILARITIES IN PENAL AND CIVIL CODES. DISCUSSES
CONSTITUTIONAL ORGANIZATION, PRE-ISLAMIC BACKGROUND, COURT
SYSTEMS, LAW SCHOOLS, AND INFLUENCE OF WESTERN JUDICIAL
PROCEDURE IN RECENT TIMES.

1211 KHAN M.Z.
"ISLAM AND INTERNATIONAL RELATIONS."
WORLD JUSTICE, 5 (MAR. 64), 293-307.
SEES RELIGION AS A VITAL DIMENSION OPERATIVE IN SPHERE
OF INTERNATIONAL RELATIONS. AIM OF ISLAM HERE IS 'AN
ASSOCIATION OF STRONG AND STABLE STATES ALLIED TOGETHER IN
PERSUANCE OF PEACE, FREEDOM OF CONSCIENCE, AND PROMOTION
OF HUMAN WELFARE.'

1212 KHOURI F.J.
"THE JORDON RIVER CONTROVERSY."
REV. POLIT., 27 (JAN. 65), 32-57.
TRACES GROWING ARAB-ISRAELI HOSTILITIES FROM EARLY 1920
ZIONIST MOVEMENTS IN PALESTINE THROUGH CREATION AND DEVELOP-
MENT OF MODERN-DAY ISRAEL. POINTING OUT THE GREAT IMPORTANCE
OF WATER TO BOTH NATIONS, CITES THE VARIOUS DISPUTES AND
ACTIONS CONCERNING THE JORDON RIVER, E.G. MAIN PLAN, ARAB
PLAN, ISRAELI PLAN. FORSEES INCREASED VIOLENCE AS TWO NA-
TIONS CONTINUE TO EXPAND AND NEED FOR WATER INCREASES.

1213 KIDDER F.E. ED., BUSHONG A.D. ED.
THESES ON PAN AMERICAN TOPICS.
WASHINGTON: PAN AMERICAN UNION, 1962, 124 PP.
UNANNOTATED LISTING OF DOCTORAL THESES FROM US AND CANADA
RELATING TO THE AMERICAS. INDEXED BY AUTHOR, SCHOOL, AND
TOPIC. TOPICS INCLUDE GENERAL HISTORY, POLITICS, INTERNA-
TIONAL RELATIONS, ECONOMICS, SOCIAL CONDITIONS, CULTURE,
GOVERNMENT, HEALTH, FINE ARTS, LAW, LANGUAGES, RELIGION,
GEOGRAPHY, AND OTHERS. THESES PERTAIN PRINCIPALLY TO CENTRAL
AND SOUTH AMERICA. CONTAINS 2,253 LISTINGS.

1214 KIM R.C.C.
"THE SUPREME COURT: ORACLE WITHOUT TRUTH."
ROCKY MOUNTAIN SOCIAL SCIENCE J., 4 (OCT. 67), 131-139.
STUDIES NEW ROLE OF COURT SYSTEMS AS ACTIVISTS IN ACTING
ON SOCIAL ISSUES. DISCUSSES INTEGRATION, PROPERTY, PRAYER,
AND CENSORSHIP DECISIONS. TREATS SUPREME COURT AS REACTOR
TO PRESSURE AND AS POLITICAL IN THAT RESPECT. URGES COURT TO
REFLECT VALUES AS THEY ARE MADE AND NOT TO HINDER FREEDOM TO
ALTER VALUES.

1215 KING D.B. ED., QUICK C.W. ED.
LEGAL ASPECTS OF THE CIVIL RIGHTS MOVEMENT.
DETROIT: WAYNE STATE U PR., 1965, 447 PP., LC#64-25183.
TOPICS INCLUDE HOUSING, EMPLOYMENT, THE LAW OF ASSOCI-
ATIONS, PUBLIC TRANSPORTATION, EDUCATION, AS WELL AS DIS-
CUSSION OF LEGAL PROCESSES AND CIVIL DISOBEDIENCE. EX-
PLORES LEGAL THEORIES, HYPOTHESES, AND NEW LEGAL DEVEL-
OPMENTS.

1216 KING W.L.
MELVILLE WESTON FULLER: CHIEF JUSTICE OF THE UNITED STATES,
1888-1910.
CHICAGO: U OF CHICAGO PRESS, 1967, 394 PP., LC#67-12152.
BIOGRAPHY OF CHIEF JUSTICE FULLER EXAMINES ISSUES BEFORE
SUPREME COURT DURING HIS TENURE AND HIS INFLUENCE. CONTRO-
VERSIAL CASES INCLUDE INCOME TAX CASE, DEBS CASE, AND INSU-
LAR CASES. TREATS VIEW OF FEDERAL POWERS, JUDICIAL SUPER-
VISION OF PUBLIC UTILITY RATE REGULATION, LABOR CASES, PULL-
MAN STRIKE, JUDICIAL REVIEW OF STATUTES, ETC. FEELS MANY
DECISIONS WERE FAILURES; ENDS WITH RELATIONS WITH HOLMES.

1217 KIRCHHEIMER O.
GEGENWARTSPROBLEME DER ASYLGEWAHRUNG.
COLOGNE: WESTDEUTSCHER VERLAG, 1959, 65 PP.
EXAMINES POLITICAL AND LEGAL IMPLICATIONS OF GRANTING
ASYLUM TO POLITICAL REFUGEES. SHOWS THAT MODERN MASS
MIGRATIONS RESULTING FROM POLITICAL UPHEAVAL AND
PERSECUTION HAVE MADE OLDER DOCTRINES INAPPLICABLE.
MAINTAINS THAT STRICT OBSERVANCE OF PRINCIPLE OF
POLITICAL ASYLUM IS NECESSARY TO PREVENT 'ARBITRARY RULE
AND DESTRUCTION OF FREEDOM.'

1219 KIRK G.
"MATERIALS FOR THE STUDY OF INTERNATIONAL RELATIONS"
WORLD POLIT., 1 (APR. 49', 426-430.
ATTEMPTS TO SET FORTH THEORY OF INTERNATIONAL RELATIONS
VIA SYSTEMATIC EXAMINATION OF CONCEPTUAL STRUCTURE WHICH
APPEARS TO BE PRESENT IN MODERN THINKING ABOUT THE SUBJECT.

1220 KIRK R.
THE CONSERVATIVE MIND.
CHICAGO: HENRY REGNERY CO, 1953, 458 PP., LC#53-5777.
DISCUSSES NATURE OF CONSERVATISM AND POLITICAL PHILOSO-
PHIES OF BURKE, ADAMS, TOCQUEVILLE, DISRAELI, SANTAYANA, AND
OTHER LEADING PHILOSOPHERS AND STATESMEN.

1221 KISER S.L.
AMERICANISM IN ACTION.
NEW YORK: EXPOSITION PRESS, 1964, 159 PP.
FAVORS STATES' RIGHTS AND LIMITED GOVERNMENT WELFARE.
CRITICAL OF US FOREIGN AID. SUGGESTS CONSTITUTIONAL AMEND-
MENTS TO CURB SUPREME COURT'S AUTHORITY.

1222 KLEIN F.J.
JUDICIAL ADMINISTRATION AND THE LEGAL PROFESSION.
NEW YORK: OCEANA PUBLISHING, 1963, 650 PP., LC#62-12025.
LIST OF 6,654 ITEMS IN ENGLISH ARRANGED BY SUBJECT ON
COURT SYSTEMS AND PROCEDURES. PUBLICATION DATES OF
LISTINGS, 1940-1962.

1223 KLESMENT J., KRIVICKAS D. ET AL.
LEGAL SOURCES AND BIBLIOGRAPHY OF THE BALTIC STATES (ESTON-
IA, LATVIA, LITHUANIA)
NEW YORK: FREDERICK PRAEGER, 1963, 197 PP., LC#63-15981.
PART OF A SERIES PREPARED BY THE MID-EUROPEAN LAW PROJECT
AND PUBLISHED BY THE MID-EUROPEAN STUDIES CENTER. PART I
COVERS PERIOD PRIOR TO 1918; PART II IS CONCERNED WITH THE
CONTINUITY OF LAW, EFFORTS TOWARD UNIFICATION OF LAW, ETC.;
PART III COVERS EACH COUNTRY SEPARATELY, BOTH TRADITIONAL
AND SPECIFIC TOPICS; PART IV CONCERNS POST-SOVIET ERA. 1207
ITEMS IN EUROPEAN LANGUAGES; INDEXED; ANNOTATED.

1224 KNEIER C.M.
"MISLEADING THE VOTERS."
NATIONAL CIVIC REV., 46 (OCT. 57), 450-455.
THIS REVIEW OF LEGAL SUITS BY VOTERS CLAIMING THAT
POLITICAL CANDIDATES OR PUBLIC OFFICIALS DELIBERATELY
MADE MISREPRESENTATIONS TO WIN ELECTIONS SHOWS THAT THE
COURTS WILL NOT BE OF MUCH ASSISTANCE TO VOTERS IN SUCH
CIRCUMSTANCES. POLITICIANS AND ELECTED OFFICIALS CAN SAY
JUST ABOUT ANYTHING AND NOT BE BOUND BY IT.

1225 KNIERIEM A.
THE NUREMBERG TRIALS.
CHICAGO: HENRY REGNERY CO, 1959, 561 PP., LC#59-8417.
WRITTEN BY GERMAN LAWYER ACQUITTED AT NUREMBERG WHO LATER
TOOK UP STUDY OF LEGAL PROBLEMS OF TRIAL. ATTEMPTS TO
DISCOVER, ANALYZE, AND CLARIFY LEGAL ISSUES OF COMPLEX
CASES. ASSERTS THAT TRIAL WAS SUCCESSFUL IN TAMING HATRED
AND REVENGE OF EUROPE AND US, BUT WAS FAILURE AS AN ATTEMPT
TO ENFORCE INTERNATIONAL LAW AND ORDER FOR THE MOMENT AND
FOR FUTURE.

1226 KONRAD F.
DIE PERSONLICHE FREIHEIT IM NATIONALSOZIALISTISCHEN DEUT-
SCHEN REICHE.
MUNICH: F. & J. VOGLRIEDER, 1936, 83 PP.
DISCUSSES CONCEPT OF PERSONAL FREEDOM FROM JURISTIC-PHIL-
OSOPHICAL POINT OF VIEW. SEEKS TO DETERMINE LIMITS OF
PERSONAL FREEDOM IN AREA OF ADMINISTRATIVE LAW (POLICE
POWER) AS WELL AS CONSTITUTIONAL LAW (CIVIL LIBERTIES).

1227 KONVITZ M.R.
THE CONSTITUTION AND CIVIL RIGHTS.
NEW YORK: COLUMBIA U PRESS, 1947, 253 PP.
DEALS WITH PRIVILEGES AND IMMUNITIES OF CITIZENS AND RE-
LATION OF THEM TO US CONSTITUTION. CRITICIZES CONSTITUTION
AS HAVING INSUFFICIENT SAFEGUARDS FOR RIGHTS OF CITIZENS.
DISCUSSES DEVELOPMENT SINCE 1866 AND PERTINENT SUPREME COURT
DECISIONS IN THIS AREA. APPENDIXES LIST STATE CIVIL RIGHTS
LAWS AS OF 1947.

1228 KONVITZ M.R.
"CIVIL LIBERTIES."
ANN. ACAD. POL. SOC. SCI., (MAY 67), 8-58.
TRACT ON CIVIL LIBERTIES CONCERNED WITH VALUES OF FREE-
DOM AND DEMOCRACY AS IDEALS, COMPARED WITH DATA INDICATING
HOW INADEQUATELY SUCH VALUES ARE FULFILLED. PROBLEM IS HOW
TO GET GUARDIANS OF GOALS TO READ INDICATORS. POINTS OUT
NEED FOR PRIVATELY FINANCED ORGANIZATION FOR RESEARCH INTO
CIVIL LIBERTIES.

1229 KOREA (REPUBLIC) SUPREME COURT
KOREAN LEGAL SYSTEM.
SEOUL: REPUBLIC OF KOREA, 1964, 151 PP.
ANALYSIS OF KOREAN LEGAL SYSTEM DESCRIBING ORGANIZATION
AND JURISDICTION OF COURTS, JUDICIAL INDEPENDENCE, CRIMINAL
SYSTEM, CIVIL PROCEDURE, AND CONSTITUTION.

1230 KRENZ F.E.
"THE REFUGEE AS A SUBJECT OF INTERNATIONAL LAW."
INT. AND COMP. LAW Q., 15 (JAN. 66), 90-116.
ADVOCATES APPROACH TO LAW OF ASYLUM TO MEET PRESENT SIT-
UATION OF INDIVIDUALS IN INTERNATIONAL LAW. SOME KIND OF
FORMAL RECOGNITION OF INDIVIDUAL RIGHT TO ASYLUM IS CALLED
FOR, PLUS THE CREATION OF AN INTERNATIONAL EXECUTIVE FOR
REFUGEES AND THEIR "LOCUS STANDI" BEFORE AN APPROPRIATE TRI-
BUNAL.

1231 KRISLOV S.
THE SUPREME COURT IN THE POLITICAL PROCESS.
NEW YORK: MACMILLAN, 1965, 155 PP., LC#65-15579.
REVEALS INTERNAL PROCESSES AND MAJOR ISSUES OF
CONSTITUTIONAL LAW THAT CONCERN SUPREME COURT. DISCUSSES
SOCIAL AND POLITICAL FORCES THAT PLAY IMPORTANT ROLE IN
DECISION-MAKING PROCESS. EXAMINES RECRUITMENT OF JUDGES,
NATURE OF THE OFFICE, SELECTION OF CASES, AND CONTROVERSIES
SURROUNDING COURT DECISIONS.

1232 KUNST H. ED., GRUNDMANN S.
EVANGELISCHES STAATSLEXIKON.
STUTTGART, KREUZ VERLAG, 1966, 2687 PP.
DICTIONARY OF CENTRAL CONCEPTS OF CHURCH LAW, POLITICAL
THEORY, SOCIOLOGY, PHILOSOPHY OF LAW, POLITICS, RELIGIOUS
HISTORY, AND POLITICAL ECONOMY. ARRANGED ALPHABETICALLY.

1233 KUNSTLER W.M.
"DEEP IN MY HEART"
NEW YORK: WILLIAM MORROW, 1966, 384 PP., LC#66-12742.
HISTORY OF CIVIL RIGHTS MOVEMENT FROM VIEWPOINT OF
"FREEDOM LAWYER." DISCUSSES BELATED PARTICIPATION OF
AMERICAN BAR IN NEGRO QUEST FOR EQUALITY. GIVES ACCOUNTS
OF SOUTHERN COURTROOM "SKIRMISHES" AND FREEDOM MOVEMENT
STRATEGY SESSIONS. STRESSES VITAL ROLE OF LAWYERS IN
FORWARDING CIVIL RIGHTS MOVEMENT.

1234 KUNZ J.
"SANCTIONS IN INTERNATIONAL LAW."
AMER. J. INT. LAW, 54 (APR. 60), 324-47.
CONTENDS THAT INTERNATIONAL LAW SANCTIONS ARE 'PRIMITIVE'
INSOFAR AS THEY OPERATE IN A DE-CENTRALIZED LEGAL ORDER.
SUCH A SYSTEM HAS NO CENTRAL INSTITUTION FOR MAKING OR
APPLYING LEGAL RULES.

1235 KUNZ J.
"THE CHANGING SCIENCE OF INTERNATIONAL LAW."
AMER. J. INT. LAW, 56 (APRIL 64), 488-499.
INTERNATIONAL LAW SHIFTING FROM THE CLASSICAL ANGLO-
AMERICAN AND CONTINENTAL METHODS. CRITICIZES THE 'NEO-
REALISTS', 'WORLD-LAW' THEORISTS AND OTHER THEORETICAL
IDEALISTS OUTSIDE THE OCCIDENT. LAW IS NECESSARY FOR REGUL-
ATING AFFAIRS OF MEN AND PROMOTING WORLD PEACE BUT DOESN'T
BELIEVE THAT THESE 'NEW CONCEPTS' WILL FURTHER DEVELOPMENT.

1236 KUPER H. ED., KUPER L. ED.
AFRICAN LAW.
BERKELEY: U OF CALIF PR, 1965, 275 PP., LC#65-24589.
ESSAYS ON AFRICAN LAW, TRADITIONAL LEGAL SYSTEMS, AND
THEIR DEVELOPMENT AND ADAPTATION TO BRITISH AND FRENCH
SYSTEMS.

1237 KUPER L.
PASSIVE RESISTANCE IN SOUTH AFRICA.
TORONTO: CLARK, IRWIN + CO, 1956.
HISTORY OF PASSIVE RESISTANCE MOVEMENTS IN SOUTH AFRICA
AFTER WWII, BEGUN BY INDIAN MINORITY, TAKEN UP BY AFRICANS
AND COLOREDS, CAUSING WHITE REACTION AND COUNTERACTION.

1238 KURL S.
ESTONIA: A SELECTED BIBLIOGRAPHY.
WASHINGTON: US GOVERNMENT, 1958, 74 PP., LC#58-60040.
ITEMS ON ESTONIA IN ENGLISH, FRENCH, GERMAN, AND
ITALIAN. PREFERENCE GIVEN TO MORE RECENT PUBLICATIONS.
INCLUDES ITEMS ON GENERAL REFERENCE AIDS; THE LAND AND
PEOPLE; HISTORY; RELIGION; LAW; POLITICS AND GOVERNMENT;
ECONOMICS; SOCIAL CONDITIONS; INTELLECTUAL LIFE; LANGUAGE
AND LITERATURE. SOME BRIEF ANNOTATIONS. 491 TITLES.

1239 KURLAND P.B.
RELIGION AND THE LAW.
CHICAGO: ALDINE PUBLISHING CO, 1961, 131 PP., LC#62-17304.
DISCUSSES ROLE OF RELIGIOUS ORGANIZATIONS IN US AS
DETERMINED BY CONSTITUTIONAL INTERPRETATION, PAST AND
PRESENT. DEVOTES SPECIAL ATTENTION TO PRESENT PROBLEM OF
AID TO EDUCATION AND CATHOLIC PRESIDENCY. DEFENDS
NON-DISCRIMINATORY AID TO PAROCHIAL SCHOOLS.

1240 KURLAND P.B. ED.
THE SUPREME COURT REVIEW.
CHICAGO: U OF CHICAGO PRESS, 1966, 400 PP., LC#60-14353.
ARTICLES STUDYING SUPREME COURT DECISIONS AND THEIR IM-
PLICATIONS FOR AMERICAN LEGAL SYSTEM, INCLUDING OBSCENITY
CASES, VOTING RIGHTS, JUVENILES, UNIONS, AND PATENTS.

1241
A BIBLIOGRAPHY OF DOCTORAL DISSERTATIONS UNDERTAKEN IN AMER-
ICAN AND CANADIAN UNIVERSITIES ON RELIGION AND POLITICS.
NEW YORK: NATL COUNC OF CHURCHES, 1963, 43 PP., LC#63-21606.
COMPILES 650 UNPUBLISHED DISSERTATIONS, 1940-62, ON COM-
BINED TOPICS OF RELIGION AND POLITICS ESPECIALLY CULTURAL
EFFECTS OF RELIGION ON POLITICS, CHURCH-STATE RELATIONS
AND FORMS OF RELIGIOUS FREEDOM.

1242 LA PONCE J.A.
THE PROTECTION OF MINORITIES.
HONOLULU: U OF HAWAII PRESS, 1960, 236 PP.
STUDY OF MINORITIES. DISCUSSES DEFINITIONS AND TYPES OF
MINORITIES; DIFFERING RIGHTS CLAIMED BY DIFFERENT
MINORITIES; TREATY GUARANTEES OF MINORITY RIGHTS; GUARANTEES
OF MINORITY RIGHTS IN CONSTITUTIONS; IMPACT OF MINORITY
GROUPS UPON FORM OF GOVERNMENT AND UPON STRUCTURE OF LEGIS-
LATIVE AND EXECUTIVE STRUCTURES; MINORITIES, ELECTORAL
SYSTEMS, AND POLITICAL PARTIES.

1243 LA PONCE J.A.
THE GOVERNMENT OF THE FIFTH REPUBLIC: FRENCH POLITICAL PAR-
TIES AND THE CONSTITUTION.
BERKELEY: U OF CALIF PR, 1961, 415 PP., LC#60-14656.
BEGINNINGS, DEVELOPMENT, PARTIES, AND PERSONALITIES OF
FIFTH FRENCH REPUBLIC, INCLUDING CHARTS AND TABLES OF VOT-
ING STATISTICS. CONCLUDES THAT REPUBLIC IN 1960 HAD REALIZED
GOALS OF FOUNDERS (SHIFT OF POWER FROM LEGISLATURE TO EXECU-
TIVE), BUT FUTURE REMAINS UNCERTAIN BECAUSE OF ALGERIAN
PROBLEM AND DEPENDENCE OF SYSTEM UPON PERSONALITY OF DE
GAULLE RATHER THAN SOUND CONSTITUTION.

1244 LAFAVE W.R. ED.
LAW AND SOVIET SOCIETY.
URBANA: U OF ILLINOIS PR, 1965, 297 PP., LC#65-19109.
CASE STUDIES DEMONSTRATE DEVELOPMENT OF SOVIET LAW UNDER
KHRUSHCHEV IN ALL BRANCHES OF CIVIL LAW. SPECIAL TOPICS
INCLUDE SPREAD OF LEGAL SYSTEM ABROAD AND RELATION OF JURIS-
PRUDENCE TO MARXISM.

1245 LAFAVE W.R. ED., HAY P. ED.
INTERNATIONAL TRADE, INVESTMENT, AND ORGANIZATION.
URBANA: U OF ILLINOIS PR, 1967, 306 PP., LC#66-25556.
ARTICLES SERVING AS AN INTRODUCTION TO IN-
TERNATIONAL TRADE AND INVESTMENT. INFORMATION ON PROBLEMS
INVOLVED, REGULATIONS BY REGIONAL INTERNATIONAL ORGANIZA-
TIONS, AND IMPACT OF THESE ORGANIZATIONS ON LEGAL NORMS. BA-
SICALLY ORIENTED TO US INVOLVEMENT, FOCUSES ON TRENDS AND
EXISTING PROBLEMS RAISED BY INCREASED INTERNATIONAL COOPERA-
TION.

1246 LALL A.S.
NEGOTIATING DISARMAMENT* THE EIGHTEEN NATION DISARMAMENT
CONFERENCE* THE FIRST TWO YEARS, 1962-1964.
ITHACA: CORNELL U PRESS, 1964, 86 PP., LC#64-25822.
INDIA'S REPRESENTATIVE TO THE EIGHTEEN NATION DISARMA-
MENT CONFERENCES COMMENTS ON THE PROCEDURES DEVELOPED FOR
NEGOTIATING DISARMAMENT, THE PROBLEMS INVOLVED, AND THE RE-
SPECTIVE ROLES OF THE US, USSR, OTHER EASTERN AND WESTERN
NATIONS, AND THE NON-ALIGNED MEMBERS OF THE CONFERENCE.

1247 LAMBERT J.D.
"CORPORATE POLITICAL SPENDING AND CAMPAIGN FINANCE."
CORP. PRACTICE COMMENTATOR, 8 (FEB. 67), 363-419.
DISCUSSES RESOURCES POLITICAL PARTIES DRAW ON TO RAISE
CAMPAIGN FUNDS. AS CAMPAIGN COSTS MOUNT - A RESULT OF INFLA-
TION, INCREASING INCOME AND VOTING POPULATION, AND TECHNO-
LOGICAL CHANGE - BOTH PARTIES HAVE TO BROADEN BASE OF FINAN-
CIAL SUPPORT. PRESENTS STATUTORY FRAMEWORK, CASES, LABOR AND
CORPORATIONS AS RESOURCES, INDIRECT EXPENDITURES, AND CON-
STITUTIONAL QUESTIONS.

1248 LANCASTER L.W.
"GOVERNMENT IN RURAL AMERICA."
PRINCETON: VAN NOSTRAND, 1952.
DESCRIBES GOVERNMENT AND ADMINISTRATION OF RURAL COUN-
TY, TOWNSHIP, AND SCHOOL DISTRICT IN US. REVIEWS AREA AND
STRUCTURE OF TOWN, COUNTY, TOWNSHIP; LEGAL ASPECTS OF RUR-
AL GOVERNMENT; PATTERN OF FISCAL RELATIONS; POLICE AND JU-
DICIAL ADMINISTRATION; PUBLIC HIGHWAYS; EDUCATION; WELFARE
AND HEALTH. BIBLIOGRAPHY CONTAINS RELATED BIBLIOGRAPHICAL
AIDS, STATISTICAL COMPILATIONS, STUDIES, AND PERIODICALS.

1249 LANDE G.R.
"THE EFFECT OF THE RESOLUTIONS OF THE UNITED NATIONS GENERAL
ASSEMBLY."
WORLD POLITICS, 19 (OCT. 66), 83-105.
RESPECT GIVEN TO UN DECISIONS CAN INDICATE REAL CHANGES
IN EFFECTIVENESS. AUTHOR SUGGESTS GENERAL ASSEMBLY RESOLU-
TIONS WHEN ANALYZED IN TERMS OF COMPLIANCE OF MEMBER STATES,
EFFECTIVENESS IN MEETING PARTICULAR OBJECTIVES, AND IN GEN-
ERALLY MOLDING BEHAVIOR -- AS SUCH AN INDICATOR. SCHEME PRE-
SENTED FOR SUCH AN ANALYSIS.

1250 LANDHEER B., VAN ESSEN J.L.F.
FUNDAMENTALS OF PUBLIC INTERNATIONAL LAW (SELECTIVE BIBLI-
OGRAPHIES OF THE LIBRARY OF THE PEACE PALACE, VOL. I; PAMPH)

LEYDEN: SYTHOFF, 1953, 85 PP.
AN ANNOTATED BIBLIOGRAPHY OF MATERIALS IN THE LIBRARY OF
THE PEACE PALACE THAT WERE PUBLISHED BETWEEN 1872-1952 ON
BOTH GENERAL AND PARTICULAR ASPECTS OF PUBLIC INTERNATIONAL
LAW. MATERIAL IS TOPICALLY ARRANGED WITHIN CATEGORIES OF
GENERAL, SPECIFIC, AND SPECIAL WORKS. SOURCES IN WESTERN
LANGUAGES ARE ANNOTATED IN LANGUAGE OF ORIGINAL PUBLICATION.
INDEXED ALPHABETICALLY BY AUTHOR.

1251 LANDHEER B., VAN ESSEN J.L.F.
RECOGNITION IN INTERNATIONAL LAW (SELECTIVE BIBLIOGRAPHIES
OF THE LIBRARY OF THE PEACE PALACE, VOL. II; PAMPHLET)
LEYDEN: SYTHOFF, 1954, 28 PP.
SYSTEMATIC, ANNOTATED BIBLIOGRAPHY OF WORKS ON RECOGNI-
TION LAW AVAILABLE AT THE PEACE PALACE LIBRARY. CLASSIFIES
MATERIAL ON RECOGNITION IN GENERAL, AS WELL AS SPECIFIC
STUDIES ON LEGAL EFFECT, PRACTICE, STIMSON DOCTRINE, ETC.
SOURCES INCLUDE ALL WESTERN-LANGUAGE PUBLICATIONS FROM 1899
TO 1953.

1252 LANOUE G.R. ED.
A BIBLIOGRAPHY OF DOCTORAL DISSERTATIONS ON POLITICS AND
RELIGION.
NEW YORK: NATL COUNC OF CHURCHES, 1963, 49 PP., LC#63-21606.
A COMPILATION OF DOCTORAL DISSERTATIONS UNDERTAKEN IN
AMERICAN AND CANADIAN UNIVERSITIES 1940-62. ENTRIES LISTED
UNDER FIVE TOPICS: PHILOSOPHY AND THEORY; FOREIGN; AMERICAN
NATIONAL; AMERICAN REGIONAL, STATE, AND LOCAL; AND AMERICAN
CONSTITUTIONAL AND LEGAL. SOME 649 DISSERTATIONS LISTED.

1253 LAPENNA I.
STATE AND LAW: SOVIET AND YUGOSLAV THEORY.
NEW HAVEN: YALE U PR, 1964, 135 PP.
DISCUSSES BASIC MARXIST VIEWS OF STATE AND LAW
ESPECIALLY FROM SOVIET AND YUGOSLAV PERSPECTIVE OF
THEORY. EXAMINES DEVELOPMENT OF THEORY OF LAW IN THESE TWO
COUNTRIES.

1254 LAPIERE R.T.
THE FREUDIAN ETHIC.
NEW YORK: DUELL, SLOAN & PEARCE, 1959, 299 PP., LC#59-12245.
RELATES GROWING POPULARITY AND ACCEPTANCE OF FREUDIAN
THEORY TO CHANGES GOING ON IN SOCIETY IN AREAS OF FAMILY,
SEX, RESPONSIBILITY, ETC. ANALYZES SOCIAL IMPLICATIONS OF
FREUDIANISM. DISCUSSES TRADITIONAL VALUES OF US SOCIETY
(PROTESTANT ETHIC, ETC.) AND COMPARES THEM TO NEW VALUES AND
ETHICS INVOLVED IN FREUDIAN CONCEPT OF MAN.

1255 LAPRADELLE ED.
ANNUAIRE DE LA VIE INTERNATIONALE: POLITIQUE, ECONOMIQUE,
JURIDIQUE.
PARIS: EDITIONS INTERNATIONALES, 1928, 598 PP.
FRENCH PUBLICATION COVERING THE YEARS 1927-28, WHICH
CLASSIFIES OFFICIAL PUBLICATIONS, SCHOLARLY AND CRITICAL
WORKS, JOURNALS, AND PERIODICAL ARTICLES ON INTERNATIONAL
RELATIONS, DIPLOMACY, AND INTERNATIONAL LAW. COMPREHENSIVE
SUBJECT AND AUTHOR TABLES PROVIDE PARTIAL CROSS REFERENCES.
BIBLIOGRAPHICAL INFORMATION GIVEN IN LANGUAGE OF PUBLICA-
TION; SOURCES IN ALL WESTERN LANGUAGES.

1256 LARROWE C.P.
SHAPE-UP AND HIRING HALL.
BERKELEY: U OF CALIF PR, 1955, 250 PP., LC#55-10806.
COMPREHENSIVE STUDY OF HIRING METHODS AND LABOR RELATIONS
ON NEW YORK AND SEATTLE WATERFRONTS. EMPHASIZES VAST DIFFER-
ENCE BETWEEN POLICIES AND SYSTEMS THAT HAVE DEVELOPED IN
THE LABOR ORGANIZATIONS OF BOTH WATERFRONTS. DISCUSSES EX-
TENT OF INVOLVEMENT OF RACKETEERING IN EAST AND WEST COAST
LONGSHOREMAN UNIONS AND THEIR DIFFICULTIES WITH AFL-CIO.

1257 LARSEN P.B.
"THE UNITED STATES-ITALY AIR TRANSPORT ARBITRATION: PROBLEMS
OF TREATY INTERPRETATION AND ENFORCEMENT."
AMER. J. OF INT. LAW, 61 (APR. 67), 496-520.
REVIEWS HISTORY OF US-ITALY AIR TRANSPORT AGREEMENT OF
1948 AND CAUSE OF DISAGREEMENT OVER INTERPRETATION IN 1963.
STUDIES INTERPRETATION PROBLEM AS CHOICE BETWEEN NARROW
TEXTUAL ANALYSIS AND BROAD CONTEXTUAL ANALYSIS. DISCUSSES
ARBITRAL DICISION MADE AND ENFORCEMENT, AND PRESENTS
VARIOUS ARBITRATION METHODS FOR AIR TRAFFIC DISPUTES.

1258 LARSON A.
WHEN NATIONS DISAGREE.
BATON ROUGE: LOUISIANA ST U PR, 1961, 249 PP.
CONSIDERS NATURE OF INTERNATIONAL LAW, ITS FOUNDATIONS,
ENFORCEMENT, AND ORGANIZATION. DISCUSSES ITS PRESENT STATE
AND MAJOR PROBLEMS THAT HAVE ARISEN WITH IT IN THE PAST.
GIVES SPECIAL EMPHASIS TO RELATION OF US TO WORLD LAW AND
ITS ROLE AS DEFENDER-ENFORCER. SUMMARIZES NECESSITIES OF
NEAR FUTURE.

1259 LASKIN B.
CANADIAN CONSTITUTIONAL LAW: TEXT AND NOTES ON
DISTRIBUTION OF LEGISLATIVE POWER (2ND ED.)
TORONTO: CARSWELL, 1960, 1061 PP.
STUDIES NATURE OF CANADIAN FEDERALISM; THE "ASPECT

DOCTRINE" OF CONSTITUTIONALITY; LEGISLATIVE RESTRICTIONS ON
POWER OF COURTS TO PASS ON CONSTITUTIONALITY OF LEGISLATION;
AND GENERAL POWER OF CANADIAN PARLIAMENT. DISCUSSES NATIONAL
AND LOCAL REGULATION OF ECONOMIC ACTIVITY; TAXING POWERS;
ADMINISTRATION OF JUSTICE; AND CANADIAN CRIMINAL LAW.
PROVIDES IMPORTANT CASES TO ILLUSTRATE TOPICS.

1260 LASLETT P. ED.
PHILOSOPHY, POLITICS AND SOCIETY.
NEW YORK: MACMILLAN, 1956, 184 PP.
ARTICLES RELATING SEVERAL POLITICAL PHILOSOPHIES TO MOD-
ERN POLITICS IN SUCH AREAS AS SOVEREIGNTY, CRIME, LAW,
SOCIALIST AND LIBERAL MORALITY, PLATO'S THEORIES,
NATURAL RIGHTS, AND ESSENCE OF POLITICS IN ATTEMPT TO
ILLUSTRATE IMPORTANCE OF STRUCTURED POLITICAL PHILOSOPHY
BEHIND ACTIONS.

1261 LASLEY J.
THE WAR SYSTEM AND YOU.
CHAPEL HILL: INST INTL STUDIES, 1965, 260 PP., LC#65-14419.
SOMEWHAT PASSIONATE STATEMENT OF THE ROLES THE NATIONAL
GOVERNMENT, INDIVIDUALS, INTERNATIONAL ORGANIZATIONS AND
PEACE MOVEMENTS PLAY IN THE "WAR SYSTEM" ALONG WITH A PRE-
SCRIPTION FOR ACTION INDIVIDUALS IN THE WEST MUST TAKE TO
DEVELOP A PEACE SYSTEM UNDER WORLD GOVERNMENT. LISTS PEACE
GROUPS AND ACTIVITIES, AND INTERNATIONAL CODES CONCERNED
WITH PEACE, DIGNITY AND WAR CRIMES.

1262 LASSWELL H.D.
"THE INTERPLAY OF ECONOMIC, POLITICAL AND SOCIAL CRITERIA IN
LEGAL POLICY."
VANDERBILT LAW REV., 14 (MAR. 61), 451-471.
CONSIDERS CRITERIA OF LEGAL POLICY IN REGARD TO ECONOMICS
IN THE FRAME OF REFERENCE PROVIDED BY VALUE ORIENTED JURIS-
PRUDENCE. ATTEMPTS TO PRESENT A MAP OF THE LEGAL-SOCIAL PRO-
ESS. TREATS THE CONTEXTUAL APPROACH AS IT IS RELEVANT TO
WEALTH, POWER PROCESS, AND SELECTIVITY.

1263 LAUTERPACHT E. ED.
"THE SUEZ CANAL SETTLEMENT."
NEW YORK: PRAEGER, 1960, 82 PP.
A COLLECTION OF PAPERS ON THE LEGALITY OF THE SUEZ
SETTLEMENT. COVERS TIME FROM OCTOBER 1956 TO MARCH 1959.

1264 LAUTERPACHT H.
PRIVATE LAW SOURCES AND ANALOGIES OF INTERNATIONAL LAW.
LONDON: LONGMANS, 1927, 326 PP.
COMMENTARY ON ARTICLE 38 OF STATUTE OR PERMANENT COURT OF
INTERNATIONAL JUSTICE WHICH RECOGNIZES GENERAL PRINCIPLES OF
LAW ACCEPTED BY CIVILIZED STATES AS BINDING, THOUGH ONLY
SUPPLEMENTARY SOURCES OF DECISION IN JUDICIAL SETTLEMENT OF
DISPUTES. AUTHOR ACCEPTS RECOURSE TO PRIVATE LAW AND REJECTS
MODERN POSITIVISM. RECOGNIZES THAT ANALOGOUS RULES OF PRIV-
ATE LAW AID IN DEVELOPING UNIVERSAL LEGAL ORDER.

1265 LAUTERPACHT H.
THE FUNCTION OF LAW IN THE INTERNATIONAL COMMUNITY.
OXFORD: CLARENDON PR., 1933, 469 PP.
DISCUSSES, THROUGH REFERENCE TO PROBLEMS OF INTERNATIONAL
JUDICIAL FUNCTION, THE PRINCIPAL ISSUES OF THE PHILOSOPHY OF
INTERNATIONAL LAW.

1266 LAUTERPACHT H.
INTERNATIONAL LAW AND HUMAN RIGHTS.
NEW YORK: PRAEGER, 1950, 475 PP.
ANALYZES LEGAL EFFECTS OF PROVISIONS OF UN CHARTER
ON ORGANS CHARGED WITH THEIR INTERPRETATION AND APPLICATION.

1267 LAVES W.H.C. ED.
INTERNATIONAL SECURITY.
CHICAGO: U. CHI. PR., 1939, 153 PP.
THESE HARRIS FOUNDATION LECTURES OF 1939 TREAT ASPECTS OF
COLLECTIVE SECURITY AND/OR LACK OF IT. EDWARD BENES EXAMINES
DEVELOPMENT AND FAILURES OF GENEVA PROTOCOL, LOCARNO PACT
AND BRIAND-KELLOGG TREATY. ARTHUR FEILER DISCUSSES GERMANY'S
FOREIGN RELATIONS 1919-1939 AND RISE OF NAZISM. RUSHTON
COULTER DEMONSTRATES BRITAIN'S FAILURE TO LEAD 1919-1939.

1268 LAVROFF D.-.G.
LES LIBERTES PUBLIQUES EN UNION SOVIETIQUE (REV. ED.)
PARIS: EDITIONS A PEDONE, 1963, 265 PP.
DISCUSSION OF FREEDOM AND ITS PHILOSOPHICAL BASIS.
EMPHASIZES INDIVIDUAL RIGHTS AND RELATIONS OF STATE AND
PUBLIC.

1269 LAW COMMISSION OF INDIA
REFORM OF JUDICIAL ADMINISTRATION.
NEW DELHI: INDIA, MIN OF LAW, 1958, 1326 PP.
FOURTEENTH REPORT ON JUDICIAL REFORM IN INDIA, BY COMMIS-
SION ESTABLISHED BY MINISTRY OF LAW. CRITICAL OF CLASS
AND ETHNIC HOMOGENEITY OF HIGH COURT JUDGES. NEW TRIAL
METHODS TO EXPEDITE FLOW OF LITIGATION SUGGESTED.

1270 LAWSON R.
INTERNATIONAL REGIONAL ORGANIZATIONS.
NEW YORK: PRAEGER, 1962, 387 PP.

DISCUSSES POSTWAR PROLIFERATION OF REGIONAL ORGANIZATIONS UNDER UN AND MEANS DEVISED TO EFFECT FUNCTIONS. LISTS SERIES OF DOCUMENTS PRINTED BY VARIOUS REGIONAL ORGANIZATIONS.

1271 LAWYERS COMM AMER POLICY VIET
VIETNAM AND INTERNATIONAL LAW: AN ANALYSIS OF THE LEGALITY OF THE US MILITARY INVOLVEMENT.
FLANDERS, N.J: O'HARE BOOKS, 1967, LC#67-19573.
COMPREHENSIVE ANALYSIS OF LEGAL ISSUES RAISED BY VIETNAM WAR, DOCUMENTING THE CONCLUSION THAT US MILITARY INVOLVEMENT VIOLATES INTERNATIONAL LAW. ISSUES DISCUSSED INCLUDE UNPRECEDENTED CHARACTER OF INVOLVEMENT, VIOLATION OF UN CHARTER, 1954 GENEVA ACCORDS, UNLAWFUL METHODS OF WARFARE, LEGAL ASPECTS OF US COMMITMENT, AND POSSIBLE PEACEFUL SOLUTIONS FOR SETTLEMENT.

1272 LAY S.H., POOLE R.E.
"EXCLUSIVE GOVERNMENTAL LIABILITY FOR SPACE ACCIDENTS."
AMER BAR ASSN., 53 (SEPT. 67), 831-836.
GAP BETWEEN SPACE TECHNOLOGY AND SPACE LAW INCLUDES THIRD-PARTY LIABILITY PROBLEMS ARISING FROM SPACE ACCIDENTS. ANALYZES CONFLICTING OBJECTIVES OF ANY SOLUTION: QUICK AND FULL COMPENSATION, POPULAR SUPPORT, PRIVATE INDUSTRIAL PARTICIPATION, PREVENTION OF ACCIDENTS, AND FAIRNESS IN DISTRIBUTION OF LOSSES. ADVOCATES GOVERNMENT LIABILITY PROGRAM AS BEST SOLUTION.

1273 LEAGUE OF NATIONS-SECRETARIAT.
THE AIMS, METHODS AND ACTIVITY OF THE LEAGUE OF NATIONS.
GENEVA: LEAG/NAT., 1938, 221 PP.
TRACES HISTORICAL EVOLUTION OF LEAGUE: PRECURSORS, COVENANT, ORGANIZATION. ENUMERATES INSTRUMENTS AND METHODS AND EVALUATES ACHIEVEMENTS.

1274 LEAGUE WOMEN VOTERS MASSACHU
THE MERIT SYSTEM IN MASSACHUSETTS (PAMPHLET)
CAMBRIDGE: LEAGUE WOMEN VOTERS, 1961, 113 PP.
STUDY OF PUBLIC PERSONNEL ADMINISTRATION THROUGH CITIZEN'S EYES. ANALYZES STRENGTHS AND WEAKNESSES OF MASSACHUSETTS SYSTEM AND COMPARES WITH OTHER STATES. SUGGESTS IMPROVEMENTS THAT WILL GIVE CITIZEN HIS JUST DUE. CONCENTRATED STUDY ON CAREER CASES NOT POLITICAL. REVIEWS OTHER STUDIES ON SUBJECT AND LAWS INVOLVED.

1275 LEAGUE WOMEN VOTERS NEW YORK
APPORTIONMENT WORKSHOP KIT.
CAMBRIDGE: LEAGUE WOMEN VOTERS, 1963, 74 PP.
EVALUATES METHODS INTENDED TO ASSURE EQUITABLE APPORTIONMENT AMONG NEW YORK STATE LEGISLATIVE AND CONGRESSIONAL DISTRICTS. APPENDIXES ON SUPREME COURT CASES, ROLE OF CONSTITUTIONAL CONVENTION, AND N. Y. ASSEMBLY AND SENATORIAL DISTRICTS.

1276 LEDERMAN W.R. ED.
THE COURTS AND THE CANDIAN CONSTITUTION.
LONDON: MCCLELLAND AND STEWART, 1964, 250 PP.
TRACES EFFECTS AND DEVELOPMENT OF CANADIAN SUPREME COURT INFLUENCES ON CONSTITUTIONALISM AND PROCESS OF INTERPRETATION. CONSIDERS MERITS OF HAVING REVIEW OF LEGISLATION AND EFFECT ON PARLIAMENT.

1277 LEE L.T.
VIENNA CONVENTION ON CONSULAR RELATIONS.
DURHAM: RULE OF LAW PRESS, 1966, 315 PP., LC#66-25083.
DESCRIBES AND ANALYZES FEATURES OF VIENNA CONVENTION ON CONSULAR RELATIONS ADOPTED AT 1963 VIENNA CONFERENCE. DISCUSSES CONSULAR RELATIONS IN GENERAL, FUNCTION OF CONSULS, PRIVILEGES AND IMMUNITIES, AND RELATIONSHIP OF CONSULS AND DIPLOMATS. MAINTAINS THAT AGREEMENT HAS FURTHERED INTERNATIONAL UNDERSTANDING AND UNITY OF LAW.

1278 LEEK J.H.
"TREASON AND THE CONSTITUTION" (BMR)"
J. OF POLITICS, 13 (NOV. 51), 605-623.
TRACES RECORD OF US CONSTITUTIONAL INTERPRETATION OF TREASON; FINDS TREND LIBERAL. BRIEFLY DISCUSSES BRITISH LAW AND ADAPTATION IN COLONIAL AMERICAN LAW. EMPHASIZES CASES CONCERNING WWII AND AFTER, AND INCLUDES DISCUSSION OF TREASON BY BROADCASTING ENEMY PROPAGANDA. CONCLUDES WITH APPLICATIONS OF SMITH ACT, WHICH FORBIDS TEACHING ARMED REVOLUTION AND VIOLENT OVERTHROW OF GOVERNMENT.

1279 LEGAULT A.
"ORGANISATION ET CONDUITE DES OPERATIONS DE MAINTIEN DE LA PAIX."
POLITIQUE ETRANGERE, 32 (1967), 369-396, 4-5.
STUDY OF THE ORGANIZATION AND OPERATING CONDUCT OF THE PEACE-KEEPING ORGANIZATIONS OF THE UN. CRITERIA FOR ORGANIZATION ARE: FORCE MUST HAVE CONSENT OF STATE TO OPERATE ON ITS TERRITORY; UN ALONE DECIDES MAKEUP OF FORCE; FORCE MUST HAVE FREEDOM OF MOVEMENT; THE GREAT POWERS CANNOT PARTICIPATE IN A PEACE-KEEPING FORCE. ANALYZES POLITICAL, JUDICIAL, AND MATERIAL PROBLEMS INVOLVED AND CONTROL OF OPERATIONS.

1280 LEGISLATIVE REFERENCE SERVICE

DIGEST OF PUBLIC GENERAL BILLS AND RESOLUTIONS.
WASHINGTON: LIBRARY OF CONGRESS, 1936.
FURNISHES A BRIEF SYNOPSIS OF ESSENTIAL FEATURES OF INTRODUCED PUBLIC BILLS AND RESOLUTIONS AND A DIGEST OF REPORTED PUBLIC BILLS AND RESOLUTIONS. INFORMS ABOUT STATUS OF BILLS AND RESOLUTIONS; LISTS PUBLIC LAWS AND INDICATES BILL AND PUBLIC LAW NUMBER; SUBJECT AND AUTHOR INDEXES; FIVE CUMULATIVE ISSUES WHILE CONGRESS IS IN SESSION AND BIWEEKLY SUPPLEMENTATS AS NEEDED. FIRST PUBLISHED IN 1936.

1281 LEHMANN L.
LEGAL UND OPPORTUN - POLITISCHE JUSTIZ IN DER BUNDESREPUBLIK.
BERLIN: VOLTAIRE VERLAG, 1966, 361 PP.
EXAMINES NATURE OF POLITICAL JUSTICE IN FEDERAL REPUBLIC OF WEST GERMANY. CENTERS ON DISCUSSION OF INVESTIGATIONS AND PERSECUTIONS OF ILLEGAL PARTIES, SUCH AS COMMUNIST PARTY AND OTHER GROUPS SUSPECTED OF SUBVERSIVE ACTIVITIES. MAINTAINS THAT COURTS AND LEGISLATURE ARE SUBVERTING JUSTICE AND PRESENTING THREAT TO DEMOCRATIC LIFE. DISCUSSES MANY INDIVIDUAL CASES.

1282 LEITZ F.
DIE PUBLIZITAT DER AKTIENGESELLSCHAFT.
FRANKFURT: F LEITZ, 1929, 291 PP.
STUDY OF PUBLIC STATEMENTS OF GERMAN CORPORATIONS CONCERNING THEIR STATUTES, FINANCIAL REPORTS, STOCK MARKET PROSPECTS, ETC. DISCUSSES THEIR LEGAL DUTIES AS WELL AS A COMPARISON WITH PRACTICES IN ENGLAND, AMERICA, FRANCE, AND BELGIUM.

1283 LENCZOWSKI G.
OIL AND STATE IN THE MIDDLE EAST.
ITHACA: CORNELL U. PR., 1960, 360 PP.
BY EMPHASIZING AND EXPLAINING CERTAIN ASPECTS OF THE MIDDLE-EASTERN OIL COMPANIES (LEGAL STATUS, CONCESSION AGREEMENTS, METHOD OF HANDLING EMPLOYEES AND GOVERNMENT OFFICIALS, AND GENERAL RELATIONSHIP TO HOST NATION) ATTEMPTS TO PROJECT THEIR FUTURE POSITION IN THESE COUNTRIES.

1284 LENG S.C.
JUSTICE IN COMMUNIST CHINA: A SURVEY OF THE JUDICIAL SYSTEM OF THE CHINESE PEOPLE'S REPUBLIC.
NEW YORK: OCEANA PUBLISHING, 1967, 196 PP., LC#67-14398.
INTRODUCTORY SURVEY OF DEVELOPMENT, ORGANIZATION, AND FUNCTIONING OF JUDICIAL SYSTEM FOCUSES ON JUDICIAL PATTERN RATHER THAN LAW; LAWS ARE TREATED ONLY WITHIN CONTEXT OF ADMINISTRATION OF JUSTICE. CONCERNED PRIMARILY WITH HISTORY OF "PEOPLE'S JUSTICE" SINCE 1920 AND WITH MACHINERY AND PROCEDURES BY WHICH JUSTICE IS ADMINISTERED. INCLUDES COURT SYSTEM, POLICE, LAWYERS, AND TRIAL SYSTEMS.

1285 LENT G.E.
"TAX INCENTIVES FOR INVESTMENT IN DEVELOPING COUNTRIES"
INTL. MONETARY FUND STAFF BUL., 14 (JULY 67), 249-323.
COMPARES VARIETY OF METHODS FOR ESTABLISHING TAX-INCENTIVE PROGRAMS TO ENCOURAGE INVESTMENT. EVALUATES MERITS OF EACH SCHEME IN ATTEMPT TO ESTABLISH BETTER STANDARDS FOR INVESTMENT CODES. DEALS WITH HARMONIZATION OF TAX-INCENTIVE LAWS IN DIFFERENT COUNTRIES AND GIVES CONCLUSIONS ON FEATURES OF INVESTMENT-INCENTIVE PLANS.

1286 LEONI B.
FREEDOM AND THE LAW.
PRINCETON: VAN NOSTRAND, 1961, 204 PP.
LEGAL DISCUSSION OF FREEDOM AS RELATED TO INDIVIDUAL IN A SOCIETY OFTEN REGULATED AND DEEPLY AFFECTED BY SOCIAL, PROBLEM-SOLVING LEGISLATION.

1287 LEPAWSKY A.
"INTERNATIONAL DEVELOPMENT OF RIVER RESOURCES."
INT. AFF., 39 (OCT. 63), 553-50.
DISCUSSES VARIOUS FORMS OF INTERNATIONAL RIVER ADMINISTRATION WHICH CAN RECONCILE CONFLICTING INTEREST OF INDEPENDENT NATIONALITIES. EMPHASIZES THE TWO EUROPEAN AUTHORITIES FOR THE DANUBE AND RHINE, THE TWO NORTH AMERICAN COMMISSIONS COVERING THE CANADIAN-U.S. AND MEXICAN-U.S. BORDERS, AND THE TWO RECENTLY-ESTABLISHED INTERNATIONAL RIVER AGENCIES IN ASIA FOR THE INDUS AND MEKONG RIVERS.

1288 LERNER M.
"CONSTITUTION AND COURT AS SYMBOLS" (BMR)"
YALE LAW J., 46 (JUNE 37), 1290-1319.
DELVES INTO NATURE OF SUPREMACY AND SOVEREIGNTY OF US CONSTITUTION AS SYMBOLS TO PUBLIC AND EXAMINES THEIR PSYCHOLOGICAL POWER. TREATS FETISHISM OF THE CONSTITUTION AND MYTH SURROUNDING IT, AND CONSIDERS "DIVINE RIGHT" OF SUPREME COURT WHICH HOLDS AMERICAN DEMOCRACY AND CAPITALISM TOGETHER. EXAMINES NEW MYTHS OF COMMON MASS IN 20TH CENTURY.

1289 LEVONTIN A.V.
THE MYTH OF INTERNATIONAL SECURITY: A JURIDICAL AND CRITICAL ANALYSIS.
JERUSALEM: MAGNES, 1957, 346 PP.
CONTENTION THAT INTERNATIONAL LAW PROVIDES SECURITY IS CRITICALLY ANALYZED AND FOUND INADEQUATE. THE BELIEF THAT

STATES CAN BE SOVEREIGN AND INDEPENDENT YET ABLE TO
ESTABLISH INTERNATIONAL SECURITY SYSTEMS IS GROUNDLESS.
ADVISES SOVEREIGN WORLD GOVERNMENT TO REPLACE SOVEREIGN
STATE SYSTEM.

1290 LEVY H.V.
LIBERDADE E JUSTICA SOCIAL (2ND ED.)
SAO PAULO: LIVRARIA MARTINS EDITORA, 1962, 203 PP.
    DISCUSSION OF SOCIAL JUSTICE AND LIBERTY UNDER MARXISM,
SOVIET SYSTEM, AND US CAPITALISM IN AUSTRIA, ENGLAND,
AND BRAZIL. INCLUDES STUDY OF RELATED DOCUMENTS OF 20TH
COMMUNIST PARTY CONGRESS OF USSR, UN, NEW CLASS BY DJILAS,
AND BRAZILIAN DELEGATION TO 48TH WORLD INTER-PARLIAMENTARY
CONFERENCE IN WARSAW.

1291 LEVY L.W.
JEFFERSON AND CIVIL LIBERTIES: THE DARKER SIDE.
CAMBRIDGE: HARVARD U PR, 1963, 225 PP., LC#63-19140.
    DISCUSSES JEFFERSON'S UNDERSTANDING OF LIBERTY AND CASES
IN WHICH HE WAS NOT CONSISTENTLY LIBERTARIAN. EXAMINES HIS
BEHAVIOR IN RELATION TO RIGHT OF POLITICAL EXPRESSION AND
DUE PROCESS DURING THE REVOLUTION; HIS FAILURE TO RESPECT
CONSTITUTIONAL RIGHTS OF THE INDIVIDUAL DURING BURR AFFAIR;
AND ABRIDGEMENTS OF INTELLECTUAL FREEDOM. PRESENTS POSSIBLE
REASONS FOR JEFFERSON'S BEHAVIOR.

1292 LEVY L.W. ED.
JUDICIAL REVIEW AND THE SUPREME COURT.
NEW YORK: HARPER & ROW, 1967, 248 PP., LC#67-10674.
    ESSAYS ON HISTORY AND DEVELOPMENT OF JUDICIAL REVIEW
IN US AND ITS RELATION TO SUPREME COURT. DISCUSSES
DEMOCRATIC CHARACTER OF JUDICIAL REVIEW, ORIGIN AND SCOPE
OF AMERICAN DOCTRINE OF CONSTITUTIONAL LAW, AND SUPREME
COURT AS NATIONAL POLICY-MAKER. DESCRIBES SEARCH FOR
OBJECTIVITY IN CONSTITUTIONAL LAW, MYTH OF NEUTRALITY IN
ADJUDICATION, AND SUPREME COURT AND FUNDAMENTAL FREEDOMS.

1293 LEWIN J.
POLITICS AND LAW IN SOUTH AFRICA.
NEW YORK: MONTHLY REVIEW PR, 1963, 115 PP.
    EXAMINATION OF RELATION OF AFRIKANER NATIONALISM, AFRICAN
NATIONALISM, AND ENGLISH ECONOMIC INTERESTS TO PRESENT FORM
OF GOVERNMENT IN SOUTH AFRICA. EXPLAINS DEVELOPMENT OF SEP-
ARATE NATIONALISM OF WHITE AFRICAN AND ATTAINMENT OF POWER
DESPITE LARGER BLACK AFRICAN POPULATION AND MORE POWERFUL
BRITISH ECONOMIC INFLUENCE.

1294 LEWIS P.R.
LITERATURE OF THE SOCIAL SCIENCES: AN INTRODUCTORY SURVEY
AND GUIDE.
LONDON: LIBRARY ASSOC, 1960, 222 PP.
    LISTS AND DISCUSSES MATERIALS PERTINENT TO SOCIAL SCI-
ENCES DATING FROM THE 1800'S FOR THE INTEREST OF THE
BRITISH READER. SURVEYS ECONOMIC THEORY AND HISTORY,
ESPECIALLY IN THE UK; STATISTICS; COMMERCE AND INDUSTRY;
POLITICAL SCIENCE, ADMINISTRATION, AND THEORY; LAW; INTER-
NATIONAL RELATIONS; AND SOCIOLOGY. INCLUDES AN INDEX AND
SUGGESTIONS FOR MAKING USE OF RESEARCH SOURCES.

1295 LIBRARY INTERNATIONAL REL
INTERNATIONAL INFORMATION SERVICE.
NEW YORK: INTL CHAMBER COMMERCE, 1963.
    QUARTERLY PUBLICATION WITH ANNOTATIONS OF BOOKS, MONO-
GRAPHS, GOVERNMENT DOCUMENTS, AND PAMPHLETS ON CONTEMPORARY
POLITICAL, ECONOMIC AND SOCIAL DEVELOPMENTS IN ALL PARTS OF
THE WORLD. BEGUN IN 1963, ENTRIES ARRANGED BY SUBJECT AND
TYPE OF PUBLICATION. INCLUDES HISTORY, POLITICS, LAW, INTER-
NATIONAL ECONOMICS AND SOCIOLOGY, ETC.

1296 LIGGETT E.
BRITISH POLITICAL ISSUES: VOLUME 1.
NEW YORK: PERGAMON PRESS, 1964, 232 PP., LC#64-8868.
    FIRST VOLUME OF FOUR VOLUME SERIES. PROVIDES GENERAL SUR-
VEY OF PARTY POLITICS AND ITS RELATIONSHIPS TO NATIONAL
GOVERNMENT AND FOREIGN POLICY, BRITISH JUDICIAL SYSTEM, AND
GOVERNMENT AGENCIES PUBLISHING POLITICAL REPORTS AND INFOR-
MATION. FOCUSES ON RECENT POLITICAL ISSUES AND DEVELOPMENTS.

1297 LILLICH R.B.
INTERNATIONAL CLAIMS: THEIR ADJUDICATION BY NATIONAL
COMMISSIONS.
SYRACUSE: U. PR., 1962, 139 PP.
    TRACES HISTORY, ORGANIZATION AND JURISPRUDENCE OF
NATIONAL COMMISSIONS AS A PROCEDURAL DEVICE FOR THE SETTLE-
MENT OF INTERNATIONAL CLAIMS. DISCUSSES SPECIFIC PARTNERSHIP
AND CORPORATE PROBLEMS, REQUIREMENTS FOR INDIVIDUAL
CLAIMANTS AND PRECEDENT-VALUE OF DECISIONS BY COMMISSIONS.

1298 LILLICH R.B.
"INTERNATIONAL CLAIMS: THEIR ADJUDICATION BY NATIONAL
COMMISSIONS."
SYRACUSE: SYRACUSE U PRESS, 1962.
    LISTS OF BOOKS, ARTICLES, INTERNATIONAL AGREEMENTS, AND
STATUTES DEALING WITH INTERNATIONAL LAW APPLICATIONS IN
STATE RESPONSIBILITY TO INDIVIDUALS AFFECTED BY GOVERNMENTAL
ACTION. ABOUT 250 ENTRIES ARE LISTED BY TYPE OF MATERIAL;

RANGE FROM 1794 TO 1961 BUT CONCENTRATED IN LAST FEW DECADES
OF PERIOD. BOOK GIVES HISTORY, ORGANIZATION, JURISPRUDENCE,
AND EVALUATION OF NATIONAL CLAIMS COMMISSIONS.

1299 LILLY W.S.
FIRST PRINCIPLES IN POLITICS.
NEW YORK: G P PUTNAM'S SONS, 1899, 322 PP.
    OFFERS MORAL LAW AS THE ONLY ETHICAL BASE FOR CREATION OF
THE STATE. TRACES HISTORICAL TRENDS REGARDING THE FOUNDING
OF STATES AND DISCUSSES BOTH GENERAL AND SPECIFIC ENDS WHICH
MAY BE ETHICALLY PURSUED BY IT. TREATS GENERAL TYPES OF
STATE FUNCTIONS AND MECHANISMS USED. DISCUSSES SANCTIONS
MORALLY AVAILABLE AND THE NATURE OF CORRUPTION WHEN IT
ENTERS OPERATION OF STATE.

1300 LIPPMAN W.
LIBERTY AND THE NEWS.
NEW YORK: MACMILLAN, 1920, 104 PP.
    DISCUSSES CENSORSHIP, GOVERNMENT CONTROL, ROLE OF
NEWSPAPERS IN PUBLIC OPINION, IMPORTANCE OF TRUTH IN JOUR-
NALISM, AND NECESSITY FOR LEGISLATION ON WRITING.

1301 LIPPMANN W.
ISOLATION AND ALLIANCES: AN AMERICAN SPEAKS TO THE BRITISH.
BOSTON: LITTLE BROWN, 1952, 56 PP., LC#52-1196.
    DISCUSSES US PUBLIC OPINION ON FOREIGN RELATIONS UNTIL
1945 AND MAINTAINS THAT ISOLATIONISM HAS BEEN DOMINANT THEME
OF US ATTITUDE. EXAMINES REALITIES OF WORLD SITUATION SINCE
WWII AND THE CHALLENGE TO TRADITIONAL US POLICIES.

1302 LIPSON L.
"AN ARGUMENT ON THE LEGALITY OF RECONNAISSANCE STATELLITES."
PROC. AMER. SOC. INT. LAW. 55(APR. 61), 174-176.
    DEALS WITH LEGAL PROBLEM TO WHICH MUCH ATTENTION HAS BEEN
DEVOTED. ATTEMPTS TO SHOW WHAT WERE THE RELEVANT DIFFERENCES
BETWEEN THE FLIGHTS OF GAGARIN AND POWERS FROM THE STAND-
POINT OF INTERNATIONAL LAW.

1303 LIPSON L.
"PEACEFUL COEXISTENCE."
LAW CONTEMP. PROBL., 29 (AUTUMN 64), 871-81.
    PRESENTS A LEGALISTIC INQUIRY INTO WHETHER OR NOT THIS
DOCTRINE IS IN REALITY THE BASIS FOR CONTEMPORARY INTERNA-
TIONAL LAW. ALSO EXAMINES SOVIET ATTITUDES TOWARDS THIS
DOCTRINE.

1304 LISSITZYN O.J.
"THE INTERNATIONAL COURT OF JUSTICE."
NEW YORK: CARNEGIE ENDOWMENT, 1951, 118 PP.
    AN APPRAISAL OF THE COURT AS INSTRUMENT OF INTERNATIONAL
PEACE, ITS PAST RECORD AND FUTURE POTENTIALITIES. FEELS
GREATEST CONDITION IS DEVELOPMENT OF INTERNATIONAL LAW.

1305 LISSITZYN O.J.
"SOME LEGAL IMPLICATIONS OF THE U-2 AND RB-47 INCIDENTS."
AMER. J. INT. LAW, 56 (JAN. 62), 135-142.
    SINCE THE LAUNCHING OF SPUTNIK I, SOVIET EXPERTS IN
INTERNATIONAL LAW HAVE SUGGESTED AN 'UPPER LIMIT TO AIR
SOVEREIGNTY' ABOVE WHICH, LAW SIMILAR TO THE LAW OF THE HIGH
SEAS, WOULD APPLY. THE U-2 CONSIDERED AN INTRUDER. NO 'UPPER
LIMIT' HAS BEEN AGREED UPON. THE RECONNAISSANCE-SATELLITE
DEVELOPMENT REDUCES LIKELIHOOD OF ANY SPACE-LAW AGREEMENT.

1306 LISSITZYN O.J.
"INTERNATIONAL LAW IN A DIVIDED WORLD."
INT. CONCIL., 542 (MAR. 63), 60 PP.
    DEALS WITH SOME OF THE MAJOR PROBLEMS PRESENTED BY THE
RESURGENCE OF INTEREST IN THE FIELD. SEES A SLOW EROSION
OF THE EXTREME HOSTILITY TO OTHER SYSTEMS OF PUBLIC ORDER
IMPLICIT IN COMMUNIST IDEOLOGY, AND A CONCOMITANT INCREASE
IN THE ROLE OF LAW IN RELATIONS BETWEEN THE WEST AND COM-
MUNIST STATES. NEWER AND LESS DEVELOPED NATIONS APPEAR TO
BE NEITHER AS MONOLITHIC IN THEIR APPROACH NOR AS ADAMANT
IN THEIR OPPOSITION TO TRADITIONAL NORMS AS ONE MIGHT FIRST
BELIEVE.

1307 LISSITZYN O.J.
"TREATIES AND CHANGED CIRCUMSTANCES (REBUS SIC STANTIBUS)"
AMER. J. OF INT. LAW, 61 (OCT. 67), 895-922.
    MAINTAINS THAT PROBLEM OF EFFECT OF CHANGE IN
CIRCUMSTANCES ON TREATY RELATIONSHIPS IS ONE OF
INTERPRETATION OF INTENTIONS AND EXPECTATIONS. PRESENTS
SEVERAL OPINIONS ON EFFECT ON CHANGE OF CIRCUMSTANCES AND
DISCUSSES SEVERAL INSTANCES. EXAMINES RELEVANT PROVISIONS OF
DRAFT ARTILLES ON LAW OF TREATIES BY INTERNATIONAL LAW
COMMISSION IN 1966.

1308 LITTLEFIELD N.
METROPOLITAN AREA PROBLEMS AND MUNICIPAL HOME RULE.
ANN ARBOR: U OF MICH LAW SCHOOL, 1962, 83 PP.
    EXAMINES LAW OF MUNICIPAL HOME RULE IN RELATION TO
METROPOLITAN AREA PROBLEMS. REEXAMINES JURISPRUDENCE OF
HOME RULE IN THE LIGHT OF INCREASING DOMINANCE OF AREA IN-
TERESTS. EXAMINES POWERS OF ANNEXATION, STATE ADMINISTRA-
TIVE CONTROL OVER LOCAL RULE, AND SOME MODEL HOME RULE
PROVISIONS.

1309 LIVELY E.
THE INVASION OF MISSISSIPPI.
BELMONT: AMER OPINION, 1963, 121 PP.
INVESTIGATION OF INTEGRATION EFFORTS IN MISSISSIPPI AND
LITTLE ROCK FOCUSING ON OXFORD, MISSISSIPPI, RIOTS. STATES
THAT FEDERAL ACTION WAS ILLEGAL, COMMUNIST-INSPIRED,
AND AN EXAMPLE OF FEDERAL GOVERNMENT'S ATTEMPTS TO REDUCE
POWER OF SOVEREIGN STATES TO AID COMMUNIST TAKE-OVER. RACIAL
PROBLEMS CAN BE SOLVED IN UNCOERCED MANNER ON MORAL
PRINCIPLES.

1310 LIVINGSTON W.S.
FEDERALISM IN THE COMMONWEALTH - A BIBLIOGRAPHICAL
COMMENTARY.
LONDON: CASSELL & CO LTD, 1963, 237 PP.
LIST OF BOOKS, PAMPHLETS, PERIODICALS, AND GOVERNMENT
PUBLICATIONS ON FEDERALISM IN CANADA, AUSTRALIA, WEST
INDIES, INDIA, PAKISTAN, MALAYA, NIGERIA, RHODESIA, AND
NYASALAND. INCLUDES FEW FOREIGN-LANGUAGE PUBLICATIONS.
ARRANGED GEOGRAPHICALLY AND BY SUBJECT. LISTS RECENT
PUBLICATIONS.

1311 LIVNEH E.
ISRAEL LEGAL BIBLIOGRAPHY IN EUROPEAN LANGUAGES.
JERUSALEM: HEBREW U PR, 1963, 85 PP.
BRIEF INTRODUCTION TO LEGAL HISTORY OF MODERN PALESTINE
AND LIST OF 311 BASIC ENTRIES DIVIDED INTO THREE SECTIONS:
LEGISLATION, LAW REPORTS, BOOKS AND ARTICLES. THIRD SEC-
ION SUBDIVIDED BY PUBLIC, CIVIL, AND CRIMINAL TOPICS. PUBLI-
CATIONS LARGELY 1948-63.

1312 LLEWELLYN K.N.
"A REALISTIC JURISPRUDENCE - THE NEXT STEP."
COLUMBIA LAW REV., 30 (APR. 30), 431-465.
DISCUSSES PROBLEM OF DEFINING LAW AND CONCLUDES THAT
"POINT OF REFERENCE" IS BEST APPROACH. EXAMINES REMEDIES,
RIGHTS, AND INTERESTS AS THEY AFFECT ANALYSIS OF LAW.
STUDIES IMPORTANCE OF PAPER RULES. EXPLORES BEHAVIOR
APPROACH AND ITS IMPLICATIONS FOR STUDY OF LAW, STRESSING
INTERACTIONS, LAYMEN'S BEHAVIOR, AND NARROW APPLICATIONS OF
LAWS. PRESENTS IDEAL LAWS.

1313 LLEWELLYN K.N.
"THE CONSTITUTION AS AN INSTITUTION" (BMR)"
COLUMBIA LAW REV., 34 (JAN. 34), 1-40.
ARGUES THAT ORTHODOX THEORY OF CONSTITUTIONAL LAW IS NO
LONGER VALID AND APPLICABLE AND SHOULD BE RECONSTRUCTED.
DISCUSSES ORTHODOX THEORY AND ITS MERITS, BACKGROUND OF
PRIVATE LAW, NATURE OF A CODE, AND NATURE OF AN INSTITUTION.
FEELS CONSTITUTION IS NO LONGER AN INSTITUTION BECAUSE NO
LONGER LIVING. DISCUSSES INTEREST GROUPS, PUBLIC, AND
SPECIALISTS.

1314 LOBINGIER C.S.
THE PEOPLE'S LAW OR POPULAR PARTICIPATION IN LAW-MAKING.
NEW YORK: MACMILLAN, 1909, 429 PP.
A STUDY OF THE EVOLUTION OF POPULAR PARTICIPATION IN
LAW-MAKING FROM ANCIENT FOLKMOOT TO MODERN REFERENDUM.
SPECIAL ATTENTION GIVEN TO ORIGINS AND DEVELOPMENT OF US
CONSTITUTION AND POPULAR RATIFICATION IN THE VARIOUS
STATES. FINAL SECTION DISCUSSES POPULAR PARTICIPATION IN
LAW-MAKING OUTSIDE THE US.

1315 LOBLE L.H., WYLIE M.
DELINQUENCY CAN BE STOPPED.
NEW YORK: MCGRAW HILL, 1967, 148 PP., LC#67-20177.
DISCUSSES FAILURES OF REFORMS TO PREVENT JUVENILE DELIN-
QUENCY. RECOMMENDS RETURN TO TIME-PROVEN METHODS OF DISCI-
PLINE. ARGUES FOR PUBLIC TRIALS OF JUVENILE OFFENDERS.

1316 LOCKE J.
TWO TREATISES OF GOVERNMENT (1690)
NEW YORK: HAFNER PUBL, 1947, 311 PP.
ATTEMPT TO JUSTIFY ENGLISH REVOLUTION OF 1688, AND CHANGE
IN LINE OF SUCCESSION, BY FOUNDING WILLIAM III'S TITLE ON
CONSENT OF PEOPLE. STRESSES CONSENT OF PEOPLE AS BASIS FOR
GOVERNMENT. MAN CONSENTS TO GOVERNMENT BECAUSE OF "INCON-
VENIENCE OF STATE OF NATURE." IMPLICATION OF POSITION IS
THAT MEN ARE EQUAL, AND THAT STATE'S FUNCTION IS TO PROVIDE
EQUAL PROTECTION OF MAN'S NATURAL RIGHTS.

1317 LOCKHART W.B., KAMISAR Y., CHOPER J.H.
CASES AND MATERIALS ON CONSTITUTIONAL RIGHTS AND LIBERTIES.
MINNEAPOLIS: WEST PUBL CO, 1964, 864 PP.
EXAMINATION OF CIVIL LIBERTIES EMPHASIZING NATURE OF DUE
PROCESS, LIMITATIONS ON GOVERNMENTAL POWER, RIGHTS OF THE
ACCUSED, FREEDOM OF SPEECH AND ASSOCIATION, CONCEPT OF STATE
ACTION, AND FRANCHISE AND APPORTIONMENT.

1318 LOEVINGER L.
"JURIMETRICS* THE METHODOLOGY OF LEGAL INQUIRY."
LAW AND CONTEMPORARY PROB., 28 (WINTER 63), 5-36.
JURIMETRICS IS DESIGNATION FOR ACTIVITIES INVOLVING SCI-
ENTIFIC INVESTIGATION OF LEGAL PROBLEMS AND IS CONCERNED NOT
WITH BASIC PHILOSOPHICAL LEGAL QUESTIONS BUT WITH QUANTITA-
TIVE ANALYSIS, ELECTRONIC RETRIEVAL OF LEGAL DATA, AND COM-

MUNICATION THEORY FOR LAW. DESCRIBES DIFFERENT METH-
ODS OF ELECTRONIC DATA RETRIEVAL, ALSO MICRO-IMAGE STORAGE
OF DOCUMENTS, AND "LEX," USED BY ANTITRUST LAWYERS.

1319 LOEWENSTEIN K.
VERFASSUNGSRECHT UND VERFASSUNGSPRAXIS DER VEREINIGTEN
STAATEN.
BERLIN: SPRINGER VERLAG, 1959, 656 PP.
TRACES US CONSTITUTIONAL HISTORY FROM COLONIAL BEGINNINGS
TO PRESENT AND EXAMINES ROLE OF POLITICAL PARTIES, CONGRESS,
EXECUTIVE, AND COURTS UNDER CONSTITUTION. DISCUSSES BASIC
FREEDOMS AS GUARANTEED BY CONSTITUTION AND BILL OF RIGHTS.

1320 LOFTON J.
JUSTICE AND THE PRESS.
BOSTON: BEACON PRESS, 1966, 462 PP., LC#66-23788.
ANALYSIS OF FUNCTIONS OF COURTS, "TO INSURE JUSTICE FOR
INDIVIDUALS; AND OF PRESS, TO INSURE PUBLIC SCRUTINY OF
COURTS AND DUE PROCESS OF LAW." BELIEVES COURT VS. PRESS
CONFLICT TO BE DUE TO HISTORY OF DISTRUST. TRACES
DEVELOPMENT FROM ANCIENT GREECE TO PRESENT, AND ANALYZES
CASE OF FREE PRESS VS. JUSTICE.

1321 LOGAN R.W.
THE AFRICAN MANDATES IN WORLD POLITICS.
WASHINGTON: PUBLIC AFFAIRS PRESS, 1948, 220 PP.
DISCUSSES INFLUENCE OF MANDATE COLONIES TAKEN FROM
GERMANY IN WWI IN WORLD POLITICS BETWEEN WARS. TRACES GERMAN
POLICY REGARDING RECOVERY OF COLONIES AFTER WWI, AND THEIR
IMPORTANCE AS A POINT OF NEGOTIATION WITH HITLER BEFORE
WWII. NOTES ROLE OF COLONIES IN POST-WWII INTERNATIONAL
AFFAIRS PARTICULARLY CITING EFFECTS ON TRUSTEE NATIONS.

1322 LONDON INSTITUTE WORLD AFFAIRS
THE YEAR BOOK OF WORLD AFFAIRS.
LONDON: LONDON INST WORLD AFFAIR.
ANNUAL COLLECTION OF ARTICLES AND REPORTS WRITTEN
PRIMARILY BY BRITISH SCHOLARS. FIRST PUBLISHED IN 1946, THE
YEARBOOK CONTAINS ABOUT TEN ANALYTICAL ESSAYS ON MAJOR PROB-
LEMS OF INTERNATIONAL RELATIONS. REPORTS ON WORLD AFFAIRS
ARE PROVIDED ALSO, INDICATING THE ECONOMIC, SOCIOLOGICAL,
PSYCHOLOGICAL, AND LEGAL ASPECTS OF VARIOUS ISSUES. EXTEN-
SIVE BIBLIOGRAPHICAL LISTINGS APPEAR IN EACH VOLUME.

1323 LONDON SCHOOL ECONOMICS-POL
ANNUAL DIGEST OF PUBLIC INTERNATIONAL LAW CASES.
LONDON: BUTTERWORTHS, 1919.
AN ANNUAL DIGEST OF DECISIONS WHICH ARE CONCERNED WITH
THE INTERPRETATION OF MUNICIPAL STATUTES ON MATTERS BEARING
UPON INTERNATIONAL LAW, IN PARTICULAR, QUESTIONS OF JURIS-
DICTION, NATIONALITY, AND EXTRADITION. SINCE 1932, 28 VOL-
UMES HAVE BEEN PUBLISHED COVERING PERIOD 1919-63. EACH VOL-
UME CONTAINS ALPHABETICAL AND GEOGRAPHICAL LISTS OF CASES,
TABLE OF TREATIES, AND BETWEEN 140-390 SUMMARIZED ENTRIES.

1324 LONG E.V.
THE INTRUDERS: THE INVASION OF PRIVACY BY GOVERNMENT AND
INDUSTRY.
NEW YORK: FREDERICK PRAEGER, 1967, 230 PP., LC#66-18907.
DESCRIPTION OF WIRETAPPING, BUGGING, AND OTHER FORMS OF
"SNOOPING" BY GOVERNMENT AND PRIVATE INDUSTRY. THE WRITER,
CHAIRMAN OF SENATE SUBCOMMITTEE ON ADMINISTRATIVE PRACTICE
AND PROCEDURE URGES LEGISLATIVE ACTION TO ASSURE INDIVIDUALS
F RIGHT TO PRIVACY.

1325 LONG H.A.
USURPERS - FOES OF FREE MAN.
NEW YORK: POST PRINT CO, 1957, 115 PP.
DEFENDS CONSTITUTIONALISM AGAINST WHAT AUTHOR SEES TO BE
ONSLAUGHT OF ADMINISTRATIONAL JURISDICTION. WARNS OF EXCESS
IN FEDERAL CENTRALIZATION OF POWER. DISCUSSES FEDERAL GOV-
ERNMENT BEFORE AND AFTER FDR. CLAIMS SUPREME COURT HAS
USURPED MUCH OF POWER OF CONGRESS THROUGH PROCESS REVERSING
INTERPRETATIONS OF THE CONSTITUTION TO SUIT JUSTICES.

1326 LONG T.G.
"THE ADMINISTRATIVE PROCESS: AGONIZING REAPPRAISAL IN THE
FTC."
G. WASH. LAW REV., 33 (MAR. 65), 671-691.
COMMISSIONER ELMAN'S DRIVE TO MAKE CEASE AND DESIST
ORDERS MORE SPECIFIC HAS RESULTED IN MUCH MORE ACTIVE
INTERST GROUP PARTICIPATION IN FTC DECISION-MAKING.

1327 LORIMER J.
THE INSTITUTES OF THE LAW OF NATIONS.
EDINBURGH: BLACKWOOD, 1880, 572 PP.
DISCUSSES NATURE AND CHARACTERISTICS OF INTERNATIONAL LAW
AND EXPLAINS IN DETAIL ITS SOURCES. ALSO SURVEYS THE ENTIRE
FIELD OF INTERNATIONAL RELATIONS AND THE ROLE OF THE LAW OF
NATURE IN THIS FIELD.

1328 LOWELL A.L.
ESSAYS ON GOVERNMENT.
BOSTON: HOUGHTON MIFFLIN, 1892, 229 PP.
A COMPENDIUM OF ESSAYS COMPARING THE ENGLISH AND AMERI-
CAN GOVERNMENTS, A LEGAL TREATISE, AND TWO ESSAYS ON THE

HISTORY OF MODERN POLITICAL PHILOSOPHY.

1329 LOWENTHAL M.
THE FEDERAL BUREAU OF INVESTIGATION.
NY: WILLIAM SLOAN ASSOCIATES, 1950, 559 PP.
DISCUSSION OF UNRESOLVED ISSUES ON THE OPERATION OF
FEDERAL BUREAU OF INVESTIGATION, NEED FOR FEDERAL POLICE
AGENCY, ITS FUNCTIONS, ROLE IN INVESTIGATING NON-CRIMINAL
PROBLEMS, CONTROL OF IT AS AGENCY, IMPACT ON AMERICAN
SOCIETY, AND NEW RESPONSIBILITY OF DEALING WITH ESPIONAGE.

1330 LOWRY C.W.
TO PRAY OR NOT TO PRAY.
THE UNIVERSITY PR OF WASH, DC, 1963, 257 PP., LC#63-14485.
DISCUSSES IMPLICATIONS OF 1962 SUPREME COURT DECISION OF
ENGEL V. VITALE, WHICH SET PRECEDENT FOR BANNING PRAYER IN
PUBLIC SCHOOLS. PARTICULARLY ATTACKS POWERS OF SUPREME COURT
IN CONTROLLING LAWS AND POSSIBILITY OF COURT'S BECOMING TOO
RADICAL OR POWERFUL THROUGH DECISIONS OF THIS TYPE.

1331 LUCE R.
LEGISLATIVE PROBLEMS.
BOSTON: HOUGHTON MIFFLIN, 1935, 732 PP., LC#36-1241.
STUDIES DEVELOPMENT, STATUS, AND TREND OF TREATMENT AND
EXERCISE OF LAWMAKING POWERS. CONSIDERS JUDICIAL PROCEDURES,
CABINET SYSTEM, BUDGET, VETO POWERS, RELATIONSHIP OF PRES-
IDENT AND CONGRESS. ANALYZES PURPOSE AND SCOPE OF LAWMAKING.

1332 LUGO-MARENCO J.J.
A STATEMENT OF THE LAWS OF NICARAGUA IN MATTERS AFFECTING
BUSINESS.
WASHINGTON: PAN AMERICAN UNION, 1965, 312 PP.
SUMMARY OF BASIC LEGISLATION CONCERNING NATIONALITY AND
IMMIGRATION, CONTRACTS, SOCIAL LEGISLATION, AND
NATURAL RESOURCES. ALSO TREATS SUCCESSION, ADMINISTRATION OF
JUSTICE, AND COPYRIGHT.

1333 LUNT D.C.
THE ROAD TO THE LAW.
NEW YORK: MCGRAW HILL, 1932, 279 PP.
TRACES DEVELOPMENT OF LAW 1500-1930, IN ENGLAND, CANADA,
AMERICA, AND AUSTRALIA AND EFFECT OF IT THERE UPON
JURISPRUDENCE IN US. PURPORTS TO DEMONSTRATE VITAL AND
CHANGEABLE NATURE OF THIS TYPE OF COMMON LAW, GIVING
MORE IMPORTANT CASES AND DECISIONS AS ILLUSTRATIVE OF
SIGNIFICANT CHANGES.

1334 LUSKY L.
"FOUR PROBLEMS IN LAWMAKING FOR PEACE."
POLIT. SCI. QUART., 80 (SEPT. 65), 341-356.
PLANS FOR WORLD ORDER THROUGH WORLD LAW, EVEN THOSE PRE-
SCRIBING "MERE SURVIVAL LAW," MUST OVERCOME FOUR INHERENT
STUMBLING BLOCKS= 1) FEAR OF MAJORITY-LEGISLATED PEACEFUL
CHANGE, 2) FEAR THAT LIMITED LEGISLATURE MAY, OVER TIME, TRY
TO BROADEN ITS POWERS, 3) FEAR THAT FULL PEACE ENFORCEMENT
WILL FORCE INTRA-SOCIETAL CHANGES, 4) PARADOX OF SUPPORTING
UNPOPULAR GOVERNMENTS OR LOSING THEIR NEEDED SUPPORT.

1335 LYONS F.S.L.
INTERNATIONALISM IN EUROPE 1815-1914.
LEYDEN: AW SIJTHOFF, 1963, 412 PP., LC#63-16252.
PRESENTS HISTORY OF INTERNATIONALISM IN EUROPE FROM
1815-1914. STUDIES MACHINERY OF INTERNATIONAL COOPERATION
AND DISCUSSES SEVERAL AREAS OF COOPERATION. THESE INCLUDE
ECONOMIC, LABOR, COMMUNICATION, LEGAL, RELIGIOUS, AND
HUMANITARIAN COOPERATION. ALSO INVESTIGATES ATTEMPTS TO
ESTABLISH PEACEFUL EXISTENCE.

1336 ROBINSON R.D.
INTERNATIONAL MANAGEMENT.
NEW YORK: HOLT RINEHART WINSTON, 1967, 178 PP., LC#67-11817.
DESIGNED FOR BASIC MANAGEMENT COURSES, TO PROVIDE THEO-
RETICAL STRUCTURE, RELEVANT DETAILS, AND CASE MATERIAL FOR
FIELD OF INTERNATIONAL MANAGEMENT. CONCERNS STRATEGY AND
INTERRELATIONSHIPS OF MARKETING, SUPPLY LABOR, MANAGEMENT,
OWNERSHIP, FINANCE, LAW, AND CONTROL.

1337 MAC CHESNEY B.
"SOME COMMENTS ON THE 'QUARANTINE' OF CUBA."
AMER. J. INT. LAW, 57 (JULY 63), 592-97.
DISCUSSES LEGAL QUESTIONS RAISED BY THE CUBAN CRISIS,
ASSERTING THAT INTERNATIONAL LAW MUST BE RE-INTERPRETED
WITHIN THE CONTEXT OF THE MID-TWENTIETH CENTURY'S POLITICS.
FEELS USA FOLLOWED DOCTRINE OF SELF-DEFENSE.

1338 MACDONALD A.F.
ELEMENTS OF POLITICAL SCIENCE RESEARCH.
ENGLEWOOD CLIFFS: PRENTICE HALL, 1928.
PRACTICAL HANDBOOK DESCRIBING CONCISELY CHIEF SOURCES
AND THEIR USES IN POLITICAL SCIENCE. COVERS MATERIAL IN
FEDERAL AND OTHER LAWS, JUDICIAL DECISIONS, CONGRESSIONAL
DEBATES AND DOCUMENTS, FOREIGN LEGISLATIVE DEBATES, EXECU-
TIVE REPORTS, ETC. CONCLUDES WITH LIST OF SOURCES FOR
COMMON POLITICAL SCIENCE COURSES.

1339 MACHOWSKI K.

"SELECTED PROBLEMS OF NATIONAL SOVEREIGNTY WITH REFERENCE
TO THE LAW OF OUTER SPACE."
PROC. AMER. SOC. INT. LAW, 55 (APR. 61), 169-74.
WARNS AGAINST POSSIBILITY OF USING OUTER SPACE FOR MILIT-
ARY PURPOSES. ASSERTS THAT ANY LEGAL SETTLEMENT ON MAN'S
ACTIVITY MUST BE BASED ON THE SAME PREMISES, NAMELY THE PRE-
SERVATION OF SECURITY OF STATES.

1340 MACIVER R.M. ED.
GREAT EXPRESSIONS OF HUMAN RIGHTS.
NEW YORK: HARPER, 1950, 321 PP.
SURVEYS MAGNA CHARTA, THE AMERICAN BILL OF RIGHTS, NATU-
RAL LAWS, THE DECLARATION OF THE RIGHTS OF MAN AND CITIZEN.
STUDIES LINCOLN'S POLITICAL ACTION. DISCUSSES THE FUNERAL
ORATION OF PERICLES. RELATES INDIVIDUAL FREEDOM TO SOCIAL
DETERMINISM.

1341 MACIVER R.M.
THE PREVENTION AND CONTROL OF DELINQUENCY.
NEW YORK: ATHERTON PRESS, 1966, 215 PP., LC#66-20835.
REVIEWS THE LITERATURE AND THE METHODOLOGY DEALING WITH
AMERICAN JUVENILE DELINQUENCY AND PROJECTS BOLD NATIONAL
STRATEGIES TO PREVENT AND CURE IT. TREATS CAUSATION AND
CONDITIONS THAT FEED ANTISOCIAL BEHAVIOR IN MINORS.

1342 MACKENZIE W.J.M.
FREE ELECTIONS: AN ELEMENTARY TEXTBOOK.
NEW YORK: RINEHART, 1958, 184 PP., $3.50.
PRESENTS GENERAL DISCUSSION OF ELECTORAL SYTEMS, AND PRO-
CEEDS TO MORE SPECIFIC DESCRIPTION OF VARIOUS COMPONENTS,
I.E. VOTING QUALIFICATIONS, VOTING SYSTEMS, AND CANDIDATES.
CONCLUDES WITH DESCRIPTION OF VARIOUS IRREGULARITIES FOUND
WITHIN THE MANY DIFFERENT ELECTORAL SYSTEMS.

1343 MACKINNON F.
"THE UNIVERSITY: COMMUNITY OR UTILITY?"
CAN. PUBLIC ADMIN., 3 (DEC. 60), 337-343.
THOUGHTS WELL APPLICABLE TO AN AMERICAN UNIVERSITY ON
THE NATURE OF UNIVERSITY ENTERPRISE AS A COMBINATION OF
SCHOLARSHIP AND BUSINESS (FINANCING) RATHER THAN AS A
SERVICE INDUSTRY. DESCRIBES DIVISION OF RESPONSIBILITY IN
MANAGEMENT, THE DEMANDS OF THE STATE AND COMMUNITY, TAX
PARTICIPATION, AND CARE FOR STUDENTS.

1344 MACLEOD R.M.
"LAW, MEDICINE AND PUBLIC OPINION: THE RESISTANCE TO COM-
PULSORY HEALTH LEGISLATION 1870-1907."
PUBLIC LAW, (SUMMER 67), 07-128.
DISCUSSES CONTROVERSY OVER COMPULSORY VACCINATION IN
1870, FACTORS THAT LED TO ABOLISHMENT, AND INTERACTION OF
LAW, MEDICINE, AND PUBLIC OPINION IN DEVELOPMENT OF
VICTORIAN MEDICAL CARE. OBJECTIONS WERE SCIENTIFIC, MORAL,
RELIGIOUS, AND CONSTITUTIONAL, AND WERE ORGANIZED UNDER
SELECT COMMITTEE OF 1871.

1345 MACMULLEN R.
ENEMIES OF THE ROMAN EMPIRE: TREASON, UNREST, AND ALIENA-
TION IN THE EMPIRE.
CAMBRIDGE: HARVARD U PR, 1966, 370 PP., LC#66-18250.
HISTORICAL ANALYSIS OF "UN-ROMAN" ACTIVITIES WITHIN THE
ROMAN EMPIRE, SHOWING SOCIAL CONDITIONS WHICH GAVE RISE TO
TREASONOUS DEEDS AND LEGAL BOUNDARIES WHICH DEFINED ACTS
AS DETRIMENTAL TO THE EMPIRE. POINTS OUT THAT OPPOSITION
AND DEVIATION POSSESSED A SHARE IN THE POWER THAT ALSO CON-
TROLLED THE ESTABLISHMENT, AND EVENTUALLY CORRUPTED AND
BROUGHT ABOUT SOCIAL DISINTEGRATION IN ROME.

1346 MACWHINNEY E.
"LES CONCEPT SOVIETIQUE DE 'COEXISTENCE PACIFIQUE' ET LES
RAPPORTS JURIDIQUES ENTRE L'URSS ET LES ETATS OCIDENTAUX."
REV. GEN. DR. INT. PUB., 34 (NO., 63), 545-62.
DEALS WITH SOVIET INTERPRETATION OF 'PEACEFUL COEX-
ISTENCE) AND ITS APPLICATION TO INTERNATIONAL LAW. STUDIES
INFLUENCE OF LAW ON TRANSFORMATION OF SOCIETIES. DISCUSSES
JURIDICAL RELATIONS BETWEEN EAST AND WEST AS VIEWED THROUGH
SOVIET DOCTRINE AND TACTICS USED TO ACHIEVE SOVIET GOALS.

1347 MAGGS P.B.
"SOVIET VIEWPOINT ON NUCLEAR WEAPONS IN INTERNATIONAL LAW."
LAW CONTEMP. PROBL., 29 (AUTUMN 64), 956-70.
EXPLAINS SOVIET APPROACH TO LEGAL PROBLEMS CONNECTED WITH
THE MILITARY USE OF NUCLEAR WEAPONS AS WELL AS THE TESTING,
CONSTRUCTION, POSSESSION, STATIONING AND TRANSFER OF SUCH
WEAPONS.

1348 MAGRATH C.P.
YAZOO; LAW AND POLITICS IN THE NEW REPUBLIC: THE CASE OF
FLETCHER V. PECK.
PROVIDENCE: BROWN U PRESS, 1966, 243 PP., LC#66-1984.
PRESENTS FULL ACCOUNT OF FLETCHER V. PECK, FIRST CONTRACT
CASE BEFORE US SUPREME COURT IN 1810, THAT FATHERED KEY
DOCTRINES. SHOWS THAT YAZOOISTS OF NEW ENGLAND MISSISSIPPI
LAND COMPANY FORMED FIRST LOBBY GROUP AGAINST SUPREME
COURT. PROVIDES INSIGHTS INTO AMERICAN CONSTITUTIONAL
POLITICS AND SUPREME COURT'S FUNCTION IN POLITICAL PROCESS.
APPENDIXES OF ALL MAJOR YAZOO DOCUMENTS.

1349 MAINE H.S.
INTERNATIONAL LAW.
LONDON: MURRAY, 1894, 234 PP.
DEALS WITH ORIGINS, SOURCES AND AUTHORITY OF INTERNATION-
AL LAW. CONSIDERS THE PROBLEM OF SANCTION. STUDIES STATE
SOVEREIGNITY AND TERRITORIAL RIGHTS. SURVEYS THE DECLARATION
OF PARIS. GIVES PROPOSAL FOR ELIMINATING WAR.

1350 MAINE H.S.
ANCIENT LAW.
NEW YORK: HOLT, 1887, 400 PP.
STUDIES ANCIENT CODES AND THEIR ECO-POLITICAL BACKGROUND.
ANALYZES THE CONCEPTS OF LAW OF NATURE AND EQUITY. CONSIDERS
ANCIENT AND MODERN IDEAS ABOUT WILLS AND SUCCESSIONS AND
EXPLORES THE EARLY HISTORY OF CONTRACTS, PROPERTY AND CRIME.

1351 MAINE H.S.
LECTURES ON THE EARLY HISTORY OF INSTITUTIONS.
NEW YORK: HENRY HOLT & CO, 1875, 412 PP.
A SOCIAL AND LEGAL HISTORY OF BASIC INSTITUTIONS IN EARLY
CULTURES. SPECIAL ATTENTION IS GIVEN TO ANCIENT IRISH
(BREHON) LAW AS APPLIED IN EARLY CELTIC SOCIETIES. DISCUSSES
KINSHIP AS BASIS OF PROPERTY OWNERSHIP, ROLE OF THE CHIEF,
DIVISIONS OF FAMILY, AND GROWTH AND DIFFUSION OF IDEAS.
FINAL CHAPTERS DEAL WITH ROMAN LAW AND CONCEPT OF SOVER-
EIGNTY AS INTERPRETED BY BENTHAM, AUSTIN, AND BLACKSTONE.

1352 MAIR L.P.
THE PROTECTION OF MINORITIES.
LONDON: CHRISTOPHERS, 1928, 232 PP.
POINTS OUT EXAMPLES OF PAST CONSIDERATION OF PROBLEM, FO-
CUSING ON MINORITIES TREATIES. DESCRIBES CONDITIONS FOR MI-
NORITIES IN ALMOST ALL EUROPEAN COUNTRIES. CONCLUDES WITH
CASE STUDIES RELATED TO NATIONALITY.

1353 MAJUMDAR B.B. ED.
PROBLEMS OF PUBLIC ADMINISTRATION IN INDIA.
BANKIPORE: BHARATI BHAWAN, 1953, 310 PP.
SCHOLARS' VIEWS ON ADMINISTRATION IN INDIA AND PUBLIC
PLANNING, PUBLIC CORPORATIONS AND GOVERNMENT CONTROL, EXEC-
UTIVES IN CIVIL SERVICE, JUDICIAL ADMINISTRATION, AND LOCAL
ADMINISTRATION AND FINANCE.

1354 MAKI J.M.
COURT AND CONSTITUTION IN JAPAN; SELECTED SUPREME COURT
DECISIONS, 1948-60.
SEATTLE: U OF WASHINGTON PR, 1964, 445 PP., LC#63-9940.
TRANSLATIONS OF SELECTED JAPANESE SUPREME COURT
CONSTITUTIONAL DECISIONS FROM 1948 TO 1960. DECISIONS DEAL
WITH LAND REFORMS, FAMILY STRUCTURE, GOVERNMENT RELATIONS,
FREEDOM, AND INDIVIDUAL RIGHTS.

1355 MAKI J.M.
COURT AND CONSTITUTION IN JAPAN: SELECTED SUPREME COURT
DECISIONS, 1948-60.
SEATTLE: U OF WASHINGTON PR, 1964, 445 PP., LC#63-9940.
TWENTY-SIX COURT DECISIONS, CHOSEN ON THE BASIS OF THEIR
BROAD SOCIAL RELEVANCE, DEALING WITH RIGHTS OF INDIVIDUAL
BEFORE THE LAW, CHANGES IN FAMILY STRUCTURE, AND ASSORTED
OTHER TOPICS. INCLUDES TRANSLATION OF JAPANESE CONSTITUTION.

1356 MANGIN G.
"LES ACCORDS DE COOPERATION EN MATIERE DE JUSTICE ENTRE LA
FRANCE ET LES ETATS AFRICAINS ET MALGACHE."
REV. JURID. POLIT. OUTREMER, 16 (JULY-SEPT. 62), 339-64.
IDENTIFIES AGREEMENTS BETWEEN FRANCE AND AFRICAN STATES
ON PROBLEMS OF JUSTICE, TRANSITIONAL DISPOSITION OF JUDICIAL
PERSONNEL. TREATS FRENCH EFFECT ON AFRICAN EVOLUTION. IN-
CLUDES LIST OF ARTICLES DEALING WITH CIVIL AND CRIMINAL LAW.

1357 MANGIN G.
"L'ORGANIZATION JUDICIAIRE DES ETATS D'AFRIQUE ET DE
MADAGASCAR."
REV. JURID. POLIT. OUTREMER, 16 (JAN.-MARCH 62), 77-134.
DESCRIBES JUDICIAL ORGANIZATION IN DEVELOPING AFRICAN
COUNTRIES, CLARIFYING DIFFERENCES AND COMMON FEATURES.
STUDIES STRUCTURE OF TRIBUNALS AND EXTENT OF POWER. CON-
CLUDES WITH STUDY OF SUPREME COURTS.

1358 MANGONE G.
"THE IDEA AND PRACTICE OF WORLD GOVERNMENT."
NEW YORK: COLUMB. U. PR., 1951, 278 PP.
ENUMERATES VARIOUS FORMS PREFERABLE FOR WORLD GOV-
ERNMENT. DESCRIBES PROBABLE SUBSEQUENT ECONOMIC AND SPIRITU-
AL PROGRESS. DENOTES PLACE OF JUSTICE AND INTERNATIONAL LAW
IN NEW WORLD ORGANIZATION.

1359 MANGONE G.
A SHORT HISTORY OF INTERNATIONAL ORGANIZATION.
NEW YORK: MCGRAW-HILL, 1954, 326 PP.
HISTORICALLY TRACES DEVELOPMENT OF INTERNATIONAL ORGANIZ-
ATIONS FROM NAPOLEONIC ERA TO THE UN. DISCUSSES INCEPTION
AND GROWTH OF INTERNATIONAL LAW.

1360 MANN S.Z.
"POLICY FORMULATION IN THE EXECUTIVE BRANCH: THE

TAFT-HARTLEY EXPERIENCE."
WESTERN POLIT. QUART., 13 (SEPT. 60), 597-608.
DISCUSSION OF CONFLICT BETWEEN NLRB, DEPARTMENT OF LABOR,
AND BUREAU OF BUDGET ON PROPOSED CHANGES IN WAGNER ACT.
SINCE THE EXECUTIVE BRANCH COULD NOT AGREE, CONGRESS PASSED
A BILL REPUGNANT TO PRESIDENT TRUMAN.

1361 MANNHEIM H.
CRIMINAL JUSTICE AND SOCIAL RECONSTRUCTION.
NEW YORK: OXFORD U PR, 1946, 290 PP.
DISCUSSION OF HOW LEGAL SYSTEM SHOULD BE MODERNIZED IN
LIGHT OF PRESENT SOCIAL CHANGE, ESPECIALLY IN AREAS OF PRO-
TECTION OF HUMAN LIFE, SEXUAL AND FAMILY RIGHTS, AND ECONOM-
ICS. IMPORTANT VALUES MUST BE CHOSEN, METHODS TO PROTECT
THEM DECIDED ON, AND CRIMINAL JUSTICE COMPLETELY REPLANNED.

1362 MANNING B.
FEDERAL CONFLICT OF INTEREST LAW.
CAMBRIDGE: HARVARD U PR, 1964, 285 PP., LC#64-21244.
DESCRIPTION OF THE FEDERAL LAW REGULATING CONFLICTS OF
INTERESTS OF FEDERAL EMPLOYEES. TECHNICAL REVIEW OF LAWS AS
MODERNIZED UP TO JANUARY, 1963.

1363 MANSERGH N., WILSON R.R. ET AL.
COMMONWEALTH PERSPECTIVES.
DURHAM: DUKE U PR, 1958, 214 PP., LC#58-11381.
ESSAYS BY ECONOMISTS, HISTORIANS, AND POLITICAL SCIEN-
TISTS ON STRUCTURE OF BRITISH COMMONWEALTH AND FORCES
PULLING FOR UNITY AND SEPARATENESS. INCLUDES TOPICS OF
MEMBERSHIP, FOREIGN POLICY FROM 1945-56, LAWS AFFECTING
MEMBER NATIONS, DEMOGRAPHY AND ITS PULL TO UNITY AND DIS-
UNITY, EMERGENCE OF GHANA, HEALTH AND WELFARE PROGRAMS IN
AUSTRALIA, AND EVOLUTION OF STERLING AREA.

1364 MANVELL R., FRAENKEL H.
THE INCOMPARABLE CRIME.
NEW YORK: G P PUTNAM'S SONS, 1967, 339 PP., LC#67-20286.
STUDY OF THE PERFECTION, MECHANIZATION, AND COMMERCIAL-
ZATION OF GENOCIDE BY THE THIRD REICH. INCLUDES ACCOUNTS OF
MURDERERS AND SURVIVORS. INVESTIGATES SIGNIFICANCE AND HIS-
TORICAL ROOTS OF GENOCIDE AND TRIES TO EXPLAIN WHY IT WAS
ACCEPTED. INCLUDES SELECTED BIBLIOGRAPHY OF APPROXIMATELY
EIGHTY ITEMS.

1365 MARITAIN J.
HUMAN RIGHTS: COMMENTS AND INTERPRETATIONS.
NEW YORK: COLUMB. U. PR., 1949, 288 PP.
ESSAYS DEALING WITH THE GENERAL PROBLEMS OF HUMAN RIGHTS.
ANALYZES IN DETAIL SUCH SUBJECTS AS: THE RESPECT OF CULTURAL
DIVERSITY, THE SOCIAL IMPLICATION OF SCIENCE, THE VALUE OF
OBJECTIVE INFORMATION, THE RIGHT TO EDUCATION, AND THE
SPECIAL POSITION OF PRIMITIVE PEOPLES.

1366 MARKE J.J. ED.
A CATALOGUE OF THE LAW COLLECTION AT NEW YORK UNIVERSITY,
WITH SELECTED ANNOTATIONS.
NEW YORK: NYU, SCHOOL OF LAW, 1953, 1372 PP., LC#53-6439.
ANNOTATED BIBLIOGRAPHICAL GUIDE TO 8000 VOLUMES CATEGOR-
IZED INTO ELEVEN SECTIONS. A SYSTEMATIC SURVEY OF PRINTED
MATERIALS IN THE LIBRARY RELATING TO ENTIRE FIELD OF LAW,
EXCLUDING FOREIGN LAW, FROM ORIGINS OF LEGAL THEORY TO
1951. ENTRIES GEOGRAPHICALLY ARRANGED WITHIN TOPICAL SEC-
TIONS.

1367 MARNELL W.H.
THE FIRST AMENDMENT: THE HISTORY OF RELIGIOUS FREEDOM IN
AMERICA.
GARDEN CITY: DOUBLEDAY, 1964, 247 PP., LC#64-16556.
TRACES CHURCH-STATE RELATIONSHIP FROM REFORMATION TO
REVEAL BELIEFS OF FOREFATHERS WHO WROTE FIRST AMENDMENT.
FEELS PROOF OF US CONCERN TO PROTECT DIVERSE "RELIGIOUS
ESTABLISHMENTS" LIES HERE. US GOVERNMENT BASED ON CLOSE
RELATION WITH CHRISTIANITY, NOT SECULARISM, AND NOT ANY ONE
STATE CHURCH. CONCENTRATES ON BELIEFS OF US PEOPLE AS OUT-
GROWTH OF CONSTITUTION. BIBLIOGRAPHY OF WORKS CITED IN TEXT.

1368 MARS D.
SUGGESTED LIBRARY IN PUBLIC ADMINISTRATION.
LOS ANGELES: U OF S CAL, PUB ADM, 1962, 133 PP.
INDEXED BIBLIOGRAPHY ON PUBLIC ADMINISTRATION AIMS AT
SELECTING MOST IMPORTANT WORKS IN THIS FIELD. ALSO INCLUDES
PERIODICALS DEALING WITH PUBLIC ADMINISTRATION AND MANAGE-
MENT. AN OUTGROWTH OF THE BERKELY BRAZIL PROJECT DESIGNED
PRIMARILY FOR OVERSEAS LIBRARIES.

1369 MARSHALL B.
FEDERALISM AND CIVIL RIGHTS.
NEW YORK: COLUMBIA U PRESS, 1964, 85 PP., LC#64-7533.
DISCUSSES ANOMALIES AND PRACTICAL QUESTIONS ARISING OUT
OF CIVIL RIGHTS STRUGGLE OF 1960'S. SHOWS HOW THESE
QUESTIONS CHALLENGE US FEDERAL, CONSTITUTIONAL SYSTEM.
ANALYZES PROBLEM OF FEDERAL POLICING OF CIVIL RIGHTS AND OF
STATE'S ABROGATION OF THEIR RESPONSIBILITY. TREATS
IMPORTANCE OF SUCH QUESTIONS FOR EVERY CITIZEN OF FEDERAL
SYSTEM.

1370 MARSHALL G.
"POLICE RESPONSIBILITY."
PUBLIC ADMINISTRATION, 38 (FALL 60), 213-226.
LOCAL POLICE OFFICIALS HAVE BOTH ADMINISTRATIVE AND
QUASI-JUDICIAL FUNCTIONS. TO PRESERVE REPRESENTATIVE
GOVERNMENT POLICE SHOULD BE FULLY RESPONSIBLE FOR
ADMINISTRATIVE FUNCTIONS TO AN ELECTED BODY.

1371 MARTENS E.
DIE HANNOVERSCHE KIRCHENKOMMISSION.
AMSTERDAM: VERLAG P SCHIPPERS, 1965, 384 PP.
EXAMINES DEVELOPMENT AND LEGAL STRUCTURE OF CHURCH COM-
MISSION OF HANNOVER, GERMANY FROM 1569 TO PRESENT. DISCUSSES
CONSTITUTIONAL BASIS, SECULAR FUNCTIONS, AND INTERNAL
ORGANIZATION.

1372 MARTIN A., YOUNG W.
"PROLIFERATION."
DISSERTATION ABSTRACTS, 3 (FALL 65), 107-134.
REJECTS FORCIBLE MEANS TO HALT PROLIFERATION AND FAVORS
UNDERGROUND TEST BAN, NON-NUCLEAR ZONES, PLUS NON-DISSEMIN-
ATION AND NON-ACQUISITION TREATIES. PROLIFERATION CAN BE
HALTED ONLY BY MASSIVE ARMS REDUCTIONS OF EXISTING NUCLEAR
POWERS.

1373 MARTIN L.J.
INTERNATIONAL PROPAGANDA: ITS LEGAL AND DIPLOMATIC CONTROL.
MINNEAPOLIS: U OF MINN PR, 1958, 284 PP., LC#58-7928.
DISCUSSES OPERATION OF PROPAGANDA AGENCIES IN VARIOUS
COUNTRIES AND ATTEMPTS MADE TO CONTROL DISSEMINATION OF PRO-
PAGANDA THROUGH MUNICIPAL LAW AND INTERNATIONAL AGREEMENTS.
INCLUDES A BRIEF HISTORICAL INTRODUCTION. CONCLUDES THAT
"INTERNATIONAL PROPAGANDA HAS LITTLE CHANCE OF BEING CON-
TROLLED AT THE INTERNATIONAL LEVEL."

1374 MARTIN L.W.
THE SEA IN MODERN STRATEGY.
NEW YORK: FREDERICK PRAEGER, 1967.
AN ANALYSIS OF THE ROLE SEA POWER PLAYS IN MODERN DIPLO-
MACY AND INTERNATIONAL POLITICS. TREATS THE GROWING ECONOMIC
IMPORTANCE OF THE SEA AND THE LEGAL CHANGES THAT SEEM LIKELY
TO OCCUR AS A RESULT. SEA POWER IS DISCUSSED IN STRATEGIC
TERMS AS A FACTOR IN GENERAL AND LIMITED WAR AND IN NON-BEL-
LIGERENT PRESSURE. DISCUSSES BLOCKADE,FUTURE OF THE AIRCRAFT
CARRIER, ANTI-SUBMARINE WARFARE, AND SEA NUCLEAR FORCES.

1375 MARX C.M.
"ADMINISTRATIVE ETHICS AND THE RULE OF LAW."
AM. POL. SCI. REV., 43 (DEC. 49), 1119-1144.
EXPLORES INTERPLAY OF ADMINISTRATIVE ETHICS AND ADMINIS-
TRATIVE LAW TO UNDERSTAND DIFFERENCE IN OUTLOOK BETWEEN AN
OFFICIAL CHARGED WITH EXECUTION OF PUBLIC POLICY AND A JUDGE
ENFORCING LEGAL RESTRAINTS. REJECTS EFFICIENCY AS AN ETHICAL
NORM; SEES AS CRITERION THE CONFORMITY BETWEEN ADMINISTRA-
TION AND THE FUNDAMENTAL VALUES OF THE POLITICAL ORDER.

1376 MASON A.T.
THE SUPREME COURT FROM TAFT TO WARREN.
BATON ROUGE: LOUISIANA ST U PR, 1958, 250 PP., LC#58-10292.
HISTORICAL DISCUSSION OF THE SUPREME COURT OVER A 40-
YEAR PERIOD, WITH SPECIAL EMPHASIS GIVEN TO JUDICIAL
CAREERS OF TAFT, HUGHES, AND STONE. CONTENDS THAT REGARDING
THE COURT AS AN INSTRUMENT OF POLITICAL POWER LIMITS ITS
EFFECTIVENESS; JUDICIAL DECISIONS HAVE BEEN RENDERED MORE
ACCEPTABLE BECAUSE OF THE BELIEF THAT THE COURT MERELY
PRONOUNCED THE LAW, DECIDING NOTHING.

1377 MASON A.T.
"THE SUPREME COURT: TEMPLE AND FORUM" (BMR)
YALE REVIEW, 48 (SUMMER 59), 524-540.
BEGINS WITH BRIEF HISTORY OF PUBLIC CONDEMNATION OF
SUPREME COURT POWER. DISCUSSES JUDICIAL SUPREMACY VERSUS
JUDICIAL REVIEW. CONCENTRATES ON WARREN COURT AND
PROTECTION OF CIVIL LIBERTIES. AUTHOR FEELS SUPREME COURT
MUST PROTECT POLITICAL RIGHTS OF MINORITIES, BUT ALLOW
MAJORITY TO RULE.

1378 MASON A.T.
THE SUPREME COURT: PALADIUM OF FREEDOM.
ANN ARBOR: U OF MICH PR, 1962, 207 PP., LC#62-18443.
COVERS HISTORY OF US POLITICAL MODELS; TREATS IN DETAIL
DECLARATION OF INDEPENDENCE, ARTICLES OF CONFEDERATION,
AND THE CONSTITUTION. STUDIES JUDICIAL REVIEW AND JUDICIAL
SUPREMACY FROM JEFFERSON AND MARSHALL TO ROOSEVELT AND
HUGHES. INCLUDES NOTES AND INDEX.

1379 MASON A.T., BEANEY W.M.
AMERICAN CONSTITUTIONAL LAW: INTRODUCTORY ESSAYS AND
SELECTED CASES (3RD ED.)
ENGLEWOOD CLIFFS: PRENTICE HALL, 1964, 588 PP., LC#64-17199.
INTRODUCTORY TEXT. EACH SECTION INTRODUCED BY ESSAY ON
HISTORICAL AND POLITICAL CONTEXTS OF THE VARIOUS CASES, AND
DEVELOPING LEGAL DOCTRINES ARE TRACED THROUGH RELEVANT
DECISIONS. SEES SUPREME COURT AS MAJOR PARTICIPANT IN
PROCESS OF GOVERNMENT, AND DECISIONS AS CHOICES BETWEEN
ALTERNATIVES, INFLUENCED BY CONTEMPORARY PRESSURES. QUOTES

DISSENTING AND CONCURRING OPINIONS.

1380 MASON H.L.
TOYNBEE'S APPROACH TO WORLD POLITICS.
NEW ORLEANS: TULANE U PR, 1958, 151 PP.
EXPLICATES TOYNBEE'S THEORY OF HISTORY AND ANALYZES PRO-
POSALS HE MAKES FOR CONSIDERING PRESENT WORLD RELATIONS.
EMPHASIZES HIS RELIGIOUS SOLUTION FOR WORLD PROBLEMS.

1381 MASON J.B.
"THE JUDICIAL SYSTEM OF THE NAZI PARTY."
AM. POL. SCI. REV., 38 (FEB. 44), 96-103.
EXAMINES ORIGIN, PURPOSE, AND LEGAL STATUS OF NAZI PARTY
COURTS; DESCRIBES STRUCTURE OF PARTY'S LOCAL, DISTRICT, AND
SUPREME COURTS. FROM AN AMERICAN LEGAL PERSPECTIVE,
EVALUATES JUDGES, JUDGMENTS, AND PARTY COURTS AS HITLER'S
INSTRUMENTS.

1382 MASSEL M.S.
THE REGULATORY PROCESS (JOURNAL REPRINT)
WASHINGTON: BROOKINGS INST, 1961, 22 PP.
SUMMARY OF CRITICISMS OF THE FEDERAL REGULATORY PROCESS.
SAYS PROCEDURAL CHANGES ALONE CANNOT SOLVE PROBLEMS: MORE
RESEARCH INTO POLITICAL NATURE OF ADMINISTRATION IS NEEDED.

1383 MASTERS R.D.
INTERNATIONAL LAW IN INTERNATIONAL COURTS.
NEW YORK: COLUMBIA U. PR., 1932, 245 PP.
'DEALS WITH THE ENFORCEMENT OF PARTICULAR AND UNIVERSAL,
CUSTOMARY AND CONVENTIONAL INTERNATIONAL LAW IN THE COURTS
OF GERMANY, SWITZERLAND, FRANCE, AND BELGIUM.'

1384 MATTHEWS D.G. ED.
"ETHIOPIAN OUTLINE: A BIBLIOGRAPHIC RESEARCH GUIDE."
AFR. BIBLIOG. CTR., SPEC. SERIES, 4 (FEB. 66), 1-17.
SUPPLEMENT TO "A CURRENT BIBLIOGRAPHY ON ETHIOPIAN AF-
FAIRS." PREPARED FOR INTERNATIONAL CONFERENCE OF ETHIOPIAN
STUDIES HELD APRIL 2-8, 1966. CONTAINS CHRONOLOGICAL AND RE-
SEARCH DATA LISTING NEW ETHIOPIAN CABINET AS OF APRIL 11,
1966. SUBJECT BIBLIOGRAPHY OF 93 UNANNOTATED ENTRIES PUB-
LISHED BETWEEN 1960-65; AUTHOR INDEX.

1385 MATTHEWS D.G. ED.
"PRELUDE-COUP D'ETAT-MILITARY GOVERNMENT: A BIBLIOGRAPHICAL
AND RESEARCH GUIDE TO NIGERIAN POL AND GOVT, JAN, 1965-66."
AFR. BIBLIOG. CTR., SPEC. SERIES, 4 (MAR. 66), 1-21.
FIRST ISSUE OF "BIBLIO-RESEARCH SERIES," DESIGNED TO
AUGMENT BIBLIOGRAPHICAL INFORMATION WITH CHRONOLOGICAL, BIO-
GRAPHICAL, AND RESEARCH DATA. CONTAINS CHRONOLOGY OF EVENTS
FROM 1965-66; LISTING OF MEMBERS OF NIGERIAN FEDERAL GOVERN-
MENT AS OF MARCH 31, 1965; LISTING OF OTHER MINISTERS AND
GOVERNORS; AND A BIBLIOGRAPHY OF GOVERNMENT MATERIALS FROM
1964-65 ARRANGED GEOGRAPHICALLY.

1386 MATTHEWS M.A.
THE AMERICAN INSTITUTE OF INTERNATIONAL LAW AND THE CODIFI-
CATION OF INTERNATIONAL LAW (PAMPHLET)
NEW YORK: CARNEGIE ENDOWMENT, 1933, 17 PP.
LIST OF OFFICIAL PUBLICATIONS OF THIS PAN AMERICAN ORGAN-
IZATION FROM 1913-32 FOLLOWED BY UNOFFICIAL REPORTS AND
ARTICLES FROM SAME PERIOD. ENTRIES IN ALL HEMISPHERIC LAN-
GUAGES WITH SOME EUROPEAN COMMENTS ON INTERNATIONAL LAW IN
AMERICAS. ARRANGED BY AUTHOR, LIST OF UNOFFICIAL PUBLICA-
TIONS IS ANNOTATED.

1387 MATTHEWS M.A.
DIPLOMACY: SELECT LIST ON DIPLOMACY, DIPLOMATIC AND CONSULAR
PRACTICE, AND FOREIGN OFFICE ORGANIZATION (PAMPHLET)
NEW YORK: CARNEGIE ENDOWMENT, 1936, 7 PP.
OVER 70 TITLES PUBLISHED OVER BROAD TIME SPAN, ARRANGED
BY AUTHOR. MOSTLY BOOKS, WITH FEW GOVERNMENT DOCUMENTS.

1388 MATTHEWS M.A.
INTERNATIONAL LAW: SELECT LIST OF WORKS IN ENGLISH ON PUBLIC
INTERNATIONAL LAW: WITH COLLECTIONS OF CASES AND OPINIONS.
NEW YORK: CARNEGIE ENDOWMENT, 1936, 21 PP.
INCLUDES BOOKS AND TREATISES PRIMARILY. SEPARATED INTO
GENERAL WORKS (NUMBERING 200) AND 21 TITLES AT END DEALING
WITH CASES AND OPINIONS. ARRANGED BY AUTHOR; BRIEF ANNO-
TATIONS. PUBLICATIONS COVER BROAD TIME SPAN, MOSTLY 20TH
CENTURY. (PAMPHLET)

1389 MATTHEWS R.O.
"THE SUEZ CANAL DISPUTE* A CASE STUDY IN PEACEFUL SETTLE-
MENT."
INTL. ORGANIZATION, 21 (WINTER 67), 79-101.
AN EXAMINATION OF THE ROLE OF THE UN AND METHODS USED FOR
SETTLING THE SUEZ CONFLICT OF 1956 PEACEFULLY. ROLES OF THE
VARIOUS GOVERNMENTS AND PERSONALITIES INVOLVED ARE PRESENT-
ED. AUTHOR HYPOTHESIZES FROM THIS CASE AS TO HOW FUTURE
INTERNATIONAL CONFLICTS MAY BE RESOLVED PEACEFULLY.

1390 MAYANJA A.
"THE GOVERNMENT'S PROPOSALS ON THE NEW CONSTITUTION."
TRANSITION, 7 (AUG.-SEPT. 67), 20-25.
CRITICIZES PROPOSED CONSTITUTION FOR UGANDA AS FALLING

FAR SHORT OF WHAT IT SHOULD BE. CLAIMS ENTIRELY TOO MUCH POWER IS INVESTED IN PRESIDENT. WARNS OF POSSIBLE EFFECTS OF THIS UPON FREEDOM AND PARLIAMENTARY PROCESS.

1391 MAYDA J. ED.
ATOMIC ENERGY AND LAW.
SAN JUAN: U OF PUERTO RICO, 1959, 254 PP.
CONSIDERS PROBLEMS OF BOTH TECHNICAL AND LEGAL ASPECTS IN USE OF ATOMIC POWER IN UNDERDEVELOPED COUNTRIES. DISCUSSES PRODUCTION, STORAGE, SALE, APPLICATION, AND DISPOSAL IN ATTEMPTING TO SET NEW POLICY FOR SOUTH AMERICAN GOVERNMENTS TO FOLLOW.

1392 MAYER A.J.
POLITICAL ORIGINS OF THE NEW DIPLOMACY, 1917-1918.
NEW HAVEN: YALE U PR, 1959, 393 PP., LC#59-6799.
SEEKS TO EXPLICATE POLITICAL DYNAMICS OF EMERGENCE OF NEW DIPLOMACY. EXAMINES POLITICS OF WAR AIMS IN WWI. ANALYZES INTERACTION BETWEEN DOMESTIC AND INTERNATIONAL POLITICS.

1393 MAYER M.
"THE IDEA OF JUSTICE AND THE POOR."
PUBLIC INTEREST, 8 (SUMMER 67), 96-115.
DISCUSSES PROBLEM OF OBTAINING LEGAL AID WITHOUT PROPER INCOME OR SOCIAL BACKGROUND. FEELS LEVELS OF INCOME NEEDED TO USE LEGAL AID SOCIETIES IN CITIES ARE UNFAIR. POINTS OUT THAT PEOPLE WHO MOST NEED LEGAL AID EITHER DO NOT KNOW ABOUT IT, OR GET CHEATED BY HAVING AVAILABLE LAWYERS FORCED ON THEM. INCLUDES CASES FROM SEVERAL LARGE CITIES TO SUPPORT VIEWS.

1394 MAYERS L.
THE AMERICAN LEGAL SYSTEM.
NEW YORK: HARPER & ROW, 1955, 589 PP., LC#54-8972.
EXAMINES ROLE AND PROCESSES OF COURTS AND ADMINISTRATIVE TRIBUNALS IN US. BRIEFLY DISCUSSES MILITARY AND VOLUNTARY ARBITRATION TRIBUNALS AND THEIR CONTROL BY COURTS. EXAMINES JUDICIAL CONTROL OF LEGISLATIVE, EXECUTIVE, AND ADMINISTRATIVE ACTION. DOES NOT INCLUDE STATE OR LOCAL ADMINISTRATIONS OF JUSTICE.

1395 MAYO L.H., JONES E.M.
"LEGAL-POLICY DECISION PROCESS: ALTERNATIVE THINKING AND THE PREDICTIVE FUNCTION."
G. WASH. LAW REV., 33 (OCT. 64), 318-456.
CREATION AND ANALYSIS OF DECISION MAKING MODELS AND THEIR RELATION TO LEGAL-POLICY SITUATIONS. DISCUSSES STUDY OF CONSEQUENCES OF RATIONAL DECISIONS.

1396 MAZZINI J.
THE DUTIES OF MAN.
NEW YORK: DUTTON, 1955, 336 PP.
'WHATEVER MEN HAVE SAID, MATERIAL INTERESTS HAVE NEVER CAUSED, AND NEVER WILL CAUSE, A REVOLUTION. REVOLUTIONS HAVE THEIR ORIGIN IN THE MIND, IN THE VERY ROOT OF LIFE: NOT IN THE BODY, IN THE MATERIAL ORGANISM. A RELIGION OR A PHILOSOPHY, LIES AT BASE OF EVERY REVOLUTION.' CONCEIVES NATIONS 'NOT AS MONSTERS LIKE THE LEVIATHAN OF HOBBES BUT AS SUBLIMATED INDIVIDUAL HUMAN BEINGS.'

1397 MC CONNELL J.P.
LAW AND BUSINESS: PATTERNS AND ISSUES IN COMMERCIAL LAW.
NEW YORK: MACMILLAN, 1966, 656 PP., LC#66-18768.
EXPLAINS AMERICAN LEGAL SYSTEM AND BUSINESS LAW WITH EMPHASIS ON INTANGIBLE RIGHTS, TORTS, AND CONTRACTS.

1398 MC REYNOLDS D.
"THE RESISTANCE."
NEW POLITICS, 6 (WINTER 67), 57-61.
EXAMINES RESISTANCE MOVEMENT IN US AGAINST SERVICE IN VIETNAM WAR. STUDIES SEVERAL ALTERNATIVES OPEN TO RESISTERS: FLIGHT TO CANADA, DESERTION, COURT MARTIAL, UNDERGROUND, AND CONSCIENTIOUS OBJECTION. DISCUSSES ORGANIZATION OF MOVEMENT IN US, DRAFT CARD TUR-INS, SUPPORT BY ADULTS, AND NEED FOR SUSTAINING IDEOLOGY TO SUPPORT EFFORTS AT RESISTANCE.

1399 MCBRIDE J.H.
THE TEST BAN TREATY: MILITARY, TECHNOLOGICAL, AND POLITICAL IMPLICATIONS.
WASHINGTON: US GOVERNMENT, 1967, 197 PP., LC#67-14660.
TRACES BACKGROUND OF TREATY, INCLUDING RELATIVE LEVELS OF NUCLEAR DEVELOPMENT IN US AND USSR. NOTES OPPOSITE CONCLUSIONS REACHED BY TWO SENATE COMMITTEES INVESTIGATING TREATY INDEPENDENTLY. ANALYZES MILITARY AND TECHNOLOGICAL ADVANTAGES AND DISADVANTAGES FOR US. DISCUSSES TESTING AND SAFEGUARDS DEMANDED BY JOINT CHIEFS. ANALYZES POLITICAL ADVANTAGES CLAIMED, NOTING ONLY ONE AS PERSUASIVE.

1400 MCCLEERY R.
"COMMUNICATION PATTERNS AS BASES OF SYSTEMS OF AUTHORITY AND POWER" IN THEORETICAL STUDIES IN SOCIAL ORGAN. OF PRISON-BMR SYDNEY: SOC SCI RES COUN AUSTRAL, 1960.
STUDIES ADMINISTRATION AND SOCIAL CHARACTERISTICS OF OLD AUTHORITARIAN PRISON. CHANGES INTRODUCED AND ADMINISTRATIVE AND SOCIAL CONSEQUENCES, AND PROCESSES OF RECONSTRUCTION IN OFFICIAL AND INTIMATE GROUPS. DISCUSSES EXERCISE OF POWER, ORGANIZATION AND COMMUNICATION, INMATE SOCIETY, AND LIBERAL MANAGEMENT POLICIES.

1401 MCCLURE W.
INTERNATIONAL EXECUTIVE AGREEMENTS.
NEW YORK: COLUMB. U. PR., 1941, 449 PP.
DEMONSTRATES INCREASED UTILIZATION OF DEMOCRATIC METHOD. COMPREHENSIVE REVIEW OF EXECUTIVE AGREEMENTS SHOWS EXTENSIVE USE OF METHOD.

1402 MCCONNELL G.
THE STEEL SEIZURE OF 1952 (PAMPHLET)
UNIVERSITY: U ALABAMA PR, 1960, 53 PP.
DESCRIBES EVENTS OF 1952 NATIONAL CRISIS IN STEEL INDUSTRY. BREAKDOWN OF NEGOTIATIONS THREATENED STRIKE. ATTEMPTS TO EVALUATE GOVERNMENTAL SEIZURE OF CONTROL IN NATIONAL INTEREST.

1403 MCDOUGAL M.S.
"THE COMPARATIVE STUDY OF LAW FOR POLICY PURPOSES."
YALE LAW J., 6 (JUNE 52), 915-946.
COMPARATIVE LAW STUDY IS VITAL IN POLICY-MAKING. POINTS OUT EXISTING INADEQUACIES IN THIS AREA AND BIDS FOR A TEAM OF SPECIALISTS TO DEVELOP REMEDIES THROUGH CONCENTRATED STUDY OF FOREIGN JUDICIAL SYSTEMS AND LAWS. EVALUATES ROLES OF STATES, ASSOCIATIONS, POLITICAL PARTIES AND PRESSURE GROUPS. SEES A BASIC DRIVE FOR POWER IN THESE GROUPS.

1404 MCDOUGAL M.S., LIPSON L.
"PERSPECTIVES FOR A LAW OF OUTER SPACE."
AMER. J. INT LAW, 2 (JULY, 58), 407-31.
DUE TO INTERDEPENDENCE OF SCIENTIFIC, MILITARY, AND COMMERCIAL OBJECTIVES, AND ACTIVITIES IN OUTER SPACE AN INTERNATIONAL CONVENTION FOR OUTER SPACE LAW IS NOT NOW POSSIBLE. FORECAST LAUNCHING OF SATELLITES FOR AND REGISTRATION BY U.N. AND UNILATERAL DISARMAMENT AS FIRST STEPS IN FUTURE CODE OF LAWS.

1405 MCDOUGAL M.S., LASSWELL H.D.
"THE IDENTIFICATION AND APPRAISAL OF DIVERSE SYSTEMS OF PUBLIC ORDER (BMR)"
AMER. J. OF INT. LAW, 53 (1959), 1-29.
DISCUSSES ROLE OF SCHOLAR IN RESEARCHING SYSTEMS OF GOVERNMENT AND MODERNIZING INTERNATIONAL LAW TO MAKE IT EFFECTIVE IN TODAY'S POLITICAL SITUATION. EXAMINES PROBLEMS OF RECONCILING DIFFERENT IDEOLOGIES TO PEACEFUL COEXISTENCE.

1406 MCDOUGAL M.S., FELICIANO F.P.
LAW AND MINIMUM WORLD PUBLIC ORDER.
NEW HAVEN: YALE U. PR., 1961, 872 PP.
STUDYING JURIDICAL PROCEDURES IN INTERNATIONAL RELATIONS, OUTLINES EXISTANT METHODS OF COERCION AND FUTURE TRENDS IN FIELD OF INTERNATIONAL CONTROL. PROCEEDS TO STUDY PROBLEM AS RELATED TO INTERPRETATION OF LAW, STATE PARTICIPATION, SANCTIONS, OPEN WARFARE (LOCAL LEVEL), AND ACTUAL MILITARY OCCUPATION.

1407 MCDOUGAL M.S., BURKE W.T.
THE PUBLIC ORDER OF THE OCEANS.
NEW HAVEN: YALE U. PR., 1962, 1226 PP.
CLARIFICATION OF 'COMMON INTEREST' IN CONTINUED MAINTENANCE OF AN INTERNATIONAL LAW OF THE SEA WHICH REJECTS ALL CLAIMS OF SPECIAL INTEREST AND UPHOLDS EVERY DECISION IN FAVOR OF INCLUSIVE RATHER THAN EXCLUSIVE INTERESTS. SURVEYS THE ARBITRAMENT PROCESSES BY WHICH GENERAL WORLD COMMUNITY ALLOCATES ACCESS TO, AND AUTHORITY OVER, THE OCEANS DURING TIMES OF RELATIVE PEACE.

1408 MCDOUGAL M.S., LASSWELL H.D.
"THE ENJOYMENT AND ACQUISITION OF RESOURCES IN OUTER SPACE."
U. PENN. LAW REV., 3 (MAR. 63), 521-636.
A COMPREHENSIVE REVIEW OF THE MORE PROMINENT FEATURES OF THE PROBABLE PROCESS OF INTERACTION FOR THEIR POTENTIAL SIGNFICANCE TO CLAIM, POLICY, AND DECISION.' THE ARTICLE COMPRISES A CHAPTER FROM THE FORTHCOMING BOOK, LAW AND PUBLIC ORDER IN SPACE. THE DESCRIPTION OF POTENTIAL SPACE RESOURCES, ESPECIALLY THE CELESTIAL BODIES AND THEIR RANGE OF POSSIBLE USES, IS UNIQUE.

1409 MCDOUGAL M.S.
"THE SOVIET-CUBAN QUARANTINE AND SELF-DEFENSE."
AMER. J. INT. LAW, 57 (JULY 63), 597-604.
ALTHOUGH USSR DID NOT EXECUTE ARMED ATTACK AGAINST USA, THE MEANS IT APPLIED INDICATED THE DANGER THAT COULD EMANATE FROM CUBAN TERRITORY. ARTICLE 51 OF THE U.N. CHARTER JUSTIFIES AMERICAN 'QUARANTINE' OF 1962.

1410 MCDOUGAL M.S., LASSWELL H.D., VLASIC I.A.
LAW AND PUBLIC ORDER IN SPACE.
NEW HAVEN: YALE U PR, 1963, 1147 PP., LC#63-13968.
ANALYSIS OF PRESENT STATUS AND LAW, AND NATIONAL POLICY RELATED TO OUTER SPACE. EXAMINES MAJOR PROBLEMS IN DECISION-MAKING REGARDING EARTH-SPACE ACTIVITY AND INTERNATIONAL RELATIONS AS MAN MORE DEEPLY EXPLORES SPACE.

1411 MCDOUGAL M.S. ED.
STUDIES IN WORLD PUBLIC ORDER.
NEW HAVEN: YALE U PR, 1964, 1058 PP., LC#60-7827.
ANTHOLOGY OF ARTICLES ABOUT INTERNATIONAL LAW IN THE
TWENTIETH CENTURY. COVERS GENERAL THEORY OF INTERNATIONAL
LAW, LAW OF THE SEA, LEGAL ASPECTS OF NUCLEAR TESTING, AND
SPACE LAW. EMPHASIZES THE DIGNITY OF MAN AS THE OVERRIDING
GOAL OF LAW. CONCLUDES WITH COMPARISON OF LEGAL THEORIES.

1412 MCDOUGAL M.S., LASSWELL H.D., MILLER J.C.
THE INTERPRETATION OF AGREEMENTS AND WORLD PUBLIC ORDER:
PRINCIPLES OF CONTENT AND PROCEDURE.
NEW HAVEN: YALE U PR, 1967, 448 PP., LC#67-13442.
RELATES INTERNATIONAL AGREEMENTS TO PROCESS OF
COMMUNICATION, AND DISCUSSES NEW APPROACHES TO THEORY OF
COMMUNICATION AND PARTICIPATION OF NEW NATIONS. APPRAISES
ADEQUACY OF TRADITIONAL PRINCIPLES OF INTERPRETATION AND
SUGGESTS A SYSTEMIZATION AND MODERIZATION OF THESE
PRINCIPLES.

1413 MCGHEE G.C.
"EAST-WEST RELATIONS TODAY."
DEPT OF STATE BULLETIN, 50 (MAR. 64), 488-496.
PRESENTS ARGUMENTS FOR AND AGAINST TWO DIFFERENT
APPROACHES TO CURRENT PROBLEMS IN EAST-WEST RELATIONS. ONE
IS TO SEARCH PATIENTLY FOR SMALL AREAS OF AGREEMENT. SECOND
IS TO REFUSE SMALL CONCESSIONS WITHOUT PROGRESS TOWARD
SOLUTIONS OF MAJOR PROBLEMS. ADVOCATES COOPERATION OF ALL
WESTERN COUNTRIES IN FORMULATING POLICY OF AGREEMENT
WHENEVER POSSIBLE.

1414 MCGRATH J.J. ED.
CHURCH AND STATE IN AMERICAN LAW.
MILWAUKEE: BRUCE, 1962, 413 PP., LC#62-19190.
CONTAINS RECORDS OF CASES DECIDED BY SUPREME AND LOWER
COURTS AFFECTING RELIGION AND CHURCH-STATE RELATIONS. AL-
THOUGH NO EVALUATION IS GIVEN OF DECISIONS, CASES ARE AR-
RANGED TOPICALLY AND FINAL CHAPTER GIVES BRIEF DISCUSSION
OF MAJOR LEGAL TRENDS IN AMERICA.

1415 MCGRATH J.J. ED.
CHURCH AND STATE IN AMERICAN LAW: CASES AND MATERIALS.
MILWAUKEE: BRUCE, 1962, 412 PP., LC#62-19190.
PRIMARY COURT CASES THAT REPRESENT US LAW ON GOVERNING
INDIVIDUAL CHURCHES, AND RELATION OF GOVERNMENT TO CHURCH
ACTIVITIES IN VARIOUS AREAS OF US LIFE. CHURCH-SCHOOLS,
PROSELYTIZING, ETC. EACH CASE GIVEN CONTEXTUAL INTRODUCTION
AND LIST OF ADDITIONAL SIMILAR CASES.

1416 MCILWAIN C.H.
THE HIGH COURT OF PARLIAMENT AND ITS SUPREMACY
B1910 1878 408.
NEW HAVEN: YALE U PR, 1910, 408 PP.
OF LAW, DEVELOPMENT OF LEGISLATION, PARLIAMENT AS A COURT
RELATION OF JUDICIARY AND LEGISLATURE, AND DEVELOPMENT
OF PARLIAMENT TO ROLE OF SUPREMACY. FOCUSES ON GROWTH OF
ENGLISH HIGH COURT DURING THE MIDDLE AGES.

1417 MCILWAIN C.H.
CONSTITUTIONALISM AND THE CHANGING WORLD.
NEW YORK: MACMILLAN, 1939, 312 PP.
ANALYZES HISTORICAL DEVELOPMENT OF GOVERNMENTAL
PROCESSES THAT ARE THE BASIS OF THE MODERN WORLD. STUDY
FOCUSES ON ENGLISH SYSTEM, AND INCLUDES DISCUSSION OF SOVER-
EIGNTY, DUE PROCESS, FUNDAMENTAL LAW BEHIND THE US
CONSTITUTION, GOVERNMENT BY LAW, AND LIBERAL AND
TOTALITARIAN IDEALS. ALSO STUDIES MAGNA CARTA, HOUSE OF
COMMONS, AND ENGLISH JUDGES.

1418 MCILWAIN C.H.
CONSTITUTIONALISM, ANCIENT AND MODERN.
ITHACA: CORNELL U PRESS, 1940, 162 PP.
BELIEVES THAT TO SECURE LIBERTY MEN MUST FIGHT FOR LEGAL
LIMITS ON ARBITRARY POWER AND FOR GOVERNMENTAL RESPON-
SIBILITY TO THE GOVERNED. DISCUSSES DEFINITIONS AND CON-
CEPTIONS OF CONSTITUTIONALISM. CONSIDERS CONSTITUTIONALISM
IN ROME, MIDDLE AGES, AND FROM MEDIEVAL TO MODERN TIMES.
DISCUSSES PROBLEMS OF MODERN CONSTITUTIONALISM.

1419 MCILWAIN C.H.
CONSTITUTIONALISM: ANCIENT AND MODERN.
ITHACA: CORNELL U PRESS, 1947, 182 PP.
TRACES DEVELOPMENT OF CONSTITUTIONALISM BY NOTING ITS
SALIENT FEATURES IN COUNTRIES WHERE ITS DEVELOPMENT IS MOST
OBVIOUS AND MOST DIRECTLY RELATED TO CONTEMPORARY SYSTEMS.
DEFINES CONSTITUTIONALISM IN MODERN USAGE. CONSIDERS ROME,
EUROPE IN MIDDLE AGES, AND BOTH EUROPE AND US NOW. OUTLINES
BASIC PROBLEMS OF MODERN CONSTITUTIONALISM.

1420 MCKAY R.B.
REAPPORTIONMENT: THE LAW AND POLITICS OF EQUAL
REPRESENTATION.
NEW YORK: TWENTIETH CENT FUND, 1965, 498 PP., LC#65-26764.
DISCUSSES STATE LEGISLATIVE APPORTIONMENT AND CONGRES-
SIONAL DISTRICTING IN US IN LIGHT OF SUPREME COURT ONE-MAN-
ONE-VOTE RULING. INCLUDES HISTORICAL BACKGROUND, PRESENT

SITUATION, AND FUTURE OF FEDERALISM.

1421 MCLAUGHLIN A.C. ED., HART A.B. ED.
CYCLOPEDIA OF AMERICAN GOVERNMENT (3 VOLS.)
NEW YORK: APPLETON, 1914.
THREE-VOLUME ENCYCLOPEDIA INTENDED FOR GENERAL READER.
INCLUDES THEORY AND PHILOSOPHY OF GOVERNMENT, FORMS OF PO-
LITICAL ORGANIZATION, METHODS AND AGENCIES BY WHICH LAW AND
GOVERNMENTAL PURPOSES ARE CARRIED OUT. TREATS INTER-
NATIONAL AND CONSTITUTIONAL LAW, PARTY ORGANIZATION AND AC-
TION, AND SIGNIFICANT AND FUNDAMENTAL PRINCIPLES OF ECONOMIC
THEORY. INCLUDES BIBLIOGRAPHIES.

1422 MCLAUGHLIN A.C.
A CONSTITUTIONAL HISTORY OF THE UNITED STATES.
NEW YORK: APPLETON, 1935, 833 PP.
PRESENTS BRIEFLY AND CLEARLY 200 YEARS OF CONSTITUTIONAL
HISTORY. TRACES CONSTITUTIONAL DEVELOPMENTS THROUGH 1932.
APPROACHES HISTORY THROUGH IMPORTANT ISSUES AND CASES.
GIVES DISPROPORTIONATELY BRIEF EMPHASIS TO FIRST THIRD OF
20TH CENTURY.

1423 MCMAHON A.H.
"INTERNATIONAL BOUNDARIES."
J. ROYAL SOC. ARTS, 84 (NOV. 25), 2-13.
ACCOUNT OF AUTHOR'S BOUNDARY-MAKING EXPERIENCES. REFERS
DISTINCTION BETWEEN DELIMITATION AND DEMARCATION. FORMER
SIGNIFY AGREEMENTS. LATTER SIGNIFY PHYSICAL MARKERS. FEELS
DEMARCATION NECESSARY TO LESSEN CHANCES OF CONFLICT.

1424 MCNAIR A.D.
THE LAW OF TREATIES: BRITISH PRACTICE AND OPINIONS.
NEW YORK: COLUMBIA U PRESS, 1938, 578 PP.
PRESENTS BRITISH PRACTICE IN THE CONCLUSION, TERMINATION,
INTERPRETATION, SCOPE, AND MODIFICATION OF TREATIES. STATES
LAWS WHICH ARE RELEVANT TO PRECEDING TOPICS. LEGAL SOURCES
WITH WHICH IT DEALS ARE PRECEDENTS OF BRITISH GOVERNMENT
AND DECISIONS OF BRITISH COURTS. AUTHOR EMPHASIZES THAT WORK
IS NOT AN OFFICIAL GOVERNMENT ONE AND THAT IT IS NOT A
TREATISE ON THE INTERNATIONAL LAW OF TREATIES.

1425 MCNAIR A.D.
THE LEGAL EFFECTS OF WAR.
NEW YORK: CAMBRIDGE U PRESS, 1966, 469 PP.
EXAMINES IMPACT OF WAR ON LEGAL POSITION OF PRIVATE PER-
SONS, WITH EMPHASIS ON ENGLISH LAW AND EFFECTS WHICH OCCUR
WHEN BRITAIN IS BELLIGERENT OR NEUTRAL. DISCUSSES IMPACT ON
TRADE, EMPLOYMENT, CONTRACTS, BILLS OF EXCHANGE, ETC.

1426 MCNAMEE B.J., PAYNE E.M.
"CONFLICT OF INTEREST: STATE GOVERNMENT EMPLOYEES."
VIRGINIA LAW REV., 47 (OCT. 61), 1034-1076.
REVIEW OF CONFLICT OF INTEREST LAWS AND PRACTICES.
SUCH LAWS ARE NECESSARY TO INSURE THAT STATE EMPLOYEES ACT
ONLY IN THE PUBLIC INTEREST.

1427 MCWHINNEY E.
"CO-EXISTENCE, THE CUBA CRISIS, AND COLD WAR-INTERNATIONAL
WAR."
INT. J., 18 (WINTER 62), 67-74.
APPRAISES THE IMMEDIATE AFTERMATH OF CUBAN MISSILE CRISIS
AND INFERS THAT CONCEPT OF CO-EXISTENCE IS SOUND. FURTHER
APPLICATION OF INTERNATIONAL LAW WILL DEPEND ON THE BALANCE
OF POWER IN THE COLD WAR ENVIRONMENT.

1428 MCWHINNEY E.
CONSTITUTIONALISM IN GERMANY AND THE FEDERAL CONSTITUTINAL
COURT.
LEYDEN: AW SIJTHOFF, 1962, 71 PP.
EXAMINES BONN CONSTITUTION AND CONSTITUTIONAL COURT
INCLUDING ITS NATURE AND ORGANIZATION, JUDICIAL EXPERIMENTA-
TION, AND ACTIVISM.

1429 MCWHINNEY E.
"PEACEFUL COEXISTENCE" AND SOVIET-WESTERN INTERNATIONAL LAW.
LEYDEN: AW SIJTHOFF, 1964, 135 PP., LC#64-22593.
COMPARES SOVIET THEORY AND PRACTICE OF "PEACEFUL
COEXISTENCE" AS DEFINED IN LAW TO POSITIONS TAKEN BY SOVIET
LEADERS IN INTERNATIONAL AFFAIRS. RELATES CURRENT SOVIET
CAMPAIGN TO SOVIET POSITION ON INTERNATIONAL LAW AND
EXAMINES WESTERN RESPONSES TO CAMPAIGN.

1430 MCWHINNEY E.
"CHANGING INTERNATIONAL LAW METHOD AND OBJECTIVES IN THE
ERA OF THE SOVIET-WESTERN DETENTE."
AMER. J. INT. LAW, 59 (JAN. 65), 1-15.
ACCOMMODATION BETWEEN SOVIET AND WEST MUTES DOCTRINAL LE-
GAL DEBATE. SHIFT DUE TO SOVIET MOVING CLOSER TO WESTERN
CONCEPT OF CLASSICAL INTERNATIONAL LAW. BOTH SIDES SHOULD
AND ARE SEEKING 'LOW-LEVEL, EMPIRICALLY-BASED, STEP-BY-STEP
APPROACH' OF 'POLITICS OF MUTUAL EXAMPLE.'

1431 MCWHINNEY E.
JUDICIAL REVIEW IN THE ENGLISH-SPEAKING WORLD (3RD ED.)
TORONTO: U OF TORONTO PRESS, 1965, 244 PP.
EXAMINES ROLE OF ENGLISH-SPEAKING COURTS FACED WITH DI-

VERSE WRITTEN CONSTITUTIONS. ADVOCATES GREATER AND MORE DY-
NAMIC PARTICIPATION IN POLICY-MAKING BY COURTS.

1432 MECHAM J.L.
THE UNITED STATES AND INTER-AMERICAN SECURITY, 1889-1960.
AUSTIN: U OF TEXAS PR, 1961, 514 PP., LC#61-1-426.
DESCRIBES POSITION OF US IN OAS. EXAMINES STRUCTURE OF
INTER-AMERICAN ALLIANCE AND CHANGES IN RELATIONS THROUGH
TWO WORLD WARS. STUDIES DEVELOPMENT OF OAS AND INTEGRATION
OF INTER-AMERICAN SYSTEM INTO UN.

1433 MEDER A.E. JR.
LEGISLATIVE APPORTIONMENT.
BOSTON: HOUGHTON MIFFLIN, 1966, 28 PP.
ANALYZES VARIOUS MATHEMATICAL METHODS USEFUL IN DETERMIN-
ATION OF APPORTIONMENT POLICY. INCLUDES APPENDIX ON MEASUR-
ING INEQUALITY OF REPRESENTATION.

1434 MEIKLEJOHN A.
FREE SPEECH AND ITS RELATION TO SELF-GOVERNMENT.
NEW YORK: HARPER & ROW, 1948, 107 PP.
ADVOCATES CAREFUL CONSIDERATION OF CONSTITUTIONAL RIGHTS
BY ALL CITIZENS, PARTICULARLY RIGHT OF FREE SPEECH. CON-
TENDS THAT CONTRARY TO FIRST AMENDMENT, AVERAGE CITIZEN'S
RIGHT TO FREE SPEECH IS CONSTANTLY IN PERIL OF CURTAILMENT
BY FEDERAL GOVERNMENT. DESCRIBES AMERICAN INDIVIDUALISM AS
IDEALIZED BY THE CONSTITUTION AND AS IT ACTUALLY IS, REG-
ULATED BY FEDERAL GOVERNMENT.

1435 MEIKLEJOHN D.
FREEDOM AND THE PUBLIC: PUBLIC AND PRIVATE MORALITY IN
AMERICA.
SYRACUSE: SYRACUSE U PRESS, 1965, 163 PP., LC#65-23650.
INQUIRY INTO RELATION BETWEEN PUBLIC AND PRIVATE INTER-
ESTS. ATTEMPTS TO RESOLVE CONFLICT BETWEEN FREEDOM (PRIVATE
INTERESTS) AND THE PUBLIC GOOD, BY BRINGING TO "BEAR UPON
THOSE DEBATES THE MOST ENDURING THEMES IN AMERICAN POLITICAL
THINKING."

1436 MENDELSON W.
"JUDICIAL REVIEW AND PARTY POLITICS" (BMR)"
VANDERBILT LAW REV., 12 (MAR. 59), 447-457.
CONTENDS THAT COURT INTRUSION UPON NATIONAL POLICY IS
STRONGEST IN PERIODS OF PARTY WEAKNESS AND IRRESPONSIBILITY.
EXAMINES CORRELATION BETWEEN JUDICIAL SUPREMACY AND PARTY
INEFFICIENCY. COMPARES US, UK, AND AUSTRALIA. CONCLUDES
THAT JUDICIAL PERSUASIVENESS MULTIPLIES WHEN POLITICAL
OPPOSITION IS LACKING.

1437 MENDELSON W.
CAPITALISM, DEMOCRACY, AND THE SUPREME COURT.
NEW YORK: APPLETON, 1960, 137 PP., LC#60-10146.
ANALYZES RECORD OF SIX SUPREME COURT JUSTICES TO SUPPORT
IMPORTANCE OF SUPREME COURT IN DETERMINING PUBLIC ATTITUDES
AND GOVERNMENT POLICY THROUGHOUT US HISTORY. CITES CHIEF
JUSTICE MARSHALL AND MERCANTILISM, CHIEF JUSTICE TANEY AND
JACKSONIAN DEMOCRACY, AND JUSTICE FIELD AND LAISSEZ-FAIRE;
ALSO THE RECORD OF HOLMES MARKED BY HUMILITY AND SKEPTICISM,
AND THE "NEW FREEDOM" WITH JUSTICES BLACK AND FRANKFURTER.

1438 MENDELSON W.
"THE NEO-BEHAVIORAL APPROACH TO THE JUDICIAL PROCESS: A CRI-
TIQUE"
AM. POL. SCI. REV., 57 (SEPT. 63), 593-603.
STUDY OF REPRESENTATIVE NEO-BEHAVIORALISTS AS THEY EXAM-
INE MINDS AND ATTITUDES OF SUPREME COURT JUDGES, NEO-BEHAV-
IORALISM BEING DEFINED AS NEW PSYCHOMETRIC RESEARCH IN JU-
DICIAL DECISION-MAKING.

1439 MENDELSON W.
JUSTICES BLACK AND FRANKFURTER: CONFLICT IN THE COURT
(2ND ED.)
CHICAGO: U OF CHICAGO PRESS, 1966, 153 PP., LC#61-5781.
EXPLORES NATURE OF JUDGE'S JOB, EMPHASIZING JUSTICES
BLACK AND FRANKFURTER BECAUSE THEY REPRESENT OPPOSING
ATTITUDES OF ACTIVISM AND ANTI-ACTIVISM. DISCUSSES PROBLEMS
OF SEPARATION OF POWERS, LIMITS OF GOVERNMENTAL CONTROL, AND
FEDERALISM.

1440 MENDELSSOHN S. ED.
MENDELSSOHN'S SOUTH AFRICA BIBLIOGRAPHY (VOL. I)
LONDON: KEGAN, PAUL& CO, 1910, 1008 PP.
COMPREHENSIVE LIST, BY AUTHOR, OF THE MENDELSSOHN LIBRARY
OF WORKS IN ENGLISH, FRENCH, GERMAN. BOOKS COVER ALL FIELDS
RELATED TO SOUTH AFRICA.

1441 MERILLAT H.C.L. ED.
LEGAL ADVISERS AND INTERNATIONAL ORGANIZATIONS.
NEW YORK: OCEANA PUBLISHING, 1966, 124 PP., LC#66-20029.
LEGAL COUNSELS TO SEVERAL INTERNATIONAL ORGANIZATIONS
COMMENT ON THE INTERACTION OF NATIONAL AND INTERNATIONAL
LAW WITHIN THESE BODIES, THE CREATION OF INTERNATIONAL LAW,
AND THE ROLES AND BACKGROUNDS OF THE ADVISERS.

1442 MERRIAM C.E., GOSNELL H.F.
THE AMERICAN PARTY SYSTEM; AN INTRODUCTION TO THE STUDY OF
POLITICAL PARTIES IN THE UNITED STATES (4TH ED.)
NEW YORK: MACMILLAN, 1950, 530 PP.
DISCUSSES PERSONAL ATTRIBUTES OF POLITICAL LEADERS,
EFFECTIVENESS OF CAMPAIGN TECHNIQUES, AND RELATIONSHIP
BETWEEN ECONOMIC, SOCIAL, AND POLITICAL CHANGES. EXAMINES
STRUGGLE TO OBTAIN RIGHT TO VOTE, EVOLUTION OF MAJOR PARTY
ISSUES, SPOILS SYSTEM, INFLUENCE OF MONEY, AND NOMINATING
SYSTEMS. PUBLIC OPINION POLLS, BALLOT AND ELECTION LAWS, AND
VOTING AND NONVOTING ARE ANALYZED.

1443 MERRITT R.L.
"SELECTED ARTICLES AND DOCUMENTS ON INTERNATIONAL LAW AND
RELATIONS."
AM. POL. SCI. REV., 59 (SEPT. 65), 764-770.
AN UNANNOTATED BIBLIOGRAPHY OF ARTICLES AND DOCUMENTS ON
INTERNATIONAL LAW AND RELATIONS. INCLUDES ENGLISH-LANGUAGE,
SOME FRENCH, GERMAN, RUSSIAN, AND SPANISH ARTICLES. GROUPED
UNDER 20 HEADINGS. MATERIAL PUBLISHED FROM 1963-65.
CONTAINS 270 ENTRIES.

1444 MERTON R.K. ED., NISBET R.A. ED.
CONTEMPORARY SOCIAL PROBLEMS: AN INTRODUCTION TO THE
SOCIOLOGY OF DEVIANT BEHAVIOR AND SOCIAL DISORGANIZATION.
NEW YORK: HARCOURT BRACE, 1961, 754 PP., LC#61-12038.
DEALS WITH SPECIAL PROBLEMS WHICH TYPIFY PATTERNS OF
DEVIANT BEHAVIOR AND SOCIAL DISORGANIZATION, ESPECIALLY
IMPORTANT IN SOCIOLOGICAL RESEARCH. INCLUDES CHAPTERS ON
CRIME, RACE RELATIONS, FAMILY AND MILITARY DISORGANIZATION,
POPULATION CRISES, COMMUNITY DISORGANIZATION, ETC.

1445 MEYER C.S.
ELIZABETH I AND THE RELIGIOUS SETTLEMENT OF 1559.   68
ST. LOUIS: CONCORDIA PUBL, 1960, 182 PP.
DISCUSSES FORMATION AND ENACTMENT OF 39 ARTICLES OF
ELIZABETHAN SETTLEMENT OF 1559 OUTLINING ANGLO-CATHOLIC RE-
LIGIOUS DOCTRINE.

1446 MEYER H.H.B. ED.
SELECT LIST OF REFERENCES ON THE INITIATIVE, REFERENDUM, AND
RECALL.
WASHINGTON: LIBRARY OF CONGRESS, 1912, 102 PP., LC#12-35001.
LIST OF 788 ARTICLES AND BOOKS, INCLUDING FOREIGN
LANGUAGE SOURCES, SEPARATED BY COUNTRY, TOPIC, AND WHETHER
PRO OR CON. INCLUDES SEPARATE SECTION ON RELEVANT CONGRES-
SIONAL SPEECHES OF 1911. ENTRIES FROM LATE 19TH CENTURY TO
1911. COMPILED FOR LIBRARY OF CONGRESS.

1447 MEYER H.H.B. ED.
LIST OF REFERENCES ON EMBARGOES (PAMPHLET)
WASHINGTON: LIBRARY OF CONGRESS, 1917, 44 PP., LC#16-26004.
LIST MAKES SPECIAL REFERENCE TO LITERATURE DEALING WITH
EARLY ATTEMPTS TO PLACE EMBARGO ON EXPORTATION OF FOOD-
STUFFS AND MUNITIONS OF WAR, ESPECIALLY DURING PERIODS 1807-
1808 AND 1812-13. INTERNATIONAL ASPECTS OF QUESTION DISCUS-
SED IN BOOKS AND ARTICLES LISTED UNDER HEADING INTERNATION-
AL LAW." DISCUSSIONS AND LITERATURE ON SUBJECT ARE ARRANGED
TOPICALLY. CONTAINS AUTHOR INDEX.

1448 MEYER H.H.B. ED.
LIST OF REFERENCES ON THE TREATY-MAKING POWER.
WASHINGTON: LIBRARY OF CONGRESS, 1920, 213 PP., LC#20-26005.
LIST OF REFERENCES TO DISCUSSIONS OF CONSTITUTIONAL
ARRANGEMENTS FOR TREATY-MAKING. CONTAINS GENERAL DISCUSSIONS
ON TREATY-MAKING AS FOUND LARGELY IN TREATISES ON INTERNA-
TIONAL LAW AND DISCUSSIONS OF PRACTICE IN OTHER COUNTRIES.
DISCUSSION ON US CONSTITUTIONAL PROVISIONS IS LARGELY HIS-
TORICAL: TREATY-MAKING UNDER CONFEDERATION, ETC. ITEMS ON
SPECIAL TREATIES GROUPED CHRONOLOGICALLY. SOME 1,010 ITEMS.

1449 MEYER P.
ADMINISTRATIVE ORGANIZATION: A COMPARATIVE STUDY OF THE
ORGANIZATION OF PUBLIC ADMINISTRATION.
LONDON: STEVENS, 1957, 323 PP.
ANALYZES THE PHENOMENA OCCURRING WITHIN PUBLIC ADMINIS-
TRATION. ATTEMPTS TO DISCOVER A COMPLEX OF PHENOMENA THAT
ARE COMMON TO ALL FORMS OF PUBLIC ADMINISTRATION, REGARDLESS
OF THEIR SOCIAL FUNCTIONS. DEFINES PUBLIC ADMINISTRATION AS
THE WORK THAT GOVERNMENT DOES TO GIVE EFFECT TO A LAW.
DISCUSSES ADMINISTRATIVE SCIENCE AND ADMINISTRATIVE DIVISION
OF WORK, AUTHORITY, HIERARCHY, AND DECENTRALIZATION.

1450 MEYERS M. ED., CAWELTI J.G. ED., KERN A. ED.
SOURCES OF THE AMERICAN REPUBLIC; A DOCUMENTARY HISTORY OF
POLITICS, SOCIETY, AND THOUGHT (VOL. I, REV. ED.)
CHICAGO: SCOTT, FORESMAN & CO, 1967, 498 PP., LC#67-22300.
SELECTED READINGS ON AMERICAN HISTORY FROM 1607-1865,
DIVIDED INTO THREE SECTIONS: COLONIAL PERIOD, 1607-1763;
REVOLUTIONARY PERIOD, 1763-1828; AND CIVIL WAR ERA, 1828-65.
INCLUDES EXCERPTS FROM EMINENT LEADERS, POLITICIANS, AND
THINKERS OF EACH PERIOD AND CONCLUDES WITH MODERN
INTERPRETATIONS OF HISTORICAL EVENTS AND IDEAS. TREATS
POLITICAL, SOCIAL, ECONOMIC, AND CULTURAL DEVELOPMENTS.

1451 MEYROWITZ H.
"LES JURISTES DEVANT L'ARME NUCLAIRE."
REV. GEN. DR. INT. PUB., 67 (63), 820-73.

SEVERAL PAPERS ON NUCLEAR WEAPONS AND LAW RELATED TO WAR. STUDIES RESPONSIBILITIES OF INTERNATIONAL BODIES TO SAFE-GUARD POSITIVE RIGHTS. EXAMINES ALTERNATIVE DECISIONS ON NUCLEAR ARMS UPON WHICH JURISTS MAY BASE AND DEVELOP A CASE THEORY.

1452 MEZERIK A.G. ED.
ATOM TESTS AND RADIATION HAZARDS (PAMPHLET)
NEW YORK: INTL REVIEW SERVICE, 1961, 59 PP.
EXAMINES POSTWAR PROBLEMS OF NUCLEAR ARMS CONTROL IN REGARD TO HEALTH DANGERS, AND UN ACTIVITIES TO LIMIT USE AND SPREAD OF NUCLEAR WEAPONS. DISCUSSES TEST BAN TREATY AND CONFERENCES ON TOPIC.

1453 MEZERIK A.G.
OUTER SPACE: UN, US, USSR (PAMPHLET)
NEW YORK: INTL REVIEW SERVICE, 1960, 52 PP.
SHORT OUTLINE OF RECENT ACTIVITIES OF US AND USSR IN AND CONCERNING SPACE EXPLORATION. SURVEYS ROLE OF UN IN ATTEMPTS AT TREATY-MAKING AND REVIEWS VARIOUS THEORIES OF SOVEREIGNTY IN SPACE, COMMITTEES AND ORGANIZATIONS CONCERNED, AND PRACTICAL AND LEGAL PROBLEMS INVOLVED.

1454 MICAUD C.A.
THE FRENCH RIGHT AND NAZI GERMANY 1933-1939: A STUDY OF PUBLIC OPINION.
DURHAM: DUKE U PR, 1943, 255 PP.
FOLLOWS THE EVOLUTION OF FOREIGN POLICY OF THE FRENCH RIGHT WITH RELATION TO NAZI GERMANY. EXPLAINS THE REVERSAL OF THE RIGHT'S POSITION FROM AN ANTI-GERMAN POLICY OF INTE-GRAL DEFENSE OF THE STATUS QUO OF THE PEACE TREATIES TO THE ACCEPTANCE OF GERMAN EXPANSION IN CENTRAL AND EASTERN EUROPE.

1455 MID-EUROPEAN LAW PROJECT
CHURCH AND STATE BEHIND THE IRON CURTAIN.
NEW YORK: FREDERICK PRAEGER, 1955, 311 PP., LC#55-8105.
ANALYSIS OF LEGAL POSITION OF CHURCH IN EACH COUNTRY BE-HIND IRON CURTAIN. COVERS HISTORY OF EACH CHURCH AND VIEWS OF CHURCH LEADERS. "HOSTILITY TOWARD RELIGION IS DEEPLY ROOTED IN COMMUNIST PHILOSOPHY." BIBLIOGRAPHIES FOR FURTHER READING ON EACH COUNTRY.

1456 MILLER A.S., HOWELL R.F.
"THE MYTH OF NEUTRALITY IN CONSTITUTIONAL ADJUDICATION."
UNIV. CHICAGO LAW REV., 27 (SUMMER 60), 661-695.
SUGGESTS THAT NEUTRALITY, SAVE ON A SUPERFICIAL AND ELE-MENTARY LEVEL, IS FUTILE QUEST: MORE USEFUL TO SEARCH FOR VALUES THAT CAN BE FURTHERED BY JUDICIAL PROCESS THAN FOR NEUTRAL OR IMPERSONAL PRINCIPLES WHICH OPERATE WITHIN PROC-ESS.

1457 MILLER B.S.
"A LAW IS PASSED: THE ATOMIC ENERGY ACT OF 1946."
UNIV. CHICAGO LAW REV., 15 (SUMMER 48), 799-821.
STUDY OF ATYPICAL LEGISLATIVE HISTORY IN WHICH DEMOCRATIC PROCESSES ARE CLEARLY PORTRAYED. ANALYSIS OF CONGRESSIONAL POLICY DECISIONS IN UNIQUE SITUATIONS.

1458 MILLER E.
"LEGAL ASPECTS OF UN ACTION IN THE CONGO."
AMER. J. INT. LAW 55 (JAN. 61), 1-28.
ATTEMPTS TO DEMONSTRATE THAT CONSIDERATIONS OF LAW AND PRINCIPLE CAN PLAY A ROLE IN INTERNATIONAL ACTION, IN SPITE OF POLITICAL CONFLICT AND TENSION.

1459 MILLER E.W. ED.
THE NEGRO IN AMERICA: A BIBLIOGRAPHY.
CAMBRIDGE: HARVARD U PR, 1966, 190 PP., LC#66-14450.
ABOUT 4,000 ENTRIES ON EVERY PHASE OF NEGRO LIFE AND HIS-TORY IN US. ARRANGED IN CHAPTERS BY SUBJECTS AND EACH CHAP-TER ALPHABETICALLY BY AUTHOR; ALPHABETICAL INDEX OF AUTHORS. ENTRIES RANGE IN PUBLICATION FROM ABOUT 1950-67.

1460 MILLER H.H.
THE CASE FOR LIBERTY.
CHAPEL HILL: U OF N CAR PR, 1965, 254 PP., LC#65-16295.
DESCRIBES NINE REPRESENTATIVE LEGAL TRIALS FROM COLONIAL AMERICA CONCERNED WITH HUMAN RIGHTS AND LEADING TO DECLARA-TIONS OF HUMAN RIGHTS BY NEW STATES IN 1776. INCLUDES FREE-DOMS OF RELIGION AND PRESS, SEARCH AND SEIZURE, DUE PROCESS, AND RIGHT TO JURY.

1461 MILLER P. ED.
THE LEGAL MIND IN AMERICA.
GARDEN CITY: DOUBLEDAY, 1962, 309 PP., LC#62-15323.
COLLECTION OF DOCUMENTS, LECTURES, AND SPEECHES ON DE-VELOPMENT OF LEGAL THOUGHT IN US FROM INDEPENDENCE TO CIVIL WAR. DISCUSSES JURISDICTION OF US COURTS, NATURE OF LAW, LEGAL REFORM, PRINCIPLES OF GOVERNMENT, FUNCTION OF LEGAL PROFESSION, ETC.

1462 MILLIS W.
AN END TO ARMS.
NEW YORK: ATHENEUM, 1965, 301 PP., LC#65-12402.
ATTEMPT TO DIFFERENTIATE A "DEMILITARIZED INTERNATIONAL SOCIETY" FROM THE PROCESS OF DISARMAMENT. COMPARES HISTORI-CAL DEVELOPMENTS IN CONCEPTS OF WAR, POWER AND LAW SEARCHING FOR A COMPROMISE METHOD FOR MOVING BEYOND HARD COLD WAR STRATEGIES TO A DEMILITARIZED SYSTEM. PRESENTS A SCENARIO FOR THE DEVELOPMENT OF SUCH A SYSTEM IN 1980.

1463 MILLIS W.
INDIVIDUAL FREEDOM AND COMMON DEFENSE (PAMPHLET)
NEW YORK: FUND FOR THE REPUBLIC, 1957, 80 PP.
DISCUSSES BALANCE OF INDIVIDUAL FREEDOM AND RESTRAINTS NECESSARY TO MAINTAIN COMMON SECURITY. EXAMINES THREE MAIN AREAS IN WHICH REQUIREMENTS OF DEFENSE ARE AT VARIANCE WITH CONSTITUTIONAL RIGHTS: OBLIGATORY MILITARY SERVICE, CONTROL OR EXTIRPATION OF SEDITION OR SUBVERSIVE BELIEF, AND STRINGENT CONTROL OF ESPIONAGE. ADVOCATES REORGANIZATION OF DRAFT AND LESS CONTROL OVER GOVERNMENT INTELLIGENCE.

1464 MINAR D.W.
IDEAS AND POLITICS: THE AMERICAN EXPERIENCE.
HOMEWOOD: DORSEY, 1964, 435 PP., LC#64-24702.
PREMISE OF THE BOOK IS THAT POLITICAL THOUGHT SHOULD BE SEEN IN TERMS OF ITS RELATIONSHIP TO OTHER VARIABLES OF PO-LITICAL LIFE: BEHAVIOR, ACTION, INSTITUTIONS, POLICY, ETC. PHILOSOPHICAL IN NATURE. BOOK DISCUSSES CONTRIBUTIONS OF THE PROTESTANT REFORMATION, REVOLUTIONARY THOUGHT IN AMERICA, JACKSONIAN POLITICS, ABOLITIONISM, AND THE THREE BRANCHES OF GOVERNMENT.

1465 MINISTERE DE L'EDUC NATIONALE
CATALOGUE DES THESES DE DOCTORAT SOUTENUES DEVANT LES UNIVERSITAIRES FRANCAISES.
PARIS: MIN DE L'EDUCATION NAT.
ANNUAL PUBLICATION SINCE 1884 LISTING DOCTORAL THESES IN FRENCH UNIVERSITIES. ITEMS ARRANGED BY UNIVERSITY AND FACULTY, THEN ALPHABETICALLY BY AUTHOR.

1466 GT BRIT MIN OVERSEAS DEV LIB
TECHNICAL CO-OPERATION -- A BIBLIOGRAPHY.
LONDON: MIN OF OVERSEAS DEVEL.
MONTHLY LISTING, FIRST PUBLISHED 1964, OF CURRENT OFFICIAL PUBLICATIONS OF THE COMMONWEALTH, DOCUMENTS, PRO-CESSED AND UNPUBLISHED MATERIALS, AND OTHER REPORTS AND BULLETINS FROM FOREIGN INSTITUTIONS. ENTRIES PERTAIN TO ECO-NOMIC, SOCIAL, LEGAL, AND STATISTICAL ASPECTS OF TECHNICAL DEVELOPMENT.

1467 MIRONENKO Y.
"A NEW EXTENSION OF CRIMINAL LIABILITY IN THE USSR."
INST. FOR STUDY OF USSR, 14 (JUNE 67), 28-32.
DISCUSSES CHANGE IN CRIMINAL STATUTES DEALING WITH PROP-AGANDA, OFFICIAL EMBLEM AND FLAG OF USSR, AND CREATION OF PUBLIC DISTURBANCES WHICH INTERFERE WITH FUNCTION OF STATE OR PUBLIC INSTITUTIONS OR ENTERPRISES. SUGGESTS REASON FOR STIFF PENALTIES DUE TO CITIZENS INCREASED FEELING OF FREEDOM TO CRITICIZE.

1468 MISHKIN P.J., MORRIS C.
ON LAW IN COURTS.
NEW YORK: FDN FOR RES ON HUM BEH, 1965, 562 PP.
INTRODUCTION TO US LEGAL SYSTEM AND LAW-MAKING FUNCTION OF COURTS. CENTERS ON CONSTRUCTION AND APPLICATION OF STATUTES, BUT INCLUDES DISCUSSION OF INFLUENCE OF LEGISLATION ON JUDICIAL LAW-MAKING.

1469 MISSISSIPPI ADVISORY COMMITTEE
REPORT ON MISSISSIPPI (PAMPHLET)
WASHINGTON: US CIVIL RIGHTS COMM, 1963, 33 PP.
REPORTS ALLEGED DENIAL OF EQUAL PROTECTION OF LAW IN MISSISSIPPI, INCLUDING TESTIMONY OF NEGRO VICTIMS ON POLICE BRUTALITY, SUMMARY OF FINDINGS BY COMMITTEE, AND RECOMMEN-DATIONS.

1470 MITAU G.T. ED., CHASE H.W. ED.
PROXIMATE SOLUTIONS: CASE PROBLEMS IN STATE AND LOCAL GOVERNMENT.
NEW YORK: CHAS SCRIBNER'S SONS, 1964, 337 PP., LC#62-10216.
CASE STUDIES CONCENTRATING ON INSTITUTIONS OF STATE AND LOCAL GOVERNMENT: INTERGOVERNMENTAL RELATIONS; CONSTITU-TIONS; LEGISLATIVE, EXECUTIVE, AND JUDICIAL POWERS. ESSAYS RAISE QUESTIONS IN EACH GROUP OF CASES.

1471 MITAU G.T. ED., CHASE H.W. ED.
INSOLUBLE PROBLEMS: CASE PROBLEMS ON THE FUNCTIONS OF STATE AND LOCAL GOVERNMENT.
NEW YORK: CHAS SCRIBNER'S SONS, 1964, 351 PP., LC#64-10217.
CASE STUDIES OF PROBLEMS INVOLVING IMPORTANT FUNCTIONS OF STATE AND LOCAL GOVERNMENT: GOVERNMENT REGULATION OF POLITICAL PARTIES; TAXING AND LICENSING, WELFARE, EDUCATION AND HOUSING; BUSINESS AND LABOR RELATIONS; LOCAL ISSUES INVOLVING AIRPORTS, ZONING, AND TORT LIABILITY. EXPLANATORY ESSAYS RAISE QUESTIONS IN EACH GROUP OF CASES.

1472 MITCHELL B., MITCHELL L.P.
A BIOGRAPHY OF THE CONSTITUTION OF THE UNITED STATES.
NEW YORK: OXFORD U PR, 1964, 384 PP., LC#64-11234.
DESCRIBES ORIGIN, FORMATION, ADOPTION, AND INTERPRETATION

OF THE US CONSTITUTION. EXAMINES DISCUSSION IN RATIFYING
CONVENTIONS IN MASSACHUSETTS, VIRGINIA, AND NEW YORK.
SELECTED CASES ARE PRESENTED TO ILLUSTRATE SUPREME COURT
INTERPRETATIONS OF THE CONSTITUTION. CONSIDERS HISTORY OF
THE CONSTITUTION, THE BILL OF RIGHTS, AND THE AMENDMENTS.

1473 MITCHELL G.E. ED., PEACE W.H. ED.
THE ANGRY BLACK SOUTH.
NEW YORK: CORINTH BOOKS, 1962, 159 PP., LC#61-15876.
COLLECTION OF ARTICLES BY NEGROES DIRECTLY INVOLVED IN
FIGHT FOR FREEDOM FROM DISCRIMINATION. DISCUSSES SECOND
CLASS CITIZENSHIP, SEGREGATED SCHOOLS, MONTGOMERY BUS BOY-
COTT, SIT-INS, AND NON-VIOLENCE.

1474 MITCHELL J.D.B.
"THE CONSTITUTIONAL IMPLICATIONS OF JUDICIAL CONTROL OF THE
ADMINISTRATION IN THE UNITED KINGDOM."
CAMBRIDGE LAW JOURNAL, (APR. 67), 46-61.
ANALYZES RELATIONSHIP BETWEEN ADMINISTRATION OR PRIME
MINISTER, PARLIAMENT, AND COURTS IN ENGLAND. SEES NEED FOR
ONE TO CONTROL OTHER (FORM OF CHECKS AND BALANCES). PROVES
THEORY BY DISCUSSING FUNCTIONS OF ALL, AS LAID DOWN IN
CONSTITUTION. SUGGESTS NEED FOR CONFORMING TO LAW IN COMPLEX
SOCIETIES.

1475 MOCKFORD J.
SOUTH-WEST AFRICA AND THE INTERNATIONAL COURT (PAMPHLET)
LONDON: DIPLOMATIC PRESS, 1950, 16 PP.
DISCUSSES STATUS OF SOUTH-WEST AFRICA AND ITS PEOPLE AS
GERMAN COLONY, UNDER BRITISH RULE, AND UNDER CONTROL OF
SOUTH AFRICA. DEALS WITH SOVEREIGNTY OF SOUTH-WEST AFRICA
AND INTERNATIONAL ATTEMPTS TO SEPARATE IT FROM SOUTH AFRICAN
DOMINATION.

1476 MOCTEZUMA A.P.
EL CONFLICTO RELIGIOSO DE 1926 (2ND ED.)
MEXICO CITY: EDITORIAL JUS, 1960, 563 PP.
STUDY OF 1926 CHURCH-STATE CONFLICT IN MEXICO. COVERS
BACKGROUND LEADING TO RELIGIOUS PERSECUTION AND REBELLION.
EXAMINES LEGAL LIMITATIONS ON CHURCH ACTIVITY AND PUBLIC
OPINION REGARDING POLICIES OF GOVERNMENT AND PROGRAMS OF
CHURCH.

1477 MODELSKI G.
"STUDY OF ALLIANCES."
J. CONFL. RESOLUT., 7 (DEC. 63), 769-76.
REVIEWS RECENT BOOKS ON ALLIANCES. FAVORS FINER DIS-
TINCTIONS BETWEEN TERMS.

1478 MOELLER R.
LUDWIG DER BAYER UND DIE KURIE IM KAMPF UM DAS REICH.
VADUZ, LIECHTENSTEIN: KRAUS REPRINT CO 1965, 254 PP.
EXAMINES RELATIONSHIP BETWEEN PAPACY AND GERMAN KINGS IN
14TH CENTURY. PROBES INTO NOTIONS ABOUT CORONATION LAWS,
LEGITIMACY OF RULE WITHOUT PAPAL APPROBATION, AND EFFORTS
OF GERMAN KINGS TO ESCAPE PAPAL AUTHORITY.

1479 MOEN N.W.
THE GOVERNMENT OF SCOTLAND 1603 - 1625.
ANN ARBOR: U MICROFILMS, INC, 1958, 468 PP., LC#58-3551.
DISCUSSES POWERS OF CROWN, OPERATION OF PRIVY COUNCIL,
AND ADMINISTRATION OF JUSTICE IN SCOTLAND FROM ACCESSION OF
JAMES I TO 1625. EXAMINES IN DETAIL EXTENSION OF ROYAL
PREROGATIVE AND CONTROL OVER SCOTTISH AFFAIRS THROUGH AB-
SENTEE GOVERNMENT OF JAMES I.

1480 MOHL R.V.
DIE GESCHICHTE UND LITERATUR DER STAATSWISSENSCHAFTEN
(3 VOLS.)
BONN: FERDINAND ENKE VERLAG, 1855, 2053 PP.
SURVEYS HISTORY OF, AND LITERATURE ON, POLITICAL SCIENCE
AND POLITICAL ECONOMY. NOT FORMALLY A BIBLIOGRAPHY, BUT AN
EXTENDED TREATMENT OF MAJOR WORKS AND DEVELOPMENTS IN THE
SCIENCE OF GOVERNMENT.

1481 MOLEY R.
POLITICS AND CRIMINAL PROSECUTION.
NEW YORK: MINTON, BALCH & CO, 1929, 241 PP.
EXAMINES POLITICAL FACTORS THAT ENTER INTO CRIMINAL-LAW
ADMINISTRATION IN THE US. EMPHASIZES ROLE OF THE PROSECUTOR
AS DOMINANT OVER MAGISTRATE-JUDGE, SHERIFF, GRAND JURY, AND
PETIT JURY. DESCRIBES PROSECUTOR'S POWER TO RESTRICT ACCESS
TO RECORDS AND DROP CASES AND RELATES THESE PREROGATIVES TO
THE POLITICAL EXIGENCIES OF THE OFFICE. ATTENTION IS FOCUSED
ON MAJOR STATE OFFENSES RATHER THAN MISDEMEANORS.

1482 MOLLARD P.T.
LE REGIME JURIDIQUE DE LA PRESSE AU MAROC.
RABAT: UNIVERSITE MOHAMMED V, 1963, 183 PP.
STUDY OF LEGAL REGULATIONS REGARDING PRESS AND PUBLICA-
TIONS IN MOROCCO. DISCUSSES RIGHTS AND LIMITATIONS ON ACTION
OF JOURNALISTS IN MOROCCAN SOCIETY AND GOVERNMENTAL POWERS
TO CONTROL PUBLICATION.

1483 MONCONDUIT F.
LA COMMISSION EUROPEENNE DES DROITS DE L'HOMME.
LEYDEN, NETHERLANDS: AW SIJTHOFF, 1965, 559 PP.
WORK UNDERTAKEN UNDER AUSPICES OF COUNCIL OF EUROPE ON
EUROPEAN COMMISSION FOR HUMAN RIGHTS, THE JUDICIAL BODY OF
THE COUNCIL. PRESENTS GENERAL THEORY ON RIGHT TO JUDGE AND
ON POWERS OF COMMISSION, SPECIFIES TERMS AND IMPORT OF
TREATY WHICH CREATED IT, AND STUDIES ITS JUDICIAL ACTIONS.

1484 MONEYPENNY P.
"UNIVERSITY PURPOSE, DISCIPLINE, AND DUE PROCESS."
NORTH DAKOTA LAW REVIEW, 43 (SUMMER 67), 739-752.
DISCUSSES ROLE OF UNIVERSITY IN SHAPING STUDENT FOR LIFE
OF SELF-GOVERNMENT AND INDEPENDENT DECISION. FEELS UNIVER-
SITY CONTROL OF NONCLASSROOM ACTIVITIES SHOULD BE MINIMAL;
STUDENT SHOULD HAVE RIGHTS OF PRIVACY AND SELF-REGULATION.
ARGUES THAT STUDENT MUST HAVE DUE PROCESS OF LAW IN CASES
INVOLVING RULE INFRACTION.

1485 MONNIER J.P.
"LA SUCCESSION D'ETATS EN MATIERE DE RESPONSABILITE
INTERNATIONALE."
ANNU. FRANC. DR. INTER., 8 (1962), 65-90.
DISCUSSES QUESTION OF LEGAL OBLIGATIONS OF MANY
STATES THAT HAVE ALTERED CONSTITUTIONAL STRUCTURE. SHOWS
THAT RECENT JURIDICAL DECISIONS HAS LEFT PROBLEM UNRESOLVED.
CONCLUDES ALTERED STATE HAS RETROACTIVE RESPONSIBILITY.

1486 MONPIED E., ZALESKI E. ET AL.
BIBLIOGRAPHIE FEDERALISTE: OUVRAGES CHOISIS (VOL. I,
MIMEOGRAPHED PAPER)
PARIS: UNION FEDER INTER-UNIV, 1950, 87 PP.
LISTS AND ANNOTATES 640 ITEMS PUBLISHED PRIOR TO, DURING,
AND SINCE WORLD WAR I DEALING WITH FEDERALISM, EUROPEAN
FEDERATION, OR WORLD GOVERNMENT. ARRANGED TOPICALLY AND
CHRONOLOGICALLY.

1487 MONPIED E., ROUSSOS G., ZALESKI E.
FEDERALIST BIBLIOGRAPHY: ARTICLES AND DOCUMENTS PUBLISHED IN
BRITISH PERIODICALS 1945-1951 (MIMEOGRAPHED)
LONDON: FED TRUST FOR ED & RES, 1951, 137 PP.
COMPILES, ANNOTATES, AND INDEXES 1,354 ARTICLES DEALING
WITH WORLD FEDERALISM, EUROPEAN UNITY, ETC. RESTRICTED TO
THOSE PUBLISHED IN UK BETWEEN 1945 AND 1951.

1488 MOODY M. ED.
CATALOG OF INTERNATIONAL LAW AND RELATIONS (20 VOLS.)
NEW YORK: OCEANA PUBLISHING, 1965, 64-0000 PP.
BOOK CATALOG OF INTERNATIONAL RELATIONS. TWENTY VOLUMES
ARRANGED ALPHABETICALLY. AUTHOR, SUBJECT AND TITLE ARRANGED
IN SINGLE ALPHABETICAL FILE. CONTAINS SOME 360,000 ITEMS IN
ALL LANGUAGES.

1489 MOOS M., ROURKE F.E.
THE CAMPUS AND THE STATE.
LONDON: OXFORD U PR, 1959, 414 PP., LC#59-10768.
ABOUT ADMINISTRATIVE CONTROLS OVER STATE-SUPPORTED
COLLEGES AND UNIVERSITIES. FRUITS OF A DISTINGUISHED
COMMITTEE ON GOVERNMENT AND HIGHER EDUCATION, BOOK PROBES
DANGERS TO THE "FREE" COLLEGE TRADITION EXAMINING THE
EFFECTS OF FINANCING AND THE ROLE OF "INDEPENDENT"LAY
BOARDS, LEGISLATIVE OVERSIGHT, THE APPLICABLE LAW, CIVIL
SERVICE PROBLEMS, AND THE EFFICIENCY OF "FREE INSTITUTIONS.

1490 MOREL E.D.
THE BRITISH CASE IN FRENCH CONGO.
LONDON: HEINEMANN, 1903, 215 PP.
CRITICISM OF DRASTIC MEASURES TAKEN BY FRENCH GOVERNMENT
IN FRENCH CONGO TO INTERFERE WITH BRITISH TRADE AND ABUSE
RIGHTS OF BRITISH MERCHANTS. ARGUES THAT CONCESSIONS DECREE
OF 1899, WHICH AUTHORIZED MEASURES, VIOLATED BERLIN ACT OF
1885 THAT ESTABLISHED RIGHT OF FREE TRADE FOR ALL NATIONS
IN CONGO BASIN. ASSESSES DAMAGE DONE TO FRENCH AND BRITISH
INTERESTS BY ACTIONS OF THE CONCESSIONNAIRE REGIME.

1491 MORELAND C.C.
EQUAL JUSTICE UNDER LAW.
NEW YORK: OCEANA PUBLISHING, 1957, 128 PP., LC#57-12805.
DISCUSSES US LEGAL SYSTEM, CONSTITUTIONAL GUARANTEES,
OPERATION AND JURISDICTION OF STATE AND FEDERAL COURTS, AND
CONCLUDES WITH BRIEF DISCUSSION OF PUBLIC DEFENDER SYSTEM,
LEGAL AID, LAWYERS' REFERRAL SYSTEM, ETC. INCLUDES DOCUMEN-
TARY APPENDIX ON CONSTITUTIONAL GUARANTEES AND CANONS OF
PROFESSIONAL ETHICS.

1492 MORENO F.J.
"THE SPANISH COLONIAL SYSTEM: A FUNCTIONAL APPROACH."
WESTERN POLIT. QUART., 20 (JUNE 67), 308-320.
ANALYZES SPANISH CONCEPT OF LAW AND POWER AS WRITTEN
IN THEORY, STRESSING ITS INABILITY TO COME TO TERMS WITH,
AND APPLY TO, REALITY. THIS UNDERSTANDING IS KEY TO
EVALUATING WRITTEN SPANISH LAW REGARDING AMERICAN COLONIES.
THIS LAW PROVIDED PERFECT CHAIN OF POWER FROM KING TO
COLONIAL RULERS, YET GOVERNMENT FUNCTIONED INEFFECTUALLY
IN REALITY AND WAS VERY UNSTABLE.

1493 MORGAN G.G.
"SOVIET ADMINISTRATIVE LEGALITY: THE ROLE OF THE ATTORNEY

GENERAL'S OFFICE."
STANFORD: STANFORD U PRESS, 1962.
STUDY OF "GENERAL SUPERVISION " FUNCTION OF USSR PROCUR-
ACY - ROLE OF EXERCISING SUPERVISION OVER LEGALITY OF SUBOR-
DINATE LEGISLATION, CERTAIN TYPES OF GOVERNMENT ENACTMENTS,
AND OFFICIAL ACTIONS OF VARIOUS GOVERNMENTAL OFFICERS.
BIBLIOGRAPHY IS, FOR MOST PART, IN RUSSIAN.

1494 MORGENTHAU H.J.
POLITICS AMONG NATIONS: THE STRUGGLE FOR POWER AND PEACE.
NEW YORK: ALFRED KNOPF, 1948, 489 PP.
ATTEMPTS TO DETECT AND UNDERSTAND FORCES THAT DETERMINE
POLITICAL RELATIONS AMONG NATIONS, AND TO COMPREHEND WAYS
THOSE FORCES ACT UPON EACH OTHER. SEEKS TO UNDERSTAND
MID-20TH CENTURY POLITICS. SHOWS THAT PEACE CAN BE
MAINTAINED ONLY BY BALANCE OF POWER, INTERNATIONAL LAW AND
MORALITY, AND WORLD PUBLIC OPINION.

1495 MORGENTHAU H.J.
"THE TWILIGHT OF INTERNATIONAL MORALITY" (BMR)"
ETHICS, 58 (JAN. 48), 79-99.
DISCUSSES ETHICAL LIMITATIONS ON INTERNATIONAL POLICIES
AND DIFFERENCES IN MORAL RESTRAINTS IN TIMES OF PEACE AND
WAR. DISCUSSES ETHIC OF PROTECTING HUMAN LIFE, HOW THIS IS
MAINTAINED, AND HOW THIS IS DISREGARDED. EXAMINES UNIVERSAL
ETHICS VERSUS NATIONALISTIC UNIVERSALISM. FINDS MORALITY HAS
DISAPPEARED IN MODERN WORLD AS EACH NATION SEEKS TO IMPOSE
ITS SYSTEM ON REST OF WORLD.

1496 MORLEY F.
THE SOCIETY OF NATIONS.
WASHINGTON: BROOKINGS INST., 1932, 678 PP.
UNDERTAKES EXAMINATION OF CONSTITUTIONAL DEVELOPMENTS OF
THE LEAGUE OF NATIONS AND OF ITS GROWTH FROM FIRST PAPER
PLANS TO THE COMPLICATED INTERNATIONAL MACHINERY ESTABLISHED
AT GENEVA.

1497 MORRIS C. ED.
THE GREAT LEGAL PHILOSOPHERS: SELECTED READINGS IN
JURISPRUDENCE.
PHILA: U OF PENN PR, 1959, 571 PP., LC#57-11955.
COMPENDIUM OF GREAT LEGAL THINKERS FROM ARISTOTLE TO
ROSCOE POUND. PROVIDES BIOGRAPHICAL PROFILES. INCLUDES
CHURCH'S PHILOSOPHERS, MEMBERS OF THE HISTORICAL SCHOOL,
UTILITARIANS, AND NEO-THOMISTS. OTHERS INCLUDED ARE HEGEL,
CARDOZO, KANT, ROUSSEAU, AND LOCKE.

1498 MORRIS R.B.
FAIR TRIAL.
NEW YORK: ALFRED KNOPF, 1952, 491 PP., LC#52-06423.
RECORDS 14 TRIALS REPRESENTING MISCARRIAGE OF JUSTICE,
TO SHOW NEED FOR REFORM IN AMERICAN JURISPRUDENCE. DISCUSSES
INFLUENCE OF JUDGES AND LAWYERS AS BEING OVERLY IMPORTANT.

1499 MORRIS R.B.
THE PEACEMAKERS: THE GREAT POWERS AND AMERICAN INDEPENDENCE.
NEW YORK: HARPER & ROW, 1965, 572 PP., LC#65-20435.
ANALYSIS OF DIPLOMATIC NEGOTIATIONS INVOLVED IN OBTAINING
PEACE AND INDEPENDENCE IN REVOLUTIONARY WAR. DEALS WITH
ACTIVITIES OF REVOLUTIONARY LEADERS AND EUROPEAN POWERS TO
END CONFLICT IN 1782-83 PEACE NEGOTIATIONS.

1500 MOSER J.J.
JOHANN JACOB MOSER'S GESAMMELTE UND ZU GEMEINNUTZIGEM
GEBRAUCH EINGERICHTETE BIBLIOTHEK.
ULM: NO PUBLISHER CITED, 1958, 416 PP.
LISTS WORKS CONTAINED IN LIBRARY OF JOHANN JAKOB MOSER
ON LAWS RELATING TO ECONOMY, TRADE, MANUFACTURING INDUSTRY,
MECHANICAL AND MINING INDUSTRY.

1501 MOSKOW M.H.
TEACHERS AND UNIONS.
PHILA: U OF PENN PR, 1966, 288 PP.
STUDIES RELATIONSHIP OF US TEACHER TO ORGANIZED LABOR.
DISCUSSES REASON FOR TEACHER MILITANCY AND PUBLIC ATTITUDES
TOWARD TEACHERS' LOBBYING AND BARGAINING. COVERS LEGAL
LIMITATION AND GENERAL POLICIES OF EDUCATIONAL
ORGANIZATIONS.

1502 MOSKOWITZ M.
HUMAN RIGHTS AND WORLD ORDER.
NEW YORK: OCEANA PUBLISHING, 1958, 239 PP., LC#58-14333.
DISCUSSES STRUGGLE FOR HUMAN RIGHTS IN UN. EXAMINES
PROGRAMS FOR PROMOTION OF HUMAN RIGHTS, AND MEANING AND
PURPOSE OF THEIR IMPLEMENTATION.

1503 MOSTECKY V. ED., BUTLER W.E. ED.
SOVIET LEGAL BIBLIOGRAPHY.
CAMBRIDGE: HARVARD LAW SCHOOL, 1965, 288 PP.
INCLUDES MATERIALS PUBLISHED IN USSR SINCE 1917 AS AC-
QUIRED BY HARVARD LAW SCHOOL LIBRARY THROUGH JANUARY 1965.
4,068 ITEMS DIVIDED BY TYPE OF MATERIAL: LEGISLATION, COURT
REPORTS, ETC., AND SUBDIVIDED BY SUBJECT. CONSTITUTIONS,
ETC.; ARRANGED CHRONOLOGICALLY. SHORT ANNOTATIONS INDICATE
SCOPE OF BOOK. CONCLUDES WITH AUTHOR INDEX.

1504 MURACCIOLE L.
"LA LOI FONDAMENTALE DE LA REPUBLIQUE DU CONGO."
REV. JURID. POLIT. OUTREMER, 16 (APR.-JUNE 62), 279-311.
ANALYZES FUNDAMENTAL LAW OF CONGO REPUBLIC ENACTED ON MAY
19, 1960. LAW DEALS WITH POLITICAL ORGANIZATION. TRACES
LAW'S EVOLUTION. COMMENTS ON ITS GENERAL CHARACTERISTICS.
OUTLINES CENTRAL CONGOLEGE INSTITUTIONS. RELATES CONGO TO
SUB-SAHARAN POLITICAL SITUATIONS.

1505 MURACCIOLE L.
"LES MODIFICATIONS DE LA CONSTITUTION MALGACHE."
REV. JURID. POLIT. OUTREMER, 16 (JULY-SEPT. 62), 424-8.
BRIEF HISTORICAL ANALYSIS OF THE CONSTITUTION OF MADAGAS-
CAR. FOCUSES ON REVISIONS OF JUNE 6, 1962. POINTS OUT ARTI-
CLES DEALING WITH FREEDOM OF SPEECH. ELABORATES LAWS AND
CONSTITUTIONAL POWERS OF REPOBLIC'S PRESIDENT. INCLUDES LIST
OF MODIFIED CONSTITUTIONAL ARTICLES.

1506 MURPHY E.F.
WATER PURITY: A STUDY IN LEGAL CONTROL OF NATURAL RESOURCES.
MADISON: U OF WISCONSIN PR, 1961, 212 PP., LC#61-5902.
STUDIES LOCAL REGULATION AND STATE ADMINISTRATION OF
WATER PURIFICATION PROGRAMS IN WISCONSIN. PRESENTS LEGAL
RESOLUTION OF ECONOMIC PROBLEMS IN NATURAL RESOURCE
CONSERVATION AND INTERPLAY OF LAW AND INTEREST GROUPS.
ANALYZES TRANSLATION OF BIOLOGICAL KNOWLEDGE INTO PUBLIC
WORKS PROGRAMS. DISCUSSES PUBLIC AND OFFICIAL ATTITUDES
TOWARD VARIOUS ASPECTS OF STATE ADMINISTRATIVE CONTROL.

1507 MURPHY T.J.
CENSORSHIP: GOVERNMENT AND OBSCENITY.
BALTIMORE: HELICON PR, 1963, 294 PP., LC#63-12095.
STUDIES THE CONTROL OF OBSCENITY AS A DEMOCRATIC FUNCTION
EXERCISED BY REPRESENTATIVE AUTHORITY. CONSIDERS ANTI-OB-
SCENITY LAWS HISTORICALLY, MORALLY, AND DEMOCRATICALLY VALID
AND ESSENTIAL TO HUMAN DIGNITY. CRITICIZES DECISION-
MAKING POWER RECENTLY GAINED BY THE JUDICIARY IN SUCH AREAS
AND SUGGESTS THIS POWER BE RELEGATED TO LEGISLATIVE
REPRESENTATIVES OF THE PUBLIC.

1508 MURPHY W.F.
"LOWER COURT CHECKS ON SUPREME COURT POWER" (BMR)"
AM. POL. SCI. REV., 53 (DEC. 59), 1018-1031.
DISCUSSES MEANS BY WHICH STATE COURTS MODIFY DECISIONS
AND CHECK POWER OF SUPREME COURT. CITES RECENT CASES OF
SCHOOL SEGREGATION IN WHICH STATES HAVE EVADED OR DEFIED
FEDERAL LAW. EXAMINES RELATIONS OF STATE COURTS AND LOWER
FEDERAL COURTS. CONCLUDES WITH STUDY OF METHOD WHICH
SUPREME COURT UTILIZES TO COUNTER LOWER COURT POWER.

1509 MURPHY W.F.
CONGRESS AND THE COURT.
CHICAGO: U OF CHICAGO PRESS, 1962, 308 PP., LC#62-9739.
EXAMINES DECISIONS OF WARREN COURT AND RESULTING RESPONSE
OF CONGRESS TO DECISIONS THEMSELVES AND TO STIMULI OF
INTEREST GROUPS. INCLUDES INTERVIEWS WITH GOVERNMENT
OFFICIALS. BEGINS WITH HISTORICAL PERSPECTIVE; DISCUSSES
JUDICIAL RESTRAINT IN PAST AND RESURGENCE OF JUDICIAL POWER.
EVALUATES JENCKS BILLS, CONGRESSIONAL ATTACK, CRISIS, AND
RESOLUTION. STUDIES STRUGGLE FOR POLITICAL SUPREMACY.

1510 MURPHY W.F.
ELEMENTS OF JUDICIAL STRATEGY.
CHICAGO: U OF CHICAGO PRESS, 1964, 249 PP., LC#64-24973.
DISCUSSION OF INNER WORKINGS OF US SUPREME COURT, POLITI-
CAL CHECKS ON ITS OPERATION, AND PROCESS OF JUDICIAL DECI-
SION-MAKING.

1511 MURPHY W.F.
WIRETAPPING ON TRIAL: A CASE STUDY IN THE JUDICIAL PROCESS.
NEW YORK: RANDOM HOUSE, INC, 1965, 176 PP., LC#65-13762.
ILLUSTRATES THE WORKINGS OF THE AMERICAN JUDICIAL PROCESS
THROUGH THE HISTORY OF OLMSTEAD VS. UNITED STATES FROM
FIRST TRIAL TO SUPREME COURT. CONSIDERS IMPACT OF THIS CASE
ON SUBSEQUENT COURT DECISIONS AND ON PUBLIC POLICY.

1512 MUSIKER R. ED.
GUIDE TO SOUTH AFRICAN REFERENCE BOOKS.
CAPETOWN: U OF CAPETOWN, 1958, 43 PP.
GENERAL REFERENCE WORKS ON SOUTH AFRICA. COVERS SOCIETY
IN GENERAL, SOCIAL, BIOLOGICAL, LEGAL, AND COMMERCIAL
ASPECTS. BRIEF.

1513 MUTHESIUS V.
DAS GESPENST DER WIRTSCHAFTLICHEN MACHT.
FRANKFURT: FRITZ KNAPP VERLAG, 1960, 176 PP.
EXAMINES PROBLEM OF ECONOMIC POWER IN PRIVATE INDUSTRY.
DISCUSSES ROLE OF BANKS, MONOPOLIES, TAX LAW, ETC. MAINTAINS
THAT ECONOMIC POWER HAS NO REAL EXISTENCE INDEPENDENT OF A
STATE'S CONFERRING THAT POWER UPON PRIVATE COMPANIES.

1514 MYERS D.P.
MANUAL OF COLLECTIONS OF TREATIES AND OF COLLECTIONS
RELATING TO TREATIES.
CAMBRIDGE: HARVARD U PR, 1922, 685 PP.
CONTAINS CONTRACTUAL AND CONVENTIONAL MATERIAL OF INTER-

NATIONAL RELATIONS TO OUTBREAK OF WWI. ARRANGEMENT
OF MATERIALS DETERMINED BY CONTENT; WITHIN SUBJECT
HEADINGS ARRANGEMENT IS CHRONOLOGICAL. APPENDIX INCLUDES
NOTES ON HISTORY OF DOCUMENTS. PRINTED IN FRENCH AND
ENGLISH. CONTAINS 3,468 ITEMS.

1515 MINNESOTA LAW REVIEW EDITORS
"UNION INVESTMENT IN BUSINESS: A SOURCE OF UNION CONFLICT
OF INTEREST."
MINN. LAW REV., 46 (JAN. 62), 573-598.
UNIONS NOW CONTROL OVER FOUR BILLION DOLLARS IN
INVESTMENT CAPITAL; PRESENT LEGISLATION AND INTERNAL
UNION CONTROLS ARE INEFFECTIVE IN COPING WITH THE RESULTANT
PROBLEMS. UNION FUNDS CAN BE USED TO EXPAND MARKETS FOR A
UNIONIZED EMPLOYER AN A CONFLICT OF INTEREST IS
CREATED. FUNDS CAN ALSO BE INVESTED IN A COMPETITOR FIRM
ON A DECISION TAKEN MOSTLY BY THE INTERNATIONAL UNION.

1516 COLUMBIA LAW REVIEW EDITORS
"QUASI-LEGISLATIVE ARBITRATION AGREEMENTS."
COLUMBIA LAW REV., 64 (JAN. 64), 109-126.
RE-EVALUATES THE ATTITUDES OF MANAGEMENT, LABOR, AND
THE COURTS TOWARD ARBITRATION AS A MEANS OF RESOLVING
DISPUTES AND AS A SUBSTITUTE FOR ECONOMIC FORCE. PROBES
LETHAL EFFECTS OF CLOSING AN ESSENTIAL INDUSTRY AND ARGUES
USE OF AGREEMENTS IN ADVANCE TO ARBITRATE FUTURE DISPUTES
NOT SETTLED DURING NEGOTIATIONS AS A BETTER REPRESENTATIONAL
TECHNIQUE THAN FORCE OR COSTLY STRIKES.

1517 NAGEL S.S.
"USING SIMPLE CALCULATIONS TO PREDICT JUDICIAL DECISIONS."
AMER. BEHAVIORAL SCIENTIST, 4 (DEC. 60), 24-28.
SUCCESSFUL PREDICTION OF JUDICIAL DECISION INHERENT IN
A TRUE RULE OF LAW. USES KEY VARIABLES FROM DECIDED CASES TO
DETERMINE THE LIKELYHOOD OF JUDGMENT IN A NEW CASE.

1518 NAGEL S.S.
"A CONCEPTUAL SCHEME OF THE JUDICIAL PROCESS."
AMER. BEHAVIORAL SCIENTIST, 7 (DEC. 63), 7-10.
STIMULUS ORGANISM RESPONSE MODEL OF LEGAL PROCESS PRO-
POSED. LEGAL POLICIES ARE CONCEIVED AS RESPONSES TO PRIOR
STIMULI AND STIMULI THAT ACT ON THOSE WHO MAKE AND APPLY
POLICY. APPLIED TO LEGAL POLICY OF SCHOOL DESEGREGATION.

1519 NAGEL S.S.
"DISPARITIES IN CRIMINAL PROCEDURE."
UCLA LAW R, 14 (AUG. 67), 1272-1305
ANALYZES DISPARITIES IN TREATMENT OF CRIMINALS OF
DIFFERENT BACKGROUNDS AT ALL STAGES OF ADMINISTRATION OF
CRIMINAL PROCEDURE AT STATE AND FEDERAL LEVEL. INCLUDES
DISPARITIES OF ECONOMIC CLASS, SEX, RACE, AGE, EDUCATION,
AND AREA OF RESIDENCE. DISCUSSES CAUSES AND REMEDIES FOR
THESE DISPARITIES.

1520 NANTWI E.K.
THE ENFORCEMENT OF INTERNATIONAL JUDICIAL DECISIONS AND
ARBITAL AWARDS IN PUBLIC INTERNATIONAL LAW.
LEYDEN: AW SIJTHOFF, 1966, 209 PP., LC#66-18228.
NOTES MAJOR CASES IN HISTORY OF INTERNATIONAL ADJUDICA-
TION. DISCUSSES CONFLICT OF NATIONAL SOVEREIGNTY WITH
SUBMISSION TO ADJUDICATION; ALSO OBLIGATIONS INDUCING STATES
TO COMPLY WITH JUDGMENTS. EXAMINES MEASURES OF ENFORCEMENT
BY SINGLE NATIONS AND THOSE OF INTERNATIONAL ORGANIZATIONS.
INCLUDES VARIOUS ORGANIZATIONS CONCERNED WITH INTERNATIONAL
DISPUTES AND THEIR RESPECTIVE FUNCTIONS; ALSO EXAMPLE CASES.

1521 NARAIN I.
THE POLITICS OF RACIALISM.
NEW YORK: VERRY LAWRENCE, 1967, 304 PP.
A STUDY OF THE INDIAN MINORITY IN SOUTH AFRICA DOWN TO
THE GANDHI-SMUTS AGREEMENT. DISCUSSES THE EMIGRATION TO NA-
TAL, THE EARLY YEARS WITHOUT DISCRIMINATION TOWARD INDIANS,
ANTI-INDIAN SENTIMENT BASED ON TRADE COMPETITION AND RACIAL
PREJUDICE, ANTI-INDIAN LEGISLATION, AND THE FAILURE OF THE
IMPERIAL GOVERNMENT IN INDIA TO AID THE INDIAN EMIGRANTS.

1522 NASA
PROCEEDINGS OF CONFERENCE ON THE LAW OF SPACE AND OF
SATELLITE COMMUNICATIONS: CHICAGO 1963.
WASHINGTON: US GOVERNMENT, 1964, 205 PP.
SURVEYS LEGAL PROBLEMS OF SPACE AGE AND FORMULATES TENTA-
TIVE LEGAL VIEWS ON SPACE. TREATS PROBLEMS OF LAW AND FOR-
EIGN DIPLOMACY THAT ARE EXPECTED IN HANDLING COMMUNICATIONS
SATELLITE, BECAUSE IT IS A "YANKEE INVENTION COMMITTED
TO FREE ENTERPRISE." INCLUDES TEXT OF SATELLITE ACT OF 1962.

1523 NATIONAL MUNICIPAL LEAGUE
COMPENDIUM ON LEGISLATIVE APPORTIONMENT.
NEW YORK: NATL MUNICIPAL LEAGUE, 1960, 150 PP.
COLLECTION OF STATISTICS AND APPRAISALS FROM LOCAL NON-
OFFICIAL AUTHORITIES IN 50 STATES RELATING TO INEQUALITIES
IN LEGISLATION AND CONGRESSIONAL REPRESENTATION.

1524 NATIONAL MUNICIPAL LEAGUE
COMPENDIUM ON LEGISLATIVE APPORTIONMENT.
NEW YORK: NATL MUNICIPAL LEAGUE, 1962, 140 PP.
COLLECTION OF STATISTICS AND APPRAISALS FROM LOCAL NON-
OFFICIAL AUTHORITIES IN 50 STATES RELATING TO INEQUALITIES
IN LEGISLATIVE AND CONGRESSIONAL REPRESENTATION.

1525 NATIONAL ASSN HOME BUILDERS
COMMUNITY FACILITIES: A LIST OF SELECTED REFERENCES (PAM-
PHLET)
WASH DC: N^TL ASSN HOME BUILDERS, 1959, 170 PP.
PARTIALLY ANNOTATED COLLECTION OF 1,400 BOOKS, ARTICLES,
US GOVERNMENT DOCUMENTS, MONOGRAPHS, AND COURT CASES PUB-
LISHED FROM 1952-59 AND ARRANGED TOPICALLY. GENERAL AIM
IS TO EXPLORE FACTORS AFFECTING COMMUNITY DEVELOPMENT SUCH
AS REVENUE-FINANCING, UTILITY INSTALLATION, ZONING, AND SUB-
DIVISION DEVELOPMENT. CONCLUDING AUTHOR INDEX.

1526 NATIONAL BOOK LEAGUE
THE COMMONWEALTH IN BOOKS: AN ANNOTATED LIST.
LONDON: NATL BOOK LEAGUE, 1964, 126 PP.
LISTS BOOKS ON GEOGRAPHY, HISTORY, SOCIOLOGY, POLITICS,
LAW, AND LOCAL GOVERNMENT; BOOKS IN FRENCH FROM CANADIAN
PUBLISHERS. ANNOTATED AND ARRANGED BY SUBJECT. CONTAINS
BOOKS PUBLISHED SINCE APPROXIMATELY 1950.

1527 NATIONAL CIVIC REVIEW
REAPPORTIONMENT: A YEAR IN REVIEW (PAMPHLET)
NEW YORK: NATL MUNICIPAL LEAGUE, 1963, 54 PP.
COLLECTION OF ARTICLES, EDITORIALS, AND BOOK REVIEWS ON
APPORTIONMENT THAT APPEARED IN NATIONAL CIVIC REVIEW FROM
MAY, 1962 TO APRIL, 1963. INCLUDES DISCUSSIONS OF BAKER V.
CARR AND OTHER COURT CASES, PLANS OF VARIOUS STATES, RURAL
VERSUS URBAN CONTROVERSY, AND EQUALITY OF RIGHTS.

1528 NATIONAL MUNICIPAL LEAGUE
COURT DECISIONS ON LEGISLATIVE APPORTIONMENT (VOL. III)
NEW YORK: NATL MUNICIPAL LEAGUE, 1962, 250 PP.
COLLECTION OF DECISIONS BY US DISTRICT COURTS AND STATE
SUPREME COURTS ON MATTERS OF LEGISLATIVE APPORTIONMENT.
ITEMS ARE ACTUAL DECISIONS AS FILED BY JUSTICES, AND ARE
ARRANGED BY STATE.

1529 NAVILLE A.
LIBERTE, EGALITE, SOLIDARITE: ESSAIS D'ANALYSE.
PARIS: LIBRAIRIE PAYOT, 1924, 124 PP.
ANALYSIS OF LIBERTY, EQUALITY, AND SOLIDARITY EMPHASIZING
FREE WILL, CIVIL AND NATURAL FREEDOM, COMMERCIAL AND SOCIAL
JUSTICE INCLUDING POLITICAL HARMONY, INTEREST CONFLICT,
DEPENDENCE, COLLABORATION, AND THE SOCIETY OF NATIONS.

1530 NEGLEY G.
POLITICAL AUTHORITY AND MORAL JUDGMENT.
DURHAM: DUKE U PR, 1965, 163 PP., LC#65-13654.
STUDIES AUTHORITY AS A LEGAL OBLIGATION AND MORAL
"FICTION," EMPHASIZING MORAL JUDGMENT, AUTHORITY AS A
POLITICAL FACT, AND ITS ADMINISTRATION.

1531 NELSON D.H.
ADMINISTRATIVE AGENCIES OF THE USA: THEIR DECISIONS AND
AUTHORITY.
DETROIT: WAYNE STATE U PR, 1964, 341 PP., LC#63-13433.
BASICALLY FORMALISTIC TEXT REVIEWING THE ADJUDICATORY
POWERS AND PROCEDURES OF ADMINISTRATIVE AGENCIES, INCLUDING
A DESCRIPTION OF ADMINISTRATIVE LAW IN THE US.

1532 NELSON H.L.
LIBEL IN NEWS OF CONGRESSIONAL INVESTIGATING COMMITTEES.
MINNEAPOLIS: U OF MINN PR, 1961, 174 PP.
QUESTIONS WHETHER A NEWSPAPER CAN REPORT A FALSE ACCUSA-
TION BEFORE THE 4OUSE COMMITTEE ON UN-AMERICAN ACTIVITIES
THOUT FEAR OF LIBEL SUIT. WOULD BE PROTECTED IF THE PRO-
CEEDING OF THE COMMITTEE WAS "OFFICIAL." HOWEVER, THE MANNER
OF DECIDING WHEN THE PROCEEDING IS OFFICIAL IS NEBULOUS.
TRIES TO ESTABLISH PRINCIPLES FOR DEFINING WHAT ARE OFFICIAL
PROCEEDINGS.

1533 NEUBURGER O.
GUIDE TO OFFICIAL PUBLICATIONS OF OTHER AMERICAN REPUBLICS:
HONDURAS (VOL. XIII)
WASHINGTON: LIBRARY OF CONGRESS, 1947, 31 PP.
PROVIDES AN ANNOTATED BIBLIOGRAPHY AND CHECKLIST OF
OFFICIAL PUBLICATIONS, SERIES, SERIALS, AND MONOGRAPHS
ISSUED SINCE 1821 BY THE REPUBLIC OF HONDURAS AND AVAILABLE
IN THE LIBRARY OF CONGRESS. ORGANIZED BY AGENCY OR DEPART-
MENT WHERE ISSUED AND INDEXED BY TITLE. PART OF A PROJECT
SPONSORED BY THE STATE DEPARTMENT.

1534 NEUBURGER O.
GUIDE TO OFFICIAL PUBLICATIONS OF THE OTHER AMERICAN REPUB-
LICS: HAITI (VOL. XII)
WASHINGTON: LIBRARY OF CONGRESS, 1947, 25 PP.
LIST OF OFFICIAL PUBLICATIONS ISSUED BY THE REPUBLIC OF
HAITI SINCE 1804; ARRANGED BY DEPARTMENT OR AGENCY OF
ISSUANCE; INDEXED ALPHABETICALLY BY TITLE, AND ANNOTATED.
SERVES AS A CHECKLIST AND GUIDE TO ALL SERIES, SERIALS, AND
MONOGRAPHS ISSUED BY THE HAITIAN GOVERNMENT SINCE INDEPEND-
ENCE AND LISTED IN LIBRARY OF CONGRESS CATALOG.

1535 NEUBURGER O.
GUIDE TO OFFICIAL PUBLICATIONS OF THE OTHER AMERICAN REPUB-
LICS: VENEZUELA (VOL. XIX)
WASHINGTON: LIBRARY OF CONGRESS, 1948, 59 PP.
COMPILES ALL STATE PUBLICATIONS PUBLISHED BY VENEZUELA
SINCE ITS INDEPENDENCE IN 1811 AND AVAILABLE IN THE LIBRARY
OF CONGRESS. PART OF A PROJECT UNDER THE AUSPICES OF THE
STATE DEPARTMENT'S INTERDEPARTMENTAL COMMITTEE ON SCIENTIFIC
AND CULTURAL COOPERATION. INCLUDES SERIALS, MONOGRAPHS, AND
BOOKS. ARRANGED BY AGENCY OR DEPARTMENT OF ISSUANCE.
PROVIDES AN INDEX TO TITLES.

1536 NEUMANN F.
THE DEMOCRATIC AND THE AUTHORITARIAN STATE: ESSAYS IN POL-
ITICAL AND LEGAL THEORY.
NEW YORK: FREE PRESS OF GLENCOE, 1957, 303 PP., LC#56-6878.
VOLUME OF PAPERS COLLECTED AND PREPARED BY FRANZ
NEUMANN WITH A FEW ADDED BY EDITOR HERBERT MARCUSE, ALL
DEALING WITH POLITICAL THEORY AND LEGAL THEORY. MAIN ATTEN-
TION ON THE CHANGE IN FUNCTION OF LAW IN MODERN SOCIETY
AND POLITICAL FREEDOM. INCLUDES WRITINGS OF
FRANZ NEUMANN: A SELECTED CHRONOLOGICAL BIBLIOGRAPHY.

1537 NEW JERSEY LEGISLATURE-SENATE
PUBLIC HEARINGS BEFORE COMMITTEE ON REVISION AND AMENDMENT
OF LAWS ON SENATE BILL NO. 8.
TRENTON: NJ STATE LEGISLATURE, 1961, 300 PP.
HEARINGS HELD FEBRUARY, 1961 ON "URBAN RENEWAL CORPORA-
TION LAW OF 1961." A BILL PROPOSING TAX RELIEF TO INCOMING
BUSINESSES IN HOPES THAT INCREASED INDUSTRIALIZATION WILL
ALLEVIATE SOME OF THE POWERTY, DISEASE, AND DELINQUENCY OF
THE CITIES. SOME DISAGREEMENT AMONG SPEAKERS AS TO HOW BEST
TO IMPLEMENT TAX RELIEF; A FEW SUGGEST SUBSIDIZING RENEWAL;
ALL AGREE RENEWAL IS NECESSARY BY SOME METHOD.

1538 NEW YORK STATE LEGISLATURE
REPORT AND DRAFT OF PROPOSED LEGISLATION ON COURT
REORGANIZATION.
WASHINGTON: US GOVERNMENT, 1962, 354 PP.
REPORTS ON REORGANIZATION OF UNIFIED COURT SYSTEM OF
NEW YORK STATE. DISCUSSES FAMILY COURT ACT, STATUTORY
AMENDMENTS INTENDED TO ABOLISH CERTAIN COUNTY COURTS,
NEW YORK CITY CIVIL COURT ACT, AND CREATION OF CRIMINAL
COURTS.

1539 NEW YORK STATE LIBRARY
CHECKLIST OF OFFICIAL PUBLICATIONS OF THE STATE OF NEW YORK.
ALBANY: U STATE NY FOR AREA STUD.
MONTHLY PUBLICATION LISITING OFFICIAL LITERATURE.
ORGANIZED ALPHABETICALLY BY DEPARTMENT ISSUING DOCUMENT.
EACH MONTH INCLUDES ABOUT 200 ITEMS.

1540 NEWBURY C.W.
BRITISH POLICY TOWARDS WEST AFRICA: SELECT DOCUMENTS
1786-1874.
LONDON: OXFORD U PR, 1965, 656 PP.
VOLUME PROVIDES MATERIALS FOR HISTORY OF EUROPEAN RELA-
TIONS WITH WEST AFRICA FOR THE PERIOD FROM THE TERMINATION
OF SLAVE TRADE UNTIL SOME TEN YEARS BEFORE INTERNATIONAL
PARTITION. MOST OF MATERIAL IS COLLECTED FROM STATE
PAPERS PUBLISHED FOR THE FIRST TIME IN THIS REFERENCE.

1541 NEWMAN E.S. ED.
THE FREEDOM READER.
NEW YORK: OCEANA PUBLISHING, 1963, 222 PP., LC#63-21226.
PRESENTS MATERIALS ON CIVIL RIGHTS AND CIVIL LIBERTIES
IN US, INCLUDING "SUPREME COURT DECISIONS AND COMMENTARY OF
EMINENT LAWYERS, GOVERNMENT OFFICIALS, POLITICAL SCIENTISTS,
AND OPINION MOULDERS." PROBLEMS COVERED ARE SECURITY IN
DEMOCRACY, PUBLIC WELFARE, AND LIBERTY VS. EQUALITY.

1542 NEWMAN E.S.
POLICE, THE LAW, AND PERSONAL FREEDOM.
NEW YORK: OCEANA PUBLISHING, 1964, 102 PP., LC#64-25441.
DESCRIBES LEGAL SYSTEM AND INDIVIDUAL IN US, INCLUDING
DEFINITION OF PERSONAL LIBERTY, POLICE METHODS AND PRAC-
TICES, FAIR TRIAL UNDER VALID STATUTES, AND FREEDOM FROM
ILLEGAL DETENTION.

1543 NEWMAN E.S.
CIVIL LIBERTY AND CIVIL RIGHTS.
NEW YORK: OCEANA PUBLISHING, 1964, 90 PP., LC#64-25410.
CONCERNED WITH PROTECTION OF PEOPLE AGAINST THEMSELVES,
RATHER THAN AGAINST GOVERNMENT. BEGINS WITH FREEDOM OF
EXPRESSION; EXAMINES PROTECTION OF PUBLIC WELFARE AND OF
NATIONAL SECURITY, PERSONAL LIBERTY, AND CIVIL RIGHTS. ENDS
WITH SEPARATION OF CHURCH AND STATE. INCLUDES CENSORSHIP,
POLICE POWER REGULATION, SEDITION AND SUBVERSION, ROLE OF
FEDERAL GOVERNMENT, AND RELIGION AND SCHOOLS.

1544 NEWMAN R.P.
RECOGNITION OF COMMUNIST CHINA? A STUDY IN ARGUMENT.
NEW YORK: MACMILLAN, 1961, 318 PP., LC#61-15184.
DISCUSSES "SHOULD US EXTEND DIPLOMATIC RECOGNITION TO
COMMUNIST CHINA?" ATTEMPTS TO DEVELOP LOGICAL
ARGUMENTS FOR VIABLE ALTERNATIVES, ASSUMING THE MORAL,

POLITICAL, AND LEGAL ISSUES. CONCLUDES THAT SOME SORT
OF MODIFICATION IS CALLED FOR.

1545 NICE R.W. ED.
TREASURY OF LAW.
NEW YORK: PHILOSOPHICAL LIB, 1964, 553 PP., LC#64-20425.
DOCUMENTS FROM ANCIENT THROUGH MODERN TIMES ON MAN'S
DETERMINATION TO GOVERN INTERPERSONAL AND INTERNATIONAL
CONDUCT THROUGH LAW. MOST REFLECT REGULATION OF PRACTICE,
DEALING WITH SPECIFIC ISSUES OF THEIR TIMES; MANY SHOW
INFLUENCE OF RELIGIOUS AND MORAL NORMS; OTHER ARE BASED
ON THE "PURE" LAW TRADITION.

1546 NICHOLS J.P.
"HAZARDS OF AMERICAN PRIVATE INVESTMENT IN UNDERDEVELOPED
COUNTRIES."
ORBIS, 4 (SUMMER 60), 174-191.
SURVEYS DEVELOPMENT OF AMERICAN INVESTMENT IN THE UNDER-
DEVELOPED NATIONS FROM EARLIER AGE OF EXPLOITATION TO THE
PRESENT AGE OF NATIONALIZATION. CONCLUDES THAT ALTHOUGH SOME
COMPANIES HAVE CREATED GOOD FEELING BY CONTRIBUTING TO LOCAL
WELFARE, RISKS TO PRIVATE INVESTMENT ARE INCREASING DUE TO
INDIGENOUS POLITICAL AND ECONOMIC FACTORS AND COMMUNISM.

1547 NICHOLS R.F.
RELIGION AND AMERICAN DEMOCRACY.
BATON ROUGE: LOUISIANA ST U PR, 1959, 107 PP., LC#59-9085.
TRACES RELIGIOUS SPIRIT IN ORIGINAL AMERICAN COLONISTS.
CONTENDS THAT THE GOVERNMENT THEY CREATED SHOWS THE
SPIRIT IF NOT FORM OF THEIR RELIGION. DISCUSSES NEW WORLD
ATMOSPHERE OF RELIGIOUS TOLERATION AND NOTES DEMOCRATIC
ASPECTS OF CHRISTIANITY. POINTS OUT RELIGIOUS NATURE OF
PARTS OF AMERICAN CONCEPT OF DEMOCRACY AND EFFECTS OF THIS
ON MORAL AND ETHICAL ATTITUDES.

1548 NICOLSON H.G.
"THE EVOLUTION OF DIPLOMATIC METHOD."
LONDON: CONSTABLE, 1954, 93 PP.
FOUR LECTURES RELATE DIPLOMATIC DEVELOPMENT THROUGH FOUR
ESSENTIAL HISTORICAL PHASES: GREEK AND ROMAN ERA, MEDIEVAL
ITALY, SEVENTEENTH THROUGH NINETEENTH CENTURY FRANCE, AND
'MODERN AGE' FROM 1919 TO THE PRESENT. CONCLUDES WITH BELIEF
THAT DIPLOMACY UNDER THE AUTHORITY OF USA WILL HAVE A
PROPITIOUS FUTURE.

1549 NIEMEYER G.
LAW WITHOUT FORCE: THE FUNCTION OF POLITICS IN INTERNATIONAL
LAW.
PRINCETON: PRINCETON U PRESS, 1941, 408 PP.
A STUDY OF THE NATURE OF LAW AND INTERNATIONAL RELATIONS.
COMPARES LEGAL THEORY AND POLITICAL REALITY. ARGUES THAT LAW
AND SOCIAL ORDER ARE CONCERNED WITH RELATIONSHIPS AND NOT
WITH SEPARATE INDIVIDUALS AND GROUPS; THEREFORE, THE
STANDARDS OF LEGAL ORDER SHOULD BE DERIVED FROM THE IDEA OF
INTERRELATED ACTIVITIES AND NOT FROM INDIVIDUALS AND GROUPS.
CONCEPT IS RELATED TO OUTBREAK OF WWII.

1550 NIVEN R.
NIGERIA.
NEW YORK: FREDERICK PRAEGER, 1967, 268 PP., LC#66-21789.
CHAPTERS 19 TO 23 MOST RELEVANT TO RESEARCHER. COVERS
POLITICAL STRUCTURE, PARTIES, CONSTITUTIONS, ADMINISTRATION,
1966 REVOLTS. ALSO HAS INFORMATION ABOUT EACH PROVINCE AND
RELATION TO NATIONAL UNITY. TRACES DEVELOPMENT FROM TRIBAL
FEDERATION TO NATIONAL STATE.

1551 NIZARD L.
"CUBAN QUESTION AND SECURITY COUNCIL."
REV. GEN. DR. INT. PUB., 66(NO.3, 62), 486-545.
CASTRO'S ACTION IN CUBA IS VIEWED AS AN IMPORTANT THREAT
TO AMERICAN INTERESTS AND SECURITY. COMPLAINTS TO SECURITY
COUNCIL, MADE BY INVOLVED PARTIES, ARE PRESENTED. DEMON-
STRATES HOW CONCEPTS OF THE UN CHARTER WERE APPLIED FOR
PROPOSING CONSTRUCTIVE SOLUTIONS.

1552 NJ LEGIS REAPPORT PLAN COMM
PUBLIC HEARING ON REDISTRICTING AND REAPPORTIONMENT.
TRENTON: NJ STATE LEGISLATURE, 1965, 147 PP.
STATEMENTS, DISCUSSIONS, AND PROPOSALS ON LEGISLATIVE RE-
APPORTIONMENT IN NEW JERSEY. INCLUDES STATEMENTS BY UNION
OFFICIALS, SENATORS, PRIVATE ASSOCIATION PRESIDENTS, ETC.

1553 NOBLEMAN E.E.
"THE DELEGATION OF PRESIDENTIAL FUNCTIONS: CONSTITUTIONAL
AND LEGAL ASPECTS."
ANN. ACAD. POL. SOC. SCI., (SEPT. 56), 134-143.
REVIEW OF FORMAL AUTHORITY OF PRESIDENT TO DELEGATE
FUNCTIONS. SAYS AUTHORITY TODAY IS SUFFICIENT. PRESIDENT CAN
DELEGATE FUNCTIONS, BUT RETAINS RESPONSIBILITY.

1554 NORDEN A.
WAR AND NAZI CRIMINALS IN WEST GERMANY: STATE, ECONOMY,
ADMINISTRATION, ARMY, JUSTICE, SCIENCE.
BERLIN: NATL FRONT DEM GERMANY, 1965, 402 PP.
CLAIMS THAT NAZI WAR CRIMINALS ARE TAKING OVER WEST GER-
MAN GOVERNMENT WHICH WILL PRECIPITATE WWIII. CASTI-

GATES BONN GOVERNMENT FOR CESSATION OF PROSECUTION OF WAR
CRIMINALS. DESCRIBES HITLER'S SECRET POLICE AND POLITICAL
MACHINE, AND HIS STAFF FOR EXTERMINATION OF JEWS. LISTS
SPECIFIC INDIVIDUALS, DESCRIBING FORMER NAZI ACTIVITIES AND
CURRENT POSITION IN GOVERNMENT.

1555 NORDSKOG J.E.
SOCIAL REFORM IN NORWAY.
LOS ANGELES: U OF S CALIF PR, 1935, 177 PP.
STUDY OF NATIONALISM AND SOCIAL DEMOCRACY IN NORWAY,
INCLUDING EMERGENCE OF NATIONAL SOCIAL UNITY, FUNCTION OF
POLITICAL PARTIES, LABOR MOVEMENT, INDUSTRIAL DISPUTES, AND
LEGISLATIVE ACHIEVEMENTS FOR SOCIAL AMELIORATION.

1556 NORGAARD C.A.
THE POSITION OF THE INDIVIDUAL IN INTERNATIONAL LAW.
COPENHAGEN: SCANDINAVIAN U BOOKS, 1962, 325 PP.
DESCRIBES AND ANALYZES BODY OF RULES THAT AFFECT LIFE
OF INDIVIDUAL. EXAMINES CRIMES AGAINST HUMANITY AND PEACE,
RIGHT OF PETITION TO UN AND INTERNATIONAL LABOR ORGANIZA-
TION, NUREMBERG TRIAL, INTERNATIONAL CRIMINAL COURTS, ETC.

1557 NORTON T.J.
LOSING LIBERTY JUDICIALLY.
NEW YORK: MACMILLAN, 1928, 252 PP.
DISCUSSES INTENTION OF FRAMERS OF US CONSTITUTION TO
LIMIT AUTHORITY OF GOVERNMENT. CITES EXAMPLES OF USURPA-
TION OF POWER BY STATE AND NATIONAL LEGISLATURES AS WELL AS
INSTANCES IN WHICH COURTS HAVE FAILED TO MAINTAIN BALANCE
BETWEEN POWERS OF GOVERNMENT AND LIBERTY OF INDIVIDUAL.

1558 NOTZ R.L.
FEDERAL GRANTS-IN-AID TO STATES: ANALYSIS OF LAWS IN FORCE
ON SEPTEMBER 10, 1956.
CHICAGO: COUNCIL OF STATE GOVTS, 1956, 108 PP.
REPORT COVERS FEDERAL GRANTS-IN-AID TO STATES. ARRANGED
IN FOUR MAIN SECTIONS: GRANTS-IN-AID FROM APPROPRIATED
FUNDS; PAYMENTS MADE FROM CERTAIN RECEIPTS OR FUNDS;
PAYMENTS IN LIEU OF TAXES; AND FEDERAL EXPENDITURES DEPEN-
DENT UPON THE MATCHING OF FEDERAL FUNDS. ITEMS ARE NUMBERED
AND PROVIDE COMPLETE REFERENCE FOR EACH LAW OR BILL
DISCUSSED.

1559 NUMELIN R.
"THE BEGINNINGS OF DIPLOMACY."
NEW YORK: PHILOSOPHICAL LIB, 1950.
SOCIOLOGICAL ESSAY BASED ON ETHNOLOGICAL FIELD RESEARCHES
OF TECHNIQUES OF DIPLOMACY OF NONLITERATE PEOPLES. EXTENSIVE
BIBLIOGRAPHY IS COMPOSED OF HISTORICAL AND PHILOSOPHICAL
LITERATURE, LITERATURE OF INTERNATIONAL LAW AND SOCIOLOGY,
ETHNOLOGICAL, ETHNO-SOCIOLOGICAL, AND GEOGRAPHICAL LITERA-
TURE IN EUROPEAN LANGUAGES.

1560 NUSSBAUM D.
A CONCISE HISTORY OF THE LAW OF NATIONS.
NEW YORK: MACMILLAN, 1954, 378 PP.
BRIEF HISTORY OF INTERNATIONAL LAW SINCE FIRST GREEK AND
ROMAN EFFORTS FOR A COMPLETE DEFINITION. DEPICTS JURIDICAL
SCIENCE IN THE MIDDLE AGES AND IN MODERN TIMES. INCLUDES
HISTORIOGRAPHY OF INTERNATIONAL RELATIONS.

1561 NWOGUGU E.I.
THE LEGAL PROBLEMS OF FOREIGN INVESTMENT IN DEVELOPING
COUNTRIES.
NEW YORK: OCEANA PUBLISHING, 1965, 320 PP., LC#63-22349.
NIGERIAN SCHOLAR DISCUSSES NATURE AND SOURCES OF
FOREIGN INVESTMENT IN UNDERDEVELOPED COUNTRIES. INCLUDES
LEGAL DETERRENTS AND INCENTIVES TO INVESTMENT, PROTECTION
BY TREATY, CONTRACTS BETWEEN STATES AND PRIVATE INVESTORS,
ROLE OF INTERNATIONAL ORGANIZATIONS, SETTLEMENT OF INVEST-
MENT DISPUTES, AND SANCTIONS FOR INJURY TO INVESTMENTS.

1562 NYC BAR ASSOCIATION RECORD
"PAPERBACKS FOR THE BAR."
RECORD OF ASSN. OF BAR OF NYC, 21 (DEC. 66), 666-672.
UNANNOTATED LIST OF PAPERBACKS PUBLISHED IN ENGLISH
COVERING TOPICS OF LEGAL INTEREST.

1563 O'BRIEN F.W.
JUSTICE REED AND THE FIRST AMENDMENT, THE RELIGION CLAUSES.
WASHINGTON: GEORGETOWN U PRESS, 1958, 260 PP., LC#58-05716.
STUDIES ROLE OF STANLEY REED, SUPREME COURT JUSTICE,
1938-57, IN INTERPRETING CONSTITUTIONAL APPLICATIONS
TO RELIGION AND ALSO GENERAL CHANGES IN INTERPRETATION
THAT TOOK PLACE, EMPHASIZING INCREASING ROLE OF FEDERAL
GOVERNMENT IN REGULATING STATES' RIGHTS.

1564 O'BRIEN W.
"THE ROLE OF FORCE IN THE INTERNATIONAL JURIDICAL ORDER."
CATH. LAWYER, 6 (WINTER 60), 22-32.
CONTENDS THAT FORCE IS IMPORTANT TO THE CONCEPT OF INTER-
NATIONAL JURIDICAL ORDER. POSTULATES ON THE IMPORTANCE OF
FORCE AS A REALITY, AS A LEGAL NECESSITY, AND AS A MORAL
MEANS OF ATTAINING WORLD PEACE. ADHERES TO SCHOLASTIC VIEW
OF JUST AND UNJUST WARS, AND CONCLUDES WITH A PLEA FOR MORE
SERIOUS STUDY OF THE LAWS OF WAR IN ORDER TO LIMIT AND REG-

ULATE IT.

1565 O'BRIEN W.V. ED.
THE NEW NATIONS IN INTERNATIONAL LAW AND DIPLOMACY* THE
YEAR BOOK OF WORLD POLITY* VOLUME III.
NEW YORK: FREDERICK PRAEGER, 1965, 323 PP., LC#65-13962.
4 ESSAYS ATTEMPT TO RECONCILE THE WESTERN CHARACTER OF
MUCH OF INTERNATIONAL LAW WITH THE POSTWAR DEVELOPMENT OF
A PLURALISTIC INTERNATIONAL SYSTEM WITH MANY NON-WESTERN
CULTURE STATES. PAPERS TREAT: "INDEPENDENCE AND PROBLEMS OF
STATE SUCCESSION, MILITARY SERVITUDE AND THE NEW NATIONS,
UNITED STATES RECOGNITION POLICY TOWARD THE NEW NATIONS,
THE NEW STATES AND THE UNITED NATIONS."

1566 O'CONNELL D.P.
INTERNATIONAL LAW (2 VOLS.)
NEW YORK: OCEANA PUBLISHING, 1965, 1213 PP.
EXAMINES INTERNATIONAL LAW AS A SYSTEM OF LAW RATHER
THAN A BRANCH OF DIPLOMACY OR POLITICAL SCIENCE. APPLIES
CRITICAL STANDARDS OF LAWYER. INCLUDES VAST DOCUMENTATION
AND VARIETY OF SOURCE MATERIALS. ATTEMPTS TO AVOID NATIONAL
APPROACH AND EMPHASIZES UNIVERSALITY OF SCOPE AND APPEAL.
PARTICULAR ATTENTION IS GIVEN TO ECONOMIC PROBLEMS AND
DISPUTES.

1567 O'HIGGINS P.
"A BIBLIOGRAPHY OF PERIODICAL LITERATURE RELATING TO IRISH
LAW."
AMER. J. OF COMPARATIVE LAW, 15 (JAN. 67), 392-393.
BOOK NOTICE OF BIBLIOGRAPHY OF ARTICLES WRITTEN ON IRISH
LAW AND ARTICLES WRITTEN BY IRISHMEN ON FOREIGN LAW.
INCLUDES 5,000 ARTICLES ARRANGED UNDER SUBJECT HEADINGS.
ALL ENTRIES ARE IN ENGLISH.

1568 O'NEILL C.E.
CHURCH AND STATE IN FRENCH COLONIAL LOUISIANA: POLICY AND
POLITICS TO 1732.
NEW HAVEN: YALE U PR, 1966, 313 PP., LC#66-21529.
STUDIES ATTITUDES AND ACTIVITIES OF CIVIL AND RELIGIOUS
INSTITUTIONS IN FRENCH COLONY OF LOUISIANA FROM BEGINNING OF
COLONY TO RETROCESSION TO KING BY COMPANY OF INDIES; THEIR
COOPERATION AND CONFLICT, AND THEIR MOTIVES.

1569 O'NEILL J.M.
CATHOLICS IN CONTROVERSY.
NEW YORK: MC MULLEN BOOKS, INC, 1954, 227 PP.
STATES CATHOLIC POSITION ON SEPARATION OF CHURCH AND
STATE, RELIGIOUS BIAS IN INTERPRETING CONSTITUTION,
EDUCATION, AND CENSORSHIP. DISCUSSES BASIC CONFLICTS
BETWEEN US POLICY AND CATHOLIC ETHICS AND RELEVANCE OF
CERTAIN SUPREME COURT CASES TO MODERN RELIGIOUS FREEDOM.

1570 OBERER W.E.
"VOLUNTARY IMPARTIAL REVIEW OF LABOR: SOME REFLECTIONS."
MICH. LAW REV., 58 (NOV. 59), 55-88.
DISCUSSES CHARACTER, FUNCTIONS, AND PROBLEMS OF VOLUNTARY
REVIEW BODIES IN LABOR UNIONS. WRITTEN JUST PRIOR TO PASSAGE
OF LANDRUM-GRIFFIN ACT, BOOK CONSIDERS UAW PUBLIC REVIEW
BOARD AS A SUPREME COURT. DISCUSSES ACLU'S LABOR UNION BILL
OF RIGHTS AND ADVANTAGES OF SUCH VOLUNTARY TRIBUNALS AND RE-
VIEW BOARDS.
ADVANTAGES OF SUCH VOLUNTARY TRIBUNALS AND REVIEW BOARDS.

1571 OBERMANN E.
VERTEIDIGUNG DER FREIHEIT.
STUTTGART: STUTTG VERL KANTOR, 1966, 614 PP.
DISCUSSES WAR AND DEFENSE OF FREEDOM IN EUROPEAN CON-
SCIOUSNESS, COMMUNIST TEACHING ON WAR AND PEACE, WESTERN AND
EASTERN MILITARY ALLIANCES, AND GERMAN CONTRIBUTION TO
EUROPEAN DEFENSE.

1572 OGDEN F.D.
THE POLL TAX IN THE SOUTH.
UNIVERSITY: U ALABAMA PR, 1958, 301 PP., LC#58-08773.
STUDIES WHAT POLL TAX IS, HOW IT OPERATES, AND ITS VALUE
AS VOTING PREREQUISITE. PRESENTS HISTORICAL SUMMARY, MEANS
OF ADMINISTERING IT, ITS EFFECTS ON VOTER PARTICIPATION AND
RELATION BETWEEN TAX AND CORRUPTION.

1573 OKINSHEVICH L.A., GOROKHOFF C.J.
LATIN AMERICA IN SOVIET WRITINGS, 1945-1958: A BIBLIOGRAPHY.
WASHINGTON: LIBRARY OF CONGRESS, 1959, 257 PP., LC#59-64248.
LISTS 2385 ITEMS ORIGINALLY WRITTEN BY RUSSIANS AND RUS-
SIAN TRANSLATIONS OF WORKS RELATING TO LATIN AMERICA BY
WRITERS OF ALL NATIONALITIES PUBLISHED IN USSR BETWEEN 1945
AND 1958. ENTRIES ARRANGED BY SUBJECT-MATTER: GENERAL REFER-
ENCE WORKS, ANTHROPOLOGY, EDUCATION, GEOGRAPHY, GOVERNMENT
AND POLITICS, HISTORY, INTERNATIONAL RELATIONS, LABOR, LAW,
SOCIAL CONDITIONS, ETC.

1574 OLIVER C.T.
"THE AMERICAN LAW INSTITUTE'S DRAFT RESTATEMENT OF THE
FOREIGN RELATIONS LAW OF THE UNITED STATES."
AMER. J. INT. LAW, 55 (NO.2, 61), 428-40.
TREATS INTERNATIONAL LAW STUDIES PROGRAM SET UP IN RE-
SPONSE TO REALIZATION THAT USA LEGAL PROFESSION INSUF-

FICIENTLY INFORMED ABOUT RELATION OF LAW TO FOREIGN AFFAIRS.

1575 OLSON W.C., SONDERMANN F.A.
THE THEORY AND PRACTICE OF INTERNATIONAL RELATIONS (2ND ED.)
ENGLEWOOD CLIFFS: PRENTICE HALL, 1966, 478 PP., LC#66-19880.
EXAMINES THEORY AND PRACTICE OF INTERNATIONAL RELATIONS.
ANALYZES STATE SYSTEM AND FACTORS WHICH DETERMINE A
STATE'S ABILITY TO ACHIEVE ITS GOALS. STUDIES VARIOUS
DIMENSIONS OF POLICY, AND DEGREE TO WHICH NATIONS HAVE
ARRIVED AT AN ORGANIZATIONAL AND LEGAL BASIS FOR WORKING
TOGETHER. STRESSES RESPONSIBILITY OF NATIONAL LEADERSHIP
IN FOREIGN POLICY.

1576 OPERATIONS AND POLICY RESEARCH
URUGUAY: ELECTION FACTBOOK: NOVEMBER 27, 1966 (PAMPHLET)
WASHINGTON: INST COMP STUDY POL, 1966, 53 PP., LC#66-29840.
ATTEMPTS TO CLARIFY ISSUES IN ELECTIONS THAT WERE COMING
WHEN THIS PAMPHLET WAS WRITTEN AND TO PUT THEM IN HISTORICAL
PERSPECTIVE. IDENTIFIES THE NUMEROUS PARTIES AND FACTIONS,
DESCRIBES THEIR PROGRAMS, AND PRESENTS BRIEF BIOGRAPHIES OF
CANDIDATES AND LEADING POLITICAL FIGURES. INCLUDES RELEVANT
DATA ON PAST ELECTION RESULTS, CURRENT ELECTORAL LAWS
SYSTEM OF REPRESENTATION, AND STRUCTURE OF GOVERNMENT.

1577 OPERATIONS AND POLICY RESEARCH
NICARAGUA: ELECTION FACTBOOK: FEBRUARY 5, 1967 (PAMPHLET)
WASHINGTON: INST COMP STUDY POL, 1967, 39 PP., LC#67-16332.
ATTEMPTS TO CLARIFY SURFACE AND UNDERLYING ISSUES IN THE
"COMING" NICARAGUAN ELECTIONS, AND TO PUT THEM IN HISTORICAL
PERSPECTIVE. IDENTIFIES THE NUMEROUS PARTIES AND FACTIONS,
DESCRIBES THEIR PROGRAMS AND PRESENTS BRIEF BIOGRAPHIES OF
CANDIDATES AND LEADING POLITICAL FIGURES. INCLUDES RELEVANT
DATA ON PAST ELECTION RESULTS, CURRENT ELECTORAL LAWS,
SYSTEM OF REPRESENTATION, AND STRUCTURE OF GOVERNMENT.

1578 OPPENHEIM L.
THE FUTURE OF INTERNATIONAL LAW.
NEW YORK: CARNEGIE ENDOWMENT, 1921, 68 PP.
SEEKS TO DEFINE ORGANIZATION OF STATES. ANALYZES PROBLEMS
TREATED IN INTERNATIONAL LEGISLATION. OFFERS PROPOSALS THAT
WOULD AID INTERPRETATION. STUDIES INTERNATIONAL ADMINISTRA-
TION OF JUSTICE.

1579 OPPENHEIM L., LAUTERPACHT H. ED.
INTERNATIONAL LAW: A TREATISE (7TH ED., 2 VOLS.)
LONDON: LONGMANS, GREEN & CO, 1953, 1891 PP.
THIS EDITION EXPANDS SECTIONS ON UN, TRUSTEESHIP SYSTEM,
AND ILO. SECTIONS ON LEAGUE OF NATIONS AND MANDATES SYSTEM
ARE REDUCED. BIBLIOGRAPHIES UPDATED. OTHER SUBJECTS COVERED
INCLUDE FOUNDATION, DEVELOPMENT, SUBJECTS, AND OBJECTS OF
LAW OF NATIONS; ORGANS OF THE STATES FOR INTERNATIONAL
RELATIONS; INTERNATIONAL TRANSACTIONS; SETTLEMENT OF
DIFFERENCES; WAR; AND NEUTRALITY.

1580 OPPENHEIMER M., LAKEY G.
A MANUAL FOR DIRECT ACTION.
CHICAGO: QUADRANGLE BOOKS, INC, 1964, 138 PP., LC#65-12781.
STRATEGY AND TACTICS FOR CIVIL RIGHTS AND ALL OTHER NON-
VIOLENT PROTEST MOVEMENTS, INCLUDING ORGANIZING, VOTER REG-
ISTRATION, WORKSHOPS IN DIRECT ACTION, AND ARREST AND THE
COURTS.

1581 ORFIELD L.B.
THE GROWTH OF SCANDINAVIAN LAW.
PHILA: U OF PENN PR, 1953, 363 PP.
DEVELOPMENT OF LAW AND LEGAL INSTITUTIONS IN DENMARK,
ICELAND, NORWAY, AND SWEDEN. CHAPTERS LISTED BY COUNTRY,
WITH HISTORICAL AND POLITICAL BACKGROUND.

1582 ORTIZ R.P.
ANNUARIO BIBLIOGRAFICO COLOMBIANO, 1951-1956.
BOGOTA: BOG INST CARA CUERNO, 1958, 334 PP.
LISTING OF BOOKS AND MONOGRAPHS PUBLISHED IN COLUMBIA OR
BY COLUMBIANS DURING PERIOD 1951-1956. MATERIAL ON
POLITICAL SCIENCE, SOCIOLOGY, STATISTICS, ECONOMICS, LAW,
PUBLIC ADMINISTRATION, SOCIAL WELFARE, EDUCATION, COMMERCE,
AND LINGUISTICS.

1583 OSSENBECK F.J. ED., KROECK P.C. ED.
OPEN SPACE AND PEACE.
STANFORD: HOOVER INSTITUTE, 1964, 227 PP., LC#64-18827.
COLLECTION OF PAPERS GIVEN AT OPEN SPACE AND PEACE SYM-
POSIUM ON SATELLITE OBSERVATION. COVERS BACKGROUND, TECH-
NOLOGY, SOCIOLOGICAL AND POLITICAL IMPLICATIONS, IMPLEMENTA-
TION OF FURTHER RESEARCH, AND FUTURE PROGRAMS IN US.

1584 OSTERMANN R.
A REPORT IN DEPTH ON CRIME IN AMERICA.
NEW YORK: DOW JONES, 1966, 174 PP.
ILLUSTRATED REPORT ON CONTEMPORARY CRIME IN US, AND WHAT
IS BEING DONE ABOUT IT. EXAMINES ACCELERATING CRIME RATE AND
ACTION TAKEN TO MEET IT. DISCUSSES CRIME IN LARGE CITIES AND
SUBURBAN COMMUNITIES, COMPUTER VS. CRIME, PSYCHIATRY AND
LAW, PENAL INSTITUTIONS, ETC.

1585 OTTENBERG M.

THE FEDERAL INVESTIGATORS.
ENGLEWOOD CLIFFS: PRENTICE HALL, 1962, 348 PP., LC#62-17427.
APPRAISES ADMINISTRATION, POWERS, STRUCTURE, AND
RESPONSIBILITIES OF VARIOUS FEDERAL INVESTIGATIVE AGENCIES
CREATED TO PROTECT THE GOVERNMENT AND PUBLIC. BEGINS WITH
FBI AS PATTERN FOR ESTABLISHING JUSTICE AND THWARTING
ESPIONAGE; COVERS INTELLIGENCE AGENCIES OF ARMED FORCES
DESIGNED TO PROTECT COMMON DEFENSE. INCLUDES AGENCIES
PROTECTING GENERAL WELFARE AND DOMESTIC TRANQUILITY.

1586 OTTOSON H.W. ED.
LAND USE POLICY AND PROBLEMS IN THE UNITED STATES.
LINCOLN: U OF NEB PR, 1963, 469 PP., LC#63-9096.
COMPREHENSIVE STUDY OF LAND POLICY IN US FROM HOMESTEAD
ACT OF 1862 TO PRESENT. PRESENTS SOCIAL FACTORS INVOLVED IN
LAND POLICY, DEMANDS FOR AND CONFLICTS OVER LAND, AND
CHANGES IN OUR POLICY, AND APPLICATION IN DEVELOPING
COUNTRIES.

1587 PACHTER H.M.
COLLISION COURSE; THE CUBAN MISSILE CRISIS AND COEXISTENCE.
NEW YORK: FREDERICK PRAEGER, 1963, 261 PP., LC#63-18528.
CURRENT HISTORY OF EVENTS INVOLVED IN THE CUBAN
MISSILE CRISIS OF OCTOBER, 1962. DISCUSSES PRINCIPAL
PERSONS INVOLVED - KHRUSHCHEV, CASTRO, KENNEDY, U THANT.
POINTS OUT FORCES WHICH MOTIVATED THEIR ACTIONS. ANALYZES
AND FORMULATES GENERAL CONCLUSIONS ABOUT POWER CONFLICTS IN
NUCLEAR AGE; PRESENTS PRINCIPLES OF COEXISTENCE WHICH
MAY PREVENT COLD WAR FROM BEING ACTIVATED.

1588 PADELFORD N.J. ED., GOODRICH L. ED.
THE UNITED NATIONS IN THE BALANCE* ACCOMPLISHMENTS AND PROS-
PECTS.
NEW YORK: FREDERICK PRAEGER, 1965, 482 PP., LC#65-24725.
THIS COLLECTION OF ESSAYS ORIGINALLY APPEARED AS A SPE-
CIAL ISSUE OF "INTERNATIONAL ORGANIZATION" IN 1965 COMMEM-
ORATING THE TWENTIETH ANNIVERSARY OF THE UNITED NATIONS.
THE PAPERS TRACE THE EVOLUTION OF THE UN AS AN INTERNATIONAL
ORGANIZATION. ASSESS ITS RECORD IN COOPERATION AND CONFLICT,
PRESENT THE UN POLICIES OF MAJOR MEMBERS AND BLOCS, AND CON-
TEMPLATE THE FUTURE.

1589 PADELFORD N.J., LINCOLN G.A.
THE DYNAMICS OF INTERNATIONAL POLITICS (2ND ED.)
NEW YORK: MACMILLAN, 1967, 640 PP.
DESCRIBES BACKGROUND OF INTERNATIONAL POLITICS AND DIS-
CUSSES MAJOR FACTORS. EMPHASIS IS PLACED ON DECISION-MAKING
PROCESS. INCLUDES INSTRUMENTS AND PATTERNS OF FOREIGN POL-
ICY, ORGANIZATION OF INTERNATIONAL COMMUNITY, ECONOMIC AND
POLITICAL PRINCIPLES, IMPACT OF TECHNOLOGICAL CHANGE, GROW-
ING POPULATION, AND SHIFTING RELATIONSHIPS WITHIN POWER
BLOCS. TEXTS TO IMPORTANT TREATIES INCLUDED.

1590 PADOVER S.K.
THE LIVING US CONSTITUTION.
NEW YORK: FREDERICK PRAEGER, 1953, 176 PP., LC#53-6442.
INCLUDES TEXT OF CONSTITUTION, STORY OF ITS COMPOSITION
AND SIGNING, SELECTED LETTERS AND PAPERS OF MEMBERS OF CON-
VENTION, PORTRAITS OF THOSE MEN WHO SIGNED. ALSO DESCRIBES
SOME SUPREME COURT DECISIONS THAT HAVE AFFECTED THE CON-
STITUTION, AND INCLUDES ALPHABETICALLY INDEXED GUIDE TO ITS
PROVISIONS.

1591 PAIKERT G.C.
THE GERMAN EXODUS.
THE HAGUE: MARTINUS NIJHOFF, 1962, 97 PP.
"SELECTIVE VISUAL STUDY ON POST WWII EXPULSION OF GERMAN POPULA-
TIONS AND ITS EFFECTS," PARTICULARLY ON WEST GERMANY. IN-
CLUDES MOTIVES AND LEGAL BASIS OF EXODUS, IMMIGRANTS' RE-
SETTLEMENT, EFFECT ON SOCIO-CULTURAL GEOGRAPHY OF WEST GER-
MANY, AND SOLUTIONS TO PROBLEMS OF INTEGRATION OF NATIONAL
MINORITIES.

1592 PALMER E.E. ED.
CIVIL LIBERTIES.
SYRACUSE: SYR U, MAXWELL SCHOOL, 1958, 162 PP.
ATTEMPTS TO RELATE CIVIL LIBERTIES TO MAINTENANCE OF
AMERICAN VALUE PRESCRIBING LATITUDE FOR EACH PERSON TO DE-
VELOP HIS INTERESTS. CONCERNED WITH DEFINING THE BOUNDARIES
OF CIVIL LIBERTIES. OBSERVING HOW THEY ARE EXERCISED, AND
EXAMINING SAFEGUARDS AND THREATS TO THEIR EXISTENCE. BEGINS
WITH PHILOSOPHICAL WRITINGS AND MOVES TO ACTUAL CASES.

1593 PALMER N.D., PERKINS H.C.
INTERNATIONAL RELATIONS.
BOSTON: HOUGHTON MIFFLIN, 1957, 860 PP.
STUDIES PATTERN OF INTERNATIONAL RELATIONS FIRST FROM
THEORETICAL VIEWPOINT. CONSIDERS BASIC INSTRUMENTS FOR
PROMOTION OF NATIONAL INTEREST: DIPLOMACY, PROPAGANDA,
ECONOMICS, WAR, AND IMPERIALISM. TREATS CONTROLS OF INTER-
STATE RELATIONS, SUCH AS BALANCE OF POWER, INTERNATIONAL
LAW, TREATIES, AND INTERNATIONAL ORGANIZATIONS. DISCUSSES
MAJOR CHANGES AFTER WWII.

1594 PALOTAI O.C.
PUBLICATIONS OF THE INSTITUTE OF GOVERNMENT, 1930-1962.

CHAPEL HILL: U OF N CAR INST GOV, 1963, 78 PP.
RECORD OF RESEARCH AND PUBLISHING ACTIVITIES OF THE
INSTITUTE OF GOVERNMENT. TOPICALLY CLASSIFIED LIST OF COM-
PARATIVE STUDIES IN THE STRUCTURE AND WORKINGS OF GOVERNMENT
AT ALL LEVELS, PRIMARILY STATE AND LOCAL ADMINISTRATION.
INCLUDES ANNOTATED SECTION ON SPECIAL STUDIES PUB-
LISHED BY THE INSTITUTE.

1595 PAN AMERICAN UNION
INFORME DE LA MISION DE ASISTENCIA TECNICA DE LA OEA A LA
REPUBLICA DE HONDURAS EN MATERIA ELECTORAL (PAMPHLET)
WASHINGTON: PAN AMERICAN UNION, 1963, 66 PP.
REPORT OF OAS TECHNICAL ASSISTANCE MISSION ON ELECTORAL
SYSTEM FOR OCTOBER 13, 1963 ELECTIONS, AND RECOMMENDATIONS
FOR FUTURE ELECTIONS. DISCUSSES POLITICAL PARTIES AND PRO-
CESS IN HONDURAS.

1596 PANHUYS H.F.
THE ROLE OF NATIONALITY IN INTERNATIONAL LAW.
LEYDEN: AW SIJTHOFF, 1959, 251 PP.
TRACES CHANGING EFFECTS OF NATIONALITY ON LEGAL RIGHTS OF
ALIENS IN INTERNATIONAL LAW AND IN TIME OF WAR, GIVING
DIGEST OF TRADITIONAL FUNCTIONS OF NATIONALITY AND PRESENT
ARRANGEMENTS.

1597 PARADIES F.
"SOBRE LA HISTORIA DE LA LOGICA Y DE LA LOGICA JURIDICA."
REV. INST. CIENC. SOC., (NO.3, 64), 264-67.
DISCUSSES CHRONOLOGICAL DEVELOPMENT OF STUDY OF LOGIC
AND JURIDICAL LOGIC. ASSAYS INFLUENCE OF LOGIC ON JUDICIAL
THOUGHT. ANALYZES RELATION OF THEORY OF LOGIC TO JUDICIAL
STUDIES AND METHODS.

1598 PARKER D., O'NEIL R.M. ET AL.
CIVIL LIBERTIES CASE STUDIES AND THE LAW.
BOSTON: HOUGHTON MIFFLIN, 1965, 242 PP.
DISCUSSES CIVIL RIGHTS AND INDIVIDUAL LIBERTIES IN TERMS
OF CASE STUDIES AND CONSTITUTIONAL FOUNDATIONS. EXAMINES
RIGHTS OF ACCUSED, ECONOMIC RIGHTS, EQUAL OPPORTUNITY,
FREEDOM OF RELIGION AND EXPRESSION, AND CONCLUDES WITH
DISCUSSION OF CIVIL RIGHTS ACTION AND ITS RELATION TO
RULE OF LAW.

1599 PARRY C.
THE SOURCES AND EVIDENCES OF INTERNATIONAL LAW.
NEW YORK: OCEANA PUBLISHING, 1965, 122 PP., LC#65-17525.
INQUIRY INTO BASES AND NATURE OF INTERNATIONAL LAW, DIS-
CUSSING TREATIES, CUSTOM AND PRECEDENTS, AND OTHER SOURCES.
CONSIDERS IMPLICATIONS AND SHORTCOMINGS OF ARTICLE 38, STAT-
UTE OF INTERNATIONAL COURT OF JUSTICE, AND CONCLUDES THAT
INTERNATIONAL LAW COMMISSION AND UN DEBATES AND ACTIONS ARE
PRESENTLY MOST IMPORTANT INFLUENCES ON INTERNATIONAL LAW.

1600 PASCUAL R.R.
PARTYLESS DEMOCRACY.
QUEZON CITY: U OF PHILIPPINES, 1952, 302 PP.
ANALYSIS OF CONCEPT OF PARTYLESS DEMOCRACY IN PHILIPPINE
POLITICAL SYSTEM. DISCUSSES POLITICAL PARTIES AND THEIR
EFFECT ON NATIONAL LIFE AND INDIVIDUAL CITIZEN AS WELL AS
LEGAL, POLITICAL, AND ECONOMIC IMPLICATIONS FOR DEMOCRACY IN
PHILIPPINES.

1601 PATON G.W.
A TEXT-BOOK OF JURISPRUDENCE.
LONDON: CLARENDON PRESS, 1946, 528 PP.
A GENERAL OUTLINE OF THE NATURE OF JURISPRUDENCE. COVERS
THE EVOLUTION AND DEFINITION OF LAW; WRITINGS, STATUTES, AND
OTHER SOURCES; DESCRIPTION OF LEGAL TECHNIQUES; AND AN
ANALYSIS OF SUCH CONCEPTS AS THE LEGAL PERSONALITY, RIGHTS,
CRIMINAL LAW, PROPERTY, POSSESSION, AND THE LAW OF
PROCEDURE.

1602 PATRA A.C.
THE ADMINISTRATION OF JUSTICE UNDER THE EAST INDIA COMPANY
IN BENGAL, BIHAR AND ORISSA.
NEW YORK: ASIA PUBL HOUSE, 1963, 233 PP.
APPRAISAL OF DISPENSATION OF JUSTICE BY PRINCIPAL JUDI-
CIAL INSTITUTIONS OPERATING UNDER EAST INDIA COMPANY IN
BENGAL. FOCUSES ON AREA OF LEGAL ADMINISTRATION.

1603 PAUL A.M.
CONSERVATIVE CRISIS AND THE RULE OF LAW.
ITHACA: CORNELL U PRESS, 1960, 256 PP.
DISCUSSES SOCIAL TENSIONS AND CONSERVATIVE ROLE OF
SUPREME COURT FROM HAYMARKET RIOT IN 1886 TO BRIAN
ELECTION CAMPAIGN IN 1896. EXAMINES DOCTRINES AND
DECISIONS OF SUPREME COURT AND CHANGING ATTITUDES OF
LAWYERS AND JUDGES.

1604 PAULSEN M.G. ED.
LEGAL INSTITUTIONS TODAY AND TOMORROW.
NEW YORK: COLUMBIA U PRESS, 1959, 346 PP., LC#59-14820.
COLLECTION OF ESSAYS ON JUDICIAL AND ADMINISTRATIVE LAW-
MAKING PROCESSES IN US. EXAMINES ROLE OF LEGAL PROFESSION,
CONGRESS, STATE LEGISLATURES, ADMINISTRATIVE AGENCIES, AND
COURTS. ALSO DISCUSSES LEGAL INSTITUTIONS IN ENGLAND.

1605 PEASLEE A.J.
CONSTITUTIONS OF NATIONS.
THE HAGUE: NIJHOFF, 1956, 3VOLS., 2435 PP.
COMPREHENSIVE COMPILATION OF CONSTITUTIONS OF BOTH MA-
JOR AND MINOR NATIONS. PRESENTS EACH CONSTITUTION IN FULL,
SUMMARIZES IT AND INCLUDES ANNOTATIONS, BIBLIOGRAPHIES AND
PERTINENT GEOGRAPHIC FACTS.

1606 PEASLEE A.J.
CONSTITUTIONS OF NATIONS* THIRD REVISED EDITION (VOLUME I*
AFRICA)
GENEVA: MARTINUS NIJHOFF, 1965, 1108 PP.
COMPILATION OF ALL AFRICAN NATIONS' CONSTITUTIONS. COM-
PLETE WITH TEXTS, SUMMARIES, ANNOTATIONS, BIBLIOGRAPHIES
AND GEOGRAPHICAL INFORMATION.

1607 PEDERSON V.L. ED.
A CHECK LIST OF THE SPECIAL AND STANDING COMMITTEES OF THE
AMERICAN BAR ASSOCIATION (VOL. II)
CHICAGO: AMERICAN BAR ASSN, 1964, 66 PP.
SECOND VOLUME OF SERIES PUBLISHED BY AMERICAN BAR FOUNDA-
TION'S CROMWELL LIBRARY. BIBLIOGRAPHICAL DESCRIPTION LISTS
ITEM IN FORM IN WHICH LIBRARY COPY EXISTS AND IS SO INDI-
CATED. BULK OF PUBLICATIONS ARE SERIES OF REPORTS SUBMITTED
TO GOVERNING BODY OF ASSOCIATION. COMMITTEES LISTED ALPHA-
BETICALLY ACCORDING TO CHARACTER.

1608 PEMBERTON J., JR.
"CONSTITUTIONAL PROBLEMS IN RESTRAINT ON THE MEDIA."
NOTRE DAME LAWYER, 42 (1967), 881-887.
INVESTIGATES CONSTITUTIONAL PROBLEMS IN AMERICAN BAR
ASSOCIATION'S PROPOSALS FOR RESTRAINT OF PRESS BEFORE AND
DURING COURT PROCEDURES. FINDS THAT CONSTITUTION GUARANTEES
RIGHT OF PROTECTION AGAINST PARTIALITY IN TRIAL AND DOES NOT
GIVE GOVERNMENT POWER TO CONTROL PRESS. BELIEVES THAT SUCH
LAWS SHOULD NOT BE PASSED UNTIL NEED FOR THEM IS FULLY
ESTABLISHED.

1609 PERKINS D.
CHARLES EVANS HUGHES AND THE AMERICAN DEMOCRATIC STATES-
MANSHIP.
BOSTON: LITTLE/BROWN, 1956, 200 PP.
OUTLINES CAREER AS POLITICIAN, U.S. SECRETARY OF STATE,
AND CHIEF JUSTICE OF THE SUPREME COURT. CREDITS HUGHES WITH
BROADENING SCOPE OF AMERICAN DIPLOMACY AFTER WORLD WAR ONE.

1610 PERKINS D.
AMERICA'S QUEST FOR PEACE.
BLOOMINGTON: INDIANA U PR, 1962, 122 PP., LC#61-13718.
ANALYSIS OF US ATTITUDE AND PROPOSALS FOR WORLD PEACE.
DISCUSSES INTERNATIONAL LAWS AND TREATIES, ORGANIZATION OF
NATIONS, AND DISARMAMENT PROPOSALS.

1611 PETKOFF D.K.
"RECOGNITION AND NON-RECOGNITION OF STATES AND GOVERNMENTS
IN INTERNATIONAL LAW."
ASSEN. CAPT. EUROP. NAT. SECRETARIAT, 5 (MAR. 62), 25-52.
DISCUSSES DECLARATIVE AND CONSTITUTIVE THEORIES ON NATURE
OF RECOGNITION UNDER INTERNATIONAL LAW. APPLIES THEORIES
TO CURRENT POLITICAL SITUATION. ANALYZES ISSUE OF RECOGNI-
TION IN REGARD TO EAST-WEST RELATIONS. MAKES POLICY RECOM-
MENDATIONS FOR INTERNATIONAL DIPLOMACY.

1612 PHILLIPS J.B.
"MODIFICATIONS OF THE JURY SYSTEM."
U. OF COLORADO STUDIES, 11 (JUNE 05), 209-219.
HISTORICAL STUDY AND CRITIQUE OF JURY SYSTEM. SEVERAL
ARGUMENTS FOR REFORM GIVEN. PRINCIPAL ARGUMENT IS CLAIM THAT
JURY GIVES ONE MAN TOO MUCH POWER DESPITE VARIOUS OPINIONS
AND CONCLUSIONS REACHED.

1613 PHILLIPS O.H.
CONSTITUTIONAL AND ADMINISTRATIVE LAW (3RD ED.)
LONDON: SWEET AND MAXWELL, LTD, 1962, 855 PP.
EXAMINES ENGLISH LAW, INCLUDING ANALYSIS OF CONSTITUTION
AND PARLIAMENT, CROWN AND CENTRAL GOVERNMENT, JUDICIAL SYS-
TEM, AND RIGHTS AND DUTIES OF CITIZENRY, AND ADMINISTRATIVE
LAW AND RELATION TO COMMONWELATH.

1614 PHILLIPSON C.
THE INTERNATIONAL LAW AND CUSTOM OF ANCIENT GREECE AND
ROME.
LONDON: MACMILLAN, 1911, 830 PP.
OFFERS A COMPREHENSIVE AND SYSTEMATIC ACCOUNT OF THE
SUBJECT. TRIES TO REVEAL THE EXISTENCE OF A SYSTEM OF INTER-
NATIONAL LAW IN THE ANCIENT WORLD. WORK IS BASED ON GREEK
AND ROMAN BASIC SOCIAL INSTITUTIONS.

1615 PICKLES D.
THE FIFTH FRENCH REPUBLIC.
NEW YORK: FREDERICK PRAEGER, 1960, 222 PP., LC#60-8738.
ANALYZES CONSTITUTION OF 4 OCT., 1958: ITS PURPOSES AND
HOW THEY WERE ACHIEVED AFTER FIRST YEAR. AUTHOR ANALYZES
POLITICAL CONTEXT OF CONSTITUTION TO CLARIFY WHY IT WAS
CONTROVERSIAL BEFORE VOTED ON, THEN DESCRIBES ESSENTIAL
PROVISIONS AND LAWS. FULL TEXT OF CONSTITUTION INCLUDED.

1616 PIERCE R.A.
RUSSIAN CENTRAL ASIA, 1867-1917: A SELECTED BIBLIOGRAPHY
(PAMPHLET)
BERKELEY: U OF CALIF PR, 1953, 28 PP.
SELECTED LIST OF MATERIAL DESIGNED TO AID SPECIALISTS IN
RESEARCH IN FIELD. MAIN STRESS IS ON DOMESTIC DEVELOPMENTS.
ITEMS ARE ARRANGED BY SUBJECT CONTENT: HISTORY, RUSSIAN CON-
QUEST, ADMINISTRATION, WWI IMPACT, ECONOMICS, ETHNOGRAPHY,
NATIVE LAW, CULTURAL DEVELOPMENT, EDUCATION, AND GEOG-
RAPHY. INCLUDES 483 ENTRIES.

1617 PINTO F.B.M.
ENRIQUECIMENTO ILICITO NO EXERCICIO DE CARGOS PUBLICOS.
RIO DE JANEIRO: COM EDIT FORENSE, 1960, 411 PP.
ANALYZES CORRUPTION AND GRAFT OF PUBLIC OFFICIALS IN
AMERICAS, WITH EMPHASIS ON BRAZIL. COMPARES LATIN AMERICAN
COUNTRIES AND US. DISCUSSES CONSTITUTIONAL AND LEGAL CONTROL
AND RESTRICTION ON PUBLIC OFFICIALS AND HOW THESE ARE
VIOLATED. EXAMINES REASONS AND ETHICAL NORMS AS BASIS FOR
DEVELOPING SYSTEM TO COMBAT ABUSE OF PUBLIC POWER AND
POSITION.

1618 PLANO J.C., RIGGS R.E.
FORGING WORLD ORDER: THE POLITICS OF INTERNATIONAL ORGANIZA-
TION.
NEW YORK: MACMILLAN, 1967, 600 PP., LC#67-18893.
INVESTIGATES CONTEMPORARY INTERNATIONAL ORGANIZATION
WITHOUT ATTACHMENT TO ANY SINGLE THEORY OF POLITICAL BEHAV-
IOR. DISCUSSION OF SETTING, PROBLEMS, AND PROCESSES OF IN-
TERNATIONAL ORGANIZATION. REVEALS INTERACTION OF POLITICAL
INSTITUTIONS AND INDIVIDUALS WHO SHAPE THEM --WHO GETS WHAT,
WHY, AND HOW.

1619 PLATE H.
PARTEIFINANZIERUNG UND GRUNDESETZ.
BERLIN: DUNCKER & HUMBLOT, 1966, 139 PP.
DISCUSSES DUTY OF POLITICAL PARTIES TO REPORT FINANCIAL
EXPENDITURES AND MAKES RECOMMENDATIONS THAT WOULD MAKE THE
CONSTITUTIONAL REQUIREMENT A REALITY. CONTAINS MATERIAL ON
INCOME OF PARTIES AND DISCUSSES VARIOUS PLANS TO FINANCE
PARTIES.

1620 PLAYFAIR R.L. ED.
"A BIBLIOGRAPHY OF MOROCCO."
LONDON: JOHN MURRAY, 1893.
ANNOTATED BIBLIOGRAPHY OF WORKS IN VARIOUS LANGUAGES
REGARDING MOROCCO FROM EARLIEST TIMES THROUGH THE END OF
1891. INCLUDES ROMAN AND GREEK WRITINGS AND EARLY EXPLORERS'
ACCOUNTS OF GEOGRAPHY, THE PEOPLE, AND THEIR CULTURE. LATER
WORKS INCLUDE HISTORY OF THE COUNTRY, ECONOMICS, SOCIAL
CONDITIONS, RELIGION, LEADERS, MILITARY SUBJECTS, INTER-
NATIONAL RELATIONS, ETC.

1621 PLISCHKE E.
AMERICAN FOREIGN RELATIONS: A BIBLIOGRAPHY OF OFFICIAL
SOURCES.
COLLEGE PARK: U MD, BUR GOVT RES, 1955, 71 PP.
INCLUSIVE AND ACCESSIBLE LISTING OF OFFICIAL SOURCES IN
AMERICAN FOREIGN RELATIONS. INCLUDES ONLY MATERIALS PUB-
LISHED IN ENGLISH WITH EMPHASIS ON RECENT MATERIALS. GUIDE
TO PUBLISHED SOURCE MATERIALS CONTAINS REFERENCES TO
VARIOUS SPECIFIC COLLECTIONS, COMPILATIONS, SERIES, AND
SPECIAL REPORTS. CONCENTRATES ON OFFICIAL SOURCES;
UNOFFICIAL DOCUMENTS OF INTEREST CONTAINED IN APPENDIX.

1622 POGANY A.H., POGANY H.L.
POLITICAL SCIENCE AND INTERNATIONAL RELATIONS, BOOKS RECOM-
MENDED FOR AMERICAN CATHOLIC COLLEGE LIBRARIES.
METUCHEN: SCARECROW PRESS, 1967, 387 PP., LC#67-10196.
UNANNOTATED LISTING OF 5,800 BOOKS PERTINENT TO POLITI-
CAL SCIENCE AND INTERNATIONAL RELATIONS. ORGANIZED AROUND
HISTORY OF WORLD POLITICAL THEORY, POLITICAL AND CONSTITU-
TIONAL HISTORY OF WORLD, GOVERNMENT ADMINISTRATION, POLITI-
CAL ECONOMY, INTERNATIONAL LAW, AND INTERNATIONAL RELATIONS.
ENTRIES PRINCIPALLY TAKEN FROM 1955-66 PERIOD. AUTHOR AND
SUBJECT INDEX.

1623 POLLACK R.S.
THE INDIVIDUAL'S RIGHTS AND INTERNATIONAL ORGANIZATION.
NORTHAMPTON: SMITH COLLEGE, 1966, 122 PP., LC#65-28710.
DISCUSSES STATUS OF INDIVIDUAL IN PUBLIC INTERNATIONAL
LAW. EXAMINES TREATIES, CONVENTIONS, COVENANTS, EUROPEAN
CONVENTION ON HUMAN RIGHTS, AND CONCLUDES WITH REFLECTIONS
ON WORLD LEGAL ORDER.

1624 POLLOCK F.
THE GENIUS OF THE COMMON LAW.
NEW YORK: COLUMBIA U PRESS, 1912, 141 PP.
EXAMINES HISTORY OF ENGLISH COMMON LAW TO DETERMINE ITS
EFFECT ON MODERN ATTITUDES. MAINTAINS THAT COMMON LAW HAD NO
SPECIFIC POINT OF BEGINNING AND THAT IT UNDERGOES CONSTANT
CHANGE. ARGUES AGAINST FORMALISM AND SLAVISHNESS TO PRECE-
DENT. WARNS AGAINST HASTY BORROWING OF FOREIGN ELEMENTS OF
LAW. DISCUSSES DANGER TO COMMON LAW, REMEDIES AND REFORM,
AND COMMON LAW IN RELATION TO TRADE.

1625 POLLOCK F.
ESSAYS IN JURISPRUDENCE AND ETHICS.
LONDON: MACMILLAN, 1882, 383 PP.
ESSAYS CONSIDER JURISPRUDENCE AS IT AFFECTS OR IS AF-
FECTED BY HISTORY, POLITICS, AND LEGISLATION. ETHICS ARE
CONSIDERED IN RELATION TO LEGAL CONCEPTIONS AND BY APPLI-
CATION OF LEGAL CONCEPTIONS TO FACT. HISTORICAL APPROACH
USED. STUDY NATURE OF JURISPRUDENCE, LAWS OF NATURE AND OF
MAN, ENGLISH LAW OF PARTNERSHIP, EMPLOYERS' LIABILITY THEORY
OF PERSECUTION, OATH OF ALLEGIANCE, AND OTHER SUBJECTS.

1626 POLLOCK F., MAITLAND F.W.
THE HISTORY OF ENGLISH LAW BEFORE THE TIME OF EDWARD I (2
VOLS, 2ND ED.)
BOSTON: LITTLE BROWN, 1898, 1379 PP.
COMPREHENSIVE STUDY FIRST CONCENTRATES ON PERIODS OF
ENGLISH LEGAL HISTORY: ANGLO-SAXON, NORMAN, ROMAN-CANON-
ICAL, AND THE AGES OF GLENVILL AND BRACTON. LONGER SECOND
PART DEALS WITH DOCTRINES AND RULES: TENURE, SORTS AND
CONDITIONS OF MEN, JURISDICTION AND COMMUNITIES, OWNERSHIP
AND POSSESSION, CONTRACT FAMILY LAW, INHERITANCE, CRIME AND
TORT, AND PROCEDURE. NEW CHAPTER I IN SECOND EDITION.

1627 POLSBY N.W.
"BOOKS IN THE FIELD: POLITICAL SCIENCE."
WILSON LIBRARY BULLETIN, 40 (JAN. 66), 432-439.
AN ANNOTATED BIBLIOGRAPHY ON POLITICAL SCIENCE. ENGLISH-
LANGUAGE MATERIAL. RANGES FROM 1956 TO 1965. CONTAINS 25
ENTRIES. OUTLINED UNDER THREE HEADINGS: PEOPLE AND THE
AMERICAN POLITICAL PROCESS, ADMINISTRATIVE STRATEGY, AND
THE SUPREME COURT.

1628 POOLEY B.J.
PLANNING AND ZONING IN THE UNITED STATES.
ANN ARBOR: U OF MICH LAW SCHOOL, 1961, 123 PP.
STUDIES ENABLING ACTS; ZONING LAWS AND THEIR ADMINISTRA-
TION; AND MODERN TRENDS IN ZONING LAWS. FEELS THAT EXISTING
TECHNIQUES OF LAND USE CONTROL ARE EQUAL TO THE PROBLEMS
POSED BY RAPID GROWTH OF URBAN AREAS, PROVIDED STATE GOVERN-
MENT IS PREPARED TO ACCEPT ITS RESPONSIBLITY. ADEQUATELY
STAFFED STATE AND LOCAL PLANNING COMMISSIONS SHOULD BE ES-
TABLISHED, ALONG WITH METROPOLITAN BOARDS OF APPEAL.

1629 PORTER K.H.
A HISTORY OF SUFFRAGE IN THE UNITED STATES.
CHICAGO: U OF CHICAGO PRESS, 1918, 260 PP.
HISTORY OF PROCESS TO OBTAIN SUFFRAGE, CONCERNED MAINLY
WITH FIGHT OF WOMEN AND NEGROES. BEGINS WITH 1776 AND
LANDED-PROPERTY QUALIFICATION TO VOTE; DISCUSSES WEAKENING
OF PROPERTY TESTS AND BEGINNING OF PROBLEM OF FOREIGNER AND
FREE NEGRO. EXAMINES END OF PROPERTY AND TAX QUALIFICATIONS;
INCLUDES ALIENS, BEGINNING OF WOMEN'S SUFFRAGE, AND SUFFRAGE
FROM CIVIL WAR TO EARLY 20TH CENTURY.

1630 POSPISIL L.
"LEGAL LEVELS AND MULTIPLICITY OF LEGAL SYSTEMS IN HUMAN
SOCIETIES."
J. OF CONFLICT RESOLUTION, 11 (MAR. 67), 2-26.
DISCUSSES MULTIPLE LEGAL SYSTEMS IN ANY GIVEN SOCIETY
THAT ARE CREATED BY SUBGROUPS OF SOCIETY. EXPLORES
HISTORICAL DEVELOPMENT OF MULTIPLICITY BY EXAMINING THEORIES
ON SUBJECT. DISCUSSES HIERARCHIES OF LEGAL LEVELS AND CENTER
OF LEGAL POWER. STUDIES HOW LEGAL LEVELS CHANGE AS SUBGROUPS
CHANGE. MAINTAINS THAT LAW MUST BE CONSIDERD AGAINST SOCIAL
STRUCTURE.

1631 POTTER P.B.
"NEUTRALITY, 1955."
AMER. J. OF INT. LAW, 50 (JAN. 56), 101-102.
EDITORIAL COMMENT REVIEWS BRIEFLY EVOLUTION OF CONCEPT OF
NEUTRALITY AND TRACES CHANGE IN ATTITUDES. RIGHT OF NATION
TO REMAIN NEUTRAL REMAINED UNCHALLENGED UNTIL 20TH CENTURY,
WHEN DOUBTS AROSE AS TO ITS JUSTIFIABILITY. LEAGUE OF
NATIONS DISCREDITED IT FURTHER; UN OUTLAWED IT. FINDS IT HAS
NOW BEEN REPLACED BY NEUTRALISM, I.E., RIGHT TO REFUSE TO
TAKE SIDES IN COLD WAR.

1632 POTTER P.B.
"OBSTACLES AND ALTERNATIVES TO INTERNATIONAL LAW."
AMER. J. INT. LAW, 3 (JULY 59), 647-651.
THE PAST 45 YEARS HAS SEEN THE REPLACEMENT OF INTERNA-
TIONAL LAW BY A SYSTEM OF INTERNATIONAL LEGISLATION AND
ADMINISTRATION. EFFORTS MUST NOW BE MADE TO INSTITUTE THESE
NEW SYSTEMS.

1633 POTTER P.B.
"RELATIVE VALUES OF INTERNATIONAL RELATIONS, LAW, AND
ORGANIZATIONS."
AMER. J. INT. LAW, 54 (APR. 60), 379-82.
VIEWS PHENOMENA OF RISE IN NUMBER OF INDEPENDENT STATES
AND ESTABLISHMENT OF INTERNATIONAL ORGANIZATIONS. STATES
THAT EFFORTS SHOULD BE MADE TO ALTER THE CURRENT USAGE OF
DIPLOMACY IN FAVOR OF INTERNATIONAL LEGISLATIVE SYSTEM.

1634 POUND R.
"THE SCOPE AND PURPOSE OF SOCIOLOGICAL JURISPRUDENCE."

HARVARD LAW REV., 24 (JUNE-DEC. 11), 591-619, 140-168.
THREE-PART ARTICLE CONCLUDED IN APRIL, 1912, VOL. 25,
PP. 489-516. DISCUSSES ANALYTICAL, HISTORICAL, AND PHILO-
SOPHICAL JURISPRUDENCE. EXAMINES SOCIAL PHILOSOPHICAL
SCHOOL, SOCIAL UTILITARIANS, NEO-KANTIANS, NEO-HEGELIANS,
FRENCH SCHOOL, ETC. STUDIES ECONOMIC INTERPRETATIONS OF
JURISPRUDENCE; MECHANICAL, BIOLOGICAL, AND PSYCHOLOGICAL,
STAGES OF JURISPRUDENCE; AND PRESENT SITUATION.

1635 POUND R.
ORGANIZATION OF THE COURTS (PAMPHLET)
CHICAGO: AMER JUDICATURE SOC, 1914, 28 PP.
BRIEFLY TRACES HISTORY OF COURT SYSTEMS IN US, INCLUDING
ORIGINS IN EUROPE AND DISTINCTIVE CHARACTER OF AMERICAN
DEVELOPMENT. POINTS UP HISTORICAL CONDITIONS AND HERITAGE
THAT CREATED ORGANIZATIONAL STRUCTURE PECULIAR TO AMERICAN
SYSTEM AND SHOWS ADVANTAGES OF SUCH A STRUCTURE. PROPOSES
CHANGES THAT WOULD CONCENTRATE JUDICIAL RESPONSIBILITY IN
A CHIEF JUSTICE AND GIVE HIM CORRESPONDING POWER.

1636 POUND R.
INTERPRETATIONS OF LEGAL HISTORY.
NEW YORK: MACMILLAN, 1923, 170 PP.
STUDIES 19TH-CENTURY HISTORICAL SCHOOL OF JURISPRUDENCE,
EXAMINING ETHICAL, POLITICAL, POSITIVIST, AND ECONOMIC IN-
TERPRETATIONS OF LEGAL HISTORY. REJECTS ORGANISMIC MODEL OF
LAW AND ASSUMPTION THAT A SINGLE CAUSE IS AT WORK IN LEGAL
DEVELOPMENT. NOTES MIXTURE OF THE RATIONAL AND IRRATIONAL
IN LAW. VIEWING LAW AS A BUILDING ERECTED AND CONTINUALLY
ALTERED BY MEN, PROPOSES ENGINEERING INTERPRETATION.

1637 POUND R.
THE FORMATIVE ERA OF AMERICAN LAW.
BOSTON: LITTLE BROWN, 1938, 188 PP.
DISCUSSES JURISTIC THEORY AS PRACTICED IN COLONIAL AND
POST-REVOLUTIONARY AMERICA. EXAMINES ORIGINS AND DEVELOPMENT
OF CHIEF LEGAL AGENCIES FROM INDEPENDENCE TO CIVIL WAR.
ANALYZES LEGAL PORTIONS OF FEDERAL AND STATE CONSTITUTIONS
AND MAJOR REFORM MOVEMENTS. DISCUSSES INFLUENCES OF CLASS
SELF-INTEREST AND INDIVIDUAL JUDICIAL PSYCHOLOGY ON THE
FORMATION OF THE LAW.

1638 POUND R.
THE DEVELOPMENT OF CONSTITUTIONAL GUARANTEES OF LIBERTY.
NEW HAVEN: YALE U PR, 1957, 207 PP., LC#57-6343.
HISTORY OF DEVELOPMENT OF US CONSTITUTIONAL GUARANTEES
OUT OF MEDIEVAL FAITH IN LAW. TRACES WAYS IDEA OF
GUARANTEES BECAME INVOLVED IN VERY IDEA OF LAW AND
MAINTAINED ITSELF AGAINST MASTERFUL MONARCHS AND IN ERAS OF
PROFOUND SOCIAL AND ECONOMIC CHANGE TO BECOME LAW OF
LAND IN FORMATIVE AMERICA.

1639 POUND R.
JUSTICE ACCORDING TO LAW.
NEW HAVEN: YALE U PR, 1958, 98 PP.
GENERAL DISCUSSION OF PURPOSE, METHODS, AND PROBLEMS IN-
VOLVED IN LEGAL ADMINISTRATION OF JUSTICE. CONSISTS OF THREE
LECTURES DEFINING JUSITCE, LAW, AND LEGAL JUSTICE. APPROACH
IS THEORETICALLY AND HISTORICALLY ORIENTED.

1640 POUNDS N.J.G. ET AL.
"THE POLITICS OF PARTITION."
J. INT. AFF., 18 (NO.2, 64), 161-252.
WHOLE ISSUE DEVOTED TO A THEORETICAL AND COMPARATIVE
ANALYSIS OF THE SOCIO-POLITICAL CONCEPT OF PARTITION. PAR-
TITION IS SEEN AS PROVIDING A KEY TO CURRENT CRISES AS WELL
AS TO AREAS OF POTENTIAL STRIFE. DEALS WITH THE CAMEROONS,
INDIA, JERUSALEM, KOREA, VIETNAM, PAKISTAN AND UNION OF
SOUTH AFRICA.

1641 POWELL T.
THE SCHOOL BUS LAW: A CASE STUDY IN EDUCATION, RELIGION, AND
POLITICS.
MIDDLETON: WESLEYAN U PR, 1960, 334 PP., LC#60-13155.
STUDIES ROLE OF RELIGIOUS GROUPS AS POLITICAL FORCE.
SPECIFICALLY ANALYZES AND CRITICIZES ACTIONS AND POLITICAL
METHODS OF CONN. CHURCH GROUPS DURING 1956-57 DISPUTE OVER
USE OF PUBLIC SERVICES FOR CHURCH SCHOOLS. SUGGESTS POSSIBLE
WAYS FOR RELIGIOUS LEADERS TO USE POLITICAL INFLUENCE
WITHOUT CREATING SEVERE COMMUNITY DIVISIONS IN FUTURE.

1642 POWELL T.R.
"THE LOGIC AND RHETORIC OF CONSTITUTIONAL LAW" (BMR)"
J. OF PHILOSOPHY, 15 (NOV. 18), 645-658.
EXAMINES THE LOGIC BEHIND THE RHETORIC OF CONSTITUTIONAL
LAW, DIRECTING HIS ATTENTION TO THE THESIS THAT THIS LOGIC
IS REPRESENTED BY THE RATIONAL JUDGMENT OF THE SUPREME
COURT. CONTENDS THAT MUCH OF OUR CONSTITUTIONAL LAW IS
MERELY GETTING AT THE COMMON SENSE OF THE MATTER, FOR FEW
QUESTIONS OF CONSTITUTIONAL LAW ARE ANSWERED BY SPECIFIC
LANGUAGE IN THE CONSTITUTION.

1643 POWERS E.
CRIME AND PUNISHMENT IN EARLY MASSACHUSETTS 1620-1692: A
DOCUMENTARY HISTORY.
BOSTON: BEACON PRESS, 1966, 647 PP., LC#66-14490.
STUDIES 17TH-CENTURY PENOLOGY IN MASSACHUSETTS COLONY.
USING WORDS OF THOSE WHO PUNISHED AND THOSE WHO WERE PUN-
ISHED, AUTHOR RELATES DOCUMENTS TO SOCIAL, RELIGIOUS, AND
POLITICAL TEMPER OF THE TIMES. OFFERS HISTORICAL PERSPECTIVE
TO PRESENT SYSTEM OF ADMINISTERING CRIMINAL JUSTICE IN THE
STATE.

1644 COLUMBIA U. BUREAU APPL SOC RES
ATTITUDES OF PROMINENT AMERICANS TOWARD "WORLD PEACE THROUGH
WORLD LAW" (SUPRA-NATL ORGANIZATION FOR WAR PREVENTION)
NEW YORK: COLUMBIA U APP SOC RES, 1959.
ANALYZES OPINION OF PERSONS LISTED IN "WHO'S WHO
IN AMERICA" CONCERNING TWO PLANS FOR AN INTERNATIONAL AGENCY
TO SETTLE NATIONAL DISPUTES IN WORLD LAW COURTS. OPINION
ANALYSIS IS BASED ON ATTITUDINAL CHARACTERISTICS AND SOCIAL
VARIABLES; EXTENSIVE USE OF TABLES AND STATISTICS.

1645 PRABHAKAR P.
"SURVEY OF RESEARCH AND SOURCE MATERIALS; THE SINO-INDIAN
BORDER DISPUTE."
INT. STUDIES, 7 (JULY 65), 120-127.
ENTRIES DEAL WITH LEGAL CLAIMS OF THE DISPUTE, CHINESE
GOALS IN THE AREA, AND THE IMPACT OF THE DISPUTE ON WORLD
POLITICS. TREATS FOREIGN POLICY OF INDIA.

1646 PRASAD B.
THE ORIGINS OF PROVINCIAL AUTONOMY.
NEW DELHI: ATMA RAM & SONS, 1960, 288 PP.
HISTORICAL DISCUSSION OF RELATIONS BETWEEN CENTRAL
GOVERNMENT AND PROVINCIAL GOVERNMENTS IN INDIA FROM 1860 TO
1919. EMPHASIS IS ON EVOLUTION OF DECENTRALIZATION IN ITS
EARLY PHASES AND TRANSFER OF GOVERNMENT AND POLITICAL
AUTHORITY TO POPULAR CONTROL IN PROVINCIAL FIELD.

1647 PRATT I.A.
MODERN EGYPT: A LIST OF REFERENCES TO MATERIAL IN THE NEW
YORK PUBLIC LIBRARY.
NEW YORK: NY PUBLIC LIBRARY, 1929, 320 PP.
EXTENSIVE LIST OF WORKS DEALING WITH ASPECTS OF MODERN
EGYPT. INCLUDES SECTIONS ON ANTHROPOLOGY AND ETHNOLOGY,
GEOGRAPHY, HISTORY, GOVERNMENT, LAW, FOREIGN RELATIONS,
ECONOMIC HISTORY, ETC. MATERIAL IS ARRANGED TOPICALLY BUT
INCLUDES AUTHOR INDEX.

1648 PRESS C., WILLIAMS O.
STATE MANUALS, BLUE BOOKS AND ELECTION RESULTS.
BERKELEY: U CAL, INST GOVT STUD, 1962, 101 PP.
COMPREHENSIVE STATE-BY-STATE SURVEY OF ALL STATE LEGIS-
LATIVE MANUALS AND BLUEBOOKS. ANALYZES AND TABULATES THEIR
CONTENTS AND INDICATES FREQUENCY OF PUBLICATION AND PRICE.
COMPILATION OF STATE ELECTIONS RESULTS DESIGNED TO PROVIDE
FACTUAL MATERIALS USEFUL IN COMPARATIVE STUDIES OF DECISION-
MAKING.

1649 PRESS C.
A BIBLIOGRAPHIC INTRODUCTION TO AMERICAN STATE GOVERNMENT
AND POLITICS (PAMPHLET)
E LANSING: MSU COMM DEV & SERV, 1964, 34 PP.
UNANNOTATED TOPICAL LISTING OF 500 BOOKS, SCHOLARLY
ARTICLES, TEXTBOOKS, CASE HISTORIES, AND BIBLIOGRAPHIES
PUBLISHED FROM 1935 TO 1964. EMPHASIS IS ON PARTY POLITICS
AND EXECUTIVE AND LEGISLATIVE BRANCHES OF GOVERNMENT.

1650 PRICE D.K.
THE SECRETARY OF STATE.
ENGLEWOOD CLIFFS: PRENTICE HALL, 1960, 200 PP.
ESSAYS CONCERNED WITH DIFFERENT FUNCTIONS OF SECRETARY OF
STATE: POLICY FORMULATION, POLICY EXECUTION, MANAGEMENT OF
STATE DEPARTMENT, LINK OF PRESIDENT AND CONGRESS.

1651 PRITCHETT C.H.
"THE PRESIDENT AND THE SUPREME COURT."
J. OF POLITICS, 11 (FEB. 49), 80-92.
"IN GENERAL THE COURT TODAY APPEARS TO PREFER THAT THE
POWERS OF THE PRESIDENT BE DEFINED BY THE POLITICAL RATHER
THAN THE JUDICIAL PROCESS, AND THAT IS AS IT SHOULD BE."

1652 PRITCHETT C.H.
CONGRESS VERSUS THE SUPREME COURT, 1957-1960.
MINNEAPOLIS: U OF MINN PR, 1961, 168 PP., LC#61-8401.
DEALS WITH THE EFFORTS IN THE 85TH AND 86TH CONGRESS TO
CURB THE SUPREME COURT. MAINTAINS THAT THE OSTENSIBLE CAUSE
OF FRICTION WAS A SERIES OF DECISIONS HANDED DOWN BY THE
COURT BETWEEN 1955 AND 1958.

1653 PRITCHETT C.H.
THE ROOSEVELT COURT.
NEW YORK: OCTAGON PUBL CO, 1963, 314 PP., LC#63-20893.
A HISTORY OF THE SUPREME COURT DURING THE PRESIDENCY
OF F. D. ROOSEVELT COVERING THE DECISIONS OF THE COURT IN
ECONOMIC REGULATION, LEGISLATIVE SUPREMACY, CIVIL
LIBERTIES, JUDICIAL SUPREMACY, CRIME AND PUNISHMENT,
BUREAUCRACY AND LABOR.

1654 PRITCHETT C.H. ED., WESTIN A.F. ED.
THE THIRD BRANCH OF GOVERNMENT.

NEW YORK: HARCOURT BRACE, 1963, 308 PP., LC#63-13250.
SURVEYS ACTIVITIES OF SUPREME COURT SINCE 1937, AND CON-
SISTS OF EIGHT ARTICLES DEALING WITH A VARIETY OF CASES,
FROM SEPARATION OF CHURCH AND STATE, TO LOYALTY-SECURITY
PROGRAMS, TO INDUSTRIAL RELATIONS.

1655 PRITCHETT C.H.
"EQUAL PROTECTION AND THE URBAN MAJORITY."
AM. POL. SCI. REV., 58 (DEC. 64), 869-875.
DISCUSSION AND DEFENSE OF THE ONE-MAN-ONE-VOTE RULE
EMBODIED IN BAKER VS. CARR AND REYNOLDS VS. SIMS. AUTHOR
SUPPORTS THE SUPREME COURT'S INITIATIVE IN THIS AREA AND
BELIEVES THE RULE "COMES CLOSER TO SUMMARIZING THE CURRENT
NOTIONS OF DEMOCRACY THAN ANY OTHER."

1656 PROEHL P.O.
FOREIGN ENTERPRISE IN NIGERIA.
CHAPEL HILL: U OF N CAR PR, 1965, 250 PP., LC#65-19387.
DISCUSSES LEGAL ENVIRONMENT FOR FOREIGN INVESTMENT IN
NIGERIA IN CONTEXT OF POLITICAL, ECONOMIC, AND SOCIAL
DEVELOPMENT. COVERS CONDITIONS OF LABOR, TAXATION, AND
NATIONALIZATION.

1657 PRYOR F.L.
THE COMMUNIST FOREIGN TRADE SYSTEM.
LONDON: ALLEN UNWIN, 1963, 234 PP.
SINCE ALL 'SYSTEMS' (DEFINED AS TOTAL NETWORK OF FOREIGN-
TRADE DECISIONS) OPERATE FUNDAMENTALLY THE SAME, THE DDR
(EAST GERMANY) CHOSEN AS CASE-STUDY TO ILLUSTRATE MAIN
PROBLEMS FACING PLANNERS AND POLICY-MAKERS. TRADITIONAL
METHODS OF ANALYSIS BY WESTERNER INAPPLICABLE BECAUSE
PRIMARY ORIENTATION TOWARDS FULFILLMENT PLAN AND CERTAIN
POLITICAL-IDEOLOGICAL GOALS.

1658 PUBLISHERS' CIRCULAR LIMITED
THE ENGLISH CATALOGUE OF BOOKS.
LONDON: PUBL CIRCULAR LTD.
YEARLY PUBLICATION SINCE 1836 LISTING ALL BOOKS PUBLISHED
IN UNITED KINGDOM DURING THAT CALENDAR YEAR. BOOKS ARE
LISTED BY AUTHOR AND TITLE AND INDEXED BY SUBJECT AT END
OF VOLUME. SEPARATE LISTING FOR PAPERBACKS. INCLUDES
MATERIALS ON ALL SUBJECTS.

1659 PUFENDORF S.
LAW OF NATURE AND OF NATIONS (ABRIDGED)
ORIGINAL PUBLISHER NOT AVAILABLE, 1716, 339 PP.
"MORAL ENTITIES" WERE DESIGNED BY GOD FOR THE REGULATION
OF HUMAN LIFE. THEY EXIST IN THE STATE, WHICH IS THAT CON-
DITION IN WHICH MEN ARE SETTLED FOR EXERCISE OF ACTIONS.
POWER IS "THAT BY WHICH A MAN IS QUALIFIED TO DO A THING
LAWFULLY AND WITH A MORAL EFFECT." DISCUSSES MORAL KNOWLEDGE
AND ACTION, STATE OF NATURE, LAW OF NATURE, DUTY OF MAN
TOWARD HIMSELF AND GOD, SELF-DEFENSE, TREATIES, AND SO ON.

1660 PUGET H. ED.
ESSAI DE BIBLIOGRAPHIE DES PRINCIPAUX OUVRAGES DE DROIT
PUBLIC... QUI ONT PARU HORS DE FRANCE DE 1945 A 1958.
PARIS: EDITIONS DE L'EPARGNE, 1961, 369 PP.
LISTING OF WORKS ON PUBLIC LAW AND ADMINISTRATION
PUBLISHED BETWEEN 1945 AND 1958 IN US AND WESTERN EUROPE.
CONTAINS 5,030 ENTRIES AND AUTHOR INDEX. SECTIONS ON
REFERENCE WORKS; CONSTITUTIONAL LAW AND POLITICAL SCIENCE;
ADMINISTRATIVE LAW AND MANAGEMENT.

1661 PUGWASH CONFERENCE
"ON BIOLOGICAL AND CHEMICAL WARFARE."
BULL. ATOM. SCI., 15 (OCT. 59), 337-39.
ASSESSMENT OF POTENTIALITIES OF CHEMICAL AND BIOLOGICAL
AGENTS AS WEAPONS AND EXPLORATION OF MEANS TO PREVENT
PRODUCTION FOR USE IN WAR. EVALUATES POSSIBILITY OF
INTERNATIONAL CONTROL BUT ENCOUNTERS DIFFICULTIES IN EXER-
CISING CONTROLS. FEELS PROPER INSPECTION BY UN SCIENTIFIC
COMMISSION TO DISPEL INTERNATIONAL SUSPICION AND TENSION.

1662 PULLEN W.R.
A CHECK LIST OF LEGISLATIVE JOURNALS ISSUED SINCE 1937 BY
THE STATES OF THE UNITED STATES OF AMERICA (PAMPHLET)
CHICAGO: AMER LIB ASSN, 1955, 60 PP., LC#55-8711.
AN UNANNOTATED BIBLIOGRAPHY ON LEGISLATIVE JOURNALS IS-
SUED SINCE 1937. MATERIAL IN ENGLISH LANGUAGE, RANGING FROM
1937-55. 1,160 ENTRIES. CONSISTS OF A CHECK LIST OF
JOURNALS OF VARIOUS STATE LEGISLATURES AND THE DATES OF IS-
SUANCE FROM 1937 TO 1955.

1663 PUSEY M.J.
CHARLES EVANS HUGHES (2 VOLS.)
NEW YORK: MACMILLAN, 1951, 829 PP.
BIOGRAPHY OF THE FORMER CHIEF JUSTICE OF THE US, BASED
ON HIS PERSONAL AND OFFICIAL PAPERS AND INTERVIEWS WITH HIS
FAMILY AND ASSOCIATES. VOLUME I DEALS WITH HIS CHILDHOOD AND
EDUCATION, FIRST YEARS AT THE BAR, GOVERNORSHIP, APPOINTMENT
TO THE SUPREME COURT BENCH, AND WORLD WAR I AND THE LEAGUE
OF NATIONS DISPUTE. VOLUME II COVERS HIS CAREERS AS SECRE-
TARY OF STATE AND CHIEF JUSTICE, AND HIS FINAL YEARS.

1664 PUTTKAMMER E.W.

WAR AND THE LAW.
CHICAGO: U. CHI. PR., 1944, 205.
ANALYZES WARTIME CIVIL LIBERTIES, THE RELATION BETWEEN
THE ARMED FORCES AND THE CIVILIAN POPULATION, THE EFFECT ON
LABOR, THE WORKING OF INTERNATIONAL CARTELS AND THE ECONO-
MICS OF WARTIME PRICE CONTROL. CONCLUDES WITH STUDY OF MILI-
TARY JUSTICE.

1665 PYLEE M.V.
CONSTITUTIONAL GOVERNMENT IN INDIA (2ND REV. ED.)
BOMBAY: ASIA PUBL HOUSE, 1965, 824 PP.
DISCUSSES RISE AND NATURE OF CONSTITUTIONAL GOVERNMENT IN
INDIA. EXAMINES FUNDAMENTAL RIGHTS, OPERATION OF NATIONAL
AND STATE GOVERNMENTS, AND FEDERAL SYSTEM.

1666 RADZINOWICZ L.
THE NEED FOR CRIMINOLOGY AND A PROPOSAL FOR AN INSTITUTE
OF CRIMINOLOGY.
LONDON: HEINEMANN, 1965, 123 PP.
DEMONSTRATES THAT THERE HAS BEEN NO CONTINUING, PERMANENT
ORGANIZATION OR INSTITUTION FOR STUDY OF CRIME AND ALL ITS
ASPECTS IN US. PROPOSES SUCH AN INSTITUTION OF EDUCATIONAL
QUALITY AND STANDING WHERE PURE, AS WELL AS APPLIED, RE-
SEARCH CAN BE CARRIED OUT. IT SHOULD EMBRACE WITHIN ITS PRO-
GRAM ALL DISCIPLINES WHICH MAY HELP UNDERSTAND NATURE, EF-
FECTS, AND CONTROL OF CRIME.

1667 RAE D.
THE POLITICAL CONSEQUENCES OF ELECTORAL LAWS.
NEW HAVEN: YALE U PR, 1967, 173 PP., LC#67-24511.
EMPLOYS MATHEMATICAL TOOLS IN DEFINING RELATIONSHIP BE-
TWEEN ELECTORAL SYSTEM AND POLITICS. STUDIES ELECTIONS 1945-
65 IN 20 DEMOCRATIC NATIONS. FINDS THAT BOTH PROPORTIONAL
AND PLURALITY SYSTEMS FAVOR LARGE PARTIES OVER MORE
SMALL ONES. MEASURES PARTY FRACTIONALIZATION AND CATEGORIZES
VARIOUS KINDS OF ELECTORAL LAWS.

1668 RAGHAVAN M.D.
INDIA IN CEYLONESE HISTORY, SOCIETY AND CULTURE.
BOMBAY: ASIA PUBL HOUSE, 1964, 190 PP.
ANALYSIS OF SOCIAL AND CULTURAL RELATIONS BETWEEN INDIA
AND CEYLON. DISCUSSES STRUCTURE OF CEYLONESE SOCIETY AND
INFLUENCE OF INDIA ON RELIGION, LANGUAGE, ART, LAW, AND
CUSTOMS.

1669 RAI H.
"DISTRICT MAGISTRATE AND POLICE SUPERINTENDENT IN INDIA: THE
CONTROVERSY OF DUAL CONTROL"
J. OF ADMINISTRATION OVERSEAS, 6 (JULY 67), 192-199.
PRESENTS BACKGROUND OF CONFLICT BETWEEN DISTRICT MAGIS-
TRATE AND POLICE SUPERINTENDENT OVER CONTROL OF POLICE
FORCE. BEGINS WITH POLICE ACT OF 1861 AND INCLUDES PRESENT
SITUATION OF MAGISTRATIVE DOMINANCE. GIVES ARGUMENTS ON BOTH
SIDES AND SUGGESTS NEW ARRANGEMENT.

1670 RAJAN M.S.
"UNITED NATIONS AND DOMESTIC JURISDICTION."
LONDON: LONGMANS, GREEN & CO, 1958.
ABOUT 350 REFERENCES TO 20TH CENTURY MATERIAL CONCERNING
LEGAL ASPECTS OF INTERNATIONAL RELATIONS ALMOST EXCLUSIVELY
IN ENGLISH. INCLUDES DOCUMENTS OF THE UN AND ITS VARIOUS
AGENCIES. MAJORITY OF WORKS ARE POST-WWII.

1671 RALSTON A.
A FRESH LOOK AT LEGISLATIVE APPORTIONMENT IN NEW JERSEY
(PAMPHLET)
LEEDS: LEEDS UNIVERSITY PRESS, 1960, 26 PP.
EXAMINES BODY OF LITERATURE ON REAPPORTIONMENT IN NEW
JERSEY FROM POINT OF VIEW OF MATHEMATICIAN. ALSO DISCUSSES
CRITERIA OF FAIRNESS IN POLITICAL SENSE.

1672 RAM J.
THE SCIENCE OF LEGAL JUDGMENT: A TREATISE...
ORIGINAL PUBLISHER NOT AVAILABLE, 1835, 146 PP.
STUDY OF THE COURTS OF WESTMINSTER HALL IN THE EARLY
19TH-CENTURY AND THE AUTHORITY AND PROCESSES BY WHICH LEGAL
JUDGMENTS ARE PASSED. OUTLINES THE GENERAL PRINCIPLES OF
ENGLISH LAW AND THE PRECEDENT ON WHICH DECISIONS ARE BASED.
DISCUSSES METHODS OF PRACTICE AND THE DUTIES OF THE JUDGE.
CIVIL LAW, CUSTOM OF MERCHANTS, THE CANON LAW, AND THE LAW
OF NATIONS ARE GIVEN SPECIAL ATTENTION.

1673 RAMUNDO B.A.
PEACEFUL COEXISTENCE: INTERNATIONAL LAW IN THE BUILDING OF
COMMUNISM.
BALTIMORE: JOHNS HOPKINS PRESS, 1967, 262 PP., LC#67-12421.
EXPLORES SOVIET POSITION ON BASIC QUESTIONS OF INTERNA-
TIONAL LAW AND LEGAL PROBLEMS. EXAMINES MANNER IN WHICH SO-
VIETS UTILIZE INTERNATIONAL LAW TO SUPPORT POLICY OBJEC-
TIVES AND COMPARES WITH OTHER COUNTRIES. FOCUSES ON IMPACT
OF LAW OF PEACEFUL COEXISTENCE UPON CONCEPTS OF INTERNATION-
AL LAW. ILLUSTRATES HOW PRINCIPLES OF PEACEFUL COEXISTENCE
ARE USED TO SUPPORT SPECIFIC SOVIET POLICIES.

1674 RAVENS J.P.
STAAT UND KATHOLISCHE KIRCHE IN PREUSSENS POLNISCHEN

TEILUNGSGEBIETEN.
WIESBADEN: OTTO HARRASSOWITZ, 1963, 181 PP.
EXAMINES DISPUTES BETWEEN PRUSSIA AND CATHOLIC CHURCH IN AREAS FORMERLY BELONGING TO POLAND BUT JOINED WITH PRUSSIA IN POLISH DIVISIONS OF 1772, 1793, AND 1795. DISCUSSES IN DETAIL POLITICAL, LEGAL, AND SOCIAL ACTIVITIES OF CATHOLIC CHURCH.

1675 READ J.S.
"CENSORED."
TRANSITION, 7 (AUG.-SEPT. 67), 37-41.
UGANDAN PUBLICATION DISCUSSES CENSORSHIP IN AFRICA. IMPORTED BOOKS MAY BE BANNED ON THE BASIS OF A MINISTER'S SUBJECTIVE JUDGMENT IN MOST COUNTRIES. IN SOME, BLANKET BANS MAY BE IMPOSED ON BOTH NATIVE AND FOREIGN AUTHORS AND PUBLISHERS. DISCUSSES PHILOSOPHY OF, AND AFRICAN HISTORY OF, CENSORSHIP. LAMENTS THE EFFECT OF STRICTNESS ON LONG-DELAYED FLOWERING OF AFRICAN LITERATURE.

1676 REALE M.
PLURALISMO E LIBERDADE.
SAO PAULO: EDICAO SARAIVO, 1963, 300 PP.
ANALYSIS OF POLITICAL AND SOCIAL PHILOSOPHY CONCERNING LIBERTY IN 20TH CENTURY. DISCUSSES RELATION OF MAN TO HIS SOCIETY, PLACE OF MAN IN DEMOCRACY, AND LEGAL RIGHTS.

1677 RECASENS SICHES S.
TRATADO GENERAL DE SOCIOLOGIA.
MEXICO CITY: EDITORIAL PORRUA, 1956, 636 PP.
GENERAL SOCIOLOGY TEXT DEALING WITH FAMILY, COMMUNITY, GROUP CONDUCT, SOCIAL CHANGE, RACES, SOCIAL INTERACTION, LANGUAGE, LAW, AND CULTURE.

1678 REDFORD E.S. ED.
PUBLIC ADMINISTRATION AND POLICY FORMATION: STUDIES IN OIL, GAS, BANKING, RIVER DEVELOPMENT AND CORPORATE INVESTIGATIONS
AUSTIN: U OF TEXAS PR, 1956, 319 PP., LC#56-7507.
FIVE CASE STUDIES OF ADMINISTRATIVE REGULATION EMPHASIZE RELATIONSHIP BETWEEN CONTROL, EFFICIENCY, AND PUBLIC INTEREST. DISCUSSES INTERRELATIONSHIPS BETWEEN AGENCIES, CLIENTELE, AND SPECIFIC INDIVIDUALS.

1679 REGALA R.
WORLD PEACE THROUGH DIPLOMACY AND LAW.
MANILA, PHIL: CENTRAL LAW BOOK, 1964, 270 PP.
DISCUSSES ROLE OF DIPLOMACY, INTERNATIONAL LAW, AND IN-TERNATIONAL ORGANIZATIONS IN THEORY AND PRACTICE OF MAIN-TAINING WORLD PEACE.

1680 REID H.D.
RECUEIL DES COURS; TOME 45: LES SERVITUDES INTERNATIONALES III.
PARIS: RECUEIL SIREY, 1933, 798 PP.
ESSAYS STUDY INTERNATIONAL RIGHTS WHICH EMPHASIZE INTERNATIONAL CONSTITUTIONAL LAW, INCLUDING COMMUNICATIONS, STRAITS, INDIVIDUAL MORALITY, AND MORALITY IN GENERAL.

1681 REIFF H.
THE UNITED STATES AND THE TREATY LAW OF THE SEA.
MINNEAPOLIS: U. MINN. PR., 1959, 451 PP.
MULTI-PARTITE AGREEMENTS BETWEEN USA AND OTHER NATIONS REGARDING THE USE OF THE SEA ARE PAINSTAKINGLY DISCUSSED. FOCUSES ON THE HISTORICAL AS WELL AS THE ETHICAL ASPECTS OF 'SEA-USAGE' AND CONCLUDES WITH OPTIMISTIC NOTE THAT THE SEA SHOULD ONE DAY BE APPLIED AS A FORCE WHICH WILL FOREVER UNIFY THE COMMUNITY OF NATIONS.

1682 REILLY T.J.
"FREEZING AND CONFISCATION OF CUBAN PROPERTY."
STANFORD LAW REV., 19. (JUNE 67), 1358-1368.
QUESTIONS US ACTIONS OF FREEZING AND CONFISCATING CUBAN NATIONALISTS' PROPERTY IN US, AND POLICY BEHIND IT, THROUGH STUDY OF COURT CASE OF SARDINO V. FEDERAL RESERVE BANK. MAINTAINS THAT POLICY IS IRRECONCILABLE WITH POLICY OF PROMOTING US INVESTMENT ABROAD.

1683 REINSCH P.
PUBLIC INTERNATIONAL UNION.
BOSTON: WORLD PEACE FOUND., 1911, 189 PP.
A SURVEY OF DEVELOPMENT AND ORGANIZATION OF INTERNATIONAL UNIONS. STUDIES ROLE IN INTERNATIONAL RELATIONS, ADMINIS-TRATIVE LAW AND WAR. FEELS INTERNATIONAL COOPERATION IS NECESSARILY INCREASING AND IS KEY TO MODERN SOCIETY.

1684 REITZEL A.M.
DAS MAINZER KRONUNGSRECHT UND DIE POLITISCHE PROBLEMATIK.
MAINZ: VERLAG HANS KRACH, 1963, 55 PP.
EXAMINES CORONATION LAWS AND ELECTION PROCEDURES OF GER-MAN KINGS IN FRAMEWORK OF CONSTITUTIONAL HISTORY OF GERMANY. DISCUSSES IN DETAIL NOMINATION AND ELECTION OF KONRAD IV IN VIENNA IN 1237. DESCRIBES ROLE OF CITY OF MAINZ IN DEVELOP-MENT OF CORONATION LAWS AND TRADITIONS.

1685 RENNER K.
MENSCH UND GESELLSCHAFT - GRUNDRISS EINER SOZIOLOGIE (2ND ED.)

VIENNA: VERL WIENER VOLKSBUCHH, 1965, 398 PP.
DISCUSSES PRINCIPLES OF HUMAN SOCIETY FROM SOCIOLOGICAL POINT OF VIEW. EXAMINES FAMILY STRUCTURE, LIFE PROCESSES AND CONSCIOUSNESS, RELATION OF INDIVIDUAL TO SOCIETY, LAW AND STATE, AND WAR AND POST-WAR ECONOMIC CONDITIONS.

1686 REOCK E.C.
PROCEDURES AND STANDARDS FOR THE APPORTIONMENT OF STATE LEGISLATURES (DOCTORAL THESIS)
NEW BRUNSWICK, NJ: RUTGERS UNIV, 1959, 231 PP.
EXAMINES RULES OF APPORTIONMENT LAID DOWN IN STATE CON-STITUTIONS IN ORDER TO DEVELOP STANDARDS CONSISTENT WITH AMERICAN POLITICAL PRACTICES. SEEKS APPLICATION TO EVALUAT-ING ANY PLAN FOR APPORTIONMENT OF STATE LEGISLATIVE BODIES. INCLUDES EXTENSIVE BIBLIOGRAPHY INCLUDING REPORTS FROM INDIVIDUAL STATES.

1687 REOCK E.C. JR.
POPULATION INEQUALITY AMONG COUNTIES IN THE NEW JERSEY LEG-ISLATURE 1791-1962.
N BRUNSWICK: RUTGERS BUR GOV RES, 1963, 29 PP.
DISCUSSES METHODS OF MEASURING POPULATION INEQUALITY AND EXAMINES INEQUALITIES IN NEW JERSEY LOWER AND UPPER HOUSE. CONCLUDES THAT TODAY "TWO HOUSES PRESENT TWO SUBSTANTIALLY DIFFERENT PICTURES OF THE STATE'S ELECTORATE."

1688 REVES E.
THE ANATOMY OF PEACE.
NEW YORK: HARPER, 1945, 293 PP.
ANAYLZES HISTORICAL SIGNIFICANCE OF SOVEREIGNTY. EXAMINES RELATIONSHIP BETWEEN INDIVIDUAL BEHAVIOR AND STATE POLICIES. POINTS OUT 'FALLACY' OF INTERNATIONALISM AND OF SELF-DETERMINISM OF NATIONS. ANALYZES PROBLEM OF NUCLEAR POWER.

1689 RHODESIA-NYASA NATL ARCHIVES
A SELECT BIBLIOGRAPHY OF RECENT PUBLICATIONS CONCERNING THE FEDERATION OF RHODESIA AND NYASALAND (PAMPHLET)
SALISBURY: NAT ARCH RHODES NYAS, 1960, 13 PP.
UNANNOTATED CLASSIFIED BIBLIOGRAPHY OF POST-1950 PUB-LICATIONS IN ENGLISH. COVERS OFFICIAL PERIODICAL PUBLICA-TIONS, GOVERNMENT PUBLICATIONS ON SPECIAL TOPICS, NEWSPA-PERS, PERIODICALS, AND BOOKS. SELECTIONS CONCERN SUBJECTS OF HISTORICAL, POLITICAL, ECONOMIC, GEOLOGICAL, AND ANTHROPO-LOGICAL INTEREST.

1690 RHYNE C.S.
"LAW AS AN INSTRUMENT FOR PEACE."
BOSTON U. LAW REV., 40 (SPRING 60), 187-196.
BELIEVES THAT LAW IS THE ONLY DEVELOPED STRUCTURE WHICH CAN REGULATE THE USE OF NEW INSTRUMENTS OF POWER SO AS TO MAKE IT A PEACEFUL RATHER THAN A DESTRUCTIVE FORCE. RECOMMENDS A WORLD LEGAL ORDER WHICH CAN BE ACHIEVED BY TAKING THE LOGIC OF SUCH A WORLD-ORDER TO THE PEOPLE ON A WORLD-WIDE BASIS. DISCUSSES THE WEAKNESSES OF THE PRESENT WORLD COURT.

1691 RICE C.E.
FREEDOM OF ASSOCIATION.
NEW YORK: NEW YORK U PR, 1962, 202 PP., LC#62-16636.
DISCUSSES PRINCIPLE OF FREEDOM OF ASSOCIATION IN AMERICAN HISTORY BEFORE AND AFTER WAR OF INDEPENDENCE, AND AS IT HAS RELATED TO FREEDOMS OF RELIGION, LIVELIHOOD, POLITICAL PARTIES AND PRESSURE GROUPS, AND SUBVERSIVE ASSOCIATIONS.

1692 RICE C.E.
THE SUPREME COURT AND PUBLIC PRAYER.
NEW YORK: FORDHAM U PR, 1964, 202 PP., LC#64-18392.
DISCUSSES US GOVERNMENT AND RELIGION, INCLUDING FEDERAL AID TO CHURCH-RELATED SCHOOLS AND TAX PRIVILEGES OF RELI-GIOUS ORGANIZATIONS. CRITICIZES DECISIONS RESTRAINING PRAYER IN SCHOOLS.

1693 RICHARDS P.G.
PATRONAGE IN BRITISH GOVERNMENT.
TORONTO: U OF TORONTO PRESS, 1963, 284 PP.
DISCUSSION OF THE INFLUENCE OF PARTY POLITICS ON GOVERNMENT APPOINTMENTS IN BRITAIN, TO THE ADMINISTRATIVE BRANCHES, THE JUDICIARY, AND THE CHURCH. SAYS THAT ALTHOUGH PATRONAGE STILL EXISTS, IT IS NOT DETRIMENTAL TO DEMOCRACY.

1694 RICHARDSON I.L.
BIBLIOGRAFIA BRASILEIRA DE ADMINISTRACAO PUBLICA E ASSUNTOS CORRELATOS.
RIO DE JAN: FUND GETULIO VARGAS, 1964, 840 PP.
BIBLIOGRAPHY OF 7,300 ITEMS ON BRAZILIAN DEVELOPMENT IN FIELD OF PUBLIC ADMINISTRATION. COVERS PERIOD 1940-61. CONTAINS REFERENCES TO CONSTITUTIONAL RIGHTS; POLITICAL THEORY; CENTRAL GOVERNMENT ORGANIZATION; INTERNATIONAL RELATIONS, LAWS, AND ORGANIZATIONS; STATE, LOCAL, AND TERRI-ORIAL GOVERNMENTS; POLITICAL PARTIES AND ELECTIONS; ADMINIS-TRATIVE LAW; PLANNING, ETC.

1695 RICHARDSON J.J.
"THE MAKING OF THE RESTRICTIVE TRADE PRACTICES ACT 1956 - A CASE STUDY OF THE POLICY PROCESS IN BRITAIN."
PARLIAMENTARY AFFAIRS, 20 (FALL 67), 350-374.

ACT WAS AN ATTEMPT BY CONSERVATIVE GOVERNMENT TO INCREASE
COMPETITION WITHIN THE BRITISH ECONOMY. TRACES HISTORY OF
RESTRICTIVE PRACTICES OF INDUSTRY. REVIEWS MONOPOLIES COM-
MISSION REPORT OF 1956 WHICH FOUND MONOPOLIES DETRIMENTAL TO
PUBLIC INTEREST. EXAMINES HOW PUBLIC OPINION, POLITICAL PAR-
TY OPINION, AND ORGANIZED INTEREST GROUPS AFFECTED THE BILL
PASSED AND POLICY-MAKING PROCESSES.

1696 RICHSTEIN A.R.
"LEGAL RULES IN NUCLEAR WEAPONS EMPLOYMENTS."
MIL. REV., 41(JULY 61), 91-98.
DESTRUCTIVE SCALE OF NUCLEAR WEAPONS AND GUIDANCE ERRORS
OF MISSILE SYSTEMS CREATE PROBLEMS AS TO EFFECTS ON
CIVILIAN NON-COMBATANS IN TARGET AREAS.

1697 RIENOW R.
INTRODUCTION TO GOVERNMENT (2ND ED.)
NEW YORK: ALFRED KNOPF, 1960, 583 PP., LC#56-6937.
TEXTBOOK OF COMPARATIVE GOVERNMENT BEGINNING WITH SURVEY
OF FRENCH, ENGLISH, AMERICAN, AND SOVIET GOVERNMENTS WITH
EMPHASIS ON US. DISCUSSES AREAS OF NATURE OF GOVERNMENT,
DIFFERENT STRUCTURES, POLITICS AND REPRESENTATIVE SYSTEM,
JUDICIAL SYSTEM, LOCAL GOVERNMENT AND INTERNATIONAL ORGANI-
ZATIONS. MAINTAINS THAT STUDENT NEEDS TO SEE PLACE OF OWN
GOVERNMENT IN WORLD TO UNDERSTAND IT.

1698 RIENOW R.
CONTEMPORARY INTERNATIONAL POLITICS.
NEW YORK: THOMAS Y CROWELL, 1961, 431 PP., LC#61-10668.
DISCUSSES FACTORS SHAPING CURRENT INTERNATIONAL POLITICS,
INCLUDING CONTEMPORARY SITUATION, INSTRUMENTS OF POWER, CON-
TROL OF POWER, PROBLEMS OF INTERNATIONAL LIFE, AND POWER AND
PEACE.

1699 RIGAUX F.
"LA SIGNIFICATION DES ACTES JUDICIARES A L'ETRANGER."
REV. CRIT. DR. INT. PRIV., 53 (NO. 3, 63), 447-74.
EXAMINES VARIOUS FACTORS INFLUENCING JURIDICAL ACTS RE-
LATED TO FOREIGNERS. EXAMINES SOLUTIONS PROPOSED BY SEVERAL
EUROPEAN CODES AND COMPARES THEM TO TRADITIONAL SOLUTIONS.
CRITICIZES INTERPRETATION OF LAW RESULTING FROM HAGUE CON-
VENTION.

1700 RIKER W.H.
"THE PARADOX OF VOTING AND CONGRESSIONAL RULES FOR VOTING ON
AMENDMENTS."
AM. POL. SCI. REV., 52 (JUNE 58), 349-366.
ANALYZES THE PROCESS OF VOTING ON AMENDMENTS, BILLS, AND
RESOLUTIONS IN CONGRESS. CONCLUDES THAT THIS PROCESS CAN IN
NO CIRCUMSTANCES BE CALLED RATIONAL BEHAVIOR. SUGGESTS RULE
TO GIVE CONGRESSIONAL VOTING SOME SEMBLANCE OF ORDER AND
LISTS THE ADVANTAGES AND DISADVANTAGES OF THE PROPOSED RULE.

1701 ROBERT H.M.
PARLIAMENTARY LAW.
NEW YORK: CENTURY CO, 1923, 588 PP.
GENERAL DISCUSSION OF METHODS OF TRANSACTING BUSINESS IN
PARLIAMENTARY BODIES - CONDUCT OF ELECTIONS, DUTIES OF
MEMBERS, BY-LAWS, MOTIONS, ETC. INCLUDES ANSWERS TO
QUESTIONS ON PARLIAMENTARY LAW AND DEFINITIONS OF
PARLIAMENTARY TERMS.

1702 ROBERT J.
LA MONARCHIE MAROCAINE.
PARIS: PICHON ET DURAND-AUZIAS, 1963, 350 PP.
RECAPITULATES STUDIES ALREADY UNDERTAKEN ON MOROCCO.
AUTHOR POINTS OUT THAT THEY ARE ALMOST NONEXISTENT SINCE
MOROCCO'S INDEPENDENCE; HENCE IMPORTANCE OF THIS WORK.
COLLATES ALL OFFICIAL TEXTS ON ADMINISTRATIVE AND
CONSTITUTIONAL MATTERS TO GAIN AN EXACT DESCRIPTION OF THE
PRINCIPAL ORGANS OF THE STATE. ILLUMINATES PAPERS ON ALL
QUESTIONS FACING MOROCCO SINCE INDEPENDENCE.

1703 ROBERTS H.L.
FOREIGN AFFAIRS BIBLIOGRAPHY, 1952-1962.
NEW YORK: RR BOWKER, 1964, 752 PP., LC#33-7094.
A SELECTED AND ANNOTATED CUMULATIVE BIBLIOGRAPHY OF BOOKS
ON INTERNATIONAL RELATIONS BASED LARGELY UPON NOTES APPEAR-
ING QUARTERLY IN "FOREIGN AFFAIRS." RETAINS SCHEMATIC CLAS-
SIFICATION OF EARLIER VOLUMES: GENERAL INTERNATIONAL RELA-
TIONS, THE WORLD SINCE 1914, AND THE WORLD BY REGIONS, EM-
PHASIZING ANALYTICAL, CHRONOLOGICAL, AND REGIONAL TREATMENTS
RESPECTIVELY. LIMITED TO WORKS PUBLISHED FROM 1953-62.

1704 ROBERTSON A.H.
THE LAW OF INTERNATIONAL INSTITUTIONS IN EUROPE.
NEW YORK: OCEANA, 1961, 140 PP.
DISCUSSES THE 'EUROPEAN IDEA' (ITS POLITICAL SIGNIFICANCE
AND IDEOLOGICAL CONNOTATION) AND TRACES HISTORICAL DEVELOP-
MENT OF THIS CONCEPT THROUGH MAJOR TREATIES, CONFERENCES AND
COOPERATIVE ORGANIZATIONS. ASSIGNS SPECIAL PLACE FOR HUMAN
RIGHTS IN COUNCIL OF EUROPE PHILOSOPHY.

1705 ROBERTSON A.H.
HUMAN RIGHTS IN EUROPE.
MANCHESTER: U. PR., 1963, 280 PP.

ANALYZES EUROPEAN CONVENTION TEN YEARS AFTER ITS CONCEP-
TION, FOCUSING ON THE APPLICATION OF THE IDEALS SET FORTH IN
THE CHARTER. STUDIES THE VARIOUS BODIES CREATED TO CARRY OUT
THE DOCTRINES, AND DRAWS CONCLUSIONS AS TO THE EFFICACY OF
THE ORGANIZATION AS A GUARANTOR OF HUMAN RIGHTS, USING
CASE STUDIES.

1706 ROBINSON R.D.
INTERNATIONAL BUSINESS POLICY.
NEW YORK: HOLT RINEHART WINSTON, 1964, 252 PP., LC#64-11210.
ATTEMPT TO DEVELOP CALCULUS WHICH, IF USED IN SELECTING
OVERSEAS PROJECTS, IN STRUCTURING INTERNATIONAL ENTERPRISES,
AND IN RESOLVING OPERATIONAL PROBLEMS, WOULD BECOME A
VIABLE INTERNATIONAL CONCEPT AND ENABLE BUSINESS TO
REDUCE CONFLICT.

1707 ROBINSON W.S.
"BIAS, PROBABILITY AND TRIAL BY JURY" (BMR)"
AMER. SOCIOLOGICAL REV., 15 (FEB. 50), 73-78.
DISCUSSES NEW SUPREME COURT IDEA THAT GRAND AND TRIAL
JURIES OUGHT TO BE BODIES TRULY REPRESENTATIVE OF
THE COMMUNITY. TRACES DEVELOPMENT OF CONCEPT IN COURT
DECISIONS, 1940-50. DESCRIBES SOCIAL AND ECONOMIC BIASES IN
PRESENT METHODS OF JURY SELECTION THAT GAVE RISE TO
PRINCIPLE OF REPRESENTATIVE JURY. STATES THAT NEW CONCEPT
WILL "WIPE OUT" PRINCIPLE OF REPRESENTATIVENESS.

1708 ROBSON W.A.
CIVILISATION AND THE GROWTH OF LAW.
NEW YORK: MACMILLAN, 1935, 354 PP.
STUDY OF THE RELATIONS BETWEEN MEN'S IDEAS ABOUT THE
UNIVERSE AND THE INSTITUTIONS OF LAW AND GOVERNMENT.
EXAMINES INFLUENCES OF MAGIC, SUPERSTITION, RELIGION, AND
SCIENCE ON LEGAL AND POLITICAL DEVELOPMENT IN PRIMITIVE AND
CIVILIZED SOCIETIES IN ANCIENT AND MODERN TIMES.

1709 ROCHE J.P.
"POLITICAL SCIENCE AND SCIENCE FICTION" (BMR)"
AM. POL. SCI. REV., 52 (DEC. 58), 1027-1029.
OBJECTS TO THE "SPELL OF NUMEROLOGY WHICH HAS FALLEN OVER
THE STUDY OF POLITICS." DISLIKES NOT QUANTIFICATION, BUT
"BOGUS QUANTIFICATION," THE ASSUMPTION THAT A SCIENTIST CAN
CREATE A MEASURABLE THING MERELY BY ASSIGNING TO IT A
NUMERICAL SYMBOL. PROPOSES POLITICAL SCIENTISTS ADHERE TO
NORMS OF LOGIC AND VALIDITY IN THEIR RESEARCH, ESPECIALLY
IN ANALYSIS OF JUDICIAL PROCESS.

1710 ROCHE J.P.
COURTS AND RIGHTS: THE AMERICAN JUDICIARY IN ACTION
(2ND ED.)
NEW YORK: RANDOM HOUSE, INC, 1961, 143 PP., LC#66-14886.
TREATS STRUCTURE OF AMERICAN FEDERAL AND STATE JUDICIAL
SYSTEM, FREQUENTLY CONTRASTING IT WITH BRITISH AND FRENCH
SYSTEMS FOR EMPHASIS. DISCUSSES PLACE OF CITIZEN - HIS
FREEDOMS AND RIGHTS IN LEGAL PROCESSES. PROVIDES OVERVIEW OF
DEVELOPMENT OF BRITISH LAW, WITH REFERENCES.

1711 ROOT E.
ADDRESSES ON INTERNATIONAL SUBJECTS.
CAMBRIDGE: HARVARD U. PR., 1916, 463 PP.
DEALS WITH THE NEED OF POPULAR UNDERSTANDING OF INTERNA-
TIONAL LAW. FOCUSES ON POLITICAL QUESTION RAISED UNDER
JAPANESE TREATY AND SAN FRANCISCO SCHOOL BOARD RESOLUTION.
EXPLAINS THE RELATIONS BETWEEN INTERNATIONAL TRIBUNALS OF
ARBITRATION AND THE JURISDICTION OF NATIONAL COURTS.

1712 ROOT E.
"THE EFFECT OF DEMOCRACY ON INTERNATIONAL LAW."
PROC. AMER. SOC. INT. LAW, (1917), 2-11.
TRIES TO ESTIMATE FUTURE POSSIBILITIES OF INTERNATIONAL
LAW AND TO FORM USEFUL OPINION ABOUT METHODS BY WHICH LAW
CAN BE MADE MORE BINDING UPON INTERNATIONAL CONDUCT.

1713 ROSE A.M. ED., ROSE C.B. ED.
MINORITY PROBLEMS: A TEXTBOOK OF READINGS IN INTERGROUP
RELATIONS.
NEW YORK: HARPER & ROW, 1965, 438 PP., LC#66-10319.
BASIC TEXT ON RACIAL MINORITIES ORGANIZED AROUND PROB-
EMS AND PROCESSES, SUCH AS ECONOMIC, HOUSING, LEGAL, POLITI-
CAL, AND SOCIAL DISCRIMINATION; GROUP IDENTIFICATION AND
PSYCHOLOGICAL PROBLEMS; DEFINITION OF RACE AND CAUSES OF
RACIAL PREJUDICE; PROPOSED MEANS TO REMOVE RACIAL MINORITY
PROBLEMS IN US AND EUROPE.

1714 ROSE R. ED., HEIDENHEIMER A. ED.
"COMPARATIVE STUDIES IN POLITICAL FINANCE: A SYMPOSIUM."
J. POLIT., 25 (NOV. 63), 643-871.
A COLLECTION OF PAPERS BY WELL-KNOWN SPECIALISTS,
EXAMINING INTENSIVELY THE PARTICULAR PATTERN OF POLITICAL
FINANCE IN EIGHT DEMOCRATIC STATES. EACH ARTICLE CONCERNS
A BASIC SET OF QUESTIONS ABOUT PARTY MEMBERSHIP, INCOME,
EXPENDITURE, SUBSIDIES, LAWS AND CAMPAIGN COSTS. INCLUDES
AUSTRALIA, BRITAIN, INDIA, ISRAEL, ITALY, JAPAN, THE
PHILIPPINES, AND WEST GERMANY.

1715 ROSENBERG M.

"POWER AND DESEGREGATION."
SOCIAL PROBLEMS, 3 (APR. 56), 215-223.
CONCLUDES THAT OF ALL THE FORMS OF POWER (PERSUASION, COERCION, CHARISMA, CONTRACT, MANIPULATION) AVAILABLE TO EFFECT DESEGREGATION, THE MOST PROMISING OVER ALL IS THE POWER BASED ON TRADITIONAL LEGITIMACY (SUPREME COURT DECISIONS).

1716 ROSENNE S.
THE INTERNATIONAL COURT OF JUSTICE.
LEIDEN: SIJTHOFF, 1957, 592 PP.
ANALYSIS OF POSITION OF THIS BODY WITHIN THE UNITED NA-TIONS SYSTEM. FOCUSES ON THE INTERPLAY OF ITS POLITICAL AND LEGAL FACTORS AND INCLUDES A COMPREHENSIVE REVIEW, WITH FRE-QUENT EVALUATIONS, OF THE ORGANIZATION, PRACTICE AND PROCE-DURE OF THE COURT.

1717 ROSENNE S.
THE WORLD COURT: WHAT IT IS AND HOW IT WORKS.
DOBBS FERRY: OCEANA, 1962, 230 PP.
TRACES HISTORY OF WORLD COURT AND DISCUSSES THE EXTENT OF ITS JURISDICTION, ITS PROCESSES AND APPROXIMATELY THREE DOZEN MAJOR CASES WHICH HAVE BEEN DECIDED BY THIS BODY.

1718 ROSENZWEIG F.
HEGEL UND DER STAAT.
AALEN: SCIENTIA VERLAG, 1962, 260 PP.
CRITICAL ANALYSIS OF HEGEL'S CONCEPT OF THE STATE AND PHILOSOPHY OF LAW. TRACES DEVELOPMENT OF HEGEL'S THOUGHT FROM EARLIEST BEGINNINGS AT STUTTAGRT AND TUBINGEN, TO MA-TURITY AND COMPLETION AT BERLIN.

1719 ROSNER G.
THE UNITED NATIONS EMERGENCY FORCE.
NEW YORK: COLUMB. U. PR., 1963, 292 PP.
COMPREHENSIVE ACCOUNT OF CREATION, ORGANIZATION, FUNC-TIONS, STATUS AND OPERATION OF THE UNITED NATIONS EMERGENCY FORCE, ANALYZING IT FROM BOTH ITS PRACTICAL AND LEGAL AS-PECTS. SEES FORCE AS SYMBOL OF GROWING COMMUNITY INTEREST IN PEACEFUL AND SETTLED WORLD.

1720 ROSS A.
TOWARDS A REALISTIC JURISPRUDENCE: A CRITICISM OF THE DUALISM IN LAW (TRANS. BY ANNIE I. FAUSBOLL)
COPENHAGEN: MUNKSGAARD INTL, 1946, 304 PP.
AN EXAMINATION OF SCANDINAVIAN AND ANGLO-AMERICAN LEGAL PHILOSOPHY. ATTEMPTS TO RE-EVALUATE AND SYNTHESIZE DUALISM IN LEGAL THEORY BETWEEN EMPIRICAL FACT AND ABSTRACT VALIDITY. EXAMINES THE CHIEF THEORIES AND SOURCES OF LAW AND THEIR ANTINOMIES.

1721 ROSS A.
CONSTITUTION OF THE UNITED NATIONS.
NEW YORK: RINEHART, 1950, 236 PP.
EXAMINES ORIGIN, GROWTH, ORGANIZATIONAL STRUCTURE, AND AIMS OF UN. DISCUSSES PRINCIPLES OF PROCEDURE AND SCOPE OF POWERS IN MAINTENANCE OF INTERNATIONAL PEACE.

1722 ROSS A.
ON LAW AND JUSTICE.
BERKELEY: U OF CALIF PR, 1959, 383 PP., LC#59-16245.
COMPARES TREND IN AMERICA AND SCANDINAVIAN COUNTRIES TO DISSOCIATE LEGAL PHILOSOPHY FROM NATURAL-LAW DOCTRINES AND RAMIFICATIONS OF CONTINENTAL PHILOSOPHY OF LAW. DISCUSSES DOMINATION OF SCANDINAVIAN JURISPRUDENCE BY PRINCIPLES OF EMPIRICAL PHILOSOPHY. COMBINES METHODOLOGICAL AND ANALYTIC DEMANDS TO CARRY OUT EMPIRICAL PRINCIPLES.

1723 ROSS P.
THE GOVERNMENT AS A SOURCE OF UNION POWER.
PROVIDENCE: BROWN U PRESS, 1965, 320 PP., LC#65-10155.
ANALYSIS OF GOVERNMENT INFLUENCE AND ACTIVITY IN LABOR-MANAGEMENT COLLECTIVE BARGAINING. DISCUSSES LEGISLATION REGARDING DUTY OF BOTH GROUPS TO BARGAIN IN GOOD FAITH.

1724 ROSSITER C.
THE SUPREME COURT AND THE COMMANDER IN CHIEF.
ITHACA: CORNELL U PRESS, 1951, 145 PP., LC#51-10308.
STUDY OF THE RELATIONSHIP BETWEEN THE PRESIDENT AND THE SUPREME COURT. SHOWS HOW CUPREME COURT IN DECIDING CASES IN-VOLVING SCOPE OF NATIONAL WAR POWERS HAS INTERPRETED PRESI-DENT'S STATUS AND AUTHORITY AS COMMANDER-IN-CHIEF. TREATS SUPREME COURT AND THE PRESIDENT'S POWER OF MARTIAL RULE AND SUPREME COURT AND OTHER ASPECTS OF THE WAR POWERS.

1725 ROSTOW E.V.
"THE DEMOCRATIC CHARACTER OF JUDICIAL REVIEW" (BMR)"
HARVARD LAW REV., 66 (DEC. 52), 193-224.
DISCUSSES CURRENT ISSUES AND PROBLEMS OF JUDICIAL REVIEW IN US. ANALYZES ACCUSATIONS THAT JUDICIAL REVIEW IS UNDEMOCRATIC. EXAMINES ALTERNATIVE WAYS TO DEFINE SUPREME COURT'S TASK IN PASSING ON CONSTITUTIONALITY OF LEGISLATION OR OFFICIAL ACTION.

1726 ROSTOW E.V.
THE SOVEREIGN PREROGATIVE: THE SUPREME COURT AND THE QUEST

FOR LAW.
NEW HAVEN: YALE U PR, 1962, 318 PP., LC#62-16240.
DISCUSSES JUDICIAL REVIEW, ITS DEMOCRATIC CHARACTER, AND ATTITUDE OF LEGAL PROFESSION. EXAMINES JAPANESE-AMERICAN RELOCATION CASE AND EXPRESSES NEED FOR "RATIONAL SECURITY PROGRAM."

1727 ROURKE F.E.
"ADMINISTRATIVE SECRECY: A CONGRESSIONAL DILEMMA."
AM. POL. SCI. REV., 54 (SEPT. 60), 684-694.
DEALS WITH THE LONG-STANDING CONGRESSIONAL RESENTMENT AGAINST ADMINISTRATIVE EFFORTS TO CONCEAL INFORMATION. GIVES SPECIFIC EXAMPLES OF LEGISLATIVE FUNCTIONS WHICH HAVE DE-MANDED ACCESS TO WHAT ONLY EXECUTIVE OFFICIALS COULD SUPPLY AND WHICH WERE HANDICAPPED BY EXECUTIVE SECRECY. YET, A WIDE RANGE OF CONGRESSIONAL STATUTES EXIST WHICH ALIGN CONGRESS ITSELF ON THE SIDE OF SECRECY.

1728 ROWAN C.T.
GO SOUTH TO SORROW.
NEW YORK: RANDOM HOUSE, INC, 1957, 246 PP., LC#57-5378.
DISCUSSION BY NEGRO AUTHOR OF DANGEROUS RESULTS OF 1954 SUPREME COURT RULING ON INTEGRATION IN SOUTH. WHITE RACISTS WERE AROUSED TO DEFEND THEIR PREVIOUSLY ACCEPTED PREJUDICES AND DID SO VIOLENTLY. MODERATION BY GOVERNMENT LED ONLY TO INCREASE IN HOSTILITIES AND NEGRO FRUSTRATIONS THAT WILL ONE DAY EXPLODE.

1729 ROYAL INSTITUTE PUBLIC ADMIN
BRITISH PUBLIC ADMINISTRATION.
LONDON: LAWRENCE BROS, LTD, 1963, 27 PP.
SELECTED BIBLIOGRAPHY LISTS ABOUT 400 ITEMS DEALING WITH VARIOUS ASPECTS OF PUBLIC ADMINISTRATION IN THE UK. ARRANGED TOPICALLY, IT DEALS WITH SUCH AREAS AS PARLAIMENT, ELEC-TIONS, PRESSURE GROUPS, PARTIES, CIVIL SERVICE, NATIONALIZED INDUSTRY, PUBLIC FINANCE, LOCAL GOVERNMENT, ADMINISTRATIVE LAW, SOCIAL SERVICES, MANAGEMENT, ETC. INCLUDES REPORTS.

1730 RUBIN A.P.
"UNITED STATES CONTEMPORARY PRACTICE RELATING TO INTERNATIONAL LAW."
AMER. J. INT. LAW, 59 (JAN. 65), 103-30.
LISTS AND BRIEFLY EXAMINES RECENT USA COURT DECISIONS IN LIGHT OF IMPACT ON INTERNATIONAL LAW - BOUNDARY CLAIMS, DIPLOMACY AND EXTRADITION. ALSO PUBLISHES EXECUTIVE DEPARTMENT VIEWS ON SUBJECTS RELATING TO INTERNATIONAL LAW.

1731 RUCKER B.W.
"WHAT SOLUTIONS DO PEOPLE ENDORSE IN FREE PRESS-FAIR TRIAL DILEMMA?"
JOURNALISM QUARTERLY, (SUMMER 67), 240-244.
REPORT ON EXPERIMENTAL STUDY WHICH IDENTIFIES FIVE DIS-TINCT GROUPS OF PEOPLE HOLDING DIVERGENT OPINIONS ON FREE PRESS-FREE TRIAL ISSUES. USES AND DESCRIBES Q TECHNIQUE OF SAMPLING AND ANALYZING PUBLIC OPINION.

1732 RUDIN H.R.
ARMISTICE 1918.
NEW HAVEN: YALE U PR, 1944, 442 PP.
STORY OF THE ARMISTICE SIGNED BY THE ENTENTE POWERS AND GERMANY. SEEKS TO TELL WHY THE GERMANS WANTED AN ARMI-STICE, HOW THE ALLIES DRAFTED THE TREATY, AND HOW THE TWO DELEGATIONS CAME TO FINAL AGREEMENT. AUTHOR BELIEVES THAT THE APPOINTMENT OF THE ARMISTICE COMMISSION WAS A CIVILIAN AFFAIR; THAT THE GERMANS IN POWER IN 1918 SINCERELY DESIRED PEACE; AND THAT WILSON'S PROGRAM SPEEDED THE END OF THE WAR.

1733 RUEDA B.
A STATEMENT OF THE LAWS OF COLOMBIA IN MATTERS AFFECTING BUSINESS (3RD ED.)
WASHINGTON: PAN AMERICAN UNION, 1961, 303 PP.
SUMMARY IN ENGLISH OF CONSTITUTIONAL, STATUTORY, AND REGULATORY PROVISIONS OF COLOMBIA RELEVANT TO COMMERCIAL CONCERNS. COVERS LAWS IN FORCE IN SPRING, 1961, BOTH CIVIL AND CRIMINAL.

1734 RUNCIMAN W.G.
RELATIVE DEPRIVATION AND SOCIAL JUSTICE: A STUDY OF ATTITUDES TO SOCIAL INEQUALITY IN TWENTIETH-CENTURY ENGLAND.
BERKELEY: U OF CALIF PR, 1966, 338 PP.
EXAMINES QUESTIONS OF RELATIONSHIP BETWEEN INSTITUTION-ALIZED INEQUALITIES AND AWARENESS OF THEM. DISCUSSES WHICH INEQUALITIES OUGHT TO BE PERCEIVED BY STANDARDS OF SOCIAL JUSTICE. VIEWS QUESTIONS IN LIGHT OF ENGLISH SOCIAL HISTORY SINCE 1918, AND THE RESULTS OF A NATIONAL SAMPLE SURVEY CARRIED OUT IN 1962.

1735 RUSSEL F.M.
THEORIES OF INTERNATIONAL RELATIONS.
LONDON: APPLETON, 1936, 651 PP.
SURVEY OF DEVELOPMENT OF IDEAS OF MAN WITH REGARD TO RELATIONSHIP BETWEEN INDEPENDENT POLITICAL COMMUNITIES. IT IS DESIGNED TO DO FOR THE FIELD OF INTERNATIONAL RELATIONS WHAT HISTORICAL SURVEYS OF POLITICAL THEORY HAVE DONE FOR THE ENTIRE FIELD OF POLITICAL THOUGHT.

1736 RUSSELL B.
WAR CRIMES IN VIETNAM.
LONDON: ALLEN & UNWIN, 1967, 178 PP., LC#67-23969.
BERTRAND RUSSELL APPEALS TO AMERICAN CONSCIENCE TO STOP
WAR CRIMES IN VIETNAM. TELLS OF NAPALM, "LAZY BOMBS,"
CHEMICALS THAT NOT ONLY DEFOLIATE BUT POISON AND KILL, AND
OF CONCENTRATION CAMPS POLITELY CALLED "RELOCATION CENTERS."
FEELS RACISM IN US HAS CREATED CLIMATE IN WHICH IT IS
DIFFICULT FOR AMERICANS TO UNDERSTAND WAR.

1737 RUSSELL R.B., MUTHER J.E.
A HISTORY OF THE UNITED NATIONS CHARTER: THE ROLE OF THE
UNITED STATES.
WASHINGTON: BROOKINGS INSTIT., 1958, 1140 PP.
OUTLINES FOUNDATION AND DEVELOPMENT OF UN CHARTER DURING
PERIOD OF WW 2 WITHIN FRAMEWORK OF U.S. POLICY. POINTS OUT
PRINCIPLE IDEAS AND PROPOSALS INITIATED BY U.S. GOVERNMENT
WHILE ESTABLISHING ITS SPECIFIC PROVISIONS FOR THE CHARTER.

1738 RUSSELL R.B.
UNITED NATIONS EXPERIENCE WITH MILITARY FORCES: POLITICAL
AND LEGAL ASPECTS.
WASHINGTON: BROOKINGS INST, 1964, 174 PP.
ANALYSIS OF UN'S INTERNATIONAL POLICE FORCE AND PEACE-
KEEPING MISSIONS. INCLUDES UNEF, UNOGIL, ONUC, AND UNSF,
WITH DISCUSSION OF AVAILABILITY OF FORCES, CHARTER
PROVISIONS CONCERNING ENFORCEMENT AND SANCTION, AND THE
NATURE OF AN INTERNATIONAL FORCE.

1739 RUTHERFORD M.L.
THE INFLUENCE OF THE AMERICAN BAR ASSOCIATION ON PUBLIC
OPINION AND LEGISLATION.
CHICAGO: FOUNDATION PRESS, INC, 1937, 393 PP.
THESIS ANALYZING HISTORICAL DEVELOPMENT OF BAR ASSOCIA-
TIONS, OBJECTIVES, ORGANIZATION, PERSONNEL, AND FINANCING.
USE OF PUBLIC RELATIONS TO INFLUENCE LEGISLATION AND ETHICS
OF PRACTICE OBSERVED.

1740 RYAN J.A.
DECLINING LIVERTY AND OTHER ESSAYS.
NEW YORK: MACMILLAN, 1927, 350 PP.
DISCUSSES DECLINE OF POLITICAL, SOCIAL, AND ECONOMIC
LIBERTY IN US, CITING INVASIONS OF LIBERTY BY EXECUTIVE
DEPARTMENT AND CONGRESS. MAINTAINS THAT A PHILOSOPHY OF
SOCIAL WORK IS "ONLY ONE COMPATIBLE WITH LASTING SOCIAL
PROGRESS."

1741 SAINT-PIERRE C.I.
SCHEME FOR LASTING PEACE (TRANS. BY H. BELLOT)
ORIGINAL PUBLISHER NOT AVAILABLE, 1738, 140 PP.
PROPOSES AN OBLIGATORY AND PERMANENT SYSTEM OF INTER-
NATIONAL ARBITRATION, ACCEPTED BY EACH COUNTRY IN EUROPE
AND IMPOSED ON RECALCITRANTS; AN INTERNATIONAL TRIBUNAL,
FOR ARBITRATION OF DISPUTES; AND AN INTERNATIONAL ARMED
FORCE TO COMPEL ACCEPTANCE OF ITS DECISIONS. CLAIMS THIS
WILL ALSO LEAD TO RISE IN COMMERCE AND PRODUCTION BY CON-
TRIBUTING TO PEACE AND FREE TRADE.

1742 SALMOND J.W.
JURISPRUDENCE.
LONDON: STEVENS AND HAYES, 1916, 1935 PP.
A TEXTBOOK ON THE SCIENCE OF LAW INTENDED FOR STUDENTS,
PROFESSIONALS, AND LAYMEN. PASSAGES OF LESSER IMPORTANCE,
GREATER DIFFICULTY, OR CONTROVERSIAL NATURE ARE PRINTED IN
SMALL TYPE AND NOT ESSENTIAL TO BASIC CONTINUITY. CONTENTS
INCLUDE SCIENCE OF LAW, KINDS OF LAW, ADMINISTRATION OF LAW,
LEGISLATION, CUSTOM, RIGHTS, OWNERSHIP, POSSESSION, TITLES,
LIABILITY, INTENTION AND NEGLIGENCE, AND SO ON.

1743 SALTER L.M.
RESOLUTION OF INTERNATIONAL CONFLICT.
NEW YORK: VINTAGE BOOKS, 1966, 142 PP., LC#66-22335.
STUDY OF US FOREIGN POLICY IN LIGHT OF TENUOUS EAST-WEST
RELATIONS. EXAMINES ROOTS OF CONTENTION. DISCUSSES PEACE
EFFORTS OF ORGANIZATIONS FROM LOCAL TO INTERNATIONAL LEVEL.
QUESTIONS ETHICS AND EFFICIENCY OF US FOREIGN POLICY. DE-
SCRIBES ROLE OF LAWYER IN WORLD PEACE EFFORTS.

1744 SAND P.T., LYON J.T., PRATT G.N.
"AN HISTORICAL SURVEY OF INTERNATIONAL AIR LAW SINCE 1944."
MCGILL LAW J., 7 (1961), 125-60.
INDICATES THE EXTENT TO WHICH AVIATION IMPINGES UPON MANY
BRANCHES OF A STATE'S LEGAL SYSTEM. FIRST SECTION EXAMINES
INTERNATIONAL CIVIL AVIATION AND PUBLIC INTERNATIONAL LAW.
SECOND SECTION DEALS WITH CONFLICTS OF LAW. INCLUDES ANALY-
SIS OF ROME CONVENTION 1952 AND HAGUE PROTOCOL 1955.

1745 SANDERS R.
"NUCLEAR DYNAMITE: A NEW DIMENSION IN FOREIGN POLICY."
ORBIS, 4 (FALL 60), 307-322.
CONTENDS THAT UNDERGROUND TESTS HAVE PROVED UNLIMITED USE
OF ATOMIC ENERGY COULD BE ULTIMATELY UTILIZED FOR PEACEFUL
PURPOSES. CONTROLLED NUCLEAR UNDERGROUND EXPLOSIONS COULD BE
MADE SAFE ENOUGH FOR THEIR APPLICATION TO VARIOUS SCIENTIFIC
PROJECTS. HOPES THAT FURTHER DEVELOPMENT OF NUCLEAR DYNAMITE
WILL DEPEND ON UNIVERSAL AGREEMENT ON TEST BAN TREATY.

1746 SARTORI G. ED.
IL PARLAMENTO ITALIANO: 1946-1963.
NAPLES: EDIZIONI SCIENTIF ITAL, 1963, 386 PP.
STUDY OF ITALIAN POLITICS AND GOVERNMENT CONDUCTED FROM
POINT OF VIEW OF POLITICAL SCIENTIST. SOCIOLOGICAL COMMEN-
TARY ON CHARACTER, NATURE, AND DEVELOPMENT OF POLITICIAN.
ONSIDERS PARTISANSHIP, BUREAUCRACY, "LEGISLATIVE INFLATION,"
AND OTHER ASPECTS OF AN EVOLVING POLITICAL SYSTEM.

1747 SARTORIUS R.E.
THE JUSTIFICATION OF THE JUDICIAL DECISION (DISSERTATION)
PRINCETON: PRIN U, DEPT OF PHIL, 1964, 325 PP.
ESSAY IN PHILOSOPHY OF LAW, DISCUSSING MEANING OF LAW,
JUSTIFICATION OF JUDICIAL DECISION IN HARD AND EASY CASES,
AND LEGAL VALIDITY AND STATUS OF RULE OF RECOGNITION.

1748 SAWYER R.A.
A LIST OF WORKS ON COUNTY GOVERNMENT.
PRINCETON: PRIN U INDUS REL CTR, 1915.
LISTS APPROXIMATELY 600 SOURCES INCLUDING BOOKS, JOURNAL
ARTICLES, AND OFFICIAL PUBLICATIONS DEALING WITH WIDE RANGE
OF POLITICAL AND LEGAL ASPECTS OF COUNTY GOVERNMENT IN US.
ARRANGED ACCORDING TO FOLLOWING TOPICS: GENERAL WORKS IN
COUNTY ADMINISTRATION, COUNTY ADMINISTRATION IN INDIVIDUAL
STATES, COUNTY OFFICES, AND COUNTY PUBLICATIONS. ALL ENTRIES
ARE IN ENGLISH AND WERE PUBLISHED FROM LATE 1800'S TO 1915.

1749 SCANLON H.L.
INTERNATIONAL LAW: A SELECTIVE LIST OF WORKS IN ENGLISH ON
PUBLIC INTERNATIONAL LAW (A PAMPHLET)
WASHINGTON: CARNEGIE ENDOWMENT, 1946, 20 PP.
INCLUDES BOOKS AND TREATISES PRIMARILY, SEPARATED INTO
GENERAL TREATISES AND COLLECTIONS, AND PARTICULAR TREATMENTS
WITH SOME REFERENCE TO CASES AT THE END. PUBLICATIONS OVER
BROAD TIME SPAN, MOSTLY 20TH CENTURY; 250 TITLES. THIS LIST
IS REVISION OF 1936 WORK. ARRANGED BY AUTHOR WITHIN DIVI-
SIONS, BRIEF ANNOTATIONS. INCLUDES JOURNAL INDEX.

1750 SCHACHTER O.
"THE ENFORCEMENT OF INTERNATIONAL JUDICIAL AND ARBITRAL
DECISIONS."
AMER. J. INT. LAW, 54, (JAN. 60), 1-24.
DISCUSSING DIFFICULTIES FOUND IN ENFORCEMENT OF WORLD
COURT DECISIONS, ANALYZES PROBLEMS AND PROCEDURES CONNECTED
WITH SUCCESSFUL PARTIES CLAIMS. OUTLINES POSSIBLE REMEDIES
AVAILABLE THROUGH INTERNATIONAL ORGANIZATIONS.

1751 SCHACHTER O.
"DAG HAMMARSKJOLD AND THE RELATION OF LAW TO POLITICS."
AMER. J. INT. LAW, 56 (JAN. 62), 1-8.
DISCUSSION DIVIDED INTO FOUR CATEGORIES: LAW AS A SOURCE
AND BASIS OF POLICY, PRINCIPLES AND FLEXIBILITY, RELATION
BETWEEN LAW AND DIPLOMACY, AND POWER AND ACTION. SEES
NEED FOR PRACTICAL ACTION WHICH WOULD IMPART A NEW DIMENSION
TO EFFORTS TO GIVE VIGOR AND EFFICACY TO A NORMATIVE
STRUCTURE BASED ON THE COMMON INTERESTS OF 'THE MANY'.

1752 SCHECHTER A.H.
INTERPRETATION OF AMBIGUOUS DOCUMENTS BY INTERNATIONAL
ADMINISTRATIVE TRIBUNALS.
NEW YORK: FREDERICK PRAEGER, 1964, 183 PP.
ANALYSIS OF INTERNATIONAL LEGAL DEVELOPMENTS SINCE WWII.
EXAMINES ACTIONS OF UN ADMINISTRATIVE TRIBUNAL, ILO ADMINIS-
TRATIVE TRIBUNAL, AND EUROPEAN COURT OF JUSTICE IN INTERPRE-
TATIONS OF INTERNATIONAL RULES AND REGULATIONS.

1753 SHEEHAN D.
"PUBLIC AND PRIVATE GROUPS AS IDENTIFIED IN THE FIELD OF
TRADE REGULATIONS."
RUTGERS LAW REV., 13 (SPRING 59), 577-588.
DISCUSSES GROUP INTERESTS IN TRADE REGULATION IN THREE
FIELDS: PATENT AND ANTI-TRUST LAW, DOMESTIC ADMINISTRATIVE
LAW, AND INTERNATIONAL LAW.

1754 SCHEIBER H.N.
THE WILSON ADMINISTRATION AND CIVIL LIBERTIES 1917-1921.
ITHACA: CORNELL U PRESS, 1960, 69 PP.
ANALYSIS OF CIVIL LIBERTIES IN US DURING WWI AND ATTITUDE
OF FEDERAL GOVERNMENT IN CONTROLLING POPULATION IN REGARD TO
NATIONAL SECURITY. EXAMINES LEGISLATION LIMITING RIGHTS AND
EXECUTIVE APPLICATION OF RESTRICTIVE LAWS.

1755 SCHEINGOLD S.A.
"THE RULE OF LAW IN EUROPEAN INTEGRATION: THE PATH OF THE
SCHUMAN PLAN."
NEW HAVEN: YALE U PR, 1965.
STUDY OF RECIPROCAL RELATIONSHIP BETWEEN LEGAL AND POLIT-
ICAL ASPECTS OF EUROPEAN INTEGRATION. SELECTIVE BIBLIOG-
RAPHY OF ABOUT 150 BOOKS, DOCUMENTS, AND ARTICLES IN FRENCH
AND ENGLISH, TO 1964. REFERENCE GIVEN TO MORE COMPLETE
BIBLIOGRAPHICAL SOURCES.

1756 SCHELLING T.C.
"ECONOMICS AND CRIMINAL ENTERPRISE."
PUBLIC INTEREST, 17 (SPRING 67), 61-79.
ECONOMIC ANALYSIS OF CRIMINAL UNDERWORLD. SUGGESTS TENTA-

TIVE TYPOLOGY OF UNDERWORLD BUSINESS AND EXAMINES INCENTIVES
TO CRIMINAL ORGANIZATION. ARGUES FOR ANALYSIS OF MARKET AD-
JUSTMENTS TO COMPARE THE COSTS OF SOCIETY TO THE GAINS OF
CRIMINALS AND BETTER UNDERSTANDING OF INSTITUTIONAL PRAC-
TICES. EXAMINES RELATION OF ORGANIZED CRIME TO ENFORCEMENT,
AND SOCIAL ADVANTAGES OF ORGANIZED CRIME.

1757 SCHLOCHAUER H.J.
OFFENTLICHES RECHT.
KARLSRUHE: VERL C F MULLER, 1957, 269 PP.
EXAMINES ORIGIN AND NATURE OF BASIC LAW OF FEDERAL REPUB-
LIC OF WEST GERMANY. EXAMINES RELATION OF NATION AND STATES
AND POSITION OF WEST GERMANY IN RELATION TO INTERNATIONAL
COMMUNITY. STUDIES CONSTITUTIONAL ORGANS, CONSTITUTIONAL
COURT, AND SYSTEM OF ADMINISTRATIVE ADJUDICATION.

1758 SCHMEISER D.A.
CIVIL LIBERTIES IN CANADA.
LONDON: OXFORD U PR, 1964, 302 PP.
"LEGAL AND HISTORICAL STUDY" OF DEVELOPMENT OF CIVIL LIB-
ERTIES IN CANADA. DISCUSSES FREEDOMS OF RELIGION, EDUCATION,
COMMUNICATION, AND RACE IN THEIR "CONSTITUTIONAL SETTING."
SOME CRITICISMS OF CHURCH-STATE CONFLICT OVER EDUCATION,
AND ANALYSIS OF CANADIAN BILL OF RIGHTS (FULL TEXT INCLU-
DED IN APPENDIX AS WELL AS TEXT OF US BILL OF RIGHTS).

1759 SCHMIDHAUSER J.R.
JUDICIAL BEHAVIOR AND THE SECTIONAL CRISIS OF 1837-1860.
J. OF POLITICS, (NOV. 61), 615-640.
EXAMINES, ESPECIALLY BY USING SCALOGRAMS, SIGNIFICANCE OF
BACKGROUND FACTORS LIKE SECTIONAL BACKGROUND AND PARTY AF-
FILIATION IN RELATION TO JUDICIAL BEHAVIOR OF SUPREME COURT
JUDGES IN PRE-CIVIL WAR ERA. ALSO BREAKS DOWN CASE ASSIGN-
MENT PROCESS UNDER CHIEF JUSTICE TANEY. COMPARES COURT AND
CONGRESS AS TO ROLE PLAYED. CONCLUDES THAT PARTY DIFFERENCES
DOMINATED REGIONAL ONES.

1760 SCHMIDHAUSER J.R.
THE SUPREME COURT: ITS POLITICS, PERSONALITIES, AND PROCE-
DURES.
NEW YORK: HOLT RINEHART WINSTON, 1960, 163 PP., LC#60-10636.
ASSESSES THE REALITIES OF THE JUDICIAL SELECTION PROCESS,
THE RELATIONSHIP OF SUPREME COURT TO STATE SUPREME COURTS
AND TO PROFESSIONAL LEGAL ORGANIZATION, AND THE EVOLUTION
AND MODERN CHARACTERISTICS OF THE DECISION-MAKING PROCESS.
EACH TOPIC TREAT HISTORICALLY.

1761 SCHMIDHAUSER J.R. ED.
CONSTITUTIONAL LAW IN THE POLITICAL PROCESS.
SKOKIE: RAND MCNALLY & CO, 1963, 544 PP., LC#63-7578.
SELECTIONS FROM ARTICLES AND ESSAYS, JUDICIAL DECISIONS,
LEGISLATIVE DEBATES, AND ELECTION CAMPAIGN DOCUMENTS.
UNIFYING THEME IS THE ROLE OF THE US SUPREME COURT IN
THE US POLITICAL PROCESS. EMPHASIS IS ON SOCIAL AND POLIT-
ICAL CONFLICT. DISCUSSES FEDERALISM, SEPARATION OF POWERS,
US COURT SYSTEM, SELECTION OF FEDERAL JUDGES, AND THE
CONSTITUTION.

1762 SCHNEIDER J.
TREATY-MAKING POWER OF INTERNATIONAL ORGANIZATIONS.
GENEVA: DROZ, 1959, 150 PP.
USING THE METHODOLOGY OF LAW, ANALYZES HISTORICAL AS WELL
AS CONTEMPORARY PRACTICES OF INTERNATIONAL ORGANIZATIONS IN
REGARD TO TREATY-MAKING POWERS. IN ESSENCE, A STUDY OF THE
CHARACTER OF AGREEMENTS MADE BY WORLD-STRUCTURES SINCE WW 2.

1763 SCHOEDER P.W.
THE AXIS ALLIANCE AND JAPANESE-AMERICAN RELATIONS 1941.
ITHACA: CORNELL U PRESS, 1958, 243 PP.
CONCENTRATES ON ASPECT OF TRIPARTITE ALLIANCE, AS IT
AFFECTED JAPANESE-AMERICAN NEGOTIATIONS PRECEDING WWII.
TRIES TO GIVE AN INTERPRETATION DIFFERENT FROM ONE CURRENTLY
PREVAILING, CONCENTRATING ON ANALYSIS MORE THAN NARRATION.

1764 SCHONS D.
BOOK CENSORSHIP IN NEW SPAIN (NEW WORLD STUDIES, BOOK II)
ANN ARBOR: EDWARDS BROTHERS, 1949, 45 PP.
REGISTER OF 96 COPIES OF LETTERS AND SUMMARIES OF LETTERS
DEALING WITH PUNITIVE CENSORSHIP OF 17TH-CENTURY BOOKS,
FILED BY SPANISH SUPREME COUNCIL OF THE INQUISITION, SUPPLE-
MENTED BY CORRESPONDENCE EXCHANGED BETWEEN THE SPANISH AND
MEXICAN INQUISITIONS. ASSERTS THAT INQUISITORIAL LETTERS
WERE NOT MERE INDEXES OF PROHIBITED BOOKS, BUT INDICATORS
OF ISSUES FACING CHURCH AND STATE IN THAT PERIOD.

1765 SCHORN H.
DER RICHTER IM DRITTEN REICH; GESCHICHTE UND DOKUMENTE.
FRANKFURT: V KLOSTERMANN, 1959, 743 PP.
INDICATES THAT IN NAZI GERMANY THERE WERE COURAGEOUS
JUDGES, THAT THERE IS A JUSTICE HIGHER THAN LAW, AND THAT
INJUSTICE REMAINS UNJUST EVEN WHEN IT IS PROMULGATED AS
LAW. BASES STUDY OF JUDGES IN NAZI GERMANY UPON MATERIALS
FROM THE MINISTRY OF JUSTICE, JUDGES, CHURCHES, THE BAR,
POLITICAL PARTIES, INCLUDING NAZI ACCUSATION AGAINST
JUDGES.

1766 SCHROEDER O. ED., SSMITH D.T. ED.
DEFACTO SEGREGATION AND CIVIL RIGHTS.
BUFFALO: WM S HEIN AND CO, 1965, 332 PP., LC#65-26876.
ESSAYS COVERING ALL ASPECTS OF CIVIL RIGHTS. SPOKESMEN
FROM MAJOR EDUCATIONAL DISCIPLINES TREAT LAW EDUCATION,
HISTORY ,AND SOCIOLOGY. THE FOURTEENTH AMMENDMENT, SCHOOL
SEGREGATION, EMPLOYMENT SEGREGATION, CIVIL RIGHTS ACT OF
1964, AND CIVIL DISOBEDIENCE ARE DISCUSSED.

1767 SCHROEDER T.
FREE SPEECH FOR RADICALS (REV. ED.)
NEW YORK: FREE SPEECH LEAGUE, 1916, 206 PP.
ESSAYS REGARDING AMERICAN INTOLERANCE AND SUPPRESSION OF
CONTROVERSIAL FIGURES AND ISSUES. INCLUDES CHARGES OF
DESPOTISM, INJUSTICE, AND THE ILLUSION OF LIBERTY.

1768 SCHROEDER T. ED.
FREE SPEECH BIBLIOGRAPHY.
NEW YORK: H W WILSON, 1922, 247 PP.
WORKS ON FREE SPEECH AND ITS SUPPRESSION, 1519-1920. HAS
SOME 5,000 ENTRIES, IN ENGLISH, GERMAN, FRENCH, AND SPANISH,
LISTED BY MOTIVE: ECONOMIC, PERSONAL, RELIGIOUS, SEX, WAR,
INCLUDING LIST OF SUPPRESSED PUBLICATIONS AND WORKS ON
SEDITION.

1769 SCHROEDER T.
METHODS OF CONSTITUTIONAL CONSTRUCTION.
NEW YORK: FREE SPEECH LEAGUE, 1956, 106 PP.
MAINTAINS THAT ALL PREDISPOSITIONS "BE SUBMITTED
TO THE CHECK AND JUSTIFICATION OF SCIENTIFIC METHOD," AND
APPLIES SYNTHETIC (SCIENTIFIC) METHODOLOGY TO ANALYSIS OF
THE FREE-SPEECH CLAUSE OF THE FEDERAL CONSTITUTION. APPENDED
ARE SUPPLEMENTS ON RIGHTS OF REVOLUTIONISTS.

1770 SCHUBERT G.
THE PUBLIC INTEREST.
NEW YORK: FREE PRESS OF GLENCOE, 1960, 244 PP., LC#60-10902.
ANALYZES AND TRACES DEVELOPMENT AND USE OF THE CONCEPT
"PUBLIC INTEREST" IN CONTEMPORARY POLITICAL SCIENCE,
IDENTIFYING THREE MAJOR SCHOOLS OF THOUGHT. SUGGESTS
THAT FOCUS ON THE MOST "REPRESENTATIVE" INSTITUTION BE
ELIMINATED, THAT THE CONCEPT OF PUBLIC INTEREST MAKES NO
"OPERATIONAL SENSE."

1771 SCHUBERT G.
"A PSYCHOMETRIC MODEL OF THE SUPREME COURT."
AMER. BEHAVIORAL SCIENTIST, 5 (NOV. 61), 14-18.
DISCUSSES POSSIBILITY OF PSYCHOLOGICAL THEORY OF SUPREME
COURT AND PRESENTS A THEORY BASED ON JUDICIAL VOTING BEHAV-
IOR IN NON-UNANIMOUS CASES, WITH A JUSTICE'S VOTE REPRESENT-
ING A RESPONSE EXPRESSING HIS ATTITUDE TOWARD A VALUE
EVOKED BY A CASE-STIMULUS. BY LOCATING JUDICIAL IDEAL-POINTS
IN PSYCHOLOGICAL SPACE AND POSITIONING SCALE AXES, CAN SEE
IF VOTES ARE ATTITUDINAL RESPONSES TO PUBLIC POLICY ISSUES.

1772 SCHUBERT G.
"THE 1960 TERM OF THE SUPREME COURT: A PSYCHOLOGICAL ANALY-
SIS."
AM. POL. SCI. REV., 56 (MAR. 62), 90-98.
AN ATTEMPT TO DESCRIBE A MULTIDIMENSIONAL MODEL OF THE
SUPREME COURT ACTION AND TO EXPLAIN ITS THEORY AND APPLI-
CATION TO THE EMPIRICAL DATA OF ONE OF THE SESSIONS OF THE
COURT. THE PURPOSE OF THE ARTICLE IS TO DEMONSTRATE THAT
THE PSYCHOLOGICAL APPROACH PROPOSED LEADS TO MORE SIGNIFI-
CANT INSIGHTS INTO THE POLITICAL BEHAVIOR OF THE COURT THAN
BY THE CASE-BY-CASE APPROACH.

1773 SCHUBERT G. ED.
"JUDICIAL DECISION-MAKING."
NEW YORK: FREE PRESS OF GLENCOE, 1963.
ANALYSIS AND EXPLANATION OF JUDICIAL DECISION-MAKING BY
MEANS OF STUDIES IN DEPTH OF LEGAL ATTITUDES AND BEHAVIOR
AND THROUGH ADVANCED BEHAVIORAL RESEARCH TECHNIQUES. USES
SOCIAL PSYCHOLOGY AND POLITICAL SOCIOLOGY WITH STATISTICAL
PREDICTION TECHNIQUES AS APPROACHES TO BEHAVIORAL ANALYSIS
STUDIES. EACH ESSAY CONTAINS NOTES AND APPENDICES ALONG
WITH GENERAL BIBLIOGRAPHY ARRANGED BY SECTION.

1774 SCHUBERT G.
THE JUDICIAL MIND: THE ATTITUDES AND IDEOLOGIES OF SUPREME
COURT JUSTICES 1946-1963.
EVANSTON: NORTHWESTERN U PRESS, 1965, 295 PP., LC#65-15472.
DATA OF STUDY CONSIST OF ALL THE INDIVIDUAL VOTES OF
THE JUSTICES IN DECISIONS WITH ONE OR MORE JUSTICES DISSENT-
ED ON SUBSTANTIVE ISSUE. USES FACTOR ANALYSIS AND CUMULATIVE
LINEAR SCALING AND CONSTRUCTS A MODEL OF THE GROUP DECISION-
MAKING FUNCTION OF THE SUPREME COURT. SHOWS THAT THOUGH THE
LIBERALS DID NOT CONSTITUTE A MAJORITY UNTIL THE FINAL TERM,
THEY OFTEN DOMINATED THE MORE HETEROGENEOUS CONSERVATIVES.

1775 SCHUBERT G. ED.
REAPPORTIONMENT.
NEW YORK: CHAS SCRIBNER'S SONS, 1965, 257 PP.
A COMPILATION OF ESSAYS ON THE SUBJECT OF APPORTIONMENT.
GENERAL AREAS OF DISCUSSION ARE THEORIES OF REPRESENTATION;
THE COMPOSITION OF STATE LEGISLATURES BEFORE AND AFTER THE

BAKER CASE; THE COMPOSITION OF CONGRESS BEFORE AND AFTER
REINOLDSV. SIMS; AND THE POLITICAL IMPLICAITONS, AT ALL
LEVELS, OF INCREASED REPRESENTATION OF URBAN AREAS IN
LEGISLATIVE COUNCILS.

1776 SCHUBERT G.
THE POLITICAL ROLE OF THE COURTS IN :JUDICIAL POLICY MAKING.
GLENVIEW, ILL: SCOTT, FORESMAN, 1965, 212 PP., LC#65-17728.
    VOLUME SHOWS THAT STRUCTURAL THEORY WHICH VIEWS JUDICIAL
REVIEWS AS MEANS WHEREBY JUDICIARY MAY IMPOSE CONSERVATIVE
CHECK ON LIBERAL TENDENCIES IS FALSE. SEEKS RATIONALLY TO
UNDERSTAND JUDICIAL BEHAVIOR. BRINGS TO BEAR UPON STUDY OF
JUDICIAL BEHAVIOR TECHNIQUES AND DATA OF BEHAVIORAL SCIENCE.

1777 SCHUBERT G.
"THE RHETORIC OF CONSTITUTIONAL CHANGE."
JOURNAL OF PUBLIC LAW, 16 (1967), 16-50.
    STUDIES THREE MODELS: CONSTITUTIONAL DOCUMENT,
INSTITUTIONS, AND CULTURE, AS THEY RELATE TO CONSTITUTIONAL
CHANGE. COMPARES THREE METHODS ON POLICIES OF EQUALITY.
DISCUSSES WHICH METHOD WOULD BE MOST EFFECTIVE IN ENFORCING
CIVIL DISARMAMENT. FINDS DOCUMENT AMENDMENT TO BE LEAST
COSTLY BUT CULTURAL CHANGE MOST EFFICIENT MEANS OF
CONSTITUTIONAL CHANGE.

1778 SCHUBERT G.A.
THE PRESIDENCY IN THE COURTS.
MINNEAPOLIS: U OF MINN PR, 1957, 391 PP., LC#57-5803.
    STUDY IN POWERS OF PRESIDENCY AS SEEN THROUGH EYES OF
COURTS. ANALYZES JUDICIAL BEHAVIOR WITH REFERENCE TO EXEC-
UTIVE BRANCH OF GOVERNMENT. EXPLORES PRESIDENTIAL MANAGE-
MENT, CONDUCT OF FOREIGN RELATIONS, MILITARY DECISIONS,
AND LEGAL SOURCES OF PRESIDENTIAL POWER.

1779 SCHUBERT G.A.
"THE STUDY OF JUDICIAL DECISION-MAKING AS AN ASPECT OF PO-
LITICAL BEHAVIOR."
AM. POL. SCI. REV., 52 (DEC. 58), 1007-1025.
    SHOWS USES OF EXPERIMENTATION IN GROUP DYNAMICS, OF COM-
MUNICATION CONTENT ANALYSIS, AND OF THEORY OF GAMES TO IL-
LUSTRATE KINDS OF QUESTIONS ABOUT JUDICIAL BEHAVIOR THAT CAN
BE INVESTIGATED WITH THEM. ANALYZES SUMMARY DECISION-MAKING;
USES BLOC ANALYSIS ON SUPREME COURT VOTES, AND ALSO CONTENT
ANALYSIS AND GAME ANALYSIS SIMILARLY.

1780 SCHUBERT G.A.
QUANTITATIVE ANALYSIS OF JUDICIAL BEHAVIOR.
NEW YORK: FREE PRESS OF GLENCOE, 1959, 392 PP., LC#59-13021.
    ANALYSIS OF LAW COURTS AS A SMALL SYSTEM OF SOCIAL INTER-
ACTIONS. EXPERIMENTATION WITH USE OF SOCIAL AND BEHAVIORAL
SCIENCE RESEARCH TECHNIQUES TO ANALYZE JUDICIAL DECISION-
MAKING BEHAVIOR. AFTER DISCUSSION OF US SUPREME COURT, ANAL-
YZES ITS SUMMARY JUDICIAL POWER. USES BLOC ANALYSIS ON MICH-
IGAN SUPREME COURT AND WARREN COURT; APPLIES GAME ANALYSIS
AND SCALOGRAM ANALYSIS IN SEVERAL VARIATIONS.

1781 SCHUBERT G.A.
CONSTITUTIONAL POLITICS: THE POLITICAL BEHAVIOR OF SUPREME
COURT JUSTICES AND THE CONSTITUTIONAL POLICIES THEY MAKE.
NEW YORK: HOLT RINEHART WINSTON, 1960, 735 PP., LC#60-11754.
    ATTEMPTS TO ESTABLISH A BEHAVIORAL FRAME OF REFERENCE FOR
POLITICAL ANALYSIS OF THE SUPREME COURT. DEALS WITH INTERRE-
LATIONSHIPS BETWEEN COURT, CONGRESS, AND EXECUTIVE BRANCH
AND LOWER COURTS, STATE AND FEDERAL. TREATS ARBITRATION OF
CONFLICTS OF INTEREST BETWEEN THE NATIONAL GOVERNMENT AND
THE STATES AND ARBITRATION OF INTEREST CONFLICTS BETWEEN
MINORITIES-INDIVIDUALS AND THE MAJORITY.

1782 SCHUBERT G.A. ED.
JUDICIAL BEHAVIOR: A READER IN THEORY AND RESEARCH.
SKOKIE: RAND MCNALLY & CO, 1964, 603 PP., LC#64-17638.
    COLLECTION OF PAPERS STUDYING PROGRESS MADE IN DEVELOP-
MENT OF THEORY AND METHOD OF STUDYING JUDICIAL BEHAVIOR AND
FINDINGS OF SUCH STUDIES. INCLUDES HISTORY OF STUDY,
DISCOVERY OF SUBCONSCIOUS AND START OF REALISM; RELATION-
SHIPS BETWEEN CULTURAL ANTHROPOLOGY, POLITICAL SOCIOLOGY,
SOCIAL PSYCHOLOGY AND JUDICIAL BEHAVIOR; PREDICTIONS OF
JUDICIAL BEHAVIOR THROUGH MODELS.

1783 SCHULZ F.
PRINCIPLES OF ROMAN LAW.
NEW YORK: OXFORD U PR, 1936, 268 PP.
    ELUCIDATES BASIC VIEW OF LAW AND JUSTICE IN ROMAN LEGAL
SYSTEM AND ITS UNDERLYING PRINCIPLES. BEGINS WITH ENACTED
STATUTES, THEN DISCUSSES PRINCIPLES OF ISOLATION, SIMPLIC-
ITY, ABSTRACTION, AND AUTHORITY. PRINCIPLE OF LIBERTY IN
CONSTITUTIONAL LAW, PRINCIPLE OF HUMANITY IN FAMILY, LEGAL
SECURITY, AND FIDELITY ARE TREATED. CLOSES WITH SEPARATION
OF PRIVATE LAW FROM LAW OF PROCEDURE.

1784 SCHUMAN S.I.
LEGAL POSITIVISM: ITS SCOPE AND LIMITATIONS.
DETROIT: WAYNE STATE U PR, 1963, 265 PP., LC#62-14874.
    PRESENTS PHILOSOPHY OF LAW, EXAMINING THE ETHICS AND
OBLIGATION OF LEGAL THEORIES AND RELATING THEM TO PURPOSIVE
CONDUCT. DISCUSSES THE DICHOTOMY BETWEEN "IS" AND "OUGHT."

STUDIES ULTIMATE GOALS, SCIENCE, AND NATURE OF MAN IN TERMS
OF POLITICAL THEORIES. CONCLUDES WITH COMPARISON AND ANALY-
SIS OF THE POLITICS OF PHILOSOPHY.

1785 SCHUSTER E.
GUIDE TO LAW AND LEGAL LITERATURE OF CENTRAL AMERICAN
REPUBLICS.
CHICAGO: AMER FOREIGN LAW ASSOC, 1937, 152 PP.
    ENTRIES INCLUDE SEVERAL TYPES OF LEGAL PUBLICATIONS DAT-
ING FROM LATE 1800'S TO 1936. COUNTRIES COVERED INCLUDE
COSTA RICA, GUATEMALA, HONDURAS, NICARAGUA, PANAMA, AND
SALVADOR. PUBLICATIONS LISTED IN SPANISH; ANNOTATIONS CON-
TAIN COMPARATIVE ANALYSIS OF RELATIONSHIPS BETWEEN LEGAL
SYSTEMS OF THE SIX COUNTRIES AND ARE IN ENGLISH. APPROXI-
MATELY 700 ENTRIES.

1786 SCHWARTZ B.
FRENCH ADMINISTRATIVE LAW AND THE COMMON-LAW WORLD.
NEW YORK: NEW YORK U PR, 1954, 367 PP., LC#54-5276.
    COMPARES FRENCH LAW WITH THE ANGLO-AMERICAN SYSTEM, WITH-
IN THE CONTEXT OF THEIR ECONOMIC, HISTORICAL, POLITICAL, AND
SOCIAL HERITAGES. PURPOSE IS TO FIND POSSIBLE AREAS OF IM-
PROVEMENT IN THE AMERICAN LEGAL SYSTEM. EMPHASIZES THE RELA-
TIONS OF THE THREE BRANCHES OF GOVERNMENT - LEGISLATIVE, EX-
ECUTIVE, AND JUDICIAL - TO EACH OTHER, AND THE INTERRELATION
OF LOCAL, STATE, AND FEDERAL GOVERNMENTS. CITES MANY CASES.

1787 SCHWARTZ L.E.
INTERNATIONAL ORGANIZATIONS AND SPACE COOPERATION.
DURHAM: DUKE U PR, 1962, 108 PP.
    COLLECTS BASIC DATA ON PUBLIC AND PRIVATE INTERNATIONAL
ORGANIZATIONS INVOLVED IN SPACE PROGRAMS. STUDIES ORIGINS,
HISTORY, AIMS, STRUCTURE, PAST ACHIEVEMENTS, AND PLANS
OF ALL BODIES WITH ROLES IN SPACE COORDINATION, INCLUDING
INTERNATIONAL COUNCIL OF SCIENTIFIC UNIONS, INTERNATIONAL
GEOPHYSICAL YEAR, COMMITTEE ON SPACE RESEARCH, UN AND ITS
COMMITTEES, AND INTERNATIONAL CIVIL AVIATION ORGANIZATION.

1788 SCHWARTZ M.D. ED.
CONFERENCE ON SPACE SCIENCE AND SPACE LAW.
S HACKENSACK: FRED B ROTHMAN CO, 1964, 176 PP.
    ARTICLES IN LAW AND SCIENCE ON FUTURE OF MAN IN SPACE,
INCLUDING PEACEFUL USES, MILITARY STRATEGY, INTERNATIONAL
COOPERATION, SPACE AND NATIONAL ECONOMY, AND LEGAL PROBLEMS.

1789 SCHWARZENBERGER G.
THE FRONTIERS OF INTERNATIONAL LAW.
LONDON: STEVENS, 1962, 320 PP.
    ATTEMPTS TO DETERMINE MODERN TEMPORAL, FUNCTIONAL, AND
ANALYTICAL FRONTIERS OF INTERNATIONAL LAW. EXPLORES SOCIAL
FACTORS UNDERLYING GROWTH OF UNIVERSAL LEGAL SYSTEM, EMPHA-
SIZES POLITICAL AND SOCIAL ENDS SERVED BY INTERNATIONAL LAW,
AND ARGUES EAST-WEST RIFT HAS FOSTERED CLOSER LEGAL INTEG-
RATION ON BIPOLAR LEVEL SINCE SOCIAL AND ECONOMIC INTERDE-
PENDENCE ARE EXPANDING WITHIN BLOC SYSTEM AND REGIONALLY.

1790 SCHWELB E.
"INTERNATIONAL CONVENTIONS ON HUMAN RIGHTS."
INT. LAW COMP. QUART., 9 (OCT. 60).
    STUDY OF MEANS TO IMPLEMENT HUMAN RIGHTS. PROVISIONS OF
UN CHARTER TRACE VARIOUS CONVENTIONS IN THE PAST WITH REGARD
TO GENOCIDE, PROTECTION OF WAR VICTIMS, CULTURAL PROPERTY,
STATE-LESS PERSONS ET AL. PRAGMATIC VIEW OF INTERNATIONAL
COMMUNITY AS IT EXISTS TODAY AND ITS CHANCES OF RESOLVING
PRACTICAL DIFFERENCES. STRESSES OPINION THAT 'ENFORCEMENT OF
HUMAN RIGHTS' IS POLITICAL-MORAL MATTER, NOT A LEGAL ISSUE.

1791 SCHWELB E.
"OPERATION OF THE EUROPEAN CONVENTION ON HUMAN RIGHTS."
INT. ORGAN., 18 (SUMMER 64), 558-85.
    EFFECTIVENESS OF EUROPEAN COMMISSION OF HUMAN RIGHTS IS
ILLUSTRATED BY SELECTED CASES WHICH DEMONSTRATE HOW THE COM-
MISSION ENSURED OBSERVANCE OF OBLIGATIONS BETWEEN VARIOUS
PARTIES. CONCLUDES WORK OF COMMISSION IS SIGNIFICANT ADVANCE
IN INTERNATIONAL PROTECTION OF HUMAN RIGHTS.

1792 SCHWELB E.
HUMAN RIGHTS AND THE INTERNATIONAL COMMUNITY.
CHICAGO: QUADRANGLE BOOKS, INC, 1964, 95 PP., LC#64-16781.
    TRACES HISTORICAL EVENTS LEADING TO UN UNIVERSAL
DECLARATION OF HUMAN RIGHTS IN 1948. EXAMINES DECLARATION AS
STANDARD FOR THE MEASUREMENT OF INTERNATIONAL RECOGNITION
OF HUMAN RIGHTS. DISCUSSES PENETRATION OF DECLARATION INTO
INTERNATIONAL LAW AND ITS EFFECTS ON INDIVIDUAL NATIONS'
HUMAN RIGHTS POLICY. REVIEWS LATER UN RESOLUTIONS REGARDING
COLONIALISM AND VARIOUS AREAS OF INTERNATIONAL COOPERATION.

1793 SCHWERIN K.
"LAW LIBRARIES AND FOREIGN LAW COLLECTION IN THE USA."
INT. AND COMP. LAW Q., 11 (APR. 62), 537-567.
    STUDIES BOTH US LAW LIBRARIES IN GENERAL AND THEIR FOR-
EIGN LAW COLLECTIONS. REVIEWS SOME MAJOR LAW LIBRARIES AND
LIBRARY FACILITIES AND SYSTEMS. SURVEYS MAJOR COLLECTIONS
OF FOREIGN LAW, AND METHODS OF DEVELOPING THESE COLLECTIONS.

1794 SCOTT A.

"TWENTY-FIVE YEARS OF OPINION ON INTEGRATION IN TEXAS."
S.W. SOCIAL SCI. QUART., 48 (SEPT. 67), 155-163.
PRESENTS RESULTS OF OPINION POLLS FROM 1940-65 IN TEXAS
ON INTEGRATION. DISCUSSES CIVIL RIGHTS STRUGGLE, ATTITUDES
OF RESIDENTS ON CHANGES, PRESENT ATTITUDES, AND TRENDS IN
PUBLIC OPINION.

1795 SCOTT A.M., WALLACE E.
POLITICS, USA; CASES ON THE AMERICAN DEMOCRATIC PROCESS.
NEW YORK: MACMILLAN, 1961, 571 PP., LC#61-6164.
COLLECTION OF CASES ON TOPICS OF STATES' RIGHTS, COURT
SYSTEM, CIVIL LIBERTIES, LOYALTY, ELECTIONS, PUBLIC RE-
LATIONS, PRESSURE GROUPS, CONGRESS, EXECUTIVE BRANCH, WEL-
FARE AND ECONOMY, FOREIGN POLICY, STATE AND LOCAL GOVERN-
MENT, AND PREJUDICE. SERVES AS DIFFERENT APPROACH TO INTRO-
DUCTORY GOVERNMENT TEXTBOOK.

1796 SCOTT A.M.
THE SUPREME COURT V. THE CONSTITUTION.
NEW YORK: EXPOSITION PRESS, 1963, 58 PP.
DISCUSSION OF ACQUISITION OF DICTATORIAL POWERS BY JUDGES
AND PRINCIPALLY BY SUPREME COURT JUSTICES. DISCUSSES
TENDENCIES OF JUDGES TO IMPROVISE, ENACT, AND FOLLOW
PERSONAL CONCEPTS AND LAWS RATHER THAN DISCHARGING THEIR
DUTIES ACCORDING TO PROVISIONS OF CONSTITUTION. ADVOCATES
ABIDING BY CONSTITUTION IN ALL LEGAL MATTERS UNDER ALL
CIRCUMSTANCES.

1797 SCOTT F.R.
CIVIL LIBERTIES AND CANADIAN FEDERALISM.
TORONTO: TORONTO UNIV PRESS, 1959, 57 PP.
LECTURES ON EVOLUTIONARY GROWTH OF CANADIAN CONSTITUTION
AS EVIDENCED BY NEW MOVEMENT TO INTRODUCE BILL OF RIGHTS.
HISTORY OF CONSTITUTION REGARDING CIVIL LIBERTIES AND HUMAN
RIGHTS.

1798 SCOTT J.B.
"LAW, THE STATE, AND THE INTERNATIONAL COMMUNITY (2 VOLS.)"
NEW YORK: COLUMBIA U PRESS, 1939.
A WORK IN TWO VOLUMES: VOLUME I IS A SURVEY AND COMMEN-
TARY ON THE DEVELOPMENT OF LEGAL, POLITICAL, AND INTERNA-
TIONAL IDEALS; VOLUME II IS A COLLECTION OF EXTRAS ILLUS-
TRATING THE GROWTH OF THEORIES AND PRINCIPLES OF JURISPRU-
DENCE, GOVERNMENT, AND THE LAW OF NATIONS. VOLUME II CON-
TAINS A GENERAL UNANNOTATED BIBLIOGRAPHY AND A BIBLIOGRAPHY
OF SOURCE MATERIALS FROM WHICH QUOTATIONS HAVE BEEN TAKEN.

1799 SEARA M.V.
"COSMIC INTERNATIONAL LAW."
DETROIT: WAYNE STATE U PR, 1965.
A GENERAL STUDY OF PROBLEMS IN INTERNATIONAL LAW AND
SPACE, MODIFIED FROM SPANISH EDITION. BIBLIOGRAPHY OF ABOUT
400 BOOKS AND PERIODICALS IN ALL MAJOR LANGUAGES, UP TO
1963. ARRANGED BY AREA, INCLUDING GENERAL AND SPECIAL
PROBLEMS OF INTERNATIONAL LAW, AIR LAW, OUTER SPACE, AND
TECHNICAL WORKS.

1800 SECKLER-HUDSON C.
BIBLIOGRAPHY ON PUBLIC ADMINISTRATION (4TH ED.)
WASHINGTON: AMERICAN U PR, 1953, 131 PP.
SELECTED, ANNOTATED, AND INDEXED BIBLIOGRAPHY OF OVER
1,100 REFERENCES TO PUBLIC ADMINISTRATION. INCLUDES GOVERN-
MENT PUBLICATIONS, PERIODICALS, REPORTS, BOOKS, AND OTHER
ITEMS ARRANGED ACCORDING TO CATEGORIES SUCH AS BUDGETARY
ADMINISTRATION, ORGANIZATION AND MANAGEMENT, PERSONNEL,
ADJUDICATION, ADMINISTRATIVE LAW, PUBLIC RELATIONS, INTER-
NATIONAL ADMINISTRATION, ETC.

1801 SEGAL R.
SANCTIONS AGAINST SOUTH AFRICA.
BALTIMORE: PENGUIN BOOKS, 1964, 272 PP.
TWENTY-TWO ARTICLES FROM INTERNATIONAL CONFERENCE ON ECO-
NOMIC SANCTIONS AGAINST SOUTH AFRICA OF 1964, DESCRIBING
ECONOMIC, RACIAL, POLITICAL, LEGAL, AND STRATEGIC ASPECTS OF
SANCTIONS.

1802 SEIDLER G.L.
"MARXIST LEGAL THOUGHT IN POLAND."
SLAVIC REVIEW, 26 (SEPT. 67), 382-394.
SINCE WWII, POLISH LEGAL THEORY HAS FOCUSED PRIMARILY ON
SOCIOLOGICAL ASPECTS OF THE LAW. RESEARCH INDICATES THAT
THIS FOCUS BENEFITED INTEREST GROUPS. AS A RESULT NEW PROB-
LEMS ARE BEING CONSIDERED. THOSE RECEIVING SPECIAL ATTEN-
TION ARE: EVALUATION OF POSITIVE LAW; RELATIONSHIP BETWEEN
LEGAL AND SOCIALIST CONSCIOUSNESS; AND COMPREHENSIVE LEGAL
RESEARCH. ARTICLE IS CONFINED TO PRESENTATION OF PROBLEMS.

1803 SEN B.
A DIPLOMAT'S HANDBOOK OF INTERNATIONAL LAW AND PRACTICE.
THE HAGUE: MARTINUS NIJHOFF, 1965, 522 PP.
ON THE ASSUMPTION THAT STATES DESIRE THEIR INTERNATIONAL
BEHAVIOR, WHENEVER POSSIBLE, TO FALL WITHIN THE BOUNDS SANC-
TIONED BY INTERNATIONAL LAW AND PUBLIC OPINION, SEN PRESENTS
A RESUME OF TOPICALLY ORGANIZED INTERNATIONAL LAW FOR THE
PRACTICING DIPLOMAT& DIPLOMATIC AND CONSULAR FUNCTIONS, IM-
MUNITIES AND PRIVILEGES, PROTECTION OF CITIZENS, PASSPORTS,
COMMERCE, RECOGNITION, AND TREATY-MAKING.

1804 SERENI A.P.
THE ITALIAN CONCEPTION OF INTERNATIONAL LAW.
NEW YORK: COLUMB. U. PR., 1943, 353 PP.
MAJOR PURPOSE IS TO SHOW THAT THE FASCISM OF THE PRE-WAR
ERA WAS A DEVIATION FROM THE NORMAL COURSE OF ITALIAN
JUSTICE AND FREEDOM.

1805 SERRANO MOSCOSO E.
A STATEMENT OF THE LAWS OF ECUADOR IN MATTERS AFFECTING
BUSINESS (2ND ED.)
WASHINGTON: PAN AMERICAN UNION, 1955, 191 PP.
SUMMARY IN ENGLISH OF CONSTITUTIONAL, STATUTORY, AND
REGULATORY PROVISIONS OF ECUADOR RELEVANT TO COMMERCIAL
CONCERNS; COVERS LAWS IN FORCE IN 1955. INCLUDES LAWS
ON MARRIAGE, TAXATION, AND COMMERCE.

1806 SETARO F.C.
A BIBLIOGRAPHY OF THE WRITINGS OF ROSCOE POUND.
CAMBRIDGE: HARVARD U PR, 1942, 193 PP.
INCLUDES ALL OF POUND'S WRITINGS PUBLISHED BEFORE
JULY 1, 1940.

1807 SEYID MUHAMMAD V.A.
THE LEGAL FRAMEWORK OF WORLD TRADE.
NEW YORK: FREDERICK PRAEGER, 1958, 348 PP., LC#58-8538.
DEALS WITH LEGAL ASPECTS OF INTERNATIONAL TRADE, EMPHA-
SIZING GENERAL AGREEMENT ON TARIFFS AND TRADE OF 1947. IN-
CLUDES RELATION OF GENERAL AGREEMENT TO INTERNATIONAL LAW
AND OTHER INTERNATIONAL ORGANIZATIONS; ORGANIZATION OF
GENERAL AGREEMENT GROUP; RULES AND PROCEDURE ON TARIFF NE-
GOTIATIONS AND OTHER ASPECTS OF WORLD TRADE; AND APPRAISAL
OF GENERAL AGREEMENT.

1808 SEYLER W.C.
"DOCTORAL DISSERTATIONS IN POLITICAL SCIENCE IN UNIVERSITIES
OF THE UNITED STATES AND CANADA."
AM. POL. SCI. REV., 60 (SEPT. 66), 778-803.
AN UNANNOTATED BIBLIOGRAPHY OF DOCTORAL DISSERTATIONS IN
POLITICAL SCIENCE. MATERIAL IS FROM LATE 1965 TO 1966.
ENGLISH LANGUAGE. CONTAINS 1,150 ENTRIES.

1809 SHAFFER T.L.
"DIRECT RESTRAINT ON THE PRESS."
NOTRE DAME LAWYER, 42 (1967), 865-880.
ADVOCATES INCREASE IN INFORMATION AVAILABLE TO PRESS AND
STRONG LAWS MAKING PREMATURE PUBLICATION OF CERTAIN KINDS
OF PREJUDICIAL INFORMATION A CRIME. SUGGESTS THAT THIS
METHOD WOULD GIVE PRESS FREEST EXPRESSION POSSIBLE.

1810 SHAPIRO J.P.
"SOVIET HISTORIOGRAPHY AND THE MOSCOW TRIALS: AFTER THIRTY
YEARS."
RUSSIAN REVIEWS, 27 (JAN. 68), 68-77.
DISCUSSES THE SOVIET PROCESS OF "REHABILITATION" OF VIC-
TIMS OF THE 1936-38 GREAT PURGE. REHABILITATION CAN BE EI-
THER PUBLIC, BY THE SOVIET PRESS'S PUBLICATION OF THE VIC-
TIM'S BIOGRAPHY, OR JUDICIAL. DISCUSSES THE "REHABILITA-
TION" OF MANY PROMINENT BOLSHEVIK LEADERS.

1811 SHAPIRO M.
LAW AND POLITICS IN THE SUPREME COURT: NEW APPROACHES TO
POLITICAL JURISPRUDENCE.
NEW YORK: FREE PRESS OF GLENCOE, 1964, 264 PP.
DESCRIBES AND EVALUATES THE POLITICAL AS DISTINCY FROM
THE CONSTITUTIONAL. CONSIDERATIONS OF THE SUPREME COURT IN
REACHING ITS DECISIONS. SHOWS HOW THE COURT ALSO ACTS AS
POLITICAL SCIENTIST, ECONOMIST, AND LABOR AND TAX LAWYER AS
WELL AS SUPREME AUTHORITY ON CONSTITUTIONAL QUESTIONS.

1812 SHAPIRO M.
FREEDOM OF SPEECH: THE SUPREME COURT AND JUDICIAL REVIEW.
ENGLEWOOD CLIFFS: PRENTICE HALL, 1966, 182 PP., LC#66-14702.
CONTENDS THAT CRUCIAL ISSUES IN THE CONSTITUTIONAL
DEBATE OVER FREEDOM OF SPEECH CAN BE RESOLVED ONLY BY PROP-
ER UNDERSTANDING OF THE PLACE OF THE SUPREME COURT IN AMER-
ICAN POLITICS. DISCUSSES CONFLICT BETWEEN THE JUDICIALLY
MODEST, WHO WANT THE COURT TO DO LITTLE TO PROTECT FREEDOM
OF SPEECH, AND THE JUDICIAL ACTIVISTS. EXAMINES THE VEHICLE
FOR ACTIVE JUDICIAL PROTECTION OF FREEDOM OF SPEECH.

1813 SHARMA M.P.
PUBLIC ADMINISTRATION IN THEORY AND PRACTICE.
ALLAHABAD, INDIA: KITAB MAHAL, 1958, 508 PP.
DISCUSSES THEORY OF PUBLIC ADMINISTRATION, ITS ORGANIZA-
TION, VARIOUS REGULATORY AGENCIES AND COMMISSIONS, PERSONNEL
ADMINISTRATION, AND ADMINISTRATIVE LAW AND RESPONSIBILITY
IN CONTEXT OF INDIAN, BRITISH, AN US EXPERIENCE.

1814 SHARMA S.A.
PARLIAMENTARY GOVERNMENT IN INDIA.
ALLAHABAD: CENTRAL BOOK DEPT, 1965, 242 PP.
SURVEYS ALL ASPECTS OF INDIAN GOVERNMENT FROM MAKING OF
CONSTITUTION TO DETAILS OF PUBLIC FINANCE AND LOCAL GOVERN-
MENTAL SYSTEMS. INCLUDES DISCUSSION OF JUDICIAL AND ADMINIS-

TRATIVE TRIBUNALS AND WORK OF PLANNING COMMISSIONS.

1815 SHARMA S.P.
"THE INDIA-CHINA BORDER DISPUTE: AN INDIAN PERSPECTIVE."
AMER. J. INT. LAW, 59 (JAN. 65), 16-47.
PRESENTS CLAIMS AND COUNTER-CLAIMS OF PARTIES IN DISPUTE.
ASSESSES PAST JURIDICAL PRACTISES. SUPPORTS INDIA'S CLAIM ON
GEOGRAPHICAL, HISTORICAL, AND LEGAL GROUNDS.

1816 SHAW C. ED.
LEGAL PROBLEMS IN INTERNATIONAL TRADE AND INVESTMENT.
NEW HAVEN: YALE U PR, 1962, 265 PP.
DESCRIBES WAYS PUBLIC AND PRIVATE INTERNATIONAL BUSINESS
TRANSACTIONS ARE CONDUCTED. INCLUDES LAWYER'S ROLE IN TRANS-
ACTIONS; PROBLEMS OF INTERNATIONAL TRADE AND INVESTMENT
BETWEEN DEVELOPED NATIONS AND UNDEVELOPED ONES OF AFRICA,
ASIA, AND SOUTH AMERICA; ANTI-TRUST PROBLEMS; REGIONAL
MARKETING AND TAX PROBLEMS.

1817 SHEEHY E.P.
"SELECTED REFERENCE BOOKS OF 1965-1966."
COLLEGE AND RESEARCH LIBRARIES, 27 (JULY 66), 304-317.
AN ANNOTATED BIBLIOGRAPHY OF REFERENCE BOOKS. MATERIAL
IN ENGLISH LANGUAGE AND SOME FRENCH, GERMAN, RUSSIAN,
SPANISH, AND FINNISH. PUBLISHED 1965 TO 1966.

1818 SHELDON C.H.
"PUBLIC OPINION AND HIGH COURTS: COMMUNIST PARTY CASES IN
FOUR CONSTITUTIONAL SYSTEMS."
WESTERN POLIT. QUART., 20 (JUNE 67), 341-360.
THEORIZES THAT IN ALL CONSTITUTIONAL SYSTEMS, HIGHEST
COURTS WILL ALWAYS RULE CONSISTENTLY WITH PUBLIC OPINION IN
CRUCIAL AREAS, E.G., IN THREATS FROM SUBVERSIVE GROUPS LIKE
COMMUNIST PARTY. ANALYZES COURT RULINGS FROM 1950-61 IN US,
CANADA, AUSTRALIA, AND WEST GERMANY TO PROVE THEORY, FOR
COURT'S OPINIONS CHANGED WITH POLITICAL TIDE DURING THIS
PERIOD.

1819 SHERMAN C.P.
"ROMAN LAW IN THE MODERN WORLD (2ND ED.) (3 VOLS.)"
NEW YORK: BAKER, VORHIS & CO, 1924.
VOLUME THREE OF STUDY CONTAINS LISTS OF PERTINENT TEXTS
OF ROMAN LAW; REFERENCES TO THE MODERN CODES AND TRANSLA-
TIONS, AND TO PERTINENT MODERN LEGAL LITERATURE. INCLUDES
A BIBLIOGRAPHY OF PRINCIPAL WORKS (MOSTLY MODERN) -
ON ROMAN LAW. LISTS MAGAZINE ARTICLES AND MINOR WORKS
TREATING ROMAN LAW.

1820 SHKLAR J.
"SELECTED ARTICLES AND DOCUMENTS ON POLITICAL THEORY."
AM. POL. SCI. REV., 60 (SEPT. 66), 715-716.
AN UNANNOTATED BIBLIOGRAPHY OF ARTICLES AND DOCUMENTS ON
POLITICAL THEORY. ENGLISH-LANGUAGE AND SOME SPANISH, FRENCH,
AND GERMAN. MATERIAL RANGES FROM 1965 TO 1966. CONTAINS
60 ENTRIES.

1821 SHKLAR J.N.
LEGALISM.
CAMBRIDGE: HARVARD U PR, 1964, 224 PP., LC#64-19584.
DEALS WITH AREA BETWEEN POLITICAL THEORY AND JURISPRU-
DENCE. ATTEMPTS TO EXPLAIN HOW LEGALISM HAS FALLEN SHORT IN
ITS APPROACH TO MORALS AND POLITICS; SUGGESTS MEANS OF
RE-ESTABLISHING RAPPORT AMONG THESE FIELDS.

1822 SIDGWICK H.
THE ELEMENTS OF POLITICS.
LONDON: MACMILLAN, 1891, 623 PP.
A COMPREHENSIVE STUDY OF POLITICAL THEORY AND PRACTICE IN
RELATION TO 19TH-CENTURY SOCIETY. THE SCOPE, CONCEPTION AND
PRINCIPLES OF POLITICS ARE BASED ON WRITINGS OF J.S. MILL
AND BENTHAM. MAJOR AREAS DISCUSSED INCLUDE JURISPRUDENCE,
INTERNATIONAL LAW, MAINTENANCE AND STRUCTURE OF GOVERNMENT,
RELATION OF JUDICIARY TO LEGISLATURE AND EXECUTIVE, LOCAL
AND FEDERAL GOVERNMENTS, AND SOVEREIGNTY AND ORDER.

1823 SIEKANOWICZ P., GSOVSKI V. ED.
LEGAL SOURCES AND BIBLIOGRAPHY OF POLAND.
NEW YORK: FREDERICK PRAEGER, 1964, 311 PP., LC#64-15524.
MATERIALS ORGANIZED CHRONOLOGICALLY AND BY SUBJECT FROM
PREPARTITION (1500'S) TO PRESENT. INCLUDE DOCUMENTS AND
SECONDARY SOURCES. ITEMS USUALLY IN POLISH WITH INDEXES TO
CURRENT LAWS, AUTHORS, SUBJECTS, AND TITLES FOLLOWING 1,750
ITEMS.

1824 SIEYES E.J., BASTID P. ED.
LES DISCOURS DE SIEYES DANS LES DEBATS CONSTITUTIONNELS DE
L'AN III (2 ET 18 THERMIDOR)
PARIS: LIB HACHETTE ET CIE, 1939, 115 PP.
SPEECHES CONCERN PROPOSED FRENCH CONSTITUTION OF 1793.
ADVOCATE ESTABLISHMENT OF JURY TO HEAR COMPLAINTS AGAINST
CONSTITUTION. TASKS OF GOVERNMENT ARE TO PROPOSE LAWS, TO
PUT THEM INTO EFFECT, AND TO MAKE THIS POSSIBLE THROUGH
ESTABLISHING EXECUTIVE POWER. PROPOSE UNICAMERAL LEGISLA-
TURE, LARGER THAN OTHER BRANCHES OF GOVERNMENT, BUT WITHOUT
POWER TO ISSUE ITS OWN DECREES.

1825 SIGLIANO R E.
THE COURTS.
BOSTON: LITTLE BROWN, 1962, 504 PP., LC#62-09512.
READER IN AMERICAN JUDICIAL PROCESS. STUDIES JUDICIAL
POWER, JUDICIAL SELECTION AND TENURE, LEGAL ENVIRONMENT,
DECISION-MAKING PROCESS, JUDICIAL FUNCTION, AND SUPREME
COURT IN AMERICAN POLITICAL SYSTEM.

1826 SILVA R.C.
"LEGISLATIVE REPESENTATION - WITH SPECIAL REFERENCE TO
NEW YORK."
LAW AND CONTEMPORARY PROB., 27 (SUMMER 62), 408-433.
ANALYSIS OF VARIOUS BASES OF REPRESENTATION, APPORTION-
MENT, DISTRICTING, AND JUDICIAL REMEDIES.

1827 SILVA R.C.
RUM, RELIGION, AND VOTES: 1928 RE-EXAMINED.
UNIVERSITY PARK: PENN STATE U PR, 1962, 76 PP., LC#62-20759.
ANALYZES POLITICAL STRENGTH OF ALFRED E. SMITH AS DEMO-
CRATIC PRESIDENTIAL CANDIDATE IN 1928, AND RELEVANCE OF HIS
RELIGION AND ATTITUDE TOWARD PROHIBITION IN VOTING BEHAVIOR.

1828 SILVING H.
"IN RE EICHMANN: A DILEMMA OF LAW AND MORALITY"
AMER. J. OF INT. LAW, 55 (APR. 61), 307-358.
EXPLORES CONFLICT OF POSITIVE-LAW CLAIM BASED ON
TERRITORIAL INVIOLABILITY WITH NATURAL-LAW HUMANISTIC
INTEREST THROUGH STUDY OF ADOLF EICHMANN CASE. DISCUSSES
CONFLICT OF LAW AND MORALITY AND ADVOCATES LESS "THING"
ORIENTATION IN INTERNATIONAL LAW AND DEVELOPMENT OF SENSE
OF MORALITY SIGNIFICANT TO MODERN MAN.

1829 SIMPSON J.L., FOX H.
INTERNATIONAL ARBITRATION: LAW AND PRACTICE.
NEW YORK: FREDERICK PRAEGER, 1959, 330 PP., LC#59-7392.
SURVEY OF SETTLEMENT BY JUDICIAL MEANS OF DISPUTES
BETWEEN NATIONS. CONCENTRATES ON PERIOD AFTER WWII, HAGUE
COURT, GERMAN TRIALS, ETC. COVERS INFORMAL ARBITRATION AND
FORMAL TRIBUNALS, BOTH PROCESSES AND RELATION TO EACH OTHER.
EMPHASIS ON ACTUAL PRACTICE OF COURTS. INCLUDES ALPHABETICAL
TABLE OF CASES AND APPENDIX OF MODEL RULES ON ARBITRAL
PROCEDURE.

1830 SINCLAIR T.C., KRISLOV S. ET AL.
THE POLITICS OF JUDICIAL REVIEW 1937-1957.
DALLAS: SOUTHERN METHODIST U PR, 1957, 46 PP.
DISCUSSES ROLE OF SUPREME COURT IN PROTECTION OF ECONOMIC
AND CIVIL RIGHTS, AND PUBLIC OPINION OF COURT BETWEEN
1937 AND 1957.

1831 SINCO V.G.
PHILIPPINE POLITICAL LAW: PRINCIPLES AND CONCEPTS (10TH
ED.)
MANILA: COMMUNITY PUBL, 1954.
EXAMINES POLITICAL LAW IN LAW SCHOOLS OF PHILIPPINES.
PRESENTS FUNDAMENTAL PRINCIPLES OF ALL ASPECTS OF
CONSTITUTION AND LEGAL PROCESSES, FUNCTIONS OF LEGAL BODIES,
ETC.

1832 SINEY M.C.
THE ALLIED BLOCKADE OF GERMANY: 1914-1916.
ANN ARBOR: U OF MICH PR, 1957, 339 PP., LC#57-5143.
ANALYSIS OF MEASURES TAKEN BY ALLIES DURING WWI TO INTER-
FERE WITH AND STOP GERMAN TRADE. CONSIDERS BLOCKADE MEASURES
ESSENTIALLY AS INSTRUMENTS OF ECONOMIC WARFARE. ALSO EXAM-
INES LEGAL ASPECTS OF BLOCKADE AND OF TRADE RESTRICTIONS
PLACED ON NEUTRAL STATES. CONCENTRATES LARGELY ON BRITISH
NEGOTIATIONS WITH SCANDIANAVIAN COUNTRIES.

1833 SINGH N., NAWAS M.K.
"THE CONTEMPORARY PRACTICE OF INDIA IN THE FIELD OF
INTERNATIONAL LAW."
INT. STUDIES, 6 (JULY 64), 69-86.
TRACES EVOLUTION OF INTERNATIONAL LAW AS IT RELATES TO
PRACTICES AND ACTIONS OF INDIA IN THE INTERNATIONAL DOMAIN
FOR 1962. CONCEPTS OF RECOGNITION, JURISDICTION AND TERR-
ITORY WERE SCRUTINIZED. LEGAL IMPLICATIONS OF COMMUNIST
CHINESE OCCUPATION OF LADAKH PROVINCE EXPLORED.

1834 SIPKOV I.
LEGAL SOURCES AND BIBLIOGRAPHY OF BULGARIA.
NEW YORK: FREDERICK PRAEGER, 1956, 199 PP., LC#57-13220.
ONE OF THE SERIES OF BIBLIOGRAPHIES PREPARED BY THE MID-
EUROPEAN LAW PROJECT AND PUBLISHED BY THE MID-EUROPEAN
STUDIES CENTER: COVERS NEW LEGAL COLLECTIONS, NEW WRITINGS,
AND NEW PERIODICALS WHICH HAVE APPEARED SINCE THE ESTABLISH-
MENT OF COMMUNIST GOVERNMENT IN BULGARIA. SURVEYS LEGAL
SOURCES, ROOTS OF THE NATIONAL LEGISLATIVE SYSTEM, AND TRAN-
SITION TO PRESENT SYSTEM. PRIMARILY RECENT PUBLICATIONS.

1835 SISSON C.H.
THE SPIRIT OF BRITISH ADMINISTRATION AND SOME EUROPEAN
COMPARISONS.
LONDON: FABER AND FABER, 1959, 162 PP.
ANALYSIS OF INDIVIDUAL IN, AND ORGANIZATION OF, BRITISH
PUBLIC ADMINISTRATION AND ITS RELATION TO LAW AND POLITICS.

COMPARES BRITISH SYSTEM WITH THAT OF FRANCE, GERMANY, AND SWEDEN.

1836 SKOLNICK J.H.
JUSTICE WITHOUT TRIAL: LAW ENFORCEMENT IN DEMOCRATIC SOCIETY
NEW YORK: JOHN WILEY, 1966, 279 PP., LC#66-17613.
SOCIOLOGICAL ANALYSIS OF PROBLEMS OF LAW ENFORCEMENT.
INVESTIGATES INNER WORKINGS OF AN ACTUAL MIDDLE-SIZED
AMERICAN POLICE DEPARTMENT. INCLUDES STUDY OF POLICEMAN'S
"WORKING PERSONALITY"; POLICE ORGANIZATION; EFFECTS OF
BUREAUCRACY ON CRIMINAL JUSTICE; NARCOTICS AND VICE IN-
VESTIGATION; INFORMER'S PAYOFF AND ITS CONSEQUENCES; RELA-

1837 SKUBISZEWSKI K.
"FORMS OF PARTICIPATION OF INTERNATIONAL ORGANIZATION IN
THE LAW MAKING PROCESS."
INT. ORGAN., 18 (AUTUMN 64), 790-805.
'THIS ARTICLE SEEKS TO LIST AND BRIEFLY ANALYZE THE
DIFFERENT WAYS AND FORMS WHEREBY CONTEMPORARY INTERNATIONAL
ORGANIZATIONS PARTICIPATE IN THE MAKING OF NEW RULES OF
PUBLIC INTERNATIONAL LAW.' TREATIES, RESOLUTIONS BEARING ON
INTERNATIONAL LAW, ENACTMENT OF INTERNAL LAW OF INTERNATION-
AL ORGANIZATION, AND LAW MAKINGS ARE DISCUSSED.

1838 SLATER J.
THE OAS AND UNITED STATES FOREIGN POLICY.
COLUMBUS: OHIO STATE U PR, 1967, 315 PP., LC#67-10162.
US POLICY OF EXCLUDING COMMUNISM FROM WESTERN HEMISPHERE
BY PRESERVING STATUS QUO PERMITTED OAS A CONSTRUCTIVE ROLE
IN PROVIDING COLLECTIVE SECURITY. AFTER 1960, US POLICY
DISCOURAGED ANY DICTATORIAL LEADERS AS PROVOCATIVE OF
COMMUNIST SYMPATHIES AMONG SUPPRESSED PEOPLES. US ATTEMPT
TO MAKE OAS AN ANTI-COMMUNIST OR ANTI-DICTATORIAL
ALLIANCE THREATENS ITS EFFECTIVENESS AS ARBITRATOR.

1839 SLESSER H.
THE ADMINISTRATION OF THE LAW.
LONDON: HUTCHINSON U LIBRARY, 1948, 144 PP.
A STUDY FOR LAYMEN OF THE ADMINISTRATION OF ENGLISH CIVIL
AND CRIMINAL LAW. DESCRIBES THE CONSTITUTION OF COURTS, THE
RECEPTION OF EVIDENCE, THE METHOD OF PROOF, AND THE MANNER
IN WHICH JUDGES ARRIVE AT DECISIONS. INCLUDES A BRIEF
OUTLINE OF BRITISH LEGAL HISTORY AND DEVELOPMENT AND OF
HISTORICAL FORMS OF ACTION AND PROSECUTION.

1840 SMITH A.
LECTURES ON JUSTICE, POLICE, REVENUE AND ARMS (1763)
LONDON: OXFORD U PR, 1896, 293 PP.
DISCUSSES THEORIES OF JURISPRUDENCE FROM LAISSEZ-FAIRE
STANDPOINT. CONSIDERS JUSTICE TO BE SECURITY FROM INJURY;
PRICE CEILINGS AN OBJECTIVE OF LAW ENFORCEMENT; AND
PREFERRED MEANS OF TAXATION TO BE THAT WHICH IS LEAST DIS-
COMFITING. CONCENTRATES ON ENGLISH JUDICIAL SYSTEM FOR
EXAMPLES. ALSO EXAMINES POSSIBILITY OF EXISTENCE OF
NATURAL LAW'S AFFECTING INTERNATIONAL RELATIONS.

1841 SMITH C. ED.
THE OMBUDSMAN: A BIBLIOGRAPHY (PAMPHLET)
RALEIGH: N CAR FRIEND COMM LEGIS, 1965, 7 PP.
LISTS 100 ENTRIES PUBLISHED BETWEEN 1957 AND 1964 IN
ENGLISH ALPHABETICALLY BY AUTHOR.

1842 SMITH E.A.
CHURCH AND STATE IN YOUR COMMUNITY.
PHILADELPHIA: WESTMINSTER PR, 1963, 90 PP., LC#63-7263.
CLARIFIES PRECISE BEARING OF GENERAL PROBLEM OF CHURCH-
STATE RELATIONS ON ACTUAL SITUATIONS THAT OCCUR IN AMERICAN
COMMUNITIES. DISCUSSES MYRIAD VIEWS OF PROBLEM: THE NA-
TION'S, HISTORY'S, PROTESTANT, ROMAN CATHOLIC, AND EVERYDAY
AMERICA'S. REALIZES THAT HONEST PROTESTANT STAND MUST BE
FOR FREEDOM FOR ALL TO LEARN ABOUT RELIGION WITHOUT BEING
FORCED. QUESTIONS FOR DISCUSSION INCLUDED AT END.

1843 SMITH E.A. ED.
CHURCH-STATE RELATIONS IN ECUMENICAL PERSPECTIVE.
PITTSBURGH: DUQUESNE U PRESS, 1966, 280 PP., LC#66-18450.
ESSAYS DEALING WITH RELATION OF ECUMENISM TO RECENT
SOCIAL CHANGE, RELIGIOUS MEANING OF COMMUNITY FOR CIVIL
LIFE, STUDIES OF PHILOSOPHY OF NATURAL LAW, STUDIES OF
AMERICAN LEGAL CONCEPTS VIS-A-VIS CHURCH-STATE RELATIONS.
ALL DEAL WITH BASIC QUESTIONS OF CHRISTIAN RESPONSIBILITY
TO CIVIL POWER.

1844 SMITH G.
A CONSTITUTIONAL AND LEGAL HISTORY OF ENGLAND.
NEW YORK: CHAS SCRIBNER'S SONS, 1955, 565 PP., LC#55-7297.
TRACES THE HISTORY OF LAW IN ENGLAND FROM EARLY ANGLO-
SAXON TIMES TO THE PRESENT. SHOWS HOW EXTENSION OF NATIONAL
TERRITORY CAUSED CREATION OF SEMI-INDEPENDENT LORDS WHO
COULD INSIST UPON CERTAIN PRINCIPLES OF JUSTICE, WHICH CAME
TO INCLUDE ALL OF LAW. EXTENSION OF THE PROPERTY BASE IN
THE 17TH-19TH CENTURIES GAVE THE MIDDLE CLASS A CLAIM TO
JUSTICE AND ITS ADMINISTRATION.

1845 SMITH J.W. ED., JAMISON A.L. ED.
RELIGIOUS PERSPECTIVES IN AMERICAN CULTURE, VOL. 2, RELIGION

IN AMERICAN LIFE.
PRINCETON: PRINCETON U PRESS, 1961, 427 PP., LC#61-5383.
TEN ESSAYS SHOWING VARIOUS WAYS IN WHICH RELIGION
INFLUENCES AMERICAN LIFE. INCLUDES APPROPRIATE
ESSAYS ON RELIGION AND EDUCATION, LAW, POLITICAL ATTITUDES,
THE ARTS, TECHNIQUES OF POLITICAL ACTION: THE STATE,
CHURCH, AND LOBBY; PLACE OF BIBLE IN AMERICAN FICTION. ALL
ESSAYS INCLUDE SOME HISTORY, WHILE MAJOR THRUST IS TO SHOW
IMPACT RELIGION HAS MADE OUTSIDE CHURCHES AND SEMINARIES.

1846 SMITH R.C.
THEY CLOSED THEIR SCHOOLS.
CHAPEL HILL: U OF N CAR PR, 1965, 281 PP., LC#65-16296.
DETAILED ANALYSIS OF ACTION OF CLOSING SCHOOLS IN PRINCE
EDWARD COUNTY, VIRGINIA, IN 1958. DISCUSSES BACKGROUND LEAD-
ING UP TO DECISION AND ITS EFFECTS ON WHITE AND NEGRO
RESIDENTS.

1847 SMITH R.H.
JUSTICE AND THE POOR.
NY: CARNEGIE ENDOW ADVANCMT TCHG, 1919, 271 PP.
STUDIES DENIAL OF JUSTICE TO THE POOR AND AGENCIES
DEDICATED TO EQUALIZE THEIR LEGAL RIGHTS. DISCUSSES DEFECTS
IN COURT PROCEDURES AND EXPENSES. EXAMINES METHODS OF
CONCILIATION AND ARBITRATION. DESCRIBES VARIOUS AGENCIES OF
LAW WITH SPECIAL ATTENTION TO LEGAL AID ORGANIZATIONS AND
THEIR FUNCTIONS.

1848 SNOW J.H.
REAPPORTIONMENT.
NEW CANAAN: LONG HOUSE, 1965, 65 PP., LC#65-26960.
AFTER WEIGHING PROS AND CONS OF 1962 SUPREME COURT DECI-
SION ON TENNESSEE APPORTIONMENT, PROPOSES RESOLUTION TO
PROBLEM OF RE-DISTRICTING IN CONNECTICUT.

1849 SOBEL N.R.
THE NEW CONFESSION STANDARDS, MIRANDA V. ARIZONA.
JAMAICA: GOULD PUBLICATIONS, 1966, 153 PP.
DISCUSSES TWO EXCLUSIONARY RULES IN LAW OF CONFESSIONS
PRIOR TO 1966, BUT WITH PRIMARY EMPHASIS ON MIRANDA V.
ARIZONA. EXAMINES "TRADITIONAL INVOLUNTARY RULE," MASSIAH
"DEFENDANT STAGE," AND ESCOBEDO "ACCUSATORY STAGE"
EXCLUSIONARY RULES. BRIEFLY STATES HOLDING OF MIRANDA CASE.

1850 SOC OF COMP LEGIS AND INT LAW
THE LAW OF THE SEA... (PAMPHLET)
LONDON: SOC COMPAR LEGISLATION, 1958, 42 PP.
CONCERNED WITH UN CONFERENCE ON LAW OF THE SEA HELD IN
GENEVA IN 1958. CONSIDERS CLAIMS TO JURISDICTION OVER
TERRITORIAL SEA, CONTIGUOUS ZONE, AND THE CONTINENTAL SHELF.
INCLUDES RESOLUTIONS ON NUCLEAR TESTS ON HIGH SEAS, HUMANE
KILLING OF MARINE LIFE, FISHERY CONSERVATION CONVENTIONS,
POLLUTION OF HIGH SEAS BY RADIOACTIVE MATERIALS, AND
OPTIONAL PROTOCOL OF SIGNATURE ON SETTLEMENT OF DISPUTES.

1851 SOCIETE DES NATIONS
TRAITES INTERNATIONAUX ET ACTES LEGISLATIFS.
PARIS: CONSEIL D'ETAT.
PUBLISHED ANNUALLY DURING 1930-40. LISTS INTERNATIONAL
TREATIES AND LEGISLATIVE ACTS OF VARIOUS COUNTRIES PERTAIN-
ING TO TREATY-MAKING. EACH ISSUE CONTAINS ABOUT 1,500 ITEMS.

1852 SOHN L.B.
CASES AND OTHER MATERIALS ON WORLD LAW.
BROOKLYN: FOUNDATION PR., 1950, 1363 PP.
OUTGROWTH OF COURSE ON WORLD ORGANIZATION AT HARVARD LAW
SCHOOL. CONTAINS CONSTITUTIONAL TEXTS, JUDICIAL DECISIONS,
AND OFFICIAL DOCUMENTS SERVING AS AN INTERPRETATION AND
APPLICATION OF THE UN CHARTER AND CONSTITUTIONS OF OTHER
INTERNATIONAL AGENCIES. SECTION ON INTERNATIONAL COURTS
INCLUDES REPRESENTATIVE CASES IN RE ARBITRATION AND
CONCILIATION. DRAFT OF WORLD CONSTITUTION.

1853 SOHN L.B.
BASIC DOCUMENTS OF THE UNITED NATIONS.
BROOKLYN: FOUND. PR., 1956, 307 PP.
COMPILATION OF DOCUMENTS INTENDED TO SERVE AS A REFERENCE
VOLUME. REPRODUCTION OF UN CHARTER ACCOMPANIED BY THIRTY-
EIGHT SUPPLEMENTARY RECORDS AND FIFTEEN EXPLANATORY NOTES.

1854 SOHN L.B. ED.
CASES ON UNITED NATIONS LAW.
BROOKLYN: FOUNDATION PRESS, 1956, 1048 PP.
CASEBOOK CENTERING ON LEGAL PROBLEMS WHICH HAVE ARISEN IN
WORK OF UN. EMPHASIZES MATERIAL WHICH PRESENTS CLEARLY THE
ARGUMENTS ON BOTH SIDES OF EACH CASE. CASES ARE GROUPED
IN A WAY THAT BRINGS TOGETHER DECISIONS WHICH ARE PARALLEL
N FACTS BUT OPPOSITE IN CONCLUSIONS OR POSITIONS. SELECTIONS
DEAL WITH PROBLEMS OF UN ORGANIZATION, FUNCTIONS AND POWERS
OF UN ORGANS, AND CURRENT PROBLEMS OF WORLD LAW.

1855 SOHN L.B.
"THE DEFINITION OF AGGRESSION."
VIRGINIA LAW REV., 45 (JUNE 59), 697-701.
DEMANDS THAT THE INTERNATIONAL COURTS BE STRENGTHENED, SO
THAT AGGRESSIVE NATIONS WILL BE PROSECUTED. FEELS THAT A

CLEARER UNDERSTANDING OF THE LAW IS NECESSARY IN ORDER TO
DO THIS.

1856 SOMMER T.
DEUTSCHLAND UND JAPAN ZWISCHEN DEN MACHTEN.
TUBINGEN: J C B MOHR, 1962, 540 PP.
DISCUSSES DIPLOMATIC RELATIONS BETWEEN GERMANY AND JAPAN
FROM ALLIANCE IN 1935 TO 1940. SEEKS TO DESTROY POPULAR NO-
TION THAT CLOSE COLLABORATION EXISTED BETWEEN THE TWO POW-
ERS. SHEDS LIGHT ON STRUCTURE AND FUNCTION OF TOTALITARIAN
DIPLOMACY.

1857 SOPER T.
EVOLVING COMMONWEALTH.
NEW YORK: PERGAMON PRESS, 1965, 141 PP., LC#65-27362.
ESSAY ON HISTORY AND DEVELOPMENT OF BRITISH EMPIRE AND
COMMONWEALTH FROM COLONIALISM TO PRESENT DAY. DISCUSSES
INDEPENDENCE OF SOME NATIONS, ADDITION OF OTHERS TO COMMON-
WEALTH; STRUCTURE OF ORGANIZATION; LAWS REGULATING GROUP
RELATIONS; AND ROLE OF COMMONWEALTH IN SUCH AREAS AS COMMON
MARKET.

1858 SOUTH AFRICA STATE LIBRARY
SOUTH AFRICAN NATIONAL BIBLIOGRAPHY, SANB.
PRETORIA: S AFRICA STATE LIB.
LISTING OF PUBLICATIONS RECEIVED BY STATE LIBRARY IN
PRETORIA DURING TWO-MONTH PERIODS. TEXTS IN ENGLISH AND
AFRIKAANS. INCLUDES ANNUAL REPORTS OF GOVERNMENTAL DEPART-
MENTS. CONTAINS LARGE SECTION ON SOCIAL SCIENCES: ECONOMICS,
LAW, PUBLIC ADMINISTRATION, EDUCATION, SOCIOLOGY, SOCIOG-
RAPHY. BIMONTHLY PUBLICATION.

1859 SOWLE C.R. ED.
POLICE POWER AND INDIVIDUAL FREEDOM: THE QUEST FOR BALANCE.
CHICAGO: ALDINE PUBLISHING CO, 1962, 287 PP., LC#62-10632.
COMPARATIVE ANALYSIS OF POLICY PRIVILEGE AND PERSONAL
RIGHTS EMPHASIZING FOREIGN LAW, SELF-INCRIMINATION, ARREST
AND DETENTION, INTERROGATION, AND THE EXCLUSIONARY RULE.

1860 SPAETH H.J.
"JUDICIAL POWER AS A VARIABLE MOTIVATING SUPREME COURT
BEHAVIOR."
MIDWEST J. OF POLI. SCI., 6 (FEB. 62), 54-82.
TRIES TO ASCERTAIN IF A DOMINANT VARIABLE EXISTS WHICH
MOTIVATES BEHAVIOR OF SUPREME COURT JUSTICES IN WHAT IS
TERMED "TRUE" JUDICIAL POWER ITEMS (THOSE IN WHICH MORE VAL-
UE-LADEN VARIABLES ARE ABSENT OR SUBORDINATE TO CONSIDERA-
TIONS OF EXERCISE OF POWER BY THE COURT). EXAMINES VOTES IN
52 CASES DECIDED BY WARREN COURT. FINDS SIGNIFICANT CONTI-
NUITY IN DECISION-MAKING IN THESE ACTIVISM-RESTRAINT CASES.

1861 SPIRO H.J.
GOVERNMENT BY CONSTITUTIONS: THE POLITICAL SYSTEMS OF
DEMOCRACY.
NEW YORK: RANDOM, 1959, 496 PP.
EXAMINES THE POLITICS, POLICIES, INSTITUTIONS, PRO-
CEDURES AND REPRESENTATION IN SYSTEMS OF CONSTITUTIONAL
GOVERNMENT. DEALS SPECIFICALLY WITH SWEDEN, ITALY,
SWITZERLAND, GERMANY, FRANCE, GREAT BRITAIN, CANADA AND THE
UNITED STATES. DISCUSSES CONDITIONS OF CONSTITUTIONAL
SUCCESS AND LOOKS AT FUTURE OF CONSTITUTIONAL SYSTEMS.

1862 SPITZ D.
DEMOCRACY AND THE CHALLANGE OF POWER.
NEW YORK: COLUMB. U. PR., 1958, 228 PP.
ASSAYS THE ABUSES OF POWER IN A DEMOCRACY, CONTENDING
THEY ARISE FROM BOTH OPPRESSIVE ACTS OF GOVERNMENT AND ARBI-
TRARY PRACTICES OF INDIVIDUALS AND GROUPS. IN A DEMOCRACY,
NON-CONFORMISTS ARE OFTEN PERSECUTED AND PUBLIC OPINION CAN
OFTEN BE TYRANNICAL. STATES CONTROL IS DIFFICULT BECAUSE OF
THE WIDE DIFFUSION OF POWERS AND RESPONSIBILITIES.

1863 SQUIBB G.D.
THE HIGH COURT OF CHIVALRY.
LONDON: OXFORD U PR, 1959, 301 PP.
DISCUSSES HISTORY OF HIGH COURT OF CHIVALRY IN ENGLAND
(ONLY SURVIVING ENGLISH CIVIL LAW COURT). DISCUSSES ITS IN-
ACTIVITY SINCE EARLY 18TH CENTURY AND ITS REVIVAL IN
1954. ATTEMPTS TO CLEAR UP MISCONCEPTIONS CONCERNING COURT'S
HISTORY AND JURISDICTION.

1864 STAAR R.F.
"ELECTIONS IN COMMUNIST POLAND."
MIDWEST. J. POLIT. SCI., 2 (MAY 58), 57-75.
BRIEF HISTORY OF POSTWAR POLAND'S ELECTIONS AND REFEREN-
DUMS. EMPHASIZES EARLY COMMUNIST TECHNIQUES OF INTIMIDATION,
COERCION AND FRAUD TO WIN ELECTIONS. CONCLUDES WITH ANALYSIS
OF MORE RECENT DEMOCRATIC MACHINERY BEING USED NOW.

1865 STANGER R.J. ED.
ESSAYS ON INTERVENTION.
COLUMBUS: OHIO STATE U PR, 1964, 125 PP., LC#64-17107.
FOUR VARIED APPROACHES TO IDEA THAT INTERNATIONAL LAW IS
"AMBIGUOUS, OUTDATED, AND INADEQUATE." ALL AGREE THAT LINE
BETWEEN INTERNAL STRIFE AND INTERNATIONAL CONFLICT THREAT-
ENING WORLD PEACE MUST BE DISTINCTLY DEFINED. ALL SEE NEED

TO UTILIZE UN MORE OFTEN AND TO GIVE IT MORE POWERS, AS
SUGGESTED.

1866 STEEL R.
"WHAT CAN THE UN DO?"
COMMENTARY, 43 (MAY 67), 84-89.
WITHIN THE FRAMEWORK OF A REVIEW OF SEVERAL BOOKS, A DIS-
CUSSION OF THE FAILURES, SUCCESSES, AND PROBLEMS OF THE UN.
THE UN, THOUGH FORCED TO BECOME SUBSERVIENT TO THE GREAT
POWERS, IS USEFUL AS A SOUNDING BOARD FOR SMALL NATIONS, FOR
ITS TOO-LITTLE RECOGNIZED SOCIAL AND ECONOMIC ACHIEVEMENTS,
AND FOR OTHER REASONS. BUT THE ANTI-RHODESIA SANCTIONS SET
A DANGEROUS PRECEDENT IN INTERFERING IN A DOMESTIC MATTER.

1867 STEIN E. ED., NICHOLSON T.L. ED.
AMERICAN ENTERPRISE IN THE EUROPEAN COMMON MARKET: A
LEGAL PROFILE.
ANN ARBOR: U. MICH. PR., 1960 2 VOLS., 1242 PP.
PROFESSORS AND INTERNATIONAL CIVIL SERVANTS IN USA AND
EUROPE CONTRIBUTE TO TREATISE ON THE SUBJECT. DOCUMENTED
EXTENSIVELY BY GOVERNING TREATIES AND INTERNATIONAL LAWS.
FIRST VOLUME SURVEYS EUROPEAN INTEGRATION AND SECOND VOLUME
PRESENTS VARIOUS LEGAL FORMS AVAILABLE TO AN ENTERPRISE IN
BUSINESS OPERATIONS.

1868 STEIN E., HAY P.
"LEGAL REMEDIES OF ENTERPRISES IN THE EUROPEAN ECONOMIC
COMMUNITY."
AMER. J. COMP. LAW, 9 (SUMMER 60), 375-424.
SURVEYS GOALS OF EEC, CONSIDERING INTEGRATION OF NATIONAL
ECONOMIES OF FRANCE, GERMANY, ITALY AND BENELUX COUNTRIES
AS PRINCIPAL OBJECTIVE. ANALYZES LAW-MAKING POWERS VESTED BY
COMMON MARKET TREATY IN COMMUNITY'S MAIN INSTITUTIONS:
COUNCIL OF MINISTERS AND EUROPEAN COMMISSION. RAISES
QUESTIONS REGARDING JURISDICTION OF COMMUNITY JUSTICE COURT.

1869 STEIN E.
"MR HAMMARSKJOLD, THE CHARTER LAW AND THE FUTURE ROLE OF
THE UNITED NATIONS SECRETARY-GENERAL."
AMER. J. INT. LAW., 56 (JAN. 62), 9-32.
PROVIDES AN ACCOUNT OF HAMMARSKJOLD'S CONCEPT OF LEGAL-
CONSTITUTIONAL FRAMEWORK WITHIN WHICH HE PERFORMED HIS HIGH
OFFICE. IT WOULD BE UNWISE FOR MEMBER-NATIONS AND FOR UN
POLITICAL ORGANS TO PLACE THE BURDEN OF THEIR RESPONSIBILIT-
IES UPON SHOULDERS OF SECRETARY-GENERAL AND TO CHARGE HIM
WITH POLITICAL TASKS WITHOUT PROPER GUIDANCE.

1870 STEIN E.
"TOWARD SUPREMACY OF TREATY-CONSTITUTION BY JUDICIAL FIAT:
ON THE MARGIN OF THE COSTA CASE."
MICH. LAW REV., 63 (JAN. 65), 491-518.
STUDY OF THE RELATIONSHIP OF NATIONAL AND INTERNATIONAL
LEGAL ORDERS ACCOMPLISHED BY ANALYSIS OF JUDGEMENTS HANDED
DOWN ON THE SAME CASE BY AN ITALIAN COURT AND THE COURT OF
THE EUROPEAN COMMUNITY. INQUIRY INTO THE CONSIDERATION OF
TREATIES AS CONSTITUTIONAL IN NATURE AND AS TAKING PRECE-
DENCE OVER NATIONAL LAW.

1871 STERN A.C. ED.
AIR POLLUTION (2 VOLS.)
NY & LONDON: ACADEMIC PRESS, 1962, 1242 PP., LC#61-18293.
A DETAILED ANALYSIS OF THE CAUSE, EFFECT, TRANSPORT,
MEASUREMENT, AND CONTROL OF AIR POLLUTION BY 45 AUTHORS.
INCLUDES CHAPTERS ON THE NATURE OF POLLUTANTS; THEIR
DISPERSAL AND EFFECTS UPON PLANTS, ANIMALS, HUMANS, MATTER,
AND VISIBILITY; AND SAMPLING, ANALYSIS, MEASURING, AND
MONITORING. DISCUSSES PRINCIPAL SOURCES, CONTROL TECHNIQUES,
AND LEGAL REGULATIONS AND THEIR ADMINISTRATION.

1872 STERN R.L., GRESSMAN E.
SUPREME COURT PRACTICE.
WASHINGTON: BUREAU NATL AFFAIRS, 1962, 691 PP., LC#62-17543.
DEFINES JURISDICTION, PROCEDURE, ARGUING AND BRIEFING
TECHNIQUES, RULES, FORMS, AND STATUTES PRACTICED IN THE SU-
PREME COURT. RELATES COURT'S JURISDICTION OVER APPEALS, AND
PROCEDURE OF APPLYING TO THE COURT TO RELEASE INDIVIDUALS ON
BAIL.

1873 STEVENS R.E.
REFERENCE BOOKS IN THE SOCIAL SCIENCES AND HUMANITIES.
CHAMPAIGN, ILL: ILLINI UNION, 1966, 166 PP.
ANNOTATED BIBLIOGRAPHY OF APPROXIMATELY 450 REFERENCE
BOOKS IN COMMON MODERN LANGUAGES PUBLISHED FROM 1920-65.
ENTRIES ARRANGED BY TYPE OF BOOK UNDER SUBJECTS OF SOCIAL
SCIENCES, EDUCATION, SOCIOLOGY AND SOCIAL WORK, PSYCHOLOGY,
ANTHROPOLOGY, ECONOMICS, STATISTICS, POLITICAL SCIENCE, LAW,
HISTORY, PHILOSOPHY, RELIGION, LITERATURE, MUSIC, ART, AND
THEATER AND DANCE.

1874 STOICOIU V.
LEGAL SOURCES AND BIBLIOGRAPHY OF ROMANIA.
NEW YORK: FREDERICK PRAEGER, 1964, 237 PP., LC#64-15523.
COMPILES, ANNOTATES, AND THOROUGHLY INDEXES BY SUBJECT
AND AUTHOR MONOGRAPHS, SERIALS, BOOKS, ARTICLES, DOCUMENTS,
ETC. CONTAINS 1,589 ITEMS DEALING WITH THE PRINCIPLES AND
DEVELOPMENT OF ROMANIAN LAW SINCE ITS ACCEPTANCE OF THE

FRENCH LEGAL SYSTEM IN 1859 AND INCLUDING THE PERIOD
FOLLOWING SOVIET OCCUPATION. WRITINGS IN ROMANIAN AND MOST
OTHER EUROPEAN LANGUAGES.

1875 STOKES A.P.
CHURCH AND STATE IN THE UNITED STATES (3 VOLS.)
NEW YORK: HARPER & ROW, 1964, 2600 PP.
SHOWS GROWTH OF RELIGIOUS FREEDOM UNDER CONSTITUTIONAL
SEPARATION OF CHURCH AND STATE, AND RESULTING INFLUENCE OF
RELIGION IN MAJOR PHASES OF NATIONAL DEVELOPMENT. ALSO
DISCUSSES STATUS OF RELIGIOUS GROUPS UNDER STATE
CONSTITUTIONS AND JUDICIAL DECISIONS.

1876 STOKES W.S.
BIBLIOGRAPHY OF STANDARD AND CLASSICAL WORKS IN THE FIELDS
OF AMERICAN POLITICAL SCIENCE.
WASHINGTON: PAN AMERICAN UNION, 1948, 30 PP.
CONTAINS 90 LISTINGS IN ENGLISH OF BOOKS AND US GOVERN-
MENT DOCUMENTS ON AMERICAN POLITICS. ARRANGED BY SUBJECT,
SELECTIVE. PUBLICATION DATES OF LISTINGS, 1900-47.

1877 STONE J.
THE PROVINCE AND FUNCTION OF LAW.
CAMBRIDGE: HARVARD U. PR., 1950, 918 PP.
CITES CURRENT DIVISIONS IN FIELD OF JURISPRUDENCE. EX-
PLORES RELATIONS BETWEEN LAW AND LOGIC AND LAW AND JUSTICE.
DEPICTS THE NEO-HEGELIAN THEORY OF JUSTICE. FOCUSES ON COR-
RELATION OF LEGAL AND SOCIAL CHANGE IN MODERN TIMES. SURVEYS
LAW IN PRESENT-DAY DEMOCRATIC SOCIETIES, AND THE SOCIAL,
ECONOMIC, AND PSYCHOLOGICAL FACTORS IN LEGAL STABILITY AND
FLUX.

1878 STONE J.
LEGAL CONTROLS OF INTERNATIONAL CONFLICT: A TREATISE ON
THE DYNAMICS OF DISPUTES AND WAR LAW.
LONDON: STEVENS, 1954, 850 PP.
PRESENTS THE GENERALLY ESTABLISHED BODY OF INTERNATIONAL
LAW AND ITS INSTITUTIONS, AND COMMENTS ON PHILOSOPHIC WRIT-
INGS AND POLITICAL ACTIONS AND ATTITUDES RELATING TO IT.

1879 STONE J.
AGGRESSION AND WORLD ORDER: A CRITIQUE OF UNITED NATIONS
THEORIES OF AGGRESSION.
BERKELEY: U OF CALIF PR, 1958, 226 PP.
EXAMINATION OF THE FOUNDATIONS AND ROLE OF THE UN IN THE
MAINTENANCE OF INTERNATIONAL PEACE. DISCUSSES PROBLEMS OF
DEFINING AGGRESSION, EXPERIENCE OF LEAGUE OF NATIONS, THE UN
CHARTER AND ROLE OF THE GENERAL ASSEMBLY, AND APPLICATIONS
OF PRINCIPLES TO THE 1956 SUEZ CRISIS. ANALYZES CONCEPT OF
AGGRESSION WITH RELATION TO POWER POLITICS, INTERNATIONAL
MORALITY, AND INDIVIDUAL CRIMINALITY.

1880 STONE J.
"CONFLICT MANAGEMENT THROUGH CONTEMPORARY INTERNATIONAL
LAW AND ORGANIZATION."
CHICAGO: NORTHWESTERN INT. REL. CONF., 1959.
THE CONSTANT CHANGE TAKING PLACE AMONG THE NATIONS HAS
PRODUCED A WEAKENING OF THE SYSTEM OF INTERNATIONAL LAW. IN
ORDER FOR THE LAW TO BECOME MORE USEFUL IN THE FUTURE, IT
MUST BE USED NOW SO THAT IT WILL ADAPT ITSELF TO THE CHANGE.

1881 STONE J.
HUMAN LAW AND HUMAN JUSTICE.
STANFORD: STANFORD U PRESS, 1965, 415 PP.
STUDIES GROWTH AND IMPORTANCE OF IDEALS OF HUMAN JUSTICE
IN RELATION TO LEGAL, SOCIAL, AND ECONOMIC CONTEXTS.
DEALS WITH THEORIES OF JUSTICE BASED ON KANTIAN AND
UTILITARIAN PRINCIPLES - THE ADJUSTMENT OF CONFLICTING
INTERESTS.

1882 STOREY R.G.
OUR UNALIENABLE RIGHTS.
SPRINGFIELD: THOMAS, 1965, 152 PP., LC#65-14174.
STUDY OF HISTORICAL AND CONSTITUTIONAL SOURCES OF RIGHTS
IN US. EXAMINES DEVELOPMENT FROM ENGLISH LAW AND INFLUENCE
OF INDEPENDENCE ON LEGAL CHANGES IN SOCIETY.

1883 STOUT H.M.
BRITISH GOVERNMENT.
NEW YORK: OXFORD U PR, 1953, 433 PP., LC#52-14156.
DESCRIPTION OF THE PRESENT-DAY STRUCTURE AND PRACTICE
OF BRITISH GOVERNMENT, INTENDED FOR AMERICAN STUDENTS. EXAM-
INES THE GOVERNMENT IN LIGHT OF POSTWAR DEVELOPMENTS - NEW
ELECTIONS, EXPANSION OF GOVERNMENTAL FUNCTIONS UNDER THE
WELFARE STATE CONCEPT, NEW COMMONWEALTH RELATIONS, ETC. DIS-
CUSSES THE CONSTITUTION AND CONSTITUTIONAL RIGHTS, STRUCTURE
OF THE PRINCIPAL INSTITUTIONS, AND POLICY FORMATION.

1884 STOWELL E.C.
INTERVENTION IN INTERNATIONAL LAW.
WASHINGTON: BYRNE, 1921, 558 PP.
SETS FORTH THE OCCASIONS WHEN A STATE, THREATENED BY A-
NOTHER NATION, IS JUSTIFIED IN USING FORCE TO INFLUENCE THE
OTHER'S CONDUCT. ANALYZES INTERNATIONAL POLICE REGULATIONS,
SURVEYS POLITICAL REASONS FOR VIOLATION OF SOVEREIGNTY,
POINTS OUT PROBLEM OF BALANCE OF POWER.

1885 STOWELL E.C.
INTERNATIONAL LAW.
NEW YORK: HOLT, 1931, 1558 PP.
ANALYZES VARIOUS GROUNDS UPON WHICH INTERNATIONAL INTER-
VENTION MAY JUSTLY BE UNDERTAKEN TO DEFEND INTERNATIONAL LAW
RIGHTS, EITHER BY WAY OF INTERPOSITION OR BY INTERNATIONAL
POLICE ACTIONS.

1886 STREET H.
FREEDOM: THE INDIVIDUAL AND THE LAW.
BALTIMORE: PENGUIN BOOKS, 1963, 316 PP.
SURVEYS PRESENT NATURE AND CONTENT OF CIVIL LIBERTIES IN
UK. EXAMINES FREEDOM OF EXPRESSION IN RADIO, TV, CINEMA,
PRESS, AND ADVERTISING. DISCUSSES FREEDOM OF RELIGION AND
MOVEMENT, PLUS RIGHT TO PROTECTION AGAINST DISCRIMINA-
TION AND "PRIVATE POWER."

1887 STRONG C.F.
MODERN POLITICAL CONSTITUTIONS.
LONDON: SIDGWICK + JACKSON, 1958, 383 PP.
INTRODUCTORY TEXT ON CONSTITUTIONAL POLITICS. CONSIDERS
MEANING OF POLITICAL CONSTITUTIONALISM, AND THE ORIGINS AND
GROWTH OF THE CONSTITUTIONAL STATE. ANALYZES IN DETAIL
COMPARATIVE CONSTITUTIONAL POLITICS. CONSIDERS DIRECT
DEMOCRATIC CHECKS, CONSTITUTIONAL CHECKS AMONG NON-EUROPEAN
PEOPLES, ECONOMIC ORGANIZATION OF THE STATE, AND THE CHARTER
OF THE UN. DISCUSSES OUTLOOK FOR CONSTITUTIONALISM.

1888 STRONG C.F.
HISTORY OF MODERN POLITICAL CONSTITUTIONS.
NEW YORK: G P PUTNAM'S SONS, 1964, 389 PP., LC#63-14083.
DEFINES POLITICAL CONSTITUTIONALISM; STUDIES ITS GROWTH
AND ORIGINS IN THE STATE; CLASSIFIES FORMS OF STATES AND
CONSTITUTION; AND DISCUSSES CONSTITUTIONAL DIVISIONS OF
GOVERNMENT. EXAMINES RISE OF NATIONALISM THROUGHOUT WORLD,
WORLDWIDE ECONOMIC ORGANIZATION, AND THE UN CHARTER.

1889 STUART G.H.
"AMERICAN DIPLOMATIC AND CONSULAR PRACTICE (2ND ED.)"
NEW YORK: APPLETON, 1952.
REVISED EDITION OF STUART'S TEXT ON THE ORGANIZATION AND
FUNCTIONING OF US CONSULAR AND DIPLOMATIC MACHINERY. EDITION
BASED LARGELY UPON MATERIAL OBTAINED IN WASHINGTON AND
ABROAD SINCE WWII. UNANNOTATED BIBLIOGRAPHY OF BOOKS IN
ENGLISH AND FRENCH PUBLISHED IN THE 19TH-20TH CENTURIES.
EMPHASIS ON POST-WWI MATERIALS.

1890 STUMPF S.E.
MORALITY AND THE LAW.
NASHVILLE: VANDERBILT U PR, 1966, 247 PP., LC#66-15286.
DETAILED EXAMINATION OF THE RELATION BETWEEN LAW AND
MORALITY. EXPLORES THE RELATION IN FIVE DIFFERENT WAYS: LAW
AS WHAT COURTS DO IN FACT, LAW AS WILL OF THE ECO-
NOMICALLY DOMINANT CLASS, LAW AS COMMAND OF THE
SOVEREIGN, A NEW KIND OF INTERNATIONAL LAW, AND
NATURAL LAW. AUTHOR INDICATES DIFFERENCES IN LAW AND MORAL-
ITY AND POINTS OUT VAST SIMILARITIES.

1891 STURZO L.
THE INTERNATIONAL COMMUNITY AND THE RIGHT OF WAR (TRANS. BY
BARBARA BARCLAY CARTER)
NEW YORK: RICHARD R SMITH, 1929, 293 PP.
STUDY OF THE SOCIOLOGICAL AND HISTORICAL ASPECTS OF WAR
AND THE FORMATION OF INTERNATIONAL STRUCTURES TOWARD THE
CONTROL AND/OR JUSTIFICATION OF WAR. ARGUES THAT THE THREE
THEORIES ADVANCED TO EXPLAIN THE RIGHT OF WAR ARE INCOMPLETE
AND CAN BE SUPPLANTED BY A FOURTH PROPOUNDING THAT WAR, LIKE
SLAVERY AND DUELS, IS NOT A NECESSARY HUMAN CONDITION AND
CAN BE ELIMINATED THROUGH CIVILIZED INTERNATIONAL LAW.

1892 SUAREZ F.
A TREATISE ON LAWS AND GOD THE LAWGIVER (1612) IN SELECTIONS
FROM THREE WORKS, VOL. II.
LONDON: OXFORD U PR, 1944, 625 PP.
ANALYZES LEGAL SYSTEMS OF EUROPE, 1500-1620, FROM VIEW-
POINT OF SCHOLASTICISM. CLAIMS LAW TO BE JUST CONCERN OF
THEOLOGY BECAUSE BOTH CONCERN RULES OF HUMAN ACTION. DECIDES
THAT LAW IS A DIVISION OF THEOLOGY. CONSIDERS LAW TO BE A
POSITIVE RATHER THAN NEGATIVE SYSTEM, ENFORCING VIRTUE AS
WELL AS PROSCRIBING SIN. CONCLUDES THAT ALL LAW STEMS FROM
GOD AND NATURAL LAW.

1893 SUMMERS R.E.
FEDERAL INFORMATION CONTROLS IN PEACETIME.
NEW YORK: H W WILSON, 1949, 301 PP.
ANALYSIS OF US GOVERNMENTAL CONTROLS ON SPREADING OF IN-
FORMATION TO PUBLIC. DEALS WITH BASIC ISSUES AND OPINIONS ON
GOVERNMENT'S ROLE AND SECRECY RELATING TO ATOMIC ENERGY,
COMMUNIST ACTIVITIES, LOYALTY, AND LEGAL ASPECTS OF CONTROL
POLICIES.

1894 SURRENCY E.C., FELD B., CREA J.
A GUIDE TO LEGAL RESEARCH.
NEW YORK: OCEANA PUBLISHING, 1959, 124 PP.
DISCUSSES METHODS OF LEGAL RESEARCH UNDER SEPARATE CHAP-
TERS ACCORDING TO TYPE OF LAW BOOKS: RESEARCH IN STATE

STATUTORY LAW, STATE DECISIONAL LAW, FEDERAL LAW, FEDERAL
ADMINISTRATIVE LAW. MENTIONS MAJOR SOURCES WHICH MIGHT BE
CONSULTED AND INCLUDES SAMPLE PAGES FROM MANY VOLUMES DIS-
CUSSED.

1895 SUTHERLAND A.E.
THE LAW AND ONE MAN AMONG MANY.
MADISON: U OF WISCONSIN PR, 1956, 101 PP., LC#56-9306.
A LAWYER'S CONSIDERATION OF THE ATTITUDE OF 20TH-CENTURY
AMERICAN LAW TOWARD SOME ASPECTS OF RELATION OF INDIVIDUAL
TO SOCIETY. DISCUSSES CONCEPTS OF "INDIVIDUALISM" THAT
HAVE BEEN FASHIONABLE OVER THE PAST FOUR CENTURIES. ANALYZES
SEVERAL RECENT CASES WHEREIN INDIVIDUAL FREEDOM HAS BEEN
UPHELD BY US COURTS. EMPHASIZES ROLE OF JUDGE IN ARBITRATING
WITHIN THE IMPRECISENESS OF THE LAW.

1896 SUTTON F.X.
"REPRESENTATION AND THE NATURE OF POLITICAL SYSTEMS."
COMP. STUD. SOC. HIST., 2 (OCT. 59), 1-10.
TRACES DEVELOPMENT OF POLITICAL REPRESENTATION FROM
PRIMITIVE SOCIETY TO MODERN INDUSTRIAL SOCIETY. ALSO
DIFFERENTIATES BETWEEN THAT WHICH IS REPRESENTATIVE ACTION
AND THAT WHICH IS AUTONOMOUS ACTIVITY OF INDIVIDUALS IN
COLLECTIVITY.

1897 SVARLIEN O.
AN INTRODUCTION TO THE LAW OF NATIONS.
NEW YORK: MCGRAW HILL, 1955, 478 PP., LC#56-6173.
INTRODUCTORY TEXT IN INTERNATIONAL LAW. TREATS EACH TOPIC
IN LIGHT OF ITS HISTORY, OF ITS LAW, AND IN TERMS OF TRENDS
AND DEVELOPMENT. INCLUDES STUDY OF THE INTERNATIONAL
COMMUNITY, THE FUNCTION OF STATES IN INTERNATIONAL LAW,
TERRITORIAL PROBLEMS, DIPLOMATIC RELATIONS, HOSTILE
RELATIONS BETWEEN NATIONS, AND THE INDIVIDUAL IN
INTERNATIONAL LAW. BIBLIOGRAPHY OF ABOUT 200 ITEMS.

1898 SWAYZE H.
POLITICAL CONTROL OF LITERATURE IN THE USSR, 1946-1959.
CAMBRIDGE: HARVARD U PR, 1962, 301 PP., LC#62-9432.
ANALYZES METHODS OF CONTROLLING IMAGINATIVE WRITING
IN USSR. OUTLINES BASIC ASSUMPTIONS AND AIMS OF SOVIET
LITERARY POLICIES, DISCUSSES PROBLEM WITH WHICH THEY HAVE
HAD TO COPE, AND DESCRIBES MAIN FEATURES OF LITERARY CONTROL
STRUCTURE.

1899 SWEET E.C.
CIVIL LIBERTIES IN AMERICA.
PRINCETON: VAN NOSTRAND, 1966, 352 PP.
STUDY OF MAJOR ISSUES OF CIVIL LIBERTIES AND RELEVANT
CASES. EXAMINES LIBERTIES REGARDING DUE PROCESS, RELIGION,
SPEECH, INVESTIGATION, ASSOCIATION, SEARCH AND SEIZURE,
RIGHT TO COUNSEL, VOTING, AND CITIZENSHIP.

1900 SWEET AND MAXWELL
A LEGAL BIBLIOGRAPHY OF THE BRITISH COMMONWEALTH OF NATIONS
(2ND ED. 7 VOLS.)
LONDON: SWEET AND MAXWELL, LTD, 1955.
SEVEN-VOLUME BIBLIOGRAPHY OF LAW WITH CUMULATIVE
SUPPLEMENTS. VOLUME I, ENGLISH LAW TO 1800, INCLUDES WORKS
PRINTED FROM 1480-1954. FURTHER VOLUMES COVER LEGAL LITERA-
TURE AND DEVELOPMENTS THROUGH 1954, CANADIAN, IRISH, NORTH
AMERICAN COLONIES, SCOTTISH, AND THE PACIFIC AREAS OF COM-
MONWEALTH, INCLUDING AUSTRALIAN LEGAL SYSTEMS. ARRANGEMENT
IS TOPICAL. CONCLUDES WITH SUBJECTS, PLACES, AUTHORS INDEX.

1901 SWISHER C.B.
THE SUPREME COURT IN MODERN ROLE.
NEW YORK: NEW YORK U PR, 1965, 221 PP., LC#65-19522.
HISTORICAL AND ANALYTICAL DISCUSSION OF SUPREME COURT IN
MODERN AMERICAN SOCIETY, STRESSING ITS VITAL IMPORTANCE IN
RELATION TO MAJOR IDEOLOGICAL ISSUES AND POLITICAL EVENTS.
DISCUSSES OBSCURING OF COURT'S ROLE AND FUNCTION IN REGARD
TO CONTROVERSIAL ISSUES WITH WHICH IT DEALS BY MASS MEDIA
AND ACTIVITY OF VARIOUS INTEREST GROUPS.

1902 SYATAUW J.J.G.
SOME NEWLY ESTABLISHED ASIAN STATES AND THE DEVELOPMENT OF
INTERNATIONAL LAW.
THE HAGUE: MARTINUS NIJHOFF, 1961, 349 PP.
STUDIES SIGNIFICANCE OF WORLD DEVELOPMENTS FOR INTER-
NATIONAL LAW, FROM VIEWPOINT OF SOME NEWLY ESTABLISHED
ASIAN STATES - INDIA, INDONESIA, BURMA, AND CEYLON. EXAMINES
CHANGES IN BIPOLARIZATION, PROGRESS, INTERDEPENDENCE, AND
EXPANSIONISM. DISCUSSES CONTRIBUTIONS OF NEW ASIAN STATES
TO DEFINITIONS OF COLONIALISM, SELF-DETERMINATION, PEACEFUL
COEXISTENCE, AND NEUTRALITY IN INTERNATIONAL LAW.

1903 SYKES G.M.
CRIME AND SOCIETY.
NEW YORK: RANDOM HOUSE, INC, 1956, 125 PP., LC#56-07692.
STUDIES RELATION BETWEEN CRIME AND CULTURE, AND EFFECTS
OF EACH ON BREAKING OF RULES. CLASSIFIES CRIME, STUDIES
BEHAVIOR OF SOCIETY TOWARDS CRIMINALS, AND RELATES AGE,
SEX, RACE, AND SOCIO-ECONOMIC STATUS TO CRIME.

1904 SZLADITS C.

BIBLIOGRAPHY ON FOREIGN AND COMPARATIVE LAW: BOOKS AND
ARTICLES IN ENGLISH (SUPPLEMENT 1962)
NEW YORK: OCEANA PUBLISHING, 1964, 134 PP., LC#55-11076.
ANNOTATES AND LISTS 3,431 ITEMS ARRANGED TOPICALLY;
BOOKS, ARTICLES, PAMPHLETS, SERIALS, DOCUMENTS, ETC.,
PERTINENT TO COMPARATIVE LAW, PUBLIC LAW, INTERNATIONAL LAW,
COMMERCIAL LAW, CRIMINAL LAW, AND PRIVATE LAW. INCLUDES
BIBLIOGRAPHIES, REFERENCES, LISTS OF INSTITUTIONS OF
COMPARATIVE LAW, ETC.

1905 SZLADITS C.
A BIBLIOGRAPHY ON FOREIGN AND COMPARATIVE LAW (SUPPLEMENT
1964)
NEW YORK: OCEANA PUBLISHING, 1966, 119 PP., LC#55-11076.
ANNOTATED BIBLIOGRAPHY ON BOOKS AND ARTICLES IN ENGLISH
FROM 1960-66. SOURCES ON COMPARATIVE LAW, GENERAL WORKS,
PRIVATE LAW, COMMERCIAL LAW, LABOR LAW, LAW OF PROCEDURE,
CRIMINAL LAW, CRIMINAL PROCEDURE, PUBLIC LAW, AND PRIVATE
INTERNATIONAL LAW. PUBLISHED FOR PARKER SCHOOL OF FOREIGN
AND COMPARATIVE LAW, COLUMBIA UNIVERSITY.

1906 TALLON D.
"L'ETUDE DU DROIT COMPARE COMME MOYEN DE RECHERCHER LES
MATIERES SUSCEPTIBLES D'UNIFICATION INTERNATIONALE."
TRAV. RECH. INST. DR. COMP. UNIV. PARIS, 22 (1963), 149-53.
CONSIDERS STUDY OF COMPARATIVE LAW MOST ADAPTIVE DISCI-
PLINE TO ACHIEVE COORDINATION OF JURIDIC PATTERNS. STUDY
BASED ON JURISPRUDENCE RESEARCH.

1907 TANENHAUS J.
"THE SUPREME COURT AND PRESIDENTIAL POWER."
ANN. ACAD. POL. SOC. SCI., 307 (SEPT. 56).
BRIEF ANALYSIS OF CASES RESTRICTING PRESIDENTIAL
AUTHORITY. COURT PERMITS PRESIDENT MORE POWER IN EMERGENCIES
AND HAS MADE CLEAR THAT PRIME RESPONSIBILITY FOR CONTROLLING
PRESIDENT RESTS WITH CONGRESS.

1908 TAPER B.
GOMILLION VERSUS LIGHTFOOT: THE TUSKEGEE GERRYMANDER CASE.
NEW YORK: MCGRAW HILL, 1962, 118 PP., LC#61-18135.
INVESTIGATION OF GERRYMANDERING IN TUSKEGEE, ALABAMA IN
ATTEMPT TO LIMIT NEGRO REPRESENTATION IN GOVERNMENT. CASE OF
CHARLES G. GOMILLION, NEGRO PROFESSOR, VERSUS PHIL M.
LIGHTFOOT, MAYOR OF TUSKEGEE DISCUSSED IN GREAT DETAIL.

1909 TAUBENFELD H.J.
"A TREATY FOR ANTARCTICA."
INT. COUNCIL., 531 (JAN. 61), 243-322.
APPRAISES SPECIAL FACTORS WHICH MADE POSSIBLE THE 1957
TWELVE-NATION AGREEMENT ON SCIENTIFIC RESEARCH. CONSIDERS
ITS POTENTIAL RELEVANCE TO POLITICAL ISSUES.

1910 TAUBENFELD H.J.
"A REGIME FOR OUTER SPACE."
NORTHWEST. U. LAW REV., 56 (MAR.-APR. 61), 129-67.
EXPLORES LEGAL CONCEPTS WHICH COULD GOVERN OUTER SPACE
TO PREVENT IT FROM BECOMING A SOURCE OF OR THEATER FOR CON-
FLICT. DISCUSSES INADEQUACY OF SEA AIR ANALOGIES, SCIENTIFIC
DELINEATION, AND GEOCENTRIC POLITICS. PROPOSES A NEW AP-
PROACH, RECOGNIZING THAT PROBLEM CANNOT BE COMPLETELY SOLVED
AS IT IS A PROJECTION OF COLD WAR.

1911 TAUBENFELD H.J. ED.
SPACE AND SOCIETY.
NEW YORK: OCEANA PUBLISHING, 1964, 172 PP., LC#64-21185.
PAPERS FROM SEMINAR ON PROBLEMS OF OUTER SPACE SPONSORED
BY CARNEGIE ENDOWMENT FOR INTERNATIONAL PEACE, CONCERNING
IMPACT OF MAN IN SPACE ON MAN'S SOCIETY ON EARTH. COVERS
TOPICS OF LAW, POLITICS, SPACE SCIENCE, VALUES AND GOALS
OF SPACE EXPLORATION, SPACE COMMUNICATION, CLAIMS TO USE
OF SPACE, MILITARY USE, AND FUTURE PROSPECTS OF SPACE
EXPLORATION.

1912 TAYLOR H.
WHY THE PENDING TREATY WITH COLOMBIA SHOULD BE RATIFIED
(PAMPHLET)
NEW YORK: LAS NOBLE DADES, 1914, 18 PP.
HISTORICAL ANALYSIS, THAT PEOPLE OF US MIGHT KNOW
FACTS OF CONTROVERSY WITH COLOMBIA OVER CANAL ZONE.
DISCUSSES TREATY OF PEACE, AMITY, NAVIGATION AND COM-
MERCE, IN 1840; SPOONER ACT AND HAY-HERRAN CONVENTION OF
1903; OPERA BOUFFE REVOLUTION OF 1903; AND COLOMBIA'S RIGHT
TO ARBITRATION.

1913 TELLADO A.
A STATEMENT OF THE LAWS OF THE DOMINICAN REPUBLIC IN MATTERS
AFFECTING BUSINESS (3RD ED.)
WASHINGTON: PAN AMERICAN UNION, 1964.
SURVEY OF BASIC LEGISLATION EMPHASIZING NATIONALITY AND
IMMIGRATION, CONTRACTS, AND ADMINISTRATION OF JUSTICE. ALSO
INCLUDES PATENTS, TRADEMARKS, AND COPYRIGHT.

1914 TENBROCK J.
EQUAL UNDER LAW.
NEW YORK: COLLIERS, 1964, 352 PP., LC#64-24351.
DOCUMENTARY ACCOUNT OF ANTISLAVERY MOVEMENT IN 19TH

CENTURY AMERICA RESULTING IN ENACTMENT OF 14TH AMENDMENT ABOLISHING SLAVERY. INCLUDES SHORT (APPROXIMATELY 60) BIBLIOGRAPHY OF SOURCES CITED: BOOKS, DIARIES, ARTICLES BOTH SECONDARY AND PRIMARY.

1915 THANT U.
TOWARD WORLD PEACE.
NEW YORK: THOMAS YOSELOFF, 1964, 404 PP., LC#64-21343.
COLLECTION OF MAJOR PUBLIC ADDRESSES OF U THANT SINCE 1961. SPEECHES ON PURPOSE OF UN, MIDDLE EAST CRISIS, EDUCATION, SMALL NATIONS AND UN, SCIENCE, ETC.

1916 THOM J.M.
GUIDE TO RESEARCH MATERIAL IN POLITICAL SCIENCE (PAMPHLET)
WASHINGTON: WASHINGTON U LIBS, 1952, 34 PP.
AN ANNOTATED BIBLIOGRAPHY IN POLITICAL SCIENCE MATERIAL. 233 ENTRIES. MATERIAL IN ENGLISH AND SOME FRENCH, GERMAN, ITALIAN AND RUSSIAN.

1917 THOMAS A.V., THOMAS A.J. JR.
NONINTERVENTION: THE LAW AND ITS IMPORT IN THE AMERICAS.
DALLAS: SOUTHERN METHODIST U PR, 1965, 476 PP., LC#56-9845.
STUDIES INTERNATIONAL NONINTERVENTION LAW IN LIGHT OF GENERAL INTERNATIONAL LAW. MAINTAINS THAT LAWS REGARDING NONINTERVENTION MUST BE ADHERED TO BY ACCEPTANCE OF VALUE OF LAW, NOT POWER. INCLUDES EVOLUTION OF DOCTRINE OF NONINTERVENTION AND WAYS IN WHICH LAW DEFINES LEGALITY OR ILLEGALITY OF INTERVENTION.

1918 THOMPSON D., MARSH N.S.
"THE UNITED KINGDOM AND THE TREATY OF ROME."
INT. COMP. LAW QUART., 11 (JAN. 62), 73-88.
ASSESSES LEGAL ARGUMENTS REGARDING THE ENTRY OF UNITED KINGDOM INTO THE COMMON MARKET UNDER THE TREATY OF ROME PROVISIONS. OUTLINES ADMINISTRATIVE AND JUDICIAL ASPECTS OF THE SYSTEM AND INDICATES WHAT ACTION PARLIAMENT MIGHT TAKE (IN VIEW OF ENGLISH COMMON LAW) WITH REGARD TO LABOR UNIONS. FORESEES A HARMONIZATION OF LAWS.

1919 THOMPSON J.M.
RUSSIA, BOLSHEVISM, AND THE VERSAILLES PEACE.
PRINCETON: PRINCETON U PRESS, 1966, 429 PP., LC#66-17712.
STUDIES ROLE OF RUSSIA AT PARIS PEACE CONFERENCE OF 1919. SHOWS THAT, THOUGH RUSSIA WAS NOT REPRESENTED AT CONFERENCE, THE PEACEMAKERS ATTACHED GREAT IMPORTANCE TO RUSSIAN QUESTION. EXAMINES HOW, AND FROM WHAT MOTIVES, PEACEMAKERS DEALT WITH THREAT OF BOLSHEVISM AND STRUGGLE FOR POWER IN RUSSIA. FOCUSES ON RELATIONSHIPS BETWEEN PEACE CONFERENCE AND SOVIET AND WHITE RUSSIAN GOVERNMENTS.

1920 THOMPSON J.W., PADOVER S.K.
SECRET DIPLOMACY: A RECORD OF ESPIONAGE AND DOUBLE-DEALING: 1500-1815.
LONDON: JARROLDS PUBLISHERS, LTD, 1937, 286 PP.
ATTEMPTS TO SHOW THAT UNDERCOVER OPERATIONS HAVE BEEN UNIVERSALLY EMPLOYED, AND THAT SPYING AND BRIBERY HAVE PLAYED A LARGER ROLE IN DIPLOMATIC HISTORY THAN HERETOFORE BELIEVED. BOOK BASED ON OFFICIAL DOCUMENTS, MEMOIRS, MEMORANDA OF MINISTERS, POLICE REPORTS, LETTERS, AND INFORMATION OF SPIES. EXTENSIVE BIBLIOGRAPHY ARRANGED ACCORDING TO CHAPTER SUBJECTS.

1921 THOMPSON K.W.
"MORAL PURPOSE IN FOREIGN POLICY: REALITIES AND ILLUSIONS."
SOC. RES., 27 (AUTUMN 60), 261-276.
RAISES QUESTION OF POLITICS AND ETHICS. ANALYZES GOALS AND PURPOSES OF BROADER INTERNATIONAL COMMUNITY IN THE FACE OF HARSH REALITIES OF INTERNATIONAL POLITICS. CONSIDERS LEGAL AND MORAL IMPLICATIONS REGARDING DELICATE SITUATIONS LIKE U2. DISUSSES FUNDAMENTAL PROBLEMS OF POLICY COORDINATION AND DECISION-MAKING IN FOREIGN AFFAIRS. QUESTIONS ROLE OF PRIVATE CITIZEN IN VAST AND SPRAWLING POLITICAL SYSTEM.

1922 THOMPSON K.W.
AMERICAN DIPLOMACY AND EMERGENT PATTERNS.
NEW YORK: N.Y.U. PR., 1962, 267 PP.
A CRITICAL ESSAY ASSERTING THAT THOSE WHO FORMULATE POLICY TODAY LABOR WITHIN AN ESTABLISHED FRAMEWORK OF INSTITUTIONS AND PRACTICES AND DRAW ON A FIXED BODY OF IDEAS AND DOCTRINE.

1923 THOREAU H.D.
CIVIL DISOBEDIENCE (1849)
ORIGINAL PUBLISHER NOT AVAILABLE, 1849, 150 PP.
SUPPORTS RIGHT OF INDIVIDUALS TO DISOBEY GOVERNMENTS WHEN THEY BEHAVE UNJUSTLY. DECLARES THIS TO BE A DUTY OF JUST MEN. ESPECIALLY CONCERNED WITH SLAVERY. DISCUSSES MEANS OF COMBATING IT THROUGH PRESSURING GOVERNMENT. SUGGESTS WITHOLDING OF TAXES AS MEANS OF COMBATING A STATE WHEN IT IS UNJUST. ADVOCATES GOING TO PRISON RATHER THAN OBEYING UNJUST LAWS.

1924 TIEDT S.W.
THE ROLE OF THE FEDERAL GOVERNMENT IN EDUCATION.
NEW YORK: OXFORD U PR, 1966, 243 PP., LC#66-14479.
ANALYZES HISTORICAL BACKGROUND OF THE ROLE OF THE FEDERAL GOVERNMENT IN EDUCATION. PRESENTS REPRESENTATIVE ARGUMENTS FOR AND AGAINST THE GOVERNMENT'S GREATER INVOLVEMENT IN EDUCATIONAL CONCERNS. DISCUSSES QUESTIONS CONCERNING AID TO PRIVATE SCHOOLS. EXAMINES PRESENT AND FUTURE ASPECTS OF THE PROBLEM.

1925 TIMASHEFF N.S.
"WHAT IS SOCIOLOGY OF LAW?" (BMR)"
AMER. J. OF SOCIOLOGY, 43 (SEPT. 37), 225-235.
INDICATES SOCIOLOGY OF LAW STUDIES HUMAN SOCIAL BEHAVIOR INSOFAR AS IT IS DETERMINED BY RECOGNIZED ETHICO-LEGAL NORMS, AND INSOFAR AS IT INFLUENCES THEM. CONVERSELY, JURISPRUDENCE STUDIES NORMS AS SUCH. STATES THAT STUDIES OF PSYCHOLOGISTS, ANTHROPOLOGISTS, PHILOSOPHERS OF LAW, AND JURISTS PERMIT FORMULATION OF DEFINITION OF LAW AS A COMPLEX INSTRUMENT OF SOCIAL COORDINATION OF ETHICS AND POWER.

1926 TIMASHEFF N.S.
AN INTRODUCTION TO THE SOCIOLOGY OF LAW.
CAMBRIDGE: HARVARD U PR, 1939.
ANALYSIS OF LAW AS A SOCIAL PHENOMENON AND ROLE OF SOCIOLOGY IN FORMULATION OF LEGAL PRACTICES. EXAMINES HISTORICAL DEVELOPMENT OF SOCIOLOGY OF LAW AND RELATION OF LAW TO ETHICAL NORMS OF SOCIETY. DISCUSSION OF INTEGRATION OF POWER OR MIGHT AND LAW. EACH CHAPTER ACCOMPANIED BY BIBLIOGRAPHICAL NOTE IN ADDITION TO EXTENSIVE GENERAL BIBLIOGRAPHY AT CONCLUSION IN RELEVANT EUROPEAN LANGUAGES.

1927 TINGSTERN H.
PEACE AND SECURITY AFTER WW II.
UPSALA: SWED. INST. INT. AFF., 1945, 191 PP.
DENOTES AIMS AND STRUCTURE OF LEAGUE OF NATIONS. DISCUSSES PROCEDURES OF CONCILIATION AND MEDIATION. EXAMINES PERMANENT COURT OF INTERNATIONAL JUSTICE AND SPECIALIZED ECONOMIC AND SOCIAL AGENCIES.

1928 TIPTON J.B.
"PARTICIPATION OF THE UNITED STATES IN THE INTERNATIONAL LABOR ORGANIZATION."
URBANA: INST. LABOR INDUS. REL./U. ILL., 1959, 150 PP.
ENVISAGES CONSTRUCTIVE ROLE FOR USA IN ILO. RAPID INDUSTRIAL DEVELOPMENT IN EMERGING NATIONS PRESENTS NEW PROBLEMS TO WHICH THE US CAN CONTRIBUTE TO THE SOLUTION FROM HER OWN EXPERIENCE. TREATS SUBJECT OF AUTOMATION AND ITS IMPACT ON LABOR RELATIONS.

1929 TODD A.
JUSTICE ON TRIAL: THE CASE OF LOUIS D. BRANDEIS.
NEW YORK: MCGRAW HILL, 1964, 275 PP., LC#64-16300.
DISCUSSES CONTROVERSY OVER APPOINTMENT OF JUSTICE BRANDEIS TO US SUPREME COURT. EXAMINES IN DETAIL POLITICAL STRUGGLE IN SENATE.

1930 TOMASEK R.D.
"THE CHILEAN-BOLIVIAN LAUCA RIVER DISPUTE AND THE OAS."
J. INTER-AMER. STUDIES, 9 (JULY 67), 351-366.
DISCUSSES STRAINED RELATIONS BETWEEN CHILE AND BOLIVIA. EXAMINES DEVELOPMENT OF DISPUTE FROM 1953, BREAKING OF DIPLOMATIC RELATIONS IN 1962, AND ATTEMPTS AT SOLUTION. ATTEMPTS TO ESTABLISH NATURE OF DISPUTE, AND WHETHER BOLIVIA'S TRUE CONCERN IS TO OPEN DEMANDS ON CHILE FOR AN OUTLET TO THE SEA. REVIEWS ROLE OF OAS.

1931 TOMPKINS D.C.
SUPREME COURT OF THE UNITED STATES: A BIBLIOGRAPHY.
BERKELEY: U CALIF, BUR PUB ADMIN, 1959, 215 PP.
ANNOTATED AND THOROUGHLY INDEXED BIBLIOGRAPHY ON THE SUPREME COURT. INCLUDES A RUNNING COMMENTARY WHICH CONNECTS, CLARIFIES, AND SUMMARIZES SOURCES. ITEMS BROADLY CATEGORIZED INTO HEADINGS SUCH AS ORGANIZATION, WORK, RELATION WITH OTHER GOVERNMENTAL BRANCHES, AND CONTROVERSIES.

1932 TOMPKINS D.C.
CONFLICT OF INTEREST IN THE FEDERAL GOVERNMENT: A BIBLIOGRAPHY.
BERKELEY: U CALIF, BUR PUB ADMIN, 1961, 66 PP.
BIBLIOGRAPHY OF CONFLICT OF INTEREST LAWS STRESSES THE PERIOD SINCE 1950 AND INCLUDES EXPLANATORY AND SUPPLEMENTARY TEXT WITH REFERENCES DRAWN FROM THE UNIVERSITY OF CALIFORNIA LIBRARIES. DEALS WITH LAWS, PERSONS AFFECTED AND EXEMPT, REGULATIONS OF EXECUTIVE EMPLOYEES' CONDUCT, ROLE OF CONGRESS, THE SHERMAN ADAMS CASE, AND THE PRESIDENT'S 1961 PROGRAM.

1933 TOMPKINS D.C.
PRESIDENTIAL SUCCESSION.
BERKELEY: U CAL, INST GOVT STUD, 1964, 29 PP., LC#64-63620.
ANNOTATED GUIDE TO RECENT PUBLICATIONS DEALING WITH PRESIDENTIAL SUCCESSION. INCLUDES RUNNING COMMENTARY EXPLAINING AND DISCUSSING ITEMS LISTED. INCLUDES CONGRESSIONAL REPORTS, REFERENCES TO "CONGRESSIONAL RECORD." BOOKS, ARTICLES, ETC. PREPARED WITH A VIEW THAT CURRENT PROCEDURE, AS EXPRESSED BY PRESIDENT TRUMAN'S POLICY, IS UNSOUND AND CALLS FOR REAPPRAISAL.

1934 TONG T.

UNITED STATES DIPLOMACY IN CHINA, 1844-1860.
SEATTLE: U OF WASHINGTON PR, 1964, 332 PP., LC#64-11051.
ANALYSIS OF DIPLOMATIC RELATIONS BETWEEN CHINA AND US IN
SPECIFIC PERIOD BEGINNING WITH TREATY OF WANGHIA. DEALS WITH
IMPERIALISM IN CHINA AND US ACTIVITIES IN POLITICAL AND
TRADE EVENTS DURING PERIOD.

1935 TOSCANO M.
THE HISTORY OF TREATIES AND INTERNATIONAL POLITICS
(REV. ED.)
BALTIMORE: JOHNS HOPKINS PRESS, 1966, 685 PP., LC#66-15525.
SOURCE BOOK FOR HISTORY OF TREATIES AND DIPLOMACY,
ENUMERATING MAJOR COLLECTIONS OF TREATIES, DOCUMENTS
RELATING TO DIPLOMACY IN WWI AND WWII, AND SOURCES OF
MEMOIRS ABOUT THESE WARS AND THEIR ORIGINS. COVERS SOURCES
FROM ALL PARTS OF WORLD AND NOT ONLY EUROPE AND US.

1936 TOTOK W., WEITZEL R.
HANDBUCH DER BIBLIOGRAPHISCHEN NACHSCHLAGEWERKE.
FRANKFURT: V KLOSTERMANN, 1954, 258 PP.
BIBLIOGRAPHY OF GERMAN BIBLIOGRAPHIES IN GENERAL
AND SPECIFIC SUBJECTS.

1937 TOWLE L.W.
INTERNATIONAL TRADE AND COMMERCIAL POLICY.
NEW YORK: HARPER, 1947, 780 PP.
STUDIES ECONOMIC BASES OF INTERNATIONAL RELATIONS AND
EFFECT ON NATIONAL INCOMES AND NATIONAL PROSPERITY. PRESENTS
MAJOR ISSUES OF INTERNATIONAL ECONOMICS AND EXAMINES THEIR
EFFECTS ON POLITICS. DISCUSSES METHODOLOGY OF ECONOMIC
ANALYSIS.

1938 TRAYNOR R.J.
"WHO CAN BEST JUDGE THE JUDGES?"
VIRGINIA LAW REV., 53 (OCT. 67), 1266-1282.
DISCUSSES METHODS OF CHOOSING JUDGES AND REVEALING PUBLIC
OPINION ABOUT THEIR DECISIONS. URGES REMOVAL OF POPULAR
ELECTION SYSTEM. STUDIES MERIT SELECTION PLAN OF APPOINTMENT
BY GOVERNOR AND COMMISSION. DESCRIBES IN DETAIL CALIFORNIA
SYSTEM OF JUDGING JUDGES.

1939 TRESOLINI R.J.
AMERICAN CONSTITUTIONAL LAW.
NEW YORK: MACMILLAN, 1965, 781 PP., LC#64-22597.
AIMED AT UNDERGRADUATES, BOOK INTRODUCES CONSTITUTIONAL
LAW IN US WITH THEORY AND CASE STUDY. CONSIDERS ROLE OF
SUPREME COURT. COORDINATES STUDY OF CASES WITH HISTORICAL
PERSPECTIVE WITHOUT USING LEGAL TERMINOLOGY, AND PROVIDES
STUDIES ON THE LIVES OF INDIVIDUAL JUSTICES.

1940 TRESOLINI R.J. ED., FROST R.T. ED.
CASES IN AMERICAN NATIONAL GOVERNMENT AND POLITICS.
ENGLEWOOD CLIFFS: PRENTICE HALL, 1966, 292 PP., LC#66-10951.
TEXT ON US GOVERNMENT USES CASE STUDIES BY VARIOUS
AUTHORS TO DEMONSTRATE OPERATIONS OF FEDERALISM, POLITICAL
PARTIES AND PRESSURE GROUPS, LEGISLATIVE PROCESS, PRESIDENT,
JUDICIAL PROCESS, CIVIL LIBERTIES, AND FOREIGN POLICY.

1941 TRISKA J.F., SLUSSER R.M.
THE THEORY, LAW, AND POLICY OF SOVIET TREATIES.
STANFORD: U. PR., 1962, 593 PP.
ATTEMPT AT A SYSTEMATIC INVESTIGATION AND ANALYSIS OF
SOVIET INTERNATIONAL LEGAL ARRANGEMENTS, COVERING CHIEFLY
THE PERIOD FROM 1917 - 1957.

1942 TRISKA J.F.
"SOVIET TREATY LAW: A QUANTITATIVE ANALYSIS."
LAW CONTEMP. PROBL., 29 (AUTUMN 64), 896-909.
STUDY OF SOVIET TREATY DATA SHOWING RECENT DEVELOPMENTS
AND TRENDS WHICH CHARACTERIZE THE SOVIET LAW OF TREATIES.
IMPLICATIONS REGARDING FURTHER GROWTH AND CHANGES IN ATTI-
TUDES ARE ASSESSED.

1943 TROTIER A.H. ED., HARMAN M. ED.
DOCTORAL DISSERTATIONS ACCEPTED BY AMERICAN UNIVERSITIES
1954-55.
NEW YORK: H W WILSON, 1955, 298 PP., LC#34-40898.
UNANNOTATED LISTING OF DOCTORAL DISSERTATIONS ACCEPTED
IN US IN 1954-55. INCLUDES STATISTICS ON DOCTORAL DEGREES
GRANTED IN ALL FIELDS FROM 1945-46 THROUGH 1954-55. INCLUDES
PHILOSOPHY, RELIGION, GEOGRAPHY, PUBLIC HEALTH, ECONOMICS,
EDUCATION, INTERNATIONAL LAW AND RELATIONS, SOCIOLOGY, ART,
ARCHEOLOGY, LANGUAGES AND LITERATURE, POLITICS, HISTORY,
AND OTHERS.

1944 TURNER R.K.
BIBLIOGRAPHY ON WORLD ORGANIZATION.
NEW YORK: W WILSON MEM LIB.
ANNOTATED BIBLIOGRAPHY OF MATERIAL ON WORLD ORGANIZA-
TION REPRINTED FROM THE QUARTERLY JOURNAL "INTERNATIONAL
ORGANIZATION," PUBLISHED BY THE WORLD PEACE FOUNDATION.
FIRST ISSUED IN SEPTEMBER 1947, THE BIBLIOGRAPHY LISTS DOCU-
MENTS, BOOKS, PAMPHLETS, AND PERIODICAL ARTICLES ON REGIONAL
ORGANIZATIONS, WAR AND TRANSITIONAL AGENCIES, AND OTHER
FUNCTIONAL ORGANIZATIONS.

1945 TUSSMAN J. ED.
THE SUPREME COURT ON CHURCH AND STATE.
NEW YORK: OXFORD U PR, 1962, 298 PP.
REVIEWS OPINIONS IN RELIGIOUS FREEDOM DECISIONS OF
SUPREME COURT 1815-1960. CASES INVOLVE USE OF GOVERNMENT
TO FURTHER RELIGIOUS ENDS, RELIGIOUS TESTS FOR POLITICAL
CANDIDATES, FREE EXERCISE, FREEDOM TO PROSELYTIZE, AND
FREEDOM OF ACTION.

1946 TUSSMAN J. ED.
THE SUPREME COURT ON RACIAL DISCRIMINATION.
NEW YORK: OXFORD U PR, 1963, 393 PP., LC#63-7870.
ANALYZES MANY SUPREME COURT DECISIONS ON RACIAL DISCRIMI-
NATION. LISTED BY TOPIC, DECISIONS INCLUDE DISCRIMINATION
IN TRAVEL, DINING, LIVELIHOOD, FREE SPEECH, EDUCATION,
RESTRICTIVE COVENANTS, AND JURIES.

1947 TWENTIETH CENTURY FUND
ONE MAN - ONE VOTE (PAMPHLET)
NEW YORK: TWENTIETH CENT FUND, 1962, 19 PP.
STATES BASIC PRINCIPLES OF LEGISLATIVE REAPPORTIONMENT
AS SEEN BY GROUP OF SCHOLARS FROM SEVERAL FIELDS. PROBLEM
BECAME ISSUE WITH BAKER V. CARR CASE RAISING QUESTIONS OF
STATE VERSUS FEDERAL JURISDICTION OVER REDISTRICTING, PROPER
METHOD, URBAN VERSUS RURAL MAJORITY, ROLE OF COURTS AND
SOLUTION TO CONTROVERSY.

1948 TYDINGS J.D.
"MODERNIZING THE ADMINISTRATION OF JUSTICE."
J. OF AM. JUDICATURE SOC., 50 (APR. 67), 258-261.
DISCUSSES IN SOME DETAIL THE KIND OF STUDY OF COURTS
WHICH MIGHT BE MADE BY MANAGEMENT CONSULTANTS AND SYSTEMS
ANALYSTS. LIMITED TO ADMINISTRATIVE STUDY, NOT JUDICIAL.
SUCH ANALYSIS WOULD DISCUSS CURRENT OPERATIONS AND BOTTLE-
NECKS IN COURT PROCEDURES, MAKE RECOMMENDATIONS FOR REFORMS,
AND SUGGEST POSSIBLE ORGANIZATIONAL CHANGES. GREATEST PROB-
LEM IS ORDERLY, STEADY FLOW OF CASES. URGES USING COMPUTERS.

1949 TYLER P. ED.
"IMMIGRATION AND THE UNITED STATES."
NEW YORK: H W WILSON, 1956.
COLLECTION OF ESSAYS ON HISTORICAL BACKGROUND OF IMMIGRA-
TION IN AMERICA. COVERS MC CARRAN WALTER ACT AND RECENT
REFUGEE REFORM PROGRAMS. UNANNOTATED BIBLIOGRAPHY OF POST-
1940 BOOKS, PAMPHLETS, AND PERIODICALS CONCERNING IMMIGRA-
TION AND IMMIGRATION POLICIES.

1950 U OF MICHIGAN LAW SCHOOL
ATOMS AND THE LAW.
ANN ARBOR: U OF MICH LAW SCHOOL, 1959, 1512 PP.
CONCERNS LEGAL PROBLEMS INVOLVED IN PEACEFUL USES OF
ATOMIC ENERGY. CONCENTRATES ON TORT LIABILITY FOR RADIATION
INJURIES, WORKMEN'S COMPENSATION, FEDERAL STATUTORY AND
ADMINISTRATIVE PROVISIONS REGULATING ATOMIC ACTIVITIES, AND
STATE REGULATION OF ATOMIC ENERGY. INCLUDES ESSAYS ON
INTERNATIONAL ASPECTS OF THE SUBJECT.

1951 ULMER S.S.
"THE ANALYSIS OF BEHAVIOR PATTERNS ON THE UNITED STATES
SUPREME COURT"
J. OF POLITICS, 22 (NOV. 60), 629-653.
ILLUSTRATES METHODS BY WHICH BEHAVIOR PATTERNS OF SUPREME
COURT JUSTICES MAY BE IDENTIFIED AND ANALYZED. STUDIES
INTERPERSONAL RELATIONSHIPS TO DISCERN EFFECT OF INDIVIDUAL
PERSONALITY ON LAW-MAKING AND DECISION-MAKING. USES CASES
RAISING QUESTIONS OF CIVIL LIBERTY IN 1958 TO SUPPORT THEORY
THAT ATTITUDE OF JUDGE HAS HIGH SIGNIFICANCE IN DECIDING
FINAL RULING.

1952 ULMER S.S.
"TOWARD A THEORY OF SUBGROUP FORMATION IN THE UNITED STATES
SUPREME COURT."
J. OF POLITICS, 27 (FEB. 65), 133-152.
USING A DISTINCTION BETWEEN CLIQUES (SMALL GROUPS HELD
TOGETHER BY COMMON VALUES) AND COALITIONS, SUGGESTS THAT
SUBGROUP FORMATION IN SUPREME COURT IS BASICALLY CLIQUE
FORMATION. REJECTS POWER AS PRIMARY MOTIVATING FORCE BEHIND
JUSTICES. APPLIES FACTOR ANALYSIS METHOD TO VOTING DATA.

1953 UN HEADQUARTERS LIBRARY
BIBLIOGRAPHIE DE LA CHARTE DES NATIONS UNIES.
NEW YORK: UNITED NATIONS, 1955, 128 PP.
COMPILES, ANNOTATES, AND INDEXES 2,059 ITEMS (BOOKS, DOC-
UMENTS, ARTICLES, PAMPHLETS, ETC.) DEALING WITH, OR DEVOTED
TO, THE HISTORY, PRINCIPLES, PURPOSES, ORGANS, MEMBERSHIP,
AND ORGANIZATION OF THE UN, AS DEFINED BY ITS CHARTER AND
THE PROPOSALS, CONFERENCES, AND COMMITTEES PRECEDING ITS
DRAFTING. ARRANGED ACCORDING TO CHARTER PROVISIONS. IN
FRENCH.

1954 UN PUB. INFORM. ORGAN.
EVERY MAN'S UNITED NATIONS.
NEW YORK: UN, 1964, 593 PP.
COMPREHENSIVE ANALYSIS OF FUNCTIONS AND ACTIVITIES OF UN.
DESCRIBES THEIR PRINCIPAL ORGANS SUCH AS GENERAL ASSEMBLY,
SECURITY COUNCIL, AND INTERNATIONAL COURT OF JUSTICE.

FOCUSES ON QUESTIONS RELATED TO PROBLEMS OF INTERNATIONAL
SECURITY. INCLUDES LIST OF INTER-GOVERNMENTAL AGENCIES CON-
NECTED WITH UN ORGANIZATION.

1955 UNCIO CONFERENCE LIBRARY
SHORT TITLE CLASSIFIED CATALOG.
NEW YORK: UNITED NATIONS, 1945, 65 PP.
UNANNOTATED BIBLIOGRAPHICAL COLLECTION OF PUBLICATIONS
FROM 1900-44 ON INTERNATIONAL AND NATIONAL POLITICAL, ECO-
NOMIC, AND SOCIAL PROBLEMS. CLASSIFIED BIOGRAPHICAL DICTIO-
NARIES, STATISTICAL YEARBOOKS, ENCYCLOPEDIAS, AND DICTIONAR-
IES. INCLUDES DOCUMENTS FROM LEAGUE OF NATIONS AND THE
HAGUE, TOGETHER WITH TREATIES AND RELEVANT NEWSPAPER, PERI-
ODICAL, AND JOURNAL INDEXES. SOURCES IN WESTERN LANGUAGES.

1956 UNECA LIBRARY
NEW ACQUISITIONS IN THE UNECA LIBRARY.
NEW YORK: UNITED NATIONS, 1962.
PERIODICAL LISTING OF RECENT BOOKS, MONOGRAPHS, SERIAL
PUBLICATIONS AND PERIODICALS COVERING CURRENT SOCIAL, ECO-
NOMIC, CULTURAL, AND TECHNICAL PROBLEMS OF WORLD WITH SPE-
CIAL ATTENTION TO AFRICA AND DEVELOPING NATIONS. FIRST PUB-
LISHED 1962. ITEMS, IN ALL LANGUAGES, ARRANGED BY SUBJECT.

1957 UNESCO
INTERNATIONAL BIBLIOGRAPHY OF POLITICAL SCIENCE
(VOLUMES 1-8)
PARIS: UNESCO.
AN ANNUAL PUBLICATION IN THE SERIES OF THE GENERAL PRO-
GRAM FOR SOCIAL SCIENCE DOCUMENTATION. AN INTERNATIONAL CUR-
RENT BIBLIOGRAPHY CONTAINING BOOKS AND PERIODICAL ARTICLES
ARRANGED IN A CLASSIFIED SCHEME WITH INDEXES BY AUTHOR AND
SUBJECT. ALSO INCLUDES RELEVANT GOVERNMENT DOCUMENTS. UNAN-
NOTATED. BEGINNING WITH VOLUME 9, 1960, PUBLISHED IN LONDON
BY STEVENS & SONS AND IN CHICAGO BY ALDINE PUBLISHING CO.

1958 UNESCO
THESES DE SCIENCES SOCIALES: CATALOGUE ANALYTIQUE INTERNA-
TIONAL DE THESES INEDITES DE DOCTORAT, 1940-1950.
PARIS: UNESCO, 1952, 236 PP.
3,215 ITEMS DESCRIBING DOCTORAL THESES IN THE SOCIAL
SCIENCES FROM 23 MEMBERS PARTICIPATING IN PROGRAM ORGAN-
IZED BY UNESCO. BILINGUAL CATALOGUE, WITH TITLES EITHER IN
FRENCH OR ENGLISH. CLASSIFICATION ACCORDING TO MAJOR DIS-
CIPLINE AS PRESCRIBED BY UNIVERSAL DECIMAL SYSTEM. CONTAINS
SUBJECT, AUTHOR, AND GEOGRAPHICAL INDEXES AND TABLE OF
LANGUAGES.

1959 UNESCO
A REGISTER OF LEGAL DOCUMENTATION IN THE WORLD.
PARIS: UNESCO, 1953, 362 PP.
A LISTING IN ENGLISH AND FRENCH OF CONSTITUTIONS,
TREATIES, LEGISLATION, EXECUTIVE ACTIONS, ADMINISTRATIVE
REPORTS, AND COURT RULINGS. ALSO INCLUDED ARE PERIODICAL
ARTICLES AND BIBLIOGRAPHIES. UNANNOTATED AND ARRANGED BY
COUNTRY. ITEMS FROM 1225 TO PRESENT.

1960 UNESCO
A REGISTER OF LEGAL DOCUMENTATION IN THE WORLD (2ND ED.)
PARIS: UNESCO, 1957, 423 PP.
A CATALOGUE OF DOCUMENTATION ON FOREIGN LEGAL SYSTEMS,
ARRANGED ALPHABETICALLY BY COUNTRY. PROVIDES INFORMATION ON
CONSTITUTIONAL LAW, LAW CODES, PERIODICALS, AND JUDICIAL
CENTERS OF ACTIVITY. AT END OF EACH TERRITORIAL UNIT, A
BIBLIOGRAPHY LISTS THE MAIN BIBLIOGRAPHICAL PUBLICATIONS
DOCUMENTING THE LEGAL SYSTEM OF THAT AREA.

1961 UNESCO
"TECHNIQUES OF MEDIATION AND CONCILIATION."
INT. SOC. SCI. BULL., 10 (NO.4, 58), 507-628.
COVERS THE ROLE OF MEDIATION IN INTERNATIONAL LAW, CIVIL
PROCEDURE AND COLLECTIVE INDUSTRIAL DISPUTES. CONCILIATION
AND MEDIATION EXPLORED AS DEVICES EMPLOYED TO ALLEVIATE
PREVALENT INTERNATIONAL CONFLICTS AND TENSIONS.

1962 UNESCO
INTERNATIONAL ORGANIZATIONS IN THE SOCIAL SCIENCES(REV. ED.)
PARIS: UNESCO, 1965, 147 PP.
SUMMARY DESCRIPTION OF THE STRUCTURE AND ACTIVITIES OF
NONGOVERNMENTAL ORGANIZATIONS SPECIALIZING IN SOCIAL
SCIENCES AND IN CONSULTATIVE RELATIONSHIP WITH UNESCO. THIS
BILINGUAL EDITION COMPRISES 14 INTERNATIONAL SOCIAL SCIENCE
ORGANIZATIONS HAVING CONSULTATIVE AND ASSOCIATE OR INFORMA-
TION AND CONSULTATIVE RELATIONS WITH UNESCO. LISTS THEIR
GEOGRAPHICAL EXTENSION, AFFILIATED BODIES, STRUCTURE, ETC.

1963 UNESCO
HANDBOOK OF INTERNATIONAL EXCHANGES.
PARIS: UNESCO, 1965.
REFERENCE SUPPLIES INFORMATION ON AIMS, PROGRAMS, AND
ACTIVITIES OF NATIONAL AND INTERNATIONAL ORGANIZATIONS;
AND ON INTERNATIONAL AGREEMENTS CONCERNING INTERNATIONAL
RELATIONS AND EXCHANGES IN THE FIELDS OF EDUCATION,
SCIENCE, CULTURE, AND MASS COMMUNICATION. CONTAINS DATA ON
THE ACTIVITIES OF 272 INTERNATIONAL AND 5,000 GOVERNMENTAL
AGENCIES; LISTS 4,200 AGREEMENTS.

1964 UNITED NATIONS
OFFICIAL RECORDS OF THE UNITED NATIONS' GENERAL ASSEMBLY.
NEW YORK: UNITED NATIONS.
OFFICIAL RECORDS OF GENERAL ASSEMBLY CONSIST OF SUMMARY
OR VERBATIM REPORTS OF PLENARY MEETINGS OF THE GENERAL
COMMITTEE, THE SIX MAIN COMMITTEES, AND SESSIONAL COMMIT-
TEES; ANNEXES OF MOST SIGNIFICANT AND PERTINENT DOCUMENTS;
SUPPLEMENTS INCLUDING RESOLUTIONS ADOPTED BY THE SESSION;
ANNUAL REPORT AND BUDGET BY THE SECRETARY-GENERAL, COUNCIL
REPORTS, COMMITTEE REPORTS, ETC. ANNUAL PUBLICATIONS.

1965 UNITED NATIONS
UNITED NATIONS PUBLICATIONS.
NEW YORK: UNITED NATIONS.
ANNUAL PUBLICATION, FIRST PUBLISHED 1945, LISTING ALL
MATERIALS PUBLISHED DURING YEAR BY ALL UN DEPARTMENTS AND
AGENCIES.

1966 UNITED NATIONS
YEARBOOK OF THE INTERNATIONAL LAW COMMISSION.
NEW YORK: UNITED NATIONS.
ANNUAL PUBLICATION COVERING SUMMARY RECORDS AND DOCUMENTS
OF SESSIONS, INCLUDING REPORTS TO COMMISSION TO THE GENERAL
ASSEMBLY, FOR PERIOD 1949-PRESENT. CUMULATIVE PUBLICATION
FIRST APPEARED IN 1956. STUDIES, SPECIAL REPORTS, PRINCIPAL
DRAFT RESOLUTIONS, AND AMENDMENTS PRESENTED TO COMMISSION
ARE PRINTED IN ORIGINAL LANGUAGES. SUMMARY RECORDS APPEAR
IN ENGLISH.

1967 UNITED NATIONS
"CAPITAL PUNISHMENT."
NEW YORK: UN PUBL. SERV., 1962, 76 PP., $0.50.
WORLD-WIDE SURVEY OF NATIONAL LAWS AND PROCEDURES RE-
LATING TO CAPITAL CRIMES. INCLUDES DATA ON THE SOCIOLOG-
ICAL AND CRIMINOLOGICAL EFFECTS OF CAPITAL PUNISHMENT AND
ITS ABOLITION.

1969 UNITED NATIONS
INTERNATIONAL SPACE BIBLIOGRAPHY.
NEW YORK: UNITED NATIONS, 1966, 166 PP.
LISTS ABOUT 3,000 BOOKS, REPORTS, BULLETINS, GOVERNMENT
DOCUMENTS, AND PERIODICALS PUBLISHED IN 1960'S IN 34 MAJOR
COUNTRIES OF THE WORLD. PREPARED TO ASSIST COMMITTEE ON
PEACEFUL PURPOSES OF OUTER SPACE. ENTRIES ARRANGED BY TYPE
OF MATERIAL UNDER COUNTRY; SUBDIVIDED BY SUBJECT.

1970 UNITED NATIONS
UNITED NATIONS PUBLICATIONS: 1945-1966.
NEW YORK: UNITED NATIONS, 1967, 175 PP.
INCLUDES UN AND INTERNATIONAL COURT OF JUSTICE SALES PUB-
LICATIONS ISSUED FROM 1945-66 AND EXCLUDES MIMEOGRAPHED DOC-
UMENTS OF THE ECONOMIC COMMISSION FOR EUROPE. ARRANGEMENT
IS TOPICAL: ECONOMIC DEVELOPMENT, WORLD ECONOMY, TRADE,
FINANCE, PUBLIC ADMINISTRATION, SOCIAL QUESTIONS, CARTOG-
RAPHY, DEMOGRAPHY, HEALTH SERVICES, UN ORGANS AND ORGANIZA-
TION, STATISTICS, LEAGUE OF NATIONS, ETC. INCLUDES APPENDIX.

1971 UNITED WORLD FEDERALISTS
UNITED WORLD FEDERALISTS; PANORAMA OF RECENT BOOKS, FILMS,
AND JOURNALS ON WORLD FEDERATION, THE UN, AND WORLD PEACE.
BOSTON: UNITED WORLD FEDERALISTS, 1960, 26 PP.
AN ANNOTATED BIBLIOGRAPHY OF 65 RECENT BOOKS, 14 FILMS,
AND 27 JOURNALS ON WORLD FEDERATION, THE UN, AND WORLD
PEACE. MOST BOOKS PUBLISHED SINCE 1955; WITH EXCEPTION OF
"THE FEDERALIST," ALL BOOKS DATE FROM 1945. ENTRIES ORGAN-
IZED TOPICALLY WITHIN NINE SUBJECT CATEGORIES AND ANNOTATED
WITH EXCERPTS FROM PUBLISHED CRITIQUES OF THE WORK.

1972 UNIVERSAL REFERENCE SYSTEM
INTERNATIONAL AFFAIRS: VOLUME I IN THE POLITICAL SCIENCE,
GOVERNMENT, AND PUBLIC POLICY SERIES.
PRINCETON: UNIVERSAL REF SYSTEM, 1965, 1205 PP., LC#65-19793
COMPUTERIZED INFORMATION RETRIEVAL SYSTEM FOR THE SOCIAL
AND BEHAVIORAL SCIENCES; ANNOTATED AND INTENSIVELY INDEXED
UTILYZING THE "TOPICAL-METHODOLOGICAL INDEX" DEVELOPED
BY PROFESSOR ALFRED DE GRAZIA. VOLUME CARRIES 3,000 REFEREN-
CES IN INTERNATIONAL AFFAIRS. QUARTERLY GAZETTES BEGAN IN
AUGUST, 1967.

1973 UNIVERSAL REFERENCE SYSTEM
BIBLIOGRAPHY OF BIBLIOGRAPHIES IN POLITICAL SCIENCE, GOVERN-
MENT, AND PUBLIC POLICY (VOLUME III)
PRINCETON* UNIV. REF. SYSTEM, 1967, 1200 PP.
COMPUTERIZED INFORMATION RETRIEVAL SYSTEM FOR THE SOCIAL
AND BEHAVIORAL SCIENCES. ANNOTATED AND INTENSIVELY INDEXED,
UTILIZING "TOPICAL-METHODOLOGICAL INDEX" DEVELOPED BY PRO-
FESSOR ALFRED DE GRAZIA. APPROXIMATELY 3,000 CITATIONS FROM
SCHOLARLY JOURNALS, BOOKS, GOVERNMENT DOCUMENTS IN ENGLISH
AND EUROPEAN LANGUAGES. INCLUDES CLASSICAL SOURCES THROUGH
1967. TO BE PUBLISHED EARLY 1968 WITH QUARTERLY GAZETTES.

1974 UNIVERSAL REFERENCE SYSTEM
CURRENT EVENTS AND PROBLEMS OF MODERN SOCIETY (VOLUME V)
PRINCETON* UNIV. REF. SYSTEM, 1967, 1200 PP.
TREATS BOOKS, ARTICLES, REPORTS, AND GOVERNMENT DOCUMENTS
CONCERNED WITH SOCIAL, POLITICAL, EDUCATIONAL, AND ECONOMIC

CONTROVERSIES OF THE PRESENT PERIOD. MAJORITY OF ITEMS ARE PUBLICATIONS OF THE 1960'S, AND ARE IN ENGLISH AND EUROPEAN LANGUAGES. ABOUT 3000 ITEMS CITED. TO BE PUBLISHED EARLY 1968. QUARTERLY GAZETTES BEGAN AUG., 1967. COMPUTERIZED INFORMATION RETRIEVAL SYSTEM.

1975 UNIVERSAL REFERENCE SYSTEM
PUBLIC POLICY AND THE MANAGEMENT OF SCIENCE (VOLUME IX)
PRINCETON* UNIV. REF. SYSTEM, 1967, 1200 PP.
ABOUT 3000 SELECTED BOOKS, ARTICLES, AND DOCUMENTS CON-
CERNED WITH INSTITUTIONAL AND BEHAVIORAL PROCESS OF SCIEN-
TIFIC DECISION-MAKING. MAJORITY OF ITEMS FROM 1960'S; IN-
CLUDES ENGLISH-LANGUAGE AND EUROPEAN SOURCES. USES PROFESSOR
ALFRED DE GRAZIA'S "TOPICAL-METHODOLOGICAL INDEX." TO BE
PUBLISHED EARLY 1968. QUARTERLY GAZETTES BEGAN AUG., 1967.

1976 UNIVERSAL REFERENCE SYSTEM
LAW, JURISPRUDENCE, AND JUDICIAL PROCESS (VOLUME VII)
PRINCETON: UNIVERSAL REF SYSTEM, 1967, 1200 PP.
COMPUTERIZED INFORMATION RETRIEVAL SYSTEM. TREATS SCIENCE
OF STUDY OF LAW AND ITS METHODOLOGY. ANNOTATED AND EXTEN-
SIVELY INDEXED USING PROFESSOR ALFRED DE GRAZIA'S "TOPICAL-
METHODOLOGICAL INDEX." APPROXIMATELY 3,000 CITATIONS FROM
ENGLISH AND EUROPEAN-LANGUAGE BOOKS, JOURNALS, DOCUMENTS
RANGING FROM CLASSICS TO PRESENT. TO BE PUBLISHED EARLY
1968. QUARTERLY GAZETTES BEGAN JUNE, 1967.

1977 US ADVISORY COMN INTERGOV REL
APPORTIONMENT OF STATE LEGISLATURES (PAMPHLET)
WASHINGTON: US GOVERNMENT, 1962, 78 PP.
CONSIDERS THE EFFECT OF MALAPPORTIONED LEGISLATURES ON
THE GOVERNING PROCESS, FACTORS TO BE CONSIDERED IN
APPORTIONMENT FORMULAS, PROCEDURES INVOLVED IN THE
APPORTIONMENT PROCESS, AND SUGGESTS GUIDELINES FOR THE
STATES.

1978 US AIR FORCE
THE MILITARY JUSTICE SYSTEM (REV. ED.)
MONTGOMERY: AIR U, 1962, 140 PP.
PRESENTS GENERAL ELEMENTS OF MILITARY JUSTICE SYSTEM.
DISCUSSES UNIFORM CODE, OFFENSES, RIGHTS OF ACCUSED,
COURT MARTIAL, TRIAL PROCEDURE, ETC.

1979 US AIR FORCE ACADEMY ASSEMBLY
OUTER SPACE: FINAL REPORT APRIL 1-4, 1964.
NEW YORK: AMERICAN ASSEMBLY, 1964, 94 PP.
SPEECHES GIVEN AT ACADEMY BY EXPERTS ON PROBLEMS OF
CONTROLLING OUTER SPACE. COVERS BOTH PEACEFUL AND HARMFUL
POSSIBILITIES FOR WORLD. EVALUATES US PROGRESS, REASONS FOR
PROJECTS, AND FUTURE PLANS.

1980 US BUREAU OF THE CENSUS
BIBLIOGRAPHY OF SOCIAL SCIENCE PERIODICALS AND MONOGRAPH
SERIES.
WASHINGTON: GOVT PR OFFICE.
ISSUED IRREGULARLY SINCE 1962. ANNOTATED, LISTING AREA
STUDIES. INCLUDES MATERIALS IN NON-WESTERN LANGUAGES AND
TRANSLATED INTO ENGLISH. ENTRIES CLASSIFIED BY SUBJECT AND
AGENCY. COVERS WORLD FROM 1950 TO PRESENT. TOPICS INCLUDE:
GENERAL SOCIAL SCIENCES, CULTURAL ANTHROPOLOGY, ECONOMICS,
EDUCATION, HISTORY, LAW. POLITICAL SCIENCE, PUBLIC HEALTH,
SOCIOLOGY, AND BIBLIOGRAPHIES.

1981 US COMMISSION GOVT SECURITY
RECOMMENDATIONS; AREA: IMMIGRANT PROGRAM.
WASHINGTON: US GOVERNMENT, 1957, 300 PP.
CONSIDERS MEASURES TO BE TAKEN TO PREVENT ENTRY INTO US
OF SUBVERSIVE ALIENS. SETS STANDARDS OF BEHAVIOR AND
SPECIFIES WHAT ACTION IS TO BE CONSIDERED AS SUBVERSIVE.
ALSO GIVES DEFINITION OF UNDESIRABLE, SPECIFIED BY
ATTORNEY GENERAL.

1982 US COMMISSION GOVT SECURITY
RECOMMENDATIONS; AREA: LEGISLATION.
WASHINGTON: US GOVERNMENT, 1957, 80 PP.
RECOMMENDS AMENDMENT TO TITLE 18 OF UNITED STATES CODE
TO DEFINE AND PUNISH UNAUTHORIZED DISCLOSURE OF CRITICAL
MILITARY SECRETS. ALSO RECOMMENDS EMPOWERING FEDERAL AGENTS
TO USE WIRETAPPING IN SECURITY MATTERS.

1983 US COMMISSION ON CIVIL RIGHTS
JUSTICE: BOOK 5, 1961 REPORT OF THE U.S. COMMISSION ON CIVIL
RIGHTS.
WASHINGTON: US GOVERNMENT, 1961, 307 PP.
STUDIES PROBLEMS OF EQUAL JUSTICE UNDER LAW, WITH PARTIC-
ULAR ATTENTION TO NEGROES, AND OF THE STATUS AND DIFFICUL-
TIES OF AMERICAN INDIANS. CONCERNING NEGROES, BOTH
POLICE AND PRIVATE VIOLENCE ARE DISCUSSED, AS WELL AS AVAIL-
ABLE FEDERAL SANCTIONS, STATE AND LOCAL LAWS AND PROGRAMS,
AND JURY EXCLUSION. LEGAL AND MINORITY STATUS OF INDIANS
AND BACKGROUND TO THIS PROBLEM ARE DISCUSSED. DOCUMENTATION.

1984 US COMMISSION ON CIVIL RIGHTS
EQUAL PROTECTION OF THE LAWS IN NORTH CAROLINA.
WASHINGTON: GOVT PR OFFICE, 1962, 251 PP.
REPORT OF NORTH CAROLINA ADVISORY COMMITTEE TO CIVIL

RIGHTS COMMISSION ON LEGAL EQUALITY IN THAT STATE'S
PRACTICES IN VOTING, ADMINISTRATION OF JUSTICE, EMPLOYMENT,
EDUCATION, HOUSING, AND MEDICAL CARE. FIND. A FEW
MALPRACTICES AND SUGGESTS REMEDIES.

1985 US COMMISSION ON CIVIL RIGHTS
HEARINGS BEFORE UNITED STATES COMMISSION ON CIVIL RIGHTS.
WASHINGTON: GOVT PR OFFICE, 1962, 489 PP.
HEARINGS HELD IN MEMPHIS, TENNESSEE, JUNE 25-6, 1962,
CONCERNING CIVIL RIGHTS AND HEALTH FACILITIES AND SERVICES,
ADMINISTRATION OF JUSTICE, EDUCATION, EMPLOYMENT, HOUSING.

1986 US COMMISSION ON CIVIL RIGHTS
FREEDOM TO THE FREE.
WASHINGTON: GOVT PR OFFICE, 1963, 246 PP.
HISTORY OF FREEDOM FOR NEGROES SINCE EMANCIPATION, 1863,
EMPHASIZING RECONSTRUCTION, BEGINNING OF CIVIL RIGHTS
MOVEMENTS, NATIONAL CRISES AND CIVIL RIGHTS, AND
BREAKTHROUGH TOWARD EQUALITY.

1987 US COMMISSION ON CIVIL RIGHTS
REPORT ON MISSISSIPPI.
WASHINGTON: US CIVIL RIGHTS COMM, 1963, 33 PP.
REPORT ON ALLEGED DENIAL OF EQUAL PROTECTION BY LAW TO
NEGROES IN MISSISSIPPI IN 1962. PROVIDES ACCOUNTS OF SEVEN
CASES IN WHICH CONSTITUTIONAL RIGHTS WERE DENIED NEGROES BY
LOCAL OFFICIALS AND EXTREME POLICE BRUTALITY WAS EVIDENCED.

1988 US SENATE COMM ON JUDICIARY
FREEDOM OF INFORMATION AND SECRECY IN GOVERNMENT (2 VOLS.)
WASHINGTON: GOVT PR OFFICE, 1958, 1022 PP.
HEARINGS BEFORE SUBCOMMITTEE ON CONSTITUTIONAL RIGHTS, OF
COMMITTEE ON JUDICIARY. DISCUSSES EXECUTIVE PRIVILEGE TO
WITHHOLD INFORMATION FROM PUBLIC, AND NEED FOR FREEDOM OF
INFORMATION IN DEMOCRACY.

1989 US SENATE COMM ON JUDICIARY
CONSTITUTIONAL RIGHTS OF THE MENTALLY ILL.
WASHINGTON: GOVT PR OFFICE, 1961, 825 PP.
HEARINGS BEFORE SUBCOMMITTEE ON CONSTITUTIONAL RIGHTS OF
THE COMMITTEE ON THE JUDICIARY HEADED BY SAM J. ERVIN, DEAL-
ING WITH CONSTITUTIONAL RIGHTS OF MENTALLY ILL. INCLUDES
TESTIMONY AND APPENDIX OF STUDIES ON SUBJECT, RESULTS OF
QUESTIONNAIRE SENT TO GOVERNMENT AGENCIES CONCERNED WITH
MENTAL ILLNESS, AND SPECIFIC CASES.

1990 US CONGRESS
COMMUNICATIONS SATELLITE LEGISLATION: HEARINGS BEFORE COMM
ON AERON AND SPACE SCIENCES ON BILLS S2550 AND 2814.
WASHINGTON: US GOVERNMENT, 1962, 485 PP.
TESTIMONIES BY GOVERNMENT OFFICIALS CONCERNING CREATION
OF WORLDWIDE COMMUNICATIONS SYSTEM, AS AMENDMENT TO NSA ACT
OF 1958. INCLUDES EVIDENCE BY REPRESENTATIVES OF PRIVATE
INDUSTRY, DISCUSSION OF PARTICIPANTS ON NEED FOR
INTERNATIONAL COOPERATION, AND SPECIFIC TESTIMONY ON
OWNERSHIP, OPERATION, AND CONTROL OF SUCH SYSTEM.

1991 US CONGRESS JT ATOM ENRGY COMM
SELECTED MATERIALS ON FEDERAL-STATE COOPERATION IN THE
ATOMIC ENERGY FIELD.
WASHINGTON: GOVT PR OFFICE, 1959, 517 PP.
OUTLINES POLICY QUESTIONS AND ALTERNATIVES FOR JOINT
COMMITTEE ON ATOMIC ENERGY. COLLECTS REPORTS AND MATERIALS
SUMMARIZING ACTIVITIES OF FEDERAL, STATE, AND LOCAL AGENCIES
AND CERTAIN NONGOVERNMENTAL ORGANIZATIONS IN ATOMIC ENERGY
FIELD. INCLUDES ARTICLES, LEGAL ANALYSES, AND A BIBLIOGRAPHY
ON FEDERAL-STATE COOPERATION IN ATOMIC ENERGY.

1992 US SENATE COMM ON JUDICIARY
HEARINGS OF THE COMMITTEE ON THE JUDICIARY.
WASHINGTON: GOVT PR OFFICE, 1963, 1185 PP.
APPENDIX VOLUME II OF HEARINGS BEFORE SUBCOMMITTEE TO
INVESTIGATE ADMINISTRATION OF INTERNAL SECURITY ACT DEALING
WITH DEPARTMENTAL AND AGENCY RULES AND REGULATIONS. COLLEC-
TION OF DOCUMENTS ON US PERSONNEL SECURITY PRACTICES. SUB-
COMMITTEE HEADED BY JAMES O. EASTMAN AND THOMAS J. DODD.

1993 US DEPARTMENT OF STATE
PUBLICATIONS OF THE DEPARTMENT OF STATE: A LIST CUMULATIVE
FROM OCTOBER 1, 1929 (PAMPHLET)
WASHINGTON: DEPT OF STATE, 1945, 35 PP.
LISTING BY DATE AND TITLE OF SERIAL PUBLICATIONS, WHICH
INCLUDE AREA, MAP, TREATY, PASSPORT, CONFERENCE, COMMERCIAL
POLICY, EXECUTIVE AGREEMENT, ARBITRATION, AND FEDERAL LAW
SERIES. DATES FROM 1929-45 AND IS FOLLOWED BY LISTING OF
NONSERIAL PUBLICATIONS BY DATE. SOME 2,400 PUBLICATIONS
INCLUDED.

1994 US DEPARTMENT OF STATE
SOVIET BIBLIOGRAPHY (PAMPHLET)
WASHINGTON: DEPT OF STATE, 1949.
SERIES OF SOME 110 SEPARATE BIBLIOGRAPHIES PUBLISHED FROM
1949 TO 1953, AVERAGING ABOUT 18 PAGES EACH, AND CON-
TAINING MORE THAN 10,000 ITEMS. PUBLISHED BIMONTHLY AND IN-
CLUDES ONLY ENGLISH-LANGUAGE WORKS SELECTED FROM SCHOLARLY
JOURNALS, SPEECHES, GOVERNMENT DOCUMENTS, AND BOOKS. AR-

RANGED TOPICALLY AND ANNOTATED. ALL MATERIALS ARE CURRENT TO DATE OF BIBLIOGRAPHY. SUBJECT INDEX.

1995 US DEPARTMENT OF STATE
RESEARCH ON EASTERN EUROPE (EXCLUDING USSR)
WASHINGTON: DEPT OF STATE, 1952.
LISTING OF COMPLETED AND IN PROGRESS RESEARCH PROJECTS REPORTED BY SCHOLARS TO EXTERNAL RESEARCH STAFF. PUBLISHED ERRATICALLY FROM 1952-58. PUBLISHED LARGELY TO INDICATE COMPLETION AND AVAILABILITY OF NEW RESEARCH. RESEARCH IS LISTED BY COUNTRY WITH WHICH IT IS CONCERNED. INCLUDES SOME PROJECTS BEGUN AS EARLY AS 1941 BUT BELIEVED NOT TO HAVE BEEN PUBLISHED. PUBLISHED IN 10 PARTS.

1996 US DEPARTMENT OF STATE
RESEARCH ON AFRICA (EXTERNAL RESEARCH LIST NO 5-25)
WASHINGTON: DEPT OF STATE, 1966, 55 PP.
LIST OF SOCIAL SCIENCE RESEARCH SUBMITTED BY PRIVATE US SCHOLARS AND RESEARCH CENTERS TO DEPT. OF STATE CURRENTLY IN PROGRESS OR COMPLETED BUT UNPUBLISHED FOR THE PERIOD AUGUST 1965 THROUGH FEBRUARY 1966. MAJORITY OF ENTRIES ANNO-TATED ITEMS TREAT ASIA IN GENERAL AND THEN INDIVIDUAL COUNTRIES. PUBLISHED ANNUALLY SINCE 1965.

1997 US DEPARTMENT OF STATE
RESEARCH ON THE USSR AND EASTERN EUROPE (EXTERNAL RESEARCH LIST NO 1-25)
WASHINGTON: DEPT OF STATE, 1966, 63 PP.
LIST OF SOCIAL SCIENCE RESEARCH SUBMITTED BY PRIVATE US SCHOLARS AND RESEARCH CENTERS TO DEPT OF STATE ON COMMUNIST COUNTRIES OF EASTERN EUROPE CURRENTLY "IN PROGRESS" OR "COM-PLETED" BUT UNPUBLISHED AS OF LATTER DATE FOR PERIOD AUGUST 1965 THROUGH FEBRUARY 1966. MAJORITY OF ENTRIES ANNOTATED. ANNUAL PUBLICATION SINCE 1965.

1998 US DEPARTMENT OF STATE
RESEARCH ON WESTERN EUROPE, GREAT BRITAIN, AND CANADA (EX-TERNAL RESEARCH LIST NO 3-25)
WASHINGTON: DEPT OF STATE, 1966, 120 PP.
SERIAL PUBLICATION OF DEPT OF STATE RECORDING SOCIAL SCIENCE RESEARCH SUBMITTED BY SCHOLARS IN US FOR PERIOD AUG-UST 1965 THROUGH FEBRUARY 1966. ENTRIES ARRANGED BY SUBJECT AND CLASSIFIED AS "IN PROGRESS" OR "COMPLETED." APPEARS AN-NUALLY SINCE 1965. MAJORITY OF ENTRIES ANNOTATED.

1999 US DEPARTMENT OF STATE
TREATIES IN FORCE.
WASHINGTON: US GOVERNMENT, 1967, 336 PP.
LIST OF TREATIES AND OTHER INTERNATIONAL AGREEMENTS TO WHICH US HAS BECOME A PARTY THAT WERE IN FORCE AS OF JANUARY 1, 1967. LIST ARRANGED IN TWO PARTS, FOLLOWED BY AN APPENDIX. PART I INCLUDES BILATERAL TREATIES LISTED BY COUN-TRY, WITH SUBJECT HEADINGS UNDER EACH COUNTRY. PART TWO IN-CLUDES MULTILATERAL TREATIES, ARRANGED BY SUBJECT HEADINGS, WITH A LIST OF PARTICIPATING STATES.

2000 US DEPARTMENT OF STATE
CATALOGUE OF WORKS RELATING TO THE LAW OF NATIONS AND DIPLO-MACY IN THE LIBRARY OF THE DEPARTMENT OF STATE (PAMPHLET)
WASHINGTON: GOVT PR OFFICE, 1897, 110 PP.
ANNOTATED AND ARRANGED BY AUTHOR WITH MANY ITEMS IN OTHER THAN ENGLISH. INCLUDES ABOUT 1,000 BOOKS, ARTICLES, AND PERIODICALS. LISTS AUTHORS ONLY THROUGH THE LETTER B. ITEMS FROM 1840 TO 1897.

2001 US FEDERAL BUREAU INVESTIGAT
BIBLIOGRAPHY OF CRIME AND KINDRED SUBJECTS (PAPER)
WASHINGTON: US GOVERNMENT, 1950, 42 PP.
LIST OF BOOKS AND PERIODICALS FOR POLICE ON CRIMINOLOGY AND TECHNICAL MATTERS OF POLICE WORK. INCLUDES APPENDICES BY AUTHORS, TITLES, AND PUBLISHERS. TITLES MOSTLY 1930-50.

2002 US HOUSE COMM FOREIGN AFFAIRS
HEARINGS ON DRAFT LEGISLATION TO AMEND FURTHER THE MUTUAL SECURITY ACT OF 1954 (PAMPHLET)
WASHINGTON: GOVT PR OFFICE, 1958, 350 PP.
STATEMENTS, TESTIMONY, AND MEMORANDA SUPPLIED BY GOVERN-MENT OFFICIALS ON DESIRABILITY OF AMENDING MUTUAL SECURITY ACT OF 1954, PLUS COST OF US TROOPS IN EUROPE, MISSILE SYSTEMS, IMPORTATION OF ARMS, ETC. INCLUDES PROPOSALS FOR LEGISLATION.

2003 US HOUSE COMM ON JUDICIARY
ESTABLISHMENT OF CONGRESSIONAL DISTRICTS.
WASHINGTON: US GOVERNMENT, 1960, 513 PP.
REPORT OF HEARINGS BEFORE SPECIAL SUBCOMMITTEE ON REAPPORTIONMENT OF COMMITTEE ON THE JUDICIARY HEADED BY WILLIAM T. BYRNE AND TEXT OF BILLS HR 2648 AND 38 REQUIRING ESTABLISHMENT OF CONGRESSIONAL DISTRICTS OF CONTIGUOUS AREAS AND MAKING MEMBERSHIP OF HOUSE OF REPRESENTATIVES 450.

2004 US HOUSE COMM ON JUDICIARY
LEGISLATION RELATING TO ORGANIZED CRIME.
WASHINGTON: US GOVERNMENT, 1961, 388 PP.
HEARINGS BEFORE SUBCOMMITTEE 5 OF HOUSE COMMITTEE ON JUDICIARY, CONCERNING PROPOSALS SUBMITTED BY ATTORNEY

GENERAL ROBERT F. KENNEDY TREATING ORGANIZED CRIME. COVERS PROHIBITION OF INTERSTATE TRAVEL SUPPORTING RACKETEERING, OF INTERSTATE USE OF WIRE COMMUNICATIONS FOR BETTING, AND OF INTERSTATE TRANSPORTATION OF GAMBLING MATERIALS; WITNESS IMMUNITY; AND EXTENSION OF FUGITIVE FELON ACT.

2005 US HOUSE COMM ON JUDICIARY
CONGRESSIONAL REDISTRICTING.
WASHINGTON: US GOVERNMENT, 1964, 157 PP.
REPORT ON HEARINGS BEFORE SUBCOMMITTEE NUMBER FIVE OF COMMITTEE OF JUDICIARY HEADED BY EMANUEL CELLER ON NEED FOR FEDERAL GUIDELINES FOR REDISTRICTING AND FOR CONTIGUOUS DISTRICTS. INCLUDES TEXT AND DISCUSSION OF BILLS ON REDISTRICTING AND REPORTS ON SUBJECT.

2006 US HOUSE COMM ON JUDICIARY
IMMIGRATION HEARINGS.
WASHINGTON: US GOVERNMENT, 1964, 1030 PP.
REPORTS DEBATE BEFORE COMMITTEE ON JUDICIARY, ON PROPOSED CHANGE OF IMMIGRATION ACT TO ABOLISH NATIONALITY QUOTAS FOR IMMIGRANTS. INCLUDES STATEMENTS BY 60 REPRESENTATIVES.

2007 US HOUSE COMM ON JUDICIARY
IMMIGRATION AND NATIONALITY.
NEW YORK: SCHOCKEN BOOKS, 1965, 259 PP.
REPRODUCES TEXT FO MCCARREN ACT OF 1952 WITH AMENDMENTS AND NOTES ON RELATED LAWS. ALSO INCLUDES SUMMARIES OF PERTINENT JUDICIAL DECISIONS CONCERNING IMMIGRATION AND NATIONALITY.

2008 US HOUSE COMM ON JUDICIARY
CIVIL COMMITMENT AND TREATMENT OF NARCOTIC ADDICTS.
WASHINGTON: GOVT PR OFFICE, 1966, 465 PP.
US CONGRESSIONAL HEARINGS STUDY CONCEPT OF CIVIL COMMITMENT OF CERTAIN ADDICTION CASES INSTEAD OF CRIMINAL PROSECUTION. DISCUSSION INCLUDES REVIEW OF SENTENCING PROCEDURES AND MEDICAL TESTIMONY ON TREATMENT AND REHABILITATION.

2009 US HOUSE RULES COMM
HEARINGS BEFORE A SPECIAL SUBCOMMITTEE: ESTABLISHMENT OF A STANDING COMMITTEE ON ADMINISTRATIVE PROCEDURE, PRACTICE.
WASHINGTON: US GOVERNMENT, 1956, 88 PP.
TRANSCRIPTS OF TESTIMONY ON HOUSE RESOLUTION 462, TO ESTABLISH STANDING COMMITTEE TO STUDY ABUSES OF ADMINIS-TRATIVE AUTHORITY, AND NEED FOR LEGISLATIVE STANDARDS TO LIMIT EXERCISE OF ADMINISTRATIVE DISCRETION IN AREAS OF DEL-EGATED POWER. STUDY PROCEDURES AND PRACTICES OF ADMINISTRA-TIVE AGENCIES, AND EVALUATE EFFECTS OF LAWS REGULATING PROCEDURES.

2010 US HOUSE UNAMER ACTIV COMM
HEARINGS ON BILLS TO MAKE PUNISHABLE ASSISTANCE TO ENEMIES OF US IN TIME OF UNDECLARED WAR.
WASHINGTON: US GOVERNMENT, 1966, 1400 PP.
INVESTIGATIVE HEARINGS, BEFORE HOUSE COMMITTEE ON UN-AMERICAN ACTIVITIES, TO DETERMINE OBJECTIVES OF GROUPS THAT ASSIST US ENEMIES OR IMPEDE US MILITARY MOVEMENTS. COLLECTS TESTIMONY ON ADVISABILITY OF PUNISHMENT FOR SUCH GROUPS AND RESTRICTION OF THEIR TRAVEL ABROAD; ON COMMUNIST PROPAGANDA IN US SUPPORTING NORTH VIETNAM; AND ON ACTIVITIES OF US CITIZENS ON BEHALF OF FOREIGN COMMUNIST PRINCIPLES.

2011 US HOUSE WAYS MEANS COMMITTEE
TRAFFIC IN, AND CONTROL OF NARCOTICS, BARBITURATES, AND AMPHETAMINES.
WASHINGTON: GOVT PR OFFICE, 1956, 1633 PP.
ILLUSTRATED HEARINGS ON DRUG TRAFFIC AND ADDICTION GIVE COMPREHENSIVE VIEW OF SITUATION IN US, WITH EMPHASIS ON VIOLATION OF DRUG LAWS, EFFECTS AND TREATMENT OF ADDICTION, PROPOSED ANTI-DRUG LEGISLATION, AND SENTENCING.

2012 US LIBRARY OF CONGRESS
SOCIAL AND CULTURAL PROBLEMS IN WARTIME: APRIL 1941-MARCH 1942.
WASHINGTON: LIBRARY OF CONGRESS, 1942, 80 PP.
SELECTED AND ANNOTATED BIBLIOGRAPHY OF WORKS RELATING TO SOCIAL GROUPS, CONDITIONS, AND INSTITUTIONS DURING WORLD WAR II. CONTAINS 625 ITEMS ARRANGED TOPICALLY UNDER HEADS SUCH AS POPULATION, PUBLIC HEALTH, CRIME, MORALE, ALIENS, RECREA-TION, YOUTH, CIVIL LIBERTIES, EDUCATION, ETC., AND INDEXED BY AUTHOR. PART OF LIBRARY OF CONGRESS SERIES CALLED "THE WORLD AT WAR" IN TEN PARTS.

2013 US LIBRARY OF CONGRESS
SOCIAL AND CULTURAL PROBLEMS IN WARTIME: APRIL-DECEMBER (SUPPLEMENT 1)
WASHINGTON: LIBRARY OF CONGRESS, 1943, 305 PP.
1,926 ITEMS ANNOTATED AND ARRANGED TOPICALLY WITH A SUB-JECT AND AUTHOR INDEX. INCLUDES BOOKS, ARTICLES, PAMPHLETS, BIBLIOGRAPHIES, REFERENCES, ETC., DEALING WITH VARIOUS SO-CIAL AND CULTURAL PROBLEMS OF WORLD WAR II. PART OF THE LEGISLATIVE REFERENCE SERIES.

2014 US LIBRARY OF CONGRESS
SOCIAL AND CULTURAL PROBLEMS IN WARTIME: JANUARY-MAY 1943

(SUPPLEMENT 2)
WASHINGTON: LIBRARY OF CONGRESS, 1943, 201 PP.
1,568-ITEM BIBLIOGRAPHY RELATING TO THE CULTURAL AND
SOCIAL PROBLEMS OF WORLD WAR II. LISTS REFERENCES TO
DEMOGRAPHY, SOCIAL TRENDS, RACE RELATIONS, CITIZENSHIP
PROBLEMS, ZIONISM, ANTI-SEMITISM, YOUTH, CHILDREN, PUBLIC
WELFARE AND HEALTH, MORALE, PROPAGANDA, CRIME, FAMILY,
COMMUNITY PLANNING, RELIGION, CIVIL RIGHTS, ARTS AND
SCIENCES, EDUCATION, ETC.

2015 US LIBRARY OF CONGRESS
RUSSIA: A CHECK LIST PRELIMINARY TO A BASIC BIBLIOGRAPHY
OF MATERIALS IN THE RUSSIAN LANGUAGE.
WASHINGTON: LIBRARY OF CONGRESS, 1944, 99 PP.
SERIES PUBLISHED IN 1944-46 LISTING RUSSIAN-LANGUAGE
MATERIALS ON "BELLES LETTRES"; FINE ARTS; LAWS AND INSTITU-
TIONS PRIOR TO 1918; FOLKLORE; LINGUISTICS, AND LITERARY
FORMS; CHURCH AND EDUCATION PRIOR TO 1918; HISTORY, IN-
CLUDING AUXILIARY SCIENCES, PRIOR TO 1918; REFERENCE BOOKS;
AND THE SOVIET UNION.

2016 US LIBRARY OF CONGRESS
CONSTITUTIONAL AND STATUTORY PROVISIONS OF THE STATES
(VOL. I)
CHICAGO: COUNCIL OF STATE GOVTS, 1945, 72 PP.
A CUMULATIVE STUDY OF STATE CONSTITUTIONAL AND STATUTORY
PROVISIONS. DEALS WITH ELECTIONS, PARDONING POWER, TAXATION,
AND STATE AND FEDERAL CONSTITUTION. ALSO INDEXES PRIOR
VOLUMES IN THE SERIES AND CLASSIFIES SPECIFIC ARTICLES
UNDER GENERAL HEADINGS.

2017 US LIBRARY OF CONGRESS
NETHERLANDS EAST INDIES.
WASHINGTON: LIBRARY OF CONGRESS, 1945, 200 PP.
ANNOTATED LISTING OF APPROXIMATELY 1,500 BOOKS PUBLISHED
AFTER 1930 AND PERIODICALS AFTER 1932 IN DUTCH AND ENGLISH
PERTINENT TO THE NETHERLANDS EAST INDIES. INCLUDES GEOG-
RAPHY, GOVERNMENT, ECONOMICS, LANGUAGES, SOCIAL CONDITIONS,
CULTURE, HISTORY, LAW, EDUCATION, AND HEALTH PROBLEMS.

2018 US LIBRARY OF CONGRESS
FREEDOM OF INFORMATION: SELECTIVE REPORT ON RECENT WRITINGS.
WASHINGTON: LIBRARY OF CONGRESS, 1949, 153 PP.
COMPILES AND SUMMARIZES BOOKS, ARTICLES, PAMPHLETS, ETC.
DEALING WITH FREE EXPRESSION AND INFORMATION. PRESENTS ATTI-
TUDES ON THE INTERNATIONAL LEVEL, AMERICAN COMMENT, AND
COMMENT FROM OTHER COUNTRIES. DEALS WITH PROPAGANDA, CENSOR-
SHIP, PRESSURE GROUPS, MASS MEDIA, AND TOTALITARIANISM.
PROVIDES AN INDEX.

2019 US LIBRARY OF CONGRESS
INDEX TO LATIN AMERICAN LEGISLATION: 1950-1960 (2 VOLS.)
WASHINGTON: LIBRARY OF CONGRESS, 1960, 1474 PP.
COMPREHENSIVE AND TOPICALLY ARRANGED INDEX TO IMPORTANT
AND RELEVANT LEGISLATION ENACTED BY LATIN AMERICAN GOVERN-
MENTS; INDEXES 30,000 ITEMS. INCLUDES "MATTERS
OF GENERAL INTEREST, BASIC CODES, AND ORGANIC LAWS WITH
THEIR AMENDMENTS"; EXCLUDES PRIVATE LEGISLATION, CONFERRING
OF HONORS, APPOINTMENTS, DISMISSALS, ETC.

2020 US LIBRARY OF CONGRESS
INTERNAL SECURITY AND SUBVERSION.
WASHINGTON: LIBRARY OF CONGRESS, 1965, 675 PP.
STUDIES CASES OF SUBVERSION AS HANDLED UNDER STATE LAWS
IN EFFECT AS OF 1964. INCLUDES CASES OF ANARCHY, SEDITION,
REGISTRATION, EXCLUSION FROM ELECTIVE PROCESS, SCREEN OF
CIVIL SERVICE WORKERS, AND TEACHER LOYALTY.

2021 US OFFICE ECONOMIC OPPORTUNITY
CATALOG OF FEDERAL PROGRAMS FOR INDIVIDUAL AND COMMUNITY
IMPROVEMENT.
WASHINGTON: US GOVERNMENT, 1965, 414 PP.
DESCRIBES NATURE AND PURPOSES OF GOVERNMENTAL PRO-
GRAMS TO HELP INDIVIDUALS AND COMMUNITIES. NOTES MAJOR
ELIGIBILITY REQUIREMENTS AND HOW TO APPLY. LISTS PRINTED
MATERIAL AVAILABLE ON PROGRAM. NOTES AUTHORIZING LEGISLATION
AND ADMINISTERING AGENCY.

2022 US PRES COMN CRIME IN DC
REPORT OF THE US PRESIDENT'S COMMISSION ON CRIME IN THE
DISTRICT OF COLUMBIA.
WASHINGTON: US GOVERNMENT, 1966, 1041 PP.
DETAILED ANALYSIS OF CRIME SITUATION EMPHASIZES
ADMINISTRATION OF JUSTICE, SENTENCING, PRETRIAL RELEASE, AND
SOCIO-ECONOMIC ROOTS OF CRIME. ALSO DISCUSSES PROBATION,
PAROLE, POLICE INTERROGATION, AND CRIMINAL CODE REVISION.

2023 US PRES COMN REGIS AND VOTING
REPORT ON REGISTRATION AND VOTING (PAMPHLET)
WASHINGTON: US GOVERNMENT, 1963, 69 PP.
INVESTIGATES REASONS FOR LOW VOTER TURNOUT BY ANALYZING
ELECTION LAWS AND PRACTICES IN 50 STATES. FINDS THAT ONE
THIRD OF ADULTS DO NOT VOTE IN PRESIDENTIAL ELECTIONS.
REASONS ARE PSYCHOLOGICAL AND LEGAL. SUGGESTS BETTER
EDUCATION IN CITIZENSHIP, COMPREHENSIVE REGISTRATION
CAMPAIGNS, STRONG TWO-PARTY SYSTEM, AND 21 STANDARDS TO
INSURE RIGHT TO VOTE.

2024 US PRES CONF ADMIN PROCEDURE
REPORT (PAMPHLET)
WASHINGTON DC: CONF. ADMIN. PROCEDURE, 1953, 94 PP.
RECOMMENDATIONS TO PRESIDENT ON WAYS TO REDUCE DELAY, EX-
PENSE, AND VOLUME OF RECORDS IN ADJUDICATORY PROCEEDINGS OF
GOVERNMENT AGENCIES, INCLUDING JUDICIAL CONFERENCE, CIVIL
SERVICE COMMISSION, GENERAL SERVICES ADMINISTRATION, AND ALL
GOVERNMENTAL AGENCIES.

2025 US PRES TASK FORCE ADMIN JUS
TASK FORCE REPORT: THE COURTS.
WASH DC: US PRES COMN LAW ENFORCE, 1967, 178 PP.
INVESTIGATES AREAS OF US COURT SYSTEM MOST IN NEED OF RE-
FORM: DISPOSITION WITHOUT TRIAL, SENTENCING, CAPITAL PUNISH-
MENT, LOWER COURTS, COURT PROCEEDINGS, COUNSEL FOR ACCUSED,
OFFICERS OF JUSTICE, ADMINISTRATION OF COURTS, LAW REFORM,
AND LIMITS OF EFFECTIVE LAW ENFORCEMENT. CONTAINS BACKGROUND
AND ANALYSIS PAPERS WRITTEN BY EXPERTS.

2026 US SENATE COMM AERO SPACE SCI
DOCUMENTS ON INTERNATIONAL ASPECTS OF EXPLORATION AND USE OF
OUTER SPACE, 1954-62: STAFF REPORT FOR COMM AERON SPACE SCI.
WASHINGTON: US GOVERNMENT, 1963, 407 PP.
EXERPTS OF OFFICIAL DOCUMENTS CONCERNING POLICY VIEWS OF
US AND RUSSIA ON SPACE MATTERS. CONTAINS ANALYSIS BY US
OFFICIALS. COVERS HISTORICAL EVENTS OF BOTH NATIONS, STATE-
MENTS BY THEIR LEADERS, AND ALL LEGISLATION CONCERNING OUTER
SPACE LAWS AND PROJECTS.

2027 US SENATE COMM AERO SPACE SCI
US INTERNATIONAL SPACE PROGRAMS, 1959-65: STAFF REPORT FOR
COMM ON AERONAUTICAL AND SPACE SCIENCES.
WASHINGTON: US GOVERNMENT, 1965, 575 PP.
COMPILATION OF EXECUIVEE AGREEMENTS, LETTERS, MEMORANDA
OF UNDERSTANDING, AND ALL INTERNATIONAL ARRANGEMENTS
CONCERNING OUTER SPACE, FROM 1959-65. AIMS TO REVEAL SCOPE
OF US SPACE EFFORTS AND METHODS OF ACHIEVING INTERNATIONAL
COOPERATION DOCUMENTS ARE ARRANGED ALPHABETICALLY BY
COUNTRY OF ORIGIN.

2028 US SENATE COMM AERO SPACE SCI
SOVIET SPACE PROGRAMS, 1962-65: GOALS AND PURPOSES, ACHIEVE-
MENTS, PLANS, AND INTERNATIONAL IMPLICATIONS.
WASHINGTON: US GOVERNMENT, 1966, 920 PP.
STAFF REPORT PREPARED FOR SENATE COMMITTEE ON AERONAUTI-
CAL AND SPACE SCIENCES. SUMMARIZES SOVIET SPACE PROGRAMS,
AND ANALYZES INTERNATIONAL, POLITICAL, AND LEGAL IMPLI-
CATIONS. DISCUSSES SOVIET GOALS, WESTERN PROJECTIONS OF FU-
TURE SOVIET SPACE PLANS AND CAPABILITIES, AND SOVIET ATTI-
TUDE TOWARD INTERNATIONAL SPACE COOPERATION.

2029 US SENATE COMM ON FOREIGN REL
REVIEW OF THE UNITED NATIONS CHARTER: A COLLECTION OF
DOCUMENTS.
WASHINGTON: US GOVERNMENT, 1954, 895 PP.
DOCUMENTS USED BY SENATE SUBCOMMITTEE ON THE UNITED
NATIONS CHARTER IN CONSIDERATION OF CONDITIONS OF ITS
RENEWAL. INCLUDES TEXT OF BASIC INTERNATIONAL INSTRUMENTS
RELATED TO ADOPTION OF CHARTER; DOCUMENTARY HISTORY OF LEG-
ISLATION SINCE 1943 WHICH RELATES TO CHARTER; ILLUSTRATIVE
SELECTION OF OFFICIAL STUDIES, ACTS, ETC., RELATED TO RE-
NEWAL AND UN MEMBERS' VIEWS ON CHARTER REVIEW.

2030 US SENATE COMM ON FOREIGN REL
ASIAN DEVELOPMENT BANK ACT.
WASHINGTON: US GOVERNMENT, 1966, 138 PP.
HEARINGS BEFORE COMMITTEE ON FOREIGN RELATIONS ON ASIAN
DEVELOPMENT BANK ACT. INCLUDES TESTIMONY BY EUGENE BLACK,
PRESIDENTIAL ADVISER ON SOUTHEASTERN ASIAN ECONOMIC AND
SOCIAL DEVELOPMENT.

2031 US SENATE COMM ON FOREIGN REL
CONSULAR CONVENTION WITH THE SOVIET UNION.
WASHINGTON: US GOVERNMENT, 1967, 374 PP.
HEARINGS BEFORE SENATE COMMITTEE ON FOREIGN RELATIONS
JANUARY AND FEBRUARY, 1967, JW FULLBRIGHT PRESIDING. DEAN
RUSK AND NICHOLAS KATZENBACH TESTIFY IN FAVOR OF RATIFI-
CATION OF CONSULAR CONVENTION WITH USSR. BOTH CLAIM THAT
SECURITY WOULD NOT BE THREATENED BY ESTABLISHMENT OF ADDI-
TIONAL SOVIET CONSULATES. SEVERAL LOBBYISTS EXPRESS OPPOSI-
TION TO CONVENTION ON GROUNDS OF ITS "THREAT TO LIBERTY."

2032 US SENATE COMM ON FOREIGN REL
TREATY ON OUTER SPACE.
WASHINGTON: US GOVERNMENT, 1967, 162 PP.
HEARINGS BEFORE SENATE COMMITTEE ON FOREIGN RELATIONS,
HEADED BY J. W. FULLBRIGHT, TO CONSIDER TREATY ON OUTER SPACE
SIGNED BY US AND 59 OTHER COUNTRIES INCLUDING USSR ON
JANUARY 27, 1967. SECRETARY OF STATE RUSK, CYRUS R. VANCE,
GENERAL EARLE WHEELER, AND AMBASSADOR TO UN ARTHUR GOLDBERG
TESTIFIED.

2033 US SENATE COMM ON FOREIGN REL
A SELECT CHRONOLOGY AND BACKGROUND DOCUMENTS RELATING TO THE

MIDDLE EAST.
WASHINGTON: US GOVERNMENT, 1967, 151 PP.
CONTAINS SUMMARY OF EVENTS IN MIDDLE EAST FROM 1946
THROUGH 1967 AND TEXTS OF BACKGROUND DOCUMENTS ON MIDDLE
EAST INCLUDING TRUMAN DOCTRINE, PLAN FOR PARTITION OF
PALESTINE, EGYPTION-ISRAELI ARMISTICE AGREEMENT, BAGHDAD
PACT, EISENHOWER DOCTRINE, AND UN DEBATES ON CRISIS UP TO
MAY 29, 1967.

2034 US SENATE COMM ON FOREIGN REL
INTER-AMERICAN DEVELOPMENT BANK ACT AMENDMENT.
WASHINGTON: US GOVERNMENT, 1967, 143 PP.
HEARINGS BEFORE SENATE COMMITTEE ON FOREIGN RELATIONS,
HEADED BY J. W. FULBRIGHT ON BILL TO AMEND INTER-AMERICAN
DEVELOPMENT BANK ACT. PURPOSE OF AMENDMENT IS TO AUTHORIZE
US PARTICIPATION IN INCREASING FUNDS AVAILABLE TO BANK.

2035 US SENATE COMM ON FOREIGN REL
UNITED STATES ARMAMENT AND DISARMAMENT PROBLEMS.
WASHINGTON: US GOVERNMENT, 1967, 181 PP.
HEARINGS BEFORE SUBCOMMITTEE ON DISARMAMENT OF COMMITTEE
ON FOREIGN RELATIONS HEADED BY ALBERT GORE. INCLUDES DIS-
CUSSION OF STATUS OF DEVELOPMENT OF BALLISTIC AND ANTI-
BALLISTIC SYSTEMS IN US AND BRIEFING ON NONPROLIFERATION
TREATY, DEPLOYMENT OF NIKE X ANTI-BALLISTIC MISSLE SYSTEM,
ARMS SALES, AND OTHER DISARMAMENT AND ARMANENT PROBLEMS.

2036 US SENATE COMM ON FOREIGN REL
FOREIGN ASSISTANCE ACT OF 1967.
WASHINGTON: US GOVERNMENT, 1967, 393 PP.
HEARINGS BEFORE SENATE COMMITTEE ON FOREIGN RELATIONS ON
FOREIGN ASSISTANCE BILL OF 1967. WITNESSES INCLUDE SECRETARY
OF DEFENSE ROBERT MC NAMARA, SECRETARY OF STATE DEAN RUSK,
AND WILLIAM E. MORAN OF INTERNATIONAL ECONOMIC POLICY ASSO-
CIATION. COVERS ALL AREAS OF FOREIGN AID IN SEVERAL PARTS OF
WORLD.

2037 US SENATE COMM ON FOREIGN REL
SURVEY OF THE ALLIANCE FOR PROGRESS: FOREIGN TRADE POLICIES
(PAMPHLET)
WASHINGTON: US GOVERNMENT, 1967, 28 PP.
STUDY OF RELATIONSHIP BETWEEN US FOREIGN TRADE POLICY AND
LATIN AMERICAN DEVELOPMENT, PREPARED AT REQUEST OF
SUBCOMMITTEE ON AMERICAN REPUBLICS AFFAIRS OF COMMITTEE ON
FOREIGN RELATIONS. DISCUSSES EFFORTS OF GATT AND UN TO COPE
WITH TRADE PROBLEMS, LAFTA DEFICIENCIES, TARIFF PREFERENCES,
LATIN AMERICAN COMMON MARKET, AND INTERNATIONAL COMMODITY
AGREEMENTS.

2038 US SENATE COMM ON FOREIGN REL
USIA FOREIGN SERVICE PERSONNEL SYSTEM.
WASHINGTON: US GOVERNMENT, 1967, 94 PP.
HEARINGS BEFORE AD HOC SUBCOMMITTEE ON A FOREIGN SERVICE
INFORMATION OFFICER CORPS OF COMMITTEE ON FOREIGN RELATIONS
ON TWO BILLS TO FORM FOREIGN SERVICE INFORMATION OFFICER
CORPS TO GIVE USIA OFFICERS STATUS OF DIPLOMATIC PERSONNEL.

2039 US SENATE COMM ON JUDICIARY
CIVIL RIGHTS - 1957.
WASHINGTON: GOVT PR OFFICE, 1957, 930 PP.
RECORD OF HEARINGS BEFORE SENATE JUDICIARY COMMITTEE ON
CIVIL RIGHTS LEGISLATION OF 1957, INCLUDING TEXT OF BILLS,
TESTIMONY OF WITNESSES, AND DOCUMENTS.

2040 US SENATE COMM ON JUDICIARY
HEARING BEFORE SUBCOMMITTEE ON COMMITTEE OF JUDICIARY,
UNITED STATES SENATE: S. J. RES. 3.
WASHINGTON: GOVT PR OFFICE, 1957, 480 PP.
JUNE 25, 1957 HEARINGS ON PROPOSED AMENDMENT TO CONSTITU-
TION RELATING TO LEGAL EFFECT OF CERTAIN TREATIES AND OTHER
INTERNATIONAL AGREEMENTS. PRESENT WERE SENATORS KEFAUVER,
HENNINGS, DIRKSEN.

2041 US SENATE COMM ON JUDICIARY
LIMITATION OF APPELLATE JURISDICTION OF THE SUPREME COURT.
WASHINGTON: US GOVERNMENT, 1957, 320 PP.
REPORTS FINDINGS OF COMMITTEE REVIEWING PROPOSED BILL,
S. 2646, LIMITING APPELLATE JURISDICTION OF SUPREME COURT
IN CASES INVOLVING COMMITTEES OF CONGRESS, ACTIONS BY
BRANCHES OF FEDERAL GOVERNMENT AFFECTING SECURITY, AND
REGULATIONS TO CONTROL SUBVERSIVES.

2042 US SENATE COMM ON JUDICIARY
EXECUTIVE PRIVILEGE.
WASHINGTON: GOVT PR OFFICE, 1959, 365 PP.
HEARINGS BEFORE SENATE SUBCOMMITTEE ON CONSTITUTIONAL
RIGHTS OF COMMITTEE ON JUDICIARY HEADED BY THOMAS C. HEN-
NINGS, JR., ON EXECUTIVE PRIVILEGE OF WITHHOLDING INFOR-
MATION FROM CONGRESS AND PUBLIC.

2043 US SENATE COMM ON JUDICIARY
FEDERAL ADMINISTRATIVE PROCEDURE.
WASHINGTON: GOVT PR OFFICE, 1960, 343 PP.
RECORD OF HEARINGS BEFORE SUBCOMMITTEE ON ADMINISTRATIVE
PRACTICE AND PROCEDURE ON PROCEDURAL PROBLEMS IN ADMINIS-
TRATIVE AGENCIES. INCLUDES TESTIMONY OF WITNESSES AND

EXHIBITS.

2044 US SENATE COMM ON JUDICIARY
ADMINISTRATIVE PROCEDURE LEGISLATION.
WASHINGTON: GOVT PR OFFICE, 1960, 429 PP.
RECORD OF HEARINGS BEFORE SUBCOMMITTEE ON ADMINISTRATIVE
PRACTICE AND PROCEDURE, ON LEGISLATION TO ESTABLISH OFFICE
OF FEDERAL ADMINISTRATIVE PRACTICE AND STANDARDS OF CONDUCT
FOR AGENCY HEARING PROCEEDINGS. INCLUDES TESTIMONY OF WIT-
NESSES AND EXHIBITS.

2045 US SENATE COMM ON JUDICIARY
LEGISLATION TO STRENGTHEN PENALTIES UNDER THE ANTITRUST LAWS
(PAMPHLET)
WASHINGTON: GOVT PR OFFICE, 1962, 218 PP.
COLLECTION OF STATEMENTS AND WITNESS TESTIMONIES FROM IN-
VESTIGATION OF SUBCOMMITTEE ON ANTITRUST AND MONOPOLY OF
SENATE COMMITTEE ON JUDICIARY INTO EXISTING MONOPOLY LAW
AND PROPOSED CHANGES.

2046 US SENATE COMM ON JUDICIARY
CONSTITUTIONAL RIGHTS OF MILITARY PERSONNEL.
WASHINGTON: US GOVERNMENT, 1962, 967 PP.
COLLECTION OF STATEMENTS MADE BY PUBLIC OFFICIALS BEFORE
SUBCOMMITTEE ON CONSTITUTIONAL RIGHTS ON MILITARY JUSTICE.
HEARINGS WERE INITIATED BECAUSE OF INCREASE IN "UNDESIRABLE
DISCHARGES" THROUGH ADMINISTRATIVE PROCESS, RAISING QUESTION
OF LEGAL SAFEGUARDS.

2047 US SENATE COMM ON JUDICIARY
ADMINISTERED PRICES.
WASHINGTON: GOVT PR OFFICE, 1963, 276 PP.
LEGAL AND ECONOMIC AUTHORITIES DISCUSS APPROPRIATE
PUBLIC POLICY WITH REGARD TO ADMINISTERED PRICES. CASE
STUDIES, CELLER-KEFAUVER ACT, AND ANTI-TRUST LAWS ARE
INCLUDED.

2048 US SENATE COMM ON JUDICIARY
ADMINISTRATIVE CONFERENCE OF THE UNITED STATES.
WASHINGTON: GOVT PR OFFICE, 1963, 151 PP.
RECORD OF HEARINGS BEFORE SUBCOMMITTEE ON ADMINISTRATIVE
PRACTICE AND PROCEDURE ON LEGISLATION TO IMPROVE ADMINIS-
TRATION OF FEDERAL AGENCIES THROUGH CREATION OF ADMINISTRA-
TIVE CONFERENCE OF US. INCLUDES TESTIMONY OF WITNESSES.

2049 US SENATE COMM ON JUDICIARY
US PERSONNEL SECURITY PRACTICES.
NEW YORK: SCHOCKEN BOOKS, 1963, 600 PP.
REPORTS HEARINGS ON ADMINISTRATION OF INTERNAL SECURITY
ACT AND OTHER SECURITY LAWS HELD BY SENATE. SPECIFIC CONCERN
IS WITH ADMINISTRATION OF DEPARTMENTAL AND AGENCY RULES
APPLYING TO PERSONNEL HIRING AND EVALUATION.

2050 US SENATE COMM ON JUDICIARY
CASTRO'S NETWORK IN THE UNITED STATES.
WASHINGTON: US GOVERNMENT, 1963, 635 PP.
HEARINGS, BEFORE SUBCOMMITTEE TO INVESTIGATE ADMINISTRA-
TION OF INTERNAL SECURITY ACT AND OTHER INTERNAL SECURITY
LAWS OF COMMITTEE ON JUDICIARY, ON CASTRO'S NETWORK IN US
OR FAIR PLAY TO CUBA COMMITTEE. CONTAINS TESTIMONY OF
VINCENT LEE, JOHN A. ROSSEN, BORIS EVANS ROSS, RICHARD
CRILEY, ROBERT TABER, JACOB ROSSEN, LYLE STUART, SIDNEY
LENS, AND WALDO FRANK.

2051 US SENATE COMM ON JUDICIARY
PACIFICA FOUNDATION.
WASHINGTON: US GOVERNMENT, 1963, 224 PP.
HEARINGS, BEFORE SUBCOMMITTEE TO INVESTIGATE ADMINISTRA-
TION OF INTERNAL SECURITY ACT AND OTHER INTERNAL SECURITY
LAWS OF COMMITTEE, ON JUDICIARY, ON ACTIVITIES OF PACIFICA
FOUNDATION AND ITS RADIO STATIONS. INCLUDES TESTIMONY OF
PETER ODEGARD, JOSEPH J. BINNS, PAULINE SCHINDLER, DOROTHY
HEALEY, AND TREVOR K. THOMAS

2052 US SENATE COMM ON JUDICIARY
HEARINGS BEFORE SUBCOMMITTEE ON ANTITRUST AND MONOPOLY:
ECONOMIC CONCENTRATION VOLUMES 1-5 JULY 1964-SEPT 1966.
WASHINGTON: US GOVERNMENT, 1964, 2163 PP.
TESTIMONIES FOR AND AGAINST EXISTING OR VIRTUAL
MONOPOLIES IN US. GIVES OVER-ALL ASPECTS. COVERS MERGERS
AND OTHER LEGAL FORMS OF CONCENTRATING, AS WELL AS NEW
INNOVATIONS. DISCUSSES EFFICIENCY OF CONCENTRATING AS
OPPOSED TO DIVIDING AND GIVES REPORTS OF COMPANIES THAT
HAVE DONE BOTH.

2053 US SENATE COMM ON JUDICIARY
CIVIL RIGHTS - THE PRESIDENT'S PROGRAM.
WASHINGTON: US GOVERNMENT, 1964, 483 PP.
SENATE HEARINGS ON CIVIL RIGHTS LEGISLATION, 1963, IN-
CLUDING TESTIMONY OF WITNESSES. BILLS BEING CONSIDERED,
NEWSPAPER EDITORIALS, COURT PROCEEDINGS, AND LETTERS.

2054 US SENATE COMM ON JUDICIARY
ADMINISTRATIVE PROCEDURE ACT.
WASHINGTON: GOVT PR OFFICE, 1964, 693 PP.
RECORD OF HEARINGS BEFORE SUBCOMMITTEE ON ADMINISTRATIVE

PRACTICE AND PROCEDURE ON AMENDMENT TO ADMINISTRATIVE PRO-
CEDURE ACT. INCLUDES TESTIMONY OF WITNESSES, TEXTS OF BILLS
UNDER DISCUSSION, AND EXHIBITS.

2055 US SENATE COMM ON JUDICIARY
HEARINGS BEFORE SUBCOMMITTEE ON ADMINISTRATIVE PRACTICE AND
PROCEDURE ABOUT ADMINISTRATIVE PROCEDURE ACT 1965.
WASHINGTON: GOVT PR OFFICE, 1965, 572 PP.
TRANSCRIPT OF HEARINGS IN MAY, 1965, ON FOUR BILLS TO
AMEND THE ADMINISTRATIVE PROCEDURE ACT OF 1946. INCLUDES
TEXTS OF BILLS, STATEMENTS OF WITNESSES, AND COMMENTS
OF FEDERAL AGENCIES, BAR ASSOCIATIONS, AND VARIOUS COM-
PANIES. BILLS CONCERN IMPROVING RULES GOVERNING PROCEDURES
BEFORE FEDERAL ADMINISTRATIVE AGENCIES, FREEDOM OF INFORMA-
TION ABOUT GOVERNMENT ACTIVITIES, ATTORNEYS' PRACTICE.

2056 US SENATE COMM ON JUDICIARY
ANTITRUST EXEMPTIONS FOR AGREEMENTS RELATING TO BALANCE OF
PAYMENTS.
WASHINGTON: US GOVERNMENT, 1965, 248 PP.
REPORT OF HEARINGS ON H RES 40, AN ACT TO PROVIDE FOR
EXEMPTIONS FROM ANTITRUST LAWS FOR COMPANIES IN INTERNATION-
AL TRADING TO ASSIST US IN MAINTAINING FAVORABLE BALANCE OF
PAYMENTS. DEBATES WHETHER ANTI-MONOPOLY LAWS OR INTERNATION-
AL MONETARY POSITION IS MORE INPORTANT.

2057 US SENATE COMM ON JUDICIARY
HEARINGS ON FREE PRESS AND FAIR TRIAL (2 VOLS.)
WASHINGTON: GOVT PR OFFICE, 1966, 762 PP.
REPORT ON RELATIONSHIP BETWEEN CONSTITUTIONAL RIGHT OF
FREE PRESS AND GUARANTEES OF IMPARTIAL TRIAL RELATING TO
BILL PROPOSED TO PROHIBIT PUBLISHING INFORMATION NOT PROPER-
LY ADMITTED IN CRIMINAL CASES.

2058 US SENATE COMM ON JUDICIARY
SCHOOL PRAYER.
WASHINGTON: US GOVERNMENT, 1966, 884 PP.
HEARINGS BEFORE SUBCOMMITTEE ON CONSTITUTIONAL
AMENDMENTS, OF COMMITTEE ON THE JUDICIARY, US SENATE.
SESSIONS DEAL WITH PRAYER IN PUBLIC SCHOOLS.

2059 US SENATE COMM ON POST OFFICE
TO PROVIDE FOR AN EFFECTIVE SYSTEM OF PERSONNEL
ADMINISTRATION.
WASHINGTON: US GOVERNMENT, 1959, 140 PP.
HEARINGS BEFORE SUBCOMMITTEE ON CIVIL SERVICE OF
COMMITTEE ON POST OFFICE AND CIVIL SERVICE OF US SENATE
HEADED BY RALPH YARBOROUGH, ON BILL S. 1638 PROVIDING FOR
EFFECTIVE SYSTEM OF PERSONNEL ADMINISTRATION FOR EXECUTIVE
BRANCH BY ESTABLISHING AGENCIES TO CONTROL MANAGEMENT OF
DEPARTMENTS.

2060 US SENATE COMM POST OFFICE
TO PROVIDE AN EFFECTIVE SYSTEM OF PERSONNEL ADMINISTRATION.
WASHINGTON: US GOVERNMENT, 1958, 195 PP.
RECORD OF HEARINGS BEFORE SENATE POST OFFICE AND CIVIL
SERVICE COMMITTEE ON BILL TO PROVIDE EFFECTIVE SYSTEM OF
PERSONNEL FOR EXECUTIVE BRANCH. INCLUDES REPORTS AND
TESTIMONY.

2061 US SENATE SPEC COMM POLIT ACT
REPORT OF SPECIAL COMMITTEE TO INVESTIGATE POLITICAL ACTIVI-
TIES, LOBBYING, AND CAMPAIGN CONTRIBUTIONS.
WASHINGTON: GOVT PR OFFICE, 1957, 339 PP.
ANALYZES ATTEMPTS BY PRESSURE GROUPS TO INFLUENCE LEGIS-
LATION AND VOTING BY LOBBYING AND AIDING ELECTORAL CAMPAIGN
FUNDS DISCUSSES SPECIFIC CASES OF LEGISLATIVE INFLUENCE
EXAMINES EXISTING AND PROPOSED LEGISLATION TO REGULATE OR
PREVENT THESE POLITICAL ACTIVITIES.

2062 US SUPERINTENDENT OF DOCUMENTS
EDUCATION (PRICE LIST 31)
WASHINGTON: GOVT PR OFFICE.
A SERIES PUBLICATION OF US GOVERNMENT PUBLICATIONS CUR-
RENTLY AVAILABLE FOR SALE. INCLUDES MATERIALS ON TOPICS SUCH
AS CIVIL DEFENSE, CIVIL RIGHTS AND EDUCATION, SECONDARY AND
HIGHER EDUCATION, FEDERAL AID, FOREIGN EDUCATION, DEBATES,
SCHOOL FINANCE, AND NATIONAL SCIENCE FOUNDATION PUBLICA-
TIONS. ENTRIES LISTED BY SUBJECT. 53 EDITIONS TO DATE. CUR-
RENT EDITION COVERS MATERIALS FROM 1958 THROUGH 1966.

2063 US SUPERINTENDENT OF DOCUMENTS
POLITICAL SCIENCE: GOVERNMENT, CRIME, DISTRICT OF COLUMBIA
(PRICE LIST 54)
WASHINGTON: GOVT PR OFFICE.
SERIES PUBLICATION LISTING US GOVERNMENT DOCUMENTS CUR-
RENTLY AVAILABLE FOR SALE. ITEMS ARRANGED BY SUBJECT COVER
TOPICS SUCH AS STATE DEPARTMENT, JUSTICE DEPARTMENT, CIVIL
PROCEDURE, CONSTITUTIONAL RIGHTS, GOVERNMENT ORGANIZATION,
SUPREME COURT, VOTING, GOVERNMENT EMPLOYEES, AND CRIME AND
CRIMINAL PROCEDURE. ITEMS ARE ARRANGED BY SUBJECT. 44 EDI-
TIONS TO DATE. CURRENT ISSUE CONTAINS 1959-66 SOURCES.

2064 US TARIFF COMMISSION
THE TARIFF: A BIBLIOGRAPHY: A SELECT LIST OF REFERENCES.
WASHINGTON: US GOVERNMENT, 1934, 980 PP.

ALPHABETICAL LISTING OF 6,500 ITEMS, BOOKS, PAMPHLETS,
AND PERIODICALS AVAILABLE IN US. INCLUDES REFERENCE TO
HISTORY, STATE, FEDERAL, AND INTERNATIONAL; THEORY AND
POLICY; PRACTICE; TREATIES, ADMINISTRATION; AND ECONOMIC
IMPLICATIONS OF TARIFF LAWS. CONTAINS AUTHOR AND SUBJECT
INDEXES. INCLUDES ANNOTATIONS WHERE WORK IS NOTABLE OR
TITLE OBSCURE.

2065 UTLEY T.E.
OCCASION FOR OMBUDSMAN.
LONDON: CHRISTOPHER JOHNSON PUBL, 1961, 160 PP.
STUDY OF INSTITUTION OF OMBUDSMEN AND NEED IN BRITAIN
FOR RECOGNIZED MEANS OF APPEALING GOVERNMENTAL ACTIONS
INJURIOUS TO PRIVATE CITIZENS. EXAMPLES OF CASES DISCUSSED
ALONG WITH PROPOSALS FOR BRITISH OMBUDSMEN.

2066 VALENZUELA G.E. ED.
BIBLIOGRAFIA GUATEMALTECA, Y CATALOG GENERAL DE LIBROS,
FOLLETOS, PERIODICOS, REVISTAS, ETC. (10 VOLS.)
GUATEMALA CITY: TIPOGRAFIA NACIONAL, 1961
AN ANNOTATED BIBLIOGRAPHY LISTING ALL TYPES OF MATERIALS
PUBLISHED IN GUATEMALA BETWEEN 1821 AND 1960. ENTRIES
ARRANGED CHRONOLOGICALLY. PERIOD FROM 1960 TO 1821. COVERED
BY LA IMPRINTA EN GUATEMALA BY JOSE TORBIO MEDINA IN-
CLUDED AS VOLS. I AND II OF SERIES.

2067 VAN CAENEGEM R.C.
ROYAL WRITS IN ENGLAND FROM THE CONQUEST TO GLANVILL.
LONDON: BERNARD QUARITCH, 1959, 556 PP.
DISCUSSES DEVELOPMENT OF ROYAL WRITS IN ENGLISH LAW BE-
TWEEN 1066 AND 1189. EXAMINES COURT PROCESSES AND ASSIMILA-
TION OF ROYAL WRIT INTO BODY OF COMMON LAW.

2068 VAN DER SPRENKEL S.
"LEGAL INSTITUTIONS IN MANCHU CHINA."
LONDON: ATHLONE PRESS, 1962.
PRELIMINARY SURVEY OF COMPLEX OF LEGAL AND QUASI-LEGAL
INSTITUTIONS OF MANCHU PERIOD. DESCRIPTION OF THEORY AND
FUNCTIONS OF GOVERNMENT IN CHINA, STRUCTURE OF ADMINISTRA-
TION. DISCUSSES CODIFIED LAW, JUDICIAL PROCEDURE, JURISDIC-
TIONAL ASPECTS OF THE "TSU" AND GUILD SYSTEM, LOCAL AND
CUSTOMARY JURISDICTION. CONCLUDING CHAPTER ON LAW AS ETHI-
CAL FOUNDATION OF SOCIETY. BIBLIOGRAPHY INCLUDED.

2069 VAN SLYCK P.
PEACE: THE CONTROL OF NATIONAL POWER.
BOSTON: BEACON PRESS, 1963, 186 PP., LC#63-21565.
SUBTITLED "A GUIDE FOR THE CONCERNED CITIZEN ON PROBLEMS
OF DISARMAMENT AND STRENGTHENING OF THE UNITED NATIONS."
ANALYZES MAJOR ISSUES IN WORLD AFFAIRS AND PROPOSALS FOR
RESTRUCTURING PRESENT WORLD. ISSUES INCLUDE CUBAN MISSILE
CRISIS, INTERNATIONAL LAW AND CONTROL OF FORCE, FINANCING
PEACE, PROBLEMS OF WORLD AUTHORITY, ROLE OF UN, AND PROB-
LEMS OF AND PROSPECTS FOR ARMS CONTROL.

2070 VANCE H.L., CLAGETT H.L.
GUIDE TO THE LAW AND LEGAL LITERATURE OF MEXICO.
WASHINGTON: LIBRARY OF CONGRESS, 1945, 269 PP.
PART OF SERIES SPONSORED BY LAW LIBRARY OF CONGRESS. SUR-
VEY OF DEVELOPMENT OF LEGAL THEORY AND PRACTICE AND LITERA-
TURE OF LAW. REVIEWS BIBLIOGRAPHIC ADVANCES, COLLECTIONS,
PERIODICALS, DICTIONARIES. SECTIONS ON PHILOSOPHY OF LAW,
COMMERCIAL, CRIMINAL AND INTERNATIONAL LAW, JUDICIAL SYSTEM,
CIVIL AND CRIMINAL PROCEDURE. INDEX OF AUTHORS INCLUDED.

2071 VANDENBOSCH A., HOGAN W.N.
THE UN: BACKGROUND, ORGANIZATION, FUNCTIONS, ACTIVITIES.
NEW YORK: MCGRAW HILL, 1952, 456 PP.
OUTLINES COMPLEX OF FACTORS INVOLVED IN UN PROCEDURES AND
PRACTISES. EMPHASIZES THAT FIRST PURPOSE OF UN SYSTEM IS
COLLECTIVE SECURITY. TRACES DEVELOPMENT OF INTERNATIONAL CO-
OPERATION TO PRESERVE HUMAN RIGHTS AND FUNDAMENTAL FREEDOMS.

2072 VANDERPOL A.
LA DOCTRINE SCOLASTIQUE DU DROIT DE GUERRE.
PARIS: A PEDONE, 1919, 534 PP.
BELIEVES THERE WAS A DOCTRINE OF WAR, FOUNDED ON
CHRISTIAN TRADITION, WHICH BEGAN IN MIDDLE AGES AND LASTED
UNTIL SEVENTEENTH CENTURY. WAR WAS CONSIDERED AN ACT OF
JUSTICE AND A PUNISHMENT OF FOREIGN EVIL-DOERS. DOCUMENTS
THEORY FROM NUMEROUS SOURCES, AND INDICATES SOURCES THAT
CONTRADICT IT. REPRODUCES IMPORTANT CHAPTERS OF AQUINAS,
VICTORIA, AND SUAREZ ON RIGHT OF WAR.

2073 VAUGHN W.P.
"SEPARATE AND UNEQUAL: THE CIVIL RIGHTS ACT OF 1875 AND
DEFEAT OF THE SCHOOL INTEGRATION CLAUSE."
S.W. SOCIAL SCI. QUART., 48 (SEPT. 67), 146-154.
LEGISLATIVE HISTORY OF SENATOR CHARLES SUMNER'S CIVIL
RIGHTS BILL EMPHASIZED DESEGREGATION OF SCHOOLS.BILLS
WAS PASSED IN 1875 WITHOUT EDUCATIONAL PROVISIONS AND WAS
INEFFECTIVE IN CHANGING RACE SITUATION.

2074 VECCHIO G.D.
THE FORMAL BASES OF LAW (TRANS. BY J. LISLE)
BOSTON: BOSTON BOOK CO, 1914, 412 PP.

CLAIMS LAW IS NEITHER FORCE ALONE NOR TRADITIONS DEVEL-
OPING OVER TIME, BUT A FORM OF "RIGHT REASON" WHICH EXISTS
IN THE NATURE OF MAN HIMSELF. LAW IS TO BE WORKED OUT IN
EXPERIENCE OF MAN BY AN INTELLIGENT PREVISION WHICH IS
INHERENT IN REASON OF MAN. COMPARES PREVIOUS NOTIONS OF
NATURAL AND COMMON LAW AND SEEKS TO SET UP LOGICAL FORM
FOR DERIVING LAWS.

2075 VIGNES D.
"L'AUTORITE DES TRAITES INTERNATIONAUX EN DROIT INTERNE."
ETUD. DR. COMP., 23 (1962), 475-85.
EMPLOYS QUANTITATIVE ANALYSIS TO ASCERTAIN FACTORS
NECESSARY TO INSURE APPLICABILITY OF AN INTERNATIONAL TREATY
TO NATIONAL LAW. INCLUDES ANALYSIS OF ARTICLE 55 OF 1958
FRENCH CONSTITUTION.

2076 VILE M.J.C.
CONSTITUTIONALISM AND THE SEPARATION OF POWERS.
LONDON: OXFORD U PR, 1967, 359 PP.
HISTORY AND POLITICAL THEORY OF SEPARATION OF POWERS.
PRESENTS BASIC DOCTRINE AND FOUNDATION OF THE THEORY AND
OF A BALANCED CONSTITUTION. STUDIES MONTESQUIEU AND THE
ENGLISH SYSTEM, ALSO THE DOCTRINE IN FRANCE AS USED BY
PARLIAMENTS AND REPUBLICS. DISCUSSES AMERICAN THEORY AND
DEVELOPMENT OF POLITICAL SCIENCE. ANALYZES BEHAVIORAL
APPROACH, AND OFFERS MODEL OF THEORY OF CONSTITUTIONALISM.

2077 VINER J.
THE INTELLECTUAL HISTORY OF LAISSEZ FAIRE (PAMPHLET)
CHICAGO: U OF CHICAGO LAW SCHOOL, 1961, 24 PP.
DISCUSSES LOGICAL AND RHETORICAL NATURE OF THE ARGUMENTS
BY WHICH EXPONENTS OF LAISSEZ-FAIRE ATTEMPTED TO WIN
CONVERTS TO THEIR CAUSE. OBSERVES ART OF PERSUASION AS USED
IN SOCIAL THOUGHT. STATES THAT DOCTRINE HAS LEGAL, ETHICAL,
AND POLITICAL ASPECTS AS WELL AS ECONOMIC ONES.

2078 VINES K.N.
"THE ROLE OF THE CIRCUIT COURT OF APPEALS IN THE FEDERAL
JUDICIAL PROCESS: A CASE STUDY."
MIDWEST J. OF POLI. SCI., 7 (NOV. 63), 305-319.
A STUDY OF ONE ASPECT OF THE FEDERAL JUDICIAL PROCESS,
THE RELATION OF THE CIRCUIT COURT OF APPEALS TO THE DISTRICT
COURTS. STUDY USES RACE RELATIONS CASES IN THE SOUTH TO SHOW
THE COMPARATIVE DISPOSITION OF CASES FOR OR AGAINST NEGRO
LITIGANTS.

2079 VINES K.N., JACOB H.
STUDIES IN JUDICIAL POLITICS: TULANE STUDIES IN POLITICAL
SCIENCE (VOL. 8)
NEW ORLEANS: TULANE U PR, 1963, 119 PP.
FOUR ESSAYS DESCRIBING POLITICAL FUNCTIONS OF JUDICIARY
AND WAYS IN WHICH OTHER PARTS OF POLITICAL SYSTEM IMPINGE ON
COURTS. FIRST IS HISTORICAL ANALYSIS OF COURTS AS POLITICAL
AGENCIES. THEN, POLITICAL FUNCTIONS OF A STATE SUPREME COURT
(LOUISIANA), FOLLOWED BY POLITICS AND CRIMINAL PROSECUTION
IN NEW ORLEANS, AND SELECTION OF JUDGES IN LOUISIANA.

2080 VINOGRADOFF P.
OUTLINES OF HISTORICAL JURISPRUDENCE (2 VOLS.)
LONDON: OXFORD U PR, 1920, 673 PP.
ANALYSIS OF METHODS AND SCHOOLS OF JURISPRUDENCE,
RELATION OF LAW TO LOGIC, PSYCHOLOGY, SOCIAL SCIENCE, AND
POLITICAL THEORY. DISCUSSION OF ORIGINS OF JURISPRUDENCE IN
PRIMITIVE SOCIETY, FAMILY, CLAN AND TRIBE, PARTICULAR
ASPECTS OF ARYAN CULTURE. SECOND VOLUME BASED ON ANALYSIS
OF GREEK JURISPRUDENCE IN AGE OF DEMOCRACY. BIBLIOGRAPHY
INCLUDED. ITEMS IN GERMAN, FRENCH, LATIN, ETC.

2081 VITTACHI T.
EMERGENCY '58.
LONDON: ANDRE DEUTSCH, 1959.
GIVES BACKGROUND AND CONDITIONS LEADING TO CEYLONESE RACE
RIOTS 1958, RELATING THEM TO LACK OF LEADERSHIP, SOCIAL
STRUCTURE, LEGAL FAILURES, AND COMMUNIST INSTIGATION.

2082 VON GLAHN G.
LAW AMONG NATIONS: AN INTRODUCTION TO PUBLIC INTERNATIONAL
LAW.
NEW YORK: MACMILLAN, 1965, 293 PP., LC#65-10402.
TEXT FOR UNDERGRADUATE INTERNATIONAL LAW COURSES. MOST OF
THE 34 CHAPTERS ARE FOLLOWED BY LISTS OF FROM FIVE TO TEN
SUGGESTED READINGS IN OTHER SOURCES. SOME ALSO LIST CASES.
INCLUDES BOOKS AND PERIODICALS, ALL IN ENGLISH. EXTENSIVE
FOOTNOTES WITH REFERENCE TO OTHER MATERIAL. SUGGESTED READ-
INGS KEPT TO MATERIAL GENERALLY AVAILABLE IN UNDERGRADUATE
LIBRARIES.

2083 VON RENESSE E.A., KRAWIETZ W., BIERKAEMPER C.
UNVOLLENDETE DEMOKRATIEN.
COLOGNE: WESTDEUTSCHER VERLAG, 1965, 429 PP.
EXAMINES FORMS OF ORGANIZATION AND STRUCTURES OF POWER IN
NON-COMMUNIST DEVELOPING NATIONS IN ASIA, AFRICA, AND NEAR
EAST. STUDIES LEGAL AND POLITICAL STATUS OF THESE LANDS
AND THEIR SOCIAL AND ECONOMIC BACKGROUNDS. EMPIRICAL-
INDUCTIVE APPROACH.

2084 VONGLAHN G.
LAW AMONG NATIONS: AN INTRODUCTION TO PUBLIC INTERNATIONAL
LAW.
NEW YORK: MACMILLAN, 1965, 768 PP., $9.95.
PRESENTS ISSUES OF FOLLOWING TOPICS: LAW OF NATIONS, IN-
TERNATIONAL LAW, LAW AND THE INDIVIDUAL, TERRITORIAL QUES-
TIONS, INTERNATIONAL TRANSACTIONS, AND WAR. GIVES FACTS, DE-
CISIONS, AND REASONING OF SIGNIFICANT CASES.

2085 VOSE C.E.
"LITIGATION AS A FORM OF PRESSURE GROUP ACTIVITY" (BMR)"
ANN. ACAD. POL. SOC. SCI., 319 (SEPT. 58), 20-31.
DISCUSSES ROLE OF ORGANIZATIONS IN COURT CASES, DRAWING
ATTENTION TO ACTIVITIES OF AMERICAN LIBERTY LEAGUE, THE
NATIONAL CONSUMERS' LEAGUE, AND NAACP. SHOWS HOW PRACTICES
OF THESE AND OTHER ORGANIZATIONS HAVE LED TO CONTROLS
DESIGNED TO ASSURE INTEGRITY OF JUDICIAL PROCESS. CONTENDS
THAT CONTROLS MUST BE CAUTIOUSLY APPLIED LEST THEY
INTERFERE WITH FREEDOM OF ASSOCIATION AND OTHER RIGHTS.

2086 VOSE C.E.
CAUCASIANS ONLY: THE SUPREME COURT, THE NAACP, AND THE
RESTRICTIVE COVENANT CASES.
BERKELEY: U OF CALIF PR, 1959, 296 PP., LC#59-8758.
DESCRIBES SOCIOLOGICAL AND POLITICAL EVENTS LEADING TO
SUPREME COURT'S DECISION IN "RESTRICTIVE COVENANT CASES."
APPRAISES PRACTICAL RESULT OF RULING. FOCUSES ON ROLE OF
INTEREST GROUPS IN DECISION-MAKING PROCESS AND INTERPLAY
OF HISTORICAL FORCES IN RECENT CONSTITUTIONAL DEVELOPMENT.

2087 WADE E.C.S., PHILLIPS G.G.
CONSTITUTIONAL LAW: AN OUTLINE OF THE LAW AND PRACTICE OF
THE CONSTITUTION.
LONDON: LONGMANS, GREEN & CO, 1950, 535 PP.
EXAMINES THE ENGLISH SYSTEM OF GOVERNMENT. BROAD STUDY
INCLUDES NATURE OF CONSTITUTION AND GENERAL PRINCIPLES FOR
AUTHORITY, PARLIAMENT, EXECUTIVE, AND JUDICIARY; DESCRIBES
GOVERNMENT ON LOCAL LEVEL. CONSIDERS ADMINISTRATIVE LAW,
CITIZEN AND STATE, MILITARY FORCES, AND RELATIONS WITH THE
COMMONWEALTH.

2088 WADE H.W.R.
TOWARDS ADMINISTRATIVE JUSTICE.
ANN ARBOR: U OF MICH PR, 1963, 138 PP., LC#63-9896.
FIVE LECTURES (THE THOMAS M. COOLEY LECTURES), DELIVERED
AT THE UNIVERSITY OF MICHIGAN IN OCTOBER, 1961, BY PROFESSOR
WADE OF OXFORD UNIVERSITY, ATTEMPT TO EXPLAIN SOME OF
PRESENT PROBLEMS OF ADMINISTRATIVE LAW IN BRITAIN AND
BRITISH ATTEMPTS TO SOLVE THEM. MAKES COMPARISONS BETWEEN
AMERICAN AND BRITISH INSTITUTIONS. INCLUDES TABLES OF
STATUTES AND CASES, AND AN INDEX.

2089 WADSWORTH J.J.
THE PRICE OF PEACE.
NEW YORK: FREDERICK PRAEGER, 1962, 127 PP., LC#62-13748.
ANALYSIS OF QUESTION OF DISARMAMENT AND INTERNATIONAL
PEACE. DISCUSSES PAST NEGOTIATIONS AND MILITARY AND POLITI-
CAL FACTORS INVOLVED IN TREATY NEGOTIATIONS AND ARMS
CONTROL.

2090 WAELBROECK M.
"THE APPLICATION OF EEC LAW BY NATIONAL COURTS."
STANFORD LAW REV., 19 (JUNE 67), 1248-1276.
DESCRIBES APPLICATION OF EEC LAW BY LEGAL SYSTEMS OF
MEMBER STATES AND POINTS OUT PROBLEMS OF APPLICATION.
GENERAL PROBLEMS INCLUDE SOURCES AND INTERPRETATION OF EEC
LAW AND CONFLICTS WITH NATIONAL LAWS. MORE SPECIFIC DIFFI-
CULTIES ARE DIRECT APPLICABILITY OF DIRECTIVES AND OF
PROVISIONS IMPOSING OBLIGATIONS ON MEMBER STATES.

2091 WAGNER W.J.
THE FEDERAL STATES AND THEIR JUDICIARY.
HAGUE: MOUTON & CO, 1959, 390 PP.
COMPARATIVE STUDY OF JUDICIARY IN FEDERAL STATES. FOCUSES
UPON DEVELOPMENTS IN US, AUSTRALIA, SWITZERLAND, CANADA,
ARGENTINA, BRAZIL, AND MEXICO. DEVELOPMENTS IN US RECEIVE
MOST ATTENTION DUE TO ITS GREATER INFLUENCE. ILLUMINATES
COMMON PROBLEMS AND COMPARES SOLUTIONS IN DIFFERENT LEGAL
SYSTEMS.

2092 WAINHOUSE D.W.
INTERNATIONAL PEACE OBSERVATION: A HISTORY AND FORECAST.
BALTIMORE: JOHNS HOPKINS PRESS, 1966, 663 PP., LC#66-14376.
CONCERNED WITH THE METHODS AND PROCEDURES THAT HAVE BEEN
TRIED SINCE 1920 TO PREVENT WAR OR LIMIT CONFLICTS. DEALS IN
PARTICULAR WITH THE USE OF THIRD-PARTY ARBITRATION. EMPHASI-
ZES WORK OF THE LEAGUE OF NATIONS, THE UN, AND THE OAS.
EVALUATES AND ANALYZES PAST PRECEDENTS AND MAKES RECOMMENDA-
TIONS FOR THE FUTURE.

2093 WALINE M.
LE CONTROLE JURIDICTIONNEL DE L'ADMINISTRATION.
CAIRO: UNIVERSITE FOUAD 1ER, 1949, 208 PP.
EXAMINES ORGANIZATION OF ADMINISTRATIVE JURISDICTION,
ESPECIALLY "COUNSEIL D'ETATS," IN FRANCE, BELGIUM, AND
EGYPT. CONSIDERS HOW ADMINISTRATIVE ACTS, WHEN BEYOND THEIR

JURISDICTION, CAN BE ANNULLED THROUGH JUDICIAL PROCESSES.

2094 WALKER H.
"THE LEGISLATIVE PROCESS; LAWMAKING IN THE UNITED STATES."
NEW YORK: RONALD PRESS, 1948.
        A DESCRIPTION OF THE MACHINERY SET UP IN THE US FOR DE-
TERMINING AND DECLARING THE WILL OF THE PEOPLE. EVALUATES
DEFECTS WITHIN THE LEGISLATIVE PROCESS AND SUGGESTS A DIREC-
TION FOR FUTURE REFORMS. UNANNOTATED BIBLIOGRAPHY OF AP-
PROXIMATELY 200 BOOKS IN ENGLISH, ARRANGED ALPHABETICALLY BY
AUTHOR WITHIN EACH CHAPTER DIVISION; LISTS WORKS PUBLISHED
FROM 1876 THROUGH 1946.

2095 WALKER H.
"THE INTERNATIONAL LAW OF COMMODITY AGREEMENTS."
LAW CONTEMP. PROBL., 28 (SPRING 63), 392-415.
        DISCUSSES GATT PROVISIONS, OBLIGATIONS TOWARD NON-MEM-
BERS, PRIMARY COMMODITY AND COTTON TEXTILE AGREEMENTS, AND
THE HAVANA CHARTER. SUGGESTS THAT GENERAL AGREEMENTS ARE
FRAMED TO PROMOTE INTERNATIONAL TRADE AND EFFICIENT DISTRI-
BUTION OF PRODUCTION BY REMOVING ARTIFICIAL BARRIERS THAT
PREVENT MARKET DETERMINATION OF FREE TRADE.

2096 WALL E.H.
THE COURT OF JUSTICE IN THE EUROPEAN COMMUNITIES:
JURISDICTION AND PROCEDURE.
LONDON, WASH, DC: BUTTERWORTHS, 1966, 321 PP.
        INTERPRETS RESULTS OF ATTEMPTS BY THE COURT OF JUSTICE
TO RECONCILE LEGAL CONCEPTS THAT DIFFER AMONG MEMBER
COUNTRIES. LOOKS INTO OPERATION OF CONTINENTAL
ADMINISTRATIVE LAW AND ITS CREATION BY EUROPEAN JUDGES.
DESCRIBES ORGANIZATION OF THE COURT, PROCEDURE BEFORE THE
COURT, AND THE GENERAL TASK OF THE COURT.

2097 WALTER P.A.F.
RACE AND CULTURE RELATIONS.
NEW YORK: MCGRAW HILL, 1952, 482 PP., LC#52-6008.
        INTERPRETATION OF RACIAL DISCRIMINATION WITHIN CONTEXTS
OF WORLD CULTURE AND ORGANIC WHOLE OF EMERGING SOCIAL
THEORY. SPECIAL REFERENCES TO SPECIFIC AREAS OF RACE RELA-
TIONS: AFRICA, LATIN AMERICA, JEWS AND ANTI-SEMITISM; ETC.
EACH CHAPTER IS FOLLOWED BY LIST OF SUGGESTED READINGS.

2098 WARD R.E. ED.
A GUIDE TO JAPANESE REFERENCE AND RESEARCH MATERIALS IN THE
FIELD OF POLITICAL SCIENCE.
ANN ARBOR: U OF MICH PR, 1950, 104 PP.
        SELECTED ANNOTATED BIBLIOGRAPHY. REFERS ONLY TO POLITICAL
DEVELOPMENTS SINCE 1868 AND INCLUDES FEW WORKS PUBLISHED
AFTER 1940. ITEMS IN FIELDS OF HISTORY, ECONOMY, METHOD-
OLOGY, AND GENERAL BACKGROUND. GREAT MAJORITY OF WORKS IN
JAPANESE WITH EXCEPTIONS IN FIELD OF METHODOLOGY. NO WORKS
ON FOREIGN RELATIONS INCLUDED. ARRANGED TOPICALLY. CONTAINS
LIST OF PUBLISHERS.

2099 WARD R.E., WATANABE H.
JAPANESE POLITICAL SCIENCE: A GUIDE TO JAPANESE REFERENCE
AND RESEARCH MATERIALS (2ND ED.)
ANN ARBOR: U OF MICH PR, 1961, 210 PP.
        A BRIEFLY ANNOTATED BIBLIOGRAPHY OF 1,759 ITEMS, LARGELY
LIMITED TO JAPANESE TITLES WHICH TREAT POLITICAL SCIENCE
SUBJECTS AND DEVELOPMENTS IN JAPAN SINCE THE MEIJI RESTORA-
TION (1868). FOCUSES UPON RESULTS OF POST-1945 SCHOLARSHIP
WHICH APPEAR IN BOOK RATHER THAN ARTICLE FORM. ARRANGED INTO
27 TOPICAL HEADINGS, AND INDEXED BY AUTHOR AND EDITOR. ANNO-
TATIONS EVALUATE UTILITY OF ITEM FOR REFERENCE PURPOSES.

2100 WASHINGTON S.H. ED.
BIBLIOGRAPHY: LABOR-MANAGEMENT RELATIONS ACT, 1947 AS AMEND-
ED BY LABOR-MANAGEMENT REPORTING AND DISCLOSURE ACT, 1959.
WASHINGTON: NATL LAB REL BOARD, 1966, 117 PP.
        BIBLIOGRAPHICAL LISTING OF MATERIALS PUBLISHED ON LABOR
LAW AND RELATED AREAS FROM 1959-1966. ENTRIES DIVIDED INTO
FIVE MAJOR CLASSIFICATIONS: GOVERNMENT PUBLICATIONS, BOOKS
AND PAMPHLETS, GENERAL AND TRADE PERIODICALS, LEGAL PERIOD-
ICAL ARTICLES, AND CASE COMMENTS-LEGAL PERIODICALS. SUBJECT
INDEX PROVIDED. SUPPLEMENTS PLANNED. CONTAINS 1,075 ENTRIES.

2101 WASSENBERGH H.A.
POST-WAR INTERNATIONAL CIVIL AVIATION POLICY AND THE LAW
OF THE AIR.
THE HAGUE: NIJHOFF, 1957, 180 PP.
        EXAMINES FACTORS GOVERNING DEVELOPMENT OF CIVIL AVIA-
TION, ESPECIALLY SINCE END OF WORLD WAR 2. ANALYZES PROBLEMS
ARISING IN FIELD OF FORCE BETWEEN POLITICS AND LAW IN
CONNECTION WITH REGULATION OF CIVIL AVIATION THROUGHOUT THE
WORLD.

2102 WASSERSTROM R.A.
THE JUDICIAL DECISION: TOWARD A THEORY OF LEGAL JUSTIFI-
CATION.
STANFORD: STANFORD U PRESS, 1961, 176 PP., LC#61-6535.
        AUTHOR ATTEMPTS TO DETERMINE HOW CONTROVERSIES PRESENTED
TO THE LEGAL SYSTEM FOR ADJUDICATION OUGHT TO BE RESOLVED.

2103 WATT A.
THE EVOLUTION OF AUSTRALIAN FOREIGN POLICY 1938-65.
NEW YORK: CAMBRIDGE U PRESS, 1967, 387 PP., LC#67-10782.
        TRACES HISTORY OF AUSTRALIAN FOREIGN POLICY BEGINNING
WITH PREWAR DIVERGENCE FROM BRITAIN THROUGH 1965. DISCUSSES
ESTABLISHMENT OF AUSTRALIAN RELATIONS IN AMERICA AND ASIA AT
BEGINNING OF WWII AND SUBSEQUENT POSTWAR INTERNATIONAL RE-
LATIONS AND AGREEMENTS. INCLUDES ACTION IN KOREA, RELATIONS
WITH INDONESIA, COMMUNIST CHINA, AND MALAYSIA. DISSECTS AND
CRITICIZES PRINCIPLES UNDERLYING AUSTRALIAN FOREIGN POLICY.

2104 WAY H.F. JR.
LIBERTY IN THE BALANCE - CURRENT ISSUES IN CIVIL LIBERTIES.
NEW YORK: MCGRAW HILL, 1964, 133 PP., LC#64-18402.
        DISCUSSES RACIAL DISCRIMINATION, CENSORSHIP AND OBSCENI-
TY, RADICAL RIGHT AND LEFT, ROLE OF SUPREME COURT, AND IDEAL
OF LIBERTY IN US.

2105 WEBSTER J.A.
A GENERAL STUDY OF THE DEPARTMENT OF DEFENSE INTERNAL
SECURITY PROGRAM.
LOS ANGELES: U OF S CALIF PR, 1960, 78 PP.
        EXAMINES ADMINISTRATIVE SUCCESS, PROBLEMS, AND FAILINGS
OF INDUSTRIAL SECURITY PROGRAM. CONSIDERS COST OF ADMIN-
ISTRATION, NEED FOR SECURITY, LEGAL ASPECTS OF SECURITY,
AND RELATION OF JUDICIAL TO EXECUTIVE BRANCHES IN THESE
PROBLEMS.

2106 WECHSLER H.
PRINCIPLES, POLITICS AND FUNDAMENTAL LAW: SELECTED ESSAYS.
CAMBRIDGE: HARVARD U. PR., 1961.
        FOUR ESSAYS ON NATIONAL EFFORTS TO GOVERN USA BY FUNDA-
MENTAL LAW. FOCUSES ON SUPREME COURT AS INTERPRETER OF CON-
STITUTION, CONSTITUTIONAL CONTROVERSIES, PHASES OF CONSTITU-
TIONALISM THAT STRUCTURE GOVERNMENT AND POLICIES, AND A DE-
FENSE OF THE NUREMBERG TRIALS.

2107 WEIL G.L. ED.
A HANDBOOK ON THE EUROPEAN ECONOMIC COMMUNITY.
NEW YORK: FREDERICK PRAEGER, 1965, 480 PP., LC#65-25594.
        COMPILATION OF BASIC DOCUMENTS ON HISTORY AND DEVELOPMENT
OF THE EEC. INCLUDES BACKGROUND DATA ON ITS INSTITUTIONS,
ASSOCIATION WITH EUROPEAN STATES, EXTERNAL RELATIONS, AND
ECONOMIC AND FINANCIAL AFFAIRS. CONSIDERS THE INTERNAL
MARKET, LABOR REGULATIONS, FAIR COMPETITION, AGRICULTURE,
TRANSPORT, AND OVERSEAS TRADE. SUMS UP PAST PROGRESS AND
LOOKS AT FUTURE GOALS.

2108 WEINSTEIN J.B.
"THE EFFECT OF THE FEDERAL REAPPORTIONMENT DECISIONS ON
COUNTIES AND OTHER FORMS OF GOVERNMENT."
COLUMBIA LAW REV., 65 (JAN. 65), 21-50.
        THIS ANALYSIS, WHICH DEALS PRIMARILY WITH COUNTY GOVERN-
MENT, CONCLUDES THAT IT IS VERY PROBABLE THAT THE ONE-MAN-
ONE-VOTE RULE WILL BE APPLIED TO GENERAL PURPOSE LOCAL
SUBDIVISIONS OF GOVERNMENT. IT ALSO CONSIDERS MEHTODS FOR
ACHIEVING FAIR REPRESENTATION.

2109 WEIS P.
NATIONALITY AND STATELESSNESS IN INTERNATIONAL LAW.
LONDON: STEVENS, 1956, 260 PP.
        TREATISE ON VARIOUS ASPECTS OF INTERNATIONAL LAW AND
BRITISH NATIONALITY LAW, CONCERNING HOW CERTAIN PRACTISES
HAVE HISTORICALLY AFFECTED AND PRESENTLY AFFECT INDIVIDUALS.
EXAMINES TREATIES, STATUTES AND CASES AS COURCES OF IMFORMA-
TION.

2110 WEISSBERG G.
"MAPS AS EVIDENCE IN INTERNATIONAL BOUNDARY DISPUTES: A RE-
APPRAISAL."
AMER. J. INT. LAW, 57 (OCT. 63), 781-803.
        DISCUSSES NEW EMPHASIS ON MAPS AS IMPORTANT EVIDENCE IN
BOUNDARY DISPUTES. GIVES 3 EXAMPLES FROM CASES IN INTERNA-
TIONAL COURT OF JUSTICE. DISCUSSES INDIA-CHINA BOUNDARY CON-
FLICT.

2111 WENGLER W.
"LES CONFLITS DE LOIS ET LE PRINCIPE D'EGALITE."
REV. CRIT. DR. INT. PRIV., 52 (NO. 3, 63), 503-27.
        STUDIES EXISTENCE OF PRIVATE LAW IN INTERNATIONAL RE-
LATIONS. FINDS PUBLIC ORDER EXPRESSION OF IDEA OF EQUALITY.
SHOWS CONFLICTS OF LAWS AND PRINCIPLE OF EQUALITY.

2112 WEST R.
CONSCIENCE AND SOCIETY: A STUDY OF THE PSYCHOLOGICAL
PREREQUISITES OF LAW AND ORDER.
NEW YORK: EMERSON BOOKS, 1945, 261 PP.
        STUDIES HUMAN NATURE IN ITS SOCIAL RELATIONSHIP, FOCUSING
ON SIGNIFICANCE OF AGGRESSIVENESS. DISCUSSES CONTROL OF
HUMAN NATURE BY LAW, SHOWING HOW LAW MAINTAINS ASCENDENCY
OF MAN'S SOCIAL INSTINCT OVER HIS SELF-ASSERTIVE INSTINCT.
STATES THAT INTERNATIONAL LAW HAS NOT SUCCEEDED IN
CONTROLLING MAN'S AGGRESSIVENESS. FORECASTS ESSENTIAL
STRUCTURE OF THE FUTURE WORLD ORDER THAT MANKIND SEEKS.

2113 WESTIN A.F.
THE ANATOMY OF A CONSTITUTIONAL LAW CASE.

NEW YORK: MACMILLAN, 1958, 183 PP., LC#58-9839.
DOCUMENTARY PRESENTATION OF "YOUNGSTOWN SHEET & TUBE CO
V. SAWYER" SUPREME COURT CASE. INTENDED TO PORTRAY THE WORK-
INGS OF THE AMERICAN CONSTITUTIONAL PROCESS. TRACES DEVELOP-
MENT OF CASE FROM ITS BEGINNING AS STEEL INDUSTRY DISPUTE IN
1952 TO AFTERMATH OF SUPREME COURT DECISION. DISCUSSES MEANS
BY WHICH POLITICAL AND SOCIAL PRESSURES ARE BROUGHT TO BEAR
ON LEGAL CASES AT SUPREME COURT LEVEL.

2114 WESTIN A.F. ED.
THE SUPREME COURT: VIEWS FROM INSIDE.
NEW YORK: W W NORTON, 1961, 192 PP., LC#61-6921.
ESSAYS BY SUPREME COURT JUSTICES CONCENTRATE ON ISSUES IN
1950'S. BEGIN WITH PLACE OF COURT IN STRUCTURE OF US
GOVERNMENT AND ROLE OF JUSTICES; CONSIDER RELATIONS WITH
CONGRESS AND STATE COURTS. COVER DESEGRATION DOCTRINES,
INTERNAL DISSENSION, AND "STARE DECISIS." STUDY CENTRAL
PROBLEMS OF JUDICIAL REVIEW, AND CONCLUDE WITH DEBATE ON
COURT REVIEW IN CIVIL LIBERTY CASES.

2115 WHEARE K.C.
MODERN CONSTITUTIONS (HOME UNIVERSITY LIBRARY)
LONDON: OXFORD U PR, 1951, 216 PP.
DEFINES CONSTITUTION. DISCUSSES HOW CONSTITUTIONS MAY BE
CLASSIFIED; WHAT THEY SHOULD CONTAIN, CONSTITUTIONAL
AUTHORITY, CONSTITUTIONAL CHANGES; AND PROSPECTS FOR
CONSTITUTIONAL GOVERNMENT. BELIEVES WAR, ABSOLUTISM, AND
THOSE WHO ABUSE CONSTITUTIONAL FREEDOMS POSE SOME OF
GREATEST THREATS TO CONSTITUTIONAL GOVERNMENT.

2116 WHEARE K.C.
GOVERNMENT BY COMMITTEE; AN ESSAY ON THE BRITISH
CONSTITUTION.
LONDON: OXFORD U PR, 1955, 264 PP.
EXAMINES CONDUCT OF GOVERNMENT THROUGH GROUPS OF PEOPLE
ACTING COLLECTIVELY IN COMMITTEES. STUDIES SIX TYPES OF
COMMITTEES ACCORDING TO THEIR FUNCTIONS - COMMITTEES TO
ADVISE, INQUIRE, NEGOTIATE, LEGISLATE, ADMINISTER, AND
CONTROL. COMPARES COMMITTEES ON THEIR EFFECTIVENESS AND
SHORTCOMINGS. ALSO COMPARES OFFICERS OF COMMITTEES. STATES
THAT WELL-LED COMMITTEES ENSURE DEMOCRACY.

2117 WHITE G.M.
THE USE OF EXPERTS BY INTERNATIONAL TRIBUNALS.
SYRACUSE: SYRACUSE U PRESS, 1965, 258 PP., LC#65-15853.
DISCUSSES NATURE OF INTERNATIONAL LEGAL PROCEEDINGS AND
ROLE OF VARIOUS EXPERTS. TRACES USE OF EXPERTS BY COURT SYS-
TEMS IN VARIOUS NATIONS AND NOTES IMPLIED RIGHT OF WORLD
TRIBUNALS TO CALL ON EXPERTS. EXAMINES INSTANCES IN WHICH
EXPERTS ARE USED MOST OFTEN, AS IN SUPPLYING IMPARTIAL OB-
SERVATION OR ACTING AS ARBITRATOR. NOTES PRIVILEGES AND
IMMUNITIES OF EXPERTS, AND COMMENTS ON FEES AND EXPENSES.

2118 WHITEMAN M.M. ED.
DIGEST OF INTERNATIONAL LAW* VOLUME 5, DEPARTMENT OF STATE
PUBLICATION 7873.
WASHINGTON: GOVT PR OFFICE, 1965, 1175 PP.
THIS IS CHAPTER XIII IN A STATE DEPARTMENT SERIES ON
WORLD PRACTICES AND LEGAL ACTIONS EMBRACING CURRENT INTERNA-
TIONAL LAW. EXTENSIVE CITATION OF POLICY STATEMENTS AND LE-
GAL DOCUMENTS. CONCERNS "RIGHTS AND DUTIES OF STATES."
OTHERS IN SERIES WHICH COMMENCED IN 1963 TREAT MANY FACETS
OF INTERNATIONAL LAW FROM RECOGNITION TO TERRITORIAL SEAS.

2119 WHITNEY S.N.
ANTITRUST POLICIES: AMERICAN EXPERIENCE IN TWENTY INDUSTRIES
NEW YORK: TWENTIETH CENT FUND, 1958, 541 PP., LC#58-9954.
CASE STUDIES AND COURT RULINGS ON FAMOUS ANTITRUST DECI-
SIONS. ANALYZES CASE IN ITS INDUSTRIAL AND HISTORICAL SET-
TING. DISCOVERS LACK OF BALANCE BETWEEN LEGISLATURE'S DETER-
MINATION OF VIOLATIONS AND SUGGESTIONS TO IMPROVE LAWS THAT
PREVENT VIOLATIONS. FEELS LEGISLATURE SHOULD STUDY EFFECTS
OF CASES' OUTCOMES ON CORPORATIONS' FUTURE ACTIONS, TO DE-
TERMINE WHETHER AND HOW MUCH TRIALS HELP FREE COMPETITION.

2120 WHITRIDGE L.I.
"LEGISLATIVE INQUESTS"
POLIT. SCI. QUART., 1 (MAR. 86), 84-102.
CONTENDS THAT STATE AND NATIONAL LEGISLATURES HAVE POWER
TO EXERCISE JUDICIAL FUNCTIONS, HOLD INQUIRIES, AND GIVE OUT
PUNISHMENTS. DENIES DISTINCTION OF DUTIES OF THREE BRANCHES
OF GOVERNMENT. CITES SPECIFIC CASES, EMPHASIZING NECESSITY
FOR LEGISLATIVE INQUIRY ON STATE AND NATIONAL LEVEL.

2121 WIGGINS J.R.
FREEDOM OR SECRECY.
NEW YORK: OXFORD U PR, 1956, 242 PP., LC#56-11115.
STUDY OF CENSORSHIP AND POPULAR INFORMATION THAT DIMIN-
ISHES WITH GROWING NATIONAL SECRECY. DEALS WITH PRIVATE
TRANSACTIONS, USE OF CAMERAS IN COURT, REPRISAL FOR
PUBLICATION, AND RIGHT OF DISTRIBUTION.

2122 WILDNER H.
DIE TECHNIK DER DIPLOMATIE.
STUTTGART: SPRINGER VERLAG, 1959, 342 PP.
DISCUSSES EVOLUTION OF DIPLOMATIC TECHNIQUES, ROLE OF

FOREIGN MINISTER, TECHNIQUES OF NEGOTIATION, DIPLOMACY OUT-
SIDE OFFICIAL FRAMEWORK, AND DIPLOMATIC APPARATUS AS SUBJECT
TO PUBLIC CRITICISM AND CONTROL.

2123 WILLIAMS S.P. ED.
TOWARD A GENUINE WORLD SECURITY SYSTEM (PAMPHLET)
BOSTON: UNITED WORLD FEDERALISTS, 1964, 65 PP., LC#64-20453.
ANNOTATED BIBLIOGRAPHY OF SOURCES FOR AREAS OF WORLD
LAW, ORDER, AND PEACE. INCLUDES INTRODUCTORY BOOKS AND SYM-
POSIA FOR THE BEGINNER, TOPICAL FOCUS ON DETAILED AREAS,
INDEX OF AUTHORS, EDITORS, PERIODICALS. CONTAINS 355
ENTRIES, MAJORITY DATED 1962-1963.

2124 WILLIG S.H.
"THE CONTROL OVER INTERSTATE DISTRIBUTION AND USE OF
INVESTIGATIONAL DRUGS (IN THE UNITED STATES)"
LEX ET SCIENTIA, 4 (APR.-JUNE 67), 110-119.
DISCUSSES FOOD AND DRUG ADMINISTRATION CONTROL OF USE OF
INVESTIGATIONAL DRUGS. DESCRIBES PROCEDURES INVOLVED IN
FILING APPLICATION FOR USE OF SUCH DRUGS, AND TRACES STEPS
WHICH MUST BE TAKEN TO TEST DRUGS' SAFETY.

2125 WILLOUGHBY W.W.
PRINCIPLES OF THE CONSTITUTIONAL LAW OF THE UNITED STATES.
NEW YORK: BAKER, VORHEES & CO, 1930, 884 PP.
ANALYSIS INCLUDES PRINCIPLES AND DEFINITIONS OF CONSTI-
TUTIONAL CONSTRUCTION, RELATION OF THE STATES TO THE
NATION, THEORY AND METHOD OF FEDERAL SUPREMACY, AND STUDY OF
MANY SPECIFIC QUESTIONS AS RELATED TO THE US GOVERNMENTAL
PROCESS. COVERS MANY PROBLEMS, CASES, AND POINTS OF
CONSTITUTIONAL LAW.

2126 WILSON G.
CASES AND MATERIALS ON CONSTITUTIONAL AND ADMINISTRATIVE LAW
NEW YORK: CAMBRIDGE U PRESS, 1966, 609 PP., LC#66-10244.
DISCUSSES PROBLEMS OF LAW IN RELATION TO ADMINISTRATION
AND CONSTITUTIONAL AUTHORITY. BASED ON ENGLISH LAW, INCLU-
DING CENTRAL GOVERNMENT, CIVIL SERVICE, PARLIAMENT, COURTS,
LIBERTIES AND ORDER, FOREIGN AFFAIRS, AND CROWN PROCEEDINGS.

2127 WILSON G.D.
"CRIMINAL SANCTIONS AGAINST PASSPORT AREA-RESTRICTION
VIOLATIONS."
STANFORD LAW REV., 19 (JUNE 67), 1369-1381.
EXAMINES ISSUES RAISED BY COURT CASES OF US V. LAUB AND
TRAVIS V. US CONCERNING TRAVEL TO RESTRICTED AREAS WITHOUT
AUTHORIZATION. DISCUSSES PROPRIETY OF ENFORCING AREA TRAVEL
RESTRICTIONS SET UP BY STATE DEPARTMENT ALONE AND SUGGESTS
THAT SUCH LAWS BE RESULT OF CONGRESSIONAL ACTION TO IMPROVE
PROTECTION OF CITIZEN'S CONSTITUTIONAL RIGHTS.

2128 WILSON G.G.
HANDBOOK OF INTERNATIONAL LAW.
ST. PAUL: WEST, 1939, 567 PP.
SETS FORTH HISTORICAL DEVELOPMENT OF BASIC PRINCIPLES
OF INTERNATIONAL LAW. EXAMINES PROBLEMS OF EXISTENCE, INDE-
PENDENCE AND EQUALITY. ANALYZES DOMAIN PROCESS. SURVEYS
DIPLOMATIC AND CONSULAR RELATIONSHIPS. CONCLUDES WITH STUDY
OF NATURE AND CONTEMPLATES CAUSES OF WAR.

2129 WILSON J.F.
CHURCH AND STATE IN AMERICAN HISTORY.
BOSTON: D C HEATH, 1965, 227 PP., LC#65-10224.
COLLECTION OF READINGS (MOSTLY PRIMARY SOURCES) ON RELA-
TIONSHIPS BETWEEN CHURCH AND STATE IN AMERICAN HISTORY,
SHOWING DERIVATION OF AMERICAN EXPERIENCE FROM EUROPEAN CIV-
ILIZATION. PLACES MAJOR EMPHASIS UPON INTERRELATIONSHIPS OF
POLITICAL, LEGAL, AND RELIGIOUS PHENOMENA IN GIVEN PERIOD,
AND INTERPRETATION PLACED UPON THESE PHENOMENA. SHOWS AS-
SUMPTIONS ON WHICH EVENTS AND DOCUMENTS WERE FRAMED.

2130 WILSON W.
CONSTITUTIONAL GOVERNMENT IN THE UNITED STATES.
NY: LEMCKE, LEMCKE & BEUCHNER, 1908, 236 PP.
WOODROW WILSON'S STUDY OF US GOVERNMENT INCLUDES
DISCUSSION OF CONSTITUTIONAL GOVERNMENT IN GENERAL, PLACE OF
US IN CONSTITUTIONAL DEVELOPMENT, BRANCHES OF GOVERNMENT,
FEDERAL-STATE RELATIONS, AND POLITICAL PARTIES.

2131 WILSON W.
THE STATE: ELEMENTS OF HISTORICAL AND PRACTICAL POLITICS.
BOSTON: D C HEATH, 1918, 554 PP.
DISCUSSES OBJECTS AND FUNCTIONS OF GOVERNMENT, NATURE OF
LAW; EXAMINES STRUCTURE OF GOVERNMENT OF MAJOR BELLIGERENT
POWERS OF WWI, INCLUDING US.

2132 WINES R.
"THE IMPERIAL CIRCLES, PRINCELY DIPLOMACY, AND IMPERIAL RE-
FORM* 1681-1714."
J. MODERN HISTORY, 39 (MAR. 67), 1-29.
DETAILED AND SCHOLARLY ACCOUNT OF HOLY ROMAN EMPIRE AFTER
WESTPHALIA TREATY. TRACES AND CLARIFIES GERMAN IMPERIAL
POLICY WITH CONSIDERABLE DOCUMENTATION FROM ORIGINAL SOURCES
AND LENGTHLY FOOTNOTES. CONCLUDES THAT EMPIRE DID NOT DIE,
BUT BECAME INCREASINGLY RESTRICTED IN AREA. PRINCELY LIBERTY
WAS COHESIVE AS WELL AS DIVISIVE FORCE IN MAINTENANCE OF

THE EMPIRE.

2133 WINFIELD P.H.
THE CHIEF SOURCES OF ENGLISH LEGAL HISTORY.
CAMBRIDGE: HARVARD U PR, 1925, 374 PP.
    A GUIDE TO THE CHIEF SOURCES OF ENGLISH LEGAL HISTORY:
BIBLIOGRAPHICAL GUIDES, SOURCES OF ANGLO-SAXON LAW, STAT-
UTES, PUBLIC RECORDS, CASE LAW, AND TEXTBOOKS. COVERS THE
PERIOD FROM THE BEGINNINGS OF ENGLISH LEGAL LITERATURE TO
BLACKSTONE. CRITICALLY AND DESCRIPTIVELY ANNOTATED.

2134 WINTERS J.M.
STATE CONSTITUTIONAL LIMITATIONS ON SOLUTIONS OF
METROPOLITAN AREA PROBLEMS.
ANN ARBOR: U OF MICH LAW SCHOOL, 1961, 169 PP.
    THE RIGHT TO LOCAL SELF-GOVERNMENT AND POSSIBLE DEVICES
FOR INCORPORATION OF METROPOLITAN UNITS ARE EXAMINED IN
A LEGAL AND POLITICAL FRAMEWORK.

2135 WINTERS J.M.
INTERSTATE METROPOLITAN AREAS.
ANN ARBOR: U OF MICH LAW SCHOOL, 1962, 110 PP.
    A STUDY OF THE LEGAL QUESTIONS POSED BY THE FEDERAL AND
STATE CONSTITUTIONS IN THE AREA OF INTERSTATE ARRANGEMENTS
DEALING WITH METROPOLITAN PROBLEMS.

2136 WOETZEL R.K.
DIE INTERNATIONALE KONTROLLE DER HOHEREN LUFTSCHICHTEN UND
DES WELTRAUMS.
BONN: BONN UNIV, 1959, 98 PP.
    DISCUSSES CONCEPT OF SOVEREIGNTY IN RELATION TO SPACE AND
EXAMINES NATIONAL LAWS ON RIGHTS OF AIR TRAVEL. STUDIES
LEGAL POSITION OF SPACE OBJECTS AND INTERNATIONAL CONTROL OF
SPACE.

2137 WOETZEL R.K.
THE INTERNATIONAL CONTROL OF AIRSPACE AND OUTERSPACE.
BAD-GOPESBERG: ASGARD, 1960, 97 PP.
    ANALYZES LEGAL ASPECTS OF SPACE PENETRATION. PROBES INTO
THE MANY UNSOLVED PROBLEMS OF SOVEREIGNTY AND SOVEREIGN
RIGHTS. CONSIDERS LEGAL CHARACTER OF SPACE IN TERMS OF
INTERNATIONAL LAW. CONCLUDES THAT AIR SPACE BE LIMITED TO
SIXTY MILES BASED ON THE LIMITING FACTOR OF CONVENTIONAL
AIRCRAFTS IMPOSED BY CONDITIONS OF NATURE. SUGGESTS SPACE
ABOVE SIXTY MILES BE CONSIDERED AS RES COMMUNIS UNDER SOME
INTERNATIONAL CONTROL.

2138 WOETZEL R.K.
THE NURENBERG TRIALS IN INTERNATIONAL LAW.
NEW YORK: PRAEGER, 1962, 287 PP.
    ATTEMPTS TO SHOW JURIDICAL BASIS FOR INTERNATIONAL MILI-
TARY TRIBUNAL, WHETHER INDIVIDUAL LIABILITY ACTUALLY EXISTED
FOR DENOTED CRIMES, I.E. WAR CRIMES, CRIMES AGAINST PEACE
AND HUMANITY, AND WHETHER THESE CRIMES CAN ACTUALLY BE CON-
SIDERED INTERNATIONAL IN SCOPE.

2139 WOLFERS A.
BRITAIN AND FRANCE BETWEEN TWO WORLD WARS.
NEW YORK: HARCOURT BRACE, 1940, 446 PP.
    DISCUSSES FOREIGN POLICIES OF BRITAIN AND FRANCE DURING
INTERIM PERIOD, 1918-38. RELATES TREATY OF VERSAILLES,
ECONOMIC TACTICS, AND POLITICAL ISOLATION TO ONSET OF WWII.
IMPLICATES US IN POLICY ERRORS OF THESE TWO COUNTRIES.

2140 WOLFF C.
JUS GENTIUM METHODO SCIENTIFICA PERTRACTATUM.
OXFORD: CLARENDON, 1934, 541 PP.
    ANALYZES OBLIGATIONS OF NATIONS. PRESENTS THEORY OF
NATIONAL OWNERSHIP, TREATIES AND OTHER AGREEMENTS. EXPLORES
INTERNATIONAL LAW OF WAR. DISCUSSES PEACE AND PEACE
TREATIES.

2141 WOLL P.
ADMINISTRATIVE LAW: THE INFORMAL PROCESS.
BERKELEY: U OF CALIF PR, 1963, 203 PP., LC#63-10409.
    DISCUSSION OF THE ADJUDICATIVE FUNCTION OF
ADMINISTRATIVE AGENCIES. SAYS THAT REQUIREMENTS OF PUBLIC
POLICY, SPEED, AND TECHNICAL SKILLS HAVE MADE
ADMINISTRATIVE ADJUDICATION LARGELY INFORMAL IN PRACTICE.

2142 WOOD J.E., THOMPSON E.B., MILLER R.T.
CHURCH AND STATE IN SCRIPTURE HISTORY AND CONSTITUTIONAL
LAW.
WACO: BAYLOR UNIV PRESS, 1958, 171 PP., LC#59-21543.
    TRACES BIBLICAL FOUNDATIONS OF CHURCH-STATE RELATIONS,
NOTING THAT THE PROBLEM IS INHERENT IN BOTH OLD AND NEW
TESTAMENTS. OUTLINES DEVELOPMENT OF PRINCIPLE
OF SEPARATION OF CHURCH AND STATE, LOOKING CLOSELY AT EURO-
PEAN AND COLONIAL BACKGROUNDS AS DECISIVE. LAST SECTION IS A
STUDY OF DEVELOPMENT OF PRINCIPLES IN CONSTITUTIONAL LAW:
COURTS AND STATES AS DELINEATORS OF CHURCH-STATE BOUNDARIES.

2143 WOOD V.
DUE PROCESS OF LAW 1932-1949: SUPREME COURT'S USE OF A
CONSTITUTIONAL TOOL.
BATON ROUGE: LOUISIANA ST U PR, 1951, 436 PP.
    COMPARISONS OF IMPORTANT COURT CASES ON DUE PROCESS OF
LAW IN 20 YEARS THAT SHIFTED THE INTERPRETATIONS FROM A
CONSERVATIVE FAVORING OF GOVERNMENT PROTECTION TO THE LIB-
ERAL POSITION RENDERING PEOPLE THEIR DUE PROCESS. CASES CON-
CERN SOCIAL, ECONOMIC, CRIMINAL, AND TAX MATTERS. CHART OF
COURT PERSONNEL AND LIST OF CASES INVOLVED.

2144 WOOLBERT R.G.
FOREIGN AFFAIRS BIBLIOGRAPHY, 1932-1942.
NEW YORK: HARPER & ROW, 1945, 705 PP., LC#33-7094.
    A SELECTED AND ANNOTATED LIST OF 10,000 BOOKS ON INTER-
NATIONAL RELATIONS COVERING THE DECADE FROM MID-1932 TO MID-
1942. INCLUDES BOOKS IN ALL WESTERN LANGUAGES AS WELL AS
TURKISH, HEBREW, ARABIC, CHINESE, AND JAPANESE. BOOKS CLAS-
SIFIED INTO ANALYTICAL, CHRONOLOGICAL, AND REGIONAL TREAT-
MENTS, AND INDEXED BY AUTHOR.

2145 WORLD PEACE FOUNDATION
"INTERNATIONAL ORGANIZATIONS: SUMMARY OF ACTIVITIES."
INT. ORGAN., 18 (SPRING 64), 302-485.
    GIVES COMPLETE BREAK-DOWN OF UN'S ORGANIZATION AND FUNC-
TIONS THROUGH A STUDY OF MEMBERS, GENERAL ASSEMBLY, SECUR-
ITY COUNCIL AND SPECIFIC EXAMPLES OF PAST POLICIES AND PRO-
CEDURES, E.G. INDIA-PAKISTAN DISPUTE, CYPRUS-TURKISH QUES-
TION.

2146 WORMUTH F.D.
THE ORIGINS OF MODERN CONSTITUTIONALISM.
NEW YORK: HARPER & ROW, 1949, 243 PP.
    ANALYZES THE CONTRIBUTIONS OF THE CROMWELLIAN CONSTITU-
TIONS TO MODERN GOVERNMENT. DESCRIBES THE INTRODUCTION INTO
POLITICAL SCIENCE OF SEPARATION OF POWERS, BICAMERALISM, THE
WRITTEN CONSTITUTION, AND JUDICIAL REVIEW. TRACES THE TRADI-
TION OF CONSTITUTIONALISM FROM ANCIENT GREECE TO 17TH-
CENTURY BRITAIN.

2147 WRAITH R.E.
"ADMINISTRATIVE CHANGE IN THE NEW AFRICA."
AFRICAN AFFAIRS, 66 (JULY 67), 231-240.
    OUTLINES TRENDS WHICH HAVE DEVELOPED SINCE INDEPENDENCE
IN THE STATES OF ENGLISH-SPEAKING AFRICA IN THE FIELD OF
PUBLIC ADMINISTRATION. DESCRIBES IMPORTANT CURRENT PROBLEMS;
CITES STUDIES THAT HAVE BEEN MADE. INCLUDES CIVIL SERVICE,
PUBLIC CORPORATIONS, LOCAL GOVERNMENT, APPLICATION OF ADMIN-
ISTRATIVE LAW. WRITTEN BEFORE MILITARY COUPS IN WEST AFRICA.

2148 WRIGHT G.
RURAL REVOLUTION IN FRANCE: THE PEASANTRY IN THE TWENTIETH
CENTURY.
STANFORD: U. PR., 1964, 271 PP., $6.00.
    TRACES GRADUAL AWAKENING OF FRENCH PEASANTRY--AT FIRST
TO A NEW SELF-CONSCIOUSNESS, AND LATER TO SYNDICALIST
ORGANIZATION AND POLITICAL ACTION. DISCUSSES RIVAL EFFORTS
OF THE COMMUNISTS AND CATHOLICS IN THE COUNTRYSIDE. CON-
CLUDES WITH AN ANALYSIS AND TENTATIVE ASSESSMENT OF THE
FIFTH REPUBLIC'S NEW COURSE IN THE AREA OF RURAL REFORM.

2149 WRIGHT Q.
"THE ENFORCEMENT OF INTERNATIONAL LAW THROUGH MUNICIPAL LAW
IN THE US."
IN (U. ILL. STUD. SOC. SCI., VOL. 5, 1916, 1-264).
    REFERRING TO THEORETICAL RELATIONSHIP BETWEEN MUNICIPAL
AND INTERNATIONAL LAW, ATTEMPTS TO DEFINE STATUS OF INTERNA-
TIONAL LAW ENFORCEMENT IN USA. ENUMERATES LEGAL OBLIGATIONS
OF BELLIGERENT TO ENEMIES.

2150 WRIGHT Q.
THE CONTROL OF AMERICAN FOREIGN RELATIONS.
NEW YORK: MACMILLAN, 1922, 412 PP.
    DRAWS PARTICULAR ATTENTION TO DIFFICULTY IN CONTROL OF
FOREIGN RELATIONS FOUND IN EVERY GOVERNMENT, PARTICULARLY IN
THOSE WHERE ORGANS CONDUCTING FOREIGN RELATIONS HAVE RE-
SPONSIBILITIES DEFINED BY INTERNATIONAL LAW AND POWERS DE-
FINED BY CONSTITUTIONAL LAW. PRESENTS ANALYTIC ACCOUNT OF
LACK OF COORDINATION BETWEEN RESPONSIBILITIES AND POWERS.
PRESENTS BOTH INTERNATIONAL AND CONSTITUTIONAL VIEWPOINT.

2151 WRIGHT Q.
MANDATES UNDER THE LEAGUE OF NATIONS.
CHICAGO: U. CHI. PR., 1930, 726 PP.
    TRACES ORIGINS AND DEVELOPMENT OF MANDATE SYSTEM. DES-
CRIBES STRUCTURE OF SYSTEM AND ACTIVITIES OF PARTICIPATING
PARTIES. SEEKS PLACE FOR SYSTEM WITHIN FRAMEWORK OF INTER-
NATIONAL LAW.

2152 WRIGHT Q.
"FUNDAMENTAL PROBLEMS OF INTERNATIONAL ORGANIZATION."
INT. CONCIL., 369 (APR. 41), 468-492.
    CONSIDERS PROBLEMS OF INTERNATIONAL ORGANIZATION IN LIGHT
OF: ORDER AND ANARCHY, SCOPE OF ORGANIZATIONS, REGIONAL AND
UNIVERSAL ORGANIZATIONS, CHANGE AND STABILITY, EVOLUTION AND
REVOLUTION, SANCTIONS, AND AUTHORITY AND CONSENT. SEES PROB-
LEM OF INTERNATIONAL ORGANIZATION AS RECOGNIZING LIMITATIONS
ON NATIONAL SOVEREIGNTY AND PROVIDING FOR EXERCISE OF ORGAN-
IZATIONS POWER WHILE CREATING WORLD CITIZENSHIP SENTIMENT.

2153 WRIGHT Q.
"CONSTITUTIONAL PROCEDURES OF THE US FOR CARRYING OUT OBLI-
GATIONS FOR MILITARY SANCTIONS."
AMER. J. INT. LAW, 138(1944), 678-684.
CALLS FOR A CONGRESSIONAL RESOLUTION AUTHORIZING THE
PRESIDENT TO USE ARMED FORCES IN COLLABORATION WITH OTHER
COUNTRIES TO SUPPRESS ACTS FOUND TO CONSTITUTE AGGRESSION
AND ARE CONTRARY TO INTERNATIONAL LAW.

2154 WRIGHT Q.
"CONGRESS AND THE TREATY-MAKING POWER."
PROC. AMER. SOC. INT. LAW, 1952, 43-69.
DEALS WITH STATEMENT CONCERNING CONSTITUTIONAL POWERS OF
THE PRESIDENT AND THE CONGRESS, INDICATING POSSIBLIITY OR
PROBABILITY OF FREQUENT CONFLICTS. PRESENTS DIRECTIONS FOR
CONSTITUTIONAL AMENDMENTS TO IMPROVE CONDUCT OF FOREIGN
RELATIONS.

2155 WRIGHT Q.
PROBLEMS OF STABILITY AND PROGRESS IN INTERNATIONAL
RELATIONSHIPS.
BERKELEY: U. CALIF. PR., 1954, 378 PP.
DISCUSSES POSSIBILITY OF USING SCIENCE, EDUCATION, ORGAN-
IZATION, LAW AND POLITICS TO CREATE GREATER HARMONY IN FIELD
OF INTERNATIONAL RELATIONS. FAVORS CENTRALIZATION OF INSTI-
TUTIONS THROUGH UN FRAMEWORK. STUDIES GROUP BEHAVIOR.

2156 WRIGHT Q.
"THE PEACEFUL ADJUSTMENT OF INTERNATIONAL RELATIONS:
PROBLEMS AND RESEARCH APPROACHES."
J. SOC. ISSUES, 11 (1955), 3-12.
SEES PROBLEM SOLUTION FOR PEACEFUL WORLD AS VARIED, AND
THEREFORE TYPES OF RESEARCH RELEVANT TO EACH CLASS OF PROB-
LEMS AS VARIED ALSO. DEVISES SCHEME OF CLASSIFICATION OF
PROBLEMS IN INTERNATIONAL RELATIONS INTO 4 TYPES, AS WELL AS
CLASSIFICATION OF 4 TYPES OF RESEARCH.

2157 WRIGHT Q.
"LEGAL ASPECTS OF THE U-2 INCIDENT."
AMER. J. INT. LAW, 54 (OCT. 60), 836-54.
CONCERNED OVER US AUTHORIZATION OF U-2 FLIGHT AND VIOLAT-
ION OF INTERNATIONAL LAW - BUT DOES NOT CONSIDER U-2 AS ACT
OF AGGRESSION. ASSERTS THAT FLIGHTS WERE MORALLY (NOT LEGAL-
LY) RIGHT ACCORDING TO RULES OF SELF-PRESERVATION AND SOVIET
ESPIONAGE ACTIVITIES ALTHOUGH CESSATION OF FLIGHTS AND APOL-
OGY WOULD HAVE BEEN APPROPRIATE. CONSIDERS USSR ACTION COR-
RECT. CITES DECISION-MAKING FLAWS OF USA GOVERNMENT.

2158 WRIGHT Q.
THE ROLE OF INTERNATIONAL LAW IN THE ELIMINATION OF WAR.
NEW YORK: OCEANA, 1961, 119 PP.
SURVEYS SCOPE OF INTERNATIONAL LAW, AND DISCUSSES ITS
HISTORY, FUNCTIONS, CONTEMPORARY CONDITIONS, RULES OF ORDER
AND FUTURE PROSPECTS.

2159 WRIGHT Q.
A STUDY OF WAR.
CHICAGO: U OF CHICAGO PRESS, 1964, 451 PP.
STUDIES PHENOMENON OF WAR, ITS HISTORY, CAUSES, AND
CONTROL. ATTEMPTS TO EXPLAIN WHY MILITARY BUDGETS RISE WHEN
WAR IS CONSIDERED "OBSOLETE." MAINTAINS THAT SOLUTION TO
PREVENTION OF WAR IS "ADAPTIVE STABILITY WITHIN WORLD-
COMMUNITY," BUT THAT TECHNICAL AND SOCIAL DEVELOPMENTS ARE
ACCENTUATING CONFLICT. INCLUDES EFFECTS OF WAR ON PEOPLE,
LEGAL ASPECTS, AND STRUGGLE FOR POWER.

2160 WRIGHT Q.
"THE ESCALATION OF INTERNATIONAL CONFLICTS."
J. OF CONFLICT RESOLUTION, 9 (DEC. 65), 434-449.
FORMULA FOR THE PREDICTION OF WAR ESCALATION PROBABILI-
TIES IS DERIVED WHICH IS A MODIFICATION OF RICHARDSON'S
ARMS RACE FORMULA. 46 CONFLICTS STUDIED FROM WORLD WAR I TO
THE PRESENT. MAGNITUDES OF KEY FACTORS AND ESCALATION PROBA-
BILITIES GIVEN FOR THESE CONFLICTS, WHICH ARE CLASSED BY
"NO HOSTILITIES," HOSTILITIES BUT NO ESCALATION, HOSTILITIES
WITH ESCALATION, AND WORLD WARS.

2161 WRONG D.H.
AMERICAN AND CANADIAN VIEWPOINTS.
WASHINGTON: AMER COUNCIL ON EDUC, 1955, 62 PP., LC#55-12179.
PRESENTS BRIEF SUMMARY OF NATIONAL VALUE SYSTEMS OF
AMERICANS AND CANADIANS. COMPARES ATTITUDES ON FAMILY,
RELIGION, EDUCATION, ECONOMIC ACTIVITIES, GOVERNMENT, SOCIAL
CLASSES, AND LAW. COMPARES TWO SIMILAR INDUSTRIAL NATIONS
TO DISCOVER DIFFERENCES.

2162 YAKOBSON S. ED.
FIVE HUNDRED RUSSIAN WORKS FOR COLLEGE LIBRARIES (PAMPHLET)
NEW YORK: AMER COUN LEARNED SOC, 1948, 38 PP.
AN ELEMENTARY BIBLIOGRAPHY SUGGESTING A BASIC LIBRARY OF
RUSSIAN WORKS DEALING WITH RUSSIA IN SUCH AREAS AS CULTURE,
POLITICAL HISTORY, GEOGRAPHY, LAW, ETC. DOES NOT INCLUDE
PERIODICALS, NEWSPAPERS, SPECIALIZED MONOGRAPHS, OR ORIGINAL
RUSSIAN BELLETRISTIC LITERATURE. PUBLISHED AS A GUIDE FOR
SMALL LIBRARIES ESTABLISHING A BASIC COLLECTION. ALL ENTRIES
PRINTED IN RUSSIAN, BUT NOT IN CYRILLIC ALPHABET.

2163 YALEM R.J.
"THE STUDY OF INTERNATIONAL ORGANIZATION, 1920-1965* A
SURVEY OF THE LITERATURE."
BACKGROUND, 10 (MAY 66), 1-56.
SELECTIVE SURVEY DIVIDES STUDY OF INTERNATIONAL ORGANIZA-
TION INTO 5 PHASES OF SCHOLARLY DEVELOPMENT, WITH MORE
ATTENTION TO THE LITERATURE SINCE 1945 THAN TO THE EARLIER
PERIOD. INCLUDED IS A BRIEF APPRAISAL OF THE STATE OF THE
FIELD AND SOME INDICATIONS AS TO FUTURE RESEARCH PRIORITIES.

2164 YANG KUNG-SUN
THE BOOK OF LORD SHANG.
LONDON: PROBSTHAIN, 1928, 346 PP.
INTRODUCES SHANG YANG AND HIS RELATION TO LEGAL
PRINCIPLES FOCUSES ON HISTORICAL AND LITERARY CRITICISM.
SHOWS SHANG TO HAVE AIDED DEVELOPMENT OF SCHOOL OF LAW.

2165 YOUNG W. ED.
EXISTING MECHANISMS OF ARMS CONTROL.
NEW YORK: PERGAMON PRESS, 1966, 150 PP., LC#65-25010.
FOR NEW ARMS CONTROL MEASURES TO WORK THEY NEED TO BE
BASED ON EXPERIENCE AS WELL AS ANALOGY AND IMAGINATION. EDI-
TOR YOUNG HAS COLLECTED ESSAYS ON EXPERIENCES OF 5 INSTITU-
TIONS IN CONTROLLING THE WARLIKE USES OF FISSIONABLE MATTER.
CONTRIBUTORS: MEN SUCH AS SEABORG EXPERIENCED IN THE OPERA-
TIONS OF THE ATOMIC ENERGY COMMISSION, EURATON, ETC.

2166 YOUNGER R.D.
THE PEOPLE'S PANEL: THE GRAND JURY IN THE UNITED STATES,
1634-1941.
PROVIDENCE: BROWN U PRESS, 1963, 263 PP., LC#63-12993.
HISTORICAL STUDY OF GRAND JURY IN US LEGAL SYSTEM FROM
COLONIAL TIMES TO WWII AND ITS RELATION TO AND IMPACT ON US
LAW DEVELOPED UNDER CONSTITUTION. VIEWS FUTURE DEVELOPMENT
OF GRAND JURY AND TRENDS RELATED TO RECENT ACTIONS TAKEN.

2167 YUKIO O.
THE VOICE OF JAPANESE DEMOCRACY, AN ESSAY ON CONSTITUTIONAL
LOYALTY (TRANS BY J. E. BECKER)
BALTIMORE: KELLY & WALSH, LTD, 1918, 108 PP.
DISCUSSES RELATIONSHIP OF JAPANESE IMPERIAL HOUSE AND
CONSTITUTIONAL GOVERNMENT BEFORE WWI. DESCRIBES NATIONAL
POLITICAL PARTIES' ORGANIZATION AND THEIR RESPONSIVENESS TO
WISHES OF PEOPLE. NOTES MEANS OF FINDING OUT POPULAR SEN-
TIMENT AND SPECIFIC PROCESSES USED IN RUNNING CONSTITUTIONAL
GOVERNMENT. DISCUSSES COMPETITION FOR LOYALTY BETWEEN IMPER-
IAL HOUSE AND CONSTITUTION.

2168 ZABEL O.H.
GOD AND CAESAR IN NEBRASKA: A STUDY OF LEGAL RELATIONSHIP
OF CHURCH AND STATE, 1854-1954.
LINCOLN: U OF NEB PR, 1955, 198 PP.
STUDIES LEGAL RELATIONSHIP OF CHURCH AND STATE FROM 1854-
1954 IN NEBRASKA. EXAMINES BOTH STATE'S RECOGNITION OF
RELIGIOUS FREEDOM AND RELIGION'S ROLE IN ADMINISTRATIVE
DECISIONS. DISCUSSES SUNDAY LAWS AND PROVIDES DETAILED
STUDY OF EDUCATION AS IT RELATES TO CHURCH AND STATE.
COMPARES NEBRASKA'S SITUATION TO THOSE OF OTHER STATES.

2169 ZAWODNY J.K.
"GUIDE TO THE STUDY OF INTERNATIONAL RELATIONS."
SAN FRANCISCO: CHANDLER, 1966.
AN ARRANGEMENT OF SELECTED SOURCES IN ENGLISH, CROSS-IN-
DEXING 500 ENTRIES WHICH ARE CLASSIFIED UNDER SUBJECT HEAD-
INGS, AND WHICH, EXCEPT FOR THE JOURNALS, HAVE BEEN ANNO-
TATED. INCLUDES CHAPTER ON BIBLIOGRAPHIES CONTAINING 55
LISTINGS OF BIBLIOGRAPHIES OF BIBLIOGRAPHIES, NATIONAL AND
SUBJECT BIBLIOGRAPHIES, AND NATIONAL LIBRARY COLLECTIONS,
PUBLISHED BETWEEN 1940-1965.

2170 ZIMMERN A.
THE LEAGUE OF NATIONS AND THE RULE OF LAW.
LONDON: MACMILLAN, 1939, 542 PP.
IGNORING CONTEMPORARY POLITICS, EXPLORES THE ABILITY OF
THE LEAGUE OF NATIONS IN DEVELOPING INTER-STATE RELATIONS.
PRESENTS HISTORICAL BACKGROUND OF LEAGUE TILL 1936, AND
TRACES AFFECTS ON PREVIOUS DIPLOMATIC METHODS.

2171 ZINN C.J.
HOW OUR LAWS ARE MADE: BROCHURE HOUSE OF REPRESENTATIVES
DOCUMENT 451.
WASHINGTON: GOVT PR OFFICE, 1956, 34 PP., LC#56-62376.
OUTLINES LEGISLATIVE BILL-MAKING PROCESS FROM ORIGIN OF
IDEA FOR A LAW THROUGH ITS ENACTMENT AND PUBLICATION AS A
STATUTE. COVERS SOURCES OF LEGISLATION, KINDS OF BILLS AND
RESOLUTIONS, COMMITTEE CONSIDERATION, CALENDARS, OBTAINING
CONSIDERATION OF MEASURES, SENATE PROCEDURES, FINAL ACTION
ON AMENDED BILL, PRESIDENTIAL ACTION, PUBLICATION.

A

AARON T.J. E0042

ABA....AMERICAN BAR ASSOCIATION

B37
RUTHERFORD M.L.,THE INFLUENCE OF THE AMERICAN BAR ATTIT
ASSOCIATION ON PUBLIC OPINION AND LEGISLATION. ADJUD
USA+45 LAW CONSTN LABOR LEGIS DOMIN EDU/PROP LEGIT PROF/ORG
CT/SYS ROUTINE...TIME/SEQ 19/20. ABA. PAGE 87 E1739 JURID

B50
HURST J.W.,THE GROWTH OF AMERICAN LAW; THE LAW LAW
MAKERS. USA-45 LOC/G NAT/G DELIB/GP JUDGE ADJUD LEGIS
ADMIN ATTIT PWR...POLICY JURID BIBLIOG 18/20 CONSTN
CONGRESS SUPREME/CT ABA PRESIDENT. PAGE 56 E1115 CT/SYS

B67
ELDRIDGE W.B.,NARCOTICS AND THE LAW: A CRITIQUE OF LAW
THE AMERICAN EXPERIMENT IN NARCOTIC DRUG CONTROL. INSPECT
PUB/INST ACT/RES PLAN LICENSE GP/REL EFFICIENCY BIO/SOC
ATTIT HEALTH...CRIMLGY HEAL STAT 20 ABA DEPT/HEW JURID
NARCO/ACT. PAGE 34 E0679

S67
SHAFFER T.L.,"DIRECT RESTRAINT ON THE PRESS." LAW
USA+45 EDU/PROP CONTROL...JURID NEW/IDEA ABA. PRESS
PAGE 90 E1809 ORD/FREE
ADJUD

ABELS J. E0043

ABILITY TESTS....SEE KNO/TEST

ABLARD C.D. E0044

ABM/DEFSYS....ANTI-BALLISTIC MISSILE DEFENSE SYSTEMS

ABORIGINES....ABORIGINES (AUSTRALIA)

ABORTION....ABORTION

ABRAHAM H.J. E0045,E0046

ABRIKOSSOV, DIMITRI....SEE ABRIKSSV/D

ABRIKSSV/D....DIMITRI ABRIKOSSOV

ACAD/ASST....ACADEMIC ASSISTANCE COUNCIL (U.K.)

ACADEM....UNIVERSITY, COLLEGE, GRADUATE SCHOOL, HIGHER
EDUCATION

N
DEUTSCHE BUCHEREI,JAHRESVERZEICHNIS DER DEUTSCHEN BIBLIOG
HOCHSCHULSCHRIFTEN. EUR+WWI GERMANY LAW ADMIN WRITING
PERSON...MGT SOC 19/20. PAGE 31 E0613 ACADEM
INTELL

N
MINISTERE DE L'EDUC NATIONALE,CATALOGUE DES THESES BIBLIOG
DE DOCTORAT SOUTENNES DEVANT LES UNIVERSITAIRES ACADEM
FRANCAISES. FRANCE LAW DIPLOM ADMIN...HUM SOC 20. KNOWL
PAGE 73 E1465 NAT/G

N
US SUPERINTENDENT OF DOCUMENTS,EDUCATION (PRICE BIBLIOG/A
LIST 31). USA+45 LAW FINAN LOC/G NAT/G DEBATE ADMIN EDU/PROP
LEAD RACE/REL FEDERAL HEALTH POLICY. PAGE 103 E2062 ACADEM
SCHOOL

N19
AMERICAN CIVIL LIBERTIES UNION,"WE HOLD THESE ORD/FREE
TRUTHS" FREEDOM, JUSTICE, EQUALITY: REPORT ON CIVIL LAW
LIBERTIES (A PERIODICAL PAMPHLET COVERING 1951-53). RACE/REL
USA+45 ACADEM NAT/G FORCES LEGIS COERCE CIVMIL/REL CONSTN
GOV/REL DISCRIM PRIVIL MARXISM...OLD/LIB 20 ACLU UN
CIVIL/LIB. PAGE 4 E0076

B28
MACDONALD A.F.,ELEMENTS OF POLITICAL SCIENCE LAW
RESEARCH. USA-45 ACADEM JUDGE EDU/PROP DEBATE ADJUD FEDERAL
EXEC...BIBLIOG METH T 20 CONGRESS. PAGE 67 E1338 DECISION
CT/SYS

B31
COLUMBIA UNIVERSITY,A BIBLIOGRAPHY OF THE FACULTY BIBLIOG
OF POLITICAL SCIENCE OF COLUMBIA UNIVERSITY, ACADEM
1880-1930. USA-45 LAW NAT/G LEGIS DIPLOM LEAD WAR PHIL/SCI
GOV/REL ATTIT...TIME/SEQ 19/20. PAGE 24 E0478

C39
HADDOW A.,"POLITICAL SCIENCE IN AMERICAN COLLEGES USA-45

AND UNIVERSITIES 1636-1900." CONSTN MORAL...POLICY LAW
INT/LAW CON/ANAL BIBLIOG T 17/20. PAGE 49 E0971 ACADEM
KNOWL

B51
HUXLEY J.,FREEDOM AND CULTURE. UNIV LAW SOCIETY R+D CULTURE
ACADEM SCHOOL CREATE SANCTION ATTIT KNOWL...HUM ORD/FREE
ANTHOL 20. PAGE 56 E1118 PHIL/SCI
IDEA/COMP

B52
UNESCO,THESES DE SCIENCES SOCIALES: CATALOGUE BIBLIOG
ANALYTIQUE INTERNATIONAL DE THESES INEDITES DE ACADEM
DOCTORAT, 1940-1950. INT/ORG DIPLOM EDU/PROP...GEOG WRITING
INT/LAW MGT PSY SOC 20. PAGE 98 E1958

B53
MARKE J.J.,A CATALOGUE OF THE LAW COLLECTION AT NEW BIBLIOG/A
YORK UNIVERSITY, WITH SELECTED ANNOTATIONS. ACADEM LAW
ADJUD CT/SYS...CONCPT BIOG 20. PAGE 68 E1366 PHIL/SCI
IDEA/COMP

B55
KHADDURI M.,LAW IN THE MIDDLE EAST. LAW CONSTN ADJUD
ACADEM FAM EDU/PROP CT/SYS SANCTION CRIME...INT/LAW JURID
GOV/COMP ANTHOL 6/20 MID/EAST. PAGE 61 E1210 ISLAM

B55
TROTIER A.H.,DOCTORAL DISSERTATIONS ACCEPTED BY BIBLIOG
AMERICAN UNIVERSITIES 1954-55. SECT DIPLOM HEALTH ACADEM
...ART/METH GEOG INT/LAW SOC LING CHARTS 20. USA+45
PAGE 97 E1943 WRITING

B57
FAIRCHILD H.P.,THE ANATOMY OF FREEDOM. USA+45 ORD/FREE
ACADEM SCHOOL SECT CAP/ISM PRESS CHOOSE SOCISM. CONCPT
PAGE 36 E0712 NAT/G
JURID

B58
AMERICAN SOCIETY PUBLIC ADMIN,STRENGTHENING ADMIN
MANAGEMENT FOR DEMOCRATIC GOVERNMENT. USA+45 ACADEM NAT/G
EX/STRUC WORKER PLAN BUDGET CONFER CT/SYS EXEC
EFFICIENCY ANTHOL. PAGE 4 E0083 MGT

B58
DEUTSCHE GESCHAFT VOLKERRECHT,DIE VOLKERRECHTLICHEN BIBLIOG
DISSERTATIONEN AN DEN WESTDEUTSCHEN UNIVERSITATEN, INT/LAW
1945-1957. GERMANY/W NAT/G DIPLOM ADJUD CT/SYS ACADEM
...POLICY 20. PAGE 31 E0616 JURID

B59
MOOS M.,THE CAMPUS AND THE STATE. LAW FINAN EDU/PROP
DELIB/GP LEGIS EXEC LOBBY GP/REL PWR...POLICY ACADEM
BIBLIOG. PAGE 74 E1489 PROVS
CONTROL

B59
SURRENCY E.C.,A GUIDE TO LEGAL RESEARCH. USA+45 NAT/G
ACADEM LEGIS ACT/RES ADMIN...DECISION METH/COMP PROVS
BIBLIOG METH. PAGE 94 E1894 ADJUD
JURID

B60
FELLMAN D.,THE SUPREME COURT AND EDUCATION. ACADEM CT/SYS
NAT/G PROVS DELIB/GP ADJUD ORD/FREE...POLICY JURID SECT
WORSHIP 20 SUPREME/CT NEGRO CHURCH/STA. PAGE 37 RACE/REL
E0731 SCHOOL

B60
FLORES R.H.,CATALOGO DE TESIS DOCTORALES DE LAS BIBLIOG
FACULTADES DE LA UNIVERSIDAD DE EL SALVADOR. ACADEM
EL/SALVADR LAW DIPLOM ADMIN LEAD GOV/REL...SOC L/A+17C
19/20. PAGE 39 E0767 NAT/G

S60
MACKINNON F.,"THE UNIVERSITY: COMMUNITY OR ACADEM
UTILITY?" CLIENT CONSTN INTELL FINAN NAT/G NEIGH MGT
EDU/PROP PARTIC REPRESENT ROLE. PAGE 67 E1343 CONTROL
SERV/IND

L61
FELLMAN D.,"ACADEMIC FREEDOM IN AMERICAN LAW." LAW ACADEM
CONSTN NAT/G VOL/ASSN PLAN PERSON KNOWL NEW/LIB. ORD/FREE
PAGE 37 E0732 LEGIS
CULTURE

B62
DAVIS F.J.,SOCIETY AND THE LAW. USA+45 CONSTN LAW
ACADEM FAM CONSULT ACT/RES GP/REL ORD/FREE SOC
ENGLSH/LAW 20. PAGE 29 E0572 CULTURE
STRUCT

B62
DUPRE J.S.,SCIENCE AND THE NATION: POLICY AND R+D
POLITICS. USA+45 LAW ACADEM FORCES ADMIN CIVMIL/REL INDUS

GOV/REL EFFICIENCY PEACE...TREND 20 SCI/ADVSRY.   TEC/DEV
PAGE 34 E0665   NUC/PWR

                                                          B62
INTERNAT CONGRESS OF JURISTS,EXECUTIVE ACTION AND   JURID
THE RULE OF RULE: REPORTION PROCEEDINGS OF INT'T   EXEC
CONGRESS OF JURISTS.-RIO DE JANEIRO, BRAZIL. WOR+45   ORD/FREE
ACADEM CONSULT JUDGE EDU/PROP ADJUD CT/SYS IN   REL   CONTROL
PERSON DEPT/DEFEN. PAGE 57 E1130

                                                          L62
SCHWERIN K.,"LAW LIBRARIES AND FOREIGN LAW   BIBLIOG
COLLECTION IN THE USA." USA+45 USA-45...INT/LAW   LAW
STAT 20. PAGE 89 E1793   ACADEM
                                                          ADMIN

                                                          B63
CHOJNACKI S.,REGISTER ON CURRENT RESEARCH ON   BIBLIOG
ETHIOPIA AND THE HORN OF AFRICA. ETHIOPIA LAW   ACT/RES
CULTURE AGRI SECT EDU/PROP ADMIN...GEOG HEAL LING   INTELL
20. PAGE 22 E0433   ACADEM

                                                          B63
A BIBLIOGRAPHY OF DOCTORAL DISSERTATIONS UNDERTAKEN   BIBLIOG
IN AMERICAN AND CANADIAN UNIVERSITIES ON RELIGION   ACADEM
AND POLITICS. LAW CONSTN DOMIN LEGIT ADJUD GP/REL   SECT
...POLICY 20. PAGE 62 E1241   JURID

                                                          B63
LEVY L.W.,JEFFERSON AND CIVIL LIBERTIES: THE DARKER   BIOG
SIDE. USA-45 LAW INTELL ACADEM FORCES PRESS REV   ORD/FREE
INGP/REL PERSON 18/19 JEFFERSN/T CIVIL/LIB. PAGE 65   CONSTN
E1291   ATTIT

                                                          S63
JOUGHIN L.,"ACADEMIC DUE PROCESS." DELIB/GP ADJUD   ACADEM
ROUTINE ORD/FREE...POLICY MAJORIT TREND. PAGE 59   LAW
E1175   PROF/ORG
                                                          CLIENT

                                                          B64
DOOLIN D.J.,COMMUNIST CHINA: THE POLITICS OF   MARXISM
STUDENT OPPOSITION. CHINA/COM ELITES STRATA ACADEM   DEBATE
NAT/G WRITING CT/SYS LEAD PARTIC COERCE TOTALISM   AGE/Y
20. PAGE 32 E0637   PWR

                                                          B64
DORMAN M.,WE SHALL OVERCOME. USA+45 ELITES ACADEM   RACE/REL
FORCES TOP/EX MURDER...JURID 20 CIV/RIGHTS   LAW
MISSISSIPP EVERS/MED CLEMSON. PAGE 32 E0638   DISCRIM

                                                          B65
CHARLTON K.,EDUCATION IN RENAISSANCE ENGLAND. ITALY   EDU/PROP
UK USA-45 WOR-45 LAW LOC/G NAT/G...IDEA/COMP 14/17   SCHOOL
HUMANISM. PAGE 21 E0423   ACADEM

                                                          B65
CONGRESSIONAL QUARTERLY SERV,FEDERAL ROLE IN   ACADEM
EDUCATION (PAMPHLET). LAW SCHOOL PLAN TAX ADJUD   DISCRIM
...CHARTS SOC/INTEG 20 PRESIDENT. PAGE 25 E0487   RECEIVE
                                                          FEDERAL

                                                          B65
NORDEN A.,WAR AND NAZI CRIMINALS IN WEST GERMANY: FASCIST
STATE, ECONOMY, ADMINISTRATION, ARMY, JUSTICE,   WAR
SCIENCE. GERMANY GERMANY/W MOD/EUR ECO/DEV ACADEM   NAT/G
EX/STRUC FORCES DOMIN ADMIN CT/SYS...POLICY MAJORIT   TOP/EX
PACIFIST 20. PAGE 77 E1554

                                                          B65
RADZINOWICZ L.,THE NEED FOR CRIMINOLOGY AND A   CRIMLGY
PROPOSAL FOR AN INSTITUTE OF CRIMINOLOGY. FUT UK   PROF/ORG
USA+45 SOCIETY ACT/RES PROB/SOLV CRIME...PSY SOC   ACADEM
BIBLIOG 20. PAGE 83 E1666   CONTROL

                                                          B65
UNESCO,HANDBOOK OF INTERNATIONAL EXCHANGES. COM/IND   INDEX
R+D ACADEM PROF/ORG VOL/ASSN CREATE TEC/DEV   INT/ORG
EDU/PROP AGREE 20 TREATY. PAGE 98 E1963   DIPLOM
                                                          PRESS

                                                          B65
US LIBRARY OF CONGRESS,INTERNAL SECURITY AND   CONTROL
SUBVERSION. USA+45 ACADEM LOC/G NAT/G PROVS   ADJUD
...POLICY ANARCH DECISION 20 CIVIL/SERV SUBVERT   LAW
SEDITION. PAGE 101 E2020   PLAN

                                                          B65
VON GLAHN G.,LAW AMONG NATIONS: AN INTRODUCTION TO   ACADEM
PUBLIC INTERNATIONAL LAW. WOR+45 WOR-45 INT/ORG   INT/LAW
NAT/G CREATE ADJUD WAR...GEOG CLASSIF TREND   GEN/LAWS
BIBLIOG. PAGE 104 E2082   LAW

                                                          C65
SEARA M.V.,"COSMIC INTERNATIONAL LAW." LAW ACADEM   SPACE
ACT/RES DIPLOM COLONIAL CONTROL NUC/PWR SOVEREIGN   INT/LAW

...GEN/LAWS BIBLIOG UN. PAGE 90 E1799   IDEA/COMP
                                                          INT/ORG

                                                          B66
BRAIBANTI R.,RESEARCH ON THE BUREAUCRACY OF   HABITAT
PAKISTAN. PAKISTAN LAW CULTURE INTELL ACADEM LOC/G   NAT/G
SECT PRESS CT/SYS...LING CHARTS 20 BUREAUCRCY.   ADMIN
PAGE 15 E0286   CONSTN

                                                          B66
FALK R.A.,THE STRATEGY OF WORLD ORDER* 4 VOLUMES.   ORD/FREE
WOR+45 ECO/UNDEV ACADEM INT/ORG ACT/RES DIPLOM   GEN/LAWS
ARMS/CONT WAR...NET/THEORY SIMUL BIBLIOG UN.   ANTHOL
PAGE 36 E0719   INT/LAW

                                                          S66
EWALD R.F.,"ONE OF MANY POSSIBLE GAMES." ACADEM   SIMUL
INT/ORG ARMS/CONT...INT/LAW GAME. PAGE 36 E0706   HYPO/EXP
                                                          PROG/TEAC
                                                          RECORD

                                                          B67
DIEGUES M.,SOCIAL SCIENCE IN LATIN AMERICA. L/A+17C   METH
...JURID SOC ANTHOL 20. PAGE 31 E0624   ACADEM
                                                          EDU/PROP
                                                          ACT/RES

                                                          L67
HITCHMAN J.M.,"THE PLATT AMENDMENT REVISITED: A   ATTIT
BIBLIOGRAPHICAL SURVEY." CUBA ACADEM DELIB/GP   DIPLOM
ORD/FREE...HIST/WRIT 20. PAGE 53 E1055   SOVEREIGN
                                                          INT/LAW

                                                          S67
MONEYPENNY P.,"UNIVERSITY PURPOSE, DISCIPLINE, AND   ACADEM
DUE PROCESS." USA+45 EDU/PROP ADJUD LEISURE   AGE/Y
ORD/FREE. PAGE 74 E1484   CONTROL
                                                          ADMIN

ACADEM/SCI....ACADEMY OF SCIENCES (U.S.S.R.)

ACBC....ACTION COUNCIL FOR BETTER CITIES

ACCOUNTING....SEE ACCT

ACCT....ACCOUNTING, BOOKKEEPING

ACCULTURATION....SEE CULTURE

ACD....UNITED STATES ARMS CONTROL AND DISARMAMENT AGENCY

ACHESON/D....DEAN ACHESON

ACLU....AMERICAN CIVIL LIBERTIES UNION

                                                          N19
IN THE SHADOW OF FEAR; AMERICAN CIVIL LIBERTIES,   ORD/FREE
1948-49 (PAMPHLET). COM LAW LEGIS BAL/PWR EDU/PROP   CONSTN
CT/SYS RACE/REL DISCRIM MARXISM SOCISM 20 COLD/WAR   POLICY
CONGRESS ACLU CIV/RIGHTS ESPIONAGE. PAGE 2 E0030

                                                          N19
AMERICAN CIVIL LIBERTIES UNION,"WE HOLD THESE   ORD/FREE
TRUTHS" FREEDOM, JUSTICE, EQUALITY: REPORT ON CIVIL   LAW
LIBERTIES (A PERIODICAL PAMPHLET COVERING 1951-53).   RACE/REL
USA+45 ACADEM NAT/G FORCES LEGIS COERCE CIVMIL/REL   CONSTN
GOV/REL DISCRIM PRIVIL MARXISM...OLD/LIB 20 ACLU UN
CIVIL/LIB. PAGE 4 E0076

ACQUAINTANCE GROUP....SEE FACE/GP

ACT/RES....RESEARCH FACILITATING SOCIAL ACTION

ACTION COUNCIL FOR BETTER CITIES....SEE ACBC

ACTION....ALLEGHENY COUNCIL TO IMPROVE OUR NEIGHBORHOODS

ACTON/LORD....LORD ACTON

ADA....AMERICANS FOR DEMOCRATIC ACTION

ADAIR D. E0991

ADAMOVITCH A. E0873

ADAMS B. E0047

ADAMS J. E0048

ADAMS/J....PRESIDENT JOHN ADAMS

ADAMS/JQ....PRESIDENT JOHN QUINCY ADAMS

ADAMS/SAM....SAMUEL ADAMS

ADDICTION....ADDICTION

ADENAUER/K....KONRAD ADENAUER

ADJUD....JUDICIAL AND ADJUDICATIVE PROCESSES

KEITT L.,AN ANNOTATED BIBLIOGRAPHY OF   N
BIBLIOGRAPHIES OF STATUTORY MATERIALS OF THE UNITED   BIBLIOG/A
STATES. CHRIST-17C USA-45 LEGIS ADJUD COLONIAL   LAW
CT/SYS...JURID 16/20. PAGE 60 E1196   CONSTN
                          PROVS

AMERICAN JOURNAL OF INTERNATIONAL LAW. WOR+45   N
WOR-45 CONSTN INT/ORG NAT/G CT/SYS ARMS/CONT WAR   BIBLIOG/A
...DECISION JURID NAT/COMP 20. PAGE 1 E0001   INT/LAW
                          DIPLOM
                          ADJUD

INDEX TO LEGAL PERIODICALS. CANADA NEW/ZEALND UK   N
USA+45 USA-45 CONSTN LEGIS JUDGE ADJUD ADMIN   BIBLIOG
CONTROL CT/SYS FEDERAL...CRIMLGY INT/LAW 20   INDEX
CMN/WLTH AUSTRAL. PAGE 1 E0006   LAW
                          JURID

INTERNATIONAL BOOK NEWS, 1928-1934. ECO/UNDEV FINAN   N
INDUS LABOR INT/TRADE CONFER ADJUD COLONIAL...HEAL   BIBLIOG/A
SOC/WK CHARTS 20 LEAGUE/NAT. PAGE 1 E0008   DIPLOM
                          INT/LAW
                          INT/ORG

ARBITRATION JOURNAL. WOR+45 LAW INDUS JUDGE DIPLOM   N
CT/SYS INGP/REL 20. PAGE 1 E0016   BIBLIOG
                          MGT
                          LABOR
                          ADJUD

HARVARD LAW SCHOOL LIBRARY,ANNUAL LEGAL   N
BIBLIOGRAPHY. USA+45 CONSTN LEGIS ADJUD CT/SYS   BIBLIOG
...POLICY 20. PAGE 50 E1005   JURID
                          LAW
                          INT/LAW

HARVARD UNIVERSITY LAW LIBRARY,CATALOG OF   N
INTERNATIONAL LAW AND RELATIONS. WOR+45 WOR-45   BIBLIOG
INT/ORG NAT/G JUDGE DIPLOM INT/TRADE ADJUD CT/SYS   INT/LAW
19/20. PAGE 51 E1007   JURID

SOCIETE DES NATIONS,TRAITES INTERNATIONAUX ET ACTES   N
LEGISLATIFS. WOR-45 INT/ORG NAT/G...INT/LAW JURID   BIBLIOG
20 LEAGUE/NAT TREATY. PAGE 92 E1851   DIPLOM
                          LEGIS
                          ADJUD

US SUPERINTENDENT OF DOCUMENTS,POLITICAL SCIENCE: N
GOVERNMENT, CRIME, DISTRICT OF COLUMBIA (PRICE LIST   BIBLIOG/A
54). USA+45 LAW CONSTN EX/STRUC WORKER ADJUD ADMIN   NAT/G
CT/SYS CHOOSE INGP/REL RACE/REL CONGRESS PRESIDENT.   CRIME
PAGE 103 E2063

LALL A.S.,NEGOTIATING DISARMAMENT* THE EIGHTEEN   B'
NATION DISARMAMENT CONFERENCE* THE FIRST TWO YEARS,   OBS
1962-1964. ASIA FRANCE INDIA USA+45 USSR PROB/SOLV   ARMS/CONT
ADJUD NEUTRAL ATTIT...IDEA/COMP COLD/WAR. PAGE 62   DIPLOM
E1246   OP/RES

                          B00
DARBY W.E.,INTERNATIONAL TRIBUNALS. WOR-45 NAT/G   INT/ORG
ECO/TAC DOMIN LEGIT CT/SYS COERCE ORD/FREE PWR   ADJUD
SOVEREIGN JURID. PAGE 29 E0567   PEACE
                          INT/LAW

                          B03
FAGUET E.,LE LIBERALISME. FRANCE PRESS ADJUD ADMIN   ORD/FREE
DISCRIM CONSERVE SOCISM...TRADIT SOC LING WORSHIP   EDU/PROP
PARLIAMENT. PAGE 36 E0711   NAT/G
                          LAW

                          B03
GRIFFIN A.P.C.,LIST OF REFERENCES ON INDUSTRIAL   BIBLIOG/A
ARBITRATION (PAMPHLET). USA-45 STRATA VOL/ASSN   INDUS
DELIB/GP WORKER ADJUD GP/REL...MGT 19/20. PAGE 46   LABOR
E0921   BARGAIN

                          B03
GRIFFIN A.P.C.,LISTS PUBLISHED 1902-03: GOVERNMENT   BIBLIOG
OWNERSHIP OF RAILROADS (PAMPHLET). USA-45 LAW NAT/G   DIST/IND
RATION GOV/REL CENTRAL SOCISM...POLICY 19/20.   CONTROL
PAGE 46 E0922   ADJUD

                          B03
GRIFFIN A.P.C.,SELECT LIST OF BOOKS ON LABOR   BIBLIOG/A

PARTICULARLY RELATING TO STRIKES. FRANCE GERMANY   GP/REL
MOD/EUR UK USA-45 LAW NAT/G DELIB/GP WORKER BARGAIN   MGT
LICENSE PAY ADJUD 19/20. PAGE 46 E0924   LABOR

                          B04
BURKE E.,A LETTER TO THE SHERIFFS OF BRISTOL   LEGIS
(1777). USA-45 LAW ECO/TAC COLONIAL CT/SYS REV   ADJUD
GP/REL ORD/FREE...POLICY 18 PARLIAMENT BURKE/EDM.   CRIME
PAGE 17 E0341

                          B04
FREUND E.,THE POLICE POWER; PUBLIC POLICY AND   CONSTN
CONSTITUTIONAL RIGHTS. USA-45 SOCIETY LOC/G NAT/G   LAW
FORCES LEGIS ADJUD CT/SYS OWN PWR...JURID 18/19   ORD/FREE
SUPREME/CT. PAGE 40 E0795   CONTROL

                          B04
GRIFFIN A.P.C.,A LIST OF BOOKS RELATING TO   BIBLIOG/A
RAILROADS IN THEIR RELATION TO THE GOVERNMENT AND   SERV/IND
THE PUBLIC (PAMPHLET). USA-45 LAW ECO/DEV NAT/G   ADJUD
TEC/DEV CAP/ISM LICENSE CENTRAL LAISSEZ...DECISION   ECO/TAC
19/20. PAGE 47 E0925

                          B05
DICEY A.V.,LECTURES ON THE RELATION BETWEEN LAW AND   LAW
PUBLIC OPINION IN ENGLAND DURING THE NINETEENTH   ADJUD
CENTURY. UK LEGIS CT/SYS...JURID 19 TORY/PARTY   ATTIT
BENTHAM/J ENGLSH/LAW. PAGE 31 E0621   IDEA/COMP

                          B07
BENTHAM J.,AN INTRODUCTION TO THE PRINCIPLES OF   LAW
MORALS AND LEGISLATION. UNIV CONSTN CULTURE SOCIETY   GEN/LAWS
NAT/G CONSULT LEGIS JUDGE ADJUD CT/SYS...JURID   CONCPT
CONCPT NEW/IDEA. PAGE 10 E0190

                          B08
GRIFFIN A.P.C.,LIST OF WORKS RELATING TO GOVERNMENT   BIBLIOG/A
REGULATION OF INSURANCE UNITED STATES AND FOREIGN   FINAN
COUNTRIES (2ND. ED.) (PAMPHLET). FRANCE GERMANY UK   LAW
USA-45 WOR-45 LG/CO LOC/G NAT/G LEGIS LICENSE ADJUD   CONTROL
LOBBY CENTRAL ORD/FREE 19/20. PAGE 47 E0933

                          B08
WILSON W.,CONSTITUTIONAL GOVERNMENT IN THE UNITED   NAT/G
STATES. USA-45 LAW POL/PAR PROVS CHIEF LEGIS   GOV/REL
BAL/PWR ADJUD EXEC FEDERAL PWR 18/20 SUPREME/CT   CONSTN
HOUSE/REP SENATE. PAGE 106 E2130   PARL/PROC

                          B09
HARVARD UNIVERSITY LAW LIBRARY,CATALOGUE OF THE   BIBLIOG/A
LIBRARY OF THE LAW SCHOOL OF HARVARD UNIVERSITY (3   LAW
VOLS.). UK USA-45 LEGIS JUDGE ADJUD CT/SYS...JURID   ADMIN
CHARTS 14/20. PAGE 51 E1008

                          B12
BEARD C.A.,THE SUPREME COURT AND THE CONSTITUTION.   CONSTN
LAW NAT/G PROVS LEGIS GOV/REL ATTIT POPULISM   CT/SYS
SUPREME/CT. PAGE 9 E0164   ADJUD
                          CONTROL

                          B12
GRIFFIN A.P.C.,SELECT LIST OF REFERENCES ON   BIBLIOG/A
IMPEACHMENT (REV. ED.) (PAMPHLET). USA-45 LAW PROVS   CONSTN
ADJUD ATTIT...JURID 19/20 NEGRO. PAGE 47 E0935   NAT/G
                          LEGIS

                          B13
BUTLER N.M.,THE INTERNATIONAL MIND. WOR-45 INT/ORG   ADJUD
LEGIT PWR...JURID CONCPT 20. PAGE 18 E0350   ORD/FREE
                          INT/LAW

                          N13
SCHMIDHAUSER J.R.,JUDICIAL BEHAVIOR AND THE   JUDGE
SECTIONAL CRISIS OF 1837-1860. USA-45 ADJUD CT/SYS   POL/PAR
INGP/REL ATTIT HABITAT...DECISION PSY STAT CHARTS   PERS/COMP
SIMUL. PAGE 88 E1759   PERSON

                          B15
HOBSON J.A.,TOWARDS INTERNATIONAL GOVERNMENT.   FUT
MOD/EUR STRUCT ECO/TAC EDU/PROP ADJUD ALL/VALS   INT/ORG
...SOCIALIST CONCPT GEN/LAWS TOT/POP 20. PAGE 53   CENTRAL
E1059

                          B15
INTERNATIONAL LAW ASSOCIATION,A FORTY YEARS'   BIBLIOG
CATALOGUE OF THE BOOKS, PAMPHLETS AND PAPERS IN THE   LAW
LIBRARY OF THE INTERNATIONAL LAW ASSOCIATION.   INT/LAW
INT/ORG DIPLOM ADJUD NEUTRAL...IDEA/COMP 19/20.
PAGE 57 E1134

                          B16
SALMOND J.W.,JURISPRUDENCE. UK LOC/G NAT/G LEGIS   LAW
PROB/SOLV LICENSE LEGIT CRIME PERS/REL OWN ORD/FREE   CT/SYS
...T 20. PAGE 87 E1742   JURID
                          ADJUD

S18

POWELL T.R.,"THE LOGIC AND RHETORIC OF CONSTN
CONSTITUTIONAL LAW" (BMR)" USA+45 USA-45 DELIB/GP LAW
PROB/SOLV ADJUD CT/SYS...DECISION 20 SUPREME/CT JURID
CON/INTERP. PAGE 82 E1642 LOG

N18

BREWER D.J.,THE MOVEMENT OF COERCION (PAMPHLET). GP/REL
CONSTN INDUS ADJUD COERCE OWN WEALTH...OLD/LIB LABOR
JURID 19 SUPREME/CT. PAGE 15 E0296 LG/CO
LAW

B19

LONDON SCHOOL ECONOMICS-POL,ANNUAL DIGEST OF PUBLIC BIBLIOG/A
INTERNATIONAL LAW CASES. INT/ORG MUNIC NAT/G PROVS INT/LAW
ADMIN NEUTRAL WAR GOV/REL PRIVIL 20. PAGE 66 E1323 ADJUD
DIPLOM

B19

SMITH R.H.,JUSTICE AND THE POOR. LAW RECEIVE ADJUD CT/SYS
CRIME GOV/REL COST...JURID SOC/WK CONCPT STAT DISCRIM
CHARTS GP/COMP 20. PAGE 92 E1847 WEALTH

N19

BRENNAN W.J. JR.,THE BILL OF RIGHTS AND THE STATES CONSTN
(PAMPHLET). USA+45 USA-45 LEGIS BAL/PWR ADJUD PROVS
CT/SYS FEDERAL PWR SOVEREIGN 18/20 SUPREME/CT GOV/REL
BILL/RIGHT. PAGE 15 E0293 ORD/FREE

N19

CARPER E.T.,LOBBYING AND THE NATURAL GAS BILL LOBBY
(PAMPHLET). USA+45 SERV/IND BARGAIN PAY DRIVE ROLE ADJUD
WEALTH 20 CONGRESS SENATE EISNHWR/DD. PAGE 20 E0389 TRIBUTE
NAT/G

N19

GIBB A.D.,JUDICIAL CORRUPTION IN THE UNITED KINGDOM MORAL
(PAMPHLET). UK DELIB/GP CT/SYS CRIME PERSON SUPEGO ATTIT
17/20 SCOTLAND. PAGE 43 E0856 ADJUD

N19

MCCONNELL G.,THE STEEL SEIZURE OF 1952 (PAMPHLET). DELIB/GP
USA+45 FINAN INDUS PROC/MFG LG/CO EX/STRUC ADJUD LABOR
CONTROL GP/REL ORD/FREE PWR 20 TRUMAN/HS PRESIDENT PROB/SOLV
CONGRESS. PAGE 70 E1402 NAT/G

N19

MISSISSIPPI ADVISORY COMMITTEE,REPORT ON RACE/REL
MISSISSIPPI (PAMPHLET). USA+45 LAW PROVS FORCES DISCRIM
ADJUD PWR...SOC/WK INT 20 MISSISSIPP NEGRO COERCE
CIV/RIGHTS. PAGE 73 E1469 ORD/FREE

N19

POUND R.,ORGANIZATION OF THE COURTS (PAMPHLET). CT/SYS
MOD/EUR UK USA-45 ADJUD PWR...GOV/COMP 10/20 JURID
EUROPE. PAGE 82 E1635 STRUCT
ADMIN

B22

COX G.C.,THE PUBLIC CONSCIENCE: A CASEBOOK IN MORAL
ETHICS....PHIL/SCI SOC CONCPT METH/COMP 20. PAGE 27 ADJUD
E0534

B22

SCHROEDER T.,FREE SPEECH BIBLIOGRAPHY. EUR+WWI BIBLIOG/A
WOR-45 NAT/G SECT ECO/TAC WRITING ADJUD ATTIT ORD/FREE
MARXISM SOCISM 16/20. PAGE 88 E1768 CONTROL
LAW

B23

HOLMES O.W. JR.,THE COMMON LAW. FUT WOR-45 CULTURE ADJUD
SOCIETY CREATE LEGIT ROUTINE ATTIT ALL/VALS...JURID CON/ANAL
METH/CNCPT TIME/SEQ GEN/LAWS TOT/POP VAL/FREE.
PAGE 55 E1087

B24

CARDOZO B.,THE GROWTH OF THE LAW. USA-45 CULTURE LAW
...JURID 20. PAGE 19 E0376 ADJUD
CT/SYS

B24

HOLDSWORTH W.S.,A HISTORY OF ENGLISH LAW; THE LAW
COMMON LAW AND ITS RIVALS (VOL. V). UK SEA EX/STRUC LEGIS
WRITING ADMIN...INT/LAW JURID CONCPT IDEA/COMP ADJUD
WORSHIP 16/17 PARLIAMENT ENGLSH/LAW COMMON/LAW. CT/SYS
PAGE 54 E1073

B24

HOLDSWORTH W.S.,A HISTORY OF ENGLISH LAW; THE LAW
COMMON LAW AND ITS RIVALS (VOL. VI). UK STRATA CONSTN
EX/STRUC ADJUD ADMIN CONTROL CT/SYS...JURID CONCPT LEGIS
GEN/LAWS 17 COMMONWLTH PARLIAMENT ENGLSH/LAW CHIEF
COMMON/LAW. PAGE 54 E1074

B24

HOLDSWORTH W.S.,A HISTORY OF ENGLISH LAW; THE LAW

LEGIS

COMMON LAW AND ITS RIVALS (VOL. IV). UK SEA AGRI CT/SYS
CHIEF ADJUD CONTROL CRIME GOV/REL...INT/LAW JURID CONSTN
NAT/COMP 16/17 PARLIAMENT COMMON/LAW CANON/LAW
ENGLSH/LAW. PAGE 54 E1075

C24

SHERMAN C.P.,"ROMAN LAW IN THE MODERN WORLD (2ND LAW
ED.) (3 VOLS.)" MEDIT-7...JURID BIBLIOG. PAGE 91 ADJUD
E1819 OWN
CONSTN

B25

WINFIELD P.H.,THE CHIEF SOURCES OF ENGLISH LEGAL BIBLIOG/A
HISTORY. UK CONSTN JUDGE ADJUD CT/SYS 13/18. JURID
PAGE 107 E2133 LAW

L25

HUDSON M.,"THE PERMANENT COURT OF INTERNATIONAL INT/ORG
JUSTICE AND THE QUESTION OF AMERICAN ADJUD
PARTICIPATION." WOR-45 LEGIT CT/SYS ORD/FREE DIPLOM
...JURID CONCPT TIME/SEQ GEN/LAWS VAL/FREE 20 ICJ. INT/LAW
PAGE 56 E1108

B26

BEALE J.H.,A BIBLIOGRAPHY OF EARLY ENGLISH LAW BIBLIOG/A
BOOKS. MOD/EUR UK PRESS ADJUD CT/SYS ATTIT...CHARTS JURID
10/16. PAGE 8 E0161 LAW

S26

HALL A.B.,"DETERMINATION OF METHODS FOR ADJUD
ASCERTAINING THE FACTORS THAT INFLUENCE JUDICIAL DECISION
DECISIONS IN CASES INVOLVING DUE PROCESS" LAW JUDGE CONSTN
DEBATE EFFICIENCY OPTIMAL UTIL...SOC CONCPT JURID
PROBABIL STAT SAMP. PAGE 49 E0981

B27

DICKINSON J.,ADMINISTRATIVE JUSTICE AND THE CT/SYS
SUPREMACY OF LAW IN THE UNITED STATES. USA-45 LAW ADJUD
INDUS DOMIN EDU/PROP CONTROL EXEC GP/REL ORD/FREE ADMIN
...POLICY JURID 19/20. PAGE 31 E0623 NAT/G

B27

LAUTERPACHT H.,PRIVATE LAW SOURCES AND ANALOGIES OF INT/ORG
INTERNATIONAL LAW. WOR-45 NAT/G DELIB/GP LEGIT ADJUD
COERCE ATTIT ORD/FREE PWR SOVEREIGN...JURID CONCPT PEACE
HIST/WRIT TIME/SEQ GEN/METH LEAGUE/NAT 20. PAGE 63 INT/LAW
E1264

B28

BENTHAM J.,A COMMENT OF THE COMMENTARIES (1765-69). LAW
MUNIC SECT ADJUD AGREE CT/SYS CONSEN HAPPINESS CONCPT
ORD/FREE 18. PAGE 10 E0191 IDEA/COMP

B28

FRANKFURTER F.,THE BUSINESS OF THE SUPREME COURT; A CT/SYS
STUDY IN THE FEDERAL JUDICIAL SYSTEM. USA-45 CONSTN ADJUD
EX/STRUC PROB/SOLV GP/REL ATTIT PWR...POLICY JURID LAW
18/20 SUPREME/CT CONGRESS. PAGE 40 E0789 FEDERAL

B28

MACDONALD A.F.,ELEMENTS OF POLITICAL SCIENCE LAW
RESEARCH. USA-45 ACADEM JUDGE EDU/PROP DEBATE ADJUD FEDERAL
EXEC...BIBLIOG METH T 20 CONGRESS. PAGE 67 E1338 DECISION
CT/SYS

B29

CAM H.M.,BIBLIOGRAPHY OF ENGLISH CONSTITUTIONAL BIBLIOG/A
HISTORY (PAMPHLET). UK LAW LOC/G NAT/G POL/PAR SECT CONSTN
DELIB/GP ADJUD ORD/FREE 19/20 PARLIAMENT. PAGE 19 ADMIN
E0369 PARL/PROC

B29

MOLEY R.,POLITICS AND CRIMINAL PROSECUTION. USA-45 PWR
POL/PAR EX/STRUC LEGIT CONTROL LEAD ROUTINE CHOOSE CT/SYS
INGP/REL...JURID CHARTS 20. PAGE 74 E1481 CRIME
ADJUD

B29

STURZO L.,THE INTERNATIONAL COMMUNITY AND THE RIGHT INT/ORG
OF WAR (TRANS. BY BARBARA BARCLAY CARTER). CULTURE PLAN
CREATE PROB/SOLV DIPLOM ADJUD CONTROL PEACE PERSON WAR
ORD/FREE....INT/LAW IDEA/COMP PACIFIST 20 CONCPT
LEAGUE/NAT. PAGE 94 E1891

B30

BIRD F.L.,THE RECALL OF PUBLIC OFFICERS; A STUDY OF REPRESENT
THE OPERATION OF RECALL IN CALIFORNIA. LOC/G MUNIC SANCTION
POL/PAR PROVS PROB/SOLV ADJUD PARTIC...CHARTS CHOOSE
METH/COMP 20 CALIFORNIA RECALL. PAGE 12 E0230 LAW

B30

WILLOUGHBY W.W.,PRINCIPLES OF THE CONSTITUTIONAL CONSTN
LAW OF THE UNITED STATES. USA-45 ADJUD FEDERAL NAT/G
SOVEREIGN 18/20 COMMON/LAW. PAGE 106 E2125 CONCPT
JURID

L30
LLEWELLYN K.N.,"A REALISTIC JURISPRUDENCE - THE LAW
NEXT STEP." PROB/SOLV ADJUD GP/REL PERS/REL CONCPT
IDEA/COMP. PAGE 66 E1312 JURID
GEN/LAWS

B32
EAGLETON C.,INTERNATIONAL GOVERNMENT. BRAZIL FRANCE INT/ORG
GERMANY ITALY UK USSR WOR-45 DELIB/GP TOP/EX PLAN JURID
ECO/TAC EDU/PROP LEGIT ADJUD ARMS/CONT DIPLOM
COERCE ATTIT PWR...GEOG MGT VAL/FREE LEAGUE/NAT 20. INT/LAW
PAGE 34 E0670

B32
GREGORY W.,LIST OF THE SERIAL PUBLICATIONS OF BIBLIOG
FOREIGN GOVERNMENTS, 1815-1931. WOR-45 DIPLOM ADJUD NAT/G
...POLICY 20. PAGE 46 E0914 LAW
JURID

B32
LUNT D.C.,THE ROAD TO THE LAW. UK USA-45 LEGIS ADJUD
EDU/PROP OWN ORD/FREE...DECISION TIME/SEQ NAT/COMP LAW
16/20 AUSTRAL ENGLSH/LAW COMMON/LAW. PAGE 67 E1333 JURID
CT/SYS

B33
AMERICAN FOREIGN LAW ASSN,BIOGRAPHICAL NOTES ON THE BIBLIOG/A
LAWS AND LEGAL LITERATURE OF URUGUAY AND CURACAO. LAW
URUGUAY CONSTN FINAN SECT FORCES JUDGE DIPLOM JURID
INT/TRADE ADJUD CT/SYS CRIME 20. PAGE 4 E0078 ADMIN

B33
ENSOR R.C.K.,COURTS AND JUDGES IN FRANCE, GERMANY, CT/SYS
AND ENGLAND. FRANCE GERMANY UK LAW PROB/SOLV ADMIN EX/STRUC
ROUTINE CRIME ROLE...METH/COMP 20 CIVIL/LAW. ADJUD
PAGE 35 E0692 NAT/COMP

B33
MATTHEWS M.A.,THE AMERICAN INSTITUTE OF BIBLIOG/A
INTERNATIONAL LAW AND THE CODIFICATION OF INT/LAW
INTERNATIONAL LAW (PAMPHLET). USA-45 CONSTN ADJUD L/A+17C
CT/SYS...JURID 20. PAGE 69 E1386 DIPLOM

B34
CULVER D.C.,BIBLIOGRAPHY OF CRIME AND CRIMINAL BIBLIOG/A
JUSTICE, 1927-1931. LAW CULTURE PUB/INST PROB/SOLV CRIMLGY
CT/SYS...PSY SOC STAT 20. PAGE 28 E0549 ADJUD
FORCES

B35
BEMIS S.F.,GUIDE TO THE DIPLOMATIC HISTORY OF THE BIBLIOG/A
UNITED STATES, 17751921. NAT/G LEGIS TOP/EX DIPLOM
PROB/SOLV CAP/ISM INT/TRADE TARIFFS ADJUD USA-45
...CON/ANAL 18/20. PAGE 10 E0184

B35
CUMMING J.,A CONTRIBUTION TOWARD A BIBLIOGRAPHY BIBLIOG
DEALING WITH CRIME AND COGNATE SUBJECTS (3RD ED.). CRIMLGY
UK LAW CULTURE PUB/INST ADJUD AGE BIO/SOC...PSY SOC FORCES
SOC/WK STAT METH/COMP 20. PAGE 28 E0552 CT/SYS

B35
HALL J.,THEFT, LAW, AND SOCIETY. SOCIETY PROB/SOLV CRIME
...CRIMLGY SOC CONCPT TREND METH/COMP 18/20 LAW
LARCENCY. PAGE 49 E0982 ADJUD
ADJUST

B35
KENNEDY W.P.,THE LAW AND CUSTOM OF THE SOUTH CT/SYS
AFRICAN CONSTITUTION. AFR SOUTH/AFR KIN LOC/G PROVS CONSTN
DIPLOM ADJUD ADMIN EXEC 20. PAGE 60 E1203 JURID
PARL/PROC

B35
MCLAUGHLIN A.C.,A CONSTITUTIONAL HISTORY OF THE CONSTN
UNITED STATES. USA+45 USA-45 LOC/G NAT/G PROVS DECISION
LEGIS JUDGE ADJUD...T 18/20. PAGE 71 E1422

B35
NORDSKOG J.E.,SOCIAL REFORM IN NORWAY. NORWAY INDUS LABOR
NAT/G POL/PAR LEGIS ADJUD...SOC BIBLIOG SOC/INTEG ADJUST
20. PAGE 78 E1555

B35
RAM J.,THE SCIENCE OF LEGAL JUDGMENT: A TREATISE... LAW
UK LAW CONSTN NAT/G LEGIS CREATE PROB/SOLV AGREE CT/SYS JURID
...INT/LAW CONCPT 19 ENGLSH/LAW CANON/LAW CIVIL/LAW EX/STRUC
CTS/WESTM. PAGE 83 E1672 ADJUD

B35
ROBSON W.A.,CIVILISATION AND THE GROWTH OF LAW. LAW
UNIV CONSTN SOCIETY LEGIS ADJUD ATTIT PERCEPT MORAL IDEA/COMP
ALL/IDEOS...CONCPT WORSHIP 20. PAGE 85 E1708 SOC

B36
EHRLICH E.,FUNDAMENTAL PRINCIPLES OF THE SOCIOLOGY LAW

OF LAW (TRANS. BY WALTER L. MOLL). UNIV SOCIETY JURID
ADJUD CT/SYS...POLICY GP/COMP GEN/LAWS GEN/METH. SOC
PAGE 34 E0678 CONCPT

B36
HUDSON M.O.,INTERNATIONAL LEGISLATION: 1929-1931. INT/LAW
WOR-45 SEA AIR AGRI FINAN LABOR DIPLOM ECO/TAC PARL/PROC
REPAR CT/SYS ARMS/CONT WAR WEAPON...JURID 20 TREATY ADJUD
LEAGUE/NAT. PAGE 56 E1112 LAW

B36
KONRAD F.,DIE PERSONLICHE FREIHEIT IM ORD/FREE
NATIONALSOZIALISTISCHEN DEUTSCHEN REICHE. GERMANY JURID
JUDGE ADJUD GP/REL FASCISM 20 CIVIL/LIB. PAGE 61 CONSTN
E1226 CONCPT

B36
MATTHEWS M.A.,INTERNATIONAL LAW: SELECT LIST OF BIBLIOG/A
WORKS IN ENGLISH ON PUBLIC INTERNATIONAL LAW: WITH INT/LAW
COLLECTIONS OF CASES AND OPINIONS. CHRIST-17C ATTIT
EUR+WWI MOD/EUR WOR-45 CONSTN ADJUD JURID. PAGE 69 DIPLOM
E1388

B36
SCHULZ F.,PRINCIPLES OF ROMAN LAW. CONSTN FAM NAT/G LAW
DOMIN CONTROL CT/SYS CRIME ISOLAT ATTIT ORD/FREE LEGIS
PWR...JURID ROME/ANC ROMAN/LAW. PAGE 89 E1783 ADJUD
CONCPT

S36
CORWIN E.S.,"THE CONSTITUTION AS INSTRUMENT AND AS CONSTN
SYMBOL." USA-45 ECO/DEV INDUS CAP/ISM SANCTION LAW
RIGID/FLEX ORD/FREE LAISSEZ OBJECTIVE 20 CONGRESS ADJUD
SUPREME/CT. PAGE 26 E0512 PWR

B37
BUREAU OF NATIONAL AFFAIRS,LABOR RELATIONS LABOR
REFERENCE MANUAL VOL 1, 1935-1937. BARGAIN DEBATE ADMIN
ROUTINE INGP/REL 20 NLRB. PAGE 17 E0335 ADJUD
NAT/G

B37
KETCHAM E.H.,PRELIMINARY SELECT BIBLIOGRAPHY OF BIBLIOG
INTERNATIONAL LAW (PAMPHLET). WOR-45 LAW INT/ORG DIPLOM
NAT/G PROB/SOLV CT/SYS NEUTRAL WAR 19/20. PAGE 60 ADJUD
E1207 INT/LAW

B37
RUTHERFORD M.L.,THE INFLUENCE OF THE AMERICAN BAR ATTIT
ASSOCIATION ON PUBLIC OPINION AND LEGISLATION. ADJUD
USA+45 LAW CONSTN LABOR LEGIS DOMIN EDU/PROP LEGIT PROF/ORG
CT/SYS ROUTINE...TIME/SEQ 19/20 ABA. PAGE 87 E1739 JURID

B37
SCHUSTER E.,GUIDE TO LAW AND LEGAL LITERATURE OF BIBLIOG/A
CENTRAL AMERICAN REPUBLICS. L/A+17C INT/ORG ADJUD REGION
SANCTION CRIME...JURID 19/20. PAGE 89 E1785 CT/SYS
LAW

B38
FIELD G.L.,THE SYNDICAL AND CORPORATIVE FASCISM
INSTITUTIONS OF ITALIAN FASCISM. ITALY CONSTN INDUS
STRATA LABOR EX/STRUC TOP/EX ADJUD ADMIN LEAD NAT/G
TOTALISM AUTHORIT...MGT 20 MUSSOLIN/B. PAGE 38 WORKER
E0746

B38
HAGUE PERMANENT CT INTL JUSTIC,WORLD COURT REPORTS: INT/ORG
COLLECTION OF THE JUDGEMENTS ORDERS AND OPINIONS CT/SYS
VOLUME 3 1932-35. WOR-45 LAW DELIB/GP CONFER WAR DIPLOM
PEACE ATTIT...DECISION ANTHOL 20 WORLD/CT CASEBOOK. ADJUD
PAGE 49 E0976

B38
HOLDSWORTH W.S.,A HISTORY OF ENGLISH LAW; THE LAW
CENTURIES OF SETTLEMENT AND REFORM (VOL. X). INDIA LOC/G
UK CONSTN NAT/G CHIEF LEGIS ADMIN COLONIAL CT/SYS EX/STRUC
CHOOSE ORD/FREE PWR...JURID 18 PARLIAMENT ADJUD
COMMONWLTH COMMON/LAW. PAGE 54 E1077

B38
HOLDSWORTH W.S.,A HISTORY OF ENGLISH LAW; THE LAW
CENTURIES OF SETTLEMENT AND REFORM (VOL. XII). UK PROF/ORG
CONSTN STRATA LEGIS JUDGE ADJUD CT/SYS ATTIT WRITING
...JURID CONCPT BIOG GEN/LAWS 18 ENGLSH/LAW IDEA/COMP
BLACKSTN/W COMMON/LAW. PAGE 54 E1078

B38
HOLDSWORTH W.S.,A HISTORY OF ENGLISH LAW; THE LAW
CENTURIES OF SETTLEMENT AND REFORM (VOL. XI). UK COLONIAL
CONSTN NAT/G EX/STRUC DIPLOM ADJUD CT/SYS LEAD LEGIS
CRIME ATTIT...INT/LAW JURID 18 CMN/WLTH PARLIAMENT PARL/PROC
ENGLSH/LAW. PAGE 54 E1079

B38
LEAGUE OF NATIONS-SECRETARIAT,THE AIMS, METHODS ADJUD

AND ACTIVITY OF THE LEAGUE OF NATIONS. WOR+45 STRUCT
DIPLOM EDU/PROP LEGIT RIGID/FLEX ALL/VALS
...TIME/SEQ LEAGUE/NAT VAL/FREE 19/20. PAGE 64
E1273

B38
MCNAIR A.D.,THE LAW OF TREATIES: BRITISH PRACTICE AGREE
AND OPINIONS. UK CREATE DIPLOM LEGIT WRITING ADJUD LAW
WAR...INT/LAW JURID TREATY. PAGE 71 E1424 CT/SYS
NAT/G

B38
POUND R.,THE FORMATIVE ERA OF AMERICAN LAW. CULTURE CONSTN
NAT/G PROVS LEGIS ADJUD CT/SYS PERSON SOVEREIGN LAW
...POLICY IDEA/COMP GEN/LAWS 18/19. PAGE 82 E1637 CREATE
JURID

B39
BALDWIN L.D.,WHISKEY REBELS; THE STORY OF A REV
FRONTIER UPRISING. USA-45 LAW ADJUD LEAD COERCE PWR POL/PAR
...BIBLIOG/A 18 PENNSYLVAN FEDERALIST. PAGE 8 E0145 TAX
TIME/SEQ

B39
CULVER D.C.,BIBLIOGRAPHY OF CRIME AND CRIMINAL BIBLIOG/A
JUSTICE, 1932-1937. USA-45 LAW CULTURE PUB/INST CRIMLGY
PROB/SOLV CT/SYS...PSY SOC STAT 20. PAGE 28 E0551 ADJUD
FORCES

B39
SIEYES E.J.,LES DISCOURS DE SIEYES DANS LES DEBATS CONSTN
CONSTITUTIONNELS DE L'AN III (2 ET 18 THERMIDOR). ADJUD
FRANCE LAW NAT/G PROB/SOLV BAL/PWR GOV/REL 18 JURY. LEGIS
PAGE 91 E1824 EX/STRUC

B40
FULLER G.H.,A SELECTED LIST OF RECENT REFERENCES ON BIBLIOG/A
THE CONSTITUTION OF THE UNITED STATES (PAMPHLET). CONSTN
CULTURE NAT/G LEGIS CONFER ADJUD GOV/REL CONSEN LAW
POPULISM...JURID CONCPT 18/20 CONGRESS. PAGE 41 USA-45
E0820

B40
HART J.,AN INTRODUCTION TO ADMINISTRATIVE LAW, WITH LAW
SELECTED CASES. USA-45 CONSTN SOCIETY NAT/G ADMIN
EX/STRUC ADJUD CT/SYS LEAD CRIME ORD/FREE LEGIS
...DECISION JURID 20 CASEBOOK. PAGE 50 E1002 PWR

B40
HOBBES T.,A DIALOGUE BETWEEN A PHILOSOPHER AND A CT/SYS
STUDENT OF THE COMMON LAWS OF ENGLAND (1667?). UK CHIEF
SECT DOMIN ADJUD CRIME INCOME OWN UTIL ORD/FREE PWR SANCTION
SOVEREIGN...JURID GEN/LAWS 17. PAGE 53 E1057

B41
CHAFEE Z. JR.,FREE SPEECH IN THE UNITED STATES. ORD/FREE
USA-45 ADJUD CONTROL CRIME WAR...BIBLIOG 20 CONSTN
FREE/SPEE AMEND/I SUPREME/CT. PAGE 21 E0413 ATTIT
JURID

B41
GELLHORN W.,FEDERAL ADMINISTRATIVE PROCEEDINGS. EX/STRUC
USA+45 CLIENT FACE/GP NAT/G LOBBY REPRESENT PWR 20. LAW
PAGE 43 E0844 ADJUD
POLICY

B41
MCCLURE W.,INTERNATIONAL EXECUTIVE AGREEMENTS. TOP/EX
USA-45 WOR-45 INT/ORG NAT/G DELIB/GP ADJUD ROUTINE DIPLOM
ORD/FREE PWR...TIME/SEQ TREND CON/ANAL. PAGE 70
E1401

B41
NIEMEYER G.,LAW WITHOUT FORCE: THE FUNCTION OF COERCE
POLITICS IN INTERNATIONAL LAW. PLAN INSPECT DIPLOM LAW
REPAR LEGIT ADJUD WAR ORD/FREE...IDEA/COMP PWR
METH/COMP GEN/LAWS 20. PAGE 77 E1549 INT/LAW

L41
COMM. STUDY ORGAN. PEACE,"ORGANIZATION OF PEACE." INT/ORG
USA-45 WOR-45 STRATA NAT/G ACT/RES DIPLOM ECO/TAC PLAN
EDU/PROP ADJUD ATTIT ORD/FREE PWR...SOC CONCPT PEACE
ANTHOL LEAGUE/NAT 20. PAGE 24 E0479

B42
FEILCHENFELD E.H.,THE INTERNATIONAL ECONOMIC LAW OF ECO/TAC
BELLIGERENT OCCUPATION. EUR+WWI MOD/EUR USA-45 INT/LAW
INT/ORG DIPLOM ADJUD ARMS/CONT LEAGUE/NAT 20. WAR
PAGE 37 E0726

B42
FULLER G.H.,DEFENSE FINANCING: A SUPPLEMENTARY LIST BIBLIOG/A
OF REFERENCES (PAMPHLET). CANADA UK USA-45 ECO/DEV FINAN
NAT/G DELIB/GP BUDGET ADJUD ARMS/CONT WEAPON COST FORCES
PEACE PWR 20 AUSTRAL CHINJAP CONGRESS. PAGE 41 DIPLOM
E0821

B42
GURVITCH G.,SOCIOLOGY OF LAW. CONSTN SOCIETY CREATE SOC
MORAL SOVEREIGN...POLICY EPIST JURID PHIL/SCI LAW
IDEA/COMP METH/COMP HOLMES/OW HOBBES/T. PAGE 48 ADJUD
E0964

B42
HAMBRO C.J.,HOW TO WIN THE PEACE. ECO/TAC EDU/PROP FUT
ADJUD PERSON ALL/VALS...SOCIALIST TREND GEN/LAWS INT/ORG
20. PAGE 50 E0987 PEACE

B42
KELSEN H.,LAW AND PEACE IN INTERNATIONAL RELATIONS. INT/ORG
FUT WOR-45 NAT/G DELIB/GP DIPLOM LEGIT RIGID/FLEX ADJUD
ORD/FREE SOVEREIGN...JURID CONCPT TREND STERTYP PEACE
GEN/LAWS LEAGUE/NAT 20. PAGE 60 E1197 INT/LAW

B43
ANDERSON R.B.,SUPPLEMENT TO BEALE'S BIBLIOGRAPHY OF BIBLIOG/A
EARLY ENGLISH LAW BOOKS. MOD/EUR UK CONSTN PRESS JURID
ADJUD...CHARTS 10/15. PAGE 5 E0091 CT/SYS
LAW

B43
BACKUS R.C.,A GUIDE TO THE LAW AND LEGAL LITERATURE BIBLIOG/A
OF COLOMBIA. FINAN INDUS LABOR FORCES ADJUD ADMIN LAW
COLONIAL CT/SYS CRIME...INT/LAW JURID 20 COLOMB. CONSTN
PAGE 7 E0127 L/A+17C

B43
CONOVER H.F.,THE BALKANS: A SELECTED LIST OF BIBLIOG
REFERENCES. ALBANIA BULGARIA ROMANIA YUGOSLAVIA EUR+WWI
INT/ORG PROB/SOLV DIPLOM LEGIT CONFER ADJUD WAR
NAT/LISM PEACE PWR 20 LEAGUE/NAT. PAGE 25 E0493

B43
HAGUE PERMANENT CT INTL JUSTIC,WORLD COURT REPORTS: INT/ORG
COLLECTION OF THE JUDGEMENTS ORDERS AND OPINIONS CT/SYS
VOLUME 4 1936-42. WOR-45 CONFER PEACE ATTIT DIPLOM
...DECISION JURID ANTHOL 20 WORLD/CT CASEBOOK. ADJUD
PAGE 49 E0977

B44
BRIERLY J.L.,THE OUTLOOK FOR INTERNATIONAL LAW. FUT INT/ORG
WOR-45 CONSTN NAT/G VOL/ASSN FORCES ECO/TAC DOMIN LAW
LEGIT ADJUD ROUTINE PEACE ORD/FREE...INT/LAW JURID
METH LEAGUE/NAT 20. PAGE 15 E0298

B44
DE HUSZAR G.B.,NEW PERSPECTIVES ON PEACE. UNIV ATTIT
CULTURE SOCIETY ECO/DEV ECO/UNDEV NAT/G FORCES MYTH
CREATE ECO/TAC DOMIN ADJUD COERCE DRIVE ORD/FREE PEACE
...GEOG JURID PSY SOC CONCPT TOT/POP. PAGE 29 E0584 WAR

B44
HUDSON M.,INTERNATIONAL TRIBUNALS PAST AND FUTURE. INT/ORG
FUT WOR-45 LAW EDU/PROP ADJUD ORD/FREE...CONCPT STRUCT
TIME/SEQ TREND GEN/LAWS TOT/POP VAL/FREE 18/20. INT/LAW
PAGE 56 E1111

S44
MASON J.B.,"THE JUDICIAL SYSTEM OF THE NAZI PARTY." FASCISM
GERMANY ELITES POL/PAR DOMIN CONTROL SANCTION CT/SYS
TOTALISM...JURID 20 HITLER/A. PAGE 69 E1381 ADJUD
LAW

B45
CLAGETT H.L.,A GUIDE TO THE LAW AND LEGAL BIBLIOG
LITERATURE OF THE MEXICAN STATES. CONSTN LEGIS JURID
JUDGE ADJUD ADMIN...INT/LAW CON/ANAL 20 MEXIC/AMER. L/A+17C
PAGE 22 E0440 LAW

B45
HILL N.,CLAIMS TO TERRITORY IN INTERNATIONAL LAW INT/ORG
AND RELATIONS. WOR-45 NAT/G DOMIN EDU/PROP LEGIT ADJUD
REGION ROUTINE ORD/FREE PWR WEALTH...GEOG INT/LAW SOVEREIGN
JURID 20. PAGE 52 E1047

B45
US DEPARTMENT OF STATE,PUBLICATIONS OF THE BIBLIOG
DEPARTMENT OF STATE: A LIST CUMULATIVE FROM OCTOBER DIPLOM
1, 1929 (PAMPHLET). ASIA EUR+WWI ISLAM L/A+17C INT/TRADE
USA-45 ADJUD...INT/LAW 20. PAGE 99 E1993

B45
VANCE H.L.,GUIDE TO THE LAW AND LEGAL LITERATURE OF BIBLIOG/A
MEXICO. LAW CONSTN FINAN LABOR FORCES ADJUD ADMIN INT/LAW
...CRIMLGY PHIL/SCI CON/ANAL 20 MEXIC/AMER. JURID
PAGE 103 E2070 CT/SYS

B46
KEETON G.W.,MAKING INTERNATIONAL LAW WORK. FUT INT/ORG
WOR-45 NAT/G DELIB/GP FORCES LEGIT COERCE PEACE ADJUD
ATTIT RIGID/FLEX ORD/FREE PWR...JURID CONCPT INT/LAW
HIST/WRIT GEN/METH LEAGUE/NAT 20. PAGE 60 E1193

CT/SYS

B46
MANNHEIM H.,CRIMINAL JUSTICE AND SOCIAL   ADJUD
RECONSTRUCTION. USA+45 EDU/PROP CRIME ANOMIE   LAW
...JURID BIBLIOG 20. PAGE 68 E1361   STRUCT
                                                          ADJUST

B46
PATON G.W.,A TEXT-BOOK OF JURISPRUDENCE. CREATE   LAW
INSPECT LEGIT CT/SYS ROUTINE CRIME INGP/REL PRIVIL   ADJUD
...CONCPT BIBLIOG 20. PAGE 80 E1601   JURID
                                                          T

B46
ROSS A.,TOWARDS A REALISTIC JURISPRUDENCE: A   LAW
CRITICISM OF THE DUALISM IN LAW (TRANS. BY ANNIE I.   CONCPT
FAUSBOLL). PLAN ADJUD CT/SYS ATTIT RIGID/FLEX   IDEA/COMP
POPULISM...JURID PHIL/SCI LOG METH/COMP GEN/LAWS 20
SCANDINAV. PAGE 86 E1720

B46
SCANLON H.L.,INTERNATIONAL LAW: A SELECTIVE LIST OF   BIBLIOG/A
WORKS IN ENGLISH ON PUBLIC INTERNATIONAL LAW (A   INT/LAW
PAMPHLET). CHRIST-17C EUR+WWI MOD/EUR WOR-45 CT/SYS   ADJUD
...JURID 20. PAGE 87 E1749   DIPLOM

B47
CLAGETT H.L.,A GUIDE TO THE LAW AND LEGAL   BIBLIOG
LITERATURE OF CHILE, 1917-1946. CHILE CONSTN LABOR   L/A+17C
JUDGE ADJUD ADMIN...CRIMLGY INT/LAW JURID CON/ANAL   LAW
20. PAGE 22 E0442   LEGIS

B47
CLAGETT H.L.,A GUIDE TO THE LAW AND LEGAL   BIBLIOG
LITERATURE OF ECUADOR. ECUADOR CONSTN LABOR LEGIS   JURID
JUDGE ADJUD ADMIN CIVMIL/REL...CRIMLGY INT/LAW   LAW
CON/ANAL 20. PAGE 22 E0443   L/A+17C

B47
CLAGETT H.L.,A GUIDE TO THE LAW AND LEGAL   BIBLIOG
LITERATURE OF VENEZUELA. VENEZUELA CONSTN LABOR   L/A+17C
LEGIS JUDGE ADJUD ADMIN CIVMIL/REL...CRIMLGY JURID   INT/LAW
CON/ANAL 20. PAGE 23 E0446   LAW

B47
INTERNATIONAL COURT OF JUSTICE,CHARTER OF THE   INT/LAW
UNITED NATIONS, STATUTE AND RULES OF COURT AND   INT/ORG
OTHER CONSTITUTIONAL DOCUMENTS. SWITZERLND LAW   CT/SYS
ADJUD INGP/REL...JURID 20 ICJ UN. PAGE 57 E1133   DIPLOM

B47
KONVITZ M.R.,THE CONSTITUTION AND CIVIL RIGHTS.   CONSTN
USA-45 NAT/G ADJUD GP/REL RACE/REL POPULISM   LAW
...MAJORIT 19/20 SUPREME/CT CIV/RIGHTS. PAGE 61   GOV/REL
E1227   ORD/FREE

S47
FRANKFURTER F.,"SOME REFLECTIONS ON THE READING OF   JURID
STATUTES" USA+45 USA-45 PROB/SOLV CT/SYS TASK   LAW
EFFICIENCY...LING 20. PAGE 40 E0791   ADJUD
                                                          WRITING

B48
BISHOP H.M.,BASIC ISSUES OF AMERICAN DEMOCRACY.   NAT/G
USA+45 USA-45 POL/PAR EX/STRUC LEGIS ADJUD FEDERAL   PARL/PROC
...BIBLIOG 18/20. PAGE 12 E0232   CONSTN

B48
CLAGETT H.L.,A GUIDE TO THE LAW AND LEGAL   BIBLIOG
LITERATURE OF ARGENTINA, 1917-1946. CONSTN LABOR   L/A+17C
JUDGE ADJUD ADMIN...CRIMLGY INT/LAW JURID CON/ANAL   LAW
20 ARGEN. PAGE 23 E0447   LEGIS

B48
CORWIN E.S.,LIBERTY AGAINST GOVERNMENT: THE RISE,   CONCPT
FLOWERING AND DECLINE OF A FAMOUS JURIDICAL   ORD/FREE
CONCEPT. LEGIS ADJUD CT/SYS SANCTION GOV/REL   JURID
FEDERAL CONSERVE NEW/LIB...OLD/LIB 18/20 ROMAN/LAW   CONSTN
COMMON/LAW. PAGE 26 E0514

B48
HOLCOMBE A.N.,HUMAN RIGHTS IN THE MODERN WORLD.   ORD/FREE
WOR+45 LEGIS DIPLOM ADJUD PERSON...INT/LAW 20 UN   INT/ORG
TREATY CIVIL/LIB BILL/RIGHT. PAGE 54 E1071   CONSTN
                                                          LAW

B48
JESSUP P.C.,A MODERN LAW OF NATIONS. FUT WOR+45   INT/ORG
WOR-45 SOCIETY NAT/G DELIB/GP LEGIS BAL/PWR   ADJUD
EDU/PROP LEGIT PWR...INT/LAW JURID TIME/SEQ
LEAGUE/NAT 20. PAGE 58 E1166

B48
KEIR D.L.,CASES IN CONSTITUTIONAL LAW. UK CHIEF   CONSTN
LEGIS DIPLOM TAX PARL/PROC CRIME GOV/REL...INT/LAW   LAW
JURID 17/20. PAGE 60 E1195   ADJUD

B48
SLESSER H.,THE ADMINISTRATION OF THE LAW. UK CONSTN   LAW
EX/STRUC OP/RES PROB/SOLV CRIME ROLE...DECISION   CT/SYS
METH/COMP 20 CIVIL/LAW ENGLSH/LAW CIVIL/LAW.   ADJUD
PAGE 92 E1839

B49
DENNING A.,FREEDOM UNDER THE LAW. MOD/EUR UK LAW   ORD/FREE
SOCIETY CHIEF EX/STRUC LEGIS ADJUD CT/SYS PERS/REL   JURID
PERSON 17/20 ENGLSH/LAW. PAGE 31 E0606   NAT/G

B49
FRANK J.,LAW AND THE MODERN MIND. UNIV LAW CT/SYS   JURID
RATIONAL ATTIT...CONCPT 20 HOLMES/OW JURY. PAGE 40   ADJUD
E0787   IDEA/COMP
                                                          MYTH

B49
JACKSON R.H.,INTERNATIONAL CONFERENCE ON MILITARY   DIPLOM
TRIALS. FRANCE GERMANY UK USA+45 USSR VOL/ASSN   INT/ORG
DELIB/GP REPAR ADJUD CT/SYS CRIME WAR 20 WAR/TRIAL.   INT/LAW
PAGE 57 E1141   CIVMIL/REL

B49
SCHONS D.,BOOK CENSORSHIP IN NEW SPAIN (NEW WORLD   CHRIST-17C
STUDIES, BOOK II). SPAIN LAW CULTURE INSPECT ADJUD   EDU/PROP
CT/SYS SANCTION GP/REL ORD/FREE 14/17. PAGE 88   CONTROL
E1764   PRESS

B49
SUMMERS R.E.,FEDERAL INFORMATION CONTROLS IN   ADJUD
PEACETIME. USA+45 COM/IND DOMIN INGP/REL ATTIT   CONTROL
ORD/FREE 20. PAGE 94 E1893   EDU/PROP
                                                          PRESS

B49
WALINE M.,LE CONTROLE JURIDICTIONNEL DE   JURID
L'ADMINISTRATION. BELGIUM FRANCE UAR JUDGE BAL/PWR   ADMIN
ADJUD CONTROL CT/SYS...GP/COMP 20. PAGE 104 E2093   PWR
                                                          ORD/FREE

B49
WORMUTH F.D.,THE ORIGINS OF MODERN   NAT/G
CONSTITUTIONALISM. GREECE UK LEGIS CREATE TEC/DEV   CONSTN
BAL/PWR DOMIN ADJUD REV WAR PWR...JURID ROMAN/REP   LAW
CROMWELL/O. PAGE 107 E2146

B50
BERMAN H.J.,JUSTICE IN RUSSIA; AN INTERPRETATION OF   JURID
SOVIET LAW. USSR LAW STRUCT LABOR FORCES AGREE   ADJUD
GP/REL ORD/FREE SOCISM...TIME/SEQ 20. PAGE 11 E0207   MARXISM
                                                          COERCE

B50
FRANK J.,COURTS ON TRIAL: MYTH AND REALITY IN   JURID
AMERICAN JUSTICE. LAW CONSULT PROB/SOLV EDU/PROP   CT/SYS
ADJUD ROUTINE ROLE ORD/FREE...GEN/LAWS T 20.   MYTH
PAGE 40 E0788   CONSTN

B50
GRAVES W.B.,PUBLIC ADMINISTRATION: A COMPREHENSIVE   BIBLIOG
BIBLIOGRAPHY ON PUBLIC ADMINISTRATION IN THE UNITED   FINAN
STATES (PAMPHLET). USA+45 USA-45 LOC/G NAT/G LEGIS   CONTROL
ADJUD INGP/REL...MGT 20. PAGE 45 E0901   ADMIN

B50
HURST J.W.,THE GROWTH OF AMERICAN LAW; THE LAW   LAW
MAKERS. USA-45 LOC/G NAT/G DELIB/GP JUDGE ADJUD   LEGIS
ADMIN ATTIT PWR...POLICY JURID BIBLIOG 18/20   CONSTN
CONGRESS SUPREME/CT ABA PRESIDENT. PAGE 56 E1115   CT/SYS

B51
ANDERSON W.,STATE AND LOCAL GOVERNMENT IN THE   LOC/G
UNITED STATES. USA+45 CONSTN POL/PAR EX/STRUC LEGIS   MUNIC
BUDGET TAX ADJUD CT/SYS CHOOSE...CHARTS T 20.   PROVS
PAGE 5 E0094   GOV/REL

B51
BECKER O.,MASTER RESEARCH GUIDE. USA+45 USA-45   BIBLIOG
PRESS...JURID INDEX 20. PAGE 9 E0171   LAW
                                                          ADJUD
                                                          CT/SYS

B51
DAVIS K.C.,ADMINISTRATIVE LAW. USA+45 USA-45 NAT/G   ADMIN
PROB/SOLV BAL/PWR CONTROL ORD/FREE...POLICY 20   JURID
SUPREME/CT. PAGE 29 E0574   EX/STRUC
                                                          ADJUD

B51
FRIEDMANN W.,LAW AND SOCIAL CHANGE IN CONTEMPORARY   LAW
BRITAIN. UK LABOR LG/CO LEGIS JUDGE CT/SYS ORD/FREE   ADJUD
NEW/LIB...DECISION JURID TREND METH/COMP BIBLIOG 20   SOCIETY
PARLIAMENT ENGLSH/LAW COMMON/LAW. PAGE 40 E0802   CONSTN

GIBBS C.R.,CONSTITUTIONAL AND STATUTORY PROVISIONS OF THE STATES (VOL. IX). USA+45 LICENSE ADJUD LEAD 20. PAGE 43 E0857
PROVS CONSTN JURID LOBBY
B51

KELSEN H.,THE LAW OF THE UNITED NATIONS. WOR+45 STRUCT RIGID/FLEX ORD/FREE...INT/LAW JURID CONCPT CON/ANAL GEN/METH UN TOT/POP VAL/FREE 20. PAGE 60 E1198
INT/ORG ADJUD
B51

PUSEY M.J.,CHARLES EVANS HUGHES (2 VOLS.). LAW CONSTN NAT/G POL/PAR DIPLOM LEGIT WAR CHOOSE PERS/REL DRIVE HEREDITY 19/20 DEPT/STATE LEAGUE/NAT SUPREME/CT HUGHES/CE WWI. PAGE 83 E1663
BIOG TOP/EX ADJUD PERSON
B51

ROSSITER C.,THE SUPREME COURT AND THE COMMANDER IN CHIEF. LAW CONSTN DELIB/GP EX/STRUC LEGIS TOP/EX ADJUD CONTROL...DECISION SOC/EXP PRESIDENT. PAGE 86 E1724
CT/SYS CHIEF WAR PWR
B51

WOOD V.,DUE PROCESS OF LAW 1932-1949: SUPREME COURT'S USE OF A CONSTITUTIONAL TOOL. USA+45 USA-45 SOCIETY TAX CRIME...POLICY CHARTS 20 SUPREME/CT. PAGE 107 E2143
CONSTN TREND ADJUD GOV/REL
B51

LISSITZYN O.J.,"THE INTERNATIONAL COURT OF JUSTICE." WOR+45 INT/ORG LEGIT ORD/FREE...CONCPT TIME/SEQ TREND GEN/LAWS VAL/FREE 20 ICJ. PAGE 65 E1304
ADJUD JURID INT/LAW
L51

COHEN M.B.,"PERSONALITY AS A FACTOR IN ADMINISTRATIVE DECISIONS." ADJUD PERS/REL ANOMIE SUPEGO...OBS SELF/OBS INT. PAGE 24 E0465
PERSON ADMIN PROB/SOLV PSY
S51

BUCKLAND W.W.,ROMAN LAW AND COMMON LAW; A COMPARISON IN OUTLINE (2ND REV. ED.). UK FAM LEGIT AGREE CT/SYS OWN...JURID ROMAN/REP ROMAN/LAW COMMON/LAW. PAGE 17 E0325
IDEA/COMP LAW ADJUD CONCPT
B52

CAHILL F.V.,JUDICIAL LEGISLATION: A STUDY IN AMERICAN LEGAL THEORY. USA+45 USA-45 LAW NAT/G GP/REL...POLICY PHIL/SCI SOC 20 HOLMES/OW. PAGE 18 E0359
JURID ADJUD LEGIS CONTROL
B52

DE GRAZIA A.,POLITICAL ORGANIZATION. CONSTN LOC/G MUNIC NAT/G CHIEF LEGIS TOP/EX ADJUD CT/SYS PERS/REL...INT/LAW MYTH UN. PAGE 29 E0581
FEDERAL LAW ADMIN
B52

FLECHTHEIM O.K.,FUNDAMENTALS OF POLITICAL SCIENCE. WOR+45 WOR-45 LAW POL/PAR EX/STRUC LEGIS ADJUD ATTIT PWR...INT/LAW. PAGE 38 E0760
NAT/G DIPLOM IDEA/COMP CONSTN
B52

JENNINGS W.I.,CONSTITUTIONAL LAWS OF THE COMMONWEALTH. UK LAW CHIEF LEGIS TAX CT/SYS PARL/PROC GOV/REL...INT/LAW 18/20 COMMONWLTH ENGLSH/LAW COMMON/LAW. PAGE 58 E1165
CONSTN JURID ADJUD COLONIAL
B52

KELSEN H.,PRINCIPLES OF INTERNATIONAL LAW. WOR+45 WOR-45 INT/ORG ORD/FREE...JURID GEN/LAWS TOT/POP 20. PAGE 60 E1200
ADJUD CONSTN INT/LAW
B52

MORRIS R.B.,FAIR TRIAL. USA-45 JUDGE ORD/FREE ...JURID 20. PAGE 75 E1498
ADJUD CT/SYS CRIME LAW
B52

THOM J.M.,GUIDE TO RESEARCH MATERIAL IN POLITICAL SCIENCE (PAMPHLET). ELITES LOC/G MUNIC NAT/G LEGIS DIPLOM ADJUD CIVMIL/REL GOV/REL PWR MGT. PAGE 96 E1916
BIBLIOG/A KNOWL
B52

ROSTOW E.V.,"THE DEMOCRATIC CHARACTER OF JUDICIAL REVIEW" (BMR)" USA+45 LAW NAT/G LEGIS TASK...JURID 20 SUPREME/CT. PAGE 86 E1725
CONSTN PROB/SOLV ADJUD CT/SYS
L52

MCDOUGAL M.S.,"THE COMPARATIVE STUDY OF LAW FOR POLICY PURPOSES." FUT NAT/G POL/PAR CONSULT ADJUD PWR SOVEREIGN...METH/CNCPT IDEA/COMP SIMUL 20. PAGE 70 E1403
PLAN JURID NAT/LISM
S52

CLAGETT H.L.,"THE ADMINISTRATION OF JUSTICE IN LATIN AMERICA." L/A+17C ADMIN FEDERAL...JURID METH/COMP BIBLIOG 20. PAGE 23 E0448
CT/SYS ADJUD JUDGE CONSTN
C52

STUART G.H.,"AMERICAN DIPLOMATIC AND CONSULAR PRACTICE (2ND ED.)" EUR+WWI MOD/EUR USA-45 DELIB/GP INT/TRADE ADJUD...BIBLIOG 20. PAGE 94 E1889
DIPLOM ADMIN INT/ORG
C52

COKE E.,INSTITUTES OF THE LAWS OF ENGLAND (1628-1658). UK LAW ADJUD PERS/REL ORD/FREE ...CRIMLGY 11/17. PAGE 24 E0471
JURID OWN CT/SYS CONSTN
B53

MAJUMDAR B.B.,PROBLEMS OF PUBLIC ADMINISTRATION IN INDIA. INDIA INDUS PLAN BUDGET ADJUD CENTRAL DEMAND WEALTH...WELF/ST ANTHOL 20 CIVIL/SERV. PAGE 68 E1353
ECO/UNDEV GOV/REL ADMIN MUNIC
B53

MARKE J.J.,A CATALOGUE OF THE LAW COLLECTION AT NEW YORK UNIVERSITY, WITH SELECTED ANNOTATIONS. ACADEM ADJUD CT/SYS...CONCPT BIOG 20. PAGE 68 E1366
BIBLIOG/A LAW PHIL/SCI IDEA/COMP
B53

OPPENHEIM L.,INTERNATIONAL LAW: A TREATISE (7TH ED., 2 VOLS.). LAW CONSTN PROB/SOLV INT/TRADE ADJUD AGREE NEUTRAL WAR ORD/FREE SOVEREIGN...BIBLIOG 20 LEAGUE/NAT UN ILO. PAGE 79 E1579
INT/LAW INT/ORG DIPLOM
B53

PADOVER S.K.,THE LIVING US CONSTITUTION. USA+45 USA-45 POL/PAR ADJUD...DECISION AUD/VIS IDEA/COMP 18/20 SUPREME/CT. PAGE 79 E1590
CONSTN LEGIS DELIB/GP BIOG
B53

SECKLER-HUDSON C.,BIBLIOGRAPHY ON PUBLIC ADMINISTRATION (4TH ED.). USA+45 LAW POL/PAR DELIB/GP BUDGET ADJUD LOBBY GOV/REL GP/REL ATTIT ...JURID 20. PAGE 90 E1800
BIBLIOG/A ADMIN NAT/G MGT
B53

US PRES CONF ADMIN PROCEDURE,REPORT (PAMPHLET). USA+45 CONFER ADJUD...METH/COMP 20 PRESIDENT. PAGE 101 E2024
NAT/G DELIB/GP ADJUST ADMIN
N53

BENTLEY A.F.,INQUIRY INTO INQUIRIES: ESSAYS IN SOCIAL THEORY. UNIV LEGIS ADJUD ADMIN LOBBY ...PHIL/SCI PSY NEW/IDEA LING METH 20. PAGE 10 E0200
EPIST SOC CONCPT
B54

HAMSON C.J.,EXECUTIVE DISCRETION AND JUDICIAL CONTROL; AN ASPECT OF THE FRENCH CONSEIL D'ETAT. EUR+WWI FRANCE MOD/EUR UK NAT/G EX/STRUC PARTIC CONSERVE...JURID BIBLIOG/A 18/20 SUPREME/CT. PAGE 50 E0992
ELITES ADJUD NAT/COMP
B54

JAMES L.F.,THE SUPREME COURT IN AMERICAN LIFE. USA+45 USA-45 CONSTN CRIME GP/REL INGP/REL RACE/REL CONSEN FEDERAL PERSON ORD/FREE 18/20 SUPREME/CT DEPRESSION CIV/RIGHTS CHURCH/STA FREE/SPEE. PAGE 58 E1147
ADJUD CT/SYS JURID DECISION
B54

SCHWARTZ B.,FRENCH ADMINISTRATIVE LAW AND THE COMMON-LAW WORLD. FRANCE CULTURE LOC/G NAT/G PROVS DELIB/GP EX/STRUC LEGIS PROB/SOLV CT/SYS EXEC GOV/REL...IDEA/COMP ENGLSH/LAW. PAGE 89 E1786
JURID LAW METH/COMP ADJUD
B54

SINCO,PHILIPPINE POLITICAL LAW: PRINCIPLES AND CONCEPTS (10TH ED.). PHILIPPINE LOC/G EX/STRUC BAL/PWR ECO/TAC TAX ADJUD ADMIN CONTROL CT/SYS SUFF ORD/FREE...T 20. PAGE 91 E1831
LAW CONSTN LEGIS
B54

WRIGHT Q.,PROBLEMS OF STABILITY AND PROGRESS IN INTERNATIONAL RELATIONSHIPS. FUT WOR+45 WOR-45 SOCIETY LEGIS CREATE TEC/DEV ECO/TAC EDU/PROP ADJUD WAR PEACE ORD/FREE PWR...KNO/TEST TREND GEN/LAWS
INT/ORG CONCPT DIPLOM
B54

20. PAGE 108 E2155

COOPER L.,"ADMINISTRATIVE JUSTICE." UK ADMIN   LAW   S54
REPRESENT PWR...POLICY 20. PAGE 25 E0502   ADJUD
                                                      CONTROL
                                                      EX/STRUC

BOWIE R.R.,"STUDIES IN FEDERALISM." AGRI FINAN   FEDERAL   C54
LABOR EX/STRUC FORCES LEGIS DIPLOM INT/TRADE ADJUD   EUR+WWI
...BIBLIOG 20 EEC. PAGE 14 E0279   INT/ORG
                                                      CONSTN

BIBLIOGRAPHY ON THE COMMUNIST PROBLEM IN THE UNITED   BIBLIOG/A   B55
STATES. USA-45 PRESS ADJUD ATTIT...BIOG 20. PAGE 2   MARXISM
E0033   POL/PAR
                                                      USA+45

BEANEY W.M.,THE RIGHT TO COUNSEL IN AMERICAN   ADJUD   B55
COURTS. UK USA+45 USA-45 LAW NAT/G PROVS COLONIAL   CONSTN
PERCEPT 18/20 SUPREME/CT AMEND/VI AMEND/XIV   CT/SYS
ENGLSH/LAW. PAGE 8 E0163

BERNSTEIN M.H.,REGULATING BUSINESS BY INDEPENDENT   DELIB/GP   B55
COMMISSION. USA+45 USA-45 LG/CO CHIEF LEGIS   CONTROL
PROB/SOLV ADJUD SANCTION GP/REL ATTIT...TIME/SEQ   CONSULT
19/20 MONOPOLY PRESIDENT CONGRESS. PAGE 11 E0214

BLOOM G.F.,ECONOMICS OF LABOR RELATIONS. USA+45 LAW   ECO/DEV   B55
CONSULT WORKER CAP/ISM PAY ADJUD CONTROL EFFICIENCY   ECO/TAC
ORD/FREE...CHARTS 19/20 AFL/CIO NLRB DEPT/LABOR.   LABOR
PAGE 13 E0249   GOV/REL

BRAUN K.,LABOR DISPUTES AND THEIR SETTLEMENT.   INDUS   B55
ECO/TAC ROUTINE TASK GP/REL...DECISION GEN/LAWS.   LABOR
PAGE 15 E0288   BARGAIN
                                                      ADJUD

CHOWDHURI R.N.,INTERNATIONAL MANDATES AND   DELIB/GP   B55
TRUSTEESHIP SYSTEMS. WOR+45 STRUCT ECO/UNDEV   PLAN
INT/ORG LEGIS DOMIN EDU/PROP LEGIT ADJUD EXEC PWR   SOVEREIGN
...CONCPT TIME/SEQ UN 20. PAGE 22 E0434

CRAIG J.,BIBLIOGRAPHY OF PUBLIC ADMINISTRATION IN   BIBLIOG   B55
AUSTRALIA. CONSTN FINAN EX/STRUC LEGIS PLAN DIPLOM   GOV/REL
RECEIVE ADJUD ROUTINE...HEAL 19/20 AUSTRAL   ADMIN
PARLIAMENT. PAGE 27 E0540   NAT/G

DE ARAGAO J.G.,LA JURIDICTION ADMINISTRATIVE AU   EX/STRUC   B55
BRESIL. BRAZIL ADJUD COLONIAL CT/SYS REV FEDERAL   ADMIN
ORD/FREE...BIBLIOG 19/20. PAGE 29 E0580   NAT/G

HOGAN W.N.,INTERNATIONAL CONFLICT AND COLLECTIVE   INT/ORG   B55
SECURITY: THE PRINCIPLE OF CONCERN IN INTERNATIONAL   WAR
ORGANIZATION. CONSTN EX/STRUC BAL/PWR DIPLOM ADJUD   ORD/FREE
CONTROL CENTRAL CONSEN PEACE...INT/LAW CONCPT   FORCES
METH/COMP 20 UN LEAGUE/NAT. PAGE 53 E1066

KHADDURI M.,WAR AND PEACE IN THE LAW OF ISLAM.   ISLAM   B55
CONSTN CULTURE SOCIETY STRATA NAT/G PROVS SECT   JURID
FORCES TOP/EX CREATE DOMIN EDU/PROP ADJUD COERCE   PEACE
ATTIT RIGID/FLEX ALL/VALS...CONCPT TIME/SEQ TOT/POP   WAR
VAL/FREE. PAGE 61 E1209

KHADDURI M.,LAW IN THE MIDDLE EAST. LAW CONSTN   ADJUD   B55
ACADEM FAM EDU/PROP CT/SYS SANCTION CRIME...INT/LAW   JURID
GOV/COMP ANTHOL 6/20 MID/EAST. PAGE 61 E1210   ISLAM

LARROWE C.P.,SHAPE-UP AND HIRING HALL. TRIBUTE   LABOR   B55
ADJUD CONTROL SANCTION COERCE CRIME GP/REL PWR   INDUS
...CHARTS 20 AFL/CIO NEWYORK/C SEATTLE. PAGE 63   WORKER
E1256   NAT/G

MAYERS L.,THE AMERICAN LEGAL SYSTEM. USA+45 USA-45   JURID   B55
NAT/G EX/STRUC ADMIN CONTROL FEDERAL 20 SUPREME/CT.   CT/SYS
PAGE 70 E1394   LEGIS
                                                      ADJUD

PULLEN W.R.,A CHECK LIST OF LEGISLATIVE JOURNALS   BIBLIOG   B55
ISSUED SINCE 1937 BY THE STATES OF THE UNITED   PROVS
STATES OF AMERICA (PAMPHLET). USA+45 USA-45 LAW   EDU/PROP

WRITING ADJUD ADMIN...JURID 20. PAGE 83 E1662   LEGIS

SMITH G.,A CONSTITUTIONAL AND LEGAL HISTORY OF   CONSTN   B55
ENGLAND. UK ELITES NAT/G LEGIS ADJUD OWN HABITAT   PARTIC
POPULISM...JURID 20 ENGLSH/LAW. PAGE 92 E1844   LAW
                                                      CT/SYS

SWEET AND MAXWELL,A LEGAL BIBLIOGRAPHY OF THE   BIBLIOG/A   B55
BRITISH COMMONWEALTH OF NATIONS (2ND ED. 7 VOLS.).   LAW
UK LOC/G MUNIC JUDGE ADJUD CRIME OWN...JURID 14/20   CONSTN
CMN/WLTH. PAGE 95 E1900   CT/SYS

WHEARE K.C.,GOVERNMENT BY COMMITTEE; AN ESSAY ON   DELIB/GP   B55
THE BRITISH CONSTITUTION. UK NAT/G LEGIS INSPECT   CONSTN
CONFER ADJUD ADMIN CONTROL TASK EFFICIENCY ROLE   LEAD
POPULISM 20. PAGE 106 E2116   GP/COMP

WRONG D.H.,AMERICAN AND CANADIAN VIEWPOINTS. CANADA   DIPLOM   B55
USA+45 CONSTN STRATA FAM SECT WORKER ECO/TAC   ATTIT
EDU/PROP ADJUD MARRIAGE...IDEA/COMP 20. PAGE 108   NAT/COMP
E2161   CULTURE

BETH L.P.,"THE CASE FOR JUDICIAL PROTECTION OF   CT/SYS   S55
CIVIL LIBERTIES" (BMR)" USA+45 CONSTN ELITES LEGIS   JUDGE
CONTROL...POLICY DECISION JURID 20 SUPREME/CT   ADJUD
CIVIL/LIB. PAGE 11 E0220   ORD/FREE

CAHN E.,"A DANGEROUS MYTH IN THE SCHOOL SEGREGATION   JURID   S55
CASES" (BMR)" USA+45 CONSTN PROVS ADJUD DISCRIM   SCHOOL
...POLICY MYTH SOC/INTEG 20 SUPREME/CT AMEND/XIV.   RACE/REL
PAGE 18 E0360

WRIGHT Q.,"THE PEACEFUL ADJUSTMENT OF INTERNATIONAL   R+D   S55
RELATIONS: PROBLEMS AND RESEARCH APPROACHES." UNIV   METH/CNCPT
INTELL EDU/PROP ADJUD ROUTINE KNOWL SKILL...INT/LAW   PEACE
JURID PHIL/SCI CLASSIF 20. PAGE 108 E2156

ALEXANDER F.,THE CRIMINAL, THE JUDGE, AND THE   CRIME   B56
PUBLIC. LAW CULTURE CONSULT LEGIT ADJUD SANCTION   CRIMLGY
ORD/FREE 20. PAGE 3 E0060   PSY
                                                      ATTIT

CALLISON I.P.,COURTS OF INJUSTICE. USA+45 PROF/ORG   CT/SYS   B56
ADJUD CRIME PERSON MORAL PWR RESPECT SKILL 20.   JUDGE
PAGE 19 E0368   JURID

DOUGLAS W.O.,WE THE JUDGES. INDIA USA+45 USA-45 LAW   ADJUD   B56
NAT/G SECT LEGIS PRESS CRIME FEDERAL ORD/FREE   CT/SYS
...POLICY GOV/COMP 19/20 WARRN/EARL MARSHALL/J   CONSTN
SUPREME/CT. PAGE 32 E0640   GOV/REL

JESSUP P.C.,TRANSNATIONAL LAW. FUT WOR+45 JUDGE   LAW   B56
CREATE ADJUD ORD/FREE...CONCPT VAL/FREE 20. PAGE 59   JURID
E1167   INT/LAW

KALNOKI BEDO A.,LEGAL SOURCES AND BIBLIOGRAPHY OF   BIBLIOG   B56
HUNGARY. COM HUNGARY CONSTN LEGIS JUDGE CT/SYS   ADJUD
SANCTION CRIME 16/20. PAGE 59 E1181   LAW
                                                      JURID

SIPKOV I.,LEGAL SOURCES AND BIBLIOGRAPHY OF   BIBLIOG   B56
BULGARIA. BULGARIA COM LEGIS WRITING ADJUD CT/SYS   LAW
...INT/LAW TREATY 20. PAGE 91 E1834   TOTALISM
                                                      MARXISM

SOHN L.B.,CASES ON UNITED NATIONS LAW. STRUCT   INT/ORG   B56
DELIB/GP WAR PEACE ORD/FREE...DECISION ANTHOL 20   INT/LAW
UN. PAGE 92 E1854   ADMIN
                                                      ADJUD

SUTHERLAND A.E.,THE LAW AND ONE MAN AMONG MANY.   JURID   B56
USA+45 INTELL ADJUD CT/SYS 20. PAGE 95 E1895   INGP/REL
                                                      ORD/FREE
                                                      CONCPT

US HOUSE RULES COMM,HEARINGS BEFORE A SPECIAL   ADMIN   B56
SUBCOMMITTEE: ESTABLISHMENT OF A STANDING COMMITTEE   DOMIN
ON ADMINISTRATIVE PROCEDURE, PRACTICE. USA+45 LAW   DELIB/GP
EX/STRUC ADJUD CONTROL EXEC GOV/REL EFFICIENCY PWR   NAT/G
...POLICY INT 20 CONGRESS. PAGE 100 E2009

WIGGINS J.R.,FREEDOM OR SECRECY. USA+45 USA-45 DELIB/GP EX/STRUC FORCES ADJUD SANCTION KNOWL PWR ...AUD/VIS CONGRESS 20. PAGE 106 E2121
B56
ORD/FREE
PRESS
NAT/G
CONTROL

CARRINGTON P.D.,"POLITICAL QUESTIONS: THE JUDICIAL CHECK ON THE EXECUTIVE." USA+45 LAW CHIEF 20. PAGE 20 E0395
L56
ADJUD
EXEC
PWR
REPRESENT

TANENHAUS J.,"THE SUPREME COURT AND PRESIDENTIAL POWER." USA+45 USA-45 NAT/G ADJUD GOV/REL FEDERAL 20 PRESIDENT. PAGE 95 E1907
S56
CT/SYS
PWR
CONTROL
CHIEF

AUMANN F.R.,"THE ISTRUMENTALITIES OF JUSTICE: THEIR FORMS, FUNCTIONS, AND LIMITATIONS." WOR+45 WOR-45 JUDGE PROB/SOLV ROUTINE ATTIT...BIBLIOG 20. PAGE 6 E0118
C56
JURID
ADMIN
CT/SYS
ADJUD

NJ LAW AND LEGISLATIVE BURE,NEW JERSEY LEGISLAVTIVE REAPPORTIONMENT (PAMPHLET). USA+45 ACT/RES ADJUD...STAT CHARTS 20 NEW/JERSEY. PAGE 2 E0041
B57
APPORT
LEGIS
CENSUS
REPRESENT

ALIGHIERI D.,ON WORLD GOVERNMENT. ROMAN/EMP LAW SOCIETY INT/ORG NAT/G POL/PAR ADJUD WAR GP/REL PEACE WORSHIP 15 WORLDUNITY DANTE. PAGE 4 E0067
B57
POLICY
CONCPT
DIPLOM
SECT

BAYITCH S.A.,A GUIDE TO INTERAMERICAN LEGAL STUDIES: A SELECTIVE BIBLIOGRAPHY OF WORKS IN ENGLISH. NAT/G LEGIS ADJUD CT/SYS CONGRESS 20. PAGE 8 E0157
B57
BIBLIOG
L/A+17C
LAW
JURID

BERNS W.,FREEDOM, VIRTUE AND THE FIRST AMENDMENT. USA+45 USA-45 CONSTN INTELL JUDGE ADJUD RIGID/FLEX MORAL...CONCPT 20 AMEND/I. PAGE 11 E0211
B57
JURID
ORD/FREE
CT/SYS
LAW

BERNS W.,FREEDOM, VIRTUE, AND THE FIRST AMENDMENT. USA-45 LAW CONSTN PROB/SOLV NEW/LIB...JURID 20 SUPREME/CT AMEND/I. PAGE 11 E0212
B57
ADJUD
CT/SYS
ORD/FREE

CHICAGO U LAW SCHOOL,CONFERENCE ON JUDICIAL ADMINISTRATION. LOC/G MUNIC NAT/G PROVS...ANTHOL 20. PAGE 22 E0429
B57
CT/SYS
ADJUD
ADMIN
GOV/REL

CONOVER H.F.,NORTH AND NORTHEAST AFRICA; A SELECTED ANNOTATED LIST OF WRITINGS. ALGERIA MOROCCO SUDAN UAR CULTURE INT/ORG PROB/SOLV ADJUD NAT/LISM PWR WEALTH...SOC 20 UN. PAGE 25 E0496
B57
BIBLIOG/A
DIPLOM
AFR
ECO/UNDEV

COOPER F.E.,THE LAWYER AND ADMINISTRATIVE AGENCIES. USA+45 CLIENT LAW PROB/SOLV CT/SYS PERSON ROLE. PAGE 25 E0500
B57
CONSULT
ADMIN
ADJUD
DELIB/GP

DIVINE R.A.,AMERICAN IMMIGRATION POLICY, 1924-52. USA+45 USA-45 VOL/ASSN DELIB/GP ADJUD WAR ADJUST DISCRIM...POLICY JURID 20 DEPRESSION MIGRATION. PAGE 32 E0630
B57
GEOG
HABITAT
LEGIS
CONTROL

DUMBAULD E.,THE BILL OF RIGHTS AND WHAT IT MEANS TODAY. USA+45 USA-45 CT/SYS...JURID STYLE TIME/SEQ BIBLIOG 18/20 BILL/RIGHT. PAGE 33 E0656
B57
CONSTN
LAW
ADJUD
ORD/FREE

HINDERLING A.,DIE REFORMATORISCHE VERWALTUNGSGERICHTSBARKEIT. GERMANY/W PROB/SOLV ADJUD SUPEGO PWR...CONCPT 20. PAGE 53 E1049
B57
ADMIN
CT/SYS
JURID
CONTROL

HISS A.,IN THE COURT OF PUBLIC OPINION. USA+45 DELIB/GP LEGIS LEGIT CT/SYS ATTIT 20 DEPT/STATE NIXON/RM HUAC HISS/ALGER. PAGE 53 E1053
B57
CRIME
MARXISM
BIOG
ADJUD

INSTITUT DE DROIT INTL,TABLEAU GENERAL DES RESOLUTIONS (1873-1956). LAW NEUTRAL CRIME WAR MARRIAGE PEACE...JURID 19/20. PAGE 56 E1124
B57
INT/LAW
DIPLOM
ORD/FREE
ADJUD

LONG H.A.,USURPERS - FOES OF FREE MAN. LAW NAT/G CHIEF LEGIS DOMIN ADJUD REPRESENT GOV/REL ORD/FREE LAISSEZ POPULISM...POLICY 18/20 SUPREME/CT ROOSEVLT/F CONGRESS CON/INTERP. PAGE 66 E1325
B57
CT/SYS
CENTRAL
FEDERAL
CONSTN

MEYER P.,ADMINISTRATIVE ORGANIZATION: A COMPARATIVE STUDY OF THE ORGANIZATION OF PUBLIC ADMINISTRATION. DENMARK FRANCE NORWAY SWEDEN UK USA+45 ELITES LOC/G CONSULT LEGIS ADJUD CONTROL LEAD PWR SKILL DECISION. PAGE 72 E1449
B57
ADMIN
METH/COMP
NAT/G
CENTRAL

MORELAND C.C.,EQUAL JUSTICE UNDER LAW. USA+45 USA-45 PROF/ORG PROVS JUDGE...POLICY JURID. PAGE 74 E1491
B57
CONSTN
ADJUD
CT/SYS
ORD/FREF

SCHUBERT G.A.,THE PRESIDENCY IN THE COURTS. CONSTN FORCES DIPLOM TARIFFS ADJUD CONTROL WAR...DECISION MGT CHARTS 18/20 PRESIDENT CONGRESS SUPREME/CT. PAGE 89 E1778
B57
PWR
CT/SYS
LEGIT
CHIEF

US SENATE COMM ON JUDICIARY,HEARING BEFORE SUBCOMMITTEE ON COMMITTEE OF JUDICIARY, UNITED STATES SENATE: S. J. RES. 3. USA+45 NAT/G CONSULT DELIB/GP DIPLOM ADJUD LOBBY REPRESENT 20 CONGRESS TREATY. PAGE 102 E2040
B57
LEGIS
CONSTN
CONFER
AGREE

US SENATE COMM ON JUDICIARY,LIMITATION OF APPELLATE JURISDICTION OF THE SUPREME COURT. USA+45 LAW NAT/G DELIB/GP PLAN ADMIN CONTROL PWR...DECISION 20 CONGRESS SUPREME/CT. PAGE 102 E2041
B57
CT/SYS
ADJUD
POLICY
GOV/REL

FRANKFURTER F.,"THE SUPREME COURT IN THE MIRROR OF JUSTICES" (BMR)" USA+45 USA-45 INTELL INSPECT EFFICIENCY ROLE KNOWL MORAL 18/20 SUPREME/CT. PAGE 40 E0792
S57
EDU/PROP
ADJUD
CT/SYS
PERSON

ALEXANDROWICZ,A BIBLIOGRAPHY OF INDIAN LAW. INDIA S/ASIA CONSTN CT/SYS...INT/LAW 19/20. PAGE 3 E0062
B58
BIBLIOG
LAW
ADJUD
JURID

BOWETT D.W.,SELF-DEFENSE IN INTERNATIONAL LAW. EUR+WWI MOD/EUR WOR+45 WOR-45 SOCIETY INT/ORG CONSULT DIPLOM LEGIT COERCE ATTIT ORD/FREE...JURID 20 UN. PAGE 14 E0276
B58
ADJUD
CONCPT
WAR
INT/LAW

BRIERLY J.L.,THE BASIS OF OBLIGATION IN INTERNATIONAL LAW, AND OTHER PAPERS. WOR+45 WOR-45 LEGIS...JURID CONCPT NAT/COMP ANTHOL 20. PAGE 15 E0299
B58
INT/LAW
DIPLOM
ADJUD
SOVEREIGN

CARPENTER W.S.,FOUNDATIONS OF MODERN JURISPRUDENCE. LAW UNIV PROB/SOLV ADJUD CT/SYS CRIME ATTIT...CONCPT 18/20. PAGE 20 E0388
B58
JURID

CAUGHEY J.W.,IN CLEAR AND PRESENT DANGER. USA+45 ADJUD COERCE ATTIT AUTHORIT...POLICY 20 COLD/WAR MCCARTHY/J. PAGE 21 E0408
B58
NAT/G
CONTROL
DOMIN
ORD/FREE

CHARLES R.,LA JUSTICE EN FRANCE. FRANCE LAW CONSTN DELIB/GP CRIME 20. PAGE 21 E0422
B58
JURID
ADMIN
CT/SYS
ADJUD

CUNNINGHAM W.B.,COMPULSORY CONCILIATION AND COLLECTIVE BARGAINING. CANADA NAT/G LEGIS ADJUD CT/SYS GP/REL...MGT 20 NEW/BRUNS STRIKE CASEBOOK. PAGE 28 E0555
B58
POLICY
BARGAIN
LABOR
INDUS

DAVIS K.C.,ADMINISTRATIVE LAW TREATISE (VOLS. I AND IV). NAT/G JUDGE PROB/SOLV ADJUD GP/REL 20 SUPREME/CT. PAGE 29 E0575
B58
ADMIN
JURID
CT/SYS
EX/STRUC

DAVIS K.C.,ADMINISTRATIVE LAW: CASES, TEXT, PROBLEMS. LAW LOC/G NAT/G TOP/EX PAY CONTROL GOV/REL INGP/REL FEDERAL 20 SUPREME/CT. PAGE 29 E0576
B58 ADJUD JURID CT/SYS ADMIN

DEUTSCHE GESCHAFT VOLKERRECHT,DIE VOLKERRECHTLICHEN DISSERTATIONEN AN DEN WESTDEUTSCHEN UNIVERSITATEN, 1945-1957. GERMANY/W NAT/G DIPLOM ADJUD CT/SYS ...POLICY 20. PAGE 31 E0616
B58 BIBLIOG INT/LAW ACADEM JURID

FELLMAN D.,THE DEFENDANT'S RIGHTS. USA+45 NAT/G CONSULT CT/SYS SUPEGO ORD/FREE...BIBLIOG SUPREME/CT CIVIL/SERV. PAGE 37 E0730
B58 CONSTN LAW CRIME ADJUD

HOOD W.C.,FINANCING OF ECONOMIC ACTIVITY IN CANADA. CANADA FUT VOL/ASSN WORKER ECO/TAC ADJUD ADMIN ...CHARTS 20. PAGE 55 E1093
B58 BUDGET FINAN GP/REL ECO/DEV

KAPLAN H.E.,THE LAW OF CIVIL SERVICE. USA+45 LAW POL/PAR CT/SYS CRIME GOV/REL...POLICY JURID 20. PAGE 59 E1183
B58 ADJUD NAT/G ADMIN CONSTN

LAW COMMISSION OF INDIA,REFORM OF JUDICIAL ADMINISTRATION. INDIA TOP/EX ADMIN DISCRIM EFFICIENCY...METH/COMP 20. PAGE 63 E1269
B58 CT/SYS ADJUD GOV/REL CONTROL

MASON A.T.,THE SUPREME COURT FROM TAFT TO WARREN. EX/STRUC LEGIS ROLE 20 SUPREME/CT TAFT/WH HUGHES/CE STONE/HF. PAGE 69 E1376
B58 CT/SYS JURID ADJUD

O'BRIEN F.W.,JUSTICE REED AND THE FIRST AMENDMENT, THE RELIGION CLAUSES. USA+45 USA-45 NAT/G PROVS CONTROL FEDERAL...POLICY JURID TIME/SEQ 20 SUPREME/CT CHRUCH/STA AMEND/I REED/STAN. PAGE 78 E1563
B58 ADJUD SECT CT/SYS

OGDEN F.D.,THE POLL TAX IN THE SOUTH. USA+45 USA-45 TAX CONSTN ADJUD ADMIN PARTIC CRIME...TIME/SEQ GOV/COMP METH/COMP 18/20 SOUTH/US. PAGE 78 E1572
B58 TAX CHOOSE RACE/REL DISCRIM

PALMER E.E.,CIVIL LIBERTIES. USA+45 ADJUD CT/SYS PARTIC OWN LAISSEZ POPULISM...JURID CONCPT ANTHOL 20 SUPREME/CT CIVIL/LIB. PAGE 79 E1592
B58 ORD/FREE CONSTN RACE/REL LAW

POUND R.,JUSTICE ACCORDING TO LAW. LAW SOCIETY CT/SYS 20. PAGE 82 E1639
B58 CONCPT JURID ADJUD ADMIN

SHARMA M.P.,PUBLIC ADMINISTRATION IN THEORY AND PRACTICE. INDIA UK USA+45 USA-45 EX/STRUC ADJUD ...POLICY CONCPT NAT/COMP 20. PAGE 90 E1813
B58 MGT ADMIN DELIB/GP JURID

SOC OF COMP LEGIS AND INT LAW,THE LAW OF THE SEA... (PAMPHLET). WOR+45 NAT/G INT/TRADE ADJUD CONTROL NUC/PWR WAR PEACE ATTIT ORD/FREE...JURID CHARTS 20 UN TREATY RESOURCE/N. PAGE 92 E1850
B58 INT/LAW INT/ORG DIPLOM SEA

SPITZ D.,DEMOCRACY AND THE CHALLANGE OF POWER. FUT USA+45 USA-45 LAW SOCIETY STRUCT LOC/G POL/PAR PROVS DELIB/GP EX/STRUC LEGIS TOP/EX ACT/RES CREATE DOMIN EDU/PROP LEGIT ADJUD ADMIN ATTIT DRIVE MORAL ORD/FREE TOT/POP. PAGE 93 E1862
B58 NAT/G PWR

STONE J.,AGGRESSION AND WORLD ORDER: A CRITIQUE OF UNITED NATIONS THEORIES OF AGGRESSION. LAW CONSTN DELIB/GP PROB/SOLV BAL/PWR DIPLOM DEBATE ADJUD CRIME PWR...POLICY IDEA/COMP 20 UN SUEZ LEAGUE/NAT. PAGE 94 E1879
B58 ORD/FREE INT/ORG WAR CONCPT

STRONG C.F.,MODERN POLITICAL CONSTITUTIONS. LAW CHIEF DELIB/GP EX/STRUC LEGIS ADJUD CHOOSE FEDERAL
B58 CONSTN IDEA/COMP

POPULISM...CONCPT BIBLIOG 20 UN. PAGE 94 E1887
NAT/G

WESTIN A.F.,THE ANATOMY OF A CONSTITUTIONAL LAW CASE. USA+45 LAW LEGIS ADMIN EXEC...DECISION MGT SOC RECORD 20 SUPREME/CT. PAGE 105 E2113
B58 CT/SYS INDUS ADJUD CONSTN

WHITNEY S.N.,ANTITRUST POLICIES: AMERICAN EXPERIENCE IN TWENTY INDUSTRIES. USA+45 USA-45 LAW DELIB/GP LEGIS ADJUD CT/SYS GOV/REL ATTIT...ANTHOL 20 MONOPOLY CASEBOOK. PAGE 106 E2119
B58 INDUS CONTROL LG/CO MARKET

WOOD J.E.,CHURCH AND STATE IN SCRIPTURE HISTORY AND CONSTITUTIONAL LAW. LAW CONSTN SOCIETY PROVS VOL/ASSN BAL/PWR COLONIAL CT/SYS ATTIT...BIBLIOG 20 SUPREME/CT CHURCH/STA BIBLE. PAGE 107 E2142
B58 GP/REL SECT NAT/G ADJUD

BEVAN W.,"JURY BEHAVIOR AS A FUNCTION OF THE PRESTIGE OF THE FOREMAN AND THE NATURE OF HIS LEADERSHIP" (BMR)" DELIB/GP DOMIN ADJUD LEAD PERS/REL ATTIT...PSY STAT INT QU CHARTS SOC/EXP 20 JURY. PAGE 11 E0221
L58 PERSON EDU/PROP DECISION CT/SYS

DAHL R.A.,"DECISION-MAKING IN A DEMOCRACY: THE SUPREME COURT AS A NATIONAL POLICY-MAKER" (BMR)" USA+45 USA-45 POL/PAR ADJUD GOV/REL PWR...POLICY JURID 19/20 SUPREME/CT. PAGE 28 E0561
S58 CT/SYS CONSTN DECISION NAT/G

ROCHE J.P.,"POLITICAL SCIENCE AND SCIENCE FICTION" (BMR)" WOR+45 INTELL OP/RES ADJUD...JURID SOC IDEA/COMP 20. PAGE 85 E1709
S58 QUANT RATIONAL MATH METH

SCHUBERT G.A.,"THE STUDY OF JUDICIAL DECISION-MAKING AS AN ASPECT OF POLITICAL BEHAVIOR." PLAN ADJUD CT/SYS INGP/REL PERSON...PHIL/SCI SOC QUANT STAT CHARTS IDEA/COMP SOC/EXP. PAGE 89 E1779
S58 JUDGE DECISION CON/ANAL GAME

STAAR R.F.,"ELECTIONS IN COMMUNIST POLAND." EUR+WWI COM SOCIETY INT/ORG NAT/G POL/PAR LEGIS ACT/RES ECO/TAC CHOOSE EDU/PROP ADJUD ADMIN ROUTINE COERCE TOTALISM ATTIT POLAND ORD/FREE PWR 20. PAGE 93 E1864
S58 COM CHOOSE POLAND

VOSE C.E.,"LITIGATION AS A FORM OF PRESSURE GROUP ACTIVITY" (BMR)" USA+45 ADJUD ORD/FREE NAACP. PAGE 104 E2085
S58 CONTROL CT/SYS VOL/ASSN LOBBY

FRIEDRICH C.J.,"AUTHORITY, REASON AND DISCRETION" IN C. FRIEDRICH'S AUTHORITY (BMR)" UNIV EX/STRUC ADJUD ADMIN CONTROL INGP/REL ATTIT PERSON PWR. PAGE 41 E0807
C58 AUTHORIT CHOOSE RATIONAL PERS/REL

ABRAHAM H.J.,COURTS AND JUDGES: AN INTRODUCTION TO THE JUDICIAL PROCESS. USA+45 CONSTN ELITES NAT/G ORD/FREE PWR 19/20 SUPREME/CT. PAGE 2 E0045
B59 CT/SYS PERSON JURID ADJUD

ANDERSON J.N.D.,ISLAMIC LAW IN THE MODERN WORLD. FAM KIN SECT LEGIT ADJUD ATTIT DRIVE...TIME/SEQ TREND GEN/LAWS 20 MUSLIM. PAGE 5 E0089
B59 ISLAM JURID

BECK C.,CONTEMPT OF CONGRESS: A STUDY OF THE PROSECUTIONS INITIATED BY THE COMMITTEE ON UN-AMERICAN ACTIVITIES. USA+45 CONSTN DEBATE EXEC. PAGE 9 E0170
B59 LEGIS DELIB/GP PWR ADJUD

BOHMER A.,LEGAL SOURCES AND BIBLIOGRAPHY OF CZECHOSLOVAKIA. COM CZECHOSLVK PARL/PROC SANCTION CRIME MARXISM 20. PAGE 13 E0261
B59 BIBLIOG ADJUD LAW JURID

BROMWICH L.,UNION CONSTITUTIONS. CONSTN EX/STRUC PRESS ADJUD CONTROL CHOOSE REPRESENT PWR SAMP. PAGE 16 E0306
B59 LABOR ROUTINE INGP/REL RACE/REL

CHRISTMAN H.M.,THE PUBLIC PAPERS OF CHIEF JUSTICE EARL WARREN. CONSTN POL/PAR EDU/PROP SANCTION HEALTH...TREND 20 SUPREME/CT WARRN/EARL. PAGE 22
B59 LAW CT/SYS PERSON

E0436   ADJUD

B59

COMM. STUDY ORGAN. PEACE,ORGANIZING PEACE IN THE   INT/ORG
NUCLEAR AGE. FUT CONSULT DELIB/GP DOMIN ADJUD   ACT/RES
ROUTINE COERCE ORD/FREE...TECHNIC INT/LAW JURID   NUC/PWR
NEW/IDEA UN COLD/WAR 20. PAGE 24 E0483

B59

CORBETT P.E.,LAW IN DIPLOMACY. UK USA+45 USSR   NAT/G
CONSTN SOCIETY INT/ORG JUDGE LEGIT ATTIT ORD/FREE   ADJUD
TOT/POP LEAGUE/NAT 20. PAGE 26 E0507   JURID
                                          DIPLOM

B59

COUNCIL OF STATE GOVERNORS,AMERICAN LEGISLATURES: LEGIS
STRUCTURE AND PROCEDURES. SUMMARY AND TABULATIONS   CHARTS
OF A 1959 SURVEY. PUERT/RICO USA+45 PAY ADJUD ADMIN   PROVS
APPORT...IDEA/COMP 20 GUAM VIRGIN/ISL. PAGE 27   REPRESENT
E0525

B59

DAVIS K.C.,ADMINISTRATIVE LAW TEXT. USA+45 NAT/G   ADJUD
DELIB/GP EX/STRUC CONTROL ORD/FREE...T 20   ADMIN
SUPREME/CT. PAGE 29 E0577   JURID
                                          CT/SYS

B59

DESMITH S.A.,JUDICIAL REVIEW OF ADMINISTRATIVE   ADJUD
ACTION. UK LOC/G CONSULT DELIB/GP ADMIN PWR   NAT/G
...DECISION JURID 20 ENGLSH/LAW. PAGE 31 E0609   PROB/SOLV
                                          CT/SYS

B59

ELLIOTT S.D.,IMPROVING OUR COURTS. LAW EX/STRUC   CT/SYS
PLAN PROB/SOLV ADJUD ADMIN TASK CRIME EFFICIENCY   JURID
ORD/FREE 20. PAGE 34 E0684   GOV/REL
                                          NAT/G

B59

GOMEZ ROBLES J.,A STATEMENT OF THE LAWS OF   JURID
GUATEMALA IN MATTERS AFFECTING BUSINESS (2ND ED.   NAT/G
REV., ENLARGED). GUATEMALA L/A+17C LAW FINAN FAM   INDUS
WORKER ACT/RES DIPLOM ADJUD ADMIN GP/REL 20 OAS.   LEGIT
PAGE 44 E0881

B59

GREENSPAN M.,THE MODERN LAW OF LAND WARFARE. WOR+45 ADJUD
INT/ORG NAT/G DELIB/GP FORCES ATTIT...POLICY   PWR
HYPO/EXP STERTYP 20. PAGE 46 E0911   WAR

B59

GSOVSKI V.,GOVERNMENT, LAW, AND COURTS IN THE   ADJUD
SOVIET UNION AND EASTERN EUROPE (2 VOLS). COM USSR   MARXISM
AGRI INDUS WORKER CT/SYS CRIME...BIBLIOG 20   CONTROL
EUROPE/E. PAGE 48 E0958   ORD/FREE

B59

HARVARD UNIVERSITY LAW SCHOOL,INTERNATIONAL   NUC/PWR
PROBLEMS OF FINANCIAL PROTECTION AGAINST NUCLEAR   ADJUD
RISK. WOR+45 NAT/G DELIB/GP PROB/SOLV DIPLOM   INDUS
CONTROL ATTIT...POLICY INT/LAW MATH 20. PAGE 51   FINAN
E1009

B59

MORRIS C.,THE GREAT LEGAL PHILOSOPHERS: SELECTED   JURID
READINGS IN JURISPRUDENCE. UNIV INTELL SOCIETY   ADJUD
EDU/PROP MAJORITY UTOPIA PERSON KNOWL...ANTHOL.   PHIL/SCI
PAGE 75 E1497   IDEA/COMP

B59

PANHUYS H.F.,THE ROLE OF NATIONALITY IN   INT/LAW
INTERNATIONAL LAW. ADJUD CRIME WAR STRANGE...JURID   NAT/LISM
TREND. PAGE 80 E1596   INGP/REL

B59

PAULSEN M.G.,LEGAL INSTITUTIONS TODAY AND TOMORROW. JURID
UK USA+45 NAT/G PROF/ORG PROVS ADMIN PARL/PROC   ADJUD
ORD/FREE NAT/COMP. PAGE 80 E1604   JUDGE
                                          LEGIS

B59

REIFF H.,THE UNITED STATES AND THE TREATY LAW OF   ADJUD
THE SEA. USA+45 USA-45 SEA SOCIETY INT/ORG CONSULT   INT/LAW
DELIB/GP LEGIS DIPLOM LEGIT ATTIT ORD/FREE PWR
WEALTH...GEOG JURID TOT/POP 20 TREATY. PAGE 84
E1681

B59

REOCK E.C.,PROCEDURES AND STANDARDS FOR THE   PROVS
APPORTIONMENT OF STATE LEGISLATURES (DOCTORAL   LOC/G
THESIS). USA+45 POL/PAR LEGIS TEC/DEV ADJUD   APPORT
BIBLIOG. PAGE 84 E1686   REPRESENT

B59

SCHORN H.,DER RICHTER IM DRITTEN REICH; GESCHICHTE   ADJUD

UND DOKUMENTE. GERMANY NAT/G LEGIT CT/SYS INGP/REL   JUDGE
MORAL ORD/FREE RESPECT...JURID GP/COMP 20. PAGE 88   FASCISM
E1765

B59

SCHUBERT G.A.,QUANTITATIVE ANALYSIS OF JUDICIAL   JUDGE
BEHAVIOR. ADJUD LEAD CHOOSE INGP/REL MAJORITY ATTIT CT/SYS
...DECISION JURID CHARTS GAME SIMUL SUPREME/CT.   PERSON
PAGE 89 E1780   QUANT

B59

SCOTT F.R.,CIVIL LIBERTIES AND CANADIAN FEDERALISM. ORD/FREE
CANADA LAW ADJUD CT/SYS GOV/REL 20 CIV/RIGHTS.   FEDERAL
PAGE 90 E1797   NAT/LISM
                                          CONSTN

B59

SIMPSON J.L.,INTERNATIONAL ARBITRATION: LAW AND   INT/LAW
PRACTICE. WOR+45 WOR-45 INT/ORG DELIB/GP ADJUD   DIPLOM
PEACE MORAL ORD/FREE...METH 18/20. PAGE 91 E1829   CT/SYS
                                          CONSULT

B59

SQUIBB G.D.,THE HIGH COURT OF CHIVALRY. UK NAT/G   CT/SYS
FORCES ADJUD WAR 14/20 PARLIAMENT ENGLSH/LAW.   PARL/PROC
PAGE 93 E1863   JURID

B59

SURRENCY E.C.,A GUIDE TO LEGAL RESEARCH. USA+45   NAT/G
ACADEM LEGIS ACT/RES ADMIN...DECISION METH/COMP   PROVS
BIBLIOG METH. PAGE 94 E1894   ADJUD
                                          JURID

B59

TOMPKINS D.C.,SUPREME COURT OF THE UNITED STATES: A BIBLIOG/A
BIBLIOGRAPHY. LAW JUDGE ADJUD GOV/REL DISCRIM   CT/SYS
...JURID 18/20 SUPREME/CT NEGRO. PAGE 96 E1931   CONSTN
                                          NAT/G

B59

US CONGRESS JT ATOM ENRGY COMM,SELECTED MATERIALS   NAT/G
ON FEDERAL-STATE COOPERATION IN THE ATOMIC ENERGY   NUC/PWR
FIELD. USA+45 LAW LOC/G PROVS CONSULT LEGIS ADJUD   GOV/REL
...POLICY BIBLIOG 20 AEC. PAGE 99 E1991   DELIB/GP

B59

VAN CAENEGEM R.C.,ROYAL WRITS IN ENGLAND FROM THE   JURID
CONQUEST TO GLANVILL. UK JUDGE...TREND IDEA/COMP   CHIEF
11/12 COMMON/LAW. PAGE 103 E2067   ADJUD
                                          CT/SYS

B59

VITTACHIT,EMERGENCY '58. CEYLON UK STRUCT NAT/G   RACE/REL
FORCES ADJUD CRIME REV NAT/LISM 20. PAGE 104 E2081   DISCRIM
                                          DIPLOM
                                          SOVEREIGN

B59

WAGNER W.J.,THE FEDERAL STATES AND THEIR JUDICIARY. ADJUD
BRAZIL CANADA SWITZERLND USA+45 CONFER CT/SYS TASK   METH/COMP
EFFICIENCY FEDERAL PWR...JURID BIBLIOG 20 AUSTRAL   PROB/SOLV
MEXIC/AMER. PAGE 104 E2091   NAT/G

I59

COWAN T.A.,"A SYMPOSIUM ON GROUP INTERESTS AND THE   ADJUD
LAW" USA+45 LAW MARKET LABOR PLAN INT/TRADE TAX   PWR
RACE/REL RIGID/FLEX...JURID ANTHOL 20. PAGE 27   INGP/REL
E0528   CREATE

L59

HECTOR L.J.,"GOVERNMENT BY ANONYMITY: WHO WRITES   ADJUD
OUR REGULATORY OPINIONS?" USA+45 NAT/G TOP/EX   REPRESENT
CONTROL EXEC. PAGE 51 E1021   EX/STRUC
                                          ADMIN

L59

OBERER W.E.,"VOLUNTARY IMPARTIAL REVIEW OF LABOR: LABOR
SOME REFLECTIONS." DELIB/GP LEGIS PROB/SOLV ADJUD   LAW
CONTROL COERCE PWR PLURISM POLICY. PAGE 78 E1570   PARTIC
                                          INGP/REL

S59

BEANEY W.B.,"CIVIL LIBERTIES AND STATUTORY   CT/SYS
CONSTRUCTION"(BMR)" USA+45 LEGIS BAL/PWR 20   ORD/FREE
SUPREME/CT. PAGE 8 E0162   ADJUD
                                          LAW

S59

CARLSTON K.S.,"NATIONALIZATION: AN ANALYTIC   INDUS
APPROACH." WOR+45 INT/ORG ECO/TAC DOMIN LEGIT ADJUD NAT/G
COERCE ORD/FREE PWR WEALTH SOCISM...JURID CONCPT   NAT/LISM
TREND STERTYP TOT/POP VAL/FREE 20. PAGE 19 E0380   SOVEREIGN

S59

CORY R.H. JR.,"INTERNATIONAL INSPECTION FROM   STRUCT
PROPOSALS TO REALIZATION." WOR+45 TEC/DEV ECO/TAC   PSY

ADJUD ORD/FREE PWR WEALTH...RECORD VAL/FREE 20.   ARMS/CONT
PAGE 26 E0516   NUC/PWR

                                                   S59
MENDELSON W.,"JUDICIAL REVIEW AND PARTY POLITICS" CT/SYS
(BMR)" UK USA+45 USA-45 NAT/G LEGIS PROB/SOLV   POL/PAR
EDU/PROP ADJUD EFFICIENCY...POLICY NAT/COMP 19/20 BAL/PWR
AUSTRAL SUPREME/CT. PAGE 72 E1436   JURID

                                                   S59
MURPHY W.F.,"LOWER COURT CHECKS ON SUPREME COURT   CT/SYS
POWER" (BMR)" USA+45 NAT/G PROVS SCHOOL GOV/REL   BAL/PWR
RACE/REL DISCRIM ATTIT...DECISION JURID 20   CONTROL
SUPREME/CT NEGRO. PAGE 75 E1508   ADJUD

                                                   S59
PUGWASH CONFERENCE,"ON BIOLOGICAL AND CHEMICAL   ACT/RES
WARFARE." WOR+45 SOCIETY PROC/MFG INT/ORG FORCES   BIO/SOC
EDU/PROP ADJUD RIGID/FLEX ORD/FREE PWR...DECISION WAR
PSY NEW/IDEA MATH VAL/FREE 20. PAGE 83 E1661   WEAPON

                                                   S59
SCHEEHAN D.,"PUBLIC AND PRIVATE GROUPS AS   LAW
IDENTIFIED IN THE FIELD OF TRADE REGULATIONS."   CONTROL
USA+45 ADMIN REPRESENT GOV/REL. PAGE 87 E1753   ADJUD
                                                   LOBBY

                                                   S59
SOHN L.B.,"THE DEFINITION OF AGGRESSION." FUT LAW INT/ORG
FORCES LEGIT ADJUD ROUTINE COERCE ORD/FREE PWR   CT/SYS
...MAJORIT JURID QUANT COLD/WAR 20. PAGE 92 E1855 DETER
                                                   SOVEREIGN

                                                   B60
ADRIAN C.R.,STATE AND LOCAL GOVERNMENTS: A STUDY IN LOC/G
THE POLITICAL PROCESS. USA+45 LAW FINAN MUNIC   PROVS
POL/PAR LEGIS ADJUD EXEC CHOOSE REPRESENT. PAGE 3   GOV/REL
E0051   ATTIT

                                                   B60
BEEM H.D.,AN INTRODUCTION TO LEGAL BIBLIOGRAPHY FOT BIBLIOG/A
THE NON-PROFESSIONAL STUDENT. LOC/G NAT/G TAX 20.   JURID
PAGE 9 E0177   METH
                                                    ADJUD

                                                   B60
CARPER E.T.,THE DEFENSE APPROPRIATIONS RIDER   GOV/REL
(PAMPHLET). USA+45 CONSTN CHIEF DELIB/GP LEGIS   ADJUD
BUDGET LOBBY CIVMIL/REL...POLICY 20 CONGRESS   LAW
EISNHWR/DD DEPT/DEFEN PRESIDENT BOSTON. PAGE 20   CONTROL
E0390

                                                   B60
CASTBERG F.,FREEDOM OF SPEECH IN THE WEST. FRANCE ORD/FREE
GERMANY USA+45 USA-45 LAW CONSTN CHIEF PRESS   SANCTION
DISCRIM...CONCPT 18/20. PAGE 21 E0406   ADJUD
                                                   NAT/COMP

                                                   B60
DAVIS K.C.,ADMINISTRATIVE LAW AND GOVERNMENT.   ADMIN
USA+45 EX/STRUC PROB/SOLV ADJUD GP/REL PWR...POLICY JURID
20 SUPREME/CT. PAGE 29 E0578   CT/SYS
                                                    NAT/G

                                                   B60
ENGEL J.,THE SECURITY OF THE FREE WORLD. USSR   COM
WOR+45 STRATA STRUC ECO/DEV ECO/UNDEV INT/ORG   TREND
DELIB/GP FORCES DOMIN LEGIT ADJUD EXEC ARMS/CONT   DIPLOM
COERCE...POLICY CONCPT NEW/IDEA TIME/SEQ GEN/LAWS
COLD/WAR WORK UN 20 NATO. PAGE 35 E0689

                                                   B60
FELLMAN D.,THE SUPREME COURT AND EDUCATION. ACADEM CT/SYS
NAT/G PROVS DELIB/GP ADJUD ORD/FREE...POLICY JURID SECT
WORSHIP 20 SUPREME/CT NEGRO CHURCH/STA. PAGE 37   RACE/REL
E0731   SCHOOL

                                                   B60
GELLHORN W.,AMERICAN RIGHTS: THE CONSTITUTION IN   ORD/FREE
ACTION. USA+45 USA-45 LEGIS ADJUD COERCE RACE/REL JURID
DISCRIM MARXISM 20 SUPREME/CT. PAGE 43 E0846   CT/SYS
                                                   CONSTN

                                                   B60
HARVARD LAW SCHOOL LIBRARY,CURRENT LEGAL   BIBLIOG
BIBLIOGRAPHY. USA+45 CONSTN LEGIS ADJUD CT/SYS   JURID
POLICY. PAGE 51 E1006   LAW
                                                   INT/LAW

                                                   B60
PAUL A.M.,CONSERVATIVE CRISIS AND THE RULE OF LAW. CONSTN
USA-45 LABOR WORKER ATTIT ORD/FREE CONSERVE LAISSEZ ADJUD
...DECISION JURID 19 SUPREME/CT. PAGE 80 E1603   STRUC
                                                   PROF/ORG

                                                   B60
PICKLES D.,THE FIFTH FRENCH REPUBLIC. ALGERIA   CONSTN
FRANCE CHOOSE GOV/REL ATTIT CONSERVE...CHARTS 20   ADJUD
DEGAULLE/C. PAGE 80 E1615   NAT/G
                                                   EFFICIENCY

                                                   B60
POWELL T.,THE SCHOOL BUS LAW: A CASE STUDY IN   JURID
EDUCATION, RELIGION, AND POLITICS. USA+45 LAW NEIGH SCHOOL
SECT LEGIS EDU/PROP ADJUD CT/SYS LOBBY CATHISM
WORSHIP 20 CONNECTICT CHURCH/STA. PAGE 82 E1641

                                                   B60
SCHMIDHAUSER J.R.,THE SUPREME COURT: ITS POLITICS, JUDGE
PERSONALITIES, AND PROCEDURES. LAW DELIB/GP   JURID
EX/STRUC TOP/EX ADJUD CT/SYS CHOOSE RATIONAL PWR   DECISION
SUPREME/CT. PAGE 88 E1760

                                                   B60
SCHUBERT G.,THE PUBLIC INTEREST. USA+45 CONSULT   POLICY
PLAN PROB/SOLV ADJUD ADMIN GP/REL PWR ALL/IDEOS 20. DELIB/GP
PAGE 88 E1770   REPRESENT
                                                   POL/PAR

                                                   B60
STEIN E.,AMERICAN ENTERPRISE IN THE EUROPEAN COMMON MARKET
MARKET: A LEGAL PROFILE. EUR+WWI FUT USA+45 SOCIETY ADJUD
STRUC ECO/DEV NAT/G VOL/ASSN CONSULT PLAN TEC/DEV INT/LAW
ECO/TAC INT/TRADE ADMIN ATTIT RIGID/FLEX PWR...MGT
NEW/IDEA STAT TREND COMPUT/IR SIMUL EEC 20. PAGE 93
E1867

                                                   B60
WEBSTER J.A.,A GENERAL STUDY OF THE DEPARTMENT OF ORD/FREE
DEFENSE INTERNAL SECURITY PROGRAM. USA+45 WORKER   PLAN
TEC/DEV ADJUD CONTROL CT/SYS EXEC GOV/REL COST   ADMIN
...POLICY DECISION MGT 20 DEPT/DEFEN SUPREME/CT.   NAT/G
PAGE 105 E2105

                                                   B60
WOETZEL R.K.,THE INTERNATIONAL CONTROL OF AIRSPACE INT/ORG
AND OUTERSPACE. FUT WOR+45 AIR CONSTN STRUC   JURID
CONSULT PLAN TEC/DEV ADJUD RIGID/FLEX KNOWL   SPACE
ORD/FREE PWR...TECHNIC GEOG MGT NEW/IDEA TREND   INT/LAW
COMPUT/IR VAL/FREE 20 TREATY. PAGE 107 E2137

                                                   L60
DEAN A.W.,"SECOND GENEVA CONFERENCE OF THE LAW OF INT/ORG
THE SEA: THE FIGHT FOR FREEDOM OF THE SEAS." FUT   JURID
USA+45 USSR WOR+45 WOR-45 SEA CONSTN STRUC PLAN   INT/LAW
INT/TRADE ADJUD ADMIN ORD/FREE...DECISION RECORD
TREND GEN/LAWS 20 TREATY. PAGE 30 E0600

                                                   L60
FUCHS R.F.,"FAIRNESS AND EFFECTIVENESS IN   EFFICIENCY
ADMINISTRATIVE AGENCY ORGANIZATION AND PROCEDURES." EX/STRUC
USA+45 ADJUD ADMIN REPRESENT. PAGE 41 E0816   EXEC
                                                   POLICY

                                                   L60
KUNZ J.,"SANCTIONS IN INTERNATIONAL LAW." WOR+45   INT/ORG
WOR-45 LEGIT ARMS/CONT COERCE PEACE ATTIT   ADJUD
...METH/CNCPT TIME/SEQ TREND 20. PAGE 62 E1234   INT/LAW

                                                   L60
MILLER A.S.,"THE MYTH OF NEUTRALITY IN   ADJUD
CONSTITUTIONAL ADJUDICATION." LAW...DECISION JURID CONSTN
LING TREND IDEA/COMP. PAGE 73 E1456   MYTH
                                                   UTIL

                                                   L60
STEIN E.,"LEGAL REMEDIES OF ENTERPRISES IN THE   MARKET
EUROPEAN ECONOMIC COMMUNITY." EUR+WWI FUT ECO/DEV ADJUD
INDUS PLAN ECO/TAC ADMIN PWR...MGT MATH STAT TREND
CON/ANAL EEC 20. PAGE 93 E1868

                                                   S60
GRACIA-MORA M.R.,"INTERNATIONAL RESPONSIBILITY FOR INT/ORG
SUBVERSIVE ACTIVITIES AND HOSTILE PROPAGANDA BY   JURID
PRIVATE PERSONS AGAINST." EUR+WWI L/A+17C UK   SOVEREIGN
USA+45 USSR WOR-45 CONSTN NAT/G LEGIT ADJUD REV
PEACE TOTALISM ORD/FREE...INT/LAW 20. PAGE 45 E0895

                                                   S60
MARSHALL G.,"POLICE RESPONSIBILITY." UK LOC/G ADJUD CONTROL
ADMIN EXEC 20. PAGE 69 E1370   REPRESENT
                                                   LAW
                                                   FORCES

                                                   S60
NICHOLS J.P.,"HAZARDS OF AMERICAN PRIVATE   FINAN
INVESTMENT IN UNDERDEVELOPED COUNTRIES." FUT   ECO/UNDEV
L/A+17C USA+45 USA-45 EXTR/IND CONSULT BAL/PWR   CAP/ISM
ECO/TAC DOMIN ADJUD ATTIT SOVEREIGN WEALTH   NAT/LISM
...HIST/WRIT TIME/SEQ TREND VAL/FREE 20. PAGE 77
E1546

S60
O'BRIEN W.,"THE ROLE OF FORCE IN THE INTERNATIONAL   INT/ORG
JURIDICAL ORDER." WOR+45 NAT/G FORCES DOMIN ADJUD   COERCE
ARMS/CONT DETER NUC/PWR WAR ATTIT PWR...CATH
INT/LAW JURID CONCPT TREND STERTYP GEN/LAWS 20.
PAGE 78 E1564

S60
POTTER P.B.,"RELATIVE VALUES OF INTERNATIONAL   INT/ORG
RELATIONS, LAW, AND ORGANIZATIONS." WOR+45 NAT/G   LEGIS
LEGIT ADJUD ORD/FREE...CONCPT TOT/POP COLD/WAR 20.   DIPLOM
PAGE 81 E1633   INT/LAW

S60
RHYNE C.S.,"LAW AS AN INSTRUMENT FOR PEACE." FUT   ADJUD
WOR+45 PLAN LEGIT ROUTINE ARMS/CONT NUC/PWR ATTIT   EDU/PROP
ORD/FREE...JURID METH/CNCPT TREND CON/ANAL HYPO/EXP INT/LAW
COLD/WAR 20. PAGE 84 E1690   PEACE

S60
SCHACHTER O.,"THE ENFORCEMENT OF INTERNATIONAL   INT/ORG
JUDICIAL AND ARBITRAL DECISIONS." WOR+45 NAT/G   ADJUD
ECO/TAC DOMIN LEGIT ROUTINE COERCE ATTIT DRIVE   INT/LAW
ALL/VALS PWR...METH/CNCPT TREND TOT/POP 20 UN.
PAGE 87 E1750

S60
SCHWELB E.,"INTERNATIONAL CONVENTIONS ON HUMAN   INT/ORG
RIGHTS." FUT WOR+45 LAW CONSTN CULTURE SOCIETY   HUM
STRUCT VOL/ASSN DELIB/GP PLAN ADJUD SUPEGO LOVE
MORAL...SOC CONCPT STAT RECORD HIST/WRIT TREND 20
UN. PAGE 89 E1790

S60
THOMPSON K.W.,"MORAL PURPOSE IN FOREIGN POLICY: MORAL
REALITIES AND ILLUSIONS." WOR+45 LAW CULTURE   JURID
SOCIETY INT/ORG PLAN ADJUD ADMIN COERCE RIGID/FLEX   DIPLOM
SUPEGO KNOWL ORD/FREE PWR...SOC TREND SOC/EXP
TOT/POP 20. PAGE 96 E1921

S60
ULMER S.S.,"THE ANALYSIS OF BEHAVIOR PATTERNS ON   ATTIT
THE UNITED STATES SUPREME COURT" USA+45 LAW CT/SYS   ADJUD
PERS/REL RACE/REL PERSON...DECISION PSY SOC TREND   PROF/ORG
METH/COMP METH 20 SUPREME/CT CIVIL/LIB. PAGE 97   INGP/REL
E1951

S60
WRIGHT Q.,"LEGAL ASPECTS OF THE U-2 INCIDENT." COM   PWR
USA+45 USSR STRUCT NAT/G FORCES PLAN TEC/DEV PLAN   POLICY
RIGID/FLEX MORAL ORD/FREE...DECISION INT/LAW JURID   SPACE
PSY TREND GEN/LAWS COLD/WAR VAL/FREE 20 U-2.
PAGE 108 E2157

C60
HAZARD J.N.,"SETTLING DISPUTES IN SOVIET SOCIETY: ADJUD
THE FORMATIVE YEARS OF LEGAL INSTITUTIONS." USSR   LAW
NAT/G PROF/ORG PROB/SOLV CONTROL CT/SYS ROUTINE REV COM
CENTRAL...JURID BIBLIOG 20. PAGE 51 E1017   POLICY

B61
ALFRED H.,PUBLIC OWNERSHIP IN THE USA: GOALS AND   CONTROL
PRIORITIES. LAW INDUS INT/TRADE ADJUD GOV/REL   OWN
EFFICIENCY PEACE SOCISM...POLICY ANTHOL 20 TVA.   ECO/DEV
PAGE 3 E0064   ECO/TAC

B61
ANAND R.P.,COMPULSORY JURISDICTION OF INTERNATIONAL INT/ORG
COURT OF JUSTICE. FUT WOR+45 SOCIETY PLAN LEGIT   COERCE
ADJUD ATTIT DRIVE PERSON ORD/FREE...JURID CONCPT   INT/LAW
TREND 20 ICJ. PAGE 5 E0086

B61
AUERBACH C.A.,THE LEGAL PROCESS. USA+45 DELIB/GP   JURID
JUDGE CONFER ADJUD CONTROL...DECISION 20   ADMIN
SUPREME/CT. PAGE 6 E0116   LEGIS
                                                     CT/SYS

B61
BAINS J.S.,STUDIES IN POLITICAL SCIENCE. INDIA   DIPLOM
WOR+45 WOR-45 CONSTN BAL/PWR ADJUD ADMIN PARL/PROC   INT/LAW
SOVEREIGN...SOC METH/COMP ANTHOL 17/20 UN. PAGE 7   NAT/G
E0137

B61
BAYITCH S.A.,LATIN AMERICA: A BIBLIOGRAPHICAL   BIBLIOG
GUIDE. LAW CONSTN LEGIS JUDGE ADJUD CT/SYS 20.   L/A+17C
PAGE 8 E0158   NAT/G
                                                     JURID

B61
BEASLEY K.E.,STATE SUPERVISION OF MUNICIPAL DEBT IN MUNIC
KANSAS - A CASE STUDY. USA+45 USA-45 FINAN PROVS   LOC/G
BUDGET TAX ADJUD ADMIN CONTROL SUPEGO. PAGE 9 E0167 LEGIS
                                                     JURID

B61
CARNELL F.,THE POLITICS OF THE NEW STATES: A SELECT BIBLIOG/A
ANNOTATED BIBLIOGRAPHY WITH SPECIAL REFERENCE TO   AFR
THE COMMONWEALTH. CONSTN ELITES LABOR NAT/G POL/PAR ASIA
EX/STRUC DIPLOM ADJUD ADMIN...GOV/COMP 20   COLONIAL
COMMONWLTH. PAGE 20 E0387

B61
CARROTHERS A.W.R.,LABOR ARBITRATION IN CANADA.   LABOR
CANADA LAW NAT/G CONSULT LEGIS WORKER ADJUD ADMIN   MGT
CT/SYS 20. PAGE 20 E0396   GP/REL
                                                     BARGAIN

B61
CHILDS M.W.,THE EROSION OF INDIVIDUAL LIBERTIES.   ADJUD
NAT/G LEGIS ATTIT...JURID SOC CONCPT IDEA/COMP 20   CT/SYS
SUPREME/CT AMEND/I. PAGE 22 E0430   ORD/FREE
                                                     CONSTN

B61
FREUND P.A.,THE SUPREME COURT OF THE UNITED STATES: CT/SYS
ITS BUSINESS, PURPOSES, AND PERFORMANCE. CONSTN   JURID
CRIME CONSEN ORD/FREE...DECISION 20 SUPREME/CT   ADJUD
CIVIL/LIB. PAGE 40 E0797   FEDERAL

B61
JACOBS C.E.,JUSTICE FRANKFURTER AND CIVIL   BIOG
LIBERTIES. USA+45 USA-45 LAW NAT/G PROB/SOLV PRESS   CONSTN
PERS/REL...JURID WORSHIP 20 SUPREME/CT FRANKFUR/F   ADJUD
CIVIL/LIB. PAGE 57 E1144   ORD/FREE

B61
JUSTICE,THE CITIZEN AND THE ADMINISTRATION: THE   INGP/REL
REDRESS OF GRIEVANCES (PAMPHLET). EUR+WWI UK LAW   CONSULT
CONSTN STRATA NAT/G CT/SYS PARTIC COERCE...NEW/IDEA ADJUD
IDEA/COMP 20 OMBUDSMAN. PAGE 59 E1176   REPRESENT

B61
KURLAND P.B.,RELIGION AND THE LAW. USA+45 USA-45   SECT
CONSTN PROVS CHIEF ADJUD SANCTION PRIVIL CATHISM   NAT/G
...POLICY 17/20 SUPREME/CT PRESIDENT CHURCH/STA.   CT/SYS
PAGE 62 E1239   GP/REL

B61
LARSON A.,WHEN NATIONS DISAGREE. USA+45 WOR+45   INT/LAW
INT/ORG ADJUD COERCE CRIME OWN SOVEREIGN...POLICY   DIPLOM
JURID 20. PAGE 63 E1258   WAR

B61
LEONI B.,FREEDOM AND THE LAW. WOR+45 SOCIETY ADJUD   JURID
INGP/REL EFFICIENCY ATTIT DRIVE. PAGE 64 E1286   ORD/FREE
                                                     LEGIS
                                                     CONTROL

B61
MASSEL M.S.,THE REGULATORY PROCESS (JOURNAL   ADJUD
REPRINT). NAT/G LOBBY REPRESENT GOV/REL 20. PAGE 69 EX/STRUC
E1382   EXEC

B61
MCDOUGAL M.S.,LAW AND MINIMUM WORLD PUBLIC ORDER.   INT/ORG
WOR+45 SOCIETY NAT/G DELIB/GP EDU/PROP LEGIT ADJUD   ORD/FREE
COERCE ATTIT PERSON...JURID CONCPT RECORD TREND   INT/LAW
TOT/POP 20. PAGE 70 E1406

B61
POOLEY B.J.,PLANNING AND ZONING IN THE UNITED   PLAN
STATES. USA+45 MUNIC DELIB/GP ACT/RES PROB/SOLV   LOC/G
TEC/DEV ADJUD ADMIN REGION 20 ZONING. PAGE 81 E1628 PROVS
                                                     LAW

B61
SMITH J.W.,RELIGIOUS PERSPECTIVES IN AMERICAN   SECT
CULTURE. VOL. 2: RELIGION IN AMERICAN LIFE. USA+45   DOMIN
CULTURE NAT/G EDU/PROP ADJUD LOBBY ATTIT...ART/METH SOCIETY
ANTHOL 20 CHURCH/STA BIBLE. PAGE 92 E1845   GP/REL

B61
TOMPKINS D.C.,CONFLICT OF INTEREST IN THE FEDERAL   BIBLIOG
GOVERNMENT: A BIBLIOGRAPHY. USA+45 EX/STRUC LEGIS   ROLE
ADJUD ADMIN CRIME CONGRESS PRESIDENT. PAGE 96 E1932 NAT/G
                                                     LAW

B61
US CONGRESS,CONSTITUTIONAL RIGHTS OF THE MENTALLY   HEALTH
ILL. USA+45 LAW PUB/INST DELIB/GP ADJUD ORD/FREE   CONSTN
...PSY QU 20 CONGRESS. PAGE 99 E1989   JURID
                                                     CONFER

B61
UTLEY T.E.,OCCASION FOR OMBUDSMAN. UK CREATE   PROB/SOLV
CONTROL 20 OMBUDSMAN. PAGE 103 E2065   INGP/REL
                                                     REPRESENT
                                                     ADJUD

B61

WASSERSTROM R.A.,THE JUDICIAL DECISION: TOWARD A   JUDGE
THEORY OF LEGAL JUSTIFICATION. ACT/RES RATIONAL   LAW
PERCEPT KNOWL OBJECTIVE...DECISION JURID. PAGE 105   ADJUD
E2102

B61

WESTIN A.F.,THE SUPREME COURT: VIEWS FROM INSIDE.   CT/SYS
USA+45 NAT/G PROF/ORG PROVS DELIB/GP INGP/REL   LAW
DISCRIM ATTIT...POLICY DECISION JURID 20   ADJUD
SUPREME/CT CONGRESS CIVIL/LIB. PAGE 106 E2114   GOV/REL

B61

WRIGHT Q.,THE ROLE OF INTERNATIONAL LAW IN THE   INT/ORG
ELIMINATION OF WAR. FUT WOR+45 WOR-45 NAT/G BAL/PWR   ADJUD
DIPLOM DOMIN LEGIT PWR...POLICY INT/LAW JURID   ARMS/CONT
CONCPT TIME/SEQ TREND GEN/LAWS COLD/WAR 20.
PAGE 108 E2158

L61

TAUBENFELD H.J.,"A REGIME FOR OUTER SPACE." FUT   INT/ORG
UNIV R+D ACT/RES PLAN BAL/PWR LEGIT ARMS/CONT   ADJUD
ORD/FREE...POLICY JURID TREND UN TOT/POP 20   SPACE
COLD/WAR. PAGE 95 E1910

S61

ABLARD C.D.,"EX PARTE CONTACTS WITH FEDERAL   EXEC
ADMINISTRATIVE AGENCIES." USA+45 CLIENT NAT/G   ADJUD
DELIB/GP ADMIN PWR 20. PAGE 2 E0044   LOBBY
                                                          REPRESENT

S61

BAER E.,"THE GENERAL ACCOUNTING OFFICE: THE FEDERAL   ADJUD
GOVERNMENT'S AUDITOR." USA+45 NAT/G REPRESENT 20   EX/STRUC
GENACCOUNT. PAGE 7 E0132   EXEC
                                                          LAW

S61

SCHUBERT G.,"A PSYCHOMETRIC MODEL OF THE SUPREME   JUDGE
COURT." DELIB/GP ADJUD CHOOSE ATTIT...DECISION   CT/SYS
JURID PSY QUANT STAT HYPO/EXP GEN/METH SUPREME/CT.   PERSON
PAGE 88 E1771   SIMUL

B62

ALEXANDROWICZ C.H.,WORLD ECONOMIC AGENCIES: LAW AND   INT/LAW
PRACTICE. WOR+45 DIST/IND FINAN LABOR CONSULT   INT/ORG
INT/TRADE TARIFFS REPRESENT HEALTH...JURID 20 UN   DIPLOM
GATT EEC OAS ECSC. PAGE 3 E0063   ADJUD

B62

AMERICAN LAW INSTITUTE,FOREIGN RELATIONS LAW OF THE   PROF/ORG
UNITED STATES: RESTATEMENT, SECOND. USA+45 NAT/G   LAW
LEGIS ADJUD EXEC ROUTINE GOV/REL...INT/LAW JURID   DIPLOM
CONCPT 20 TREATY. PAGE 4 E0082   ORD/FREE

B62

BEBR G.,JUDICIAL CONTROL OF THE EUROPEAN   ADJUD
COMMUNITIES. EUR+WWI INT/ORG NAT/G DOMIN LEGIT PWR   VOL/ASSN
...JURID CONCPT GEN/LAWS GEN/METH EEC 20. PAGE 9   INT/LAW
E0168

B62

BIBLIOTHEQUE PALAIS DE LA PAIX,CATALOGUE OF THE   BIBLIOG
PEACE PALACE LIBRARY, SUPPLEMENT 1937-1952 (7   INT/LAW
VOLS.). WOR+45 WOR-45 INT/ORG NAT/G ADJUD WAR PEACE   DIPLOM
...JURID 20. PAGE 12 E0225

B62

BICKEL A.,THE LEAST DANGEROUS BRANCH. USA+45 USA-45   LAW
CONSTN SCHOOL LEGIS ADJUD RACE/REL DISCRIM ORD/FREE   NAT/G
...JURID 18/20 SUPREME/CT CONGRESS MARSHALL/J   CT/SYS
HOLMES/OW FRANKFUR/F. PAGE 12 E0226

B62

BORKIN J.,THE CORRUPT JUDGE. USA+45 CT/SYS ATTIT   ADJUD
SUPEGO MORAL RESPECT...BIBLIOG + SUPREME/CT   TRIBUTE
MANTON/M DAVIS/W JOHNSN/ALB. PAGE 14 E0271   CRIME

B62

COLOMBOS C.J.,THE INTERNATIONAL LAW OF THE SEA.   INT/LAW
WOR+45 EXTR/IND DIPLOM INT/TRADE TARIFFS AGREE WAR   SEA
...TIME/SEQ 20 TREATY. PAGE 24 E0476   JURID
                                                          ADJUD

B62

DELANY V.T.H.,THE ADMINISTRATION OF JUSTICE IN   ADMIN
IRELAND. IRELAND CONSTN FINAN JUDGE COLONIAL CRIME   JURID
...CRIMLGY 19/20. PAGE 30 E0604   CT/SYS
                                                          ADJUD

B62

DIESING P.,REASON IN SOCIETY; FIVE TYPES OF   RATIONAL
DECISIONS AND THEIR SOCIAL CONDITIONS. SOCIETY   METH/COMP
STRUCT LABOR CREATE TEC/DEV BARGAIN ADJUD ROLE   DECISION
...JURID BIBLIOG 20. PAGE 31 E0625   CONCPT

B62

DONNELLY R.C.,CRIMINAL LAW: PROBLEMS FOR DECISION   CRIME
IN THE PROMULGATION, INVOCATION AND ADMINISTRATION   LAW
OF A LAW OF CRIMES. USA+45 SANCTION BIO/SOC   ADJUD
...DECISION JURID BIBLIOG 20. PAGE 32 E0636   PROB/SOLV

B62

EVAN W.M.,LAW AND SOCIOLOGY: EXPLORATORY ESSAYS.   JURID
CONSULT ACT/RES OP/RES PROB/SOLV EDU/PROP LEGIT   SOC
ADJUD CT/SYS GP/REL...PHIL/SCI ANTHOL SOC/INTEG 20.   PROF/ORG
PAGE 35 E0703

B62

FATOUROS A.A.,GOVERNMENT GUARANTEES TO FOREIGN   NAT/G
INVESTORS. WOR+45 ECO/UNDEV INDUS WORKER ADJUD   FINAN
...NAT/COMP BIBLIOG TREATY. PAGE 36 E0722   INT/TRADE
                                                          ECO/DEV

B62

FRIEDRICH C.J.,NOMOS V: THE PUBLIC INTEREST. UNIV   METH/CNCPT
ECO/TAC ADJUD UTIL ATTIT...POLICY LING LOG GEN/LAWS   CONCPT
20. PAGE 41 E0808   LAW
                                                          IDEA/COMP

B62

GROGAN V.,ADMINISTRATIVE TRIBUNALS IN THE PUBLIC   ADMIN
SERVICE. IRELAND UK NAT/G CONTROL CT/SYS...JURID   LAW
GOV/COMP 20. PAGE 48 E0945   ADJUD
                                                          DELIB/GP

B62

GRZYBOWSKI K.,SOVIET LEGAL INSTITUTIONS. USA+45   ADJUD
USSR ECO/DEV NAT/G EDU/PROP CONTROL CT/SYS CRIME   LAW
OWN ATTIT PWR SOCISM...NAT/COMP 20. PAGE 48 E0955   JURID

B62

HIRSCHFIELD R.S.,THE CONSTITUTION AND THE COURT.   ADJUD
SCHOOL WAR RACE/REL EQUILIB ORD/FREE...POLICY   PWR
MAJORIT DECISION JURID 18/20 PRESIDENT COLD/WAR   CONSTN
CIVIL/LIB SUPREME/CT CONGRESS. PAGE 53 E1051   LAW

B62

INTERNAT CONGRESS OF JURISTS,EXECUTIVE ACTION AND   JURID
THE RULE OF RULE: REPORTION PROCEEDINGS OF INT'T   EXEC
CONGRESS OF JURISTS,-RIO DE JANEIRO, BRAZIL. WOR+45   ORD/FREE
ACADEM CONSULT JUDGE EDU/PROP ADJUD CT/SYS INGP/REL   CONTROL
PERSON DEPT/DEFEN. PAGE 57 E1130

B62

JACOBINI H.B.,INTERNATIONAL LAW: A TEXT. DIPLOM   INT/LAW
ADJUD NEUTRAL WAR PEACE T. PAGE 57 E1143   CT/SYS
                                                          CONCPT

B62

JENKS C.W.,THE PROPER LAW OF INTERNATIONAL   LAW
ORGANISATIONS. DIPLOM LEGIT AGREE CT/SYS SANCTION   INT/ORG
REPRESENT SOVEREIGN...GEN/LAWS 20 UN UNESCO ILO   ADJUD
NATO OAS. PAGE 58 E1158   INT/LAW

B62

KAUPER P.G.,CIVIL LIBERTIES AND THE CONSTITUTION.   LAW
USA+45 SECT EDU/PROP WRITING ADJUD SEX ORD/FREE 20   CONSTN
SUPREME/CT CIVIL/LIB CHURCH/STA. PAGE 60 E1188   CT/SYS
                                                          DECISION

B62

LILLICH R.B.,INTERNATIONAL CLAIMS: THEIR   ADJUD
ADJUDICATION BY NATIONAL COMMISSIONS. WOR+45 WOR-45   JURID
INT/ORG LEGIT CT/SYS TOT/POP 20. PAGE 65 E1297   INT/LAW

B62

MARS D.,SUGGESTED LIBRARY IN PUBLIC ADMINISTRATION.   BIBLIOG
FINAN DELIB/GP EX/STRUC WORKER COMPUTER ADJUD   ADMIN
...DECISION PSY SOC METH/COMP 20. PAGE 68 E1368   METH
                                                          MGT

B62

MASON A.T.,THE SUPREME COURT: PALADIUM OF FREEDOM.   CONSTN
USA-45 NAT/G POL/PAR CHIEF LEGIS ADJUD PARL/PROC   CT/SYS
FEDERAL PWR...POLICY BIOG 18/20 SUPREME/CT   JURID
ROOSEVLT/F JEFFERSN/T MARSHALL/J HUGHES/CE. PAGE 69
E1378

B62

MCDOUGAL M.S.,THE PUBLIC ORDER OF THE OCEANS.   ADJUD
WOR+45 WOR-45 SEA INT/ORG NAT/G CONSULT DELIB/GP   ORD/FREE
DIPLOM LEGIT PEACE RIGID/FLEX...GEOG INT/LAW JURID
RECORD TOT/POP 20 TREATY. PAGE 70 E1407

B62

MCGRATH J.J.,CHURCH AND STATE IN AMERICAN LAW. LAW   SECT
PROVS SCHOOL TAX GIVE CT/SYS GP/REL...POLICY ANTHOL   ADJUD
18/20 SUPREME/CT CHURCH/STA CASEBOOK. PAGE 71 E1414   CONSTN
                                                          NAT/G

MCGRATH J.J.,CHURCH AND STATE IN AMERICAN LAW: CASES AND MATERIALS. USA+45 USA-45 LEGIS EDU/PROP ADJUD CT/SYS PWR...ANTHOL 18/20 CHURCH/STA. PAGE 71 E1415
B62
LAW GOV/REL SECT

MCWHINNEY E.,CONSTITUTIONALISM IN GERMANY AND THE FEDERAL CONSTITUTINAL COURT. GERMANY/W POL/PAR TV ADJUD CHOOSE EFFICIENCY ATTIT ORD/FREE MARXISM ...NEW/IDEA BIBLIOG 20. PAGE 71 E1428
B62
CONSTN CT/SYS CONTROL NAT/G

MILLER P.,THE LEGAL MIND IN AMERICA. PROF/ORG JUDGE ADJUD CT/SYS 18/19 SUPREME/CT. PAGE 73 E1461
B62
JURID CONSTN NAT/G CONCPT

MURPHY W.F.,CONGRESS AND THE COURT. USA+45 LAW LOBBY GP/REL RACE/REL ATTIT PWR...JURID INT BIBLIOG CONGRESS SUPREME/CT WARRN/EARL. PAGE 75 E1509
B62
LEGIS CT/SYS GOV/REL ADJUD

NATIONAL MUNICIPAL LEAGUE,COURT DECISIONS ON LEGISLATIVE APPORTIONMENT (VOL. III). USA+45 JUDGE ADJUD CONTROL ATTIT...DECISION JURID COURT/DIST CASEBOOK. PAGE 76 E1528
B62
PROVS CT/SYS APPORT LEGIS

NEW YORK STATE LEGISLATURE,REPORT AND DRAFT OF PROPOSED LEGISLATION ON COURT REORGANIZATION. LAW PROVS DELIB/GP CREATE ADJUD 20 NEW/YORK. PAGE 77 E1538
B62
CT/SYS JURID MUNIC LOC/G

PHILLIPS O.H.,CONSTITUTIONAL AND ADMINISTRATIVE LAW (3RD ED.). UK INT/ORG LOC/G CHIEF EX/STRUC LEGIS BAL/PWR ADJUD COLONIAL CT/SYS PWR...CHARTS 20. PAGE 80 E1613
B62
JURID ADMIN CONSTN NAT/G

ROSENNE S.,THE WORLD COURT: WHAT IT IS AND HOW IT WORKS. WOR+45 WOR-45 LAW CONSTN JUDGE ADJUD LEGIT ROUTINE CHOOSE PEACE ORD/FREE...JURID OBS TIME/SEQ CHARTS UN TOT/POP VAL/FREE 20. PAGE 86 E1717
B62
INT/ORG ADJUD INT/LAW

SIGLIANO R E.,THE COURTS. USA+45 USA-45 LAW CONSTN NAT/G ROUTINE CHOOSE 18/20 SUPREME/CT. PAGE 91 E1825
B62
ADJUD PROB/SOLV CT/SYS JUDGE

STERN R.L.,SUPREME COURT PRACTICE. USA+45 USA-45 OP/RES...STYLE METH 20 SUPREME/CT. PAGE 93 E1872
B62
CT/SYS ADJUD JURID ROUTINE

TAPER B.,GOMILLION VERSUS LIGHTFOOT: THE TUSKEGEE GERRYMANDER CASE. USA+45 LAW CONSTN LOC/G MUNIC CT/SYS 20 NEGRO CIV/RIGHTS GOMILLN/CG LIGHTFT/PM TUSKEGEE. PAGE 95 E1908
B62
APPORT REPRESENT RACE/REL ADJUD

TUSSMAN J.,THE SUPREME COURT ON CHURCH AND STATE. USA+45 USA-45 SANCTION PRIVIL...POLICY JURID 19/20 SUPREME/CT CHURCH/STA. PAGE 97 E1945
B62
CT/SYS SECT ADJUD

US AIR FORCE,THE MILITARY JUSTICE SYSTEM (REV. ED.). USA+45 DELIB/GP...IDEA/COMP 20. PAGE 99 E1978
B62
JURID FORCES ADJUD ORD/FREE

US COMMISSION ON CIVIL RIGHTS,EQUAL PROTECTION OF THE LAWS IN NORTH CAROLINA. USA+45 LOC/G NAT/G CONSULT LEGIS WORKER PROB/SOLV EDU/PROP ADJUD CHOOSE DISCRIM HEALTH 20 NEGRO NORTH/CAR CIV/RIGHTS. PAGE 99 E1984
B62
ORD/FREE RESPECT LAW PROVS

US COMMISSION ON CIVIL RIGHTS,HEARINGS BEFORE UNITED STATES COMMISSION ON CIVIL RIGHTS. USA+45 ECO/DEV NAT/G CONSULT WORKER EDU/PROP ADJUD DISCRIM ISOLAT HABITAT HEALTH RESPECT 20 NEGRO CIV/RIGHTS. PAGE 99 E1985
B62
ORD/FREE LAW ADMIN LEGIS

US CONGRESS,COMMUNICATIONS SATELLITE LEGISLATION: HEARINGS BEFORE COMM ON AERON AND SPACE SCIENCES ON BILLS 52550 AND 2814. WOR+45 LAW VOL/ASSN PLAN
B62
SPACE COM/IND ADJUD

DIPLOM CONTROL OWN PEACE...NEW/IDEA CONGRESS NASA. PAGE 99 E1990
GOV/REL

WOETZEL R.K.,THE NURENBERG TRIALS IN INTERNATIONAL LAW. CHRIST-17C MOD/EUR WOR+45 SOCIETY NAT/G DELIB/GP DOMIN LEGIT ROUTINE ATTIT DRIVE PERSON SUPEGO MORAL ORD/FREE...POLICY MAJORIT JURID PSY SOC SELF/OBS RECORD NAZI TOT/POP. PAGE 107 E2138
B62
INT/ORG ADJUD WAR

ERDMANN H.H.,"ADMINISTRATIVE LAW AND FARM ECONOMICS." USA+45 LOC/G NAT/G PLAN PROB/SOLV LOBBY ...DECISION ANTHOL 20. PAGE 35 E0695
L62
AGRI ADMIN ADJUD POLICY

MURACCIOLE L.,"LA LOI FONDAMENTALE DE LA REPUBLIQUE DU CONGO." WOR+45 SOCIETY ECO/UNDEV INT/ORG NAT/G LEGIS PLAN LEGIT ADJUD COLONIAL ROUTINE ATTIT SOVEREIGN 20 CONGO. PAGE 75 E1504
L62
AFR CONSTN

SPAETH H.J.,"JUDICIAL POWER AS A VARIABLE MOTIVATING SUPREME COURT BEHAVIOR." DELIB/GP ADJUD RATIONAL ATTIT PERSON ORD/FREE...CLASSIF STAT GEN/METH. PAGE 93 E1860
L62
JUDGE DECISION PERS/COMP PSY

FALK R.A.,"THE REALITY OF INTERNATIONAL LAW." WOR+45 NAT/G LEGIT COERCE DETER WAR MORAL ORD/FREE PWR SOVEREIGN...JURID CONCPT VAL/FREE COLD/WAR 20. PAGE 36 E0714
S62
INT/ORG ADJUD NUC/PWR INT/LAW

FENWICK C.G.,"ISSUES AT PUNTA DEL ESTE: NON-INTERVENTION VS COLLECTIVE SECURITY." L/A+17C USA+45 VOL/ASSN DELIB/GP ECO/TAC LEGIT ADJUD REGION ORD/FREE OAS COLD/WAR 20. PAGE 37 E0738
S62
INT/ORG CUBA

FINKELSTEIN L.S.,"THE UNITED NATIONS AND ORGANIZATIONS FOR CONTROL OF ARMAMENT." FUT WOR+45 VOL/ASSN DELIB/GP TOP/EX CREATE EDU/PROP LEGIT ADJUD NUC/PWR ATTIT RIGID/FLEX ORD/FREE...POLICY DECISION CONCPT OBS TREND GEN/LAWS TOT/POP COLD/WAR. PAGE 38 E0752
S62
INT/ORG PWR ARMS/CONT

MONNIER J.P.,"LA SUCCESSION D'ETATS EN MATIERE DE RESPONSABILITE INTERNATIONALE." UNIV CONSTN INTELL SOCIETY ADJUD ROUTINE PERCEPT SUPEGO...GEN/LAWS TOT/POP 20. PAGE 74 E1485
S62
NAT/G JURID INT/LAW

SCHACHTER O.,"DAG HAMMARSKJOLD AND THE RELATION OF LAW TO POLITICS." FUT WOR+45 INT/ORG CONSULT PLAN TEC/DEV BAL/PWR DIPLOM LEGIT ATTIT PERCEPT ORD/FREE ...POLICY JURID CONCPT OBS TESTS STERTYP GEN/LAWS 20 HAMMARSK/D. PAGE 87 E1751
S62
ACT/RES ADJUD

THOMPSON D.,"THE UNITED KINGDOM AND THE TREATY OF ROME." EUR+WWI INT/ORG NAT/G DELIB/GP LEGIS INT/TRADE RIGID/FLEX...CONCPT EEC PARLIAMENT CMN/WLTH 20. PAGE 96 E1918
S62
ADJUD JURID

ABRAHAM H.J.,"THE JUDICIAL PROCESS." USA+45 USA-45 LAW NAT/G ADMIN CT/SYS INGP/REL RACE/REL DISCRIM ...JURID IDEA/COMP 19/20. PAGE 2 E0046
C62
BIBLIOG CONSTN JUDGE ADJUD

BACON F.,"OF JUDICATURE" (1612) IN F. BACON, ESSAYS." ADJUD ADMIN SANCTION CRIME PWR...JURID GEN/LAWS. PAGE 7 E0128
C62
CT/SYS LEGIS LAW

LILLICH R.B.,"INTERNATIONAL CLAIMS: THEIR ADJUDICATION BY NATIONAL COMMISSIONS." WOR+45 WOR-45 NAT/G ADJUD...JURID BIBLIOG 18/20. PAGE 65 E1298
C62
INT/LAW DIPLOM PROB/SOLV

VAN DER SPRENKEL S.,"LEGAL INSTITUTIONS IN MANCHU CHINA." ASIA STRUCT CT/SYS ROUTINE GOV/REL GP/REL ...CONCPT BIBLIOG 17/20. PAGE 103 E2068
C62
LAW JURID ADMIN ADJUD

US SENATE COMM ON JUDICIARY,LEGISLATION TO STRENGTHEN PENALTIES UNDER THE ANTITRUST LAWS (PAMPHLET). USA+45 LG/CO CONFER CONTROL SANCTION ORD/FREE 20 SENATE MONOPOLY. PAGE 102 E2045
N62
LEAD ADJUD INDUS ECO/TAC

BLOCK E.B.,THE VINDICATORS. LAW FORCES CT/SYS
DISCRIM 19/20. PAGE 13 E0247
B63
ATTIT
CRIME
ADJUD
CRIMLGY

BOWETT D.W.,THE LAW OF INTERNATIONAL INSTITUTIONS.
WOR+45 WOR-45 CONSTN DELIB/GP EX/STRUC JUDGE
EDU/PROP LEGIT CT/SYS EXEC ROUTINE RIGID/FLEX
ORD/FREE PWR...JURID CONCPT ORG/CHARTS GEN/METH
LEAGUE/NAT OAS OEEC 20 UN. PAGE 14 E0277
B63
INT/ORG
ADJUD
DIPLOM

BOWIE R.R.,GOVERNMENT REGULATION OF BUSINESS: CASES
FROM THE NATIONAL REPORTER SYSTEM. USA+45 USA-45
NAT/G ECO/TAC ADJUD...ANTHOL 19/20 SUPREME/CT FTC
FAIR/LABOR MONOPOLY. PAGE 14 E0280
B63
LAW
CONTROL
INDUS
CT/SYS

BROWN R.M.,THE SOUTH CAROLINA REGULATORS. USA-45
LEGIS LEGIT ADJUD COLONIAL CONTROL WAR...BIBLIOG/A
18 CHARLESTON SOUTH/CAR. PAGE 16 E0315
B63
ORD/FREE
JURID
PWR
PROVS

BURRUS B.R.,ADMINSTRATIVE LAW AND LOCAL GOVERNMENT.
USA+45 PROVS LEGIS LICENSE ADJUD ORD/FREE 20.
PAGE 18 E0347
B63
EX/STRUC
LOC/G
JURID
CONSTN

COUNCIL OF STATE GOVERNMENTS,INCREASED RIGHTS FOR
DEFENDANTS IN STATE CRIMINAL PROSECUTIONS. USA+45
GOV/REL INGP/REL FEDERAL ORD/FREE...JURID 20
SUPREME/CT. PAGE 26 E0522
B63
CT/SYS
ADJUD
PROVS
CRIME

DE GRAZIA A.,APPORTIONMENT AND REPRESENTATIVE
GOVERNMENT. CONSTN POL/PAR LEGIS PLAN ADJUD DISCRIM
RATIONAL...CONCPT STAT PREDICT TREND IDEA/COMP.
PAGE 29 E0583
B63
REPRESENT
APPORT
NAT/G
MUNIC

DILLIARD I.,ONE MAN'S STAND FOR FREEDOM: MR.
JUSTICE BLACK AND THE BILL OF RIGHTS. USA+45
POL/PAR SECT DELIB/GP FORCES ADJUD CONTROL WAR
DISCRIM MORAL...BIBLIOG 20 NEGRO SUPREME/CT
BILL/RIGHT BLACK/HL. PAGE 32 E0628
B63
CONSTN
JURID
JUDGE
ORD/FREE

DRINAN R.F.,RELIGION, THE COURTS, AND PUBLIC
POLICY. USA+45 CONSTN BUDGET TAX GIVE ADJUD
SANCTION GP/REL PRIVIL 20 CHURCH/STA. PAGE 33 E0649
B63
SECT
CT/SYS
POLICY
SCHOOL

DUNHAM A.,MR. JUSTICE. ADJUD PWR...JURID ANTHOL
18/20 SUPREME/CT. PAGE 33 E0659
B63
BIOG
PERSON
LAW
CT/SYS

ECOLE NATIONALE D'ADMIN,BIBLIOGRAPHIE SELECTIVE
D'OUVRAGES DE LANGUE FRANCAISE TRAITANT DES
PROBLEMES GOUVERNEMENTAUX ET ADMINISTRATIFS. NAT/G
FORCES ACT/RES OP/RES PLAN PROB/SOLV BUDGET ADJUD
COLONIAL LEAD 20. PAGE 34 E0672
B63
BIBLIOG
AFR
ADMIN
EX/STRUC

EDDY J.P.,JUSTICE OF THE PEACE. UK LAW CONSTN
CULTURE 14/20 COMMON/LAW. PAGE 34 E0674
B63
CRIME
JURID
CT/SYS
ADJUD

ELIAS T.O.,THE NIGERIAN LEGAL SYSTEM. NIGERIA LAW
FAM KIN SECT ADMIN NAT/LISM...JURID 18/20
ENGLSH/LAW COMMON/LAW. PAGE 34 E0682
B63
CT/SYS
ADJUD
COLONIAL
PROF/ORG

FALK R.A.,LAW, MORALITY, AND WAR IN THE
CONTEMPORARY WORLD. WOR+45 LAW INT/ORG EX/STRUC
FORCES EDU/PROP LEGIT DETER NUC/PWR MORAL ORD/FREE
...JURID TOT/POP 20. PAGE 36 E0715
B63
ADJUD
ARMS/CONT
PEACE
INT/LAW

FAWCETT J.E.S.,THE BRITISH COMMONWEALTH IN
INTERNATIONAL LAW. LAW INT/ORG NAT/G VOL/ASSN
OP/RES DIPLOM ADJUD CENTRAL CONSEN...NET/THEORY
CMN/WLTH TREATY. PAGE 36 E0723
B63
INT/LAW
STRUCT
COLONIAL

FRAENKEL O.K.,THE SUPREME COURT AND CIVIL
LIBERTIES: HOW THE COURT HAS PROTECTED THE BILL OF
B63
ORD/FREE
CONSTN

RIGHTS. NAT/G CT/SYS CHOOSE PERS/REL RACE/REL
DISCRIM PERSON...DECISION 20 SUPREME/CT CIVIL/LIB
BILL/RIGHT. PAGE 39 E0782
B63
ADJUD
JURID

FRIEDRICH C.J.,JUSTICE: NOMOS VI. UNIV LAW SANCTION
CRIME...CONCPT ANTHOL MARX/KARL LOCKE/JOHN
AQUINAS/T. PAGE 41 E0809
B63
LEGIT
ADJUD
ORD/FREF
JURID

FRIEDRICH C.J.,MAN AND HIS GOVERNMENT: AN EMPIRICAL
THEORY OF POLITICS. UNIV LOC/G NAT/G ADJUD REV
INGP/REL DISCRIM PWR BIBLIOG. PAGE 41 E0810
B63
PERSON
ORD/FREE
PARTIC
CONTROL

GALLAGHER J.F.,SUPERVISORIAL DISTRICTING IN
CALIFORNIA COUNTIES: 1960-1963 (PAMPHLET). USA+45
ADJUD ADMIN PARTIC CHOOSE GP/REL...CENSUS 20
CALIFORNIA. PAGE 42 E0828
B63
APPORT
REGION
REPRESENT
LOC/G

GARNER U.F.,ADMINISTRATIVE LAW. UK LAW LOC/G NAT/G
EX/STRUC LEGIS JUDGE BAL/PWR BUDGET ADJUD CONTROL
CT/SYS...BIBLIOG 20. PAGE 42 E0840
B63
ADMIN
JURID
PWR
GOV/REL

GINZBERG E.,DEMOCRATIC VALUES AND THE RIGHTS OF
MANAGEMENT. LAW CONSTN REPRESENT GP/REL ROLE PWR
RESPECT POLICY. PAGE 44 E0870
B63
LABOR
MGT
DELIB/GP
ADJUD

GRIFFITH J.A.G.,PRINCIPLES OF ADMINISTRATIVE LAW
(3RD ED.). UK CONSTN EX/STRUC LEGIS ADJUD CONTROL
CT/SYS PWR...CHARTS 20. PAGE 47 E0940
B63
JURID
ADMIN
NAT/G
BAL/PWR

GSOUSKI V.,LEGAL SOURCES AND BIBLIOGRAPHY OF THE
BALTIC STATES (ESTONIA, LATVIA, LITHUANIA). COM
ESTONIA LATVIA LITHUANIA NAT/G LEGIS CT/SYS
SANCTION CRIME 20. PAGE 48 E0957
B63
BIBLIOG
ADJUD
LAW
JURID

HYNEMAN C.S.,THE SUPREME COURT ON TRIAL. ADJUD LEAD
GP/REL FEDERAL...IDEA/COMP 20 SUPREME/CT. PAGE 56
E1120
B63
CT/SYS
JURID
POLICY
NAT/G

JENKS C.W.,LAW, FREEDOM, AND WELFARE. WOR+45 GIVE
ADJUD WAR PEACE HABITAT ORD/FREE. PAGE 58 E1159
B63
INT/LAW
DIPLOM
SOVEREIGN
PROB/SOLV

KLEIN F.J.,JUDICIAL ADMINISTRATION AND THE LEGAL
PROFESSION. USA+45 ADMIN CONTROL EFFICIENCY
...POLICY 20. PAGE 61 E1222
B63
BIBLIOG/A
CT/SYS
ADJUD
JUDGE

KLESMENT J.,LEGAL SOURCES AND BIBLIOGRAPHY OF THE
BALTIC STATES (ESTONIA, LATVIA, LITHUANIA). COM
ESTONIA LATVIA LITHUANIA LAW FINAN ADJUD CT/SYS
REGION CENTRAL MARXISM 19/20. PAGE 61 E1223
B63
BIBLIOG/A
JURID
CONSTN
ADMIN

A BIBLIOGRAPHY OF DOCTORAL DISSERTATIONS UNDERTAKEN
IN AMERICAN AND CANADIAN UNIVERSITIES ON RELIGION
AND POLITICS. LAW CONSTN DOMIN LEGIT ADJUD GP/REL
...POLICY 20. PAGE 62 E1241
B63
BIBLIOG
ACADEM
SECT
JURID

LOWRY C.W.,TO PRAY OR NOT TO PRAY. ADJUD SANCTION
GP/REL ORD/FREE PWR CATHISM WORSHIP 20 SUPREME/CT
CHRISTIAN CHRUCH/STA. PAGE 67 E1330
B63
SECT
CT/SYS
CONSTN
PRIVIL

MCDOUGAL M.S.,LAW AND PUBLIC ORDER IN SPACE. FUT
USA+45 ACT/RES TEC/DEV ADJUD...POLICY INT/LAW JURID
20. PAGE 70 E1410
B63
SPACE
ORD/FREE
DIPLOM
DECISION

NEWMAN E.S.,THE FREEDOM READER. USA+45 LEGIS TOP/EX
PLAN ADJUD CONTROL CT/SYS DISCRIM...DECISION ANTHOL
20 SUPREME/CT CIV/RIGHTS. PAGE 77 E1541
B63
RACE/REL
LAW
POLICY
ORD/FREE

PATRA A.C.,THE ADMINISTRATION OF JUSTICE UNDER THE
B63
ADMIN

EAST INDIA COMPANY IN BENGAL, BIHAR AND ORISSA. JURID
INDIA UK LG/CO CAP/ISM INT/TRADE ADJUD COLONIAL CONCPT
CONTROL CT/SYS...POLICY 20. PAGE 80 E1602

B63
PRITCHETT C.H.,THE THIRD BRANCH OF GOVERNMENT. JURID
USA+45 USA-45 CONSTN SOCIETY INDUS SECT LEGIS JUDGE NAT/G
PROB/SOLV GOV/REL 20 SUPREME/CT CHURCH/STA. PAGE 82 ADJUD
E1654 CT/SYS

B63
ROBERTSON A.H.,HUMAN RIGHTS IN EUROPE. CONSTN EUR+WWI
SOCIETY INT/ORG NAT/G VOL/ASSN DELIB/GP ACT/RES PERSON
PLAN ADJUD REGION ROUTINE ATTIT LOVE ORD/FREE
RESPECT...JURID SOC CONCPT SOC/EXP UN 20. PAGE 85
E1705

B63
SCHMIDHAUSER J.R.,CONSTITUTIONAL LAW IN THE LAW
POLITICAL PROCESS. SOCIETY LEGIS ADJUD CT/SYS CONSTN
FEDERAL...SOC TREND IDEA/COMP ANTHOL T SUPREME/CT JURID
SENATE CONGRESS HOUSE/REP. PAGE 88 E1761

B63
TUSSMAN J.,THE SUPREME COURT ON RACIAL CT/SYS
DISCRIMINATION. USA+45 USA-45 NAT/G PROB/SOLV ADJUD DISCRIM
RACE/REL ORD/FREE...JURID 20 SUPREME/CT CIV/RIGHTS. ATTIT
PAGE 97 E1946 LAW

B63
US SENATE COMM ON JUDICIARY,ADMINISTERED PRICES. LG/CO
USA+45 RATION ADJUD CONTROL LOBBY...POLICY 20 PRICE
SENATE MONOPOLY. PAGE 102 E2047 ADMIN
DECISION

B63
US SENATE COMM ON JUDICIARY,US PERSONNEL SECURITY PLAN
PRACTICES. USA+45 DELIB/GP ADJUD ADMIN ORD/FREE NAT/G
...CHARTS 20 CONGRESS CIVIL/SERV. PAGE 102 E2049 CONTROL
WORKER

B63
VINES K.N.,STUDIES IN JUDICIAL POLITICS: TULANE CT/SYS
STUDIES IN POLITICAL SCIENCE (VOL. 8). POL/PAR GOV/REL
JUDGE ADJUD SANCTION CRIME CHOOSE PWR...JURID STAT PROVS
TIME/SEQ CHARTS. PAGE 104 E2079

B63
WADE H.W.R.,TOWARDS ADMINISTRATIVE JUSTICE. UK ADJUD
USA+45 CONSTN CONSULT PROB/SOLV CT/SYS PARL/PROC IDEA/COMP
...POLICY JURID METH/COMP 20 ENGLSH/LAW. PAGE 104 ADMIN
E2088

B63
WOLL P.,ADMINISTRATIVE LAW: THE INFORMAL PROCESS. ADMIN
USA+45 NAT/G CONTROL EFFICIENCY 20. PAGE 107 E2141 ADJUD
REPRESENT
EX/STRUC

L63
BOLGAR V.,"THE PUBLIC INTEREST: A JURISPRUDENTIAL CONCPT
AND COMPARATIVE OVERVIEW OF SYMPOSIUM ON ORD/FREE
FUNDAMENTAL CONCEPTS OF PUBLIC LAW" COM FRANCE CONTROL
GERMANY SWITZERLND LAW ADJUD ADMIN AGREE LAISSEZ NAT/COMP
...JURID GEN/LAWS 20 EUROPE/E. PAGE 14 E0264

L63
LISSITZYN O.J.,"INTERNATIONAL LAW IN A DIVIDED INT/ORG
WORLD." FUT WOR+45 CONSTN CULTURE ECO/DEV ECO/UNDEV LAW
DIST/IND NAT/G FORCES ECO/TAC LEGIT ADJUD ADMIN
COERCE ATTIT HEALTH MORAL ORD/FREE PWR RESPECT
WEALTH VAL/FREE. PAGE 65 E1306

L63
LOEVINGER L.,"JURIMETRICS* THE METHODOLOGY OF LEGAL COMPUT/IR
INQUIRY." COMPUTER CREATE PLAN TEC/DEV AUTOMAT JURID
CT/SYS EFFICIENCY...DECISION PHIL/SCI NEW/IDEA GEN/METH
QUANT PREDICT. PAGE 66 E1318 ADJUD

S63
BOHN L.,"WHOSE NUCLEAR TEST: NON-PHYSICAL ADJUD
INSPECTION AND TEST BAN." WOR+45 R+D INT/ORG ARMS/CONT
VOL/ASSN ORD/FREE...GEN/LAWS GEN/METH COLD/WAR 20. TEC/DEV
PAGE 13 E0262 NUC/PWR

S63
GIRAUD E.,"L'INTERDICTION DU RECOURS A LA FORCE, LA INT/ORG
THEORIE ET LA PRATIQUE DES NATIONS UNIES." ALGERIA FORCES
COM CUBA HUNGARY WOR+45 ADJUD TOTALISM ATTIT DIPLOM
RIGID/FLEX PWR...POLICY JURID CONCPT UN 20 CONGO.
PAGE 44 E0872

S63
JOUGHIN L.,"ACADEMIC DUE PROCESS." DELIB/GP ADJUD ACADEM
ROUTINE ORD/FREE...POLICY MAJORIT TREND. PAGE 59 LAW
E1175 PROF/ORG

S63
LEPAWSKY A.,"INTERNATIONAL DEVELOPMENT OF RIVER INT/ORG
RESOURCES." CANADA EUR+WWI S/ASIA USA+45 SEA LEGIT DELIB/GP
ADJUD ORD/FREE PWR WEALTH...MGT TIME/SEQ VAL/FREE
MEXIC/AMER 20. PAGE 64 E1287

S63
MENDELSON W.,"THE NEO-BEHAVIORAL APPROACH TO THE DECISION
JUDICIAL PROCESS: A CRITIQUE" ADJUD PERSON...SOC JURID
RECORD IDEA/COMP. PAGE 72 E1438 JUDGE

S63
MEYROWITZ H.,"LES JURISTES DEVANT L'ARME NUCLEAIRE." ACT/RES
FUT WOR+45 INTELL SOCIETY BAL/PWR DETER WAR...JURID ADJUD
CONCPT 20. PAGE 72 E1451 INT/LAW
NUC/PWR

S63
NAGEL S.S.,"A CONCEPTUAL SCHEME OF THE JUDICIAL POLICY
PROCESS." ADJUD...DECISION NEW/IDEA AVERAGE MODAL LAW
CHARTS. PAGE 76 E1518 JURID
DISCRIM

S63
VINES K.N.,"THE ROLE OF THE CIRCUIT COURT OF REGION
APPEALS IN THE FEDERAL JUDICIAL PROCESS: A CASE ADJUD
STUDY." USA+45 STRATA JUDGE RESPECT...DECISION CT/SYS
JURID CHARTS GP/COMP. PAGE 104 E2078 RACE/REL

C63
SCHUBERT G.,"JUDICIAL DECISION-MAKING." FORCES LEAD ADJUD
ATTIT DRIVE...POLICY PSY STAT CHARTS ANTHOL BIBLIOG DECISION
20. PAGE 88 E1773 JUDGE
CT/SYS

B64
BENNETT H.A.,THE COMMISSION AND THE COMMON LAW: A ADJUD
STUDY IN ADMINISTRATIVE ADJUDICATION. LAW ADMIN DELIB/GP
CT/SYS LOBBY SANCTION GOV/REL 20 COMMON/LAW. DIST/IND
PAGE 10 E0188 POLICY

B64
BERWANGER E.H.,WESTERN ANTI-NEGRO SENTIMENT AND RACE/REL
LAWS 1846-60: A FACTOR IN THE SLAVERY EXTENSION REGION
CONTROVERSY (PAPER). USA-45 LAW CONSTN LEGIS ADJUD DISCRIM
...BIBLIOG 19 NEGRO. PAGE 11 E0218 ORD/FREE

B64
BLOUSTEIN E.J.,NUCLEAR ENERGY, PUBLIC POLICY, AND TEC/DEV
THE LAW. USA+45 NAT/G ADJUD ADMIN GP/REL OWN PEACE LAW
ATTIT HEALTH...ANTHOL 20. PAGE 13 E0251 POLICY
NUC/PWR

B64
BREVER E.H.,LEARNED HAND, JANUARY 27, 1872-AUGUST BIBLIOG/A
18, 1961 (PAMPHLET). USA+45 USA-45 LAW CONSTN ADJUD JUDGE
...DECISION BIOG 19/20. PAGE 15 E0295 CT/SYS
JURID

B64
BROOKS T.R.,TOIL AND TROUBLE, A HISTORY OF AMERICAN INDUS
LABOR. WORKER BARGAIN CAP/ISM ADJUD AUTOMAT EXEC LABOR
GP/REL RACE/REL EFFICIENCY INCOME PROFIT MARXISM LEGIS
17/20 KENNEDY/JF AFL/CIO NEGRO. PAGE 16 E0310

B64
BUREAU OF NATIONAL AFFAIRS,STATE FAIR EMPLOYMENT PROVS
LAWS AND THEIR ADMINISTRATION. INDUS ADJUD PERS/REL DISCRIM
RACE/REL ATTIT ORD/FREE WEALTH 20. PAGE 17 E0338 WORKER
JURID

B64
DIAS R.W.M.,A BIBLIOGRAPHY OF JURISPRUDENCE (2ND BIBLIOG/A
ED.). VOL/ASSN LEGIS ADJUD CT/SYS OWN...INT/LAW JURID
18/20. PAGE 31 E0619 LAW
CONCPT

B64
DRESSLER D.,READINGS IN CRIMINOLOGY AND PENOLOGY. CRIMLGY
UNIV CULTURE PUB/INST FORCES ACT/RES PROB/SOLV CRIME
ANOMIE BIO/SOC SUPEGO...GEOG PSY ANTHOL 20. PAGE 33 ADJUD
E0648 ADJUST

B64
DUBISSON M.,LA COUR INTERNATIONALE DE JUSTICE. CT/SYS
FRANCE LAW CONSTN JUDGE DOMIN ADJUD...INT/LAW INT/ORG
CLASSIF RECORD ORG/CHARTS UN. PAGE 33 E0651

B64
ENDACOTT G.B.,GOVERNMENT AND PEOPLE IN HONG KONG CONSTN
1841-1962: A CONSTITUTIONAL HISTORY. UK LEGIS ADJUD COLONIAL
REPRESENT ATTIT 19/20 HONG/KONG. PAGE 35 E0688 CONTROL
ADMIN

CLIENT

B64

FEIFER G.,JUSTICE IN MOSCOW. USSR LAW CRIME   ADJUD
...RECORD 20. PAGE 37 E0725   JURID
                                                     CT/SYS
                                                     MARXISM

B64

FRIEDMANN W.G.,THE CHANGING STRUCTURE OF   ADJUD
INTERNATIONAL LAW. WOR+45 INT/ORG NAT/G PROVS LEGIT TREND
ORD/FREE PWR...JURID CONCPT GEN/LAWS TOT/POP UN 20. INT/LAW
PAGE 41 E0805

B64

GJUPANOVIC H.,LEGAL SOURCES AND BIBLIOGRAPHY OF   BIBLIOG/A
YUGOSLAVIA. COM YUGOSLAVIA LAW LEGIS DIPLOM ADMIN   JURID
PARL/PROC REGION CRIME CENTRAL 20. PAGE 44 E0873   CONSTN
                                                     ADJUD

B64

GRZYBOWSKI K.,THE SOCIALIST COMMONWEALTH OF   INT/LAW
NATIONS: ORGANIZATIONS AND INSTITUTIONS. FORCES   COM
DIPLOM INT/TRADE ADJUD ADMIN LEAD WAR MARXISM   REGION
SOCISM...BIBLIOG 20 COMECON WARSAW/P. PAGE 48 E0956 INT/ORG

B64

HALLER W.,DER SCHWEDISCHE JUSTITIEOMBUDSMAN.   JURID
DENMARK FINLAND NORWAY SWEDEN LEGIS ADJUD CONTROL   PARL/PROC
PERSON ORD/FREE...NAT/COMP 20 OMBUDSMAN. PAGE 50   ADMIN
E0986   CHIEF

B64

HENDERSON D.F.,CONCILIATION AND JAPANESE LAW (VOL.   CONCPT
II). LAW SOCIETY...BIBLIOG 17/20 CHINJAP. PAGE 52   CT/SYS
E1028   ADJUD
                                                     POLICY

B64

HENDERSON D.F.,CONCILIATION AND JAPANESE LAW (VOL.   CT/SYS
I). LAW SOCIETY 17/19 CHINJAP. PAGE 52 E1029   CONCPT
                                                     ADJUD
                                                     POLICY

B64

HOHFELD W.N.,FUNDAMENTAL LEGAL CONCEPTIONS.   JURID
PROB/SOLV OWN PWR...DECISION LING IDEA/COMP   ADJUD
GEN/METH. PAGE 54 E1069   LAW
                                                     METH/CNCPT

B64

HOLDSWORTH W.S.,A HISTORY OF ENGLISH LAW; THE   LAW
CENTURIES OF DEVELOPMENT AND REFORM (VOL. XIV). UK   LEGIS
CONSTN LOC/G NAT/G POL/PAR CHIEF EX/STRUC ADJUD   LEAD
COLONIAL ATTIT...INT/LAW JURID 18/19 TORY/PARTY   CT/SYS
COMMONWLTH WHIG/PARTY COMMON/LAW. PAGE 54 E1081

B64

HURST W.H.,JUSTICE HOLMES ON LEGAL HISTORY. USA-45   ADJUD
LAW SOCIETY NAT/G WRITING...POLICY PHIL/SCI SOC   JURID
CONCPT 20 HOLMES/OW SUPREME/CT ENGLSH/LAW. PAGE 56   BIOG
E1117

B64

IKLE F.C.,HOW NATIONS NEGOTIATE. COM EUR+WWI USA+45 NAT/G
INTELL INT/ORG VOL/ASSN DELIB/GP ACT/RES CREATE   PWR
DOMIN EDU/PROP ADJUD ROUTINE ATTIT PERSON ORD/FREE   POLICY
RESPECT SKILL...PSY SOC OBS VAL/FREE. PAGE 56 E1122

B64

JACKSON R.M.,THE MACHINERY OF JUSTICE IN ENGLAND.   CT/SYS
UK EDU/PROP CONTROL COST ORD/FREE...MGT 20   ADJUD
ENGLSH/LAW. PAGE 57 E1142   JUDGE
                                                     JURID

B64

JENKS C.W.,THE PROSPECTS OF INTERNATIONAL   INT/LAW
ADJUDICATION. WOR+45 WOR-45 NAT/G DIPLOM CONTROL   ADJUD
PWR...POLICY JURID CONCPT METH/COMP 19/20 ICJ   CT/SYS
LEAGUE/NAT UN TREATY. PAGE 58 E1160   INT/ORG

B64

KAHNG T.J.,LAW, POLITICS, AND THE SECURITY COUNCIL* DELIB/GP
AN INQUIRY INTO THE HANDLING OF LEGAL QUESTIONS.   ADJUD
LAW CONSTN NAT/G ACT/RES OP/RES CT/SYS TASK PWR   ROUTINE
...INT/LAW BIBLIOG UN. PAGE 59 E1180

B64

LIGGETT E.,BRITISH POLITICAL ISSUES: VOLUME 1. UK   POL/PAR
LAW CONSTN LOC/G NAT/G ADJUD 20. PAGE 65 E1296   GOV/REL
                                                     CT/SYS
                                                     DIPLOM

B64

MASON A.T.,AMERICAN CONSTITUTIONAL LAW: CONSTN
INTRODUCTORY ESSAYS AND SELECTED CASES (3RD ED.).   CT/SYS
LAW LEGIS TAX ADJUD GOV/REL FEDERAL ORD/FREE PWR   JURID
...TIME/SEQ BIBLIOG T 19/20 SUPREME/CT. PAGE 69

E1379

B64

MINAR D.W.,IDEAS AND POLITICS: THE AMERICAN   CONSTN
EXPERIENCE. SECT CHIEF LEGIS CREATE ADJUD EXEC REV   NAT/G
PWR...PHIL/SCI CONCPT IDEA/COMP 18/20 HAMILTON/A   FEDERAL
JEFFERSN/T DECLAR/IND JACKSON/A PRESIDENT. PAGE 73
E1464

B64

MITAU G.T.,PROXIMATE SOLUTIONS: CASE PROBLEMS IN   PROVS
STATE AND LOCAL GOVERNMENT. USA+45 CONSTN NAT/G   LOC/G
CHIEF LEGIS CT/SYS EXEC GOV/REL GP/REL PWR 20   ADJUD
CASEBOOK. PAGE 73 E1470

B64

MITAU G.T.,INSOLUBLE PROBLEMS: CASE PROBLEMS ON THE ADJUD
FUNCTIONS OF STATE AND LOCAL GOVERNMENT. USA+45 AIR LOC/G
FINAN LABOR POL/PAR PROB/SOLV TAX RECEIVE CONTROL   PROVS
GP/REL 20 CASEBOOK ZONING. PAGE 73 E1471

B64

MITCHELL B.,A BIOGRAPHY OF THE CONSTITUTION OF THE   CONSTN
UNITED STATES. USA+45 USA-45 PROVS CHIEF LEGIS   LAW
DEBATE ADJUD SUFF FEDERAL...SOC 18/20 SUPREME/CT   JURID
CONGRESS SENATE HOUSE/REP PRESIDENT. PAGE 73 E1472

B64

MURPHY W.F.,ELEMENTS OF JUDICIAL STRATEGY. CONSTN   CT/SYS
JUDGE PERS/REL PERSON 19/20 SUPREME/CT. PAGE 75   ADJUD
E1510   JURID

B64

NASA,PROCEEDINGS OF CONFERENCE ON THE LAW OF SPACE   SPACE
AND OF SATELLITE COMMUNICATIONS: CHICAGO 1963. FUT   COM/IND
WOR+45 DELIB/GP PROB/SOLV TEC/DEV CONFER ADJUD   LAW
NUC/PWR...POLICY IDEA/COMP 20 NASA. PAGE 76 E1522   DIPLOM

B64

NELSON D.H.,ADMINISTRATIVE AGENCIES OF THE USA: ADMIN
THEIR DECISIONS AND AUTHORITY. USA+45 NAT/G CONTROL EX/STRUC
CT/SYS REPRESENT...DECISION 20. PAGE 76 E1531   ADJUD
                                                     LAW

B64

NEWMAN E.S.,POLICE, THE LAW, AND PERSONAL FREEDOM.   JURID
USA+45 CONSTN JUDGE CT/SYS CRIME PERS/REL RESPECT   FORCES
...CRIMLGY 20. PAGE 77 E1542   ORD/FREE
                                                     ADJUD

B64

NICE R.W.,TREASURY OF LAW. WOR+45 WOR-45 SECT ADJUD LAW
MORAL ORD/FREE...INT/LAW JURID PHIL/SCI ANTHOL.   WRITING
PAGE 77 E1545   PERS/REL
                                                     DIPLOM

B64

OPPENHEIMER M.,A MANUAL FOR DIRECT ACTION. USA+45   PLAN
SCHOOL FORCES ADJUD CT/SYS SUFF RACE/REL DISCRIM   VOL/ASSN
...POLICY CHARTS 20. PAGE 79 E1580   JURID
                                                     LEAD

B64

PRESS C.,A BIBLIOGRAPHIC INTRODUCTION TO AMERICAN   BIBLIOG
STATE GOVERNMENT AND POLITICS (PAMPHLET). USA+45   LEGIS
USA-45 EX/STRUC ADJUD INGP/REL FEDERAL ORD/FREE 20. LOC/G
PAGE 82 E1649   POL/PAR

B64

REGALA R.,WORLD PEACE THROUGH DIPLOMACY AND LAW.   DIPLOM
S/ASIA WOR+45 ECO/UNDEV INT/ORG FORCES PLAN   PEACE
PROB/SOLV FOR/AID NUC/PWR WAR...POLICY INT/LAW 20.   ADJUD
PAGE 84 E1679

B64

SARTORIUS R.E.,THE JUSTIFICATION OF THE JUDICIAL   LAW
DECISION (DISSERTATION). PROB/SOLV LEGIT...JURID   PHIL/SCI
GEN/LAWS BIBLIOG 20. PAGE 87 E1747   CT/SYS
                                                     ADJUD

B64

SCHECHTER A.H.,INTERPRETATION OF AMBIGUOUS   INT/LAW
DOCUMENTS BY INTERNATIONAL ADMINISTRATIVE   DIPLOM
TRIBUNALS. WOR+45 EX/STRUC INT/TRADE CT/SYS   INT/ORG
SOVEREIGN 20 UN ILO EURCT/JUST. PAGE 87 E1752   ADJUD

B64

SCHMEISER D.A.,CIVIL LIBERTIES IN CANADA. CANADA   ORD/FREE
LAW SECT PRESS RACE/REL NAT/LISM PRIVIL 20   CONSTN
COMMONWLTH PARLIAMENT CIVIL/LIB CHURCH/STA. PAGE 88 ADJUD
E1758   EDU/PROP

B64

SCHUBERT G.A.,JUDICIAL BEHAVIOR: A READER IN THEORY ATTIT
AND RESEARCH. POL/PAR CT/SYS ROLE SUPEGO PWR   PERSON
...DECISION JURID REGRESS CHARTS SIMUL ANTHOL 20.   ADJUD

ACT/RES

E1303

PEACE

B64
SIEKANOWICZ P.,LEGAL SOURCES AND BIBLIOGRAPHY OF
POLAND. COM POLAND CONSTN NAT/G PARL/PROC SANCTION
CRIME MARXISM 16/20. PAGE 91 E1823

BIBLIOG
ADJUD
LAW
JURID

B64
STANGER R.J.,ESSAYS ON INTERVENTION. PLAN PROB/SOLV
BAL/PWR ADJUD COERCE WAR ROLE PWR...INT/LAW CONCPT
20 UN INTERVENT. PAGE 93 E1865

SOVEREIGN
DIPLOM
POLICY
LEGIT

B64
STOICOIU V.,LEGAL SOURCES AND BIBLIOGRAPHY OF
ROMANIA. COM ROMANIA LAW FINAN POL/PAR LEGIS JUDGE
ADJUD CT/SYS PARL/PROC MARXISM 20. PAGE 93 E1874

BIBLIOG/A
JURID
CONSTN
ADMIN

B64
SZLADITS C.,BIBLIOGRAPHY ON FOREIGN AND COMPARATIVE
LAW: BOOKS AND ARTICLES IN ENGLISH (SUPPLEMENT
1962). FINAN INDUS JUDGE LICENSE ADMIN CT/SYS
PARL/PROC OWN...INT/LAW CLASSIF METH/COMP NAT/COMP
20. PAGE 95 E1904

BIBLIOG/A
JURID
ADJUD
LAW

B64
TAUBENFELD H.J.,SPACE AND SOCIETY. USA+45 LAW
FORCES CREATE TEC/DEV ADJUD CONTROL COST PEACE
...PREDICT ANTHOL 20. PAGE 95 E1911

SPACE
SOCIETY
ADJUST
DIPLOM

B64
TOMPKINS D.C.,PRESIDENTIAL SUCCESSION. USA+45 CHIEF
ADJUD 20 PRESIDENT CONGRESS. PAGE 96 E1933

BIBLIOG/A
EX/STRUC
CONSTN
TOP/EX

B64
US SENATE COMM ON JUDICIARY,HEARINGS BEFORE
SUBCOMMITTEE ON ANTITRUST AND MONOPOLY: ECONOMIC
CONCENTRATION VOLUMES 1-5 JULY 1964-SEPT 1966.
USA+45 LAW FINAN ECO/TAC ADJUD COST EFFICIENCY
PRODUC...STAT CHARTS 20 CONGRESS MONOPOLY. PAGE 102
E2052

ECO/DEV
CONTROL
MARKET
LG/CO

B64
US SENATE COMM ON JUDICIARY,CIVIL RIGHTS - THE
PRESIDENT'S PROGRAM. USA+45 LAW PROB/SOLV PRESS
ADJUD GOV/REL RACE/REL ORD/FREE PWR...JURID 20
SUPREME/CT SENATE CIV/RIGHTS PRESIDENT. PAGE 102
E2053

INT
LEGIS
DISCRIM
PARL/PROC

S64
CARNEGIE ENDOWMENT INT. PEACE,"LEGAL QUESTIONS
(ISSUES BEFORE THE NINETEENTH GENERAL ASSEMBLY)."
WOR+45 CONSTN NAT/G DELIB/GP ADJUD PEACE MORAL
ORD/FREE...RECORD UN 20 TREATY. PAGE 20 E0386

INT/ORG
LAW
INT/LAW

S64
COHEN M.,"BASIC PRINCIPLES OF INTERNATIONAL LAW."
UNIV WOR+45 WOR-45 BAL/PWR LEGIT ADJUD WAR ATTIT
MORAL ORD/FREE PWR...JURID CONCPT MYTH TOT/POP 20.
PAGE 23 E0463

INT/ORG
INT/LAW

S64
GARDNER R.N.,"THE SOVIET UNION AND THE UNITED
NATIONS." WOR+45 FINAN POL/PAR VOL/ASSN FORCES
ECO/TAC DOMIN EDU/PROP LEGIT ADJUD ADMIN ARMS/CONT
COERCE ATTIT ALL/VALS...POLICY MAJORIT CONCPT OBS
TIME/SEQ TREND STERTYP UN. PAGE 42 E0838

COM
INT/ORG
USSR

S64
HICKEY D.,"THE PHILOSOPHICAL ARGUMENT FOR WORLD
GOVERNMENT." WOR+45 SOCIETY ACT/RES PLAN LEGIT
ADJUD PEACE PERCEPT PERSON ORD/FREE...HUM JURID
PHIL/SCI METH/CNCPT CON/ANAL STERTYP GEN/LAWS
TOT/POP 20. PAGE 52 E1039

FUT
INT/ORG

S64
KARPOV P.V.,"PEACEFUL COEXISTENCE AND INTERNATIONAL
LAW." WOR+45 LAW SOCIETY INT/ORG VOL/ASSN FORCES
CREATE CAP/ISM DIPLOM ADJUD NUC/PWR PEACE MORAL
ORD/FREE PWR MARXISM...MARXIST JURID CONCPT OBS
TREND COLD/WAR MARX/KARL 20. PAGE 59 E1186

COM
ATTIT
INT/LAW
USSR

S64
KUNZ J.,"THE CHANGING SCIENCE OF INTERNATIONAL
LAW." FUT WOR+45 WOR-45 INT/ORG LEGIT ORD/FREE
...JURID TIME/SEQ GEN/LAWS 20. PAGE 62 E1235

ADJUD
CONCPT
INT/LAW

S64
LIPSON L.,"PEACEFUL COEXISTENCE." COM USSR WOR+45
LAW INT/ORG DIPLOM LEGIT ADJUD ORD/FREE...CONCPT
OBS TREND GEN/LAWS VAL/FREE COLD/WAR 20. PAGE 65

ATTIT
JURID
INT/LAW

S64
MCGHEE G.C.,"EAST-WEST RELATIONS TODAY." WOR+45
PROB/SOLV BAL/PWR PEACE 20 COLD/WAR. PAGE 71 E1413

IDEA/COMP
DIPLOM
ADJUD

S64
N.,"QUASI-LEGISLATIVE ARBITRATION AGREEMENTS." LAW
LG/CO ECO/TAC SANCTION ATTIT POLICY. PAGE 76 E1516

ADJUD
ADJUST
LABOR
GP/REL

S64
PARADIES F.,"SOBRE LA HISTORIA DE LA LOGICA Y DE LA
LOGICA JURIDICA." LEGIT KNOWL...JURID METH/CNCPT
HIST/WRIT 20. PAGE 80 E1597

ADJUD

S64
SCHWELB E.,"OPERATION OF THE EUROPEAN CONVENTION ON
HUMAN RIGHTS." EUR+WWI LAW SOCIETY CREATE EDU/PROP
ADJUD ADMIN PEACE ATTIT ORD/FREE PWR...POLICY
INT/LAW CONCPT OBS GEN/LAWS UN VAL/FREE ILO 20
ECHR. PAGE 89 E1791

INT/ORG
MORAL

C64
BECKER T.L.,"POLITICAL BEHAVIORALISM AND MODERN
JURISPRUDENCE." LEGIS JUDGE OP/RES ADJUD CT/SYS
ATTIT PWR...BIBLIOG 20. PAGE 9 E0173

DECISION
PROB/SOLV
JURID
GEN/LAWS

C64
CORWIN E.S.,"AMERICAN CONSTITUTIONAL HISTORY." LAW
NAT/G PROB/SOLV EQUILIB FEDERAL ATTIT PWR...JURID
BIBLIOG 20. PAGE 26 E0515

ANTHOL
JUDGE
ADJUD
CT/SYS

B65
AMERICAN ASSEMBLY COLUMBIA U,THE COURTS, THE
PUBLIC, AND THE LAW EXPLOSION. USA+45 ELITES PROVS
EDU/PROP CRIME CHOOSE PERSON ORD/FREE PWR 20.
PAGE 4 E0074

CT/SYS
ADJUD
NAT/G

B65
ANDRUS H.L.,LIBERALISM, CONSERVATISM, MORMONISM.
USA+45 PLAN ADJUD CONTROL HAPPINESS ORD/FREE
CONSERVE NEW/LIB WORSHIP 20. PAGE 5 E0097

SECT
UTOPIA
MORAL

B65
ASSOCIATION BAR OF NYC,RADIO, TELEVISION, AND THE
ADMINISTRATION OF JUSTICE: A DOCUMENTED SURVEY OF
MATERIALS. USA+45 DELIB/GP FORCES PRESS ADJUD
CONTROL CT/SYS CRIME...INT IDEA/COMP BIBLIOG.
PAGE 6 E0109

AUD/VIS
ATTIT
ORD/FREE

B65
BARKER L.J.,FREEDOM, COURTS, POLITICS: STUDIES IN
CIVIL LIBERTIES. USA+45 LEGIS CREATE DOMIN PRESS
ADJUD LOBBY CRIME GP/REL RACE/REL MARXISM 20
CIVIL/LIB. PAGE 8 E0148

JURID
CT/SYS
ATTIT
ORD/FREE

B65
BEGGS D.W.,AMERICA'S SCHOOLS AND CHURCHES: PARTNERS
IN CONFLICT. USA+45 PROVS EDU/PROP ADJUD DISCRIM
ATTIT...IDEA/COMP ANTHOL BIBLIOG WORSHIP 20
CHURCH/STA. PAGE 9 E0179

SECT
GP/REL
SCHOOL
NAT/G

B65
BELL J.,THE JOHNSON TREATMENT: HOW LYNDON JOHNSON
TOOK OVER THE PRESIDENCY AND MADE IT HIS OWN.
USA+45 DELIB/GP DIPLOM ADJUD MURDER CHOOSE PERSON
PWR...POLICY OBS INT TIME 20 JOHNSON/LB KENNEDY/JF
PRESIDENT CONGRESS. PAGE 10 E0183

INGP/REL
TOP/EX
CONTROL
NAT/G

B65
BREITEL C.D.,THE LAWMAKERS. USA+45 EX/STRUC LEGIS
JUDGE ATTIT ORD/FREE JURID. PAGE 15 E0290

CT/SYS
ADJUD
FEDERAL
NAT/G

B65
BRIGGS H.W.,THE INTERNATIONAL LAW COMMISSION. LAW
CONSTN LEGIS CREATE ADJUD CT/SYS ROUTINE TASK
EFFICIENCY...CLASSIF OBS UN. PAGE 15 E0302

INT/LAW
DELIB/GP

B65
BROMBERG W.,CRIME AND THE MIND. LAW LEGIT ADJUD
CRIME MURDER AGE/Y ANOMIE BIO/SOC DRIVE SEX PSY.
PAGE 16 E0305

CRIMLGY
SOC
HEALTH
COERCE

B65
CALIFORNIA LEGISLATURE,COMMITTEE ON ELECTIONS AND
REAPPORTIONMENT, FINAL REPORT. USA+45 LAW COMPUTER
TEC/DEV CHOOSE JURID. PAGE 19 E0366

DELIB/GP
APPORT
LEGIS
ADJUD

B65
CAVERS D.F.,THE CHOICE-OF-LAW PROCESS. PROB/SOLV   JURID
ADJUD CT/SYS CHOOSE RATIONAL...IDEA/COMP 16/20   DECISION
TREATY. PAGE 21 E0411   METH/COMP
                                                     ADMIN

B65
CONGRESSIONAL QUARTERLY SERV,FEDERAL ROLE IN   ACADEM
EDUCATION (PAMPHLET). LAW SCHOOL PLAN TAX ADJUD   DISCRIM
...CHARTS SOC/INTEG 20 PRESIDENT. PAGE 25 E0487   RECEIVE
                                                     FEDERAL

B65
CONGRESSIONAL QUARTERLY SERV,REVOLUTION IN CIVIL   LAW
RIGHTS. USA+45 USA-45 LEGIS ADJUD CT/SYS CHOOSE   CONSTN
DISCRIM...DECISION CONGRESS SUPREME/CT. PAGE 25   RACE/REL
E0488   LOBBY

B65
COOPER F.E.,STATE ADMINISTRATIVE LAW (2 VOLS.). LAW JURID
LEGIS PLAN TAX ADJUD CT/SYS FEDERAL PWR...CONCPT   CONSTN
20. PAGE 25 E0501   ADMIN
                                                     PROVS

B65
EHLE J.,THE FREE MEN. USA+45 NAT/G PROVS FORCES   RACE/REL
JUDGE ADJUD ATTIT...POLICY SOC SOC/INTEG 20 NEGRO.   ORD/FREE
PAGE 34 E0677   DISCRIM

B65
FALK R.A.,THE AFTERMATH OF SABBATINO: BACKGROUND   SOVEREIGN
PAPERS AND PROCEEDINGS OF SEVENTH HAMMARSKJOLD   CT/SYS
FORUM. USA+45 LAW ACT/RES ADJUD ROLE...BIBLIOG 20   INT/LAW
EXPROPRIAT SABBATINO HARLAN/JM. PAGE 36 E0718   OWN

B65
FELLMAN D.,RELIGION IN AMERICAN PUBLIC LAW. USA+45   SECT
USA-45 NAT/G PROVS ADJUD SANCTION GP/REL PRIVIL   CONSTN
ORD/FREE...JURID TIME/SEQ 18/20 SUPREME/CT   LAW
CHURCH/STA. PAGE 37 E0733   POLICY

B65
FLEMING R.W.,THE LABOR ARBITRATION PROCESS. USA+45   GP/REL
LAW BARGAIN ADJUD ROUTINE SANCTION COST...PREDICT   LABOR
CHARTS TIME 20. PAGE 38 E0763   CONSULT
                                                     DELIB/GP

B65
FRIEDMAN L.,SOUTHERN JUSTICE. USA+45 PUB/INST LEGIT ADJUD
ADMIN CT/SYS DISCRIM...DECISION ANTHOL 20 NEGRO   LAW
SOUTH/US CIV/RIGHTS. PAGE 40 E0800   CONSTN
                                                     RACE/REL

B65
FRYE R.J.,HOUSING AND URBAN RENEWAL IN ALABAMA.   MUNIC
USA+45 NEIGH LEGIS BUDGET ADJUD ADMIN PARTIC...MGT   PROB/SOLV
20 ALABAMA URBAN/RNWL. PAGE 41 E0815   PLAN
                                                     GOV/REL

B65
GAJENDRAGADKAR P.B.,LAW, LIBERTY AND SOCIAL   ORD/FREE
JUSTICE. INDIA CONSTN NAT/G SECT PLAN ECO/TAC PRESS LAW
POPULISM...SOC METH/COMP 20 HINDU. PAGE 42 E0826   ADJUD
                                                     JURID

B65
GINSBERG M.,ON JUSTICE IN SOCIETY. LAW EDU/PROP   ADJUD
LEGIT CT/SYS INGP/REL PRIVIL RATIONAL ATTIT MORAL   ROLE
ORD/FREE...JURID 20. PAGE 44 E0867   CONCPT

B65
GLUECK S.,ROSCOE POUND AND CRIMINAL JUSTICE.   CT/SYS
SOCIETY FAM GOV/REL AGE/Y ATTIT ORD/FREE...CRIMLGY   CRIME
BIOG ANTHOL SOC/INTEG 19/20. PAGE 44 E0875   LAW
                                                     ADJUD

B65
HAEFELE E.T.,GOVERNMENT CONTROLS ON TRANSPORT. AFR   ECO/UNDEV
RHODESIA TANZANIA DIPLOM ECO/TAC TARIFFS PRICE   DIST/IND
ADJUD CONTROL REGION EFFICIENCY...POLICY 20 CONGO.   FINAN
PAGE 49 E0973   NAT/G

B65
HIGHSAW R.B.,CONFLICT AND CHANGE IN LOCAL   GOV/REL
GOVERNMENT. USA+45 BUDGET ECO/TAC LEGIT ADJUD   PROB/SOLV
ALABAMA. PAGE 52 E1044   LOC/G
                                                     BAL/PWR

B65
HOLDSWORTH W.S.,A HISTORY OF ENGLISH LAW; THE   LAW
CENTURIES OF SETTLEMENT AND REFORM (VOL. XV). UK   INDUS
CONSTN SECT LEGIS JUDGE WRITING ADJUD CT/SYS CRIME   PROF/ORG
OWN...JURID IDEA/COMP 18 PARLIAMENT ENGLSH/LAW   ATTIT
COMMON/LAW. PAGE 54 E1082

B65
INST INTL DES CIVILISATION DIF,THE CONSTITUTIONS   CONSTN
AND ADMINISTRATIVE INSTITUTIONS OF THE NEW STATES.   ADMIN
AFR ISLAM S/ASIA NAT/G POL/PAR DELIB/GP EX/STRUC   ADJUD
CONFER EFFICIENCY NAT/LISM...JURID SOC 20. PAGE 56   ECO/UNDEV
E1123

B65
KAAS L.,DIE GEISTLICHE GERICHTSBARKEIT DER   JURID
KATHOLISCHEN KIRCHE IN PREUSSEN (2 VOLS.). PRUSSIA   CATHISM
CONSTN NAT/G PROVS SECT ADJUD ADMIN ATTIT 16/20.   GP/REL
PAGE 59 E1178   CT/SYS

B65
KARIS T.,THE TREASON TRIAL IN SOUTH AFRICA: A GUIDE BIBLIOG/A
TO THE MICROFILM RECORD OF THE TRIAL. SOUTH/AFR LAW ADJUD
ELITES NAT/G LEGIT CT/SYS RACE/REL DISCRIM...SOC   CRIME
20. PAGE 59 E1185   AFR

B65
KING D.B.,LEGAL ASPECTS OF THE CIVIL RIGHTS   LAW
MOVEMENT. SERV/IND VOL/ASSN LEGIS EDU/PROP ADJUD   DISCRIM
PARTIC CHOOSE...JURID SEGREGAT WORK. PAGE 61 E1215   TREND

B65
KRISLOV S.,THE SUPREME COURT IN THE POLITICAL   ADJUD
PROCESS. USA+45 LAW SOCIETY STRUCT WORKER ADMIN   DECISION
ROLE...JURID SOC 20 SUPREME/CT. PAGE 62 E1231   CT/SYS
                                                     CONSTN

B65
KUPER H.,AFRICAN LAW. LAW FAM KIN SECT JUDGE ADJUST AFR
NAT/LISM 17/20. PAGE 62 E1236   CT/SYS
                                                     ADJUD
                                                     COLONIAL

B65
LAFAVE W.R.,LAW AND SOVIET SOCIETY. EX/STRUC DIPLOM JURID
DOMIN EDU/PROP PRESS ADMIN CRIME OWN MARXISM 20   CT/SYS
KHRUSH/N. PAGE 62 E1244   ADJUD
                                                     GOV/REL

B65
MCKAY R.B.,REAPPORTIONMENT: THE LAW AND POLITICS OF APPORT
EQUAL REPRESENTATION. FUT USA+45 PROVS BAL/PWR   MAJORIT
ADJUD CHOOSE REPRESENT GOV/REL FEDERAL...JURID   LEGIS
BIBLIOG 20 SUPREME/CT CONGRESS. PAGE 71 E1420   PWR

B65
MCWHINNEY E.,JUDICIAL REVIEW IN THE ENGLISH-   GOV/COMP
SPEAKING WORLD (3RD ED.). CANADA UK WOR+45 LEGIS   CT/SYS
CONTROL EXEC PARTIC...JURID 20 AUSTRAL. PAGE 71   ADJUD
E1431   CONSTN

B65
MISHKIN P.J.,ON LAW IN COURTS. USA+45 LEGIS CREATE   LAW
ROLE 20. PAGE 73 E1468   CT/SYS
                                                     ADJUD
                                                     CONSTN

B65
MONCONDUIT F.,LA COMMISSION EUROPEENNE DES DROITS   INT/LAW
DE L'HOMME. DIPLOM AGREE GP/REL ORD/FREE PWR   INT/ORG
...BIBLIOG 20 TREATY. PAGE 74 E1483   ADJUD
                                                     JURID

B65
MOODY M.,CATALOG OF INTERNATIONAL LAW AND RELATIONS BIBLIOG
(20 VOLS.). WOR+45 INT/ORG NAT/G ADJUD ADMIN CT/SYS INT/LAW
POLICY. PAGE 74 E1488   DIPLOM

B65
MOSTECKY V.,SOVIET LEGAL BIBLIOGRAPHY. USSR LEGIS   BIBLIOG/A
PRESS WRITING CONFER ADJUD CT/SYS REV MARXISM   LAW
...INT/LAW JURID DICTIONARY 20. PAGE 75 E1503   COM
                                                     CONSTN

B65
NWOGUGU E.I.,THE LEGAL PROBLEMS OF FOREIGN   FOR/AID
INVESTMENT IN DEVELOPING COUNTRIES. WOR+45 INT/ORG   FINAN
DELIB/GP LEGIS PROB/SOLV INT/TRADE TAX ADJUD   INT/LAW
SANCTION...BIBLIOG 20 TREATY. PAGE 78 E1561   ECO/UNDEV

B65
PARKER D.,CIVIL LIBERTIES CASE STUDIES AND THE LAW. ORD/FREE
SECT ADJUD...CONCPT WORSHIP 20 SUPREME/CT   JURID
CIV/RIGHTS FREE/SPEE. PAGE 80 E1598   CONSTN
                                                     JUDGE

B65
PARRY C.,THE SOURCES AND EVIDENCES OF INTERNATIONAL INT/LAW
LAW. WOR+45 WOR-45 DIPLOM AGREE SOVEREIGN...METH 20 ADJUD
TREATY UN LEAGUE/NAT. PAGE 80 E1599   INT/ORG
                                                     CT/SYS

B65

SMITH C.,THE OMBUDSMAN: A BIBLIOGRAPHY (PAMPHLET). BIBLIOG
DENMARK SWEDEN USA+45 LAW LEGIS JUDGE GOV/REL ADMIN
GP/REL...JURID 20. PAGE 92 E1841 CT/SYS
ADJUD

B65

SMITH R.C.,THEY CLOSED THEIR SCHOOLS. USA+45 NEIGH RACE/REL
ADJUD CROWD CONSEN WEALTH...DECISION OBS INT 20 DISCRIM
NEGRO VIRGINIA. PAGE 92 E1846 LOC/G
SCHOOL

B65

SNOW J.H.,REAPPORTIONMENT. LAW CONSTN NAT/G GOV/REL APPORT
ORD/FREE...JURID 20 SUPREME/CT CONNECTICT. PAGE 92 ADJUD
E1848 LEGIS
PROVS

B65

SWISHER C.B.,THE SUPREME COURT IN MODERN ROLE. COM DELIB/GP
COM/IND NAT/G FORCES LEGIS LOBBY PARTIC RACE/REL 20 ATTIT
SUPREME/CT. PAGE 95 E1901 CT/SYS
ADJUD

B65

THOMAS A.V.,NONINTERVENTION: THE LAW AND ITS IMPORT INT/LAW
IN THE AMERICAS. L/A+17C USA+45 USA-45 WOR+45 PWR
DIPLOM ADJUD...JURID IDEA/COMP 20 UN INTERVENT. COERCE
PAGE 96 E1917

B65

TRESOLINI R.J.,AMERICAN CONSTITUTIONAL LAW. USA+45 CONSTN
USA-45 NAT/G ADJUD ORD/FREE PWR...POLICY BIOG 20 CT/SYS
SUPREME/CT CASEBOOK. PAGE 97 E1939 JURID
LAW

B65

US LIBRARY OF CONGRESS,INTERNAL SECURITY AND CONTROL
SUBVERSION. USA+45 ACADEM LOC/G NAT/G PROVS ADJUD
...POLICY ANARCH DECISION 20 CIVIL/SERV SUBVERT LAW
SEDITION. PAGE 101 E2020 PLAN

B65

US SENATE COMM ON JUDICIARY,HEARINGS BEFORE ROUTINE
SUBCOMMITTEE ON ADMINISTRATIVE PRACTICE AND DELIB/GP
PROCEDURE ABOUT ADMINISTRATIVE PROCEDURE ACT 1965. ADMIN
USA+45 LEGIS EDU/PROP ADJUD GOV/REL INGP/REL NAT/G
EFFICIENCY...POLICY INT 20 CONGRESS. PAGE 103 E2055

B65

US SENATE COMM ON JUDICIARY,ANTITRUST EXEMPTIONS BAL/PAY
FOR AGREEMENTS RELATING TO BALANCE OF PAYMENTS. ADJUD
FINAN ECO/TAC CONTROL WEALTH...POLICY 20 CONGRESS. MARKET
PAGE 103 E2056 INT/TRADE

B65

VON GLAHN G.,LAW AMONG NATIONS: AN INTRODUCTION TO ACADEM
PUBLIC INTERNATIONAL LAW. WOR+45 WOR-45 INT/ORG INT/LAW
NAT/G CREATE ADJUD WAR...GEOG CLASSIF TREND GEN/LAWS
BIBLIOG. PAGE 104 E2082 LAW

B65

WHITE G.M.,THE USE OF EXPERTS BY INTERNATIONAL INT/LAW
TRIBUNALS. WOR+45 WOR-45 INT/ORG NAT/G PAY ADJUD ROUTINE
COST...OBS BIBLIOG 20. PAGE 106 E2117 CONSULT
CT/SYS

B65

WILSON J.F.,CHURCH AND STATE IN AMERICAN HISTORY. SECT
USA+45 USA-45 ADJUD CT/SYS ORD/FREE SOVEREIGN NAT/G
...ANTHOL BIBLIOG/A 17/20 CHURCH/STA. PAGE 106 GP/REL
E2129 CONTROL

L65

FORTE W.E.,"THE FOOD AND DRUG ADMINISTRATION, THE CONTROL
FEDERAL TRADE COMMISSION AND THE DECEPTIVE HEALTH
PACKAGING." ROUTINE...JURID 20 FTC. PAGE 39 E0772 ADJUD
INDUS

S65

AMRAM P.W.,"REPORT ON THE TENTH SESSION OF THE VOL/ASSN
HAGUE CONFERENCE ON PRIVATE INTERNATIONAL LAW." DELIB/GP
USA+45 WOR+45 INT/ORG CREATE LEGIT ADJUD ALL/VALS INT/LAW
...JURID CONCPT METH/CNCPT OBS GEN/METH 20. PAGE 4
E0085

S65

FRIEDHEIM R.,"THE 'SATISFIED' AND 'DISSATISFIED' INT/LAW
STATES NEGOTIATE INTERNATIONAL LAW* A CASE STUDY." RECORD
DIPLOM CONFER ADJUD CONSEN PEACE ATTIT UN. PAGE 40
E0799

S65

GROSS L.,"PROBLEMS OF INTERNATIONAL ADJUDICATION LAW
AND COMPLIANCE WITH INTERNATIONAL LAW: SOME SIMPLE METH/CNCPT
SOLUTIONS." WOR+45 SOCIETY NAT/G DOMIN LEGIT ADJUD INT/LAW

CT/SYS RIGID/FLEX HEALTH PWR...JURID NEW/IDEA
COLD/WAR 20. PAGE 48 E0951

S65

HAZARD J.N.,"CO-EXISTENCE LAW BOWS OUT." WOR+45 R+D PROF/ORG
INT/ORG VOL/ASSN CONSULT DELIB/GP ACT/RES CREATE ADJUD
PEACE KNOWL...JURID CONCPT COLD/WAR VAL/FREE 20.
PAGE 51 E1018

S65

LONG T.G.,"THE ADMINISTRATIVE PROCESS: AGONIZING ADJUD
REAPPRAISAL IN THE FTC." NAT/G REPRESENT 20 FTC. LOBBY
PAGE 66 E1326 ADMIN
EX/STRUC

S65

LUSKY L.,"FOUR PROBLEMS IN LAWMAKING FOR PEACE." ORD/FREE
FORCES LEGIS CREATE ADJUD COERCE WAR MAJORITY PEACE INT/LAW
PWR. PAGE 67 E1334 UTOPIA
RECORD

S65

STEIN E.,"TOWARD SUPREMACY OF TREATY-CONSTITUTION ADJUD
BY JUDICIAL FIAT: ON THE MARGIN OF THE COSTA CASE." CONSTN
EUR+WWI ITALY WOR+45 INT/ORG NAT/G LEGIT REGION SOVEREIGN
NAT/LISM PWR...JURID CONCPT TREND TOT/POP VAL/FREE INT/LAW
20. PAGE 93 E1870

S65

ULMER S.S.,"TOWARD A THEORY OF SUBGROUP FORMATION CT/SYS
IN THE UNITED STATES SUPREME COURT." USA+45 ROUTINE ADJUD
CHOOSE PWR...JURID STAT CON/ANAL SIMUL SUPREME/CT. ELITES
PAGE 97 E1952 INGP/REL

C65

SCHEINGOLD S.A.,"THE RULE OF LAW IN EUROPEAN INT/LAW
INTEGRATION: THE PATH OF THE SCHUMAN PLAN." EUR+WWI CT/SYS
JUDGE ADJUD FEDERAL ATTIT PWR...RECORD INT BIBLIOG REGION
EEC ECSC. PAGE 87 E1755 CENTRAL

B66

BAKER G.E.,THE REAPPORTIONMENT REVOLUTION: LEGIS
REPRESENTATION, POLITICAL POWER, AND THE SUPREME APPORT
COURT. USA+45 MUNIC NAT/G POL/PAR PROVS PROB/SOLV REPRESENT
CHOOSE ORD/FREE POPULISM...CONCPT CHARTS 20 ADJUD
SUPREME/CT. PAGE 7 E0140

B66

BAXTER M.G.,DANIEL WEBSTER & THE SUPREME COURT. LAW CONSTN
NAT/G PROF/ORG DEBATE ADJUD LEAD FEDERAL PERSON. CT/SYS
PAGE 8 E0156 JURID

B66

BEDI A.S.,FREEDOM OF EXPRESSION AND SECURITY: METH
COMPARATIVE STUDY OF FUNCTIONS OF SUPREME COURTS IN CT/SYS
UNITED STATES AND INDIA. INDIA USA+45 LAW CONSTN ADJUD
PROB/SOLV...DECISION JURID BIBLIOG 20 SUPREME/CT ORD/FREE
FREE/SPEE AMEND/I. PAGE 9 E0175

B66

BEELEY A.L.,THE BAIL SYSTEM IN CHICAGO. LAW MUNIC JURID
PUB/INST EFFICIENCY MORAL...CRIMLGY METH/CNCPT STAT CT/SYS
20 CHICAGO. PAGE 9 E0176 CRIME
ADJUD

B66

BEISER E.N.,THE TREATMENT OF LEGISLATIVE CT/SYS
APPORTIONMENT BY THE STATE AND FEDERAL COURTS APPORT
(DISSERTATION). USA+45 CONSTN NAT/G PROVS LEGIS ADJUD
CHOOSE REPRESENT ATTIT...POLICY BIBLIOG 20 CONGRESS PWR
SUPREME/CT. PAGE 9 E0181

B66

BRENNAN J.T.,THE COST OF THE AMERICAN JUDICIAL COST
SYSTEM. USA+45 PROF/ORG TV ADMIN EFFICIENCY. CT/SYS
PAGE 15 E0292 ADJUD
JURID

B66

BROWNLIE I.,PRINCIPLES OF PUBLIC INTERNATIONAL LAW. INT/LAW
WOR+45 WOR-45 LAW JUDGE REPAR ADJUD SOVEREIGN DIPLOM
...JURID T. PAGE 16 E0319 INT/ORG

B66

CAHN E.,CONFRONTING INJUSTICE. USA+45 PROB/SOLV TAX ORD/FREE
EDU/PROP PRESS CT/SYS GP/REL DISCRIM BIO/SOC CONSTN
...IDEA/COMP BIBLIOG WORSHIP 20 BILL/RIGHT. PAGE 18 ADJUD
E0362

B66

CANFIELD L.H.,THE PRESIDENCY OF WOODROW WILSON: PERSON
PRELUDE TO A WORLD IN CRISIS. USA-45 ADJUD NEUTRAL POLICY
WAR CHOOSE INGP/REL PEACE ORD/FREE 20 WILSON/W DIPLOM
PRESIDENT TREATY LEAGUE/NAT. PAGE 19 E0373 GOV/REL

CLARK G.,WORLD PEACE THROUGH WORLD LAW; TWO
ALTERNATIVE PLANS. WOR+45 DELIB/GP FORCES TAX
CONFER ADJUD SANCTION ARMS/CONT WAR CHOOSE PRIVIL
20 UN COLD/WAR. PAGE 23 E0450

B66
INT/LAW
PEACE
PLAN
INT/ORG

COPLIN W.D.,THE FUNCTIONS OF INTERNATIONAL LAW.
WOR+45 ECO/DEV ECO/UNDEV ADJUD COLONIAL WAR OWN
SOVEREIGN...POLICY GEN/LAWS 20. PAGE 25 E0503

B66
INT/LAW
DIPLOM
INT/ORG

COUNCIL OF EUROPE,EUROPEAN CONVENTION ON HUMAN
RIGHTS - COLLECTED TEXTS (5TH ED.). EUR+WWI DIPLOM
ADJUD CT/SYS...INT/LAW 20 ECHR. PAGE 26 E0520

B66
ORD/FREE
DELIB/GP
INT/ORG
JURID

DOUGLAS W.O.,THE BIBLE AND THE SCHOOLS. USA+45
CULTURE ADJUD INGP/REL AGE/C AGE/Y ATTIT KNOWL
WORSHIP 20 SUPREME/CT CHURCH/STA BIBLE CHRISTIAN.
PAGE 32 E0644

B66
SECT
NAT/G
SCHOOL
GP/REL

FELSHER H.,JUSTICE USA? USA+45 COM/IND JUDGE CT/SYS ADJUD
MORAL ORD/FREE...SAMP/SIZ HYPO/EXP. PAGE 37 E0735

B66
EDU/PROP
LOBBY

GARCON M.,LETTRE OUVERTE A LA JUSTICE. FRANCE NAT/G ORD/FREE
PROB/SOLV PAY EFFICIENCY MORAL 20. PAGE 42 E0834

B66
ADJUD
CT/SYS

GILLMOR D.M.,FREE PRESS AND FAIR TRIAL. UK USA+45
CONSTN PROB/SOLV PRESS CONTROL CRIME DISCRIM
RESPECT...AUD/VIS 20 CIVIL/LIB. PAGE 44 E0865

B66
ORD/FREE
ADJUD
ATTIT
EDU/PROP

HAMILTON H.D.,REAPPORTIONING LEGISLATURES. USA+45
CONSTN POL/PAR PROVS LEGIS COMPUTER ADJUD CHOOSE
ATTIT...ANTHOL 20 SUPREME/CT CONGRESS. PAGE 50
E0989

B66
APPORT
REPRESENT
PHIL/SCI
PWR

HAUSNER G.,JUSTICE IN JERUSALEM. GERMANY ISRAEL
SOCIETY KIN DIPLOM LEGIT CT/SYS PARTIC MURDER
MAJORITY ATTIT FASCISM...INT/LAW JURID 20 JEWS
WAR/TRIAL. PAGE 51 E1013

B66
ADJUD
CRIME
RACE/REL
COERCE

HAYS P.R.,LABOR ARBITRATION: A DISSENTING VIEW.
USA+45 LAW DELIB/GP BARGAIN ADJUD...PREDICT 20.
PAGE 51 E1016

B66
GP/REL
LABOR
CONSULT
CT/SYS

HOLMES O.W.,JUSTICE HOLMES, EX CATHEDRA. USA+45
USA-45 LAW INTELL ADMIN ATTIT...BIBLIOG 20
SUPREME/CT HOLMES/OW. PAGE 55 E1088

B66
BIOG
PERSON
CT/SYS
ADJUD

HOLTZMAN A.,INTEREST GROUPS AND LOBBYING. USA+45
CHIEF ACT/RES ADJUD LEAD PARTIC CHOOSE...POLICY 20
CONGRESS. PAGE 55 E1092

B66
LOBBY
NAT/G
EDU/PROP
GP/REL

INTL ATOMIC ENERGY AGENCY,INTERNATIONAL CONVENTIONS DIPLOM
ON CIVIL LIABILITY FOR NUCLEAR DAMAGE. FUT WOR+45
ADJUD WAR COST PEACE SOVEREIGN...JURID 20. PAGE 57
E1135

B66
INT/ORG
DELIB/GP
NUC/PWR

KEAY E.A.,THE NATIVE AND CUSTOMARY COURTS OF
NIGERIA. NIGERIA CONSTN ELITES NAT/G TOP/EX PARTIC
REGION...DECISION JURID 19/20. PAGE 60 E1190

B66
AFR
ADJUD
LAW

KUNSTLER W.M.,"DEEP IN MY HEART" USA+45 LAW
PROF/ORG SECT LOBBY PARTIC CROWD DISCRIM ROLE
...BIOG 20 KING/MAR/L NEGRO CIV/RIGHTS SOUTH/US.
PAGE 62 E1233

B66
CT/SYS
RACE/REL
ADJUD
CONSULT

KURLAND P.B.,THE SUPREME COURT REVIEW. USA+45
USA-45 LAW LABOR SUFF...ANTHOL 20 SUPREME/CT.
PAGE 62 E1240

B66
JURID
PROB/SOLV
ADJUD
NAT/G

LEHMANN L.,LEGAL UND OPPORTUN - POLITISCHE JUSTIZ
IN DER BUNDESREPUBLIK. GERMANY/W EDU/PROP ADJUD
CONTROL PARL/PROC COERCE TOTALISM ATTIT 20

B66
ORD/FREE
POL/PAR
JURID

COM/PARTY. PAGE 64 E1281

LEGIS

MACMULLEN R.,ENEMIES OF THE ROMAN EMPIRE: TREASON,
UNREST, AND ALIENATION IN THE EMPIRE. ROMAN/EMP
MUNIC CONTROL LEAD ATTIT PERSON MYSTISM...PHIL/SCI
BIBLIOG. PAGE 67 E1345

B66
CRIME
ADJUD
MORAL
SOCIETY

MC CONNELL J.P.,LAW AND BUSINESS: PATTERNS AND
ISSUES IN COMMERCIAL LAW. USA+45 USA-45 LOC/G
WORKER LICENSE CRIME REPRESENT GP/REL 20. PAGE 70
E1397

B66
ECO/DEV
JURID
ADJUD
MGT

MENDELSON W.,JUSTICES BLACK AND FRANKFURTER:
CONFLICT IN THE COURT (2ND ED.). NAT/G PROVS
PROB/SOLV BAL/PWR CONTROL FEDERAL ISOLAT ANOMIE
ORD/FREE...DECISION 20 SUPREME/CT BLACK/HL
FRANKFUR/F. PAGE 72 E1439

B66
JURID
ADJUD
IDEA/COMP
ROLE

MERILLAT H.C.L.,LEGAL ADVISERS AND INTERNATIONAL
ORGANIZATIONS. LAW NAT/G CONSULT OP/RES ADJUD
SANCTION TASK CONSEN ORG/CHARTS. PAGE 72 E1441

B66
INT/ORG
INT/LAW
CREATE
OBS

MOSKOW M.H.,TEACHERS AND UNIONS. SCHOOL WORKER
ADJUD LOBBY ATTIT ORD/FREE 20. PAGE 75 E1501

B66
EDU/PROP
PROF/ORG
LABOR
BARGAIN

NANTWI E.K.,THE ENFORCEMENT OF INTERNATIONAL
JUDICIAL DECISIONS AND ARBITAL AWARDS IN PUBLIC
INTERNATIONAL LAW. WOR+45 WOR-45 JUDGE PROB/SOLV
DIPLOM CT/SYS SUPEGO MORAL PWR RESPECT...METH/CNCPT INT/ORG
18/20 CASEBOOK. PAGE 76 E1520

B66
INT/LAW
ADJUD
SOVEREIGN

O'NEILL C.E.,CHURCH AND STATE IN FRENCH COLONIAL
LOUISIANA: POLICY AND POLITICS TO 1732. PROVS
VOL/ASSN DELIB/GP ADJUD ADMIN GP/REL ATTIT DRIVE
...POLICY BIBLIOG 17/18 LOUISIANA CHURCH/STA.
PAGE 78 E1568

B66
COLONIAL
NAT/G
SECT
PWR

POWERS E.,CRIME AND PUNISHMENT IN EARLY
MASSACHUSETTS 1620-1692: A DOCUMENTARY HISTORY.
USA-45 SECT LEGIS COLONIAL ATTIT ORD/FREE MYSTISM
17 PRE/US/AM MASSACHU. PAGE 82 E1643

B66
CRIME
ADJUD
CT/SYS
PROVS

SMITH E.A.,CHURCH-STATE RELATIONS IN ECUMENICAL
PERSPECTIVE. WOR+45 LAW MUNIC INGP/REL DISCRIM
ATTIT SUPEGO ORD/FREE CATHISM...PHIL/SCI IDEA/COMP
20 PROTESTANT ECUMENIC CHURCH/STA CHRISTIAN.
PAGE 92 E1843

B66
NAT/G
SECT
GP/REL
ADJUD

SOBEL N.R.,THE NEW CONFESSION STANDARDS, MIRANDA V.
ARIZONA. USA+45 USA-45 LAW PROF/ORG EDU/PROP 20
SUPREME/CT. PAGE 92 E1849

B66
JURID
CT/SYS
ORD/FREE
ADJUD

STUMPF S.E.,MORALITY AND THE LAW. USA+45 LAW
CULTURE PROB/SOLV DOMIN ADJUD CONTROL ADJUST
ALL/IDEOS MARXISM...INT/LAW 20 SUPREME/CT. PAGE 94
E1890

B66
JURID
MORAL
CT/SYS

SWEET E.C.,CIVIL LIBERTIES IN AMERICA. LAW CONSTN
NAT/G PRESS CT/SYS DISCRIM ATTIT WORSHIP 20
CIVIL/LIB. PAGE 95 E1899

B66
ADJUD
ORD/FREE
SUFF
COERCE

TRESOLINI R.J.,CASES IN AMERICAN NATIONAL
GOVERNMENT AND POLITICS. LAW DIPLOM ADJUD LOBBY
FEDERAL ORD/FREE WEALTH...DECISION ANTHOL 20
PRESIDENT. PAGE 97 E1940

B66
NAT/G
LEGIS
CT/SYS
POL/PAR

US PRES COMN CRIME IN DC,REPORT OF THE US
PRESIDENT'S COMMISSION ON CRIME IN THE DISTRICT OF
COLUMBIA. LEGIS WORKER EDU/PROP ADJUD CONTROL
CT/SYS GP/REL BIO/SOC HEALTH...CRIMLGY NEW/IDEA
STAT 20. PAGE 101 E2022

B66
CRIME
FORCES
AGE/Y
SANCTION

US SENATE COMM AERO SPACE SCI,SOVIET SPACE
PROGRAMS, 1962-65; GOALS AND PURPOSES,
ACHIEVEMENTS, PLANS, AND INTERNATIONAL
IMPLICATIONS. USA+45 USSR R+D FORCES PLAN EDU/PROP

B66
CONSULT
SPACE
FUT
DIPLOM

PRESS ADJUD ARMS/CONT ATTIT MARXISM. PAGE 101 E2028

B66
US SENATE COMM ON JUDICIARY,SCHOOL PRAYER. USA+45   SCHOOL
LAW LOC/G SECT ADJUD WORSHIP 20 SENATE DEITY.   JURID
PAGE 103 E2058   NAT/G

B66
WALL E.H.,THE COURT OF JUSTICE IN THE EUROPEAN   CT/SYS
COMMUNITIES: JURISDICTION AND PROCEDURE. EUR+WWI   INT/ORG
DIPLOM ADJUD ADMIN ROUTINE TASK...CONCPT LING 20.   LAW
PAGE 105 E2096   OP/RES

B66
WASHINGTON S.H.,BIBLIOGRAPHY: LABOR-MANAGEMENT   BIBLIOG
RELATIONS ACT, 1947 AS AMENDED BY LABOR-MANAGEMENT   LAW
REPORTING AND DISCLOSURE ACT, 1959. USA+45 CONSTN   LABOR
INDUS DELIB/GP LEGIS WORKER BARGAIN ECO/TAC ADJUD   MGT
GP/REL NEW/LIB...JURID CONGRESS. PAGE 105 E2100

B66
WILSON G.,CASES AND MATERIALS ON CONSTITUTIONAL AND   JURID
ADMINISTRATIVE LAW. UK LAW NAT/G EX/STRUC LEGIS   ADMIN
BAL/PWR BUDGET DIPLOM ADJUD CONTROL CT/SYS GOV/REL   CONSTN
ORD/FREE 20 PARLIAMENT ENGLSH/LAW. PAGE 106 E2126   PWR

L66
GREIG D.W.,"THE ADVISORY JURISDICTION OF THE   INT/LAW
INTERNATIONAL COURT AND THE SETTLEMENT OF DISPUTES   CT/SYS
BETWEEN STATES." ISRAEL KOREA FORCES BUDGET DOMIN
LEGIT ADJUD COST...RECORD UN CONGO/LEOP TREATY.
PAGE 46 E0915

L66
HIGGINS R.,"THE INTERNATIONAL COURT AND SOUTH WEST   SOUTH/AFR
AFRICA* SOME IMPLICATIONS OF THE JUDGMENT." AFR LAW   COLONIAL
ECO/UNDEV JUDGE RACE/REL COST PWR...INT/LAW TREND   CT/SYS
UN TREATY. PAGE 52 E1043   ADJUD

L66
HOLSTI K.J.,"RESOLVING INTERNATIONAL CONFLICTS* A   DIPLOM
TAXONOMY OF BEHAVIOR AND SOME FIGURES ON   PROB/SOLV
PROCEDURES." WOR+45 WOR-45 INT/ORG ADJUD EFFICIENCY   WAR
...STAT IDEA/COMP. PAGE 55 E1089   CLASSIF

L66
KRENZ F.E.,"THE REFUGEE AS A SUBJECT OF   INT/LAW
INTERNATIONAL LAW." FUT LAW NAT/G CREATE ADJUD   DISCRIM
ISOLAT STRANGE...RECORD UN. PAGE 62 E1230   NEW/IDEA

S66
ANAND R.P.,"ATTITUDE OF THE ASIAN-AFRICAN STATES   INT/LAW
TOWARD CERTAIN PROBLEMS OF INTERNATIONAL LAW."   ATTIT
L/A+17C S/ASIA ECO/UNDEV CREATE CONFER ADJUD   ASIA
COLONIAL...RECORD GP/COMP UN. PAGE 5 E0087   AFR

S66
FINE R.I.,"PEACE-KEEPING COSTS AND ARTICLE 19 OF   FORCES
THE UN CHARTER* AN INVITATION TO RESPONSIBILITY."   COST
INT/ORG NAT/G ADJUD CT/SYS CHOOSE CONSEN...RECORD   CONSTN
IDEA/COMP UN. PAGE 38 E0750

S66
NYC BAR ASSOCIATION RECORD,"PAPERBACKS FOR THE   BIBLIOG
BAR." USA+45 LEGIS ADJUD CT/SYS. PAGE 78 E1562   JURID
                                                       LAW
                                                       WRITING

S66
POLSBY N.W.,"BOOKS IN THE FIELD: POLITICAL   BIBLIOG/A
SCIENCE." LAW CONSTN LOC/G NAT/G LEGIS ADJUD PWR 20   ATTIT
SUPREME/CT. PAGE 81 E1627   ADMIN
                                                       JURID

S66
SHKLAR J.,"SELECTED ARTICLES AND DOCUMENTS ON   BIBLIOG
POLITICAL THEORY." ADJUD REV...JURID PHIL/SCI   ELITES
IDEA/COMP. PAGE 91 E1820   PWR

B67
ASCH S.H.,POLICE AUTHORITY AND THE RIGHTS OF THE   FORCES
INDIVIDUAL. CONSTN DOMIN ADJUD CT/SYS...JURID 20.   OP/RES
PAGE 6 E0106   ORD/FREE

B67
BAKKE E.W.,UNIONS, MANAGEMENT AND THE PUBLIC*   LABOR
READINGS AND TEXT. WORKER LOBBY...POLICY JURID   INDUS
ANTHOL T. PAGE 7 E0143   ADJUD
                                                       GP/REL

B67
BEAL E.F.,THE PRACTICE OF COLLECTIVE BARGAINING   BARGAIN
(3RD ED.). USA+45 WOR+45 ECO/DEV INDUS LG/CO   MGT
PROF/ORG WORKER ECO/TAC GP/REL WEALTH...JURID   LABOR
METH/CNCPT. PAGE 8 E0160   ADJUD

B67
BOHANNAN P.,LAW AND WARFARE. CULTURE CT/SYS COERCE   METH/COMP
REV PEACE...JURID SOC CONCPT ANTHOL 20. PAGE 13   ADJUD
E0259   WAR
                                                       LAW

B67
BOLES D.E.,THE TWO SWORDS. USA+45 USA-45 LAW CONSTN   SCHOOL
SOCIETY FINAN PRESS CT/SYS...HEAL JURID BIBLIOG   EDU/PROP
WORSHIP 20 SUPREME/CT CHURCH/STA. PAGE 13 E0263   ADJUD

B67
BOULTON D.,OBJECTION OVERRULED. UK LAW POL/PAR   FORCES
DIPLOM ADJUD SANCTION DEATH WAR CIVMIL/REL 20.   SOCISM
PAGE 14 E0273   SECT

B67
CAVES R.,AMERICAN INDUSTRY: STRUCTURE, CONDUCT,   ECO/DEV
PERFORMANCE (2ND ED.). USA+45 MARKET NAT/G ADJUD   INDUS
CONTROL GP/REL DEMAND WEALTH 20. PAGE 21 E0412   POLICY
                                                       ECO/TAC

B67
ESTEY M.,THE UNIONS: STRUCTURE, DEVELOPMENT, AND   LABOR
MANAGEMENT. FUT USA+45 ADJUD CONTROL INGP/REL DRIVE   EX/STRUC
...DECISION T 20 AFL/CIO. PAGE 35 E0699   ADMIN
                                                       GOV/REL

B67
GELLHORN W.,OMBUDSMEN AND OTHERS: CITIZENS'   NAT/COMP
PROTECTORS IN NINE COUNTRIES. WOR+45 LAW CONSTN   REPRESENT
LEGIS INSPECT ADJUD ADMIN CONTROL CT/SYS CHOOSE   INGP/REL
PERS/REL...STAT CHARTS 20. PAGE 43 E0847   PROB/SOLV

B67
HEWITT W.H.,ADMINISTRATION OF CRIMINAL JUSTICE IN   CRIME
NEW YORK. LAW PROB/SOLV ADJUD ADMIN...CRIMLGY   ROLE
CHARTS T 20 NEW/YORK. PAGE 52 E1035   CT/SYS
                                                       FORCES

B67
KING W.L.,MELVILLE WESTON FULLER: CHIEF JUSTICE OF   BIOG
THE UNITED STATES, 1888-1910. USA-45 CONSTN FINAN   CT/SYS
LABOR TAX GOV/REL PERS/REL ATTIT PERSON PWR...JURID   LAW
BIBLIOG 19/20 SUPREME/CT FULLER/MW HOLMES/OW.   ADJUD
PAGE 61 E1216

B67
LAWYERS COMM AMER POLICY VIET,VIETNAM AND   INT/LAW
INTERNATIONAL LAW: AN ANALYSIS OF THE LEGALITY OF   DIPLOM
THE US MILITARY INVOLVEMENT. VIETNAM LAW INT/ORG   ADJUD
COERCE WEAPON PEACE ORD/FREE 20 UN SEATO TREATY.   WAR
PAGE 64 E1271

B67
LENG S.C.,JUSTICE IN COMMUNIST CHINA: A SURVEY OF   CT/SYS
THE JUDICIAL SYSTEM OF THE CHINESE PEOPLE'S   ADJUD
REPUBLIC. CHINA/COM LAW CONSTN LOC/G NAT/G PROF/ORG   JURID
CONSULT FORCES ADMIN CRIME ORD/FREE...BIBLIOG 20   MARXISM
MAO. PAGE 64 E1284

B67
LEVY L.W.,JUDICIAL REVIEW AND THE SUPREME COURT.   ADJUD
USA+45 USA-45 NEUTRAL ATTIT ORD/FREE...POLICY   CONSTN
DECISION BIBLIOG 18/20 BILL/RIGHT SUPREME/CT.   LAW
PAGE 65 E1292   CT/SYS

B67
LOBLE L.H.,DELINQUENCY CAN BE STOPPED. FAM PUB/INST   AGE/Y
CT/SYS ADJUST ATTIT...NEW/IDEA METH/COMP 20.   PROB/SOLV
PAGE 66 E1315   ADJUD
                                                       CRIME

B67
RAE D.,THE POLITICAL CONSEQUENCES OF ELECTORAL   POL/PAR
LAWS. EUR+WWI ICELAND ISRAEL NEW/ZEALND UK USA+45   CHOOSE
ADJUD APPORT GP/REL MAJORITY...MATH STAT CENSUS   NAT/COMP
CHARTS BIBLIOG 20 AUSTRAL. PAGE 83 E1667   REPRESENT

B67
SLATER J.,THE OAS AND UNITED STATES FOREIGN POLICY.   INT/ORG
KOREA L/A+17C USA+45 VOL/ASSN RISK COERCE PEACE   DIPLOM
ORD/FREE MARXISM...TREND 20 OAS. PAGE 92 E1838   ALL/IDEOS
                                                       ADJUD

B67
UNIVERSAL REFERENCE SYSTEM,LAW, JURISPRUDENCE, AND   BIBLIOG/A
JUDICIAL PROCESS (VOLUME VII). WOR+45 WOR-45 CONSTN   LAW
NAT/G LEGIS JUDGE CT/SYS...INT/LAW COMPUT/IR   JURID
GEN/METH METH. PAGE 99 E1976   ADJUD

B67
US PRES TASK FORCE ADMIN JUS,TASK FORCE REPORT: THE   CT/SYS
COURTS. USA+45 CONSULT CONFER...JURID CHARTS.   ADJUD
PAGE 101 E2025   ROUTINE
                                                       ADMIN

B67

VILE M.J.C.,CONSTITUTIONALISM AND THE SEPARATION OF CONSTN
POWERS. FRANCE UK USA+45 USA-45 NAT/G ADJUD CONTROL BAL/PWR
GOV/REL...POLICY DECISION JURID GEN/LAWS 15/20 CONCPT
MONTESQ. PAGE 104 E2076   LAW

L67

"A PROPOS DES INCITATIONS FINANCIERES AUX   LOC/G
GROUPEMENTS DES COMMUNES: ESSAI D'INTERPRETATION."   ECO/TAC
FRANCE NAT/G LEGIS ADMIN GOV/REL CENTRAL 20. PAGE 2 APPORT
E0037   ADJUD

L67

BAADE H.W.,"THE ACQUIRED RIGHTS OF INTERNATIONAL   INT/ORG
PUBLIC SERVANTS; A CASE STUDY IN RECEPTION OF   WORKER
PUBLIC LAW." WOR+45 DELIB/GP DIPLOM ORD/FREE   ADJUD
...INT/LAW JURID UN. PAGE 7 E0125   LAW

L67

BARRON J.A.,"ACCESS TO THE PRESS." USA+45 TEC/DEV   ORD/FREE
PRESS TV ADJUD AUD/VIS. PAGE 8 E0152   COM/IND
                                                     EDU/PROP
                                                     LAW

L67

BLUMBERG A.S.,"THE PRACTICE OF LAW AS CONFIDENCE   CT/SYS
GAME: ORGANIZATIONAL COOPTATION OF A PROFESSION."   ADJUD
USA+45 CLIENT SOCIETY CONSULT ROLE JURID. PAGE 13   GP/REL
E0252   ADMIN

L67

CARMICHAEL D.M.,"FORTY YEARS OF WATER POLLUTION   HEALTH
CONTROL IN WISCONSIN: A CASE STUDY." LAW EXTR/IND   CONTROL
INDUS MUNIC DELIB/GP PLAN PROB/SOLV SANCTION   ADMIN
...CENSUS CHARTS 20 WISCONSIN. PAGE 20 E0384   ADJUD

L67

FRANCK T.M.,"SOME PSYCHOLOGICAL FACTORS IN   DIPLOM
INTERNATIONAL THIRD-PARTY DECISION-MAKING." UNIV   ADJUD
SOCIETY PROB/SOLV DISCRIM ATTIT HABITAT...DECISION   PERSON
PSY. PAGE 40 E0786   CONSULT

L67

HOWARD A.E.D.,"MR. JUSTICE BLACK: THE NEGRO PROTEST ADJUD
MOVEMENT AND THE RULE OF LAW." USA+45 CONSTN CT/SYS JUDGE
CHOOSE GP/REL...DECISION JURID NEGRO SUPREME/CT.   LAW
PAGE 55 E1100   REPRESENT

L67

LAMBERT J.D.,"CORPORATE POLITICAL SPENDING AND   USA+45
CAMPAIGN FINANCE." LAW CONSTN FINAN LABOR LG/CO   POL/PAR
LOC/G NAT/G VOL/ASSN TEC/DEV ADJUD ADMIN PARTIC.   CHOOSE
PAGE 62 E1247   COST

L67

LEGAULT A.,"ORGANISATION ET CONDUITE DES OPERATIONS INT/ORG
DE MAINTIEN DE LA PAIX." FORCES ACT/RES ADJUD AGREE PEACE
CONTROL NEUTRAL TASK PRIVIL ORD/FREE 20. UN. PAGE 64 WAR
E1279   INT/LAW

L67

NAGEL S.S.,"DISPARITIES IN CRIMINAL PROCEDURE."   ADJUD
STRATA NAT/G PROVS EDU/PROP RACE/REL AGE HABITAT   DISCRIM
SEX...JURID CHARTS 20. PAGE 76 E1519   STRUCT
                                                     ACT/RES

L67

SCHUBERT G.,"THE RHETORIC OF CONSTITUTIONAL   CONSTN
CHANGE." USA+45 LAW CULTURE CHIEF LEGIS ADJUD   METH/COMP
CT/SYS ARMS/CONT ADJUST...CHARTS SIMUL. PAGE 89   ORD/FREE
E1777

S67

"THE STATE OF ZONING ADMINISTRATION IN ILLINOIS: ADMIN
PROCEDURAL REQUIREMENTS OF JUDICIAL INTERVENTION."   CONTROL
USA+45 LAW CONSTN DELIB/GP ADJUD CT/SYS ORD/FREE   HABITAT
ILLINOIS. PAGE 2 E0038   PLAN

S67

ADOKO A.,"THE CONSTITUTION OF UGANDA." AFR UGANDA   NAT/G
LOC/G CHIEF FORCES LEGIS ADJUD EXEC CHOOSE NAT/LISM CONSTN
...IDEA/COMP 20. PAGE 3 E0050   ORD/FREE
                                                     LAW

S67

BLUMSTEIN A.,"POLICE TECHNOLOGY." USA+45 DELIB/GP   TEC/DEV
COMPUTER EDU/PROP CRIME COMPUT/IR. PAGE 13 E0253   FORCES
                                                     CRIMLGY
                                                     ADJUD

S67

BOHANNAN P.,"INSTITUTIONS OF DIVORCE, FAMILY, AND   FAM
THE LAW." WOR+45 LAW CONSULT...JURID SOC. PAGE 13   MARRIAGE
E0258   ADJUD
                                                     SOCIETY

S67

CARTER R.M.,"SOME FACTORS IN SENTENCING POLICY."   ADJUD
LAW PUB/INST CRIME PERS/REL...POLICY JURID SOC   CT/SYS
TREND CON/ANAL CHARTS SOC/EXP 20. PAGE 20 E0403   ADMIN

S67

CHAMBLISS W.J.,"TYPES OF DEVIANCE AND THE   CRIME
EFFECTIVENESS OF LEGAL SANCTIONS" SOCIETY PROB/SOLV SANCTION
ADJUD CONTROL DETER. PAGE 21 E0417   EFFICIENCY
                                                     LAW

S67

COHN K.,"CRIMES AGAINST HUMANITY." GERMANY INT/ORG   WAR
SANCTION ATTIT ORD/FREE...MARXIST CRIMLGY 20 UN.   INT/LAW
PAGE 24 E0469   CRIME
                                                     ADJUD

S67

DALFEN C.M.,"THE WORLD COURT IN IDLE SPLENDOUR: THE CT/SYS
BASIS OF STATES' ATTITUDES." WOR+45 LAW ADJUD   INT/ORG
COERCE...JURID 20 UN WORLD/CT. PAGE 28 E0562   INT/LAW
                                                     DIPLOM

S67

DEUTSCH E.P.,"A JUDICIAL PATH TO WORLD PEACE." FUT   INT/LAW
WOR+45 CONSTN PROB/SOLV DIPLOM LICENSE ADJUD   INT/ORG
SANCTION CHOOSE REPRESENT NAT/LISM SOVEREIGN 20   JURID
ICJ. PAGE 31 E0611   PEACE

S67

GIBSON G.H.,"LABOR PIRACY ON THE BRANDYWINE."   ECO/TAC
USA-45 INDUS R+D VOL/ASSN CAP/ISM ADJUD DRIVE...PSY CREATE
19. PAGE 43 E0859   TEC/DEV
                                                     WORKER

S67

GOSSETT W.T.,"ELECTING THE PRESIDENT: NEW HOPE FOR   CONSTN
AN OLD IDEAL." FUT USA+45 USA-45 PROVS LEGIS   CHIEF
PROB/SOLV WRITING DEBATE ADJUD REPRESENT...MAJORIT   CHOOSE
DECISION 20 HOUSE/REP PRESIDENT. PAGE 45 E0892   NAT/G

S67

GRIFFIN H.C.,"PREJUDICIAL PUBLICITY: SEARCH FOR A   LAW
CIVIL REMEDY." EDU/PROP CONTROL DISCRIM...JURID 20. SANCTION
PAGE 47 E0937   PRESS
                                                     ADJUD

S67

HAMILTON H.D.,"LEGISLATIVE CONSTITUENCIES: SINGLE-   LEGIS
MEMBER DISTRICTS, MULTI-MEMBER DISTRICTS, AND   REPRESENT
FLOTERAL DISTRICTS." USA+45 LAW POL/PAR ADJUD   APPORT
RACE/REL...CHARTS METH/COMP 20. PAGE 50 E0990   PLAN

S67

HILL D.G.,"HUMAN RIGHTS LEGISLATION IN ONTARIO."   DELIB/GP
CANADA R+D VOL/ASSN CONSULT INSPECT EDU/PROP ADJUD   ORD/FREE
AGREE TASK GP/REL INGP/REL DISCRIM 20 CIV/RIGHTS   LAW
ONTARIO CIVIL/LIB. PAGE 52 E1045   POLICY

S67

HUBERT C.J.,"PLANNED UNIT DEVELOPMENT" LAW VOL/ASSN PLAN
LEGIS EDU/PROP CT/SYS GOV/REL...NEW/IDEA 20   MUNIC
PLAN/UNIT. PAGE 56 E1107   HABITAT
                                                     ADJUD

S67

KETCHAM O.W.,"GUIDELINES FROM GAULT: REVOLUTIONARY   ADJUD
REQUIREMENTS AND REAPPRAISAL." LAW CONSTN CREATE   AGE/Y
LEGIT ROUTINE SANCTION CRIME DISCRIM PRIVIL ROLE   CT/SYS
...JURID NEW/IDEA 20 SUPREME/CT. PAGE 60 E1208

S67

KIM R.C.C.,"THE SUPREME COURT: ORALLE WITHOUT   CT/SYS
TRUTH." USA+45 EDU/PROP RACE/REL ADJUST ALL/VALS   PROB/SOLV
ORD/FREE...DECISION WORSHIP SUPREME/CT. PAGE 61   ADJUD
E1214   REPRESENT

S67

LARSEN P.B.,"THE UNITED STATES-ITALY AIR TRANSPORT   INT/LAW
ARBITRATION: PROBLEMS OF TREATY INTERPRETATION AND   ADJUD
ENFORCEMENT." ITALY USA+45 AIR PROB/SOLV DIPLOM   INT/TRADE
DEBATE CONTROL CT/SYS...DECISION TREATY. PAGE 63   DIST/IND
E1257

S67

LAY S.H.,"EXCLUSIVE GOVERNMENTAL LIABILITY FOR   NAT/G
SPACE ACCIDENTS." USA+45 LAW FINAN SERV/IND TEC/DEV SUPEGO
ADJUD. PAGE 64 E1272   SPACE
                                                     PROB/SOLV

S67

MATTHEWS R.O.,"THE SUEZ CANAL DISPUTE* A CASE STUDY PEACE
IN PEACEFUL SETTLEMENT." FRANCE ISRAEL UAR UK NAT/G DIPLOM
CONTROL LEAD COERCE WAR NAT/LISM ROLE ORD/FREE PWR   ADJUD
...INT/LAW UN 20. PAGE 69 E1389

S67

MAYANJA A.,"THE GOVERNMENT'S PROPOSALS ON THE NEW CONSTITUTION." AFR UGANDA LAW CHIEF LEGIS ADJUD REPRESENT FEDERAL PWR 20. PAGE 69 E1390
CONSTN
CONFER
ORD/FREE
NAT/G

S67

MAYER M.,"THE IDEA OF JUSTICE AND THE POOR." USA+45 INCOME CLIENT CONSULT RENT ADJUD DISCRIM KNOWL 20. PAGE 70 E1393
INCOME
WEALTH
LAW
ORD/FREE

S67

MC REYNOLDS D.,"THE RESISTANCE." USA+45 LAW ADJUD SANCTION INGP/REL PEACE 20. PAGE 70 E1398
ATTIT
WAR
LEGIT
FORCES

S67

MIRONENKO Y.,"A NEW EXTENSION OF CRIMINAL LIABILITY ADJUD IN THE USSR." COM USSR DOMIN EDU/PROP 20. PAGE 73 E1467
ADJUD
SANCTION
CRIME
MARXISM

S67

MITCHELL J.D.B.,"THE CONSTITUTIONAL IMPLICATIONS OF JUDICIAL CONTROL OF THE ADMINISTRATION IN THE UNITED KINGDOM." UK LAW ADJUD ADMIN GOV/REL ROLE ...GP/COMP 20. PAGE 74 E1474
CONSTN
CT/SYS
CONTROL
EX/STRUC

S67

MONEYPENNY P.,"UNIVERSITY PURPOSE, DISCIPLINE, AND DUE PROCESS." USA+45 EDU/PROP ADJUD LEISURE ORD/FREE. PAGE 74 E1484
ACADEM
AGE/Y
CONTROL
ADMIN

S67

MORENO F.J.,"THE SPANISH COLONIAL SYSTEM: A FUNCTIONAL APPROACH." SPAIN WOR-45 LAW CHIEF DIPLOM ADJUD CIVMIL/REL AUTHORIT ROLE PWR...CONCPT 17/20. PAGE 74 E1492
COLONIAL
CONTROL
NAT/G
OP/RES

S67

O'HIGGINS P.,"A BIBLIOGRAPHY OF PERIODICAL LITERATURE RELATING TO IRISH LAW." IRELAND...JURID 20. PAGE 78 E1567
BIBLIOG
LAW
ADJUD

S67

READ J.S.,"CENSORED." UGANDA CONSTN INTELL SOCIETY NAT/G DIPLOM PRESS WRITING ADJUD ADMIN COLONIAL RISK...IDEA/COMP 20. PAGE 84 E1675
EDU/PROP
AFR
CREATE

S67

REILLY T.J.,"FREEZING AND CONFISCATION OF CUBAN PROPERTY." CUBA USA+45 LAW DIPLOM LEGIT ADJUD CONTROL. PAGE 84 E1682
STRANGE
OWN
ECO/TAC

S67

RICHARDSON J.J.,"THE MAKING OF THE RESTRICTIVE TRADE PRACTICES ACT 1956 A CASE STUDY OF THE POLICY PROCESS IN BRITAIN." UK FINAN MARKET LG/CO POL/PAR CONSULT PRESS ADJUD ADMIN AGREE LOBBY SANCTION ATTIT 20. PAGE 84 E1695
LEGIS
ECO/TAC
POLICY
INDUS

S67

RUCKER B.W.,"WHAT SOLUTIONS DO PEOPLE ENDORSE IN FREE PRESS-FAIR TRIAL DILEMMA?" LAW NAT/G CT/SYS ATTIT...NET/THEORY SAMP CHARTS IDEA/COMP METH 20. PAGE 86 E1731
CONCPT
PRESS
ADJUD
ORD/FREE

S67

SEIDLER G.L.,"MARXIST LEGAL THOUGHT IN POLAND." POLAND SOCIETY R+D LOC/G NAT/G ACT/RES ADJUD CT/SYS SUPEGO PWR...SOC TREND 20 MARX/KARL. PAGE 90 E1802
MARXISM
LAW
CONCPT
EFFICIENCY

S67

SHAFFER T.L.,"DIRECT RESTRAINT ON THE PRESS." USA+45 EDU/PROP CONTROL...JURID NEW/IDEA ABA. PAGE 90 E1809
LAW
PRESS
ORD/FREE
ADJUD

S67

TOMASEK R.D.,"THE CHILEAN-BOLIVIAN LAUCA RIVER DISPUTE AND THE OAS." CHILE L/A+17C PROB/SOLV ADJUD CONTROL PEACE 20 BOLIV OAS. PAGE 96 E1930
INT/ORG
DIPLOM
GEOG
WAR

S67

TRAYNOR R.J.,"WHO CAN BEST JUDGE THE JUDGES?" USA+45 PLAN PROB/SOLV ATTIT...DECISION JURID 20. PAGE 97 E1938
CHOOSE
ADJUD
REPRESENT
CT/SYS

S67

WILSON G.D.,"CRIMINAL SANCTIONS AGAINST PASSPORT AREA-RESTRICTION VIOLATIONS." USA+45 ADJUD CRIME GOV/REL DEPT/STATE CONGRESS. PAGE 106 E2127
LAW
SANCTION
LICENSE
POLICY

S67

WINES R.,"THE IMPERIAL CIRCLES, PRINCELY DIPLOMACY, AND IMPERIAL REFORM* 1681-1714." MOD/EUR DELIB/GP BAL/PWR CONFER ADJUD PARL/PROC PARTIC ATTIT PWR 17/18. PAGE 106 E2132
NAT/G
NAT/LISM
CENTRAL
REGION

S67

WRAITH R.E.,"ADMINISTRATIVE CHANGE IN THE NEW AFRICA." AFR LG/CO ADJUD INGP/REL PWR...RECORD GP/COMP 20. PAGE 107 E2147
ADMIN
NAT/G
LOC/G
ECO/UNDEV

L68

CHIU H.,"COMMUNIST CHINA'S ATTITUDE TOWARD THE UNITED NATIONS: A LEGAL ANALYSIS." CHINA/COM WOR+45 LAW NAT/G DIPLOM CONFER ADJUD PARTIC ATTIT...POLICY TREND 20 UN. PAGE 22 E0432
INT/LAW
SOVEREIGN
INT/ORG
REPRESENT

S68

DUGARD J.,"THE REVOCATION OF THE MANDATE FOR SOUTH WEST AFRICA." SOUTH/AFR WOR+45 STRATA NAT/G DELIB/GP DIPLOM ADJUD SANCTION CHOOSE RACE/REL ...POLICY NAT/COMP 20 AFRICA/SW UN TRUST/TERR LEAGUE/NAT. PAGE 33 E0654
AFR
INT/ORG
DISCRIM
COLONIAL

S68

DUPRE L.,"TILL DEATH DO US PART?" UNIV FAM INSPECT LEGIT ADJUD SANCTION PERS/REL ANOMIE RIGID/FLEX SEX ...JURID IDEA/COMP 20 CHURCH/STA BIBLE CANON/LAW CIVIL/LAW. PAGE 34 E0666
MARRIAGE
CATH
LAW

S68

SHAPIRO J.P.,"SOVIET HISTORIOGRAPHY AND THE MOSCOW TRIALS: AFTER THIRTY YEARS." USSR NAT/G LEGIT PRESS CONTROL LEAD ATTIT MARXISM...NEW/IDEA METH 20 TROTSKY/L STALIN/J KHRUSH/N. PAGE 90 E1810
HIST/WRIT
EDU/PROP
SANCTION
ADJUD

B70

BLACKSTONE W.,COMMENTARIES ON THE LAWS OF ENGLAND (4 VOLS.) (4TH ED.). UK CHIEF DELIB/GP LEGIS WORKER CT/SYS SANCTION CRIME OWN...CRIMLGY 18 ENGLSH/LAW. PAGE 12 E0238
LAW
JURID
ADJUD
CONSTN

B73

AUSTIN J.,LECTURES ON JURISPRUDENCE OR THE PHILOSOPHY OF POSITIVE LAW (VOL. II) (4TH ED., REV.). UK CONSTN STRUCT PROB/SOLV LEGIT CT/SYS SANCTION CRIME INGP/REL OWN SUPEGO ORD/FREE...T 19. PAGE 6 E0120
LAW
ADJUD
JURID
METH/CNCPT

B77

CADWALDER J.L.,DIGEST OF THE PUBLISHED OPINIONS OF THE ATTORNEYS-GENERAL, AND OF THE LEADING DECISIONS OF THE FEDERAL COURTS (REV ED). USA-45 NAT/G JUDGE PROB/SOLV DIPLOM ATTIT...POLICY INT/LAW ANTHOL 19. PAGE 18 E0356
BIBLIOG
CT/SYS
DECISION
ADJUD

L86

GOODNOW F.J.,"AN EXECUTIVE AND THE COURTS: JUDICIAL REMEDIES AGAINST ADMINISTRATIVE ACTION" FRANCE UK USA-45 WOR-45 LAW CONSTN SANCTION ORD/FREE 19. PAGE 45 E0888
CT/SYS
GOV/REL
ADMIN
ADJUD

L86

WHITRIDGE L.I.,"LEGISLATIVE INQUESTS" USA-45 ADJUD GOV/REL SOVEREIGN 19/20 CONGRESS. PAGE 106 E2120
CT/SYS
LEGIS
JURID
CONSTN

B89

FICHTE J.G.,THE SCIENCE OF RIGHTS (TRANS. BY A.E. KROEGER). WOR-45 FAM MUNIC NAT/G PROVS ADJUD CRIME CHOOSE MARRIAGE SEX POPULISM 19 FICHTE/JG NATURL/LAW. PAGE 37 E0744
ORD/FREE
CONSTN
LAW
CONCPT

B90

BURGESS J.W.,POLITICAL SCIENCE AND COMPARATIVE CONSTITUTIONAL LAW. FRANCE GERMANY UK USA-45 LEGIS DIPLOM ADJUD REPRESENT...CONCPT 19. PAGE 17 E0340
CONSTN
LAW
LOC/G
NAT/G

B91

SIDGWICK H.,THE ELEMENTS OF POLITICS. LOC/G NAT/G LEGIS DIPLOM ADJUD CONTROL EXEC PARL/PROC REPRESENT GOV/REL SOVEREIGN ALL/IDEOS 19 MILL/JS BENTHAM/J. PAGE 91 E1822
POLICY
LAW
CONCPT

B92

LOWELL A.L.,ESSAYS ON GOVERNMENT. UK USA-45 LEGIS PARL/PROC...POLICY PREDICT 19. PAGE 66 E1328
CONSTN
ADJUD

CT/SYS
NAT/G

B96
ESMEIN A.,ELEMENTS DE DROIT CONSTITUTIONNEL. FRANCE LAW
UK CHIEF EX/STRUC LEGIS ADJUD CT/SYS PARL/PROC REV CONSTN
GOV/REL ORD/FREE...JURID METH/COMP 18/19. PAGE 35 NAT/G
E0697 CONCPT

B97
US DEPARTMENT OF STATE,CATALOGUE OF WORKS RELATING BIBLIOG/A
TO THE LAW OF NATIONS AND DIPLOMACY IN THE LIBRARY DIPLOM
OF THE DEPARTMENT OF STATE (PAMPHLET). WOR-45 NAT/G LAW
ADJUD CT/SYS...INT/LAW JURID 19. PAGE 100 E2000

B98
POLLOCK F.,THE HISTORY OF ENGLISH LAW BEFORE THE LAW
TIME OF EDWARD I (2 VOLS, 2ND ED.). UK CULTURE ADJUD
LOC/G LEGIS LICENSE AGREE CONTROL CT/SYS SANCTION JURID
CRIME...TIME/SEQ 13 COMMON/LAW CANON/LAW. PAGE 81
E1626

B99
LILLY W.S.,FIRST PRINCIPLES IN POLITICS. UNIV LAW NAT/G
LEGIS DOMIN ADJUD INGP/REL ORD/FREE SOVEREIGN CONSTN
...JURID CONCPT 19 NATURL/LAW. PAGE 65 E1299 MORAL
POLICY

ADJUST....SOCIAL ADJUSTMENT, SOCIALIZATION. SEE ALSO INGP/REL

C01
BERKELEY G.,"DISCOURSE ON PASSIVE OBEDIENCE" (1712) INGP/REL
THE WORKS... (VOL. IV)" UNIV DOMIN LEGIT CONTROL SANCTION
CRIME ADJUST CENTRAL MORAL ORD/FREE...POLICY RESPECT
WORSHIP. PAGE 10 E0202 GEN/LAWS

B06
GRIFFIN A.P.C.,SELECT LIST OF REFERENCES ON THE BIBLIOG/A
NEGRO QUESTION (REV. ED.). USA-45 CONSTN SCHOOL RACE/REL
SUFF ADJUST...JURID SOC/INTEG 19/20 NEGRO. PAGE 47 DISCRIM
E0930 ATTIT

B35
HALL J.,THEFT, LAW, AND SOCIETY. SOCIETY PROB/SOLV CRIME
...CRIMLGY SOC CONCPT TREND METH/COMP 18/20 LAW
LARCENCY. PAGE 49 E0982 ADJUD
ADJUST

B35
NORDSKOG J.E.,SOCIAL REFORM IN NORWAY. NORWAY INDUS LABOR
NAT/G POL/PAR LEGIS ADJUD...SOC BIBLIOG SOC/INTEG ADJUST
20. PAGE 78 E1555

B42
GILLETTE J.M.,PROBLEMS OF A CHANGING SOCIAL ORDER. BIO/SOC
USA+45 STRATA FAM CONTROL CRIME RACE/REL HEALTH ADJUST
WEALTH...GEOG GP/COMP. PAGE 43 E0862 ATTIT
SOC/WK

B46
GILLIN J.L.,SOCIAL PATHOLOGY. SOCIETY SECT CRIME SOC
ANOMIE DISPL ORD/FREE WEALTH...CRIMLGY PSY WORSHIP. ADJUST
PAGE 44 E0864 CULTURE
INGP/REL

B46
MANNHEIM H.,CRIMINAL JUSTICE AND SOCIAL ADJUD
RECONSTRUCTION. USA+45 EDU/PROP CRIME ANOMIE LAW
...JURID BIBLIOG 20. PAGE 68 E1361 STRUCT
ADJUST

S47
ANGELL R.C.,"THE SOCIAL INTEGRATION OF AMERICAN MUNIC
CITIES OF MORE THAN 1000,000 POPULATION" (BMR)" CENSUS
USA+45 SOCIETY CRIME ADJUST WEALTH...GEOG SOC GP/REL
CONCPT INDICATOR SAMP CHARTS SOC/INTEG 20. PAGE 5
E0098

N53
US PRES CONF ADMIN PROCEDURE,REPORT (PAMPHLET). NAT/G
USA+45 CONFER ADJUD...METH/COMP 20 PRESIDENT. DELIB/GP
PAGE 101 E2024 ADJUST
ADMIN

B57
DIVINE R.A.,AMERICAN IMMIGRATION POLICY, 1924-52. GEOG
USA+45 USA-45 VOL/ASSN DELIB/GP ADJUD WAR ADJUST HABITAT
DISCRIM...POLICY JURID 20 DEPRESSION MIGRATION. LEGIS
PAGE 32 E0630 CONTROL

B59
COUNCIL OF STATE GOVERNMENTS,STATE GOVERNMENT: AN BIBLIOG/A
ANNOTATED BIBLIOGRAPHY (PAMPHLET). USA+45 LAW AGRI PROVS
INDUS WORKER PLAN TAX ADJUST AGE/Y ORD/FREE...HEAL LOC/G
MGT 20. PAGE 26 E0521 ADMIN

B59
LAPIERE R.,THE FREUDIAN ETHIC. USA+45 FAM EDU/PROP PSY
CONTROL CRIME ADJUST AGE DRIVE PERCEPT PERSON SEX ORD/FREE
...SOC 20 FREUD/S. PAGE 63 E1254 SOCIETY

S59
CLOWARD R.A.,"ILLEGITIMATE MEANS, ANOMIE, AND ANOMIE
DEVIANT BEHAVIOR" STRUCT CRIME DRIVE PERSON...SOC CRIMLGY
CONCPT NEW/IDEA 20 DURKHEIM/E MERTON/R. PAGE 23 LEGIT
E0459 ADJUST

B60
CONANT M.,ANTITRUST IN THE MOTION PICTURE INDUSTRY: PRICE
ECONOMIC AND LEGAL ANALYSIS. USA+45 MARKET ADJUST CONTROL
DEMAND BIBLIOG. PAGE 24 E0484 LAW
ART/METH

B61
COWEN D.V.,THE FOUNDATIONS OF FREEDOM. AFR CONSTN
SOUTH/AFR DOMIN LEGIT ADJUST DISCRIM TOTALISM ATTIT ELITES
ORD/FREE...MAJORIT JURID SOC/INTEG WORSHIP 20 RACE/REL
NEGRO. PAGE 27 E0529

B61
SYATAUW J.J.G.,SOME NEWLY ESTABLISHED ASIAN STATES INT/LAW
AND THE DEVELOPMENT OF INTERNATIONAL LAW. BURMA ADJUST
CEYLON INDIA INDONESIA ECO/UNDEV COLONIAL NEUTRAL SOCIETY
WAR PEACE SOVEREIGN...CHARTS 19/20. PAGE 95 E1902 S/ASIA

L61
SILVING H.,"IN RE EICHMANN: A DILEMMA OF LAW AND CT/SYS
MORALITY" WOR+45 INSPECT ADJUST MORAL...JURID 20 INT/LAW
WAR/TRIAL EICHMANN/A NATURL/LAW. PAGE 91 E1828 CONCPT

S61
AGNEW P.C.,"INTRODUCING CHANGE IN A MENTAL ORD/FREE
HOSPITAL." CLIENT WORKER PROB/SOLV INGP/REL PUB/INST
PERS/REL ADJUST. PAGE 3 E0054 PSY
ADMIN

B62
MITCHELL G.E.,THE ANGRY BLACK SOUTH. USA+45 LAW RACE/REL
CONSTN SCHOOL DELIB/GP EDU/PROP CONTROL SUFF ANOMIE DISCRIM
DRIVE...ANTHOL 20 NEGRO CIV/RIGHTS SOUTH/US. ADJUST
PAGE 74 E1473 ORD/FREE

B63
REALE M.,PLURALISMO E LIBERDADE. STRUCT ADJUST CONCPT
ATTIT 20 CIVIL/LIB. PAGE 84 E1676 ORD/FREE
JURID
INGP/REL

B64
DRESSLER D.,READINGS IN CRIMINOLOGY AND PENOLOGY. CRIMLGY
UNIV CULTURE PUB/INST FORCES ACT/RES PROB/SOLV CRIME
ANOMIE BIO/SOC SUPEGO...GEOG PSY ANTHOL 20. PAGE 33 ADJUD
E0648 ADJUST

B64
TAUBENFELD H.J.,SPACE AND SOCIETY. USA+45 LAW SPACE
FORCES CREATE TEC/DEV ADJUD CONTROL COST PEACE SOCIETY
...PREDICT ANTHOL 20. PAGE 95 E1911 ADJUST
DIPLOM

S64
N,"QUASI-LEGISLATIVE ARBITRATION AGREEMENTS." LAW ADJUD
LG/CO ECO/TAC SANCTION ATTIT POLICY. PAGE 76 E1516 LAW
LABOR
GP/REL

B65
HIGGINS R.,CONFLICT OF INTERESTS* INTERNATIONAL LAW INT/LAW
IN A DIVIDED WORLD. ASIA USSR ECO/DEV ECO/UNDEV IDEA/COMP
SECT INT/TRADE COLD/WAR WORSHIP. PAGE 52 E1042 ADJUST

B65
KUPER H.,AFRICAN LAW. LAW FAM KIN SECT JUDGE ADJUST AFR
NAT/LISM 17/20. PAGE 62 E1236 CT/SYS
ADJUD
COLONIAL

B65
SEN B.,A DIPLOMAT'S HANDBOOK OF INTERNATIONAL LAW DIPLOM
AND PRACTICE. WOR+45 NAT/G ADJUST. PAGE 90 E1803 INT/LAW
TASK
LAW

S65
MARTIN A.,"PROLIFERATION." FUT WOR+45 PROB/SOLV RECORD
REGION ADJUST...PREDICT NAT/COMP UN TREATY. PAGE 69 NUC/PWR
E1372 ARMS/CONT
VOL/ASSN

B66
MACIVER R.M.,THE PREVENTION AND CONTROL OF AGE/Y
DELINQUENCY. USA+45 STRATA PUB/INST ANOMIE ATTIT PLAN

HABITAT PERSON HEALTH...CRIMLGY PSY SOC METH.
PAGE 67 E1341
ADJUST
CRIME

B66
MILLER E.W.,THE NEGRO IN AMERICA: A BIBLIOGRAPHY.
USA+45 LAW EDU/PROP REV GOV/REL GP/REL INGP/REL
ADJUST HABITAT PERSON HEALTH ORD/FREE SOC/INTEG 20
NEGRO. PAGE 73 E1459
BIBLIOG
DISCRIM
RACE/REL

B66
STUMPF S.E.,MORALITY AND THE LAW. USA+45 LAW
CULTURE PROB/SOLV DOMIN ADJUD CONTROL ADJUST
ALL/IDEOS MARXISM...INT/LAW 20 SUPREME/CT. PAGE 94
E1890
JURID
MORAL
CT/SYS

B67
LOBLE L.H.,DELINQUENCY CAN BE STOPPED. FAM PUB/INST
CT/SYS ADJUST ATTIT...NEW/IDEA METH/COMP 20.
PAGE 66 E1315
AGE/Y
PROB/SOLV
ADJUD
CRIME

L67
SCHUBERT G.,"THE RHETORIC OF CONSTITUTIONAL
CHANGE." USA+45 LAW CULTURE CHIEF LEGIS ADJUD
CT/SYS ARMS/CONT ADJUST...CHARTS SIMUL. PAGE 89
E1777
CONSTN
METH/COMP
ORD/FREE

S67
KENNEDY R.F.,"TOWARD A NATION WHERE THE LAW IS
KING." PLAN CT/SYS CRIME INGP/REL...JURID SOC.
PAGE 60 E1202
CRIMLGY
ADJUST
LAW
PUB/INST

S67
KIM R.C.C.,"THE SUPREME COURT: ORALLE WITHOUT
TRUTH." USA+45 EDU/PROP RACE/REL ADJUST ALL/VALS
ORD/FREE...DECISION WORSHIP SUPREME/CT. PAGE 61
E1214
CT/SYS
PROB/SOLV
ADJUD
REPRESENT

S67
SCHELLING T.C.,"ECONOMICS AND CRIMINAL ENTERPRISE."
LAW FORCES BARGAIN ECO/TAC CONTROL GAMBLE ROUTINE
ADJUST DEMAND INCOME PROFIT CRIMLGY. PAGE 87 E1756
CRIME
PROB/SOLV
CONCPT

S67
SCOTT A.,"TWENTY-FIVE YEARS OF OPINION ON
INTEGRATION IN TEXAS." USA+45 USA-45 DISCRIM
...KNO/TEST TREND CHARTS 20 TEXAS. PAGE 89 E1794
ATTIT
ADJUST
RACE/REL
LAW

B97
JENKS E.J.,LAW AND POLITICS IN THE MIDDLE AGES.
CHRIST-17C CULTURE STRUCT KIN NAT/G SECT CT/SYS
GP/REL...CLASSIF CHARTS IDEA/COMP BIBLIOG 8/16.
PAGE 58 E1162
LAW
SOCIETY
ADJUST

ADJUSTMENT, SOCIAL....SEE ADJUST

ADLER M.J. E0049

ADLER/A....ALFRED ADLER

ADMIN....ORGANIZATIONAL BEHAVIOR, NONEXECUTIVE

N
CONOVER H.F.,OFFICIAL PUBLICATIONS OF BRITISH EAST
AFRICA (PAMPHLET). UK LAW ECO/UNDEV AGRI EXTR/IND
SECT LEGIS BUDGET TAX...HEAL STAT 20. PAGE 25 E0491
BIBLIOG/A
AFR
ADMIN
COLONIAL

B
DEUTSCHE BIBLIOTH FRANKF A M,DEUTSCHE
BIBLIOGRAPHIE. EUR+WWI GERMANY ECO/DEV FORCES
DIPLOM LEAD...POLICY PHIL/SCI SOC 20. PAGE 31 E0612
BIBLIOG
LAW
ADMIN
NAT/G

N
AMERICAN POLITICAL SCIENCE REVIEW. USA+45 USA-45
WOR+45 WOR-45 INT/ORG ADMIN...INT/LAW PHIL/SCI
CONCPT METH 20 UN. PAGE 1 E0002
BIBLIOG/A
DIPLOM
NAT/G
GOV/COMP

N
INDEX TO LEGAL PERIODICALS. CANADA NEW/ZEALND UK
USA+45 USA-45 CONSTN LEGIS JUDGE ADJUD ADMIN
CONTROL CT/SYS FEDERAL...CRIMLGY INT/LAW 20
CMN/WLTH AUSTRAL. PAGE 1 E0006
BIBLIOG
INDEX
LAW
JURID

N
ADVANCED MANAGEMENT. INDUS EX/STRUC WORKER OP/RES
...DECISION BIBLIOG/A 20. PAGE 1 E0015
MGT
ADMIN
LABOR
GP/REL

N
DEUTSCHE BIBLIOGRAPHIE, HALBJAHRESVERZEICHNIS.
BIBLIOG

WOR+45 LAW ADMIN PERSON. PAGE 1 E0020
NAT/G
DIPLOM

HANDBOOK OF LATIN AMERICAN STUDIES. LAW CULTURE
ECO/UNDEV POL/PAR ADMIN LEAD...SOC 20. PAGE 1 E0022
BIBLIOG/A
L/A+17C
NAT/G
DIPLOM

THE JAPAN SCIENCE REVIEW: LAW AND POLITICS: LIST OF
BOOKS AND ARTICLES ON LAW AND POLITICS. CONSTN AGRI
INDUS LABOR DIPLOM TAX ADMIN CRIME...INT/LAW SOC 20
CHINJAP. PAGE 2 E0027
BIBLIOG
LAW
S/ASIA
PHIL/SCI

NEUE POLITISCHE LITERATUR; BERICHTE UBER DAS
INTERNATIONALE SCHRIFTTUM ZUR POLITIK. WOR+45 LAW
CONSTN POL/PAR ADMIN LEAD GOV/REL...POLICY
IDEA/COMP. PAGE 2 E0028
BIBLIOG/A
DIPLOM
NAT/G
NAT/COMP

N
PERSONNEL. USA+45 LAW LABOR LG/CO WORKER CREATE
GOV/REL PERS/REL ATTIT WEALTH. PAGE 2 E0029
BIBLIOG/A
ADMIN
MGT
GP/REL

N
CATHERINE R.,LA REVUE ADMINISTRATIVE. FRANCE LAW
NAT/G LEGIS...JURID BIBLIOG/A 20. PAGE 21 E0407
ADMIN
MGT
FINAN
METH/COMP

N
DEUTSCHE BUCHEREI,JAHRESVERZEICHNIS DER DEUTSCHEN
HOCHSCHULSCHRIFTEN. EUR+WWI GERMANY LAW ADMIN
PERSON...MGT SOC 19/20. PAGE 31 E0613
BIBLIOG
WRITING
ACADEM
INTELL

N
DEUTSCHE BUCHEREI,JAHRESVERZEICHNIS DES DEUTSCHEN
SCHRIFTUMS. AUSTRIA EUR+WWI GERMANY SWITZERLND LAW
LOC/G DIPLOM ADMIN...MGT SOC 19/20. PAGE 31 E0614
BIBLIOG
WRITING
NAT/G

N
DEUTSCHE BUCHEREI,DEUTSCHES BUCHERVERZEICHNIS.
GERMANY LAW CULTURE POL/PAR ADMIN LEAD ATTIT PERSON
...SOC 20. PAGE 31 E0615
BIBLIOG
NAT/G
DIPLOM
ECO/DEV

N
MINISTERE DE L'EDUC NATIONALE,CATALOGUE DES THESES
DE DOCTORAT SOUTENNES DEVANT LES UNIVERSITAIRES
FRANCAISES. FRANCE LAW DIPLOM ADMIN...HUM SOC 20.
PAGE 73 E1465
BIBLIOG
ACADEM
KNOWL
NAT/G

N
PUBLISHERS' CIRCULAR LIMITED,THE ENGLISH CATALOGUE
OF BOOKS. UK WOR+45 WOR-45 LAW CULTURE LOC/G NAT/G
ADMIN LEAD...MGT 19/20. PAGE 83 E1658
BIBLIOG
ALL/VALS
ALL/IDEOS
SOCIETY

N
UNESCO,INTERNATIONAL BIBLIOGRAPHY OF POLITICAL
SCIENCE (VOLUMES 1-8). WOR+45 LAW NAT/G EX/STRUC
LEGIS PROB/SOLV DIPLOM ADMIN GOV/REL 20 UNESCO.
PAGE 98 E1957
BIBLIOG
CONCPT
IDEA/COMP

N
UNITED NATIONS,OFFICIAL RECORDS OF THE UNITED
NATIONS' GENERAL ASSEMBLY. WOR+45 BUDGET DIPLOM
ADMIN 20 UN. PAGE 98 E1964
INT/ORG
DELIB/GP
INT/LAW
WRITING

N
UNITED NATIONS,UNITED NATIONS PUBLICATIONS. WOR+45
ECO/UNDEV AGRI FINAN FORCES ADMIN LEAD WAR PEACE
...POLICY INT/LAW 20 UN. PAGE 98 E1965
BIBLIOG
INT/ORG
DIPLOM

US SUPERINTENDENT OF DOCUMENTS,EDUCATION (PRICE
LIST 31). USA+45 LAW FINAN LOC/G NAT/G DEBATE ADMIN
LEAD RACE/REL FEDERAL HEALTH POLICY. PAGE 103 E2062
BIBLIOG/A
EDU/PROP
ACADEM
SCHOOL

N
US SUPERINTENDENT OF DOCUMENTS,POLITICAL SCIENCE:
GOVERNMENT, CRIME, DISTRICT OF COLUMBIA (PRICE LIST
54). USA+45 LAW CONSTN EX/STRUC WORKER ADJUD ADMIN
CT/SYS CHOOSE INGP/REL RACE/REL CONGRESS PRESIDENT.
PAGE 103 E2063
BIBLIOG/A
NAT/G
CRIME

B00
GRIFFIN A.P.C.,LIST OF BOOKS RELATING TO THE THEORY
OF COLONIZATION, GOVERNMENT OF DEPENDENCIES,
PROTECTORATES, AND RELATED TOPICS. FRANCE GERMANY
BIBLIOG/A
COLONIAL
GOV/REL

ITALY SPAIN UK USA-45 WOR-45 ECO/TAC ADMIN CONTROL   DOMIN
REGION NAT/LISM ALL/VALS PWR...INT/LAW SOC 16/19.
PAGE 46 E0917

                                                       B03
FAGUET E.,LE LIBERALISME. FRANCE PRESS ADJUD ADMIN   ORD/FREE
DISCRIM CONSERVE SOCISM...TRADIT SOC LING WORSHIP   EDU/PROP
PARLIAMENT. PAGE 36 E0711   NAT/G
                                                       LAW

                                                       B05
GOODNOW F.J.,THE PRINCIPLES OF THE ADMINISTRATIVE   ADMIN
LAW OF THE UNITED STATES. USA-45 LAW STRUCT   NAT/G
EX/STRUC LEGIS BAL/PWR CONTROL GOV/REL PWR...JURID   PROVS
19/20 CIVIL/SERV. PAGE 45 E0887   LOC/G

                                                       B05
GRIFFIN A.P.C.,LIST OF BOOKS ON RAILROADS IN   BIBLIOG/A
FOREIGN COUNTRIES. MOD/EUR ECO/DEV NAT/G CONTROL   SERV/IND
SOCISM...JURID 19/20 RAILROAD. PAGE 47 E0927   ADMIN
                                                       DIST/IND

                                                       B06
FOSTER J.W.,THE PRACTICE OF DIPLOMACY AS   DIPLOM
ILLUSTRATED IN THE FOREIGN RELATIONS OF THE UNITED   ROUTINE
STATES. MOD/EUR USA-45 NAT/G EX/STRUC ADMIN   PHIL/SCI
...POLICY INT/LAW BIBLIOG 19/20. PAGE 39 E0777

                                                       B09
HARVARD UNIVERSITY LAW LIBRARY,CATALOGUE OF THE   BIBLIOG/A
LIBRARY OF THE LAW SCHOOL OF HARVARD UNIVERSITY (3   LAW
VOLS.). UK USA-45 LEGIS JUDGE ADJUD CT/SYS...JURID   ADMIN
CHARTS 14/20. PAGE 51 E1008

                                                       B10
COLORADO CIVIL SERVICE COMN,SECOND BIENNIAL REPORT   PROVS
TO THE GOVERNOR, 1909-1910. USA+45 DELIB/GP LEGIS   LOC/G
LICENSE PAY 20 COLORADO CIVIL/SERV. PAGE 24 E0477   ADMIN
                                                       WORKER

                                                       B12
FOUAD M.,LE REGIME DE LA PRESSE EN EGYPTE: THESE   ORD/FREE
POUR LE DOCTORAT. UAR LICENSE EDU/PROP ADMIN   LEGIS
SANCTION CRIME SUPEGO PWR...ART/METH JURID 19/20.   CONTROL
PAGE 39 E0778   PRESS

                                                       B12
POLLOCK F.,THE GENIUS OF THE COMMON LAW. CHRIST-17C   LAW
UK FINAN CHIEF ACT/RES ADMIN GP/REL ATTIT SOCISM   CULTURE
...ANARCH JURID. PAGE 81 E1624   CREATE

                                                       B14
MCLAUGHLIN A.C.,CYCLOPEDIA OF AMERICAN GOVERNMENT   USA+45
(3 VOLS.). LAW CONSTN POL/PAR ADMIN ROUTINE   NAT/G
...INT/LAW CONCPT BIBLIOG METH 20. PAGE 71 E1421   DICTIONARY

                                                       B15
SAWYER R.A.,A LIST OF WORKS ON COUNTY GOVERNMENT.   BIBLIOG/A
LAW FINAN MUNIC TOP/EX ROUTINE CRIME...CLASSIF   LOC/G
RECORD 19/20. PAGE 87 E1748   GOV/REL
                                                       ADMIN

                                                       B19
LONDON SCHOOL ECONOMICS-POL,ANNUAL DIGEST OF PUBLIC   BIBLIOG/A
INTERNATIONAL LAW CASES. INT/ORG MUNIC NAT/G PROVS   INT/LAW
ADMIN NEUTRAL WAR GOV/REL PRIVIL 20. PAGE 66 E1323   ADJUD
                                                       DIPLOM

                                                       N19
ARNOW K.,SELF-INSURANCE IN THE TREASURY (PAMPHLET).   ADMIN
USA+45 LAW RIGID/FLEX...POLICY METH/COMP 20   PLAN
DEPT/TREAS. PAGE 5 E0104   EFFICIENCY
                                                       NAT/G

                                                       N19
BURRUS B.R.,INVESTIGATION AND DISCOVERY IN STATE   NAT/G
ANTITRUST (PAMPHLET). USA+45 USA-45 LEGIS ECO/TAC   PROVS
ADMIN CONTROL CT/SYS CRIME GOV/REL PWR...JURID   LAW
CHARTS 19/20 FTC MONOPOLY. PAGE 18 E0346   INSPECT

                                                       N19
POUND R.,ORGANIZATION OF THE COURTS (PAMPHLET).   CT/SYS
MOD/EUR UK USA-45 ADJUD PWR...GOV/COMP 10/20   JURID
EUROPE. PAGE 82 E1635   STRUCT
                                                       ADMIN

                                                       C20
BLACHLY F.F.,"THE GOVERNMENT AND ADMINISTRATION OF   NAT/G
GERMANY." GERMANY CONSTN LOC/G PROVS DELIB/GP   GOV/REL
EX/STRUC FORCES LEGIS TOP/EX CT/SYS...BIBLIOG/A   ADMIN
19/20. PAGE 12 E0235   PHIL/SCI

                                                       B22
MYERS D.P.,MANUAL OF COLLECTIONS OF TREATIES AND OF   BIBLIOG/A
COLLECTIONS RELATING TO TREATIES. MOD/EUR INT/ORG   DIPLOM
LEGIS WRITING ADMIN SOVEREIGN...INT/LAW 19/20.   CONFER

PAGE 75 E1514

                                                       B24
HOLDSWORTH W.S.,A HISTORY OF ENGLISH LAW; THE   LAW
COMMON LAW AND ITS RIVALS (VOL. V). UK SEA EX/STRUC   LEGIS
WRITING ADMIN...INT/LAW JURID CONCPT IDEA/COMP   ADJUD
WORSHIP 16/17 PARLIAMENT ENGLSH/LAW COMMON/LAW.   CT/SYS
PAGE 54 E1073

                                                       B24
HOLDSWORTH W.S.,A HISTORY OF ENGLISH LAW; THE   LAW
COMMON LAW AND ITS RIVALS (VOL. VI). UK STRATA   CONSTN
EX/STRUC ADJUD ADMIN CONTROL CT/SYS...JURID CONCPT   LEGIS
GEN/LAWS 17 COMMONWLTH PARLIAMENT ENGLSH/LAW   CHIEF
COMMON/LAW. PAGE 54 E1074

                                                       B26
FORTESCUE J.,THE GOVERNANCE OF ENGLAND (1471-76).   CONSERVE
UK LAW FINAN SECT LEGIS PROB/SOLV TAX DOMIN ADMIN   CONSTN
GP/REL COST ORD/FREE PWR 14/15. PAGE 39 E0776   CHIEF
                                                       NAT/G

                                                       B27
DICKINSON J.,ADMINISTRATIVE JUSTICE AND THE   CT/SYS
SUPREMACY OF LAW IN THE UNITED STATES. USA-45 LAW   ADJUD
INDUS DOMIN EDU/PROP CONTROL EXEC GP/REL ORD/FREE   ADMIN
...POLICY JURID 19/20. PAGE 31 E0623   NAT/G

                                                       B29
BUELL R.,INTERNATIONAL RELATIONS. WOR+45 WOR-45   INT/ORG
CONSTN STRATA FORCES TOP/EX ADMIN ATTIT DRIVE   BAL/PWR
SUPEGO MORAL ORD/FREE PWR SOVEREIGN...JURID SOC   DIPLOM
CONCPT 20. PAGE 17 E0326

                                                       B29
CAM H.M.,BIBLIOGRAPHY OF ENGLISH CONSTITUTIONAL   BIBLIOG/A
HISTORY (PAMPHLET). UK LAW LOC/G NAT/G POL/PAR SECT   CONSTN
DELIB/GP ADJUD ORD/FREE 19/20 PARLIAMENT. PAGE 19   ADMIN
E0369   PARL/PROC

                                                       C29
BUCK A.E.,"PUBLIC BUDGETING." USA-45 FINAN LOC/G   BUDGET
NAT/G LEGIS BAL/PAY COST...JURID TREND BIBLIOG/A   ROUTINE
20. PAGE 17 E0324   ADMIN

                                                       B30
FAIRLIE J.A.,COUNTY GOVERNMENT AND ADMINISTRATION.   ADMIN
UK USA-45 NAT/G SCHOOL FORCES BUDGET TAX CT/SYS   GOV/REL
CHOOSE...JURID BIBLIOG 11/20. PAGE 36 E0713   LOC/G
                                                       MUNIC

                                                       B31
BORCHARD E.H.,GUIDE TO THE LAW AND LEGAL LITERATURE   BIBLIOG/A
OF FRANCE. FRANCE FINAN INDUS LABOR SECT LEGIS   LAW
ADMIN COLONIAL CRIME OWN...INT/LAW 20. PAGE 14   CONSTN
E0266   METH

                                                       B33
AMERICAN FOREIGN LAW ASSN,BIOGRAPHICAL NOTES ON THE   BIBLIOG/A
LAWS AND LEGAL LITERATURE OF URUGUAY AND CURACAO.   LAW
URUGUAY CONSTN FINAN SECT FORCES JUDGE DIPLOM   JURID
INT/TRADE ADJUD CT/SYS CRIME 20. PAGE 4 E0078   ADMIN

                                                       B33
ENSOR R.C.K.,COURTS AND JUDGES IN FRANCE, GERMANY,   CT/SYS
AND ENGLAND. FRANCE GERMANY UK LAW PROB/SOLV ADMIN   EX/STRUC
ROUTINE CRIME ROLE...METH/COMP 20 CIVIL/LAW.   ADJUD
PAGE 35 E0692   NAT/COMP

                                                       B34
CUMMINGS H.,LIBERTY UNDER LAW AND ADMINISTRATION.   ORD/FREE
MOD/EUR USA-45 ADMIN ATTIT...JURID PHIL/SCI.   LAW
PAGE 28 E0553   NAT/G
                                                       SOCIETY

                                                       B34
US TARIFF COMMISSION,THE TARIFF: A BIBLIOGRAPHY: A   BIBLIOG/A
SELECT LIST OF REFERENCES. USA-45 LAW DIPLOM TAX   TARIFFS
ADMIN...POLICY TREATY 20. PAGE 103 E2064   ECO/TAC

                                                       B35
BURCHFIELD L.,STUDENT'S GUIDE TO MATERIALS IN   BIBLIOG
POLITICAL SCIENCE. FINAN INT/ORG NAT/G POL/PAR   INDEX
DIPLOM PRESS ADMIN...BIOG 18/19. PAGE 17 E0328   LAW

                                                       B35
KENNEDY W.P.,THE LAW AND CUSTOM OF THE SOUTH   CT/SYS
AFRICAN CONSTITUTION. AFR SOUTH/AFR KIN LOC/G PROVS   CONSTN
DIPLOM ADJUD ADMIN EXEC 20. PAGE 60 E1203   JURID
                                                       PARL/PROC

                                                       B35
LUCE R.,LEGISLATIVE PROBLEMS. CONSTN CHIEF JUDGE   TREND
BUDGET CONFER ETIQUET CONTROL MORAL PWR NEW/LIB   ADMIN
CONGRESS. PAGE 67 E1331   LEGIS

B36
GRAVES W.B.,AMERICAN STATE GOVERNMENT. CONSTN FINAN NAT/G
EX/STRUC FORCES LEGIS BUDGET TAX CT/SYS REPRESENT PROVS
GOV/REL...BIBLIOG/A 19/20. PAGE 45 E0900 ADMIN
FEDERAL

B36
HERRING E.P.,PUBLIC ADMINISTRATION AND THE PUBLIC GP/REL
INTEREST. LABOR NAT/G PARTIC EFFICIENCY 20. PAGE 52 DECISION
E1033 PROB/SOLV
ADMIN

B37
BUREAU OF NATIONAL AFFAIRS,LABOR RELATIONS LABOR
REFERENCE MANUAL VOL 1, 1935-1937. BARGAIN DEBATE ADMIN
ROUTINE INGP/REL 20 NLRB. PAGE 17 E0335 ADJUD
NAT/G

B38
FIELD G.L.,THE SYNDICAL AND CORPORATIVE FASCISM
INSTITUTIONS OF ITALIAN FASCISM. ITALY CONSTN INDUS
STRATA LABOR EX/STRUC TOP/EX ADJUD ADMIN LEAD NAT/G
TOTALISM AUTHORIT...MGT 20 MUSSOLIN/B. PAGE 38 WORKER
E0746

B38
HARPER S.N.,THE GOVERNMENT OF THE SOVIET UNION. COM MARXISM
USSR LAW CONSTN ECO/DEV PLAN TEC/DEV DIPLOM NAT/G
INT/TRADE ADMIN REV NAT/LISM...POLICY 20. PAGE 50 LEAD
E1001 POL/PAR

B38
HOLDSWORTH W.S.,A HISTORY OF ENGLISH LAW; THE LAW
CENTURIES OF SETTLEMENT AND REFORM (VOL. X). INDIA LOC/G
UK CONSTN NAT/G CHIEF LEGIS ADMIN COLONIAL CT/SYS EX/STRUC
CHOOSE ORD/FREE PWR...JURID 18 PARLIAMENT ADJUD
COMMONWLTH COMMON/LAW. PAGE 54 E1077

B40
ANDERSON W.,FUNDAMENTALS OF AMERICAN GOVERNMENT. NAT/G
USA-45 LAW POL/PAR CHIEF EX/STRUC BUDGET ADMIN LOC/G
CT/SYS PARL/PROC CHOOSE FEDERAL...BIBLIOG 20. GOV/REL
PAGE 5 E0093 CONSTN

B40
HART J.,AN INTRODUCTION TO ADMINISTRATIVE LAW, WITH LAW
SELECTED CASES. USA-45 CONSTN SOCIETY NAT/G ADMIN
EX/STRUC ADJUD CT/SYS LEAD CRIME ORD/FREE LEGIS
...DECISION JURID 20 CASEBOOK. PAGE 50 E1002 PWR

S40
GERTH H.,"THE NAZI PARTY: ITS LEADERSHIP AND POL/PAR
COMPOSITION" (BMR) GERMANY ELITES STRATA STRUCT DOMIN
EX/STRUC FORCES ECO/TAC CT/SYS CHOOSE TOTALISM LEAD
AGE/Y AUTHORIT PWR 20. PAGE 43 E0851 ADMIN

N40
COUNTY GOVERNMENT IN THE UNITED STATES: A LIST OF BIBLIOG/A
RECENT REFERENCES (PAMPHLET). USA-45 LAW PUB/INST LOC/G
PLAN BUDGET CT/SYS CENTRAL 20. PAGE 52 E1027 ADMIN
MUNIC

B41
EVANS C.,AMERICAN BIBLIOGRAPHY... (12 VOLUMES). BIBLIOG
USA-45 LAW DIPLOM ADMIN PERSON...HUM SOC 17/18. NAT/G
PAGE 35 E0704 ALL/VALS
ALL/IDEOS

B43
BACKUS R.C.,A GUIDE TO THE LAW AND LEGAL LITERATURE BIBLIOG/A
OF COLOMBIA. FINAN INDUS LABOR FORCES ADJUD ADMIN LAW
COLONIAL CT/SYS CRIME...INT/LAW JURID 20 COLOMB. CONSTN
PAGE 7 E0127 L/A+17C

B43
CLAGETT H.L.,A GUIDE TO THE LAW AND LEGAL BIBLIOG
LITERATURE OF PARAGUAY. PARAGUAY CONSTN COM/IND JURID
LABOR MUNIC JUDGE ADMIN CT/SYS...CRIMLGY INT/LAW LAW
CON/ANAL 20. PAGE 22 E0439 L/A+17C

B44
FULLER G.H.,MILITARY GOVERNMENT: A LIST OF BIBLIOG
REFERENCES (A PAMPHLET). ITALY UK USA-45 WOR-45 LAW DIPLOM
FORCES DOMIN ADMIN ARMS/CONT ORD/FREE PWR CIVMIL/REL
...DECISION 20 CHINJAP. PAGE 41 E0822 SOVEREIGN

S44
GRIFFITH E.S.,"THE CHANGING PATTERN OF PUBLIC LAW
POLICY FORMATION." MOD/EUR WOR-45 FINAN CHIEF POLICY
CONFER ADMIN LEAD CONSERVE SOCISM TECHRACY...SOC TEC/DEV
CHARTS CONGRESS. PAGE 47 E0938

B45
CLAGETT H.L.,A GUIDE TO THE LAW AND LEGAL BIBLIOG
LITERATURE OF THE MEXICAN STATES. CONSTN LEGIS JURID
JUDGE ADJUD ADMIN...INT/LAW CON/ANAL 20 MEXIC/AMER. L/A+17C

PAGE 22 E0440

LAW

B45
CONOVER H.F.,THE GOVERNMENTS OF THE MAJOR FOREIGN BIBLIOG
POWERS: A BIBLIOGRAPHY. FRANCE GERMANY ITALY UK NAT/G
USSR CONSTN LOC/G POL/PAR EX/STRUC FORCES ADMIN DIPLOM
CT/SYS CIVMIL/REL TOTALISM...POLICY 19/20. PAGE 25
E0494

B45
GALLOWAY E.,ABSTRACTS OF POSTWAR LITERATURE (VOL. BIBLIOG/A
IV) JAN.-JULY, 1945 NOS. 901-1074. POLAND USA+45 NUC/PWR
USSR WOR+45 INDUS LABOR PLAN ECO/TAC INT/TRADE TAX NAT/G
EDU/PROP ADMIN COLONIAL INT/LAW. PAGE 42 E0829 DIPLOM

B45
VANCE H.L.,GUIDE TO THE LAW AND LEGAL LITERATURE OF BIBLIOG/A
MEXICO. LAW CONSTN FINAN LABOR FORCES ADJUD ADMIN INT/LAW
...CRIMLGY PHIL/SCI CON/ANAL 20 MEXIC/AMER. JURID
PAGE 103 E2070 CT/SYS

B46
AMERICAN DOCUMENTATION INST,CATALOGUE OF AUXILIARY BIBLIOG
PUBLICATIONS IN MICROFILMS AND PHOTOPRINTS. USA-45 EDU/PROP
LAW AGRI CREATE TEC/DEV ADMIN...GEOG LING MATH 20. PSY
PAGE 4 E0077

B46
GRIFFIN G.G.,A GUIDE TO MANUSCRIPTS RELATING TO BIBLIOG/A
AMERICAN HISTORY IN BRITISH DEPOSITORIES. CANADA ALL/VALS
IRELAND MOD/EUR UK USA-45 LAW DIPLOM ADMIN COLONIAL NAT/G
WAR NAT/LISM SOVEREIGN...GEOG INT/LAW 15/19
CMN/WLTH. PAGE 47 E0936

C46
GOODRICH L.M.,"CHARTER OF THE UNITED NATIONS: CONSTN
COMMENTARY AND DOCUMENTS." EX/STRUC ADMIN...INT/LAW INT/ORG
CON/ANAL BIBLIOG 20 UN. PAGE 45 E0890 DIPLOM

B47
BORGESE G.,COMMON CAUSE. LAW CONSTN SOCIETY STRATA WOR+45
ECO/DEV INT/ORG POL/PAR FORCES LEGIS TOP/EX CAP/ISM NAT/G
DIPLOM ADMIN EXEC ATTIT PWR 20. PAGE 14 E0269 SOVEREIGN
REGION

B47
CLAGETT H.L.,A GUIDE TO THE LAW AND LEGAL BIBLIOG/A
LITERATURE OF BOLIVIA. L/A+17C CONSTN LABOR LEGIS JURID
ADMIN...CRIMLGY INT/LAW PHIL/SCI 16/20 BOLIV. LAW
PAGE 22 E0441 CT/SYS

B47
CLAGETT H.L.,A GUIDE TO THE LAW AND LEGAL BIBLIOG
LITERATURE OF CHILE, 1917-1946. CHILE CONSTN LABOR L/A+17C
JUDGE ADJUD ADMIN...CRIMLGY INT/LAW JURID CON/ANAL LAW
20. PAGE 22 E0442 LEGIS

B47
CLAGETT H.L.,A GUIDE TO THE LAW AND LEGAL BIBLIOG
LITERATURE OF ECUADOR. ECUADOR CONSTN LABOR LEGIS JURID
JUDGE ADJUD ADMIN CIVMIL/REL...CRIMLGY INT/LAW LAW
CON/ANAL 20. PAGE 22 E0443 L/A+17C

B47
CLAGETT H.L.,A GUIDE TO THE LAW AND LEGAL BIBLIOG
LITERATURE OF PERU. PERU CONSTN COM/IND LABOR MUNIC L/A+17C
JUDGE ADMIN CT/SYS...CRIMLGY INT/LAW JURID 20. PHIL/SCI
PAGE 23 E0444 LAW

B47
CLAGETT H.L.,A GUIDE TO THE LAW AND LEGAL BIBLIOG
LITERATURE OF URUGUAY. URUGUAY CONSTN COM/IND FINAN LAW
LABOR MUNIC JUDGE PRESS ADMIN CT/SYS...INT/LAW JURID
PHIL/SCI 20. PAGE 23 E0445 L/A+17C

B47
CLAGETT H.L.,A GUIDE TO THE LAW AND LEGAL BIBLIOG
LITERATURE OF VENEZUELA. VENEZUELA CONSTN LABOR L/A+17C
LEGIS JUDGE ADJUD ADMIN CIVMIL/REL...CRIMLGY JURID INT/LAW
CON/ANAL 20. PAGE 23 E0446 LAW

B47
DE NOIA J.,GUIDE TO OFFICIAL PUBLICATIONS OF THE BIBLIOG/A
OTHER AMERICAN REPUBLICS: EL SALVADOR. EL/SALVADR CONSTN
LAW LEGIS EDU/PROP CT/SYS 20. PAGE 30 E0590 NAT/G
ADMIN

B47
DE NOIA J.,GUIDE TO OFFICIAL PUBLICATIONS OF THE BIBLIOG/A
OTHER AMERICAN REPUBLICS: NICARAGUA (VOL. XIV). EDU/PROP
NICARAGUA LAW LEGIS ADMIN CT/SYS...JURID 19/20. NAT/G
PAGE 30 E0591 CONSTN

B47
DE NOIA J.,GUIDE TO OFFICIAL PUBLICATIONS OF THE BIBLIOG/A
OTHER AMERICAN REPUBLICS: PANAMA (VOL. XV). PANAMA CONSTN

LAW LEGIS EDU/PROP CT/SYS 20. PAGE 30 E0592 — ADMIN NAT/G

HILL M.,IMMUNITIES AND PRIVILEGES OF INTERNATIONAL OFFICIALS. CANADA EUR+WWI NETHERLND SWITZERLND LAW LEGIS DIPLOM LEGIT RESPECT...TIME/SEQ LEAGUE/NAT UN VAL/FREE 20. PAGE 52 E1046 — B47 INT/ORG ADMIN

HIRSHBERG H.S.,SUBJECT GUIDE TO UNITED STATES GOVERNMENT PUBLICATIONS. USA+45 USA-45 LAW ADMIN ...SOC 20. PAGE 53 E1052 — B47 BIBLIOG NAT/G DIPLOM LOC/G

NEUBURGER O.,GUIDE TO OFFICIAL PUBLICATIONS OF OTHER AMERICAN REPUBLICS: HONDURAS (VOL. XIII). HONDURAS LAW LEGIS ADMIN CT/SYS...JURID 19/20. PAGE 76 E1533 — B47 BIBLIOG/A NAT/G EDU/PROP CONSTN

CLAGETT H.L.,A GUIDE TO THE LAW AND LEGAL LITERATURE OF ARGENTINA, 1917-1946. CONSTN LABOR JUDGE ADJUD ADMIN...CRIMLGY INT/LAW JURID CON/ANAL 20 ARGEN. PAGE 23 E0447 — B48 BIBLIOG L/A+17C LAW LEGIS

DE NOIA J.,GUIDE TO OFFICIAL PUBLICATIONS OF OTHER AMERICAN REPUBLICS: PERU (VOL. XVII). PERU LAW LEGIS ADMIN CT/SYS...JURID 19/20. PAGE 30 E0593 — B48 BIBLIOG/A CONSTN NAT/G EDU/PROP

STOKES W.S.,BIBLIOGRAPHY OF STANDARD AND CLASSICAL WORKS IN THE FIELDS OF AMERICAN POLITICAL SCIENCE. USA+45 USA-45 POL/PAR PROVS FORCES DIPLOM ADMIN CT/SYS APPORT 20 CONGRESS PRESIDENT. PAGE 94 E1876 — B48 BIBLIOG NAT/G LOC/G CONSTN

APPLEBY P.H.,POLICY AND ADMINISTRATION. USA+45 NAT/G LOBBY PWR 20. PAGE 5 E0101 — B49 REPRESENT EXEC ADMIN CLIENT

BOYD A.M.,UNITED STATES GOVERNMENT PUBLICATIONS (3RD ED.). USA+45 EX/STRUC LEGIS ADMIN...JURID CHARTS 20. PAGE 14 E0281 — B49 BIBLIOG/A PRESS NAT/G EDU/PROP

WALINE M.,LE CONTROLE JURIDICTIONNEL DE L'ADMINISTRATION. BELGIUM FRANCE UAR JUDGE BAL/PWR ADJUD CONTROL CT/SYS...GP/COMP 20. PAGE 104 E2093 — B49 JURID ADMIN PWR ORD/FREE

MARX C.M.,"ADMINISTRATIVE ETHICS AND THE RULE OF LAW." USA+45 ELITES ACT/RES DOMIN NEUTRAL ROUTINE INGP/REL ORD/FREE...JURID IDEA/COMP. PAGE 69 E1375 — L49 ADMIN LAW

BROWN E.S.,MANUAL OF GOVERNMENT PUBLICATIONS. WOR+45 WOR-45 CONSTN INT/ORG MUNIC PROVS DIPLOM ADMIN 20. PAGE 16 E0313 — B50 BIBLIOG/A NAT/G LAW

GRAVES W.B.,PUBLIC ADMINISTRATION: A COMPREHENSIVE BIBLIOGRAPHY ON PUBLIC ADMINISTRATION IN THE UNITED STATES (PAMPHLET). USA+45 USA-45 LOC/G NAT/G LEGIS ADJUD INGP/REL...MGT 20. PAGE 45 E0901 — B50 BIBLIOG FINAN CONTROL ADMIN

HURST J.W.,THE GROWTH OF AMERICAN LAW; THE LAW MAKERS. USA-45 LOC/G NAT/G DELIB/GP JUDGE ADJUD ADMIN ATTIT PWR...POLICY JURID BIBLIOG 18/20 CONGRESS SUPREME/CT ABA PRESIDENT. PAGE 56 E1115 — B50 LAW LEGIS CONSTN CT/SYS

JENKINS W.S.,A GUIDE TO THE MICROFILM COLLECTION OF EARLY STATE RECORDS. USA+45 CONSTN MUNIC LEGIS PRESS ADMIN CT/SYS 18/20. PAGE 58 E1152 — B50 BIBLIOG PROVS AUD/VIS

LOWENTHAL M.,THE FEDERAL BUREAU OF INVESTIGATION. USA+45 SOCIETY ADMIN TASK CRIME INGP/REL...CRIMLGY 20 FBI ESPIONAGE. PAGE 67 E1329 — B50 FORCES NAT/G ATTIT LAW

MONPIED E.,BIBLIOGRAPHIE FEDERALISTE: OUVRAGES CHOISIS (VOL. I; MIMEOGRAPHED PAPER). EUR+WWI DIPLOM ADMIN REGION ATTIT PACIFISM SOCISM...INT/LAW 19/20. PAGE 74 E1486 — B50 BIBLIOG/A FEDERAL CENTRAL INT/ORG

WADE E.C.S.,CONSTITUTIONAL LAW; AN OUTLINE OF THE LAW AND PRACTICE OF THE CONSTITUTION. UK LEGIS DOMIN ADMIN GP/REL 16/20 CMN/WLTH PARLIAMENT ENGLSH/LAW. PAGE 104 E2087 — B50 CONSTN NAT/G PARL/PROC LAW

WARD R.E.,A GUIDE TO JAPANESE REFERENCE AND RESEARCH MATERIALS IN THE FIELD OF POLITICAL SCIENCE. LAW CONSTN LOC/G PRESS ADMIN...SOC CON/ANAL METH 19/20 CHINJAP. PAGE 105 E2098 — B50 BIBLIOG/A ASIA NAT/G

HOLCOMBE A.,"OUR MORE PERFECT UNION." USA+45 USA-45 POL/PAR JUDGE CT/SYS EQUILIB FEDERAL PWR...MAJORIT TREND BIBLIOG 18/20 CONGRESS PRESIDENT. PAGE 54 E1070 — C50 CONSTN NAT/G ADMIN PLAN

DAVIS K.C.,ADMINISTRATIVE LAW. USA+45 USA-45 NAT/G PROB/SOLV BAL/PWR CONTROL ORD/FREE...POLICY 20 SUPREME/CT. PAGE 29 E0574 — B51 ADMIN JURID EX/STRUC ADJUD

COHEN M.B.,"PERSONALITY AS A FACTOR IN ADMINISTRATIVE DECISIONS." ADJUD PERS/REL ANOMIE SUPEGO...OBS SELF/OBS INT. PAGE 24 E0465 — S51 PERSON ADMIN PROB/SOLV PSY

ANDREWS F.E.,CORPORATION GIVING. LAW TAX EDU/PROP ADMIN...POLICY STAT CHARTS. PAGE 5 E0096 — B52 LG/CO GIVE SML/CO FINAN

APPLEBY P.H.,MORALITY AND ADMINISTRATION IN DEMOCRATIC GOVERNMENT. USA+45 CLIENT NAT/G EXEC EFFICIENCY 20. PAGE 5 E0102 — B52 REPRESENT LOBBY ADMIN EX/STRUC

COUNCIL STATE GOVERNMENTS,OCCUPATIONAL LICENSING IN THE STATES. USA+45 PROVS ADMIN EXEC LOBBY 20. PAGE 27 E0526 — B52 PROF/ORG LICENSE REPRESENT EX/STRUC

DE GRAZIA A.,POLITICAL ORGANIZATION. CONSTN LOC/G MUNIC NAT/G CHIEF LEGIS TOP/EX ADJUD CT/SYS PERS/REL...INT/LAW MYTH UN. PAGE 29 E0581 — B52 FEDERAL LAW ADMIN

US DEPARTMENT OF STATE,RESEARCH ON EASTERN EUROPE (EXCLUDING USSR). EUR+WWI LAW ECO/DEV NAT/G PROB/SOLV DIPLOM ADMIN LEAD MARXISM...TREND 19/20. PAGE 100 E1995 — B52 BIBLIOG R+D ACT/RES COM

CLAGETT H.L.,"THE ADMINISTRATION OF JUSTICE IN LATIN AMERICA." L/A+17C ADMIN FEDERAL...JURID METH/COMP BIBLIOG 20. PAGE 23 E0448 — C52 CT/SYS ADJUD JUDGE CONSTN

LANCASTER L.W.,"GOVERNMENT IN RURAL AMERICA." USA+45 ECO/DEV AGRI SCHOOL FORCES LEGIS JUDGE BUDGET TAX CT/SYS...CHARTS BIBLIOG. PAGE 62 E1248 — C52 GOV/REL LOC/G MUNIC ADMIN

STUART G.H.,"AMERICAN DIPLOMATIC AND CONSULAR PRACTICE (2ND ED.)" EUR+WWI MOD/EUR USA-45 DELIB/GP INT/TRADE ADJUD...BIBLIOG 20. PAGE 94 E1889 — C52 DIPLOM ADMIN INT/ORG

CALDWELL L.K.,RESEARCH METHODS IN PUBLIC ADMINISTRATION; AN OUTLINE OF TOPICS AND READINGS (PAMPHLET). LAW ACT/RES COMPUTER KNOWL...SOC STAT GEN/METH 20. PAGE 18 E0364 — B53 BIBLIOG/A METH/COMP ADMIN OP/RES

GROSS B.M.,THE LEGISLATIVE STRUGGLE: A STUDY IN SOCIAL COMBAT. STRUCT LOC/G POL/PAR JUDGE EDU/PROP DEBATE ETIQUET ADMIN LOBBY CHOOSE GOV/REL INGP/REL HEREDITY ALL/VALS...SOC PRESIDENT. PAGE 48 E0948 — B53 LEGIS DECISION PERSON LEAD

MAJUMDAR B.B.,PROBLEMS OF PUBLIC ADMINISTRATION IN INDIA. INDIA INDUS PLAN BUDGET ADJUD CENTRAL DEMAND WEALTH...WELF/ST ANTHOL 20 CIVIL/SERV. PAGE 68 E1353 — B53 ECO/UNDEV GOV/REL ADMIN MUNIC

PIERCE R.A.,RUSSIAN CENTRAL ASIA, 1867-1917: A — B53 BIBLIOG

SELECTED BIBLIOGRAPHY (PAMPHLET). USSR LAW CULTURE   COLONIAL
NAT/G EDU/PROP WAR...GEOG SOC 19/20. PAGE 81 E1616   ADMIN
   COM

   B53
SECKLER-HUDSON C.,BIBLIOGRAPHY ON PUBLIC   BIBLIOG/A
ADMINISTRATION (4TH ED.). USA+45 LAW POL/PAR   ADMIN
DELIB/GP BUDGET ADJUD LOBBY GOV/REL GP/REL ATTIT   NAT/G
...JURID 20. PAGE 90 E1800   MGT

   B53
STOUT H.M.,BRITISH GOVERNMENT. UK FINAN LOC/G   NAT/G
POL/PAR DELIB/GP DIPLOM ADMIN COLONIAL CHOOSE   PARL/PROC
ORD/FREE...JURID BIBLIOG 20 COMMONWLTH. PAGE 94   CONSTN
E1883   NEW/LIB

   N53
US PRES CONF ADMIN PROCEDURE,REPORT (PAMPHLET).   NAT/G
USA+45 CONFER ADJUD...METH/COMP 20 PRESIDENT.   DELIB/GP
PAGE 101 E2024   ADJUST
   ADMIN

   B54
BENTLEY A.F.,INQUIRY INTO INQUIRIES: ESSAYS IN   EPIST
SOCIAL THEORY. UNIV LEGIS ADJUD ADMIN LOBBY   SOC
...PHIL/SCI PSY NEW/IDEA LING METH 20. PAGE 10   CONCPT
E0200

   B54
BINANI G.D.,INDIA AT A GLANCE (REV. ED.). INDIA   INDEX
COM/IND FINAN INDUS LABOR PROVS SCHOOL PLAN DIPLOM   CON/ANAL
INT/TRADE ADMIN...JURID 20. PAGE 12 E0229   NAT/G
   ECO/UNDEV

   B54
SINCO,PHILIPPINE POLITICAL LAW: PRINCIPLES AND   LAW
CONCEPTS (10TH ED.). PHILIPPINE LOC/G EX/STRUC   CONSTN
BAL/PWR ECO/TAC TAX ADJUD ADMIN CONTROL CT/SYS SUFF   LEGIS
ORD/FREE...T 20. PAGE 91 E1831

   B54
TOTOK W.,HANDBUCH DER BIBLIOGRAPHISCHEN   BIBLIOG/A
NACHSCHLAGEWERKE. GERMANY LAW CULTURE ADMIN...SOC   NAT/G
20. PAGE 97 E1936   DIPLOM
   POLICY

US SENATE COMM ON FOREIGN REL,REVIEW OF THE UNITED   BIBLIOG
NATIONS CHARTER: A COLLECTION OF DOCUMENTS. LEGIS   CONSTN
DIPLOM ADMIN ARMS/CONT WAR REPRESENT SOVEREIGN   INT/ORG
...INT/LAW 20 UN. PAGE 101 E2029   DEBATE

   S54
COOPER L.,"ADMINISTRATIVE JUSTICE." UK ADMIN   LAW
REPRESENT PWR...POLICY 20. PAGE 25 E0502   ADJUD
   CONTROL
   EX/STRUC

   S54
HART J.,"ADMINISTRATION AND THE COURTS." USA+45   ADMIN
NAT/G REPRESENT 20. PAGE 50 E1003   GOV/REL
   CT/SYS
   FEDERAL

   C54
CALDWELL L.K.,"THE GOVERNMENT AND ADMINISTRATION OF   PROVS
NEW YORK." LOC/G MUNIC POL/PAR SCHOOL CHIEF LEGIS   ADMIN
PLAN TAX CT/SYS...MGT SOC/WK BIBLIOG 20 NEWYORK/C.   CONSTN
PAGE 19 E0365   EX/STRUC

   B55
CRAIG J.,BIBLIOGRAPHY OF PUBLIC ADMINISTRATION IN   BIBLIOG
AUSTRALIA. CONSTN FINAN EX/STRUC LEGIS PLAN DIPLOM   GOV/REL
RECEIVE ADJUD ROUTINE...HEAL 19/20 AUSTRAL   ADMIN
PARLIAMENT. PAGE 27 E0540   NAT/G

   B55
DE ARAGAO J.G.,LA JURIDICTION ADMINISTRATIVE AU   EX/STRUC
BRESIL. BRAZIL ADJUD COLONIAL CT/SYS REV FEDERAL   ADMIN
ORD/FREE...BIBLIOG 19/20. PAGE 29 E0580   NAT/G

   B55
FLIESS P.J.,FREEDOM OF THE PRESS IN THE GERMAN   EDU/PROP
REPUBLIC. 1918-1933. GERMANY LAW CONSTN POL/PAR   ORD/FREE
LEGIS WRITING ADMIN COERCE MURDER MARXISM...POLICY   JURID
BIBLIOG 20 WEIMAR/REP. PAGE 39 E0765   PRESS

   B55
GUAITA A.,BIBLIOGRAFIA ESPANOLA DE DERECHO   BIBLIOG
ADMINISTRATIVO (PAMPHLET). SPAIN LOC/G MUNIC NAT/G   ADMIN
PROVS JUDGE BAL/PWR GOV/REL OWN...JURID 18/19.   CONSTN
PAGE 48 E0959   PWR

   B55
JAPAN MOMBUSHO DAIGAKU GAKIYUT,BIBLIOGRAPHY OF THE   BIBLIOG
STUDIES ON LAW AND POLITICS (PAMPHLET). CONSTN   LAW

INDUS LABOR DIPLOM TAX ADMIN...CRIMLGY INT/LAW 20   PHIL/SCI
CHINJAP. PAGE 58 E1150

   B55
MAYERS L.,THE AMERICAN LEGAL SYSTEM. USA+45 USA-45   JURID
NAT/G EX/STRUC ADMIN CONTROL FEDERAL 20 SUPREME/CT.   CT/SYS
PAGE 70 E1394   LEGIS
   ADJUD

   B55
PULLEN W.R.,A CHECK LIST OF LEGISLATIVE JOURNALS   BIBLIOG
ISSUED SINCE 1937 BY THE STATES OF THE UNITED   PROVS
STATES OF AMERICA (PAMPHLET). USA+45 USA-45 LAW   EDU/PROP
WRITING ADJUD ADMIN...JURID 20. PAGE 83 E1662   LEGIS

   B55
SVARLIEN O.,AN INTRODUCTION TO THE LAW OF NATIONS.   INT/LAW
SEA AIR INT/ORG NAT/G CHIEF ADMIN AGREE WAR PRIVIL   DIPLOM
ORD/FREE SOVEREIGN...BIBLIOG 16/20. PAGE 95 E1897

   B55
UN HEADQUARTERS LIBRARY,BIBLIOQRAPHIE DE LA CHARTE   BIBLIOG/A
DES NATIONS UNIES. CHINA/COM KOREA WOR+45 VOL/ASSN   INT/ORG
CONFER ADMIN COERCE PEACE ATTIT ORD/FREE SOVEREIGN   DIPLOM
...INT/LAW 20 UNESCO UN. PAGE 97 E1953

   B55
WHEARE K.C.,GOVERNMENT BY COMMITTEE; AN ESSAY ON   DELIB/GP
THE BRITISH CONSTITUTION. UK NAT/G LEGIS INSPECT   CONSTN
CONFER ADJUD ADMIN CONTROL TASK EFFICIENCY ROLE   LEAD
POPULISM 20. PAGE 106 E2116   GP/COMP

   B55
ZABEL O.H.,GOD AND CAESAR IN NEBRASKA: A STUDY OF   SECT
LEGAL RELATIONSHIP OF CHURCH AND STATE, 1854-1954.   PROVS
TAX GIVE ADMIN CONTROL GP/REL ROLE...GP/COMP 19/20   LAW
NEBRASKA. PAGE 108 E2168   EDU/PROP

   B56
ABELS J.,THE TRUMAN SCANDALS. USA+45 USA-45 POL/PAR   CRIME
TAX LEGIT CT/SYS CHOOSE PRIVIL MORAL WEALTH 20   ADMIN
TRUMAN/HS PRESIDENT CONGRESS. PAGE 2 E0043   CHIEF
   TRIBUTE

   B56
BROWNE D.G.,THE RISE OF SCOTLAND YARD: A HISTORY OF   CRIMLGY
THE METROPOLITAN POLICE. UK MUNIC CHIEF ADMIN CRIME   LEGIS
GP/REL 19/20. PAGE 16 E0316   CONTROL
   FORCES

   B56
DUNNILL F.,THE CIVIL SERVICE. UK LAW PLAN ADMIN   PERSON
EFFICIENCY DRIVE NEW/LIB...STAT CHARTS 20   WORKER
PARLIAMENT CIVIL/SERV. PAGE 33 E0662   STRATA
   SOC/WK

   B56
FRANCIS R.G.,SERVICE AND PROCEDURE IN BUREAUCRACY.   CLIENT
EXEC LEAD ROUTINE...QU 20. PAGE 39 E0784   ADMIN
   INGP/REL
   REPRESENT

   B56
HURST J.W.,LAW AND THE CONDITIONS OF FREEDOM IN THE   LAW
NINETEENTH CENTURY UNITED STATES. USA-45 CONSTN   ORD/FREE
STRUCT ADMIN GP/REL FEDERAL HABITAT...JURID 19.   POLICY
PAGE 56 E1116   NAT/G

   B56
REDFORD E.S.,PUBLIC ADMINISTRATION AND POLICY   EX/STRUC
FORMATION: STUDIES IN OIL, GAS, BANKING, RIVER   PROB/SOLV
DEVELOPMENT AND CORPORATE INVESTIGATIONS. USA+45   CONTROL
CLIENT NAT/G ADMIN LOBBY REPRESENT GOV/REL INGP/REL   EXEC
20. PAGE 84 E1678

   B56
SOHN L.B.,CASES ON UNITED NATIONS LAW. STRUCT   INT/ORG
DELIB/GP WAR PEACE ORD/FREE...DECISION ANTHOL 20   INT/LAW
UN. PAGE 92 E1854   ADMIN
   ADJUD

   B56
US HOUSE RULES COMM,HEARINGS BEFORE A SPECIAL   ADMIN
SUBCOMMITTEE: ESTABLISHMENT OF A STANDING COMMITTEE   DOMIN
ON ADMINISTRATIVE PROCEDURE, PRACTICE. USA+45 LAW   DELIB/GP
EX/STRUC ADJUD CONTROL EXEC GOV/REL EFFICIENCY PWR   NAT/G
...POLICY INT 20 CONGRESS. PAGE 100 E2009

   C56
AUMANN F.R.,"THE ISTRUMENTALITIES OF JUSTICE: THEIR   JURID
FORMS, FUNCTIONS, AND LIMITATIONS." WOR+45 WOR-45   ADMIN
JUDGE PROB/SOLV ROUTINE ATTIT...BIBLIOG 20. PAGE 6   CT/SYS
E0118   ADJUD

   C56
FALL B.B.,"THE VIET-MINH REGIME." VIETNAM LAW   NAT/G

ECO/UNDEV POL/PAR FORCES DOMIN WAR ATTIT MARXISM ...BIOG PREDICT BIBLIOG/A 20. PAGE 36 E0720
ADMIN
EX/STRUC
LEAD

B57
CHICAGO U LAW SCHOOL, CONFERENCE ON JUDICIAL ADMINISTRATION. LOC/G MUNIC NAT/G PROVS...ANTHOL 20. PAGE 22 E0429
CT/SYS
ADJUD
ADMIN
GOV/REL

B57
COOPER F.E., THE LAWYER AND ADMINISTRATIVE AGENCIES. USA+45 CLIENT LAW PROB/SOLV CT/SYS PERSON ROLE. PAGE 25 E0500
CONSULT
ADMIN
ADJUD
DELIB/GP

B57
DONALDSON A.G., SOME COMPARATIVE ASPECTS OF IRISH LAW. IRELAND NAT/G DIPLOM ADMIN CT/SYS LEAD ATTIT SOVEREIGN...JURID BIBLIOG/A 12/20 CMN/WLTH. PAGE 32 E0635
CONSTN
LAW
NAT/COMP
INT/LAW

B57
HINDERLING A., DIE REFORMATORISCHE VERWALTUNGSGERICHTSBARKEIT. GERMANY/W PROB/SOLV ADJUD SUPEGO PWR...CONCPT 20. PAGE 53 E1049
ADMIN
CT/SYS
JURID
CONTROL

B57
MEYER P., ADMINISTRATIVE ORGANIZATION: A COMPARATIVE STUDY OF THE ORGANIZATION OF PUBLIC ADMINISTRATION. DENMARK FRANCE NORWAY SWEDEN UK USA+45 ELITES LOC/G CONSULT LEGIS ADJUD CONTROL LEAD PWR SKILL DECISION. PAGE 72 E1449
ADMIN
METH/COMP
NAT/G
CENTRAL

B57
SCHLOCHAUER H.J., OFFENTLICHES RECHT. GERMANY/W FINAN EX/STRUC LEGIS DIPLOM FEDERAL ORD/FREE ...INT/LAW 20. PAGE 88 E1757
CONSTN
JURID
ADMIN
CT/SYS

B57
US COMMISSION GOVT SECURITY, RECOMMENDATIONS; AREA: IMMIGRANT PROGRAM. USA+45 LAW WORKER DIPLOM EDU/PROP WRITING ADMIN PEACE ATTIT...CONCPT ANTHOL 20 MIGRATION SUBVERT. PAGE 99 E1981
POLICY
CONTROL
PLAN
NAT/G

B57
US SENATE COMM ON JUDICIARY, LIMITATION OF APPELLATE JURISDICTION OF THE SUPREME COURT. USA+45 LAW NAT/G DELIB/GP PLAN ADMIN CONTROL PWR...DECISION 20 CONGRESS SUPREME/CT. PAGE 102 E2041
CT/SYS
ADJUD
POLICY
GOV/REL

B58
AMERICAN SOCIETY PUBLIC ADMIN, STRENGTHENING MANAGEMENT FOR DEMOCRATIC GOVERNMENT. USA+45 ACADEM EX/STRUC WORKER PLAN BUDGET CONFER CT/SYS EFFICIENCY ANTHOL. PAGE 4 E0083
ADMIN
NAT/G
EXEC
MGT

B58
BUGEDA LANZAS J., A STATEMENT OF THE LAWS OF CUBA IN MATTERS AFFECTING BUSINESS (2ND ED. REV., ENLARGED). CUBA L/A+17C LAW FINAN FAM LEGIS ACT/RES ADMIN GP/REL...BIBLIOG 20 OAS. PAGE 17 E0327
JURID
NAT/G
INDUS
WORKER

B58
CHARLES R., LA JUSTICE EN FRANCE. FRANCE LAW CONSTN DELIB/GP CRIME 20. PAGE 21 E0422
JURID
ADMIN
CT/SYS
ADJUD

B58
DAVIS K.C., ADMINISTRATIVE LAW TREATISE (VOLS. I AND IV). NAT/G JUDGE PROB/SOLV ADJUD GP/REL 20 SUPREME/CT. PAGE 29 E0575
ADMIN
JURID
CT/SYS
EX/STRUC

B58
DAVIS K.C., ADMINISTRATIVE LAW; CASES, TEXT, PROBLEMS. LAW LOC/G NAT/G TOP/EX PAY CONTROL GOV/REL INGP/REL FEDERAL 20 SUPREME/CT. PAGE 29 E0576
ADJUD
JURID
CT/SYS
ADMIN

B58
DEVLIN P., THE CRIMINAL PROSECUTION IN ENGLAND. UK NAT/G ADMIN ROUTINE EFFICIENCY...JURID SOC 20. PAGE 31 E0617
CRIME
LAW
METH
CT/SYS

B58
HOOD W.C., FINANCING OF ECONOMIC ACTIVITY IN CANADA. CANADA FUT VOL/ASSN WORKER ECO/TAC ADJUD ADMIN ...CHARTS 20. PAGE 55 E1093
BUDGET
FINAN
GP/REL
ECO/DEV

B58
JAPAN MINISTRY OF JUSTICE, CRIMINAL JUSTICE IN JAPAN. LAW PROF/ORG PUB/INST FORCES CONTROL CT/SYS PARL/PROC 20 CHINJAP. PAGE 58 E1149
CONSTN
CRIME
JURID
ADMIN

B58
KAPLAN H.E., THE LAW OF CIVIL SERVICE. USA+45 LAW POL/PAR CT/SYS CRIME GOV/REL...POLICY JURID 20. PAGE 59 E1183
ADJUD
NAT/G
ADMIN
CONSTN

B58
LAW COMMISSION OF INDIA, REFORM OF JUDICIAL ADMINISTRATION. INDIA TOP/EX ADMIN DISCRIM EFFICIENCY...METH/COMP 20. PAGE 63 E1269
CT/SYS
ADJUD
GOV/REL
CONTROL

B58
MOEN N.W., THE GOVERNMENT OF SCOTLAND 1603 - 1625. UK JUDGE ADMIN GP/REL PWR 17 SCOTLAND COMMON/LAW. PAGE 74 E1479
CHIEF
JURID
CONTROL
PARL/PROC

B58
OGDEN F.D., THE POLL TAX IN THE SOUTH. USA+45 USA-45 CONSTN ADJUD ADMIN PARTIC CRIME...TIME/SEQ GOV/COMP METH/COMP 18/20 SOUTH/US. PAGE 78 E1572
TAX
CHOOSE
RACE/REL
DISCRIM

B58
ORTIZ R.P., ANNUARIO BIBLIOGRAFICO COLOMBIANO, 1951-1956. LAW RECEIVE EDU/PROP ADMIN...LING STAT 20 COLOMB. PAGE 79 E1582
BIBLIOG
SOC

B58
POUND R., JUSTICE ACCORDING TO LAW. LAW SOCIETY CT/SYS 20. PAGE 82 E1639
CONCPT
JURID
ADJUD
ADMIN

B58
SHARMA M.P., PUBLIC ADMINISTRATION IN THEORY AND PRACTICE. INDIA UK USA+45 USA-45 EX/STRUC ADJUD ...POLICY CONCPT NAT/COMP 20. PAGE 90 E1813
MGT
ADMIN
DELIB/GP
JURID

B58
SPITZ D., DEMOCRACY AND THE CHALLANGE OF POWER. FUT USA+45 USA-45 LAW SOCIETY STRUCT LOC/G POL/PAR PROVS DELIB/GP EX/STRUC LEGIS TOP/EX ACT/RES CREATE DOMIN EDU/PROP LEGIT ADJUD ADMIN ATTIT DRIVE MORAL ORD/FREE TOT/POP. PAGE 93 E1862
NAT/G
PWR

B58
US SENATE COMM POST OFFICE, TO PROVIDE AN EFFECTIVE SYSTEM OF PERSONNEL ADMINISTRATION. USA+45 NAT/G EX/STRUC PARL/PROC GOV/REL...JURID 20 SENATE CIVIL/SERV. PAGE 103 E2060
INT
LEGIS
CONFER
ADMIN

B58
WESTIN A.F., THE ANATOMY OF A CONSTITUTIONAL LAW CASE. USA+45 LAW LEGIS ADMIN EXEC...DECISION MGT SOC RECORD 20 SUPREME/CT. PAGE 105 E2113
CT/SYS
INDUS
ADJUD
CONSTN

S58
STAAR R.F., "ELECTIONS IN COMMUNIST POLAND." EUR+WWI SOCIETY INT/ORG NAT/G POL/PAR LEGIS ACT/RES ECO/TAC EDU/PROP ADJUD ADMIN ROUTINE COERCE TOTALISM ATTIT ORD/FREE PWR 20. PAGE 93 E1864
COM
CHOOSE
POLAND

C58
FRIEDRICH C.J., "AUTHORITY, REASON AND DISCRETION" IN C. FRIEDRICH'S AUTHORITY (BMR)" UNIV EX/STRUC ADJUD ADMIN CONTROL INGP/REL ATTIT PERSON PWR. PAGE 41 E0807
AUTHORIT
CHOOSE
RATIONAL
PERS/REL

B59
COUNCIL OF STATE GOVERNMENTS, STATE GOVERNMENT: AN ANNOTATED BIBLIOGRAPHY (PAMPHLET). USA+45 LAW AGRI INDUS WORKER PLAN TAX ADJUST AGE/Y ORD/FREE...HEAL MGT 20. PAGE 26 E0521
BIBLIOG/A
PROVS
LOC/G
ADMIN

B59
COUNCIL OF STATE GOVERNORS, AMERICAN LEGISLATURES: STRUCTURE AND PROCEDURES. SUMMARY AND TABULATIONS OF A 1959 SURVEY. PUERT/RICO USA+45 PAY ADJUD ADMIN APPORT...IDEA/COMP 20 GUAM VIRGIN/ISL. PAGE 27 E0525
LEGIS
CHARTS
PROVS
REPRESENT

B59
DAVIS K.C., ADMINISTRATIVE LAW TEXT. USA+45 NAT/G DELIB/GP EX/STRUC CONTROL ORD/FREE...T 20 SUPREME/CT. PAGE 29 E0577
ADJUD
ADMIN
JURID
CT/SYS

DESMITH S.A.,JUDICIAL REVIEW OF ADMINISTRATIVE
ACTION. UK LOC/G CONSULT DELIB/GP ADMIN PWR
...DECISION JURID 20 ENGLSH/LAW. PAGE 31 E0609
B59
ADJUD
NAT/G
PROB/SOLV
CT/SYS

ELLIOTT S.D.,IMPROVING OUR COURTS. LAW EX/STRUC
PLAN PROB/SOLV ADJUD ADMIN TASK CRIME EFFICIENCY
ORD/FREE 20. PAGE 34 E0684
B59
CT/SYS
JURID
GOV/REL
NAT/G

EPSTEIN F.T.,EAST GERMANY: A SELECTED BIBLIOGRAPHY
(PAMPHLET). COM GERMANY/E LAW AGRI FINAN INDUS
LABOR POL/PAR EDU/PROP ADMIN AGE/Y 20. PAGE 35
E0693
B59
BIBLIOG/A
INTELL
MARXISM
NAT/G

GINSBURG M.,LAW AND OPINION IN ENGLAND. UK CULTURE
KIN LABOR LEGIS EDU/PROP ADMIN CT/SYS CRIME OWN
HEALTH...ANTHOL 20 ENGLSH/LAW. PAGE 44 E0868
B59
JURID
POLICY
ECO/TAC

GOMEZ ROBLES J.,A STATEMENT OF THE LAWS OF
GUATEMALA IN MATTERS AFFECTING BUSINESS (2ND ED.
REV., ENLARGED). GUATEMALA L/A+17C LAW FINAN FAM
WORKER ACT/RES DIPLOM ADJUD ADMIN GP/REL 20 OAS.
PAGE 44 E0881
B59
JURID
NAT/G
INDUS
LEGIT

MAYDA J.,ATOMIC ENERGY AND LAW. ECO/UNDEV FINAN
TEC/DEV FOR/AID EFFICIENCY PRODUC WEALTH...POLICY
TECHNIC 20. PAGE 70 E1391
B59
NUC/PWR
L/A+17C
LAW
ADMIN

PAULSEN M.G.,LEGAL INSTITUTIONS TODAY AND TOMORROW.
UK USA+45 NAT/G PROF/ORG PROVS ADMIN PARL/PROC
ORD/FREE NAT/COMP. PAGE 80 E1604
B59
JURID
ADJUD
JUDGE
LEGIS

SISSON C.H.,THE SPIRIT OF BRITISH ADMINISTRATION
AND SOME EUROPEAN COMPARISONS. FRANCE GERMANY/W
SWEDEN UK LAW EX/STRUC INGP/REL EFFICIENCY ORD/FREE
...DECISION 20. PAGE 91 E1835
B59
GOV/COMP
ADMIN
ELITES
ATTIT

SPIRO H.J.,GOVERNMENT BY CONSTITUTIONS: THE
POLITICAL SYSTEMS OF DEMOCRACY. CANADA EUR+WWI FUT
USA+45 WOR+45 WOR-45 LEGIS TOP/EX LEGIT ADMIN
CT/SYS ORD/FREE PWR...TREND TOT/POP VAL/FREE 20.
PAGE 93 E1861
B59
NAT/G
CONSTN

SURRENCY E.C.,A GUIDE TO LEGAL RESEARCH. USA+45
ACADEM LEGIS ACT/RES ADMIN...DECISION METH/COMP
BIBLIOG METH. PAGE 94 E1894
B59
NAT/G
PROVS
ADJUD
JURID

U OF MICHIGAN LAW SCHOOL,ATOMS AND THE LAW. USA+45
PROVS WORKER PROB/SOLV DIPLOM ADMIN GOV/REL ANTHOL.
PAGE 97 E1950
B59
NUC/PWR
NAT/G
CONTROL
LAW

US SENATE COMM ON POST OFFICE,TO PROVIDE FOR AN
EFFECTIVE SYSTEM OF PERSONNEL ADMINISTRATION.
EFFICIENCY...MGT 20 CONGRESS CIVIL/SERV POSTAL/SYS
YARBROGH/R. PAGE 103 E2059
B59
ADMIN
NAT/G
EX/STRUC
LAW

HECTOR L.J.,"GOVERNMENT BY ANONYMITY: WHO WRITES
OUR REGULATORY OPINIONS?" USA+45 NAT/G TOP/EX
CONTROL EXEC. PAGE 51 E1021
L59
ADJUD
REPRESENT
EX/STRUC
ADMIN

CHAPMAN B.,"THE FRENCH CONSEIL D'ETAT." FRANCE
NAT/G CONSULT OP/RES PROB/SOLV PWR...OBS 20.
PAGE 21 E0421
S59
ADMIN
LAW
CT/SYS
LEGIS

DWYER R.J.,"THE ADMINISTRATIVE ROLE IN
DESEGREGATION." USA+45 LAW PROB/SOLV LEAD RACE/REL
ISOLAT STRANGE ROLE...POLICY SOC/INTEG MISSOURI
NEGRO CIV/RIGHTS. PAGE 34 E0668
S59
ADMIN
SCHOOL
DISCRIM
ATTIT

SCHEEHAN D.,"PUBLIC AND PRIVATE GROUPS AS
IDENTIFIED IN THE FIELD OF TRADE REGULATIONS."
USA+45 ADMIN REPRESENT GOV/REL. PAGE 87 E1753
S59
LAW
CONTROL
ADJUD

TIPTON J.B.,"PARTICIPATION OF THE UNITED STATES IN
THE INTERNATIONAL LABOR ORGANIZATION." USA+45 LAW
STRUCT ECO/DEV ECO/UNDEV INDUS TEC/DEV ECO/TAC
ADMIN PERCEPT ORD/FREE SKILL...STAT HIST/WRIT
GEN/METH ILO WORK 20. PAGE 96 E1928
S59
LABOR
INT/ORG

COLLINS I.,"THE GOVERNMENT AND THE NEWSPAPER PRESS
IN FRANCE, 1814-1881. FRANCE LAW ADMIN CT/SYS
...CON/ANAL BIBLIOG 19. PAGE 24 E0475
C59
PRESS
ORD/FREE
NAT/G
EDU/PROP

JUNZ A.J.,PRESENT TRENDS IN AMERICAN NATIONAL
GOVERNMENT. LEGIS DIPLOM ADMIN CT/SYS ORD/FREE
...CONCPT ANTHOL 20 CONGRESS PRESIDENT SUPREME/CT.
PAGE 2 E0040
B60
POL/PAR
CHOOSE
CONSTN
NAT/G

ALBI F.,TRATADO DE LOS MODOS DE GESTION DE LAS
CORPORACIONES LOCALES. SPAIN FINAN NAT/G BUDGET
CONTROL EXEC ROUTINE GOV/REL ORD/FREE SOVEREIGN
...MGT 20. PAGE 3 E0057
B60
LOC/G
LAW
ADMIN
MUNIC

CLARK G.,WORLD PEACE THROUGH WORLD LAW. FUT WOR+45
CONSULT FORCES ACT/RES CREATE PLAN ADMIN ROUTINE
ARMS/CONT DETER ATTIT PWR...JURID VAL/FREE UNESCO
20 UN. PAGE 23 E0449
B60
INT/ORG
LAW
PEACE
INT/LAW

DAVIS K.C.,ADMINISTRATIVE LAW AND GOVERNMENT.
USA+45 EX/STRUC PROB/SOLV ADJUD GP/REL PWR...POLICY
20 SUPREME/CT. PAGE 29 E0578
B60
ADMIN
JURID
CT/SYS
NAT/G

DILEY A.V.,INTRODUCTION TO THE STUDY OF THE LAW OF
THE CONSTITUTION. FRANCE UK USA+45 USA-45 CONSULT
FORCES TAX ADMIN FEDERAL ORD/FREE SOVEREIGN
...IDEA/COMP 20 ENGLSH/LAW CON/INTERP PARLIAMENT.
PAGE 32 E0627
B60
CONSTN
LAW
LEGIS
GEN/LAWS

DUMON F.,LA COMMUNAUTE FRANCO-AFRO-MALGACHE: SES
ORIGINES, SES INSTITUTIONS, SON EVOLUTION. FRANCE
MADAGASCAR POL/PAR DIPLOM ADMIN ATTIT...TREND T 20.
PAGE 33 E0657
B60
JURID
INT/ORG
AFR
CONSTN

FLORES R.H.,CATALOGO DE TESIS DOCTORALES DE LAS
FACULTADES DE LA UNIVERSIDAD DE EL SALVADOR.
EL/SALVADR LAW DIPLOM ADMIN LEAD GOV/REL...SOC
19/20. PAGE 39 E0767
B60
BIBLIOG
ACADEM
L/A+17C
NAT/G

HEAP D.,AN OUTLINE OF PLANNING LAW (3RD ED.). UK
LAW PROB/SOLV ADMIN CONTROL 20. PAGE 51 E1020
B60
MUNIC
PLAN
JURID
LOC/G

LENCZOWSKI G.,OIL AND STATE IN THE MIDDLE EAST. FUT
IRAN LAW ECO/UNDEV EXTR/IND NAT/G TOP/EX PLAN
TEC/DEV ECO/TAC LEGIT ADMIN COERCE ATTIT ALL/VALS
PWR...CHARTS 20. PAGE 64 E1283
B60
ISLAM
INDUS
NAT/LISM

LEWIS P.R.,LITERATURE OF THE SOCIAL SCIENCES: AN
INTRODUCTORY SURVEY AND GUIDE. UK LAW INDUS DIPLOM
INT/TRADE ADMIN...MGT 19/20. PAGE 65 E1294
B60
BIBLIOG/A
SOC

PINTO F.B.M.,ENRIQUECIMENTO ILICITO NO EXERCICIO DE
CARGOS PUBLICOS. BRAZIL L/A+17C USA+45 ELITES
TRIBUTE CONTROL INGP/REL ORD/FREE PWR...NAT/COMP
20. PAGE 81 E1617
B60
ADMIN
NAT/G
CRIME
LAW

RIENOW R.,INTRODUCTION TO GOVERNMENT (2ND ED.). UK
USA+45 USSR POL/PAR ADMIN REV CHOOSE SUFF FEDERAL
PWR...JURID GOV/COMP T 20. PAGE 85 E1697
B60
CONSTN
PARL/PROC
REPRESENT
AUTHORIT

SCHUBERT G.,THE PUBLIC INTEREST. USA+45 CONSULT
PLAN PROB/SOLV ADJUD ADMIN GP/REL PWR ALL/IDEOS 20.
PAGE 88 E1770
B60
POLICY
DELIB/GP
REPRESENT
POL/PAR

STEIN E.,AMERICAN ENTERPRISE IN THE EUROPEAN COMMON
MARKET: A LEGAL PROFILE. EUR+WWI FUT USA+45 SOCIETY
B60
MARKET
ADJUD

STRUCT ECO/DEV NAT/G VOL/ASSN CONSULT PLAN TEC/DEV INT/LAW
ECO/TAC INT/TRADE ADMIN ATTIT RIGID/FLEX PWR...MGT
NEW/IDEA STAT TREND COMPUT/IR SIMUL EEC 20. PAGE 93
E1867

B60
US LIBRARY OF CONGRESS,INDEX TO LATIN AMERICAN BIBLIOG/A
LEGISLATION: 1950-1960 (2 VOLS.). NAT/G DELIB/GP LEGIS
ADMIN PARL/PROC 20. PAGE 101 E2019 L/A+17C
  JURID

B60
US SENATE COMM ON JUDICIARY,FEDERAL ADMINISTRATIVE PARL/PROC
PROCEDURE. USA+45 CONSTN NAT/G PROB/SOLV CONFER LEGIS
GOV/REL...JURID INT 20 SENATE. PAGE 102 E2043 ADMIN
  LAW

B60
US SENATE COMM ON JUDICIARY,ADMINISTRATIVE PARL/PROC
PROCEDURE LEGISLATION. USA+45 CONSTN NAT/G LEGIS
PROB/SOLV CONFER ROUTINE GOV/REL...INT 20 SENATE. ADMIN
PAGE 102 E2044 JURID

B60
WEBSTER J.A.,A GENERAL STUDY OF THE DEPARTMENT OF ORD/FREE
DEFENSE INTERNAL SECURITY PROGRAM. USA+45 WORKER PLAN
TEC/DEV ADJUD CONTROL CT/SYS EXEC GOV/REL COST ADMIN
...POLICY DECISION MGT 20 DEPT/DEFEN SUPREME/CT. NAT/G
PAGE 105 E2105

L60
DEAN A.W.,"SECOND GENEVA CONFERENCE OF THE LAW OF INT/ORG
THE SEA: THE FIGHT FOR FREEDOM OF THE SEAS." FUT JURID
USA+45 USSR WOR+45 WOR-45 SEA CONSTN STRUCT PLAN INT/LAW
INT/TRADE ADJUD ADMIN ORD/FREE...DECISION RECORD
TREND GEN/LAWS 20 TREATY. PAGE 30 E0600

L60
FUCHS R.F.,"FAIRNESS AND EFFECTIVENESS IN EFFICIENCY
ADMINISTRATIVE AGENCY ORGANIZATION AND PROCEDURES." EX/STRUC
USA+45 ADJUD ADMIN REPRESENT. PAGE 41 E0816 EXEC
  POLICY

L60
STEIN E.,"LEGAL REMEDIES OF ENTERPRISES IN THE MARKET
EUROPEAN ECONOMIC COMMUNITY." EUR+WWI FUT ECO/DEV ADJUD
INDUS PLAN ECO/TAC ADMIN PWR...MGT MATH STAT TREND
CON/ANAL EEC 20. PAGE 93 E1868

S60
MARSHALL G.,"POLICE RESPONSIBILITY." UK LOC/G ADJUD CONTROL
ADMIN EXEC 20. PAGE 69 E1370 REPRESENT
  LAW
  FORCES

S60
THOMPSON K.W.,"MORAL PURPOSE IN FOREIGN POLICY: MORAL
REALITIES AND ILLUSIONS." WOR+45 WOR-45 LAW CULTURE JURID
SOCIETY INT/ORG PLAN ADJUD ADMIN COERCE RIGID/FLEX DIPLOM
SUPEGO KNOWL ORD/FREE PWR...SOC TREND SOC/EXP
TOT/POP 20. PAGE 96 E1921

C60
MCCLEERY R.,"COMMUNICATION PATTERNS AS BASES OF PERS/REL
SYSTEMS OF AUTHORITY AND POWER" IN THEORETICAL PUB/INST
STUDIES IN SOCIAL ORGAN. OF PRISON-BMR. USA+45 PWR
SOCIETY STRUCT EDU/PROP ADMIN CONTROL COERCE CRIME DOMIN
GP/REL AUTHORIT...SOC 20. PAGE 70 E1400

N60
RHODESIA-NYASA NATL ARCHIVES,A SELECT BIBLIOGRAPHY BIBLIOG
OF RECENT PUBLICATIONS CONCERNING THE FEDERATION OF ADMIN
RHODESIA AND NYASALAND (PAMPHLET). MALAWI RHODESIA ORD/FREE
LAW CULTURE STRUCT ECO/UNDEV LEGIS...GEOG 20. NAT/G
PAGE 84 E1689

B61
AUERBACH C.A.,THE LEGAL PROCESS. USA+45 DELIB/GP JURID
JUDGE CONFER ADJUD CONTROL...DECISION 20 ADMIN
SUPREME/CT. PAGE 6 E0116 LEGIS
  CT/SYS

B61
AVERY M.W.,GOVERNMENT OF WASHINGTON STATE. USA+45 PROVS
MUNIC DELIB/GP EX/STRUC LEGIS GIVE CT/SYS PARTIC LOC/G
REGION EFFICIENCY 20 WASHINGT/G GOVERNOR. PAGE 6 ADMIN
E0121 GOV/REL

B61
AYLMER G.,THE KING'S SERVANTS. UK ELITES CHIEF PAY ADMIN
CT/SYS WEALTH 17 CROMWELL/O CHARLES/I. PAGE 6 E0122 ROUTINE
  EX/STRUC
  NAT/G

B61
BAINS J.S.,STUDIES IN POLITICAL SCIENCE. INDIA DIPLOM

WOR+45 WOR-45 CONSTN BAL/PWR ADJUD ADMIN PARL/PROC INT/LAW
SOVEREIGN...SOC METH/COMP ANTHOL 17/20 UN. PAGE 7 NAT/G
E0137

B61
BEASLEY K.E.,STATE SUPERVISION OF MUNICIPAL DEBT IN MUNIC
KANSAS - A CASE STUDY. USA+45 USA-45 FINAN PROVS LOC/G
BUDGET TAX ADJUD ADMIN CONTROL SUPEGO. PAGE 9 E0167 LEGIS
  JURID

B61
BURDETTE F.L.,POLITICAL SCIENCE: A SELECTED BIBLIOG/A
BIBLIOGRAPHY OF BOOKS IN PRINT, WITH ANNOTATIONS GOV/COMP
(PAMPHLET). LAW LOC/G NAT/G POL/PAR PROVS DIPLOM CONCPT
EDU/PROP ADMIN CHOOSE ATTIT 20. PAGE 17 E0330 ROUTINE

B61
CARNELL F.,THE POLITICS OF THE NEW STATES: A SELECT BIBLIOG/A
ANNOTATED BIBLIOGRAPHY WITH SPECIAL REFERENCE TO AFR
THE COMMONWEALTH. CONSTN ELITES LABOR NAT/G POL/PAR ASIA
EX/STRUC DIPLOM ADJUD ADMIN...GOV/COMP 20 COLONIAL
COMMONWLTH. PAGE 20 E0387

B61
CARROTHERS A.W.R.,LABOR ARBITRATION IN CANADA. LABOR
CANADA LAW NAT/G CONSULT LEGIS WORKER ADJUD ADMIN MGT
CT/SYS 20. PAGE 20 E0396 GP/REL
  BARGAIN

B61
JENKS C.W.,INTERNATIONAL IMMUNITIES. PLAN EDU/PROP INT/ORG
ADMIN PERCEPT...OLD/LIB JURID CONCPT TREND TOT/POP. DIPLOM
PAGE 58 E1157

B61
POOLEY B.J.,PLANNING AND ZONING IN THE UNITED PLAN
STATES. USA+45 MUNIC DELIB/GP ACT/RES PROB/SOLV LOC/G
TEC/DEV ADJUD ADMIN REGION 20 ZONING. PAGE 81 E1628 PROVS
  LAW

B61
PUGET H.,ESSAI DE BIBLIOGRAPHIE DES PRINCIPAUX BIBLIOG
OUVRAGES DE DROIT PUBLIC... QUI ONT PARU HORS DE MGT
FRANCE DE 1945 A 1958. EUR+WWI USA+45 CONSTN LOC/G ADMIN
...METH 20. PAGE 83 E1660 LAW

B61
TOMPKINS D.C.,CONFLICT OF INTEREST IN THE FEDERAL BIBLIOG
GOVERNMENT: A BIBLIOGRAPHY. USA+45 EX/STRUC LEGIS ROLE
ADJUD ADMIN CRIME CONGRESS PRESIDENT. PAGE 96 E1932 NAT/G
  LAW

B61
WARD R.E.,JAPANESE POLITICAL SCIENCE: A GUIDE TO BIBLIOG/A
JAPANESE REFERENCE AND RESEARCH MATERIALS (2ND PHIL/SCI
ED.). LAW CONSTN STRATA NAT/G POL/PAR DELIB/GP
LEGIS ADMIN CHOOSE GP/REL...INT/LAW 19/20 CHINJAP.
PAGE 105 E2099

L61
GERWIG R.,"PUBLIC AUTHORITIES IN THE UNITED LOC/G
STATES." LAW CONSTN PROVS TAX ADMIN FEDERAL. MUNIC
PAGE 43 E0852 GOV/REL
  PWR

L61
MCNAMEE B.J.,"CONFLICT OF INTEREST: STATE LAW
GOVERNMENT EMPLOYEES." USA+45 PROVS 20. PAGE 71 REPRESENT
E1426 ADMIN
  CONTROL

S61
ABLARD C.D.,"EX PARTE CONTACTS WITH FEDERAL EXEC
ADMINISTRATIVE AGENCIES." USA+45 CLIENT NAT/G ADJUD
DELIB/GP ADMIN PWR 20. PAGE 2 E0044 LOBBY
  REPRESENT

S61
AGNEW P.C.,"INTRODUCING CHANGE IN A MENTAL ORD/FREE
HOSPITAL." CLIENT WORKER PROB/SOLV INGP/REL PUB/INST
PERS/REL ADJUST. PAGE 3 E0054 PSY
  ADMIN

S61
MILLER E.,"LEGAL ASPECTS OF UN ACTION IN THE INT/ORG
CONGO." AFR CULTURE ADMIN PEACE DRIVE RIGID/FLEX LEGIT
ORD/FREE...WELF/ST JURID OBS UN CONGO 20. PAGE 73
E1458

B62
CARPER E.T.,ILLINOIS GOES TO CONGRESS FOR ARMY ADMIN
LAND. USA+45 LAW EXTR/IND PROVS REGION CIVMIL/REL LOBBY
GOV/REL FEDERAL ATTIT 20 ILLINOIS SENATE CONGRESS GEOG
DIRKSEN/E DOUGLAS/P. PAGE 20 E0391 LEGIS

B62
CARSON P.,MATERIALS FOR WEST AFRICAN HISTORY IN THE BIBLIOG/A
ARCHIVES OF BELGIUM AND HOLLAND. CLIENT INDUS COLONIAL
INT/TRADE ADMIN 17/19. PAGE 20 E0397 AFR
ECO/UNDEV

B62
COSTA RICA UNIVERSIDAD BIBL,LISTA DE TESIS DE GRADO BIBLIOG/A
DE LA UNIVERSIDAD DE COSTA RICA. COSTA/RICA LAW NAT/G
LOC/G ADMIN LEAD...SOC 20. PAGE 26 E0518 DIPLOM
ECO/UNDEV

B62
DELANY V.T.H.,THE ADMINISTRATION OF JUSTICE IN ADMIN
IRELAND. IRELAND CONSTN FINAN JUDGE COLONIAL CRIME JURID
...CRIMLGY 19/20. PAGE 30 E0604 CT/SYS
ADJUD

B62
DUPRE J.S.,SCIENCE AND THE NATION: POLICY AND R+D
POLITICS. USA+45 LAW ACADEM FORCES ADMIN CIVMIL/REL INDUS
GOV/REL EFFICIENCY PEACE...TREND 20 SCI/ADVSRY. TEC/DEV
PAGE 34 E0665 NUC/PWR

B62
GROGAN V.,ADMINISTRATIVE TRIBUNALS IN THE PUBLIC ADMIN
SERVICE. IRELAND UK NAT/G CONTROL CT/SYS...JURID LAW
GOV/COMP 20. PAGE 48 E0945 ADJUD
DELIB/GP

B62
HADWEN J.G.,HOW UNITED NATIONS DECISIONS ARE MADE. INT/ORG
WOR+45 LAW EDU/PROP LEGIT ADMIN PWR...DECISION ROUTINE
SELF/OBS GEN/LAWS UN 20. PAGE 49 E0972

B62
HSUEH S.--S.,GOVERNMENT AND ADMINISTRATION OF HONG ADMIN
KONG. CHIEF DELIB/GP LEGIS CT/SYS REPRESENT GOV/REL LOC/G
20 HONG/KONG CITY/MGT CIVIL/SERV GOVERNOR. PAGE 55 COLONIAL
E1106 EX/STRUC

B62
INSTITUTE JUDICIAL ADMIN,JUDGES: THEIR TEMPORARY NAT/G
APPOINTMENT, ASSIGNMENT AND TRANSFER: SURVEY OF FED LOC/G
AND STATE CONSTN'S STATUTES, ROLES OF CT. USA+45 JUDGE
CONSTN PROVS CT/SYS GOV/REL PWR JURID. PAGE 57 ADMIN
E1128

B62
LAWSON R.,INTERNATIONAL REGIONAL ORGANIZATIONS. INT/ORG
WOR+45 NAT/G VOL/ASSN CONSULT LEGIS EDU/PROP LEGIT DELIB/GP
ADMIN EXEC ROUTINE HEALTH PWR WEALTH...JURID EEC REGION
COLD/WAR 20 UN. PAGE 63 E1270

B62
LITTLEFIELD N.,METROPOLITAN AREA PROBLEMS AND LOC/G
MUNICIPAL HOME RULE. USA+45 PROVS ADMIN CONTROL SOVEREIGN
GP/REL PWR. PAGE 65 E1308 JURID
LEGIS

B62
MARS D.,SUGGESTED LIBRARY IN PUBLIC ADMINISTRATION. BIBLIOG
FINAN DELIB/GP EX/STRUC WORKER COMPUTER ADJUD ADMIN
...DECISION PSY SOC METH/COMP 20. PAGE 68 E1368 METH
MGT

B62
PHILLIPS O.H.,CONSTITUTIONAL AND ADMINISTRATIVE LAW JURID
(3RD ED.). UK INT/ORG LOC/G CHIEF EX/STRUC LEGIS ADMIN
BAL/PWR ADJUD COLONIAL CT/SYS PWR...CHARTS 20. CONSTN
PAGE 80 E1613 NAT/G

B62
PRESS C.,STATE MANUALS, BLUE BOOKS AND ELECTION BIBLIOG
RESULTS. LAW LOC/G MUNIC LEGIS WRITING FEDERAL PROVS
SOVEREIGN...DECISION STAT CHARTS 20. PAGE 82 E1648 ADMIN
CHOOSE

B62
UNECA LIBRARY,NEW ACQUISITIONS IN THE UNECA BIBLIOG
LIBRARY. LAW NAT/G PLAN PROB/SOLV TEC/DEV ADMIN AFR
REGION...GEOG SOC 20 UN. PAGE 98 E1956 ECO/UNDEV
INT/ORG

B62
US COMMISSION ON CIVIL RIGHTS,HEARINGS BEFORE ORD/FREE
UNITED STATES COMMISSION ON CIVIL RIGHTS. USA+45 LAW
ECO/DEV NAT/G CONSULT WORKER EDU/PROP ADJUD DISCRIM ADMIN
ISOLAT HABITAT HEALTH RESPECT 20 NEGRO CIV/RIGHTS. LEGIS
PAGE 99 E1985

L62
CAVERS D.F.,"ADMINISTRATIVE DECISION-MAKING IN REPRESENT
NUCLEAR FACILITIES LICENSING." USA+45 CLIENT ADMIN LOBBY
EXEC 20 AEC. PAGE 21 E0410 PWR
CONTROL

L62
ERDMANN H.H.,"ADMINISTRATIVE LAW AND FARM AGRI
ECONOMICS." USA+45 LOC/G NAT/G PLAN PROB/SOLV LOBBY ADMIN
...DECISION ANTHOL 20. PAGE 35 E0695 ADJUD
POLICY

L62
SCHWERIN K.,"LAW LIBRARIES AND FOREIGN LAW BIBLIOG
COLLECTION IN THE USA." USA+45 USA-45...INT/LAW LAW
STAT 20. PAGE 89 E1793 ACADEM
ADMIN

C62
ABRAHAM H.J.,"THE JUDICIAL PROCESS." USA+45 USA-45 BIBLIOG
LAW NAT/G ADMIN CT/SYS INGP/REL RACE/REL DISCRIM CONSTN
...JURID IDEA/COMP 19/20. PAGE 2 E0046 JUDGE
ADJUD

C62
BACON F.,"OF JUDICATURE" (1612) IN F. BACON, CT/SYS
ESSAYS." ADJUD ADMIN SANCTION CRIME PWR...JURID LEGIS
GEN/LAWS. PAGE 7 E0128 LAW

C62
MORGAN G.G.,"SOVIET ADMINISTRATIVE LEGALITY: THE LAW
ROLE OF THE ATTORNEY GENERAL'S OFFICE." COM USSR CONSTN
CONTROL ROUTINE...CONCPT BIBLIOG 18/20. PAGE 74 LEGIS
E1493 ADMIN

C62
VAN DER SPRENKEL S.,"LEGAL INSTITUTIONS IN MANCHU LAW
CHINA." ASIA STRUCT CT/SYS ROUTINE GOV/REL GP/REL JURID
...CONCPT BIBLIOG 17/20. PAGE 103 E2068 ADMIN
ADJUD

B63
ADRIAN C.R.,GOVERNING OVER FIFTY STATES AND THEIR PROVS
COMMUNITIES. USA+45 CONSTN FINAN MUNIC NAT/G LOC/G
POL/PAR EX/STRUC LEGIS ADMIN CONTROL CT/SYS GOV/REL
...CHARTS 20. PAGE 3 E0052 GOV/COMP

B63
CHOJNACKI S.,REGISTER ON CURRENT RESEARCH ON BIBLIOG
ETHIOPIA AND THE HORN OF AFRICA. ETHIOPIA LAW ACT/RES
CULTURE AGRI SECT EDU/PROP ADMIN...GEOG HEAL LING INTELL
20. PAGE 22 E0433 ACADEM

B63
CORLEY R.N.,THE LEGAL ENVIRONMENT OF BUSINESS. NAT/G
CONSTN LEGIS TAX ADMIN CT/SYS DISCRIM ATTIT PWR INDUS
...TREND 18/20. PAGE 26 E0509 JURID
DECISION

B63
ECOLE NATIONALE D'ADMIN,BIBLIOGRAPHIE SELECTIVE BIBLIOG
D'OUVRAGES DE LANGUE FRANCAISE TRAITANT DES AFR
PROBLEMES GOUVERNEMENTAUX ET ADMINISTRATIFS. NAT/G ADMIN
FORCES ACT/RES OP/RES PLAN PROB/SOLV BUDGET ADJUD EX/STRUC
COLONIAL LEAD 20. PAGE 34 E0672

B63
ELIAS T.O.,THE NIGERIAN LEGAL SYSTEM. NIGERIA LAW CT/SYS
FAM KIN SECT ADMIN NAT/LISM...JURID 18/20 ADJUD
ENGLSH/LAW COMMON/LAW. PAGE 34 E0682 COLONIAL
PROF/ORG

B63
FORTES A.B.,HISTORIA ADMINISTRATIVA, JUDICIARIA E PROVS
ECLESIASTICA DO RIO GRANDE DO SUL. BRAZIL L/A+17C ADMIN
LOC/G SECT COLONIAL CT/SYS ORD/FREE CATHISM 16/20. JURID
PAGE 39 E0773

B63
GALLAGHER J.F.,SUPERVISORIAL DISTRICTING IN APPORT
CALIFORNIA COUNTIES: 1960-1963 (PAMPHLET). USA+45 REGION
ADJUD ADMIN PARTIC CHOOSE GP/REL...CENSUS 20 REPRESENT
CALIFORNIA. PAGE 42 E0828 LOC/G

B63
GARNER J.F.,ADMINISTRATIVE LAW. UK LAW LOC/G NAT/G ADMIN
EX/STRUC LEGIS JUDGE BAL/PWR BUDGET ADJUD CONTROL JURID
CT/SYS...BIBLIOG 20. PAGE 42 E0840 PWR
GOV/REL

B63
GOURNAY B.,PUBLIC ADMINISTRATION. FRANCE LAW CONSTN BIBLIOG/A
AGRI FINAN LABOR SCHOOL EX/STRUC CHOOSE...MGT ADMIN
METH/COMP 20. PAGE 45 E0894 NAT/G
LOC/G

B63
GRANT D.R.,STATE AND LOCAL GOVERNMENT IN AMERICA. PROVS
USA+45 FINAN LOC/G MUNIC EX/STRUC FORCES EDU/PROP POL/PAR
ADMIN CHOOSE FEDERAL ATTIT...JURID 20. PAGE 45 LEGIS
E0897 CONSTN

GRIFFITH J.A.G.,PRINCIPLES OF ADMINISTRATIVE LAW (3RD ED.). UK CONSTN EX/STRUC LEGIS ADJUD CONTROL CT/SYS PWR...CHARTS 20. PAGE 47 E0940
B63
JURID
ADMIN
NAT/G
BAL/PWR

KLEIN F.J.,JUDICIAL ADMINISTRATION AND THE LEGAL PROFESSION. USA+45 ADMIN CONTROL EFFICIENCY ...POLICY 20. PAGE 61 E1222
B63
BIBLIOG/A
CT/SYS
ADJUD
JUDGE

KLESMENT J.,LEGAL SOURCES AND BIBLIOGRAPHY OF THE BALTIC STATES (ESTONIA, LATVIA, LITHUANIA). COM ESTONIA LATVIA LITHUANIA LAW FINAN ADJUD CT/SYS REGION CENTRAL MARXISM 19/20. PAGE 61 E1223
B63
BIBLIOG/A
JURID
CONSTN
ADMIN

PALOTAI O.C.,PUBLICATIONS OF THE INSTITUTE OF GOVERNMENT, 1930-1962. LAW PROVS SCHOOL WORKER ACT/RES OP/RES CT/SYS GOV/REL...CRIMLGY SOC/WK. PAGE 79 E1594
B63
BIBLIOG/A
ADMIN
LOC/G
FINAN

PATRA A.C.,THE ADMINISTRATION OF JUSTICE UNDER THE EAST INDIA COMPANY IN BENGAL, BIHAR AND ORISSA. INDIA UK LG/CO CAP/ISM INT/TRADE ADJUD COLONIAL CONTROL CT/SYS...POLICY 20. PAGE 80 E1602
B63
ADMIN
JURID
CONCPT

RICHARDS P.G.,PATRONAGE IN BRITISH GOVERNMENT. ELITES DELIB/GP TOP/EX PROB/SOLV CONTROL CT/SYS EXEC PWR. PAGE 84 E1693
B63
EX/STRUC
REPRESENT
POL/PAR
ADMIN

ROBERT J.,LA MONARCHIE MAROCAINE. MOROCCO LABOR MUNIC POL/PAR EX/STRUC ORD/FREE PWR...JURID TREND T 20. PAGE 85 E1702
B63
CHIEF
CONSERVE
ADMIN
CONSTN

ROYAL INSTITUTE PUBLIC ADMIN,BRITISH PUBLIC ADMINISTRATION. UK LAW FINAN INDUS LOC/G POL/PAR LEGIS LOBBY PARL/PROC CHOOSE JURID. PAGE 86 E1729
B63
BIBLIOG
ADMIN
MGT
NAT/G

US CONGRESS: SENATE,HEARINGS OF THE COMMITTEE ON THE JUDICIARY. USA+45 CONSTN NAT/G ADMIN GOV/REL 20 CONGRESS. PAGE 99 E1992
B63
LEGIS
LAW
ORD/FREE
DELIB/GP

US SENATE COMM ON JUDICIARY,ADMINISTERED PRICES. USA+45 RATION ADJUD CONTROL LOBBY...POLICY 20 SENATE MONOPOLY. PAGE 102 E2047
B63
LG/CO
PRICE
ADMIN
DECISION

US SENATE COMM ON JUDICIARY,ADMINISTRATIVE CONFERENCE OF THE UNITED STATES. USA+45 CONSTN NAT/G PROB/SOLV CONFER GOV/REL...INT 20 SENATE. PAGE 102 E2048
B63
PARL/PROC
JURID
ADMIN
LEGIS

US SENATE COMM ON JUDICIARY,US PERSONNEL SECURITY PRACTICES. USA+45 DELIB/GP ADJUD ADMIN ORD/FREE ...CHARTS 20 CONGRESS CIVIL/SERV. PAGE 102 E2049
B63
PLAN
NAT/G
CONTROL
WORKER

VAN SLYCK P.,PEACE: THE CONTROL OF NATIONAL POWER. CUBA WOR+45 FINAN NAT/G FORCES PROB/SOLV TEC/DEV BAL/PWR ADMIN CONTROL ORD/FREE...POLICY INT/LAW UN COLD/WAR TREATY. PAGE 103 E2069
B63
ARMS/CONT
PEACE
INT/ORG
DIPLOM

WADE H.W.R.,TOWARDS ADMINISTRATIVE JUSTICE. UK USA+45 CONSTN CONSULT PROB/SOLV CT/SYS PARL/PROC ...POLICY JURID METH/COMP 20 ENGLSH/LAW. PAGE 104 E2088
B63
ADJUD
IDEA/COMP
ADMIN

WOLL P.,ADMINISTRATIVE LAW: THE INFORMAL PROCESS. USA+45 NAT/G CONTROL EFFICIENCY 20. PAGE 107 E2141
B63
ADMIN
ADJUD
REPRESENT
EX/STRUC

BOLGAR V.,"THE PUBLIC INTEREST: A JURISPRUDENTIAL AND COMPARATIVE OVERVIEW OF SYMPOSIUM ON FUNDAMENTAL CONCEPTS OF PUBLIC LAW" COM FRANCE GERMANY SWITZERLND LAW ADJUD ADMIN AGREE LAISSEZ
L63
CONCPT
ORD/FREE
CONTROL
NAT/COMP

...JURID GEN/LAWS 20 EUROPE/E. PAGE 14 E0264

LISSITZYN O.J.,"INTERNATIONAL LAW IN A DIVIDED WORLD." FUT WOR+45 CONSTN CULTURE ECO/DEV ECO/UNDEV DIST/IND NAT/G FORCES ECO/TAC LEGIT ADJUD ADMIN COERCE ATTIT HEALTH MORAL ORD/FREE PWR RESPECT WEALTH VAL/FREE. PAGE 65 E1306
L63
INT/ORG
LAW

HILLS R.J.,"THE REPRESENTATIVE FUNCTION: NEGLECTED DIMENSION OF LEADERSHIP BEHAVIOR" USA+45 CLIENT STRUCT SCHOOL PERS/REL...STAT QU SAMP LAB/EXP 20. PAGE 53 E1048
S63
LEAD
ADMIN
EXEC
ACT/RES

MODELSKI G.,"STUDY OF ALLIANCES." WOR+45 WOR-45 INT/ORG NAT/G FORCES LEGIT ADMIN CHOOSE ALL/VALS PWR SKILL...INT/LAW CONCPT GEN/LAWS 20 TREATY. PAGE 74 E1477
S63
VOL/ASSN
CON/ANAL
DIPLOM

BENNETT H.A.,THE COMMISSION AND THE COMMON LAW: A STUDY IN ADMINISTRATIVE ADJUDICATION. LAW ADMIN CT/SYS LOBBY SANCTION GOV/REL 20 COMMON/LAW. PAGE 10 E0188
B64
ADJUD
DELIB/GP
DIST/IND
POLICY

BERNSTEIN H.,A BOOKSHELF ON BRAZIL. BRAZIL ADMIN COLONIAL...HUM JURID SOC 20. PAGE 11 E0213
B64
BIBLIOG/A
NAT/G
L/A+17C
ECO/UNDEV

BLOUSTEIN E.J.,NUCLEAR ENERGY, PUBLIC POLICY, AND THE LAW. USA+45 NAT/G ADJUD ADMIN GP/REL OWN PEACE ATTIT HEALTH...ANTHOL 20. PAGE 13 E0251
B64
TEC/DEV
LAW
POLICY
NUC/PWR

BOUVIER-AJAM M.,MANUEL TECHNIQUE ET PRATIQUE DU MAIRE ET DES ELUS ET AGENTS COMMUNAUX. FRANCE LOC/G BUDGET CHOOSE GP/REL SUPEGO...JURID BIBLIOG 20 MAYOR COMMUNES. PAGE 14 E0274
B64
MUNIC
ADMIN
CHIEF
NEIGH

ENDACOTT G.B.,GOVERNMENT AND PEOPLE IN HONG KONG 1841-1962: A CONSTITUTIONAL HISTORY. UK LEGIS ADJUD REPRESENT ATTIT 19/20 HONG/KONG. PAGE 35 E0688
B64
CONSTN
COLONIAL
CONTROL
ADMIN

FISK W.M.,ADMINISTRATIVE PROCEDURE IN A REGULATORY AGENCY: THE CAB AND THE NEW YORK-CHICAGO CASE (PAMPHLET). USA+45 DIST/IND ADMIN CONTROL LOBBY GP/REL ROLE ORD/FREE NEWYORK/C CHICAGO CAB. PAGE 38 E0758
B64
SERV/IND
ECO/DEV
AIR
JURID

FORBES A.H.,CURRENT RESEARCH IN BRITISH STUDIES. UK CONSTN CULTURE POL/PAR SECT DIPLOM ADMIN...JURID BIOG WORSHIP 20. PAGE 39 E0769
B64
BIBLIOG
PERSON
NAT/G
PARL/PROC

FRANCK T.M.,EAST AFRICAN UNITY THROUGH LAW. MALAWI TANZANIA UGANDA UK ZAMBIA CONSTN INT/ORG NAT/G ADMIN ROUTINE TASK NAT/LISM ATTIT SOVEREIGN ...RECORD IDEA/COMP NAT/COMP. PAGE 40 E0785
B64
AFR
FEDERAL
REGION
INT/LAW

GESELLSCHAFT RECHTSVERGLEICH,BIBLIOGRAPHIE DES DEUTSCHEN RECHTS (BIBLIOGRAPHY OF GERMAN LAW, TRANS. BY COURTLAND PETERSON). GERMANY FINAN INDUS LABOR SECT FORCES CT/SYS PARL/PROC CRIME...INT/LAW SOC NAT/COMP 20. PAGE 43 E0853
B64
BIBLIOG/A
JURID
CONSTN
ADMIN

GJUPANOVIC H.,LEGAL SOURCES AND BIBLIOGRAPHY OF YUGOSLAVIA. COM YUGOSLAVIA LAW LEGIS DIPLOM ADMIN PARL/PROC REGION CRIME CENTRAL 20. PAGE 44 E0873
B64
BIBLIOG/A
JURID
CONSTN
ADJUD

GOODNOW H.F.,THE CIVIL SERVICE OF PAKISTAN: BUREAUCRACY IN A NEW NATION. INDIA PAKISTAN S/ASIA ECO/UNDEV PROVS CHIEF PARTIC CHOOSE EFFICIENCY PWR ...BIBLIOG 20. PAGE 45 E0889
B64
ADMIN
GOV/REL
LAW
NAT/G

GRZYBOWSKI K.,THE SOCIALIST COMMONWEALTH OF NATIONS: ORGANIZATIONS AND INSTITUTIONS. FORCES DIPLOM INT/TRADE ADJUD ADMIN LEAD WAR MARXISM SOCISM...BIBLIOG 20 COMECON WARSAW/P. PAGE 48 E0956
B64
INT/LAW
COM
REGION
INT/ORG

HALLER W.,DER SCHWEDISCHE JUSTITIEOMBUDSMAN.
DENMARK FINLAND NORWAY SWEDEN LEGIS ADJUD CONTROL
PERSON ORD/FREE...NAT/COMP 20 OMBUDSMAN. PAGE 50
E0986
JURID
PARL/PROC
ADMIN
CHIEF
B64

HOLT S.,THE DICTIONARY OF AMERICAN GOVERNMENT.
USA+45 LOC/G MUNIC PROVS LEGIS ADMIN JURID. PAGE 55
E1091
DICTIONARY
INDEX
LAW
NAT/G
B64

KEEFE W.J.,THE AMERICAN LEGISLATIVE PROCESS:
CONGRESS AND THE STATES. USA+45 LAW POL/PAR
DELIB/GP DEBATE ADMIN LOBBY REPRESENT CONGRESS
PRESIDENT. PAGE 60 E1191
LEGIS
DECISION
PWR
PROVS
B64

MAKI J.M.,COURT AND CONSTITUTION IN JAPAN: SELECTED
SUPREME COURT DECISIONS, 1948-60. LAW AGRI FAM
LEGIS BAL/PWR ADMIN CHOOSE...SOC ANTHOL CABINET 20
CHINJAP CIVIL/LIB. PAGE 68 E1355
CONSTN
JURID
CT/SYS
CRIME
B64

MANNING B.,FEDERAL CONFLICT OF INTEREST LAW. USA+45
NAT/G PWR 20. PAGE 68 E1362
LAW
CONTROL
ADMIN
JURID
B64

NATIONAL BOOK LEAGUE,THE COMMONWEALTH IN BOOKS: AN
ANNOTATED LIST. CANADA UK LOC/G SECT ADMIN...SOC
BIOG 20 CMN/WLTH. PAGE 76 E1526
BIBLIOG/A
JURID
NAT/G
B64

NELSON D.H.,ADMINISTRATIVE AGENCIES OF THE USA:
THEIR DECISIONS AND AUTHORITY. USA+45 NAT/G CONTROL
CT/SYS REPRESENT...DECISION 20. PAGE 76 E1531
ADMIN
EX/STRUC
ADJUD
LAW
B64

RICHARDSON I.L.,BIBLIOGRAFIA BRASILEIRA DE
ADMINISTRACAO PUBLICA E ASSUNTOS CORRELATOS. BRAZIL
CONSTN FINAN LOC/G NAT/G POL/PAR PLAN DIPLOM
RECEIVE ATTIT...METH 20. PAGE 84 E1694
BIBLIOG
MGT
ADMIN
LAW
B64

RUSSELL R.B.,UNITED NATIONS EXPERIENCE WITH
MILITARY FORCES: POLITICAL AND LEGAL ASPECTS. AFR
KOREA WOR+45 LEGIS PROB/SOLV ADMIN CONTROL
EFFICIENCY PEACE...POLICY INT/LAW BIBLIOG UN.
PAGE 87 E1738
FORCES
DIPLOM
SANCTION
ORD/FREE
B64

STOICOIU V.,LEGAL SOURCES AND BIBLIOGRAPHY OF
ROMANIA. COM ROMANIA LAW FINAN POL/PAR LEGIS JUDGE
ADJUD CT/SYS PARL/PROC MARXISM 20. PAGE 93 E1874
BIBLIOG/A
JURID
CONSTN
ADMIN
B64

SZLADITS C.,BIBLIOGRAPHY ON FOREIGN AND COMPARATIVE
LAW: BOOKS AND ARTICLES IN ENGLISH (SUPPLEMENT
1962). FINAN INDUS JUDGE LICENSE ADMIN CT/SYS
PARL/PROC OWN...INT/LAW CLASSIF METH/COMP NAT/COMP
20. PAGE 95 E1904
BIBLIOG/A
JURID
ADJUD
LAW
B64

US SENATE COMM ON JUDICIARY,ADMINISTRATIVE
PROCEDURE ACT. USA+45 CONSTN NAT/G PROB/SOLV CONFER
GOV/REL PWR...INT 20 SENATE. PAGE 102 E2054
PARL/PROC
LEGIS
JURID
ADMIN
B64

GARDNER R.N.,"THE SOVIET UNION AND THE UNITED
NATIONS." WOR+45 FINAN POL/PAR VOL/ASSN FORCES
ECO/TAC DOMIN EDU/PROP LEGIT ADJUD ADMIN ARMS/CONT
COERCE ATTIT ALL/VALS...POLICY MAJORIT CONCPT OBS
TIME/SEQ TREND STERTYP UN. PAGE 42 E0838
COM
INT/ORG
USSR
S64

SCHWELB E.,"OPERATION OF THE EUROPEAN CONVENTION ON
HUMAN RIGHTS." EUR+WWI LAW SOCIETY CREATE EDU/PROP
ADJUD ADMIN PEACE ATTIT ORD/FREE PWR...POLICY
INT/LAW CONCPT OBS GEN/LAWS UN VAL/FREE ILO 20
ECHR. PAGE 89 E1791
INT/ORG
MORAL
S64

BOCK E.,GOVERNMENT REGULATION OF BUSINESS. USA+45
LAW EX/STRUC LEGIS EXEC ORD/FREE PWR...ANTHOL
CONGRESS. PAGE 13 E0255
MGT
ADMIN
NAT/G
CONTROL
B65

CAVERS D.F.,THE CHOICE-OF-LAW PROCESS. PROB/SOLV
ADJUD CT/SYS CHOOSE RATIONAL...IDEA/COMP 16/20
JURID
DECISION
B65

TREATY. PAGE 21 E0411
METH/COMP
ADMIN

COHN H.J.,THE GOVERNMENT OF THE RHINE PALATINATE IN
THE FIFTEENTH CENTURY. GERMANY FINAN LOC/G DELIB/GP
LEGIS CT/SYS CHOOSE CATHISM 14/15 PALATINATE.
PAGE 24 E0468
PROVS
JURID
GP/REL
ADMIN
B65

COOPER F.E.,STATE ADMINISTRATIVE LAW (2 VOLS.). LAW
LEGIS PLAN TAX ADJUD CT/SYS FEDERAL PWR...CONCPT
20. PAGE 25 E0501
JURID
CONSTN
ADMIN
PROVS
B65

FISCHER F.C.,THE GOVERNMENT OF MICHIGAN. USA+45
NAT/G PUB/INST EX/STRUC LEGIS BUDGET GIVE EDU/PROP
CT/SYS CHOOSE GOV/REL...T MICHIGAN. PAGE 38 E0753
PROVS
LOC/G
ADMIN
CONSTN
B65

FRIEDMAN L.,SOUTHERN JUSTICE. USA+45 PUB/INST LEGIT
ADMIN CT/SYS DISCRIM...DECISION ANTHOL 20 NEGRO
SOUTH/US CIV/RIGHTS. PAGE 40 E0800
ADJUD
LAW
CONSTN
RACE/REL
B65

FRYE R.J.,HOUSING AND URBAN RENEWAL IN ALABAMA.
USA+45 NEIGH LEGIS BUDGET ADJUD ADMIN PARTIC...MGT
20 ALABAMA URBAN/RNWL. PAGE 41 E0815
MUNIC
PROB/SOLV
PLAN
GOV/REL
B65

GOTLIEB A.,DISARMAMENT AND INTERNATIONAL LAW* A
STUDY OF THE ROLE OF LAW IN THE DISARMAMENT
PROCESS. USA+45 USSR PROB/SOLV CONFER ADMIN ROUTINE
NUC/PWR ORD/FREE SOVEREIGN UN TREATY. PAGE 45 E0893
INT/LAW
INT/ORG
ARMS/CONT
IDEA/COMP
B65

HOWE R.,THE STORY OF SCOTLAND YARD: A HISTORY OF
THE CID FROM THE EARLIEST TIMES TO THE PRESENT DAY.
UK MUNIC EDU/PROP 6/20 SCOT/YARD. PAGE 55 E1104
CRIMLGY
CRIME
FORCES
ADMIN
B65

INST INTL DES CIVILISATION DIF,THE CONSTITUTIONS
AND ADMINISTRATIVE INSTITUTIONS OF THE NEW STATES.
AFR ISLAM S/ASIA NAT/G POL/PAR DELIB/GP EX/STRUC
CONFER EFFICIENCY NAT/LISM...JURID SOC 20. PAGE 56
E1123
CONSTN
ADMIN
ADJUD
ECO/UNDEV
B65

KAAS L.,DIE GEISTLICHE GERICHTSBARKEIT DER
KATHOLISCHEN KIRCHE IN PREUSSEN (2 VOLS.). PRUSSIA
CONSTN NAT/G PROVS SECT ADJUD ADMIN ATTIT 16/20.
PAGE 59 E1178
JURID
CATHISM
GP/REL
CT/SYS
B65

KRISLOV S.,THE SUPREME COURT IN THE POLITICAL
PROCESS. USA+45 LAW SOCIETY STRUCT WORKER ADMIN
ROLE...JURID SOC 20 SUPREME/CT. PAGE 62 E1231
ADJUD
DECISION
CT/SYS
CONSTN
B65

LAFAVE W.R.,LAW AND SOVIET SOCIETY. EX/STRUC DIPLOM
DOMIN EDU/PROP PRESS ADMIN CRIME OWN MARXISM 20
KHRUSH/N. PAGE 62 E1244
JURID
CT/SYS
ADJUD
GOV/REL
B65

MOODY M.,CATALOG OF INTERNATIONAL LAW AND RELATIONS
(20 VOLS.). WOR+45 INT/ORG NAT/G ADJUD ADMIN CT/SYS
POLICY. PAGE 74 E1488
BIBLIOG
INT/LAW
DIPLOM
B65

NEWBURY C.W.,BRITISH POLICY TOWARDS WEST AFRICA:
SELECT DOCUMENTS 1786-1874. AFR UK INT/TRADE DOMIN
ADMIN COLONIAL CT/SYS COERCE ORD/FREE...BIBLIOG/A
18/19. PAGE 77 E1540
DIPLOM
POLICY
NAT/G
WRITING
B65

NORDEN A.,WAR AND NAZI CRIMINALS IN WEST GERMANY:
STATE, ECONOMY, ADMINISTRATION, ARMY, JUSTICE,
SCIENCE. GERMANY GERMANY/W MOD/EUR ECO/DEV ACADEM
EX/STRUC FORCES DOMIN ADMIN CT/SYS...POLICY MAJORIT
PACIFIST 20. PAGE 77 E1554
FASCIST
WAR
NAT/G
TOP/EX
B65

PADELFORD N.,THE UNITED NATIONS IN THE BALANCE*
ACCOMPLISHMENTS AND PROSPECTS. NAT/G VOL/ASSN
DIPLOM ADMIN COLONIAL CT/SYS REGION WAR ORD/FREE
...ANTHOL UN. PAGE 79 E1588
INT/ORG
CONTROL
B65

SHARMA S.A.,PARLIAMENTARY GOVERNMENT IN INDIA.
NAT/G
B65

INDIA FINAN LOC/G PROVS DELIB/GP PLAN ADMIN CT/SYS   CONSTN
FEDERAL...JURID 20. PAGE 90 E1814   PARL/PROC
                                                           LEGIS

                                                           B65
SMITH C.,THE OMBUDSMAN: A BIBLIOGRAPHY (PAMPHLET).   BIBLIOG
DENMARK SWEDEN USA+45 LAW LEGIS JUDGE GOV/REL   ADMIN
GP/REL...JURID 20. PAGE 92 E1841   CT/SYS
                                                           ADJUD

                                                           B65
UNESCO,INTERNATIONAL ORGANIZATIONS IN THE SOCIAL   INT/ORG
SCIENCES(REV. ED.). LAW ADMIN ATTIT...CRIMLGY GEOG   R+D
INT/LAW PSY SOC STAT 20 UNESCO. PAGE 98 E1962   PROF/ORG
                                                          ACT/RES

                                                          B65
US OFFICE ECONOMIC OPPORTUNITY,CATALOG OF FEDERAL   BIBLIOG
PROGRAMS FOR INDIVIDUAL AND COMMUNITY IMPROVEMENT.   CLIENT
USA+45 GIVE RECEIVE ADMIN HEALTH KNOWL SKILL WEALTH   ECO/TAC
CHARTS. PAGE 101 E2021   MUNIC

                                                          B65
US SENATE COMM ON JUDICIARY,HEARINGS BEFORE   ROUTINE
SUBCOMMITTEE ON ADMINISTRATIVE PRACTICE AND   DELIB/GP
PROCEDURE ABOUT ADMINISTRATIVE PROCEDURE ACT 1965.   ADMIN
USA+45 LEGIS EDU/PROP ADJUD GOV/REL INGP/REL   NAT/G
EFFICIENCY...POLICY INT 20 CONGRESS. PAGE 103 E2055

                                                          S65
LONG T.G.,"THE ADMINISTRATIVE PROCESS: AGONIZING   ADJUD
REAPPRAISAL IN THE FTC." NAT/G REPRESENT 20 FTC.   LOBBY
PAGE 66 E1326   ADMIN
                                                          EX/STRUC

                                                          B66
AARON T.J.,THE CONTROL OF POLICE DISCRETION: THE   CONTROL
DANISH EXPERIENCE. DENMARK LAW CREATE ADMIN   FORCES
INGP/REL SUPEGO PWR 20 OMBUDSMAN. PAGE 2 E0042   REPRESENT
                                                         PROB/SOLV

                                                          B66
ANDERSON S.V.,CANADIAN OMBUDSMAN PROPOSALS. CANADA   NAT/G
LEGIS DEBATE PARL/PROC...MAJORIT JURID TIME/SEQ   CREATE
IDEA/COMP 20 OMBUDSMAN PARLIAMENT. PAGE 5 E0092   ADMIN
                                                         POL/PAR

                                                          B66
BESTERMAN T.,A WORLD BIBLIOGRAPHY OF BIBLIOGRAPHIES BIBLIOG/A
(4TH ED.). WOR+45 WOR-45 LAW INT/ORG ADMIN   DIPLOM
CON/ANAL. PAGE 11 E0219

                                                          B66
BRAIBANTI R.,RESEARCH ON THE BUREAUCRACY OF   HABITAT
PAKISTAN. PAKISTAN LAW CULTURE INTELL ACADEM LOC/G   NAT/G
SECT PRESS CT/SYS...LING CHARTS 20 BUREAUCRCY.   ADMIN
PAGE 15 E0286   CONSTN

                                                          B66
BRENNAN J.T.,THE COST OF THE AMERICAN JUDICIAL   COST
SYSTEM. USA+45 PROF/ORG TV ADMIN EFFICIENCY.   CT/SYS
PAGE 15 E0292   ADJUD
                                                         JURID

                                                          B66
DAVIS K.,BUSINESS AND ITS ENVIRONMENT. LAW ECO/DEV   EX/STRUC
INDUS OP/RES ADMIN CONTROL ROUTINE GP/REL PROFIT   PROB/SOLV
POLICY. PAGE 29 E0573   CAP/ISM
                                                         EXEC

                                                          B66
EPSTEIN F.T.,THE AMERICAN BIBLIOGRAPHY OF RUSSIAN   BIBLIOG
AND EAST EUROPEAN STUDIES FOR 1964. USSR LOC/G   COM
NAT/G POL/PAR FORCES ADMIN ARMS/CONT...JURID CONCPT MARXISM
20 UN. PAGE 35 E0694   DIPLOM

                                                          B66
FENN DH J.R.,BUSINESS DECISION MAKING AND   DECISION
GOVERNMENT POLICY. SERV/IND LEGIS LICENSE ADMIN   PLAN
CONTROL GP/REL INGP/REL 20 CASEBOOK. PAGE 37 E0736   NAT/G
                                                         LG/CO

                                                          B66
FINK M.,A SELECTIVE BIBLIOGRAPHY ON STATE   BIBLIOG
CONSTITUTIONAL REVISION (PAMPHLET). USA+45 FINAN   PROVS
EX/STRUC LEGIS EDU/PROP ADMIN CT/SYS APPORT CHOOSE   LOC/G
GOV/REL 20. PAGE 38 E0751   CONSTN

                                                          B66
GREENE L.E.,GOVERNMENT IN TENNESSEE (2ND ED.).   PROVS
USA+45 DIST/IND INDUS POL/PAR EX/STRUC LEGIS PLAN   LOC/G
BUDGET GIVE CT/SYS...MGT T 20 TENNESSEE. PAGE 46   CONSTN
E0909   ADMIN

                                                          B66
HOLMES O.W.,JUSTICE HOLMES, EX CATHEDRA. USA+45   BIOG

USA-45 LAW INTELL ADMIN ATTIT...BIBLIOG 20   PERSON
SUPREME/CT HOLMES/OW. PAGE 55 E1088   CT/SYS
                                                         ADJUD

                                                          B66
LEE L.T.,VIENNA CONVENTION ON CONSULAR RELATIONS.   AGREE
WOR+45 LAW INT/ORG CONFER GP/REL PRIVIL...INT/LAW   DIPLOM
20 TREATY VIENNA/CNV. PAGE 64 E1277   ADMIN

                                                          B66
O'NEILL C.E.,CHURCH AND STATE IN FRENCH COLONIAL   COLONIAL
LOUISIANA: POLICY AND POLITICS TO 1732. PROVS   NAT/G
VOL/ASSN DELIB/GP ADJUD ADMIN GP/REL ATTIT DRIVE   SECT
...POLICY BIBLIOG 17/18 LOUISIANA CHURCH/STA.   PWR
PAGE 78 E1568

                                                          B66
SZLADITS C.,A BIBLIOGRAPHY ON FOREIGN AND   BIBLIOG/A
COMPARATIVE LAW (SUPPLEMENT 1964). FINAN FAM LABOR   CT/SYS
LG/CO LEGIS JUDGE ADMIN CRIME...CRIMLGY 20. PAGE 95 INT/LAW
E1905

                                                          B66
WALL E.H.,THE COURT OF JUSTICE IN THE EUROPEAN   CT/SYS
COMMUNITIES: JURISDICTION AND PROCEDURE. EUR+WWI   INT/ORG
DIPLOM ADJUD ADMIN ROUTINE TASK...CONCPT LING 20.   LAW
PAGE 105 E2096   OP/RES

                                                          B66
WILSON G.,CASES AND MATERIALS ON CONSTITUTIONAL AND JURID
ADMINISTRATIVE LAW. UK LAW NAT/G EX/STRUC LEGIS   ADMIN
BAL/PWR BUDGET DIPLOM ADJUD CONTROL CT/SYS GOV/REL   CONSTN
ORD/FREE 20 PARLIAMENT ENGLSH/LAW. PAGE 106 E2126   PWR

                                                          B66
YOUNG W.,EXISTING MECHANISMS OF ARMS CONTROL.   ARMS/CONT
PROC/MFG OP/RES DIPLOM TASK CENTRAL...MGT TREATY.   ADMIN
PAGE 108 E2165   NUC/PWR
                                                         ROUTINE

                                                          L66
SEYLER W.C.,"DOCTORAL DISSERTATIONS IN POLITICAL   BIBLIOG
SCIENCE IN UNIVERSITIES OF THE UNITED STATES AND   LAW
CANADA." INT/ORG LOC/G ADMIN...INT/LAW MGT   NAT/G
GOV/COMP. PAGE 90 E1808

                                                          S66
BURDETTE F.L.,"SELECTED ARTICLES AND DOCUMENTS ON   BIBLIOG
AMERICAN GOVERNMENT AND POLITICS." LAW LOC/G MUNIC   USA+45
NAT/G POL/PAR PROVS LEGIS BAL/PWR ADMIN EXEC   JURID
REPRESENT MGT. PAGE 17 E0331   CONSTN

                                                          S66
MATTHEWS D.G.,"ETHIOPIAN OUTLINE: A BIBLIOGRAPHIC   BIBLIOG
RESEARCH GUIDE." ETHIOPIA LAW STRUCT ECO/UNDEV AGRI   NAT/G
LABOR SECT CHIEF DELIB/GP EX/STRUC ADMIN...LING   DIPLOM
ORG/CHARTS 20. PAGE 69 E1384   POL/PAR

                                                          S66
MATTHEWS D.G.,"PRELUDE-COUP D'ETAT-MILITARY   BIBLIOG
GOVERNMENT: A BIBLIOGRAPHICAL AND RESEARCH GUIDE TO NAT/G
NIGERIAN POL AND GOVT, JAN, 1965-66." AFR NIGER LAW ADMIN
CONSTN POL/PAR LEGIS CIVMIL/REL GOV/REL...STAT 20.   CHOOSE
PAGE 69 E1385

                                                          S66
POLSBY N.W.,"BOOKS IN THE FIELD: POLITICAL   BIBLIOG/A
SCIENCE." LAW CONSTN LOC/G NAT/G LEGIS ADJUD PWR 20 ATTIT
SUPREME/CT. PAGE 81 E1627   ADMIN
                                                         JURID

                                                          N66
BACHELDER G.L.,THE LITERATURE OF FEDERALISM: A   BIBLIOG
SELECTED BIBLIOGRAPHY (REV ED) (A PAMPHLET). USA+45 FEDERAL
USA-45 WOR+45 WOR-45 LAW CONSTN PROVS ADMIN CT/SYS NAT/G
GOV/REL ROLE...CONCPT 19/20. PAGE 7 E0126   LOC/G

                                                          B67
BUREAU GOVERNMENT RES AND SERV,COUNTY GOVERNMENT   BIBLIOG/A
REORGANIZATION - A SELECTED ANNOTATED BIBLIOGRAPHY   APPORT
(PAPER). USA+45 USA-45 LAW CONSTN MUNIC PROVS   LOC/G
EX/STRUC CREATE PLAN PROB/SOLV REPRESENT GOV/REL   ADMIN
20. PAGE 17 E0332

                                                          B67
CAHIER P.,LE DROIT DIPLOMATIQUE CONTEMPORAIN.   INT/LAW
INT/ORG CHIEF ADMIN...T 20. PAGE 18 E0358   DIPLOM
                                                         JURID

                                                          B67
ESTEY M.,THE UNIONS: STRUCTURE, DEVELOPMENT, AND   LABOR
MANAGEMENT. FUT USA+45 ADJUD CONTROL INGP/REL DRIVE EX/STRUC
...DECISION T 20 AFL/CIO. PAGE 35 E0699   ADMIN
                                                         GOV/REL

FESLER J.W.,THE FIFTY STATES AND THEIR LOCAL
GOVERNMENTS. FUT USA+45 POL/PAR LEGIS PROB/SOLV
ADMIN CT/SYS CHOOSE GOV/REL FEDERAL...POLICY CHARTS
20 SUPREME/CT. PAGE 37 E0743
B67 PROVS LOC/G

GABRIEL P.P.,THE INTERNATIONAL TRANSFER OF
CORPORATE SKILLS: MANAGEMENT CONTRACTS IN LESS
DEVELOPED COUNTRIES. CLIENT INDUS LG/CO PLAN
PROB/SOLV CAP/ISM ECO/TAC FOR/AID INT/TRADE RENT
ADMIN SKILL 20. PAGE 42 E0825
B67 ECO/UNDEV AGREE MGT CONSULT

GELLHORN W.,OMBUDSMEN AND OTHERS: CITIZENS'
PROTECTORS IN NINE COUNTRIES. WOR+45 LAW CONSTN
LEGIS INSPECT ADJUD ADMIN CONTROL CT/SYS CHOOSE
PERS/REL...STAT CHARTS 20. PAGE 43 E0847
B67 NAT/COMP REPRESENT INGP/REL PROB/SOLV

GREENE L.S.,AMERICAN GOVERNMENT POLICIES AND
FUNCTIONS. USA+45 LAW AGRI DIST/IND LABOR MUNIC
BUDGET DIPLOM EDU/PROP ORD/FREE...BIBLIOG T 20.
PAGE 46 E0910
B67 POLICY NAT/G ADMIN DECISION

HEWITT W.H.,ADMINISTRATION OF CRIMINAL JUSTICE IN
NEW YORK. LAW PROB/SOLV ADJUD ADMIN...CRIMLGY
CHARTS T 20 NEW/YORK. PAGE 52 E1035
B67 CRIME ROLE CT/SYS FORCES

LENG S.C.,JUSTICE IN COMMUNIST CHINA: A SURVEY OF
THE JUDICIAL SYSTEM OF THE CHINESE PEOPLE'S
REPUBLIC. CHINA/COM LAW CONSTN LOC/G NAT/G PROF/ORG
CONSULT FORCES ADMIN CRIME ORD/FREE...BIBLIOG 20
MAO. PAGE 64 E1284
B67 CT/SYS ADJUD JURID MARXISM

PLANO J.C.,FORGING WORLD ORDER: THE POLITICS OF
INTERNATIONAL ORGANIZATION. PROB/SOLV DIPLOM
CONTROL CENTRAL RATIONAL ORD/FREE...INT/LAW CHARTS
BIBLIOG 20 UN LEAGUE/NAT. PAGE 81 E1618
B67 INT/ORG ADMIN JURID

UNITED NATIONS,UNITED NATIONS PUBLICATIONS:
1945-1966. WOR+45 COM/IND DIST/IND FINAN TEC/DEV
ADMIN...POLICY INT/LAW MGT CHARTS 20 UN UNESCO.
PAGE 98 E1970
B67 BIBLIOG/A INT/ORG DIPLOM WRITING

UNIVERSAL REFERENCE SYSTEM,BIBLIOGRAPHY OF
BIBLIOGRAPHIES IN POLITICAL SCIENCE, GOVERNMENT,
AND PUBLIC POLICY (VOLUME III). WOR+45 WOR-45 LAW
ADMIN...SOC CON/ANAL COMPUT/IR GEN/METH. PAGE 98
E1973
B67 BIBLIOG/A NAT/G DIPLOM POLICY

US PRES TASK FORCE ADMIN JUS,TASK FORCE REPORT: THE
COURTS. USA+45 CONSULT CONFER...JURID CHARTS.
PAGE 101 E2025
B67 CT/SYS ADJUD ROUTINE ADMIN

US SENATE COMM ON FOREIGN REL,USIA FOREIGN SERVICE
PERSONNEL SYSTEM. USA+45 LAW CONSULT ADMIN 20 USIA.
PAGE 102 E2038
B67 DIPLOM EDU/PROP PRIVIL PROF/ORG

"A PROPOS DES INCITATIONS FINANCIERES AUX
GROUPEMENTS DES COMMUNES: ESSAI D'INTERPRETATION."
FRANCE NAT/G LEGIS ADMIN GOV/REL CENTRAL 20. PAGE 2
E0037
L67 LOC/G ECO/TAC APPORT ADJUD

BLUMBERG A.S.,"THE PRACTICE OF LAW AS CONFIDENCE
GAME; ORGANIZATIONAL COOPTATION OF A PROFESSION."
USA+45 CLIENT SOCIETY CONSULT ROLE JURID. PAGE 13
E0252
L67 CT/SYS ADJUD GP/REL ADMIN

CARMICHAEL D.M.,"FORTY YEARS OF WATER POLLUTION
CONTROL IN WISCONSIN: A CASE STUDY." LAW EXTR/IND
INDUS MUNIC DELIB/GP PLAN PROB/SOLV SANCTION
...CENSUS CHARTS 20 WISCONSIN. PAGE 20 E0384
L67 HEALTH CONTROL ADMIN ADJUD

LAMBERT J.D.,"CORPORATE POLITICAL SPENDING AND
CAMPAIGN FINANCE." LAW CONSTN FINAN LABOR LG/CO
LOC/G NAT/G VOL/ASSN TEC/DEV ADJUD ADMIN PARTIC.
PAGE 62 E1247
L67 USA+45 POL/PAR CHOOSE COST

LENT G.E.,"TAX INCENTIVES FOR INVESTMENT IN
DEVELOPING COUNTRIES" WOR+45 LAW INDUS PLAN BUDGET
L67 ECO/UNDEV TAX

TARIFFS ADMIN...METH/COMP 20. PAGE 64 E1285
FINAN ECO/TAC

"THE STATE OF ZONING ADMINISTRATION IN ILLINOIS:
PROCEDURAL REQUIREMENTS OF JUDICIAL INTERVENTION."
USA+45 LAW CONSTN DELIB/GP ADJUD CT/SYS ORD/FREE
ILLINOIS. PAGE 2 E0038
S67 ADMIN CONTROL HABITAT PLAN

BERRODIN E.F.,"AT THE BARGAINING TABLE." LABOR
DIPLOM ECO/TAC ADMIN...MGT 20 MICHIGAN. PAGE 11
E0216
S67 PROVS WORKER LAW BARGAIN

BLAKEY G.R.,"ORGANIZED CRIME IN THE UNITED STATES."
USA+45 USA-45 STRUCT LABOR NAT/G VOL/ASSN ADMIN
PERS/REL PWR...CRIMLGY INT 17/20. PAGE 12 E0240
S67 CRIME ELITES CONTROL

BRADLEY A.W.,"CONSTITUTION-MAKING IN UGANDA."
UGANDA LAW CHIEF DELIB/GP LEGIS ADMIN EXEC
PARL/PROC RACE/REL ORD/FREE...GOV/COMP 20. PAGE 15
E0284
S67 NAT/G CREATE CONSTN FEDERAL

CARTER R.M.,"SOME FACTORS IN SENTENCING POLICY."
LAW PUB/INST CRIME PERS/REL...POLICY JURID SOC
TREND CON/ANAL CHARTS SOC/EXP 20. PAGE 20 E0403
S67 ADJUD CT/SYS ADMIN

GANZ G.,"THE CONTROL OF INDUSTRY BY ADMINISTRATIVE
PROCESS." UK DELIB/GP WORKER 20. PAGE 42 E0832
S67 INDUS LAW ADMIN CONTROL

MITCHELL J.D.B.,"THE CONSTITUTIONAL IMPLICATIONS OF
JUDICIAL CONTROL OF THE ADMINISTRATION IN THE
UNITED KINGDOM." UK LAW ADJUD ADMIN GOV/REL ROLE
...GP/COMP 20. PAGE 74 E1474
S67 CONSTN CT/SYS CONTROL EX/STRUC

MONEYPENNY P.,"UNIVERSITY PURPOSE, DISCIPLINE, AND
DUE PROCESS." USA+45 EDU/PROP ADJUD LEISURE
ORD/FREE. PAGE 74 E1484
S67 ACADEM AGE/Y CONTROL ADMIN

RAI H.,"DISTRICT MAGISTRATE AND POLICE
SUPERINTENDENT IN INDIA: THE CONTROVERSY OF DUAL
CONTROL" INDIA LAW PROVS ADMIN PWR 19/20. PAGE 83
E1669
S67 STRUCT CONTROL ROLE FORCES

READ J.S.,"CENSORED." UGANDA CONSTN INTELL SOCIETY
NAT/G DIPLOM PRESS WRITING ADJUD ADMIN COLONIAL
RISK...IDEA/COMP 20. PAGE 84 E1675
S67 EDU/PROP AFR CREATE

RICHARDSON J.J.,"THE MAKING OF THE RESTRICTIVE
TRADE PRACTICES ACT 1956 A CASE STUDY OF THE POLICY
PROCESS IN BRITAIN." UK FINAN MARKET LG/CO POL/PAR
CONSULT PRESS ADJUD ADMIN AGREE LOBBY SANCTION
ATTIT 20. PAGE 84 E1695
S67 LEGIS ECO/TAC POLICY INDUS

TYDINGS J.D.,"MODERNIZING THE ADMINISTRATION OF
JUSTICE." PLAN ADMIN ROUTINE EFFICIENCY...JURID
SIMUL. PAGE 97 E1948
S67 CT/SYS MGT COMPUTER CONSULT

WRAITH R.E.,"ADMINISTRATIVE CHANGE IN THE NEW
AFRICA." AFR LG/CO ADJUD INGP/REL PWR...RECORD
GP/COMP 20. PAGE 107 E2147
S67 ADMIN NAT/G LOC/G ECO/UNDEV

ELLMAKER E.G.,"REVELATION OF RIGHTS." JUDGE DISCRIM
SUPEGO...JURID PHIL/SCI CONCPT 17/18. PAGE 35 E0685
L84 ORD/FREE ADMIN MORAL NAT/G

GOODNOW F.J.,"AN EXECUTIVE AND THE COURTS: JUDICIAL
REMEDIES AGAINST ADMINISTRATIVE ACTION" FRANCE UK
USA-45 WOR-45 LAW CONSTN SANCTION ORD/FREE 19.
PAGE 45 E0888
L86 CT/SYS GOV/REL ADMIN ADJUD

ADMINISTRATIVE MANAGEMENT....SEE MGT

ADOKO A. E0050

ADOLESCENCE....SEE AGE/Y

ADRIAN C.R. E0051,E0052

ADVERT/ADV....ADVERTISING ADVISORY COMMISSION

ADVERTISING....SEE SERV/IND+EDU/PROP; SEE ALSO TV, PRESS

AEA....ATOMIC ENERGY AUTHORITY OF UN; SEE ALSO NUC/PWR

AEC....ATOMIC ENERGY COMMISSION; SEE ALSO NUC/PWR

N19
ATOMIC INDUSTRIAL FORUM,COMMENTARY ON LEGISLATION   NUC/PWR
TO PERMIT PRIVATE OWNERSHIP OF SPECIAL NUCLEAR   MARKET
MATERIAL (PAMPHLET). USA+45 DELIB/GP LEGIS PLAN OWN INDUS
...POLICY 20 AEC CONGRESS. PAGE 6 E0111   LAW

B59
US CONGRESS JT ATOM ENRGY COMM,SELECTED MATERIALS NAT/G
ON FEDERAL-STATE COOPERATION IN THE ATOMIC ENERGY NUC/PWR
FIELD. USA+45 LAW LOC/G PROVS CONSULT LEGIS ADJUD GOV/REL
...POLICY BIBLIOG 20 AEC. PAGE 99 E1991   DELIB/GP

L62
CAVERS D.F.,"ADMINISTRATIVE DECISION-MAKING IN   REPRESENT
NUCLEAR FACILITIES LICENSING." USA+45 CLIENT ADMIN LOBBY
EXEC 20 AEC. PAGE 21 E0410   PWR
  CONTROL

S67
EYRAUD M.,"LA FRANCE FACE A UN EVENTUEL TRAITE DE NUC/PWR
NON DISSEMINATION DES ARMES NUCLEAIRES." FRANCE ARMS/CONT
USA+45 EXTR/IND INDUS R+D INT/ORG ACT/RES TEC/DEV POLICY
AGREE PRODUC ATTIT 20 TREATY AEC EURATOM. PAGE 36
E0708

AFGHANISTN....SEE ALSO ISLAM, ASIA

AFL/CIO....AMERICAN FEDERATION OF LABOR, CONGRESS OF
  INDUSTRIAL ORGANIZATIONS

B55
BLOOM G.F.,ECONOMICS OF LABOR RELATIONS. USA+45 LAW ECO/DEV
CONSULT WORKER CAP/ISM PAY ADJUD CONTROL EFFICIENCY ECO/TAC
ORD/FREE...CHARTS 19/20 AFL/CIO NLRB DEPT/LABOR. LABOR
PAGE 13 E0249   GOV/REL

B55
LARROWE C.P.,SHAPE-UP AND HIRING HALL. TRIBUTE   LABOR
ADJUD CONTROL SANCTION COERCE CRIME GP/REL PWR   INDUS
...CHARTS 20 AFL/CIO NEWYORK/C SEATTLE. PAGE 63 WORKER
E1256   NAT/G

B58
BUREAU OF NATIONAL AFFAIRS,THE MCCLELLAN COMMITTEE DELIB/GP
HEARINGS - 1957. USA+45 LEGIS CONTROL CRIME   CONFER
...CHARTS 20 CONGRESS AFL/CIO MCCLELLN/J. PAGE 17 LABOR
E0336   MGT

B64
BROOKS T.R.,TOIL AND TROUBLE, A HISTORY OF AMERICAN INDUS
LABOR. WORKER BARGAIN CAP/ISM ADJUD AUTOMAT EXEC LABOR
GP/REL RACE/REL EFFICIENCY INCOME PROFIT MARXISM LEGIS
17/20 KENNEDY/JF AFL/CIO NEGRO. PAGE 16 E0310

B67
ESTEY M.,THE UNIONS: STRUCTURE, DEVELOPMENT, AND LABOR
MANAGEMENT. FUT USA+45 ADJUD CONTROL INGP/REL DRIVE EX/STRUC
...DECISION T 20 AFL/CIO. PAGE 35 E0699   ADMIN
  GOV/REL

AFLAK/M....MICHEL AFLAK

AFR....AFRICA

N
CONOVER H.F.,OFFICIAL PUBLICATIONS OF BRITISH EAST BIBLIOG/A
AFRICA (PAMPHLET). UK LAW ECO/UNDEV AGRI EXTR/IND AFR
SECT LEGIS BUDGET TAX...HEAL STAT 20. PAGE 25 E0491 ADMIN
  COLONIAL

N
INTERNATIONAL COMN JURISTS,AFRICAN CONFERENCE ON CT/SYS
THE RULE OF LAW. AFR INT/ORG LEGIS DIPLOM CONFER JURID
COLONIAL ORD/FREE...CONCPT METH/COMP 20. PAGE 57 DELIB/GP
E1131

N
ANNALS OF THE AMERICAN ACADEMY OF POLITICAL AND BIBLIOG/A
SOCIAL SCIENCE. AFR ASIA S/ASIA WOR+45 POL/PAR NAT/G
DIPLOM CRIME REV...SOC BIOG 20. PAGE 1 E0003   CULTURE
  ATTIT

N
AFRICAN BIBLIOGRAPHIC CENTER,A CURRENT BIBLIOGRAPHY BIBLIOG/A
ON AFRICAN AFFAIRS. LAW CULTURE ECO/UNDEV LABOR AFR
SECT DIPLOM FOR/AID COLONIAL NAT/LISM...LING 20. NAT/G
PAGE 3 E0053   REGION

B00
BATY T.,INTERNATIONAL LAW IN SOUTH AFRICA. AFR JURID
SOUTH/AFR LAW CONFER 19/20. PAGE 8 E0155   WAR
  SOVEREIGN
  COLONIAL

B01
GRONING J.,BIBLIOTHECA JURIS GENTIUM COMMUNIS, QUA BIBLIOG
PRAECIPUORUM, ASIAE, AFRICAE, ET AMERICAE,   JURID
POPULORUM DE JURIS NATURAE... AFR ASIA S/ASIA LAW
USA-45 16/17. PAGE 48 E0946   NAT/G

B03
GRONING J.,BIBLIOTHECA JURIS GENTIUM EXOTICA. AFR BIBLIOG
ASIA S/ASIA USA-45 16/17. PAGE 48 E0947   JURID
  NAT/G
  LAW

B03
MOREL E.D.,THE BRITISH CASE IN FRENCH CONGO. DIPLOM
CONGO/BRAZ FRANCE UK COERCE MORAL WEALTH...POLICY INT/TRADE
INT/LAW 20 CONGO/LEOP. PAGE 74 E1490   COLONIAL
  AFR

B34
EVANS I.L.,NATIVE POLICY IN SOUTHERN AFRICA. AFR
RHODESIA SOUTH/AFR UK STRUCT PARTIC RACE/REL ATTIT COLONIAL
WEALTH SOC/INTEG AFRICA/SW. PAGE 35 E0705   DOMIN
  LAW

B35
KENNEDY W.P.,THE LAW AND CUSTOM OF THE SOUTH CT/SYS
AFRICAN CONSTITUTION. AFR SOUTH/AFR KIN LOC/G PROVS CONSTN
DIPLOM ADJUD ADMIN EXEC 20. PAGE 60 E1203   JURID
  PARL/PROC

B42
CROWE S.E.,THE BERLIN WEST AFRICA CONFERENCE, AFR
1884-85. GERMANY ELITES MARKET INT/ORG DELIB/GP CONFER
FORCES PROB/SOLV BAL/PWR CAP/ISM DOMIN COLONIAL INT/TRADE
...INT/LAW 19. PAGE 28 E0548   DIPLOM

B48
LOGAN R.W.,THE AFRICAN MANDATES IN WORLD POLITICS. WAR
EUR+WWI GERMANY ISLAM INT/ORG BARGAIN...POLICY COLONIAL
INT/LAW 20. PAGE 66 E1321   AFR
  DIPLOM

B50
MOCKFORD J.,SOUTH-WEST AFRICA AND THE INTERNATIONAL COLONIAL
COURT (PAMPHLET). AFR GERMANY SOUTH/AFR UK   SOVEREIGN
ECO/UNDEV DIPLOM CONTROL DISCRIM...DECISION JURID INT/LAW
20 AFRICA/SW. PAGE 74 E1475   DOMIN

B52
DU BOIS W.E.B.,IN BATTLE FOR PEACE. AFR USA+45 PEACE
COLONIAL CT/SYS PERS/REL PERSON ORD/FREE...JURID 20 RACE/REL
NEGRO CIVIL/LIB. PAGE 33 E0650   DISCRIM
  BIOG

B54
BATTEN T.R.,PROBLEMS OF AFRICAN DEVELOPMENT (2ND ECO/UNDEV
ED.). AFR LAW SOCIETY SCHOOL ECO/TAC TAX...GEOG AGRI
HEAL SOC 20. PAGE 8 E0154   LOC/G
  PROB/SOLV

B54
ELIAS T.O.,GROUNDWORK OF NIGERIAN LAW. AFR LEAD JURID
CRIME INGP/REL ORD/FREE 17/20. PAGE 34 E0680 CT/SYS
  CONSTN
  CONSULT

B57
CONOVER H.F.,NORTH AND NORTHEAST AFRICA; A SELECTED BIBLIOG/A
ANNOTATED LIST OF WRITINGS. ALGERIA MOROCCO SUDAN DIPLOM
UAR CULTURE INT/ORG PROB/SOLV ADJUD NAT/LISM PWR AFR
WEALTH...SOC 20 UN. PAGE 25 E0496   ECO/UNDEV

B58
MASON H.L.,TOYNBEE'S APPROACH TO WORLD POLITICS. DIPLOM
AFR USA+45 USSR LAW WAR NAT/LISM ALL/IDEOS...HUM CONCPT
BIBLIOG. PAGE 69 E1380   PHIL/SCI
  SECT

B60
DUMON F.,LA COMMUNAUTE FRANCO-AFRO-MALGACHE: SES JURID
ORIGINES, SES INSTITUTIONS, SON EVOLUTION. FRANCE INT/ORG
MADAGASCAR POL/PAR DIPLOM ADMIN ATTIT...TREND T 20. AFR
PAGE 33 E0657   CONSTN

LAW

B60
HEYSE T.,PROBLEMS FONCIERS ET REGIME DES TERRES   BIBLIOG
(ASPECTS ECONOMIQUES, JURIDIQUES ET SOCIAUX). AFR   AGRI
CONGO/BRAZ INT/ORG DIPLOM SOVEREIGN...GEOG TREATY   ECO/UNDEV
20. PAGE 52 E1037   LEGIS

B61
BENNETT G.,THE KENYATTA ELECTION: KENYA 1960-1961.   CHOOSE
AFR INGP/REL RACE/REL CONSEN ATTIT 20 KENYATTA.   POL/PAR
PAGE 10 E0187   LAW
                                                         SUFF

B61
CARNELL F.,THE POLITICS OF THE NEW STATES: A SELECT   BIBLIOG/A
ANNOTATED BIBLIOGRAPHY WITH SPECIAL REFERENCE TO   AFR
THE COMMONWEALTH. CONSTN ELITES LABOR NAT/G POL/PAR   ASIA
EX/STRUC DIPLOM ADJUD ADMIN...GOV/COMP 20   COLONIAL
COMMONWLTH. PAGE 20 E0387

B61
COWEN D.V.,THE FOUNDATIONS OF FREEDOM. AFR   CONSTN
SOUTH/AFR DOMIN LEGIT ADJUST DISCRIM TOTALISM ATTIT   ELITES
ORD/FREE...MAJORIT JURID SOC/INTEG WORSHIP 20   RACE/REL
NEGRO. PAGE 27 E0529

S61
MILLER E.,"LEGAL ASPECTS OF UN ACTION IN THE   INT/ORG
CONGO." AFR CULTURE ADMIN PEACE DRIVE RIGID/FLEX   LEGIT
ORD/FREE...WELF/ST JURID OBS UN CONGO 20. PAGE 73
E1458

B62
ALLOTT A.N.,JUDICIAL AND LEGAL SYSTEMS IN AFRICA.   CT/SYS
LAW CONSTN JUDGE CONTROL...METH/CNCPT CLASSIF   AFR
CHARTS 20 COMMON/LAW. PAGE 4 E0070   JURID
                                                         COLONIAL

B62
CARSON P.,MATERIALS FOR WEST AFRICAN HISTORY IN THE   BIBLIOG/A
ARCHIVES OF BELGIUM AND HOLLAND. CLIENT INDUS   COLONIAL
INT/TRADE ADMIN 17/19. PAGE 20 E0397   AFR
                                                         ECO/UNDEV

B62
UNECA LIBRARY,NEW ACQUISITIONS IN THE UNECA   BIBLIOG
LIBRARY. LAW NAT/G PLAN PROB/SOLV TEC/DEV ADMIN   AFR
REGION...GEOG SOC 20 UN. PAGE 98 E1956   ECO/UNDEV
                                                         INT/ORG

L62
"AMERICAN BEHAVIORAL SCIENTIST." USSR LAW NAT/G   BIBLIOG
...SOC 20 UN. PAGE 2 E0034   AFR
                                                         R+D

L62
MANGIN G.,"L'ORGANIZATION JUDICIAIRE DES ETATS   AFR
D'AFRIQUE ET DE MADAGASCAR." ISLAM WOR+45 STRATA   LEGIS
STRUCT ECO/UNDEV NAT/G LEGIT EXEC...JURID TIME/SEQ   COLONIAL
TOT/POP 20 SUPREME/CT. PAGE 68 E1357   MADAGASCAR

L62
MURACCIOLE L.,"LA LOI FONDAMENTALE DE LA REPUBLIQUE   AFR
DU CONGO." WOR+45 SOCIETY ECO/UNDEV INT/ORG NAT/G   CONSTN
LEGIS PLAN LEGIT ADJUD COLONIAL ROUTINE ATTIT
SOVEREIGN 20 CONGO. PAGE 75 E1504

S62
GANDOLFI A.,"REFLEXIONS SUR L'IMPOT DE CAPITATION   AFR
EN AFRIQUE NOIRE." GHANA SENEGAL LAW FINAN ACT/RES   CHOOSE
TEC/DEV ECO/TAC WEALTH...MGT TREND 20. PAGE 42
E0830

S62
MANGIN G.,"LES ACCORDS DE COOPERATION EN MATIERE DE   INT/ORG
JUSTICE ENTRE LA FRANCE ET LES ETATS AFRICAINS ET   LAW
MALGACHE." AFR ISLAM WOR+45 STRUCT ECO/UNDEV NAT/G   FRANCE
DELIB/GP PERCEPT ALL/VALS...JURID MGT TIME/SEQ 20.
PAGE 68 E1356

S62
MURACCIOLE L.,"LES MODIFICATIONS DE LA CONSTITUTION   NAT/G
MALGACHE." AFR WOR+45 ECO/UNDEV LEGIT EXEC ALL/VALS   STRUCT
...JURID 20. PAGE 75 E1505   SOVEREIGN
                                                         MADAGASCAR

B63
CARTER G.M.,FIVE AFRICAN STATES: RESPONSES TO   AFR
DIVERSITY. CONSTN CULTURE STRATA LEGIS PLAN ECO/TAC   SOCIETY
DOMIN EDU/PROP CT/SYS EXEC CHOOSE ATTIT HEALTH
ORD/FREE PWR...TIME/SEQ TOT/POP VAL/FREE. PAGE 20
E0398

B63
DECOTTIGNIES R.,LES NATIONALITES AFRICAINES. AFR   NAT/LISM
NAT/G PROB/SOLV DIPLOM COLONIAL ORD/FREE...CHARTS   JURID
GOV/COMP 20. PAGE 30 E0602   LEGIS

B63
ECOLE NATIONALE D'ADMIN.BIBLIOGRAPHIE SELECTIVE   BIBLIOG
D'OUVRAGES DE LANGUE FRANCAISE TRAITANT DES   AFR
PROBLEMES GOUVERNEMENTAUX ET ADMINISTRATIFS. NAT/G   ADMIN
FORCES ACT/RES OP/RES PLAN PROB/SOLV BUDGET ADJUD   EX/STRUC
COLONIAL LEAD 20. PAGE 34 E0672

B63
ELIAS T.O.,GOVERNMENT AND POLITICS IN AFRICA.   AFR
CONSTN CULTURE SOCIETY NAT/G POL/PAR DIPLOM   NAT/LISM
REPRESENT PERSON...SOC TREND BIBLIOG 4/20. PAGE 34   COLONIAL
E0681   LAW

B63
GEERTZ C.,OLD SOCIETIES AND NEW STATES: THE QUEST   ECO/UNDEV
FOR MODERNITY IN ASIA AND AFRICA. AFR ASIA LAW   TEC/DEV
CULTURE SECT EDU/PROP REV...GOV/COMP NAT/COMP 20.   NAT/LISM
PAGE 42 E0842   SOVEREIGN

B63
HAUSMAN W.H.,MANAGING ECONOMIC DEVELOPMENT IN   ECO/UNDEV
AFRICA. AFR USA+45 LAW FINAN WORKER TEC/DEV WEALTH   PLAN
...ANTHOL 20. PAGE 51 E1012   FOR/AID
                                                         MGT

B63
JOSEPH H.,IF THIS BE TREASON. SOUTH/AFR 20. PAGE 59   AFR
E1174   LAW
                                                         CT/SYS
                                                         CRIME

S63
BRAUSCH G.E.,"AFRICAN ETHNOCRACIES: SOME   LAW
SOCIOLOGICAL IMPLICATIONS OF CONSTITUTIONAL CHANGE   SOC
IN EMERGENT TERRITORIES OF AFRICA." AFR CONSTN   ELITES
FACE/GP MUNIC NAT/G DOMIN ATTIT ALL/VALS
...HIST/WRIT GEN/LAWS VAL/FREE 20. PAGE 15 E0289

S63
HARNETTY P.,"CANADA, SOUTH AFRICA AND THE   AFR
COMMONWEALTH." CANADA SOUTH/AFR LAW INT/ORG   ATTIT
VOL/ASSN DELIB/GP LEGIS TOP/EX ECO/TAC LEGIT DRIVE
MORAL...CONCPT CMN/WLTH 20. PAGE 50 E1000

B64
CURRIE D.P.,FEDERALISM AND THE NEW NATIONS OF   FEDERAL
AFRICA. CANADA USA+45 INT/TRADE TAX GP/REL   AFR
...NAT/COMP SOC/INTEG 20. PAGE 28 E0556   ECO/UNDEV
                                                         INT/LAW

B64
FRANCK T.M.,EAST AFRICAN UNITY THROUGH LAW. MALAWI   AFR
TANZANIA UGANDA UK ZAMBIA CONSTN INT/ORG NAT/G   FEDERAL
ADMIN ROUTINE TASK NAT/LISM ATTIT SOVEREIGN   REGION
...RECORD IDEA/COMP NAT/COMP. PAGE 40 E0785   INT/LAW

B64
HANNA W.J.,POLITICS IN BLACK AFRICA: A SELECTIVE   BIBLIOG
BIBLIOGRAPHY OF RELEVANT PERIODICAL LITERATURE. AFR   NAT/LISM
LAW LOC/G MUNIC NAT/G POL/PAR LOBBY CHOOSE RACE/REL   COLONIAL
SOVEREIGN 20. PAGE 50 E0995

B64
ROBINSON R.D.,INTERNATIONAL BUSINESS POLICY. AFR   ECO/TAC
INDIA L/A+17C USA+45 ELITES AGRI FOR/AID COERCE   DIST/IND
BAL/PAY...DECISION INT/LAW MGT 20. PAGE 85 E1706   COLONIAL
                                                         FINAN

B64
RUSSELL R.B.,UNITED NATIONS EXPERIENCE WITH   FORCES
MILITARY FORCES: POLITICAL AND LEGAL ASPECTS. AFR   DIPLOM
KOREA WOR+45 LEGIS PROB/SOLV ADMIN CONTROL   SANCTION
EFFICIENCY PEACE...POLICY INT/LAW BIBLIOG UN.   ORD/FREE
PAGE 87 E1738

B64
SEGAL R.,SANCTIONS AGAINST SOUTH AFRICA. AFR   SANCTION
SOUTH/AFR NAT/G INT/TRADE RACE/REL PEACE PWR   DISCRIM
...INT/LAW ANTHOL 20 UN. PAGE 90 E1801   ECO/TAC
                                                         POLICY

L64
POUNDS N.J.G.,"THE POLITICS OF PARTITION." AFR ASIA   NAT/G
COM EUR+WWI FUT ISLAM S/ASIA USA-45 LAW ECO/DEV   NAT/LISM
ECO/UNDEV AGRI INDUS INT/ORG POL/PAR PROVS SECT
FORCES TOP/EX EDU/PROP LEGIT ATTIT MORAL ORD/FREE
PWR RESPECT WEALTH. PAGE 82 E1640

S64
CARNEGIE ENDOWMENT INT. PEACE,"HUMAN RIGHTS (ISSUES   INT/ORG
BEFORE THE NINETEENTH GENERAL ASSEMBLY)." AFR   PERSON
WOR+45 LAW CONSTN NAT/G EDU/PROP GP/REL DISCRIM   RACE/REL
PEACE ATTIT MORAL ORD/FREE...INT/LAW PSY CONCPT
RECORD UN 20. PAGE 20 E0385

BOVY L.,LE MOUVEMENT SYNDICAL OUEST AFRICAIN D'EXPRESSION FRANCAISE. AFR SECT...JURID SOC 20. PAGE 14 E0275
B65
BIBLIOG
SOCISM
ECO/UNDEV
IDEA/COMP

HAEFELE E.T.,GOVERNMENT CONTROLS ON TRANSPORT. AFR RHODESIA TANZANIA DIPLOM ECO/TAC TARIFFS PRICE ADJUD CONTROL REGION EFFICIENCY...POLICY 20 CONGO. PAGE 49 E0973
B65
ECO/UNDEV
DIST/IND
FINAN
NAT/G

INST INTL DES CIVILISATION DIF,THE CONSTITUTIONS AND ADMINISTRATIVE INSTITUTIONS OF THE NEW STATES. AFR ISLAM S/ASIA NAT/G POL/PAR DELIB/GP EX/STRUC CONFER EFFICIENCY NAT/LISM...JURID SOC 20. PAGE 56 E1123
B65
CONSTN
ADMIN
ADJUD
ECO/UNDEV

KARIS T.,THE TREASON TRIAL IN SOUTH AFRICA: A GUIDE TO THE MICROFILM RECORD OF THE TRIAL. SOUTH/AFR LAW ELITES NAT/G LEGIT CT/SYS RACE/REL DISCRIM...SOC 20. PAGE 59 E1185
B65
BIBLIOG/A
ADJUD
CRIME
AFR

KUPER H.,AFRICAN LAW. LAW FAM KIN SECT JUDGE ADJUST NAT/LISM 17/20. PAGE 62 E1236
B65
AFR
CT/SYS
ADJUD
COLONIAL

NEWBURY C.W.,BRITISH POLICY TOWARDS WEST AFRICA: SELECT DOCUMENTS 1786-1874. AFR UK INT/TRADE DOMIN ADMIN COLONIAL CT/SYS COERCE ORD/FREE...BIBLIOG/A 18/19. PAGE 77 E1540
B65
DIPLOM
POLICY
NAT/G
WRITING

PEASLEE A.J.,CONSTITUTIONS OF NATIONS* THIRD REVISED EDITION (VOLUME I* AFRICA). LAW EX/STRUC LEGIS TOP/EX LEGIT CT/SYS ROUTINE ORD/FREE PWR SOVEREIGN...CON/ANAL CHARTS. PAGE 80 E1606
B65
AFR
CHOOSE
CONSTN
NAT/G

SOPER T.,EVOLVING COMMONWEALTH. AFR CANADA INDIA IRELAND UK LAW CONSTN POL/PAR DOMIN CONTROL WAR PWR ...AUD/VIS 18/20 COMMONWLTH OEEC. PAGE 93 E1857
B65
INT/ORG
COLONIAL
VOL/ASSN

VON RENESSE E.A.,UNVOLLENDETE DEMOKRATIEN. AFR ISLAM S/ASIA SOCIETY ACT/RES COLONIAL...JURID CHARTS BIBLIOG METH 13/20. PAGE 104 E2083
B65
ECO/UNDEV
NAT/COMP
SOVEREIGN

HARVEY W.B.,LAW AND SOCIAL CHANGE IN GHANA. AFR GHANA CONSULT CONTROL CT/SYS INGP/REL 20. PAGE 51 E1011
B66
JURID
CONSTN
LEAD
ORD/FREE

KEAY E.A.,THE NATIVE AND CUSTOMARY COURTS OF NIGERIA. NIGERIA CONSTN ELITES NAT/G TOP/EX PARTIC REGION...DECISION JURID 19/20. PAGE 60 E1190
B66
AFR
ADJUD
LAW

HIGGINS R.,"THE INTERNATIONAL COURT AND SOUTH WEST AFRICA* SOME IMPLICATIONS OF THE JUDGMENT." AFR LAW ECO/UNDEV JUDGE RACE/REL COST PWR...INT/LAW TREND UN TREATY. PAGE 52 E1043
L66
SOUTH/AFR
COLONIAL
CT/SYS
ADJUD

ANAND R.P.,"ATTITUDE OF THE ASIAN-AFRICAN STATES TOWARD CERTAIN PROBLEMS OF INTERNATIONAL LAW." L/A+17C S/ASIA ECO/UNDEV CREATE CONFER ADJUD COLONIAL...RECORD GP/COMP UN. PAGE 5 E0087
S66
INT/LAW
ATTIT
ASIA
AFR

GREEN L.C.,"RHODESIAN OIL: BOOTLEGGERS OR PIRATES?" AFR RHODESIA UK WOR+45 INT/ORG NAT/G DIPLOM LEGIT COLONIAL SOVEREIGN 20 UN OAU. PAGE 46 E0907
S66
INT/TRADE
SANCTION
INT/LAW
POLICY

MATTHEWS D.G.,"PRELUDE-COUP D'ETAT-MILITARY GOVERNMENT: A BIBLIOGRAPHICAL AND RESEARCH GUIDE TO NIGERIAN POL AND GOVT. JAN. 1965-66." AFR NIGER LAW CONSTN POL/PAR LEGIS CIVMIL/REL GOV/REL...STAT 20. PAGE 69 E1385
S66
BIBLIOG
NAT/G
ADMIN
CHOOSE

ADOKO A.,"THE CONSTITUTION OF UGANDA." AFR UGANDA LOC/G CHIEF FORCES LEGIS ADJUD EXEC CHOOSE NAT/LISM ...IDEA/COMP 20. PAGE 3 E0050
S67
NAT/G
CONSTN
ORD/FREE
LAW

MAYANJA A.,"THE GOVERNMENT'S PROPOSALS ON THE NEW CONSTITUTION." AFR UGANDA LAW CHIEF LEGIS ADJUD REPRESENT FEDERAL PWR 20. PAGE 69 E1390
S67
CONSTN
CONFER
ORD/FREE
NAT/G

READ J.S.,"CENSORED." UGANDA CONSTN INTELL SOCIETY NAT/G DIPLOM PRESS WRITING ADJUD ADMIN COLONIAL RISK...IDEA/COMP 20. PAGE 84 E1675
S67
EDU/PROP
AFR
CREATE

WRAITH R.E.,"ADMINISTRATIVE CHANGE IN THE NEW AFRICA." AFR LG/CO ADJUD INGP/REL PWR...RECORD GP/COMP 20. PAGE 107 E2147
S67
ADMIN
NAT/G
LOC/G
ECO/UNDEV

DUGARD J.,"THE REVOCATION OF THE MANDATE FOR SOUTH WEST AFRICA." AFR/SW WOR+45 STRATA NAT/G DELIB/GP DIPLOM ADJUD SANCTION CHOOSE RACE/REL ...POLICY NAT/COMP 20 AFRICA/SW UN TRUST/TERR LEAGUE/NAT. PAGE 33 E0654
S68
AFR
INT/ORG
DISCRIM
COLONIAL

BROOKS S.,BRITAIN AND THE BOERS. AFR SOUTH/AFR UK CULTURE INSPECT LEGIT...INT/LAW 19/20 BOER/WAR. PAGE 16 E0309
B99
WAR
DIPLOM
NAT/G

AFR/STATES....ORGANIZATION OF AFRICAN STATES

AFRICA/CEN....CENTRAL AFRICA

AFRICA/E....EAST AFRICA

AFRICA/N....NORTH AFRICA

AFRICA/SW....SOUTH WEST AFRICA

EVANS I.L.,NATIVE POLICY IN SOUTHERN AFRICA. RHODESIA SOUTH/AFR UK STRUCT PARTIC RACE/REL ATTIT WEALTH SOC/INTEG AFRICA/SW. PAGE 35 E0705
B34
AFR
COLONIAL
DOMIN
LAW

MOCKFORD J.,SOUTH-WEST AFRICA AND THE INTERNATIONAL COURT (PAMPHLET). AFR GERMANY SOUTH/AFR UK ECO/UNDEV DIPLOM CONTROL DISCRIM...DECISION JURID 20 AFRICA/SW. PAGE 74 E1475
B50
COLONIAL
SOVEREIGN
INT/LAW
DOMIN

DUGARD J.,"THE REVOCATION OF THE MANDATE FOR SOUTH WEST AFRICA." SOUTH/AFR WOR+45 STRATA NAT/G DELIB/GP DIPLOM ADJUD SANCTION CHOOSE RACE/REL ...POLICY NAT/COMP 20 AFRICA/SW UN TRUST/TERR LEAGUE/NAT. PAGE 33 E0654
S68
AFR
INT/ORG
DISCRIM
COLONIAL

AFRICA/W....WEST AFRICA

AFRICAN BIBLIOGRAPHIC CENTER E0053

AFTA....ATLANTIC FREE TRADE AREA

AGE....AGE FACTORS

CUMMING J.,A CONTRIBUTION TOWARD A BIBLIOGRAPHY DEALING WITH CRIME AND COGNATE SUBJECTS (3RD ED.). UK LAW CULTURE PUB/INST ADJUD AGE BIO/SOC...PSY SOC SOC/WK STAT METH/COMP 20. PAGE 28 E0552
B35
BIBLIOG
CRIMLGY
FORCES
CT/SYS

LAPIERE R.,THE FREUDIAN ETHIC. USA+45 FAM EDU/PROP CONTROL CRIME ADJUST AGE DRIVE PERCEPT PERSON SEX ...SOC 20 FREUD/S. PAGE 63 E1254
B59
PSY
ORD/FREE
SOCIETY

DERGE D.R.,"THE LAWYER AS DECISION-MAKER IN THE AMERICAN STATE LEGISLATURE." INTELL LOC/G POL/PAR CHOOSE AGE HEREDITY PERSON CONSERVE...JURID STAT CHARTS. PAGE 31 E0607
S59
LEGIS
LAW
DECISION
LEAD

FEINE H.E.,DIE BESETZUNG DER REICHSBISTUMER VOM WESTFALISCHEN FRIEDEN BIS ZUR SAKULARISATION. GERMANY EDU/PROP GP/REL AGE 17/19. PAGE 37 E0727
B64
CHOOSE
SECT
JURID
PROVS

NAGEL S.S.,"DISPARITIES IN CRIMINAL PROCEDURE." STRATA NAT/G PROVS EDU/PROP RACE/REL AGE HABITAT SEX...JURID CHARTS 20. PAGE 76 E1519
L67
ADJUD
DISCRIM
STRUCT
ACT/RES

AGE/A....ADULTS

AGE/C....INFANTS AND CHILDREN

B06
GRIFFIN A.P.C.,LIST OF BOOKS RELATING TO CHILD
LABOR (PAMPHLET). BELGIUM FRANCE GERMANY MOD/EUR UK
USA-45 ECO/DEV INDUS WORKER CAP/ISM PAY ROUTINE
ALL/IDEOS...MGT SOC 19/20. PAGE 47 E0929
BIBLIOG/A
LAW
LABOR
AGE/C

B66
BAHRO H.,DAS KINDSCHAFTSRECHT IN DER UNION DER
SOZIALISTITSCHEN SOWJETREPUBLIKEN. USSR SECT
EDU/PROP CONTROL PWR...SOC/WK 20. PAGE 7 E0133
JURID
AGE/C
PERS/REL
SUPEGO

B66
DOUGLAS W.O.,THE BIBLE AND THE SCHOOLS. USA+45
CULTURE ADJUD INGP/REL AGE/C AGE/Y ATTIT KNOWL
WORSHIP 20 SUPREME/CT CHURCH/STA BIBLE CHRISTIAN.
PAGE 32 E0644
SECT
NAT/G
SCHOOL
GP/REL

AGE/O....OLD PEOPLE

B62
BUREAU OF NATIONAL AFFAIRS,FEDERAL-STATE REGULATION
OF WELFARE FUNDS (REV. ED.). USA+45 LAW LEGIS
DEBATE AGE/O 20 CONGRESS. PAGE 17 E0337
WELF/ST
WEALTH
PLAN
SOC/WK

AGE/Y....YOUTH AND ADOLESCENCE

N
INTERNATIONAL BIBLIOGRAPHY ON CRIME AND
DELINQUENCY. USA+45 LAW FORCES PROB/SOLV AGE/Y 20.
PAGE 1 E0023
BIBLIOG/A
CRIME
ANOMIE
CRIMLGY

B33
GILLETTE J.M.,CURRENT SOCIAL PROBLEMS. CONTROL
CRIME AGE/Y BIO/SOC...SOC 20. PAGE 43 E0861
GEOG
HEALTH
RACE/REL
FAM

S40
GERTH H.,"THE NAZI PARTY: ITS LEADERSHIP AND
COMPOSITION" (BMR)" GERMANY ELITES STRATA STRUCT
EX/STRUC FORCES ECO/TAC CT/SYS CHOOSE TOTALISM
AGE/Y AUTHORIT PWR 20. PAGE 43 E0851
POL/PAR
DOMIN
LEAD
ADMIN

B55
CAVAN R.S.,CRIMINOLOGY (2ND ED.). USA+45 LAW FAM
PUB/INST FORCES PLAN WAR AGE/Y PERSON ROLE SUPEGO
...CHARTS 20 FBI. PAGE 21 E0409
DRIVE
CRIMLGY
CONTROL
METH/COMP

B56
COHEN A.,THE SUTHERLAND PAPERS. USA+45 USA-45 LAW
CONTROL CRIME AGE/Y...TREND ANTHOL BIBLIOG 20.
PAGE 23 E0461
CRIMLGY
PHIL/SCI
ACT/RES
METH

B56
HOGAN J.D.,AMERICAN SOCIAL LEGISLATION. USA+45 FAM
AGE/Y ATTIT...JURID CONCPT TREND. PAGE 53 E1065
STRUCT
RECEIVE
LEGIS
LABOR

B58
ALLEN C.K.,ASPECTS OF JUSTICE. UK FAM COERCE CRIME
MARRIAGE AGE/Y LOVE 20 ENGLSH/LAW. PAGE 4 E0068
JURID
MORAL
ORD/FREE

B59
COUNCIL OF STATE GOVERNMENTS,STATE GOVERNMENT: AN
ANNOTATED BIBLIOGRAPHY (PAMPHLET). USA+45 LAW AGRI
INDUS WORKER PLAN TAX ADJUST AGE/Y ORD/FREE...HEAL
MGT 20. PAGE 26 E0521
BIBLIOG/A
PROVS
LOC/G
ADMIN

B59
EPSTEIN F.T.,EAST GERMANY: A SELECTED BIBLIOGRAPHY
(PAMPHLET). COM GERMANY/E LAW AGRI FINAN INDUS
LABOR POL/PAR EDU/PROP ADMIN AGE/Y 20. PAGE 35
E0693
BIBLIOG/A
INTELL
MARXISM
NAT/G

B59
KERREMANS-RAMIOULL,LE PROBLEME DE LA DELINQUENCE
JUVENILE (2ND ED.). FAM PUB/INST SCHOOL FORCES
LEGIS MORAL...CRIMLGY SOC 20. PAGE 60 E1205
BIBLIOG
CRIME
AGE/Y
SOC/WK

B64
CHEIN I.,THE ROAD TO H; NARCOTICS, DELINQUENCY, AND
SOCIAL POLICY. USA+45 NEIGH CRIME INGP/REL ATTIT
PERSON...SOC/WK 20 NEWYORK/C. PAGE 22 E0426
BIO/SOC
AGE/Y
POLICY
ANOMIE

B64
DOOLIN D.J.,COMMUNIST CHINA: THE POLITICS OF
STUDENT OPPOSITION. CHINA/COM ELITES STRATA ACADEM
NAT/G WRITING CT/SYS LEAD PARTIC COERCE TOTALISM
20. PAGE 32 E0637
MARXISM
DEBATE
AGE/Y
PWR

B65
BROMBERG W.,CRIME AND THE MIND. LAW LEGIT ADJUD
CRIME MURDER AGE/Y ANOMIE BIO/SOC DRIVE SEX PSY.
PAGE 16 E0305
CRIMLGY
SOC
HEALTH
COERCE

B65
GLUECK S.,ROSCOE POUND AND CRIMINAL JUSTICE.
SOCIETY FAM GOV/REL AGE/Y ATTIT ORD/FREE...CRIMLGY
BIOG ANTHOL SOC/INTEG 19/20. PAGE 44 E0875
CT/SYS
CRIME
LAW
ADJUD

B65
HARTUNG F.E.,CRIME, LAW, AND SOCIETY. LAW PUB/INST
CRIME PERS/REL AGE/Y BIO/SOC PERSON ROLE SUPEGO
...LING GP/COMP GEN/LAWS 20. PAGE 50 E1004
PERCEPT
CRIMLGY
DRIVE
CONTROL

B66
COUNCIL OF STATE GOVERNMENTS,THE HANDBOOK ON
INTERSTATE CRIME CONTROL. USA+45 PUB/INST DELIB/GP
AGREE AGE/Y 20 INTST/CRIM. PAGE 27 E0524
CRIME
GOV/REL
CONTROL
JURID

B66
DOUGLAS W.O.,THE BIBLE AND THE SCHOOLS. USA+45
CULTURE ADJUD INGP/REL AGE/C AGE/Y ATTIT KNOWL
WORSHIP 20 SUPREME/CT CHURCH/STA BIBLE CHRISTIAN.
PAGE 32 E0644
SECT
NAT/G
SCHOOL
GP/REL

B66
FLEISCHER B.M.,THE ECONOMICS OF DELINQUENCY. UNIV
WORKER STRANGE ANOMIE...STAT CHARTS 20. PAGE 38
E0762
STRATA
INCOME
AGE/Y
CRIME

B66
MACIVER R.M.,THE PREVENTION AND CONTROL OF
DELINQUENCY. USA+45 STRATA PUB/INST ANOMIE ATTIT
HABITAT PERSON HEALTH...CRIMLGY PSY SOC METH.
PAGE 67 E1341
AGE/Y
PLAN
ADJUST
CRIME

B66
US PRES COMN CRIME IN DC,REPORT OF THE US
PRESIDENT'S COMMISSION ON CRIME IN THE DISTRICT OF
COLUMBIA. LEGIS WORKER EDU/PROP ADJUD CONTROL
CT/SYS GP/REL BIO/SOC HEALTH...CRIMLGY NEW/IDEA
STAT 20. PAGE 101 E2022
CRIME
FORCES
AGE/Y
SANCTION

B67
AMDS W.E.,DELINQUENCY PREVENTION: THEORY AND
PRACTICE. USA+45 SOCIETY FAM SCHOOL SECT FORCES
PROB/SOLV...HEAL JURID PREDICT ANTHOL. PAGE 4 E0071
AGE/Y
CRIME
PUB/INST
LAW

B67
BERNSTEIN S.,ALTERNATIVES TO VIOLENCE: ALIENATED
YOUTH AND RIOTS, RACE AND POVERTY. MUNIC PUB/INST
SCHOOL INGP/REL RACE/REL UTOPIA DRIVE HABITAT ROLE
WEALTH...INT 20. PAGE 11 E0215
AGE/Y
SOC/WK
NEIGH
CRIME

B67
CLINARD M.B.,CRIMINAL BEHAVIOR SYSTEMS: A TYPOLOGY.
WOR+45 LAW SOCIETY STRUCT R+D AGE/Y ATTIT WEALTH
...CLASSIF CHARTS METH/COMP METH. PAGE 23 E0457
BIBLIOG
CRIME
CRIMLGY
PERSON

B67
LOBLE L.H.,DELINQUENCY CAN BE STOPPED. FAM PUB/INST
CT/SYS ADJUST ATTIT...NEW/IDEA METH/COMP 20.
PAGE 66 E1315
AGE/Y
PROB/SOLV
ADJUD
CRIME

S67
KETCHAM O.W.,"GUIDELINES FROM GAULT: REVOLUTIONARY
REQUIREMENTS AND REAPPRAISAL." LAW CONSTN CREATE
LEGIT ROUTINE SANCTION CRIME DISCRIM PRIVIL ROLE
...JURID NEW/IDEA 20 SUPREME/CT. PAGE 60 E1208
ADJUD
AGE/Y
CT/SYS

S67
MONEYPENNY P.,"UNIVERSITY PURPOSE, DISCIPLINE, AND
DUE PROCESS." USA+45 EDU/PROP ADJUD LEISURE
ORD/FREE. PAGE 74 E1484
ACADEM
AGE/Y
CONTROL
ADMIN

AGGRESSION....SEE WAR, COERCE+DIPLOM

AGGRESSION, PHYSICAL....SEE COERCE, DRIVE

AGNEW P.C. E0054

AGREE....AGREEMENTS, CONTRACTS, TREATIES, CONCORDATS,
INTERSTATE COMPACTS

N

TOSCANO M.,THE HISTORY OF TREATIES AND   DIPLOM
INTERNATIONAL POLITICS (REV. ED.). WOR-45 AGREE WAR INT/ORG
...BIOG 19/20 TREATY WWI. PAGE 97 E1935

B16

PUFENDORF S.,LAW OF NATURE AND OF NATIONS   CONCPT
(ABRIDGED). UNIV LAW NAT/G DIPLOM AGREE WAR PERSON INT/LAW
ALL/VALS PWR...POLICY 18 DEITY NATURL/LAW. PAGE 83   SECT
E1659   MORAL

B28

BENTHAM J.,A COMMENT OF THE COMMENTARIES (1765-69). LAW
MUNIC SECT ADJUD AGREE CT/SYS CONSEN HAPPINESS   CONCPT
ORD/FREE 18. PAGE 10 E0191   IDEA/COMP

B28

HOBBES T.,THE ELEMENTS OF LAW, NATURAL AND POLITIC   PERSON
(1650). STRATA NAT/G SECT CHIEF AGREE ATTIT   LAW
ALL/VALS MORAL ORD/FREE POPULISM...POLICY CONCPT.   SOVEREIGN
PAGE 53 E1056   CONSERVE

B30

BURLAMAQUI J.J.,PRINCIPLES OF NATURAL AND POLITIC   LAW
LAW (2 VOLS.) (1747-51). EX/STRUC LEGIS AGREE   NAT/G
CT/SYS CHOOSE ROLE SOVEREIGN 18 NATURL/LAW. PAGE 17 ORD/FREE
E0342   CONCPT

B33

GENTILI A.,DE JURE BELLI, LIBRI TRES (1612) (VOL.   WAR
2). FORCES DIPLOM AGREE PEACE SOVEREIGN. PAGE 43   INT/LAW
E0849   MORAL
                                                     SUPEGO

B35

RAM J.,THE SCIENCE OF LEGAL JUDGMENT: A TREATISE... LAW
UK CONSTN NAT/G LEGIS CREATE PROB/SOLV AGREE CT/SYS JURID
...INT/LAW CONCPT 19 ENGLSH/LAW CANON/LAW CIVIL/LAW EX/STRUC
CTS/WESTM. PAGE 83 E1672   ADJUD

B36

BRIERLY J.L.,THE LAW OF NATIONS (2ND ED.). WOR+45   DIPLOM
WOR-45 INT/ORG AGREE CONTROL COERCE WAR NAT/LISM   INT/LAW
PEACE PWR 16/20 TREATY LEAGUE/NAT. PAGE 15 E0297   NAT/G

B38

MCNAIR A.D.,THE LAW OF TREATIES: BRITISH PRACTICE   AGREE
AND OPINIONS. UK CREATE DIPLOM LEGIT WRITING ADJUD   LAW
WAR...INT/LAW JURID TREATY. PAGE 71 E1424   CT/SYS
                                                     NAT/G

B38

SAINT-PIERRE C.I.,SCHEME FOR LASTING PEACE (TRANS.   INT/ORG
BY H. BELLOT). INDUS NAT/G CHIEF FORCES INT/TRADE   PEACE
CT/SYS WAR PWR SOVEREIGN WEALTH...POLICY 18.   AGREE
PAGE 87 E1741   INT/LAW

B40

WOLFERS A.,BRITAIN AND FRANCE BETWEEN TWO WORLD   DIPLOM
WARS. FRANCE UK INT/ORG NAT/G PLAN BARGAIN ECO/TAC   WAR
AGREE ISOLAT ALL/IDEOS...DECISION GEOG 20 TREATY   POLICY
VERSAILLES INTERVENT. PAGE 107 E2139

B42

HEGEL G.W.F.,PHILOSOPHY OF RIGHT. UNIV FAM SECT   NAT/G
CHIEF AGREE WAR MARRIAGE OWN ORD/FREE...POLICY   LAW
CONCPT. PAGE 51 E1023   RATIONAL

B43

BEMIS S.F.,THE LATIN AMERICAN POLICY OF THE UNITED   DIPLOM
STATES: AN HISTORICAL INTERPRETATION. INT/ORG AGREE SOVEREIGN
COLONIAL WAR PEACE ATTIT ORD/FREE...POLICY INT/LAW   USA-45
CHARTS 18/20 MEXIC/AMER WILSON/W MONROE/DOC.   L/A+17C
PAGE 10 E0185

B43

MICAUD C.A.,THE FRENCH RIGHT AND NAZI GERMANY   DIPLOM
1933-1939: A STUDY OF PUBLIC OPINION. GERMANY UK   AGREE
USSR POL/PAR ARMS/CONT COERCE DETER PEACE
RIGID/FLEX PWR MARXISM...FASCIST TREND 20
LEAGUE/NAT TREATY. PAGE 73 E1454

B44

RUDIN H.R.,ARMISTICE 1918. FRANCE GERMANY MOD/EUR   AGREE
UK USA-45 NAT/G CHIEF DELIB/GP FORCES BAL/PWR REPAR WAR
ARMS/CONT 20 WILSON/W TREATY. PAGE 86 E1732   PEACE
                                                     DIPLOM

B47

LOCKE J.,TWO TREATISES OF GOVERNMENT (1690). UK LAW CONCPT
SOCIETY LEGIS LEGIT AGREE REV OWN HEREDITY MORAL   ORD/FREE
CONSERVE...POLICY MAJORIT 17 WILLIAM/3 NATURL/LAW.   NAT/G
PAGE 66 E1316   CONSEN

N47

FOX W.T.R.,UNITED STATES POLICY IN A TWO POWER   DIPLOM
WORLD. COM USA+45 USSR FORCES DOMIN AGREE NEUTRAL   FOR/AID
NUC/PWR ORD/FREE SOVEREIGN 20 COLD/WAR TREATY   POLICY
EUROPE/W INTERVENT. PAGE 39 E0780

S48

GROSS L.,"THE PEACE OF WESTPHALIA, 1648-1948."   INT/LAW
WOR+45 WOR-45 CONSTN BAL/PWR FEDERAL 17/20 TREATY   AGREE
WESTPHALIA. PAGE 48 E0949   CONCPT
                                                     DIPLOM

B50

BERMAN H.J.,JUSTICE IN RUSSIA; AN INTERPRETATION OF JURID
SOVIET LAW. USSR LAW STRUCT LABOR FORCES AGREE   ADJUD
GP/REL ORD/FREE SOCISM...TIME/SEQ 20. PAGE 11 E0207 MARXISM
                                                     COERCE

B52

BUCKLAND W.W.,ROMAN LAW AND COMMON LAW; A   IDEA/COMP
COMPARISON IN OUTLINE (2ND REV. ED.). UK FAM LEGIT   LAW
AGREE CT/SYS OWN...JURID ROMAN/REP ROMAN/LAW   ADJUD
COMMON/LAW. PAGE 17 E0325   CONCPT

B52

FERRELL R.H.,PEACE IN THEIR TIME. FRANCE UK USA-45   PEACE
INT/ORG NAT/G FORCES CREATE AGREE ARMS/CONT COERCE   DIPLOM
WAR TREATY 20 WILSON/W LEAGUE/NAT BRIAND/A. PAGE 37
E0741

B52

LIPPMANN W.,ISOLATION AND ALLIANCES: AN AMERICAN   DIPLOM
SPEAKS TO THE BRITISH. USA+45 USA-45 INT/ORG AGREE   SOVEREIGN
COERCE DETER WAR PEACE MORAL 20 TREATY INTERVENT.   COLONIAL
PAGE 65 E1301   ATTIT

B53

OPPENHEIM L.,INTERNATIONAL LAW: A TREATISE (7TH   INT/LAW
ED., 2 VOLS.). LAW CONSTN PROB/SOLV INT/TRADE ADJUD INT/ORG
AGREE NEUTRAL WAR ORD/FREE SOVEREIGN...BIBLIOG 20   DIPLOM
LEAGUE/NAT UN ILO. PAGE 79 E1579

B55

SVARLIEN O.,AN INTRODUCTION TO THE LAW OF NATIONS.   INT/LAW
SEA AIR INT/ORG NAT/G CHIEF ADMIN AGREE WAR PRIVIL   DIPLOM
ORD/FREE SOVEREIGN...BIBLIOG 16/20. PAGE 95 E1897

B57

US SENATE COMM ON JUDICIARY,HEARING BEFORE   LEGIS
SUBCOMMITTEE ON COMMITTEE OF JUDICIARY, UNITED   CONSTN
STATES SENATE: S. J. RES. 3. USA+45 NAT/G CONSULT   CONFER
DELIB/GP DIPLOM ADJUD LOBBY REPRESENT 20 CONGRESS   AGREE
TREATY. PAGE 102 E2040

B58

SCHOEDER P.W.,THE AXIS ALLIANCE AND JAPANESE-   AGREE
AMERICAN RELATIONS 1941. ASIA GERMANY UK USA-45   DIPLOM
PEACE ATTIT...POLICY BIBLIOG 20 CHINJAP TREATY.   WAR
PAGE 88 E1763

B62

BISHOP W.W. JR.,INTERNATIONAL LAW: CASES AND   INT/LAW
MATERIALS. WOR+45 INT/ORG FORCES PROB/SOLV AGREE   DIPLOM
WAR...JURID IDEA/COMP T 20 TREATY. PAGE 12 E0233   CONCPT
                                                     CT/SYS

B62

COLOMBOS C.J.,THE INTERNATIONAL LAW OF THE SEA.   INT/LAW
WOR+45 EXTR/IND DIPLOM INT/TRADE TARIFFS AGREE WAR   SEA
...TIME/SEQ 20 TREATY. PAGE 24 E0476   JURID
                                                     ADJUD

B62

JENKS C.W.,THE PROPER LAW OF INTERNATIONAL   LAW
ORGANISATIONS. DIPLOM LEGIT AGREE CT/SYS SANCTION   INT/ORG
REPRESENT SOVEREIGN...GEN/LAWS 20 UN UNESCO ILO   ADJUD
NATO OAS. PAGE 58 E1158   INT/LAW

B62

SOMMER T.,DEUTSCHLAND UND JAPAN ZWISCHEN DEN   DIPLOM
MACHTEN. GERMANY DELIB/GP BAL/PWR AGREE COERCE   WAR
TOTALISM PWR 20 CHINJAP TREATY. PAGE 93 E1856   ATTIT

B63

DEENER D.R.,CANADA - UNITED STATES TREATY   DIPLOM
RELATIONS. CANADA USA+45 USA-45 NAT/G FORCES PLAN   INT/LAW
PROB/SOLV AGREE NUC/PWR...TREND 18/20 TREATY.   POLICY
PAGE 30 E0603

B63

HIGGINS R.,THE DEVELOPMENT OF INTERNATIONAL LAW   INT/ORG
THROUGH THE POLITICAL ORGANS OF THE UNITED NATIONS. INT/LAW
WOR+45 FORCES DIPLOM AGREE COERCE ATTIT SOVEREIGN   TEC/DEV
...BIBLIOG 20 UN TREATY. PAGE 52 E1041   JURID

L63
BOLGAR V.,"THE PUBLIC INTEREST: A JURISPRUDENTIAL   CONCPT
AND COMPARATIVE OVERVIEW OF SYMPOSIUM ON   ORD/FREE
FUNDAMENTAL CONCEPTS OF PUBLIC LAW" COM FRANCE   CONTROL
GERMANY SWITZERLND LAW ADJUD ADMIN AGREE LAISSEZ   NAT/COMP
...JURID GEN/LAWS 20 EUROPE/E. PAGE 14 E0264

B64
MCDOUGAL M.S.,STUDIES IN WORLD PUBLIC ORDER. SPACE   INT/LAW
SEA INT/ORG CREATE AGREE NUC/PWR...POLICY PHIL/SCI   SOC
IDEA/COMP ANTHOL METH 20 UN. PAGE 71 E1411   DIPLOM

B65
HABERLER G.,A SURVEY OF INTERNATIONAL TRADE THEORY.   INT/TRADE
CANADA FRANCE GERMANY ECO/TAC TARIFFS AGREE COST   BAL/PAY
DEMAND WEALTH...ECOMETRIC 19/20 MONOPOLY TREATY.   DIPLOM
PAGE 49 E0968   POLICY

B65
MONCONDUIT F.,LA COMMISSION EUROPEENNE DES DROITS   INT/LAW
DE L'HOMME. DIPLOM AGREE GP/REL ORD/FREE PWR   INT/ORG
...BIBLIOG 20 TREATY. PAGE 74 E1483   ADJUD
                                                     JURID

B65
O'CONNELL D.P.,INTERNATIONAL LAW (2 VOLS.). WOR+45   INT/LAW
WOR-45 ECO/DEV ECO/UNDEV INT/ORG NAT/G AGREE   DIPLOM
...POLICY JURID CONCPT NAT/COMP 20 TREATY. PAGE 78   CT/SYS
E1566

B65
PARRY C.,THE SOURCES AND EVIDENCES OF INTERNATIONAL   INT/LAW
LAW. WOR+45 WOR-45 DIPLOM AGREE SOVEREIGN...METH 20   ADJUD
TREATY UN LEAGUE/NAT. PAGE 80 E1599   INT/ORG
                                                     CT/SYS

B65
UNESCO,HANDBOOK OF INTERNATIONAL EXCHANGES. COM/IND   INDEX
R+D ACADEM PROF/ORG VOL/ASSN CREATE TEC/DEV   INT/ORG
EDU/PROP AGREE 20 TREATY. PAGE 98 E1963   DIPLOM
                                                     PRESS

B66
COUNCIL OF STATE GOVERNMENTS,THE HANDBOOK ON   CRIME
INTERSTATE CRIME CONTROL. USA+45 PUB/INST DELIB/GP   GOV/REL
AGREE AGE/Y 20 INTST/CRIM. PAGE 27 E0524   CONTROL
                                                     JURID

B66
LEE L.T.,VIENNA CONVENTION ON CONSULAR RELATIONS.   AGREE
WOR+45 LAW INT/ORG CONFER GP/REL PRIVIL...INT/LAW   DIPLOM
20 TREATY VIENNA/CNV. PAGE 64 E1277   ADMIN

B66
THOMPSON J.M.,RUSSIA, BOLSHEVISM, AND THE   DIPLOM
VERSAILLES PEACE. RUSSIA USSR INT/ORG NAT/G   PEACE
DELIB/GP AGREE REV WAR PWR 20 TREATY VERSAILLES   MARXISM
BOLSHEVISM. PAGE 96 E1919

B66
WAINHOUSE D.W.,INTERNATIONAL PEACE OBSERVATION: A   PEACE
HISTORY AND FORECAST. INT/ORG PROB/SOLV BAL/PWR   DIPLOM
AGREE ARMS/CONT COERCE NUC/PWR...PREDICT METH/COMP
20 UN LEAGUE/NAT OAS TREATY. PAGE 104 E2092

B67
GABRIEL P.P.,THE INTERNATIONAL TRANSFER OF   ECO/UNDEV
CORPORATE SKILLS: MANAGEMENT CONTRACTS IN LESS   AGREE
DEVELOPED COUNTRIES. CLIENT INDUS LG/CO PLAN   MGT
PROB/SOLV CAP/ISM ECO/TAC FOR/AID INT/TRADE RENT   CONSULT
ADMIN SKILL 20. PAGE 42 E0825

B67
US DEPARTMENT OF STATE,TREATIES IN FORCE. USA+45   BIBLIOG
WOR+45 AGREE WAR PEACE 20 TREATY. PAGE 100 E1999   DIPLOM
                                                     INT/ORG
                                                     DETER

L67
LEGAULT A.,"ORGANISATION ET CONDUITE DES OPERATIONS   INT/ORG
DE MAINTIEN DE LA PAIX." FORCES ACT/RES ADJUD AGREE   PEACE
CONTROL NEUTRAL TASK PRIVIL ORD/FREE 20 UN. PAGE 64   WAR
E1279   INT/LAW

L67
LISSITZYN O.J.,"TREATIES AND CHANGED CIRCUMSTANCES   AGREE
(REBUS SIC STANTIBUS)" WOR+45 CONSEN...JURID 20.   DIPLOM
PAGE 65 E1307   INT/LAW

S67
EYRAUD M.,"LA FRANCE FACE A UN EVENTUEL TRAITE DE   NUC/PWR
NON DISSEMINATION DES ARMES NUCLEAIRES." FRANCE   ARMS/CONT
USA+45 EXTR/IND INDUS R+D INT/ORG ACT/RES TEC/DEV   POLICY
AGREE PRODUC ATTIT 20 TREATY AEC EURATOM. PAGE 36
E0708

S67
HILL D.G.,"HUMAN RIGHTS LEGISLATION IN ONTARIO."   DELIB/GP
CANADA R+D VOL/ASSN CONSULT INSPECT EDU/PROP ADJUD   ORD/FREE
AGREE TASK GP/REL INGP/REL DISCRIM 20 CIV/RIGHTS   LAW
ONTARIO CIVIL/LIB. PAGE 52 E1045   POLICY

S67
RICHARDSON J.J.,"THE MAKING OF THE RESTRICTIVE   LEGIS
TRADE PRACTICES ACT 1956 A CASE STUDY OF THE POLICY   ECO/TAC
PROCESS IN BRITAIN." UK FINAN MARKET LG/CO POL/PAR   POLICY
CONSULT PRESS ADJUD ADMIN AGREE LOBBY SANCTION   INDUS
ATTIT 20. PAGE 84 E1695

N67
US SENATE COMM ON FOREIGN REL,SURVEY OF THE   INT/TRADE
ALLIANCE FOR PROGRESS: FOREIGN TRADE POLICIES   REGION
(PAMPHLET). L/A+17C LAW ECO/UNDEV ECO/TAC TARIFFS   AGREE
20 GATT LAFTA UN. PAGE 102 E2037   INT/ORG

B68
GREGG R.W.,INTERNATIONAL ORGANIZATION IN THE   INT/ORG
WESTERN HEMISPHERE. L/A+17C USA+45 CULTURE PLAN   DIPLOM
DOMIN AGREE CONTROL DETER PWR...GEOG 20 OAS TREATY.   ECO/UNDEV
PAGE 46 E0913

B68
HULL R.H.,LAW AND VIETNAM. COM VIETNAM CONSTN   POLICY
INT/ORG FORCES DIPLOM AGREE COERCE DETER WEAPON   LAW
PEACE ATTIT 20 UN TREATY. PAGE 56 E1113   INT/LAW

B91
BENTHAM J.,A FRAGMENT ON GOVERNMENT (1776). CONSTN   SOVEREIGN
MUNIC NAT/G SECT AGREE HAPPINESS UTIL MORAL   LAW
ORD/FREE...JURID CONCPT. PAGE 10 E0198   DOMIN

B96
DE VATTEL E.,THE LAW OF NATIONS. AGRI FINAN CHIEF   LAW
DIPLOM INT/TRADE AGREE OWN ALL/VALS MORAL ORD/FREE   CONCPT
SOVEREIGN...GEN/LAWS 18 NATURL/LAW WOLFF/C. PAGE 30   NAT/G
E0597   INT/LAW

B96
SMITH A.,LECTURES ON JUSTICE, POLICE, REVENUE AND   DIPLOM
ARMS (1763). UK LAW FAM FORCES TARIFFS AGREE COERCE   JURID
INCOME OWN WEALTH LAISSEZ...GEN/LAWS 17/18. PAGE 92   OLD/LIB
E1840   TAX

B98
POLLOCK F.,THE HISTORY OF ENGLISH LAW BEFORE THE   LAW
TIME OF EDWARD I (2 VOLS, 2ND ED.). UK CULTURE   ADJUD
LOC/G LEGIS LICENSE AGREE CONTROL CT/SYS SANCTION   JURID
CRIME...TIME/SEQ 13 COMMON/LAW CANON/LAW. PAGE 81
E1626

AGRI....AGRICULTURE (INCLUDING HUNTING AND GATHERING)

N
CONOVER H.F.,OFFICIAL PUBLICATIONS OF BRITISH EAST   BIBLIOG/A
AFRICA (PAMPHLET). UK LAW ECO/UNDEV AGRI EXTR/IND   AFR
SECT LEGIS BUDGET TAX...HEAL STAT 20. PAGE 25 E0491   ADMIN
                                                     COLONIAL

N
FULLER G.A.,DEMOBILIZATION: A SELECTED LIST OF   BIBLIOG/A
REFERENCES. USA+45 LAW AGRI LABOR WORKER ECO/TAC   INDUS
RATION RECEIVE EDU/PROP ROUTINE ARMS/CONT ALL/VALS   FORCES
20. PAGE 41 E0819   NAT/G

N
CANADIAN GOVERNMENT PUBLICATIONS (1955-). CANADA   BIBLIOG/A
AGRI FINAN LABOR FORCES INT/TRADE HEALTH...JURID 20   NAT/G
PARLIAMENT. PAGE 1 E0005   DIPLOM
                                                     INT/ORG

N
THE JAPAN SCIENCE REVIEW: LAW AND POLITICS: LIST OF   BIBLIOG
BOOKS AND ARTICLES ON LAW AND POLITICS. CONSTN AGRI   LAW
INDUS LABOR DIPLOM TAX ADMIN CRIME...INT/LAW SOC 20   S/ASIA
CHINJAP. PAGE 2 E0027   PHIL/SCI

N
UNITED NATIONS,UNITED NATIONS PUBLICATIONS. WOR+45   BIBLIOG
ECO/UNDEV AGRI FINAN FORCES ADMIN LEAD WAR PEACE   INT/ORG
...POLICY INT/LAW 20 UN. PAGE 98 E1965   DIPLOM

B14
CRAIG J.,ELEMENTS OF POLITICAL SCIENCE (3 VOLS.).   PHIL/SCI
CONSTN AGRI INDUS SCHOOL FORCES TAX CT/SYS SUFF   NAT/G
MORAL WEALTH...CONCPT 19 CIVIL/LIB. PAGE 27 E0539   ORD/FREE

B17
MEYER H.H.B.,LIST OF REFERENCES ON EMBARGOES   BIBLIOG
(PAMPHLET). USA-45 AGRI DIPLOM WRITING DEBATE   DIST/IND
WEAPON...INT/LAW 18/20 CONGRESS. PAGE 72 E1447   ECO/TAC
                                                     INT/TRADE

N19

HOGARTY R.A.,NEW JERSEY FARMERS AND MIGRANT HOUSING AGRI
RULES (PAMPHLET). USA+45 LAW ELITES FACE/GP LABOR PROVS
PROF/ORG LOBBY PERS/REL RIGID/FLEX ROLE 20 WORKER
NEW/JERSEY. PAGE 53 E1067 HEALTH

B24

HOLDSWORTH W.S.,A HISTORY OF ENGLISH LAW; THE LAW
COMMON LAW AND ITS RIVALS (VOL. IV). UK SEA AGRI LEGIS
CHIEF ADJUD CONTROL CRIME GOV/REL...INT/LAW JURID CT/SYS
NAT/COMP 16/17 PARLIAMENT COMMON/LAW CANON/LAW CONSTN
ENGLSH/LAW. PAGE 54 E1075

B30

GREEN F.M.,CONSTITUTIONAL DEVELOPMENT IN THE SOUTH CONSTN
ATLANTIC STATES, 1776-1860; A STUDY IN THE PROVS
EVOLUTION OF DEMOCRACY. USA-45 ELITES SOCIETY PLURISM
STRATA ECO/DEV AGRI POL/PAR EX/STRUC LEGIS CT/SYS REPRESENT
REGION...BIBLIOG 18/19 MARYLAND VIRGINIA GEORGIA
NORTH/CAR SOUTH/CAR. PAGE 46 E0905

B36

HUDSON M.O.,INTERNATIONAL LEGISLATION: 1929-1931. INT/LAW
WOR-45 SEA AIR AGRI FINAN LABOR DIPLOM ECO/TAC PARL/PROC
REPAR CT/SYS ARMS/CONT WAR WEAPON...JURID 20 TREATY ADJUD
LEAGUE/NAT. PAGE 56 E1112 LAW

B42

BLANCHARD L.R.,MARTINIQUE: A SELECTED LIST OF BIBLIOG/A
REFERENCES (PAMPHLET). WEST/IND AGRI LOC/G SCHOOL SOCIETY
...ART/METH GEOG JURID CHARTS 20. PAGE 12 E0241 CULTURE
COLONIAL

B44

FULLER G.H.,TURKEY: A SELECTED LIST OF REFERENCES. BIBLIOG/A
ISLAM TURKEY CULTURE ECO/UNDEV AGRI DIPLOM NAT/LISM ALL/VALS
CONSERVE...GEOG HUM INT/LAW SOC 7/20 MAPS. PAGE 42
E0824

B45

US LIBRARY OF CONGRESS,NETHERLANDS EAST INDIES. BIBLIOG/A
INDONESIA LAW CULTURE AGRI INDUS SCHOOL COLONIAL S/ASIA
HEALTH...GEOG JURID SOC 19/20 NETH/IND. PAGE 101 NAT/G
E2017

B46

AMERICAN DOCUMENTATION INST.CATALOGUE OF AUXILIARY BIBLIOG
PUBLICATIONS IN MICROFILMS AND PHOTOPRINTS. USA-45 EDU/PROP
LAW AGRI CREATE TEC/DEV ADMIN...GEOG LING MATH 20. PSY
PAGE 4 E0077

B49

US DEPARTMENT OF STATE,SOVIET BIBLIOGRAPHY BIBLIOG/A
(PAMPHLET). CHINA/COM COM USSR LAW AGRI INT/ORG MARXISM
ECO/TAC EDU/PROP...POLICY GEOG 20. PAGE 99 E1994 CULTURE
DIPLOM

C49

BLODGETT R.H.,"COMPARATIVE ECONOMIC SYSTEMS (REV. METH/COMP
ED.)" WOR-45 AGRI FINAN MARKET LABOR NAT/G PLAN CONCPT
INT/TRADE PRICE...POLICY DECISION BIBLIOG 20. ROUTINE
PAGE 13 E0248

B50

COUNCIL BRITISH NATIONAL BIB,BRITISH NATIONAL BIBLIOG/A
BIBLIOGRAPHY. UK AGRI CONSTRUC PERF/ART POL/PAR NAT/G
SECT CREATE INT/TRADE LEAD...HUM JURID PHIL/SCI 20. TEC/DEV
PAGE 26 E0519 DIPLOM

B50

DOROSH J.T.,GUIDE TO SOVIET BIBLIOGRAPHIES. USSR BIBLIOG
LAW AGRI SCHOOL SECT FORCES TEC/DEV...ART/METH GEOG METH
HUM SOC 20. PAGE 32 E0639 CON/ANAL

B51

BISSAINTHE M.,DICTIONNAIRE DE BIBLIOGRAPHIE BIBLIOG
HAITIENNE. HAITI ELITES AGRI LEGIS DIPLOM INT/TRADE L/A+17C
WRITING ORD/FREE CATHISM...ART/METH GEOG 19/20 SOCIETY
NEGRO TREATY. PAGE 12 E0234 NAT/G

C52

LANCASTER L.W.,"GOVERNMENT IN RURAL AMERICA." GOV/REL
USA+45 ECO/DEV AGRI SCHOOL FORCES LEGIS JUDGE LOC/G
BUDGET TAX CT/SYS...CHARTS BIBLIOG. PAGE 62 E1248 MUNIC
ADMIN

B54

BATTEN T.R.,PROBLEMS OF AFRICAN DEVELOPMENT (2ND ECO/UNDEV
ED.). AFR LAW SOCIETY SCHOOL ECO/TAC TAX...GEOG AGRI
HEAL SOC 20. PAGE 8 E0154 LOC/G
PROB/SOLV

B54

CARTER P.G.,STATISTICAL BULLETINS: AN ANNOTATED BIBLIOG/A
BIBLIOGRAPHY OF THE GENERAL STATISTICAL BULLETINS WOR+45

AND MAJOR POL SUBDIV OF WORLD. CULTURE AGRI FINAN NAT/G
INDUS LABOR TEC/DEV INT/TRADE CT/SYS WEALTH STAT
...CRIMLGY SOC 20. PAGE 20 E0400

C54

BOWIE R.R.,"STUDIES IN FEDERALISM." AGRI FINAN FEDERAL
LABOR EX/STRUC FORCES LEGIS DIPLOM INT/TRADE ADJUD EUR+WWI
...BIBLIOG 20 EEC. PAGE 14 E0279 INT/ORG
CONSTN

B59

COUNCIL OF STATE GOVERNMENTS,STATE GOVERNMENT: AN BIBLIOG/A
ANNOTATED BIBLIOGRAPHY (PAMPHLET). USA+45 LAW AGRI PROVS
INDUS WORKER PLAN TAX ADJUST AGE/Y ORD/FREE...HEAL LOC/G
MGT 20. PAGE 26 E0521 ADMIN

B59

EPSTEIN F.T.,EAST GERMANY: A SELECTED BIBLIOGRAPHY BIBLIOG/A
(PAMPHLET). COM GERMANY/E LAW AGRI FINAN INDUS INTELL
LABOR POL/PAR EDU/PROP ADMIN AGE/Y 20. PAGE 35 MARXISM
E0693 NAT/G

B59

GSOVSKI V.,GOVERNMENT, LAW, AND COURTS IN THE ADJUD
SOVIET UNION AND EASTERN EUROPE (2 VOLS.). COM USSR MARXISM
AGRI INDUS WORKER CT/SYS CRIME...BIBLIOG 20 CONTROL
EUROPE/E. PAGE 48 E0958 ORD/FREE

B60

GONZALEZ NAVARRO M.,LA COLONIZACION EN MEXICO, ECO/UNDEV
1877-1910. AGRI NAT/G PLAN PROB/SOLV INCOME GEOG
...POLICY JURID CENSUS 19/20 MEXIC/AMER MIGRATION. HABITAT
PAGE 44 E0883 COLONIAL

B60

HEYSE T.,PROBLEMS FONCIERS ET REGIME DES TERRES BIBLIOG
(ASPECTS ECONOMIQUES, JURIDIQUES ET SOCIAUX). AFR AGRI
CONGO/BRAZ INT/ORG DIPLOM SOVEREIGN...GEOG TREATY ECO/UNDEV
20. PAGE 52 E1037 LEGIS

B61

FLINN M.W.,AN ECONOMIC AND SOCIAL HISTORY OF SOCIETY
BRITAIN, 1066-1939. UK LAW STRATA STRUCT AGRI SOC
DIST/IND INDUS WORKER INT/TRADE WAR...CENSUS 11/20.
PAGE 39 E0766

B62

INTNTL COTTON ADVISORY COMMITT,GOVERNMENT ECO/TAC
REGULATIONS ON COTTON, 1962 (PAMPHLET). WOR+45 LAW
RATION PRODUC...CHARTS 20. PAGE 57 E1136 CONTROL
AGRI

L62

ERDMANN H.H.,"ADMINISTRATIVE LAW AND FARM AGRI
ECONOMICS." USA+45 LOC/G NAT/G PLAN PROB/SOLV LOBBY ADMIN
...DECISION ANTHOL 20. PAGE 35 E0695 ADJUD
POLICY

B63

CHOJNACKI S.,REGISTER ON CURRENT RESEARCH ON BIBLIOG
ETHIOPIA AND THE HORN OF AFRICA. ETHIOPIA LAW ACT/RES
CULTURE AGRI SECT EDU/PROP ADMIN...GEOG HEAL LING INTELL
20. PAGE 22 E0433 ACADEM

B63

GOURNAY B.,PUBLIC ADMINISTRATION. FRANCE LAW CONSTN BIBLIOG/A
AGRI FINAN LABOR SCHOOL EX/STRUC CHOOSE...MGT ADMIN
METH/COMP 20. PAGE 45 E0894 NAT/G
LOC/G

B63

LYONS F.S.L.,INTERNATIONALISM IN EUROPE 1815-1914. DIPLOM
LAW AGRI COM/IND DIST/IND LABOR SECT INT/TRADE MOD/EUR
TARIFFS...BIBLIOG 19/20. PAGE 67 E1335 INT/ORG

B63

OTTOSON H.W.,LAND USE POLICY AND PROBLEMS IN THE PROB/SOLV
UNITED STATES. USA+45 USA-45 LAW AGRI INDUS NAT/G UTIL
GP/REL...CHARTS ANTHOL 19/20 HOMEST/ACT. PAGE 79 HABITAT
E1586 POLICY

B64

MAKI J.M.,COURT AND CONSTITUTION IN JAPAN: SELECTED CONSTN
SUPREME COURT DECISIONS, 1948-60. LAW AGRI FAM JURID
LEGIS BAL/PWR ADMIN CHOOSE...SOC ANTHOL CABINET 20 CT/SYS
CHINJAP CIVIL/LIB. PAGE 68 E1355 CRIME

B64

ROBINSON R.D.,INTERNATIONAL BUSINESS POLICY. AFR ECO/TAC
INDIA L/A+17C USA+45 ELITES AGRI FOR/AID COERCE DIST/IND
BAL/PAY...DECISION INT/LAW MGT 20. PAGE 85 E1706 COLONIAL
FINAN

B64

TELLADO A.,A STATEMENT OF THE LAWS OF THE DOMINICAN CONSTN
REPUBLIC IN MATTERS AFFECTING BUSINESS (3RD ED.). LEGIS

DOMIN/REP AGRI DIST/IND EXTR/IND FINAN FAM WORKER   NAT/G
ECO/TAC TAX CT/SYS MARRIAGE OWN...BIBLIOG 20   INDUS
MIGRATION. PAGE 95 E1913

                                                    B64
WRIGHT G.,RURAL REVOLUTION IN FRANCE: THE PEASANTRY PWR
IN THE TWENTIETH CENTURY. EUR+WWI MOD/EUR LAW   STRATA
CULTURE AGRI POL/PAR DELIB/GP LEGIS ECO/TAC   FRANCE
EDU/PROP COERCE CHOOSE ATTIT RIGID/FLEX HEALTH   REV
...STAT CENSUS CHARTS VAL/FREE 20. PAGE 107 E2148

                                                    L64
POUNDS N.J.G.,"THE POLITICS OF PARTITION." AFR ASIA NAT/G
COM EUR+WWI FUT ISLAM S/ASIA USA-45 LAW ECO/DEV   NAT/LISM
ECO/UNDEV AGRI INDUS INT/ORG POL/PAR PROVS SECT
FORCES TOP/EX EDU/PROP LEGIT ATTIT MORAL ORD/FREE
PWR RESPECT WEALTH. PAGE 82 E1640

                                                    S64
TRISKA J.F.,"SOVIET TREATY LAW: A QUANTITATIVE   COM
ANALYSIS." WOR+45 LAW ECO/UNDEV AGRI COM/IND INDUS   ECO/TAC
CREATE TEC/DEV DIPLOM ATTIT PWR WEALTH...JURID SAMP   INT/LAW
TIME/SEQ TREND CHARTS VAL/FREE 20 TREATY. PAGE 97   USSR
E1942

                                                    B65
LUGO-MARENCO J.J.,A STATEMENT OF THE LAWS OF   CONSTN
NICARAGUA IN MATTERS AFFECTING BUSINESS. NICARAGUA   NAT/G
AGRI DIST/IND EXTR/IND FINAN INDUS FAM WORKER   LEGIS
INT/TRADE TAX MARRIAGE OWN BIO/SOC 20 TREATY   JURID
RESOURCE/N MIGRATION. PAGE 67 E1332

                                                    S65
KHOURI F.J.,"THE JORDON RIVER CONTROVERSY." LAW   ISLAM
SOCIETY ECO/UNDEV AGRI FINAN INDUS SECT FORCES   INT/ORG
ACT/RES PLAN TEC/DEV ECO/TAC EDU/PROP COERCE ATTIT   ISRAEL
DRIVE PERCEPT RIGID/FLEX ALL/VALS...GEOG SOC MYTH   JORDAN
WORK. PAGE 61 E1212

                                                    B66
HOGUE A.R.,ORIGINS OF THE COMMON LAW. UK STRUCT   LAW
AGRI CT/SYS SANCTION CONSERVE 12/14 ENGLSH/LAW   SOCIETY
COMMON/LAW. PAGE 54 E1068   CONSTN

                                                    S66
MATTHEWS D.G.,"ETHIOPIAN OUTLINE: A BIBLIOGRAPHIC   BIBLIOG
RESEARCH GUIDE." ETHIOPIA LAW STRUCT ECO/UNDEV AGRI   NAT/G
LABOR SECT CHIEF DELIB/GP EX/STRUC ADMIN...LING   DIPLOM
ORG/CHARTS 20. PAGE 69 E1384   POL/PAR

                                                    S66
SHEEHY E.P.,"SELECTED REFERENCE BOOKS OF   BIBLIOG/A
1965-1966." AGRI PERF/ART PRESS...GEOG HUM JURID   INDEX
SOC LING WORSHIP. PAGE 91 E1817   CLASSIF

                                                    B67
GREENE L.S.,AMERICAN GOVERNMENT POLICIES AND   POLICY
FUNCTIONS. USA+45 LAW AGRI DIST/IND LABOR MUNIC   NAT/G
BUDGET DIPLOM EDU/PROP ORD/FREE...BIBLIOG T 20.   ADMIN
PAGE 46 E0910   DECISION

                                                    S67
"THE FEDERAL AGRICULTURAL STABILIZATION PROGRAM AND   AGRI
THE NEGRO." LAW CONSTN PLAN REPRESENT DISCRIM   CONTROL
ORD/FREE 20 NEGRO CONGRESS. PAGE 2 E0039   NAT/G
                                                     RACE/REL

                                                    C93
PLAYFAIR R.L.,"A BIBLIOGRAPHY OF MOROCCO." MOROCCO   BIBLIOG
CULTURE AGRI FORCES DIPLOM WAR HEALTH...GEOG JURID   ISLAM
SOC CHARTS. PAGE 81 E1620   MEDIT-7

                                                    B96
DE VATTEL E.,THE LAW OF NATIONS. AGRI FINAN CHIEF   LAW
DIPLOM INT/TRADE AGREE OWN ALL/VALS MORAL ORD/FREE   CONCPT
SOVEREIGN...GEN/LAWS 18 NATURL/LAW WOLFF/C. PAGE 30   NAT/G
E0597   INT/LAW

AGRICULTURE....SEE AGRI

AHLUWALIA K. E0055

AHRCO....ALLEGHENY HOUSING REHABILITATION CORPORATION

AIR POLLUTION....SEE POLLUTION

AIR....LOCALE OF SUBJECT ACTIVITY IS AERIAL

                                                    B36
HUDSON M.O.,INTERNATIONAL LEGISLATION: 1929-1931.   INT/LAW
WOR-45 SEA AIR AGRI FINAN LABOR DIPLOM ECO/TAC   PARL/PROC
REPAR CT/SYS ARMS/CONT WAR WEAPON...JURID 20 TREATY   ADJUD
LEAGUE/NAT. PAGE 56 E1112   LAW

                                                    B55
SVARLIEN O.,AN INTRODUCTION TO THE LAW OF NATIONS.   INT/LAW

SEA AIR INT/ORG NAT/G CHIEF ADMIN AGREE WAR PRIVIL   DIPLOM
ORD/FREE SOVEREIGN...BIBLIOG 16/20. PAGE 95 E1897

                                                    B57
WASSENBERGH H.A.,POST-WAR INTERNATIONAL CIVIL   COM/IND
AVIATION POLICY AND THE LAW OF THE AIR. WOR+45 AIR   NAT/G
INT/ORG DOMIN LEGIT PEACE ORD/FREE...POLICY JURID   INT/LAW
NEW/IDEA OBS TIME/SEQ TREND CHARTS 20 TREATY.
PAGE 105 E2101

                                                    S58
MCDOUGAL M.S.,"PERSPECTIVES FOR A LAW OF OUTER   INT/ORG
SPACE." FUT WOR+45 AIR CONSULT DELIB/GP TEC/DEV   SPACE
CT/SYS ORD/FREE...POLICY JURID 20 UN. PAGE 70 E1404   INT/LAW

                                                    B60
GOLDSEN J.M.,INTERNATIONAL POLITICAL IMPLICATIONS   R+D
OF ACTIVITIES IN OUTER SPACE. FUT USA+45 WOR+45 AIR   SPACE
LAW ACT/RES LEGIT ATTIT KNOWL ORD/FREE PWR...CONCPT
20. PAGE 44 E0879

                                                    B60
WOETZEL R.K.,THE INTERNATIONAL CONTROL OF AIRSPACE   INT/ORG
AND OUTERSPACE. FUT WOR+45 AIR CONSTN STRUCT   JURID
CONSULT PLAN TEC/DEV ADJUD RIGID/FLEX KNOWL   SPACE
ORD/FREE PWR...TECHNIC GEOG MGT NEW/IDEA TREND   INT/LAW
COMPUT/IR VAL/FREE 20 TREATY. PAGE 107 E2137

                                                    S61
LIPSON L.,"AN ARGUMENT ON THE LEGALITY OF   INT/ORG
RECONNAISSANCE STATELLITES." COM USA+45 USSR WOR+45   LAW
AIR INTELL NAT/G CONSULT PLAN DIPLOM LEGIT ROUTINE   SPACE
ATTIT...INT/LAW JURID CONCPT METH/CNCPT TREND
COLD/WAR 20. PAGE 65 E1302

                                                    S61
MACHOWSKI K.,"SELECTED PROBLEMS OF NATIONAL   UNIV
SOVEREIGNTY WITH REFERENCE TO THE LAW OF OUTER   ACT/RES
SPACE." FUT WOR+45 AIR LAW INTELL SOCIETY ECO/DEV   NUC/PWR
PLAN EDU/PROP DETER DRIVE PERCEPT SOVEREIGN   SPACE
...POLICY INT/LAW OBS TREND TOT/POP 20. PAGE 67
E1339

                                                    B62
STERN A.C.,AIR POLLUTION (2 VOLS.). LAW INDUS   AIR
PROB/SOLV TEC/DEV INSPECT RISK BIO/SOC HABITAT   OP/RES
...OBS/ENVIR TESTS SAMP 20 POLLUTION. PAGE 93 E1871   CONTROL
                                                     HEALTH

                                                    S62
CRANE R.D.,"LAW AND STRATEGY IN SPACE." FUT USA+45   CONCPT
WOR+45 AIR LAW INT/ORG NAT/G FORCES ACT/RES PLAN   SPACE
BAL/PWR LEGIT ARMS/CONT COERCE ORD/FREE...POLICY
INT/LAW JURID SOC/EXP 20 TREATY. PAGE 27 E0542

                                                    S62
CRANE R.D.,"SOVIET ATTITUDE TOWARD INTERNATIONAL   LAW
SPACE LAW." COM FUT USA+45 USSR AIR CONSTN DELIB/GP   ATTIT
DOMIN PWR...JURID TREND TOT/POP 20. PAGE 27 E0543   INT/LAW
                                                     SPACE

                                                    S62
LISSITZYN O.J.,"SOME LEGAL IMPLICATIONS OF THE U-2   LAW
AND RB-47 INCIDENTS." FUT USA+45 USSR WOR+45 AIR   CONCPT
NAT/G DIPLOM LEGIT MORAL ORD/FREE SOVEREIGN...JURID   SPACE
GEN/LAWS GEN/METH COLD/WAR 20 U-2. PAGE 65 E1305   INT/LAW

                                                    S63
GARDNER R.N.,"COOPERATION IN OUTER SPACE." FUT USSR   INT/ORG
WOR+45 AIR LAW COM/IND CONSULT DELIB/GP CREATE   ACT/RES
KNOWL 20 TREATY. PAGE 42 E0837   PEACE
                                                     SPACE

                                                    B64
FISK W.M.,ADMINISTRATIVE PROCEDURE IN A REGULATORY   SERV/IND
AGENCY: THE CAB AND THE NEW YORK-CHICAGO CASE   ECO/DEV
(PAMPHLET). USA+45 DIST/IND ADMIN CONTROL LOBBY   AIR
GP/REL ROLE ORD/FREE NEWYORK/C CHICAGO CAB. PAGE 38   JURID
E0758

                                                    B64
MITAU G.T.,INSOLUBLE PROBLEMS: CASE PROBLEMS ON THE   ADJUD
FUNCTIONS OF STATE AND LOCAL GOVERNMENT. USA+45 AIR   LOC/G
FINAN LABOR POL/PAR PROB/SOLV TAX RECEIVE CONTROL   PROVS
GP/REL 20 CASEBOOK ZONING. PAGE 73 E1471

                                                    S64
CRANE R.D.,"BASIC PRINCIPLES IN SOVIET SPACE LAW."   COM
FUT WOR+45 AIR INT/ORG DIPLOM DOMIN ARMS/CONT   LAW
COERCE NUC/PWR PEACE ATTIT DRIVE PWR...INT/LAW   USSR
METH/CNCPT NEW/IDEA OBS TREND GEN/LAWS VAL/FREE   SPACE
MARX/KARL 20. PAGE 27 E0544

                                                    B67
US SENATE COMM ON FOREIGN REL,TREATY ON OUTER   SPACE
SPACE. WOR+45 AIR FORCES PROB/SOLV NUC/PWR SENATE   DIPLOM

TREATY UN. PAGE 101 E2032   ARMS/CONT
                                                            LAW

                                                            B67
US SENATE COMM ON FOREIGN REL,UNITED STATES   ARMS/CONT
ARMAMENT AND DISARMAMENT PROBLEMS. USA+45 AIR   WEAPON
BAL/PWR DIPLOM FOR/AID NUC/PWR ORD/FREE SENATE   FORCES
TREATY. PAGE 102 E2035   PROB/SOLV

                                                            S67
LARSEN P.B.,"THE UNITED STATES-ITALY AIR TRANSPORT   INT/LAW
ARBITRATION: PROBLEMS OF TREATY INTERPRETATION AND   ADJUD
ENFORCEMENT." ITALY USA+45 AIR PROB/SOLV DIPLOM   INT/TRADE
DEBATE CONTROL CT/SYS...DECISION TREATY. PAGE 63   DIST/IND
E1257

AIR UNIVERSITY LIBRARY E0056

AJAO/A....ADEROGBA AJAO

ALABAMA....ALABAMA

                                                            B65
FRYE R.J.,HOUSING AND URBAN RENEWAL IN ALABAMA.   MUNIC
USA+45 NEIGH LEGIS BUDGET ADJUD ADMIN PARTIC...MGT   PROB/SOLV
20 ALABAMA URBAN/RNWL. PAGE 41 E0815   PLAN
                                                            GOV/REL

                                                            B65
HIGHSAW R.B.,CONFLICT AND CHANGE IN LOCAL   GOV/REL
GOVERNMENT. USA+45 BUDGET ECO/TAC LEGIT ADJUD   PROB/SOLV
ALABAMA. PAGE 52 E1044   LOC/G
                                                            BAL/PWR

ALASKA....ALASKA

ALBANIA....SEE ALSO COM

                                                            B43
CONOVER H.F.,THE BALKANS: A SELECTED LIST OF   BIBLIOG
REFERENCES. ALBANIA BULGARIA ROMANIA YUGOSLAVIA   EUR+WWI
INT/ORG PROB/SOLV DIPLOM LEGIT CONFER ADJUD WAR
NAT/LISM PEACE PWR 20 LEAGUE/NAT. PAGE 25 E0493

ALBERT R.S. E0221

ALBERTA....ALBERTA

ALBI F. E0057

ALCOHOLISM....SEE BIO/SOC

ALDRICH W.A. E0058

ALEMBERT/J....JEAN LE ROND D'ALEMBERT

                                                            B23
DE MONTESQUIEU C.,THE SPIRIT OF LAWS (2 VOLS.)   JURID
(TRANS. BY THOMAS NUGENT). FRANCE FINAN SECT   LAW
INT/TRADE TAX COERCE REV DISCRIM HABITAT ORD/FREE   CONCPT
19 ALEMBERT/J CIVIL/LAW. PAGE 30 E0588   GEN/LAWS

ALEXANDER B. E0059

ALEXANDER F. E0060

ALEXANDER L. E0061

ALEXANDROWICZ E0062

ALEXANDROWICZ C.H. E0063

ALFRED H. E0064

ALGER C.F. E0065,E0066

ALGERIA....SEE ALSO ISLAM

                                                            B57
CONOVER H.F.,NORTH AND NORTHEAST AFRICA; A SELECTED   BIBLIOG/A
ANNOTATED LIST OF WRITINGS. ALGERIA MOROCCO SUDAN   DIPLOM
UAR CULTURE INT/ORG PROB/SOLV ADJUD NAT/LISM PWR   AFR
WEALTH...SOC 20 UN. PAGE 25 E0496   ECO/UNDEV

                                                            B60
PICKLES D.,THE FIFTH FRENCH REPUBLIC. ALGERIA   CONSTN
FRANCE CHOOSE GOV/REL ATTIT CONSERVE...CHARTS 20   ADJUD
DEGAULLE/C. PAGE 80 E1615   NAT/G
                                                            EFFICIENCY

                                                            B61
LA PONCE J.A.,THE GOVERNMENT OF THE FIFTH REPUBLIC: PWR
FRENCH POLITICAL PARTIES AND THE CONSTITUTION.   POL/PAR
ALGERIA FRANCE LAW NAT/G DELIB/GP LEGIS ECO/TAC   CONSTN
MARXISM SOCISM...CHARTS BIBLIOG/A 20 DEGAULLE/C.   CHIEF
PAGE 62 E1243

                                                            S63
GIRAUD E.,"L'INTERDICTION DU RECOURS A LA FORCE. LA   INT/ORG
THEORIE ET LA PRATIQUE DES NATIONS UNIES." ALGERIA   FORCES
COM CUBA HUNGARY WOR+45 ADJUD TOTALISM ATTIT   DIPLOM
RIGID/FLEX PWR...POLICY JURID CONCPT UN 20 CONGO.
PAGE 44 E0872

ALGIER/CHR....CHARTER OF ALGIERS

ALIENATION....SEE STRANGE

ALIGHIERI D. E0067

ALL/IDEOS....CONCERNS THREE OR MORE OF THE TERMS LISTED IN
            THE IDEOLOGICAL TOPIC INDEX, P. XIII

                                                            N
JOURNAL OF INTERNATIONAL AFFAIRS. WOR+45 ECO/UNDEV   BIBLIOG
POL/PAR ECO/TAC WAR PEACE PERSON ALL/IDEOS   DIPLOM
...INT/LAW TREND. PAGE 1 E0010   INT/ORG
                                                            NAT/G

                                                            N
TEXTBOOKS IN PRINT. WOR+45 WOR-45 LAW DIPLOM   BIBLIOG
ALL/VALS ALL/IDEOS...SOC T 19/20. PAGE 1 E0014   SCHOOL
                                                            KNOWL

                                                            N
PUBLISHERS' CIRCULAR LIMITED,THE ENGLISH CATALOGUE   BIBLIOG
OF BOOKS. UK WOR+45 WOR-45 LAW CULTURE LOC/G NAT/G   ALL/VALS
ADMIN LEAD...MGT 19/20. PAGE 83 E1658   ALL/IDEOS
                                                            SOCIETY

                                                            B01
GRIFFIN A.P.C.,LIST OF BOOKS ON SAMOA (PAMPHLET).   BIBLIOG/A
GERMANY S/ASIA UK USA-45 WOR-45 ECO/UNDEV REGION   COLONIAL
ALL/VALS ORD/FREE ALL/IDEOS...GEOG INT/LAW 19 SAMOA   DIPLOM
GUAM. PAGE 46 E0918

                                                            B06
GRIFFIN A.P.C.,LIST OF BOOKS RELATING TO CHILD   BIBLIOG/A
LABOR (PAMPHLET). BELGIUM FRANCE GERMANY MOD/EUR UK   LAW
USA-45 ECO/DEV INDUS WORKER CAP/ISM PAY ROUTINE   LABOR
ALL/IDEOS...MGT SOC 19/20. PAGE 47 E0929   AGE/C

                                                            B35
ROBSON W.A.,CIVILISATION AND THE GROWTH OF LAW.   LAW
UNIV CONSTN SOCIETY LEGIS ADJUD ATTIT PERCEPT MORAL   IDEA/COMP
ALL/IDEOS...CONCPT WORSHIP 20. PAGE 85 E1708   SOC

                                                            B40
WOLFERS A.,BRITAIN AND FRANCE BETWEEN TWO WORLD   DIPLOM
WARS. FRANCE UK INT/ORG NAT/G PLAN BARGAIN ECO/TAC   WAR
AGREE ISOLAT ALL/IDEOS...DECISION GEOG 20 TREATY   POLICY
VERSAILLES INTERVENT. PAGE 107 E2139

                                                            B41
EVANS C.,AMERICAN BIBLIOGRAPHY... (12 VOLUMES).   BIBLIOG
USA-45 LAW DIPLOM ADMIN PERSON...HUM SOC 17/18.   NAT/G
PAGE 35 E0704   ALL/VALS
                                                            ALL/IDEOS

                                                            B57
NEUMANN F.,THE DEMOCRATIC AND THE AUTHORITARIAN   DOMIN
STATE: ESSAYS IN POLITICAL AND LEGAL THEORY. USA+45   NAT/G
USA-45 CONTROL REV GOV/REL PEACE ALL/IDEOS   ORD/FREE
...INT/LAW CONCPT GEN/LAWS BIBLIOG 20. PAGE 77   POLICY
E1536

                                                            B58
MASON H.L.,TOYNBEE'S APPROACH TO WORLD POLITICS.   DIPLOM
AFR USA+45 USSR LAW WAR NAT/LISM ALL/IDEOS...HUM   CONCPT
BIBLIOG. PAGE 69 E1380   PHIL/SCI
                                                            SECT

                                                            L59
MCDOUGAL M.S.,"THE IDENTIFICATION AND APPRAISAL OF   INT/LAW
DIVERSE SYSTEMS OF PUBLIC ORDER (BMR)" WOR+45 NAT/G   DIPLOM
CONSULT EDU/PROP POLICY. PAGE 70 E1405   ALL/IDEOS

                                                            B60
SCHUBERT G.,THE PUBLIC INTEREST. USA+45 CONSULT   POLICY
PLAN PROB/SOLV ADJUD ADMIN GP/REL PWR ALL/IDEOS 20.   DELIB/GP
PAGE 88 E1770   REPRESENT
                                                            POL/PAR

                                                            B62
BRANDT R.B.,SOCIAL JUSTICE. UNIV LAW GP/REL PWR   ORD/FREE
ALL/IDEOS...POLICY SOC ANTHOL 20. PAGE 15 E0287   CONSTN
                                                            CONCPT

                                                            B62
GYORGY A.,PROBLEMS IN INTERNATIONAL RELATIONS. COM   DIPLOM

CT/SYS NUC/PWR ALL/IDEOS 20 UN EEC ECSC. PAGE 49   NEUTRAL
E0966   BAL/PWR
                                                     REV

                                                     B66
FRIED R.C.,COMPARATIVE POLITICAL INSTITUTIONS. USSR NAT/G
EX/STRUC FORCES LEGIS JUDGE CONTROL REPRESENT   PWR
ALL/IDEOS 20 CONGRESS BUREAUCRCY. PAGE 40 E0798   EFFICIENCY
                                                     GOV/COMP

                                                     B66
STUMPF S.E.,MORALITY AND THE LAW. USA+45 LAW   JURID
CULTURE PROB/SOLV DOMIN ADJUD CONTROL ADJUST   MORAL
ALL/IDEOS MARXISM...INT/LAW 20 SUPREME/CT. PAGE 94   CT/SYS
E1890

                                                     B67
PADELFORD N.J.,THE DYNAMICS OF INTERNATIONAL   DIPLOM
POLITICS (2ND ED.). WOR+45 LAW INT/ORG FORCES   NAT/G
TEC/DEV REGION NAT/LISM PEACE ATTIT PWR ALL/IDEOS   POLICY
UN COLD/WAR NATO TREATY. PAGE 79 E1589   DECISION

                                                     B67
SLATER J.,THE OAS AND UNITED STATES FOREIGN POLICY. INT/ORG
KOREA L/A+17C USA+45 VOL/ASSN RISK COERCE PEACE   DIPLOM
ORD/FREE MARXISM...TREND 20 OAS. PAGE 92 E1838   ALL/IDEOS
                                                     ADJUD

                                                     B91
SIDGWICK H.,THE ELEMENTS OF POLITICS. LOC/G NAT/G   POLICY
LEGIS DIPLOM ADJUD CONTROL EXEC PARL/PROC REPRESENT LAW
GOV/REL SOVEREIGN ALL/IDEOS 19 MILL/JS BENTHAM/J.   CONCPT
PAGE 91 E1822

ALL/PROG....ALLIANCE FOR PROGRESS

ALL/VALS....CONCERNS SIX OR MORE OF THE TERMS LISTED IN
    THE VALUES INDEX. P. XIII

                                                     N
FULLER G.A.,DEMOBILIZATION: A SELECTED LIST OF   BIBLIOG/A
REFERENCES. USA+45 LAW AGRI LABOR WORKER ECO/TAC   INDUS
RATION RECEIVE EDU/PROP ROUTINE ARMS/CONT ALL/VALS   FORCES
20. PAGE 41 E0819   NAT/G

                                                     N
TEXTBOOKS IN PRINT. WOR+45 WOR-45 LAW DIPLOM   BIBLIOG
ALL/VALS ALL/IDEOS...SOC T 19/20. PAGE 1 E0014   SCHOOL
                                                     KNOWL

                                                     N
PUBLISHERS' CIRCULAR LIMITED,THE ENGLISH CATALOGUE   BIBLIOG
OF BOOKS. UK WOR+45 WOR-45 LAW CULTURE LOC/G NAT/G   ALL/VALS
ADMIN LEAD...MGT 19/20. PAGE 83 E1658   ALL/IDEOS
                                                     SOCIETY

                                                     B00
GRIFFIN A.P.C.,LIST OF BOOKS RELATING TO THE THEORY BIBLIOG/A
OF COLONIZATION, GOVERNMENT OF DEPENDENCIES,   COLONIAL
PROTECTORATES, AND RELATED TOPICS. FRANCE GERMANY   GOV/REL
ITALY SPAIN UK USA-45 WOR-45 ECO/TAC ADMIN CONTROL   DOMIN
REGION NAT/LISM ALL/VALS PWR...INT/LAW SOC 16/19.
PAGE 46 E0917

                                                     B00
MAINE H.S.,INTERNATIONAL LAW. MOD/EUR UNIV SOCIETY   INT/ORG
STRUCT ACT/RES EXEC WAR ATTIT PERSON ALL/VALS   LAW
...POLICY JURID CONCPT OBS TIME/SEQ TOT/POP.   PEACE
PAGE 68 E1349   INT/LAW

                                                     B01
GRIFFIN A.P.C.,LIST OF BOOKS ON SAMOA (PAMPHLET).   BIBLIOG/A
GERMANY S/ASIA UK USA-45 WOR-45 ECO/UNDEV REGION   COLONIAL
ALL/VALS ORD/FREE ALL/IDEOS...GEOG INT/LAW 19 SAMOA DIPLOM
GUAM. PAGE 46 E0918

                                                     B03
CHANNING W.E.,DISCOURSES ON WAR (1820-1840). LAW   WAR
SECT DIPLOM INT/TRADE ALL/VALS. PAGE 21 E0418   PLAN
                                                     LOVE
                                                     ORD/FREE

                                                     B11
REINSCH P.,PUBLIC INTERNATIONAL UNION. WOR+45 LAW   FUT
LABOR INT/TRADE LEGIT PERSON ALL/VALS...SOCIALIST   INT/ORG
CONCPT TIME/SEQ TREND GEN/LAWS 19/20. PAGE 84 E1683 DIPLOM

                                                     B15
HOBSON J.A.,TOWARDS INTERNATIONAL GOVERNMENT.   FUT
MOD/EUR STRUCT ECO/TAC EDU/PROP ADJUD ALL/VALS   INT/ORG
...SOCIALIST CONCPT GEN/LAWS TOT/POP 20. PAGE 53   CENTRAL
E1059

                                                     B16
PUFENDORF S.,LAW OF NATURE AND OF NATIONS   CONCPT
(ABRIDGED). UNIV LAW NAT/G DIPLOM AGREE WAR PERSON   INT/LAW

ALL/VALS PWR...POLICY 18 DEITY NATURL/LAW. PAGE 83   SECT
E1659   MORAL

                                                     B16
ROOT E.,ADDRESSES ON INTERNATIONAL SUBJECTS.   INT/ORG
MOD/EUR UNIV USA-45 LAW SOCIETY EXEC ATTIT ALL/VALS ACT/RES
...POLICY JURID CONCPT 20 CHINJAP. PAGE 85 E1711   PEACE
                                                     INT/LAW

                                                     L16
WRIGHT Q.,"THE ENFORCEMENT OF INTERNATIONAL LAW   INT/ORG
THROUGH MUNICIPAL LAW IN THE US." USA-45 LOC/G   LAW
NAT/G PUB/INST FORCES LEGIT CT/SYS PERCEPT ALL/VALS INT/LAW
...JURID 20. PAGE 107 E2149   WAR

                                                     B20
DICKINSON E.,THE EQUALITY OF STATES IN   LAW
INTERNATIONAL LAW. WOR-45 INT/ORG NAT/G DIPLOM   CONCPT
EDU/PROP LEGIT PEACE ATTIT ALL/VALS...JURID   SOVEREIGN
TIME/SEQ LEAGUE/NAT. PAGE 31 E0622

                                                     B22
BRYCE J.,INTERNATIONAL RELATIONS. CHRIST-17C   INT/ORG
EUR+WWI MOD/EUR CULTURE INTELL NAT/G DELIB/GP   POLICY
CREATE BAL/PWR DIPLOM ATTIT DRIVE RIGID/FLEX
ALL/VALS...PLURIST JURID CONCPT TIME/SEQ GEN/LAWS
TOT/POP. PAGE 16 E0323

                                                     B23
HOLMES O.W. JR.,THE COMMON LAW. FUT WOR-45 CULTURE   ADJUD
SOCIETY CREATE LEGIT ROUTINE ATTIT ALL/VALS...JURID CON/ANAL
METH/CNCPT TIME/SEQ GEN/LAWS TOT/POP VAL/FREE.
PAGE 55 E1087

                                                     B26
HOCKING W.E.,PRESENT STATUS OF THE PHILOSOPHY OF   JURID
LAW AND OF RIGHTS. UNIV CULTURE INTELL SOCIETY   PHIL/SCI
NAT/G CREATE LEGIT SANCTION ALL/VALS SOC/INTEG   ORD/FREE
18/20. PAGE 53 E1060

                                                     B28
HOBBES T.,THE ELEMENTS OF LAW, NATURAL AND POLITIC   PERSON
(1650). STRATA NAT/G SECT CHIEF AGREE ATTIT   LAW
ALL/VALS MORAL ORD/FREE POPULISM...POLICY CONCPT.   SOVEREIGN
PAGE 53 E1056   CONSERVE

                                                     B30
WRIGHT Q.,MANDATES UNDER THE LEAGUE OF NATIONS.   INT/ORG
WOR-45 CONSTN ECO/DEV ECO/UNDEV NAT/G DELIB/GP   LAW
TOP/EX LEGIT ALL/VALS...JURID CONCPT LEAGUE/NAT 20. INT/LAW
PAGE 107 E2151

                                                     B32
MASTERS R.D.,INTERNATIONAL LAW IN INTERNATIONAL   INT/ORG
COURTS. BELGIUM EUR+WWI FRANCE GERMANY MOD/EUR   LAW
SWITZERLND WOR-45 SOCIETY STRATA STRUCT LEGIT EXEC   INT/LAW
ALL/VALS...JURID HIST/WRIT TIME/SEQ TREND GEN/LAWS
20. PAGE 69 E1383

                                                     B38
LEAGUE OF NATIONS-SECRETARIAT.,THE AIMS, METHODS   ADJUD
AND ACTIVITY OF THE LEAGUE OF NATIONS. WOR+45   STRUCT
DIPLOM EDU/PROP LEGIT RIGID/FLEX ALL/VALS
...TIME/SEQ LEAGUE/NAT VAL/FREE 19/20. PAGE 64
E1273

                                                     B39
WILSON G.G.,HANDBOOK OF INTERNATIONAL LAW. FUT UNIV INT/ORG
USA-45 WOR-45 SOCIETY LEGIT ATTIT DISPL DRIVE   LAW
ALL/VALS...INT/LAW TIME/SEQ TREND. PAGE 106 E2128   CONCPT
                                                     WAR

                                                     B40
CARR E.H.,THE TWENTY YEARS' CRISIS 1919-1939. FUT   INT/ORG
WOR-45 BAL/PWR ECO/TAC LEGIT TOTALISM ATTIT   DIPLOM
ALL/VALS...POLICY JURID CONCPT TIME/SEQ TREND   PEACE
GEN/LAWS TOT/POP 20. PAGE 20 E0393

                                                     B41
EVANS C.,AMERICAN BIBLIOGRAPHY... (12 VOLUMES).   BIBLIOG
USA-45 LAW DIPLOM ADMIN PERSON...HUM SOC 17/18.   NAT/G
PAGE 35 E0704   ALL/VALS
                                                     ALL/IDEOS

                                                     B42
HAMBRO C.J.,HOW TO WIN THE PEACE. ECO/TAC EDU/PROP   FUT
ADJUD PERSON ALL/VALS...SOCIALIST TREND GEN/LAWS   INT/ORG
20. PAGE 50 E0987   PEACE

                                                     B44
FULLER G.H.,TURKEY: A SELECTED LIST OF REFERENCES.   BIBLIOG/A
ISLAM TURKEY CULTURE ECO/UNDEV AGRI DIPLOM NAT/LISM ALL/VALS
CONSERVE...GEOG HUM INT/LAW SOC 7/20 MAPS. PAGE 42
E0824

B44

PUTTKAMMER E.W.,WAR AND THE LAW. UNIV USA-45 CONSTN INT/ORG
CULTURE SOCIETY NAT/G POL/PAR ROUTINE ALL/VALS   LAW
...JURID CONCPT OBS WORK VAL/FREE 20. PAGE 83 E1664   WAR
                                                        INT/LAW

B45

REVES E.,THE ANATOMY OF PEACE. WOR-45 LAW CULTURE   ACT/RES
NAT/G PLAN TEC/DEV EDU/PROP WAR NAT/LISM ATTIT   CONCPT
ALL/VALS SOVEREIGN...POLICY HUM TIME/SEQ 20.   NUC/PWR
PAGE 84 E1688   PEACE

B46

GRIFFIN G.G.,A GUIDE TO MANUSCRIPTS RELATING TO   BIBLIOG/A
AMERICAN HISTORY IN BRITISH DEPOSITORIES. CANADA   ALL/VALS
IRELAND MOD/EUR UK USA-45 LAW DIPLOM ADMIN COLONIAL   NAT/G
WAR NAT/LISM SOVEREIGN...GEOG INT/LAW 15/19
CMN/WLTH. PAGE 47 E0936

B49

MARITAIN J.,HUMAN RIGHTS: COMMENTS AND   INT/ORG
INTERPRETATIONS. COM UNIV WOR+45 LAW CONSTN CULTURE   CONCPT
SOCIETY ECO/DEV ECO/UNDEV SCHOOL DELIB/GP EDU/PROP
ATTIT PERCEPT ALL/VALS...HUM SOC TREND UNESCO 20.
PAGE 68 E1365

B50

LAUTERPACHT H.,INTERNATIONAL LAW AND HUMAN RIGHTS.   DELIB/GP
USA+45 CONSTN STRUCT INT/ORG ACT/RES EDU/PROP PEACE   LAW
PERSON ALL/VALS...CONCPT CON/ANAL GEN/LAWS UN 20.   INT/LAW
PAGE 63 E1266

B52

VANDENBOSCH A.,THE UN: BACKGROUND, ORGANIZATION,   DELIB/GP
FUNCTIONS, ACTIVITIES. WOR+45 LAW CONSTN STRUCT   TIME/SEQ
INT/ORG CONSULT BAL/PWR EDU/PROP EXEC ALL/VALS   PEACE
...POLICY CONCPT UN 20. PAGE 103 E2071

B53

GROSS B.M.,THE LEGISLATIVE STRUGGLE: A STUDY IN   LEGIS
SOCIAL COMBAT. STRUCT LOC/G POL/PAR JUDGE EDU/PROP   DECISION
DEBATE ETIQUET ADMIN LOBBY CHOOSE GOV/REL INGP/REL   PERSON
HEREDITY ALL/VALS...SOC PRESIDENT. PAGE 48 E0948   LEAD

B54

CAPLOW T.,THE SOCIOLOGY OF WORK. USA+45 USA-45   LABOR
STRATA MARKET FAM GP/REL INGP/REL ALL/VALS   WORKER
...DECISION STAT BIBLIOG SOC/INTEG 20. PAGE 19   INDUS
E0375   ROLE

B54

NUSSBAUM D.,A CONCISE HISTORY OF THE LAW OF   INT/ORG
NATIONS. ASIA CHRIST-17C EUR+WWI ISLAM MEDIT-7   LAW
MOD/EUR S/ASIA UNIV WOR+45 WOR-45 SOCIETY STRUCT   PEACE
EXEC ATTIT ALL/VALS...CONCPT HIST/WRIT TIME/SEQ.   INT/LAW
PAGE 78 E1560

B55

KHADDURI M.,WAR AND PEACE IN THE LAW OF ISLAM.   ISLAM
CONSTN CULTURE SOCIETY STRATA UNIV LAW PROVS SECT   JURID
FORCES TOP/EX CREATE DOMIN EDU/PROP ADJUD COERCE   PEACE
ATTIT RIGID/FLEX ALL/VALS...CONCPT TIME/SEQ TOT/POP   WAR
VAL/FREE. PAGE 61 E1209

B55

MAZZINI J.,THE DUTIES OF MAN. MOD/EUR LAW SOCIETY   SUPEGO
FAM NAT/G POL/PAR SECT VOL/ASSN EX/STRUC ACT/RES   CONCPT
CREATE REV PEACE ATTIT ALL/VALS...GEN/LAWS WORK 19.   NAT/LISM
PAGE 70 E1396

B60

LENCZOWSKI G.,OIL AND STATE IN THE MIDDLE EAST. FUT   ISLAM
IRAN LAW ECO/UNDEV EXTR/IND NAT/G TOP/EX PLAN   INDUS
TEC/DEV ECO/TAC LEGIT ADMIN COERCE ATTIT ALL/VALS   NAT/LISM
PWR...CHARTS 20. PAGE 64 E1283

S60

SCHACHTER O.,"THE ENFORCEMENT OF INTERNATIONAL   INT/ORG
JUDICIAL AND ARBITRAL DECISIONS." WOR+45 NAT/G   ADJUD
ECO/TAC DOMIN LEGIT ROUTINE COERCE ATTIT DRIVE   INT/LAW
ALL/VALS PWR...METH/CNCPT TREND TOT/POP 20 UN.
PAGE 87 E1750

S61

ALGER C.F.,"NON-RESOLUTION CONSEQUENCES OF THE   INT/ORG
UNITED NATIONS AND THEIR EFFECT ON INTERNATIONAL   DRIVE
CONFLICT." WOR+45 CONSTN ECO/DEV NAT/G CONSULT   BAL/PWR
DELIB/GP TOP/EX ACT/RES PLAN DIPLOM EDU/PROP
ROUTINE ATTIT ALL/VALS...INT/LAW TOT/POP UN 20.
PAGE 3 E0065

B62

HOOK S.,THE PARADOXES OF FREEDOM. UNIV CONSTN   CONCPT
INTELL LEGIS CONTROL REV CHOOSE SUPEGO...POLICY   MAJORIT
JURID IDEA/COMP 19/20 CIV/RIGHTS. PAGE 55 E1095   ORD/FREE
                                                       ALL/VALS

L62

CORET A.,"L'INDEPENDANCE DU SAMOA OCCIDENTAL."   NAT/G
S/ASIA LAW INT/ORG EXEC ALL/VALS SAMOA UN 20.   STRUCT
PAGE 26 E0508   SOVEREIGN

S62

MANGIN G.,"LES ACCORDS DE COOPERATION EN MATIERE DE   INT/ORG
JUSTICE ENTRE LA FRANCE ET LES ETATS AFRICAINS ET   LAW
MALGACHE." AFR ISLAM WOR+45 STRUCT ECO/UNDEV NAT/G   FRANCE
DELIB/GP PERCEPT ALL/VALS...JURID MGT TIME/SEQ 20.
PAGE 68 E1356

S62

MURACCIOLE L.,"LES MODIFICATIONS DE LA CONSTITUTION   NAT/G
MALGACHE." AFR WOR+45 ECO/UNDEV LEGIT EXEC ALL/VALS   STRUCT
...JURID 20. PAGE 75 E1505   SOVEREIGN
                                                       MADAGASCAR

S62

VIGNES D.,"L'AUTORITE DES TRAITES INTERNATIONAUX EN   STRUCT
DROIT INTERNE." EUR+WWI UNIV LAW CONSTN INTELL   LEGIT
NAT/G POL/PAR DIPLOM ATTIT PERCEPT ALL/VALS   FRANCE
...POLICY INT/LAW JURID CONCPT TIME/SEQ 20 TREATY.
PAGE 104 E2075

S63

BERMAN H.J.,"THE DILEMMA OF SOVIET LAW REFORM."   COM
NAT/G POL/PAR CT/SYS ALL/VALS ORD/FREE PWR...POLICY   LAW
JURID VAL/FREE 20. PAGE 11 E0208   USSR

S63

BRAUSCH G.E.,"AFRICAN ETHNOCRACIES: SOME   LAW
SOCIOLOGICAL IMPLICATIONS OF CONSTITUTIONAL CHANGE   SOC
IN EMERGENT TERRITORIES OF AFRICA." AFR CONSTN   ELITES
FACE/GP MUNIC NAT/G DOMIN ATTIT ALL/VALS
...HIST/WRIT GEN/LAWS VAL/FREE 20. PAGE 15 E0289

S63

MODELSKI G.,"STUDY OF ALLIANCES." WOR+45 WOR-45   VOL/ASSN
INT/ORG NAT/G FORCES LEGIT ADMIN CHOOSE ALL/VALS   CON/ANAL
PWR SKILL...INT/LAW CONCPT GEN/LAWS 20 TREATY.   DIPLOM
PAGE 74 E1477

B64

GARDNER R.N.,IN PURSUIT OF WORLD ORDER* US FOREIGN   OBS
POLICY AND INTERNATIONAL ORGANIZATIONS. USA+45 USSR   INT/ORG
ECO/UNDEV FORCES LEGIS DIPLOM FOR/AID INT/TRADE   ALL/VALS
PEACE...INT/LAW PREDICT UN. PAGE 42 E0839

B64

SHAPIRO M.,LAW AND POLITICS IN THE SUPREME COURT: LEGIS
NEW APPROACHES TO POLITICAL JURISPRUDENCE. JUDGE   CT/SYS
PROB/SOLV LEGIT EXEC ROUTINE ATTIT ALL/VALS   LAW
...DECISION SOC. PAGE 90 E1811   JURID

B64

UN PUB. INFORM. ORGAN.,EVERY MAN'S UNITED NATIONS.   INT/ORG
UNIV WOR+45 CONSTN CULTURE SOCIETY ECO/DEV   ROUTINE
ECO/UNDEV NAT/G ACT/RES PLAN ECO/TAC INT/TRADE
EDU/PROP LEGIT PEACE ATTIT ALL/VALS...POLICY HUM
INT/LAW CONCPT CHARTS UN TOT/POP 20. PAGE 97 E1954

L64

BERKS R.N.,"THE US AND WEAPONS CONTROL." WOR+45 LAW   USA+45
INT/ORG NAT/G LEGIS EXEC COERCE PEACE ATTIT   PLAN
RIGID/FLEX ALL/VALS PWR...POLICY TOT/POP 20.   ARMS/CONT
PAGE 11 E0204

S64

GARDNER R.N.,"THE SOVIET UNION AND THE UNITED   COM
NATIONS." WOR+45 FINAN POL/PAR VOL/ASSN FORCES   INT/ORG
ECO/TAC DOMIN EDU/PROP LEGIT ADJUD ADMIN ARMS/CONT   USSR
COERCE ATTIT ALL/VALS...POLICY MAJORIT CONCPT OBS
TIME/SEQ TREND STERTYP UN. PAGE 42 E0838

S64

GREENBERG S.,"JUDAISM AND WORLD JUSTICE." MEDIT-7   SECT
WOR+45 LAW CULTURE SOCIETY INT/ORG NAT/G FORCES   JURID
EDU/PROP ATTIT DRIVE PERSON SUPEGO ALL/VALS   PEACE
...POLICY PSY CONCPT GEN/LAWS JEWS. PAGE 46 E0908

S64

KHAN M.Z.,"ISLAM AND INTERNATIONAL RELATIONS." FUT   ISLAM
WOR+45 LAW CULTURE SOCIETY NAT/G SECT DELIB/GP   INT/ORG
FORCES EDU/PROP ATTIT PERSON SUPEGO ALL/VALS   DIPLOM
...POLICY PSY CONCPT MYTH HIST/WRIT GEN/LAWS.
PAGE 61 E1211

S65

AMRAM P.W.,"REPORT ON THE TENTH SESSION OF THE   VOL/ASSN
HAGUE CONFERENCE ON PRIVATE INTERNATIONAL LAW."   DELIB/GP
USA+45 WOR+45 INT/ORG CREATE LEGIT ADJUD ALL/VALS   INT/LAW
...JURID CONCPT METH/CNCPT OBS GEN/METH 20. PAGE 4
E0085

SUPREME/CT AMEND/I. PAGE 11 E0212   ORD/FREE

KHOURI F.J.,"THE JORDON RIVER CONTROVERSY." LAW   ISLAM
SOCIETY ECO/UNDEV AGRI FINAN INDUS SECT FORCES   INT/ORG
ACT/RES PLAN TEC/DEV ECO/TAC EDU/PROP COERCE ATTIT   ISRAEL
DRIVE PERCEPT RIGID/FLEX ALL/VALS...GEOG SOC MYTH   JORDAN
WORK. PAGE 61 E1212

                                                        S65

WRIGHT Q.,"THE ESCALATION OF INTERNATIONAL   WAR
CONFLICTS." WOR+45 WOR-45 FORCES DIPLOM RISK COST   PERCEPT
ATTIT ALL/VALS...INT/LAW QUANT STAT NAT/COMP.   PREDICT
PAGE 108 E2160   MATH

                                                        B66

BUTTERFIELD H.,DIPLOMATIC INVESTIGATIONS* ESSAYS IN   GEN/LAWS
THE THEORY OF INTERNATIONAL POLITICS. LAW INT/ORG   UK
FORCES BAL/PWR ARMS/CONT WAR ALL/VALS...HUM   DIPLOM
INT/LAW. PAGE 18 E0351

                                                        B67

BONGER W.A.,CRIMINALITY AND ECONOMIC CONDITIONS.   PERSON
MOD/EUR STRUCT INDUS WORKER EDU/PROP CRIME HABITAT   CRIMLGY
ALL/VALS...JURID SOC 20 REFORMERS. PAGE 14 E0265   IDEA/COMP
                                                        ANOMIE

                                                        S67

KIM R.C.C.,"THE SUPREME COURT: ORALLE WITHOUT   CT/SYS
TRUTH." USA+45 EDU/PROP RACE/REL ADJUST ALL/VALS   PROB/SOLV
ORD/FREE...DECISION WORSHIP SUPREME/CT. PAGE 61   ADJUD
E1214   REPRESENT

                                                        B96

DE VATTEL E.,THE LAW OF NATIONS. AGRI FINAN CHIEF   LAW
DIPLOM INT/TRADE AGREE OWN ALL/VALS MORAL ORD/FREE   CONCPT
SOVEREIGN...GEN/LAWS 18 NATURL/LAW WOLFF/C. PAGE 30   NAT/G
E0597   INT/LAW

ALLEGHENY HOUSING REHABILITATION CORPORATION....SEE AHRCO

ALLEN C.K. E0068,E0069

ALLIANCES, MILITARY....SEE FORCES+DIPLOM

ALLOTT A.N. E0070

ALTO/ADIGE....ALTO-ADIGE REGION OF ITALY

AM/LEGION....AMERICAN LEGION

AMA....AMERICAN MEDICAL ASSOCIATION

AMBITION....SEE DRIVE

AMDS W.E. E0071

AMEND/I....CONCERNED WITH FREEDOMS GRANTED IN THE
     FIRST AMENDMENT

                                                        B36

HANSON L.,GOVERNMENT AND THE PRESS 1695-1763. UK   LAW
LOC/G LEGIS LICENSE CONTROL SANCTION CRIME   JURID
ORD/FREE 17/18 PARLIAMENT AMEND/I. PAGE 50 E0996   PRESS
                                                        POLICY

                                                        B41

CHAFEE Z. JR.,FREE SPEECH IN THE UNITED STATES.   ORD/FREE
USA-45 ADJUD CONTROL CRIME WAR...BIBLIOG 20   CONSTN
FREE/SPEE AMEND/I SUPREME/CT. PAGE 21 E0413   ATTIT
                                                        JURID

                                                        B47

HOCKING W.E.,FREEDOM OF THE PRESS: A FRAMEWORK OF   ORD/FREE
PRINCIPLE. WOR-45 SOCIETY NAT/G PROB/SOLV DEBATE   CONSTN
LOBBY...JURID PSY 20 AMEND/I. PAGE 53 E1061   PRESS
                                                        LAW

                                                        B48

MEIKLEJOHN A.,FREE SPEECH AND ITS RELATION TO SELF-   LEGIS
GOVERNMENT. USA+45 USA-45 LAW DOMIN PRESS ORD/FREE   NAT/G
20 AMEND/I. PAGE 72 E1434   CONSTN
                                                        PRIVIL

                                                        B57

BERNS W.,FREEDOM, VIRTUE AND THE FIRST AMENDMENT.   JURID
USA+45 USA-45 CONSTN INTELL JUDGE ADJUD RIGID/FLEX   ORD/FREE
MORAL...CONCPT 20 AMEND/I. PAGE 11 E0211   CT/SYS
                                                        LAW

                                                        B57

BERNS W.,FREEDOM, VIRTUE, AND THE FIRST AMENDMENT.   ADJUD
USA-45 LAW CONSTN PROB/SOLV NEW/LIB...JURID 20   CT/SYS

O'BRIEN F.W.,JUSTICE REED AND THE FIRST AMENDMENT,   ADJUD
THE RELIGION CLAUSES. USA+45 USA-45 NAT/G PROVS   SECT
CONTROL FEDERAL...POLICY JURID TIME/SEQ 20   CT/SYS
SUPREME/CT CHRUCH/STA AMEND/I REED/STAN. PAGE 78
E1563

                                                        B59

GINZBURG B.,REDEDICATION TO FREEDOM. DELIB/GP LEGIS   JURID
ATTIT MARXISM 20 SUPREME/CT CON/INTERP HUAC AMEND/I   ORD/FREE
FBI. PAGE 44 E0871   CONSTN
                                                        NAT/G

                                                        B61

CHILDS M.W.,THE EROSION OF INDIVIDUAL LIBERTIES.   ADJUD
NAT/G LEGIS ATTIT...JURID SOC CONCPT IDEA/COMP 20   CT/SYS
SUPREME/CT AMEND/I. PAGE 22 E0430   ORD/FREE
                                                        CONSTN

                                                        B64

ANASTAPLO G.,NOTES ON THE FIRST AMENDMENT TO THE   ORD/FREE
CONSTITUTION OF THE UNITED STATES (PART TWO).   CONSTN
USA+45 USA-45 NAT/G JUDGE DEBATE SUPEGO PWR   CT/SYS
SOVEREIGN 18/20 SUPREME/CT CONGRESS AMEND/I. PAGE 5   ATTIT
E0088

                                                        B66

BEDI A.S.,FREEDOM OF EXPRESSION AND SECURITY;   METH
COMPARATIVE STUDY OF FUNCTIONS OF SUPREME COURTS IN   CT/SYS
UNITED STATES AND INDIA. INDIA USA+45 LAW CONSTN   ADJUD
PROB/SOLV...DECISION JURID BIBLIOG 20 SUPREME/CT   ORD/FREE
FREE/SPEE AMEND/I. PAGE 9 E0175

AMEND/IV....CONCERNED WITH FREEDOMS GRANTED IN THE
     FOURTH AMENDMENT

AMEND/V....CONCERNED WITH FREEDOMS GRANTED IN THE
     FIFTH AMENDMENT

                                                        B58

HAND L.,THE BILL OF RIGHTS. USA+45 USA-45 CHIEF   CONSTN
LEGIS BAL/PWR ROLE PWR 18/20 SUPREME/CT CONGRESS   JURID
AMEND/V PRESIDENT AMEND/XIV. PAGE 50 E0994   ORD/FREE
                                                        CT/SYS

AMEND/VI....CONCERNED WITH FREEDOMS GRANTED IN THE
     SIXTH AMENDMENT

                                                        B55

BEANEY W.M.,THE RIGHT TO COUNSEL IN AMERICAN   ADJUD
COURTS. UK USA+45 USA-45 LAW NAT/G PROVS COLONIAL   CONSTN
PERCEPT 18/20 SUPREME/CT AMEND/VI AMEND/XIV   CT/SYS
ENGLSH/LAW. PAGE 8 E0163

AMEND/XIV....CONCERNED WITH FREEDOMS GRANTED IN THE
     FOURTEENTH AMENDMENT

                                                        B48

CORWIN E.S.,LIBERTY AGAINST GOVERNMENT. UK USA-45   JURID
ROMAN/EMP LAW CONSTN PERS/REL OWN ATTIT 1/20   ORD/FREE
ROMAN/LAW ENGLSH/LAW AMEND/XIV. PAGE 26 E0513   CONCPT

                                                        B55

BEANEY W.M.,THE RIGHT TO COUNSEL IN AMERICAN   ADJUD
COURTS. UK USA+45 USA-45 LAW NAT/G PROVS COLONIAL   CONSTN
PERCEPT 18/20 SUPREME/CT AMEND/VI AMEND/XIV   CT/SYS
ENGLSH/LAW. PAGE 8 E0163

                                                        S55

CAHN E.,"A DANGEROUS MYTH IN THE SCHOOL SEGREGATION   JURID
CASES" (BMR)" USA+45 CONSTN PROVS ADJUD DISCRIM   SCHOOL
...POLICY MYTH SOC/INTEG 20 SUPREME/CT AMEND/XIV.   RACE/REL
PAGE 18 E0360

                                                        B58

HAND L.,THE BILL OF RIGHTS. USA+45 USA-45 CHIEF   CONSTN
LEGIS BAL/PWR ROLE PWR 18/20 SUPREME/CT CONGRESS   JURID
AMEND/V PRESIDENT AMEND/XIV. PAGE 50 E0994   ORD/FREE
                                                        CT/SYS

                                                        B64

TENBROCK J.,EQUAL UNDER LAW. USA-45 CONSTN POL/PAR   LEGIS
EDU/PROP PARL/PROC ORD/FREE...BIBLIOG 19 AMEND/XIV.   LAW
PAGE 95 E1914   DISCRIM
                                                        DOMIN

AMER COUNCIL OF LEARNED SOCIET E0072

AMER SOCIETY POL & LEGAL PHIL E0073

AMERICAN BAR ASSOCIATION....SEE ABA

AMERICAN CIVIL LIBERTIES UNION....SEE ACLU

AMERICAN FEDERATION OF LABOR, CONGRESS OF INDUSTRIAL
    ORGANIZATIONS....SEE AFL/CIO, LABOR

AMERICAN INDIANS....SEE INDIAN/AM

AMERICAN POLITICAL SCIENCE ASSOCIATION....SEE APSA

AMERICAN TELEPHONE AND TELEGRAPH....SEE AT+T

AMERICAN ASSEMBLY COLUMBIA U E0074

AMERICAN ASSOCIATION LAW LIB E0075

AMERICAN CIVIL LIBERTIES UNION E0076
AMERICAN COUNCIL LEARNED SOC
AMERICAN DOCUMENTATION INST E0077

AMERICAN FOREIGN LAW ASSN E0078

AMERICAN JEWISH COMMITTEE E0079,E0080

AMERICAN JOURNAL COMP LAW E0081

AMERICAN LAW INSTITUTE E0082

AMERICAN SOCIETY PUBLIC ADMIN E0083

AMERICAN UNIVERSITY IN CAIRO E0084

AMERICAS, PRE/EUROPEAN....SEE PRE/AMER

AMMAN/MAX....MAX AMMAN

AMRAM P.W. E0085

ANAND R.P. E0086,E0087

ANARCH....ANARCHISM; SEE ALSO ATTIT, VALUES INDEX

                                                              B12
    POLLOCK F.,THE GENIUS OF THE COMMON LAW. CHRIST-17C LAW
    UK FINAN CHIEF ACT/RES ADMIN GP/REL ATTIT SOCISM   CULTURE
    ...ANARCH JURID. PAGE 81 E1624   CREATE

                                                              B27
    GOOCH G.P.,ENGLISH DEMOCRATIC IDEAS IN THE   IDEA/COMP
    SEVENTEENTH CENTURY (2ND ED.). UK LAW SECT FORCES   MAJORIT
    DIPLOM LEAD PARL/PROC REV ATTIT AUTHORIT...ANARCH   EX/STRUC
    CONCPT 17 PARLIAMENT CMN/WLTH REFORMERS. PAGE 45   CONSERVE
    E0885

                                                              B65
    US LIBRARY OF CONGRESS,INTERNAL SECURITY AND   CONTROL
    SUBVERSION. USA+45 ACADEM LOC/G NAT/G PROVS   ADJUD
    ...POLICY ANARCH DECISION 20 CIVIL/SERV SUBVERT   LAW
    SEDITION. PAGE 101 E2020   PLAN

ANARCHISM....SEE ANARCH

ANASTAPLO G. E0088

ANDALUSIA....SEE ALSO SPAIN

ANDERSON J.N.D. E0089

ANDERSON J.W. E0090

ANDERSON R.B. E0091

ANDERSON S.V. E0092

ANDERSON W. E0093,E0094,E0095

ANDORRA....SEE ALSO APPROPRIATE TIME/SPACE/CULTURE INDEX

ANDREWS F.E. E0096

ANDRUS H.L. E0097

ANGELL R.C. E0098

ANGLO/SAX....ANGLO-SAXON

ANGOLA....ANGOLA

ANNEXATION....ANNEXATION

ANOMIE....GENERALIZED PERSONAL ANXIETY; SEE DISPL

                                                              N
    INTERNATIONAL BIBLIOGRAPHY ON CRIME AND   BIBLIOG/A
    DELINQUENCY. USA+45 LAW FORCES PROB/SOLV AGE/Y 20. CRIME
    PAGE 1 E0023   ANOMIE
                                                        CRIMLGY

                                                              B39
    TIMASHEFF N.S.,AN INTRODUCTION TO THE SOCIOLOGY OF SOC
    LAW. CRIME ANOMIE ATTIT DRIVE ORD/FREE...JURID PSY BIBLIOG
    CONCPT. PAGE 96 E1926   PWR

                                                              B46
    GILLIN J.L.,SOCIAL PATHOLOGY. SOCIETY SECT CRIME   SOC
    ANOMIE DISPL ORD/FREE WEALTH...CRIMLGY PSY WORSHIP. ADJUST
    PAGE 44 E0864   CULTURE
                                                        INGP/REL

                                                              B46
    MANNHEIM H.,CRIMINAL JUSTICE AND SOCIAL   ADJUD
    RECONSTRUCTION. USA+45 EDU/PROP CRIME ANOMIE   LAW
    ...JURID BIBLIOG 20. PAGE 68 E1361   STRUCT
                                                        ADJUST

                                                              B51
    BIDDLE F.,THE FEAR OF FREEDOM. USA+45 LAW NAT/G   ANOMIE
    PUB/INST PROB/SOLV DOMIN CONTROL SANCTION REV   INGP/REL
    NAT/LISM 20. PAGE 12 E0227   VOL/ASSN
                                                        ORD/FREE

                                                              S51
    COHEN M.B.,"PERSONALITY AS A FACTOR IN   PERSON
    ADMINISTRATIVE DECISIONS." ADJUD PERS/REL ANOMIE   ADMIN
    SUPEGO...OBS SELF/OBS INT. PAGE 24 E0465   PROB/SOLV
                                                        PSY

                                                              B56
    SYKES G.M.,CRIME AND SOCIETY. LAW STRATA STRUCT   CRIMLGY
    ACT/RES ROUTINE ANOMIE WEALTH...POLICY SOC/INTEG   CRIME
    20. PAGE 95 E1903   CULTURE
                                                        INGP/REL

                                                              B57
    CLINARD M.B.,SOCIOLOGY OF DEVIANT BEHAVIOR. FAM   BIO/SOC
    CONTROL MURDER DISCRIM PERSON...PSY SOC T SOC/INTEG CRIME
    20. PAGE 23 E0455   SEX
                                                        ANOMIE

                                                              B57
    ROWAN C.T.,GO SOUTH TO SORROW. USA+45 STRUCT NAT/G RACE/REL
    EDU/PROP LEAD COERCE ISOLAT DRIVE SUPEGO RESPECT   DISCRIM
    ...PREDICT 20 NEGRO SUPREME/CT SOUTH/US CIV/RIGHTS. ANOMIE
    PAGE 86 E1728   LAW

                                                              S58
    CRESSEY D.R.,"ACHIEVEMENT OF AN UNSTATED   PUB/INST
    ORGANIZATIONAL GOAL: AN OBSERVATION ON PRISONS."   CLIENT
    OP/RES PROB/SOLV PERS/REL ANOMIE ATTIT ROLE RESPECT NEIGH
    CRIMLGY. PAGE 28 E0546   INGP/REL

                                                              S59
    CLOWARD R.A.,"ILLEGITIMATE MEANS, ANOMIE, AND   ANOMIE
    DEVIANT BEHAVIOR" STRUCT CRIME DRIVE PERSON...SOC   CRIMLGY
    CONCPT NEW/IDEA 20 DURKHEIM/E MERTON/R. PAGE 23   LEGIT
    E0459   ADJUST

                                                              B60
    GIBNEY F.,THE OPERATORS. USA+45 LAW STRATA BIO/SOC CRIME
    MORAL ORD/FREE SOC. PAGE 43 E0858   CULTURE
                                                        ANOMIE
                                                        CRIMLGY

                                                              B61
    DAVIS B.F.,THE DESPERATE AND THE DAMNED. USA+45 LAW PUB/INST
    DEATH ANOMIE...CRIMLGY 20 SAN/QUENTN. PAGE 29 E0571 SANCTION
                                                        CRIME

                                                              B61
    MERTON R.K.,CONTEMPORARY SOCIAL PROBLEMS: AN   CRIME
    INTRODUCTION TO THE SOCIOLOGY OF DEVIANT BEHAVIOR   ANOMIE
    AND SOCIAL DISORGANIZATION. FAM MUNIC FORCES WORKER STRANGE
    PROB/SOLV INGP/REL RACE/REL ISOLAT...CRIMLGY GEOG   SOC
    PSY T 20 NEGRO. PAGE 72 E1444

                                                              B62
    MITCHELL G.E.,THE ANGRY BLACK SOUTH. USA+45 LAW   RACE/REL
    CONSTN SCHOOL DELIB/GP EDU/PROP CONTROL SUFF ANOMIE DISCRIM
    DRIVE...ANTHOL 20 NEGRO CIV/RIGHTS SOUTH/US.   ADJUST
    PAGE 74 E1473   ORD/FREE

                                                              B64
    CHEIN I.,THE ROAD TO H: NARCOTICS, DELINQUENCY, AND BIO/SOC
    SOCIAL POLICY. USA+45 NEIGH CRIME INGP/REL ATTIT   AGE/Y
    PERSON...SOC/WK 20 NEWYORK/C. PAGE 22 E0426   POLICY
                                                        ANOMIE

CLINARD M.B.,ANOMIE AND DEVIANT BEHAVIOR: A DISCUSSION AND CRITIQUE. SOCIETY FACE/GP CRIME STRANGE ATTIT BIO/SOC DISPL RIGID/FLEX HEALTH...PSY CONCPT BIBLIOG 20 MERTON/R. PAGE 23 E0456
B64
PERSON
ANOMIE
KIN
NEIGH

DRESSLER D.,READINGS IN CRIMINOLOGY AND PENOLOGY. UNIV CULTURE PUB/INST FORCES ACT/RES PROB/SOLV ANOMIE BIO/SOC SUPEGO...GEOG PSY ANTHOL 20. PAGE 33 E0648
B64
CRIMLGY
CRIME
ADJUD
ADJUST

BROMBERG W.,CRIME AND THE MIND. LAW LEGIT ADJUD CRIME MURDER AGE/Y ANOMIE BIO/SOC DRIVE SEX PSY. PAGE 16 E0305
B65
CRIMLGY
SOC
HEALTH
COERCE

FLEISCHER B.M.,THE ECONOMICS OF DELINQUENCY. UNIV WORKER STRANGE ANOMIE...STAT CHARTS 20. PAGE 38 E0762
B66
STRATA
INCOME
AGE/Y
CRIME

MACIVER R.M.,THE PREVENTION AND CONTROL OF DELINQUENCY. USA+45 STRATA PUB/INST ANOMIE ATTIT HABITAT PERSON HEALTH...CRIMLGY PSY SOC METH. PAGE 67 E1341
B66
AGE/Y
PLAN
ADJUST
CRIME

MENDELSON W.,JUSTICES BLACK AND FRANKFURTER: CONFLICT IN THE COURT (2ND ED.). NAT/G PROVS PROB/SOLV BAL/PWR CONTROL FEDERAL ISOLAT ANOMIE ORD/FREE...DECISION 20 SUPREME/CT BLACK/HL FRANKFUR/F. PAGE 72 E1439
B66
JURID
ADJUD
IDEA/COMP
ROLE

BONGER W.A.,CRIMINALITY AND ECONOMIC CONDITIONS. MOD/EUR STRUCT INDUS WORKER EDU/PROP CRIME HABITAT ALL/VALS...JURID SOC 20 REFORMERS. PAGE 14 E0265
B67
PERSON
CRIMLGY
IDEA/COMP
ANOMIE

DUPRE L.,"TILL DEATH DO US PART?" UNIV FAM INSPECT LEGIT ADJUD SANCTION PERS/REL ANOMIE RIGID/FLEX SEX ...JURID IDEA/COMP 20 CHURCH/STA BIBLE CANON/LAW CIVIL/LAW. PAGE 34 E0666
S68
MARRIAGE
CATH
LAW

ANROD C.W. E0143

ANTARCTICA

TAUBENFELD H.J.,"A TREATY FOR ANTARCTICA." FUT USA+45 INTELL INT/ORG LABOR 20 TREATY ANTARCTICA. PAGE 95 E1909
L61
R+D
ACT/RES
DIPLOM

ANTHOL....ANTHOLOGY, SYMPOSIUM, PANEL OF WRITERS

EYBERS G.W.,SELECT CONSTITUTIONAL DOCUMENTS ILLUSTRATING SOUTH AFRICAN HISTORY 1795-1910. SOUTH/AFR LOC/G LEGIS CT/SYS...JURID ANTHOL 18/20 NATAL CAPE/HOPE ORANGE/STA. PAGE 36 E0707
B18
CONSTN
LAW
NAT/G
COLONIAL

THOMPSON J.W.,SECRET DIPLOMACY: A RECORD OF ESPIONAGE AND DOUBLE-DEALING: 1500-1815. CHRIST-17C MOD/EUR NAT/G WRITING RISK MORAL...ANTHOL BIBLIOG 16/19 ESPIONAGE. PAGE 96 E1920
B37
DIPLOM
CRIME

HAGUE PERMANENT CT INTL JUSTIC,WORLD COURT REPORTS: COLLECTION OF THE JUDGEMENTS ORDERS AND OPINIONS VOLUME 3 1932-35. WOR-45 LAW DELIB/GP CONFER WAR PEACE ATTIT...DECISION ANTHOL 20 WORLD/CT CASEBOOK. PAGE 49 E0976
B38
INT/ORG
CT/SYS
DIPLOM
ADJUD

COMM. STUDY ORGAN. PEACE,"ORGANIZATION OF PEACE." USA-45 WOR-45 STRATA NAT/G ACT/RES DIPLOM ECO/TAC EDU/PROP ADJUD ATTIT ORD/FREE PWR...SOC CONCPT ANTHOL LEAGUE/NAT 20. PAGE 24 E0479
L41
INT/ORG
PLAN
PEACE

HAGUE PERMANENT CT INTL JUSTIC,WORLD COURT REPORTS: COLLECTION OF THE JUDGEMENTS ORDERS AND OPINIONS VOLUME 4 1936-42. WOR-45 CONFER PEACE ATTIT ...DECISION JURID ANTHOL 20 WORLD/CT CASEBOOK. PAGE 49 E0977
B43
INT/ORG
CT/SYS
DIPLOM
ADJUD

GRIFFITH E.S.,RESEARCH IN POLITICAL SCIENCE: THE WORK OF PANELS OF RESEARCH COMMITTEE, APSA. WOR+45 WOR-45 COM/IND R+D FORCES ACT/RES WAR...GOV/COMP
B48
BIBLIOG
PHIL/SCI
DIPLOM

ANTHOL 20. PAGE 47 E0939
JURID

DE HUSZAR G.B.,EQUALITY IN AMERICA: THE ISSUE OF MINORITY RIGHTS. USA+45 USA-45 LAW NEIGH SCHOOL LEGIS ACT/RES CHOOSE ATTIT RESPECT...ANTHOL 20 NEGRO. PAGE 29 E0585
B49
DISCRIM
RACE/REL
ORD/FREE
PROB/SOLV

HUXLEY J.,FREEDOM AND CULTURE. UNIV LAW SOCIETY R+D ACADEM SCHOOL CREATE SANCTION ATTIT KNOWL...HUM ANTHOL 20. PAGE 56 E1118
B51
CULTURE
ORD/FREE
PHIL/SCI
IDEA/COMP

BRIGGS H.W.,THE LAW OF NATIONS (2ND ED.). WOR+45 WOR-45 NAT/G LEGIS WAR...ANTHOL 20 TREATY. PAGE 15 E0301
B52
INT/LAW
DIPLOM
JURID

MAJUMDAR B.B.,PROBLEMS OF PUBLIC ADMINISTRATION IN INDIA. INDIA INDUS PLAN BUDGET ADJUD CENTRAL DEMAND WEALTH...WELF/ST ANTHOL 20 CIVIL/SERV. PAGE 68 E1353
B53
ECO/UNDEV
GOV/REL
ADMIN
MUNIC

FRIEDMAN W.,THE PUBLIC CORPORATION: A COMPARATIVE SYMPOSIUM (UNIVERSITY OF TORONTO SCHOOL OF LAW COMPARATIVE LAW SERIES. VOL. I). SWEDEN USA+45 INDUS INT/ORG NAT/G REGION CENTRAL FEDERAL...POLICY JURID IDEA/COMP NAT/COMP ANTHOL 20 COMMONWLTH MONOPOLY EUROPE. PAGE 40 E0801
B54
LAW
SOCISM
LG/CO
OWN

BENTON W.E.,NUREMBERG: GERMAN VIEWS OF THE WAR TRIALS. EUR+WWI GERMANY VOL/ASSN LEAD PARTIC COERCE INGP/REL RACE/REL TOTALISM SUPEGO ORD/FREE...ANTHOL NUREMBERG. PAGE 10 E0201
B55
CRIME
WAR
LAW
JURID

CHARMATZ J.P.,COMPARATIVE STUDIES IN COMMUNITY PROPERTY LAW. FRANCE USA+45...JURID GOV/COMP ANTHOL 20. PAGE 22 E0424
B55
MARRIAGE
LAW
OWN
MUNIC

KHADDURI M.,LAW IN THE MIDDLE EAST. LAW CONSTN ACADEM FAM EDU/PROP CT/SYS SANCTION CRIME...INT/LAW GOV/COMP ANTHOL 6/20 MID/EAST. PAGE 61 E1210
B55
ADJUD
JURID
ISLAM

MID-EUROPEAN LAW PROJECT,CHURCH AND STATE BEHIND THE IRON CURTAIN. COM CZECHOSLVK HUNGARY POLAND USSR CULTURE SECT EDU/PROP GOV/REL CATHISM...CHARTS ANTHOL BIBLIOG WORSHIP 20 CHURCH/STA. PAGE 73 E1455
B55
LAW
MARXISM
POLICY

COHEN A.,THE SUTHERLAND PAPERS. USA+45 USA-45 LAW CONTROL CRIME AGE/Y...TREND ANTHOL BIBLIOG 20. PAGE 23 E0461
B56
CRIMLGY
PHIL/SCI
ACT/RES
METH

LASLETT P.,PHILOSOPHY, POLITICS AND SOCIETY. UNIV CRIME SOVEREIGN...JURID PHIL/SCI ANTHOL PLATO NATURL/LAW. PAGE 63 E1260
B56
CONSTN
ATTIT
CONCPT
GEN/LAWS

SOHN L.B.,BASIC DOCUMENTS OF THE UNITED NATIONS. WOR+45 LAW INT/ORG LEGIT EXEC ROUTINE CHOOSE PWR ...JURID CONCPT GEN/LAWS ANTHOL UN TOT/POP OAS FAO ILO 20. PAGE 92 E1853
B56
DELIB/GP
CONSTN

SOHN L.B.,CASES ON UNITED NATIONS LAW. STRUCT DELIB/GP WAR PEACE ORD/FREE...DECISION ANTHOL 20 UN. PAGE 92 E1854
B56
INT/ORG
INT/LAW
ADMIN
ADJUD

CHICAGO U LAW SCHOOL,CONFERENCE ON JUDICIAL ADMINISTRATION. LOC/G MUNIC NAT/G PROVS...ANTHOL 20. PAGE 22 E0429
B57
CT/SYS
ADJUD
ADMIN
GOV/REL

US COMMISSION GOVT SECURITY,RECOMMENDATIONS; AREA: IMMIGRANT PROGRAM. USA+45 LAW WORKER DIPLOM EDU/PROP WRITING ADMIN PEACE ATTIT...CONCPT ANTHOL 20 MIGRATION SUBVERT. PAGE 99 E1981
B57
POLICY
CONTROL
PLAN
NAT/G

AMERICAN SOCIETY PUBLIC ADMIN,STRENGTHENING MANAGEMENT FOR DEMOCRATIC GOVERNMENT. USA+45 ACADEM EX/STRUC WORKER PLAN BUDGET CONFER CT/SYS
B58
ADMIN
NAT/G
EXEC

EFFICIENCY ANTHOL. PAGE 4 E0083   MGT

B58
ATOMIC INDUSTRIAL FORUM,MANAGEMENT AND ATOMIC   NUC/PWR
ENERGY. WOR+45 SEA LAW MARKET NAT/G TEC/DEV INSPECT INDUS
INT/TRADE CONFER PEACE HEALTH...ANTHOL 20. PAGE 6   MGT
E0112   ECO/TAC

B58
BRIERLY J.L.,THE BASIS OF OBLIGATION IN   INT/LAW
INTERNATIONAL LAW, AND OTHER PAPERS. WOR+45 WOR-45 DIPLOM
LEGIS...JURID CONCPT NAT/COMP ANTHOL 20. PAGE 15 ADJUD
E0299   SOVEREIGN

B58
MANSERGH N.,COMMONWEALTH PERSPECTIVES. GHANA UK LAW DIPLOM
VOL/ASSN CONFER HEALTH SOVEREIGN...GEOG CHARTS   COLONIAL
ANTHOL 20 CMN/WLTH AUSTRAL. PAGE 68 E1363   INT/ORG
                                         INGP/REL

B58
PALMER E.E.,CIVIL LIBERTIES. USA+45 ADJUD CT/SYS   ORD/FREE
PARTIC OWN LAISSEZ POPULISM...JURID CONCPT ANTHOL CONSTN
20 SUPREME/CT CIVIL/LIB. PAGE 79 E1592   RACE/REL
                                         LAW

B58
WHITNEY S.N.,ANTITRUST POLICIES: AMERICAN   INDUS
EXPERIENCE IN TWENTY INDUSTRIES. USA+45 USA-45 LAW CONTROL
DELIB/GP LEGIS ADJUD CT/SYS GOV/REL ATTIT...ANTHOL LG/CO
20 MONOPOLY CASEBOOK. PAGE 106 E2119   MARKET

B59
BRIGGS A.,CHARTIST STUDIES. UK LAW NAT/G WORKER   INDUS
EDU/PROP COERCE SUFF GP/REL ATTIT...ANTHOL 19.   STRATA
PAGE 15 E0300   LABOR
                                         POLICY

B59
GINSBURG M.,LAW AND OPINION IN ENGLAND. UK CULTURE JURID
KIN LABOR LEGIS EDU/PROP ADMIN CT/SYS CRIME OWN   POLICY
HEALTH...ANTHOL 20 ENGLSH/LAW. PAGE 44 E0868   ECO/TAC

B59
HALEY A.G.,FIRST COLLOQUIUM ON THE LAW OF OUTER   SPACE
SPACE. WOR+45 INT/ORG ACT/RES PLAN BAL/PWR CONFER LAW
ATTIT PWR...POLICY JURID CHARTS ANTHOL 20. PAGE 49 SOVEREIGN
E0979   CONTROL

B59
MORRIS C.,THE GREAT LEGAL PHILOSOPHERS: SELECTED   JURID
READINGS IN JURISPRUDENCE. UNIV INTELL SOCIETY   ADJUD
EDU/PROP MAJORITY UTOPIA PERSON KNOWL...ANTHOL.   PHIL/SCI
PAGE 75 E1497   IDEA/COMP

B59
U OF MICHIGAN LAW SCHOOL,ATOMS AND THE LAW. USA+45 NUC/PWR
PROVS WORKER PROB/SOLV DIPLOM ADMIN GOV/REL ANTHOL. NAT/G
PAGE 97 E1950   CONTROL
                                         LAW

L59
COWAN T.A.,"A SYMPOSIUM ON GROUP INTERESTS AND THE ADJUD
LAW" USA+45 LAW MARKET LABOR PLAN INT/TRADE TAX   PWR
RACE/REL RIGID/FLEX...JURID ANTHOL 20. PAGE 27   INGP/REL
E0528   CREATE

B60
JUNZ A.J.,PRESENT TRENDS IN AMERICAN NATIONAL   POL/PAR
GOVERNMENT. LEGIS DIPLOM ADMIN CT/SYS ORD/FREE   CHOOSE
...CONCPT ANTHOL 20 CONGRESS PRESIDENT SUPREME/CT. CONSTN
PAGE 2 E0040   NAT/G

B60
ATOMIC INDUSTRIAL FORUM,ATOMS FOR INDUSTRY: WORLD NUC/PWR
FORUM. WOR+45 FINAN COST UTIL...JURID ANTHOL 20.   INDUS
PAGE 6 E0113   PLAN
                                       PROB/SOLV

L60
LAUTERPACHT E.,"THE SUEZ CANAL SETTLEMENT." FRANCE INT/ORG
ISLAM ISRAEL UAR UK BAL/PWR DIPLOM LEGIT...JURID   LAW
GEN/LAWS ANTHOL SUEZ VAL/FREE 20. PAGE 63 E1263

B61
ALFRED H.,PUBLIC OWNERSHIP IN THE USA: GOALS AND   CONTROL
PRIORITIES. LAW INDUS INT/TRADE ADJUD GOV/REL   OWN
EFFICIENCY PEACE SOCISM...POLICY ANTHOL 20 TVA.   ECO/DEV
PAGE 3 E0064   ECO/TAC

B61
BAINS J.S.,STUDIES IN POLITICAL SCIENCE. INDIA   DIPLOM
WOR+45 WOR-45 CONSTN BAL/PWR ADJUD ADMIN PARL/PROC INT/LAW
SOVEREIGN...SOC METH/COMP ANTHOL 17/20 UN. PAGE 7 NAT/G
E0137

B61
BRENNAN D.G.,ARMS CONTROL, DISARMAMENT, AND   ARMS/CONT
NATIONAL SECURITY. WOR+45 NAT/G FORCES CREATE   ORD/FREE
PROB/SOLV PARTIC WAR PEACE...DECISION INT/LAW   DIPLOM
ANTHOL BIBLIOG 20. PAGE 15 E0291   POLICY

B61
SCOTT A.M.,POLITICS, USA: CASES ON THE AMERICAN   CT/SYS
DEMOCRATIC PROCESS. USA+45 CHIEF FORCES DIPLOM   CONSTN
LOBBY CHOOSE RACE/REL FEDERAL ATTIT...JURID ANTHOL NAT/G
T 20 PRESIDENT CONGRESS CIVIL/LIB. PAGE 90 E1795 PLAN

B61
SMITH J.W.,RELIGIOUS PERSPECTIVES IN AMERICAN   SECT
CULTURE. VOL. 2, RELIGION IN AMERICAN LIFE. USA+45 DOMIN
CULTURE NAT/G EDU/PROP ADJUD LOBBY ATTIT...ART/METH SOCIETY
ANTHOL 20 CHURCH/STA BIBLE. PAGE 92 E1845   GP/REL

B61
WESTIN A.F.,THE SUPREME COURT: VIEWS FROM INSIDE. CT/SYS
USA+45 NAT/G PROF/ORG PROVS DELIB/GP INGP/REL   LAW
DISCRIM ATTIT...POLICY DECISION JURID ANTHOL 20   ADJUD
SUPREME/CT CONGRESS CIVIL/LIB. PAGE 106 E2114   GOV/REL

N61
DELEGACION NACIONAL DE PRENSA,FALANGE ESPANOL   EDU/PROP
TRADICIONALISTA Y DE LAS JUNTAS OFENSIVAS   FASCIST
NACIONALES SINDICALISTAS. IX CONSEJO NACIONAL   CONFER
(PAMPHLET). LAW VOL/ASSN TOTALISM AUTHORIT ORD/FREE POL/PAR
FASCISM...ANTHOL 20 FRANCO/F FALANGIST. PAGE 31
E0605

B62
AMER SOCIETY POL & LEGAL PHIL,THE PUBLIC INTEREST: CONCPT
NOMOS V. LAW EDU/PROP...SOC METH/CNCPT ANTHOL.   ATTIT
PAGE 4 E0073   PWR
                                       GEN/LAWS

B62
BOCHENSKI J.M.,HANDBOOK ON COMMUNISM. USSR WOR+45 COM
LAW SOCIETY NAT/G POL/PAR SECT CRIME PERSON MARXISM DIPLOM
...SOC ANTHOL 20. PAGE 13 E0254   POLICY
                                       CONCPT

B62
BRANDT R.B.,SOCIAL JUSTICE. UNIV LAW GP/REL PWR   ORD/FREE
ALL/IDEOS...POLICY SOC ANTHOL 20. PAGE 15 E0287   CONSTN
                                         CONCPT

B62
EVAN W.M.,LAW AND SOCIOLOGY: EXPLORATORY ESSAYS. JURID
CONSULT ACT/RES OP/RES PROB/SOLV EDU/PROP LEGIT   SOC
ADJUD CT/SYS GP/REL...PHIL/SCI ANTHOL SOC/INTEG 20. PROF/ORG
PAGE 35 E0703

B62
MCGRATH J.J.,CHURCH AND STATE IN AMERICAN LAW. LAW SECT
PROVS SCHOOL TAX GIVE CT/SYS GP/REL...POLICY ANTHOL ADJUD
18/20 SUPREME/CT CHURCH/STA CASEBOOK. PAGE 71 E1414 CONSTN
                                         NAT/G

B62
MCGRATH J.J.,CHURCH AND STATE IN AMERICAN LAW: LAW
CASES AND MATERIALS. USA+45 USA-45 LEGIS EDU/PROP GOV/REL
ADJUD CT/SYS PWR...ANTHOL 18/20 CHURCH/STA. PAGE 71 SECT
E1415

B62
MITCHELL G.E.,THE ANGRY BLACK SOUTH. USA+45 LAW   RACE/REL
CONSTN SCHOOL DELIB/GP EDU/PROP CONTROL SUFF ANOMIE DISCRIM
DRIVE...ANTHOL 20 NEGRO CIV/RIGHTS SOUTH/US.   ADJUST
PAGE 74 E1473   ORD/FREE

B62
SHAW C.,LEGAL PROBLEMS IN INTERNATIONAL TRADE AND INT/LAW
INVESTMENT. WOR+45 ECO/DEV ECO/UNDEV MARKET DIPLOM INT/TRADE
TAX INCOME ROLE...ANTHOL BIBLIOG 20 TREATY UN IMF FINAN
GATT. PAGE 91 E1816   ECO/TAC

L62
ERDMANN H.H.,"ADMINISTRATIVE LAW AND FARM   AGRI
ECONOMICS." USA+45 LOC/G NAT/G PLAN PROB/SOLV LOBBY ADMIN
...DECISION ANTHOL 20. PAGE 35 E0695   ADJUD
                                         POLICY

B63
BOWIE R.R.,GOVERNMENT REGULATION OF BUSINESS: CASES LAW
FROM THE NATIONAL REPORTER SYSTEM. USA+45 USA-45   CONTROL
NAT/G ECO/TAC ADJUD...ANTHOL 19/20 SUPREME/CT FTC INDUS
FAIR/LABOR MONOPOLY. PAGE 14 E0280   CT/SYS

B63
CAHN E.,THE GREAT RIGHTS. USA+45 NAT/G PROVS   CONSTN
CIVMIL/REL...IDEA/COMP ANTHOL BIBLIOG 18/20   LAW
MADISON/J BILL/RIGHT CIV/RIGHTS WARRN/EARL   ORD/FREE
BLACK/HL. PAGE 18 E0361   INGP/REL

DUNHAM A.,MR. JUSTICE. ADJUD PWR...JURID ANTHOL
18/20 SUPREME/CT. PAGE 33 E0659

B63
BIOG
PERSON
LAW
CT/SYS

FRIEDRICH C.J.,JUSTICE: NOMOS VI. UNIV LAW SANCTION LEGIT
CRIME...CONCPT ANTHOL MARX/KARL LOCKE/JOHN
AQUINAS/T. PAGE 41 E0809

B63
LEGIT
ADJUD
ORD/FREE
JURID

HABERMAS J.,THEORIE UND PRAXIS. RATIONAL PERSON
...PHIL/SCI ANTHOL 19/20 HEGEL/GWF MARX/KARL BLOCH
LOWITH. PAGE 49 E0969

B63
JURID
REV
GEN/LAWS
MARXISM

HAUSMAN W.H.,MANAGING ECONOMIC DEVELOPMENT IN
AFRICA. AFR USA+45 LAW FINAN WORKER TEC/DEV WEALTH
...ANTHOL 20. PAGE 51 E1012

B63
ECO/UNDEV
PLAN
FOR/AID
MGT

NATIONAL CIVIC REVIEW,REAPPORTIONMENT: A YEAR IN
REVIEW (PAMPHLET). USA+45 LAW CT/SYS CHOOSE
ORD/FREE PWR...ANTHOL 20 CONGRESS. PAGE 76 E1527

B63
APPORT
REPRESENT
LEGIS
CONSTN

NEWMAN E.S.,THE FREEDOM READER. USA+45 LEGIS TOP/EX
PLAN ADJUD CONTROL CT/SYS DISCRIM...DECISION ANTHOL
20 SUPREME/CT CIV/RIGHTS. PAGE 77 E1541

B63
RACE/REL
LAW
POLICY
ORD/FREE

OTTOSON H.W.,LAND USE POLICY AND PROBLEMS IN THE
UNITED STATES. USA+45 USA-45 LAW AGRI INDUS NAT/G
GP/REL...CHARTS ANTHOL 19/20 HOMEST/ACT. PAGE 79
E1586

B63
PROB/SOLV
UTIL
HABITAT
POLICY

SCHMIDHAUSER J.R.,CONSTITUTIONAL LAW IN THE
POLITICAL PROCESS. SOCIETY LEGIS ADJUD CT/SYS
FEDERAL...SOC TREND IDEA/COMP ANTHOL T SUPREME/CT
SENATE CONGRESS HOUSE/REP. PAGE 88 E1761

B63
LAW
CONSTN
JURID

US SENATE,DOCUMENTS ON INTERNATIONAL AS"ECTS OF
EXPLORATION AND USE OF OUTER SPACE, 1954-62: STAFF
REPORT FOR COMM AERON SPACE SCI. USA+45 USSR LEGIS
LEAD CIVMIL/REL PEACE...POLICY INT/LAW ANTHOL 20
CONGRESS NASA KHRUSH/N. PAGE 101 E2026

B63
SPACE
UTIL
GOV/REL
DIPLOM

ROSE R.,"COMPARATIVE STUDIES IN POLITICAL FINANCE:
A SYMPOSIUM." ASIA EUR+WWI S/ASIA LAW CULTURE
DELIB/GP LEGIS ACT/RES ECO/TAC EDU/PROP CHOOSE
ATTIT RIGID/FLEX SUPEGO PWR SKILL WEALTH...STAT
ANTHOL VAL/FREE. PAGE 85 E1714

L63
FINAN
POL/PAR

SCHUBERT G.,"JUDICIAL DECISION-MAKING." FORCES LEAD
ATTIT DRIVE...POLICY PSY STAT CHARTS ANTHOL BIBLIOG
20. PAGE 88 E1773

C63
ADJUD
DECISION
JUDGE
CT/SYS

BLOUSTEIN E.J.,NUCLEAR ENERGY, PUBLIC POLICY, AND
THE LAW. USA+45 NAT/G ADJUD ADMIN GP/REL OWN PEACE
ATTIT HEALTH...ANTHOL 20. PAGE 13 E0251

B64
TEC/DEV
LAW
POLICY
NUC/PWR

DIETZE G.,ESSAYS ON THE AMERICAN CONSTITUTION: A
COMMEMORATIVE VOLUME IN HONOR OF ALPHEUS T. MASON.
USA+45 USA-45 LAW INTELL...POLICY BIOG IDEA/COMP
ANTHOL SUPREME/CT. PAGE 32 E0626

B64
FEDERAL
CONSTN
DIPLOM
CT/SYS

DRESSLER D.,READINGS IN CRIMINOLOGY AND PENOLOGY.
UNIV CULTURE PUB/INST FORCES ACT/RES PROB/SOLV
ANOMIE BIO/SOC SUPEGO...GEOG PSY ANTHOL 20. PAGE 33
E0648

B64
CRIMLGY
CRIME
ADJUD
ADJUST

ENGEL S.,LAW, STATE, AND INTERNATIONAL LEGAL ORDER.
WOR+45 NAT/G ORD/FREE RELATISM...INT/LAW IDEA/COMP
ANTHOL 20 KELSEN/H. PAGE 35 E0690

B64
JURID
OBJECTIVE
CONCPT
DEBATE

GUTTMANN A.,COMMUNISM, THE COURTS, AND THE
CONSTITUTION. USA+45 CT/SYS ORD/FREE...ANTHOL 20

B64
MARXISM
POL/PAR

COM/PARTY CIV/RIGHTS. PAGE 48 E0965

CONSTN
LAW

LEDERMAN W.R.,THE COURTS AND THE CANDIAN
CONSTITUTION. CANADA PARL/PROC...POLICY JURID
GOV/COMP ANTHOL 19/20 SUPREME/CT PARLIAMENT.
PAGE 64 E1276

B64
CONSTN
CT/SYS
LEGIS
LAW

MAKI J.M.,COURT AND CONSTITUTION IN JAPAN: SELECTED
SUPREME COURT DECISIONS, 1948-60. LAW AGRI FAM
LEGIS BAL/PWR ADMIN CHOOSE...SOC ANTHOL CABINET 20
CHINJAP CIVIL/LIB. PAGE 68 E1355

B64
CONSTN
JURID
CT/SYS
CRIME

MCDOUGAL M.S.,STUDIES IN WORLD PUBLIC ORDER. SPACE
SEA INT/ORG CREATE AGREE NUC/PWR...POLICY PHIL/SCI
IDEA/COMP ANTHOL METH 20 UN. PAGE 71 E1411

B64
INT/LAW
SOC
DIPLOM

NICE R.W.,TREASURY OF LAW. WOR+45 WOR-45 SECT ADJUD
MORAL ORD/FREE...INT/LAW JURID PHIL/SCI ANTHOL.
PAGE 77 E1545

B64
LAW
WRITING
PERS/REL
DIPLOM

OSSENBECK F.J.,OPEN SPACE AND PEACE. CHINA/COM FUT
USA+45 USSR LAW PROB/SOLV TEC/DEV EDU/PROP NEUTRAL
PEACE...AUD/VIS ANTHOL 20. PAGE 79 E1583

B64
SPACE
ORD/FREE
DIPLOM
CREATE

SCHUBERT G.A.,JUDICIAL BEHAVIOR: A READER IN THEORY
AND RESEARCH. POL/PAR CT/SYS ROLE SUPEGO PWR
...DECISION JURID REGRESS CHARTS SIMUL ANTHOL 20.
PAGE 89 E1782

B64
ATTIT
PERSON
ADJUD
ACT/RES

SCHWARTZ M.D.,CONFERENCE ON SPACE SCIENCE AND SPACE
LAW. FUT COM/IND NAT/G FORCES ACT/RES PLAN BUDGET
DIPLOM NUC/PWR WEAPON...POLICY ANTHOL 20. PAGE 89
E1788

B64
SPACE
LAW
PEACE
TEC/DEV

SEGAL R.,SANCTIONS AGAINST SOUTH AFRICA. AFR
SOUTH/AFR NAT/G INT/TRADE RACE/REL PEACE PWR
...INT/LAW ANTHOL 20 UN. PAGE 90 E1801

B64
SANCTION
DISCRIM
ECO/TAC
POLICY

TAUBENFELD H.J.,SPACE AND SOCIETY. USA+45 LAW
FORCES CREATE TEC/DEV ADJUD CONTROL COST PEACE
...PREDICT ANTHOL 20. PAGE 95 E1911

B64
SPACE
SOCIETY
ADJUST
DIPLOM

US AIR FORCE ACADEMY ASSEMBLY,OUTER SPACE: FINAL
REPORT APRIL 1-4, 1964. FUT USA+45 WOR+45 LAW
DELIB/GP CONFER ARMS/CONT WAR PEACE ATTIT MORAL
...ANTHOL 20 NASA. PAGE 99 E1979

B64
SPACE
CIVMIL/REL
NUC/PWR
DIPLOM

CORWIN E.S.,"AMERICAN CONSTITUTIONAL HISTORY." LAW
NAT/G PROB/SOLV EQUILIB FEDERAL ATTIT PWR...JURID
BIBLIOG 20. PAGE 26 E0515

C64
ANTHOL
JUDGE
ADJUD
CT/SYS

BAADE H.,THE SOVIET IMPACT ON INTERNATIONAL LAW.
INT/ORG INT/TRADE LEGIT COLONIAL ARMS/CONT REV WAR
...CON/ANAL ANTHOL TREATY. PAGE 6 E0124

B65
INT/LAW
USSR
CREATE
ORD/FREE

BEGGS D.W.,AMERICA'S SCHOOLS AND CHURCHES: PARTNERS
IN CONFLICT. USA+45 PROVS EDU/PROP ADJUD DISCRIM
ATTIT...IDEA/COMP ANTHOL BIBLIOG WORSHIP 20
CHURCH/STA. PAGE 9 E0179

B65
SECT
GP/REL
SCHOOL
NAT/G

BERKOWITZ M.,AMERICAN NATIONAL SECURITY: A READER
IN THEORY AND POLICY. USA+45 INT/ORG FORCES BAL/PWR
DIPLOM ECO/TAC DETER PWR...INT/LAW ANTHOL BIBLIOG
20 UN. PAGE 11 E0203

B65
ORD/FREE
WAR
ARMS/CONT
POLICY

BLITZ L.F.,THE POLITICS AND ADMINISTRATION OF
NIGERIAN GOVERNMENT. NIGER CULTURE LOC/G LEGIS
DIPLOM COLONIAL CT/SYS SOVEREIGN...GEOG SOC ANTHOL
20. PAGE 13 E0245

B65
NAT/G
GOV/REL
POL/PAR

BOCK E.,GOVERNMENT REGULATION OF BUSINESS. USA+45
LAW EX/STRUC LEGIS EXEC ORD/FREE PWR...ANTHOL
CONGRESS. PAGE 13 E0255

B65
MGT
ADMIN
NAT/G

CONTROL

E0989   PWR

B65
CARTER G.M.,POLITICS IN EUROPE. EUR+WWI FRANCE   GOV/COMP
GERMANY/W UK USSR LAW CONSTN POL/PAR VOL/ASSN PRESS   OP/RES
LOBBY PWR...ANTHOL SOC/INTEG EEC. PAGE 20 E0399   ECO/DEV

B66
KURLAND P.B.,THE SUPREME COURT REVIEW. USA+45   JURID
USA-45 LAW LABOR SUFF...ANTHOL 20 SUPREME/CT.   PROB/SOLV
PAGE 62 E1240   ADJUD
                                                       NAT/G

B65
FRIEDMAN L.,SOUTHERN JUSTICE. USA+45 PUB/INST LEGIT   ADJUD
ADMIN CT/SYS DISCRIM...DECISION ANTHOL 20 NEGRO   LAW
SOUTH/US CIV/RIGHTS. PAGE 40 E0800   CONSTN
                                                       RACE/REL

B66
TRESOLINI R.J.,CASES IN AMERICAN NATIONAL   NAT/G
GOVERNMENT AND POLITICS. LAW DIPLOM ADJUD LOBBY   LEGIS
FEDERAL ORD/FREE WEALTH...DECISION ANTHOL 20   CT/SYS
PRESIDENT. PAGE 97 E1940   POL/PAR

B65
GLUECK S.,ROSCOE POUND AND CRIMINAL JUSTICE.   CT/SYS
SOCIETY FAM GOV/REL AGE/Y ATTIT ORD/FREE...CRIMLGY   CRIME
BIOG ANTHOL SOC/INTEG 19/20. PAGE 44 E0875   LAW
                                                       ADJUD

B67
AMDS W.E.,DELINQUENCY PREVENTION: THEORY AND   AGE/Y
PRACTICE. USA+45 SOCIETY FAM SCHOOL SECT FORCES   CRIME
PROB/SOLV...HEAL JURID PREDICT ANTHOL. PAGE 4 E0071   PUB/INST
                                                       LAW

B65
O'BRIEN W.V.,THE NEW NATIONS IN INTERNATIONAL LAW   INT/LAW
AND DIPLOMACY* THE YEAR BOOK OF WORLD POLITY*   CULTURE
VOLUME III. USA+45 ECO/UNDEV INT/ORG FORCES DIPLOM   SOVEREIGN
COLONIAL NEUTRAL REV NAT/LISM ATTIT RESPECT.   ANTHOL
PAGE 78 E1565

B67
BAKKE E.W.,UNIONS, MANAGEMENT AND THE PUBLIC*   LABOR
READINGS AND TEXT. WORKER LOBBY...POLICY JURID   INDUS
ANTHOL T. PAGE 7 E0143   ADJUD
                                                       GP/REL

B65
PADELFORD N.,THE UNITED NATIONS IN THE BALANCE*   INT/ORG
ACCOMPLISHMENTS AND PROSPECTS. NAT/G VOL/ASSN   CONTROL
DIPLOM ADMIN COLONIAL CT/SYS REGION WAR ORD/FREE
...ANTHOL UN. PAGE 79 E1588

B67
BOHANNAN P.,LAW AND WARFARE. CULTURE CT/SYS COERCE   METH/COMP
REV PEACE...JURID SOC CONCPT ANTHOL 20. PAGE 13   ADJUD
E0259   WAR
                                                       LAW

B65
ROSE A.M.,MINORITY PROBLEMS: A TEXTBOOK OF READINGS   RACE/REL
IN INTERGROUP RELATIONS. UNIV USA+45 LAW SCHOOL   DISCRIM
WORKER PROB/SOLV GP/REL PERSON...PSY ANTHOL WORSHIP   ISOLAT
20 NEGRO INDIAN/AM JEWS EUROPE. PAGE 85 E1713   ACT/RES

B67
BRAGER G.A.,COMMUNITY ACTION AGAINST POVERTY.   NEIGH
USA+45 LAW STRATA INGP/REL INCOME NEW/LIB...POLICY   WEALTH
WELF/ST ANTHOL. PAGE 15 E0285   SOC/WK
                                                       CREATE

B65
SCHROEDER O.,DEFACTO SEGREGATION AND CIVIL RIGHTS.   ANTHOL
LAW PROVS SCHOOL WORKER ATTIT HABITAT HEALTH WEALTH   DISCRIM
...JURID CHARTS 19/20 NEGRO SUPREME/CT KKK. PAGE 88   RACE/REL
E1766   ORD/FREE

B67
DEBOLD R.C.,LSD, MAN AND SOCIETY. USA+45 LAW   HEALTH
SOCIETY SECT CONTROL SANCTION STRANGE ATTIT...HEAL   DRIVE
CHARTS ANTHOL BIBLIOG. PAGE 30 E0601   PERSON
                                                       BIO/SOC

B65
WILSON J.F.,CHURCH AND STATE IN AMERICAN HISTORY.   SECT
USA+45 USA-45 ADJUD CT/SYS ORD/FREE SOVEREIGN   NAT/G
...ANTHOL BIBLIOG/A 17/20 CHURCH/STA. PAGE 106   GP/REL
E2129   CONTROL

B67
DIEGUES M.,SOCIAL SCIENCE IN LATIN AMERICA. L/A+17C   METH
...JURID SOC ANTHOL 20. PAGE 31 E0624   ACADEM
                                                       EDU/PROP
                                                       ACT/RES

B66
AMERICAN JOURNAL COMP LAW,THE AMERICAN JOURNAL OF   IDEA/COMP
COMPARATIVE LAW READER. EUR+WWI USA+45 USA-45 LAW   JURID
CONSTN LOC/G MUNIC NAT/G DIPLOM...ANTHOL 20   INT/LAW
SUPREME/CT EURCT/JUST. PAGE 4 E0081   CT/SYS

B67
GARCIA ROBLES A.,THE DENUCLEARIZATION OF LATIN   NUC/PWR
AMERICA (TRANS. BY MARJORIE URQUIDI). LAW PLAN   ARMS/CONT
DIPLOM...ANTHOL 20 TREATY UN. PAGE 42 E0833   L/A+17C
                                                       INT/ORG

B66
BURNS A.C.,PARLIAMENT AS AN EXPORT. WOR+45 CONSTN   PARL/PROC
BARGAIN DEBATE ROUTINE GOV/REL EFFICIENCY...ANTHOL   POL/PAR
COMMONWLTH PARLIAMENT. PAGE 17 E0343   CT/SYS
                                                       CHIEF

B67
LAFAVE W.R.,INTERNATIONAL TRADE, INVESTMENT, AND   INT/TRADE
ORGANIZATION. INDUS PROB/SOLV TARIFFS CONTROL   INT/LAW
...TREND ANTHOL BIBLIOG 20 EEC. PAGE 62 E1245   INT/ORG

B66
COLEMAN-NORTON P.R.,ROMAN STATE AND CHRISTIAN   GP/REL
CHURCH: A COLLECTION OF LEGAL DOCUMENTS TO A.D. 535   NAT/G
(3 VOLS.). CHRIST-17C ROMAN/EMP...ANTHOL DICTIONARY   SECT
6 CHRISTIAN CHURCH/STA. PAGE 24 E0473   LAW

B67
MEYERS M.,SOURCES OF THE AMERICAN REPUBLIC; A   COLONIAL
DOCUMENTARY HISTORY OF POLITICS, SOCIETY, AND   REV
THOUGHT (VOL. I, REV. ED.). USA-45 CULTURE STRUCT   WAR
NAT/G LEGIS LEAD ATTIT...JURID SOC ANTHOL 17/19
PRESIDENT. PAGE 72 E1450

B66
DALLIN A.,POLITICS IN THE SOVIET UNION: 7 CASES.   MARXISM
COM USSR LAW POL/PAR CHIEF FORCES WRITING CONTROL   DOMIN
PARL/PROC CIVMIL/REL TOTALISM...ANTHOL 20 KHRUSH/N   ORD/FREE
STALIN/J CASEBOOK COM/PARTY. PAGE 28 E0563   GOV/REL

B77
CADWALDER J.L.,DIGEST OF THE PUBLISHED OPINIONS OF   BIBLIOG
THE ATTORNEYS-GENERAL, AND OF THE LEADING DECISIONS   CT/SYS
OF THE FEDERAL COURTS (REV ED). USA-45 NAT/G JUDGE   DECISION
PROB/SOLV DIPLOM ATTIT...POLICY INT/LAW ANTHOL 19.   ADJUD
PAGE 18 E0356

B66
FALK R.A.,THE STRATEGY OF WORLD ORDER* 4 VOLUMES.   ORD/FREE
WOR+45 ECO/UNDEV ACADEM INT/ORG ACT/RES DIPLOM   GEN/LAWS
ARMS/CONT WAR...NET/THEORY SIMUL BIBLIOG UN.   ANTHOL
PAGE 36 E0719   INT/LAW

ANTHROPOLOGY, CULTURAL....SEE SOC

ANTHROPOLOGY, PSYCHOLOGICAL....SEE PSY

ANTI/SEMIT....ANTI-SEMITISM; SEE ALSO JEWS, GP/REL

B66
GOLDWIN R.A.,APPORTIONMENT AND REPRESENTATION.   APPORT
MUNIC CT/SYS GP/REL ORD/FREE...POLICY ANTHOL 20   REPRESENT
SUPREME/CT. PAGE 44 E0880   LEGIS
                                                       CONSTN

B62
HEYDECKER J.J.,THE NUREMBERG TRIAL: HISTORY OF NAZI   LAW
GERMANY AS REVEALED THROUGH THE TESTIMONY AT   CRIME
NUREMBERG. EUR+WWI GERMANY VOL/ASSN LEAD COERCE   PARTIC
CROWD INGP/REL RACE/REL SUPEGO ORD/FREE...CONCPT 20   TOTALISM
NAZI ANTI/SEMIT NUREMBERG JEWS. PAGE 52 E1036

B66
GRUNEWALD D.,PUBLIC POLICY AND THE MODERN   LG/CO
COOPERATION: SELECTED READINGS. USA+45 LAW MARKET   POLICY
VOL/ASSN CAP/ISM INT/TRADE CENTRAL OWN...SOC ANTHOL   NAT/G
20. PAGE 48 E0954   CONTROL

ANTIEU C.J. E0099

ANTI-SEMITISM....SEE JEWS, GP/REL, ANTI/SEMIT

B66
HAMILTON H.D.,REAPPORTIONING LEGISLATURES. USA+45   APPORT
CONSTN POL/PAR PROVS LEGIS COMPUTER ADJUD CHOOSE   REPRESENT
ATTIT...ANTHOL 20 SUPREME/CT CONGRESS. PAGE 50   PHIL/SCI

ANTI-TRUST ACTIONS....SEE MONOPOLY, INDUS, CONTROL

ANXIETY....SEE ANOMIE

APACHE....APACHE INDIANS

APARTHEID....APARTHEID

APPADORAI A. E0100

APPALACHIA

APPELLATE COURT SYSTEM....SEE CT/APPEALS, CT/SYS

APPLEBY P.H. E0101,E0102

APPORT....DELINEATION OF LEGISLATIVE DISTRICTS

B08
GRIFFIN A.P.C.,REFERENCES ON CORRUPT PRACTICES IN BIBLIOG/A
ELECTIONS (PAMPHLET). USA-45 LAW CONSTN TRIBUTE CHOOSE
CRIME REPRESENT...JURID 19/20. PAGE 47 E0934 SUFF
APPORT

N19
RALSTON A.,A FRESH LOOK AT LEGISLATIVE APPORT
APPORTIONMENT IN NEW JERSEY (PAMPHLET). USA+45 REPRESENT
CONSTN LEGIS OBJECTIVE...MATH METH 20 NEW/JERSEY. PROVS
PAGE 83 E1671 JURID

B48
STOKES W.S.,BIBLIOGRAPHY OF STANDARD AND CLASSICAL BIBLIOG
WORKS IN THE FIELDS OF AMERICAN POLITICAL SCIENCE. NAT/G
USA+45 USA-45 POL/PAR PROVS FORCES DIPLOM ADMIN LOC/G
CT/SYS APPORT 20 CONGRESS PRESIDENT. PAGE 94 E1876 CONSTN

S52
DE GRAZIA A.,"GENERAL THEORY OF APPORTIONMENT" APPORT
(BMR)" USA+45 USA-45 CONSTN ELITES DELIB/GP PARTIC LEGIS
REV CHOOSE...JURID 20. PAGE 29 E0582 PROVS
REPRESENT

B57
NJ LAW AND LEGISLATIVE BURE,NEW JERSEY APPORT
LEGISLAVTIVE REAPPORTIONMENT (PAMPHLET). USA+45 LEGIS
ACT/RES ADJUD...STAT CHARTS 20 NEW/JERSEY. PAGE 2 CENSUS
E0041 REPRESENT

B59
COUNCIL OF STATE GOVERNORS,AMERICAN LEGISLATURES: LEGIS
STRUCTURE AND PROCEDURES. SUMMARY AND TABULATIONS CHARTS
OF A 1959 SURVEY. PUERT/RICO USA+45 PAY ADJUD ADMIN PROVS
APPORT...IDEA/COMP 20 GUAM VIRGIN/ISL. PAGE 27 REPRESENT
E0525

B59
REOCK E.C.,PROCEDURES AND STANDARDS FOR THE PROVS
APPORTIONMENT OF STATE LEGISLATURES (DOCTORAL LOC/G
THESIS). USA+45 POL/PAR LEGIS TEC/DEV ADJUD APPORT
BIBLIOG. PAGE 84 E1686 REPRESENT

B60
BAKER G.E.,STATE CONSTITUTIONS - REAPPORTIONMENT. APPORT
USA+45 USA-45 CONSTN CHOOSE ATTIT ORD/FREE...JURID REPRESENT
20. PAGE 7 E0138 PROVS
LEGIS

B60
BAKER G.E.,THE POLITICS OF REAPPORTIONMENT IN VOL/ASSN
WASHINGTON STATE. LAW POL/PAR CREATE EDU/PROP APPORT
PARL/PROC CHOOSE INGP/REL...CHARTS METH/COMP 20 PROVS
WASHINGT/G LEAGUE/WV. PAGE 7 E0139 LEGIS

B60
NAT'L MUNICIPAL LEAGUE,COMPENDIUM ON LEGISLATIVE APPORT
APPORTIONMENT. USA+45 LOC/G NAT/G POL/PAR PROVS REPRESENT
CT/SYS CHOOSE 20 SUPREME/CT CONGRESS. PAGE 76 E1523 LEGIS
STAT

B60
US HOUSE COMM ON JUDICIARY,ESTABLISHMENT OF APPORT
CONGRESSIONAL DISTRICTS. USA+45 PROB/SOLV 20 REPRESENT
CONGRESS HOUSE/REP. PAGE 100 E2003 LEGIS
LAW

B62
BOYD W.J.,PATTERNS OF APPORTIONMENT (PAMPHLET). LAW MUNIC
CONSTN CHOOSE GOV/COMP. PAGE 14 E0282 PROVS
REPRESENT
APPORT

B62
NAT'L MUNICIPAL LEAGUE,COMPENDIUM ON LEGISLATIVE APPORT
APPORTIONMENT. USA+45 LOC/G NAT/G POL/PAR PROVS REPRESENT
CT/SYS CHOOSE 20 SUPREME/CT CONGRESS. PAGE 76 E1524 LEGIS
STAT

B62
NATIONAL MUNICIPAL LEAGUE,COURT DECISIONS ON PROVS
LEGISLATIVE APPORTIONMENT (VOL. III). USA+45 JUDGE CT/SYS
ADJUD CONTROL ATTIT...DECISION JURID COURT/DIST APPORT
CASEBOOK. PAGE 76 E1528 LEGIS

B62
TAPER B.,GOMILLION VERSUS LIGHTFOOT: THE TUSKEGEE APPORT
GERRYMANDER CASE. USA+45 LAW CONSTN LOC/G MUNIC REPRESENT
CT/SYS 20 NEGRO CIV/RIGHTS GOMILLN/CG LIGHTFT/PM RACE/REL
TUSKEGEE. PAGE 95 E1908 ADJUD

S62
SILVA R.C.,"LEGISLATIVE REPESENTATION - WITH MUNIC
SPECIAL REFERENCE TO NEW YORK." LAW CONSTN LOC/G LEGIS
NAT/G PROVS. PAGE 91 E1826 REPRESENT
APPORT

N62
TWENTIETH CENTURY FUND,ONE MAN - ONE VOTE APPORT
(PAMPHLET). USA+45 CONSTN CONFER CT/SYS REGION LEGIS
CONSEN FEDERAL ROLE...CENSUS 20 CONGRESS. PAGE 97 REPRESENT
E1947 PROVS

N62
US ADVISORY COMN INTERGOV REL,APPORTIONMENT OF MUNIC
STATE LEGISLATURES (PAMPHLET). LAW CONSTN EX/STRUC PROVS
LEGIS LEAD MAJORITY. PAGE 99 E1977 REPRESENT
APPORT

B63
DE GRAZIA A.,APPORTIONMENT AND REPRESENTATIVE REPRESENT
GOVERNMENT. CONSTN POL/PAR LEGIS PLAN ADJUD DISCRIM APPORT
RATIONAL...CONCPT STAT PREDICT TREND IDEA/COMP. NAT/G
PAGE 29 E0583 MUNIC

B63
GALLAGHER J.F.,SUPERVISORIAL DISTRICTING IN APPORT
CALIFORNIA COUNTIES: 1960-1963 (PAMPHLET). USA+45 REGION
ADJUD ADMIN PARTIC CHOOSE GP/REL...CENSUS 20 REPRESENT
CALIFORNIA. PAGE 42 E0828 LOC/G

B63
HACKER A.,CONGRESSIONAL DISTRICTING: THE ISSUE OF LEGIS
EQUAL REPRESENTATION. FUT CT/SYS GEOG. PAGE 49 REPRESENT
E0970 APPORT

B63
LEAGUE WOMEN VOTERS NEW YORK,APPORTIONMENT WORKSHOP APPORT
KIT. USA+45 VOL/ASSN DELIB/GP LEGIS ATTIT ORD/FREE REPRESENT
...METH/COMP 20 SUPREME/CT NEW/YORK. PAGE 64 E1275 PROVS
JURID

B63
NATIONAL CIVIC REVIEW,REAPPORTIONMENT: A YEAR IN APPORT
REVIEW (PAMPHLET). USA+45 LAW CT/SYS CHOOSE REPRESENT
ORD/FREE PWR...ANTHOL 20 CONGRESS. PAGE 76 E1527 LEGIS
CONSTN

B63
REOCK E.C. JR.,POPULATION INEQUALITY AMONG COUNTIES APPORT
IN THE NEW JERSEY LEGISLATURE 1791-1962. PROVS REPRESENT
ORD/FREE...CENSUS CHARTS 18/20 NEW/JERSEY. PAGE 84 LEGIS
E1687 JURID

B64
COUNCIL OF STATE GOVERNMENTS,LEGISLATIVE LOC/G
APPORTIONMENT: A SUMMARY OF STATE ACTION. USA+45 PROVS
LEGIS REPRESENT...POLICY SUPREME/CT. PAGE 26 E0523 APPORT
CT/SYS

B64
HAMILTON H.D.,LEGISLATIVE APPORTIONMENT; KEY TO APPORT
POWER. USA+45 LAW CONSTN PROVS LOBBY CHOOSE ATTIT CT/SYS
SUPREME/CT. PAGE 50 E0988 LEAD
REPRESENT

B64
HANSON R.,FAIR REPRESENTATION COMES TO MARYLAND APPORT
(PAMPHLET). BAL/PWR CT/SYS CHOOSE GOV/REL 20 REPRESENT
MARYLAND SUPREME/CT. PAGE 50 E0997 PROVS
LEGIS

B64
IRION F.C.,APPORTIONMENT OF THE NEW MEXICO APPORT
LEGISLATURE. NAT/G LEGIS PRESS CT/SYS ATTIT REPRESENT
...POLICY TIME/SEQ 19/20 SUPREME/CT. PAGE 57 E1137 GOV/REL
PROVS

B64
US HOUSE COMM ON JUDICIARY,CONGRESSIONAL APPORT
REDISTRICTING. USA+45 PROVS DELIB/GP 20 CONGRESS. REPRESENT
PAGE 100 E2005 LEGIS
LAW

S64
PRITCHETT C.H.,"EQUAL PROTECTION AND THE URBAN   MUNIC
MAJORITY." POL/PAR LEAD CHOOSE GP/REL PWR...MAJORIT   LAW
DECISION. PAGE 83 E1655   REPRESENT
                                                       APPORT

B65
CALIFORNIA LEGISLATURE,COMMITTEE ON ELECTIONS AND   DELIB/GP
REAPPORTIONMENT. FINAL REPORT. USA+45 LAW COMPUTER   APPORT
TEC/DEV CHOOSE JURID. PAGE 19 E0366   LEGIS
                                                       ADJUD

B65
CONGRESSIONAL QUARTERLY SERV,POLITICS IN AMERICA,   CHOOSE
1945-1964: THE POLITICS AND ISSUES OF THE POSTWAR   REPRESENT
YEARS. USA+45 LAW FINAN CHIEF DIPLOM APPORT SUFF   POL/PAR
...POLICY STAT TREND CHARTS 20 CONGRESS PRESIDENT.   LEGIS
PAGE 25 E0489

B65
FERRELL J.S.,CASES AND MATERIALS ON LOCAL   APPORT
APPORTIONMENT. CONSTN LEAD GP/REL...DECISION   LOC/G
GOV/COMP. PAGE 37 E0740   REPRESENT
                                                       LAW

B65
MCKAY R.B.,REAPPORTIONMENT: THE LAW AND POLITICS OF   APPORT
EQUAL REPRESENTATION. FUT USA+45 PROVS BAL/PWR   MAJORIT
ADJUD CHOOSE REPRESENT GOV/REL FEDERAL...JURID   LEGIS
BIBLIOG 20 SUPREME/CT CONGRESS. PAGE 71 E1420   PWR

B65
NJ LEGIS REAPPORT PLAN COMM,PUBLIC HEARING ON   APPORT
REDISTRICTING AND REAPPORTIONMENT. USA+45 CONSTN   REPRESENT
VOL/ASSN LEGIS DEBATE...POLICY GEOG CENSUS 20   PROVS
NEW/JERSEY. PAGE 77 E1552   JURID

B65
SCHUBERT G.,REAPPORTIONMENT. LAW MUNIC POL/PAR PWR   REPRESENT
GOV/COMP. PAGE 88 E1775   LOC/G
                                                       APPORT
                                                       LEGIS

B65
SNOW J.H.,REAPPORTIONMENT. LAW CONSTN NAT/G GOV/REL   APPORT
ORD/FREE...JURID 20 SUPREME/CT CONNECTICT. PAGE 92   ADJUD
E1848   LEGIS
                                                       PROVS

L65
WEINSTEIN J.B.,"THE EFFECT OF THE FEDERAL   MUNIC
REAPPORTIONMENT DECISIONS ON COUNTIES AND OTHER   LOC/G
FORMS OF GOVERNMENT." LAW CONSTN LEGIS CHOOSE   APPORT
GOV/COMP. PAGE 105 E2108   REPRESENT

S65
DIXON R.G.,"NEW CONSTITUTIONAL FORMS FOR   MUNIC
METROPOLIS: REAPPORTIONED COUNTY BOARDS; LOCAL   REGION
COUNCILS OF GOVERNMENT." LAW CONSTN LEAD APPORT   GOV/COMP
REPRESENT DECISION. PAGE 32 E0631   PLAN

B66
BAKER G.E.,THE REAPPORTIONMENT REVOLUTION;   LEGIS
REPRESENTATION, POLITICAL POWER, AND THE SUPREME   APPORT
COURT. USA+45 MUNIC NAT/G POL/PAR PROVS PROB/SOLV   REPRESENT
CHOOSE ORD/FREE POPULISM...CONCPT CHARTS 20   ADJUD
SUPREME/CT. PAGE 7 E0140

B66
BEISER E.N.,THE TREATMENT OF LEGISLATIVE   CT/SYS
APPORTIONMENT BY THE STATE AND FEDERAL COURTS   APPORT
(DISSERTATION). USA+45 CONSTN NAT/G PROVS LEGIS   ADJUD
CHOOSE REPRESENT ATTIT...POLICY BIBLIOG 20 CONGRESS   PWR
SUPREME/CT. PAGE 9 E0181

B66
CALIFORNIA STATE LIBRARY,REAPPORTIONMENT, A   BIBLIOG
SELECTIVE BIBLIOGRAPHY. USA+45 LEGIS CT/SYS   APPORT
REPRESENT GOV/REL. PAGE 19 E0367   NAT/G
                                                       PROVS

B66
CONG QUARTERLY SERVICE,REPRESENTATION AND   APPORT
APPORTIONMENT. USA+45 USA-45 POL/PAR CT/SYS SUFF   LEGIS
...POLICY 20 CONGRESS SUPREME/CT. PAGE 25 E0486   REPRESENT
                                                       CONSTN

B66
FINK M.,A SELECTIVE BIBLIOGRAPHY ON STATE   BIBLIOG
CONSTITUTIONAL REVISION (PAMPHLET). USA+45 FINAN   PROVS
EX/STRUC LEGIS EDU/PROP ADMIN CT/SYS APPORT CHOOSE   LOC/G
GOV/REL 20. PAGE 38 E0751   CONSTN

B66
GOLDWIN R.A.,APPORTIONMENT AND REPRESENTATION.   APPORT
MUNIC CT/SYS GP/REL ORD/FREE...POLICY ANTHOL 20   REPRESENT

SUPREME/CT. PAGE 44 E0880   LEGIS
                                                       CONSTN

B66
HAMILTON H.D.,REAPPORTIONING LEGISLATURES. USA+45   APPORT
CONSTN POL/PAR PROVS LEGIS COMPUTER ADJUD CHOOSE   REPRESENT
ATTIT...ANTHOL 20 SUPREME/CT CONGRESS. PAGE 50   PHIL/SCI
E0989   PWR

B66
HANSON R.,THE POLITICAL THICKET. USA+45 MUNIC   APPORT
POL/PAR LEGIS EXEC LOBBY CHOOSE...MAJORIT DECISION.   LAW
PAGE 50 E0998   CONSTN
                                                       REPRESENT

B66
MEDER A.E. JR.,LEGISLATIVE APPORTIONMENT. USA+45   APPORT
BAL/PWR REPRESENT ORD/FREE PWR...JURID 20   LEGIS
SUPREME/CT. PAGE 72 E1433   MATH
                                                       POLICY

B67
BUREAU GOVERNMENT RES AND SERV,COUNTY GOVERNMENT   BIBLIOG/A
REORGANIZATION - A SELECTED ANNOTATED BIBLIOGRAPHY   APPORT
(PAPER). USA+45 USA-45 LAW CONSTN MUNIC PROVS   LOC/G
EX/STRUC CREATE PLAN PROB/SOLV REPRESENT GOV/REL   ADMIN
20. PAGE 17 E0332

B67
RAE D.,THE POLITICAL CONSEQUENCES OF ELECTORAL   POL/PAR
LAWS. EUR+WWI ICELAND ISRAEL NEW/ZEALND UK USA+45   CHOOSE
ADJUD APPORT GP/REL MAJORITY...MATH STAT CENSUS   NAT/COMP
CHARTS BIBLIOG 20 AUSTRAL. PAGE 83 E1667   REPRESENT

L67
"A PROPOS DES INCITATIONS FINANCIERES AUX   LOC/G
GROUPEMENTS DES COMMUNES: ESSAI D'INTERPRETATION."   ECO/TAC
FRANCE NAT/G LEGIS ADMIN GOV/REL CENTRAL 20. PAGE 2   APPORT
E0037   ADJUD

S67
HAMILTON H.D.,"LEGISLATIVE CONSTITUENCIES: SINGLE-   LEGIS
MEMBER DISTRICTS, MULTI-MEMBER DISTRICTS, AND   REPRESENT
FLOTERAL DISTRICTS." USA+45 LAW POL/PAR ADJUD   APPORT
RACE/REL...CHARTS METH/COMP 20. PAGE 50 E0990   PLAN

APRA.....ALIANZA POPULAR REVOLUCIONARIA AMERICANA, A PERUVIAN
    POLITICAL PARTY

APSA.....AMERICAN POLITICAL SCIENCE ASSOCIATION

APT/TEST....APTITUDE TESTS

APTITUDE TESTS....SEE APT/TEST

AQUINAS/T....SAINT THOMAS AQUINAS

B19
VANDERPOL A.,LA DOCTRINE SCOLASTIQUE DU DROIT DE   WAR
GUERRE. CHRIST-17C FORCES DIPLOM LEGIT SUPEGO MORAL   SECT
...BIOG AQUINAS/T SUAREZ/F CHRISTIAN. PAGE 103   INT/LAW
E2072

B63
FRIEDRICH C.J.,JUSTICE: NOMOS VI. UNIV LAW SANCTION   LEGIT
CRIME...CONCPT ANTHOL MARX/KARL LOCKE/JOHN   ADJUD
AQUINAS/T. PAGE 41 E0809   ORD/FREE
                                                       JURID

ARA.....AREA REDEVELOPMENT ACT

ARABIA/SOU....SOUTH ARABIA

ARABS....ARAB WORLD, INCLUDING ITS CULTURE

B63
BADI J.,THE GOVERNMENT OF THE STATE OF ISRAEL: A   NAT/G
CRITICAL ACCOUNT OF ITS PARLIAMENT, EXECUTIVE, AND   CONSTN
JUDICIARY. ISRAEL ECO/DEV CHIEF DELIB/GP LEGIS   EX/STRUC
DIPLOM CT/SYS INGP/REL PEACE ORD/FREE...BIBLIOG 20   POL/PAR
PARLIAMENT ARABS MIGRATION. PAGE 7 E0131

ARBITRATION....SEE DELIB/GP, CONSULT, AND FUNCTIONAL GROUP
    CONCERNED (E.G., LABOR)

ARCHER P. E0103

AREA STUDIES....SEE NAT/COMP

ARGEN ....ARGENTINA

B48
CLAGETT H.L.,A GUIDE TO THE LAW AND LEGAL   BIBLIOG
LITERATURE OF ARGENTINA, 1917-1946. CONSTN LABOR   L/A+17C
JUDGE ADJUD ADMIN...CRIMLGY INT/LAW JURID CON/ANAL   LAW
20 ARGEN. PAGE 23 E0447   LEGIS

COSSIO C.,LA POLITICA COMO CONCIENCIA; MEDITACION
SOBRE LA ARGENTINA DE 1955. WOR+45 LEGIS EDU/PROP
PARL/PROC PARTIC ATTIT PWR CATHISM 20 ARGEN
PERON/JUAN. PAGE 26 E0517
POL/PAR
REV
TOTALISM
JURID
B57

ARISTOCRATIC....SEE TRADIT, STRATA, ELITES

ARISTOTLE....ARISTOTLE

ARIZONA....ARIZONA

ARKANSAS....ARKANSAS

ARMED FORCES....SEE FORCES

ARMS CONTROL....SEE ARMS/CONT

ARMS/CONT....ARMS CONTROL, DISARMAMENT

FULLER G.A.,DEMOBILIZATION: A SELECTED LIST OF
REFERENCES. USA+45 LAW AGRI LABOR WORKER ECO/TAC
RATION RECEIVE EDU/PROP ROUTINE ARMS/CONT ALL/VALS
20. PAGE 41 E0819
BIBLIOG/A
INDUS
FORCES
NAT/G
N

LONDON INSTITUTE WORLD AFFAIRS,THE YEAR BOOK OF
WORLD AFFAIRS. FINAN BAL/PWR ARMS/CONT WAR
...INT/LAW BIBLIOG 20. PAGE 66 E1322
DIPLOM
FOR/AID
INT/ORG
N

AMERICAN JOURNAL OF INTERNATIONAL LAW. WOR+45
WOR-45 CONSTN INT/ORG NAT/G CT/SYS ARMS/CONT WAR
...DECISION JURID NAT/COMP 20. PAGE 1 E0001
BIBLIOG/A
INT/LAW
DIPLOM
ADJUD
N

FOREIGN AFFAIRS. SPACE WOR+45 WOR-45 CULTURE
ECO/UNDEV FINAN NAT/G TEC/DEV INT/TRADE ARMS/CONT
NUC/PWR...POLICY 20 UN EURATOM ECSC EEC. PAGE 1
E0021
BIBLIOG
DIPLOM
INT/ORG
INT/LAW
N

AIR UNIVERSITY LIBRARY,INDEX TO MILITARY
PERIODICALS. FUT SPACE WOR+45 REGION ARMS/CONT
NUC/PWR WAR PEACE INT/LAW. PAGE 3 E0056
BIBLIOG/A
FORCES
NAT/G
DIPLOM
N

ATLANTIC INSTITUTE,ATLANTIC STUDIES. COM EUR+WWI
USA+45 CULTURE STRUCT ECO/DEV FORCES LEAD ARMS/CONT
...INT/LAW JURID SOC. PAGE 6 E0110
BIBLIOG/A
DIPLOM
POLICY
GOV/REL
N

TURNER R.K.,BIBLIOGRAPHY ON WORLD ORGANIZATION.
INT/TRADE CT/SYS ARMS/CONT WEALTH...INT/LAW 20.
PAGE 97 E1944
BIBLIOG/A
INT/ORG
PEACE
WAR
N

LALL A.S.,NEGOTIATING DISARMAMENT* THE EIGHTEEN
NATION DISARMAMENT CONFERENCE* THE FIRST TWO YEARS,
1962-1964. ASIA FRANCE INDIA USA+45 USSR PROB/SOLV
ADJUD NEUTRAL ATTIT...IDEA/COMP COLD/WAR. PAGE 62
E1246
OBS
ARMS/CONT
DIPLOM
OP/RES
B*

GRIFFIN A.P.C.,LIST OF REFERENCES ON INTERNATIONAL
ARBITRATION. FRANCE L/A+17C USA+45 WOR+45 DIPLOM
CONFER COLONIAL ARMS/CONT BAL/PAY EQUILIB SOVEREIGN
...DECISION 19/20 MEXIC/AMER. PAGE 47 E0932
BIBLIOG/A
INT/ORG
INT/LAW
DELIB/GP
B08

BAILEY S.D.,VETO IN THE SECURITY COUNCIL
(PAMPHLET). COM USSR WOR+45 BAL/PWR PARL/PROC
ARMS/CONT PRIVIL PWR...INT/LAW TREND CHARTS 20 UN
SUEZ. PAGE 7 E0135
DELIB/GP
INT/ORG
DIPLOM
N19

MEZERIK A.G.,ATOM TESTS AND RADIATION HAZARDS
(PAMPHLET). WOR+45 INT/ORG DIPLOM DETER 20 UN
TREATY. PAGE 73 E1452
NUC/PWR
ARMS/CONT
CONFER
HEALTH
N19

LAPRADELLE,ANNUAIRE DE LA VIE INTERNATIONALE:
POLITIQUE, ECONOMIQUE, JURIDIQUE. INT/ORG CONFER
ARMS/CONT 20. PAGE 63 E1255
BIBLIOG
DIPLOM
INT/LAW
B28

CONWELL-EVANS T.P.,THE LEAGUE COUNCIL IN ACTION.
EUR+WWI TURKEY UK USSR WOR-45 INT/ORG FORCES JUDGE
ECO/TAC EDU/PROP LEGIT ROUTINE ARMS/CONT COERCE
ATTIT PWR...MAJORIT GEOG JURID CONCPT LEAGUE/NAT
TOT/POP VAL/FREE TUNIS 20. PAGE 25 E0498
DELIB/GP
INT/LAW
B29

FEIS H.,"RESEARCH ACTIVITIES OF THE LEAGUE OF
NATIONS." EUR+WWI WOR-45 R+D INT/ORG CT/SYS
ARMS/CONT WEALTH...OBS RECORD LEAGUE/NAT ILO 20.
PAGE 37 E0729
CONSULT
KNOWL
PEACE
L29

EAGLETON C.,INTERNATIONAL GOVERNMENT. BRAZIL FRANCE
GERMANY ITALY UK USSR WOR-45 DELIB/GP TOP/EX PLAN
ECO/TAC EDU/PROP LEGIT ADJUD REGION ARMS/CONT
COERCE ATTIT PWR...GEOG MGT VAL/FREE LEAGUE/NAT 20.
PAGE 34 E0670
INT/ORG
JURID
DIPLOM
INT/LAW
B32

FOREIGN AFFAIRS BIBLIOGRAPHY: A SELECTED AND
ANNOTATED LIST OF BOOKS ON INTERNATIONAL RELATIONS
1919-1962 (4 VOLS.). CONSTN FORCES COLONIAL
ARMS/CONT WAR NAT/LISM PEACE ATTIT DRIVE...POLICY
INT/LAW 20. PAGE 2 E0032
BIBLIOG/A
DIPLOM
INT/ORG
B35

HUDSON M.O.,INTERNATIONAL LEGISLATION: 1929-1931.
WOR-45 SEA AIR AGRI FINAN LABOR DIPLOM ECO/TAC
REPAR CT/SYS ARMS/CONT WAR WEAPON...JURID 20 TREATY
LEAGUE/NAT. PAGE 56 E1112
INT/LAW
PARL/PROC
ADJUD
LAW
B36

LAVES W.H.C.,INTERNATIONAL SECURITY. EUR+WWI
GERMANY UK USA-45 LAW NAT/G DELIB/GP TOP/EX COERCE
PWR...POLICY FASCIST CONCPT HIST/WRIT GEN/LAWS
LEAGUE/NAT NAZI 20. PAGE 63 E1267
ORD/FREE
LEGIT
ARMS/CONT
BAL/PWR
B39

FEILCHENFELD E.H.,THE INTERNATIONAL ECONOMIC LAW OF
BELLIGERENT OCCUPATION. EUR+WWI MOD/EUR USA+45
INT/ORG DIPLOM ADJUD ARMS/CONT LEAGUE/NAT 20.
PAGE 37 E0726
ECO/TAC
INT/LAW
WAR
B42

FULLER G.H.,DEFENSE FINANCING: A SUPPLEMENTARY LIST
OF REFERENCES (PAMPHLET). CANADA UK USA+45 ECO/DEV
NAT/G DELIB/GP BUDGET ADJUD ARMS/CONT WEAPON COST
PEACE PWR 20 AUSTRAL CHINJAP CONGRESS. PAGE 41
E0821
BIBLIOG/A
FINAN
FORCES
DIPLOM
B42

MICAUD C.A.,THE FRENCH RIGHT AND NAZI GERMANY
1933-1939: A STUDY OF PUBLIC OPINION. GERMANY UK
USSR POL/PAR ARMS/CONT COERCE DETER PEACE
RIGID/FLEX PWR MARXISM...FASCIST TREND 20
LEAGUE/NAT TREATY. PAGE 73 E1454
DIPLOM
AGREE
B43

ADLER M.J.,HOW TO THINK ABOUT WAR AND PEACE. WOR-45
LAW SOCIETY EX/STRUC DIPLOM KNOWL ORD/FREE...POLICY
TREND GEN/LAWS 20. PAGE 3 E0049
INT/ORG
CREATE
ARMS/CONT
PEACE
B44

FULLER G.H.,MILITARY GOVERNMENT: A LIST OF
REFERENCES (A PAMPHLET). ITALY UK USA-45 WOR-45 LAW
FORCES DOMIN ADMIN ARMS/CONT ORD/FREE PWR
...DECISION 20 CHINJAP. PAGE 41 E0822
BIBLIOG
DIPLOM
CIVMIL/REL
SOVEREIGN
B44

RUDIN H.R.,ARMISTICE 1918. FRANCE GERMANY MOD/EUR
UK USA+45 NAT/G CHIEF DELIB/GP FORCES BAL/PWR REPAR
ARMS/CONT 20 WILSON/W TREATY. PAGE 86 E1732
AGREE
WAR
PEACE
DIPLOM
B44

FERRELL R.H.,PEACE IN THEIR TIME. FRANCE UK USA-45
INT/ORG NAT/G FORCES CREATE AGREE ARMS/CONT COERCE
WAR TREATY 20 WILSON/W LEAGUE/NAT BRIAND/A. PAGE 37
E0741
PEACE
DIPLOM
B52

BRETTON H.L.,STRESEMANN AND THE REVISION OF
VERSAILLES: A FIGHT FOR REASON. EUR+WWI GERMANY
FORCES BUDGET ARMS/CONT WAR SUPEGO...BIBLIOG 20
TREATY VERSAILLES STRESEMN/G. PAGE 15 E0294
POLICY
DIPLOM
BIOG
B53

US SENATE COMM ON FOREIGN REL,REVIEW OF THE UNITED
NATIONS CHARTER: A COLLECTION OF DOCUMENTS. LEGIS
DIPLOM ADMIN ARMS/CONT WAR REPRESENT SOVEREIGN
...INT/LAW 20 UN. PAGE 101 E2029
BIBLIOG
CONSTN
INT/ORG
DEBATE
B54

B55

COMM. STUDY ORGAN. PEACE,REPORTS. WOR-45 ECO/DEV   WOR+45
ECO/UNDEV VOL/ASSN CONSULT FORCES PLAN TEC/DEV   INT/ORG
DOMIN EDU/PROP NUC/PWR ATTIT PWR WEALTH...JURID   ARMS/CONT
STERTYP FAO ILO 20 UN. PAGE 24 E0481

B56

CORBETT P.E.,MORALS LAW, AND POWER IN INTERNATIONAL SUPEGO
RELATIONS. WOR+45 INT/ORG VOL/ASSN DELIB/GP   CONCPT
CREATE BAL/PWR DIPLOM LEGIT ARMS/CONT MORAL...JURID   POLICY
GEN/LAWS TOT/POP LEAGUE/NAT 20. PAGE 26 E0506   INT/LAW

B58

HENKIN L.,ARMS CONTROL AND INSPECTION IN AMERICAN   USA+45
LAW. LAW CONSTN INT/ORG LOC/G MUNIC NAT/G PROVS   JURID
EDU/PROP LEGIT EXEC NUC/PWR KNOWL ORD/FREE...OBS   ARMS/CONT
TOT/POP CONGRESS 20. PAGE 52 E1032

B58

JENKS C.W.,THE COMMON LAW OF MANKIND. EUR+WWI   JURID
MOD/EUR SPACE WOR+45 INT/ORG BAL/PWR ARMS/CONT   SOVEREIGN
COERCE SUPEGO MORAL...TREND 20. PAGE 58 E1154

S59

CORY R.H. JR.,"INTERNATIONAL INSPECTION FROM   STRUCT
PROPOSALS TO REALIZATION." WOR+45 TEC/DEV ECO/TAC   PSY
ADJUD ORD/FREE PWR WEALTH...RECORD VAL/FREE 20.   ARMS/CONT
PAGE 26 E0516   NUC/PWR

B60

CLARK G.,WORLD PEACE THROUGH WORLD LAW. FUT WOR+45   INT/ORG
CONSULT FORCES ACT/RES CREATE PLAN ADMIN ROUTINE   LAW
ARMS/CONT DETER ATTIT PWR...JURID VAL/FREE UNESCO   PEACE
20 UN. PAGE 23 E0449   INT/LAW

B60

ENGEL J.,THE SECURITY OF THE FREE WORLD. USSR   COM
WOR+45 STRATA STRUCT ECO/DEV ECO/UNDEV INT/ORG   TREND
DELIB/GP FORCES DOMIN LEGIT ADJUD EXEC ARMS/CONT   DIPLOM
COERCE...POLICY CONCPT NEW/IDEA TIME/SEQ GEN/LAWS
COLD/WAR WORK UN 20 NATO. PAGE 35 E0689

B60

FISCHER L.,THE SOVIETS IN WORLD AFFAIRS. CHINA/COM   DIPLOM
COM EUR+WWI USSR INT/ORG CONFER LEAD ARMS/CONT REV   NAT/G
PWR...CHARTS 20 TREATY VERSAILLES. PAGE 38 E0755   POLICY
                                                    MARXISM

B60

UNITED WORLD FEDERALISTS,UNITED WORLD FEDERALISTS;   BIBLIOG/A
PANORAMA OF RECENT BOOKS, FILMS, AND JOURNALS ON   DIPLOM
WORLD FEDERATION. THE UN, AND WORLD PEACE. CULTURE   INT/ORG
ECO/UNDEV PROB/SOLV FOR/AID ARMS/CONT NUC/PWR   PEACE
...INT/LAW PHIL/SCI 20 UN. PAGE 98 E1971

L60

KUNZ J.,"SANCTIONS IN INTERNATIONAL LAW." WOR+45   INT/ORG
WOR-45 LEGIT ARMS/CONT COERCE PEACE ATTIT   ADJUD
...METH/CNCPT TIME/SEQ TREND 20. PAGE 62 E1234   INT/LAW

S60

O'BRIEN W.,"THE ROLE OF FORCE IN THE INTERNATIONAL   INT/ORG
JURIDICAL ORDER." WOR+45 NAT/G FORCES DOMIN ADJUD   COERCE
ARMS/CONT DETER NUC/PWR WAR ATTIT PWR...CATH
INT/LAW JURID CONCPT TREND STERTYP GEN/LAWS 20.
PAGE 78 E1564

S60

RHYNE C.S.,"LAW AS AN INSTRUMENT FOR PEACE." FUT   ADJUD
WOR+45 PLAN LEGIT ROUTINE ARMS/CONT NUC/PWR ATTIT   EDU/PROP
ORD/FREE...JURID METH/CNCPT TREND CON/ANAL HYPO/EXP INT/LAW
COLD/WAR 20. PAGE 84 E1690   PEACE

B61

BRENNAN D.G.,ARMS CONTROL, DISARMAMENT, AND   ARMS/CONT
NATIONAL SECURITY. WOR+45 NAT/G FORCES CREATE   ORD/FREE
PROB/SOLV PARTIC WAR PEACE...DECISION INT/LAW   DIPLOM
ANTHOL BIBLIOG 20. PAGE 15 E0291   POLICY

B61

WRIGHT Q.,THE ROLE OF INTERNATIONAL LAW IN THE   INT/ORG
ELIMINATION OF WAR. FUT WOR+45 NAT/G BAL/PWR   ADJUD
DIPLOM DOMIN LEGIT PWR...POLICY INT/LAW JURID   ARMS/CONT
CONCPT TIME/SEQ TREND GEN/LAWS COLD/WAR 20.
PAGE 108 E2158

L61

TAUBENFELD H.J.,"A REGIME FOR OUTER SPACE." FUT   INT/ORG
UNIV R+D ACT/RES PLAN BAL/PWR LEGIT ARMS/CONT   ADJUD
ORD/FREE...POLICY JURID TREND UN TOT/POP 20   SPACE
COLD/WAR. PAGE 95 E1910

S61

RICHSTEIN A.R.,"LEGAL RULES IN NUCLEAR WEAPONS   NUC/PWR
EMPLOYMENTS." FUT WOR+45 LAW SOCIETY FORCES PLAN   TEC/DEV
WEAPON RIGID/FLEX...HEAL CONCPT TREND VAL/FREE 20.   MORAL

PAGE 85 E1696   ARMS/CONT

B62

DUROSELLE J.B.,HISTOIRE DIPLOMATIQUE DE 1919 A NOS DIPLOM
JOURS (3RD ED.). FRANCE INT/ORG CHIEF FORCES CONFER WOR+45
ARMS/CONT WAR PEACE ORD/FREE...T TREATY 20   WOR-45
COLD/WAR. PAGE 34 E0667

B62

PERKINS D.,AMERICA'S QUEST FOR PEACE. USA+45 WOR+45 INT/LAW
DIPLOM CONFER NAT/LISM ATTIT 20 UN TREATY. PAGE 80   INT/ORG
E1610   ARMS/CONT
                                                    PEACE

B62

WADSWORTH J.J.,THE PRICE OF PEACE. WOR+45 TEC/DEV   DIPLOM
CONTROL NUC/PWR PEACE ATTIT TREATY 20. PAGE 104   INT/ORG
E2089   ARMS/CONT
                                                    POLICY

S62

CRANE R.D.,"LAW AND STRATEGY IN SPACE." FUT USA+45   CONCPT
WOR+45 AIR LAW INT/ORG NAT/G FORCES ACT/RES PLAN   SPACE
BAL/PWR LEGIT ARMS/CONT COERCE ORD/FREE...POLICY
INT/LAW JURID SOC/EXP 20 TREATY. PAGE 27 E0542

S62

FINKELSTEIN L.S.,"THE UNITED NATIONS AND   INT/ORG
ORGANIZATIONS FOR CONTROL OF ARMAMENT." FUT WOR+45   PWR
VOL/ASSN DELIB/GP TOP/EX CREATE EDU/PROP LEGIT   ARMS/CONT
ADJUD NUC/PWR ATTIT RIGID/FLEX ORD/FREE...POLICY
DECISION CONCPT OBS TREND GEN/LAWS TOT/POP
COLD/WAR. PAGE 38 E0752

B63

FALK R.A.,LAW, MORALITY, AND WAR IN THE   ADJUD
CONTEMPORARY WORLD. WOR+45 LAW INT/ORG EX/STRUC   ARMS/CONT
FORCES EDU/PROP LEGIT DETER NUC/PWR MORAL ORD/FREE   PEACE
...JURID TOT/POP 20. PAGE 36 E0715   INT/LAW

B63

PACHTER H.M.,COLLISION COURSE; THE CUBAN MISSILE   WAR
CRISIS AND COEXISTENCE. CUBA USA+45 DIPLOM   BAL/PWR
ARMS/CONT PEACE MARXISM...DECISION INT/LAW 20   NUC/PWR
COLD/WAR KHRUSH/N KENNEDY/JF CASTRO/F. PAGE 79   DETER
E1587

B63

VAN SLYCK P.,PEACE: THE CONTROL OF NATIONAL POWER.   ARMS/CONT
CUBA WOR+45 FINAN NAT/G FORCES PROB/SOLV TEC/DEV   PEACE
BAL/PWR ADMIN CONTROL ORD/FREE...POLICY INT/LAW UN   INT/ORG
COLD/WAR TREATY. PAGE 103 E2069   DIPLOM

S63

BECHHOEFER B.G.,"UNITED NATIONS PROCEDURES IN CASE   INT/ORG
OF VIOLATIONS OF DISARMAMENT AGREEMENTS." COM   DELIB/GP
USA+45 USSR LAW CONSTN NAT/G EX/STRUC FORCES LEGIS
BAL/PWR EDU/PROP CT/SYS ARMS/CONT ORD/FREE PWR
...POLICY STERTYP UN VAL/FREE 20. PAGE 9 E0169

S63

BOHN L.,"WHOSE NUCLEAR TEST: NON-PHYSICAL   ADJUD
INSPECTION AND TEST BAN." WOR+45 R+D INT/ORG   ARMS/CONT
VOL/ASSN ORD/FREE...GEN/LAWS GEN/METH COLD/WAR 20.   TEC/DEV
PAGE 13 E0262   NUC/PWR

B64

BOWETT D.W.,UNITED NATIONS FORCES* A LEGAL STUDY.   OP/RES
CYPRUS ISRAEL KOREA LAW CONSTN ACT/RES CREATE   FORCES
BUDGET CONTROL TASK PWR...INT/LAW IDEA/COMP UN   ARMS/CONT
CONGO/LEOP SUEZ. PAGE 14 E0278

B64

ROBERTS HL,FOREIGN AFFAIRS BIBLIOGRAPHY, 1952-1962. BIBLIOG/A
ECO/DEV SECT PLAN FOR/AID INT/TRADE ARMS/CONT   DIPLOM
NAT/LISM ATTIT...INT/LAW GOV/COMP IDEA/COMP 20.   INT/ORG
PAGE 85 E1703   WAR

B64

US AIR FORCE ACADEMY ASSEMBLY,OUTER SPACE: FINAL   SPACE
REPORT APRIL 1-4, 1964. FUT USA+45 WOR+45 LAW   CIVMIL/REL
DELIB/GP CONFER ARMS/CONT WAR PEACE ATTIT MORAL   NUC/PWR
...ANTHOL 20 NASA. PAGE 99 E1979   DIPLOM

B64

WILLIAMS S.P.,TOWARD A GENUINE WORLD SECURITY   BIBLIOG/A
SYSTEM (PAMPHLET). WOR+45 INT/ORG FORCES PLAN   ARMS/CONT
NUC/PWR ORD/FREE...INT/LAW CONCPT UN PRESIDENT.   DIPLOM
PAGE 106 E2123   PEACE

L64

BERKS R.N.,"THE US AND WEAPONS CONTROL." WOR+45 LAW USA+45
INT/ORG NAT/G LEGIS EXEC COERCE PEACE ATTIT   PLAN
RIGID/FLEX ALL/VALS PWR...POLICY TOT/POP 20.   ARMS/CONT
PAGE 11 E0204

CRANE R.D.,"BASIC PRINCIPLES IN SOVIET SPACE LAW." COM
FUT WOR+45 AIR INT/ORG DIPLOM DOMIN ARMS/CONT LAW
COERCE NUC/PWR PEACE ATTIT DRIVE PWR...INT/LAW USSR
METH/CNCPT NEW/IDEA OBS TREND GEN/LAWS VAL/FREE SPACE
MARX/KARL 20. PAGE 27 E0544
S64

GARDNER R.N.,"THE SOVIET UNION AND THE UNITED COM
NATIONS." WOR+45 FINAN POL/PAR VOL/ASSN FORCES INT/ORG
ECO/TAC DOMIN EDU/PROP LEGIT ADJUD ADMIN ARMS/CONT USSR
COERCE ATTIT ALL/VALS...POLICY MAJORIT CONCPT OBS
TIME/SEQ TREND STERTYP UN. PAGE 42 E0838
S64

MAGGS P.B.,"SOVIET VIEWPOINT ON NUCLEAR WEAPONS IN COM
INTERNATIONAL LAW." USSR WOR+45 INT/ORG FORCES LAW
DIPLOM ARMS/CONT ATTIT ORD/FREE PWR...POLICY JURID INT/LAW
CONCPT OBS TREND CON/ANAL GEN/LAWS VAL/FREE 20. NUC/PWR
PAGE 67 E1347
S64

BAADE H.,THE SOVIET IMPACT ON INTERNATIONAL LAW. INT/LAW
INT/ORG INT/TRADE LEGIT COLONIAL ARMS/CONT REV WAR USSR
...CON/ANAL ANTHOL TREATY. PAGE 6 E0124 CREATE
ORD/FREE
B65

BERKOWITZ M.,AMERICAN NATIONAL SECURITY: A READER ORD/FREE
IN THEORY AND POLICY. USA+45 INT/ORG FORCES BAL/PWR WAR
DIPLOM ECO/TAC DETER PWR...INT/LAW ANTHOL BIBLIOG ARMS/CONT
20 UN. PAGE 11 E0203 POLICY
B65

GOTLIEB A.,DISARMAMENT AND INTERNATIONAL LAW* A INT/LAW
STUDY OF THE ROLE OF LAW IN THE DISARMAMENT INT/ORG
PROCESS. USA+45 USSR PROB/SOLV CONFER ADMIN ROUTINE ARMS/CONT
NUC/PWR ORD/FREE SOVEREIGN UN TREATY. PAGE 45 E0893 IDEA/COMP
B65

HAENSCH G.,PAN-AFRICANISM IN ACTION: AN ACCOUNT OF DICTIONARY
THE UAM TIC AND ALPHABETICAL IN GERMAN, ENGLISH, DIPLOM
FRENCH AND SPANISH. WOR+45 INT/ORG NAT/G ARMS/CONT LING
WAR...INT/LAW IDEA/COMP TREATY. PAGE 49 E0974
B65

LASLEY J.,THE WAR SYSTEM AND YOU. LAW FORCES MORAL
ARMS/CONT NUC/PWR NAT/LISM ATTIT...MAJORIT PERSON
IDEA/COMP UN WORSHIP. PAGE 63 E1261 DIPLOM
WAR
B65

MILLIS W.,AN END TO ARMS. LAW INT/ORG FORCES FUT
ACT/RES CREATE DIPLOM WAR...POLICY HUM NEW/IDEA PWR
HYPO/EXP. PAGE 73 E1462 ARMS/CONT
ORD/FREE
B65

HIBBS A.R.,"SPACE TECHNOLOGY* THE THREAT AND THE SPACE
PROMISE." FUT VOL/ASSN TEC/DEV NUC/PWR COST ARMS/CONT
EFFICIENCY UTIL UN TREATY. PAGE 52 E1038 PREDICT
S65

MARTIN A.,"PROLIFERATION." FUT WOR+45 PROB/SOLV RECORD
REGION ADJUST...PREDICT NAT/COMP UN TREATY. PAGE 69 NUC/PWR
E1372 ARMS/CONT
VOL/ASSN
S65

BUTTERFIELD H.,DIPLOMATIC INVESTIGATIONS* ESSAYS IN GEN/LAWS
THE THEORY OF INTERNATIONAL POLITICS. LAW INT/ORG UK
FORCES BAL/PWR ARMS/CONT WAR ALL/VALS...HUM DIPLOM
INT/LAW. PAGE 18 E0351
B66

CLARK G.,WORLD PEACE THROUGH WORLD LAW: TWO INT/LAW
ALTERNATIVE PLANS. WOR+45 DELIB/GP FORCES TAX PEACE
CONFER ADJUD SANCTION ARMS/CONT WAR CHOOSE PRIVIL PLAN
20 UN COLD/WAR. PAGE 23 E0450 INT/ORG
B66

EPSTEIN F.T.,THE AMERICAN BIBLIOGRAPHY OF RUSSIAN BIBLIOG
AND EAST EUROPEAN STUDIES FOR 1964. USSR LOC/G COM
NAT/G POL/PAR FORCES ADMIN ARMS/CONT...JURID CONCPT MARXISM
20 UN. PAGE 35 E0694 DIPLOM
B66

FALK R.A.,THE STRATEGY OF WORLD ORDER* 4 VOLUMES. ORD/FREE
WOR+45 ECO/UNDEV ACADEM INT/ORG ACT/RES DIPLOM GEN/LAWS
ARMS/CONT WAR...NET/THEORY SIMUL BIBLIOG UN. ANTHOL
PAGE 36 E0719 INT/LAW
B66

JACOBSON H.K.,DIPLOMATS, SCIENTISTS, AND DIPLOM
POLITICIANS* THE UNITED STATES AND THE NUCLEAR TEST ARMS/CONT
BAN NEGOTIATIONS. USA+45 USSR ACT/RES PLAN CONFER TECHRACY

DETER NUC/PWR CONSEN ORD/FREE...INT TREATY. PAGE 57 INT/ORG
E1146

UNITED NATIONS,INTERNATIONAL SPACE BIBLIOGRAPHY. BIBLIOG
FUT INT/ORG TEC/DEV DIPLOM ARMS/CONT NUC/PWR SPACE
...JURID SOC UN. PAGE 98 E1969 PEACE
R+D
B66

US SENATE COMM AERO SPACE SCI,SOVIET SPACE CONSULT
PROGRAMS, 1962-65; GOALS AND PURPOSES, SPACE
ACHIEVEMENTS, PLANS, AND INTERNATIONAL FUT
IMPLICATIONS. USA+45 USSR R+D FORCES PLAN EDU/PROP DIPLOM
PRESS ADJUD ARMS/CONT ATTIT MARXISM. PAGE 101 E2028
B66

WAINHOUSE D.W.,INTERNATIONAL PEACE OBSERVATION: A PEACE
HISTORY AND FORECAST. INT/ORG PROB/SOLV BAL/PWR DIPLOM
AGREE ARMS/CONT COERCE NUC/PWR...PREDICT METH/COMP
20 UN LEAGUE/NAT OAS TREATY. PAGE 104 E2092
B66

YOUNG W.,EXISTING MECHANISMS OF ARMS CONTROL. ARMS/CONT
PROC/MFG OP/RES DIPLOM TASK CENTRAL...MGT TREATY. ADMIN
PAGE 108 E2165 NUC/PWR
ROUTINE
B66

BROWNLIE I.,"NUCLEAR PROLIFERATION* SOME PROBLEMS NUC/PWR
OF CONTROL." USA+45 USSR ECO/UNDEV INT/ORG FORCES ARMS/CONT
TEC/DEV REGION CONSEN...RECORD TREATY. PAGE 16 VOL/ASSN
E0318 ORD/FREE
S66

EWALD R.F.,"ONE OF MANY POSSIBLE GAMES." ACADEM SIMUL
INT/ORG ARMS/CONT...INT/LAW GAME. PAGE 36 E0706 HYPO/EXP
PROG/TEAC
RECORD
S66

BLAISDELL D.C.,"INTERNATIONAL ORGANIZATION." FUT BIBLIOG
WOR+45 ECO/DEV DELIB/GP FORCES EFFICIENCY PEACE INT/ORG
ORD/FREE...INT/LAW 20 UN LEAGUE/NAT NATO. PAGE 12 DIPLOM
E0239 ARMS/CONT
C66

GARCIA ROBLES A.,THE DENUCLEARIZATION OF LATIN NUC/PWR
AMERICA (TRANS. BY MARJORIE URQUIDI). LAW PLAN ARMS/CONT
DIPLOM...ANTHOL 20 TREATY UN. PAGE 42 E0833 L/A+17C
INT/ORG
B67

HOLCOMBE A.N.,A STRATEGY OF PEACE IN A CHANGING PEACE
WORLD. USA+45 WOR+45 LAW NAT/G CREATE DIPLOM PLAN
ARMS/CONT WAR...CHARTS 20 UN COLD/WAR. PAGE 54 INT/ORG
E1072 INT/LAW
B67

MCBRIDE J.H.,THE TEST BAN TREATY: MILITARY, ARMS/CONT
TECHNOLOGICAL, AND POLITICAL IMPLICATIONS. USA+45 DIPLOM
USSR DELIB/GP FORCES LEGIS TEC/DEV BAL/PWR TREATY. NUC/PWR
PAGE 70 E1399
B67

RAMUNDO B.A.,PEACEFUL COEXISTENCE: INTERNATIONAL INT/LAW
LAW IN THE BUILDING OF COMMUNISM. USSR INT/ORG PEACE
DIPLOM COLONIAL ARMS/CONT ROLE SOVEREIGN...POLICY MARXISM
METH/COMP NAT/COMP BIBLIOG. PAGE 83 E1673 METH/CNCPT
B67

US SENATE COMM ON FOREIGN REL,TREATY ON OUTER SPACE
SPACE. WOR+45 AIR FORCES PROB/SOLV NUC/PWR SENATE DIPLOM
TREATY UN. PAGE 101 E2032 ARMS/CONT
LAW
B67

US SENATE COMM ON FOREIGN REL,UNITED STATES ARMS/CONT
ARMAMENT AND DISARMAMENT PROBLEMS. USA+45 AIR WEAPON
BAL/PWR DIPLOM FOR/AID NUC/PWR ORD/FREE SENATE FORCES
TREATY. PAGE 102 E2035 PROB/SOLV
B67

SCHUBERT G.,"THE RHETORIC OF CONSTITUTIONAL CONSTN
CHANGE." USA+45 LAW CULTURE CHIEF LEGIS ADJUD METH/COMP
CT/SYS ARMS/CONT ADJUST...CHARTS SIMUL. PAGE 89 ORD/FREE
E1777
L67

EYRAUD M.,"LA FRANCE FACE A UN EVENTUEL TRAITE DE NUC/PWR
NON DISSEMINATION DES ARMES NUCLEAIRES." FRANCE ARMS/CONT
USA+45 EXTR/IND INDUS R+D INT/ORG ACT/RES TEC/DEV POLICY
AGREE PRODUC ATTIT 20 TREATY AEC EURATOM. PAGE 36
E0708
S67

ARMY....ARMY (ALL NATIONS)

ARNOLD T. E1182

ARNOLD/M....MATTHEW ARNOLD

ARNOW K. E0104

ART/METH....FINE AND PERFORMING ARTS

N
VALENZUELE G.,BIBLIOGRAFIA GUATEMALTECA, Y CATALOG BIBLIOG/A
GENERAL DE LIBROS, FOLLETOS, PERIODICOS, REVISTAS,   L/A+17C
ETC. (10 VOLS.). GUATEMALA LAW...ART/METH 17/20.
PAGE 103 E2066

B12
FOUAD M.,LE REGIME DE LA PRESSE EN EGYPTE: THESE   ORD/FREE
POUR LE DOCTORAT. UAR LICENSE EDU/PROP ADMIN   LEGIS
SANCTION CRIME SUPEGO PWR...ART/METH JURID 19/20.   CONTROL
PAGE 39 E0778   PRESS

L21
HALDEMAN E.,"SERIALS OF AN INTERNATIONAL   BIBLIOG
CHARACTER." WOR-45 DIPLOM...ART/METH GEOG HEAL HUM   PHIL/SCI
INT/LAW JURID PSY SOC. PAGE 49 E0978

B42
BLANCHARD L.R.,MARTINIQUE: A SELECTED LIST OF   BIBLIOG/A
REFERENCES (PAMPHLET). WEST/IND AGRI LOC/G SCHOOL   SOCIETY
...ART/METH GEOG JURID CHARTS 20. PAGE 12 E0241   CULTURE
                                                     COLONIAL

B44
US LIBRARY OF CONGRESS,RUSSIA: A CHECK LIST   BIBLIOG
PRELIMINARY TO A BASIC BIBLIOGRAPHY OF MATERIALS IN LAW
THE RUSSIAN LANGUAGE. COM USSR CULTURE EDU/PROP   SECT
MARXISM...ART/METH HUM LING 19/20. PAGE 101 E2015

B48
YAKOBSON S.,FIVE HUNDRED RUSSIAN WORKS FOR COLLEGE   BIBLIOG
LIBRARIES (PAMPHLET). MOD/EUR USSR MARXISM SOCISM   NAT/G
...ART/METH GEOG HUM JURID SOC 13/20. PAGE 108   CULTURE
E2162   COM

B50
DOROSH J.T.,GUIDE TO SOVIET BIBLIOGRAPHIES. USSR   BIBLIOG
LAW AGRI SCHOOL SECT FORCES TEC/DEV...ART/METH GEOG METH
HUM SOC 20. PAGE 32 E0639   CON/ANAL

B51
BISSAINTHE M.,DICTIONNAIRE DE BIBLIOGRAPHIE   BIBLIOG
HAITIENNE. HAITI ELITES AGRI LEGIS DIPLOM INT/TRADE L/A+17C
WRITING ORD/FREE CATHISM...ART/METH GEOG 19/20   SOCIETY
NEGRO TREATY. PAGE 12 E0234   NAT/G

B52
ETTINGHAUSEN R.,SELECTED AND ANNOTATED BIBLIOGRAPHY BIBLIOG/A
OF BOOKS AND PERIODICALS IN WESTERN LANGUAGES   ISLAM
DEALING WITH NEAR AND MIDDLE EAST. LAW CULTURE SECT MEDIT-7
...ART/METH GEOG SOC. PAGE 35 E0700

B53
AYMARD A.,HISTOIRE GENERALE DES CIVILISATIONS (7   BIBLIOG/A
VOLS.). WOR+45 WOR-45 LAW SECT CREATE ATTIT   SOC
...ART/METH WORSHIP. PAGE 6 E0123

B55
TROTIER A.H.,DOCTORAL DISSERTATIONS ACCEPTED BY   BIBLIOG
AMERICAN UNIVERSITIES 1954-55. SECT DIPLOM HEALTH   ACADEM
...ART/METH GEOG INT/LAW SOC LING CHARTS 20.   USA+45
PAGE 97 E1943   WRITING

B57
BYRNES R.F.,BIBLIOGRAPHY OF AMERICAN PUBLICATIONS   BIBLIOG/A
ON EAST CENTRAL EUROPE, 1945-1957 (VOL. XXII). SECT COM
DIPLOM EDU/PROP RACE/REL...ART/METH GEOG JURID SOC   MARXISM
LING 20 JEWS. PAGE 18 E0354   NAT/G

B58
KURL S.,ESTONIA: A SELECTED BIBLIOGRAPHY. USSR   BIBLIOG
ESTONIA LAW INTELL SECT...ART/METH GEOG HUM SOC 20. CULTURE
PAGE 62 E1238   NAT/G

B60
CONANT M.,ANTITRUST IN THE MOTION PICTURE INDUSTRY: PRICE
ECONOMIC AND LEGAL ANALYSIS. USA+45 MARKET ADJUST   CONTROL
DEMAND BIBLIOG. PAGE 24 E0484   LAW
                                                     ART/METH

B61
SMITH J.W.,RELIGIOUS PERSPECTIVES IN AMERICAN   SECT
CULTURE, VOL. 2: RELIGION IN AMERICAN LIFE. USA+45   DOMIN
CULTURE NAT/G EDU/PROP ADJUD LOBBY ATTIT...ART/METH SOCIETY
ANTHOL 20 CHURCH/STA BIBLE. PAGE 92 E1845   GP/REL

B62
KIDDER F.E.,THESES ON PAN AMERICAN TOPICS. LAW   BIBLIOG

CULTURE NAT/G SECT DIPLOM HEALTH...ART/METH GEOG   CHRIST-17C
SOC 13/20. PAGE 61 E1213   L/A+17C
                                                     SOCIETY

B63
CRAIG A.,SUPPRESSED BOOKS: A HISTORY OF THE   BIBLIOG/A
CONCEPTION OF LITERARY OBSCENITY. WOR+45 WOR-45   LAW
CREATE EDU/PROP LITERACY ATTIT...ART/METH PSY   SEX
CONCPT 20. PAGE 27 E0538   CONTROL

B64
RAGHAVAN M.D.,INDIA IN CEYLONESE HISTORY, SOCIETY   DIPLOM
AND CULTURE. CEYLON INDIA S/ASIA LAW SOCIETY   CULTURE
INT/TRADE ATTIT...ART/METH JURID SOC LING 20.   SECT
PAGE 83 E1668   STRUCT

B66
CARMEN I.H.,MOVIES, CENSORSHIP, AND THE LAW. LOC/G   EDU/PROP
NAT/G ATTIT ORD/FREE...DECISION INT IDEA/COMP   LAW
BIBLIOG 20 SUPREME/CT FILM. PAGE 19 E0383   ART/METH
                                                     CONSTN

B66
STEVENS R.E.,REFERENCE BOOKS IN THE SOCIAL SCIENCES BIBLIOG/A
AND HUMANITIES. CULTURE PERF/ART SECT EDU/PROP   SOC
...JURID PSY SOC/WK STAT 20 MUSIC. PAGE 93 E1873   HUM
                                                     ART/METH

ARTHUR/CA....PRESIDENT CHESTER ALAN ARTHUR

ARTISTIC ACHIEVEMENT....SEE CREATE

ASAMOAH O.Y. E0105

ASCH S.H. E0106

ASIA....SEE ALSO APPROPRIATE TIME/SPACE/CULTURE INDEX

N
ANNALS OF THE AMERICAN ACADEMY OF POLITICAL AND   BIBLIOG/A
SOCIAL SCIENCE. AFR ASIA S/ASIA WOR+45 POL/PAR   NAT/G
DIPLOM CRIME REV...SOC BIOG 20. PAGE 1 E0003   CULTURE
                                                     ATTIT

N
INTERNATIONAL STUDIES. ASIA S/ASIA WOR+45 ECO/UNDEV BIBLIOG/A
INT/ORG NAT/G LEAD ATTIT WEALTH...SOC 20. PAGE 1   DIPLOM
E0009   INT/LAW
                                                     INT/TRADE

N
ASIA FOUNDATION,LIBRARY NOTES. LAW CONSTN CULTURE   BIBLIOG/A
SOCIETY ECO/UNDEV INT/ORG NAT/G COLONIAL LEAD   ASIA
REGION NAT/LISM ATTIT 20 UN. PAGE 6 E0107   S/ASIA
                                                     DIPLOM

B'
LALL A.S.,NEGOTIATING DISARMAMENT* THE EIGHTEEN   OBS
NATION DISARMAMENT CONFERENCE* THE FIRST TWO YEARS, ARMS/CONT
1962-1964. ASIA FRANCE INDIA USA+45 USSR PROB/SOLV   DIPLOM
ADJUD NEUTRAL ATTIT...IDEA/COMP COLD/WAR. PAGE 62   OP/RES
E1246

B01
GRONING J.,BIBLIOTHECA JURIS GENTIUM COMMUNIS, QUA   BIBLIOG
PRAECIPUORUM, ASIAE, AFRICAE, ET AMERICAE,   JURID
POPULORUM DE JURIS NATURAE... AFR ASIA S/ASIA   LAW
USA-45 16/17. PAGE 48 E0946   NAT/G

B03
GRONING J.,BIBLIOTHECA JURIS GENTIUM EXOTICA. AFR   BIBLIOG
ASIA S/ASIA USA-45 16/17. PAGE 48 E0947   JURID
                                                     NAT/G
                                                     LAW

B18
YUKIO O.,THE VOICE OF JAPANESE DEMOCRACY, AN ESSAY   CONSTN
ON CONSTITUTIONAL LOYALTY (TRANS BY J. E. BECKER).   MAJORIT
ASIA POL/PAR DELIB/GP EX/STRUC RIGID/FLEX ORD/FREE   CHOOSE
PWR...POLICY JURID METH/COMP 19/20 CHINJAP.   NAT/G
PAGE 108 E2167

B28
YANG KUNG-SUN,THE BOOK OF LORD SHANG. LAW ECO/UNDEV ASIA
LOC/G NAT/G NEIGH PLAN ECO/TAC LEGIT ATTIT SKILL   JURID
...CONCPT CON/ANAL WORK TOT/POP. PAGE 108 E2164

B38
GRISWOLD A.W.,THE FAR EASTERN POLICY OF THE UNITED   DIPLOM
STATES. ASIA S/ASIA USA-45 INT/ORG INT/TRADE WAR   POLICY
NAT/LISM...BIBLIOG 19/20 LEAGUE/NAT ROOSEVLT/T   CHIEF
ROOSEVLT/F WILSON/W TREATY. PAGE 47 E0943

B40
CONOVER H.F.,FOREIGN RELATIONS OF THE UNITED
STATES: A LIST OF RECENT BOOKS (PAMPHLET). ASIA
CANADA L/A+17C UK INT/ORG INT/TRADE TARIFFS NEUTRAL
WAR PEACE...INT/LAW CON/ANAL 20 CHINJAP. PAGE 25
E0492
BIBLIOG/A
USA-45
DIPLOM

B45
US DEPARTMENT OF STATE,PUBLICATIONS OF THE
DEPARTMENT OF STATE: A LIST CUMULATIVE FROM OCTOBER
1, 1929 (PAMPHLET). ASIA EUR+WWI ISLAM L/A+17C
USA-45 ADJUD...INT/LAW 20. PAGE 99 E1993
BIBLIOG
DIPLOM
INT/TRADE

B50
WARD R.E.,A GUIDE TO JAPANESE REFERENCE AND
RESEARCH MATERIALS IN THE FIELD OF POLITICAL
SCIENCE. LAW CONSTN LOC/G PRESS ADMIN...SOC
CON/ANAL METH 19/20 CHINJAP. PAGE 105 E2098
BIBLIOG/A
ASIA
NAT/G

B54
NUSSBAUM D.,A CONCISE HISTORY OF THE LAW OF
NATIONS. ASIA CHRIST-17C EUR+WWI ISLAM MEDIT-7
MOD/EUR S/ASIA UNIV WOR+45 WOR-45 SOCIETY STRUCT
EXEC ATTIT ALL/VALS...CONCPT HIST/WRIT TIME/SEQ.
PAGE 78 E1560
INT/ORG
LAW
PEACE
INT/LAW

B58
SCHOEDER P.W.,THE AXIS ALLIANCE AND JAPANESE-
AMERICAN RELATIONS 1941. ASIA GERMANY UK USA-45
PEACE ATTIT...POLICY BIBLIOG 20 CHINJAP TREATY.
PAGE 88 E1763
AGREE
DIPLOM
WAR

B61
CARNELL F.,THE POLITICS OF THE NEW STATES: A SELECT
ANNOTATED BIBLIOGRAPHY WITH SPECIAL REFERENCE TO
THE COMMONWEALTH. CONSTN ELITES LABOR NAT/G POL/PAR
EX/STRUC DIPLOM ADJUD ADMIN...GOV/COMP 20
COMMONWLTH. PAGE 20 E0387
BIBLIOG/A
AFR
ASIA
COLONIAL

L62
PETKOFF D.K.,"RECOGNITION AND NON-RECOGNITION OF
STATES AND GOVERNMENTS IN INTERNATIONAL LAW." ASIA
COM USA+45 WOR+45 NAT/G ACT/RES DIPLOM DOMIN LEGIT
COERCE ORD/FREE PWR...CONCPT GEN/LAWS 20. PAGE 80
E1611
INT/ORG
LAW
INT/LAW

C62
VAN DER SPRENKEL S.,"LEGAL INSTITUTIONS IN MANCHU
CHINA." ASIA STRUCT CT/SYS ROUTINE GOV/REL GP/REL
...CONCPT BIBLIOG 17/20. PAGE 103 E2068
LAW
JURID
ADMIN
ADJUD

B63
DUNN F.S.,PEACE-MAKING AND THE SETTLEMENT WITH
JAPAN. ASIA USA+45 USA-45 FORCES BAL/PWR ECO/TAC
CONFER WAR PWR SOVEREIGN 20 CHINJAP COLD/WAR
TREATY. PAGE 33 E0661
POLICY
PEACE
PLAN
DIPLOM

B63
GEERTZ C.,OLD SOCIETIES AND NEW STATES: THE QUEST
FOR MODERNITY IN ASIA AND AFRICA. AFR ASIA LAW
CULTURE SECT EDU/PROP REV...GOV/COMP NAT/COMP 20.
PAGE 42 E0842
ECO/UNDEV
TEC/DEV
NAT/LISM
SOVEREIGN

L63
ROSE R.,"COMPARATIVE STUDIES IN POLITICAL FINANCE:
A SYMPOSIUM." ASIA EUR+WWI S/ASIA LAW CULTURE
DELIB/GP LEGIS ACT/RES ECO/TAC EDU/PROP CHOOSE
ATTIT RIGID/FLEX SUPEGO PWR SKILL WEALTH...STAT
ANTHOL VAL/FREE. PAGE 85 E1714
FINAN
POL/PAR

B64
GRIFFITH W.E.,THE SINO-SOVIET RIFT. ASIA CHINA/COM
COM CUBA USSR YUGOSLAVIA NAT/G POL/PAR VOL/ASSN
DELIB/GP FORCES TOP/EX DIPLOM EDU/PROP DRIVE PERSON
PWR...TREND 20 TREATY. PAGE 47 E0941
ATTIT
TIME/SEQ
BAL/PWR
SOCISM

B64
TONG T.,UNITED STATES DIPLOMACY IN CHINA,
1844-1860. ASIA USA-45 ECO/UNDEV ECO/TAC COERCE
GP/REL...INT/LAW 19 TREATY. PAGE 96 E1934
DIPLOM
INT/TRADE
COLONIAL

L64
POUNDS N.J.G.,"THE POLITICS OF PARTITION." AFR ASIA
COM EUR+WWI FUT ISLAM S/ASIA USA-45 LAW ECO/DEV
ECO/UNDEV AGRI INDUS INT/ORG POL/PAR PROVS SECT
FORCES TOP/EX EDU/PROP LEGIT ATTIT MORAL ORD/FREE
PWR RESPECT WEALTH. PAGE 82 E1640
NAT/G
NAT/LISM

B65
HIGGINS R.,CONFLICT OF INTERESTS* INTERNATIONAL LAW
IN A DIVIDED WORLD. ASIA USSR ECO/DEV ECO/UNDEV
SECT INT/TRADE COLD/WAR WORSHIP. PAGE 52 E1042
INT/LAW
IDEA/COMP
ADJUST

L65
SHARMA S.P.,"THE INDIA-CHINA BORDER DISPUTE: AN
LAW

INDIAN PERSPECTIVE." ASIA CHINA/COM S/ASIA NAT/G
LEGIT CT/SYS NAT/LISM DRIVE MORAL ORD/FREE PWR 20.
PAGE 91 E1815
ATTIT
SOVEREIGN
INDIA

S65
PRABHAKAR P.,"SURVEY OF RESEARCH AND SOURCE
MATERIALS: THE SINO-INDIAN BORDER DISPUTE."
CHINA/COM INDIA LAW NAT/G PLAN BAL/PWR WAR...POLICY
20 COLD/WAR. PAGE 82 E1645
BIBLIOG
ASIA
S/ASIA
DIPLOM

B66
BEER U.,FRUCHTBARKEITSREGELUNG ALS KONSEQUENZ
VERANTWORTLICHER ELTERNSCHAFT. ASIA GERMANY/W INDIA
LAW ECO/DEV ECO/UNDEV TEC/DEV ECO/TAC BIO/SOC SEX
CATHISM...METH/COMP 20 CHINJAP BIRTH/CON. PAGE 9
E0178
CONTROL
GEOG
FAM
SECT

B66
US DEPARTMENT OF STATE,RESEARCH ON AFRICA (EXTERNAL
RESEARCH LIST NO 5-25). LAW CULTURE ECO/UNDEV
POL/PAR DIPLOM EDU/PROP LEAD REGION MARXISM...GEOG
LING WORSHIP 20. PAGE 100 E1996
BIBLIOG/A
ASIA
S/ASIA
NAT/G

S66
ANAND R.P.,"ATTITUDE OF THE ASIAN-AFRICAN STATES
TOWARD CERTAIN PROBLEMS OF INTERNATIONAL LAW."
L/A+17C S/ASIA ECO/UNDEV CREATE CONFER ADJUD
COLONIAL...RECORD GP/COMP UN. PAGE 5 E0087
INT/LAW
ATTIT
ASIA
AFR

B67
WATT A.,THE EVOLUTION OF AUSTRALIAN FOREIGN POLICY
1938-65. ASIA S/ASIA USA+45 USA-45 INT/ORG NAT/G
FORCES FOR/AID TREATY 20 AUSTRAL. PAGE 105 E2103
DIPLOM
WAR

ASIA FOUNDATION E0107

ASIANS....ASIANS, ASIAN MINORITIES

ASQUITH/HH....HERBERT HENRY ASQUITH

ASSASSINATION....SEE MURDER

ASSIMILATION....SEE GP/REL+INGP/REL

ASSOCIATION BAR OF NYC E0108,E0109

ASSOCIATIONS....SEE VOL/ASSN

AT+T....AMERICAN TELEPHONE AND TELEGRAPH

ATATURK/MK....MUSTAFA KEMAL ATATURK

ATHENS....ATHENS, GREECE

ATLAN/ALL....ATLANTIC ALLIANCE

ATLANTA....ATLANTA, GEORGIA

ATLANTIC INSTITUTE E0110

ATLASES....SEE MAPS

ATOM BOMB....SEE NUC/PWR

ATOMIC ENERGY COMMISSION....SEE AEC + COUNTRY'S NAME

ATOMIC INDUSTRIAL FORUM E0111,E0112,E0113

ATTENTION....SEE PERCEPT

ATTIA G.E.D. E0114

ATTIA G.E.O. E0115

ATTIT....ATTITUDES, OPINIONS, IDEOLOGY

N
ANNALS OF THE AMERICAN ACADEMY OF POLITICAL AND
SOCIAL SCIENCE. AFR ASIA S/ASIA WOR+45 POL/PAR
DIPLOM CRIME REV...SOC BIOG 20. PAGE 1 E0003
BIBLIOG/A
NAT/G
CULTURE
ATTIT

N
BACKGROUND: JOURNAL OF INTERNATIONAL STUDIES
ASSOCIATION. INT/ORG FORCES ACT/RES EDU/PROP COERCE
NAT/LISM PEACE ATTIT...INT/LAW CONCPT 20. PAGE 1
E0004
BIBLIOG
DIPLOM
POLICY

N
INTERNATIONAL STUDIES. ASIA S/ASIA WOR+45 ECO/UNDEV BIBLIOG/A

INT/ORG NAT/G LEAD ATTIT WEALTH...SOC 20. PAGE 1   DIPLOM
E0009   INT/LAW
                                                         INT/TRADE

                                                         N
MIDWEST JOURNAL OF POLITICAL SCIENCE. USA+45 CONSTN   BIBLIOG/A
ECO/DEV LEGIS PROB/SOLV CT/SYS LEAD GOV/REL ATTIT   NAT/G
POLICY. PAGE 1 E0012   DIPLOM
                                                         POL/PAR

                                                         N
PUBLISHERS' CIRCULAR, THE OFFICIAL ORGAN OF THE   BIBLIOG
PUBLISHERS' ASSOCIATION OF GREAT BRITAIN AND   NAT/G
IRELAND. EUR+WWI MOD/EUR UK LAW PROB/SOLV DIPLOM   WRITING
COLONIAL ATTIT...HUM 19/20 CMN/WLTH. PAGE 2 E0025   LEAD

                                                         N
CANON LAW ABSTRACTS. LEGIT CONFER CT/SYS INGP/REL   BIBLIOG/A
MARRIAGE ATTIT MORAL WORSHIP 20. PAGE 2 E0026   CATHISM
                                                         SECT
                                                         LAW

                                                         N
PERSONNEL. USA+45 LAW LABOR LG/CO WORKER CREATE   BIBLIOG/A
GOV/REL PERS/REL ATTIT WEALTH. PAGE 2 E0029   ADMIN
                                                         MGT
                                                         GP/REL

                                                         N
ASIA FOUNDATION,LIBRARY NOTES. LAW CONSTN CULTURE   BIBLIOG/A
SOCIETY ECO/UNDEV INT/ORG NAT/G COLONIAL LEAD   ASIA
REGION NAT/LISM ATTIT 20 UN. PAGE 6 E0107   S/ASIA
                                                         DIPLOM

                                                         N
DEUTSCHE BUCHEREI,DEUTSCHES BUCHERVERZEICHNIS.   BIBLIOG
GERMANY LAW CULTURE POL/PAR ADMIN LEAD ATTIT PERSON   NAT/G
...SOC 20. PAGE 31 E0615   DIPLOM
                                                         ECO/DEV

                                                         N
NEW YORK STATE LIBRARY,CHECKLIST OF OFFICIAL   BIBLIOG
PUBLICATIONS OF THE STATE OF NEW YORK. USA+45   PROVS
USA-45 LAW PROB/SOLV LEAD ATTIT 19/20. PAGE 77   WRITING
E1539   GOV/REL

                                                         B*
LALL A.S.,NEGOTIATING DISARMAMENT* THE EIGHTEEN   OBS
NATION DISARMAMENT CONFERENCE* THE FIRST TWO YEARS,   ARMS/CONT
1962-1964. ASIA FRANCE INDIA USA+45 USSR PROB/SOLV   DIPLOM
ADJUD NEUTRAL ATTIT...IDEA/COMP COLD/WAR. PAGE 62   OP/RES
E1246

                                                         B00
BERNARD M.,FOUR LECTURES ON SUBJECTS CONNECTED WITH   LAW
DIPLOMACY. WOR-45 NAT/G VOL/ASSN RIGID/FLEX MORAL   ATTIT
PWR...JURID OBS GEN/LAWS GEN/METH 20 TREATY.   DIPLOM
PAGE 11 E0209

                                                         B00
DE TOCQUEVILLE A.,DEMOCRACY IN AMERICA (VOLUME   USA-45
ONE). LAW SOCIETY STRUCT NAT/G POL/PAR PROVS FORCES   TREND
LEGIS TOP/EX DIPLOM LEGIT WAR PEACE ATTIT SOVEREIGN
...SELF/OBS TIME/SEQ CONGRESS 19. PAGE 30 E0594

                                                         B00
GREELY A.W.,PUBLIC DOCUMENTS OF THE FIRST FOURTEEN   BIBLIOG/A
CONGRESSES, 1789-1817. USA-45 LEAD REPRESENT ATTIT   NAT/G
18/19 CONGRESS. PAGE 45 E0904   LAW
                                                         LEGIS

                                                         B00
MAINE H.S.,INTERNATIONAL LAW. MOD/EUR UNIV SOCIETY   INT/ORG
STRUCT ACT/RES EXEC WAR ATTIT PERSON ALL/VALS   LAW
...POLICY JURID CONCPT OBS TIME/SEQ TOT/POP.   PEACE
PAGE 68 E1349   INT/LAW

                                                         B04
GRIFFIN A.P.C.,REFERENCES ON CHINESE IMMIGRATIONS   BIBLIOG/A
(PAMPHLET). USA-45 KIN NAT/LISM ATTIT...SOC 19/20.   STRANGE
PAGE 47 E0926   JURID
                                                         RACE/REL

                                                         B05
DICEY A.,LAW AND PUBLIC OPINION IN ENGLAND. LAW   ATTIT
CULTURE INTELL SOCIETY NAT/G SECT JUDGE LEGIT   UK
CHOOSE RIGID/FLEX KNOWL...OLD/LIB CONCPT STERTYP
GEN/LAWS 20. PAGE 31 E0620

                                                         B05
DICEY A.V.,LECTURES ON THE RELATION BETWEEN LAW AND   LAW
PUBLIC OPINION IN ENGLAND DURING THE NINETEENTH   ADJUD
CENTURY. UK LEGIS CT/SYS...JURID 19 TORY/PARTY   ATTIT
BENTHAM/J ENGLSH/LAW. PAGE 31 E0621   IDEA/COMP

                                                         S05
PHILLIPS J.B.,"MODIFICATIONS OF THE JURY SYSTEM."   JURID
PARTIC EFFICIENCY ATTIT PERCEPT...TREND 19   DELIB/GP
SUPREME/CT JURY. PAGE 80 E1612   PERS/REL
                                                         POLICY

                                                         B06
GRIFFIN A.P.C.,SELECT LIST OF REFERENCES ON THE   BIBLIOG/A
NEGRO QUESTION (REV. ED.). USA-45 CONSTN SCHOOL   RACE/REL
SUFF ADJUST...JURID SOC/INTEG 19/20 NEGRO. PAGE 47   DISCRIM
E0930   ATTIT

                                                         B12
BEARD C.A.,THE SUPREME COURT AND THE CONSTITUTION.   CONSTN
LAW NAT/G PROVS LEGIS GOV/REL ATTIT POPULISM   CT/SYS
SUPREME/CT. PAGE 9 E0164   ADJUD
                                                         CONTROL

                                                         B12
GRIFFIN A.P.C.,SELECT LIST OF REFERENCES ON   BIBLIOG/A
IMPEACHMENT (REV. ED.) (PAMPHLET). USA-45 LAW PROVS   CONSTN
ADJUD ATTIT...JURID 19/20 NEGRO. PAGE 47 E0935   NAT/G
                                                         LEGIS

                                                         B12
POLLOCK F.,THE GENIUS OF THE COMMON LAW. CHRIST-17C   LAW
UK FINAN CHIEF ACT/RES ADMIN GP/REL ATTIT SOCISM   CULTURE
...ANARCH JURID. PAGE 81 E1624   CREATE

                                                         N13
SCHMIDHAUSER J.R.,JUDICIAL BEHAVIOR AND THE   JUDGE
SECTIONAL CRISIS OF 1837-1860. USA-45 ADJUD CT/SYS   POL/PAR
INGP/REL ATTIT HABITAT...DECISION PSY STAT CHARTS   PERS/COMP
SIMUL. PAGE 88 E1759   PERSON

                                                         B16
ROOT E.,ADDRESSES ON INTERNATIONAL SUBJECTS.   INT/ORG
MOD/EUR UNIV USA-45 LAW SOCIETY EXEC ATTIT ALL/VALS   ACT/RES
...POLICY JURID CONCPT 20 CHINJAP. PAGE 85 E1711   PEACE
                                                         INT/LAW

                                                         B16
SCHROEDER T.,FREE SPEECH FOR RADICALS (REV. ED.).   ORD/FREE
USA-45 CONSTN INDUS LOC/G FORCES SANCTION WAR ATTIT   CONTROL
SEX...JURID REFORMERS 20 FREE/SPEE. PAGE 88 E1767   LAW
                                                         PRESS

                                                         B18
PORTER K.H.,A HISTORY OF SUFFRAGE IN THE UNITED   SUFF
STATES. USA-45 LAW CONSTN LOC/G NAT/G POL/PAR WAR   REPRESENT
DISCRIM OWN ATTIT SEX 18/20 NEGRO FEMALE/SEX.   CHOOSE
PAGE 81 E1629   PARTIC

                                                         N19
COUTROT A.,THE FIGHT OVER THE 1959 PRIVATE   SCHOOL
EDUCATION LAW IN FRANCE (PAMPHLET). FRANCE NAT/G   PARL/PROC
SECT GIVE EDU/PROP GP/REL ATTIT RIGID/FLEX ORD/FREE   CATHISM
20 CHURCH/STA. PAGE 27 E0527   LAW

                                                         N19
GIBB A.D.,JUDICIAL CORRUPTION IN THE UNITED KINGDOM   MORAL
(PAMPHLET). UK DELIB/GP CT/SYS CRIME PERSON SUPEGO   ATTIT
17/20 SCOTLAND. PAGE 43 E0856   ADJUD

                                                         N19
JANOWITZ M.,SOCIAL CONTROL OF ESCALATED RIOTS   CROWD
(PAMPHLET). USA+45 USA-45 LAW SOCIETY MUNIC FORCES   ORD/FREE
PROB/SOLV EDU/PROP TV CRIME ATTIT...BIBLIOG 20   CONTROL
NEGRO CIV/RIGHTS. PAGE 58 E1148   RACE/REL

                                                         N19
OPERATIONS AND POLICY RESEARCH,URUGUAY: ELECTION   POL/PAR
FACTBOOK: NOVEMBER 27, 1966 (PAMPHLET). URUGUAY LAW   CHOOSE
NAT/G LEAD REPRESENT...STAT BIOG CHARTS 20. PAGE 79   PLAN
E1576   ATTIT

                                                         B20
DICKINSON E.,THE EQUALITY OF STATES IN   LAW
INTERNATIONAL LAW. WOR-45 INT/ORG NAT/G DIPLOM   CONCPT
EDU/PROP LEGIT PEACE ATTIT ALL/VALS...JURID   SOVEREIGN
TIME/SEQ LEAGUE/NAT. PAGE 31 E0622

                                                         B20
LIPPMAN W.,LIBERTY AND THE NEWS. USA+45 USA-45 LAW   ORD/FREE
LEGIS DOMIN LEGIT ATTIT...POLICY SOC IDEA/COMP   PRESS
METH/COMP 19/20. PAGE 65 E1300   COM/IND
                                                         EDU/PROP

                                                         B22
BRYCE J.,INTERNATIONAL RELATIONS. CHRIST-17C   INT/ORG
EUR+WWI MOD/EUR CULTURE INTELL NAT/G DELIB/GP   POLICY
CREATE BAL/PWR DIPLOM ATTIT DRIVE RIGID/FLEX
ALL/VALS...PLURIST JURID CONCPT TIME/SEQ GEN/LAWS
TOT/POP. PAGE 16 E0323

SCHROEDER T.,FREE SPEECH BIBLIOGRAPHY. EUR+WWI WOR-45 NAT/G SECT ECO/TAC WRITING ADJUD ATTIT MARXISM SOCISM 16/20. PAGE 88 E1768
B22
BIBLIOG/A
ORD/FREE
CONTROL
LAW

HOLMES O.W. JR.,THE COMMON LAW. FUT WOR-45 CULTURE SOCIETY CREATE LEGIT ROUTINE ATTIT ALL/VALS...JURID METH/CNCPT TIME/SEQ GEN/LAWS TOT/POP VAL/FREE. PAGE 55 E1087
B23
ADJUD
CON/ANAL

BEALE J.H.,A BIBLIOGRAPHY OF EARLY ENGLISH LAW BOOKS. MOD/EUR UK PRESS ADJUD CT/SYS ATTIT...CHARTS 10/16. PAGE 8 E0161
B26
BIBLIOG/A
JURID
LAW

GOOCH G.P.,ENGLISH DEMOCRATIC IDEAS IN THE SEVENTEENTH CENTURY (2ND ED.). UK LAW SECT FORCES DIPLOM LEAD PARL/PROC REV ATTIT AUTHORIT...ANARCH CONCPT 17 PARLIAMENT CMN/WLTH REFORMERS. PAGE 45 E0885
B27
IDEA/COMP
MAJORIT
EX/STRUC
CONSERVE

LAUTERPACHT H.,PRIVATE LAW SOURCES AND ANALOGIES OF INTERNATIONAL LAW. WOR-45 NAT/G DELIB/GP LEGIT COERCE ATTIT ORD/FREE PWR SOVEREIGN...JURID CONCPT HIST/WRIT TIME/SEQ GEN/METH LEAGUE/NAT 20. PAGE 63 E1264
B27
INT/ORG
ADJUD
PEACE
INT/LAW

RYAN J.A.,DECLINING LIVERTY AND OTHER ESSAYS. USA-45 SECT DELIB/GP ATTIT PWR SOCISM 20 SUPREME/CT. PAGE 87 E1740
B27
ORD/FREE
LEGIS
JURID
NAT/G

FRANKFURTER F.,THE BUSINESS OF THE SUPREME COURT; A STUDY IN THE FEDERAL JUDICIAL SYSTEM. USA-45 CONSTN EX/STRUC PROB/SOLV GP/REL ATTIT PWR...POLICY JURID 18/20 SUPREME/CT CONGRESS. PAGE 40 E0789
B28
CT/SYS
ADJUD
LAW
FEDERAL

HOBBES T.,THE ELEMENTS OF LAW, NATURAL AND POLITIC (1650). STRATA NAT/G SECT CHIEF AGREE ATTIT ALL/VALS MORAL ORD/FREE POPULISM...POLICY CONCPT. PAGE 53 E1056
B28
PERSON
LAW
SOVEREIGN
CONSERVE

YANG KUNG-SUN,THE BOOK OF LORD SHANG. LAW ECO/UNDEV LOC/G NAT/G NEIGH PLAN ECO/TAC LEGIT ATTIT SKILL ...CONCPT CON/ANAL WORK TOT/POP. PAGE 108 E2164
B28
ASIA
JURID

HUDSON M.,"THE TEACHING OF INTERNATIONAL LAW IN AMERICA." USA-45 LAW CONSULT ACT/RES CREATE EDU/PROP ATTIT RIGID/FLEX...JURID CONCPT RECORD HIST/WRIT TREND GEN/LAWS 18/20. PAGE 56 E1109
L28
PERCEPT
KNOWL
INT/LAW

BUELL R.,INTERNATIONAL RELATIONS. WOR+45 WOR-45 CONSTN STRATA FORCES TOP/EX ADMIN ATTIT DRIVE SUPEGO MORAL ORD/FREE PWR SOVEREIGN...JURID SOC CONCPT 20. PAGE 17 E0326
B29
INT/ORG
BAL/PWR
DIPLOM

CONWELL-EVANS T.P.,THE LEAGUE COUNCIL IN ACTION. EUR+WWI TURKEY UK USSR WOR+45 INT/ORG FORCES JUDGE ECO/TAC EDU/PROP LEGIT ROUTINE ARMS/CONT COERCE ATTIT PWR...MAJORIT GEOG JURID CONCPT LEAGUE/NAT TOT/POP VAL/FREE TUNIS 20. PAGE 25 E0498
B29
DELIB/GP
INT/LAW

BYNKERSHOEK C.,QUAESTIONUM JURIS PUBLICI LIBRI DUO. CHRIST-17C MOD/EUR CONSTN ELITES SOCIETY NAT/G PROVS EX/STRUC FORCES TOP/EX BAL/PWR DIPLOM ATTIT MORAL...TRADIT CONCPT. PAGE 18 E0352
B30
INT/ORG
LAW
NAT/LISM
INT/LAW

JORDAN E.,THEORY OF LEGISLATION: AN ESSAY ON THE DYNAMICS OF PUBLIC MIND. NAT/G CREATE REPRESENT MAJORITY ATTIT GEN/LAWS. PAGE 59 E1173
B30
LEGIS
CONCPT
JURID
CT/SYS

COLUMBIA UNIVERSITY,A BIBLIOGRAPHY OF THE FACULTY OF POLITICAL SCIENCE OF COLUMBIA UNIVERSITY, 1880-1930. USA-45 LAW NAT/G LEGIS DIPLOM LEAD WAR GOV/REL ATTIT...TIME/SEQ 19/20. PAGE 24 E0478
B31
BIBLIOG
ACADEM
PHIL/SCI

EAGLETON C.,INTERNATIONAL GOVERNMENT. BRAZIL FRANCE GERMANY ITALY UK USSR WOR-45 DELIB/GP TOP/EX PLAN ECO/TAC EDU/PROP LEGIT ADJUD REGION ARMS/CONT COERCE ATTIT PWR...GEOG MGT VAL/FREE LEAGUE/NAT 20. INT/LAW
B32
INT/ORG
JURID
DIPLOM

PAGE 34 E0670

FLEMMING D.,THE UNITED STATES AND THE LEAGUE OF NATIONS, 1918-1920. FUT USA-45 NAT/G LEGIS TOP/EX DEBATE CHOOSE PEACE ATTIT SOVEREIGN...TIME/SEQ CON/ANAL CONGRESS LEAGUE/NAT 20 TREATY. PAGE 39 E0764
B32
INT/ORG
EDU/PROP

DANGERFIELD R.,IN DEFENSE OF THE SENATE. USA-45 CONSTN NAT/G EX/STRUC TOP/EX ATTIT KNOWL ...METH/CNCPT STAT TIME/SEQ TREND CON/ANAL CHARTS CONGRESS 20 TREATY. PAGE 28 E0565
B33
LEGIS
DELIB/GP
DIPLOM

LAUTERPACHT H.,THE FUNCTION OF LAW IN THE INTERNATIONAL COMMUNITY. WOR-45 NAT/G FORCES CREATE DOMIN LEGIT COERCE WAR PEACE ATTIT ORD/FREE PWR SOVEREIGN...JURID CONCPT METH/CNCPT TIME/SEQ GEN/LAWS GEN/METH LEAGUE/NAT TOT/POP VAL/FREE 20. PAGE 63 E1265
B33
INT/ORG
LAW
INT/LAW

CLYDE W.M.,THE STRUGGLE FOR THE FREEDOM OF THE PRESS FROM CAXTON TO CROMWELL. UK LAW LOC/G SECT FORCES LICENSE WRITING SANCTION REV ATTIT PWR ...POLICY 15/17 PARLIAMENT CROMWELL/O MILTON/J. PAGE 23 E0460
B34
PRESS
ORD/FREE
CONTROL

CUMMINGS H.,LIBERTY UNDER LAW AND ADMINISTRATION. MOD/EUR USA-45 ADMIN ATTIT...JURID PHIL/SCI. PAGE 28 E0553
B34
ORD/FREE
LAW
NAT/G
SOCIETY

EVANS I.L.,NATIVE POLICY IN SOUTHERN AFRICA. RHODESIA SOUTH/AFR UK STRUCT PARTIC RACE/REL ATTIT WEALTH SOC/INTEG AFRICA/SW. PAGE 35 E0705
B34
AFR
COLONIAL
DOMIN
LAW

GONZALEZ PALENCIA A,ESTUDIO HISTORICO SOBRE LA CENSURA GUBERNATIVA EN ESPANA 1800-1833. NAT/G COERCE INGP/REL ATTIT AUTHORIT KNOWL...POLICY JURID 19. PAGE 44 E0884
B34
LEGIT
EDU/PROP
PRESS
CONTROL

WOLFF C.,JUS GENTIUM METHODO SCIENTIFICA PERTRACTATUM. MOD/EUR INT/ORG VOL/ASSN LEGIT PEACE ATTIT...JURID 20. PAGE 107 E2140
B34
NAT/G
LAW
INT/LAW
WAR

FOREIGN AFFAIRS BIBLIOGRAPHY: A SELECTED AND ANNOTATED LIST OF BOOKS ON INTERNATIONAL RELATIONS 1919-1962 (4 VOLS.). CONSTN FORCES COLONIAL ARMS/CONT WAR NAT/LISM PEACE ATTIT DRIVE...POLICY INT/LAW 20. PAGE 2 E0032
B35
BIBLIOG/A
DIPLOM
INT/ORG

DE TOCQUEVILLE A.,DEMOCRACY IN AMERICA (4 VOLS.) (TRANS. BY HENRY REEVE). CONSTN STRUCT LOC/G NAT/G POL/PAR PROVS ETIQUET CT/SYS MAJORITY ATTIT 18/19. PAGE 30 E0595
B35
POPULISM
MAJORIT
ORD/FREE
SOCIETY

ROBSON W.A.,CIVILISATION AND THE GROWTH OF LAW. UNIV CONSTN SOCIETY LEGIS ADJUD ATTIT PERCEPT MORAL ALL/IDEOS...CONCPT WORSHIP 20. PAGE 85 E1708
B35
LAW
IDEA/COMP
SOC

HANSON L.,GOVERNMENT AND THE PRESS 1695-1763. UK LOC/G LEGIS LICENSE CONTROL SANCTION CRIME ATTIT ORD/FREE 17/18 PARLIAMENT AMEND/I. PAGE 50 E0996
B36
LAW
JURID
PRESS
POLICY

MATTHEWS M.A.,INTERNATIONAL LAW: SELECT LIST OF WORKS IN ENGLISH ON PUBLIC INTERNATIONAL LAW: WITH COLLECTIONS OF CASES AND OPINIONS. CHRIST-17C EUR+WWI MOD/EUR WOR-45 CONSTN ADJUD JURID. PAGE 69 E1388
B36
BIBLIOG/A
INT/LAW
ATTIT
DIPLOM

SCHULZ F.,PRINCIPLES OF ROMAN LAW. CONSTN FAM NAT/G DOMIN CONTROL CT/SYS CRIME ISOLAT ATTIT ORD/FREE PWR...JURID ROME/ANC ROMAN/LAW. PAGE 89 E1783
B36
LAW
LEGIS
ADJUD
CONCPT

RUTHERFORD M.L.,THE INFLUENCE OF THE AMERICAN BAR ASSOCIATION ON PUBLIC OPINION AND LEGISLATION. USA+45 LAW CONSTN LABOR LEGIS DOMIN EDU/PROP LEGIT CT/SYS ROUTINE...TIME/SEQ 19/20 ABA. PAGE 87 E1739
B37
ATTIT
ADJUD
PROF/ORG
JURID

LERNER M.,"CONSTITUTION AND COURT AS SYMBOLS" CONSTN L37
(BMR)" USA+45 USA-45 DOMIN PWR SOVEREIGN...PSY MYTH CT/SYS
18/20 SUPREME/CT. PAGE 64 E1288 ATTIT
EDU/PROP

FRANKFURTER F.,MR. JUSTICE HOLMES AND THE SUPREME CREATE B38
COURT. USA-45 CONSTN SOCIETY FEDERAL OWN ATTIT CT/SYS
ORD/FREE PWR...POLICY JURID 20 SUPREME/CT HOLMES/OW DECISION
BILL/RIGHT. PAGE 40 E0790 LAW

HAGUE PERMANENT CT INTL JUSTIC,WORLD COURT REPORTS: INT/ORG B38
COLLECTION OF THE JUDGEMENTS ORDERS AND OPINIONS CT/SYS
VOLUME 3 1932-35. WOR-45 LAW DELIB/GP CONFER WAR DIPLOM
PEACE ATTIT...DECISION ANTHOL 20 WORLD/CT CASEBOOK. ADJUD
PAGE 49 E0976

HELLMAN F.S.,THE SUPREME COURT ISSUE: SELECTED LIST BIBLIOG/A B38
OF REFERENCES. USA-45 NAT/G CHIEF EX/STRUC JUDGE CONSTN
ATTIT...JURID 20 PRESIDENT ROOSEVLT/F SUPREME/CT. CT/SYS
PAGE 51 E1026 LAW

HOLDSWORTH W.S.,A HISTORY OF ENGLISH LAW; THE LAW B38
CENTURIES OF SETTLEMENT AND REFORM (VOL. XII). UK PROF/ORG
CONSTN STRATA LEGIS JUDGE ADJUD CT/SYS ATTIT WRITING
...JURID CONCPT BIOG GEN/LAWS 18 ENGLSH/LAW IDEA/COMP
BLACKSTN/W COMMON/LAW. PAGE 54 E1078

HOLDSWORTH W.S.,A HISTORY OF ENGLISH LAW; THE LAW B38
CENTURIES OF SETTLEMENT AND REFORM (VOL. XI). UK COLONIAL
CONSTN NAT/G EX/STRUC DIPLOM ADJUD CT/SYS LEAD LEGIS
CRIME ATTIT...INT/LAW JURID 18 CMN/WLTH PARLIAMENT PARL/PROC
ENGLSH/LAW. PAGE 54 E1079

BENES E.,INTERNATIONAL SECURITY. GERMANY UK NAT/G EUR+WWI B39
DELIB/GP PLAN BAL/PWR ATTIT ORD/FREE PWR LEAGUE/NAT INT/ORG
20 TREATY. PAGE 10 E0186 WAR

TIMASHEFF N.S.,AN INTRODUCTION TO THE SOCIOLOGY OF SOC B39
LAW. CRIME ANOMIE ATTIT DRIVE ORD/FREE...JURID PSY BIBLIOG
CONCPT. PAGE 96 E1926 PWR

WILSON G.G.,HANDBOOK OF INTERNATIONAL LAW. FUT UNIV INT/ORG B39
USA-45 WOR-45 SOCIETY LEGIT ATTIT DISPL DRIVE LAW
ALL/VALS...INT/LAW TIME/SEQ TREND. PAGE 106 E2128 CONCPT
WAR

BROWN A.D.,COMPULSORY MILITARY TRAINING: SELECT BIBLIOG/A B40
LIST OF REFERENCES (PAMPHLET). USA-45 CONSTN FORCES
VOL/ASSN COERCE 20. PAGE 16 E0311 JURID
ATTIT

CARR E.H.,THE TWENTY YEARS' CRISIS 1919-1939. FUT INT/ORG B40
WOR-45 BAL/PWR ECO/TAC LEGIT TOTALISM ATTIT DIPLOM
ALL/VALS...POLICY JURID CONCPT TIME/SEQ TREND PEACE
GEN/LAWS TOT/POP 20. PAGE 20 E0393

FLORIN J.,"BOLSHEVIST AND NATIONAL SOCIALIST LAW S40
DOCTRINES OF INTERNATIONAL LAW." EUR+WWI GERMANY ATTIT
USSR R+D INT/ORG NAT/G DIPLOM DOMIN EDU/PROP SOCISM TOTALISM
...CONCPT TIME/SEQ 20. PAGE 39 E0768 INT/LAW

CHAFEE Z. JR.,FREE SPEECH IN THE UNITED STATES. ORD/FREE B41
USA-45 ADJUD CONTROL CRIME WAR...BIBLIOG 20 CONSTN
FREE/SPEE AMEND/I SUPREME/CT. PAGE 21 E0413 ATTIT
JURID

COMM. STUDY ORGAN. PEACE,"ORGANIZATION OF PEACE." INT/ORG L41
USA-45 WOR-45 STRATA NAT/G ACT/RES DIPLOM ECO/TAC PLAN
EDU/PROP ADJUD ATTIT ORD/FREE PWR...SOC CONCPT PEACE
ANTHOL LEAGUE/NAT 20. PAGE 24 E0479

WRIGHT Q.,"FUNDAMENTAL PROBLEMS OF INTERNATIONAL INT/ORG S41
ORGANIZATION." UNIV WOR-45 STRUCT FORCES ACT/RES ATTIT
CREATE DOMIN EDU/PROP LEGIT REGION NAT/LISM PEACE
ORD/FREE PWR RESPECT SOVEREIGN...JURID SOC CONCPT
METH/CNCPT TIME/SEQ 20. PAGE 107 E2152

CARR R.K.,THE SUPREME COURT AND JUDICIAL REVIEW. CT/SYS B42
NAT/G CHIEF LEGIS OP/RES LEAD GOV/REL GP/REL ATTIT CONSTN

...POLICY DECISION 18/20 SUPREME/CT PRESIDENT JURID
CONGRESS. PAGE 20 E0394 PWR

GILLETTE J.M.,PROBLEMS OF A CHANGING SOCIAL ORDER. BIO/SOC B42
USA+45 STRATA FAM CONTROL CRIME RACE/REL HEALTH ADJUST
WEALTH...GEOG GP/COMP. PAGE 43 E0862 ATTIT
SOC/WK

SETARO F.C.,A BIBLIOGRAPHY OF THE WRITINGS OF BIBLIOG B42
ROSCOE POUND. USA-45 CT/SYS 20. PAGE 90 E1806 LAW
ATTIT
JUDGE

US LIBRARY OF CONGRESS,SOCIAL AND CULTURAL PROBLEMS BIBLIOG/A B42
IN WARTIME: APRIL 1941-MARCH 1942. WOR-45 CLIENT WAR
SECT EDU/PROP CRIME LEISURE RACE/REL STRANGE ATTIT SOC
DRIVE HEALTH...GEOG 20. PAGE 100 E2012 CULTURE

BEMIS S.F.,THE LATIN AMERICAN POLICY OF THE UNITED DIPLOM B43
STATES: AN HISTORICAL INTERPRETATION. INT/ORG AGREE SOVEREIGN
COLONIAL WAR PEACE ATTIT ORD/FREE...POLICY INT/LAW USA-45
CHARTS 18/20 MEXIC/AMER WILSON/W MONROE/DOC. L/A+17C
PAGE 10 E0185

HAGUE PERMANENT CT INTL JUSTIC,WORLD COURT REPORTS: INT/ORG B43
COLLECTION OF THE JUDGEMENTS ORDERS AND OPINIONS CT/SYS
VOLUME 4 1936-42. WOR-45 CONFER PEACE ATTIT DIPLOM
...DECISION JURID ANTHOL 20 WORLD/CT CASEBOOK. ADJUD
PAGE 49 E0977

US LIBRARY OF CONGRESS,SOCIAL AND CULTURAL PROBLEMS BIBLIOG/A B43
IN WARTIME: APRIL-DECEMBER (SUPPLEMENT 1). WOR-45 WAR
SECT EDU/PROP CRIME LEISURE CIVMIL/REL RACE/REL SOC
ATTIT DRIVE HEALTH...GEOG 20. PAGE 100 E2013 CULTURE

DE HUSZAR G.B.,NEW PERSPECTIVES ON PEACE. UNIV ATTIT B44
CULTURE SOCIETY ECO/DEV ECO/UNDEV NAT/G FORCES MYTH
CREATE ECO/TAC DOMIN ADJUD COERCE DRIVE ORD/FREE PEACE
...GEOG JURID PSY SOC CONCPT TOT/POP. PAGE 29 E0584 WAR

FRAENKEL O.K.,OUR CIVIL LIBERTIES. USA-45...JURID CONSTN B44
CONCPT 18/20 BILL/RIGHT. PAGE 39 E0781 LAW
ATTIT

BEVERIDGE W.,THE PRICE OF PEACE. GERMANY UK WOR+45 INT/ORG B45
WOR-45 NAT/G FORCES CREATE LEGIT REGION WAR ATTIT TREND
KNOWL ORD/FREE PWR...POLICY NEW/IDEA GEN/LAWS PEACE
LEAGUE/NAT 20 TREATY. PAGE 12 E0223

REVES E.,THE ANATOMY OF PEACE. WOR-45 LAW CULTURE ACT/RES B45
NAT/G PLAN TEC/DEV EDU/PROP WAR NAT/LISM ATTIT CONCPT
ALL/VALS SOVEREIGN...POLICY HUM TIME/SEQ 20. NUC/PWR
PAGE 84 E1688 PEACE

TINGSTERN H.,PEACE AND SECURITY AFTER WW II. WOR-45 INT/ORG B45
DELIB/GP TOP/EX LEGIT CT/SYS COERCE PEACE ATTIT ORD/FREE
PERCEPT...CONCPT LEAGUE/NAT 20. PAGE 96 E1927 WAR
INT/LAW

KEETON G.W.,MAKING INTERNATIONAL LAW WORK. FUT INT/ORG B46
WOR-45 NAT/G DELIB/GP FORCES LEGIT COERCE PEACE ADJUD
ATTIT RIGID/FLEX ORD/FREE PWR...JURID CONCPT INT/LAW
HIST/WRIT GEN/METH LEAGUE/NAT 20. PAGE 60 E1193

ROSS A.,TOWARDS A REALISTIC JURISPRUDENCE: A LAW B46
CRITICISM OF THE DUALISM IN LAW (TRANS. BY ANNIE I. CONCPT
FAUSBOLL). PLAN ADJUD CT/SYS ATTIT RIGID/FLEX IDEA/COMP
POPULISM...JURID PHIL/SCI LOG METH/COMP GEN/LAWS 20
SCANDINAV. PAGE 86 E1720

CANTWELL F.V.,"PUBLIC OPINION AND THE LEGISLATIVE CHARTS S46
PROCESS" USA+45 USA-45 NAT/G CT/SYS EXEC LEAD DEBATE
DECISION. PAGE 19 E0374 LEGIS
ATTIT

BORGESE G.,COMMON CAUSE. LAW CONSTN SOCIETY STRATA WOR+45 B47
ECO/DEV INT/ORG POL/PAR FORCES LEGIS TOP/EX CAP/ISM NAT/G
DIPLOM ADMIN EXEC ATTIT PWR 20. PAGE 14 E0269 SOVEREIGN
REGION

B48
CORWIN E.S.,LIBERTY AGAINST GOVERNMENT. UK USA-45   JURID
ROMAN/EMP LAW CONSTN PERS/REL OWN ATTIT 1/20   ORD/FREE
ROMAN/LAW ENGLSH/LAW AMEND/XIV. PAGE 26 E0513   CONCPT

B48
MORGENTHAL H.J.,POLITICS AMONG NATIONS: THE   DIPLOM
STRUGGLE FOR POWER AND PEACE. FUT WOR+45 INT/ORG   PEACE
OP/RES PROB/SOLV BAL/PWR CONTROL ATTIT MORAL   PWR
...INT/LAW BIBLIOG 20 COLD/WAR. PAGE 75 E1494   POLICY

S48
ALEXANDER L.,"WAR CRIMES, THEIR SOCIAL-   DRIVE
PSYCHOLOGICAL ASPECTS." EUR+WWI GERMANY LAW CULTURE   WAR
ELITES KIN POL/PAR PUB/INST FORCES DOMIN EDU/PROP
COERCE CRIME ATTIT SUPEGO HEALTH MORAL PWR FASCISM
...PSY OBS TREND GEN/LAWS NAZI 20. PAGE 3 E0061

S48
MILLER B.S.,"A LAW IS PASSED: THE ATOMIC ENERGY ACT   TEC/DEV
OF 1946." POL/PAR CHIEF CONFER DEBATE CONTROL   LEGIS
PARL/PROC ATTIT KNOWL...POLICY CONGRESS. PAGE 73   DECISION
E1457   LAW

B49
DE HUSZAR G.B.,EQUALITY IN AMERICA: THE ISSUE OF   DISCRIM
MINORITY RIGHTS. USA+45 USA-45 LAW NEIGH SCHOOL   RACE/REL
LEGIS ACT/RES CHOOSE ATTIT RESPECT...ANTHOL 20   ORD/FREE
NEGRO. PAGE 29 E0585   PROB/SOLV

B49
FRANK J.,LAW AND THE MODERN MIND. UNIV LAW CT/SYS   JURID
RATIONAL ATTIT...CONCPT 20 HOLMES/OW JURY. PAGE 40   ADJUD
E0787   IDEA/COMP
  MYTH

B49
KAFKA G.,FREIHEIT UND ANARCHIE. SECT COERCE DETER   CONCPT
WAR ATTIT...IDEA/COMP 20 NATO. PAGE 59 E1179   ORD/FREE
  JURID
  INT/ORG

B49
MARITAIN J.,HUMAN RIGHTS: COMMENTS AND   INT/ORG
INTERPRETATIONS. COM UNIV WOR+45 LAW CONSTN CULTURE   CONCPT
SOCIETY ECO/DEV ECO/UNDEV SCHOOL DELIB/GP EDU/PROP
ATTIT PERCEPT ALL/VALS...HUM SOC TREND UNESCO 20.
PAGE 68 E1365

B49
SUMMERS R.E.,FEDERAL INFORMATION CONTROLS IN   ADJUD
PEACETIME. USA+45 COM/IND DOMIN INGP/REL ATTIT   CONTROL
ORD/FREE 20. PAGE 94 E1893   EDU/PROP
  PRESS

B49
US LIBRARY OF CONGRESS,FREEDOM OF INFORMATION: BIBLIOG/A
SELECTIVE REPORT ON RECENT WRITINGS. USA+45 LAW   ORD/FREE
CONSTN ELITES EDU/PROP PRESS LOBBY WAR TOTALISM   LICENSE
ATTIT 20 UN UNESCO COLD/WAR. PAGE 101 E2018   COM/IND

S49
KIRK G.,"MATERIALS FOR THE STUDY OF INTERNATIONAL   INT/ORG
RELATIONS." FUT UNIV WOR+45 INTELL EDU/PROP ROUTINE   ACT/RES
PEACE ATTIT...INT/LAW JURID CONCPT OBS. PAGE 61   DIPLOM
E1219

B50
BURDETTE F.L.,LOBBYISTS IN ACTION (PAMPHLET).   LOBBY
CONSULT TEC/DEV INSPECT BARGAIN PARL/PROC SANCTION   ATTIT
20 CONGRESS. PAGE 17 E0329   POLICY
  LAW

B50
FRAGA IRIBARNE M.,RAZAS Y RACISMO IN NORTEAMERICA.   RACE/REL
USA+45 CONSTN STRATA NAT/G PROVS ATTIT...SOC CONCPT   JURID
19/20 NEGRO. PAGE 39 E0783   LAW
  DISCRIM

B50
HURST J.W.,THE GROWTH OF AMERICAN LAW; THE LAW   LAW
MAKERS. USA-45 LOC/G NAT/G DELIB/GP JUDGE ADJUD   LEGIS
ADMIN ATTIT PWR...POLICY JURID BIBLIOG 18/20   CONSTN
CONGRESS SUPREME/CT ABA PRESIDENT. PAGE 56 E1115   CT/SYS

B50
LOWENTHAL M.,THE FEDERAL BUREAU OF INVESTIGATION.   FORCES
USA+45 SOCIETY ADMIN TASK CRIME INGP/REL...CRIMLGY   NAT/G
20 FBI ESPIONAGE. PAGE 67 E1329   ATTIT
  LAW

B50
MACIVER R.M.,GREAT EXPRESSIONS OF HUMAN RIGHTS. LAW   UNIV
CONSTN CULTURE INTELL SOCIETY R+D INT/ORG ATTIT   CONCPT
DRIVE...JURID OBS HIST/WRIT GEN/LAWS. PAGE 67 E1340

B50
MERRIAM C.E.,THE AMERICAN PARTY SYSTEM; AN   POL/PAR
INTRODUCTION TO THE STUDY OF POLITICAL PARTIES IN   CHOOSE
THE UNITED STATES (4TH ED.). USA+45 USA-45 LAW   SUFF
FINAN LOC/G NAT/G PROVS LEAD PARTIC CRIME ATTIT   REPRESENT
18/20 NEGRO CONGRESS PRESIDENT. PAGE 72 E1442

B50
MONPIED E.,BIBLIOGRAPHIE FEDERALISTE: OUVRAGES   BIBLIOG/A
CHOISIS (VOL. I, MIMEOGRAPHED PAPER). EUR+WWI   FEDERAL
DIPLOM ADMIN REGION ATTIT PACIFISM SOCISM...INT/LAW   CENTRAL
19/20. PAGE 74 E1486   INT/ORG

B50
STONE J.,THE PROVINCE AND FUNCTION OF LAW. UNIV   INT/ORG
WOR+45 WOR-45 CULTURE INTELL SOCIETY ECO/DEV   LAW
ECO/UNDEV NAT/G LEGIT ROUTINE ATTIT PERCEPT PERSON
...JURID CONCPT GEN/LAWS GEN/METH 20. PAGE 94 E1877

C50
NUMELIN R.,"THE BEGINNINGS OF DIPLOMACY." INT/TRADE   DIPLOM
WAR GP/REL PEACE STRANGE ATTIT...INT/LAW CONCPT   KIN
BIBLIOG. PAGE 78 E1559   CULTURE
  LAW

N51
MONPIED E.,FEDERALIST BIBLIOGRAPHY: ARTICLES AND   BIBLIOG/A
DOCUMENTS PUBLISHED IN BRITISH PERIODICALS   INT/ORG
1945-1951 (MIMEOGRAPHED). EUR+WWI UK WOR+45 DIPLOM   FEDERAL
REGION ATTIT SOCISM...INT/LAW 20. PAGE 74 E1487   CENTRAL

B51
HUXLEY J.,FREEDOM AND CULTURE. UNIV LAW SOCIETY R+D   CULTURE
ACADEM SCHOOL CREATE SANCTION ATTIT KNOWL...HUM   ORD/FREE
ANTHOL 20. PAGE 56 E1118   PHIL/SCI
  IDEA/COMP

L51
MANGONE G.,"THE IDEA AND PRACTICE OF WORLD   INT/ORG
GOVERNMENT." FUT WOR+45 WOR-45 ECO/DEV LEGIS CREATE   SOCIETY
LEGIT ROUTINE ATTIT MORAL PWR WEALTH...CONCPT   INT/LAW
GEN/LAWS 20. PAGE 68 E1358

S51
LEEK J.H.,"TREASON AND THE CONSTITUTION" (BMR)"   CONSTN
USA+45 USA-45 EDU/PROP COLONIAL CT/SYS REV WAR   JURID
ATTIT...TREND 18/20 SUPREME/CT CON/INTERP SMITH/ACT   CRIME
COMMON/LAW. PAGE 64 E1278   NAT/G

B52
BENTHAM A.,HANDBOOK OF POLITICAL FALLACIES. FUT   POL/PAR
MOD/EUR LAW INTELL LOC/G MUNIC NAT/G DELIB/GP LEGIS
CREATE EDU/PROP CT/SYS ATTIT RIGID/FLEX KNOWL PWR
...RELATIV PSY SOC CONCPT SELF/OBS TREND STERTYP
TOT/POP. PAGE 10 E0189

B52
FLECHTHEIM O.K.,FUNDAMENTALS OF POLITICAL SCIENCE.   NAT/G
WOR+45 WOR-45 LAW POL/PAR EX/STRUC LEGIS ADJUD   DIPLOM
ATTIT PWR...INT/LAW. PAGE 38 E0760   IDEA/COMP
  CONSTN

B52
FORSTER A.,THE TROUBLE MAKERS. USA+45 LAW CULTURE   DISCRIM
SOCIETY STRUCT VOL/ASSN CROWD GP/REL MORAL...PSY   SECT
SOC CONCPT 20 NEGRO JEWS. PAGE 39 E0771   RACE/REL
  ATTIT

B52
GELLHORN W.,THE STATES AND SUBVERSION. USA+45   PROVS
USA-45 LOC/G DELIB/GP LEGIS EDU/PROP LEGIT CT/SYS   JURID
REGION PEACE ATTIT ORD/FREE SOCISM...INT CON/ANAL
20 CALIFORNIA MARYLAND ILLINOIS MICHIGAN NEW/YORK.
PAGE 43 E0845

B52
HOLDSWORTH W.S.,A HISTORY OF ENGLISH LAW; THE   LAW
CENTURIES OF SETTLEMENT AND REFORM, 1701-1875 (VOL.   CONSTN
XIII). UK POL/PAR PROF/ORG LEGIS JUDGE WRITING   IDEA/COMP
ATTIT...JURID CONCPT BIOG GEN/LAWS 18/19 PARLIAMENT   CT/SYS
REFORMERS ENGLSH/LAW COMMON/LAW. PAGE 54 E1080

B52
LIPPMANN W.,ISOLATION AND ALLIANCES: AN AMERICAN   DIPLOM
SPEAKS TO THE BRITISH. USA+45 USA-45 INT/ORG AGREE   SOVEREIGN
COERCE DETER WAR PEACE MORAL 20 TREATY INTERVENT.   COLONIAL
PAGE 65 E1301   ATTIT

B52
PASCUAL R.R.,PARTYLESS DEMOCRACY. PHILIPPINE   POL/PAR
BARGAIN LOBBY CHOOSE EFFICIENCY ATTIT 20. PAGE 80   ORD/FREE
E1600   JURID
  ECO/UNDEV

B53
AYMARD A.,HISTOIRE GENERALE DES CIVILISATIONS (7   BIBLIOG/A

VOLS.). WOR+45 WOR-45 LAW SECT CREATE ATTIT
...ART/METH WORSHIP. PAGE 6 E0123
SOC

B53
SECKLER-HUDSON C.,BIBLIOGRAPHY ON PUBLIC
ADMINISTRATION (4TH ED.). USA+45 LAW POL/PAR
DELIB/GP BUDGET ADJUD LOBBY GOV/REL GP/REL ATTIT
...JURID 20. PAGE 90 E1800
BIBLIOG/A
ADMIN
NAT/G
MGT

B54
NUSSBAUM D.,A CONCISE HISTORY OF THE LAW OF
NATIONS. ASIA CHRIST-17C EUR+WWI ISLAM MEDIT-7
MOD/EUR S/ASIA UNIV WOR+45 WOR-45 SOCIETY STRUCT
EXEC ATTIT ALL/VALS...CONCPT HIST/WRIT TIME/SEQ.
PAGE 78 E1560
INT/ORG
LAW
PEACE
INT/LAW

L54
NICOLSON H.,"THE EVOLUTION OF DIPLOMATIC METHOD."
CHRIST-17C EUR+WWI FRANCE FUT ITALY MEDIT-7 MOD/EUR
USA+45 USA-45 LAW NAT/G CREATE EDU/PROP LEGIT PEACE
ATTIT ORD/FREE RESPECT SOVEREIGN. PAGE 77 E1548
RIGID/FLEX
METH/CNCPT
DIPLOM

B55
BIBLIOGRAPHY ON THE COMMUNIST PROBLEM IN THE UNITED
STATES. USA-45 PRESS ADJUD ATTIT...BIOG 20. PAGE 2
E0033
BIBLIOG/A
MARXISM
POL/PAR
USA+45

B55
BERNSTEIN M.H.,REGULATING BUSINESS BY INDEPENDENT
COMMISSION. USA+45 USA-45 LG/CO CHIEF LEGIS
PROB/SOLV ADJUD SANCTION GP/REL ATTIT...TIME/SEQ
19/20 MONOPOLY PRESIDENT CONGRESS. PAGE 11 E0214
DELIB/GP
CONTROL
CONSULT

B55
COMM. STUDY ORGAN. PEACE,REPORTS. WOR-45 ECO/DEV
ECO/UNDEV VOL/ASSN CONSULT FORCES PLAN TEC/DEV
DOMIN EDU/PROP NUC/PWR ATTIT PWR WEALTH...JURID
STERTYP FAO ILO 20 UN. PAGE 24 E0481
WOR+45
INT/ORG
ARMS/CONT

B55
KHADDURI M.,WAR AND PEACE IN THE LAW OF ISLAM.
CONSTN CULTURE SOCIETY STRATA NAT/G PROVS SECT
FORCES TOP/EX CREATE DOMIN EDU/PROP ADJUD COERCE
ATTIT RIGID/FLEX ALL/VALS...CONCPT TIME/SEQ TOT/POP
VAL/FREE. PAGE 61 E1209
ISLAM
JURID
PEACE
WAR

B55
MAZZINI J.,THE DUTIES OF MAN. MOD/EUR LAW SOCIETY
FAM NAT/G POL/PAR SECT VOL/ASSN EX/STRUC ACT/RES
CREATE REV PEACE ATTIT ALL/VALS...GEN/LAWS WORK 19.
PAGE 70 E1396
SUPEGO
CONCPT
NAT/LISM

B55
UN HEADQUARTERS LIBRARY,BIBLIOGRAPHIE DE LA CHARTE
DES NATIONS UNIES. CHINA/COM KOREA WOR+45 VOL/ASSN
CONFER ADMIN COERCE PEACE ATTIT ORD/FREE SOVEREIGN
...INT/LAW 20 UNESCO UN. PAGE 97 E1953
BIBLIOG/A
INT/ORG
DIPLOM

B55
WRONG D.H.,AMERICAN AND CANADIAN VIEWPOINTS. CANADA
USA+45 CONSTN STRATA FAM SECT WORKER ECO/TAC
EDU/PROP ADJUD MARRIAGE...IDEA/COMP 20. PAGE 108
E2161
DIPLOM
ATTIT
NAT/COMP
CULTURE

B56
ALEXANDER F.,THE CRIMINAL, THE JUDGE, AND THE
PUBLIC. LAW CULTURE CONSULT LEGIT ADJUD SANCTION
ORD/FREE 20. PAGE 3 E0060
CRIME
CRIMLGY
PSY
ATTIT

B56
CARLSTON K.S.,LAW AND STRUCTURES OF SOCIAL ACTION.
LAW SOCIETY ECO/DEV DIPLOM CONTROL ATTIT...DECISION
CONCPT 20. PAGE 19 E0379
JURID
INT/LAW
INGP/REL
STRUCT

B56
HOGAN J.D.,AMERICAN SOCIAL LEGISLATION. USA+45 FAM
AGE/Y ATTIT...JURID CONCPT TREND. PAGE 53 E1065
STRUCT
RECEIVE
LEGIS
LABOR

B56
KUPER L.,PASSIVE RESISTANCE IN SOUTH AFRICA.
SOUTH/AFR LAW NAT/G POL/PAR VOL/ASSN DISCRIM
...POLICY SOC AUD/VIS 20. PAGE 62 E1237
ORD/FREE
RACE/REL
ATTIT

B56
LASLETT P.,PHILOSOPHY, POLITICS AND SOCIETY. UNIV
CRIME SOVEREIGN...JURID PHIL/SCI ANTHOL PLATO
NATURL/LAW. PAGE 63 E1260
CONSTN
ATTIT
CONCPT
GEN/LAWS

S56
POTTER P.B.,"NEUTRALITY, 1955." WOR+45 WOR-45
NEUTRAL

INT/ORG NAT/G WAR ATTIT...POLICY IDEA/COMP 17/20
LEAGUE/NAT UN COLD/WAR. PAGE 81 E1631
INT/LAW
DIPLOM
CONCPT

C56
AUMANN F.R.,"THE ISTRUMENTALITIES OF JUSTICE: THEIR
FORMS, FUNCTIONS, AND LIMITATIONS." WOR+45 WOR-45
JUDGE PROB/SOLV ROUTINE ATTIT...BIBLIOG 20. PAGE 6
E0118
JURID
ADMIN
CT/SYS
ADJUD

C56
FALL B.B.,"THE VIET-MINH REGIME." VIETNAM LAW
ECO/UNDEV POL/PAR FORCES DOMIN WAR ATTIT MARXISM
...BIOG PREDICT BIBLIOG/A 20. PAGE 36 E0720
NAT/G
ADMIN
EX/STRUC
LEAD

C56
TYLER P.,"IMMIGRATION AND THE UNITED STATES."
USA+45 USA-45 LAW SECT INGP/REL RACE/REL NAT/LISM
ATTIT...BIBLIOG SOC/INTEG 19/20. PAGE 97 E1949
CULTURE
GP/REL
DISCRIM

B57
BLOOMFIELD L.M.,EGYPT, ISRAEL AND THE GULF OF
AQABA: IN INTERNATIONAL LAW. LAW NAT/G CONSULT
FORCES PLAN ECO/TAC ROUTINE COERCE ATTIT DRIVE
PERCEPT PERSON RIGID/FLEX LOVE PWR WEALTH...GEOG
CONCPT MYTH TREND. PAGE 13 E0250
ISLAM
INT/LAW
UAR

B57
COSSIO C.,LA POLITICA COMO CONCIENCIA; MEDITACION
SOBRE LA ARGENTINA DE 1955. WOR+45 LEGIS EDU/PROP
PARL/PROC PARTIC ATTIT PWR CATHISM 20 ARGEN
PERON/JUAN. PAGE 26 E0517
POL/PAR
REV
TOTALISM
JURID

B57
DE VISSCHER C.,THEORY AND REALITY IN PUBLIC
INTERNATIONAL LAW. WOR+45 WOR-45 SOCIETY NAT/G
CT/SYS ATTIT MORAL ORD/FREE PWR...JURID CONCPT
METH/CNCPT TIME/SEQ GEN/LAWS LEAGUE/NAT TOT/POP
VAL/FREE COLD/WAR. PAGE 30 E0599
INT/ORG
LAW
INT/LAW

B57
DONALDSON A.G.,SOME COMPARATIVE ASPECTS OF IRISH
LAW. IRELAND NAT/G DIPLOM ADMIN CT/SYS LEAD ATTIT
SOVEREIGN...JURID BIBLIOG/A 12/20 CMN/WLTH. PAGE 32
E0635
CONSTN
LAW
NAT/COMP
INT/LAW

B57
HISS A.,IN THE COURT OF PUBLIC OPINION. USA+45
DELIB/GP LEGIS LEGIT CT/SYS ATTIT 20 DEPT/STATE
NIXON/RM HUAC HISS/ALGER. PAGE 53 E1053
CRIME
MARXISM
BIOG
ADJUD

B57
LEVONTIN A.V.,THE MYTH OF INTERNATIONAL SECURITY: A
JURIDICAL AND CRITICAL ANALYSIS. FUT WOR+45 WOR-45
LAW NAT/G VOL/ASSN ACT/RES BAL/PWR ATTIT ORD/FREE
...JURID METH/CNCPT TIME/SEQ TREND STERTYP 20.
PAGE 64 E1289
INT/ORG
INT/LAW
SOVEREIGN
MYTH

B57
POUND R.,THE DEVELOPMENT OF CONSTITUTIONAL
GUARANTEES OF LIBERTY. UK USA-45 CHIEF COLONIAL REV
...JURID CONCPT 15/20. PAGE 82 E1638
LAW
CONSTN
ORD/FREE
ATTIT

B57
SINCLAIR T.C.,THE POLITICS OF JUDICIAL REVIEW
1937-1957. USA+45 USA-45 NAT/G 20 SUPREME/CT
CIVIL/LIB. PAGE 91 E1830
JURID
ATTIT
ORD/FREE
RACE/REL

B57
US COMMISSION GOVT SECURITY,RECOMMENDATIONS; AREA:
IMMIGRANT PROGRAM. USA+45 LAW WORKER DIPLOM
EDU/PROP WRITING ADMIN PEACE ATTIT...CONCPT ANTHOL
20 MIGRATION SUBVERT. PAGE 99 E1981
POLICY
CONTROL
PLAN
NAT/G

B57
US SENATE SPEC COMM POLIT ACT,REPORT OF SPECIAL
COMMITTEE TO INVESTIGATE POLITICAL ACTIVITIES,
LOBBYING, AND CAMPAIGN CONTRIBUTIONS. USA+45
BARGAIN CRIME ATTIT...DECISION 20 CONGRESS.
PAGE 103 E2061
LOBBY
LAW
ECO/TAC
PARL/PROC

S57
KNEIER C.M.,"MISLEADING THE VOTERS." CONSTN LEAD
CHOOSE PERS/REL. PAGE 61 E1224
MUNIC
REPRESENT
LAW
ATTIT

B58
ALLEN C.K.,LAW IN THE MAKING. LEGIS ATTIT ORD/FREE
SOVEREIGN POPULISM...JURID IDEA/COMP NAT/COMP
GEN/LAWS 20 ENGLSH/LAW. PAGE 4 E0069
LAW
CREATE
CONSTN
SOCIETY

BOWETT D.W.,SELF-DEFENSE IN INTERNATIONAL LAW. EUR+WWI MOD/EUR WOR+45 WOR-45 SOCIETY INT/ORG CONSULT DIPLOM LEGIT COERCE ATTIT ORD/FREE...JURID 20 UN. PAGE 14 E0276
ADJUD CONCPT WAR INT/LAW
B58

CARPENTER W.S.,FOUNDATIONS OF MODERN JURISPRUDENCE. UNIV PROB/SOLV ADJUD CT/SYS CRIME ATTIT...CONCPT 18/20. PAGE 20 E0388
LAW JURID
B58

CAUGHEY J.W.,IN CLEAR AND PRESENT DANGER. USA+45 ADJUD COERCE ATTIT AUTHORIT...POLICY 20 COLD/WAR MCCARTHY/J. PAGE 21 E0408
NAT/G CONTROL DOMIN ORD/FREE
B58

HERRMANN K.,DAS STAATSDENKEN BEI LEIBNIZ. GP/REL ATTIT ORD/FREE...CONCPT IDEA/COMP 17 LEIBNITZ/G CHURCH/STA. PAGE 52 E1034
NAT/G JURID SECT EDU/PROP
B58

MACKENZIE W.J.M.,FREE ELECTIONS: AN ELEMENTARY TEXTBOOK. WOR+45 NAT/G POL/PAR LEGIS TOP/EX EDU/PROP LEGIT CT/SYS ATTIT PWR...OBS CHARTS STERTYP T CONGRESS PARLIAMENT 20. PAGE 67 E1342
EX/STRUC CHOOSE
B58

MARTIN L.J.,INTERNATIONAL PROPAGANDA: ITS LEGAL AND DIPLOMATIC CONTROL. UK USA+45 USSR CONSULT DELIB/GP DOMIN CONTROL 20. PAGE 69 E1373
EDU/PROP DIPLOM INT/LAW ATTIT
B58

RUSSELL R.B.,A HISTORY OF THE UNITED NATIONS CHARTER: THE ROLE OF THE UNITED STATES. SOCIETY NAT/G CONSULT DOMIN LEGIT ATTIT ORD/FREE PWR ...POLICY JURID CONCPT UN LEAGUE/NAT. PAGE 87 E1737
USA-45 INT/ORG CONSTN
B58

SCHOEDER P.W.,THE AXIS ALLIANCE AND JAPANESE- AMERICAN RELATIONS 1941. ASIA GERMANY UK USA-45 PEACE ATTIT...POLICY BIBLIOG 20 CHINJAP TREATY. PAGE 88 E1763
AGREE DIPLOM WAR
B58

SOC OF COMP LEGIS AND INT LAW,THE LAW OF THE SEA... (PAMPHLET). WOR+45 NAT/G INT/TRADE ADJUD CONTROL NUC/PWR WAR PEACE ATTIT ORD/FREE...JURID CHARTS 20 UN TREATY RESOURCE/N. PAGE 92 E1850
INT/LAW INT/ORG DIPLOM SEA
B58

SPITZ D.,DEMOCRACY AND THE CHALLANGE OF POWER. FUT USA+45 USA-45 LAW SOCIETY STRUCT LOC/G POL/PAR PROVS DELIB/GP EX/STRUC LEGIS TOP/EX ACT/RES CREATE DOMIN EDU/PROP LEGIT ADJUD ADMIN ATTIT DRIVE MORAL ORD/FREE TOT/POP. PAGE 93 E1862
NAT/G PWR
B58

WHITNEY S.N.,ANTITRUST POLICIES: AMERICAN EXPERIENCE IN TWENTY INDUSTRIES. USA+45 USA-45 LAW DELIB/GP LEGIS ADJUD CT/SYS GOV/REL ATTIT...ANTHOL 20 MONOPOLY CASEBOOK. PAGE 106 E2119
INDUS CONTROL LG/CO MARKET
B58

WOOD J.E.,CHURCH AND STATE IN SCRIPTURE HISTORY AND CONSTITUTIONAL LAW. LAW CONSTN SOCIETY PROVS VOL/ASSN BAL/PWR COLONIAL CT/SYS ATTIT...BIBLIOG 20 SUPREME/CT CHURCH/STA BIBLE. PAGE 107 E2142
GP/REL SECT NAT/G ADJUD
B58

BEVAN W.,"JURY BEHAVIOR AS A FUNCTION OF THE PRESTIGE OF THE FOREMAN AND THE NATURE OF HIS LEADERSHIP" (BMR)" DELIB/GP DOMIN ADJUD LEAD PERS/REL ATTIT...PSY STAT INT QU CHARTS SOC/EXP 20 JURY. PAGE 11 E0221
PERSON EDU/PROP DECISION CT/SYS
L58

INT. SOC. SCI. BULL.,"TECHNIQUES OF MEDIATION AND CONCILIATION." EUR+WWI USA+45 SOCIETY INDUS INT/ORG LABOR NAT/G LEGIS DIPLOM EDU/PROP CHOOSE ATTIT RIGID/FLEX...JURID CONCPT GEN/LAWS 20. PAGE 57 E1129
VOL/ASSN DELIB/GP INT/LAW
L58

CRESSEY D.R.,"ACHIEVEMENT OF AN UNSTATED ORGANIZATIONAL GOAL: AN OBSERVATION ON PRISONS." OP/RES PROB/SOLV PERS/REL ANOMIE ATTIT ROLE RESPECT CRIMLGY. PAGE 28 E0546
PUB/INST CLIENT NEIGH INGP/REL
S58

FISHER F.M.,"THE MATHEMATICAL ANALYSIS OF SUPREME COURT DECISIONS: THE USE AND ABUSE OF QUANTITATIVE
PROB/SOLV CT/SYS
S58

METHODS." USA+45 LAW EX/STRUC LEGIS JUDGE ROUTINE ATTIT DECISION. PAGE 38 E0757
JURID MATH

RIKER W.H.,"THE PARADOX OF VOTING AND CONGRESSIONAL RULES FOR VOTING ON AMENDMENTS." LAW DELIB/GP EX/STRUC PROB/SOLV CONFER DEBATE EFFICIENCY ATTIT HOUSE/REP CONGRESS SENATE. PAGE 85 E1700
PARL/PROC DECISION LEGIS RATIONAL
S58

STAAR R.F.,"ELECTIONS IN COMMUNIST POLAND." EUR+WWI SOCIETY INT/ORG NAT/G POL/PAR LEGIS ACT/RES ECO/TAC EDU/PROP ADJUD ADMIN ROUTINE COERCE TOTALISM ATTIT ORD/FREE PWR 20. PAGE 93 E1864
COM CHOOSE POLAND
S58

FRIEDRICH C.J.,"AUTHORITY, REASON AND DISCRETION" IN C. FRIEDRICH'S AUTHORITY (BMR)" UNIV EX/STRUC ADJUD ADMIN CONTROL INGP/REL ATTIT PERSON PWR. PAGE 41 E0807
AUTHORIT CHOOSE RATIONAL PERS/REL
C58

ANDERSON J.N.D.,ISLAMIC LAW IN THE MODERN WORLD. FAM KIN SECT LEGIT ADJUD ATTIT DRIVE...TIME/SEQ TREND GEN/LAWS 20 MUSLIM. PAGE 5 E0089
ISLAM JURID
B59

BRIGGS A.,CHARTIST STUDIES. UK LAW NAT/G WORKER EDU/PROP COERCE SUFF GP/REL ATTIT...ANTHOL 19. PAGE 15 E0300
INDUS STRATA LABOR POLICY
B59

CORBETT P.E.,LAW IN DIPLOMACY. UK USA+45 USSR CONSTN SOCIETY INT/ORG JUDGE LEGIT ATTIT ORD/FREE TOT/POP LEAGUE/NAT 20. PAGE 26 E0507
NAT/G ADJUD JURID DIPLOM
B59

FRIEDMANN W.G.,LAW IN A CHANGING SOCIETY. FUT WOR+45 WOR-45 LAW SOCIETY STRUCT INT/TRADE LEGIT ATTIT BIO/SOC HEALTH ORD/FREE SOVEREIGN...CONCPT GEN/LAWS ILO 20. PAGE 41 E0803
SOC JURID
B59

GINZBURG B.,REDEDICATION TO FREEDOM. DELIB/GP LEGIS ATTIT MARXISM 20 SUPREME/CT CON/INTERP HUAC AMEND/I FBI. PAGE 44 E0871
JURID ORD/FREE CONSTN NAT/G
B59

GREENSPAN M.,THE MODERN LAW OF LAND WARFARE. WOR+45 INT/ORG NAT/G DELIB/GP FORCES ATTIT...POLICY HYPO/EXP STERTYP 20. PAGE 46 E0911
ADJUD PWR WAR
B59

HALEY A.G.,FIRST COLLOQUIUM ON THE LAW OF OUTER SPACE. WOR+45 INT/ORG ACT/RES PLAN BAL/PWR CONFER ATTIT PWR...POLICY JURID CHARTS ANTHOL 20. PAGE 49 E0979
SPACE LAW SOVEREIGN CONTROL
B59

HARVARD UNIVERSITY LAW SCHOOL,INTERNATIONAL PROBLEMS OF FINANCIAL PROTECTION AGAINST NUCLEAR RISK. WOR+45 NAT/G DELIB/GP PROB/SOLV DIPLOM CONTROL ATTIT...POLICY INT/LAW MATH 20. PAGE 51 E1009
NUC/PWR ADJUD INDUS FINAN
B59

KIRCHHEIMER O.,GEGENWARTSPROBLEME DER ASYLGEWAHRUNG. DOMIN GP/REL ATTIT...NAT/COMP 20. PAGE 61 E1217
DIPLOM INT/LAW JURID ORD/FREE
B59

PO414COLUMBIA BUR OF APP SOC R,ATTITUDES OF PROMINENT AMERICANS TOWARD "WORLD PEACE THROUGH WORLD LAW" (SUPRA-NATL ORGANIZATION FOR WAR PREVENTION). USA+45 USSR ELITES FORCES PLAN PROB/SOLV CONTROL WAR PWR...POLICY SOC QU IDEA/COMP 20 UN. PAGE 82 E1644
ATTIT ACT/RES INT/LAW STAT
B59

REIFF H.,THE UNITED STATES AND THE TREATY LAW OF THE SEA. USA+45 USA-45 SEA SOCIETY INT/ORG CONSULT DELIB/GP LEGIS DIPLOM LEGIT ATTIT ORD/FREE PWR WEALTH...GEOG JURID TOT/POP 20 TREATY. PAGE 84 E1681
ADJUD INT/LAW
B59

SCHUBERT G.A.,QUANTITATIVE ANALYSIS OF JUDICIAL BEHAVIOR. ADJUD LEAD CHOOSE INGP/REL MAJORITY ATTIT ...DECISION JURID CHARTS GAME SIMUL SUPREME/CT. PAGE 89 E1780
JUDGE CT/SYS PERSON QUANT
B59

SISSON C.H.,THE SPIRIT OF BRITISH ADMINISTRATION
AND SOME EUROPEAN COMPARISONS. FRANCE GERMANY/W
SWEDEN UK LAW EX/STRUC INGP/REL EFFICIENCY ORD/FREE
...DECISION 20. PAGE 91 E1835
GOV/COMP
ADMIN
ELITES
ATTIT
B59

DWYER R.J.,"THE ADMINISTRATIVE ROLE IN
DESEGREGATION." USA+45 LAW PROB/SOLV LEAD RACE/REL
ISOLAT STRANGE ROLE...POLICY SOC/INTEG MISSOURI
NEGRO CIV/RIGHTS. PAGE 34 E0668
ADMIN
SCHOOL
DISCRIM
ATTIT
S59

JENKS C.W.,"THE CHALLENGE OF UNIVERSALITY." FUT
UNIV CONSTN CULTURE CONSULT CREATE PLAN LEGIT ATTIT
MORAL ORD/FREE RESPECT...MAJORIT JURID 20. PAGE 58
E1155
INT/ORG
LAW
PEACE
INT/LAW
S59

MASON A.T.,"THE SUPREME COURT: TEMPLE AND FORUM"
(BMR)" USA+45 USA-45 CONSTN DELIB/GP RACE/REL
MAJORITY ORD/FREE...DECISION SOC/INTEG 19/20
SUPREME/CT WARRN/EARL CIV/RIGHTS. PAGE 69 E1377
CT/SYS
JURID
PWR
ATTIT
S59

MURPHY W.F.,"LOWER COURT CHECKS ON SUPREME COURT
POWER" (BMR)" USA+45 NAT/G PROVS SCHOOL GOV/REL
RACE/REL DISCRIM ATTIT...DECISION JURID 20
SUPREME/CT NEGRO. PAGE 75 E1508
CT/SYS
BAL/PWR
CONTROL
ADJUD
S59

STONE J.,"CONFLICT MANAGEMENT THROUGH CONTEMPORARY
INTERNATIONAL LAW AND ORGANIZATION." WOR+45 LAW
NAT/G CREATE BAL/PWR DOMIN LEGIT ROUTINE COERCE
ATTIT ORD/FREE PWR SOVEREIGN...JURID 20. PAGE 94
E1880
INT/ORG
INT/LAW
S59

SUTTON F.X.,"REPRESENTATION AND THE NATURE OF
POLITICAL SYSTEMS." UNIV WOR-45 CULTURE SOCIETY
STRATA INT/ORG FORCES JUDGE DOMIN LEGIT EXEC REGION
REPRESENT ATTIT ORD/FREE RESPECT...SOC HIST/WRIT
TIME/SEQ. PAGE 95 E1896
NAT/G
CONCPT
S59

ADRIAN C.R.,STATE AND LOCAL GOVERNMENTS: A STUDY IN
THE POLITICAL PROCESS. USA+45 LAW FINAN MUNIC
POL/PAR LEGIS ADJUD EXEC CHOOSE REPRESENT. PAGE 3
E0051
LOC/G
PROVS
GOV/REL
ATTIT
B60

BAKER G.E.,STATE CONSTITUTIONS - REAPPORTIONMENT.
USA+45 USA-45 CONSTN CHOOSE ATTIT ORD/FREE...JURID
20. PAGE 7 E0138
APPORT
REPRESENT
PROVS
LEGIS
B60

BLANSHARD P.,GOD AND MAN IN WASHINGTON. USA+45
CHIEF LEGIS LEGIT CT/SYS PRIVIL ATTIT ORD/FREE
...POLICY CONCPT 20 SUPREME/CT CONGRESS PRESIDENT
CHURCH/STA. PAGE 12 E0242
NAT/G
SECT
GP/REL
POL/PAR
B60

BORGATTA E.F.,SOCIAL WORKERS' PERCEPTIONS OF
CLIENTS. SERV/IND ROUTINE PERS/REL DRIVE PERSON
RESPECT...SOC PERS/COMP 20. PAGE 14 E0268
SOC/WK
ATTIT
CLIENT
PROB/SOLV
B60

CLARK G.,WORLD PEACE THROUGH WORLD LAW. FUT WOR+45
CONSULT FORCES ACT/RES CREATE PLAN ADMIN ROUTINE
ARMS/CONT DETER ATTIT PWR...JURID VAL/FREE UNESCO
20 UN. PAGE 23 E0449
INT/ORG
LAW
PEACE
INT/LAW
B60

DUMON F.,LA COMMUNAUTE FRANCO-AFRO-MALGACHE: SES
ORIGINES, SES INSTITUTIONS, SON EVOLUTION. FRANCE
MADAGASCAR POL/PAR DIPLOM ADMIN ATTIT...TREND T 20.
PAGE 33 E0657
JURID
INT/ORG
AFR
CONSTN
B60

GOLDSEN J.M.,INTERNATIONAL POLITICAL IMPLICATIONS
OF ACTIVITIES IN OUTER SPACE. FUT USA+45 WOR+45 AIR
LAW ACT/RES LEGIT ATTIT KNOWL ORD/FREE PWR...CONCPT
20. PAGE 44 E0879
R+D
SPACE
B60

JENNINGS R.,PROGRESS OF INTERNATIONAL LAW. FUT
WOR+45 WOR-45 SOCIETY NAT/G VOL/ASSN DELIB/GP
DIPLOM EDU/PROP LEGIT COERCE ATTIT DRIVE MORAL
ORD/FREE...JURID CONCPT OBS TIME/SEQ TREND
GEN/LAWS. PAGE 58 E1164
INT/ORG
LAW
INT/LAW
B60

LENCZOWSKI G.,OIL AND STATE IN THE MIDDLE EAST. FUT
IRAN LAW ECO/UNDEV EXTR/IND NAT/G TOP/EX PLAN
ISLAM
INDUS
B60

TEC/DEV ECO/TAC LEGIT ADMIN COERCE ATTIT ALL/VALS
PWR...CHARTS 20. PAGE 64 E1283
NAT/LISM

MENDELSON W.,CAPITALISM, DEMOCRACY, AND THE SUPREME
COURT. USA+45 USA-45 CONSTN DIPLOM GOV/REL ATTIT
ORD/FREE LAISSEZ...POLICY CHARTS PERS/COMP 18/20
SUPREME/CT MARSHALL/J HOLMES/OW TANEY/RB FIELD/JJ.
PAGE 72 E1437
JUDGE
CT/SYS
JURID
NAT/G
B60

MOCTEZUMA A.P.,EL CONFLICTO RELIGIOSO DE 1926 (2ND
ED.). L/A+17C LAW NAT/G LOBBY COERCE GP/REL ATTIT
...POLICY 20 MEXIC/AMER CHURCH/STA. PAGE 74 E1476
SECT
ORD/FREE
DISCRIM
REV
B60

PAUL A.M.,CONSERVATIVE CRISIS AND THE RULE OF LAW.
USA-45 LABOR WORKER ATTIT ORD/FREE CONSERVE LAISSEZ
...DECISION JURID 19 SUPREME/CT. PAGE 80 E1603
CONSTN
ADJUD
STRUCT
PROF/ORG
B60

PICKLES D.,THE FIFTH FRENCH REPUBLIC. ALGERIA
FRANCE CHOOSE GOV/REL ATTIT CONSERVE...CHARTS 20
DEGAULLE/C. PAGE 80 E1615
CONSTN
ADJUD
NAT/G
EFFICIENCY
B60

PRICE D.,THE SECRETARY OF STATE. USA+45 CONSTN
ELITES INTELL CHIEF EX/STRUC TOP/EX LEGIT ATTIT PWR
SKILL...DECISION 20 CONGRESS. PAGE 82 E1650
CONSULT
DIPLOM
INT/LAW
B60

SCHEIBER H.N.,THE WILSON ADMINISTRATION AND CIVIL
LIBERTIES 1917-1921. LAW GOV/REL ATTIT 20 WILSON/W
CIVIL/LIB. PAGE 87 E1754
ORD/FREE
WAR
NAT/G
CONTROL
B60

STEIN E.,AMERICAN ENTERPRISE IN THE EUROPEAN COMMON
MARKET: A LEGAL PROFILE. EUR+WWI FUT USA+45 SOCIETY
STRUCT ECO/DEV NAT/G VOL/ASSN CONSULT PLAN TEC/DEV
ECO/TAC INT/TRADE ADMIN ATTIT RIGID/FLEX PWR...MGT
NEW/IDEA STAT TREND COMPUT/IR SIMUL EEC 20. PAGE 93
E1867
MARKET
ADJUD
INT/LAW
B60

KUNZ J.,"SANCTIONS IN INTERNATIONAL LAW." WOR+45
WOR-45 LEGIT ARMS/CONT COERCE PEACE ATTIT
...METH/CNCPT TIME/SEQ TREND 20. PAGE 62 E1234
INT/ORG
ADJUD
INT/LAW
L60

NAGEL S.S.,"USING SIMPLE CALCULATIONS TO PREDICT
JUDICIAL DECISIONS." ATTIT PERSON MATH. PAGE 76
E1517
JURID
LAW
DECISION
COMPUTER
S60

NICHOLS J.P.,"HAZARDS OF AMERICAN PRIVATE
INVESTMENT IN UNDERDEVELOPED COUNTRIES." FUT
L/A+17C USA+45 USA-45 EXTR/IND CONSULT BAL/PWR
ECO/TAC DOMIN ADJUD ATTIT SOVEREIGN WEALTH
...HIST/WRIT TIME/SEQ TREND VAL/FREE 20. PAGE 77
E1546
FINAN
ECO/UNDEV
CAP/ISM
NAT/LISM
S60

O'BRIEN W.,"THE ROLE OF FORCE IN THE INTERNATIONAL
JURIDICAL ORDER." WOR+45 NAT/G FORCES DOMIN ADJUD
ARMS/CONT DETER NUC/PWR WAR ATTIT PWR...CATH
INT/LAW JURID CONCPT TREND STERTYP GEN/LAWS 20.
PAGE 78 E1564
INT/ORG
COERCE
S60

RHYNE C.S.,"LAW AS AN INSTRUMENT FOR PEACE." FUT
WOR+45 PLAN LEGIT ROUTINE ARMS/CONT NUC/PWR ATTIT
ORD/FREE...JURID METH/CNCPT TREND CON/ANAL HYPO/EXP
COLD/WAR 20. PAGE 84 E1690
ADJUD
EDU/PROP
INT/LAW
PEACE
S60

ROURKE F.E.,"ADMINISTRATIVE SECRECY: A
CONGRESSIONAL DILEMMA." DELIB/GP CT/SYS ATTIT
...MAJORIT DECISION JURID. PAGE 86 E1727
LEGIS
EXEC
ORD/FREE
POLICY
S60

SCHACHTER O.,"THE ENFORCEMENT OF INTERNATIONAL
JUDICIAL AND ARBITRAL DECISIONS." WOR+45 NAT/G
ECO/TAC DOMIN LEGIT ROUTINE COERCE ATTIT DRIVE
ALL/VALS PWR...METH/CNCPT TREND TOT/POP 20 UN.
PAGE 87 E1750
INT/ORG
ADJUD
INT/LAW
S60

ULMER S.S.,"THE ANALYSIS OF BEHAVIOR PATTERNS ON
THE UNITED STATES SUPREME COURT" USA+45 LAW CT/SYS
PERS/REL RACE/REL PERSON...DECISION PSY SOC TREND
ATTIT
ADJUD
PROF/ORG
S60

METH/COMP METH 20 SUPREME/CT CIVIL/LIB. PAGE 97   INGP/REL
E1951

B61

ANAND R.P.,COMPULSORY JURISDICTION OF INTERNATIONAL   INT/ORG
COURT OF JUSTICE. FUT WOR+45 SOCIETY PLAN LEGIT   COERCE
ADJUD ATTIT DRIVE PERSON ORD/FREE...JURID CONCPT   INT/LAW
TREND 20 ICJ. PAGE 5 E0086

B61

BENNETT G.,THE KENYATTA ELECTION: KENYA 1960-1961.   CHOOSE
AFR INGP/REL RACE/REL CONSEN ATTIT 20 KENYATTA.   POL/PAR
PAGE 10 E0187   LAW
    SUFF

B61

BURDETTE F.L.,POLITICAL SCIENCE: A SELECTED   BIBLIOG/A
BIBLIOGRAPHY OF BOOKS IN PRINT, WITH ANNOTATIONS   GOV/COMP
(PAMPHLET). LAW LOC/G NAT/G POL/PAR PROVS DIPLOM   CONCPT
EDU/PROP ADMIN CHOOSE ATTIT 20. PAGE 17 E0330   ROUTINE

B61

CHILDS M.W.,THE EROSION OF INDIVIDUAL LIBERTIES.   ADJUD
NAT/G LEGIS ATTIT...JURID SOC CONCPT IDEA/COMP 20   CT/SYS
SUPREME/CT AMEND/I. PAGE 22 E0430   ORD/FREE
    CONSTN

B61

COWEN D.V.,THE FOUNDATIONS OF FREEDOM. AFR   CONSTN
SOUTH/AFR DOMIN LEGIT ADJUST DISCRIM TOTALSM ATTIT   ELITES
ORD/FREE...MAJORIT JURID SOC/INTEG WORSHIP 20   RACE/REL
NEGRO. PAGE 27 E0529

B61

LEONI B.,FREEDOM AND THE LAW. WOR+45 SOCIETY ADJUD   JURID
INGP/REL EFFICIENCY ATTIT DRIVE. PAGE 64 E1286   ORD/FREE
    LEGIS
    CONTROL

B61

MCDOUGAL M.S.,LAW AND MINIMUM WORLD PUBLIC ORDER.   INT/ORG
WOR+45 SOCIETY NAT/G DELIB/GP EDU/PROP LEGIT ADJUD   ORD/FREE
COERCE ATTIT PERSON...JURID CONCPT RECORD TREND   INT/LAW
TOT/POP 20. PAGE 70 E1406

B61

MECHAM J.L.,THE UNITED STATES AND INTER-AMERICAN   DIPLOM
SECURITY, 1889-1960. L/A+17C USA+45 USA-45 CONSTN   WAR
FORCES INT/TRADE PEACE TOTALSM ATTIT...JURID 19/20   ORD/FREE
UN OAS. PAGE 72 E1432   INT/ORG

B61

MURPHY E.F.,WATER PURITY: A STUDY IN LEGAL CONTROL   SEA
OF NATURAL RESOURCES. LOC/G ACT/RES PLAN TEC/DEV   LAW
LOBBY GP/REL COST ATTIT HEALTH ORD/FREE...HEAL   PROVS
JURID 20 WISCONSIN WATER. PAGE 75 E1506   CONTROL

B61

NEWMAN R.P.,RECOGNITION OF COMMUNIST CHINA? A STUDY   MARXISM
IN ARGUMENT. CHINA/COM NAT/G PROB/SOLV RATIONAL   ATTIT
...INT/LAW LOG IDEA/COMP BIBLIOG 20. PAGE 77 E1544   DIPLOM
    POLICY

B61

SCOTT A.M.,POLITICS, USA; CASES ON THE AMERICAN   CT/SYS
DEMOCRATIC PROCESS. USA+45 CHIEF FORCES DIPLOM   CONSTN
LOBBY CHOOSE RACE/REL FEDERAL ATTIT...JURID ANTHOL   NAT/G
T 20 PRESIDENT CONGRESS CIVIL/LIB. PAGE 90 E1795   PLAN

B61

SMITH J.W.,RELIGIOUS PERSPECTIVES IN AMERICAN   SECT
CULTURE, VOL. 2: RELIGION IN AMERICAN LIFE. USA+45   DOMIN
CULTURE NAT/G EDU/PROP ADJUD LOBBY ATTIT...ART/METH   SOCIETY
ANTHOL 20 CHURCH/STA BIBLE. PAGE 92 E1845   GP/REL

B61

WESTIN A.F.,THE SUPREME COURT: VIEWS FROM INSIDE.   CT/SYS
USA+45 NAT/G PROF/ORG PROVS DELIB/GP INGP/REL   LAW
DISCRIM ATTIT...POLICY DECISION JURID ANTHOL 20   ADJUD
SUPREME/CT CONGRESS CIVIL/LIB. PAGE 106 E2114   GOV/REL

S61

ALGER C.F.,"NON-RESOLUTION CONSEQUENCES OF THE   INT/ORG
UNITED NATIONS AND THEIR EFFECT ON INTERNATIONAL   DRIVE
CONFLICT." WOR+45 CONSTN ECO/DEV NAT/G CONSULT   BAL/PWR
DELIB/GP TOP/EX ACT/RES PLAN DIPLOM EDU/PROP
ROUTINE ATTIT ALL/VALS...INT/LAW TOT/POP UN 20.
PAGE 3 E0065

S61

LIPSON L.,"AN ARGUMENT ON THE LEGALITY OF   INT/ORG
RECONNAISSANCE STATELLITES." COM USA+45 USSR WOR+45   LAW
AIR INTELL NAT/G CONSULT PLAN DIPLOM LEGIT ROUTINE   SPACE
ATTIT...INT/LAW JURID CONCPT METH/CNCPT TREND
COLD/WAR 20. PAGE 65 E1302

S61

SCHUBERT G.,"A PSYCHOMETRIC MODEL OF THE SUPREME   JUDGE
COURT." DELIB/GP ADJUD CHOOSE ATTIT...DECISION   CT/SYS
JURID PSY QUANT STAT HYPO/EXP GEN/METH SUPREME/CT.   PERSON
PAGE 88 E1771   SIMUL

N61

VINER J.,THE INTELLECTUAL HISTORY OF LAISSEZ FAIRE   ATTIT
(PAMPHLET). WOR+45 WOR-45 LAW INTELL...POLICY LING   EDU/PROP
LOG 19/20. PAGE 104 E2077   LAISSEZ
    ECO/TAC

B62

AMER SOCIETY POL & LEGAL PHIL,THE PUBLIC INTEREST: CONCPT
NOMOS V. LAW EDU/PROP...SOC METH/CNCPT ANTHOL.   ATTIT
PAGE 4 E0073   PWR
    GEN/LAWS

B62

BARLOW R.B.,CITIZENSHIP AND CONSCIENCE: STUDIES IN   SECT
THEORY AND PRACTICE OF RELIGIOUS TOLERATION IN   LEGIS
ENGLAND DURING EIGHTEENTH CENTURY. UK LAW VOL/ASSN   DISCRIM
EDU/PROP SANCTION REV GP/REL MAJORITY ATTIT
ORD/FREE...BIBLIOG WORSHIP 18. PAGE 8 E0150

B62

BORKIN J.,THE CORRUPT JUDGE. USA+45 CT/SYS ATTIT   ADJUD
SUPEGO MORAL RESPECT...BIBLIOG + SUPREME/CT   TRIBUTE
MANTON/M DAVIS/W JOHNSN/ALB. PAGE 14 E0271   CRIME

B62

CARPER E.T.,ILLINOIS GOES TO CONGRESS FOR ARMY   ADMIN
LAND. USA+45 LAW EXTR/IND PROVS REGION CIVMIL/REL   LOBBY
GOV/REL FEDERAL ATTIT 20 ILLINOIS SENATE CONGRESS   GEOG
DIRKSEN/E DOUGLAS/P. PAGE 20 E0391   LEGIS

B62

CURRY J.E.,RACE TENSIONS AND THE POLICE. LAW MUNIC   FORCES
NEIGH TEC/DEV RUMOR CONTROL COERCE GP/REL ATTIT   RACE/REL
...SOC 20 NEGRO. PAGE 28 E0558   CROWD
    ORD/FREE

B62

FRIEDRICH C.J.,NOMOS V: THE PUBLIC INTEREST. UNIV   METH/CNCPT
ECO/TAC ADJUD UTIL ATTIT...POLICY LING LOG GEN/LAWS   CONCPT
20. PAGE 41 E0808   LAW
    IDEA/COMP

B62

GONNER R.,DAS KIRCHENPATRONATRECHT IM   JURID
GROSSHERZOGTUM BADEN. GERMANY LAW PROVS DEBATE   SECT
ATTIT CATHISM 14/19 PROTESTANT CHRISTIAN CHURCH/STA   NAT/G
BADEN. PAGE 44 E0882   GP/REL

B62

GRZYBOWSKI K.,SOVIET LEGAL INSTITUTIONS. USA+45   ADJUD
USSR ECO/DEV NAT/G EDU/PROP CONTROL CT/SYS CRIME   LAW
OWN ATTIT PWR SOCISM...NAT/COMP 20. PAGE 48 E0955   JURID

B62

MCWHINNEY E.,CONSTITUTIONALISM IN GERMANY AND THE   CONSTN
FEDERAL CONSTITUTINAL COURT. GERMANY/W POL/PAR TV   CT/SYS
ADJUD CHOOSE EFFICIENCY ATTIT ORD/FREE MARXISM   CONTROL
...NEW/IDEA BIBLIOG 20. PAGE 71 E1428   NAT/G

B62

MURPHY W.F.,CONGRESS AND THE COURT. USA+45 LAW   LEGIS
LOBBY GP/REL RACE/REL ATTIT PWR...JURID INT BIBLIOG   CT/SYS
CONGRESS SUPREME/CT WARRN/EARL. PAGE 75 E1509   GOV/REL
    ADJUD

B62

NATIONAL MUNICIPAL LEAGUE,COURT DECISIONS ON   PROVS
LEGISLATIVE APPORTIONMENT (VOL. III). USA+45 JUDGE   CT/SYS
ADJUD CONTROL ATTIT...DECISION JURID COURT/DIST   APPORT
CASEBOOK. PAGE 76 E1528   LEGIS

B62

PERKINS D.,AMERICA'S QUEST FOR PEACE. USA+45 WOR+45   INT/LAW
DIPLOM CONFER NAT/LISM ATTIT 20 UN TREATY. PAGE 80   INT/ORG
E1610   ARMS/CONT
    PEACE

B62

ROSTOW E.V.,THE SOVEREIGN PREROGATIVE: THE SUPREME   JURID
COURT AND THE QUEST FOR LAW. CONSTN CT/SYS FEDERAL   PROF/ORG
MORAL SOVEREIGN 20 SUPREME/CT. PAGE 86 E1726   ATTIT
    ORD/FREE

B62

SILVA R.C.,RUM, RELIGION, AND VOTES: 1928 RE-   POL/PAR
EXAMINED. USA-45 LAW SECT DISCRIM CATHISM...CORREL   CHOOSE
STAT 20 PRESIDENT SMITH/ALF DEMOCRAT. PAGE 91 E1827   GP/COMP
    ATTIT

SOMMER T.,DEUTSCHLAND UND JAPAN ZWISCHEN DEN   DIPLOM   B62
MACHTEN. GERMANY DELIB/GP BAL/PWR AGREE COERCE   WAR
TOTALISM PWR 20 CHINJAP TREATY. PAGE 93 E1856   ATTIT

THOMPSON K.W.,AMERICAN DIPLOMACY AND EMERGENT   NAT/G   B62
PATTERNS. USA+45 USA-45 WOR+45 WOR-45 LAW DELIB/GP   BAL/PWR
FORCES TOP/EX DIPLOM ATTIT DRIVE RIGID/FLEX
ORD/FREE PWR SOVEREIGN...POLICY 20. PAGE 96 E1922

TRISKA J.F.,THE THEORY, LAW, AND POLICY OF SOVIET   COM   B62
TREATIES. WOR+45 WOR-45 CONSTN INT/ORG NAT/G   LAW
VOL/ASSN DOMIN LEGIT COERCE ATTIT PWR RESPECT   INT/LAW
...POLICY JURID CONCPT OBS SAMP TIME/SEQ TREND   USSR
GEN/LAWS 20. PAGE 97 E1941

WADSWORTH J.J.,THE PRICE OF PEACE. WOR+45 TEC/DEV   DIPLOM   B62
CONTROL NUC/PWR PEACE ATTIT TREATY 20. PAGE 104   INT/ORG
E2089   ARMS/CONT
   POLICY

WOETZEL R.K.,THE NURENBERG TRIALS IN INTERNATIONAL   INT/ORG   B62
LAW. CHRIST-17C MOD/EUR WOR+45 SOCIETY NAT/G   ADJUD
DELIB/GP DOMIN LEGIT ROUTINE ATTIT DRIVE PERSON   WAR
SUPEGO MORAL ORD/FREE...POLICY MAJORIT JURID PSY
SOC SELF/OBS RECORD NAZI TOT/POP. PAGE 107 E2138

MURACCIOLE L.,"LA LOI FONDAMENTALE DE LA REPUBLIQUE   AFR   L62
DU CONGO." WOR+45 SOCIETY ECO/UNDEV INT/ORG NAT/G   CONSTN
LEGIS PLAN LEGIT ADJUD COLONIAL ROUTINE ATTIT
SOVEREIGN 20 CONGO. PAGE 75 E1504

SPAETH H.J.,"JUDICIAL POWER AS A VARIABLE   JUDGE   L62
MOTIVATING SUPREME COURT BEHAVIOR." DELIB/GP ADJUD   DECISION
RATIONAL ATTIT PERSON ORD/FREE...CLASSIF STAT   PERS/COMP
GEN/METH. PAGE 93 E1860   PSY

BIERZANECK R.,"LA NON-RECONAISSANCE ET LE DROIT   EDU/PROP   S62
INTERNATIONAL CONTEMPORAIN." EUR+WWI FUT WOR+45 LAW   JURID
ECO/DEV ATTIT RIGID/FLEX...CONCPT TIME/SEQ TOT/POP   DIPLOM
20. PAGE 12 E0228   INT/LAW

CRANE R.D.,"SOVIET ATTITUDE TOWARD INTERNATIONAL   LAW   S62
SPACE LAW." COM FUT USA+45 USSR AIR CONSTN DELIB/GP   ATTIT
DOMIN PWR...JURID TREND TOT/POP 20. PAGE 27 E0543   INT/LAW
   SPACE

FINKELSTEIN L.S.,"THE UNITED NATIONS AND   INT/ORG   S62
ORGANIZATIONS FOR CONTROL OF ARMAMENT." FUT WOR+45   PWR
VOL/ASSN DELIB/GP TOP/EX CREATE EDU/PROP LEGIT   ARMS/CONT
ADJUD NUC/PWR ATTIT RIGID/FLEX ORD/FREE...POLICY
DECISION CONCPT OBS TREND GEN/LAWS TOT/POP
COLD/WAR. PAGE 38 E0752

GRAVEN J.,"LE MOUVEAU DROIT PENAL INTERNATIONAL."   CT/SYS   S62
UNIV STRUCT LEGIS ACT/RES CRIME ATTIT PERCEPT   PUB/INST
PERSON...JURID CONCPT 20. PAGE 45 E0899   INT/ORG
   INT/LAW

SCHACHTER O.,"DAG HAMMARSKJOLD AND THE RELATION OF   ACT/RES   S62
LAW TO POLITICS." FUT WOR+45 INT/ORG CONSULT PLAN   ADJUD
TEC/DEV BAL/PWR DIPLOM LEGIT ATTIT PERCEPT ORD/FREE
...POLICY JURID CONCPT OBS TESTS STERTYP GEN/LAWS
20 HAMMARSK/D. PAGE 87 E1751

VIGNES D.,"L'AUTORITE DES TRAITES INTERNATIONAUX EN   STRUCT   S62
DROIT INTERNE." EUR+WWI UNIV LAW CONSTN INTELL   LEGIT
NAT/G POL/PAR DIPLOM ATTIT PERCEPT ALL/VALS   FRANCE
...POLICY INT/LAW JURID CONCPT TIME/SEQ 20 TREATY.
PAGE 104 E2075

BLACK C.L. JR.,THE OCCASIONS OF JUSTICE: ESSAYS   JURID   B63
MOSTLY ON LAW. USA+45 JUDGE RACE/REL DISCRIM ATTIT   CONSTN
MORAL ORD/FREE 20 SUPREME/CT BLACK. PAGE 12 E0236   CT/SYS
   LAW

BLOCK E.B.,THE VINDICATORS. LAW FORCES CT/SYS   ATTIT   B63
DISCRIM 19/20. PAGE 13 E0247   CRIME
   ADJUD
   CRIMLGY

CARTER G.M.,FIVE AFRICAN STATES: RESPONSES TO   AFR   B63
DIVERSITY. CONSTN CULTURE STRATA LEGIS PLAN ECO/TAC   SOCIETY
DOMIN EDU/PROP CT/SYS EXEC CHOOSE ATTIT HEALTH
ORD/FREE PWR...TIME/SEQ TOT/POP VAL/FREE. PAGE 20
E0398

CORLEY R.N.,THE LEGAL ENVIRONMENT OF BUSINESS.   NAT/G   B63
CONSTN LEGIS TAX ADMIN CT/SYS DISCRIM ATTIT PWR   INDUS
...TREND 18/20. PAGE 26 E0509   JURID
   DECISION

CRAIG A.,SUPPRESSED BOOKS: A HISTORY OF THE   BIBLIOG/A   B63
CONCEPTION OF LITERARY OBSCENITY. WOR+45 WOR-45   LAW
CREATE EDU/PROP LITERACY ATTIT...ART/METH PSY   SEX
CONCPT 20. PAGE 27 E0538   CONTROL

DAY R.E.,CIVIL RIGHTS USA: PUBLIC SCHOOLS, SOUTHERN   EDU/PROP   B63
STATES - NORTH CAROLINA, 1963. USA+45 LOC/G NEIGH   ORD/FREE
LEGIS CREATE CT/SYS COERCE DISCRIM ATTIT...QU   RACE/REL
CHARTS 20 NORTH/CAR NEGRO KKK CIV/RIGHTS. PAGE 29   SANCTION
E0579

ELLERT R.B.,NATO 'FAIR TRIAL' SAFEGUARDS: PRECURSOR   JURID   B63
TO AN INTERNATIONAL BILL OF PROCEDURAL RIGHTS.   INT/LAW
WOR+45 FORCES CRIME CIVMIL/REL ATTIT ORD/FREE 20   INT/ORG
NATO. PAGE 34 E0683   CT/SYS

GRANT D.R.,STATE AND LOCAL GOVERNMENT IN AMERICA.   PROVS   B63
USA+45 FINAN LOC/G MUNIC EX/STRUC FORCES EDU/PROP   POL/PAR
ADMIN CHOOSE FEDERAL ATTIT...JURID 20. PAGE 45   LEGIS
E0897   CONSTN

HALEY A.G.,SPACE LAW AND GOVERNMENT. FUT USA+45   INT/ORG   B63
WOR+45 LEGIS ACT/RES CREATE ATTIT RIGID/FLEX   LAW
ORD/FREE PWR SOVEREIGN...POLICY JURID CONCPT CHARTS   SPACE
VAL/FREE 20. PAGE 49 E0980

HIGGINS R.,THE DEVELOPMENT OF INTERNATIONAL LAW   INT/ORG   B63
THROUGH THE POLITICAL ORGANS OF THE UNITED NATIONS.   INT/LAW
WOR+45 FORCES DIPLOM AGREE COERCE ATTIT SOVEREIGN   TEC/DEV
...BIBLIOG 20 UN TREATY. PAGE 52 E1041   JURID

JACOBS P.,STATE OF UNIONS. USA+45 STRATA TOP/EX   LABOR   B63
GP/REL RACE/REL DEMAND DISCRIM ATTIT PWR 20   ECO/TAC
CONGRESS NEGRO HOFFA/J. PAGE 57 E1145   BARGAIN
   DECISION

LAVROFF D.-.G.,LES LIBERTES PUBLIQUES EN UNION   ORD/FREE   B63
SOVIETIQUE (REV. ED.). USSR NAT/G WORKER SANCTION   LAW
CRIME MARXISM NEW/LIB...JURID BIBLIOG WORSHIP 20.   ATTIT
PAGE 63 E1268   COM

LEAGUE WOMEN VOTERS NEW YORK,APPORTIONMENT WORKSHOP   APPORT   B63
KIT. USA+45 VOL/ASSN DELIB/GP LEGIS ATTIT ORD/FREE   REPRESENT
...METH/COMP 20 SUPREME/CT NEW/YORK. PAGE 64 E1275   PROVS
   JURID

LEVY L.W.,JEFFERSON AND CIVIL LIBERTIES: THE DARKER   BIOG   B63
SIDE. USA-45 LAW INTELL ACADEM FORCES PRESS REV   ORD/FREE
INGP/REL PERSON 18/19 JEFFERSN/T CIVIL/LIB. PAGE 65   CONSTN
E1291   ATTIT

PRYOR F.L.,THE COMMUNIST FOREIGN TRADE SYSTEM. COM   ATTIT   B63
CZECHOSLVK GERMANY YUGOSLAVIA LAW ECO/DEV DIST/IND   ECO/TAC
POL/PAR PLAN DOMIN TOTALISM DRIVE RIGID/FLEX WEALTH
...STAT STAND/INT CHARTS 20. PAGE 83 E1657

REALE M.,PLURALISMO E LIBERDADE. STRUCT ADJUST   CONCPT   B63
ATTIT 20 CIVIL/LIB. PAGE 84 E1676   ORD/FREE
   JURID
   INGP/REL

ROBERTSON A.H.,HUMAN RIGHTS IN EUROPE. CONSTN   EUR+WWI   B63
SOCIETY INT/ORG NAT/G VOL/ASSN DELIB/GP ACT/RES   PERSON
PLAN ADJUD REGION ROUTINE ATTIT LOVE ORD/FREE
RESPECT...JURID SOC CONCPT SOC/EXP UN 20. PAGE 85
E1705

SARTORI G.,IL PARLAMENTO ITALIANO: 1946-1963. LAW   LEGIS   B63
CONSTN ELITES POL/PAR LOBBY PRIVIL ATTIT PERSON   PARL/PROC

MORAL PWR SOC. PAGE 87 E1746   REPRESENT

B63
SCOTT A.M.,THE SUPREME COURT V. THE CONSTITUTION.   PWR
USA+45 CONTROL ATTIT ROLE...POLICY CONCPT 20   CT/SYS
SUPREME/CT. PAGE 90 E1796   NAT/G
  CONSTN

B63
SMITH E.A.,CHURCH AND STATE IN YOUR COMMUNITY.   GP/REL
USA+45 PROVS SCHOOL ACT/RES CT/SYS PARTIC ATTIT   SECT
MORAL ORD/FREE CATHISM 20 PROTESTANT CHURCH/STA.   NAT/G
PAGE 92 E1842   NEIGH

B63
TUSSMAN J.,THE SUPREME COURT ON RACIAL   CT/SYS
DISCRIMINATION. USA+45 USA-45 NAT/G PROB/SOLV ADJUD   DISCRIM
RACE/REL ORD/FREE...JURID 20 SUPREME/CT CIV/RIGHTS.   ATTIT
PAGE 97 E1946   LAW

B63
US COMMISSION ON CIVIL RIGHTS,FREEDOM TO THE FREE.   RACE/REL
USA+45 USA-45 LAW VOL/ASSN CT/SYS ATTIT PWR...JURID   DISCRIM
BIBLIOG 17/20 SUPREME/CT NEGRO CIV/RIGHTS. PAGE 99   NAT/G
E1986   POLICY

B63
US SENATE COMM ON JUDICIARY,PACIFICA FOUNDATION.   DELIB/GP
USA+45 LAW COM/IND 20 ODEGARD/P BINNS/JJ SCHINDLR/P   EDU/PROP
HEALEY/D THOMAS/TK. PAGE 102 E2051   ORD/FREE
  ATTIT

L63
LISSITZYN O.J.,"INTERNATIONAL LAW IN A DIVIDED   INT/ORG
WORLD." FUT WOR+45 CONSTN CULTURE ECO/DEV ECO/UNDEV   LAW
DIST/IND NAT/G FORCES ECO/TAC LEGIT ADJUD ADMIN
COERCE ATTIT HEALTH MORAL ORD/FREE PWR RESPECT
WEALTH VAL/FREE. PAGE 65 E1306

L63
ROSE R.,"COMPARATIVE STUDIES IN POLITICAL FINANCE: FINAN
A SYMPOSIUM." ASIA EUR+WWI S/ASIA LAW CULTURE   POL/PAR
DELIB/GP LEGIS ACT/RES ECO/TAC EDU/PROP CHOOSE
ATTIT RIGID/FLEX SUPEGO PWR SKILL WEALTH...STAT
ANTHOL VAL/FREE. PAGE 85 E1714

S63
BRAUSCH G.E.,"AFRICAN ETHNOCRACIES: SOME   LAW
SOCIOLOGICAL IMPLICATIONS OF CONSTITUTIONAL CHANGE   SOC
IN EMERGENT TERRITORIES OF AFRICA." AFR CONSTN   ELITES
FACE/GP MUNIC NAT/G DOMIN ATTIT ALL/VALS
...HIST/WRIT GEN/LAWS VAL/FREE 20. PAGE 15 E0289

S63
CAHIER P.,"LE DROIT INTERNE DES ORGANISATIONS   INT/ORG
INTERNATIONALES." UNIV CONSTN SOCIETY ECO/DEV R+D   JURID
NAT/G TOP/EX LEGIT ATTIT PERCEPT...TIME/SEQ 19/20.   DIPLOM
PAGE 18 E0357   INT/LAW

S63
GIRAUD E.,"L'INTERDICTION DU RECOURS A LA FORCE, LA   INT/ORG
THEORIE ET LA PRATIQUE DES NATIONS UNIES." ALGERIA   FORCES
COM CUBA HUNGARY WOR+45 ADJUD TOTALISM ATTIT   DIPLOM
RIGID/FLEX PWR...POLICY JURID CONCPT UN 20 CONGO.
PAGE 44 E0872

S63
HARNETTY P.,"CANADA, SOUTH AFRICA AND THE   AFR
COMMONWEALTH." CANADA SOUTH/AFR LAW INT/ORG   ATTIT
VOL/ASSN DELIB/GP LEGIS TOP/EX ECO/TAC LEGIT DRIVE
MORAL...CONCPT CMN/WLTH 20. PAGE 50 E1000

S63
MCDOUGAL M.S.,"THE SOVIET-CUBAN QUARANTINE AND   ORD/FREE
SELF-DEFENSE." CUBA USA+45 USSR WOR+45 INT/ORG   LEGIT
NAT/G BAL/PWR NUC/PWR ATTIT...JURID CONCPT. PAGE 70   SOVEREIGN
E1409

S63
WALKER H.,"THE INTERNATIONAL LAW OF COMMODITY   MARKET
AGREEMENTS." FUT WOR+45 ECO/DEV ECO/UNDEV FINAN   VOL/ASSN
INT/ORG NAT/G CONSULT CREATE PLAN ECO/TAC ATTIT   INT/LAW
PERCEPT...CONCPT GEN/LAWS TOT/POP GATT 20. PAGE 105   INT/TRADE
E2095

S63
WENGLER W.,"LES CONFLITS DE LOIS ET LE PRINCIPE   JURID
D'EGALITE." UNIV LAW SOCIETY ACT/RES LEGIT ATTIT   CONCPT
PERCEPT 20. PAGE 105 E2111   INT/LAW

C63
SCHUBERT G.,"JUDICIAL DECISION-MAKING." FORCES LEAD   ADJUD
ATTIT DRIVE...POLICY PSY STAT CHARTS ANTHOL BIBLIOG   DECISION
20. PAGE 88 E1773   JUDGE
  CT/SYS

N63
US PRES COMN REGIS AND VOTING,REPORT ON   CHOOSE
REGISTRATION AND VOTING (PAMPHLET). USA+45 POL/PAR   LAW
CHIEF EDU/PROP PARTIC REPRESENT ATTIT...PSY CHARTS   SUFF
20. PAGE 101 E2023   INSPECT

B64
ANASTAPLO G.,NOTES ON THE FIRST AMENDMENT TO THE   ORD/FREE
CONSTITUTION OF THE UNITED STATES (PART TWO).   CONSTN
USA+45 USA-45 NAT/G JUDGE DEBATE SUPEGO PWR   CT/SYS
SOVEREIGN 18/20 SUPREME/CT CONGRESS AMEND/I. PAGE 5   ATTIT
E0088

B64
BLOUSTEIN E.J.,NUCLEAR ENERGY, PUBLIC POLICY, AND   TEC/DEV
THE LAW. USA+45 NAT/G ADJUD ADMIN GP/REL OWN PEACE   LAW
ATTIT HEALTH...ANTHOL 20. PAGE 13 E0251   POLICY
  NUC/PWR

B64
BUREAU OF NATIONAL AFFAIRS,STATE FAIR EMPLOYMENT   PROVS
LAWS AND THEIR ADMINISTRATION. INDUS ADJUD PERS/REL   DISCRIM
RACE/REL ATTIT ORD/FREE WEALTH 20. PAGE 17 E0338   WORKER
  JURID

B64
CHEIN I.,THE ROAD TO H; NARCOTICS, DELINQUENCY, AND   BIO/SOC
SOCIAL POLICY. USA+45 NEIGH CRIME INGP/REL ATTIT   AGE/Y
PERSON...SOC/WK 20 NEWYORK/C. PAGE 22 E0426   POLICY
  ANOMIE

B64
CLINARD M.B.,ANOMIE AND DEVIANT BEHAVIOR: A   PERSON
DISCUSSION AND CRITIQUE. SOCIETY FACE/GP CRIME   ANOMIE
STRANGE ATTIT BIO/SOC DISPL RIGID/FLEX HEALTH...PSY   KIN
CONCPT BIBLIOG 20 MERTON/R. PAGE 23 E0456   NEIGH

B64
COHEN M.,LAW AND POLITICS IN SPACE: SPECIFIC AND   DELIB/GP
URGENT PROBLEMS IN THE LAW OF OUTER SPACE.   LAW
CHINA/COM COM USA+45 USSR WOR+45 COM/IND INT/ORG   INT/LAW
NAT/G LEGIT NUC/PWR ATTIT BIO/SOC...JURID CONCPT   SPACE
CONGRESS 20 STALIN/J. PAGE 24 E0464

B64
ENDACOTT G.B.,GOVERNMENT AND PEOPLE IN HONG KONG   CONSTN
1841-1962: A CONSTITUTIONAL HISTORY. UK LEGIS ADJUD   COLONIAL
REPRESENT ATTIT 19/20 HONG/KONG. PAGE 35 E0688   CONTROL
  ADMIN

B64
EULAU H.,LAWYERS IN POLITICS: A STUDY IN   PROF/ORG
PROFESSIONAL CONVERGENCE. USA+45 POL/PAR DELIB/GP   JURID
GP/REL...QU 20. PAGE 35 E0701   LEGIS
  ATTIT

B64
FRANCK T.M.,EAST AFRICAN UNITY THROUGH LAW. MALAWI   AFR
TANZANIA UGANDA UK ZAMBIA CONSTN INT/ORG NAT/G   FEDERAL
ADMIN ROUTINE TASK NAT/LISM ATTIT SOVEREIGN   REGION
...RECORD IDEA/COMP NAT/COMP. PAGE 40 E0785   INT/LAW

B64
FREUD A.,OF HUMAN SOVEREIGNTY. WOR+45 INDUS SECT   NAT/LISM
ECO/TAC CRIME CHOOSE ATTIT MORAL MARXISM...POLICY   DIPLOM
BIBLIOG 20. PAGE 40 E0794   WAR
  PEACE

B64
FULBRIGHT J.W.,OLD MYTHS AND NEW REALITIES. USA+45   DIPLOM
USSR LEGIS INT/TRADE DETER ATTIT...POLICY 20   INT/ORG
COLD/WAR TREATY. PAGE 41 E0818   ORD/FREE

B64
GRIFFITH W.E.,THE SINO-SOVIET RIFT. ASIA CHINA/COM   ATTIT
COM CUBA USSR YUGOSLAVIA NAT/G POL/PAR VOL/ASSN   TIME/SEQ
DELIB/GP FORCES TOP/EX DIPLOM EDU/PROP DRIVE PERSON   BAL/PWR
PWR...TREND 20 TREATY. PAGE 47 E0941   SOCISM

B64
HAMILTON H.D.,LEGISLATIVE APPORTIONMENT; KEY TO   APPORT
POWER. USA+45 LAW CONSTN PROVS LOBBY CHOOSE ATTIT   CT/SYS
SUPREME/CT. PAGE 50 E0988   LEAD
  REPRESENT

B64
HOLDSWORTH W.S.,A HISTORY OF ENGLISH LAW; THE   LAW
CENTURIES OF DEVELOPMENT AND REFORM (VOL. XIV). UK   LEGIS
CONSTN LOC/G NAT/G POL/PAR CHIEF EX/STRUC ADJUD   LEAD
COLONIAL ATTIT...INT/LAW JURID 18/19 TORY/PARTY   CT/SYS
COMMONWLTH WHIG/PARTY COMMON/LAW. PAGE 54 E1081

B64
IKLE F.C.,HOW NATIONS NEGOTIATE. COM EUR+WWI USA+45   NAT/G
INTELL INT/ORG VOL/ASSN DELIB/GP ACT/RES CREATE   PWR
DOMIN EDU/PROP ADJUD ROUTINE ATTIT PERSON ORD/FREE   POLICY

RESPECT SKILL...PSY SOC OBS VAL/FREE. PAGE 56 E1122

B64

IRION F.C.,APPORTIONMENT OF THE NEW MEXICO
LEGISLATURE. NAT/G LEGIS PRESS CT/SYS ATTIT
...POLICY TIME/SEQ 19/20 SUPREME/CT. PAGE 57 E1137
APPORT
REPRESENT
GOV/REL
PROVS

B64

KAUPER P.G.,RELIGION AND THE CONSTITUTION. USA+45
USA-45 LAW NAT/G SCHOOL SECT GP/REL ATTIT...BIBLIOG
WORSHIP 18/20 SUPREME/CT FREE/SPEE CHURCH/STA.
PAGE 60 E1189
CONSTN
JURID
ORD/FREE

B64

KISER S.L.,AMERICANISM IN ACTION. USA+45 LAW PROVS
CAP/ISM DIPLOM RECEIVE CONTROL CT/SYS WAR FEDERAL
ATTIT WEALTH 20 SUPREME/CT. PAGE 61 E1221
OLD/LIB
FOR/AID
MARXISM
CONSTN

B64

MCWHINNEY E.,"PEACEFUL COEXISTENCE" AND SOVIET-
WESTERN INTERNATIONAL LAW. USSR DIPLOM LEAD...JURID
20 COLD/WAR. PAGE 71 E1429
PEACE
IDEA/COMP
INT/LAW
ATTIT

B64

NEWMAN E.S.,CIVIL LIBERTY AND CIVIL RIGHTS. USA+45
USA-45 CONSTN PROVS FORCES LEGIS CT/SYS RACE/REL
ATTIT...MAJORIT JURID WORSHIP 20 SUPREME/CT NEGRO
CIV/RIGHTS CHURCH/STA. PAGE 77 E1543
ORD/FREE
LAW
CONTROL
NAT/G

B64

RAGHAVAN M.D.,INDIA IN CEYLONESE HISTORY, SOCIETY
AND CULTURE. CEYLON INDIA S/ASIA LAW SOCIETY
INT/TRADE ATTIT...ART/METH JURID SOC LING 20.
PAGE 83 E1668
DIPLOM
CULTURE
SECT
STRUCT

B64

RICE C.E.,THE SUPREME COURT AND PUBLIC PRAYER.
CONSTN SCHOOL SECT PROB/SOLV TAX ATTIT WORSHIP
18/20 SUPREME/CT CHURCH/STA. PAGE 84 E1692
JURID
POLICY
NAT/G

B64

RICHARDSON I.L.,BIBLIOGRAFIA BRASILEIRA DE
ADMINISTRACAO PUBLICA E ASSUNTOS CORRELATOS. BRAZIL
CONSTN FINAN LOC/G NAT/G POL/PAR PLAN DIPLOM
RECEIVE ATTIT...METH 20. PAGE 84 E1694
BIBLIOG
MGT
ADMIN
LAW

B64

ROBERTS HL,FOREIGN AFFAIRS BIBLIOGRAPHY. 1952-1962.
ECO/DEV SECT PLAN FOR/AID INT/TRADE ARMS/CONT
NAT/LISM ATTIT...INT/LAW GOV/COMP IDEA/COMP 20.
PAGE 85 E1703
BIBLIOG/A
DIPLOM
INT/ORG
WAR

B64

SCHUBERT G.A.,JUDICIAL BEHAVIOR: A READER IN THEORY
AND RESEARCH. POL/PAR CT/SYS ROLE SUPEGO PWR
...DECISION JURID REGRESS CHARTS SIMUL ANTHOL 20.
PAGE 89 E1782
ATTIT
PERSON
ADJUD
ACT/RES

B64

SHAPIRO M.,LAW AND POLITICS IN THE SUPREME COURT:
NEW APPROACHES TO POLITICAL JURISPRUDENCE. JUDGE
PROB/SOLV LEGIT EXEC ROUTINE ATTIT ALL/VALS
...DECISION SOC. PAGE 90 E1811
LEGIS
CT/SYS
LAW
JURID

B64

UN PUB. INFORM. ORGAN.,EVERY MAN'S UNITED NATIONS.
UNIV WOR+45 CONSTN CULTURE SOCIETY ECO/DEV
ECO/UNDEV NAT/G ACT/RES PLAN ECO/TAC INT/TRADE
EDU/PROP LEGIT PEACE ATTIT ALL/VALS...POLICY HUM
INT/LAW CONCPT CHARTS UN TOT/POP 20. PAGE 97 E1954
INT/ORG
ROUTINE

B64

US AIR FORCE ACADEMY ASSEMBLY,OUTER SPACE: FINAL
REPORT APRIL 1-4, 1964. FUT USA+45 WOR+45 LAW
DELIB/GP CONFER ARMS/CONT WAR PEACE ATTIT MORAL
...ANTHOL 20 NASA. PAGE 99 E1979
SPACE
CIVMIL/REL
NUC/PWR
DIPLOM

B64

WRIGHT G.,RURAL REVOLUTION IN FRANCE: THE PEASANTRY
IN THE TWENTIETH CENTURY. EUR+WWI MOD/EUR LAW
CULTURE AGRI POL/PAR DELIB/GP LEGIS ECO/TAC
EDU/PROP COERCE CHOOSE ATTIT RIGID/FLEX HEALTH
...STAT CENSUS CHARTS VAL/FREE 20. PAGE 107 E2148
PWR
STRATA
FRANCE
REV

B64

WRIGHT Q.,A STUDY OF WAR. LAW NAT/G PROB/SOLV
BAL/PWR NAT/LISM PEACE ATTIT SOVEREIGN...CENSUS
SOC/INTEG. PAGE 108 E2159
WAR
CONCPT
DIPLOM
CONTROL

L64

BERKS R.N.,"THE US AND WEAPONS CONTROL." WOR+45 LAW
INT/ORG NAT/G LEGIS EXEC COERCE PEACE ATTIT
USA+45
PLAN

RIGID/FLEX ALL/VALS PWR...POLICY TOT/POP 20.
PAGE 11 E0204
ARMS/CONT

L64

POUNDS N.J.G.,"THE POLITICS OF PARTITION." AFR ASIA
COM EUR+WWI FUT ISLAM S/ASIA USA-45 LAW ECO/DEV
ECO/UNDEV AGRI INDUS INT/ORG POL/PAR PROVS SECT
FORCES TOP/EX EDU/PROP LEGIT ATTIT MORAL ORD/FREE
PWR RESPECT WEALTH. PAGE 82 E1640
NAT/G
NAT/LISM

S64

BAKER H.R.,"INMATE SELF-GOVERNMENT." ACT/RES CREATE
CONTROL PARTIC ATTIT RIGID/FLEX QU. PAGE 7 E0141
PUB/INST
CRIME
INGP/REL
REPRESENT

S64

CARNEGIE ENDOWMENT INT. PEACE,"HUMAN RIGHTS (ISSUES
BEFORE THE NINETEENTH GENERAL ASSEMBLY)." AFR
WOR+45 LAW CONSTN NAT/G EDU/PROP GP/REL DISCRIM
PEACE ATTIT MORAL ORD/FREE...INT/LAW PSY CONCPT
RECORD UN 20. PAGE 20 E0385
INT/ORG
PERSON
RACE/REL

S64

COHEN M.,"BASIC PRINCIPLES OF INTERNATIONAL LAW."
UNIV WOR+45 BAL/PWR LEGIT ADJUD WAR ATTIT
MORAL ORD/FREE PWR...JURID CONCPT MYTH TOT/POP 20.
PAGE 23 E0463
INT/ORG
INT/LAW

S64

CRANE R.D.,"BASIC PRINCIPLES IN SOVIET SPACE LAW."
FUT WOR+45 AIR INT/ORG DIPLOM DOMIN ARMS/CONT
COERCE NUC/PWR PEACE ATTIT DRIVE PWR...INT/LAW
METH/CNCPT NEW/IDEA OBS TREND GEN/LAWS VAL/FREE
MARX/KARL 20. PAGE 27 E0544
COM
LAW
USSR
SPACE

S64

DERWINSKI E.J.,"THE COST OF THE INTERNATIONAL
COFFEE AGREEMENT." L/A+17C USA+45 WOR+45 ECO/UNDEV
NAT/G VOL/ASSN LEGIS DIPLOM ECO/TAC FOR/AID LEGIT
ATTIT...TIME/SEQ CONGRESS 20 TREATY. PAGE 31 E0608
MARKET
DELIB/GP
INT/TRADE

S64

GARDNER R.N.,"THE SOVIET UNION AND THE UNITED
NATIONS." WOR+45 FINAN POL/PAR VOL/ASSN FORCES
ECO/TAC DOMIN EDU/PROP LEGIT ADJUD ADMIN ARMS/CONT
COERCE ATTIT ALL/VALS...POLICY MAJORIT CONCPT OBS
TIME/SEQ TREND STERTYP UN. PAGE 42 E0838
COM
INT/ORG
USSR

S64

GINSBURGS G.,"WARS OF NATIONAL LIBERATION - THE
SOVIET THESIS." COM USSR WOR+45 WOR-45 LAW CULTURE
INT/ORG DIPLOM LEGIT COLONIAL GUERRILLA WAR
NAT/LISM ATTIT PERSON MORAL PWR...JURID OBS TREND
MARX/KARL 20. PAGE 44 E0869
COERCE
CONCPT
INT/LAW
REV

S64

GREENBERG S.,"JUDAISM AND WORLD JUSTICE." MEDIT-7
WOR+45 LAW CULTURE SOCIETY INT/ORG NAT/G FORCES
EDU/PROP ATTIT DRIVE PERSON SUPEGO ALL/VALS
...POLICY PSY CONCPT GEN/LAWS JEWS. PAGE 46 E0908
SECT
JURID
PEACE

S64

KARPOV P.V.,"PEACEFUL COEXISTENCE AND INTERNATIONAL
LAW." WOR+45 LAW SOCIETY INT/ORG VOL/ASSN FORCES
CREATE CAP/ISM DIPLOM ADJUD NUC/PWR PEACE MORAL
ORD/FREE PWR MARXISM...MARXIST JURID CONCPT OBS
TREND COLD/WAR MARX/KARL 20. PAGE 59 E1186
COM
ATTIT
INT/LAW
USSR

S64

KHAN M.Z.,"ISLAM AND INTERNATIONAL RELATIONS." FUT
WOR+45 LAW CULTURE SOCIETY NAT/G SECT DELIB/GP
FORCES EDU/PROP ATTIT PERSON SUPEGO ALL/VALS
...POLICY PSY CONCPT MYTH HIST/WRIT GEN/LAWS.
PAGE 61 E1211
ISLAM
INT/ORG
DIPLOM

S64

LIPSON L.,"PEACEFUL COEXISTENCE." COM USSR WOR+45
LAW INT/ORG DIPLOM LEGIT ADJUD ORD/FREE...CONCPT
OBS TREND GEN/LAWS VAL/FREE COLD/WAR 20. PAGE 65
E1303
ATTIT
JURID
INT/LAW
PEACE

S64

MAGGS P.B.,"SOVIET VIEWPOINT ON NUCLEAR WEAPONS IN
INTERNATIONAL LAW." USSR WOR+45 INT/ORG FORCES
DIPLOM ARMS/CONT ATTIT ORD/FREE PWR...POLICY JURID
CONCPT OBS TREND CON/ANAL GEN/LAWS VAL/FREE 20.
PAGE 67 E1347
COM
LAW
INT/LAW
NUC/PWR

S64

N.,"QUASI-LEGISLATIVE ARBITRATION AGREEMENTS." LAW
LG/CO ECO/TAC SANCTION ATTIT POLICY. PAGE 76 E1516
ADJUD
ADJUST
LABOR
GP/REL

SCHWELB E.,"OPERATION OF THE EUROPEAN CONVENTION ON HUMAN RIGHTS." EUR+WWI LAW SOCIETY CREATE EDU/PROP ADJUD ADMIN PEACE ATTIT ORD/FREE PWR...POLICY INT/LAW CONCPT OBS GEN/LAWS UN VAL/FREE ILO 20 ECHR. PAGE 89 E1791
INT/ORG
MORAL
S64

SINGH N.,"THE CONTEMPORARY PRACTICE OF INDIA IN THE FIELD OF INTERNATIONAL LAW." INDIA S/ASIA INT/ORG NAT/G DOMIN EDU/PROP LEGIT KNOWL...CONCPT TOT/POP 20. PAGE 91 E1833
LAW
ATTIT
DIPLOM
INT/LAW
S64

TRISKA J.F.,"SOVIET TREATY LAW: A QUANTITATIVE ANALYSIS." WOR+45 LAW ECO/UNDEV AGRI COM/IND INDUS CREATE TEC/DEV DIPLOM ATTIT PWR WEALTH...JURID SAMP TIME/SEQ TREND CHARTS VAL/FREE 20 TREATY. PAGE 97 E1942
COM
ECO/TAC
INT/LAW
USSR
S64

BECKER T.L.,"POLITICAL BEHAVIORALISM AND MODERN JURISPRUDENCE." LEGIS JUDGE OP/RES ADJUD CT/SYS ATTIT PWR...BIBLIOG 20. PAGE 9 E0173
DECISION
PROB/SOLV
JURID
GEN/LAWS
C64

CORWIN E.S.,"AMERICAN CONSTITUTIONAL HISTORY." LAW NAT/G PROB/SOLV EQUILIB FEDERAL ATTIT PWR...JURID BIBLIOG 20. PAGE 26 E0515
ANTHOL
JUDGE
ADJUD
CT/SYS
C64

ASSOCIATION BAR OF NYC,RADIO, TELEVISION, AND THE ADMINISTRATION OF JUSTICE: A DOCUMENTED SURVEY OF MATERIALS. USA+45 DELIB/GP FORCES PRESS ADJUD CONTROL CT/SYS CRIME...INT IDEA/COMP BIBLIOG. PAGE 6 E0109
AUD/VIS
ATTIT
ORD/FREE
B65

BARKER L.J.,FREEDOM, COURTS, POLITICS: STUDIES IN CIVIL LIBERTIES. USA+45 LEGIS CREATE DOMIN PRESS ADJUD LOBBY CRIME GP/REL RACE/REL MARXISM 20 CIVIL/LIB. PAGE 8 E0148
JURID
CT/SYS
ATTIT
ORD/FREE
B65

BEGGS D.W.,AMERICA'S SCHOOLS AND CHURCHES: PARTNERS IN CONFLICT. USA+45 PROVS EDU/PROP ADJUD DISCRIM ATTIT...IDEA/COMP ANTHOL BIBLIOG WORSHIP 20 CHURCH/STA. PAGE 9 E0179
SECT
GP/REL
SCHOOL
NAT/G
B65

BREITEL C.D.,THE LAWMAKERS. USA+45 EX/STRUC LEGIS JUDGE ATTIT ORD/FREE JURID. PAGE 15 E0290
CT/SYS
ADJUD
FEDERAL
NAT/G
B65

EHLE J.,THE FREE MEN. USA+45 NAT/G PROVS FORCES JUDGE ADJUD ATTIT...POLICY SOC SOC/INTEG 20 NEGRO. PAGE 34 E0677
RACE/REL
ORD/FREE
DISCRIM
B65

GINSBERG M.,ON JUSTICE IN SOCIETY. LAW EDU/PROP LEGIT CT/SYS INGP/REL PRIVIL RATIONAL ATTIT MORAL ORD/FREE...JURID 20. PAGE 44 E0867
ADJUD
ROLE
CONCPT
B65

GLUECK S.,ROSCOE POUND AND CRIMINAL JUSTICE. SOCIETY FAM GOV/REL AGE/Y ATTIT ORD/FREE...CRIMLGY BIOG ANTHOL SOC/INTEG 19/20. PAGE 44 E0875
CT/SYS
CRIME
LAW
ADJUD
B65

HOLDSWORTH W.S.,A HISTORY OF ENGLISH LAW; THE CENTURIES OF SETTLEMENT AND REFORM (VOL. XV). UK CONSTN SECT LEGIS JUDGE WRITING ADJUD CT/SYS CRIME OWN...JURID IDEA/COMP 18 PARLIAMENT ENGLSH/LAW COMMON/LAW. PAGE 54 E1082
LAW
INDUS
PROF/ORG
ATTIT
B65

KAAS L.,DIE GEISTLICHE GERICHTSBARKEIT DER KATHOLISCHEN KIRCHE IN PREUSSEN (2 VOLS.). PRUSSIA CONSTN NAT/G PROVS SECT ADJUD ADMIN ATTIT 16/20. PAGE 59 E1178
JURID
CATHISM
GP/REL
CT/SYS
B65

KEEFE W.J.,THE AMERICAN LEGISLATIVE PROCESS. USA+45 CONSTN POL/PAR CT/SYS REPRESENT FEDERAL ATTIT PLURISM...MAJORIT 20 CONGRESS PRESIDENT. PAGE 60 E1192
LEGIS
NAT/G
CHIEF
GOV/REL
B65

LASLEY J.,THE WAR SYSTEM AND YOU. LAW FORCES ARMS/CONT NUC/PWR NAT/LISM ATTIT...MAJORIT IDEA/COMP UN WORSHIP. PAGE 63 E1261
MORAL
PERSON
DIPLOM
B65

O'BRIEN W.V.,THE NEW NATIONS IN INTERNATIONAL LAW AND DIPLOMACY* THE YEAR BOOK OF WORLD POLITY* VOLUME III. USA+45 ECO/UNDEV INT/ORG FORCES DIPLOM COLONIAL NEUTRAL REV NAT/LISM ATTIT RESPECT. PAGE 78 E1565
INT/LAW
CULTURE
SOVEREIGN
ANTHOL
B65

SCHROEDER O.,DEFACTO SEGREGATION AND CIVIL RIGHTS. LAW PROVS SCHOOL WORKER ATTIT HABITAT HEALTH WEALTH ...JURID CHARTS 19/20 NEGRO SUPREME/CT KKK. PAGE 88 E1766
ANTHOL
DISCRIM
RACE/REL
ORD/FREE
B65

SCHUBERT G.,THE JUDICIAL MIND: THE ATTITUDES AND IDEOLOGIES OF SUPREME COURT JUSTICES 1946-1963. USA+45 ELITES NAT/G CONTROL PERS/REL MAJORITY CONSERVE...DECISION JURID MODAL STAT TREND GP/COMP GAME. PAGE 88 E1774
CT/SYS
JUDGE
ATTIT
NEW/LIB
B65

SWISHER C.B.,THE SUPREME COURT IN MODERN ROLE. COM COM/IND NAT/G FORCES LEGIS LOBBY PARTIC RACE/REL 20 SUPREME/CT. PAGE 95 E1901
DELIB/GP
ATTIT
CT/SYS
ADJUD
B65

UNESCO,INTERNATIONAL ORGANIZATIONS IN THE SOCIAL SCIENCES(REV. ED.). LAW ADMIN ATTIT...CRIMLGY GEOG INT/LAW PSY SOC STAT 20 UNESCO. PAGE 98 E1962
INT/ORG
R+D
PROF/ORG
ACT/RES
B65

SHARMA S.P.,"THE INDIA-CHINA BORDER DISPUTE: AN INDIAN PERSPECTIVE." ASIA CHINA/COM S/ASIA NAT/G LEGIT CT/SYS NAT/LISM DRIVE MORAL ORD/FREE PWR 20. PAGE 91 E1815
LAW
ATTIT
SOVEREIGN
INDIA
L65

FALK R.A.,"INTERNATIONAL LEGAL ORDER." USA+45 INTELL FACE/GP INT/ORG LEGIT KNOWL...CONCPT METH/CNCPT STYLE RECORD GEN/METH 20. PAGE 36 E0717
ATTIT
GEN/LAWS
INT/LAW
S65

FRIEDHEIM R.,"THE 'SATISFIED' AND 'DISSATISFIED' STATES NEGOTIATE INTERNATIONAL LAW* A CASE STUDY." DIPLOM CONFER ADJUD CONSEN PEACE ATTIT UN. PAGE 40 E0799
INT/LAW
RECORD
S65

KHOURI F.J.,"THE JORDON RIVER CONTROVERSY." LAW SOCIETY ECO/UNDEV AGRI FINAN INDUS SECT FORCES ACT/RES PLAN TEC/DEV ECO/TAC EDU/PROP COERCE ATTIT DRIVE PERCEPT RIGID/FLEX ALL/VALS...GEOG SOC MYTH WORK. PAGE 61 E1212
ISLAM
INT/ORG
ISRAEL
JORDAN
S65

MAC CHESNEY B.,"SOME COMMENTS ON THE 'QUARANTINE' OF CUBA." USA+45 WOR+45 NAT/G BAL/PWR DIPLOM LEGIT ROUTINE ATTIT ORD/FREE...JURID METH/CNCPT 20. PAGE 67 E1337
INT/ORG
LAW
CUBA
USSR
S65

MCWHINNEY E.,"CHANGING INTERNATIONAL LAW METHOD AND OBJECTIVES IN THE ERA OF THE SOVIET-WESTERN DETENTE." COM USA+45 NAT/G BAL/PWR CT/SYS ATTIT ORD/FREE...HUM JURID NEW/IDEA COLD/WAR VAL/FREE 20. PAGE 71 E1430
LAW
TREND
S65

WRIGHT Q.,"THE ESCALATION OF INTERNATIONAL CONFLICTS." WOR+45 WOR-45 FORCES DIPLOM RISK COST ATTIT ALL/VALS...INT/LAW QUANT STAT NAT/COMP. PAGE 108 E2160
WAR
PERCEPT
PREDICT
MATH
S65

SCHEINGOLD S.A.,"THE RULE OF LAW IN EUROPEAN INTEGRATION: THE PATH OF THE SCHUMAN PLAN." EUR+WWI JUDGE ADJUD FEDERAL ATTIT PWR...RECORD INT BIBLIOG EEC ECSC. PAGE 87 E1755
INT/LAW
CT/SYS
REGION
CENTRAL
C65

AMERICAN JEWISH COMMITTEE,GROUP RELATIONS IN THE UNITED STATES: PROBLEMS AND PERSPECTIVES: A SELECTED, ANNOTATED BIBLIOGRAPHY (PAMPHLET). LAW CONSTN STRATA SCHOOL SECT PROB/SOLV ATTIT...POLICY WELF/ST SOC/WK 20. PAGE 4 E0079
BIBLIOG/A
USA+45
STRUCT
GP/REL
B66

BEISER E.N.,THE TREATMENT OF LEGISLATIVE APPORTIONMENT BY THE STATE AND FEDERAL COURTS (DISSERTATION). USA+45 CONSTN NAT/G PROVS LEGIS CHOOSE REPRESENT ATTIT...POLICY BIBLIOG 20 CONGRESS SUPREME/CT. PAGE 9 E0181
CT/SYS
APPORT
ADJUD
PWR
B66

B66

CARLIN J.E.,LAWYER'S ETHICS. CLIENT STRUCT CONSULT ATTIT
PERS/REL PWR...JURID OBS CHARTS 20. PAGE 19 E0378   PROF/ORG
                                                      INT

B66

CARMEN I.H.,MOVIES, CENSORSHIP, AND THE LAW. LOC/G   EDU/PROP
NAT/G ATTIT ORD/FREE...DECISION INT IDEA/COMP   LAW
BIBLIOG 20 SUPREME/CT FILM. PAGE 19 E0383   ART/METH
                                                      CONSTN

B66

DOUGLAS W.O.,THE BIBLE AND THE SCHOOLS. USA+45   SECT
CULTURE ADJUD INGP/REL AGE/C AGE/Y ATTIT KNOWL   NAT/G
WORSHIP 20 SUPREME/CT CHURCH/STA BIBLE CHRISTIAN.   SCHOOL
PAGE 32 E0644   GP/REL

B66

DYCK H.V.,WEIMAR GERMANY AND SOVIET RUSSIA   DIPLOM
1926-1933. EUR+WWI GERMANY UK USSR ECO/TAC   GOV/REL
INT/TRADE NEUTRAL WAR ATTIT 20 WEIMAR/REP TREATY.   POLICY
PAGE 34 E0669

B66

FEINE H.E.,REICH UND KIRCHE. CHRIST-17C MOD/EUR   JURID
ROMAN/EMP LAW CHOOSE ATTIT 10/19 CHURCH/STA   SECT
ROMAN/LAW. PAGE 37 E0728   NAT/G
                                                      GP/REL

B66

FISCHER H.,EINER IM VORDERGRUND: TARAS   FASCISM
BORODAJKEWYCZ. AUSTRIA POL/PAR PROF/ORG EDU/PROP   LAW
CT/SYS ORD/FREE 20 NAZI. PAGE 38 E0754   ATTIT
                                                      PRESS

B66

GILLMOR D.M.,FREE PRESS AND FAIR TRIAL. UK USA+45   ORD/FREE
CONSTN PROB/SOLV PRESS CONTROL CRIME DISCRIM   ADJUD
RESPECT...AUD/VIS 20 CIVIL/LIB. PAGE 44 E0865   ATTIT
                                                      EDU/PROP

B66

HAMILTON H.D.,REAPPORTIONING LEGISLATURES. USA+45   APPORT
CONSTN POL/PAR PROVS LEGIS COMPUTER ADJUD CHOOSE   REPRESENT
ATTIT...ANTHOL 20 SUPREME/CT CONGRESS. PAGE 50   PHIL/SCI
E0989   PWR

B66

HAUSNER G.,JUSTICE IN JERUSALEM. GERMANY ISRAEL   ADJUD
SOCIETY KIN DIPLOM LEGIT CT/SYS PARTIC MURDER   CRIME
MAJORITY ATTIT FASCISM...INT/LAW JURID 20 JEWS   RACE/REL
WAR/TRIAL. PAGE 51 E1013   COERCE

B66

HIDAYATULLAH M.,DEMOCRACY IN INDIA AND THE JUDICIAL   NAT/G
PROCESS. INDIA EX/STRUC LEGIS LEAD GOV/REL ATTIT   CT/SYS
ORD/FREE...MAJORIT CONCPT 20 NEHRU/J. PAGE 52 E1040   CONSTN
                                                      JURID

B66

HOLDSWORTH W.S.,A HISTORY OF ENGLISH LAW; THE   BIOG
CENTURIES OF SETTLEMENT AND REFORM (VOL. XVI). UK   PERSON
LOC/G NAT/G EX/STRUC LEGIS CT/SYS LEAD ATTIT   PROF/ORG
...POLICY DECISION JURID IDEA/COMP 18 PARLIAMENT.   LAW
PAGE 54 E1083

B66

HOLMES O.W.,JUSTICE HOLMES, EX CATHEDRA. USA+45   BIOG
USA-45 LAW INTELL ADMIN ATTIT...BIBLIOG 20   PERSON
SUPREME/CT HOLMES/OW. PAGE 55 E1088   CT/SYS
                                                      ADJUD

B66

LEHMANN L.,LEGAL UND OPPORTUN - POLITISCHE JUSTIZ   ORD/FREE
IN DER BUNDESREPUB. GERMANY/W EDU/PROP ADJUD   POL/PAR
CONTROL PARL/PROC COERCE TOTALISM ATTIT 20   JURID
COM/PARTY. PAGE 64 E1281   LEGIS

B66

MACIVER R.M.,THE PREVENTION AND CONTROL OF   AGE/Y
DELINQUENCY. USA+45 STRATA PUB/INST ANOMIE ATTIT   PLAN
HABITAT PERSON HEALTH...CRIMLGY PSY SOC METH.   ADJUST
PAGE 67 E1341   CRIME

B66

MACMULLEN R.,ENEMIES OF THE ROMAN EMPIRE: TREASON,   CRIME
UNREST, AND ALIENATION IN THE EMPIRE. ROMAN/EMP   ADJUD
MUNIC CONTROL LEAD ATTIT PERSON MYSTISM...PHIL/SCI   MORAL
BIBLIOG. PAGE 67 E1345   SOCIETY

B66

MOSKOW M.H.,TEACHERS AND UNIONS. SCHOOL WORKER   EDU/PROP
ADJUD LOBBY ATTIT ORD/FREE 20. PAGE 75 E1501   PROF/ORG
                                                      LABOR
                                                      BARGAIN

B66

O'NEILL C.E.,CHURCH AND STATE IN FRENCH COLONIAL   COLONIAL
LOUISIANA: POLICY AND POLITICS TO 1732. PROVS   NAT/G
VOL/ASSN DELIB/GP ADJUD ADMIN GP/REL ATTIT DRIVE   SECT
...POLICY BIBLIOG 17/18 LOUISIANA CHURCH/STA.   PWR
PAGE 78 E1568

B66

OSTERMANN R.,A REPORT IN DEPTH ON CRIME IN AMERICA.   CRIME
FUT USA+45 MUNIC PUB/INST TEC/DEV MURDER EFFICIENCY   FORCES
ATTIT BIO/SOC...PSY 20. PAGE 79 E1584   CONTROL
                                                      LAW

B66

POWERS E.,CRIME AND PUNISHMENT IN EARLY   CRIME
MASSACHUSETTS 1620-1692: A DOCUMENTARY HISTORY.   ADJUD
USA-45 SECT LEGIS COLONIAL ATTIT ORD/FREE MYSTISM   CT/SYS
17 PRE/US/AM MASSACHU. PAGE 82 E1643   PROVS

B66

RUNCIMAN W.G.,RELATIVE DEPRIVATION AND SOCIAL   STRATA
JUSTICE: A STUDY OF ATTITUDES TO SOCIAL INEQUALITY   STRUCT
IN TWENTIETH-CENTURY ENGLAND. UK LAW POL/PAR PWR   DISCRIM
...CONCPT NEW/IDEA SAMP METH 19/20. PAGE 86 E1734   ATTIT

B66

SMITH E.A.,CHURCH-STATE RELATIONS IN ECUMENICAL   NAT/G
PERSPECTIVE. WOR+45 LAW MUNIC INGP/REL DISCRIM   SECT
ATTIT SUPEGO ORD/FREE CATHISM...PHIL/SCI IDEA/COMP   GP/REL
20 PROTESTANT ECUMENIC CHURCH/STA CHRISTIAN.   ADJUD
PAGE 92 E1843

B66

SWEET E.C.,CIVIL LIBERTIES IN AMERICA. LAW CONSTN   ADJUD
NAT/G PRESS CT/SYS DISCRIM ATTIT WORSHIP 20   ORD/FREE
CIVIL/LIB. PAGE 95 E1899   SUFF
                                                      COERCE

B66

US SENATE COMM AERO SPACE SCI,SOVIET SPACE   CONSULT
PROGRAMS, 1962-65; GOALS AND PURPOSES,   SPACE
ACHIEVEMENTS, PLANS, AND INTERNATIONAL   FUT
IMPLICATIONS. USA+45 USSR R+D FORCES PLAN EDU/PROP   DIPLOM
PRESS ADJUD ARMS/CONT ATTIT MARXISM. PAGE 101 E2028

S66

ANAND R.P.,"ATTITUDE OF THE ASIAN-AFRICAN STATES   INT/LAW
TOWARD CERTAIN PROBLEMS OF INTERNATIONAL LAW."   ATTIT
L/A+17C S/ASIA ECO/UNDEV CREATE CONFER ADJUD   ASIA
COLONIAL...RECORD GP/COMP UN. PAGE 5 E0087   AFR

S66

LANDE G.R.,"THE EFFECT OF THE RESOLUTIONS OF THE   LEGIS
UNITED NATIONS GENERAL ASSEMBLY." WOR+45 LAW   EFFICIENCY
INT/ORG NAT/G CHOOSE ISOLAT ATTIT...CLASSIF   RESPECT
GEN/METH UN. PAGE 62 E1249

S66

POLSBY N.W.,"BOOKS IN THE FIELD: POLITICAL   BIBLIOG/A
SCIENCE." LAW CONSTN LOC/G NAT/G LEGIS ADJUD PWR 20   ATTIT
SUPREME/CT. PAGE 81 E1627   ADMIN
                                                      JURID

B67

BAILEY N.A.,LATIN AMERICA IN WORLD POLITICS. PWR   L/A+17C
CONSERVE MARXISM...INT/LAW TREND BIBLIOG/A T OAS   DIPLOM
COLD/WAR. PAGE 7 E0134   INT/ORG
                                                      ATTIT

B67

CLINARD M.B.,CRIMINAL BEHAVIOR SYSTEMS: A TYPOLOGY.   BIBLIOG
WOR+45 LAW SOCIETY STRUCT R+D AGE/Y ATTIT WEALTH   CRIME
...CLASSIF CHARTS METH/COMP METH. PAGE 23 E0457   CRIMLGY
                                                      PERSON

B67

COHEN M.R.,LAW AND THE SOCIAL ORDER: ESSAYS IN   JURID
LEGAL PHILOSOPHY. USA-45 CONSULT WORKER ECO/TAC   LABOR
ATTIT WEALTH...POLICY WELF/ST SOC 20 NEW/DEAL   IDEA/COMP
DEPRESSION. PAGE 24 E0467

B67

COWLING M.,1867 DISRAELI, GLADSTONE, AND   PARL/PROC
REVOLUTION; THE PASSING OF THE SECOND REFORM BILL.   POL/PAR
UK LEGIS LEAD LOBBY GP/REL INGP/REL...DECISION   ATTIT
BIBLIOG 19 REFORMERS. PAGE 27 E0531   LAW

B67

COX A.,CIVIL RIGHTS, THE CONSTITUTION, AND THE   LAW
COURTS. CONSTN EDU/PROP CRIME DISCRIM ATTIT...JURID   FEDERAL
20. PAGE 27 E0533   RACE/REL
                                                      PRESS

B67

DEBOLD R.C.,LSD, MAN AND SOCIETY. USA+45 LAW   HEALTH

SOCIETY SECT CONTROL SANCTION STRANGE ATTIT...HEAL   DRIVE
CHARTS ANTHOL BIBLIOG. PAGE 30 E0601   PERSON
                                                      BIO/SOC

                                                        B67
ELDRIDGE W.B.,NARCOTICS AND THE LAW: A CRITIQUE OF   LAW
THE AMERICAN EXPERIMENT IN NARCOTIC DRUG CONTROL.   INSPECT
PUB/INST ACT/RES PLAN LICENSE GP/REL EFFICIENCY   BIO/SOC
ATTIT HEALTH...CRIMLGY HEAL STAT 20 ABA DEPT/HEW   JURID
NARCO/ACT. PAGE 34 E0679

                                                        B67
GRAHAM H.D.,CRISIS IN PRINT: DESEGREGATION AND THE   PRESS
PRESS IN TENNESSEE. LAW SOCIETY MUNIC POL/PAR   PROVS
EDU/PROP LEAD REPRESENT DISCRIM ATTIT...IDEA/COMP   POLICY
BIBLIOG/A SOC/INTEG 20 TENNESSEE SUPREME/CT   RACE/REL
SOUTH/US. PAGE 45 E0896

                                                        B67
HODGKINSON R.G.,THE ORIGINS OF THE NATIONAL HEALTH   HEAL
SERVICE: THE MEDICAL SERVICES OF THE NEW POOR LAW,   NAT/G
1834-1871. UK INDUS MUNIC WORKER PROB/SOLV   POLICY
EFFICIENCY ATTIT HEALTH WEALTH SOCISM...JURID   LAW
SOC/WK 19/20. PAGE 53 E1062

                                                        B67
KING W.L.,MELVILLE WESTON FULLER: CHIEF JUSTICE OF   BIOG
THE UNITED STATES, 1888-1910. USA+45 CONSTN FINAN   CT/SYS
LABOR TAX GOV/REL PERS/REL ATTIT PERSON PWR...JURID   LAW
BIBLIOG 19/20 SUPREME/CT FULLER/MW HOLMES/OW.   ADJUD
PAGE 61 E1216

                                                        B67
LEVY L.W.,JUDICIAL REVIEW AND THE SUPREME COURT.   ADJUD
USA+45 USA-45 NEUTRAL ATTIT ORD/FREE...POLICY   CONSTN
DECISION BIBLIOG 18/20 BILL/RIGHT SUPREME/CT.   LAW
PAGE 65 E1292   CT/SYS

                                                        B67
LOBLE L.H.,DELINQUENCY CAN BE STOPPED. FAM PUB/INST   AGE/Y
CT/SYS ADJUST ATTIT...NEW/IDEA METH/COMP 20.   PROB/SOLV
PAGE 66 E1315   ADJUD
                                                      CRIME

                                                        B67
MEYERS M.,SOURCES OF THE AMERICAN REPUBLIC; A   COLONIAL
DOCUMENTARY HISTORY OF POLITICS, SOCIETY, AND   REV
THOUGHT (VOL. I, REV. ED.). USA-45 CULTURE STRUCT   WAR
NAT/G LEGIS LEAD ATTIT...JURID SOC ANTHOL 17/19
PRESIDENT. PAGE 72 E1450

                                                        B67
NARAIN I.,THE POLITICS OF RACIALISM. INDIA   DISCRIM
SOUTH/AFR LAW NAT/G RACE/REL ATTIT 20. PAGE 76   COLONIAL
E1521   HIST/WRIT

                                                        B67
OPERATIONS AND POLICY RESEARCH,NICARAGUA: ELECTION   POL/PAR
FACTBOOK: FEBRUARY 5, 1967 (PAMPHLET). NICARAGUA   CHOOSE
LAW NAT/G LEAD REPRESENT...STAT BIOG CHARTS 20.   PLAN
PAGE 79 E1577   ATTIT

                                                        B67
PADELFORD N.J.,THE DYNAMICS OF INTERNATIONAL   DIPLOM
POLITICS (2ND ED.). WOR+45 LAW INT/ORG FORCES   NAT/G
TEC/DEV REGION NAT/LISM PEACE ATTIT PWR ALL/IDEOS   POLICY
UN COLD/WAR NATO TREATY. PAGE 79 E1589   DECISION

                                                        B67
RUSSELL B.,WAR CRIMES IN VIETNAM. USA+45 VIETNAM   WAR
FORCES DIPLOM WEAPON RACE/REL DISCRIM ISOLAT   CRIME
BIO/SOC 20 COLD/WAR RUSSELL/B. PAGE 87 E1736   ATTIT
                                                      POLICY

                                                        B67
UNIVERSAL REFERENCE SYSTEM,CURRENT EVENTS AND   BIBLIOG/A
PROBLEMS OF MODERN SOCIETY (VOLUME V). WOR+45 LOC/G   SOCIETY
MUNIC NAT/G PLAN EDU/PROP CRIME RACE/REL WEALTH   PROB/SOLV
...COMPUT/IR GEN/METH. PAGE 98 E1974   ATTIT

                                                        B67
US SENATE COMM ON FOREIGN REL,CONSULAR CONVENTION   LEGIS
WITH THE SOVIET UNION. USA+45 USSR DELIB/GP LEAD   LOBBY
REPRESENT ATTIT ORD/FREE CONGRESS TREATY. PAGE 101   DIPLOM
E2031

                                                        B67
US SENATE COMM ON FOREIGN REL,A SELECT CHRONOLOGY   ISLAM
AND BACKGROUND DOCUMENTS RELATING TO THE MIDDLE   TIME/SEQ
EAST. ISRAEL UAR LAW INT/ORG FORCES PROB/SOLV   DIPLOM
CONFER CONSEN PEACE ATTIT...POLICY 20 UN SENATE
TRUMAN/HS. PAGE 101 E2033

                                                        L67
FRANCK T.M.,"SOME PSYCHOLOGICAL FACTORS IN   DIPLOM
INTERNATIONAL THIRD-PARTY DECISION-MAKING." UNIV   ADJUD

SOCIETY PROB/SOLV DISCRIM ATTIT HABITAT...DECISION   PERSON
PSY. PAGE 40 E0786   CONSULT

                                                        L67
HITCHMAN J.M.,"THE PLATT AMENDMENT REVISITED: A   ATTIT
BIBLIOGRAPHICAL SURVEY." CUBA ACADEM DELIB/GP   DIPLOM
ORD/FREE...HIST/WRIT 20. PAGE 53 E1055   SOVEREIGN
                                                      INT/LAW

                                                        S67
CHAMBERLAIN N.W.,"STRIKES IN CONTEMPORARY CONTEXT."   LABOR
LAW INDUS NAT/G CHIEF CONFER COST ATTIT ORD/FREE   BARGAIN
...POLICY MGT 20. PAGE 21 E0415   EFFICIENCY
                                                      PROB/SOLV

                                                        S67
CLOGGER T.J.,"THE BIG EAR." UK USA+45 USSR LAW   DIPLOM
LEGIS CRIME GP/REL INGP/REL ATTIT 20 FBI ESPIONAGE.   ORD/FREE
PAGE 23 E0458   COM/IND
                                                      INSPECT

                                                        S67
COHN K.,"CRIMES AGAINST HUMANITY." GERMANY INT/ORG   WAR
SANCTION ATTIT ORD/FREE...MARXIST CRIMLGY 20 UN.   INT/LAW
PAGE 24 E0469   CRIME
                                                      ADJUD

                                                        S67
EYRAUD M.,"LA FRANCE FACE A UN EVENTUEL TRAITE DE   NUC/PWR
NON DISSEMINATION DES ARMES NUCLEAIRES." FRANCE   ARMS/CONT
USA+45 EXTR/IND INDUS R+D INT/ORG ACT/RES TEC/DEV   POLICY
AGREE PRODUC ATTIT 20 TREATY AEC EURATOM. PAGE 36
E0708

                                                        S67
FLECHTHEIM O.K.,"BLOC FORMATION VS. DIALOGUE."   FUT
CONSTN ECO/DEV BAL/PWR PEACE ATTIT PWR COLD/WAR.   CAP/ISM
PAGE 38 E0761   MARXISM
                                                      DEBATE

                                                        S67
GREY D.L.,"INTERVIEWING AT THE COURT." USA+45   JUDGE
ELITES COM/IND ACT/RES PRESS CT/SYS PERSON...SOC   ATTIT
INT 20. SUPREME/CT. PAGE 46 E0916   PERS/COMP
                                                      GP/COMP

                                                        S67
MACLEOD R.M.,"LAW, MEDICINE AND PUBLIC OPINION: THE   LAW
RESISTANCE TO COMPULSORY HEALTH LEGISLATION   HEALTH
1870-1907." UK CONSTN SECT DELIB/GP DEBATE   ATTIT
PARL/PROC GP/REL MORAL 19. PAGE 67 E1344

                                                        S67
MC REYNOLDS D.,"THE RESISTANCE." USA+45 LAW ADJUD   ATTIT
SANCTION INGP/REL PEACE 20. PAGE 70 E1398   WAR
                                                      LEGIT
                                                      FORCES

                                                        S67
RICHARDSON J.J.,"THE MAKING OF THE RESTRICTIVE   LEGIS
TRADE PRACTICES ACT 1956 A CASE STUDY OF THE POLICY   ECO/TAC
PROCESS IN BRITAIN." UK FINAN MARKET LG/CO POL/PAR   POLICY
CONSULT PRESS ADJUD ADMIN AGREE LOBBY SANCTION   INDUS
ATTIT 20. PAGE 84 E1695

                                                        S67
RUCKER B.W.,"WHAT SOLUTIONS DO PEOPLE ENDORSE IN   CONCPT
FREE PRESS-FAIR TRIAL DILEMMA?" LAW NAT/G CT/SYS   PRESS
ATTIT...NET/THEORY SAMP CHARTS IDEA/COMP METH 20.   ADJUD
PAGE 86 E1731   ORD/FREE

                                                        S67
SCOTT A.,"TWENTY-FIVE YEARS OF OPINION ON   ATTIT
INTEGRATION IN TEXAS." USA+45 USA-45 DISCRIM   ADJUST
...KNO/TEST TREND CHARTS 20 TEXAS. PAGE 89 E1794   RACE/REL
                                                      LAW

                                                        S67
SHELDON C.H.,"PUBLIC OPINION AND HIGH COURTS: ATTIT
COMMUNIST PARTY CASES IN FOUR CONSTITUTIONAL   CT/SYS
SYSTEMS." CANADA GERMANY/W WOR+45 POL/PAR MARXISM   CONSTN
...METH/COMP NAT/COMP 20 AUSTRAL. PAGE 91 E1818   DECISION

                                                        S67
TRAYNOR R.J.,"WHO CAN BEST JUDGE THE JUDGES?"   CHOOSE
USA+45 PLAN PROB/SOLV ATTIT...DECISION JURID 20.   ADJUD
PAGE 97 E1938   REPRESENT
                                                      CT/SYS

                                                        S67
WINES R.,"THE IMPERIAL CIRCLES, PRINCELY DIPLOMACY,   NAT/G
AND IMPERIAL REFORM* 1681-1714." MOD/EUR DELIB/GP   NAT/LISM
BAL/PWR CONFER ADJUD PARL/PROC PARTIC ATTIT PWR   CENTRAL
17/18. PAGE 106 E2132   REGION

B68
HULL R.H.,LAW AND VIETNAM. COM VIETNAM CONSTN   POLICY
INT/ORG FORCES DIPLOM AGREE COERCE DETER WEAPON   LAW
PEACE ATTIT 20 UN TREATY. PAGE 56 E1113   WAR
                                                      INT/LAW

L68
CHIU H.,"COMMUNIST CHINA'S ATTITUDE TOWARD THE   INT/LAW
UNITED NATIONS: A LEGAL ANALYSIS." CHINA/COM WOR+45   SOVEREIGN
LAW NAT/G DIPLOM CONFER ADJUD PARTIC ATTIT...POLICY   INT/ORG
TREND 20 UN. PAGE 22 E0432   REPRESENT

S68
SHAPIRO J.P.,"SOVIET HISTORIOGRAPHY AND THE MOSCOW   HIST/WRIT
TRIALS: AFTER THIRTY YEARS." USSR NAT/G LEGIT PRESS   EDU/PROP
CONTROL LEAD ATTIT MARXISM...NEW/IDEA METH 20   SANCTION
TROTSKY/L STALIN/J KHRUSH/N. PAGE 90 E1810   ADJUD

B76
BENTHAM J.,THE THEORY OF LEGISLATION. UK CREATE   LEGIS
CRIME ATTIT ORD/FREE...CONCPT 18 REFORMERS. PAGE 10   LAW
E0196   CRIMLGY
                                                      UTIL

B77
CADWALDER J.L.,DIGEST OF THE PUBLISHED OPINIONS OF   BIBLIOG
THE ATTORNEYS-GENERAL, AND OF THE LEADING DECISIONS   CT/SYS
OF THE FEDERAL COURTS (REV ED). USA-45 NAT/G JUDGE   DECISION
PROB/SOLV DIPLOM ATTIT...POLICY INT/LAW ANTHOL 19.   ADJUD
PAGE 18 E0356

B88
BENTHAM J.,DEFENCE OF USURY (1787). UK LAW NAT/G   TAX
TEC/DEV ECO/TAC CONTROL ATTIT...CONCPT IDEA/COMP 18   FINAN
SMITH/ADAM. PAGE 10 E0197   ECO/DEV
                                                      POLICY

B89
FERNEUIL T.,LES PRINCIPES DE 1789 ET LA SCIENCE   CONSTN
SOCIALE. FRANCE NAT/G REV ATTIT...CONCPT TREND   POLICY
IDEA/COMP 18/19. PAGE 37 E0739   LAW

B91
DOLE C.F.,THE AMERICAN CITIZEN. USA-45 LAW PARTIC   NAT/G
ATTIT...INT/LAW 19. PAGE 32 E0633   MORAL
                                                      NAT/LISM
                                                      MAJORITY

ATTLEE/C....CLEMENT ATLEE

ATTORNEY GENERAL....SEE ATTRNY/GEN

ATTRNY/GEN....ATTORNEY GENERAL

AUBOYER J. E0123

AUD/VIS....FILM AND SOUND (INCLUDING PHOTOGRAPHY)

B50
JENKINS W.S.,A GUIDE TO THE MICROFILM COLLECTION OF   BIBLIOG
EARLY STATE RECORDS. USA+45 CONSTN MUNIC LEGIS   PROVS
PRESS ADMIN CT/SYS 18/20. PAGE 58 E1152   AUD/VIS

B51
KEFAUVER E.,CRIME IN AMERICA. USA+45 USA-45 MUNIC   ELITES
NEIGH DELIB/GP FORCES TRIBUTE GAMBLE LOBBY SANCTION   CRIME
...AUD/VIS 20 CAPONE/AL MAFIA MIAMI CHICAGO   PWR
DETROIT. PAGE 60 E1194   FORCES

B53
PADOVER S.K.,THE LIVING US CONSTITUTION. USA+45   CONSTN
USA-45 POL/PAR ADJUD...DECISION AUD/VIS IDEA/COMP   LEGIS
18/20 SUPREME/CT. PAGE 79 E1590   DELIB/GP
                                                      BIOG

B56
KUPER L.,PASSIVE RESISTANCE IN SOUTH AFRICA.   ORD/FREE
SOUTH/AFR LAW NAT/G POL/PAR VOL/ASSN DISCRIM   RACE/REL
...POLICY SOC AUD/VIS 20. PAGE 62 E1237   ATTIT

B56
WIGGINS J.R.,FREEDOM OR SECRECY. USA+45 USA-45   ORD/FREE
DELIB/GP EX/STRUC FORCES ADJUD SANCTION KNOWL PWR   PRESS
...AUD/VIS CONGRESS 20. PAGE 106 E2121   NAT/G
                                                      CONTROL

B64
HOPKINSON T.,SOUTH AFRICA. SOUTH/AFR UK NAT/G   SOCIETY
POL/PAR LEGIS ECO/TAC PARL/PROC WAR...JURID AUD/VIS   RACE/REL
19/20. PAGE 55 E1097   DISCRIM

B64
LOCKHART W.B.,CASES AND MATERIALS ON CONSTITUTIONAL   ORD/FREE
RIGHTS AND LIBERTIES. USA+45 FORCES LEGIS DIPLOM   CONSTN
PRESS CONTROL CRIME WAR PWR...AUD/VIS T WORSHIP 20   NAT/G
NEGRO. PAGE 66 E1317

B64
OSSENBECK F.J.,OPEN SPACE AND PEACE. CHINA/COM FUT   SPACE
USA+45 USSR LAW PROB/SOLV TEC/DEV EDU/PROP NEUTRAL   ORD/FREE
PEACE...AUD/VIS ANTHOL 20. PAGE 79 E1583   DIPLOM
                                                      CREATE

B65
ASSOCIATION BAR OF NYC,RADIO, TELEVISION, AND THE   AUD/VIS
ADMINISTRATION OF JUSTICE: A DOCUMENTED SURVEY OF   ATTIT
MATERIALS. USA+45 DELIB/GP FORCES PRESS ADJUD   ORD/FREE
CONTROL CT/SYS CRIME...INT IDEA/COMP BIBLIOG.
PAGE 6 E0109

B65
MILLER H.H.,THE CASE FOR LIBERTY. USA-45 LAW JUDGE   COLONIAL
CT/SYS...AUD/VIS 18 PRE/US/AM CASEBOOK. PAGE 73   JURID
E1460   PROB/SOLV

B65
SOPER T.,EVOLVING COMMONWEALTH. AFR CANADA INDIA   INT/ORG
IRELAND UK LAW CONSTN POL/PAR DOMIN CONTROL WAR PWR   COLONIAL
...AUD/VIS 18/20 COMMONWLTH OEEC. PAGE 93 E1857   VOL/ASSN

B66
DIZARD W.P.,TELEVISION* A WORLD VIEW. WOR+45   COM/IND
ECO/UNDEV TEC/DEV LICENSE LITERACY...STAT OBS INT   ACT/RES
QU TREND AUD/VIS BIBLIOG. PAGE 32 E0632   EDU/PROP
                                                      CREATE

B66
GILLMOR D.M.,FREE PRESS AND FAIR TRIAL. UK USA+45   ORD/FREE
CONSTN PROB/SOLV PRESS CONTROL CRIME DISCRIM   ADJUD
RESPECT...AUD/VIS 20 CIVIL/LIB. PAGE 44 E0865   ATTIT
                                                      EDU/PROP

L67
BARRON J.A.,"ACCESS TO THE PRESS." USA+45 TEC/DEV   ORD/FREE
PRESS TV ADJUD AUD/VIS. PAGE 8 E0152   COM/IND
                                                      EDU/PROP
                                                      LAW

AUERBACH C.A. E0116

AUERBACH J.S. E0117

AUGUSTINE....SAINT AUGUSTINE

B64
GRASMUCK E.L.,COERCITIO STAAT UND KIRCHE IM   GP/REL
DONATISTENSTREIT. CHRIST-17C ROMAN/EMP LAW PROVS   NAT/G
DEBATE PERSON SOVEREIGN...JURID CONCPT 4/5   SECT
AUGUSTINE CHURCH/STA ROMAN/LAW. PAGE 45 E0898   COERCE

AUMANN F.R. E0118

AUST/HUNG....AUSTRIA-HUNGARY

AUSTIN J. E0119,E0120

AUSTRAL ....AUSTRALIA

N
INDEX TO LEGAL PERIODICALS. CANADA NEW/ZEALND UK   BIBLIOG
USA+45 USA-45 CONSTN LEGIS JUDGE ADJUD ADMIN   INDEX
CONTROL CT/SYS FEDERAL...CRIMLGY INT/LAW 20   LAW
CMN/WLTH AUSTRAL. PAGE 1 E0006   JURID

N
AUSTRALIAN PUBLIC AFFAIRS INFORMATION SERVICE. LAW   BIBLIOG
...HEAL HUM MGT SOC CON/ANAL 20 AUSTRAL. PAGE 1   NAT/G
E0017   CULTURE
                                                      DIPLOM

B21
BRYCE J.,MODERN DEMOCRACIES. FUT NEW/ZEALND USA-45   NAT/G
LAW CONSTN POL/PAR PROVS VOL/ASSN EX/STRUC LEGIS   TREND
LEGIT CT/SYS EXEC KNOWL CONGRESS AUSTRAL 20.
PAGE 16 E0322

B32
LUNT D.C.,THE ROAD TO THE LAW. UK USA-45 LEGIS   ADJUD
EDU/PROP OWN ORD/FREE...DECISION TIME/SEQ NAT/COMP   LAW
16/20 AUSTRAL ENGLSH/LAW COMMON/LAW. PAGE 67 E1333   JURID
                                                      CT/SYS

B42
FULLER G.H.,DEFENSE FINANCING: A SUPPLEMENTARY LIST   BIBLIOG/A
OF REFERENCES (PAMPHLET). CANADA UK USA-45 ECO/DEV   FINAN
NAT/G DELIB/GP BUDGET ADJUD ARMS/CONT WEAPON COST   FORCES
PEACE PWR 20 AUSTRAL CHINJAP CONGRESS. PAGE 41   DIPLOM
E0821

B55
CRAIG J.,BIBLIOGRAPHY OF PUBLIC ADMINISTRATION IN   BIBLIOG
AUSTRALIA. CONSTN FINAN EX/STRUC LEGIS PLAN DIPLOM   GOV/REL

RECEIVE ADJUD ROUTINE...HEAL 19/20 AUSTRAL   ADMIN
PARLIAMENT. PAGE 27 E0540   NAT/G

                                                             B58
MANSERGH N.,COMMONWEALTH PERSPECTIVES. GHANA UK LAW   DIPLOM
VOL/ASSN CONFER HEALTH SOVEREIGN...GEOG CHARTS   COLONIAL
ANTHOL 20 CMN/WLTH AUSTRAL. PAGE 68 E1363   INT/ORG
                                                             INGP/REL

                                                             B59
WAGNER W.J.,THE FEDERAL STATES AND THEIR JUDICIARY.   ADJUD
BRAZIL CANADA SWITZERLND USA+45 CONFER CT/SYS TASK   METH/COMP
EFFICIENCY FEDERAL PWR...JURID BIBLIOG 20 AUSTRAL   PROB/SOLV
MEXIC/AMER. PAGE 104 E2091   NAT/G

                                                             S59
MENDELSON W.,"JUDICIAL REVIEW AND PARTY POLITICS"   CT/SYS
(BMR)" UK USA+45 USA-45 NAT/G LEGIS PROB/SOLV   POL/PAR
EDU/PROP ADJUD EFFICIENCY...POLICY NAT/COMP 19/20   BAL/PWR
AUSTRAL SUPREME/CT. PAGE 72 E1436   JURID

                                                             B63
LIVINGSTON W.S.,FEDERALISM IN THE COMMONWEALTH - A   BIBLIOG
BIBLIOGRAPHICAL COMMENTARY. CANADA INDIA PAKISTAN   JURID
UK STRUCT LOC/G NAT/G POL/PAR...NAT/COMP 20   FEDERAL
AUSTRAL. PAGE 66 E1310   CONSTN

                                                             B65
MCWHINNEY E.,JUDICIAL REVIEW IN THE ENGLISH-   GOV/COMP
SPEAKING WORLD (3RD ED.). CANADA UK WOR+45 LEGIS   CT/SYS
CONTROL EXEC PARTIC...JURID 20 AUSTRAL. PAGE 71   ADJUD
E1431   CONSTN

                                                             B66
CAMPBELL E.,PARLIAMENTARY PRIVILEGE IN AUSTRALIA.   LEGIS
UK LAW CONSTN COLONIAL ROLE ORD/FREE SOVEREIGN   PARL/PROC
18/20 COMMONWLTH AUSTRAL FREE/SPEE PARLIAMENT.   JURID
PAGE 19 E0370   PRIVIL

                                                             B67
RAE D.,THE POLITICAL CONSEQUENCES OF ELECTORAL   POL/PAR
LAWS. EUR+WWI ICELAND ISRAEL NEW/ZEALND UK USA+45   CHOOSE
ADJUD APPORT GP/REL MAJORITY...MATH STAT CENSUS   NAT/COMP
CHARTS BIBLIOG 20 AUSTRAL. PAGE 83 E1667   REPRESENT

                                                             B67
WATT A.,THE EVOLUTION OF AUSTRALIAN FOREIGN POLICY   DIPLOM
1938-65. ASIA S/ASIA USA+45 USA-45 INT/ORG NAT/G   WAR
FORCES FOR/AID TREATY 20 AUSTRAL. PAGE 105 E2103

                                                             S67
SHELDON C.H.,"PUBLIC OPINION AND HIGH COURTS: ATTIT
COMMUNIST PARTY CASES IN FOUR CONSTITUTIONAL   CT/SYS
SYSTEMS." CANADA GERMANY/W WOR+45 POL/PAR MARXISM   CONSTN
...METH/COMP NAT/COMP 20 AUSTRAL. PAGE 91 E1818   DECISION

AUSTRIA....SEE ALSO APPROPRIATE TIME/SPACE/CULTURE INDEX

                                                             N
DEUTSCHE BUCHEREI,JAHRESVERZEICHNIS DES DEUTSCHEN   BIBLIOG
SCHRIFTUMS. AUSTRIA EUR+WWI GERMANY SWITZERLND LAW   WRITING
LOC/G DIPLOM ADMIN...MGT SOC 19/20. PAGE 31 E0614   NAT/G

                                                             B61
BEDFORD S.,THE FACES OF JUSTICE: A TRAVELLER'S   CT/SYS
REPORT. AUSTRIA FRANCE GERMANY/W SWITZERLND UK UNIV   ORD/FREE
WOR+45 WOR-45 CULTURE PARTIC GOV/REL MORAL...JURID   PERSON
OBS GOV/COMP 20. PAGE 9 E0174   LAW

                                                             B66
FISCHER H.,EINER IM VORDERGRUND: TARAS   FASCISM
BORODAJKEWYCZ. AUSTRIA POL/PAR PROF/ORG EDU/PROP   LAW
CT/SYS ORD/FREE 20 NAZI. PAGE 38 E0754   ATTIT
                                                          PRESS

                                                             B66
HOEVELER H.J.,INTERNATIONALE BEKAMPFUNG DES   CRIMLGY
VERBRECHENS. AUSTRIA SWITZERLND WOR+45 INT/ORG   CRIME
CONTROL BIO/SOC...METH/COMP NAT/COMP 20 MAFIA   DIPLOM
SCOT/YARD FBI. PAGE 53 E1064   INT/LAW

AUSTRIA-HUNGARY....SEE AUST/HUNG

AUTHORIT....AUTHORITARIANISM, PERSONAL; SEE ALSO DOMIN

                                                             B27
GOOCH G.P.,ENGLISH DEMOCRATIC IDEAS IN THE   IDEA/COMP
SEVENTEENTH CENTURY (2ND ED.). UK LAW SECT FORCES   MAJORIT
DIPLOM LEAD PARL/PROC REV ATTIT AUTHORIT...ANARCH   EX/STRUC
CONCPT 17 PARLIAMENT CMN/WLTH REFORMERS. PAGE 45   CONSERVE
E0885

                                                             B34
GONZALEZ PALENCIA A.ESTUDIO HISTORICO SOBRE LA   LEGIT

CENSURA GUBERNATIVA EN ESPANA 1800-1833. NAT/G   EDU/PROP
COERCE INGP/REL ATTIT AUTHORIT KNOWL...POLICY JURID   PRESS
19. PAGE 44 E0884   CONTROL

                                                             B38
FIELD G.L.,THE SYNDICAL AND CORPORATIVE   FASCISM
INSTITUTIONS OF ITALIAN FASCISM. ITALY CONSTN   INDUS
STRATA LABOR EX/STRUC TOP/EX ADJUD ADMIN LEAD   NAT/G
TOTALISM AUTHORIT...MGT 20 MUSSOLIN/B. PAGE 38   WORKER
E0746

                                                             B39
MCILWAIN C.H.,CONSTITUTIONALISM AND THE CHANGING   CONSTN
WORLD. UK USA-45 LEGIS PRIVIL AUTHORIT SOVEREIGN   POLICY
...GOV/COMP 15/20 MAGNA/CART HOUSE/CMNS. PAGE 71   JURID
E1417

                                                             B40
MCILWAIN C.H.,CONSTITUTIONALISM, ANCIENT AND   CONSTN
MODERN. CHRIST-17C MOD/EUR NAT/G CHIEF PROB/SOLV   GEN/LAWS
INSPECT AUTHORIT ORD/FREE PWR...TIME/SEQ ROMAN/REP.   LAW
PAGE 71 E1418

                                                             S40
GERTH H.,"THE NAZI PARTY: ITS LEADERSHIP AND   POL/PAR
COMPOSITION" (BMR)" GERMANY ELITES STRATA STRUCT   DOMIN
EX/STRUC FORCES ECO/TAC CT/SYS CHOOSE TOTALISM   LEAD
AGE/Y AUTHORIT PWR 20. PAGE 43 E0851   ADMIN

                                                             C43
BENTHAM J.,"ON THE LIBERTY OF THE PRESS, AND PUBLIC   ORD/FREE
DISCUSSION" IN J. BOWRING, ED., THE WORKS OF JEREMY   PRESS
BENTHAM." SPAIN UK LAW ELITES NAT/G LEGIS INSPECT   CONFER
LEGIT WRITING CONTROL PRIVIL TOTALISM AUTHORIT   CONSERVE
...TRADIT 19 FREE/SPEE. PAGE 10 E0193

                                                             B58
CAUGHEY J.W.,IN CLEAR AND PRESENT DANGER. USA+45   NAT/G
ADJUD COERCE ATTIT AUTHORIT...POLICY 20 COLD/WAR   CONTROL
MCCARTHY/J. PAGE 21 E0408   DOMIN
                                                      ORD/FREE

                                                             C58
FRIEDRICH C.J.,"AUTHORITY, REASON AND DISCRETION"   AUTHORIT
IN C. FRIEDRICH'S AUTHORITY (BMR)" UNIV EX/STRUC   CHOOSE
ADJUD ADMIN CONTROL INGP/REL ATTIT PERSON PWR.   RATIONAL
PAGE 41 E0807   PERS/REL

                                                             B60
RIENOW R.,INTRODUCTION TO GOVERNMENT (2ND ED.). UK   CONSTN
USA+45 USSR POL/PAR ADMIN REV CHOOSE SUFF FEDERAL   PARL/PROC
PWR...JURID GOV/COMP T 20. PAGE 85 E1697   REPRESENT
                                                      AUTHORIT

                                                             C60
MCCLEERY R.,"COMMUNICATION PATTERNS AS BASES OF   PERS/REL
SYSTEMS OF AUTHORITY AND POWER" IN THEORETICAL   PUB/INST
STUDIES IN SOCIAL ORGAN. OF PRISON-BMR. USA+45   PWR
SOCIETY STRUCT EDU/PROP ADMIN CONTROL COERCE CRIME   DOMIN
GP/REL AUTHORIT...SOC 20. PAGE 70 E1400

                                                             N61
DELEGACION NACIONAL DE PRENSA,FALANGE ESPANOL   EDU/PROP
TRADICIONALISTA Y DE LAS JUNTAS OFENSIVAS   FASCIST
NACIONALES SINDICALISTAS. IX CONSEJO NACIONAL   CONFER
(PAMPHLET). LAW VOL/ASSN TOTALISM AUTHORIT ORD/FREE POL/PAR
FASCISM...ANTHOL 20 FRANCO/F FALANGIST. PAGE 31
E0605

                                                             S67
MORENO F.J.,"THE SPANISH COLONIAL SYSTEM: A   COLONIAL
FUNCTIONAL APPROACH." SPAIN WOR-45 LAW CHIEF DIPLOM CONTROL
ADJUD CIVMIL/REL AUTHORIT ROLE PWR...CONCPT 17/20.   NAT/G
PAGE 74 E1492   OP/RES

AUTHORITY....SEE DOMIN

AUTOMAT....AUTOMATION; SEE ALSO COMPUTER, PLAN

                                                             L63
LOEVINGER L.,"JURIMETRICS* THE METHODOLOGY OF LEGAL COMPUT/IR
INQUIRY." COMPUTER CREATE PLAN TEC/DEV AUTOMAT   JURID
CT/SYS EFFICIENCY...DECISION PHIL/SCI NEW/IDEA   GEN/METH
QUANT PREDICT. PAGE 66 E1318   ADJUD

                                                             B64
BROOKS T.R.,TOIL AND TROUBLE, A HISTORY OF AMERICAN INDUS
LABOR. WORKER BARGAIN CAP/ISM ADJUD AUTOMAT EXEC   LABOR
GP/REL RACE/REL EFFICIENCY INCOME PROFIT MARXISM   LEGIS
17/20 KENNEDY/JF AFL/CIO NEGRO. PAGE 16 E0310

AUTOMOBILE....AUTOMOBILE

AVERAGE....MEAN, AVERAGE BEHAVIORS

NAGEL S.S.,"A CONCEPTUAL SCHEME OF THE JUDICIAL   POLICY   S63
PROCESS." ADJUD...DECISION NEW/IDEA AVERAGE MODAL   LAW
CHARTS. PAGE 76 E1518   JURID
                                                        DISCRIM

AVERY M.W. E0121

AVERY R.S. E0909

AYLMER G. E0122

AYMARD A. E0123

AZERBAIJAN.....AZERBAIJAN, IRAN
                                       B
BA/MBUTI.....BA MBUTI - THE FOREST PEOPLE (CONGO)

BAADE H. E0124

BAADE H.W. E0125

BABIES.....SEE AGE/C

BACHELDER G.L. E0126

BACKUS R.C. E0127

BACKUS/I.....ISAAC BACKUS

BACON F. E0128,E0129

BACON/F.....FRANCIS BACON

BADEN A.L. E0130

BADEN.....BADEN

GONNER R.,DAS KIRCHENPATRONATRECHT IM   JURID   B62
GROSSHERZOGTUM BADEN. GERMANY LAW PROVS DEBATE   SECT
ATTIT CATHISM 14/19 PROTESTANT CHRISTIAN CHURCH/STA   NAT/G
BADEN. PAGE 44 E0882   GP/REL

BADI J. E0131

BAER E. E0132

BAGHDAD.....BAGHDAD, IRAQ

BAHAWALPUR.....BAHAWALPUR, PAKISTAN

BAHIA.....BAHIA

BAHRO H. E0133

BAIL.....BAIL

BAILEY N.A. E0134

BAILEY S.D. E0135

BAILEY S.K. E0136

BAILEY/JM.....JOHN MORAN BAILEY

BAILEY/S.....S. BAILEY

BAILEY/T.....THOMAS BAILEY

BAINS J.S. E0137

BAKER G.E. E0138,E0139,E0140

BAKER H.R. E0141

BAKER L. E0142

BAKKE E.W. E0143

BAKUBA.....BAKUBA TRIBE

BAL/PAY.....BALANCE OF PAYMENTS

GRIFFIN A.P.C.,LIST OF REFERENCES ON INTERNATIONAL   BIBLIOG/A B08
ARBITRATION. FRANCE L/A+17C USA-45 WOR-45 DIPLOM   INT/ORG
CONFER COLONIAL ARMS/CONT BAL/PAY EQUILIB SOVEREIGN   INT/LAW
...DECISION 19/20 MEXIC/AMER. PAGE 47 E0932   DELIB/GP

BUCK A.E.,"PUBLIC BUDGETING." USA-45 FINAN LOC/G   BUDGET   C29
NAT/G LEGIS BAL/PAY COST...JURID TREND BIBLIOG/A   ROUTINE
20. PAGE 17 E0324   ADMIN

ENKE S.,INTERNATIONAL ECONOMICS. UK USA+45 USSR   INT/TRADE B47
INT/ORG BAL/PWR BARGAIN CAP/ISM BAL/PAY...NAT/COMP   FINAN
20 TREATY. PAGE 35 E0691   TARIFFS
                                                        ECO/TAC

ROBINSON R.D.,INTERNATIONAL BUSINESS POLICY. AFR   ECO/TAC   B64
INDIA L/A+17C USA+45 ELITES AGRI FOR/AID COERCE   DIST/IND
BAL/PAY...DECISION INT/LAW MGT 20. PAGE 85 E1706   COLONIAL
                                                        FINAN

HABERLER G.,A SURVEY OF INTERNATIONAL TRADE THEORY.   INT/TRADE B65
CANADA FRANCE GERMANY ECO/TAC AGREE COST   BAL/PAY
DEMAND WEALTH...ECOMETRIC 19/20 MONOPOLY TREATY.   DIPLOM
PAGE 49 E0968   POLICY

US SENATE COMM ON JUDICIARY,ANTITRUST EXEMPTIONS   BAL/PAY   B65
FOR AGREEMENTS RELATING TO BALANCE OF PAYMENTS.   ADJUD
FINAN ECO/TAC CONTROL WEALTH...POLICY 20 CONGRESS.   MARKET
PAGE 103 E2056   INT/TRADE

FRIEDMANN W.G.,INTERNATIONAL FINANCIAL AID. USA+45   INT/ORG   B66
ECO/DEV ECO/UNDEV NAT/G VOL/ASSN EX/STRUC PLAN RENT   FOR/AID
GIVE BAL/PAY PWR...GEOG INT/LAW STAT TREND UN EEC   TEC/DEV
COMECON. PAGE 41 E0806   ECO/TAC

US SENATE COMM ON FOREIGN REL,INTER-AMERICAN   LAW   B67
DEVELOPMENT BANK ACT AMENDMENT. L/A+17C USA+45   FINAN
DELIB/GP DIPLOM FOR/AID BAL/PAY...CHARTS SENATE.   INT/ORG
PAGE 102 E2034   ECO/UNDEV

US SENATE COMM ON FOREIGN REL,FOREIGN ASSISTANCE   FOR/AID   B67
ACT OF 1967. VIETNAM WOR+45 DELIB/GP CONFER CONTROL   LAW
WAR WEAPON BAL/PAY...CENSUS CHARTS SENATE. PAGE 102   DIPLOM
E2036   POLICY

BARTLETT J.L.,"AMERICAN BOND ISSUES IN THE EUROPEAN   LAW   S67
ECONOMIC COMMUNITY." EUR+WWI LUXEMBOURG USA+45   ECO/TAC
DIPLOM CONTROL BAL/PAY EEC. PAGE 8 E0153   FINAN
                                                        TAX

BAL/PWR.....BALANCE OF POWER

LONDON INSTITUTE WORLD AFFAIRS,THE YEAR BOOK OF   DIPLOM   N
WORLD AFFAIRS. FINAN BAL/PWR ARMS/CONT WAR   FOR/AID
...INT/LAW BIBLIOG 20. PAGE 66 E1322   INT/ORG

GOODNOW F.J.,THE PRINCIPLES OF THE ADMINISTRATIVE   ADMIN   B05
LAW OF THE UNITED STATES. USA-45 LAW STRUCT   NAT/G
EX/STRUC LEGIS BAL/PWR CONTROL GOV/REL PWR...JURID   PROVS
19/20 CIVIL/SERV. PAGE 45 E0887   LOC/G

WILSON W.,CONSTITUTIONAL GOVERNMENT IN THE UNITED   NAT/G   B08
STATES. USA-45 LAW POL/PAR PROVS CHIEF LEGIS   GOV/REL
BAL/PWR ADJUD EXEC FEDERAL PWR 18/20 SUPREME/CT   CONSTN
HOUSE/REP SENATE. PAGE 106 E2130   PARL/PROC

FIGGIS J.N.,CHURCHES IN THE MODERN STATE (2ND ED.).   SECT   B14
LAW CHIEF BAL/PWR PWR...CONCPT CHURCH/STA POPE.   NAT/G
PAGE 38 E0748   SOCIETY
                                                        ORD/FREE

IN THE SHADOW OF FEAR; AMERICAN CIVIL LIBERTIES,   ORD/FREE   N19
1948-49 (PAMPHLET). COM LAW LEGIS BAL/PWR EDU/PROP   CONSTN
CT/SYS RACE/REL DISCRIM MARXISM SOCISM 20 COLD/WAR   POLICY
CONGRESS ACLU CIV/RIGHTS ESPIONAGE. PAGE 2 E0030

BAILEY S.D.,VETO IN THE SECURITY COUNCIL   DELIB/GP   N19
(PAMPHLET). COM USSR WOR+45 BAL/PWR PARL/PROC   INT/ORG
ARMS/CONT PRIVIL PWR...INT/LAW TREND CHARTS 20 UN   DIPLOM
SUEZ. PAGE 7 E0135

BRENNAN W.J. JR.,THE BILL OF RIGHTS AND THE STATES   CONSTN   N19
(PAMPHLET). USA+45 USA-45 LEGIS BAL/PWR ADJUD   PROVS
CT/SYS FEDERAL PWR SOVEREIGN 18/20 SUPREME/CT   GOV/REL
BILL/RIGHT. PAGE 15 E0293   ORD/FREE

STOWELL E.C.,INTERVENTION IN INTERNATIONAL LAW.   BAL/PWR   B21
UNIV LAW SOCIETY INT/ORG ACT/RES PLAN LEGIT ROUTINE   SOVEREIGN
WAR...JURID OBS GEN/LAWS 20. PAGE 94 E1884

BRYCE J.,INTERNATIONAL RELATIONS. CHRIST-17C
EUR+WWI MOD/EUR CULTURE INTELL NAT/G DELIB/GP
CREATE BAL/PWR DIPLOM ATTIT DRIVE RIGID/FLEX
ALL/VALS...PLURIST JURID CONCPT TIME/SEQ GEN/LAWS
TOT/POP. PAGE 16 E0323
INT/ORG
POLICY
B22

NORTON T.J.,LOSING LIBERTY JUDICIALLY. PROVS LEGIS
BAL/PWR CT/SYS...JURID 18/20 SUPREME/CT CIV/RIGHTS
CONGRESS. PAGE 78 E1557
NAT/G
ORD/FREE
CONSTN
JUDGE
B28

BUELL R.,INTERNATIONAL RELATIONS. WOR+45 WOR-45
CONSTN STRATA FORCES TOP/EX ADMIN ATTIT DRIVE
SUPEGO MORAL ORD/FREE PWR SOVEREIGN...JURID SOC
CONCPT 20. PAGE 17 E0326
INT/ORG
BAL/PWR
DIPLOM
B29

BYNKERSHOEK C.,QUAESTIONUM JURIS PUBLICI LIBRI DUO.
CHRIST-17C MOD/EUR CONSTN ELITES SOCIETY NAT/G
PROVS EX/STRUC FORCES TOP/EX BAL/PWR DIPLOM ATTIT
MORAL...TRADIT CONCPT. PAGE 18 E0352
INT/ORG
LAW
NAT/LISM
INT/LAW
B30

RUSSEL F.M.,THEORIES OF INTERNATIONAL RELATIONS.
EUR+WWI FUT MOD/EUR USA-45 INT/ORG DIPLOM...JURID
CONCPT. PAGE 86 E1735
PWR
POLICY
BAL/PWR
SOVEREIGN
B36

BENES E.,INTERNATIONAL SECURITY. GERMANY UK NAT/G
DELIB/GP PLAN BAL/PWR ATTIT ORD/FREE PWR LEAGUE/NAT
20 TREATY. PAGE 10 E0186
EUR+WWI
INT/ORG
WAR
B39

LAVES W.H.C.,INTERNATIONAL SECURITY. EUR+WWI
GERMANY UK USA-45 LAW NAT/G DELIB/GP TOP/EX COERCE
PWR...POLICY FASCIST CONCPT HIST/WRIT GEN/LAWS
LEAGUE/NAT NAZI 20. PAGE 63 E1267
ORD/FREE
LEGIT
ARMS/CONT
BAL/PWR
B39

SIEYES E.J.,LES DISCOURS DE SIEYES DANS LES DEBATS
CONSTITUTIONNELS DE L'AN III (2 ET 18 THERMIDOR).
FRANCE LAW NAT/G PROB/SOLV BAL/PWR GOV/REL 18 JURY.
PAGE 91 E1824
CONSTN
ADJUD
LEGIS
EX/STRUC
B39

ZIMMERN A.,THE LEAGUE OF NATIONS AND THE RULE OF
LAW. WOR-45 STRUCT NAT/G DELIB/GP EX/STRUC BAL/PWR
DOMIN LEGIT COERCE ORD/FREE PWR...POLICY RECORD
LEAGUE/NAT TOT/POP VAL/FREE 20 LEAGUE/NAT. PAGE 108
E2170
INT/ORG
LAW
DIPLOM
B39

CARR E.H.,THE TWENTY YEARS' CRISIS 1919-1939. FUT
WOR-45 BAL/PWR ECO/TAC LEGIT TOTALISM ATTIT
ALL/VALS...POLICY JURID CONCPT TIME/SEQ TREND
GEN/LAWS TOT/POP 20. PAGE 20 E0393
INT/ORG
DIPLOM
PEACE
B40

CROWE S.E.,THE BERLIN WEST AFRICA CONFERENCE,
1884-85. GERMANY ELITES MARKET INT/ORG DELIB/GP
FORCES PROB/SOLV BAL/PWR CAP/ISM DOMIN COLONIAL
...INT/LAW 19. PAGE 28 E0548
AFR
CONFER
INT/TRADE
DIPLOM
B42

FULLER G.H.,RENEGOTIATION OF WAR CONTRACTS: A
SELECTED LIST OF REFERENCES (PAMPHLET). USA-45
ECO/DEV LG/CO NAT/G OP/RES PLAN BAL/PWR LEGIT
CONTROL...MGT 20. PAGE 42 E0823
BIBLIOG
WAR
LAW
FINAN
B44

RUDIN H.R.,ARMISTICE 1918. FRANCE GERMANY MOD/EUR
UK USA-45 NAT/G CHIEF DELIB/GP FORCES BAL/PWR REPAR
ARMS/CONT 20 WILSON/W TREATY. PAGE 86 E1732
AGREE
WAR
PEACE
DIPLOM
B44

ENKE S.,INTERNATIONAL ECONOMICS. UK USA+45 USSR
INT/ORG BAL/PWR BARGAIN CAP/ISM BAL/PAY...NAT/COMP
20 TREATY. PAGE 35 E0691
INT/TRADE
FINAN
TARIFFS
ECO/TAC
B47

JESSUP P.C.,A MODERN LAW OF NATIONS. FUT WOR+45
WOR-45 SOCIETY NAT/G DELIB/GP LEGIS BAL/PWR
EDU/PROP LEGIT PWR...INT/LAW JURID TIME/SEQ
LEAGUE/NAT 20. PAGE 58 E1166
INT/ORG
ADJUD
B48

MORGENTHAL H.J.,POLITICS AMONG NATIONS: THE
STRUGGLE FOR POWER AND PEACE. FUT WOR+45 INT/ORG
OP/RES PROB/SOLV BAL/PWR CONTROL ATTIT MORAL
...INT/LAW BIBLIOG 20 COLD/WAR. PAGE 75 E1494
DIPLOM
PEACE
PWR
POLICY
B48

GROSS L.,"THE PEACE OF WESTPHALIA, 1648-1948."
WOR+45 WOR-45 CONSTN BAL/PWR FEDERAL 17/20 TREATY
WESTPHALIA. PAGE 48 E0949
INT/LAW
AGREE
CONCPT
DIPLOM
S48

MORGENTHAU H.J.,"THE TWILIGHT OF INTERNATIONAL
MORALITY" (BMR)" WOR+45 WOR-45 BAL/PWR WAR NAT/LISM
PEACE...POLICY INT/LAW IDEA/COMP 15/20 TREATY
INTERVENT. PAGE 75 E1495
MORAL
DIPLOM
NAT/G
S48

WALINE M.,LE CONTROLE JURIDICTIONNEL DE
L'ADMINISTRATION. BELGIUM FRANCE UAR JUDGE BAL/PWR
ADJUD CONTROL CT/SYS...GP/COMP 20. PAGE 104 E2093
JURID
ADMIN
PWR
ORD/FREE
B49

WORMUTH F.D.,THE ORIGINS OF MODERN
CONSTITUTIONALISM. GREECE UK LEGIS CREATE TEC/DEV
BAL/PWR DOMIN ADJUD REV WAR PWR...JURID ROMAN/REP
CROMWELL/O. PAGE 107 E2146
NAT/G
CONSTN
LAW
B49

DAVIS K.C.,ADMINISTRATIVE LAW. USA+45 USA-45 NAT/G
PROB/SOLV BAL/PWR CONTROL ORD/FREE...POLICY 20
SUPREME/CT. PAGE 29 E0574
ADMIN
JURID
EX/STRUC
ADJUD
B51

VANDENBOSCH A.,THE UN: BACKGROUND, ORGANIZATION,
FUNCTIONS, ACTIVITIES. WOR+45 LAW CONSTN STRUCT
INT/ORG CONSULT BAL/PWR EDU/PROP EXEC ALL/VALS
...POLICY CONCPT UN 20. PAGE 103 E2071
DELIB/GP
TIME/SEQ
PEACE
B52

SINCO,PHILIPPINE POLITICAL LAW: PRINCIPLES AND
CONCEPTS (10TH ED.). PHILIPPINE LOC/G EX/STRUC
BAL/PWR ECO/TAC TAX ADJUD ADMIN CONTROL CT/SYS SUFF
ORD/FREE...T 20. PAGE 91 E1831
LAW
CONSTN
LEGIS
B54

BURR R.N.,DOCUMENTS ON INTER-AMERICAN COOPERATION:
VOL. I, 1810-1881; VOL. II, 1881-1948. DELIB/GP
BAL/PWR INT/TRADE REPRESENT NAT/LISM PEACE HABITAT
ORD/FREE PWR SOVEREIGN...INT/LAW 20 OAS. PAGE 18
E0345
BIBLIOG
DIPLOM
INT/ORG
L/A+17C
B55

GUAITA A.,BIBLIOGRAFIA ESPANOLA DE DERECHO
ADMINISTRATIVO (PAMPHLET). SPAIN LOC/G MUNIC NAT/G
PROVS JUDGE BAL/PWR GOV/REL OWN...JURID 18/19.
PAGE 48 E0959
BIBLIOG
ADMIN
CONSTN
PWR
B55

HOGAN W.N.,INTERNATIONAL CONFLICT AND COLLECTIVE
SECURITY: THE PRINCIPLE OF CONCERN IN INTERNATIONAL
ORGANIZATION. CONSTN EX/STRUC BAL/PWR DIPLOM ADJUD
CONTROL CENTRAL CONSEN PEACE...INT/LAW CONCPT
METH/COMP 20 UN LEAGUE/NAT. PAGE 53 E1066
INT/ORG
WAR
ORD/FREE
FORCES
B55

CORBETT P.E.,MORALS LAW, AND POWER IN INTERNATIONAL
RELATIONS. WOR+45 WOR-45 INT/ORG VOL/ASSN DELIB/GP
CREATE BAL/PWR DIPLOM LEGIT ARMS/CONT MORAL...JURID
GEN/LAWS TOT/POP LEAGUE/NAT 20. PAGE 26 E0506
SUPEGO
CONCPT
POLICY
INT/LAW
B56

LEVONTIN A.V.,THE MYTH OF INTERNATIONAL SECURITY: A
JURIDICAL AND CRITICAL ANALYSIS. FUT WOR+45 WOR-45
LAW NAT/G VOL/ASSN ACT/RES BAL/PWR ATTIT ORD/FREE
...JURID METH/CNCPT TIME/SEQ TREND STERTYP 20.
PAGE 64 E1289
INT/ORG
INT/LAW
SOVEREIGN
MYTH
B57

PALMER N.D.,INTERNATIONAL RELATIONS. WOR+45 INT/ORG
NAT/G ECO/TAC EDU/PROP COLONIAL WAR PWR SOVEREIGN
...POLICY T 20 TREATY. PAGE 79 E1593
DIPLOM
BAL/PWR
NAT/COMP
B57

BLOCH J.,STATES' RIGHTS: THE LAW OF THE LAND.
USA+45 USA-45 LAW CONSTN LEGIS CONTROL CT/SYS
FEDERAL ORD/FREE...PREDICT 17/20 CONGRESS
SUPREME/CT. PAGE 13 E0246
PROVS
NAT/G
BAL/PWR
CENTRAL
B58

HAND L.,THE BILL OF RIGHTS. USA+45 USA-45 CHIEF
LEGIS BAL/PWR ROLE PWR 18/20 SUPREME/CT CONGRESS
AMEND/V PRESIDENT AMEND/XIV. PAGE 50 E0994
CONSTN
JURID
ORD/FREE
CT/SYS
B58

JENKS C.W.,THE COMMON LAW OF MANKIND. EUR+WWI
MOD/EUR SPACE WOR+45 INT/ORG BAL/PWR ARMS/CONT
JURID
SOVEREIGN
B58

COERCE SUPEGO MORAL...TREND 20. PAGE 58 E1154

PAGE 3 E0065

STONE J.,AGGRESSION AND WORLD ORDER: A CRITIQUE OF UNITED NATIONS THEORIES OF AGGRESSION. LAW CONSTN DELIB/GP PROB/SOLV BAL/PWR DIPLOM DEBATE ADJUD CRIME PWR...POLICY IDEA/COMP 20 UN SUEZ LEAGUE/NAT. PAGE 94 E1879
B58
ORD/FREE
INT/ORG
WAR
CONCPT

WOOD J.E.,CHURCH AND STATE IN SCRIPTURE HISTORY AND CONSTITUTIONAL LAW. LAW CONSTN SOCIETY PROVS VOL/ASSN BAL/PWR COLONIAL CT/SYS ATTIT...BIBLIOG 20 SUPREME/CT CHURCH/STA BIBLE. PAGE 107 E2142
B58
GP/REL
SECT
NAT/G
ADJUD

HALEY A.G.,FIRST COLLOQUIUM ON THE LAW OF OUTER SPACE. WOR+45 INT/ORG ACT/RES PLAN BAL/PWR CONFER ATTIT PWR...POLICY JURID CHARTS ANTHOL 20. PAGE 49 E0979
B59
SPACE
LAW
SOVEREIGN
CONTROL

BEANEY W.B.,"CIVIL LIBERTIES AND STATUTORY CONSTRUCTION"(BMR)" USA+45 LEGIS BAL/PWR 20 SUPREME/CT. PAGE 8 E0162
S59
CT/SYS
ORD/FREE
ADJUD
LAW

MENDELSON W.,"JUDICIAL REVIEW AND PARTY POLITICS" (BMR)" UK USA+45 USA-45 NAT/G LEGIS PROB/SOLV EDU/PROP ADJUD EFFICIENCY...POLICY NAT/COMP 19/20 AUSTRAL SUPREME/CT. PAGE 72 E1436
S59
CT/SYS
POL/PAR
BAL/PWR
JURID

MURPHY W.F.,"LOWER COURT CHECKS ON SUPREME COURT POWER" (BMR)" USA+45 NAT/G PROVS SCHOOL GOV/REL RACE/REL DISCRIM ATTIT...DECISION JURID 20 SUPREME/CT NEGRO. PAGE 75 E1508
S59
CT/SYS
BAL/PWR
CONTROL
ADJUD

POTTER P.B.,"OBSTACLES AND ALTERNATIVES TO INTERNATIONAL LAW." WOR+45 NAT/G VOL/ASSN DELIB/GP BAL/PWR DOMIN ROUTINE...JURID VAL/FREE 20. PAGE 81 E1632
S59
INT/ORG
NAT/G
DIPLOM
INT/LAW

STONE J.,"CONFLICT MANAGEMENT THROUGH CONTEMPORARY INTERNATIONAL LAW AND ORGANIZATION." WOR+45 LAW NAT/G CREATE BAL/PWR DOMIN LEGIT ROUTINE COERCE ATTIT ORD/FREE PWR SOVEREIGN...JURID 20. PAGE 94 E1880
S59
INT/ORG
INT/LAW

LAUTERPACHT E.,"THE SUEZ CANAL SETTLEMENT." FRANCE ISLAM ISRAEL UAR UK BAL/PWR DIPLOM LEGIT...JURID GEN/LAWS ANTHOL SUEZ VAL/FREE 20. PAGE 63 E1263
L60
INT/ORG
LAW

NICHOLS J.P.,"HAZARDS OF AMERICAN PRIVATE INVESTMENT IN UNDERDEVELOPED COUNTRIES." FUT L/A+17C USA+45 USA-45 EXTR/IND CONSULT BAL/PWR ECO/TAC DOMIN ADJUD ATTIT SOVEREIGN WEALTH ...HIST/WRIT TIME/SEQ TREND VAL/FREE 20. PAGE 77 E1546
S60
FINAN
ECO/UNDEV
CAP/ISM
NAT/LISM

BAINS J.S.,STUDIES IN POLITICAL SCIENCE. INDIA WOR+45 WOR-45 CONSTN BAL/PWR ADJUD ADMIN PARL/PROC SOVEREIGN...SOC METH/COMP ANTHOL 17/20 UN. PAGE 7 E0137
B61
DIPLOM
INT/LAW
NAT/G

RIENOW R.,CONTEMPORARY INTERNATIONAL POLITICS. WOR+45 INT/ORG BAL/PWR EDU/PROP COLONIAL NEUTRAL REGION WAR PEACE...INT/LAW 20 COLD/WAR UN. PAGE 85 E1698
B61
DIPLOM
PWR
POLICY
NAT/G

WRIGHT Q.,THE ROLE OF INTERNATIONAL LAW IN THE ELIMINATION OF WAR. FUT WOR+45 WOR-45 NAT/G BAL/PWR DIPLOM DOMIN LEGIT PWR...POLICY INT/LAW JURID CONCPT TIME/SEQ TREND GEN/LAWS COLD/WAR 20. PAGE 108 E2158
B61
INT/ORG
ADJUD
ARMS/CONT

TAUBENFELD H.J.,"A REGIME FOR OUTER SPACE." FUT UNIV R+D ACT/RES PLAN BAL/PWR LEGIT ARMS/CONT ORD/FREE...POLICY JURID TREND UN TOT/POP 20 COLD/WAR. PAGE 95 E1910
L61
INT/ORG
ADJUD
SPACE

ALGER C.F.,"NON-RESOLUTION CONSEQUENCES OF THE UNITED NATIONS AND THEIR EFFECT ON INTERNATIONAL CONFLICT." WOR+45 CONSTN ECO/DEV NAT/G CONSULT DELIB/GP TOP/EX ACT/RES PLAN DIPLOM EDU/PROP ROUTINE ATTIT ALL/VALS...INT/LAW TOT/POP UN 20.
S61
INT/ORG
DRIVE
BAL/PWR

GYORGY A.,PROBLEMS IN INTERNATIONAL RELATIONS. COM CT/SYS NUC/PWR ALL/IDEOS 20 UN EEC ECSC. PAGE 49 E0966
B62
DIPLOM
NEUTRAL
BAL/PWR
REV

PHILLIPS O.H.,CONSTITUTIONAL AND ADMINISTRATIVE LAW (3RD ED.). UK INT/ORG LOC/G CHIEF EX/STRUC LEGIS BAL/PWR ADJUD COLONIAL CT/SYS PWR...CHARTS 20. PAGE 80 E1613
B62
JURID
ADMIN
CONSTN
NAT/G

SOMMER T.,DEUTSCHLAND UND JAPAN ZWISCHEN DEN MACHTEN. GERMANY DELIB/GP BAL/PWR AGREE COERCE TOTALISM PWR 20 CHINJAP TREATY. PAGE 93 E1856
B62
DIPLOM
WAR
ATTIT

THOMPSON K.W.,AMERICAN DIPLOMACY AND EMERGENT PATTERNS. USA+45 USA-45 WOR+45 WOR-45 LAW DELIB/GP FORCES TOP/EX DIPLOM ATTIT DRIVE RIGID/FLEX ORD/FREE PWR SOVEREIGN...POLICY 20. PAGE 96 E1922
B62
NAT/G
BAL/PWR

STEIN E.,"MR HAMMARSKJOLD, THE CHARTER LAW AND THE FUTURE ROLE OF THE UNITED NATIONS SECRETARY-GENERAL." WOR+45 CONSTN INT/ORG DELIB/GP FORCES TOP/EX BAL/PWR LEGIT ROUTINE RIGID/FLEX PWR ...POLICY JURID OBS STERTYP UN COLD/WAR 20 HAMMARSK/D. PAGE 93 E1869
L62
CONCPT
BIOG

CRANE R.D.,"LAW AND STRATEGY IN SPACE." FUT USA+45 WOR+45 AIR LAW INT/ORG NAT/G FORCES ACT/RES PLAN BAL/PWR LEGIT ARMS/CONT COERCE ORD/FREE...POLICY INT/LAW JURID SOC/EXP 20 TREATY. PAGE 27 E0542
S62
CONCPT
SPACE

MCWHINNEY E.,"CO-EXISTENCE, THE CUBA CRISIS, AND COLD WAR-INTERNATIONAL WAR." CUBA USA+45 USSR WOR+45 NAT/G TOP/EX BAL/PWR DIPLOM DOMIN LEGIT PEACE RIGID/FLEX ORD/FREE...STERTYP COLD/WAR 20. PAGE 71 E1427
S62
CONCPT
INT/LAW

SCHACHTER O.,"DAG HAMMARSKJOLD AND THE RELATION OF LAW TO POLITICS." FUT WOR+45 INT/ORG CONSULT PLAN TEC/DEV BAL/PWR DIPLOM LEGIT ATTIT PERCEPT ORD/FREE ...POLICY JURID CONCPT OBS TESTS STERTYP GEN/LAWS 20 HAMMARSK/D. PAGE 87 E1751
S62
ACT/RES
ADJUD

DUNN F.S.,PEACE-MAKING AND THE SETTLEMENT WITH JAPAN. ASIA USA+45 USA-45 FORCES BAL/PWR ECO/TAC CONFER WAR PWR SOVEREIGN 20 CHINJAP COLD/WAR TREATY. PAGE 33 E0661
B63
POLICY
PEACE
PLAN
DIPLOM

GARNER U.F.,ADMINISTRATIVE LAW. UK LAW LOC/G NAT/G EX/STRUC LEGIS JUDGE BAL/PWR BUDGET ADJUD CONTROL CT/SYS...BIBLIOG 20. PAGE 42 E0840
B63
ADMIN
JURID
PWR
GOV/REL

GRIFFITH J.A.G.,PRINCIPLES OF ADMINISTRATIVE LAW (3RD ED.). UK CONSTN EX/STRUC LEGIS ADJUD CONTROL CT/SYS PWR...CHARTS 20. PAGE 47 E0940
B63
JURID
ADMIN
NAT/G
BAL/PWR

LEWIN J.,POLITICS AND LAW IN SOUTH AFRICA. SOUTH/AFR UK POL/PAR BAL/PWR ECO/TAC COLONIAL CONTROL GP/REL DISCRIM PWR 20 NEGRO. PAGE 65 E1293
B63
NAT/LISM
POLICY
LAW
RACE/REL

PACHTER H.M.,COLLISION COURSE: THE CUBAN MISSILE CRISIS AND COEXISTENCE. CUBA USA+45 DIPLOM ARMS/CONT PEACE MARXISM...DECISION INT/LAW 20 COLD/WAR KHRUSH/N KENNEDY/JF CASTRO/F. PAGE 79 E1587
B63
WAR
BAL/PWR
NUC/PWR
DETER

VAN SLYCK P.,PEACE: THE CONTROL OF NATIONAL POWER. CUBA WOR+45 FINAN NAT/G FORCES PROB/SOLV TEC/DEV BAL/PWR ADMIN CONTROL ORD/FREE...POLICY INT/LAW UN COLD/WAR TREATY. PAGE 103 E2069
B63
ARMS/CONT
PEACE
INT/ORG
DIPLOM

BECHHOEFER B.G.,"UNITED NATIONS PROCEDURES IN CASE OF VIOLATIONS OF DISARMAMENT AGREEMENTS." COM USA+45 USSR LAW CONSTN NAT/G EX/STRUC FORCES LEGIS BAL/PWR EDU/PROP CT/SYS ARMS/CONT ORD/FREE PWR ...POLICY STERTYP UN VAL/FREE 20. PAGE 9 E0169
S63
INT/ORG
DELIB/GP

S63
MACWHINNEY E.,"LES CONCEPT SOVIETIQUE DE NAT/G
'COEXISTENCE PACIFIQUE' ET LES RAPPORTS JURIDIQUES CONCPT
ENTRE L'URSS ET LES ETATS OCIDENTAUX." COM FUT DIPLOM
WOR+45 LAW CULTURE INTELL POL/PAR ACT/RES BAL/PWR USSR
...INT/LAW 20. PAGE 67 E1346

S63
MCDOUGAL M.S.,"THE SOVIET-CUBAN QUARANTINE AND ORD/FREE
SELF-DEFENSE." CUBA USA+45 USSR WOR+45 INT/ORG LEGIT
NAT/G BAL/PWR NUC/PWR ATTIT...JURID CONCPT. PAGE 70 SOVEREIGN
E1409

S63
MEYROWITZ H.,"LES JURISTES DEVANT L'ARME NUCLAIRE." ACT/RES
FUT WOR+45 INTELL SOCIETY BAL/PWR DETER WAR...JURID ADJUD
CONCPT 20. PAGE 72 E1451 INT/LAW
NUC/PWR

B64
GRIFFITH W.E.,THE SINO-SOVIET RIFT. ASIA CHINA/COM ATTIT
COM CUBA USSR YUGOSLAVIA NAT/G POL/PAR VOL/ASSN TIME/SEQ
DELIB/GP FORCES TOP/EX DIPLOM EDU/PROP DRIVE PERSON BAL/PWR
PWR...TREND 20 TREATY. PAGE 47 E0941 SOCISM

B64
HANSON R.,FAIR REPRESENTATION COMES TO MARYLAND APPORT
(PAMPHLET). BAL/PWR CT/SYS CHOOSE GOV/REL 20 REPRESENT
MARYLAND SUPREME/CT. PAGE 50 E0997 PROVS
LEGIS

B64
HEKHUIS D.J.,INTERNATIONAL STABILITY: MILITARY, TEC/DEV
ECONOMIC AND POLITICAL DIMENSIONS. FUT WOR+45 LAW DETER
ECO/UNDEV INT/ORG NAT/G VOL/ASSN FORCES ACT/RES REGION
BAL/PWR PWR WEALTH...STAT UN 20. PAGE 51 E1024

B64
MAKI J.M.,COURT AND CONSTITUTION IN JAPAN: SELECTED CONSTN
SUPREME COURT DECISIONS, 1948-60. LAW AGRI FAM JURID
LEGIS BAL/PWR ADMIN CHOOSE...SOC ANTHOL CABINET 20 CT/SYS
CHINJAP CIVIL/LIB. PAGE 68 E1355 CRIME

B64
MARSHALL B.,FEDERALISM AND CIVIL RIGHTS. USA+45 FEDERAL
PROVS BAL/PWR CONTROL CT/SYS PARTIC SOVEREIGN ORD/FREE
...JURID 20 NEGRO CIV/RIGHTS. PAGE 68 E1369 CONSTN
FORCES

B64
STANGER R.J.,ESSAYS ON INTERVENTION. PLAN PROB/SOLV SOVEREIGN
BAL/PWR ADJUD COERCE WAR ROLE PWR...INT/LAW CONCPT DIPLOM
20 UN INTERVENT. PAGE 93 E1865 POLICY
LEGIT

B64
WRIGHT Q.,A STUDY OF WAR. LAW NAT/G PROB/SOLV WAR
BAL/PWR NAT/LISM PEACE ATTIT SOVEREIGN...CENSUS CONCPT
SOC/INTEG. PAGE 108 E2159 DIPLOM
CONTROL

S64
COHEN M.,"BASIC PRINCIPLES OF INTERNATIONAL LAW." INT/ORG
UNIV WOR+45 WOR-45 BAL/PWR LEGIT ADJUD WAR ATTIT INT/LAW
MORAL ORD/FREE PWR...JURID CONCPT MYTH TOT/POP 20.
PAGE 23 E0463

S64
MCGHEE G.C.,"EAST-WEST RELATIONS TODAY." WOR+45 IDEA/COMP
PROB/SOLV BAL/PWR PEACE 20 COLD/WAR. PAGE 71 E1413 DIPLOM
ADJUD

B65
BERKOWITZ M.,AMERICAN NATIONAL SECURITY: A READER ORD/FREE
IN THEORY AND POLICY. USA+45 INT/ORG FORCES BAL/PWR WAR
DIPLOM ECO/TAC DETER PWR...INT/LAW ANTHOL BIBLIOG ARMS/CONT
20 UN. PAGE 11 E0203 POLICY

B65
CHRIMES S.B.,ENGLISH CONSTITUTIONAL HISTORY (3RD CONSTN
ED.). UK CHIEF CONSULT DELIB/GP LEGIS CT/SYS 15/20 BAL/PWR
COMMON/LAW PARLIAMENT. PAGE 22 E0435 NAT/G

B65
HIGHSAW R.B.,CONFLICT AND CHANGE IN LOCAL GOV/REL
GOVERNMENT. USA+45 BUDGET ECO/TAC LEGIT ADJUD PROB/SOLV
ALABAMA. PAGE 52 E1044 LOC/G
BAL/PWR

B65
MCKAY R.B.,REAPPORTIONMENT: THE LAW AND POLITICS OF APPORT
EQUAL REPRESENTATION. FUT USA+45 BAL/PWR MAJORIT
ADJUD CHOOSE REPRESENT GOV/REL FEDERAL...JURID LEGIS
BIBLIOG 20 SUPREME/CT CONGRESS. PAGE 71 E1420 PWR

B65
MORRIS R.B.,THE PEACEMAKERS; THE GREAT POWERS AND SOVEREIGN
AMERICAN INDEPENDENCE. BAL/PWR CONFER COLONIAL REV
NEUTRAL PEACE ORD/FREE TREATY 18 PRE/US/AM. PAGE 75 DIPLOM
E1499

S65
MAC CHESNEY B.,"SOME COMMENTS ON THE 'QUARANTINE' INT/ORG
OF CUBA." USA+45 WOR+45 NAT/G BAL/PWR DIPLOM LEGIT LAW
ROUTINE ATTIT ORD/FREE...JURID METH/CNCPT 20. CUBA
PAGE 67 E1337 USSR

S65
MCWHINNEY E.,"CHANGING INTERNATIONAL LAW METHOD AND LAW
OBJECTIVES IN THE ERA OF THE SOVIET-WESTERN TREND
DETENTE." COM USA+45 NAT/G BAL/PWR CT/SYS ATTIT
ORD/FREE...HUM JURID NEW/IDEA COLD/WAR VAL/FREE 20.
PAGE 71 E1430

S65
PRABHAKAR P.,"SURVEY OF RESEARCH AND SOURCE BIBLIOG
MATERIALS; THE SINO-INDIAN BORDER DISPUTE." ASIA
CHINA/COM INDIA LAW NAT/G PLAN BAL/PWR WAR...POLICY S/ASIA
20 COLD/WAR. PAGE 82 E1645 DIPLOM

B66
BUTTERFIELD H.,DIPLOMATIC INVESTIGATIONS* ESSAYS IN GEN/LAWS
THE THEORY OF INTERNATIONAL POLITICS. LAW INT/ORG UK
FORCES BAL/PWR ARMS/CONT WAR ALL/VALS...HUM DIPLOM
INT/LAW. PAGE 18 E0351

B66
HOYT E.C.,NATIONAL POLICY AND INTERNATIONAL LAW* INT/LAW
CASE STUDIES FROM AMERICAN CANAL POLICY* MONOGRAPH USA-45
NO. 1 -- 1966-1967. PANAMA UK ELITES BAL/PWR DIPLOM
EFFICIENCY...CLASSIF NAT/COMP SOC/EXP COLOMB PWR
TREATY. PAGE 55 E1105

B66
MEDER A.E. JR.,LEGISLATIVE APPORTIONMENT. USA+45 APPORT
BAL/PWR REPRESENT ORD/FREE PWR...JURID 20 LEGIS
SUPREME/CT. PAGE 72 E1433 MATH
POLICY

B66
MENDELSON W.,JUSTICES BLACK AND FRANKFURTER: JURID
CONFLICT IN THE COURT (2ND ED.). NAT/G PROVS ADJUD
PROB/SOLV BAL/PWR CONTROL FEDERAL ISOLAT ANOMIE IDEA/COMP
ORD/FREE...DECISION 20 SUPREME/CT BLACK/HL ROLE
FRANKFUR/F. PAGE 72 E1439

B66
WAINHOUSE D.W.,INTERNATIONAL PEACE OBSERVATION: A PEACE
HISTORY AND FORECAST. INT/ORG PROB/SOLV BAL/PWR DIPLOM
AGREE ARMS/CONT COERCE NUC/PWR...PREDICT METH/COMP
20 UN LEAGUE/NAT OAS TREATY. PAGE 104 E2092

B66
WILSON G.,CASES AND MATERIALS ON CONSTITUTIONAL AND JURID
ADMINISTRATIVE LAW. UK LAW NAT/G EX/STRUC LEGIS ADMIN
BAL/PWR BUDGET DIPLOM ADJUD CONTROL CT/SYS GOV/REL CONSTN
ORD/FREE 20 PARLIAMENT ENGLSH/LAW. PAGE 106 E2126 PWR

S66
BURDETTE F.L.,"SELECTED ARTICLES AND DOCUMENTS ON BIBLIOG
AMERICAN GOVERNMENT AND POLITICS." LAW LOC/G MUNIC USA+45
NAT/G POL/PAR PROVS LEGIS BAL/PWR ADMIN EXEC JURID
REPRESENT MGT. PAGE 17 E0331 CONSTN

B67
INTERNATIONAL CONCILIATION,ISSUES BEFORE THE 22ND PROB/SOLV
GENERAL ASSEMBLY. WOR+45 ECO/UNDEV FINAN BAL/PWR INT/ORG
BUDGET INT/TRADE STRANGE ORD/FREE...INT/LAW 20 UN DIPLOM
COLD/WAR. PAGE 57 E1132 PEACE

B67
MCBRIDE J.H.,THE TEST BAN TREATY: MILITARY, ARMS/CONT
TECHNOLOGICAL, AND POLITICAL IMPLICATIONS. USA+45 DIPLOM
USSR DELIB/GP FORCES LEGIS TEC/DEV BAL/PWR TREATY. NUC/PWR
PAGE 70 E1399

B67
POGANY A.H.,POLITICAL SCIENCE AND INTERNATIONAL BIBLIOG
RELATIONS. BOOKS RECOMMENDED FOR AMERICAN CATHOLIC DIPLOM
COLLEGE LIBRARIES. INT/ORG LOC/G NAT/G FORCES
BAL/PWR ECO/TAC NUC/PWR...CATH INT/LAW TREATY 20.
PAGE 81 E1622

B67
US SENATE COMM ON FOREIGN REL,UNITED STATES ARMS/CONT
ARMAMENT AND DISARMAMENT PROBLEMS. USA+45 AIR WEAPON
BAL/PWR DIPLOM FOR/AID NUC/PWR ORD/FREE SENATE FORCES
TREATY. PAGE 102 E2035 PROB/SOLV

B67
VILE M.J.C.,CONSTITUTIONALISM AND THE SEPARATION OF CONSTN

POWERS. FRANCE UK USA+45 USA-45 NAT/G ADJUD CONTROL BAL/PWR
GOV/REL...POLICY DECISION JURID GEN/LAWS 15/20 CONCPT
MONTESQ. PAGE 104 E2076 LAW

S67
ALDRICH W.A.,"THE SUEZ CRISIS." UAR UK USA+45 DIPLOM
DELIB/GP FORCES BAL/PWR INT/TRADE CONFER CONTROL INT/TRADE
COERCE DETER 20. PAGE 3 E0058 COLONIAL

S67
FLECHTHEIM O.K.,"BLOC FORMATION VS. DIALOGUE." FUT
CONSTN ECO/DEV BAL/PWR PEACE ATTIT PWR COLD/WAR. CAP/ISM
PAGE 38 E0761 MARXISM
DEBATE

S67
STEEL R.,"WHAT CAN THE UN DO?" RHODESIA ECO/UNDEV INT/ORG
DIPLOM ECO/TAC SANCTION...INT/LAW UN. PAGE 93 E1866 BAL/PWR
PEACE
FOR/AID

S67
WINES R.,"THE IMPERIAL CIRCLES. PRINCELY DIPLOMACY, NAT/G
AND IMPERIAL REFORM* 1681-1714." MOD/EUR DELIB/GP NAT/LISM
BAL/PWR CONFER ADJUD PARL/PROC PARTIC ATTIT PWR CENTRAL
17/18. PAGE 106 E2132 REGION

B87
ADAMS J.,A DEFENSE OF THE CONSTITUTIONS OF CONSTN
GOVERNMENT OF THE UNITED STATES OF AMERICA. USA-45 BAL/PWR
STRATA CHIEF EX/STRUC LEGIS CT/SYS CONSERVE PWR
POPULISM...CONCPT CON/ANAL GOV/COMP. PAGE 3 E0048 NAT/G

BALANCE OF PAYMENTS....SEE BAL/PAY

BALANCE OF POWER....SEE BAL/PWR

BALDWIN G.B. E0144

BALDWIN L.D. E0145

BALDWIN/J....JAMES BALDWIN

BALKANS....BALKANS

BALTIMORE....BALTIMORE, MD.

BANDA/HK....H.K. BANDA, PRIME MINISTER OF MALAWI

BANK/ENGL....THE BANK OF ENGLAND

BANKING....SEE FINAN

BANKRUPTCY....BANKRUPTCY

BANTU....BANTU NATION AND CULTURE

BANTUSTANS....BANTUSTANS, REPUBLIC OF SOUTH AFRICA

BAO/DAI....BAO DAI

BAR ASSOCIATION OF ST LOUIS E0146

BARBARIAN....BARBARIAN

BARBASH J. E0147

BARGAIN....BARGAINING; SEE ALSO ECO/TAC, MARKET, DIPLOM

B03
GRIFFIN A.P.C.,LIST OF REFERENCES ON INDUSTRIAL BIBLIOG/A
ARBITRATION (PAMPHLET). USA-45 STRATA VOL/ASSN INDUS
DELIB/GP WORKER ADJUD GP/REL...MGT 19/20. PAGE 46 LABOR
E0921 BARGAIN

B03
GRIFFIN A.P.C.,LISTS PUBLISHED 1902-03: LABOR BIBLIOG/A
PARTICULARLY RELATING TO STRIKES (PAMPHLET). UK LABOR
USA-45 FINAN WORKER PLAN BARGAIN CRIME GOV/REL GP/REL
...POLICY 19/20 PARLIAMENT. PAGE 46 E0923 ECO/TAC

B03
GRIFFIN A.P.C.,SELECT LIST OF BOOKS ON LABOR BIBLIOG/A
PARTICULARLY RELATING TO STRIKES. FRANCE GERMANY GP/REL
MOD/EUR UK USA-45 LAW NAT/G DELIB/GP WORKER BARGAIN MGT
LICENSE PAY ADJUD 19/20. PAGE 46 E0924 LABOR

N19
CARPER E.T.,LOBBYING AND THE NATURAL GAS BILL LOBBY
(PAMPHLET). USA+45 SERV/IND BARGAIN PAY DRIVE ROLE ADJUD
WEALTH 20 CONGRESS SENATE EISNHWR/DD. PAGE 20 E0389 TRIBUTE
NAT/G

B37
BUREAU OF NATIONAL AFFAIRS,LABOR RELATIONS LABOR
REFERENCE MANUAL VOL 1, 1935-1937. BARGAIN DEBATE ADMIN

ROUTINE INGP/REL 20 NLRB. PAGE 17 E0335 ADJUD
NAT/G

B40
WOLFERS A.,BRITAIN AND FRANCE BETWEEN TWO WORLD DIPLOM
WARS. FRANCE UK INT/ORG NAT/G PLAN BARGAIN ECO/TAC WAR
AGREE ISOLAT ALL/IDEOS...DECISION GEOG 20 TREATY POLICY
VERSAILLES INTERVENT. PAGE 107 E2139

B44
CHENEY F.,CARTELS, COMBINES, AND TRUSTS: A SELECTED BIBLIOG/A
LIST OF REFERENCES. GERMANY UK USA-45 WOR-45 LG/CO
DELIB/GP OP/RES BARGAIN CAP/ISM ECO/TAC INT/TRADE ECO/DEV
LICENSE LEGIT CONFER PRICE 20. PAGE 22 E0428 INDUS

B47
ENKE S.,INTERNATIONAL ECONOMICS. UK USA+45 USSR INT/TRADE
INT/ORG BAL/PWR BARGAIN CAP/ISM BAL/PAY...NAT/COMP FINAN
20 TREATY. PAGE 35 E0691 TARIFFS
ECO/TAC

B48
LOGAN R.W.,THE AFRICAN MANDATES IN WORLD POLITICS. WAR
EUR+WWI GERMANY ISLAM INT/ORG BARGAIN...POLICY COLONIAL
INT/LAW 20. PAGE 66 E1321 AFR
DIPLOM

B50
BURDETTE F.L.,LOBBYISTS IN ACTION (PAMPHLET). LOBBY
CONSULT TEC/DEV INSPECT BARGAIN PARL/PROC SANCTION ATTIT
20 CONGRESS. PAGE 17 E0329 POLICY
LAW

B52
PASCUAL R.R.,PARTYLESS DEMOCRACY. PHILIPPINE POL/PAR
BARGAIN LOBBY CHOOSE EFFICIENCY ATTIT 20. PAGE 80 ORD/FREE
E1600 JURID
ECO/UNDEV

B55
BRAUN K.,LABOR DISPUTES AND THEIR SETTLEMENT. INDUS
ECO/TAC ROUTINE TASK GP/REL...DECISION GEN/LAWS. LABOR
PAGE 15 E0288 BARGAIN
ADJUD

B57
US SENATE SPEC COMM POLIT ACT,REPORT OF SPECIAL LOBBY
COMMITTEE TO INVESTIGATE POLITICAL ACTIVITIES, LAW
LOBBYING, AND CAMPAIGN CONTRIBUTIONS. USA+45 ECO/TAC
BARGAIN CRIME ATTIT...DECISION 20 CONGRESS. PARL/PROC
PAGE 103 E2061

B58
CHAMBERLIN E.H.,LABOR UNIONS AND PUBLIC POLICY. LABOR
PLAN BARGAIN SANCTION INGP/REL JURID. PAGE 21 E0416 WEALTH
PWR
NAT/G

B58
CUNNINGHAM W.B.,COMPULSORY CONCILIATION AND POLICY
COLLECTIVE BARGAINING. CANADA NAT/G LEGIS ADJUD BARGAIN
CT/SYS GP/REL...MGT 20 NEW/BRUNS STRIKE CASEBOOK. LABOR
PAGE 28 E0555 INDUS

B61
CARROTHERS A.W.R.,LABOR ARBITRATION IN CANADA. LABOR
CANADA LAW NAT/G CONSULT LEGIS WORKER ADJUD ADMIN MGT
CT/SYS 20. PAGE 20 E0396 GP/REL
BARGAIN

B62
DIESING P.,REASON IN SOCIETY: FIVE TYPES OF RATIONAL
DECISIONS AND THEIR SOCIAL CONDITIONS. SOCIETY METH/COMP
STRUCT LABOR CREATE TEC/DEV BARGAIN ADJUD ROLE DECISION
...JURID BIBLIOG 20. PAGE 31 E0625 CONCPT

B63
JACOBS P.,STATE OF UNIONS. USA+45 STRATA TOP/EX LABOR
GP/REL RACE/REL DEMAND DISCRIM ATTIT PWR 20 ECO/TAC
CONGRESS NEGRO HOFFA/J. PAGE 57 E1145 BARGAIN
DECISION

B64
BROOKS T.R.,TOIL AND TROUBLE. A HISTORY OF AMERICAN INDUS
LABOR. WORKER BARGAIN CAP/ISM ADJUD AUTOMAT EXEC LABOR
GP/REL RACE/REL EFFICIENCY INCOME PROFIT MARXISM LEGIS
17/20 KENNEDY/JF AFL/CIO NEGRO. PAGE 16 E0310

S64
BARKUN M.,"CONFLICT RESOLUTION THROUGH IMPLICIT CONSULT
MEDIATION." UNIV BARGAIN CONSEN FEDERAL JURID. CENTRAL
PAGE 8 E0149 INT/LAW
IDEA/COMP

B65
FLEMING R.W.,THE LABOR ARBITRATION PROCESS. USA+45 GP/REL

LAW BARGAIN ADJUD ROUTINE SANCTION COST...PREDICT
CHARTS TIME 20. PAGE 38 E0763
LABOR
CONSULT
DELIB/GP

B65
ROSS P.,THE GOVERNMENT AS A SOURCE OF UNION POWER.
USA+45 LAW ECO/DEV PROB/SOLV ECO/TAC LEAD GP/REL
...MGT 20. PAGE 86 E1723
LABOR
BARGAIN
POLICY
NAT/G

B66
BURNS A.C.,PARLIAMENT AS AN EXPORT. WOR+45 CONSTN
BARGAIN DEBATE ROUTINE GOV/REL EFFICIENCY...ANTHOL
COMMONWLTH PARLIAMENT. PAGE 17 E0343
PARL/PROC
POL/PAR
CT/SYS
CHIEF

B66
HAYS P.R.,LABOR ARBITRATION: A DISSENTING VIEW.
USA+45 LAW DELIB/GP BARGAIN ADJUD...PREDICT 20.
PAGE 51 E1016
GP/REL
LABOR
CONSULT
CT/SYS

B66
MOSKOW M.H.,TEACHERS AND UNIONS. SCHOOL WORKER
ADJUD LOBBY ATTIT ORD/FREE 20. PAGE 75 E1501
EDU/PROP
PROF/ORG
LABOR
BARGAIN

B66
WASHINGTON S.H.,BIBLIOGRAPHY: LABOR-MANAGEMENT
RELATIONS ACT, 1947 AS AMENDED BY LABOR+MANAGEMENT
REPORTING AND DISCLOSURE ACT, 1959. USA+45 CONSTN
INDUS DELIB/GP LEGIS WORKER BARGAIN ECO/TAC ADJUD
GP/REL NEW/LIB...JURID CONGRESS. PAGE 105 E2100
BIBLIOG
LAW
LABOR
MGT

B67
BEAL E.F.,THE PRACTICE OF COLLECTIVE BARGAINING
(3RD ED.). USA+45 WOR+45 ECO/DEV INDUS LG/CO
PROF/ORG WORKER ECO/TAC GP/REL WEALTH...JURID
METH/CNCPT. PAGE 8 E0160
BARGAIN
MGT
LABOR
ADJUD

B67
HOLSTI K.J.,INTERNATIONAL POLITICS* A FRAMEWORK FOR
ANALYSIS. WOR+45 WOR-45 NAT/G EDU/PROP DETER WAR
WEAPON PWR BIBLIOG. PAGE 55 E1090
DIPLOM
BARGAIN
POLICY
INT/LAW

S67
BERRODIN E.F.,"AT THE BARGAINING TABLE." LABOR
DIPLOM ECO/TAC ADMIN...MGT 20 MICHIGAN. PAGE 11
E0216
PROVS
WORKER
LAW
BARGAIN

S67
CHAMBERLAIN N.W.,"STRIKES IN CONTEMPORARY CONTEXT." LABOR
LAW INDUS NAT/G CHIEF CONFER COST ATTIT ORD/FREE
...POLICY MGT 20. PAGE 21 E0415
BARGAIN
EFFICIENCY
PROB/SOLV

S67
SCHELLING T.C.,"ECONOMICS AND CRIMINAL ENTERPRISE." CRIME
LAW FORCES BARGAIN ECO/TAC CONTROL GAMBLE ROUTINE
ADJUST DEMAND INCOME PROFIT CRIMLGY. PAGE 87 E1756
PROB/SOLV
CONCPT

BARKER L.J. E0148

BARKER T.W. E0148

BARKUN M. E0149

BARLOW R.B. E0150

BARNES H.E. E0151

BARNETT/R....ROSS BARNETT

BAROTSE....BAROTSE TRIBE OF RHODESIA

BARRON J.A. E0152

BARTLETT J.L. E0153

BASHILELE....BASHILELE TRIBE

BASS H.L. E0954

BASSET E. E0978

BASTID P. E1824

BATAK....BATAK TRIBE, PHILIPPINES

BATISTA/J....JUAN BATISTA

BATTEN T.R. E0154

BATY T. E0155

BAVARIA....BAVARIA

BAWONGO....BAWONGO TRIBE

BAXTER M.G. E0156

BAYESIAN INFLUENCE....SEE SIMUL

BAYITCH S.A. E0157,E0158

BAYLEY D.H. E0159

BEAL E.F. E0160

BEALE J.H. E0161

BEANEY W.B. E0162

BEANEY W.M. E0163,E1379

BEARD C.A. E0164,E0165

BEARD/CA....CHARLES A. BEARD

S66
GASS O.,"THE LITERATURE OF AMERICAN GOVERNMENT."
CONSTN DRIVE ORD/FREE...JURID CONCPT METH/CNCPT
IDEA/COMP 20 WILSON/W BEARD/CA LINK/AS. PAGE 42
E0841
NEW/LIB
CT/SYS
NAT/G

BEARDSLEY A.R. E0166

BEASLEY K.E. E0167

BEBR G. E0168

BECCARIA/C....CAESARE BONESARA BECCARIA

BECHHOEFER B.G. E0169

BECK C. E0170

BECKER O. E0171

BECKER T.L. E0172,E0173

BECKER/E....ERNEST BECKER

BEDFORD S. E0174

BEDI A.S. E0175

BEELEY A.L. E0176

BEEM H.D. E0177

BEER U. E0178

BEGGS D.W. E0179

BEHAV/SCI....BEHAVIORAL SCIENCES

BEHAVIORSM....BEHAVIORISM

BEISEL A.R. E0180

BEISER E.N. E0181

BELGIUM....BELGIUM

B06
GRIFFIN A.P.C.,LIST OF BOOKS RELATING TO CHILD
LABOR (PAMPHLET). BELGIUM FRANCE GERMANY MOD/EUR UK
USA-45 ECO/DEV INDUS WORKER CAP/ISM PAY ROUTINE
ALL/IDEOS...MGT SOC 19/20. PAGE 47 E0929
BIBLIOG/A
LAW
LABOR
AGE/C

B29
LEITZ F.,DIE PUBLIZITAT DER AKTIENGESELLSCHAFT.
BELGIUM FRANCE GERMANY UK FINAN PRESS GP/REL PROFIT
KNOWL 20. PAGE 64 E1282
LG/CO
JURID
ECO/TAC
NAT/COMP

B32
MASTERS R.D.,INTERNATIONAL LAW IN INTERNATIONAL
COURTS. BELGIUM EUR+WWI FRANCE GERMANY MOD/EUR
SWITZERLND WOR-45 SOCIETY STRATA STRUCT LEGIT EXEC
ALL/VALS...JURID HIST/WRIT TIME/SEQ TREND GEN/LAWS
20. PAGE 69 E1383
INT/ORG
LAW
INT/LAW

B49
WALINE M.,LE CONTROLE JURIDICTIONNEL DE   JURID
L'ADMINISTRATION. BELGIUM FRANCE UAR JUDGE BAL/PWR ADMIN
ADJUD CONTROL CT/SYS...GP/COMP 20. PAGE 104 E2093 PWR
                                                   ORD/FREE

B51
INSTITUTE DES RELATIONS INTL,LES ASPECTS   WEAPON
ECONOMIQUES DU REARMEMENT (ETUDE DE L'INSTITUT DES DEMAND
RELATIONS INTERNATIONALES A BRUXELLES). BELGIUM UK ECO/TAC
USA+45 EXTR/IND FINAN FORCES WORKER PROB/SOLV   INT/TRADE
DIPLOM PRICE...POLICY 20 TREATY. PAGE 57 E1127

B65
WEIL G.L.,A HANDBOOK ON THE EUROPEAN ECONOMIC   INT/TRADE
COMMUNITY. BELGIUM EUR+WWI FRANCE GERMANY/W ITALY   INT/ORG
CONSTN ECO/DEV CREATE PARTIC GP/REL...DECISION MGT TEC/DEV
CHARTS 20 EEC. PAGE 105 E2107   INT/LAW

BELIEF....SEE SECT, ATTIT

BELL D. E0182

BELL J. E0183

BELLAS/HES....NATIONAL BELLAS HESS

BEMIS S.F. E0184,E0185

BEN/BELLA....AHMED BEN BELLA

BENES E. E0186

BENESE....BENES

BENGAL....BENGAL + BENGALIS

BENIN....BENIN - DISTRICT IN NIGERIA

BENNETT G. E0187

BENNETT H.A. E0188

BENTHAM A. E0189

BENTHAM J. E0190,E0191,E0192,E0193,E0194,E0195,E0196,E0197 ,
     E0198

BENTHAM/J....JEREMY BENTHAM

B05
DICEY A.V.,LECTURES ON THE RELATION BETWEEN LAW AND LAW
PUBLIC OPINION IN ENGLAND DURING THE NINETEENTH   ADJUD
CENTURY. UK LEGIS CT/SYS...JURID 19 TORY/PARTY   ATTIT
BENTHAM/J ENGLSH/LAW. PAGE 31 E0621   IDEA/COMP

B75
MAINE H.S.,LECTURES ON THE EARLY HISTORY OF   CULTURE
INSTITUTIONS. IRELAND UK CONSTN ELITES STRUCT FAM LAW
KIN CHIEF LEGIS CT/SYS OWN SOVEREIGN...CONCPT 16   INGP/REL
BENTHAM/J BREHON ROMAN/LAW. PAGE 68 E1351

B91
SIDGWICK H.,THE ELEMENTS OF POLITICS. LOC/G NAT/G POLICY
LEGIS DIPLOM ADJUD CONTROL EXEC PARL/PROC REPRESENT LAW
GOV/REL SOVEREIGN ALL/IDEOS 19 MILL/JS BENTHAM/J. CONCPT
PAGE 91 E1822

BENTLEY A.F. E0200

BENTLEY/AF....ARTHUR F. BENTLEY

BENTON W.E. E0201

BERGSON/H....HENRI BERGSON

BERGSON/WJ....W. JAMES BERGSON

BERKELEY G. E0202

BERKELEY....BERKELEY, CALIFORNIA

BERKOWITZ M. E0203

BERKS R.N. E0204

BERLE A.A. E0205

BERLIN....BERLIN

BERLIN/BLO....BERLIN BLOCKADE

BERMAN D.M. E0206

BERMAN H.J. E0207,E0208

BERNARD M. E0209

BERNAYS/EL....EDWARD L. BERNAYS

BERNHARD R.C. E0210

BERNS W. E0211,E0212

BERNSTEIN H. E0213

BERNSTEIN M.H. E0214

BERNSTEIN S. E0215

BERRODIN E.F. E0216

BERTHOLD O. E0217

BERWANGER E.H. E0218

BESSARABIA....BESSARABIA; SEE ALSO USSR

BESTERMAN T. E0219

BETH L.P. E0220

BEVAN W. E0221

BEVANS C.I. E0222

BEVERIDGE W. E0223

BHUMIBOL/A....BHUMIBOL ADULYADEJ

BHUTAN....SEE ALSO ASIA

BIAFRA....BIAFRA

BIBBY J. E0224

BIBLE....BIBLE: OLD AND NEW TESTAMENTS

B57
KELSEN H.,WHAT IS JUSTICE. WOR+45 WOR-45...CONCPT JURID
BIBLE. PAGE 60 E1201   ORD/FREE
                                                  OBJECTIVE
                                                  PHIL/SCI

B58
WOOD J.E.,CHURCH AND STATE IN SCRIPTURE HISTORY AND GP/REL
CONSTITUTIONAL LAW. LAW CONSTN SOCIETY PROVS   SECT
VOL/ASSN BAL/PWR COLONIAL CT/SYS ATTIT...BIBLIOG 20 NAT/G
SUPREME/CT CHURCH/STA BIBLE. PAGE 107 E2142   ADJUD

B61
SMITH J.W.,RELIGIOUS PERSPECTIVES IN AMERICAN   SECT
CULTURE. VOL. 2. RELIGION IN AMERICAN LIFE. USA+45 DOMIN
CULTURE NAT/G EDU/PROP ADJUD LOBBY ATTIT...ART/METH SOCIETY
ANTHOL 20 CHURCH/STA BIBLE. PAGE 92 E1845   GP/REL

B66
DOUGLAS W.O.,THE BIBLE AND THE SCHOOLS. USA+45   SECT
CULTURE ADJUD INGP/REL AGE/C AGE/Y ATTIT KNOWL   NAT/G
WORSHIP 20 SUPREME/CT CHURCH/STA BIBLE CHRISTIAN. SCHOOL
PAGE 32 E0644   GP/REL

S68
DUPRE L.,"TILL DEATH DO US PART?" UNIV FAM INSPECT MARRIAGE
LEGIT ADJUD SANCTION PERS/REL ANOMIE RIGID/FLEX SEX CATH
...JURID IDEA/COMP 20 CHURCH/STA BIBLE CANON/LAW   LAW
CIVIL/LAW. PAGE 34 E0666

BIBLIOG....BIBLIOGRAPHY OVER 50 ITEMS

N
LONDON INSTITUTE WORLD AFFAIRS,THE YEAR BOOK OF DIPLOM
WORLD AFFAIRS. FINAN BAL/PWR ARMS/CONT WAR   FOR/AID
...INT/LAW BIBLIOG 20. PAGE 66 E1322   INT/ORG

B
DEUTSCHE BIBLIOTH FRANKF A M,DEUTSCHE   BIBLIOG
BIBLIOGRAPHIE. EUR+WWI GERMANY ECO/DEV FORCES   LAW
DIPLOM LEAD...POLICY PHIL/SCI SOC 20. PAGE 31 E0612 ADMIN
                                                  NAT/G

N
BACKGROUND; JOURNAL OF INTERNATIONAL STUDIES   BIBLIOG
ASSOCIATION. INT/ORG FORCES ACT/RES EDU/PROP COERCE DIPLOM
NAT/LISM PEACE ATTIT...INT/LAW CONCPT 20. PAGE 1   POLICY
E0004

N
INDEX TO LEGAL PERIODICALS. CANADA NEW/ZEALND UK BIBLIOG
USA+45 USA-45 CONSTN LEGIS JUDGE ADJUD ADMIN   INDEX
CONTROL CT/SYS FEDERAL...CRIMLGY INT/LAW 20   LAW
CMN/WLTH AUSTRAL. PAGE 1 E0006   JURID

JOURNAL OF INTERNATIONAL AFFAIRS. WOR+45 ECO/UNDEV POL/PAR ECO/TAC WAR PEACE PERSON ALL/IDEOS ...INT/LAW TREND. PAGE 1 E0010
N
BIBLIOG DIPLOM INT/ORG NAT/G

TEXTBOOKS IN PRINT. WOR+45 WOR-45 LAW DIPLOM ALL/VALS ALL/IDEOS...SOC T 19/20. PAGE 1 E0014
N
BIBLIOG SCHOOL KNOWL

ARBITRATION JOURNAL. WOR+45 LAW INDUS JUDGE DIPLOM CT/SYS INGP/REL 20. PAGE 1 E0016
N
BIBLIOG MGT LABOR ADJUD

AUSTRALIAN PUBLIC AFFAIRS INFORMATION SERVICE. LAW ...HEAL HUM MGT SOC CON/ANAL 20 AUSTRAL. PAGE 1 E0017
N
BIBLIOG NAT/G CULTURE DIPLOM

BIBLIOGRAPHIE DER SOZIALWISSENSCHAFTEN. WOR-45 CONSTN SOCIETY ECO/DEV ECO/UNDEV DIPLOM LEAD WAR PEACE...PHIL/SCI SOC 19/20. PAGE 1 E0019
N
BIBLIOG LAW CONCPT NAT/G

DEUTSCHE BIBLIOGRAPHIE, HALBJAHRESVERZEICHNIS. WOR+45 LAW ADMIN PERSON. PAGE 1 E0020
N
BIBLIOG NAT/G DIPLOM

FOREIGN AFFAIRS. SPACE WOR+45 WOR-45 CULTURE ECO/UNDEV FINAN NAT/G TEC/DEV INT/TRADE ARMS/CONT NUC/PWR...POLICY 20 UN EURATOM ECSC EEC. PAGE 1 E0021
N
BIBLIOG DIPLOM INT/ORG INT/LAW

PUBLISHERS' CIRCULAR, THE OFFICIAL ORGAN OF THE PUBLISHERS' ASSOCIATION OF GREAT BRITAIN AND IRELAND. EUR+WWI MOD/EUR UK LAW PROB/SOLV DIPLOM COLONIAL ATTIT...HUM 19/20 CMN/WLTH. PAGE 2 E0025
N
BIBLIOG NAT/G WRITING LEAD

THE JAPAN SCIENCE REVIEW: LAW AND POLITICS: LIST OF BOOKS AND ARTICLES ON LAW AND POLITICS. CONSTN AGRI INDUS LABOR DIPLOM TAX ADMIN CRIME...INT/LAW SOC 20 CHINJAP. PAGE 2 E0027
N
BIBLIOG LAW S/ASIA PHIL/SCI

CORNELL UNIVERSITY LIBRARY,SOUTHEAST ASIA ACCESSIONS LIST. LAW SOCIETY STRUCT ECO/UNDEV POL/PAR TEC/DEV DIPLOM LEAD REGION. PAGE 26 E0510
N
BIBLIOG S/ASIA NAT/G CULTURE

DE MARTENS G.F.,RECUEIL GENERALE DE TRAITES ET AUTRES ACTES RELATIFS AUX RAPPORTS DE DROIT INTERNATIONAL (41 VOLS.). EUR+WWI MOD/EUR USA-45 ...INDEX TREATY 18/20. PAGE 30 E0587
N
BIBLIOG INT/LAW DIPLOM

DEUTSCHE BUCHEREI,JAHRESVERZEICHNIS DER DEUTSCHEN HOCHSCHULSCHRIFTEN. EUR+WWI GERMANY LAW ADMIN PERSON...MGT SOC 19/20. PAGE 31 E0613
N
BIBLIOG WRITING ACADEM INTELL

DEUTSCHE BUCHEREI,JAHRESVERZEICHNIS DES DEUTSCHEN SCHRIFTUMS. AUSTRIA EUR+WWI GERMANY SWITZERLND LAW LOC/G DIPLOM ADMIN...MGT SOC 19/20. PAGE 31 E0614
N
BIBLIOG WRITING NAT/G

DEUTSCHE BUCHEREI,DEUTSCHES BUCHERVERZEICHNIS. GERMANY LAW CULTURE POL/PAR ADMIN LEAD ATTIT PERSON ...SOC 20. PAGE 31 E0615
N
BIBLIOG NAT/G DIPLOM ECO/DEV

HARVARD LAW SCHOOL LIBRARY,ANNUAL LEGAL BIBLIOGRAPHY. USA+45 CONSTN LEGIS ADJUD CT/SYS ...POLICY 20. PAGE 50 E1005
N
BIBLIOG JURID LAW INT/LAW

HARVARD UNIVERSITY LAW LIBRARY,CATALOG OF INTERNATIONAL LAW AND RELATIONS. WOR+45 WOR-45 INT/ORG NAT/G JUDGE DIPLOM INT/TRADE ADJUD CT/SYS 19/20. PAGE 51 E1007
N
BIBLIOG INT/LAW JURID

MINISTERE DE L'EDUC NATIONALE,CATALOGUE DES THESES
N
BIBLIOG

DE DOCTORAT SOUTENNES DEVANT LES UNIVERSITAIRES FRANCAISES. FRANCE LAW DIPLOM ADMIN...HUM SOC 20. PAGE 73 E1465
ACADEM KNOWL NAT/G

MINISTRY OF OVERSEAS DEVELOPME,TECHNICAL CO-OPERATION -- A BIBLIOGRAPHY. UK LAW SOCIETY DIPLOM ECO/TAC FOR/AID...STAT 20 CMN/WLTH. PAGE 73 E1466
N
BIBLIOG TEC/DEV ECO/DEV NAT/G

NEW YORK STATE LIBRARY,CHECKLIST OF OFFICIAL PUBLICATIONS OF THE STATE OF NEW YORK. USA+45 USA-45 LAW PROB/SOLV LEAD ATTIT 19/20. PAGE 77 E1539
N
BIBLIOG PROVS WRITING GOV/REL

PUBLISHERS' CIRCULAR LIMITED,THE ENGLISH CATALOGUE OF BOOKS. UK WOR+45 WOR-45 LAW CULTURE LOC/G NAT/G ADMIN LEAD...MGT 19/20. PAGE 83 E1658
N
BIBLIOG ALL/VALS ALL/IDEOS SOCIETY

SOCIETE DES NATIONS,TRAITES INTERNATIONAUX ET ACTES LEGISLATIFS. WOR-45 INT/ORG NAT/G...INT/LAW JURID 20 LEAGUE/NAT TREATY. PAGE 92 E1851
N
BIBLIOG DIPLOM LEGIS ADJUD

SOUTH AFRICA STATE LIBRARY,SOUTH AFRICAN NATIONAL BIBLIOGRAPHY, SANB. SOUTH/AFR LAW NAT/G EDU/PROP ...MGT PSY SOC 20. PAGE 93 E1858
N
BIBLIOG PRESS WRITING

UNESCO,INTERNATIONAL BIBLIOGRAPHY OF POLITICAL SCIENCE (VOLUMES 1-8). WOR+45 LAW NAT/G EX/STRUC LEGIS PROB/SOLV DIPLOM ADMIN GOV/REL 20 UNESCO. PAGE 98 E1957
N
BIBLIOG CONCPT IDEA/COMP

UNITED NATIONS,UNITED NATIONS PUBLICATIONS. WOR+45 ECO/UNDEV AGRI FINAN FORCES ADMIN LEAD WAR PEACE ...POLICY INT/LAW 20 UN. PAGE 98 E1965
N
BIBLIOG INT/ORG DIPLOM

UNITED NATIONS,YEARBOOK OF THE INTERNATIONAL LAW COMMISSION....CON/ANAL 20 UN. PAGE 98 E1966
N
BIBLIOG INT/ORG INT/LAW DELIB/GP

GRONING J.,BIBLIOTHECA JURIS GENTIUM COMMUNIS, QUA PRAECIPUORUM, ASIAE, AFRICAE, ET AMERICAE, POPULORUM DE JURIS NATURAE... AFR ASIA S/ASIA USA-45 16/17. PAGE 48 E0946
B01
BIBLIOG JURID LAW NAT/G

FORTESCUE G.K.,SUBJECT INDEX OF THE MODERN WORKS ADDED TO THE LIBRARY OF THE BRITISH MUSEUM IN THE YEARS 1881-1900 (3 VOLS.). UK LAW CONSTN FINAN NAT/G FORCES INT/TRADE COLONIAL 19. PAGE 39 E0775
B03
BIBLIOG INDEX WRITING

GRIFFIN A.P.C.,LISTS PUBLISHED 1902-03: GOVERNMENT OWNERSHIP OF RAILROADS (PAMPHLET). USA-45 LAW NAT/G RATION GOV/REL CENTRAL SOCISM...POLICY 19/20. PAGE 46 E0922
B03
BIBLIOG DIST/IND CONTROL ADJUD

GRONING J.,BIBLIOTHECA JURIS GENTIUM EXOTICA. AFR ASIA S/ASIA USA-45 16/17. PAGE 48 E0947
B03
BIBLIOG JURID NAT/G LAW

DUNNING W.A.,"HISTORY OF POLITICAL THEORIES FROM LUTHER TO MONTESQUIEU." LAW NAT/G SECT DIPLOM REV WAR ORD/FREE SOVEREIGN CONSERVE...TRADIT BIBLIOG 16/18. PAGE 33 E0663
C05
PHIL/SCI CONCPT GEN/LAWS

FOSTER J.W.,THE PRACTICE OF DIPLOMACY AS ILLUSTRATED IN THE FOREIGN RELATIONS OF THE UNITED STATES. MOD/EUR USA-45 NAT/G EX/STRUC ADMIN ...POLICY INT/LAW BIBLIOG 19/20. PAGE 39 E0777
B06
DIPLOM ROUTINE PHIL/SCI

LOBINGIER C.S.,THE PEOPLE'S LAW OR POPULAR PARTICIPATION IN LAW-MAKING. FRANCE SWITZERLND UK LOC/G NAT/G PROVS LEGIS SUFF MAJORITY PWR POPULISM ...GOV/COMP BIBLIOG 19. PAGE 66 E1314
B09
CONSTN LAW PARTIC

BORCHARD E.M.,BIBLIOGRAPHY OF INTERNATIONAL LAW AND CONTINENTAL LAW. EUR+WWI MOD/EUR UK LAW INT/TRADE WAR PEACE...GOV/COMP NAT/COMP 19/20. PAGE 14 E0267
B13
BIBLIOG INT/LAW JURID

DIPLOM

B14
MCLAUGHLIN A.C.,CYCLOPEDIA OF AMERICAN GOVERNMENT USA+45
(3 VOLS.). LAW CONSTN POL/PAR ADMIN ROUTINE NAT/G
...INT/LAW CONCPT BIBLIOG METH 20. PAGE 71 E1421 DICTIONARY

B15
INTERNATIONAL LAW ASSOCIATION,A FORTY YEARS' BIBLIOG
CATALOGUE OF THE BOOKS, PAMPHLETS AND PAPERS IN THE LAW
LIBRARY OF THE INTERNATIONAL LAW ASSOCIATION. INT/LAW
INT/ORG DIPLOM ADJUD NEUTRAL...IDEA/COMP 19/20.
PAGE 57 E1134

B17
MEYER H.H.B.,LIST OF REFERENCES ON EMBARGOES BIBLIOG
(PAMPHLET). USA-45 AGRI DIPLOM WRITING DEBATE DIST/IND
WEAPON...INT/LAW 18/20 CONGRESS. PAGE 72 E1447 ECO/TAC
INT/TRADE

N19
JANOWITZ M.,SOCIAL CONTROL OF ESCALATED RIOTS CROWD
(PAMPHLET). USA+45 LAW SOCIETY MUNIC FORCES ORD/FREE
PROB/SOLV EDU/PROP TV CRIME ATTIT...BIBLIOG 20 CONTROL
NEGRO CIV/RIGHTS. PAGE 58 E1148 RACE/REL

B20
MEYER H.H.B.,LIST OF REFERENCES ON THE TREATY- BIBLIOG
MAKING POWER. USA-45 CONTROL PWR...INT/LAW TIME/SEQ DIPLOM
18/20 TREATY. PAGE 72 E1448 CONSTN

B20
VINOGRADOFF P.,OUTLINES OF HISTORICAL JURISPRUDENCE JURID
(2 VOLS.). GREECE MEDIT-7 LAW CONSTN FACE/GP FAM METH
KIN MUNIC CRIME OWN...INT/LAW IDEA/COMP BIBLIOG.
PAGE 104 E2080

C20
DUNNING W.A.,"A HISTORY OF POLITICAL THINKERS FROM IDEA/COMP
ROUSSEAU TO SPENCER." NAT/G REV NAT/LISM UTIL PHIL/SCI
CONSERVE MARXISM POPULISM...JURID BIBLIOG 18/19. CONCPT
PAGE 33 E0664 GEN/LAWS

L21
HALDEMAN E.,"SERIALS OF AN INTERNATIONAL BIBLIOG
CHARACTER." WOR-45 DIPLOM...ART/METH GEOG HEAL HUM PHIL/SCI
INT/LAW JURID PSY SOC. PAGE 49 E0978

B23
HEADICAR B.M.,CATALOGUE OF THE BOOKS, PAMPHLETS, BIBLIOG
AND OTHER DOCUMENTS IN THE EDWARD FRY LIBRARY OF INT/LAW
INTERNATIONAL LAW... UK INT/ORG 20. PAGE 51 E1019 DIPLOM

C24
BARNES H.E.,"SOCIOLOGY AND POLITICAL THEORY: A CONCPT
CONSIDERATION OF THE SOCIOLOGICAL BASIS OF STRUCT
POLITICS." LAW CONSTN NAT/G DIPLOM DOMIN ROUTINE SOC
REV ORD/FREE SOVEREIGN...PHIL/SCI CLASSIF BIBLIOG
18/20. PAGE 8 E0151

C24
SHERMAN C.P.,"ROMAN LAW IN THE MODERN WORLD (2ND LAW
ED.) (3 VOLS.)" MEDIT-7...JURID BIBLIOG. PAGE 91 ADJUD
E1819 OWN
CONSTN

B26
INSTITUT INTERMEDIAIRE INTL,REPERTOIRE GENERAL DES BIBLIOG
TRAITES ET AUTRES ACTES DIPLOMATIQUES CONCLUS DIPLOM
DEPUIS 1895 JUSQU'EN 1920. MOD/EUR WOR-45 INT/ORG
VOL/ASSN DELIB/GP INT/TRADE WAR TREATY 19/20.
PAGE 56 E1125

B28
LAPRADELLE,ANNUAIRE DE LA VIE INTERNATIONALE: BIBLIOG
POLITIQUE, ECONOMIQUE, JURIDIQUE. INT/ORG CONFER DIPLOM
ARMS/CONT 20. PAGE 63 E1255 INT/LAW

B28
MACDONALD A.F.,ELEMENTS OF POLITICAL SCIENCE LAW
RESEARCH. USA-45 ACADEM JUDGE EDU/PROP DEBATE ADJUD FEDERAL
EXEC...BIBLIOG METH T 20 CONGRESS. PAGE 67 E1338 DECISION
CT/SYS

B29
PRATT I.A.,MODERN EGYPT: A LIST OF REFERENCES TO BIBLIOG
MATERIAL IN THE NEW YORK PUBLIC LIBRARY. UAR ISLAM
ECO/UNDEV...GEOG JURID SOC LING 20. PAGE 82 E1647 DIPLOM
NAT/G

B30
FAIRLIE J.A.,COUNTY GOVERNMENT AND ADMINISTRATION. ADMIN
UK USA+45 NAT/G SCHOOL FORCES BUDGET TAX CT/SYS GOV/REL
CHOOSE...JURID BIBLIOG 11/20. PAGE 36 E0713 LOC/G
MUNIC

B30
GREEN F.M.,CONSTITUTIONAL DEVELOPMENT IN THE SOUTH CONSTN
ATLANTIC STATES, 1776-1860; A STUDY IN THE PROVS
EVOLUTION OF DEMOCRACY. USA-45 ELITES SOCIETY PLURISM
STRATA ECO/DEV AGRI POL/PAR EX/STRUC LEGIS CT/SYS REPRESENT
REGION...BIBLIOG 18/19 MARYLAND VIRGINIA GEORGIA
NORTH/CAR SOUTH/CAR. PAGE 46 E0905

B31
COLUMBIA UNIVERSITY,A BIBLIOGRAPHY OF THE FACULTY BIBLIOG
OF POLITICAL SCIENCE OF COLUMBIA UNIVERSITY, ACADEM
1880-1930. USA-45 LAW NAT/G LEGIS DIPLOM LEAD WAR PHIL/SCI
GOV/REL ATTIT...TIME/SEQ 19/20. PAGE 24 E0478

B32
GREGORY W.,LIST OF THE SERIAL PUBLICATIONS OF BIBLIOG
FOREIGN GOVERNMENTS, 1815-1931. WOR-45 DIPLOM ADJUD NAT/G
...POLICY 20. PAGE 46 E0914 LAW
JURID

B35
BURCHFIELD L.,STUDENT'S GUIDE TO MATERIALS IN BIBLIOG
POLITICAL SCIENCE. FINAN INT/ORG NAT/G POL/PAR INDEX
DIPLOM PRESS ADMIN...BIOG 18/19. PAGE 17 E0328 LAW

B35
CUMMING J.,A CONTRIBUTION TOWARD A BIBLIOGRAPHY BIBLIOG
DEALING WITH CRIME AND COGNATE SUBJECTS (3RD ED.). CRIMLGY
UK LAW CULTURE PUB/INST ADJUD AGE BIO/SOC...PSY SOC FORCES
SOC/WK STAT METH/COMP 20. PAGE 28 E0552 CT/SYS

B35
NORDSKOG J.E.,SOCIAL REFORM IN NORWAY. NORWAY INDUS LABOR
NAT/G POL/PAR LEGIS ADJUD...SOC BIBLIOG SOC/INTEG ADJUST
20. PAGE 78 E1555

B37
BADEN A.L.,IMMIGRATION AND ITS RESTRICTION IN THE BIBLIOG
US (PAMPHLET). USA-45 NAT/G LEGIS...GEOG 20 STRANGE
CONGRESS. PAGE 7 E0130 CONTROL
LAW

B37
BEARDSLEY A.R.,LEGAL BIBLIOGRAPHY AND THE USE OF BIBLIOG
LAW BOOKS. CONSTN CREATE PROB/SOLV...DECISION JURID LAW
LAB/EXP. PAGE 9 E0166 METH
OP/RES

B37
KETCHAM E.H.,PRELIMINARY SELECT BIBLIOGRAPHY OF BIBLIOG
INTERNATIONAL LAW (PAMPHLET). WOR-45 LAW INT/ORG DIPLOM
NAT/G PROB/SOLV CT/SYS NEUTRAL WAR 19/20. PAGE 60 ADJUD
E1207 INT/LAW

B37
THOMPSON J.W.,SECRET DIPLOMACY: A RECORD OF DIPLOM
ESPIONAGE AND DOUBLE-DEALING: 1500-1815. CHRIST-17C CRIME
MOD/EUR NAT/G WRITING RISK MORAL...ANTHOL BIBLIOG
16/19 ESPIONAGE. PAGE 96 E1920

B38
CLARK J.P.,THE RISE OF A NEW FEDERALISM. LEGIS FEDERAL
TARIFFS EFFICIENCY NAT/LISM UTIL...JURID SOC PROVS
GEN/LAWS BIBLIOG 19/20. PAGE 23 E0451 NAT/G
GOV/REL

B38
GRISWOLD A.W.,THE FAR EASTERN POLICY OF THE UNITED DIPLOM
STATES. ASIA S/ASIA USA-45 INT/ORG INT/TRADE WAR POLICY
NAT/LISM...BIBLIOG 19/20 LEAGUE/NAT ROOSEVLT/T CHIEF
ROOSEVLT/F WILSON/W TREATY. PAGE 47 E0943

B39
TIMASHEFF N.S.,AN INTRODUCTION TO THE SOCIOLOGY OF SOC
LAW. CRIME ANOMIE ATTIT DRIVE ORD/FREE...JURID PSY BIBLIOG
CONCPT. PAGE 96 E1926 PWR

C39
HADDOW A.,"POLITICAL SCIENCE IN AMERICAN COLLEGES USA-45
AND UNIVERSITIES 1636-1900." CONSTN MORAL...POLICY LAW
INT/LAW CON/ANAL BIBLIOG T 17/20. PAGE 49 E0971 ACADEM
KNOWL

C39
SCOTT J.B.,"LAW, THE STATE, AND THE INTERNATIONAL LAW
COMMUNITY (2 VOLS.)" INTELL INT/ORG NAT/G SECT PHIL/SCI
INT/TRADE WAR...INT/LAW GEN/LAWS BIBLIOG. PAGE 90 DIPLOM
E1798 CONCPT

B40
ANDERSON W.,FUNDAMENTALS OF AMERICAN GOVERNMENT. NAT/G
USA-45 LAW POL/PAR CHIEF EX/STRUC BUDGET ADMIN LOC/G
CT/SYS PARL/PROC CHOOSE FEDERAL...BIBLIOG 20. GOV/REL
PAGE 5 E0093 CONSTN

B41

BIRDSALL P.,VERSAILLES TWENTY YEARS AFTER. MOD/EUR DIPLOM
POL/PAR CHIEF CONSULT FORCES LEGIS REPAR PEACE NAT/LISM
ORD/FREE...BIBLIOG 20 PRESIDENT TREATY. PAGE 12 WAR
E0231

B41

CHAFEE Z. JR.,FREE SPEECH IN THE UNITED STATES. ORD/FREE
USA-45 ADJUD CONTROL CRIME WAR...BIBLIOG 20 CONSTN
FREE/SPEE AMEND/I SUPREME/CT. PAGE 21 E0413 ATTIT
JURID

B41

EVANS C.,AMERICAN BIBLIOGRAPHY... (12 VOLUMES). BIBLIOG
USA-45 LAW DIPLOM ADMIN PERSON...HUM SOC 17/18. NAT/G
PAGE 35 E0704 ALL/VALS
ALL/IDEOS

B41

GILMORE M.P.,ARGUMENT FROM ROMAN LAW IN POLITICAL JURID
THOUGHT, 1200-1600. INTELL LICENSE CONTROL CT/SYS LAW
GOV/REL PRIVIL PWR...IDEA/COMP BIBLIOG 13/16. CONCPT
PAGE 44 E0866 NAT/G

B42

CRAIG A.,ABOVE ALL LIBERTIES. FRANCE UK USA-45 LAW ORD/FREE
CONSTN CULTURE INTELL NAT/G SECT JUDGE...IDEA/COMP MORAL
BIBLIOG 18/20. PAGE 27 E0536 WRITING
EDU/PROP

B42

SETARO F.C.,A BIBLIOGRAPHY OF THE WRITINGS OF BIBLIOG
ROSCOE POUND. USA-45 CT/SYS 20. PAGE 90 E1806 LAW
ATTIT
JUDGE

B43

CLAGETT H.L.,A GUIDE TO THE LAW AND LEGAL BIBLIOG
LITERATURE OF PARAGUAY. PARAGUAY CONSTN COM/IND JURID
LABOR MUNIC JUDGE ADMIN CT/SYS...CRIMLGY INT/LAW LAW
CON/ANAL 20. PAGE 22 E0439 L/A+17C

B43

CONOVER H.F.,THE BALKANS: A SELECTED LIST OF BIBLIOG
REFERENCES. ALBANIA BULGARIA ROMANIA YUGOSLAVIA EUR+WWI
INT/ORG PROB/SOLV DIPLOM LEGIT CONFER ADJUD WAR
NAT/LISM PEACE PWR 20 LEAGUE/NAT. PAGE 25 E0493

B44

BEARD C.A.,AMERICAN GOVERNMENT AND POLITICS (REV. LEAD
ED.). CONSTN MUNIC POL/PAR PROVS EX/STRUC LEGIS USA-45
TOP/EX CT/SYS GOV/REL...BIBLIOG T 18/20. PAGE 9 NAT/G
E0165 LOC/G

B44

FULLER G.H.,MILITARY GOVERNMENT: A LIST OF BIBLIOG
REFERENCES (A PAMPHLET). ITALY UK USA-45 WOR-45 LAW DIPLOM
FORCES DOMIN ADMIN ARMS/CONT ORD/FREE PWR CIVMIL/REL
...DECISION 20 CHINJAP. PAGE 41 E0822 SOVEREIGN

B44

FULLER G.H.,RENEGOTIATION OF WAR CONTRACTS: A BIBLIOG
SELECTED LIST OF REFERENCES (PAMPHLET). USA-45 WAR
ECO/DEV LG/CO NAT/G OP/RES PLAN BAL/PWR LEGIT LAW
CONTROL...MGT 20. PAGE 42 E0823 FINAN

B44

US LIBRARY OF CONGRESS,RUSSIA: A CHECK LIST BIBLIOG
PRELIMINARY TO A BASIC BIBLIOGRAPHY OF MATERIALS IN LAW
THE RUSSIAN LANGUAGE. COM USSR CULTURE EDU/PROP SECT
MARXISM...ART/METH HUM LING 19/20. PAGE 101 E2015

B45

CLAGETT H.L.,A GUIDE TO THE LAW AND LEGAL BIBLIOG
LITERATURE OF THE MEXICAN STATES. CONSTN LEGIS JURID
JUDGE ADJUD ADMIN...INT/LAW CON/ANAL 20 MEXIC/AMER. L/A+17C
PAGE 22 E0440 LAW

B45

CONOVER H.F.,THE GOVERNMENTS OF THE MAJOR FOREIGN BIBLIOG
POWERS: A BIBLIOGRAPHY. FRANCE GERMANY ITALY UK NAT/G
USSR CONSTN LOC/G POL/PAR EX/STRUC FORCES ADMIN DIPLOM
CT/SYS CIVMIL/REL TOTALISM...POLICY 19/20. PAGE 25
E049

B45

CONOVER H.F.,THE NAZI STATE: WAR CRIMES AND WAR BIBLIOG
CRIMINALS. GERMANY CULTURE NAT/G SECT FORCES DIPLOM WAR
INT/TRADE EDU/PROP...INT/LAW BIOG HIST/WRIT CRIME
TIME/SEQ 20. PAGE 25 E0495

B45

UNCIO CONFERENCE LIBRARY,SHORT TITLE CLASSIFIED BIBLIOG
CATALOG. WOR-45 DOMIN COLONIAL WAR...SOC/WK 20 DIPLOM
LEAGUE/NAT UN. PAGE 98 E1955 INT/ORG
INT/LAW

B45

US DEPARTMENT OF STATE,PUBLICATIONS OF THE BIBLIOG
DEPARTMENT OF STATE: A LIST CUMULATIVE FROM OCTOBER DIPLOM
1, 1929 (PAMPHLET). ASIA EUR+WWI ISLAM L/A+17C INT/TRADE
USA-45 ADJUD...INT/LAW 20. PAGE 99 E1993

B46

AMERICAN DOCUMENTATION INST,CATALOGUE OF AUXILIARY BIBLIOG
PUBLICATIONS IN MICROFILMS AND PHOTOPRINTS. USA-45 EDU/PROP
LAW AGRI CREATE TEC/DEV ADMIN...GEOG LING MATH 20. PSY
PAGE 4 E0077

B46

MANNHEIM H.,CRIMINAL JUSTICE AND SOCIAL ADJUD
RECONSTRUCTION. USA+45 EDU/PROP CRIME ANOMIE LAW
...JURID BIBLIOG 20. PAGE 68 E1361 STRUCT
ADJUST

B46

PATON G.W.,A TEXT-BOOK OF JURISPRUDENCE. CREATE LAW
INSPECT LEGIT CT/SYS ROUTINE CRIME INGP/REL PRIVIL ADJUD
...CONCPT BIBLIOG 20. PAGE 80 E1601 JURID
T

L46

ERNST M.L.,"THE FIRST FREEDOM." USA-45 LAW R+D BIBLIOG
PRESS 20. PAGE 35 E0696 EDU/PROP
ORD/FREE
COM/IND

C46

GOODRICH L.M.,"CHARTER OF THE UNITED NATIONS: CONSTN
COMMENTARY AND DOCUMENTS." EX/STRUC ADMIN...INT/LAW INT/ORG
CON/ANAL BIBLIOG 20 UN. PAGE 45 E0890 DIPLOM

B47

CLAGETT H.L.,A GUIDE TO THE LAW AND LEGAL BIBLIOG
LITERATURE OF CHILE, 1917-1946. CHILE CONSTN LABOR L/A+17C
JUDGE ADJUD ADMIN...CRIMLGY INT/LAW JURID CON/ANAL LAW
20. PAGE 22 E0442 LEGIS

B47

CLAGETT H.L.,A GUIDE TO THE LAW AND LEGAL BIBLIOG
LITERATURE OF ECUADOR. ECUADOR CONSTN LABOR LEGIS JURID
JUDGE ADJUD ADMIN CIVMIL/REL...CRIMLGY INT/LAW LAW
CON/ANAL 20. PAGE 22 E0443 L/A+17C

B47

CLAGETT H.L.,A GUIDE TO THE LAW AND LEGAL BIBLIOG
LITERATURE OF PERU. PERU CONSTN COM/IND LABOR MUNIC L/A+17C
JUDGE ADMIN CT/SYS...CRIMLGY INT/LAW JURID 20. PHIL/SCI
PAGE 23 E0444 LAW

B47

CLAGETT H.L.,A GUIDE TO THE LAW AND LEGAL BIBLIOG
LITERATURE OF URUGUAY. URUGUAY CONSTN COM/IND FINAN LAW
LABOR MUNIC JUDGE PRESS ADMIN CT/SYS...INT/LAW JURID
PHIL/SCI 20. PAGE 23 E0445 L/A+17C

B47

CLAGETT H.L.,A GUIDE TO THE LAW AND LEGAL BIBLIOG
LITERATURE OF VENEZUELA. VENEZUELA CONSTN LABOR L/A+17C
LEGIS JUDGE ADJUD ADMIN CIVMIL/REL...CRIMLGY JURID INT/LAW
CON/ANAL 20. PAGE 23 E0446 LAW

B47

HIRSHBERG H.S.,SUBJECT GUIDE TO UNITED STATES BIBLIOG
GOVERNMENT PUBLICATIONS. USA+45 USA-45 LAW ADMIN NAT/G
...SOC 20. PAGE 53 E1052 DIPLOM
LOC/G

B48

BISHOP H.M.,BASIC ISSUES OF AMERICAN DEMOCRACY. NAT/G
USA+45 USA-45 POL/PAR EX/STRUC LEGIS ADJUD FEDERAL PARL/PROC
...BIBLIOG 18/20. PAGE 12 E0232 CONSTN

B48

CLAGETT H.L.,A GUIDE TO THE LAW AND LEGAL BIBLIOG
LITERATURE OF ARGENTINA, 1917-1946. CONSTN LABOR L/A+17C
JUDGE ADJUD ADMIN...CRIMLGY INT/LAW JURID CON/ANAL LAW
20 ARGEN. PAGE 23 E0447 LEGIS

B48

GRIFFITH E.S.,RESEARCH IN POLITICAL SCIENCE: THE BIBLIOG
WORK OF PANELS OF RESEARCH COMMITTEE, APSA. WOR+45 PHIL/SCI
WOR-45 COM/IND R+D FORCES ACT/RES WAR...GOV/COMP DIPLOM
ANTHOL 20. PAGE 47 E0939 JURID

B48

MORGENTHAU H.J.,POLITICS AMONG NATIONS: THE DIPLOM
STRUGGLE FOR POWER AND PEACE. FUT WOR+45 INT/ORG PEACE
OP/RES PROB/SOLV BAL/PWR CONTROL ATTIT MORAL PWR
...INT/LAW BIBLIOG 20 COLD/WAR. PAGE 75 E1494 POLICY

STOKES W.S.,BIBLIOGRAPHY OF STANDARD AND CLASSICAL WORKS IN THE FIELDS OF AMERICAN POLITICAL SCIENCE. USA+45 USA-45 POL/PAR PROVS FORCES DIPLOM ADMIN CT/SYS APPORT 20 CONGRESS PRESIDENT. PAGE 94 E1876
B48
BIBLIOG
NAT/G
LOC/G
CONSTN

YAKOBSON S.,FIVE HUNDRED RUSSIAN WORKS FOR COLLEGE LIBRARIES (PAMPHLET). MOD/EUR USSR MARXISM SOCISM ...ART/METH GEOG HUM JURID SOC 13/20. PAGE 108 E2162
B48
BIBLIOG
NAT/G
CULTURE
COM

WALKER H.,"THE LEGISLATIVE PROCESS; LAWMAKING IN THE UNITED STATES." NAT/G POL/PAR PROVS EX/STRUC OP/RES PROB/SOLV CT/SYS LOBBY GOV/REL...CHARTS BIBLIOG T 18/20 CONGRESS. PAGE 105 E2094
C48
PARL/PROC
LEGIS
LAW
CONSTN

BRUCKER H.,FREEDOM OF INFORMATION. USA-45 LAW LOC/G PRESS ECO/TAC DOMIN PWR...NEW/IDEA BIBLIOG 17/20. PAGE 16 E0320
B49
PRESS
COM/IND
ORD/FREE
NAT/G

GROB F.,THE RELATIVITY OF WAR AND PEACE: A STUDY IN LAW, HISTORY, AND POLLTICS. WOR+45 WOR-45 LAW DIPLOM DEBATE...CONCPT LING IDEA/COMP BIBLIOG 18/20. PAGE 48 E0944
B49
WAR
PEACE
INT/LAW
STYLE

BLODGETT R.H.,"COMPARATIVE ECONOMIC SYSTEMS (REV. ED.)" WOR-45 AGRI FINAN MARKET LABOR NAT/G PLAN INT/TRADE PRICE...POLICY DECISION BIBLIOG 20. PAGE 13 E0248
C49
METH/COMP
CONCPT
ROUTINE

BOHATTA H.,INTERNATIONALE BIBLIOGRAPHIE. WOR+45 LAW CULTURE PRESS. PAGE 13 E0260
B50
BIBLIOG
DIPLOM
NAT/G
WRITING

DOROSH J.T.,GUIDE TO SOVIET BIBLIOGRAPHIES. USSR LAW AGRI SCHOOL SECT FORCES TEC/DEV...ART/METH GEOG HUM SOC 20. PAGE 32 E0639
B50
BIBLIOG
METH
CON/ANAL

GRAVES W.B.,PUBLIC ADMINISTRATION: A COMPREHENSIVE BIBLIOGRAPHY ON PUBLIC ADMINISTRATION IN THE UNITED STATES (PAMPHLET). USA+45 USA-45 LOC/G NAT/G LEGIS ADJUD INGP/REL...MGT 20. PAGE 45 E0901
B50
BIBLIOG
FINAN
CONTROL
ADMIN

HURST J.W.,THE GROWTH OF AMERICAN LAW; THE LAW MAKERS. USA-45 LOC/G NAT/G DELIB/GP JUDGE ADJUD ADMIN ATTIT PWR...POLICY JURID BIBLIOG 18/20 CONGRESS SUPREME/CT ABA PRESIDENT. PAGE 56 E1115
B50
LAW
LEGIS
CONSTN
CT/SYS

JENKINS W.S.,A GUIDE TO THE MICROFILM COLLECTION OF EARLY STATE RECORDS. USA+45 CONSTN MUNIC LEGIS PRESS ADMIN CT/SYS 18/20. PAGE 58 E1152
B50
BIBLIOG
PROVS
AUD/VIS

HOLCOMBE A.,"OUR MORE PERFECT UNION." USA+45 USA-45 POL/PAR JUDGE CT/SYS EQUILIB FEDERAL PWR...MAJORIT TREND BIBLIOG 18/20 CONGRESS PRESIDENT. PAGE 54 E1070
C50
CONSTN
NAT/G
ADMIN
PLAN

NUMELIN R.,"THE BEGINNINGS OF DIPLOMACY." INT/TRADE WAR GP/REL PEACE STRANGE ATTIT...INT/LAW CONCPT BIBLIOG. PAGE 78 E1559
C50
DIPLOM
KIN
CULTURE
LAW

BECKER O.,MASTER RESEARCH GUIDE. USA+45 USA-45 PRESS...JURID INDEX 20. PAGE 9 E0171
B51
BIBLIOG
LAW
ADJUD
CT/SYS

BISSAINTHE M.,DICTIONNAIRE DE BIBLIOGRAPHIE HAITIENNE. HAITI ELITES AGRI LEGIS DIPLOM INT/TRADE WRITING ORD/FREE CATHISM...ART/METH GEOG 19/20 NEGRO TREATY. PAGE 12 E0234
B51
BIBLIOG
L/A+17C
SOCIETY
NAT/G

CAMPBELL E.H.,UNITED STATES CITIZENSHIP AND QUALIFICATIONS FOR VOTING IN WASHINGTON. USA+45 NAT/G PROVS...CHARTS BIBLIOG 20 WASHINGT/G. PAGE 19 E0371
B51
LAW
CONSTN
SUFF
CHOOSE

FRIEDMANN W.,LAW AND SOCIAL CHANGE IN CONTEMPORARY
B51
LAW

BRITAIN. UK LABOR LG/CO LEGIS JUDGE CT/SYS ORD/FREE NEW/LIB...DECISION JURID TREND METH/COMP BIBLIOG 20 PARLIAMENT ENGLSH/LAW COMMON/LAW. PAGE 40 E0802
ADJUD
SOCIETY
CONSTN

WHEARE K.C.,MODERN CONSTITUTIONS (HOME UNIVERSITY LIBRARY). UNIV LAW NAT/G LEGIS...CONCPT TREND BIBLIOG. PAGE 106 E2115
B51
CONSTN
CLASSIF
PWR
CREATE

APPADORAI A.,THE SUBSTANCE OF POLITICS (6TH ED.). EX/STRUC LEGIS DIPLOM CT/SYS CHOOSE FASCISM MARXISM SOCISM...BIBLIOG T. PAGE 5 E0100
B52
PHIL/SCI
NAT/G

DILLON D.R.,LATIN AMERICA, 1935-1949; A SELECTED BIBLIOGRAPHY. LAW EDU/PROP...SOC 20. PAGE 32 E0629
B52
BIBLIOG
L/A+17C
NAT/G
DIPLOM

GELLER M.A.,ADVERTISING AT THE CROSSROADS: FEDERAL REGULATION VS. VOLUNTARY CONTROLS. USA+45 JUDGE ECO/TAC...POLICY JURID BIBLIOG 20 FTC. PAGE 43 E0843
B52
EDU/PROP
NAT/G
CONSTN
COM/IND

UNESCO,THESES DE SCIENCES SOCIALES: CATALOGUE ANALYTIQUE INTERNATIONAL DE THESES INEDITES DE DOCTORAT, 1940-1950. INT/ORG DIPLOM EDU/PROP...GEOG INT/LAW MGT PSY SOC 20. PAGE 98 E1958
B52
BIBLIOG
ACADEM
WRITING

US DEPARTMENT OF STATE,RESEARCH ON EASTERN EUROPE (EXCLUDING USSR). EUR+WWI LAW ECO/DEV NAT/G PROB/SOLV DIPLOM ADMIN LEAD MARXISM...TREND 19/20. PAGE 100 E1995
B52
BIBLIOG
R+D
ACT/RES
COM

WALTER P.A.F.,RACE AND CULTURE RELATIONS. FAM HEALTH WEALTH...POLICY CRIMLGY GEOG BIBLIOG T 20. PAGE 105 E2097
B52
RACE/REL
DISCRIM
GP/REL
CONCPT

CLAGETT H.L.,"THE ADMINISTRATION OF JUSTICE IN LATIN AMERICA." L/A+17C ADMIN FEDERAL...JURID METH/COMP BIBLIOG 20. PAGE 23 E0448
C52
CT/SYS
ADJUD
JUDGE
CONSTN

LANCASTER L.W.,"GOVERNMENT IN RURAL AMERICA." USA+45 ECO/DEV AGRI SCHOOL FORCES LEGIS JUDGE BUDGET TAX CT/SYS...CHARTS BIBLIOG. PAGE 62 E1248
C52
GOV/REL
LOC/G
MUNIC
ADMIN

STUART G.H.,"AMERICAN DIPLOMATIC AND CONSULAR PRACTICE (2ND ED.)" EUR+WWI MOD/EUR USA-45 DELIB/GP INT/TRADE ADJUD...BIBLIOG 20. PAGE 94 E1889
C52
DIPLOM
ADMIN
INT/ORG

BRETTON H.L.,STRESEMANN AND THE REVISION OF VERSAILLES: A FIGHT FOR REASON. EUR+WWI GERMANY FORCES BUDGET ARMS/CONT WAR SUPEGO...BIBLIOG 20 TREATY VERSAILLES STRESEMN/G. PAGE 15 E0294
B53
POLICY
DIPLOM
BIOG

BUTLER D.E.,THE ELECTORAL SYSTEM IN BRITAIN, 1918-1951. UK LAW POL/PAR SUFF...STAT BIBLIOG 20 PARLIAMENT. PAGE 18 E0348
B53
CHOOSE
LEGIS
REPRESENT
PARTIC

OPPENHEIM L.,INTERNATIONAL LAW: A TREATISE (7TH ED., 2 VOLS.). LAW CONSTN PROB/SOLV INT/TRADE AGREE NEUTRAL WAR ORD/FREE SOVEREIGN...BIBLIOG 20 LEAGUE/NAT UN ILO. PAGE 79 E1579
B53
INT/LAW
INT/ORG
DIPLOM

ORFIELD L.B.,THE GROWTH OF SCANDINAVIAN LAW. DENMARK ICELAND NORWAY SWEDEN LAW DIPLOM...BIBLIOG 9/20. PAGE 79 E1581
B53
JURID
CT/SYS
NAT/G

PIERCE R.A.,RUSSIAN CENTRAL ASIA, 1867-1917: A SELECTED BIBLIOGRAPHY (PAMPHLET). USSR LAW CULTURE NAT/G EDU/PROP WAR...GEOG SOC 19/20. PAGE 81 E1616
B53
BIBLIOG
COLONIAL
ADMIN
COM

STOUT H.M.,BRITISH GOVERNMENT. UK FINAN LOC/G POL/PAR DELIB/GP DIPLOM ADMIN COLONIAL CHOOSE ORD/FREE...JURID BIBLIOG 20 COMMONWLTH. PAGE 94 E1883
B53
NAT/G
PARL/PROC
CONSTN
NEW/LIB

B53
UNESCO,A REGISTER OF LEGAL DOCUMENTATION IN THE WORLD. WOR+45 WOR-45 NAT/G PROVS DELIB/GP LEGIS 13/20. PAGE 98 E1959
BIBLIOG
CONSTN
LAW
JURID

B54
BROGAN D.W.,POLITICS IN AMERICA. LAW POL/PAR CHIEF LEGIS LOBBY CHOOSE REPRESENT GP/REL RACE/REL FEDERAL MORAL...BIBLIOG 20 PRESIDENT CONGRESS. PAGE 16 E0304
NAT/G
CONSTN
USA+45

B54
CAPLOW T.,THE SOCIOLOGY OF WORK. USA+45 USA-45 STRATA MARKET FAM GP/REL INGP/REL ALL/VALS ...DECISION STAT BIBLIOG SOC/INTEG 20. PAGE 19 E0375
LABOR
WORKER
INDUS
ROLE

B54
US SENATE COMM ON FOREIGN REL,REVIEW OF THE UNITED NATIONS CHARTER: A COLLECTION OF DOCUMENTS. LEGIS DIPLOM ADMIN ARMS/CONT WAR REPRESENT SOVEREIGN ...INT/LAW 20 UN. PAGE 101 E2029
BIBLIOG
CONSTN
INT/ORG
DEBATE

C54
BOWIE R.R.,"STUDIES IN FEDERALISM." AGRI FINAN LABOR EX/STRUC FORCES LEGIS DIPLOM INT/TRADE ADJUD ...BIBLIOG 20 EEC. PAGE 14 E0279
FEDERAL
EUR+WWI
INT/ORG
CONSTN

C54
CALDWELL L.K.,"THE GOVERNMENT AND ADMINISTRATION OF NEW YORK." LOC/G MUNIC POL/PAR SCHOOL CHIEF LEGIS PLAN TAX CT/SYS...MGT SOC/WK BIBLIOG 20 NEWYORK/C. PAGE 19 E0365
PROVS
ADMIN
CONSTN
EX/STRUC

C54
GUINS G.C.,"SOVIET LAW AND SOVIET SOCIETY." COM USSR STRATA FAM NAT/G WORKER DOMIN RACE/REL ...BIBLIOG 20. PAGE 48 E0960
LAW
STRUCT
PLAN

B55
BURR R.N.,DOCUMENTS ON INTER-AMERICAN COOPERATION: VOL. I, 1810-1881; VOL. II, 1881-1948. DELIB/GP BAL/PWR INT/TRADE REPRESENT NAT/LISM PEACE HABITAT ORD/FREE PWR SOVEREIGN...INT/LAW 20 OAS. PAGE 18 E0345
BIBLIOG
DIPLOM
INT/ORG
L/A+17C

B55
CRAIG J.,BIBLIOGRAPHY OF PUBLIC ADMINISTRATION IN AUSTRALIA. CONSTN FINAN EX/STRUC LEGIS PLAN DIPLOM RECEIVE ADJUD ROUTINE...HEAL 19/20 AUSTRAL PARLIAMENT. PAGE 27 E0540
BIBLIOG
GOV/REL
ADMIN
NAT/G

B55
DE ARAGAO J.G.,LA JURIDICTION ADMINISTRATIVE AU BRESIL. BRAZIL ADJUD COLONIAL CT/SYS REV FEDERAL ORD/FREE...BIBLIOG 19/20. PAGE 29 E0580
EX/STRUC
ADMIN
NAT/G

B55
FLIESS P.J.,FREEDOM OF THE PRESS IN THE GERMAN REPUBLIC, 1918-1933. GERMANY LAW CONSTN POL/PAR LEGIS WRITING ADMIN COERCE MURDER MARXISM...POLICY BIBLIOG 20 WEIMAR/REP. PAGE 39 E0765
EDU/PROP
ORD/FREE
JURID
PRESS

B55
GUAITA A.,BIBLIOGRAFIA ESPANOLA DE DERECHO ADMINISTRATIVO (PAMPHLET). SPAIN LOC/G MUNIC NAT/G PROVS JUDGE BAL/PWR GOV/REL OWN...JURID 18/19. PAGE 48 E0959
BIBLIOG
ADMIN
CONSTN
PWR

B55
JAPAN MOMBUSHO DAIGAKU GAKIYUT,BIBLIOGRAPHY OF THE STUDIES ON LAW AND POLITICS (PAMPHLET). CONSTN INDUS LABOR DIPLOM TAX ADMIN...CRIMLGY INT/LAW 20 CHINJAP. PAGE 58 E1150
BIBLIOG
LAW
PHIL/SCI

B55
MID-EUROPEAN LAW PROJECT,CHURCH AND STATE BEHIND THE IRON CURTAIN. COM CZECHOSLVK HUNGARY POLAND USSR CULTURE SECT EDU/PROP GOV/REL CATHISM...CHARTS ANTHOL BIBLIOG WORSHIP 20 CHURCH/STA. PAGE 73 E1455
LAW
MARXISM
POLICY

B55
PULLEN W.R.,A CHECK LIST OF LEGISLATIVE JOURNALS ISSUED SINCE 1937 BY THE STATES OF THE UNITED STATES OF AMERICA (PAMPHLET). USA+45 USA-45 LAW WRITING ADJUD ADMIN...JURID 20. PAGE 83 E1662
BIBLIOG
PROVS
EDU/PROP
LEGIS

B55
SVARLIEN O.,AN INTRODUCTION TO THE LAW OF NATIONS. SEA AIR INT/ORG NAT/G CHIEF ADMIN AGREE WAR PRIVIL ORD/FREE SOVEREIGN...BIBLIOG 16/20. PAGE 95 E1897
INT/LAW
DIPLOM

B55
TROTIER A.H.,DOCTORAL DISSERTATIONS ACCEPTED BY AMERICAN UNIVERSITIES 1954-55. SECT DIPLOM HEALTH ...ART/METH GEOG INT/LAW SOC LING CHARTS 20. PAGE 97 E1943
BIBLIOG
ACADEM
USA+45
WRITING

B56
COHEN A.,THE SUTHERLAND PAPERS. USA+45 USA-45 LAW CONTROL CRIME AGE/Y...TREND ANTHOL BIBLIOG 20. PAGE 23 E0461
CRIMLGY
PHIL/SCI
ACT/RES
METH

B56
KALNOKI BEDO A.,LEGAL SOURCES AND BIBLIOGRAPHY OF HUNGARY. COM HUNGARY CONSTN LEGIS JUDGE CT/SYS SANCTION CRIME 16/20. PAGE 59 E1181
BIBLIOG
ADJUD
LAW
JURID

B56
SIPKOV I.,LEGAL SOURCES AND BIBLIOGRAPHY OF BULGARIA. BULGARIA COM LEGIS WRITING ADJUD CT/SYS ...INT/LAW TREATY 20. PAGE 91 E1834
BIBLIOG
LAW
TOTALISM
MARXISM

C56
AUMANN F.R.,"THE ISTRUMENTALITIES OF JUSTICE: THEIR FORMS, FUNCTIONS, AND LIMITATIONS." WOR+45 WOR-45 JUDGE PROB/SOLV ROUTINE ATTIT...BIBLIOG 20. PAGE 6 E0118
JURID
ADMIN
CT/SYS
ADJUD

C56
TYLER P.,"IMMIGRATION AND THE UNITED STATES." USA+45 USA-45 LAW SECT INGP/REL RACE/REL NAT/LISM ATTIT...BIBLIOG SOC/INTEG 19/20. PAGE 97 E1949
CULTURE
GP/REL
DISCRIM

B57
BAYITCH S.A.,A GUIDE TO INTERAMERICAN LEGAL STUDIES: A SELECTIVE BIBLIOGRAPHY OF WORKS IN ENGLISH. NAT/G LEGIS ADJUD CT/SYS CONGRESS 20. PAGE 8 E0157
BIBLIOG
L/A+17C
LAW
JURID

B57
DUMBAULD E.,THE BILL OF RIGHTS AND WHAT IT MEANS TODAY. USA+45 USA-45 CT/SYS...JURID STYLE TIME/SEQ BIBLIOG 18/20 BILL/RIGHT. PAGE 33 E0656
CONSTN
LAW
ADJUD
ORD/FREE

B57
NEUMANN F.,THE DEMOCRATIC AND THE AUTHORITARIAN STATE: ESSAYS IN POLITICAL AND LEGAL THEORY. USA+45 USA-45 CONTROL REV GOV/REL PEACE ALL/IDEOS ...INT/LAW CONCPT GEN/LAWS BIBLIOG 20. PAGE 77 E1536
DOMIN
NAT/G
ORD/FREE
POLICY

B57
UNESCO,A REGISTER OF LEGAL DOCUMENTATION IN THE WORLD (2ND ED.). CT/SYS...JURID IDEA/COMP METH/COMP NAT/COMP 20. PAGE 98 E1960
BIBLIOG
LAW
INT/LAW
CONSTN

B58
ALEXANDROWICZ,A BIBLIOGRAPHY OF INDIAN LAW. INDIA S/ASIA CONSTN CT/SYS...INT/LAW 19/20. PAGE 3 E0062
BIBLIOG
LAW
ADJUD
JURID

B58
BUGEDA LANZAS J.,A STATEMENT OF THE LAWS OF CUBA IN MATTERS AFFECTING BUSINESS (2ND ED. REV., ENLARGED). CUBA L/A+17C LAW FINAN FAM LEGIS ACT/RES ADMIN GP/REL...BIBLIOG 20 OAS. PAGE 17 E0327
JURID
NAT/G
INDUS
WORKER

B58
DEUTSCHE GESCHAFT VOLKERRECHT,DIE VOLKERRECHTLICHEN DISSERTATIONEN AN DEN WESTDEUTSCHEN UNIVERSITATEN, 1945-1957. GERMANY/W NAT/G DIPLOM ADJUD CT/SYS ...POLICY 20. PAGE 31 E0616
BIBLIOG
INT/LAW
ACADEM
JURID

B58
EUSDEN J.D.,PURITANS, LAWYERS, AND POLITICS IN EARLY SEVENTEENTH-CENTURY ENGLAND. UK CT/SYS PARL/PROC RATIONAL PWR SOVEREIGN...IDEA/COMP BIBLIOG 17 PURITAN COMMON/LAW. PAGE 35 E0702
GP/REL
SECT
NAT/G
LAW

B58
FELLMAN D.,THE DEFENDANT'S RIGHTS. USA+45 NAT/G CONSULT CT/SYS SUPEGO ORD/FREE...BIBLIOG SUPREME/CT CIVIL/SERV. PAGE 37 E0730
CONSTN
LAW
CRIME
ADJUD

B58
HUNT B.I.,BIPARTISANSHIP: A CASE STUDY OF THE FOREIGN ASSISTANCE PROGRAM, 1947-56 (DOCTORAL THESIS). USA+45 INT/ORG CONSULT LEGIS TEC/DEV ...BIBLIOG PRESIDENT TREATY NATO TRUMAN/HS EISNHWR/DD CONGRESS. PAGE 56 E1114
FOR/AID
POL/PAR
GP/REL
DIPLOM

B58
KURL S.,ESTONIA: A SELECTED BIBLIOGRAPHY. USSR   BIBLIOG
ESTONIA LAW INTELL SECT...ART/METH GEOG HUM SOC 20.   CULTURE
PAGE 62 E1238   NAT/G

B58
MASON H.L.,TOYNBEE'S APPROACH TO WORLD POLITICS.   DIPLOM
AFR USA+45 USSR LAW WAR NAT/LISM ALL/IDEOS...HUM   CONCPT
BIBLIOG. PAGE 69 E1380   PHIL/SCI
                                                        SECT

B58
MOSER J.J.,JOHANN JACOB MOSER'S GESAMMELTE UND ZU   BIBLIOG
GEMEINNUTZIGEM GEBRAUCH EINGERICHTETE BIBLIOTHEK.   EXTR/IND
GERMANY PROC/MFG INT/TRADE...POLICY JURID MGT 18.   INDUS
PAGE 75 E1500

B58
ORTIZ R.P.,ANNUARIO BIBLIOGRAFICO COLOMBIANO,   BIBLIOG
1951-1956. LAW RECEIVE EDU/PROP ADMIN...LING STAT   SOC
20 COLOMB. PAGE 79 E1582

B58
SCHOEDER P.W.,THE AXIS ALLIANCE AND JAPANESE-   AGREE
AMERICAN RELATIONS 1941. ASIA GERMANY UK USA-45   DIPLOM
PEACE ATTIT...POLICY BIBLIOG 20 CHINJAP TREATY.   WAR
PAGE 88 E1763

B58
SEYID MUHAMMAD V.A.,THE LEGAL FRAMEWORK OF WORLD   INT/LAW
TRADE. WOR+45 INT/ORG DIPLOM CONTROL...BIBLIOG 20   VOL/ASSN
TREATY UN IMF GATT. PAGE 90 E1807   INT/TRADE
                                                        TARIFFS

B58
STRONG C.F.,MODERN POLITICAL CONSTITUTIONS. LAW   CONSTN
CHIEF DELIB/GP EX/STRUC LEGIS ADJUD CHOOSE FEDERAL   IDEA/COMP
POPULISM...CONCPT BIBLIOG 20 UN. PAGE 94 E1887   NAT/G

B58
WOOD J.E.,CHURCH AND STATE IN SCRIPTURE HISTORY AND   GP/REL
CONSTITUTIONAL LAW. LAW CONSTN SOCIETY PROVS   SECT
VOL/ASSN BAL/PWR COLONIAL CT/SYS ATTIT...BIBLIOG 20   NAT/G
SUPREME/CT CHURCH/STA BIBLE. PAGE 107 E2142   ADJUD

C58
RAJAN M.S.,"UNITED NATIONS AND DOMESTIC   INT/LAW
JURISDICTION." WOR+45 WOR-45 PARL/PROC...IDEA/COMP   DIPLOM
BIBLIOG 20 UN. PAGE 83 E1670   CONSTN
                                                        INT/ORG

B59
BOHMER A.,LEGAL SOURCES AND BIBLIOGRAPHY OF   BIBLIOG
CZECHOSLOVAKIA. COM CZECHOSLVK PARL/PROC SANCTION   ADJUD
CRIME MARXISM 20. PAGE 13 E0261   LAW
                                                        JURID

B59
GSOVSKI V.,GOVERNMENT, LAW, AND COURTS IN THE   ADJUD
SOVIET UNION AND EASTERN EUROPE (2 VOLS.). COM USSR   MARXISM
AGRI INDUS WORKER CT/SYS CRIME...BIBLIOG 20   CONTROL
EUROPE/E. PAGE 48 E0958   ORD/FREE

B59
KERREMANS-RAMIOULL,LE PROBLEME DE LA DELINQUENCE   BIBLIOG
JUVENILE (2ND ED.). FAM PUB/INST SCHOOL FORCES   CRIME
LEGIS MORAL...CRIMLGY SOC 20. PAGE 60 E1205   AGE/Y
                                                        SOC/WK

B59
MAYER A.J.,POLITICAL ORIGINS OF THE NEW DIPLOMACY,   TREND
1917-1918. EUR+WWI MOD/EUR USA-45 WAR PWR...POLICY   DIPLOM
INT/LAW BIBLIOG. PAGE 70 E1392

B59
MOOS M.,THE CAMPUS AND THE STATE. LAW FINAN   EDU/PROP
DELIB/GP LEGIS EXEC LOBBY GP/REL PWR...POLICY   ACADEM
BIBLIOG. PAGE 74 E1489   PROVS
                                                        CONTROL

B59
NICHOLS R.F.,RELIGION AND AMERICAN DEMOCRACY.   NAT/G
USA+45 USA-45 LAW CHOOSE SUFF MORAL ORD/FREE   SECT
POPULISM...POLICY BIBLIOG 16/20 PRE/US/AM   CONSTN
CHRISTIAN. PAGE 77 E1547   CONCPT

B59
OKINSHEVICH L.A.,LATIN AMERICA IN SOVIET WRITINGS,   BIBLIOG
1945-1958: A BIBLIOGRAPHY. USSR LAW ECO/UNDEV LABOR   WRITING
DIPLOM EDU/PROP REV...GEOG SOC 20. PAGE 78 E1573   COM
                                                        L/A+17C

B59
REOCK E.C.,PROCEDURES AND STANDARDS FOR THE   PROVS
APPORTIONMENT OF STATE LEGISLATURES (DOCTORAL   LOC/G

THESIS). USA+45 POL/PAR LEGIS TEC/DEV ADJUD   APPORT
BIBLIOG. PAGE 84 E1686   REPRESENT

B59
SURRENCY E.C.,A GUIDE TO LEGAL RESEARCH. USA+45   NAT/G
ACADEM LEGIS ACT/RES ADMIN...DECISION METH/COMP   PROVS
BIBLIOG METH. PAGE 94 E1894   ADJUD
                                                        JURID

B59
US CONGRESS JT ATOM ENRGY COMM,SELECTED MATERIALS   NAT/G
ON FEDERAL-STATE COOPERATION IN THE ATOMIC ENERGY   NUC/PWR
FIELD. USA+45 LAW LOC/G PROVS CONSULT LEGIS ADJUD   GOV/REL
...POLICY BIBLIOG 20 AEC. PAGE 99 E1991   DELIB/GP

B59
WAGNER W.J.,THE FEDERAL STATES AND THEIR JUDICIARY.   ADJUD
BRAZIL CANADA SWITZERLND USA+45 CONFER CT/SYS TASK   METH/COMP
EFFICIENCY FEDERAL PWR...JURID BIBLIOG 20 AUSTRAL   PROB/SOLV
MEXIC/AMER. PAGE 104 E2091   NAT/G

C59
COLLINS I.,"THE GOVERNMENT AND THE NEWSPAPER PRESS   PRESS
IN FRANCE, 1814-1881. FRANCE LAW ADMIN CT/SYS   ORD/FREE
...CON/ANAL BIBLIOG 19. PAGE 24 E0475   NAT/G
                                                        EDU/PROP

B60
BYRD E.M. JR.,TREATIES AND EXECUTIVE AGREEMENTS IN   CHIEF
THE UNITED STATES: THEIR SEPARATE ROLES AND   INT/LAW
LIMITATIONS. USA+45 USA-45 EX/STRUC TARIFFS CT/SYS   DIPLOM
GOV/REL FEDERAL...IDEA/COMP BIBLIOG SUPREME/CT
SENATE CONGRESS. PAGE 18 E0353

B60
CONANT M.,ANTITRUST IN THE MOTION PICTURE INDUSTRY: PRICE
ECONOMIC AND LEGAL ANALYSIS. USA+45 MARKET ADJUST   CONTROL
DEMAND BIBLIOG. PAGE 24 E0484   LAW
                                                        ART/METH

B60
FLORES R.H.,CATALOGO DE TESIS DOCTORALES DE LAS   BIBLIOG
FACULTADES DE LA UNIVERSIDAD DE EL SALVADOR.   ACADEM
EL/SALVADR LAW DIPLOM ADMIN LEAD GOV/REL...SOC   L/A+17C
19/20. PAGE 39 E0767   NAT/G

B60
HARVARD LAW SCHOOL LIBRARY,CURRENT LEGAL   BIBLIOG
BIBLIOGRAPHY. USA+45 CONSTN LEGIS ADJUD CT/SYS   JURID
POLICY. PAGE 51 E1006   LAW
                                                        INT/LAW

B60
HEYSE T.,PROBLEMS FONCIERS ET REGIME DES TERRES   BIBLIOG
(ASPECTS ECONOMIQUES, JURIDIQUES ET SOCIAUX). AFR   AGRI
CONGO/BRAZ INT/ORG DIPLOM SOVEREIGN...GEOG TREATY   ECO/UNDEV
20. PAGE 52 E1037   LEGIS

B60
LA PONCE J.A.,THE PROTECTION OF MINORITIES. WOR+45   INGP/REL
WOR-45 NAT/G POL/PAR SUFF...INT/LAW CLASSIF GP/COMP   DOMIN
GOV/COMP BIBLIOG 17/20 CIVIL/LIB CIV/RIGHTS.   SOCIETY
PAGE 62 E1242   RACE/REL

C60
HAZARD J.N.,"SETTLING DISPUTES IN SOVIET SOCIETY: ADJUD
THE FORMATIVE YEARS OF LEGAL INSTITUTIONS." USSR   LAW
NAT/G PROF/ORG PROB/SOLV CONTROL CT/SYS ROUTINE REV   COM
CENTRAL...JURID BIBLIOG 20. PAGE 51 E1017   POLICY

N60
RHODESIA-NYASA NATL ARCHIVES,A SELECT BIBLIOGRAPHY   BIBLIOG
OF RECENT PUBLICATIONS CONCERNING THE FEDERATION OF   ADMIN
RHODESIA AND NYASALAND (PAMPHLET). MALAWI RHODESIA   ORD/FREE
LAW CULTURE STRUCT ECO/UNDEV LEGIS...GEOG 20.   NAT/G
PAGE 84 E1689

B61
BARBASH J.,LABOR'S GRASS ROOTS. CONSTN NAT/G   LABOR
EX/STRUC LEGIS WORKER LEAD...MAJORIT BIBLIOG.   INGP/REL
PAGE 8 E0147   GP/REL
                                                        LAW

B61
BAYITCH S.A.,LATIN AMERICA: A BIBLIOGRAPHICAL   BIBLIOG
GUIDE. LAW CONSTN LEGIS JUDGE ADJUD CT/SYS 20.   L/A+17C
PAGE 8 E0158   NAT/G
                                                        JURID

B61
BRENNAN D.G.,ARMS CONTROL, DISARMAMENT, AND   ARMS/CONT
NATIONAL SECURITY. WOR+45 NAT/G FORCES CREATE   ORD/FREE
PROB/SOLV PARTIC WAR PEACE...DECISION INT/LAW   DIPLOM
ANTHOL BIBLIOG 20. PAGE 15 E0291   POLICY

B61
CASSINELLI C.W.,THE POLITICS OF FREEDOM. FUT UNIV   MAJORIT
LAW POL/PAR CHOOSE ORD/FREE...POLICY CONCPT MYTH   NAT/G
BIBLIOG. PAGE 21 E0404   PARL/PROC
                                                            PARTIC

B61
NEWMAN R.P.,RECOGNITION OF COMMUNIST CHINA? A STUDY   MARXISM
IN ARGUMENT. CHINA/COM NAT/G PROB/SOLV RATIONAL   ATTIT
...INT/LAW LOG IDEA/COMP BIBLIOG 20. PAGE 77 E1544   DIPLOM
                                                            POLICY

B61
PUGET H.,ESSAI DE BIBLIOGRAPHIE DES PRINCIPAUX   BIBLIOG
OUVRAGES DE DROIT PUBLIC... QUI ONT PARU HORS DE   MGT
FRANCE DE 1945 A 1958. EUR+WWI USA+45 CONSTN LOC/G   ADMIN
...METH 20. PAGE 83 E1660   LAW

B61
TOMPKINS D.C.,CONFLICT OF INTEREST IN THE FEDERAL   BIBLIOG
GOVERNMENT: A BIBLIOGRAPHY. USA+45 EX/STRUC LEGIS   ROLE
ADJUD ADMIN CRIME CONGRESS PRESIDENT. PAGE 96 E1932   NAT/G
                                                            LAW

N61
LEAGUE WOMEN VOTERS MASSACHU,THE MERIT SYSTEM IN   LOC/G
MASSACHUSETTS (PAMPHLET). USA+45 PROVS LEGIT PARTIC   LAW
CHOOSE REPRESENT GOV/REL EFFICIENCY...POLICY   SENIOR
GOV/COMP BIBLIOG 20 MASSACHU. PAGE 64 E1274   PROF/ORG

B62
BARLOW R.B.,CITIZENSHIP AND CONSCIENCE: STUDIES IN   SECT
THEORY AND PRACTICE OF RELIGIOUS TOLERATION IN   LEGIS
ENGLAND DURING EIGHTEENTH CENTURY. UK LAW VOL/ASSN   DISCRIM
EDU/PROP SANCTION REV GP/REL MAJORITY ATTIT
ORD/FREE...BIBLIOG WORSHIP 18. PAGE 8 E0150

B62
BIBLIOTHEQUE PALAIS DE LA PAIX,CATALOGUE OF THE   BIBLIOG
PEACE PALACE LIBRARY, SUPPLEMENT 1937-1952 (7   INT/LAW
VOLS.). WOR+45 WOR-45 INT/ORG NAT/G ADJUD WAR PEACE   DIPLOM
...JURID 20. PAGE 12 E0225

B62
BLAUSTEIN A.P.,MANUAL ON FOREIGN LEGAL PERIODICALS   BIBLIOG
AND THEIR INDEX. WOR+45 DIPLOM 20. PAGE 13 E0244   INDEX
                                                            LAW
                                                            JURID

B62
BORKIN J.,THE CORRUPT JUDGE. USA+45 CT/SYS ATTIT   ADJUD
SUPEGO MORAL RESPECT...BIBLIOG + SUPREME/CT   TRIBUTE
MANTON/M DAVIS/W JOHNSN/ALB. PAGE 14 E0271   CRIME

B62
DIESING P.,REASON IN SOCIETY; FIVE TYPES OF   RATIONAL
DECISIONS AND THEIR SOCIAL CONDITIONS. SOCIETY   METH/COMP
STRUCT LABOR CREATE TEC/DEV BARGAIN ADJUD ROLE   DECISION
...JURID BIBLIOG 20. PAGE 31 E0625   CONCPT

B62
DONNELLY R.C.,CRIMINAL LAW: PROBLEMS FOR DECISION   CRIME
IN THE PROMULGATION, INVOCATION AND ADMINISTRATION   LAW
OF A LAW OF CRIMES. USA+45 SANCTION BIO/SOC   ADJUD
...DECISION JURID BIBLIOG 20. PAGE 32 E0636   PROB/SOLV

B62
FATOUROS A.A.,GOVERNMENT GUARANTEES TO FOREIGN   NAT/G
INVESTORS. WOR+45 ECO/UNDEV INDUS WORKER ADJUD   FINAN
...NAT/COMP BIBLIOG TREATY. PAGE 36 E0722   INT/TRADE
                                                            ECO/DEV

B62
GANJI M.,INTERNATIONAL PROTECTION OF HUMAN RIGHTS.   ORD/FREE
WOR+45 CONSTN INT/TRADE CT/SYS SANCTION CRIME WAR   DISCRIM
RACE/REL...CHARTS IDEA/COMP NAT/COMP BIBLIOG 20   LEGIS
TREATY NEGRO LEAGUE/NAT UN CIVIL/LIB. PAGE 42 E0831   DELIB/GP

B62
HENDERSON W.O.,THE GENESIS OF THE COMMON MARKET.   ECO/DEV
EUR+WWI FRANCE MOD/EUR UK SEA COM/IND EXTR/IND   INT/TRADE
COLONIAL DISCRIM...TIME/SEQ CHARTS BIBLIOG 18/20   DIPLOM
EEC TREATY. PAGE 52 E1030

B62
KIDDER F.E.,THESES ON PAN AMERICAN TOPICS. LAW   BIBLIOG
CULTURE NAT/G SECT DIPLOM HEALTH...ART/METH GEOG   CHRIST-17C
SOC 13/20. PAGE 61 E1213   L/A+17C
                                                            SOCIETY

B62
MARS D.,SUGGESTED LIBRARY IN PUBLIC ADMINISTRATION.   BIBLIOG
FINAN DELIB/GP EX/STRUC WORKER COMPUTER ADJUD   ADMIN
...DECISION PSY SOC METH/COMP 20. PAGE 68 E1368   METH
                                                            MGT

B62
MCWHINNEY E.,CONSTITUTIONALISM IN GERMANY AND THE   CONSTN
FEDERAL CONSTITUTINAL COURT. GERMANY/W POL/PAR TV   CT/SYS
ADJUD CHOOSE EFFICIENCY ATTIT ORD/FREE MARXISM   CONTROL
...NEW/IDEA BIBLIOG 20. PAGE 71 E1428   NAT/G

B62
MURPHY W.F.,CONGRESS AND THE COURT. USA+45 LAW   LEGIS
LOBBY GP/REL RACE/REL ATTIT PWR...JURID INT BIBLIOG   CT/SYS
CONGRESS SUPREME/CT WARRN/EARL. PAGE 75 E1509   GOV/REL
                                                            ADJUD

B62
PAIKERT G.C.,THE GERMAN EXODUS. EUR+WWI GERMANY/W   INGP/REL
LAW CULTURE SOCIETY STRUCT INDUS NAT/LISM RESPECT   STRANGE
SOVEREIGN...CHARTS BIBLIOG SOC/INTEG 20 MIGRATION.   GEOG
PAGE 79 E1591   GP/REL

B62
PRESS C.,STATE MANUALS, BLUE BOOKS AND ELECTION   BIBLIOG
RESULTS. LAW LOC/G MUNIC LEGIS WRITING FEDERAL   PROVS
SOVEREIGN...DECISION STAT CHARTS 20. PAGE 82 E1648   ADMIN
                                                            CHOOSE

B62
RICE C.E.,FREEDOM OF ASSOCIATION. USA+45 USA-45   LAW
POL/PAR LOBBY GP/REL...JURID BIBLIOG 18/20   NAT/G
SUPREME/CT PRE/US/AM. PAGE 84 E1691   CONSTN

B62
SHAW C.,LEGAL PROBLEMS IN INTERNATIONAL TRADE AND   INT/LAW
INVESTMENT. WOR+45 ECO/DEV ECO/UNDEV MARKET DIPLOM   INT/TRADE
TAX INCOME ROLE...ANTHOL BIBLIOG 20 TREATY UN IMF   FINAN
GATT. PAGE 91 E1816   ECO/TAC

B62
UNECA LIBRARY,NEW ACQUISITIONS IN THE UNECA   BIBLIOG
LIBRARY. LAW NAT/G PLAN PROB/SOLV TEC/DEV ADMIN   AFR
REGION...GEOG SOC 20 UN. PAGE 98 E1956   ECO/UNDEV
                                                            INT/ORG

L62
"AMERICAN BEHAVIORAL SCIENTIST." USSR LAW NAT/G   BIBLIOG
...SOC 20 UN. PAGE 2 E0034   AFR
                                                            R+D

L62
SCHWERIN K.,"LAW LIBRARIES AND FOREIGN LAW   BIBLIOG
COLLECTION IN THE USA." USA+45 USA-45...INT/LAW   LAW
STAT 20. PAGE 89 E1793   ACADEM
                                                            ADMIN

C62
ABRAHAM H.J.,"THE JUDICIAL PROCESS." USA+45 USA-45   BIBLIOG
LAW NAT/G ADMIN CT/SYS INGP/REL RACE/REL DISCRIM   CONSTN
...JURID IDEA/COMP 19/20. PAGE 2 E0046   JUDGE
                                                            ADJUD

C62
LILLICH R.B.,"INTERNATIONAL CLAIMS: THEIR   INT/LAW
ADJUDICATION BY NATIONAL COMMISSIONS." WOR+45   DIPLOM
WOR-45 NAT/G ADJUD...JURID BIBLIOG 18/20. PAGE 65   PROB/SOLV
E1298

C62
MORGAN G.G.,"SOVIET ADMINISTRATIVE LEGALITY: THE   LAW
ROLE OF THE ATTORNEY GENERAL'S OFFICE." COM USSR   CONSTN
CONTROL ROUTINE...CONCPT BIBLIOG 18/20. PAGE 74   LEGIS
E1493   ADMIN

C62
VAN DER SPRENKEL S.,"LEGAL INSTITUTIONS IN MANCHU   LAW
CHINA." ASIA STRUCT CT/SYS ROUTINE GOV/REL GP/REL   JURID
...CONCPT BIBLIOG 17/20. PAGE 103 E2068   ADMIN
                                                          ADJUD

B63
ATTIA G.E.D.,LES FORCES ARMEES DES NATIONS UNIES EN   FORCES
COREE ET AU MOYENORIENT. KOREA CONSTN NAT/G   INT/LAW
DELIB/GP LEGIS PWR...IDEA/COMP NAT/COMP BIBLIOG UN
SUEZ. PAGE 6 E0114

B63
BADI J.,THE GOVERNMENT OF THE STATE OF ISRAEL: A   NAT/G
CRITICAL ACCOUNT OF ITS PARLIAMENT, EXECUTIVE, AND   CONSTN
JUDICIARY. ISRAEL ECO/DEV CHIEF DELIB/GP LEGIS   EX/STRUC
DIPLOM CT/SYS INGP/REL PEACE ORD/FREE...BIBLIOG 20   POL/PAR
PARLIAMENT ARABS MIGRATION. PAGE 7 E0131

B63
CAHN E.,THE GREAT RIGHTS. USA+45 NAT/G PROVS   CONSTN
CIVMIL/REL...IDEA/COMP ANTHOL BIBLIOG 18/20   LAW
MADISON/J BILL/RIGHT CIV/RIGHTS WARRN/EARL   ORD/FREE
BLACK/HL. PAGE 18 E0361   INGP/REL

B63
CHOJNACKI S.,REGISTER ON CURRENT RESEARCH ON
ETHIOPIA AND THE HORN OF AFRICA. ETHIOPIA LAW
CULTURE AGRI SECT EDU/PROP ADMIN...GEOG HEAL LING
20. PAGE 22 E0433
BIBLIOG
ACT/RES
INTELL
ACADEM

B63
DILLIARD I.,ONE MAN'S STAND FOR FREEDOM: MR.
JUSTICE BLACK AND THE BILL OF RIGHTS. USA+45
POL/PAR SECT DELIB/GP FORCES ADJUD CONTROL WAR
DISCRIM MORAL...BIBLIOG 20 NEGRO SUPREME/CT
BILL/RIGHT BLACK/HL. PAGE 32 E0628
CONSTN
JURID
JUDGE
ORD/FREE

B63
ECOLE NATIONALE D'ADMIN,BIBLIOGRAPHIE SELECTIVE
D'OUVRAGES DE LANGUE FRANCAISE TRAITANT DES
PROBLEMES GOUVERNEMENTAUX ET ADMINISTRATIFS. NAT/G
FORCES ACT/RES OP/RES PLAN PROB/SOLV BUDGET ADJUD
COLONIAL LEAD 20. PAGE 34 E0672
BIBLIOG
AFR
ADMIN
EX/STRUC

B63
ELIAS T.O.,GOVERNMENT AND POLITICS IN AFRICA.
CONSTN CULTURE SOCIETY NAT/G POL/PAR DIPLOM
REPRESENT PERSON...SOC TREND BIBLIOG 4/20. PAGE 34
E0681
AFR
NAT/LISM
COLONIAL
LAW

B63
FRIEDRICH C.J.,MAN AND HIS GOVERNMENT: AN EMPIRICAL
THEORY OF POLITICS. UNIV LOC/G NAT/G ADJUD REV
INGP/REL DISCRIM PWR BIBLIOG. PAGE 41 E0810
PERSON
ORD/FREE
PARTIC
CONTROL

B63
GARNER U.F.,ADMINISTRATIVE LAW. UK LAW LOC/G NAT/G
EX/STRUC LEGIS JUDGE BAL/PWR BUDGET ADJUD CONTROL
CT/SYS...BIBLIOG 20. PAGE 42 E0840
ADMIN
JURID
PWR
GOV/REL

B63
GSOUSKI V.,LEGAL SOURCES AND BIBLIOGRAPHY OF THE
BALTIC STATES (ESTONIA, LATVIA, LITHUANIA). COM
ESTONIA LATVIA LITHUANIA NAT/G LEGIS CT/SYS
SANCTION CRIME 20. PAGE 48 E0957
BIBLIOG
ADJUD
LAW
JURID

B63
HIGGINS R.,THE DEVELOPMENT OF INTERNATIONAL LAW
THROUGH THE POLITICAL ORGANS OF THE UNITED NATIONS.
WOR+45 FORCES DIPLOM AGREE COERCE ATTIT SOVEREIGN
...BIBLIOG 20 UN TREATY. PAGE 52 E1041
INT/ORG
INT/LAW
TEC/DEV
JURID

B63
A BIBLIOGRAPHY OF DOCTORAL DISSERTATIONS UNDERTAKEN
IN AMERICAN AND CANADIAN UNIVERSITIES ON RELIGION
AND POLITICS. LAW CONSTN DOMIN LEGIT ADJUD GP/REL
...POLICY 20. PAGE 62 E1241
BIBLIOG
ACADEM
SECT
JURID

B63
LANOUE G.R.,A BIBLIOGRAPHY OF DOCTORAL
DISSERTATIONS ON POLITICS AND RELIGION. USA+45
USA-45 CONSTN PROVS DIPLOM CT/SYS MORAL...POLICY
JURID CONCPT 20. PAGE 63 E1252
BIBLIOG
NAT/G
LOC/G
SECT

B63
LAVROFF D.-.G.,LES LIBERTES PUBLIQUES EN UNION
SOVIETIQUE (REV. ED.). USSR NAT/G WORKER SANCTION
CRIME MARXISM NEW/LIB...JURID BIBLIOG WORSHIP 20.
PAGE 63 E1268
ORD/FREE
LAW
ATTIT
COM

B63
LIVINGSTON W.S.,FEDERALISM IN THE COMMONWEALTH - A
BIBLIOGRAPHICAL COMMENTARY. CANADA INDIA PAKISTAN
UK STRUCT LOC/G NAT/G POL/PAR...NAT/COMP 20
AUSTRAL. PAGE 66 E1310
BIBLIOG
JURID
FEDERAL
CONSTN

B63
LIVNEH E.,ISRAEL LEGAL BIBLIOGRAPHY IN EUROPEAN
LANGUAGES. ISRAEL LOC/G JUDGE TAX...INT/LAW 20.
PAGE 66 E1311
BIBLIOG
LAW
NAT/G
CONSTN

B63
LYONS F.S.L.,INTERNATIONALISM IN EUROPE 1815-1914.
LAW AGRI COM/IND DIST/IND LABOR SECT INT/TRADE
TARIFFS...BIBLIOG 19/20. PAGE 67 E1335
DIPLOM
MOD/EUR
INT/ORG

B63
ROYAL INSTITUTE PUBLIC ADMIN,BRITISH PUBLIC
ADMINISTRATION. UK LAW FINAN INDUS LOC/G POL/PAR
LEGIS LOBBY PARL/PROC CHOOSE JURID. PAGE 86 E1729
BIBLIOG
ADMIN
MGT
NAT/G

B63
US COMMISSION ON CIVIL RIGHTS,FREEDOM TO THE FREE.
USA+45 USA-45 LAW VOL/ASSN CT/SYS ATTIT PWR...JURID
BIBLIOG 17/20 SUPREME/CT NEGRO CIV/RIGHTS. PAGE 99
E1986
RACE/REL
DISCRIM
NAT/G
POLICY

C63
ATTIA G.E.O.,"LES FORCES ARMEES DES NATIONS UNIES
EN COREE ET AU MOYENORIENT." KOREA CONSTN DELIB/GP
LEGIS PWR...IDEA/COMP NAT/COMP BIBLIOG UN SUEZ.
PAGE 6 E0115
FORCES
NAT/G
INT/LAW

C63
SCHUBERT G.,"JUDICIAL DECISION-MAKING." FORCES LEAD
ATTIT DRIVE...POLICY PSY STAT CHARTS ANTHOL BIBLIOG
20. PAGE 88 E1773
ADJUD
DECISION
JUDGE
CT/SYS

B64
BERWANGER E.H.,WESTERN ANTI-NEGRO SENTIMENT AND
LAWS 1846-60: A FACTOR IN THE SLAVERY EXTENSION
CONTROVERSY (PAPER). USA-45 LAW CONSTN LEGIS ADJUD
...BIBLIOG 19 NEGRO. PAGE 11 E0218
RACE/REL
REGION
DISCRIM
ORD/FREE

B64
BOUVIER-AJAM M.,MANUEL TECHNIQUE ET PRATIQUE DU
MAIRE ET DES ELUS ET AGENTS COMMUNAUX. FRANCE LOC/G
BUDGET CHOOSE GP/REL SUPEGO...JURID BIBLIOG 20
MAYOR COMMUNES. PAGE 14 E0274
MUNIC
ADMIN
CHIEF
NEIGH

B64
CHAPIN B.,THE AMERICAN LAW OF TREASON. USA-45 LAW
NAT/G JUDGE CRIME REV...BIBLIOG 18. PAGE 21 E0419
LEGIS
JURID
CONSTN
POLICY

B64
CLINARD M.B.,ANOMIE AND DEVIANT BEHAVIOR: A
DISCUSSION AND CRITIQUE. SOCIETY FACE/GP CRIME
STRANGE ATTIT BIO/SOC DISPL RIGID/FLEX HEALTH...PSY
CONCPT BIBLIOG 20 MERTON/R. PAGE 23 E0456
PERSON
ANOMIE
KIN
NEIGH

B64
FORBES A.H.,CURRENT RESEARCH IN BRITISH STUDIES. UK
CONSTN CULTURE POL/PAR SECT DIPLOM ADMIN...JURID
BIOG WORSHIP 20. PAGE 39 E0769
BIBLIOG
PERSON
NAT/G
PARL/PROC

B64
FREUD A.,OF HUMAN SOVEREIGNTY. WOR+45 INDUS SECT
ECO/TAC CRIME CHOOSE ATTIT MORAL MARXISM...POLICY
BIBLIOG 20. PAGE 40 E0794
NAT/LISM
DIPLOM
WAR
PEACE

B64
GOODNOW H.F.,THE CIVIL SERVICE OF PAKISTAN:
BUREAUCRACY IN A NEW NATION. INDIA PAKISTAN S/ASIA
ECO/UNDEV PROVS CHIEF PARTIC CHOOSE EFFICIENCY PWR
...BIBLIOG 20. PAGE 45 E0889
ADMIN
GOV/REL
LAW
NAT/G

B64
GRZYBOWSKI K.,THE SOCIALIST COMMONWEALTH OF
NATIONS: ORGANIZATIONS AND INSTITUTIONS. FORCES
DIPLOM INT/TRADE ADJUD ADMIN LEAD WAR MARXISM
SOCISM...BIBLIOG 20 COMECON WARSAW/P. PAGE 48 E0956
INT/LAW
COM
REGION
INT/ORG

B64
HANNA W.J.,POLITICS IN BLACK AFRICA: A SELECTIVE
BIBLIOGRAPHY OF RELEVANT PERIODICAL LITERATURE. AFR
LAW LOC/G MUNIC NAT/G POL/PAR LOBBY CHOOSE RACE/REL
SOVEREIGN 20. PAGE 50 E0995
BIBLIOG
NAT/LISM
COLONIAL

B64
HENDERSON D.F.,CONCILIATION AND JAPANESE LAW (VOL.
II). LAW SOCIETY...BIBLIOG 17/20 CHINJAP. PAGE 52
E1028
CONCPT
CT/SYS
ADJUD
POLICY

B64
KAHNG T.J.,LAW, POLITICS, AND THE SECURITY COUNCIL*
AN INQUIRY INTO THE HANDLING OF LEGAL QUESTIONS.
LAW CONSTN NAT/G ACT/RES OP/RES CT/SYS TASK PWR
...INT/LAW BIBLIOG UN. PAGE 59 E1180
DELIB/GP
ADJUD
ROUTINE

B64
KAUPER P.G.,RELIGION AND THE CONSTITUTION. USA+45
USA-45 LAW NAT/G SCHOOL SECT GP/REL ATTIT...BIBLIOG
WORSHIP 18/20 SUPREME/CT FREE/SPEE CHURCH/STA.
PAGE 60 E1189
CONSTN
JURID
ORD/FREE

B64
MASON A.T.,AMERICAN CONSTITUTIONAL LAW:
INTRODUCTORY ESSAYS AND SELECTED CASES (3RD ED.).
LAW LEGIS TAX ADJUD GOV/REL FEDERAL ORD/FREE PWR
...TIME/SEQ BIBLIOG T 19/20 SUPREME/CT. PAGE 69
E1379
CONSTN
CT/SYS
JURID

B64
A CHECK LIST OF THE SPECIAL AND STANDING COMMITTEES
OF THE AMERICAN BAR ASSOCIATION (VOL. II). USA+45
LEGIS PRESS CONFER...JURID CON/ANAL. PAGE 80 E1607
BIBLIOG
LAW
VOL/ASSN

B64
PRESS C.,A BIBLIOGRAPHIC INTRODUCTION TO AMERICAN BIBLIOG
STATE GOVERNMENT AND POLITICS (PAMPHLET). USA+45 LEGIS
USA-45 EX/STRUC ADJUD INGP/REL FEDERAL ORD/FREE 20. LOC/G
PAGE 82 E1649 POL/PAR

B64
RICHARDSON I.L.,BIBLIOGRAFIA BRASILEIRA DE BIBLIOG
ADMINISTRACAO PUBLICA E ASSUNTOS CORRELATOS. BRAZIL MGT
CONSTN FINAN LOC/G NAT/G POL/PAR PLAN DIPLOM ADMIN
RECEIVE ATTIT...METH 20. PAGE 84 E1694 LAW

B64
RUSSELL R.B.,UNITED NATIONS EXPERIENCE WITH FORCES
MILITARY FORCES: POLITICAL AND LEGAL ASPECTS. AFR DIPLOM
KOREA WOR+45 LEGIS PROB/SOLV ADMIN CONTROL SANCTION
EFFICIENCY PEACE...POLICY INT/LAW BIBLIOG UN. ORD/FREE
PAGE 87 E1738

B64
SARTORIUS R.E.,THE JUSTIFICATION OF THE JUDICIAL LAW
DECISION (DISSERTATION). PROB/SOLV LEGIT...JURID PHIL/SCI
GEN/LAWS BIBLIOG 20. PAGE 87 E1747 CT/SYS
ADJUD

B64
SIEKANOWICZ P.,LEGAL SOURCES AND BIBLIOGRAPHY OF BIBLIOG
POLAND. COM POLAND CONSTN NAT/G PARL/PROC SANCTION ADJUD
CRIME MARXISM 16/20. PAGE 91 E1823 LAW
JURID

B64
TELLADO A.,A STATEMENT OF THE LAWS OF THE DOMINICAN CONSTN
REPUBLIC IN MATTERS AFFECTING BUSINESS (3RD ED.). LEGIS
DOMIN/REP AGRI DIST/IND EXTR/IND FINAN FAM WORKER NAT/G
ECO/TAC TAX CT/SYS MARRIAGE OWN...BIBLIOG 20 INDUS
MIGRATION. PAGE 95 E1913

B64
TENBROCK J.,EQUAL UNDER LAW. USA-45 CONSTN POL/PAR LEGIS
EDU/PROP PARL/PROC ORD/FREE...BIBLIOG 19 AMEND/XIV. LAW
PAGE 95 E1914 DISCRIM
DOMIN

C64
BECKER T.L.,"POLITICAL BEHAVIORALISM AND MODERN DECISION
JURISPRUDENCE." LEGIS JUDGE OP/RES ADJUD CT/SYS PROB/SOLV
ATTIT PWR...BIBLIOG 20. PAGE 9 E0173 JURID
GEN/LAWS

C64
CORWIN E.S.,"AMERICAN CONSTITUTIONAL HISTORY." LAW ANTHOL
NAT/G PROB/SOLV EQUILIB FEDERAL ATTIT PWR...JURID JUDGE
BIBLIOG 20. PAGE 26 E0515 ADJUD
CT/SYS

B65
AMERICAN UNIVERSITY IN CAIRO,GUIDE TO UAR BIBLIOG
GOVERNMENT PUBLICATIONS AT THE AUC LIBRARY NAT/G
(PAMPHLET). ISLAM UAR USA+45 ECO/UNDEV...SOC STAT LEGIS
20. PAGE 4 E0084 LAW

B65
ASSOCIATION BAR OF NYC,RADIO, TELEVISION, AND THE AUD/VIS
ADMINISTRATION OF JUSTICE: A DOCUMENTED SURVEY OF ATTIT
MATERIALS. USA+45 DELIB/GP FORCES PRESS ADJUD ORD/FREE
CONTROL CT/SYS CRIME...INT IDEA/COMP BIBLIOG.
PAGE 6 E0109

B65
BEGGS D.W.,AMERICA'S SCHOOLS AND CHURCHES: PARTNERS SECT
IN CONFLICT. USA+45 PROVS EDU/PROP ADJUD DISCRIM GP/REL
ATTIT...IDEA/COMP ANTHOL BIBLIOG WORSHIP 20 SCHOOL
CHURCH/STA. PAGE 9 E0179 NAT/G

B65
BERKOWITZ M.,AMERICAN NATIONAL SECURITY: A READER ORD/FREE
IN THEORY AND POLICY. USA+45 INT/ORG FORCES BAL/PWR WAR
DIPLOM ECO/TAC DETER PWR...INT/LAW ANTHOL BIBLIOG ARMS/CONT
20 UN. PAGE 11 E0203 POLICY

B65
BOVY L.,LE MOUVEMENT SYNDICAL OUEST AFRICAIN BIBLIOG
D'EXPRESSION FRANCAISE. AFR SECT...JURID SOC 20. SOCISM
PAGE 14 E0275 ECO/UNDEV
IDEA/COMP

B65
CAMPBELL E.H.,SURVEYS, SUBDIVISIONS AND PLATTING, CONSTN
AND BOUNDARIES: WASHINGTON STATE LAW AND JUDICIAL PLAN
DECISIONS. USA+45 LAW LOC/G...DECISION JURID GEOG
CON/ANAL BIBLIOG WASHINGT/G PARTITION WATER. PROVS
PAGE 19 E0372

B65
FALK R.A.,THE AFTERMATH OF SABBATINO: BACKGROUND SOVEREIGN
PAPERS AND PROCEEDINGS OF SEVENTH HAMMARSKJOLD CT/SYS
FORUM. USA+45 LAW ACT/RES ADJUD ROLE...BIBLIOG 20 INT/LAW
EXPROPRIAT SABBATINO HARLAN/JM. PAGE 36 E0718 OWN

B65
FEERICK J.D.,FROM FAILING HANDS: THE STUDY OF EX/STRUC
PRESIDENTIAL SUCCESSION. CONSTN NAT/G PROB/SOLV CHIEF
LEAD PARL/PROC MURDER CHOOSE...NEW/IDEA BIBLIOG 20 LAW
KENNEDY/JF JOHNSON/LB PRESIDENT PRE/US/AM LEGIS
VICE/PRES. PAGE 36 E0724

B65
HOWARD C.G.,LAW: ITS NATURE, FUNCTIONS, AND LIMITS. LAW
USA+45 CONSTN LEGIS CREATE SANCTION ORD/FREE JURID
...BIBLIOG 20. PAGE 55 E1101 CONTROL
SOCIETY

B65
MCKAY R.B.,REAPPORTIONMENT: THE LAW AND POLITICS OF APPORT
EQUAL REPRESENTATION. FUT USA+45 PROVS BAL/PWR MAJORIT
ADJUD CHOOSE REPRESENT GOV/REL FEDERAL...JURID LEGIS
BIBLIOG 20 SUPREME/CT CONGRESS. PAGE 71 E1420 PWR

B65
MONCONDUIT F.,LA COMMISSION EUROPEENNE DES DROITS INT/LAW
DE L'HOMME. DIPLOM AGREE GP/REL ORD/FREE PWR INT/ORG
...BIBLIOG 20 TREATY. PAGE 74 E1483 ADJUD
JURID

B65
MOODY M.,CATALOG OF INTERNATIONAL LAW AND RELATIONS BIBLIOG
(20 VOLS.). WOR+45 INT/ORG NAT/G ADJUD ADMIN CT/SYS INT/LAW
POLICY. PAGE 74 E1488 DIPLOM

B65
NWOGUGU E.I.,THE LEGAL PROBLEMS OF FOREIGN FOR/AID
INVESTMENT IN DEVELOPING COUNTRIES. WOR+45 INT/ORG FINAN
DELIB/GP LEGIS PROB/SOLV INT/TRADE TAX ADJUD INT/LAW
SANCTION...BIBLIOG 20 TREATY. PAGE 78 E1561 ECO/UNDEV

B65
RADZINOWICZ L.,THE NEED FOR CRIMINOLOGY AND A CRIMLGY
PROPOSAL FOR AN INSTITUTE OF CRIMINOLOGY. FUT UK PROF/ORG
USA+45 SOCIETY ACT/RES PROB/SOLV CRIME...PSY SOC ACADEM
BIBLIOG 20. PAGE 83 E1666 CONTROL

B65
SMITH C.,THE OMBUDSMAN: A BIBLIOGRAPHY (PAMPHLET). BIBLIOG
DENMARK SWEDEN USA+45 LAW LEGIS JUDGE GOV/REL ADMIN
GP/REL...JURID 20. PAGE 92 E1841 CT/SYS
ADJUD

B65
US OFFICE ECONOMIC OPPORTUNITY,CATALOG OF FEDERAL BIBLIOG
PROGRAMS FOR INDIVIDUAL AND COMMUNITY IMPROVEMENT. CLIENT
USA+45 GIVE RECEIVE ADMIN HEALTH KNOWL SKILL WEALTH ECO/TAC
CHARTS. PAGE 101 E2021 MUNIC

B65
VON GLAHN G.,LAW AMONG NATIONS: AN INTRODUCTION TO ACADEM
PUBLIC INTERNATIONAL LAW. WOR+45 WOR-45 INT/ORG INT/LAW
NAT/G CREATE ADJUD WAR...GEOG CLASSIF TREND GEN/LAWS
BIBLIOG. PAGE 104 E2082 LAW

B65
VON RENESSE E.A.,UNVOLLENDETE DEMOKRATIEN. AFR ECO/UNDEV
ISLAM S/ASIA SOCIETY ACT/RES COLONIAL...JURID NAT/COMP
CHARTS BIBLIOG METH 13/20. PAGE 104 E2083 SOVEREIGN

B65
WHITE G.M.,THE USE OF EXPERTS BY INTERNATIONAL INT/LAW
TRIBUNALS. WOR+45 WOR-45 INT/ORG NAT/G PAY ADJUD ROUTINE
COST...OBS BIBLIOG 20. PAGE 106 E2117 CONSULT
CT/SYS

S65
MERRITT R.L.,"SELECTED ARTICLES AND DOCUMENTS ON BIBLIOG
INTERNATIONAL LAW AND RELATIONS." WOR+45 INT/ORG DIPLOM
FORCES INT/TRADE. PAGE 72 E1443 INT/LAW
GOV/REL

S65
PRABHAKAR P.,"SURVEY OF RESEARCH AND SOURCE BIBLIOG
MATERIALS; THE SINO-INDIAN BORDER DISPUTE." ASIA
CHINA/COM INDIA LAW NAT/G PLAN BAL/PWR WAR...POLICY S/ASIA
20 COLD/WAR. PAGE 82 E1645 DIPLOM

C65
SCHEINGOLD S.A.,"THE RULE OF LAW IN EUROPEAN INT/LAW
INTEGRATION: THE PATH OF THE SCHUMAN PLAN." EUR+WWI CT/SYS
JUDGE ADJUD FEDERAL ATTIT PWR...RECORD INT BIBLIOG REGION
EEC ECSC. PAGE 87 E1755 CENTRAL

C65

SEARA M.V.,"COSMIC INTERNATIONAL LAW." LAW ACADEM SPACE
ACT/RES DIPLOM COLONIAL CONTROL NUC/PWR SOVEREIGN INT/LAW
...GEN/LAWS BIBLIOG UN. PAGE 90 E1799 IDEA/COMP
INT/ORG

B66

ASAMOAH O.Y.,THE LEGAL SIGNIFICANCE OF THE INT/LAW
DECLARATIONS OF THE GENERAL ASSEMBLY OF THE UNITED INT/ORG
NATIONS. WOR+45 CREATE CONTROL...BIBLIOG 20 UN. DIPLOM
PAGE 5 E0105

B66

AUERBACH J.S.,LABOR AND LIBERTY; THE LA FOLLETTE DELIB/GP
COMMITTEE AND THE NEW DEAL. USA+45 LAW LEAD RESPECT LABOR
SOCISM...BIBLIOG 20 CONGRESS BILL/RIGHT LAFOLLET/R CONSTN
NEW/DEAL. PAGE 6 E0117 ORD/FREE

B66

BEDI A.S.,FREEDOM OF EXPRESSION AND SECURITY; METH
COMPARATIVE STUDY OF FUNCTIONS OF SUPREME COURTS IN CT/SYS
UNITED STATES AND INDIA. INDIA USA+45 LAW CONSTN ADJUD
PROB/SOLV...DECISION JURID BIBLIOG 20 SUPREME/CT ORD/FREE
FREE/SPEE AMEND/I. PAGE 9 E0175

B66

BEISER E.N.,THE TREATMENT OF LEGISLATIVE CT/SYS
APPORTIONMENT BY THE STATE AND FEDERAL COURTS APPORT
(DISSERTATION). USA+45 CONSTN NAT/G PROVS LEGIS ADJUD
CHOOSE REPRESENT ATTIT...POLICY BIBLIOG 20 CONGRESS PWR
SUPREME/CT. PAGE 9 E0181

B66

CAHN E.,CONFRONTING INJUSTICE. USA+45 PROB/SOLV TAX ORD/FREE
EDU/PROP PRESS CT/SYS GP/REL DISCRIM BIO/SOC CONSTN
...IDEA/COMP BIBLIOG WORSHIP 20 BILL/RIGHT. PAGE 18 ADJUD
E0362

B66

CALIFORNIA STATE LIBRARY,REAPPORTIONMENT, A BIBLIOG
SELECTIVE BIBLIOGRAPHY. USA+45 LEGIS CT/SYS APPORT
REPRESENT GOV/REL. PAGE 19 E0367 NAT/G
PROVS

B66

CARMEN I.H.,MOVIES, CENSORSHIP, AND THE LAW. LOC/G EDU/PROP
NAT/G ATTIT ORD/FREE...DECISION INT IDEA/COMP LAW
BIBLIOG 20 SUPREME/CT FILM. PAGE 19 E0383 ART/METH
CONSTN

B66

DIZARD W.P.,TELEVISION* A WORLD VIEW. WOR+45 COM/IND
ECO/UNDEV TEC/DEV LICENSE LITERACY...STAT OBS INT ACT/RES
QU TREND AUD/VIS BIBLIOG. PAGE 32 E0632 EDU/PROP
CREATE

B66

EPSTEIN F.T.,THE AMERICAN BIBLIOGRAPHY OF RUSSIAN BIBLIOG
AND EAST EUROPEAN STUDIES FOR 1964. USSR LOC/G COM
NAT/G POL/PAR FORCES ADMIN ARMS/CONT...JURID CONCPT MARXISM
20 UN. PAGE 35 E0694 DIPLOM

B66

FALK R.A.,THE STRATEGY OF WORLD ORDER* 4 VOLUMES. ORD/FREE
WOR+45 ECO/UNDEV ACADEM INT/ORG ACT/RES DIPLOM GEN/LAWS
ARMS/CONT WAR...NET/THEORY SIMUL BIBLIOG UN. ANTHOL
PAGE 36 E0719 INT/LAW

B66

FINK M.,A SELECTIVE BIBLIOGRAPHY ON STATE BIBLIOG
CONSTITUTIONAL REVISION (PAMPHLET). USA+45 FINAN PROVS
EX/STRUC LEGIS EDU/PROP ADMIN CT/SYS APPORT CHOOSE LOC/G
GOV/REL 20. PAGE 38 E0751 CONSTN

B66

HOLMES O.W.,JUSTICE HOLMES, EX CATHEDRA. USA+45 BIOG
USA-45 LAW INTELL ADMIN ATTIT...BIBLIOG 20 PERSON
SUPREME/CT HOLMES/OW. PAGE 55 E1088 CT/SYS
ADJUD

B66

KERR M.H.,ISLAMIC REFORM: THE POLITICAL AND LEGAL LAW
THEORIES OF MUHAMMAD 'ABDUH AND RASHID RIDA. NAT/G CONCPT
SECT LEAD SOVEREIGN CONSERVE...JURID BIBLIOG ISLAM
WORSHIP 20. PAGE 60 E1204

B66

MACMULLEN R.,ENEMIES OF THE ROMAN EMPIRE: TREASON, CRIME
UNREST, AND ALIENATION IN THE EMPIRE. ROMAN/EMP ADJUD
MUNIC CONTROL LEAD ATTIT PERSON MYSTISM...PHIL/SCI MORAL
BIBLIOG. PAGE 67 E1345 SOCIETY

B66

MAGRATH C.P.,YAZOO; LAW AND POLITICS IN THE NEW CT/SYS
REPUBLIC: THE CASE OF FLETCHER V. PECK. USA-45 LAW DECISION
...BIBLIOG 19 SUPREME/CT YAZOO. PAGE 67 E1348 CONSTN

LOBBY

B66

MILLER E.W.,THE NEGRO IN AMERICA: A BIBLIOGRAPHY. BIBLIOG
USA+45 LAW EDU/PROP REV GOV/REL GP/REL INGP/REL DISCRIM
ADJUST HABITAT PERSON HEALTH ORD/FREE SOC/INTEG 20 RACE/REL
NEGRO. PAGE 73 E1459

B66

O'NEILL C.E.,CHURCH AND STATE IN FRENCH COLONIAL COLONIAL
LOUISIANA: POLICY AND POLITICS TO 1732. PROVS NAT/G
VOL/ASSN DELIB/GP ADJUD ADMIN GP/REL ATTIT DRIVE SECT
...POLICY BIBLIOG 17/18 LOUISIANA CHURCH/STA. PWR
PAGE 78 E1568

B66

UNITED NATIONS,INTERNATIONAL SPACE BIBLIOGRAPHY. BIBLIOG
FUT INT/ORG TEC/DEV DIPLOM ARMS/CONT NUC/PWR SPACE
...JURID SOC UN. PAGE 98 E1969 PEACE
R+D

B66

WASHINGTON S.H.,BIBLIOGRAPHY: LABOR-MANAGEMENT BIBLIOG
RELATIONS ACT, 1947 AS AMENDED BY LABOR-MANAGEMENT LAW
REPORTING AND DISCLOSURE ACT, 1959. USA+45 CONSTN LABOR
INDUS DELIB/GP LEGIS WORKER BARGAIN ECO/TAC ADJUD MGT
GP/REL NEW/LIB...JURID CONGRESS. PAGE 105 E2100

L66

SEYLER W.C.,"DOCTORAL DISSERTATIONS IN POLITICAL BIBLIOG
SCIENCE IN UNIVERSITIES OF THE UNITED STATES AND LAW
CANADA." INT/ORG LOC/G ADMIN...INT/LAW MGT NAT/G
GOV/COMP. PAGE 90 E1808

S66

BURDETTE F.L.,"SELECTED ARTICLES AND DOCUMENTS ON BIBLIOG
AMERICAN GOVERNMENT AND POLITICS." LAW LOC/G MUNIC USA+45
NAT/G POL/PAR PROVS LEGIS BAL/PWR ADMIN EXEC JURID
REPRESENT MGT. PAGE 17 E0331 CONSTN

S66

MATTHEWS D.G.,"ETHIOPIAN OUTLINE: A BIBLIOGRAPHIC BIBLIOG
RESEARCH GUIDE." ETHIOPIA LAW STRUCT ECO/UNDEV AGRI NAT/G
LABOR SECT CHIEF DELIB/GP EX/STRUC ADMIN...LING DIPLOM
ORG/CHARTS 20. PAGE 69 E1384 POL/PAR

S66

MATTHEWS D.G.,"PRELUDE-COUP D'ETAT-MILITARY BIBLIOG
GOVERNMENT: A BIBLIOGRAPHICAL AND RESEARCH GUIDE TO NAT/G
NIGERIAN POL AND GOVT, JAN, 1965-66." AFR NIGER LAW ADMIN
CONSTN POL/PAR LEGIS CIVMIL/REL GOV/REL...STAT 20. CHOOSE
PAGE 69 E1385

S66

NYC BAR ASSOCIATION RECORD,"PAPERBACKS FOR THE BIBLIOG
BAR." USA+45 LEGIS ADJUD CT/SYS. PAGE 78 E1562 JURID
LAW
WRITING

S66

SHKLAR J.,"SELECTED ARTICLES AND DOCUMENTS ON BIBLIOG
POLITICAL THEORY." ADJUD REV...JURID PHIL/SCI ELITES
IDEA/COMP. PAGE 91 E1820 PWR

C66

BLAISDELL D.C.,"INTERNATIONAL ORGANIZATION." FUT BIBLIOG
WOR+45 ECO/DEV DELIB/GP FORCES EFFICIENCY PEACE INT/ORG
ORD/FREE...INT/LAW 20 UN LEAGUE/NAT NATO. PAGE 12 DIPLOM
E0239 ARMS/CONT

N66

BACHELDER G.L.,THE LITERATURE OF FEDERALISM: A BIBLIOG
SELECTED BIBLIOGRAPHY (REV ED) (A PAMPHLET). USA+45 FEDERAL
USA-45 WOR+45 WOR-45 LAW CONSTN PROVS ADMIN CT/SYS NAT/G
GOV/REL ROLE...CONCPT 19/20. PAGE 7 E0126 LOC/G

B67

BIBBY J.,ON CAPITOL HILL. POL/PAR LOBBY PARL/PROC CONFER
GOV/REL PERS/REL...JURID PHIL/SCI OBS INT BIBLIOG LEGIS
20 CONGRESS PRESIDENT. PAGE 12 E0224 CREATE
LEAD

B67

BOLES D.E.,THE TWO SWORDS. USA+45 USA-45 LAW CONSTN SCHOOL
SOCIETY FINAN PRESS CT/SYS...HEAL JURID BIBLIOG EDU/PROP
WORSHIP 20 SUPREME/CT CHURCH/STA. PAGE 13 E0263 ADJUD

B67

CHAPIN F.S. JR.,SELECTED REFERENCES ON URBAN BIBLIOG
PLANNING METHODS AND TECHNIQUES. USA+45 LAW ECO/DEV NEIGH
LOC/G NAT/G SCHOOL CONSULT CREATE PROB/SOLV TEC/DEV MUNIC
SOC/WK. PAGE 21 E0420 PLAN

B67

CLINARD M.B.,CRIMINAL BEHAVIOR SYSTEMS: A TYPOLOGY. BIBLIOG
WOR+45 LAW SOCIETY STRUCT R+D AGE/Y ATTIT WEALTH CRIME

...CLASSIF CHARTS METH/COMP METH. PAGE 23 E0457
CRIMLGY
PERSON

B67
COWLING M.,1867 DISRAELI, GLADSTONE, AND
REVOLUTION; THE PASSING OF THE SECOND REFORM BILL.
UK LEGIS LEAD LOBBY GP/REL INGP/REL...DECISION
BIBLIOG 19 REFORMERS. PAGE 27 E0531
PARL/PROC
POL/PAR
ATTIT
LAW

B67
DEBOLD R.C.,LSD, MAN AND SOCIETY. USA+45 LAW
SOCIETY SECT CONTROL SANCTION STRANGE ATTIT...HEAL
CHARTS ANTHOL BIBLIOG. PAGE 30 E0601
HEALTH
DRIVE
PERSON
BIO/SOC

B67
FINCHER F.,THE GOVERNMENT OF THE UNITED STATES.
USA+45 USA-45 POL/PAR CHIEF CT/SYS LOBBY GP/REL
INGP/REL...CONCPT CHARTS BIBLIOG T 18/20 PRESIDENT
CONGRESS SUPREME/CT. PAGE 38 E0749
NAT/G
EX/STRUC
LEGIS
OP/RES

B67
GREENE L.S.,AMERICAN GOVERNMENT POLICIES AND
FUNCTIONS. USA+45 LAW AGRI DIST/IND LABOR MUNIC
BUDGET DIPLOM EDU/PROP ORD/FREE...BIBLIOG T 20.
PAGE 46 E0910
POLICY
NAT/G
ADMIN
DECISION

B67
HOLSTI K.J.,INTERNATIONAL POLITICS* A FRAMEWORK FOR
ANALYSIS. WOR+45 WOR-45 NAT/G EDU/PROP DETER WAR
WEAPON PWR BIBLIOG. PAGE 55 E1090
DIPLOM
BARGAIN
POLICY
INT/LAW

B67
KING W.L.,MELVILLE WESTON FULLER: CHIEF JUSTICE OF
THE UNITED STATES, 1888-1910. USA-45 CONSTN FINAN
LABOR TAX GOV/REL PERS/REL ATTIT PERSON PWR...JURID
BIBLIOG 19/20 SUPREME/CT FULLER/MW HOLMES/OW.
PAGE 61 E1216
BIOG
CT/SYS
LAW
ADJUD

B67
LAFAVE W.R.,INTERNATIONAL TRADE, INVESTMENT, AND
ORGANIZATION. INDUS PROB/SOLV TARIFFS CONTROL
...TREND ANTHOL BIBLIOG 20 EEC. PAGE 62 E1245
INT/TRADE
INT/LAW
INT/ORG

B67
LENG S.C.,JUSTICE IN COMMUNIST CHINA: A SURVEY OF
THE JUDICIAL SYSTEM OF THE CHINESE PEOPLE'S
REPUBLIC. CHINA/COM LAW CONSTN LOC/G NAT/G PROF/ORG
CONSULT FORCES ADMIN CRIME ORD/FREE...BIBLIOG 20
MAO. PAGE 64 E1284
CT/SYS
ADJUD
JURID
MARXISM

B67
LEVY L.W.,JUDICIAL REVIEW AND THE SUPREME COURT.
USA+45 USA-45 NEUTRAL ATTIT ORD/FREE...POLICY
DECISION BIBLIOG 18/20 BILL/RIGHT SUPREME/CT.
PAGE 65 E1292
ADJUD
CONSTN
LAW
CT/SYS

B67
MANVELL R.,THE INCOMPARABLE CRIME. GERMANY ACT/RES
DEATH...BIBLIOG 20 JEWS. PAGE 68 E1364
MURDER
CRIME
WAR
HIST/WRIT

B67
PLANO J.C.,FORGING WORLD ORDER: THE POLITICS OF
INTERNATIONAL ORGANIZATION. PROB/SOLV DIPLOM
CONTROL CENTRAL RATIONAL ORD/FREE...INT/LAW CHARTS
BIBLIOG 20 UN LEAGUE/NAT. PAGE 81 E1618
INT/ORG
ADMIN
JURID

B67
POGANY A.H.,POLITICAL SCIENCE AND INTERNATIONAL
RELATIONS. BOOKS RECOMMENDED FOR AMERICAN CATHOLIC
COLLEGE LIBRARIES. INT/ORG LOC/G NAT/G FORCES
BAL/PWR ECO/TAC NUC/PWR...CATH INT/LAW TREATY 20.
PAGE 81 E1622
BIBLIOG
DIPLOM

B67
RAE D.,THE POLITICAL CONSEQUENCES OF ELECTORAL
LAWS. EUR+WWI ICELAND ISRAEL NEW/ZEALND UK USA+45
ADJUD APPORT GP/REL MAJORITY...MATH STAT CENSUS
CHARTS BIBLIOG 20 AUSTRAL. PAGE 83 E1667
POL/PAR
CHOOSE
NAT/COMP
REPRESENT

B67
RAMUNDO B.A.,PEACEFUL COEXISTENCE: INTERNATIONAL
LAW IN THE BUILDING OF COMMUNISM. USSR INT/ORG
DIPLOM COLONIAL ARMS/CONT ROLE SOVEREIGN...POLICY
METH/COMP NAT/COMP BIBLIOG. PAGE 83 E1673
INT/LAW
PEACE
MARXISM
METH/CNCPT

B67
US DEPARTMENT OF STATE,TREATIES IN FORCE. USA+45
WOR+45 AGREE WAR PEACE 20 TREATY. PAGE 100 E1999
BIBLIOG
DIPLOM
INT/ORG
DETER

L67
"FOCUS ON WORLD LAW." WOR+45 NAT/G CT/SYS PEACE
...BIBLIOG 20 UN. PAGE 2 E0036
INT/LAW
INT/ORG
PROB/SOLV
CONCPT

S67
O'HIGGINS P.,"A BIBLIOGRAPHY OF PERIODICAL
LITERATURE RELATING TO IRISH LAW." IRELAND...JURID
20. PAGE 78 E1567
BIBLIOG
LAW
ADJUD

B77
CADWALDER J.L.,DIGEST OF THE PUBLISHED OPINIONS OF
THE ATTORNEYS-GENERAL, AND OF THE LEADING DECISIONS
OF THE FEDERAL COURTS (REV ED). USA-45 NAT/G JUDGE
PROB/SOLV DIPLOM ATTIT...POLICY INT/LAW ANTHOL 19.
PAGE 18 E0356
BIBLIOG
CT/SYS
DECISION
ADJUD

C93
PLAYFAIR R.L.,"A BIBLIOGRAPHY OF MOROCCO." MOROCCO
CULTURE AGRI FORCES DIPLOM WAR HEALTH...GEOG JURID
SOC CHARTS. PAGE 81 E1620
BIBLIOG
ISLAM
MEDIT-7

B97
JENKS E.J.,LAW AND POLITICS IN THE MIDDLE AGES.
CHRIST-17C CULTURE STRUCT KIN NAT/G SECT CT/SYS
GP/REL...CLASSIF CHARTS IDEA/COMP BIBLIOG 8/16.
PAGE 58 E1162
LAW
SOCIETY
ADJUST

BIBLIOG/A....BIBLIOGRAPHY OVER 50 ITEMS ANNOTATED

N
CONOVER H.F.,OFFICIAL PUBLICATIONS OF BRITISH EAST
AFRICA (PAMPHLET). UK LAW ECO/UNDEV AGRI EXTR/IND
SECT LEGIS BUDGET TAX...HEAL STAT 20. PAGE 25 E0491
BIBLIOG/A
AFR
ADMIN
COLONIAL

N
FULLER G.A.,DEMOBILIZATION: A SELECTED LIST OF
REFERENCES. USA+45 LAW AGRI LABOR WORKER ECO/TAC
RATION RECEIVE EDU/PROP ROUTINE ARMS/CONT ALL/VALS
20. PAGE 41 E0819
BIBLIOG/A
INDUS
FORCES
NAT/G

N
KEITT L.,AN ANNOTATED BIBLIOGRAPHY OF
BIBLIOGRAPHIES OF STATUTORY MATERIALS OF THE UNITED
STATES. CHRIST-17C USA-45 LEGIS ADJUD COLONIAL
CT/SYS...JURID 16/20. PAGE 60 E1196
BIBLIOG/A
LAW
CONSTN
PROVS

N
LIBRARY INTERNATIONAL REL,INTERNATIONAL INFORMATION
SERVICE. WOR+45 CULTURE INT/ORG FORCES...GEOG HUM
SOC. PAGE 65 E1295
BIBLIOG/A
DIPLOM
INT/TRADE
INT/LAW

N
VALENZUELE G.,BIBLIOGRAFIA GUATEMALTECA, Y CATALOG
GENERAL DE LIBROS, FOLLETOS, PERIODICOS, REVISTAS,
ETC. (10 VOLS.). GUATEMALA LAW...ART/METH 17/20.
PAGE 103 E2066
BIBLIOG/A
L/A+17C

N
AMERICAN JOURNAL OF INTERNATIONAL LAW. WOR+45
WOR-45 CONSTN INT/ORG NAT/G CT/SYS ARMS/CONT WAR
...DECISION JURID NAT/COMP 20. PAGE 1 E0001
BIBLIOG/A
INT/LAW
DIPLOM
ADJUD

N
AMERICAN POLITICAL SCIENCE REVIEW. USA+45 USA-45
WOR+45 WOR-45 INT/ORG ADMIN...INT/LAW PHIL/SCI
CONCPT METH 20 UN. PAGE 1 E0002
BIBLIOG/A
DIPLOM
NAT/G
GOV/COMP

N
ANNALS OF THE AMERICAN ACADEMY OF POLITICAL AND
SOCIAL SCIENCE. AFR ASIA S/ASIA WOR+45 POL/PAR
DIPLOM CRIME REV...SOC BIOG 20. PAGE 1 E0003
BIBLIOG/A
NAT/G
CULTURE
ATTIT

N
CANADIAN GOVERNMENT PUBLICATIONS (1955-). CANADA
AGRI FINAN LABOR FORCES INT/TRADE HEALTH...JURID 20
PARLIAMENT. PAGE 1 E0005
BIBLIOG/A
NAT/G
DIPLOM
INT/ORG

N
INTERNATIONAL AFFAIRS. WOR+45 WOR-45 ECO/UNDEV
INT/ORG NAT/G PROB/SOLV FOR/AID WAR...POLICY 20.
PAGE 1 E0007
BIBLIOG/A
DIPLOM
INT/LAW
INT/TRADE

N
INTERNATIONAL BOOK NEWS, 1928-1934. ECO/UNDEV FINAN
INDUS LABOR INT/TRADE CONFER ADJUD COLONIAL...HEAL
SOC/WK CHARTS 20 LEAGUE/NAT. PAGE 1 E0008
BIBLIOG/A
DIPLOM
INT/LAW
INT/ORG

INTERNATIONAL STUDIES. ASIA S/ASIA WOR+45 ECO/UNDEV BIBLIOG/A
INT/ORG NAT/G LEAD ATTIT WEALTH...SOC 20. PAGE 1 DIPLOM
E0009 INT/LAW
INT/TRADE

N

JOURNAL OF POLITICS. USA+45 USA-45 CONSTN POL/PAR BIBLIOG/A
EX/STRUC LEGIS PROB/SOLV DIPLOM CT/SYS CHOOSE NAT/G
RACE/REL 20. PAGE 1 E0011 LAW
LOC/G

N

MIDWEST JOURNAL OF POLITICAL SCIENCE. USA+45 CONSTN BIBLIOG/A
ECO/DEV LEGIS PROB/SOLV CT/SYS LEAD GOV/REL ATTIT NAT/G
POLICY. PAGE 1 E0012 DIPLOM
POL/PAR

N

POLITICAL SCIENCE QUARTERLY. USA+45 USA-45 LAW BIBLIOG/A
CONSTN ECO/DEV INT/ORG LOC/G POL/PAR LEGIS LEAD NAT/G
NUC/PWR...CONCPT 20. PAGE 1 E0013 DIPLOM
POLICY

N

ADVANCED MANAGEMENT. INDUS EX/STRUC WORKER OP/RES MGT
...DECISION BIBLIOG/A 20. PAGE 1 E0015 ADMIN
LABOR
GP/REL

N

BIBLIOGRAPHIE DE LA PHILOSOPHIE. LAW CULTURE SECT BIBLIOG/A
EDU/PROP MORAL...HUM METH/CNCPT 20. PAGE 1 E0018 PHIL/SCI
CONCPT
LOG

N

HANDBOOK OF LATIN AMERICAN STUDIES. LAW CULTURE BIBLIOG/A
ECO/UNDEV POL/PAR ADMIN LEAD...SOC 20. PAGE 1 E0022 L/A+17C
NAT/G
DIPLOM

N

INTERNATIONAL BIBLIOGRAPHY ON CRIME AND BIBLIOG/A
DELINQUENCY. USA+45 LAW FORCES PROB/SOLV AGE/Y 20. CRIME
PAGE 1 E0023 ANOMIE
CRIMLGY

N

LATIN AMERICA IN PERIODICAL LITERATURE. LAW TEC/DEV BIBLIOG/A
DIPLOM RECEIVE EDU/PROP...GEOG HUM MGT 20. PAGE 2 L/A+17C
E0024 SOCIETY
ECO/UNDEV

N

CANON LAW ABSTRACTS. LEGIT CONFER CT/SYS INGP/REL BIBLIOG/A
MARRIAGE ATTIT MORAL WORSHIP 20. PAGE 2 E0026 CATHISM
SECT
LAW

N

NEUE POLITISCHE LITERATUR; BERICHTE UBER DAS BIBLIOG/A
INTERNATIONALE SCHRIFTTUM ZUR POLITIK. WOR+45 LAW DIPLOM
CONSTN POL/PAR ADMIN LEAD GOV/REL...POLICY NAT/G
IDEA/COMP. PAGE 2 E0028 NAT/COMP

N

PERSONNEL. USA+45 LAW LABOR LG/CO WORKER CREATE BIBLIOG/A
GOV/REL PERS/REL ATTIT WEALTH. PAGE 2 E0029 ADMIN
MGT
GP/REL

N

AFRICAN BIBLIOGRAPHIC CENTER,A CURRENT BIBLIOGRAPHY BIBLIOG/A
ON AFRICAN AFFAIRS. LAW CULTURE ECO/UNDEV LABOR AFR
SECT DIPLOM FOR/AID COLONIAL NAT/LISM...LING 20. NAT/G
PAGE 3 E0053 REGION

N

AIR UNIVERSITY LIBRARY,INDEX TO MILITARY BIBLIOG/A
PERIODICALS. FUT SPACE WOR+45 REGION ARMS/CONT FORCES
NUC/PWR WAR PEACE INT/LAW. PAGE 3 E0056 NAT/G
DIPLOM

N

AMER COUNCIL OF LEARNED SOCIET,THE ACLS CONSTITUENT BIBLIOG/A
SOCIETY JOURNAL PROJECT. FUT USA+45 LAW NAT/G PLAN HUM
DIPLOM PHIL/SCI. PAGE 4 E0072 COMPUT/IR
COMPUTER

N

ASIA FOUNDATION,LIBRARY NOTES. LAW CONSTN CULTURE BIBLIOG/A
SOCIETY ECO/UNDEV INT/ORG NAT/G COLONIAL LEAD ASIA
REGION NAT/LISM ATTIT 20 UN. PAGE 6 E0107 S/ASIA
DIPLOM

N

ATLANTIC INSTITUTE,ATLANTIC STUDIES. COM EUR+WWI BIBLIOG/A
USA+45 CULTURE STRUCT ECO/DEV FORCES LEAD ARMS/CONT DIPLOM
...INT/LAW JURID SOC. PAGE 6 E0110 POLICY
GOV/REL

N

CATHERINE R.,LA REVUE ADMINISTRATIVE. FRANCE LAW ADMIN
NAT/G LEGIS...JURID BIBLIOG/A 20. PAGE 21 E0407 MGT
FINAN
METH/COMP

N

TURNER R.K.,BIBLIOGRAPHY ON WORLD ORGANIZATION. BIBLIOG/A
INT/TRADE CT/SYS ARMS/CONT WEALTH...INT/LAW 20. INT/ORG
PAGE 97 E1944 PEACE
WAR

N

US BUREAU OF THE CENSUS,BIBLIOGRAPHY OF SOCIAL BIBLIOG/A
SCIENCE PERIODICALS AND MONOGRAPH SERIES. WOR+45 CULTURE
LAW DIPLOM EDU/PROP HEALTH...PSY SOC LING STAT. NAT/G
PAGE 99 E1980 SOCIETY

N

US SUPERINTENDENT OF DOCUMENTS,EDUCATION (PRICE BIBLIOG/A
LIST 31). USA+45 LAW FINAN LOC/G NAT/G DEBATE ADMIN EDU/PROP
LEAD RACE/REL FEDERAL HEALTH POLICY. PAGE 103 E2062 ACADEM
SCHOOL

N

US SUPERINTENDENT OF DOCUMENTS,POLITICAL SCIENCE: BIBLIOG/A
GOVERNMENT, CRIME, DISTRICT OF COLUMBIA (PRICE LIST NAT/G
54). USA+45 LAW CONSTN EX/STRUC WORKER ADJUD ADMIN CRIME
CT/SYS CHOOSE INGP/REL RACE/REL CONGRESS PRESIDENT.
PAGE 103 E2063

B00

GREELY A.W.,PUBLIC DOCUMENTS OF THE FIRST FOURTEEN BIBLIOG/A
CONGRESSES, 1789-1817. USA-45 LEAD REPRESENT ATTIT NAT/G
18/19 CONGRESS. PAGE 45 E0904 LAW
LEGIS

B00

GRIFFIN A.P.C.,LIST OF BOOKS RELATING TO THE THEORY BIBLIOG/A
OF COLONIZATION, GOVERNMENT OF DEPENDENCIES, COLONIAL
PROTECTORATES, AND RELATED TOPICS. FRANCE GERMANY GOV/REL
ITALY SPAIN UK USA-45 WOR-45 ECO/TAC ADMIN CONTROL DOMIN
REGION NAT/LISM ALL/VALS PWR...INT/LAW SOC 16/19.
PAGE 46 E0917

B01

GRIFFIN A.P.C.,LIST OF BOOKS ON SAMOA (PAMPHLET). BIBLIOG/A
GERMANY S/ASIA UK USA-45 WOR-45 ECO/UNDEV REGION COLONIAL
ALL/VALS ORD/FREE ALL/IDEOS...GEOG INT/LAW 19 SAMOA DIPLOM
GUAM. PAGE 46 E0918

B02

GRIFFIN A.P.C.,A LIST OF BOOKS RELATING TO TRUSTS BIBLIOG/A
(2ND REV. ED.) (PAMPHLET). FRANCE GERMANY UK USA-45 JURID
WOR-45 LAW ECO/DEV INDUS LG/CO NAT/G CAP/ISM ECO/TAC
CENTRAL DISCRIM PWR LAISSEZ 19/20. PAGE 46 E0919 VOL/ASSN

B03

GRIFFIN A.P.C.,LIST OF BOOKS ON THE CONSTITUTION OF BIBLIOG/A
THE UNITED STATES (PAMPHLET). USA-45 NAT/G EX/STRUC CONSTN
JUDGE TOP/EX CT/SYS 18/20 CONGRESS PRESIDENT LAW
SUPREME/CT. PAGE 46 E0920 JURID

B03

GRIFFIN A.P.C.,LIST OF REFERENCES ON INDUSTRIAL BIBLIOG/A
ARBITRATION (PAMPHLET). USA-45 STRATA VOL/ASSN INDUS
DELIB/GP WORKER ADJUD GP/REL...MGT 19/20. PAGE 46 LABOR
E0921 BARGAIN

B03

GRIFFIN A.P.C.,LISTS PUBLISHED 1902-03: LABOR BIBLIOG/A
PARTICULARLY RELATING TO STRIKES (PAMPHLET). UK LABOR
USA-45 FINAN WORKER PLAN BARGAIN CRIME GOV/REL GP/REL
...POLICY 19/20 PARLIAMENT. PAGE 46 E0923 ECO/TAC

B03

GRIFFIN A.P.C.,SELECT LIST OF BOOKS ON LABOR BIBLIOG/A
PARTICULARLY RELATING TO STRIKES. FRANCE GERMANY GP/REL
MOD/EUR UK USA-45 LAW NAT/G DELIB/GP WORKER BARGAIN MGT
LICENSE PAY ADJUD 19/20. PAGE 46 E0924 LABOR

B04

GRIFFIN A.P.C.,A LIST OF BOOKS RELATING TO BIBLIOG/A
RAILROADS IN THEIR RELATION TO THE GOVERNMENT AND SERV/IND
THE PUBLIC (PAMPHLET). USA-45 LAW ECO/DEV NAT/G ADJUD
TEC/DEV CAP/ISM LICENSE CENTRAL LAISSEZ...DECISION ECO/TAC
19/20. PAGE 47 E0925

GRIFFIN A.P.C.,REFERENCES ON CHINESE IMMIGRATIONS (PAMPHLET). USA-45 KIN NAT/LISM ATTIT...SOC 19/20. PAGE 47 E0926
B04
BIBLIOG/A
STRANGE
JURID
RACE/REL

GRIFFIN A.P.C.,LIST OF BOOKS ON RAILROADS IN FOREIGN COUNTRIES. MOD/EUR ECO/DEV NAT/G CONTROL SOCISM...JURID 19/20 RAILROAD. PAGE 47 E0927
B05
BIBLIOG/A
SERV/IND
ADMIN
DIST/IND

GRIFFIN A.P.C.,LIST OF REFERENCES ON PRIMARY ELECTIONS (PAMPHLET). USA-45 LAW LOC/G DELIB/GP LEGIS OP/RES TASK REPRESENT CONSEN...DECISION 19/20 CONGRESS. PAGE 47 E0928
B05
BIBLIOG/A
POL/PAR
CHOOSE
POPULISM

GRIFFIN A.P.C.,LIST OF BOOKS RELATING TO CHILD LABOR (PAMPHLET). BELGIUM FRANCE GERMANY MOD/EUR UK USA-45 ECO/DEV INDUS WORKER CAP/ISM PAY ROUTINE ALL/IDEOS...MGT SOC 19/20. PAGE 47 E0929
B06
BIBLIOG/A
LAW
LABOR
AGE/C

GRIFFIN A.P.C.,SELECT LIST OF REFERENCES ON THE NEGRO QUESTION (REV. ED.). USA-45 CONSTN SCHOOL SUFF ADJUST...JURID SOC/INTEG 19/20 NEGRO. PAGE 47 E0930
B06
BIBLIOG/A
RACE/REL
DISCRIM
ATTIT

GRIFFIN A.P.C.,LIST OF MORE RECENT WORKS ON FEDERAL CONTROL OF COMMERCE AND CORPORATIONS (PAMPHLET). USA-45 LAW ECO/DEV FINAN LG/CO TARIFFS TAX LICENSE CENTRAL ORD/FREE WEALTH LAISSEZ 19/20. PAGE 47 E0931
B07
BIBLIOG/A
NAT/G
JURID
ECO/TAC

GRIFFIN A.P.C.,LIST OF REFERENCES ON INTERNATIONAL ARBITRATION. FRANCE L/A+17C USA-45 WOR-45 DIPLOM CONFER COLONIAL ARMS/CONT BAL/PAY EQUILIB SOVEREIGN ...DECISION 19/20 MEXIC/AMER. PAGE 47 E0932
B08
BIBLIOG/A
INT/ORG
INT/LAW
DELIB/GP

GRIFFIN A.P.C.,LIST OF WORKS RELATING TO GOVERNMENT REGULATION OF INSURANCE UNITED STATES AND FOREIGN COUNTRIES (2ND. ED.) (PAMPHLET). FRANCE GERMANY UK USA-45 WOR-45 LG/CO LOC/G NAT/G LEGIS LICENSE ADJUD LOBBY CENTRAL ORD/FREE 19/20. PAGE 47 E0933
B08
BIBLIOG/A
FINAN
LAW
CONTROL

GRIFFIN A.P.C.,REFERENCES ON CORRUPT PRACTICES IN ELECTIONS (PAMPHLET). USA-45 LAW CONSTN TRIBUTE CRIME REPRESENT...JURID 19/20. PAGE 47 E0934
B08
BIBLIOG/A
CHOOSE
SUFF
APPORT

HARVARD UNIVERSITY LAW LIBRARY,CATALOGUE OF THE LIBRARY OF THE LAW SCHOOL OF HARVARD UNIVERSITY (3 VOLS.). UK USA-45 LEGIS JUDGE ADJUD CT/SYS...JURID CHARTS 14/20. PAGE 51 E1008
B09
BIBLIOG/A
LAW
ADMIN

MENDELSSOHN S.,MENDELSSOHN'S SOUTH AFRICA BIBLIOGRAPHY (VOL. I). SOUTH/AFR RACE/REL...GEOG JURID 19/20. PAGE 72 E1440
B10
BIBLIOG/A
CULTURE

GRIFFIN A.P.C.,SELECT LIST OF REFERENCES ON IMPEACHMENT (REV. ED.) (PAMPHLET). USA-45 LAW PROVS ADJUD ATTIT...JURID 19/20 NEGRO. PAGE 47 E0935
B12
BIBLIOG/A
CONSTN
NAT/G
LEGIS

MEYER H.H.B.,SELECT LIST OF REFERENCES ON THE INITIATIVE, REFERENDUM, AND RECALL. MOD/EUR USA-45 LAW LOC/G MUNIC REPRESENT POPULISM 20 CONGRESS. PAGE 72 E1446
B12
BIBLIOG/A
NAT/G
LEGIS
CHOOSE

SAWYER R.A.,A LIST OF WORKS ON COUNTY GOVERNMENT. LAW FINAN MUNIC TOP/EX ROUTINE CRIME...CLASSIF RECORD 19/20. PAGE 87 E1748
B15
BIBLIOG/A
LOC/G
GOV/REL
ADMIN

CARLYLE A.J.,BIBLIOGRAPHY OF POLITICAL THEORY (PAMPHLET). FRANCE GERMANY UK USA-45...JURID 9/19. PAGE 19 E0382
B16
BIBLIOG/A
CONCPT
PHIL/SCI

LONDON SCHOOL ECONOMICS-POL,ANNUAL DIGEST OF PUBLIC INTERNATIONAL LAW CASES. INT/ORG MUNIC NAT/G PROVS ADMIN NEUTRAL WAR GOV/REL PRIVIL 20. PAGE 66 E1323
B19
BIBLIOG/A
INT/LAW
ADJUD
DIPLOM

BLACHLY F.F.,"THE GOVERNMENT AND ADMINISTRATION OF GERMANY." GERMANY CONSTN LOC/G PROVS DELIB/GP EX/STRUC FORCES LEGIS TOP/EX CT/SYS...BIBLIOG/A 19/20. PAGE 12 E0235
C20
NAT/G
GOV/REL
ADMIN
PHIL/SCI

MYERS D.P.,MANUAL OF COLLECTIONS OF TREATIES AND OF COLLECTIONS RELATING TO TREATIES. MOD/EUR INT/ORG LEGIS WRITING ADMIN SOVEREIGN...INT/LAW 19/20. PAGE 75 E1514
B22
BIBLIOG/A
DIPLOM
CONFER

SCHROEDER T.,FREE SPEECH BIBLIOGRAPHY. EUR+WWI WOR-45 NAT/G SECT ECO/TAC WRITING ADJUD ATTIT MARXISM SOCISM 16/20. PAGE 88 E1768
B22
BIBLIOG/A
ORD/FREE
CONTROL
LAW

GODET M.,INDEX BIBLIOGRAPHICUS: INTERNATIONAL CATALOGUE OF SOURCES OF CURRENT BIBLIOGRAPHIC INFORMATION. EUR+WWI MOD/EUR SOCIETY SECT TAX ...JURID PHIL/SCI SOC MATH. PAGE 44 E0876
B25
BIBLIOG/A
DIPLOM
EDU/PROP
LAW

WINFIELD P.H.,THE CHIEF SOURCES OF ENGLISH LEGAL HISTORY. UK CONSTN JUDGE ADJUD CT/SYS 13/18. PAGE 107 E2133
B25
BIBLIOG/A
JURID
LAW

BEALE J.H.,A BIBLIOGRAPHY OF EARLY ENGLISH LAW BOOKS. MOD/EUR UK PRESS ADJUD CT/SYS ATTIT...CHARTS 10/16. PAGE 8 E0161
B26
BIBLIOG/A
JURID
LAW

CAM H.M.,BIBLIOGRAPHY OF ENGLISH CONSTITUTIONAL HISTORY (PAMPHLET). UK LAW LOC/G NAT/G POL/PAR SECT DELIB/GP ADJUD ORD/FREE 19/20 PARLIAMENT. PAGE 19 E0369
B29
BIBLIOG/A
CONSTN
ADMIN
PARL/PROC

BUCK A.E.,"PUBLIC BUDGETING." USA-45 FINAN LOC/G NAT/G LEGIS BAL/PAY COST...JURID TREND BIBLIOG/A 20. PAGE 17 E0324
C29
BUDGET
ROUTINE
ADMIN

BORCHARD E.H.,GUIDE TO THE LAW AND LEGAL LITERATURE OF FRANCE. FRANCE FINAN INDUS LABOR SECT LEGIS ADMIN COLONIAL CRIME OWN...INT/LAW 20. PAGE 14 E0266
B31
BIBLIOG/A
LAW
CONSTN
METH

AMERICAN FOREIGN LAW ASSN,BIOGRAPHICAL NOTES ON THE LAWS AND LEGAL LITERATURE OF URUGUAY AND CURACAO. URUGUAY CONSTN FINAN SECT FORCES JUDGE DIPLOM INT/TRADE ADJUD CT/SYS CRIME 20. PAGE 4 E0078
B33
BIBLIOG/A
LAW
JURID
ADMIN

HELLMAN F.S.,SELECTED LIST OF REFERENCES ON THE CONSTITUTIONAL POWERS OF THE PRESIDENT INCLUDING POWERS RECENTLY DELEGATED. USA-45 NAT/G EX/STRUC TOP/EX CENTRAL FEDERAL PWR 20 PRESIDENT. PAGE 51 E1025
B33
BIBLIOG/A
JURID
LAW
CONSTN

MATTHEWS M.A.,THE AMERICAN INSTITUTE OF INTERNATIONAL LAW AND THE CODIFICATION OF INTERNATIONAL LAW (PAMPHLET). USA-45 CONSTN ADJUD CT/SYS...JURID 20. PAGE 69 E1386
B33
BIBLIOG/A
INT/LAW
L/A+17C
DIPLOM

CULVER D.C.,BIBLIOGRAPHY OF CRIME AND CRIMINAL JUSTICE, 1927-1931. LAW CULTURE PUB/INST PROB/SOLV CT/SYS...PSY SOC STAT 20. PAGE 28 E0549
B34
BIBLIOG/A
CRIMLGY
ADJUD
FORCES

US TARIFF COMMISSION,THE TARIFF: A BIBLIOGRAPHY: A SELECT LIST OF REFERENCES. USA-45 LAW DIPLOM TAX ADMIN...POLICY TREATY 20. PAGE 103 E2064
B34
BIBLIOG/A
TARIFFS
ECO/TAC

FOREIGN AFFAIRS BIBLIOGRAPHY: A SELECTED AND ANNOTATED LIST OF BOOKS ON INTERNATIONAL RELATIONS 1919-1962 (4 VOLS.). CONSTN FORCES COLONIAL ARMS/CONT WAR NAT/LISM PEACE ATTIT DRIVE...POLICY INT/LAW 20. PAGE 2 E0032
B35
BIBLIOG/A
DIPLOM
INT/ORG

BEMIS S.F.,GUIDE TO THE DIPLOMATIC HISTORY OF THE UNITED STATES, 17751921. NAT/G LEGIS TOP/EX PROB/SOLV CAP/ISM INT/TRADE TARIFFS ADJUD ...CON/ANAL 18/20. PAGE 10 E0184
B35
BIBLIOG/A
DIPLOM
USA-45

CULVER D.C.,METHODOLOGY OF SOCIAL SCIENCE RESEARCH:
B36
BIBLIOG/A

A BIBLIOGRAPHY. LAW CULTURE...CRIMLGY GEOG STAT OBS METH
INT QU HIST/WRIT CHARTS 20. PAGE 28 E0550   SOC

B36
GRAVES W.B.,AMERICAN STATE GOVERNMENT. CONSTN FINAN   NAT/G
EX/STRUC FORCES LEGIS BUDGET TAX CT/SYS REPRESENT   PROVS
GOV/REL...BIBLIOG/A 19/20. PAGE 45 E0900   ADMIN
                                                      FEDERAL

B36
MATTHEWS M.A.,DIPLOMACY: SELECT LIST ON DIPLOMACY,   BIBLIOG/A
DIPLOMATIC AND CONSULAR PRACTICE, AND FOREIGN   DIPLOM
OFFICE ORGANIZATION (PAMPHLET). EUR+WWI MOD/EUR   NAT/G
USA-45 WOR-45...INT/LAW 20. PAGE 69 E1387

B36
MATTHEWS M.A.,INTERNATIONAL LAW: SELECT LIST OF   BIBLIOG/A
WORKS IN ENGLISH ON PUBLIC INTERNATIONAL LAW: WITH   INT/LAW
COLLECTIONS OF CASES AND OPINIONS. CHRIST-17C   ATTIT
EUR+WWI MOD/EUR WOR-45 CONSTN ADJUD JURID. PAGE 69   DIPLOM
E1388

B37
SCHUSTER E.,GUIDE TO LAW AND LEGAL LITERATURE OF   BIBLIOG/A
CENTRAL AMERICAN REPUBLICS. L/A+17C INT/ORG ADJUD   REGION
SANCTION CRIME...JURID 19/20. PAGE 89 E1785   CT/SYS
                                                      LAW

B38
HELLMAN F.S.,THE SUPREME COURT ISSUE: SELECTED LIST   BIBLIOG/A
OF REFERENCES. USA-45 NAT/G CHIEF EX/STRUC JUDGE   CONSTN
ATTIT...JURID 20 PRESIDENT ROOSEVLT/F SUPREME/CT.   CT/SYS
PAGE 51 E1026   LAW

B39
BALDWIN L.D.,WHISKEY REBELS: THE STORY OF A   REV
FRONTIER UPRISING. USA-45 LAW ADJUD LEAD COERCE PWR   POL/PAR
...BIBLIOG/A 18 PENNSYLVAN FEDERALIST. PAGE 8 E0145   TAX
                                                      TIME/SEQ

B39
CULVER D.C.,BIBLIOGRAPHY OF CRIME AND CRIMINAL   BIBLIOG/A
JUSTICE, 1932-1937. USA-45 LAW CULTURE PUB/INST   CRIMLGY
PROB/SOLV CT/SYS...PSY SOC STAT 20. PAGE 28 E0551   ADJUD
                                                      FORCES

B40
BROWN A.D.,COMPULSORY MILITARY TRAINING: SELECT   BIBLIOG/A
LIST OF REFERENCES (PAMPHLET). USA-45 CONSTN   FORCES
VOL/ASSN COERCE 20. PAGE 16 E0311   JURID
                                                      ATTIT

B40
CONOVER H.F.,FOREIGN RELATIONS OF THE UNITED   BIBLIOG/A
STATES: A LIST OF RECENT BOOKS (PAMPHLET). ASIA   USA-45
CANADA L/A+17C UK INT/ORG INT/TRADE TARIFFS NEUTRAL   DIPLOM
WAR PEACE...INT/LAW CON/ANAL 20 CHINJAP. PAGE 25
E0492

B40
FULLER G.H.,A SELECTED LIST OF RECENT REFERENCES ON   BIBLIOG/A
THE CONSTITUTION OF THE UNITED STATES (PAMPHLET).   CONSTN
CULTURE NAT/G LEGIS CONFER ADJUD GOV/REL CONSEN   LAW
POPULISM...JURID CONCPT 18/20 CONGRESS. PAGE 41   USA-45
E0820

N40
COUNTY GOVERNMENT IN THE UNITED STATES: A LIST OF   BIBLIOG/A
RECENT REFERENCES (PAMPHLET). USA-45 LAW PUB/INST   LOC/G
PLAN BUDGET CT/SYS CENTRAL 20. PAGE 52 E1027   ADMIN
                                                      MUNIC

B42
BLANCHARD L.R.,MARTINIQUE: A SELECTED LIST OF   BIBLIOG/A
REFERENCES (PAMPHLET). WEST/IND AGRI LOC/G SCHOOL   SOCIETY
...ART/METH GEOG JURID CHARTS 20. PAGE 12 E0241   CULTURE
                                                      COLONIAL

B42
FULLER G.H.,DEFENSE FINANCING: A SUPPLEMENTARY LIST   BIBLIOG/A
OF REFERENCES (PAMPHLET). CANADA UK USA-45 ECO/DEV   FINAN
NAT/G DELIB/GP BUDGET ADJUD ARMS/CONT WEAPON COST   FORCES
PEACE PWR 20 AUSTRAL CHINJAP CONGRESS. PAGE 41   DIPLOM
E0821

B42
US LIBRARY OF CONGRESS,SOCIAL AND CULTURAL PROBLEMS   BIBLIOG/A
IN WARTIME: APRIL 1941-MARCH 1942. WOR-45 CLIENT   WAR
SECT EDU/PROP CRIME LEISURE RACE/REL STRANGE ATTIT   SOC
DRIVE HEALTH...GEOG 20. PAGE 100 E2012   CULTURE

C42
CRAIG A.,"ABOVE ALL LIBERTIES." FRANCE UK LAW   BIBLIOG/A
CULTURE INTELL SECT ORD/FREE 18/20. PAGE 27 E0537   EDU/PROP
                                                      WRITING
                                                      MORAL

B43
ANDERSON R.B.,SUPPLEMENT TO BEALE'S BIBLIOGRAPHY OF   BIBLIOG/A
EARLY ENGLISH LAW BOOKS. MOD/EUR UK CONSTN PRESS   JURID
ADJUD...CHARTS 10/15. PAGE 5 E0091   CT/SYS
                                                      LAW

B43
BACKUS R.C.,A GUIDE TO THE LAW AND LEGAL LITERATURE   BIBLIOG/A
OF COLOMBIA. FINAN INDUS LABOR FORCES ADJUD ADMIN   LAW
COLONIAL CT/SYS CRIME...INT/LAW JURID 20 COLOMB.   CONSTN
PAGE 7 E0127   L/A+17C

B43
US LIBRARY OF CONGRESS,SOCIAL AND CULTURAL PROBLEMS   BIBLIOG/A
IN WARTIME: APRIL-DECEMBER (SUPPLEMENT 1). WOR-45   WAR
SECT EDU/PROP CRIME LEISURE CIVMIL/REL RACE/REL   SOC
ATTIT DRIVE HEALTH...GEOG 20. PAGE 100 E2013   CULTURE

B43
US LIBRARY OF CONGRESS,SOCIAL AND CULTURAL PROBLEMS   BIBLIOG/A
IN WARTIME: JANUARY-MAY 1943 (SUPPLEMENT 2). WOR-45   WAR
FAM SECT PLAN EDU/PROP CRIME LEISURE RACE/REL DRIVE   SOC
HEALTH...GEOG 20 JEWS. PAGE 100 E2014   CULTURE

B44
CHENEY F.,CARTELS, COMBINES, AND TRUSTS: A SELECTED   BIBLIOG/A
LIST OF REFERENCES. GERMANY UK USA-45 WOR-45   LG/CO
DELIB/GP OP/RES BARGAIN CAP/ISM ECO/TAC INT/TRADE   ECO/DEV
LICENSE LEGIT CONFER PRICE 20. PAGE 22 E0428   INDUS

B44
FULLER G.H.,TURKEY: A SELECTED LIST OF REFERENCES.   BIBLIOG/A
ISLAM TURKEY CULTURE ECO/UNDEV AGRI DIPLOM NAT/LISM   ALL/VALS
CONSERVE...GEOG HUM INT/LAW SOC 7/20 MAPS. PAGE 42
E0824

B45
GALLOWAY E.,ABSTRACTS OF POSTWAR LITERATURE (VOL.   BIBLIOG/A
IV) JAN.-JULY, 1945 NOS. 901-1074. POLAND USA+45   NUC/PWR
USSR WOR+45 INDUS LABOR PLAN ECO/TAC INT/TRADE TAX   NAT/G
EDU/PROP ADMIN COLONIAL INT/LAW. PAGE 42 E0829   DIPLOM

B45
US LIBRARY OF CONGRESS,NETHERLANDS EAST INDIES.   BIBLIOG/A
INDONESIA LAW CULTURE AGRI INDUS SCHOOL COLONIAL   S/ASIA
HEALTH...GEOG JURID SOC 19/20 NETH/IND. PAGE 101   NAT/G
E2017

B45
VANCE H.L.,GUIDE TO THE LAW AND LEGAL LITERATURE OF   BIBLIOG/A
MEXICO. LAW CONSTN FINAN LABOR FORCES ADJUD ADMIN   INT/LAW
...CRIMLGY PHIL/SCI CON/ANAL 20 MEXIC/AMER.   JURID
PAGE 103 E2070   CT/SYS

B45
WOOLBERT R.G.,FOREIGN AFFAIRS BIBLIOGRAPHY,   BIBLIOG/A
1932-1942. INT/ORG SECT INT/TRADE COLONIAL RACE/REL   DIPLOM
NAT/LISM...GEOG INT/LAW GOV/COMP IDEA/COMP 20.   WAR
PAGE 107 E2144

B46
GRIFFIN G.G.,A GUIDE TO MANUSCRIPTS RELATING TO   BIBLIOG/A
AMERICAN HISTORY IN BRITISH DEPOSITORIES. CANADA   ALL/VALS
IRELAND MOD/EUR UK USA-45 LAW DIPLOM ADMIN COLONIAL   NAT/G
WAR NAT/LISM SOVEREIGN...GEOG INT/LAW 15/19
CMN/WLTH. PAGE 47 E0936

B46
SCANLON H.L.,INTERNATIONAL LAW: A SELECTIVE LIST OF   BIBLIOG/A
WORKS IN ENGLISH ON PUBLIC INTERNATIONAL LAW (A   INT/LAW
PAMPHLET). CHRIST-17C EUR+WWI MOD/EUR WOR-45 CT/SYS   ADJUD
...JURID 20. PAGE 87 E1749   DIPLOM

B47
CLAGETT H.L.,A GUIDE TO THE LAW AND LEGAL   BIBLIOG/A
LITERATURE OF BOLIVIA. L/A+17C CONSTN LABOR LEGIS   JURID
ADMIN...CRIMLGY INT/LAW PHIL/SCI 16/20 BOLIV.   LAW
PAGE 22 E0441   CT/SYS

B47
DE NOIA J.,GUIDE TO OFFICIAL PUBLICATIONS OF OTHER   BIBLIOG/A
AMERICAN REPUBLICS: ECUADOR (VOL. IX). ECUADOR LAW   CONSTN
FINAN LEGIS BUDGET CT/SYS 19/20. PAGE 30 E0589   NAT/G
                                                      EDU/PROP

B47
DE NOIA J.,GUIDE TO OFFICIAL PUBLICATIONS OF THE   BIBLIOG/A
OTHER AMERICAN REPUBLICS: EL SALVADOR. EL/SALVADR   CONSTN
LAW LEGIS EDU/PROP CT/SYS 20. PAGE 30 E0590   NAT/G
                                                      ADMIN

B47
DE NOIA J.,GUIDE TO OFFICIAL PUBLICATIONS OF THE   BIBLIOG/A
OTHER AMERICAN REPUBLICS: NICARAGUA (VOL. XIV).   EDU/PROP
NICARAGUA LAW LEGIS ADMIN CT/SYS...JURID 19/20.   NAT/G

CONSTN

B47
DE NOIA J.,GUIDE TO OFFICIAL PUBLICATIONS OF THE
OTHER AMERICAN REPUBLICS: PANAMA (VOL. XV). PANAMA
LAW LEGIS EDU/PROP CT/SYS 20. PAGE 30 E0592
BIBLIOG/A
CONSTN
ADMIN
NAT/G

B47
HARGRETT L.,A BIBLIOGRAPHY OF THE CONSTITUTIONS AND
LAWS OF THE AMERICAN INDIANS. USA-45 LOC/G GOV/REL
GP/REL 19/20 INDIAN/AM. PAGE 50 E0999
BIBLIOG/A
CONSTN
LAW
NAT/G

B47
NEUBURGER O.,GUIDE TO OFFICIAL PUBLICATIONS OF
OTHER AMERICAN REPUBLICS: HONDURAS (VOL. XIII).
HONDURAS LAW LEGIS ADMIN CT/SYS...JURID 19/20.
PAGE 76 E1533
BIBLIOG/A
NAT/G
EDU/PROP
CONSTN

B47
NEUBURGER O.,GUIDE TO OFFICIAL PUBLICATIONS OF THE
OTHER AMERICAN REPUBLICS: HAITI (VOL. XII). HAITI
LAW FINAN LEGIS PRESS...JURID 20. PAGE 76 E1534
BIBLIOG/A
CONSTN
NAT/G
EDU/PROP

B48
DE NOIA J.,GUIDE TO OFFICIAL PUBLICATIONS OF OTHER
AMERICAN REPUBLICS: PERU (VOL. XVII). PERU LAW
LEGIS ADMIN CT/SYS...JURID 19/20. PAGE 30 E0593
BIBLIOG/A
CONSTN
NAT/G
EDU/PROP

B48
NEUBURGER O.,GUIDE TO OFFICIAL PUBLICATIONS OF THE
OTHER AMERICAN REPUBLICS: VENEZUELA (VOL. XIX).
VENEZUELA FINAN LEGIS PLAN BUDGET DIPLOM CT/SYS
PARL/PROC 19/20. PAGE 77 E1535
BIBLIOG/A
NAT/G
CONSTN
LAW

B49
BOYD A.M.,UNITED STATES GOVERNMENT PUBLICATIONS
(3RD ED.). USA+45 EX/STRUC LEGIS ADMIN...JURID
CHARTS 20. PAGE 14 E0281
BIBLIOG/A
PRESS
NAT/G
EDU/PROP

B49
US DEPARTMENT OF STATE,SOVIET BIBLIOGRAPHY
(PAMPHLET). CHINA/COM COM USSR LAW AGRI INT/ORG
ECO/TAC EDU/PROP...POLICY GEOG 20. PAGE 99 E1994
BIBLIOG/A
MARXISM
CULTURE
DIPLOM

B49
US LIBRARY OF CONGRESS,FREEDOM OF INFORMATION:
SELECTIVE REPORT ON RECENT WRITINGS. USA+45 LAW
CONSTN ELITES EDU/PROP PRESS LOBBY WAR TOTALISM
ATTIT 20 UN UNESCO COLD/WAR. PAGE 101 E2018
BIBLIOG/A
ORD/FREE
LICENSE
COM/IND

B50
BROWN E.S.,MANUAL OF GOVERNMENT PUBLICATIONS.
WOR+45 WOR-45 CONSTN INT/ORG MUNIC PROVS DIPLOM
ADMIN 20. PAGE 16 E0313
BIBLIOG/A
NAT/G
LAW

B50
COUNCIL BRITISH NATIONAL BIB,BRITISH NATIONAL
BIBLIOGRAPHY. UK AGRI CONSTRUC PERF/ART POL/PAR
SECT CREATE INT/TRADE LEAD...HUM JURID PHIL/SCI 20.
PAGE 26 E0519
BIBLIOG/A
NAT/G
TEC/DEV
DIPLOM

B50
EMBREE J.F.,BIBLIOGRAPHY OF THE PEOPLES AND
CULTURES OF MAINLAND SOUTHEAST ASIA. CAMBODIA LAOS
THAILAND VIETNAM LAW...GEOG HUM SOC MYTH LING
CHARTS WORSHIP 20. PAGE 35 E0686
BIBLIOG/A
CULTURE
S/ASIA

B50
MONPIED E.,BIBLIOGRAPHIE FEDERALISTE: OUVRAGES
CHOISIS (VOL. I, MIMEOGRAPHED PAPER). EUR+WWI
DIPLOM ADMIN REGION ATTIT PACIFISM SOCISM...INT/LAW
19/20. PAGE 74 E1486
BIBLIOG/A
FEDERAL
CENTRAL
INT/ORG

B50
US FEDERAL BUREAU INVESTIGAT,BIBLIOGRAPHY OF CRIME
AND KINDRED SUBJECTS (PAPER). USA+45 PROB/SOLV
TREND. PAGE 100 E2001
BIBLIOG/A
CRIME
LAW
CRIMLGY

B50
WARD R.E.,A GUIDE TO JAPANESE REFERENCE AND
RESEARCH MATERIALS IN THE FIELD OF POLITICAL
SCIENCE. LAW CONSTN LOC/G PRESS ADMIN...SOC
CON/ANAL METH 19/20 CHINJAP. PAGE 105 E2098
BIBLIOG/A
ASIA
NAT/G

N51
MONPIED E.,FEDERALIST BIBLIOGRAPHY: ARTICLES AND
DOCUMENTS PUBLISHED IN BRITISH PERIODICALS
1945-1951 (MIMEOGRAPHED). EUR+WWI UK WOR+45 DIPLOM
REGION ATTIT SOCISM...INT/LAW 20. PAGE 74 E1487
BIBLIOG/A
INT/ORG
FEDERAL
CENTRAL

B52
DUNN F.S.,CURRENT RESEARCH IN INTERNATIONAL
AFFAIRS. UK USA+45...POLICY TREATY. PAGE 33 E0660
BIBLIOG/A
DIPLOM
INT/LAW

B52
ETTINGHAUSEN R.,SELECTED AND ANNOTATED BIBLIOGRAPHY
OF BOOKS AND PERIODICALS IN WESTERN LANGUAGES
DEALING WITH NEAR AND MIDDLE EAST. LAW CULTURE SECT
...ART/METH GEOG SOC. PAGE 35 E0700
BIBLIOG/A
ISLAM
MEDIT-7

B52
THOM J.M.,GUIDE TO RESEARCH MATERIAL IN POLITICAL
SCIENCE (PAMPHLET). ELITES LOC/G MUNIC NAT/G LEGIS
DIPLOM ADJUD CIVMIL/REL GOV/REL PWR MGT. PAGE 96
E1916
BIBLIOG/A
KNOWL

B53
AYMARD A.,HISTOIRE GENERALE DES CIVILISATIONS (7
VOLS.). WOR+45 WOR-45 LAW SECT CREATE ATTIT
...ART/METH WORSHIP. PAGE 6 E0123
BIBLIOG/A
SOC

B53
CALDWELL L.K.,RESEARCH METHODS IN PUBLIC
ADMINISTRATION: AN OUTLINE OF TOPICS AND READINGS
(PAMPHLET). LAW ACT/RES COMPUTER KNOWL...SOC STAT
GEN/METH 20. PAGE 18 E0364
BIBLIOG/A
METH/COMP
ADMIN
OP/RES

B53
CURRIER T.F.,A BIBLIOGRAPHY OF OLIVER WENDELL
HOLMES. USA-45...BIOG 19/20. PAGE 28 E0557
BIBLIOG/A
HUM
JURID
JUDGE

B53
LANDHEER B.,FUNDAMENTALS OF PUBLIC INTERNATIONAL
LAW (SELECTIVE BIBLIOGRAPHIES OF THE LIBRARY OF THE
PEACE PALACE, VOL. I; PAMPH). INT/ORG OP/RES PEACE
...IDEA/COMP 20. PAGE 62 E1250
BIBLIOG/A
INT/LAW
DIPLOM
PHIL/SCI

B53
MARKE J.J.,A CATALOGUE OF THE LAW COLLECTION AT NEW
YORK UNIVERSITY, WITH SELECTED ANNOTATIONS. ACADEM
ADJUD CT/SYS...CONCPT BIOG 20. PAGE 68 E1366
BIBLIOG/A
LAW
PHIL/SCI
IDEA/COMP

B53
SECKLER-HUDSON C.,BIBLIOGRAPHY ON PUBLIC
ADMINISTRATION (4TH ED.). USA+45 LAW POL/PAR
DELIB/GP BUDGET ADJUD LOBBY GOV/REL GP/REL ATTIT
...JURID 20. PAGE 90 E1800
BIBLIOG/A
ADMIN
NAT/G
MGT

B54
CARTER P.G.,STATISTICAL BULLETINS: AN ANNOTATED
BIBLIOGRAPHY OF THE GENERAL STATISTICAL BULLETINS
AND MAJOR POL SUBDIV OF WORLD. CULTURE AGRI FINAN
INDUS LABOR TEC/DEV INT/TRADE CT/SYS WEALTH
...CRIMLGY SOC 20. PAGE 20 E0400
BIBLIOG/A
WOR+45
NAT/G
STAT

B54
HAMSON C.J.,EXECUTIVE DISCRETION AND JUDICIAL
CONTROL; AN ASPECT OF THE FRENCH CONSEIL D'ETAT.
EUR+WWI FRANCE MOD/EUR UK NAT/G EX/STRUC PARTIC
CONSERVE...JURID BIBLIOG/A 18/20 SUPREME/CT.
PAGE 50 E0992
ELITES
ADJUD
NAT/COMP

B54
LANDHEER B.,RECOGNITION IN INTERNATIONAL LAW
(SELECTIVE BIBLIOGRAPHIES OF THE LIBRARY OF THE
PEACE PALACE, VOL. II; PAMPHLET). NAT/G LEGIT
SANCTION 20. PAGE 63 E1251
BIBLIOG/A
INT/LAW
INT/ORG
DIPLOM

B54
TOTOK W.,HANDBUCH DER BIBLIOGRAPHISCHEN
NACHSCHLAGEWERKE. GERMANY LAW CULTURE ADMIN...SOC
20. PAGE 97 E1936
BIBLIOG/A
NAT/G
DIPLOM
POLICY

B55
BIBLIOGRAPHY ON THE COMMUNIST PROBLEM IN THE UNITED
STATES. USA-45 PRESS ADJUD ATTIT...BIOG 20. PAGE 2
E0033
BIBLIOG/A
MARXISM
POL/PAR
USA+45

B55
PLISCHKE E.,AMERICAN FOREIGN RELATIONS: A
BIBLIOGRAPHY OF OFFICIAL SOURCES. USA+45 USA-45
INT/ORG FORCES PRESS WRITING DEBATE EXEC...POLICY
INT/LAW 18/20 CONGRESS. PAGE 81 E1621
BIBLIOG/A
DIPLOM
NAT/G

B55
SWEET AND MAXWELL,A LEGAL BIBLIOGRAPHY OF THE
BRITISH COMMONWEALTH OF NATIONS (2ND ED. 7 VOLS.).
UK LOC/G MUNIC JUDGE ADJUD CRIME OWN...JURID 14/20
CMN/WLTH. PAGE 95 E1900
BIBLIOG/A
LAW
CONSTN
CT/SYS

B55
UN HEADQUARTERS LIBRARY,BIBLIOGRAPHIE DE LA CHARTE   BIBLIOG/A
DES NATIONS UNIES. CHINA/COM KOREA WOR+45 VOL/ASSN   INT/ORG
CONFER ADMIN COERCE PEACE ATTIT ORD/FREE SOVEREIGN   DIPLOM
...INT/LAW 20 UNESCO UN. PAGE 97 E1953

B56
ESTEP R.,AN AIR POWER BIBLIOGRAPHY. USA+45 TEC/DEV   BIBLIOG/A
BUDGET DIPLOM EDU/PROP DETER CIVMIL/REL...DECISION   FORCES
INT/LAW 20. PAGE 35 E0698   WEAPON
                                                      PLAN

C56
FALL B.B.,"THE VIET-MINH REGIME." VIETNAM LAW   NAT/G
ECO/UNDEV POL/PAR FORCES DOMIN WAR ATTIT MARXISM   ADMIN
...BIOG PREDICT BIBLIOG/A 20. PAGE 36 E0720   EX/STRUC
                                                      LEAD

B57
BYRNES R.F.,BIBLIOGRAPHY OF AMERICAN PUBLICATIONS   BIBLIOG/A
ON EAST CENTRAL EUROPE, 1945-1957 (VOL. XXII). SECT   COM
DIPLOM EDU/PROP RACE/REL...ART/METH GEOG JURID SOC   MARXISM
LING 20 JEWS. PAGE 18 E0354   NAT/G

B57
CONOVER H.F.,NORTH AND NORTHEAST AFRICA; A SELECTED   BIBLIOG/A
ANNOTATED LIST OF WRITINGS. ALGERIA MOROCCO SUDAN   DIPLOM
UAR CULTURE INT/ORG PROB/SOLV ADJUD NAT/LISM PWR   AFR
WEALTH...SOC 20 UN. PAGE 25 E0496   ECO/UNDEV

B57
DONALDSON A.G.,SOME COMPARATIVE ASPECTS OF IRISH   CONSTN
LAW. IRELAND NAT/G DIPLOM ADMIN CT/SYS LEAD ATTIT   LAW
SOVEREIGN...JURID BIBLIOG/A 12/20 CMN/WLTH. PAGE 32   NAT/COMP
E0635   INT/LAW

B58
MUSIKER R.,GUIDE TO SOUTH AFRICAN REFERENCE BOOKS.   BIBLIOG/A
SOUTH/AFR SOCIETY SECT EDU/PROP PRESS RACE/REL   SOC
...JURID SOC/WK 20. PAGE 75 E1512   GEOG

B59
COUNCIL OF STATE GOVERNMENTS,STATE GOVERNMENT: AN   BIBLIOG/A
ANNOTATED BIBLIOGRAPHY (PAMPHLET). USA+45 LAW AGRI   PROVS
INDUS WORKER PLAN TAX ADJUST AGE/Y ORD/FREE...HEAL   LOC/G
MGT 20. PAGE 26 E0521   ADMIN

B59
EPSTEIN F.T.,EAST GERMANY: A SELECTED BIBLIOGRAPHY   BIBLIOG/A
(PAMPHLET). COM GERMANY/E LAW AGRI FINAN INDUS   INTELL
LABOR POL/PAR EDU/PROP ADMIN AGE/Y 20. PAGE 35   MARXISM
E0693   NAT/G

B59
TOMPKINS D.C.,SUPREME COURT OF THE UNITED STATES: A   BIBLIOG/A
BIBLIOGRAPHY. LAW JUDGE ADJUD GOV/REL DISCRIM   CT/SYS
...JURID 18/20 SUPREME/CT NEGRO. PAGE 96 E1931   CONSTN
                                                      NAT/G

C59
EASTON D.,"POLITICAL ANTHROPOLOGY" IN BIENNIAL   SOC
REVIEW OF ANTHROPOLOGY" UNIV LAW CULTURE ELITES   BIBLIOG/A
SOCIETY CREATE...PSY CONCPT GP/COMP GEN/METH 20.   NEW/IDEA
PAGE 34 E0671

N59
NATIONAL ASSN HOME BUILDERS,COMMUNITY FACILITIES: A   BIBLIOG/A
LIST OF SELECTED REFERENCES (PAMPHLET). USA+45   PLAN
DIST/IND FINAN SERV/IND SCHOOL CREATE CONTROL   LOC/G
FEDERAL...JURID 20. PAGE 76 E1525   MUNIC

B60
BEEM H.D.,AN INTRODUCTION TO LEGAL BIBLIOGRAPHY FOT   BIBLIOG/A
THE NON-PROFESSIONAL STUDENT. LOC/G NAT/G TAX 20.   JURID
PAGE 9 E0177   METH
                                                      ADJUD

B60
LEWIS P.R.,LITERATURE OF THE SOCIAL SCIENCES: AN   BIBLIOG/A
INTRODUCTORY SURVEY AND GUIDE. UK LAW INDUS DIPLOM   SOC
INT/TRADE ADMIN...MGT 19/20. PAGE 65 E1294

B60
UNITED WORLD FEDERALISTS,UNITED WORLD FEDERALISTS;   BIBLIOG/A
PANORAMA OF RECENT BOOKS, FILMS, AND JOURNALS ON   DIPLOM
WORLD FEDERATION, THE UN, AND WORLD PEACE. CULTURE   INT/ORG
ECO/UNDEV PROB/SOLV FOR/AID ARMS/CONT NUC/PWR   PEACE
...INT/LAW PHIL/SCI 20 UN. PAGE 98 E1971

B60
US LIBRARY OF CONGRESS,INDEX TO LATIN AMERICAN   BIBLIOG/A
LEGISLATION: 1950-1960 (2 VOLS.). NAT/G DELIB/GP   LEGIS
ADMIN PARL/PROC 20. PAGE 101 E2019   L/A+17C
                                                      JURID

B61
BURDETTE F.L.,POLITICAL SCIENCE: A SELECTED   BIBLIOG/A
BIBLIOGRAPHY OF BOOKS IN PRINT, WITH ANNOTATIONS   GOV/COMP
(PAMPHLET). LAW LOC/G NAT/G POL/PAR PROVS DIPLOM   CONCPT
EDU/PROP ADMIN CHOOSE ATTIT 20. PAGE 17 E0330   ROUTINE

B61
CARNELL F.,THE POLITICS OF THE NEW STATES: A SELECT   BIBLIOG/A
ANNOTATED BIBLIOGRAPHY WITH SPECIAL REFERENCE TO   AFR
THE COMMONWEALTH. CONSTN ELITES LABOR NAT/G POL/PAR   ASIA
EX/STRUC DIPLOM ADJUD ADMIN...GOV/COMP 20   COLONIAL
COMMONWLTH. PAGE 20 E0387

B61
CONFERENCE ATLANTIC COMMUNITY,AN INTRODUCTORY   BIBLIOG/A
BIBLIOGRAPHY. COM WOR+45 FORCES DIPLOM ECO/TAC WAR   CON/ANAL
...INT/LAW HIST/WRIT COLD/WAR NATO. PAGE 25 E0485   INT/ORG

B61
LA PONCE J.A.,THE GOVERNMENT OF THE FIFTH REPUBLIC: PWR
FRENCH POLITICAL PARTIES AND THE CONSTITUTION.   POL/PAR
ALGERIA FRANCE LAW NAT/G DELIB/GP LEGIS ECO/TAC   CONSTN
MARXISM SOCISM...CHARTS BIBLIOG/A 20 DEGAULLE/C.   CHIEF
PAGE 62 E1243

B61
WARD R.E.,JAPANESE POLITICAL SCIENCE: A GUIDE TO   BIBLIOG/A
JAPANESE REFERENCE AND RESEARCH MATERIALS (2ND   PHIL/SCI
ED.). LAW CONSTN STRATA NAT/G POL/PAR DELIB/GP
LEGIS ADMIN CHOOSE GP/REL...INT/LAW 19/20 CHINJAP.
PAGE 105 E2099

B62
CARSON P.,MATERIALS FOR WEST AFRICAN HISTORY IN THE   BIBLIOG/A
ARCHIVES OF BELGIUM AND HOLLAND. CLIENT INDUS   COLONIAL
INT/TRADE ADMIN 17/19. PAGE 20 E0397   AFR
                                                      ECO/UNDEV

B62
COSTA RICA UNIVERSIDAD BIBL,LISTA DE TESIS DE GRADO   BIBLIOG/A
DE LA UNIVERSIDAD DE COSTA RICA. COSTA/RICA LAW   NAT/G
LOC/G ADMIN LEAD...SOC 20. PAGE 26 E0518   DIPLOM
                                                      ECO/UNDEV

B63
BROWN R.M.,THE SOUTH CAROLINA REGULATORS. USA-45   ORD/FREE
LEGIS LEGIT ADJUD COLONIAL CONTROL WAR...BIBLIOG/A   JURID
18 CHARLESTON SOUTH/CAR. PAGE 16 E0315   PWR
                                                      PROVS

B63
CRAIG A.,SUPPRESSED BOOKS: A HISTORY OF THE   BIBLIOG/A
CONCEPTION OF LITERARY OBSCENITY. WOR+45 WOR-45   LAW
CREATE EDU/PROP LITERACY ATTIT...ART/METH PSY   SEX
CONCPT 20. PAGE 27 E0538   CONTROL

B63
FISCHER-GALATI S.A.,RUMANIA; A BIBLIOGRAPHIC GUIDE   BIBLIOG/A
(PAMPHLET). ROMANIA INTELL ECO/DEV LABOR SECT   NAT/G
WEALTH...GEOG SOC/WK LING 20. PAGE 38 E0756   COM
                                                      LAW

B63
GOURNAY B.,PUBLIC ADMINISTRATION. FRANCE LAW CONSTN   BIBLIOG/A
AGRI FINAN LABOR SCHOOL EX/STRUC CHOOSE...MGT   ADMIN
METH/COMP 20. PAGE 45 E0894   NAT/G
                                                      LOC/G

B63
HOWARD W.S.,AMERICAN SLAVERS AND THE FEDERAL LAW: DIST/IND
1837-1862. USA-45 NAT/G LEGIT COERCE RACE/REL   CRIMLGY
WEALTH...POLICY BIBLIOG/A 19. PAGE 55 E1102   LAW
                                                      EXEC

B63
KLEIN F.J.,JUDICIAL ADMINISTRATION AND THE LEGAL   BIBLIOG/A
PROFESSION. USA+45 ADMIN CONTROL EFFICIENCY   CT/SYS
...POLICY 20. PAGE 61 E1222   ADJUD
                                                      JUDGE

B63
KLESMENT J.,LEGAL SOURCES AND BIBLIOGRAPHY OF THE   BIBLIOG/A
BALTIC STATES (ESTONIA, LATVIA, LITHUANIA). COM   JURID
ESTONIA LATVIA LITHUANIA LAW FINAN ADJUD CT/SYS   CONSTN
REGION CENTRAL MARXISM 19/20. PAGE 61 E1223   ADMIN

B63
LEGISLATIVE REFERENCE SERVICE,DIGEST OF PUBLIC   BIBLIOG/A
GENERAL BILLS AND RESOLUTIONS. LAW COM/IND EDU/PROP   LEGIS
GOV/REL INGP/REL KNOWL...JURID 20 CONGRESS. PAGE 64   DELIB/GP
E1280   NAT/G

B63
PALOTAI O.C.,PUBLICATIONS OF THE INSTITUTE OF   BIBLIOG/A
GOVERNMENT, 1930-1962. LAW PROVS SCHOOL WORKER   ADMIN
ACT/RES OP/RES CT/SYS GOV/REL...CRIMLGY SOC/WK.   LOC/G

PAGE 79 E1594   FINAN

B64
BERNSTEIN H.,A BOOKSHELF ON BRAZIL. BRAZIL ADMIN   BIBLIOG/A
COLONIAL...HUM JURID SOC 20. PAGE 11 E0213   NAT/G
                                                   L/A+17C
                                                   ECO/UNDEV

B64
BREVER E.H.,LEARNED HAND, JANUARY 27, 1872-AUGUST   BIBLIOG/A
18, 1961 (PAMPHLET). USA+45 USA-45 LAW CONSTN ADJUD   JUDGE
...DECISION BIOG 19/20. PAGE 15 E0295   CT/SYS
                                                   JURID

B64
COHEN M.L.,SELECTED BIBLIOGRAPHY OF FOREIGN AND   BIBLIOG/A
INTERNATIONAL LAW....IDEA/COMP METH/COMP 20.   JURID
PAGE 24 E0466   LAW
                                                   INT/LAW

B64
DIAS R.W.M.,A BIBLIOGRAPHY OF JURISPRUDENCE (2ND   BIBLIOG/A
ED.). VOL/ASSN LEGIS ADJUD CT/SYS OWN...INT/LAW   JURID
18/20. PAGE 31 E0619   LAW
                                                   CONCPT

B64
GESELLSCHAFT RECHTSVERGLEICH.BIBLIOGRAPHIE DES   BIBLIOG/A
DEUTSCHEN RECHTS (BIBLIOGRAPHY OF GERMAN LAW,   JURID
TRANS. BY COURTLAND PETERSON). GERMANY FINAN INDUS   CONSTN
LABOR SECT FORCES CT/SYS PARL/PROC CRIME...INT/LAW   ADMIN
SOC NAT/COMP 20. PAGE 43 E0853

B64
GIANNELLA D.A.,RELIGION AND THE PUBLIC ORDER: AN   SECT
ANNUAL REVIEW OF CHURCH AND STATE, AND OF RELIGION,   NAT/G
LAW, AND SOCIETY. USA+45 LAW SOCIETY FAM POL/PAR   CONSTN
SCHOOL GIVE EDU/PROP GP/REL...JURID GEN/LAWS   ORD/FREE
BIBLIOG/A 20 CHURCH/STA BIRTH/CON CONSCN/OBJ
NATURL/LAW. PAGE 43 E0855

B64
GJUPANOVIC H.,LEGAL SOURCES AND BIBLIOGRAPHY OF   BIBLIOG/A
YUGOSLAVIA. COM YUGOSLAVIA LAW LEGIS DIPLOM ADMIN   JURID
PARL/PROC REGION CRIME CENTRAL 20. PAGE 44 E0873   CONSTN
                                                   ADJUD

B64
MARNELL W.H.,THE FIRST AMENDMENT: THE HISTORY OF   CONSTN
RELIGIOUS FREEDOM IN AMERICA. WOR+45 WOR-45 PROVS   SECT
CREATE CT/SYS...POLICY BIBLIOG/A WORSHIP 16/20.   ORD/FREE
PAGE 68 E1367   GOV/REL

NATIONAL BOOK LEAGUE,THE COMMONWEALTH IN BOOKS: AN   BIBLIOG/A
ANNOTATED LIST. CANADA UK LOC/G SECT ADMIN...SOC   JURID
BIOG 20 CMN/WLTH. PAGE 76 E1526   NAT/G

B64
ROBERTS HL,FOREIGN AFFAIRS BIBLIOGRAPHY, 1952-1962.   BIBLIOG/A
ECO/DEV SECT PLAN FOR/AID INT/TRADE ARMS/CONT   DIPLOM
NAT/LISM ATTIT...INT/LAW GOV/COMP IDEA/COMP 20.   INT/ORG
PAGE 85 E1703   WAR

STOICOIU V.,LEGAL SOURCES AND BIBLIOGRAPHY OF   BIBLIOG/A
ROMANIA. COM ROMANIA LAW FINAN POL/PAR LEGIS JUDGE   JURID
ADJUD CT/SYS PARL/PROC MARXISM 20. PAGE 93 E1874   CONSTN
                                                   ADMIN

B64
SZLADITS C.,BIBLIOGRAPHY ON FOREIGN AND COMPARATIVE   BIBLIOG/A
LAW: BOOKS AND ARTICLES IN ENGLISH (SUPPLEMENT   JURID
1962). FINAN INDUS JUDGE LICENSE ADMIN CT/SYS   ADJUD
PARL/PROC OWN...INT/LAW CLASSIF METH/COMP NAT/COMP   LAW
20. PAGE 95 E1904

B64
TOMPKINS D.C.,PRESIDENTIAL SUCCESSION. USA+45 CHIEF   BIBLIOG/A
ADJUD 20 PRESIDENT CONGRESS. PAGE 96 E1933   EX/STRUC
                                                   CONSTN
                                                   TOP/EX

B64
WILLIAMS S.P.,TOWARD A GENUINE WORLD SECURITY   BIBLIOG/A
SYSTEM (PAMPHLET). WOR+45 INT/ORG FORCES PLAN   ARMS/CONT
NUC/PWR ORD/FREE...INT/LAW CONCPT UN PRESIDENT.   DIPLOM
PAGE 106 E2123   PEACE

B65
KARIS T.,THE TREASON TRIAL IN SOUTH AFRICA: A GUIDE   BIBLIOG/A
TO THE MICROFILM RECORD OF THE TRIAL. SOUTH/AFR LAW   ADJUD
ELITES NAT/G LEGIT CT/SYS RACE/REL DISCRIM...SOC   CRIME
20. PAGE 59 E1185   AFR

B65
MOSTECKY V.,SOVIET LEGAL BIBLIOGRAPHY. USSR LEGIS   BIBLIOG/A
PRESS WRITING CONFER ADJUD CT/SYS REV MARXISM   LAW
...INT/LAW JURID DICTIONARY 20. PAGE 75 E1503   COM
                                                   CONSTN

B65
NEWBURY C.W.,BRITISH POLICY TOWARDS WEST AFRICA: DIPLOM
SELECT DOCUMENTS 1786-1874. AFR UK INT/TRADE DOMIN   POLICY
ADMIN COLONIAL CT/SYS COERCE ORD/FREE...BIBLIOG/A   NAT/G
18/19. PAGE 77 E1540   WRITING

B65
SCHUBERT G.,THE POLITICAL ROLE OF THE COURTS IN   CT/SYS
JUDICIAL POLICY MAKING. USA+45 CONSTN JUDGE   POLICY
FEEDBACK CHOOSE RACE/REL ORD/FREE...TRADIT PSY   DECISION
BIBLIOG/A 20 KENNEDY/JF SUPREME/CT. PAGE 89 E1776

B65
UNIVERSAL REFERENCE SYSTEM,INTERNATIONAL AFFAIRS: BIBLIOG/A
VOLUME I IN THE POLITICAL SCIENCE, GOVERNMENT, AND   GEN/METH
PUBLIC POLICY SERIES....DECISION ECOMETRIC GEOG   COMPUT/IR
INT/LAW JURID MGT PHIL/SCI PSY SOC. PAGE 98 E1972   DIPLOM

B65
WILSON J.F.,CHURCH AND STATE IN AMERICAN HISTORY.   SECT
USA+45 USA-45 ADJUD CT/SYS ORD/FREE SOVEREIGN   NAT/G
...ANTHOL BIBLIOG/A 17/20 CHURCH/STA. PAGE 106   GP/REL
E2129   CONTROL

B66
AMERICAN JEWISH COMMITTEE,GROUP RELATIONS IN THE   BIBLIOG/A
UNITED STATES: PROBLEMS AND PERSPECTIVES: A   USA+45
SELECTED, ANNOTATED BIBLIOGRAPHY (PAMPHLET). LAW   STRUCT
CONSTN STRATA SCHOOL SECT PROB/SOLV ATTIT...POLICY   GP/REL
WELF/ST SOC/WK 20. PAGE 4 E0079

B66
AMERICAN JEWISH COMMITTEE,THE TYRANNY OF POVERTY   BIBLIOG/A
(PAMPHLET). USA+45 LAW ECO/DEV LOC/G MUNIC NAT/G   WEALTH
PUB/INST WORKER EDU/PROP CRIME...SOC/WK 20. PAGE 4   WELF/ST
E0080   PROB/SOLV

B66
BESTERMAN T.,A WORLD BIBLIOGRAPHY OF BIBLIOGRAPHIES   BIBLIOG/A
(4TH ED.). WOR+45 WOR-45 LAW INT/ORG ADMIN   DIPLOM
CON/ANAL. PAGE 11 E0219

B66
DOUMA J.,BIBLIOGRAPHY ON THE INTERNATIONAL COURT   BIBLIOG/A
INCLUDING THE PERMANENT COURT, 1918-1964. WOR+45   INT/ORG
WOR-45 DELIB/GP WAR PRIVIL...JURID NAT/COMP 20 UN   CT/SYS
LEAGUE/NAT. PAGE 33 E0645   DIPLOM

B66
HOPKINS J.F.K.,ARABIC PERIODICAL LITERATURE, 1961.   BIBLIOG/A
ISLAM LAW CULTURE SECT...GEOG HEAL PHIL/SCI PSY SOC   NAT/LISM
20. PAGE 55 E1096   TEC/DEV
                                                   INDUS

B66
STEVENS R.E.,REFERENCE BOOKS IN THE SOCIAL SCIENCES   BIBLIOG/A
AND HUMANITIES. CULTURE PERF/ART SECT EDU/PROP   SOC
...JURID PSY SOC/WK STAT 20 MUSIC. PAGE 93 E1873   HUM
                                                   ART/METH

B66
SZLADITS C.,A BIBLIOGRAPHY ON FOREIGN AND   BIBLIOG/A
COMPARATIVE LAW (SUPPLEMENT 1964). FINAN FAM LABOR   CT/SYS
LG/CO LEGIS JUDGE ADMIN CRIME...CRIMLGY 20. PAGE 95   INT/LAW
E1905

B66
US DEPARTMENT OF STATE,RESEARCH ON AFRICA (EXTERNAL   BIBLIOG/A
RESEARCH LIST NO 5-25). LAW CULTURE ECO/UNDEV   ASIA
POL/PAR DIPLOM EDU/PROP LEAD REGION MARXISM...GEOG   S/ASIA
LING WORSHIP 20. PAGE 100 E1996   NAT/G

B66
US DEPARTMENT OF STATE,RESEARCH ON THE USSR AND   BIBLIOG/A
EASTERN EUROPE (EXTERNAL RESEARCH LIST NO 1-25).   EUR+WWI
USSR LAW CULTURE SOCIETY NAT/G TEC/DEV DIPLOM   COM
EDU/PROP REGION...GEOG LING. PAGE 100 E1997   MARXISM

B66
US DEPARTMENT OF STATE,RESEARCH ON WESTERN EUROPE,   BIBLIOG/A
GREAT BRITAIN, AND CANADA (EXTERNAL RESEARCH LIST   EUR+WWI
NO 3-25). CANADA GERMANY/W UK LAW CULTURE NAT/G   DIPLOM
POL/PAR FORCES EDU/PROP REGION MARXISM...GEOG SOC
WORSHIP 20 CMN/WLTH. PAGE 100 E1998

L66
YALEM R.J.,"THE STUDY OF INTERNATIONAL   VOL/ASSN
ORGANIZATION, 1920-1965* A SURVEY OF THE   INT/ORG
LITERATURE." WOR+45 WOR-45 REGION...INT/LAW CLASSIF   BIBLIOG/A
RECORD HIST/WRIT CON/ANAL IDEA/COMP UN. PAGE 108

E2163

POLSBY N.W.,"BOOKS IN THE FIELD: POLITICAL   BIBLIOG/A
SCIENCE." LAW CONSTN LOC/G NAT/G LEGIS ADJUD PWR 20 ATTIT
SUPREME/CT. PAGE 81 E1627   ADMIN
                                                 JURID
                                                        S66

SHEEHY E.P.,"SELECTED REFERENCE BOOKS OF   BIBLIOG/A
1965-1966." AGRI PERF/ART PRESS...GEOG HUM JURID INDEX
SOC LING WORSHIP. PAGE 91 E1817   CLASSIF
                                                        S66

ZAWODNY J.K.,"GUIDE TO THE STUDY OF INTERNATIONAL BIBLIOG/A
RELATIONS." OP/RES PRESS...STAT INT 20. PAGE 108 DIPLOM
E2169   INT/LAW
                                                 INT/ORG
                                                        C66

BAILEY N.A.,LATIN AMERICA IN WORLD POLITICS. PWR L/A+17C
CONSERVE MARXISM...INT/LAW TREND BIBLIOG/A T OAS DIPLOM
COLD/WAR. PAGE 7 E0134   INT/ORG
                                                 ATTIT
                                                        B67

BUREAU GOVERNMENT RES AND SERV,COUNTY GOVERNMENT BIBLIOG/A
REORGANIZATION - A SELECTED ANNOTATED BIBLIOGRAPHY APPORT
(PAPER). USA+45 USA-45 LAW CONSTN MUNIC PROVS   LOC/G
EX/STRUC CREATE PLAN PROB/SOLV REPRESENT GOV/REL ADMIN
20. PAGE 17 E0332
                                                        B67

GRAHAM H.D.,CRISIS IN PRINT: DESEGREGATION AND THE PRESS
PRESS IN TENNESSEE. LAW SOCIETY MUNIC POL/PAR   PROVS
EDU/PROP LEAD REPRESENT DISCRIM ATTIT...IDEA/COMP POLICY
BIBLIOG/A SOC/INTEG 20 TENNESSEE SUPREME/CT   RACE/REL
SOUTH/US. PAGE 45 E0896
                                                        B67

UNITED NATIONS,UNITED NATIONS PUBLICATIONS: BIBLIOG/A
1945-1966. WOR+45 COM/IND DIST/IND FINAN TEC/DEV INT/ORG
ADMIN...POLICY INT/LAW MGT CHARTS 20 UN UNESCO.   DIPLOM
PAGE 98 E1970   WRITING
                                                        B67

UNIVERSAL REFERENCE SYSTEM,BIBLIOGRAPHY OF   BIBLIOG/A
BIBLIOGRAPHIES IN POLITICAL SCIENCE, GOVERNMENT, NAT/G
AND PUBLIC POLICY (VOLUME III). WOR+45 WOR-45 LAW DIPLOM
ADMIN...SOC CON/ANAL COMPUT/IR GEN/METH. PAGE 98 POLICY
E1973
                                                        B67

UNIVERSAL REFERENCE SYSTEM,CURRENT EVENTS AND   BIBLIOG/A
PROBLEMS OF MODERN SOCIETY (VOLUME V). WOR+45 LOC/G SOCIETY
MUNIC NAT/G PLAN EDU/PROP CRIME RACE/REL WEALTH   PROB/SOLV
...COMPUT/IR GEN/METH. PAGE 98 E1974   ATTIT
                                                        B67

UNIVERSAL REFERENCE SYSTEM,PUBLIC POLICY AND THE BIBLIOG/A
MANAGEMENT OF SCIENCE (VOLUME IX). FUT SPACE WOR+45 POLICY
LAW NAT/G TEC/DEV CONTROL NUC/PWR GOV/REL   MGT
...COMPUT/IR GEN/METH. PAGE 99 E1975   PHIL/SCI
                                                        B67

UNIVERSAL REFERENCE SYSTEM,LAW, JURISPRUDENCE, AND BIBLIOG/A
JUDICIAL PROCESS (VOLUME VII). WOR+45 WOR-45 CONSTN LAW
NAT/G LEGIS JUDGE CT/SYS...INT/LAW COMPUT/IR   JURID
GEN/METH METH. PAGE 99 E1976   ADJUD
                                                        B97

US DEPARTMENT OF STATE,CATALOGUE OF WORKS RELATING BIBLIOG/A
TO THE LAW OF NATIONS AND DIPLOMACY IN THE LIBRARY DIPLOM
OF THE DEPARTMENT OF STATE (PAMPHLET). WOR-45 NAT/G LAW
ADJUD CT/SYS...INT/LAW JURID 19. PAGE 100 E2000

BIBLIOTHEQUE PALAIS DE LA PAIX E0225

BICAMERALISM....SEE LEGIS, CONGRESS, HOUSE/REP, SENATE

BICKEL A. E0226

BIDDLE F. E0227

BIERKAEMPER C. E2083

BIERZANECK R. E0228

BIEVILLE MARC D.E. E0602

BIGLER/W....WILLIAM BIGLER

BILL/RIGHT....BILL OF RIGHTS
                                                        N19

THE REGIONAL DIRECTOR AND THE PRESS (PAMPHLET). PRESS

USA-45 COM/IND LOBBY ROLE 20 NLRB CINCINNATI   LABOR
BILL/RIGHT. PAGE 2 E0031   ORD/FREE
                                                 EDU/PROP
                                                        N19

BRENNAN W.J. JR.,THE BILL OF RIGHTS AND THE STATES CONSTN
(PAMPHLET). USA+45 USA-45 LEGIS BAL/PWR ADJUD   PROVS
CT/SYS FEDERAL PWR SOVEREIGN 18/20 SUPREME/CT   GOV/REL
BILL/RIGHT. PAGE 15 E0293   ORD/FREE
                                                        B38

FRANKFURTER F.,MR. JUSTICE HOLMES AND THE SUPREME CREATE
COURT. USA-45 CONSTN SOCIETY FEDERAL OWN ATTIT   CT/SYS
ORD/FREE PWR...POLICY JURID 20 SUPREME/CT HOLMES/OW DECISION
BILL/RIGHT. PAGE 40 E0790   LAW
                                                        B44

FRAENKEL O.K.,OUR CIVIL LIBERTIES. USA+45...JURID CONSTN
CONCPT 18/20 BILL/RIGHT. PAGE 39 E0781   LAW
                                                 ATTIT
                                                        B48

HOLCOMBE A.N.,HUMAN RIGHTS IN THE MODERN WORLD. ORD/FREE
WOR+45 LEGIS DIPLOM ADJUD PERSON...INT/LAW 20 UN INT/ORG
TREATY CIVIL/LIB BILL/RIGHT. PAGE 54 E1071   CONSTN
                                                 LAW
                                                        B57

DUMBAULD E.,THE BILL OF RIGHTS AND WHAT IT MEANS CONSTN
TODAY. USA+45 USA-45 CT/SYS...JURID STYLE TIME/SEQ LAW
BIBLIOG 18/20 BILL/RIGHT. PAGE 33 E0656   ADJUD
                                                 ORD/FREE
                                                        B59

LOEWENSTEIN K.,VERFASSUNGSRECHT UND   CONSTN
VERFASSUNGSPRAXIS DER VEREINIGTEN STAATEN. USA+45 POL/PAR
USA-45 COLONIAL CT/SYS GP/REL RACE/REL ORD/FREE   EX/STRUC
...JURID 18/20 SUPREME/CT CONGRESS PRESIDENT   NAT/G
BILL/RIGHT CIVIL/LIB. PAGE 66 E1319
                                                        S60

BLACK H.,"THE BILL OF RIGHTS" (BMR)" USA+45 USA-45 CONSTN
LAW LEGIS CT/SYS FEDERAL PWR 18/20 CONGRESS   ORD/FREE
SUPREME/CT BILL/RIGHT CIV/RIGHTS. PAGE 12 E0237   NAT/G
                                                 JURID
                                                        B63

CAHN E.,THE GREAT RIGHTS. USA+45 NAT/G PROVS   CONSTN
CIVMIL/REL...IDEA/COMP ANTHOL BIBLIOG 18/20   LAW
MADISON/J BILL/RIGHT CIV/RIGHTS WARRN/EARL   ORD/FREE
BLACK/HL. PAGE 18 E0361   INGP/REL
                                                        B63

DILLIARD I.,ONE MAN'S STAND FOR FREEDOM: MR.   CONSTN
JUSTICE BLACK AND THE BILL OF RIGHTS. USA+45   JURID
POL/PAR SECT DELIB/GP FORCES ADJUD CONTROL WAR   JUDGE
DISCRIM MORAL...BIBLIOG 20 NEGRO SUPREME/CT   ORD/FREE
BILL/RIGHT BLACK/HL. PAGE 32 E0628
                                                        B63

FRAENKEL O.K.,THE SUPREME COURT AND CIVIL   ORD/FREE
LIBERTIES: HOW THE COURT HAS PROTECTED THE BILL OF CONSTN
RIGHTS. NAT/G CT/SYS CHOOSE PERS/REL RACE/REL   ADJUD
DISCRIM PERSON...DECISION 20 SUPREME/CT CIVIL/LIB JURID
BILL/RIGHT. PAGE 39 E0782
                                                        B66

AUERBACH J.S.,LABOR AND LIBERTY: THE LA FOLLETTE DELIB/GP
COMMITTEE AND THE NEW DEAL. USA-45 LAW LEAD RESPECT LABOR
SOCISM...BIBLIOG 20 CONGRESS BILL/RIGHT LAFOLLET/R CONSTN
NEW/DEAL. PAGE 6 E0117   ORD/FREE
                                                        B66

CAHN E.,CONFRONTING INJUSTICE. USA+45 PROB/SOLV TAX ORD/FREE
EDU/PROP PRESS CT/SYS GP/REL DISCRIM BIO/SOC   CONSTN
...IDEA/COMP BIBLIOG WORSHIP 20 BILL/RIGHT. PAGE 18 ADJUD
E0362
                                                        B67

LEVY L.W.,JUDICIAL REVIEW AND THE SUPREME COURT. ADJUD
USA+45 USA-45 NEUTRAL ATTIT ORD/FREE...POLICY   CONSTN
DECISION BIBLIOG 18/20 BILL/RIGHT SUPREME/CT.   LAW
PAGE 65 E1292   CT/SYS

BINANI G.D. E0229

BINNS/JJ....JOSEPH J. BINNS
                                                        B63

US SENATE COMM ON JUDICIARY,PACIFICA FOUNDATION. DELIB/GP
USA+45 LAW COM/IND 20 ODEGARD/P BINNS/JJ SCHINDLR/P EDU/PROP
HEALEY/D THOMAS/TK. PAGE 102 E2051   ORD/FREE
                                                 ATTIT

BIO/SOC....BIO-SOCIAL PROCESSES, DRUGS, SEXUALITY

L29
DARWIN L.."WHAT IS EUGENICS." USA-45 LAW SOCIETY | PLAN
FACE/GP FAM ACT/RES ECO/TAC HEALTH...HEAL TREND | BIO/SOC
STERTYP 20. PAGE 29 E0568

B33
GILLETTE J.M.,CURRENT SOCIAL PROBLEMS. CONTROL | GEOG
CRIME AGE/Y BIO/SOC...SOC 20. PAGE 43 E0861 | HEALTH
| RACE/REL
| FAM

B35
CUMMING J.,A CONTRIBUTION TOWARD A BIBLIOGRAPHY | BIBLIOG
DEALING WITH CRIME AND COGNATE SUBJECTS (3RD ED.). | CRIMLGY
UK LAW CULTURE PUB/INST ADJUD AGE BIO/SOC...PSY SOC | FORCES
SOC/WK STAT METH/COMP 20. PAGE 28 E0552 | CT/SYS

B42
GILLETTE J.M.,PROBLEMS OF A CHANGING SOCIAL ORDER. | BIO/SOC
USA+45 STRATA FAM CONTROL CRIME RACE/REL HEALTH | ADJUST
WEALTH...GEOG GP/COMP. PAGE 43 E0862 | ATTIT
| SOC/WK

B56
US HOUSE WAYS MEANS COMMITTEE,TRAFFIC IN, AND | BIO/SOC
CONTROL OF NARCOTICS, BARBITURATES, AND | CONTROL
AMPHETAMINES. CHINA/COM USA+45 SOCIETY LEGIS | PROB/SOLV
ACT/RES EDU/PROP CT/SYS SANCTION PROFIT HEALTH | CRIME
...HEAL PSY STAT 20. PAGE 100 E2011

B57
CLINARD M.B.,SOCIOLOGY OF DEVIANT BEHAVIOR. FAM | BIO/SOC
CONTROL MURDER DISCRIM PERSON...PSY SOC T SOC/INTEG | CRIME
20. PAGE 23 E0455 | SEX
| ANOMIE

B59
FRIEDMANN W.G.,LAW IN A CHANGING SOCIETY. FUT | SOC
WOR+45 WOR-45 LAW SOCIETY STRUCT INT/TRADE LEGIT | JURID
ATTIT BIO/SOC HEALTH ORD/FREE SOVEREIGN...CONCPT
GEN/LAWS ILO 20. PAGE 41 E0803

S59
PUGWASH CONFERENCE,"ON BIOLOGICAL AND CHEMICAL | ACT/RES
WARFARE." WOR+45 SOCIETY PROC/MFG INT/ORG FORCES | BIO/SOC
EDU/PROP ADJUD RIGID/FLEX ORD/FREE PWR...DECISION | WAR
PSY NEW/IDEA MATH VAL/FREE 20. PAGE 83 E1661 | WEAPON

B60
GIBNEY F.,THE OPERATORS. USA+45 LAW STRATA BIO/SOC | CRIME
MORAL ORD/FREE SOC. PAGE 43 E0858 | CULTURE
| ANOMIE
| CRIMLGY

B62
DONNELLY R.C.,CRIMINAL LAW: PROBLEMS FOR DECISION | CRIME
IN THE PROMULGATION, INVOCATION AND ADMINISTRATION | LAW
OF A LAW OF CRIMES. USA+45 SANCTION BIO/SOC | ADJUD
...DECISION JURID BIBLIOG 20. PAGE 32 E0636 | PROB/SOLV

B62
STERN A.C.,AIR POLLUTION (2 VOLS.). LAW INDUS | AIR
PROB/SOLV TEC/DEV INSPECT RISK BIO/SOC HABITAT | OP/RES
...OBS/ENVIR TESTS SAMP 20 POLLUTION. PAGE 93 E1871 | CONTROL
| HEALTH

B64
CHEIN I.,THE ROAD TO H; NARCOTICS, DELINQUENCY, AND | BIO/SOC
SOCIAL POLICY. USA+45 NEIGH CRIME INGP/REL ATTIT | AGE/Y
PERSON...SOC/WK 20 NEWYORK/C. PAGE 22 E0426 | POLICY
| ANOMIE

B64
CLINARD M.B.,ANOMIE AND DEVIANT BEHAVIOR: A | PERSON
DISCUSSION AND CRITIQUE. SOCIETY FACE/GP CRIME | ANOMIE
STRANGE ATTIT BIO/SOC DISPL RIGID/FLEX HEALTH...PSY | KIN
CONCPT BIBLIOG 20 MERTON/R. PAGE 23 E0456 | NEIGH

B64
COHEN M.,LAW AND POLITICS IN SPACE: SPECIFIC AND | DELIB/GP
URGENT PROBLEMS IN THE LAW OF OUTER SPACE. | LAW
CHINA/COM COM USA+45 USSR WOR+45 COM/IND INT/ORG | INT/LAW
NAT/G LEGIT NUC/PWR ATTIT BIO/SOC...JURID CONCPT | SPACE
CONGRESS 20 STALIN/J. PAGE 24 E0464

B64
DRESSLER D.,READINGS IN CRIMINOLOGY AND PENOLOGY. | CRIMLGY
UNIV CULTURE PUB/INST FORCES ACT/RES PROB/SOLV | CRIME
ANOMIE BIO/SOC SUPEGO...GEOG PSY ANTHOL 20. PAGE 33 | ADJUD
E0648 | ADJUST

B65
BROMBERG W.,CRIME AND THE MIND. LAW LEGIT ADJUD | CRIMLGY
CRIME MURDER AGE/Y ANOMIE BIO/SOC DRIVE SEX PSY. | SOC
PAGE 16 E0305 | HEALTH
| COERCE

B65
HARTUNG F.E.,CRIME, LAW, AND SOCIETY. LAW PUB/INST | PERCEPT
CRIME PERS/REL AGE/Y BIO/SOC PERSON ROLE SUPEGO | CRIMLGY
...LING GP/COMP GEN/LAWS 20. PAGE 50 E1004 | DRIVE
| CONTROL

B65
LUGO-MARENCO J.J.,A STATEMENT OF THE LAWS OF | CONSTN
NICARAGUA IN MATTERS AFFECTING BUSINESS. NICARAGUA | NAT/G
AGRI DIST/IND EXTR/IND FINAN INDUS FAM WORKER | LEGIS
INT/TRADE TAX MARRIAGE OWN BIO/SOC 20 TREATY | JURID
RESOURCE/N MIGRATION. PAGE 67 E1332

B66
BEER U.,FRUCHTBARKEITSREGELUNG ALS KONSEQUENZ | CONTROL
VERANTWORTLICHER ELTERNSCHAFT. ASIA GERMANY/W INDIA | GEOG
LAW ECO/DEV ECO/UNDEV TEC/DEV ECO/TAC BIO/SOC SEX | FAM
CATHISM...METH/COMP 20 CHINJAP BIRTH/CON. PAGE 9 | SECT
E0178

B66
CAHN E.,CONFRONTING INJUSTICE. USA+45 PROB/SOLV TAX | ORD/FREE
EDU/PROP PRESS CT/SYS GP/REL DISCRIM BIO/SOC | CONSTN
...IDEA/COMP BIBLIOG WORSHIP 20 BILL/RIGHT. PAGE 18 | ADJUD
E0362

B66
HOEVELER H.J.,INTERNATIONALE BEKAMPFUNG DES | CRIMLGY
VERBRECHENS. AUSTRIA SWITZERLND WOR+45 INT/ORG | CRIME
CONTROL BIO/SOC...METH/COMP NAT/COMP 20 MAFIA | DIPLOM
SCOT/YARD FBI. PAGE 53 E1064 | INT/LAW

B66
OSTERMANN R.,A REPORT IN DEPTH ON CRIME IN AMERICA. | CRIME
FUT USA+45 MUNIC PUB/INST TEC/DEV MURDER EFFICIENCY | FORCES
ATTIT BIO/SOC...PSY 20. PAGE 79 E1584 | CONTROL
| LAW

B66
SKOLNICK J.H.,JUSTICE WITHOUT TRIAL: LAW | FORCES
ENFORCEMENT IN DEMOCRATIC SOCIETY. USA+45 LAW | CRIMLGY
TRIBUTE RACE/REL BIO/SOC PERSON...PSY SOC 20 NEGRO | CRIME
BUREAUCRCY PROSTITUTN. PAGE 92 E1836

B66
US HOUSE COMM ON JUDICIARY,CIVIL COMMITMENT AND | BIO/SOC
TREATMENT OF NARCOTIC ADDICTS. USA+45 SOCIETY FINAN | CRIME
LEGIS PROB/SOLV GIVE CT/SYS SANCTION HEALTH | IDEA/COMP
...POLICY HEAL 20. PAGE 100 E2008 | CONTROL

B66
US PRES COMN CRIME IN DC,REPORT OF THE US | CRIME
PRESIDENT'S COMMISSION ON CRIME IN THE DISTRICT OF | FORCES
COLUMBIA. LEGIS WORKER EDU/PROP ADJUD CONTROL | AGE/Y
CT/SYS GP/REL BIO/SOC HEALTH...CRIMLGY NEW/IDEA | SANCTION
STAT 20. PAGE 101 E2022

B67
DEBOLD R.C.,LSD, MAN AND SOCIETY. USA+45 LAW | HEALTH
SOCIETY SECT CONTROL SANCTION STRANGE ATTIT...HEAL | DRIVE
CHARTS ANTHOL BIBLIOG. PAGE 30 E0601 | PERSON
| BIO/SOC

B67
ELDRIDGE W.B.,NARCOTICS AND THE LAW: A CRITIQUE OF | LAW
THE AMERICAN EXPERIMENT IN NARCOTIC DRUG CONTROL. | INSPECT
PUB/INST ACT/RES PLAN LICENSE GP/REL EFFICIENCY | BIO/SOC
ATTIT HEALTH...CRIMLGY HEAL STAT 20 ABA DEPT/HEW | JURID
NARCO/ACT. PAGE 34 E0679

B67
RUSSELL B.,WAR CRIMES IN VIETNAM. USA+45 VIETNAM | WAR
FORCES DIPLOM WEAPON RACE/REL DISCRIM ISOLAT | CRIME
BIO/SOC 20 COLD/WAR RUSSELL/B. PAGE 87 E1736 | ATTIT
| POLICY

BIOG....BIOGRAPHY (INCLUDES PSYCHOANALYSIS)

N
TOSCANO M.,THE HISTORY OF TREATIES AND | DIPLOM
INTERNATIONAL POLITICS (REV. ED.). WOR-45 AGREE WAR | INT/ORG
...BIOG 19/20 TREATY WWI. PAGE 97 E1935

N
ANNALS OF THE AMERICAN ACADEMY OF POLITICAL AND | BIBLIOG/A
SOCIAL SCIENCE. AFR ASIA S/ASIA WOR+45 POL/PAR | NAT/G
DIPLOM CRIME REV...SOC BIOG 20. PAGE 1 E0003 | CULTURE
| ATTIT

B19
VANDERPOL A.,LA DOCTRINE SCOLASTIQUE DU DROIT DE | WAR
GUERRE. CHRIST-17C FORCES DIPLOM LEGIT SUPEGO MORAL | SECT
...BIOG AQUINAS/T SUAREZ/F CHRISTIAN. PAGE 103 | INT/LAW
E2072

N19
OPERATIONS AND POLICY RESEARCH,URUGUAY: ELECTION FACTBOOK: NOVEMBER 27, 1966 (PAMPHLET). URUGUAY LAW NAT/G LEAD REPRESENT...STAT BIOG CHARTS 20. PAGE 79 E1576
POL/PAR CHOOSE PLAN ATTIT

B28
HOLDSWORTH W.S.,THE HISTORIANS OF ANGLO-AMERICAN LAW. UK USA-45 INTELL LEGIS RESPECT...BIOG NAT/COMP 17/20 COMMON/LAW. PAGE 54 E1076
HIST/WRIT LAW JURID

B35
BURCHFIELD L.,STUDENT'S GUIDE TO MATERIALS IN POLITICAL SCIENCE. FINAN INT/ORG NAT/G POL/PAR DIPLOM PRESS ADMIN...BIOG 18/19. PAGE 17 E0328
BIBLIOG INDEX LAW

B38
HOLDSWORTH W.S.,A HISTORY OF ENGLISH LAW; THE CENTURIES OF SETTLEMENT AND REFORM (VOL. XII). UK CONSTN STRATA LEGIS JUDGE ADJUD CT/SYS ATTIT ...JURID CONCPT BIOG GEN/LAWS 18 ENGLSH/LAW BLACKSTN/W COMMON/LAW. PAGE 54 E1078
LAW PROF/ORG WRITING IDEA/COMP

B45
CONOVER H.F.,THE NAZI STATE: WAR CRIMES AND WAR CRIMINALS. GERMANY CULTURE NAT/G SECT FORCES DIPLOM INT/TRADE EDU/PROP...INT/LAW BIOG HIST/WRIT TIME/SEQ 20. PAGE 25 E0495
BIBLIOG WAR CRIME

B51
PUSEY M.J.,CHARLES EVANS HUGHES (2 VOLS.). LAW CONSTN NAT/G POL/PAR DIPLOM LEGIT WAR CHOOSE PERS/REL DRIVE HEREDITY 19/20 DEPT/STATE LEAGUE/NAT SUPREME/CT HUGHES/CE WWI. PAGE 83 E1663
BIOG TOP/EX ADJUD PERSON

B52
DU BOIS W.E.B.,IN BATTLE FOR PEACE. AFR USA+45 COLONIAL CT/SYS PERS/REL PERSON ORD/FREE...JURID 20 NEGRO CIVIL/LIB. PAGE 33 E0650
PEACE RACE/REL DISCRIM BIOG

B52
HOLDSWORTH W.S.,A HISTORY OF ENGLISH LAW; THE CENTURIES OF SETTLEMENT AND REFORM, 1701-1875 (VOL. XIII). UK POL/PAR PROF/ORG LEGIS JUDGE WRITING ATTIT...JURID CONCPT BIOG GEN/LAWS 18/19 PARLIAMENT REFORMERS ENGLSH/LAW COMMON/LAW. PAGE 54 E1080
LAW CONSTN IDEA/COMP CT/SYS

B53
BRETTON H.L.,STRESEMANN AND THE REVISION OF VERSAILLES: A FIGHT FOR REASON. EUR+WWI GERMANY FORCES BUDGET ARMS/CONT WAR SUPEGO...BIBLIOG 20 TREATY VERSAILLES STRESEMN/G. PAGE 15 E0294
POLICY DIPLOM BIOG

B53
CURRIER T.F.,A BIBLIOGRAPHY OF OLIVER WENDELL HOLMES. USA-45...BIOG 19/20. PAGE 28 E0557
BIBLIOG/A HUM JURID JUDGE

B53
MARKE J.J.,A CATALOGUE OF THE LAW COLLECTION AT NEW YORK UNIVERSITY, WITH SELECTED ANNOTATIONS. ACADEM ADJUD CT/SYS...CONCPT BIOG 20. PAGE 68 E1366
BIBLIOG/A LAW PHIL/SCI IDEA/COMP

B53
PADOVER S.K.,THE LIVING US CONSTITUTION. USA+45 USA-45 POL/PAR ADJUD...DECISION AUD/VIS IDEA/COMP 18/20 SUPREME/CT. PAGE 79 E1590
CONSTN LEGIS DELIB/GP BIOG

B55
BIBLIOGRAPHY ON THE COMMUNIST PROBLEM IN THE UNITED STATES. USA-45 PRESS ADJUD ATTIT...BIOG 20. PAGE 2 E0033
BIBLIOG/A MARXISM POL/PAR USA+45

B56
PERKINS D.,CHARLES EVANS HUGHES AND THE AMERICAN DEMOCRATIC STATESMANSHIP. USA+45 USA-45 NAT/G POL/PAR DELIB/GP JUDGE PLAN MORAL PWR...HIST/WRIT LEAGUE/NAT 20. PAGE 80 E1609
PERSON BIOG DIPLOM

C56
FALL B.B.,"THE VIET-MINH REGIME." VIETNAM LAW ECO/UNDEV POL/PAR FORCES DOMIN WAR ATTIT MARXISM ...BIOG PREDICT BIBLIOG/A 20. PAGE 36 E0720
NAT/G ADMIN EX/STRUC LEAD

B57
HISS A.,IN THE COURT OF PUBLIC OPINION. USA+45 DELIB/GP LEGIS LEGIT CT/SYS ATTIT 20 DEPT/STATE NIXON/RM HUAC HISS/ALGER. PAGE 53 E1053
CRIME MARXISM BIOG ADJUD

B59
HAYS B.,A SOUTHERN MODERATE SPEAKS. LAW PROVS SCHOOL KNOWL...JURID SOC SELF/OBS BIOG 20 NEGRO SUPREME/CT. PAGE 51 E1015
SECT DISCRIM CT/SYS RACE/REL

B61
JACOBS C.E.,JUSTICE FRANKFURTER AND CIVIL LIBERTIES. USA+45 USA-45 LAW NAT/G PROB/SOLV PRESS PERS/REL...JURID WORSHIP 20 SUPREME/CT FRANKFUR/F CIVIL/LIB. PAGE 57 E1144
BIOG CONSTN ADJUD ORD/FREE

B62
MASON A.T.,THE SUPREME COURT: PALADIUM OF FREEDOM. USA-45 NAT/G POL/PAR CHIEF LEGIS ADJUD PARL/PROC FEDERAL PWR...POLICY BIOG 18/20 SUPREME/CT ROOSEVLT/F JEFFERSN/T MARSHALL/J HUGHES/CE. PAGE 69 E1378
CONSTN CT/SYS JURID

B62
ROSENZWEIG F.,HEGEL UND DER STAAT. GERMANY SOCIETY FAM POL/PAR NAT/LISM...BIOG 19. PAGE 86 E1718
JURID NAT/G CONCPT PHIL/SCI

L62
STEIN E.,"MR HAMMARSKJOLD, THE CHARTER LAW AND THE FUTURE ROLE OF THE UNITED NATIONS SECRETARY-GENERAL." WOR+45 CONSTN INT/ORG DELIB/GP FORCES TOP/EX BAL/PWR LEGIT ROUTINE RIGID/FLEX PWR ...POLICY JURID OBS STERTYP UN COLD/WAR 20 HAMMARSK/D. PAGE 93 E1869
CONCPT BIOG

B63
DUNHAM A.,MR. JUSTICE. ADJUD PWR...JURID ANTHOL 18/20 SUPREME/CT. PAGE 33 E0659
BIOG PERSON LAW CT/SYS

B63
LEVY L.W.,JEFFERSON AND CIVIL LIBERTIES: THE DARKER SIDE. USA-45 LAW INTELL ACADEM FORCES PRESS REV INGP/REL PERSON 18/19 JEFFERSN/T CIVIL/LIB. PAGE 65 E1291
BIOG ORD/FREE CONSTN ATTIT

B64
BREVER E.H.,LEARNED HAND, JANUARY 27, 1872-AUGUST 18, 1961 (PAMPHLET). USA+45 USA-45 LAW CONSTN ADJUD ...DECISION BIOG 19/20. PAGE 15 E0295
BIBLIOG/A JUDGE CT/SYS JURID

B64
DANELSKI D.J.,A SUPREME COURT JUSTICE IS APPOINTED. CHIEF LEGIS CONFER DEBATE EXEC PERSON PWR...BIOG 20 CONGRESS PRESIDENT. PAGE 28 E0564
CHOOSE JUDGE DECISION

B64
DIETZE G.,ESSAYS ON THE AMERICAN CONSTITUTION: A COMMEMORATIVE VOLUME IN HONOR OF ALPHEUS T. MASON. USA+45 USA-45 LAW INTELL...POLICY BIOG IDEA/COMP ANTHOL SUPREME/CT. PAGE 32 E0626
FEDERAL CONSTN DIPLOM CT/SYS

B64
FORBES A.H.,CURRENT RESEARCH IN BRITISH STUDIES. UK CONSTN CULTURE POL/PAR SECT DIPLOM ADMIN...JURID BIOG WORSHIP 20. PAGE 39 E0769
BIBLIOG PERSON NAT/G PARL/PROC

B64
HEGEL G.W.,HEGEL'S POLITICAL WRITINGS (TRANS. BY T.M. KNOX). GERMANY UK FINAN FORCES PARL/PROC CHOOSE REPRESENT...BIOG 19. PAGE 51 E1022
CONSTN LEGIS JURID

B64
HURST W.H.,JUSTICE HOLMES ON LEGAL HISTORY. USA-45 LAW SOCIETY NAT/G WRITING...POLICY PHIL/SCI SOC CONCPT 20 HOLMES/OW SUPREME/CT ENGLSH/LAW. PAGE 56 E1117
ADJUD JURID BIOG

B64
NATIONAL BOOK LEAGUE,THE COMMONWEALTH IN BOOKS: AN ANNOTATED LIST. CANADA UK LOC/G SECT ADMIN...SOC BIOG 20 CMN/WLTH. PAGE 76 E1526
BIBLIOG/A JURID NAT/G

B64
THANT U.,TOWARD WORLD PEACE. DELIB/GP TEC/DEV EDU/PROP WAR SOVEREIGN...INT/LAW 20 UN MID/EAST. PAGE 96 E1915
DIPLOM BIOG PEACE COERCE

B65
GLUECK S.,ROSCOE POUND AND CRIMINAL JUSTICE. SOCIETY FAM GOV/REL AGE/Y ATTIT ORD/FREE...CRIMLGY BIOG ANTHOL SOC/INTEG 19/20. PAGE 44 E0875
CT/SYS CRIME LAW ADJUD

B65
TRESOLINI R.J.,AMERICAN CONSTITUTIONAL LAW. USA+45   CONSTN
USA-45 NAT/G ADJUD ORD/FREE PWR...POLICY BIOG 20   CT/SYS
SUPREME/CT CASEBOOK. PAGE 97 E1939   JURID
                                                      LAW

B66
HOLDSWORTH W.S.,A HISTORY OF ENGLISH LAW; THE   BIOG
CENTURIES OF SETTLEMENT AND REFORM (VOL. XVI). UK   PERSON
LOC/G NAT/G EX/STRUC LEGIS CT/SYS LEAD ATTIT   PROF/ORG
...POLICY DECISION JURID IDEA/COMP 18 PARLIAMENT.   LAW
PAGE 54 E1083

B66
HOLMES O.W.,JUSTICE HOLMES, EX CATHEDRA. USA+45   BIOG
USA-45 LAW INTELL ADMIN ATTIT...BIBLIOG 20   PERSON
SUPREME/CT HOLMES/OW. PAGE 55 E1088   CT/SYS
                                                      ADJUD

B66
KUNSTLER W.M.,"DEEP IN MY HEART" USA+45 LAW   CT/SYS
PROF/ORG SECT LOBBY PARTIC CROWD DISCRIM ROLE   RACE/REL
...BIOG 20 KING/MAR/L NEGRO CIV/RIGHTS SOUTH/US.   ADJUD
PAGE 62 E1233   CONSULT

B67
KING W.L.,MELVILLE WESTON FULLER: CHIEF JUSTICE OF   BIOG
THE UNITED STATES, 1888-1910. USA-45 CONSTN FINAN   CT/SYS
LABOR TAX GOV/REL PERS/REL ATTIT PERSON PWR...JURID   LAW
BIBLIOG 19/20 SUPREME/CT FULLER/MW HOLMES/OW.   ADJUD
PAGE 61 E1216

B67
OPERATIONS AND POLICY RESEARCH,NICARAGUA: ELECTION   POL/PAR
FACTBOOK: FEBRUARY 5, 1967 (PAMPHLET). NICARAGUA   CHOOSE
LAW NAT/G LEAD REPRESENT...STAT BIOG CHARTS 20.   PLAN
PAGE 79 E1577   ATTIT

BIRCH/SOC....JOHN BIRCH SOCIETY

BIRD F.L. E0230

BIRDSALL P. E0231

BIRTH/CON....BIRTH CONTROL POLICIES AND TECHNIQUES

B64
GIANNELLA D.A.,RELIGION AND THE PUBLIC ORDER: AN   SECT
ANNUAL REVIEW OF CHURCH AND STATE, AND OF RELIGION,   NAT/G
LAW, AND SOCIETY. USA+45 LAW SOCIETY FAM POL/PAR   CONSTN
SCHOOL GIVE EDU/PROP GP/REL...JURID GEN/LAWS   ORD/FREE
BIBLIOG/A 20 CHURCH/STA BIRTH/CON CONSCN/OBJ
NATURL/LAW. PAGE 43 E0855

B66
BEER U.,FRUCHTBARKEITSREGELUNG ALS KONSEQUENZ   CONTROL
VERANTWORTLICHER ELTERNSCHAFT. ASIA GERMANY/W INDIA   GEOG
LAW ECO/DEV ECO/UNDEV TEC/DEV ECO/TAC BIO/SOC SEX   FAM
CATHISM...METH/COMP 20 CHINJAP BIRTH/CON. PAGE 9   SECT
E0178

BISHOP H.M. E0232

BISHOP W.W. E0233

BISMARCK/O....OTTO VON BISMARCK

BISSAINTHE M. E0234

BLACHLY F.F. E0235

BLACK C.L. E0236

BLACK H. E0237

BLACK R.L. E0509

BLACK

B63
BLACK C.L. JR.,THE OCCASIONS OF JUSTICE: ESSAYS   JURID
MOSTLY ON LAW. USA+45 JUDGE RACE/REL DISCRIM ATTIT   CONSTN
MORAL ORD/FREE 20 SUPREME/CT BLACK. PAGE 12 E0236   CT/SYS
                                                      LAW

BLACK/EUG....EUGENE BLACK

B66
US SENATE COMM ON FOREIGN REL,ASIAN DEVELOPMENT   FOR/AID
BANK ACT. USA+45 LAW DIPLOM...CHARTS 20 BLACK/EUG   FINAN
S/EASTASIA. PAGE 101 E2030   ECO/UNDEV
                                                      S/ASIA

BLACK/HL....HUGO L. BLACK

B63
CAHN E.,THE GREAT RIGHTS. USA+45 NAT/G PROVS   CONSTN
CIVMIL/REL...IDEA/COMP ANTHOL BIBLIOG 18/20   LAW
MADISON/J BILL/RIGHT CIV/RIGHTS WARRN/EARL   ORD/FREE
BLACK/HL. PAGE 18 E0361   INGP/REL

B63
DILLIARD I.,ONE MAN'S STAND FOR FREEDOM: MR.   CONSTN
JUSTICE BLACK AND THE BILL OF RIGHTS. USA+45   JURID
POL/PAR SECT DELIB/GP FORCES ADJUD CONTROL WAR   JUDGE
DISCRIM MORAL...BIBLIOG 20 NEGRO SUPREME/CT   ORD/FREE
BILL/RIGHT BLACK/HL. PAGE 32 E0628

B66
MENDELSON W.,JUSTICES BLACK AND FRANKFURTER: JURID
CONFLICT IN THE COURT (2ND ED.). NAT/G. PROVS   ADJUD
PROB/SOLV BAL/PWR CONTROL FEDERAL ISOLAT ANOMIE   IDEA/COMP
ORD/FREE...DECISION 20 SUPREME/CT BLACK/HL   ROLE
FRANKFUR/F. PAGE 72 E1439

BLACK/MUS....BLACK MUSLIMS

BLACK/PWR....BLACK POWER; SEE ALSO NEGRO

BLACK/ZION....BLACK ZIONISM

BLACKSTN/W....SIR WILLIAM BLACKSTONE

B38
HOLDSWORTH W.S.,A HISTORY OF ENGLISH LAW; THE   LAW
CENTURIES OF SETTLEMENT AND REFORM (VOL. XII). UK   PROF/ORG
CONSTN STRATA LEGIS JUDGE ADJUD CT/SYS ATTIT   WRITING
...JURID CONCPT BIOG GEN/LAWS 18 ENGLSH/LAW   IDEA/COMP
BLACKSTN/W COMMON/LAW. PAGE 54 E1078

BLACKSTONE W. E0238

BLACKSTONE, SIR WILLIAM....SEE BLACKSTN/W

BLAISDELL D.C. E0239

BLAKEY G.R. E0240

BLANCHARD L.R. E0241

BLANSHARD P. E0242

BLAUSTEIN A.P. E0244

BLITZ L.F. E0245

BLOCH J. E0246

BLOCH E.

B63
HABERMAS J.,THEORIE UND PRAXIS. RATIONAL PERSON   JURID
...PHIL/SCI ANTHOL 19/20 HEGEL/GWF MARX/KARL BLOCH   REV
LOWITH. PAGE 49 E0969   GEN/LAWS
                                                      MARXISM

BLOCH/E....ERNEST BLOCH

BLOCK E.B. E0247

BLODGETT R.H. E0248

BLOMSTROM R.L. E0573

BLOOM G.F. E0249

BLOOMFIELD L.M. E0250

BLOUSTEIN E.J. E0251

BLUMBERG A.S. E0252

BLUMSTEIN A. E0253

BMA....BRITISH MEDICAL ASSOCIATION

BOARD....SEE DELIB/GP

BOARD/MDCN....BOARD ON MEDICINE

BOAS/FRANZ....FRANZ BOAS

BOCHENSKI J.M. E0254

BOCK E. E0255

BOCK E.A. E0256

BOCK P.G. E0203

BODIN/JEAN....JEAN BODIN

BOER/WAR....BOER WAR

B99
BROOKS S.,BRITAIN AND THE BOERS. AFR SOUTH/AFR UK   WAR
CULTURE INSPECT LEGIT...INT/LAW 19/20 BOER/WAR.   DIPLOM
PAGE 16 E0309   NAT/G

BOGARDUS....BOGARDUS SCALE

BOGEN J.I. E0257

BOHANNAN P. E0258,E0259

BOHATTA H. E0260

BOHME/H....HELMUT BOHME

BOHMER A. E0261

BOHN L. E0262

BOLES D.E. E0263

BOLGAR V. E0264

BOLIVIA....SEE ALSO L/A+17C

B47
CLAGETT H.L.,A GUIDE TO THE LAW AND LEGAL   BIBLIOG/A
LITERATURE OF BOLIVIA. L/A+17C CONSTN LABOR LEGIS   JURID
ADMIN...CRIMLGY INT/LAW PHIL/SCI 16/20 BOLIV.   LAW
PAGE 22 E0441   CT/SYS

S67
TOMASEK R.D.,"THE CHILEAN-BOLIVIAN LAUCA RIVER   INT/ORG
DISPUTE AND THE OAS." CHILE L/A+17C PROB/SOLV ADJUD DIPLOM
CONTROL PEACE 20 BOLIV OAS. PAGE 96 E1930   GEOG
                                                     WAR

BOLSHEVISM....BOLSHEVISM AND BOLSHEVISTS

B66
THOMPSON J.M.,RUSSIA, BOLSHEVISM, AND THE   DIPLOM
VERSAILLES PEACE. RUSSIA USSR INT/ORG NAT/G   PEACE
DELIB/GP AGREE REV WAR PWR 20 TREATY VERSAILLES   MARXISM
BOLSHEVISM. PAGE 96 E1919

BONAPART/L....LOUIS BONAPARTE (KING OF HOLLAND)

BONGER W.A. E0265

BONTOC....BONTOC, A MOUNTAIN TRIBE OF LUZON, PHILIPPINES

BOONE/DANL....DANIEL BOONE

BORCHARD E.H. E0266

BORCHARD E.M. E0267

BORDEN/R....SIR ROBERT BORDEN

BORGATTA E.F. E0268

BORGESE G. E0269

BORGESE G.A. E0270

BORK R.H. E0280

BORKIN J. E0271

BORNEO....SEE ALSO S/ASIA

BOSCH/JUAN....JUAN BOSCH

BOSSISM....BOSSISM; MONOPOLY OF POLITICAL POWER (U.S.)

BOSTON....BOSTON, MASSACHUSETTS

B60
CARPER E.T.,THE DEFENSE APPROPRIATIONS RIDER   GOV/REL
(PAMPHLET). USA+45 CONSTN CHIEF DELIB/GP LEGIS   ADJUD
BUDGET LOBBY CIVMIL/REL...POLICY 20 CONGRESS   LAW
EISNHWR/DD DEPT/DEFEN PRESIDENT BOSTON. PAGE 20   CONTROL
E0390

BOTERO G. E0272

BOTSWANA....BOTSWANA

BOULDER....BOULDER, COLORADO

BOULTON D. E0273

BOURASSA/H....HENRI BOURASSA

BOUVIER-AJAM M. E0274

BOVY L. E0275

BOWETT D.W. E0276,E0277,E0278

BOWIE R.R. E0279,E0280

BOXER/REBL....BOXER REBELLION

BOYD A.M. E0281

BOYD W.J. E0282

BRADEN G.D. E0283

BRADLEY A.W. E0284

BRADLEY P.H. E0416

BRADLEY/FH....FRANCIS HERBERT BRADLEY

BRAGER G.A. E0285

BRAHMIN....BRAHMIN CASTE

BRAIBANTI R. E0286

BRAINWASHING....SEE EDU/PROP

BRANDEIS/L....LOUIS BRANDEIS

B64
TODD A.,JUSTICE ON TRIAL: THE CASE OF LOUIS D.   PERSON
BRANDEIS. TOP/EX DISCRIM...JURID 20 WILSON/W   RACE/REL
CONGRESS SUPREME/CT BRANDEIS/L SENATE. PAGE 96   PERS/REL
E1929   NAT/G

BRANDT R.B. E0287

BRANNAN/C....CHARLES BRANNAN (SECRETARY OF AGRICULTURE)

BRAUN K. E0288

BRAUSCH G.E. E0289

BRAZIL....SEE ALSO L/A+17C

B32
EAGLETON C.,INTERNATIONAL GOVERNMENT. BRAZIL FRANCE INT/ORG
GERMANY ITALY UK USSR WOR-45 DELIB/GP TOP/EX PLAN   JURID
ECO/TAC EDU/PROP LEGIT ADJUD REGION ARMS/CONT   DIPLOM
COERCE ATTIT PWR...GEOG MGT VAL/FREE LEAGUE/NAT 20. INT/LAW
PAGE 34 E0670

B55
DE ARAGAO J.G.,LA JURIDICTION ADMINISTRATIVE AU   EX/STRUC
BRESIL. BRAZIL ADJUD COLONIAL CT/SYS REV FEDERAL   ADMIN
ORD/FREE...BIBLIOG 19/20. PAGE 29 E0580   NAT/G

B59
WAGNER W.J.,THE FEDERAL STATES AND THEIR JUDICIARY. ADJUD
BRAZIL CANADA SWITZERLND USA+45 CONFER CT/SYS TASK   METH/COMP
EFFICIENCY FEDERAL PWR...JURID BIBLIOG 20 AUSTRAL   PROB/SOLV
MEXIC/AMER. PAGE 104 E2091   NAT/G

B60
PINTO F.B.M.,ENRIQUECIMENTO ILICITO NO EXERCICIO DE ADMIN
CARGOS PUBLICOS. BRAZIL L/A+17C USA+45 ELITES   NAT/G
TRIBUTE CONTROL INGP/REL ORD/FREE PWR...NAT/COMP   CRIME
20. PAGE 81 E1617   LAW

B62
LEVY H.V.,LIBERDADE E JUSTICA SOCIAL (2ND ED.).   ORD/FREE
BRAZIL COM L/A+17C USSR INT/ORG PARTIC GP/REL   MARXISM
WEALTH 20 UN COM/PARTY. PAGE 65 E1290   CAP/ISM
                                                     LAW

B63
FORTES A.B.,HISTORIA ADMINISTRATIVA, JUDICIARIA E   PROVS
ECLESIASTICA DO RIO GRANDE DO SUL. BRAZIL L/A+17C   ADMIN
LOC/G SECT COLONIAL CT/SYS ORD/FREE CATHISM 16/20.   JURID
PAGE 39 E0773

B64
BERNSTEIN H.,A BOOKSHELF ON BRAZIL. BRAZIL ADMIN   BIBLIOG/A
COLONIAL...HUM JURID SOC 20. PAGE 11 E0213   NAT/G
                                                     L/A+17C
                                                     ECO/UNDEV

B64
DUMON F.,LE BRESIL; SES INSTITUTIONS POLITIQUES ET   CONSTN
JUDICIARIES. BRAZIL POL/PAR CHIEF LEGIS ORD/FREE   JURID
19/20. PAGE 33 E0658   CT/SYS
                                                       GOV/REL

B64
RICHARDSON I.L.,BIBLIOGRAFIA BRASILEIRA DE   BIBLIOG
ADMINISTRACAO PUBLICA E ASSUNTOS CORRELATOS. BRAZIL   MGT
CONSTN FINAN LOC/G NAT/G POL/PAR PLAN DIPLOM   ADMIN
RECEIVE ATTIT...METH 20. PAGE 84 E1694   LAW

BREHON....BREHON LAW (ANCIENT CELTIC)

B75
MAINE H.S.,LECTURES ON THE EARLY HISTORY OF   CULTURE
INSTITUTIONS. IRELAND UK CONSTN ELITES STRUCT FAM   LAW
KIN CHIEF LEGIS CT/SYS OWN SOVEREIGN...CONCPT 16   INGP/REL
BENTHAM/J BREHON ROMAN/LAW. PAGE 68 E1351

BREITEL C.D. E0290

BRENNAN D.G. E0291

BRENNAN J.T. E0292

BRENNAN W.J. E0293

BRETTON H.L. E0294

BREUER E.H. E0295

BREWER D.J. E0296

BRIAND/A....ARISTIDE BRIAND

B52
FERRELL R.H.,PEACE IN THEIR TIME. FRANCE UK USA-45   PEACE
INT/ORG NAT/G FORCES CREATE AGREE ARMS/CONT COERCE   DIPLOM
WAR TREATY 20 WILSON/W LEAGUE/NAT BRIAND/A. PAGE 37
E0741

BRIDGEPORT....BRIDGEPORT, CONNECTICUT

BRIERLY J.L. E0297,E0298,E0299

BRIGGS A. E0300

BRIGGS H.W. E0301,E0302

BRIT/COLUM....BRITISH COLUMBIA, CANADA

BRITISH COMMONWEALTH OF NATIONS....SEE COMMONWLTH

BRITISH MEDICAL ASSOCIATION....SEE BMA

BRODEN T.F. E0303

BROGAN D.W. E0304

BROMBERG W. E0305

BROMWICH L. E0306

BROOK/EDGR....EDGAR H. BROOKES

BROOKES E.H. E0307,E0308

BROOKINGS....BROOKINGS INSTITUTION, THE

BROOKS S. E0309

BROOKS T.R. E0310

BROWN A.D. E0311

BROWN D.M. E0312

BROWN E.S. E0313

BROWN L.N. E0314

BROWN R.M. E0315

BROWN/JOHN....JOHN BROWN

BROWNE D.G. E0316

BROWNELL/H....HERBERT BROWNELL

B64
ANDERSON J.W.,EISENHOWER, BROWNELL, AND THE   LAW

CONGRESS - THE TANGLED ORIGINS OF THE CIVIL RIGHTS   CONSTN
BILL OF 1956-1957. USA+45 POL/PAR LEGIS CREATE   POLICY
PROB/SOLV LOBBY GOV/REL RIGID/FLEX...NEW/IDEA 20   NAT/G
EISNHWR/DD CONGRESS BROWNELL/H CIV/RIGHTS. PAGE 5
E0090

BROWNLIE I. E0317,E0318,E0319

BRUCKER H. E0320

BRYAN/WJ....WILLIAM JENNINGS BRYAN

BRYCE J. E0321,E0322,E0323

BRYCE/J....JAMES BRYCE

BRZEZNSK/Z....ZBIGNIEW K. BRZEZINSKI

BUCHANAN/J....PRESIDENT JAMES BUCHANAN

BUCK A.E. E0324

BUCKLAND W.W. E0325

BUCKLEY/WF....WILLIAM F. BUCKLEY

BUDDHISM....BUDDHISM

BUDGET....BUDGETING, BUDGETS, FISCAL PLANNING

N
CONOVER H.F.,OFFICIAL PUBLICATIONS OF BRITISH EAST   BIBLIOG/A
AFRICA (PAMPHLET). UK LAW ECO/UNDEV AGRI EXTR/IND   AFR
SECT LEGIS BUDGET TAX...HEAL STAT 20. PAGE 25 E0491   ADMIN
                                                      COLONIAL

N
UNITED NATIONS,OFFICIAL RECORDS OF THE UNITED   INT/ORG
NATIONS' GENERAL ASSEMBLY. WOR+45 BUDGET DIPLOM   DELIB/GP
ADMIN 20 UN. PAGE 98 E1964   INT/LAW
                                                      WRITING

C29
BUCK A.E.,"PUBLIC BUDGETING." USA-45 FINAN LOC/G   BUDGET
NAT/G LEGIS BAL/PAY COST...JURID TREND BIBLIOG/A   ROUTINE
20. PAGE 17 E0324   ADMIN

B30
FAIRLIE J.A.,COUNTY GOVERNMENT AND ADMINISTRATION.   ADMIN
UK USA-45 NAT/G SCHOOL FORCES BUDGET TAX CT/SYS   GOV/REL
CHOOSE...JURID BIBLIOG 11/20. PAGE 36 E0713   LOC/G
                                                      MUNIC

B35
LUCE R.,LEGISLATIVE PROBLEMS. CONSTN CHIEF JUDGE   TREND
BUDGET CONFER ETIQUET CONTROL MORAL PWR NEW/LIB   ADMIN
CONGRESS. PAGE 67 E1331   LEGIS

B36
GRAVES W.B.,AMERICAN STATE GOVERNMENT. CONSTN FINAN   NAT/G
EX/STRUC FORCES LEGIS BUDGET TAX CT/SYS REPRESENT   PROVS
GOV/REL...BIBLIOG/A 19/20. PAGE 45 E0900   ADMIN
                                                      FEDERAL

B40
ANDERSON W.,FUNDAMENTALS OF AMERICAN GOVERNMENT.   NAT/G
USA-45 LAW POL/PAR CHIEF EX/STRUC BUDGET ADMIN   LOC/G
CT/SYS PARL/PROC CHOOSE FEDERAL...BIBLIOG 20.   GOV/REL
PAGE 5 E0093   CONSTN

N40
COUNTY GOVERNMENT IN THE UNITED STATES: A LIST OF   BIBLIOG/A
RECENT REFERENCES (PAMPHLET). USA-45 LAW PUB/INST   LOC/G
PLAN BUDGET CT/SYS CENTRAL 20. PAGE 52 E1027   ADMIN
                                                      MUNIC

B42
FULLER G.H.,DEFENSE FINANCING: A SUPPLEMENTARY LIST   BIBLIOG/A
OF REFERENCES (PAMPHLET). CANADA UK USA-45 ECO/DEV   FINAN
NAT/G DELIB/GP BUDGET ADJUD ARMS/CONT WEAPON COST   FORCES
PEACE PWR 20 AUSTRAL CHINJAP CONGRESS. PAGE 41   DIPLOM
E0821

B47
DE NOIA J.,GUIDE TO OFFICIAL PUBLICATIONS OF OTHER   BIBLIOG/A
AMERICAN REPUBLICS: ECUADOR (VOL. IX). ECUADOR LAW   CONSTN
FINAN LEGIS BUDGET CT/SYS 19/20. PAGE 30 E0589   NAT/G
                                                      EDU/PROP

B48
NEUBURGER O.,GUIDE TO OFFICIAL PUBLICATIONS OF THE   BIBLIOG/A
OTHER AMERICAN REPUBLICS: VENEZUELA (VOL. XIX).   NAT/G
VENEZUELA FINAN LEGIS PLAN BUDGET DIPLOM CT/SYS   CONSTN
PARL/PROC 19/20. PAGE 77 E1535   LAW

ANDERSON W.,STATE AND LOCAL GOVERNMENT IN THE   LOC/G
UNITED STATES. USA+45 CONSTN POL/PAR EX/STRUC LEGIS   MUNIC
BUDGET TAX ADJUD CT/SYS CHOOSE...CHARTS T 20.   PROVS
PAGE 5 E0094   GOV/REL
B51

LANCASTER L.W.,"GOVERNMENT IN RURAL AMERICA."   GOV/REL
USA+45 ECO/DEV AGRI SCHOOL FORCES LEGIS JUDGE   LOC/G
BUDGET TAX CT/SYS...CHARTS BIBLIOG. PAGE 62 E1248 MUNIC
                                          ADMIN
C52

BRETTON H.L.,STRESEMANN AND THE REVISION OF   POLICY
VERSAILLES: A FIGHT FOR REASON. EUR+WWI GERMANY   DIPLOM
FORCES BUDGET ARMS/CONT WAR SUPEGO...BIBLIOG 20   BIOG
TREATY VERSAILLES STRESEMN/G. PAGE 15 E0294
B53

MAJUMDAR B.B.,PROBLEMS OF PUBLIC ADMINISTRATION IN ECO/UNDEV
INDIA. INDIA INDUS PLAN BUDGET ADJUD CENTRAL DEMAND GOV/REL
WEALTH...WELF/ST ANTHOL 20 CIVIL/SERV. PAGE 68   ADMIN
E1353   MUNIC
B53

SECKLER-HUDSON C.,BIBLIOGRAPHY ON PUBLIC   BIBLIOG/A
ADMINISTRATION (4TH ED.). USA+45 LAW POL/PAR   ADMIN
DELIB/GP BUDGET ADJUD LOBBY GOV/REL GP/REL ATTIT NAT/G
...JURID 20. PAGE 90 E1800   MGT
B53

ESTEP R.,AN AIR POWER BIBLIOGRAPHY. USA+45 TEC/DEV BIBLIOG/A
BUDGET DIPLOM EDU/PROP DETER CIVMIL/REL...DECISION FORCES
INT/LAW 20. PAGE 35 E0698   WEAPON
                                          PLAN
B56

AMERICAN SOCIETY PUBLIC ADMIN,STRENGTHENING   ADMIN
MANAGEMENT FOR DEMOCRATIC GOVERNMENT. USA+45 ACADEM NAT/G
EX/STRUC WORKER PLAN BUDGET CONFER CT/SYS   EXEC
EFFICIENCY ANTHOL. PAGE 4 E0083   MGT
B58

HOOD W.C.,FINANCING OF ECONOMIC ACTIVITY IN CANADA. BUDGET
CANADA FUT VOL/ASSN WORKER ECO/TAC ADJUD ADMIN   FINAN
...CHARTS 20. PAGE 55 E1093   GP/REL
                                          ECO/DEV
B58

US HOUSE COMM FOREIGN AFFAIRS,HEARINGS ON DRAFT   LEGIS
LEGISLATION TO AMEND FURTHER THE MUTUAL SECURITY   DELIB/GP
ACT OF 1954 (PAMPHLET). USA+45 CONSULT FORCES   CONFER
BUDGET DIPLOM DETER COST ORD/FREE...JURID 20   WEAPON
DEPT/DEFEN UN DEPT/STATE. PAGE 100 E2002
N58

ALBI F.,TRATADO DE LOS MODOS DE GESTION DE LAS   LOC/G
CORPORACIONES LOCALES. SPAIN FINAN NAT/G BUDGET   LAW
CONTROL EXEC ROUTINE GOV/REL ORD/FREE SOVEREIGN   ADMIN
...MGT 20. PAGE 3 E0057   MUNIC
B60

CARPER E.T.,THE DEFENSE APPROPRIATIONS RIDER   GOV/REL
(PAMPHLET). USA+45 CONSTN CHIEF DELIB/GP LEGIS   ADJUD
BUDGET LOBBY CIVMIL/REL...POLICY 20 CONGRESS   LAW
EISNHWR/DD DEPT/DEFEN PRESIDENT BOSTON. PAGE 20   CONTROL
E0390
B60

CARTER R.F.,COMMUNITIES AND THEIR SCHOOLS. USA+45 SCHOOL
LAW FINAN PROVS BUDGET TAX LEAD PARTIC CHOOSE...SOC ACT/RES
INT QU 20. PAGE 20 E0401   NEIGH
                                          INGP/REL
B60

BEASLEY K.E.,STATE SUPERVISION OF MUNICIPAL DEBT IN MUNIC
KANSAS - A CASE STUDY. USA+45 USA-45 FINAN PROVS   LOC/G
BUDGET TAX ADJUD ADMIN CONTROL SUPEGO. PAGE 9 E0167 LEGIS
                                          JURID
B61

NEW JERSEY LEGISLATURE-SENATE,PUBLIC HEARINGS   LEGIS
BEFORE COMMITTEE ON REVISION AND AMENDMENT OF LAWS MUNIC
ON SENATE BILL NO. 8. USA+45 FINAN PROVS WORKER   INDUS
ACT/RES PLAN BUDGET TAX CRIME...IDEA/COMP 20   PROB/SOLV
NEW/JERSEY URBAN/RNWL. PAGE 77 E1537
B61

DRINAN R.F.,RELIGION, THE COURTS, AND PUBLIC   SECT
POLICY. USA+45 CONSTN BUDGET TAX GIVE ADJUD   CT/SYS
SANCTION GP/REL PRIVIL 20 CHURCH/STA. PAGE 33 E0649 POLICY
                                          SCHOOL
B63

ECOLE NATIONALE D'ADMIN,BIBLIOGRAPHIE SELECTIVE   BIBLIOG
D'OUVRAGES DE LANGUE FRANCAISE TRAITANT DES   AFR
B63

PROBLEMES GOUVERNEMENTAUX ET ADMINISTRATIFS. NAT/G ADMIN
FORCES ACT/RES OP/RES PLAN PROB/SOLV BUDGET ADJUD EX/STRUC
COLONIAL LEAD 20. PAGE 34 E0672

GARNER U.F.,ADMINISTRATIVE LAW. UK LAW LOC/G NAT/G ADMIN
EX/STRUC LEGIS JUDGE BAL/PWR BUDGET ADJUD CONTROL JURID
CT/SYS...BIBLIOG 20. PAGE 42 E0840   PWR
                                          GOV/REL
B63

BOUVIER-AJAM M.,MANUEL TECHNIQUE ET PRATIQUE DU   MUNIC
MAIRE ET DES ELUS ET AGENTS COMMUNAUX. FRANCE LOC/G ADMIN
BUDGET CHOOSE GP/REL SUPEGO...JURID BIBLIOG 20   CHIEF
MAYOR COMMUNES. PAGE 14 E0274   NEIGH
B64

BOWETT D.W.,UNITED NATIONS FORCES* A LEGAL STUDY. OP/RES
CYPRUS ISRAEL KOREA LAW CONSTN ACT/RES CREATE   FORCES
BUDGET CONTROL TASK PWR...INT/LAW IDEA/COMP UN   ARMS/CONT
CONGO/LEOP SUEZ. PAGE 14 E0278
B64

HAAR C.M.,LAW AND LAND: ANGLO-AMERICAN PLANNING   LAW
PRACTICE. UK USA+45 NAT/G TEC/DEV BUDGET CT/SYS   PLAN
INGP/REL EFFICIENCY OWN...JURID 20. PAGE 49 E0967 MUNIC
                                          NAT/COMP
B64

SCHWARTZ M.D.,CONFERENCE ON SPACE SCIENCE AND SPACE SPACE
LAW. FUT COM/IND NAT/G FORCES ACT/RES PLAN BUDGET LAW
DIPLOM NUC/PWR WEAPON...POLICY ANTHOL 20. PAGE 89 PEACE
E1788   TEC/DEV
B64

FISCHER F.C.,THE GOVERNMENT OF MICHIGAN. USA+45   PROVS
NAT/G PUB/INST EX/STRUC LEGIS BUDGET GIVE EDU/PROP LOC/G
CT/SYS CHOOSE GOV/REL...T MICHIGAN. PAGE 38 E0753 ADMIN
                                          CONSTN
B65

FRYE R.J.,HOUSING AND URBAN RENEWAL IN ALABAMA.   MUNIC
USA+45 NEIGH LEGIS BUDGET ADJUD ADMIN PARTIC...MGT PROB/SOLV
20 ALABAMA URBAN/RNWL. PAGE 41 E0815   PLAN
                                          GOV/REL
B65

HIGHSAW R.B.,CONFLICT AND CHANGE IN LOCAL   GOV/REL
GOVERNMENT. USA+45 BUDGET ECO/TAC LEGIT ADJUD   PROB/SOLV
ALABAMA. PAGE 52 E1044   LOC/G
                                          BAL/PWR
B65

FOX A.B.,"NATO AND CONGRESS." CONSTN DELIB/GP   CONTROL
EX/STRUC FORCES TOP/EX BUDGET NUC/PWR GOV/REL   DIPLOM
...GP/COMP CONGRESS NATO TREATY. PAGE 39 E0779
S65

GHOSH P.K.,THE CONSTITUTION OF INDIA: HOW IT HAS   CONSTN
BEEN FRAMED. INDIA LOC/G DELIB/GP EX/STRUC   NAT/G
PROB/SOLV BUDGET INT/TRADE CT/SYS CHOOSE...LING 20. LEGIS
PAGE 43 E0854   FEDERAL
B66

GREENE L.E.,GOVERNMENT IN TENNESSEE (2ND ED.).   PROVS
USA+45 DIST/IND INDUS POL/PAR EX/STRUC LEGIS PLAN LOC/G
BUDGET GIVE CT/SYS...MGT T 20 TENNESSEE. PAGE 46   CONSTN
E0909   ADMIN
B66

TIEDT S.W.,THE ROLE OF THE FEDERAL GOVERNMENT IN   NAT/G
EDUCATION. FUT USA+45 USA-45 CONSTN SECT BUDGET   EDU/PROP
CT/SYS GOV/REL 18/20 SUPREME/CT. PAGE 96 E1924   GIVE
                                          SCHOOL
B66

WILSON G.,CASES AND MATERIALS ON CONSTITUTIONAL AND JURID
ADMINISTRATIVE LAW. UK LAW NAT/G EX/STRUC LEGIS   ADMIN
BAL/PWR BUDGET DIPLOM ADJUD CONTROL CT/SYS GOV/REL CONSTN
ORD/FREE 20 PARLIAMENT ENGLSH/LAW. PAGE 106 E2126 PWR
B66

GREIG D.W.,"THE ADVISORY JURISDICTION OF THE   INT/LAW
INTERNATIONAL COURT AND THE SETTLEMENT OF DISPUTES CT/SYS
BETWEEN STATES." ISRAEL KOREA FORCES BUDGET DOMIN
LEGIT ADJUD COST...RECORD UN CONGO/LEOP TREATY.
PAGE 46 E0915
L66

GREENE L.S.,AMERICAN GOVERNMENT POLICIES AND   POLICY
FUNCTIONS. USA+45 LAW AGRI DIST/IND LABOR MUNIC   NAT/G
BUDGET DIPLOM EDU/PROP ORD/FREE...BIBLIOG T 20.   ADMIN
PAGE 46 E0910   DECISION
B67

INTERNATIONAL CONCILIATION,ISSUES BEFORE THE 22ND PROB/SOLV
B67

GENERAL ASSEMBLY. WOR+45 ECO/UNDEV FINAN BAL/PWR   INT/ORG
BUDGET INT/TRADE STRANGE ORD/FREE...INT/LAW 20 UN   DIPLOM
COLD/WAR. PAGE 57 E1132   PEACE

                                                     L67
LENT G.E.,"TAX INCENTIVES FOR INVESTMENT IN   ECO/UNDEV
DEVELOPING COUNTRIES" WOR+45 LAW INDUS PLAN BUDGET   TAX
TARIFFS ADMIN...METH/COMP 20. PAGE 64 E1285   FINAN
                                                          ECO/TAC

                                                     S67
ANDERSON W.,"THE PERILS OF 'SHARING'." USA+45   BUDGET
ECO/TAC RECEIVE LOBBY GOV/REL CENTRAL COST INCOME   TAX
...POLICY PLURIST CONGRESS. PAGE 5 E0095   FEDERAL
                                                          LAW

                                                     S67
DOUTY H.M.," REFERENCE TO DEVELOPING COUNTRIES."   TAX
JAMAICA MALAYSIA UK WOR+45 LAW FINAN ACT/RES BUDGET   ECO/UNDEV
CAP/ISM ECO/TAC TARIFFS RISK EFFICIENCY PROFIT   NAT/G
...CHARTS 20. PAGE 33 E0646

BUELL R. E0326

BUENOS/AIR....BUENOS AIRES, ARGENTINA

BUGANDA....BUGANDA, UGANDA

BUGEDA LANZAS J. E0327

BUKHARIN/N....NIKOLAI BUKHARIN

BULGARIA....BULGARIA; SEE ALSO COM

                                                     B43
CONOVER H.F.,THE BALKANS: A SELECTED LIST OF   BIBLIOG
REFERENCES. ALBANIA BULGARIA ROMANIA YUGOSLAVIA   EUR+WWI
INT/ORG PROB/SOLV DIPLOM LEGIT CONFER ADJUD WAR
NAT/LISM PEACE PWR 20 LEAGUE/NAT. PAGE 25 E0493

                                                     B56
SIPKOV I.,LEGAL SOURCES AND BIBLIOGRAPHY OF   BIBLIOG
BULGARIA. BULGARIA COM LEGIS WRITING ADJUD CT/SYS   LAW
...INT/LAW TREATY 20. PAGE 91 E1834   TOTALISM
                                                          MARXISM

BULLITT/WC....WILLIAM C. BULLITT

BUNCHE/R....RALPH BUNCHE

BUNDY/M....MCGEORGE BUNDY

BUR/BUDGET....BUREAU OF THE BUDGET

BUR/STNDRD....BUREAU OF STANDARDS

BURAGR/ECO....BUREAU OF AGRICULTURAL ECONOMICS

BURCHFIELD L. E0328

BURDETTE F.L. E0329,E0330,E0331

BUREAU OF STANDARDS....SEE BUR/STNDRD

BUREAU OF THE BUDGET....SEE BUR/BUDGET

BUREAU GOVERNMENT RES AND SERV E0332

BUREAU OF NATIONAL AFFAIRS E0333,E0334,E0335,E0336,E0337,E0338

BUREAUCRCY....BUREAUCRACY; SEE ALSO ADMIN

                                                     B66
BRAIBANTI R.,RESEARCH ON THE BUREAUCRACY OF   HABITAT
PAKISTAN. PAKISTAN LAW CULTURE INTELL ACADEM LOC/G   NAT/G
SECT PRESS CT/SYS...LING CHARTS 20 BUREAUCRCY.   ADMIN
PAGE 15 E0286   CONSTN

                                                     B66
FRIED R.C.,COMPARATIVE POLITICAL INSTITUTIONS. USSR   NAT/G
EX/STRUC FORCES LEGIS JUDGE CONTROL REPRESENT   PWR
ALL/IDEOS 20 CONGRESS BUREAUCRCY. PAGE 40 E0798   EFFICIENCY
                                                          GOV/COMP

                                                     B66
SKOLNICK J.H.,JUSTICE WITHOUT TRIAL: LAW   FORCES
ENFORCEMENT IN DEMOCRATIC SOCIETY. USA+45 LAW   CRIMLGY
TRIBUTE RACE/REL BIO/SOC PERSON...PSY SOC 20 NEGRO   CRIME

BUREAUCRCY PROSTITUTN. PAGE 92 E1836

BURGESS J.W. E0339,E0340

BURKE E. E0341

BURKE T.C. E0099

BURKE W.T. E1407

BURKE/EDM....EDMUND BURKE

                                                     B04
BURKE E.,A LETTER TO THE SHERIFFS OF BRISTOL   LEGIS
(1777). USA-45 LAW ECO/TAC COLONIAL CT/SYS REV   ADJUD
GP/REL ORD/FREE...POLICY 18 PARLIAMENT BURKE/EDM.   CRIME
PAGE 17 E0341

BURLAMAQUI J.J. E0342

BURMA....BURMA

                                                     B61
SYATAUW J.J.G.,SOME NEWLY ESTABLISHED ASIAN STATES   INT/LAW
AND THE DEVELOPMENT OF INTERNATIONAL LAW. BURMA   ADJUST
CEYLON INDIA INDONESIA ECO/UNDEV COLONIAL NEUTRAL   SOCIETY
WAR PEACE SOVEREIGN...CHARTS 19/20. PAGE 95 E1902   S/ASIA

BURNS A.C. E0343

BURNS A.L. E1024

BURNS C.D. E0344

BURR R.N. E0345

BURR/AARON....AARON BURR

BURRUS B.R. E0346,E0347

BURUNDI....SEE ALSO AFR

BUSHONG E1213

BUSINESS CYCLE....SEE ECO, FINAN

BUSINESS MANAGEMENT....SEE MGT

BUTLER D.E. E0348

BUTLER G. E0349

BUTLER N.M. E0350

BUTLER W.E. E1503

BUTTERFIELD H. E0351

BYNKERSHOEK C. E0352

BYRD E.M. E0353

BYRNES R.F. E0354

BYZANTINE....BYZANTINE EMPIRE   C

CAB....CIVIL AERONAUTICS BOARD

                                                     B64
FISK W.M.,ADMINISTRATIVE PROCEDURE IN A REGULATORY   SERV/IND
AGENCY: THE CAB AND THE NEW YORK-CHICAGO CASE   ECO/DEV
(PAMPHLET). USA+45 DIST/IND ADMIN CONTROL LOBBY   AIR
GP/REL ROLE ORD/FREE NEWYORK/C CHICAGO CAB. PAGE 38   JURID
E0758

CABINET....SEE ALSO EX/STRUC, DELIB/GP, CONSULT

                                                     B64
MAKI J.M.,COURT AND CONSTITUTION IN JAPAN: SELECTED   CONSTN
SUPREME COURT DECISIONS, 1948-60. LAW AGRI FAM   JURID
LEGIS BAL/PWR ADMIN CHOOSE...SOC ANTHOL CABINET 20   CT/SYS
CHINJAP CIVIL/LIB. PAGE 68 E1355   CRIME

CABLE G.W. E0355

CADWALDER J.L. E0356

CAESAR/JUL....JULIUS CAESAR

CAHIER P. E0357,E0358

CAHILL F.V. E0359

CAHN E. E0360,E0361,E0362

CAIRO....CAIRO, EGYPT

CALCUTTA....CALCUTTA, INDIA

CALDWELL L.K. E0364,E0365

CALHOUN/JC....JOHN C. CALHOUN

CALIFORNIA LEGISLATURE E0366

CALIFORNIA STATE LIBRARY E0367

CALIFORNIA....CALIFORNIA

B30
BIRD F.L.,THE RECALL OF PUBLIC OFFICERS: A STUDY OF REPRESENT
THE OPERATION OF RECALL IN CALIFORNIA. LOC/G MUNIC SANCTION
POL/PAR PROVS PROB/SOLV ADJUD PARTIC...CHARTS CHOOSE
METH/COMP 20 CALIFORNIA RECALL. PAGE 12 E0230 LAW

B52
GELLHORN W.,THE STATES AND SUBVERSION. USA+45 PROVS
USA-45 LOC/G DELIB/GP LEGIS EDU/PROP LEGIT CT/SYS JURID
REGION PEACE ATTIT ORD/FREE SOCISM...INT CON/ANAL
20 CALIFORNIA MARYLAND ILLINOIS MICHIGAN NEW/YORK.
PAGE 43 E0845

B63
GALLAGHER J.F.,SUPERVISORIAL DISTRICTING IN APPORT
CALIFORNIA COUNTIES: 1960-1963 (PAMPHLET). USA+45 REGION
ADJUD ADMIN PARTIC CHOOSE GP/REL...CENSUS 20 REPRESENT
CALIFORNIA. PAGE 42 E0828 LOC/G

CALLISON I.P. E0368

CALVIN/J....JOHN CALVIN

CAM H.M. E0369

CAMB/SOMER....CAMBRIDGE-SOMERVILLE YOUTH STUDY

CAMBODIA....SEE ALSO S/ASIA

B50
EMBREE J.F.,BIBLIOGRAPHY OF THE PEOPLES AND BIBLIOG/A
CULTURES OF MAINLAND SOUTHEAST ASIA. CAMBODIA LAOS CULTURE
THAILAND VIETNAM LAW...GEOG HUM SOC MYTH LING S/ASIA
CHARTS WORSHIP 20. PAGE 35 E0686

CAMBRIDGE-SOMERVILLE YOUTH STUDY....SEE CAMB/SOMER

CAMELOT....PROJECT CAMELOT (CHILE)

CAMEROON....SEE ALSO AFR

CAMPBELL A.K. E0256

CAMPBELL E. E0370

CAMPBELL E.H. E0371,E0372

CAMPBELL R. E0120

CANAD/CRWN....CANADIAN CROWN CORPORATIONS

CANADA....SEE ALSO COMMONWLTH

N
CANADIAN GOVERNMENT PUBLICATIONS (1955-). CANADA BIBLIOG/A
AGRI FINAN LABOR FORCES INT/TRADE HEALTH...JURID 20 NAT/G
PARLIAMENT. PAGE 1 E0005 DIPLOM
INT/ORG

N
INDEX TO LEGAL PERIODICALS. CANADA NEW/ZEALND UK BIBLIOG
USA+45 USA-45 CONSTN LEGIS JUDGE ADJUD ADMIN INDEX
CONTROL CT/SYS FEDERAL...CRIMLGY INT/LAW 20 LAW
CMN/WLTH AUSTRAL. PAGE 1 E0006 JURID

B28
CORBETT P.E.,CANADA AND WORLD POLITICS. LAW CULTURE NAT/G
SOCIETY STRUCT MARKET INT/ORG FORCES ACT/RES PLAN CANADA
ECO/TAC LEGIT ORD/FREE PWR RESPECT...SOC CONCPT
TIME/SEQ TREND CMN/WLTH 20 LEAGUE/NAT. PAGE 26
E0504

B40
CONOVER H.F.,FOREIGN RELATIONS OF THE UNITED BIBLIOG/A
STATES: A LIST OF RECENT BOOKS (PAMPHLET). ASIA USA-45
CANADA L/A+17C UK INT/ORG INT/TRADE TARIFFS NEUTRAL DIPLOM
WAR PEACE...INT/LAW CON/ANAL 20 CHINJAP. PAGE 25
E0492

B42
FULLER G.H.,DEFENSE FINANCING: A SUPPLEMENTARY LIST BIBLIOG/A
OF REFERENCES (PAMPHLET). CANADA UK USA-45 ECO/DEV FINAN
NAT/G DELIB/GP BUDGET ADJUD ARMS/CONT WEAPON COST FORCES
PEACE PWR 20 AUSTRAL CHINJAP CONGRESS. PAGE 41 DIPLOM

E0821

B46
GRIFFIN G.G.,A GUIDE TO MANUSCRIPTS RELATING TO BIBLIOG/A
AMERICAN HISTORY IN BRITISH DEPOSITORIES. CANADA ALL/VALS
IRELAND MOD/EUR UK USA-45 LAW DIPLOM ADMIN COLONIAL NAT/G
WAR NAT/LISM SOVEREIGN...GEOG INT/LAW 15/19
CMN/WLTH. PAGE 47 E0936

B47
HILL M.,IMMUNITIES AND PRIVILEGES OF INTERNATIONAL INT/ORG
OFFICIALS. CANADA EUR+WWI NETHERLAND SWITZERLND LAW ADMIN
LEGIS DIPLOM LEGIT RESPECT...TIME/SEQ LEAGUE/NAT UN
VAL/FREE 20. PAGE 52 E1046

B55
WRONG D.H.,AMERICAN AND CANADIAN VIEWPOINTS. CANADA DIPLOM
USA+45 CONSTN STRATA FAM SECT WORKER ECO/TAC ATTIT
EDU/PROP ADJUD MARRIAGE...IDEA/COMP 20. PAGE 108 NAT/COMP
E2161 CULTURE

B58
CUNNINGHAM W.B.,COMPULSORY CONCILIATION AND POLICY
COLLECTIVE BARGAINING. CANADA NAT/G LEGIS ADJUD BARGAIN
CT/SYS GP/REL...MGT 20 NEW/BRUNS STRIKE CASEBOOK. LABOR
PAGE 28 E0555 INDUS

B58
HOOD W.C.,FINANCING OF ECONOMIC ACTIVITY IN CANADA. BUDGET
CANADA FUT VOL/ASSN WORKER ECO/TAC ADJUD ADMIN FINAN
...CHARTS 20. PAGE 55 E1093 GP/REL
ECO/DEV

B59
SCOTT F.R.,CIVIL LIBERTIES AND CANADIAN FEDERALISM. ORD/FREE
CANADA LAW ADJUD CT/SYS GOV/REL 20 CIV/RIGHTS. FEDERAL
PAGE 90 E1797 NAT/LISM
CONSTN

B59
SPIRO H.J.,GOVERNMENT BY CONSTITUTIONS: THE NAT/G
POLITICAL SYSTEMS OF DEMOCRACY. CANADA EUR+WWI FUT CONSTN
USA+45 WOR+45 WOR-45 LEGIS TOP/EX LEGIT ADMIN
CT/SYS ORD/FREE PWR...TREND TOT/POP VAL/FREE 20.
PAGE 93 E1861

B59
WAGNER W.J.,THE FEDERAL STATES AND THEIR JUDICIARY. ADJUD
BRAZIL CANADA SWITZERLND USA+45 CONFER CT/SYS TASK METH/COMP
EFFICIENCY FEDERAL PWR...JURID BIBLIOG 20 AUSTRAL PROB/SOLV
MEXIC/AMER. PAGE 104 E2091 NAT/G

B60
LASKIN B.,CANADIAN CONSTITUTIONAL LAW: TEXT AND CONSTN
NOTES ON DISTRIBUTION OF LEGISLATIVE POWER (2ND NAT/G
ED.). CANADA LOC/G ECO/TAC TAX CONTROL CT/SYS CRIME LAW
FEDERAL PWR...JURID 20 PARLIAMENT. PAGE 63 E1259 LEGIS

B61
CARROTHERS A.W.R.,LABOR ARBITRATION IN CANADA. LABOR
CANADA LAW NAT/G CONSULT LEGIS WORKER ADJUD ADMIN MGT
CT/SYS 20. PAGE 20 E0396 GP/REL
BARGAIN

B62
SOWLE C.R.,POLICE POWER AND INDIVIDUAL FREEDOM: THE FORCES
QUEST FOR BALANCE. CANADA EUR+WWI ISRAEL NORWAY ORD/FREE
USA+45 LAW CONSTN SOCIETY CONTROL ROUTINE SANCTION IDEA/COMP
GP/REL 20 CHINJAP. PAGE 93 E1859

B63
DEENER D.R.,CANADA - UNITED STATES TREATY DIPLOM
RELATIONS. CANADA USA+45 USA-45 NAT/G FORCES PLAN INT/LAW
PROB/SOLV AGREE NUC/PWR...TREND 18/20 TREATY. POLICY
PAGE 30 E0603

B63
LIVINGSTON W.S.,FEDERALISM IN THE COMMONWEALTH - A BIBLIOG
BIBLIOGRAPHICAL COMMENTARY. CANADA INDIA PAKISTAN JURID
UK STRUCT LOC/G NAT/G POL/PAR...NAT/COMP 20 FEDERAL
AUSTRAL. PAGE 66 E1310 CONSTN

S63
HARNETTY P.,"CANADA, SOUTH AFRICA AND THE AFR
COMMONWEALTH." CANADA SOUTH/AFR LAW INT/ORG ATTIT
VOL/ASSN DELIB/GP LEGIS TOP/EX ECO/TAC LEGIT DRIVE
MORAL...CONCPT CMN/WLTH 20. PAGE 50 E1000

S63
LEPAWSKY A.,"INTERNATIONAL DEVELOPMENT OF RIVER INT/ORG
RESOURCES." CANADA EUR+WWI S/ASIA USA+45 SEA LEGIT DELIB/GP
ADJUD ORD/FREE PWR WEALTH...MGT TIME/SEQ VAL/FREE
MEXIC/AMER 20. PAGE 64 E1287

B64
CURRIE D.P.,FEDERALISM AND THE NEW NATIONS OF FEDERAL

AFRICA. CANADA USA+45 INT/TRADE TAX GP/REL ...NAT/COMP SOC/INTEG 20. PAGE 28 E0556
AFR ECO/UNDEV INT/LAW

B64
LEDERMAN W.R.,THE COURTS AND THE CANDIAN CONSTITUTION. CANADA PARL/PROC...POLICY JURID GOV/COMP ANTHOL 19/20 SUPREME/CT PARLIAMENT. PAGE 64 E1276
CONSTN CT/SYS LEGIS LAW

B64
NATIONAL BOOK LEAGUE,THE COMMONWEALTH IN BOOKS: AN ANNOTATED LIST. CANADA UK LOC/G SECT ADMIN...SOC BIOG 20 CMN/WLTH. PAGE 76 E1526
BIBLIOG/A JURID NAT/G

B64
SCHMEISER D.A.,CIVIL LIBERTIES IN CANADA. CANADA LAW SECT PRESS RACE/REL NAT/LISM PRIVIL 20 COMMONWLTH PARLIAMENT CIVIL/LIB CHURCH/STA. PAGE 88 E1758
ORD/FREE CONSTN ADJUD EDU/PROP

B65
HABERLER G.,A SURVEY OF INTERNATIONAL TRADE THEORY. CANADA FRANCE GERMANY ECO/TAC TARIFFS AGREE COST DEMAND WEALTH...ECOMETRIC 19/20 MONOPOLY TREATY. PAGE 49 E0968
INT/TRADE BAL/PAY DIPLOM POLICY

B65
MCWHINNEY E.,JUDICIAL REVIEW IN THE ENGLISH-SPEAKING WORLD (3RD ED.). CANADA UK WOR+45 LEGIS CONTROL EXEC PARTIC...JURID 20 AUSTRAL. PAGE 71 E1431
GOV/COMP CT/SYS ADJUD CONSTN

B65
SOPER T.,EVOLVING COMMONWEALTH. AFR CANADA INDIA IRELAND UK LAW CONSTN POL/PAR DOMIN CONTROL WAR PWR ...AUD/VIS 18/20 COMMONWLTH OEEC. PAGE 93 E1857
INT/ORG COLONIAL VOL/ASSN

B66
ANDERSON S.V.,CANADIAN OMBUDSMAN PROPOSALS. CANADA LEGIS DEBATE PARL/PROC...MAJORIT JURID TIME/SEQ IDEA/COMP 20 OMBUDSMAN PARLIAMENT. PAGE 5 E0092
NAT/G CREATE ADMIN POL/PAR

B66
US DEPARTMENT OF STATE,RESEARCH ON WESTERN EUROPE, GREAT BRITAIN, AND CANADA (EXTERNAL RESEARCH LIST NO 3-25). CANADA GERMANY/W UK LAW CULTURE NAT/G POL/PAR FORCES EDU/PROP REGION MARXISM...GEOG SOC WORSHIP 20 CMN/WLTH. PAGE 100 E1998
BIBLIOG/A EUR+WWI DIPLOM

S67
HILL D.G.,"HUMAN RIGHTS LEGISLATION IN ONTARIO." CANADA R+D VOL/ASSN CONSULT INSPECT EDU/PROP ADJUD AGREE TASK GP/REL INGP/REL DISCRIM 20 CIV/RIGHTS ONTARIO CIVIL/LIB. PAGE 52 E1045
DELIB/GP ORD/FREE LAW POLICY

S67
SHELDON C.H.,"PUBLIC OPINION AND HIGH COURTS: COMMUNIST PARTY CASES IN FOUR CONSTITUTIONAL SYSTEMS." CANADA GERMANY/W WOR+45 POL/PAR MARXISM ...METH/COMP NAT/COMP 20 AUSTRAL. PAGE 91 E1818
ATTIT CT/SYS CONSTN DECISION

CANAL/ZONE....CANAL ZONE

B64
DUBOIS J.,DANGER OVER PANAMA. FUT PANAMA SCHOOL PROB/SOLV EDU/PROP MARXISM...POLICY 19/20 TREATY INTERVENT CANAL/ZONE. PAGE 33 E0652
DIPLOM COERCE

CANFIELD L.H. E0373

CANNON/JG....JOSEPH G. CANNON

CANON/LAW....CANON LAW

B24
HOLDSWORTH W.S.,A HISTORY OF ENGLISH LAW: THE COMMON LAW AND ITS RIVALS (VOL. IV). UK SEA AGRI CHIEF ADJUD CONTROL CRIME GOV/REL...INT/LAW JURID NAT/COMP 16/17 PARLIAMENT COMMON/LAW CANON/LAW ENGLSH/LAW. PAGE 54 E1075
LAW LEGIS CT/SYS CONSTN

B35
RAM J.,THE SCIENCE OF LEGAL JUDGMENT: A TREATISE... UK CONSTN NAT/G LEGIS CREATE PROB/SOLV AGREE CT/SYS ...INT/LAW CONCPT 19 ENGLSH/LAW CANON/LAW CIVIL/LAW CTS/WESTM. PAGE 83 E1672
LAW JURID EX/STRUC ADJUD

S68
DUPRE L.,"TILL DEATH DO US PART?" UNIV FAM INSPECT LEGIT ADJUD SANCTION PERS/REL ANOMIE RIGID/FLEX SEX
MARRIAGE CATH

...JURID IDEA/COMP 20 CHURCH/STA BIBLE CANON/LAW CIVIL/LAW. PAGE 34 E0666
LAW

B98
POLLOCK F.,THE HISTORY OF ENGLISH LAW BEFORE THE TIME OF EDWARD I (2 VOLS, 2ND ED.). UK CULTURE LOC/G LEGIS LICENSE AGREE CONTROL CT/SYS SANCTION CRIME...TIME/SEQ 13 COMMON/LAW CANON/LAW. PAGE 81 E1626
LAW ADJUD JURID

CANTRIL/H....HADLEY CANTRIL

CANTWELL F.V. E0374

CAP/ISM....CAPITALISM

B02
GRIFFIN A.P.C.,A LIST OF BOOKS RELATING TO TRUSTS (2ND REV. ED.) (PAMPHLET). FRANCE GERMANY UK USA+45 WOR-45 LAW ECO/DEV INDUS LG/CO NAT/G CAP/ISM CENTRAL DISCRIM PWR LAISSEZ 19/20. PAGE 46 E0919
BIBLIOG/A JURID ECO/TAC VOL/ASSN

B04
GRIFFIN A.P.C.,A LIST OF BOOKS RELATING TO RAILROADS IN THEIR RELATION TO THE GOVERNMENT AND THE PUBLIC (PAMPHLET). USA-45 LAW ECO/DEV NAT/G TEC/DEV CAP/ISM LICENSE CENTRAL LAISSEZ...DECISION 19/20. PAGE 47 E0925
BIBLIOG/A SERV/IND ADJUD ECO/TAC

B06
GRIFFIN A.P.C.,LIST OF BOOKS RELATING TO CHILD LABOR (PAMPHLET). BELGIUM FRANCE GERMANY MOD/EUR UK USA-45 ECO/DEV INDUS WORKER CAP/ISM PAY ROUTINE ALL/IDEOS...MGT SOC 19/20. PAGE 47 E0929
BIBLIOG/A LAW LABOR AGE/C

B13
ADAMS B.,THE THEORY OF SOCIAL REVOLUTIONS. FUT USA-45 GP/REL PEACE...NEW/IDEA 20. PAGE 3 E0047
CAP/ISM REV SOCIETY CT/SYS

B35
BEMIS S.F.,GUIDE TO THE DIPLOMATIC HISTORY OF THE UNITED STATES, 1775·1921. NAT/G LEGIS TOP/EX PROB/SOLV CAP/ISM INT/TRADE TARIFFS ADJUD ...CON/ANAL 18/20. PAGE 10 E0184
BIBLIOG/A DIPLOM USA-45

S36
CORWIN E.S.,"THE CONSTITUTION AS INSTRUMENT AND AS SYMBOL." USA-45 ECO/DEV INDUS CAP/ISM SANCTION RIGID/FLEX ORD/FREE LAISSEZ OBJECTIVE 20 CONGRESS SUPREME/CT. PAGE 26 E0512
CONSTN LAW ADJUD PWR

B42
CROWE S.E.,THE BERLIN WEST AFRICA CONFERENCE, 1884-85. GERMANY ELITES MARKET INT/ORG DELIB/GP FORCES PROB/SOLV BAL/PWR CAP/ISM DOMIN COLONIAL ...INT/LAW 19. PAGE 28 E0548
AFR CONFER INT/TRADE DIPLOM

B44
CHENEY F.,CARTELS, COMBINES, AND TRUSTS: A SELECTED LIST OF REFERENCES. GERMANY UK USA+45 WOR-45 DELIB/GP OP/RES BARGAIN CAP/ISM ECO/TAC INT/TRADE LICENSE LEGIT CONFER PRICE 20. PAGE 22 E0428
BIBLIOG/A LG/CO ECO/DEV INDUS

B47
BORGESE G.,COMMON CAUSE. LAW CONSTN SOCIETY STRATA ECO/DEV INT/ORG POL/PAR FORCES LEGIS TOP/EX CAP/ISM DIPLOM ADMIN EXEC ATTIT PWR 20. PAGE 14 E0269
WOR+45 NAT/G SOVEREIGN REGION

B47
ENKE S.,INTERNATIONAL ECONOMICS. UK USA+45 USSR INT/ORG BAL/PWR BARGAIN CAP/ISM BAL/PAY...NAT/COMP 20 TREATY. PAGE 35 E0691
INT/TRADE FINAN TARIFFS ECO/TAC

B51
COOKE C.A.,CORPORATION TRUST AND COMPANY: AN ESSAY IN LEGAL HISTORY. UK STRUCT LEGIS CAP/ISM GP/REL PROFIT 13/20 COMPNY/ACT. PAGE 25 E0499
LG/CO FINAN ECO/TAC JURID

B55
BLOOM G.F.,ECONOMICS OF LABOR RELATIONS. USA+45 LAW CONSULT WORKER CAP/ISM PAY ADJUD CONTROL EFFICIENCY ORD/FREE...CHARTS 19/20 AFL/CIO NLRB DEPT/LABOR. PAGE 13 E0249
ECO/DEV ECO/TAC LABOR GOV/REL

B57
BERLE A.A. JR.,ECONOMIC POWER AND FREE SOCIETY (PAMPHLET). CLIENT CONSTN EX/STRUC ECO/TAC CONTROL PARTIC PWR WEALTH MAJORIT. PAGE 11 E0205
LG/CO CAP/ISM INGP/REL LEGIT

FAIRCHILD H.P.,THE ANATOMY OF FREEDOM. USA+45   B57   ORD/FREE
ACADEM SCHOOL SECT CAP/ISM PRESS CHOOSE SOCISM.   CONCPT
PAGE 36 E0712   NAT/G
                                                        JURID

NICHOLS J.P.,"HAZARDS OF AMERICAN PRIVATE   S60   FINAN
INVESTMENT IN UNDERDEVELOPED COUNTRIES." FUT   ECO/UNDEV
L/A+17C USA+45 USA-45 EXTR/IND CONSULT BAL/PWR   CAP/ISM
ECO/TAC DOMIN ADJUD ATTIT SOVEREIGN WEALTH   NAT/LISM
...HIST/WRIT TIME/SEQ TREND VAL/FREE 20. PAGE 77
E1546

LEVY H.V.,LIBERDADE E JUSTICA SOCIAL (2ND ED.). B62   ORD/FREE
BRAZIL COM L/A+17C USSR INT/ORG PARTIC GP/REL   MARXISM
WEALTH 20 UN COM/PARTY. PAGE 65 E1290   CAP/ISM
                                                        LAW

PATRA A.C.,THE ADMINISTRATION OF JUSTICE UNDER THE B63 ADMIN
EAST INDIA COMPANY IN BENGAL, BIHAR AND ORISSA.   JURID
INDIA UK LG/CO CAP/ISM INT/TRADE ADJUD COLONIAL   CONCPT
CONTROL CT/SYS...POLICY 20. PAGE 80 E1602

BROOKS T.R.,TOIL AND TROUBLE, A HISTORY OF AMERICAN B64 INDUS
LABOR. WORKER BARGAIN CAP/ISM ADJUD AUTOMAT EXEC   LABOR
GP/REL RACE/REL EFFICIENCY INCOME PROFIT MARXISM   LEGIS
17/20 KENNEDY/JF AFL/CIO NEGRO. PAGE 16 E0310

KISER S.L.,AMERICANISM IN ACTION. USA+45 LAW PROVS B64 OLD/LIB
CAP/ISM DIPLOM RECEIVE CONTROL CT/SYS WAR FEDERAL   FOR/AID
ATTIT WEALTH 20 SUPREME/CT. PAGE 61 E1221   MARXISM
                                                        CONSTN

KARPOV P.V.,"PEACEFUL COEXISTENCE AND INTERNATIONAL S64 COM
LAW." WOR+45 LAW SOCIETY INT/ORG VOL/ASSN FORCES   ATTIT
CREATE CAP/ISM DIPLOM ADJUD NUC/PWR PEACE MORAL   INT/LAW
ORD/FREE PWR MARXISM...MARXIST JURID CONCPT OBS   USSR
TREND COLD/WAR MARX/KARL 20. PAGE 59 E1186

PROEHL P.O.,FOREIGN ENTERPRISE IN NIGERIA. NIGERIA B65 ECO/UNDEV
FINAN LABOR NAT/G TAX 20. PAGE 83 E1656   ECO/TAC
                                                        JURID
                                                        CAP/ISM

DAVIS K.,BUSINESS AND ITS ENVIRONMENT. LAW ECO/DEV B66 EX/STRUC
INDUS OP/RES ADMIN CONTROL ROUTINE GP/REL PROFIT   PROB/SOLV
POLICY. PAGE 29 E0573   CAP/ISM
                                                        EXEC

EDWARDS C.D.,TRADE REGULATIONS OVERSEAS. IRELAND B66   INT/TRADE
NEW/ZEALND SOUTH/AFR NAT/G CAP/ISM TARIFFS CONTROL   DIPLOM
...POLICY JURID 20 EEC CHINJAP. PAGE 34 E0676   INT/LAW
                                                        ECO/TAC

GRUNEWALD D.,PUBLIC POLICY AND THE MODERN   B66   LG/CO
COOPERATION: SELECTED READINGS. USA+45 LAW MARKET   POLICY
VOL/ASSN CAP/ISM INT/TRADE CENTRAL OWN...SOC ANTHOL   NAT/G
20. PAGE 48 E0954   CONTROL

GABRIEL P.P.,THE INTERNATIONAL TRANSFER OF   B67   ECO/UNDEV
CORPORATE SKILLS: MANAGEMENT CONTRACTS IN LESS   AGREE
DEVELOPED COUNTRIES. CLIENT INDUS LG/CO PLAN   MGT
PROB/SOLV CAP/ISM ECO/TAC FOR/AID INT/TRADE RENT   CONSULT
ADMIN SKILL 20. PAGE 42 E0825

DOUTY H.M.," REFERENCE TO DEVELOPING COUNTRIES." S67   TAX
JAMAICA MALAYSIA UK WOR+45 LAW FINAN ACT/RES BUDGET   ECO/UNDEV
CAP/ISM ECO/TAC TARIFFS RISK EFFICIENCY PROFIT   NAT/G
...CHARTS 20. PAGE 33 E0646

FLECHTHEIM O.K.,"BLOC FORMATION VS. DIALOGUE."   S67   FUT
CONSTN ECO/DEV BAL/PWR PEACE ATTIT PWR COLD/WAR.   CAP/ISM
PAGE 38 E0761   MARXISM
                                                        DEBATE

GIBSON G.H.,"LABOR PIRACY ON THE BRANDYWINE."   S67   ECO/TAC
USA-45 INDUS R+D VOL/ASSN CAP/ISM ADJUD DRIVE...PSY   CREATE
19. PAGE 43 E0859   TEC/DEV
                                                        WORKER

CAPE/HOPE....CAPE OF GOOD HOPE

EYBERS G.W.,SELECT CONSTITUTIONAL DOCUMENTS   B18   CONSTN
ILLUSTRATING SOUTH AFRICAN HISTORY 1795-1910.   LAW
SOUTH/AFR LOC/G LEGIS CT/SYS...JURID ANTHOL 18/20   NAT/G
NATAL CAPE HOPE ORANGE/STA. PAGE 36 E0707   COLONIAL

CAPITAL....SEE FINAN

CAPITALISM....SEE CAP/ISM

CAPLOW T. E0375

CAPODIST/J....JOHN CAPODISTRIAS

CAPONE/AL....AL CAPONE

KEFAUVER E.,CRIME IN AMERICA. USA+45 USA-45 MUNIC B51   ELITES
NEIGH DELIB/GP TRIBUTE GAMBLE LOBBY SANCTION   CRIME
...AUD/VIS 20 CAPONE/AL MAFIA MIAMI CHICAGO   PWR
DETROIT. PAGE 60 E1194   FORCES

CARDOZA/JN....JACOB N. CARDOZA

CARDOZO B. E0376

CARDOZO B.N. E0377

CARIBBEAN....CARIBBEAN

CARLIN J.E. E0378

CARLSTON K.S. E0379,E0380,E0381

CARLYLE A.J. E0382

CARMEN I.H. E0383

CARMICHAEL D.M. E0384

CARNEG/COM....CARNEGIE COMMISSION

CARNEGIE COMMISSION....SEE CARNEG/COM

CARNEGIE ENDOWMENT INT. PEACE E0385,E0386

CARNELL F. E0387

CARPENTER W.S. E0388

CARPER E.T. E0389,E0390,E0391

CARR C. E0392

CARR E.H. E0393

CARR R.K. E0394

CARRANZA/V....VENUSTIANZO CARRANZA

CARRINGTON P.D. E0395

CARROLL P.M. E0099

CARROTHERS A.W.R. E0396

CARSON P. E0397

CARTER G.M. E0398,E0399

CARTER P.G. E0400

CARTER R.F. E0401

CARTER R.L. E0402

CARTER R.M. E0403

CASE STUDIES....CARRIED UNDER THE SPECIAL TECHNIQUES USED,
    OR TOPICS COVERED

CASEBOOK....CASEBOOK, SUCH AS LEGAL OR SOCIOLOGICAL CASEBOOK

HAGUE PERMANENT CT INTL JUSTIC,WORLD COURT REPORTS: INT/ORG B38
COLLECTION OF THE JUDGEMENTS ORDERS AND OPINIONS   CT/SYS
VOLUME 3 1932-35. WOR-45 LAW DELIB/GP CONFER WAR   DIPLOM
PEACE ATTIT...DECISION ANTHOL 20 WORLD/CT CASEBOOK.   ADJUD
PAGE 49 E0976

HART J.,AN INTRODUCTION TO ADMINISTRATIVE LAW, WITH B40 LAW
SELECTED CASES. USA-45 CONSTN SOCIETY NAT/G   ADMIN
EX/STRUC ADJUD CT/SYS LEAD CRIME ORD/FREE   LEGIS
...DECISION JURID 20 CASEBOOK. PAGE 50 E1002   PWR

B43
HAGUE PERMANENT CT INTL JUSTIC,WORLD COURT REPORTS: INT/ORG
COLLECTION OF THE JUDGEMENTS ORDERS AND OPINIONS   CT/SYS
VOLUME 4 1936-42. WOR-45 CONFER PEACE ATTIT   DIPLOM
...DECISION JURID ANTHOL 20 WORLD/CT CASEBOOK.   ADJUD
PAGE 49 E0977

B55
CUSHMAN R.E.,LEADING CONSTITUTIONAL DECISIONS.   CONSTN
USA+45 USA-45 NAT/G EX/STRUC LEGIS JUDGE TAX   PROB/SOLV
FEDERAL...DECISION 20 SUPREME/CT CASEBOOK. PAGE 28   JURID
E0559   CT/SYS

B58
CUNNINGHAM W.B.,COMPULSORY CONCILIATION AND   POLICY
COLLECTIVE BARGAINING. CANADA NAT/G LEGIS ADJUD   BARGAIN
CT/SYS GP/REL...MGT 20 NEW/BRUNS STRIKE CASEBOOK.   LABOR
PAGE 28 E0555   INDUS

B58
WHITNEY S.N.,ANTITRUST POLICIES: AMERICAN   INDUS
EXPERIENCE IN TWENTY INDUSTRIES. USA+45 USA-45 LAW   CONTROL
DELIB/GP LEGIS ADJUD CT/SYS GOV/REL ATTIT...ANTHOL   LG/CO
20 MONOPOLY CASEBOOK. PAGE 106 E2119   MARKET

B62
BOCK E.A.,CASE STUDIES IN AMERICAN GOVERNMENT.   POLICY
USA+45 ECO/DEV CHIEF EDU/PROP CT/SYS RACE/REL   LEGIS
ORD/FREE...JURID MGT PHIL/SCI PRESIDENT CASEBOOK.   IDEA/COMP
PAGE 13 E0256   NAT/G

B62
MCGRATH J.J.,CHURCH AND STATE IN AMERICAN LAW. LAW   SECT
PROVS SCHOOL TAX GIVE CT/SYS GP/REL...POLICY ANTHOL ADJUD
18/20 SUPREME/CT CHURCH/STA CASEBOOK. PAGE 71 E1414 CONSTN
                                                     NAT/G

B62
NATIONAL MUNICIPAL LEAGUE,COURT DECISIONS ON   PROVS
LEGISLATIVE APPORTIONMENT (VOL. III). USA+45 JUDGE   CT/SYS
ADJUD CONTROL ATTIT...DECISION JURID COURT/DIST   APPORT
CASEBOOK. PAGE 76 E1528   LEGIS

B64
MITAU G.T.,PROXIMATE SOLUTIONS: CASE PROBLEMS IN   PROVS
STATE AND LOCAL GOVERNMENT. USA+45 CONSTN NAT/G   LOC/G
CHIEF LEGIS CT/SYS EXEC GOV/REL GP/REL PWR 20   ADJUD
CASEBOOK. PAGE 73 E1470

B64
MITAU G.T.,INSOLUBLE PROBLEMS: CASE PROBLEMS ON THE ADJUD
FUNCTIONS OF STATE AND LOCAL GOVERNMENT. USA+45 AIR LOC/G
FINAN LABOR POL/PAR PROB/SOLV TAX RECEIVE CONTROL   PROVS
GP/REL 20 CASEBOOK ZONING. PAGE 73 E1471

B65
MILLER H.H.,THE CASE FOR LIBERTY. USA-45 LAW JUDGE   COLONIAL
CT/SYS...AUD/VIS 18 PRE/US/AM CASEBOOK. PAGE 73   JURID
E1460   PROB/SOLV

B65
TRESOLINI R.J.,AMERICAN CONSTITUTIONAL LAW. USA+45   CONSTN
USA-45 NAT/G ADJUD ORD/FREE PWR...POLICY BIOG 20   CT/SYS
SUPREME/CT CASEBOOK. PAGE 97 E1939   JURID
                                                     LAW

B66
DALLIN A.,POLITICS IN THE SOVIET UNION: 7 CASES.   MARXISM
COM USSR LAW POL/PAR CHIEF FORCES WRITING CONTROL   DOMIN
PARL/PROC CIVMIL/REL TOTALISM...ANTHOL 20 KHRUSH/N   ORD/FREE
STALIN/J CASEBOOK COM/PARTY. PAGE 28 E0563   GOV/REL

B66
FENN DH J.R.,BUSINESS DECISION MAKING AND   DECISION
GOVERNMENT POLICY. SERV/IND LEGIS LICENSE ADMIN   PLAN
CONTROL GP/REL INGP/REL 20 CASEBOOK. PAGE 37 E0736   NAT/G
                                                     LG/CO

B66
NANTWI E.K.,THE ENFORCEMENT OF INTERNATIONAL   INT/LAW
JUDICIAL DECISIONS AND ARBITAL AWARDS IN PUBLIC   ADJUD
INTERNATIONAL LAW. WOR+45 WOR-45 JUDGE PROB/SOLV   SOVEREIGN
DIPLOM CT/SYS SUPEGO MORAL PWR RESPECT...METH/CNCPT INT/ORG
18/20 CASEBOOK. PAGE 76 E1520

B63
PACHTER H.M.,COLLISION COURSE; THE CUBAN MISSILE   WAR
CRISIS AND COEXISTENCE. CUBA USA+45 DIPLOM   BAL/PWR
ARMS/CONT PEACE MARXISM...DECISION INT/LAW 20   NUC/PWR
COLD/WAR KHRUSH/N KENNEDY/JF CASTRO/F. PAGE 79   DETER
E1587

B63
US SENATE COMM ON JUDICIARY,CASTRO'S NETWORK IN THE PRESS
UNITED STATES. CUBA LAW DELIB/GP 20 SENATE   MARXISM
CASTRO/F. PAGE 102 E2050   DIPLOM
                                                     INSPECT

CATH....ROMAN CATHOLIC

B24
GENTILI A.,DE LEGATIONIBUS. CHRIST-17C NAT/G SECT   DIPLOM
CONSULT LEGIT...POLICY CATH JURID CONCPT MYTH.   INT/LAW
PAGE 43 E0848   INT/ORG
                                                     LAW

B27
JOHN OF SALISBURY,THE STATESMAN'S BOOK (1159)   NAT/G
(TRANS. BY J. DICKINSON). DOMIN GP/REL MORAL   SECT
ORD/FREE PWR CONSERVE...CATH CONCPT 12. PAGE 59   CHIEF
E1169   LAW

B44
SUAREZ F.,A TREATISE ON LAWS AND GOD THE LAWGIVER   LAW
(1612) IN SELECTIONS FROM THREE WORKS. VOL. II.   JURID
FRANCE ITALY UK CULTURE NAT/G SECT CHIEF LEGIS   GEN/LAWS
DOMIN LEGIT CT/SYS ORD/FREE PWR WORSHIP 16/17.   CATH
PAGE 94 E1892

S60
O'BRIEN W.,"THE ROLE OF FORCE IN THE INTERNATIONAL   INT/ORG
JURIDICAL ORDER." WOR+45 NAT/G FORCES DOMIN ADJUD   COERCE
ARMS/CONT DETER NUC/PWR WAR ATTIT PWR...CATH
INT/LAW JURID CONCPT TREND STERTYP GEN/LAWS 20.
PAGE 78 E1564

B63
MURPHY T.J.,CENSORSHIP: GOVERNMENT AND OBSCENITY.   ORD/FREE
USA+45 CULTURE LEGIS JUDGE EDU/PROP CONTROL   MORAL
INGP/REL RATIONAL POPULISM...CATH JURID 20. PAGE 75 LAW
E1507   CONSEN

B67
POGANY A.H.,POLITICAL SCIENCE AND INTERNATIONAL   BIBLIOG
RELATIONS, BOOKS RECOMMENDED FOR AMERICAN CATHOLIC   DIPLOM
COLLEGE LIBRARIES. INT/ORG LOC/G NAT/G FORCES
BAL/PWR ECO/TAC NUC/PWR...CATH INT/LAW TREATY 20.
PAGE 81 E1622

S68
DUPRE L.,"TILL DEATH DO US PART?" UNIV FAM INSPECT   MARRIAGE
LEGIT ADJUD SANCTION PERS/REL ANOMIE RIGID/FLEX SEX CATH
...JURID IDEA/COMP 20 CHURCH/STA BIBLE CANON/LAW   LAW
CIVIL/LAW. PAGE 34 E0666

N
CANON LAW ABSTRACTS. LEGIT CONFER CT/SYS INGP/REL   BIBLIOG/A
MARRIAGE ATTIT MORAL WORSHIP 20. PAGE 2 E0026   CATHISM
                                                     SECT
                                                     LAW

NRE
MEYER C.S.,ELIZABETH I AND THE RELIGIOUS SETTLEMENT GP/REL
OF 1559. UK ELITES CHIEF LEGIS DISCRIM CATHISM 16   SECT
CHURCH/STA ELIZABTH/I. PAGE 72 E1445   LAW
                                                     PARL/PROC

N19
COUTROT A.,THE FIGHT OVER THE 1959 PRIVATE   SCHOOL
EDUCATION LAW IN FRANCE (PAMPHLET). FRANCE NAT/G   PARL/PROC
SECT GIVE EDU/PROP GP/REL ATTIT RIGID/FLEX ORD/FREE CATHISM
20 CHURCH/STA. PAGE 27 E0527   LAW

B49
HOLLERAN M.P.,CHURCH AND STATE IN GUATEMALA.   SECT
GUATEMALA LAW STRUCT CATHISM...SOC SOC/INTEG 17/20   NAT/G
CHURCH/STA. PAGE 55 E1086   GP/REL
                                                     CULTURE

B51
BISSAINTHE M.,DICTIONNAIRE DE BIBLIOGRAPHIE   BIBLIOG
HAITIENNE. HAITI ELITES AGRI LEGIS DIPLOM INT/TRADE L/A+17C
WRITING ORD/FREE CATHISM...ART/METH GEOG 19/20   SOCIETY
NEGRO TREATY. PAGE 12 E0234   NAT/G

B54

O'NEILL J.M., CATHOLICS IN CONTROVERSY. USA+45 NAT/G CATHISM
PROVS SCHOOL SECT EDU/PROP LEGIT CT/SYS SANCTION CONSTN
GP/REL 20 SUPREME/CT CHURCH/STA. PAGE 78 E1569 POLICY
LAW

B55

MID-EUROPEAN LAW PROJECT, CHURCH AND STATE BEHIND LAW
THE IRON CURTAIN. COM CZECHOSLVK HUNGARY POLAND MARXISM
USSR CULTURE SECT EDU/PROP GOV/REL CATHISM...CHARTS POLICY
ANTHOL BIBLIOG WORSHIP 20 CHURCH/STA. PAGE 73 E1455

B57

COSSIO C., LA POLITICA COMO CONCIENCIA; MEDITACION POL/PAR
SOBRE LA ARGENTINA DE 1955. WOR+45 LEGIS EDU/PROP REV
PARL/PROC PARTIC ATTIT PWR CATHISM 20 ARGEN TOTALISM
PERON/JUAN. PAGE 26 E0517 JURID

B58

GARDINER H.C., CATHOLIC VIEWPOINT ON CENSORSHIP. WRITING
DEBATE COERCE GP/REL...JURID CONCPT 20. PAGE 42 LOBBY
E0835 CATHISM
EDU/PROP

B60

BERTHOLD O., KAISER, VOLK UND AVIGNON. GERMANY CHIEF DIPLOM
LEGIT LEAD NAT/LISM CONSERVE 14 POPE CHRUCH/STA CATHISM
LUDWIG/BAV JOHN/XXII. PAGE 11 E0217 JURID

B60

POWELL T., THE SCHOOL BUS LAW: A CASE STUDY IN JURID
EDUCATION, RELIGION, AND POLITICS. USA+45 LAW NEIGH SCHOOL
SECT LEGIS EDU/PROP ADJUD CT/SYS LOBBY CATHISM
WORSHIP 20 CONNECTICT CHURCH/STA. PAGE 82 E1641

B61

HAGEN A., STAAT UND KATHOLISCHE KIRCHE IN SECT
WURTTEMBERG IN DEN JAHREN 1848-1862 (2 VOLS.). PROVS
GERMANY DELIB/GP EDU/PROP MARRIAGE CATHISM 19 GP/REL
CHURCH/STA. PAGE 49 E0975 JURID

B61

KURLAND P.B., RELIGION AND THE LAW. USA+45 USA-45 SECT
CONSTN PROVS CHIEF ADJUD SANCTION PRIVIL CATHISM NAT/G
...POLICY 17/20 SUPREME/CT PRESIDENT CHURCH/STA. CT/SYS
PAGE 62 E1239 GP/REL

B62

GONNER R., DAS KIRCHENPATRONATRECHT IM JURID
GROSSHERZOGTUM BADEN. GERMANY LAW PROVS DEBATE SECT
ATTIT CATHISM 14/19 PROTESTANT CHRISTIAN CHURCH/STA NAT/G
BADEN. PAGE 44 E0882 GP/REL

B62

SILVA R.C., RUM, RELIGION, AND VOTES: 1928 RE- POL/PAR
EXAMINED. USA-45 LAW SECT DISCRIM CATHISM...CORREL CHOOSE
STAT 20 PRESIDENT SMITH/ALF DEMOCRAT. PAGE 91 E1827 GP/COMP
ATTIT

B63

FORTES A.B., HISTORIA ADMINISTRATIVA, JUDICIARIA E PROVS
ECLESIASTICA DO RIO GRANDE DO SUL. BRAZIL L/A+17C ADMIN
LOC/G SECT COLONIAL CT/SYS ORD/FREE CATHISM 16/20. JURID
PAGE 39 E0773

B63

LOWRY C.W., TO PRAY OR NOT TO PRAY. ADJUD SANCTION SECT
GP/REL ORD/FREE PWR CATHISM WORSHIP 20 SUPREME/CT CT/SYS
CHRISTIAN CHRUCH/STA. PAGE 67 E1330 CONSTN
PRIVIL

B63

RAVENS J.P., STAAT UND KATHOLISCHE KIRCHE IN GP/REL
PREUSSENS POLNISCHEN TEILUNGSGEBIETEN. GERMANY CATHISM
POLAND PRUSSIA PROVS DIPLOM EDU/PROP DEBATE SECT
NAT/LISM...JURID 18 CHURCH/STA. PAGE 83 E1674 NAT/G

B63

REITZEL A.M., DAS MAINZER KRONUNGSRECHT UND DIE CHIEF
POLITISCHE PROBLEMATIK. GERMANY MUNIC LEGIT CATHISM JURID
12/13. PAGE 84 E1684 CHOOSE
SECT

B63

SMITH E.A., CHURCH AND STATE IN YOUR COMMUNITY. GP/REL
USA+45 PROVS SCHOOL ACT/RES CT/SYS PARTIC ATTIT SECT
MORAL ORD/FREE CATHISM 20 PROTESTANT CHURCH/STA. NAT/G
PAGE 92 E1842 NEIGH

B64

FREISEN J., STAAT UND KATHOLISCHE KIRCHE IN DEN SECT
DEUTSCHEN BUNDESSTAATEN (2 VOLS.). GERMANY LAW FAM CATHISM
NAT/G EDU/PROP GP/REL MARRIAGE WEALTH 19/20 JURID
CHURCH/STA. PAGE 40 E0793 PROVS

B65

CHARNAY J.P., LE SUFFRAGE POLITIQUE EN FRANCE; CHOOSE
ELECTIONS PARLEMENTAIRES, ELECTION PRESIDENTIELLE, SUFF
REFERENDUMS. FRANCE CONSTN CHIEF DELIB/GP ECO/TAC NAT/G
EDU/PROP CRIME INGP/REL MORAL ORD/FREE PWR CATHISM LEGIS
20 PARLIAMENT PRESIDENT. PAGE 22 E0425

B65

COHN H.J., THE GOVERNMENT OF THE RHINE PALATINATE IN PROVS
THE FIFTEENTH CENTURY. GERMANY FINAN LOC/G DELIB/GP JURID
LEGIS CT/SYS CHOOSE CATHISM 14/15 PALATINATE. GP/REL
PAGE 24 E0468 ADMIN

B65

KAAS L., DIE GEISTLICHE GERICHTSBARKEIT DER JURID
KATHOLISCHEN KIRCHE IN PREUSSEN (2 VOLS.). PRUSSIA CATHISM
CONSTN NAT/G PROVS SECT ADJUD ADMIN ATTIT 16/20. GP/REL
PAGE 59 E1178 CT/SYS

B65

MARTENS E., DIE HANNOVERSCHE KIRCHENKOMMISSION. JURID
GERMANY LAW INT/ORG PROVS SECT CONFER GP/REL DELIB/GP
CATHISM 16/20. PAGE 69 E1371 CONSTN
PROF/ORG

B65

MOELLER R., LUDWIG DER BAYER UND DIE KURIE IM KAMPF JURID
UM DAS REICH. GERMANY LAW SECT LEGIT LEAD GP/REL CHIEF
CATHISM CONSERVE 14 LUDWIG/BAV POPE CHURCH/STA. CHOOSE
PAGE 74 E1478 NAT/LISM

B66

BEER U., FRUCHTBARKEITSREGELUNG ALS KONSEQUENZ CONTROL
VERANTWORTLICHER ELTERNSCHAFT. ASIA GERMANY/W INDIA GEOG
LAW ECO/DEV ECO/UNDEV TEC/DEV ECO/TAC BIO/SOC SEX FAM
CATHISM...METH/COMP 20 CHINJAP BIRTH/CON. PAGE 9 SECT
E0178

B66

SMITH E.A., CHURCH-STATE RELATIONS IN ECUMENICAL NAT/G
PERSPECTIVE. WOR+45 LAW MUNIC INGP/REL DISCRIM SECT
ATTIT SUPEGO ORD/FREE CATHISM...PHIL/SCI IDEA/COMP GP/REL
20 PROTESTANT ECUMENIC CHURCH/STA CHRISTIAN. ADJUD
PAGE 92 E1843

CATHOLICISM....SEE CATH, CATHISM

CAUCUS....SEE PARL/PROC

CAUGHEY J.W. E0408

CAVAN R.S. E0409

CAVERS D.F. E0410,E0411

CAVES R. E0412

CAWELTI J.G. E1450

CED....COMMITTEE FOR ECONOMIC DEVELOPMENT

CENSORSHIP....SEE EDU/PROP

CENSUS....POPULATION ENUMERATION

S47

ANGELL R.C., "THE SOCIAL INTEGRATION OF AMERICAN MUNIC
CITIES OF MORE THAN 1000,000 POPULATION" (BMR)" CENSUS
USA+45 SOCIETY CRIME ADJUST WEALTH...GEOG SOC GP/REL
CONCPT INDICATOR SAMP CHARTS SOC/INTEG 20. PAGE 5
E0098

B57

NJ LAW AND LEGISLATIVE BURE, NEW JERSEY APPORT
LEGISLAVTIVE REAPPORTIONMENT (PAMPHLET). USA+45 LEGIS
ACT/RES ADJUD...STAT CHARTS 20 NEW/JERSEY. PAGE 2 CENSUS
E0041 REPRESENT

B60

GONZALEZ NAVARRO M., LA COLONIZACION EN MEXICO, ECO/UNDEV
1877-1910. AGRI NAT/G PLAN PROB/SOLV INCOME GEOG
...POLICY JURID CENSUS 19/20 MEXIC/AMER MIGRATION. HABITAT
PAGE 44 E0883 COLONIAL

B61

FLINN M.W., AN ECONOMIC AND SOCIAL HISTORY OF SOCIETY
BRITAIN, 1066-1939. UK LAW STRATA STRUCT AGRI SOC
DIST/IND INDUS WORKER INT/TRADE WAR...CENSUS 11/20.
PAGE 39 E0766

N62

TWENTIETH CENTURY FUND, ONE MAN - ONE VOTE APPORT
(PAMPHLET). USA+45 CONSTN CONFER CT/SYS REGION LEGIS
CONSEN FEDERAL ROLE...CENSUS 20 CONGRESS. PAGE 97 REPRESENT
E1947 PROVS

B63
GALLAGHER J.F.,SUPERVISORIAL DISTRICTING IN			APPORT
CALIFORNIA COUNTIES: 1960-1963 (PAMPHLET). USA+45		REGION
ADJUD ADMIN PARTIC CHOOSE GP/REL...CENSUS 20			REPRESENT
CALIFORNIA. PAGE 42 E0828								LOC/G

B63
REOCK E.C. JR.,POPULATION INEQUALITY AMONG COUNTIES	APPORT
IN THE NEW JERSEY LEGISLATURE 1791-1962. PROVS			REPRESENT
ORD/FREE...CENSUS CHARTS 18/20 NEW/JERSEY. PAGE 84		LEGIS
E1687													JURID

B64
WRIGHT G.,RURAL REVOLUTION IN FRANCE: THE PEASANTRY	PWR
IN THE TWENTIETH CENTURY. EUR+WWI MOD/EUR LAW			STRATA
CULTURE AGRI POL/PAR DELIB/GP LEGIS ECO/TAC			FRANCE
EDU/PROP COERCE CHOOSE ATTIT RIGID/FLEX HEALTH			REV
...STAT CENSUS CHARTS VAL/FREE 20. PAGE 107 E2148

B64
WRIGHT Q.,A STUDY OF WAR. LAW NAT/G PROB/SOLV			WAR
BAL/PWR NAT/LISM PEACE ATTIT SOVEREIGN...CENSUS			CONCPT
SOC/INTEG. PAGE 108 E2159								DIPLOM
														CONTROL

B65
NJ LEGIS REAPPORT PLAN COMM,PUBLIC HEARING ON			APPORT
REDISTRICTING AND REAPPORTIONMENT. USA+45 CONSTN		REPRESENT
VOL/ASSN LEGIS DEBATE...POLICY GEOG CENSUS 20			PROVS
NEW/JERSEY. PAGE 77 E1552								JURID

B67
RAE D.,THE POLITICAL CONSEQUENCES OF ELECTORAL			POL/PAR
LAWS. EUR+WWI ICELAND ISRAEL NEW/ZEALND UK USA+45		CHOOSE
ADJUD APPORT GP/REL MAJORITY...MATH STAT CENSUS			NAT/COMP
CHARTS BIBLIOG 20 AUSTRAL. PAGE 83 E1667				REPRESENT

B67
US SENATE COMM ON FOREIGN REL,FOREIGN ASSISTANCE		FOR/AID
ACT OF 1967. VIETNAM WOR+45 DELIB/GP CONFER CONTROL	LAW
WAR WEAPON BAL/PAY...CENSUS CHARTS SENATE. PAGE 102	DIPLOM
E2036													POLICY

L67
CARMICHAEL D.M.,"FORTY YEARS OF WATER POLLUTION		HEALTH
CONTROL IN WISCONSIN: A CASE STUDY." LAW EXTR/IND		CONTROL
INDUS MUNIC DELIB/GP PLAN PROB/SOLV SANCTION			ADMIN
...CENSUS CHARTS 20 WISCONSIN. PAGE 20 E0384			ADJUD

CENTER/PAR....CENTER PARTY (ALL NATIONS)

CENTO....CENTRAL TREATY ORGANIZATION

CENTRAL AFRICA....SEE AFRICA/CEN

CENTRAL AFRICAN REPUBLIC....SEE CENTRL/AFR

CENTRAL INTELLIGENCE AGENCY....SEE CIA

CENTRAL....CENTRALIZATION

C01
BERKELEY G.,"DISCOURSE ON PASSIVE OBEDIENCE" (1712)	INGP/REL
THE WORKS... (VOL. IV)" UNIV DOMIN LEGIT CONTROL		SANCTION
CRIME ADJUST CENTRAL MORAL ORD/FREE...POLICY			RESPECT
WORSHIP. PAGE 10 E0202									GEN/LAWS

B02
GRIFFIN A.P.C.,A LIST OF BOOKS RELATING TO TRUSTS		BIBLIOG/A
(2ND REV. ED.) (PAMPHLET). FRANCE GERMANY UK USA-45	JURID
WOR-45 LAW ECO/DEV INDUS LG/CO NAT/G CAP/ISM			ECO/TAC
CENTRAL DISCRIM PWR LAISSEZ 19/20. PAGE 46 E0919		VOL/ASSN

B03
GRIFFIN A.P.C.,LISTS PUBLISHED 1902-03: GOVERNMENT	BIBLIOG
OWNERSHIP OF RAILROADS (PAMPHLET). USA-45 LAW NAT/G	DIST/IND
RATION GOV/REL CENTRAL SOCISM...POLICY 19/20.			CONTROL
PAGE 46 E0922											ADJUD

B04
GRIFFIN A.P.C.,A LIST OF BOOKS RELATING TO				BIBLIOG/A
RAILROADS IN THEIR RELATION TO THE GOVERNMENT AND		SERV/IND
THE PUBLIC (PAMPHLET). USA-45 LAW ECO/DEV NAT/G		ADJUD
TEC/DEV CAP/ISM LICENSE CENTRAL LAISSEZ...DECISION	ECO/TAC
19/20. PAGE 47 E0925

B07
GRIFFIN A.P.C.,LIST OF MORE RECENT WORKS ON FEDERAL	BIBLIOG/A
CONTROL OF COMMERCE AND CORPORATIONS (PAMPHLET).		NAT/G
USA-45 LAW ECO/DEV FINAN LG/CO TARIFFS TAX LICENSE	JURID
CENTRAL ORD/FREE WEALTH LAISSEZ 19/20. PAGE 47			ECO/TAC
E0931

B08
GRIFFIN A.P.C.,LIST OF WORKS RELATING TO GOVERNMENT	BIBLIOG/A
REGULATION OF INSURANCE UNITED STATES AND FOREIGN		FINAN
COUNTRIES (2ND. ED.) (PAMPHLET). FRANCE GERMANY UK	LAW
USA-45 WOR-45 LG/CO LOC/G NAT/G LEGIS LICENSE ADJUD	CONTROL
LOBBY CENTRAL ORD/FREE 19/20. PAGE 47 E0933

B15
HOBSON J.A.,TOWARDS INTERNATIONAL GOVERNMENT.			FUT
MOD/EUR STRUCT ECO/TAC EDU/PROP ADJUD ALL/VALS			INT/ORG
...SOCIALIST CONCPT GEN/LAWS TOT/POP 20. PAGE 53		CENTRAL
E1059

B33
HELLMAN F.S.,SELECTED LIST OF REFERENCES ON THE		BIBLIOG/A
CONSTITUTIONAL POWERS OF THE PRESIDENT INCLUDING		JURID
POWERS RECENTLY DELEGATED. USA-45 NAT/G EX/STRUC		LAW
TOP/EX CENTRAL FEDERAL PWR 20 PRESIDENT. PAGE 51		CONSTN
E1025

N40
COUNTY GOVERNMENT IN THE UNITED STATES: A LIST OF		BIBLIOG/A
RECENT REFERENCES (PAMPHLET). USA-45 LAW PUB/INST		LOC/G
PLAN BUDGET CT/SYS CENTRAL 20. PAGE 52 E1027			ADMIN
														MUNIC

B50
MONPIED E.,BIBLIOGRAPHIE FEDERALISTE: OUVRAGES			BIBLIOG/A
CHOISIS (VOL. I, MIMEOGRAPHED PAPER). EUR+WWI			FEDERAL
DIPLOM ADMIN REGION ATTIT PACIFISM SOCISM...INT/LAW	CENTRAL
19/20. PAGE 74 E1486									INT/ORG

N51
MONPIED E.,FEDERALIST BIBLIOGRAPHY: ARTICLES AND		BIBLIOG/A
DOCUMENTS PUBLISHED IN BRITISH PERIODICALS				INT/ORG
1945-1951 (MIMEOGRAPHED). EUR+WWI UK WOR+45 DIPLOM	FEDERAL
REGION ATTIT SOCISM...INT/LAW 20. PAGE 74 E1487		CENTRAL

B53
MAJUMDAR B.B.,PROBLEMS OF PUBLIC ADMINISTRATION IN	ECO/UNDEV
INDIA. INDIA INDUS PLAN BUDGET ADJUD CENTRAL DEMAND	GOV/REL
WEALTH...WELF/ST ANTHOL 20 CIVIL/SERV. PAGE 68			ADMIN
E1353													MUNIC

B54
FRIEDMAN W.,THE PUBLIC CORPORATION: A COMPARATIVE		LAW
SYMPOSIUM (UNIVERSITY OF TORONTO SCHOOL OF LAW			SOCISM
COMPARATIVE LAW SERIES, VOL. I). SWEDEN USA+45			LG/CO
INDUS INT/ORG NAT/G REGION CENTRAL FEDERAL...POLICY	OWN
JURID IDEA/COMP NAT/COMP ANTHOL 20 COMMONWLTH
MONOPOLY EUROPE. PAGE 40 E0801

B55
HOGAN W.N.,INTERNATIONAL CONFLICT AND COLLECTIVE		INT/ORG
SECURITY: THE PRINCIPLE OF CONCERN IN INTERNATIONAL	WAR
ORGANIZATION. CONSTN EX/STRUC BAL/PWR DIPLOM ADJUD	ORD/FREE
CONTROL CENTRAL CONSEN PEACE...INT/LAW CONCPT			FORCES
METH/COMP 20 UN LEAGUE/NAT. PAGE 53 E1066

B57
LONG H.A.,USURPERS - FOES OF FREE MAN. LAW NAT/G		CT/SYS
CHIEF LEGIS DOMIN ADJUD REPRESENT GOV/REL ORD/FREE	CENTRAL
LAISSEZ POPULISM...POLICY 18/20 SUPREME/CT				FEDERAL
ROOSEVLT/F CONGRESS CON/INTERP. PAGE 66 E1325			CONSTN

B57
MEYER P.,ADMINISTRATIVE ORGANIZATION: A COMPARATIVE	ADMIN
STUDY OF THE ORGANIZATION OF PUBLIC ADMINISTRATION.	METH/COMP
DENMARK FRANCE NORWAY SWEDEN UK USA+45 ELITES LOC/G	NAT/G
CONSULT LEGIS ADJUD CONTROL LEAD PWR SKILL				CENTRAL
DECISION. PAGE 72 E1449

B58
BLOCH J.,STATES' RIGHTS: THE LAW OF THE LAND.			PROVS
USA+45 USA-45 LAW CONSTN LEGIS CONTROL CT/SYS			NAT/G
FEDERAL ORD/FREE...PREDICT 17/20 CONGRESS				BAL/PWR
SUPREME/CT. PAGE 13 E0246								CENTRAL

B60
PRASAD B.,THE ORIGINS OF PROVINCIAL AUTONOMY. INDIA	CENTRAL
UK FINAN LOC/G FORCES LEGIS CONTROL CT/SYS PWR			PROVS
...JURID 19/20. PAGE 82 E1646							COLONIAL
														NAT/G

C60
HAZARD J.N.,"SETTLING DISPUTES IN SOVIET SOCIETY:		ADJUD
THE FORMATIVE YEARS OF LEGAL INSTITUTIONS." USSR		LAW
NAT/G PROF/ORG PROB/SOLV CONTROL CT/SYS ROUTINE REV	COM
CENTRAL...JURID BIBLIOG 20. PAGE 51 E1017				POLICY

B63
FAWCETT J.E.S.,THE BRITISH COMMONWEALTH IN				INT/LAW
INTERNATIONAL LAW. LAW INT/ORG NAT/G VOL/ASSN			STRUCT
OP/RES DIPLOM ADJUD CENTRAL CONSEN...NET/THEORY		COLONIAL
CMN/WLTH TREATY. PAGE 36 E0723

KLESMENT J.,LEGAL SOURCES AND BIBLIOGRAPHY OF THE
BALTIC STATES (ESTONIA, LATVIA, LITHUANIA). COM
ESTONIA LATVIA LITHUANIA LAW FINAN ADJUD CT/SYS
REGION CENTRAL MARXISM 19/20. PAGE 61 E1223
B63
BIBLIOG/A
JURID
CONSTN
ADMIN

GJUPANOVIC H.,LEGAL SOURCES AND BIBLIOGRAPHY OF
YUGOSLAVIA. COM YUGOSLAVIA LAW LEGIS DIPLOM ADMIN
PARL/PROC REGION CRIME CENTRAL 20. PAGE 44 E0873
B64
BIBLIOG/A
JURID
CONSTN
ADJUD

BARKUN M.,"CONFLICT RESOLUTION THROUGH IMPLICIT
MEDIATION." UNIV BARGAIN CONSEN FEDERAL JURID.
PAGE 8 E0149
S64
CONSULT
CENTRAL
INT/LAW
IDEA/COMP

SCHEINGOLD S.A.,"THE RULE OF LAW IN EUROPEAN
INTEGRATION: THE PATH OF THE SCHUMAN PLAN." EUR+WWI
JUDGE ADJUD FEDERAL ATTIT PWR...RECORD INT BIBLIOG
EEC ECSC. PAGE 87 E1755
C65
INT/LAW
CT/SYS
REGION
CENTRAL

GRUNEWALD D.,PUBLIC POLICY AND THE MODERN
COOPERATION: SELECTED READINGS. USA+45 LAW MARKET
VOL/ASSN CAP/ISM INT/TRADE CENTRAL OWN...SOC ANTHOL
20. PAGE 48 E0954
B66
LG/CO
POLICY
NAT/G
CONTROL

YOUNG W.,EXISTING MECHANISMS OF ARMS CONTROL.
PROC/MFG OP/RES DIPLOM TASK CENTRAL...MGT TREATY.
PAGE 108 E2165
B66
ARMS/CONT
ADMIN
NUC/PWR
ROUTINE

PLANO J.C.,FORGING WORLD ORDER: THE POLITICS OF
INTERNATIONAL ORGANIZATION. PROB/SOLV DIPLOM
CONTROL CENTRAL RATIONAL ORD/FREE...INT/LAW CHARTS
BIBLIOG 20 UN LEAGUE/NAT. PAGE 81 E1618
B67
INT/ORG
ADMIN
JURID

"A PROPOS DES INCITATIONS FINANCIERES AUX
GROUPEMENTS DES COMMUNES: ESSAI D'INTERPRETATION."
FRANCE NAT/G LEGIS ADMIN GOV/REL CENTRAL 20. PAGE 2
E0037
L67
LOC/G
ECO/TAC
APPORT
ADJUD

ANDERSON W.,"THE PERILS OF 'SHARING'." USA+45
ECO/TAC RECEIVE LOBBY GOV/REL CENTRAL COST INCOME
...POLICY PLURIST CONGRESS. PAGE 5 E0095
S67
BUDGET
TAX
FEDERAL
LAW

POSPISIL L.,"LEGAL LEVELS AND MULTIPLICITY OF LEGAL
SYSTEMS IN HUMAN SOCIETIES." WOR+45 CENTRAL PWR
...SOC CHARTS GP/COMP GEN/LAWS. PAGE 81 E1630
S67
LAW
STRATA
JURID
STRUCT

WINES R.,"THE IMPERIAL CIRCLES, PRINCELY DIPLOMACY,
AND IMPERIAL REFORM* 1681-1714." MOD/EUR DELIB/GP
BAL/PWR CONFER ADJUD PARL/PROC PARTIC ATTIT PWR
17/18. PAGE 106 E2132
S67
NAT/G
NAT/LISM
CENTRAL
REGION

CENTRAL/AM....CENTRAL AMERICA

CENTRL/AFR....CENTRAL AFRICAN REPUBLIC

CERMAK/AJ....ANTON J. CERMAK

CEWA....CEWA (AFRICAN TRIBE)

CEYLON....CEYLON

VITTACHIT,EMERGENCY '58. CEYLON UK STRUCT NAT/G
FORCES ADJUD CRIME REV NAT/LISM 20. PAGE 104 E2081
B59
RACE/REL
DISCRIM
DIPLOM
SOVEREIGN

SYATAUW J.J.G.,SOME NEWLY ESTABLISHED ASIAN STATES
AND THE DEVELOPMENT OF INTERNATIONAL LAW. BURMA
CEYLON INDIA INDONESIA ECO/UNDEV COLONIAL NEUTRAL
WAR PEACE SOVEREIGN...CHARTS 19/20. PAGE 95 E1902
B61
INT/LAW
ADJUST
SOCIETY
S/ASIA

RAGHAVAN M.D.,INDIA IN CEYLONESE HISTORY, SOCIETY
AND CULTURE. CEYLON INDIA S/ASIA LAW SOCIETY
INT/TRADE ATTIT...ART/METH JURID SOC LING 20.
PAGE 83 E1668
B64
DIPLOM
CULTURE
SECT
STRUCT

CHACO/WAR....CHACO WAR

CHAD....SEE ALSO AFR

CHAFEE Z. E0413

CHAMBERLAIN J.P. E0414

CHAMBERLAIN N.W. E0415

CHAMBERLIN E.H. E0416

CHAMBERS/J....JORDAN CHAMBERS

CHAMBLISS W.J. E0417

CHAMBR/DEP....CHAMBER OF DEPUTIES (FRANCE)

CHAMBRLN/J....JOSEPH CHAMBERLAIN

CHAMBRLN/N....NEVILLE CHAMBERLAIN

CHANGE (AS GOAL)....SEE ORD/FREE

CHANGE (AS INNOVATION)....SEE CREATE

CHANGE (SOCIAL MOBILITY)....SEE GEOG, STRATA

CHANNING W.E. E0418

CHAPIN B. E0419

CHAPIN F.S. E0420

CHAPMAN B. E0421

CHAPMAN J.W. E0809

CHARACTER....SEE PERSON

CHARISMA....CHARISMA

CHARLES R. E0422

CHARLES/I....CHARLES I OF ENGLAND

AYLMER G.,THE KING'S SERVANTS. UK ELITES CHIEF PAY
CT/SYS WEALTH 17 CROMWELL/O CHARLES/I. PAGE 6 E0122
B61
ADMIN
ROUTINE
EX/STRUC
NAT/G

CHARLESTON....CHARLESTON,SOUTH CAROLINA

BROWN R.M.,THE SOUTH CAROLINA REGULATORS. USA-45
LEGIS LEGIT ADJUD COLONIAL CONTROL WAR...BIBLIOG/A
18 CHARLESTON SOUTH/CAR. PAGE 16 E0315
B63
ORD/FREE
JURID
PWR
PROVS

CHARLTON K. E0423

CHARMATZ J.P. E0424

CHARNAY J.P. E0425

CHARTISM....CHARTISM

CHARTS....GRAPHS, CHARTS, DIAGRAMS, MAPS

CHASE H.W. E1470,E1471

CHASE/S....STUART CHASE

CHATEAUB/F....VICOMTE FRANCOIS RENE DE CHATEAUBRIAND

CHATTANOOG....CHATTANOOGA, TENNESSEE

CHECKS AND BALANCES SYSTEM....SEE BAL/PWR

CHEIN I. E0426

CHEN/YUN....CH'EN YUN

CHENERY W.L. E0427

CHENEY F. E0428

CHIANG....CHIANG KAI-SHEK

CHICAGO....CHICAGO, ILLINOIS

KEFAUVER E.,CRIME IN AMERICA. USA+45 USA-45 MUNIC
NEIGH DELIB/GP TRIBUTE GAMBLE LOBBY SANCTION
...AUD/VIS 20 CAPONE/AL MAFIA MIAMI CHICAGO
DETROIT. PAGE 60 E1194
B51
ELITES
CRIME
PWR
FORCES

B64
FISK W.M.,ADMINISTRATIVE PROCEDURE IN A REGULATORY
AGENCY: THE CAB AND THE NEW YORK-CHICAGO CASE
(PAMPHLET). USA+45 DIST/IND ADMIN CONTROL LOBBY
GP/REL ROLE ORD/FREE NEWYORK/C CHICAGO CAB. PAGE 38
E0758
SERV/IND
ECO/DEV
AIR
JURID

B66
BEELEY A.L.,THE BAIL SYSTEM IN CHICAGO. LAW MUNIC
PUB/INST EFFICIENCY MORAL...CRIMLGY METH/CNCPT STAT
20 CHICAGO. PAGE 9 E0176
JURID
CT/SYS
CRIME
ADJUD

CHICAGO U LAW SCHOOL E0429

CHIEF....PRESIDENT, MONARCH, PRESIDENCY, PREMIER, CHIEF
OFFICER OF ANY GOVERNMENT

NRE
MEYER C.S.,ELIZABETH I AND THE RELIGIOUS SETTLEMENT
OF 1559. UK ELITES CHIEF LEGIS DISCRIM CATHISM 16
CHURCH/STA ELIZABTH/I. PAGE 72 E1445
GP/REL
SECT
LAW
PARL/PROC

B08
WILSON W.,CONSTITUTIONAL GOVERNMENT IN THE UNITED
STATES. USA-45 LAW POL/PAR PROVS CHIEF LEGIS
BAL/PWR ADJUD EXEC FEDERAL PWR 18/20 SUPREME/CT
HOUSE/REP SENATE. PAGE 106 E2130
NAT/G
GOV/REL
CONSTN
PARL/PROC

B12
POLLOCK F.,THE GENIUS OF THE COMMON LAW. CHRIST-17C
UK FINAN CHIEF ACT/RES ADMIN GP/REL ATTIT SOCISM
...ANARCH JURID. PAGE 81 E1624
LAW
CULTURE
CREATE

B14
FIGGIS J.N.,CHURCHES IN THE MODERN STATE (2ND ED.).
LAW CHIEF BAL/PWR PWR...CONCPT CHURCH/STA POPE.
PAGE 38 E0748
SECT
NAT/G
SOCIETY
ORD/FREE

B17
DE VICTORIA F.,DE INDIS ET DE JURE BELLI (1557) IN
F. DE VICTORIA, DE INDIS ET DE JURE BELLI
REFLECTIONES. UNIV NAT/G SECT CHIEF PARTIC COERCE
PEACE MORAL...POLICY 16 INDIAN/AM CHRISTIAN
CONSCN/OBJ. PAGE 30 E0598
WAR
INT/LAW
OWN

B24
HOLDSWORTH W.S.,A HISTORY OF ENGLISH LAW; THE
COMMON LAW AND ITS RIVALS (VOL. VI). UK STRATA
EX/STRUC ADJUD ADMIN CONTROL CT/SYS...JURID CONCPT
GEN/LAWS 17 COMMONWLTH PARLIAMENT ENGLSH/LAW
COMMON/LAW. PAGE 54 E1074
LAW
CONSTN
LEGIS
CHIEF

B24
HOLDSWORTH W.S.,A HISTORY OF ENGLISH LAW; THE
COMMON LAW AND ITS RIVALS (VOL. IV). UK SEA AGRI
CHIEF ADJUD CONTROL CRIME GOV/REL...INT/LAW JURID
NAT/COMP 16/17 PARLIAMENT COMMON/LAW CANON/LAW
ENGLSH/LAW. PAGE 54 E1075
LAW
LEGIS
CT/SYS
CONSTN

B26
FORTESCUE J.,THE GOVERNANCE OF ENGLAND (1471-76).
UK LAW FINAN SECT LEGIS PROB/SOLV TAX DOMIN ADMIN
GP/REL COST ORD/FREE PWR 14/15. PAGE 39 E0776
CONSERVE
CONSTN
CHIEF
NAT/G

B27
JOHN OF SALISBURY,THE STATESMAN'S BOOK (1159)
(TRANS. BY J. DICKINSON). DOMIN GP/REL MORAL
ORD/FREE PWR CONSERVE...CATH CONCPT 12. PAGE 59
E1169
NAT/G
SECT
CHIEF
LAW

B28
HOBBES T.,THE ELEMENTS OF LAW, NATURAL AND POLITIC
(1650). STRATA NAT/G SECT CHIEF AGREE ATTIT
ALL/VALS MORAL ORD/FREE POPULISM...POLICY CONCPT.
PAGE 53 E1056
PERSON
LAW
SOVEREIGN
CONSERVE

B35
LUCE R.,LEGISLATIVE PROBLEMS. CONSTN CHIEF JUDGE
BUDGET CONFER ETIQUET CONTROL MORAL PWR NEW/LIB
CONGRESS. PAGE 67 E1331
TREND
ADMIN
LEGIS

B38
GRISWOLD A.W.,THE FAR EASTERN POLICY OF THE UNITED
STATES. ASIA S/ASIA USA-45 INT/ORG INT/TRADE WAR
NAT/LISM...BIBLIOG 19/20 LEAGUE/NAT ROOSEVLT/T
ROOSEVLT/F WILSON/W TREATY. PAGE 47 E0943
DIPLOM
POLICY
CHIEF

B38
HELLMAN F.S.,THE SUPREME COURT ISSUE: SELECTED LIST
OF REFERENCES. USA-45 NAT/G CHIEF EX/STRUC JUDGE
ATTIT...JURID 20 PRESIDENT ROOSEVLT/F SUPREME/CT.
PAGE 51 E1026
BIBLIOG/A
CONSTN
CT/SYS
LAW

B38
HOLDSWORTH W.S.,A HISTORY OF ENGLISH LAW; THE
CENTURIES OF SETTLEMENT AND REFORM (VOL. X). INDIA
UK CONSTN NAT/G CHIEF LEGIS ADMIN COLONIAL CT/SYS
CHOOSE ORD/FREE PWR...JURID 18 PARLIAMENT
COMMONWLTH COMMON/LAW. PAGE 54 E1077
LAW
LOC/G
EX/STRUC
ADJUD

B38
SAINT-PIERRE C.I.,SCHEME FOR LASTING PEACE (TRANS.
BY H. BELLOT). INDUS NAT/G CHIEF FORCES INT/TRADE
CT/SYS WAR PWR SOVEREIGN WEALTH...POLICY 18.
PAGE 87 E1741
INT/ORG
PEACE
AGREE
INT/LAW

B40
ANDERSON W.,FUNDAMENTALS OF AMERICAN GOVERNMENT.
USA-45 LAW POL/PAR CHIEF EX/STRUC BUDGET ADMIN
CT/SYS PARL/PROC CHOOSE FEDERAL...BIBLIOG 20.
PAGE 5 E0093
NAT/G
LOC/G
GOV/REL
CONSTN

B40
HOBBES T.,A DIALOGUE BETWEEN A PHILOSOPHER AND A
STUDENT OF THE COMMON LAWS OF ENGLAND (1667?). UK
SECT DOMIN ADJUD CRIME INCOME OWN UTIL ORD/FREE PWR
SOVEREIGN...JURID GEN/LAWS 17. PAGE 53 E1057
CT/SYS
CHIEF
SANCTION

B40
MCILWAIN C.H.,CONSTITUTIONALISM, ANCIENT AND
MODERN. CHRIST-17C MOD/EUR NAT/G CHIEF PROB/SOLV
INSPECT AUTHORIT ORD/FREE PWR...TIME/SEQ ROMAN/REP.
PAGE 71 E1418
CONSTN
GEN/LAWS
LAW

B41
BIRDSALL P.,VERSAILLES TWENTY YEARS AFTER. MOD/EUR
POL/PAR CHIEF CONSULT FORCES LEGIS REPAR PEACE
ORD/FREE...BIBLIOG 20 PRESIDENT TREATY. PAGE 12
E0231
DIPLOM
NAT/LISM
WAR

B42
CARR R.K.,THE SUPREME COURT AND JUDICIAL REVIEW.
NAT/G CHIEF LEGIS OP/RES LEAD GOV/REL GP/REL ATTIT
...POLICY DECISION 18/20 SUPREME/CT PRESIDENT
CONGRESS. PAGE 20 E0394
CT/SYS
CONSTN
JURID
PWR

B42
FORTESCU J.,IN PRAISE OF ENGLISH LAW (1464) (TRANS.
BY S.B. CHRIMES). UK ELITES CHIEF FORCES CT/SYS
COERCE CRIME GOV/REL ILLEGIT...JURID GOV/COMP
GEN/LAWS 15. PAGE 39 E0774
LAW
CONSTN
LEGIS
ORD/FREE

B42
HEGEL G.W.F.,PHILOSOPHY OF RIGHT. UNIV FAM SECT
CHIEF AGREE WAR MARRIAGE OWN ORD/FREE...POLICY
CONCPT. PAGE 51 E1023
NAT/G
LAW
RATIONAL

B44
RUDIN H.R.,ARMISTICE 1918. FRANCE GERMANY MOD/EUR
UK USA-45 NAT/G CHIEF DELIB/GP FORCES BAL/PWR REPAR
ARMS/CONT 20 WILSON/W TREATY. PAGE 86 E1732
AGREE
WAR
PEACE
DIPLOM

B44
SUAREZ F.,A TREATISE ON LAWS AND GOD THE LAWGIVER
(1612) IN SELECTIONS FROM THREE WORKS, VOL. II.
FRANCE ITALY UK CULTURE NAT/G SECT CHIEF LEGIS
DOMIN LEGIT CT/SYS ORD/FREE PWR WORSHIP 16/17.
PAGE 94 E1892
LAW
JURID
GEN/LAWS
CATH

S44
GRIFFITH E.S.,"THE CHANGING PATTERN OF PUBLIC
POLICY FORMATION." MOD/EUR WOR+45 FINAN CHIEF
CONFER ADMIN LEAD CONSERVE SOCISM TECHRACY...SOC
CHARTS CONGRESS. PAGE 47 E0938
LAW
POLICY
TEC/DEV

B47
MCILWAIN C.H.,CONSTITUTIONALISM: ANCIENT AND
MODERN. USA+45 ROMAN/EMP LAW CHIEF LEGIS CT/SYS
GP/REL ORD/FREE SOVEREIGN...POLICY TIME/SEQ
ROMAN/REP EUROPE. PAGE 71 E1419
CONSTN
NAT/G
PARL/PROC
GOV/COMP

B48
KEIR D.L.,CASES IN CONSTITUTIONAL LAW. UK CHIEF
LEGIS DIPLOM TAX PARL/PROC CRIME GOV/REL...INT/LAW
JURID 17/20. PAGE 60 E1195
CONSTN
LAW
ADJUD
CT/SYS

S48
MILLER B.S.,"A LAW IS PASSED: THE ATOMIC ENERGY ACT
OF 1946." POL/PAR CHIEF CONFER DEBATE CONTROL
PARL/PROC ATTIT KNOWL...POLICY CONGRESS. PAGE 73
E1457
TEC/DEV
LEGIS
DECISION
LAW

B49
DENNING A.,FREEDOM UNDER THE LAW. MOD/EUR UK LAW
SOCIETY CHIEF EX/STRUC LEGIS ADJUD CT/SYS PERS/REL
PERSON 17/20 ENGLSH/LAW. PAGE 31 E0606
ORD/FREE
JURID
NAT/G

S49
PRITCHETT C.H.,"THE PRESIDENT AND THE SUPREME   GOV/REL
COURT." NAT/G CONTROL REPRESENT FEDERAL 20. PAGE 82 CT/SYS
E1651   CHIEF

B51
ROSSITER C.,THE SUPREME COURT AND THE COMMANDER IN CT/SYS
CHIEF. LAW CONSTN DELIB/GP EX/STRUC LEGIS TOP/EX   CHIEF
ADJUD CONTROL...DECISION SOC/EXP PRESIDENT. PAGE 86 WAR
E1724   PWR

B52
DE GRAZIA A.,POLITICAL ORGANIZATION. CONSTN LOC/G   FEDERAL
MUNIC NAT/G CHIEF LEGIS TOP/EX ADJUD CT/SYS   LAW
PERS/REL...INT/LAW MYTH UN. PAGE 29 E0581   ADMIN

B52
JENNINGS W.I.,CONSTITUTIONAL LAWS OF THE   CONSTN
COMMONWEALTH. UK LAW CHIEF LEGIS TAX CT/SYS   JURID
PARL/PROC GOV/REL...INT/LAW 18/20 COMMONWLTH   ADJUD
ENGLSH/LAW COMMON/LAW. PAGE 58 E1165   COLONIAL

L52
WRIGHT Q.,"CONGRESS AND THE TREATY-MAKING POWER."   ROUTINE
USA+45 WOR+45 CONSTN INTELL NAT/G CHIEF CONSULT   DIPLOM
EX/STRUC LEGIS TOP/EX CREATE GOV/REL DISPL DRIVE   INT/LAW
RIGID/FLEX...TREND TOT/POP CONGRESS CONGRESS 20   DELIB/GP
TREATY. PAGE 108 E2154

B54
BROGAN D.W.,POLITICS IN AMERICA. LAW POL/PAR CHIEF NAT/G
LEGIS LOBBY CHOOSE REPRESENT GP/REL RACE/REL   CONSTN
FEDERAL MORAL...BIBLIOG 20 PRESIDENT CONGRESS.   USA+45
PAGE 16 E0304

C54
CALDWELL L.K.,"THE GOVERNMENT AND ADMINISTRATION OF PROVS
NEW YORK." LOC/G MUNIC POL/PAR SCHOOL CHIEF LEGIS   ADMIN
PLAN TAX CT/SYS...MGT SOC/WK BIBLIOG 20 NEWYORK/C. CONSTN
PAGE 19 E0365   EX/STRUC

B55
BERNSTEIN M.H.,REGULATING BUSINESS BY INDEPENDENT   DELIB/GP
COMMISSION. USA+45 USA-45 LG/CO CHIEF LEGIS   CONTROL
PROB/SOLV ADJUD SANCTION GP/REL ATTIT...TIME/SEQ   CONSULT
19/20 MONOPOLY PRESIDENT CONGRESS. PAGE 11 E0214

B55
SVARLIEN O.,AN INTRODUCTION TO THE LAW OF NATIONS. INT/LAW
SEA AIR INT/ORG NAT/G CHIEF ADMIN AGREE WAR PRIVIL DIPLOM
ORD/FREE SOVEREIGN...BIBLIOG 16/20. PAGE 95 E1897

B56
ABELS J.,THE TRUMAN SCANDALS. USA+45 USA-45 POL/PAR CRIME
TAX LEGIT CT/SYS CHOOSE PRIVIL MORAL WEALTH 20   ADMIN
TRUMAN/HS PRESIDENT CONGRESS. PAGE 2 E0043   CHIEF
                                                    TRIBUTE

B56
BOTERO G.,THE REASON OF STATE AND THE GREATNESS OF PHIL/SCI
CITIES. SECT CHIEF FORCES PLAN LEAD WAR MORAL   NEW/IDEA
...POLICY 16 MACHIAVELL TREATY. PAGE 14 E0272   CONTROL

B56
BROWNE D.G.,THE RISE OF SCOTLAND YARD: A HISTORY OF CRIMLGY
THE METROPOLITAN POLICE. UK MUNIC CHIEF ADMIN CRIME LEGIS
GP/REL 19/20. PAGE 16 E0316   CONTROL
                                                    FORCES

B56
ZINN C.J.,HOW OUR LAWS ARE MADE: BROCHURE HOUSE OF LEGIS
REPRESENTATIVES DOCUMENT 451. LAW CONSTN CHIEF   DELIB/GP
EX/STRUC PROB/SOLV HOUSE/REP SENATE. PAGE 108 E2171 PARL/PROC
                                                    ROUTINE

L56
CARRINGTON P.D.,"POLITICAL QUESTIONS: THE JUDICIAL ADJUD
CHECK ON THE EXECUTIVE." USA+45 LAW CHIEF 20.   EXEC
PAGE 20 E0395   PWR
                                                    REPRESENT

S56
NOBLEMAN E.E.,"THE DELEGATION OF PRESIDENTIAL   CHIEF
FUNCTIONS: CONSTITUTIONAL AND LEGAL ASPECTS."   REPRESENT
USA+45 CONSTN NAT/G CONTROL 20. PAGE 77 E1553   EX/STRUC
                                                    LAW

S56
TANENHAUS J.,"THE SUPREME COURT AND PRESIDENTIAL   CT/SYS
POWER." USA+45 USA-45 NAT/G ADJUD GOV/REL FEDERAL   PWR
20 PRESIDENT. PAGE 95 E1907   CONTROL
                                                    CHIEF

B57
LONG H.A.,USURPERS - FOES OF FREE MAN. LAW NAT/G   CT/SYS

CHIEF LEGIS DOMIN ADJUD REPRESENT GOV/REL ORD/FREE CENTRAL
LAISSEZ POPULISM...POLICY 18/20 SUPREME/CT   FEDERAL
ROOSEVLT/F CONGRESS CON/INTERP. PAGE 66 E1325   CONSTN

B57
POUND R.,THE DEVELOPMENT OF CONSTITUTIONAL   LAW
GUARANTEES OF LIBERTY. UK USA-45 CHIEF COLONIAL REV CONSTN
...JURID CONCPT 15/20. PAGE 82 E1638   ORD/FREE
                                                    ATTIT

B57
SCHUBERT G.A.,THE PRESIDENCY IN THE COURTS. CONSTN PWR
FORCES DIPLOM TARIFFS ADJUD CONTROL WAR...DECISION CT/SYS
MGT CHARTS 18/20 PRESIDENT CONGRESS SUPREME/CT.   LEGIT
PAGE 89 E1778   CHIEF

B58
HAND L.,THE BILL OF RIGHTS. USA+45 USA-45 CHIEF   CONSTN
LEGIS BAL/PWR ROLE PWR 18/20 SUPREME/CT CONGRESS   JURID
AMEND/V PRESIDENT AMEND/XIV. PAGE 50 E0994   ORD/FREE
                                                    CT/SYS

B58
MOEN N.W.,THE GOVERNMENT OF SCOTLAND 1603 - 1625.   CHIEF
UK JUDGE ADMIN GP/REL PWR 17 SCOTLAND COMMON/LAW.   JURID
PAGE 74 E1479   CONTROL
                                                    PARL/PROC

B58
STRONG C.F.,MODERN POLITICAL CONSTITUTIONS. LAW   CONSTN
CHIEF DELIB/GP EX/STRUC LEGIS ADJUD CHOOSE FEDERAL IDEA/COMP
POPULISM...CONCPT BIBLIOG 20 UN. PAGE 94 E1887   NAT/G

B58
US CONGRESS,FREEDOM OF INFORMATION AND SECRECY IN   CHIEF
GOVERNMENT (2 VOLS.). USA+45 DELIB/GP EX/STRUC   PRIVIL
EDU/PROP PWR 20 CONGRESS PRESIDENT. PAGE 99 E1988   CONSTN
                                                    LAW

B59
US SENATE COMM ON JUDICIARY,EXECUTIVE PRIVILEGE.   CHIEF
USA+45 DELIB/GP CONTROL KNOWL PWR 20 CONGRESS   PRIVIL
PRESIDENT. PAGE 102 E2042   CONSTN
                                                    LAW

B59
VAN CAENEGEM R.C.,ROYAL WRITS IN ENGLAND FROM THE   JURID
CONQUEST TO GLANVILL. UK JUDGE...TREND IDEA/COMP   CHIEF
11/12 COMMON/LAW. PAGE 103 E2067   ADJUD
                                                    CT/SYS

B60
BERTHOLD O.,KAISER, VOLK UND AVIGNON. GERMANY CHIEF DIPLOM
LEGIT LEAD NAT/LISM CONSERVE 14 POPE CHRUCH/STA   CATHISM
LUDWIG/BAV JOHN/XXII. PAGE 11 E0217   JURID

B60
BLANSHARD P.,GOD AND MAN IN WASHINGTON. USA+45   NAT/G
CHIEF LEGIS LEGIT CT/SYS PRIVIL ATTIT ORD/FREE   SECT
...POLICY CONCPT 20 SUPREME/CT CONGRESS PRESIDENT   GP/REL
CHURCH/STA. PAGE 12 E0242   POL/PAR

B60
BYRD E.M. JR.,TREATIES AND EXECUTIVE AGREEMENTS IN CHIEF
THE UNITED STATES: THEIR SEPARATE ROLES AND   INT/LAW
LIMITATIONS. USA+45 USA-45 EX/STRUC TARIFFS CT/SYS DIPLOM
GOV/REL FEDERAL...IDEA/COMP BIBLIOG SUPREME/CT
SENATE CONGRESS. PAGE 18 E0353

B60
CARPER E.T.,THE DEFENSE APPROPRIATIONS RIDER   GOV/REL
(PAMPHLET). USA+45 CONSTN CHIEF DELIB/GP LEGIS   ADJUD
BUDGET LOBBY CIVMIL/REL...POLICY 20 CONGRESS   LAW
EISNHWR/DD DEPT/DEFEN PRESIDENT BOSTON. PAGE 20   CONTROL
E0390

B60
CASTBERG F.,FREEDOM OF SPEECH IN THE WEST. FRANCE   ORD/FREE
GERMANY USA+45 USA-45 LAW CONSTN CHIEF PRESS   SANCTION
DISCRIM...CONCPT 18/20. PAGE 21 E0406   ADJUD
                                                    NAT/COMP

B60
PRICE D.,THE SECRETARY OF STATE. USA+45 CONSTN   CONSULT
ELITES INTELL CHIEF EX/STRUC TOP/EX LEGIT ATTIT PWR DIPLOM
SKILL...DECISION 20 CONGRESS. PAGE 82 E1650   INT/LAW

B60
SCHUBERT G.A.,CONSTITUTIONAL POLITICS: THE   CONSTN
POLITICAL BEHAVIOR OF SUPREME COURT JUSTICES AND   CT/SYS
THE CONSTITUTIONAL POLICIES THEY MAKE. LAW ELITES   JURID
CHIEF DELIB/GP EX/STRUC LEGIS DISCRIM ORD/FREE PWR DECISION
...POLICY MAJORIT CHARTS SUPREME/CT CONGRESS.
PAGE 89 E1781

S60

MANN S.Z.,"POLICY FORMULATION IN THE EXECUTIVE
BRANCH: THE TAFT-HARTLEY EXPERIENCE." USA+45 LABOR
CHIEF INGP/REL 20 NLRB. PAGE 68 E1360

EXEC
GOV/REL
EX/STRUC
PROB/SOLV

B61

AYLMER G.,THE KING'S SERVANTS. UK ELITES CHIEF PAY
CT/SYS WEALTH 17 CROMWELL/O CHARLES/I. PAGE 6 E0122

ADMIN
ROUTINE
EX/STRUC
NAT/G

B61

GUIZOT F.P.G.,HISTORY OF THE ORIGIN OF
REPRESENTATIVE GOVERNMENT IN EUROPE. CHRIST-17C
FRANCE MOD/EUR SPAIN UK LAW CHIEF FORCES POPULISM
...MAJORIT TIME/SEQ GOV/COMP NAT/COMP 4/19
PARLIAMENT. PAGE 48 E0961

LEGIS
REPRESENT
CONSTN
NAT/G

B61

KURLAND P.B.,RELIGION AND THE LAW. USA+45 USA-45
CONSTN PROVS CHIEF ADJUD SANCTION PRIVIL CATHISM
...POLICY 17/20 SUPREME/CT PRESIDENT CHURCH/STA.
PAGE 62 E1239

SECT
NAT/G
CT/SYS
GP/REL

B61

LA PONCE J.A.,THE GOVERNMENT OF THE FIFTH REPUBLIC:
FRENCH POLITICAL PARTIES AND THE CONSTITUTION.
ALGERIA FRANCE LAW NAT/G DELIB/GP LEGIS ECO/TAC
MARXISM SOCISM...CHARTS BIBLIOG/A 20 DEGAULLE/C.
PAGE 62 E1243

PWR
POL/PAR
CONSTN
CHIEF

B61

SCOTT A.M.,POLITICS, USA; CASES ON THE AMERICAN
DEMOCRATIC PROCESS. USA+45 CHIEF FORCES DIPLOM
LOBBY CHOOSE RACE/REL FEDERAL ATTIT...JURID ANTHOL
T 20 PRESIDENT CONGRESS CIVIL/LIB. PAGE 90 E1795

CT/SYS
CONSTN
NAT/G
PLAN

B62

BOCK E.A.,CASE STUDIES IN AMERICAN GOVERNMENT.
USA+45 ECO/DEV CHIEF EDU/PROP CT/SYS RACE/REL
ORD/FREE...JURID MGT PHIL/SCI PRESIDENT CASEBOOK.
PAGE 13 E0256

POLICY
LEGIS
IDEA/COMP
NAT/G

B62

DUROSELLE J.B.,HISTOIRE DIPLOMATIQUE DE 1919 A NOS
JOURS (3RD ED.). FRANCE INT/ORG CHIEF FORCES CONFER
ARMS/CONT WAR PEACE ORD/FREE...T TREATY 20
COLD/WAR. PAGE 34 E0667

DIPLOM
WOR+45
WOR-45

B62

FROMAN L.A. JR.,PEOPLE AND POLITICS: AN ANALYSIS OF
THE AMERICAN POLITICAL SYSTEM. USA+45 CHIEF
DELIB/GP EX/STRUC LEGIS TOP/EX CT/SYS LOBBY
PERS/REL PWR...POLICY DECISION. PAGE 41 E0813

POL/PAR
PROB/SOLV
GOV/REL

B62

HSUEH S.--S.,GOVERNMENT AND ADMINISTRATION OF HONG
KONG. CHIEF DELIB/GP LEGIS CT/SYS REPRESENT GOV/REL
20 HONG/KONG CITY/MGT CIVIL/SERV GOVERNOR. PAGE 55
E1106

ADMIN
LOC/G
COLONIAL
EX/STRUC

B62

MASON A.T.,THE SUPREME COURT: PALADIUM OF FREEDOM.
USA-45 NAT/G POL/PAR CHIEF LEGIS ADJUD PARL/PROC
FEDERAL PWR...POLICY BIOG 18/20 SUPREME/CT
ROOSEVLT/F JEFFERSN/T MARSHALL/J HUGHES/CE. PAGE 69
E1378

CONSTN
CT/SYS
JURID

B62

PHILLIPS O.H.,CONSTITUTIONAL AND ADMINISTRATIVE LAW
(3RD ED.). UK INT/ORG LOC/G CHIEF EX/STRUC LEGIS
BAL/PWR ADJUD COLONIAL CT/SYS PWR...CHARTS 20.
PAGE 80 E1613

JURID
ADMIN
CONSTN
NAT/G

B63

BADI J.,THE GOVERNMENT OF THE STATE OF ISRAEL: A
CRITICAL ACCOUNT OF ITS PARLIAMENT, EXECUTIVE, AND
JUDICIARY. ISRAEL ECO/DEV CHIEF DELIB/GP LEGIS
DIPLOM CT/SYS INGP/REL PEACE ORD/FREE...BIBLIOG 20
PARLIAMENT ARABS MIGRATION. PAGE 7 E0131

NAT/G
CONSTN
EX/STRUC
POL/PAR

B63

REITZEL A.M.,DAS MAINZER KRONUNGSRECHT UND DIE
POLITISCHE PROBLEMATIK. GERMANY MUNIC LEGIT CATHISM
12/13. PAGE 84 E1684

CHIEF
JURID
CHOOSE
SECT

B63

ROBERT J.,LA MONARCHIE MAROCAINE. MOROCCO LABOR
MUNIC POL/PAR EX/STRUC ORD/FREE PWR...JURID TREND T
20. PAGE 85 E1702

CHIEF
CONSERVE
ADMIN
CONSTN

N63

US PRES COMN REGIS AND VOTING,REPORT ON

CHOOSE

REGISTRATION AND VOTING (PAMPHLET). USA+45 POL/PAR
CHIEF EDU/PROP PARTIC REPRESENT ATTIT...PSY CHARTS
20. PAGE 101 E2023

LAW
SUFF
INSPECT

B64

BOUVIER-AJAM M.,MANUEL TECHNIQUE ET PRATIQUE DU
MAIRE ET DES ELUS ET AGENTS COMMUNAUX. FRANCE LOC/G
BUDGET CHOOSE GP/REL SUPEGO...JURID BIBLIOG 20
MAYOR COMMUNES. PAGE 14 E0274

MUNIC
ADMIN
CHIEF
NEIGH

B64

DANELSKI D.J.,A SUPREME COURT JUSTICE IS APPOINTED.
CHIEF LEGIS CONFER DEBATE EXEC PERSON PWR...BIOG 20
CONGRESS PRESIDENT. PAGE 28 E0564

CHOOSE
JUDGE
DECISION

B64

DUMON F.,LE BRESIL; SES INSTITUTIONS POLITIQUES ET
JUDICIARIES. BRAZIL POL/PAR CHIEF LEGIS ORD/FREE
19/20. PAGE 33 E0658

CONSTN
JURID
CT/SYS
GOV/REL

B64

GOODNOW H.F.,THE CIVIL SERVICE OF PAKISTAN:
BUREAUCRACY IN A NEW NATION. INDIA PAKISTAN S/ASIA
ECO/UNDEV PROVS CHIEF PARTIC CHOOSE EFFICIENCY PWR
...BIBLIOG 20. PAGE 45 E0889

ADMIN
GOV/REL
LAW
NAT/G

B64

GROVES H.E.,THE CONSTITUTION OF MALAYSIA. MALAYSIA
POL/PAR CHIEF CONSULT DELIB/GP CT/SYS PARL/PROC
CHOOSE FEDERAL ORD/FREE 20. PAGE 48 E0953

CONSTN
NAT/G
LAW

B64

HALLER W.,DER SCHWEDISCHE JUSTITIEOMBUDSMAN.
DENMARK FINLAND NORWAY SWEDEN LEGIS ADJUD CONTROL
PERSON ORD/FREE...NAT/COMP 20 OMBUDSMAN. PAGE 50
E0986

JURID
PARL/PROC
ADMIN
CHIEF

B64

HOLDSWORTH W.S.,A HISTORY OF ENGLISH LAW; THE
CENTURIES OF DEVELOPMENT AND REFORM (VOL. XIV). UK
CONSTN LOC/G NAT/G POL/PAR CHIEF EX/STRUC ADJUD
COLONIAL ATTIT...INT/LAW JURID 18/19 TORY/PARTY
COMMONWLTH WHIG/PARTY COMMON/LAW. PAGE 54 E1081

LAW
LEGIS
LEAD
CT/SYS

B64

MINAR D.W.,IDEAS AND POLITICS: THE AMERICAN
EXPERIENCE. SECT CHIEF LEGIS CREATE ADJUD EXEC REV
PWR...PHIL/SCI CONCPT IDEA/COMP 18/20 HAMILTON/A
JEFFERSN/T DECLAR/IND JACKSON/A PRESIDENT. PAGE 73
E1464

CONSTN
NAT/G
FEDERAL

B64

MITAU G.T.,PROXIMATE SOLUTIONS: CASE PROBLEMS IN
STATE AND LOCAL GOVERNMENT. USA+45 CONSTN NAT/G
CHIEF LEGIS CT/SYS EXEC GOV/REL GP/REL PWR 20
CASEBOOK. PAGE 73 E1470

PROVS
LOC/G
ADJUD

B64

MITCHELL B.,A BIOGRAPHY OF THE CONSTITUTION OF THE
UNITED STATES. USA+45 USA-45 PROVS CHIEF LEGIS
DEBATE ADJUD SUFF FEDERAL...SOC 18/20 SUPREME/CT
CONGRESS SENATE HOUSE/REP PRESIDENT. PAGE 73 E1472

CONSTN
LAW
JURID

B64

TOMPKINS D.C.,PRESIDENTIAL SUCCESSION. USA+45 CHIEF
ADJUD 20 PRESIDENT CONGRESS. PAGE 96 E1933

BIBLIOG/A
EX/STRUC
CONSTN
TOP/EX

B65

CHARNAY J.P.,LE SUFFRAGE POLITIQUE EN FRANCE;
ELECTIONS PARLEMENTAIRES, ELECTION PRESIDENTIELLE,
REFERENDUMS. FRANCE CONSTN CHIEF DELIB/GP ECO/TAC
EDU/PROP CRIME INGP/REL MORAL ORD/FREE PWR CATHISM
20 PARLIAMENT PRESIDENT. PAGE 22 E0425

CHOOSE
SUFF
NAT/G
LEGIS

B65

CHRIMES S.B.,ENGLISH CONSTITUTIONAL HISTORY (3RD
ED.). UK CHIEF CONSULT DELIB/GP LEGIS CT/SYS 15/20
COMMON/LAW PARLIAMENT. PAGE 22 E0435

CONSTN
BAL/PWR
NAT/G

B65

CONGRESSIONAL QUARTERLY SERV,POLITICS IN AMERICA,
1945-1964: THE POLITICS AND ISSUES OF THE POSTWAR
YEARS. USA+45 LAW FINAN CHIEF DIPLOM APPORT SUFF
...POLICY STAT TREND CHARTS 20 CONGRESS PRESIDENT.
PAGE 25 E0489

CHOOSE
REPRESENT
POL/PAR
LEGIS

B65

FEERICK J.D.,FROM FAILING HANDS: THE STUDY OF
PRESIDENTIAL SUCCESSION. CONSTN NAT/G PROB/SOLV
LEAD PARL/PROC MURDER CHOOSE...NEW/IDEA BIBLIOG 20
KENNEDY/JF JOHNSON/LB PRESIDENT PRE/US/AM
VICE/PRES. PAGE 36 E0724

EX/STRUC
CHIEF
LAW
LEGIS

B65
KEEFE W.J.,THE AMERICAN LEGISLATIVE PROCESS. USA+45   LEGIS
CONSTN POL/PAR CT/SYS REPRESENT FEDERAL ATTIT   NAT/G
PLURISM...MAJORIT 20 CONGRESS PRESIDENT. PAGE 60   CHIEF
E1192   GOV/REL

B65
MOELLER R.,LUDWIG DER BAYER UND DIE KURIE IM KAMPF   JURID
UM DAS REICH. GERMANY LAW SECT LEGIT LEAD GP/REL   CHIEF
CATHISM CONSERVE 14 LUDWIG/BAV POPE CHURCH/STA.   CHOOSE
PAGE 74 E1478   NAT/LISM

B66
BURNS A.C.,PARLIAMENT AS AN EXPORT. WOR+45 CONSTN   PARL/PROC
BARGAIN DEBATE ROUTINE GOV/REL EFFICIENCY...ANTHOL   POL/PAR
COMMONWLTH PARLIAMENT. PAGE 17 E0343   CT/SYS
                                                           CHIEF

B66
DALLIN A.,POLITICS IN THE SOVIET UNION: 7 CASES.   MARXISM
COM USSR LAW POL/PAR CHIEF FORCES WRITING CONTROL   DOMIN
PARL/PROC CIVMIL/REL TOTALISM...ANTHOL 20 KHRUSH/N   ORD/FREE
STALIN/J CASEBOOK COM/PARTY. PAGE 28 E0563   GOV/REL

B66
HOLTZMAN A.,INTEREST GROUPS AND LOBBYING. USA+45   LOBBY
CHIEF ACT/RES ADJUD LEAD PARTIC CHOOSE...POLICY 20   NAT/G
CONGRESS. PAGE 55 E1092   EDU/PROP
                                                           GP/REL

S66
MATTHEWS D.G.,"ETHIOPIAN OUTLINE: A BIBLIOGRAPHIC   BIBLIOG
RESEARCH GUIDE." ETHIOPIA LAW STRUCT ECO/UNDEV AGRI   NAT/G
LABOR SECT CHIEF DELIB/GP EX/STRUC ADMIN...LING   DIPLOM
ORG/CHARTS 20. PAGE 69 E1384   POL/PAR

B67
BAKER L.,BACK TO BACK: THE DUEL BETWEEN FDR AND THE   CHIEF
SUPREME COURT. ELITES LEGIS CREATE DOMIN INGP/REL   CT/SYS
PERSON PWR NEW/LIB 20 ROOSEVLT/F SUPREME/CT SENATE.   PARL/PROC
PAGE 7 E0142   GOV/REL

B67
CAHIER P.,LE DROIT DIPLOMATIQUE CONTEMPORAIN.   INT/LAW
INT/ORG CHIEF ADMIN...T 20. PAGE 18 E0358   DIPLOM
                                                           JURID

B67
FINCHER F.,THE GOVERNMENT OF THE UNITED STATES.   NAT/G
USA+45 USA-45 POL/PAR CHIEF CT/SYS LOBBY GP/REL   EX/STRUC
INGP/REL...CONCPT CHARTS BIBLIOG T 18/20 PRESIDENT   LEGIS
CONGRESS SUPREME/CT. PAGE 38 E0749   OP/RES

L67
SCHUBERT G.,"THE RHETORIC OF CONSTITUTIONAL   CONSTN
CHANGE." USA+45 LAW CULTURE CHIEF LEGIS ADJUD   METH/COMP
CT/SYS ARMS/CONT ADJUST...CHARTS SIMUL. PAGE 89   ORD/FREE
E1777

S67
ADOKO A.,"THE CONSTITUTION OF UGANDA." AFR UGANDA   NAT/G
LOC/G CHIEF FORCES LEGIS ADJUD EXEC CHOOSE NAT/LISM   CONSTN
...IDEA/COMP 20. PAGE 3 E0050   ORD/FREE
                                                           LAW

S67
BRADLEY A.W.,"CONSTITUTION-MAKING IN UGANDA."   NAT/G
UGANDA LAW CHIEF DELIB/GP LEGIS ADMIN EXEC   CREATE
PARL/PROC RACE/REL ORD/FREE...GOV/COMP 20. PAGE 15   CONSTN
E0284   FEDERAL

S67
CHAMBERLAIN N.W.,"STRIKES IN CONTEMPORARY CONTEXT."   LABOR
LAW INDUS NAT/G CHIEF CONFER COST ATTIT ORD/FREE   BARGAIN
...POLICY MGT 20. PAGE 21 E0415   EFFICIENCY
                                                           PROB/SOLV

S67
GOSSETT W.T.,"ELECTING THE PRESIDENT: NEW HOPE FOR   CONSTN
AN OLD IDEAL." FUT USA+45 USA-45 PROVS LEGIS   CHIEF
PROB/SOLV WRITING DEBATE ADJUD REPRESENT...MAJORIT   CHOOSE
DECISION 20 HOUSE/REP PRESIDENT. PAGE 45 E0892   NAT/G

S67
MAYANJA A.,"THE GOVERNMENT'S PROPOSALS ON THE NEW   CONSTN
CONSTITUTION." AFR UGANDA LAW CHIEF LEGIS ADJUD   CONFER
REPRESENT FEDERAL PWR 20. PAGE 69 E1390   ORD/FREE
                                                           NAT/G

S67
MORENO F.J.,"THE SPANISH COLONIAL SYSTEM: A   COLONIAL
FUNCTIONAL APPROACH." SPAIN WOR-45 LAW CHIEF DIPLOM   CONTROL
ADJUD CIVMIL/REL AUTHORIT ROLE PWR...CONCPT 17/20.   NAT/G
PAGE 74 E1492   OP/RES

B70
BLACKSTONE W.,COMMENTARIES ON THE LAWS OF ENGLAND   LAW
(4 VOLS.) (4TH ED.). UK CHIEF DELIB/GP LEGIS WORKER   JURID
CT/SYS SANCTION CRIME OWN...CRIMLGY 18 ENGLSH/LAW.   ADJUD
PAGE 12 E0238   CONSTN

B75
MAINE H.S.,LECTURES ON THE EARLY HISTORY OF   CULTURE
INSTITUTIONS. IRELAND UK CONSTN ELITES STRUCT FAM   LAW
KIN CHIEF LEGIS CT/SYS OWN SOVEREIGN...CONCPT 16   INGP/REL
BENTHAM/J BREHON ROMAN/LAW. PAGE 68 E1351

B87
ADAMS J.,A DEFENSE OF THE CONSTITUTIONS OF   CONSTN
GOVERNMENT OF THE UNITED STATES OF AMERICA. USA-45   BAL/PWR
STRATA CHIEF EX/STRUC LEGIS CT/SYS CONSERVE   PWR
POPULISM...CONCPT CON/ANAL GOV/COMP. PAGE 3 E0048   NAT/G

B96
DE VATTEL E.,THE LAW OF NATIONS. AGRI FINAN CHIEF   LAW
DIPLOM INT/TRADE AGREE OWN ALL/VALS MORAL ORD/FREE   CONCPT
SOVEREIGN...GEN/LAWS 18 NATURL/LAW WOLFF/C. PAGE 30   NAT/G
E0597   INT/LAW

B96
ESMEIN A.,ELEMENTS DE DROIT CONSTITUTIONNEL. FRANCE   LAW
UK CHIEF EX/STRUC LEGIS ADJUD CT/SYS PARL/PROC REV   CONSTN
GOV/REL ORD/FREE...JURID METH/COMP 18/19. PAGE 35   NAT/G
E0697   CONCPT

CHILDREN....SEE AGE/C

CHILDS J.B. E0590

CHILDS M.W. E0430

CHILDS/RS....RICHARD SPENCER CHILDS

CHILE....SEE ALSO L/A+17C

B47
CLAGETT H.L.,A GUIDE TO THE LAW AND LEGAL   BIBLIOG
LITERATURE OF CHILE, 1917-1946. CHILE CONSTN LABOR   L/A+17C
JUDGE ADJUD ADMIN...CRIMLGY INT/LAW JURID CON/ANAL   LAW
20. PAGE 22 E0442   LEGIS

S67
TOMASEK R.D.,"THE CHILEAN-BOLIVIAN LAUCA RIVER   INT/ORG
DISPUTE AND THE OAS." CHILE L/A+17C PROB/SOLV ADJUD   DIPLOM
CONTROL PEACE 20 BOLIV OAS. PAGE 96 E1930   GEOG
                                                           WAR

CHINA....CHINA IN GENERAL; SEE ALSO ASIA

CHINA/COM....COMMUNIST CHINA

B49
US DEPARTMENT OF STATE,SOVIET BIBLIOGRAPHY   BIBLIOG/A
(PAMPHLET). CHINA/COM COM USSR LAW AGRI INT/ORG   MARXISM
ECO/TAC EDU/PROP...POLICY GEOG 20. PAGE 99 E1994   CULTURE
                                                           DIPLOM

B55
UN HEADQUARTERS LIBRARY,BIBLIOGRAPHIE DE LA CHARTE   BIBLIOG/A
DES NATIONS UNIES. CHINA/COM KOREA WOR+45 VOL/ASSN   INT/ORG
CONFER ADMIN COERCE PEACE ATTIT ORD/FREE SOVEREIGN   DIPLOM
...INT/LAW 20 UNESCO UN. PAGE 97 E1953

B56
US HOUSE WAYS MEANS COMMITTEE,TRAFFIC IN, AND   BIO/SOC
CONTROL OF NARCOTICS, BARBITURATES, AND   CONTROL
AMPHETAMINES. CHINA/COM USA+45 SOCIETY LEGIS   PROB/SOLV
ACT/RES EDU/PROP CT/SYS SANCTION PROFIT HEALTH   CRIME
...HEAL PSY STAT 20. PAGE 100 E2011

B60
FISCHER L.,THE SOVIETS IN WORLD AFFAIRS. CHINA/COM   DIPLOM
COM EUR+WWI USSR INT/ORG CONFER LEAD ARMS/CONT REV   NAT/G
PWR...CHARTS 20 TREATY VERSAILLES. PAGE 38 E0755   POLICY
                                                           MARXISM

B61
NEWMAN R.P.,RECOGNITION OF COMMUNIST CHINA? A STUDY   MARXISM
IN ARGUMENT. CHINA/COM NAT/G PROB/SOLV RATIONAL   ATTIT
...INT/LAW LOG IDEA/COMP BIBLIOG 20. PAGE 77 E1544   DIPLOM
                                                           POLICY

S63
WEISSBERG G.,"MAPS AS EVIDENCE IN INTERNATIONAL   LAW
BOUNDARY DISPUTES: A REAPPRAISAL." CHINA/COM   GEOG
EUR+WWI INDIA MOD/EUR S/ASIA INT/ORG NAT/G LEGIT   SOVEREIGN
PERCEPT...JURID CHARTS 20. PAGE 105 E2110

B64
COHEN M.,LAW AND POLITICS IN SPACE: SPECIFIC AND   DELIB/GP
URGENT PROBLEMS IN THE LAW OF OUTER SPACE.   LAW

CHINA/COM COM USA+45 USSR WOR+45 COM/IND INT/ORG   INT/LAW
NAT/G LEGIT NUC/PWR ATTIT BIO/SOC...JURID CONCPT   SPACE
CONGRESS 20 STALIN/J. PAGE 24 E0464

                                                   B64
DOOLIN D.J.,COMMUNIST CHINA: THE POLITICS OF   MARXISM
STUDENT OPPOSITION. CHINA/COM ELITES STRATA ACADEM DEBATE
NAT/G WRITING CT/SYS LEAD PARTIC COERCE TOTALISM   AGE/Y
20. PAGE 32 E0637   PWR

                                                   B64
GRIFFITH W.E.,THE SINO-SOVIET RIFT. ASIA CHINA/COM ATTIT
COM CUBA USSR YUGOSLAVIA NAT/G POL/PAR VOL/ASSN   TIME/SEQ
DELIB/GP FORCES TOP/EX DIPLOM EDU/PROP DRIVE PERSON BAL/PWR
PWR...TREND 20 TREATY. PAGE 47 E0941   SOCISM

                                                   B64
OSSENBECK F.J.,OPEN SPACE AND PEACE. CHINA/COM FUT SPACE
USA+45 USSR LAW PROB/SOLV TEC/DEV EDU/PROP NEUTRAL ORD/FREE
PEACE...AUD/VIS ANTHOL 20. PAGE 79 E1583   DIPLOM
                                                   CREATE

                                                   L65
SHARMA S.P.,"THE INDIA-CHINA BORDER DISPUTE: AN   LAW
INDIAN PERSPECTIVE." ASIA CHINA/COM S/ASIA NAT/G   ATTIT
LEGIT CT/SYS NAT/LISM DRIVE MORAL ORD/FREE PWR 20. SOVEREIGN
PAGE 91 E1815   INDIA

                                                   S65
PRABHAKAR P.,"SURVEY OF RESEARCH AND SOURCE   BIBLIOG
MATERIALS; THE SINO-INDIAN BORDER DISPUTE." ASIA
CHINA/COM INDIA LAW NAT/G PLAN BAL/PWR WAR...POLICY S/ASIA
20 COLD/WAR. PAGE 82 E1645   DIPLOM

                                                   S66
CHIU H.,"COMMUNIST CHINA'S ATTITUDE TOWARD   INT/LAW
INTERNATIONAL LAW" CHINA/COM USSR LAW CONSTN DIPLOM MARXISM
GP/REL 20 LENIN/VI. PAGE 22 E0431   CONCPT
                                                   IDEA/COMP

                                                   B67
LENG S.C.,JUSTICE IN COMMUNIST CHINA: A SURVEY OF   CT/SYS
THE JUDICIAL SYSTEM OF THE CHINESE PEOPLE'S   ADJUD
REPUBLIC. CHINA/COM LAW CONSTN LOC/G NAT/G PROF/ORG JURID
CONSULT FORCES ADMIN CRIME ORD/FREE...BIBLIOG 20   MARXISM
MAO. PAGE 64 E1284

                                                   L68
CHIU H.,"COMMUNIST CHINA'S ATTITUDE TOWARD THE   INT/LAW
UNITED NATIONS: A LEGAL ANALYSIS." CHINA/COM WOR+45 SOVEREIGN
LAW NAT/G DIPLOM CONFER ADJUD PARTIC ATTIT...POLICY INT/ORG
TREND 20 UN. PAGE 22 E0432   REPRESENT

CHINESE/AM....CHINESE IMMIGRANTS TO US AND THEIR DESCENDANTS

CHITTAGONG....CHITTAGONG HILL TRIBES

CHIU H. E0431,E0432

CHOICE (IN DECISION-MAKING)....SEE PROB/SOLV

CHOJNACKI S. E0433

CHOOSE....CHOICE, ELECTION

                                                   N
JOURNAL OF POLITICS. USA+45 USA-45 CONSTN POL/PAR   BIBLIOG/A
EX/STRUC LEGIS PROB/SOLV DIPLOM CT/SYS CHOOSE   NAT/G
RACE/REL 20. PAGE 1 E0011   LAW
                                                   LOC/G

                                                   N
US SUPERINTENDENT OF DOCUMENTS,POLITICAL SCIENCE: BIBLIOG/A
GOVERNMENT, CRIME, DISTRICT OF COLUMBIA (PRICE LIST NAT/G
54). USA+45 LAW CONSTN EX/STRUC WORKER ADJUD ADMIN CRIME
CT/SYS CHOOSE INGP/REL RACE/REL CONGRESS PRESIDENT.
PAGE 103 E2063

                                                   B05
DICEY A.,LAW AND PUBLIC OPINION IN ENGLAND. LAW   ATTIT
CULTURE INTELL SOCIETY NAT/G SECT JUDGE LEGIT   UK
CHOOSE RIGID/FLEX KNOWL...OLD/LIB CONCPT STERTYP
GEN/LAWS 20. PAGE 31 E0620

                                                   B05
GRIFFIN A.P.C.,LIST OF REFERENCES ON PRIMARY   BIBLIOG/A
ELECTIONS (PAMPHLET). USA-45 LAW LOC/G DELIB/GP   POL/PAR
LEGIS OP/RES TASK REPRESENT CONSEN...DECISION 19/20 CHOOSE
CONGRESS. PAGE 47 E0928   POPULISM

                                                   B08
GRIFFIN A.P.C.,REFERENCES ON CORRUPT PRACTICES IN   BIBLIOG/A
ELECTIONS (PAMPHLET). USA-45 LAW CONSTN TRIBUTE   CHOOSE
CRIME REPRESENT...JURID 19/20. PAGE 47 E0934   SUFF
                                                   APPORT

                                                   B12
MEYER H.H.B.,SELECT LIST OF REFERENCES ON THE   BIBLIOG/A
INITIATIVE, REFERENDUM, AND RECALL. MOD/EUR USA-45 NAT/G
LAW LOC/G MUNIC REPRESENT POPULISM 20 CONGRESS.   LEGIS
PAGE 72 E1446   CHOOSE

                                                   B18
PORTER K.H.,A HISTORY OF SUFFRAGE IN THE UNITED   SUFF
STATES. USA-45 LAW CONSTN LOC/G NAT/G POL/PAR WAR   REPRESENT
DISCRIM OWN ATTIT SEX 18/20 NEGRO FEMALE/SEX.   CHOOSE
PAGE 81 E1629   PARTIC

                                                   B18
YUKIO O.,THE VOICE OF JAPANESE DEMOCRACY, AN ESSAY CONSTN
ON CONSTITUTIONAL LOYALTY (TRANS BY J. E. BECKER). MAJORIT
ASIA POL/PAR DELIB/GP EX/STRUC RIGID/FLEX ORD/FREE CHOOSE
PWR...POLICY JURID METH/COMP 19/20 CHINJAP.   NAT/G
PAGE 108 E2167

                                                   N19
OPERATIONS AND POLICY RESEARCH,URUGUAY: ELECTION   POL/PAR
FACTBOOK: NOVEMBER 27, 1966 (PAMPHLET). URUGUAY LAW CHOOSE
NAT/G LEAD REPRESENT...STAT BIOG CHARTS 20. PAGE 79 PLAN
E1576   ATTIT

                                                   N19
PAN AMERICAN UNION,INFORME DE LA MISION DE   CHOOSE
ASISTENCIA TECNICA DE LA OEA A LA REPUBLICA DE   SUFF
HONDURAS EN MATERIA ELECTORAL (PAMPHLET). HONDURAS POL/PAR
CONSTN ORD/FREE...JURID OBS 20 OAS. PAGE 80 E1595   NAT/G

                                                   B23
ROBERT H.M.,PARLIAMENTARY LAW. POL/PAR LEGIS PARTIC PARL/PROC
CHOOSE REPRESENT GP/REL. PAGE 85 E1701   DELIB/GP
                                                   NAT/G
                                                   JURID

                                                   B29
MOLEY R.,POLITICS AND CRIMINAL PROSECUTION. USA-45 PWR
POL/PAR EX/STRUC LEGIT CONTROL LEAD ROUTINE CHOOSE CT/SYS
INGP/REL...JURID CHARTS 20. PAGE 74 E1481   CRIME
                                                   ADJUD

                                                   B30
BIRD F.L.,THE RECALL OF PUBLIC OFFICERS; A STUDY OF REPRESENT
THE OPERATION OF RECALL IN CALIFORNIA. LOC/G MUNIC SANCTION
POL/PAR PROVS PROB/SOLV ADJUD PARTIC...CHARTS   CHOOSE
METH/COMP 20 CALIFORNIA RECALL. PAGE 12 E0230   LAW

                                                   B30
BURLAMAQUI J.J.,PRINCIPLES OF NATURAL AND POLITIC   LAW
LAW (2 VOLS.) (1747-51). EX/STRUC LEGIS AGREE   NAT/G
CT/SYS CHOOSE ROLE SOVEREIGN 18 NATURL/LAW. PAGE 17 ORD/FREE
E0342   CONCPT

                                                   B30
FAIRLIE J.A.,COUNTY GOVERNMENT AND ADMINISTRATION. ADMIN
UK USA-45 NAT/G SCHOOL FORCES BUDGET TAX CT/SYS   GOV/REL
CHOOSE...JURID BIBLIOG 11/20. PAGE 36 E0713   LOC/G
                                                   MUNIC

                                                   B32
FLEMMING D.,THE UNITED STATES AND THE LEAGUE OF   INT/ORG
NATIONS, 1918-1920. FUT USA-45 NAT/G LEGIS TOP/EX   EDU/PROP
DEBATE CHOOSE PEACE ATTIT SOVEREIGN...TIME/SEQ
CON/ANAL CONGRESS LEAGUE/NAT 20 TREATY. PAGE 39
E0764

                                                   B33
REID H.D.,RECUEIL DES COURS; TOME 45: LES   ORD/FREE
SERVITUDES INTERNATIONALES III. FRANCE CONSTN   DIPLOM
DELIB/GP PRESS CONTROL REV WAR CHOOSE PEACE MORAL   LAW
MARITIME TREATY. PAGE 84 E1680

                                                   B38
HOLDSWORTH W.S.,A HISTORY OF ENGLISH LAW; THE   LAW
CENTURIES OF SETTLEMENT AND REFORM (VOL. X). INDIA LOC/G
UK CONSTN NAT/G CHIEF LEGIS ADMIN COLONIAL CT/SYS   EX/STRUC
CHOOSE ORD/FREE PWR...JURID 18 PARLIAMENT   ADJUD
COMMONWLTH COMMON/LAW. PAGE 54 E1077

                                                   S38
CLEMMER D.,"LEADERSHIP PHENOMENA IN A PRISON   PUB/INST
COMMUNITY." NEIGH PLAN CHOOSE PERSON ROLE...OBS   CRIMLGY
INT. PAGE 23 E0452   LEAD
                                                   CLIENT

                                                   B40
ANDERSON W.,FUNDAMENTALS OF AMERICAN GOVERNMENT.   NAT/G
USA-45 LAW POL/PAR CHIEF EX/STRUC BUDGET ADMIN   LOC/G
CT/SYS PARL/PROC CHOOSE FEDERAL...BIBLIOG 20.   GOV/REL
PAGE 5 E0093   CONSTN

                                                   S40
GERTH H.,"THE NAZI PARTY: ITS LEADERSHIP AND   POL/PAR
COMPOSITION" (BMR)" GERMANY ELITES STRATA STRUCT   DOMIN

EX/STRUC FORCES ECO/TAC CT/SYS CHOOSE TOTALISM   LEAD
AGE/Y AUTHORIT PWR 20. PAGE 43 E0851   ADMIN

                                                        C44
JEFFERSON T.,"DEMOCRACY" (1816) IN BASIC WRITINGS."   POPULISM
USA-45 LOC/G NAT/G TAX CT/SYS CHOOSE ORD/FREE   MAJORIT
...GEN/LAWS 18/19 JEFFERSN/T. PAGE 58 E1151   REPRESENT
                                                        CONSTN

                                                        B45
US LIBRARY OF CONGRESS,CONSTITUTIONAL AND STATUTORY   CONSTN
PROVISIONS OF THE STATES (VOL. I). USA-45 CREATE   FEDERAL
TAX CT/SYS CHOOSE SUFF INCOME PWR 20. PAGE 101   PROVS
E2016   JURID

                                                        B49
DE HUSZAR G.B.,EQUALITY IN AMERICA: THE ISSUE OF   DISCRIM
MINORITY RIGHTS. USA+45 USA-45 LAW NEIGH SCHOOL   RACE/REL
LEGIS ACT/RES CHOOSE ATTIT RESPECT...ANTHOL 20   ORD/FREE
NEGRO. PAGE 29 E0585   PROB/SOLV

                                                        B50
JIMENEZ E.,VOTING AND HANDLING OF DISPUTES IN THE   DELIB/GP
SECURITY COUNCIL. WOR+45 CONSTN INT/ORG DIPLOM   ROUTINE
LEGIT DETER CHOOSE MORAL ORD/FREE PWR...JURID
TIME/SEQ COLD/WAR UN 20. PAGE 59 E1168

                                                        B50
MERRIAM C.E.,THE AMERICAN PARTY SYSTEM; AN   POL/PAR
INTRODUCTION TO THE STUDY OF POLITICAL PARTIES IN   CHOOSE
THE UNITED STATES (4TH ED.). USA+45 USA-45 LAW   SUFF
FINAN LOC/G NAT/G PROVS LEAD PARTIC CRIME ATTIT   REPRESENT
18/20 NEGRO CONGRESS PRESIDENT. PAGE 72 E1442

                                                        B51
ANDERSON W.,STATE AND LOCAL GOVERNMENT IN THE   LOC/G
UNITED STATES. USA+45 CONSTN POL/PAR EX/STRUC LEGIS   MUNIC
BUDGET TAX ADJUD CT/SYS CHOOSE...CHARTS T 20.   PROVS
PAGE 5 E0094   GOV/REL

                                                        B51
CAMPBELL E.H.,UNITED STATES CITIZENSHIP AND   LAW
QUALIFICATIONS FOR VOTING IN WASHINGTON. USA+45   CONSTN
NAT/G PROVS...CHARTS BIBLIOG 20 WASHINGT/G. PAGE 19   SUFF
E0371   CHOOSE

                                                        B51
PUSEY M.J.,CHARLES EVANS HUGHES (2 VOLS.). LAW   BIOG
CONSTN NAT/G POL/PAR DIPLOM LEGIT WAR CHOOSE   TOP/EX
PERS/REL DRIVE HEREDITY 19/20 DEPT/STATE LEAGUE/NAT   ADJUD
SUPREME/CT HUGHES/CE WWI. PAGE 83 E1663   PERSON

                                                        B52
APPADORAI A.,THE SUBSTANCE OF POLITICS (6TH ED.).   PHIL/SCI
EX/STRUC LEGIS DIPLOM CT/SYS CHOOSE FASCISM MARXISM   NAT/G
SOCISM...BIBLIOG T. PAGE 5 E0100

                                                        B52
PASCUAL R.R.,PARTYLESS DEMOCRACY. PHILIPPINE   POL/PAR
BARGAIN LOBBY CHOOSE EFFICIENCY ATTIT 20. PAGE 80   ORD/FREE
E1600   JURID
                                                        ECO/UNDEV

                                                        S52
DE GRAZIA A.,"GENERAL THEORY OF APPORTIONMENT"   APPORT
(BMR)" USA+45 USA-45 CONSTN ELITES DELIB/GP PARTIC   LEGIS
REV CHOOSE...JURID 20. PAGE 29 E0582   PROVS
                                                        REPRESENT

                                                        B53
BUTLER D.E.,THE ELECTORAL SYSTEM IN BRITAIN.   CHOOSE
1918-1951. UK LAW POL/PAR SUFF...STAT BIBLIOG 20   LEGIS
PARLIAMENT. PAGE 18 E0348   REPRESENT
                                                        PARTIC

                                                        B53
GROSS B.M.,THE LEGISLATIVE STRUGGLE: A STUDY IN   LEGIS
SOCIAL COMBAT. STRUCT LOC/G POL/PAR JUDGE EDU/PROP   DECISION
DEBATE ETIQUET ADMIN LOBBY CHOOSE GOV/REL INGP/REL   PERSON
HEREDITY ALL/VALS...SOC PRESIDENT. PAGE 48 E0948   LEAD

                                                        B53
STOUT H.M.,BRITISH GOVERNMENT. UK FINAN LOC/G   NAT/G
POL/PAR DELIB/GP DIPLOM ADMIN COLONIAL CHOOSE   PARL/PROC
ORD/FREE...JURID BIBLIOG 20 COMMONWLTH. PAGE 94   CONSTN
E1883   NEW/LIB

                                                        B54
BROGAN D.W.,POLITICS IN AMERICA. LAW POL/PAR CHIEF   NAT/G
LEGIS LOBBY CHOOSE REPRESENT GP/REL RACE/REL   CONSTN
FEDERAL MORAL...BIBLIOG 20 PRESIDENT CONGRESS.   USA+45
PAGE 16 E0304

                                                        B56
ABELS J.,THE TRUMAN SCANDALS. USA+45 USA-45 POL/PAR   CRIME
TAX LEGIT CT/SYS CHOOSE PRIVIL MORAL WEALTH 20   ADMIN

TRUMAN/HS PRESIDENT CONGRESS. PAGE 2 E0043   CHIEF
                                                        TRIBUTE

                                                        B56
PEASLEE A.J.,CONSTITUTIONS OF NATIONS. WOR+45 LAW   CONSTN
NAT/G EX/STRUC LEGIS TOP/EX LEGIT CT/SYS ROUTINE   CON/ANAL
CHOOSE ORD/FREE PWR SOVEREIGN...CHARTS TOT/POP.
PAGE 80 E1605

                                                        B56
SOHN L.B.,BASIC DOCUMENTS OF THE UNITED NATIONS.   DELIB/GP
WOR+45 LAW INT/ORG LEGIT EXEC ROUTINE CHOOSE PWR   CONSTN
...JURID CONCPT GEN/LAWS ANTHOL UN TOT/POP OAS FAO
ILO 20. PAGE 92 E1853

                                                        B57
FAIRCHILD H.P.,THE ANATOMY OF FREEDOM. USA+45   ORD/FREE
ACADEM SCHOOL SECT CAP/ISM PRESS CHOOSE SOCISM.   CONCPT
PAGE 36 E0712   NAT/G
                                                        JURID

                                                        B57
MILLS W.,INDIVIDUAL FREEDOM AND COMMON DEFENSE   ORD/FREE
(PAMPHLET). USA+45 USSR NAT/G EDU/PROP CRIME CHOOSE   CONSTN
20 COLD/WAR. PAGE 73 E1463   INGP/REL
                                                        FORCES

                                                        S57
KNEIER C.M.,"MISLEADING THE VOTERS." CONSTN LEAD   MUNIC
CHOOSE PERS/REL. PAGE 61 E1224   REPRESENT
                                                        LAW
                                                        ATTIT

                                                        B58
CABLE G.W.,THE NEGRO QUESTION: A SELECTION OF   RACE/REL
WRITINGS ON CIVIL RIGHTS IN THE SOUTH. USA+45   CULTURE
STRATA LOC/G POL/PAR GIVE EDU/PROP WRITING CT/SYS   DISCRIM
SANCTION CRIME CHOOSE WORSHIP 20 NEGRO CIV/RIGHTS   ORD/FREE
CONV/LEASE SOUTH/US. PAGE 18 E0355

                                                        B58
MACKENZIE W.J.M.,FREE ELECTIONS: AN ELEMENTARY   EX/STRUC
TEXTBOOK. WOR+45 NAT/G POL/PAR LEGIS TOP/EX   CHOOSE
EDU/PROP LEGIT CT/SYS ATTIT PWR...OBS CHARTS
STERTYP T CONGRESS PARLIAMENT 20. PAGE 67 E1342

                                                        B58
OGDEN F.D.,THE POLL TAX IN THE SOUTH. USA+45 USA-45   TAX
CONSTN ADJUD ADMIN PARTIC CRIME...TIME/SEQ GOV/COMP   CHOOSE
METH/COMP 18/20 SOUTH/US. PAGE 78 E1572   RACE/REL
                                                        DISCRIM

                                                        B58
STRONG C.F.,MODERN POLITICAL CONSTITUTIONS. LAW   CONSTN
CHIEF DELIB/GP EX/STRUC LEGIS ADJUD CHOOSE FEDERAL   IDEA/COMP
POPULISM...CONCPT BIBLIOG 20 UN. PAGE 94 E1887   NAT/G

                                                        L58
INT. SOC. SCI. BULL.,"TECHNIQUES OF MEDIATION AND   VOL/ASSN
CONCILIATION." EUR+WWI USA+45 SOCIETY INDUS INT/ORG   DELIB/GP
LABOR NAT/G LEGIS DIPLOM EDU/PROP CHOOSE ATTIT   INT/LAW
RIGID/FLEX...JURID CONCPT GEN/LAWS 20. PAGE 57
E1129

                                                        S58
STAAR R.F.,"ELECTIONS IN COMMUNIST POLAND." EUR+WWI   COM
SOCIETY INT/ORG NAT/G POL/PAR LEGIS ACT/RES ECO/TAC   CHOOSE
EDU/PROP ADJUD ADMIN ROUTINE COERCE TOTALISM ATTIT   POLAND
ORD/FREE PWR 20. PAGE 93 E1864

                                                        C58
FRIEDRICH C.J.,"AUTHORITY, REASON AND DISCRETION"   AUTHORIT
IN C. FRIEDRICH'S AUTHORITY (BMR)" UNIV EX/STRUC   CHOOSE
ADJUD ADMIN CONTROL INGP/REL ATTIT PERSON PWR.   RATIONAL
PAGE 41 E0807   PERS/REL

                                                        B59
BROMWICH L.,UNION CONSTITUTIONS. CONSTN EX/STRUC   LABOR
PRESS ADJUD CONTROL CHOOSE REPRESENT PWR SAMP.   ROUTINE
PAGE 16 E0306   INGP/REL
                                                        RACE/REL

                                                        B59
HOOK S.,POLITICAL POWER AND PERSONAL FREEDOM: ORD/FREE
CRITICAL STUDIES IN DEMOCRACY, COMMUNISM AND CIVIL   PWR
RIGHTS. UNIV LAW SOCIETY DIPLOM TOTALISM MARXISM   WELF/ST
SOCISM...PHIL/SCI IDEA/COMP 20 CIV/RIGHTS. PAGE 55   CHOOSE
E1094

                                                        B59
NICHOLS R.F.,RELIGION AND AMERICAN DEMOCRACY.   NAT/G
USA+45 USA-45 LAW CHOOSE SUFF MORAL ORD/FREE   SECT
POPULISM...POLICY BIBLIOG 16/20 PRE/US/AM   CONSTN
CHRISTIAN. PAGE 77 E1547   CONCPT

SCHUBERT G.A.,QUANTITATIVE ANALYSIS OF JUDICIAL   JUDGE
BEHAVIOR. ADJUD LEAD CHOOSE INGP/REL MAJORITY ATTIT   CT/SYS
...DECISION JURID CHARTS GAME SIMUL SUPREME/CT.   PERSON
PAGE 89 E1780   QUANT

                                                          B59

COX A.,"THE ROLE OF LAW IN PRESERVING UNION   LABOR
DEMOCRACY." EX/STRUC LEGIS PARTIC ROUTINE CHOOSE   REPRESENT
INGP/REL ORD/FREE. PAGE 27 E0532   LAW
                                                        MAJORIT
                                                          L59

DERGE D.R.,"THE LAWYER AS DECISION-MAKER IN THE   LEGIS
AMERICAN STATE LEGISLATURE." INTELL LOC/G POL/PAR   LAW
CHOOSE AGE HEREDITY PERSON CONSERVE...JURID STAT   DECISION
CHARTS. PAGE 31 E0607   LEAD
                                                          S59

JUNZ A.J.,PRESENT TRENDS IN AMERICAN NATIONAL   POL/PAR
GOVERNMENT. LEGIS DIPLOM ADMIN CT/SYS ORD/FREE   CHOOSE
...CONCPT ANTHOL 20 CONGRESS PRESIDENT SUPREME/CT.   CONSTN
PAGE 2 E0040   NAT/G
                                                          B60

ADRIAN C.R.,STATE AND LOCAL GOVERNMENTS: A STUDY IN   LOC/G
THE POLITICAL PROCESS. USA+45 LAW FINAN MUNIC   PROVS
POL/PAR LEGIS ADJUD EXEC CHOOSE REPRESENT. PAGE 3   GOV/REL
E0051   ATTIT
                                                          B60

BAKER G.E.,STATE CONSTITUTIONS - REAPPORTIONMENT.   APPORT
USA+45 USA-45 CONSTN CHOOSE ATTIT ORD/FREE...JURID   REPRESENT
20. PAGE 7 E0138   PROVS
                                                        LEGIS
                                                          B60

BAKER G.E.,THE POLITICS OF REAPPORTIONMENT IN   VOL/ASSN
WASHINGTON STATE. LAW POL/PAR CREATE EDU/PROP   APPORT
PARL/PROC CHOOSE INGP/REL...CHARTS METH/COMP 20   PROVS
WASHINGT/G LEAGUE/WV. PAGE 7 E0139   LEGIS
                                                          B60

CARTER R.F.,COMMUNITIES AND THEIR SCHOOLS. USA+45   SCHOOL
LAW FINAN PROVS BUDGET TAX LEAD PARTIC CHOOSE...SOC   ACT/RES
INT QU 20. PAGE 20 E0401   NEIGH
                                                        INGP/REL
                                                          B60

NAT'L MUNICIPAL LEAGUE,COMPENDIUM ON LEGISLATIVE   APPORT
APPORTIONMENT. USA+45 LOC/G NAT/G POL/PAR PROVS   REPRESENT
CT/SYS CHOOSE 20 SUPREME/CT CONGRESS. PAGE 76 E1523   LEGIS
                                                        STAT
                                                          B60

PICKLES D.,THE FIFTH FRENCH REPUBLIC. ALGERIA   CONSTN
FRANCE CHOOSE GOV/REL ATTIT CONSERVE...CHARTS 20   ADJUD
DEGAULLE/C. PAGE 80 E1615   NAT/G
                                                        EFFICIENCY
                                                          B60

RIENOW R.,INTRODUCTION TO GOVERNMENT (2ND ED.). UK   CONSTN
USA+45 USSR POL/PAR ADMIN REV CHOOSE SUFF FEDERAL   PARL/PROC
PWR...JURID GOV/COMP T 20. PAGE 85 E1697   REPRESENT
                                                        AUTHORIT
                                                          B60

SCHMIDHAUSER J.R.,THE SUPREME COURT: ITS POLITICS,   JUDGE
PERSONALITIES, AND PROCEDURES. LAW DELIB/GP   JURID
EX/STRUC TOP/EX ADJUD CT/SYS CHOOSE RATIONAL PWR   DECISION
SUPREME/CT. PAGE 88 E1760
                                                          B61

BENNETT G.,THE KENYATTA ELECTION: KENYA 1960-1961.   CHOOSE
AFR INGP/REL RACE/REL CONSEN ATTIT 20 KENYATTA.   POL/PAR
PAGE 10 E0187   LAW
                                                        SUFF
                                                          B61

BURDETTE F.L.,POLITICAL SCIENCE: A SELECTED   BIBLIOG/A
BIBLIOGRAPHY OF BOOKS IN PRINT, WITH ANNOTATIONS   GOV/COMP
(PAMPHLET). LAW LOC/G NAT/G POL/PAR PROVS DIPLOM   CONCPT
EDU/PROP ADMIN CHOOSE ATTIT 20. PAGE 17 E0330   ROUTINE
                                                          B61

CASSINELLI C.W.,THE POLITICS OF FREEDOM. FUT UNIV   MAJORIT
LAW POL/PAR CHOOSE ORD/FREE...POLICY CONCPT MYTH   NAT/G
BIBLIOG. PAGE 21 E0404   PARL/PROC
                                                        PARTIC
                                                          B61

SCOTT A.M.,POLITICS, USA; CASES ON THE AMERICAN   CT/SYS
DEMOCRATIC PROCESS. USA+45 CHIEF FORCES DIPLOM   CONSTN
LOBBY CHOOSE RACE/REL FEDERAL ATTIT...JURID ANTHOL   NAT/G
T 20 PRESIDENT CONGRESS CIVIL/LIB. PAGE 90 E1795   PLAN

WARD R.E.,JAPANESE POLITICAL SCIENCE: A GUIDE TO   BIBLIOG/A
JAPANESE REFERENCE AND RESEARCH MATERIALS (2ND   PHIL/SCI
ED.). LAW CONSTN STRATA NAT/G POL/PAR DELIB/GP
LEGIS ADMIN CHOOSE GP/REL...INT/LAW 19/20 CHINJAP.
PAGE 105 E2099
                                                          B61

SCHUBERT G.,"A PSYCHOMETRIC MODEL OF THE SUPREME   JUDGE
COURT." DELIB/GP ADJUD CHOOSE ATTIT...DECISION   CT/SYS
JURID PSY QUANT STAT HYPO/EXP GEN/METH SUPREME/CT.   PERSON
PAGE 88 E1771   SIMUL
                                                          S61

LEAGUE WOMEN VOTERS MASSACHU,THE MERIT SYSTEM IN   LOC/G
MASSACHUSETTS (PAMPHLET). USA+45 PROVS LEGIT PARTIC   LAW
CHOOSE REPRESENT GOV/REL EFFICIENCY...POLICY   SENIOR
GOV/COMP BIBLIOG 20 MASSACHU. PAGE 64 E1274   PROF/ORG
                                                          N61

BOYD W.J.,PATTERNS OF APPORTIONMENT (PAMPHLET). LAW   MUNIC
CONSTN CHOOSE GOV/COMP. PAGE 14 E0282   PROVS
                                                        REPRESENT
                                                        APPORT
                                                          B62

HOOK S.,THE PARADOXES OF FREEDOM. UNIV CONSTN   CONCPT
INTELL LEGIS CONTROL REV CHOOSE SUPEGO...POLICY   MAJORIT
JURID IDEA/COMP 19/20 CIV/RIGHTS. PAGE 55 E1095   ORD/FREE
                                                        ALL/VALS
                                                          B62

MCWHINNEY E.,CONSTITUTIONALISM IN GERMANY AND THE   CONSTN
FEDERAL CONSTITUTIONAL COURT. GERMANY/W POL/PAR TV   CT/SYS
ADJUD CHOOSE EFFICIENCY ATTIT ORD/FREE MARXISM   CONTROL
...NEW/IDEA BIBLIOG 20. PAGE 71 E1428   NAT/G
                                                          B62

NAT'L MUNICIPAL LEAGUE,COMPENDIUM ON LEGISLATIVE   APPORT
APPORTIONMENT. USA+45 LOC/G NAT/G POL/PAR PROVS   REPRESENT
CT/SYS CHOOSE 20 SUPREME/CT CONGRESS. PAGE 76 E1524   LEGIS
                                                        STAT
                                                          B62

PRESS C.,STATE MANUALS, BLUE BOOKS AND ELECTION   BIBLIOG
RESULTS. LAW LOC/G MUNIC LEGIS WRITING FEDERAL   PROVS
SOVEREIGN...DECISION STAT CHARTS 20. PAGE 82 E1648   ADMIN
                                                        CHOOSE
                                                          B62

ROSENNE S.,THE WORLD COURT: WHAT IT IS AND HOW IT   INT/ORG
WORKS. WOR+45 WOR-45 LAW CONSTN JUDGE EDU/PROP   ADJUD
LEGIT ROUTINE CHOOSE PEACE ORD/FREE...JURID OBS   INT/LAW
TIME/SEQ CHARTS UN TOT/POP VAL/FREE 20. PAGE 86
E1717
                                                          B62

SIGLIANO R E.,THE COURTS. USA+45 USA-45 LAW CONSTN   ADJUD
NAT/G ROUTINE CHOOSE 18/20 SUPREME/CT. PAGE 91   PROB/SOLV
E1825   CT/SYS
                                                        JUDGE
                                                          B62

SILVA R.C.,RUM, RELIGION, AND VOTES: 1928 RE-   POL/PAR
EXAMINED. USA-45 LAW SECT DISCRIM CATHISM...CORREL   CHOOSE
STAT 20 PRESIDENT SMITH/ALF DEMOCRAT. PAGE 91 E1827   GP/COMP
                                                        ATTIT
                                                          B62

US COMMISSION ON CIVIL RIGHTS,EQUAL PROTECTION OF   ORD/FREE
THE LAWS IN NORTH CAROLINA. USA+45 LOC/G NAT/G   RESPECT
CONSULT LEGIS WORKER PROB/SOLV EDU/PROP ADJUD   LAW
CHOOSE DISCRIM HEALTH 20 NEGRO NORTH/CAR   PROVS
CIV/RIGHTS. PAGE 99 E1984
                                                          B62

WINTERS J.M.,INTERSTATE METROPOLITAN AREAS. CONSTN   MUNIC
LEAD CHOOSE PWR DECISION. PAGE 107 E2135   LAW
                                                        REGION
                                                        GOV/REL
                                                          B62

GANDOLFI A.,"REFLEXIONS SUR L'IMPOT DE CAPITATION   AFR
EN AFRIQUE NOIRE." GHANA SENEGAL LAW FINAN ACT/RES   CHOOSE
TEC/DEV ECO/TAC WEALTH...MGT TREND 20. PAGE 42
E0830
                                                          S62

CARTER G.M.,FIVE AFRICAN STATES: RESPONSES TO   AFR
DIVERSITY. CONSTN CULTURE STRATA LEGIS PLAN ECO/TAC   SOCIETY
DOMIN EDU/PROP CT/SYS EXEC CHOOSE ATTIT HEALTH
ORD/FREE PWR...TIME/SEQ TOT/POP VAL/FREE. PAGE 20
E0398
                                                          B63

FRAENKEL O.K.,THE SUPREME COURT AND CIVIL   ORD/FREE

LIBERTIES: HOW THE COURT HAS PROTECTED THE BILL OF RIGHTS. NAT/G CT/SYS CHOOSE PERS/REL RACE/REL DISCRIM PERSON...DECISION 20 SUPREME/CT CIVIL/LIB BILL/RIGHT. PAGE 39 E0782 — CONSTN ADJUD JURID

B63
GALLAGHER J.F.,SUPERVISORIAL DISTRICTING IN CALIFORNIA COUNTIES: 1960-1963 (PAMPHLET). USA+45 ADJUD ADMIN PARTIC CHOOSE GP/REL...CENSUS 20 CALIFORNIA. PAGE 42 E0828 — APPORT REGION REPRESENT LOC/G

B63
GOURNAY B.,PUBLIC ADMINISTRATION. FRANCE LAW CONSTN AGRI FINAN LABOR SCHOOL EX/STRUC CHOOSE...MGT METH/COMP 20. PAGE 45 E0894 — BIBLIOG/A ADMIN NAT/G LOC/G

B63
GRANT D.R.,STATE AND LOCAL GOVERNMENT IN AMERICA. USA+45 FINAN LOC/G MUNIC EX/STRUC FORCES EDU/PROP ADMIN CHOOSE FEDERAL ATTIT...JURID 20. PAGE 45 E0897 — PROVS POL/PAR LEGIS CONSTN

B63
NATIONAL CIVIC REVIEW,REAPPORTIONMENT: A YEAR IN REVIEW (PAMPHLET). USA+45 LAW CT/SYS CHOOSE ORD/FREE PWR...ANTHOL 20 CONGRESS. PAGE 76 E1527 — APPORT REPRESENT LEGIS CONSTN

B63
REITZEL A.M.,DAS MAINZER KRONUNGSRECHT UND DIE POLITISCHE PROBLEMATIK. GERMANY MUNIC LEGIT CATHISM 12/13. PAGE 84 E1684 — CHIEF JURID CHOOSE SECT

B63
ROYAL INSTITUTE PUBLIC ADMIN,BRITISH PUBLIC ADMINISTRATION. UK LAW FINAN INDUS LOC/G POL/PAR LEGIS LOBBY PARL/PROC CHOOSE JURID. PAGE 86 E1729 — BIBLIOG ADMIN MGT NAT/G

B63
VINES K.N.,STUDIES IN JUDICIAL POLITICS: TULANE STUDIES IN POLITICAL SCIENCE (VOL. 8). POL/PAR JUDGE ADJUD SANCTION CRIME CHOOSE PWR...JURID STAT TIME/SEQ CHARTS. PAGE 104 E2079 — CT/SYS GOV/REL PROVS

L63
ROSE R.,"COMPARATIVE STUDIES IN POLITICAL FINANCE: A SYMPOSIUM." ASIA EUR+WWI S/ASIA LAW CULTURE DELIB/GP LEGIS ACT/RES ECO/TAC EDU/PROP CHOOSE ATTIT RIGID/FLEX SUPEGO PWR SKILL WEALTH...STAT ANTHOL VAL/FREE. PAGE 85 E1714 — FINAN POL/PAR

S63
MODELSKI G.,"STUDY OF ALLIANCES." WOR+45 WOR-45 INT/ORG NAT/G FORCES LEGIT ADMIN CHOOSE ALL/VALS PWR SKILL...INT/LAW CONCPT GEN/LAWS 20 TREATY. PAGE 74 E1477 — VOL/ASSN CON/ANAL DIPLOM

N63
US PRES COMN REGIS AND VOTING,REPORT ON REGISTRATION AND VOTING (PAMPHLET). USA+45 POL/PAR CHIEF EDU/PROP PARTIC REPRESENT ATTIT...PSY CHARTS 20. PAGE 101 E2023 — CHOOSE LAW SUFF INSPECT

B64
BOUVIER-AJAM M.,MANUEL TECHNIQUE ET PRATIQUE DU MAIRE ET DES ELUS ET AGENTS COMMUNAUX. FRANCE LOC/G BUDGET CHOOSE GP/REL SUPEGO...JURID BIBLIOG 20 MAYOR COMMUNES. PAGE 14 E0274 — MUNIC ADMIN CHIEF NEIGH

B64
DANELSKI D.J.,A SUPREME COURT JUSTICE IS APPOINTED. CHIEF LEGIS CONFER DEBATE EXEC PERSON PWR...BIOG 20 CONGRESS PRESIDENT. PAGE 28 E0564 — CHOOSE JUDGE DECISION

B64
FEINE H.E.,DIE BESETZUNG DER REICHSBISTUMER VOM WESTFALISCHEN FRIEDEN BIS ZUR SAKULARISATION. GERMANY EDU/PROP GP/REL AGE 17/19. PAGE 37 E0727 — CHOOSE SECT JURID PROVS

B64
FREUD A.,OF HUMAN SOVEREIGNTY. WOR+45 INDUS SECT ECO/TAC CRIME CHOOSE ATTIT MORAL MARXISM...POLICY BIBLIOG 20. PAGE 40 E0794 — NAT/LISM DIPLOM WAR PEACE

B64
GOODNOW H.F.,THE CIVIL SERVICE OF PAKISTAN: BUREAUCRACY IN A NEW NATION. INDIA PAKISTAN S/ASIA ECO/UNDEV PROVS CHIEF PARTIC CHOOSE EFFICIENCY PWR ...BIBLIOG 20. PAGE 45 E0889 — ADMIN GOV/REL LAW NAT/G

B64
GROVES H.E.,THE CONSTITUTION OF MALAYSIA. MALAYSIA POL/PAR CHIEF CONSULT DELIB/GP CT/SYS PARL/PROC CHOOSE FEDERAL ORD/FREE 20. PAGE 48 E0953 — CONSTN NAT/G LAW

B64
HAMILTON H.D.,LEGISLATIVE APPORTIONMENT: KEY TO POWER. USA+45 LAW CONSTN PROVS LOBBY CHOOSE ATTIT SUPREME/CT. PAGE 50 E0988 — APPORT CT/SYS LEAD REPRESENT

B64
HANNA W.J.,POLITICS IN BLACK AFRICA: A SELECTIVE BIBLIOGRAPHY OF RELEVANT PERIODICAL LITERATURE. AFR LAW LOC/G MUNIC NAT/G POL/PAR LOBBY CHOOSE RACE/REL SOVEREIGN 20. PAGE 50 E0995 — BIBLIOG NAT/LISM COLONIAL

B64
HANSON R.,FAIR REPRESENTATION COMES TO MARYLAND (PAMPHLET). BAL/PWR CT/SYS CHOOSE GOV/REL 20 MARYLAND SUPREME/CT. PAGE 50 E0997 — APPORT REPRESENT PROVS LEGIS

B64
HEGEL G.W.,HEGEL'S POLITICAL WRITINGS (TRANS. BY T.M. KNOX). GERMANY UK FINAN FORCES PARL/PROC CHOOSE REPRESENT...BIOG 19. PAGE 51 E1022 — CONSTN LEGIS JURID

B64
MAKI J.M.,COURT AND CONSTITUTION IN JAPAN: SELECTED SUPREME COURT DECISIONS, 1948-60. LAW AGRI FAM LEGIS BAL/PWR ADMIN CHOOSE...SOC ANTHOL CABINET 20 CHINJAP CIVIL/LIB. PAGE 68 E1355 — CONSTN JURID CT/SYS CRIME

B64
WRIGHT G.,RURAL REVOLUTION IN FRANCE: THE PEASANTRY IN THE TWENTIETH CENTURY. EUR+WWI MOD/EUR LAW CULTURE AGRI POL/PAR DELIB/GP LEGIS ECO/TAC EDU/PROP COERCE CHOOSE ATTIT RIGID/FLEX HEALTH ...STAT CENSUS CHARTS VAL/FREE 20. PAGE 107 E2148 — PWR STRATA FRANCE REV

S64
PRITCHETT C.H.,"EQUAL PROTECTION AND THE URBAN MAJORITY." POL/PAR LEAD CHOOSE GP/REL PWR...MAJORIT DECISION. PAGE 83 E1655 — MUNIC LAW REPRESENT APPORT

B65
AMERICAN ASSEMBLY COLUMBIA U,THE COURTS, THE PUBLIC, AND THE LAW EXPLOSION. USA+45 ELITES PROVS EDU/PROP CRIME CHOOSE PERSON ORD/FREE PWR 20. PAGE 4 E0074 — CT/SYS ADJUD NAT/G

B65
BELL J.,THE JOHNSON TREATMENT: HOW LYNDON JOHNSON TOOK OVER THE PRESIDENCY AND MADE IT HIS OWN. USA+45 DELIB/GP DIPLOM ADJUD MURDER CHOOSE PERSON PWR...POLICY OBS INT TIME 20 JOHNSON/LB KENNEDY/JF PRESIDENT CONGRESS. PAGE 10 E0183 — INGP/REL TOP/EX CONTROL NAT/G

B65
CALIFORNIA LEGISLATURE,COMMITTEE ON ELECTIONS AND REAPPORTIONMENT, FINAL REPORT. USA+45 LAW COMPUTER TEC/DEV CHOOSE JURID. PAGE 19 E0366 — DELIB/GP APPORT LEGIS ADJUD

B65
CAVERS D.F.,THE CHOICE-OF-LAW PROCESS. PROB/SOLV ADJUD CT/SYS CHOOSE RATIONAL...IDEA/COMP 16/20 TREATY. PAGE 21 E0411 — JURID DECISION METH/COMP ADMIN

B65
CHARNAY J.P.,LE SUFFRAGE POLITIQUE EN FRANCE; ELECTIONS PARLEMENTAIRES, ELECTION PRESIDENTIELLE, REFERENDUMS. FRANCE CONSTN CHIEF DELIB/GP ECO/TAC EDU/PROP CRIME INGP/REL MORAL ORD/FREE PWR CATHISM 20 PARLIAMENT PRESIDENT. PAGE 22 E0425 — CHOOSE SUFF NAT/G LEGIS

B65
COHN H.J.,THE GOVERNMENT OF THE RHINE PALATINATE IN THE FIFTEENTH CENTURY. GERMANY FINAN LOC/G DELIB/GP LEGIS CT/SYS CHOOSE CATHISM 14/15 PALATINATE. PAGE 24 E0468 — PROVS JURID GP/REL ADMIN

B65
COLGNE A.B.,STATUTE MAKING (2ND ED.). LOC/G PROVS CHOOSE MAJORITY...CHARTS DICTIONARY 20. PAGE 24 E0474 — LEGIS LAW CONSTN NAT/G

B65
CONGRESSIONAL QUARTERLY SERV,REVOLUTION IN CIVIL RIGHTS. USA+45 USA-45 LEGIS ADJUD CT/SYS CHOOSE DISCRIM...DECISION CONGRESS SUPREME/CT. PAGE 25 E0488 — LAW CONSTN RACE/REL LOBBY

B65
CONGRESSIONAL QUARTERLY SERV,POLITICS IN AMERICA, CHOOSE
1945-1964: THE POLITICS AND ISSUES OF THE POSTWAR REPRESENT
YEARS. USA+45 LAW FINAN CHIEF DIPLOM APPORT SUFF POL/PAR
...POLICY STAT TREND CHARTS 20 CONGRESS PRESIDENT. LEGIS
PAGE 25 E0489

B65
FEERICK J.D.,FROM FAILING HANDS: THE STUDY OF EX/STRUC
PRESIDENTIAL SUCCESSION. CONSTN NAT/G PROB/SOLV CHIEF
LEAD PARL/PROC MURDER CHOOSE...NEW/IDEA BIBLIOG 20 LAW
KENNEDY/JF JOHNSON/LB PRESIDENT PRE/US/AM LEGIS
VICE/PRES. PAGE 36 E0724

B65
FISCHER F.C.,THE GOVERNMENT OF MICHIGAN. USA+45 PROVS
NAT/G PUB/INST EX/STRUC LEGIS BUDGET GIVE EDU/PROP LOC/G
CT/SYS CHOOSE GOV/REL...T MICHIGAN. PAGE 38 E0753 ADMIN
CONSTN

B65
KING D.B.,LEGAL ASPECTS OF THE CIVIL RIGHTS LAW
MOVEMENT. SERV/IND VOL/ASSN LEGIS EDU/PROP ADJUD DISCRIM
PARTIC CHOOSE...JURID SEGREGAT WORK. PAGE 61 E1215 TREND

B65
MCKAY R.B.,REAPPORTIONMENT: THE LAW AND POLITICS OF APPORT
EQUAL REPRESENTATION. FUT USA+45 PROVS BAL/PWR MAJORIT
ADJUD CHOOSE REPRESENT GOV/REL FEDERAL...JURID LEGIS
BIBLIOG 20 SUPREME/CT CONGRESS. PAGE 71 E1420 PWR

B65
MOELLER R.,LUDWIG DER BAYER UND DIE KURIE IM KAMPF JURID
UM DAS REICH. GERMANY LAW SECT LEGIT LEAD GP/REL CHIEF
CATHISM CONSERVE 14 LUDWIG/BAV POPE CHURCH/STA. CHOOSE
PAGE 74 E1478 NAT/LISM

B65
PEASLEE A.J.,CONSTITUTIONS OF NATIONS* THIRD AFR
REVISED EDITION (VOLUME I* AFRICA). LAW EX/STRUC CHOOSE
LEGIS TOP/EX LEGIT CT/SYS ROUTINE ORD/FREE PWR CONSTN
SOVEREIGN...CON/ANAL CHARTS. PAGE 80 E1606 NAT/G

B65
SCHUBERT G.,THE POLITICAL ROLE OF THE COURTS IN CT/SYS
JUDICIAL POLICY MAKING. USA+45 CONSTN JUDGE POLICY
FEEDBACK CHOOSE RACE/REL ORD/FREE...TRADIT PSY DECISION
BIBLIOG/A 20 KENNEDY/JF SUPREME/CT. PAGE 89 E1776

L65
WEINSTEIN J.B.,"THE EFFECT OF THE FEDERAL MUNIC
REAPPORTIONMENT DECISIONS ON COUNTIES AND OTHER LOC/G
FORMS OF GOVERNMENT." LAW CONSTN LEGIS CHOOSE APPORT
GOV/COMP. PAGE 105 E2108 REPRESENT

S65
ULMER S.S.,"TOWARD A THEORY OF SUBGROUP FORMATION CT/SYS
IN THE UNITED STATES SUPREME COURT." USA+45 ROUTINE ADJUD
CHOOSE PWR...JURID STAT CON/ANAL SIMUL SUPREME/CT. ELITES
PAGE 97 E1952 INGP/REL

B66
BAKER G.E.,THE REAPPORTIONMENT REVOLUTION: LEGIS
REPRESENTATION, POLITICAL POWER, AND THE SUPREME APPORT
COURT. USA+45 MUNIC NAT/G POL/PAR PROVS PROB/SOLV REPRESENT
CHOOSE ORD/FREE POPULISM...CONCPT CHARTS 20 ADJUD
SUPREME/CT. PAGE 7 E0140

B66
BEISER E.N.,THE TREATMENT OF LEGISLATIVE CT/SYS
APPORTIONMENT BY THE STATE AND FEDERAL COURTS APPORT
(DISSERTATION). USA+45 CONSTN NAT/G PROVS LEGIS ADJUD
CHOOSE REPRESENT ATTIT...POLICY BIBLIOG 20 CONGRESS PWR
SUPREME/CT. PAGE 9 E0181

B66
CANFIELD L.H.,THE PRESIDENCY OF WOODROW WILSON: PERSON
PRELUDE TO A WORLD IN CRISIS. USA-45 ADJUD NEUTRAL POLICY
WAR CHOOSE INGP/REL PEACE ORD/FREE 20 WILSON/W DIPLOM
PRESIDENT TREATY LEAGUE/NAT. PAGE 19 E0373 GOV/REL

B66
CLARK G.,WORLD PEACE THROUGH WORLD LAW: TWO INT/LAW
ALTERNATIVE PLANS. WOR+45 DELIB/GP FORCES TAX PEACE
CONFER ADJUD SANCTION ARMS/CONT WAR CHOOSE PRIVIL PLAN
20 UN COLD/WAR. PAGE 23 E0450 INT/ORG

B66
FEINE H.E.,REICH UND KIRCHE. CHRIST-17C MOD/EUR JURID
ROMAN/EMP LAW CHOOSE ATTIT 10/19 CHURCH/STA SECT
ROMAN/LAW. PAGE 37 E0728 NAT/G
GP/REL

B66
FINK M.,A SELECTIVE BIBLIOGRAPHY ON STATE BIBLIOG

B65
CONSTITUTIONAL REVISION (PAMPHLET). USA+45 FINAN PROVS
EX/STRUC LEGIS EDU/PROP ADMIN CT/SYS APPORT CHOOSE LOC/G
GOV/REL 20. PAGE 38 E0751 CONSTN

B66
GHOSH P.K.,THE CONSTITUTION OF INDIA: HOW IT HAS CONSTN
BEEN FRAMED. INDIA LOC/G DELIB/GP EX/STRUC NAT/G
PROB/SOLV BUDGET INT/TRADE CT/SYS CHOOSE...LING 20. LEGIS
PAGE 43 E0854 FEDERAL

B66
HAMILTON H.D.,REAPPORTIONING LEGISLATURES. USA+45 APPORT
CONSTN POL/PAR PROVS LEGIS COMPUTER ADJUD CHOOSE REPRESENT
ATTIT...ANTHOL 20 SUPREME/CT CONGRESS. PAGE 50 PHIL/SCI
E0989 PWR

B66
HANSON R.,THE POLITICAL THICKET. USA+45 MUNIC APPORT
POL/PAR LEGIS EXEC LOBBY CHOOSE...MAJORIT DECISION. LAW
PAGE 50 E0998 CONSTN
REPRESENT

B66
HOLTZMAN A.,INTEREST GROUPS AND LOBBYING. USA+45 LOBBY
CHIEF ACT/RES ADJUD LEAD PARTIC CHOOSE...POLICY 20 NAT/G
CONGRESS. PAGE 55 E1092 EDU/PROP
GP/REL

B66
INSTITUTE COMP STUDY POL SYS,DOMINICAN REPUBLIC SUFF
ELECTION FACT BOOK. DOMIN/REP LAW LEGIS REPRESENT CHOOSE
...JURID CHARTS 20. PAGE 57 E1126 POL/PAR
NAT/G

S66
FINE R.I.,"PEACE-KEEPING COSTS AND ARTICLE 19 OF FORCES
THE UN CHARTER* AN INVITATION TO RESPONSIBILITY." COST
INT/ORG NAT/G ADJUD CT/SYS CHOOSE CONSEN...RECORD CONSTN
IDEA/COMP UN. PAGE 38 E0750

S66
LANDE G.R.,"THE EFFECT OF THE RESOLUTIONS OF THE LEGIS
UNITED NATIONS GENERAL ASSEMBLY." WOR+45 LAW EFFICIENCY
INT/ORG NAT/G CHOOSE ISOLAT ATTIT...CLASSIF RESPECT
GEN/METH UN. PAGE 62 E1249

S66
MATTHEWS D.G.,"PRELUDE-COUP D'ETAT-MILITARY BIBLIOG
GOVERNMENT: A BIBLIOGRAPHICAL AND RESEARCH GUIDE TO NAT/G
NIGERIAN POL AND GOVT, JAN, 1965-66." AFR NIGER LAW ADMIN
CONSTN POL/PAR LEGIS CIVMIL/REL GOV/REL...STAT 20. CHOOSE
PAGE 69 E1385

B67
FESLER J.W.,THE FIFTY STATES AND THEIR LOCAL PROVS
GOVERNMENTS. FUT USA+45 POL/PAR LEGIS PROB/SOLV LOC/G
ADMIN CT/SYS CHOOSE GOV/REL FEDERAL...POLICY CHARTS
20 SUPREME/CT. PAGE 37 E0743

B67
GELLHORN W.,OMBUDSMEN AND OTHERS: CITIZENS' NAT/COMP
PROTECTORS IN NINE COUNTRIES. WOR+45 LAW CONSTN REPRESENT
LEGIS INSPECT ADJUD ADMIN CONTROL CT/SYS CHOOSE INGP/REL
PERS/REL...STAT CHARTS 20. PAGE 43 E0847 PROB/SOLV

B67
JONES C.O.,EVERY SECOND YEAR: CONGRESSIONAL EFFICIENCY
BEHAVIOR AND THE TWO-YEAR TERM. LAW POL/PAR LEGIS
PROB/SOLV DEBATE CHOOSE PERS/REL COST FEDERAL PWR TIME/SEQ
...CHARTS 20 CONGRESS SENATE HOUSE/REP. PAGE 59 NAT/G
E1172

B67
NIVEN R.,NIGERIA. NIGERIA CONSTN INDUS EX/STRUC NAT/G
COLONIAL REV NAT/LISM...CHARTS 19/20. PAGE 77 E1550 REGION
CHOOSE
GP/REL

B67
OPERATIONS AND POLICY RESEARCH,NICARAGUA: ELECTION POL/PAR
FACTBOOK: FEBRUARY 5, 1967 (PAMPHLET). NICARAGUA CHOOSE
LAW NAT/G LEAD REPRESENT...STAT BIOG CHARTS 20. PLAN
PAGE 79 E1577 ATTIT

B67
RAE D.,THE POLITICAL CONSEQUENCES OF ELECTORAL POL/PAR
LAWS. EUR+WWI ICELAND ISRAEL NEW/ZEALND UK USA+45 CHOOSE
ADJUD APPORT GP/REL MAJORITY...MATH STAT CENSUS NAT/COMP
CHARTS BIBLIOG 20 AUSTRAL. PAGE 83 E1667 REPRESENT

L67
HOWARD A.E.D.,"MR. JUSTICE BLACK: THE NEGRO PROTEST ADJUD
MOVEMENT AND THE RULE OF LAW." USA+45 CONSTN CT/SYS JUDGE
CHOOSE GP/REL...DECISION JURID NEGRO SUPREME/CT. LAW
PAGE 55 E1100 REPRESENT

LAMBERT J.D.,"CORPORATE POLITICAL SPENDING AND   L67
CAMPAIGN FINANCE." LAW CONSTN FINAN LABOR LG/CO   USA+45
LOC/G NAT/G VOL/ASSN TEC/DEV ADJUD ADMIN PARTIC.   POL/PAR
PAGE 62 E1247   CHOOSE
  COST

ADOKO A.,"THE CONSTITUTION OF UGANDA." AFR UGANDA   S67
LOC/G CHIEF FORCES LEGIS ADJUD EXEC CHOOSE NAT/LISM   NAT/G
...IDEA/COMP 20. PAGE 3 E0050   CONSTN
  ORD/FREE
  LAW

DEUTSCH E.P.,"A JUDICIAL PATH TO WORLD PEACE." FUT   S67
WOR+45 CONSTN PROB/SOLV DIPLOM LICENSE ADJUD   INT/LAW
SANCTION CHOOSE REPRESENT NAT/LISM SOVEREIGN 20   INT/ORG
ICJ. PAGE 31 E0611   JURID
  PEACE

GOSSETT W.T.,"ELECTING THE PRESIDENT: NEW HOPE FOR   S67
AN OLD IDEAL." FUT USA+45 USA-45 PROVS LEGIS   CONSTN
PROB/SOLV WRITING DEBATE ADJUD REPRESENT...MAJORIT   CHIEF
DECISION 20 HOUSE/REP PRESIDENT. PAGE 45 E0892   CHOOSE
  NAT/G

TRAYNOR R.J.,"WHO CAN BEST JUDGE THE JUDGES?"   CHOOSE
USA+45 PLAN PROB/SOLV ATTIT...DECISION JURID 20.   ADJUD
PAGE 97 E1938   REPRESENT
  CT/SYS

DUGARD J.,"THE REVOCATION OF THE MANDATE FOR SOUTH   S68
WEST AFRICA." SOUTH/AFR WOR+45 STRATA NAT/G   AFR
DELIB/GP DIPLOM ADJUD SANCTION CHOOSE RACE/REL   INT/ORG
...POLICY NAT/COMP 20 AFRICA/SW UN TRUST/TERR   DISCRIM
LEAGUE/NAT. PAGE 33 E0654   COLONIAL

FICHTE J.G.,THE SCIENCE OF RIGHTS (TRANS. BY A.E.   B89
KROEGER). WOR-45 FAM MUNIC NAT/G PROVS ADJUD CRIME   ORD/FREE
CHOOSE MARRIAGE SEX POPULISM 19 FICHTE/JG   CONSTN
NATURL/LAW. PAGE 37 E0744   LAW
  CONCPT

CHOPER J.H. E1317

CHOU/ENLAI....CHOU EN-LAI

CHOWDHURI R.N. E0434

CHRIMES S.B. E0435

CHRIS/DEM....CHRISTIAN DEMOCRATIC PARTY (ALL NATIONS)

CHRISTIAN DEMOCRATIC PARTY....SEE CHRIS/DEM

CHRISTIAN....CHRISTIAN BELIEFS OR CHURCHES

DE VICTORIA F.,DE INDIS ET DE JURE BELLI (1557) IN   B17
F. DE VICTORIA, DE INDIS ET DE JURE BELLI   WAR
REFLECTIONES. UNIV NAT/G SECT CHIEF PARTIC COERCE   INT/LAW
PEACE MORAL...POLICY 16 INDIAN/AM CHRISTIAN   OWN
CONSCN/OBJ. PAGE 30 E0598

VANDERPOL A.,LA DOCTRINE SCOLASTIQUE DU DROIT DE   B19
GUERRE. CHRIST-17C FORCES DIPLOM LEGIT SUPEGO MORAL   WAR
...BIOG AQUINAS/T SUAREZ/F CHRISTIAN. PAGE 103   INT/LAW
E2072

NICHOLS R.F.,RELIGION AND AMERICAN DEMOCRACY.   B59
USA+45 USA-45 LAW CHOOSE SUFF MORAL ORD/FREE   NAT/G
POPULISM...POLICY BIBLIOG 16/20 PRE/US/AM   SECT
CHRISTIAN. PAGE 77 E1547   CONSTN
  CONCPT

GONNER R.,DAS KIRCHENPATRONATRECHT IM   B62
GROSSHERZOGTUM BADEN. GERMANY LAW PROVS DEBATE   JURID
ATTIT CATHISM 14/19 PROTESTANT CHRISTIAN CHURCH/STA   SECT
BADEN. PAGE 44 E0882   NAT/G
  GP/REL

LOWRY C.W.,TO PRAY OR NOT TO PRAY. ADJUD SANCTION   B63
GP/REL ORD/FREE PWR CATHISM WORSHIP 20 SUPREME/CT   SECT
CHRISTIAN CHRUCH/STA. PAGE 67 E1330   CT/SYS
  CONSTN
  PRIVIL

COLEMAN-NORTON P.R.,ROMAN STATE AND CHRISTIAN   B66
CHURCH: A COLLECTION OF LEGAL DOCUMENTS TO A.D. 535   GP/REL
(3 VOLS.). CHRIST-17C ROMAN/EMP...ANTHOL DICTIONARY   NAT/G
6 CHRISTIAN CHURCH/STA. PAGE 24 E0473   SECT
  LAW

DOUGLAS W.O.,THE BIBLE AND THE SCHOOLS. USA+45   B66
  SECT

CULTURE ADJUD INGP/REL AGE/C AGE/Y ATTIT KNOWL   NAT/G
WORSHIP 20 SUPREME/CT CHURCH/STA BIBLE CHRISTIAN.   SCHOOL
PAGE 32 E0644   GP/REL

FUCHS W.P.,STAAT UND KIRCHE IM WANDEL DER   B66
JAHRHUNDERTE. EUR+WWI MOD/EUR UK REV...JURID CONCPT   SECT
4/20 EUROPE CHRISTIAN CHURCH/STA. PAGE 41 E0817   NAT/G
  ORD/FREE
  GP/REL

SMITH E.A.,CHURCH-STATE RELATIONS IN ECUMENICAL   B66
PERSPECTIVE. WOR+45 LAW MUNIC INGP/REL DISCRIM   NAT/G
ATTIT SUPEGO ORD/FREE CATHISM...PHIL/SCI IDEA/COMP   SECT
20 PROTESTANT ECUMENIC CHURCH/STA CHRISTIAN.   GP/REL
PAGE 92 E1843   ADJUD

CHRIST-17C.... CHRISTENDOM TO 1700

KEITT L.,AN ANNOTATED BIBLIOGRAPHY OF   N
BIBLIOGRAPHIES OF STATUTORY MATERIALS OF THE UNITED   BIBLIOG/A
STATES. CHRIST-17C USA-45 LEGIS ADJUD COLONIAL   LAW
CT/SYS...JURID 16/20. PAGE 60 E1196   CONSTN
  PROVS

GROTIUS H.,DE JURE BELLI AC PACIS. CHRIST-17C UNIV   B00
LAW SOCIETY PROVS LEGIT PEACE PERCEPT MORAL PWR   JURID
...CONCPT CON/ANAL GEN/LAWS. PAGE 48 E0952   INT/LAW
  WAR

POLLOCK F.,THE GENIUS OF THE COMMON LAW. CHRIST-17C   B12
LAW UK FINAN CHIEF ACT/RES ADMIN GP/REL ATTIT SOCISM   LAW
...ANARCH JURID. PAGE 81 E1624   CULTURE
  CREATE

VANDERPOL A.,LA DOCTRINE SCOLASTIQUE DU DROIT DE   B19
GUERRE. CHRIST-17C FORCES DIPLOM LEGIT SUPEGO MORAL   WAR
...BIOG AQUINAS/T SUAREZ/F CHRISTIAN. PAGE 103   SECT
E2072   INT/LAW

BRYCE J.,INTERNATIONAL RELATIONS. CHRIST-17C   B22
EUR+WWI MOD/EUR CULTURE INTELL NAT/G DELIB/GP   INT/ORG
CREATE BAL/PWR DIPLOM ATTIT DRIVE RIGID/FLEX   POLICY
ALL/VALS...PLURIST JURID CONCPT TIME/SEQ GEN/LAWS
TOT/POP. PAGE 16 E0323

GENTILI A.,DE LEGATIONIBUS. CHRIST-17C NAT/G SECT   B24
CONSULT LEGIT...POLICY CATH JURID CONCPT MYTH.   DIPLOM
PAGE 43 E0848   INT/LAW
  INT/ORG
  LAW

BYNKERSHOEK C.,QUAESTIONUM JURIS PUBLICI LIBRI DUO.   B30
CHRIST-17C MOD/EUR CONSTN ELITES SOCIETY NAT/G   INT/ORG
PROVS EX/STRUC FORCES TOP/EX BAL/PWR DIPLOM ATTIT   LAW
MORAL...TRADIT CONCPT. PAGE 18 E0352   NAT/LISM
  INT/LAW

MATTHEWS M.A.,INTERNATIONAL LAW: SELECT LIST OF   B36
WORKS IN ENGLISH ON PUBLIC INTERNATIONAL LAW: WITH   BIBLIOG/A
COLLECTIONS OF CASES AND OPINIONS. CHRIST-17C   INT/LAW
EUR+WWI MOD/EUR WOR-45 CONSTN ADJUD JURID. PAGE 69   ATTIT
E1388   DIPLOM

THOMPSON J.W.,SECRET DIPLOMACY: A RECORD OF   B37
ESPIONAGE AND DOUBLE-DEALING: 1500-1815. CHRIST-17C   DIPLOM
MOD/EUR NAT/G WRITING RISK MORAL...ANTHOL BIBLIOG   CRIME
16/19 ESPIONAGE. PAGE 96 E1920

MCILWAIN C.H.,CONSTITUTIONALISM, ANCIENT AND   B40
MODERN. CHRIST-17C MOD/EUR NAT/G CHIEF PROB/SOLV   CONSTN
INSPECT AUTHORIT ORD/FREE PWR...TIME/SEQ ROMAN/REP.   GEN/LAWS
PAGE 71 E1418   LAW

SCANLON H.L.,INTERNATIONAL LAW: A SELECTIVE LIST OF   B46
WORKS IN ENGLISH ON PUBLIC INTERNATIONAL LAW (A   BIBLIOG/A
PAMPHLET). CHRIST-17C EUR+WWI MOD/EUR WOR-45 CT/SYS   INT/LAW
...JURID 20. PAGE 87 E1749   ADJUD
  DIPLOM

SCHONS D.,BOOK CENSORSHIP IN NEW SPAIN (NEW WORLD   B49
STUDIES, BOOK II). SPAIN LAW CULTURE INSPECT ADJUD   CHRIST-17C
CT/SYS SANCTION GP/REL ORD/FREE 14/17. PAGE 88   EDU/PROP
E1764   CONTROL
  PRESS

NUSSBAUM D.,A CONCISE HISTORY OF THE LAW OF   B54
NATIONS. ASIA CHRIST-17C EUR+WWI ISLAM MEDIT-7   INT/ORG
MOD/EUR S/ASIA UNIV WOR+45 WOR-45 SOCIETY STRUCT   LAW
EXEC ATTIT ALL/VALS...CONCPT HIST/WRIT TIME/SEQ.   PEACE
  INT/LAW

PAGE 78 E1560

L54
NICOLSON H.,"THE EVOLUTION OF DIPLOMATIC METHOD." RIGID/FLEX
CHRIST-17C EUR+WWI FRANCE FUT ITALY MEDIT-7 MOD/EUR METH/CNCPT
USA+45 USA-45 LAW NAT/G CREATE EDU/PROP LEGIT PEACE DIPLOM
ATTIT ORD/FREE RESPECT SOVEREIGN. PAGE 77 E1548

B61
GUIZOT F.P.G.,HISTORY OF THE ORIGIN OF LEGIS
REPRESENTATIVE GOVERNMENT IN EUROPE. CHRIST-17C REPRESENT
FRANCE MOD/EUR SPAIN UK LAW CHIEF FORCES POPULISM CONSTN
...MAJORIT TIME/SEQ GOV/COMP NAT/COMP 4/19 NAT/G
PARLIAMENT. PAGE 48 E0961

B62
KIDDER F.E.,THESES ON PAN AMERICAN TOPICS. LAW BIBLIOG
CULTURE NAT/G SECT DIPLOM HEALTH...ART/METH GEOG CHRIST-17C
SOC 13/20. PAGE 61 E1213 L/A+17C
SOCIETY

B62
WOETZEL R.K.,THE NURENBERG TRIALS IN INTERNATIONAL INT/ORG
LAW. CHRIST-17C MOD/EUR WOR+45 SOCIETY NAT/G ADJUD
DELIB/GP DOMIN LEGIT ROUTINE ATTIT DRIVE PERSON WAR
SUPEGO MORAL ORD/FREE...POLICY MAJORIT JURID PSY
SOC SELF/OBS RECORD NAZI TOT/POP. PAGE 107 E2138

S62
JOHNSON O.H.,"THE ENGLISH TRADITION IN LAW
INTERNATIONAL LAW." CHRIST-17C MOD/EUR EDU/PROP INT/LAW
LEGIT CT/SYS ORD/FREE...JURID CONCPT TIME/SEQ. UK
PAGE 59 E1170

L63
MCDOUGAL M.S.,"THE ENJOYMENT AND ACQUISITION OF PLAN
RESOURCES IN OUTER SPACE." CHRIST-17C FUT WOR+45 TREND
WOR-45 LAW EXTR/IND INT/ORG ACT/RES CREATE TEC/DEV
ECO/TAC LEGIT COERCE HEALTH KNOWL ORD/FREE PWR
WEALTH...JURID HIST/WRIT VAL/FREE. PAGE 70 E1408

B64
GRASMUCK E.L.,COERCITIO STAAT UND KIRCHE IM GP/REL
DONATISTENSTREIT. CHRIST-17C ROMAN/EMP LAW PROVS NAT/G
DEBATE PERSON SOVEREIGN...JURID CONCPT 4/5 SECT
AUGUSTINE CHURCH/STA ROMAN/LAW. PAGE 45 E0898 COERCE

B66
COLEMAN-NORTON P.R.,ROMAN STATE AND CHRISTIAN GP/REL
CHURCH: A COLLECTION OF LEGAL DOCUMENTS TO A.D. 535 NAT/G
(3 VOLS.). CHRIST-17C ROMAN/EMP...ANTHOL DICTIONARY SECT
6 CHRISTIAN CHURCH/STA. PAGE 24 E0473 LAW

B66
FEINE H.E.,REICH UND KIRCHE. CHRIST-17C MOD/EUR JURID
ROMAN/EMP LAW CHOOSE ATTIT 10/19 CHURCH/STA SECT
ROMAN/LAW. PAGE 37 E0728 NAT/G
GP/REL

B97
JENKS E.J.,LAW AND POLITICS IN THE MIDDLE AGES. LAW
CHRIST-17C CULTURE STRUCT KIN NAT/G SECT CT/SYS SOCIETY
GP/REL...CLASSIF CHARTS IDEA/COMP BIBLIOG 8/16. ADJUST
PAGE 58 E1162

CHRISTMAN H.M. E0436

CHRONOLOGY....SEE TIME/SEQ

CHROUST A.H. E0437

CHURCH....SEE SECT

CHURCH/STA....CHURCH-STATE RELATIONS (ALL NATIONS)

B58
O'BRIEN F.W.,JUSTICE REED AND THE FIRST AMENDMENT, ADJUD
THE RELIGION CLAUSES. USA+45 USA-45 NAT/G PROVS SECT
CONTROL FEDERAL...POLICY JURID TIME/SEQ 20 CT/SYS
SUPREME/CT CHRUCH/STA AMEND/I REED/STAN. PAGE 78
E1563

B60
BERTHOLD O.,KAISER, VOLK UND AVIGNON. GERMANY CHIEF DIPLOM
LEGIT LEAD NAT/LISM CONSERVE 14 POPE CHRUCH/STA CATHISM
LUDWIG/BAV JOHN/XXII. PAGE 11 E0217 JURID

B63
LOWRY C.W.,TO PRAY OR NOT TO PRAY. ADJUD SANCTION SECT
GP/REL ORD/FREE PWR CATHISM WORSHIP 20 SUPREME/CT CT/SYS
CHRISTIAN CHRUCH/STA. PAGE 67 E1330 CONSTN
PRIVIL

NRE
MEYER C.S.,ELIZABETH I AND THE RELIGIOUS SETTLEMENT GP/REL
OF 1559. UK ELITES CHIEF LEGIS DISCRIM CATHISM 16 SECT
CHURCH/STA ELIZABTH/I. PAGE 72 E1445 LAW
PARL/PROC

B14
FIGGIS J.N.,CHURCHES IN THE MODERN STATE (2ND ED.). SECT
LAW CHIEF BAL/PWR PWR...CONCPT CHURCH/STA POPE. NAT/G
PAGE 38 E0748 SOCIETY
ORD/FREE

N19
COUTROT A.,THE FIGHT OVER THE 1959 PRIVATE SCHOOL
EDUCATION LAW IN FRANCE (PAMPHLET). FRANCE NAT/G PARL/PROC
SECT GIVE EDU/PROP GP/REL ATTIT RIGID/FLEX ORD/FREE CATHISM
20 CHURCH/STA. PAGE 27 E0527 LAW

B49
HOLLERAN M.P.,CHURCH AND STATE IN GUATEMALA. SECT
GUATEMALA LAW STRUCT CATHISM...SOC SOC/INTEG 17/20 NAT/G
CHURCH/STA. PAGE 55 E1086 GP/REL
CULTURE

B54
JAMES L.F.,THE SUPREME COURT IN AMERICAN LIFE. ADJUD
USA+45 USA-45 CONSTN CRIME GP/REL INGP/REL RACE/REL CT/SYS
CONSEN FEDERAL PERSON ORD/FREE 18/20 SUPREME/CT JURID
DEPRESSION CIV/RIGHTS CHURCH/STA FREE/SPEE. PAGE 58 DECISION
E1147

B54
O'NEILL J.M.,CATHOLICS IN CONTROVERSY. USA+45 NAT/G CATHISM
PROVS SCHOOL SECT EDU/PROP LEGIT CT/SYS SANCTION CONSTN
GP/REL 20 SUPREME/CT CHURCH/STA. PAGE 78 E1569 POLICY
LAW

B55
MID-EUROPEAN LAW PROJECT,CHURCH AND STATE BEHIND LAW
THE IRON CURTAIN. COM CZECHOSLVK HUNGARY POLAND MARXISM
USSR CULTURE SECT EDU/PROP GOV/REL CATHISM...CHARTS POLICY
ANTHOL BIBLIOG WORSHIP 20 CHURCH/STA. PAGE 73 E1455

B58
HERRMANN K.,DAS STAATSDENKEN BEI LEIBNIZ. GP/REL NAT/G
ATTIT ORD/FREE...CONCPT IDEA/COMP 17 LEIBNITZ/G JURID
CHURCH/STA. PAGE 52 E1034 SECT
EDU/PROP

B58
WOOD J.E.,CHURCH AND STATE IN SCRIPTURE HISTORY AND GP/REL
CONSTITUTIONAL LAW. LAW CONSTN SOCIETY PROVS SECT
VOL/ASSN BAL/PWR COLONIAL CT/SYS ATTIT...BIBLIOG 20 NAT/G
SUPREME/CT CHURCH/STA BIBLE. PAGE 107 E2142 ADJUD

B60
BLANSHARD P.,GOD AND MAN IN WASHINGTON. USA+45 NAT/G
CHIEF LEGIS LEGIT CT/SYS PRIVIL ATTIT ORD/FREE SECT
...POLICY CONCPT 20 SUPREME/CT CONGRESS PRESIDENT GP/REL
CHURCH/STA. PAGE 12 E0242 POL/PAR

B60
FELLMAN D.,THE SUPREME COURT AND EDUCATION. ACADEM CT/SYS
NAT/G PROVS DELIB/GP ADJUD ORD/FREE...POLICY JURID SECT
WORSHIP 20 SUPREME/CT NEGRO CHURCH/STA. PAGE 37 RACE/REL
E0731 SCHOOL

B60
MOCTEZUMA A.P.,EL CONFLICTO RELIGIOSO DE 1926 (2ND SECT
ED.). L/A+17C LAW NAT/G LOBBY COERCE GP/REL ATTIT ORD/FREE
...POLICY 20 MEXIC/AMER CHURCH/STA. PAGE 74 E1476 DISCRIM
REV

B60
POWELL T.,THE SCHOOL BUS LAW: A CASE STUDY IN JURID
EDUCATION, RELIGION, AND POLITICS. USA+45 LAW NEIGH SCHOOL
SECT LEGIS EDU/PROP ADJUD CT/SYS LOBBY CATHISM
WORSHIP 20 CONNECTICT CHURCH/STA. PAGE 82 E1641

B61
HAGEN A.,STAAT UND KATHOLISCHE KIRCHE IN SECT
WURTTEMBERG IN DEN JAHREN 1848-1862 (2 VOLS.). PROVS
GERMANY DELIB/GP EDU/PROP MARRIAGE CATHISM 19 GP/REL
CHURCH/STA. PAGE 49 E0975 JURID

B61
KURLAND P.B.,RELIGION AND THE LAW. USA+45 USA-45 SECT
CONSTN PROVS CHIEF ADJUD SANCTION PRIVIL CATHISM NAT/G
...POLICY 17/20 SUPREME/CT PRESIDENT CHURCH/STA. CT/SYS
PAGE 62 E1239 GP/REL

B61
SMITH J.W.,RELIGIOUS PERSPECTIVES IN AMERICAN SECT
CULTURE, VOL. 2, RELIGION IN AMERICAN LIFE. USA+45 DOMIN
CULTURE NAT/G EDU/PROP ADJUD LOBBY ATTIT...ART/METH SOCIETY
ANTHOL 20 CHURCH/STA BIBLE. PAGE 92 E1845 GP/REL

GONNER R.,DAS KIRCHENPATRONATRECHT IM
GROSSHERZOGTUM BADEN. GERMANY LAW PROVS DEBATE
ATTIT CATHISM 14/19 PROTESTANT CHRISTIAN CHURCH/STA
BADEN. PAGE 44 E0882
JURID
SECT
NAT/G
GP/REL
B62

KAUPER P.G.,CIVIL LIBERTIES AND THE CONSTITUTION.
USA+45 SECT EDU/PROP WRITING ADJUD SEX ORD/FREE 20
SUPREME/CT CIVIL/LIB CHURCH/STA. PAGE 60 E1188
LAW
CONSTN
CT/SYS
DECISION
B62

MCGRATH J.J.,CHURCH AND STATE IN AMERICAN LAW.
PROVS SCHOOL TAX GIVE CT/SYS GP/REL...POLICY ANTHOL
18/20 SUPREME/CT CHURCH/STA CASEBOOK. PAGE 71 E1414
LAW
SECT
ADJUD
CONSTN
NAT/G
B62

MCGRATH J.J.,CHURCH AND STATE IN AMERICAN LAW:
CASES AND MATERIALS. USA+45 USA-45 LEGIS EDU/PROP
ADJUD CT/SYS PWR...ANTHOL 18/20 CHURCH/STA. PAGE 71
E1415
LAW
GOV/REL
SECT
B62

TUSSMAN J.,THE SUPREME COURT ON CHURCH AND STATE.
USA+45 USA-45 SANCTION PRIVIL...POLICY JURID 19/20
SUPREME/CT CHURCH/STA. PAGE 97 E1945
CT/SYS
SECT
ADJUD
B62

DRINAN R.F.,RELIGION, THE COURTS, AND PUBLIC
POLICY. USA+45 CONSTN BUDGET TAX GIVE ADJUD
SANCTION GP/REL PRIVIL 20 CHURCH/STA. PAGE 33 E0649
SECT
CT/SYS
POLICY
SCHOOL
B63

PRITCHETT C.H.,THE THIRD BRANCH OF GOVERNMENT.
USA+45 USA-45 CONSTN SOCIETY INDUS SECT LEGIS JUDGE
PROB/SOLV GOV/REL 20 SUPREME/CT CHURCH/STA. PAGE 82
E1654
JURID
NAT/G
ADJUD
CT/SYS
B63

RAVENS J.P.,STAAT UND KATHOLISCHE KIRCHE IN
PREUSSENS POLNISCHEN TEILUNGSGEBIETEN. GERMANY
POLAND PRUSSIA PROVS DIPLOM EDU/PROP DEBATE
NAT/LISM...JURID 18 CHURCH/STA. PAGE 83 E1674
GP/REL
CATHISM
SECT
NAT/G
B63

SMITH E.A.,CHURCH AND STATE IN YOUR COMMUNITY.
USA+45 PROVS SCHOOL ACT/RES CT/SYS PARTIC ATTIT
MORAL ORD/FREE CATHISM 20 PROTESTANT CHURCH/STA.
PAGE 92 E1842
GP/REL
SECT
NAT/G
NEIGH
B63

FREISEN J.,STAAT UND KATHOLISCHE KIRCHE IN DEN
DEUTSCHEN BUNDESSTAATEN (2 VOLS.). GERMANY LAW FAM
NAT/G EDU/PROP GP/REL MARRIAGE WEALTH 19/20
CHURCH/STA. PAGE 40 E0793
SECT
CATHISM
JURID
PROVS
B64

GIANNELLA D.A.,RELIGION AND THE PUBLIC ORDER: AN
ANNUAL REVIEW OF CHURCH AND STATE, AND OF RELIGION,
LAW, AND SOCIETY. USA+45 LAW SOCIETY FAM POL/PAR
SCHOOL GIVE EDU/PROP GP/REL...JURID GEN/LAWS
BIBLIOG/A 20 CHURCH/STA BIRTH/CON CONSCN/OBJ
NATURL/LAW. PAGE 43 E0855
SECT
NAT/G
CONSTN
ORD/FREE
B64

GRASMUCK E.L.,COERCITIO STAAT UND KIRCHE IM
DONATISTENSTREIT. CHRIST-17C ROMAN/EMP LAW PROVS
DEBATE PERSON SOVEREIGN...JURID CONCPT 4/5
AUGUSTINE CHURCH/STA ROMAN/LAW. PAGE 45 E0898
GP/REL
NAT/G
SECT
COERCE
B64

KAUPER P.G.,RELIGION AND THE CONSTITUTION. USA+45
USA-45 LAW NAT/G SCHOOL SECT GP/REL ATTIT...BIBLIOG
WORSHIP 18/20 SUPREME/CT FREE/SPEE CHURCH/STA.
PAGE 60 E1189
CONSTN
JURID
ORD/FREE
B64

NEWMAN E.S.,CIVIL LIBERTY AND CIVIL RIGHTS. USA+45
USA-45 CONSTN PROVS FORCES LEGIS CT/SYS RACE/REL
ATTIT...MAJORIT JURID WORSHIP 20 SUPREME/CT NEGRO
CIV/RIGHTS CHURCH/STA. PAGE 77 E1543
ORD/FREE
LAW
CONTROL
NAT/G
B64

RICE C.E.,THE SUPREME COURT AND PUBLIC PRAYER.
CONSTN SCHOOL SECT PROB/SOLV TAX ATTIT WORSHIP
18/20 SUPREME/CT CHURCH/STA. PAGE 84 E1692
JURID
POLICY
NAT/G
B64

SCHMEISER D.A.,CIVIL LIBERTIES IN CANADA. CANADA
LAW SECT PRESS RACE/REL NAT/LISM PRIVIL 20
COMMONWLTH PARLIAMENT CIVIL/LIB CHURCH/STA. PAGE 88
E1758
ORD/FREE
CONSTN
ADJUD
EDU/PROP
B64

STOKES A.P.,CHURCH AND STATE IN THE UNITED STATES
(3 VOLS.). USA+45 USA-45 NAT/G PROVS LEGIS CT/SYS
SANCTION PRIVIL ORD/FREE 17/20 CHURCH/STA. PAGE 94
E1875
SECT
CONSTN
POLICY
B64

ANTIEU C.J.,RELIGION UNDER THE STATE CONSTITUTIONS.
USA+45 LAW SCHOOL TAX SANCTION PRIVIL ORD/FREE
...JURID 20 SUPREME/CT CHURCH/STA. PAGE 5 E0099
SECT
CONSTN
PROVS
GP/REL
B65

BEGGS D.W.,AMERICA'S SCHOOLS AND CHURCHES: PARTNERS
IN CONFLICT. USA+45 PROVS EDU/PROP ADJUD DISCRIM
ATTIT...IDEA/COMP ANTHOL BIBLIOG WORSHIP 20
CHURCH/STA. PAGE 9 E0179
SECT
GP/REL
SCHOOL
NAT/G
B65

CONRING E.,KIRCHE UND STAAT NACH DER LEHRE DER
NIEDERLANDISCHEN CALVINISTEN IN DER ERSTEN HALFTE
DES 17. JAHRHUNDERTS. NETHERLAND GP/REL...CONCPT 17
CHURCH/STA. PAGE 25 E0497
SECT
JURID
NAT/G
ORD/FREE
B65

FELLMAN D.,RELIGION IN AMERICAN PUBLIC LAW. USA+45
USA-45 NAT/G PROVS ADJUD SANCTION GP/REL PRIVIL
ORD/FREE...JURID TIME/SEQ 18/20 SUPREME/CT
CHURCH/STA. PAGE 37 E0733
SECT
CONSTN
LAW
POLICY
B65

HOWE M.D.W.,THE GARDEN AND THE WILDERNESS. USA+45
LAW GIVE EDU/PROP LEGIT NAT/LISM ORD/FREE...POLICY
JURID SUPREME/CT CHURCH/STA. PAGE 55 E1103
CONSTN
SECT
NAT/G
GP/REL
B65

MOELLER R.,LUDWIG DER BAYER UND DIE KURIE IM KAMPF
UM DAS REICH. GERMANY LAW SECT LEGIT LEAD GP/REL
CATHISM CONSERVE 14 LUDWIG/BAV POPE CHURCH/STA.
PAGE 74 E1478
JURID
CHIEF
CHOOSE
NAT/LISM
B65

WILSON J.F.,CHURCH AND STATE IN AMERICAN HISTORY.
USA+45 USA-45 ADJUD CT/SYS ORD/FREE SOVEREIGN
...ANTHOL BIBLIOG/A 17/20 CHURCH/STA. PAGE 106
E2129
SECT
NAT/G
GP/REL
CONTROL
B65

COLEMAN-NORTON P.R.,ROMAN STATE AND CHRISTIAN
CHURCH: A COLLECTION OF LEGAL DOCUMENTS TO A.D. 535
(3 VOLS.). CHRIST-17C ROMAN/EMP...ANTHOL DICTIONARY
6 CHRISTIAN CHURCH/STA. PAGE 24 E0473
GP/REL
NAT/G
SECT
LAW
B66

DOUGLAS W.O.,THE BIBLE AND THE SCHOOLS. USA+45
CULTURE ADJUD INGP/REL AGE/C AGE/Y ATTIT KNOWL
WORSHIP 20 SUPREME/CT CHURCH/STA BIBLE CHRISTIAN.
PAGE 32 E0644
SECT
NAT/G
SCHOOL
GP/REL
B66

FEINE H.E.,REICH UND KIRCHE. CHRIST-17C MOD/EUR
ROMAN/EMP LAW CHOOSE ATTIT 10/19 CHURCH/STA
ROMAN/LAW. PAGE 37 E0728
JURID
SECT
NAT/G
GP/REL
B66

FUCHS W.P.,STAAT UND KIRCHE IM WANDEL DER
JAHRHUNDERTE. EUR+WWI MOD/EUR UK REV...JURID CONCPT
4/20 EUROPE CHRISTIAN CHURCH/STA. PAGE 41 E0817
SECT
NAT/G
ORD/FREE
GP/REL
B66

O'NEILL C.E.,CHURCH AND STATE IN FRENCH COLONIAL
LOUISIANA: POLICY AND POLITICS TO 1732. PROVS
VOL/ASSN DELIB/GP ADJUD ADMIN GP/REL ATTIT DRIVE
...POLICY BIBLIOG 17/18 LOUISIANA CHURCH/STA.
PAGE 78 E1568
COLONIAL
NAT/G
SECT
PWR
B66

SMITH E.A.,CHURCH-STATE RELATIONS IN ECUMENICAL
PERSPECTIVE. WOR+45 LAW MUNIC INGP/REL DISCRIM
ATTIT SUPEGO ORD/FREE CATHISM...PHIL/SCI IDEA/COMP
20 PROTESTANT ECUMENIC CHURCH/STA CHRISTIAN.
PAGE 92 E1843
NAT/G
SECT
GP/REL
ADJUD
B66

BOLES D.E.,THE TWO SWORDS. USA+45 USA-45 LAW CONSTN
SOCIETY FINAN PRESS CT/SYS...HEAL JURID BIBLIOG
WORSHIP 20 SUPREME/CT CHURCH/STA. PAGE 13 E0263
SCHOOL
EDU/PROP
ADJUD
B67

DUPRE L.,"TILL DEATH DO US PART?" UNIV FAM INSPECT
LEGIT ADJUD SANCTION PERS/REL ANOMIE RIGID/FLEX SEX
...JURID IDEA/COMP 20 CHURCH/STA BIBLE CANON/LAW
MARRIAGE
CATH
LAW
S68

CIVIL/LAW. PAGE 34 E0666

CHURCHLL/W....SIR WINSTON CHURCHILL

CIA....CENTRAL INTELLIGENCE AGENCY

B62
OTTENBERG M.,THE FEDERAL INVESTIGATORS. USA+45 LAW FORCES
COM/IND DIST/IND WORKER DIPLOM INT/TRADE CONTROL INSPECT
FEDERAL HEALTH ORD/FREE FBI CIA FTC SEC FDA. NAT/G
PAGE 79 E1585 CRIME

CICERO....CICERO

CICOUREL A.V. E0438

CINCINNATI....CINCINNATI, OHIO

N19
THE REGIONAL DIRECTOR AND THE PRESS (PAMPHLET). PRESS
USA-45 COM/IND LOBBY ROLE 20 NLRB CINCINNATI LABOR
BILL/RIGHT. PAGE 2 E0031 ORD/FREE
 EDU/PROP

CINEMA....SEE FILM

CITIES....SEE MUNIC

CITY/MGT....CITY MANAGEMENT, CITY MANAGERS; SEE ALSO MUNIC,
 ADMIN, MGT, LOC/G

B62
HSUEH S.-S.,GOVERNMENT AND ADMINISTRATION OF HONG ADMIN
KONG. CHIEF DELIB/GP LEGIS CT/SYS REPRESENT GOV/REL LOC/G
20 HONG/KONG CITY/MGT CIVIL/SERV GOVERNOR. PAGE 55 COLONIAL
E1106 EX/STRUC

CIV/DEFENS....CIVIL DEFENSE (SYSTEMS, PLANNING, AND

CIV/DISOBD....CIVIL DISOBEDIENCE

CIV/RIGHTS....CIVIL RIGHTS: CONTEMPORARY CIVIL RIGHTS
 MOVEMENTS; SEE ALSO RACE/REL, CONSTN + LAW

N19
IN THE SHADOW OF FEAR; AMERICAN CIVIL LIBERTIES, ORD/FREE
1948-49 (PAMPHLET). COM LAW LEGIS BAL/PWR EDU/PROP CONSTN
CT/SYS RACE/REL DISCRIM MARXISM SOCISM 20 COLD/WAR POLICY
CONGRESS ACLU CIV/RIGHTS ESPIONAGE. PAGE 2 E0030

N19
BUREAU OF NAT'L AFFAIRS INC.,A CURRENT LOOK AT: DISCRIM
(1) THE NEGRO AND TITLE VII, (2) SEX AND TITLE VII SEX
(PAMPHLET). LAW LG/CO SML/CO RACE/REL...POLICY SOC WORKER
STAT DEEP/QU TREND CON/ANAL CHARTS 20 NEGRO MGT
CIV/RIGHTS. PAGE 17 E0334

N19
JANOWITZ M.,SOCIAL CONTROL OF ESCALATED RIOTS CROWD
(PAMPHLET). USA+45 USA-45 LAW SOCIETY MUNIC FORCES ORD/FREE
PROB/SOLV EDU/PROP TV CRIME ATTIT...BIBLIOG 20 CONTROL
NEGRO CIV/RIGHTS. PAGE 58 E1148 RACE/REL

N19
MISSISSIPPI ADVISORY COMMITTEE,REPORT ON RACE/REL
MISSISSIPPI (PAMPHLET). USA+45 LAW PROVS FORCES DISCRIM
ADJUD PWR...SOC/WK INT 20 MISSISSIPP NEGRO COERCE
CIV/RIGHTS. PAGE 73 E1469 ORD/FREE

B28
NORTON T.J.,LOSING LIBERTY JUDICIALLY. PROVS LEGIS NAT/G
BAL/PWR CT/SYS...JURID 18/20 SUPREME/CT CIV/RIGHTS ORD/FREE
CONGRESS. PAGE 78 E1557 CONSTN
 JUDGE

B47
KONVITZ M.R.,THE CONSTITUTION AND CIVIL RIGHTS. CONSTN
USA-45 NAT/G ADJUD GP/REL RACE/REL POPULISM LAW
...MAJORIT 19/20 SUPREME/CT CIV/RIGHTS. PAGE 61 GOV/REL
E1227 ORD/FREE

B54
JAMES L.F.,THE SUPREME COURT IN AMERICAN LIFE. ADJUD
USA+45 USA-45 CONSTN CRIME GP/REL INGP/REL RACE/REL CT/SYS
CONSEN FEDERAL PERSON ORD/FREE 18/20 SUPREME/CT JURID
DEPRESSION CIV/RIGHTS CHURCH/STA FREE/SPEE. PAGE 58 DECISION
E1147

B57
ROWAN C.T.,GO SOUTH TO SORROW. USA+45 STRUCT NAT/G RACE/REL
EDU/PROP LEAD COERCE ISOLAT DRIVE SUPEGO RESPECT DISCRIM
...PREDICT 20 NEGRO SUPREME/CT SOUTH/US CIV/RIGHTS. ANOMIE

PAGE 86 E1728 LAW

B57
US SENATE COMM ON JUDICIARY,CIVIL RIGHTS - 1957. INT
USA+45 LAW NAT/G CONFER GOV/REL RACE/REL ORD/FREE LEGIS
PWR...JURID 20 SENATE CIV/RIGHTS. PAGE 102 E2039 DISCRIM
 PARL/PROC

B58
CABLE G.W.,THE NEGRO QUESTION: A SELECTION OF RACE/REL
WRITINGS ON CIVIL RIGHTS IN THE SOUTH. USA+45 CULTURE
STRATA LOC/G POL/PAR GIVE EDU/PROP WRITING CT/SYS DISCRIM
SANCTION CRIME CHOOSE WORSHIP 20 NEGRO CIV/RIGHTS ORD/FREE
CONV/LEASE SOUTH/US. PAGE 18 E0355

B58
MOSKOWITZ M.,HUMAN RIGHTS AND WORLD ORDER. INT/ORG DIPLOM
PLAN GP/REL NAT/LISM SOVEREIGN...CONCPT 20 UN INT/LAW
TREATY CIV/RIGHTS. PAGE 75 E1502 ORD/FREE

B59
HOOK S.,POLITICAL POWER AND PERSONAL FREEDOM: ORD/FREE
CRITICAL STUDIES IN DEMOCRACY, COMMUNISM AND CIVIL PWR
RIGHTS. UNIV LAW SOCIETY DIPLOM TOTALISM MARXISM WELF/ST
SOCISM...PHIL/SCI IDEA/COMP 20 CIV/RIGHTS. PAGE 55 CHOOSE
E1094

B59
SCOTT F.R.,CIVIL LIBERTIES AND CANADIAN FEDERALISM. ORD/FREE
CANADA LAW ADJUD CT/SYS GOV/REL 20 CIV/RIGHTS. FEDERAL
PAGE 90 E1797 NAT/LISM
 CONSTN

S59
DWYER R.J.,"THE ADMINISTRATIVE ROLE IN ADMIN
DESEGREGATION." USA+45 LAW PROB/SOLV LEAD RACE/REL SCHOOL
ISOLAT STRANGE ROLE...POLICY SOC/INTEG MISSOURI DISCRIM
NEGRO CIV/RIGHTS. PAGE 34 E0668 ATTIT

S59
MASON A.T.,"THE SUPREME COURT: TEMPLE AND FORUM" CT/SYS
(BMR)" USA+45 USA-45 CONSTN DELIB/GP RACE/REL JURID
MAJORITY ORD/FREE...DECISION SOC/INTEG 19/20 PWR
SUPREME/CT WARRN/EARL CIV/RIGHTS. PAGE 69 E1377 ATTIT

B60
LA PONCE J.A.,THE PROTECTION OF MINORITIES. WOR+45 INGP/REL
WOR-45 NAT/G POL/PAR SUFF...INT/LAW CLASSIF GP/COMP DOMIN
GOV/COMP BIBLIOG 17/20 CIVIL/LIB CIV/RIGHTS. SOCIETY
PAGE 62 E1242 RACE/REL

S60
BLACK H.,"THE BILL OF RIGHTS" (BMR)" USA+45 USA-45 CONSTN
LAW LEGIS CT/SYS FEDERAL PWR 18/20 CONGRESS ORD/FREE
SUPREME/CT BILL/RIGHT CIV/RIGHTS. PAGE 12 E0237 NAT/G
 JURID

B61
US COMMISSION ON CIVIL RIGHTS,JUSTICE: BOOK 5, 1961 DISCRIM
REPORT OF THE U.S. COMMISSION ON CIVIL RIGHTS. LAW
LOC/G NAT/G RACE/REL...JURID 20 NEGRO CIV/RIGHTS FORCES
INDIAN/AM JURY INDIAN/AM. PAGE 99 E1983

B62
BERMAN D.M.,A BILL BECOMES A LAW: THE CIVIL RIGHTS DISCRIM
ACT OF 1960. USA+45 LAW POL/PAR LOBBY RACE/REL PARL/PROC
KNOWL...CHARTS 20 CONGRESS NEGRO CIV/RIGHTS. JURID
PAGE 11 E0206 GOV/REL

B62
HOOK S.,THE PARADOXES OF FREEDOM. UNIV CONSTN CONCPT
INTELL LEGIS CONTROL REV CHOOSE SUPEGO...POLICY MAJORIT
JURID IDEA/COMP 19/20 CIV/RIGHTS. PAGE 55 E1095 ORD/FREE
 ALL/VALS

B62
MITCHELL G.E.,THE ANGRY BLACK SOUTH. USA+45 LAW RACE/REL
CONSTN SCHOOL DELIB/GP EDU/PROP CONTROL SUFF ANOMIE DISCRIM
DRIVE...ANTHOL 20 NEGRO CIV/RIGHTS SOUTH/US. ADJUST
PAGE 74 E1473 ORD/FREE

B62
TAPER B.,GOMILLION VERSUS LIGHTFOOT: THE TUSKEGEE APPORT
GERRYMANDER CASE. USA+45 LAW CONSTN LOC/G MUNIC REPRESENT
CT/SYS 20 NEGRO CIV/RIGHTS GOMILLN/CG LIGHTFT/PM RACE/REL
TUSKEGEE. PAGE 95 E1908 ADJUD

B62
US COMMISSION ON CIVIL RIGHTS,EQUAL PROTECTION OF ORD/FREE
THE LAWS IN NORTH CAROLINA. USA+45 LOC/G NAT/G RESPECT
CONSULT LEGIS WORKER PROB/SOLV EDU/PROP ADJUD LAW
CHOOSE DISCRIM HEALTH 20 NEGRO NORTH/CAR PROVS
CIV/RIGHTS. PAGE 99 E1984

B62
US COMMISSION ON CIVIL RIGHTS,HEARINGS BEFORE ORD/FREE

UNITED STATES COMMISSION ON CIVIL RIGHTS. USA+45   LAW
ECO/DEV NAT/G CONSULT WORKER EDU/PROP ADJUD DISCRIM ADMIN
ISOLAT HABITAT HEALTH RESPECT 20 NEGRO CIV/RIGHTS. LEGIS
PAGE 99 E1985

B63
CAHN E.,THE GREAT RIGHTS. USA+45 NAT/G PROVS   CONSTN
CIVMIL/REL...IDEA/COMP ANTHOL BIBLIOG 18/20   LAW
MADISON/J BILL/RIGHT CIV/RIGHTS WARRN/EARL   ORD/FREE
BLACK/HL. PAGE 18 E0361   INGP/REL

B63
DAY R.E.,CIVIL RIGHTS USA: PUBLIC SCHOOLS, SOUTHERN EDU/PROP
STATES - NORTH CAROLINA, 1963. USA+45 LOC/G NEIGH ORD/FREE
LEGIS CREATE CT/SYS COERCE DISCRIM ATTIT...QU   RACE/REL
CHARTS 20 NORTH/CAR NEGRO KKK CIV/RIGHTS. PAGE 29 SANCTION
E0579

B63
NEWMAN E.S.,THE FREEDOM READER. USA+45 LEGIS TOP/EX RACE/REL
PLAN ADJUD CONTROL CT/SYS DISCRIM...DECISION ANTHOL LAW
20 SUPREME/CT CIV/RIGHTS. PAGE 77 E1541   POLICY
                                   ORD/FREE

B63
TUSSMAN J.,THE SUPREME COURT ON RACIAL   CT/SYS
DISCRIMINATION. USA+45 USA-45 NAT/G PROB/SOLV ADJUD DISCRIM
RACE/REL ORD/FREE...JURID 20 SUPREME/CT CIV/RIGHTS. ATTIT
PAGE 97 E1946   LAW

B63
US COMMISSION ON CIVIL RIGHTS,FREEDOM TO THE FREE. RACE/REL
USA+45 USA-45 LAW VOL/ASSN CT/SYS ATTIT PWR...JURID DISCRIM
BIBLIOG 17/20 SUPREME/CT NEGRO CIV/RIGHTS. PAGE 99 NAT/G
E1986   POLICY

B64
ANDERSON J.W.,EISENHOWER, BROWNELL, AND THE   LAW
CONGRESS - THE TANGLED ORIGINS OF THE CIVIL RIGHTS CONSTN
BILL OF 1956-1957. USA+45 POL/PAR LEGIS CREATE   POLICY
PROB/SOLV LOBBY GOV/REL RIGID/FLEX...NEW/IDEA 20 NAT/G
EISNHWR/DD CONGRESS BROWNELL/H CIV/RIGHTS. PAGE 5
E0090

B64
BUREAU OF NAT'L AFFAIRS,THE CIVIL RIGHTS ACT OF LEGIS
1964. USA+45 LOC/G NAT/G DELIB/GP CONFER DEBATE   RACE/REL
DISCRIM...JURID 20 CONGRESS SUPREME/CT CIV/RIGHTS. LAW
PAGE 17 E0333   CONSTN

B64
DORMAN M.,WE SHALL OVERCOME. USA+45 ELITES ACADEM RACE/REL
FORCES TOP/EX MURDER...JURID 20 CIV/RIGHTS   LAW
MISSISSIPP EVERS/MED CLEMSON. PAGE 32 E0638   DISCRIM

B64
FACTS ON FILE, INC.,CIVIL RIGHTS 1960-63: THE NEGRO DISCRIM
CAMPAIGN TO WIN EQUAL RIGHTS AND OPPORTUNITIES IN PRESS
THE UNITED STATES. LAW CONSTN PARTIC SUFF 20 NEGRO RACE/REL
CIV/RIGHTS MISSISSIPP. PAGE 36 E0710

B64
GUTTMANN A.,COMMUNISM, THE COURTS, AND THE   MARXISM
CONSTITUTION. USA+45 CT/SYS ORD/FREE...ANTHOL 20 POL/PAR
COM/PARTY CIV/RIGHTS. PAGE 48 E0965   CONSTN
                                   LAW

B64
MAKI J.M.,COURT AND CONSTITUTION IN JAPAN; SELECTED CT/SYS
SUPREME COURT DECISIONS, 1948-60. FAM LABOR GOV/REL CONSTN
HABITAT ORD/FREE...DECISION JURID 20 CHINJAP   PROB/SOLV
SUPREME/CT CIV/RIGHTS. PAGE 68 E1354   LAW

B64
MARSHALL B.,FEDERALISM AND CIVIL RIGHTS. USA+45 FEDERAL
PROVS BAL/PWR CONTROL CT/SYS PARTIC SOVEREIGN   ORD/FREE
...JURID 20 NEGRO CIV/RIGHTS. PAGE 68 E1369   CONSTN
                                   FORCES

B64
NEWMAN E.S.,CIVIL LIBERTY AND CIVIL RIGHTS. USA+45 ORD/FREE
USA-45 CONSTN PROVS FORCES LEGIS CT/SYS RACE/REL LAW
ATTIT...MAJORIT JURID WORSHIP 20 SUPREME/CT NEGRO CONTROL
CIV/RIGHTS CHURCH/STA. PAGE 77 E1543   NAT/G

B64
US SENATE COMM ON JUDICIARY,CIVIL RIGHTS - THE   INT
PRESIDENT'S PROGRAM. USA+45 LAW PROB/SOLV PRESS   LEGIS
ADJUD GOV/REL RACE/REL ORD/FREE PWR...JURID 20   DISCRIM
SUPREME/CT SENATE CIV/RIGHTS PRESIDENT. PAGE 102 PARL/PROC
E2053

B65
BAR ASSOCIATION OF ST LOUIS,CONSTITUTIONAL FREEDOM ORD/FREE
AND THE LAW. USA+45 LAW LABOR LEGIS EDU/PROP   CONSTN
...JURID CONCPT SUPREME/CT CIVIL/LIB CIV/RIGHTS. RACE/REL

PAGE 8 E0146   NAT/G

B65
FRIEDMAN L.,SOUTHERN JUSTICE. USA+45 PUB/INST LEGIT ADJUD
ADMIN CT/SYS DISCRIM...DECISION ANTHOL 20 NEGRO   LAW
SOUTH/US CIV/RIGHTS. PAGE 40 E0800   CONSTN
                                   RACE/REL

B65
IANNIELLO L.,MILESTONES ALONG THE MARCH: TWELVE RACE/REL
HISTORIC CIVIL RIGHTS DOCUMENTS--FROM WORLD WAR II DISCRIM
TO SELMA. USA+45 LAW FORCES TOP/EX PARTIC SUFF...T CONSTN
20 NEGRO CIV/RIGHTS TRUMAN/HS SUPREME/CT   NAT/G
KENNEDY/JF. PAGE 56 E1121

B65
KAMISAR Y.,CRIMINAL JUSTICE IN OUR TIME. USA+45 ORD/FREE
FORCES JUDGE PROB/SOLV COERCE MORAL 20 CIVIL/LIB CRIME
CIV/RIGHTS. PAGE 59 E1182   CT/SYS
                                   LAW

B65
PARKER D.,CIVIL LIBERTIES CASE STUDIES AND THE LAW. ORD/FREE
SECT ADJUD...CONCPT WORSHIP 20 SUPREME/CT   JURID
CIV/RIGHTS FREE/SPEE. PAGE 80 E1598   CONSTN
                                   JUDGE

B66
KUNSTLER W.M.,"DEEP IN MY HEART" USA+45 LAW   CT/SYS
PROF/ORG SECT LOBBY PARTIC CROWD DISCRIM ROLE   RACE/REL
...BIOG 20 KING/MAR/L NEGRO CIV/RIGHTS SOUTH/US. ADJUD
PAGE 62 E1233   CONSULT

S67
EDGEWORTH A.B. JR.,"CIVIL RIGHTS PLUS THREE YEARS: WORKER
BANKS AND THE ANTI-DISCRIMINATION LAW" USA+45   DISCRIM
SOCIETY DELIB/GP RACE/REL EFFICIENCY 20 NEGRO   FINAN
CIV/RIGHTS. PAGE 34 E0675   LAW

S67
HILL D.G.,"HUMAN RIGHTS LEGISLATION IN ONTARIO." DELIB/GP
CANADA R+D VOL/ASSN CONSULT INSPECT EDU/PROP ADJUD ORD/FREE
AGREE TASK GP/REL INGP/REL DISCRIM 20 CIV/RIGHTS LAW
ONTARIO CIVIL/LIB. PAGE 52 E1045   POLICY

CIVIL AERONAUTICS BOARD....SEE CAB

CIVIL DISOBEDIENCE....SEE CIV/DISOBD

CIVIL RIGHTS....SEE CIV/RIGHTS

CIVIL SERVICE....SEE ADMIN

CIVIL/CODE....CIVIL CODE (FRANCE)

CIVIL/LAW....CIVIL LAW

B09
JUSTINIAN,THE DIGEST (DIGESTA CORPUS JURIS CIVILIS) JURID
(2 VOLS.) (TRANS. BY C. H. MONRO). ROMAN/EMP LAW CT/SYS
FAM LOC/G LEGIS EDU/PROP CONTROL MARRIAGE OWN ROLE NAT/G
CIVIL/LAW. PAGE 59 E1177   STRATA

B23
DE MONTESQUIEU C.,THE SPIRIT OF LAWS (2 VOLS.)   JURID
(TRANS. BY THOMAS NUGENT). FRANCE FINAN SECT   LAW
INT/TRADE TAX COERCE REV DISCRIM HABITAT ORD/FREE CONCPT
19 ALEMBERT/J CIVIL/LAW. PAGE 30 E0588   GEN/LAWS

B33
ENSOR R.C.K.,COURTS AND JUDGES IN FRANCE, GERMANY, CT/SYS
AND ENGLAND. FRANCE GERMANY UK LAW PROB/SOLV ADMIN EX/STRUC
ROUTINE CRIME ROLE...METH/COMP 20 CIVIL/LAW.   ADJUD
PAGE 35 E0692   NAT/COMP

B35
RAM J.,THE SCIENCE OF LEGAL JUDGMENT: A TREATISE... LAW
UK CONSTN NAT/G LEGIS CREATE PROB/SOLV AGREE CT/SYS JURID
...INT/LAW CONCPT 19 ENGLSH/LAW CANON/LAW CIVIL/LAW EX/STRUC
CTS/WESTM. PAGE 83 E1672   ADJUD

B48
SLESSER H.,THE ADMINISTRATION OF THE LAW. UK CONSTN LAW
EX/STRUC OP/RES PROB/SOLV CRIME ROLE...DECISION CT/SYS
METH/COMP 20 CIVIL/LAW ENGLSH/LAW CIVIL/LAW.   ADJUD
PAGE 92 E1839

B48
SLESSER H.,THE ADMINISTRATION OF THE LAW. UK CONSTN LAW
EX/STRUC OP/RES PROB/SOLV CRIME ROLE...DECISION CT/SYS
METH/COMP 20 CIVIL/LAW ENGLSH/LAW CIVIL/LAW.   ADJUD
PAGE 92 E1839

DUPRE L.,"TILL DEATH DO US PART?" UNIV FAM INSPECT MARRIAGE
LEGIT ADJUD SANCTION PERS/REL ANOMIE RIGID/FLEX SEX CATH
...JURID IDEA/COMP 20 CHURCH/STA BIBLE CANON/LAW LAW
CIVIL/LAW. PAGE 34 E0666   S68

CIVIL/LIB....CIVIL LIBERTIES; SEE ALSO CONSTN + LAW

CRAIG J.,ELEMENTS OF POLITICAL SCIENCE (3 VOLS.). PHIL/SCI
CONSTN AGRI INDUS SCHOOL FORCES TAX CT/SYS SUFF NAT/G
MORAL WEALTH...CONCPT 19 CIVIL/LIB. PAGE 27 E0539 ORD/FREE   B14

AMERICAN CIVIL LIBERTIES UNION,"WE HOLD THESE ORD/FREE
TRUTHS" FREEDOM, JUSTICE, EQUALITY: REPORT ON CIVIL LAW
LIBERTIES (A PERIODICAL PAMPHLET COVERING 1951-53). RACE/REL
USA+45 ACADEM NAT/G FORCES LEGIS COERCE CIVMIL/REL CONSTN
GOV/REL DISCRIM PRIVIL MARXISM...OLD/LIB 20 ACLU UN
CIVIL/LIB. PAGE 4 E0076   N19

KONRAD F.,DIE PERSONLICHE FREIHEIT IM ORD/FREE
NATIONALSOZIALISTISCHEN DEUTSCHEN REICHE. GERMANY JURID
JUDGE ADJUD GP/REL FASCISM 20 CIVIL/LIB. PAGE 61 CONSTN
E1226   CONCPT   B36

HOLCOMBE A.N.,HUMAN RIGHTS IN THE MODERN WORLD. ORD/FREE
WOR+45 LEGIS DIPLOM ADJUD PERSON...INT/LAW 20 UN INT/ORG
TREATY CIVIL/LIB BILL/RIGHT. PAGE 54 E1071 CONSTN
                                                LAW   B48

DU BOIS W.E.B.,IN BATTLE FOR PEACE. AFR USA+45 PEACE
COLONIAL CT/SYS PERS/REL PERSON ORD/FREE...JURID 20 RACE/REL
NEGRO CIVIL/LIB. PAGE 33 E0650 DISCRIM
                                                BIOG   B52

BETH L.P.,"THE CASE FOR JUDICIAL PROTECTION OF CT/SYS
CIVIL LIBERTIES" (BMR)" USA+45 CONSTN ELITES LEGIS JUDGE
CONTROL...POLICY DECISION JURID 20 SUPREME/CT ADJUD
CIVIL/LIB. PAGE 11 E0220 ORD/FREE   S55

SINCLAIR T.C.,THE POLITICS OF JUDICIAL REVIEW JURID
1937-1957. USA+45 USA-45 NAT/G 20 SUPREME/CT ATTIT
CIVIL/LIB. PAGE 91 E1830 ORD/FREE
                                                RACE/REL   B57

PALMER E.E.,CIVIL LIBERTIES. USA+45 ADJUD CT/SYS ORD/FREE
PARTIC OWN LAISSEZ POPULISM...JURID CONCPT ANTHOL CONSTN
20 SUPREME/CT CIVIL/LIB. PAGE 79 E1592 RACE/REL
                                                LAW   B58

LOEWENSTEIN K.,VERFASSUNGSRECHT UND CONSTN
VERFASSUNGSPRAXIS DER VEREINIGTEN STAATEN. USA+45 POL/PAR
USA-45 COLONIAL CT/SYS GP/REL RACE/REL ORD/FREE EX/STRUC
...JURID 18/20 SUPREME/CT CONGRESS PRESIDENT NAT/G
BILL/RIGHT CIVIL/LIB. PAGE 66 E1319   B59

LA PONCE J.A.,THE PROTECTION OF MINORITIES. WOR+45 INGP/REL
WOR-45 NAT/G POL/PAR SUFF...INT/LAW CLASSIF GP/COMP DOMIN
GOV/COMP BIBLIOG 17/20 CIVIL/LIB CIV/RIGHTS. SOCIETY
PAGE 62 E1242 RACE/REL   B60

SCHEIBER H.N.,THE WILSON ADMINISTRATION AND CIVIL ORD/FREE
LIBERTIES 1917-1921. LAW GOV/REL ATTIT 20 WILSON/W WAR
CIVIL/LIB. PAGE 87 E1754 NAT/G
                                                CONTROL   B60

ULMER S.S.,"THE ANALYSIS OF BEHAVIOR PATTERNS ON ATTIT
THE UNITED STATES SUPREME COURT" USA+45 LAW CT/SYS ADJUD
PERS/REL RACE/REL PERSON...DECISION PSY SOC TREND PROF/ORG
METH/COMP METH 20 SUPREME/CT CIVIL/LIB. PAGE 97 INGP/REL
E1951   S60

FREUND P.A.,THE SUPREME COURT OF THE UNITED STATES: CT/SYS
ITS BUSINESS, PURPOSES, AND PERFORMANCE. CONSTN JURID
CRIME CONSEN ORD/FREE...DECISION 20 SUPREME/CT ADJUD
CIVIL/LIB. PAGE 40 E0797 FEDERAL   B61

JACOBS C.E.,JUSTICE FRANKFURTER AND CIVIL BIOG
LIBERTIES. USA+45 USA-45 LAW NAT/G PROB/SOLV PRESS CONSTN
PERS/REL...JURID WORSHIP 20 SUPREME/CT FRANKFUR/F ADJUD
CIVIL/LIB. PAGE 57 E1144 ORD/FREE   B61

SCOTT A.M.,POLITICS, USA; CASES ON THE AMERICAN CT/SYS
DEMOCRATIC PROCESS. USA+45 CHIEF FORCES DIPLOM CONSTN
LOBBY CHOOSE RACE/REL FEDERAL ATTIT...JURID ANTHOL NAT/G
T 20 PRESIDENT CONGRESS CIVIL/LIB. PAGE 90 E1795 PLAN   B61

WESTIN A.F.,THE SUPREME COURT: VIEWS FROM INSIDE. CT/SYS
USA+45 NAT/G PROF/ORG PROVS DELIB/GP INGP/REL LAW
DISCRIM ATTIT...POLICY DECISION JURID ANTHOL 20 ADJUD
SUPREME/CT CONGRESS CIVIL/LIB. PAGE 106 E2114 GOV/REL   B61

GANJI M.,INTERNATIONAL PROTECTION OF HUMAN RIGHTS. ORD/FREE
WOR+45 CONSTN INT/TRADE CT/SYS SANCTION CRIME WAR DISCRIM
RACE/REL...CHARTS IDEA/COMP NAT/COMP BIBLIOG 20 LEGIS
TREATY NEGRO LEAGUE/NAT UN CIVIL/LIB. PAGE 42 E0831 DELIB/GP B62

HIRSCHFIELD R.S.,THE CONSTITUTION AND THE COURT. ADJUD
SCHOOL WAR RACE/REL EQUILIB ORD/FREE...POLICY PWR
MAJORIT DECISION JURID 18/20 PRESIDENT COLD/WAR CONSTN
CIVIL/LIB SUPREME/CT CONGRESS. PAGE 53 E1051 LAW   B62

KAUPER P.G.,CIVIL LIBERTIES AND THE CONSTITUTION. LAW
USA+45 SECT EDU/PROP WRITING ADJUD SEX ORD/FREE 20 CONSTN
SUPREME/CT CIVIL/LIB CHURCH/STA. PAGE 60 E1188 CT/SYS
                                                DECISION   B62

FRAENKEL O.K.,THE SUPREME COURT AND CIVIL ORD/FREE
LIBERTIES: HOW THE COURT HAS PROTECTED THE BILL OF CONSTN
RIGHTS. NAT/G CT/SYS CHOOSE PERS/REL RACE/REL ADJUD
DISCRIM PERSON...DECISION 20 SUPREME/CT CIVIL/LIB JURID
BILL/RIGHT. PAGE 39 E0782   B63

LEVY L.W.,JEFFERSON AND CIVIL LIBERTIES: THE DARKER BIOG
SIDE. USA+45 LAW INTELL ACADEM FORCES PRESS REV ORD/FREE
INGP/REL PERSON 18/19 JEFFERSN/T CIVIL/LIB. PAGE 65 CONSTN
E1291 ATTIT   B63

REALE M.,PLURALISMO E LIBERDADE. STRUCT ADJUST CONCPT
ATTIT 20 CIVIL/LIB. PAGE 84 E1676 ORD/FREE
                                                JURID
                                                INGP/REL   B63

STREET H.,FREEDOM: THE INDIVIDUAL AND THE LAW. UK ORD/FREE
COM/IND EDU/PROP PRESS RUMOR TV PWR 20 CIVIL/LIB NAT/G
FILM. PAGE 94 E1886 JURID
                                                PARL/PROC B63

MAKI J.M.,COURT AND CONSTITUTION IN JAPAN: SELECTED CONSTN
SUPREME COURT DECISIONS, 1948-60. LAW AGRI FAM JURID
LEGIS BAL/PWR ADMIN CHOOSE...SOC ANTHOL CABINET 20 CT/SYS
CHINJAP CIVIL/LIB. PAGE 68 E1355 CRIME   B64

SCHMEISER D.A.,CIVIL LIBERTIES IN CANADA. CANADA ORD/FREE
LAW SECT PRESS RACE/REL NAT/LISM PRIVIL 20 CONSTN
COMMONWLTH PARLIAMENT CIVIL/LIB CHURCH/STA. PAGE 88 ADJUD
E1758 EDU/PROP   B64

WAY H.F. JR.,LIBERTY IN THE BALANCE - CURRENT ORD/FREE
ISSUES IN CIVIL LIBERTIES. USA+45 USA-45 DELIB/GP EDU/PROP
RACE/REL DISCRIM TOTALISM MARXISM SOCISM...CONCPT NAT/G
20 CONGRESS SUPREME/CT CIVIL/LIB. PAGE 105 E2104 JURID   B64

BAR ASSOCIATION OF ST LOUIS,CONSTITUTIONAL FREEDOM ORD/FREE
AND THE LAW. USA+45 LAW LABOR LEGIS EDU/PROP CONSTN
...JURID CONCPT SUPREME/CT CIVIL/LIB CIV/RIGHTS. RACE/REL
PAGE 8 E0146 NAT/G   B65

BARKER L.J.,FREEDOM, COURTS, POLITICS: STUDIES IN JURID
CIVIL LIBERTIES. USA+45 LEGIS CREATE DOMIN PRESS CT/SYS
ADJUD LOBBY CRIME GP/REL RACE/REL MARXISM 20 ATTIT
CIVIL/LIB. PAGE 8 E0148 ORD/FREE   B65

KAMISAR Y.,CRIMINAL JUSTICE IN OUR TIME. USA+45 ORD/FREE
FORCES JUDGE PROB/SOLV COERCE MORAL 20 CIVIL/LIB CRIME
CIV/RIGHTS. PAGE 59 E1182 CT/SYS
                                                LAW   B65

STOREY R.G.,OUR UNALIENABLE RIGHTS. LAW SECT CT/SYS CONSTN
SUFF DISCRIM 17/20 CIVIL/LIB ENGLSH/LAW. PAGE 94 JURID
E1882 ORD/FREE
                                                LEGIS   B65

CIVMIL/REL....CIVIL-MILITARY RELATIONS

B66
ARCHER P.,FREEDOM AT STAKE. UK LAW NAT/G LEGIS — ORD/FREE
JUDGE CRIME MORAL...CONCPT 20 CIVIL/LIB. PAGE 5 — NAT/COMP
E0103 — POLICY

B66
GILLMOR D.M.,FREE PRESS AND FAIR TRIAL. UK USA+45 — ORD/FREE
CONSTN PROB/SOLV PRESS CONTROL CRIME DISCRIM — ADJUD
RESPECT...AUD/VIS 20 CIVIL/LIB. PAGE 44 E0865 — ATTIT
— EDU/PROP

B66
SWEET E.C.,CIVIL LIBERTIES IN AMERICA. LAW CONSTN — ADJUD
NAT/G PRESS CT/SYS DISCRIM ATTIT WORSHIP 20 — ORD/FREE
CIVIL/LIB. PAGE 95 E1899 — SUFF
— COERCE

S67
HILL D.G.,"HUMAN RIGHTS LEGISLATION IN ONTARIO." — DELIB/GP
CANADA R+D VOL/ASSN CONSULT INSPECT EDU/PROP ADJUD — ORD/FREE
AGREE TASK GP/REL INGP/REL DISCRIM 20 CIV/RIGHTS — LAW
ONTARIO CIVIL/LIB. PAGE 52 E1045 — POLICY

CIVIL/SERV....CIVIL SERVICE; SEE ALSO ADMIN

B05
GOODNOW F.J.,THE PRINCIPLES OF THE ADMINISTRATIVE — ADMIN
LAW OF THE UNITED STATES. USA-45 LAW STRUCT — NAT/G
EX/STRUC LEGIS BAL/PWR CONTROL GOV/REL PWR...JURID — PROVS
19/20 CIVIL/SERV. PAGE 45 E0887 — LOC/G

B10
COLORADO CIVIL SERVICE COMN,SECOND BIENNIAL REPORT — PROVS
TO THE GOVERNOR, 1909-1910. USA+45 DELIB/GP LEGIS — LOC/G
LICENSE PAY 20 COLORADO CIVIL/SERV. PAGE 24 E0477 — ADMIN
— WORKER

B53
MAJUMDAR B.B.,PROBLEMS OF PUBLIC ADMINISTRATION IN — ECO/UNDEV
INDIA. INDIA INDUS PLAN BUDGET ADJUD CENTRAL DEMAND — GOV/REL
WEALTH...WELF/ST ANTHOL 20 CIVIL/SERV. PAGE 68 — ADMIN
E1353 — MUNIC

B56
DUNNILL F.,THE CIVIL SERVICE. UK LAW PLAN ADMIN — PERSON
EFFICIENCY DRIVE NEW/LIB...STAT CHARTS 20 — WORKER
PARLIAMENT CIVIL/SERV. PAGE 33 E0662 — STRATA
— SOC/WK

B58
FELLMAN D.,THE DEFENDANT'S RIGHTS. USA+45 NAT/G — CONSTN
CONSULT CT/SYS SUPEGO ORD/FREE...BIBLIOG SUPREME/CT — LAW
CIVIL/SERV. PAGE 37 E0730 — CRIME
— ADJUD

B58
US SENATE COMM POST OFFICE,TO PROVIDE AN EFFECTIVE — INT
SYSTEM OF PERSONNEL ADMINISTRATION. USA+45 NAT/G — LEGIS
EX/STRUC PARL/PROC GOV/REL...JURID 20 SENATE — CONFER
CIVIL/SERV. PAGE 103 E2060 — ADMIN

B59
US SENATE COMM ON POST OFFICE,TO PROVIDE FOR AN — ADMIN
EFFECTIVE SYSTEM OF PERSONNEL ADMINISTRATION. — NAT/G
EFFICIENCY...MGT 20 CONGRESS CIVIL/SERV POSTAL/SYS — EX/STRUC
YARBROGH/R. PAGE 103 E2059 — LAW

B62
HSUEH S.-.S.,GOVERNMENT AND ADMINISTRATION OF HONG — ADMIN
KONG. CHIEF DELIB/GP LEGIS CT/SYS REPRESENT GOV/REL — LOC/G
20 HONG/KONG CITY/MGT CIVIL/SERV GOVERNOR. PAGE 55 — COLONIAL
E1106 — EX/STRUC

B63
US SENATE COMM ON JUDICIARY,US PERSONNEL SECURITY — PLAN
PRACTICES. USA+45 DELIB/GP ADJUD ADMIN ORD/FREE — NAT/G
...CHARTS 20 CONGRESS CIVIL/SERV. PAGE 102 E2049 — CONTROL
— WORKER

B65
US LIBRARY OF CONGRESS,INTERNAL SECURITY AND — CONTROL
SUBVERSION. USA+45 ACADEM LOC/G NAT/G PROVS — ADJUD
...POLICY ANARCH DECISION 20 CIVIL/SERV SUBVERT — LAW
SEDITION. PAGE 101 E2020 — PLAN

CIVIL/WAR....CIVIL WAR

L00
HISTORICUS,"LETTERS AND SOME QUESTIONS OF — WEALTH
INTERNATIONAL LAW." FRANCE NETHERLAND UK USA-45 — JURID
WOR-45 LAW NAT/G COERCE...SOC CONCPT GEN/LAWS — WAR
TOT/POP 19 CIVIL/WAR. PAGE 53 E1054 — INT/LAW

CIVIL-MILITARY RELATIONS....SEE CIVMIL/REL

N19
AMERICAN CIVIL LIBERTIES UNION,"WE HOLD THESE — ORD/FREE
TRUTHS" FREEDOM, JUSTICE, EQUALITY: REPORT ON CIVIL — LAW
LIBERTIES (A PERIODICAL PAMPHLET COVERING 1951-53). — RACE/REL
USA+45 ACADEM NAT/G FORCES LEGIS COERCE CIVMIL/REL — CONSTN
GOV/REL DISCRIM PRIVIL MARXISM...OLD/LIB 20 ACLU UN
CIVIL/LIB. PAGE 4 E0076

B43
US LIBRARY OF CONGRESS,SOCIAL AND CULTURAL PROBLEMS — BIBLIOG/A
IN WARTIME: APRIL-DECEMBER (SUPPLEMENT 1). WOR-45 — WAR
SECT EDU/PROP CRIME LEISURE CIVMIL/REL RACE/REL — SOC
ATTIT DRIVE HEALTH...GEOG 20. PAGE 100 E2013 — CULTURE

B44
FULLER G.H.,MILITARY GOVERNMENT: A LIST OF — BIBLIOG
REFERENCES (A PAMPHLET). ITALY UK USA-45 WOR-45 LAW — DIPLOM
FORCES DOMIN ADMIN ARMS/CONT ORD/FREE PWR — CIVMIL/REL
...DECISION 20 CHINJAP. PAGE 41 E0822 — SOVEREIGN

B45
CONOVER H.F.,THE GOVERNMENTS OF THE MAJOR FOREIGN — BIBLIOG
POWERS: A BIBLIOGRAPHY. FRANCE GERMANY ITALY UK — NAT/G
USSR CONSTN LOC/G POL/PAR EX/STRUC FORCES ADMIN — DIPLOM
CT/SYS CIVMIL/REL TOTALISM...POLICY 19/20. PAGE 25
E0494

B47
CLAGETT H.L.,A GUIDE TO THE LAW AND LEGAL — BIBLIOG
LITERATURE OF ECUADOR. ECUADOR CONSTN LABOR LEGIS — JURID
JUDGE ADJUD ADMIN CIVMIL/REL...CRIMLGY INT/LAW — LAW
CON/ANAL 20. PAGE 22 E0443 — L/A+17C

B47
CLAGETT H.L.,A GUIDE TO THE LAW AND LEGAL — BIBLIOG
LITERATURE OF VENEZUELA. VENEZUELA CONSTN LABOR — L/A+17C
LEGIS JUDGE ADJUD ADMIN CIVMIL/REL...CRIMLGY JURID — INT/LAW
CON/ANAL 20. PAGE 23 E0446 — LAW

B49
JACKSON R.H.,INTERNATIONAL CONFERENCE ON MILITARY — DIPLOM
TRIALS. FRANCE GERMANY UK USA+45 USSR VOL/ASSN — INT/ORG
DELIB/GP REPAR ADJUD CT/SYS CRIME WAR 20 WAR/TRIAL. — INT/LAW
PAGE 57 E1141 — CIVMIL/REL

S49
BROWN D.M.,"RECENT JAPANESE POLITICAL AND — WAR
HISTORICAL MATERIALS." ELITES CT/SYS CIVMIL/REL 20 — FORCES
CHINJAP. PAGE 16 E0312

B52
THOM J.M.,GUIDE TO RESEARCH MATERIAL IN POLITICAL — BIBLIOG/A
SCIENCE (PAMPHLET). ELITES LOC/G MUNIC NAT/G LEGIS — KNOWL
DIPLOM ADJUD CIVMIL/REL GOV/REL PWR MGT. PAGE 96
E1916

B56
ESTEP R.,AN AIR POWER BIBLIOGRAPHY. USA+45 TEC/DEV — BIBLIOG/A
BUDGET DIPLOM EDU/PROP DETER CIVMIL/REL...DECISION — FORCES
INT/LAW 20. PAGE 35 E0698 — WEAPON
— PLAN

B57
US COMMISSION GOVT SECURITY,RECOMMENDATIONS; AREA: — LEGIS
LEGISLATION. USA+45 USA-45 DELIB/GP PLAN TEC/DEV — SANCTION
CIVMIL/REL ORD/FREE...POLICY DECISION 20 PRIVACY. — CRIME
PAGE 99 E1982 — CONTROL

B58
DOUGLAS W.O.,THE RIGHT OF THE PEOPLE. USA+45 — ORD/FREE
EDU/PROP CONTROL REPRESENT PRIVIL...IDEA/COMP 20. — CONSTN
PAGE 32 E0641 — CT/SYS
— CIVMIL/REL

B60
CARPER E.T.,THE DEFENSE APPROPRIATIONS RIDER — GOV/REL
(PAMPHLET). USA+45 CONSTN CHIEF DELIB/GP LEGIS — ADJUD
BUDGET LOBBY CIVMIL/REL...POLICY 20 CONGRESS — LAW
EISNHWR/DD DEPT/DEFEN PRESIDENT BOSTON. PAGE 20 — CONTROL
E0390

B62
CARPER E.T.,ILLINOIS GOES TO CONGRESS FOR ARMY — ADMIN
LAND. USA+45 LAW EXTR/IND PROVS REGION CIVMIL/REL — LOBBY
GOV/REL FEDERAL ATTIT 20 ILLINOIS SENATE CONGRESS — GEOG
DIRKSEN/E DOUGLAS/P. PAGE 20 E0391 — LEGIS

B62
DUPRE J.S.,SCIENCE AND THE NATION: POLICY AND — R+D
POLITICS. USA+45 LAW ACADEM FORCES ADMIN CIVMIL/REL — INDUS
GOV/REL EFFICIENCY PEACE...TREND 20 SCI/ADVSRY. — TEC/DEV
PAGE 34 E0665 — NUC/PWR

B63
CAHN E.,THE GREAT RIGHTS. USA+45 NAT/G PROVS   CONSTN
CIVMIL/REL...IDEA/COMP ANTHOL BIBLIOG 18/20   LAW
MADISON/J BILL/RIGHT CIV/RIGHTS WARRN/EARL   ORD/FREE
BLACK/HL. PAGE 18 E0361   INGP/REL

B63
ELLERT R.B.,NATO 'FAIR TRIAL' SAFEGUARDS: PRECURSOR   JURID
TO AN INTERNATIONAL BILL OF PROCEDURAL RIGHTS.   INT/LAW
WOR+45 FORCES CRIME CIVMIL/REL ATTIT ORD/FREE 20   INT/ORG
NATO. PAGE 34 E0683   CT/SYS

B63
US SENATE,DOCUMENTS ON INTERNATIONAL AS"ECTS OF   SPACE
EXPLORATION AND USE OF OUTER SPACE, 1954-62: STAFF   UTIL
REPORT FOR COMM AERON SPACE SCI. USA+45 USSR LEGIS   GOV/REL
LEAD CIVMIL/REL PEACE...POLICY INT/LAW ANTHOL 20   DIPLOM
CONGRESS NASA KHRUSH/N. PAGE 101 E2026

B64
US AIR FORCE ACADEMY ASSEMBLY,OUTER SPACE: FINAL   SPACE
REPORT APRIL 1-4, 1964. FUT USA+45 WOR+45 LAW   CIVMIL/REL
DELIB/GP CONFER ARMS/CONT WAR PEACE ATTIT MORAL   NUC/PWR
...ANTHOL 20 NASA. PAGE 99 E1979   DIPLOM

B65
US SENATE,US INTERNATIONAL SPACE PROGRAMS, 1959-65:   SPACE
STAFF REPORT FOR COMM ON AERONAUTICAL AND SPACE   DIPLOM
SCIENCES. WOR+45 VOL/ASSN CIVMIL/REL 20 CONGRESS   PLAN
NASA TREATY. PAGE 101 E2027   GOV/REL

B66
DALLIN A.,POLITICS IN THE SOVIET UNION: 7 CASES.   MARXISM
COM USSR LAW POL/PAR CHIEF FORCES WRITING CONTROL   DOMIN
PARL/PROC CIVMIL/REL TOTALISM...ANTHOL 20 KHRUSH/N   ORD/FREE
STALIN/J CASEBOOK COM/PARTY. PAGE 28 E0563   GOV/REL

S66
MATTHEWS D.G.,"PRELUDE-COUP D'ETAT-MILITARY   BIBLIOG
GOVERNMENT: A BIBLIOGRAPHICAL AND RESEARCH GUIDE TO   NAT/G
NIGERIAN POL AND GOVT, JAN, 1965-66." AFR NIGER LAW   ADMIN
CONSTN POL/PAR LEGIS CIVMIL/REL GOV/REL...STAT 20.   CHOOSE
PAGE 69 E1385

B67
BOULTON D.,OBJECTION OVERRULED. UK LAW POL/PAR   FORCES
DIPLOM ADJUD SANCTION DEATH WAR CIVMIL/REL 20.   SOCISM
PAGE 14 E0273   SECT

S67
MORENO F.J.,"THE SPANISH COLONIAL SYSTEM: A   COLONIAL
FUNCTIONAL APPROACH." SPAIN WOR-45 LAW CHIEF DIPLOM   CONTROL
ADJUD CIVMIL/REL AUTHORIT ROLE PWR...CONCPT 17/20.   NAT/G
PAGE 74 E1492   OP/RES

CLAGETT H.L. E0439,E0440,E0441,E0442,E0443,E0444,E0445,E0446 ,
    E0447,E0448,E2070

CLAN....SEE KIN

CLARK G. E0449,E0450

CLARK J.P. E0451

CLARK/JB....JOHN BATES CLARK

CLASS DIVISION....SEE STRATA

CLASS, SOCIAL....SEE STRATA

CLASSIF....CLASSIFICATION, TYPOLOGY, SET THEORY

B15
SAWYER R.A.,A LIST OF WORKS ON COUNTY GOVERNMENT.   BIBLIOG/A
LAW FINAN MUNIC TOP/EX ROUTINE CRIME...CLASSIF   LOC/G
RECORD 19/20. PAGE 87 E1748   GOV/REL
                                                     ADMIN

B23
POUND R.,INTERPRETATIONS OF LEGAL HISTORY. CULTURE   LAW
...PHIL/SCI NEW/IDEA CLASSIF SIMUL GEN/LAWS 19/20.   IDEA/COMP
PAGE 82 E1636   JURID

C24
BARNES H.E.,"SOCIOLOGY AND POLITICAL THEORY: A   CONCPT
CONSIDERATION OF THE SOCIOLOGICAL BASIS OF   STRUCT
POLITICS." LAW CONSTN NAT/G DIPLOM DOMIN ROUTINE   SOC
REV ORD/FREE SOVEREIGN...PHIL/SCI CLASSIF BIBLIOG
18/20. PAGE 8 E0151

S40
GILL N.N.,"PERMANENT ADVISORY COMMISSIONS IN THE   DELIB/GP
FEDERAL GOVERNMENT." CLIENT FINAN OP/RES EDU/PROP   NAT/G
PARTIC ROUTINE INGP/REL KNOWL SKILL...CLASSIF   DECISION
TREND. PAGE 43 E0860

B51
WHEARE K.C.,MODERN CONSTITUTIONS (HOME UNIVERSITY   CONSTN
LIBRARY). UNIV LAW NAT/G LEGIS...CONCPT TREND   CLASSIF
BIBLIOG. PAGE 106 E2115   PWR
                                                     CREATE

B54
AUSTIN J.,THE PROVINCE OF JURISPRUDENCE DETERMINED   CONCPT
AND THE USES OF THE STUDY OF JURISPRUDENCE. MORAL   LAW
...CLASSIF LING STYLE 19. PAGE 6 E0119   JURID
                                                     GEN/LAWS

S55
WRIGHT Q.,"THE PEACEFUL ADJUSTMENT OF INTERNATIONAL   R+D
RELATIONS: PROBLEMS AND RESEARCH APPROACHES." UNIV   METH/CNCPT
INTELL EDU/PROP ADJUD ROUTINE KNOWL SKILL...INT/LAW   PEACE
JURID PHIL/SCI CLASSIF 20. PAGE 108 E2156

B60
LA PONCE J.A.,THE PROTECTION OF MINORITIES. WOR+45   INGP/REL
WOR-45 NAT/G POL/PAR SUFF...INT/LAW CLASSIF GP/COMP   DOMIN
GOV/COMP BIBLIOG 17/20 CIVIL/LIB CIV/RIGHTS.   SOCIETY
PAGE 62 E1242   RACE/REL

B62
ALLOTT A.N.,JUDICIAL AND LEGAL SYSTEMS IN AFRICA.   CT/SYS
LAW CONSTN JUDGE CONTROL...METH/CNCPT CLASSIF   AFR
CHARTS 20 COMMON/LAW. PAGE 4 E0070   JURID
                                                     COLONIAL

L62
SPAETH H.J.,"JUDICIAL POWER AS A VARIABLE   JUDGE
MOTIVATING SUPREME COURT BEHAVIOR." DELIB/GP ADJUD   DECISION
RATIONAL ATTIT PERSON ORD/FREE...CLASSIF STAT   PERS/COMP
GEN/METH. PAGE 93 E1860   PSY

B64
DUBISSON M.,LA COUR INTERNATIONALE DE JUSTICE.   CT/SYS
FRANCE LAW CONSTN JUDGE DOMIN ADJUD...INT/LAW   INT/ORG
CLASSIF RECORD ORG/CHARTS UN. PAGE 33 E0651

B64
SZLADITS C.,BIBLIOGRAPHY ON FOREIGN AND COMPARATIVE   BIBLIOG/A
LAW: BOOKS AND ARTICLES IN ENGLISH (SUPPLEMENT   JURID
1962). FINAN INDUS JUDGE LICENSE ADMIN CT/SYS   ADJUD
PARL/PROC OWN...INT/LAW CLASSIF METH/COMP NAT/COMP   LAW
20. PAGE 95 E1904

B65
BRIGGS H.W.,THE INTERNATIONAL LAW COMMISSION. LAW   INT/LAW
CONSTN LEGIS CREATE ADJUD CT/SYS ROUTINE TASK   DELIB/GP
EFFICIENCY...CLASSIF OBS UN. PAGE 15 E0302

B65
RENNER K.,MENSCH UND GESELLSCHAFT - GRUNDRISS EINER   SOC
SOZIOLOGIE (2ND ED.). STRATA FAM LABOR PROF/ORG WAR   STRUCT
...JURID CLASSIF 20. PAGE 84 E1685   NAT/G
                                                     SOCIETY

B65
VON GLAHN G.,LAW AMONG NATIONS: AN INTRODUCTION TO   ACADEM
PUBLIC INTERNATIONAL LAW. WOR+45 WOR-45 INT/ORG   INT/LAW
NAT/G CREATE ADJUD WAR...GEOG CLASSIF TREND   GEN/LAWS
BIBLIOG. PAGE 104 E2082   LAW

B65
WHITEMAN M.M.,DIGEST OF INTERNATIONAL LAW* VOLUME   INT/LAW
5. DEPARTMENT OF STATE PUBLICATION 7873. USA+45   NAT/G
WOR+45 OP/RES...CONCPT CLASSIF RECORD IDEA/COMP.   NAT/COMP
PAGE 106 E2118

B66
HOYT E.C.,NATIONAL POLICY AND INTERNATIONAL LAW*   INT/LAW
CASE STUDIES FROM AMERICAN CANAL POLICY* MONOGRAPH   USA-45
NO. 1 -- 1966-1967. PANAMA UK ELITES BAL/PWR   DIPLOM
EFFICIENCY...CLASSIF NAT/COMP SOC/EXP COLOMB   PWR
TREATY. PAGE 55 E1105

L66
HOLSTI K.J.,"RESOLVING INTERNATIONAL CONFLICTS* A   DIPLOM
TAXONOMY OF BEHAVIOR AND SOME FIGURES ON   PROB/SOLV
PROCEDURES." WOR+45 WOR-45 INT/ORG ADJUD EFFICIENCY   WAR
...STAT IDEA/COMP. PAGE 55 E1089   CLASSIF

L66
YALEM R.J.,"THE STUDY OF INTERNATIONAL   VOL/ASSN
ORGANIZATION, 1920-1965* A SURVEY OF THE   INT/ORG
LITERATURE." WOR+45 WOR-45 REGION...INT/LAW CLASSIF   BIBLIOG/A
RECORD HIST/WRIT CON/ANAL IDEA/COMP UN. PAGE 108
E2163

S66
LANDE G.R.,"THE EFFECT OF THE RESOLUTIONS OF THE   LEGIS
UNITED NATIONS GENERAL ASSEMBLY." WOR+45 LAW   EFFICIENCY
INT/ORG NAT/G CHOOSE ISOLAT ATTIT...CLASSIF   RESPECT
GEN/METH UN. PAGE 62 E1249

SHEEHY E.P.,"SELECTED REFERENCE BOOKS OF   S66
1965-1966." AGRI PERF/ART PRESS...GEOG HUM JURID   BIBLIOG/A
SOC LING WORSHIP. PAGE 91 E1817   INDEX
                                                     CLASSIF

                                                          B67
CLINARD M.B.,CRIMINAL BEHAVIOR SYSTEMS: A TYPOLOGY. BIBLIOG
WOR+45 LAW SOCIETY STRUCT R+D AGE/Y ATTIT WEALTH   CRIME
...CLASSIF CHARTS METH/COMP METH. PAGE 23 E0457   CRIMLGY
                                                     PERSON

                                                          B97
JENKS E.J.,LAW AND POLITICS IN THE MIDDLE AGES.   LAW
CHRIST-17C CULTURE STRUCT KIN NAT/G SECT CT/SYS   SOCIETY
GP/REL...CLASSIF CHARTS IDEA/COMP BIBLIOG 8/16.   ADJUST
PAGE 58 E1162

CLAUSWTZ/K....KARL VON CLAUSEWITZ

CLEMENCE/G....GEORGES CLEMENCEAU

CLEMENCEAU, GEORGES....SEE CLEMENCE/G

CLEMMER D. E0452,E0453

CLEMSON....CLEMSON UNIVERSITY

                                                          B64
DORMAN M.,WE SHALL OVERCOME. USA+45 ELITES ACADEM   RACE/REL
FORCES TOP/EX MURDER...JURID 20 CIV/RIGHTS   LAW
MISSISSIPP EVERS/MED CLEMSON. PAGE 32 E0638   DISCRIM

CLEVELAND H. E0454

CLEVELAND....CLEVELAND, OHIO

CLEVELND/G....PRESIDENT GROVER CLEVELAND

CLIENT....CLIENTS, CLIENTELE (BUT NOT CUSTOMERS)

                                                          S38
CLEMMER D.,"LEADERSHIP PHENOMENA IN A PRISON   PUB/INST
COMMUNITY." NEIGH PLAN CHOOSE PERSON ROLE...OBS   CRIMLGY
INT. PAGE 23 E0452   LEAD
                                                     CLIENT

                                                          S40
GILL N.N.,"PERMANENT ADVISORY COMMISSIONS IN THE   DELIB/GP
FEDERAL GOVERNMENT." CLIENT FINAN OP/RES EDU/PROP   NAT/G
PARTIC ROUTINE INGP/REL KNOWL SKILL...CLASSIF   DECISION
TREND. PAGE 43 E0860

                                                          B41
GELLHORN W.,FEDERAL ADMINISTRATIVE PROCEEDINGS.   EX/STRUC
USA+45 CLIENT FACE/GP NAT/G LOBBY REPRESENT PWR 20. LAW
PAGE 43 E0844   ADJUD
                                                     POLICY

                                                          B42
US LIBRARY OF CONGRESS,SOCIAL AND CULTURAL PROBLEMS BIBLIOG/A
IN WARTIME: APRIL 1941-MARCH 1942. WOR-45 CLIENT   WAR
SECT EDU/PROP CRIME LEISURE RACE/REL STRANGE ATTIT   SOC
DRIVE HEALTH...GEOG 20. PAGE 100 E2012   CULTURE

                                                          B49
APPLEBY P.H.,POLICY AND ADMINISTRATION. USA+45   REPRESENT
NAT/G LOBBY PWR 20. PAGE 5 E0101   EXEC
                                                     ADMIN
                                                     CLIENT

                                                          B52
APPLEBY P.H.,MORALITY AND ADMINISTRATION IN   REPRESENT
DEMOCRATIC GOVERNMENT. USA+45 CLIENT NAT/G EXEC   LOBBY
EFFICIENCY 20. PAGE 5 E0102   ADMIN
                                                     EX/STRUC

                                                          B56
FRANCIS R.G.,SERVICE AND PROCEDURE IN BUREAUCRACY.   CLIENT
EXEC LEAD ROUTINE...QU 20. PAGE 39 E0784   ADMIN
                                                     INGP/REL
                                                     REPRESENT

                                                          B56
REDFORD E.S.,PUBLIC ADMINISTRATION AND POLICY   EX/STRUC
FORMATION: STUDIES IN OIL, GAS, BANKING, RIVER   PROB/SOLV
DEVELOPMENT AND CORPORATE INVESTIGATIONS. USA+45   CONTROL
CLIENT NAT/G ADMIN LOBBY REPRESENT GOV/REL INGP/REL EXEC
20. PAGE 84 E1678

                                                          B57
BERLE A.A. JR.,ECONOMIC POWER AND FREE SOCIETY   LG/CO
(PAMPHLET). CLIENT CONSTN EX/STRUC ECO/TAC CONTROL   CAP/ISM
PARTIC PWR WEALTH MAJORIT. PAGE 11 E0205   INGP/REL
                                                     LEGIT

                                                          B57
COOPER F.E.,THE LAWYER AND ADMINISTRATIVE AGENCIES. CONSULT
USA+45 CLIENT LAW PROB/SOLV CT/SYS PERSON ROLE.   ADMIN
PAGE 25 E0500   ADJUD
                                                     DELIB/GP

                                                          S57
GOODE W.J.,"COMMUNITY WITHIN A COMMUNITY: THE   PROF/ORG
PROFESSIONS." STRATA STRUCT SANCTION INGP/REL...SOC NEIGH
GP/COMP. PAGE 45 E0886   CLIENT
                                                     CONTROL

                                                          B58
CLEMMER D.,THE PRISON COMMUNITY. CULTURE CONTROL   PUB/INST
LEAD ROUTINE PERS/REL PERSON...SOC METH/CNCPT.   CRIMLGY
PAGE 23 E0453   CLIENT
                                                     INGP/REL

                                                          S58
CRESSEY D.R.,"ACHIEVEMENT OF AN UNSTATED   PUB/INST
ORGANIZATIONAL GOAL: AN OBSERVATION ON PRISONS."   CLIENT
OP/RES PROB/SOLV PERS/REL ANOMIE ATTIT ROLE RESPECT NEIGH
CRIMLGY. PAGE 28 E0546   INGP/REL

                                                          B59
FERRY W.H.,THE CORPORATION AND THE ECONOMY. CLIENT   LG/CO
LAW CONSTN LABOR NAT/G PLAN INT/TRADE PARTIC CONSEN CONTROL
ORD/FREE PWR POLICY. PAGE 37 E0742   REPRESENT

                                                          B60
BORGATTA E.F.,SOCIAL WORKERS' PERCEPTIONS OF   SOC/WK
CLIENTS. SERV/IND ROUTINE PERS/REL DRIVE PERSON   ATTIT
RESPECT...SOC PERS/COMP 20. PAGE 14 E0268   CLIENT
                                                     PROB/SOLV

                                                          S60
MACKINNON F.,"THE UNIVERSITY: COMMUNITY OR   ACADEM
UTILITY?" CLIENT CONSTN INTELL FINAN NAT/G NEIGH   MGT
EDU/PROP PARTIC REPRESENT ROLE. PAGE 67 E1343   CONTROL
                                                     SERV/IND

                                                          S61
ABLARD C.D.,"EX PARTE CONTACTS WITH FEDERAL   EXEC
ADMINISTRATIVE AGENCIES." USA+45 CLIENT NAT/G   ADJUD
DELIB/GP ADMIN PWR 20. PAGE 2 E0044   LOBBY
                                                     REPRESENT

                                                          S61
AGNEW P.C.,"INTRODUCING CHANGE IN A MENTAL   ORD/FREE
HOSPITAL." CLIENT WORKER PROB/SOLV INGP/REL   PUB/INST
PERS/REL ADJUST. PAGE 3 E0054   PSY
                                                     ADMIN

                                                          B62
ASSOCIATION BAR OF NYC,REPORT ON ADMISSION   PUB/INST
PROCEDURES TO NEW YORK STATE MENTAL HOSPITALS. LAW   HEALTH
CONSTN INGP/REL RESPECT...PSY OBS RECORD. PAGE 6   CLIENT
E0108   ROUTINE

                                                          B62
CARSON P.,MATERIALS FOR WEST AFRICAN HISTORY IN THE BIBLIOG/A
ARCHIVES OF BELGIUM AND HOLLAND. CLIENT INDUS   COLONIAL
INT/TRADE ADMIN 17/19. PAGE 20 E0397   AFR
                                                     ECO/UNDEV

                                                          L62
CAVERS D.F.,"ADMINISTRATIVE DECISION-MAKING IN   REPRESENT
NUCLEAR FACILITIES LICENSING." USA+45 CLIENT ADMIN   LOBBY
EXEC 20 AEC. PAGE 21 E0410   PWR
                                                     CONTROL

                                                          S63
HILLS R.J.,"THE REPRESENTATIVE FUNCTION: NEGLECTED   LEAD
DIMENSION OF LEADERSHIP BEHAVIOR" USA+45 CLIENT   ADMIN
STRUCT SCHOOL PERS/REL...STAT QU SAMP LAB/EXP 20.   EXEC
PAGE 53 E1048   ACT/RES

                                                          S63
JOUGHIN L.,"ACADEMIC DUE PROCESS." DELIB/GP ADJUD   ACADEM
ROUTINE ORD/FREE...POLICY MAJORIT TREND. PAGE 59   LAW
E1175   PROF/ORG
                                                     CLIENT

                                                          B65
US OFFICE ECONOMIC OPPORTUNITY,CATALOG OF FEDERAL   BIBLIOG
PROGRAMS FOR INDIVIDUAL AND COMMUNITY IMPROVEMENT.   CLIENT
USA+45 GIVE RECEIVE ADMIN HEALTH KNOWL SKILL WEALTH ECO/TAC
CHARTS. PAGE 101 E2021   MUNIC

                                                          B66
CARLIN J.E.,LAWYER'S ETHICS. CLIENT STRUCT CONSULT   ATTIT
PERS/REL PWR...JURID OBS CHARTS 20. PAGE 19 E0378   PROF/ORG
                                                     INT

                                                          B67
GABRIEL P.P.,THE INTERNATIONAL TRANSFER OF   ECO/UNDEV

CORPORATE SKILLS: MANAGEMENT CONTRACTS IN LESS   AGREE
DEVELOPED COUNTRIES. CLIENT INDUS LG/CO PLAN   MGT
PROB/SOLV CAP/ISM ECO/TAC FOR/AID INT/TRADE RENT   CONSULT
ADMIN SKILL 20. PAGE 42 E0825

                                                   L67
BLUMBERG A.S.,"THE PRACTICE OF LAW AS CONFIDENCE   CT/SYS
GAME; ORGANIZATIONAL COOPTATION OF A PROFESSION." ADJUD
USA+45 CLIENT SOCIETY CONSULT ROLE JURID. PAGE 13 GP/REL
E0252   ADMIN

                                                   S67
MAYER M.,"THE IDEA OF JUSTICE AND THE POOR." USA+45 INCOME
CLIENT CONSULT RENT ADJUD DISCRIM KNOWL 20. PAGE 70 WEALTH
E1393   LAW
                                                   ORD/FREE

CLIFFORD/C....CLARK CLIFFORD

CLINARD M.B. E0455,E0456,E0457

CLIQUES....SEE FACE/GP

CLOGGER T.J. E0458

CLOWARD R.A. E0459

CLUBS....SEE VOL/ASSN, FACE/GP

CLYDE W.M. E0460

CMA....CANADIAN MEDICAL ASSOCIATION

CMN/WLTH....BRITISH COMMONWEALTH OF NATIONS; SEE
    ALSO VOL/ASSN, APPROPRIATE NATIONS, COMMONWLTH

                                                   N
INDEX TO LEGAL PERIODICALS. CANADA NEW/ZEALND UK   BIBLIOG
USA+45 USA-45 CONSTN LEGIS JUDGE ADJUD ADMIN   INDEX
CONTROL CT/SYS FEDERAL...CRIMLGY INT/LAW 20   LAW
CMN/WLTH AUSTRAL. PAGE 1 E0006   JURID

                                                   N
PUBLISHERS' CIRCULAR, THE OFFICIAL ORGAN OF THE   BIBLIOG
PUBLISHERS' ASSOCIATION OF GREAT BRITAIN AND   NAT/G
IRELAND. EUR+WWI MOD/EUR UK LAW PROB/SOLV DIPLOM   WRITING
COLONIAL ATTIT...HUM 19/20 CMN/WLTH. PAGE 2 E0025 LEAD

                                                   N
MINISTRY OF OVERSEAS DEVELOPME,TECHNICAL CO-   BIBLIOG
OPERATION -- A BIBLIOGRAPHY. UK LAW SOCIETY DIPLOM TEC/DEV
ECO/TAC FOR/AID...STAT 20 CMN/WLTH. PAGE 73 E1466 ECO/DEV
                                                   NAT/G

                                                   B27
GOOCH G.P.,ENGLISH DEMOCRATIC IDEAS IN THE   IDEA/COMP
SEVENTEENTH CENTURY (2ND ED.). UK LAW SECT FORCES MAJORIT
DIPLOM LEAD PARL/PROC REV ATTIT AUTHORIT...ANARCH EX/STRUC
CONCPT 17 PARLIAMENT CMN/WLTH REFORMERS. PAGE 45   CONSERVE
E0885

                                                   B28
CORBETT P.E.,CANADA AND WORLD POLITICS. LAW CULTURE NAT/G
SOCIETY STRUCT MARKET INT/ORG FORCES PLAN   CANADA
ECO/TAC LEGIT ORD/FREE PWR RESPECT...SOC CONCPT
TIME/SEQ TREND CMN/WLTH 20 LEAGUE/NAT. PAGE 26
E0504

                                                   B38
HOLDSWORTH W.S.,A HISTORY OF ENGLISH LAW; THE   LAW
CENTURIES OF SETTLEMENT AND REFORM (VOL. XI). UK   COLONIAL
CONSTN NAT/G EX/STRUC DIPLOM ADJUD CT/SYS LEAD   LEGIS
CRIME ATTIT...INT/LAW JURID 18 CMN/WLTH PARLIAMENT PARL/PROC
ENGLSH/LAW. PAGE 54 E1079

                                                   B46
GRIFFIN G.G.,A GUIDE TO MANUSCRIPTS RELATING TO   BIBLIOG/A
AMERICAN HISTORY IN BRITISH DEPOSITORIES. CANADA   ALL/VALS
IRELAND MOD/EUR UK USA+45 LAW DIPLOM ADMIN COLONIAL NAT/G
WAR NAT/LISM SOVEREIGN...GEOG INT/LAW 15/19
CMN/WLTH. PAGE 47 E0936

                                                   B50
WADE E.C.S.,CONSTITUTIONAL LAW; AN OUTLINE OF THE CONSTN
LAW AND PRACTICE OF THE CONSTITUTION. UK LEGIS   NAT/G
DOMIN ADMIN GP/REL 16/20 CMN/WLTH PARLIAMENT   PARL/PROC
ENGLSH/LAW. PAGE 104 E2087   LAW

                                                   B55
SWEET AND MAXWELL,A LEGAL BIBLIOGRAPHY OF THE   BIBLIOG/A
BRITISH COMMONWEALTH OF NATIONS (2ND ED. 7 VOLS.). LAW
UK LOC/G MUNIC JUDGE ADJUD CRIME OWN...JURID 14/20 CONSTN
CMN/WLTH. PAGE 95 E1900   CT/SYS

                                                   B56
WEIS P.,NATIONALITY AND STATELESSNESS IN   INT/ORG
INTERNATIONAL LAW. UK WOR+45 WOR-45 LAW CONSTN   SOVEREIGN

NAT/G DIPLOM EDU/PROP LEGIT ROUTINE RIGID/FLEX   INT/LAW
...JURID RECORD CMN/WLTH 20. PAGE 105 E2109

                                                   B57
DONALDSON A.G.,SOME COMPARATIVE ASPECTS OF IRISH   CONSTN
LAW. IRELAND NAT/G DIPLOM ADMIN CT/SYS LEAD ATTIT LAW
SOVEREIGN...JURID BIBLIOG/A 12/20 CMN/WLTH. PAGE 32 NAT/COMP
E0635   INT/LAW

                                                   B58
MANSERGH N.,COMMONWEALTH PERSPECTIVES. GHANA UK LAW DIPLOM
VOL/ASSN CONFER HEALTH SOVEREIGN...GEOG CHARTS   COLONIAL
ANTHOL 20 CMN/WLTH AUSTRAL. PAGE 68 E1363   INT/ORG
                                                   INGP/REL

                                                   S62
THOMPSON D.,"THE UNITED KINGDOM AND THE TREATY OF ADJUD
ROME." EUR+WWI INT/ORG NAT/G DELIB/GP LEGIS   JURID
INT/TRADE RIGID/FLEX...CONCPT EEC PARLIAMENT
CMN/WLTH 20. PAGE 96 E1918

                                                   B63
FAWCETT J.E.S.,THE BRITISH COMMONWEALTH IN   INT/LAW
INTERNATIONAL LAW. LAW INT/ORG NAT/G VOL/ASSN   STRUCT
OP/RES DIPLOM ADJUD CENTRAL CONSEN...NET/THEORY   COLONIAL
CMN/WLTH TREATY. PAGE 36 E0723

                                                   S63
HARNETTY P.,"CANADA, SOUTH AFRICA AND THE   AFR
COMMONWEALTH." CANADA SOUTH/AFR LAW INT/ORG   ATTIT
VOL/ASSN DELIB/GP LEGIS TOP/EX ECO/TAC LEGIT DRIVE
MORAL...CONCPT CMN/WLTH 20. PAGE 50 E1000

                                                   B64
NATIONAL BOOK LEAGUE,THE COMMONWEALTH IN BOOKS: AN BIBLIOG/A
ANNOTATED LIST. CANADA UK LOC/G SECT ADMIN...SOC   JURID
BIOG 20 CMN/WLTH. PAGE 76 E1526   NAT/G

                                                   B66
US DEPARTMENT OF STATE,RESEARCH ON WESTERN EUROPE, BIBLIOG/A
GREAT BRITAIN, AND CANADA (EXTERNAL RESEARCH LIST EUR+WWI
NO 3-25). CANADA GERMANY/W UK LAW CULTURE NAT/G   DIPLOM
POL/PAR FORCES EDU/PROP REGION MARXISM...GEOG SOC
WORSHIP 20 CMN/WLTH. PAGE 100 E1998

COALITIONS....SEE VOL/ASSN

COASTGUARD....COAST GUARD

COBB/HOWLL....HOWELL COBB

COERCE....COERCION, VIOLENCE; SEE ALSO FORCES,
    PROCESSES AND PRACTICES INDEX, PART G, P. XIII

                                                   N
BACKGROUND; JOURNAL OF INTERNATIONAL STUDIES   BIBLIOG
ASSOCIATION. INT/ORG FORCES ACT/RES EDU/PROP COERCE DIPLOM
NAT/LISM PEACE ATTIT...INT/LAW CONCPT 20. PAGE 1   POLICY
E0004

                                                   B00
DARBY W.E.,INTERNATIONAL TRIBUNALS. WOR-45 NAT/G   INT/ORG
ECO/TAC DOMIN LEGIT CT/SYS COERCE ORD/FREE PWR   ADJUD
SOVEREIGN JURID. PAGE 29 E0567   PEACE
                                                   INT/LAW

                                                   B00
HOLLAND T.E.,STUDIES IN INTERNATIONAL LAW. TURKEY INT/ORG
USSR WOR-45 CONSTN NAT/G DIPLOM DOMIN LEGIT COERCE LAW
WAR PEACE ORD/FREE PWR SOVEREIGN...JURID CHARTS 20 INT/LAW
PARLIAMENT SUEZ TREATY. PAGE 54 E1084

                                                   L00
HISTORICUS,"LETTERS AND SOME QUESTIONS OF   WEALTH
INTERNATIONAL LAW." FRANCE NETHERLAND UK USA-45   JURID
WOR-45 LAW NAT/G COERCE...SOC CONCPT GEN/LAWS   WAR
TOT/POP 19 CIVIL/WAR. PAGE 53 E1054   INT/LAW

                                                   B03
MOREL E.D.,THE BRITISH CASE IN FRENCH CONGO.   DIPLOM
CONGO/BRAZ FRANCE UK COERCE MORAL WEALTH...POLICY INT/TRADE
INT/LAW 20 CONGO/LEOP. PAGE 74 E1490   COLONIAL
                                                   AFR

                                                   B09
HOLLAND T.E.,LETTERS UPON WAR AND NEUTRALITY.   LAW
WOR-45 NAT/G FORCES JUDGE ECO/TAC LEGIT CT/SYS   INT/LAW
NEUTRAL ROUTINE COERCE...JURID TIME/SEQ 20. PAGE 55 INT/ORG
E1085   WAR

                                                   B14
VECCHIO G.D.,THE FORMAL BASES OF LAW (TRANS. BY J. LAW
LISLE). DOMIN LEGIT CONTROL COERCE UTIL MORAL PWR JURID
...CONCPT TIME/SEQ 17/20 COMMON/LAW NATURL/LAW.   GEN/LAWS

PAGE 103 E2074   IDEA/COMP

                                                           B17
DE VICTORIA F.,DE INDIS ET DE JURE BELLI (1557) IN   WAR
F. DE VICTORIA, DE INDIS ET DE JURE BELLI   INT/LAW
REFLECTIONES. UNIV NAT/G SECT CHIEF PARTIC COERCE   OWN
PEACE MORAL...POLICY 16 INDIAN/AM CHRISTIAN
CONSCN/OBJ. PAGE 30 E0598

                                                           N18
BREWER D.J.,THE MOVEMENT OF COERCION (PAMPHLET).   GP/REL
CONSTN INDUS ADJUD COERCE OWN WEALTH...OLD/LIB   LABOR
JURID 19 SUPREME/CT. PAGE 15 E0296   LG/CO
                                                     LAW

                                                           N19
AMERICAN CIVIL LIBERTIES UNION,"WE HOLD THESE   ORD/FREE
TRUTHS" FREEDOM, JUSTICE, EQUALITY: REPORT ON CIVIL LAW
LIBERTIES (A PERIODICAL PAMPHLET COVERING 1951-53). RACE/REL
USA+45 ACADEM NAT/G FORCES LEGIS COERCE CIVMIL/REL   CONSTN
GOV/REL DISCRIM PRIVIL MARXISM...OLD/LIB 20 ACLU UN
CIVIL/LIB. PAGE 4 E0076

                                                           N19
MISSISSIPPI ADVISORY COMMITTEE,REPORT ON   RACE/REL
MISSISSIPPI (PAMPHLET). USA+45 LAW PROVS FORCES   DISCRIM
ADJUD PWR...SOC/WK INT 20 MISSISSIPP NEGRO   COERCE
CIV/RIGHTS. PAGE 73 E1469   ORD/FREE

                                                           B23
DE MONTESQUIEU C.,THE SPIRIT OF LAWS (2 VOLS.)   JURID
(TRANS. BY THOMAS NUGENT). FRANCE FINAN SECT   LAW
INT/TRADE TAX COERCE REV DISCRIM HABITAT ORD/FREE   CONCPT
19 ALEMBERT/J CIVIL/LAW. PAGE 30 E0588   GEN/LAWS

                                                           B27
LAUTERPACHT H.,PRIVATE LAW SOURCES AND ANALOGIES OF INT/ORG
INTERNATIONAL LAW. WOR-45 NAT/G DELIB/GP LEGIT   ADJUD
COERCE ATTIT ORD/FREE PWR SOVEREIGN...JURID CONCPT   PEACE
HIST/WRIT TIME/SEQ GEN/METH LEAGUE/NAT 20. PAGE 63   INT/LAW
E1264

                                                           B29
CONWELL-EVANS T.P.,THE LEAGUE COUNCIL IN ACTION.   DELIB/GP
EUR+WWI TURKEY UK USSR WOR-45 INT/ORG FORCES JUDGE   INT/LAW
ECO/TAC EDU/PROP LEGIT ROUTINE ARMS/CONT COERCE
ATTIT PWR...MAJORIT GEOG JURID CONCPT LEAGUE/NAT
TOT/POP VAL/FREE TUNIS 20. PAGE 25 E0498

                                                           B30
BENTHAM J.,THE RATIONALE OF PUNISHMENT. UK LAW   CRIME
LOC/G NAT/G LEGIS CONTROL...JURID GEN/LAWS   SANCTION
COURT/SYS 19. PAGE 10 E0192   COERCE
                                                     ORD/FREE

                                                           B32
EAGLETON C.,INTERNATIONAL GOVERNMENT. BRAZIL FRANCE INT/ORG
GERMANY ITALY UK USSR WOR-45 DELIB/GP TOP/EX PLAN   JURID
ECO/TAC EDU/PROP LEGIT ADJUD REGION ARMS/CONT   DIPLOM
COERCE ATTIT PWR...GEOG MGT VAL/FREE LEAGUE/NAT 20. INT/LAW
PAGE 34 E0670

                                                           B33
LAUTERPACHT H.,THE FUNCTION OF LAW IN THE   INT/ORG
INTERNATIONAL COMMUNITY. WOR-45 NAT/G FORCES CREATE LAW
DOMIN LEGIT COERCE WAR PEACE ATTIT ORD/FREE PWR   INT/LAW
SOVEREIGN...JURID CONCPT METH/CNCPT TIME/SEQ
GEN/LAWS GEN/METH LEAGUE/NAT TOT/POP VAL/FREE 20.
PAGE 63 E1265

                                                           B34
GONZALEZ PALENCIA A.,ESTUDIO HISTORICO SOBRE LA   LEGIT
CENSURA GUBERNATIVA EN ESPANA 1800-1833. NAT/G   EDU/PROP
COERCE INGP/REL ATTIT AUTHORIT KNOWL...POLICY JURID PRESS
19. PAGE 44 E0884   CONTROL

                                                           B36
BRIERLY J.L.,THE LAW OF NATIONS (2ND ED.). WOR+45   DIPLOM
WOR-45 INT/ORG AGREE CONTROL COERCE WAR NAT/LISM   INT/LAW
PEACE PWR 16/20 TREATY LEAGUE/NAT. PAGE 15 E0297   NAT/G

                                                           B39
BALDWIN L.D.,WHISKEY REBELS; THE STORY OF A   REV
FRONTIER UPRISING. USA-45 LAW ADJUD LEAD COERCE PWR POL/PAR
...BIBLIOG/A 18 PENNSYLVAN FEDERALIST. PAGE 8 E0145 TAX
                                                     TIME/SEQ

                                                           B39
LAVES W.H.C.,INTERNATIONAL SECURITY. EUR+WWI   ORD/FREE
GERMANY UK USA-45 LAW NAT/G DELIB/GP TOP/EX COERCE   LEGIT
PWR...POLICY FASCIST CONCPT HIST/WRIT GEN/LAWS   ARMS/CONT
LEAGUE/NAT NAZI 20. PAGE 63 E1267   BAL/PWR

                                                           B39
ZIMMERN A.,THE LEAGUE OF NATIONS AND THE RULE OF   INT/ORG
LAW. WOR-45 STRUCT NAT/G DELIB/GP EX/STRUC BAL/PWR   LAW

DOMIN LEGIT COERCE ORD/FREE PWR...POLICY RECORD   DIPLOM
LEAGUE/NAT TOT/POP VAL/FREE 20 LEAGUE/NAT. PAGE 108
E2170

                                                           B40
BROWN A.D.,COMPULSORY MILITARY TRAINING: SELECT   BIBLIOG/A
LIST OF REFERENCES (PAMPHLET). USA-45 CONSTN   FORCES
VOL/ASSN COERCE 20. PAGE 16 E0311   JURID
                                                     ATTIT

                                                           B41
NIEMEYER G.,LAW WITHOUT FORCE: THE FUNCTION OF   COERCE
POLITICS IN INTERNATIONAL LAW. PLAN INSPECT DIPLOM   LAW
REPAR LEGIT ADJUD WAR ORD/FREE...IDEA/COMP   PWR
METH/COMP GEN/LAWS 20. PAGE 77 E1549   INT/LAW

                                                           B42
FORTESCU J.,IN PRAISE OF ENGLISH LAW (1464) (TRANS. LAW
BY S.B. CHRIMES). UK ELITES CHIEF FORCES CT/SYS   CONSTN
COERCE CRIME GOV/REL ILLEGIT...JURID GOV/COMP   LEGIS
GEN/LAWS 15. PAGE 39 E0774   ORD/FREE

                                                           B43
MICAUD C.A.,THE FRENCH RIGHT AND NAZI GERMANY   DIPLOM
1933-1939: A STUDY OF PUBLIC OPINION. GERMANY UK   AGREE
USSR POL/PAR ARMS/CONT COERCE DETER PEACE
RIGID/FLEX PWR MARXISM...FASCIST TREND 20
LEAGUE/NAT TREATY. PAGE 73 E1454

                                                           B43
SERENI A.P.,THE ITALIAN CONCEPTION OF INTERNATIONAL LAW
LAW. EUR+WWI MOD/EUR INT/ORG NAT/G DOMIN COERCE   TIME/SEQ
ORD/FREE FASCISM...OBS/ENVIR TREND 20. PAGE 90   INT/LAW
E1804   ITALY

                                                           B44
DE HUSZAR G.B.,NEW PERSPECTIVES ON PEACE. UNIV   ATTIT
CULTURE SOCIETY ECO/DEV ECO/UNDEV NAT/G FORCES   MYTH
CREATE ECO/TAC DOMIN ADJUD COERCE DRIVE ORD/FREE   PEACE
...GEOG JURID PSY SOC CONCPT TOT/POP. PAGE 29 E0584 WAR

                                                           B45
TINGSTERN H.,PEACE AND SECURITY AFTER WW II. WOR-45 INT/ORG
DELIB/GP TOP/EX LEGIT CT/SYS COERCE PEACE ATTIT   ORD/FREE
PERCEPT...CONCPT LEAGUE/NAT 20. PAGE 96 E1927   WAR
                                                     INT/LAW

                                                           B45
WEST R.,CONSCIENCE AND SOCIETY: A STUDY OF THE   COERCE
PSYCHOLOGICAL PREREQUISITES OF LAW AND ORDER. FUT   INT/LAW
UNIV LAW SOCIETY STRUCT DIPLOM WAR PERS/REL SUPEGO   ORD/FREE
...SOC 20. PAGE 105 E2112   PERSON

                                                           S45
DAVIS A.,"CASTE, ECONOMY, AND VIOLENCE" (BMR)"   STRATA
USA-45 LAW SOCIETY STRUCT SECT SANCTION COERCE   RACE/REL
MARRIAGE SEX...PSY SOC SOC/INTEG 18/20 NEGRO   DISCRIM
MISCEGEN SOUTH/US. PAGE 29 E0570

                                                           B46
KEETON G.W.,MAKING INTERNATIONAL LAW WORK. FUT   INT/ORG
WOR-45 NAT/G DELIB/GP FORCES LEGIT COERCE PEACE   ADJUD
ATTIT RIGID/FLEX ORD/FREE PWR...JURID CONCPT   INT/LAW
HIST/WRIT GEN/METH LEAGUE/NAT 20. PAGE 60 E1193

                                                           S48
ALEXANDER L.,"WAR CRIMES, THEIR SOCIAL-   DRIVE
PSYCHOLOGICAL ASPECTS." EUR+WWI GERMANY LAW CULTURE WAR
ELITES KIN POL/PAR PUB/INST FORCES DOMIN EDU/PROP
COERCE CRIME ATTIT SUPEGO HEALTH MORAL PWR FASCISM
...PSY OBS TREND GEN/LAWS NAZI 20. PAGE 3 E0061

                                                           B49
KAFKA G.,FREIHEIT UND ANARCHIE. SECT COERCE DETER   CONCPT
WAR ATTIT...IDEA/COMP 20 NATO. PAGE 59 E1179   ORD/FREE
                                                     JURID
                                                     INT/ORG

                                                           B49
THOREAU H.D.,CIVIL DISOBEDIENCE (1849). USA-45 LAW   GEN/LAWS
CONSTN TAX COERCE REPRESENT GP/REL SUPEGO...MAJORIT ORD/FREE
CONCPT 19. PAGE 96 E1923   POLICY

                                                           B50
BERMAN H.J.,JUSTICE IN RUSSIA; AN INTERPRETATION OF JURID
SOVIET LAW. USSR LAW STRUCT LABOR FORCES AGREE   ADJUD
GP/REL ORD/FREE SOCISM...TIME/SEQ 20. PAGE 11 E0207 MARXISM
                                                     COERCE

                                                           B51
FITCH R.E.,THE LIMITS OF LIBERTY. COERCE...JURID   ORD/FREE
GEN/LAWS. PAGE 38 E0759   CONCPT
                                                     PWR

                                                           B52
COLEMAN J.W. JR.,DEATH AT THE COURT-HOUSE. CONTROL   CROWD

COERCE 20 KENTUCKY. PAGE 24 E0472 — ORD/FREE CRIME CT/SYS

B52
FERRELL R.H.,PEACE IN THEIR TIME. FRANCE UK USA+45 INT/ORG NAT/G FORCES CREATE AGREE ARMS/CONT COERCE WAR TREATY 20 WILSON/W LEAGUE/NAT BRIAND/A. PAGE 37 E0741 — PEACE DIPLOM

B52
LIPPMANN W.,ISOLATION AND ALLIANCES: AN AMERICAN SPEAKS TO THE BRITISH. USA+45 USA-45 INT/ORG AGREE COERCE DETER WAR PEACE MORAL 20 TREATY INTERVENT. PAGE 65 E1301 — DIPLOM SOVEREIGN COLONIAL ATTIT

B55
BENTON W.E.,NUREMBERG: GERMAN VIEWS OF THE WAR TRIALS. EUR+WWI GERMANY VOL/ASSN LEAD PARTIC COERCE INGP/REL RACE/REL TOTALISM SUPEGO ORD/FREE...ANTHOL NUREMBERG. PAGE 10 E0201 — CRIME WAR LAW JURID

B55
FLIESS P.J.,FREEDOM OF THE PRESS IN THE GERMAN REPUBLIC, 1918-1933. GERMANY LAW CONSTN POL/PAR LEGIS WRITING ADMIN COERCE MURDER MARXISM...POLICY BIBLIOG 20 WEIMAR/REP. PAGE 39 E0765 — EDU/PROP ORD/FREE JURID PRESS

B55
KHADDURI M.,WAR AND PEACE IN THE LAW OF ISLAM. CONSTN CULTURE SOCIETY STRATA NAT/G PROVS SECT FORCES TOP/EX CREATE DOMIN EDU/PROP ADJUD COERCE ATTIT RIGID/FLEX ALL/VALS...CONCPT TIME/SEQ TOT/POP VAL/FREE. PAGE 61 E1209 — ISLAM JURID PEACE WAR

B55
LARROWE C.P.,SHAPE-UP AND HIRING HALL. TRIBUTE ADJUD CONTROL SANCTION COERCE CRIME GP/REL PWR ...CHARTS 20 AFL/CIO NEWYORK/C SEATTLE. PAGE 63 E1256 — LABOR INDUS WORKER NAT/G

B55
UN HEADQUARTERS LIBRARY,BIBLIOGRAPHIE DE LA CHARTE DES NATIONS UNIES. CHINA/COM KOREA WOR+45 VOL/ASSN CONFER ADMIN COERCE PEACE ATTIT ORD/FREE SOVEREIGN ...INT/LAW 20 UNESCO UN. PAGE 97 E1953 — BIBLIOG/A INT/ORG DIPLOM

B57
BLOOMFIELD L.M.,EGYPT, ISRAEL AND THE GULF OF AQABA: IN INTERNATIONAL LAW. LAW NAT/G CONSULT FORCES PLAN ECO/TAC ROUTINE COERCE ATTIT DRIVE PERCEPT PERSON RIGID/FLEX LOVE PWR WEALTH...GEOG CONCPT MYTH TREND. PAGE 13 E0250 — ISLAM INT/LAW UAR

B57
COMM. STUDY ORGAN. PEACE,STRENGTHENING THE UNITED NATIONS. FUT USA+45 WOR+45 CONSTN NAT/G DELIB/GP FORCES LEGIS ECO/TAC LEGIT COERCE PEACE...JURID CONCPT UN COLD/WAR 20. PAGE 24 E0482 — INT/ORG ORD/FREE

B57
ROWAN C.T.,GO SOUTH TO SORROW. USA+45 STRUCT NAT/G EDU/PROP LEAD COERCE ISOLAT DRIVE SUPEGO RESPECT ...PREDICT 20 NEGRO SUPREME/CT SOUTH/US CIV/RIGHTS. PAGE 86 E1728 — RACE/REL DISCRIM ANOMIE LAW

B58
ALLEN C.K.,ASPECTS OF JUSTICE. UK FAM COERCE CRIME MARRIAGE AGE/Y LOVE 20 ENGLSH/LAW. PAGE 4 E0068 — JURID MORAL ORD/FREE

B58
BOWETT D.W.,SELF-DEFENSE IN INTERNATIONAL LAW. EUR+WWI MOD/EUR WOR+45 WOR-45 SOCIETY INT/ORG CONSULT DIPLOM LEGIT COERCE ATTIT ORD/FREE...JURID 20 UN. PAGE 14 E0276 — ADJUD CONCPT WAR INT/LAW

B58
CAUGHEY J.W.,IN CLEAR AND PRESENT DANGER. USA+45 ADJUD COERCE ATTIT AUTHORIT...POLICY 20 COLD/WAR MCCARTHY/J. PAGE 21 E0408 — NAT/G CONTROL DOMIN ORD/FREE

B58
DUCLOUX L.,FROM BLACKMAIL TO TREASON. FRANCE PLAN DIPLOM EDU/PROP PRESS RUMOR NAT/LISM...CRIMLGY 20. PAGE 33 E0653 — COERCE CRIME NAT/G PWR

B58
GARDINER H.C.,CATHOLIC VIEWPOINT ON CENSORSHIP. DEBATE COERCE GP/REL...JURID CONCPT 20. PAGE 42 E0835 — WRITING LOBBY CATHISM EDU/PROP

B58
JENKS C.W.,THE COMMON LAW OF MANKIND. EUR+WWI MOD/EUR SPACE WOR+45 INT/ORG BAL/PWR ARMS/CONT COERCE SUPEGO MORAL...TREND 20. PAGE 58 E1154 — JURID SOVEREIGN

S58
STAAR R.F.,"ELECTIONS IN COMMUNIST POLAND." EUR+WWI SOCIETY INT/ORG NAT/G POL/PAR LEGIS ACT/RES ECO/TAC EDU/PROP ADJUD ADMIN ROUTINE COERCE TOTALISM ATTIT ORD/FREE PWR 20. PAGE 93 E1864 — COM CHOOSE POLAND

B59
BRIGGS A.,CHARTIST STUDIES. UK LAW NAT/G WORKER EDU/PROP COERCE SUFF GP/REL ATTIT...ANTHOL 19. PAGE 15 E0300 — INDUS STRATA LABOR POLICY

B59
COMM. STUDY ORGAN. PEACE,ORGANIZING PEACE IN THE NUCLEAR AGE. FUT CONSULT DELIB/GP DOMIN ADJUD ROUTINE COERCE ORD/FREE...TECHNIC INT/LAW JURID NEW/IDEA UN COLD/WAR 20. PAGE 24 E0483 — INT/ORG ACT/RES NUC/PWR

B59
KNIERIEM A.,THE NUREMBERG TRIALS. EUR+WWI GERMANY VOL/ASSN LEAD COERCE WAR INGP/REL TOTALISM SUPEGO ORD/FREE...CONCPT METH/COMP. PAGE 61 E1225 — INT/LAW CRIME PARTIC JURID

L59
OBERER W.E.,"VOLUNTARY IMPARTIAL REVIEW OF LABOR: SOME REFLECTIONS." DELIB/GP LEGIS PROB/SOLV ADJUD CONTROL COERCE PWR PLURISM POLICY. PAGE 78 E1570 — LABOR LAW PARTIC INGP/REL

S59
CARLSTON K.S.,"NATIONALIZATION: AN ANALYTIC APPROACH." WOR+45 INT/ORG ECO/TAC DOMIN LEGIT ADJUD COERCE ORD/FREE PWR WEALTH SOCISM...JURID CONCPT TREND STERTYP TOT/POP VAL/FREE 20. PAGE 19 E0380 — INDUS NAT/G NAT/LISM SOVEREIGN

S59
SOHN L.B.,"THE DEFINITION OF AGGRESSION." FUT LAW FORCES LEGIT ADJUD ROUTINE COERCE ORD/FREE PWR ...MAJORIT JURID QUANT COLD/WAR 20. PAGE 92 E1855 — INT/ORG CT/SYS DETER SOVEREIGN

S59
STONE J.,"CONFLICT MANAGEMENT THROUGH CONTEMPORARY INTERNATIONAL LAW AND ORGANIZATION." WOR+45 LAW NAT/G CREATE BAL/PWR DOMIN LEGIT ROUTINE COERCE ATTIT ORD/FREE PWR SOVEREIGN...JURID 20. PAGE 94 E1880 — INT/ORG INT/LAW

B60
BAYLEY D.H.,VIOLENT AGITATION AND THE DEMOCRATIC PROCESS IN INDIA. INDIA LAW POL/PAR 20. PAGE 8 E0159 — COERCE CROWD CONSTN PROB/SOLV

B60
ENGEL J.,THE SECURITY OF THE FREE WORLD. USSR WOR+45 STRATA STRUCT ECO/DEV ECO/UNDEV INT/ORG DELIB/GP FORCES DOMIN LEGIT ADJUD EXEC ARMS/CONT COERCE...POLICY CONCPT NEW/IDEA TIME/SEQ GEN/LAWS COLD/WAR WORK UN 20 NATO. PAGE 35 E0689 — COM TREND DIPLOM

B60
GELLHORN W.,AMERICAN RIGHTS: THE CONSTITUTION IN ACTION. USA+45 USA-45 LEGIS ADJUD COERCE RACE/REL DISCRIM MARXISM 20 SUPREME/CT. PAGE 43 E0846 — ORD/FREE JURID CT/SYS CONSTN

B60
JENNINGS R.,PROGRESS OF INTERNATIONAL LAW. FUT WOR+45 WOR-45 SOCIETY NAT/G VOL/ASSN DELIB/GP DIPLOM EDU/PROP LEGIT COERCE ATTIT DRIVE MORAL ORD/FREE...JURID CONCPT OBS TIME/SEQ TREND GEN/LAWS. PAGE 58 E1164 — INT/ORG LAW INT/LAW

B60
LENCZOWSKI G.,OIL AND STATE IN THE MIDDLE EAST. FUT IRAN LAW ECO/UNDEV EXTR/IND NAT/G TOP/EX PLAN TEC/DEV ECO/TAC LEGIT ADMIN COERCE ATTIT ALL/VALS PWR...CHARTS 20. PAGE 64 E1283 — ISLAM INDUS NAT/LISM

B60
MOCTEZUMA A.P.,EL CONFLICTO RELIGIOSO DE 1926 (2ND ED.). L/A+17C LAW NAT/G LOBBY COERCE GP/REL ATTIT ...POLICY 20 MEXIC/AMER CHURCH/STA. PAGE 74 E1476 — SECT ORD/FREE DISCRIM REV

L60
KUNZ J.,"SANCTIONS IN INTERNATIONAL LAW." WOR+45 WOR-45 LEGIT ARMS/CONT COERCE PEACE ATTIT ...METH/CNCPT TIME/SEQ TREND 20. PAGE 62 E1234 — INT/ORG ADJUD INT/LAW

S60
O'BRIEN W.,"THE ROLE OF FORCE IN THE INTERNATIONAL INT/ORG
JURIDICAL ORDER." WOR+45 NAT/G FORCES DOMIN ADJUD COERCE
ARMS/CONT DETER NUC/PWR WAR ATTIT PWR...CATH
INT/LAW JURID CONCPT TREND STERTYP GEN/LAWS 20.
PAGE 78 E1564

S60
SCHACHTER O.,"THE ENFORCEMENT OF INTERNATIONAL INT/ORG
JUDICIAL AND ARBITRAL DECISIONS." WOR+45 NAT/G ADJUD
ECO/TAC DOMIN LEGIT ROUTINE COERCE ATTIT DRIVE INT/LAW
ALL/VALS PWR...METH/CNCPT TREND TOT/POP 20 UN.
PAGE 87 E1750

S60
THOMPSON K.W.,"MORAL PURPOSE IN FOREIGN POLICY: MORAL
REALITIES AND ILLUSIONS." WOR+45 WOR-45 LAW CULTURE JURID
SOCIETY INT/ORG PLAN ADJUD ADMIN COERCE RIGID/FLEX DIPLOM
SUPEGO KNOWL ORD/FREE PWR...SOC TREND SOC/EXP
TOT/POP 20. PAGE 96 E1921

C60
MCCLEERY R.,"COMMUNICATION PATTERNS AS BASES OF PERS/REL
SYSTEMS OF AUTHORITY AND POWER" IN THEORETICAL PUB/INST
STUDIES IN SOCIAL ORGAN. OF PRISON-BMR. USA+45 PWR
SOCIETY STRUCT EDU/PROP ADMIN CONTROL COERCE CRIME DOMIN
GP/REL AUTHORIT...SOC 20. PAGE 70 E1400

B61
ANAND R.P.,COMPULSORY JURISDICTION OF INTERNATIONAL INT/ORG
COURT OF JUSTICE. FUT WOR+45 SOCIETY PLAN LEGIT COERCE
ADJUD ATTIT DRIVE PERSON ORD/FREE...JURID CONCPT INT/LAW
TREND 20 ICJ. PAGE 5 E0086

B61
JUSTICE,THE CITIZEN AND THE ADMINISTRATION: THE INGP/REL
REDRESS OF GRIEVANCES (PAMPHLET). EUR+WWI UK LAW CONSULT
CONSTN STRATA NAT/G CT/SYS PARTIC COERCE...NEW/IDEA ADJUD
IDEA/COMP 20 OMBUDSMAN. PAGE 59 E1176 REPRESENT

B61
LARSON A.,WHEN NATIONS DISAGREE. USA+45 WOR+45 INT/LAW
INT/ORG ADJUD COERCE CRIME OWN SOVEREIGN...POLICY DIPLOM
JURID 20. PAGE 63 E1258 WAR

B61
MCDOUGAL M.S.,LAW AND MINIMUM WORLD PUBLIC ORDER. INT/ORG
WOR+45 SOCIETY NAT/G DELIB/GP EDU/PROP LEGIT ADJUD ORD/FREE
COERCE ATTIT PERSON...JURID CONCPT RECORD TREND INT/LAW
TOT/POP 20. PAGE 70 E1406

B62
CARLSTON K.S.,LAW AND ORGANIZATION IN WORLD INT/ORG
SOCIETY. WOR+45 FINAN ECO/TAC DOMIN LEGIT CT/SYS LAW
ROUTINE COERCE ORD/FREE PWR WEALTH...PLURIST
DECISION JURID MGT METH/CNCPT GEN/LAWS 20. PAGE 19
E0381

B62
CURRY J.E.,RACE TENSIONS AND THE POLICE. LAW MUNIC FORCES
NEIGH TEC/DEV RUMOR CONTROL COERCE GP/REL ATTIT RACE/REL
...SOC 20 NEGRO. PAGE 28 E0558 CROWD
ORD/FREE

B62
HEYDECKER J.J.,THE NUREMBERG TRIAL: HISTORY OF NAZI LAW
GERMANY AS REVEALED THROUGH THE TESTIMONY AT CRIME
NUREMBERG. EUR+WWI GERMANY VOL/ASSN LEAD COERCE PARTIC
CROWD INGP/REL RACE/REL SUPEGO ORD/FREE...CONCPT 20 TOTALISM
NAZI ANTI/SEMIT NUREMBERG JEWS. PAGE 52 E1036

B62
SOMMER T.,DEUTSCHLAND UND JAPAN ZWISCHEN DEN DIPLOM
MACHTEN. GERMANY DELIB/GP BAL/PWR AGREE COERCE WAR
TOTALISM PWR 20 CHINJAP TREATY. PAGE 93 E1856 ATTIT

B62
TRISKA J.F.,THE THEORY, LAW, AND POLICY OF SOVIET COM
TREATIES. WOR+45 WOR-45 CONSTN INT/ORG NAT/G LAW
VOL/ASSN DOMIN LEGIT COERCE ATTIT PWR RESPECT INT/LAW
...POLICY JURID CONCPT OBS SAMP TIME/SEQ TREND USSR
GEN/LAWS 20. PAGE 97 E1941

L62
PETKOFF D.K.,"RECOGNITION AND NON-RECOGNITION OF INT/ORG
STATES AND GOVERNMENTS IN INTERNATIONAL LAW." ASIA LAW
COM USA+45 WOR+45 NAT/G ACT/RES DIPLOM DOMIN LEGIT INT/LAW
COERCE ORD/FREE PWR...CONCPT GEN/LAWS 20. PAGE 80
E1611

L62
UNITED NATIONS,"CAPITAL PUNISHMENT." WOR+45 CULTURE LAW
NAT/G ROUTINE COERCE HEALTH PWR...POLICY SOC QU STAT
CHARTS VAL/FREE 20. PAGE 98 E1967

S62
CRANE R.D.,"LAW AND STRATEGY IN SPACE." FUT USA+45 CONCPT
WOR+45 AIR LAW INT/ORG NAT/G FORCES ACT/RES PLAN SPACE
BAL/PWR LEGIT ARMS/CONT COERCE ORD/FREE...POLICY
INT/LAW JURID SOC/EXP 20 TREATY. PAGE 27 E0542

S62
FALK R.A.,"THE REALITY OF INTERNATIONAL LAW." INT/ORG
WOR+45 NAT/G LEGIT COERCE DETER WAR MORAL ORD/FREE ADJUD
PWR SOVEREIGN...JURID CONCPT VAL/FREE COLD/WAR 20. NUC/PWR
PAGE 36 E0714 INT/LAW

S62
GREENSPAN M.,"INTERNATIONAL LAW AND ITS PROTECTION FORCES
FOR PARTICIPANTS IN UNCONVENTIONAL WARFARE." WOR+45 JURID
LAW INT/ORG NAT/G POL/PAR COERCE REV ORD/FREE GUERRILLA
...INT/LAW TOT/POP 20. PAGE 46 E0912 WAR

B63
DAY R.E.,CIVIL RIGHTS USA: PUBLIC SCHOOLS, SOUTHERN EDU/PROP
STATES - NORTH CAROLINA, 1963. USA+45 LOC/G NEIGH ORD/FREE
LEGIS CREATE CT/SYS COERCE DISCRIM ATTIT...QU RACE/REL
CHARTS 20 NORTH/CAR NEGRO KKK CIV/RIGHTS. PAGE 29 SANCTION
E0579

B63
HIGGINS R.,THE DEVELOPMENT OF INTERNATIONAL LAW INT/ORG
THROUGH THE POLITICAL ORGANS OF THE UNITED NATIONS. INT/LAW
WOR+45 FORCES DIPLOM AGREE COERCE ATTIT SOVEREIGN TEC/DEV
...BIBLIOG 20 UN TREATY. PAGE 52 E1041 JURID

B63
HOWARD W.S.,AMERICAN SLAVERS AND THE FEDERAL LAW: DIST/IND
1837-1862. USA-45 NAT/G LEGIT COERCE RACE/REL CRIMLGY
WEALTH...POLICY BIBLIOG/A 19. PAGE 55 E1102 LAW
EXEC

B63
LIVELY E.,THE INVASION OF MISSISSIPPI. USA+45 LAW RACE/REL
CONSTN NAT/G PROVS CT/SYS GOV/REL FEDERAL CONSERVE CROWD
...TRADIT 20 MISSISSIPP NEGRO NAACP WARRN/EARL COERCE
KENNEDY/JF. PAGE 66 E1309 MARXISM

B63
US COMN CIVIL RIGHTS,REPORT ON MISSISSIPPI. LAW RACE/REL
LOC/G NAT/G LEGIS PLAN PROB/SOLV DISCRIM SOC/INTEG CONSTN
20 MISSISSIPP NEGRO. PAGE 99 E1987 ORD/FREE
COERCE

L63
LISSITZYN O.J.,"INTERNATIONAL LAW IN A DIVIDED INT/ORG
WORLD." FUT WOR+45 CONSTN CULTURE ECO/DEV ECO/UNDEV LAW
DIST/IND NAT/G FORCES ECO/TAC LEGIT ADJUD ADMIN
COERCE ATTIT HEALTH MORAL ORD/FREE PWR RESPECT
WEALTH VAL/FREE. PAGE 65 E1306

L63
MCDOUGAL M.S.,"THE ENJOYMENT AND ACQUISITION OF PLAN
RESOURCES IN OUTER SPACE." CHRIST-17C FUT WOR+45 TREND
WOR-45 LAW EXTR/IND INT/ORG ACT/RES CREATE TEC/DEV
ECO/TAC LEGIT COERCE HEALTH KNOWL ORD/FREE PWR
WEALTH...JURID HIST/WRIT VAL/FREE. PAGE 70 E1408

B64
DOOLIN D.J.,COMMUNIST CHINA: THE POLITICS OF MARXISM
STUDENT OPPOSITION. CHINA/COM ELITES STRATA ACADEM DEBATE
NAT/G WRITING CT/SYS LEAD PARTIC COERCE TOTALISM AGE/Y
20. PAGE 32 E0637 PWR

B64
DUBOIS J.,DANGER OVER PANAMA. FUT PANAMA SCHOOL DIPLOM
PROB/SOLV EDU/PROP MARXISM...POLICY 19/20 TREATY COERCE
INTERVENT CANAL/ZONE. PAGE 33 E0652

B64
FRYDENSBERG P.,PEACE-KEEPING: EXPERIENCE AND INT/ORG
EVALUATION: THE OSLO PAPERS. NORWAY FORCES PLAN DIPLOM
CONTROL...INT/LAW 20 UN. PAGE 41 E0814 PEACE
COERCE

B64
GRASMUCK E.L.,COERCITIO STAAT UND KIRCHE IM GP/REL
DONATISTENSTREIT. CHRIST-17C ROMAN/EMP LAW PROVS NAT/G
DEBATE PERSON SOVEREIGN...JURID CONCPT 4/5 SECT
AUGUSTINE CHURCH/STA ROMAN/LAW. PAGE 45 E0898 COERCE

B64
LAPENNA I.,STATE AND LAW: SOVIET AND YUGOSLAV JURID
THEORY. USSR YUGOSLAVIA STRATA STRUCT NAT/G DOMIN COM
COERCE MARXISM...GOV/COMP IDEA/COMP 20. PAGE 63 LAW
E1253 SOVEREIGN

B64
ROBINSON R.D.,INTERNATIONAL BUSINESS POLICY. AFR ECO/TAC
INDIA L/A+17C USA+45 ELITES AGRI FOR/AID COERCE DIST/IND
BAL/PAY...DECISION INT/LAW MGT 20. PAGE 85 E1706 COLONIAL

FINAN

B64
STANGER R.J.,ESSAYS ON INTERVENTION. PLAN PROB/SOLV SOVEREIGN
BAL/PWR ADJUD COERCE WAR ROLE PWR...INT/LAW CONCPT DIPLOM
20 UN INTERVENT. PAGE 93 E1865 POLICY
LEGIT

B64
THANT U.,TOWARD WORLD PEACE. DELIB/GP TEC/DEV DIPLOM
EDU/PROP WAR SOVEREIGN...INT/LAW 20 UN MID/EAST. BIOG
PAGE 96 E1915 PEACE
COERCE

B64
TONG T.,UNITED STATES DIPLOMACY IN CHINA, DIPLOM
1844-1860. ASIA USA-45 ECO/UNDEV ECO/TAC COERCE INT/TRADE
GP/REL...INT/LAW 19 TREATY. PAGE 96 E1934 COLONIAL

B64
WRIGHT G.,RURAL REVOLUTION IN FRANCE: THE PEASANTRY PWR
IN THE TWENTIETH CENTURY. EUR+WWI MOD/EUR LAW STRATA
CULTURE AGRI POL/PAR DELIB/GP LEGIS ECO/TAC FRANCE
EDU/PROP COERCE CHOOSE ATTIT RIGID/FLEX HEALTH REV
...STAT CENSUS CHARTS VAL/FREE 20. PAGE 107 E2148

L64
BERKS R.N.,"THE US AND WEAPONS CONTROL." WOR+45 LAW USA+45
INT/ORG NAT/G LEGIS EXEC COERCE PEACE ATTIT PLAN
RIGID/FLEX ALL/VALS...POLICY TOT/POP 20. ARMS/CONT
PAGE 11 E0204

S64
CRANE R.D.,"BASIC PRINCIPLES IN SOVIET SPACE LAW." COM
FUT WOR+45 AIR INT/ORG DIPLOM DOMIN ARMS/CONT LAW
COERCE NUC/PWR PEACE ATTIT DRIVE PWR...INT/LAW USSR
METH/CNCPT NEW/IDEA OBS TREND GEN/LAWS VAL/FREE SPACE
MARX/KARL 20. PAGE 27 E0544

S64
GARDNER R.N.,"THE SOVIET UNION AND THE UNITED COM
NATIONS." WOR+45 FINAN POL/PAR VOL/ASSN FORCES INT/ORG
ECO/TAC DOMIN EDU/PROP LEGIT ADJUD ADMIN ARMS/CONT USSR
COERCE ATTIT ALL/VALS...POLICY MAJORIT CONCPT OBS
TIME/SEQ TREND STERTYP UN. PAGE 42 E0838

S64
GINSBURGS G.,"WARS OF NATIONAL LIBERATION - THE COERCE
SOVIET THESIS." COM USSR WOR+45 WOR-45 LAW CULTURE CONCPT
INT/ORG DIPLOM LEGIT COLONIAL GUERRILLA WAR INT/LAW
NAT/LISM ATTIT PERSON MORAL PWR...JURID OBS TREND REV
MARX/KARL 20. PAGE 44 E0869

B65
MISSISSIPPI BLACK PAPER: (FIFTY-SEVEN NEGRO AND COERCE
WHITE CITIZENS' TESTIMONY OF POLICE BRUTALITY...). RACE/REL
USA+45 LAW SOCIETY CT/SYS SANCTION CRIME MORAL DISCRIM
ORD/FREE RESPECT 20 NEGRO. PAGE 2 E0035 FORCES

B65
BROMBERG W.,CRIME AND THE MIND. LAW LEGIT ADJUD CRIMLGY
CRIME MURDER AGE/Y ANOMIE BIO/SOC DRIVE SEX PSY. SOC
PAGE 16 E0305 HEALTH
COERCE

B65
KAMISAR Y.,CRIMINAL JUSTICE IN OUR TIME. USA+45 ORD/FREE
FORCES JUDGE PROB/SOLV COERCE MORAL 20 CIVIL/LIB CRIME
CIV/RIGHTS. PAGE 59 E1182 CT/SYS
LAW

B65
NEWBURY C.W.,BRITISH POLICY TOWARDS WEST AFRICA: DIPLOM
SELECT DOCUMENTS 1786-1874. AFR UK INT/TRADE DOMIN POLICY
ADMIN COLONIAL CT/SYS COERCE ORD/FREE...BIBLIOG/A NAT/G
18/19. PAGE 77 E1540 WRITING

B65
THOMAS A.V.,NONINTERVENTION: THE LAW AND ITS IMPORT INT/LAW
IN THE AMERICAS. L/A+17C USA+45 USA-45 WOR+45 PWR
DIPLOM ADJUD...JURID IDEA/COMP 20 UN INTERVENT. COERCE
PAGE 96 E1917

S65
KHOURI F.J.,"THE JORDON RIVER CONTROVERSY." LAW ISLAM
SOCIETY ECO/UNDEV AGRI FINAN INDUS SECT FORCES INT/ORG
ACT/RES PLAN TEC/DEV ECO/TAC EDU/PROP COERCE ATTIT ISRAEL
DRIVE PERCEPT RIGID/FLEX ALL/VALS...GEOG SOC MYTH JORDAN
WORK. PAGE 61 E1212

S65
LUSKY L.,"FOUR PROBLEMS IN LAWMAKING FOR PEACE." ORD/FREE
FORCES LEGIS CREATE ADJUD COERCE WAR MAJORITY PEACE INT/LAW
PWR. PAGE 67 E1334 UTOPIA
RECORD

B66
HAUSNER G.,JUSTICE IN JERUSALEM. GERMANY ISRAEL ADJUD
SOCIETY KIN DIPLOM LEGIT CT/SYS PARTIC MURDER CRIME
MAJORITY ATTIT FASCISM...INT/LAW JURID 20 JEWS RACE/REL
WAR/TRIAL. PAGE 51 E1013 COERCE

B66
LEHMANN L.,LEGAL UND OPPORTUN - POLITISCHE JUSTIZ ORD/FREE
IN DER BUNDESREPUBLIK. GERMANY/W EDU/PROP ADJUD POL/PAR
CONTROL PARL/PROC COERCE TOTALISM ATTIT 20 JURID
COM/PARTY. PAGE 64 E1281 LEGIS

B66
OBERMANN E.,VERTEIDIGUNG PER FREIHEIT. GERMANY/W FORCES
WOR+45 INT/ORG COERCE NUC/PWR WEAPON MARXISM 20 UN ORD/FREE
NATO WARSAW/P TREATY. PAGE 78 E1571 WAR
PEACE

B66
SWEET E.C.,CIVIL LIBERTIES IN AMERICA. LAW CONSTN ADJUD
NAT/G PRESS CT/SYS DISCRIM ATTIT WORSHIP 20 ORD/FREE
CIVIL/LIB. PAGE 95 E1899 SUFF
COERCE

B66
WAINHOUSE D.W.,INTERNATIONAL PEACE OBSERVATION: A PEACE
HISTORY AND FORECAST. INT/ORG PROB/SOLV BAL/PWR DIPLOM
AGREE ARMS/CONT COERCE NUC/PWR...PREDICT METH/COMP
20 UN LEAGUE/NAT OAS TREATY. PAGE 104 E2092

S66
DETTER I.,"THE PROBLEM OF UNEQUAL TREATIES." CONSTN SOVEREIGN
NAT/G LEGIS COLONIAL COERCE PWR...GEOG UN TIME DOMIN
TREATY. PAGE 31 E0610 INT/LAW
ECO/UNDEV

B67
BOHANNAN P.,LAW AND WARFARE. CULTURE CT/SYS COERCE METH/COMP
REV PEACE...JURID SOC CONCPT ANTHOL 20. PAGE 13 ADJUD
E0259 WAR
LAW

B67
LAWYERS COMM AMER POLICY VIET,VIETNAM AND INT/LAW
INTERNATIONAL LAW: AN ANALYSIS OF THE LEGALITY OF DIPLOM
THE US MILITARY INVOLVEMENT. VIETNAM LAW INT/ORG ADJUD
COERCE WEAPON PEACE ORD/FREE 20 UN SEATO TREATY. WAR
PAGE 64 E1271

B67
SLATER J.,THE OAS AND UNITED STATES FOREIGN POLICY. INT/ORG
KOREA L/A+17C USA+45 VOL/ASSN RISK COERCE PEACE DIPLOM
ORD/FREE MARXISM...TREND 20 OAS. PAGE 92 E1838 ALL/IDEOS
ADJUD

S67
ALDRICH W.A.,"THE SUEZ CRISIS." UAR UK USA+45 DIPLOM
DELIB/GP FORCES BAL/PWR INT/TRADE CONFER CONTROL INT/LAW
COERCE DETER 20. PAGE 3 E0058 COLONIAL

S67
DALFEN C.M.,"THE WORLD COURT IN IDLE SPLENDOUR: THE CT/SYS
BASIS OF STATES' ATTITUDES." WOR+45 LAW ADJUD INT/ORG
COERCE...JURID 20 UN WORLD/CT. PAGE 28 E0562 INT/LAW
DIPLOM

S67
MATTHEWS R.O.,"THE SUEZ CANAL DISPUTE* A CASE STUDY PEACE
IN PEACEFUL SETTLEMENT." FRANCE ISRAEL UAR UK NAT/G DIPLOM
CONTROL LEAD COERCE WAR NAT/LISM ROLE ORD/FREE PWR ADJUD
...INT/LAW UN 20. PAGE 69 E1389

B68
HULL R.H.,LAW AND VIETNAM. COM VIETNAM CONSTN POLICY
INT/ORG FORCES DIPLOM AGREE COERCE DETER WEAPON LAW
PEACE ATTIT 20 UN TREATY. PAGE 56 E1113 WAR
INT/LAW

B96
SMITH A.,LECTURES ON JUSTICE, POLICE, REVENUE AND DIPLOM
ARMS (1763). UK LAW FAM FORCES TARIFFS AGREE COERCE JURID
INCOME OWN WEALTH LAISSEZ...GEN/LAWS 17/18. PAGE 92 OLD/LIB
E1840 TAX

COERCION....SEE COERCE

COEXIST....COEXISTENCE; SEE ALSO COLD/WAR, PEACE

COEXISTENCE....SEE COLD/WAR, PEACE

COFFIN/WS....WILLIAM SLOANE COFFIN, JR.

COGNITION....SEE PERCEPT

COGNITIVE DISSONANCE....SEE PERCEPT, ROLE

COHEN A. E0461

COHEN M. E0463,E0464

COHEN M.B. E0465

COHEN M.L. E0466

COHEN M.R. E0467

COHEN R.A. E0465

COHESION....SEE CONSEN

COHN H.J. E0468

COHN K. E0469

COHN M.M. E0470
COIGNE A.B. E0474
COKE E. E0471

COLD/WAR....COLD WAR

LALL A.S.,NEGOTIATING DISARMAMENT* THE EIGHTEEN NATION DISARMAMENT CONFERENCE* THE FIRST TWO YEARS, 1962-1964. ASIA FRANCE INDIA USA+45 USSR PROB/SOLV ADJUD NEUTRAL ATTIT...IDEA/COMP COLD/WAR. PAGE 62 E1246
OBS
ARMS/CONT
DIPLOM
OP/RES
B'

IN THE SHADOW OF FEAR; AMERICAN CIVIL LIBERTIES, 1948-49 (PAMPHLET). COM LAW LEGIS BAL/PWR EDU/PROP CT/SYS RACE/REL DISCRIM MARXISM SOCISM 20 COLD/WAR CONGRESS ACLU CIV/RIGHTS ESPIONAGE. PAGE 2 E0030
ORD/FREE
CONSTN
POLICY
N19

FOX W.T.R.,UNITED STATES POLICY IN A TWO POWER WORLD. COM USA+45 USSR FORCES DOMIN AGREE NEUTRAL NUC/PWR ORD/FREE SOVEREIGN 20 COLD/WAR TREATY EUROPE/W INTERVENT. PAGE 39 E0780
DIPLOM
FOR/AID
POLICY
N47

MORGENTHAL H.J.,POLITICS AMONG NATIONS: THE STRUGGLE FOR POWER AND PEACE. FUT WOR+45 INT/ORG OP/RES PROB/SOLV BAL/PWR CONTROL ATTIT MORAL ...INT/LAW BIBLIOG 20 COLD/WAR. PAGE 75 E1494
DIPLOM
PEACE
PWR
POLICY
B48

US LIBRARY OF CONGRESS,FREEDOM OF INFORMATION: SELECTIVE REPORT ON RECENT WRITINGS. USA+45 LAW CONSTN ELITES EDU/PROP PRESS LOBBY WAR TOTALISM ATTIT 20 UN UNESCO COLD/WAR. PAGE 101 E2018
BIBLIOG/A
ORD/FREE
LICENSE
COM/IND
B49

JIMENEZ E.,VOTING AND HANDLING OF DISPUTES IN THE SECURITY COUNCIL. WOR+45 CONSTN INT/ORG DIPLOM LEGIT DETER CHOOSE MORAL ORD/FREE PWR...JURID TIME/SEQ COLD/WAR UN 20. PAGE 59 E1168
DELIB/GP
ROUTINE
B50

STONE J.,LEGAL CONTROLS OF INTERNATIONAL CONFLICT: A TREATISE ON THE DYNAMICS OF DISPUTES AND WAR LAW. WOR+45 WOR-45 NAT/G DIPLOM CT/SYS SOVEREIGN...JURID CONCPT METH/CNCPT GEN/LAWS TOT/POP VAL/FREE COLD/WAR LEAGUE/NAT 20. PAGE 94 E1878
INT/ORG
LAW
WAR
INT/LAW
B54

POTTER P.B.,"NEUTRALITY, 1955." WOR+45 WOR-45 INT/ORG NAT/G WAR ATTIT...POLICY IDEA/COMP 17/20 LEAGUE/NAT UN COLD/WAR. PAGE 81 E1631
NEUTRAL
INT/LAW
DIPLOM
CONCPT
S56

COMM. STUDY ORGAN. PEACE,STRENGTHENING THE UNITED NATIONS. FUT USA+45 WOR+45 CONSTN NAT/G DELIB/GP FORCES LEGIS ECO/TAC LEGIT COERCE PEACE...JURID CONCPT UN COLD/WAR 20. PAGE 24 E0482
INT/ORG
ORD/FREE
B57

DE VISSCHER C.,THEORY AND REALITY IN PUBLIC INTERNATIONAL LAW. WOR+45 WOR-45 SOCIETY NAT/G CT/SYS ATTIT MORAL ORD/FREE PWR...JURID CONCPT METH/CNCPT TIME/SEQ GEN/LAWS LEAGUE/NAT TOT/POP VAL/FREE COLD/WAR. PAGE 30 E0599
INT/ORG
LAW
INT/LAW
B57

MILLS W.,INDIVIDUAL FREEDOM AND COMMON DEFENSE (PAMPHLET). USA+45 USSR NAT/G EDU/PROP CRIME CHOOSE 20 COLD/WAR. PAGE 73 E1463
ORD/FREE
CONSTN
INGP/REL
FORCES
B57

CAUGHEY J.W.,IN CLEAR AND PRESENT DANGER. USA+45 ADJUD COERCE ATTIT AUTHORIT...POLICY 20 COLD/WAR
NAT/G
CONTROL
B58

MCCARTHY/J. PAGE 21 E0408
DOMIN
ORD/FREE

COMM. STUDY ORGAN. PEACE,ORGANIZING PEACE IN THE NUCLEAR AGE. FUT CONSULT DELIB/GP DOMIN ADJUD ROUTINE COERCE ORD/FREE...TECHNIC INT/LAW JURID NEW/IDEA UN COLD/WAR 20. PAGE 24 E0483
INT/ORG
ACT/RES
NUC/PWR
B59

SOHN L.B.,"THE DEFINITION OF AGGRESSION." FUT LAW FORCES LEGIT ADJUD ROUTINE COERCE ORD/FREE PWR ...MAJORIT JURID QUANT COLD/WAR 20. PAGE 92 E1855
INT/ORG
CT/SYS
DETER
SOVEREIGN
S59

ENGEL J.,THE SECURITY OF THE FREE WORLD. USSR WOR+45 STRATA STRUCT ECO/DEV ECO/UNDEV INT/ORG DELIB/GP FORCES DOMIN LEGIT ADJUD EXEC ARMS/CONT COERCE...POLICY CONCPT NEW/IDEA TIME/SEQ GEN/LAWS COLD/WAR WORK UN 20 NATO. PAGE 35 E0689
COM
TREND
DIPLOM
B60

POTTER P.B.,"RELATIVE VALUES OF INTERNATIONAL RELATIONS, LAW, AND ORGANIZATIONS." WOR+45 NAT/G LEGIT ADJUD ORD/FREE...CONCPT TOT/POP COLD/WAR 20. PAGE 81 E1633
INT/ORG
LEGIS
DIPLOM
INT/LAW
S60

RHYNE C.S.,"LAW AS AN INSTRUMENT FOR PEACE." FUT WOR+45 PLAN LEGIT ROUTINE ARMS/CONT NUC/PWR ATTIT ORD/FREE...JURID METH/CNCPT TREND CON/ANAL HYPO/EXP COLD/WAR 20. PAGE 84 E1690
ADJUD
EDU/PROP
INT/LAW
PEACE
S60

WRIGHT Q.,"LEGAL ASPECTS OF THE U-2 INCIDENT." COM USA+45 USSR STRUCT NAT/G FORCES PLAN TEC/DEV ADJUD RIGID/FLEX MORAL ORD/FREE...DECISION INT/LAW JURID PSY TREND GEN/LAWS COLD/WAR VAL/FREE 20 U-2. PAGE 108 E2157
PWR
POLICY
SPACE
S60

CONFERENCE ATLANTIC COMMUNITY,AN INTRODUCTORY BIBLIOGRAPHY. COM WOR+45 FORCES DIPLOM ECO/TAC WAR ...INT/LAW HIST/WRIT COLD/WAR NATO. PAGE 25 E0485
BIBLIOG/A
CON/ANAL
INT/ORG
B61

RIENOW R.,CONTEMPORARY INTERNATIONAL POLITICS. WOR+45 INT/ORG BAL/PWR EDU/PROP COLONIAL NEUTRAL REGION WAR PEACE...INT/LAW 20 COLD/WAR UN. PAGE 85 E1698
DIPLOM
PWR
POLICY
NAT/G
B61

WRIGHT Q.,THE ROLE OF INTERNATIONAL LAW IN THE ELIMINATION OF WAR. FUT WOR+45 WOR-45 BAL/PWR DIPLOM DOMIN LEGIT PWR...POLICY INT/LAW JURID CONCPT TIME/SEQ TREND GEN/LAWS COLD/WAR 20. PAGE 108 E2158
INT/ORG
ADJUD
ARMS/CONT
B61

TAUBENFELD H.J.,"A REGIME FOR OUTER SPACE." FUT UNIV R+D ACT/RES PLAN BAL/PWR LEGIT ARMS/CONT ORD/FREE...POLICY JURID TREND UN TOT/POP 20 COLD/WAR. PAGE 95 E1910
INT/ORG
ADJUD
SPACE
L61

LIPSON L.,"AN ARGUMENT ON THE LEGALITY OF RECONNAISSANCE SATELLITES." COM USA+45 USSR WOR+45 AIR INTELL NAT/G CONSULT PLAN DIPLOM LEGIT ROUTINE ATTIT...INT/LAW JURID CONCPT METH/CNCPT TREND COLD/WAR 20. PAGE 65 E1302
INT/ORG
LAW
SPACE
S61

DUROSELLE J.B.,HISTOIRE DIPLOMATIQUE DE 1919 A NOS JOURS (3RD ED.). FRANCE INT/ORG CHIEF FORCES CONFER ARMS/CONT WAR PEACE ORD/FREE...T TREATY 20 COLD/WAR. PAGE 34 E0667
DIPLOM
WOR+45
WOR-45
B62

HIRSCHFIELD R.S.,THE CONSTITUTION AND THE COURT. SCHOOL WAR RACE/REL EQUILIB ORD/FREE...POLICY MAJORIT DECISION JURID 18/20 PRESIDENT COLD/WAR CIVIL/LIB SUPREME/CT CONGRESS. PAGE 53 E1051
ADJUD
PWR
CONSTN
LAW
B62

LAWSON R.,INTERNATIONAL REGIONAL ORGANIZATIONS. WOR+45 NAT/G VOL/ASSN CONSULT LEGIS EDU/PROP LEGIT ADMIN EXEC ROUTINE HEALTH PWR WEALTH...JURID EEC COLD/WAR 20 UN. PAGE 63 E1270
INT/ORG
DELIB/GP
REGION
B62

SCHWARZENBERGER G.,THE FRONTIERS OF INTERNATIONAL LAW. WOR+45 WOR-45 NAT/G LEGIT CT/SYS ROUTINE MORAL ORD/FREE PWR...JURID SOC GEN/METH 20 COLD/WAR. PAGE 89 E1789
INT/ORG
LAW
INT/LAW
B62

L62

STEIN E.,"MR HAMMARSKJOLD, THE CHARTER LAW AND THE   CONCPT
FUTURE ROLE OF THE UNITED NATIONS SECRETARY-   BIOG
GENERAL." WOR+45 CONSTN INT/ORG DELIB/GP FORCES
TOP/EX BAL/PWR LEGIT ROUTINE RIGID/FLEX PWR
...POLICY JURID OBS STERTYP UN COLD/WAR 20
HAMMARSK/D. PAGE 93 E1869

S62

FALK R.A.,"THE REALITY OF INTERNATIONAL LAW."   INT/ORG
WOR+45 NAT/G LEGIT COERCE DETER WAR MORAL ORD/FREE   ADJUD
PWR SOVEREIGN...JURID CONCPT VAL/FREE COLD/WAR 20.   NUC/PWR
PAGE 36 E0714   INT/LAW

S62

FENWICK C.G.,"ISSUES AT PUNTA DEL ESTE: NON-   INT/ORG
INTERVENTION VS COLLECTIVE SECURITY." L/A+17C   CUBA
USA+45 VOL/ASSN DELIB/GP ECO/TAC LEGIT ADJUD REGION
ORD/FREE OAS COLD/WAR 20. PAGE 37 E0738

S62

FINKELSTEIN L.S.,"THE UNITED NATIONS AND   INT/ORG
ORGANIZATIONS FOR CONTROL OF ARMAMENT." FUT WOR+45   PWR
VOL/ASSN DELIB/GP TOP/EX CREATE EDU/PROP LEGIT   ARMS/CONT
ADJUD NUC/PWR ATTIT RIGID/FLEX ORD/FREE...POLICY
DECISION CONCPT OBS TREND GEN/LAWS TOT/POP
COLD/WAR. PAGE 38 E0752

S62

LISSITZYN O.J.,"SOME LEGAL IMPLICATIONS OF THE U-2   LAW
AND RB-47 INCIDENTS." FUT USA+45 USSR WOR+45 AIR   CONCPT
NAT/G DIPLOM LEGIT MORAL ORD/FREE SOVEREIGN...JURID   SPACE
GEN/LAWS GEN/METH COLD/WAR 20 U-2. PAGE 65 E1305   INT/LAW

S62

MCWHINNEY E.,"CO-EXISTENCE, THE CUBA CRISIS, AND   CONCPT
COLD WAR-INTERNATIONAL WAR." CUBA USA+45 USSR   INT/LAW
WOR+45 NAT/G TOP/EX BAL/PWR DIPLOM DOMIN LEGIT
PEACE RIGID/FLEX ORD/FREE...STERTYP COLD/WAR 20.
PAGE 71 E1427

B63

DUNN F.S.,PEACE-MAKING AND THE SETTLEMENT WITH   POLICY
JAPAN. ASIA USA+45 USA-45 FORCES BAL/PWR ECO/TAC   PEACE
CONFER WAR PWR SOVEREIGN 20 CHINJAP COLD/WAR   PLAN
TREATY. PAGE 33 E0661   DIPLOM

B63

PACHTER H.M.,COLLISION COURSE; THE CUBAN MISSILE   WAR
CRISIS AND COEXISTENCE. CUBA USA+45 DIPLOM   BAL/PWR
ARMS/CONT PEACE MARXISM...DECISION INT/LAW 20   NUC/PWR
COLD/WAR KHRUSH/N KENNEDY/JF CASTRO/F. PAGE 79   DETER
E1587

B63

VAN SLYCK P.,PEACE: THE CONTROL OF NATIONAL POWER.   ARMS/CONT
CUBA WOR+45 FINAN NAT/G FORCES PROB/SOLV TEC/DEV   PEACE
BAL/PWR ADMIN CONTROL ORD/FREE...POLICY INT/LAW UN   INT/ORG
COLD/WAR TREATY. PAGE 103 E2069   DIPLOM

S63

BOHN L.,"WHOSE NUCLEAR TEST: NON-PHYSICAL   ADJUD
INSPECTION AND TEST BAN." WOR+45 R+D INT/ORG   ARMS/CONT
VOL/ASSN ORD/FREE...GEN/LAWS GEN/METH COLD/WAR 20.   TEC/DEV
PAGE 13 E0262   NUC/PWR

B64

FULBRIGHT J.W.,OLD MYTHS AND NEW REALITIES. USA+45   DIPLOM
USSR LEGIS INT/TRADE DETER ATTIT...POLICY 20   INT/ORG
COLD/WAR TREATY. PAGE 41 E0818   ORD/FREE

B64

MCWHINNEY E.,"PEACEFUL COEXISTENCE" AND SOVIET-   PEACE
WESTERN INTERNATIONAL LAW. USSR DIPLOM LEAD...JURID   IDEA/COMP
20 COLD/WAR. PAGE 71 E1429   INT/LAW
                                                         ATTIT

S64

KARPOV P.V.,"PEACEFUL COEXISTENCE AND INTERNATIONAL   COM
LAW." WOR+45 LAW SOCIETY INT/ORG VOL/ASSN FORCES   ATTIT
CREATE CAP/ISM DIPLOM ADJUD NUC/PWR PEACE MORAL   INT/LAW
ORD/FREE PWR MARXISM...MARXIST JURID CONCPT OBS   USSR
TREND COLD/WAR MARX/KARL 20. PAGE 59 E1186

S64

LIPSON L.,"PEACEFUL COEXISTENCE." COM USSR WOR+45   ATTIT
LAW INT/ORG DIPLOM LEGIT ADJUD ORD/FREE...JURID   JURID
OBS TREND GEN/LAWS VAL/FREE COLD/WAR 20. PAGE 65   INT/LAW
E1303   PEACE

S64

MCGHEE G.C.,"EAST-WEST RELATIONS TODAY." WOR+45   IDEA/COMP
PROB/SOLV BAL/PWR PEACE 20 COLD/WAR. PAGE 71 E1413   DIPLOM
                                                         ADJUD

B65

HIGGINS R.,CONFLICT OF INTERESTS* INTERNATIONAL LAW   INT/LAW
IN A DIVIDED WORLD. ASIA USSR ECO/DEV ECO/UNDEV   IDEA/COMP
SECT INT/TRADE COLD/WAR WORSHIP. PAGE 52 E1042   ADJUST

L65

RUBIN A.P.,"UNITED STATES CONTEMPORARY PRACTICE   LAW
RELATING TO INTERNATIONAL LAW." USA+45 WOR+45   LEGIT
CONSTN INT/ORG NAT/G DELIB/GP EX/STRUC DIPLOM DOMIN   INT/LAW
CT/SYS ROUTINE ORD/FREE...CONCPT COLD/WAR 20.
PAGE 86 E1730

S65

GROSS L.,"PROBLEMS OF INTERNATIONAL ADJUDICATION   LAW
AND COMPLIANCE WITH INTERNATIONAL LAW: SOME SIMPLE   METH/CNCPT
SOLUTIONS." WOR+45 SOCIETY NAT/G DOMIN LEGIT ADJUD   INT/LAW
CT/SYS RIGID/FLEX HEALTH PWR...JURID NEW/IDEA
COLD/WAR 20. PAGE 48 E0951

S65

HAZARD J.N.,"CO-EXISTENCE LAW BOWS OUT." WOR+45 R+D   PROF/ORG
INT/ORG VOL/ASSN CONSULT DELIB/GP ACT/RES CREATE   ADJUD
PEACE KNOWL...JURID CONCPT COLD/WAR VAL/FREE 20.
PAGE 51 E1018

S65

MCWHINNEY E.,"CHANGING INTERNATIONAL LAW METHOD AND   LAW
OBJECTIVES IN THE ERA OF THE SOVIET-WESTERN   TREND
DETENTE." COM USA+45 NAT/G BAL/PWR CT/SYS ATTIT
ORD/FREE...HUM JURID NEW/IDEA COLD/WAR VAL/FREE 20.
PAGE 71 E1430

S65

PRABHAKAR P.,"SURVEY OF RESEARCH AND SOURCE   BIBLIOG
MATERIALS; THE SINO-INDIAN BORDER DISPUTE."   ASIA
CHINA/COM INDIA LAW NAT/G PLAN BAL/PWR WAR...POLICY   S/ASIA
20 COLD/WAR. PAGE 82 E1645   DIPLOM

B66

CLARK G.,WORLD PEACE THROUGH WORLD LAW; TWO   INT/LAW
ALTERNATIVE PLANS. WOR+45 DELIB/GP FORCES TAX   PEACE
CONFER ADJUD SANCTION ARMS/CONT WAR CHOOSE PRIVIL   PLAN
20 UN COLD/WAR. PAGE 23 E0450   INT/ORG

B67

BAILEY N.A.,LATIN AMERICA IN WORLD POLITICS. PWR   L/A+17C
CONSERVE MARXISM...INT/LAW TREND BIBLIOG/A T OAS   DIPLOM
COLD/WAR. PAGE 7 E0134   INT/ORG
                                                         ATTIT

B67

HOLCOMBE A.N.,A STRATEGY OF PEACE IN A CHANGING   PEACE
WORLD. USA+45 WOR+45 LAW NAT/G CREATE DIPLOM   PLAN
ARMS/CONT WAR...CHARTS 20 UN COLD/WAR. PAGE 54   INT/ORG
E1072   INT/LAW

B67

INTERNATIONAL CONCILIATION.ISSUES BEFORE THE 22ND   PROB/SOLV
GENERAL ASSEMBLY. WOR+45 ECO/UNDEV FINAN BAL/PWR   INT/ORG
BUDGET INT/TRADE STRANGE ORD/FREE...INT/LAW 20 UN   DIPLOM
COLD/WAR. PAGE 57 E1132   PEACE

B67

PADELFORD N.J.,THE DYNAMICS OF INTERNATIONAL   DIPLOM
POLITICS (2ND ED.). WOR+45 LAW INT/ORG FORCES   NAT/G
TEC/DEV REGION NAT/LISM PEACE ATTIT PWR ALL/IDEOS   POLICY
UN COLD/WAR NATO TREATY. PAGE 79 E1589   DECISION

B67

RUSSELL B.,WAR CRIMES IN VIETNAM. USA+45 VIETNAM   WAR
FORCES DIPLOM WEAPON RACE/REL DISCRIM ISOLAT   CRIME
BIO/SOC 20 COLD/WAR RUSSELL/B. PAGE 87 E1736   ATTIT
                                                         POLICY

S67

FLECHTHEIM O.K.,"BLOC FORMATION VS. DIALOGUE."   FUT
CONSTN ECO/DEV BAL/PWR PEACE ATTIT PWR COLD/WAR.   CAP/ISM
PAGE 38 E0761   MARXISM
                                                         DEBATE

COLE/GEO....GEORGE COLE

COLEMAN J.W. E0472

COLEMAN-NORTON P.R. E0473

COLLECTIVE BARGAINING....SEE BARGAIN+LABOR+GP/REL

COLLECTIVE SECURITY....SEE INT/ORG+FORCES

COLLEGES....SEE ACADEM

COLLINS I. E0475

COLOMBIA....SEE ALSO L/A&17C

N19
TAYLOR H.,WHY THE PENDING TREATY WITH COLOMBIA   INT/LAW
SHOULD BE RATIFIED (PAMPHLET). PANAMA USA-45   DIPLOM
DELIB/GP INT/TRADE REV ORD/FREE...JURID TREATY
18/19 ROOSEVLT/T TAFT/WH COLOMB. PAGE 95 E1912

B43
BACKUS R.C.,A GUIDE TO THE LAW AND LEGAL LITERATURE BIBLIOG/A
OF COLOMBIA. FINAN INDUS LABOR FORCES ADJUD ADMIN LAW
COLONIAL CT/SYS CRIME...INT/LAW JURID 20 COLOMB.   CONSTN
PAGE 7 E0127   L/A+17C

B58
ORTIZ R.P.,ANNUARIO BIBLIOGRAFICO COLOMBIANO,   BIBLIOG
1951-1956. LAW RECEIVE EDU/PROP ADMIN...LING STAT SOC
20 COLOMB. PAGE 79 E1582

B61
RUEDA B.,A STATEMENT OF THE LAWS OF COLOMBIA IN   FINAN
MATTERS AFFECTING BUSINESS (3RD ED.). INDUS FAM   ECO/UNDEV
LABOR LG/CO NAT/G LEGIS TAX CONTROL MARRIAGE 20   LAW
COLOMB. PAGE 86 E1733   CONSTN

B66
HOYT E.C.,NATIONAL POLICY AND INTERNATIONAL LAW* INT/LAW
CASE STUDIES FROM AMERICAN CANAL POLICY* MONOGRAPH USA-45
NO. 1 -- 1966-1967. PANAMA UK ELITES BAL/PWR   DIPLOM
EFFICIENCY...CLASSIF NAT/COMP SOC/EXP COLOMB   PWR
TREATY. PAGE 55 E1105

S67
FABREGA J.,"ANTECEDENTES EXTRANJEROS EN LA   CONSTN
CONSTITUCION PANAMENA." CUBA L/A+17C PANAMA URUGUAY JURID
EX/STRUC LEGIS DIPLOM ORD/FREE 19/20 COLOMB   NAT/G
MEXIC/AMER. PAGE 36 E0709   PARL/PROC

COLOMBOS C.J. E0476

COLONIAL AMERICA....SEE PRE/US/AM

COLONIAL....COLONIALISM; SEE ALSO DOMIN

N
CONOVER H.F.,OFFICIAL PUBLICATIONS OF BRITISH EAST BIBLIOG/A
AFRICA (PAMPHLET). UK LAW ECO/UNDEV AGRI EXTR/IND AFR
SECT LEGIS BUDGET TAX...HEAL STAT 20. PAGE 25 E0491 ADMIN
                                                    COLONIAL

N
INTERNATIONAL COMN JURISTS,AFRICAN CONFERENCE ON CT/SYS
THE RULE OF LAW. AFR INT/ORG LEGIS DIPLOM CONFER   JURID
COLONIAL ORD/FREE...CONCPT METH/COMP 20. PAGE 57   DELIB/GP
E1131

N
KEITT L.,AN ANNOTATED BIBLIOGRAPHY OF   BIBLIOG/A
BIBLIOGRAPHIES OF STATUTORY MATERIALS OF THE UNITED LAW
STATES. CHRIST-17C USA-45 LEGIS ADJUD COLONIAL   CONSTN
CT/SYS...JURID 16/20. PAGE 60 E1196   PROVS

N
INTERNATIONAL BOOK NEWS, 1928-1934. ECO/UNDEV FINAN BIBLIOG/A
INDUS LABOR INT/TRADE CONFER ADJUD COLONIAL...HEAL DIPLOM
SOC/WK CHARTS 20 LEAGUE/NAT. PAGE 1 E0008   INT/LAW
                                                    INT/ORG

N
PUBLISHERS' CIRCULAR, THE OFFICIAL ORGAN OF THE   BIBLIOG
PUBLISHERS' ASSOCIATION OF GREAT BRITAIN AND   NAT/G
IRELAND. EUR+WWI MOD/EUR UK LAW PROB/SOLV DIPLOM   WRITING
COLONIAL ATTIT...HUM 19/20 CMN/WLTH. PAGE 2 E0025 LEAD

N
AFRICAN BIBLIOGRAPHIC CENTER,A CURRENT BIBLIOGRAPHY BIBLIOG/A
ON AFRICAN AFFAIRS. LAW CULTURE ECO/UNDEV LABOR   AFR
SECT DIPLOM FOR/AID COLONIAL NAT/LISM...LING 20.   NAT/G
PAGE 3 E0053   REGION

N
ASIA FOUNDATION,LIBRARY NOTES. LAW CONSTN CULTURE BIBLIOG/A
SOCIETY ECO/UNDEV INT/ORG NAT/G COLONIAL LEAD   ASIA
REGION NAT/LISM ATTIT 20 UN. PAGE 6 E0107   S/ASIA
                                                   DIPLOM

B00
BATY T.,INTERNATIONAL LAW IN SOUTH AFRICA. AFR   JURID
SOUTH/AFR LAW CONFER 19/20. PAGE 8 E0155   WAR
                                                  SOVEREIGN
                                                  COLONIAL

B00
GRIFFIN A.P.C.,LIST OF BOOKS RELATING TO THE THEORY BIBLIOG/A

OF COLONIZATION, GOVERNMENT OF DEPENDENCIES,   COLONIAL
PROTECTORATES, AND RELATED TOPICS. FRANCE GERMANY GOV/REL
ITALY SPAIN UK USA-45 WOR-45 ECO/TAC ADMIN CONTROL DOMIN
REGION NAT/LISM ALL/VALS PWR...INT/LAW SOC 16/19.
PAGE 46 E0917

B01
GRIFFIN A.P.C.,LIST OF BOOKS ON SAMOA (PAMPHLET). BIBLIOG/A
GERMANY S/ASIA UK USA-45 WOR-45 ECO/UNDEV REGION   COLONIAL
ALL/VALS ORD/FREE ALL/IDEOS...GEOG INT/LAW 19 SAMOA DIPLOM
GUAM. PAGE 46 E0918

B03
FORTESCUE G.K.,SUBJECT INDEX OF THE MODERN WORKS BIBLIOG
ADDED TO THE LIBRARY OF THE BRITISH MUSEUM IN THE INDEX
YEARS 1881-1900 (3 VOLS.). UK LAW CONSTN FINAN   WRITING
NAT/G FORCES INT/TRADE COLONIAL 19. PAGE 39 E0775

B03
MOREL E.D.,THE BRITISH CASE IN FRENCH CONGO.   DIPLOM
CONGO/BRAZ FRANCE UK COERCE MORAL WEALTH...POLICY INT/TRADE
INT/LAW 20 CONGO/LEOP. PAGE 74 E1490   COLONIAL
                                                   AFR

B04
BURKE E.,A LETTER TO THE SHERIFFS OF BRISTOL   LEGIS
(1777). USA-45 LAW ECO/TAC COLONIAL CT/SYS REV   ADJUD
GP/REL ORD/FREE...POLICY 18 PARLIAMENT BURKE/EDM. CRIME
PAGE 17 E0341

B08
GRIFFIN A.P.C.,LIST OF REFERENCES ON INTERNATIONAL BIBLIOG/A
ARBITRATION. FRANCE L/A+17C USA-45 WOR-45 DIPLOM   INT/ORG
CONFER COLONIAL ARMS/CONT BAL/PAY EQUILIB SOVEREIGN INT/LAW
...DECISION 19/20 MEXIC/AMER. PAGE 47 E0932   DELIB/GP

B18
EYBERS G.W.,SELECT CONSTITUTIONAL DOCUMENTS   CONSTN
ILLUSTRATING SOUTH AFRICAN HISTORY 1795-1910.   LAW
SOUTH/AFR LOC/G LEGIS CT/SYS...JURID ANTHOL 18/20 NAT/G
NATAL CAPE/HOPE ORANGE/STA. PAGE 36 E0707   COLONIAL

B31
BORCHARD E.H.,GUIDE TO THE LAW AND LEGAL LITERATURE BIBLIOG/A
OF FRANCE. FRANCE FINAN INDUS LABOR SECT LEGIS   LAW
ADMIN COLONIAL CRIME OWN...INT/LAW 20. PAGE 14   CONSTN
E0266   METH

B34
EVANS I.L.,NATIVE POLICY IN SOUTHERN AFRICA.   AFR
RHODESIA SOUTH/AFR UK STRUCT PARTIC RACE/REL ATTIT COLONIAL
WEALTH SOC/INTEG AFRICA/SW. PAGE 35 E0705   DOMIN
                                                   LAW

B35
FOREIGN AFFAIRS BIBLIOGRAPHY: A SELECTED AND   BIBLIOG/A
ANNOTATED LIST OF BOOKS ON INTERNATIONAL RELATIONS DIPLOM
1919-1962 (4 VOLS.). CONSTN FORCES COLONIAL   INT/ORG
ARMS/CONT WAR NAT/LISM PEACE ATTIT DRIVE...POLICY
INT/LAW 20. PAGE 2 E0032

B38
HOLDSWORTH W.S.,A HISTORY OF ENGLISH LAW; THE   LAW
CENTURIES OF SETTLEMENT AND REFORM (VOL. X). INDIA LOC/G
UK CONSTN NAT/G CHIEF LEGIS ADMIN COLONIAL CT/SYS EX/STRUC
CHOOSE ORD/FREE PWR...JURID 18 PARLIAMENT   ADJUD
COMMONWLTH COMMON/LAW. PAGE 54 E1077

B38
HOLDSWORTH W.S.,A HISTORY OF ENGLISH LAW; THE   LAW
CENTURIES OF SETTLEMENT AND REFORM (VOL. XI). UK   COLONIAL
CONSTN NAT/G EX/STRUC DIPLOM ADJUD CT/SYS LEAD   LEGIS
CRIME ATTIT...INT/LAW JURID 18 CMN/WLTH PARLIAMENT PARL/PROC
ENGLSH/LAW. PAGE 54 E1079

B42
BLANCHARD L.R.,MARTINIQUE: A SELECTED LIST OF   BIBLIOG/A
REFERENCES (PAMPHLET). WEST/IND AGRI LOC/G SCHOOL SOCIETY
...ART/METH GEOG JURID CHARTS 20. PAGE 12 E0241   CULTURE
                                                   COLONIAL

B42
CROWE S.E.,THE BERLIN WEST AFRICA CONFERENCE,   AFR
1884-85. GERMANY S/ASIA UK INT/ORG DELIB/GP   CONFER
FORCES PROB/SOLV BAL/PWR CAP/ISM DOMIN COLONIAL   INT/TRADE
...INT/LAW 19. PAGE 28 E0548   DIPLOM

B43
BACKUS R.C.,A GUIDE TO THE LAW AND LEGAL LITERATURE BIBLIOG/A
OF COLOMBIA. FINAN INDUS LABOR FORCES ADJUD ADMIN LAW
COLONIAL CT/SYS CRIME...INT/LAW JURID 20 COLOMB.   CONSTN
PAGE 7 E0127   L/A+17C

B43
BEMIS S.F.,THE LATIN AMERICAN POLICY OF THE UNITED DIPLOM
STATES: AN HISTORICAL INTERPRETATION. INT/ORG AGREE SOVEREIGN

COLONIAL WAR PEACE ATTIT ORD/FREE...POLICY INT/LAW   USA-45
CHARTS 18/20 MEXIC/AMER WILSON/W MONROE/DOC.   L/A+17C
PAGE 10 E0185

B45
GALLOWAY E.,ABSTRACTS OF POSTWAR LITERATURE (VOL.   BIBLIOG/A
IV) JAN.-JULY, 1945 NOS. 901-1074. POLAND USA+45   NUC/PWR
USSR WOR+45 INDUS LABOR PLAN ECO/TAC INT/TRADE TAX   NAT/G
EDU/PROP ADMIN COLONIAL INT/LAW. PAGE 42 E0829   DIPLOM

B45
UNCIO CONFERENCE LIBRARY,SHORT TITLE CLASSIFIED   BIBLIOG
CATALOG. WOR-45 DOMIN COLONIAL WAR...SOC/WK 20   DIPLOM
LEAGUE/NAT UN. PAGE 98 E1955   INT/ORG
                                                     INT/LAW

B45
US LIBRARY OF CONGRESS,NETHERLANDS EAST INDIES.   BIBLIOG/A
INDONESIA LAW CULTURE AGRI INDUS SCHOOL COLONIAL   S/ASIA
HEALTH...GEOG JURID SOC 19/20 NETH/IND. PAGE 101   NAT/G
E2017

B45
WOOLBERT R.G.,FOREIGN AFFAIRS BIBLIOGRAPHY,   BIBLIOG/A
1932-1942. INT/ORG SECT INT/TRADE COLONIAL RACE/REL DIPLOM
NAT/LISM...GEOG INT/LAW GOV/COMP IDEA/COMP 20.   WAR
PAGE 107 E2144

B46
GRIFFIN G.G.,A GUIDE TO MANUSCRIPTS RELATING TO   BIBLIOG/A
AMERICAN HISTORY IN BRITISH DEPOSITORIES. CANADA   ALL/VALS
IRELAND MOD/EUR UK USA-45 LAW DIPLOM ADMIN COLONIAL NAT/G
WAR NAT/LISM SOVEREIGN...GEOG INT/LAW 15/19
CMN/WLTH. PAGE 47 E0936

B48
LOGAN R.W.,THE AFRICAN MANDATES IN WORLD POLITICS.   WAR
EUR+WWI GERMANY ISLAM INT/ORG BARGAIN...POLICY   COLONIAL
INT/LAW 20. PAGE 66 E1321   AFR
                                                     DIPLOM

B50
MOCKFORD J.,SOUTH-WEST AFRICA AND THE INTERNATIONAL COLONIAL
COURT (PAMPHLET). AFR GERMANY SOUTH/AFR UK   SOVEREIGN
ECO/UNDEV DIPLOM CONTROL DISCRIM...DECISION JURID   INT/LAW
20 AFRICA/SW. PAGE 74 E1475   DOMIN

S51
LEEK J.H.,"TREASON AND THE CONSTITUTION" (BMR)"   CONSTN
USA+45 USA-45 EDU/PROP COLONIAL CT/SYS REV WAR   JURID
ATTIT...TREND 18/20 SUPREME/CT CON/INTERP SMITH/ACT CRIME
COMMON/LAW. PAGE 64 E1278   NAT/G

B52
DU BOIS W.E.B.,IN BATTLE FOR PEACE. AFR USA+45   PEACE
COLONIAL CT/SYS PERS/REL PERSON ORD/FREE...JURID 20 RACE/REL
NEGRO CIVIL/LIB. PAGE 33 E0650   DISCRIM
                                                     BIOG

B52
JENNINGS W.I.,CONSTITUTIONAL LAWS OF THE   CONSTN
COMMONWEALTH. UK LAW CHIEF LEGIS TAX CT/SYS   JURID
PARL/PROC GOV/REL...INT/LAW 18/20 COMMONWLTH   ADJUD
ENGLSH/LAW COMMON/LAW. PAGE 58 E1165   COLONIAL

B52
LIPPMANN W.,ISOLATION AND ALLIANCES: AN AMERICAN   DIPLOM
SPEAKS TO THE BRITISH. USA+45 USA-45 INT/ORG AGREE   SOVEREIGN
COERCE DETER WAR PEACE MORAL 20 TREATY INTERVENT.   COLONIAL
PAGE 65 E1301   ATTIT

B53
PIERCE R.A.,RUSSIAN CENTRAL ASIA, 1867-1917: A   BIBLIOG
SELECTED BIBLIOGRAPHY (PAMPHLET). USSR LAW CULTURE   COLONIAL
NAT/G EDU/PROP WAR...GEOG SOC 19/20. PAGE 81 E1616   ADMIN
                                                     COM

B53
STOUT H.M.,BRITISH GOVERNMENT. UK FINAN LOC/G   NAT/G
POL/PAR DELIB/GP DIPLOM ADMIN COLONIAL CHOOSE   PARL/PROC
ORD/FREE...JURID BIBLIOG 20 COMMONWLTH. PAGE 94   CONSTN
E1883   NEW/LIB

B55
BEANEY W.M.,THE RIGHT TO COUNSEL IN AMERICAN   ADJUD
COURTS. UK USA+45 USA-45 LAW NAT/G PROVS COLONIAL   CONSTN
PERCEPT 18/20 SUPREME/CT AMEND/VI AMEND/XIV   CT/SYS
ENGLSH/LAW. PAGE 8 E0163

B55
DE ARAGAO J.G.,LA JURIDICTION ADMINISTRATIVE AU   EX/STRUC
BRESIL. BRAZIL ADJUD COLONIAL CT/SYS REV FEDERAL   ADMIN
ORD/FREE...BIBLIOG 19/20. PAGE 29 E0580   NAT/G

B57
PALMER N.D.,INTERNATIONAL RELATIONS. WOR+45 INT/ORG DIPLOM

NAT/G ECO/TAC EDU/PROP COLONIAL WAR PWR SOVEREIGN   BAL/PWR
...POLICY T 20 TREATY. PAGE 79 E1593   NAT/COMP

B57
POUND R.,THE DEVELOPMENT OF CONSTITUTIONAL   LAW
GUARANTEES OF LIBERTY. UK USA-45 CHIEF COLONIAL REV CONSTN
...JURID CONCPT 15/20. PAGE 82 E1638   ORD/FREE
                                                     ATTIT

B58
MANSERGH N.,COMMONWEALTH PERSPECTIVES. GHANA UK LAW DIPLOM
VOL/ASSN CONFER HEALTH SOVEREIGN...GEOG CHARTS   COLONIAL
ANTHOL 20 CMN/WLTH AUSTRAL. PAGE 68 E1363   INT/ORG
                                                     INGP/REL

B58
WOOD J.E.,CHURCH AND STATE IN SCRIPTURE HISTORY AND GP/REL
CONSTITUTIONAL LAW. LAW CONSTN SOCIETY PROVS   SECT
VOL/ASSN BAL/PWR COLONIAL CT/SYS ATTIT...BIBLIOG 20 NAT/G
SUPREME/CT CHURCH/STA BIBLE. PAGE 107 E2142   ADJUD

B59
LOEWENSTEIN K.,VERFASSUNGSRECHT UND   CONSTN
VERFASSUNGSPRAXIS DER VEREINIGTEN STAATEN. USA+45   POL/PAR
USA-45 COLONIAL CT/SYS GP/REL RACE/REL ORD/FREE   EX/STRUC
...JURID 18/20 SUPREME/CT CONGRESS PRESIDENT   NAT/G
BILL/RIGHT CIVIL/LIB. PAGE 66 E1319

B60
GONZALEZ NAVARRO M.,LA COLONIZACION EN MEXICO,   ECO/UNDEV
1877-1910. AGRI NAT/G PLAN PROB/SOLV INCOME   GEOG
...POLICY JURID CENSUS 19/20 MEXIC/AMER MIGRATION.   HABITAT
PAGE 44 E0883   COLONIAL

B60
PRASAD B.,THE ORIGINS OF PROVINCIAL AUTONOMY. INDIA CENTRAL
UK FINAN LOC/G FORCES LEGIS CONTROL CT/SYS PWR   PROVS
...JURID 19/20. PAGE 82 E1646   COLONIAL
                                                     NAT/G

B61
CARNELL F.,THE POLITICS OF THE NEW STATES: A SELECT BIBLIOG/A
ANNOTATED BIBLIOGRAPHY WITH SPECIAL REFERENCE TO   AFR
THE COMMONWEALTH. CONSTN ELITES LABOR NAT/G POL/PAR ASIA
EX/STRUC DIPLOM ADJUD ADMIN...GOV/COMP 20   COLONIAL
COMMONWLTH. PAGE 20 E0387

B61
RIENOW R.,CONTEMPORARY INTERNATIONAL POLITICS.   DIPLOM
WOR+45 INT/ORG BAL/PWR EDU/PROP COLONIAL NEUTRAL   PWR
REGION WAR PEACE...INT/LAW 20 COLD/WAR UN. PAGE 85   POLICY
E1698   NAT/G

B61
SYATAUW J.J.G.,SOME NEWLY ESTABLISHED ASIAN STATES   INT/LAW
AND THE DEVELOPMENT OF INTERNATIONAL LAW. BURMA   ADJUST
CEYLON INDIA INDONESIA ECO/UNDEV COLONIAL NEUTRAL   SOCIETY
WAR PEACE SOVEREIGN...CHARTS 19/20. PAGE 95 E1902   S/ASIA

B62
ALLOTT A.N.,JUDICIAL AND LEGAL SYSTEMS IN AFRICA.   CT/SYS
LAW CONSTN JUDGE CONTROL...METH/CNCPT CLASSIF   AFR
CHARTS 20 COMMON/LAW. PAGE 4 E0070   JURID
                                                     COLONIAL

B62
CARSON P.,MATERIALS FOR WEST AFRICAN HISTORY IN THE BIBLIOG/A
ARCHIVES OF BELGIUM AND HOLLAND. CLIENT INDUS   COLONIAL
INT/TRADE ADMIN 17/19. PAGE 20 E0397   AFR
                                                     ECO/UNDEV

B62
DELANY V.T.H.,THE ADMINISTRATION OF JUSTICE IN   ADMIN
IRELAND. IRELAND CONSTN FINAN JUDGE COLONIAL CRIME   JURID
...CRIMLGY 19/20. PAGE 30 E0604   CT/SYS
                                                     ADJUD

B62
HENDERSON W.O.,THE GENESIS OF THE COMMON MARKET.   ECO/DEV
EUR+WWI FRANCE MOD/EUR UK SEA COM/IND EXTR/IND   INT/TRADE
COLONIAL DISCRIM...TIME/SEQ CHARTS BIBLIOG 18/20   DIPLOM
EEC TREATY. PAGE 52 E1030

B62
HSUEH S.-S.,GOVERNMENT AND ADMINISTRATION OF HONG   ADMIN
KONG. CHIEF DELIB/GP LEGIS CT/SYS REPRESENT GOV/REL LOC/G
20 HONG/KONG CITY/MGT CIVIL/SERV GOVERNOR. PAGE 55   COLONIAL
E1106   EX/STRUC

B62
PHILLIPS O.H.,CONSTITUTIONAL AND ADMINISTRATIVE LAW JURID
(3RD ED.). UK INT/ORG LOC/G CHIEF EX/STRUC LEGIS   ADMIN
BAL/PWR ADJUD COLONIAL CT/SYS PWR...CHARTS 20.   CONSTN
PAGE 80 E1613   NAT/G

MANGIN G.,"L'ORGANIZATION JUDICIAIRE DES ETATS   L62
D'AFRIQUE ET DE MADAGASCAR." ISLAM WOR+45 STRATA   AFR
STRUCT ECO/UNDEV NAT/G LEGIT EXEC...JURID TIME/SEQ   LEGIS
TOT/POP 20 SUPREME/CT. PAGE 68 E1357   COLONIAL
                                                        MADAGASCAR

                                                        L62
MURACCIOLE L.,"LA LOI FONDAMENTALE DE LA REPUBLIQUE   AFR
DU CONGO." WOR+45 SOCIETY ECO/UNDEV INT/ORG NAT/G   CONSTN
LEGIS PLAN LEGIT ADJUD COLONIAL ROUTINE ATTIT
SOVEREIGN 20 CONGO. PAGE 75 E1504

                                                        B63
BROWN R.M.,THE SOUTH CAROLINA REGULATORS. USA-45   ORD/FREE
LEGIS LEGIT ADJUD COLONIAL CONTROL WAR...BIBLIOG/A   JURID
18 CHARLESTON SOUTH/CAR. PAGE 16 E0315   PWR
                                                        PROVS

                                                        B63
DECOTTIGNIES R.,LES NATIONALITES AFRICAINES. AFR   NAT/LISM
NAT/G PROB/SOLV DIPLOM COLONIAL ORD/FREE...CHARTS   JURID
GOV/COMP 20. PAGE 30 E0602   LEGIS
                                                        LAW

                                                        B63
ECOLE NATIONALE D'ADMIN,BIBLIOGRAPHIE SELECTIVE   BIBLIOG
D'OUVRAGES DE LANGUE FRANCAISE TRAITANT DES   AFR
PROBLEMES GOUVERNEMENTAUX ET ADMINISTRATIFS. NAT/G   ADMIN
FORCES ACT/RES OP/RES PLAN PROB/SOLV BUDGET ADJUD   EX/STRUC
COLONIAL LEAD 20. PAGE 34 E0672

                                                        B63
ELIAS T.O.,GOVERNMENT AND POLITICS IN AFRICA.   AFR
CONSTN CULTURE SOCIETY NAT/G POL/PAR DIPLOM   NAT/LISM
REPRESENT PERSON...SOC TREND BIBLIOG 4/20. PAGE 34   COLONIAL
E0681   LAW

                                                        B63
ELIAS T.O.,THE NIGERIAN LEGAL SYSTEM. NIGERIA LAW   CT/SYS
FAM KIN SECT ADMIN NAT/LISM...JURID 18/20   ADJUD
ENGLSH/LAW COMMON/LAW. PAGE 34 E0682   COLONIAL
                                                        PROF/ORG

                                                        B63
FAWCETT J.E.S.,THE BRITISH COMMONWEALTH IN   INT/LAW
INTERNATIONAL LAW. LAW INT/ORG NAT/G VOL/ASSN   STRUCT
OP/RES DIPLOM ADJUD CENTRAL CONSEN...NET/THEORY   COLONIAL
CMN/WLTH TREATY. PAGE 36 E0723

                                                        B63
FORTES A.B.,HISTORIA ADMINISTRATIVA, JUDICIARIA E   PROVS
ECLESIASTICA DO RIO GRANDE DO SUL. BRAZIL L/A+17C   ADMIN
LOC/G SECT COLONIAL CT/SYS ORD/FREE CATHISM 16/20.   JURID
PAGE 39 E0773

                                                        B63
LEWIN J.,POLITICS AND LAW IN SOUTH AFRICA.   NAT/LISM
SOUTH/AFR UK POL/PAR BAL/PWR ECO/TAC COLONIAL   POLICY
CONTROL GP/REL DISCRIM PWR 20 NEGRO. PAGE 65 E1293   LAW
                                                        RACE/REL

                                                        B63
PATRA A.C.,THE ADMINISTRATION OF JUSTICE UNDER THE   ADMIN
EAST INDIA COMPANY IN BENGAL, BIHAR AND ORISSA.   JURID
INDIA UK LG/CO CAP/ISM INT/TRADE ADJUD COLONIAL   CONCPT
CONTROL CT/SYS...POLICY 20. PAGE 80 E1602

                                                        B64
BERNSTEIN H.,A BOOKSHELF ON BRAZIL. BRAZIL ADMIN   BIBLIOG/A
COLONIAL...HUM JURID SOC 20. PAGE 11 E0213   NAT/G
                                                        L/A+17C
                                                        ECO/UNDEV

                                                        B64
ENDACOTT G.B.,GOVERNMENT AND PEOPLE IN HONG KONG   CONSTN
1841-1962: A CONSTITUTIONAL HISTORY. UK LEGIS ADJUD   COLONIAL
REPRESENT ATTIT 19/20 HONG/KONG. PAGE 35 E0688   CONTROL
                                                        ADMIN

                                                        B64
HANNA W.J.,POLITICS IN BLACK AFRICA: A SELECTIVE   BIBLIOG
BIBLIOGRAPHY OF RELEVANT PERIODICAL LITERATURE. AFR   NAT/LISM
LAW LOC/G MUNIC NAT/G POL/PAR LOBBY CHOOSE RACE/REL   COLONIAL
SOVEREIGN 20. PAGE 50 E0995

                                                        B64
HOLDSWORTH W.S.,A HISTORY OF ENGLISH LAW; THE   LAW
CENTURIES OF DEVELOPMENT AND REFORM (VOL. XIV). UK   LEGIS
CONSTN LOC/G NAT/G POL/PAR CHIEF EX/STRUC ADJUD   LEAD
COLONIAL ATTIT...INT/LAW JURID 18/19 TORY/PARTY   CT/SYS
COMMONWLTH WHIG/PARTY COMMON/LAW. PAGE 54 E1081

                                                        B64
ROBINSON R.D.,INTERNATIONAL BUSINESS POLICY. AFR   ECO/TAC
INDIA L/A+17C USA+45 ELITES AGRI FOR/AID COERCE   DIST/IND
BAL/PAY...DECISION INT/LAW MGT 20. PAGE 85 E1706   COLONIAL

                                                        B64
TONG T.,UNITED STATES DIPLOMACY IN CHINA,   DIPLOM
1844-1860. ASIA USA-45 ECO/UNDEV ECO/TAC COERCE   INT/TRADE
GP/REL...INT/LAW 19 TREATY. PAGE 96 E1934   COLONIAL

                                                        S64
GINSBURGS G.,"WARS OF NATIONAL LIBERATION - THE   COERCE
SOVIET THESIS." COM USSR WOR+45 WOR-45 LAW CULTURE   CONCPT
INT/ORG DIPLOM LEGIT COLONIAL GUERRILLA WAR   INT/LAW
NAT/LISM ATTIT PERSON MORAL PWR...JURID OBS TREND   REV
MARX/KARL 20. PAGE 44 E0869

                                                        B65
BAADE H.,THE SOVIET IMPACT ON INTERNATIONAL LAW.   INT/LAW
INT/ORG INT/TRADE LEGIT COLONIAL ARMS/CONT REV WAR   USSR
...CON/ANAL ANTHOL TREATY. PAGE 6 E0124   CREATE
                                                        ORD/FREE

                                                        B65
BLITZ L.F.,THE POLITICS AND ADMINISTRATION OF   NAT/G
NIGERIAN GOVERNMENT. NIGER CULTURE LOC/G LEGIS   GOV/REL
DIPLOM COLONIAL CT/SYS SOVEREIGN...GEOG SOC ANTHOL   POL/PAR
20. PAGE 13 E0245

                                                        B65
CHROUST A.H.,THE RISE OF THE LEGAL PROFESSION IN   JURID
AMERICA (3 VOLS.). STRATA STRUCT POL/PAR PROF/ORG   USA-45
COLONIAL LEAD REV SKILL...SOC 17/20. PAGE 22 E0437   CT/SYS
                                                        LAW

                                                        B65
COWEN Z.,THE BRITISH COMMONWEALTH OF NATIONS IN A   JURID
CHANGING WORLD. UK ECO/UNDEV INT/ORG ECO/TAC   DIPLOM
INT/TRADE COLONIAL WAR GP/REL RACE/REL SOVEREIGN   PARL/PROC
SOC/INTEG 20 TREATY EEC COMMONWLTH. PAGE 27 E0530   NAT/LISM

                                                        B65
KUPER H.,AFRICAN LAW. LAW FAM KIN SECT JUDGE ADJUST   AFR
NAT/LISM 17/20. PAGE 62 E1236   CT/SYS
                                                        ADJUD
                                                        COLONIAL

                                                        B65
MILLER H.H.,THE CASE FOR LIBERTY. USA-45 LAW JUDGE   COLONIAL
CT/SYS...AUD/VIS 18 PRE/US/AM CASEBOOK. PAGE 73   JURID
E1460   PROB/SOLV

                                                        B65
MORRIS R.B.,THE PEACEMAKERS; THE GREAT POWERS AND   SOVEREIGN
AMERICAN INDEPENDENCE. BAL/PWR CONFER COLONIAL   REV
NEUTRAL PEACE ORD/FREE TREATY 18 PRE/US/AM. PAGE 75   DIPLOM
E1499

                                                        B65
NEWBURY C.W.,BRITISH POLICY TOWARDS WEST AFRICA: DIPLOM
SELECT DOCUMENTS 1786-1874. AFR UK INT/TRADE DOMIN   POLICY
ADMIN COLONIAL CT/SYS COERCE ORD/FREE...BIBLIOG/A   NAT/G
18/19. PAGE 77 E1540   WRITING

                                                        B65
O'BRIEN W.V.,THE NEW NATIONS IN INTERNATIONAL LAW   INT/LAW
AND DIPLOMACY* THE YEAR BOOK OF WORLD POLITY*   CULTURE
VOLUME III. USA+45 ECO/UNDEV INT/ORG FORCES DIPLOM   SOVEREIGN
COLONIAL NEUTRAL REV NAT/LISM ATTIT RESPECT.   ANTHOL
PAGE 78 E1565

                                                        B65
PADELFORD N.,THE UNITED NATIONS IN THE BALANCE*   INT/ORG
ACCOMPLISHMENTS AND PROSPECTS. NAT/G VOL/ASSN   CONTROL
DIPLOM ADMIN COLONIAL CT/SYS REGION WAR ORD/FREE
...ANTHOL UN. PAGE 79 E1588

                                                        B65
PYLEE M.V.,CONSTITUTIONAL GOVERNMENT IN INDIA (2ND   CONSTN
REV. ED.). INDIA POL/PAR EX/STRUC DIPLOM COLONIAL   NAT/G
CT/SYS PARL/PROC PRIVIL...JURID 16/20. PAGE 83   PROVS
E1665   FEDERAL

                                                        B65
SOPER T.,EVOLVING COMMONWEALTH. AFR CANADA INDIA   INT/ORG
IRELAND UK LAW CONSTN POL/PAR DOMIN CONTROL WAR PWR   COLONIAL
...AUD/VIS 18/20 COMMONWLTH OEEC. PAGE 93 E1857   VOL/ASSN

                                                        B65
VON RENESSE E.A.,UNVOLLENDETE DEMOKRATIEN. AFR   ECO/UNDEV
ISLAM S/ASIA SOCIETY ACT/RES COLONIAL...JURID   NAT/COMP
CHARTS BIBLIOG METH 13/20. PAGE 104 E2083   SOVEREIGN

                                                        C65
SEARA M.V.,"COSMIC INTERNATIONAL LAW." LAW ACADEM   SPACE
ACT/RES DIPLOM COLONIAL CONTROL NUC/PWR SOVEREIGN   INT/LAW
...GEN/LAWS BIBLIOG UN. PAGE 90 E1799   IDEA/COMP
                                                        INT/ORG

CAMPBELL E.,PARLIAMENTARY PRIVILEGE IN AUSTRALIA. LEGIS
UK LAW CONSTN COLONIAL ROLE ORD/FREE SOVEREIGN PARL/PROC
18/20 COMMONWLTH AUSTRAL FREE/SPEE PARLIAMENT. JURID
PAGE 19 E0370 PRIVIL
B66

COPLIN W.D.,THE FUNCTIONS OF INTERNATIONAL LAW. INT/LAW
WOR+45 ECO/DEV ECO/UNDEV ADJUD COLONIAL WAR OWN DIPLOM
SOVEREIGN...POLICY GEN/LAWS 20. PAGE 25 E0503 INT/ORG
B66

O'NEILL C.E.,CHURCH AND STATE IN FRENCH COLONIAL COLONIAL
LOUISIANA: POLICY AND POLITICS TO 1732. PROVS NAT/G
VOL/ASSN DELIB/GP ADJUD ADMIN GP/REL ATTIT DRIVE SECT
...POLICY BIBLIOG 17/18 LOUISIANA CHURCH/STA. PWR
PAGE 78 E1568
B66

POWERS E.,CRIME AND PUNISHMENT IN EARLY CRIME
MASSACHUSETTS 1620-1692: A DOCUMENTARY HISTORY. ADJUD
USA-45 SECT LEGIS COLONIAL ATTIT ORD/FREE MYSTISM CT/SYS
17 PRE/US/AM MASSACHU. PAGE 82 E1643 PROVS
L66

HIGGINS R.,"THE INTERNATIONAL COURT AND SOUTH WEST SOUTH/AFR
AFRICA* SOME IMPLICATIONS OF THE JUDGMENT." AFR LAW COLONIAL
ECO/UNDEV JUDGE RACE/REL COST PWR...INT/LAW TREND CT/SYS
UN TREATY. PAGE 52 E1043 ADJUD
S66

ANAND R.P.,"ATTITUDE OF THE ASIAN-AFRICAN STATES INT/LAW
TOWARD CERTAIN PROBLEMS OF INTERNATIONAL LAW." ATTIT
L/A+17C S/ASIA ECO/UNDEV CREATE CONFER ADJUD ASIA
COLONIAL...RECORD GP/COMP UN. PAGE 5 E0087 AFR
S66

DETTER I.,"THE PROBLEM OF UNEQUAL TREATIES." CONSTN SOVEREIGN
NAT/G LEGIS COLONIAL COERCE PWR...GEOG UN TIME DOMIN
TREATY. PAGE 31 E0610 INT/LAW
ECO/UNDEV
S66

GREEN L.C.,"RHODESIAN OIL: BOOTLEGGERS OR PIRATES?" INT/TRADE
AFR RHODESIA UK WOR+45 INT/ORG NAT/G DIPLOM LEGIT SANCTION
COLONIAL SOVEREIGN 20 UN OAU. PAGE 46 E0907 INT/LAW
POLICY
B67

MEYERS M.,SOURCES OF THE AMERICAN REPUBLIC; A COLONIAL
DOCUMENTARY HISTORY OF POLITICS, SOCIETY, AND REV
THOUGHT (VOL. I, REV. ED.). USA-45 CULTURE STRUCT WAR
NAT/G LEGIS LEAD ATTIT...JURID SOC ANTHOL 17/19
PRESIDENT. PAGE 72 E1450
B67

NARAIN I.,THE POLITICS OF RACIALISM. INDIA DISCRIM
SOUTH/AFR LAW NAT/G RACE/REL ATTIT 20. PAGE 76 COLONIAL
E1521 HIST/WRIT
B67

NIVEN R.,NIGERIA. NIGERIA CONSTN INDUS EX/STRUC NAT/G
COLONIAL REV NAT/LISM...CHARTS 19/20. PAGE 77 E1550 REGION
CHOOSE
GP/REL
B67

RAMUNDO B.A.,PEACEFUL COEXISTENCE: INTERNATIONAL INT/LAW
LAW IN THE BUILDING OF COMMUNISM. USSR INT/ORG PEACE
DIPLOM COLONIAL ARMS/CONT ROLE SOVEREIGN...POLICY MARXISM
METH/COMP NAT/COMP BIBLIOG. PAGE 83 E1673 METH/CNCPT
S67

ALDRICH W.A.,"THE SUEZ CRISIS." UAR UK USA+45 DIPLOM
DELIB/GP FORCES BAL/PWR INT/TRADE CONFER CONTROL INT/LAW
COERCE DETER 20. PAGE 3 E0058 COLONIAL
S67

MORENO F.J.,"THE SPANISH COLONIAL SYSTEM: A COLONIAL
FUNCTIONAL APPROACH." SPAIN WOR-45 LAW CHIEF DIPLOM CONTROL
ADJUD CIVMIL/REL AUTHORIT ROLE PWR...CONCPT 17/20. NAT/G
PAGE 74 E1492 OP/RES
S67

READ J.S.,"CENSORED." UGANDA CONSTN INTELL SOCIETY EDU/PROP
NAT/G DIPLOM PRESS WRITING ADJUD ADMIN COLONIAL AFR
RISK...IDEA/COMP 20. PAGE 84 E1675 CREATE
S68

DUGARD J.,"THE REVOCATION OF THE MANDATE FOR SOUTH AFR
WEST AFRICA." SOUTH/AFR WOR+45 STRATA NAT/G INT/ORG
DELIB/GP DIPLOM ADJUD SANCTION CHOOSE RACE/REL DISCRIM
...POLICY NAT/COMP 20 AFRICA/SW UN TRUST/TERR COLONIAL
LEAGUE/NAT. PAGE 33 E0654

COLORADO....COLORADO

COLORADO CIVIL SERVICE COMN,SECOND BIENNIAL REPORT PROVS
TO THE GOVERNOR, 1909-1910. USA+45 DELIB/GP LEGIS LOC/G
LICENSE PAY 20 COLORADO CIVIL/SERV. PAGE 24 E0477 ADMIN
WORKER
B10

COLORADO CIVIL SERVICE COMN E0477

COLUMBIA UNIVERSITY E0478

COLUMBIA/U....COLUMBIA UNIVERSITY

COM....COMMUNIST COUNTRIES, EXCEPT CHINA; SEE ALSO
APPROPRIATE NATIONS, MARXISM

ATLANTIC INSTITUTE,ATLANTIC STUDIES. COM EUR+WWI BIBLIOG/A
USA+45 CULTURE STRUCT ECO/DEV FORCES LEAD ARMS/CONT DIPLOM
...INT/LAW JURID SOC. PAGE 6 E0110 POLICY
GOV/REL
N

IN THE SHADOW OF FEAR; AMERICAN CIVIL LIBERTIES, ORD/FREE
1948-49 (PAMPHLET). COM LAW LEGIS BAL/PWR EDU/PROP CONSTN
CT/SYS RACE/REL DISCRIM MARXISM SOCISM 20 COLD/WAR POLICY
CONGRESS ACLU CIV/RIGHTS ESPIONAGE. PAGE 2 E0030
N19

BAILEY S.D.,VETO IN THE SECURITY COUNCIL DELIB/GP
(PAMPHLET). COM USSR WOR+45 BAL/PWR PARL/PROC INT/ORG
ARMS/CONT PRIVIL PWR...INT/LAW TREND CHARTS 20 UN DIPLOM
SUEZ. PAGE 7 E0135
N19

HARPER S.N.,THE GOVERNMENT OF THE SOVIET UNION. COM MARXISM
USSR LAW CONSTN ECO/DEV PLAN TEC/DEV DIPLOM NAT/G
INT/TRADE ADMIN REV NAT/LISM...POLICY 20. PAGE 50 LEAD
E1001 POL/PAR
B38

US LIBRARY OF CONGRESS,RUSSIA: A CHECK LIST BIBLIOG
PRELIMINARY TO A BASIC BIBLIOGRAPHY OF MATERIALS IN LAW
THE RUSSIAN LANGUAGE. COM USSR CULTURE EDU/PROP SECT
MARXISM...ART/METH HUM LING 19/20. PAGE 101 E2015
B44

FOX W.T.R.,UNITED STATES POLICY IN A TWO POWER DIPLOM
WORLD. COM USA+45 USSR FORCES DOMIN AGREE NEUTRAL FOR/AID
NUC/PWR ORD/FREE SOVEREIGN 20 COLD/WAR TREATY POLICY
EUROPE/W INTERVENT. PAGE 39 E0780
N47

YAKOBSON S.,FIVE HUNDRED RUSSIAN WORKS FOR COLLEGE BIBLIOG
LIBRARIES (PAMPHLET). MOD/EUR USSR MARXISM SOCISM NAT/G
...ART/METH GEOG HUM JURID SOC 13/20. PAGE 108 CULTURE
E2162 COM
B48

MARITAIN J.,HUMAN RIGHTS: COMMENTS AND INT/ORG
INTERPRETATIONS. COM UNIV WOR+45 LAW CONSTN CULTURE CONCPT
SOCIETY ECO/DEV ECO/UNDEV SCHOOL DELIB/GP EDU/PROP
ATTIT PERCEPT ALL/VALS...HUM SOC TREND UNESCO 20.
PAGE 68 E1365
B49

US DEPARTMENT OF STATE,SOVIET BIBLIOGRAPHY BIBLIOG/A
(PAMPHLET). CHINA/COM COM USSR LAW AGRI INT/ORG MARXISM
ECO/TAC EDU/PROP...POLICY GEOG 20. PAGE 99 E1994 CULTURE
DIPLOM
B49

US DEPARTMENT OF STATE,RESEARCH ON EASTERN EUROPE BIBLIOG
(EXCLUDING USSR). EUR+WWI LAW ECO/DEV NAT/G R+D
PROB/SOLV DIPLOM ADMIN LEAD MARXISM...TREND 19/20. ACT/RES
PAGE 100 E1995 COM
B52

PIERCE R.A.,RUSSIAN CENTRAL ASIA, 1867-1917: A BIBLIOG
SELECTED BIBLIOGRAPHY (PAMPHLET). USSR LAW CULTURE COLONIAL
NAT/G EDU/PROP WAR...GEOG SOC 19/20. PAGE 81 E1616 ADMIN
COM
B53

GUINS G.C.,"SOVIET LAW AND SOVIET SOCIETY." COM LAW
USSR LAW STRATA FAM NAT/G WORKER DOMIN RACE/REL STRUCT
...BIBLIOG 20. PAGE 48 E0960 PLAN
C54

MID-EUROPEAN LAW PROJECT,CHURCH AND STATE BEHIND LAW
THE IRON CURTAIN. COM CZECHOSLVK HUNGARY POLAND MARXISM
USSR CULTURE SECT EDU/PROP GOV/REL CATHISM...CHARTS POLICY
ANTHOL BIBLIOG WORSHIP 20 CHURCH/STA. PAGE 73 E1455
B55

KALNOKI BEDO A.,LEGAL SOURCES AND BIBLIOGRAPHY OF BIBLIOG
HUNGARY. COM HUNGARY CONSTN LEGIS JUDGE CT/SYS ADJUD
B56

SANCTION CRIME 16/20. PAGE 59 E1181 — LAW JURID

B56
SIPKOV I., LEGAL SOURCES AND BIBLIOGRAPHY OF BULGARIA. BULGARIA COM LEGIS WRITING ADJUD CT/SYS ...INT/LAW TREATY 20. PAGE 91 E1834 — BIBLIOG LAW TOTALISM MARXISM

B57
BYRNES R.F., BIBLIOGRAPHY OF AMERICAN PUBLICATIONS ON EAST CENTRAL EUROPE, 1945-1957 (VOL. XXII). SECT DIPLOM EDU/PROP RACE/REL...ART/METH GEOG JURID SOC LING 20 JEWS. PAGE 18 E0354 — BIBLIOG/A COM MARXISM NAT/G

S58
STAAR R.F., "ELECTIONS IN COMMUNIST POLAND." EUR+WWI SOCIETY INT/ORG NAT/G POL/PAR LEGIS ACT/RES ECO/TAC EDU/PROP ADJUD ADMIN ROUTINE COERCE TOTALISM ATTIT ORD/FREE PWR 20. PAGE 93 E1864 — COM CHOOSE POLAND

B59
BOHMER A., LEGAL SOURCES AND BIBLIOGRAPHY OF CZECHOSLOVAKIA. COM CZECHOSLVK PARL/PROC SANCTION CRIME MARXISM 20. PAGE 13 E0261 — BIBLIOG ADJUD LAW JURID

B59
EPSTEIN F.T., EAST GERMANY: A SELECTED BIBLIOGRAPHY (PAMPHLET). COM GERMANY/E LAW AGRI FINAN INDUS LABOR POL/PAR EDU/PROP ADMIN AGE/Y 20. PAGE 35 E0693 — BIBLIOG/A INTELL MARXISM NAT/G

B59
GSOVSKI V., GOVERNMENT, LAW, AND COURTS IN THE SOVIET UNION AND EASTERN EUROPE (2 VOLS.). COM USSR AGRI INDUS WORKER CT/SYS CRIME...BIBLIOG 20 EUROPE/E. PAGE 48 E0958 — ADJUD MARXISM CONTROL ORD/FREE

B59
OKINSHEVICH L.A., LATIN AMERICA IN SOVIET WRITINGS, 1945-1958: A BIBLIOGRAPHY. USSR LAW ECO/UNDEV LABOR DIPLOM EDU/PROP REV...GEOG SOC 20. PAGE 78 E1573 — BIBLIOG WRITING COM L/A+17C

B60
ENGEL J., THE SECURITY OF THE FREE WORLD. USSR WOR+45 STRATA STRUCT ECO/DEV ECO/UNDEV INT/ORG DELIB/GP FORCES DOMIN LEGIT ADJUD EXEC ARMS/CONT COERCE...POLICY CONCPT NEW/IDEA TIME/SEQ GEN/LAWS COLD/WAR WORK UN 20 NATO. PAGE 35 E0689 — COM TREND DIPLOM

B60
FISCHER L., THE SOVIETS IN WORLD AFFAIRS. CHINA/COM COM EUR+WWI USSR INT/ORG CONFER LEAD ARMS/CONT REV PWR...CHARTS 20 TREATY VERSAILLES. PAGE 38 E0755 — DIPLOM NAT/G POLICY MARXISM

S60
GRACIA-MORA M.R., "INTERNATIONAL RESPONSIBILITY FOR SUBVERSIVE ACTIVITIES AND HOSTILE PROPAGANDA BY PRIVATE PERSONS AGAINST." COM EUR+WWI L/A+17C UK USA+45 USSR WOR-45 CONSTN NAT/G LEGIT ADJUD REV PEACE TOTALISM ORD/FREE...INT/LAW 20. PAGE 45 E0895 — INT/ORG JURID SOVEREIGN

S60
WRIGHT Q., "LEGAL ASPECTS OF THE U-2 INCIDENT." COM USA+45 USSR STRUCT NAT/G FORCES PLAN TEC/DEV ADJUD RIGID/FLEX MORAL ORD/FREE...DECISION INT/LAW JURID PSY TREND GEN/LAWS COLD/WAR VAL/FREE 20 U-2. PAGE 108 E2157 — PWR POLICY SPACE

C60
HAZARD J.N., "SETTLING DISPUTES IN SOVIET SOCIETY: THE FORMATIVE YEARS OF LEGAL INSTITUTIONS." USSR NAT/G PROF/ORG PROB/SOLV CONTROL CT/SYS ROUTINE REV CENTRAL...JURID BIBLIOG 20. PAGE 51 E1017 — ADJUD LAW COM POLICY

B61
CONFERENCE ATLANTIC COMMUNITY, AN INTRODUCTORY BIBLIOGRAPHY. COM WOR+45 FORCES DIPLOM ECO/TAC WAR ...INT/LAW HIST/WRIT COLD/WAR NATO. PAGE 25 E0485 — BIBLIOG/A CON/ANAL INT/ORG

S61
LIPSON L., "AN ARGUMENT ON THE LEGALITY OF RECONNAISSANCE STATELLITES." COM USA+45 USSR WOR+45 AIR INTELL NAT/G CONSULT PLAN DIPLOM LEGIT ROUTINE ATTIT...INT/LAW JURID CONCPT METH/CNCPT TREND COLD/WAR 20. PAGE 65 E1302 — INT/ORG LAW SPACE

B62
BOCHENSKI J.M., HANDBOOK ON COMMUNISM. USSR WOR+45 LAW SOCIETY NAT/G POL/PAR SECT CRIME PERSON MARXISM ...SOC ANTHOL 20. PAGE 13 E0254 — COM DIPLOM POLICY CONCPT

B62
DOUGLAS W.O., DEMOCRACY'S MANIFESTO. COM USA+45 ECO/UNDEV INT/ORG FORCES PLAN NEUTRAL TASK MARXISM ...JURID 20 NATO SEATO. PAGE 32 E0642 — DIPLOM POLICY NAT/G ORD/FREE

B62
GYORGY A., PROBLEMS IN INTERNATIONAL RELATIONS. COM CT/SYS NUC/PWR ALL/IDEOS 20 UN EEC ECSC. PAGE 49 E0966 — DIPLOM NEUTRAL BAL/PWR REV

B62
LEVY H.V., LIBERDADE E JUSTICA SOCIAL (2ND ED.). BRAZIL COM L/A+17C USSR INT/ORG PARTIC GP/REL WEALTH 20 UN COM/PARTY. PAGE 65 E1290 — ORD/FREE MARXISM CAP/ISM LAW

B62
TRISKA J.F., THE THEORY, LAW, AND POLICY OF SOVIET TREATIES. WOR+45 WOR-45 CONSTN INT/ORG NAT/G VOL/ASSN DOMIN LEGIT COERCE ATTIT PWR RESPECT ...POLICY JURID CONCPT OBS SAMP TIME/SEQ TREND GEN/LAWS 20. PAGE 97 E1941 — COM LAW INT/LAW USSR

L62
PETKOFF D.K., "RECOGNITION AND NON-RECOGNITION OF STATES AND GOVERNMENTS IN INTERNATIONAL LAW." ASIA COM USA+45 WOR+45 NAT/G ACT/RES DIPLOM DOMIN LEGIT COERCE ORD/FREE PWR...CONCPT GEN/LAWS 20. PAGE 80 E1611 — INT/ORG LAW INT/LAW

S62
CRANE R.D., "SOVIET ATTITUDE TOWARD INTERNATIONAL SPACE LAW." COM FUT USA+45 USSR AIR CONSTN DELIB/GP DOMIN PWR...JURID TREND TOT/POP 20. PAGE 27 E0543 — LAW ATTIT INT/LAW SPACE

C62
MORGAN G.G., "SOVIET ADMINISTRATIVE LEGALITY: THE ROLE OF THE ATTORNEY GENERAL'S OFFICE." COM USSR CONTROL ROUTINE...CONCPT BIBLIOG 18/20. PAGE 74 E1493 — LAW CONSTN LEGIS ADMIN

B63
FISCHER-GALATI S.A., RUMANIA: A BIBLIOGRAPHIC GUIDE (PAMPHLET). ROMANIA INTELL ECO/DEV LABOR SECT WEALTH...GEOG SOC/WK LING 20. PAGE 38 E0756 — BIBLIOG/A NAT/G COM LAW

B63
GSOUSKI V., LEGAL SOURCES AND BIBLIOGRAPHY OF THE BALTIC STATES (ESTONIA, LATVIA, LITHUANIA). COM ESTONIA LATVIA LITHUANIA NAT/G LEGIS CT/SYS SANCTION CRIME 20. PAGE 48 E0957 — BIBLIOG ADJUD LAW JURID

B63
KLESMENT J., LEGAL SOURCES AND BIBLIOGRAPHY OF THE BALTIC STATES (ESTONIA, LATVIA, LITHUANIA). COM ESTONIA LATVIA LITHUANIA LAW FINAN ADJUD CT/SYS REGION CENTRAL MARXISM 19/20. PAGE 61 E1223 — BIBLIOG/A JURID CONSTN ADMIN

B63
LAVROFF D.-G., LES LIBERTES PUBLIQUES EN UNION SOVIETIQUE (REV. ED.). USSR NAT/G WORKER SANCTION CRIME MARXISM NEW/LIB...JURID BIBLIOG WORSHIP 20. PAGE 63 E1268 — ORD/FREE LAW ATTIT COM

B63
PRYOR F.L., THE COMMUNIST FOREIGN TRADE SYSTEM. COM CZECHOSLVK GERMANY YUGOSLAVIA LAW ECO/DEV DIST/IND POL/PAR PLAN DOMIN TOTALISM DRIVE RIGID/FLEX WEALTH ...STAT STAND/INT CHARTS 20. PAGE 83 E1657 — ATTIT ECO/TAC

L63
BOLGAR V., "THE PUBLIC INTEREST: A JURISPRUDENTIAL AND COMPARATIVE OVERVIEW OF SYMPOSIUM ON FUNDAMENTAL CONCEPTS OF PUBLIC LAW" COM FRANCE GERMANY SWITZERLND LAW ADJUD ADMIN AGREE LAISSEZ ...JURID GEN/LAWS 20 EUROPE/E. PAGE 14 E0264 — CONCPT ORD/FREE CONTROL NAT/COMP

S63
BECHHOEFER B.G., "UNITED NATIONS PROCEDURES IN CASE OF VIOLATIONS OF DISARMAMENT AGREEMENTS." COM USA+45 USSR LAW CONSTN NAT/G EX/STRUC FORCES LEGIS BAL/PWR EDU/PROP CT/SYS ARMS/CONT ORD/FREE PWR ...POLICY STERTYP UN VAL/FREE 20. PAGE 9 E0169 — INT/ORG DELIB/GP

S63
BERMAN H.J., "THE DILEMMA OF SOVIET LAW REFORM." NAT/G POL/PAR CT/SYS ALL/VALS ORD/FREE PWR...POLICY JURID VAL/FREE 20. PAGE 11 E0208 — COM LAW USSR

S63
GIRAUD E., "L'INTERDICTION DU RECOURS A LA FORCE, LA THEORIE ET LA PRATIQUE DES NATIONS UNIES." ALGERIA — INT/ORG FORCES

COM CUBA HUNGARY WOR+45 ADJUD TOTALISM ATTIT   DIPLOM
RIGID/FLEX PWR...POLICY JURID CONCPT UN 20 CONGO.
PAGE 44 E0872

                                                    S63
MACWHINNEY E.,"LES CONCEPT SOVIETIQUE DE   NAT/G
'COEXISTENCE PACIFIQUE' ET LES RAPPORTS JURIDIQUES   CONCPT
ENTRE L'URSS ET LES ETATS OCIDENTAUX." COM FUT   DIPLOM
WOR+45 LAW CULTURE INTELL POL/PAR ACT/RES BAL/PWR   USSR
...INT/LAW 20. PAGE 67 E1346

                                                    B64
COHEN M.,LAW AND POLITICS IN SPACE: SPECIFIC AND   DELIB/GP
URGENT PROBLEMS IN THE LAW OF OUTER SPACE.   LAW
CHINA/COM COM USA+45 USSR WOR+45 COM/IND INT/ORG   INT/LAW
NAT/G LEGIT NUC/PWR ATTIT BIO/SOC...JURID CONCPT   SPACE
CONGRESS 20 STALIN/J. PAGE 24 E0464

                                                    B64
GJUPANOVIC H.,LEGAL SOURCES AND BIBLIOGRAPHY OF   BIBLIOG/A
YUGOSLAVIA. COM YUGOSLAVIA LAW LEGIS DIPLOM ADMIN   JURID
PARL/PROC REGION CRIME CENTRAL 20. PAGE 44 E0873   CONSTN
                                                    ADJUD

                                                    B64
GRIFFITH W.E.,THE SINO-SOVIET RIFT. ASIA CHINA/COM ATTIT
COM CUBA USSR YUGOSLAVIA NAT/G POL/PAR VOL/ASSN   TIME/SEQ
DELIB/GP FORCES TOP/EX DIPLOM EDU/PROP DRIVE PERSON BAL/PWR
PWR...TREND 20 TREATY. PAGE 47 E0941   SOCISM

                                                    B64
GRZYBOWSKI K.,THE SOCIALIST COMMONWEALTH OF   INT/LAW
NATIONS: ORGANIZATIONS AND INSTITUTIONS. FORCES   COM
DIPLOM INT/TRADE ADJUD ADMIN LEAD WAR MARXISM   REGION
SOCISM...BIBLIOG 20 COMECON WARSAW/P. PAGE 48 E0956 INT/ORG

                                                    B64
IKLE F.C.,HOW NATIONS NEGOTIATE. COM EUR+WWI USA+45 NAT/G
INTELL INT/ORG VOL/ASSN DELIB/GP ACT/RES CREATE   PWR
DOMIN EDU/PROP ADJUD ROUTINE ATTIT PERSON ORD/FREE POLICY
RESPECT SKILL...PSY SOC OBS VAL/FREE. PAGE 56 E1122

                                                    B64
LAPENNA I.,STATE AND LAW: SOVIET AND YUGOSLAV   JURID
THEORY. USSR YUGOSLAVIA STRATA STRUCT NAT/G DOMIN   COM
COERCE MARXISM...GOV/COMP IDEA/COMP 20. PAGE 63   LAW
E1253   SOVEREIGN

                                                    B64
SIEKANOWICZ P.,LEGAL SOURCES AND BIBLIOGRAPHY OF   BIBLIOG
POLAND. COM POLAND CONSTN NAT/G PARL/PROC SANCTION ADJUD
CRIME MARXISM 16/20. PAGE 91 E1823   LAW
                                                    JURID

                                                    B64
STOICOIU V.,LEGAL SOURCES AND BIBLIOGRAPHY OF   BIBLIOG/A
ROMANIA. COM ROMANIA LAW FINAN POL/PAR LEGIS JUDGE JURID
ADJUD CT/SYS PARL/PROC MARXISM 20. PAGE 93 E1874   CONSTN
                                                    ADMIN

                                                    L64
POUNDS N.J.G.,"THE POLITICS OF PARTITION." AFR ASIA NAT/G
COM EUR+WWI FUT ISLAM S/ASIA USA-45 LAW ECO/DEV   NAT/LISM
ECO/UNDEV AGRI INDUS INT/ORG POL/PAR PROVS SECT
FORCES TOP/EX EDU/PROP LEGIT ATTIT MORAL ORD/FREE
PWR RESPECT WEALTH. PAGE 82 E1640

                                                    S64
CRANE R.D.,"BASIC PRINCIPLES IN SOVIET SPACE LAW." COM
FUT WOR+45 AIR INT/ORG DIPLOM DOMIN ARMS/CONT   LAW
COERCE NUC/PWR PEACE ATTIT DRIVE PWR...INT/LAW   USSR
METH/CNCPT NEW/IDEA OBS TREND GEN/LAWS VAL/FREE   SPACE
MARX/KARL 20. PAGE 27 E0544

                                                    S64
GARDNER R.N.,"THE SOVIET UNION AND THE UNITED   COM
NATIONS." WOR+45 FINAN POL/PAR VOL/ASSN FORCES   INT/ORG
ECO/TAC DOMIN EDU/PROP LEGIT ADJUD ADMIN ARMS/CONT USSR
COERCE ATTIT ALL/VALS...POLICY MAJORIT CONCPT OBS
TIME/SEQ TREND STERTYP UN. PAGE 42 E0838

                                                    S64
GINSBURGS G.,"WARS OF NATIONAL LIBERATION - THE   COERCE
SOVIET THESIS." COM USSR WOR+45 WOR-45 LAW CULTURE CONCPT
INT/ORG DIPLOM LEGIT COLONIAL GUERRILLA WAR   INT/LAW
NAT/LISM ATTIT PERSON MORAL PWR...JURID OBS TREND   REV
MARX/KARL 20. PAGE 44 E0869

                                                    S64
KARPOV P.V.,"PEACEFUL COEXISTENCE AND INTERNATIONAL COM
LAW." WOR+45 LAW SOCIETY INT/ORG VOL/ASSN FORCES   ATTIT
CREATE CAP/ISM DIPLOM ADJUD NUC/PWR PEACE MORAL   INT/LAW
ORD/FREE PWR MARXISM...MARXIST JURID CONCPT OBS   USSR
TREND COLD/WAR MARX/KARL 20. PAGE 59 E1186

                                                    S64
LIPSON L.,"PEACEFUL COEXISTENCE." COM USSR WOR+45   ATTIT
LAW INT/ORG DIPLOM LEGIT ADJUD ORD/FREE...CONCPT   JURID
OBS TREND GEN/LAWS VAL/FREE COLD/WAR 20. PAGE 65   INT/LAW
E1303   PEACE

                                                    S64
MAGGS P.B.,"SOVIET VIEWPOINT ON NUCLEAR WEAPONS IN COM
INTERNATIONAL LAW." USSR WOR+45 INT/ORG FORCES   LAW
DIPLOM ARMS/CONT ATTIT ORD/FREE PWR...POLICY JURID INT/LAW
CONCPT OBS TREND CON/ANAL GEN/LAWS VAL/FREE 20.   NUC/PWR
PAGE 67 E1347

                                                    S64
TRISKA J.F.,"SOVIET TREATY LAW: A QUANTITATIVE   COM
ANALYSIS." WOR+45 LAW ECO/UNDEV AGRI COM/IND INDUS ECO/TAC
CREATE TEC/DEV DIPLOM ATTIT PWR WEALTH...JURID SAMP INT/LAW
TIME/SEQ TREND CHARTS VAL/FREE 20 TREATY. PAGE 97   USSR
E1942

                                                    B65
MOSTECKY V.,SOVIET LEGAL BIBLIOGRAPHY. USSR LEGIS   BIBLIOG/A
PRESS WRITING CONFER ADJUD CT/SYS REV MARXISM   LAW
...INT/LAW JURID DICTIONARY 20. PAGE 75 E1503   COM
                                                    CONSTN

                                                    B65
SWISHER C.B.,THE SUPREME COURT IN MODERN ROLE. COM DELIB/GP
COM/IND NAT/G FORCES LEGIS LOBBY PARTIC RACE/REL 20 ATTIT
SUPREME/CT. PAGE 95 E1901   CT/SYS
                                                    ADJUD

                                                    S65
MCWHINNEY E.,"CHANGING INTERNATIONAL LAW METHOD AND LAW
OBJECTIVES IN THE ERA OF THE SOVIET-WESTERN   TREND
DETENTE." COM USA+45 NAT/G BAL/PWR CT/SYS ATTIT
ORD/FREE...HUM JURID NEW/IDEA COLD/WAR VAL/FREE 20.
PAGE 71 E1430

                                                    B66
DALLIN A.,POLITICS IN THE SOVIET UNION: 7 CASES.   MARXISM
COM USSR LAW POL/PAR CHIEF FORCES WRITING CONTROL   DOMIN
PARL/PROC CIVMIL/REL TOTALISM...ANTHOL 20 KHRUSH/N ORD/FREE
STALIN/J CASEBOOK COM/PARTY. PAGE 28 E0563   GOV/REL

                                                    B66
EPSTEIN F.T.,THE AMERICAN BIBLIOGRAPHY OF RUSSIAN   BIBLIOG
AND EAST EUROPEAN STUDIES FOR 1964. USSR LOC/G   COM
NAT/G POL/PAR FORCES ADMIN ARMS/CONT...JURID CONCPT MARXISM
20 UN. PAGE 35 E0694   DIPLOM

                                                    B66
US DEPARTMENT OF STATE,RESEARCH ON THE USSR AND   BIBLIOG/A
EASTERN EUROPE (EXTERNAL RESEARCH LIST NO 1-25).   EUR+WWI
USSR LAW CULTURE SOCIETY NAT/G TEC/DEV DIPLOM   COM
EDU/PROP REGION...GEOG LING. PAGE 100 E1997   MARXISM

                                                    S67
MIRONENKO Y.,"A NEW EXTENSION OF CRIMINAL LIABILITY ADJUD
IN THE USSR." COM USSR DOMIN EDU/PROP 20. PAGE 73   SANCTION
E1467   CRIME
                                                    MARXISM

                                                    B68
HULL R.H.,LAW AND VIETNAM. COM VIETNAM CONSTN   POLICY
INT/ORG FORCES DIPLOM AGREE COERCE DETER WEAPON   LAW
PEACE ATTIT 20 UN TREATY. PAGE 56 E1113   WAR
                                                    INT/LAW

COM/IND....COMMUNICATIONS INDUSTRY

                                                    N19
THE REGIONAL DIRECTOR AND THE PRESS (PAMPHLET).   PRESS
USA-45 COM/IND LOBBY ROLE 20 NLRB CINCINNATI   LABOR
BILL/RIGHT. PAGE 2 E0031   ORD/FREE
                                                    EDU/PROP

                                                    B20
LIPPMAN W.,LIBERTY AND THE NEWS. USA+45 USA-45 LAW ORD/FREE
LEGIS DOMIN LEGIT ATTIT...POLICY SOC IDEA/COMP   PRESS
METH/COMP 19/20. PAGE 65 E1300   COM/IND
                                                    EDU/PROP

                                                    B43
CLAGETT H.L.,A GUIDE TO THE LAW AND LEGAL   BIBLIOG
LITERATURE OF PARAGUAY. PARAGUAY CONSTN COM/IND   JURID
LABOR MUNIC JUDGE ADMIN CT/SYS...CRIMLGY INT/LAW   LAW
CON/ANAL 20. PAGE 22 E0439   L/A+17C

                                                    L46
ERNST M.L.,"THE FIRST FREEDOM." USA-45 LAW R+D   BIBLIOG
PRESS 20. PAGE 35 E0696   EDU/PROP
                                                    ORD/FREE
                                                    COM/IND

CLAGETT H.L.,A GUIDE TO THE LAW AND LEGAL LITERATURE OF PERU. PERU CONSTN COM/IND LABOR MUNIC JUDGE ADMIN CT/SYS...CRIMLGY INT/LAW JURID 20. PAGE 23 E0444
B47
BIBLIOG
L/A+17C
PHIL/SCI
LAW

CLAGETT H.L.,A GUIDE TO THE LAW AND LEGAL LITERATURE OF URUGUAY. URUGUAY CONSTN COM/IND FINAN LABOR MUNIC JUDGE PRESS ADMIN CT/SYS...INT/LAW PHIL/SCI 20. PAGE 23 E0445
B47
BIBLIOG
LAW
JURID
L/A+17C

GRIFFITH E.S.,RESEARCH IN POLITICAL SCIENCE: THE WORK OF PANELS OF RESEARCH COMMITTEE, APSA. WOR+45 WOR-45 COM/IND R+D FORCES ACT/RES WAR...GOV/COMP ANTHOL 20. PAGE 47 E0939
B48
BIBLIOG
PHIL/SCI
DIPLOM
JURID

BRUCKER H.,FREEDOM OF INFORMATION. USA-45 LAW LOC/G ECO/TAC DOMIN PWR...NEW/IDEA BIBLIOG 17/20. PAGE 16 E0320
B49
PRESS
COM/IND
ORD/FREE
NAT/G

SUMMERS R.E.,FEDERAL INFORMATION CONTROLS IN PEACETIME. USA+45 COM/IND DOMIN INGP/REL ATTIT ORD/FREE 20. PAGE 94 E1893
B49
ADJUD
CONTROL
EDU/PROP
PRESS

US LIBRARY OF CONGRESS,FREEDOM OF INFORMATION: SELECTIVE REPORT ON RECENT WRITINGS. USA+45 LAW CONSTN ELITES EDU/PROP PRESS LOBBY WAR TOTALSM ATTIT 20 UN UNESCO COLD/WAR. PAGE 101 E2018
B49
BIBLIOG/A
ORD/FREE
LICENSE
COM/IND

GELLER M.A.,ADVERTISING AT THE CROSSROADS: FEDERAL REGULATION VS. VOLUNTARY CONTROLS. USA+45 JUDGE ECO/TAC...POLICY JURID BIBLIOG 20 FTC. PAGE 43 E0843
B52
EDU/PROP
NAT/G
CONSTN
COM/IND

BINANI G.D.,INDIA AT A GLANCE (REV. ED.). INDIA COM/IND FINAN INDUS LABOR PROVS SCHOOL PLAN DIPLOM INT/TRADE ADMIN...JURID 20. PAGE 12 E0229
B54
INDEX
CON/ANAL
NAT/G
ECO/UNDEV

CHENERY W.L.,FREEDOM OF THE PRESS. USA+45 USA-45 LAW NAT/G DOMIN EDU/PROP 17/20. PAGE 22 E0427
B55
ORD/FREE
COM/IND
PRESS
CONSTN

WASSENBERGH H.A.,POST-WAR INTERNATIONAL CIVIL AVIATION POLICY AND THE LAW OF THE AIR. WOR+45 AIR INT/ORG DOMIN LEGIT PEACE ORD/FREE...POLICY JURID NEW/IDEA OBS TIME/SEQ TREND CHARTS 20 TREATY. PAGE 105 E2101
B57
COM/IND
NAT/G
INT/LAW

HENDERSON W.O.,THE GENESIS OF THE COMMON MARKET. EUR+WWI FRANCE MOD/EUR UK SEA COM/IND EXTR/IND COLONIAL DISCRIM...TIME/SEQ CHARTS BIBLIOG 18/20 EEC TREATY. PAGE 52 E1030
B62
ECO/DEV
INT/TRADE
DIPLOM

OTTENBERG M.,THE FEDERAL INVESTIGATORS. USA+45 LAW COM/IND DIST/IND WORKER DIPLOM INT/TRADE CONTROL FEDERAL HEALTH ORD/FREE FBI CIA FTC SEC FDA. PAGE 79 E1585
B62
FORCES
INSPECT
NAT/G
CRIME

US CONGRESS,COMMUNICATIONS SATELLITE LEGISLATION: HEARINGS BEFORE COMM ON AERON AND SPACE SCIENCES ON BILLS S2550 AND 2814. WOR+45 LAW VOL/ASSN PLAN DIPLOM CONTROL OWN PEACE...NEW/IDEA CONGRESS NASA. PAGE 99 E1990
B62
SPACE
COM/IND
ADJUD
GOV/REL

LEGISLATIVE REFERENCE SERVICE,DIGEST OF PUBLIC GENERAL BILLS AND RESOLUTIONS. LAW COM/IND EDU/PROP GOV/REL INGP/REL KNOWL...JURID 20 CONGRESS. PAGE 64 E1280
B63
BIBLIOG/A
LEGIS
DELIB/GP
NAT/G

LYONS F.S.L.,INTERNATIONALISM IN EUROPE 1815-1914. LAW AGRI COM/IND DIST/IND LABOR SECT INT/TRADE TARIFFS...BIBLIOG 19/20. PAGE 67 E1335
B63
DIPLOM
MOD/EUR
INT/ORG

STREET H.,FREEDOM: THE INDIVIDUAL AND THE LAW. UK COM/IND EDU/PROP PRESS RUMOR TV PWR 20 CIVIL/LIB FILM. PAGE 94 E1886
B63
ORD/FREE
NAT/G
JURID
PARL/PROC

US SENATE COMM ON JUDICIARY,PACIFICA FOUNDATION. USA+45 LAW COM/IND 20 ODEGARD/P BINNS/JJ SCHINDLR/P HEALEY/D THOMAS/TK. PAGE 102 E2051
B63
DELIB/GP
EDU/PROP
ORD/FREE
ATTIT

GARDNER R.N.,"COOPERATION IN OUTER SPACE." FUT USSR WOR+45 AIR LAW COM/IND CONSULT DELIB/GP CREATE KNOWL 20 TREATY. PAGE 42 E0837
S63
INT/ORG
ACT/RES
PEACE
SPACE

COHEN M.,LAW AND POLITICS IN SPACE: SPECIFIC AND URGENT PROBLEMS IN THE LAW OF OUTER SPACE. CHINA/COM COM USA+45 USSR WOR+45 INT/ORG NAT/G LEGIT NUC/PWR ATTIT BIO/SOC...JURID CONCPT CONGRESS 20 STALIN/J. PAGE 24 E0464
B64
DELIB/GP
LAW
INT/LAW
SPACE

NASA,PROCEEDINGS OF CONFERENCE ON THE LAW OF SPACE AND OF SATELLITE COMMUNICATIONS: CHICAGO 1963. FUT WOR+45 DELIB/GP PROB/SOLV TEC/DEV CONFER ADJUD NUC/PWR...POLICY IDEA/COMP 20 NASA. PAGE 76 E1522
B64
SPACE
COM/IND
LAW
DIPLOM

SCHWARTZ M.D.,CONFERENCE ON SPACE SCIENCE AND SPACE LAW. FUT COM/IND NAT/G FORCES ACT/RES PLAN BUDGET DIPLOM NUC/PWR WEAPON...POLICY ANTHOL 20. PAGE 89 E1788
B64
SPACE
LAW
PEACE
TEC/DEV

TRISKA J.F.,"SOVIET TREATY LAW: A QUANTITATIVE ANALYSIS." WOR+45 LAW ECO/UNDEV AGRI COM/IND INDUS CREATE TEC/DEV DIPLOM ATTIT PWR WEALTH...JURID SAMP TIME/SEQ TREND CHARTS VAL/FREE 20 TREATY. PAGE 97 E1942
S64
COM
ECO/TAC
INT/LAW
USSR

SWISHER C.B.,THE SUPREME COURT IN MODERN ROLE. COM COM/IND NAT/G FORCES LEGIS LOBBY PARTIC RACE/REL 20 SUPREME/CT. PAGE 95 E1901
B65
DELIB/GP
ATTIT
CT/SYS
ADJUD

UNESCO,HANDBOOK OF INTERNATIONAL EXCHANGES. COM/IND R+D ACADEM PROF/ORG VOL/ASSN CREATE TEC/DEV EDU/PROP AGREE 20 TREATY. PAGE 98 E1963
B65
INDEX
INT/ORG
DIPLOM
PRESS

DIZARD W.P.,TELEVISION* A WORLD VIEW. WOR+45 ECO/UNDEV TEC/DEV LICENSE LITERACY...STAT OBS INT QU TREND AUD/VIS BIBLIOG. PAGE 32 E0632
B66
COM/IND
ACT/RES
EDU/PROP
CREATE

FELSHER H.,JUSTICE USA? USA+45 COM/IND JUDGE CT/SYS MORAL ORD/FREE...SAMP/SIZ HYPO/EXP. PAGE 37 E0735
B66
ADJUD
EDU/PROP
LOBBY

LONG E.V.,THE INTRUDERS: THE INVASION OF PRIVACY BY GOVERNMENT AND INDUSTRY. USA+45 COM/IND INDUS LEGIS TASK PERS/REL...JURID 20 CONGRESS. PAGE 66 E1324
B67
LAW
PARTIC
NAT/G

UNITED NATIONS,UNITED NATIONS PUBLICATIONS: 1945-1966. WOR+45 COM/IND DIST/IND FINAN TEC/DEV ADMIN...POLICY INT/LAW MGT CHARTS 20 UN UNESCO. PAGE 98 E1970
B67
BIBLIOG/A
INT/ORG
DIPLOM
WRITING

BARRON J.A.,"ACCESS TO THE PRESS." USA+45 TEC/DEV PRESS TV ADJUD AUD/VIS. PAGE 8 E0152
L67
ORD/FREE
COM/IND
EDU/PROP
LAW

CLOGGER T.J.,"THE BIG EAR." UK USA+45 USSR LAW LEGIS CRIME GP/REL INGP/REL ATTIT 20 FBI ESPIONAGE. PAGE 23 E0458
S67
DIPLOM
ORD/FREE
COM/IND
INSPECT

DOYLE S.E.,"COMMUNICATION SATELLITES* INTERNAL ORGANIZATION FOR DEVELOPMENT AND CONTROL." USA+45 R+D ACT/RES DIPLOM NAT/LISM...POLICY INT/LAW PREDICT UN. PAGE 33 E0647
S67
TEC/DEV
SPACE
COM/IND
INT/ORG

GREY D.L.,"INTERVIEWING AT THE COURT." USA+45 ELITES COM/IND ACT/RES PRESS CT/SYS PERSON...SOC INT 20 SUPREME/CT. PAGE 46 E0916
S67
JUDGE
ATTIT
PERS/COMP
GP/COMP

COM/PARTY....COMMUNIST PARTY (ALL NATIONS)

LEVY H.V.,LIBERDADE E JUSTICA SOCIAL (2ND ED.). ORD/FREE
BRAZIL COM L/A+17C USSR INT/ORG PARTIC GP/REL MARXISM
WEALTH 20 UN COM/PARTY. PAGE 65 E1290 CAP/ISM
LAW
B62

GUTTMANN A.,COMMUNISM, THE COURTS, AND THE MARXISM
CONSTITUTION. USA+45 CT/SYS ORD/FREE...ANTHOL 20 POL/PAR
COM/PARTY CIV/RIGHTS. PAGE 48 E0965 CONSTN
LAW
B64

DALLIN A.,POLITICS IN THE SOVIET UNION: 7 CASES. MARXISM
COM USSR LAW POL/PAR CHIEF FORCES WRITING CONTROL DOMIN
PARL/PROC CIVMIL/REL TOTALISM...ANTHOL 20 KHRUSH/N ORD/FREE
STALIN/J CASEBOOK COM/PARTY. PAGE 28 E0563 GOV/REL
B66

LEHMANN L.,LEGAL UND OPPORTUN - POLITISCHE JUSTIZ ORD/FREE
IN DER BUNDESREPUBLIK. GERMANY/W EDU/PROP ADJUD POL/PAR
CONTROL PARL/PROC COERCE TOTALISM ATTIT 20 JURID
COM/PARTY. PAGE 64 E1281 LEGIS
B66

COM/SCITEC....COMMITTEE ON SCIENCE AND TECHNOLOGY (OF

COMECON....COMMUNIST ECONOMIC ORGANIZATION EAST EUROPE

GRZYBOWSKI K.,THE SOCIALIST COMMONWEALTH OF INT/LAW
NATIONS: ORGANIZATIONS AND INSTITUTIONS. FORCES COM
DIPLOM INT/TRADE ADJUD ADMIN LEAD WAR MARXISM REGION
SOCISM...BIBLIOG 20 COMECON WARSAW/P. PAGE 48 E0956 INT/ORG
B64

FRIEDMANN W.G.,INTERNATIONAL FINANCIAL AID. USA+45 INT/ORG
ECO/DEV ECO/UNDEV NAT/G VOL/ASSN EX/STRUC PLAN RENT FOR/AID
GIVE BAL/PAY PWR...GEOG INT/LAW STAT TREND UN EEC TEC/DEV
COMECON. PAGE 41 E0806 ECO/TAC
B66

COMINFORM....COMMUNIST INFORMATION BUREAU

COMINTERN....COMMUNIST THIRD INTERNATIONAL

COMM. STUDY ORGAN. PEACE E0479,E0480,E0481,E0482,E0483

COMM/SPACE....COMMITTEE ON SPACE RESEARCH

COMMANDS....SEE LEAD, DOMIN

COMMISSIONS....SEE CONFER, DELIB/GP

COMMITTEE FOR ECONOMIC DEVELOPMENT....SEE CED

COMMITTEES....SEE CONFER, DELIB/GP

COMMON/LAW....COMMON LAW

VECCHIO G.D.,THE FORMAL BASES OF LAW (TRANS. BY J. LAW
LISLE). DOMIN LEGIT CONTROL COERCE UTIL MORAL PWR JURID
...CONCPT TIME/SEQ 17/20 COMMON/LAW NATURL/LAW. GEN/LAWS
PAGE 103 E2074 IDEA/COMP
B14

HOLDSWORTH W.S.,A HISTORY OF ENGLISH LAW; THE LAW
COMMON LAW AND ITS RIVALS (VOL. V). UK SEA EX/STRUC LEGIS
WRITING ADMIN...INT/LAW JURID CONCPT IDEA/COMP ADJUD
WORSHIP 16/17 PARLIAMENT ENGLSH/LAW COMMON/LAW. CT/SYS
PAGE 54 E1073
B24

HOLDSWORTH W.S.,A HISTORY OF ENGLISH LAW; THE LAW
COMMON LAW AND ITS RIVALS (VOL. VI). UK STRATA CONSTN
EX/STRUC ADJUD ADMIN CONTROL CT/SYS...JURID CONCPT LEGIS
GEN/LAWS 17 COMMONWLTH PARLIAMENT ENGLSH/LAW CHIEF
COMMON/LAW. PAGE 54 E1074
B24

HOLDSWORTH W.S.,A HISTORY OF ENGLISH LAW; THE LAW
COMMON LAW AND ITS RIVALS (VOL. IV). UK SEA AGRI LEGIS
CHIEF ADJUD CONTROL CRIME GOV/REL...INT/LAW JURID CT/SYS
NAT/COMP 16/17 PARLIAMENT COMMON/LAW CANON/LAW CONSTN
ENGLSH/LAW. PAGE 54 E1075
B24

HOLDSWORTH W.S.,THE HISTORIANS OF ANGLO-AMERICAN HIST/WRIT
LAW. UK USA-45 INTELL LEGIS RESPECT...BIOG NAT/COMP LAW
17/20 COMMON/LAW. PAGE 54 E1076 JURID
B28

WILLOUGHBY W.W.,PRINCIPLES OF THE CONSTITUTIONAL CONSTN
LAW OF THE UNITED STATES. USA-45 ADJUD FEDERAL NAT/G
SOVEREIGN 18/20 COMMON/LAW. PAGE 106 E2125 CONCPT
JURID
B30

LUNT D.C.,THE ROAD TO THE LAW. UK USA-45 LEGIS ADJUD
EDU/PROP OWN ORD/FREE...DECISION TIME/SEQ NAT/COMP LAW
16/20 AUSTRAL ENGLSH/LAW COMMON/LAW. PAGE 67 E1333 JURID
CT/SYS
B32

HOLDSWORTH W.S.,A HISTORY OF ENGLISH LAW; THE LAW
CENTURIES OF SETTLEMENT AND REFORM (VOL. X). INDIA LOC/G
UK CONSTN NAT/G CHIEF LEGIS ADMIN COLONIAL CT/SYS EX/STRUC
CHOOSE ORD/FREE PWR...JURID 18 PARLIAMENT ADJUD
COMMONWLTH COMMON/LAW. PAGE 54 E1077
B38

HOLDSWORTH W.S.,A HISTORY OF ENGLISH LAW; THE LAW
CENTURIES OF SETTLEMENT AND REFORM (VOL. XII). UK PROF/ORG
CONSTN STRATA LEGIS JUDGE ADJUD CT/SYS ATTIT WRITING
...JURID CONCPT BIOG GEN/LAWS 18 ENGLSH/LAW IDEA/COMP
BLACKSTN/W COMMON/LAW. PAGE 54 E1078
B38

CORWIN E.S.,LIBERTY AGAINST GOVERNMENT: THE RISE, CONCPT
FLOWERING AND DECLINE OF A FAMOUS JURIDICAL ORD/FREE
CONCEPT. LEGIS ADJUD CT/SYS SANCTION GOV/REL JURID
FEDERAL CONSERVE NEW/LIB...OLD/LIB 18/20 ROMAN/LAW CONSTN
COMMON/LAW. PAGE 26 E0514
B48

FRIEDMANN W.,LAW AND SOCIAL CHANGE IN CONTEMPORARY LAW
BRITAIN. UK LABOR LG/CO LEGIS JUDGE ADJUD ORD/FREE ADJUD
NEW/LIB...DECISION JURID TREND METH/COMP BIBLIOG 20 SOCIETY
PARLIAMENT ENGLSH/LAW COMMON/LAW. PAGE 40 E0802 CONSTN
B51

LEEK J.H.,"TREASON AND THE CONSTITUTION" (BMR)" CONSTN
USA+45 USA-45 EDU/PROP COLONIAL CT/SYS REV WAR JURID
ATTIT...TREND 18/20 SUPREME/CT CON/INTERP SMITH/ACT CRIME
COMMON/LAW. PAGE 64 E1278 NAT/G
S51

BUCKLAND W.W.,ROMAN LAW AND COMMON LAW; A IDEA/COMP
COMPARISON IN OUTLINE (2ND REV. ED.). UK FAM LEGIT LAW
AGREE CT/SYS OWN...JURID ROMAN/REP ROMAN/LAW ADJUD
COMMON/LAW. PAGE 17 E0325 CONCPT
B52

HOLDSWORTH W.S.,A HISTORY OF ENGLISH LAW; THE LAW
CENTURIES OF SETTLEMENT AND REFORM, 1701-1875 (VOL. CONSTN
XIII). UK POL/PAR PROF/ORG LEGIS JUDGE WRITING IDEA/COMP
ATTIT...JURID CONCPT BIOG GEN/LAWS 18/19 PARLIAMENT CT/SYS
REFORMERS ENGLSH/LAW COMMON/LAW. PAGE 54 E1080
B52

JENNINGS W.I.,CONSTITUTIONAL LAWS OF THE CONSTN
COMMONWEALTH. UK LAW CHIEF LEGIS TAX CT/SYS JURID
PARL/PROC GOV/REL...INT/LAW 18/20 COMMONWLTH ADJUD
ENGLSH/LAW COMMON/LAW. PAGE 58 E1165 COLONIAL
B52

EUSDEN J.D.,PURITANS, LAWYERS, AND POLITICS IN GP/REL
EARLY SEVENTEENTH-CENTURY ENGLAND. UK CT/SYS SECT
PARL/PROC RATIONAL PWR SOVEREIGN...IDEA/COMP NAT/G
BIBLIOG 17 PURITAN COMMON/LAW. PAGE 35 E0702 LAW
B58

MOEN N.W.,THE GOVERNMENT OF SCOTLAND 1603 - 1625. CHIEF
UK JUDGE ADMIN GP/REL PWR 17 SCOTLAND COMMON/LAW. JURID
PAGE 74 E1479 CONTROL
PARL/PROC
B58

VAN CAENEGEM R.C.,ROYAL WRITS IN ENGLAND FROM THE JURID
CONQUEST TO GLANVILL. UK JUDGE...TREND IDEA/COMP CHIEF
11/12 COMMON/LAW. PAGE 103 E2067 ADJUD
CT/SYS
B59

HANBURY H.G.,ENGLISH COURTS OF LAW. UK EX/STRUC JURID
LEGIS CRIME ROLE 12/20 COMMON/LAW ENGLSH/LAW. CT/SYS
PAGE 50 E0993 CONSTN
GOV/REL
B60

ALLOTT A.N.,JUDICIAL AND LEGAL SYSTEMS IN AFRICA. CT/SYS
LAW CONSTN JUDGE CONTROL...METH/CNCPT CLASSIF AFR
CHARTS 20 COMMON/LAW. PAGE 4 E0070 JURID
COLONIAL
B62

EDDY J.P.,JUSTICE OF THE PEACE. UK LAW CONSTN CRIME
B63

CULTURE 14/20 COMMON/LAW. PAGE 34 E0674   JURID
                                                          CT/SYS
                                                          ADJUD

                                                          B63
ELIAS T.O.,THE NIGERIAN LEGAL SYSTEM. NIGERIA LAW   CT/SYS
FAM KIN SECT ADMIN NAT/LISM...JURID 18/20   ADJUD
ENGLSH/LAW COMMON/LAW. PAGE 34 E0682   COLONIAL
                                                          PROF/ORG

                                                          B64
BENNETT H.A.,THE COMMISSION AND THE COMMON LAW: A   ADJUD
STUDY IN ADMINISTRATIVE ADJUDICATION. LAW ADMIN   DELIB/GP
CT/SYS LOBBY SANCTION GOV/REL 20 COMMON/LAW.   DIST/IND
PAGE 10 E0188   POLICY

                                                          B64
HOLDSWORTH W.S.,A HISTORY OF ENGLISH LAW; THE   LAW
CENTURIES OF DEVELOPMENT AND REFORM (VOL. XIV). UK   LEGIS
CONSTN LOC/G NAT/G POL/PAR CHIEF EX/STRUC ADJUD   LEAD
COLONIAL ATTIT...INT/LAW JURID 18/19 TORY/PARTY   CT/SYS
COMMONWLTH WHIG/PARTY COMMON/LAW. PAGE 54 E1081

                                                          B65
CHRIMES S.B.,ENGLISH CONSTITUTIONAL HISTORY (3RD   CONSTN
ED.). UK CHIEF CONSULT DELIB/GP LEGIS CT/SYS 15/20   BAL/PWR
COMMON/LAW PARLIAMENT. PAGE 22 E0435   NAT/G

                                                          B65
HOLDSWORTH W.S.,A HISTORY OF ENGLISH LAW; THE   LAW
CENTURIES OF SETTLEMENT AND REFORM (VOL. XV). UK   INDUS
CONSTN SECT LEGIS JUDGE WRITING ADJUD CT/SYS CRIME   PROF/ORG
OWN...JURID IDEA/COMP 18 PARLIAMENT ENGLSH/LAW   ATTIT
COMMON/LAW. PAGE 54 E1082

                                                          B66
HOGUE A.R.,ORIGINS OF THE COMMON LAW. UK STRUCT   LAW
AGRI CT/SYS SANCTION CONSERVE 12/14 ENGLSH/LAW   SOCIETY
COMMON/LAW. PAGE 54 E1068   CONSTN

                                                          B98
POLLOCK F.,THE HISTORY OF ENGLISH LAW BEFORE THE   LAW
TIME OF EDWARD I (2 VOLS, 2ND ED.). UK CULTURE   ADJUD
LOC/G LEGIS LICENSE AGREE CONTROL CT/SYS SANCTION   JURID
CRIME...TIME/SEQ 13 COMMON/LAW CANON/LAW. PAGE 81
E1626

COMMONWEALTH....SEE COMMONWLTH

COMMONWLTH....BRITISH COMMONWEALTH OF NATIONS; SEE ALSO
     VOL/ASSN AND APPROPRIATE NATIONS

                                                          B24
HOLDSWORTH W.S.,A HISTORY OF ENGLISH LAW; THE   LAW
COMMON LAW AND ITS RIVALS (VOL. VI). UK STRATA   CONSTN
EX/STRUC ADJUD ADMIN CONTROL CT/SYS...JURID CONCPT   LEGIS
GEN/LAWS 17 COMMONWLTH PARLIAMENT ENGLSH/LAW   CHIEF
COMMON/LAW. PAGE 54 E1074

                                                          B38
HOLDSWORTH W.S.,A HISTORY OF ENGLISH LAW; THE   LAW
CENTURIES OF SETTLEMENT AND REFORM (VOL. X). INDIA   LOC/G
UK CONSTN NAT/G CHIEF LEGIS ADMIN COLONIAL CT/SYS   EX/STRUC
CHOOSE ORD/FREE PWR...JURID 18 PARLIAMENT   ADJUD
COMMONWLTH COMMON/LAW. PAGE 54 E1077

                                                          B52
JENNINGS W.I.,CONSTITUTIONAL LAWS OF THE   CONSTN
COMMONWEALTH. UK LAW CHIEF LEGIS TAX CT/SYS   JURID
PARL/PROC GOV/REL...INT/LAW 18/20 COMMONWLTH   ADJUD
ENGLSH/LAW COMMON/LAW. PAGE 58 E1165   COLONIAL

                                                          B53
STOUT H.M.,BRITISH GOVERNMENT. UK FINAN LOC/G   NAT/G
POL/PAR DELIB/GP DIPLOM ADMIN COLONIAL CHOOSE   PARL/PROC
ORD/FREE...JURID BIBLIOG 20 COMMONWLTH. PAGE 94   CONSTN
E1883   NEW/LIB

                                                          B54
FRIEDMAN W.,THE PUBLIC CORPORATION: A COMPARATIVE   LAW
SYMPOSIUM (UNIVERSITY OF TORONTO SCHOOL OF LAW   SOCISM
COMPARATIVE LAW SERIES, VOL. I). SWEDEN USA+45   LG/CO
INDUS INT/ORG NAT/G REGION CENTRAL FEDERAL...POLICY   OWN
JURID IDEA/COMP NAT/COMP ANTHOL 20 COMMONWLTH
MONOPOLY EUROPE. PAGE 40 E0801

                                                          B61
CARNELL F.,THE POLITICS OF THE NEW STATES: A SELECT   BIBLIOG/A
ANNOTATED BIBLIOGRAPHY WITH SPECIAL REFERENCE TO   AFR
THE COMMONWEALTH. CONSTN ELITES LABOR NAT/G POL/PAR   ASIA
EX/STRUC DIPLOM ADJUD ADMIN...GOV/COMP 20   COLONIAL
COMMONWLTH. PAGE 20 E0387

                                                          B64
HOLDSWORTH W.S.,A HISTORY OF ENGLISH LAW; THE   LAW
CENTURIES OF DEVELOPMENT AND REFORM (VOL. XIV). UK   LEGIS

CONSTN LOC/G NAT/G POL/PAR CHIEF EX/STRUC ADJUD   LEAD
COLONIAL ATTIT...INT/LAW JURID 18/19 TORY/PARTY   CT/SYS
COMMONWLTH WHIG/PARTY COMMON/LAW. PAGE 54 E1081

                                                          B64
SCHMEISER D.A.,CIVIL LIBERTIES IN CANADA. CANADA   ORD/FREE
LAW SECT PRESS RACE/REL NAT/LISM PRIVIL 20   CONSTN
COMMONWLTH PARLIAMENT CIVIL/LIB CHURCH/STA. PAGE 88   ADJUD
E1758   EDU/PROP

                                                          B65
COWEN Z.,THE BRITISH COMMONWEALTH OF NATIONS IN A   JURID
CHANGING WORLD. UK ECO/UNDEV INT/ORG ECO/TAC   DIPLOM
INT/TRADE COLONIAL WAR GP/REL RACE/REL SOVEREIGN   PARL/PROC
SOC/INTEG 20 TREATY EEC COMMONWLTH. PAGE 27 E0530   NAT/LISM

                                                          B65
SOPER T.,EVOLVING COMMONWEALTH. AFR CANADA INDIA   INT/ORG
IRELAND UK LAW CONSTN POL/PAR DOMIN CONTROL WAR PWR   COLONIAL
...AUD/VIS 18/20 COMMONWLTH OEEC. PAGE 93 E1857   VOL/ASSN

                                                          B66
BURNS A.C.,PARLIAMENT AS AN EXPORT. WOR+45 CONSTN   PARL/PROC
BARGAIN DEBATE ROUTINE GOV/REL EFFICIENCY...ANTHOL   POL/PAR
COMMONWLTH PARLIAMENT. PAGE 17 E0343   CT/SYS
                                                          CHIEF

                                                          B66
CAMPBELL E.,PARLIAMENTARY PRIVILEGE IN AUSTRALIA.   LEGIS
UK LAW CONSTN COLONIAL ROLE ORD/FREE SOVEREIGN   PARL/PROC
18/20 COMMONWLTH AUSTRAL FREE/SPEE PARLIAMENT.   JURID
PAGE 19 E0370   PRIVIL

COMMUN/DEV....COMMUNITY DEVELOPMENT MOVEMENT IN INDIA

COMMUNES....COMMUNES

                                                          B64
BOUVIER-AJAM M.,MANUEL TECHNIQUE ET PRATIQUE DU   MUNIC
MAIRE ET DES ELUS ET AGENTS COMMUNAUX. FRANCE LOC/G   ADMIN
BUDGET CHOOSE GP/REL SUPEGO...JURID BIBLIOG 20   CHIEF
MAYOR COMMUNES. PAGE 14 E0274   NEIGH

COMMUNICATION, MASS....SEE EDU/PROP

COMMUNICATION, PERSONAL....SEE PERS/REL

COMMUNICATION, POLITICAL....SEE EDU/PROP

COMMUNICATIONS INDUSTRY....SEE COM/IND

COMMUNISM....SEE MARXISM

COMMUNIST CHINA....SEE CHINA/COM

COMMUNIST COUNTRIES (EXCEPT CHINA)....SEE COM

COMMUNIST ECONOMIC ORGANIZATION....SEE COMECON

COMMUNITY....SEE NEIGH

COMPANY, LARGE....SEE LG/CO

COMPANY, SMALL....SEE SML/CO

COMPARATIVE....SEE APPROPRIATE COMPARATIVE ANALYSIS INDEX

COMPETITION....SEE APPROPRIATE RELATIONS AND VALUES INDEXES

COMPNY/ACT....COMPANIES ACT (U.K., 1882)

                                                          B51
COOKE C.A.,CORPORATION TRUST AND COMPANY: AN ESSAY   LG/CO
IN LEGAL HISTORY. UK STRUCT LEGIS CAP/ISM GP/REL   FINAN
PROFIT 13/20 COMPNY/ACT. PAGE 25 E0499   ECO/TAC
                                                          JURID

COMPUT/IR....INFORMATION RETRIEVAL

                                                          N
AMER COUNCIL OF LEARNED SOCIET,THE ACLS CONSTITUENT   BIBLIOG/A
SOCIETY JOURNAL PROJECT. FUT USA+45 LAW NAT/G PLAN   HUM
DIPLOM PHIL/SCI. PAGE 4 E0072   COMPUT/IR
                                                          COMPUTER

                                                          B60
STEIN E.,AMERICAN ENTERPRISE IN THE EUROPEAN COMMON   MARKET
MARKET: A LEGAL PROFILE. EUR+WWI FUT USA+45 SOCIETY   ADJUD
STRUCT ECO/DEV NAT/G VOL/ASSN CONSULT PLAN TEC/DEV   INT/LAW
ECO/TAC INT/TRADE ADMIN ATTIT RIGID/FLEX PWR...MGT

NEW/IDEA STAT TREND COMPUT/IR SIMUL EEC 20. PAGE 93
E1867

BLUMSTEIN A.,"POLICE TECHNOLOGY." USA+45 DELIB/GP
COMPUTER EDU/PROP CRIME COMPUT/IR. PAGE 13 E0253
   S67
TEC/DEV
FORCES
CRIMLGY
ADJUD

WOETZEL R.K.,THE INTERNATIONAL CONTROL OF AIRSPACE
AND OUTERSPACE. FUT WOR+45 AIR CONSTN STRUCT
CONSULT PLAN TEC/DEV ADJUD RIGID/FLEX KNOWL
ORD/FREE PWR...TECHNIC GEOG MGT NEW/IDEA TREND
COMPUT/IR VAL/FREE 20 TREATY. PAGE 107 E2137
   B60
INT/ORG
JURID
SPACE
INT/LAW

TYDINGS J.D.,"MODERNIZING THE ADMINISTRATION OF
JUSTICE." PLAN ADMIN ROUTINE EFFICIENCY...JURID
SIMUL. PAGE 97 E1948
   S67
CT/SYS
MGT
COMPUTER
CONSULT

LOEVINGER L.,"JURIMETRICS* THE METHODOLOGY OF LEGAL
INQUIRY." COMPUTER CREATE PLAN TEC/DEV AUTOMAT
CT/SYS EFFICIENCY...DECISION PHIL/SCI NEW/IDEA
QUANT PREDICT. PAGE 66 E1318
   L63
COMPUT/IR
JURID
GEN/METH
ADJUD

COMTE/A....AUGUST COMTE

CON/ANAL....QUANTITATIVE CONTENT ANALYSIS

UNIVERSAL REFERENCE SYSTEM,INTERNATIONAL AFFAIRS:
VOLUME I IN THE POLITICAL SCIENCE, GOVERNMENT, AND
PUBLIC POLICY SERIES....DECISION ECOMETRIC GEOG
INT/LAW JURID MGT PHIL/SCI PSY SOC. PAGE 98 E1972
   B65
BIBLIOG/A
GEN/METH
COMPUT/IR
DIPLOM

AUSTRALIAN PUBLIC AFFAIRS INFORMATION SERVICE. LAW
...HEAL HUM MGT SOC CON/ANAL 20 AUSTRAL. PAGE 1
E0017
   N
BIBLIOG
NAT/G
CULTURE
DIPLOM

UNIVERSAL REFERENCE SYSTEM,BIBLIOGRAPHY OF
BIBLIOGRAPHIES IN POLITICAL SCIENCE, GOVERNMENT,
AND PUBLIC POLICY (VOLUME III). WOR+45 WOR-45 LAW
ADMIN...SOC CON/ANAL COMPUT/IR GEN/METH. PAGE 98
E1973
   B67
BIBLIOG/A
NAT/G
DIPLOM
POLICY

UNITED NATIONS,YEARBOOK OF THE INTERNATIONAL LAW
COMMISSION....CON/ANAL 20 UN. PAGE 98 E1966
   N
BIBLIOG
INT/ORG
INT/LAW
DELIB/GP

UNIVERSAL REFERENCE SYSTEM,CURRENT EVENTS AND
PROBLEMS OF MODERN SOCIETY (VOLUME V). WOR+45 LOC/G
MUNIC NAT/G PLAN EDU/PROP CRIME RACE/REL WEALTH
...COMPUT/IR GEN/METH. PAGE 98 E1974
   B67
BIBLIOG/A
SOCIETY
PROB/SOLV
ATTIT

GROTIUS H.,DE JURE BELLI AC PACIS. CHRIST-17C UNIV
LAW SOCIETY PROVS LEGIT PEACE PERCEPT MORAL PWR
...CONCPT CON/ANAL GEN/LAWS. PAGE 48 E0952
   B00
JURID
INT/LAW
WAR

UNIVERSAL REFERENCE SYSTEM,PUBLIC POLICY AND THE
MANAGEMENT OF SCIENCE (VOLUME IX). FUT SPACE WOR+45
LAW NAT/G TEC/DEV CONTROL NUC/PWR GOV/REL
...COMPUT/IR GEN/METH. PAGE 99 E1975
   B67
BIBLIOG/A
POLICY
MGT
PHIL/SCI

MAINE H.S.,ANCIENT LAW. MEDIT-7 CULTURE SOCIETY KIN
SECT LEGIS LEGIT ROUTINE...JURID HIST/WRIT CON/ANAL
TOT/POP VAL/FREE. PAGE 68 E1350
   B00
FAM
LAW

UNIVERSAL REFERENCE SYSTEM,LAW, JURISPRUDENCE, AND
JUDICIAL PROCESS (VOLUME VII). WOR+45 WOR-45 CONSTN
NAT/G LEGIS JUDGE CT/SYS...INT/LAW COMPUT/IR
GEN/METH METH. PAGE 99 E1976
   B67
BIBLIOG/A
LAW
JURID
ADJUD

PHILLIPSON C.,THE INTERNATIONAL LAW AND CUSTOM OF
ANCIENT GREECE AND ROME. MEDIT-7 UNIV INTELL
SOCIETY STRUCT NAT/G LEGIS EXEC PERSON...CONCPT OBS
CON/ANAL ROM/EMP. PAGE 80 E1614
   B11
INT/ORG
LAW
INT/LAW

BLUMSTEIN A.,"POLICE TECHNOLOGY." USA+45 DELIB/GP
COMPUTER EDU/PROP CRIME COMPUT/IR. PAGE 13 E0253
   S67
TEC/DEV
FORCES
CRIMLGY
ADJUD

BUREAU OF NAT'L AFFAIRS INC.,A CURRENT LOOK AT:
(1) THE NEGRO AND TITLE VII, (2) SEX AND TITLE VII
(PAMPHLET). LAW LG/CO SML/CO RACE/REL...POLICY SOC
STAT DEEP/QU TREND CON/ANAL CHARTS 20 NEGRO
CIV/RIGHTS. PAGE 17 E0334
   N19
DISCRIM
SEX
WORKER
MGT

COMPUTER....COMPUTER TECHNIQUES AND TECHNOLOGY

HOLMES O.W. JR.,THE COMMON LAW. FUT WOR-45 CULTURE
SOCIETY CREATE LEGIT ROUTINE ATTIT ALL/VALS...JURID
METH/CNCPT TIME/SEQ GEN/LAWS TOT/POP VAL/FREE.
PAGE 55 E1087
   B23
ADJUD
CON/ANAL

AMER COUNCIL OF LEARNED SOCIET,THE ACLS CONSTITUENT
SOCIETY JOURNAL PROJECT. FUT USA+45 LAW NAT/G PLAN
DIPLOM PHIL/SCI. PAGE 4 E0072
   N
BIBLIOG/A
HUM
COMPUT/IR
COMPUTER

YANG KUNG-SUN,THE BOOK OF LORD SHANG. LAW ECO/UNDEV
LOC/G NAT/G NEIGH PLAN ECO/TAC LEGIT ATTIT SKILL
...CONCPT CON/ANAL WORK TOT/POP. PAGE 108 E2164
   B28
ASIA
JURID

CALDWELL L.K.,RESEARCH METHODS IN PUBLIC
ADMINISTRATION; AN OUTLINE OF TOPICS AND READINGS
(PAMPHLET). LAW ACT/RES COMPUTER KNOWL...SOC STAT
GEN/METH 20. PAGE 18 E0364
   B53
BIBLIOG/A
METH/COMP
ADMIN
OP/RES

FLEMMING D.,THE UNITED STATES AND THE LEAGUE OF
NATIONS, 1918-1920. FUT USA-45 NAT/G LEGIS TOP/EX
DEBATE CHOOSE PEACE ATTIT SOVEREIGN...TIME/SEQ
CON/ANAL CONGRESS LEAGUE/NAT 20 TREATY. PAGE 39
E0764
   B32
INT/ORG
EDU/PROP

NAGEL S.S.,"USING SIMPLE CALCULATIONS TO PREDICT
JUDICIAL DECISIONS." ATTIT PERSON MATH. PAGE 76
E1517
   S60
JURID
LAW
DECISION
COMPUTER

DANGERFIELD R.,IN DEFENSE OF THE SENATE. USA-45
CONSTN NAT/G EX/STRUC TOP/EX ATTIT KNOWL
...METH/CNCPT STAT TIME/SEQ TREND CON/ANAL CHARTS
CONGRESS 20 TREATY. PAGE 28 E0565
   B33
LEGIS
DELIB/GP
DIPLOM

MARS D.,SUGGESTED LIBRARY IN PUBLIC ADMINISTRATION.
FINAN DELIB/GP EX/STRUC WORKER COMPUTER ADJUD
...DECISION PSY SOC METH/COMP 20. PAGE 68 E1368
   B62
BIBLIOG
ADMIN
METH
MGT

BEMIS S.F.,GUIDE TO THE DIPLOMATIC HISTORY OF THE
UNITED STATES, 17751921. NAT/G LEGIS TOP/EX
PROB/SOLV CAP/ISM INT/TRADE TARIFFS ADJUD
...CON/ANAL 18/20. PAGE 10 E0184
   B35
BIBLIOG/A
DIPLOM
USA-45

LOEVINGER L.,"JURIMETRICS* THE METHODOLOGY OF LEGAL
INQUIRY." COMPUTER CREATE PLAN TEC/DEV AUTOMAT
CT/SYS EFFICIENCY...DECISION PHIL/SCI NEW/IDEA
QUANT PREDICT. PAGE 66 E1318
   L63
COMPUT/IR
JURID
GEN/METH
ADJUD

CHAMBERLAIN J.P.,LEGISLATIVE PROCESS: NATION AND
STATE. LAW DELIB/GP ROUTINE. PAGE 21 E0414
   B36
CON/ANAL
PROVS
LEGIS
NAT/G

CALIFORNIA LEGISLATURE,COMMITTEE ON ELECTIONS AND
REAPPORTIONMENT, FINAL REPORT. USA+45 LAW COMPUTER
TEC/DEV CHOOSE JURID. PAGE 19 E0366
   B65
DELIB/GP
APPORT
LEGIS
ADJUD

HADDOW A.,"POLITICAL SCIENCE IN AMERICAN COLLEGES
AND UNIVERSITIES 1636-1900." CONSTN MORAL...POLICY
INT/LAW CON/ANAL BIBLIOG T 17/20. PAGE 49 E0971
   C39
USA-45
LAW
ACADEM
KNOWL

HAMILTON H.D.,REAPPORTIONING LEGISLATURES. USA+45
CONSTN POL/PAR PROVS LEGIS COMPUTER ADJUD CHOOSE
ATTIT...ANTHOL 20 SUPREME/CT CONGRESS. PAGE 50
E0989
   B66
APPORT
REPRESENT
PHIL/SCI
PWR

CONOVER H.F.,FOREIGN RELATIONS OF THE UNITED
   B40
BIBLIOG/A

STATES: A LIST OF RECENT BOOKS (PAMPHLET). ASIA CANADA L/A+17C UK INT/ORG INT/TRADE TARIFFS NEUTRAL WAR PEACE...INT/LAW CON/ANAL 20 CHINJAP. PAGE 25 E0492
USA-45 DIPLOM

B41
MCCLURE W.,INTERNATIONAL EXECUTIVE AGREEMENTS. USA-45 WOR-45 INT/ORG NAT/G DELIB/GP ADJUD ROUTINE ORD/FREE PWR...TIME/SEQ TREND CON/ANAL. PAGE 70 E1401
TOP/EX DIPLOM

B43
CLAGETT H.L.,A GUIDE TO THE LAW AND LEGAL LITERATURE OF PARAGUAY. PARAGUAY CONSTN COM/IND LABOR MUNIC JUDGE ADMIN CT/SYS...CRIMLGY INT/LAW CON/ANAL 20. PAGE 22 E0439
BIBLIOG JURID LAW L/A+17C

B45
CLAGETT H.L.,A GUIDE TO THE LAW AND LEGAL LITERATURE OF THE MEXICAN STATES. CONSTN LEGIS JUDGE ADJUD ADMIN...INT/LAW CON/ANAL 20 MEXIC/AMER. PAGE 22 E0440
BIBLIOG JURID L/A+17C LAW

B45
VANCE H.L.,GUIDE TO THE LAW AND LEGAL LITERATURE OF MEXICO. LAW CONSTN FINAN LABOR FORCES ADJUD ADMIN ...CRIMLGY PHIL/SCI CON/ANAL 20 MEXIC/AMER. PAGE 103 E2070
BIBLIOG/A INT/LAW JURID CT/SYS

C46
GOODRICH L.M.,"CHARTER OF THE UNITED NATIONS: COMMENTARY AND DOCUMENTS." EX/STRUC ADMIN...INT/LAW CON/ANAL BIBLIOG 20 UN. PAGE 45 E0890
CONSTN INT/ORG DIPLOM

B47
CLAGETT H.L.,A GUIDE TO THE LAW AND LEGAL LITERATURE OF CHILE, 1917-1946. CHILE CONSTN LABOR JUDGE ADJUD ADMIN...CRIMLGY INT/LAW JURID CON/ANAL 20. PAGE 22 E0442
BIBLIOG L/A+17C LAW LEGIS

B47
CLAGETT H.L.,A GUIDE TO THE LAW AND LEGAL LITERATURE OF ECUADOR. ECUADOR CONSTN LABOR LEGIS JUDGE ADJUD ADMIN CIVMIL/REL...CRIMLGY INT/LAW CON/ANAL 20. PAGE 22 E0443
BIBLIOG JURID LAW L/A+17C

B47
CLAGETT H.L.,A GUIDE TO THE LAW AND LEGAL LITERATURE OF VENEZUELA. VENEZUELA CONSTN LABOR LEGIS JUDGE ADJUD ADMIN CIVMIL/REL...CRIMLGY JURID CON/ANAL 20. PAGE 23 E0446
BIBLIOG L/A+17C INT/LAW LAW

B48
CLAGETT H.L.,A GUIDE TO THE LAW AND LEGAL LITERATURE OF ARGENTINA, 1917-1946. CONSTN LABOR JUDGE ADJUD ADMIN...CRIMLGY INT/LAW JURID CON/ANAL 20 ARGEN. PAGE 23 E0447
BIBLIOG L/A+17C LAW LEGIS

B50
DOROSH J.T.,GUIDE TO SOVIET BIBLIOGRAPHIES. USSR LAW AGRI SCHOOL SECT FORCES TEC/DEV...ART/METH GEOG HUM SOC 20. PAGE 32 E0639
BIBLIOG METH CON/ANAL

B50
LAUTERPACHT H.,INTERNATIONAL LAW AND HUMAN RIGHTS. USA+45 CONSTN STRUCT INT/ORG ACT/RES EDU/PROP PEACE PERSON ALL/VALS...CONCPT CON/ANAL GEN/LAWS UN 20. PAGE 63 E1266
DELIB/GP LAW INT/LAW

B50
WARD R.E.,A GUIDE TO JAPANESE REFERENCE AND RESEARCH MATERIALS IN THE FIELD OF POLITICAL SCIENCE. LAW CONSTN LOC/G PRESS ADMIN...SOC CON/ANAL METH 19/20 CHINJAP. PAGE 105 E2098
BIBLIOG/A ASIA NAT/G

B51
KELSEN H.,THE LAW OF THE UNITED NATIONS. WOR+45 STRUCT RIGID/FLEX ORD/FREE...INT/LAW JURID CONCPT CON/ANAL GEN/METH UN TOT/POP VAL/FREE 20. PAGE 60 E1198
INT/ORG ADJUD

L51
KELSEN H.,"RECENT TRENDS IN THE LAW OF THE UNITED NATIONS." KOREA WOR+45 CONSTN LEGIS DIPLOM LEGIT DETER WAR RIGID/FLEX HEALTH ORD/FREE RESPECT ...JURID CON/ANAL UN VAL/FREE 20 NATO. PAGE 60 E1199
INT/ORG LAW INT/LAW

B52
GELLHORN W.,THE STATES AND SUBVERSION. USA+45 USA-45 LOC/G DELIB/GP LEGIS EDU/PROP LEGIT CT/SYS REGION PEACE ATTIT ORD/FREE SOCISM...INT CON/ANAL 20 CALIFORNIA MARYLAND ILLINOIS MICHIGAN NEW/YORK. PAGE 43 E0845
PROVS JURID

B54
BINANI G.D.,INDIA AT A GLANCE (REV. ED.). INDIA COM/IND FINAN INDUS LABOR PROVS SCHOOL PLAN DIPLOM INT/TRADE ADMIN...JURID 20. PAGE 12 E0229
INDEX CON/ANAL NAT/G ECO/UNDEV

B56
PEASLEE A.J.,CONSTITUTIONS OF NATIONS. WOR+45 LAW NAT/G EX/STRUC LEGIS TOP/EX LEGIT CT/SYS ROUTINE CHOOSE ORD/FREE PWR SOVEREIGN...CHARTS TOT/POP. PAGE 80 E1605
CONSTN CON/ANAL

B57
ROSENNE S.,THE INTERNATIONAL COURT OF JUSTICE. WOR+45 LAW DOMIN LEGIT PEACE PWR SOVEREIGN...JURID CONCPT RECORD TIME/SEQ CON/ANAL CHARTS UN TOT/POP VAL/FREE LEAGUE/NAT 20 ICJ. PAGE 86 E1716
INT/ORG CT/SYS INT/LAW

S58
SCHUBERT G.A.,"THE STUDY OF JUDICIAL DECISION-MAKING AS AN ASPECT OF POLITICAL BEHAVIOR." PLAN ADJUD CT/SYS INGP/REL PERSON...PHIL/SCI SOC QUANT STAT CHARTS IDEA/COMP SOC/EXP. PAGE 89 E1779
JUDGE DECISION CON/ANAL GAME

C59
COLLINS I.,"THE GOVERNMENT AND THE NEWSPAPER PRESS IN FRANCE, 1814-1881. FRANCE LAW ADMIN CT/SYS ...CON/ANAL BIBLIOG 19. PAGE 24 E0475
PRESS ORD/FREE NAT/G EDU/PROP

L60
STEIN E.,"LEGAL REMEDIES OF ENTERPRISES IN THE EUROPEAN ECONOMIC COMMUNITY." EUR+WWI FUT ECO/DEV INDUS PLAN ECO/TAC ADMIN PWR...MGT MATH STAT TREND CON/ANAL EEC 20. PAGE 93 E1868
MARKET ADJUD

S60
RHYNE C.S.,"LAW AS AN INSTRUMENT FOR PEACE." FUT WOR+45 PLAN LEGIT ROUTINE ARMS/CONT NUC/PWR ATTIT ORD/FREE...JURID METH/CNCPT TREND CON/ANAL HYPO/EXP COLD/WAR 20. PAGE 84 E1690
ADJUD EDU/PROP INT/LAW PEACE

B61
CONFERENCE ATLANTIC COMMUNITY,AN INTRODUCTORY BIBLIOGRAPHY. COM WOR+45 FORCES DIPLOM ECO/TAC WAR ...INT/LAW HIST/WRIT COLD/WAR NATO. PAGE 25 E0485
BIBLIOG/A CON/ANAL INT/ORG

S63
MODELSKI G.,"STUDY OF ALLIANCES." WOR+45 WOR-45 INT/ORG NAT/G FORCES LEGIT ADMIN CHOOSE ALL/VALS PWR SKILL...INT/LAW CONCPT GEN/LAWS 20 TREATY. PAGE 74 E1477
VOL/ASSN CON/ANAL DIPLOM

B64
A CHECK LIST OF THE SPECIAL AND STANDING COMMITTEES OF THE AMERICAN BAR ASSOCIATION (VOL. II). USA+45 LEGIS PRESS CONFER...JURID CON/ANAL. PAGE 80 E1607
BIBLIOG LAW VOL/ASSN

S64
HICKEY D.,"THE PHILOSOPHICAL ARGUMENT FOR WORLD GOVERNMENT." WOR+45 SOCIETY ACT/RES PLAN LEGIT ADJUD PEACE PERCEPT PERSON ORD/FREE...HUM JURID PHIL/SCI METH/CNCPT CON/ANAL STERTYP GEN/LAWS TOT/POP 20. PAGE 52 E1039
FUT INT/ORG

S64
MAGGS P.B.,"SOVIET VIEWPOINT ON NUCLEAR WEAPONS IN INTERNATIONAL LAW." USSR WOR+45 INT/ORG FORCES DIPLOM ARMS/CONT ATTIT ORD/FREE PWR...POLICY JURID CONCPT OBS TREND CON/ANAL GEN/LAWS VAL/FREE 20. PAGE 67 E1347
COM LAW INT/LAW NUC/PWR

B65
BAADE H.,THE SOVIET IMPACT ON INTERNATIONAL LAW. INT/ORG INT/TRADE LEGIT COLONIAL ARMS/CONT REV WAR ...CON/ANAL ANTHOL TREATY. PAGE 6 E0124
INT/LAW USSR CREATE ORD/FREE

B65
CAMPBELL E.H.,SURVEYS, SUBDIVISIONS AND PLATTING, AND BOUNDARIES: WASHINGTON STATE LAW AND JUDICIAL DECISIONS. USA+45 LAW LOC/G...DECISION JURID CON/ANAL BIBLIOG WASHINGT/G PARTITION WATER. PAGE 19 E0372
CONSTN PLAN GEOG PROVS

B65
PEASLEE A.J.,CONSTITUTIONS OF NATIONS* THIRD REVISED EDITION (VOLUME I* AFRICA). LAW EX/STRUC LEGIS TOP/EX LEGIT CT/SYS ROUTINE ORD/FREE PWR SOVEREIGN...CON/ANAL CHARTS. PAGE 80 E1606
AFR CHOOSE CONSTN NAT/G

S65
ULMER S.S.,"TOWARD A THEORY OF SUBGROUP FORMATION IN THE UNITED STATES SUPREME COURT." USA+45 ROUTINE CHOOSE PWR...JURID STAT CON/ANAL SIMUL SUPREME/CT. PAGE 97 E1952
CT/SYS ADJUD ELITES INGP/REL

E1131

BESTERMAN T.,A WORLD BIBLIOGRAPHY OF BIBLIOGRAPHIES BIBLIOG/A
(4TH ED.). WOR+45 WOR-45 LAW INT/ORG ADMIN   DIPLOM
CON/ANAL. PAGE 11 E0219   B66

INTERNATIONAL BOOK NEWS, 1928-1934. ECO/UNDEV FINAN BIBLIOG/A
INDUS LABOR INT/TRADE CONFER ADJUD COLONIAL...HEAL   DIPLOM
SOC/WK CHARTS 20 LEAGUE/NAT. PAGE 1 E0008   INT/LAW
                                                     INT/ORG   N

YALEM R.J.,"THE STUDY OF INTERNATIONAL   VOL/ASSN
ORGANIZATION, 1920-1965: A SURVEY OF THE   INT/ORG
LITERATURE." WOR+45 WOR-45 REGION...INT/LAW CLASSIF BIBLIOG/A
RECORD HIST/WRIT CON/ANAL IDEA/COMP UN. PAGE 108
E2163   L66

CANON LAW ABSTRACTS. LEGIT CONFER CT/SYS INGP/REL   BIBLIOG/A
MARRIAGE ATTIT MORAL WORSHIP 20. PAGE 2 E0026   CATHISM
                                                   SECT
                                                   LAW   N

MCDOUGAL M.S.,THE INTERPRETATION OF AGREEMENTS AND INT/LAW
WORLD PUBLIC ORDER: PRINCIPLES OF CONTENT AND   STRUCT
PROCEDURE. WOR+45 CONSTN PROB/SOLV TEC/DEV   ECO/UNDEV
...CON/ANAL TREATY. PAGE 71 E1412   DIPLOM
                                                     B67

BATY T.,INTERNATIONAL LAW IN SOUTH AFRICA. AFR   JURID
SOUTH/AFR LAW CONFER 19/20. PAGE 8 E0155   WAR
                                                   SOVEREIGN
                                                   COLONIAL   B00

UNIVERSAL REFERENCE SYSTEM,BIBLIOGRAPHY OF   BIBLIOG/A
BIBLIOGRAPHIES IN POLITICAL SCIENCE, GOVERNMENT,   NAT/G
AND PUBLIC POLICY (VOLUME III). WOR+45 WOR-45 LAW DIPLOM
ADMIN...SOC CON/ANAL COMPUT/IR GEN/METH. PAGE 98 POLICY
E1973   B67

GRIFFIN A.P.C.,LIST OF REFERENCES ON INTERNATIONAL BIBLIOG/A
ARBITRATION. FRANCE L/A+17C USA-45 WOR-45 DIPLOM   INT/ORG
CONFER COLONIAL ARMS/CONT BAL/PAY EQUILIB SOVEREIGN INT/LAW
...DECISION 19/20 MEXIC/AMER. PAGE 47 E0932   DELIB/GP   B08

CARTER R.M.,"SOME FACTORS IN SENTENCING POLICY."   ADJUD
LAW PUB/INST CRIME PERS/REL...POLICY JURID SOC   CT/SYS
TREND CON/ANAL CHARTS SOC/EXP 20. PAGE 20 E0403   ADMIN
                                                     S67

MEZERIK A.G.,ATOM TESTS AND RADIATION HAZARDS   NUC/PWR
(PAMPHLET). WOR+45 INT/ORG DIPLOM DETER 20 UN   ARMS/CONT
TREATY. PAGE 73 E1452   CONFER
                                                   HEALTH   N19

GLASER D.,"NATIONAL GOALS AND INDICATORS FOR THE   CRIME
REDUCTION OF CRIME AND DELINQUENCY." FUT USA+45   CRIMLGY
NAT/G...CON/ANAL METH 20. PAGE 44 E0874   LAW
                                                   STAT   S67

MYERS D.P.,MANUAL OF COLLECTIONS OF TREATIES AND OF BIBLIOG/A
COLLECTIONS RELATING TO TREATIES. MOD/EUR INT/ORG DIPLOM
LEGIS WRITING ADMIN SOVEREIGN...INT/LAW 19/20.   CONFER
PAGE 75 E1514   B22

ADAMS J.,A DEFENSE OF THE CONSTITUTIONS OF   CONSTN
GOVERNMENT OF THE UNITED STATES OF AMERICA. USA-45 BAL/PWR
STRATA CHIEF EX/STRUC LEGIS CT/SYS CONSERVE   PWR
POPULISM...CONCPT CON/ANAL GOV/COMP. PAGE 3 E0048 NAT/G   B87

LAPRADELLE,ANNUAIRE DE LA VIE INTERNATIONALE: BIBLIOG
POLITIQUE, ECONOMIQUE, JURIDIQUE. INT/ORG CONFER   DIPLOM
ARMS/CONT 20. PAGE 63 E1255   INT/LAW   B28

CON/INTERP....CONSTITUTIONAL INTERPRETATION

LUCE R.,LEGISLATIVE PROBLEMS. CONSTN CHIEF JUDGE   TREND
BUDGET CONFER ETIQUET CONTROL MORAL PWR NEW/LIB   ADMIN
CONGRESS. PAGE 67 E1331   LEGIS   B35

POWELL T.R.,"THE LOGIC AND RHETORIC OF   CONSTN
CONSTITUTIONAL LAW" (BMR) USA+45 USA-45 DELIB/GP   LAW
PROB/SOLV ADJUD CT/SYS...DECISION 20 SUPREME/CT   JURID
CON/INTERP. PAGE 82 E1642   LOG   S18

HAGUE PERMANENT CT INTL JUSTIC,WORLD COURT REPORTS: INT/ORG
COLLECTION OF THE JUDGEMENTS ORDERS AND OPINIONS   CT/SYS
VOLUME 3 1932-35. WOR-45 LAW DELIB/GP CONFER WAR   DIPLOM
PEACE ATTIT...DECISION ANTHOL 20 WORLD/CT CASEBOOK. ADJUD
PAGE 49 E0976   B38

LEEK J.H.,"TREASON AND THE CONSTITUTION" (BMR)"   CONSTN
USA+45 USA-45 EDU/PROP COLONIAL CT/SYS REV WAR   JURID
ATTIT...TREND 18/20 SUPREME/CT CON/INTERP SMITH/ACT CRIME
COMMON/LAW. PAGE 64 E1278   NAT/G   S51

FULLER G.H.,A SELECTED LIST OF RECENT REFERENCES ON BIBLIOG/A
THE CONSTITUTION OF THE UNITED STATES (PAMPHLET). CONSTN
CULTURE NAT/G LEGIS CONFER ADJUD GOV/REL CONSEN   LAW
POPULISM...JURID CONCPT 18/20 CONGRESS. PAGE 41   USA-45
E0820   B40

LONG H.A.,USURPERS - FOES OF FREE MAN. LAW NAT/G   CT/SYS
CHIEF LEGIS DOMIN ADJUD REPRESENT GOV/REL ORD/FREE CENTRAL
LAISSEZ POPULISM...POLICY 18/20 SUPREME/CT   FEDERAL
ROOSEVLT/F CONGRESS CON/INTERP. PAGE 66 E1325   CONSTN   B57

CROWE S.E.,THE BERLIN WEST AFRICA CONFERENCE,   AFR
1884-85. GERMANY ELITES MARKET INT/ORG DELIB/GP   CONFER
FORCES PROB/SOLV BAL/PWR CAP/ISM DOMIN COLONIAL   INT/TRADE
...INT/LAW 19. PAGE 28 E0548   DIPLOM   B42

GINZBURG B.,REDEDICATION TO FREEDOM. DELIB/GP LEGIS JURID
ATTIT MARXISM 20 SUPREME/CT CON/INTERP HUAC AMEND/I ORD/FREE
FBI. PAGE 44 E0871   CONSTN
                                                   NAT/G   B59

CONOVER H.F.,THE BALKANS: A SELECTED LIST OF   BIBLIOG
REFERENCES. ALBANIA BULGARIA ROMANIA YUGOSLAVIA   EUR+WWI
INT/ORG PROB/SOLV DIPLOM LEGIT CONFER ADJUD WAR
NAT/LISM PEACE PWR 20 LEAGUE/NAT. PAGE 25 E0493   B43

DILEY A.V.,INTRODUCTION TO THE STUDY OF THE LAW OF CONSTN
THE CONSTITUTION. FRANCE UK USA+45 USA-45 CONSULT LAW
FORCES TAX ADMIN FEDERAL ORD/FREE SOVEREIGN   LEGIS
...IDEA/COMP 20 ENGLSH/LAW CON/INTERP PARLIAMENT. GEN/LAWS
PAGE 32 E0627   B60

HAGUE PERMANENT CT INTL JUSTIC,WORLD COURT REPORTS: INT/ORG
COLLECTION OF THE JUDGEMENTS ORDERS AND OPINIONS   CT/SYS
VOLUME 4 1936-42. WOR-45 CONFER PEACE ATTIT   DIPLOM
...DECISION JURID ANTHOL 20 WORLD/CT CASEBOOK.   ADJUD
PAGE 49 E0977   B43

CONANT M. E0484

CONCEN/CMP....CONCENTRATION CAMPS

CONCEPT....SEE CONCPT

CONCPT....SUBJECT-MATTER CONCEPTS

CONDEMNATION OF LAND OR PROPERTY....SEE CONDEMNATN

CONDEMNATN....CONDEMNATION OF LAND OR PROPERTY

CONDOTTIER....CONDOTTIERI - HIRED MILITIA

CONFER....CONFERENCES; SEE ALSO DELIB/GP

BENTHAM J.,"ON THE LIBERTY OF THE PRESS, AND PUBLIC ORD/FREE
DISCUSSION" IN J. BOWRING, ED., THE WORKS OF JEREMY PRESS
BENTHAM." SPAIN UK LAW ELITES NAT/G LEGIS INSPECT CONFER
LEGIT WRITING CONTROL PRIVIL TOTALISM AUTHORIT   CONSERVE
...TRADIT 19 FREE/SPEE. PAGE 10 E0193   C43

INTERNATIONAL COMN JURISTS,AFRICAN CONFERENCE ON   CT/SYS
THE RULE OF LAW. AFR INT/ORG LEGIS DIPLOM CONFER   JURID
COLONIAL ORD/FREE...CONCPT METH/COMP 20. PAGE 57   DELIB/GP   N

CHENEY F.,CARTELS, COMBINES, AND TRUSTS: A SELECTED BIBLIOG/A
LIST OF REFERENCES. GERMANY UK USA-45 WOR-45   LG/CO
DELIB/GP OP/RES BARGAIN CAP/ISM ECO/TAC INT/TRADE ECO/DEV
LICENSE LEGIT CONFER PRICE 20. PAGE 22 E0428   INDUS   B44

GRIFFITH E.S.,"THE CHANGING PATTERN OF PUBLIC   LAW   S44

POLICY FORMATION." MOD/EUR WOR+45 FINAN CHIEF   POLICY
CONFER ADMIN LEAD CONSERVE SOCISM TECHRACY...SOC   TEC/DEV
CHARTS CONGRESS. PAGE 47 E0938

                                                S48
MILLER B.S.,"A LAW IS PASSED: THE ATOMIC ENERGY ACT   TEC/DEV
OF 1946." POL/PAR CHIEF CONFER DEBATE CONTROL   LEGIS
PARL/PROC ATTIT KNOWL...POLICY CONGRESS. PAGE 73   DECISION
E1457   LAW

                                                N53
US PRES CONF ADMIN PROCEDURE,REPORT (PAMPHLET).   NAT/G
USA+45 CONFER ADJUD...METH/COMP 20 PRESIDENT.   DELIB/GP
PAGE 101 E2024   ADJUST
                                                       ADMIN

                                                B55
UN HEADQUARTERS LIBRARY,BIBLIOGRAPHIE DE LA CHARTE   BIBLIOG/A
DES NATIONS UNIES. CHINA/COM KOREA WOR+45 VOL/ASSN   INT/ORG
CONFER ADMIN COERCE PEACE ATTIT ORD/FREE SOVEREIGN   DIPLOM
...INT/LAW 20 UNESCO UN. PAGE 97 E1953

                                                B55
WHEARE K.C.,GOVERNMENT BY COMMITTEE; AN ESSAY ON   DELIB/GP
THE BRITISH CONSTITUTION. UK NAT/G LEGIS INSPECT   CONSTN
CONFER ADJUD ADMIN CONTROL TASK EFFICIENCY ROLE   LEAD
POPULISM 20. PAGE 106 E2116   GP/COMP

                                                B57
US SENATE COMM ON JUDICIARY,CIVIL RIGHTS - 1957.   INT
USA+45 LAW NAT/G CONFER GOV/REL RACE/REL ORD/FREE   LEGIS
PWR...JURID 20 SENATE CIV/RIGHTS. PAGE 102 E2039   DISCRIM
                                                       PARL/PROC

                                                B57
US SENATE COMM ON JUDICIARY,HEARING BEFORE   LEGIS
SUBCOMMITTEE ON COMMITTEE OF JUDICIARY, UNITED   CONSTN
STATES SENATE: S. J. RES. 3. USA+45 NAT/G CONSULT   CONFER
DELIB/GP DIPLOM ADJUD LOBBY REPRESENT 20 CONGRESS   AGREE
TREATY. PAGE 102 E2040

                                                B58
AMERICAN SOCIETY PUBLIC ADMIN,STRENGTHENING   ADMIN
MANAGEMENT FOR DEMOCRATIC GOVERNMENT. USA+45 ACADEM   NAT/G
EX/STRUC WORKER PLAN BUDGET CONFER CT/SYS   EXEC
EFFICIENCY ANTHOL. PAGE 4 E0083   MGT

                                                B58
ATOMIC INDUSTRIAL FORUM,MANAGEMENT AND ATOMIC   NUC/PWR
ENERGY. WOR+45 SEA LAW MARKET NAT/G TEC/DEV INSPECT   INDUS
INT/TRADE CONFER PEACE HEALTH...ANTHOL 20. PAGE 6   MGT
E0112   ECO/TAC

                                                B58
BUREAU OF NATIONAL AFFAIRS,THE MCCLELLAN COMMITTEE   DELIB/GP
HEARINGS - 1957. USA+45 LEGIS CONTROL CRIME   CONFER
...CHARTS 20 CONGRESS AFL/CIO MCCLELLN/J. PAGE 17   LABOR
E0336   MGT

                                                B58
MANSERGH N.,COMMONWEALTH PERSPECTIVES. GHANA UK LAW   DIPLOM
VOL/ASSN CONFER HEALTH SOVEREIGN...GEOG CHARTS   COLONIAL
ANTHOL 20 CMN/WLTH AUSTRAL. PAGE 68 E1363   INT/ORG
                                                       INGP/REL

                                                B58
US SENATE COMM POST OFFICE,TO PROVIDE AN EFFECTIVE   INT
SYSTEM OF PERSONNEL ADMINISTRATION. USA+45 NAT/G   LEGIS
EX/STRUC PARL/PROC GOV/REL...JURID 20 SENATE   CONFER
CIVIL/SERV. PAGE 103 E2060   ADMIN

                                                S58
RIKER W.H.,"THE PARADOX OF VOTING AND CONGRESSIONAL   PARL/PROC
RULES FOR VOTING ON AMENDMENTS." LAW DELIB/GP   DECISION
EX/STRUC PROB/SOLV CONFER DEBATE EFFICIENCY ATTIT   LEGIS
HOUSE/REP CONGRESS SENATE. PAGE 85 E1700   RATIONAL

                                                N58
US HOUSE COMM FOREIGN AFFAIRS,HEARINGS ON DRAFT   LEGIS
LEGISLATION TO AMEND FURTHER THE MUTUAL SECURITY   DELIB/GP
ACT OF 1954 (PAMPHLET). USA+45 CONSULT FORCES   CONFER
BUDGET DIPLOM DETER COST ORD/FREE...JURID 20   WEAPON
DEPT/DEFEN UN DEPT/STATE. PAGE 100 E2002

                                                B59
HALEY A.G.,FIRST COLLOQUIUM ON THE LAW OF OUTER   SPACE
SPACE. WOR+45 INT/ORG ACT/RES PLAN BAL/PWR CONFER   LAW
ATTIT PWR...POLICY JURID CHARTS ANTHOL 20. PAGE 49   SOVEREIGN
E0979   CONTROL

                                                B59
WAGNER W.J.,THE FEDERAL STATES AND THEIR JUDICIARY.   ADJUD
BRAZIL CANADA SWITZERLND USA+45 CONFER CT/SYS TASK   METH/COMP
EFFICIENCY FEDERAL PWR...JURID BIBLIOG 20 AUSTRAL   PROB/SOLV
MEXIC/AMER. PAGE 104 E2091   NAT/G

                                                B60
FISCHER L.,THE SOVIETS IN WORLD AFFAIRS. CHINA/COM   DIPLOM
COM EUR+WWI USSR INT/ORG CONFER LEAD ARMS/CONT REV   NAT/G
PWR...CHARTS 20 TREATY VERSAILLES. PAGE 38 E0755   POLICY
                                                       MARXISM

                                                B60
US SENATE COMM ON JUDICIARY,FEDERAL ADMINISTRATIVE   PARL/PROC
PROCEDURE. USA+45 CONSTN NAT/G PROB/SOLV CONFER   LEGIS
GOV/REL...JURID INT 20 SENATE. PAGE 102 E2043   ADMIN
                                                       LAW

                                                B60
US SENATE COMM ON JUDICIARY,ADMINISTRATIVE   PARL/PROC
PROCEDURE LEGISLATION. USA+45 CONSTN NAT/G   LEGIS
PROB/SOLV CONFER ROUTINE GOV/REL...INT 20 SENATE.   ADMIN
PAGE 102 E2044   JURID

                                                B61
AUERBACH C.A.,THE LEGAL PROCESS. USA+45 DELIB/GP   JURID
JUDGE CONFER ADJUD CONTROL...DECISION 20   ADMIN
SUPREME/CT. PAGE 6 E0116   LEGIS
                                                       CT/SYS

                                                B61
US CONGRESS,CONSTITUTIONAL RIGHTS OF THE MENTALLY   HEALTH
ILL. USA+45 LAW PUB/INST DELIB/GP ADJUD ORD/FREE   CONSTN
...PSY QU 20 CONGRESS. PAGE 99 E1989   JURID
                                                       CONFER

                                                N61
DELEGACION NACIONAL DE PRENSA,FALANGE ESPANOL   EDU/PROP
TRADICIONALISTA Y DE LAS JUNTAS OFENSIVAS   FASCIST
NACIONALES SINDICALISTAS. IX CONSEJO NACIONAL   CONFER
(PAMPHLET). LAW VOL/ASSN TOTALISM AUTHORIT ORD/FREE POL/PAR
FASCISM...ANTHOL 20 FRANCO/F FALANGIST. PAGE 31
E0605

                                                B62
DUROSELLE J.B.,HISTOIRE DIPLOMATIQUE DE 1919 A NOS DIPLOM
JOURS (3RD ED.). FRANCE INT/ORG CHIEF FORCES CONFER WOR+45
ARMS/CONT WAR PEACE ORD/FREE...T TREATY 20   WOR-45
COLD/WAR. PAGE 34 E0667

                                                B62
PERKINS D.,AMERICA'S QUEST FOR PEACE. USA+45 WOR+45   INT/LAW
DIPLOM CONFER NAT/LISM ATTIT 20 UN TREATY. PAGE 80   INT/ORG
E1610   ARMS/CONT
                                                      PEACE

                                                N62
TWENTIETH CENTURY FUND,ONE MAN - ONE VOTE   APPORT
(PAMPHLET). USA+45 CONSTN CONFER CT/SYS REGION   LEGIS
CONSEN FEDERAL ROLE...CENSUS 20 CONGRESS. PAGE 97   REPRESENT
E1947   PROVS

                                                N62
US SENATE COMM ON JUDICIARY,LEGISLATION TO   LEAD
STRENGTHEN PENALTIES UNDER THE ANTITRUST LAWS   ADJUD
(PAMPHLET). USA+45 LG/CO CONFER CONTROL SANCTION   INDUS
ORD/FREE 20 SENATE MONOPOLY. PAGE 102 E2045   ECO/TAC

                                                B63
DUNN F.S.,PEACE-MAKING AND THE SETTLEMENT WITH   POLICY
JAPAN. ASIA USA+45 USA-45 FORCES BAL/PWR ECO/TAC   PEACE
CONFER WAR PWR SOVEREIGN 20 CHINJAP COLD/WAR   PLAN
TREATY. PAGE 33 E0661   DIPLOM

                                                B63
US SENATE COMM ON JUDICIARY,ADMINISTRATIVE   PARL/PROC
CONFERENCE OF THE UNITED STATES. USA+45 CONSTN   JURID
NAT/G PROB/SOLV CONFER GOV/REL...INT 20 SENATE.   ADMIN
PAGE 102 E2048   LEGIS

                                                B64
BUREAU OF NAT'L AFFAIRS,THE CIVIL RIGHTS ACT OF   LEGIS
1964. USA+45 LOC/G NAT/G DELIB/GP CONFER DEBATE   RACE/REL
DISCRIM...JURID 20 CONGRESS SUPREME/CT CIV/RIGHTS.   LAW
PAGE 17 E0333   CONSTN

                                                B64
DANELSKI D.J.,A SUPREME COURT JUSTICE IS APPOINTED.   CHOOSE
CHIEF LEGIS CONFER DEBATE EXEC PERSON PWR...BIOG 20   JUDGE
CONGRESS PRESIDENT. PAGE 28 E0564   DECISION

                                                B64
NASA,PROCEEDINGS OF CONFERENCE ON THE LAW OF SPACE   SPACE
AND OF SATELLITE COMMUNICATIONS: CHICAGO 1963. FUT   COM/IND
WOR+45 DELIB/GP PROB/SOLV TEC/DEV CONFER ADJUD   LAW
NUC/PWR...POLICY IDEA/COMP 20 NASA. PAGE 76 E1522   DIPLOM

                                                B64
A CHECK LIST OF THE SPECIAL AND STANDING COMMITTEES   BIBLIOG
OF THE AMERICAN BAR ASSOCIATION (VOL. II). USA+45   LAW
LEGIS PRESS CONFER...JURID CON/ANAL. PAGE 80 E1607   VOL/ASSN

US AIR FORCE ACADEMY ASSEMBLY,OUTER SPACE: FINAL REPORT APRIL 1-4, 1964. FUT USA+45 WOR+45 LAW DELIB/GP CONFER ARMS/CONT WAR PEACE ATTIT MORAL ...ANTHOL 20 NASA. PAGE 99 E1979
B64
SPACE
CIVMIL/REL
NUC/PWR
DIPLOM

US SENATE COMM ON JUDICIARY,ADMINISTRATIVE PROCEDURE ACT. USA+45 CONSTN NAT/G PROB/SOLV CONFER GOV/REL PWR...INT 20 SENATE. PAGE 102 E2054
B64
PARL/PROC
LEGIS
JURID
ADMIN

GOTLIEB A.,DISARMAMENT AND INTERNATIONAL LAW* A STUDY OF THE ROLE OF LAW IN THE DISARMAMENT PROCESS. USA+45 USSR PROB/SOLV CONFER ADMIN ROUTINE NUC/PWR ORD/FREE SOVEREIGN UN TREATY. PAGE 45 E0893
B65
INT/LAW
INT/ORG
ARMS/CONT
IDEA/COMP

INST INTL DES CIVILISATION DIF,THE CONSTITUTIONS AND ADMINISTRATIVE INSTITUTIONS OF THE NEW STATES. AFR ISLAM S/ASIA NAT/G POL/PAR DELIB/GP EX/STRUC CONFER EFFICIENCY NAT/LISM...JURID SOC 20. PAGE 56 E1123
B65
CONSTN
ADMIN
ADJUD
ECO/UNDEV

MARTENS E.,DIE HANNOVERSCHE KIRCHENKOMMISSION. GERMANY LAW INT/ORG PROVS SECT CONFER GP/REL CATHISM 16/20. PAGE 69 E1371
B65
JURID
DELIB/GP
CONSTN
PROF/ORG

MORRIS R.B.,THE PEACEMAKERS; THE GREAT POWERS AND AMERICAN INDEPENDENCE. BAL/PWR CONFER COLONIAL NEUTRAL PEACE ORD/FREE TREATY 18 PRE/US/AM. PAGE 75 E1499
B65
SOVEREIGN
REV
DIPLOM

MOSTECKY V.,SOVIET LEGAL BIBLIOGRAPHY. USSR LEGIS PRESS WRITING CONFER ADJUD CT/SYS REV MARXISM ...INT/LAW JURID DICTIONARY 20. PAGE 75 E1503
B65
BIBLIOG/A
LAW
COM
CONSTN

FRIEDHEIM R.,"THE 'SATISFIED' AND 'DISSATISFIED' STATES NEGOTIATE INTERNATIONAL LAW* A CASE STUDY." DIPLOM CONFER ADJUD CONSEN PEACE ATTIT UN. PAGE 40 E0799
S65
INT/LAW
RECORD

CLARK G.,WORLD PEACE THROUGH WORLD LAW; TWO ALTERNATIVE PLANS. WOR+45 DELIB/GP FORCES TAX CONFER ADJUD SANCTION ARMS/CONT WAR CHOOSE PRIVIL 20 UN COLD/WAR. PAGE 23 E0450
B66
INT/LAW
PEACE
PLAN
INT/ORG

JACOBSON H.K.,DIPLOMATS, SCIENTISTS, AND POLITICIANS* THE UNITED STATES AND THE NUCLEAR TEST BAN NEGOTIATIONS. USA+45 USSR ACT/RES PLAN CONFER DETER NUC/PWR CONSEN ORD/FREE...INT TREATY. PAGE 57 E1146
B66
DIPLOM
ARMS/CONT
TECHRACY
INT/ORG

LEE L.T.,VIENNA CONVENTION ON CONSULAR RELATIONS. WOR+45 LAW INT/ORG CONFER GP/REL PRIVIL...INT/LAW 20 TREATY VIENNA/CNV. PAGE 64 E1277
B66
AGREE
DIPLOM
ADMIN

ANAND R.P.,"ATTITUDE OF THE ASIAN-AFRICAN STATES TOWARD CERTAIN PROBLEMS OF INTERNATIONAL LAW." L/A+17C S/ASIA ECO/UNDEV CREATE CONFER ADJUD COLONIAL...RECORD GP/COMP UN. PAGE 5 E0087
S66
INT/LAW
ATTIT
ASIA
AFR

BIBBY J.,ON CAPITOL HILL. POL/PAR LOBBY PARL/PROC GOV/REL PERS/REL...JURID PHIL/SCI OBS INT BIBLIOG 20 CONGRESS PRESIDENT. PAGE 12 E0224
B67
CONFER
LEGIS
CREATE
LEAD

US PRES TASK FORCE ADMIN JUS,TASK FORCE REPORT: THE COURTS. USA+45 CONSULT CONFER...JURID CHARTS. PAGE 101 E2025
B67
CT/SYS
ADJUD
ROUTINE
ADMIN

US SENATE COMM ON FOREIGN REL,A SELECT CHRONOLOGY AND BACKGROUND DOCUMENTS RELATING TO THE MIDDLE EAST. ISRAEL UAR LAW INT/ORG FORCES PROB/SOLV CONFER CONSEN PEACE ATTIT...POLICY 20 UN SENATE TRUMAN/HS. PAGE 101 E2033
B67
ISLAM
TIME/SEQ
DIPLOM

US SENATE COMM ON FOREIGN REL,FOREIGN ASSISTANCE ACT OF 1967. VIETNAM WOR+45 DELIB/GP CONFER CONTROL WAR WEAPON BAL/PAY...CENSUS CHARTS SENATE. PAGE 102 E2033
B67
FOR/AID
LAW
DIPLOM

E2036
POLICY

ALDRICH W.A.,"THE SUEZ CRISIS." UAR UK USA+45 DELIB/GP FORCES BAL/PWR INT/TRADE CONFER CONTROL COERCE DETER 20. PAGE 3 E0058
S67
DIPLOM
INT/LAW
COLONIAL

CHAMBERLAIN N.W.,"STRIKES IN CONTEMPORARY CONTEXT." LAW INDUS NAT/G CHIEF CONFER COST ATTIT ORD/FREE ...POLICY MGT 20. PAGE 21 E0415
S67
LABOR
BARGAIN
EFFICIENCY
PROB/SOLV

CUMMINS L.,"THE FORMULATION OF THE "PLATT" AMENDMENT." CUBA L/A+17C NAT/G DELIB/GP CONFER ...POLICY 20. PAGE 28 E0554
S67
DIPLOM
INT/LAW
LEGIS

MAYANJA A.,"THE GOVERNMENT'S PROPOSALS ON THE NEW CONSTITUTION." AFR UGANDA LAW CHIEF LEGIS ADJUD REPRESENT FEDERAL PWR 20. PAGE 69 E1390
S67
CONSTN
CONFER
ORD/FREE
NAT/G

PEMBERTON J., JR.,"CONSTITUTIONAL PROBLEMS IN RESTRAINT ON THE MEDIA." CONSTN PROB/SOLV EDU/PROP CONFER CONTROL JURID. PAGE 80 E1608
S67
LAW
PRESS
ORD/FREE

WINES R.,"THE IMPERIAL CIRCLES, PRINCELY DIPLOMACY, AND IMPERIAL REFORM* 1681-1714." MOD/EUR DELIB/GP BAL/PWR CONFER ADJUD PARL/PROC PARTIC ATTIT PWR 17/18. PAGE 106 E2132
S67
NAT/G
NAT/LISM
CENTRAL
REGION

CHIU H.,"COMMUNIST CHINA'S ATTITUDE TOWARD THE UNITED NATIONS: A LEGAL ANALYSIS." CHINA/COM WOR+45 LAW NAT/G DIPLOM CONFER ADJUD PARTIC ATTIT...POLICY TREND 20 UN. PAGE 22 E0432
L68
INT/LAW
SOVEREIGN
INT/ORG
REPRESENT

CONFERENCE ATLANTIC COMMUNITY E0485

CONFERENCES....SEE CONFER, DELIB/GP

CONFIDENCE, PERSONAL....SEE SUPEGO

CONFLICT, MILITARY....SEE WAR, FORCES+COERCE

CONFLICT, PERSONAL....SEE PERS/REL, ROLE

CONFLICT....CONFLICT THEORY

CONFORMITY....SEE CONSEN, DOMIN

CONFRONTATION....SEE CONFRONTN

CONFRONTN....CONFRONTATION

CONFUCIUS....CONFUCIUS

CONGRESSIONAL QUARTERLY SERV

CONGO....CONGO, PRE-INDEPENDENCE OR GENERAL

MILLER E.,"LEGAL ASPECTS OF UN ACTION IN THE CONGO." AFR CULTURE ADMIN PEACE DRIVE RIGID/FLEX ORD/FREE...WELF/ST JURID OBS UN CONGO 20. PAGE 73 E1458
S61
INT/ORG
LEGIT

MURACCIOLE L.,"LA LOI FONDAMENTALE DE LA REPUBLIQUE DU CONGO." WOR+45 SOCIETY ECO/UNDEV INT/ORG NAT/G LEGIS PLAN LEGIT ADJUD COLONIAL ROUTINE ATTIT SOVEREIGN 20 CONGO. PAGE 75 E1504
L62
AFR
CONSTN

GIRAUD E.,"L'INTERDICTION DU RECOURS A LA FORCE, LA THEORIE ET LA PRATIQUE DES NATIONS UNIES." ALGERIA COM CUBA HUNGARY WOR+45 ADJUD TOTALISM ATTIT RIGID/FLEX PWR...POLICY JURID CONCPT UN 20 CONGO. PAGE 44 E0872
S63
INT/ORG
FORCES
DIPLOM

HAEFELE E.T.,GOVERNMENT CONTROLS ON TRANSPORT. AFR RHODESIA TANZANIA DIPLOM ECO/TAC TARIFFS PRICE ADJUD CONTROL REGION EFFICIENCY...POLICY 20 CONGO. PAGE 49 E0973
B65
ECO/UNDEV
DIST/IND
FINAN
NAT/G

CONGO/BRAZ....CONGO, BRAZZAVILLE; SEE ALSO AFR

MOREL E.D.,THE BRITISH CASE IN FRENCH CONGO. CONGO/BRAZ FRANCE UK COERCE MORAL WEALTH...POLICY INT/LAW 20 CONGO/LEOP. PAGE 74 E1490
B03
DIPLOM
INT/TRADE
COLONIAL

HEYSE T.,PROBLEMS FONCIERS ET REGIME DES TERRES (ASPECTS ECONOMIQUES, JURIDIQUES ET SOCIAUX). AFR CONGO/BRAZ INT/ORG DIPLOM SOVEREIGN...GEOG TREATY 20. PAGE 52 E1037
AFR
B60
BIBLIOG
AGRI
ECO/UNDEV
LEGIS

CONGO/KINS....CONGO, KINSHASA; SEE ALSO AFR

MOREL E.D.,THE BRITISH CASE IN FRENCH CONGO. CONGO/BRAZ FRANCE UK COERCE MORAL WEALTH...POLICY INT/LAW 20 CONGO/LEOP. PAGE 74 E1490
B03
DIPLOM
INT/TRADE
COLONIAL
AFR

BOWETT D.W.,UNITED NATIONS FORCES* A LEGAL STUDY. CYPRUS ISRAEL KOREA LAW CONSTN ACT/RES CREATE BUDGET CONTROL TASK PWR...INT/LAW IDEA/COMP UN CONGO/LEOP SUEZ. PAGE 14 E0278
B64
OP/RES
FORCES
ARMS/CONT

GREIG D.W.,"THE ADVISORY JURISDICTION OF THE INTERNATIONAL COURT AND THE SETTLEMENT OF DISPUTES BETWEEN STATES." ISRAEL KOREA FORCES BUDGET DOMIN LEGIT ADJUD COST...RECORD UN CONGO/LEOP TREATY. PAGE 46 E0915
L66
INT/LAW
CT/SYS

CONGRESS OF RACIAL EQUALITY....SEE CORE

CONGRESS....CONGRESS (ALL NATIONS); SEE ALSO LEGIS, HOUSE/REP, SENATE, DELIB/GP

US SUPERINTENDENT OF DOCUMENTS,POLITICAL SCIENCE: GOVERNMENT, CRIME, DISTRICT OF COLUMBIA (PRICE LIST 54). USA+45 LAW CONSTN EX/STRUC WORKER ADJUD ADMIN CT/SYS CHOOSE INGP/REL RACE/REL CONGRESS PRESIDENT. PAGE 103 E2063
N
BIBLIOG/A
NAT/G
CRIME

DE TOCQUEVILLE A.,DEMOCRACY IN AMERICA (VOLUME ONE). LAW SOCIETY STRUCT NAT/G POL/PAR PROVS FORCES LEGIS TOP/EX DIPLOM LEGIT WAR PEACE ATTIT SOVEREIGN ...SELF/OBS TIME/SEQ CONGRESS 19. PAGE 30 E0594
B00
USA-45
TREND

GREELY A.W.,PUBLIC DOCUMENTS OF THE FIRST FOURTEEN CONGRESSES, 1789-1817. USA-45 LEAD REPRESENT ATTIT 18/19 CONGRESS. PAGE 45 E0904
B00
BIBLIOG/A
NAT/G
LAW
LEGIS

GRIFFIN A.P.C.,LIST OF BOOKS ON THE CONSTITUTION OF THE UNITED STATES (PAMPHLET). USA-45 NAT/G EX/STRUC JUDGE TOP/EX CT/SYS 18/20 CONGRESS PRESIDENT SUPREME/CT. PAGE 46 E0920
B03
BIBLIOG/A
CONSTN
LAW
JURID

CRANDALL S.B.,TREATIES: THEIR MAKING AND ENFORCEMENT. MOD/EUR USA-45 CONSTN INT/ORG NAT/G LEGIS EDU/PROP LEGIT EXEC PEACE KNOWL MORAL...JURID CONGRESS 19/20 TREATY. PAGE 27 E0541
B04
LAW

GRIFFIN A.P.C.,LIST OF REFERENCES ON PRIMARY ELECTIONS (PAMPHLET). USA-45 LAW LOC/G DELIB/GP LEGIS OP/RES TASK REPRESENT CONSEN...DECISION 19/20 CONGRESS. PAGE 47 E0928
B05
BIBLIOG/A
POL/PAR
CHOOSE
POPULISM

MEYER H.H.B.,SELECT LIST OF REFERENCES ON THE INITIATIVE, REFERENDUM, AND RECALL. MOD/EUR USA-45 LAW LOC/G MUNIC REPRESENT POPULISM 20 CONGRESS. PAGE 72 E1446
B12
BIBLIOG/A
NAT/G
LEGIS
CHOOSE

MEYER H.H.B.,LIST OF REFERENCES ON EMBARGOES (PAMPHLET). USA-45 AGRI DIPLOM WRITING DEBATE WEAPON...INT/LAW 18/20 CONGRESS. PAGE 72 E1447
B17
BIBLIOG
DIST/IND
ECO/TAC
INT/TRADE

IN THE SHADOW OF FEAR; AMERICAN CIVIL LIBERTIES, 1948-49 (PAMPHLET). COM LAW LEGIS BAL/PWR EDU/PROP CT/SYS RACE/REL DISCRIM MARXISM SOCISM 20 COLD/WAR CONGRESS ACLU CIV/RIGHTS ESPIONAGE. PAGE 2 E0030
N19
ORD/FREE
CONSTN
POLICY

ATOMIC INDUSTRIAL FORUM,COMMENTARY ON LEGISLATION TO PERMIT PRIVATE OWNERSHIP OF SPECIAL NUCLEAR MATERIAL (PAMPHLET). USA+45 DELIB/GP LEGIS PLAN OWN ...POLICY 20 AEC CONGRESS. PAGE 6 E0111
N19
NUC/PWR
MARKET
INDUS
LAW

CARPER E.T.,LOBBYING AND THE NATURAL GAS BILL (PAMPHLET). USA+45 SERV/IND BARGAIN PAY DRIVE ROLE WEALTH 20 CONGRESS SENATE EISNHWR/DD. PAGE 20 E0389
N19
LOBBY
ADJUD
TRIBUTE
NAT/G

MCCONNELL G.,THE STEEL SEIZURE OF 1952 (PAMPHLET). USA+45 FINAN INDUS PROC/MFG LG/CO EX/STRUC ADJUD CONTROL GP/REL ORD/FREE PWR 20 TRUMAN/HS PRESIDENT CONGRESS. PAGE 70 E1402
N19
DELIB/GP
LABOR
PROB/SOLV
NAT/G

BRYCE J.,MODERN DEMOCRACIES. FUT NEW/ZEALND USA-45 LAW CONSTN POL/PAR PROVS VOL/ASSN EX/STRUC LEGIS LEGIT CT/SYS EXEC KNOWL CONGRESS AUSTRAL 20. PAGE 16 E0322
B21
NAT/G
TREND

FRANKFURTER F.,THE BUSINESS OF THE SUPREME COURT; A STUDY IN THE FEDERAL JUDICIAL SYSTEM. USA-45 CONSTN EX/STRUC PROB/SOLV GP/REL ATTIT PWR...POLICY JURID 18/20 SUPREME/CT CONGRESS. PAGE 40 E0789
B28
CT/SYS
ADJUD
LAW
FEDERAL

MACDONALD A.F.,ELEMENTS OF POLITICAL SCIENCE RESEARCH. USA-45 ACADEM JUDGE EDU/PROP DEBATE ADJUD EXEC...BIBLIOG METH T 20 CONGRESS. PAGE 67 E1338
B28
LAW
FEDERAL
DECISION
CT/SYS

NORTON T.J.,LOSING LIBERTY JUDICIALLY. PROVS LEGIS BAL/PWR CT/SYS...JURID 18/20 SUPREME/CT CIV/RIGHTS CONGRESS. PAGE 78 E1557
B28
NAT/G
ORD/FREE
CONSTN
JUDGE

FLEMMING D.,THE UNITED STATES AND THE LEAGUE OF NATIONS, 1918-1920. FUT USA-45 NAT/G LEGIS TOP/EX DEBATE CHOOSE PEACE ATTIT SOVEREIGN...TIME/SEQ CON/ANAL CONGRESS LEAGUE/NAT 20 TREATY. PAGE 39 E0764
B32
INT/ORG
EDU/PROP

DANGERFIELD R.,IN DEFENSE OF THE SENATE. USA-45 CONSTN NAT/G EX/STRUC TOP/EX ATTIT KNOWL ...METH/CNCPT STAT TIME/SEQ TREND CON/ANAL CHARTS CONGRESS 20 TREATY. PAGE 28 E0565
B33
LEGIS
DELIB/GP
DIPLOM

LUCE R.,LEGISLATIVE PROBLEMS. CONSTN CHIEF JUDGE BUDGET CONFER ETIQUET CONTROL MORAL PWR NEW/LIB CONGRESS. PAGE 67 E1331
B35
TREND
ADMIN
LEGIS

CORWIN E.S.,"THE CONSTITUTION AS INSTRUMENT AND AS SYMBOL." USA-45 ECO/DEV INDUS CAP/ISM SANCTION RIGID/FLEX ORD/FREE LAISSEZ OBJECTIVE 20 CONGRESS SUPREME/CT. PAGE 26 E0512
S36
CONSTN
LAW
ADJUD
PWR

BADEN A.L.,IMMIGRATION AND ITS RESTRICTION IN THE US (PAMPHLET). USA-45 NAT/G LEGIS...GEOG 20 CONGRESS. PAGE 7 E0130
B37
BIBLIOG
STRANGE
CONTROL
LAW

FULLER G.H.,A SELECTED LIST OF RECENT REFERENCES ON THE CONSTITUTION OF THE UNITED STATES (PAMPHLET). CULTURE NAT/G LEGIS CONFER ADJUD GOV/REL CONSEN POPULISM...JURID CONCPT 18/20 CONGRESS. PAGE 41 E0820
B40
BIBLIOG/A
CONSTN
LAW
USA-45

CARR R.K.,THE SUPREME COURT AND JUDICIAL REVIEW. NAT/G CHIEF LEGIS OP/RES LEAD GOV/REL GP/REL ATTIT ...POLICY DECISION 18/20 SUPREME/CT PRESIDENT CONGRESS. PAGE 20 E0394
B42
CT/SYS
CONSTN
JURID
PWR

FULLER G.H.,DEFENSE FINANCING: A SUPPLEMENTARY LIST OF REFERENCES (PAMPHLET). CANADA UK USA-45 ECO/DEV NAT/G DELIB/GP BUDGET ADJUD ARMS/CONT WEAPON COST PEACE PWR 20 AUSTRAL CHINJAP CONGRESS. PAGE 41 E0821
B42
BIBLIOG/A
FINAN
FORCES
DIPLOM

GRIFFITH E.S.,"THE CHANGING PATTERN OF PUBLIC POLICY FORMATION." MOD/EUR WOR+45 FINAN CHIEF CONFER ADMIN LEAD CONSERVE SOCISM TECHRACY...SOC CHARTS CONGRESS. PAGE 47 E0938
S44
LAW
POLICY
TEC/DEV

STOKES W.S.,BIBLIOGRAPHY OF STANDARD AND CLASSICAL WORKS IN THE FIELDS OF AMERICAN POLITICAL SCIENCE.
B48
BIBLIOG
NAT/G

USA+45 USA-45 POL/PAR PROVS FORCES DIPLOM ADMIN   LOC/G
CT/SYS APPORT 20 CONGRESS PRESIDENT. PAGE 94 E1876   CONSTN

                                                        S48
MILLER B.S.,"A LAW IS PASSED: THE ATOMIC ENERGY ACT   TEC/DEV
OF 1946." POL/PAR CHIEF CONFER DEBATE CONTROL   LEGIS
PARL/PROC ATTIT KNOWL...POLICY CONGRESS. PAGE 73   DECISION
E1457   LAW

                                                        C48
WALKER H.,"THE LEGISLATIVE PROCESS; LAWMAKING IN   PARL/PROC
THE UNITED STATES." NAT/G POL/PAR PROVS EX/STRUC   LEGIS
OP/RES PROB/SOLV CT/SYS LOBBY GOV/REL...CHARTS   LAW
BIBLIOG T 18/20 CONGRESS. PAGE 105 E2094   CONSTN

                                                        B50
BURDETTE F.L.,LOBBYISTS IN ACTION (PAMPHLET).   LOBBY
CONSULT TEC/DEV INSPECT BARGAIN PARL/PROC SANCTION   ATTIT
20 CONGRESS. PAGE 17 E0329   POLICY
                                                        LAW

                                                        B50
HURST J.W.,THE GROWTH OF AMERICAN LAW; THE LAW   LAW
MAKERS. USA-45 LOC/G NAT/G DELIB/GP JUDGE ADJUD   LEGIS
ADMIN ATTIT PWR...POLICY JURID BIBLIOG 18/20   CONSTN
CONGRESS SUPREME/CT ABA PRESIDENT. PAGE 56 E1115   CT/SYS

                                                        B50
MERRIAM C.E.,THE AMERICAN PARTY SYSTEM; AN   POL/PAR
INTRODUCTION TO THE STUDY OF POLITICAL PARTIES IN   CHOOSE
THE UNITED STATES (4TH ED.). USA+45 USA-45 LAW   SUFF
FINAN LOC/G NAT/G PROVS LEAD PARTIC CRIME ATTIT   REPRESENT
18/20 NEGRO CONGRESS PRESIDENT. PAGE 72 E1442

                                                        C50
HOLCOMBE A.,"OUR MORE PERFECT UNION." USA+45 USA-45   CONSTN
POL/PAR JUDGE CT/SYS EQUILIB FEDERAL PWR...MAJORIT   NAT/G
TREND BIBLIOG 18/20 CONGRESS PRESIDENT. PAGE 54   ADMIN
E1070   PLAN

                                                        L52
WRIGHT Q.,"CONGRESS AND THE TREATY-MAKING POWER."   ROUTINE
USA+45 WOR+45 CONSTN INTELL NAT/G CHIEF CONSULT   DIPLOM
EX/STRUC LEGIS TOP/EX CREATE GOV/REL DISPL DRIVE   INT/LAW
RIGID/FLEX...TREND TOT/POP CONGRESS CONGRESS 20   DELIB/GP
TREATY. PAGE 108 E2154

                                                        L52
WRIGHT Q.,"CONGRESS AND THE TREATY-MAKING POWER."   ROUTINE
USA+45 WOR+45 CONSTN INTELL NAT/G CHIEF CONSULT   DIPLOM
EX/STRUC LEGIS TOP/EX CREATE GOV/REL DISPL DRIVE   INT/LAW
RIGID/FLEX...TREND TOT/POP CONGRESS CONGRESS 20   DELIB/GP
TREATY. PAGE 108 E2154

                                                        B54
BROGAN D.W.,POLITICS IN AMERICA. LAW POL/PAR CHIEF   NAT/G
LEGIS LOBBY CHOOSE REPRESENT GP/REL RACE/REL   CONSTN
FEDERAL MORAL...BIBLIOG 20 PRESIDENT CONGRESS.   USA+45
PAGE 16 E0304

                                                        B55
BERNSTEIN M.H.,REGULATING BUSINESS BY INDEPENDENT   DELIB/GP
COMMISSION. USA+45 USA-45 LG/CO CHIEF LEGIS   CONTROL
PROB/SOLV ADJUD SANCTION GP/REL ATTIT...TIME/SEQ   CONSULT
19/20 MONOPOLY PRESIDENT CONGRESS. PAGE 11 E0214

                                                        B55
PLISCHKE E.,AMERICAN FOREIGN RELATIONS: A   BIBLIOG/A
BIBLIOGRAPHY OF OFFICIAL SOURCES. USA+45 USA-45   DIPLOM
INT/ORG FORCES PRESS WRITING DEBATE EXEC...POLICY   NAT/G
INT/LAW 18/20 CONGRESS. PAGE 81 E1621

                                                        B56
ABELS J.,THE TRUMAN SCANDALS. USA+45 USA-45 POL/PAR   CRIME
TAX LEGIT CT/SYS CHOOSE PRIVIL MORAL WEALTH 20   ADMIN
TRUMAN/HS PRESIDENT CONGRESS. PAGE 2 E0043   CHIEF
                                                        TRIBUTE

                                                        B56
US HOUSE RULES COMM,HEARINGS BEFORE A SPECIAL   ADMIN
SUBCOMMITTEE: ESTABLISHMENT OF A STANDING COMMITTEE   DOMIN
ON ADMINISTRATIVE PROCEDURE, PRACTICE. USA+45 LAW   DELIB/GP
EX/STRUC ADJUD CONTROL EXEC GOV/REL EFFICIENCY PWR   NAT/G
...POLICY INT 20 CONGRESS. PAGE 100 E2009

                                                        B56
WIGGINS J.R.,FREEDOM OR SECRECY. USA+45 USA-45   ORD/FREE
DELIB/GP EX/STRUC FORCES ADJUD SANCTION KNOWL PWR   PRESS
...AUD/VIS CONGRESS 20. PAGE 106 E2121   NAT/G
                                                        CONTROL

                                                        B57
BAYITCH S.A.,A GUIDE TO INTERAMERICAN LEGAL   BIBLIOG
STUDIES: A SELECTIVE BIBLIOGRAPHY OF WORKS IN   L/A+17C
ENGLISH. NAT/G LEGIS ADJUD CT/SYS CONGRESS 20.   LAW
PAGE 8 E0157   JURID

                                                        B57
LONG H.A.,USURPERS - FOES OF FREE MAN. LAW NAT/G   CT/SYS
CHIEF LEGIS DOMIN ADJUD REPRESENT GOV/REL ORD/FREE   CENTRAL
LAISSEZ POPULISM...POLICY 18/20 SUPREME/CT   FEDERAL
ROOSEVLT/F CONGRESS CON/INTERP. PAGE 66 E1325   CONSTN

                                                        B57
SCHUBERT G.A.,THE PRESIDENCY IN THE COURTS. CONSTN   PWR
FORCES DIPLOM TARIFFS ADJUD CONTROL WAR...DECISION   CT/SYS
MGT CHARTS 18/20 PRESIDENT CONGRESS SUPREME/CT.   LEGIT
PAGE 89 E1778   CHIEF

                                                        B57
US SENATE COMM ON JUDICIARY,HEARING BEFORE   LEGIS
SUBCOMMITTEE ON COMMITTEE OF JUDICIARY, UNITED   CONSTN
STATES SENATE: S. J. RES. 3. USA+45 NAT/G CONSULT   CONFER
DELIB/GP DIPLOM ADJUD LOBBY REPRESENT 20 CONGRESS   AGREE
TREATY. PAGE 102 E2040

                                                        B57
US SENATE COMM ON JUDICIARY,LIMITATION OF APPELLATE   CT/SYS
JURISDICTION OF THE SUPREME COURT. USA+45 LAW NAT/G   ADJUD
DELIB/GP PLAN ADMIN CONTROL PWR...DECISION 20   POLICY
CONGRESS SUPREME/CT. PAGE 102 E2041   GOV/REL

                                                        B57
US SENATE SPEC COMM POLIT ACT,REPORT OF SPECIAL   LOBBY
COMMITTEE TO INVESTIGATE POLITICAL ACTIVITIES,   LAW
LOBBYING, AND CAMPAIGN CONTRIBUTIONS. USA+45   ECO/TAC
BARGAIN CRIME ATTIT...DECISION 20 CONGRESS.   PARL/PROC
PAGE 103 E2061

                                                        B58
BLOCH J.,STATES' RIGHTS: THE LAW OF THE LAND.   PROVS
USA+45 USA-45 LAW CONSTN LEGIS CONTROL CT/SYS   NAT/G
FEDERAL ORD/FREE...PREDICT 17/20 CONGRESS   BAL/PWR
SUPREME/CT. PAGE 13 E0246   CENTRAL

                                                        B58
BUREAU OF NATIONAL AFFAIRS,THE MCCLELLAN COMMITTEE   DELIB/GP
HEARINGS - 1957. USA+45 LEGIS CONTROL CRIME   CONFER
...CHARTS 20 CONGRESS AFL/CIO MCCLELLN/J. PAGE 17   LABOR
E0336   MGT

                                                        B58
HAND L.,THE BILL OF RIGHTS. USA+45 USA-45 CHIEF   CONSTN
LEGIS BAL/PWR ROLE PWR 18/20 SUPREME/CT CONGRESS   JURID
AMEND/V PRESIDENT AMEND/XIV. PAGE 50 E0994   ORD/FREE
                                                        CT/SYS

                                                        B58
HENKIN L.,ARMS CONTROL AND INSPECTION IN AMERICAN   USA+45
LAW. LAW CONSTN INT/ORG LOC/G MUNIC NAT/G PROVS   JURID
EDU/PROP LEGIT EXEC NUC/PWR KNOWL ORD/FREE...OBS   ARMS/CONT
TOT/POP CONGRESS 20. PAGE 52 E1032

                                                        B58
HUNT B.I.,BIPARTISANSHIP: A CASE STUDY OF THE   FOR/AID
FOREIGN ASSISTANCE PROGRAM, 1947-56 (DOCTORAL   POL/PAR
THESIS). USA+45 INT/ORG CONSULT LEGIS TEC/DEV   GP/REL
...BIBLIOG PRESIDENT TREATY NATO TRUMAN/HS   DIPLOM
EISNHWR/DD CONGRESS. PAGE 56 E1114

                                                        B58
MACKENZIE W.J.M.,FREE ELECTIONS: AN ELEMENTARY   EX/STRUC
TEXTBOOK. WOR+45 NAT/G POL/PAR LEGIS TOP/EX   CHOOSE
EDU/PROP LEGIT CT/SYS ATTIT PWR...OBS CHARTS
STERTYP T CONGRESS PARLIAMENT 20. PAGE 67 E1342

                                                        B58
US CONGRESS,FREEDOM OF INFORMATION AND SECRECY IN   CHIEF
GOVERNMENT (2 VOLS.). USA+45 DELIB/GP EX/STRUC   PRIVIL
EDU/PROP PWR 20 CONGRESS PRESIDENT. PAGE 99 E1988   CONSTN
                                                        LAW

                                                        S58
RIKER W.H.,"THE PARADOX OF VOTING AND CONGRESSIONAL   PARL/PROC
RULES FOR VOTING ON AMENDMENTS." LAW DELIB/GP   DECISION
EX/STRUC PROB/SOLV CONFER DEBATE EFFICIENCY ATTIT   LEGIS
HOUSE/REP CONGRESS SENATE. PAGE 85 E1700   RATIONAL

                                                        B59
LOEWENSTEIN K.,VERFASSUNGSRECHT UND   CONSTN
VERFASSUNGSPRAXIS DER VEREINIGTEN STAATEN. USA+45   POL/PAR
USA-45 COLONIAL CT/SYS GP/REL RACE/REL ORD/FREE   EX/STRUC
...JURID 18/20 SUPREME/CT CONGRESS PRESIDENT   NAT/G
BILL/RIGHT CIVIL/LIB. PAGE 66 E1319

                                                        B59
US SENATE COMM ON JUDICIARY,EXECUTIVE PRIVILEGE.   CHIEF
USA+45 DELIB/GP CONTROL KNOWL PWR 20 CONGRESS   PRIVIL
PRESIDENT. PAGE 102 E2042   CONSTN
                                                        LAW

B59

US SENATE COMM ON POST OFFICE,TO PROVIDE FOR AN
EFFECTIVE SYSTEM OF PERSONNEL ADMINISTRATION.
EFFICIENCY...MGT 20 CONGRESS CIVIL/SERV POSTAL/SYS
YARBROGH/R. PAGE 103 E2059
ADMIN
NAT/G
EX/STRUC
LAW

B60

)B JUNZ A.J.,PRESENT TRENDS IN AMERICAN NATIONAL
GOVERNMENT. LEGIS DIPLOM ADMIN CT/SYS ORD/FREE
...CONCPT ANTHOL 20 CONGRESS PRESIDENT SUPREME/CT.
PAGE 2 E0040
POL/PAR
CHOOSE
CONSTN
NAT/G

B60

BLANSHARD P.,GOD AND MAN IN WASHINGTON. USA+45
CHIEF LEGIS LEGIT CT/SYS PRIVIL ATTIT ORD/FREE
...POLICY CONCPT 20 SUPREME/CT CONGRESS PRESIDENT
CHURCH/STA. PAGE 12 E0242
NAT/G
SECT
GP/REL
POL/PAR

B60

BYRD E.M. JR.,TREATIES AND EXECUTIVE AGREEMENTS IN
THE UNITED STATES: THEIR SEPARATE ROLES AND
LIMITATIONS. USA+45 USA-45 EX/STRUC TARIFFS CT/SYS
GOV/REL FEDERAL...IDEA/COMP BIBLIOG SUPREME/CT
SENATE CONGRESS. PAGE 18 E0353
CHIEF
INT/LAW
DIPLOM

B60

CARPER E.T.,THE DEFENSE APPROPRIATIONS RIDER
(PAMPHLET). USA+45 CONSTN CHIEF DELIB/GP LEGIS
BUDGET LOBBY CIVMIL/REL...POLICY 20 CONGRESS
EISNHWR/DD DEPT/DEFEN PRESIDENT BOSTON. PAGE 20
E0390
GOV/REL
ADJUD
LAW
CONTROL

B60

NAT'L MUNICIPAL LEAGUE,COMPENDIUM ON LEGISLATIVE
APPORTIONMENT. USA+45 LOC/G NAT/G POL/PAR PROVS
CT/SYS CHOOSE 20 SUPREME/CT CONGRESS. PAGE 76 E1523
APPORT
REPRESENT
LEGIS
STAT

B60

PRICE D.,THE SECRETARY OF STATE. USA+45 CONSTN
ELITES INTELL CHIEF EX/STRUC TOP/EX LEGIT ATTIT PWR
SKILL...DECISION 20 CONGRESS. PAGE 82 E1650
CONSULT
DIPLOM
INT/LAW

B60

SCHUBERT G.A.,CONSTITUTIONAL POLITICS: THE
POLITICAL BEHAVIOR OF SUPREME COURT JUSTICES AND
THE CONSTITUTIONAL POLICIES THEY MAKE. LAW ELITES
CHIEF DELIB/GP EX/STRUC LEGIS DISCRIM ORD/FREE PWR
...POLICY MAJORIT CHARTS SUPREME/CT CONGRESS.
PAGE 89 E1781
CONSTN
CT/SYS
JURID
DECISION

B60

US HOUSE COMM ON JUDICIARY,ESTABLISHMENT OF
CONGRESSIONAL DISTRICTS. USA+45 PROB/SOLV 20
CONGRESS HOUSE/REP. PAGE 100 E2003
APPORT
REPRESENT
LEGIS
LAW

S60

BLACK H.,"THE BILL OF RIGHTS" (BMR)" USA+45 USA-45
LAW LEGIS CT/SYS FEDERAL PWR 18/20 CONGRESS
SUPREME/CT BILL/RIGHT CIV/RIGHTS. PAGE 12 E0237
CONSTN
ORD/FREE
NAT/G
JURID

B61

PRITCHETT C.H.,CONGRESS VERSUS THE SUPREME COURT,
1957-1960. PROB/SOLV DOMIN EXEC GP/REL DISCRIM PWR
CONGRESS SUPREME/CT SUPREME/CT. PAGE 82 E1652
LEGIS
JURID
LAW

B61

SCOTT A.M.,POLITICS, USA; CASES ON THE AMERICAN
DEMOCRATIC PROCESS. USA+45 CHIEF FORCES DIPLOM
LOBBY CHOOSE RACE/REL FEDERAL ATTIT...JURID ANTHOL
T 20 PRESIDENT CONGRESS CIVIL/LIB. PAGE 90 E1795
CT/SYS
CONSTN
NAT/G
PLAN

B61

TOMPKINS D.C.,CONFLICT OF INTEREST IN THE FEDERAL
GOVERNMENT: A BIBLIOGRAPHY. USA+45 EX/STRUC LEGIS
ADJUD ADMIN CRIME CONGRESS PRESIDENT. PAGE 96 E1932
BIBLIOG
ROLE
NAT/G
LAW

B61

US CONGRESS,CONSTITUTIONAL RIGHTS OF THE MENTALLY
ILL. USA+45 LAW PUB/INST DELIB/GP ADJUD ORD/FREE
...PSY QU 20 CONGRESS. PAGE 99 E1989
HEALTH
CONSTN
JURID
CONFER

B61

WESTIN A.F.,THE SUPREME COURT: VIEWS FROM INSIDE.
USA+45 NAT/G PROF/ORG PROVS DELIB/GP INGP/REL
DISCRIM ATTIT...POLICY DECISION JURID ANTHOL 20
SUPREME/CT CONGRESS CIVIL/LIB. PAGE 106 E2114
CT/SYS
LAW
ADJUD
GOV/REL

B62

BERMAN D.M.,A BILL BECOMES A LAW: THE CIVIL RIGHTS
ACT OF 1960. USA+45 LAW POL/PAR LOBBY RACE/REL
KNOWL...CHARTS 20 CONGRESS NEGRO CIV/RIGHTS.
DISCRIM
PARL/PROC
JURID

GOV/REL

B62

BICKEL A.,THE LEAST DANGEROUS BRANCH. USA+45 USA-45
CONSTN SCHOOL LEGIS ADJUD RACE/REL ORD/FREE
...JURID 18/20 SUPREME/CT CONGRESS MARSHALL/J
HOLMES/OW FRANKFUR/F. PAGE 12 E0226
LAW
NAT/G
CT/SYS

B62

BUREAU OF NATIONAL AFFAIRS,FEDERAL-STATE REGULATION
OF WELFARE FUNDS (REV. ED.). USA+45 LAW LEGIS
DEBATE AGE/O 20 CONGRESS. PAGE 17 E0337
WELF/ST
WEALTH
PLAN
SOC/WK

B62

CARPER E.T.,ILLINOIS GOES TO CONGRESS FOR ARMY
LAND. USA+45 LAW EXTR/IND PROVS REGION CIVMIL/REL
GOV/REL FEDERAL ATTIT 20 ILLINOIS SENATE CONGRESS
DIRKSEN/E DOUGLAS/P. PAGE 20 E0391
ADMIN
LOBBY
GEOG
LEGIS

B62

HIRSCHFIELD R.S.,THE CONSTITUTION AND THE COURT.
SCHOOL WAR RACE/REL EQUILIB ORD/FREE...POLICY
MAJORIT DECISION JURID 18/20 PRESIDENT COLD/WAR
CIVIL/LIB SUPREME/CT CONGRESS. PAGE 53 E1051
ADJUD
PWR
CONSTN
LAW

B62

MURPHY W.F.,CONGRESS AND THE COURT. USA+45 LAW
LOBBY GP/REL RACE/REL ATTIT PWR...JURID INT BIBLIOG
CONGRESS SUPREME/CT WARRN/EARL. PAGE 75 E1509
LEGIS
CT/SYS
GOV/REL
ADJUD

B62

NAT'L MUNICIPAL LEAGUE,COMPENDIUM ON LEGISLATIVE
APPORTIONMENT. USA+45 LOC/G NAT/G POL/PAR PROVS
CT/SYS CHOOSE 20 SUPREME/CT CONGRESS. PAGE 76 E1524
APPORT
REPRESENT
LEGIS
STAT

B62

US CONGRESS,COMMUNICATIONS SATELLITE LEGISLATION:
HEARINGS BEFORE COMM ON AERON AND SPACE SCIENCES ON
BILLS S2550 AND 2814. WOR+45 LAW VOL/ASSN PLAN
DIPLOM CONTROL OWN PEACE...NEW/IDEA CONGRESS NASA.
PAGE 99 E1990
SPACE
COM/IND
ADJUD
GOV/REL

B62

US SENATE COMM ON JUDICIARY,CONSTITUTIONAL RIGHTS
OF MILITARY PERSONNEL. USA+45 USA-45 FORCES DIPLOM
WAR CONGRESS. PAGE 102 E2046
CONSTN
ORD/FREE
JURID
CT/SYS

N62

TWENTIETH CENTURY FUND,ONE MAN - ONE VOTE
(PAMPHLET). USA+45 CONSTN CONFER CT/SYS REGION
CONSEN FEDERAL ROLE...CENSUS 20 CONGRESS. PAGE 97
E1947
APPORT
LEGIS
REPRESENT
PROVS

B63

JACOBS P.,STATE OF UNIONS. USA+45 STRATA TOP/EX
GP/REL RACE/REL DEMAND DISCRIM ATTIT PWR 20
CONGRESS NEGRO HOFFA/J. PAGE 57 E1145
LABOR
ECO/TAC
BARGAIN
DECISION

B63

LEGISLATIVE REFERENCE SERVICE,DIGEST OF PUBLIC
GENERAL BILLS AND RESOLUTIONS. LAW COM/IND EDU/PROP
GOV/REL INGP/REL KNOWL...JURID 20 CONGRESS. PAGE 64
E1280
BIBLIOG/A
LEGIS
DELIB/GP
NAT/G

B63

NATIONAL CIVIC REVIEW,REAPPORTIONMENT: A YEAR IN
REVIEW (PAMPHLET). USA+45 LAW CT/SYS CHOOSE
ORD/FREE PWR...ANTHOL 20 CONGRESS. PAGE 76 E1527
APPORT
REPRESENT
LEGIS
CONSTN

B63

SCHMIDHAUSER J.R.,CONSTITUTIONAL LAW IN THE
POLITICAL PROCESS. SOCIETY LEGIS ADJUD CT/SYS
FEDERAL...SOC TREND IDEA/COMP ANTHOL T SUPREME/CT
SENATE CONGRESS HOUSE/REP. PAGE 88 E1761
LAW
CONSTN
JURID

B63

US CONGRESS: SENATE,HEARINGS OF THE COMMITTEE ON
THE JUDICIARY. USA+45 CONSTN NAT/G ADMIN GOV/REL 20
CONGRESS. PAGE 99 E1992
LEGIS
LAW
ORD/FREE
DELIB/GP

B63

US SENATE,DOCUMENTS ON INTERNATIONAL AS"ECTS OF
EXPLORATION AND USE OF OUTER SPACE, 1954-62: STAFF
REPORT FOR COMM AERON SPACE SCI. USA+45 USSR LEGIS
LEAD CIVMIL/REL PEACE...POLICY INT/LAW ANTHOL 20
CONGRESS NASA KHRUSH/N. PAGE 101 E2026
SPACE
UTIL
GOV/REL
DIPLOM

B63

US SENATE COMM ON JUDICIARY,US PERSONNEL SECURITY
PLAN

PRACTICES. USA+45 DELIB/GP ADJUD ADMIN ORD/FREE ...CHARTS 20 CONGRESS CIVIL/SERV. PAGE 102 E2049
NAT/G CONTROL WORKER

B64
ANASTAPLO G.,NOTES ON THE FIRST AMENDMENT TO THE CONSTITUTION OF THE UNITED STATES (PART TWO). USA+45 USA-45 NAT/G JUDGE DEBATE SUPEGO PWR SOVEREIGN 18/20 SUPREME/CT CONGRESS AMEND/I. PAGE 5 E0088
ORD/FREE CONSTN CT/SYS ATTIT

B64
ANDERSON J.W.,EISENHOWER, BROWNELL, AND THE CONGRESS - THE TANGLED ORIGINS OF THE CIVIL RIGHTS BILL OF 1956-1957. USA+45 POL/PAR LEGIS CREATE PROB/SOLV LOBBY GOV/REL RIGID/FLEX...NEW/IDEA 20 EISNHWR/DD CONGRESS BROWNELL/H CIV/RIGHTS. PAGE 5 E0090
LAW CONSTN POLICY NAT/G

B64
BUREAU OF NAT'L AFFAIRS,THE CIVIL RIGHTS ACT OF 1964. USA+45 LOC/G NAT/G DELIB/GP CONFER DEBATE DISCRIM...JURID 20 CONGRESS SUPREME/CT CIV/RIGHTS. PAGE 17 E0333
LEGIS RACE/REL LAW CONSTN

B64
COHEN M.,LAW AND POLITICS IN SPACE: SPECIFIC AND URGENT PROBLEMS IN THE LAW OF OUTER SPACE. CHINA/COM COM USA+45 USSR WOR+45 COM/IND INT/ORG NAT/G LEGIT NUC/PWR ATTIT BIO/SOC...JURID CONCPT CONGRESS 20 STALIN/J. PAGE 24 E0464
DELIB/GP LAW INT/LAW SPACE

B64
DANELSKI D.J.,A SUPREME COURT JUSTICE IS APPOINTED. CHIEF LEGIS CONFER DEBATE EXEC PERSON PWR...BIOG 20 CONGRESS PRESIDENT. PAGE 28 E0564
CHOOSE JUDGE DECISION

B64
KEEFE W.J.,THE AMERICAN LEGISLATIVE PROCESS: CONGRESS AND THE STATES. USA+45 LAW POL/PAR DELIB/GP DEBATE ADMIN LOBBY REPRESENT CONGRESS PRESIDENT. PAGE 60 E1191
LEGIS DECISION PWR PROVS

B64
MITCHELL B.,A BIOGRAPHY OF THE CONSTITUTION OF THE UNITED STATES. USA+45 USA-45 PROVS CHIEF LEGIS DEBATE ADJUD SUFF FEDERAL...SOC 18/20 SUPREME/CT CONGRESS SENATE HOUSE/REP PRESIDENT. PAGE 73 E1472
CONSTN LAW JURID

B64
TODD A.,JUSTICE ON TRIAL: THE CASE OF LOUIS D. BRANDEIS. TOP/EX DISCRIM...JURID 20 WILSON/W CONGRESS SUPREME/CT BRANDEIS/L SENATE. PAGE 96 E1929
PERSON RACE/REL PERS/REL NAT/G

B64
TOMPKINS D.C.,PRESIDENTIAL SUCCESSION. USA+45 CHIEF ADJUD 20 PRESIDENT CONGRESS. PAGE 96 E1933
BIBLIOG/A EX/STRUC CONSTN TOP/EX

B64
US HOUSE COMM ON JUDICIARY,CONGRESSIONAL REDISTRICTING. USA+45 PROVS DELIB/GP 20 CONGRESS. PAGE 100 E2005
APPORT REPRESENT LEGIS LAW

B64
US HOUSE COMM ON JUDICIARY,IMMIGRATION HEARINGS. DELIB/GP STRANGE HABITAT...GEOG JURID 20 CONGRESS MIGRATION. PAGE 100 E2006
NAT/G POLICY DIPLOM NAT/LISM

B64
US SENATE COMM ON JUDICIARY,HEARINGS BEFORE SUBCOMMITTEE ON ANTITRUST AND MONOPOLY: ECONOMIC CONCENTRATION VOLUMES 1-5 JULY 1964-SEPT 1966. USA+45 LAW FINAN ECO/TAC ADJUD COST EFFICIENCY PRODUC...STAT CHARTS 20 CONGRESS MONOPOLY. PAGE 102 E2052
ECO/DEV CONTROL MARKET LG/CO

B64
WAY H.F. JR.,LIBERTY IN THE BALANCE - CURRENT ISSUES IN CIVIL LIBERTIES. USA+45 USA-45 DELIB/GP RACE/REL DISCRIM TOTALISM MARXISM SOCISM...CONCPT 20 CONGRESS SUPREME/CT CIVIL/LIB. PAGE 105 E2104
ORD/FREE EDU/PROP NAT/G JURID

S64
DERWINSKI E.J.,"THE COST OF THE INTERNATIONAL COFFEE AGREEMENT." L/A+17C USA+45 WOR+45 ECO/UNDEV NAT/G VOL/ASSN LEGIS DIPLOM ECO/TAC FOR/AID LEGIT ATTIT...TIME/SEQ CONGRESS 20 TREATY. PAGE 31 E0608
MARKET DELIB/GP INT/TRADE

B65
BELL J.,THE JOHNSON TREATMENT: HOW LYNDON JOHNSON TOOK OVER THE PRESIDENCY AND MADE IT HIS OWN.
INGP/REL TOP/EX

USA+45 DELIB/GP DIPLOM ADJUD MURDER CHOOSE PERSON PWR...POLICY OBS INT TIME 20 JOHNSON/LB KENNEDY/JF PRESIDENT CONGRESS. PAGE 10 E0183
CONTROL NAT/G

B65
BOCK E.,GOVERNMENT REGULATION OF BUSINESS. USA+45 LAW EX/STRUC LEGIS EXEC ORD/FREE PWR...ANTHOL CONGRESS. PAGE 13 E0255
MGT ADMIN NAT/G CONTROL

B65
CONGRESSIONAL QUARTERLY SERV,REVOLUTION IN CIVIL RIGHTS. USA+45 USA-45 LEGIS ADJUD CT/SYS CHOOSE DISCRIM...DECISION CONGRESS SUPREME/CT. PAGE 25 E0488
LAW CONSTN RACE/REL LOBBY

B65
CONGRESSIONAL QUARTERLY SERV,POLITICS IN AMERICA, 1945-1964: THE POLITICS AND ISSUES OF THE POSTWAR YEARS. USA+45 LAW FINAN CHIEF DIPLOM APPORT SUFF ...POLICY STAT TREND CHARTS 20 CONGRESS PRESIDENT. PAGE 25 E0489
CHOOSE REPRESENT POL/PAR LEGIS

B65
GILLETTE W.,THE RIGHT TO VOTE: POLITICS AND THE PASSAGE OF THE FIFTEENTH AMENDMENT. USA-45 LAW LEAD DISCRIM SEGREGAT CONGRESS. PAGE 44 E0863
RACE/REL CONSTN

B65
KEEFE W.J.,THE AMERICAN LEGISLATIVE PROCESS. USA+45 CONSTN POL/PAR CT/SYS REPRESENT FEDERAL ATTIT PLURISM...MAJORIT 20 CONGRESS PRESIDENT. PAGE 60 E1192
LEGIS NAT/G CHIEF GOV/REL

B65
MCKAY R.B.,REAPPORTIONMENT: THE LAW AND POLITICS OF EQUAL REPRESENTATION. FUT USA+45 PROVS BAL/PWR ADJUD CHOOSE REPRESENT GOV/REL FEDERAL...JURID BIBLIOG 20 SUPREME/CT CONGRESS. PAGE 71 E1420
APPORT MAJORIT LEGIS PWR

B65
US SENATE,US INTERNATIONAL SPACE PROGRAMS, 1959-65: STAFF REPORT FOR COMM ON AERONAUTICAL AND SPACE SCIENCES. WOR+45 VOL/ASSN CIVMIL/REL 20 CONGRESS NASA TREATY. PAGE 101 E2027
SPACE DIPLOM PLAN GOV/REL

B65
US SENATE COMM ON JUDICIARY,HEARINGS BEFORE SUBCOMMITTEE ON ADMINISTRATIVE PRACTICE AND PROCEDURE ABOUT ADMINISTRATIVE PROCEDURE ACT 1965. USA+45 LEGIS EDU/PROP ADJUD GOV/REL INGP/REL EFFICIENCY...POLICY INT 20 CONGRESS. PAGE 103 E2055
ROUTINE DELIB/GP ADMIN NAT/G

B65
US SENATE COMM ON JUDICIARY,ANTITRUST EXEMPTIONS FOR AGREEMENTS RELATING TO BALANCE OF PAYMENTS. FINAN ECO/TAC CONTROL WEALTH...POLICY 20 CONGRESS. PAGE 103 E2056
BAL/PAY ADJUD MARKET INT/TRADE

S65
FOX A.B.,"NATO AND CONGRESS." CONSTN DELIB/GP EX/STRUC FORCES TOP/EX BUDGET NUC/PWR GOV/REL ...GP/COMP CONGRESS NATO TREATY. PAGE 39 E0779
CONTROL DIPLOM

B66
AUERBACH J.S.,LABOR AND LIBERTY; THE LA FOLLETTE COMMITTEE AND THE NEW DEAL. USA-45 LAW LEAD RESPECT SOCISM...BIBLIOG 20 CONGRESS BILL/RIGHT LAFOLLET/R NEW/DEAL. PAGE 6 E0117
DELIB/GP LABOR CONSTN ORD/FREE

B66
BEISER E.N.,THE TREATMENT OF LEGISLATIVE APPORTIONMENT BY THE STATE AND FEDERAL COURTS (DISSERTATION). USA+45 CONSTN NAT/G PROVS LEGIS CHOOSE REPRESENT ATTIT...POLICY BIBLIOG 20 CONGRESS SUPREME/CT. PAGE 9 E0181
CT/SYS APPORT ADJUD PWR

B66
CONG QUARTERLY SERVICE,REPRESENTATION AND APPORTIONMENT. USA+45 USA-45 POL/PAR CT/SYS SUFF ...POLICY 20 CONGRESS SUPREME/CT. PAGE 25 E0486
APPORT LEGIS REPRESENT CONSTN

B66
FRIED R.C.,COMPARATIVE POLITICAL INSTITUTIONS. USSR EX/STRUC FORCES LEGIS JUDGE CONTROL REPRESENT ALL/IDEOS 20 CONGRESS BUREAUCRCY. PAGE 40 E0798
NAT/G PWR EFFICIENCY GOV/COMP

B66
HAMILTON H.D.,REAPPORTIONING LEGISLATURES. USA+45 CONSTN POL/PAR PROVS LEGIS COMPUTER ADJUD CHOOSE ATTIT...ANTHOL 20 SUPREME/CT CONGRESS. PAGE 50 E0989
APPORT REPRESENT PHIL/SCI PWR

B66
HOLTZMAN A.,INTEREST GROUPS AND LOBBYING. USA+45   LOBBY
CHIEF ACT/RES ADJUD LEAD PARTIC CHOOSE...POLICY 20   NAT/G
CONGRESS. PAGE 55 E1092   EDU/PROP
                                                    GP/REL

B66
US SENATE COMM ON JUDICIARY,HEARINGS ON FREE PRESS   PRESS
AND FAIR TRIAL (2 VOLS.). USA+45 CONSTN ELITES   LAW
LEGIS EDU/PROP CT/SYS LEAD CONGRESS. PAGE 103 E2057 CRIME
                                                    ORD/FREE

B66
WASHINGTON S.H.,BIBLIOGRAPHY: LABOR-MANAGEMENT   BIBLIOG
RELATIONS ACT, 1947 AS AMENDED BY LABOR-MANAGEMENT   LAW
REPORTING AND DISCLOSURE ACT, 1959. USA+45 CONSTN   LABOR
INDUS DELIB/GP LEGIS WORKER BARGAIN ECO/TAC ADJUD   MGT
GP/REL NEW/LIB...JURID CONGRESS. PAGE 105 E2100

B67
BIBBY J.,ON CAPITOL HILL. POL/PAR LOBBY PARL/PROC   CONFER
GOV/REL PERS/REL...JURID PHIL/SCI OBS INT BIBLIOG   LEGIS
20 CONGRESS PRESIDENT. PAGE 12 E0224   CREATE
                                                    LEAD

B67
FINCHER F.,THE GOVERNMENT OF THE UNITED STATES.   NAT/G
USA+45 USA-45 POL/PAR CHIEF CT/SYS LOBBY GP/REL   EX/STRUC
INGP/REL...CONCPT CHARTS BIBLIOG T 18/20 PRESIDENT   LEGIS
CONGRESS SUPREME/CT. PAGE 38 E0749   OP/RES

B67
JONES C.O.,EVERY SECOND YEAR: CONGRESSIONAL   EFFICIENCY
BEHAVIOR AND THE TWO-YEAR TERM. LAW POL/PAR   LEGIS
PROB/SOLV DEBATE CHOOSE PERS/REL COST FEDERAL PWR   TIME/SEQ
...CHARTS 20 CONGRESS SENATE HOUSE/REP. PAGE 59   NAT/G
E1172

B67
LONG E.V.,THE INTRUDERS: THE INVASION OF PRIVACY BY LAW
GOVERNMENT AND INDUSTRY. USA+45 COM/IND INDUS LEGIS PARTIC
TASK PERS/REL...JURID 20 CONGRESS. PAGE 66 E1324   NAT/G

B67
US SENATE COMM ON FOREIGN REL,CONSULAR CONVENTION   LEGIS
WITH THE SOVIET UNION. USA+45 USSR DELIB/GP LEAD   LOBBY
REPRESENT ATTIT ORD/FREE CONGRESS TREATY. PAGE 101   DIPLOM
E2031

S67
"THE FEDERAL AGRICULTURAL STABILIZATION PROGRAM AND AGRI
THE NEGRO." LAW CONSTN PLAN REPRESENT DISCRIM   CONTROL
ORD/FREE 20 NEGRO CONGRESS. PAGE 2 E0039   NAT/G
                                                    RACE/REL

S67
ANDERSON W.,"THE PERILS OF 'SHARING'." USA+45   BUDGET
ECO/TAC RECEIVE LOBBY GOV/REL CENTRAL COST INCOME   TAX
...POLICY PLURIST CONGRESS. PAGE 5 E0095   FEDERAL
                                                    LAW

S67
VAUGHN W.P.,"SEPARATE AND UNEQUAL: THE CIVIL RIGHTS LAW
ACT OF 1875 AND DEFEAT OF THE SCHOOL INTEGRATION   DISCRIM
CLAUSE." USA-45 LEGIS RACE/REL 19 CONGRESS.   EDU/PROP
PAGE 103 E2073   PARL/PROC

S67
WILSON G.D.,"CRIMINAL SANCTIONS AGAINST PASSPORT   LAW
AREA-RESTRICTION VIOLATIONS." USA+45 ADJUD CRIME   SANCTION
GOV/REL DEPT/STATE CONGRESS. PAGE 106 E2127   LICENSE
                                                    POLICY

L86
WHITRIDGE L.I.,"LEGISLATIVE INQUESTS" USA-45 ADJUD   CT/SYS
GOV/REL SOVEREIGN 19/20 CONGRESS. PAGE 106 E2120   LEGIS
                                                    JURID
                                                    CONSTN

CONGRESS/P....CONGRESS PARTY (ALL NATIONS)

CONGRESSIONAL QUARTERLY SERV E0487,E0488,E0489,E0490

CONNECTICT....CONNECTICUT

B60
POWELL T.,THE SCHOOL BUS LAW: A CASE STUDY IN   JURID
EDUCATION, RELIGION, AND POLITICS. USA+45 LAW NEIGH SCHOOL
SECT LEGIS EDU/PROP ADJUD CT/SYS LOBBY CATHISM
WORSHIP 20 CONNECTICT CHURCH/STA. PAGE 82 E1641

B65
SNOW J.H.,REAPPORTIONMENT. LAW CONSTN NAT/G GOV/REL APPORT
ORD/FREE...JURID 20 SUPREME/CT CONNECTICT. PAGE 92   ADJUD
E1848   LEGIS
                                                    PROVS

CONOVER H.F. E0491,E0492,E0493,E0494,E0495,E0496

CONRAD/JOS....JOSEPH CONRAD

CONRING E. E0497

CONSCIENCE....SEE SUPEGO

CONSCN/OBJ....CONSCIENTIOUS OBJECTION TO WAR AND KILLING

B17
DE VICTORIA F.,DE INDIS ET DE JURE BELLI (1557) IN   WAR
F. DE VICTORIA, DE INDIS ET DE JURE BELLI   INT/LAW
REFLECTIONES. UNIV NAT/G SECT CHIEF PARTIC COERCE   OWN
PEACE MORAL...POLICY 16 INDIAN/AM CHRISTIAN
CONSCN/OBJ. PAGE 30 E0598

B64
GIANNELLA D.A.,RELIGION AND THE PUBLIC ORDER: AN   SECT
ANNUAL REVIEW OF CHURCH AND STATE, AND OF RELIGION, NAT/G
LAW, AND SOCIETY. USA+45 LAW SOCIETY FAM POL/PAR   CONSTN
SCHOOL GIVE EDU/PROP GP/REL...JURID GEN/LAWS   ORD/FREE
BIBLIOG/A 20 CHURCH/STA BIRTH/CON CONSCN/OBJ
NATURL/LAW. PAGE 43 E0855

CONSCRIPTN....CONSCRIPTION

CONSEN....CONSENSUS

B05
GRIFFIN A.P.C.,LIST OF REFERENCES ON PRIMARY   BIBLIOG/A
ELECTIONS (PAMPHLET). USA-45 LAW LOC/G DELIB/GP   POL/PAR
LEGIS OP/RES TASK REPRESENT CONSEN...DECISION 19/20 CHOOSE
CONGRESS. PAGE 47 E0928   POPULISM

B28
BENTHAM J.,A COMMENT OF THE COMMENTARIES (1765-69). LAW
MUNIC SECT ADJUD AGREE CT/SYS CONSEN HAPPINESS   CONCPT
ORD/FREE 18. PAGE 10 E0191   IDEA/COMP

B40
FULLER G.H.,A SELECTED LIST OF RECENT REFERENCES ON BIBLIOG/A
THE CONSTITUTION OF THE UNITED STATES (PAMPHLET).   CONSTN
CULTURE NAT/G LEGIS CONFER ADJUD GOV/REL CONSEN   LAW
POPULISM...JURID CONCPT 18/20 CONGRESS. PAGE 41   USA-45
E0820

B47
LOCKE J.,TWO TREATISES OF GOVERNMENT (1690). UK LAW CONCPT
SOCIETY LEGIS LEGIT AGREE REV OWN HEREDITY MORAL   ORD/FREE
CONSERVE...POLICY MAJORIT 17 WILLIAM/3 NATURL/LAW.   NAT/G
PAGE 66 E1316   CONSEN

B54
JAMES L.F.,THE SUPREME COURT IN AMERICAN LIFE.   ADJUD
USA+45 USA-45 CONSTN CRIME GP/REL INGP/REL RACE/REL CT/SYS
CONSEN FEDERAL PERSON ORD/FREE 18/20 SUPREME/CT   JURID
DEPRESSION CIV/RIGHTS CHURCH/STA FREE/SPEE. PAGE 58 DECISION
E1147

B55
HOGAN W.N.,INTERNATIONAL CONFLICT AND COLLECTIVE   INT/ORG
SECURITY: THE PRINCIPLE OF CONCERN IN INTERNATIONAL WAR
ORGANIZATION. CONSTN EX/STRUC BAL/PWR DIPLOM ADJUD   ORD/FREE
CONTROL CENTRAL CONSEN PEACE...INT/LAW CONCPT   FORCES
METH/COMP 20 UN LEAGUE/NAT. PAGE 53 E1066

B59
FERRY W.H.,THE CORPORATION AND THE ECONOMY. CLIENT   LG/CO
LAW CONSTN LABOR NAT/G PLAN INT/TRADE PARTIC CONSEN CONTROL
ORD/FREE PWR POLICY. PAGE 37 E0742   REPRESENT

B61
BENNETT G.,THE KENYATTA ELECTION: KENYA 1960-1961.   CHOOSE
AFR INGP/REL RACE/REL CONSEN ATTIT 20 KENYATTA.   POL/PAR
PAGE 10 E0187   LAW
                                                    SUFF

B61
FREUND P.A.,THE SUPREME COURT OF THE UNITED STATES: CT/SYS
ITS BUSINESS, PURPOSES, AND PERFORMANCE. CONSTN   JURID
CRIME CONSEN ORD/FREE...DECISION 20 SUPREME/CT   ADJUD
CIVIL/LIB. PAGE 40 E0797   FEDERAL

N62
TWENTIETH CENTURY FUND,ONE MAN - ONE VOTE   APPORT
(PAMPHLET). USA+45 CONSTN CONFER CT/SYS REGION   LEGIS
CONSEN FEDERAL ROLE...CENSUS 20 CONGRESS. PAGE 97   REPRESENT
E1947   PROVS

B63
FAWCETT J.E.S.,THE BRITISH COMMONWEALTH IN   INT/LAW
INTERNATIONAL LAW. LAW INT/ORG NAT/G VOL/ASSN   STRUCT
OP/RES DIPLOM ADJUD CENTRAL CONSEN...NET/THEORY   COLONIAL
CMN/WLTH TREATY. PAGE 36 E0723

B63
MURPHY T.J.,CENSORSHIP: GOVERNMENT AND OBSCENITY. ORD/FREE
USA+45 CULTURE LEGIS JUDGE EDU/PROP CONTROL MORAL
INGP/REL RATIONAL POPULISM...CATH JURID 20. PAGE 75 LAW
E1507 CONSEN

S64
BARKUN M.,"CONFLICT RESOLUTION THROUGH IMPLICIT CONSULT
MEDIATION." UNIV BARGAIN CONSEN FEDERAL JURID. CENTRAL
PAGE 8 E0149 INT/LAW
IDEA/COMP

B65
SMITH R.C.,THEY CLOSED THEIR SCHOOLS. USA+45 NEIGH RACE/REL
ADJUD CROWD CONSEN WEALTH...DECISION OBS INT 20 DISCRIM
NEGRO VIRGINIA. PAGE 92 E1846 LOC/G
SCHOOL

S65
FRIEDHEIM R.,"THE 'SATISFIED' AND 'DISSATISFIED' INT/LAW
STATES NEGOTIATE INTERNATIONAL LAW* A CASE STUDY." RECORD
DIPLOM CONFER ADJUD CONSEN PEACE ATTIT UN. PAGE 40
E0799

B66
JACOBSON H.K.,DIPLOMATS, SCIENTISTS, AND DIPLOM
POLITICIANS* THE UNITED STATES AND THE NUCLEAR TEST ARMS/CONT
BAN NEGOTIATIONS. USA+45 USSR ACT/RES PLAN CONFER TECHRACY
DETER NUC/PWR CONSEN ORD/FREE...INT TREATY. PAGE 57 INT/ORG
E1146

B66
MERILLAT H.C.L.,LEGAL ADVISERS AND INTERNATIONAL INT/ORG
ORGANIZATIONS. LAW NAT/G CONSULT OP/RES ADJUD INT/LAW
SANCTION TASK CONSEN ORG/CHARTS. PAGE 72 E1441 CREATE
OBS

S66
BROWNLIE I.,"NUCLEAR PROLIFERATION* SOME PROBLEMS NUC/PWR
OF CONTROL." USA+45 USSR ECO/UNDEV INT/ORG FORCES ARMS/CONT
TEC/DEV REGION CONSEN...RECORD TREATY. PAGE 16 VOL/ASSN
E0318 ORD/FREE

S66
FINE R.I.,"PEACE-KEEPING COSTS AND ARTICLE 19 OF FORCES
THE UN CHARTER* AN INVITATION TO RESPONSIBILITY." COST
INT/ORG NAT/G ADJUD CT/SYS CHOOSE CONSEN...RECORD CONSTN
IDEA/COMP UN. PAGE 38 E0750

B67
US SENATE COMM ON FOREIGN REL,A SELECT CHRONOLOGY ISLAM
AND BACKGROUND DOCUMENTS RELATING TO THE MIDDLE TIME/SEQ
EAST. ISRAEL UAR LAW INT/ORG FORCES PROB/SOLV DIPLOM
CONFER CONSEN PEACE ATTIT...POLICY 20 UN SENATE
TRUMAN/HS. PAGE 101 E2033

L67
LISSITZYN O.J.,"TREATIES AND CHANGED CIRCUMSTANCES AGREE
(REBUS SIC STANTIBUS)" WOR+45 CONSEN...JURID 20. DIPLOM
PAGE 65 E1307 INT/LAW

CONSENSUS....SEE CONSEN

CONSERVATISM....SEE CONSERVE

CONSERVE....TRADITIONALISM

B03
FAGUET E.,LE LIBERALISME. FRANCE PRESS ADJUD ADMIN ORD/FREE
DISCRIM CONSERVE SOCISM...TRADIT SOC LING WORSHIP EDU/PROP
PARLIAMENT. PAGE 36 E0711 NAT/G
LAW

C05
DUNNING W.A.,"HISTORY OF POLITICAL THEORIES FROM PHIL/SCI
LUTHER TO MONTESQUIEU." LAW NAT/G SECT DIPLOM REV CONCPT
WAR ORD/FREE SOVEREIGN CONSERVE...TRADIT BIBLIOG GEN/LAWS
16/18. PAGE 33 E0663

C20
DUNNING W.A.,"A HISTORY OF POLITICAL THINKERS FROM IDEA/COMP
ROUSSEAU TO SPENCER." NAT/G REV NAT/LISM UTIL PHIL/SCI
CONSERVE MARXISM POPULISM...JURID BIBLIOG 18/19. CONCPT
PAGE 33 E0664 GEN/LAWS

B26
FORTESCUE J.,THE GOVERNANCE OF ENGLAND (1471-76). CONSERVE
UK LAW FINAN SECT LEGIS PROB/SOLV TAX DOMIN ADMIN CONSTN
GP/REL COST ORD/FREE PWR 14/15. PAGE 39 E0776 CHIEF
NAT/G

B27
GOOCH G.P.,ENGLISH DEMOCRATIC IDEAS IN THE IDEA/COMP
SEVENTEENTH CENTURY (2ND ED.). UK LAW SECT FORCES MAJORIT
DIPLOM LEAD PARL/PROC REV ATTIT AUTHORIT...ANARCH EX/STRUC
CONCPT 17 PARLIAMENT CMN/WLTH REFORMERS. PAGE 45 CONSERVE

E0885

B27
JOHN OF SALISBURY,THE STATESMAN'S BOOK (1159) NAT/G
(TRANS. BY J. DICKINSON). DOMIN GP/REL MORAL SECT
ORD/FREE PWR CONSERVE...CATH CONCPT 12. PAGE 59 CHIEF
E1169 LAW

B28
HOBBES T.,THE ELEMENTS OF LAW, NATURAL AND POLITIC PERSON
(1650). STRATA NAT/G SECT CHIEF AGREE ATTIT LAW
ALL/VALS MORAL ORD/FREE POPULISM...POLICY CONCPT. SOVEREIGN
PAGE 53 E1056 CONSERVE

C43
BENTHAM J.,"ON THE LIBERTY OF THE PRESS, AND PUBLIC ORD/FREE
DISCUSSION" IN J. BOWRING, ED., THE WORKS OF JEREMY PRESS
BENTHAM." SPAIN UK LAW ELITES NAT/G LEGIS INSPECT CONFER
LEGIT WRITING CONTROL PRIVIL TOTALISM AUTHORIT CONSERVE
...TRADIT 19 FREE/SPEE. PAGE 10 E0193

B44
FULLER G.H.,TURKEY: A SELECTED LIST OF REFERENCES. BIBLIOG/A
ISLAM TURKEY CULTURE ECO/UNDEV AGRI DIPLOM NAT/LISM ALL/VALS
CONSERVE...GEOG HUM INT/LAW SOC 7/20 MAPS. PAGE 42 CONSERVE
E0824

S44
GRIFFITH E.S.,"THE CHANGING PATTERN OF PUBLIC LAW
POLICY FORMATION." MOD/EUR WOR+45 FINAN CHIEF POLICY
CONFER ADMIN LEAD CONSERVE SOCISM TECHRACY...SOC TEC/DEV
CHARTS CONGRESS. PAGE 47 E0938

B47
LOCKE J.,TWO TREATISES OF GOVERNMENT (1690). UK LAW CONCPT
SOCIETY LEGIS LEGIT AGREE REV OWN HEREDITY MORAL ORD/FREE
CONSERVE...POLICY MAJORIT 17 WILLIAM/3 NATURL/LAW. NAT/G
PAGE 66 E1316 CONSEN

B48
CORWIN E.S.,LIBERTY AGAINST GOVERNMENT: THE RISE, CONCPT
FLOWERING AND DECLINE OF A FAMOUS JURIDICAL ORD/FREE
CONCEPT. LEGIS ADJUD CT/SYS SANCTION GOV/REL JURID
FEDERAL CONSERVE NEW/LIB...OLD/LIB 18/20 ROMAN/LAW CONSTN
COMMON/LAW. PAGE 26 E0514

B53
KIRK R.,THE CONSERVATIVE MIND. POL/PAR ORD/FREE CONSERVE
...JURID CONCPT 18/20. PAGE 61 E1220 PERSON
PHIL/SCI
IDEA/COMP

B54
HAMSON C.J.,EXECUTIVE DISCRETION AND JUDICIAL ELITES
CONTROL; AN ASPECT OF THE FRENCH CONSEIL D'ETAT. ADJUD
EUR+WWI FRANCE MOD/EUR UK NAT/G EX/STRUC PARTIC NAT/COMP
CONSERVE...JURID BIBLIOG/A 18/20 SUPREME/CT.
PAGE 50 E0992

S59
DERGE D.R.,"THE LAWYER AS DECISION-MAKER IN THE LEGIS
AMERICAN STATE LEGISLATURE." INTELL LOC/G POL/PAR LAW
CHOOSE AGE HEREDITY PERSON CONSERVE...JURID STAT DECISION
CHARTS. PAGE 31 E0607 LEAD

B60
BERTHOLD O.,KAISER, VOLK UND AVIGNON. GERMANY CHIEF DIPLOM
LEGIT LEAD NAT/LISM CONSERVE 14 POPE CHRUCH/STA CATHISM
LUDWIG/BAV JOHN/XXII. PAGE 11 E0217 JURID

B60
PAUL A.M.,CONSERVATIVE CRISIS AND THE RULE OF LAW. CONSTN
USA-45 LABOR WORKER ATTIT ORD/FREE CONSERVE LAISSEZ ADJUD
...DECISION JURID 19 SUPREME/CT. PAGE 80 E1603 STRUCT
PROF/ORG

B60
PICKLES D.,THE FIFTH FRENCH REPUBLIC. ALGERIA CONSTN
FRANCE CHOOSE GOV/REL ATTIT CONSERVE...CHARTS 20 ADJUD
DEGAULLE/C. PAGE 80 E1615 NAT/G
EFFICIENCY

B63
LIVELY E.,THE INVASION OF MISSISSIPPI. USA+45 LAW RACE/REL
CONSTN NAT/G PROVS CT/SYS GOV/REL FEDERAL CONSERVE CROWD
...TRADIT 20 MISSISSIPP NEGRO NAACP WARRN/EARL COERCE
KENNEDY/JF. PAGE 66 E1309 MARXISM

B63
ROBERT J.,LA MONARCHIE MAROCAINE. MOROCCO LABOR CHIEF
MUNIC POL/PAR EX/STRUC ORD/FREE PWR...JURID TREND T CONSERVE
20. PAGE 85 E1702 ADMIN
CONSTN

B65
ANDRUS H.L.,LIBERALISM, CONSERVATISM, MORMONISM. SECT

USA+45 PLAN ADJUD CONTROL HAPPINESS ORD/FREE
CONSERVE NEW/LIB WORSHIP 20. PAGE 5 E0097
UTOPIA
MORAL

B65

MOELLER R.,LUDWIG DER BAYER UND DIE KURIE IM KAMPF
UM DAS REICH. GERMANY LAW SECT LEGIT LEAD GP/REL
CATHISM CONSERVE 14 LUDWIG/BAV POPE CHURCH/STA.
PAGE 74 E1478
JURID
CHIEF
CHOOSE
NAT/LISM

B65

SCHUBERT G.,THE JUDICIAL MIND: THE ATTITUDES AND
IDEOLOGIES OF SUPREME COURT JUSTICES 1946-1963.
USA+45 ELITES NAT/G CONTROL PERS/REL MAJORITY
CONSERVE...DECISION JURID MODAL STAT TREND GP/COMP
GAME. PAGE 88 E1774
CT/SYS
JUDGE
ATTIT
NEW/LIB

B66

HOGUE A.R.,ORIGINS OF THE COMMON LAW. UK STRUCT
AGRI CT/SYS SANCTION CONSERVE 12/14 ENGLSH/LAW
COMMON/LAW. PAGE 54 E1068
LAW
SOCIETY
CONSTN

B66

KERR M.H.,ISLAMIC REFORM: THE POLITICAL AND LEGAL
THEORIES OF MUHAMMAD 'ABDUH AND RASHID RIDA. NAT/G
SECT LEAD SOVEREIGN CONSERVE...JURID BIBLIOG
WORSHIP 20. PAGE 60 E1204
LAW
CONCPT
ISLAM

B67

BAILEY N.A.,LATIN AMERICA IN WORLD POLITICS. PWR
CONSERVE MARXISM...INT/LAW TREND BIBLIOG/A T OAS
COLD/WAR. PAGE 7 E0134
L/A+17C
DIPLOM
INT/ORG
ATTIT

B87

ADAMS J.,A DEFENSE OF THE CONSTITUTIONS OF
GOVERNMENT OF THE UNITED STATES OF AMERICA. USA-45
STRATA CHIEF EX/STRUC LEGIS CT/SYS CONSERVE
POPULISM...CONCPT CON/ANAL GOV/COMP. PAGE 3 E0048
CONSTN
BAL/PWR
PWR
NAT/G

CONSRV/PAR....CONSERVATIVE PARTY (ALL NATIONS)

CONSTITUTION....SEE CONSTN

CONSTN....CONSTITUTIONS

N

KEITT L.,AN ANNOTATED BIBLIOGRAPHY OF
BIBLIOGRAPHIES OF STATUTORY MATERIALS OF THE UNITED
STATES. CHRIST-17C USA-45 LEGIS ADJUD COLONIAL
CT/SYS...JURID 16/20. PAGE 60 E1196
BIBLIOG/A
LAW
CONSTN
PROVS

N

AMERICAN JOURNAL OF INTERNATIONAL LAW. WOR+45
WOR-45 CONSTN INT/ORG NAT/G CT/SYS ARMS/CONT WAR
...DECISION JURID NAT/COMP 20. PAGE 1 E0001
BIBLIOG/A
INT/LAW
DIPLOM
ADJUD

N

INDEX TO LEGAL PERIODICALS. CANADA NEW/ZEALND UK
USA+45 USA-45 CONSTN LEGIS JUDGE ADJUD ADMIN
CONTROL CT/SYS FEDERAL...CRIMLGY INT/LAW 20
CMN/WLTH AUSTRAL. PAGE 1 E0006
BIBLIOG
INDEX
LAW
JURID

N

JOURNAL OF POLITICS. USA+45 USA-45 CONSTN POL/PAR
EX/STRUC LEGIS PROB/SOLV DIPLOM CT/SYS CHOOSE
RACE/REL 20. PAGE 1 E0011
BIBLIOG/A
NAT/G
LAW
LOC/G

N

MIDWEST JOURNAL OF POLITICAL SCIENCE. USA+45 CONSTN
ECO/DEV LEGIS PROB/SOLV CT/SYS LEAD GOV/REL ATTIT
POLICY. PAGE 1 E0012
BIBLIOG/A
NAT/G
DIPLOM
POL/PAR

N

POLITICAL SCIENCE QUARTERLY. USA+45 USA-45 LAW
CONSTN ECO/DEV INT/ORG LOC/G POL/PAR LEGIS LEAD
NUC/PWR...CONCPT 20. PAGE 1 E0013
BIBLIOG/A
NAT/G
DIPLOM
POLICY

N

BIBLIOGRAPHIE DER SOZIALWISSENSCHAFTEN. WOR-45
CONSTN SOCIETY ECO/DEV ECO/UNDEV DIPLOM LEAD WAR
PEACE...PHIL/SCI SOC 19/20. PAGE 1 E0019
BIBLIOG
LAW
CONCPT
NAT/G

N

THE JAPAN SCIENCE REVIEW: LAW AND POLITICS: LIST OF
BOOKS AND ARTICLES ON LAW AND POLITICS. CONSTN AGRI
INDUS LABOR DIPLOM TAX ADMIN CRIME...INT/LAW SOC 20
CHINJAP. PAGE 2 E0027
BIBLIOG
LAW
S/ASIA
PHIL/SCI

N

NEUE POLITISCHE LITERATUR; BERICHTE UBER DAS
INTERNATIONALE SCHRIFTTUM ZUR POLITIK. WOR+45 LAW
BIBLIOG/A
DIPLOM

CONSTN POL/PAR ADMIN LEAD GOV/REL...POLICY
IDEA/COMP. PAGE 2 E0028
NAT/G
NAT/COMP

N

ASIA FOUNDATION,LIBRARY NOTES. LAW CONSTN CULTURE
SOCIETY ECO/UNDEV INT/ORG NAT/G COLONIAL LEAD
REGION NAT/LISM ATTIT 20 UN. PAGE 6 E0107
BIBLIOG/A
ASIA
S/ASIA
DIPLOM

N

HARVARD LAW SCHOOL LIBRARY,ANNUAL LEGAL
BIBLIOGRAPHY. USA+45 CONSTN LEGIS ADJUD CT/SYS
...POLICY 20. PAGE 50 E1005
BIBLIOG
JURID
LAW
INT/LAW

N

US SUPERINTENDENT OF DOCUMENTS,POLITICAL SCIENCE:
GOVERNMENT, CRIME, DISTRICT OF COLUMBIA (PRICE LIST
54). USA+45 LAW CONSTN EX/STRUC WORKER ADJUD ADMIN
CT/SYS CHOOSE INGP/REL RACE/REL CONGRESS PRESIDENT.
PAGE 103 E2063
BIBLIOG/A
NAT/G
CRIME

B00

HOLLAND T.E.,STUDIES IN INTERNATIONAL LAW. TURKEY
USSR WOR-45 CONSTN NAT/G DIPLOM DOMIN LEGIT COERCE
WAR PEACE ORD/FREE PWR SOVEREIGN...JURID CHARTS 20
PARLIAMENT SUEZ TREATY. PAGE 54 E1084
INT/ORG
LAW
INT/LAW

B01

BRYCE J.,STUDIES IN HISTORY AND JURISPRUDENCE (2
VOLS.). ICELAND SOUTH/AFR UK LAW PROB/SOLV
SOVEREIGN...PHIL/SCI NAT/COMP ROME/ANC ROMAN/LAW.
PAGE 16 E0321
IDEA/COMP
CONSTN
JURID

B03

FORTESCUE G.K.,SUBJECT INDEX OF THE MODERN WORKS
ADDED TO THE LIBRARY OF THE BRITISH MUSEUM IN THE
YEARS 1881-1900 (3 VOLS.). UK LAW CONSTN FINAN
NAT/G FORCES INT/TRADE COLONIAL 19. PAGE 39 E0775
BIBLIOG
INDEX
WRITING

B03

GRIFFIN A.P.C.,LIST OF BOOKS ON THE CONSTITUTION OF
THE UNITED STATES (PAMPHLET). USA-45 NAT/G EX/STRUC
JUDGE TOP/EX CT/SYS 18/20 CONGRESS PRESIDENT
SUPREME/CT. PAGE 46 E0920
BIBLIOG/A
CONSTN
LAW
JURID

B04

CRANDALL S.B.,TREATIES: THEIR MAKING AND
ENFORCEMENT. MOD/EUR USA+45 CONSTN INT/ORG NAT/G
LEGIS EDU/PROP LEGIT EXEC PEACE KNOWL MORAL...JURID
CONGRESS 19/20 TREATY. PAGE 27 E0541
LAW

B04

FREUND E.,THE POLICE POWER; PUBLIC POLICY AND
CONSTITUTIONAL RIGHTS. USA-45 SOCIETY LOC/G NAT/G
FORCES LEGIS ADJUD CT/SYS OWN PWR...JURID 18/19
SUPREME/CT. PAGE 40 E0795
CONSTN
LAW
ORD/FREE
CONTROL

B06

GRIFFIN A.P.C.,SELECT LIST OF REFERENCES ON THE
NEGRO QUESTION (REV. ED.). USA+45 CONSTN SCHOOL
SUFF ADJUST...JURID SOC/INTEG 19/20 NEGRO. PAGE 47
E0930
BIBLIOG/A
RACE/REL
DISCRIM
ATTIT

B07

BENTHAM J.,AN INTRODUCTION TO THE PRINCIPLES OF
MORALS AND LEGISLATION. UNIV CONSTN CULTURE SOCIETY
NAT/G CONSULT LEGIS JUDGE ADJUD CT/SYS...JURID
CONCPT NEW/IDEA. PAGE 10 E0190
LAW
GEN/LAWS

B08

GRIFFIN A.P.C.,REFERENCES ON CORRUPT PRACTICES IN
ELECTIONS (PAMPHLET). USA-45 LAW CONSTN TRIBUTE
CRIME REPRESENT...JURID 19/20. PAGE 47 E0934
BIBLIOG/A
CHOOSE
SUFF
APPORT

B08

WILSON W.,CONSTITUTIONAL GOVERNMENT IN THE UNITED
STATES. USA-45 LAW POL/PAR PROVS CHIEF LEGIS
BAL/PWR ADJUD EXEC FEDERAL PWR 18/20 SUPREME/CT
HOUSE/REP SENATE. PAGE 106 E2130
NAT/G
GOV/REL
CONSTN
PARL/PROC

B09

LOBINGIER C.S.,THE PEOPLE'S LAW OR POPULAR
PARTICIPATION IN LAW-MAKING. FRANCE SWITZERLND UK
LOC/G NAT/G PROVS LEGIS SUFF MAJORITY PWR POPULISM
...GOV/COMP BIBLIOG 19. PAGE 66 E1314
CONSTN
LAW
PARTIC

B10

MCILWAIN C.H.,THE HIGH COURT OF PARLIAMENT AND ITS
SUPREMACY B1910 1878 408. UK EX/STRUC PARL/PROC
GOV/REL INGP/REL PRIVIL 12/20 PARLIAMENT
ENGLSH/LAW. PAGE 71 E1416
LAW
LEGIS
CONSTN
NAT/G

B12

BEARD C.A.,THE SUPREME COURT AND THE CONSTITUTION.   CONSTN

LAW NAT/G PROVS LEGIS GOV/REL ATTIT POPULISM
SUPREME/CT. PAGE 9 E0164
CT/SYS
ADJUD
CONTROL

B12
GRIFFIN A.P.C.,SELECT LIST OF REFERENCES ON
IMPEACHMENT (REV. ED.) (PAMPHLET). USA-45 LAW PROVS
ADJUD ATTIT...JURID 19/20 NEGRO. PAGE 47 E0935
BIBLIOG/A
CONSTN
NAT/G
LEGIS

B14
CRAIG J.,ELEMENTS OF POLITICAL SCIENCE (3 VOLS.).
CONSTN AGRI INDUS SCHOOL FORCES TAX CT/SYS SUFF
MORAL WEALTH...CONCPT 19 CIVIL/LIB. PAGE 27 E0539
PHIL/SCI
NAT/G
ORD/FREE

B14
MCLAUGHLIN A.C.,CYCLOPEDIA OF AMERICAN GOVERNMENT
(3 VOLS.). LAW CONSTN POL/PAR ADMIN ROUTINE
...INT/LAW CONCPT BIBLIOG METH 20. PAGE 71 E1421
USA+45
NAT/G
DICTIONARY

B16
SCHROEDER T.,FREE SPEECH FOR RADICALS (REV. ED.).
USA-45 CONSTN INDUS LOC/G FORCES SANCTION WAR ATTIT
SEX...JURID REFORMERS 20 FREE/SPEE. PAGE 88 E1767
ORD/FREE
CONTROL
LAW
PRESS

B18
EYBERS G.W.,SELECT CONSTITUTIONAL DOCUMENTS
ILLUSTRATING SOUTH AFRICAN HISTORY 1795-1910.
SOUTH/AFR LOC/G LEGIS CT/SYS...JURID ANTHOL 18/20
NATAL CAPE/HOPE ORANGE/STA. PAGE 36 E0707
CONSTN
LAW
NAT/G
COLONIAL

B18
PORTER K.H.,A HISTORY OF SUFFRAGE IN THE UNITED
STATES. USA-45 LAW CONSTN LOC/G NAT/G POL/PAR WAR
DISCRIM OWN ATTIT SEX 18/20 NEGRO FEMALE/SEX.
PAGE 81 E1629
SUFF
REPRESENT
CHOOSE
PARTIC

B18
WILSON W.,THE STATE: ELEMENTS OF HISTORICAL AND
PRACTICAL POLITICS. FRANCE GERMANY ITALY UK USSR
CONSTN EX/STRUC LEGIS CT/SYS WAR PWR...POLICY
GOV/COMP 20. PAGE 106 E2131
NAT/G
JURID
CONCPT
NAT/COMP

B18
YUKIO O.,THE VOICE OF JAPANESE DEMOCRACY, AN ESSAY
ON CONSTITUTIONAL LOYALTY (TRANS BY J. E. BECKER).
ASIA POL/PAR DELIB/GP EX/STRUC RIGID/FLEX ORD/FREE
PWR...POLICY JURID METH/COMP 19/20 CHINJAP.
PAGE 108 E2167
CONSTN
MAJORIT
CHOOSE
NAT/G

S18
POWELL T.R.,"THE LOGIC AND RHETORIC OF
CONSTITUTIONAL LAW" (BMR)" USA+45 USA-45 DELIB/GP
PROB/SOLV ADJUD CT/SYS...DECISION 20 SUPREME/CT
CON/INTERP. PAGE 82 E1642
CONSTN
LAW
JURID
LOG

N18
BREWER D.J.,THE MOVEMENT OF COERCION (PAMPHLET).
CONSTN INDUS ADJUD COERCE OWN WEALTH...OLD/LIB
JURID 19 SUPREME/CT. PAGE 15 E0296
GP/REL
LABOR
LG/CO
LAW

B19
DUGUIT L.,LAW IN THE MODERN STATE (TRANS. BY FRIDA
AND HAROLD LASKI). CONSTN SOCIETY STRUCT MORAL
ORD/FREE SOVEREIGN 20. PAGE 33 E0655
GEN/LAWS
CONCPT
NAT/G
LAW

N19
IN THE SHADOW OF FEAR; AMERICAN CIVIL LIBERTIES,
1948-49 (PAMPHLET). COM LAW LEGIS BAL/PWR EDU/PROP
CT/SYS RACE/REL DISCRIM MARXISM SOCISM 20 COLD/WAR
CONGRESS ACLU CIV/RIGHTS ESPIONAGE. PAGE 2 E0030
ORD/FREE
CONSTN
POLICY

N19
AMERICAN CIVIL LIBERTIES UNION,"WE HOLD THESE
TRUTHS" FREEDOM, JUSTICE, EQUALITY: REPORT ON CIVIL
LIBERTIES (A PERIODICAL PAMPHLET COVERING 1951-53).
USA+45 ACADEM NAT/G FORCES LEGIS COERCE CIVMIL/REL
GOV/REL DISCRIM PRIVIL MARXISM...OLD/LIB 20 ACLU UN
CIVIL/LIB. PAGE 4 E0076
ORD/FREE
LAW
RACE/REL
CONSTN

N19
BRENNAN W.J. JR.,THE BILL OF RIGHTS AND THE STATES
(PAMPHLET). USA+45 USA-45 LEGIS BAL/PWR ADJUD
CT/SYS FEDERAL PWR SOVEREIGN 18/20 SUPREME/CT
BILL/RIGHT. PAGE 15 E0293
CONSTN
PROVS
GOV/REL
ORD/FREE

N19
PAN AMERICAN UNION,INFORME DE LA MISION DE
ASISTENCIA TECNICA DE LA OEA A LA REPUBLICA DE
HONDURAS EN MATERIA ELECTORAL (PAMPHLET). HONDURAS
CONSTN ORD/FREE...JURID OBS 20 OAS. PAGE 80 E1595
CHOOSE
SUFF
POL/PAR
NAT/G

N19
RALSTON A.,A FRESH LOOK AT LEGISLATIVE
APPORTIONMENT IN NEW JERSEY (PAMPHLET). USA+45
CONSTN LEGIS OBJECTIVE...MATH METH 20 NEW/JERSEY.
PAGE 83 E1671
APPORT
REPRESENT
PROVS
JURID

B20
MEYER H.H.B.,LIST OF REFERENCES ON THE TREATY-
MAKING POWER. USA-45 CONTROL PWR...INT/LAW TIME/SEQ
18/20 TREATY. PAGE 72 E1448
BIBLIOG
DIPLOM
CONSTN

B20
VINOGRADOFF P.,OUTLINES OF HISTORICAL JURISPRUDENCE
(2 VOLS.). GREECE MEDIT-7 LAW CONSTN FACE/GP FAM
KIN MUNIC CRIME OWN...INT/LAW IDEA/COMP BIBLIOG.
PAGE 104 E2080
JURID
METH

C20
BLACHLY F.F.,"THE GOVERNMENT AND ADMINISTRATION OF
GERMANY." GERMANY CONSTN LOC/G PROVS DELIB/GP
EX/STRUC FORCES LEGIS TOP/EX CT/SYS...BIBLIOG/A
19/20. PAGE 12 E0235
NAT/G
GOV/REL
ADMIN
PHIL/SCI

B21
BRYCE J.,MODERN DEMOCRACIES. FUT NEW/ZEALND USA-45
LAW CONSTN POL/PAR PROVS VOL/ASSN EX/STRUC LEGIS
LEGIT CT/SYS EXEC KNOWL CONGRESS AUSTRAL 20.
PAGE 16 E0322
NAT/G
TREND

B22
FARRAND M.,THE FRAMING OF THE CONSTITUTION OF THE
UNITED STATES (1913). USA-45 EX/STRUC PROB/SOLV
PERSON. PAGE 36 E0721
CONSTN
DELIB/GP
LEGIS
CT/SYS

B22
WRIGHT Q.,THE CONTROL OF AMERICAN FOREIGN
RELATIONS. USA-45 WOR-45 CONSTN INT/ORG CONSULT
LEGIS LEGIT ROUTINE ORD/FREE PWR...POLICY JURID
CONCPT METH/CNCPT RECORD LEAGUE/NAT 20. PAGE 107
E2150
NAT/G
EXEC
DIPLOM

B24
HALL W.E.,A TREATISE ON INTERNATIONAL LAW. WOR-45
CONSTN INT/ORG NAT/G DIPLOM ORD/FREE LEAGUE/NAT 20
TREATY. PAGE 49 E0985
PWR
JURID
WAR
INT/LAW

B24
HOLDSWORTH W.S.,A HISTORY OF ENGLISH LAW; THE
COMMON LAW AND ITS RIVALS (VOL. VI). UK STRATA
EX/STRUC ADJUD ADMIN CONTROL CT/SYS...JURID CONCPT
GEN/LAWS 17 COMMONWLTH PARLIAMENT ENGLSH/LAW
COMMON/LAW. PAGE 54 E1074
LAW
CONSTN
LEGIS
CHIEF

B24
HOLDSWORTH W.S.,A HISTORY OF ENGLISH LAW; THE
COMMON LAW AND ITS RIVALS (VOL. IV). UK SEA AGRI
CHIEF ADJUD CONTROL CRIME GOV/REL...INT/LAW JURID
NAT/COMP 16/17 PARLIAMENT COMMON/LAW CANON/LAW
ENGLSH/LAW. PAGE 54 E1075
LAW
LEGIS
CT/SYS
CONSTN

C24
BARNES H.E.,"SOCIOLOGY AND POLITICAL THEORY: A
CONSIDERATION OF THE SOCIOLOGICAL BASIS OF
POLITICS." LAW CONSTN NAT/G DIPLOM DOMIN ROUTINE
REV ORD/FREE SOVEREIGN...PHIL/SCI CLASSIF BIBLIOG
18/20. PAGE 8 E0151
CONCPT
STRUCT
SOC

C24
SHERMAN C.P.,"ROMAN LAW IN THE MODERN WORLD (2ND
ED.) (3 VOLS.)" MEDIT-7...JURID BIBLIOG. PAGE 91
E1819
LAW
ADJUD
OWN
CONSTN

B25
WINFIELD P.H.,THE CHIEF SOURCES OF ENGLISH LEGAL
HISTORY. UK CONSTN JUDGE ADJUD CT/SYS 13/18.
PAGE 107 E2133
BIBLIOG/A
JURID
LAW

B26
FORTESCUE J.,THE GOVERNANCE OF ENGLAND (1471-76).
UK LAW FINAN SECT LEGIS PROB/SOLV TAX DOMIN ADMIN
GP/REL COST ORD/FREE PWR 14/15. PAGE 39 E0776
CONSERVE
CONSTN
CHIEF
NAT/G

S26
HALL A.B.,"DETERMINATION OF METHODS FOR
ASCERTAINING THE FACTORS THAT INFLUENCE JUDICIAL
DECISIONS IN CASES INVOLVING DUE PROCESS" LAW JUDGE
DEBATE EFFICIENCY OPTIMAL UTIL...SOC CONCPT
PROBABIL STAT SAMP. PAGE 49 E0981
ADJUD
DECISION
CONSTN
JURID

B28
FRANKFURTER F.,THE BUSINESS OF THE SUPREME COURT; A
STUDY IN THE FEDERAL JUDICIAL SYSTEM. USA-45 CONSTN
CT/SYS
ADJUD

EX/STRUC PROB/SOLV GP/REL ATTIT PWR...POLICY JURID LAW
18/20 SUPREME/CT CONGRESS. PAGE 40 E0789   FEDERAL

                                                         B28
MAIR L.P.,THE PROTECTION OF MINORITIES. EUR+WWI   LAW
WOR-45 CONSTN INT/ORG NAT/G LEGIT CT/SYS GP/REL   SOVEREIGN
RACE/REL DISCRIM ORD/FREE RESPECT...JURID CONCPT
TIME/SEQ 20. PAGE 68 E1352

                                                         B28
NORTON T.J.,LOSING LIBERTY JUDICIALLY. PROVS LEGIS   NAT/G
BAL/PWR CT/SYS...JURID 18/20 SUPREME/CT CIV/RIGHTS   ORD/FREE
CONGRESS. PAGE 78 E1557   CONSTN
                                                         JUDGE

                                                         B29
BUELL R.,INTERNATIONAL RELATIONS. WOR+45 WOR-45   INT/ORG
CONSTN STRATA FORCES TOP/EX ADMIN ATTIT DRIVE   BAL/PWR
SUPEGO MORAL ORD/FREE PWR SOVEREIGN...JURID SOC   DIPLOM
CONCPT 20. PAGE 17 E0326

                                                         B29
CAM H.M.,BIBLIOGRAPHY OF ENGLISH CONSTITUTIONAL   BIBLIOG/A
HISTORY (PAMPHLET). UK LAW LOC/G NAT/G POL/PAR SECT   CONSTN
DELIB/GP ADJUD ORD/FREE 19/20 PARLIAMENT. PAGE 19   ADMIN
E0369   PARL/PROC

                                                         B30
BYNKERSHOEK C.,QUAESTIONUM JURIS PUBLICI LIBRI DUO.   INT/ORG
CHRIST-17C MOD/EUR CONSTN ELITES SOCIETY NAT/G   LAW
PROVS EX/STRUC FORCES TOP/EX BAL/PWR DIPLOM ATTIT   NAT/LISM
MORAL...TRADIT CONCPT. PAGE 18 E0352   INT/LAW

                                                         B30
GREEN F.M.,CONSTITUTIONAL DEVELOPMENT IN THE SOUTH   CONSTN
ATLANTIC STATES, 1776-1860; A STUDY IN THE   PROVS
EVOLUTION OF DEMOCRACY. USA-45 ELITES SOCIETY   PLURISM
STRATA ECO/DEV AGRI POL/PAR EX/STRUC LEGIS CT/SYS   REPRESENT
REGION...BIBLIOG 18/19 MARYLAND VIRGINIA GEORGIA
NORTH/CAR SOUTH/CAR. PAGE 46 E0905

                                                         B30
WILLOUGHBY W.W.,PRINCIPLES OF THE CONSTITUTIONAL   CONSTN
LAW OF THE UNITED STATES. USA-45 ADJUD FEDERAL   NAT/G
SOVEREIGN 18/20 COMMON/LAW. PAGE 106 E2125   CONCPT
                                                         JURID

                                                         B30
WRIGHT Q.,MANDATES UNDER THE LEAGUE OF NATIONS.   INT/ORG
WOR-45 DEV ECO/UNDEV NAT/G DELIB/GP   LAW
TOP/EX LEGIT ALL/VALS...JURID CONCPT LEAGUE/NAT 20.   INT/LAW
PAGE 107 E2151

                                                         B31
BORCHARD E.H.,GUIDE TO THE LAW AND LEGAL LITERATURE   BIBLIOG/A
OF FRANCE. FRANCE FINAN INDUS LABOR SECT LEGIS   LAW
ADMIN COLONIAL CRIME OWN...INT/LAW 20. PAGE 14   CONSTN
E0266   METH

                                                         B32
GREAT BRIT COMM MINISTERS PWR,REPORT. UK LAW CONSTN EX/STRUC
CONSULT LEGIS PARL/PROC SANCTION SOVEREIGN   NAT/G
...DECISION JURID 20 PARLIAMENT. PAGE 45 E0902   PWR
                                                         CONTROL

                                                         B32
MORLEY F.,THE SOCIETY OF NATIONS. EUR+WWI UNIV   INT/ORG
WOR-45 LAW CONSTN ACT/RES PLAN EDU/PROP LEGIT   CONCPT
ROUTINE...POLICY TIME/SEQ LEAGUE/NAT TOT/POP 20.
PAGE 75 E1496

                                                         B33
AMERICAN FOREIGN LAW ASSN,BIOGRAPHICAL NOTES ON THE BIBLIOG/A
LAWS AND LEGAL LITERATURE OF URUGUAY AND CURACAO.   LAW
URUGUAY CONSTN FINAN SECT FORCES JUDGE DIPLOM   JURID
INT/TRADE ADJUD CT/SYS CRIME 20. PAGE 4 E0078   ADMIN

                                                         B33
DANGERFIELD R.,IN DEFENSE OF THE SENATE. USA-45   LEGIS
CONSTN NAT/G EX/STRUC TOP/EX ATTIT KNOWL   DELIB/GP
...METH/CNCPT STAT TIME/SEQ TREND CON/ANAL CHARTS   DIPLOM
CONGRESS 20 TREATY. PAGE 28 E0565

                                                         B33
HELLMAN F.S.,SELECTED LIST OF REFERENCES ON THE   BIBLIOG/A
CONSTITUTIONAL POWERS OF THE PRESIDENT INCLUDING   JURID
POWERS RECENTLY DELEGATED. USA-45 NAT/G EX/STRUC   LAW
TOP/EX CENTRAL FEDERAL PWR 20 PRESIDENT. PAGE 51   CONSTN
E1025

                                                         B33
MATTHEWS M.A.,THE AMERICAN INSTITUTE OF   BIBLIOG/A
INTERNATIONAL LAW AND THE CODIFICATION OF   INT/LAW
INTERNATIONAL LAW (PAMPHLET). USA-45 CONSTN ADJUD   L/A+17C
CT/SYS...JURID 20. PAGE 69 E1386   DIPLOM

                                                         B33
REID H.D.,RECUEIL DES COURS; TOME 45: LES   ORD/FREE
SERVITUDES INTERNATIONALES III. FRANCE CONSTN   DIPLOM
DELIB/GP PRESS CONTROL REV WAR CHOOSE PEACE MORAL   LAW
MARITIME TREATY. PAGE 84 E1680

                                                         L34
LLEWELLYN K.N.,"THE CONSTITUTION AS AN INSTITUTION"   CONSTN
(BMR)" USA-45 PROB/SOLV LOBBY REPRESENT...DECISION   LAW
JURID 18/20 SUPREME/CT. PAGE 66 E1313   CONCPT
                                                         CT/SYS

                                                         B35
FOREIGN AFFAIRS BIBLIOGRAPHY: A SELECTED AND   BIBLIOG/A
ANNOTATED LIST OF BOOKS ON INTERNATIONAL RELATIONS   DIPLOM
1919-1962 (4 VOLS.). CONSTN FORCES COLONIAL   INT/ORG
ARMS/CONT WAR NAT/LISM PEACE ATTIT DRIVE...POLICY
INT/LAW 20. PAGE 2 E0032

                                                         B35
DE TOCQUEVILLE A.,DEMOCRACY IN AMERICA (4 VOLS.)   POPULISM
(TRANS. BY HENRY REEVE). CONSTN STRUCT LOC/G NAT/G   MAJORIT
POL/PAR PROVS ETIQUET CT/SYS MAJORITY ATTIT 18/19.   ORD/FREE
PAGE 30 E0595   SOCIETY

                                                         B35
KENNEDY W.P.,THE LAW AND CUSTOM OF THE SOUTH   CT/SYS
AFRICAN CONSTITUTION. AFR SOUTH/AFR KIN LOC/G PROVS   CONSTN
DIPLOM ADJUD ADMIN EXEC 20. PAGE 60 E1203   JURID
                                                         PARL/PROC

                                                         B35
LUCE R.,LEGISLATIVE PROBLEMS. CONSTN CHIEF JUDGE   TREND
BUDGET CONFER ETIQUET CONTROL MORAL PWR NEW/LIB   ADMIN
CONGRESS. PAGE 67 E1331   LEGIS

                                                         B35
MCLAUGHLIN A.C.,A CONSTITUTIONAL HISTORY OF THE   CONSTN
UNITED STATES. USA+45 USA-45 LOC/G NAT/G PROVS   DECISION
LEGIS JUDGE ADJUD...T 18/20. PAGE 71 E1422

                                                         B35
RAM J.,THE SCIENCE OF LEGAL JUDGMENT: A TREATISE...   LAW
UK CONSTN NAT/G LEGIS CREATE PROB/SOLV AGREE CT/SYS   JURID
...INT/LAW CONCPT 19 ENGLSH/LAW CANON/LAW CIVIL/LAW   EX/STRUC
CTS/WESTM. PAGE 83 E1672   ADJUD

                                                         B35
ROBSON W.A.,CIVILISATION AND THE GROWTH OF LAW.   LAW
UNIV CONSTN SOCIETY LEGIS ADJUD ATTIT PERCEPT MORAL   IDEA/COMP
ALL/IDEOS...CONCPT WORSHIP 20. PAGE 85 E1708   SOC

                                                         B36
GRAVES W.B.,AMERICAN STATE GOVERNMENT. CONSTN FINAN   NAT/G
EX/STRUC FORCES LEGIS BUDGET TAX CT/SYS REPRESENT   PROVS
GOV/REL...BIBLIOG/A 19/20. PAGE 45 E0900   ADMIN
                                                         FEDERAL

                                                         B36
KONRAD F.,DIE PERSONLICHE FREIHEIT IM   ORD/FREE
NATIONALSOZIALISTISCHEN DEUTSCHEN REICHE. GERMANY   JURID
JUDGE ADJUD GP/REL FASCISM 20 CIVIL/LIB. PAGE 61   CONSTN
E1226   CONCPT

                                                         B36
MATTHEWS M.A.,INTERNATIONAL LAW: SELECT LIST OF   BIBLIOG/A
WORKS IN ENGLISH ON PUBLIC INTERNATIONAL LAW: WITH   INT/LAW
COLLECTIONS OF CASES AND OPINIONS. CHRIST-17C   ATTIT
EUR+WWI MOD/EUR WOR-45 CONSTN ADJUD JURID. PAGE 69   DIPLOM
E1388

                                                         B36
SCHULZ F.,PRINCIPLES OF ROMAN LAW. CONSTN FAM NAT/G   LAW
DOMIN CONTROL CT/SYS CRIME ISOLAT ATTIT ORD/FREE   LEGIS
PWR...JURID ROME/ANC ROMAN/LAW. PAGE 89 E1783   ADJUD
                                                         CONCPT

                                                         S36
CORWIN E.S.,"THE CONSTITUTION AS INSTRUMENT AND AS   CONSTN
SYMBOL." USA-45 ECO/DEV INDUS CAP/ISM SANCTION   LAW
RIGID/FLEX ORD/FREE LAISSEZ OBJECTIVE 20 CONGRESS   ADJUD
SUPREME/CT. PAGE 26 E0512   PWR

                                                         B37
BEARDSLEY A.R.,LEGAL BIBLIOGRAPHY AND THE USE OF   BIBLIOG
LAW BOOKS. CONSTN CREATE PROB/SOLV...DECISION JURID   LAW
LAB/EXP. PAGE 9 E0166   METH
                                                         OP/RES

                                                         B37
HAMILTON W.H.,THE POWER TO GOVERN. ECO/DEV FINAN   LING
INDUS ECO/TAC INT/TRADE TARIFFS TAX CONTROL CT/SYS   CONSTN
WAR COST PWR 18/20 SUPREME/CT. PAGE 50 E0991   NAT/G
                                                         POLICY

B37
RUTHERFORD M.L.,THE INFLUENCE OF THE AMERICAN BAR ATTIT
ASSOCIATION ON PUBLIC OPINION AND LEGISLATION. ADJUD
USA+45 LAW CONSTN LABOR LEGIS DOMIN EDU/PROP LEGIT PROF/ORG
CT/SYS ROUTINE...TIME/SEQ 19/20 ABA. PAGE 87 E1739 JURID

L37
LERNER M.,"CONSTITUTION AND COURT AS SYMBOLS" CONSTN
(BMR)" USA+45 USA-45 DOMIN PWR SOVEREIGN...PSY MYTH CT/SYS
18/20 SUPREME/CT. PAGE 64 E1288 ATTIT
EDU/PROP

B38
FIELD G.L.,THE SYNDICAL AND CORPORATIVE FASCISM
INSTITUTIONS OF ITALIAN FASCISM. ITALY CONSTN INDUS
STRATA LABOR EX/STRUC TOP/EX ADJUD ADMIN LEAD NAT/G
TOTALISM AUTHORIT...MGT 20 MUSSOLIN/B. PAGE 38 WORKER
E0746

B38
FRANKFURTER F.,MR. JUSTICE HOLMES AND THE SUPREME CREATE
COURT. USA-45 CONSTN SOCIETY FEDERAL OWN ATTIT CT/SYS
ORD/FREE PWR...POLICY JURID 20 SUPREME/CT HOLMES/OW DECISION
BILL/RIGHT. PAGE 40 E0790 LAW

B38
HARPER S.N.,THE GOVERNMENT OF THE SOVIET UNION. COM MARXISM
USSR LAW CONSTN ECO/DEV PLAN TEC/DEV DIPLOM NAT/G
INT/TRADE ADMIN REV NAT/LISM...POLICY 20. PAGE 50 LEAD
E1001 POL/PAR

B38
HELLMAN F.S.,THE SUPREME COURT ISSUE: SELECTED LIST BIBLIOG/A
OF REFERENCES. USA-45 NAT/G CHIEF EX/STRUC JUDGE CONSTN
ATTIT...JURID 20 PRESIDENT ROOSEVLT/F SUPREME/CT. CT/SYS
PAGE 51 E1026 LAW

B38
HOLDSWORTH W.S.,A HISTORY OF ENGLISH LAW; THE LAW
CENTURIES OF SETTLEMENT AND REFORM (VOL. X). INDIA LOC/G
UK CONSTN NAT/G CHIEF LEGIS ADMIN COLONIAL CT/SYS EX/STRUC
CHOOSE ORD/FREE PWR...JURID 18 PARLIAMENT ADJUD
COMMONWLTH COMMON/LAW. PAGE 54 E1077

B38
HOLDSWORTH W.S.,A HISTORY OF ENGLISH LAW; THE LAW
CENTURIES OF SETTLEMENT AND REFORM (VOL. XII). UK PROF/ORG
CONSTN STRATA LEGIS JUDGE ADJUD CT/SYS ATTIT WRITING
...JURID CONCPT BIOG GEN/LAWS 18 ENGLSH/LAW IDEA/COMP
BLACKSTN/W COMMON/LAW. PAGE 54 E1078

B38
HOLDSWORTH W.S.,A HISTORY OF ENGLISH LAW; THE LAW
CENTURIES OF SETTLEMENT AND REFORM (VOL. XI). UK COLONIAL
CONSTN NAT/G EX/STRUC DIPLOM ADJUD CT/SYS LEAD LEGIS
CRIME ATTIT...INT/LAW JURID 18 CMN/WLTH PARLIAMENT PARL/PROC
ENGLSH/LAW. PAGE 54 E1079

B38
POUND R.,THE FORMATIVE ERA OF AMERICAN LAW. CULTURE CONSTN
NAT/G PROVS LEGIS ADJUD CT/SYS PERSON SOVEREIGN LAW
...POLICY IDEA/COMP GEN/LAWS 18/19. PAGE 82 E1637 CREATE
JURID

B39
MCILWAIN C.H.,CONSTITUTIONALISM AND THE CHANGING CONSTN
WORLD. UK USA-45 LEGIS PRIVIL AUTHORIT SOVEREIGN POLICY
...GOV/COMP 15/20 MAGNA/CART HOUSE/CMNS. PAGE 71 JURID
E1417

B39
SIEYES E.J.,LES DISCOURS DE SIEYES DANS LES DEBATS CONSTN
CONSTITUTIONNELS DE L'AN III (2 ET 18 THERMIDOR). ADJUD
FRANCE LAW NAT/G PROB/SOLV BAL/PWR GOV/REL 18 JURY. LEGIS
PAGE 91 E1824 EX/STRUC

C39
HADDOW A.,"POLITICAL SCIENCE IN AMERICAN COLLEGES USA-45
AND UNIVERSITIES 1636-1900." CONSTN MORAL...POLICY LAW
INT/LAW CON/ANAL BIBLIOG T 17/20. PAGE 49 E0971 ACADEM
KNOWL

B40
ANDERSON W.,FUNDAMENTALS OF AMERICAN GOVERNMENT. NAT/G
USA-45 LAW POL/PAR CHIEF EX/STRUC BUDGET ADMIN LOC/G
CT/SYS PARL/PROC CHOOSE FEDERAL...BIBLIOG 20. GOV/REL
PAGE 5 E0093 CONSTN

B40
BROWN A.D.,COMPULSORY MILITARY TRAINING: SELECT BIBLIOG/A
LIST OF REFERENCES (PAMPHLET). USA-45 CONSTN FORCES
VOL/ASSN COERCE 20. PAGE 16 E0311 JURID
ATTIT

B40
FULLER G.H.,A SELECTED LIST OF RECENT REFERENCES ON BIBLIOG/A

THE CONSTITUTION OF THE UNITED STATES (PAMPHLET). CONSTN
CULTURE NAT/G LEGIS CONFER ADJUD GOV/REL CONSEN LAW
POPULISM...JURID CONCPT 18/20 CONGRESS. PAGE 41 USA-45
E0820

B40
HART J.,AN INTRODUCTION TO ADMINISTRATIVE LAW, WITH LAW
SELECTED CASES. USA-45 CONSTN SOCIETY NAT/G ADMIN
EX/STRUC ADJUD CT/SYS LEAD CRIME ORD/FREE LEGIS
...DECISION JURID 20 CASEBOOK. PAGE 50 E1002 PWR

B40
MCILWAIN C.H.,CONSTITUTIONALISM, ANCIENT AND CONSTN
MODERN. CHRIST-17C MOD/EUR NAT/G CHIEF PROB/SOLV GEN/LAWS
INSPECT AUTHORIT ORD/FREE PWR...TIME/SEQ ROMAN/REP. LAW
PAGE 71 E1418

B41
CHAFEE Z. JR.,FREE SPEECH IN THE UNITED STATES. ORD/FREE
USA-45 ADJUD CONTROL CRIME WAR...BIBLIOG 20 CONSTN
FREE/SPEE AMEND/I SUPREME/CT. PAGE 21 E0413 ATTIT
JURID

B42
CARR R.K.,THE SUPREME COURT AND JUDICIAL REVIEW. CT/SYS
NAT/G CHIEF LEGIS OP/RES LEAD GOV/REL GP/REL ATTIT CONSTN
...POLICY DECISION 18/20 SUPREME/CT PRESIDENT JURID
CONGRESS. PAGE 20 E0394 PWR

B42
CRAIG A.,ABOVE ALL LIBERTIES. FRANCE UK USA-45 LAW ORD/FREE
CONSTN CULTURE INTELL NAT/G SECT JUDGE...IDEA/COMP MORAL
BIBLIOG 18/20. PAGE 27 E0536 WRITING
EDU/PROP

B42
FORTESCU J.,IN PRAISE OF ENGLISH LAW (1464) (TRANS. LAW
BY S.B. CHRIMES). UK ELITES CHIEF FORCES CT/SYS CONSTN
COERCE CRIME GOV/REL ILLEGIT...JURID GOV/COMP LEGIS
GEN/LAWS 15. PAGE 39 E0774 ORD/FREE

B42
GURVITCH G.,SOCIOLOGY OF LAW. CONSTN SOCIETY CREATE SOC
MORAL SOVEREIGN...POLICY EPIST JURID PHIL/SCI LAW
IDEA/COMP METH/COMP HOLMES/OW HOBBES/T. PAGE 48 ADJUD
E0964

B43
ANDERSON R.B.,SUPPLEMENT TO BEALE'S BIBLIOGRAPHY OF BIBLIOG/A
EARLY ENGLISH LAW BOOKS. MOD/EUR UK CONSTN PRESS JURID
ADJUD...CHARTS 10/15. PAGE 5 E0091 CT/SYS
LAW

B43
BACKUS R.C.,A GUIDE TO THE LAW AND LEGAL LITERATURE BIBLIOG/A
OF COLOMBIA. FINAN INDUS LABOR FORCES ADJUD ADMIN LAW
COLONIAL CT/SYS CRIME...INT/LAW JURID 20 COLOMB. CONSTN
PAGE 7 E0127 L/A+17C

B43
CLAGETT H.L.,A GUIDE TO THE LAW AND LEGAL BIBLIOG
LITERATURE OF PARAGUAY. PARAGUAY CONSTN COM/IND JURID
LABOR MUNIC JUDGE ADMIN CT/SYS...CRIMLGY INT/LAW LAW
CON/ANAL 20. PAGE 22 E0439 L/A+17C

B44
BEARD C.A.,AMERICAN GOVERNMENT AND POLITICS (REV. LEAD
ED.). CONSTN MUNIC POL/PAR PROVS EX/STRUC LEGIS USA-45
TOP/EX CT/SYS GOV/REL...BIBLIOG T 18/20. PAGE 9 NAT/G
E0165 LOC/G

B44
BRIERLY J.L.,THE OUTLOOK FOR INTERNATIONAL LAW. FUT INT/ORG
WOR-45 CONSTN NAT/G VOL/ASSN FORCES ECO/TAC DOMIN LAW
LEGIT ADJUD ROUTINE PEACE ORD/FREE...INT/LAW JURID
METH LEAGUE/NAT 20. PAGE 15 E0298

B44
FRAENKEL O.K.,OUR CIVIL LIBERTIES. USA-45...JURID CONSTN
CONCPT 18/20 BILL/RIGHT. PAGE 39 E0781 LAW
ATTIT

B44
PUTTKAMMER E.W.,WAR AND THE LAW. UNIV USA-45 CONSTN INT/ORG
CULTURE SOCIETY NAT/G POL/PAR ROUTINE ALL/VALS LAW
...JURID CONCPT OBS WORK VAL/FREE 20. PAGE 83 E1664 WAR
INT/LAW

S44
WRIGHT G.,"CONSTITUTIONAL PROCEDURES OF THE US FOR TOP/EX
CARRYING OUT OBLIGATIONS FOR MILITARY SANCTIONS." FORCES
EUR+WWI FUT USA-45 WOR-45 CONSTN INTELL NAT/G INT/LAW
CONSULT EX/STRUC LEGIS ROUTINE DRIVE...POLICY JURID WAR
CONCPT OBS TREND TOT/POP 20. PAGE 108 E2153

JEFFERSON T.,"DEMOCRACY" (1816) IN BASIC WRITINGS." USA-45 LOC/G NAT/G TAX CT/SYS CHOOSE ORD/FREE ...GEN/LAWS 18/19 JEFFERSN/T. PAGE 58 E1151
POPULISM MAJORIT REPRESENT CONSTN
C44

CLAGETT H.L.,A GUIDE TO THE LAW AND LEGAL LITERATURE OF THE MEXICAN STATES. CONSTN LEGIS JUDGE ADJUD ADMIN...INT/LAW CON/ANAL 20 MEXIC/AMER. PAGE 22 E0440
BIBLIOG JURID L/A+17C LAW
B45

CONOVER H.F.,THE GOVERNMENTS OF THE MAJOR FOREIGN POWERS: A BIBLIOGRAPHY. FRANCE GERMANY ITALY UK USSR CONSTN LOC/G POL/PAR EX/STRUC FORCES ADMIN CT/SYS CIVMIL/REL TOTALISM...POLICY 19/20. PAGE 25 E0494
BIBLIOG NAT/G DIPLOM
B45

US LIBRARY OF CONGRESS,CONSTITUTIONAL AND STATUTORY PROVISIONS OF THE STATES (VOL. I). USA-45 CREATE TAX CT/SYS CHOOSE SUFF INCOME PWR 20. PAGE 101 E2016
CONSTN FEDERAL PROVS JURID
B45

VANCE H.L.,GUIDE TO THE LAW AND LEGAL LITERATURE OF MEXICO. LAW CONSTN FINAN LABOR FORCES ADJUD ADMIN ...CRIMLGY PHIL/SCI CON/ANAL 20 MEXIC/AMER. PAGE 103 E2070
BIBLIOG/A INT/LAW JURID CT/SYS
B45

CORRY J.A.,DEMOCRATIC GOVERNMENT AND POLITICS. WOR-45 EX/STRUC LOBBY TOTALISM...MAJORIT CONCPT METH/COMP NAT/COMP 20. PAGE 26 E0511
NAT/G CONSTN POL/PAR JURID
B46

GOODRICH L.M.,"CHARTER OF THE UNITED NATIONS: COMMENTARY AND DOCUMENTS." EX/STRUC ADMIN...INT/LAW CON/ANAL BIBLIOG 20 UN. PAGE 45 E0890
CONSTN INT/ORG DIPLOM
C46

BORGESE G.,COMMON CAUSE. LAW CONSTN SOCIETY STRATA ECO/DEV INT/ORG POL/PAR FORCES LEGIS TOP/EX CAP/ISM DIPLOM ADMIN EXEC ATTIT PWR 20. PAGE 14 E0269
WOR+45 NAT/G SOVEREIGN REGION
B47

CLAGETT H.L.,A GUIDE TO THE LAW AND LEGAL LITERATURE OF BOLIVIA. L/A+17C CONSTN LABOR LEGIS ADMIN...CRIMLGY INT/LAW PHIL/SCI 16/20 BOLIV. PAGE 22 E0441
BIBLIOG/A JURID LAW CT/SYS
B47

CLAGETT H.L.,A GUIDE TO THE LAW AND LEGAL LITERATURE OF CHILE, 1917-1946. CHILE CONSTN LABOR JUDGE ADJUD ADMIN...CRIMLGY INT/LAW JURID CON/ANAL 20. PAGE 22 E0442
BIBLIOG L/A+17C LAW LEGIS
B47

CLAGETT H.L.,A GUIDE TO THE LAW AND LEGAL LITERATURE OF ECUADOR. ECUADOR CONSTN LABOR LEGIS JUDGE ADJUD ADMIN CIVMIL/REL...CRIMLGY INT/LAW CON/ANAL 20. PAGE 22 E0443
BIBLIOG JURID LAW L/A+17C
B47

CLAGETT H.L.,A GUIDE TO THE LAW AND LEGAL LITERATURE OF PERU. PERU CONSTN COM/IND LABOR MUNIC JUDGE ADMIN CT/SYS...CRIMLGY INT/LAW JURID 20. PAGE 23 E0444
BIBLIOG L/A+17C PHIL/SCI LAW
B47

CLAGETT H.L.,A GUIDE TO THE LAW AND LEGAL LITERATURE OF URUGUAY. URUGUAY CONSTN COM/IND FINAN LABOR MUNIC JUDGE PRESS ADMIN CT/SYS...INT/LAW PHIL/SCI 20. PAGE 23 E0445
BIBLIOG LAW JURID L/A+17C
B47

CLAGETT H.L.,A GUIDE TO THE LAW AND LEGAL LITERATURE OF VENEZUELA. VENEZUELA CONSTN LABOR LEGIS JUDGE ADJUD ADMIN CIVMIL/REL...CRIMLGY JURID CON/ANAL 20. PAGE 23 E0446
BIBLIOG L/A+17C INT/LAW LAW
B47

DE NOIA J.,GUIDE TO OFFICIAL PUBLICATIONS OF OTHER AMERICAN REPUBLICS: ECUADOR (VOL. IX). ECUADOR LAW FINAN LEGIS BUDGET CT/SYS 19/20. PAGE 30 E0589
BIBLIOG/A CONSTN NAT/G EDU/PROP
B47

DE NOIA J.,GUIDE TO OFFICIAL PUBLICATIONS OF THE OTHER AMERICAN REPUBLICS: EL SALVADOR. EL/SALVADR LAW LEGIS EDU/PROP CT/SYS 20. PAGE 30 E0590
BIBLIOG/A CONSTN NAT/G ADMIN
B47

DE NOIA J.,GUIDE TO OFFICIAL PUBLICATIONS OF THE OTHER AMERICAN REPUBLICS: NICARAGUA (VOL. XIV). NICARAGUA LAW LEGIS ADMIN CT/SYS...JURID 19/20. PAGE 30 E0591
BIBLIOG/A EDU/PROP NAT/G CONSTN
B47

DE NOIA J.,GUIDE TO OFFICIAL PUBLICATIONS OF THE OTHER AMERICAN REPUBLICS: PANAMA (VOL. XV). PANAMA LAW LEGIS EDU/PROP CT/SYS 20. PAGE 30 E0592
BIBLIOG/A CONSTN ADMIN NAT/G
B47

HARGRETT L.,A BIBLIOGRAPHY OF THE CONSTITUTIONS AND LAWS OF THE AMERICAN INDIANS. USA-45 LOC/G GOV/REL GP/REL 19/20 INDIAN/AM. PAGE 50 E0999
BIBLIOG/A CONSTN LAW NAT/G
B47

HOCKING W.E.,FREEDOM OF THE PRESS: A FRAMEWORK OF PRINCIPLE. WOR-45 SOCIETY NAT/G PROB/SOLV DEBATE LOBBY...JURID PSY 20 AMEND/I. PAGE 53 E1061
ORD/FREE CONSTN PRESS .AW
B47

KONVITZ M.R.,THE CONSTITUTION AND CIVIL RIGHTS. USA-45 NAT/G ADJUD GP/REL RACE/REL POPULISM ...MAJORIT 19/20 SUPREME/CT CIV/RIGHTS. PAGE 61 E1227
CONSTN LAW GOV/REL ORD/FREE
B47

MCILWAIN C.H.,CONSTITUTIONALISM: ANCIENT AND MODERN. USA+45 ROMAN/EMP LAW CHIEF LEGIS CT/SYS GP/REL ORD/FREE SOVEREIGN...POLICY TIME/SEQ ROMAN/REP EUROPE. PAGE 71 E1419
CONSTN NAT/G PARL/PROC GOV/COMP
B47

NEUBURGER O.,GUIDE TO OFFICIAL PUBLICATIONS OF OTHER AMERICAN REPUBLICS: HONDURAS (VOL. XIII). HONDURAS LAW LEGIS ADMIN CT/SYS...JURID 19/20. PAGE 76 E1533
BIBLIOG/A NAT/G EDU/PROP CONSTN
B47

NEUBURGER O.,GUIDE TO OFFICIAL PUBLICATIONS OF THE OTHER AMERICAN REPUBLICS: HAITI (VOL. XII). HAITI LAW FINAN LEGIS PRESS...JURID 20. PAGE 76 E1534
BIBLIOG/A CONSTN NAT/G EDU/PROP
B47

BISHOP H.M.,BASIC ISSUES OF AMERICAN DEMOCRACY. USA+45 USA-45 POL/PAR EX/STRUC LEGIS ADJUD FEDERAL ...BIBLIOG 18/20. PAGE 12 E0232
NAT/G PARL/PROC CONSTN
B48

CLAGETT H.L.,A GUIDE TO THE LAW AND LEGAL LITERATURE OF ARGENTINA, 1917-1946. CONSTN LABOR JUDGE ADJUD ADMIN...CRIMLGY INT/LAW JURID CON/ANAL 20 ARGEN. PAGE 23 E0447
BIBLIOG L/A+17C LAW LEGIS
B48

CORWIN E.S.,LIBERTY AGAINST GOVERNMENT. UK USA-45 ROMAN/EMP LAW CONSTN PERS/REL OWN ATTIT 1/20 ROMAN/LAW ENGLSH/LAW AMEND/XIV. PAGE 26 E0513
JURID ORD/FREE CONCPT
B48

CORWIN E.S.,LIBERTY AGAINST GOVERNMENT: THE RISE, FLOWERING AND DECLINE OF A FAMOUS JURIDICAL CONCEPT. LEGIS ADJUD CT/SYS SANCTION GOV/REL FEDERAL CONSERVE NEW/LIB...OLD/LIB 18/20 ROMAN/LAW COMMON/LAW. PAGE 26 E0514
CONCPT ORD/FREE JURID CONSTN
B48

DE NOIA J.,GUIDE TO OFFICIAL PUBLICATIONS OF OTHER AMERICAN REPUBLICS: PERU (VOL. XVII). PERU LAW LEGIS ADMIN CT/SYS...JURID 19/20. PAGE 30 E0593
BIBLIOG/A CONSTN NAT/G EDU/PROP
B48

FENWICK C.G.,INTERNATIONAL LAW. WOR+45 WOR-45 CONSTN NAT/G LEGIT CT/SYS REGION...CONCPT LEAGUE/NAT UN 20. PAGE 37 E0737
INT/ORG JURID INT/LAW
B48

HOLCOMBE A.N.,HUMAN RIGHTS IN THE MODERN WORLD. WOR+45 LEGIS DIPLOM ADJUD PERSON...INT/LAW 20 UN TREATY CIVIL/LIB BILL/RIGHT. PAGE 54 E1071
ORD/FREE INT/ORG CONSTN LAW
B48

KEIR D.L.,CASES IN CONSTITUTIONAL LAW. UK CHIEF LEGIS DIPLOM TAX PARL/PROC CRIME GOV/REL...INT/LAW JURID 17/20. PAGE 60 E1195
CONSTN LAW ADJUD CT/SYS
B48

MEIKLEJOHN A.,FREE SPEECH AND ITS RELATION TO SELF-
LEGIS
B48

GOVERNMENT. USA+45 USA-45 LAW DOMIN PRESS ORD/FREE   NAT/G
20 AMEND/I. PAGE 72 E1434   CONSTN
                                                         PRIVIL

                                                         B48
NEUBURGER O.,GUIDE TO OFFICIAL PUBLICATIONS OF THE   BIBLIOG/A
OTHER AMERICAN REPUBLICS: VENEZUELA (VOL. XIX).   NAT/G
VENEZUELA FINAN LEGIS PLAN BUDGET DIPLOM CT/SYS   CONSTN
PARL/PROC 19/20. PAGE 77 E1535   LAW

                                                         B48
SLESSER H.,THE ADMINISTRATION OF THE LAW. UK CONSTN LAW
EX/STRUC OP/RES PROB/SOLV CRIME ROLE...DECISION   CT/SYS
METH/COMP 20 CIVIL/LAW ENGLSH/LAW CIVIL/LAW.   ADJUD
PAGE 92 E1839

                                                         B48
STOKES W.S.,BIBLIOGRAPHY OF STANDARD AND CLASSICAL   BIBLIOG
WORKS IN THE FIELDS OF AMERICAN POLITICAL SCIENCE.   NAT/G
USA+45 USA-45 POL/PAR PROVS FORCES DIPLOM ADMIN   LOC/G
CT/SYS APPORT 20 CONGRESS PRESIDENT. PAGE 94 E1876   CONSTN

                                                         S48
BRADEN G.D.,"THE SEARCH FOR OBJECTIVITY IN   CONSTN
CONSTITUTIONAL LAW" (BMR)" USA+45 USA-45 LAW NAT/G   CT/SYS
CONTROL ORD/FREE PWR OBJECTIVE...JURID 20   IDEA/COMP
SUPREME/CT. PAGE 15 E0283   POLICY

                                                         S48
GROSS L.,"THE PEACE OF WESTPHALIA, 1648-1948."   INT/LAW
WOR+45 WOR-45 CONSTN BAL/PWR FEDERAL 17/20 TREATY   AGREE
WESTPHALIA. PAGE 48 E0949   CONCPT
                                                         DIPLOM

                                                         C48
WALKER H.,"THE LEGISLATIVE PROCESS; LAWMAKING IN   PARL/PROC
THE UNITED STATES." NAT/G POL/PAR PROVS EX/STRUC   LEGIS
OP/RES PROB/SOLV CT/SYS LOBBY GOV/REL...CHARTS   LAW
BIBLIOG T 18/20 CONGRESS. PAGE 105 E2094   CONSTN

                                                         B49
MARITAIN J.,HUMAN RIGHTS: COMMENTS AND   INT/ORG
INTERPRETATIONS. COM UNIV WOR+45 LAW CONSTN CULTURE CONCPT
SOCIETY ECO/DEV ECO/UNDEV SCHOOL DELIB/GP EDU/PROP
ATTIT PERCEPT ALL/VALS...HUM SOC TREND UNESCO 20.
PAGE 68 E1365

                                                         B49
THOREAU H.D.,CIVIL DISOBEDIENCE (1849). USA+45 LAW   GEN/LAWS
CONSTN TAX COERCE REPRESENT GP/REL SUPEGO...MAJORIT   ORD/FREE
CONCPT 19. PAGE 96 E1923   POLICY

                                                         B49
US LIBRARY OF CONGRESS,FREEDOM OF INFORMATION: BIBLIOG/A
SELECTIVE REPORT ON RECENT WRITINGS. USA+45 LAW   ORD/FREE
CONSTN ELITES EDU/PROP PRESS LOBBY WAR TOTALSM   LICENSE
ATTIT 20 UN UNESCO COLD/WAR. PAGE 101 E2018   COM/IND

                                                         B49
WORMUTH F.D.,THE ORIGINS OF MODERN   NAT/G
CONSTITUTIONALISM. GREECE UK LEGIS CREATE TEC/DEV   CONSTN
BAL/PWR DOMIN ADJUD REV WAR PWR...JURID ROMAN/REP   LAW
CROMWELL/O. PAGE 107 E2146

                                                         L49
COMM. STUDY ORGAN. PEACE,"A TEN YEAR RECORD,   INT/ORG
1939-1949." FUT WOR+45 LAW R+D CONSULT DELIB/GP   CONSTN
CREATE LEGIT ROUTINE ORD/FREE...TIME/SEQ UN 20.   PEACE
PAGE 24 E0480

                                                         B50
BROWN E.S.,MANUAL OF GOVERNMENT PUBLICATIONS.   BIBLIOG/A
WOR+45 WOR-45 CONSTN INT/ORG MUNIC PROVS DIPLOM   NAT/G
ADMIN 20. PAGE 16 E0313   LAW

                                                         B50
FRAGA IRIBARNE M.,RAZAS Y RACISMO EN NORTEAMERICA.   RACE/REL
USA+45 CONSTN STRATA NAT/G PROVS ATTIT...SOC CONCPT   JURID
19/20 NEGRO. PAGE 39 E0783   LAW
                                                         DISCRIM

                                                         B50
FRANK J.,COURTS ON TRIAL: MYTH AND REALITY IN   JURID
AMERICAN JUSTICE. LAW CONSULT PROB/SOLV EDU/PROP   CT/SYS
ADJUD ROUTINE ROLE ORD/FREE...GEN/LAWS T 20.   MYTH
PAGE 40 E0788   CONSTN

                                                         B50
HURST J.W.,THE GROWTH OF AMERICAN LAW; THE LAW   LAW
MAKERS. USA-45 LOC/G NAT/G DELIB/GP JUDGE ADJUD   LEGIS
ADMIN ATTIT PWR...POLICY JURID BIBLIOG 18/20   CONSTN
CONGRESS SUPREME/CT ABA PRESIDENT. PAGE 56 E1115   CT/SYS

                                                         B50
JENKINS W.S.,A GUIDE TO THE MICROFILM COLLECTION OF BIBLIOG
EARLY STATE RECORDS. USA+45 CONSTN MUNIC LEGIS   PROVS

PRESS ADMIN CT/SYS 18/20. PAGE 58 E1152   AUD/VIS

                                                         B50
JIMENEZ E.,VOTING AND HANDLING OF DISPUTES IN THE   DELIB/GP
SECURITY COUNCIL. WOR+45 CONSTN INT/ORG DIPLOM   ROUTINE
LEGIT DETER CHOOSE MORAL ORD/FREE PWR...JURID
TIME/SEQ COLD/WAR UN 20. PAGE 59 E1168

                                                         B50
LAUTERPACHT H.,INTERNATIONAL LAW AND HUMAN RIGHTS.   DELIB/GP
USA+45 CONSTN STRUCT INT/ORG ACT/RES EDU/PROP PEACE LAW
PERSON ALL/VALS...CONCPT CON/ANAL GEN/LAWS UN 20.   INT/LAW
PAGE 63 E1266

                                                         B50
MACIVER R.M.,GREAT EXPRESSIONS OF HUMAN RIGHTS. LAW UNIV
CONSTN CULTURE INTELL SOCIETY R+D INT/ORG ATTIT   CONCPT
DRIVE...JURID OBS HIST/WRIT GEN/LAWS. PAGE 67 E1340

                                                         B50
ROSS A.,CONSTITUTION OF THE UNITED NATIONS. CONSTN   PEACE
CONSULT DELIB/GP ECO/TAC...INT/LAW JURID 20 UN   DIPLOM
LEAGUE/NAT. PAGE 86 E1721   ORD/FREE
                                                         INT/ORG

                                                         B50
SOHN L.B.,CASES AND OTHER MATERIALS ON WORLD LAW.   CT/SYS
FUT WOR+45 LAW INT/ORG...INT/LAW JURID METH/CNCPT   CONSTN
20 UN. PAGE 92 E1852

                                                         B50
WADE E.C.S.,CONSTITUTIONAL LAW; AN OUTLINE OF THE   CONSTN
LAW AND PRACTICE OF THE CONSTITUTION. UK LEGIS   NAT/G
DOMIN ADMIN GP/REL 16/20 CMN/WLTH PARLIAMENT   PARL/PROC
ENGLSH/LAW. PAGE 104 E2087   LAW

                                                         B50
WARD R.E.,A GUIDE TO JAPANESE REFERENCE AND   BIBLIOG/A
RESEARCH MATERIALS IN THE FIELD OF POLITICAL   ASIA
SCIENCE. LAW CONSTN LOC/G PRESS ADMIN...SOC   NAT/G
CON/ANAL METH 19/20 CHINJAP. PAGE 105 E2098

                                                         C50
HOLCOMBE A.,"OUR MORE PERFECT UNION." USA+45 USA-45 CONSTN
POL/PAR JUDGE CT/SYS EQUILIB FEDERAL PWR...MAJORIT   NAT/G
TREND BIBLIOG 18/20 CONGRESS PRESIDENT. PAGE 54   ADMIN
E1070   PLAN

                                                         B51
ANDERSON W.,STATE AND LOCAL GOVERNMENT IN THE   LOC/G
UNITED STATES. USA+45 CONSTN POL/PAR EX/STRUC LEGIS MUNIC
BUDGET TAX ADJUD CT/SYS CHOOSE...CHARTS T 20.   PROVS
PAGE 5 E0094   GOV/REL

                                                         B51
CAMPBELL E.H.,UNITED STATES CITIZENSHIP AND   LAW
QUALIFICATIONS FOR VOTING IN WASHINGTON. USA+45   CONSTN
NAT/G PROVS...CHARTS BIBLIOG 20 WASHINGT/G. PAGE 19 SUFF
E0371   CHOOSE

                                                         B51
FRIEDMANN W.,LAW AND SOCIAL CHANGE IN CONTEMPORARY LAW
BRITAIN. UK LABOR LG/CO LEGIS JUDGE CT/SYS ORD/FREE ADJUD
NEW/LIB...DECISION JURID TREND METH/COMP BIBLIOG 20 SOCIETY
PARLIAMENT ENGLSH/LAW COMMON/LAW. PAGE 40 E0802   CONSTN

                                                         B51
GIBBS C.R.,CONSTITUTIONAL AND STATUTORY PROVISIONS   PROVS
OF THE STATES (VOL. IX). USA+45 LICENSE ADJUD LEAD   CONSTN
20. PAGE 43 E0857   JURID
                                                         LOBBY

                                                         B51
PUSEY M.J.,CHARLES EVANS HUGHES (2 VOLS.). LAW   BIOG
CONSTN NAT/G POL/PAR DIPLOM LEGIT WAR CHOOSE   TOP/EX
PERS/REL DRIVE HEREDITY 19/20 DEPT/STATE LEAGUE/NAT ADJUD
SUPREME/CT HUGHES/CE WWI. PAGE 83 E1663   PERSON

                                                         B51
ROSSITER C.,THE SUPREME COURT AND THE COMMANDER IN   CT/SYS
CHIEF. LAW CONSTN DELIB/GP EX/STRUC LEGIS TOP/EX   CHIEF
ADJUD CONTROL...DECISION SOC/EXP PRESIDENT. PAGE 86 WAR
E1724   PWR

                                                         B51
WHEARE K.C.,MODERN CONSTITUTIONS (HOME UNIVERSITY   CONSTN
LIBRARY). UNIV LAW NAT/G LEGIS...CONCPT TREND   CLASSIF
BIBLIOG. PAGE 106 E2115   PWR
                                                         CREATE

                                                         B51
WOOD V.,DUE PROCESS OF LAW 1932-1949: SUPREME   CONSTN
COURT'S USE OF A CONSTITUTIONAL TOOL. USA+45 USA-45 TREND
SOCIETY TAX CRIME...POLICY CHARTS 20 SUPREME/CT.   ADJUD
PAGE 107 E2143   GOV/REL

KELSEN H.,"RECENT TRENDS IN THE LAW OF THE UNITED
NATIONS." KOREA WOR+45 CONSTN LEGIS DIPLOM LEGIT
DETER WAR RIGID/FLEX HEALTH ORD/FREE RESPECT
...JURID CON/ANAL UN VAL/FREE 20 NATO. PAGE 60
E1199
L51
INT/ORG
LAW
INT/LAW

LEEK J.H.,"TREASON AND THE CONSTITUTION" (BMR)"
USA+45 USA-45 EDU/PROP COLONIAL CT/SYS REV WAR
ATTIT...TREND 18/20 SUPREME/CT CON/INTERP SMITH/ACT
COMMON/LAW. PAGE 64 E1278
S51
CONSTN
JURID
CRIME
NAT/G

DE GRAZIA A.,POLITICAL ORGANIZATION. CONSTN LOC/G
MUNIC NAT/G CHIEF LEGIS TOP/EX ADJUD CT/SYS
PERS/REL...INT/LAW MYTH UN. PAGE 29 E0581
B52
FEDERAL
LAW
ADMIN

FLECHTHEIM O.K.,FUNDAMENTALS OF POLITICAL SCIENCE.
WOR+45 WOR-45 LAW POL/PAR EX/STRUC LEGIS ADJUD
ATTIT PWR...INT/LAW. PAGE 38 E0760
B52
NAT/G
DIPLOM
IDEA/COMP
CONSTN

GELLER M.A.,ADVERTISING AT THE CROSSROADS: FEDERAL
REGULATION VS. VOLUNTARY CONTROLS. USA+45 JUDGE
ECO/TAC...POLICY JURID BIBLIOG 20 FTC. PAGE 43
E0843
B52
EDU/PROP
NAT/G
CONSTN
COM/IND

HOLDSWORTH W.S.,A HISTORY OF ENGLISH LAW; THE
CENTURIES OF SETTLEMENT AND REFORM, 1701-1875 (VOL.
XIII). UK POL/PAR PROF/ORG LEGIS JUDGE WRITING
ATTIT...JURID CONCPT BIOG GEN/LAWS 18/19 PARLIAMENT
REFORMERS ENGLSH/LAW COMMON/LAW. PAGE 54 E1080
B52
LAW
CONSTN
IDEA/COMP
CT/SYS

JENNINGS W.I.,CONSTITUTIONAL LAWS OF THE
COMMONWEALTH. UK LAW CHIEF LEGIS TAX CT/SYS
PARL/PROC GOV/REL...INT/LAW 18/20 COMMONWLTH
ENGLSH/LAW COMMON/LAW. PAGE 58 E1165
B52
CONSTN
JURID
ADJUD
COLONIAL

KELSEN H.,PRINCIPLES OF INTERNATIONAL LAW. WOR+45
WOR-45 INT/ORG ORD/FREE...JURID GEN/LAWS TOT/POP
20. PAGE 60 E1200
B52
ADJUD
CONSTN
INT/LAW

VANDENBOSCH A.,THE UN: BACKGROUND, ORGANIZATION,
FUNCTIONS, ACTIVITIES. WOR+45 LAW CONSTN STRUCT
INT/ORG CONSULT BAL/PWR EDU/PROP EXEC ALL/VALS
...POLICY CONCPT UN 20. PAGE 103 E2071
B52
DELIB/GP
TIME/SEQ
PEACE

ROSTOW E.V.,"THE DEMOCRATIC CHARACTER OF JUDICIAL
REVIEW" (BMR)" USA+45 LAW NAT/G LEGIS TASK...JURID
20 SUPREME/CT. PAGE 86 E1725
L52
CONSTN
PROB/SOLV
ADJUD
CT/SYS

WRIGHT Q.,"CONGRESS AND THE TREATY-MAKING POWER."
USA+45 WOR+45 CONSTN NAT/G CHIEF CONSULT
EX/STRUC LEGIS TOP/EX CREATE GOV/REL DISPL DRIVE
RIGID/FLEX...TREND TOT/POP CONGRESS CONGRESS 20
TREATY. PAGE 108 E2154
L52
ROUTINE
DIPLOM
INT/LAW
DELIB/GP

DE GRAZIA A.,"GENERAL THEORY OF APPORTIONMENT"
(BMR)" USA+45 USA-45 CONSTN ELITES DELIB/GP PARTIC
REV CHOOSE...JURID 20. PAGE 29 E0582
S52
APPORT
LEGIS
PROVS
REPRESENT

CLAGETT H.L.,"THE ADMINISTRATION OF JUSTICE IN
LATIN AMERICA." L/A+17C ADMIN FEDERAL...JURID
METH/COMP BIBLIOG 20. PAGE 23 E0448
C52
CT/SYS
ADJUD
JUDGE
CONSTN

COKE E.,INSTITUTES OF THE LAWS OF ENGLAND
(1628-1658). UK LAW ADJUD PERS/REL ORD/FREE
...CRIMLGY 11/17. PAGE 24 E0471
B53
JURID
OWN
CT/SYS
CONSTN

OPPENHEIM L.,INTERNATIONAL LAW: A TREATISE (7TH
ED., 2 VOLS.). UK LAW CONSTN INTELL INT/TRADE ADJUD
AGREE NEUTRAL WAR ORD/FREE SOVEREIGN...BIBLIOG 20
LEAGUE/NAT UN ILO. PAGE 79 E1579
B53
INT/LAW
INT/ORG
DIPLOM

PADOVER S.K.,THE LIVING US CONSTITUTION. USA+45
USA-45 POL/PAR ADJUD...DECISION AUD/VIS IDEA/COMP
18/20 SUPREME/CT. PAGE 79 E1590
B53
CONSTN
LEGIS
DELIB/GP
BIOG

STOUT H.M.,BRITISH GOVERNMENT. UK FINAN LOC/G
POL/PAR DELIB/GP DIPLOM ADMIN COLONIAL CHOOSE
ORD/FREE...JURID BIBLIOG 20 COMMONWLTH. PAGE 94
E1883
B53
NAT/G
PARL/PROC
CONSTN
NEW/LIB

UNESCO,A REGISTER OF LEGAL DOCUMENTATION IN THE
WORLD. WOR+45 WOR-45 NAT/G PROVS DELIB/GP LEGIS
13/20. PAGE 98 E1959
B53
BIBLIOG
CONSTN
LAW
JURID

BROGAN D.W.,POLITICS IN AMERICA. LAW POL/PAR CHIEF
LEGIS LOBBY CHOOSE REPRESENT GP/REL RACE/REL
FEDERAL MORAL...BIBLIOG 20 PRESIDENT CONGRESS.
PAGE 16 E0304
B54
NAT/G
CONSTN
USA+45

ELIAS T.O.,GROUNDWORK OF NIGERIAN LAW. AFR LEAD
CRIME INGP/REL ORD/FREE 17/20. PAGE 34 E0680
B54
JURID
CT/SYS
CONSTN
CONSULT

JAMES L.F.,THE SUPREME COURT IN AMERICAN LIFE.
USA+45 USA-45 CONSTN CRIME GP/REL INGP/REL RACE/REL
CONSEN FEDERAL PERSON ORD/FREE 18/20 SUPREME/CT
DEPRESSION CIV/RIGHTS CHURCH/STA FREE/SPEE. PAGE 58
E1147
B54
ADJUD
CT/SYS
JURID
DECISION

O'NEILL J.M.,CATHOLICS IN CONTROVERSY. USA+45 NAT/G
PROVS SCHOOL SECT EDU/PROP LEGIT CT/SYS SANCTION
GP/REL 20 SUPREME/CT CHURCH/STA. PAGE 78 E1569
B54
CATHISM
CONSTN
POLICY
LAW

SINCO,PHILIPPINE POLITICAL LAW: PRINCIPLES AND
CONCEPTS (10TH ED.). PHILIPPINE LOC/G EX/STRUC
BAL/PWR ECO/TAC TAX ADJUD ADMIN CONTROL CT/SYS SUFF
ORD/FREE...T 20. PAGE 91 E1831
B54
LAW
CONSTN
LEGIS

US SENATE COMM ON FOREIGN REL,REVIEW OF THE UNITED
NATIONS CHARTER: A COLLECTION OF DOCUMENTS. LEGIS
DIPLOM ADMIN ARMS/CONT WAR REPRESENT SOVEREIGN
...INT/LAW 20 UN. PAGE 101 E2029
B54
BIBLIOG
CONSTN
INT/ORG
DEBATE

BOWIE R.R.,"STUDIES IN FEDERALISM." AGRI FINAN
LABOR EX/STRUC FORCES LEGIS DIPLOM INT/TRADE ADJUD
...BIBLIOG 20 EEC. PAGE 14 E0279
C54
FEDERAL
EUR+WWI
INT/ORG
CONSTN

CALDWELL L.K.,"THE GOVERNMENT AND ADMINISTRATION OF
NEW YORK." LOC/G MUNIC POL/PAR SCHOOL CHIEF LEGIS
PLAN TAX CT/SYS...MGT SOC/WK BIBLIOG 20 NEWYORK/C.
PAGE 19 E0365
C54
PROVS
ADMIN
CONSTN
EX/STRUC

BEANEY W.M.,THE RIGHT TO COUNSEL IN AMERICAN
COURTS. UK USA+45 USA-45 LAW NAT/G PROVS COLONIAL
PERCEPT 18/20 SUPREME/CT AMEND/VI AMEND/XIV
ENGLSH/LAW. PAGE 8 E0163
B55
ADJUD
CONSTN
CT/SYS

BEISEL A.R.,CONTROL OVER ILLEGAL ENFORCEMENT OF THE
CRIMINAL LAW: ROLE OF THE SUPREME COURT. CONSTN
ROUTINE MORAL PWR...SOC 20 SUPREME/CT. PAGE 9 E0180
B55
ORD/FREE
LAW
CRIME

CHENERY W.L.,FREEDOM OF THE PRESS. USA+45 USA-45
LAW NAT/G DOMIN EDU/PROP 17/20. PAGE 22 E0427
B55
ORD/FREE
COM/IND
PRESS
CONSTN

CRAIG J.,BIBLIOGRAPHY OF PUBLIC ADMINISTRATION IN
AUSTRALIA. CONSTN FINAN EX/STRUC LEGIS PLAN DIPLOM
RECEIVE ADJUD ROUTINE...HEAL 19/20 AUSTRAL
PARLIAMENT. PAGE 27 E0540
B55
BIBLIOG
GOV/REL
ADMIN
NAT/G

CUSHMAN R.E.,LEADING CONSTITUTIONAL DECISIONS.
USA+45 USA-45 NAT/G EX/STRUC LEGIS JUDGE TAX
FEDERAL...DECISION 20 SUPREME/CT CASEBOOK. PAGE 28
E0559
B55
CONSTN
PROB/SOLV
JURID
CT/SYS

FLIESS P.J.,FREEDOM OF THE PRESS IN THE GERMAN
REPUBLIC, 1918-1933. GERMANY LAW CONSTN POL/PAR
LEGIS WRITING ADMIN COERCE MURDER MARXISM...POLICY
BIBLIOG 20 WEIMAR/REP. PAGE 39 E0765
B55
EDU/PROP
ORD/FREE
JURID
PRESS

GUAITA A.,BIBLIOGRAFIA ESPANOLA DE DERECHO ADMINISTRATIVO (PAMPHLET). SPAIN LOC/G MUNIC NAT/G PROVS JUDGE BAL/PWR GOV/REL OWN...JURID 18/19. PAGE 48 E0959
B55 BIBLIOG ADMIN CONSTN PWR

HOGAN W.N.,INTERNATIONAL CONFLICT AND COLLECTIVE SECURITY: THE PRINCIPLE OF CONCERN IN INTERNATIONAL ORGANIZATION. CONSTN EX/STRUC BAL/PWR DIPLOM ADJUD CONTROL CENTRAL CONSEN PEACE...INT/LAW CONCPT METH/COMP 20 UN LEAGUE/NAT. PAGE 53 E1066
B55 INT/ORG WAR ORD/FREE FORCES

JAPAN MOMBUSHO DAIGAKU GAKIYUT,BIBLIOGRAPHY OF THE STUDIES ON LAW AND POLITICS (PAMPHLET). CONSTN INDUS LABOR DIPLOM TAX ADMIN...CRIMLGY INT/LAW 20 CHINJAP. PAGE 58 E1150
B55 BIBLIOG LAW PHIL/SCI

KHADDURI M.,WAR AND PEACE IN THE LAW OF ISLAM. CONSTN CULTURE SOCIETY STRATA NAT/G PROVS SECT FORCES TOP/EX CREATE DOMIN EDU/PROP ADJUD COERCE ATTIT RIGID/FLEX ALL/VALS...CONCPT TIME/SEQ TOT/POP VAL/FREE. PAGE 61 E1209
B55 ISLAM JURID PEACE WAR

KHADDURI M.,LAW IN THE MIDDLE EAST. LAW CONSTN ACADEM FAM EDU/PROP CT/SYS SANCTION CRIME...INT/LAW GOV/COMP ANTHOL 6/20 MID/EAST. PAGE 61 E1210
B55 ADJUD JURID ISLAM

SERRANO MOSCOSO E.,A STATEMENT OF THE LAWS OF ECUADOR IN MATTERS AFFECTING BUSINESS (2ND ED.). ECUADOR INDUS LABOR LG/CO NAT/G LEGIS TAX CONTROL MARRIAGE 20. PAGE 90 E1805
B55 FINAN ECO/UNDEV LAW CONSTN

SMITH G.,A CONSTITUTIONAL AND LEGAL HISTORY OF ENGLAND. UK ELITES NAT/G LEGIS ADJUD OWN HABITAT POPULISM...JURID 20 ENGLSH/LAW. PAGE 92 E1844
B55 CONSTN PARTIC LAW CT/SYS

SWEET AND MAXWELL,A LEGAL BIBLIOGRAPHY OF THE BRITISH COMMONWEALTH OF NATIONS (2ND ED. 7 VOLS.). UK LOC/G MUNIC JUDGE ADJUD CRIME OWN...JURID 14/20 CMN/WLTH. PAGE 95 E1900
B55 BIBLIOG/A LAW CONSTN CT/SYS

WHEARE K.C.,GOVERNMENT BY COMMITTEE: AN ESSAY ON THE BRITISH CONSTITUTION. UK NAT/G LEGIS INSPECT CONFER ADJUD ADMIN CONTROL TASK EFFICIENCY ROLE POPULISM 20. PAGE 106 E2116
B55 DELIB/GP CONSTN LEAD GP/COMP

WRONG D.H.,AMERICAN AND CANADIAN VIEWPOINTS. CANADA USA+45 CONSTN STRATA FAM SECT WORKER ECO/TAC EDU/PROP ADJUD MARRIAGE...IDEA/COMP 20. PAGE 108 E2161
B55 DIPLOM ATTIT NAT/COMP CULTURE

BETH L.P.,"THE CASE FOR JUDICIAL PROTECTION OF CIVIL LIBERTIES" (BMR)" USA+45 CONSTN ELITES LEGIS CONTROL...POLICY DECISION JURID 20 SUPREME/CT CIVIL/LIB. PAGE 11 E0220
S55 CT/SYS JUDGE ADJUD ORD/FREE

CAHN E.,"A DANGEROUS MYTH IN THE SCHOOL SEGREGATION CASES" (BMR)" USA+45 CONSTN PROVS ADJUD DISCRIM ...POLICY MYTH SOC/INTEG 20 SUPREME/CT AMEND/XIV. PAGE 18 E0360
S55 JURID SCHOOL RACE/REL

DOUGLAS W.O.,WE THE JUDGES. INDIA USA+45 USA-45 LAW NAT/G SECT LEGIS PRESS CRIME FEDERAL ORD/FREE ...POLICY GOV/COMP 19/20 WARRN/EARL MARSHALL/J SUPREME/CT. PAGE 32 E0640
B56 ADJUD CT/SYS CONSTN GOV/REL

EMDEN C.S.,THE PEOPLE AND THE CONSTITUTION (2ND ED.). UK LEGIS POPULISM 17/20 PARLIAMENT. PAGE 35 E0687
B56 CONSTN PARL/PROC NAT/G LAW

HURST J.W.,LAW AND THE CONDITIONS OF FREEDOM IN THE NINETEENTH CENTURY UNITED STATES. USA-45 CONSTN STRUCT ADMIN GP/REL FEDERAL HABITAT...JURID 19. PAGE 56 E1116
B56 LAW ORD/FREE POLICY NAT/G

KALNOKI BEDO A.,LEGAL SOURCES AND BIBLIOGRAPHY OF HUNGARY. COM HUNGARY CONSTN LEGIS JUDGE CT/SYS SANCTION CRIME 16/20. PAGE 59 E1181
B56 BIBLIOG ADJUD LAW

LASLETT P.,PHILOSOPHY, POLITICS AND SOCIETY. UNIV CRIME SOVEREIGN...JURID PHIL/SCI ANTHOL PLATO NATURL/LAW. PAGE 63 E1260
B56 CONSTN ATTIT CONCPT GEN/LAWS

PEASLEE A.J.,CONSTITUTIONS OF NATIONS. WOR+45 LAW NAT/G EX/STRUC LEGIS TOP/EX LEGIT CT/SYS ROUTINE CHOOSE ORD/FREE PWR SOVEREIGN...CHARTS TOT/POP. PAGE 80 E1605
B56 CONSTN CON/ANAL

SCHROEDER T.,METHODS OF CONSTITUTIONAL CONSTRUCTION. LAW...METH 20. PAGE 88 E1769
B56 ORD/FREE CONSTN JURID EDU/PROP

SOHN L.B.,BASIC DOCUMENTS OF THE UNITED NATIONS. WOR+45 LAW INT/ORG LEGIT EXEC ROUTINE CHOOSE PWR ...JURID CONCPT GEN/LAWS ANTHOL UN TOT/POP OAS FAO ILO 20. PAGE 92 E1853
B56 DELIB/GP CONSTN

WEIS P.,NATIONALITY AND STATELESSNESS IN INTERNATIONAL LAW. UK WOR+45 WOR-45 LAW CONSTN NAT/G DIPLOM EDU/PROP LEGIT ROUTINE RIGID/FLEX ...JURID RECORD CMN/WLTH 20. PAGE 105 E2109
B56 INT/ORG SOVEREIGN INT/LAW

ZINN C.J.,HOW OUR LAWS ARE MADE: BROCHURE HOUSE OF REPRESENTATIVES DOCUMENT 451. LAW CONSTN CHIEF EX/STRUC PROB/SOLV HOUSE/REP SENATE. PAGE 108 E2171
B56 LEGIS DELIB/GP PARL/PROC ROUTINE

NOBLEMAN E.E.,"THE DELEGATION OF PRESIDENTIAL FUNCTIONS: CONSTITUTIONAL AND LEGAL ASPECTS." USA+45 CONSTN NAT/G CONTROL 20. PAGE 77 E1553
S56 CHIEF REPRESENT EX/STRUC LAW

BERLE A.A. JR.,ECONOMIC POWER AND FREE SOCIETY (PAMPHLET). CLIENT CONSTN EX/STRUC ECO/TAC CONTROL PARTIC PWR WEALTH MAJORIT. PAGE 11 E0205
B57 LG/CO CAP/ISM INGP/REL LEGIT

BERNS W.,FREEDOM, VIRTUE AND THE FIRST AMENDMENT. USA+45 USA-45 CONSTN INTELL JUDGE ADJUD RIGID/FLEX MORAL...CONCPT 20 AMEND/I. PAGE 11 E0211
B57 JURID ORD/FREE CT/SYS LAW

BERNS W.,FREEDOM, VIRTUE, AND THE FIRST AMENDMENT. USA-45 LAW CONSTN PROB/SOLV NEW/LIB...JURID 20 SUPREME/CT AMEND/I. PAGE 11 E0212
B57 ADJUD CT/SYS ORD/FREE

COMM. STUDY ORGAN. PEACE,STRENGTHENING THE UNITED NATIONS. FUT USA+45 WOR+45 CONSTN NAT/G DELIB/GP FORCES LEGIS ECO/TAC LEGIT COERCE PEACE...JURID CONCPT UN COLD/WAR 20. PAGE 24 E0482
B57 INT/ORG ORD/FREE

DONALDSON A.G.,SOME COMPARATIVE ASPECTS OF IRISH LAW. IRELAND NAT/G DIPLOM ADMIN CT/SYS LEAD ATTIT SOVEREIGN...JURID BIBLIOG/A 12/20 CMN/WLTH. PAGE 32 E0635
B57 CONSTN LAW NAT/COMP INT/LAW

DUMBAULD E.,THE BILL OF RIGHTS AND WHAT IT MEANS TODAY. USA+45 USA-45 CT/SYS...JURID STYLE TIME/SEQ BIBLIOG 18/20 BILL/RIGHT. PAGE 33 E0656
B57 CONSTN LAW ADJUD ORD/FREE

LONG H.A.,USURPERS - FOES OF FREE MAN. LAW NAT/G CHIEF LEGIS DOMIN ADJUD REPRESENT GOV/REL ORD/FREE LAISSEZ POPULISM...POLICY 18/20 SUPREME/CT ROOSEVLT/F CONGRESS CON/INTERP. PAGE 66 E1325
B57 CT/SYS CENTRAL FEDERAL CONSTN

MILLS W.,INDIVIDUAL FREEDOM AND COMMON DEFENSE (PAMPHLET). USA+45 USSR NAT/G EDU/PROP CRIME CHOOSE 20 COLD/WAR. PAGE 73 E1463
B57 ORD/FREE CONSTN INGP/REL FORCES

MORELAND C.C.,EQUAL JUSTICE UNDER LAW. USA+45 USA-45 PROF/ORG PROVS JUDGE...POLICY JURID. PAGE 74 E1491
B57 CONSTN ADJUD CT/SYS ORD/FREE

POUND R.,THE DEVELOPMENT OF CONSTITUTIONAL
GUARANTEES OF LIBERTY. UK USA-45 CHIEF COLONIAL REV
...JURID CONCPT 15/20. PAGE 82 E1638
B57
LAW
CONSTN
ORD/FREE
ATTIT

SCHLOCHAUER H.J.,OFFENTLICHES RECHT. GERMANY/W
FINAN EX/STRUC LEGIS DIPLOM FEDERAL ORD/FREE
...INT/LAW 20. PAGE 88 E1757
B57
CONSTN
JURID
ADMIN
CT/SYS

SCHUBERT G.A.,THE PRESIDENCY IN THE COURTS. CONSTN
FORCES DIPLOM TARIFFS ADJUD CONTROL WAR...DECISION
MGT CHARTS 18/20 PRESIDENT CONGRESS SUPREME/CT.
PAGE 89 E1778
B57
PWR
CT/SYS
LEGIT
CHIEF

UNESCO,A REGISTER OF LEGAL DOCUMENTATION IN THE
WORLD (2ND ED.). CT/SYS...JURID IDEA/COMP METH/COMP
NAT/COMP 20. PAGE 98 E1960
B57
BIBLIOG
LAW
INT/LAW
CONSTN

US SENATE COMM ON JUDICIARY,HEARING BEFORE
SUBCOMMITTEE ON COMMITTEE OF JUDICIARY, UNITED
STATES SENATE: S. J. RES. 3. USA+45 NAT/G CONSULT
DELIB/GP DIPLOM ADJUD LOBBY REPRESENT 20 CONGRESS
TREATY. PAGE 102 E2040
B57
LEGIS
CONSTN
CONFER
AGREE

KNEIER C.M.,"MISLEADING THE VOTERS." CONSTN LEAD
CHOOSE PERS/REL. PAGE 61 E1224
S57
MUNIC
REPRESENT
LAW
ATTIT

ALEXANDROWICZ,A BIBLIOGRAPHY OF INDIAN LAW. INDIA
S/ASIA CONSTN CT/SYS...INT/LAW 19/20. PAGE 3 E0062
B58
BIBLIOG
LAW
ADJUD
JURID

ALLEN C.K.,LAW IN THE MAKING. LEGIS ATTIT ORD/FREE
SOVEREIGN POPULISM...JURID IDEA/COMP NAT/COMP
GEN/LAWS 20 ENGLSH/LAW. PAGE 4 E0069
B58
LAW
CREATE
CONSTN
SOCIETY

BLOCH J.,STATES' RIGHTS: THE LAW OF THE LAND.
USA+45 USA-45 LAW CONSTN LEGIS CONTROL CT/SYS
FEDERAL ORD/FREE...PREDICT 17/20 CONGRESS
SUPREME/CT. PAGE 13 E0246
B58
PROVS
NAT/G
BAL/PWR
CENTRAL

CHARLES R.,LA JUSTICE EN FRANCE. FRANCE LAW CONSTN
DELIB/GP CRIME 20. PAGE 21 E0422
B58
JURID
ADMIN
CT/SYS
ADJUD

DOUGLAS W.O.,THE RIGHT OF THE PEOPLE. USA+45
EDU/PROP CONTROL REPRESENT PRIVIL...IDEA/COMP 20.
PAGE 32 E0641
B58
ORD/FREE
CONSTN
CT/SYS
CIVMIL/REL

FELLMAN D.,THE DEFENDANT'S RIGHTS. USA+45 NAT/G
CONSULT CT/SYS SUPEGO ORD/FREE...BIBLIOG SUPREME/CT
CIVIL/SERV. PAGE 37 E0730
B58
CONSTN
LAW
CRIME
ADJUD

HAND L.,THE BILL OF RIGHTS. USA+45 USA-45 CHIEF
LEGIS BAL/PWR ROLE PWR 18/20 SUPREME/CT CONGRESS
AMEND/V PRESIDENT AMEND/XIV. PAGE 50 E0994
B58
CONSTN
JURID
ORD/FREE
CT/SYS

HENKIN L.,ARMS CONTROL AND INSPECTION IN AMERICAN
LAW. LAW CONSTN INT/ORG LOC/G MUNIC NAT/G PROVS
EDU/PROP LEGIT EXEC NUC/PWR KNOWL ORD/FREE...OBS
TOT/POP CONGRESS 20. PAGE 52 E1032
B58
USA+45
JURID
ARMS/CONT

JAPAN MINISTRY OF JUSTICE,CRIMINAL JUSTICE IN
JAPAN. LAW PROF/ORG PUB/INST FORCES CONTROL CT/SYS
PARL/PROC 20 CHINJAP. PAGE 58 E1149
B58
CONSTN
CRIME
JURID
ADMIN

KAPLAN H.E.,THE LAW OF CIVIL SERVICE. USA+45 LAW
POL/PAR CT/SYS CRIME GOV/REL...POLICY JURID 20.
PAGE 59 E1183
B58
ADJUD
NAT/G
ADMIN

OGDEN F.D.,THE POLL TAX IN THE SOUTH. USA+45 USA-45
CONSTN ADJUD ADMIN PARTIC CRIME...TIME/SEQ GOV/COMP
METH/COMP 18/20 SOUTH/US. PAGE 78 E1572
B58
TAX
CHOOSE
RACE/REL
DISCRIM

PALMER E.E.,CIVIL LIBERTIES. USA+45 ADJUD CT/SYS
PARTIC OWN LAISSEZ POPULISM...JURID CONCPT ANTHOL
20 SUPREME/CT CIVIL/LIB. PAGE 79 E1592
B58
ORD/FREE
CONSTN
RACE/REL
LAW

RUSSELL R.B.,A HISTORY OF THE UNITED NATIONS
CHARTER: THE ROLE OF THE UNITED STATES. SOCIETY
NAT/G CONSULT DOMIN LEGIT ATTIT ORD/FREE PWR
...POLICY JURID CONCPT UN LEAGUE/NAT. PAGE 87 E1737
B58
USA-45
INT/ORG
CONSTN

STONE J.,AGGRESSION AND WORLD ORDER: A CRITIQUE OF
UNITED NATIONS THEORIES OF AGGRESSION. LAW CONSTN
DELIB/GP PROB/SOLV BAL/PWR DIPLOM DEBATE ADJUD
CRIME PWR...POLICY IDEA/COMP 20 UN SUEZ LEAGUE/NAT.
PAGE 94 E1879
B58
ORD/FREE
INT/ORG
WAR
CONCPT

STRONG C.F.,MODERN POLITICAL CONSTITUTIONS. LAW
CHIEF DELIB/GP EX/STRUC LEGIS ADJUD CHOOSE FEDERAL
POPULISM...CONCPT BIBLIOG 20 UN. PAGE 94 E1887
B58
CONSTN
IDEA/COMP
NAT/G

US CONGRESS,FREEDOM OF INFORMATION AND SECRECY IN
GOVERNMENT (2 VOLS.). USA+45 DELIB/GP EX/STRUC
EDU/PROP PWR 20 CONGRESS PRESIDENT. PAGE 99 E1988
B58
CHIEF
PRIVIL
CONSTN
LAW

WESTIN A.F.,THE ANATOMY OF A CONSTITUTIONAL LAW
CASE. USA+45 LAW LEGIS ADMIN EXEC...DECISION MGT
SOC RECORD 20 SUPREME/CT. PAGE 105 E2113
B58
CT/SYS
INDUS
ADJUD
CONSTN

WOOD J.E.,CHURCH AND STATE IN SCRIPTURE HISTORY AND
CONSTITUTIONAL LAW. LAW CONSTN SOCIETY PROVS
VOL/ASSN BAL/PWR COLONIAL CT/SYS ATTIT...BIBLIOG 20
SUPREME/CT CHURCH/STA BIBLE. PAGE 107 E2142
B58
GP/REL
SECT
NAT/G
ADJUD

DAHL R.A.,"DECISION-MAKING IN A DEMOCRACY: THE
SUPREME COURT AS A NATIONAL POLICY-MAKER" (BMR)"
USA+45 USA-45 POL/PAR ADJUD GOV/REL PWR...POLICY
JURID 19/20 SUPREME/CT. PAGE 28 E0561
S58
CT/SYS
CONSTN
DECISION
NAT/G

RAJAN M.S.,"UNITED NATIONS AND DOMESTIC
JURISDICTION." WOR+45 WOR-45 PARL/PROC...IDEA/COMP
BIBLIOG 20 UN. PAGE 83 E1670
C58
INT/LAW
DIPLOM
CONSTN
INT/ORG

ABRAHAM H.J.,COURTS AND JUDGES: AN INTRODUCTION TO
THE JUDICIAL PROCESS. USA+45 CONSTN ELITES NAT/G
ORD/FREE PWR 19/20 SUPREME/CT. PAGE 2 E0045
B59
CT/SYS
PERSON
JURID
ADJUD

BECK C.,CONTEMPT OF CONGRESS: A STUDY OF THE
PROSECUTIONS INITIATED BY THE COMMITTEE ON UN-
AMERICAN ACTIVITIES. USA+45 CONSTN DEBATE EXEC.
PAGE 9 E0170
B59
LEGIS
DELIB/GP
PWR
ADJUD

BROMWICH L.,UNION CONSTITUTIONS. CONSTN EX/STRUC
PRESS ADJUD CONTROL CHOOSE REPRESENT PWR SAMP.
PAGE 16 E0306
B59
LABOR
ROUTINE
INGP/REL
RACE/REL

CHRISTMAN H.M.,THE PUBLIC PAPERS OF CHIEF JUSTICE
EARL WARREN. CONSTN POL/PAR EDU/PROP SANCTION
HEALTH...TREND 20 SUPREME/CT WARRN/EARL. PAGE 22
E0436
B59
LAW
CT/SYS
PERSON
ADJUD

CORBETT P.E.,LAW IN DIPLOMACY. UK USA+45 USSR
CONSTN SOCIETY INT/ORG JUDGE LEGIT ATTIT ORD/FREE
TOT/POP LEAGUE/NAT 20. PAGE 26 E0507
B59
NAT/G
ADJUD
JURID
DIPLOM

FELLMANN D.,THE LIMITS OF FREEDOM. USA+45 USA-45
NAT/G SECT ROLE ORD/FREE WORSHIP 18/20 FREE/SPEE.
PAGE 37 E0734
B59
CONCPT
JURID
CONSTN

B59
FERRY W.H.,THE CORPORATION AND THE ECONOMY. CLIENT LG/CO
LAW CONSTN LABOR NAT/G PLAN INT/TRADE PARTIC CONSEN CONTROL
ORD/FREE PWR POLICY. PAGE 37 E0742 REPRESENT

B59
GINZBURG B.,REDEDICATION TO FREEDOM. DELIB/GP LEGIS JURID
ATTIT MARXISM 20 SUPREME/CT CON/INTERP HUAC AMEND/I ORD/FREE
FBI. PAGE 44 E0871 CONSTN
NAT/G

B59
LOEWENSTEIN K.,VERFASSUNGSRECHT UND CONSTN
VERFASSUNGSPRAXIS DER VEREINIGTEN STAATEN. USA+45 POL/PAR
USA-45 COLONIAL CT/SYS GP/REL RACE/REL ORD/FREE EX/STRUC
...JURID 18/20 SUPREME/CT CONGRESS PRESIDENT NAT/G
BILL/RIGHT CIVIL/LIB. PAGE 66 E1319

B59
NICHOLS R.F.,RELIGION AND AMERICAN DEMOCRACY. NAT/G
USA+45 USA-45 LAW CHOOSE SUFF MORAL ORD/FREE SECT
POPULISM...POLICY BIBLIOG 16/20 PRE/US/AM CONSTN
CHRISTIAN. PAGE 77 E1547 CONCPT

B59
SCOTT F.R.,CIVIL LIBERTIES AND CANADIAN FEDERALISM. ORD/FREE
CANADA LAW ADJUD CT/SYS GOV/REL 20 CIV/RIGHTS. FEDERAL
PAGE 90 E1797 NAT/LISM
CONSTN

B59
SPIRO H.J.,GOVERNMENT BY CONSTITUTIONS: THE NAT/G
POLITICAL SYSTEMS OF DEMOCRACY. CANADA EUR+WWI FUT CONSTN
USA+45 WOR+45 WOR-45 LEGIS TOP/EX LEGIT ADMIN
CT/SYS ORD/FREE PWR...TREND TOT/POP VAL/FREE 20.
PAGE 93 E1861

B59
TOMPKINS D.C.,SUPREME COURT OF THE UNITED STATES: A BIBLIOG/A
BIBLIOGRAPHY. LAW JUDGE ADJUD GOV/REL DISCRIM CT/SYS
...JURID 18/20 SUPREME/CT NEGRO. PAGE 96 E1931 CONSTN
NAT/G

B59
US SENATE COMM ON JUDICIARY,EXECUTIVE PRIVILEGE. CHIEF
USA+45 DELIB/GP CONTROL KNOWL PWR 20 CONGRESS PRIVIL
PRESIDENT. PAGE 102 E2042 CONSTN
LAW

B59
VOSE C.E.,CAUCASIANS ONLY: THE SUPREME COURT, THE CT/SYS
NAACP, AND THE RESTRICTIVE COVENANT CASES. USA+45 RACE/REL
LAW CONSTN LOBBY...SOC 20 NAACP SUPREME/CT NEGRO. DISCRIM
PAGE 104 E2086

S59
JENKS C.W.,"THE CHALLENGE OF UNIVERSALITY." FUT INT/ORG
UNIV CONSTN CULTURE CONSULT CREATE PLAN LEGIT ATTIT LAW
MORAL ORD/FREE RESPECT...MAJORIT JURID 20. PAGE 58 PEACE
E1155 INT/LAW

S59
MASON A.T.,"THE SUPREME COURT: TEMPLE AND FORUM" CT/SYS
(BMR)" USA+45 USA-45 CONSTN DELIB/GP RACE/REL JURID
MAJORITY ORD/FREE...DECISION SOC/INTEG 19/20 PWR
SUPREME/CT WARRN/EARL CIV/RIGHTS. PAGE 69 E1377 ATTIT

B60
JUNZ A.J.,PRESENT TRENDS IN AMERICAN NATIONAL POL/PAR
GOVERNMENT. LEGIS DIPLOM ADMIN CT/SYS ORD/FREE CHOOSE
...CONCPT ANTHOL 20 CONGRESS PRESIDENT SUPREME/CT. CONSTN
PAGE 2 E0040 NAT/G

B60
BAKER G.E.,STATE CONSTITUTIONS - REAPPORTIONMENT. APPORT
USA+45 USA-45 CONSTN CHOOSE ATTIT ORD/FREE...JURID REPRESENT
20. PAGE 7 E0138 PROVS
LEGIS

B60
BAYLEY D.H.,VIOLENT AGITATION AND THE DEMOCRATIC COERCE
PROCESS IN INDIA. INDIA LAW POL/PAR 20. PAGE 8 CROWD
E0159 CONSTN
PROB/SOLV

B60
CARPER E.T.,THE DEFENSE APPROPRIATIONS RIDER GOV/REL
(PAMPHLET). USA+45 CONSTN CHIEF DELIB/GP LEGIS ADJUD
BUDGET LOBBY CIVMIL/REL...POLICY 20 CONGRESS LAW
EISNHWR/DD DEPT/DEFEN PRESIDENT BOSTON. PAGE 20 CONTROL
E0390

B60
CASTBERG F.,FREEDOM OF SPEECH IN THE WEST. FRANCE ORD/FREE
GERMANY USA+45 USA-45 LAW CONSTN CHIEF PRESS SANCTION

DISCRIM...CONCPT 18/20. PAGE 21 E0406 ADJUD
NAT/COMP

B60
DILEY A.V.,INTRODUCTION TO THE STUDY OF THE LAW OF CONSTN
THE CONSTITUTION. FRANCE UK USA+45 USA-45 CONSULT LAW
FORCES TAX ADMIN FEDERAL ORD/FREE SOVEREIGN LEGIS
...IDEA/COMP 20 ENGLSH/LAW CON/INTERP PARLIAMENT. GEN/LAWS
PAGE 32 E0627

B60
DUMON F.,LA COMMUNAUTE FRANCO-AFRO-MALGACHE: SES JURID
ORIGINES, SES INSTITUTIONS, SON EVOLUTION. FRANCE INT/ORG
MADAGASCAR POL/PAR DIPLOM ADMIN ATTIT...TREND T 20. AFR
PAGE 33 E0657 CONSTN

B60
GELLHORN W.,AMERICAN RIGHTS: THE CONSTITUTION IN ORD/FREE
ACTION. USA+45 USA-45 LEGIS ADJUD COERCE RACE/REL JURID
DISCRIM MARXISM 20 SUPREME/CT. PAGE 43 E0846 CT/SYS
CONSTN

B60
HANBURY H.G.,ENGLISH COURTS OF LAW. UK EX/STRUC JURID
LEGIS CRIME ROLE 12/20 COMMON/LAW ENGLSH/LAW. CT/SYS
PAGE 50 E0993 CONSTN
GOV/REL

B60
HARVARD LAW SCHOOL LIBRARY,CURRENT LEGAL BIBLIOG
BIBLIOGRAPHY. USA+45 CONSTN LEGIS ADJUD CT/SYS JURID
POLICY. PAGE 51 E1006 LAW
INT/LAW

B60
JENKS C.W.,HUMAN RIGHTS AND INTERNATIONAL LABOR CONCPT
STANDARDS. WOR+45 CONSTN LABOR VOL/ASSN DELIB/GP
ACT/RES EDU/PROP MORAL RESPECT...JURID SOC TREND
GEN/LAWS WORK ILO 20. PAGE 58 E1156

B60
LASKIN B.,CANADIAN CONSTITUTIONAL LAW: TEXT AND CONSTN
NOTES ON DISTRIBUTION OF LEGISLATIVE POWER (2ND NAT/G
ED.). CANADA LOC/G ECO/TAC TAX CONTROL CT/SYS CRIME LAW
FEDERAL PWR...JURID 20 PARLIAMENT. PAGE 63 E1259 LEGIS

B60
MENDELSON W.,CAPITALISM, DEMOCRACY, AND THE SUPREME JUDGE
COURT. USA+45 USA-45 CONSTN DIPLOM GOV/REL ATTIT CT/SYS
ORD/FREE LAISSEZ...POLICY CHARTS PERS/COMP 18/20 JURID
SUPREME/CT MARSHALL/J HOLMES/OW TANEY/RB FIELD/JJ. NAT/G
PAGE 72 E1437

B60
PAUL A.M.,CONSERVATIVE CRISIS AND THE RULE OF LAW. CONSTN
USA-45 LABOR WORKER ATTIT ORD/FREE CONSERVE LAISSEZ ADJUD
...DECISION JURID 19 SUPREME/CT. PAGE 80 E1603 STRUCT
PROF/ORG

B60
PICKLES D.,THE FIFTH FRENCH REPUBLIC. ALGERIA CONSTN
FRANCE CHOOSE GOV/REL ATTIT CONSERVE...CHARTS 20 ADJUD
DEGAULLE/C. PAGE 80 E1615 NAT/G
EFFICIENCY

B60
PRICE D.,THE SECRETARY OF STATE. USA+45 CONSTN CONSULT
ELITES INTELL CHIEF EX/STRUC TOP/EX LEGIT ATTIT PWR DIPLOM
SKILL...DECISION 20 CONGRESS. PAGE 82 E1650 INT/LAW

B60
RIENOW R.,INTRODUCTION TO GOVERNMENT (2ND ED.). UK CONSTN
USA+45 USSR POL/PAR ADMIN REV CHOOSE SUFF FEDERAL PARL/PROC
PWR...JURID GOV/COMP T 20. PAGE 85 E1697 REPRESENT
AUTHORIT

B60
SCHUBERT G.A.,CONSTITUTIONAL POLITICS: THE CONSTN
POLITICAL BEHAVIOR OF SUPREME COURT JUSTICES AND CT/SYS
THE CONSTITUTIONAL POLICIES THEY MAKE. LAW ELITES JURID
CHIEF DELIB/GP EX/STRUC LEGIS DISCRIM ORD/FREE PWR DECISION
...POLICY MAJORIT CHARTS SUPREME/CT CONGRESS.
PAGE 89 E1781

B60
US SENATE COMM ON JUDICIARY,FEDERAL ADMINISTRATIVE PARL/PROC
PROCEDURE. USA+45 CONSTN NAT/G PROB/SOLV CONFER LEGIS
GOV/REL...JURID INT 20 SENATE. PAGE 102 E2043 ADMIN
LAW

B60
US SENATE COMM ON JUDICIARY,ADMINISTRATIVE PARL/PROC
PROCEDURE LEGISLATION. USA+45 CONSTN NAT/G LEGIS
PROB/SOLV CONFER ROUTINE GOV/REL...INT 20 SENATE. ADMIN
PAGE 102 E2044 JURID

B60

WOETZEL R.K.,THE INTERNATIONAL CONTROL OF AIRSPACE AND OUTERSPACE. FUT WOR+45 AIR CONSTN STRUCT CONSULT PLAN TEC/DEV ADJUD RIGID/FLEX KNOWL ORD/FREE PWR...TECHNIC GEOG MGT NEW/IDEA TREND COMPUT/IR VAL/FREE 20 TREATY. PAGE 107 E2137
INT/ORG
JURID
SPACE
INT/LAW

L60

DEAN A.W.,"SECOND GENEVA CONFERENCE OF THE LAW OF THE SEA: THE FIGHT FOR FREEDOM OF THE SEAS." FUT USA+45 USSR WOR+45 WOR-45 SEA CONSTN STRUCT PLAN INT/TRADE ADJUD ADMIN ORD/FREE...DECISION RECORD TREND GEN/LAWS 20 TREATY. PAGE 30 E0600
INT/ORG
JURID
INT/LAW

L60

MILLER A.S.,"THE MYTH OF NEUTRALITY IN CONSTITUTIONAL ADJUDICATION." LAW...DECISION JURID LING TREND IDEA/COMP. PAGE 73 E1456
ADJUD
CONSTN
MYTH
UTIL

S60

BLACK H.,"THE BILL OF RIGHTS" (BMR)" USA+45 USA-45 LAW LEGIS CT/SYS FEDERAL PWR 18/20 CONGRESS SUPREME/CT BILL/RIGHT CIV/RIGHTS. PAGE 12 E0237
CONSTN
ORD/FREE
NAT/G
JURID

S60

GRACIA-MORA M.R.,"INTERNATIONAL RESPONSIBILITY FOR SUBVERSIVE ACTIVITIES AND HOSTILE PROPAGANDA BY PRIVATE PERSONS AGAINST." COM EUR+WWI L/A+17C UK USA+45 USSR WOR-45 CONSTN NAT/G LEGIT ADJUD REV PEACE TOTALISM ORD/FREE...INT/LAW 20. PAGE 45 E0895
INT/ORG
JURID
SOVEREIGN

S60

MACKINNON F.,"THE UNIVERSITY: COMMUNITY OR UTILITY?" CLIENT CONSTN INTELL FINAN NAT/G NEIGH EDU/PROP PARTIC REPRESENT ROLE. PAGE 67 E1343
ACADEM
MGT
CONTROL
SERV/IND

S60

SCHWELB E.,"INTERNATIONAL CONVENTIONS ON HUMAN RIGHTS." FUT WOR+45 LAW CONSTN CULTURE SOCIETY STRUCT VOL/ASSN DELIB/GP PLAN ADJUD SUPEGO LOVE MORAL...SOC CONCPT STAT RECORD HIST/WRIT TREND 20 UN. PAGE 89 E1790
INT/ORG
HUM

B61

BAINS J.S.,STUDIES IN POLITICAL SCIENCE. INDIA WOR+45 WOR-45 CONSTN BAL/PWR ADJUD ADMIN PARL/PROC SOVEREIGN...SOC METH/COMP ANTHOL 17/20 UN. PAGE 7 E0137
DIPLOM
INT/LAW
NAT/G

B61

BARBASH J.,LABOR'S GRASS ROOTS. CONSTN NAT/G EX/STRUC LEGIS WORKER LEAD...MAJORIT BIBLIOG. PAGE 8 E0147
LABOR
INGP/REL
GP/REL
LAW

B61

BAYITCH S.A.,LATIN AMERICA: A BIBLIOGRAPHICAL GUIDE. LAW CONSTN LEGIS JUDGE ADJUD CT/SYS 20. PAGE 8 E0158
BIBLIOG
L/A+17C
NAT/G
JURID

B61

CARNELL F.,THE POLITICS OF THE NEW STATES: A SELECT ANNOTATED BIBLIOGRAPHY WITH SPECIAL REFERENCE TO THE COMMONWEALTH. CONSTN ELITES LABOR NAT/G POL/PAR EX/STRUC DIPLOM ADJUD ADMIN...GOV/COMP 20 COMMONWLTH. PAGE 20 E0387
BIBLIOG/A
AFR
ASIA
COLONIAL

B61

CHILDS M.W.,THE EROSION OF INDIVIDUAL LIBERTIES. NAT/G LEGIS ATTIT...JURID SOC CONCPT IDEA/COMP 20 SUPREME/CT AMEND/I. PAGE 22 E0430
ADJUD
CT/SYS
ORD/FREE
CONSTN

B61

COWEN D.V.,THE FOUNDATIONS OF FREEDOM. AFR SOUTH/AFR DOMIN LEGIT ADJUST DISCRIM TOTALISM ATTIT ORD/FREE...MAJORIT JURID SOC/INTEG WORSHIP 20 NEGRO. PAGE 27 E0529
CONSTN
ELITES
RACE/REL

B61

FREUND P.A.,THE SUPREME COURT OF THE UNITED STATES: ITS BUSINESS, PURPOSES, AND PERFORMANCE. CONSTN CRIME CONSEN ORD/FREE...DECISION 20 SUPREME/CT CIVIL/LIB. PAGE 40 E0797
CT/SYS
JURID
ADJUD
FEDERAL

B61

GUIZOT F.P.G.,HISTORY OF THE ORIGIN OF REPRESENTATIVE GOVERNMENT IN EUROPE. CHRIST-17C FRANCE MOD/EUR SPAIN UK LAW CHIEF FORCES POPULISM ...MAJORIT TIME/SEQ GOV/COMP NAT/COMP 4/19 PARLIAMENT. PAGE 48 E0961
LEGIS
REPRESENT
CONSTN
NAT/G

B61

JACOBS C.E.,JUSTICE FRANKFURTER AND CIVIL LIBERTIES. USA+45 USA-45 LAW NAT/G PROB/SOLV PRESS PERS/REL...JURID WORSHIP 20 SUPREME/CT FRANKFUR/F CIVIL/LIB. PAGE 57 E1144
BIOG
CONSTN
ADJUD
ORD/FREE

B61

JUSTICE,THE CITIZEN AND THE ADMINISTRATION: THE REDRESS OF GRIEVANCES (PAMPHLET). EUR+WWI UK LAW CONSTN STRATA NAT/G CT/SYS PARTIC COERCE...NEW/IDEA IDEA/COMP 20 OMBUDSMAN. PAGE 59 E1176
INGP/REL
CONSULT
ADJUD
REPRESENT

B61

KURLAND P.B.,RELIGION AND THE LAW. USA+45 USA-45 CONSTN PROVS CHIEF ADJUD SANCTION PRIVIL CATHISM ...POLICY 17/20 SUPREME/CT PRESIDENT CHURCH/STA. PAGE 62 E1239
SECT
NAT/G
CT/SYS
GP/REL

B61

LA PONCE J.A.,THE GOVERNMENT OF THE FIFTH REPUBLIC: FRENCH POLITICAL PARTIES AND THE CONSTITUTION. ALGERIA FRANCE LAW NAT/G DELIB/GP LEGIS ECO/TAC MARXISM SOCISM...CHARTS BIBLIOG/A 20 DEGAULLE/C. PAGE 62 E1243
PWR
POL/PAR
CONSTN
CHIEF

B61

MECHAM J.L.,THE UNITED STATES AND INTER-AMERICAN SECURITY, 1889-1960. L/A+17C USA+45 USA-45 CONSTN FORCES INT/TRADE PEACE TOTALISM ATTIT...JURID 19/20 UN OAS. PAGE 72 E1432
DIPLOM
WAR
ORD/FREE
INT/ORG

B61

PUGET H.,ESSAI DE BIBLIOGRAPHIE DES PRINCIPAUX OUVRAGES DE DROIT PUBLIC... QUI ONT PARU HORS DE FRANCE DE 1945 A 1958. EUR+WWI USA+45 CONSTN LOC/G ...METH 20. PAGE 83 E1660
BIBLIOG
MGT
ADMIN
LAW

B61

RUEDA B.,A STATEMENT OF THE LAWS OF COLOMBIA IN MATTERS AFFECTING BUSINESS (3RD ED.). INDUS FAM LABOR LG/CO NAT/G LEGIS TAX CONTROL MARRIAGE 20 COLOMB. PAGE 86 E1733
FINAN
ECO/UNDEV
LAW
CONSTN

B61

SCOTT A.M.,POLITICS, USA; CASES ON THE AMERICAN DEMOCRATIC PROCESS. USA+45 CHIEF FORCES DIPLOM LOBBY CHOOSE RACE/REL FEDERAL ATTIT...JURID ANTHOL T 20 PRESIDENT CONGRESS CIVIL/LIB. PAGE 90 E1795
CT/SYS
CONSTN
NAT/G
PLAN

B61

US CONGRESS,CONSTITUTIONAL RIGHTS OF THE MENTALLY ILL. USA+45 LAW PUB/INST DELIB/GP ADJUD ORD/FREE ...PSY QU 20 CONGRESS. PAGE 99 E1989
HEALTH
CONSTN
JURID
CONFER

B61

WARD R.E.,JAPANESE POLITICAL SCIENCE: A GUIDE TO JAPANESE REFERENCE AND RESEARCH MATERIALS (2ND ED.). LAW CONSTN STRATA NAT/G POL/PAR DELIB/GP LEGIS ADMIN CHOOSE GP/REL...INT/LAW 19/20 CHINJAP. PAGE 105 E2099
BIBLIOG/A
PHIL/SCI

B61

WECHSLER H.,PRINCIPLES, POLITICS AND FUNDAMENTAL LAW: SELECTED ESSAYS. USA+45 USA-45 LAW SOCIETY NAT/G PROVS DELIB/GP EX/STRUC ACT/RES LEGIT PERSON KNOWL PWR...JURID 20 NUREMBERG. PAGE 105 E2106
CT/SYS
CONSTN
INT/LAW

B61

WINTERS J.M.,STATE CONSTITUTIONAL LIMITATIONS ON SOLUTIONS OF METROPOLITAN AREA PROBLEMS. CONSTN LEGIS LEAD REPRESENT DECISION. PAGE 107 E2134
MUNIC
REGION
LOC/G
LAW

L61

FELLMAN D.,"ACADEMIC FREEDOM IN AMERICAN LAW." LAW CONSTN NAT/G VOL/ASSN PLAN PERSON KNOWL NEW/LIB. PAGE 37 E0732
ACADEM
ORD/FREE
LEGIS
CULTURE

L61

GERWIG R.,"PUBLIC AUTHORITIES IN THE UNITED STATES." LAW CONSTN PROVS TAX ADMIN FEDERAL. PAGE 43 E0852
LOC/G
MUNIC
GOV/REL
PWR

L61

KAUPER P.G.,"CHURCH AND STATE: COOPERATIVE SEPARATISM." NAT/G LEGIS OP/RES TAX EDU/PROP GP/REL TREND. PAGE 59 E1187
SECT
CONSTN
LAW
POLICY

S61

ALGER C.F.,"NON-RESOLUTION CONSEQUENCES OF THE UNITED NATIONS AND THEIR EFFECT ON INTERNATIONAL CONFLICT." WOR+45 CONSTN ECO/DEV NAT/G CONSULT
INT/ORG
DRIVE
BAL/PWR

DELIB/GP TOP/EX ACT/RES PLAN DIPLOM EDU/PROP
ROUTINE ATTIT ALL/VALS...INT/LAW TOT/POP UN 20.
PAGE 3 E0065

S61
JACKSON E.,"THE FUTURE DEVELOPMENT OF THE UNITED   INT/ORG
NATIONS: SOME SUGGESTIONS FOR RESEARCH." FUT LAW   PWR
CONSTN ECO/DEV FINAN PEACE WEALTH...WELF/ST CONCPT
UN 20. PAGE 57 E1140

B62
ALLOTT A.N.,JUDICIAL AND LEGAL SYSTEMS IN AFRICA.   CT/SYS
LAW CONSTN JUDGE CONTROL...METH/CNCPT CLASSIF   AFR
CHARTS 20 COMMON/LAW. PAGE 4 E0070   JURID
                                                     COLONIAL

B62
ASSOCIATION BAR OF NYC,REPORT ON ADMISSION   PUB/INST
PROCEDURES TO NEW YORK STATE MENTAL HOSPITALS. LAW HEALTH
CONSTN INGP/REL RESPECT...PSY OBS RECORD. PAGE 6   CLIENT
E0108   ROUTINE

B62
BICKEL A.,THE LEAST DANGEROUS BRANCH. USA+45 USA-45 LAW
CONSTN SCHOOL LEGIS ADJUD RACE/REL DISCRIM ORD/FREE NAT/G
...JURID 18/20 SUPREME/CT CONGRESS MARSHALL/J   CT/SYS
HOLMES/OW FRANKFUR/F. PAGE 12 E0226

B62
BOYD W.J.,PATTERNS OF APPORTIONMENT (PAMPHLET). LAW MUNIC
CONSTN CHOOSE GOV/COMP. PAGE 14 E0282   PROVS
                                                     REPRESENT
                                                     APPORT

B62
BRANDT R.B.,SOCIAL JUSTICE. UNIV LAW GP/REL PWR   ORD/FREE
ALL/IDEOS...POLICY SOC ANTHOL 20. PAGE 15 E0287   CONSTN
                                                     CONCPT

B62
DAVIS F.J.,SOCIETY AND THE LAW. USA+45 CONSTN   LAW
ACADEM FAM CONSULT ACT/RES GP/REL ORD/FREE   SOC
ENGLSH/LAW 20. PAGE 29 E0572   CULTURE
                                                     STRUCT

B62
DE LAVALLE H.,A STATEMENT OF THE LAWS OF PERU IN   CONSTN
MATTERS AFFECTING BUSINESS (3RD ED.). PERU WORKER   JURID
INT/TRADE INCOME ORD/FREE...INT/LAW 20. PAGE 30   FINAN
E0586   TAX

B62
DELANY V.T.H.,THE ADMINISTRATION OF JUSTICE IN   ADMIN
IRELAND. IRELAND CONSTN FINAN JUDGE COLONIAL CRIME   JURID
...CRIMLGY 19/20. PAGE 30 E0604   CT/SYS
                                                     ADJUD

B62
GALENSON W.,TRADE UNIONS MONOGRAPH SERIES (A SERIES LABOR
OF NINE TEXTS). DELIB/GP LEAD PARTIC...DECISION   INGP/REL
ORG/CHARTS. PAGE 42 E0827   CONSTN
                                                     REPRESENT

B62
GANJI M.,INTERNATIONAL PROTECTION OF HUMAN RIGHTS.   ORD/FREE
WOR+45 CONSTN INT/TRADE CT/SYS SANCTION CRIME WAR   DISCRIM
RACE/REL...CHARTS IDEA/COMP NAT/COMP BIBLIOG 20   LEGIS
TREATY NEGRO LEAGUE/NAT UN CIVIL/LIB. PAGE 42 E0831 DELIB/GP

B62
HIRSCHFIELD R.S.,THE CONSTITUTION AND THE COURT.   ADJUD
SCHOOL WAR RACE/REL EQUILIB ORD/FREE...POLICY   PWR
MAJORIT DECISION JURID 18/20 PRESIDENT COLD/WAR   CONSTN
CIVIL/LIB SUPREME/CT CONGRESS. PAGE 53 E1051   LAW

B62
HOOK S.,THE PARADOXES OF FREEDOM. UNIV CONSTN   CONCPT
INTELL LEGIS CONTROL REV CHOOSE SUPEGO...POLICY   MAJORIT
JURID IDEA/COMP 19/20 CIV/RIGHTS. PAGE 55 E1095   ORD/FREE
                                                     ALL/VALS

B62
INSTITUTE JUDICIAL ADMIN,JUDGES: THEIR TEMPORARY   NAT/G
APPOINTMENT, ASSIGNMENT AND TRANSFER: SURVEY OF FED LOC/G
AND STATE CONSTN'S STATUTES, ROLES OF CT. USA+45   JUDGE
CONSTN PROVS CT/SYS GOV/REL PWR JURID. PAGE 57   ADMIN
E1128

B62
KAUPER P.G.,CIVIL LIBERTIES AND THE CONSTITUTION.   LAW
USA+45 SECT EDU/PROP WRITING ADJUD SEX ORD/FREE 20   CONSTN
SUPREME/CT CIVIL/LIB CHURCH/STA. PAGE 60 E1188   CT/SYS
                                                     DECISION

B62
MASON A.T.,THE SUPREME COURT: PALADIUM OF FREEDOM.   CONSTN

USA-45 NAT/G POL/PAR CHIEF LEGIS ADJUD PARL/PROC   CT/SYS
FEDERAL PWR...POLICY BIOG 18/20 SUPREME/CT   JURID
ROOSEVLT/F JEFFERSN/T MARSHALL/J HUGHES/CE. PAGE 69
E1378

B62
MCGRATH J.J.,CHURCH AND STATE IN AMERICAN LAW. LAW   SECT
PROVS SCHOOL TAX GIVE CT/SYS GP/REL...POLICY ANTHOL ADJUD
18/20 SUPREME/CT CHURCH/STA CASEBOOK. PAGE 71 E1414 CONSTN
                                                     NAT/G

B62
MCWHINNEY E.,CONSTITUTIONALISM IN GERMANY AND THE   CONSTN
FEDERAL CONSTITUTINAL COURT. GERMANY/W POL/PAR TV   CT/SYS
ADJUD CHOOSE EFFICIENCY ATTIT ORD/FREE MARXISM   CONTROL
...NEW/IDEA BIBLIOG 20. PAGE 71 E1428   NAT/G

B62
MILLER P.,THE LEGAL MIND IN AMERICA. PROF/ORG JUDGE JURID
ADJUD CT/SYS 18/19 SUPREME/CT. PAGE 73 E1461   CONSTN
                                                     NAT/G
                                                     CONCPT

B62
MITCHELL G.E.,THE ANGRY BLACK SOUTH. USA+45 LAW   RACE/REL
CONSTN SCHOOL DELIB/GP EDU/PROP CONTROL SUFF ANOMIE DISCRIM
DRIVE...ANTHOL 20 NEGRO CIV/RIGHTS SOUTH/US.   ADJUST
PAGE 74 E1473   ORD/FREE

B62
PHILLIPS O.H.,CONSTITUTIONAL AND ADMINISTRATIVE LAW JURID
(3RD ED.). UK INT/ORG LOC/G CHIEF EX/STRUC LEGIS   ADMIN
BAL/PWR ADJUD COLONIAL CT/SYS PWR...CHARTS 20.   CONSTN
PAGE 80 E1613   NAT/G

B62
RICE C.E.,FREEDOM OF ASSOCIATION. USA+45 USA-45   LAW
POL/PAR LOBBY GP/REL...JURID BIBLIOG 18/20   NAT/G
SUPREME/CT PRE/US/AM. PAGE 84 E1691   CONSTN

B62
ROSENNE S.,THE WORLD COURT: WHAT IT IS AND HOW IT   INT/ORG
WORKS. WOR+45 WOR-45 LAW CONSTN JUDGE EDU/PROP   ADJUD
LEGIT ROUTINE CHOOSE PEACE ORD/FREE...JURID OBS   INT/LAW
TIME/SEQ CHARTS UN TOT/POP VAL/FREE 20. PAGE 86
E1717

B62
ROSTOW E.V.,THE SOVEREIGN PREROGATIVE: THE SUPREME   JURID
COURT AND THE QUEST FOR LAW. CONSTN CT/SYS FEDERAL   PROF/ORG
MORAL SOVEREIGN 20 SUPREME/CT. PAGE 86 E1726   ATTIT
                                                     ORD/FREE

B62
SIGLIANO R E.,THE COURTS. USA+45 USA-45 LAW CONSTN   ADJUD
NAT/G ROUTINE CHOOSE 18/20 SUPREME/CT. PAGE 91   PROB/SOLV
E1825   CT/SYS
                                                     JUDGE

B62
SOWLE C.R.,POLICE POWER AND INDIVIDUAL FREEDOM: THE FORCES
QUEST FOR BALANCE. CANADA EUR+WWI ISRAEL NORWAY   ORD/FREE
USA+45 LAW CONSTN SOCIETY CONTROL ROUTINE SANCTION   IDEA/COMP
GP/REL 20 CHINJAP. PAGE 93 E1859

B62
TAPER B.,GOMILLION VERSUS LIGHTFOOT: THE TUSKEGEE   APPORT
GERRYMANDER CASE. USA+45 LAW CONSTN LOC/G MUNIC   REPRESENT
CT/SYS 20 NEGRO CIV/RIGHTS GOMILLN/CG LIGHTFT/PM   RACE/REL
TUSKEGEE. PAGE 95 E1908   ADJUD

B62
TRISKA J.F.,THE THEORY, LAW, AND POLICY OF SOVIET   COM
TREATIES. WOR+45 WOR-45 CONSTN INT/ORG NAT/G   LAW
VOL/ASSN DOMIN LEGIT COERCE ATTIT PWR RESPECT   INT/LAW
...POLICY JURID CONCPT OBS SAMP TIME/SEQ TREND   USSR
GEN/LAWS 20. PAGE 97 E1941

B62
US SENATE COMM ON JUDICIARY,CONSTITUTIONAL RIGHTS   CONSTN
OF MILITARY PERSONNEL. USA+45 USA-45 FORCES DIPLOM   ORD/FREE
WAR CONGRESS. PAGE 102 E2046   JURID
                                                     CT/SYS

B62
WINTERS J.M.,INTERSTATE METROPOLITAN AREAS. CONSTN   MUNIC
LEAD CHOOSE PWR DECISION. PAGE 107 E2135   LAW
                                                     REGION
                                                     GOV/REL

L62
MURACCIOLE L.,"LA LOI FONDAMENTALE DE LA REPUBLIQUE AFR
DU CONGO." WOR+45 SOCIETY ECO/UNDEV INT/ORG NAT/G   CONSTN
LEGIS PLAN LEGIT ADJUD COLONIAL ROUTINE ATTIT
SOVEREIGN 20 CONGO. PAGE 75 E1504

L62

STEIN E.,"MR HAMMARSKJOLD, THE CHARTER LAW AND THE   CONCPT
FUTURE ROLE OF THE UNITED NATIONS SECRETARY-   BIOG
GENERAL." WOR+45 CONSTN INT/ORG DELIB/GP FORCES
TOP/EX BAL/PWR LEGIT ROUTINE RIGID/FLEX PWR
...POLICY JURID OBS STERTYP UN COLD/WAR 20
HAMMARSK/D. PAGE 93 E1869

S62

CRANE R.D.,"SOVIET ATTITUDE TOWARD INTERNATIONAL   LAW
SPACE LAW." COM FUT USA+45 USSR AIR CONSTN DELIB/GP   ATTIT
DOMIN PWR...JURID TREND TOT/POP 20. PAGE 27 E0543   INT/LAW
                                                     SPACE

S62

MONNIER J.P.,"LA SUCCESSION D'ETATS EN MATIERE DE   NAT/G
RESPONSABILITE INTERNATIONALE." UNIV CONSTN INTELL   JURID
SOCIETY ADJUD ROUTINE PERCEPT SUPEGO...GEN/LAWS   INT/LAW
TOT/POP 20. PAGE 74 E1485

S62

SILVA R.C.,"LEGISLATIVE REPESENTATION - WITH   MUNIC
SPECIAL REFERENCE TO NEW YORK." LAW CONSTN LOC/G   LEGIS
NAT/G PROVS. PAGE 91 E1826   REPRESENT
                                                     APPORT

S62

VIGNES D.,"L'AUTORITE DES TRAITES INTERNATIONAUX EN   STRUCT
DROIT INTERNE." EUR+WWI UNIV CONSTN INTELL   LEGIT
NAT/G POL/PAR DIPLOM ATTIT PERCEPT ALL/VALS   FRANCE
...POLICY INT/LAW JURID CONCPT TIME/SEQ 20 TREATY.
PAGE 104 E2075

C62

ABRAHAM H.J.,"THE JUDICIAL PROCESS." USA+45 USA-45   BIBLIOG
LAW NAT/G ADMIN CT/SYS INGP/REL RACE/REL DISCRIM   CONSTN
...JURID IDEA/COMP 19/20. PAGE 2 E0046   JUDGE
                                                     ADJUD

C62

BACON F.,"OF THE TRUE GREATNESS OF KINGDOMS AND   WAR
ESTATES" (1612) IN F. BACON, ESSAYS." ELITES FORCES   PWR
DOMIN EDU/PROP LEGIT...POLICY GEN/LAWS 16/17   DIPLOM
TREATY. PAGE 7 E0129   CONSTN

C62

MORGAN G.G.,"SOVIET ADMINISTRATIVE LEGALITY: THE   LAW
ROLE OF THE ATTORNEY GENERAL'S OFFICE." COM USSR   CONSTN
CONTROL ROUTINE...CONCPT BIBLIOG 18/20. PAGE 74   LEGIS
E1493   ADMIN

N62

TWENTIETH CENTURY FUND,ONE MAN - ONE VOTE   APPORT
(PAMPHLET). USA+45 CONSTN CONFER CT/SYS REGION   LEGIS
CONSEN FEDERAL ROLE...CENSUS 20 CONGRESS. PAGE 97   REPRESENT
E1947   PROVS

N62

US ADVISORY COMN INTERGOV REL,APPORTIONMENT OF   MUNIC
STATE LEGISLATURES (PAMPHLET). LAW CONSTN EX/STRUC   PROVS
LEGIS LEAD MAJORITY. PAGE 99 E1977   REPRESENT
                                                     APPORT

B63

ADRIAN C.R.,GOVERNING OVER FIFTY STATES AND THEIR   PROVS
COMMUNITIES. USA+45 CONSTN FINAN MUNIC NAT/G   LOC/G
POL/PAR EX/STRUC LEGIS ADMIN CONTROL CT/SYS   GOV/REL
...CHARTS 20. PAGE 3 E0052   GOV/COMP

B63

ATTIA G.E.D.,LES FORCES ARMEES DES NATIONS UNIES EN   FORCES
COREE ET AU MOYENORIENT. KOREA CONSTN NAT/G   INT/LAW
DELIB/GP LEGIS PWR...IDEA/COMP NAT/COMP BIBLIOG UN
SUEZ. PAGE 6 E0114

B63

BADI J.,THE GOVERNMENT OF THE STATE OF ISRAEL: A   NAT/G
CRITICAL ACCOUNT OF ITS PARLIAMENT, EXECUTIVE, AND   CONSTN
JUDICIARY. ISRAEL ECO/DEV CHIEF DELIB/GP LEGIS   EX/STRUC
DIPLOM CT/SYS INGP/REL PEACE ORD/FREE...BIBLIOG 20   POL/PAR
PARLIAMENT ARABS MIGRATION. PAGE 7 E0131

B63

BLACK C.L. JR.,THE OCCASIONS OF JUSTICE: ESSAYS   JURID
MOSTLY ON LAW. USA+45 JUDGE RACE/REL DISCRIM ATTIT   CONSTN
MORAL ORD/FREE 20 SUPREME/CT BLACK. PAGE 12 E0236   CT/SYS
                                                     LAW

B63

BOWETT D.W.,THE LAW OF INTERNATIONAL INSTITUTIONS.   INT/ORG
WOR+45 WOR-45 CONSTN DELIB/GP EX/STRUC JUDGE   ADJUD
EDU/PROP LEGIT CT/SYS EXEC ROUTINE RIGID/FLEX   DIPLOM
ORD/FREE PWR...JURID CONCPT ORG/CHARTS GEN/METH
LEAGUE/NAT OAS OEEC 20 UN. PAGE 14 E0277

B63

BURRUS B.R.,ADMINSTRATIVE LAW AND LOCAL GOVERNMENT.   EX/STRUC
USA+45 PROVS LEGIS LICENSE ADJUD ORD/FREE 20.   LOC/G
PAGE 18 E0347   JURID
                                                     CONSTN

B63

CAHN E.,THE GREAT RIGHTS. USA+45 NAT/G PROVS   CONSTN
CIVMIL/REL...IDEA/COMP ANTHOL BIBLIOG 18/20   LAW
MADISON/J BILL/RIGHT CIV/RIGHTS WARRN/EARL   ORD/FREE
BLACK/HL. PAGE 18 E0361   INGP/REL

B63

CARTER G.M.,FIVE AFRICAN STATES: RESPONSES TO   AFR
DIVERSITY. CONSTN CULTURE STRATA LEGIS PLAN ECO/TAC   SOCIETY
DOMIN EDU/PROP CT/SYS EXEC CHOOSE ATTIT HEALTH
ORD/FREE PWR...TIME/SEQ TOT/POP VAL/FREE. PAGE 20
E0398

B63

CORLEY R.N.,THE LEGAL ENVIRONMENT OF BUSINESS.   NAT/G
CONSTN LEGIS TAX ADMIN CT/SYS DISCRIM ATTIT PWR   INDUS
...TREND 18/20. PAGE 26 E0509   JURID
                                                     DECISION

B63

DE GRAZIA A.,APPORTIONMENT AND REPRESENTATIVE   REPRESENT
GOVERNMENT. CONSTN POL/PAR LEGIS PLAN ADJUD DISCRIM   APPORT
RATIONAL...CONCPT STAT PREDICT TREND IDEA/COMP.   NAT/G
PAGE 29 E0583   MUNIC

B63

DILLIARD I.,ONE MAN'S STAND FOR FREEDOM: MR.   CONSTN
JUSTICE BLACK AND THE BILL OF RIGHTS. USA+45   JURID
POL/PAR SECT DELIB/GP FORCES ADJUD CONTROL WAR   JUDGE
DISCRIM MORAL...BIBLIOG 20 NEGRO SUPREME/CT   ORD/FREE
BILL/RIGHT BLACK/HL. PAGE 32 E0628

B63

DRINAN R.F.,RELIGION, THE COURTS, AND PUBLIC   SECT
POLICY. USA+45 CONSTN BUDGET TAX GIVE ADJUD   CT/SYS
SANCTION GP/REL PRIVIL 20 CHURCH/STA. PAGE 33 E0649   POLICY
                                                     SCHOOL

B63

EDDY J.P.,JUSTICE OF THE PEACE. UK LAW CONSTN   CRIME
CULTURE 14/20 COMMON/LAW. PAGE 34 E0674   JURID
                                                     CT/SYS
                                                     ADJUD

B63

ELIAS T.O.,GOVERNMENT AND POLITICS IN AFRICA.   AFR
CONSTN CULTURE SOCIETY NAT/G POL/PAR DIPLOM   NAT/LISM
REPRESENT PERSON...SOC TREND BIBLIOG 4/20. PAGE 34   COLONIAL
E0681   LAW

B63

FRAENKEL O.K.,THE SUPREME COURT AND CIVIL   ORD/FREE
LIBERTIES: HOW THE COURT HAS PROTECTED THE BILL OF   CONSTN
RIGHTS. NAT/G CT/SYS CHOOSE PERS/REL RACE/REL   ADJUD
DISCRIM PERSON...DECISION 20 SUPREME/CT CIVIL/LIB   JURID
BILL/RIGHT. PAGE 39 E0782

B63

GINZBERG E.,DEMOCRATIC VALUES AND THE RIGHTS OF   LABOR
MANAGEMENT. LAW CONSTN REPRESENT GP/REL ROLE PWR   MGT
RESPECT POLICY. PAGE 44 E0870   DELIB/GP
                                                     ADJUD

B63

GOURNAY B.,PUBLIC ADMINISTRATION. FRANCE LAW CONSTN   BIBLIOG/A
AGRI FINAN LABOR SCHOOL EX/STRUC CHOOSE...MGT   ADMIN
METH/COMP 20. PAGE 45 E0894   NAT/G
                                                     LOC/G

B63

GRANT D.R.,STATE AND LOCAL GOVERNMENT IN AMERICA.   PROVS
USA+45 FINAN LOC/G MUNIC EX/STRUC FORCES EDU/PROP   POL/PAR
ADMIN CHOOSE FEDERAL ATTIT...JURID 20. PAGE 45   LEGIS
E0897   CONSTN

B63

GRIFFITH J.A.G.,PRINCIPLES OF ADMINISTRATIVE LAW   JURID
(3RD ED.). UK CONSTN EX/STRUC LEGIS ADJUD CONTROL   ADMIN
CT/SYS PWR...CHARTS 20. PAGE 47 E0940   NAT/G
                                                     BAL/PWR

B63

HALL J.,COMPARATIVE LAW AND SOCIAL THEORY. WOR+45   LAW
CONSTN CULTURE DOMIN CT/SYS ORD/FREE...PLURIST   SOC
JURID CONCPT NEW/IDEA GEN/LAWS VAL/FREE. PAGE 49
E0984

B63

KLESMENT J.,LEGAL SOURCES AND BIBLIOGRAPHY OF THE   BIBLIOG/A
BALTIC STATES (ESTONIA, LATVIA, LITHUANIA). COM   JURID

ESTONIA LATVIA LITHUANIA LAW FINAN ADJUD CT/SYS CONSTN REGION CENTRAL MARXISM 19/20. PAGE 61 E1223 ADMIN

B63
A BIBLIOGRAPHY OF DOCTORAL DISSERTATIONS UNDERTAKEN BIBLIOG IN AMERICAN AND CANADIAN UNIVERSITIES ON RELIGION ACADEM AND POLITICS. LAW CONSTN DOMIN LEGIT ADJUD GP/REL SECT ...POLICY 20. PAGE 62 E1241 JURID

B63
LANOUE G.R.,A BIBLIOGRAPHY OF DOCTORAL BIBLIOG DISSERTATIONS ON POLITICS AND RELIGION. USA+45 NAT/G USA-45 CONSTN PROVS DIPLOM CT/SYS MORAL...POLICY LOC/G JURID CONCPT 20. PAGE 63 E1252 SECT

B63
LEVY L.W.,JEFFERSON AND CIVIL LIBERTIES: THE DARKER BIOG SIDE. USA-45 LAW INTELL ACADEM FORCES PRESS REV ORD/FREE INGP/REL PERSON 18/19 JEFFERSN/T CIVIL/LIB. PAGE 65 CONSTN E1291 ATTIT

B63
LIVELY E.,THE INVASION OF MISSISSIPPI. USA+45 LAW RACE/REL CONSTN NAT/G PROVS CT/SYS GOV/REL FEDERAL CONSERVE CROWD ...TRADIT 20 MISSISSIPP NEGRO NAACP WARRN/EARL COERCE KENNEDY/JF. PAGE 66 E1309 MARXISM

B63
LIVINGSTON W.S.,FEDERALISM IN THE COMMONWEALTH - A BIBLIOG BIBLIOGRAPHICAL COMMENTARY. CANADA INDIA PAKISTAN JURID UK STRUCT LOC/G NAT/G POL/PAR...NAT/COMP 20 FEDERAL AUSTRAL. PAGE 66 E1310 CONSTN

B63
LIVNEH E.,ISRAEL LEGAL BIBLIOGRAPHY IN EUROPEAN BIBLIOG LANGUAGES. ISRAEL LOC/G JUDGE TAX...INT/LAW 20. LAW PAGE 66 E1311 NAT/G CONSTN

B63
LOWRY C.W.,TO PRAY OR NOT TO PRAY. ADJUD SANCTION SECT GP/REL ORD/FREE PWR CATHISM WORSHIP 20 SUPREME/CT CT/SYS CHRISTIAN CHRUCH/STA. PAGE 67 E1330 CONSTN PRIVIL

B63
NATIONAL CIVIC REVIEW,REAPPORTIONMENT: A YEAR IN APPORT REVIEW (PAMPHLET). USA+45 LAW CT/SYS CHOOSE REPRESENT ORD/FREE PWR...ANTHOL 20 CONGRESS. PAGE 76 E1527 LEGIS CONSTN

B63
PRITCHETT C.H.,THE THIRD BRANCH OF GOVERNMENT. JURID USA+45 USA-45 CONSTN SOCIETY INDUS SECT LEGIS JUDGE NAT/G PROB/SOLV GOV/REL 20 SUPREME/CT CHURCH/STA. PAGE 82 ADJUD E1654 CT/SYS

B63
ROBERT J.,LA MONARCHIE MAROCAINE. MOROCCO LABOR CHIEF MUNIC POL/PAR EX/STRUC ORD/FREE PWR...JURID TREND T CONSERVE 20. PAGE 85 E1702 ADMIN CONSTN

B63
ROBERTSON A.H.,HUMAN RIGHTS IN EUROPE. CONSTN EUR+WWI SOCIETY INT/ORG NAT/G VOL/ASSN DELIB/GP ACT/RES PERSON PLAN ADJUD REGION ROUTINE ATTIT LOVE ORD/FREE RESPECT...JURID SOC CONCPT SOC/EXP UN 20. PAGE 85 E1705

B63
SARTORI G.,IL PARLAMENTO ITALIANO: 1946-1963. LAW LEGIS CONSTN ELITES POL/PAR LOBBY PRIVIL ATTIT PERSON PARL/PROC MORAL PWR SOC. PAGE 87 E1746 REPRESENT

B63
SCHMIDHAUSER J.R.,CONSTITUTIONAL LAW IN THE LAW POLITICAL PROCESS. SOCIETY LEGIS ADJUD CT/SYS CONSTN FEDERAL...SOC TREND IDEA/COMP ANTHOL T SUPREME/CT JURID SENATE CONGRESS HOUSE/REP. PAGE 88 E1761

B63
SCHUMAN S.I.,LEGAL POSITIVISM: ITS SCOPE AND GEN/METH LIMITATIONS. CONSTN NAT/G DIPLOM PARTIC UTOPIA LAW ...POLICY DECISION PHIL/SCI CONCPT 20. PAGE 89 METH/COMP E1784

B63
SCOTT A.M.,THE SUPREME COURT V. THE CONSTITUTION. PWR USA+45 CONTROL ATTIT ROLE...POLICY CONCPT 20 CT/SYS SUPREME/CT. PAGE 90 E1796 NAT/G CONSTN

B63
US COMN CIVIL RIGHTS,REPORT ON MISSISSIPPI. LAW RACE/REL LOC/G NAT/G LEGIS PLAN PROB/SOLV DISCRIM SOC/INTEG CONSTN

20 MISSISSIPP NEGRO. PAGE 99 E1987 ORD/FREE COERCE

B63
US CONGRESS: SENATE,HEARINGS OF THE COMMITTEE ON LEGIS THE JUDICIARY. USA+45 CONSTN NAT/G ADMIN GOV/REL 20 LAW CONGRESS. PAGE 99 E1992 ORD/FREE DELIB/GP

B63
US SENATE COMM ON JUDICIARY,ADMINISTRATIVE PARL/PROC CONFERENCE OF THE UNITED STATES. USA+45 CONSTN JURID NAT/G PROB/SOLV CONFER GOV/REL...INT 20 SENATE. ADMIN PAGE 102 E2048 LEGIS

B63
WADE H.W.R.,TOWARDS ADMINISTRATIVE JUSTICE. UK ADJUD USA+45 CONSTN CONSULT PROB/SOLV CT/SYS PARL/PROC IDEA/COMP ...POLICY JURID METH/COMP 20 ENGLSH/LAW. PAGE 104 ADMIN E2088

B63
YOUNGER R.D.,THE PEOPLE'S PANEL: THE GRAND JURY IN CT/SYS THE UNITED STATES, 1634-1941. USA-45 LAW LEGIT JURID CONTROL TASK GP/REL ROLE...TREND 17/20 GRAND/JURY. CONSTN PAGE 108 E2166 LOC/G

L63
LISSITZYN O.J.,"INTERNATIONAL LAW IN A DIVIDED INT/ORG WORLD." FUT WOR+45 CONSTN CULTURE ECO/DEV ECO/UNDEV LAW DIST/IND NAT/G FORCES ECO/TAC LEGIT ADJUD ADMIN COERCE ATTIT HEALTH MORAL ORD/FREE PWR RESPECT WEALTH VAL/FREE. PAGE 65 E1306

S63
BECHHOEFER B.G.,"UNITED NATIONS PROCEDURES IN CASE INT/ORG OF VIOLATIONS OF DISARMAMENT AGREEMENTS." COM DELIB/GP USA+45 USSR LAW CONSTN NAT/G EX/STRUC FORCES LEGIS BAL/PWR EDU/PROP CT/SYS ARMS/CONT ORD/FREE PWR ...POLICY STERTYP UN VAL/FREE 20. PAGE 9 E0169

S63
BRAUSCH G.E.,"AFRICAN ETHNOCRACIES: SOME LAW SOCIOLOGICAL IMPLICATIONS OF CONSTITUTIONAL CHANGE SOC IN EMERGENT TERRITORIES OF AFRICA." AFR CONSTN ELITES FACE/GP MUNIC NAT/G DOMIN ATTIT ALL/VALS ...HIST/WRIT GEN/LAWS VAL/FREE 20. PAGE 15 E0289

S63
CAHIER P.,"LE DROIT INTERNE DES ORGANISATIONS INT/ORG INTERNATIONALES." UNIV CONSTN SOCIETY ECO/DEV R+D JURID NAT/G TOP/EX LEGIT ATTIT PERCEPT...TIME/SEQ 19/20. DIPLOM PAGE 18 E0357 INT/LAW

C63
ATTIA G.E.O.,"LES FORCES ARMEES DES NATIONS UNIES FORCES EN COREE ET AU MOYENORIENT." KOREA CONSTN DELIB/GP NAT/G LEGIS PWR...IDEA/COMP NAT/COMP BIBLIOG UN SUEZ. INT/LAW PAGE 6 E0115

B64
ANASTAPLO G.,NOTES ON THE FIRST AMENDMENT TO THE ORD/FREE CONSTITUTION OF THE UNITED STATES (PART TWO). CONSTN USA+45 USA-45 NAT/G JUDGE DEBATE SUPEGO PWR CT/SYS SOVEREIGN 18/20 SUPREME/CT CONGRESS AMEND/I. PAGE 5 ATTIT E0088

B64
ANDERSON J.W.,EISENHOWER, BROWNELL, AND THE LAW CONGRESS - THE TANGLED ORIGINS OF THE CIVIL RIGHTS CONSTN BILL OF 1956-1957. USA+45 POL/PAR LEGIS CREATE POLICY PROB/SOLV LOBBY GOV/REL RIGID/FLEX...NEW/IDEA 20 NAT/G EISNHWR/DD CONGRESS BROWNELL/H CIV/RIGHTS. PAGE 5 E0090

B64
BECKER T.L.,POLITICAL BEHAVIORALISM AND MODERN JUDGE JURISPRUDENCE* A WORKING THEORY AND STUDY IN LAW JUDICIAL DECISION-MAKING. CONSTN...JURID STAT DECISION GEN/METH INDEX. PAGE 9 E0172 CT/SYS

B64
BERWANGER E.H.,WESTERN ANTI-NEGRO SENTIMENT AND RACE/REL LAWS 1846-60: A FACTOR IN THE SLAVERY EXTENSION REGION CONTROVERSY (PAPER). USA-45 LAW CONSTN LEGIS ADJUD DISCRIM ...BIBLIOG 19 NEGRO. PAGE 11 E0218 ORD/FREE

B64
BOWETT D.W.,UNITED NATIONS FORCES* A LEGAL STUDY. OP/RES CYPRUS ISRAEL KOREA LAW CONSTN ACT/RES CREATE FORCES BUDGET CONTROL TASK PWR...INT/LAW IDEA/COMP UN ARMS/CONT CONGO/LEOP SUEZ. PAGE 14 E0278

B64
BREVER E.H.,LEARNED HAND. JANUARY 27, 1872-AUGUST BIBLIOG/A 18, 1961 (PAMPHLET). USA+45 USA-45 LAW CONSTN ADJUD JUDGE

...DECISION BIOG 19/20. PAGE 15 E0295   CT/SYS
                                                         JURID

B64

BUREAU OF NAT'L AFFAIRS,THE CIVIL RIGHTS ACT OF   LEGIS
1964. USA+45 LOC/G NAT/G DELIB/GP CONFER DEBATE   RACE/REL
DISCRIM...JURID 20 CONGRESS SUPREME/CT CIV/RIGHTS.   LAW
PAGE 17 E0333   CONSTN

B64

CHAPIN B.,THE AMERICAN LAW OF TREASON. USA-45 LAW   LEGIS
NAT/G JUDGE CRIME REV...BIBLIOG 18. PAGE 21 E0419   JURID
                                                       CONSTN
                                                       POLICY

B64

DIETZE G.,ESSAYS ON THE AMERICAN CONSTITUTION: A   FEDERAL
COMMEMORATIVE VOLUME IN HONOR OF ALPHEUS T. MASON.   CONSTN
USA+45 USA-45 LAW INTELL...POLICY BIOG IDEA/COMP   DIPLOM
ANTHOL SUPREME/CT. PAGE 32 E0626   CT/SYS

B64

DUBISSON M.,LA COUR INTERNATIONALE DE JUSTICE.   CT/SYS
FRANCE LAW CONSTN JUDGE DOMIN ADJUD...INT/LAW   INT/ORG
CLASSIF RECORD ORG/CHARTS UN. PAGE 33 E0651

B64

DUMON F.,LE BRESIL; SES INSTITUTIONS POLITIQUES ET   CONSTN
JUDICIARIES. BRAZIL POL/PAR CHIEF LEGIS ORD/FREE   JURID
19/20. PAGE 33 E0658   CT/SYS
                                                       GOV/REL

B64

ENDACOTT G.B.,GOVERNMENT AND PEOPLE IN HONG KONG   CONSTN
1841-1962: A CONSTITUTIONAL HISTORY. UK LEGIS ADJUD   COLONIAL
REPRESENT ATTIT 19/20 HONG/KONG. PAGE 35 E0688   CONTROL
                                                       ADMIN

B64

FACTS ON FILE, INC.,CIVIL RIGHTS 1960-63: THE NEGRO   DISCRIM
CAMPAIGN TO WIN EQUAL RIGHTS AND OPPORTUNITIES IN   PRESS
THE UNITED STATES. LAW CONSTN PARTIC SUFF 20 NEGRO   RACE/REL
CIV/RIGHTS MISSISSIPP. PAGE 36 E0710

B64

FORBES A.H.,CURRENT RESEARCH IN BRITISH STUDIES. UK   BIBLIOG
CONSTN CULTURE POL/PAR SECT DIPLOM ADMIN...JURID   PERSON
BIOG WORSHIP 20. PAGE 39 E0769   NAT/G
                                                       PARL/PROC

B64

FRANCK T.M.,EAST AFRICAN UNITY THROUGH LAW. MALAWI   AFR
TANZANIA UGANDA UK ZAMBIA CONSTN INT/ORG NAT/G   FEDERAL
ADMIN ROUTINE TASK NAT/LISM ATTIT SOVEREIGN   REGION
...RECORD IDEA/COMP NAT/COMP. PAGE 40 E0785   INT/LAW

B64

GESELLSCHAFT RECHTSVERGLEICH,BIBLIOGRAPHIE DES   BIBLIOG/A
DEUTSCHEN RECHTS (BIBLIOGRAPHY OF GERMAN LAW,   JURID
TRANS. BY COURTLAND PETERSON). GERMANY FINAN INDUS   CONSTN
LABOR SECT FORCES CT/SYS PARL/PROC CRIME...INT/LAW   ADMIN
SOC NAT/COMP 20. PAGE 43 E0853

B64

GIANNELLA D.A.,RELIGION AND THE PUBLIC ORDER: AN   SECT
ANNUAL REVIEW OF CHURCH AND STATE, AND OF RELIGION,   NAT/G
LAW, AND SOCIETY. USA+45 LAW SOCIETY FAM POL/PAR   CONSTN
SCHOOL GIVE EDU/PROP GP/REL...JURID GEN/LAWS   ORD/FREE
BIBLIOG/A 20 CHURCH/STA BIRTH/CON CONSCN/OBJ
NATURL/LAW. PAGE 43 E0855

B64

GJUPANOVIC H.,LEGAL SOURCES AND BIBLIOGRAPHY OF   BIBLIOG/A
YUGOSLAVIA. COM YUGOSLAVIA LAW LEGIS DIPLOM ADMIN   JURID
PARL/PROC REGION CRIME CENTRAL 20. PAGE 44 E0873   CONSTN
                                                       ADJUD

B64

GROVES H.E.,THE CONSTITUTION OF MALAYSIA. MALAYSIA   CONSTN
POL/PAR CHIEF CONSULT DELIB/GP CT/SYS PARL/PROC   NAT/G
CHOOSE FEDERAL ORD/FREE 20. PAGE 48 E0953   LAW

B64

GUTTMANN A.,COMMUNISM, THE COURTS, AND THE   MARXISM
CONSTITUTION. USA+45 CT/SYS ORD/FREE...ANTHOL 20   POL/PAR
COM/PARTY CIV/RIGHTS. PAGE 48 E0965   CONSTN
                                                       LAW

B64

HAMILTON H.D.,LEGISLATIVE APPORTIONMENT; KEY TO   APPORT
POWER. USA+45 LAW CONSTN PROVS LOBBY CHOOSE ATTIT   CT/SYS
SUPREME/CT. PAGE 50 E0988   LEAD
                                                       REPRESENT

B64

HEGEL G.W.,HEGEL'S POLITICAL WRITINGS (TRANS. BY   CONSTN

T.M. KNOX). GERMANY UK FINAN FORCES PARL/PROC   LEGIS
CHOOSE REPRESENT...BIOG 19. PAGE 51 E1022   JURID

B64

HENKE W.,DAS RECHT DER POLITISCHEN PARTEIEN.   POL/PAR
GERMANY/W LAW CT/SYS GP/REL SUPEGO 20. PAGE 52   JURID
E1031   CONSTN
                                                       NAT/G

B64

HOLDSWORTH W.S.,A HISTORY OF ENGLISH LAW; THE   LAW
CENTURIES OF DEVELOPMENT AND REFORM (VOL. XIV). UK   LEGIS
CONSTN LOC/G NAT/G POL/PAR CHIEF EX/STRUC ADJUD   LEAD
COLONIAL ATTIT...INT/LAW JURID 18/19 TORY/PARTY   CT/SYS
COMMONWLTH WHIG/PARTY COMMON/LAW. PAGE 54 E1081

B64

KAHNG T.J.,LAW, POLITICS, AND THE SECURITY COUNCIL*   DELIB/GP
AN INQUIRY INTO THE HANDLING OF LEGAL QUESTIONS.   ADJUD
LAW CONSTN NAT/G ACT/RES OP/RES CT/SYS TASK PWR   ROUTINE
...INT/LAW BIBLIOG UN. PAGE 59 E1180

B64

KAUPER P.G.,RELIGION AND THE CONSTITUTION. USA+45   CONSTN
USA-45 LAW NAT/G SCHOOL SECT GP/REL ATTIT...BIBLIOG   JURID
WORSHIP 18/20 SUPREME/CT FREE/SPEE CHURCH/STA.   ORD/FREE
PAGE 60 E1189

B64

KISER S.L.,AMERICANISM IN ACTION. USA+45 LAW PROVS   OLD/LIB
CAP/ISM DIPLOM RECEIVE CONTROL CT/SYS WAR FEDERAL   FOR/AID
ATTIT WEALTH 20 SUPREME/CT. PAGE 61 E1221   MARXISM
                                                       CONSTN

B64

KOREA (REPUBLIC) SUPREME COURT,KOREAN LEGAL SYSTEM.   JURID
KOREA/S WOR+45 LAW LEAD ROUTINE GOV/REL ORD/FREE 20   CT/SYS
SUPREME/CT. PAGE 61 E1229   CONSTN
                                                       CRIME

B64

LEDERMAN W.R.,THE COURTS AND THE CANDIAN   CONSTN
CONSTITUTION. CANADA PARL/PROC...POLICY JURID   CT/SYS
GOV/COMP ANTHOL 19/20 SUPREME/CT PARLIAMENT.   LEGIS
PAGE 64 E1276   LAW

B64

LIGGETT E.,BRITISH POLITICAL ISSUES: VOLUME 1. UK   POL/PAR
LAW CONSTN LOC/G NAT/G ADJUD 20. PAGE 65 E1296   GOV/REL
                                                       CT/SYS
                                                       DIPLOM

B64

LOCKHART W.B.,CASES AND MATERIALS ON CONSTITUTIONAL   ORD/FREE
RIGHTS AND LIBERTIES. USA+45 FORCES LEGIS DIPLOM   CONSTN
PRESS CONTROL CRIME WAR PWR...AUD/VIS T WORSHIP 20   NAT/G
NEGRO. PAGE 66 E1317

B64

MAKI J.M.,COURT AND CONSTITUTION IN JAPAN; SELECTED   CT/SYS
SUPREME COURT DECISIONS, 1948-60. FAM LABOR GOV/REL   CONSTN
HABITAT ORD/FREE...DECISION JURID 20 CHINJAP   PROB/SOLV
SUPREME/CT CIV/RIGHTS. PAGE 68 E1354   LAW

B64

MAKI J.M.,COURT AND CONSTITUTION IN JAPAN: SELECTED   CONSTN
SUPREME COURT DECISIONS, 1948-60. LAW AGRI FAM   JURID
LEGIS BAL/PWR ADMIN CHOOSE...SOC ANTHOL CABINET 20   CT/SYS
CHINJAP CIVIL/LIB. PAGE 68 E1355   CRIME

B64

MARNELL W.H.,THE FIRST AMENDMENT: THE HISTORY OF   CONSTN
RELIGIOUS FREEDOM IN AMERICA. WOR+45 WOR-45 PROVS   SECT
CREATE CT/SYS...POLICY BIBLIOG/A WORSHIP 16/20.   ORD/FREE
PAGE 68 E1367   GOV/REL

B64

MARSHALL B.,FEDERALISM AND CIVIL RIGHTS. USA+45   FEDERAL
PROVS BAL/PWR CONTROL CT/SYS PARTIC SOVEREIGN   ORD/FREE
...JURID 20 NEGRO CIV/RIGHTS. PAGE 68 E1369   CONSTN
                                                       FORCES

B64

MASON A.T.,AMERICAN CONSTITUTIONAL LAW: CONSTN
INTRODUCTORY ESSAYS AND SELECTED CASES (3RD ED.).   CT/SYS
LAW LEGIS TAX ADJUD GOV/REL FEDERAL ORD/FREE PWR   JURID
...TIME/SEQ BIBLIOG T 19/20 SUPREME/CT. PAGE 69
E1379

B64

MINAR D.W.,IDEAS AND POLITICS: THE AMERICAN   CONSTN
EXPERIENCE. SECT CHIEF LEGIS CREATE ADJUD EXEC REV   NAT/G
PWR...PHIL/SCI CONCPT IDEA/COMP 18/20 HAMILTON/A   FEDERAL
JEFFERSN/T DECLAR/IND JACKSON/A PRESIDENT. PAGE 73
E1464

MITAU G.T.,PROXIMATE SOLUTIONS: CASE PROBLEMS IN STATE AND LOCAL GOVERNMENT. USA+45 CONSTN NAT/G CHIEF LEGIS CT/SYS EXEC GOV/REL GP/REL PWR 20 CASEBOOK. PAGE 73 E1470
PROVS LOC/G ADJUD
B64

MITCHELL B.,A BIOGRAPHY OF THE CONSTITUTION OF THE UNITED STATES. USA+45 USA-45 PROVS CHIEF LEGIS DEBATE ADJUD SUFF FEDERAL...SOC 18/20 SUPREME/CT CONGRESS SENATE HOUSE/REP PRESIDENT. PAGE 73 E1472
CONSTN LAW JURID
B64

MURPHY W.F.,ELEMENTS OF JUDICIAL STRATEGY. CONSTN JUDGE PERS/REL PERSON 19/20 SUPREME/CT. PAGE 75 E1510
CT/SYS ADJUD JURID
B64

NEWMAN E.S.,POLICE, THE LAW, AND PERSONAL FREEDOM. USA+45 CONSTN JUDGE CT/SYS CRIME PERS/REL RESPECT ...CRIMLGY 20. PAGE 77 E1542
JURID FORCES ORD/FREE ADJUD
B64

NEWMAN E.S.,CIVIL LIBERTY AND CIVIL RIGHTS. USA+45 USA-45 CONSTN PROVS FORCES LEGIS CT/SYS RACE/REL ATTIT...MAJORIT JURID WORSHIP 20 SUPREME/CT NEGRO CIV/RIGHTS CHURCH/STA. PAGE 77 E1543
ORD/FREE LAW CONTROL NAT/G
B64

RICE C.E.,THE SUPREME COURT AND PUBLIC PRAYER. CONSTN SCHOOL SECT PROB/SOLV TAX ATTIT WORSHIP 18/20 SUPREME/CT CHURCH/STA. PAGE 84 E1692
JURID POLICY NAT/G
B64

RICHARDSON I.L.,BIBLIOGRAFIA BRASILEIRA DE ADMINISTRACAO PUBLICA E ASSUNTOS CORRELATOS. BRAZIL CONSTN FINAN LOC/G NAT/G POL/PAR PLAN DIPLOM RECEIVE ATTIT...METH 20. PAGE 84 E1694
BIBLIOG MGT ADMIN LAW
B64

SCHMEISER D.A.,CIVIL LIBERTIES IN CANADA. CANADA LAW SECT PRESS RACE/REL NAT/LISM PRIVIL 20 COMMONWLTH PARLIAMENT CIVIL/LIB CHURCH/STA. PAGE 88 E1758
ORD/FREE CONSTN ADJUD EDU/PROP
B64

SIEKANOWICZ P.,LEGAL SOURCES AND BIBLIOGRAPHY OF POLAND. COM POLAND CONSTN NAT/G PARL/PROC SANCTION CRIME MARXISM 16/20. PAGE 91 E1823
BIBLIOG ADJUD LAW JURID
B64

STOICOIU V.,LEGAL SOURCES AND BIBLIOGRAPHY OF ROMANIA. COM ROMANIA LAW FINAN POL/PAR LEGIS JUDGE ADJUD CT/SYS PARL/PROC MARXISM 20. PAGE 93 E1874
BIBLIOG/A JURID CONSTN ADMIN
B64

STOKES A.P.,CHURCH AND STATE IN THE UNITED STATES (3 VOLS.). USA+45 USA-45 NAT/G PROVS LEGIS CT/SYS SANCTION PRIVIL ORD/FREE 17/20 CHURCH/STA. PAGE 94 E1875
SECT CONSTN POLICY
B64

STRONG C.F.,HISTORY OF MODERN POLITICAL CONSTITUTIONS. STRUCT INT/ORG NAT/G LEGIS TEC/DEV DIPLOM INT/TRADE CT/SYS EXEC...METH/COMP T 12/20 UN. PAGE 94 E1888
CONSTN CONCPT
B64

TELLADO A.,A STATEMENT OF THE LAWS OF THE DOMINICAN REPUBLIC IN MATTERS AFFECTING BUSINESS (3RD ED.). DOMIN/REP AGRI DIST/IND EXTR/IND FINAN FAM WORKER ECO/TAC TAX CT/SYS MARRIAGE OWN...BIBLIOG 20 MIGRATION. PAGE 95 E1913
CONSTN LEGIS NAT/G INDUS
B64

TENBROCK J.,EQUAL UNDER LAW. USA-45 CONSTN POL/PAR EDU/PROP PARL/PROC ORD/FREE...BIBLIOG 19 AMEND/XIV. PAGE 95 E1914
LEGIS LAW DISCRIM DOMIN
B64

TOMPKINS D.C.,PRESIDENTIAL SUCCESSION. USA+45 CHIEF ADJUD 20 PRESIDENT CONGRESS. PAGE 96 E1933
BIBLIOG/A EX/STRUC CONSTN TOP/EX
B64

UN PUB. INFORM. ORGAN.,EVERY MAN'S UNITED NATIONS. UNIV WOR+45 CONSTN CULTURE SOCIETY ECO/DEV ECO/UNDEV NAT/G ACT/RES PLAN ECO/TAC INT/TRADE EDU/PROP LEGIT PEACE ATTIT ALL/VALS...POLICY HUM INT/LAW CONCPT CHARTS UN TOT/POP 20. PAGE 97 E1954
INT/ORG ROUTINE
B64

US SENATE COMM ON JUDICIARY,ADMINISTRATIVE PROCEDURE ACT. USA+45 CONSTN NAT/G PROB/SOLV CONFER GOV/REL PWR...INT 20 SENATE. PAGE 102 E2054
PARL/PROC LEGIS JURID ADMIN
B64

WORLD PEACE FOUNDATION,"INTERNATIONAL ORGANIZATIONS: SUMMARY OF ACTIVITIES." INDIA PAKISTAN TURKEY WOR+45 CONSTN CONSULT EX/STRUC ECO/TAC EDU/PROP LEGIT ORD/FREE...JURID SOC UN 20 CYPRESS. PAGE 107 E2145
INT/ORG ROUTINE
L64

CARNEGIE ENDOWMENT INT. PEACE,"HUMAN RIGHTS (ISSUES BEFORE THE NINETEENTH GENERAL ASSEMBLY)." AFR WOR+45 LAW CONSTN NAT/G EDU/PROP GP/REL DISCRIM PEACE ATTIT MORAL ORD/FREE...INT/LAW PSY CONCPT RECORD UN 20. PAGE 20 E0385
INT/ORG PERSON RACE/REL
S64

CARNEGIE ENDOWMENT INT. PEACE,"LEGAL QUESTIONS (ISSUES BEFORE THE NINETEENTH GENERAL ASSEMBLY)." WOR+45 CONSTN NAT/G DELIB/GP ADJUD PEACE MORAL ORD/FREE...RECORD UN 20 TREATY. PAGE 20 E0386
INT/ORG LAW INT/LAW
S64

ANTIEU C.J.,RELIGION UNDER THE STATE CONSTITUTIONS. USA+45 LAW SCHOOL TAX SANCTION PRIVIL ORD/FREE ...JURID 20 SUPREME/CT CHURCH/STA. PAGE 5 E0099
SECT CONSTN PROVS GP/REL
B65

BAR ASSOCIATION OF ST LOUIS,CONSTITUTIONAL FREEDOM AND THE LAW. USA+45 LAW LABOR LEGIS EDU/PROP ...JURID CONCPT SUPREME/CT CIVIL/LIB CIV/RIGHTS. PAGE 8 E0146
ORD/FREE CONSTN RACE/REL NAT/G
B65

BRIGGS H.W.,THE INTERNATIONAL LAW COMMISSION. LAW CONSTN LEGIS CREATE ADJUD CT/SYS ROUTINE TASK EFFICIENCY...CLASSIF OBS UN. PAGE 15 E0302
INT/LAW DELIB/GP
B65

CAMPBELL E.H.,SURVEYS, SUBDIVISIONS AND PLATTING, AND BOUNDARIES: WASHINGTON STATE LAW AND JUDICIAL DECISIONS. USA+45 LAW LOC/G...DECISION JURID CON/ANAL BIBLIOG WASHINGT/G PARTITION WATER. PAGE 19 E0372
CONSTN PLAN GEOG PROVS
B65

CARTER G.M.,POLITICS IN EUROPE. EUR+WWI FRANCE GERMANY/W UK USSR LAW CONSTN POL/PAR VOL/ASSN PRESS LOBBY PWR...ANTHOL SOC/INTEG EEC. PAGE 20 E0399
GOV/COMP OP/RES ECO/DEV
B65

CHARNAY J.P.,LE SUFFRAGE POLITIQUE EN FRANCE; ELECTIONS PARLEMENTAIRES, ELECTION PRESIDENTIELLE, REFERENDUMS. FRANCE CONSTN CHIEF DELIB/GP ECO/TAC EDU/PROP CRIME INGP/REL MORAL ORD/FREE PWR CATHISM 20 PARLIAMENT PRESIDENT. PAGE 22 E0425
CHOOSE SUFF NAT/G LEGIS
B65

CHRIMES S.B.,ENGLISH CONSTITUTIONAL HISTORY (3RD ED.). UK CHIEF CONSULT DELIB/GP LEGIS CT/SYS 15/20 COMMON/LAW PARLIAMENT. PAGE 22 E0435
CONSTN BAL/PWR NAT/G
B65

COLGNE A.B.,STATUTE MAKING (2ND ED.). LOC/G PROVS CHOOSE MAJORITY...CHARTS DICTIONARY 20. PAGE 24 E0474
LEGIS LAW CONSTN NAT/G
B65

CONGRESSIONAL QUARTERLY SERV,REVOLUTION IN CIVIL RIGHTS. USA+45 USA-45 LEGIS ADJUD CT/SYS CHOOSE DISCRIM...DECISION CONGRESS SUPREME/CT. PAGE 25 E0488
LAW CONSTN RACE/REL LOBBY
B65

COOPER F.E.,STATE ADMINISTRATIVE LAW (2 VOLS.). LAW LEGIS PLAN TAX ADJUD CT/SYS FEDERAL PWR...CONCPT 20. PAGE 25 E0501
JURID CONSTN ADMIN PROVS
B65

FEERICK J.D.,FROM FAILING HANDS: THE STUDY OF PRESIDENTIAL SUCCESSION. CONSTN NAT/G PROB/SOLV LEAD PARL/PROC MURDER CHOOSE...NEW/IDEA BIBLIOG 20 KENNEDY/JF JOHNSON/LB PRESIDENT PRE/US/AM VICE/PRES. PAGE 36 E0724
EX/STRUC CHIEF LAW LEGIS
B65

FELLMAN D.,RELIGION IN AMERICAN PUBLIC LAW. USA+45 USA-45 NAT/G PROVS ADJUD SANCTION GP/REL PRIVIL ORD/FREE...JURID TIME/SEQ 18/20 SUPREME/CT
SECT CONSTN LAW
B65

CHURCH/STA. PAGE 37 E0733   POLICY

B65
FERRELL J.S.,CASES AND MATERIALS ON LOCAL
APPORTIONMENT. CONSTN LEAD GP/REL...DECISION
GOV/COMP. PAGE 37 E0740
APPORT
LOC/G
REPRESENT
LAW

B65
FISCHER F.C.,THE GOVERNMENT OF MICHIGAN. USA+45
NAT/G PUB/INST EX/STRUC LEGIS BUDGET GIVE EDU/PROP
CT/SYS CHOOSE GOV/REL...T MICHIGAN. PAGE 38 E0753
PROVS
LOC/G
ADMIN
CONSTN

B65
FRIEDMAN L.,SOUTHERN JUSTICE. USA+45 PUB/INST LEGIT
ADMIN CT/SYS DISCRIM...DECISION ANTHOL 20 NEGRO
SOUTH/US CIV/RIGHTS. PAGE 40 E0800
ADJUD
LAW
CONSTN
RACE/REL

B65
GAJENDRAGADKAR P.B.,LAW, LIBERTY AND SOCIAL
JUSTICE. INDIA CONSTN NAT/G SECT PLAN ECO/TAC PRESS
POPULISM...SOC METH/COMP 20 HINDU. PAGE 42 E0826
ORD/FREE
LAW
ADJUD
JURID

B65
GILLETTE W.,THE RIGHT TO VOTE: POLITICS AND THE
PASSAGE OF THE FIFTEENTH AMENDMENT. USA-45 LAW LEAD
DISCRIM SEGREGAT CONGRESS. PAGE 44 E0863
RACE/REL
CONSTN

B65
HOLDSWORTH W.S.,A HISTORY OF ENGLISH LAW; THE
CENTURIES OF SETTLEMENT AND REFORM (VOL. XV). UK
CONSTN SECT LEGIS JUDGE WRITING ADJUD CT/SYS CRIME
OWN...JURID IDEA/COMP 18 PARLIAMENT ENGLSH/LAW
COMMON/LAW. PAGE 54 E1082
LAW
INDUS
PROF/ORG
ATTIT

B65
HOWARD C.G.,LAW: ITS NATURE, FUNCTIONS, AND LIMITS.
USA+45 CONSTN LEGIS CREATE SANCTION ORD/FREE
...BIBLIOG 20. PAGE 55 E1101
LAW
JURID
CONTROL
SOCIETY

B65
HOWE M.D.W.,THE GARDEN AND THE WILDERNESS. USA+45
LAW GIVE EDU/PROP LEGIT NAT/LISM ORD/FREE...POLICY
JURID SUPREME/CT CHURCH/STA. PAGE 55 E1103
CONSTN
SECT
NAT/G
GP/REL

B65
IANNIELLO L.,MILESTONES ALONG THE MARCH: TWELVE
HISTORIC CIVIL RIGHTS DOCUMENTS--FROM WORLD WAR II
TO SELMA. USA+45 LAW FORCES TOP/EX PARTIC SUFF...T
20 NEGRO CIV/RIGHTS TRUMAN/HS SUPREME/CT
KENNEDY/JF. PAGE 56 E1121
RACE/REL
DISCRIM
CONSTN
NAT/G

B65
INST INTL DES CIVILISATION DIF,THE CONSTITUTIONS
AND ADMINISTRATIVE INSTITUTIONS OF THE NEW STATES.
AFR ISLAM S/ASIA NAT/G POL/PAR DELIB/GP EX/STRUC
CONFER EFFICIENCY NAT/LISM...JURID SOC 20. PAGE 56
E1123
CONSTN
ADMIN
ADJUD
ECO/UNDEV

B65
KAAS L.,DIE GEISTLICHE GERICHTSBARKEIT DER
KATHOLISCHEN KIRCHE IN PREUSSEN (2 VOLS.). PRUSSIA
CONSTN NAT/G PROVS SECT ADJUD ADMIN ATTIT 16/20.
PAGE 59 E1178
JURID
CATHISM
GP/REL
CT/SYS

B65
KEEFE W.J.,THE AMERICAN LEGISLATIVE PROCESS. USA+45
CONSTN POL/PAR CT/SYS REPRESENT FEDERAL ATTIT
PLURISM...MAJORIT 20 CONGRESS PRESIDENT. PAGE 60
E1192
LEGIS
NAT/G
CHIEF
GOV/REL

B65
KRISLOV S.,THE SUPREME COURT IN THE POLITICAL
PROCESS. USA+45 LAW SOCIETY STRUCT WORKER ADMIN
ROLE...JURID SOC 20 SUPREME/CT. PAGE 62 E1231
ADJUD
DECISION
CT/SYS
CONSTN

B65
LUGO-MARENCO J.J.,A STATEMENT OF THE LAWS OF
NICARAGUA IN MATTERS AFFECTING BUSINESS. NICARAGUA
AGRI DIST/IND EXTR/IND FINAN INDUS FAM WORKER
INT/TRADE TAX MARRIAGE OWN BIO/SOC 20 TREATY
RESOURCE/N MIGRATION. PAGE 67 E1332
CONSTN
NAT/G
LEGIS
JURID

B65
MARTENS E.,DIE HANNOVERSCHE KIRCHENKOMMISSION.
GERMANY LAW INT/ORG PROVS SECT CONFER GP/REL
CATHISM 16/20. PAGE 69 E1371
JURID
DELIB/GP
CONSTN
PROF/ORG

B65
MCWHINNEY E.,JUDICIAL REVIEW IN THE ENGLISH-
SPEAKING WORLD (3RD ED.). CANADA UK WOR+45 LEGIS
CONTROL EXEC PARTIC...JURID 20 AUSTRAL. PAGE 71
E1431
GOV/COMP
CT/SYS
ADJUD
CONSTN

B65
MISHKIN P.J.,ON LAW IN COURTS. USA+45 LEGIS CREATE
ROLE 20. PAGE 73 E1468
LAW
CT/SYS
ADJUD
CONSTN

B65
MOSTECKY V.,SOVIET LEGAL BIBLIOGRAPHY. USSR LEGIS
PRESS WRITING CONFER ADJUD CT/SYS REV MARXISM
...INT/LAW JURID DICTIONARY 20. PAGE 75 E1503
BIBLIOG/A
LAW
COM
CONSTN

B65
MURPHY W.F.,WIRETAPPING ON TRIAL: A CASE STUDY IN
THE JUDICIAL PROCESS. CONSTN ELITES CT/SYS CRIME
MORAL ORD/FREE...DECISION SUPREME/CT. PAGE 75 E1511
JURID
LAW
POLICY

B65
NJ LEGIS REAPPORT PLAN COMM,PUBLIC HEARING ON
REDISTRICTING AND REAPPORTIONMENT. USA+45 CONSTN
VOL/ASSN LEGIS DEBATE...POLICY GEOG CENSUS 20
NEW/JERSEY. PAGE 77 E1552
APPORT
REPRESENT
PROVS
JURID

B65
PARKER D.,CIVIL LIBERTIES CASE STUDIES AND THE LAW.
SECT ADJUD...CONCPT WORSHIP 20 SUPREME/CT
CIV/RIGHTS FREE/SPEE. PAGE 80 E1598
ORD/FREE
JURID
CONSTN
JUDGE

B65
PEASLEE A.J.,CONSTITUTIONS OF NATIONS* THIRD
REVISED EDITION (VOLUME I* AFRICA). LAW EX/STRUC
LEGIS TOP/EX LEGIT CT/SYS ROUTINE ORD/FREE PWR
SOVEREIGN...CON/ANAL CHARTS. PAGE 80 E1606
AFR
CHOOSE
CONSTN
NAT/G

B65
PYLEE M.V.,CONSTITUTIONAL GOVERNMENT IN INDIA (2ND
REV. ED.). INDIA POL/PAR EX/STRUC DIPLOM COLONIAL
CT/SYS PARL/PROC PRIVIL...JURID 16/20. PAGE 83
E1665
CONSTN
NAT/G
PROVS
FEDERAL

B65
SCHUBERT G.,THE POLITICAL ROLE OF THE COURTS IN
JUDICIAL POLICY MAKING. USA+45 CONSTN JUDGE
FEEDBACK CHOOSE RACE/REL ORD/FREE...TRADIT PSY
BIBLIOG/A 20 KENNEDY/JF SUPREME/CT. PAGE 89 E1776
CT/SYS
POLICY
DECISION

B65
SHARMA S.A.,PARLIAMENTARY GOVERNMENT IN INDIA.
INDIA FINAN LOC/G PROVS DELIB/GP PLAN ADMIN CT/SYS
FEDERAL...JURID 20. PAGE 90 E1814
NAT/G
CONSTN
PARL/PROC
LEGIS

B65
SNOW J.H.,REAPPORTIONMENT. LAW CONSTN NAT/G GOV/REL
ORD/FREE...JURID 20 SUPREME/CT CONNECTICT. PAGE 92
E1848
APPORT
ADJUD
LEGIS
PROVS

B65
SOPER T.,EVOLVING COMMONWEALTH. AFR CANADA INDIA
IRELAND UK LAW CONSTN POL/PAR DOMIN CONTROL WAR PWR
...AUD/VIS 18/20 COMMONWLTH OEEC. PAGE 93 E1857
INT/ORG
COLONIAL
VOL/ASSN

B65
STOREY R.G.,OUR UNALIENABLE RIGHTS. LAW SECT CT/SYS
SUFF DISCRIM 17/20 CIVIL/LIB ENGLSH/LAW. PAGE 94
E1882
CONSTN
JURID
ORD/FREE
LEGIS

B65
TRESOLINI R.J.,AMERICAN CONSTITUTIONAL LAW. USA+45
USA-45 NAT/G ADJUD ORD/FREE PWR...POLICY BIOG 20
SUPREME/CT CASEBOOK. PAGE 97 E1939
CONSTN
CT/SYS
JURID
LAW

B65
VONGLAHN G.,LAW AMONG NATIONS: AN INTRODUCTION TO
PUBLIC INTERNATIONAL LAW. UNIV WOR+45 LAW INT/ORG
NAT/G LEGIT EXEC RIGID/FLEX...CONCPT TIME/SEQ
GEN/LAWS UN TOT/POP 20. PAGE 104 E2084
CONSTN
JURID
INT/LAW

B65
WEIL G.L.,A HANDBOOK ON THE EUROPEAN ECONOMIC
COMMUNITY. BELGIUM EUR+WWI FRANCE GERMANY/W ITALY
CONSTN ECO/DEV CREATE PARTIC GP/REL...DECISION MGT
CHARTS 20 EEC. PAGE 105 E2107
INT/TRADE
INT/ORG
TEC/DEV
INT/LAW

L65
RUBIN A.P.,"UNITED STATES CONTEMPORARY PRACTICE   LAW

RELATING TO INTERNATIONAL LAW." USA+45 WOR+45   LEGIT
CONSTN INT/ORG NAT/G DELIB/GP EX/STRUC DIPLOM DOMIN   INT/LAW
CT/SYS ROUTINE ORD/FREE...CONCPT COLD/WAR 20.
PAGE 86 E1730

L65
WEINSTEIN J.B.,"THE EFFECT OF THE FEDERAL   MUNIC
REAPPORTIONMENT DECISIONS ON COUNTIES AND OTHER   LOC/G
FORMS OF GOVERNMENT." LAW CONSTN LEGIS CHOOSE   APPORT
GOV/COMP. PAGE 105 E2108   REPRESENT

S65
DIXON R.G.,"NEW CONSTITUTIONAL FORMS FOR   MUNIC
METROPOLIS: REAPPORTIONED COUNTY BOARDS; LOCAL   REGION
COUNCILS OF GOVERNMENT." LAW CONSTN LEAD APPORT   GOV/COMP
REPRESENT DECISION. PAGE 32 E0631   PLAN

S65
FOX A.B.,"NATO AND CONGRESS." CONSTN DELIB/GP   CONTROL
EX/STRUC FORCES TOP/EX BUDGET NUC/PWR GOV/REL   DIPLOM
...GP/COMP CONGRESS NATO TREATY. PAGE 39 E0779

S65
STEIN E.,"TOWARD SUPREMACY OF TREATY-CONSTITUTION   ADJUD
BY JUDICIAL FIAT: ON THE MARGIN OF THE COSTA CASE."   CONSTN
EUR+WWI ITALY WOR+45 INT/ORG NAT/G LEGIT REGION   SOVEREIGN
NAT/LISM PWR...JURID CONCPT TREND TOT/POP VAL/FREE   INT/LAW
20. PAGE 93 E1870

B66
AMERICAN JEWISH COMMITTEE,GROUP RELATIONS IN THE   BIBLIOG/A
UNITED STATES: PROBLEMS AND PERSPECTIVES: A   USA+45
SELECTED, ANNOTATED BIBLIOGRAPHY (PAMPHLET). LAW   STRUCT
CONSTN STRATA SCHOOL SECT PROB/SOLV ATTIT...POLICY   GP/REL
WELF/ST SOC/WK 20. PAGE 4 E0079

B66
AMERICAN JOURNAL COMP LAW,THE AMERICAN JOURNAL OF   IDEA/COMP
COMPARATIVE LAW READER. EUR+WWI USA+45 USA-45 LAW   JURID
CONSTN LOC/G MUNIC NAT/G DIPLOM...ANTHOL 20   INT/LAW
SUPREME/CT EURCT/JUST. PAGE 4 E0081   CT/SYS

B66
AUERBACH J.S.,LABOR AND LIBERTY; THE LA FOLLETTE   DELIB/GP
COMMITTEE AND THE NEW DEAL. USA-45 LAW LEAD RESPECT   LABOR
SOCISM...BIBLIOG 20 CONGRESS BILL/RIGHT LAFOLLET/R   CONSTN
NEW/DEAL. PAGE 6 E0117   ORD/FREE

B66
BAXTER M.G.,DANIEL WEBSTER & THE SUPREME COURT. LAW   CONSTN
NAT/G PROF/ORG DEBATE ADJUD LEAD FEDERAL PERSON.   CT/SYS
PAGE 8 E0156   JURID

B66
BEDI A.S.,FREEDOM OF EXPRESSION AND SECURITY;   METH
COMPARATIVE STUDY OF FUNCTIONS OF SUPREME COURTS IN   CT/SYS
UNITED STATES AND INDIA. INDIA USA+45 LAW CONSTN   ADJUD
PROB/SOLV...DECISION JURID BIBLIOG 20 SUPREME/CT   ORD/FREE
FREE/SPEE AMEND/I. PAGE 9 E0175

B66
BEISER E.N.,THE TREATMENT OF LEGISLATIVE   CT/SYS
APPORTIONMENT BY THE STATE AND FEDERAL COURTS   APPORT
(DISSERTATION). USA+45 CONSTN NAT/G PROVS LEGIS   ADJUD
CHOOSE REPRESENT ATTIT...POLICY BIBLIOG 20 CONGRESS   PWR
SUPREME/CT. PAGE 9 E0181

B66
BRAIBANTI R.,RESEARCH ON THE BUREAUCRACY OF   HABITAT
PAKISTAN. PAKISTAN LAW CULTURE INTELL ACADEM LOC/G   NAT/G
SECT PRESS CT/SYS...LING CHARTS 20 BUREAUCRCY.   ADMIN
PAGE 15 E0286   CONSTN

B66
BURNS A.C.,PARLIAMENT AS AN EXPORT. WOR+45 CONSTN   PARL/PROC
BARGAIN DEBATE ROUTINE GOV/REL EFFICIENCY...ANTHOL   POL/PAR
COMMONWLTH PARLIAMENT. PAGE 17 E0343   CT/SYS
     CHIEF

B66
CAHN E.,CONFRONTING INJUSTICE. USA+45 PROB/SOLV TAX   ORD/FREE
EDU/PROP PRESS CT/SYS GP/REL DISCRIM BIO/SOC   CONSTN
...IDEA/COMP BIBLIOG WORSHIP 20 BILL/RIGHT. PAGE 18   ADJUD
E0362

B66
CAMPBELL E.,PARLIAMENTARY PRIVILEGE IN AUSTRALIA.   LEGIS
UK LAW CONSTN COLONIAL ROLE ORD/FREE SOVEREIGN   PARL/PROC
18/20 COMMONWLTH AUSTRAL FREE/SPEE PARLIAMENT.   JURID
PAGE 19 E0370   PRIVIL

B66
CARMEN I.H.,MOVIES, CENSORSHIP, AND THE LAW. LOC/G   EDU/PROP
NAT/G ATTIT ORD/FREE...DECISION INT IDEA/COMP   LAW
BIBLIOG 20 SUPREME/CT FILM. PAGE 19 E0383   ART/METH
     CONSTN

B66
CONG QUARTERLY SERVICE,REPRESENTATION AND   APPORT
APPORTIONMENT. USA+45 USA-45 POL/PAR CT/SYS SUFF   LEGIS
...POLICY 20 CONGRESS SUPREME/CT. PAGE 25 E0486   REPRESENT
     CONSTN

B66
DE TOCQUEVILLE A,DEMOCRACY IN AMERICA (1834-1840)   POPULISM
(2 VOLS. IN I; TRANS. BY G. LAWRENCE). FRANCE   USA+45
CULTURE STRATA POL/PAR CT/SYS REPRESENT FEDERAL   CONSTN
ORD/FREE SOVEREIGN...MAJORIT TREND GEN/LAWS 18/19.   NAT/COMP
PAGE 30 E0596

B66
FINK M.,A SELECTIVE BIBLIOGRAPHY ON STATE   BIBLIOG
CONSTITUTIONAL REVISION (PAMPHLET). USA+45 FINAN   PROVS
EX/STRUC LEGIS EDU/PROP ADMIN CT/SYS APPORT CHOOSE   LOC/G
GOV/REL 20. PAGE 38 E0751   CONSTN

B66
GHOSH P.K.,THE CONSTITUTION OF INDIA: HOW IT HAS   CONSTN
BEEN FRAMED. INDIA LOC/G DELIB/GP EX/STRUC   NAT/G
PROB/SOLV BUDGET INT/TRADE CT/SYS CHOOSE...LING 20.   LEGIS
PAGE 43 E0854   FEDERAL

B66
GILLMOR D.M.,FREE PRESS AND FAIR TRIAL. UK USA+45   ORD/FREE
CONSTN PROB/SOLV PRESS CONTROL CRIME DISCRIM   ADJUD
RESPECT...AUD/VIS 20 CIVIL/LIB. PAGE 44 E0865   ATTIT
     EDU/PROP

B66
GOLDWIN R.A.,APPORTIONMENT AND REPRESENTATION.   APPORT
MUNIC CT/SYS GP/REL ORD/FREE...POLICY ANTHOL 20   REPRESENT
SUPREME/CT. PAGE 44 E0880   LEGIS
     CONSTN

B66
GREENE L.E.,GOVERNMENT IN TENNESSEE (2ND ED.).   PROVS
USA+45 DIST/IND INDUS POL/PAR EX/STRUC LEGIS PLAN   LOC/G
BUDGET GIVE CT/SYS...MGT T 20 TENNESSEE. PAGE 46   CONSTN
E0909   ADMIN

B66
HAMILTON H.D.,REAPPORTIONING LEGISLATURES. USA+45   APPORT
CONSTN POL/PAR PROVS LEGIS COMPUTER ADJUD CHOOSE   REPRESENT
ATTIT...ANTHOL 20 SUPREME/CT CONGRESS. PAGE 50   PHIL/SCI
E0989   PWR

B66
HANSON R.,THE POLITICAL THICKET. USA+45 MUNIC   APPORT
POL/PAR LEGIS EXEC LOBBY CHOOSE...MAJORIT DECISION.   LAW
PAGE 50 E0998   CONSTN
     REPRESENT

B66
HARVEY W.B.,LAW AND SOCIAL CHANGE IN GHANA. AFR   JURID
GHANA CONSULT CONTROL CT/SYS INGP/REL 20. PAGE 51   CONSTN
E1011   LEAD
     ORD/FREE

B66
HIDAYATULLAH M.,DEMOCRACY IN INDIA AND THE JUDICIAL   NAT/G
PROCESS. INDIA EX/STRUC LEGIS LEAD GOV/REL ATTIT   CT/SYS
ORD/FREE...MAJORIT CONCPT 20 NEHRU/J. PAGE 52 E1040   CONSTN
     JURID

B66
HOGUE A.R.,ORIGINS OF THE COMMON LAW. UK STRUCT   LAW
AGRI CT/SYS SANCTION CONSERVE 12/14 ENGLSH/LAW   SOCIETY
COMMON/LAW. PAGE 54 E1068   CONSTN

B66
KEAY E.A.,THE NATIVE AND CUSTOMARY COURTS OF   AFR
NIGERIA. NIGERIA CONSTN ELITES NAT/G TOP/EX PARTIC   ADJUD
REGION...DECISION JURID 19/20. PAGE 60 E1190   LAW

B66
KUNST H.,EVANGELISCHES STAATSLEXIKON. LAW CONSTN   JURID
POL/PAR...PHIL/SCI CONCPT DICTIONARY. PAGE 62 E1232   SECT
     SOC
     NAT/G

B66
MAGRATH C.P.,YAZOO; LAW AND POLITICS IN THE NEW   CT/SYS
REPUBLIC: THE CASE OF FLETCHER V. PECK. USA-45 LAW   DECISION
...BIBLIOG 19 SUPREME/CT YAZOO. PAGE 67 E1348   CONSTN
     LOBBY

B66
PLATE H.,PARTEIFINANZIERUNG UND GRUNDESETZ. GERMANY   POL/PAR
NAT/G PLAN GIVE PAY INCOME WEALTH...JURID 20.   CONSTN
PAGE 81 E1619   FINAN

B66
SHAPIRO M.,FREEDOM OF SPEECH: THE SUPREME COURT AND CT/SYS
JUDICIAL REVIEW. USA+45 LEGIS...CHARTS 20 ORD/FREE
SUPREME/CT FREE/SPEE. PAGE 90 E1812 CONSTN
JURID

B66
SWEET E.C.,CIVIL LIBERTIES IN AMERICA. LAW CONSTN ADJUD
NAT/G PRESS CT/SYS DISCRIM ATTIT WORSHIP 20 ORD/FREE
CIVIL/LIB. PAGE 95 E1899 SUFF
COERCE

B66
TIEDT S.W.,THE ROLE OF THE FEDERAL GOVERNMENT IN NAT/G
EDUCATION. FUT USA+45 USA-45 CONSTN SECT BUDGET EDU/PROP
CT/SYS GOV/REL 18/20 SUPREME/CT. PAGE 96 E1924 GIVE
SCHOOL

B66
US SENATE COMM ON JUDICIARY,HEARINGS ON FREE PRESS PRESS
AND FAIR TRIAL (2 VOLS.). USA+45 CONSTN ELITES LAW
LEGIS EDU/PROP CT/SYS LEAD CONGRESS. PAGE 103 E2057 CRIME
ORD/FREE

B66
WASHINGTON S.H.,BIBLIOGRAPHY: LABOR-MANAGEMENT BIBLIOG
RELATIONS ACT, 1947 AS AMENDED BY LABOR-MANAGEMENT LAW
REPORTING AND DISCLOSURE ACT, 1959. USA+45 CONSTN LABOR
INDUS DELIB/GP LEGIS WORKER BARGAIN ECO/TAC ADJUD MGT
GP/REL NEW/LIB...JURID CONGRESS. PAGE 105 E2100

B66
WILSON G.,CASES AND MATERIALS ON CONSTITUTIONAL AND JURID
ADMINISTRATIVE LAW. UK LAW NAT/G EX/STRUC LEGIS ADMIN
BAL/PWR BUDGET DIPLOM ADJUD CONTROL CT/SYS GOV/REL CONSTN
ORD/FREE 20 PARLIAMENT ENGLSH/LAW. PAGE 106 E2126 PWR

S66
BURDETTE F.L.,"SELECTED ARTICLES AND DOCUMENTS ON BIBLIOG
AMERICAN GOVERNMENT AND POLITICS." LAW LOC/G MUNIC USA+45
NAT/G POL/PAR PROVS LEGIS BAL/PWR ADMIN EXEC JURID
REPRESENT MGT. PAGE 17 E0331 CONSTN

S66
CHIU H.,"COMMUNIST CHINA'S ATTITUDE TOWARD INT/LAW
INTERNATIONAL LAW" CHINA/COM USSR LAW CONSTN DIPLOM MARXISM
GP/REL 20 LENIN/VI. PAGE 22 E0431 CONCPT
IDEA/COMP

S66
DETTER I.,"THE PROBLEM OF UNEQUAL TREATIES." CONSTN SOVEREIGN
NAT/G LEGIS COLONIAL COERCE PWR...GEOG UN TIME DOMIN
TREATY. PAGE 31 E0610 INT/LAW
ECO/UNDEV

S66
FINE R.I.,"PEACE-KEEPING COSTS AND ARTICLE 19 OF FORCES
THE UN CHARTER* AN INVITATION TO RESPONSIBILITY." COST
INT/ORG NAT/G ADJUD CT/SYS CHOOSE CONSEN...RECORD CONSTN
IDEA/COMP UN. PAGE 38 E0750

S66
GASS O.,"THE LITERATURE OF AMERICAN GOVERNMENT." NEW/LIB
CONSTN DRIVE ORD/FREE...JURID CONCPT METH/CNCPT CT/SYS
IDEA/COMP 20 WILSON/W BEARD/CA LINK/AS. PAGE 42 NAT/G
E0841

S66
MATTHEWS D.G.,"PRELUDE-COUP D'ETAT-MILITARY BIBLIOG
GOVERNMENT: A BIBLIOGRAPHICAL AND RESEARCH GUIDE TO NAT/G
NIGERIAN POL AND GOVT, JAN, 1965-66." AFR NIGER LAW ADMIN
CONSTN POL/PAR LEGIS CIVMIL/REL GOV/REL...STAT 20. CHOOSE
PAGE 69 E1385

S66
POLSBY N.W.,"BOOKS IN THE FIELD: POLITICAL BIBLIOG/A
SCIENCE." LAW CONSTN LOC/G NAT/G LEGIS ADJUD PWR 20 ATTIT
SUPREME/CT. PAGE 81 E1627 ADMIN
JURID

N66
BACHELDER G.L.,THE LITERATURE OF FEDERALISM: A BIBLIOG
SELECTED BIBLIOGRAPHY (REV ED) (A PAMPHLET). USA+45 FEDERAL
USA-45 WOR+45 WOR-45 LAW CONSTN PROVS ADMIN CT/SYS NAT/G
GOV/REL ROLE...CONCPT 19/20. PAGE 7 E0126 LOC/G

B67
ASCH S.H.,POLICE AUTHORITY AND THE RIGHTS OF THE FORCES
INDIVIDUAL. CONSTN DOMIN ADJUD CT/SYS...JURID 20. OP/RES
PAGE 6 E0106 ORD/FREE

B67
BOLES D.E.,THE TWO SWORDS. USA+45 USA-45 LAW CONSTN SCHOOL
SOCIETY FINAN PRESS CT/SYS...HEAL JURID BIBLIOG EDU/PROP
WORSHIP 20 SUPREME/CT CHURCH/STA. PAGE 13 E0263 ADJUD

B67
BROWN L.N.,FRENCH ADMINISTRATIVE LAW. FRANCE UK EX/STRUC
CONSTN NAT/G LEGIS DOMIN CONTROL EXEC PARL/PROC PWR LAW
...JURID METH/COMP GEN/METH. PAGE 16 E0314 IDEA/COMP
CT/SYS

B67
BUREAU GOVERNMENT RES AND SERV,COUNTY GOVERNMENT BIBLIOG/A
REORGANIZATION - A SELECTED ANNOTATED BIBLIOGRAPHY APPORT
(PAPER). USA+45 USA-45 LAW CONSTN MUNIC PROVS LOC/G
EX/STRUC CREATE PLAN PROB/SOLV REPRESENT GOV/REL ADMIN
20. PAGE 17 E0332

B67
COX A.,CIVIL RIGHTS, THE CONSTITUTION, AND THE LAW
COURTS. CONSTN EDU/PROP CRIME DISCRIM ATTIT...JURID FEDERAL
20. PAGE 27 E0533 RACE/REL
PRESS

B67
GELLHORN W.,OMBUDSMEN AND OTHERS: CITIZENS' NAT/COMP
PROTECTORS IN NINE COUNTRIES. WOR+45 LAW CONSTN REPRESENT
LEGIS INSPECT ADJUD ADMIN CONTROL CT/SYS CHOOSE INGP/REL
PERS/REL...STAT CHARTS 20. PAGE 43 E0847 PROB/SOLV

B67
KING W.L.,MELVILLE WESTON FULLER: CHIEF JUSTICE OF BIOG
THE UNITED STATES, 1888-1910. USA-45 CONSTN FINAN CT/SYS
LABOR TAX GOV/REL PERS/REL ATTIT PERSON PWR...JURID LAW
BIBLIOG 19/20 SUPREME/CT FULLER/MW HOLMES/OW. ADJUD
PAGE 61 E1216

B67
LENG S.C.,JUSTICE IN COMMUNIST CHINA: A SURVEY OF CT/SYS
THE JUDICIAL SYSTEM OF THE CHINESE PEOPLE'S ADJUD
REPUBLIC. CHINA/COM LAW CONSTN LOC/G NAT/G PROF/ORG JURID
CONSULT FORCES ADMIN CRIME ORD/FREE...BIBLIOG 20 MARXISM
MAO. PAGE 64 E1284

B67
LEVY L.W.,JUDICIAL REVIEW AND THE SUPREME COURT. ADJUD
USA+45 USA-45 NEUTRAL ATTIT ORD/FREE...POLICY CONSTN
DECISION BIBLIOG 18/20 BILL/RIGHT SUPREME/CT. LAW
PAGE 65 E1292 CT/SYS

B67
MCDOUGAL M.S.,THE INTERPRETATION OF AGREEMENTS AND INT/LAW
WORLD PUBLIC ORDER: PRINCIPLES OF CONTENT AND STRUCT
PROCEDURE. WOR+45 CONSTN PROB/SOLV TEC/DEV ECO/UNDEV
...CON/ANAL TREATY. PAGE 71 E1412 DIPLOM

B67
NIVEN R.,NIGERIA. NIGERIA CONSTN INDUS EX/STRUC NAT/G
COLONIAL REV NAT/LISM...CHARTS 19/20. PAGE 77 E1550 REGION
CHOOSE
GP/REL

B67
UNIVERSAL REFERENCE SYSTEM,LAW, JURISPRUDENCE, AND BIBLIOG/A
JUDICIAL PROCESS (VOLUME VII). WOR+45 WOR-45 CONSTN LAW
NAT/G LEGIS JUDGE CT/SYS...INT/LAW COMPUT/IR JURID
GEN/METH METH. PAGE 99 E1976 ADJUD

B67
VILE M.J.C.,CONSTITUTIONALISM AND THE SEPARATION OF CONSTN
POWERS. FRANCE UK USA+45 USA-45 NAT/G ADJUD CONTROL BAL/PWR
GOV/REL...POLICY DECISION JURID GEN/LAWS 15/20 CONCPT
MONTESQ. PAGE 104 E2076 LAW

L67
HOWARD A.E.D.,"MR. JUSTICE BLACK: THE NEGRO PROTEST ADJUD
MOVEMENT AND THE RULE OF LAW." USA+45 CONSTN CT/SYS JUDGE
CHOOSE GP/REL...DECISION JURID NEGRO SUPREME/CT. LAW
PAGE 55 E1100 REPRESENT

L67
LAMBERT J.D.,"CORPORATE POLITICAL SPENDING AND USA+45
CAMPAIGN FINANCE." LAW CONSTN FINAN LABOR LG/CO POL/PAR
LOC/G NAT/G VOL/ASSN TEC/DEV ADJUD ADMIN PARTIC. CHOOSE
PAGE 62 E1247 COST

L67
SCHUBERT G.,"THE RHETORIC OF CONSTITUTIONAL CONSTN
CHANGE." USA+45 LAW CULTURE CHIEF LEGIS ADJUD METH/COMP
CT/SYS ARMS/CONT ADJUST...CHARTS SIMUL. PAGE 89 ORD/FREE
E1777

S67
"THE STATE OF ZONING ADMINISTRATION IN ILLINOIS: ADMIN
PROCEDURAL REQUIREMENTS OF JUDICIAL INTERVENTION." CONTROL
USA+45 LAW CONSTN DELIB/GP ADJUD CT/SYS ORD/FREE HABITAT
ILLINOIS. PAGE 2 E0038 PLAN

S67
"THE FEDERAL AGRICULTURAL STABILIZATION PROGRAM AND AGRI
THE NEGRO." LAW CONSTN PLAN REPRESENT DISCRIM CONTROL

ORD/FREE 20 NEGRO CONGRESS. PAGE 2 E0039   NAT/G
RACE/REL

S67
ADOKO A.,"THE CONSTITUTION OF UGANDA." AFR UGANDA   NAT/G
LOC/G CHIEF FORCES LEGIS ADJUD EXEC CHOOSE NAT/LISM   CONSTN
...IDEA/COMP 20. PAGE 3 E0050   ORD/FREE
LAW

S67
ALEXANDER B.,"GIBRALTAR" SPAIN UK CONSTN WORKER   DIPLOM
PROB/SOLV FOR/AID RECEIVE CONTROL 20. PAGE 3 E0059   INT/ORG
ORD/FREE
ECO/TAC

S67
BRADLEY A.W.,"CONSTITUTION-MAKING IN UGANDA."   NAT/G
UGANDA LAW CHIEF DELIB/GP LEGIS ADMIN EXEC   CREATE
PARL/PROC RACE/REL ORD/FREE...GOV/COMP 20. PAGE 15   CONSTN
E0284   FEDERAL

S67
DEUTSCH E.P.,"A JUDICIAL PATH TO WORLD PEACE." FUT   INT/LAW
WOR+45 CONSTN PROB/SOLV DIPLOM LICENSE ADJUD   INT/ORG
SANCTION CHOOSE REPRESENT NAT/LISM SOVEREIGN 20   JURID
ICJ. PAGE 31 E0611   PEACE

S67
FABREGA J.,"ANTECEDENTES EXTRANJEROS EN LA   CONSTN
CONSTITUCION PANAMENA." CUBA L/A+17C PANAMA URUGUAY   JURID
EX/STRUC LEGIS DIPLOM ORD/FREE 19/20 COLOMB   NAT/G
MEXIC/AMER. PAGE 36 E0709   PARL/PROC

S67
FLECHTHEIM O.K.,"BLOC FORMATION VS. DIALOGUE."   FUT
CONSTN ECO/DEV BAL/PWR PEACE ATTIT PWR COLD/WAR.   CAP/ISM
PAGE 38 E0761   MARXISM
DEBATE

S67
GOSSETT W.T.,"ELECTING THE PRESIDENT: NEW HOPE FOR   CONSTN
AN OLD IDEAL." FUT USA+45 USA-45 PROVS LEGIS   CHIEF
PROB/SOLV WRITING DEBATE ADJUD REPRESENT...MAJORIT   CHOOSE
DECISION 20 HOUSE/REP PRESIDENT. PAGE 45 E0892   NAT/G

S67
KETCHAM O.W.,"GUIDELINES FROM GAULT: REVOLUTIONARY   ADJUD
REQUIREMENTS AND REAPPRAISAL." LAW CONSTN CREATE   AGE/Y
LEGIT ROUTINE SANCTION CRIME DISCRIM PRIVIL ROLE   CT/SYS
...JURID NEW/IDEA 20 SUPREME/CT. PAGE 60 E1208

S67
MACLEOD R.M.,"LAW, MEDICINE AND PUBLIC OPINION: THE   LAW
RESISTANCE TO COMPULSORY HEALTH LEGISLATION   HEALTH
1870-1907." UK CONSTN SECT DELIB/GP DEBATE   ATTIT
PARL/PROC GP/REL MORAL 19. PAGE 67 E1344

S67
MAYANJA A.,"THE GOVERNMENT'S PROPOSALS ON THE NEW   CONSTN
CONSTITUTION." AFR UGANDA LAW CHIEF LEGIS ADJUD   CONFER
REPRESENT FEDERAL PWR 20. PAGE 69 E1390   ORD/FREE
NAT/G

S67
MITCHELL J.D.B.,"THE CONSTITUTIONAL IMPLICATIONS OF   CONSTN
JUDICIAL CONTROL OF THE ADMINISTRATION IN THE   CT/SYS
UNITED KINGDOM." UK LAW ADJUD ADMIN GOV/REL ROLE   CONTROL
...GP/COMP 20. PAGE 74 E1474   EX/STRUC

S67
PEMBERTON J., JR.,"CONSTITUTIONAL PROBLEMS IN   LAW
RESTRAINT ON THE MEDIA." CONSTN PROB/SOLV EDU/PROP   PRESS
CONFER CONTROL JURID. PAGE 80 E1608   ORD/FREE

S67
READ J.S.,"CENSORED." UGANDA CONSTN INTELL SOCIETY   EDU/PROP
NAT/G DIPLOM PRESS WRITING ADJUD ADMIN COLONIAL   AFR
RISK...IDEA/COMP 20. PAGE 84 E1675   CREATE

S67
SHELDON C.H.,"PUBLIC OPINION AND HIGH COURTS: ATTIT
COMMUNIST PARTY CASES IN FOUR CONSTITUTIONAL   CT/SYS
SYSTEMS." CANADA GERMANY/W WOR+45 POL/PAR MARXISM   CONSTN
...METH/COMP NAT/COMP 20 AUSTRAL. PAGE 91 E1818   DECISION

B68
HULL R.H.,LAW AND VIETNAM. COM VIETNAM CONSTN   POLICY
INT/ORG FORCES DIPLOM AGREE COERCE DETER WEAPON   LAW
PEACE ATTIT 20 UN TREATY. PAGE 56 E1113   WAR
INT/LAW

B68
BURGESS J.W.,"VON HOLST'S PUBLIC LAW OF THE UNITED   CONSTN
STATES" USA-45 LAW GOV/REL...GOV/COMP IDEA/COMP 19.   FEDERAL
PAGE 17 E0339   NAT/G
JURID

B70
BLACKSTONE W.,COMMENTARIES ON THE LAWS OF ENGLAND   LAW
(4 VOLS.) (4TH ED.). UK CHIEF DELIB/GP LEGIS WORKER   JURID
CT/SYS SANCTION CRIME OWN...CRIMLGY 18 ENGLSH/LAW.   ADJUD
PAGE 12 E0238   CONSTN

B73
AUSTIN J.,LECTURES ON JURISPRUDENCE OR THE   LAW
PHILOSOPHY OF POSITIVE LAW (VOL. II) (4TH ED.,   ADJUD
REV.). UK CONSTN STRUCT PROB/SOLV LEGIT CT/SYS   JURID
SANCTION CRIME INGP/REL OWN SUPEGO ORD/FREE...T 19.   METH/CNCPT
PAGE 6 E0120

B75
MAINE H.S.,LECTURES ON THE EARLY HISTORY OF   CULTURE
INSTITUTIONS. IRELAND UK CONSTN ELITES STRUCT FAM   LAW
KIN CHIEF LEGIS CT/SYS OWN SOVEREIGN...CONCPT 16   INGP/REL
BENTHAM/J BREHON ROMAN/LAW. PAGE 68 E1351

L86
GOODNOW F.J.,"AN EXECUTIVE AND THE COURTS: JUDICIAL   CT/SYS
REMEDIES AGAINST ADMINISTRATIVE ACTION" FRANCE UK   GOV/REL
USA-45 WOR-45 LAW CONSTN SANCTION ORD/FREE 19.   ADMIN
PAGE 45 E0888   ADJUD

L86
WHITRIDGE L.I.,"LEGISLATIVE INQUESTS" USA-45 ADJUD   CT/SYS
GOV/REL SOVEREIGN 19/20 CONGRESS. PAGE 106 E2120   LEGIS
JURID
CONSTN

B87
ADAMS J.,A DEFENSE OF THE CONSTITUTIONS OF   CONSTN
GOVERNMENT OF THE UNITED STATES OF AMERICA. USA-45   BAL/PWR
STRATA CHIEF EX/STRUC LEGIS CT/SYS CONSERVE   PWR
POPULISM...CONCPT CON/ANAL GOV/COMP. PAGE 3 E0048   NAT/G

B89
FERNEUIL T.,LES PRINCIPES DE 1789 ET LA SCIENCE   CONSTN
SOCIALE. FRANCE NAT/G REV ATTIT...CONCPT TREND   POLICY
IDEA/COMP 18/19. PAGE 37 E0739   LAW

B89
FICHTE J.G.,THE SCIENCE OF RIGHTS (TRANS. BY A.E.   ORD/FREE
KROEGER). WOR-45 FAM MUNIC NAT/G PROVS ADJUD CRIME   CONSTN
CHOOSE MARRIAGE SEX POPULISM 19 FICHTE/JG   LAW
NATURL/LAW. PAGE 37 E0744   CONCPT

B90
BURGESS J.W.,POLITICAL SCIENCE AND COMPARATIVE   CONSTN
CONSTITUTIONAL LAW. FRANCE GERMANY UK USA-45 LEGIS   LAW
DIPLOM ADJUD REPRESENT...CONCPT 19. PAGE 17 E0340   LOC/G
NAT/G

B91
BENTHAM J.,A FRAGMENT ON GOVERNMENT (1776). CONSTN   SOVEREIGN
MUNIC NAT/G SECT AGREE HAPPINESS UTIL MORAL   LAW
ORD/FREE...JURID CONCPT. PAGE 10 E0198   DOMIN

B92
COHN M.M.,AN INTRODUCTION TO THE STUDY OF THE   CONSTN
CONSTITUTION. USA+45 USA-45 SOCIETY NAT/G EX/STRUC   JURID
HABITAT...PSY CONCPT 18/20. PAGE 24 E0470   OLD/LIB

B92
LOWELL A.L.,ESSAYS ON GOVERNMENT. UK USA-45 LEGIS   CONSTN
PARL/PROC...POLICY PREDICT 19. PAGE 66 E1328   ADJUD
CT/SYS
NAT/G

B96
ESMEIN A.,ELEMENTS DE DROIT CONSTITUTIONNEL. FRANCE   LAW
UK CHIEF EX/STRUC LEGIS ADJUD CT/SYS PARL/PROC REV   CONSTN
GOV/REL ORD/FREE...JURID METH/COMP 18/19. PAGE 35   NAT/G
E0697   CONCPT

B99
LILLY W.S.,FIRST PRINCIPLES IN POLITICS. UNIV LAW   NAT/G
LEGIS DOMIN ADJUD INGP/REL ORD/FREE SOVEREIGN   CONSTN
...JURID CONCPT 19 NATURL/LAW. PAGE 65 E1299   MORAL
POLICY

CONSTN/CNV....CONSTITUTIONAL CONVENTION

CONSTRUC....CONSTRUCTION INDUSTRY

B50
COUNCIL BRITISH NATIONAL BIB,BRITISH NATIONAL   BIBLIOG/A
BIBLIOGRAPHY. UK AGRI CONSTRUC PERF/ART POL/PAR   NAT/G
SECT CREATE INT/TRADE LEAD...HUM JURID PHIL/SCI 20.   TEC/DEV
PAGE 26 E0519   DIPLOM

S67
CREYKE G. JR.,"THE PAYMENT GAP IN FEDERAL   CONSTRUC
CONSTRUCTION CONTRACTS." USA+45 LAW FINAN ECO/TAC   PAY

CONTROL CT/SYS SUPREME/CT. PAGE 28 E0547   COST NAT/G

CONSTRUCTION INDUSTRY....SEE CONSTRUC

CONSULT....CONSULTANTS

B07
BENTHAM J.,AN INTRODUCTION TO THE PRINCIPLES OF   LAW
MORALS AND LEGISLATION. UNIV CONSTN CULTURE SOCIETY   GEN/LAWS
NAT/G CONSULT LEGIS JUDGE ADJUD CT/SYS...JURID
CONCPT NEW/IDEA. PAGE 10 E0190

S17
ROOT E.,"THE EFFECT OF DEMOCRACY ON INTERNATIONAL   LEGIS
LAW." USA-45 WOR-45 INTELL SOCIETY INT/ORG NAT/G   JURID
CONSULT ACT/RES CREATE PLAN EDU/PROP PEACE SKILL   INT/LAW
...CONCPT METH/CNCPT OBS 20. PAGE 85 E1712

B22
WRIGHT Q.,THE CONTROL OF AMERICAN FOREIGN   NAT/G
RELATIONS. USA-45 WOR-45 CONSTN INT/ORG CONSULT   EXEC
LEGIS LEGIT ROUTINE ORD/FREE PWR...POLICY JURID   DIPLOM
CONCPT METH/CNCPT RECORD LEAGUE/NAT 20. PAGE 107
E2150

B24
GENTILI A.,DE LEGATIONIBUS. CHRIST-17C NAT/G SECT   DIPLOM
CONSULT LEGIT...POLICY CATH JURID CONCPT MYTH.   INT/LAW
PAGE 43 E0848   INT/ORG
                                      LAW

L28
HUDSON M.,"THE TEACHING OF INTERNATIONAL LAW IN   PERCEPT
AMERICA." USA-45 LAW CONSULT ACT/RES CREATE   KNOWL
EDU/PROP ATTIT RIGID/FLEX...JURID CONCPT RECORD   INT/LAW
HIST/WRIT TREND GEN/LAWS 18/20. PAGE 56 E1109

L29
FEIS H.,"RESEARCH ACTIVITIES OF THE LEAGUE OF   CONSULT
NATIONS." EUR+WWI WOR-45 R+D INT/ORG CT/SYS   KNOWL
ARMS/CONT WEALTH...OBS RECORD LEAGUE/NAT ILO 20.   PEACE
PAGE 37 E0729

B31
STOWELL E.C.,INTERNATIONAL LAW. FUT UNIV WOR-45   INT/ORG
SOCIETY CONSULT EX/STRUC FORCES ACT/RES PLAN DIPLOM   ROUTINE
EDU/PROP LEGIT DISPL PWR SKILL...POLICY CONCPT OBS   INT/LAW
TREND TOT/POP 20. PAGE 94 E1885

B32
GREAT BRIT COMM MINISTERS PWR,REPORT. UK LAW CONSTN   EX/STRUC
CONSULT LEGIS PARL/PROC SANCTION SOVEREIGN   NAT/G
...DECISION JURID 20 PARLIAMENT. PAGE 45 E0902   PWR
                                        CONTROL

B41
BIRDSALL P.,VERSAILLES TWENTY YEARS AFTER. MOD/EUR   DIPLOM
POL/PAR CHIEF CONSULT FORCES LEGIS REPAR PEACE   NAT/LISM
ORD/FREE...BIBLIOG 20 PRESIDENT TREATY. PAGE 12   WAR
E0231

S44
WRIGHT Q.,"CONSTITUTIONAL PROCEDURES OF THE US FOR   TOP/EX
CARRYING OUT OBLIGATIONS FOR MILITARY SANCTIONS."   FORCES
EUR+WWI FUT USA-45 WOR-45 CONSTN INTELL NAT/G   INT/LAW
CONSULT EX/STRUC LEGIS ROUTINE DRIVE...POLICY JURID   WAR
CONCPT OBS TREND TOT/POP 20. PAGE 108 E2153

B47
GORDON D.L.,THE HIDDEN WEAPON: THE STORY OF   INT/ORG
ECONOMIC WARFARE. EUR+WWI USA-45 LAW FINAN INDUS   ECO/TAC
NAT/G CONSULT FORCES PLAN DOMIN PWR WEALTH   INT/TRADE
...INT/LAW CONCPT OBS TOT/POP NAZI 20. PAGE 45   WAR
E0891

L49
COMM. STUDY ORGAN. PEACE,"A TEN YEAR RECORD,   INT/ORG
1939-1949." FUT WOR+45 LAW R+D CONSULT DELIB/GP   CONSTN
CREATE LEGIT ROUTINE ORD/FREE...TIME/SEQ UN 20.   PEACE
PAGE 24 E0480

B50
BURDETTE F.L.,LOBBYISTS IN ACTION (PAMPHLET).   LOBBY
CONSULT TEC/DEV INSPECT BARGAIN PARL/PROC SANCTION   ATTIT
20 CONGRESS. PAGE 17 E0329   POLICY
                                        LAW

B50
FRANK J.,COURTS ON TRIAL: MYTH AND REALITY IN   JURID
AMERICAN JUSTICE. LAW CONSULT PROB/SOLV EDU/PROP   CT/SYS
ADJUD ROUTINE ROLE ORD/FREE...GEN/LAWS T 20.   MYTH
PAGE 40 E0788   CONSTN

B50
ROSS A.,CONSTITUTION OF THE UNITED NATIONS. CONSTN   PEACE

CONSULT DELIB/GP ECO/TAC...INT/LAW JURID 20 UN   DIPLOM
LEAGUE/NAT. PAGE 86 E1721   ORD/FREE
                                        INT/ORG

B52
VANDENBOSCH A.,THE UN: BACKGROUND, ORGANIZATION,   DELIB/GP
FUNCTIONS, ACTIVITIES. WOR+45 LAW CONSTN STRUCT   TIME/SEQ
INT/ORG CONSULT BAL/PWR EDU/PROP EXEC ALL/VALS   PEACE
...POLICY CONCPT UN 20. PAGE 103 E2071

L52
WRIGHT Q.,"CONGRESS AND THE TREATY-MAKING POWER."   ROUTINE
USA+45 WOR+45 CONSTN INTELL NAT/G CHIEF CONSULT   DIPLOM
EX/STRUC LEGIS TOP/EX CREATE GOV/REL DISPL DRIVE   INT/LAW
RIGID/FLEX...TREND TOT/POP CONGRESS CONGRESS 20   DELIB/GP
TREATY. PAGE 108 E2154

S52
MCDOUGAL M.S.,"THE COMPARATIVE STUDY OF LAW FOR   PLAN
POLICY PURPOSES." FUT NAT/G POL/PAR CONSULT ADJUD   JURID
PWR SOVEREIGN...METH/CNCPT IDEA/COMP SIMUL 20.   NAT/LISM
PAGE 70 E1403

B54
ELIAS T.O.,GROUNDWORK OF NIGERIAN LAW. AFR LEAD   JURID
CRIME INGP/REL ORD/FREE 17/20. PAGE 34 E0680   CT/SYS
                                        CONSTN
                                        CONSULT

B55
BERNSTEIN M.H.,REGULATING BUSINESS BY INDEPENDENT   DELIB/GP
COMMISSION. USA+45 USA-45 LG/CO CHIEF LEGIS   CONTROL
PROB/SOLV ADJUD SANCTION GP/REL ATTIT...TIME/SEQ   CONSULT
19/20 MONOPOLY PRESIDENT CONGRESS. PAGE 11 E0214

B55
BLOOM G.F.,ECONOMICS OF LABOR RELATIONS. USA+45 LAW   ECO/DEV
CONSULT WORKER CAP/ISM PAY ADJUD CONTROL EFFICIENCY   ECO/TAC
ORD/FREE...CHARTS 19/20 AFL/CIO NLRB DEPT/LABOR.   LABOR
PAGE 13 E0249   GOV/REL

B55
COMM. STUDY ORGAN. PEACE,REPORTS. WOR-45 ECO/DEV   WOR+45
ECO/UNDEV VOL/ASSN CONSULT FORCES PLAN TEC/DEV   INT/ORG
DOMIN EDU/PROP NUC/PWR ATTIT PWR WEALTH...JURID   ARMS/CONT
STERTYP FAO ILO 20 UN. PAGE 24 E0481

B56
ALEXANDER F.,THE CRIMINAL, THE JUDGE, AND THE   CRIME
PUBLIC. LAW CULTURE CONSULT LEGIT ADJUD SANCTION   CRIMLGY
ORD/FREE 20. PAGE 3 E0060   PSY
                                        ATTIT

B57
BLOOMFIELD L.M.,EGYPT, ISRAEL AND THE GULF OF   ISLAM
AQABA: IN INTERNATIONAL LAW. LAW NAT/G CONSULT   INT/LAW
FORCES PLAN ECO/TAC ROUTINE COERCE ATTIT DRIVE   UAR
PERCEPT PERSON RIGID/FLEX LOVE PWR WEALTH...GEOG
CONCPT MYTH TREND. PAGE 13 E0250

B57
COOPER F.E.,THE LAWYER AND ADMINISTRATIVE AGENCIES.   CONSULT
USA+45 CLIENT LAW PROB/SOLV CT/SYS PERSON ROLE.   ADMIN
PAGE 25 E0500   ADJUD
                                        DELIB/GP

B57
MEYER P.,ADMINISTRATIVE ORGANIZATION: A COMPARATIVE   ADMIN
STUDY OF THE ORGANIZATION OF PUBLIC ADMINISTRATION.   METH/COMP
DENMARK FRANCE NORWAY SWEDEN UK USA+45 ELITES LOC/G   NAT/G
CONSULT LEGIS ADJUD CONTROL LEAD PWR SKILL   CENTRAL
DECISION. PAGE 72 E1449

B57
US SENATE COMM ON JUDICIARY,HEARING BEFORE   LEGIS
SUBCOMMITTEE ON COMMITTEE OF JUDICIARY, UNITED   CONSTN
STATES SENATE: S. J. RES. 3. USA+45 NAT/G CONSULT   CONFER
DELIB/GP DIPLOM ADJUD LOBBY REPRESENT 20 CONGRESS   AGREE
TREATY. PAGE 102 E2040

B58
BOWETT D.W.,SELF-DEFENSE IN INTERNATIONAL LAW.   ADJUD
EUR+WWI MOD/EUR WOR+45 WOR-45 SOCIETY INT/ORG   CONCPT
CONSULT DIPLOM LEGIT COERCE ATTIT ORD/FREE...JURID   WAR
20 UN. PAGE 14 E0276   INT/LAW

B58
FELLMAN D.,THE DEFENDANT'S RIGHTS. USA+45 NAT/G   CONSTN
CONSULT CT/SYS SUPEGO ORD/FREE...BIBLIOG SUPREME/CT   LAW
CIVIL/SERV. PAGE 37 E0730   CRIME
                                        ADJUD

B58
HUNT B.I.,BIPARTISANSHIP: A CASE STUDY OF THE   FOR/AID
FOREIGN ASSISTANCE PROGRAM, 1947-56 (DOCTORAL   POL/PAR
THESIS). USA+45 INT/ORG CONSULT LEGIS TEC/DEV   GP/REL

...BIBLIOG PRESIDENT TREATY NATO TRUMAN/HS
EISNHWR/DD CONGRESS. PAGE 56 E1114   DIPLOM

B58
MARTIN L.J.,INTERNATIONAL PROPAGANDA: ITS LEGAL AND EDU/PROP
DIPLOMATIC CONTROL. UK USA+45 USSR CONSULT DELIB/GP DIPLOM
DOMIN CONTROL 20. PAGE 69 E1373   INT/LAW
                                                     ATTIT

B58
RUSSELL R.B.,A HISTORY OF THE UNITED NATIONS   USA-45
CHARTER: THE ROLE OF THE UNITED STATES. SOCIETY   INT/ORG
NAT/G CONSULT DOMIN LEGIT ATTIT ORD/FREE PWR   CONSTN
...POLICY JURID CONCPT UN LEAGUE/NAT. PAGE 87 E1737

L58
UNESCO,"TECHNIQUES OF MEDIATION AND CONCILIATION."   INT/ORG
EUR+WWI USA+45 WOR+45 INDUS FACE/GP EX/STRUC   CONSULT
EDU/PROP LEGIT PEACE ORD/FREE...INT/LAW TIME/SEQ   DIPLOM
LEAGUE/NAT 20. PAGE 98 E1961

S58
MCDOUGAL M.S.,"PERSPECTIVES FOR A LAW OF OUTER   INT/ORG
SPACE." FUT WOR+45 AIR CONSULT DELIB/GP TEC/DEV   SPACE
CT/SYS ORD/FREE...POLICY JURID 20 UN. PAGE 70 E1404 INT/LAW

N58
US HOUSE COMM FOREIGN AFFAIRS,HEARINGS ON DRAFT   LEGIS
LEGISLATION TO AMEND FURTHER THE MUTUAL SECURITY   DELIB/GP
ACT OF 1954 (PAMPHLET). USA+45 CONSULT FORCES   CONFER
BUDGET DIPLOM DETER COST ORD/FREE...JURID 20   WEAPON
DEPT/DEFEN UN DEPT/STATE. PAGE 100 E2002

B59
COMM. STUDY ORGAN. PEACE,ORGANIZING PEACE IN THE   INT/ORG
NUCLEAR AGE. FUT CONSULT DELIB/GP DOMIN ADJUD   ACT/RES
ROUTINE COERCE ORD/FREE...TECHNIC INT/LAW JURID   NUC/PWR
NEW/IDEA UN COLD/WAR 20. PAGE 24 E0483

B59
DESMITH S.A.,JUDICIAL REVIEW OF ADMINISTRATIVE   ADJUD
ACTION. UK LOC/G CONSULT DELIB/GP ADMIN PWR   NAT/G
...DECISION JURID 20 ENGLSH/LAW. PAGE 31 E0609   PROB/SOLV
                                                     CT/SYS

B59
REIFF H.,THE UNITED STATES AND THE TREATY LAW OF   ADJUD
THE SEA. USA+45 USA-45 SEA SOCIETY INT/ORG CONSULT   INT/LAW
DELIB/GP LEGIS DIPLOM LEGIT ATTIT ORD/FREE PWR
WEALTH...GEOG JURID TOT/POP 20 TREATY. PAGE 84
E1681

B59
SIMPSON J.L.,INTERNATIONAL ARBITRATION: LAW AND   INT/LAW
PRACTICE. WOR+45 WOR-45 INT/ORG DELIB/GP ADJUD   DIPLOM
PEACE MORAL ORD/FREE...METH 18/20. PAGE 91 E1829   CT/SYS
                                                     CONSULT

B59
US CONGRESS JT ATOM ENRGY COMM,SELECTED MATERIALS   NAT/G
ON FEDERAL-STATE COOPERATION IN THE ATOMIC ENERGY   NUC/PWR
FIELD. USA+45 LAW LOC/G PROVS CONSULT LEGIS ADJUD   GOV/REL
...POLICY BIBLIOG 20 AEC. PAGE 99 E1991   DELIB/GP

L59
MCDOUGAL M.S.,"THE IDENTIFICATION AND APPRAISAL OF   INT/LAW
DIVERSE SYSTEMS OF PUBLIC ORDER (BMR)" WOR+45 NAT/G DIPLOM
CONSULT EDU/PROP POLICY. PAGE 70 E1405   ALL/IDEOS

S59
CHAPMAN B.,"THE FRENCH CONSEIL D'ETAT." FRANCE   ADMIN
NAT/G CONSULT OP/RES PROB/SOLV PWR...OBS 20.   LAW
PAGE 21 E0421   CT/SYS
                                                     LEGIS

S59
DOMKE M.,"THE SETTLEMENT OF DISPUTES IN   CONSULT
INTERNATIONAL TRADE." USA+45 LAW STRATA STRUCT   LEGIT
JUDGE EDU/PROP PWR...METH/CNCPT 20. PAGE 32 E0634   INT/TRADE

S59
JENKS C.W.,"THE CHALLENGE OF UNIVERSALITY." FUT   INT/ORG
UNIV CONSTN CULTURE CONSULT CREATE PLAN LEGIT ATTIT LAW
MORAL ORD/FREE RESPECT...MAJORIT JURID 20. PAGE 58   PEACE
E1155   INT/LAW

B60
CLARK G.,WORLD PEACE THROUGH WORLD LAW. FUT WOR+45   INT/ORG
CONSULT FORCES ACT/RES CREATE PLAN ADMIN ROUTINE   LAW
ARMS/CONT DETER ATTIT PWR...JURID VAL/FREE UNESCO   PEACE
20 UN. PAGE 23 E0449   INT/LAW

B60
DILEY A.V.,INTRODUCTION TO THE STUDY OF THE LAW OF   CONSTN
THE CONSTITUTION. FRANCE UK USA+45 USA-45 CONSULT   LAW
FORCES TAX ADMIN FEDERAL ORD/FREE SOVEREIGN   LEGIS

...IDEA/COMP 20 ENGLSH/LAW CON/INTERP PARLIAMENT.   GEN/LAWS
PAGE 32 E0627

B60
PRICE D.,THE SECRETARY OF STATE. USA+45 CONSTN   CONSULT
ELITES INTELL CHIEF EX/STRUC TOP/EX LEGIT ATTIT PWR DIPLOM
SKILL...DECISION 20 CONGRESS. PAGE 82 E1650   INT/LAW

B60
SCHUBERT G.,THE PUBLIC INTEREST. USA+45 CONSULT   POLICY
PLAN PROB/SOLV ADJUD ADMIN GP/REL PWR ALL/IDEOS 20. DELIB/GP
PAGE 88 E1770   REPRESENT
                                                     POL/PAR

B60
STEIN E.,AMERICAN ENTERPRISE IN THE EUROPEAN COMMON MARKET
MARKET: A LEGAL PROFILE. EUR+WWI FUT USA+45 SOCIETY ADJUD
STRUCT ECO/DEV NAT/G VOL/ASSN CONSULT PLAN TEC/DEV   INT/LAW
ECO/TAC INT/TRADE ADMIN ATTIT RIGID/FLEX PWR...MGT
NEW/IDEA STAT TREND COMPUT/IR SIMUL EEC 20. PAGE 93
E1867

B60
WOETZEL R.K.,THE INTERNATIONAL CONTROL OF AIRSPACE   INT/ORG
AND OUTERSPACE. FUT WOR+45 AIR CONSTN STRUCT   JURID
CONSULT PLAN TEC/DEV ADJUD RIGID/FLEX KNOWL   SPACE
ORD/FREE PWR...TECHNIC GEOG MGT NEW/IDEA TREND   INT/LAW
COMPUT/IR VAL/FREE 20 TREATY. PAGE 107 E2137

S60
NICHOLS J.P.,"HAZARDS OF AMERICAN PRIVATE   FINAN
INVESTMENT IN UNDERDEVELOPED COUNTRIES." FUT   ECO/UNDEV
L/A+17C USA+45 USA-45 EXTR/IND CONSULT BAL/PWR   CAP/ISM
ECO/TAC DOMIN ADJUD ATTIT SOVEREIGN WEALTH   NAT/LISM
...HIST/WRIT TIME/SEQ TREND VAL/FREE 20. PAGE 77
E1546

S60
SANDERS R.,"NUCLEAR DYNAMITE: A NEW DIMENSION IN   INDUS
FOREIGN POLICY." FUT WOR+45 ECO/DEV CONSULT TEC/DEV PWR
PERCEPT...CONT/OBS TIME/SEQ TREND GEN/LAWS TOT/POP   DIPLOM
20 TREATY. PAGE 87 E1745   NUC/PWR

B61
CARROTHERS A.W.R.,LABOR ARBITRATION IN CANADA.   LABOR
CANADA LAW NAT/G CONSULT LEGIS WORKER ADJUD ADMIN   MGT
CT/SYS 20. PAGE 20 E0396   GP/REL
                                                     BARGAIN

B61
JUSTICE,THE CITIZEN AND THE ADMINISTRATION: THE   INGP/REL
REDRESS OF GRIEVANCES (PAMPHLET). EUR+WWI UK LAW   CONSULT
CONSTN STRATA NAT/G CT/SYS PARTIC COERCE...NEW/IDEA ADJUD
IDEA/COMP 20 OMBUDSMAN. PAGE 59 E1176   REPRESENT

L61
SAND P.T.,"AN HISTORICAL SURVEY OF INTERNATIONAL   INT/ORG
AIR LAW SINCE 1944." USA+45 USA-45 WOR+45 WOR-45   LAW
SOCIETY ECO/DEV NAT/G CONSULT EX/STRUC ACT/RES PLAN INT/LAW
LEGIT ROUTINE...JURID CONCPT METH/CNCPT TREND 20.   SPACE
PAGE 87 E1744

S61
ALGER C.F.,"NON-RESOLUTION CONSEQUENCES OF THE   INT/ORG
UNITED NATIONS AND THEIR EFFECT ON INTERNATIONAL   DRIVE
CONFLICT." WOR+45 CONSTN ECO/DEV NAT/G CONSULT   BAL/PWR
DELIB/GP TOP/EX ACT/RES PLAN DIPLOM EDU/PROP
ROUTINE ATTIT ALL/VALS...INT/LAW TOT/POP UN 20.
PAGE 3 E0065

S61
LIPSON L.,"AN ARGUMENT ON THE LEGALITY OF   INT/ORG
RECONNAISSANCE STATELLITES." COM USA+45 USSR WOR+45 LAW
AIR INTELL NAT/G CONSULT PLAN DIPLOM LEGIT ROUTINE   SPACE
ATTIT...INT/LAW JURID CONCPT METH/CNCPT TREND
COLD/WAR 20. PAGE 65 E1302

S61
OLIVER C.T.,"THE AMERICAN LAW INSTITUTE'S DRAFT   KNOWL
RESTATEMENT OF THE FOREIGN RELATIONS LAW OF THE   JURID
UNITED STATES." FUT USA+45 SOCIETY CONSULT   DIPLOM
EDU/PROP. PAGE 78 E1574

B62
ALEXANDROWICZ C.H.,WORLD ECONOMIC AGENCIES: LAW AND INT/LAW
PRACTICE. WOR+45 DIST/IND FINAN LABOR CONSULT   INT/ORG
INT/TRADE TARIFFS REPRESENT HEALTH...JURID 20 UN   DIPLOM
GATT EEC OAS ECSC. PAGE 3 E0063   ADJUD

B62
DAVIS F.J.,SOCIETY AND THE LAW. USA+45 CONSTN   LAW
ACADEM FAM CONSULT ACT/RES GP/REL ORD/FREE   SOC
ENGLSH/LAW 20. PAGE 29 E0572   CULTURE
                                                     STRUCT

EVAN W.M.,LAW AND SOCIOLOGY: EXPLORATORY ESSAYS. JURID B62
CONSULT ACT/RES OP/RES PROB/SOLV EDU/PROP LEGIT SOC
ADJUD CT/SYS GP/REL...PHIL/SCI ANTHOL SOC/INTEG 20. PROF/ORG
PAGE 35 E0703

INTERNAT CONGRESS OF JURISTS,EXECUTIVE ACTION AND JURID B62
THE RULE OF RULE: REPORTION PROCEEDINGS OF INT'T EXEC
CONGRESS OF JURISTS,-RIO DE JANEIRO, BRAZIL. WOR+45 ORD/FREE
ACADEM CONSULT JUDGE EDU/PROP ADJUD CT/SYS INGP/REL CONTROL
PERSON DEPT/DEFEN. PAGE 57 E1130

LAWSON R.,INTERNATIONAL REGIONAL ORGANIZATIONS. INT/ORG B62
WOR+45 NAT/G VOL/ASSN CONSULT LEGIS EDU/PROP LEGIT DELIB/GP
ADMIN EXEC ROUTINE HEALTH PWR WEALTH...JURID EEC REGION
COLD/WAR 20 UN. PAGE 63 E1270

MCDOUGAL M.S.,THE PUBLIC ORDER OF THE OCEANS. ADJUD B62
WOR+45 WOR-45 SEA INT/ORG NAT/G CONSULT DELIB/GP ORD/FREE
DIPLOM LEGIT PEACE RIGID/FLEX...GEOG INT/LAW JURID
RECORD TOT/POP 20 TREATY. PAGE 70 E1407

SCHWARTZ L.E.,INTERNATIONAL ORGANIZATIONS AND SPACE INT/ORG B62
COOPERATION. VOL/ASSN CONSULT CREATE TEC/DEV DIPLOM
SANCTION...POLICY INT/LAW PHIL/SCI 20 UN. PAGE 89 R+D
E1787 SPACE

US COMMISSION ON CIVIL RIGHTS,EQUAL PROTECTION OF ORD/FREE B62
THE LAWS IN NORTH CAROLINA. USA+45 LOC/G NAT/G RESPECT
CONSULT LEGIS WORKER PROB/SOLV EDU/PROP ADJUD LAW
CHOOSE DISCRIM HEALTH 20 NEGRO NORTH/CAR PROVS
CIV/RIGHTS. PAGE 99 E1984

US COMMISSION ON CIVIL RIGHTS,HEARINGS BEFORE ORD/FREE B62
UNITED STATES COMMISSION ON CIVIL RIGHTS. USA+45 LAW
ECO/DEV NAT/G CONSULT WORKER EDU/PROP ADJUD DISCRIM ADMIN
ISOLAT HABITAT HEALTH RESPECT 20 NEGRO CIV/RIGHTS. LEGIS
PAGE 99 E1985

GROSS L.,"IMMUNITIES AND PRIVILEGES OF DELIGATIONS INT/ORG L62
TO THE UNITED NATIONS." USA+45 WOR+45 STRATA NAT/G LAW
VOL/ASSN CONSULT DIPLOM EDU/PROP ROUTINE RESPECT ELITES
...POLICY INT/LAW CONCPT UN 20. PAGE 48 E0950

SCHACHTER O.,"DAG HAMMARSKJOLD AND THE RELATION OF ACT/RES S62
LAW TO POLITICS." FUT WOR+45 INT/ORG CONSULT PLAN ADJUD
TEC/DEV BAL/PWR DIPLOM LEGIT ATTIT PERCEPT ORD/FREE
...POLICY JURID CONCPT OBS TESTS STERTYP GEN/LAWS
20 HAMMARSK/D. PAGE 87 E1751

WADE H.W.R.,TOWARDS ADMINISTRATIVE JUSTICE. UK ADJUD B63
USA+45 CONSTN CONSULT PROB/SOLV CT/SYS PARL/PROC IDEA/COMP
...POLICY JURID METH/COMP 20 ENGLSH/LAW. PAGE 104 ADMIN
E2088

GARDNER R.N.,"COOPERATION IN OUTER SPACE." FUT USSR INT/ORG S63
WOR+45 AIR LAW COM/IND CONSULT DELIB/GP CREATE ACT/RES
KNOWL 20 TREATY. PAGE 42 E0837 PEACE
SPACE

RIGAUX F.,"LA SIGNIFICATION DES ACTES JUDICIARES A CONSULT S63
L'ETRANGER." EUR+WWI ITALY NETHERLAND LAW ACT/RES CT/SYS
DRIVE...JURID GEN/LAWS TOT/POP 20. PAGE 85 E1699 GERMANY

TALLON D.,"L'ETUDE DU DROIT COMPARE COMME MOYEN DE INT/ORG S63
RECHERCHER LES MATIERES SUSCEPTIBLES D'UNIFICATION JURID
INTERNATIONALE." WOR+45 LAW SOCIETY VOL/ASSN INT/LAW
CONSULT LEGIT CT/SYS RIGID/FLEX KNOWL 20. PAGE 95
E1906

WALKER H.,"THE INTERNATIONAL LAW OF COMMODITY MARKET S63
AGREEMENTS." FUT WOR+45 ECO/DEV ECO/UNDEV FINAN VOL/ASSN
INT/ORG NAT/G CONSULT CREATE PLAN ECO/TAC ATTIT INT/LAW
PERCEPT...CONCPT GEN/LAWS TOT/POP GATT 20. PAGE 105 INT/TRADE
E2095

AHLUWALIA K.,THE LEGAL STATUS, PRIVILEGES AND PRIVIL B64
IMMUNITIES OF SPECIALIZED AGENCIES OF UN AND DIPLOM
CERTAIN OTHER INTERNATIONAL ORGANIZATIONS. WOR+45 INT/ORG
LAW CONSULT DELIB/GP FORCES. PAGE 3 E0055 INT/LAW

GROVES H.E.,THE CONSTITUTION OF MALAYSIA. MALAYSIA CONSTN B64
POL/PAR CHIEF CONSULT DELIB/GP CT/SYS PARL/PROC NAT/G
CHOOSE FEDERAL ORD/FREE 20. PAGE 48 E0953 LAW

WORLD PEACE FOUNDATION,"INTERNATIONAL INT/ORG L64
ORGANIZATIONS: SUMMARY OF ACTIVITIES." INDIA ROUTINE
PAKISTAN TURKEY WOR+45 CONSTN CONSULT EX/STRUC
ECO/TAC EDU/PROP LEGIT ORD/FREE...JURID SOC UN 20
CYPRESS. PAGE 107 E2145

BARKUN M.,"CONFLICT RESOLUTION THROUGH IMPLICIT CONSULT S64
MEDIATION." UNIV BARGAIN CONSEN FEDERAL JURID. CENTRAL
PAGE 8 E0149 INT/LAW
IDEA/COMP

CHRIMES S.B.,ENGLISH CONSTITUTIONAL HISTORY (3RD CONSTN B65
ED.). UK CHIEF CONSULT DELIB/GP LEGIS CT/SYS 15/20 BAL/PWR
COMMON/LAW PARLIAMENT. PAGE 22 E0435 NAT/G

FLEMING R.W.,THE LABOR ARBITRATION PROCESS. USA+45 GP/REL B65
LAW BARGAIN ADJUD ROUTINE SANCTION COST...PREDICT LABOR
CHARTS TIME 20. PAGE 38 E0763 CONSULT
DELIB/GP

WHITE G.M.,THE USE OF EXPERTS BY INTERNATIONAL INT/LAW B65
TRIBUNALS. WOR+45 WOR-45 INT/ORG NAT/G PAY ADJUD ROUTINE
COST...OBS BIBLIOG 20. PAGE 106 E2117 CONSULT
CT/SYS

HAZARD J.N.,"CO-EXISTENCE LAW BOWS OUT." WOR+45 R+D PROF/ORG S65
INT/ORG VOL/ASSN CONSULT DELIB/GP ACT/RES CREATE ADJUD
PEACE KNOWL...JURID CONCPT COLD/WAR VAL/FREE 20.
PAGE 51 E1018

CARLIN J.E.,LAWYER'S ETHICS. CLIENT STRUCT CONSULT ATTIT B66
PERS/REL PWR...JURID OBS CHARTS 20. PAGE 19 E0378 PROF/ORG
INT

HARVEY W.B.,LAW AND SOCIAL CHANGE IN GHANA. AFR JURID B66
GHANA CONSULT CONTROL CT/SYS INGP/REL 20. PAGE 51 CONSTN
E1011 LEAD
ORD/FREE

HAYS P.R.,LABOR ARBITRATION: A DISSENTING VIEW. GP/REL B66
USA+45 LAW DELIB/GP BARGAIN ADJUD...PREDICT 20. LABOR
PAGE 51 E1016 CONSULT
CT/SYS

KUNSTLER W.M.,"DEEP IN MY HEART" USA+45 LAW CT/SYS B66
PROF/ORG SECT LOBBY PARTIC CROWD DISCRIM ROLE RACE/REL
...BIOG 20 KING/MAR/L NEGRO CIV/RIGHTS SOUTH/US. ADJUD
PAGE 62 E1233 CONSULT

MERILLAT H.C.L.,LEGAL ADVISERS AND INTERNATIONAL INT/ORG B66
ORGANIZATIONS. LAW NAT/G CONSULT OP/RES ADJUD INT/LAW
SANCTION TASK CONSEN ORG/CHARTS. PAGE 72 E1441 CREATE
OBS

US SENATE COMM AERO SPACE SCI,SOVIET SPACE CONSULT B66
PROGRAMS, 1962-65: GOALS AND PURPOSES, SPACE
ACHIEVEMENTS, PLANS, AND INTERNATIONAL FUT
IMPLICATIONS. USA+45 USSR R+D FORCES PLAN EDU/PROP DIPLOM
PRESS ADJUD ARMS/CONT ATTIT MARXISM. PAGE 101 E2028

CHAPIN F.S. JR.,SELECTED REFERENCES ON URBAN BIBLIOG B67
PLANNING METHODS AND TECHNIQUES. USA+45 LAW ECO/DEV NEIGH
LOC/G NAT/G SCHOOL CONSULT CREATE PROB/SOLV TEC/DEV MUNIC
SOC/WK. PAGE 21 E0420 PLAN

COHEN M.R.,LAW AND THE SOCIAL ORDER: ESSAYS IN JURID B67
LEGAL PHILOSOPHY. USA-45 CONSULT WORKER ECO/TAC LABOR
ATTIT WEALTH...POLICY WELF/ST SOC 20 NEW/DEAL IDEA/COMP
DEPRESSION. PAGE 24 E0467

GABRIEL P.P.,THE INTERNATIONAL TRANSFER OF ECO/UNDEV B67
CORPORATE SKILLS: MANAGEMENT CONTRACTS IN LESS AGREE
DEVELOPED COUNTRIES. CLIENT INDUS LG/CO PLAN MGT
PROB/SOLV CAP/ISM ECO/TAC FOR/AID INT/TRADE RENT CONSULT
ADMIN SKILL 20. PAGE 42 E0825

B67
LENG S.C.,JUSTICE IN COMMUNIST CHINA: A SURVEY OF   CT/SYS
THE JUDICIAL SYSTEM OF THE CHINESE PEOPLE'S   ADJUD
REPUBLIC. CHINA/COM LAW CONSTN LOC/G NAT/G PROF/ORG   JURID
CONSULT FORCES ADMIN CRIME ORD/FREE...BIBLIOG 20   MARXISM
MAO. PAGE 64 E1284

B67
US PRES TASK FORCE ADMIN JUS,TASK FORCE REPORT: THE   CT/SYS
COURTS. USA+45 CONSULT CONFER...JURID CHARTS.   ADJUD
PAGE 101 E2025   ROUTINE
                                                          ADMIN

B67
US SENATE COMM ON FOREIGN REL,USIA FOREIGN SERVICE   DIPLOM
PERSONNEL SYSTEM. USA+45 LAW CONSULT ADMIN 20 USIA.   EDU/PROP
PAGE 102 E2038   PRIVIL
                                                          PROF/ORG

L67
BLUMBERG A.S.,"THE PRACTICE OF LAW AS CONFIDENCE   CT/SYS
GAME; ORGANIZATIONAL COOPTATION OF A PROFESSION."   ADJUD
USA+45 CLIENT SOCIETY CONSULT ROLE JURID. PAGE 13   GP/REL
E0252   ADMIN

L67
FRANCK T.M.,"SOME PSYCHOLOGICAL FACTORS IN   DIPLOM
INTERNATIONAL THIRD-PARTY DECISION-MAKING." UNIV   ADJUD
SOCIETY PROB/SOLV DISCRIM ATTIT HABITAT...DECISION   PERSON
PSY. PAGE 40 E0786   CONSULT

S67
BOHANNAN P.,"INSTITUTIONS OF DIVORCE, FAMILY, AND   FAM
THE LAW." WOR+45 LAW CONSULT...JURID SOC. PAGE 13   MARRIAGE
E0258   ADJUD
                                                          SOCIETY

S67
HILL D.G.,"HUMAN RIGHTS LEGISLATION IN ONTARIO."   DELIB/GP
CANADA R+D VOL/ASSN CONSULT INSPECT EDU/PROP ADJUD   ORD/FREE
AGREE TASK GP/REL INGP/REL DISCRIM 20 CIV/RIGHTS   LAW
ONTARIO CIVIL/LIB. PAGE 52 E1045   POLICY

S67
MAYER M.,"THE IDEA OF JUSTICE AND THE POOR." USA+45   INCOME
CLIENT CONSULT RENT ADJUD DISCRIM KNOWL 20. PAGE 70   WEALTH
E1393   LAW
                                                          ORD/FREE

S67
RICHARDSON J.J.,"THE MAKING OF THE RESTRICTIVE   LEGIS
TRADE PRACTICES ACT 1956 A CASE STUDY OF THE POLICY   ECO/TAC
PROCESS IN BRITAIN." UK FINAN MARKET LG/CO POL/PAR   POLICY
CONSULT PRESS ADJUD ADMIN AGREE LOBBY SANCTION   INDUS
ATTIT 20. PAGE 84 E1695

S67
TYDINGS J.D.,"MODERNIZING THE ADMINISTRATION OF   CT/SYS
JUSTICE." PLAN ADMIN ROUTINE EFFICIENCY...JURID   MGT
SIMUL. PAGE 97 E1948   COMPUTER
                                                          CONSULT

CONSULTANTS....SEE CONSULT

CONT/OBS....CONTROLLED DIRECT OBSERVATION

S60
SANDERS R.,"NUCLEAR DYNAMITE: A NEW DIMENSION IN   INDUS
FOREIGN POLICY." FUT WOR+45 ECO/DEV CONSULT TEC/DEV   PWR
PERCEPT...CONT/OBS TIME/SEQ TREND GEN/LAWS TOT/POP   DIPLOM
20 TREATY. PAGE 87 E1745   NUC/PWR

CONTEMPT....SEE RESPECT

CONTENT ANALYSIS....SEE CON/ANAL

CONTROL....CONTROL OF HUMAN GROUP OPERATIONS

N
INDEX TO LEGAL PERIODICALS. CANADA NEW/ZEALND UK   BIBLIOG
USA+45 USA-45 CONSTN LEGIS JUDGE ADJUD ADMIN   INDEX
CONTROL CT/SYS FEDERAL...CRIMLGY INT/LAW 20   LAW
CMN/WLTH AUSTRAL. PAGE 1 E0006   JURID

B00
GRIFFIN A.P.C.,LIST OF BOOKS RELATING TO THE THEORY   BIBLIOG/A
OF COLONIZATION, GOVERNMENT OF DEPENDENCIES,   COLONIAL
PROTECTORATES, AND RELATED TOPICS. FRANCE GERMANY   GOV/REL
ITALY SPAIN UK USA-45 WOR-45 ECO/TAC ADMIN CONTROL   DOMIN
REGION NAT/LISM ALL/VALS PWR...INT/LAW SOC 16/19.
PAGE 46 E0917

C01
BERKELEY G.,"DISCOURSE ON PASSIVE OBEDIENCE" (1712) INGP/REL

THE WORKS... (VOL. IV)" UNIV DOMIN LEGIT CONTROL   SANCTION
CRIME ADJUST CENTRAL MORAL ORD/FREE...POLICY   RESPECT
WORSHIP. PAGE 10 E0202   GEN/LAWS

B03
GRIFFIN A.P.C.,LISTS PUBLISHED 1902-03: GOVERNMENT   BIBLIOG
OWNERSHIP OF RAILROADS (PAMPHLET). USA-45 LAW NAT/G   DIST/IND
RATION GOV/REL CENTRAL SOCISM...POLICY 19/20.   CONTROL
PAGE 46 E0922   ADJUD

B04
FREUND E.,THE POLICE POWER; PUBLIC POLICY AND   CONSTN
CONSTITUTIONAL RIGHTS. USA-45 SOCIETY LOC/G NAT/G   LAW
FORCES LEGIS ADJUD CT/SYS OWN PWR...JURID 18/19   ORD/FREE
SUPREME/CT. PAGE 40 E0795   CONTROL

B05
GOODNOW F.J.,THE PRINCIPLES OF THE ADMINISTRATIVE   ADMIN
LAW OF THE UNITED STATES. USA-45 LAW STRUCT   NAT/G
EX/STRUC LEGIS BAL/PWR CONTROL GOV/REL PWR...JURID   PROVS
19/20 CIVIL/SERV. PAGE 45 E0887   LOC/G

B05
GRIFFIN A.P.C.,LIST OF BOOKS ON RAILROADS IN   BIBLIOG/A
FOREIGN COUNTRIES. MOD/EUR ECO/DEV NAT/G CONTROL   SERV/IND
SOCISM...JURID 19/20 RAILROAD. PAGE 47 E0927   ADMIN
                                                        DIST/IND

B08
GRIFFIN A.P.C.,LIST OF WORKS RELATING TO GOVERNMENT   BIBLIOG/A
REGULATION OF INSURANCE UNITED STATES AND FOREIGN   FINAN
COUNTRIES (2ND. ED.) (PAMPHLET). FRANCE GERMANY UK   LAW
USA-45 WOR-45 LG/CO LOC/G NAT/G LEGIS LICENSE ADJUD   CONTROL
LOBBY CENTRAL ORD/FREE 19/20. PAGE 47 E0933

B09
JUSTINIAN,THE DIGEST (DIGESTA CORPUS JURIS CIVILIS)   JURID
(2 VOLS.) (TRANS. BY C. H. MONRO). ROMAN/EMP LAW   CT/SYS
FAM LOC/G LEGIS EDU/PROP CONTROL MARRIAGE OWN ROLE   NAT/G
CIVIL/LAW. PAGE 59 E1177   STRATA

B12
BEARD C.A.,THE SUPREME COURT AND THE CONSTITUTION.   CONSTN
LAW NAT/G PROVS LEGIS GOV/REL ATTIT POPULISM   CT/SYS
SUPREME/CT. PAGE 9 E0164   ADJUD
                                                        CONTROL

B12
FOUAD M.,LE REGIME DE LA PRESSE EN EGYPTE: THESE   ORD/FREE
POUR LE DOCTORAT. UAR LICENSE EDU/PROP ADMIN   LEGIS
SANCTION CRIME SUPEGO PWR...ART/METH JURID 19/20.   CONTROL
PAGE 39 E0778   PRESS

B14
VECCHIO G.D.,THE FORMAL BASES OF LAW (TRANS. BY J.   LAW
LISLE). DOMIN LEGIT CONTROL COERCE UTIL MORAL PWR   JURID
...CONCPT TIME/SEQ 17/20 COMMON/LAW NATURL/LAW.   GEN/LAWS
PAGE 103 E2074   IDEA/COMP

B16
SCHROEDER T.,FREE SPEECH FOR RADICALS (REV. ED.).   ORD/FREE
USA-45 CONSTN INDUS LOC/G FORCES SANCTION WAR ATTIT   CONTROL
SEX...JURID REFORMERS 20 FREE/SPEE. PAGE 88 E1767   LAW
                                                        PRESS

N19
BURRUS B.R.,INVESTIGATION AND DISCOVERY IN STATE   NAT/G
ANTITRUST (PAMPHLET). USA+45 USA-45 LEGIS ECO/TAC   PROVS
ADMIN CONTROL CT/SYS CRIME GOV/REL PWR...JURID   LAW
CHARTS 19/20 FTC MONOPOLY. PAGE 18 E0346   INSPECT

N19
JANOWITZ M.,SOCIAL CONTROL OF ESCALATED RIOTS   CROWD
(PAMPHLET). USA+45 USA-45 LAW SOCIETY MUNIC FORCES   ORD/FREE
PROB/SOLV EDU/PROP TV CRIME ATTIT...BIBLIOG 20   CONTROL
NEGRO CIV/RIGHTS. PAGE 58 E1148   RACE/REL

N19
MCCONNELL G.,THE STEEL SEIZURE OF 1952 (PAMPHLET).   DELIB/GP
USA+45 FINAN INDUS PROC/MFG LG/CO EX/STRUC ADJUD   LABOR
CONTROL GP/REL ORD/FREE PWR 20 TRUMAN/HS PRESIDENT   PROB/SOLV
CONGRESS. PAGE 70 E1402   NAT/G

N19
MEZERIK AG,OUTER SPACE: UN, US, USSR (PAMPHLET).   SPACE
USSR DELIB/GP FORCES DETER NUC/PWR SOVEREIGN   CONTROL
...POLICY 20 UN TREATY. PAGE 73 E1453   DIPLOM
                                                        INT/ORG

B20
MEYER H.H.B.,LIST OF REFERENCES ON THE TREATY-   BIBLIOG
MAKING POWER. USA-45 CONTROL PWR...INT/LAW TIME/SEQ   DIPLOM
18/20 TREATY. PAGE 72 E1448   CONSTN

B22
SCHROEDER T.,FREE SPEECH BIBLIOGRAPHY. EUR+WWI   BIBLIOG/A

WOR-45 NAT/G SECT ECO/TAC WRITING ADJUD ATTIT   ORD/FREE
MARXISM SOCISM 16/20. PAGE 88 E1768   CONTROL
                                                        LAW

                                                        B24
HOLDSWORTH W.S.,A HISTORY OF ENGLISH LAW; THE   LAW
COMMON LAW AND ITS RIVALS (VOL. VI). UK STRATA   CONSTN
EX/STRUC ADJUD ADMIN CONTROL CT/SYS...JURID CONCPT   LEGIS
GEN/LAWS 17 COMMONWLTH PARLIAMENT ENGLSH/LAW   CHIEF
COMMON/LAW. PAGE 54 E1074

                                                        B24
HOLDSWORTH W.S.,A HISTORY OF ENGLISH LAW; THE   LAW
COMMON LAW AND ITS RIVALS (VOL. IV). UK SEA AGRI   LEGIS
CHIEF ADJUD CONTROL CRIME GOV/REL...INT/LAW JURID   CT/SYS
NAT/COMP 16/17 PARLIAMENT COMMON/LAW CANON/LAW   CONSTN
ENGLSH/LAW. PAGE 54 E1075

                                                        B27
DICKINSON J.,ADMINISTRATIVE JUSTICE AND THE   CT/SYS
SUPREMACY OF LAW IN THE UNITED STATES. USA-45 LAW   ADJUD
INDUS DOMIN EDU/PROP CONTROL EXEC GP/REL ORD/FREE   ADMIN
...POLICY JURID 19/20. PAGE 31 E0623   NAT/G

                                                        B29
MOLEY R.,POLITICS AND CRIMINAL PROSECUTION. USA-45   PWR
POL/PAR EX/STRUC LEGIT CONTROL LEAD ROUTINE CHOOSE   CT/SYS
INGP/REL...JURID CHARTS 20. PAGE 74 E1481   CRIME
                                                        ADJUD

                                                        B29
STURZO L.,THE INTERNATIONAL COMMUNITY AND THE RIGHT   INT/ORG
OF WAR (TRANS. BY BARBARA BARCLAY CARTER). CULTURE   PLAN
CREATE PROB/SOLV DIPLOM ADJUD CONTROL PEACE PERSON   WAR
ORD/FREE...INT/LAW IDEA/COMP PACIFIST 20   CONCPT
LEAGUE/NAT. PAGE 94 E1891

                                                        B30
BENTHAM J.,THE RATIONALE OF PUNISHMENT. UK LAW   CRIME
LOC/G NAT/G LEGIS CONTROL...JURID GEN/LAWS   SANCTION
COURT/SYS 19. PAGE 10 E0192   COERCE
                                                        ORD/FREE

                                                        B32
GREAT BRIT COMM MINISTERS PWR,REPORT. UK LAW CONSTN   EX/STRUC
CONSULT LEGIS PARL/PROC SANCTION SOVEREIGN   NAT/G
...DECISION JURID 20 PARLIAMENT. PAGE 45 E0902   PWR
                                                        CONTROL

                                                        B33
GILLETTE J.M.,CURRENT SOCIAL PROBLEMS. CONTROL   GEOG
CRIME AGE/Y BIO/SOC...SOC 20. PAGE 43 E0861   HEALTH
                                                        RACE/REL
                                                        FAM

                                                        B33
REID H.D.,RECUEIL DES COURS; TOME 45: LES   ORD/FREE
SERVITUDES INTERNATIONALES III. FRANCE CONSTN   DIPLOM
DELIB/GP PRESS CONTROL REV WAR CHOOSE PEACE MORAL   LAW
MARITIME TREATY. PAGE 84 E1680

                                                        B34
CLYDE W.M.,THE STRUGGLE FOR THE FREEDOM OF THE   PRESS
PRESS FROM CAXTON TO CROMWELL. UK LAW LOC/G SECT   ORD/FREE
FORCES LICENSE WRITING SANCTION REV ATTIT PWR   CONTROL
...POLICY 15/17 PARLIAMENT CROMWELL/O MILTON/J.
PAGE 23 E0460

                                                        B34
GONZALEZ PALENCIA A.,ESTUDIO HISTORICO SOBRE LA   LEGIT
CENSURA GUBERNATIVA EN ESPANA 1800-1833. NAT/G   EDU/PROP
COERCE INGP/REL ATTIT AUTHORIT KNOWL...POLICY JURID   PRESS
19. PAGE 44 E0884   CONTROL

                                                        B35
LUCE R.,LEGISLATIVE PROBLEMS. CONSTN CHIEF JUDGE   TREND
BUDGET CONFER ETIQUET CONTROL MORAL PWR NEW/LIB   ADMIN
CONGRESS. PAGE 67 E1331   LEGIS

                                                        B36
BRIERLY J.L.,THE LAW OF NATIONS (2ND ED.). WOR+45   DIPLOM
WOR-45 INT/ORG AGREE CONTROL COERCE WAR NAT/LISM   INT/LAW
PEACE PWR 16/20 TREATY LEAGUE/NAT. PAGE 15 E0297   NAT/G

                                                        B36
HANSON L.,GOVERNMENT AND THE PRESS 1695-1763. UK   LAW
LOC/G LEGIS LICENSE CONTROL SANCTION CRIME ATTIT   JURID
ORD/FREE 17/18 PARLIAMENT AMEND/I. PAGE 50 E0996   PRESS
                                                        POLICY

                                                        B36
SCHULZ F.,PRINCIPLES OF ROMAN LAW. CONSTN FAM NAT/G   LAW
DOMIN CONTROL CT/SYS CRIME ISOLAT ATTIT ORD/FREE   LEGIS
PWR...JURID ROME/ANC ROMAN/LAW. PAGE 89 E1783   ADJUD
                                                        CONCPT

                                                        B37
BADEN A.L.,IMMIGRATION AND ITS RESTRICTION IN THE   BIBLIOG
US (PAMPHLET). USA-45 NAT/G LEGIS...GEOG 20   STRANGE
CONGRESS. PAGE 7 E0130   CONTROL
                                                        LAW

                                                        B37
HAMILTON W.H.,THE POWER TO GOVERN. ECO/DEV FINAN   LING
INDUS ECO/TAC INT/TRADE TARIFFS TAX CONTROL CT/SYS   CONSTN
WAR COST PWR 18/20 SUPREME/CT. PAGE 50 E0991   NAT/G
                                                        POLICY

                                                        B41
CHAFEE Z. JR.,FREE SPEECH IN THE UNITED STATES.   ORD/FREE
USA-45 ADJUD CONTROL CRIME WAR...BIBLIOG 20   CONSTN
FREE/SPEE AMEND/I SUPREME/CT. PAGE 21 E0413   ATTIT
                                                        JURID

                                                        B41
GILMORE M.P.,ARGUMENT FROM ROMAN LAW IN POLITICAL   JURID
THOUGHT, 1200-1600. INTELL LICENSE CONTROL CT/SYS   LAW
GOV/REL PRIVIL PWR...IDEA/COMP BIBLIOG 13/16.   CONCPT
PAGE 44 E0866   NAT/G

                                                        B42
GILLETTE J.M.,PROBLEMS OF A CHANGING SOCIAL ORDER.   BIO/SOC
USA+45 STRATA FAM CONTROL CRIME RACE/REL HEALTH   ADJUST
WEALTH...GEOG GP/COMP. PAGE 43 E0862   ATTIT
                                                        SOC/WK

                                                        C43
BENTHAM J.,"ON THE LIBERTY OF THE PRESS, AND PUBLIC   ORD/FREE
DISCUSSION" IN J. BOWRING, ED., THE WORKS OF JEREMY   PRESS
BENTHAM." SPAIN UK LAW ELITES NAT/G LEGIS INSPECT   CONFER
LEGIT WRITING CONTROL PRIVIL TOTALISM AUTHORIT   CONSERVE
...TRADIT 19 FREE/SPEE. PAGE 10 E0193

                                                        C43
BENTHAM J.,"PRINCIPLES OF INTERNATIONAL LAW" IN J.   INT/LAW
BOWRING, ED., THE WORKS OF JEREMY BENTHAM." UNIV   JURID
NAT/G PLAN PROB/SOLV DIPLOM CONTROL SANCTION MORAL   WAR
ORD/FREE PWR SOVEREIGN 19. PAGE 10 E0194   PEACE

                                                        B44
FULLER G.H.,RENEGOTIATION OF WAR CONTRACTS: A   BIBLIOG
SELECTED LIST OF REFERENCES (PAMPHLET). USA-45   WAR
ECO/DEV LG/CO NAT/G OP/RES PLAN BAL/PWR LEGIT   LAW
CONTROL...MGT 20. PAGE 42 E0823   FINAN

                                                        S44
MASON J.B.,"THE JUDICIAL SYSTEM OF THE NAZI PARTY."   FASCISM
GERMANY ELITES POL/PAR DOMIN CONTROL SANCTION   CT/SYS
TOTALISM...JURID 20 HITLER/A. PAGE 69 E1381   ADJUD
                                                        LAW

                                                        B48
MORGENTHAL H.J.,POLITICS AMONG NATIONS: THE   DIPLOM
STRUGGLE FOR POWER AND PEACE. FUT WOR+45 INT/ORG   PEACE
OP/RES PROB/SOLV BAL/PWR CONTROL ATTIT MORAL   PWR
...INT/LAW BIBLIOG 20 COLD/WAR. PAGE 75 E1494   POLICY

                                                        S48
BRADEN G.D.,"THE SEARCH FOR OBJECTIVITY IN   CONSTN
CONSTITUTIONAL LAW" (BMR)" USA+45 USA-45 LAW NAT/G   CT/SYS
CONTROL ORD/FREE PWR OBJECTIVE...JURID 20   IDEA/COMP
SUPREME/CT. PAGE 15 E0283   POLICY

                                                        S48
MILLER B.S.,"A LAW IS PASSED: THE ATOMIC ENERGY ACT   TEC/DEV
OF 1946." POL/PAR CHIEF CONFER DEBATE CONTROL   LEGIS
PARL/PROC ATTIT KNOWL...POLICY CONGRESS. PAGE 73   DECISION
E1457   LAW

                                                        B49
SCHONS D.,BOOK CENSORSHIP IN NEW SPAIN (NEW WORLD   CHRIST-17C
STUDIES, BOOK II). SPAIN LAW CULTURE INSPECT ADJUD   EDU/PROP
CT/SYS SANCTION GP/REL ORD/FREE 14/17. PAGE 88   CONTROL
E1764   PRESS

                                                        B49
SUMMERS R.E.,FEDERAL INFORMATION CONTROLS IN   ADJUD
PEACETIME. USA+45 COM/IND DOMIN INGP/REL ATTIT   CONTROL
ORD/FREE 20. PAGE 94 E1893   EDU/PROP
                                                        PRESS

                                                        B49
WALINE M.,LE CONTROLE JURIDICTIONNEL DE   JURID
L'ADMINISTRATION. BELGIUM FRANCE UAR JUDGE BAL/PWR   ADMIN
ADJUD CONTROL CT/SYS...GP/COMP 20. PAGE 104 E2093   PWR
                                                        ORD/FREE

                                                        S49
PRITCHETT C.H.,"THE PRESIDENT AND THE SUPREME   GOV/REL
COURT." NAT/G CONTROL REPRESENT FEDERAL 20. PAGE 82   CT/SYS
E1651   CHIEF

GRAVES W.B.,PUBLIC ADMINISTRATION: A COMPREHENSIVE   BIBLIOG   B50
BIBLIOGRAPHY ON PUBLIC ADMINISTRATION IN THE UNITED   FINAN
STATES (PAMPHLET). USA+45 USA-45 LOC/G NAT/G LEGIS   CONTROL
ADJUD INGP/REL...MGT 20. PAGE 45 E0901   ADMIN

MOCKFORD J.,SOUTH-WEST AFRICA AND THE INTERNATIONAL   COLONIAL   B50
COURT (PAMPHLET). AFR GERMANY SOUTH/AFR UK   SOVEREIGN
ECO/UNDEV DIPLOM CONTROL DISCRIM...DECISION JURID   INT/LAW
20 AFRICA/SW. PAGE 74 E1475   DOMIN

BIDDLE F.,THE FEAR OF FREEDOM. USA+45 LAW NAT/G   ANOMIE   B51
PUB/INST PROB/SOLV DOMIN CONTROL SANCTION REV   INGP/REL
NAT/LISM 20. PAGE 12 E0227   VOL/ASSN
                                                         ORD/FREE

CORBETT P.E.,LAW AND SOCIETY IN THE RELATIONS OF   INT/LAW   B51
STATES. FUT WOR+45 WOR-45 CONTROL WAR PEACE PWR   DIPLOM
...POLICY JURID 16/20 TREATY. PAGE 26 E0505   INT/ORG

DAVIS K.C.,ADMINISTRATIVE LAW. USA+45 USA-45 NAT/G   ADMIN   B51
PROB/SOLV BAL/PWR CONTROL ORD/FREE...POLICY 20   JURID
SUPREME/CT. PAGE 29 E0574   EX/STRUC
                                                         ADJUD

ROSSITER C.,THE SUPREME COURT AND THE COMMANDER IN   CT/SYS   B51
CHIEF. LAW CONSTN DELIB/GP EX/STRUC LEGIS TOP/EX   CHIEF
ADJUD CONTROL...DECISION SOC/EXP PRESIDENT. PAGE 86   WAR
E1724   PWR

CAHILL F.V.,JUDICIAL LEGISLATION: A STUDY IN   JURID   B52
AMERICAN LEGAL THEORY. USA+45 USA-45 LAW NAT/G   ADJUD
GP/REL...POLICY PHIL/SCI SOC 20 HOLMES/OW. PAGE 18   LEGIS
E0359   CONTROL

COLEMAN J.W. JR.,DEATH AT THE COURT-HOUSE. CONTROL   CROWD   B52
COERCE 20 KENTUCKY. PAGE 24 E0472   ORD/FREE
                                                         CRIME
                                                         CT/SYS

SINCO,PHILIPPINE POLITICAL LAW: PRINCIPLES AND   LAW   B54
CONCEPTS (10TH ED.). PHILIPPINE LOC/G EX/STRUC   CONSTN
BAL/PWR ECO/TAC TAX ADJUD ADMIN CONTROL CT/SYS SUFF   LEGIS
ORD/FREE...T 20. PAGE 91 E1831

COOPER L.,"ADMINISTRATIVE JUSTICE." UK ADMIN   LAW   S54
REPRESENT PWR...POLICY 20. PAGE 25 E0502   ADJUD
                                                         CONTROL
                                                         EX/STRUC

BERNSTEIN M.H.,REGULATING BUSINESS BY INDEPENDENT   DELIB/GP   B55
COMMISSION. USA+45 USA-45 LG/CO CHIEF LEGIS   CONTROL
PROB/SOLV ADJUD SANCTION GP/REL ATTIT...TIME/SEQ   CONSULT
19/20 MONOPOLY PRESIDENT CONGRESS. PAGE 11 E0214

BLOOM G.F.,ECONOMICS OF LABOR RELATIONS. USA+45 LAW   ECO/DEV   B55
CONSULT WORKER CAP/ISM PAY ADJUD CONTROL EFFICIENCY   ECO/TAC
ORD/FREE...CHARTS 19/20 AFL/CIO NLRB DEPT/LABOR.   LABOR
PAGE 13 E0249   GOV/REL

CAVAN R.S.,CRIMINOLOGY (2ND ED.). USA+45 LAW FAM   DRIVE   B55
PUB/INST FORCES PLAN WAR AGE/Y PERSON ROLE SUPEGO   CRIMLGY
...CHARTS 20 FBI. PAGE 21 E0409   CONTROL
                                                         METH/COMP

HOGAN W.N.,INTERNATIONAL CONFLICT AND COLLECTIVE   INT/ORG   B55
SECURITY: THE PRINCIPLE OF CONCERN IN INTERNATIONAL   WAR
ORGANIZATION. CONSTN EX/STRUC BAL/PWR DIPLOM ADJUD   ORD/FREE
CONTROL CENTRAL CONSEN PEACE...INT/LAW CONCPT   FORCES
METH/COMP 20 UN LEAGUE/NAT. PAGE 53 E1066

LARROWE C.P.,SHAPE-UP AND HIRING HALL. TRIBUTE   LABOR   B55
ADJUD CONTROL SANCTION COERCE CRIME GP/REL PWR   INDUS
...CHARTS 20 AFL/CIO NEWYORK/C SEATTLE. PAGE 63   WORKER
E1256   NAT/G

MAYERS L.,THE AMERICAN LEGAL SYSTEM. USA+45 USA-45   JURID   B55
NAT/G EX/STRUC ADMIN CONTROL FEDERAL 20 SUPREME/CT.   CT/SYS
PAGE 70 E1394   LEGIS
                                                         ADJUD

SERRANO MOSCOSO E.,A STATEMENT OF THE LAWS OF   FINAN   B55
ECUADOR IN MATTERS AFFECTING BUSINESS (2ND ED.).   ECO/UNDEV
ECUADOR INDUS LABOR LG/CO NAT/G LEGIS TAX CONTROL   LAW
MARRIAGE 20. PAGE 90 E1805   CONSTN

WHEARE K.C.,GOVERNMENT BY COMMITTEE; AN ESSAY ON   DELIB/GP   B55
THE BRITISH CONSTITUTION. UK NAT/G LEGIS INSPECT   CONSTN
CONFER ADJUD ADMIN CONTROL TASK EFFICIENCY ROLE   LEAD
POPULISM 20. PAGE 106 E2116   GP/COMP

ZABEL O.H.,GOD AND CAESAR IN NEBRASKA: A STUDY OF   SECT   B55
LEGAL RELATIONSHIP OF CHURCH AND STATE, 1854-1954.   PROVS
TAX GIVE ADMIN CONTROL GP/REL ROLE...GP/COMP 19/20   LAW
NEBRASKA. PAGE 108 E2168   EDU/PROP

BETH L.P.,"THE CASE FOR JUDICIAL PROTECTION OF   CT/SYS   S55
CIVIL LIBERTIES" (BMR)" USA+45 CONSTN ELITES LEGIS   JUDGE
CONTROL...POLICY DECISION JURID 20 SUPREME/CT   ADJUD
CIVIL/LIB. PAGE 11 E0220   ORD/FREE

CARR C.,"LEGISLATIVE CONTROL OF ADMINISTRATIVE   EXEC   S55
RULES AND REGULATIONS: PARLIAMENTARY SUPERVISION IN   REPRESENT
BRITAIN." DELIB/GP CONTROL ROLE PWR PARLIAMENT.   JURID
PAGE 20 E0392

BOTERO G.,THE REASON OF STATE AND THE GREATNESS OF   PHIL/SCI   B56
CITIES. SECT CHIEF FORCES PLAN LEAD WAR MORAL   NEW/IDEA
...POLICY 16 MACHIAVELL TREATY. PAGE 14 E0272   CONTROL

BROWNE D.G.,THE RISE OF SCOTLAND YARD: A HISTORY OF   CRIMLGY   B56
THE METROPOLITAN POLICE. UK MUNIC CHIEF ADMIN CRIME   LEGIS
GP/REL 19/20. PAGE 16 E0316   CONTROL
                                                         FORCES

CARLSTON K.S.,LAW AND STRUCTURES OF SOCIAL ACTION.   JURID   B56
LAW SOCIETY ECO/DEV DIPLOM CONTROL ATTIT...DECISION   INT/LAW
CONCPT 20. PAGE 19 E0379   INGP/REL
                                                         STRUCT

COHEN A.,THE SUTHERLAND PAPERS. USA+45 USA-45 LAW   CRIMLGY   B56
CONTROL CRIME AGE/Y...TREND ANTHOL BIBLIOG 20.   PHIL/SCI
PAGE 23 E0461   ACT/RES
                                                         METH

REDFORD E.S.,PUBLIC ADMINISTRATION AND POLICY   EX/STRUC   B56
FORMATION: STUDIES IN OIL, GAS, BANKING, RIVER   PROB/SOLV
DEVELOPMENT AND CORPORATE INVESTIGATIONS. USA+45   CONTROL
CLIENT NAT/G ADMIN LOBBY REPRESENT GOV/REL INGP/REL   EXEC
20. PAGE 84 E1678

US HOUSE RULES COMM,HEARINGS BEFORE A SPECIAL   ADMIN   B56
SUBCOMMITTEE: ESTABLISHMENT OF A STANDING COMMITTEE   DOMIN
ON ADMINISTRATIVE PROCEDURE, PRACTICE. USA+45 LAW   DELIB/GP
EX/STRUC ADJUD CONTROL EXEC GOV/REL EFFICIENCY PWR   NAT/G
...POLICY INT 20 CONGRESS. PAGE 100 E2009

US HOUSE WAYS MEANS COMMITTEE,TRAFFIC IN, AND   BIO/SOC   B56
CONTROL OF NARCOTICS, BARBITURATES, AND   CONTROL
AMPHETAMINES. CHINA/COM USA+45 SOCIETY LEGIS   PROB/SOLV
ACT/RES EDU/PROP CT/SYS SANCTION PROFIT HEALTH   CRIME
...HEAL PSY STAT 20. PAGE 100 E2011

WIGGINS J.R.,FREEDOM OR SECRECY. USA+45 USA-45   ORD/FREE   B56
DELIB/GP EX/STRUC FORCES ADJUD SANCTION KNOWL PWR   PRESS
...AUD/VIS CONGRESS 20. PAGE 106 E2121   NAT/G
                                                         CONTROL

NOBLEMAN E.E.,"THE DELEGATION OF PRESIDENTIAL   CHIEF   S56
FUNCTIONS: CONSTITUTIONAL AND LEGAL ASPECTS."   REPRESENT
USA+45 CONSTN NAT/G CONTROL 20. PAGE 77 E1553   EX/STRUC
                                                         LAW

TANENHAUS J.,"THE SUPREME COURT AND PRESIDENTIAL   CT/SYS   S56
POWER." USA+45 USA-45 NAT/G ADJUD GOV/REL FEDERAL   PWR
20 PRESIDENT. PAGE 95 E1907   CONTROL
                                                         CHIEF

BERLE A.A. JR.,ECONOMIC POWER AND FREE SOCIETY   LG/CO   B57
(PAMPHLET). CLIENT CONSTN EX/STRUC ECO/TAC CONTROL   CAP/ISM
PARTIC PWR WEALTH MAJORIT. PAGE 11 E0205   INGP/REL

LEGIT

MCCARTHY/J. PAGE 21 E0408

DOMIN
ORD/FREE

B57

CLINARD M.B.,SOCIOLOGY OF DEVIANT BEHAVIOR. FAM
CONTROL MURDER DISCRIM PERSON...PSY SOC T SOC/INTEG
20. PAGE 23 E0455

BIO/SOC
CRIME
SEX
ANOMIE

B58

CLEMMER D.,THE PRISON COMMUNITY. CULTURE CONTROL
LEAD ROUTINE PERS/REL PERSON...SOC METH/CNCPT.
PAGE 23 E0453

PUB/INST
CRIMLGY
CLIENT
INGP/REL

B57

DIVINE R.A.,AMERICAN IMMIGRATION POLICY. 1924-52.
USA+45 USA-45 VOL/ASSN DELIB/GP ADJUD WAR ADJUST
DISCRIM...POLICY JURID 20 DEPRESSION MIGRATION.
PAGE 32 E0630

GEOG
HABITAT
LEGIS
CONTROL

B58

DAVIS K.C.,ADMINISTRATIVE LAW; CASES, TEXT,
PROBLEMS. LAW LOC/G NAT/G TOP/EX PAY CONTROL
GOV/REL INGP/REL FEDERAL 20 SUPREME/CT. PAGE 29
E0576

ADJUD
JURID
CT/SYS
ADMIN

B57

FREUND G.,UNHOLY ALLIANCE. EUR+WWI GERMANY USSR
FORCES ECO/TAC CONTROL WAR PWR...TREND TREATY.
PAGE 40 E0796

DIPLOM
PLAN
POLICY

B58

DOUGLAS W.O.,THE RIGHT OF THE PEOPLE. USA+45
EDU/PROP CONTROL REPRESENT PRIVIL...IDEA/COMP 20.
PAGE 32 E0641

ORD/FREE
CONSTN
CT/SYS
CIVMIL/REL

B57

HINDERLING A.,DIE REFORMATORISCHE
VERWALTUNGSGERICHTSBARKEIT. GERMANY/W PROB/SOLV
ADJUD SUPEGO PWR...CONCPT 20. PAGE 53 E1049

ADMIN
CT/SYS
JURID
CONTROL

B58

JAPAN MINISTRY OF JUSTICE,CRIMINAL JUSTICE IN
JAPAN. LAW PROF/ORG PUB/INST FORCES CONTROL CT/SYS
PARL/PROC 20 CHINJAP. PAGE 58 E1149

CONSTN
CRIME
JURID
ADMIN

B57

JENNINGS I.,PARLIAMENT. UK FINAN INDUS POL/PAR
DELIB/GP EX/STRUC PLAN CONTROL...MAJORIT JURID
PARLIAMENT. PAGE 58 E1163

PARL/PROC
TOP/EX
MGT
LEGIS

B58

LAW COMMISSION OF INDIA,REFORM OF JUDICIAL
ADMINISTRATION. INDIA TOP/EX ADMIN DISCRIM
EFFICIENCY...METH/COMP 20. PAGE 63 E1269

CT/SYS
ADJUD
GOV/REL
CONTROL

B57

MEYER P.,ADMINISTRATIVE ORGANIZATION: A COMPARATIVE
STUDY OF THE ORGANIZATION OF PUBLIC ADMINISTRATION.
DENMARK FRANCE NORWAY SWEDEN UK USA+45 ELITES LOC/G
CONSULT LEGIS ADJUD CONTROL LEAD PWR SKILL
DECISION. PAGE 72 E1449

ADMIN
METH/COMP
NAT/G
CENTRAL

B58

MARTIN L.J.,INTERNATIONAL PROPAGANDA: ITS LEGAL AND
DIPLOMATIC CONTROL. UK USA+45 USSR CONSULT DELIB/GP
DOMIN CONTROL 20. PAGE 69 E1373

EDU/PROP
DIPLOM
INT/LAW
ATTIT

B57

NEUMANN F.,THE DEMOCRATIC AND THE AUTHORITARIAN
STATE: ESSAYS IN POLITICAL AND LEGAL THEORY. USA+45
USA-45 CONTROL REV GOV/REL PEACE ALL/IDEOS
...INT/LAW CONCPT GEN/LAWS BIBLIOG 20. PAGE 77
E1536

DOMIN
NAT/G
ORD/FREE
POLICY

B58

MOEN N.W.,THE GOVERNMENT OF SCOTLAND 1603 - 1625.
UK JUDGE ADMIN GP/REL PWR 17 SCOTLAND COMMON/LAW.
PAGE 74 E1479

CHIEF
JURID
CONTROL
PARL/PROC

B57

SCHUBERT G.A.,THE PRESIDENCY IN THE COURTS. CONSTN
FORCES DIPLOM TARIFFS ADJUD CONTROL WAR...DECISION
MGT CHARTS 18/20 PRESIDENT CONGRESS SUPREME/CT.
PAGE 89 E1778

PWR
CT/SYS
LEGIT
CHIEF

B58

O'BRIEN F.W.,JUSTICE REED AND THE FIRST AMENDMENT,
THE RELIGION CLAUSES. USA+45 USA-45 NAT/G PROVS
CONTROL FEDERAL...POLICY JURID TIME/SEQ 20
SUPREME/CT CHRUCH/STA AMEND/I REED/STAN. PAGE 78
E1563

ADJUD
SECT
CT/SYS

B57

SINEY M.C.,THE ALLIED BLOCKADE OF GERMANY:
1914-1916. EUR+WWI GERMANY MOD/EUR USA-45 DIPLOM
CONTROL NEUTRAL PWR 20. PAGE 91 E1832

DETER
INT/TRADE
INT/LAW
WAR

B58

SEYID MUHAMMAD V.A.,THE LEGAL FRAMEWORK OF WORLD
TRADE. WOR+45 INT/ORG DIPLOM CONTROL...BIBLIOG 20
TREATY UN IMF GATT. PAGE 90 E1807

INT/LAW
VOL/ASSN
INT/TRADE
TARIFFS

B57

US COMMISSION GOVT SECURITY,RECOMMENDATIONS; AREA:
IMMIGRANT PROGRAM. USA+45 LAW WORKER DIPLOM
EDU/PROP WRITING ADMIN PEACE ATTIT...CONCPT ANTHOL
20 MIGRATION SUBVERT. PAGE 99 E1981

POLICY
CONTROL
PLAN
NAT/G

B58

SOC OF COMP LEGIS AND INT LAW,THE LAW OF THE SEA...
(PAMPHLET). WOR+45 NAT/G INT/TRADE ADJUD CONTROL
NUC/PWR WAR PEACE ATTIT ORD/FREE...JURID CHARTS 20
UN TREATY RESOURCE/N. PAGE 92 E1850

INT/LAW
INT/ORG
DIPLOM
SEA

B57

US COMMISSION GOVT SECURITY,RECOMMENDATIONS; AREA:
LEGISLATION. USA+45 USA-45 DELIB/GP PLAN TEC/DEV
CIVMIL/REL ORD/FREE...POLICY DECISION 20 PRIVACY.
PAGE 99 E1982

LEGIS
SANCTION
CRIME
CONTROL

B58

WHITNEY S.N.,ANTITRUST POLICIES: AMERICAN
EXPERIENCE IN TWENTY INDUSTRIES. USA+45 USA-45 LAW
DELIB/GP LEGIS ADJUD CT/SYS GOV/REL ATTIT...ANTHOL
20 MONOPOLY CASEBOOK. PAGE 106 E2119

INDUS
CONTROL
LG/CO
MARKET

B57

US SENATE COMM ON JUDICIARY,LIMITATION OF APPELLATE
JURISDICTION OF THE SUPREME COURT. USA+45 LAW NAT/G
DELIB/GP PLAN ADMIN CONTROL PWR...DECISION 20
CONGRESS SUPREME/CT. PAGE 102 E2041

CT/SYS
ADJUD
POLICY
GOV/REL

358

VOSE C.E.,"LITIGATION AS A FORM OF PRESSURE GROUP
ACTIVITY" (BMR)" USA+45 ADJUD ORD/FREE NAACP.
PAGE 104 E2085

CONTROL
CT/SYS
VOL/ASSN
LOBBY

S57

GOODE W.J.,"COMMUNITY WITHIN A COMMUNITY: THE
PROFESSIONS." STRATA STRUCT SANCTION INGP/REL...SOC
GP/COMP. PAGE 45 E0886

PROF/ORG
NEIGH
CLIENT
CONTROL

C58

FRIEDRICH C.J.,"AUTHORITY, REASON AND DISCRETION"
IN C. FRIEDRICH'S AUTHORITY (BMR)" UNIV EX/STRUC
ADJUD ADMIN CONTROL INGP/REL ATTIT PERSON PWR.
PAGE 41 E0807

AUTHORIT
CHOOSE
RATIONAL
PERS/REL

B58

BLOCH J.,STATES' RIGHTS: THE LAW OF THE LAND.
USA+45 USA-45 LAW CONSTN LEGIS CONTROL CT/SYS
FEDERAL ORD/FREE...PREDICT 17/20 CONGRESS
SUPREME/CT. PAGE 13 E0246

PROVS
NAT/G
BAL/PWR
CENTRAL

B59

BROMWICH L.,UNION CONSTITUTIONS. CONSTN EX/STRUC
PRESS ADJUD CONTROL CHOOSE REPRESENT PWR SAMP.
PAGE 16 E0306

LABOR
ROUTINE
INGP/REL
RACE/REL

B58

BUREAU OF NATIONAL AFFAIRS,THE MCCLELLAN COMMITTEE
HEARINGS - 1957. USA+45 LEGIS CONTROL CRIME
...CHARTS 20 CONGRESS AFL/CIO MCCLELLN/J. PAGE 17
E0336

DELIB/GP
CONFER
LABOR
MGT

B59

DASH S.,THE EAVESDROPPERS. USA+45 DELIB/GP TEC/DEV
ORD/FREE...POLICY CRIMLGY JURID 20 PRIVACY. PAGE 29
E0569

CRIME
CONTROL
ACT/RES
LAW

B58

CAUGHEY J.W.,IN CLEAR AND PRESENT DANGER. USA+45
ADJUD COERCE ATTIT AUTHORIT...POLICY 20 COLD/WAR

NAT/G
CONTROL

B59

DAVIS K.C.,ADMINISTRATIVE LAW TEXT. USA+45 NAT/G

ADJUD

DELIB/GP EX/STRUC CONTROL ORD/FREE...T 20 ADMIN
SUPREME/CT. PAGE 29 E0577 JURID
CT/SYS

B59
FERRY W.H.,THE CORPORATION AND THE ECONOMY. CLIENT LG/CO
LAW CONSTN LABOR NAT/G PLAN INT/TRADE PARTIC CONSEN CONTROL
ORD/FREE PWR POLICY. PAGE 37 E0742 REPRESENT

B59
GSOVSKI V.,GOVERNMENT, LAW, AND COURTS IN THE ADJUD
SOVIET UNION AND EASTERN EUROPE (2 VOLS.). COM USSR MARXISM
AGRI INDUS WORKER CT/SYS CRIME...BIBLIOG 20 CONTROL
EUROPE/E. PAGE 48 E0958 ORD/FREE

B59
HALEY A.G.,FIRST COLLOQUIUM ON THE LAW OF OUTER SPACE
SPACE. WOR+45 INT/ORG ACT/RES PLAN BAL/PWR CONFER LAW
ATTIT PWR...POLICY JURID CHARTS ANTHOL 20. PAGE 49 SOVEREIGN
E0979 CONTROL

B59
HARVARD UNIVERSITY LAW SCHOOL,INTERNATIONAL NUC/PWR
PROBLEMS OF FINANCIAL PROTECTION AGAINST NUCLEAR ADJUD
RISK. WOR+45 NAT/G DELIB/GP PROB/SOLV DIPLOM INDUS
CONTROL ATTIT...POLICY INT/LAW MATH 20. PAGE 51 FINAN
E1009

B59
LAPIERE R.,THE FREUDIAN ETHIC. USA+45 FAM EDU/PROP PSY
CONTROL CRIME ADJUST AGE DRIVE PERCEPT PERSON SEX ORD/FREE
...SOC 20 FREUD/S. PAGE 63 E1254 SOCIETY

B59
MOOS M.,THE CAMPUS AND THE STATE. LAW FINAN EDU/PROP
DELIB/GP LEGIS EXEC LOBBY GP/REL PWR...POLICY ACADEM
BIBLIOG. PAGE 74 E1489 PROVS
CONTROL

B59
COLUMBIA U. BUREAU OF APPL SOC RES, ATTITUDES OF ATTIT
PROMINENT AMERICANS TOWARD "WORLD PEACE THROUGH ACT/RES
WORLD LAW" (SUPRA-NATL ORGANIZATION FOR WAR INT/LAW
PREVENTION). USA+45 USSR ELITES FORCES PLAN STAT
PROB/SOLV CONTROL WAR PWR...POLICY SOC QU IDEA/COMP
20 UN. PAGE 82 E1644

B59
U OF MICHIGAN LAW SCHOOL,ATOMS AND THE LAW. USA+45 NUC/PWR
PROVS WORKER PROB/SOLV DIPLOM ADMIN GOV/REL ANTHOL. NAT/G
PAGE 97 E1950 CONTROL
LAW

B59
US SENATE COMM ON JUDICIARY,EXECUTIVE PRIVILEGE. CHIEF
USA+45 DELIB/GP CONTROL KNOWL PWR 20 CONGRESS PRIVIL
PRESIDENT. PAGE 102 E2042 CONSTN
LAW

B59
WOETZEL R.K.,DIE INTERNATIONALE KONTROLLE DER SPACE
HOHEREN LUFTSCHICHTEN UND DES WELTRAUMS. INT/ORG INT/LAW
NAT/G CONTROL SUPEGO...JURID CONCPT 20. PAGE 107 DIPLOM
E2136 SOVEREIGN

L59
HECTOR L.J.,"GOVERNMENT BY ANONYMITY: WHO WRITES ADJUD
OUR REGULATORY OPINIONS?" USA+45 NAT/G TOP/EX REPRESENT
CONTROL EXEC. PAGE 51 E1021 EX/STRUC
ADMIN

L59
OBERER W.E.,"VOLUNTARY IMPARTIAL REVIEW OF LABOR: LABOR
SOME REFLECTIONS." DELIB/GP LEGIS PROB/SOLV ADJUD LAW
CONTROL COERCE PWR PLURISM POLICY. PAGE 78 E1570 PARTIC
INGP/REL

S59
MURPHY W.F.,"LOWER COURT CHECKS ON SUPREME COURT CT/SYS
POWER" (BMR)" USA+45 NAT/G PROVS SCHOOL GOV/REL BAL/PWR
RACE/REL DISCRIM ATTIT...DECISION JURID 20 CONTROL
SUPREME/CT NEGRO. PAGE 75 E1508 ADJUD

S59
SCHEEHAN D.,"PUBLIC AND PRIVATE GROUPS AS LAW
IDENTIFIED IN THE FIELD OF TRADE REGULATIONS." CONTROL
USA+45 ADMIN REPRESENT GOV/REL. PAGE 87 E1753 ADJUD
LOBBY

N59
NATIONAL ASSN HOME BUILDERS,COMMUNITY FACILITIES: A BIBLIOG/A
LIST OF SELECTED REFERENCES (PAMPHLET). USA+45 PLAN
DIST/IND FINAN SERV/IND SCHOOL CREATE CONTROL LOC/G
FEDERAL...JURID 20. PAGE 76 E1525 MUNIC

B60
ALBI F.,TRATADO DE LOS MODOS DE GESTION DE LAS LOC/G
CORPORACIONES LOCALES. SPAIN FINAN NAT/G BUDGET LAW
CONTROL EXEC ROUTINE GOV/REL ORD/FREE SOVEREIGN ADMIN
...MGT 20. PAGE 3 E0057 MUNIC

B60
CARPER E.T.,THE DEFENSE APPROPRIATIONS RIDER GOV/REL
(PAMPHLET). USA+45 CONSTN CHIEF DELIB/GP LEGIS ADJUD
BUDGET LOBBY CIVMIL/REL...POLICY 20 CONGRESS LAW
EISNHWR/DD DEPT/DEFEN PRESIDENT BOSTON. PAGE 20 CONTROL
E0390

B60
CONANT M.,ANTITRUST IN THE MOTION PICTURE INDUSTRY: PRICE
ECONOMIC AND LEGAL ANALYSIS. USA+45 MARKET ADJUST CONTROL
DEMAND BIBLIOG. PAGE 24 E0484 LAW
ART/METH

B60
HEAP D.,AN OUTLINE OF PLANNING LAW (3RD ED.). UK MUNIC
LAW PROB/SOLV ADMIN CONTROL 20. PAGE 51 E1020 PLAN
JURID
LOC/G

B60
LASKIN B.,CANADIAN CONSTITUTIONAL LAW: TEXT AND CONSTN
NOTES ON DISTRIBUTION OF LEGISLATIVE POWER (2ND NAT/G
ED.). CANADA LOC/G ECO/TAC TAX CONTROL CT/SYS CRIME LAW
FEDERAL PWR...JURID 20 PARLIAMENT. PAGE 63 E1259 LEGIS

B60
PINTO F.B.M.,ENRIQUECIMENTO ILICITO NO EXERCICIO DE ADMIN
CARGOS PUBLICOS. BRAZIL L/A+17C USA+45 ELITES NAT/G
TRIBUTE CONTROL INGP/REL ORD/FREE PWR...NAT/COMP CRIME
20. PAGE 81 E1617 LAW

B60
PRASAD B.,THE ORIGINS OF PROVINCIAL AUTONOMY. INDIA CENTRAL
UK FINAN LOC/G FORCES LEGIS CONTROL CT/SYS PWR PROVS
...JURID 19/20. PAGE 82 E1646 COLONIAL
NAT/G

B60
SCHEIBER H.N.,THE WILSON ADMINISTRATION AND CIVIL ORD/FREE
LIBERTIES 1917-1921. LAW GOV/REL ATTIT 20 WILSON/W WAR
CIVIL/LIB. PAGE 87 E1754 NAT/G
CONTROL

B60
WEBSTER J.A.,A GENERAL STUDY OF THE DEPARTMENT OF ORD/FREE
DEFENSE INTERNAL SECURITY PROGRAM. USA+45 WORKER PLAN
TEC/DEV ADJUD CONTROL CT/SYS EXEC GOV/REL COST ADMIN
...POLICY DECISION MGT 20 DEPT/DEFEN SUPREME/CT. NAT/G
PAGE 105 E2105

S60
MACKINNON F.,"THE UNIVERSITY: COMMUNITY OR ACADEM
UTILITY?" CLIENT CONSTN INTELL FINAN NAT/G NEIGH MGT
EDU/PROP PARTIC REPRESENT ROLE. PAGE 67 E1343 CONTROL
SERV/IND

S60
MARSHALL G.,"POLICE RESPONSIBILITY." UK LOC/G ADJUD CONTROL
ADMIN EXEC 20. PAGE 69 E1370 REPRESENT
LAW
FORCES

C60
HAZARD J.N.,"SETTLING DISPUTES IN SOVIET SOCIETY: ADJUD
THE FORMATIVE YEARS OF LEGAL INSTITUTIONS." USSR LAW
NAT/G PROF/ORG PROB/SOLV CONTROL CT/SYS ROUTINE REV COM
CENTRAL...JURID BIBLIOG 20. PAGE 51 E1017 POLICY

C60
MCCLEERY R.,"COMMUNICATION PATTERNS AS BASES OF PERS/REL
SYSTEMS OF AUTHORITY AND POWER" IN THEORETICAL PUB/INST
STUDIES IN SOCIAL ORGAN. OF PRISON-BMR. USA+45 PWR
SOCIETY STRUCT EDU/PROP ADMIN CONTROL COERCE CRIME DOMIN
GP/REL AUTHORIT...SOC 20. PAGE 70 E1400

B61
ALFRED H.,PUBLIC OWNERSHIP IN THE USA: GOALS AND CONTROL
PRIORITIES. LAW INDUS INT/TRADE ADJUD GOV/REL OWN
EFFICIENCY PEACE SOCISM...POLICY ANTHOL 20 TVA. ECO/DEV
PAGE 3 E0064 ECO/TAC

B61
AUERBACH C.A.,THE LEGAL PROCESS. USA+45 DELIB/GP JURID
JUDGE CONFER ADJUD CONTROL...DECISION 20 ADMIN
SUPREME/CT. PAGE 6 E0116 LEGIS
CT/SYS

B61
BEASLEY K.E.,STATE SUPERVISION OF MUNICIPAL DEBT IN MUNIC
KANSAS - A CASE STUDY. USA+45 USA-45 FINAN PROVS LOC/G

BUDGET TAX ADJUD ADMIN CONTROL SUPEGO. PAGE 9 E0167 LEGIS
JURID

B61
LEONI B.,FREEDOM AND THE LAW. WOR+45 SOCIETY ADJUD   JURID
INGP/REL EFFICIENCY ATTIT DRIVE. PAGE 64 E1286   ORD/FREE
LEGIS
CONTROL

B61
MURPHY E.F.,WATER PURITY: A STUDY IN LEGAL CONTROL   SEA
OF NATURAL RESOURCES. LOC/G ACT/RES PLAN TEC/DEV   LAW
LOBBY GP/REL COST ATTIT HEALTH ORD/FREE...HEAL   PROVS
JURID 20 WISCONSIN WATER. PAGE 75 E1506   CONTROL

B61
RUEDA B.,A STATEMENT OF THE LAWS OF COLOMBIA IN   FINAN
MATTERS AFFECTING BUSINESS (3RD ED.). INDUS FAM   ECO/UNDEV
LABOR LG/CO NAT/G LEGIS TAX CONTROL MARRIAGE 20   LAW
COLOMB. PAGE 86 E1733   CONSTN

B61
US HOUSE COMM ON JUDICIARY,LEGISLATION RELATING TO   LEGIS
ORGANIZED CRIME. USA+45 DIST/IND DELIB/GP GAMBLE   CONTROL
SANCTION HOUSE/REP. PAGE 100 E2004   CRIME
LAW

B61
UTLEY T.E.,OCCASION FOR OMBUDSMAN. UK CREATE   PROB/SOLV
CONTROL 20 OMBUDSMAN. PAGE 103 E2065   INGP/REL
REPRESENT
ADJUD

L61
MCNAMEE B.J.,"CONFLICT OF INTEREST: STATE   LAW
GOVERNMENT EMPLOYEES." USA+45 PROVS 20. PAGE 71   REPRESENT
E1426   ADMIN
CONTROL

B62
ALLOTT A.N.,JUDICIAL AND LEGAL SYSTEMS IN AFRICA.   CT/SYS
LAW CONSTN JUDGE CONTROL...METH/CNCPT CLASSIF   AFR
CHARTS 20 COMMON/LAW. PAGE 4 E0070   JURID
COLONIAL

B62
CURRY J.E.,RACE TENSIONS AND THE POLICE. LAW MUNIC   FORCES
NEIGH TEC/DEV RUMOR CONTROL COERCE GP/REL ATTIT   RACE/REL
...SOC 20 NEGRO. PAGE 28 E0558   CROWD
ORD/FREE

B62
GROGAN V.,ADMINISTRATIVE TRIBUNALS IN THE PUBLIC   ADMIN
SERVICE. IRELAND UK NAT/G CONTROL CT/SYS...JURID   LAW
GOV/COMP 20. PAGE 48 E0945   ADJUD
DELIB/GP

B62
GRZYBOWSKI K.,SOVIET LEGAL INSTITUTIONS. USA+45   ADJUD
USSR ECO/DEV NAT/G EDU/PROP CONTROL CT/SYS CRIME   LAW
OWN ATTIT PWR SOCISM...NAT/COMP 20. PAGE 48 E0955   JURID

B62
HOOK S.,THE PARADOXES OF FREEDOM. UNIV CONSTN   CONCPT
INTELL LEGIS CONTROL REV CHOOSE SUPEGO...POLICY   MAJORIT
JURID IDEA/COMP 19/20 CIV/RIGHTS. PAGE 55 E1095   ORD/FREE
ALL/VALS

B62
INTERNAT CONGRESS OF JURISTS,EXECUTIVE ACTION AND   JURID
THE RULE OF RULE: REPORTION PROCEEDINGS OF INT'T   EXEC
CONGRESS OF JURISTS,-RIO DE JANEIRO, BRAZIL. WOR+45   ORD/FREE
ACADEM CONSULT JUDGE EDU/PROP ADJUD CT/SYS INGP/REL   CONTROL
PERSON DEPT/DEFEN. PAGE 57 E1130

B62
INTNTL COTTON ADVISORY COMMITT,GOVERNMENT   ECO/TAC
REGULATIONS ON COTTON, 1962 (PAMPHLET). WOR+45   LAW
RATION PRODUC...CHARTS 20. PAGE 57 E1136   CONTROL
AGRI

B62
LITTLEFIELD N.,METROPOLITAN AREA PROBLEMS AND   LOC/G
MUNICIPAL HOME RULE. USA+45 PROVS ADMIN CONTROL   SOVEREIGN
GP/REL PWR. PAGE 65 E1308   JURID
LEGIS

B62
MCWHINNEY E.,CONSTITUTIONALISM IN GERMANY AND THE   CONSTN
FEDERAL CONSTITUTINAL COURT. GERMANY/W POL/PAR TV   CT/SYS
ADJUD CHOOSE EFFICIENCY ATTIT ORD/FREE MARXISM   CONTROL
...NEW/IDEA BIBLIOG 20. PAGE 71 E1428   NAT/G

B62
MITCHELL G.E.,THE ANGRY BLACK SOUTH. USA+45 LAW   RACE/REL
CONSTN SCHOOL DELIB/GP EDU/PROP CONTROL SUFF ANOMIE   DISCRIM

DRIVE...ANTHOL 20 NEGRO CIV/RIGHTS SOUTH/US.   ADJUST
PAGE 74 E1473   ORD/FREE

B62
NATIONAL MUNICIPAL LEAGUE,COURT DECISIONS ON   PROVS
LEGISLATIVE APPORTIONMENT (VOL. III). USA+45 JUDGE   CT/SYS
ADJUD CONTROL ATTIT...DECISION JURID COURT/DIST   APPORT
CASEBOOK. PAGE 76 E1528   LEGIS

B62
OTTENBERG M.,THE FEDERAL INVESTIGATORS. USA+45 LAW   FORCES
COM/IND DIST/IND WORKER DIPLOM INT/TRADE CONTROL   INSPECT
FEDERAL HEALTH ORD/FREE FBI CIA FTC SEC FDA.   NAT/G
PAGE 79 E1585   CRIME

B62
SOWLE C.R.,POLICE POWER AND INDIVIDUAL FREEDOM: THE   FORCES
QUEST FOR BALANCE. CANADA EUR+WWI ISRAEL NORWAY   ORD/FREE
USA+45 LAW CONSTN SOCIETY CONTROL ROUTINE SANCTION   IDEA/COMP
GP/REL 20 CHINJAP. PAGE 93 E1859

B62
STERN A.C.,AIR POLLUTION (2 VOLS.). LAW INDUS   AIR
PROB/SOLV TEC/DEV INSPECT RISK BIO/SOC HABITAT   OP/RES
...OBS/ENVIR TESTS SAMP 20 POLLUTION. PAGE 93 E1871   CONTROL
HEALTH

B62
SWAYZE H.,POLITICAL CONTROL OF LITERATURE IN THE   MARXISM
USSR, 1946-1959. USSR NAT/G CREATE LICENSE...JURID   WRITING
20. PAGE 95 E1898   CONTROL
DOMIN

B62
US CONGRESS,COMMUNICATIONS SATELLITE LEGISLATION: SPACE
HEARINGS BEFORE COMM ON AERON AND SPACE SCIENCES ON   COM/IND
BILLS S2550 AND 2814. WOR+45 LAW VOL/ASSN PLAN   ADJUD
DIPLOM CONTROL OWN PEACE...NEW/IDEA CONGRESS NASA.   GOV/REL
PAGE 99 E1990

B62
WADSWORTH J.J.,THE PRICE OF PEACE. WOR+45 TEC/DEV   DIPLOM
CONTROL NUC/PWR PEACE ATTIT TREATY 20. PAGE 104   INT/ORG
E2089   ARMS/CONT
POLICY

L62
CAVERS D.F.,"ADMINISTRATIVE DECISION-MAKING IN   REPRESENT
NUCLEAR FACILITIES LICENSING." USA+45 CLIENT ADMIN   LOBBY
EXEC 20 AEC. PAGE 21 E0410   PWR
CONTROL

L62
N,"UNION INVESTMENT IN BUSINESS: A SOURCE OF UNION   LABOR
CONFLICT OF INTEREST." LAW NAT/G LEGIS CONTROL   POLICY
GP/REL INGP/REL DECISION. PAGE 76 E1515   FINAN
LG/CO

C62
MORGAN G.G.,"SOVIET ADMINISTRATIVE LEGALITY: THE   LAW
ROLE OF THE ATTORNEY GENERAL'S OFFICE." COM USSR   CONSTN
CONTROL ROUTINE...CONCPT BIBLIOG 18/20. PAGE 74   LEGIS
E1493   ADMIN

N62
US SENATE COMM ON JUDICIARY,LEGISLATION TO   LEAD
STRENGTHEN PENALTIES UNDER THE ANTITRUST LAWS   ADJUD
(PAMPHLET). USA+45 LG/CO CONFER CONTROL SANCTION   INDUS
ORD/FREE 20 SENATE MONOPOLY. PAGE 102 E2045   ECO/TAC

B63
ADRIAN C.R.,GOVERNING OVER FIFTY STATES AND THEIR   PROVS
COMMUNITIES. USA+45 CONSTN FINAN MUNIC NAT/G   LOC/G
POL/PAR EX/STRUC LEGIS ADMIN CONTROL CT/SYS   GOV/REL
...CHARTS 20. PAGE 3 E0052   GOV/COMP

B63
BOWIE R.R.,GOVERNMENT REGULATION OF BUSINESS: CASES LAW
FROM THE NATIONAL REPORTER SYSTEM. USA+45 USA-45   CONTROL
NAT/G ECO/TAC ADJUD...ANTHOL 19/20 SUPREME/CT FTC   INDUS
FAIR/LABOR MONOPOLY. PAGE 14 E0280   CT/SYS

B63
BROWN R.M.,THE SOUTH CAROLINA REGULATORS. USA-45   ORD/FREE
LEGIS LEGIT ADJUD COLONIAL CONTROL WAR...BIBLIOG/A   JURID
18 CHARLESTON SOUTH/CAR. PAGE 16 E0315   PWR
PROVS

B63
CRAIG A.,SUPPRESSED BOOKS: A HISTORY OF THE   BIBLIOG/A
CONCEPTION OF LITERARY OBSCENITY. WOR+45 WOR-45   LAW
CREATE EDU/PROP LITERACY ATTIT...ART/METH PSY   SEX
CONCPT 20. PAGE 27 E0538   CONTROL

B63
DILLIARD I.,ONE MAN'S STAND FOR FREEDOM: MR.   CONSTN

JUSTICE BLACK AND THE BILL OF RIGHTS. USA+45 JURID
POL/PAR SECT DELIB/GP FORCES ADJUD CONTROL WAR JUDGE
DISCRIM MORAL...BIBLIOG 20 NEGRO SUPREME/CT ORD/FREE
BILL/RIGHT BLACK/HL. PAGE 32 E0628

B63
FRIEDRICH C.J.,MAN AND HIS GOVERNMENT: AN EMPIRICAL PERSON
THEORY OF POLITICS. UNIV LOC/G NAT/G ADJUD REV ORD/FREE
INGP/REL DISCRIM PWR BIBLIOG. PAGE 41 E0810 PARTIC
CONTROL

B63
GARNER U.F.,ADMINISTRATIVE LAW. UK LAW LOC/G NAT/G ADMIN
EX/STRUC LEGIS JUDGE BAL/PWR BUDGET ADJUD CONTROL JURID
CT/SYS...BIBLIOG 20. PAGE 42 E0840 PWR
GOV/REL

B63
GRIFFITH J.A.G.,PRINCIPLES OF ADMINISTRATIVE LAW JURID
(3RD ED.). UK CONSTN EX/STRUC LEGIS ADJUD CONTROL ADMIN
CT/SYS PWR...CHARTS 20. PAGE 47 E0940 NAT/G
BAL/PWR

B63
HORRELL M.,LEGISLATION AND RACE RELATIONS LAW
(PAMPHLET). SOUTH/AFR SCHOOL TAX DOMIN CONTROL 20. RACE/REL
PAGE 55 E1098 DISCRIM
PARTIC

B63
KLEIN F.J.,JUDICIAL ADMINISTRATION AND THE LEGAL BIBLIOG/A
PROFESSION. USA+45 ADMIN CONTROL EFFICIENCY CT/SYS
...POLICY 20. PAGE 61 E1222 ADJUD
JUDGE

B63
LEWIN J.,POLITICS AND LAW IN SOUTH AFRICA. NAT/LISM
SOUTH/AFR UK POL/PAR BAL/PWR ECO/TAC COLONIAL POLICY
CONTROL GP/REL DISCRIM PWR 20 NEGRO. PAGE 65 E1293 LAW
RACE/REL

B63
MOLLARD P.T.,LE REGIME JURIDIQUE DE LA PRESSE AU PRESS
MAROC. MOROCCO CONTROL CRIME GP/REL ORD/FREE 20. LAW
PAGE 74 E1482 LEAD
LEGIT

B63
MURPHY T.J.,CENSORSHIP: GOVERNMENT AND OBSCENITY. ORD/FREE
USA+45 CULTURE LEGIS JUDGE EDU/PROP CONTROL MORAL
INGP/REL RATIONAL POPULISM...CATH JURID 20. PAGE 75 LAW
E1507 CONSEN

B63
NEWMAN E.S.,THE FREEDOM READER. USA+45 LEGIS TOP/EX RACE/REL
PLAN ADJUD CONTROL CT/SYS DISCRIM...DECISION ANTHOL LAW
20 SUPREME/CT CIV/RIGHTS. PAGE 77 E1541 POLICY
ORD/FREE

B63
PATRA A.C.,THE ADMINISTRATION OF JUSTICE UNDER THE ADMIN
EAST INDIA COMPANY IN BENGAL, BIHAR AND ORISSA. JURID
INDIA UK LG/CO CAP/ISM INT/TRADE ADJUD COLONIAL CONCPT
CONTROL CT/SYS...POLICY 20. PAGE 80 E1602

B63
RICHARDS P.G.,PATRONAGE IN BRITISH GOVERNMENT. EX/STRUC
ELITES DELIB/GP TOP/EX PROB/SOLV CONTROL CT/SYS REPRESENT
EXEC PWR. PAGE 84 E1693 POL/PAR
ADMIN

B63
SCOTT A.M.,THE SUPREME COURT V. THE CONSTITUTION. PWR
USA+45 CONTROL ATTIT ROLE...POLICY CONCPT 20 CT/SYS
SUPREME/CT. PAGE 90 E1796 NAT/G
CONSTN

B63
US SENATE COMM ON JUDICIARY,ADMINISTERED PRICES. LG/CO
USA+45 RATION ADJUD CONTROL LOBBY...POLICY 20 PRICE
SENATE MONOPOLY. PAGE 102 E2047 ADMIN
DECISION

B63
US SENATE COMM ON JUDICIARY,US PERSONNEL SECURITY PLAN
PRACTICES. USA+45 DELIB/GP ADJUD ADMIN ORD/FREE NAT/G
...CHARTS 20 CONGRESS CIVIL/SERV. PAGE 102 E2049 CONTROL
WORKER

B63
VAN SLYCK P.,PEACE: THE CONTROL OF NATIONAL POWER. ARMS/CONT
CUBA WOR+45 FINAN NAT/G FORCES PROB/SOLV TEC/DEV PEACE
BAL/PWR ADMIN CONTROL ORD/FREE...POLICY INT/LAW UN INT/ORG
COLD/WAR TREATY. PAGE 103 E2069 DIPLOM

B63
WOLL P.,ADMINISTRATIVE LAW: THE INFORMAL PROCESS. ADMIN
USA+45 NAT/G CONTROL EFFICIENCY 20. PAGE 107 E2141 ADJUD
REPRESENT
EX/STRUC

B63
YOUNGER R.D.,THE PEOPLE'S PANEL: THE GRAND JURY IN CT/SYS
THE UNITED STATES, 1634-1941. USA-45 LAW LEGIT JURID
CONTROL TASK GP/REL ROLE...TREND 17/20 GRAND/JURY. CONSTN
PAGE 108 E2166 LOC/G

L63
BOLGAR V.,"THE PUBLIC INTEREST: A JURISPRUDENTIAL CONCPT
AND COMPARATIVE OVERVIEW OF SYMPOSIUM ON ORD/FREE
FUNDAMENTAL CONCEPTS OF PUBLIC LAW" COM FRANCE CONTROL
GERMANY SWITZERLND LAW ADJUD ADMIN AGREE LAISSEZ NAT/COMP
...JURID GEN/LAWS 20 EUROPE/E. PAGE 14 E0264

B64
BOWETT D.W.,UNITED NATIONS FORCES* A LEGAL STUDY. OP/RES
CYPRUS ISRAEL KOREA LAW CONSTN ACT/RES CREATE FORCES
BUDGET CONTROL TASK PWR...INT/LAW IDEA/COMP UN ARMS/CONT
CONGO/LEOP SUEZ. PAGE 14 E0278

B64
ENDACOTT G.B.,GOVERNMENT AND PEOPLE IN HONG KONG CONSTN
1841-1962: A CONSTITUTIONAL HISTORY. UK LEGIS ADJUD COLONIAL
REPRESENT ATTIT 19/20 HONG/KONG. PAGE 35 E0688 CONTROL
ADMIN

B64
FISK W.M.,ADMINISTRATIVE PROCEDURE IN A REGULATORY SERV/IND
AGENCY: THE CAB AND THE NEW YORK-CHICAGO CASE ECO/DEV
(PAMPHLET). USA+45 DIST/IND ADMIN CONTROL LOBBY AIR
GP/REL ROLE ORD/FREE NEWYORK/C CHICAGO CAB. PAGE 38 JURID
E0758

B64
FRYDENSBERG P.,PEACE-KEEPING: EXPERIENCE AND INT/ORG
EVALUATION: THE OSLO PAPERS. NORWAY FORCES PLAN DIPLOM
CONTROL...INT/LAW 20 UN. PAGE 41 E0814 PEACE
COERCE

B64
HALLER W.,DER SCHWEDISCHE JUSTITIEOMBUDSMAN. JURID
DENMARK FINLAND NORWAY SWEDEN LEGIS ADJUD CONTROL PARL/PROC
PERSON ORD/FREE...NAT/COMP 20 OMBUDSMAN. PAGE 50 ADMIN
E0986 CHIEF

B64
JACKSON R.M.,THE MACHINERY OF JUSTICE IN ENGLAND. CT/SYS
UK EDU/PROP CONTROL COST ORD/FREE...MGT 20 ADJUD
ENGLSH/LAW. PAGE 57 E1142 JUDGE
JURID

B64
JENKS C.W.,THE PROSPECTS OF INTERNATIONAL INT/LAW
ADJUDICATION. WOR+45 WOR-45 NAT/G DIPLOM CONTROL ADJUD
PWR...POLICY JURID CONCPT METH/COMP 19/20 ICJ CT/SYS
LEAGUE/NAT UN TREATY. PAGE 58 E1160 INT/ORG

B64
KISER S.L.,AMERICANISM IN ACTION. USA+45 LAW PROVS OLD/LIB
CAP/ISM DIPLOM RECEIVE CONTROL CT/SYS WAR FEDERAL FOR/AID
ATTIT WEALTH 20 SUPREME/CT. PAGE 61 E1221 MARXISM
CONSTN

B64
LOCKHART W.B.,CASES AND MATERIALS ON CONSTITUTIONAL ORD/FREE
RIGHTS AND LIBERTIES. USA+45 FORCES LEGIS DIPLOM CONSTN
PRESS CONTROL CRIME WAR PWR...AUD/VIS T WORSHIP 20 NAT/G
NEGRO. PAGE 66 E1317

B64
MANNING B.,FEDERAL CONFLICT OF INTEREST LAW. USA+45 LAW
NAT/G PWR 20. PAGE 68 E1362 CONTROL
ADMIN
JURID

B64
MARSHALL B.,FEDERALISM AND CIVIL RIGHTS. USA+45 FEDERAL
PROVS BAL/PWR CONTROL CT/SYS PARTIC SOVEREIGN ORD/FREE
...JURID 20 NEGRO CIV/RIGHTS. PAGE 68 E1369 CONSTN
FORCES

B64
MITAU G.T.,INSOLUBLE PROBLEMS: CASE PROBLEMS ON THE ADJUD
FUNCTIONS OF STATE AND LOCAL GOVERNMENT. USA+45 AIR LOC/G
FINAN LABOR POL/PAR PROB/SOLV TAX RECEIVE CONTROL PROVS
GP/REL 20 CASEBOOK ZONING. PAGE 73 E1471

B64
NELSON D.H.,ADMINISTRATIVE AGENCIES OF THE USA: ADMIN
THEIR DECISIONS AND AUTHORITY. USA+45 NAT/G CONTROL EX/STRUC
CT/SYS REPRESENT...DECISION 20. PAGE 76 E1531 ADJUD

LAW

B64

NEWMAN E.S.,CIVIL LIBERTY AND CIVIL RIGHTS. USA+45
USA-45 CONSTN PROVS FORCES LEGIS CT/SYS RACE/REL
ATTIT...MAJORIT JURID WORSHIP 20 SUPREME/CT NEGRO
CIV/RIGHTS CHURCH/STA. PAGE 77 E1543
ORD/FREE
LAW
CONTROL
NAT/G

B64

RUSSELL R.B.,UNITED NATIONS EXPERIENCE WITH
MILITARY FORCES: POLITICAL AND LEGAL ASPECTS. AFR
KOREA WOR+45 LEGIS PROB/SOLV ADMIN CONTROL
EFFICIENCY PEACE...POLICY INT/LAW BIBLIOG UN.
PAGE 87 E1738
FORCES
DIPLOM
SANCTION
ORD/FREE

B64

TAUBENFELD H.J.,SPACE AND SOCIETY. USA+45 LAW
FORCES CREATE TEC/DEV ADJUD CONTROL COST PEACE
...PREDICT ANTHOL 20. PAGE 95 E1911
SPACE
SOCIETY
ADJUST
DIPLOM

B64

US SENATE COMM ON JUDICIARY,HEARINGS BEFORE
SUBCOMMITTEE ON ANTITRUST AND MONOPOLY: ECONOMIC
CONCENTRATION VOLUMES 1-5 JULY 1964-SEPT 1966.
USA+45 LAW FINAN ECO/TAC ADJUD COST EFFICIENCY
PRODUC...STAT CHARTS 20 CONGRESS MONOPOLY. PAGE 102
E2052
ECO/DEV
CONTROL
MARKET
LG/CO

B64

WRIGHT Q.,A STUDY OF WAR. LAW NAT/G PROB/SOLV
BAL/PWR NAT/LISM PEACE ATTIT SOVEREIGN...CENSUS
SOC/INTEG. PAGE 108 E2159
WAR
CONCPT
DIPLOM
CONTROL

S64

BAKER H.R.,"INMATE SELF-GOVERNMENT." ACT/RES CREATE
CONTROL PARTIC ATTIT RIGID/FLEX QU. PAGE 7 E0141
PUB/INST
CRIME
INGP/REL
REPRESENT

B65

ANDRUS H.L.,LIBERALISM, CONSERVATISM, MORMONISM.
USA+45 PLAN ADJUD CONTROL HAPPINESS ORD/FREE
CONSERVE NEW/LIB WORSHIP 20. PAGE 5 E0097
SECT
UTOPIA
MORAL

B65

ASSOCIATION BAR OF NYC,RADIO, TELEVISION, AND THE
ADMINISTRATION OF JUSTICE: A DOCUMENTED SURVEY OF
MATERIALS. USA+45 DELIB/GP FORCES PRESS ADJUD
CONTROL CT/SYS CRIME...INT IDEA/COMP BIBLIOG.
PAGE 6 E0109
AUD/VIS
ATTIT
ORD/FREE

B65

BELL J.,THE JOHNSON TREATMENT: HOW LYNDON JOHNSON
TOOK OVER THE PRESIDENCY AND MADE IT HIS OWN.
USA+45 DELIB/GP DIPLOM ADJUD MURDER CHOOSE PERSON
PWR...POLICY OBS INT TIME 20 JOHNSON/LB KENNEDY/JF
PRESIDENT CONGRESS. PAGE 10 E0183
INGP/REL
TOP/EX
CONTROL
NAT/G

B65

BOCK E.,GOVERNMENT REGULATION OF BUSINESS. USA+45
LAW EX/STRUC LEGIS EXEC ORD/FREE PWR...ANTHOL
CONGRESS. PAGE 13 E0255
MGT
ADMIN
NAT/G
CONTROL

B65

HAEFELE E.T.,GOVERNMENT CONTROLS ON TRANSPORT. AFR
RHODESIA TANZANIA DIPLOM ECO/TAC TARIFFS PRICE
ADJUD CONTROL REGION EFFICIENCY...POLICY 20 CONGO.
PAGE 49 E0973
ECO/DEV
DIST/IND
FINAN
NAT/G

B65

HARTUNG F.E.,CRIME, LAW, AND SOCIETY. LAW PUB/INST
CRIME PERS/REL AGE/Y BIO/SOC PERSON ROLE SUPEGO
...LING GP/COMP GEN/LAWS 20. PAGE 50 E1004
PERCEPT
CRIMLGY
DRIVE
CONTROL

B65

HOWARD C.G.,LAW: ITS NATURE, FUNCTIONS, AND LIMITS.
USA+45 CONSTN LEGIS CREATE SANCTION ORD/FREE
...BIBLIOG 20. PAGE 55 E1101
LAW
JURID
CONTROL
SOCIETY

B65

JENKS C.W.,SPACE LAW. DIPLOM DEBATE CONTROL
ORD/FREE TREATY 20 UN. PAGE 58 E1161
SPACE
INT/LAW
JURID
INT/ORG

B65

JOHNSTON D.M.,THE INTERNATIONAL LAW OF FISHERIES: A
FRAMEWORK FOR POLICYORIENTED INQUIRIES. WOR+45
ACT/RES PLAN PROB/SOLV CONTROL SOVEREIGN. PAGE 59
E1171
CONCPT
EXTR/IND
JURID
DIPLOM

B65

MCWHINNEY E.,JUDICIAL REVIEW IN THE ENGLISH-
SPEAKING WORLD (3RD ED.). CANADA UK WOR+45 LEGIS
CONTROL EXEC PARTIC...JURID 20 AUSTRAL. PAGE 71
E1431
GOV/COMP
CT/SYS
ADJUD
CONSTN

B65

NEGLEY G.,POLITICAL AUTHORITY AND MORAL JUDGMENT.
INTELL SOCIETY LEGIS SANCTION UTOPIA SOVEREIGN
MARXISM...INT/LAW LOG 20. PAGE 76 E1530
MORAL
PWR
CONTROL

B65

PADELFORD N.,THE UNITED NATIONS IN THE BALANCE*
ACCOMPLISHMENTS AND PROSPECTS. NAT/G VOL/ASSN
DIPLOM ADMIN COLONIAL CT/SYS REGION WAR ORD/FREE
...ANTHOL UN. PAGE 79 E1588
INT/ORG
CONTROL

B65

RADZINOWICZ L.,THE NEED FOR CRIMINOLOGY AND A
PROPOSAL FOR AN INSTITUTE OF CRIMINOLOGY. FUT UK
USA+45 SOCIETY ACT/RES PROB/SOLV CRIME...PSY SOC
BIBLIOG 20. PAGE 83 E1666
CRIMLGY
PROF/ORG
ACADEM
CONTROL

B65

SCHUBERT G.,THE JUDICIAL MIND: THE ATTITUDES AND
IDEOLOGIES OF SUPREME COURT JUSTICES 1946-1963.
USA+45 ELITES NAT/G CONTROL PERS/REL MAJORITY
CONSERVE...DECISION JURID MODAL STAT TREND GP/COMP
GAME. PAGE 88 E1774
CT/SYS
JUDGE
ATTIT
NEW/LIB

B65

SOPER T.,EVOLVING COMMONWEALTH. AFR CANADA INDIA
IRELAND UK LAW CONSTN POL/PAR DOMIN CONTROL WAR PWR
...AUD/VIS 18/20 COMMONWLTH OEEC. PAGE 93 E1857
INT/ORG
COLONIAL
VOL/ASSN

B65

US LIBRARY OF CONGRESS,INTERNAL SECURITY AND
SUBVERSION. USA+45 ACADEM LOC/G NAT/G PROVS
...POLICY ANARCH DECISION 20 CIVIL/SERV SUBVERT
SEDITION. PAGE 101 E2020
CONTROL
ADJUD
LAW
PLAN

B65

US SENATE COMM ON JUDICIARY,ANTITRUST EXEMPTIONS
FOR AGREEMENTS RELATING TO BALANCE OF PAYMENTS.
FINAN ECO/TAC CONTROL WEALTH...POLICY 20 CONGRESS.
PAGE 103 E2056
BAL/PAY
ADJUD
MARKET
INT/TRADE

B65

WILSON J.F.,CHURCH AND STATE IN AMERICAN HISTORY.
USA+45 USA-45 ADJUD CT/SYS ORD/FREE SOVEREIGN
...ANTHOL BIBLIOG/A 17/20 CHURCH/STA. PAGE 106
E2129
SECT
NAT/G
GP/REL
CONTROL

L65

FORTE W.E.,"THE FOOD AND DRUG ADMINISTRATION, THE
FEDERAL TRADE COMMISSION AND THE DECEPTIVE
PACKAGING." ROUTINE...JURID 20 FTC. PAGE 39 E0772
CONTROL
HEALTH
ADJUD
INDUS

S65

FOX A.B.,"NATO AND CONGRESS." CONSTN DELIB/GP
EX/STRUC FORCES TOP/EX BUDGET NUC/PWR GOV/REL
...GP/COMP CONGRESS NATO TREATY. PAGE 39 E0779
CONTROL
DIPLOM

C65

SEARA M.V.,"COSMIC INTERNATIONAL LAW." LAW ACADEM
ACT/RES DIPLOM COLONIAL CONTROL NUC/PWR SOVEREIGN
...GEN/LAWS BIBLIOG UN. PAGE 90 E1799
SPACE
INT/LAW
IDEA/COMP
INT/ORG

B66

AARON T.J.,THE CONTROL OF POLICE DISCRETION: THE
DANISH EXPERIENCE. DENMARK LAW CREATE ADMIN
INGP/REL SUPEGO PWR 20 OMBUDSMAN. PAGE 2 E0042
CONTROL
FORCES
REPRESENT
PROB/SOLV

B66

ASAMOAH O.Y.,THE LEGAL SIGNIFICANCE OF THE
DECLARATIONS OF THE GENERAL ASSEMBLY OF THE UNITED
NATIONS. WOR+45 CREATE CONTROL...BIBLIOG 20 UN.
PAGE 5 E0105
INT/LAW
INT/ORG
DIPLOM

B66

BAHRO H.,DAS KINDSCHAFTSRECHT IN DER UNION DER
SOZIALISTITSCHEN SOWJETREPUBLIKEN. USSR SECT
EDU/PROP CONTROL PWR...SOC/WK 20. PAGE 7 E0133
JURID
AGE/C
PERS/REL
SUPEGO

B66

BEER U.,FRUCHTBARKEITSREGELUNG ALS KONSEQUENZ
VERANTWORTLICHER ELTERNSCHAFT. ASIA GERMANY/W INDIA
LAW ECO/DEV ECO/UNDEV TEC/DEV ECO/TAC BIO/SOC SEX
CATHISM...METH/COMP 20 CHINJAP BIRTH/CON. PAGE 9
E0178
CONTROL
GEOG
FAM
SECT

B66
COUNCIL OF STATE GOVERNMENTS,THE HANDBOOK ON   CRIME
INTERSTATE CRIME CONTROL. USA+45 PUB/INST DELIB/GP   GOV/REL
AGREE AGE/Y 20 INTST/CRIM. PAGE 27 E0524   CONTROL
                                                     JURID

B66
DALLIN A.,POLITICS IN THE SOVIET UNION: 7 CASES.   MARXISM
COM USSR LAW POL/PAR CHIEF FORCES WRITING CONTROL   DOMIN
PARL/PROC CIVMIL/REL TOTALISM...ANTHOL 20 KHRUSH/N   ORD/FREE
STALIN/J CASEBOOK COM/PARTY. PAGE 28 E0563   GOV/REL

B66
DAVIS K.,BUSINESS AND ITS ENVIRONMENT. LAW ECO/DEV   EX/STRUC
INDUS OP/RES ADMIN CONTROL ROUTINE GP/REL PROFIT   PROB/SOLV
POLICY. PAGE 29 E0573   CAP/ISM
                                                     EXEC

B66
EDWARDS C.D.,TRADE REGULATIONS OVERSEAS. IRELAND   INT/TRADE
NEW/ZEALND SOUTH/AFR NAT/G CAP/ISM TARIFFS CONTROL   DIPLOM
...POLICY JURID 20 EEC CHINJAP. PAGE 34 E0676   INT/LAW
                                                     ECO/TAC

B66
FENN DH J.R.,BUSINESS DECISION MAKING AND   DECISION
GOVERNMENT POLICY. SERV/IND LEGIS LICENSE ADMIN   PLAN
CONTROL GP/REL INGP/REL 20 CASEBOOK. PAGE 37 E0736   NAT/G
                                                     LG/CO

B66
FRIED R.C.,COMPARATIVE POLITICAL INSTITUTIONS. USSR NAT/G
EX/STRUC FORCES LEGIS JUDGE CONTROL REPRESENT   PWR
ALL/IDEOS 20 CONGRESS BUREAUCRCY. PAGE 40 E0798   EFFICIENCY
                                                     GOV/COMP

B66
GILLMOR D.M.,FREE PRESS AND FAIR TRIAL. UK USA+45   ORD/FREE
CONSTN PROB/SOLV PRESS CONTROL CRIME DISCRIM   ADJUD
RESPECT...AUD/VIS 20 CIVIL/LIB. PAGE 44 E0865   ATTIT
                                                     EDU/PROP

B66
GRUNEWALD D.,PUBLIC POLICY AND THE MODERN   LG/CO
COOPERATION: SELECTED READINGS. USA+45 LAW MARKET   POLICY
VOL/ASSN CAP/ISM INT/TRADE CENTRAL OWN...SOC ANTHOL NAT/G
20. PAGE 48 E0954   CONTROL

B66
HARVEY W.B.,LAW AND SOCIAL CHANGE IN GHANA. AFR   JURID
GHANA CONSULT CONTROL CT/SYS INGP/REL 20. PAGE 51   CONSTN
E1011   LEAD
                                                     ORD/FREE

B66
HOEVELER H.J.,INTERNATIONALE BEKAMPFUNG DES   CRIMLGY
VERBRECHENS. AUSTRIA SWITZERLND WOR+45 INT/ORG   CRIME
CONTROL BIO/SOC...METH/COMP NAT/COMP 20 MAFIA   DIPLOM
SCOT/YARD FBI. PAGE 53 E1064   INT/LAW

B66
LEHMANN L.,LEGAL UND OPPORTUN - POLITISCHE JUSTIZ   ORD/FREE
IN DER BUNDESREPUBLIK. GERMANY/W EDU/PROP ADJUD   POL/PAR
CONTROL PARL/PROC COERCE TOTALISM ATTIT 20   JURID
COM/PARTY. PAGE 64 E1281   LEGIS

B66
MACMULLEN R.,ENEMIES OF THE ROMAN EMPIRE: TREASON,   CRIME
UNREST, AND ALIENATION IN THE EMPIRE. ROMAN/EMP   ADJUD
MUNIC CONTROL LEAD ATTIT PERSON MYSTISM...PHIL/SCI   MORAL
BIBLIOG. PAGE 67 E1345   SOCIETY

B66
MENDELSON W.,JUSTICES BLACK AND FRANKFURTER: JURID
CONFLICT IN THE COURT (2ND ED.). NAT/G PROVS   ADJUD
PROB/SOLV BAL/PWR CONTROL FEDERAL ISOLAT ANOMIE   IDEA/COMP
ORD/FREE...DECISION 20 SUPREME/CT BLACK/HL   ROLE
FRANKFUR/F. PAGE 72 E1439

B66
OSTERMANN R.,A REPORT IN DEPTH ON CRIME IN AMERICA. CRIME
FUT USA+45 MUNIC PUB/INST TEC/DEV MURDER EFFICIENCY FORCES
ATTIT BIO/SOC...PSY 20. PAGE 79 E1584   CONTROL
                                                     LAW

B66
STUMPF S.E.,MORALITY AND THE LAW. USA+45 LAW   JURID
CULTURE PROB/SOLV DOMIN ADJUD CONTROL ADJUST   MORAL
ALL/IDEOS MARXISM...INT/LAW 20 SUPREME/CT. PAGE 94   CT/SYS
E1890

B66
US HOUSE COMM ON JUDICIARY,CIVIL COMMITMENT AND   BIO/SOC
TREATMENT OF NARCOTIC ADDICTS. USA+45 SOCIETY FINAN CRIME
LEGIS PROB/SOLV GIVE CT/SYS SANCTION HEALTH   IDEA/COMP
...POLICY HEAL 20. PAGE 100 E2008   CONTROL

B66
US HOUSE UNAMER ACTIV COMM,HEARINGS ON BILLS TO   LAW
MAKE PUNISHABLE ASSISTANCE TO ENEMIES OF US IN TIME SANCTION
OF UNDECLARED WAR. USA+45 VIETNAM/N EDU/PROP   VOL/ASSN
CONTROL WAR MARXISM HOUSE/REP. PAGE 100 E2010   GIVE

B66
US PRES COMN CRIME IN DC,REPORT OF THE US   CRIME
PRESIDENT'S COMMISSION ON CRIME IN THE DISTRICT OF   FORCES
COLUMBIA. LEGIS WORKER EDU/PROP ADJUD CONTROL   AGE/Y
CT/SYS GP/REL BIO/SOC HEALTH...CRIMLGY NEW/IDEA   SANCTION
STAT 20. PAGE 101 E2022

B66
WILSON G.,CASES AND MATERIALS ON CONSTITUTIONAL AND JURID
ADMINISTRATIVE LAW. UK LAW NAT/G EX/STRUC LEGIS   ADMIN
BAL/PWR BUDGET DIPLOM ADJUD CONTROL CT/SYS GOV/REL   CONSTN
ORD/FREE 20 PARLIAMENT ENGLSH/LAW. PAGE 106 E2126   PWR

B67
BROWN L.N.,FRENCH ADMINISTRATIVE LAW. FRANCE UK   EX/STRUC
CONSTN NAT/G LEGIS DOMIN CONTROL EXEC PARL/PROC PWR LAW
...JURID METH/COMP GEN/METH. PAGE 16 E0314   IDEA/COMP
                                                     CT/SYS

B67
CAVES R.,AMERICAN INDUSTRY: STRUCTURE, CONDUCT,   ECO/DEV
PERFORMANCE (2ND ED.). USA+45 MARKET NAT/G ADJUD   INDUS
CONTROL GP/REL DEMAND WEALTH 20. PAGE 21 E0412   POLICY
                                                     ECO/TAC

B67
DEBOLD R.C.,LSD, MAN AND SOCIETY. USA+45 LAW   HEALTH
SOCIETY SECT CONTROL SANCTION STRANGE ATTIT...HEAL   DRIVE
CHARTS ANTHOL BIBLIOG. PAGE 30 E0601   PERSON
                                                     BIO/SOC

B67
ESTEY M.,THE UNIONS: STRUCTURE, DEVELOPMENT, AND   LABOR
MANAGEMENT. FUT USA+45 ADJUD CONTROL INGP/REL DRIVE EX/STRUC
...DECISION T 20 AFL/CIO. PAGE 35 E0699   ADMIN
                                                     GOV/REL

B67
GELLHORN W.,OMBUDSMEN AND OTHERS: CITIZENS'   NAT/COMP
PROTECTORS IN NINE COUNTRIES. WOR+45 LAW CONSTN   REPRESENT
LEGIS INSPECT ADJUD ADMIN CONTROL CT/SYS CHOOSE   INGP/REL
PERS/REL...STAT CHARTS 20. PAGE 43 E0847   PROB/SOLV

B67
LAFAVE W.R.,INTERNATIONAL TRADE, INVESTMENT, AND   INT/TRADE
ORGANIZATION. INDUS PROB/SOLV TARIFFS CONTROL   INT/LAW
...TREND ANTHOL BIBLIOG 20 EEC. PAGE 62 E1245   INT/ORG

B67
PLANO J.C.,FORGING WORLD ORDER: THE POLITICS OF   INT/ORG
INTERNATIONAL ORGANIZATION. PROB/SOLV DIPLOM   ADMIN
CONTROL CENTRAL RATIONAL ORD/FREE...INT/LAW CHARTS   JURID
BIBLIOG 20 UN LEAGUE/NAT. PAGE 81 E1618

B67
UNIVERSAL REFERENCE SYSTEM,PUBLIC POLICY AND THE   BIBLIOG/A
MANAGEMENT OF SCIENCE (VOLUME IX). FUT SPACE WOR+45 POLICY
LAW NAT/G TEC/DEV CONTROL NUC/PWR GOV/REL   MGT
...COMPUT/IR GEN/METH. PAGE 99 E1975   PHIL/SCI

B67
US SENATE COMM ON FOREIGN REL,FOREIGN ASSISTANCE   FOR/AID
ACT OF 1967. VIETNAM WOR+45 DELIB/GP CONFER CONTROL LAW
WAR WEAPON BAL/PAY...CENSUS CHARTS SENATE. PAGE 102 DIPLOM
E2036   POLICY

B67
VILE M.J.C.,CONSTITUTIONALISM AND THE SEPARATION OF CONSTN
POWERS. FRANCE UK USA+45 USA-45 NAT/G ADJUD CONTROL BAL/PWR
GOV/REL...POLICY DECISION JURID GEN/LAWS 15/20   CONCPT
MONTESQ. PAGE 104 E2076   LAW

L67
BERNHARD R.C.,"COMPETITION IN LAW AND ECONOMICS."   MARKET
LAW PLAN PRICE CONTROL PRODUC PROFIT...METH/CNCPT   POLICY
IDEA/COMP GEN/LAWS 20. PAGE 11 E0210   NAT/G
                                                     CT/SYS

L67
CARMICHAEL D.M.,"FORTY YEARS OF WATER POLLUTION   HEALTH
CONTROL IN WISCONSIN: A CASE STUDY." LAW EXTR/IND   CONTROL
INDUS MUNIC DELIB/GP PLAN PROB/SOLV SANCTION   ADMIN
...CENSUS CHARTS 20 WISCONSIN. PAGE 20 E0384   ADJUD

L67
LEGAULT A.,"ORGANISATION ET CONDUITE DES OPERATIONS INT/ORG
DE MAINTIEN DE LA PAIX." FORCES ACT/RES ADJUD AGREE PEACE
CONTROL NEUTRAL TASK PRIVIL ORD/FREE 20 UN. PAGE 64 WAR
E1279   INT/LAW

S67
"THE STATE OF ZONING ADMINISTRATION IN ILLINOIS: ADMIN
PROCEDURAL REQUIREMENTS OF JUDICIAL INTERVENTION." CONTROL
USA+45 LAW CONSTN DELIB/GP ADJUD CT/SYS ORD/FREE HABITAT
ILLINOIS. PAGE 2 E0038 PLAN

S67
"THE FEDERAL AGRICULTURAL STABILIZATION PROGRAM AND AGRI
THE NEGRO." LAW CONSTN PLAN REPRESENT DISCRIM CONTROL
ORD/FREE 20 NEGRO CONGRESS. PAGE 2 E0039 NAT/G
RACE/REL

S67
ALDRICH W.A.,"THE SUEZ CRISIS." UAR UK USA+45 DIPLOM
DELIB/GP FORCES BAL/PWR INT/TRADE CONFER CONTROL INT/LAW
COERCE DETER 20. PAGE 3 E0058 COLONIAL

S67
ALEXANDER B.,"GIBRALTAR" SPAIN UK CONSTN WORKER DIPLOM
PROB/SOLV FOR/AID RECEIVE CONTROL 20. PAGE 3 E0059 INT/ORG
ORD/FREE
ECO/TAC

S67
BARTLETT J.L.,"AMERICAN BOND ISSUES IN THE EUROPEAN LAW
ECONOMIC COMMUNITY." EUR+WWI LUXEMBOURG USA+45 ECO/TAC
DIPLOM CONTROL BAL/PAY EEC. PAGE 8 E0153 FINAN
TAX

S67
BLAKEY G.R.,"ORGANIZED CRIME IN THE UNITED STATES." CRIME
USA+45 USA-45 STRUCT LABOR NAT/G VOL/ASSN ADMIN ELITES
PERS/REL PWR...CRIMLGY INT 17/20. PAGE 12 E0240 CONTROL

S67
CHAMBLISS W.J.,"TYPES OF DEVIANCE AND THE CRIME
EFFECTIVENESS OF LEGAL SANCTIONS" SOCIETY PROB/SOLV SANCTION
ADJUD CONTROL DETER. PAGE 21 E0417 EFFICIENCY
LAW

S67
CREYKE G. JR.,"THE PAYMENT GAP IN FEDERAL CONSTRUC
CONSTRUCTION CONTRACTS." USA+45 LAW FINAN ECO/TAC PAY
CONTROL CT/SYS SUPREME/CT. PAGE 28 E0547 COST
NAT/G

S67
GANZ G.,"THE CONTROL OF INDUSTRY BY ADMINISTRATIVE INDUS
PROCESS." UK DELIB/GP WORKER 20. PAGE 42 E0832 LAW
ADMIN
CONTROL

S67
GRIFFIN H.C.,"PREJUDICIAL PUBLICITY: SEARCH FOR A LAW
CIVIL REMEDY." EDU/PROP CONTROL DISCRIM...JURID 20. SANCTION
PAGE 47 E0937 PRESS
ADJUD

S67
LARSEN P.B.,"THE UNITED STATES-ITALY AIR TRANSPORT INT/LAW
ARBITRATION: PROBLEMS OF TREATY INTERPRETATION AND ADJUD
ENFORCEMENT." ITALY USA+45 AIR PROB/SOLV DIPLOM INT/TRADE
DEBATE CONTROL CT/SYS...DECISION TREATY. PAGE 63 DIST/IND
E1257

S67
MATTHEWS R.O.,"THE SUEZ CANAL DISPUTE* A CASE STUDY PEACE
IN PEACEFUL SETTLEMENT." FRANCE ISRAEL UAR UK NAT/G DIPLOM
CONTROL LEAD COERCE WAR NAT/LISM ROLE ORD/FREE PWR ADJUD
...INT/LAW UN 20. PAGE 69 E1389

S67
MITCHELL J.D.B.,"THE CONSTITUTIONAL IMPLICATIONS OF CONSTN
JUDICIAL CONTROL OF THE ADMINISTRATION IN THE CT/SYS
UNITED KINGDOM." UK LAW ADJUD ADMIN GOV/REL ROLE CONTROL
...GP/COMP 20. PAGE 74 E1474 EX/STRUC

S67
MONEYPENNY P.,"UNIVERSITY PURPOSE, DISCIPLINE, AND ACADEM
DUE PROCESS." USA+45 EDU/PROP ADJUD LEISURE AGE/Y
ORD/FREE. PAGE 74 E1484 CONTROL
ADMIN

S67
MORENO F.J.,"THE SPANISH COLONIAL SYSTEM: A COLONIAL
FUNCTIONAL APPROACH." SPAIN WOR-45 LAW CHIEF DIPLOM CONTROL
ADJUD CIVMIL/REL AUTHORIT ROLE PWR...CONCPT 17/20. NAT/G
PAGE 74 E1492 OP/RES

S67
PEMBERTON J., JR.,"CONSTITUTIONAL PROBLEMS IN LAW
RESTRAINT ON THE MEDIA." CONSTN PROB/SOLV EDU/PROP PRESS
CONFER CONTROL JURID. PAGE 80 E1608 ORD/FREE

S67
RAI H.,"DISTRICT MAGISTRATE AND POLICE STRUCT
SUPERINTENDENT IN INDIA: THE CONTROVERSY OF DUAL CONTROL
CONTROL" INDIA LAW PROVS ADMIN PWR 19/20. PAGE 83 ROLE
E1669 FORCES

S67
REILLY T.J.,"FREEZING AND CONFISCATION OF CUBAN STRANGE
PROPERTY." CUBA USA+45 LAW DIPLOM LEGIT ADJUD OWN
CONTROL. PAGE 84 E1682 ECO/TAC

S67
SCHELLING T.C.,"ECONOMICS AND CRIMINAL ENTERPRISE." CRIME
LAW FORCES BARGAIN ECO/TAC CONTROL GAMBLE ROUTINE PROB/SOLV
ADJUST DEMAND INCOME PROFIT CRIMLGY. PAGE 87 E1756 CONCPT

S67
SHAFFER T.L.,"DIRECT RESTRAINT ON THE PRESS." LAW
USA+45 EDU/PROP CONTROL...JURID NEW/IDEA ABA. PRESS
PAGE 90 E1809 ORD/FREE
ADJUD

S67
TOMASEK R.D.,"THE CHILEAN-BOLIVIAN LAUCA RIVER INT/ORG
DISPUTE AND THE OAS." CHILE L/A+17C PROB/SOLV ADJUD DIPLOM
CONTROL PEACE 20 BOLIV OAS. PAGE 96 E1930 GEOG
WAR

S67
WILLIG S.H.,"THE CONTROL OVER INTERSTATE DIST/IND
DISTRIBUTION AND USE OF INVESTIGATIONAL DRUGS (IN HEALTH
THE UNITED STATES)" USA+45 NAT/G INT/TRADE LICENSE. CONTROL
PAGE 106 E2124 DELIB/GP

B68
GREGG R.W.,INTERNATIONAL ORGANIZATION IN THE INT/ORG
WESTERN HEMISPHERE. L/A+17C USA+45 CULTURE PLAN DIPLOM
DOMIN AGREE CONTROL DETER PWR...GEOG 20 OAS TREATY. ECO/UNDEV
PAGE 46 E0913

S68
SHAPIRO J.P.,"SOVIET HISTORIOGRAPHY AND THE MOSCOW HIST/WRIT
TRIALS: AFTER THIRTY YEARS." USSR NAT/G LEGIT PRESS EDU/PROP
CONTROL LEAD ATTIT MARXISM...NEW/IDEA METH 20 SANCTION
TROTSKY/L STALIN/J KHRUSH/N. PAGE 90 E1810 ADJUD

B88
BENTHAM J.,DEFENCE OF USURY (1787). UK LAW NAT/G TAX
TEC/DEV ECO/TAC CONTROL ATTIT...CONCPT IDEA/COMP 18 FINAN
SMITH/ADAM. PAGE 10 E0197 ECO/DEV
POLICY

B91
SIDGWICK H.,THE ELEMENTS OF POLITICS. LOC/G NAT/G POLICY
LEGIS DIPLOM ADJUD CONTROL EXEC PARL/PROC REPRESENT LAW
GOV/REL SOVEREIGN ALL/IDEOS 19 MILL/JS BENTHAM/J. CONCPT
PAGE 91 E1822

B98
POLLOCK F.,THE HISTORY OF ENGLISH LAW BEFORE THE LAW
TIME OF EDWARD I (2 VOLS. 2ND ED.). UK CULTURE ADJUD
LOC/G LEGIS LICENSE AGREE CONTROL CT/SYS SANCTION JURID
CRIME...TIME/SEQ 13 COMMON/LAW CANON/LAW. PAGE 81
E1626

CONTROLLED DIRECT OBSERVATION....SEE CONT/OBS

CONV/LEASE....CONVICT LEASE SYSTEM IN SOUTH

B58
CABLE G.W.,THE NEGRO QUESTION: A SELECTION OF RACE/REL
WRITINGS ON CIVIL RIGHTS IN THE SOUTH. USA+45 CULTURE
STRATA LOC/G POL/PAR GIVE EDU/PROP WRITING CT/SYS DISCRIM
SANCTION CRIME CHOOSE WORSHIP 20 NEGRO CIV/RIGHTS ORD/FREE
CONV/LEASE SOUTH/US. PAGE 18 E0355

CONVNTL....CONVENTIONAL

CONWELL-EVANS T.P. E0498

COOKE C.A. E0499

COOLIDGE/C....CALVIN COOLIDGE

COOPER F.E. E0500,E0501

COOPER L. E0502

COOPERATION....SEE AGREE

COOPERATIVE....SEE VOL/ASSN

COPLIN W.D. E0503

COPYRIGHT....COPYRIGHT

CORBETT P.E. E0504,E0505,E0506,E0507

CORE....CONGRESS OF RACIAL EQUALITY

CORET A. E0508

CORLEY R.N. E0509

CORN/LAWS....CORN LAWS (U.K.)

CORNELL UNIVERSITY LIBRARY E0510

CORNELL/U....CORNELL UNIVERSITY

CORONATIONS....SEE INAUGURATE

CORPORATION....SEE CORPORATN

CORPORATN....CORPORATION

CORRECTIONAL INSTITUTION....SEE PUB/INST

CORREL....STATISTICAL CORRELATIONS

B62
SILVA R.C.,RUM, RELIGION, AND VOTES: 1928 RE-   POL/PAR
EXAMINED. USA-45 LAW SECT DISCRIM CATHISM...CORREL   CHOOSE
STAT 20 PRESIDENT SMITH/ALF DEMOCRAT. PAGE 91 E1827   GP/COMP
                                                          ATTIT

CORRY J.A. E0511

CORWIN E.S. E0512,E0513,E0514,E0515

CORY R.H. E0516

COSSIO C. E0517

COST....ECONOMIC VALUE; SEE ALSO PROFIT

B19
SMITH R.H.,JUSTICE AND THE POOR. LAW RECEIVE ADJUD   CT/SYS
CRIME GOV/REL COST...JURID SOC/WK CONCPT STAT   DISCRIM
CHARTS GP/COMP 20. PAGE 92 E1847   WEALTH

B26
FORTESCUE J.,THE GOVERNANCE OF ENGLAND (1471-76).   CONSERVE
UK LAW FINAN SECT LEGIS PROB/SOLV TAX DOMIN ADMIN   CONSTN
GP/REL COST ORD/FREE PWR 14/15. PAGE 39 E0776   CHIEF
                                                          NAT/G

C29
BUCK A.E.,"PUBLIC BUDGETING." USA-45 FINAN LOC/G   BUDGET
NAT/G LEGIS BAL/PAY COST...JURID TREND BIBLIOG/A   ROUTINE
20. PAGE 17 E0324   ADMIN

B37
HAMILTON W.H.,THE POWER TO GOVERN. ECO/DEV FINAN   LING
INDUS ECO/TAC INT/TRADE TARIFFS TAX CONTROL CT/SYS   CONSTN
WAR COST PWR 18/20 SUPREME/CT. PAGE 50 E0991   NAT/G
                                                          POLICY

B42
FULLER G.H.,DEFENSE FINANCING: A SUPPLEMENTARY LIST   BIBLIOG/A
OF REFERENCES (PAMPHLET). CANADA UK USA-45 ECO/DEV   FINAN
NAT/G DELIB/GP BUDGET ADJUD ARMS/CONT WEAPON COST   FORCES
PEACE PWR 20 AUSTRAL CHINJAP CONGRESS. PAGE 41   DIPLOM
E0821

N58
US HOUSE COMM FOREIGN AFFAIRS,HEARINGS ON DRAFT   LEGIS
LEGISLATION TO AMEND FURTHER THE MUTUAL SECURITY   DELIB/GP
ACT OF 1954 (PAMPHLET). USA+45 CONSULT FORCES   CONFER
BUDGET DIPLOM DETER COST ORD/FREE...JURID 20   WEAPON
DEPT/DEFEN UN DEPT/STATE. PAGE 100 E2002

B60
ATOMIC INDUSTRIAL FORUM,ATOMS FOR INDUSTRY: WORLD   NUC/PWR
FORUM. WOR+45 FINAN COST UTIL...JURID ANTHOL 20.   INDUS
PAGE 6 E0113   PLAN
                                                          PROB/SOLV

B60
WEBSTER J.A.,A GENERAL STUDY OF THE DEPARTMENT OF   ORD/FREE
DEFENSE INTERNAL SECURITY PROGRAM. USA+45 WORKER   PLAN
TEC/DEV ADJUD CONTROL CT/SYS EXEC GOV/REL COST   ADMIN
...POLICY DECISION MGT 20 DEPT/DEFEN SUPREME/CT.   NAT/G
PAGE 105 E2105

B61
MURPHY E.F.,WATER PURITY: A STUDY IN LEGAL CONTROL   SEA
OF NATURAL RESOURCES. LOC/G ACT/RES PLAN TEC/DEV   LAW

LOBBY GP/REL COST ATTIT HEALTH ORD/FREE...HEAL   PROVS
JURID 20 WISCONSIN WATER. PAGE 75 E1506   CONTROL

B64
JACKSON R.M.,THE MACHINERY OF JUSTICE IN ENGLAND.   CT/SYS
UK EDU/PROP CONTROL COST ORD/FREE...MGT 20   ADJUD
ENGLSH/LAW. PAGE 57 E1142   JUDGE
                                                          JURID

B64
TAUBENFELD H.J.,SPACE AND SOCIETY. USA+45 LAW   SPACE
FORCES CREATE TEC/DEV ADJUD CONTROL COST PEACE   SOCIETY
...PREDICT ANTHOL 20. PAGE 95 E1911   ADJUST
                                                          DIPLOM

B64
US SENATE COMM ON JUDICIARY,HEARINGS BEFORE   ECO/DEV
SUBCOMMITTEE ON ANTITRUST AND MONOPOLY: ECONOMIC   CONTROL
CONCENTRATION VOLUMES 1-5 JULY 1964-SEPT 1966.   MARKET
USA+45 LAW FINAN ECO/TAC ADJUD COST EFFICIENCY   LG/CO
PRODUC...STAT CHARTS 20 CONGRESS MONOPOLY. PAGE 102
E2052

B65
FLEMING R.W.,THE LABOR ARBITRATION PROCESS. USA+45   GP/REL
LAW BARGAIN ADJUD ROUTINE SANCTION COST...PREDICT   LABOR
CHARTS TIME 20. PAGE 38 E0763   CONSULT
                                                          DELIB/GP

B65
HABERLER G.,A SURVEY OF INTERNATIONAL TRADE THEORY.   INT/TRADE
CANADA FRANCE GERMANY ECO/TAC TARIFFS AGREE COST   BAL/PAY
DEMAND WEALTH...ECOMETRIC 19/20 MONOPOLY TREATY.   DIPLOM
PAGE 49 E0968   POLICY

B65
WHITE G.M.,THE USE OF EXPERTS BY INTERNATIONAL   INT/LAW
TRIBUNALS. WOR+45 WOR-45 INT/ORG NAT/G PAY ADJUD   ROUTINE
COST...OBS BIBLIOG 20. PAGE 106 E2117   CONSULT
                                                          CT/SYS

S65
HIBBS A.R.,"SPACE TECHNOLOGY* THE THREAT AND THE   SPACE
PROMISE." FUT VOL/ASSN TEC/DEV NUC/PWR COST   ARMS/CONT
EFFICIENCY UTIL UN TREATY. PAGE 52 E1038   PREDICT

S65
WRIGHT Q.,"THE ESCALATION OF INTERNATIONAL   WAR
CONFLICTS." WOR+45 WOR-45 FORCES DIPLOM RISK COST   PERCEPT
ATTIT ALL/VALS...INT/LAW QUANT STAT NAT/COMP.   PREDICT
PAGE 108 E2160   MATH

B66
BRENNAN J.T.,THE COST OF THE AMERICAN JUDICIAL   COST
SYSTEM. USA+45 PROF/ORG TV ADMIN EFFICIENCY.   CT/SYS
PAGE 15 E0292   ADJUD
                                                          JURID

B66
INTL ATOMIC ENERGY AGENCY,INTERNATIONAL CONVENTIONS DIPLOM
ON CIVIL LIABILITY FOR NUCLEAR DAMAGE. FUT WOR+45   INT/ORG
ADJUD WAR COST PEACE SOVEREIGN...JURID 20. PAGE 57   DELIB/GP
E1135   NUC/PWR

L66
GREIG D.W.,"THE ADVISORY JURISDICTION OF THE   INT/LAW
INTERNATIONAL COURT AND THE SETTLEMENT OF DISPUTES   CT/SYS
BETWEEN STATES." ISRAEL KOREA FORCES BUDGET DOMIN
LEGIT ADJUD COST...RECORD UN CONGO/LEOP TREATY.
PAGE 46 E0915

L66
HIGGINS R.,"THE INTERNATIONAL COURT AND SOUTH WEST   SOUTH/AFR
AFRICA* SOME IMPLICATIONS OF THE JUDGMENT." AFR LAW   COLONIAL
ECO/UNDEV JUDGE RACE/REL COST PWR...INT/LAW TREND   CT/SYS
UN TREATY. PAGE 52 E1043   ADJUD

S66
FINE R.I.,"PEACE-KEEPING COSTS AND ARTICLE 19 OF   FORCES
THE UN CHARTER* AN INVITATION TO RESPONSIBILITY."   COST
INT/ORG NAT/G ADJUD CT/SYS CHOOSE CONSEN...RECORD   CONSTN
IDEA/COMP UN. PAGE 38 E0750

B67
JONES C.O.,EVERY SECOND YEAR: CONGRESSIONAL   EFFICIENCY
BEHAVIOR AND THE TWO-YEAR TERM. LAW POL/PAR   LEGIS
PROB/SOLV DEBATE CHOOSE PERS/REL COST FEDERAL PWR   TIME/SEQ
...CHARTS 20 CONGRESS SENATE HOUSE/REP. PAGE 59   NAT/G
E1172

L67
LAMBERT J.D.,"CORPORATE POLITICAL SPENDING AND   USA+45
CAMPAIGN FINANCE." LAW CONSTN FINAN LABOR LG/CO   POL/PAR
LOC/G NAT/G VOL/ASSN TEC/DEV ADJUD ADMIN PARTIC.   CHOOSE
PAGE 62 E1247   COST

ANDERSON W.,"THE PERILS OF 'SHARING'." USA+45
ECO/TAC RECEIVE LOBBY GOV/REL CENTRAL COST INCOME
...POLICY PLURIST CONGRESS. PAGE 5 E0095
S67
BUDGET
TAX
FEDERAL
LAW

CHAMBERLAIN N.W.,"STRIKES IN CONTEMPORARY CONTEXT."
LAW INDUS NAT/G CHIEF CONFER COST ATTIT ORD/FREE
...POLICY MGT 20. PAGE 21 E0415
S67
LABOR
BARGAIN
EFFICIENCY
PROB/SOLV

CREYKE G. JR.,"THE PAYMENT GAP IN FEDERAL
CONSTRUCTION CONTRACTS." USA+45 LAW FINAN ECO/TAC
CONTROL CT/SYS SUPREME/CT. PAGE 28 E0547
S67
CONSTRUC
PAY
COST
NAT/G

COSTA RICA UNIVERSIDAD BIBL E0518

COSTA/RICA....SEE ALSO L/A+17C

COSTA RICA UNIVERSIDAD BIBL,LISTA DE TESIS DE GRADO
DE LA UNIVERSIDAD DE COSTA RICA. COSTA/RICA LAW
LOC/G ADMIN LEAD...SOC 20. PAGE 26 E0518
B62
BIBLIOG/A
NAT/G
DIPLOM
ECO/UNDEV

COUGHLIN/C....CHARLES EDWARD COUGHLIN

COUNCIL BRITISH NATIONAL BIB E0519

COUNCIL OF EUROPE E0520

COUNCIL OF STATE GOVERNMENTS E0521,E0522,E0523,E0524

COUNCIL OF STATE GOVERNMENTS E0525

COUNCIL OF STATE GOVERNMENTS E0526

COUNCL/EUR....COUNCIL OF EUROPE

ECONOMIDES C.P.,LE POUVOIR DE DECISION DES
ORGANISATIONS INTERNATIONALES EUROPEENNES. DIPLOM
DOMIN INGP/REL EFFICIENCY...INT/LAW JURID 20 NATO
OEEC EEC COUNCL/EUR EURATOM. PAGE 34 E0673
B64
INT/ORG
PWR
DECISION
GP/COMP

COUNCL/MGR....COUNCIL-MANAGER SYSTEM OF LOCAL GOVERNMENT

COUNTIES....SEE LOC/G

COUNTY AGRICULTURAL AGENT....SEE COUNTY/AGT

COUNTY/AGT....COUNTY AGRICULTURAL AGENT

COURAGE....SEE DRIVE

COURT OF APPEALS....SEE CT/APPEALS

COURT SYSTEMS....SEE CT/SYS

COURT/DIST....DISTRICT COURTS

NATIONAL MUNICIPAL LEAGUE,COURT DECISIONS ON
LEGISLATIVE APPORTIONMENT (VOL. III). USA+45 JUDGE
ADJUD CONTROL ATTIT...DECISION JURID COURT/DIST
CASEBOOK. PAGE 76 E1528
B62
PROVS
CT/SYS
APPORT
LEGIS

COURT/SYS....COURT SYSTEM ; SEE ALSO CT/SYS

BENTHAM J.,THE RATIONALE OF PUNISHMENT. UK LAW
LOC/G NAT/G LEGIS CONTROL...JURID GEN/LAWS
COURT/SYS 19. PAGE 10 E0192
B30
CRIME
SANCTION
COERCE
ORD/FREE

COURTS OF WESTMINSTER HALL....SEE CTS/WESTM

COUTROT A. E0527

COWAN T.A. E0528

COWEN D.V. E0529

COWEN Z. E0530

COWLING M. E0531

COWPER/W....WILLIAM COWPER

COX A. E0532,E0533

COX G.C. E0534

COX H. E0535

CRAIG A. E0536,E0537,E0538

CRAIG J. E0539,E0540

CRANDALL S.B. E0541

CRANE R.D. E0542,E0543,E0544

CRANSTON M. E0545

CREA J. E1894

CREATE....CREATIVE PROCESSES

PERSONNEL. USA+45 LAW LABOR LG/CO WORKER CREATE
GOV/REL PERS/REL ATTIT WEALTH. PAGE 2 E0029
N
BIBLIOG/A
ADMIN
MGT
GP/REL

POLLOCK F.,THE GENIUS OF THE COMMON LAW. CHRIST-17C
UK FINAN CHIEF ACT/RES ADMIN GP/REL ATTIT SOCISM
...ANARCH JURID. PAGE 81 E1624
B12
LAW
CULTURE
CREATE

ROOT E.,"THE EFFECT OF DEMOCRACY ON INTERNATIONAL
LAW." USA-45 WOR-45 INTELL SOCIETY INT/ORG NAT/G
CONSULT ACT/RES CREATE PLAN EDU/PROP PEACE SKILL
...CONCPT METH/CNCPT OBS 20. PAGE 85 E1712
S17
LEGIS
JURID
INT/LAW

BRYCE J.,INTERNATIONAL RELATIONS. CHRIST-17C
EUR+WWI MOD/EUR CULTURE INTELL NAT/G DELIB/GP
CREATE BAL/PWR DIPLOM ATTIT DRIVE RIGID/FLEX
ALL/VALS...PLURIST JURID CONCPT TIME/SEQ GEN/LAWS
TOT/POP. PAGE 16 E0323
B22
INT/ORG
POLICY

HOLMES O.W. JR.,THE COMMON LAW. FUT WOR-45 CULTURE
SOCIETY CREATE LEGIT ROUTINE ATTIT ALL/VALS...JURID
METH/CNCPT TIME/SEQ GEN/LAWS TOT/POP VAL/FREE.
PAGE 55 E1087
B23
ADJUD
CON/ANAL

HOCKING W.E.,PRESENT STATUS OF THE PHILOSOPHY OF
LAW AND OF RIGHTS. UNIV CULTURE INTELL SOCIETY
NAT/G CREATE LEGIT SANCTION ALL/VALS SOC/INTEG
18/20. PAGE 53 E1060
B26
JURID
PHIL/SCI
ORD/FREE

HUDSON M.,"THE TEACHING OF INTERNATIONAL LAW IN
AMERICA." USA-45 LAW CONSULT ACT/RES CREATE
EDU/PROP ATTIT RIGID/FLEX...JURID CONCPT RECORD
HIST/WRIT TREND GEN/LAWS 18/20. PAGE 56 E1109
L28
PERCEPT
KNOWL
INT/LAW

STURZO L.,THE INTERNATIONAL COMMUNITY AND THE RIGHT
OF WAR (TRANS. BY BARBARA BARCLAY CARTER). CULTURE
CREATE PROB/SOLV DIPLOM ADJUD CONTROL PEACE PERSON
ORD/FREE...INT/LAW IDEA/COMP PACIFIST 20
LEAGUE/NAT. PAGE 94 E1891
B29
INT/ORG
PLAN
WAR
CONCPT

JORDAN E.,THEORY OF LEGISLATION: AN ESSAY ON THE
DYNAMICS OF PUBLIC MIND. NAT/G CREATE REPRESENT
MAJORITY ATTIT GEN/LAWS. PAGE 59 E1173
B30
LEGIS
CONCPT
JURID
CT/SYS

LAUTERPACHT H.,THE FUNCTION OF LAW IN THE
INTERNATIONAL COMMUNITY. WOR-45 NAT/G FORCES CREATE
DOMIN LEGIT COERCE WAR PEACE ATTIT ORD/FREE PWR
SOVEREIGN...JURID CONCPT METH/CNCPT TIME/SEQ
GEN/LAWS GEN/METH LEAGUE/NAT TOT/POP VAL/FREE 20.
PAGE 63 E1265
B33
INT/ORG
LAW
INT/LAW

RAM J.,THE SCIENCE OF LEGAL JUDGMENT: A TREATISE...
UK CONSTN NAT/G LEGIS CREATE PROB/SOLV AGREE CT/SYS
...INT/LAW CONCPT 19 ENGLSH/LAW CANON/LAW CIVIL/LAW
CTS/WESTM. PAGE 83 E1672
B35
LAW
JURID
EX/STRUC
ADJUD

BEARDSLEY A.R.,LEGAL BIBLIOGRAPHY AND THE USE OF
LAW BOOKS. CONSTN CREATE PROB/SOLV...DECISION JURID
LAB/EXP. PAGE 9 E0166
B37
BIBLIOG
LAW
METH
OP/RES

FRANKFURTER F.,MR. JUSTICE HOLMES AND THE SUPREME
COURT. USA-45 CONSTN SOCIETY FEDERAL OWN ATTIT
B38
CREATE
CT/SYS

ORD/FREE PWR...POLICY JURID 20 SUPREME/CT HOLMES/OW DECISION
BILL/RIGHT. PAGE 40 E0790   LAW

B38
MCNAIR A.D.,THE LAW OF TREATIES: BRITISH PRACTICE   AGREE
AND OPINIONS. UK CREATE DIPLOM LEGIT WRITING ADJUD   LAW
WAR...INT/LAW JURID TREATY. PAGE 71 E1424   CT/SYS
NAT/G

B38
POUND R.,THE FORMATIVE ERA OF AMERICAN LAW. CULTURE   CONSTN
NAT/G PROVS LEGIS ADJUD CT/SYS PERSON SOVEREIGN   LAW
...POLICY IDEA/COMP GEN/LAWS 18/19. PAGE 82 E1637   CREATE
JURID

S41
WRIGHT Q.,"FUNDAMENTAL PROBLEMS OF INTERNATIONAL   INT/ORG
ORGANIZATION." UNIV WOR-45 STRUCT FORCES ACT/RES   ATTIT
CREATE DOMIN EDU/PROP LEGIT REGION NAT/LISM   PEACE
ORD/FREE PWR RESPECT SOVEREIGN...JURID SOC CONCPT
METH/CNCPT TIME/SEQ 20. PAGE 107 E2152

B42
GURVITCH G.,SOCIOLOGY OF LAW. CONSTN SOCIETY CREATE   SOC
MORAL SOVEREIGN...POLICY EPIST JURID PHIL/SCI   LAW
IDEA/COMP METH/COMP HOLMES/OW HOBBES/T. PAGE 48   ADJUD
E0964

C43
BENTHAM J.,"THE RATIONALE OF REWARD" IN J. BOWRING,   SANCTION
ED., THE WORKS OF JEREMY BENTHAM (VOL. 2)" LAW   ECO/TAC
WORKER CREATE INSPECT PAY ROUTINE HAPPINESS PRODUC   INCOME
SUPEGO WEALTH METH/CNCPT. PAGE 10 E0195   PWR

B44
ADLER M.J.,HOW TO THINK ABOUT WAR AND PEACE. WOR-45   INT/ORG
LAW SOCIETY EX/STRUC DIPLOM KNOWL ORD/FREE...POLICY   CREATE
TREND GEN/LAWS 20. PAGE 3 E0049   ARMS/CONT
PEACE

B44
DE HUSZAR G.B.,NEW PERSPECTIVES ON PEACE. UNIV   ATTIT
CULTURE SOCIETY ECO/DEV ECO/UNDEV NAT/G FORCES   MYTH
CREATE ECO/TAC DOMIN ADJUD COERCE DRIVE ORD/FREE   PEACE
...GEOG JURID PSY SOC CONCPT TOT/POP. PAGE 29 E0584   WAR

B45
BEVERIDGE W.,THE PRICE OF PEACE. GERMANY UK WOR+45   INT/ORG
WOR-45 NAT/G FORCES CREATE LEGIT REGION WAR ATTIT   TREND
KNOWL ORD/FREE PWR...POLICY NEW/IDEA GEN/LAWS   PEACE
LEAGUE/NAT 20 TREATY. PAGE 12 E0223

B45
US LIBRARY OF CONGRESS,CONSTITUTIONAL AND STATUTORY   CONSTN
PROVISIONS OF THE STATES (VOL. I). USA-45 CREATE   FEDERAL
TAX CT/SYS CHOOSE SUFF INCOME PWR 20. PAGE 101   PROVS
E2016   JURID

B46
AMERICAN DOCUMENTATION INST,CATALOGUE OF AUXILIARY   BIBLIOG
PUBLICATIONS IN MICROFILMS AND PHOTOPRINTS. USA-45   EDU/PROP
LAW AGRI CREATE TEC/DEV ADMIN...GEOG LING MATH 20.   PSY
PAGE 4 E0077

B46
PATON G.W.,A TEXT-BOOK OF JURISPRUDENCE. CREATE   LAW
INSPECT LEGIT CT/SYS ROUTINE CRIME INGP/REL PRIVIL   ADJUD
...CONCPT BIBLIOG 20. PAGE 80 E1601   JURID
T

B49
WORMUTH F.D.,THE ORIGINS OF MODERN   NAT/G
CONSTITUTIONALISM. GREECE UK LEGIS CREATE TEC/DEV   CONSTN
BAL/PWR DOMIN ADJUD REV WAR PWR...JURID ROMAN/REP   LAW
CROMWELL/O. PAGE 107 E2146

L49
COMM. STUDY ORGAN. PEACE,"A TEN YEAR RECORD,   INT/ORG
1939-1949." FUT WOR+45 LAW R+D CONSULT DELIB/GP   CONSTN
CREATE LEGIT ROUTINE ORD/FREE...TIME/SEQ UN 20.   PEACE
PAGE 24 E0480

B50
COUNCIL BRITISH NATIONAL BIB,BRITISH NATIONAL   BIBLIOG/A
BIBLIOGRAPHY. UK AGRI CONSTRUC PERF/ART POL/PAR   NAT/G
SECT CREATE INT/TRADE LEAD...HUM JURID PHIL/SCI 20.   TEC/DEV
PAGE 26 E0519   DIPLOM

B51
HUXLEY J.,FREEDOM AND CULTURE. UNIV LAW SOCIETY R+D   CULTURE
ACADEM SCHOOL CREATE SANCTION ATTIT KNOWL...HUM   ORD/FREE
ANTHOL 20. PAGE 56 E1118   PHIL/SCI
IDEA/COMP

B51
WHEARE K.C.,MODERN CONSTITUTIONS (HOME UNIVERSITY   CONSTN

LIBRARY). UNIV LAW NAT/G LEGIS...CONCPT TREND   CLASSIF
BIBLIOG. PAGE 106 E2115   PWR
CREATE

L51
MANGONE G.,"THE IDEA AND PRACTICE OF WORLD   INT/ORG
GOVERNMENT." FUT WOR+45 WOR-45 ECO/DEV LEGIS CREATE   SOCIETY
LEGIT ROUTINE ATTIT MORAL PWR WEALTH...CONCPT   INT/LAW
GEN/LAWS 20. PAGE 68 E1358

B52
BENTHAM A.,HANDBOOK OF POLITICAL FALLACIES. FUT   POL/PAR
MOD/EUR LAW INTELL LOC/G MUNIC NAT/G DELIB/GP LEGIS
CREATE EDU/PROP CT/SYS ATTIT RIGID/FLEX KNOWL PWR
...RELATIV PSY SOC CONCPT SELF/OBS TREND STERTYP
TOT/POP. PAGE 10 E0189

B52
FERRELL R.H.,PEACE IN THEIR TIME. FRANCE UK USA-45   PEACE
INT/ORG NAT/G FORCES CREATE AGREE ARMS/CONT COERCE   DIPLOM
WAR TREATY 20 WILSON/W LEAGUE/NAT BRIAND/A. PAGE 37
E0741

L52
WRIGHT Q.,"CONGRESS AND THE TREATY-MAKING POWER."   ROUTINE
USA+45 WOR+45 CONSTN INTELL NAT/G CHIEF CONSULT   DIPLOM
EX/STRUC LEGIS TOP/EX CREATE GOV/REL DISPL DRIVE   INT/LAW
RIGID/FLEX...TREND TOT/POP CONGRESS CONGRESS 20   DELIB/GP
TREATY. PAGE 108 E2154

B53
AYMARD A.,HISTOIRE GENERALE DES CIVILISATIONS (7   BIBLIOG/A
VOLS.). WOR+45 WOR-45 LAW SECT CREATE ATTIT   SOC
...ART/METH WORSHIP. PAGE 6 E0123

B54
MANGONE G.,A SHORT HISTORY OF INTERNATIONAL   INT/ORG
ORGANIZATION. MOD/EUR USA+45 USA-45 WOR+45 WOR-45   INT/LAW
LAW LEGIS CREATE LEGIT ROUTINE RIGID/FLEX PWR
...JURID CONCPT OBS TIME/SEQ STERTYP GEN/LAWS UN
TOT/POP VAL/FREE 18/20. PAGE 68 E1359

B54
WRIGHT Q.,PROBLEMS OF STABILITY AND PROGRESS IN   INT/ORG
INTERNATIONAL RELATIONSHIPS. FUT WOR+45 WOR-45   CONCPT
SOCIETY LEGIS CREATE TEC/DEV ECO/TAC EDU/PROP ADJUD   DIPLOM
WAR PEACE ORD/FREE PWR...KNO/TEST TREND GEN/LAWS
20. PAGE 108 E2155

L54
NICOLSON H.,"THE EVOLUTION OF DIPLOMATIC METHOD."   RIGID/FLEX
CHRIST-17C EUR+WWI FRANCE FUT ITALY MEDIT-7 MOD/EUR   METH/CNCPT
USA+45 USA-45 LAW NAT/G CREATE EDU/PROP LEGIT PEACE   DIPLOM
ATTIT ORD/FREE RESPECT SOVEREIGN. PAGE 77 E1548

B55
KHADDURI M.,WAR AND PEACE IN THE LAW OF ISLAM.   ISLAM
CONSTN CULTURE SOCIETY STRATA NAT/G PROVS SECT   JURID
FORCES TOP/EX CREATE DOMIN EDU/PROP ADJUD COERCE   PEACE
ATTIT RIGID/FLEX ALL/VALS...CONCPT TIME/SEQ TOT/POP   WAR
VAL/FREE. PAGE 61 E1209

B55
MAZZINI J.,THE DUTIES OF MAN. MOD/EUR LAW SOCIETY   SUPEGO
FAM NAT/G POL/PAR SECT VOL/ASSN EX/STRUC ACT/RES   CONCPT
CREATE REV PEACE ATTIT ALL/VALS...GEN/LAWS WORK 19.   NAT/LISM
PAGE 70 E1396

B56
CORBETT P.E.,MORALS LAW, AND POWER IN INTERNATIONAL   SUPEGO
RELATIONS. WOR+45 WOR-45 INT/ORG VOL/ASSN DELIB/GP   CONCPT
CREATE BAL/PWR DIPLOM LEGIT ARMS/CONT MORAL...JURID   POLICY
GEN/LAWS TOT/POP LEAGUE/NAT 20. PAGE 26 E0506   INT/LAW

B56
JESSUP P.C.,TRANSNATIONAL LAW. FUT WOR+45 JUDGE   LAW
CREATE ADJUD ORD/FREE...CONCPT VAL/FREE 20. PAGE 59   JURID
E1167   INT/LAW

B58
ALLEN C.K.,LAW IN THE MAKING. LEGIS ATTIT ORD/FREE   LAW
SOVEREIGN POPULISM...JURID IDEA/COMP NAT/COMP   CREATE
GEN/LAWS 20 ENGLSH/LAW. PAGE 4 E0069   CONSTN
SOCIETY

B58
HALL J.,STUDIES IN JURISPRUDENCE AND CRIMINAL   JURID
THEORY. USA-45 LAW CULTURE CREATE SUPEGO...CRIMLGY   CRIME
PSY /20 PLATO. PAGE 49 E0983   CONCPT
CT/SYS

B58
SPITZ D.,DEMOCRACY AND THE CHALLANGE OF POWER. FUT   NAT/G
USA+45 USA-45 LAW SOCIETY STRUCT LOC/G POL/PAR   PWR
PROVS DELIB/GP EX/STRUC LEGIS TOP/EX ACT/RES CREATE
DOMIN EDU/PROP LEGIT ADJUD ADMIN ATTIT DRIVE MORAL

ORD/FREE TOT/POP. PAGE 93 E1862

L59

COWAN T.A.,"A SYMPOSIUM ON GROUP INTERESTS AND THE LAW" USA+45 LAW MARKET LABOR PLAN INT/TRADE TAX RACE/REL RIGID/FLEX...JURID ANTHOL 20. PAGE 27 E0528 — ADJUD PWR INGP/REL CREATE

S59

JENKS C.W.,"THE CHALLENGE OF UNIVERSALITY." FUT UNIV CONSTN CULTURE CONSULT CREATE PLAN LEGIT ATTIT MORAL ORD/FREE RESPECT...MAJORIT JURID 20. PAGE 58 E1155 — INT/ORG LAW PEACE INT/LAW

S59

STONE J.,"CONFLICT MANAGEMENT THROUGH CONTEMPORARY INTERNATIONAL LAW AND ORGANIZATION." WOR+45 LAW NAT/G CREATE BAL/PWR DOMIN LEGIT ROUTINE COERCE ATTIT ORD/FREE PWR SOVEREIGN...JURID 20. PAGE 94 E1880 — INT/ORG INT/LAW

C59

EASTON D.,"POLITICAL ANTHROPOLOGY" IN BIENNIAL REVIEW OF ANTHROPOLOGY" UNIV LAW CULTURE ELITES SOCIETY CREATE...PSY CONCPT GP/COMP GEN/METH 20. PAGE 34 E0671 — SOC BIBLIOG/A NEW/IDEA

N59

NATIONAL ASSN HOME BUILDERS,COMMUNITY FACILITIES: A LIST OF SELECTED REFERENCES (PAMPHLET). USA+45 DIST/IND FINAN SERV/IND SCHOOL CREATE CONTROL FEDERAL...JURID 20. PAGE 76 E1525 — BIBLIOG/A PLAN LOC/G MUNIC

B60

BAKER G.E.,THE POLITICS OF REAPPORTIONMENT IN WASHINGTON STATE. LAW POL/PAR CREATE EDU/PROP PARL/PROC CHOOSE INGP/REL...CHARTS METH/COMP 20 WASHINGT/G LEAGUE/WV. PAGE 7 E0139 — VOL/ASSN APPORT PROVS LEGIS

B60

CLARK G.,WORLD PEACE THROUGH WORLD LAW. FUT WOR+45 CONSULT FORCES ACT/RES CREATE PLAN ADMIN ROUTINE ARMS/CONT DETER ATTIT PWR...JURID VAL/FREE UNESCO 20 UN. PAGE 23 E0449 — INT/ORG LAW PEACE INT/LAW

B61

BRENNAN D.G.,ARMS CONTROL, DISARMAMENT, AND NATIONAL SECURITY. WOR+45 NAT/G FORCES CREATE PROB/SOLV PARTIC WAR PEACE...DECISION INT/LAW ANTHOL BIBLIOG 20. PAGE 15 E0291 — ARMS/CONT ORD/FREE DIPLOM POLICY

B61

UTLEY T.E.,OCCASION FOR OMBUDSMAN. UK CREATE CONTROL 20 OMBUDSMAN. PAGE 103 E2065 — PROB/SOLV INGP/REL REPRESENT ADJUD

B62

DIESING P.,REASON IN SOCIETY; FIVE TYPES OF DECISIONS AND THEIR SOCIAL CONDITIONS. SOCIETY STRUCT LABOR CREATE TEC/DEV BARGAIN ADJUD ROLE ...JURID BIBLIOG 20. PAGE 31 E0625 — RATIONAL METH/COMP DECISION CONCPT

B62

NEW YORK STATE LEGISLATURE,REPORT AND DRAFT OF PROPOSED LEGISLATION ON COURT REORGANIZATION. LAW PROVS DELIB/GP CREATE ADJUD 20 NEW/YORK. PAGE 77 E1538 — CT/SYS JURID MUNIC LOC/G

B62

SCHWARTZ L.E.,INTERNATIONAL ORGANIZATIONS AND SPACE COOPERATION. VOL/ASSN CONSULT CREATE TEC/DEV SANCTION...POLICY INT/LAW PHIL/SCI 20 UN. PAGE 89 E1787 — INT/ORG DIPLOM R+D SPACE

B62

SWAYZE H.,POLITICAL CONTROL OF LITERATURE IN THE USSR, 1946-1959. USSR NAT/G CREATE LICENSE...JURID 20. PAGE 95 E1898 — MARXISM WRITING CONTROL DOMIN

S62

FINKELSTEIN L.S.,"THE UNITED NATIONS AND ORGANIZATIONS FOR CONTROL OF ARMAMENT." FUT WOR+45 VOL/ASSN DELIB/GP TOP/EX CREATE EDU/PROP LEGIT ADJUD NUC/PWR ATTIT RIGID/FLEX ORD/FREE...POLICY DECISION CONCPT OBS TREND GEN/LAWS TOT/POP COLD/WAR. PAGE 38 E0752 — INT/ORG PWR ARMS/CONT

B63

CRAIG A.,SUPPRESSED BOOKS: A HISTORY OF THE CONCEPTION OF LITERARY OBSCENITY. WOR+45 WOR-45 CREATE EDU/PROP LITERACY ATTIT...ART/METH PSY CONCPT 20. PAGE 27 E0538 — BIBLIOG/A LAW SEX CONTROL

B63

DAY R.E.,CIVIL RIGHTS USA: PUBLIC SCHOOLS, SOUTHERN STATES - NORTH CAROLINA, 1963. USA+45 LOC/G NEIGH LEGIS CREATE CT/SYS COERCE DISCRIM ATTIT...QU CHARTS 20 NORTH/CAR NEGRO KKK CIV/RIGHTS. PAGE 29 E0579 — EDU/PROP ORD/FREE RACE/REL SANCTION

B63

HALEY A.G.,SPACE LAW AND GOVERNMENT. FUT USA+45 WOR+45 LEGIS ACT/RES CREATE ATTIT RIGID/FLEX ORD/FREE PWR SOVEREIGN...POLICY JURID CONCPT CHARTS VAL/FREE 20. PAGE 49 E0980 — INT/ORG LAW SPACE

B63

ROSNER G.,THE UNITED NATIONS EMERGENCY FORCE. FRANCE ISRAEL UAR UK WOR+45 CREATE WAR PEACE ORD/FREE PWR...INT/LAW JURID HIST/WRIT TIME/SEQ UN. PAGE 86 E1719 — INT/ORG FORCES

L63

LOEVINGER L.,"JURIMETRICS* THE METHODOLOGY OF LEGAL INQUIRY." COMPUTER CREATE PLAN TEC/DEV AUTOMAT CT/SYS EFFICIENCY...DECISION PHIL/SCI NEW/IDEA QUANT PREDICT. PAGE 66 E1318 — COMPUT/IR JURID GEN/METH ADJUD

L63

MCDOUGAL M.S.,"THE ENJOYMENT AND ACQUISITION OF RESOURCES IN OUTER SPACE." CHRIST-17C FUT WOR+45 WOR-45 LAW EXTR/IND INT/ORG ACT/RES CREATE TEC/DEV ECO/TAC LEGIT COERCE HEALTH KNOWL ORD/FREE PWR WEALTH...JURID HIST/WRIT VAL/FREE. PAGE 70 E1408 — PLAN TREND

S63

GARDNER R.N.,"COOPERATION IN OUTER SPACE." FUT USSR WOR+45 AIR LAW COM/IND CONSULT DELIB/GP CREATE KNOWL 20 TREATY. PAGE 42 E0837 — INT/ORG ACT/RES PEACE SPACE

S63

WALKER H.,"THE INTERNATIONAL LAW OF COMMODITY AGREEMENTS." FUT WOR+45 ECO/DEV ECO/UNDEV FINAN INT/ORG NAT/G CONSULT CREATE PLAN ECO/TAC ATTIT PERCEPT...CONCPT GEN/LAWS TOT/POP GATT 20. PAGE 105 E2095 — MARKET VOL/ASSN INT/LAW INT/TRADE

B64

ANDERSON J.W.,EISENHOWER, BROWNELL, AND THE CONGRESS - THE TANGLED ORIGINS OF THE CIVIL RIGHTS BILL OF 1956-1957. USA+45 POL/PAR LEGIS CREATE PROB/SOLV LOBBY GOV/REL RIGID/FLEX...NEW/IDEA 20 EISNHWR/DD CONGRESS BROWNELL/H CIV/RIGHTS. PAGE 5 E0090 — LAW CONSTN POLICY NAT/G

B64

BOWETT D.W.,UNITED NATIONS FORCES* A LEGAL STUDY. CYPRUS ISRAEL KOREA LAW CONSTN ACT/RES CREATE BUDGET CONTROL TASK PWR...INT/LAW IDEA/COMP UN CONGO/LEOP SUEZ. PAGE 14 E0278 — OP/RES FORCES ARMS/CONT

B64

IKLE F.C.,HOW NATIONS NEGOTIATE. COM EUR+WWI USA+45 INTELL INT/ORG VOL/ASSN DELIB/GP ACT/RES CREATE DOMIN EDU/PROP ADJUD ROUTINE ATTIT PERSON ORD/FREE RESPECT SKILL...PSY SOC OBS VAL/FREE. PAGE 56 E1122 — NAT/G PWR POLICY

B64

MARNELL W.H.,THE FIRST AMENDMENT: THE HISTORY OF RELIGIOUS FREEDOM IN AMERICA. WOR+45 WOR-45 PROVS CREATE CT/SYS...POLICY BIBLIOG/A WORSHIP 16/20. PAGE 68 E1367 — CONSTN SECT ORD/FREE GOV/REL

B64

MCDOUGAL M.S.,STUDIES IN WORLD PUBLIC ORDER. SPACE SEA INT/ORG CREATE AGREE NUC/PWR...POLICY PHIL/SCI IDEA/COMP ANTHOL METH 20 UN. PAGE 71 E1411 — INT/LAW SOC DIPLOM

B64

MINAR D.W.,IDEAS AND POLITICS: THE AMERICAN EXPERIENCE. SECT CHIEF LEGIS CREATE ADJUD EXEC REV PWR...PHIL/SCI CONCPT IDEA/COMP 18/20 HAMILTON/A JEFFERSN/T DECLAR/IND JACKSON/A PRESIDENT. PAGE 73 E1464 — CONSTN NAT/G FEDERAL

B64

OSSENBECK F.J.,OPEN SPACE AND PEACE. CHINA/COM FUT USA+45 USSR LAW PROB/SOLV TEC/DEV EDU/PROP NEUTRAL PEACE...AUD/VIS ANTHOL 20. PAGE 79 E1583 — SPACE ORD/FREE DIPLOM CREATE

B64

SHKLAR J.N.,LEGALISM. CREATE PROB/SOLV CT/SYS ...POLICY CRIMLGY DECISION JURID METH/CNCPT. PAGE 91 E1821 — MORAL LAW NEW/IDEA

B64

TAUBENFELD H.J.,SPACE AND SOCIETY. USA+45 LAW — SPACE

FORCES CREATE TEC/DEV ADJUD CONTROL COST PEACE ...PREDICT ANTHOL 20. PAGE 95 E1911
SOCIETY
ADJUST
DIPLOM

S64
BAKER H.R.,"INMATE SELF-GOVERNMENT." ACT/RES CREATE CONTROL PARTIC ATTIT RIGID/FLEX QU. PAGE 7 E0141
PUB/INST
CRIME
INGP/REL
REPRESENT

S64
KARPOV P.V.,"PEACEFUL COEXISTENCE AND INTERNATIONAL LAW." WOR+45 LAW SOCIETY INT/ORG VOL/ASSN FORCES CREATE CAP/ISM DIPLOM ADJUD NUC/PWR PEACE MORAL ORD/FREE PWR MARXISM...MARXIST JURID CONCPT OBS TREND COLD/WAR MARX/KARL 20. PAGE 59 E1186
COM
ATTIT
INT/LAW
USSR

S64
SCHWELB E.,"OPERATION OF THE EUROPEAN CONVENTION ON HUMAN RIGHTS." EUR+WWI LAW SOCIETY CREATE EDU/PROP ADJUD ADMIN PEACE ATTIT ORD/FREE PWR...POLICY INT/LAW CONCPT OBS GEN/LAWS UN VAL/FREE ILO 20 ECHR. PAGE 89 E1791
INT/ORG
MORAL

S64
TRISKA J.F.,"SOVIET TREATY LAW: A QUANTITATIVE ANALYSIS." WOR+45 LAW ECO/UNDEV AGRI COM/IND INDUS CREATE TEC/DEV DIPLOM ATTIT PWR WEALTH...JURID SAMP TIME/SEQ TREND CHARTS VAL/FREE 20 TREATY. PAGE 97 E1942
COM
ECO/TAC
INT/LAW
USSR

B65
BAADE H.,THE SOVIET IMPACT ON INTERNATIONAL LAW. INT/ORG INT/TRADE LEGIT COLONIAL ARMS/CONT REV WAR ...CON/ANAL ANTHOL TREATY. PAGE 6 E0124
INT/LAW
USSR
CREATE
ORD/FREE

B65
BARKER L.J.,FREEDOM, COURTS, POLITICS: STUDIES IN CIVIL LIBERTIES. USA+45 LEGIS CREATE DOMIN PRESS ADJUD LOBBY CRIME GP/REL RACE/REL MARXISM 20 CIVIL/LIB. PAGE 8 E0148
JURID
CT/SYS
ATTIT
ORD/FREE

B65
BRIGGS H.W.,THE INTERNATIONAL LAW COMMISSION. LAW CONSTN LEGIS CREATE ADJUD CT/SYS ROUTINE TASK EFFICIENCY...CLASSIF OBS UN. PAGE 15 E0302
INT/LAW
DELIB/GP

B65
CARTER R.L.,EQUALITY. LAW LABOR NEIGH SCHOOL RACE/REL 20 NEGRO. PAGE 20 E0402
POLICY
DISCRIM
PLAN
CREATE

B65
HOWARD C.G.,LAW: ITS NATURE, FUNCTIONS, AND LIMITS. USA+45 CONSTN LEGIS CREATE SANCTION ORD/FREE ...BIBLIOG 20. PAGE 55 E1101
LAW
JURID
CONTROL
SOCIETY

B65
MILLIS W.,AN END TO ARMS. LAW INT/ORG FORCES ACT/RES CREATE DIPLOM WAR...POLICY HUM NEW/IDEA HYPO/EXP. PAGE 73 E1462
FUT
PWR
ARMS/CONT
ORD/FREE

B65
MISHKIN P.J.,ON LAW IN COURTS. USA+45 LEGIS CREATE ROLE 20. PAGE 73 E1468
LAW
CT/SYS
ADJUD
CONSTN

B65
UNESCO,HANDBOOK OF INTERNATIONAL EXCHANGES. COM/IND R+D ACADEM PROF/ORG VOL/ASSN CREATE TEC/DEV EDU/PROP AGREE 20 TREATY. PAGE 98 E1963
INDEX
INT/ORG
DIPLOM
PRESS

B65
VON GLAHN G.,LAW AMONG NATIONS: AN INTRODUCTION TO PUBLIC INTERNATIONAL LAW. WOR+45 WOR-45 INT/ORG NAT/G CREATE ADJUD WAR...GEOG CLASSIF TREND BIBLIOG. PAGE 104 E2082
ACADEM
INT/LAW
GEN/LAWS
LAW

B65
WEIL G.L.,A HANDBOOK ON THE EUROPEAN ECONOMIC COMMUNITY. BELGIUM EUR+WWI FRANCE GERMANY/W ITALY CONSTN ECO/DEV CREATE PARTIC GP/REL...DECISION MGT CHARTS 20 EEC. PAGE 105 E2107
INT/TRADE
INT/ORG
TEC/DEV
INT/LAW

S65
AMRAM P.W.,"REPORT ON THE TENTH SESSION OF THE HAGUE CONFERENCE ON PRIVATE INTERNATIONAL LAW." USA+45 WOR+45 INT/ORG CREATE LEGIT ADJUD ALL/VALS ...JURID CONCPT METH/CNCPT OBS GEN/METH 20. PAGE 4 E0085
VOL/ASSN
DELIB/GP
INT/LAW

S65
HAZARD J.N.,"CO-EXISTENCE LAW BOWS OUT." WOR+45 R+D INT/ORG VOL/ASSN CONSULT DELIB/GP ACT/RES CREATE PEACE KNOWL...JURID CONCPT COLD/WAR VAL/FREE 20. PAGE 51 E1018
PROF/ORG
ADJUD

S65
LUSKY L.,"FOUR PROBLEMS IN LAWMAKING FOR PEACE." FORCES LEGIS CREATE ADJUD COERCE WAR MAJORITY PEACE PWR. PAGE 67 E1334
ORD/FREE
INT/LAW
UTOPIA
RECORD

B66
AARON T.J.,THE CONTROL OF POLICE DISCRETION: THE DANISH EXPERIENCE. DENMARK LAW CREATE ADMIN INGP/REL SUPEGO PWR 20 OMBUDSMAN. PAGE 2 E0042
CONTROL
FORCES
REPRESENT
PROB/SOLV

B66
ANDERSON S.V.,CANADIAN OMBUDSMAN PROPOSALS. CANADA LEGIS DEBATE PARL/PROC...MAJORIT JURID TIME/SEQ IDEA/COMP 20 OMBUDSMAN PARLIAMENT. PAGE 5 E0092
NAT/G
CREATE
ADMIN
POL/PAR

B66
ASAMOAH O.Y.,THE LEGAL SIGNIFICANCE OF THE DECLARATIONS OF THE GENERAL ASSEMBLY OF THE UNITED NATIONS. WOR+45 CREATE CONTROL...BIBLIOG 20 UN. PAGE 5 E0105
INT/LAW
INT/ORG
DIPLOM

B66
DIZARD W.P.,TELEVISION* A WORLD VIEW. WOR+45 ECO/UNDEV TEC/DEV LICENSE LITERACY...STAT OBS INT QU TREND AUD/VIS BIBLIOG. PAGE 32 E0632
COM/IND
ACT/RES
EDU/PROP
CREATE

B66
MERILLAT H.C.L.,LEGAL ADVISERS AND INTERNATIONAL ORGANIZATIONS. LAW NAT/G CONSULT OP/RES ADJUD SANCTION TASK CONSEN ORG/CHARTS. PAGE 72 E1441
INT/ORG
INT/LAW
CREATE
OBS

L66
KRENZ F.E.,"THE REFUGEE AS A SUBJECT OF INTERNATIONAL LAW." FUT LAW NAT/G CREATE ADJUD ISOLAT STRANGE...RECORD UN. PAGE 62 E1230
INT/LAW
DISCRIM
NEW/IDEA

S66
ANAND R.P.,"ATTITUDE OF THE ASIAN-AFRICAN STATES TOWARD CERTAIN PROBLEMS OF INTERNATIONAL LAW." L/A+17C S/ASIA ECO/UNDEV CREATE CONFER ADJUD COLONIAL...RECORD GP/COMP UN. PAGE 5 E0087
INT/LAW
ATTIT
ASIA
AFR

B67
BAKER L.,BACK TO BACK: THE DUEL BETWEEN FDR AND THE SUPREME COURT. ELITES LEGIS CREATE DOMIN INGP/REL PERSON PWR NEW/LIB 20 ROOSEVLT/F SUPREME/CT SENATE. PAGE 7 E0142
CHIEF
CT/SYS
PARL/PROC
GOV/REL

B67
BIBBY J.,ON CAPITOL HILL. POL/PAR LOBBY PARL/PROC GOV/REL PERS/REL...JURID PHIL/SCI OBS INT BIBLIOG 20 CONGRESS PRESIDENT. PAGE 12 E0224
CONFER
LEGIS
CREATE
LEAD

B67
BRAGER G.A.,COMMUNITY ACTION AGAINST POVERTY. USA+45 LAW STRATA INGP/REL INCOME NEW/LIB...POLICY WELF/ST ANTHOL. PAGE 15 E0285
NEIGH
WEALTH
SOC/WK
CREATE

B67
BUREAU GOVERNMENT RES AND SERV,COUNTY GOVERNMENT REORGANIZATION - A SELECTED ANNOTATED BIBLIOGRAPHY (PAPER). USA+45 USA-45 LAW CONSTN MUNIC PROVS EX/STRUC CREATE PLAN PROB/SOLV REPRESENT GOV/REL 20. PAGE 17 E0332
BIBLIOG/A
APPORT
LOC/G
ADMIN

B67
CHAPIN F.S. JR.,SELECTED REFERENCES ON URBAN PLANNING METHODS AND TECHNIQUES. USA+45 LAW ECO/DEV LOC/G NAT/G SCHOOL CONSULT CREATE PROB/SOLV TEC/DEV SOC/WK. PAGE 21 E0420
BIBLIOG
NEIGH
MUNIC
PLAN

B67
HOLCOMBE A.N.,A STRATEGY OF PEACE IN A CHANGING WORLD. USA+45 WOR+45 LAW NAT/G CREATE DIPLOM ARMS/CONT WAR...CHARTS 20 UN COLD/WAR. PAGE 54 E1072
PEACE
PLAN
INT/ORG
INT/LAW

B67
BRADLEY A.W.,"CONSTITUTION-MAKING IN UGANDA." UGANDA LAW CHIEF DELIB/GP LEGIS ADMIN EXEC PARL/PROC RACE/REL ORD/FREE...GOV/COMP 20. PAGE 15 E0284
NAT/G
CREATE
CONSTN
FEDERAL

GIBSON G.H.,"LABOR PIRACY ON THE BRANDYWINE." USA-45 INDUS R+D VOL/ASSN CAP/ISM ADJUD DRIVE...PSY 19. PAGE 43 E0859
S67
ECO/TAC
CREATE
TEC/DEV
WORKER

KETCHAM O.W.,"GUIDELINES FROM GAULT: REVOLUTIONARY REQUIREMENTS AND REAPPRAISAL." LAW CONSTN CREATE LEGIT ROUTINE SANCTION CRIME DISCRIM PRIVIL ROLE ...JURID NEW/IDEA 20 SUPREME/CT. PAGE 60 E1208
S67
ADJUD
AGE/Y
CT/SYS

READ J.S.,"CENSORED." UGANDA CONSTN INTELL SOCIETY NAT/G DIPLOM PRESS WRITING ADJUD ADMIN COLONIAL RISK...IDEA/COMP 20. PAGE 84 E1675
S67
EDU/PROP
AFR
CREATE

BENTHAM J.,THE THEORY OF LEGISLATION. UK CREATE CRIME ATTIT ORD/FREE...CONCPT 18 REFORMERS. PAGE 10 E0196
B76
LEGIS
LAW
CRIMLGY
UTIL

CREDIT....CREDIT

CRESSEY D.R. E0546

CREYKE G. E0547

CRIME....SEE ALSO ANOMIE

ANNALS OF THE AMERICAN ACADEMY OF POLITICAL AND SOCIAL SCIENCE. AFR ASIA S/ASIA WOR+45 POL/PAR DIPLOM CRIME REV...SOC BIOG 20. PAGE 1 E0003
N
BIBLIOG/A
NAT/G
CULTURE
ATTIT

INTERNATIONAL BIBLIOGRAPHY ON CRIME AND DELINQUENCY. USA+45 LAW FORCES PROB/SOLV AGE/Y 20. PAGE 1 E0023
N
BIBLIOG/A
CRIME
ANOMIE
CRIMLGY

THE JAPAN SCIENCE REVIEW: LAW AND POLITICS: LIST OF BOOKS AND ARTICLES ON LAW AND POLITICS. CONSTN AGRI INDUS LABOR DIPLOM TAX ADMIN CRIME...INT/LAW SOC 20 CHINJAP. PAGE 2 E0027
N
BIBLIOG
LAW
S/ASIA
PHIL/SCI

US SUPERINTENDENT OF DOCUMENTS,POLITICAL SCIENCE: GOVERNMENT, CRIME, DISTRICT OF COLUMBIA (PRICE LIST 54). USA+45 LAW CONSTN EX/STRUC WORKER ADJUD ADMIN CT/SYS CHOOSE INGP/REL RACE/REL CONGRESS PRESIDENT. PAGE 103 E2063
N
BIBLIOG/A
NAT/G
CRIME

BERKELEY G.,"DISCOURSE ON PASSIVE OBEDIENCE" (1712) THE WORKS... (VOL. IV)" UNIV DOMIN LEGIT CONTROL CRIME ADJUST CENTRAL MORAL ORD/FREE...POLICY WORSHIP. PAGE 10 E0202
C01
INGP/REL
SANCTION
RESPECT
GEN/LAWS

GRIFFIN A.P.C.,LISTS PUBLISHED 1902-03: LABOR PARTICULARLY RELATING TO STRIKES (PAMPHLET). UK USA-45 FINAN WORKER PLAN BARGAIN CRIME GOV/REL ...POLICY 19/20 PARLIAMENT. PAGE 46 E0923
B03
BIBLIOG/A
LABOR
GP/REL
ECO/TAC

BURKE E.,A LETTER TO THE SHERIFFS OF BRISTOL (1777). USA-45 LAW ECO/TAC COLONIAL CT/SYS REV GP/REL ORD/FREE...POLICY 18 PARLIAMENT BURKE/EDM. PAGE 17 E0341
B04
LEGIS
ADJUD
CRIME

GRIFFIN A.P.C.,REFERENCES ON CORRUPT PRACTICES IN ELECTIONS (PAMPHLET). USA-45 LAW CONSTN TRIBUTE CRIME REPRESENT...JURID 19/20. PAGE 47 E0934
B08
BIBLIOG/A
CHOOSE
SUFF
APPORT

FOUAD M.,LE REGIME DE LA PRESSE EN EGYPTE: THESE POUR LE DOCTORAT. UAR LICENSE EDU/PROP ADMIN SANCTION CRIME SUPEGO PWR...ART/METH JURID 19/20. PAGE 39 E0778
B12
ORD/FREE
LEGIS
CONTROL
PRESS

SAWYER R.A.,A LIST OF WORKS ON COUNTY GOVERNMENT. LAW FINAN MUNIC TOP/EX ROUTINE CRIME...CLASSIF RECORD 19/20. PAGE 87 E1748
B15
BIBLIOG/A
LOC/G
GOV/REL
ADMIN

SALMOND J.W.,JURISPRUDENCE. UK LOC/G NAT/G LEGIS PROB/SOLV LICENSE LEGIT CRIME PERS/REL OWN ORD/FREE
B16
LAW
CT/SYS

...T 20. PAGE 87 E1742
JURID
ADJUD

SMITH R.H.,JUSTICE AND THE POOR. LAW RECEIVE ADJUD CRIME GOV/REL COST...JURID SOC/WK CONCPT STAT CHARTS GP/COMP 20. PAGE 92 E1847
B19
CT/SYS
DISCRIM
WEALTH

BURRUS B.R.,INVESTIGATION AND DISCOVERY IN STATE ANTITRUST (PAMPHLET). USA+45 USA-45 LEGIS ECO/TAC ADMIN CONTROL CT/SYS CRIME GOV/REL PWR...JURID CHARTS 19/20 FTC MONOPOLY. PAGE 18 E0346
N19
NAT/G
PROVS
LAW
INSPECT

GIBB A.D.,JUDICIAL CORRUPTION IN THE UNITED KINGDOM (PAMPHLET). UK DELIB/GP CT/SYS CRIME PERSON SUPEGO 17/20 SCOTLAND. PAGE 43 E0856
N19
MORAL
ATTIT
ADJUD

JANOWITZ M.,SOCIAL CONTROL OF ESCALATED RIOTS (PAMPHLET). USA+45 USA-45 LAW SOCIETY MUNIC FORCES PROB/SOLV EDU/PROP TV CRIME ATTIT...BIBLIOG 20 NEGRO CIV/RIGHTS. PAGE 58 E1148
N19
CROWD
ORD/FREE
CONTROL
RACE/REL

VINOGRADOFF P.,OUTLINES OF HISTORICAL JURISPRUDENCE (2 VOLS.). GREECE MEDIT-7 LAW CONSTN FACE/GP FAM KIN MUNIC CRIME OWN...INT/LAW IDEA/COMP BIBLIOG. PAGE 104 E2080
B20
JURID
METH

HOLDSWORTH W.S.,A HISTORY OF ENGLISH LAW; THE COMMON LAW AND ITS RIVALS (VOL. IV). UK SEA AGRI CHIEF ADJUD CONTROL CRIME GOV/REL...INT/LAW JURID NAT/COMP 16/17 PARLIAMENT COMMON/LAW CANON/LAW ENGLSH/LAW. PAGE 54 E1075
B24
LAW
LEGIS
CT/SYS
CONSTN

MOLEY R.,POLITICS AND CRIMINAL PROSECUTION. USA-45 POL/PAR EX/STRUC LEGIT CONTROL LEAD ROUTINE CHOOSE INGP/REL...JURID CHARTS 20. PAGE 74 E1481
B29
PWR
CT/SYS
CRIME
ADJUD

BENTHAM J.,THE RATIONALE OF PUNISHMENT. UK LAW LOC/G NAT/G LEGIS CONTROL...JURID GEN/LAWS COURT/SYS 19. PAGE 10 E0192
B30
CRIME
SANCTION
COERCE
ORD/FREE

BORCHARD E.H.,GUIDE TO THE LAW AND LEGAL LITERATURE OF FRANCE. FRANCE FINAN INDUS LABOR SECT LEGIS ADMIN COLONIAL CRIME OWN...INT/LAW 20. PAGE 14 E0266
B31
BIBLIOG/A
LAW
CONSTN
METH

AMERICAN FOREIGN LAW ASSN,BIOGRAPHICAL NOTES ON THE LAWS AND LEGAL LITERATURE OF URUGUAY AND CURACAO. URUGUAY CONSTN FINAN SECT FORCES JUDGE DIPLOM INT/TRADE ADJUD CT/SYS CRIME 20. PAGE 4 E0078
B33
BIBLIOG/A
LAW
JURID
ADMIN

ENSOR R.C.K.,COURTS AND JUDGES IN FRANCE, GERMANY, AND ENGLAND. FRANCE GERMANY UK LAW PROB/SOLV ADMIN ROUTINE CRIME ROLE...METH/COMP 20 CIVIL/LAW. PAGE 35 E0692
B33
CT/SYS
EX/STRUC
ADJUD
NAT/COMP

GILLETTE J.M.,CURRENT SOCIAL PROBLEMS. CONTROL CRIME AGE/Y BIO/SOC...SOC 20. PAGE 43 E0861
B33
GEOG
HEALTH
RACE/REL
FAM

HALL J.,THEFT, LAW, AND SOCIETY. SOCIETY PROB/SOLV ...CRIMLGY SOC CONCPT TREND METH/COMP 18/20 LARCENY. PAGE 49 E0982
B35
CRIME
LAW
ADJUD
ADJUST

HANSON L.,GOVERNMENT AND THE PRESS 1695-1763. UK LOC/G NAT/G LEGIS LICENSE CONTROL SANCTION CRIME ATTIT ORD/FREE 17/18 PARLIAMENT AMEND/I. PAGE 50 E0996
B36
LAW
JURID
PRESS
POLICY

SCHULZ F.,PRINCIPLES OF ROMAN LAW. CONSTN FAM NAT/G DOMIN CONTROL CT/SYS CRIME ISOLAT ATTIT ORD/FREE PWR...JURID ROME/ANC ROMAN/LAW. PAGE 89 E1783
B36
LAW
LEGIS
ADJUD
CONCPT

SCHUSTER E.,GUIDE TO LAW AND LEGAL LITERATURE OF CENTRAL AMERICAN REPUBLICS. L/A+17C INT/ORG ADJUD SANCTION CRIME...JURID 19/20. PAGE 89 E1785
B37
BIBLIOG/A
REGION
CT/SYS

LAW   T

B37

THOMPSON J.W.,SECRET DIPLOMACY: A RECORD OF   DIPLOM
ESPIONAGE AND DOUBLE-DEALING: 1500-1815. CHRIST-17C CRIME
MOD/EUR NAT/G WRITING RISK MORAL...ANTHOL BIBLIOG
16/19 ESPIONAGE. PAGE 96 E1920

B38

HOLDSWORTH W.S.,A HISTORY OF ENGLISH LAW; THE   LAW
CENTURIES OF SETTLEMENT AND REFORM (VOL. XI). UK   COLONIAL
CONSTN NAT/G EX/STRUC DIPLOM ADJUD CT/SYS LEAD   LEGIS
CRIME ATTIT...INT/LAW JURID 18 CMN/WLTH PARLIAMENT   PARL/PROC
ENGLSH/LAW. PAGE 54 E1079

B39

TIMASHEFF N.S.,AN INTRODUCTION TO THE SOCIOLOGY OF   SOC
LAW. CRIME ANOMIE ATTIT DRIVE ORD/FREE...JURID PSY   BIBLIOG
CONCPT. PAGE 96 E1926   PWR

B40

HART J.,AN INTRODUCTION TO ADMINISTRATIVE LAW, WITH LAW
SELECTED CASES. USA-45 CONSTN SOCIETY NAT/G   ADMIN
EX/STRUC ADJUD CT/SYS LEAD CRIME ORD/FREE   LEGIS
...DECISION JURID 20 CASEBOOK. PAGE 50 E1002   PWR

B40

HOBBES T.,A DIALOGUE BETWEEN A PHILOSOPHER AND A   CT/SYS
STUDENT OF THE COMMON LAWS OF ENGLAND (1667?). UK   CHIEF
SECT DOMIN ADJUD CRIME INCOME OWN UTIL ORD/FREE PWR SANCTION
SOVEREIGN...JURID GEN/LAWS 17. PAGE 53 E1057

B41

CHAFEE Z. JR.,FREE SPEECH IN THE UNITED STATES.   ORD/FREE
USA-45 ADJUD CONTROL CRIME WAR...BIBLIOG 20   CONSTN
FREE/SPEE AMEND/I SUPREME/CT. PAGE 21 E0413   ATTIT
                                                     JURID

B42

FORTESCU J.,IN PRAISE OF ENGLISH LAW (1464) (TRANS. LAW
BY S.B. CHRIMES). UK ELITES CHIEF FORCES CT/SYS   CONSTN
COERCE CRIME GOV/REL ILLEGIT...JURID GOV/COMP   LEGIS
GEN/LAWS 15. PAGE 39 E0774   ORD/FREE

B42

GILLETTE J.M.,PROBLEMS OF A CHANGING SOCIAL ORDER.   BIO/SOC
USA+45 STRATA FAM CONTROL CRIME RACE/REL HEALTH   ADJUST
WEALTH...GEOG GP/COMP. PAGE 43 E0862   ATTIT
                                                     SOC/WK

B42

US LIBRARY OF CONGRESS,SOCIAL AND CULTURAL PROBLEMS BIBLIOG/A
IN WARTIME: APRIL 1941-MARCH 1942. WOR-45 CLIENT   WAR
SECT EDU/PROP LEISURE RACE/REL STRANGE ATTIT   SOC
DRIVE HEALTH...GEOG 20. PAGE 100 E2012   CULTURE

B43

BACKUS R.C.,A GUIDE TO THE LAW AND LEGAL LITERATURE BIBLIOG/A
OF COLOMBIA. FINAN INDUS LABOR FORCES ADJUD ADMIN   LAW
COLONIAL CT/SYS CRIME...INT/LAW JURID 20 COLOMB.   CONSTN
PAGE 7 E0127   L/A+17C

B43

US LIBRARY OF CONGRESS,SOCIAL AND CULTURAL PROBLEMS BIBLIOG/A
IN WARTIME: APRIL-DECEMBER (SUPPLEMENT 1). WOR-45   WAR
SECT EDU/PROP CRIME LEISURE CIVMIL/REL RACE/REL   SOC
ATTIT DRIVE HEALTH...GEOG 20. PAGE 100 E2013   CULTURE

B43

US LIBRARY OF CONGRESS,SOCIAL AND CULTURAL PROBLEMS BIBLIOG/A
IN WARTIME: JANUARY-MAY 1943 (SUPPLEMENT 2). WOR-45 WAR
FAM SECT PLAN EDU/PROP CRIME LEISURE RACE/REL DRIVE SOC
HEALTH...GEOG 20 JEWS. PAGE 100 E2014   CULTURE

B45

CONOVER H.F.,THE NAZI STATE: WAR CRIMES AND WAR   BIBLIOG
CRIMINALS. GERMANY CULTURE NAT/G SECT FORCES DIPLOM WAR
INT/TRADE EDU/PROP...INT/LAW BIOG HIST/WRIT   CRIME
TIME/SEQ 20. PAGE 25 E0495

B46

GILLIN J.L.,SOCIAL PATHOLOGY. SOCIETY SECT CRIME   SOC
ANOMIE DISPL ORD/FREE WEALTH...CRIMLGY PSY WORSHIP. ADJUST
PAGE 44 E0864   CULTURE
                                                     INGP/REL

B46

MANNHEIM H.,CRIMINAL JUSTICE AND SOCIAL   ADJUD
RECONSTRUCTION. USA+45 EDU/PROP CRIME ANOMIE   LAW
...JURID BIBLIOG 20. PAGE 68 E1361   STRUCT
                                                     ADJUST

B46

PATON G.W.,A TEXT-BOOK OF JURISPRUDENCE. CREATE   LAW
INSPECT LEGIT CT/SYS ROUTINE CRIME INGP/REL PRIVIL   ADJUD
...CONCPT BIBLIOG 20. PAGE 80 E1601   JURID

S47

ANGELL R.C.,"THE SOCIAL INTEGRATION OF AMERICAN   MUNIC
CITIES OF MORE THAN 1,000,000 POPULATION" (BMR)"   CENSUS
USA+45 SOCIETY CRIME ADJUST WEALTH...GEOG SOC   GP/REL
CONCPT INDICATOR SAMP CHARTS SOC/INTEG 20. PAGE 5
E0098

B48

KEIR D.L.,CASES IN CONSTITUTIONAL LAW. UK CHIEF   CONSTN
LEGIS DIPLOM TAX PARL/PROC CRIME GOV/REL...INT/LAW   LAW
JURID 17/20. PAGE 60 E1195   ADJUD
                                                     CT/SYS

B48

SLESSER H.,THE ADMINISTRATION OF THE LAW. UK CONSTN LAW
EX/STRUC OP/RES PROB/SOLV CRIME ROLE...DECISION   CT/SYS
METH/COMP 20 CIVIL/LAW ENGLSH/LAW CIVIL/LAW.   ADJUD
PAGE 92 E1839

S48

ALEXANDER L.,"WAR CRIMES, THEIR SOCIAL-   DRIVE
PSYCHOLOGICAL ASPECTS." EUR+WWI GERMANY LAW CULTURE WAR
ELITES KIN POL/PAR PUB/INST FORCES DOMIN EDU/PROP
COERCE CRIME ATTIT SUPEGO HEALTH MORAL PWR FASCISM
...PSY OBS TREND GEN/LAWS NAZI 20. PAGE 3 E0061

B49

JACKSON R.H.,INTERNATIONAL CONFERENCE ON MILITARY   DIPLOM
TRIALS. FRANCE GERMANY UK USA+45 USSR VOL/ASSN   INT/ORG
DELIB/GP REPAR ADJUD CT/SYS CRIME WAR 20 WAR/TRIAL. INT/LAW
PAGE 57 E1141   CIVMIL/REL

B50

LOWENTHAL M.,THE FEDERAL BUREAU OF INVESTIGATION.   FORCES
USA+45 SOCIETY ADMIN TASK CRIME INGP/REL...CRIMLGY   NAT/G
20 FBI ESPIONAGE. PAGE 67 E1329   ATTIT
                                                     LAW

B50

MERRIAM C.E.,THE AMERICAN PARTY SYSTEM; AN   POL/PAR
INTRODUCTION TO THE STUDY OF POLITICAL PARTIES IN   CHOOSE
THE UNITED STATES (4TH ED.). USA+45 USA-45 LAW   SUFF
FINAN LOC/G NAT/G PROVS LEAD PARTIC CRIME ATTIT   REPRESENT
18/20 NEGRO CONGRESS PRESIDENT. PAGE 72 E1442

B50

US FEDERAL BUREAU INVESTIGAT,BIBLIOGRAPHY OF CRIME   BIBLIOG/A
AND KINDRED SUBJECTS (PAPER). USA+45 PROB/SOLV   CRIME
TREND. PAGE 100 E2001   LAW
                                                     CRIMLGY

B51

KEFAUVER E.,CRIME IN AMERICA. USA+45 USA-45 MUNIC   ELITES
NEIGH DELIB/GP TRIBUTE GAMBLE LOBBY SANCTION   CRIME
...AUD/VIS 20 CAPONE/AL MAFIA MIAMI CHICAGO   PWR
DETROIT. PAGE 60 E1194   FORCES

B51

WOOD V.,DUE PROCESS OF LAW 1932-1949: SUPREME   CONSTN
COURT'S USE OF A CONSTITUTIONAL TOOL. USA+45 USA-45 TREND
SOCIETY TAX CRIME...POLICY CHARTS 20 SUPREME/CT.   ADJUD
PAGE 107 E2143   GOV/REL

S51

LEEK J.H.,"TREASON AND THE CONSTITUTION" (BMR)"   CONSTN
USA+45 USA-45 EDU/PROP COLONIAL CT/SYS REV WAR   JURID
ATTIT...TREND 18/20 SUPREME/CT CON/INTERP SMITH/ACT CRIME
COMMON/LAW. PAGE 64 E1278   NAT/G

B52

COLEMAN J.W. JR.,DEATH AT THE COURT-HOUSE. CONTROL   CROWD
COERCE 20 KENTUCKY. PAGE 24 E0472   ORD/FREE
                                                     CRIME
                                                     CT/SYS

B52

MORRIS R.B.,FAIR TRIAL. USA-45 JUDGE ORD/FREE   ADJUD
...JURID 20. PAGE 75 E1498   CT/SYS
                                                     CRIME
                                                     LAW

B54

ELIAS T.O.,GROUNDWORK OF NIGERIAN LAW. AFR LEAD   JURID
CRIME INGP/REL ORD/FREE 17/20. PAGE 34 E0680   CT/SYS
                                                     CONSTN
                                                     CONSULT

B54

JAMES L.F.,THE SUPREME COURT IN AMERICAN LIFE.   ADJUD
USA+45 USA-45 CONSTN CRIME GP/REL INGP/REL RACE/REL CT/SYS
CONSEN FEDERAL PERSON ORD/FREE 18/20 SUPREME/CT   JURID
DEPRESSION CIV/RIGHTS CHURCH/STA FREE/SPEE. PAGE 58 DECISION
E1147

B55
BEISEL A.R.,CONTROL OVER ILLEGAL ENFORCEMENT OF THE ORD/FREE
CRIMINAL LAW: ROLE OF THE SUPREME COURT. CONSTN   LAW
ROUTINE MORAL PWR...SOC 20 SUPREME/CT. PAGE 9 E0180 CRIME

B55
BENTON W.E.,NUREMBERG: GERMAN VIEWS OF THE WAR   CRIME
TRIALS. EUR+WWI GERMANY VOL/ASSN LEAD PARTIC COERCE WAR
INGP/REL RACE/REL TOTALSM SUPEGO ORD/FREE...ANTHOL LAW
NUREMBERG. PAGE 10 E0201   JURID

B55
KHADDURI M.,LAW IN THE MIDDLE EAST. LAW CONSTN   ADJUD
ACADEM FAM EDU/PROP CT/SYS SANCTION CRIME...INT/LAW JURID
GOV/COMP ANTHOL 6/20 MID/EAST. PAGE 61 E1210   ISLAM

B55
LARROWE C.P.,SHAPE-UP AND HIRING HALL. TRIBUTE   LABOR
ADJUD CONTROL SANCTION COERCE CRIME GP/REL PWR   INDUS
...CHARTS 20 AFL/CIO NEWYORK/C SEATTLE. PAGE 63   WORKER
E1256   NAT/G

B55
SWEET AND MAXWELL,A LEGAL BIBLIOGRAPHY OF THE   BIBLIOG/A
BRITISH COMMONWEALTH OF NATIONS (2ND ED. 7 VOLS.). LAW
UK LOC/G MUNIC JUDGE ADJUD CRIME OWN...JURID 14/20 CONSTN
CMN/WLTH. PAGE 95 E1900   CT/SYS

B56
ABELS J.,THE TRUMAN SCANDALS. USA+45 USA-45 POL/PAR CRIME
TAX LEGIT CT/SYS CHOOSE PRIVIL MORAL WEALTH 20   ADMIN
TRUMAN/HS PRESIDENT CONGRESS. PAGE 2 E0043   CHIEF
                                                   TRIBUTE

B56
ALEXANDER F.,THE CRIMINAL, THE JUDGE, AND THE   CRIME
PUBLIC. LAW CULTURE CONSULT LEGIT ADJUD SANCTION   CRIMLGY
ORD/FREE 20. PAGE 3 E0060   PSY
                                                   ATTIT

B56
BROWNE D.G.,THE RISE OF SCOTLAND YARD: A HISTORY OF CRIMLGY
THE METROPOLITAN POLICE. UK MUNIC CHIEF ADMIN CRIME LEGIS
GP/REL 19/20. PAGE 16 E0316   CONTROL
                                                   FORCES

B56
CALLISON I.P.,COURTS OF INJUSTICE. USA+45 PROF/ORG CT/SYS
ADJUD CRIME PERSON MORAL PWR RESPECT SKILL 20.   JUDGE
PAGE 19 E0368   JURID

B56
COHEN A.,THE SUTHERLAND PAPERS. USA+45 USA-45 LAW   CRIMLGY
CONTROL CRIME AGE/Y...TREND ANTHOL BIBLIOG 20.   PHIL/SCI
PAGE 23 E0461   ACT/RES
                                                   METH

B56
DOUGLAS W.O.,WE THE JUDGES. INDIA USA+45 USA-45 LAW ADJUD
NAT/G SECT LEGIS PRESS CRIME FEDERAL ORD/FREE   CT/SYS
...POLICY GOV/COMP 19/20 WARRN/EARL MARSHALL/J   CONSTN
SUPREME/CT. PAGE 32 E0640   GOV/REL

B56
KALNOKI BEDO A.,LEGAL SOURCES AND BIBLIOGRAPHY OF   BIBLIOG
HUNGARY. COM HUNGARY CONSTN LEGIS JUDGE CT/SYS   ADJUD
SANCTION CRIME 16/20. PAGE 59 E1181   LAW
                                                   JURID

B56
LASLETT P.,PHILOSOPHY, POLITICS AND SOCIETY. UNIV   CONSTN
CRIME SOVEREIGN...JURID PHIL/SCI ANTHOL PLATO   ATTIT
NATURL/LAW. PAGE 63 E1260   CONCPT
                                                   GEN/LAWS

B56
SYKES G.M.,CRIME AND SOCIETY. LAW STRATA STRUCT   CRIMLGY
ACT/RES ROUTINE ANOMIE WEALTH...POLICY SOC/INTEG   CRIME
20. PAGE 95 E1903   CULTURE
                                                   INGP/REL

B56
US HOUSE WAYS MEANS COMMITTEE,TRAFFIC IN, AND   BIO/SOC
CONTROL OF NARCOTICS, BARBITURATES, AND   CONTROL
AMPHETAMINES. CHINA/COM USA+45 SOCIETY LEGIS   PROB/SOLV
ACT/RES EDU/PROP CT/SYS SANCTION PROFIT HEALTH   CRIME
...HEAL PSY STAT 20. PAGE 100 E2011

B57
CLINARD M.B.,SOCIOLOGY OF DEVIANT BEHAVIOR. FAM   BIO/SOC
CONTROL MURDER DISCRIM PERSON...PSY SOC T SOC/INTEG CRIME
20. PAGE 23 E0455   SEX
                                                   ANOMIE

B57
HISS A.,IN THE COURT OF PUBLIC OPINION. USA+45   CRIME

B57
DELIB/GP LEGIS LEGIT CT/SYS ATTIT 20 DEPT/STATE   MARXISM
NIXON/RM HUAC HISS/ALGER. PAGE 53 E1053   BIOG
                                                   ADJUD

B57
INSTITUT DE DROIT INTL,TABLEAU GENERAL DES   INT/LAW
RESOLUTIONS (1873-1956). LAW NEUTRAL CRIME WAR   DIPLOM
MARRIAGE PEACE...JURID 19/20. PAGE 56 E1124   ORD/FREE
                                                   ADJUD

B57
MILLS W.,INDIVIDUAL FREEDOM AND COMMON DEFENSE   ORD/FREE
(PAMPHLET). USA+45 USSR NAT/G EDU/PROP CRIME CHOOSE CONSTN
20 COLD/WAR. PAGE 73 E1463   INGP/REL
                                                   FORCES

B57
US COMMISSION GOVT SECURITY,RECOMMENDATIONS; AREA: LEGIS
LEGISLATION. USA+45 USA-45 DELIB/GP PLAN TEC/DEV   SANCTION
CIVMIL/REL ORD/FREE...POLICY DECISION 20 PRIVACY.   CRIME
PAGE 99 E1982   CONTROL

B57
US SENATE SPEC COMM POLIT ACT,REPORT OF SPECIAL   LOBBY
COMMITTEE TO INVESTIGATE POLITICAL ACTIVITIES,   LAW
LOBBYING, AND CAMPAIGN CONTRIBUTIONS. USA+45   ECO/TAC
BARGAIN CRIME ATTIT...DECISION 20 CONGRESS.   PARL/PROC
PAGE 103 E2061

B58
ALLEN C.K.,ASPECTS OF JUSTICE. UK FAM COERCE CRIME JURID
MARRIAGE AGE/Y LOVE 20 ENGLSH/LAW. PAGE 4 E0068   MORAL
                                                   ORD/FREE

B58
BUREAU OF NATIONAL AFFAIRS,THE MCCLELLAN COMMITTEE DELIB/GP
HEARINGS - 1957. USA+45 LEGIS CONTROL CRIME   CONFER
...CHARTS 20 CONGRESS AFL/CIO MCCLELLN/J. PAGE 17   LABOR
E0336   MGT

B58
CABLE G.W.,THE NEGRO QUESTION: A SELECTION OF   RACE/REL
WRITINGS ON CIVIL RIGHTS IN THE SOUTH. USA+45   CULTURE
STRATA LOC/G POL/PAR GIVE EDU/PROP WRITING CT/SYS   DISCRIM
SANCTION CRIME CHOOSE WORSHIP 20 NEGRO CIV/RIGHTS   ORD/FREE
CONV/LEASE SOUTH/US. PAGE 18 E0355

B58
CARPENTER W.S.,FOUNDATIONS OF MODERN JURISPRUDENCE. LAW
UNIV PROB/SOLV ADJUD CT/SYS CRIME ATTIT...CONCPT   JURID
18/20. PAGE 20 E0388

B58
CHARLES R.,LA JUSTICE EN FRANCE. FRANCE LAW CONSTN JURID
DELIB/GP CRIME 20. PAGE 21 E0422   ADMIN
                                                   CT/SYS
                                                   ADJUD

B58
DEVLIN P.,THE CRIMINAL PROSECUTION IN ENGLAND. UK   CRIME
NAT/G ADMIN ROUTINE EFFICIENCY...JURID SOC 20.   LAW
PAGE 31 E0617   METH
                                                   CT/SYS

B58
DUCLOUX L.,FROM BLACKMAIL TO TREASON. FRANCE PLAN   COERCE
DIPLOM EDU/PROP PRESS RUMOR NAT/LISM...CRIMLGY 20. CRIME
PAGE 33 E0653   NAT/G
                                                   PWR

B58
FELLMAN D.,THE DEFENDANT'S RIGHTS. USA+45 NAT/G   CONSTN
CONSULT CT/SYS SUPEGO ORD/FREE...BIBLIOG SUPREME/CT LAW
CIVIL/SERV. PAGE 37 E0730   CRIME
                                                   ADJUD

B58
HALL J.,STUDIES IN JURISPRUDENCE AND CRIMINAL   JURID
THEORY. USA-45 LAW CULTURE CREATE SUPEGO...CRIMLGY CRIME
PSY /20 PLATO. PAGE 49 E0983   CONCPT
                                                   CT/SYS

B58
JAPAN MINISTRY OF JUSTICE,CRIMINAL JUSTICE IN   CONSTN
JAPAN. LAW PROF/ORG PUB/INST FORCES CONTROL CT/SYS CRIME
PARL/PROC 20 CHINJAP. PAGE 58 E1149   JURID
                                                   ADMIN

B58
KAPLAN H.E.,THE LAW OF CIVIL SERVICE. USA+45 LAW   ADJUD
POL/PAR CT/SYS CRIME GOV/REL...POLICY JURID 20.   NAT/G
PAGE 59 E1183   ADMIN
                                                   CONSTN

B58
OGDEN F.D.,THE POLL TAX IN THE SOUTH. USA+45 USA-45 TAX

CONSTN ADJUD ADMIN PARTIC CRIME...TIME/SEQ GOV/COMP CHOOSE
METH/COMP 18/20 SOUTH/US. PAGE 78 E1572 RACE/REL
DISCRIM

B58
STONE J.,AGGRESSION AND WORLD ORDER: A CRITIQUE OF ORD/FREE
UNITED NATIONS THEORIES OF AGGRESSION. LAW CONSTN INT/ORG
DELIB/GP PROB/SOLV BAL/PWR DIPLOM DEBATE ADJUD WAR
CRIME PWR...POLICY IDEA/COMP 20 UN SUEZ LEAGUE/NAT. CONCPT
PAGE 94 E1879

B59
BOHMER A.,LEGAL SOURCES AND BIBLIOGRAPHY OF BIBLIOG
CZECHOSLOVAKIA. COM CZECHOSLVK PARL/PROC SANCTION ADJUD
CRIME MARXISM 20. PAGE 13 E0261 LAW
JURID

B59
DASH S.,THE EAVESDROPPERS. USA+45 DELIB/GP TEC/DEV CRIME
ORD/FREE...POLICY CRIMLGY JURID 20 PRIVACY. PAGE 29 CONTROL
E0569 ACT/RES
LAW

B59
ELLIOTT S.D.,IMPROVING OUR COURTS. LAW EX/STRUC CT/SYS
PLAN PROB/SOLV ADJUD ADMIN TASK CRIME EFFICIENCY JURID
ORD/FREE 20. PAGE 34 E0684 GOV/REL
NAT/G

B59
GINSBURG M.,LAW AND OPINION IN ENGLAND. UK CULTURE JURID
KIN LABOR LEGIS EDU/PROP ADMIN CT/SYS CRIME OWN POLICY
HEALTH...ANTHOL 20 ENGLSH/LAW. PAGE 44 E0868 ECO/TAC

B59
GSOVSKI V.,GOVERNMENT, LAW, AND COURTS IN THE ADJUD
SOVIET UNION AND EASTERN EUROPE (2 VOLS.). COM USSR MARXISM
AGRI INDUS WORKER CT/SYS CRIME...BIBLIOG 20 CONTROL
EUROPE/E. PAGE 48 E0958 ORD/FREE

B59
HOBSBAWM E.J.,PRIMITIVE REBELS; STUDIES IN ARCHAIC SOCIETY
FORMS OF SOCIAL MOVEMENT IN THE 19TH AND 20TH CRIME
CENTURIES. ITALY SPAIN CULTURE VOL/ASSN RISK CROWD REV
GP/REL INGP/REL ISOLAT TOTALISM...PSY SOC 18/20. GUERRILLA
PAGE 53 E1058

B59
KERREMANS-RAMIOULL.LE PROBLEME DE LA DELINQUENCE BIBLIOG
JUVENILE (2ND ED.). FAM PUB/INST SCHOOL FORCES CRIME
LEGIS MORAL...CRIMLGY SOC 20. PAGE 60 E1205 AGE/Y
SOC/WK

B59
KNIERIEM A.,THE NUREMBERG TRIALS. EUR+WWI GERMANY INT/LAW
VOL/ASSN LEAD COERCE WAR INGP/REL TOTALISM SUPEGO CRIME
ORD/FREE...CONCPT METH/COMP. PAGE 61 E1225 PARTIC
JURID

B59
LAPIERE R.,THE FREUDIAN ETHIC. USA+45 FAM EDU/PROP PSY
CONTROL CRIME ADJUST AGE DRIVE PERCEPT PERSON SEX ORD/FREE
...SOC 20 FREUD/S. PAGE 63 E1254 SOCIETY

B59
PANHUYS H.F.,THE ROLE OF NATIONALITY IN INT/LAW
INTERNATIONAL LAW. ADJUD CRIME WAR STRANGE...JURID NAT/LISM
TREND. PAGE 80 E1596 INGP/REL

B59
VITTACHIT.EMERGENCY '58. CEYLON UK STRUCT NAT/G RACE/REL
FORCES ADJUD CRIME REV NAT/LISM 20. PAGE 104 E2081 DISCRIM
DIPLOM
SOVEREIGN

S59
BELL D.,"THE RACKET RIDDEN LONGSHOREMEN" (BMR)" CRIME
USA+45 SEA WORKER MURDER ROLE...SOC 20 NEWYORK/C. LABOR
PAGE 9 E0182 DIST/IND
ELITES

S59
CLOWARD R.A.,"ILLEGITIMATE MEANS, ANOMIE, AND ANOMIE
DEVIANT BEHAVIOR" STRUCT CRIME DRIVE PERSON...SOC CRIMLGY
CONCPT NEW/IDEA 20 DURKHEIM/E MERTON/R. PAGE 23 LEGIT
E0459 ADJUST

B60
GIBNEY F.,THE OPERATORS. USA+45 LAW STRATA BIO/SOC CRIME
MORAL ORD/FREE SOC. PAGE 43 E0858 CULTURE
ANOMIE
CRIMLGY

B60
HANBURY H.G.,ENGLISH COURTS OF LAW. UK EX/STRUC JURID
LEGIS CRIME ROLE 12/20 COMMON/LAW ENGLSH/LAW. CT/SYS

PAGE 50 E0993 CONSTN
GOV/REL

B60
LASKIN B.,CANADIAN CONSTITUTIONAL LAW: TEXT AND CONSTN
NOTES ON DISTRIBUTION OF LEGISLATIVE POWER (2ND NAT/G
ED.). CANADA LOC/G ECO/TAC TAX CONTROL CT/SYS CRIME LAW
FEDERAL PWR...JURID 20 PARLIAMENT. PAGE 63 E1259 LEGIS

B60
PINTO F.B.M.,ENRIQUECIMENTO ILICITO NO EXERCICIO DE ADMIN
CARGOS PUBLICOS. BRAZIL L/A+17C USA+45 ELITES NAT/G
TRIBUTE CONTROL INGP/REL ORD/FREE PWR...NAT/COMP CRIME
20. PAGE 81 E1617 LAW

C60
MCCLEERY R.,"COMMUNICATION PATTERNS AS BASES OF PERS/REL
SYSTEMS OF AUTHORITY AND POWER" IN THEORETICAL PUB/INST
STUDIES IN SOCIAL ORGAN. OF PRISON-BMR. USA+45 PWR
SOCIETY STRUCT EDU/PROP ADMIN CONTROL COERCE CRIME DOMIN
GP/REL AUTHORIT...SOC 20. PAGE 70 E1400

B61
DAVIS B.F.,THE DESPERATE AND THE DAMNED. USA+45 LAW PUB/INST
DEATH ANOMIE...CRIMLGY 20 SAN/QUENTN. PAGE 29 E0571 SANCTION
CRIME

B61
FREUND P.A.,THE SUPREME COURT OF THE UNITED STATES: CT/SYS
ITS BUSINESS, PURPOSES, AND PERFORMANCE. CONSTN JURID
CRIME CONSEN ORD/FREE...DECISION 20 SUPREME/CT ADJUD
CIVIL/LIB. PAGE 40 E0797 FEDERAL

B61
LARSON A.,WHEN NATIONS DISAGREE. USA+45 WOR+45 INT/LAW
INT/ORG ADJUD COERCE CRIME OWN SOVEREIGN...POLICY DIPLOM
JURID 20. PAGE 63 E1258 WAR

B61
MERTON R.K.,CONTEMPORARY SOCIAL PROBLEMS: AN CRIME
INTRODUCTION TO THE SOCIOLOGY OF DEVIANT BEHAVIOR ANOMIE
AND SOCIAL DISORGANIZATION. FAM MUNIC FORCES WORKER STRANGE
PROB/SOLV INGP/REL RACE/REL ISOLAT...CRIMLGY GEOG SOC
PSY T 20 NEGRO. PAGE 72 E1444

B61
NEW JERSEY LEGISLATURE-SENATE,PUBLIC HEARINGS LEGIS
BEFORE COMMITTEE ON REVISION AND AMENDMENT OF LAWS MUNIC
ON SENATE BILL NO. 8. USA+45 FINAN PROVS WORKER INDUS
ACT/RES PLAN BUDGET TAX CRIME...IDEA/COMP 20 PROB/SOLV
NEW/JERSEY URBAN/RNWL. PAGE 77 E1537

B61
TOMPKINS D.C.,CONFLICT OF INTEREST IN THE FEDERAL BIBLIOG
GOVERNMENT: A BIBLIOGRAPHY. USA+45 EX/STRUC LEGIS ROLE
ADJUD ADMIN CRIME CONGRESS PRESIDENT. PAGE 96 E1932 NAT/G
LAW

B61
US HOUSE COMM ON JUDICIARY,LEGISLATION RELATING TO LEGIS
ORGANIZED CRIME. USA+45 DIST/IND DELIB/GP GAMBLE CONTROL
SANCTION HOUSE/REP. PAGE 100 E2004 CRIME
LAW

B62
BOCHENSKI J.M.,HANDBOOK ON COMMUNISM. USSR WOR+45 COM
LAW SOCIETY NAT/G POL/PAR SECT CRIME PERSON MARXISM DIPLOM
...SOC ANTHOL 20. PAGE 13 E0254 POLICY
CONCPT

B62
BORKIN J.,THE CORRUPT JUDGE. USA+45 CT/SYS ATTIT ADJUD
SUPEGO MORAL RESPECT...BIBLIOG + SUPREME/CT TRIBUTE
MANTON/M DAVIS/W JOHNSN/ALB. PAGE 14 E0271 CRIME

B62
DELANY V.T.H.,THE ADMINISTRATION OF JUSTICE IN ADMIN
IRELAND. IRELAND CONSTN FINAN JUDGE COLONIAL CRIME JURID
...CRIMLGY 19/20. PAGE 30 E0604 CT/SYS
ADJUD

B62
DONNELLY R.C.,CRIMINAL LAW: PROBLEMS FOR DECISION CRIME
IN THE PROMULGATION, INVOCATION AND ADMINISTRATION LAW
OF A LAW OF CRIMES. USA+45 SANCTION BIO/SOC ADJUD
...DECISION JURID BIBLIOG 20. PAGE 32 E0636 PROB/SOLV

B62
GANJI M.,INTERNATIONAL PROTECTION OF HUMAN RIGHTS. ORD/FREE
WOR+45 CONSTN INT/TRADE CT/SYS SANCTION CRIME WAR DISCRIM
RACE/REL...CHARTS IDEA/COMP NAT/COMP BIBLIOG 20 LEGIS
TREATY NEGRO LEAGUE/NAT UN CIVIL/LIB. PAGE 42 E0831 DELIB/GP

B62
GRZYBOWSKI K.,SOVIET LEGAL INSTITUTIONS. USA+45 ADJUD
USSR ECO/DEV NAT/G EDU/PROP CONTROL CT/SYS CRIME LAW

OWN ATTIT PWR SOCISM...NAT/COMP 20. PAGE 48 E0955   JURID

B62
HEYDECKER J.J.,THE NUREMBERG TRIAL: HISTORY OF NAZI LAW
GERMANY AS REVEALED THROUGH THE TESTIMONY AT   CRIME
NUREMBERG. EUR+WWI GERMANY VOL/ASSN LEAD COERCE   PARTIC
CROWD INGP/REL RACE/REL SUPEGO ORD/FREE...CONCPT 20 TOTALISM
NAZI ANTI/SEMIT NUREMBERG JEWS. PAGE 52 E1036

B62
NORGAARD C.A.,THE POSITION OF THE INDIVIDUAL IN   INT/LAW
INTERNATIONAL LAW. INT/ORG SUPEGO ORD/FREE   DIPLOM
SOVEREIGN...CONCPT 20 UN. PAGE 78 E1556   CRIME
                                                    JURID

B62
OTTENBERG M.,THE FEDERAL INVESTIGATORS. USA+45 LAW FORCES
COM/IND DIST/IND WORKER DIPLOM INT/TRADE CONTROL   INSPECT
FEDERAL HEALTH ORD/FREE FBI CIA FTC SEC FDA.   NAT/G
PAGE 79 E1585   CRIME

S62
GRAVEN J.,"LE MOUVEAU DROIT PENAL INTERNATIONAL."   CT/SYS
UNIV STRUCT LEGIS ACT/RES CRIME ATTIT PERCEPT   PUB/INST
PERSON...JURID CONCPT 20. PAGE 45 E0899   INT/ORG
                                                    INT/LAW

C62
BACON F.,"OF JUDICATURE" (1612) IN F. BACON,   CT/SYS
ESSAYS." ADJUD ADMIN SANCTION CRIME PWR...JURID   LEGIS
GEN/LAWS. PAGE 7 E0128   LAW

B63
BLOCK E.B.,THE VINDICATORS. LAW FORCES CT/SYS   ATTIT
DISCRIM 19/20. PAGE 13 E0247   CRIME
                                                    ADJUD
                                                    CRIMLGY

B63
COUNCIL OF STATE GOVERNMENTS,INCREASED RIGHTS FOR   CT/SYS
DEFENDANTS IN STATE CRIMINAL PROSECUTIONS. USA+45   ADJUD
GOV/REL INGP/REL FEDERAL ORD/FREE...JURID 20   PROVS
SUPREME/CT. PAGE 26 E0522   CRIME

B63
EDDY J.P.,JUSTICE OF THE PEACE. UK LAW CONSTN   CRIME
CULTURE 14/20 COMMON/LAW. PAGE 34 E0674   JURID
                                                    CT/SYS
                                                    ADJUD

B63
ELLERT R.B.,NATO 'FAIR TRIAL' SAFEGUARDS: PRECURSOR JURID
TO AN INTERNATIONAL BILL OF PROCEDURAL RIGHTS.   INT/LAW
WOR+45 FORCES CRIME CIVMIL/REL ATTIT ORD/FREE 20   INT/ORG
NATO. PAGE 34 E0683   CT/SYS

B63
FRIEDRICH C.J.,JUSTICE: NOMOS VI. UNIV LAW SANCTION LEGIT
CRIME...CONCPT ANTHOL MARX/KARL LOCKE/JOHN   ADJUD
AQUINAS/T. PAGE 41 E0809   ORD/FREE
                                                    JURID

B63
GSOUSKI V.,LEGAL SOURCES AND BIBLIOGRAPHY OF THE   BIBLIOG
BALTIC STATES (ESTONIA, LATVIA, LITHUANIA). COM   ADJUD
ESTONIA LATVIA LITHUANIA NAT/G LEGIS CT/SYS   LAW
SANCTION CRIME 20. PAGE 48 E0957   JURID

B63
JOSEPH H.,IF THIS BE TREASON. SOUTH/AFR 20. PAGE 59 AFR
E1174   LAW
                                                    CT/SYS
                                                    CRIME

B63
LAVROFF D.-.G.,LES LIBERTES PUBLIQUES EN UNION   ORD/FREE
SOVIETIQUE (REV. ED.). USSR NAT/G WORKER SANCTION   LAW
CRIME MARXISM NEW/LIB...JURID BIBLIOG WORSHIP 20.   ATTIT
PAGE 63 E1268   COM

B63
MOLLARD P.T.,LE REGIME JURIDIQUE DE LA PRESSE AU   PRESS
MAROC. MOROCCO CONTROL CRIME GP/REL ORD/FREE 20.   LAW
PAGE 74 E1482   LEAD
                                                    LEGIT

B63
VINES K.N.,STUDIES IN JUDICIAL POLITICS: TULANE   CT/SYS
STUDIES IN POLITICAL SCIENCE (VOL. 8). POL/PAR   GOV/REL
JUDGE ADJUD SANCTION CRIME CHOOSE PWR...JURID STAT PROVS
TIME/SEQ CHARTS. PAGE 104 E2079

B64
CHAPIN B.,THE AMERICAN LAW OF TREASON. USA-45 LAW   LEGIS
NAT/G JUDGE CRIME REV...BIBLIOG 18. PAGE 21 E0419   JURID
                                                    CONSTN

B64
CHEIN I.,THE ROAD TO H; NARCOTICS, DELINQUENCY, AND BIO/SOC
SOCIAL POLICY. USA+45 NEIGH CRIME INGP/REL ATTIT   AGE/Y
PERSON...SOC/WK 20 NEWYORK/C. PAGE 22 E0426   POLICY
                                                    ANOMIE

B64
CLINARD M.B.,ANOMIE AND DEVIANT BEHAVIOR: A   PERSON
DISCUSSION AND CRITIQUE. SOCIETY FACE/GP CRIME   ANOMIE
STRANGE ATTIT BIO/SOC DISPL RIGID/FLEX HEALTH...PSY KIN
CONCPT BIBLIOG 20 MERTON/R. PAGE 23 E0456   NEIGH

B64
DRESSLER D.,READINGS IN CRIMINOLOGY AND PENOLOGY.   CRIMLGY
UNIV CULTURE PUB/INST FORCES ACT/RES PROB/SOLV   CRIME
ANOMIE BIO/SOC SUPEGO...GEOG PSY ANTHOL 20. PAGE 33 ADJUD
E0648   ADJUST

B64
FEIFER G.,JUSTICE IN MOSCOW. USSR LAW CRIME   ADJUD
...RECORD 20. PAGE 37 E0725   JURID
                                                    CT/SYS
                                                    MARXISM

B64
FREUD A.,OF HUMAN SOVEREIGNTY. WOR+45 INDUS SECT   NAT/LISM
ECO/TAC CRIME CHOOSE ATTIT MORAL MARXISM...POLICY   DIPLOM
BIBLIOG 20. PAGE 40 E0794   WAR
                                                    PEACE

B64
GESELLSCHAFT RECHTSVERGLEICH,BIBLIOGRAPHIE DES   BIBLIOG/A
DEUTSCHEN RECHTS (BIBLIOGRAPHY OF GERMAN LAW,   JURID
TRANS. BY COURTLAND PETERSON). GERMANY FINAN INDUS CONSTN
LABOR SECT FORCES CT/SYS PARL/PROC CRIME...INT/LAW ADMIN
SOC NAT/COMP 20. PAGE 43 E0853

B64
GJUPANOVIC H.,LEGAL SOURCES AND BIBLIOGRAPHY OF   BIBLIOG/A
YUGOSLAVIA. COM YUGOSLAVIA LAW LEGIS DIPLOM ADMIN   JURID
PARL/PROC REGION CRIME CENTRAL 20. PAGE 44 E0873   CONSTN
                                                    ADJUD

B64
KOREA (REPUBLIC) SUPREME COURT,KOREAN LEGAL SYSTEM. JURID
KOREA/S WOR+45 LAW LEAD ROUTINE GOV/REL ORD/FREE 20 CT/SYS
SUPREME/CT. PAGE 61 E1229   CONSTN
                                                    CRIME

B64
LOCKHART W.B.,CASES AND MATERIALS ON CONSTITUTIONAL ORD/FREE
RIGHTS AND LIBERTIES. USA+45 FORCES LEGIS DIPLOM   CONSTN
PRESS CONTROL CRIME WAR PWR...AUD/VIS T WORSHIP 20 NAT/G
NEGRO. PAGE 66 E1317

B64
MAKI J.M.,COURT AND CONSTITUTION IN JAPAN: SELECTED CONSTN
SUPREME COURT DECISIONS, 1948-60. LAW AGRI FAM   JURID
LEGIS BAL/PWR ADMIN CHOOSE...SOC ANTHOL CABINET 20 CT/SYS
CHINJAP CIVIL/LIB. PAGE 68 E1355   CRIME

B64
NEWMAN E.S.,POLICE, THE LAW, AND PERSONAL FREEDOM. JURID
USA+45 CONSTN JUDGE CT/SYS CRIME PERS/REL RESPECT   FORCES
...CRIMLGY 20. PAGE 77 E1542   ORD/FREE
                                                    ADJUD

B64
SIEKANOWICZ P.,LEGAL SOURCES AND BIBLIOGRAPHY OF   BIBLIOG
POLAND. COM POLAND CONSTN NAT/G PARL/PROC SANCTION ADJUD
CRIME MARXISM 16/20. PAGE 91 E1823   LAW
                                                    JURID

S64
BAKER H.R.,"INMATE SELF-GOVERNMENT." ACT/RES CREATE PUB/INST
CONTROL PARTIC ATTIT RIGID/FLEX QU. PAGE 7 E0141   CRIME
                                                    INGP/REL
                                                    REPRESENT

B65
MISSISSIPPI BLACK PAPER: (FIFTY-SEVEN NEGRO AND   COERCE
WHITE CITIZENS' TESTIMONY OF POLICE BRUTALITY...). RACE/REL
USA+45 LAW SOCIETY CT/SYS SANCTION CRIME MORAL   DISCRIM
ORD/FREE RESPECT 20 NEGRO. PAGE 2 E0035   FORCES

B65
AMERICAN ASSEMBLY COLUMBIA U,THE COURTS, THE   CT/SYS
PUBLIC, AND THE LAW EXPLOSION. USA+45 ELITES PROVS ADJUD
EDU/PROP CRIME CHOOSE PERSON ORD/FREE PWR 20.   NAT/G
PAGE 4 E0074

B65
ASSOCIATION BAR OF NYC,RADIO, TELEVISION, AND THE   AUD/VIS
ADMINISTRATION OF JUSTICE: A DOCUMENTED SURVEY OF   ATTIT

MATERIALS. USA+45 DELIB/GP FORCES PRESS ADJUD ORD/FREE
CONTROL CT/SYS CRIME...INT IDEA/COMP BIBLIOG.
PAGE 6 E0109

B65
BARKER L.J.,FREEDOM, COURTS, POLITICS: STUDIES IN JURID
CIVIL LIBERTIES. USA+45 LEGIS CREATE DOMIN PRESS CT/SYS
ADJUD LOBBY CRIME GP/REL RACE/REL MARXISM 20 ATTIT
CIVIL/LIB. PAGE 8 E0148 ORD/FREE

B65
BROMBERG W.,CRIME AND THE MIND. LAW LEGIT ADJUD CRIMLGY
CRIME MURDER AGE/Y ANOMIE BIO/SOC DRIVE SEX PSY. SOC
PAGE 16 E0305 HEALTH
COERCE

B65
CHARNAY J.P.,LE SUFFRAGE POLITIQUE EN FRANCE; CHOOSE
ELECTIONS PARLEMENTAIRES, ELECTION PRESIDENTIELLE, SUFF
REFERENDUMS. FRANCE CONSTN CHIEF DELIB/GP ECO/TAC NAT/G
EDU/PROP CRIME INGP/REL MORAL ORD/FREE PWR CATHISM LEGIS
20 PARLIAMENT PRESIDENT. PAGE 22 E0425

B65
GLUECK S.,ROSCOE POUND AND CRIMINAL JUSTICE. CT/SYS
SOCIETY FAM GOV/REL AGE/Y ATTIT ORD/FREE...CRIMLGY CRIME
BIOG ANTHOL SOC/INTEG 19/20. PAGE 44 E0875 LAW
ADJUD

B65
HARTUNG F.E.,CRIME, LAW, AND SOCIETY. LAW PUB/INST PERCEPT
CRIME PERS/REL AGE/Y BIO/SOC PERSON ROLE SUPEGO CRIMLGY
...LING GP/COMP GEN/LAWS 20. PAGE 50 E1004 DRIVE
CONTROL

B65
HOLDSWORTH W.S.,A HISTORY OF ENGLISH LAW; THE LAW
CENTURIES OF SETTLEMENT AND REFORM (VOL. XV). UK INDUS
CONSTN SECT LEGIS JUDGE WRITING ADJUD CT/SYS CRIME PROF/ORG
OWN...JURID IDEA/COMP 18 PARLIAMENT ENGLSH/LAW ATTIT
COMMON/LAW. PAGE 54 E1082

B65
HOWE R.,THE STORY OF SCOTLAND YARD: A HISTORY OF CRIMLGY
THE CID FROM THE EARLIEST TIMES TO THE PRESENT DAY. CRIME
UK MUNIC EDU/PROP 6/20 SCOT/YARD. PAGE 55 E1104 FORCES
ADMIN

B65
ISORNI J.,LES CAS DE CONSCIENCE DE L'AVOCAT. SUPEGO
FRANCE LAW ACT/RES CT/SYS PARTIC ROLE MORAL 20. JURID
PAGE 57 E1138 CRIME

B65
KAMISAR Y.,CRIMINAL JUSTICE IN OUR TIME. USA+45 ORD/FREE
FORCES JUDGE PROB/SOLV COERCE MORAL 20 CIVIL/LIB CRIME
CIV/RIGHTS. PAGE 59 E1182 CT/SYS
LAW

B65
KARIS T.,THE TREASON TRIAL IN SOUTH AFRICA: A GUIDE BIBLIOG/A
TO THE MICROFILM RECORD OF THE TRIAL. SOUTH/AFR LAW ADJUD
ELITES NAT/G LEGIT CT/SYS RACE/REL DISCRIM...SOC CRIME
20. PAGE 59 E1185 AFR

B65
LAFAVE W.R.,LAW AND SOVIET SOCIETY. EX/STRUC DIPLOM JURID
DOMIN EDU/PROP PRESS ADMIN CRIME OWN MARXISM 20 CT/SYS
KHRUSH/N. PAGE 62 E1244 ADJUD
GOV/REL

B65
MURPHY W.F.,WIRETAPPING ON TRIAL: A CASE STUDY IN JURID
THE JUDICIAL PROCESS. CONSTN ELITES CT/SYS CRIME LAW
MORAL ORD/FREE...DECISION SUPREME/CT. PAGE 75 E1511 POLICY

B65
RADZINOWICZ L.,THE NEED FOR CRIMINOLOGY AND A CRIMLGY
PROPOSAL FOR AN INSTITUTE OF CRIMINOLOGY. FUT UK PROF/ORG
USA+45 SOCIETY ACT/RES PROB/SOLV CRIME...PSY SOC ACADEM
BIBLIOG 20. PAGE 83 E1666 CONTROL

B66
AMERICAN JEWISH COMMITTEE,THE TYRANNY OF POVERTY BIBLIOG/A
(PAMPHLET). USA+45 LAW ECO/DEV LOC/G MUNIC NAT/G WEALTH
PUB/INST WORKER EDU/PROP CRIME...SOC/WK 20. PAGE 4 WELF/ST
E0080 PROB/SOLV

B66
ARCHER P.,FREEDOM AT STAKE. UK LAW NAT/G LEGIS ORD/FREE
JUDGE CRIME MORAL...CONCPT 20 CIVIL/LIB. PAGE 5 NAT/COMP
E0103 POLICY

B66
BEELEY A.L.,THE BAIL SYSTEM IN CHICAGO. LAW MUNIC JURID
PUB/INST EFFICIENCY MORAL...CRIMLGY METH/CNCPT STAT CT/SYS

20 CHICAGO. PAGE 9 E0176 CRIME
ADJUD

B66
COUNCIL OF STATE GOVERNMENTS,THE HANDBOOK ON CRIME
INTERSTATE CRIME CONTROL. USA+45 PUB/INST DELIB/GP GOV/REL
AGREE AGE/Y 20 INTST/CRIM. PAGE 27 E0524 CONTROL
JURID

B66
FLEISCHER B.M.,THE ECONOMICS OF DELINQUENCY. UNIV STRATA
WORKER STRANGE ANOMIE...STAT CHARTS 20. PAGE 38 INCOME
E0762 AGE/Y
CRIME

B66
GILLMOR D.M.,FREE PRESS AND FAIR TRIAL. UK USA+45 ORD/FREE
CONSTN PROB/SOLV PRESS CONTROL CRIME DISCRIM ADJUD
RESPECT...AUD/VIS 20 CIVIL/LIB. PAGE 44 E0865 ATTIT
EDU/PROP

B66
HAUSNER G.,JUSTICE IN JERUSALEM. GERMANY ISRAEL ADJUD
SOCIETY KIN DIPLOM LEGIT CT/SYS PARTIC MURDER CRIME
MAJORITY ATTIT FASCISM...INT/LAW JURID 20 JEWS RACE/REL
WAR/TRIAL. PAGE 51 E1013 COERCE

B66
HOEVELER H.J.,INTERNATIONALE BEKAMPFUNG DES CRIMLGY
VERBRECHENS. AUSTRIA SWITZERLND WOR+45 INT/ORG CRIME
CONTROL BIO/SOC...METH/COMP NAT/COMP 20 MAFIA DIPLOM
SCOT/YARD FBI. PAGE 53 E1064 INT/LAW

B66
MACIVER R.M.,THE PREVENTION AND CONTROL OF AGE/Y
DELINQUENCY. USA+45 STRATA PUB/INST ANOMIE ATTIT PLAN
HABITAT PERSON HEALTH...CRIMLGY PSY SOC METH. ADJUST
PAGE 67 E1341 CRIME

B66
MACMULLEN R.,ENEMIES OF THE ROMAN EMPIRE: TREASON, CRIME
UNREST, AND ALIENATION IN THE EMPIRE. ROMAN/EMP ADJUD
MUNIC CONTROL LEAD ATTIT PERSON MYSTISM...PHIL/SCI MORAL
BIBLIOG. PAGE 67 E1345 SOCIETY

B66
MC CONNELL J.P.,LAW AND BUSINESS: PATTERNS AND ECO/DEV
ISSUES IN COMMERCIAL LAW. USA+45 USA-45 LOC/G JURID
WORKER LICENSE CRIME REPRESENT GP/REL 20. PAGE 70 ADJUD
E1397 MGT

B66
OSTERMANN R.,A REPORT IN DEPTH ON CRIME IN AMERICA. CRIME
FUT USA+45 MUNIC PUB/INST TEC/DEV MURDER EFFICIENCY FORCES
ATTIT BIO/SOC...PSY 20. PAGE 79 E1584 CONTROL
LAW

B66
POWERS E.,CRIME AND PUNISHMENT IN EARLY CRIME
MASSACHUSETTS 1620-1692: A DOCUMENTARY HISTORY. ADJUD
USA-45 SECT LEGIS COLONIAL ATTIT ORD/FREE MYSTISM CT/SYS
17 PRE/US/AM MASSACHU. PAGE 82 E1643 PROVS

B66
SKOLNICK J.H.,JUSTICE WITHOUT TRIAL: LAW FORCES
ENFORCEMENT IN DEMOCRATIC SOCIETY. USA+45 LAW CRIMLGY
TRIBUTE RACE/REL BIO/SOC PERSON...PSY SOC 20 NEGRO CRIME
BUREAUCRCY PROSTITUTN. PAGE 92 E1836

B66
SZLADITS C.,A BIBLIOGRAPHY ON FOREIGN AND BIBLIOG/A
COMPARATIVE LAW (SUPPLEMENT 1964). FINAN FAM LABOR CT/SYS
LG/CO LEGIS JUDGE ADMIN CRIME...CRIMLGY 20. PAGE 95 INT/LAW
E1905

B66
US HOUSE COMM ON JUDICIARY,CIVIL COMMITMENT AND BIO/SOC
TREATMENT OF NARCOTIC ADDICTS. USA+45 SOCIETY FINAN CRIME
LEGIS PROB/SOLV GIVE CT/SYS SANCTION HEALTH IDEA/COMP
...POLICY HEAL 20. PAGE 100 E2008 CONTROL

B66
US PRES COMN CRIME IN DC,REPORT OF THE US CRIME
PRESIDENT'S COMMISSION ON CRIME IN THE DISTRICT OF FORCES
COLUMBIA. LEGIS WORKER EDU/PROP ADJUD CONTROL AGE/Y
CT/SYS GP/REL BIO/SOC HEALTH...CRIMLGY NEW/IDEA SANCTION
STAT 20. PAGE 101 E2022

B66
US SENATE COMM ON JUDICIARY,HEARINGS ON FREE PRESS PRESS
AND FAIR TRIAL (2 VOLS.). USA+45 CONSTN ELITES LAW
LEGIS EDU/PROP CT/SYS LEAD CONGRESS. PAGE 103 E2057 CRIME
ORD/FREE

B67
AMDS W.E.,DELINQUENCY PREVENTION: THEORY AND AGE/Y

PRACTICE. USA+45 SOCIETY FAM SCHOOL SECT FORCES
PROB/SOLV...HEAL JURID PREDICT ANTHOL. PAGE 4 E0071
CRIME
PUB/INST
LAW

B67
BERNSTEIN S.,ALTERNATIVES TO VIOLENCE: ALIENATED
YOUTH AND RIOTS, RACE AND POVERTY. MUNIC PUB/INST
SCHOOL INGP/REL RACE/REL UTOPIA DRIVE HABITAT ROLE
WEALTH...INT 20. PAGE 11 E0215
AGE/Y
SOC/WK
NEIGH
CRIME

B67
BONGER W.A.,CRIMINALITY AND ECONOMIC CONDITIONS.
MOD/EUR STRUCT INDUS WORKER EDU/PROP CRIME HABITAT
ALL/VALS...JURID SOC 20 REFORMERS. PAGE 14 E0265
PERSON
CRIMLGY
IDEA/COMP
ANOMIE

B67
CLINARD M.B.,CRIMINAL BEHAVIOR SYSTEMS: A TYPOLOGY.
WOR+45 LAW SOCIETY STRUCT R+D AGE/Y ATTIT WEALTH
...CLASSIF CHARTS METH/COMP METH. PAGE 23 E0457
BIBLIOG
CRIME
CRIMLGY
PERSON

B67
COX A.,CIVIL RIGHTS, THE CONSTITUTION, AND THE
COURTS. CONSTN EDU/PROP CRIME DISCRIM ATTIT...JURID
20. PAGE 27 E0533
LAW
FEDERAL
RACE/REL
PRESS

B67
FRIENDLY A.,CRIME AND PUBLICITY. TV CT/SYS SUPEGO
20. PAGE 41 E0811
PRESS
CRIME
ROLE
LAW

B67
HEWITT W.H.,ADMINISTRATION OF CRIMINAL JUSTICE IN
NEW YORK. LAW PROB/SOLV ADJUD ADMIN...CRIMLGY
CHARTS T 20 NEW/YORK. PAGE 52 E1035
CRIME
ROLE
CT/SYS
FORCES

B67
LENG S.C.,JUSTICE IN COMMUNIST CHINA: A SURVEY OF
THE JUDICIAL SYSTEM OF THE CHINESE PEOPLE'S
REPUBLIC. CHINA/COM LAW CONSTN LOC/G NAT/G PROF/ORG
CONSULT FORCES ADMIN CRIME ORD/FREE...BIBLIOG 20
MAO. PAGE 64 E1284
CT/SYS
ADJUD
JURID
MARXISM

B67
LOBLE L.H.,DELINQUENCY CAN BE STOPPED. FAM PUB/INST
CT/SYS ADJUST ATTIT...NEW/IDEA METH/COMP 20.
PAGE 66 E1315
AGE/Y
PROB/SOLV
ADJUD
CRIME

B67
MANVELL R.,THE INCOMPARABLE CRIME. GERMANY ACT/RES
DEATH...BIBLIOG 20 JEWS. PAGE 68 E1364
MURDER
CRIME
WAR
HIST/WRIT

B67
RUSSELL B.,WAR CRIMES IN VIETNAM. USA+45 VIETNAM
FORCES DIPLOM WEAPON RACE/REL DISCRIM ISOLAT
BIO/SOC 20 COLD/WAR RUSSELL/B. PAGE 87 E1736
WAR
CRIME
ATTIT
POLICY

B67
UNIVERSAL REFERENCE SYSTEM,CURRENT EVENTS AND
PROBLEMS OF MODERN SOCIETY (VOLUME V). WOR+45 LOC/G
MUNIC NAT/G PLAN EDU/PROP CRIME RACE/REL WEALTH
...COMPUT/IR GEN/METH. PAGE 98 E1974
BIBLIOG/A
SOCIETY
PROB/SOLV
ATTIT

S67
BLAKEY G.R.,"ORGANIZED CRIME IN THE UNITED STATES."
USA+45 USA-45 STRUCT LABOR NAT/G VOL/ASSN ADMIN
PERS/REL PWR...CRIMLGY INT 17/20. PAGE 12 E0240
CRIME
ELITES
CONTROL

S67
BLUMSTEIN A.,"POLICE TECHNOLOGY." USA+45 DELIB/GP
COMPUTER EDU/PROP CRIME COMPUT/IR. PAGE 13 E0253
TEC/DEV
FORCES
CRIMLGY
ADJUD

S67
CARTER R.M.,"SOME FACTORS IN SENTENCING POLICY."
LAW PUB/INST CRIME PERS/REL...POLICY JURID SOC
TREND CON/ANAL CHARTS SOC/EXP 20. PAGE 20 E0403
ADJUD
CT/SYS
ADMIN

S67
CHAMBLISS W.J.,"TYPES OF DEVIANCE AND THE
EFFECTIVENESS OF LEGAL SANCTIONS" SOCIETY PROB/SOLV
ADJUD CONTROL DETER. PAGE 21 E0417
CRIME
SANCTION
EFFICIENCY
LAW

S67
CLOGGER T.J.,"THE BIG EAR." UK USA+45 USSR LAW
LEGIS CRIME GP/REL INGP/REL ATTIT 20 FBI ESPIONAGE.
DIPLOM
ORD/FREE

PAGE 23 E0458
COM/IND
INSPECT

S67
COHN K.,"CRIMES AGAINST HUMANITY." GERMANY INT/ORG
SANCTION ATTIT ORD/FREE...MARXIST CRIMLGY 20 UN.
PAGE 24 E0469
WAR
INT/LAW
CRIME
ADJUD

S67
GLASER D.,"NATIONAL GOALS AND INDICATORS FOR THE
REDUCTION OF CRIME AND DELINQUENCY." FUT USA+45
NAT/G...CON/ANAL METH 20. PAGE 44 E0874
CRIME
CRIMLGY
LAW
STAT

S67
KENNEDY R.F.,"TOWARD A NATION WHERE THE LAW IS
KING." PLAN CT/SYS CRIME INGP/REL...JURID SOC.
PAGE 60 E1202
CRIMLGY
ADJUST
LAW
PUB/INST

S67
KETCHAM O.W.,"GUIDELINES FROM GAULT: REVOLUTIONARY
REQUIREMENTS AND REAPPRAISAL." LAW CONSTN CREATE
LEGIT ROUTINE SANCTION CRIME DISCRIM PRIVIL ROLE
...JURID NEW/IDEA 20 SUPREME/CT. PAGE 60 E1208
ADJUD
AGE/Y
CT/SYS

S67
MIRONENKO Y.,"A NEW EXTENSION OF CRIMINAL LIABILITY
IN THE USSR." COM USSR DOMIN EDU/PROP 20. PAGE 73
E1467
ADJUD
SANCTION
CRIME
MARXISM

S67
SCHELLING T.C.,"ECONOMICS AND CRIMINAL ENTERPRISE."
LAW FORCES BARGAIN ECO/TAC CONTROL GAMBLE ROUTINE
ADJUST DEMAND INCOME PROFIT CRIMLGY. PAGE 87 E1756
CRIME
PROB/SOLV
CONCPT

S67
WILSON G.D.,"CRIMINAL SANCTIONS AGAINST PASSPORT
AREA-RESTRICTION VIOLATIONS." USA+45 ADJUD CRIME
GOV/REL DEPT/STATE CONGRESS. PAGE 106 E2127
LAW
SANCTION
LICENSE
POLICY

B70
BLACKSTONE W.,COMMENTARIES ON THE LAWS OF ENGLAND
(4 VOLS.) (4TH ED.). UK CHIEF DELIB/GP LEGIS WORKER
CT/SYS SANCTION CRIME OWN...CRIMLGY 18 ENGLSH/LAW.
PAGE 12 E0238
LAW
JURID
ADJUD
CONSTN

B73
AUSTIN J.,LECTURES ON JURISPRUDENCE OR THE
PHILOSOPHY OF POSITIVE LAW (VOL. II) (4TH ED.,
REV.). UK CONSTN STRUCT PROB/SOLV LEGIT CT/SYS
SANCTION CRIME INGP/REL OWN SUPEGO ORD/FREE...T 19.
PAGE 6 E0120
LAW
ADJUD
JURID
METH/CNCPT

B76
BENTHAM J.,THE THEORY OF LEGISLATION. UK CREATE
CRIME ATTIT ORD/FREE...CONCPT 18 REFORMERS. PAGE 10
E0196
LEGIS
LAW
CRIMLGY
UTIL

B89
FICHTE J.G.,THE SCIENCE OF RIGHTS (TRANS. BY A.E.
KROEGER). WOR+45 FAM MUNIC NAT/G PROVS ADJUD CRIME
CHOOSE MARRIAGE SEX POPULISM 19 FICHTE/JG
NATURL/LAW. PAGE 37 E0744
ORD/FREE
CONSTN
LAW
CONCPT

B98
POLLOCK F.,THE HISTORY OF ENGLISH LAW BEFORE THE
TIME OF EDWARD I (2 VOLS, 2ND ED.). UK CULTURE
LOC/G LEGIS LICENSE AGREE CONTROL CT/SYS SANCTION
CRIME...TIME/SEQ 13 COMMON/LAW CANON/LAW. PAGE 81
E1626
LAW
ADJUD
JURID

CRIMINOLOGY....SEE CRIMLGY

CRIMLGY....CRIMINOLOGY

N
INDEX TO LEGAL PERIODICALS. CANADA NEW/ZEALND UK
USA+45 USA-45 CONSTN LEGIS JUDGE ADJUD ADMIN
CONTROL CT/SYS FEDERAL...CRIMLGY INT/LAW 20
CMN/WLTH AUSTRAL. PAGE 1 E0006
BIBLIOG
INDEX
LAW
JURID

N
INTERNATIONAL BIBLIOGRAPHY ON CRIME AND
DELINQUENCY. USA+45 LAW FORCES PROB/SOLV AGE/Y 20.
PAGE 1 E0023
BIBLIOG/A
CRIME
ANOMIE
CRIMLGY

B34
CULVER D.C.,BIBLIOGRAPHY OF CRIME AND CRIMINAL
JUSTICE, 1927-1931. LAW CULTURE PUB/INST PROB/SOLV
CT/SYS...PSY SOC STAT 20. PAGE 28 E0549
BIBLIOG/A
CRIMLGY
ADJUD

FORCES

CUMMING J.,A CONTRIBUTION TOWARD A BIBLIOGRAPHY
DEALING WITH CRIME AND COGNATE SUBJECTS (3RD ED.).
UK LAW CULTURE PUB/INST ADJUD AGE BIO/SOC...PSY SOC
SOC/WK STAT METH/COMP 20. PAGE 28 E0552
B35
BIBLIOG
CRIMLGY
FORCES
CT/SYS

HALL J.,THEFT, LAW, AND SOCIETY. SOCIETY PROB/SOLV
...CRIMLGY SOC CONCPT TREND METH/COMP 18/20
LARCENCY. PAGE 49 E0982
B35
CRIME
LAW
ADJUD
ADJUST

CULVER D.C.,METHODOLOGY OF SOCIAL SCIENCE RESEARCH:
A BIBLIOGRAPHY. LAW CULTURE...CRIMLGY GEOG STAT OBS
INT QU HIST/WRIT CHARTS 20. PAGE 28 E0550
B36
BIBLIOG/A
METH
SOC

CLEMMER D.,"LEADERSHIP PHENOMENA IN A PRISON
COMMUNITY." NEIGH PLAN CHOOSE PERSON ROLE...OBS
INT. PAGE 23 E0452
S38
PUB/INST
CRIMLGY
LEAD
CLIENT

CULVER D.C.,BIBLIOGRAPHY OF CRIME AND CRIMINAL
JUSTICE, 1932-1937. USA-45 LAW CULTURE PUB/INST
PROB/SOLV CT/SYS...PSY SOC STAT 20. PAGE 28 E0551
B39
BIBLIOG/A
CRIMLGY
ADJUD
FORCES

CLAGETT H.L.,A GUIDE TO THE LAW AND LEGAL
LITERATURE OF PARAGUAY. PARAGUAY CONSTN COM/IND
LABOR MUNIC JUDGE ADMIN CT/SYS...CRIMLGY INT/LAW
CON/ANAL 20. PAGE 22 E0439
B43
BIBLIOG
JURID
LAW
L/A+17C

VANCE H.L.,GUIDE TO THE LAW AND LEGAL LITERATURE OF
MEXICO. LAW CONSTN FINAN LABOR FORCES ADJUD ADMIN
...CRIMLGY PHIL/SCI CON/ANAL 20 MEXIC/AMER.
PAGE 103 E2070
B45
BIBLIOG/A
INT/LAW
JURID
CT/SYS

GILLIN J.L.,SOCIAL PATHOLOGY. SOCIETY SECT CRIME
ANOMIE DISPL ORD/FREE WEALTH...CRIMLGY PSY WORSHIP.
PAGE 44 E0864
B46
SOC
ADJUST
CULTURE
INGP/REL

CLAGETT H.L.,A GUIDE TO THE LAW AND LEGAL
LITERATURE OF BOLIVIA. L/A+17C CONSTN LABOR LEGIS
ADMIN...CRIMLGY INT/LAW PHIL/SCI 16/20 BOLIV.
PAGE 22 E0441
B47
BIBLIOG/A
JURID
LAW
CT/SYS

CLAGETT H.L.,A GUIDE TO THE LAW AND LEGAL
LITERATURE OF CHILE, 1917-1946. CHILE CONSTN LABOR
JUDGE ADJUD ADMIN...CRIMLGY INT/LAW JURID CON/ANAL
20. PAGE 22 E0442
B47
BIBLIOG
L/A+17C
LAW
LEGIS

CLAGETT H.L.,A GUIDE TO THE LAW AND LEGAL
LITERATURE OF ECUADOR. ECUADOR CONSTN LABOR LEGIS
JUDGE ADJUD ADMIN CIVMIL/REL...CRIMLGY INT/LAW
CON/ANAL 20. PAGE 22 E0443
B47
BIBLIOG
JURID
LAW
L/A+17C

CLAGETT H.L.,A GUIDE TO THE LAW AND LEGAL
LITERATURE OF PERU. PERU CONSTN COM/IND LABOR MUNIC
JUDGE ADMIN CT/SYS...CRIMLGY INT/LAW JURID 20.
PAGE 23 E0444
B47
BIBLIOG
L/A+17C
PHIL/SCI
LAW

CLAGETT H.L.,A GUIDE TO THE LAW AND LEGAL
LITERATURE OF VENEZUELA. VENEZUELA CONSTN LABOR
LEGIS JUDGE ADJUD ADMIN CIVMIL/REL...CRIMLGY JURID
CON/ANAL 20. PAGE 23 E0446
B47
BIBLIOG
L/A+17C
INT/LAW
LAW

CLAGETT H.L.,A GUIDE TO THE LAW AND LEGAL
LITERATURE OF ARGENTINA, 1917-1946. CONSTN LABOR
JUDGE ADJUD ADMIN...CRIMLGY INT/LAW JURID CON/ANAL
20 ARGEN. PAGE 23 E0447
B48
BIBLIOG
L/A+17C
LAW
LEGIS

LOWENTHAL M.,THE FEDERAL BUREAU OF INVESTIGATION.
USA+45 SOCIETY ADMIN TASK CRIME INGP/REL...CRIMLGY
20 FBI ESPIONAGE. PAGE 67 E1329
B50
FORCES
NAT/G
ATTIT
LAW

US FEDERAL BUREAU INVESTIGAT,BIBLIOGRAPHY OF CRIME
AND KINDRED SUBJECTS (PAPER). USA+45 PROB/SOLV
TREND. PAGE 100 E2001
B50
BIBLIOG/A
CRIME
LAW
CRIMLGY

WALTER P.A.F.,RACE AND CULTURE RELATIONS. FAM
HEALTH WEALTH...POLICY CRIMLGY GEOG BIBLIOG T 20.
PAGE 105 E2097
B52
RACE/REL
DISCRIM
GP/REL
CONCPT

COKE E.,INSTITUTES OF THE LAWS OF ENGLAND
(1628-1658). UK LAW ADJUD PERS/REL ORD/FREE
...CRIMLGY 11/17. PAGE 24 E0471
B53
JURID
OWN
CT/SYS
CONSTN

CARTER P.G.,STATISTICAL BULLETINS: AN ANNOTATED
BIBLIOGRAPHY OF THE GENERAL STATISTICAL BULLETINS
AND MAJOR POL SUBDIV OF WORLD. CULTURE AGRI FINAN
INDUS LABOR TEC/DEV INT/TRADE CT/SYS WEALTH
...CRIMLGY SOC 20. PAGE 20 E0400
B54
BIBLIOG/A
WOR+45
NAT/G
STAT

CAVAN R.S.,CRIMINOLOGY (2ND ED.). USA+45 LAW FAM
PUB/INST FORCES PLAN WAR AGE/Y PERSON ROLE SUPEGO
...CHARTS 20 FBI. PAGE 21 E0409
B55
DRIVE
CRIMLGY
CONTROL
METH/COMP

JAPAN MOMBUSHO DAIGAKU GAKIYUT,BIBLIOGRAPHY OF THE
STUDIES ON LAW AND POLITICS (PAMPHLET). CONSTN
INDUS LABOR DIPLOM TAX ADMIN...CRIMLGY INT/LAW 20
CHINJAP. PAGE 58 E1150
B55
BIBLIOG
LAW
PHIL/SCI

ALEXANDER F.,THE CRIMINAL, THE JUDGE, AND THE
PUBLIC. LAW CULTURE CONSULT LEGIT ADJUD SANCTION
ORD/FREE 20. PAGE 3 E0060
B56
CRIME
CRIMLGY
PSY
ATTIT

BROWNE D.G.,THE RISE OF SCOTLAND YARD: A HISTORY OF
THE METROPOLITAN POLICE. UK MUNIC CHIEF ADMIN CRIME
GP/REL 19/20. PAGE 16 E0316
B56
CRIMLGY
LEGIS
CONTROL
FORCES

COHEN A.,THE SUTHERLAND PAPERS. USA+45 USA-45 LAW
CONTROL CRIME AGE/Y...TREND ANTHOL BIBLIOG 20.
PAGE 23 E0461
B56
CRIMLGY
PHIL/SCI
ACT/RES
METH

SYKES G.M.,CRIME AND SOCIETY. LAW STRATA STRUCT
ACT/RES ROUTINE ANOMIE WEALTH...POLICY SOC/INTEG
20. PAGE 95 E1903
B56
CRIMLGY
CRIME
CULTURE
INGP/REL

CLEMMER D.,THE PRISON COMMUNITY. CULTURE CONTROL
LEAD ROUTINE PERS/REL PERSON...SOC METH/CNCPT.
PAGE 23 E0453
B58
PUB/INST
CRIMLGY
CLIENT
INGP/REL

DUCLOUX L.,FROM BLACKMAIL TO TREASON. FRANCE PLAN
DIPLOM EDU/PROP PRESS RUMOR NAT/LISM...CRIMLGY 20.
PAGE 33 E0653
B58
COERCE
CRIME
NAT/G
PWR

HALL J.,STUDIES IN JURISPRUDENCE AND CRIMINAL
THEORY. USA-45 LAW CULTURE CREATE SUPEGO...CRIMLGY
PSY /20 PLATO. PAGE 49 E0983
B58
JURID
CRIME
CONCPT
CT/SYS

CRESSEY D.R.,"ACHIEVEMENT OF AN UNSTATED
ORGANIZATIONAL GOAL: AN OBSERVATION ON PRISONS."
OP/RES PROB/SOLV PERS/REL ANOMIE ATTIT ROLE RESPECT
CRIMLGY. PAGE 28 E0546
S58
PUB/INST
CLIENT
NEIGH
INGP/REL

DASH S.,THE EAVESDROPPERS. USA+45 DELIB/GP TEC/DEV
ORD/FREE...POLICY CRIMLGY JURID 20 PRIVACY. PAGE 29
E0569
B59
CRIME
CONTROL
ACT/RES
LAW

KERREMANS-RAMIOULL,LE PROBLEME DE LA DELINQUENCE
JUVENILE (2ND ED.). FAM PUB/INST SCHOOL FORCES
LEGIS MORAL...CRIMLGY SOC 20. PAGE 60 E1205
B59
BIBLIOG
CRIME
AGE/Y
SOC/WK

CLOWARD R.A.,"ILLEGITIMATE MEANS, ANOMIE, AND
DEVIANT BEHAVIOR" STRUCT CRIME DRIVE PERSON...SOC
CONCPT NEW/IDEA 20 DURKHEIM/E MERTON/R. PAGE 23
S59
ANOMIE
CRIMLGY
LEGIT

E0459   ADJUST

B60

GIBNEY F.,THE OPERATORS. USA+45 LAW STRATA BIO/SOC   CRIME
MORAL ORD/FREE SOC. PAGE 43 E0858   CULTURE
                                                      ANOMIE
                                                      CRIMLGY

B61

DAVIS B.F.,THE DESPERATE AND THE DAMNED. USA+45 LAW   PUB/INST
DEATH ANOMIE...CRIMLGY 20 SAN/QUENTN. PAGE 29 E0571   SANCTION
                                                      CRIME

B61

MERTON R.K.,CONTEMPORARY SOCIAL PROBLEMS: AN   CRIME
INTRODUCTION TO THE SOCIOLOGY OF DEVIANT BEHAVIOR   ANOMIE
AND SOCIAL DISORGANIZATION. FAM MUNIC FORCES WORKER   STRANGE
PROB/SOLV INGP/REL RACE/REL ISOLAT...CRIMLGY GEOG   SOC
PSY T 20 NEGRO. PAGE 72 E1444

B62

DELANY V.T.H.,THE ADMINISTRATION OF JUSTICE IN   ADMIN
IRELAND. IRELAND CONSTN FINAN JUDGE COLONIAL CRIME   JURID
...CRIMLGY 19/20. PAGE 30 E0604   CT/SYS
                                                      ADJUD

B63

BLOCK E.B.,THE VINDICATORS. LAW FORCES CT/SYS   ATTIT
DISCRIM 19/20. PAGE 13 E0247   CRIME
                                                      ADJUD
                                                      CRIMLGY

B63

HOWARD W.S.,AMERICAN SLAVERS AND THE FEDERAL LAW: DIST/IND
1837-1862. USA-45 NAT/G LEGIT COERCE RACE/REL   CRIMLGY
WEALTH...POLICY BIBLIOG/A 19. PAGE 55 E1102   LAW
                                                      EXEC

B63

PALOTAI O.C.,PUBLICATIONS OF THE INSTITUTE OF   BIBLIOG/A
GOVERNMENT, 1930-1962. LAW PROVS SCHOOL WORKER   ADMIN
ACT/RES OP/RES CT/SYS GOV/REL...CRIMLGY SOC/WK.   LOC/G
PAGE 79 E1594   FINAN

B64

DRESSLER D.,READINGS IN CRIMINOLOGY AND PENOLOGY.   CRIMLGY
UNIV CULTURE PUB/INST FORCES ACT/RES PROB/SOLV   CRIME
ANOMIE BIO/SOC SUPEGO...GEOG PSY ANTHOL 20. PAGE 33   ADJUD
E0648   ADJUST

B64

NEWMAN E.S.,POLICE, THE LAW, AND PERSONAL FREEDOM.   JURID
USA+45 CONSTN JUDGE CT/SYS CRIME PERS/REL RESPECT   FORCES
...CRIMLGY 20. PAGE 77 E1542   ORD/FREE
                                                      ADJUD

B64

SHKLAR J.N.,LEGALISM. CREATE PROB/SOLV CT/SYS   MORAL
...POLICY CRIMLGY DECISION JURID METH/CNCPT.   LAW
PAGE 91 E1821   NEW/IDEA

B65

BROMBERG W.,CRIME AND THE MIND. LAW LEGIT ADJUD   CRIMLGY
CRIME MURDER AGE/Y ANOMIE BIO/SOC DRIVE SEX PSY.   SOC
PAGE 16 E0305   HEALTH
                                                      COERCE

B65

GLUECK S.,ROSCOE POUND AND CRIMINAL JUSTICE.   CT/SYS
SOCIETY FAM GOV/REL AGE/Y ATTIT ORD/FREE...CRIMLGY   CRIME
BIOG ANTHOL SOC/INTEG 19/20. PAGE 44 E0875   LAW
                                                      ADJUD

B65

HARTUNG F.E.,CRIME, LAW, AND SOCIETY. LAW PUB/INST   PERCEPT
CRIME PERS/REL AGE/Y BIO/SOC PERSON ROLE SUPEGO   CRIMLGY
...LING GP/COMP GEN/LAWS 20. PAGE 50 E1004   DRIVE
                                                      CONTROL

B65

HOWE R.,THE STORY OF SCOTLAND YARD: A HISTORY OF   CRIMLGY
THE CID FROM THE EARLIEST TIMES TO THE PRESENT DAY.   CRIME
UK MUNIC EDU/PROP 6/20 SCOT/YARD. PAGE 55 E1104   FORCES
                                                      ADMIN

B65

RADZINOWICZ L.,THE NEED FOR CRIMINOLOGY AND A   CRIMLGY
PROPOSAL FOR AN INSTITUTE OF CRIMINOLOGY. FUT UK   PROF/ORG
USA+45 SOCIETY ACT/RES PROB/SOLV CRIME...PSY SOC   ACADEM
BIBLIOG 20. PAGE 83 E1666   CONTROL

B65

UNESCO,INTERNATIONAL ORGANIZATIONS IN THE SOCIAL   INT/ORG
SCIENCES(REV. ED.). LAW ADMIN ATTIT...CRIMLGY GEOG   R+D
INT/LAW PSY SOC STAT 20 UNESCO. PAGE 98 E1962   PROF/ORG
                                                      ACT/RES

B66

BEELEY A.L.,THE BAIL SYSTEM IN CHICAGO. LAW MUNIC   JURID
PUB/INST EFFICIENCY MORAL...CRIMLGY METH/CNCPT STAT   CT/SYS
20 CHICAGO. PAGE 9 E0176   CRIME
                                                      ADJUD

B66

HOEVELER H.J.,INTERNATIONALE BEKAMPFUNG DES   CRIMLGY
VERBRECHENS. AUSTRIA SWITZERLND WOR+45 INT/ORG   CRIME
CONTROL BIO/SOC...METH/COMP NAT/COMP 20 MAFIA   DIPLOM
SCOT/YARD FBI. PAGE 53 E1064   INT/LAW

B66

MACIVER R.M.,THE PREVENTION AND CONTROL OF   AGE/Y
DELINQUENCY. USA+45 STRATA PUB/INST ANOMIE ATTIT   PLAN
HABITAT PERSON HEALTH...CRIMLGY PSY SOC METH.   ADJUST
PAGE 67 E1341   CRIME

B66

SKOLNICK J.H.,JUSTICE WITHOUT TRIAL: LAW   FORCES
ENFORCEMENT IN DEMOCRATIC SOCIETY. USA+45 LAW   CRIMLGY
TRIBUTE RACE/REL BIO/SOC PERSON...PSY SOC 20 NEGRO   CRIME
BUREAUCRCY PROSTITUTN. PAGE 92 E1836

B66

SZLADITS C.,A BIBLIOGRAPHY ON FOREIGN AND   BIBLIOG/A
COMPARATIVE LAW (SUPPLEMENT 1964). FINAN FAM LABOR   CT/SYS
LG/CO LEGIS JUDGE ADMIN CRIME...CRIMLGY 20. PAGE 95   INT/LAW
E1905

B66

US PRES COMN CRIME IN DC,REPORT OF THE US   CRIME
PRESIDENT'S COMMISSION ON CRIME IN THE DISTRICT OF   FORCES
COLUMBIA. LEGIS WORKER EDU/PROP ADJUD CONTROL   AGE/Y
CT/SYS GP/REL BIO/SOC HEALTH...CRIMLGY NEW/IDEA   SANCTION
STAT 20. PAGE 101 E2022

B67

BONGER W.A.,CRIMINALITY AND ECONOMIC CONDITIONS.   PERSON
MOD/EUR STRUCT INDUS WORKER EDU/PROP CRIME HABITAT   CRIMLGY
ALL/VALS...JURID SOC 20 REFORMERS. PAGE 14 E0265   IDEA/COMP
                                                      ANOMIE

B67

CLINARD M.B.,CRIMINAL BEHAVIOR SYSTEMS: A TYPOLOGY.   BIBLIOG
WOR+45 LAW SOCIETY STRUCT R+D AGE/Y ATTIT WEALTH   CRIME
...CLASSIF CHARTS METH/COMP METH. PAGE 23 E0457   CRIMLGY
                                                      PERSON

B67

ELDRIDGE W.B.,NARCOTICS AND THE LAW: A CRITIQUE OF   LAW
THE AMERICAN EXPERIMENT IN NARCOTIC DRUG CONTROL.   INSPECT
PUB/INST ACT/RES PLAN LICENSE GP/REL EFFICIENCY   BIO/SOC
ATTIT HEALTH...CRIMLGY HEAL STAT 20 ABA DEPT/HEW   JURID
NARCO/ACT. PAGE 34 E0679

B67

HEWITT W.H.,ADMINISTRATION OF CRIMINAL JUSTICE IN   CRIME
NEW YORK. LAW PROB/SOLV ADJUD ADMIN...CRIMLGY   ROLE
CHARTS T 20 NEW/YORK. PAGE 52 E1035   CT/SYS
                                                      FORCES

S67

BLAKEY G.R.,"ORGANIZED CRIME IN THE UNITED STATES."   CRIME
USA+45 USA-45 STRUCT LABOR NAT/G VOL/ASSN ADMIN   ELITES
PERS/REL PWR...CRIMLGY INT 17/20. PAGE 12 E0240   CONTROL

S67

BLUMSTEIN A.,"POLICE TECHNOLOGY." USA+45 DELIB/GP   TEC/DEV
COMPUTER EDU/PROP CRIME COMPUT/IR. PAGE 13 E0253   FORCES
                                                      CRIMLGY
                                                      ADJUD

S67

COHN K.,"CRIMES AGAINST HUMANITY." GERMANY INT/ORG   WAR
SANCTION ATTIT ORD/FREE...MARXIST CRIMLGY 20 UN.   INT/LAW
PAGE 24 E0469   CRIME
                                                      ADJUD

S67

GLASER D.,"NATIONAL GOALS AND INDICATORS FOR THE   CRIME
REDUCTION OF CRIME AND DELINQUENCY." FUT USA+45   CRIMLGY
NAT/G...CON/ANAL METH 20. PAGE 44 E0874   LAW
                                                      STAT

S67

KENNEDY R.F.,"TOWARD A NATION WHERE THE LAW IS   CRIMLGY
KING." PLAN CT/SYS CRIME INGP/REL...JURID SOC.   ADJUST
PAGE 60 E1202   LAW
                                                      PUB/INST

S67

SCHELLING T.C.,"ECONOMICS AND CRIMINAL ENTERPRISE."   CRIME
LAW FORCES BARGAIN ECO/TAC CONTROL GAMBLE ROUTINE   PROB/SOLV
ADJUST DEMAND INCOME PROFIT CRIMLGY. PAGE 87 E1756   CONCPT

B70
BLACKSTONE W.,COMMENTARIES ON THE LAWS OF ENGLAND   LAW
(4 VOLS.) (4TH ED.). UK CHIEF DELIB/GP LEGIS WORKER JURID
CT/SYS SANCTION CRIME OWN...CRIMLGY 18 ENGLSH/LAW.   ADJUD
PAGE 12 E0238   CONSTN

B76
BENTHAM J.,THE THEORY OF LEGISLATION. UK CREATE   LEGIS
CRIME ATTIT ORD/FREE...CONCPT 18 REFORMERS. PAGE 10 LAW
E0196   CRIMLGY
UTIL

CRIMNL/LAW....CRIMINAL LAW

CROMWELL/O....OLIVER CROMWELL

B34
CLYDE W.M.,THE STRUGGLE FOR THE FREEDOM OF THE   PRESS
PRESS FROM CAXTON TO CROMWELL. UK LAW LOC/G SECT   ORD/FREE
FORCES LICENSE WRITING SANCTION REV ATTIT PWR   CONTROL
...POLICY 15/17 PARLIAMENT CROMWELL/O MILTON/J.
PAGE 23 E0460

B49
WORMUTH F.D.,THE ORIGINS OF MODERN   NAT/G
CONSTITUTIONALISM. GREECE UK LEGIS CREATE TEC/DEV   CONSTN
BAL/PWR DOMIN ADJUD REV WAR PWR...JURID ROMAN/REP   LAW
CROMWELL/O. PAGE 107 E2146

B61
AYLMER G.,THE KING'S SERVANTS. UK ELITES CHIEF PAY   ADMIN
CT/SYS WEALTH 17 CROMWELL/O CHARLES/I. PAGE 6 E0122 ROUTINE
EX/STRUC
NAT/G

CROSS-PRESSURES .... SEE ROLE

CROUZET M. E0123

CROWD....MOB BEHAVIOR, MASS BEHAVIOR

N19
JANOWITZ M.,SOCIAL CONTROL OF ESCALATED RIOTS   CROWD
(PAMPHLET). USA+45 USA-45 LAW SOCIETY MUNIC FORCES   ORD/FREE
PROB/SOLV EDU/PROP TV CRIME ATTIT...BIBLIOG 20   CONTROL
NEGRO CIV/RIGHTS. PAGE 58 E1148   RACE/REL

B52
COLEMAN J.W. JR.,DEATH AT THE COURT-HOUSE. CONTROL   CROWD
COERCE 20 KENTUCKY. PAGE 24 E0472   ORD/FREE
CRIME
CT/SYS

B52
FORSTER A.,THE TROUBLE MAKERS. USA+45 LAW CULTURE   DISCRIM
SOCIETY STRUCT VOL/ASSN CROWD GP/REL MORAL...PSY   SECT
SOC CONCPT 20 NEGRO JEWS. PAGE 39 E0771   RACE/REL
ATTIT

B59
HOBSBAWM E.J.,PRIMITIVE REBELS: STUDIES IN ARCHAIC   SOCIETY
FORMS OF SOCIAL MOVEMENT IN THE 19TH AND 20TH   CRIME
CENTURIES. ITALY SPAIN CULTURE VOL/ASSN RISK CROWD   REV
GP/REL INGP/REL ISOLAT TOTALISM...PSY SOC 18/20.   GUERRILLA
PAGE 53 E1058

B60
BAYLEY D.H.,VIOLENT AGITATION AND THE DEMOCRATIC   COERCE
PROCESS IN INDIA. INDIA LAW POL/PAR 20. PAGE 8   CROWD
E0159   CONSTN
PROB/SOLV

B62
CURRY J.E.,RACE TENSIONS AND THE POLICE. LAW MUNIC   FORCES
NEIGH TEC/DEV RUMOR CONTROL COERCE GP/REL ATTIT   RACE/REL
...SOC 20 NEGRO. PAGE 28 E0558   CROWD
ORD/FREE

B62
HEYDECKER J.J.,THE NUREMBERG TRIAL: HISTORY OF NAZI LAW
GERMANY AS REVEALED THROUGH THE TESTIMONY AT   CRIME
NUREMBERG. EUR+WWI GERMANY VOL/ASSN LEAD COERCE   PARTIC
CROWD INGP/REL RACE/REL SUPEGO ORD/FREE...CONCPT 20 TOTALISM
NAZI ANTI/SEMIT NUREMBERG JEWS. PAGE 52 E1036

B63
LIVELY E.,THE INVASION OF MISSISSIPPI. USA+45 LAW   RACE/REL
CONSTN NAT/G PROVS CT/SYS GOV/REL FEDERAL CONSERVE   CROWD
...TRADIT 20 MISSISSIPP NEGRO NAACP WARRN/EARL   COERCE
KENNEDY/JF. PAGE 66 E1309   MARXISM

B65
SMITH R.C.,THEY CLOSED THEIR SCHOOLS. USA+45 NEIGH   RACE/REL
ADJUD CROWD CONSEN WEALTH...DECISION OBS INT 20   DISCRIM
NEGRO VIRGINIA. PAGE 92 E1846   LOC/G

B66
KUNSTLER W.M.,"DEEP IN MY HEART" USA+45 LAW   CT/SYS
PROF/ORG SECT LOBBY PARTIC CROWD DISCRIM ROLE   RACE/REL
...BIOG 20 KING/MAR/L NEGRO CIV/RIGHTS SOUTH/US.   ADJUD
PAGE 62 E1233   CONSULT

CROWE S.E. E0548

CRUMP/ED....EDWARD H. CRUMP

CRUSADES....CRUSADES, CRUSADERS OF HOLY WARS

CT/APPEALS....COURT OF APPEALS AND APPELLATE COURT SYSTEM

CT/SYS....COURT SYSTEMS;SEE ALSO COURT/SYS

N
INTERNATIONAL COMN JURISTS,AFRICAN CONFERENCE ON   CT/SYS
THE RULE OF LAW. AFR INT/ORG LEGIS DIPLOM CONFER   JURID
COLONIAL ORD/FREE...CONCPT METH/COMP 20. PAGE 57   DELIB/GP
E1131

N
KEITT L.,AN ANNOTATED BIBLIOGRAPHY OF   BIBLIOG/A
BIBLIOGRAPHIES OF STATUTORY MATERIALS OF THE UNITED LAW
STATES. CHRIST-17C USA-45 LEGIS ADJUD COLONIAL   CONSTN
CT/SYS...JURID 16/20. PAGE 60 E1196   PROVS

N
AMERICAN JOURNAL OF INTERNATIONAL LAW. WOR+45   BIBLIOG/A
WOR-45 CONSTN INT/ORG NAT/G CT/SYS ARMS/CONT WAR   INT/LAW
...DECISION JURID NAT/COMP 20. PAGE 1 E0001   DIPLOM
ADJUD

N
INDEX TO LEGAL PERIODICALS. CANADA NEW/ZEALND UK   BIBLIOG
USA+45 USA-45 CONSTN LEGIS JUDGE ADMIN   INDEX
CONTROL CT/SYS FEDERAL...CRIMLGY INT/LAW 20   LAW
CMN/WLTH AUSTRAL. PAGE 1 E0006   JURID

N
JOURNAL OF POLITICS. USA+45 USA-45 CONSTN POL/PAR   BIBLIOG/A
EX/STRUC LEGIS PROB/SOLV DIPLOM CT/SYS CHOOSE   NAT/G
RACE/REL 20. PAGE 1 E0011   LAW
LOC/G

N
MIDWEST JOURNAL OF POLITICAL SCIENCE. USA+45 CONSTN BIBLIOG/A
ECO/DEV LEGIS PROB/SOLV CT/SYS LEAD GOV/REL ATTIT   NAT/G
POLICY. PAGE 1 E0012   DIPLOM
POL/PAR

N
ARBITRATION JOURNAL. WOR+45 LAW INDUS JUDGE DIPLOM   BIBLIOG
CT/SYS INGP/REL 20. PAGE 1 E0016   MGT
LABOR
ADJUD

N
CANON LAW ABSTRACTS. LEGIT CONFER CT/SYS INGP/REL   BIBLIOG/A
MARRIAGE ATTIT MORAL WORSHIP 20. PAGE 2 E0026   CATHISM
SECT
LAW

N
HARVARD LAW SCHOOL LIBRARY,ANNUAL LEGAL   BIBLIOG
BIBLIOGRAPHY. USA+45 CONSTN LEGIS ADJUD CT/SYS   JURID
...POLICY 20. PAGE 50 E1005   LAW
INT/LAW

N
HARVARD UNIVERSITY LAW LIBRARY,CATALOG OF   BIBLIOG
INTERNATIONAL LAW AND RELATIONS. WOR+45 WOR-45   INT/LAW
INT/ORG NAT/G JUDGE DIPLOM INT/TRADE ADJUD CT/SYS   JURID
19/20. PAGE 51 E1007

N
TURNER R.K.,BIBLIOGRAPHY ON WORLD ORGANIZATION.   BIBLIOG/A
INT/TRADE CT/SYS ARMS/CONT WEALTH...INT/LAW 20.   INT/ORG
PAGE 97 E1944   PEACE
WAR

N
US SUPERINTENDENT OF DOCUMENTS,POLITICAL SCIENCE: BIBLIOG/A
GOVERNMENT. CRIME. DISTRICT OF COLUMBIA (PRICE LIST NAT/G
54). USA+45 LAW CONSTN EX/STRUC WORKER ADJUD ADMIN   CRIME
CT/SYS CHOOSE INGP/REL RACE/REL CONGRESS PRESIDENT.
PAGE 103 E2063

B00
DARBY W.E.,INTERNATIONAL TRIBUNALS. WOR-45 NAT/G   INT/ORG
ECO/TAC DOMIN LEGIT CT/SYS COERCE ORD/FREE PWR   ADJUD
SOVEREIGN JURID. PAGE 29 E0567   PEACE
INT/LAW

B03
GRIFFIN A.P.C.,LIST OF BOOKS ON THE CONSTITUTION OF   BIBLIOG/A
THE UNITED STATES (PAMPHLET). USA-45 NAT/G EX/STRUC   CONSTN
JUDGE TOP/EX CT/SYS 18/20 CONGRESS PRESIDENT   LAW
SUPREME/CT. PAGE 46 E0920   JURID

B04
BURKE E.,A LETTER TO THE SHERIFFS OF BRISTOL   LEGIS
(1777). USA-45 LAW ECO/TAC COLONIAL CT/SYS REV   ADJUD
GP/REL ORD/FREE...POLICY 18 PARLIAMENT BURKE/EDM.   CRIME
PAGE 17 E0341

B04
FREUND E.,THE POLICE POWER; PUBLIC POLICY AND   CONSTN
CONSTITUTIONAL RIGHTS. USA-45 SOCIETY LOC/G NAT/G   LAW
FORCES LEGIS ADJUD CT/SYS OWN PWR...JURID 18/19   ORD/FREE
SUPREME/CT. PAGE 40 E0795   CONTROL

B05
DICEY A.V.,LECTURES ON THE RELATION BETWEEN LAW AND   LAW
PUBLIC OPINION IN ENGLAND DURING THE NINETEENTH   ADJUD
CENTURY. UK LEGIS CT/SYS...JURID 19 TORY/PARTY   ATTIT
BENTHAM/J ENGLSH/LAW. PAGE 31 E0621   IDEA/COMP

B07
BENTHAM J.,AN INTRODUCTION TO THE PRINCIPLES OF   LAW
MORALS AND LEGISLATION. UNIV CONSTN CULTURE SOCIETY   GEN/LAWS
NAT/G CONSULT LEGIS JUDGE ADJUD CT/SYS...JURID
CONCPT NEW/IDEA. PAGE 10 E0190

B09
HARVARD UNIVERSITY LAW LIBRARY,CATALOGUE OF THE   BIBLIOG/A
LIBRARY OF THE LAW SCHOOL OF HARVARD UNIVERSITY (3   LAW
VOLS.). UK USA-45 LEGIS JUDGE ADJUD CT/SYS...JURID   ADMIN
CHARTS 14/20. PAGE 51 E1008

B09
HOLLAND T.E.,LETTERS UPON WAR AND NEUTRALITY.   LAW
WOR-45 NAT/G FORCES JUDGE ECO/TAC LEGIT CT/SYS   INT/LAW
NEUTRAL ROUTINE COERCE...JURID TIME/SEQ 20. PAGE 55   INT/ORG
E1085   WAR

B09
JUSTINIAN,THE DIGEST (DIGESTA CORPUS JURIS CIVILIS)   JURID
(2 VOLS.) (TRANS. BY C. H. MONRO). ROMAN/EMP LAW   CT/SYS
FAM LOC/G LEGIS EDU/PROP CONTROL MARRIAGE OWN ROLE   NAT/G
CIVIL/LAW. PAGE 59 E1177   STRATA

B12
BEARD C.A.,THE SUPREME COURT AND THE CONSTITUTION.   CONSTN
LAW NAT/G PROVS LEGIS GOV/REL ATTIT POPULISM   CT/SYS
SUPREME/CT. PAGE 9 E0164   ADJUD
                                                      CONTROL

B13
ADAMS B.,THE THEORY OF SOCIAL REVOLUTIONS. FUT   CAP/ISM
USA-45 GP/REL PEACE...NEW/IDEA 20. PAGE 3 E0047   REV
                                                      SOCIETY
                                                      CT/SYS

N13
SCHMIDHAUSER J.R.,JUDICIAL BEHAVIOR AND THE   JUDGE
SECTIONAL CRISIS OF 1837-1860. USA-45 ADJUD CT/SYS   POL/PAR
INGP/REL ATTIT HABITAT...DECISION PSY STAT CHARTS   PERS/COMP
SIMUL. PAGE 88 E1759   PERSON

B14
CRAIG J.,ELEMENTS OF POLITICAL SCIENCE (3 VOLS.).   PHIL/SCI
CONSTN AGRI INDUS SCHOOL FORCES TAX CT/SYS SUFF   NAT/G
MORAL WEALTH...CONCPT 19 CIVIL/LIB. PAGE 27 E0539   ORD/FREE

B16
SALMOND J.W.,JURISPRUDENCE. UK LOC/G NAT/G LEGIS   LAW
PROB/SOLV LICENSE LEGIT CRIME PERS/REL OWN ORD/FREE   CT/SYS
...T 20. PAGE 87 E1742   JURID
                                                      ADJUD

L16
WRIGHT Q.,"THE ENFORCEMENT OF INTERNATIONAL LAW   INT/ORG
THROUGH MUNICIPAL LAW IN THE US." USA-45 LOC/G   LAW
NAT/G PUB/INST FORCES LEGIT CT/SYS PERCEPT ALL/VALS   INT/LAW
...JURID 20. PAGE 107 E2149   WAR

B18
EYBERS G.W.,SELECT CONSTITUTIONAL DOCUMENTS   CONSTN
ILLUSTRATING SOUTH AFRICAN HISTORY 1795-1910.   LAW
SOUTH/AFR LOC/G LEGIS CT/SYS...JURID ANTHOL 18/20   NAT/G
NATAL CAPE/HOPE ORANGE/STA. PAGE 36 E0707   COLONIAL

B18
WILSON W.,THE STATE: ELEMENTS OF HISTORICAL AND   NAT/G
PRACTICAL POLITICS. FRANCE GERMANY ITALY UK USSR   JURID
CONSTN EX/STRUC LEGIS CT/SYS WAR PWR...POLICY   CONCPT
GOV/COMP 20. PAGE 106 E2131   NAT/COMP

S18
POWELL T.R.,"THE LOGIC AND RHETORIC OF   CONSTN
CONSTITUTIONAL LAW" (BMR)" USA+45 USA-45 DELIB/GP   LAW
PROB/SOLV ADJUD CT/SYS...DECISION 20 SUPREME/CT   JURID
CON/INTERP. PAGE 82 E1642   LOG

B19
SMITH R.H.,JUSTICE AND THE POOR. LAW RECEIVE ADJUD   CT/SYS
CRIME GOV/REL COST...JURID SOC/WK CONCPT STAT   DISCRIM
CHARTS GP/COMP 20. PAGE 92 E1847   WEALTH

N19
IN THE SHADOW OF FEAR; AMERICAN CIVIL LIBERTIES,   ORD/FREE
1948-49 (PAMPHLET). COM LAW LEGIS BAL/PWR EDU/PROP   CONSTN
CT/SYS RACE/REL DISCRIM MARXISM SOCISM 20 COLD/WAR   POLICY
CONGRESS ACLU CIV/RIGHTS ESPIONAGE. PAGE 2 E0030

N19
BRENNAN W.J. JR.,THE BILL OF RIGHTS AND THE STATES   CONSTN
(PAMPHLET). USA+45 USA-45 LEGIS BAL/PWR ADJUD   PROVS
CT/SYS FEDERAL PWR SOVEREIGN 18/20 SUPREME/CT   GOV/REL
BILL/RIGHT. PAGE 15 E0293   ORD/FREE

N19
BURRUS B.R.,INVESTIGATION AND DISCOVERY IN STATE   NAT/G
ANTITRUST (PAMPHLET). USA+45 USA-45 LEGIS ECO/TAC   PROVS
ADMIN CONTROL CT/SYS CRIME GOV/REL PWR...JURID   LAW
CHARTS 19/20 FTC MONOPOLY. PAGE 18 E0346   INSPECT

N19
GIBB A.D.,JUDICIAL CORRUPTION IN THE UNITED KINGDOM   MORAL
(PAMPHLET). UK DELIB/GP CT/SYS CRIME PERSON SUPEGO   ATTIT
17/20 SCOTLAND. PAGE 43 E0856   ADJUD

N19
POUND R.,ORGANIZATION OF THE COURTS (PAMPHLET).   CT/SYS
MOD/EUR UK USA-45 ADJUD PWR...GOV/COMP 10/20   JURID
EUROPE. PAGE 82 E1635   STRUCT
                                                      ADMIN

C20
BLACHLY F.F.,"THE GOVERNMENT AND ADMINISTRATION OF   NAT/G
GERMANY." GERMANY CONSTN LOC/G PROVS DELIB/GP   GOV/REL
EX/STRUC FORCES LEGIS TOP/EX CT/SYS...BIBLIOG/A   ADMIN
19/20. PAGE 12 E0235   PHIL/SCI

B21
BRYCE J.,MODERN DEMOCRACIES. FUT NEW/ZEALND USA-45   NAT/G
LAW CONSTN POL/PAR PROVS VOL/ASSN EX/STRUC LEGIS   TREND
LEGIT CT/SYS EXEC KNOWL CONGRESS AUSTRAL 20.
PAGE 16 E0322

B21
CARDOZO B.N.,THE NATURE OF THE JUDICIAL PROCESS.   JURID
ROUTINE ORD/FREE...POLICY 20. PAGE 19 E0377   CT/SYS
                                                      LEAD
                                                      DECISION

B21
OPPENHEIM L.,THE FUTURE OF INTERNATIONAL LAW.   INT/ORG
EUR+WWI MOD/EUR LAW LEGIS JUDGE LEGIT ORD/FREE   CT/SYS
...JURID TIME/SEQ GEN/LAWS 20. PAGE 79 E1578   INT/LAW

B22
FARRAND M.,THE FRAMING OF THE CONSTITUTION OF THE   CONSTN
UNITED STATES (1913). USA-45 EX/STRUC PROB/SOLV   DELIB/GP
PERSON. PAGE 36 E0721   LEGIS
                                                      CT/SYS

B24
CARDOZO B.,THE GROWTH OF THE LAW. USA-45 CULTURE   LAW
...JURID 20. PAGE 19 E0376   ADJUD
                                                      CT/SYS

B24
HOLDSWORTH W.S.,A HISTORY OF ENGLISH LAW; THE   LAW
COMMON LAW AND ITS RIVALS (VOL. V). UK SEA EX/STRUC   LEGIS
WRITING ADMIN...INT/LAW JURID CONCPT IDEA/COMP   ADJUD
WORSHIP 16/17 PARLIAMENT ENGLSH/LAW COMMON/LAW.   CT/SYS
PAGE 54 E1073

B24
HOLDSWORTH W.S.,A HISTORY OF ENGLISH LAW; THE   LAW
COMMON LAW AND ITS RIVALS (VOL. VI). UK STRATA   CONSTN
EX/STRUC ADJUD CONTROL CT/SYS...JURID CONCPT   LEGIS
GEN/LAWS 17 COMMONWLTH PARLIAMENT ENGLSH/LAW   CHIEF
COMMON/LAW. PAGE 54 E1074

B24
HOLDSWORTH W.S.,A HISTORY OF ENGLISH LAW; THE   LAW
COMMON LAW AND ITS RIVALS (VOL. IV). UK SEA AGRI   LEGIS
CHIEF ADJUD CONTROL CRIME GOV/REL...INT/LAW JURID   CT/SYS
NAT/COMP 16/17 PARLIAMENT COMMON/LAW CANON/LAW   CONSTN
ENGLSH/LAW. PAGE 54 E1075

B25
WINFIELD P.H.,THE CHIEF SOURCES OF ENGLISH LEGAL   BIBLIOG/A
HISTORY. UK CONSTN JUDGE ADJUD CT/SYS 13/18.   JURID
PAGE 107 E2133   LAW

L25
HUDSON M.,"THE PERMANENT COURT OF INTERNATIONAL   INT/ORG
JUSTICE AND THE QUESTION OF AMERICAN   ADJUD
PARTICIPATION." WOR-45 LEGIT CT/SYS ORD/FREE   DIPLOM
...JURID CONCPT TIME/SEQ GEN/LAWS VAL/FREE 20 ICJ. INT/LAW
PAGE 56 E1108

B26
BEALE J.H.,A BIBLIOGRAPHY OF EARLY ENGLISH LAW   BIBLIOG/A
BOOKS. MOD/EUR UK PRESS ADJUD CT/SYS ATTIT...CHARTS JURID
10/16. PAGE 8 E0161   LAW

B27
DICKINSON J.,ADMINISTRATIVE JUSTICE AND THE   CT/SYS
SUPREMACY OF LAW IN THE UNITED STATES. USA-45 LAW   ADJUD
INDUS DOMIN EDU/PROP CONTROL EXEC GP/REL ORD/FREE   ADMIN
...POLICY JURID 19/20. PAGE 31 E0623   NAT/G

B28
BENTHAM J.,A COMMENT OF THE COMMENTARIES (1765-69). LAW
MUNIC SECT ADJUD AGREE CT/SYS CONSEN HAPPINESS   CONCPT
ORD/FREE 18. PAGE 10 E0191   IDEA/COMP

B28
FRANKFURTER F.,THE BUSINESS OF THE SUPREME COURT; A CT/SYS
STUDY IN THE FEDERAL JUDICIAL SYSTEM. USA-45 CONSTN ADJUD
EX/STRUC PROB/SOLV GP/REL ATTIT PWR...POLICY JURID LAW
18/20 SUPREME/CT CONGRESS. PAGE 40 E0789   FEDERAL

B28
MACDONALD A.F.,ELEMENTS OF POLITICAL SCIENCE   LAW
RESEARCH. USA-45 ACADEM JUDGE EDU/PROP DEBATE ADJUD FEDERAL
EXEC...BIBLIOG METH T 20 CONGRESS. PAGE 67 E1338   DECISION
                                                    CT/SYS

B28
MAIR L.P.,THE PROTECTION OF MINORITIES. EUR+WWI   LAW
WOR-45 CONSTN INT/ORG NAT/G LEGIT CT/SYS GP/REL   SOVEREIGN
RACE/REL DISCRIM ORD/FREE RESPECT...JURID CONCPT
TIME/SEQ 20. PAGE 68 E1352

B28
NORTON T.J.,LOSING LIBERTY JUDICIALLY. PROVS LEGIS NAT/G
BAL/PWR CT/SYS...JURID 18/20 SUPREME/CT CIV/RIGHTS ORD/FREE
CONGRESS. PAGE 78 E1557   CONSTN
                                                    JUDGE

B29
MOLEY R.,POLITICS AND CRIMINAL PROSECUTION. USA-45 PWR
POL/PAR EX/STRUC LEGIT CONTROL LEAD ROUTINE CHOOSE CT/SYS
INGP/REL...JURID CHARTS 20. PAGE 74 E1481   CRIME
                                                    ADJUD

L29
FEIS H.,"RESEARCH ACTIVITIES OF THE LEAGUE OF   CONSULT
NATIONS." EUR+WWI WOR-45 R+D INT/ORG CT/SYS   KNOWL
ARMS/CONT WEALTH...OBS RECORD LEAGUE/NAT ILO 20.   PEACE
PAGE 37 E0729

B30
BURLAMAQUI J.J.,PRINCIPLES OF NATURAL AND POLITIC   LAW
LAW (2 VOLS.) (1747-51). EX/STRUC LEGIS AGREE   NAT/G
CT/SYS CHOOSE ROLE SOVEREIGN 18 NATURL/LAW. PAGE 17 ORD/FREE
E0342   CONCPT

B30
FAIRLIE J.A.,COUNTY GOVERNMENT AND ADMINISTRATION. ADMIN
UK USA-45 NAT/G SCHOOL FORCES BUDGET TAX CT/SYS   GOV/REL
CHOOSE...JURID BIBLIOG 11/20. PAGE 36 E0713   LOC/G
                                                    MUNIC

B30
GREEN F.M.,CONSTITUTIONAL DEVELOPMENT IN THE SOUTH CONSTN
ATLANTIC STATES, 1776-1860; A STUDY IN THE   PROVS
EVOLUTION OF DEMOCRACY. USA-45 ELITES SOCIETY   PLURISM
STRATA ECO/DEV AGRI POL/PAR EX/STRUC LEGIS CT/SYS   REPRESENT
REGION...BIBLIOG 18/19 MARYLAND VIRGINIA GEORGIA
NORTH/CAR SOUTH/CAR. PAGE 46 E0905

B30
JORDAN E.,THEORY OF LEGISLATION: AN ESSAY ON THE   LEGIS
DYNAMICS OF PUBLIC MIND. NAT/G CREATE REPRESENT   CONCPT
MAJORITY ATTIT GEN/LAWS. PAGE 59 E1173   JURID
                                                    CT/SYS

B32
LUNT D.C.,THE ROAD TO THE LAW. UK USA-45 LEGIS   ADJUD
EDU/PROP OWN ORD/FREE...DECISION TIME/SEQ NAT/COMP LAW
16/20 AUSTRAL ENGLSH/LAW COMMON/LAW. PAGE 67 E1333 JURID
                                                    CT/SYS

B33
AMERICAN FOREIGN LAW ASSN,BIOGRAPHICAL NOTES ON THE BIBLIOG/A
LAWS AND LEGAL LITERATURE OF URUGUAY AND CURACAO.   LAW
URUGUAY CONSTN FINAN SECT FORCES JUDGE DIPLOM   JURID
INT/TRADE ADJUD CT/SYS CRIME 20. PAGE 4 E0078   ADMIN

B33
ENSOR R.C.K.,COURTS AND JUDGES IN FRANCE, GERMANY, CT/SYS
AND ENGLAND. FRANCE GERMANY UK LAW PROB/SOLV ADMIN EX/STRUC
ROUTINE CRIME ROLE...METH/COMP 20 CIVIL/LAW.   ADJUD
PAGE 35 E0692   NAT/COMP

B33
MATTHEWS M.A.,THE AMERICAN INSTITUTE OF   BIBLIOG/A
INTERNATIONAL LAW AND THE CODIFICATION OF   INT/LAW
INTERNATIONAL LAW (PAMPHLET). USA-45 CONSTN ADJUD   L/A+17C
CT/SYS...JURID 20. PAGE 69 E1386   DIPLOM

B34
CULVER D.C.,BIBLIOGRAPHY OF CRIME AND CRIMINAL   BIBLIOG/A
JUSTICE, 1927-1931. LAW CULTURE PUB/INST PROB/SOLV CRIMLGY
CT/SYS...PSY SOC STAT 20. PAGE 28 E0549   ADJUD
                                                    FORCES

L34
LLEWELLYN K.N.,"THE CONSTITUTION AS AN INSTITUTION" CONSTN
(BMR)" USA-45 PROB/SOLV LOBBY REPRESENT...DECISION LAW
JURID 18/20 SUPREME/CT. PAGE 66 E1313   CONCPT
                                                    CT/SYS

B35
CUMMING J.,A CONTRIBUTION TOWARD A BIBLIOGRAPHY   BIBLIOG
DEALING WITH CRIME AND COGNATE SUBJECTS (3RD ED.). CRIMLGY
UK LAW CULTURE PUB/INST ADJUD AGE BIO/SOC...PSY SOC FORCES
SOC/WK STAT METH/COMP 20. PAGE 28 E0552   CT/SYS

B35
DE TOCQUEVILLE A.,DEMOCRACY IN AMERICA (4 VOLS.)   POPULISM
(TRANS. BY HENRY REEVE). CONSTN STRUCT LOC/G NAT/G MAJORIT
POL/PAR PROVS ETIQUET CT/SYS MAJORITY ATTIT 18/19. ORD/FREE
PAGE 30 E0595   SOCIETY

B35
HUDSON M.,BY PACIFIC MEANS. WOR-45 EDU/PROP   INT/ORG
ORD/FREE...CONCPT TIME/SEQ GEN/LAWS LEAGUE/NAT   CT/SYS
TOT/POP 20 TREATY. PAGE 56 E1110   PEACE

B35
KENNEDY W.P.,THE LAW AND CUSTOM OF THE SOUTH   CT/SYS
AFRICAN CONSTITUTION. AFR SOUTH/AFR KIN LOC/G PROVS CONSTN
DIPLOM ADJUD ADMIN EXEC 20. PAGE 60 E1203   JURID
                                                    PARL/PROC

B35
RAM J.,THE SCIENCE OF LEGAL JUDGMENT: A TREATISE... LAW
UK CONSTN NAT/G LEGIS CREATE PROB/SOLV AGREE CT/SYS JURID
...INT/LAW CONCPT 19 ENGLSH/LAW CANON/LAW CIVIL/LAW EX/STRUC
CTS/WESTM. PAGE 83 E1672   ADJUD

B36
EHRLICH E.,FUNDAMENTAL PRINCIPLES OF THE SOCIOLOGY LAW
OF LAW (TRANS. BY WALTER L. MOLL). UNIV SOCIETY   JURID
ADJUD CT/SYS...POLICY GP/COMP GEN/LAWS GEN/METH.   SOC
PAGE 34 E0678   CONCPT

B36
GRAVES W.B.,AMERICAN STATE GOVERNMENT. CONSTN FINAN NAT/G
EX/STRUC FORCES LEGIS BUDGET TAX CT/SYS REPRESENT   PROVS
GOV/REL...BIBLIOG/A 19/20. PAGE 45 E0900   ADMIN
                                                    FEDERAL

B36
HUDSON M.O.,INTERNATIONAL LEGISLATION: 1929-1931.   INT/LAW
WOR-45 SEA AIR AGRI FINAN LABOR DIPLOM ECO/TAC   PARL/PROC
REPAR CT/SYS ARMS/CONT WAR WEAPON...JURID 20 TREATY ADJUD
LEAGUE/NAT. PAGE 56 E1112   LAW

B36
SCHULZ F.,PRINCIPLES OF ROMAN LAW. CONSTN FAM NAT/G LAW
DOMIN CONTROL CT/SYS CRIME ISOLAT ATTIT ORD/FREE   LEGIS
PWR...JURID ROME/ANC ROMAN/LAW. PAGE 89 E1783   ADJUD
                                                    CONCPT

B37
HAMILTON W.H.,THE POWER TO GOVERN. ECO/DEV FINAN   LING
INDUS ECO/TAC INT/TRADE TARIFFS TAX CONTROL CT/SYS CONSTN
WAR COST PWR 18/20 SUPREME/CT. PAGE 50 E0991   NAT/G
                                                    POLICY

B37
KETCHAM E.H.,PRELIMINARY SELECT BIBLIOGRAPHY OF   BIBLIOG
INTERNATIONAL LAW (PAMPHLET). WOR-45 LAW INT/ORG   DIPLOM
NAT/G PROB/SOLV CT/SYS NEUTRAL WAR 19/20. PAGE 60   ADJUD
E1207   INT/LAW

RUTHERFORD M.L.,THE INFLUENCE OF THE AMERICAN BAR ASSOCIATION ON PUBLIC OPINION AND LEGISLATION. USA+45 LAW CONSTN LABOR LEGIS DOMIN EDU/PROP LEGIT CT/SYS ROUTINE...TIME/SEQ 19/20 ABA. PAGE 87 E1739
ATTIT ADJUD PROF/ORG JURID
B37

SCHUSTER E.,GUIDE TO LAW AND LEGAL LITERATURE OF CENTRAL AMERICAN REPUBLICS. L/A+17C INT/ORG ADJUD SANCTION CRIME...JURID 19/20. PAGE 89 E1785
BIBLIOG/A REGION CT/SYS LAW
B37

LERNER M.,"CONSTITUTION AND COURT AS SYMBOLS" (BMR)" USA+45 USA-45 DOMIN PWR SOVEREIGN...PSY MYTH 18/20 SUPREME/CT. PAGE 64 E1288
CONSTN CT/SYS ATTIT EDU/PROP
L37

FRANKFURTER F.,MR. JUSTICE HOLMES AND THE SUPREME COURT. USA-45 CONSTN SOCIETY FEDERAL OWN ATTIT ORD/FREE PWR...POLICY JURID 20 SUPREME/CT HOLMES/OW BILL/RIGHT. PAGE 40 E0790
CREATE CT/SYS DECISION LAW
B38

HAGUE PERMANENT CT INTL JUSTIC,WORLD COURT REPORTS: COLLECTION OF THE JUDGEMENTS ORDERS AND OPINIONS VOLUME 3 1932-35. WOR-45 LAW DELIB/GP CONFER WAR PEACE ATTIT...DECISION ANTHOL 20 WORLD/CT CASEBOOK. PAGE 49 E0976
INT/ORG CT/SYS DIPLOM ADJUD
B38

HELLMAN F.S.,THE SUPREME COURT ISSUE: SELECTED LIST OF REFERENCES. USA-45 NAT/G CHIEF EX/STRUC JUDGE ATTIT...JURID 20 PRESIDENT ROOSEVLT/F SUPREME/CT. PAGE 51 E1026
BIBLIOG/A CONSTN CT/SYS LAW
B38

HOLDSWORTH W.S.,A HISTORY OF ENGLISH LAW; THE CENTURIES OF SETTLEMENT AND REFORM (VOL. X). INDIA UK CONSTN NAT/G CHIEF LEGIS ADMIN COLONIAL CT/SYS CHOOSE ORD/FREE PWR...JURID 18 PARLIAMENT COMMONWLTH COMMON/LAW. PAGE 54 E1077
LAW LOC/G EX/STRUC ADJUD
B38

HOLDSWORTH W.S.,A HISTORY OF ENGLISH LAW; THE CENTURIES OF SETTLEMENT AND REFORM (VOL. XII). UK CONSTN STRATA LEGIS JUDGE ADJUD CT/SYS ATTIT ...JURID CONCPT BIOG GEN/LAWS 18 ENGLSH/LAW BLACKSTN/W COMMON/LAW. PAGE 54 E1078
LAW PROF/ORG WRITING IDEA/COMP
B38

HOLDSWORTH W.S.,A HISTORY OF ENGLISH LAW; THE CENTURIES OF SETTLEMENT AND REFORM (VOL. XI). UK CONSTN NAT/G EX/STRUC DIPLOM ADJUD CT/SYS LEAD CRIME ATTIT...INT/LAW JURID 18 CMN/WLTH PARLIAMENT ENGLSH/LAW. PAGE 54 E1079
LAW COLONIAL LEGIS PARL/PROC
B38

MCNAIR A.D.,THE LAW OF TREATIES: BRITISH PRACTICE AND OPINIONS. UK CREATE DIPLOM LEGIT WRITING ADJUD WAR...INT/LAW JURID TREATY. PAGE 71 E1424
AGREE LAW CT/SYS NAT/G
B38

POUND R.,THE FORMATIVE ERA OF AMERICAN LAW. CULTURE NAT/G PROVS LEGIS ADJUD CT/SYS PERSON SOVEREIGN ...POLICY IDEA/COMP GEN/LAWS 18/19. PAGE 82 E1637
CONSTN LAW CREATE JURID
B38

SAINT-PIERRE C.I.,SCHEME FOR LASTING PEACE (TRANS. BY H. BELLOT). INDUS NAT/G CHIEF FORCES INT/TRADE CT/SYS WAR PWR SOVEREIGN WEALTH...POLICY 18. PAGE 87 E1741
INT/ORG PEACE AGREE INT/LAW
B38

CULVER D.C.,BIBLIOGRAPHY OF CRIME AND CRIMINAL JUSTICE, 1932-1937. USA-45 LAW CULTURE PUB/INST PROB/SOLV CT/SYS...PSY SOC STAT 20. PAGE 28 E0551
BIBLIOG/A CRIMLGY ADJUD FORCES
B39

ANDERSON W.,FUNDAMENTALS OF AMERICAN GOVERNMENT. USA-45 LAW POL/PAR CHIEF EX/STRUC BUDGET ADMIN CT/SYS PARL/PROC CHOOSE FEDERAL...BIBLIOG 20. PAGE 5 E0093
NAT/G LOC/G GOV/REL CONSTN
B40

HART J.,AN INTRODUCTION TO ADMINISTRATIVE LAW, WITH SELECTED CASES. USA-45 CONSTN SOCIETY NAT/G EX/STRUC ADJUD CT/SYS LEAD CRIME ORD/FREE ...DECISION JURID 20 CASEBOOK. PAGE 50 E1002
LAW ADMIN LEGIS PWR
B40

HOBBES T.,A DIALOGUE BETWEEN A PHILOSOPHER AND A
CT/SYS
B40

STUDENT OF THE COMMON LAWS OF ENGLAND (1667?). UK SECT DOMIN ADJUD CRIME INCOME OWN UTIL ORD/FREE PWR SOVEREIGN...JURID GEN/LAWS 17. PAGE 53 E1057
CHIEF SANCTION

GERTH H.,"THE NAZI PARTY: ITS LEADERSHIP AND COMPOSITION" (BMR)" GERMANY ELITES STRATA STRUCT EX/STRUC FORCES ECO/TAC CT/SYS CHOOSE TOTALISM AGE/Y AUTHORIT PWR 20. PAGE 43 E0851
POL/PAR DOMIN LEAD ADMIN
S40

COUNTY GOVERNMENT IN THE UNITED STATES: A LIST OF RECENT REFERENCES (PAMPHLET). USA-45 LAW PUB/INST PLAN BUDGET CT/SYS CENTRAL 20. PAGE 52 E1027
BIBLIOG/A LOC/G ADMIN MUNIC
N40

GILMORE M.P.,ARGUMENT FROM ROMAN LAW IN POLITICAL THOUGHT, 1200-1600. INTELL LICENSE CONTROL CT/SYS GOV/REL PRIVIL PWR...IDEA/COMP BIBLIOG 13/16. PAGE 44 E0866
JURID LAW CONCPT NAT/G
B41

CARR R.K.,THE SUPREME COURT AND JUDICIAL REVIEW. NAT/G CHIEF LEGIS OP/RES LEAD GOV/REL GP/REL ATTIT ...POLICY DECISION 18/20 SUPREME/CT PRESIDENT CONGRESS. PAGE 20 E0394
CT/SYS CONSTN JURID PWR
B42

FORTESCU J.,IN PRAISE OF ENGLISH LAW (1464) (TRANS. BY S.B. CHRIMES). UK ELITES CHIEF FORCES CT/SYS COERCE CRIME GOV/REL ILLEGIT...JURID GOV/COMP GEN/LAWS 15. PAGE 39 E0774
LAW CONSTN LEGIS ORD/FREE
B42

SETARO F.C.,A BIBLIOGRAPHY OF THE WRITINGS OF ROSCOE POUND. USA-45 CT/SYS 20. PAGE 90 E1806
BIBLIOG LAW ATTIT JUDGE
B42

ANDERSON R.B.,SUPPLEMENT TO BEALE'S BIBLIOGRAPHY OF EARLY ENGLISH LAW BOOKS. MOD/EUR UK CONSTN PRESS ADJUD...CHARTS 10/15. PAGE 5 E0091
BIBLIOG/A JURID CT/SYS LAW
B43

BACKUS R.C.,A GUIDE TO THE LAW AND LEGAL LITERATURE OF COLOMBIA. FINAN INDUS LABOR FORCES ADJUD ADMIN COLONIAL CT/SYS CRIME...INT/LAW JURID 20 COLOMB. PAGE 7 E0127
BIBLIOG/A LAW CONSTN L/A+17C
B43

CLAGETT H.L.,A GUIDE TO THE LAW AND LEGAL LITERATURE OF PARAGUAY. PARAGUAY CONSTN COM/IND LABOR MUNIC JUDGE ADMIN CT/SYS...CRIMLGY INT/LAW CON/ANAL 20. PAGE 22 E0439
BIBLIOG JURID LAW L/A+17C
B43

HAGUE PERMANENT CT INTL JUSTIC,WORLD COURT REPORTS: COLLECTION OF THE JUDGEMENTS ORDERS AND OPINIONS VOLUME 4 1936-42. WOR-45 CONFER PEACE ATTIT ...DECISION JURID ANTHOL 20 WORLD/CT CASEBOOK. PAGE 49 E0977
INT/ORG CT/SYS DIPLOM ADJUD
B43

BEARD C.A.,AMERICAN GOVERNMENT AND POLITICS (REV. ED.). CONSTN MUNIC POL/PAR PROVS EX/STRUC LEGIS TOP/EX CT/SYS GOV/REL...BIBLIOG T 18/20. PAGE 9 E0165
LEAD USA-45 NAT/G LOC/G
B44

SUAREZ F.,A TREATISE ON LAWS AND GOD THE LAWGIVER (1612) IN SELECTIONS FROM THREE WORKS, VOL. II. FRANCE ITALY UK CULTURE NAT/G SECT CHIEF LEGIS DOMIN LEGIT CT/SYS ORD/FREE PWR WORSHIP 16/17. PAGE 94 E1892
LAW JURID GEN/LAWS CATH
B44

MASON J.B.,"THE JUDICIAL SYSTEM OF THE NAZI PARTY." GERMANY ELITES POL/PAR DOMIN CONTROL SANCTION TOTALISM...JURID 20 HITLER/A. PAGE 69 E1381
FASCISM CT/SYS ADJUD LAW
S44

JEFFERSON T.,"DEMOCRACY" (1816) IN BASIC WRITINGS." USA-45 LOC/G NAT/G TAX CT/SYS CHOOSE ORD/FREE ...GEN/LAWS 18/19 JEFFERSN/T. PAGE 58 E1151
POPULISM MAJORIT REPRESENT CONSTN
C44

CONOVER H.F.,THE GOVERNMENTS OF THE MAJOR FOREIGN POWERS: A BIBLIOGRAPHY. FRANCE GERMANY ITALY UK USSR CONSTN LOC/G POL/PAR EX/STRUC FORCES ADMIN CT/SYS CIVMIL/REL TOTALISM...POLICY 19/20. PAGE 25 E0494
BIBLIOG NAT/G DIPLOM
B45

B45
TINGSTERN H.,PEACE AND SECURITY AFTER WW II. WOR-45 INT/ORG
DELIB/GP TOP/EX LEGIT CT/SYS COERCE PEACE ATTIT ORD/FREE
PERCEPT...CONCPT LEAGUE/NAT 20. PAGE 96 E1927 WAR
INT/LAW

B45
US LIBRARY OF CONGRESS,CONSTITUTIONAL AND STATUTORY CONSTN
PROVISIONS OF THE STATES (VOL. I). USA-45 CREATE FEDERAL
TAX CT/SYS CHOOSE SUFF INCOME PWR 20. PAGE 101 PROVS
E2016 JURID

B45
VANCE H.L.,GUIDE TO THE LAW AND LEGAL LITERATURE OF BIBLIOG/A
MEXICO. LAW CONSTN FINAN LABOR FORCES ADJUD ADMIN INT/LAW
...CRIMLGY PHIL/SCI CON/ANAL 20 MEXIC/AMER. JURID
PAGE 103 E2070 CT/SYS

B46
PATON G.W.,A TEXT-BOOK OF JURISPRUDENCE. CREATE LAW
INSPECT LEGIT CT/SYS ROUTINE CRIME INGP/REL PRIVIL ADJUD
...CONCPT BIBLIOG 20. PAGE 80 E1601 JURID
T

B46
ROSS A.,TOWARDS A REALISTIC JURISPRUDENCE: A LAW
CRITICISM OF THE DUALISM IN LAW (TRANS. BY ANNIE I. CONCPT
FAUSBOLL). PLAN ADJUD CT/SYS ATTIT RIGID/FLEX IDEA/COMP
POPULISM...JURID PHIL/SCI LOG METH/COMP GEN/LAWS 20
SCANDINAV. PAGE 86 E1720

B46
SCANLON H.L.,INTERNATIONAL LAW: A SELECTIVE LIST OF BIBLIOG/A
WORKS IN ENGLISH ON PUBLIC INTERNATIONAL LAW (A INT/LAW
PAMPHLET). CHRIST-17C EUR+WWI MOD/EUR WOR-45 CT/SYS ADJUD
...JURID 20. PAGE 87 E1749 DIPLOM

S46
CANTWELL F.V.,"PUBLIC OPINION AND THE LEGISLATIVE CHARTS
PROCESS" USA+45 USA-45 NAT/G CT/SYS EXEC LEAD DEBATE
DECISION. PAGE 19 E0374 LEGIS
ATTIT

B47
CLAGETT H.L.,A GUIDE TO THE LAW AND LEGAL BIBLIOG/A
LITERATURE OF BOLIVIA. L/A+17C CONSTN LABOR LEGIS JURID
ADMIN...CRIMLGY INT/LAW PHIL/SCI 16/20 BOLIV. LAW
PAGE 22 E0441 CT/SYS

B47
CLAGETT H.L.,A GUIDE TO THE LAW AND LEGAL BIBLIOG
LITERATURE OF PERU. PERU CONSTN COM/IND LABOR MUNIC L/A+17C
JUDGE ADMIN CT/SYS...CRIMLGY INT/LAW JURID 20. PHIL/SCI
PAGE 23 E0444 LAW

B47
CLAGETT H.L.,A GUIDE TO THE LAW AND LEGAL BIBLIOG
LITERATURE OF URUGUAY. URUGUAY CONSTN COM/IND FINAN LAW
LABOR MUNIC JUDGE PRESS ADMIN CT/SYS...INT/LAW JURID
PHIL/SCI 20. PAGE 23 E0445 L/A+17C

B47
DE NOIA J.,GUIDE TO OFFICIAL PUBLICATIONS OF OTHER BIBLIOG/A
AMERICAN REPUBLICS: ECUADOR (VOL. IX). ECUADOR LAW CONSTN
FINAN LEGIS BUDGET CT/SYS 19/20. PAGE 30 E0589 NAT/G
EDU/PROP

B47
DE NOIA J.,GUIDE TO OFFICIAL PUBLICATIONS OF THE BIBLIOG/A
OTHER AMERICAN REPUBLICS: EL SALVADOR. EL/SALVADR CONSTN
LAW LEGIS EDU/PROP CT/SYS 20. PAGE 30 E0590 NAT/G
ADMIN

B47
DE NOIA J.,GUIDE TO OFFICIAL PUBLICATIONS OF THE BIBLIOG/A
OTHER AMERICAN REPUBLICS: NICARAGUA (VOL. XIV). EDU/PROP
NICARAGUA LAW LEGIS ADMIN CT/SYS...JURID 19/20. NAT/G
PAGE 30 E0591 CONSTN

B47
DE NOIA J.,GUIDE TO OFFICIAL PUBLICATIONS OF THE BIBLIOG/A
OTHER AMERICAN REPUBLICS: PANAMA (VOL. XV). PANAMA CONSTN
LAW LEGIS EDU/PROP CT/SYS 20. PAGE 30 E0592 ADMIN
NAT/G

B47
HYDE C.C.,INTERNATIONAL LAW, CHIEFLY AS INTERPRETED INT/LAW
AND APPLIED BY THE UNITED STATES (3 VOLS., 2ND REV. DIPLOM
ED.). USA-45 WOR+45 WOR-45 INT/ORG CT/SYS WAR NAT/G
NAT/LISM PEACE ORD/FREE...JURID 19/20 TREATY. POLICY
PAGE 56 E1119

B47
INTERNATIONAL COURT OF JUSTICE,CHARTER OF THE INT/LAW
UNITED NATIONS, STATUTE AND RULES OF COURT AND INT/ORG

CT/SYS
OTHER CONSTITUTIONAL DOCUMENTS. SWITZERLND LAW DIPLOM
ADJUD INGP/REL...JURID 20 ICJ UN. PAGE 57 E1133

B47
MCILWAIN C.H.,CONSTITUTIONALISM: ANCIENT AND CONSTN
MODERN. USA+45 ROMAN/EMP LAW CHIEF LEGIS CT/SYS NAT/G
GP/REL ORD/FREE SOVEREIGN...POLICY TIME/SEQ PARL/PROC
ROMAN/REP EUROPE. PAGE 71 E1419 GOV/COMP

B47
NEUBURGER O.,GUIDE TO OFFICIAL PUBLICATIONS OF BIBLIOG/A
OTHER AMERICAN REPUBLICS: HONDURAS (VOL. XIII). NAT/G
HONDURAS LAW LEGIS ADMIN CT/SYS...JURID 19/20. EDU/PROP
PAGE 76 E1533 CONSTN

S47
FRANKFURTER F.,"SOME REFLECTIONS ON THE READING OF JURID
STATUTES" USA+45 USA-45 PROB/SOLV CT/SYS TASK LAW
EFFICIENCY...LING 20. PAGE 40 E0791 ADJUD
WRITING

B48
CORWIN E.S.,LIBERTY AGAINST GOVERNMENT: THE RISE, CONCPT
FLOWERING AND DECLINE OF A FAMOUS JURIDICAL ORD/FREE
CONCEPT. LEGIS ADJUD CT/SYS SANCTION GOV/REL JURID
FEDERAL CONSERVE NEW/LIB...OLD/LIB 18/20 ROMAN/LAW CONSTN
COMMON/LAW. PAGE 26 E0514

B48
DE NOIA J.,GUIDE TO OFFICIAL PUBLICATIONS OF OTHER BIBLIOG/A
AMERICAN REPUBLICS: PERU (VOL. XVII). PERU LAW CONSTN
LEGIS ADMIN CT/SYS...JURID 19/20. PAGE 30 E0593 NAT/G
EDU/PROP

B48
FENWICK C.G.,INTERNATIONAL LAW. WOR+45 WOR-45 INT/ORG
CONSTN NAT/G LEGIT CT/SYS REGION...CONCPT JURID
LEAGUE/NAT UN 20. PAGE 37 E0737 INT/LAW

B48
KEIR D.L.,CASES IN CONSTITUTIONAL LAW. UK CHIEF CONSTN
LEGIS DIPLOM TAX PARL/PROC CRIME GOV/REL...INT/LAW LAW
JURID 17/20. PAGE 60 E1195 ADJUD
CT/SYS

B48
NEUBURGER O.,GUIDE TO OFFICIAL PUBLICATIONS OF THE BIBLIOG/A
OTHER AMERICAN REPUBLICS: VENEZUELA (VOL. XIX). NAT/G
VENEZUELA FINAN LEGIS PLAN BUDGET DIPLOM CT/SYS CONSTN
PARL/PROC 19/20. PAGE 77 E1535 LAW

B48
SLESSER H.,THE ADMINISTRATION OF THE LAW. UK CONSTN LAW
EX/STRUC OP/RES PROB/SOLV CRIME ROLE...DECISION CT/SYS
METH/COMP 20 CIVIL/LAW ENGLSH/LAW CIVIL/LAW. ADJUD
PAGE 92 E1839

B48
STOKES W.S.,BIBLIOGRAPHY OF STANDARD AND CLASSICAL BIBLIOG
WORKS IN THE FIELDS OF AMERICAN POLITICAL SCIENCE. NAT/G
USA+45 USA-45 POL/PAR PROVS FORCES DIPLOM ADJUD LOC/G
CT/SYS APPORT 20 CONGRESS PRESIDENT. PAGE 94 E1876 CONSTN

S48
BRADEN G.D.,"THE SEARCH FOR OBJECTIVITY IN CONSTN
CONSTITUTIONAL LAW" (BMR)" USA+45 USA-45 LAW NAT/G CT/SYS
CONTROL ORD/FREE PWR OBJECTIVE...JURID 20 IDEA/COMP
SUPREME/CT. PAGE 15 E0283 POLICY

C48
WALKER H.,"THE LEGISLATIVE PROCESS; LAWMAKING IN PARL/PROC
THE UNITED STATES." NAT/G POL/PAR PROVS EX/STRUC LEGIS
OP/RES PROB/SOLV CT/SYS LOBBY GOV/REL...CHARTS LAW
BIBLIOG T 18/20 CONGRESS. PAGE 105 E2094 CONSTN

B49
DENNING A.,FREEDOM UNDER THE LAW. MOD/EUR UK LAW ORD/FREE
SOCIETY CHIEF EX/STRUC LEGIS ADJUD CT/SYS PERS/REL JURID
PERSON 17/20 ENGLSH/LAW. PAGE 31 E0606 NAT/G

B49
FRANK J.,LAW AND THE MODERN MIND. UNIV LAW CT/SYS JURID
RATIONAL ATTIT...CONCPT 20 HOLMES/OW JURY. PAGE 40 ADJUD
E0787 IDEA/COMP
MYTH

B49
JACKSON R.H.,INTERNATIONAL CONFERENCE ON MILITARY DIPLOM
TRIALS. FRANCE GERMANY UK USA+45 USSR VOL/ASSN INT/ORG
DELIB/GP REPAR ADJUD CT/SYS CRIME WAR 20 WAR/TRIAL. INT/LAW
PAGE 57 E1141 CIVMIL/REL

B49
SCHONS D.,BOOK CENSORSHIP IN NEW SPAIN (NEW WORLD CHRIST-17C
STUDIES, BOOK II). SPAIN LAW CULTURE INSPECT ADJUD EDU/PROP
CT/SYS SANCTION GP/REL ORD/FREE 14/17. PAGE 88 CONTROL

E1764   PRESS

                                               B49
WALINE M., LE CONTROLE JURIDICTIONNEL DE   JURID
L'ADMINISTRATION. BELGIUM FRANCE UAR JUDGE BAL/PWR ADMIN
ADJUD CONTROL CT/SYS...GP/COMP 20. PAGE 104 E2093   PWR
                                               ORD/FREE

                                               S49
BROWN D.M., "RECENT JAPANESE POLITICAL AND   WAR
HISTORICAL MATERIALS." ELITES CT/SYS CIVMIL/REL 20 FORCES
CHINJAP. PAGE 16 E0312

                                               S49
PRITCHETT C.H., "THE PRESIDENT AND THE SUPREME GOV/REL
COURT." NAT/G CONTROL REPRESENT FEDERAL 20. PAGE 82 CT/SYS
E1651   CHIEF

                                               B50
FRANK J., COURTS ON TRIAL: MYTH AND REALITY IN JURID
AMERICAN JUSTICE. LAW CONSULT PROB/SOLV EDU/PROP   CT/SYS
ADJUD ROUTINE ROLE ORD/FREE...GEN/LAWS T 20.   MYTH
PAGE 40 E0788   CONSTN

                                               B50
HURST J.W., THE GROWTH OF AMERICAN LAW; THE LAW LAW
MAKERS. USA+45 LOC/G NAT/G DELIB/GP JUDGE ADJUD LEGIS
ADMIN ATTIT PWR...POLICY JURID BIBLIOG 18/20   CONSTN
CONGRESS SUPREME/CT ABA PRESIDENT. PAGE 56 E1115 CT/SYS

                                               B50
JENKINS W.S., A GUIDE TO THE MICROFILM COLLECTION OF BIBLIOG
EARLY STATE RECORDS. USA+45 CONSTN MUNIC LEGIS   PROVS
PRESS ADMIN CT/SYS 18/20. PAGE 58 E1152   AUD/VIS

                                               B50
SOHN L.B., CASES AND OTHER MATERIALS ON WORLD LAW. CT/SYS
FUT WOR+45 LAW INT/ORG...INT/LAW JURID METH/CNCPT CONSTN
20 UN. PAGE 92 E1852

                                               S50
ROBINSON W.S., "BIAS, PROBABILITY AND TRIAL BY JURY" REPRESENT
(BMR)" USA+45 USA-45 SOCIETY...SOC CONCPT. PAGE 85 JURID
E1707   CT/SYS
                                               DECISION

                                               C50
HOLCOMBE A., "OUR MORE PERFECT UNION." USA+45 USA-45 CONSTN
POL/PAR JUDGE CT/SYS EQUILIB FEDERAL PWR...MAJORIT NAT/G
TREND BIBLIOG 18/20 CONGRESS PRESIDENT. PAGE 54 ADMIN
E1070   PLAN

                                               B51
ANDERSON W., STATE AND LOCAL GOVERNMENT IN THE LOC/G
UNITED STATES. USA+45 CONSTN POL/PAR EX/STRUC LEGIS MUNIC
BUDGET TAX ADJUD CT/SYS CHOOSE...CHARTS T 20.   PROVS
PAGE 5 E0094   GOV/REL

                                               B51
BECKER O., MASTER RESEARCH GUIDE. USA+45 USA-45 BIBLIOG
PRESS...JURID INDEX 20. PAGE 9 E0171   LAW
                                               ADJUD
                                               CT/SYS

                                               B51
FRIEDMANN W., LAW AND SOCIAL CHANGE IN CONTEMPORARY LAW
BRITAIN. UK LABOR LG/CO LEGIS JUDGE CT/SYS ORD/FREE ADJUD
NEW/LIB...DECISION JURID TREND METH/COMP BIBLIOG 20 SOCIETY
PARLIAMENT ENGLSH/LAW COMMON/LAW. PAGE 40 E0802 CONSTN

                                               B51
ROSSITER C., THE SUPREME COURT AND THE COMMANDER IN CT/SYS
CHIEF. LAW CONSTN DELIB/GP EX/STRUC LEGIS TOP/EX CHIEF
ADJUD CONTROL...DECISION SOC/EXP PRESIDENT. PAGE 86 WAR
E1724   PWR

                                               S51
LEEK J.H., "TREASON AND THE CONSTITUTION" (BMR)" CONSTN
USA+45 USA-45 EDU/PROP COLONIAL CT/SYS REV WAR   JURID
ATTIT...TREND 18/20 SUPREME/CT CON/INTERP SMITH/ACT CRIME
COMMON/LAW. PAGE 64 E1278   NAT/G

                                               B52
APPADORAI A., THE SUBSTANCE OF POLITICS (6TH ED.). PHIL/SCI
EX/STRUC LEGIS DIPLOM CT/SYS CHOOSE FASCISM MARXISM NAT/G
SOCISM...BIBLIOG T. PAGE 5 E0100

                                               B52
BENTHAM A., HANDBOOK OF POLITICAL FALLACIES. FUT POL/PAR
MOD/EUR LAW INTELL LOC/G MUNIC NAT/G DELIB/GP LEGIS
CREATE EDU/PROP CT/SYS ATTIT RIGID/FLEX KNOWL PWR
...RELATIV PSY SOC CONCPT SELF/OBS TREND STERTYP
TOT/POP. PAGE 10 E0189

                                               B52
BUCKLAND W.W., ROMAN LAW AND COMMON LAW; A   IDEA/COMP

COMPARISON IN OUTLINE (2ND REV. ED.). UK FAM LEGIT LAW
AGREE CT/SYS OWN...JURID ROMAN/REP ROMAN/LAW   ADJUD
COMMON/LAW. PAGE 17 E0325   CONCPT

                                               B52
COLEMAN J.W. JR., DEATH AT THE COURT-HOUSE. CONTROL CROWD
COERCE 20 KENTUCKY. PAGE 24 E0472   ORD/FREE
                                               CRIME
                                               CT/SYS

                                               B52
DE GRAZIA A., POLITICAL ORGANIZATION. CONSTN LOC/G FEDERAL
MUNIC NAT/G CHIEF LEGIS TOP/EX ADJUD CT/SYS   LAW
PERS/REL...INT/LAW MYTH UN. PAGE 29 E0581   ADMIN

                                               B52
DU BOIS W.E.B., IN BATTLE FOR PEACE. AFR USA+45 PEACE
COLONIAL CT/SYS PERS/REL PERSON ORD/FREE...JURID 20 RACE/REL
NEGRO CIVIL/LIB. PAGE 33 E0650   DISCRIM
                                               BIOG

                                               B52
GELLHORN W., THE STATES AND SUBVERSION. USA+45   PROVS
USA-45 LOC/G DELIB/GP LEGIS EDU/PROP LEGIT CT/SYS JURID
REGION PEACE ATTIT ORD/FREE SOCISM...INT CON/ANAL
20 CALIFORNIA MARYLAND ILLINOIS MICHIGAN NEW/YORK.
PAGE 43 E0845

                                               B52
HOLDSWORTH W.S., A HISTORY OF ENGLISH LAW; THE   LAW
CENTURIES OF SETTLEMENT AND REFORM, 1701-1875 (VOL. CONSTN
XIII). UK POL/PAR PROF/ORG LEGIS JUDGE WRITING   IDEA/COMP
ATTIT...JURID CONCPT BIOG GEN/LAWS 18/19 PARLIAMENT CT/SYS
REFORMERS ENGLSH/LAW COMMON/LAW. PAGE 54 E1080

                                               B52
JENNINGS W.I., CONSTITUTIONAL LAWS OF THE   CONSTN
COMMONWEALTH. UK LAW CHIEF LEGIS TAX CT/SYS   JURID
PARL/PROC GOV/REL...INT/LAW 18/20 COMMONWLTH   ADJUD
ENGLSH/LAW COMMON/LAW. PAGE 58 E1165   COLONIAL

                                               B52
MORRIS R.B., FAIR TRIAL. USA-45 JUDGE ORD/FREE   ADJUD
...JURID 20. PAGE 75 E1498   CT/SYS
                                               CRIME
                                               LAW

                                               L52
ROSTOW E.V., "THE DEMOCRATIC CHARACTER OF JUDICIAL CONSTN
REVIEW" (BMR)" USA+45 LAW NAT/G LEGIS TASK...JURID PROB/SOLV
20 SUPREME/CT. PAGE 86 E1725   ADJUD
                                               CT/SYS

                                               C52
CLAGETT H.L., "THE ADMINISTRATION OF JUSTICE IN CT/SYS
LATIN AMERICA." L/A+17C ADMIN FEDERAL...JURID   ADJUD
METH/COMP BIBLIOG 20. PAGE 23 E0448   JUDGE
                                               CONSTN

                                               C52
LANCASTER L.W., "GOVERNMENT IN RURAL AMERICA."   GOV/REL
USA+45 ECO/DEV AGRI SCHOOL FORCES LEGIS JUDGE   LOC/G
BUDGET TAX CT/SYS...CHARTS BIBLIOG. PAGE 62 E1248 MUNIC
                                               ADMIN

                                               B53
COKE E., INSTITUTES OF THE LAWS OF ENGLAND   JURID
(1628-1658). UK LAW ADJUD PERS/REL ORD/FREE   OWN
...CRIMLGY 11/17. PAGE 24 E0471   CT/SYS
                                               CONSTN

                                               B53
MARKE J.J., A CATALOGUE OF THE LAW COLLECTION AT NEW BIBLIOG/A
YORK UNIVERSITY, WITH SELECTED ANNOTATIONS. ACADEM LAW
ADJUD CT/SYS...CONCPT BIOG 20. PAGE 68 E1366   PHIL/SCI
                                               IDEA/COMP

                                               B53
ORFIELD L.B., THE GROWTH OF SCANDINAVIAN LAW.   JURID
DENMARK ICELAND NORWAY SWEDEN LAW DIPLOM...BIBLIOG CT/SYS
9/20. PAGE 79 E1581   NAT/G

                                               B54
CARTER P.G., STATISTICAL BULLETINS: AN ANNOTATED BIBLIOG/A
BIBLIOGRAPHY OF THE GENERAL STATISTICAL BULLETINS WOR+45
AND MAJOR POL SUBDIV OF WORLD. CULTURE AGRI FINAN NAT/G
INDUS LABOR TEC/DEV INT/TRADE CT/SYS WEALTH   STAT
...CRIMLGY SOC 20. PAGE 20 E0400

                                               B54
ELIAS T.O., GROUNDWORK OF NIGERIAN LAW. AFR LEAD JURID
CRIME INGP/REL ORD/FREE 17/20. PAGE 34 E0680   CT/SYS
                                               CONSTN
                                               CONSULT

B54

JAMES L.F.,THE SUPREME COURT IN AMERICAN LIFE.   ADJUD
USA+45 USA-45 CONSTN CRIME GP/REL INGP/REL RACE/REL   CT/SYS
CONSEN FEDERAL PERSON ORD/FREE 18/20 SUPREME/CT   JURID
DEPRESSION CIV/RIGHTS CHURCH/STA FREE/SPEE. PAGE 58   DECISION
E1147

B54

O'NEILL J.M.,CATHOLICS IN CONTROVERSY. USA+45 NAT/G   CATHISM
PROVS SCHOOL SECT EDU/PROP LEGIT CT/SYS SANCTION   CONSTN
GP/REL 20 SUPREME/CT CHURCH/STA. PAGE 78 E1569   POLICY
                                                        LAW

B54

SCHWARTZ B.,FRENCH ADMINISTRATIVE LAW AND THE   JURID
COMMON-LAW WORLD. FRANCE CULTURE LOC/G NAT/G PROVS   LAW
DELIB/GP EX/STRUC LEGIS PROB/SOLV CT/SYS EXEC   METH/COMP
GOV/REL...IDEA/COMP ENGLSH/LAW. PAGE 89 E1786   ADJUD

B54

SINCO,PHILIPPINE POLITICAL LAW: PRINCIPLES AND   LAW
CONCEPTS (10TH ED.). PHILIPPINE LOC/G EX/STRUC   CONSTN
BAL/PWR ECO/TAC TAX ADJUD ADMIN CONTROL CT/SYS SUFF   LEGIS
ORD/FREE...T 20. PAGE 91 E1831

B54

STONE J.,LEGAL CONTROLS OF INTERNATIONAL CONFLICT: INT/ORG
A TREATISE ON THE DYNAMICS OF DISPUTES AND WAR LAW.   LAW
WOR+45 WOR-45 NAT/G DIPLOM CT/SYS SOVEREIGN...JURID   WAR
CONCPT METH/CNCPT GEN/LAWS TOT/POP VAL/FREE   INT/LAW
COLD/WAR LEAGUE/NAT 20. PAGE 94 E1878

S54

HART J.,"ADMINISTRATION AND THE COURTS." USA+45   ADMIN
NAT/G REPRESENT 20. PAGE 50 E1003   GOV/REL
                                                        CT/SYS
                                                        FEDERAL

C54

CALDWELL L.K.,"THE GOVERNMENT AND ADMINISTRATION OF   PROVS
NEW YORK." LOC/G MUNIC POL/PAR SCHOOL CHIEF LEGIS   ADMIN
PLAN TAX CT/SYS...MGT SOC/WK BIBLIOG 20 NEWYORK/C.   CONSTN
PAGE 19 E0365   EX/STRUC

B55

BEANEY W.M.,THE RIGHT TO COUNSEL IN AMERICAN   ADJUD
COURTS. UK USA+45 USA-45 LAW NAT/G PROVS COLONIAL   CONSTN
PERCEPT 18/20 SUPREME/CT AMEND/VI AMEND/XIV   CT/SYS
ENGLSH/LAW. PAGE 8 E0163

B55

CUSHMAN R.E.,LEADING CONSTITUTIONAL DECISIONS.   CONSTN
USA+45 USA-45 NAT/G EX/STRUC LEGIS JUDGE TAX   PROB/SOLV
FEDERAL...DECISION 20 SUPREME/CT CASEBOOK. PAGE 28   JURID
E0559   CT/SYS

B55

DE ARAGAO J.G.,LA JURIDICTION ADMINISTRATIVE AU   EX/STRUC
BRESIL. BRAZIL ADJUD COLONIAL CT/SYS REV FEDERAL   ADMIN
ORD/FREE...BIBLIOG 19/20. PAGE 29 E0580   NAT/G

B55

KHADDURI M.,LAW IN THE MIDDLE EAST. LAW CONSTN   ADJUD
ACADEM FAM EDU/PROP CT/SYS SANCTION CRIME...INT/LAW   JURID
GOV/COMP ANTHOL 6/20 MID/EAST. PAGE 61 E1210   ISLAM

B55

MAYERS L.,THE AMERICAN LEGAL SYSTEM. USA+45 USA-45   JURID
NAT/G EX/STRUC ADMIN CONTROL FEDERAL 20 SUPREME/CT.   CT/SYS
PAGE 70 E1394   LEGIS
                                                        ADJUD

B55

SMITH G.,A CONSTITUTIONAL AND LEGAL HISTORY OF   CONSTN
ENGLAND. UK ELITES NAT/G LEGIS ADJUD OWN HABITAT   PARTIC
POPULISM...JURID 20 ENGLSH/LAW. PAGE 92 E1844   LAW
                                                        CT/SYS

B55

SWEET AND MAXWELL,A LEGAL BIBLIOGRAPHY OF THE   BIBLIOG/A
BRITISH COMMONWEALTH OF NATIONS (2ND ED. 7 VOLS.).   LAW
UK LOC/G MUNIC JUDGE ADJUD CRIME OWN...JURID 14/20   CONSTN
CMN/WLTH. PAGE 95 E1900   CT/SYS

S55

BETH L.P.,"THE CASE FOR JUDICIAL PROTECTION OF   CT/SYS
CIVIL LIBERTIES" (BMR)" USA+45 CONSTN ELITES LEGIS   JUDGE
CONTROL...POLICY DECISION JURID 20 SUPREME/CT   ADJUD
CIVIL/LIB. PAGE 11 E0220   ORD/FREE

B56

ABELS J.,THE TRUMAN SCANDALS. USA+45 USA-45 POL/PAR   CRIME
TAX LEGIT CT/SYS CHOOSE PRIVIL MORAL WEALTH 20   ADMIN
TRUMAN/HS PRESIDENT CONGRESS. PAGE 2 E0043   CHIEF
                                                        TRIBUTE

B56

CALLISON I.P.,COURTS OF INJUSTICE. USA+45 PROF/ORG   CT/SYS
ADJUD CRIME PERSON MORAL PWR RESPECT SKILL 20.   JUDGE
PAGE 19 E0368   JURID

B56

DOUGLAS W.O.,WE THE JUDGES. INDIA USA+45 USA-45 LAW   ADJUD
NAT/G SECT LEGIS PRESS CRIME FEDERAL ORD/FREE   CT/SYS
...POLICY GOV/COMP 19/20 WARRN/EARL MARSHALL/J   CONSTN
SUPREME/CT. PAGE 32 E0640   GOV/REL

B56

KALNOKI BEDO A.,LEGAL SOURCES AND BIBLIOGRAPHY OF   BIBLIOG
HUNGARY. COM HUNGARY CONSTN LEGIS JUDGE CT/SYS   ADJUD
SANCTION CRIME 16/20. PAGE 59 E1181   LAW
                                                        JURID

B56

PEASLEE A.J.,CONSTITUTIONS OF NATIONS. WOR+45 LAW   CONSTN
NAT/G EX/STRUC LEGIS TOP/EX LEGIT CT/SYS ROUTINE   CON/ANAL
CHOOSE ORD/FREE PWR SOVEREIGN...CHARTS TOT/POP.
PAGE 80 E1605

B56

SIPKOV I.,LEGAL SOURCES AND BIBLIOGRAPHY OF   BIBLIOG
BULGARIA. BULGARIA COM LEGIS WRITING ADJUD CT/SYS   LAW
...INT/LAW TREATY 20. PAGE 91 E1834   TOTALISM
                                                        MARXISM

B56

SUTHERLAND A.E.,THE LAW AND ONE MAN AMONG MANY.   JURID
USA+45 INTELL ADJUD CT/SYS 20. PAGE 95 E1895   INGP/REL
                                                        ORD/FREE
                                                        CONCPT

B56

US HOUSE WAYS MEANS COMMITTEE,TRAFFIC IN, AND   BIO/SOC
CONTROL OF NARCOTICS, BARBITURATES, AND   CONTROL
AMPHETAMINES. CHINA/COM USA+45 SOCIETY LEGIS   PROB/SOLV
ACT/RES EDU/PROP CT/SYS SANCTION PROFIT HEALTH   CRIME
...HEAL PSY STAT 20. PAGE 100 E2011

S56

TANENHAUS J.,"THE SUPREME COURT AND PRESIDENTIAL   CT/SYS
POWER." USA+45 USA-45 NAT/G ADJUD GOV/REL FEDERAL   PWR
20 PRESIDENT. PAGE 95 E1907   CONTROL
                                                        CHIEF

C56

AUMANN F.R.,"THE ISTRUMENTALITIES OF JUSTICE: THEIR   JURID
FORMS, FUNCTIONS, AND LIMITATIONS." WOR+45 WOR-45   ADMIN
JUDGE PROB/SOLV ROUTINE ATTIT...BIBLIOG 20. PAGE 6   CT/SYS
E0118   ADJUD

B57

BAYITCH S.A.,A GUIDE TO INTERAMERICAN LEGAL   BIBLIOG
STUDIES: A SELECTIVE BIBLIOGRAPHY OF WORKS IN   L/A+17C
ENGLISH. NAT/G LEGIS ADJUD CT/SYS CONGRESS 20.   LAW
PAGE 8 E0157   JURID

B57

BERNS W.,FREEDOM, VIRTUE AND THE FIRST AMENDMENT.   JURID
USA+45 USA-45 CONSTN INTELL JUDGE ADJUD RIGID/FLEX   ORD/FREE
MORAL...CONCPT 20 AMEND/I. PAGE 11 E0211   CT/SYS
                                                        LAW

B57

BERNS W.,FREEDOM, VIRTUE, AND THE FIRST AMENDMENT.   ADJUD
USA-45 LAW CONSTN PROB/SOLV NEW/LIB...JURID 20   CT/SYS
SUPREME/CT AMEND/I. PAGE 11 E0212   ORD/FREE

B57

CHICAGO U LAW SCHOOL,CONFERENCE ON JUDICIAL   CT/SYS
ADMINISTRATION. LOC/G MUNIC NAT/G PROVS...ANTHOL   ADJUD
20. PAGE 22 E0429   ADMIN
                                                        GOV/REL

B57

COOPER F.E.,THE LAWYER AND ADMINISTRATIVE AGENCIES.   CONSULT
USA+45 CLIENT LAW PROB/SOLV CT/SYS PERSON ROLE.   ADMIN
PAGE 25 E0500   ADJUD
                                                        DELIB/GP

B57

DE VISSCHER C.,THEORY AND REALITY IN PUBLIC   INT/ORG
INTERNATIONAL LAW. WOR+45 WOR-45 SOCIETY NAT/G   LAW
CT/SYS ATTIT MORAL ORD/FREE PWR...JURID CONCPT   INT/LAW
METH/CNCPT TIME/SEQ GEN/LAWS LEAGUE/NAT TOT/POP
VAL/FREE COLD/WAR. PAGE 30 E0599

B57

DONALDSON A.G.,SOME COMPARATIVE ASPECTS OF IRISH   CONSTN
LAW. IRELAND NAT/G DIPLOM ADMIN CT/SYS LEAD ATTIT   LAW
SOVEREIGN...JURID BIBLIOG/A 12/20 CMN/WLTH. PAGE 32   NAT/COMP
E0635   INT/LAW

DUMBAULD E.,THE BILL OF RIGHTS AND WHAT IT MEANS
TODAY. USA+45 USA-45 CT/SYS...JURID STYLE TIME/SEQ
BIBLIOG 18/20 BILL/RIGHT. PAGE 33 E0656
B57
CONSTN
LAW
ADJUD
ORD/FREE

HINDERLING A.,DIE REFORMATORISCHE
VERWALTUNGSGERICHTSBARKEIT. GERMANY/W PROB/SOLV
ADJUD SUPEGO PWR...CONCPT 20. PAGE 53 E1049
B57
ADMIN
CT/SYS
JURID
CONTROL

HISS A.,IN THE COURT OF PUBLIC OPINION. USA+45
DELIB/GP LEGIS LEGIT CT/SYS ATTIT 20 DEPT/STATE
NIXON/RM HUAC HISS/ALGER. PAGE 53 E1053
B57
CRIME
MARXISM
BIOG
ADJUD

JENKS C.W.,THE INTERNATIONAL PROTECTION OF TRADE
UNION FREEDOM. FUT WOR+45 WOR-45 VOL/ASSN DELIB/GP
CT/SYS REGION ROUTINE...JURID METH/CNCPT RECORD
TIME/SEQ CHARTS ILO WORK OAS 20. PAGE 58 E1153
B57
LABOR
INT/ORG

LONG H.A.,USURPERS - FOES OF FREE MAN. LAW NAT/G
CHIEF LEGIS DOMIN ADJUD REPRESENT GOV/REL ORD/FREE
LAISSEZ POPULISM...POLICY 18/20 SUPREME/CT
ROOSEVLT/F CONGRESS CON/INTERP. PAGE 66 E1325
B57
CT/SYS
CENTRAL
FEDERAL
CONSTN

MORELAND C.C.,EQUAL JUSTICE UNDER LAW. USA+45
USA-45 PROF/ORG PROVS JUDGE...POLICY JURID. PAGE 74
E1491
B57
CONSTN
ADJUD
CT/SYS
ORD/FREE

ROSENNE S.,THE INTERNATIONAL COURT OF JUSTICE.
WOR+45 LAW DOMIN LEGIT PEACE PWR SOVEREIGN...JURID
CONCPT RECORD TIME/SEQ CON/ANAL CHARTS UN TOT/POP
VAL/FREE LEAGUE/NAT 20 ICJ. PAGE 86 E1716
B57
INT/ORG
CT/SYS
INT/LAW

SCHLOCHAUER H.J.,OFFENTLICHES RECHT. GERMANY/W
FINAN EX/STRUC LEGIS DIPLOM FEDERAL ORD/FREE
...INT/LAW 20. PAGE 88 E1757
B57
CONSTN
JURID
ADMIN
CT/SYS

SCHUBERT G.A.,THE PRESIDENCY IN THE COURTS. CONSTN
FORCES DIPLOM TARIFFS ADJUD CONTROL WAR...DECISION
MGT CHARTS 18/20 PRESIDENT CONGRESS SUPREME/CT.
PAGE 89 E1778
B57
PWR
CT/SYS
LEGIT
CHIEF

UNESCO,A REGISTER OF LEGAL DOCUMENTATION IN THE
WORLD (2ND ED.). CT/SYS...JURID IDEA/COMP METH/COMP
NAT/COMP 20. PAGE 98 E1960
B57
BIBLIOG
LAW
INT/LAW
CONSTN

US SENATE COMM ON JUDICIARY,LIMITATION OF APPELLATE
JURISDICTION OF THE SUPREME COURT. USA+45 LAW NAT/G
DELIB/GP PLAN ADMIN CONTROL PWR...DECISION 20
CONGRESS SUPREME/CT. PAGE 102 E2041
B57
CT/SYS
ADJUD
POLICY
GOV/REL

FRANKFURTER F.,"THE SUPREME COURT IN THE MIRROR OF
JUSTICES" (BMR)" USA+45 USA-45 INTELL INSPECT
EFFICIENCY ROLE KNOWL MORAL 18/20 SUPREME/CT.
PAGE 40 E0792
S57
EDU/PROP
ADJUD
CT/SYS
PERSON

ALEXANDROWICZ,A BIBLIOGRAPHY OF INDIAN LAW. INDIA
S/ASIA CONSTN CT/SYS...INT/LAW 19/20. PAGE 3 E0062
B58
BIBLIOG
LAW
ADJUD
JURID

AMERICAN SOCIETY PUBLIC ADMIN,STRENGTHENING
MANAGEMENT FOR DEMOCRATIC GOVERNMENT. USA+45 ACADEM
EX/STRUC WORKER PLAN BUDGET CONFER CT/SYS
EFFICIENCY ANTHOL. PAGE 4 E0083
B58
ADMIN
NAT/G
EXEC
MGT

BLOCH J.,STATES' RIGHTS: THE LAW OF THE LAND.
USA+45 USA-45 LAW CONSTN LEGIS CONTROL CT/SYS
FEDERAL ORD/FREE...PREDICT 17/20 CONGRESS
SUPREME/CT. PAGE 13 E0246
B58
PROVS
NAT/G
BAL/PWR
CENTRAL

CABLE G.W.,THE NEGRO QUESTION: A SELECTION OF
WRITINGS ON CIVIL RIGHTS IN THE SOUTH. USA+45
STRATA LOC/G POL/PAR GIVE EDU/PROP WRITING CT/SYS
SANCTION CRIME CHOOSE WORSHIP 20 NEGRO CIV/RIGHTS
CONV/LEASE SOUTH/US. PAGE 18 E0355
B58
RACE/REL
CULTURE
DISCRIM
ORD/FREE

CARPENTER W.S.,FOUNDATIONS OF MODERN JURISPRUDENCE. LAW
UNIV PROB/SOLV ADJUD CT/SYS CRIME ATTIT...CONCPT
18/20. PAGE 20 E0388
B58
JURID

CHARLES R.,LA JUSTICE EN FRANCE. FRANCE LAW CONSTN
DELIB/GP CRIME 20. PAGE 21 E0422
B58
JURID
ADMIN
CT/SYS
ADJUD

CUNNINGHAM W.B.,COMPULSORY CONCILIATION AND
COLLECTIVE BARGAINING. CANADA NAT/G LEGIS ADJUD
CT/SYS GP/REL...MGT 20 NEW/BRUNS STRIKE CASEBOOK.
PAGE 28 E0555
B58
POLICY
BARGAIN
LABOR
INDUS

DAVIS K.C.,ADMINISTRATIVE LAW TREATISE (VOLS. I AND
IV). NAT/G JUDGE PROB/SOLV ADJUD GP/REL 20
SUPREME/CT. PAGE 29 E0575
B58
ADMIN
JURID
CT/SYS
EX/STRUC

DAVIS K.C.,ADMINISTRATIVE LAW; CASES, TEXT,
PROBLEMS. LAW LOC/G NAT/G TOP/EX PAY CONTROL
GOV/REL INGP/REL FEDERAL 20 SUPREME/CT. PAGE 29
E0576
B58
ADJUD
JURID
CT/SYS
ADMIN

DEUTSCHE GESCHAFT VOLKERRECHT,DIE VOLKERRECHTLICHEN
DISSERTATIONEN AN DEN WESTDEUTSCHEN UNIVERSITATEN,
1945-1957. GERMANY/W NAT/G DIPLOM ADJUD CT/SYS
...POLICY 20. PAGE 31 E0616
B58
BIBLIOG
INT/LAW
ACADEM
JURID

DEVLIN P.,THE CRIMINAL PROSECUTION IN ENGLAND. UK
NAT/G ADMIN ROUTINE EFFICIENCY...JURID SOC 20.
PAGE 31 E0617
B58
CRIME
LAW
METH
CT/SYS

DOUGLAS W.O.,THE RIGHT OF THE PEOPLE. USA+45
EDU/PROP CONTROL REPRESENT PRIVIL...IDEA/COMP 20.
PAGE 32 E0641
B58
ORD/FREE
CONSTN
CT/SYS
CIVMIL/REL

EUSDEN J.D.,PURITANS, LAWYERS, AND POLITICS IN
EARLY SEVENTEENTH-CENTURY ENGLAND. UK CT/SYS
PARL/PROC RATIONAL PWR SOVEREIGN...IDEA/COMP
BIBLIOG 17 PURITAN COMMON/LAW. PAGE 35 E0702
B58
GP/REL
SECT
NAT/G
LAW

FELLMAN D.,THE DEFENDANT'S RIGHTS. USA+45 NAT/G
CONSULT CT/SYS SUPEGO ORD/FREE...BIBLIOG SUPREME/CT
CIVIL/SERV. PAGE 37 E0730
B58
CONSTN
LAW
CRIME
ADJUD

HALL J.,STUDIES IN JURISPRUDENCE AND CRIMINAL
THEORY. USA-45 LAW CULTURE CREATE SUPEGO...CRIMLGY
PSY /20 PLATO. PAGE 49 E0983
B58
JURID
CRIME
CONCPT
CT/SYS

HAND L.,THE BILL OF RIGHTS. USA+45 USA-45 CHIEF
LEGIS BAL/PWR ROLE PWR 18/20 SUPREME/CT CONGRESS
AMEND/V PRESIDENT AMEND/XIV. PAGE 50 E0994
B58
CONSTN
JURID
ORD/FREE
CT/SYS

JAPAN MINISTRY OF JUSTICE,CRIMINAL JUSTICE IN
JAPAN. LAW PROF/ORG PUB/INST FORCES CONTROL CT/SYS
PARL/PROC 20 CHINJAP. PAGE 58 E1149
B58
CONSTN
CRIME
JURID
ADMIN

KAPLAN H.E.,THE LAW OF CIVIL SERVICE. USA+45 LAW
POL/PAR CT/SYS CRIME GOV/REL...POLICY JURID 20.
PAGE 59 E1183
B58
ADJUD
NAT/G
ADMIN
CONSTN

LAW COMMISSION OF INDIA,REFORM OF JUDICIAL
ADMINISTRATION. INDIA TOP/EX ADMIN DISCRIM
EFFICIENCY...METH/COMP 20. PAGE 63 E1269
B58
CT/SYS
ADJUD
GOV/REL
CONTROL

MACKENZIE W.J.M.,FREE ELECTIONS: AN ELEMENTARY
TEXTBOOK. WOR+45 NAT/G POL/PAR LEGIS TOP/EX
EDU/PROP LEGIT CT/SYS ATTIT PWR...OBS CHARTS
STERTYP T CONGRESS PARLIAMENT 20. PAGE 67 E1342
B58
EX/STRUC
CHOOSE

B58

MASON A.T.,THE SUPREME COURT FROM TAFT TO WARREN.   CT/SYS
EX/STRUC LEGIS ROLE 20 SUPREME/CT TAFT/WH HUGHES/CE   JURID
STONE/HF. PAGE 69 E1376   ADJUD

B58

O'BRIEN F.W.,JUSTICE REED AND THE FIRST AMENDMENT,   ADJUD
THE RELIGION CLAUSES. USA+45 USA-45 NAT/G PROVS   SECT
CONTROL FEDERAL...POLICY JURID TIME/SEQ 20   CT/SYS
SUPREME/CT CHRUCH/STA AMEND/I REED/STAN. PAGE 78
E1563

B58

PALMER E.E.,CIVIL LIBERTIES. USA+45 ADJUD CT/SYS   ORD/FREE
PARTIC OWN LAISSEZ POPULISM...JURID CONCPT ANTHOL   CONSTN
20 SUPREME/CT CIVIL/LIB. PAGE 79 E1592   RACE/REL
                                                          LAW

B58

POUND R.,JUSTICE ACCORDING TO LAW. LAW SOCIETY   CONCPT
CT/SYS 20. PAGE 82 E1639   JURID
                                                          ADJUD
                                                          ADMIN

B58

WESTIN A.F.,THE ANATOMY OF A CONSTITUTIONAL LAW   CT/SYS
CASE. USA+45 LAW LEGIS ADMIN EXEC...DECISION MGT   INDUS
SOC RECORD 20 SUPREME/CT. PAGE 105 E2113   ADJUD
                                                          CONSTN

B58

WHITNEY S.N.,ANTITRUST POLICIES: AMERICAN   INDUS
EXPERIENCE IN TWENTY INDUSTRIES. USA+45 USA-45 LAW   CONTROL
DELIB/GP LEGIS ADJUD CT/SYS GOV/REL ATTIT...ANTHOL   LG/CO
20 MONOPOLY CASEBOOK. PAGE 106 E2119   MARKET

B58

WOOD J.E.,CHURCH AND STATE IN SCRIPTURE HISTORY AND   GP/REL
CONSTITUTIONAL LAW. LAW CONSTN SOCIETY PROVS   SECT
VOL/ASSN BAL/PWR COLONIAL CT/SYS ATTIT...BIBLIOG 20   NAT/G
SUPREME/CT CHURCH/STA BIBLE. PAGE 107 E2142   ADJUD

L58

BEVAN W.,"JURY BEHAVIOR AS A FUNCTION OF THE   PERSON
PRESTIGE OF THE FOREMAN AND THE NATURE OF HIS   EDU/PROP
LEADERSHIP" (BMR)" DELIB/GP DOMIN ADJUD LEAD   DECISION
PERS/REL ATTIT...PSY STAT INT QU CHARTS SOC/EXP 20   CT/SYS
JURY. PAGE 11 E0221

S58

DAHL R.A.,"DECISION-MAKING IN A DEMOCRACY: THE   CT/SYS
SUPREME COURT AS A NATIONAL POLICY-MAKER" (BMR)"   CONSTN
USA+45 USA-45 POL/PAR ADJUD GOV/REL PWR...POLICY   DECISION
JURID 19/20 SUPREME/CT. PAGE 28 E0561   NAT/G

S58

FISHER F.M.,"THE MATHEMATICAL ANALYSIS OF SUPREME   PROB/SOLV
COURT DECISIONS: THE USE AND ABUSE OF QUANTITATIVE   CT/SYS
METHODS." USA+45 LAW EX/STRUC LEGIS JUDGE ROUTINE   JURID
ATTIT DECISION. PAGE 38 E0757   MATH

S58

MCDOUGAL M.S.,"PERSPECTIVES FOR A LAW OF OUTER   INT/ORG
SPACE." FUT WOR+45 AIR CONSULT DELIB/GP TEC/DEV   SPACE
CT/SYS ORD/FREE...POLICY JURID 20 UN. PAGE 70 E1404   INT/LAW

S58

SCHUBERT G.A.,"THE STUDY OF JUDICIAL DECISION-   JUDGE
MAKING AS AN ASPECT OF POLITICAL BEHAVIOR." PLAN   DECISION
ADJUD CT/SYS INGP/REL PERSON...PHIL/SCI SOC QUANT   CON/ANAL
STAT CHARTS IDEA/COMP SOC/EXP. PAGE 89 E1779   GAME

S58

VOSE C.E.,"LITIGATION AS A FORM OF PRESSURE GROUP   CONTROL
ACTIVITY" (BMR)" USA+45 ADJUD ORD/FREE NAACP.   CT/SYS
PAGE 104 E2085   VOL/ASSN
                                                          LOBBY

B59

ABRAHAM H.J.,COURTS AND JUDGES: AN INTRODUCTION TO   CT/SYS
THE JUDICIAL PROCESS. USA+45 CONSTN ELITES NAT/G   PERSON
ORD/FREE PWR 19/20 SUPREME/CT. PAGE 2 E0045   JURID
                                                          ADJUD

B59

CHRISTMAN H.M.,THE PUBLIC PAPERS OF CHIEF JUSTICE   LAW
EARL WARREN. CONSTN POL/PAR EDU/PROP SANCTION   CT/SYS
HEALTH...TREND 20 SUPREME/CT WARRN/EARL. PAGE 22   PERSON
E0436   ADJUD

B59

DAVIS K.C.,ADMINISTRATIVE LAW TEXT. USA+45 NAT/G   ADJUD
DELIB/GP EX/STRUC CONTROL ORD/FREE...T 20   ADMIN
SUPREME/CT. PAGE 29 E0577   JURID
                                                          CT/SYS

B59

DESMITH S.A.,JUDICIAL REVIEW OF ADMINISTRATIVE   ADJUD
ACTION. UK LOC/G CONSULT DELIB/GP ADMIN PWR   NAT/G
...DECISION JURID 20 ENGLSH/LAW. PAGE 31 E0609   PROB/SOLV
                                                          CT/SYS

B59

ELLIOTT S.D.,IMPROVING OUR COURTS. LAW EX/STRUC   CT/SYS
PLAN PROB/SOLV ADJUD ADMIN TASK CRIME EFFICIENCY   JURID
ORD/FREE 20. PAGE 34 E0684   GOV/REL
                                                          NAT/G

B59

GINSBURG M.,LAW AND OPINION IN ENGLAND. UK CULTURE   JURID
KIN LABOR LEGIS EDU/PROP ADMIN CT/SYS CRIME OWN   POLICY
HEALTH...ANTHOL 20 ENGLSH/LAW. PAGE 44 E0868   ECO/TAC

B59

GSOVSKI V.,GOVERNMENT, LAW, AND COURTS IN THE   ADJUD
SOVIET UNION AND EASTERN EUROPE (2 VOLS.). COM USSR   MARXISM
AGRI INDUS WORKER CT/SYS CRIME...BIBLIOG 20   CONTROL
EUROPE/E. PAGE 48 E0958   ORD/FREE

B59

HAYS B.,A SOUTHERN MODERATE SPEAKS. LAW PROVS   SECT
SCHOOL KNOWL...JURID SOC SELF/OBS BIOG 20 NEGRO   DISCRIM
SUPREME/CT. PAGE 51 E1015   CT/SYS
                                                          RACE/REL

B59

LOEWENSTEIN K.,VERFASSUNGSRECHT UND   CONSTN
VERFASSUNGSPRAXIS DER VEREINIGTEN STAATEN. USA+45   POL/PAR
USA-45 COLONIAL CT/SYS GP/REL RACE/REL ORD/FREE   EX/STRUC
...JURID 18/20 SUPREME/CT CONGRESS PRESIDENT   NAT/G
BILL/RIGHT CIVIL/LIB. PAGE 66 E1319

B59

SCHNEIDER J.,TREATY-MAKING POWER OF INTERNATIONAL   INT/ORG
ORGANIZATIONS. FUT WOR+45 WOR-45 LAW NAT/G JUDGE   ROUTINE
DIPLOM LEGIT CT/SYS ORD/FREE PWR...INT/LAW JURID
GEN/LAWS TOT/POP UNESCO 20 TREATY. PAGE 88 E1762

B59

SCHORN H.,DER RICHTER IM DRITTEN REICH: GESCHICHTE   ADJUD
UND DOKUMENTE. GERMANY NAT/G LEGIT CT/SYS INGP/REL   JUDGE
MORAL ORD/FREE RESPECT...JURID GP/COMP 20. PAGE 88   FASCISM
E1765

B59

SCHUBERT G.A.,QUANTITATIVE ANALYSIS OF JUDICIAL   JUDGE
BEHAVIOR. ADJUD LEAD CHOOSE INGP/REL MAJORITY ATTIT   CT/SYS
...DECISION JURID CHARTS GAME SIMUL SUPREME/CT.   PERSON
PAGE 89 E1780   QUANT

B59

SCOTT F.R.,CIVIL LIBERTIES AND CANADIAN FEDERALISM.   ORD/FREE
CANADA LAW ADJUD CT/SYS GOV/REL 20 CIV/RIGHTS.   FEDERAL
PAGE 90 E1797   NAT/LISM
                                                          CONSTN

B59

SIMPSON J.L.,INTERNATIONAL ARBITRATION: LAW AND   INT/LAW
PRACTICE. WOR+45 WOR-45 INT/ORG DELIB/GP ADJUD   DIPLOM
PEACE MORAL ORD/FREE...METH 18/20. PAGE 91 E1829   CT/SYS
                                                          CONSULT

B59

SPIRO H.J.,GOVERNMENT BY CONSTITUTIONS: THE   NAT/G
POLITICAL SYSTEMS OF DEMOCRACY. CANADA EUR+WWI FUT   CONSTN
USA+45 WOR+45 LEGIS TOP/EX LEGIT ADMIN
CT/SYS ORD/FREE PWR...TREND TOT/POP VAL/FREE 20.
PAGE 93 E1861

B59

SQUIBB G.D.,THE HIGH COURT OF CHIVALRY. UK NAT/G   CT/SYS
FORCES ADJUD WAR 14/20 PARLIAMENT ENGLSH/LAW.   PARL/PROC
PAGE 93 E1863   JURID

B59

TOMPKINS D.C.,SUPREME COURT OF THE UNITED STATES: A   BIBLIOG/A
BIBLIOGRAPHY. LAW JUDGE ADJUD GOV/REL DISCRIM   CT/SYS
...JURID 18/20 SUPREME/CT NEGRO. PAGE 96 E1931   CONSTN
                                                          NAT/G

B59

VAN CAENEGEM R.C.,ROYAL WRITS IN ENGLAND FROM THE   JURID
CONQUEST TO GLANVILL. UK JUDGE...TREND IDEA/COMP   CHIEF
11/12 COMMON/LAW. PAGE 103 E2067   ADJUD
                                                          CT/SYS

B59

VOSE C.E.,CAUCASIANS ONLY: THE SUPREME COURT, THE   CT/SYS
NAACP, AND THE RESTRICTIVE COVENANT CASES. USA+45   RACE/REL
LAW CONSTN LOBBY...SOC 20 NAACP SUPREME/CT NEGRO.   DISCRIM
PAGE 104 E2086

WAGNER W.J.,THE FEDERAL STATES AND THEIR JUDICIARY. ADJUD
BRAZIL CANADA SWITZERLND USA+45 CONFER CT/SYS TASK METH/COMP
EFFICIENCY FEDERAL PWR...JURID BIBLIOG 20 AUSTRAL PROB/SOLV
MEXIC/AMER. PAGE 104 E2091 NAT/G
B59

BEANEY W.B.,"CIVIL LIBERTIES AND STATUTORY CT/SYS
CONSTRUCTION"(BMR)" USA+45 LEGIS BAL/PWR 20 ORD/FREE
SUPREME/CT. PAGE 8 E0162 ADJUD
LAW
S59

CHAPMAN B.,"THE FRENCH CONSEIL D'ETAT." FRANCE ADMIN
NAT/G CONSULT OP/RES PROB/SOLV PWR...OBS 20. LAW
PAGE 21 E0421 CT/SYS
LEGIS
S59

MASON A.T.,"THE SUPREME COURT: TEMPLE AND FORUM" CT/SYS
(BMR)" USA+45 USA-45 CONSTN DELIB/GP RACE/REL JURID
MAJORITY ORD/FREE...DECISION SOC/INTEG 19/20 PWR
SUPREME/CT WARRN/EARL CIV/RIGHTS. PAGE 69 E1377 ATTIT
S59

MENDELSON W.,"JUDICIAL REVIEW AND PARTY POLITICS" CT/SYS
(BMR)" UK USA+45 USA-45 NAT/G LEGIS PROB/SOLV POL/PAR
EDU/PROP ADJUD EFFICIENCY...POLICY NAT/COMP 19/20 BAL/PWR
AUSTRAL SUPREME/CT. PAGE 72 E1436 JURID
S59

MURPHY W.F.,"LOWER COURT CHECKS ON SUPREME COURT CT/SYS
POWER" (BMR)" USA+45 NAT/G PROVS SCHOOL GOV/REL BAL/PWR
RACE/REL DISCRIM ATTIT...DECISION JURID 20 CONTROL
SUPREME/CT NEGRO. PAGE 75 E1508 ADJUD
S59

SOHN L.B.,"THE DEFINITION OF AGGRESSION." FUT LAW INT/ORG
FORCES LEGIT ADJUD ROUTINE COERCE ORD/FREE PWR CT/SYS
...MAJORIT JURID QUANT COLD/WAR 20. PAGE 92 E1855 DETER
SOVEREIGN
C59

COLLINS I.,"THE GOVERNMENT AND THE NEWSPAPER PRESS PRESS
IN FRANCE, 1814-1881. FRANCE LAW ADMIN CT/SYS ORD/FREE
...CON/ANAL BIBLIOG 19. PAGE 24 E0475 NAT/G
EDU/PROP
B60

JUNZ A.J.,PRESENT TRENDS IN AMERICAN NATIONAL POL/PAR
GOVERNMENT. LEGIS DIPLOM ADMIN CT/SYS ORD/FREE CHOOSE
...CONCPT ANTHOL 20 CONGRESS PRESIDENT SUPREME/CT. CONSTN
PAGE 2 E0040 NAT/G
B60

BLANSHARD P.,GOD AND MAN IN WASHINGTON. USA+45 NAT/G
CHIEF LEGIS LEGIT CT/SYS PRIVIL ATTIT ORD/FREE SECT
...POLICY CONCPT 20 SUPREME/CT CONGRESS PRESIDENT GP/REL
CHURCH/STA. PAGE 12 E0242 POL/PAR
B60

BYRD E.M. JR.,TREATIES AND EXECUTIVE AGREEMENTS IN CHIEF
THE UNITED STATES: THEIR SEPARATE ROLES AND INT/LAW
LIMITATIONS. USA+45 USA-45 EX/STRUC TARIFFS CT/SYS DIPLOM
GOV/REL FEDERAL...IDEA/COMP BIBLIOG SUPREME/CT
SENATE CONGRESS. PAGE 18 E0353
B60

DAVIS K.C.,ADMINISTRATIVE LAW AND GOVERNMENT. ADMIN
USA+45 EX/STRUC PROB/SOLV ADJUD GP/REL PWR...POLICY JURID
20 SUPREME/CT. PAGE 29 E0578 CT/SYS
NAT/G
B60

FELLMAN D.,THE SUPREME COURT AND EDUCATION. ACADEM CT/SYS
NAT/G PROVS DELIB/GP ADJUD ORD/FREE...POLICY JURID SECT
WORSHIP 20 SUPREME/CT NEGRO CHURCH/STA. PAGE 37 RACE/REL
E0731 SCHOOL
B60

GELLHORN W.,AMERICAN RIGHTS: THE CONSTITUTION IN ORD/FREE
ACTION. USA+45 USA-45 LEGIS ADJUD COERCE RACE/REL JURID
DISCRIM MARXISM 20 SUPREME/CT. PAGE 43 E0846 CT/SYS
CONSTN
B60

HANBURY H.G.,ENGLISH COURTS OF LAW. UK EX/STRUC JURID
LEGIS CRIME ROLE 12/20 COMMON/LAW ENGLSH/LAW. CT/SYS
PAGE 50 E0993 CONSTN
GOV/REL
B60

HARVARD LAW SCHOOL LIBRARY,CURRENT LEGAL BIBLIOG
BIBLIOGRAPHY. USA+45 CONSTN LEGIS ADJUD CT/SYS JURID
POLICY. PAGE 51 E1006 LAW
INT/LAW

LASKIN B.,CANADIAN CONSTITUTIONAL LAW: TEXT AND CONSTN
NOTES ON DISTRIBUTION OF LEGISLATIVE POWER (2ND NAT/G
ED.). CANADA LOC/G ECO/TAC TAX CONTROL CT/SYS CRIME LAW
FEDERAL PWR...JURID 20 PARLIAMENT. PAGE 63 E1259 LEGIS
B60

MENDELSON W.,CAPITALISM, DEMOCRACY, AND THE SUPREME JUDGE
COURT. USA+45 USA-45 CONSTN DIPLOM GOV/REL ATTIT CT/SYS
ORD/FREE LAISSEZ...POLICY CHARTS PERS/COMP 18/20 JURID
SUPREME/CT MARSHALL/J HOLMES/OW TANEY/RB FIELD/JJ. NAT/G
PAGE 72 E1437
B60

NAT'L MUNICIPAL LEAGUE,COMPENDIUM ON LEGISLATIVE APPORT
APPORTIONMENT. USA+45 LOC/G NAT/G POL/PAR PROVS REPRESENT
CT/SYS CHOOSE 20 SUPREME/CT CONGRESS. PAGE 76 E1523 LEGIS
STAT
B60

POWELL T.,THE SCHOOL BUS LAW: A CASE STUDY IN JURID
EDUCATION, RELIGION, AND POLITICS. USA+45 LAW NEIGH SCHOOL
SECT LEGIS EDU/PROP ADJUD CT/SYS LOBBY CATHISM
WORSHIP 20 CONNECTICT CHURCH/STA. PAGE 82 E1641
B60

PRASAD B.,THE ORIGINS OF PROVINCIAL AUTONOMY. INDIA CENTRAL
UK FINAN LOC/G FORCES LEGIS CONTROL CT/SYS PWR PROVS
...JURID 19/20. PAGE 82 E1646 COLONIAL
NAT/G
B60

SCHMIDHAUSER J.R.,THE SUPREME COURT: ITS POLITICS, JUDGE
PERSONALITIES, AND PROCEDURES. LAW DELIB/GP JURID
EX/STRUC TOP/EX ADJUD CT/SYS CHOOSE RATIONAL PWR DECISION
SUPREME/CT. PAGE 88 E1760
B60

SCHUBERT G.A.,CONSTITUTIONAL POLITICS: THE CONSTN
POLITICAL BEHAVIOR OF SUPREME COURT JUSTICES AND CT/SYS
THE CONSTITUTIONAL POLICIES THEY MAKE. LAW ELITES JURID
CHIEF DELIB/GP EX/STRUC LEGIS DISCRIM ORD/FREE PWR DECISION
...POLICY MAJORIT CHARTS SUPREME/CT CONGRESS.
PAGE 89 E1781
B60

WEBSTER J.A.,A GENERAL STUDY OF THE DEPARTMENT OF ORD/FREE
DEFENSE INTERNAL SECURITY PROGRAM. USA+45 WORKER PLAN
TEC/DEV ADJUD CONTROL CT/SYS EXEC GOV/REL COST ADMIN
...POLICY DECISION MGT 20 DEPT/DEFEN SUPREME/CT. NAT/G
PAGE 105 E2105
S60

BLACK H.,"THE BILL OF RIGHTS" (BMR)" USA+45 USA-45 CONSTN
LAW LEGIS CT/SYS FEDERAL PWR 18/20 CONGRESS ORD/FREE
SUPREME/CT BILL/RIGHT CIV/RIGHTS. PAGE 12 E0237 NAT/G
JURID
S60

ROURKE F.E.,"ADMINISTRATIVE SECRECY: A LEGIS
CONGRESSIONAL DILEMMA." DELIB/GP CT/SYS ATTIT EXEC
...MAJORIT DECISION JURID. PAGE 86 E1727 ORD/FREE
POLICY
S60

ULMER S.S.,"THE ANALYSIS OF BEHAVIOR PATTERNS ON ATTIT
THE UNITED STATES SUPREME COURT" USA+45 LAW CT/SYS ADJUD
PERS/REL RACE/REL PERSON...DECISION PSY SOC TREND PROF/ORG
METH/COMP METH 20 SUPREME/CT CIVIL/LIB. PAGE 97 INGP/REL
E1951
C60

HAZARD J.N.,"SETTLING DISPUTES IN SOVIET SOCIETY: ADJUD
THE FORMATIVE YEARS OF LEGAL INSTITUTIONS." USSR LAW
NAT/G PROF/ORG PROB/SOLV CONTROL CT/SYS ROUTINE REV COM
CENTRAL...JURID BIBLIOG 20. PAGE 51 E1017 POLICY
B61

AUERBACH C.A.,THE LEGAL PROCESS. USA+45 DELIB/GP JURID
JUDGE CONFER ADJUD CONTROL...DECISION 20 ADMIN
SUPREME/CT. PAGE 6 E0116 LEGIS
CT/SYS
B61

AVERY M.W.,GOVERNMENT OF WASHINGTON STATE. USA+45 PROVS
MUNIC DELIB/GP EX/STRUC LEGIS GIVE CT/SYS PARTIC LOC/G
REGION EFFICIENCY 20 WASHINGT/G GOVERNOR. PAGE 6 ADMIN
E0121 GOV/REL
B61

AYLMER G.,THE KING'S SERVANTS. UK ELITES CHIEF PAY ADMIN
CT/SYS WEALTH 17 CROMWELL/O CHARLES/I. PAGE 6 E0122 ROUTINE
EX/STRUC
NAT/G

BAYITCH S.A.,LATIN AMERICA: A BIBLIOGRAPHICAL
GUIDE. LAW CONSTN LEGIS JUDGE ADJUD CT/SYS 20.
PAGE 8 E0158
B61
BIBLIOG
L/A+17C
NAT/G
JURID

BEDFORD S.,THE FACES OF JUSTICE: A TRAVELLER'S
REPORT. AUSTRIA FRANCE GERMANY/W SWITZERLND UK UNIV
WOR+45 WOR-45 CULTURE PARTIC GOV/REL MORAL...JURID
OBS GOV/COMP 20. PAGE 9 E0174
B61
CT/SYS
ORD/FREE
PERSON
LAW

CARROTHERS A.W.R.,LABOR ARBITRATION IN CANADA.
CANADA LAW NAT/G CONSULT LEGIS WORKER ADJUD ADMIN
CT/SYS 20. PAGE 20 E0396
B61
LABOR
MGT
GP/REL
BARGAIN

CHILDS M.W.,THE EROSION OF INDIVIDUAL LIBERTIES.
NAT/G LEGIS ATTIT...JURID SOC CONCPT IDEA/COMP 20
SUPREME/CT AMEND/I. PAGE 22 E0430
B61
ADJUD
CT/SYS
ORD/FREE
CONSTN

FREUND P.A.,THE SUPREME COURT OF THE UNITED STATES:
ITS BUSINESS, PURPOSES, AND PERFORMANCE. CONSTN
CRIME CONSEN ORD/FREE...DECISION 20 SUPREME/CT
CIVIL/LIB. PAGE 40 E0797
B61
CT/SYS
JURID
ADJUD
FEDERAL

JUSTICE,THE CITIZEN AND THE ADMINISTRATION: THE
REDRESS OF GRIEVANCES (PAMPHLET). EUR+WWI UK LAW
CONSTN STRATA NAT/G CT/SYS PARTIC COERCE...NEW/IDEA
IDEA/COMP 20 OMBUDSMAN. PAGE 59 E1176
B61
INGP/REL
CONSULT
ADJUD
REPRESENT

KURLAND P.B.,RELIGION AND THE LAW. USA+45 USA-45
CONSTN PROVS CHIEF ADJUD SANCTION PRIVIL CATHISM
...POLICY 17/20 SUPREME/CT PRESIDENT CHURCH/STA.
PAGE 62 E1239
B61
SECT
NAT/G
CT/SYS
GP/REL

ROCHE J.P.,COURTS AND RIGHTS: THE AMERICAN
JUDICIARY IN ACTION (2ND ED.). UK USA+45 USA-45
STRUCT TEC/DEV SANCTION PERS/REL RACE/REL ORD/FREE
...METH/CNCPT GOV/COMP METH/COMP T 13/20. PAGE 85
E1710
B61
JURID
CT/SYS
NAT/G
PROVS

SCOTT A.M.,POLITICS, USA: CASES ON THE AMERICAN
DEMOCRATIC PROCESS. USA+45 CHIEF FORCES DIPLOM
LOBBY CHOOSE RACE/REL FEDERAL ATTIT...JURID ANTHOL
T 20 PRESIDENT CONGRESS CIVIL/LIB. PAGE 90 E1795
B61
CT/SYS
CONSTN
NAT/G
PLAN

WECHSLER H.,PRINCIPLES, POLITICS AND FUNDAMENTAL
LAW: SELECTED ESSAYS. USA+45 USA-45 LAW SOCIETY
NAT/G PROVS DELIB/GP EX/STRUC ACT/RES LEGIT PERSON
KNOWL PWR...JURID 20 NUREMBERG. PAGE 105 E2106
B61
CT/SYS
CONSTN
INT/LAW

WESTIN A.F.,THE SUPREME COURT: VIEWS FROM INSIDE.
USA+45 NAT/G PROF/ORG PROVS DELIB/GP INGP/REL
DISCRIM ATTIT...POLICY DECISION JURID ANTHOL 20
SUPREME/CT CONGRESS CIVIL/LIB. PAGE 106 E2114
B61
CT/SYS
LAW
ADJUD
GOV/REL

SILVING H.,"IN RE EICHMANN: A DILEMMA OF LAW AND
MORALITY" WOR+45 INSPECT ADJUST MORAL...JURID 20
WAR/TRIAL EICHMANN/A NATURL/LAW. PAGE 91 E1828
L61
CT/SYS
INT/LAW
CONCPT

SCHUBERT G.,"A PSYCHOMETRIC MODEL OF THE SUPREME
COURT." DELIB/GP ADJUD CHOOSE ATTIT...DECISION
JURID PSY QUANT STAT HYPO/EXP GEN/METH SUPREME/CT.
PAGE 88 E1771
S61
JUDGE
CT/SYS
PERSON
SIMUL

ALLOTT A.N.,JUDICIAL AND LEGAL SYSTEMS IN AFRICA.
LAW CONSTN JUDGE CONTROL...METH/CNCPT CLASSIF
CHARTS 20 COMMON/LAW. PAGE 4 E0070
B62
CT/SYS
AFR
JURID
COLONIAL

BICKEL A.,THE LEAST DANGEROUS BRANCH. USA+45 USA-45
CONSTN SCHOOL LEGIS ADJUD RACE/REL DISCRIM ORD/FREE
...JURID 18/20 SUPREME/CT CONGRESS MARSHALL/J
HOLMES/OW FRANKFUR/F. PAGE 12 E0226
B62
LAW
NAT/G
CT/SYS

BISHOP W.W. JR.,INTERNATIONAL LAW: CASES AND
MATERIALS. WOR+45 INT/ORG FORCES PROB/SOLV AGREE
WAR...JURID IDEA/COMP T 20 TREATY. PAGE 12 E0233
B62
INT/LAW
DIPLOM
CONCPT
CT/SYS

BOCK E.A.,CASE STUDIES IN AMERICAN GOVERNMENT.
USA+45 ECO/DEV CHIEF EDU/PROP CT/SYS RACE/REL
ORD/FREE...JURID MGT PHIL/SCI PRESIDENT CASEBOOK.
PAGE 13 E0256
B62
POLICY
LEGIS
IDEA/COMP
NAT/G

BORKIN J.,THE CORRUPT JUDGE. USA+45 CT/SYS ATTIT
SUPEGO MORAL RESPECT...BIBLIOG + SUPREME/CT
MANTON/M DAVIS/W JOHNSN/ALB. PAGE 14 E0271
B62
ADJUD
TRIBUTE
CRIME

CARLSTON K.S.,LAW AND ORGANIZATION IN WORLD
SOCIETY. WOR+45 FINAN ECO/TAC DOMIN LEGIT CT/SYS
ROUTINE COERCE ORD/FREE PWR WEALTH...PLURIST
DECISION JURID MGT METH/CNCPT GEN/LAWS 20. PAGE 19
E0381
B62
INT/ORG
LAW

DELANY V.T.H.,THE ADMINISTRATION OF JUSTICE IN
IRELAND. IRELAND CONSTN FINAN JUDGE COLONIAL CRIME
...CRIMLGY 19/20. PAGE 30 E0604
B62
ADMIN
JURID
CT/SYS
ADJUD

EVAN W.M.,LAW AND SOCIOLOGY: EXPLORATORY ESSAYS.
CONSULT ACT/RES OP/RES PROB/SOLV EDU/PROP LEGIT
ADJUD CT/SYS GP/REL...PHIL/SCI ANTHOL SOC/INTEG 20.
PAGE 35 E0703
B62
JURID
SOC
PROF/ORG

FROMAN L.A. JR.,PEOPLE AND POLITICS: AN ANALYSIS OF
THE AMERICAN POLITICAL SYSTEM. USA+45 CHIEF
DELIB/GP EX/STRUC LEGIS TOP/EX CT/SYS LOBBY
PERS/REL PWR...POLICY DECISION. PAGE 41 E0813
B62
POL/PAR
PROB/SOLV
GOV/REL

GANJI M.,INTERNATIONAL PROTECTION OF HUMAN RIGHTS.
WOR+45 CONSTN INT/TRADE CT/SYS SANCTION CRIME WAR
RACE/REL...CHARTS IDEA/COMP NAT/COMP BIBLIOG 20
TREATY NEGRO LEAGUE/NAT UN CIVIL/LIB. PAGE 42 E0831
B62
ORD/FREE
DISCRIM
LEGIS
DELIB/GP

GROGAN V.,ADMINISTRATIVE TRIBUNALS IN THE PUBLIC
SERVICE. IRELAND UK NAT/G CONTROL CT/SYS...JURID
GOV/COMP 20. PAGE 48 E0945
B62
ADMIN
LAW
ADJUD
DELIB/GP

GRZYBOWSKI K.,SOVIET LEGAL INSTITUTIONS. USA+45
USSR ECO/DEV NAT/G EDU/PROP CONTROL CT/SYS CRIME
OWN ATTIT PWR SOCISM...NAT/COMP 20. PAGE 48 E0955
B62
ADJUD
LAW
JURID

GYORGY A.,PROBLEMS IN INTERNATIONAL RELATIONS. COM
CT/SYS NUC/PWR ALL/IDEOS 20 UN EEC ECSC. PAGE 49
E0966
B62
DIPLOM
NEUTRAL
BAL/PWR
REV

HSUEH S.-.S.,GOVERNMENT AND ADMINISTRATION OF HONG
KONG. CHIEF DELIB/GP LEGIS CT/SYS REPRESENT GOV/REL
20 HONG/KONG CITY/MGT CIVIL/SERV GOVERNOR. PAGE 55
E1106
B62
ADMIN
LOC/G
COLONIAL
EX/STRUC

INSTITUTE JUDICIAL ADMIN,JUDGES: THEIR TEMPORARY
APPOINTMENT, ASSIGNMENT AND TRANSFER: SURVEY OF FED
AND STATE CONSTN'S STATUTES, ROLES OF CT. USA+45
CONSTN PROVS CT/SYS GOV/REL PWR JURID. PAGE 57
E1128
B62
NAT/G
LOC/G
JUDGE
ADMIN

INTERNAT CONGRESS OF JURISTS,EXECUTIVE ACTION AND
THE RULE OF RULE: REPORTION PROCEEDINGS OF INT'T
CONGRESS OF JURISTS--RIO DE JANEIRO, BRAZIL. WOR+45
ACADEM CONSULT JUDGE EDU/PROP ADJUD CT/SYS INGP/REL
PERSON DEPT/DEFEN. PAGE 57 E1130
B62
JURID
EXEC
ORD/FREE
CONTROL

JACOBINI H.B.,INTERNATIONAL LAW: A TEXT. DIPLOM
ADJUD NEUTRAL WAR PEACE T. PAGE 57 E1143
B62
INT/LAW
CT/SYS
CONCPT

JENKS C.W.,THE PROPER LAW OF INTERNATIONAL
ORGANISATIONS. DIPLOM LEGIT AGREE CT/SYS SANCTION
REPRESENT SOVEREIGN...GEN/LAWS 20 UN UNESCO ILO
NATO OAS. PAGE 58 E1158
B62
LAW
INT/ORG
ADJUD
INT/LAW

KAUPER P.G.,CIVIL LIBERTIES AND THE CONSTITUTION.
USA+45 SECT EDU/PROP WRITING ADJUD SEX ORD/FREE 20
SUPREME/CT CIVIL/LIB CHURCH/STA. PAGE 60 E1188
B62
LAW
CONSTN
CT/SYS
DECISION

LILLICH R.B.,INTERNATIONAL CLAIMS: THEIR   B62   ADJUD
ADJUDICATION BY NATIONAL COMMISSIONS. WOR+45 WOR-45   JURID
INT/ORG LEGIT CT/SYS TOT/POP 20. PAGE 65 E1297   INT/LAW

MASON A.T.,THE SUPREME COURT: PALADIUM OF FREEDOM. B62   CONSTN
USA+45 NAT/G POL/PAR CHIEF LEGIS ADJUD PARL/PROC   CT/SYS
FEDERAL PWR...POLICY BIOG 18/20 SUPREME/CT   JURID
ROOSEVLT/F JEFFERSN/T MARSHALL/J HUGHES/CE. PAGE 69
E1378

MCGRATH J.J.,CHURCH AND STATE IN AMERICAN LAW. LAW B62   SECT
PROVS SCHOOL TAX GIVE CT/SYS GP/REL...POLICY ANTHOL   ADJUD
18/20 SUPREME/CT CHURCH/STA CASEBOOK. PAGE 71 E1414   CONSTN
                                                           NAT/G

MCGRATH J.J.,CHURCH AND STATE IN AMERICAN LAW: B62   LAW
CASES AND MATERIALS. USA+45 USA-45 LEGIS EDU/PROP   GOV/REL
ADJUD CT/SYS PWR...ANTHOL 18/20 CHURCH/STA. PAGE 71   SECT
E1415

MCWHINNEY E.,CONSTITUTIONALISM IN GERMANY AND THE   B62   CONSTN
FEDERAL CONSTITUTINAL COURT. GERMANY/W POL/PAR TV   CT/SYS
ADJUD CHOOSE EFFICIENCY ATTIT ORD/FREE MARXISM   CONTROL
...NEW/IDEA BIBLIOG 20. PAGE 71 E1428   NAT/G

MILLER P.,THE LEGAL MIND IN AMERICA. PROF/ORG JUDGE B62   JURID
ADJUD CT/SYS 18/19 SUPREME/CT. PAGE 73 E1461   CONSTN
                                                           NAT/G
                                                          CONCPT

MURPHY W.F.,CONGRESS AND THE COURT. USA+45 LAW   B62   LEGIS
LOBBY GP/REL RACE/REL ATTIT PWR...JURID INT BIBLIOG   CT/SYS
CONGRESS SUPREME/CT WARRN/EARL. PAGE 75 E1509   GOV/REL
                                                          ADJUD

NAT'L MUNICIPAL LEAGUE,COMPENDIUM ON LEGISLATIVE   B62   APPORT
APPORTIONMENT. USA+45 LOC/G NAT/G POL/PAR PROVS   REPRESENT
CT/SYS CHOOSE 20 SUPREME/CT CONGRESS. PAGE 76 E1524   LEGIS
                                                          STAT

NATIONAL MUNICIPAL LEAGUE,COURT DECISIONS ON   B62   PROVS
LEGISLATIVE APPORTIONMENT (VOL. III). USA+45 JUDGE   CT/SYS
ADJUD CONTROL ATTIT...DECISION JURID COURT/DIST   APPORT
CASEBOOK. PAGE 76 E1528   LEGIS

NEW YORK STATE LEGISLATURE,REPORT AND DRAFT OF   B62   CT/SYS
PROPOSED LEGISLATION ON COURT REORGANIZATION. LAW   JURID
PROVS DELIB/GP CREATE ADJUD 20 NEW/YORK. PAGE 77   MUNIC
E1538   LOC/G

PHILLIPS O.H.,CONSTITUTIONAL AND ADMINISTRATIVE LAW B62   JURID
(3RD ED.). UK INT/ORG LOC/G CHIEF EX/STRUC LEGIS   ADMIN
BAL/PWR ADJUD COLONIAL CT/SYS PWR...CHARTS 20.   CONSTN
PAGE 80 E1613   NAT/G

ROSTOW E.V.,THE SOVEREIGN PREROGATIVE: THE SUPREME B62   JURID
COURT AND THE QUEST FOR LAW. CONSTN CT/SYS FEDERAL   PROF/ORG
MORAL SOVEREIGN 20 SUPREME/CT. PAGE 86 E1726   ATTIT
                                                          ORD/FREE

SCHWARZENBERGER G.,THE FRONTIERS OF INTERNATIONAL   B62   INT/ORG
LAW. WOR+45 WOR-45 NAT/G LEGIT CT/SYS ROUTINE MORAL   LAW
ORD/FREE PWR...JURID SOC GEN/METH 20 COLD/WAR.   INT/LAW
PAGE 89 E1789

SIGLIANO R E.,THE COURTS. USA+45 USA-45 LAW CONSTN B62   ADJUD
NAT/G ROUTINE CHOOSE 18/20 SUPREME/CT. PAGE 91   PROB/SOLV
E1825   CT/SYS
                                                          JUDGE

STERN R.L.,SUPREME COURT PRACTICE. USA+45 USA-45   B62   CT/SYS
OP/RES...STYLE METH 20 SUPREME/CT. PAGE 93 E1872   ADJUD
                                                          JURID
                                                          ROUTINE

TAPER B.,GOMILLION VERSUS LIGHTFOOT: THE TUSKEGEE   B62   APPORT
GERRYMANDER CASE. USA+45 LAW CONSTN LOC/G MUNIC   REPRESENT
CT/SYS 20 NEGRO CIV/RIGHTS GOMILLN/CG LIGHTFT/PM   RACE/REL
TUSKEGEE. PAGE 95 E1908   ADJUD

TUSSMAN J.,THE SUPREME COURT ON CHURCH AND STATE.   B62   CT/SYS
USA+45 USA-45 SANCTION PRIVIL...POLICY JURID 19/20   SECT
SUPREME/CT CHURCH/STA. PAGE 97 E1945   ADJUD

US SENATE COMM ON JUDICIARY,CONSTITUTIONAL RIGHTS   B62   CONSTN
OF MILITARY PERSONNEL. USA+45 USA-45 FORCES DIPLOM   ORD/FREE
WAR CONGRESS. PAGE 102 E2046   JURID
                                                          CT/SYS

GRAVEN J.,"LE MOUVEAU DROIT PENAL INTERNATIONAL."   S62   CT/SYS
UNIV STRUCT LEGIS ACT/RES CRIME ATTIT PERCEPT   PUB/INST
PERSON...JURID CONCPT 20. PAGE 45 E0899   INT/ORG
                                                          INT/LAW

JOHNSON O.H.,"THE ENGLISH TRADITION IN   S62   LAW
INTERNATIONAL LAW." CHRIST-17C MOD/EUR EDU/PROP   INT/LAW
LEGIT CT/SYS ORD/FREE...JURID CONCPT TIME/SEQ.   UK
PAGE 59 E1170

SCHUBERT G.,"THE 1960 TERM OF THE SUPREME COURT: A S62   DECISION
PSYCHOLOGICAL ANALYSIS." USA+45 LAW CT/SYS...STAT   LEGIS
SUPREME/CT. PAGE 88 E1772   JUDGE
                                                          EX/STRUC

ABRAHAM H.J.,"THE JUDICIAL PROCESS." USA+45 USA-45 C62   BIBLIOG
LAW NAT/G ADMIN CT/SYS INGP/REL RACE/REL DISCRIM   CONSTN
...JURID IDEA/COMP 19/20. PAGE 2 E0046   JUDGE
                                                          ADJUD

BACON F.,"OF JUDICATURE" (1612) IN F. BACON,   C62   CT/SYS
ESSAYS." ADJUD ADMIN SANCTION CRIME PWR...JURID   LEGIS
GEN/LAWS. PAGE 7 E0128   LAW

VAN DER SPRENKEL S.,"LEGAL INSTITUTIONS IN MANCHU   C62   LAW
CHINA." ASIA STRUCT CT/SYS ROUTINE GOV/REL GP/REL   JURID
...CONCPT BIBLIOG 17/20. PAGE 103 E2068   ADMIN
                                                          ADJUD

TWENTIETH CENTURY FUND,ONE MAN - ONE VOTE   N62   APPORT
(PAMPHLET). USA+45 CONSTN CONFER CT/SYS REGION   LEGIS
CONSEN FEDERAL ROLE...CENSUS 20 CONGRESS. PAGE 97   REPRESENT
E1947   PROVS

ADRIAN C.R.,GOVERNING OVER FIFTY STATES AND THEIR   B63   PROVS
COMMUNITIES. USA+45 CONSTN FINAN MUNIC NAT/G   LOC/G
POL/PAR EX/STRUC LEGIS ADMIN CONTROL CT/SYS   GOV/REL
...CHARTS 20. PAGE 3 E0052   GOV/COMP

BADI J.,THE GOVERNMENT OF THE STATE OF ISRAEL: A   B63   NAT/G
CRITICAL ACCOUNT OF ITS PARLIAMENT, EXECUTIVE, AND   CONSTN
JUDICIARY. ISRAEL ECO/DEV CHIEF DELIB/GP LEGIS   EX/STRUC
DIPLOM CT/SYS INGP/REL PEACE ORD/FREE...BIBLIOG 20   POL/PAR
PARLIAMENT ARABS MIGRATION. PAGE 7 E0131

BLACK C.L. JR.,THE OCCASIONS OF JUSTICE: ESSAYS   B63   JURID
MOSTLY ON LAW. USA+45 JUDGE RACE/REL DISCRIM ATTIT   CONSTN
MORAL ORD/FREE 20 SUPREME/CT BLACK. PAGE 12 E0236   CT/SYS
                                                          LAW

BLOCK E.B.,THE VINDICATORS. LAW FORCES CT/SYS   B63   ATTIT
DISCRIM 19/20. PAGE 13 E0247   CRIME
                                                          ADJUD
                                                          CRIMLGY

BOWETT D.W.,THE LAW OF INTERNATIONAL INSTITUTIONS. B63   INT/ORG
WOR+45 WOR-45 CONSTN DELIB/GP EX/STRUC JUDGE   ADJUD
EDU/PROP LEGIT CT/SYS EXEC ROUTINE RIGID/FLEX   DIPLOM
ORD/FREE PWR...JURID CONCPT ORG/CHARTS GEN/METH
LEAGUE/NAT OAS OEEC 20 UN. PAGE 14 E0277

BOWIE R.R.,GOVERNMENT REGULATION OF BUSINESS: CASES B63 LAW
FROM THE NATIONAL REPORTER SYSTEM. USA+45 USA-45   CONTROL
NAT/G ECO/TAC ADJUD...ANTHOL 19/20 SUPREME/CT FTC   INDUS
FAIR/LABOR MONOPOLY. PAGE 14 E0280   CT/SYS

CARTER G.M.,FIVE AFRICAN STATES: RESPONSES TO   B63   AFR
DIVERSITY. CONSTN CULTURE STRATA LEGIS PLAN ECO/TAC   SOCIETY
DOMIN EDU/PROP CT/SYS EXEC CHOOSE ATTIT HEALTH
ORD/FREE PWR...TIME/SEQ TOT/POP VAL/FREE. PAGE 20
E0398

B63

CORLEY R.N.,THE LEGAL ENVIRONMENT OF BUSINESS.   NAT/G
CONSTN LEGIS TAX ADMIN CT/SYS DISCRIM ATTIT PWR   INDUS
...TREND 18/20. PAGE 26 E0509   JURID
  DECISION

B63

JOSEPH H.,IF THIS BE TREASON. SOUTH/AFR 20. PAGE 59 AFR
E1174   LAW
  CT/SYS
  CRIME

B63

COUNCIL OF STATE GOVERNMENTS,INCREASED RIGHTS FOR CT/SYS
DEFENDANTS IN STATE CRIMINAL PROSECUTIONS. USA+45 ADJUD
GOV/REL INGP/REL FEDERAL ORD/FREE...JURID 20   PROVS
SUPREME/CT. PAGE 26 E0522   CRIME

B63

KLEIN F.J.,JUDICIAL ADMINISTRATION AND THE LEGAL BIBLIOG/A
PROFESSION. USA+45 ADMIN CONTROL EFFICIENCY   CT/SYS
...POLICY 20. PAGE 61 E1222   ADJUD
  JUDGE

B63

DAY R.E.,CIVIL RIGHTS USA: PUBLIC SCHOOLS, SOUTHERN EDU/PROP
STATES - NORTH CAROLINA, 1963. USA+45 LOC/G NEIGH ORD/FREE
LEGIS CREATE CT/SYS COERCE DISCRIM ATTIT...QU   RACE/REL
CHARTS 20 NORTH/CAR NEGRO KKK CIV/RIGHTS. PAGE 29 SANCTION
E0579

B63

KLESMENT J.,LEGAL SOURCES AND BIBLIOGRAPHY OF THE BIBLIOG/A
BALTIC STATES (ESTONIA, LATVIA, LITHUANIA). COM JURID
ESTONIA LATVIA LITHUANIA LAW FINAN ADJUD CT/SYS CONSTN
REGION CENTRAL MARXISM 19/20. PAGE 61 E1223   ADMIN

B63

DRINAN R.F.,RELIGION, THE COURTS, AND PUBLIC   SECT
POLICY. USA+45 CONSTN BUDGET TAX GIVE ADJUD   CT/SYS
SANCTION GP/REL PRIVIL 20 CHURCH/STA. PAGE 33 E0649 POLICY
  SCHOOL

B63

LANOUE G.R.,A BIBLIOGRAPHY OF DOCTORAL   BIBLIOG
DISSERTATIONS ON POLITICS AND RELIGION. USA+45 NAT/G
USA-45 CONSTN PROVS DIPLOM CT/SYS MORAL...POLICY LOC/G
JURID CONCPT 20. PAGE 63 E1252   SECT

B63

DUNHAM A.,MR. JUSTICE. ADJUD PWR...JURID ANTHOL BIOG
18/20 SUPREME/CT. PAGE 33 E0659   PERSON
  LAW
  CT/SYS

B63

LIVELY E.,THE INVASION OF MISSISSIPPI. USA+45 LAW RACE/REL
CONSTN NAT/G PROVS CT/SYS GOV/REL FEDERAL CONSERVE CROWD
...TRADIT 20 MISSISSIPP NEGRO NAACP WARRN/EARL COERCE
KENNEDY/JF. PAGE 66 E1309   MARXISM

B63

EDDY J.P.,JUSTICE OF THE PEACE. UK LAW CONSTN CRIME
CULTURE 14/20 COMMON/LAW. PAGE 34 E0674   JURID
  CT/SYS
  ADJUD

B63

LOWRY C.W.,TO PRAY OR NOT TO PRAY. ADJUD SANCTION SECT
GP/REL ORD/FREE PWR CATHISM WORSHIP 20 SUPREME/CT CT/SYS
CHRISTIAN CHRUCH/STA. PAGE 67 E1330   CONSTN
  PRIVIL

B63

ELIAS T.O.,THE NIGERIAN LEGAL SYSTEM. NIGERIA LAW CT/SYS
FAM KIN SECT ADMIN NAT/LISM...JURID 18/20   ADJUD
ENGLSH/LAW COMMON/LAW. PAGE 34 E0682   COLONIAL
  PROF/ORG

B63

NATIONAL CIVIC REVIEW,REAPPORTIONMENT: A YEAR IN APPORT
REVIEW (PAMPHLET). USA+45 LAW CT/SYS CHOOSE REPRESENT
ORD/FREE PWR...ANTHOL 20 CONGRESS. PAGE 76 E1527 LEGIS
  CONSTN

B63

ELLERT R.B.,NATO 'FAIR TRIAL' SAFEGUARDS: PRECURSOR JURID
TO AN INTERNATIONAL BILL OF PROCEDURAL RIGHTS. INT/LAW
WOR+45 FORCES CRIME CIVMIL/REL ATTIT ORD/FREE 20 INT/ORG
NATO. PAGE 34 E0683   CT/SYS

B63

NEWMAN E.S.,THE FREEDOM READER. USA+45 LEGIS TOP/EX RACE/REL
PLAN ADJUD CONTROL CT/SYS DISCRIM...DECISION ANTHOL LAW
20 SUPREME/CT CIV/RIGHTS. PAGE 77 E1541   POLICY
  ORD/FREE

B63

FORTES A.B.,HISTORIA ADMINISTRATIVA, JUDICIARIA E PROVS
ECLESIASTICA DO RIO GRANDE DO SUL, BRAZIL L/A+17C ADMIN
LOC/G SECT COLONIAL CT/SYS ORD/FREE CATHISM 16/20. JURID
PAGE 39 E0773

B63

PALOTAI O.C.,PUBLICATIONS OF THE INSTITUTE OF BIBLIOG/A
GOVERNMENT, 1930-1962. LAW PROVS SCHOOL WORKER ADMIN
ACT/RES OP/RES CT/SYS GOV/REL...CRIMLGY SOC/WK. LOC/G
PAGE 79 E1594   FINAN

B63

FRAENKEL O.K.,THE SUPREME COURT AND CIVIL   ORD/FREE
LIBERTIES: HOW THE COURT HAS PROTECTED THE BILL OF CONSTN
RIGHTS. NAT/G CT/SYS CHOOSE PERS/REL RACE/REL ADJUD
DISCRIM PERSON...DECISION 20 SUPREME/CT CIVIL/LIB JURID
BILL/RIGHT. PAGE 39 E0782

B63

PATRA A.C.,THE ADMINISTRATION OF JUSTICE UNDER THE ADMIN
EAST INDIA COMPANY IN BENGAL, BIHAR AND ORISSA. JURID
INDIA UK LG/CO CAP/ISM INT/TRADE ADJUD COLONIAL CONCPT
CONTROL CT/SYS...POLICY 20. PAGE 80 E1602

B63

GARNER U.F.,ADMINISTRATIVE LAW. UK LAW LOC/G NAT/G ADMIN
EX/STRUC LEGIS JUDGE BAL/PWR BUDGET ADJUD CONTROL JURID
CT/SYS...BIBLIOG 20. PAGE 42 E0840   PWR
  GOV/REL

B63

PRITCHETT C.H.,THE ROOSEVELT COURT. USA-45 LAW DECISION
INGP/REL...CHARTS 20 SUPREME/CT. PAGE 82 E1653 PROB/SOLV
  CT/SYS
  JURID

B63

GRIFFITH J.A.G.,PRINCIPLES OF ADMINISTRATIVE LAW JURID
(3RD ED.) UK CONSTN EX/STRUC LEGIS ADJUD CONTROL ADMIN
CT/SYS PWR...CHARTS 20. PAGE 47 E0940   NAT/G
  BAL/PWR

B63

PRITCHETT C.H.,THE THIRD BRANCH OF GOVERNMENT. JURID
USA+45 USA-45 CONSTN SOCIETY INDUS SECT LEGIS JUDGE NAT/G
PROB/SOLV GOV/REL 20 SUPREME/CT CHURCH/STA. PAGE 82 ADJUD
E1654   CT/SYS

B63

GSOUSKI V.,LEGAL SOURCES AND BIBLIOGRAPHY OF THE BIBLIOG
BALTIC STATES (ESTONIA, LATVIA, LITHUANIA). COM ADJUD
ESTONIA LATVIA LITHUANIA NAT/G LEGIS CT/SYS LAW
SANCTION CRIME 20. PAGE 48 E0957   JURID

B63

RICHARDS P.G.,PATRONAGE IN BRITISH GOVERNMENT. EX/STRUC
ELITES DELIB/GP TOP/EX PROB/SOLV CONTROL CT/SYS REPRESENT
EXEC PWR. PAGE 84 E1693   POL/PAR
  ADMIN

B63

HACKER A.,CONGRESSIONAL DISTRICTING: THE ISSUE OF LEGIS
EQUAL REPRESENTATION. FUT CT/SYS GEOG. PAGE 49 REPRESENT
E0970   APPORT

B63

SCHMIDHAUSER J.R.,CONSTITUTIONAL LAW IN THE LAW
POLITICAL PROCESS. SOCIETY LEGIS ADJUD CT/SYS CONSTN
FEDERAL...SOC TREND IDEA/COMP ANTHOL T SUPREME/CT JURID
SENATE CONGRESS HOUSE/REP. PAGE 88 E1761

B63

HALL J.,COMPARATIVE LAW AND SOCIAL THEORY. WOR+45 LAW
CONSTN CULTURE DOMIN CT/SYS ORD/FREE...PLURIST SOC
JURID CONCPT NEW/IDEA GEN/LAWS VAL/FREE. PAGE 49
E0984

B63

SCOTT A.M.,THE SUPREME COURT V. THE CONSTITUTION. PWR
USA+45 CONTROL ATTIT ROLE...POLICY CONCPT 20 CT/SYS
SUPREME/CT. PAGE 90 E1796   NAT/G
  CONSTN

B63

HYNEMAN C.S.,THE SUPREME COURT ON TRIAL. ADJUD LEAD CT/SYS
GP/REL FEDERAL...IDEA/COMP 20 SUPREME/CT. PAGE 56 JURID
E1120   POLICY

B63

SMITH E.A.,CHURCH AND STATE IN YOUR COMMUNITY. GP/REL
USA+45 PROVS SCHOOL ACT/RES CT/SYS PARTIC ATTIT SECT
MORAL ORD/FREE CATHISM 20 PROTESTANT CHURCH/STA. NAT/G

PAGE 92 E1842   NEIGH

                                                        B63
TUSSMAN J.,THE SUPREME COURT ON RACIAL   CT/SYS
DISCRIMINATION. USA+45 USA-45 NAT/G PROB/SOLV ADJUD DISCRIM
RACE/REL ORD/FREE...JURID 20 SUPREME/CT CIV/RIGHTS. ATTIT
PAGE 97 E1946   LAW

                                                        B63
US COMMISSION ON CIVIL RIGHTS,FREEDOM TO THE FREE. RACE/REL
USA+45 USA-45 LAW VOL/ASSN CT/SYS ATTIT PWR...JURID DISCRIM
BIBLIOG 17/20 SUPREME/CT NEGRO CIV/RIGHTS. PAGE 99 NAT/G
E1986   POLICY

                                                        B63
VINES K.N.,STUDIES IN JUDICIAL POLITICS: TULANE   CT/SYS
STUDIES IN POLITICAL SCIENCE (VOL. 8). POL/PAR   GOV/REL
JUDGE ADJUD SANCTION CRIME CHOOSE PWR...JURID STAT PROVS
TIME/SEQ CHARTS. PAGE 104 E2079

                                                        B63
WADE H.W.R.,TOWARDS ADMINISTRATIVE JUSTICE. UK   ADJUD
USA+45 CONSTN CONSULT PROB/SOLV CT/SYS PARL/PROC   IDEA/COMP
...POLICY JURID METH/COMP 20 ENGLSH/LAW. PAGE 104   ADMIN
E2088

                                                        B63
YOUNGER R.D.,THE PEOPLE'S PANEL: THE GRAND JURY IN CT/SYS
THE UNITED STATES, 1634-1941. USA-45 LAW LEGIT   JURID
CONTROL TASK GP/REL ROLE...TREND 17/20 GRAND/JURY. CONSTN
PAGE 108 E2166   LOC/G

                                                        L63
LOEVINGER L.,"JURIMETRICS* THE METHODOLOGY OF LEGAL COMPUT/IR
INQUIRY." COMPUTER CREATE PLAN TEC/DEV AUTOMAT   JURID
CT/SYS EFFICIENCY...DECISION PHIL/SCI NEW/IDEA   GEN/METH
QUANT PREDICT. PAGE 66 E1318   ADJUD

                                                        S63
BECHHOEFER B.G.,"UNITED NATIONS PROCEDURES IN CASE INT/ORG
OF VIOLATIONS OF DISARMAMENT AGREEMENTS." COM   DELIB/GP
USA+45 USSR LAW CONSTN NAT/G EX/STRUC FORCES LEGIS
BAL/PWR EDU/PROP CT/SYS ARMS/CONT ORD/FREE PWR
...POLICY STERTYP UN VAL/FREE 20. PAGE 9 E0169

                                                        S63
BERMAN H.J.,"THE DILEMMA OF SOVIET LAW REFORM."   COM
NAT/G POL/PAR CT/SYS ALL/VALS ORD/FREE PWR...POLICY LAW
JURID VAL/FREE 20. PAGE 11 E0208   USSR

                                                        S63
RIGAUX F.,"LA SIGNIFICATION DES ACTES JUDICIARES A CONSULT
L'ETRANGER." EUR+WWI ITALY NETHERLAND LAW ACT/RES   CT/SYS
DRIVE...JURID GEN/LAWS TOT/POP 20. PAGE 85 E1699   GERMANY

                                                        S63
TALLON D.,"L'ETUDE DU DROIT COMPARE COMME MOYEN DE INT/ORG
RECHERCHER LES MATIERES SUSCEPTIBLES D'UNIFICATION JURID
INTERNATIONALE." WOR+45 LAW SOCIETY VOL/ASSN   INT/LAW
CONSULT LEGIT CT/SYS RIGID/FLEX KNOWL 20. PAGE 95
E1906

                                                        S63
VINES K.N.,"THE ROLE OF THE CIRCUIT COURT OF   REGION
APPEALS IN THE FEDERAL JUDICIAL PROCESS: A CASE   ADJUD
STUDY." USA+45 STRATA JUDGE RESPECT...DECISION   CT/SYS
JURID CHARTS GP/COMP. PAGE 104 E2078   RACE/REL

                                                        C63
SCHUBERT G.,"JUDICIAL DECISION-MAKING." FORCES LEAD ADJUD
ATTIT DRIVE...POLICY PSY STAT CHARTS ANTHOL BIBLIOG DECISION
20. PAGE 88 E1773   JUDGE
                                                    CT/SYS

                                                        B64
ANASTAPLO G.,NOTES ON THE FIRST AMENDMENT TO THE   ORD/FREE
CONSTITUTION OF THE UNITED STATES (PART TWO).   CONSTN
USA+45 USA-45 NAT/G JUDGE DEBATE SUPEGO PWR   CT/SYS
SOVEREIGN 18/20 SUPREME/CT CONGRESS AMEND/I. PAGE 5 ATTIT
E0088

                                                        B64
BECKER T.L.,POLITICAL BEHAVIORALISM AND MODERN   JUDGE
JURISPRUDENCE* A WORKING THEORY AND STUDY IN   LAW
JUDICIAL DECISION-MAKING. CONSTN...JURID STAT   DECISION
GEN/METH INDEX. PAGE 9 E0172   CT/SYS

                                                        B64
BENNETT H.A.,THE COMMISSION AND THE COMMON LAW: A   ADJUD
STUDY IN ADMINISTRATIVE ADJUDICATION. LAW ADMIN   DELIB/GP
CT/SYS LOBBY SANCTION GOV/REL 20 COMMON/LAW.   DIST/IND
PAGE 10 E0188   POLICY

                                                        B64
BREVER E.H.,LEARNED HAND, JANUARY 27, 1872-AUGUST   BIBLIOG/A
18, 1961 (PAMPHLET). USA+45 USA-45 LAW CONSTN ADJUD JUDGE

...DECISION BIOG 19/20. PAGE 15 E0295   CT/SYS
                                                    JURID

                                                        B64
COUNCIL OF STATE GOVERNMENTS,LEGISLATIVE   LOC/G
APPORTIONMENT: A SUMMARY OF STATE ACTION. USA+45   PROVS
LEGIS REPRESENT...POLICY SUPREME/CT. PAGE 26 E0523 APPORT
                                                    CT/SYS

                                                        B64
DIAS R.W.M.,A BIBLIOGRAPHY OF JURISPRUDENCE (2ND   BIBLIOG/A
ED.). VOL/ASSN LEGIS ADJUD CT/SYS OWN...INT/LAW   JURID
18/20. PAGE 31 E0619   LAW
                                                    CONCPT

                                                        B64
DIETZE G.,ESSAYS ON THE AMERICAN CONSTITUTION: A   FEDERAL
COMMEMORATIVE VOLUME IN HONOR OF ALPHEUS T. MASON. CONSTN
USA+45 USA-45 LAW INTELL...POLICY BIOG IDEA/COMP   DIPLOM
ANTHOL SUPREME/CT. PAGE 32 E0626   CT/SYS

                                                        B64
DOOLIN D.J.,COMMUNIST CHINA: THE POLITICS OF   MARXISM
STUDENT OPPOSITION. CHINA/COM ELITES STRATA ACADEM DEBATE
NAT/G WRITING CT/SYS LEAD PARTIC COERCE TOTALISM   AGE/Y
20. PAGE 32 E0637   PWR

                                                        B64
DUBISSON M.,LA COUR INTERNATIONALE DE JUSTICE.   CT/SYS
FRANCE LAW CONSTN JUDGE DOMIN ADJUD...INT/LAW   INT/ORG
CLASSIF RECORD ORG/CHARTS UN. PAGE 33 E0651

                                                        B64
DUMON F.,LE BRESIL: SES INSTITUTIONS POLITIQUES ET CONSTN
JUDICIARIES. BRAZIL POL/PAR CHIEF LEGIS ORD/FREE   JURID
19/20. PAGE 33 E0658   CT/SYS
                                                    GOV/REL

                                                        B64
FALK R.A.,THE ROLE OF DOMESTIC COURTS IN THE   LAW
INTERNATIONAL LEGAL ORDER. FUT WOR+45 INT/ORG NAT/G INT/LAW
JUDGE EDU/PROP LEGIT CT/SYS...POLICY RELATIV JURID
CONCPT GEN/LAWS 20. PAGE 36 E0716

                                                        B64
FEIFER G.,JUSTICE IN MOSCOW. USSR LAW CRIME   ADJUD
...RECORD 20. PAGE 37 E0725   JURID
                                                    CT/SYS
                                                    MARXISM

                                                        B64
GESELLSCHAFT RECHTSVERGLEICH,BIBLIOGRAPHIE DES   BIBLIOG/A
DEUTSCHEN RECHTS (BIBLIOGRAPHY OF GERMAN LAW,   JURID
TRANS. BY COURTLAND PETERSON). GERMANY FINAN INDUS CONSTN
LABOR SECT FORCES CT/SYS PARL/PROC CRIME...INT/LAW ADMIN
SOC NAT/COMP 20. PAGE 43 E0853

                                                        B64
GROVES H.E.,THE CONSTITUTION OF MALAYSIA. MALAYSIA CONSTN
POL/PAR CHIEF CONSULT DELIB/GP CT/SYS PARL/PROC   NAT/G
CHOOSE FEDERAL ORD/FREE 20. PAGE 48 E0953   LAW

                                                        B64
GUTTMANN A.,COMMUNISM, THE COURTS, AND THE   MARXISM
CONSTITUTION. USA+45 CT/SYS ORD/FREE...ANTHOL 20   POL/PAR
COM/PARTY CIV/RIGHTS. PAGE 48 E0965   CONSTN
                                                    LAW

                                                        B64
HAAR C.M.,LAW AND LAND: ANGLO-AMERICAN PLANNING   LAW
PRACTICE. UK USA+45 NAT/G TEC/DEV BUDGET CT/SYS   PLAN
INGP/REL EFFICIENCY OWN...JURID 20. PAGE 49 E0967   MUNIC
                                                    NAT/COMP

                                                        B64
HAMILTON H.D.,LEGISLATIVE APPORTIONMENT: KEY TO   APPORT
POWER. USA+45 LAW CONSTN PROVS LOBBY CHOOSE ATTIT   CT/SYS
SUPREME/CT. PAGE 50 E0988   LEAD
                                                    REPRESENT

                                                        B64
HANSON R.,FAIR REPRESENTATION COMES TO MARYLAND   APPORT
(PAMPHLET). BAL/PWR CT/SYS CHOOSE GOV/REL 20   REPRESENT
MARYLAND SUPREME/CT. PAGE 50 E0997   PROVS
                                                    LEGIS

                                                        B64
HENDERSON D.F.,CONCILIATION AND JAPANESE LAW (VOL. CONCPT
II). LAW SOCIETY...BIBLIOG 17/20 CHINJAP. PAGE 52   CT/SYS
E1028   ADJUD
                                                    POLICY

                                                        B64
HENDERSON D.F.,CONCILIATION AND JAPANESE LAW (VOL. CT/SYS
I). LAW SOCIETY 17/19 CHINJAP. PAGE 52 E1029   CONCPT
                                                    ADJUD

POLICY

B64
HENKE W.,DAS RECHT DER POLITISCHEN PARTEIEN. POL/PAR
GERMANY/W LAW CT/SYS GP/REL SUPEGO 20. PAGE 52 JURID
E1031 CONSTN
NAT/G

B64
HOLDSWORTH W.S.,A HISTORY OF ENGLISH LAW; THE LAW
CENTURIES OF DEVELOPMENT AND REFORM (VOL. XIV). UK LEGIS
CONSTN LOC/G NAT/G POL/PAR CHIEF EX/STRUC ADJUD LEAD
COLONIAL ATTIT...INT/LAW JURID 18/19 TORY/PARTY CT/SYS
COMMONWLTH WHIG/PARTY COMMON/LAW. PAGE 54 E1081

B64
IRION F.C.,APPORTIONMENT OF THE NEW MEXICO APPORT
LEGISLATURE. NAT/G LEGIS PRESS CT/SYS ATTIT REPRESENT
...POLICY TIME/SEQ 19/20 SUPREME/CT. PAGE 57 E1137 GOV/REL
PROVS

B64
JACKSON R.M.,THE MACHINERY OF JUSTICE IN ENGLAND. CT/SYS
UK EDU/PROP CONTROL COST ORD/FREE...MGT 20 ADJUD
ENGLSH/LAW. PAGE 57 E1142 JUDGE
JURID

B64
JENKS C.W.,THE PROSPECTS OF INTERNATIONAL INT/LAW
ADJUDICATION. WOR+45 NAT/G DIPLOM CONTROL ADJUD
PWR...POLICY JURID CONCPT METH/COMP 19/20 ICJ CT/SYS
LEAGUE/NAT UN TREATY. PAGE 58 E1160 INT/ORG

B64
KAHNG T.J.,LAW, POLITICS, AND THE SECURITY COUNCIL* DELIB/GP
AN INQUIRY INTO THE HANDLING OF LEGAL QUESTIONS. ADJUD
LAW CONSTN NAT/G ACT/RES OP/RES CT/SYS TASK PWR ROUTINE
...INT/LAW BIBLIOG UN. PAGE 59 E1180

B64
KISER S.L.,AMERICANISM IN ACTION. USA+45 LAW PROVS OLD/LIB
CAP/ISM DIPLOM RECEIVE CONTROL CT/SYS WAR FEDERAL FOR/AID
ATTIT WEALTH 20 SUPREME/CT. PAGE 61 E1221 MARXISM
CONSTN

B64
KOREA (REPUBLIC) SUPREME COURT,KOREAN LEGAL SYSTEM. JURID
KOREA/S WOR+45 LAW LEAD ROUTINE GOV/REL ORD/FREE 20 CT/SYS
SUPREME/CT. PAGE 61 E1229 CONSTN
CRIME

B64
LEDERMAN W.R.,THE COURTS AND THE CANDIAN CONSTN
CONSTITUTION. CANADA PARL/PROC...POLICY JURID CT/SYS
GOV/COMP ANTHOL 19/20 SUPREME/CT PARLIAMENT. LEGIS
PAGE 64 E1276 LAW

B64
LIGGETT E.,BRITISH POLITICAL ISSUES: VOLUME 1. UK POL/PAR
LAW CONSTN LOC/G NAT/G ADJUD 20. PAGE 65 E1296 GOV/REL
CT/SYS
DIPLOM

B64
MAKI J.M.,COURT AND CONSTITUTION IN JAPAN; SELECTED CT/SYS
SUPREME COURT DECISIONS, 1948-60. FAM LABOR GOV/REL CONSTN
HABITAT ORD/FREE...DECISION JURID 20 CHINJAP PROB/SOLV
SUPREME/CT CIV/RIGHTS. PAGE 68 E1354 LAW

B64
MAKI J.M.,COURT AND CONSTITUTION IN JAPAN: SELECTED CONSTN
SUPREME COURT DECISIONS, 1948-60. LAW AGRI FAM JURID
LEGIS BAL/PWR ADMIN CHOOSE...SOC ANTHOL CABINET 20 CT/SYS
CHINJAP CIVIL/LIB. PAGE 68 E1355 CRIME

B64
MARNELL W.H.,THE FIRST AMENDMENT: THE HISTORY OF CONSTN
RELIGIOUS FREEDOM IN AMERICA. WOR+45 WOR-45 PROVS SECT
CREATE CT/SYS...POLICY BIBLIOG/A WORSHIP 16/20. ORD/FREE
PAGE 68 E1367 GOV/REL

B64
MARSHALL B.,FEDERALISM AND CIVIL RIGHTS. USA+45 FEDERAL
PROVS BAL/PWR CONTROL CT/SYS PARTIC SOVEREIGN ORD/FREE
...JURID 20 NEGRO CIV/RIGHTS. PAGE 68 E1369 CONSTN
FORCES

B64
MASON A.T.,AMERICAN CONSTITUTIONAL LAW: CONSTN
INTRODUCTORY ESSAYS AND SELECTED CASES (3RD ED.). CT/SYS
LAW LEGIS TAX ADJUD GOV/REL FEDERAL ORD/FREE PWR JURID
...TIME/SEQ BIBLIOG T 19/20 SUPREME/CT. PAGE 69
E1379

B64
MITAU G.T.,PROXIMATE SOLUTIONS: CASE PROBLEMS IN PROVS

B64
STATE AND LOCAL GOVERNMENT. USA+45 CONSTN NAT/G LOC/G
CHIEF LEGIS CT/SYS EXEC GOV/REL GP/REL PWR 20 ADJUD
CASEBOOK. PAGE 73 E1470

B64
MURPHY W.F.,ELEMENTS OF JUDICIAL STRATEGY. CONSTN CT/SYS
JUDGE PERS/REL PERSON 19/20 SUPREME/CT. PAGE 75 ADJUD
E1510 JURID

B64
NELSON D.H.,ADMINISTRATIVE AGENCIES OF THE USA: ADMIN
THEIR DECISIONS AND AUTHORITY. USA+45 NAT/G CONTROL EX/STRUC
CT/SYS REPRESENT...DECISION 20. PAGE 76 E1531 ADJUD
LAW

B64
NEWMAN E.S.,POLICE, THE LAW, AND PERSONAL FREEDOM. JURID
USA+45 CONSTN JUDGE CT/SYS CRIME PERS/REL RESPECT FORCES
...CRIMLGY 20. PAGE 77 E1542 ORD/FREE
ADJUD

B64
NEWMAN E.S.,CIVIL LIBERTY AND CIVIL RIGHTS. USA+45 ORD/FREE
USA-45 CONSTN PROVS FORCES LEGIS CT/SYS RACE/REL LAW
ATTIT...MAJORIT JURID WORSHIP 20 SUPREME/CT NEGRO CONTROL
CIV/RIGHTS CHURCH/STA. PAGE 77 E1543 NAT/G

B64
OPPENHEIMER M.,A MANUAL FOR DIRECT ACTION. USA+45 PLAN
SCHOOL FORCES ADJUD CT/SYS SUFF RACE/REL DISCRIM VOL/ASSN
...POLICY CHARTS 20. PAGE 79 E1580 JURID
LEAD

B64
SARTORIUS R.E.,THE JUSTIFICATION OF THE JUDICIAL LAW
DECISION (DISSERTATION). PROB/SOLV LEGIT...JURID PHIL/SCI
GEN/LAWS BIBLIOG 20. PAGE 87 E1747 CT/SYS
ADJUD

B64
SCHECHTER A.H.,INTERPRETATION OF AMBIGUOUS INT/LAW
DOCUMENTS BY INTERNATIONAL ADMINISTRATIVE DIPLOM
TRIBUNALS. WOR+45 EX/STRUC INT/TRADE CT/SYS INT/ORG
SOVEREIGN 20 UN ILO EURCT/JUST. PAGE 87 E1752 ADJUD

B64
SCHUBERT G.A.,JUDICIAL BEHAVIOR: A READER IN THEORY ATTIT
AND RESEARCH. POL/PAR CT/SYS ROLE SUPEGO PWR PERSON
...DECISION JURID REGRESS CHARTS SIMUL ANTHOL 20. ADJUD
PAGE 89 E1782 ACT/RES

B64
SHAPIRO M.,LAW AND POLITICS IN THE SUPREME COURT: LEGIS
NEW APPROACHES TO POLITICAL JURISPRUDENCE. JUDGE CT/SYS
PROB/SOLV LEGIT EXEC ROUTINE ATTIT ALL/VALS LAW
...DECISION SOC. PAGE 90 E1811 JURID

B64
SHKLAR J.N.,LEGALISM. CREATE PROB/SOLV CT/SYS MORAL
...POLICY CRIMLGY DECISION JURID METH/CNCPT. LAW
PAGE 91 E1821 NEW/IDEA

B64
STOICOIU V.,LEGAL SOURCES AND BIBLIOGRAPHY OF BIBLIOG/A
ROMANIA. COM ROMANIA LAW FINAN POL/PAR LEGIS JUDGE JURID
ADJUD CT/SYS PARL/PROC MARXISM 20. PAGE 93 E1874 CONSTN
ADMIN

B64
STOKES A.P.,CHURCH AND STATE IN THE UNITED STATES SECT
(3 VOLS.). USA+45 USA-45 NAT/G PROVS LEGIS CT/SYS CONSTN
SANCTION PRIVIL ORD/FREE 17/20 CHURCH/STA. PAGE 94 POLICY
E1875

B64
STRONG C.F.,HISTORY OF MODERN POLITICAL CONSTN
CONSTITUTIONS. STRUCT INT/ORG NAT/G LEGIS TEC/DEV CONCPT
DIPLOM INT/TRADE CT/SYS EXEC...METH/COMP T 12/20
UN. PAGE 94 E1888

B64
SZLADITS C.,BIBLIOGRAPHY ON FOREIGN AND COMPARATIVE BIBLIOG/A
LAW: BOOKS AND ARTICLES IN ENGLISH (SUPPLEMENT JURID
1962). FINAN INDUS JUDGE LICENSE ADMIN CT/SYS ADJUD
PARL/PROC OWN...INT/LAW CLASSIF METH/COMP NAT/COMP LAW
20. PAGE 95 E1904

B64
TELLADO A.,A STATEMENT OF THE LAWS OF THE DOMINICAN CONSTN
REPUBLIC IN MATTERS AFFECTING BUSINESS (3RD ED.). LEGIS
DOMIN/REP AGRI DIST/IND EXTR/IND FINAN FAM WORKER NAT/G
ECO/TAC TAX CT/SYS MARRIAGE OWN...BIBLIOG 20 INDUS
MIGRATION. PAGE 95 E1913

C64
BECKER T.L.,"POLITICAL BEHAVIORALISM AND MODERN DECISION

JURISPRUDENCE." LEGIS JUDGE OP/RES ADJUD CT/SYS   PROB/SOLV
ATTIT PWR...BIBLIOG 20. PAGE 9 E0173   JURID
                                                     GEN/LAWS

                                              C64
CORWIN E.S.,"AMERICAN CONSTITUTIONAL HISTORY." LAW   ANTHOL
NAT/G PROB/SOLV EQUILIB FEDERAL ATTIT PWR...JURID   JUDGE
BIBLIOG 20. PAGE 26 E0515   ADJUD
                                                     CT/SYS

                                              B65
MISSISSIPPI BLACK PAPER: (FIFTY-SEVEN NEGRO AND   COERCE
WHITE CITIZENS' TESTIMONY OF POLICE BRUTALITY...).   RACE/REL
USA+45 LAW SOCIETY CT/SYS SANCTION CRIME MORAL   DISCRIM
ORD/FREE RESPECT 20 NEGRO. PAGE 2 E0035   FORCES

                                              B65
AMERICAN ASSEMBLY COLUMBIA U.THE COURTS, THE   CT/SYS
PUBLIC, AND THE LAW EXPLOSION. USA+45 ELITES PROVS   ADJUD
EDU/PROP CRIME CHOOSE PERSON ORD/FREE PWR 20.   NAT/G
PAGE 4 E0074

                                              B65
ASSOCIATION BAR OF NYC,RADIO, TELEVISION, AND THE   AUD/VIS
ADMINISTRATION OF JUSTICE: A DOCUMENTED SURVEY OF   ATTIT
MATERIALS. USA+45 DELIB/GP FORCES PRESS ADJUD   ORD/FREE
CONTROL CT/SYS CRIME...INT IDEA/COMP BIBLIOG.
PAGE 6 E0109

                                              B65
BARKER L.J.,FREEDOM, COURTS, POLITICS: STUDIES IN   JURID
CIVIL LIBERTIES. USA+45 LEGIS CREATE DOMIN PRESS   CT/SYS
ADJUD LOBBY CRIME GP/REL RACE/REL MARXISM 20   ATTIT
CIVIL/LIB. PAGE 8 E0148   ORD/FREE

                                              B65
BLITZ L.F.,THE POLITICS AND ADMINISTRATION OF   NAT/G
NIGERIAN GOVERNMENT. NIGER CULTURE LOC/G LEGIS   GOV/REL
DIPLOM COLONIAL CT/SYS SOVEREIGN...GEOG SOC ANTHOL   POL/PAR
20. PAGE 13 E0245

                                              B65
BREITEL C.D.,THE LAWMAKERS. USA+45 EX/STRUC LEGIS   CT/SYS
JUDGE ATTIT ORD/FREE JURID. PAGE 15 E0290   ADJUD
                                                     FEDERAL
                                                     NAT/G

                                              B65
BRIGGS H.W.,THE INTERNATIONAL LAW COMMISSION. LAW   INT/LAW
CONSTN LEGIS CREATE ADJUD CT/SYS ROUTINE TASK   DELIB/GP
EFFICIENCY...CLASSIF OBS UN. PAGE 15 E0302

                                              B65
CAVERS D.F.,THE CHOICE-OF-LAW PROCESS. PROB/SOLV   JURID
ADJUD CT/SYS CHOOSE RATIONAL...IDEA/COMP 16/20   DECISION
TREATY. PAGE 21 E0411   METH/COMP
                                                     ADMIN

                                              B65
CHRIMES S.B.,ENGLISH CONSTITUTIONAL HISTORY (3RD   CONSTN
ED.). UK CHIEF CONSULT DELIB/GP LEGIS CT/SYS 15/20   BAL/PWR
COMMON/LAW PARLIAMENT. PAGE 22 E0435   NAT/G

                                              B65
CHROUST A.H.,THE RISE OF THE LEGAL PROFESSION IN   JURID
AMERICA (3 VOLS.). STRATA STRUCT POL/PAR PROF/ORG   USA-45
COLONIAL LEAD REV SKILL...SOC 17/20. PAGE 22 E0437   CT/SYS
                                                     LAW

                                              B65
COHN H.J.,THE GOVERNMENT OF THE RHINE PALATINATE IN PROVS
THE FIFTEENTH CENTURY. GERMANY FINAN LOC/G DELIB/GP JURID
LEGIS CT/SYS CHOOSE CATHISM 14/15 PALATINATE.   GP/REL
PAGE 24 E0468   ADMIN

                                              B65
CONGRESSIONAL QUARTERLY SERV,REVOLUTION IN CIVIL   LAW
RIGHTS. USA+45 USA-45 LEGIS ADJUD CT/SYS CHOOSE   CONSTN
DISCRIM...DECISION CONGRESS SUPREME/CT. PAGE 25   RACE/REL
E0488   LOBBY

                                              B65
COOPER F.E.,STATE ADMINISTRATIVE LAW (2 VOLS.). LAW JURID
LEGIS PLAN TAX ADJUD CT/SYS FEDERAL PWR...CONCPT   CONSTN
20. PAGE 25 E0501   ADMIN
                                                     PROVS

                                              B65
FALK R.A.,THE AFTERMATH OF SABBATINO: BACKGROUND   SOVEREIGN
PAPERS AND PROCEEDINGS OF SEVENTH HAMMARSKJOLD   CT/SYS
FORUM. USA+45 LAW ACT/RES ADJUD ROLE...BIBLIOG 20   INT/LAW
EXPROPRIAT SABBATINO HARLAN/JM. PAGE 36 E0718   OWN

                                              B65
FISCHER F.C.,THE GOVERNMENT OF MICHIGAN. USA+45   PROVS
NAT/G PUB/INST EX/STRUC LEGIS BUDGET GIVE EDU/PROP   LOC/G

CT/SYS CHOOSE GOV/REL...T MICHIGAN. PAGE 38 E0753   ADMIN
                                                     CONSTN

                                              B65
FRIEDMAN L.,SOUTHERN JUSTICE. USA+45 PUB/INST LEGIT ADJUD
ADMIN CT/SYS DISCRIM...DECISION ANTHOL 20 NEGRO   LAW
SOUTH/US CIV/RIGHTS. PAGE 40 E0800   CONSTN
                                                     RACE/REL

                                              B65
GINSBERG M.,ON JUSTICE IN SOCIETY. LAW EDU/PROP   ADJUD
LEGIT CT/SYS INGP/REL PRIVIL RATIONAL ATTIT MORAL   ROLE
ORD/FREE...JURID 20. PAGE 44 E0867   CONCPT

                                              B65
GLUECK S.,ROSCOE POUND AND CRIMINAL JUSTICE.   CT/SYS
SOCIETY FAM GOV/REL AGE/Y ATTIT ORD/FREE...CRIMLGY   CRIME
BIOG ANTHOL SOC/INTEG 19/20. PAGE 44 E0875   LAW
                                                     ADJUD

                                              B65
HOLDSWORTH W.S.,A HISTORY OF ENGLISH LAW: THE   LAW
CENTURIES OF SETTLEMENT AND REFORM (VOL. XV). UK   INDUS
CONSTN SECT LEGIS JUDGE WRITING ADJUD CT/SYS CRIME   PROF/ORG
OWN...JURID IDEA/COMP 18 PARLIAMENT ENGLSH/LAW   ATTIT
COMMON/LAW. PAGE 54 E1082

                                              B65
ISORNI J.,LES CAS DE CONSCIENCE DE L'AVOCAT.   SUPEGO
FRANCE LAW ACT/RES CT/SYS PARTIC ROLE MORAL 20.   JURID
PAGE 57 E1138   CRIME

                                              B65
KAAS L.,DIE GEISTLICHE GERICHTSBARKEIT DER   JURID
KATHOLISCHEN KIRCHE IN PREUSSEN (2 VOLS.). PRUSSIA   CATHISM
CONSTN NAT/G PROVS SECT ADJUD ADMIN ATTIT 16/20.   GP/REL
PAGE 59 E1178   CT/SYS

                                              B65
KAMISAR Y.,CRIMINAL JUSTICE IN OUR TIME. USA+45   ORD/FREE
FORCES JUDGE PROB/SOLV COERCE MORAL 20 CIVIL/LIB   CRIME
CIV/RIGHTS. PAGE 59 E1182   CT/SYS
                                                     LAW

                                              B65
KARIS T.,THE TREASON TRIAL IN SOUTH AFRICA: A GUIDE BIBLIOG/A
TO THE MICROFILM RECORD OF THE TRIAL. SOUTH/AFR LAW ADJUD
ELITES NAT/G LEGIT CT/SYS RACE/REL DISCRIM...SOC   CRIME
20. PAGE 59 E1185   AFR

                                              B65
KEEFE W.J.,THE AMERICAN LEGISLATIVE PROCESS. USA+45 LEGIS
CONSTN POL/PAR CT/SYS REPRESENT FEDERAL ATTIT   NAT/G
PLURISM...MAJORIT 20 CONGRESS PRESIDENT. PAGE 60   CHIEF
E1192   GOV/REL

                                              B65
KRISLOV S.,THE SUPREME COURT IN THE POLITICAL   ADJUD
PROCESS. USA+45 LAW SOCIETY STRUCT WORKER ADMIN   DECISION
ROLE...JURID SOC 20 SUPREME/CT. PAGE 62 E1231   CT/SYS
                                                     CONSTN

                                              B65
KUPER H.,AFRICAN LAW. LAW FAM KIN SECT JUDGE ADJUST AFR
NAT/LISM 17/20. PAGE 62 E1236   CT/SYS
                                                     ADJUD
                                                     COLONIAL

                                              B65
LAFAVE W.R.,LAW AND SOVIET SOCIETY. EX/STRUC DIPLOM JURID
DOMIN EDU/PROP PRESS ADMIN CRIME OWN MARXISM 20   CT/SYS
KHRUSH/N. PAGE 62 E1244   ADJUD
                                                     GOV/REL

                                              B65
MCWHINNEY E.,JUDICIAL REVIEW IN THE ENGLISH-   GOV/COMP
SPEAKING WORLD (3RD ED.). CANADA UK WOR+45 LEGIS   CT/SYS
CONTROL EXEC PARTIC...JURID 20 AUSTRAL. PAGE 71   ADJUD
E1431   CONSTN

                                              B65
MILLER H.H.,THE CASE FOR LIBERTY. USA-45 LAW JUDGE   COLONIAL
CT/SYS...AUD/VIS 18 PRE/US/AM CASEBOOK. PAGE 73   JURID
E1460   PROB/SOLV

                                              B65
MISHKIN P.J.,ON LAW IN COURTS. USA+45 LEGIS CREATE   LAW
ROLE 20. PAGE 73 E1468   CT/SYS
                                                     ADJUD
                                                     CONSTN

                                              B65
MOODY M.,CATALOG OF INTERNATIONAL LAW AND RELATIONS BIBLIOG
(20 VOLS.). WOR+45 INT/ORG NAT/G ADJUD ADMIN CT/SYS INT/LAW
POLICY. PAGE 74 E1488   DIPLOM

MOSTECKY V.,SOVIET LEGAL BIBLIOGRAPHY. USSR LEGIS
PRESS WRITING CONFER ADJUD CT/SYS REV MARXISM
...INT/LAW JURID DICTIONARY 20. PAGE 75 E1503
B65
BIBLIOG/A
LAW
COM
CONSTN

MURPHY W.F.,WIRETAPPING ON TRIAL: A CASE STUDY IN
THE JUDICIAL PROCESS. CONSTN ELITES CT/SYS CRIME
MORAL ORD/FREE...DECISION SUPREME/CT. PAGE 75 E1511
B65
JURID
LAW
POLICY

NEWBURY C.W.,BRITISH POLICY TOWARDS WEST AFRICA:
SELECT DOCUMENTS 1786-1874. AFR UK INT/TRADE DOMIN
ADMIN COLONIAL CT/SYS COERCE ORD/FREE...BIBLIOG/A
18/19. PAGE 77 E1540
B65
DIPLOM
POLICY
NAT/G
WRITING

NORDEN A.,WAR AND NAZI CRIMINALS IN WEST GERMANY:
STATE, ECONOMY, ADMINISTRATION, ARMY, JUSTICE,
SCIENCE. GERMANY GERMANY/W MOD/EUR ECO/DEV ACADEM
EX/STRUC FORCES DOMIN ADMIN CT/SYS...POLICY MAJORIT
PACIFIST 20. PAGE 77 E1554
B65
FASCIST
WAR
NAT/G
TOP/EX

O'CONNELL D.P.,INTERNATIONAL LAW (2 VOLS.). WOR+45
WOR-45 ECO/DEV ECO/UNDEV INT/ORG NAT/G AGREE
...POLICY JURID CONCPT NAT/COMP 20 TREATY. PAGE 78
E1566
B65
INT/LAW
DIPLOM
CT/SYS

PADELFORD N.,THE UNITED NATIONS IN THE BALANCE*
ACCOMPLISHMENTS AND PROSPECTS. NAT/G VOL/ASSN
DIPLOM ADMIN COLONIAL CT/SYS REGION WAR ORD/FREE
...ANTHOL UN. PAGE 79 E1588
B65
INT/ORG
CONTROL

PARRY C.,THE SOURCES AND EVIDENCES OF INTERNATIONAL
LAW. WOR+45 WOR-45 DIPLOM AGREE SOVEREIGN...METH 20
TREATY UN LEAGUE/NAT. PAGE 80 E1599
B65
INT/LAW
ADJUD
INT/ORG
CT/SYS

PEASLEE A.J.,CONSTITUTIONS OF NATIONS* THIRD
REVISED EDITION (VOLUME I* AFRICA). LAW EX/STRUC
LEGIS TOP/EX LEGIT CT/SYS ROUTINE ORD/FREE PWR
SOVEREIGN...CON/ANAL CHARTS. PAGE 80 E1606
B65
AFR
CHOOSE
CONSTN
NAT/G

PYLEE M.V.,CONSTITUTIONAL GOVERNMENT IN INDIA (2ND
REV. ED.). INDIA POL/PAR EX/STRUC DIPLOM COLONIAL
CT/SYS PARL/PROC PRIVIL...JURID 16/20. PAGE 83
E1665
B65
CONSTN
NAT/G
PROVS
FEDERAL

SCHUBERT G.,THE JUDICIAL MIND: THE ATTITUDES AND
IDEOLOGIES OF SUPREME COURT JUSTICES 1946-1963.
USA+45 ELITES NAT/G CONTROL PERS/REL MAJORITY
CONSERVE...DECISION JURID MODAL STAT TREND GP/COMP
GAME. PAGE 88 E1774
B65
CT/SYS
JUDGE
ATTIT
NEW/LIB

SCHUBERT G.,THE POLITICAL ROLE OF THE COURTS IN
JUDICIAL POLICY MAKING. USA+45 CONSTN JUDGE
FEEDBACK CHOOSE RACE/REL ORD/FREE...TRADIT PSY
BIBLIOG/A 20 KENNEDY/JF SUPREME/CT. PAGE 89 E1776
B65
CT/SYS
POLICY
DECISION

SHARMA S.A.,PARLIAMENTARY GOVERNMENT IN INDIA.
INDIA FINAN LOC/G PROVS DELIB/GP PLAN ADMIN CT/SYS
FEDERAL...JURID 20. PAGE 90 E1814
B65
NAT/G
CONSTN
PARL/PROC
LEGIS

SMITH C.,THE OMBUDSMAN: A BIBLIOGRAPHY (PAMPHLET).
DENMARK SWEDEN USA+45 LAW LEGIS JUDGE GOV/REL
GP/REL...JURID 20. PAGE 92 E1841
B65
BIBLIOG
ADMIN
CT/SYS
ADJUD

STOREY R.G.,OUR UNALIENABLE RIGHTS. LAW SECT CT/SYS
SUFF DISCRIM 17/20 CIVIL/LIB ENGLSH/LAW. PAGE 94
E1882
B65
CONSTN
JURID
ORD/FREE
LEGIS

SWISHER C.B.,THE SUPREME COURT IN MODERN ROLE. COM
COM/IND NAT/G FORCES LEGIS LOBBY PARTIC RACE/REL 20
SUPREME/CT. PAGE 95 E1901
B65
DELIB/GP
ATTIT
CT/SYS
ADJUD

TRESOLINI R.J.,AMERICAN CONSTITUTIONAL LAW. USA+45
USA-45 NAT/G ADJUD ORD/FREE PWR...POLICY BIOG 20
SUPREME/CT CASEBOOK. PAGE 97 E1939
B65
CONSTN
CT/SYS
JURID
LAW

WHITE G.M.,THE USE OF EXPERTS BY INTERNATIONAL
TRIBUNALS. WOR+45 WOR-45 INT/ORG NAT/G PAY ADJUD
COST...OBS BIBLIOG 20. PAGE 106 E2117
B65
INT/LAW
ROUTINE
CONSULT
CT/SYS

WILSON J.F.,CHURCH AND STATE IN AMERICAN HISTORY.
USA+45 USA-45 ADJUD CT/SYS ORD/FREE SOVEREIGN
...ANTHOL BIBLIOG/A 17/20 CHURCH/STA. PAGE 106
E2129
B65
SECT
NAT/G
GP/REL
CONTROL

RUBIN A.P.,"UNITED STATES CONTEMPORARY PRACTICE
RELATING TO INTERNATIONAL LAW." USA+45 WOR+45
CONSTN INT/ORG NAT/G DELIB/GP EX/STRUC DIPLOM DOMIN
CT/SYS ROUTINE ORD/FREE...CONCPT COLD/WAR 20.
PAGE 86 E1730
L65
LAW
LEGIT
INT/LAW

SHARMA S.P.,"THE INDIA-CHINA BORDER DISPUTE: AN
INDIAN PERSPECTIVE." ASIA CHINA/COM S/ASIA NAT/G
LEGIT CT/SYS NAT/LISM DRIVE MORAL ORD/FREE PWR 20.
PAGE 91 E1815
L65
LAW
ATTIT
SOVEREIGN
INDIA

GROSS L.,"PROBLEMS OF INTERNATIONAL ADJUDICATION
AND COMPLIANCE WITH INTERNATIONAL LAW: SOME SIMPLE
SOLUTIONS." WOR+45 SOCIETY NAT/G DOMIN LEGIT ADJUD
CT/SYS RIGID/FLEX HEALTH PWR...JURID NEW/IDEA
COLD/WAR 20. PAGE 48 E0951
S65
LAW
METH/CNCPT
INT/LAW

MCWHINNEY E.,"CHANGING INTERNATIONAL LAW METHOD AND
OBJECTIVES IN THE ERA OF THE SOVIET-WESTERN
DETENTE." COM USA+45 NAT/G BAL/PWR CT/SYS ATTIT
ORD/FREE...HUM JURID NEW/IDEA COLD/WAR VAL/FREE 20.
PAGE 71 E1430
S65
LAW
TREND

ULMER S.S.,"TOWARD A THEORY OF SUBGROUP FORMATION
IN THE UNITED STATES SUPREME COURT." USA+45 ROUTINE
CHOOSE PWR...JURID STAT CON/ANAL SIMUL SUPREME/CT.
PAGE 97 E1952
S65
CT/SYS
ADJUD
ELITES
INGP/REL

SCHEINGOLD S.A.,"THE RULE OF LAW IN EUROPEAN
INTEGRATION: THE PATH OF THE SCHUMAN PLAN." EUR+WWI
JUDGE ADJUD FEDERAL ATTIT PWR...RECORD INT BIBLIOG
EEC ECSC. PAGE 87 E1755
C65
INT/LAW
CT/SYS
REGION
CENTRAL

AMERICAN JOURNAL COMP LAW,THE AMERICAN JOURNAL OF
COMPARATIVE LAW READER. EUR+WWI USA+45 USA-45 LAW
CONSTN LOC/G MUNIC NAT/G DIPLOM...ANTHOL 20
SUPREME/CT EURCT/JUST. PAGE 4 E0081
B66
IDEA/COMP
JURID
INT/LAW
CT/SYS

BAXTER M.G.,DANIEL WEBSTER & THE SUPREME COURT. LAW
NAT/G PROF/ORG DEBATE ADJUD LEAD FEDERAL PERSON.
PAGE 8 E0156
B66
CONSTN
CT/SYS
JURID

BEDI A.S.,FREEDOM OF EXPRESSION AND SECURITY;
COMPARATIVE STUDY OF FUNCTIONS OF SUPREME COURTS IN
UNITED STATES AND INDIA. INDIA USA+45 LAW CONSTN
PROB/SOLV...DECISION JURID BIBLIOG 20 SUPREME/CT
FREE/SPEE AMEND/I. PAGE 9 E0175
B66
METH
CT/SYS
ADJUD
ORD/FREE

BEELEY A.L.,THE BAIL SYSTEM IN CHICAGO. LAW MUNIC
PUB/INST EFFICIENCY MORAL...CRIMLGY METH/CNCPT STAT
20 CHICAGO. PAGE 9 E0176
B66
JURID
CT/SYS
CRIME
ADJUD

BEISER E.N.,THE TREATMENT OF LEGISLATIVE
APPORTIONMENT BY THE STATE AND FEDERAL COURTS
(DISSERTATION). USA+45 CONSTN NAT/G PROVS LEGIS
CHOOSE REPRESENT ATTIT...POLICY BIBLIOG 20 CONGRESS
SUPREME/CT. PAGE 9 E0181
B66
CT/SYS
APPORT
ADJUD
PWR

BRAIBANTI R.,RESEARCH ON THE BUREAUCRACY OF
PAKISTAN. PAKISTAN LAW CULTURE INTELL ACADEM LOC/G
SECT PRESS CT/SYS...LING CHARTS 20 BUREAUCRCY.
PAGE 15 E0286
B66
HABITAT
NAT/G
ADMIN
CONSTN

BRENNAN J.T.,THE COST OF THE AMERICAN JUDICIAL
SYSTEM. USA+45 PROF/ORG TV ADMIN EFFICIENCY.
PAGE 15 E0292
B66
COST
CT/SYS
ADJUD
JURID

BURNS A.C.,PARLIAMENT AS AN EXPORT. WOR+45 CONSTN BARGAIN DEBATE ROUTINE GOV/REL EFFICIENCY...ANTHOL COMMONWLTH PARLIAMENT. PAGE 17 E0343
B66
PARL/PROC
POL/PAR
CT/SYS
CHIEF

CAHN E.,CONFRONTING INJUSTICE. USA+45 PROB/SOLV TAX EDU/PROP PRESS CT/SYS GP/REL DISCRIM BIO/SOC ...IDEA/COMP BIBLIOG WORSHIP 20 BILL/RIGHT. PAGE 18 E0362
B66
ORD/FREE
CONSTN
ADJUD

CALIFORNIA STATE LIBRARY,REAPPORTIONMENT, A SELECTIVE BIBLIOGRAPHY. USA+45 LEGIS CT/SYS REPRESENT GOV/REL. PAGE 19 E0367
B66
BIBLIOG
APPORT
NAT/G
PROVS

CONG QUARTERLY SERVICE,REPRESENTATION AND APPORTIONMENT. USA+45 USA-45 POL/PAR CT/SYS SUFF ...POLICY 20 CONGRESS SUPREME/CT. PAGE 25 E0486
B66
APPORT
LEGIS
REPRESENT
CONSTN

COUNCIL OF EUROPE,EUROPEAN CONVENTION ON HUMAN RIGHTS - COLLECTED TEXTS (5TH ED.). EUR+WWI DIPLOM ADJUD CT/SYS...INT/LAW 20 ECHR. PAGE 26 E0520
B66
ORD/FREE
DELIB/GP
INT/ORG
JURID

DE TOCQUEVILLE A,DEMOCRACY IN AMERICA (1834-1840) (2 VOLS. IN I; TRANS. BY G. LAWRENCE). FRANCE CULTURE STRATA POL/PAR CT/SYS REPRESENT FEDERAL ORD/FREE SOVEREIGN...MAJORIT TREND GEN/LAWS 18/19. PAGE 30 E0596
B66
POPULISM
USA-45
CONSTN
NAT/COMP

DOUMA J.,BIBLIOGRAPHY ON THE INTERNATIONAL COURT INCLUDING THE PERMANENT COURT, 1918-1964. WOR+45 WOR-45 DELIB/GP WAR PRIVIL...JURID NAT/COMP 20 UN LEAGUE/NAT. PAGE 33 E0645
B66
BIBLIOG/A
INT/ORG
CT/SYS
DIPLOM

FELSHER H.,JUSTICE USA? USA+45 COM/IND JUDGE CT/SYS MORAL ORD/FREE...SAMP/SIZ HYPO/EXP. PAGE 37 E0735
B66
ADJUD
EDU/PROP
LOBBY

FINK M.,A SELECTIVE BIBLIOGRAPHY ON STATE CONSTITUTIONAL REVISION (PAMPHLET). USA+45 FINAN EX/STRUC LEGIS EDU/PROP ADMIN CT/SYS APPORT CHOOSE GOV/REL 20. PAGE 38 E0751
B66
BIBLIOG
PROVS
LOC/G
CONSTN

FISCHER H.,EINER IM VORDERGRUND: TARAS BORODAJKEWYCZ. AUSTRIA POL/PAR PROF/ORG EDU/PROP CT/SYS ORD/FREE 20 NAZI. PAGE 38 E0754
B66
FASCISM
LAW
ATTIT
PRESS

GARCON M.,LETTRE OUVERTE A LA JUSTICE. FRANCE NAT/G PROB/SOLV PAY EFFICIENCY MORAL 20. PAGE 42 E0834
B66
ORD/FREE
ADJUD
CT/SYS

GHOSH P.K.,THE CONSTITUTION OF INDIA: HOW IT HAS BEEN FRAMED. INDIA LOC/G DELIB/GP EX/STRUC PROB/SOLV BUDGET INT/TRADE CT/SYS CHOOSE...LING 20. PAGE 43 E0854
B66
CONSTN
NAT/G
LEGIS
FEDERAL

GOLDWIN R.A.,APPORTIONMENT AND REPRESENTATION. MUNIC CT/SYS GP/REL ORD/FREE...POLICY ANTHOL 20 SUPREME/CT. PAGE 44 E0880
B66
APPORT
REPRESENT
LEGIS
CONSTN

GREENE L.E.,GOVERNMENT IN TENNESSEE (2ND ED.). USA+45 DIST/IND INDUS POL/PAR EX/STRUC LEGIS PLAN BUDGET GIVE CT/SYS...MGT T 20 TENNESSEE. PAGE 46 E0909
B66
PROVS
LOC/G
CONSTN
ADMIN

HARVEY W.B.,LAW AND SOCIAL CHANGE IN GHANA. AFR GHANA CONSULT CONTROL CT/SYS INGP/REL 20. PAGE 51 E1011
B66
JURID
CONSTN
LEAD
ORD/FREE

HAUSNER G.,JUSTICE IN JERUSALEM. GERMANY ISRAEL SOCIETY KIN DIPLOM LEGIT CT/SYS PARTIC MURDER MAJORITY ATTIT FASCISM...INT/LAW JURID 20 JEWS WAR/TRIAL. PAGE 51 E1013
B66
ADJUD
CRIME
RACE/REL
COERCE

HAYS P.R.,LABOR ARBITRATION: A DISSENTING VIEW. USA+45 LAW DELIB/GP BARGAIN ADJUD...PREDICT 20. PAGE 51 E1016
B66
GP/REL
LABOR
CONSULT
CT/SYS

HIDAYATULLAH M.,DEMOCRACY IN INDIA AND THE JUDICIAL PROCESS. INDIA EX/STRUC LEGIS LEAD GOV/REL ATTIT ORD/FREE...MAJORIT CONCPT 20 NEHRU/J. PAGE 52 E1040
B66
NAT/G
CT/SYS
CONSTN
JURID

HOGUE A.R.,ORIGINS OF THE COMMON LAW. UK STRUCT AGRI CT/SYS SANCTION CONSERVE 12/14 ENGLSH/LAW COMMON/LAW. PAGE 54 E1068
B66
LAW
SOCIETY
CONSTN

HOLDSWORTH W.S.,A HISTORY OF ENGLISH LAW; THE CENTURIES OF SETTLEMENT AND REFORM (VOL. XVI). UK LOC/G NAT/G EX/STRUC LEGIS CT/SYS LEAD ATTIT ...POLICY DECISION JURID IDEA/COMP 18 PARLIAMENT. PAGE 54 E1083
B66
BIOG
PERSON
PROF/ORG
LAW

HOLMES O.W.,JUSTICE HOLMES, EX CATHEDRA. USA+45 USA-45 LAW INTELL ADMIN ATTIT...BIBLIOG 20 SUPREME/CT HOLMES/OW. PAGE 55 E1088
B66
BIOG
PERSON
CT/SYS
ADJUD

KUNSTLER W.M.,"DEEP IN MY HEART" USA+45 LAW PROF/ORG SECT LOBBY PARTIC CROWD DISCRIM ROLE ...BIOG 20 KING/MAR/L NEGRO CIV/RIGHTS SOUTH/US. PAGE 62 E1233
B66
CT/SYS
RACE/REL
ADJUD
CONSULT

LOFTON J.,JUSTICE AND THE PRESS. EDU/PROP GOV/REL MORAL 20. PAGE 66 E1320
B66
PRESS
JURID
CT/SYS
ORD/FREE

MAGRATH C.P.,YAZOO: LAW AND POLITICS IN THE NEW REPUBLIC: THE CASE OF FLETCHER V. PECK. USA-45 LAW ...BIBLIOG 19 SUPREME/CT YAZOO. PAGE 67 E1348
B66
CT/SYS
DECISION
CONSTN
LOBBY

NANTWI E.K.,THE ENFORCEMENT OF INTERNATIONAL JUDICIAL DECISIONS AND ARBITAL AWARDS IN PUBLIC INTERNATIONAL LAW. WOR+45 WOR-45 JUDGE PROB/SOLV DIPLOM CT/SYS SUPEGO MORAL PWR RESPECT...METH/CNCPT 18/20 CASEBOOK. PAGE 76 E1520
B66
INT/LAW
ADJUD
SOVEREIGN
INT/ORG

POWERS E.,CRIME AND PUNISHMENT IN EARLY MASSACHUSETTS 1620-1692: A DOCUMENTARY HISTORY. USA-45 SECT LEGIS COLONIAL ATTIT ORD/FREE MYSTISM 17 PRE/US/AM MASSACHU. PAGE 82 E1643
B66
CRIME
ADJUD
CT/SYS
PROVS

SHAPIRO M.,FREEDOM OF SPEECH: THE SUPREME COURT AND JUDICIAL REVIEW. USA+45 LEGIS...CHARTS 20 SUPREME/CT FREE/SPEE. PAGE 90 E1812
B66
CT/SYS
ORD/FREE
CONSTN
JURID

SOBEL N.R.,THE NEW CONFESSION STANDARDS, MIRANDA V. ARIZONA. USA+45 USA-45 LAW PROF/ORG EDU/PROP 20 SUPREME/CT. PAGE 92 E1849
B66
JURID
CT/SYS
ORD/FREE
ADJUD

STUMPF S.E.,MORALITY AND THE LAW. USA+45 LAW CULTURE PROB/SOLV DOMIN ADJUD CONTROL ADJUST ALL/IDEOS MARXISM...INT/LAW 20 SUPREME/CT. PAGE 94 E1890
B66
JURID
MORAL
CT/SYS

SWEET E.C.,CIVIL LIBERTIES IN AMERICA. LAW CONSTN NAT/G PRESS CT/SYS DISCRIM ATTIT WORSHIP 20 CIVIL/LIB. PAGE 95 E1899
B66
ADJUD
ORD/FREE
SUFF
COERCE

SZLADITS C.,A BIBLIOGRAPHY ON FOREIGN AND COMPARATIVE LAW (SUPPLEMENT 1964). FINAN FAM LABOR LG/CO LEGIS JUDGE ADMIN CRIME...CRIMLGY 20. PAGE 95 E1905
B66
BIBLIOG/A
CT/SYS
INT/LAW

TIEDT S.W.,THE ROLE OF THE FEDERAL GOVERNMENT IN EDUCATION. FUT USA+45 USA-45 CONSTN SECT BUDGET CT/SYS GOV/REL 18/20 SUPREME/CT. PAGE 96 E1924
B66
NAT/G
EDU/PROP
GIVE
SCHOOL

TRESOLINI R.J.,CASES IN AMERICAN NATIONAL
GOVERNMENT AND POLITICS. LAW DIPLOM ADJUD LOBBY
FEDERAL ORD/FREE WEALTH...DECISION ANTHOL 20
PRESIDENT. PAGE 97 E1940

B66
NAT/G
LEGIS
CT/SYS
POL/PAR

US HOUSE COMM ON JUDICIARY,CIVIL COMMITMENT AND
TREATMENT OF NARCOTIC ADDICTS. USA+45 SOCIETY FINAN
LEGIS PROB/SOLV GIVE CT/SYS SANCTION HEALTH
...POLICY HEAL 20. PAGE 100 E2008

B66
BIO/SOC
CRIME
IDEA/COMP
CONTROL

US PRES COMN CRIME IN DC,REPORT OF THE US
PRESIDENT'S COMMISSION ON CRIME IN THE DISTRICT OF
COLUMBIA. LEGIS WORKER EDU/PROP ADJUD CONTROL
CT/SYS GP/REL BIO/SOC HEALTH...CRIMLGY NEW/IDEA
STAT 20. PAGE 101 E2022

B66
CRIME
FORCES
AGE/Y
SANCTION

US SENATE COMM ON JUDICIARY,HEARINGS ON FREE PRESS
AND FAIR TRIAL (2 VOLS.). USA+45 CONSTN ELITES
LEGIS EDU/PROP CT/SYS LEAD CONGRESS. PAGE 103 E2057

B66
PRESS
LAW
CRIME
ORD/FREE

WALL E.H.,THE COURT OF JUSTICE IN THE EUROPEAN
COMMUNITIES: JURISDICTION AND PROCEDURE. EUR+WWI
DIPLOM ADJUD ADMIN ROUTINE TASK...CONCPT LING 20.
PAGE 105 E2096

B66
CT/SYS
INT/ORG
LAW
OP/RES

WILSON G.,CASES AND MATERIALS ON CONSTITUTIONAL AND
ADMINISTRATIVE LAW. UK LAW NAT/G EX/STRUC LEGIS
BAL/PWR BUDGET DIPLOM ADJUD CONTROL CT/SYS GOV/REL
ORD/FREE 20 PARLIAMENT ENGLSH/LAW. PAGE 106 E2126

B66
JURID
ADMIN
CONSTN
PWR

GREIG D.W.,"THE ADVISORY JURISDICTION OF THE
INTERNATIONAL COURT AND THE SETTLEMENT OF DISPUTES
BETWEEN STATES." ISRAEL KOREA FORCES BUDGET DOMIN
LEGIT ADJUD COST...RECORD UN CONGO/LEOP TREATY.
PAGE 46 E0915

L66
INT/LAW
CT/SYS

HIGGINS R.,"THE INTERNATIONAL COURT AND SOUTH WEST
AFRICA* SOME IMPLICATIONS OF THE JUDGMENT." AFR LAW
ECO/UNDEV JUDGE RACE/REL COST PWR...INT/LAW TREND
UN TREATY. PAGE 52 E1043

L66
SOUTH/AFR
COLONIAL
CT/SYS
ADJUD

FINE R.I.,"PEACE-KEEPING COSTS AND ARTICLE 19 OF
THE UN CHARTER* AN INVITATION TO RESPONSIBILITY."
INT/ORG NAT/G ADJUD CT/SYS CHOOSE CONSEN...RECORD
IDEA/COMP UN. PAGE 38 E0750

S66
FORCES
COST
CONSTN

GASS O.,"THE LITERATURE OF AMERICAN GOVERNMENT."
CONSTN DRIVE ORD/FREE...JURID CONCPT METH/CNCPT
IDEA/COMP 20 WILSON/W BEARD/CA LINK/AS. PAGE 42
E0841

S66
NEW/LIB
CT/SYS
NAT/G

NYC BAR ASSOCIATION RECORD,"PAPERBACKS FOR THE
BAR." USA+45 LEGIS ADJUD CT/SYS. PAGE 78 E1562

S66
BIBLIOG
JURID
LAW
WRITING

BACHELDER G.L.,THE LITERATURE OF FEDERALISM: A
SELECTED BIBLIOGRAPHY (REV ED) (A PAMPHLET). USA+45
USA-45 WOR+45 WOR-45 LAW CONSTN PROVS ADMIN CT/SYS
GOV/REL ROLE...CONCPT 19/20. PAGE 7 E0126

N66
BIBLIOG
FEDERAL
NAT/G
LOC/G

ASCH S.H.,POLICE AUTHORITY AND THE RIGHTS OF THE
INDIVIDUAL. CONSTN DOMIN ADJUD CT/SYS...JURID 20.
PAGE 6 E0106

B67
FORCES
OP/RES
ORD/FREE

BAKER L.,BACK TO BACK: THE DUEL BETWEEN FDR AND THE
SUPREME COURT. ELITES LEGIS CREATE DOMIN INGP/REL
PERSON PWR NEW/LIB 20 ROOSEVLT/F SUPREME/CT SENATE.
PAGE 7 E0142

B67
CHIEF
CT/SYS
PARL/PROC
GOV/REL

BOHANNAN P.,LAW AND WARFARE. CULTURE CT/SYS COERCE
REV PEACE...JURID SOC CONCPT ANTHOL 20. PAGE 13
E0259

B67
METH/COMP
ADJUD
WAR
LAW

BOLES D.E.,THE TWO SWORDS. USA+45 USA-45 LAW CONSTN
SOCIETY FINAN PRESS CT/SYS...HEAL JURID BIBLIOG
WORSHIP 20 SUPREME/CT CHURCH/STA. PAGE 13 E0263

B67
SCHOOL
EDU/PROP
ADJUD

BROWN L.N.,FRENCH ADMINISTRATIVE LAW. FRANCE UK
CONSTN NAT/G LEGIS DOMIN CONTROL EXEC PARL/PROC PWR
...JURID METH/COMP GEN/METH. PAGE 16 E0314

B67
EX/STRUC
LAW
IDEA/COMP
CT/SYS

FESLER J.W.,THE FIFTY STATES AND THEIR LOCAL
GOVERNMENTS. FUT USA+45 POL/PAR LEGIS PROB/SOLV
ADMIN CT/SYS CHOOSE GOV/REL FEDERAL...POLICY CHARTS
20 SUPREME/CT. PAGE 37 E0743

B67
PROVS
LOC/G

FINCHER F.,THE GOVERNMENT OF THE UNITED STATES.
USA+45 USA-45 POL/PAR CHIEF CT/SYS LOBBY GP/REL
INGP/REL...CONCPT CHARTS BIBLIOG T 18/20 PRESIDENT
CONGRESS SUPREME/CT. PAGE 38 E0749

B67
NAT/G
EX/STRUC
LEGIS
OP/RES

FRIENDLY A.,CRIME AND PUBLICITY. TV CT/SYS SUPEGO
20. PAGE 41 E0811

B67
PRESS
CRIME
ROLE
LAW

GELLHORN W.,OMBUDSMEN AND OTHERS: CITIZENS'
PROTECTORS IN NINE COUNTRIES. WOR+45 LAW CONSTN
LEGIS INSPECT ADJUD ADMIN CONTROL CT/SYS CHOOSE
PERS/REL...STAT CHARTS 20. PAGE 43 E0847

B67
NAT/COMP
REPRESENT
INGP/REL
PROB/SOLV

HEWITT W.H.,ADMINISTRATION OF CRIMINAL JUSTICE IN
NEW YORK. LAW PROB/SOLV ADJUD ADMIN...CRIMLGY
CHARTS T 20 NEW/YORK. PAGE 52 E1035

B67
CRIME
ROLE
CT/SYS
FORCES

KING W.L.,MELVILLE WESTON FULLER: CHIEF JUSTICE OF
THE UNITED STATES, 1888-1910. USA-45 CONSTN FINAN
LABOR TAX GOV/REL PERS/REL ATTIT PERSON PWR...JURID
BIBLIOG 19/20 SUPREME/CT FULLER/MW HOLMES/OW.
PAGE 61 E1216

B67
BIOG
CT/SYS
LAW
ADJUD

LENG S.C.,JUSTICE IN COMMUNIST CHINA: A SURVEY OF
THE JUDICIAL SYSTEM OF THE CHINESE PEOPLE'S
REPUBLIC. CHINA/COM LAW CONSTN LOC/G NAT/G PROF/ORG
CONSULT FORCES ADMIN CRIME ORD/FREE...BIBLIOG 20
MAO. PAGE 64 E1284

B67
CT/SYS
ADJUD
JURID
MARXISM

LEVY L.W.,JUDICIAL REVIEW AND THE SUPREME COURT.
USA+45 USA-45 NEUTRAL ATTIT ORD/FREE...POLICY
DECISION BIBLIOG 18/20 BILL/RIGHT SUPREME/CT.
PAGE 65 E1292

B67
ADJUD
CONSTN
LAW
CT/SYS

LOBLE L.H.,DELINQUENCY CAN BE STOPPED. FAM PUB/INST
CT/SYS ADJUST ATTIT...NEW/IDEA METH/COMP 20.
PAGE 66 E1315

B67
AGE/Y
PROB/SOLV
ADJUD
CRIME

UNIVERSAL REFERENCE SYSTEM,LAW, JURISPRUDENCE, AND
JUDICIAL PROCESS (VOLUME VII). WOR+45 WOR-45 CONSTN
NAT/G LEGIS JUDGE CT/SYS...INT/LAW COMPUT/IR
GEN/METH METH. PAGE 99 E1976

B67
BIBLIOG/A
LAW
JURID
ADJUD

US PRES TASK FORCE ADMIN JUS,TASK FORCE REPORT: THE
COURTS. USA+45 CONSULT CONFER...JURID CHARTS.
PAGE 101 E2025

B67
CT/SYS
ADJUD
ROUTINE
ADMIN

"FOCUS ON WORLD LAW." WOR+45 NAT/G CT/SYS PEACE
...BIBLIOG 20 UN. PAGE 2 E0036

L67
INT/LAW
INT/ORG
PROB/SOLV
CONCPT

BERNHARD R.C.,"COMPETITION IN LAW AND ECONOMICS."
LAW PLAN PRICE CONTROL PRODUC PROFIT...METH/CNCPT
IDEA/COMP GEN/LAWS 20. PAGE 11 E0210

L67
MARKET
POLICY
NAT/G
CT/SYS

BLUMBERG A.S.,"THE PRACTICE OF LAW AS CONFIDENCE
GAME: ORGANIZATIONAL COOPTATION OF A PROFESSION."
USA+45 CLIENT SOCIETY CONSULT ROLE JURID. PAGE 13
E0252

L67
CT/SYS
ADJUD
GP/REL
ADMIN

HOWARD A.E.D.,"MR. JUSTICE BLACK: THE NEGRO PROTEST
MOVEMENT AND THE RULE OF LAW." USA+45 CONSTN CT/SYS

L67
ADJUD
JUDGE

CHOOSE GP/REL...DECISION JURID NEGRO SUPREME/CT.
PAGE 55 E1100

LAW
REPRESENT

L67

SCHUBERT G.,"THE RHETORIC OF CONSTITUTIONAL
CHANGE." USA+45 LAW CULTURE CHIEF LEGIS ADJUD
CT/SYS ARMS/CONT ADJUST...CHARTS SIMUL. PAGE 89
E1777

CONSTN
METH/COMP
ORD/FREE

L67

WAELBROECK M.,"THE APPLICATION OF EEC LAW BY
NATIONAL COURTS." EUR+WWI INT/ORG CT/SYS...JURID
EEC TREATY. PAGE 104 E2090

INT/LAW
NAT/G
LAW
PROB/SOLV

S67

"THE STATE OF ZONING ADMINISTRATION IN ILLINOIS:
PROCEDURAL REQUIREMENTS OF JUDICIAL INTERVENTION."
USA+45 LAW CONSTN DELIB/GP ADJUD CT/SYS ORD/FREE
ILLINOIS. PAGE 2 E0038

ADMIN
CONTROL
HABITAT
PLAN

S67

CARTER R.M.,"SOME FACTORS IN SENTENCING POLICY."
LAW PUB/INST CRIME PERS/REL...POLICY JURID SOC
TREND CON/ANAL CHARTS SOC/EXP 20. PAGE 20 E0403

ADJUD
CT/SYS
ADMIN

S67

CREYKE G. JR.,"THE PAYMENT GAP IN FEDERAL
CONSTRUCTION CONTRACTS." USA+45 LAW FINAN ECO/TAC
CONTROL CT/SYS SUPREME/CT. PAGE 28 E0547

CONSTRUC
PAY
COST
NAT/G

S67

DALFEN C.M.,"THE WORLD COURT IN IDLE SPLENDOUR: THE
BASIS OF STATES' ATTITUDES." WOR+45 LAW ADJUD
COERCE...JURID 20 UN WORLD/CT. PAGE 28 E0562

CT/SYS
INT/ORG
INT/LAW
DIPLOM

S67

GREY D.L.,"INTERVIEWING AT THE COURT." USA+45
ELITES COM/IND ACT/RES PRESS CT/SYS PERSON...SOC
INT 20 SUPREME/CT. PAGE 46 E0916

JUDGE
ATTIT
PERS/COMP
GP/COMP

S67

HUBERT C.J.,"PLANNED UNIT DEVELOPMENT" LAW VOL/ASSN
LEGIS EDU/PROP CT/SYS GOV/REL...NEW/IDEA 20
PLAN/UNIT. PAGE 56 E1107

PLAN
MUNIC
HABITAT
ADJUD

S67

KENNEDY R.F.,"TOWARD A NATION WHERE THE LAW IS
KING." PLAN CT/SYS CRIME INGP/REL...JURID SOC.
PAGE 60 E1202

CRIMLGY
ADJUST
LAW
PUB/INST

S67

KETCHAM O.W.,"GUIDELINES FROM GAULT: REVOLUTIONARY
REQUIREMENTS AND REAPPRAISAL." LAW CONSTN CREATE
LEGIT ROUTINE SANCTION CRIME DISCRIM PRIVIL ROLE
...JURID NEW/IDEA 20 SUPREME/CT. PAGE 60 E1208

ADJUD
AGE/Y
CT/SYS

S67

KIM R.C.C.,"THE SUPREME COURT: ORALLE WITHOUT
TRUTH." USA+45 EDU/PROP RACE/REL ADJUST ALL/VALS
ORD/FREE...DECISION WORSHIP SUPREME/CT. PAGE 61
E1214

CT/SYS
PROB/SOLV
ADJUD
REPRESENT

S67

LARSEN P.B.,"THE UNITED STATES-ITALY AIR TRANSPORT
ARBITRATION: PROBLEMS OF TREATY INTERPRETATION AND
ENFORCEMENT." ITALY USA+45 AIR PROB/SOLV DIPLOM
DEBATE CONTROL CT/SYS...DECISION TREATY. PAGE 63
E1257

INT/LAW
ADJUD
INT/TRADE
DIST/IND

S67

MITCHELL J.D.B.,"THE CONSTITUTIONAL IMPLICATIONS OF
JUDICIAL CONTROL OF THE ADMINISTRATION IN THE
UNITED KINGDOM." UK LAW ADJUD ADMIN GOV/REL ROLE
...GP/COMP 20. PAGE 74 E1474

CONSTN
CT/SYS
CONTROL
EX/STRUC

S67

RUCKER B.W.,"WHAT SOLUTIONS DO PEOPLE ENDORSE IN
FREE PRESS-FAIR TRIAL DILEMMA?" LAW NAT/G CT/SYS
ATTIT...NET/THEORY SAMP CHARTS IDEA/COMP METH 20.
PAGE 86 E1731

CONCPT
PRESS
ADJUD
ORD/FREE

S67

SEIDLER G.L.,"MARXIST LEGAL THOUGHT IN POLAND."
POLAND SOCIETY R+D LOC/G NAT/G ACT/RES ADJUD CT/SYS
SUPEGO PWR...SOC TREND 20 MARX/KARL. PAGE 90 E1802

MARXISM
LAW
CONCPT
EFFICIENCY

S67

SHELDON C.H.,"PUBLIC OPINION AND HIGH COURTS:
COMMUNIST PARTY CASES IN FOUR CONSTITUTIONAL

ATTIT
CT/SYS

SYSTEMS." CANADA GERMANY/W WOR+45 POL/PAR MARXISM
...METH/COMP NAT/COMP 20 AUSTRAL. PAGE 91 E1818

CONSTN
DECISION

S67

TRAYNOR R.J.,"WHO CAN BEST JUDGE THE JUDGES?"
USA+45 PLAN PROB/SOLV ATTIT...DECISION JURID 20.
PAGE 97 E1938

CHOOSE
ADJUD
REPRESENT
CT/SYS

S67

TYDINGS J.D.,"MODERNIZING THE ADMINISTRATION OF
JUSTICE." PLAN ADMIN ROUTINE EFFICIENCY...JURID
SIMUL. PAGE 97 E1948

CT/SYS
MGT
COMPUTER
CONSULT

B70

BLACKSTONE W.,COMMENTARIES ON THE LAWS OF ENGLAND
(4 VOLS.) (4TH ED.). UK CHIEF DELIB/GP LEGIS WORKER
CT/SYS SANCTION CRIME OWN...CRIMLGY 18 ENGLSH/LAW.
PAGE 12 E0238

LAW
JURID
ADJUD
CONSTN

B73

AUSTIN J.,LECTURES ON JURISPRUDENCE OR THE
PHILOSOPHY OF POSITIVE LAW (VOL. II) (4TH ED.,
REV.). UK CONSTN STRUCT PROB/SOLV LEGIT CT/SYS
SANCTION CRIME INGP/REL OWN SUPEGO ORD/FREE...T 19.
PAGE 6 E0120

LAW
ADJUD
JURID
METH/CNCPT

B75

MAINE H.S.,LECTURES ON THE EARLY HISTORY OF
INSTITUTIONS. IRELAND UK CONSTN ELITES STRUCT FAM
KIN CHIEF LEGIS CT/SYS OWN SOVEREIGN...CONCPT 16
BENTHAM/J BREHON ROMAN/LAW. PAGE 68 E1351

CULTURE
LAW
INGP/REL

B77

CADWALDER J.L.,DIGEST OF THE PUBLISHED OPINIONS OF
THE ATTORNEYS-GENERAL, AND OF THE LEADING DECISIONS
OF THE FEDERAL COURTS (REV ED). USA-45 NAT/G JUDGE
PROB/SOLV DIPLOM ATTIT...POLICY INT/LAW ANTHOL 19.
PAGE 18 E0356

BIBLIOG
CT/SYS
DECISION
ADJUD

L86

GOODNOW F.J.,"AN EXECUTIVE AND THE COURTS: JUDICIAL
REMEDIES AGAINST ADMINISTRATIVE ACTION" FRANCE UK
USA-45 WOR-45 LAW CONSTN SANCTION ORD/FREE 19.
PAGE 45 E0888

CT/SYS
GOV/REL
ADMIN
ADJUD

L86

WHITRIDGE L.I.,"LEGISLATIVE INQUESTS" USA-45 ADJUD
GOV/REL SOVEREIGN 19/20 CONGRESS. PAGE 106 E2120

CT/SYS
LEGIS
JURID
CONSTN

B87

ADAMS J.,A DEFENSE OF THE CONSTITUTIONS OF
GOVERNMENT OF THE UNITED STATES OF AMERICA. USA-45
STRATA CHIEF EX/STRUC LEGIS CT/SYS CONSERVE
POPULISM...CONCPT CON/ANAL GOV/COMP. PAGE 3 E0048

CONSTN
BAL/PWR
PWR
NAT/G

B92

LOWELL A.L.,ESSAYS ON GOVERNMENT. UK USA-45 LEGIS
PARL/PROC...POLICY PREDICT 19. PAGE 66 E1328

CONSTN
ADJUD
CT/SYS
NAT/G

B96

ESMEIN A.,ELEMENTS DE DROIT CONSTITUTIONNEL. FRANCE
UK CHIEF EX/STRUC LEGIS ADJUD CT/SYS PARL/PROC REV
GOV/REL ORD/FREE...JURID METH/COMP 18/19. PAGE 35
E0697

LAW
CONSTN
NAT/G
CONCPT

B97

JENKS E.J.,LAW AND POLITICS IN THE MIDDLE AGES.
CHRIST-17C CULTURE STRUCT KIN NAT/G SECT CT/SYS
GP/REL...CLASSIF CHARTS IDEA/COMP BIBLIOG 8/16.
PAGE 58 E1162

LAW
SOCIETY
ADJUST

B97

US DEPARTMENT OF STATE,CATALOGUE OF WORKS RELATING
TO THE LAW OF NATIONS AND DIPLOMACY IN THE LIBRARY
OF THE DEPARTMENT OF STATE (PAMPHLET). WOR-45 NAT/G
ADJUD CT/SYS...INT/LAW JURID 19. PAGE 100 E2000

BIBLIOG/A
DIPLOM
LAW

B98

POLLOCK F.,THE HISTORY OF ENGLISH LAW BEFORE THE
TIME OF EDWARD I (2 VOLS. 2ND ED.). UK CULTURE
LOC/G LEGIS LICENSE AGREE CONTROL CT/SYS SANCTION
CRIME...TIME/SEQ 13 COMMON/LAW CANON/LAW. PAGE 81
E1626

LAW
ADJUD
JURID

CTS/WESTM....COURTS OF WESTMINSTER HALL

B35

RAM J.,THE SCIENCE OF LEGAL JUDGMENT: A TREATISE...
UK CONSTN NAT/G LEGIS CREATE PROB/SOLV AGREE CT/SYS
...INT/LAW CONCPT 19 ENGLSH/LAW CANON/LAW CIVIL/LAW

LAW
JURID
EX/STRUC

CTS/WESTM. PAGE 83 E1672   ADJUD

CUBA....SEE ALSO L/A+17C

B58
BUGEDA LANZAS J.,A STATEMENT OF THE LAWS OF CUBA IN JURID
MATTERS AFFECTING BUSINESS (2ND ED. REV.,   NAT/G
ENLARGED). CUBA L/A+17C LAW FINAN FAM LEGIS ACT/RES INDUS
ADMIN GP/REL...BIBLIOG 20 OAS. PAGE 17 E0327   WORKER

L62
NIZARD L.,"CUBAN QUESTION AND SECURITY COUNCIL."   INT/ORG
L/A+17C USA+45 ECO/UNDEV NAT/G POL/PAR DELIB/GP   JURID
ECO/TAC PWR...RELATIV OBS TIME/SEQ TREND GEN/LAWS   DIPLOM
UN 20 UN. PAGE 77 E1551   CUBA

S62
FENWICK C.G.,"ISSUES AT PUNTA DEL ESTE: NON-   INT/ORG
INTERVENTION VS COLLECTIVE SECURITY." L/A+17C   CUBA
USA+45 VOL/ASSN DELIB/GP ECO/TAC LEGIT ADJUD REGION
ORD/FREE OAS COLD/WAR 20. PAGE 37 E0738

S62
MCWHINNEY E.,"CO-EXISTENCE, THE CUBA CRISIS, AND   CONCPT
COLD WAR-INTERNATIONAL WAR." CUBA USA+45 USSR   INT/LAW
WOR+45 NAT/G TOP/EX BAL/PWR DIPLOM DOMIN LEGIT
PEACE RIGID/FLEX ORD/FREE...STERTYP COLD/WAR 20.
PAGE 71 E1427

B63
PACHTER H.M.,COLLISION COURSE; THE CUBAN MISSILE   WAR
CRISIS AND COEXISTENCE. CUBA USA+45 DIPLOM   BAL/PWR
ARMS/CONT PEACE MARXISM...DECISION INT/LAW 20   NUC/PWR
COLD/WAR KHRUSH/N KENNEDY/JF CASTRO/F. PAGE 79   DETER
E1587

B63
US SENATE COMM ON JUDICIARY,CASTRO'S NETWORK IN THE PRESS
UNITED STATES. CUBA LAW DELIB/GP 20 SENATE   MARXISM
CASTRO/F. PAGE 102 E2050   DIPLOM
                                                    INSPECT

B63
VAN SLYCK P.,PEACE: THE CONTROL OF NATIONAL POWER. ARMS/CONT
CUBA WOR+45 FINAN NAT/G FORCES PROB/SOLV TEC/DEV   PEACE
BAL/PWR ADMIN CONTROL ORD/FREE...POLICY INT/LAW UN INT/ORG
COLD/WAR TREATY. PAGE 103 E2069   DIPLOM

S63
GIRAUD E.,"L'INTERDICTION DU RECOURS A LA FORCE, LA INT/ORG
THEORIE ET LA PRATIQUE DES NATIONS UNIES." ALGERIA FORCES
COM CUBA HUNGARY WOR+45 ADJUD TOTALISM ATTIT   DIPLOM
RIGID/FLEX PWR...POLICY JURID CONCPT UN 20 CONGO.
PAGE 44 E0872

S63
MCDOUGAL M.S.,"THE SOVIET-CUBAN QUARANTINE AND   ORD/FREE
SELF-DEFENSE." CUBA USA+45 USSR WOR+45 INT/ORG   LEGIT
NAT/G BAL/PWR NUC/PWR ATTIT...JURID CONCPT. PAGE 70 SOVEREIGN
E1409

B64
GRIFFITH W.E.,THE SINO-SOVIET RIFT. ASIA CHINA/COM ATTIT
COM CUBA USSR YUGOSLAVIA NAT/G POL/PAR VOL/ASSN   TIME/SEQ
DELIB/GP FORCES TOP/EX DIPLOM EDU/PROP DRIVE PERSON BAL/PWR
PWR...TREND 20 TREATY. PAGE 47 E0941   SOCISM

S65
MAC CHESNEY B.,"SOME COMMENTS ON THE 'QUARANTINE'   INT/ORG
OF CUBA." USA+45 WOR+45 NAT/G BAL/PWR DIPLOM LEGIT LAW
ROUTINE ATTIT ORD/FREE...JURID METH/CNCPT 20.   CUBA
PAGE 67 E1337   USSR

L67
HITCHMAN J.M.,"THE PLATT AMENDMENT REVISITED: A   ATTIT
BIBLIOGRAPHICAL SURVEY." CUBA ACADEM DELIB/GP   DIPLOM
ORD/FREE...HIST/WRIT 20. PAGE 53 E1055   SOVEREIGN
                                                    INT/LAW

S67
CUMMINS L.,"THE FORMULATION OF THE "PLATT"   DIPLOM
AMENDMENT." CUBA L/A+17C NAT/G DELIB/GP CONFER   INT/LAW
...POLICY 20. PAGE 28 E0554   LEGIS

S67
FABREGA J.,"ANTECEDENTES EXTRANJEROS EN LA   CONSTN
CONSTITUCION PANAMENA." CUBA L/A+17C PANAMA URUGUAY JURID
EX/STRUC LEGIS DIPLOM ORD/FREE 19/20 COLOMB   NAT/G
MEXIC/AMER. PAGE 36 E0709   PARL/PROC

S67
REILLY T.J.,"FREEZING AND CONFISCATION OF CUBAN   STRANGE
PROPERTY." CUBA USA+45 LAW DIPLOM LEGIT ADJUD   OWN
CONTROL. PAGE 84 E1682   ECO/TAC

CUBAN CRISIS....SEE INT/REL+APPROPRIATE NATIONS+COLD WAR

CULTS....SEE SECT

CULTUR/REV....CULTURAL REVOLUTION IN CHINA

CULTURE....CULTURAL PATTERNS

N
LIBRARY INTERNATIONAL REL,INTERNATIONAL INFORMATION BIBLIOG/A
SERVICE. WOR+45 CULTURE INT/ORG FORCES...GEOG HUM   DIPLOM
SOC. PAGE 65 E1295   INT/TRADE
                                                    INT/LAW

N
ANNALS OF THE AMERICAN ACADEMY OF POLITICAL AND   BIBLIOG/A
SOCIAL SCIENCE. AFR ASIA S/ASIA WOR+45 POL/PAR   NAT/G
DIPLOM CRIME REV...SOC BIOG 20. PAGE 1 E0003   CULTURE
                                                    ATTIT

N
AUSTRALIAN PUBLIC AFFAIRS INFORMATION SERVICE. LAW BIBLIOG
...HEAL HUM MGT SOC CON/ANAL 20 AUSTRAL. PAGE 1   NAT/G
E0017   CULTURE
                                                    DIPLOM

N
BIBLIOGRAPHIE DE LA PHILOSOPHIE. LAW CULTURE SECT   BIBLIOG/A
EDU/PROP MORAL...HUM METH/CNCPT 20. PAGE 1 E0018   PHIL/SCI
                                                    CONCPT
                                                    LOG

N
FOREIGN AFFAIRS. SPACE WOR+45 WOR-45 CULTURE   BIBLIOG
ECO/UNDEV FINAN NAT/G TEC/DEV INT/TRADE ARMS/CONT   DIPLOM
NUC/PWR...POLICY 20 UN EURATOM ECSC EEC. PAGE 1   INT/ORG
E0021   INT/LAW

N
HANDBOOK OF LATIN AMERICAN STUDIES. LAW CULTURE   BIBLIOG/A
ECO/UNDEV POL/PAR ADMIN LEAD...SOC 20. PAGE 1 E0022 L/A+17C
                                                    NAT/G
                                                    DIPLOM

N
AFRICAN BIBLIOGRAPHIC CENTER,A CURRENT BIBLIOGRAPHY BIBLIOG/A
ON AFRICAN AFFAIRS. LAW CULTURE ECO/UNDEV LABOR   AFR
SECT DIPLOM FOR/AID COLONIAL NAT/LISM...LING 20.   NAT/G
PAGE 3 E0053   REGION

N
ASIA FOUNDATION,LIBRARY NOTES. LAW CONSTN CULTURE   BIBLIOG/A
SOCIETY ECO/UNDEV INT/ORG NAT/G COLONIAL LEAD   ASIA
REGION NAT/LISM ATTIT 20 UN. PAGE 6 E0107   S/ASIA
                                                    DIPLOM

N
ATLANTIC INSTITUTE,ATLANTIC STUDIES. COM EUR+WWI   BIBLIOG/A
USA+45 CULTURE STRUCT ECO/DEV FORCES LEAD ARMS/CONT DIPLOM
...INT/LAW JURID SOC. PAGE 6 E0110   POLICY
                                                    GOV/REL

N
CORNELL UNIVERSITY LIBRARY,SOUTHEAST ASIA   BIBLIOG
ACCESSIONS LIST. LAW SOCIETY STRUCT ECO/UNDEV   S/ASIA
POL/PAR TEC/DEV DIPLOM LEAD REGION. PAGE 26 E0510   NAT/G
                                                    CULTURE

N
DEUTSCHE BUCHEREI,DEUTSCHES BUCHERVERZEICHNIS.   BIBLIOG
GERMANY LAW CULTURE POL/PAR ADMIN LEAD ATTIT PERSON NAT/G
...SOC 20. PAGE 31 E0615   DIPLOM
                                                    ECO/DEV

N
PUBLISHERS' CIRCULAR LIMITED,THE ENGLISH CATALOGUE BIBLIOG
OF BOOKS. UK WOR+45 WOR-45 LAW CULTURE LOC/G NAT/G ALL/VALS
ADMIN LEAD...MGT 19/20. PAGE 83 E1658   ALL/IDEOS
                                                    SOCIETY

N
US BUREAU OF THE CENSUS,BIBLIOGRAPHY OF SOCIAL   BIBLIOG/A
SCIENCE PERIODICALS AND MONOGRAPH SERIES. WOR+45   CULTURE
LAW DIPLOM EDU/PROP HEALTH...PSY SOC LING STAT.   NAT/G
PAGE 99 E1980   SOCIETY

B00
LORIMER J.,THE INSTITUTES OF THE LAW OF NATIONS.   INT/ORG
WOR-45 CULTURE SOCIETY NAT/G VOL/ASSN DIPLOM LEGIT LAW
WAR PEACE DRIVE ORD/FREE SOVEREIGN...CONCPT RECORD INT/LAW
INT TREND HYPO/EXP GEN/METH TOT/POP VAL/FREE 20.
PAGE 66 E1327

B00
MAINE H.S.,ANCIENT LAW. MEDIT-7 CULTURE SOCIETY KIN FAM
SECT LEGIS LEGIT ROUTINE...JURID HIST/WRIT CON/ANAL LAW

TOT/POP VAL/FREE. PAGE 68 E1350

B05
DICEY A.,LAW AND PUBLIC OPINION IN ENGLAND. LAW ATTIT
CULTURE INTELL SOCIETY NAT/G SECT JUDGE LEGIT UK
CHOOSE RIGID/FLEX KNOWL...OLD/LIB CONCPT STERTYP
GEN/LAWS 20. PAGE 31 E0620

B07
BENTHAM J.,AN INTRODUCTION TO THE PRINCIPLES OF LAW
MORALS AND LEGISLATION. UNIV CONSTN CULTURE SOCIETY GEN/LAWS
NAT/G CONSULT LEGIS JUDGE ADJUD CT/SYS...JURID
CONCPT NEW/IDEA. PAGE 10 E0190

B10
MENDELSSOHN S.,MENDELSSOHN'S SOUTH AFRICA BIBLIOG/A
BIBLIOGRAPHY (VOL. I). SOUTH/AFR RACE/REL...GEOG CULTURE
JURID 19/20. PAGE 72 E1440

B12
POLLOCK F.,THE GENIUS OF THE COMMON LAW. CHRIST-17C LAW
UK FINAN CHIEF ACT/RES ADMIN GP/REL ATTIT SOCISM CULTURE
...ANARCH JURID. PAGE 81 E1624 CREATE

B22
BRYCE J.,INTERNATIONAL RELATIONS. CHRIST-17C INT/ORG
EUR+WWI MOD/EUR CULTURE INTELL NAT/G DELIB/GP POLICY
CREATE BAL/PWR DIPLOM ATTIT DRIVE RIGID/FLEX
ALL/VALS...PLURIST JURID CONCPT TIME/SEQ GEN/LAWS
TOT/POP. PAGE 16 E0323

B23
HOLMES O.W. JR.,THE COMMON LAW. FUT WOR-45 CULTURE ADJUD
SOCIETY CREATE LEGIT ROUTINE ATTIT ALL/VALS...JURID CON/ANAL
METH/CNCPT TIME/SEQ GEN/LAWS TOT/POP VAL/FREE.
PAGE 55 E1087

B23
POUND R.,INTERPRETATIONS OF LEGAL HISTORY. CULTURE LAW
...PHIL/SCI NEW/IDEA CLASSIF SIMUL GEN/LAWS 19/20. IDEA/COMP
PAGE 82 E1636 JURID

B24
CARDOZO B.,THE GROWTH OF THE LAW. USA-45 CULTURE LAW
...JURID 20. PAGE 19 E0376 ADJUD
CT/SYS

B26
HOCKING W.E.,PRESENT STATUS OF THE PHILOSOPHY OF JURID
LAW AND OF RIGHTS. UNIV CULTURE INTELL SOCIETY PHIL/SCI
NAT/G CREATE LEGIT SANCTION ALL/VALS SOC/INTEG ORD/FREE
18/20. PAGE 53 E1060

B28
CORBETT P.E.,CANADA AND WORLD POLITICS. LAW CULTURE NAT/G
SOCIETY STRUCT MARKET INT/ORG FORCES ACT/RES PLAN CANADA
ECO/TAC LEGIT ORD/FREE PWR RESPECT...SOC CONCPT
TIME/SEQ TREND CMN/WLTH 20 LEAGUE/NAT. PAGE 26
E0504

B29
BURNS C.D.,POLITICAL IDEALS. WOR-45 LAW CULTURE CONCPT
SOCIETY INT/ORG HEALTH MORAL...POLICY TOT/POP 20. GEN/LAWS
PAGE 18 E0344

B29
STURZO L.,THE INTERNATIONAL COMMUNITY AND THE RIGHT INT/ORG
OF WAR (TRANS. BY BARBARA BARCLAY CARTER). CULTURE PLAN
CREATE PROB/SOLV DIPLOM ADJUD CONTROL PEACE PERSON WAR
ORD/FREE...INT/LAW IDEA/COMP PACIFIST 20 CONCPT
LEAGUE/NAT. PAGE 94 E1891

B34
CULVER D.C.,BIBLIOGRAPHY OF CRIME AND CRIMINAL BIBLIOG/A
JUSTICE, 1927-1931. LAW CULTURE PUB/INST PROB/SOLV CRIMLGY
CT/SYS...PSY SOC STAT 20. PAGE 28 E0549 ADJUD
FORCES

B35
CUMMING J.,A CONTRIBUTION TOWARD A BIBLIOGRAPHY BIBLIOG
DEALING WITH CRIME AND COGNATE SUBJECTS (3RD ED.). CRIMLGY
UK LAW CULTURE PUB/INST ADJUD AGE BIO/SOC...PSY SOC FORCES
SOC/WK STAT METH/COMP 20. PAGE 28 E0552 CT/SYS

B36
CULVER D.C.,METHODOLOGY OF SOCIAL SCIENCE RESEARCH: BIBLIOG/A
A BIBLIOGRAPHY. LAW CULTURE...CRIMLGY GEOG STAT OBS METH
INT QU HIST/WRIT CHARTS 20. PAGE 28 E0550 SOC

B38
POUND R.,THE FORMATIVE ERA OF AMERICAN LAW. CULTURE CONSTN
NAT/G PROVS LEGIS ADJUD CT/SYS PERSON SOVEREIGN LAW
...POLICY IDEA/COMP GEN/LAWS 18/19. PAGE 82 E1637 CREATE
JURID

B39
CULVER D.C.,BIBLIOGRAPHY OF CRIME AND CRIMINAL BIBLIOG/A
JUSTICE, 1932-1937. USA-45 LAW CULTURE PUB/INST CRIMLGY
PROB/SOLV CT/SYS...PSY SOC STAT 20. PAGE 28 E0551 ADJUD
FORCES

B40
FULLER G.H.,A SELECTED LIST OF RECENT REFERENCES ON BIBLIOG/A
THE CONSTITUTION OF THE UNITED STATES (PAMPHLET). CONSTN
CULTURE NAT/G LEGIS CONFER ADJUD GOV/REL CONSEN LAW
POPULISM...JURID CONCPT 18/20 CONGRESS. PAGE 41 USA-45
E0820

S40
GURVITCH G.,"MAJOR PROBLEMS OF THE SOCIOLOGY OF SOC
LAW." CULTURE SANCTION KNOWL MORAL...POLICY EPIST LAW
JURID WORSHIP. PAGE 48 E0963 PHIL/SCI

B42
BLANCHARD L.R.,MARTINIQUE: A SELECTED LIST OF BIBLIOG/A
REFERENCES (PAMPHLET). WEST/IND AGRI LOC/G SCHOOL SOCIETY
...ART/METH GEOG JURID CHARTS 20. PAGE 12 E0241 CULTURE
COLONIAL

B42
CRAIG A.,ABOVE ALL LIBERTIES. FRANCE UK USA-45 LAW ORD/FREE
CONSTN CULTURE INTELL NAT/G SECT JUDGE...IDEA/COMP MORAL
BIBLIOG 18/20. PAGE 27 E0536 WRITING
EDU/PROP

B42
US LIBRARY OF CONGRESS,SOCIAL AND CULTURAL PROBLEMS BIBLIOG/A
IN WARTIME: APRIL 1941-MARCH 1942. WOR-45 CLIENT WAR
SECT EDU/PROP CRIME LEISURE RACE/REL STRANGE ATTIT SOC
DRIVE HEALTH...GEOG 20. PAGE 100 E2012 CULTURE

C42
CRAIG A.,"ABOVE ALL LIBERTIES." FRANCE UK LAW BIBLIOG/A
CULTURE INTELL SECT ORD/FREE 18/20. PAGE 27 E0537 EDU/PROP
WRITING
MORAL

B43
US LIBRARY OF CONGRESS,SOCIAL AND CULTURAL PROBLEMS BIBLIOG/A
IN WARTIME: APRIL-DECEMBER (SUPPLEMENT 1). WOR-45 WAR
SECT EDU/PROP CRIME LEISURE CIVMIL/REL RACE/REL SOC
ATTIT DRIVE HEALTH...GEOG 20. PAGE 100 E2013 CULTURE

B43
US LIBRARY OF CONGRESS,SOCIAL AND CULTURAL PROBLEMS BIBLIOG/A
IN WARTIME: JANUARY-MAY 1943 (SUPPLEMENT 2). WOR-45 WAR
FAM SECT PLAN EDU/PROP CRIME LEISURE RACE/REL DRIVE SOC
HEALTH...GEOG 20 JEWS. PAGE 100 E2014 CULTURE

B44
DE HUSZAR G.B.,NEW PERSPECTIVES ON PEACE. UNIV ATTIT
CULTURE SOCIETY ECO/DEV ECO/UNDEV NAT/G FORCES MYTH
CREATE ECO/TAC DOMIN ADJUD COERCE DRIVE ORD/FREE PEACE
...GEOG JURID PSY SOC CONCPT TOT/POP. PAGE 29 E0584 WAR

B44
FULLER G.H.,TURKEY: A SELECTED LIST OF REFERENCES. BIBLIOG/A
ISLAM TURKEY CULTURE ECO/UNDEV AGRI DIPLOM NAT/LISM ALL/VALS
CONSERVE...GEOG HUM INT/LAW SOC 7/20 MAPS. PAGE 42
E0824

B44
PUTTKAMMER E.W.,WAR AND THE LAW. UNIV USA-45 CONSTN INT/ORG
CULTURE SOCIETY NAT/G POL/PAR ROUTINE ALL/VALS LAW
...JURID CONCPT OBS WORK VAL/FREE 20. PAGE 83 E1664 WAR
INT/LAW

B44
SUAREZ F.,A TREATISE ON LAWS AND GOD THE LAWGIVER LAW
(1612) IN SELECTIONS FROM THREE WORKS, VOL. II. JURID
FRANCE ITALY UK CULTURE NAT/G SECT CHIEF LEGIS GEN/LAWS
DOMIN LEGIT CT/SYS ORD/FREE PWR WORSHIP 16/17. CATH
PAGE 94 E1892

B44
US LIBRARY OF CONGRESS,RUSSIA: A CHECK LIST BIBLIOG
PRELIMINARY TO A BASIC BIBLIOGRAPHY OF MATERIALS IN LAW
THE RUSSIAN LANGUAGE. COM USSR CULTURE EDU/PROP SECT
MARXISM...ART/METH HUM LING 19/20. PAGE 101 E2015

B45
CONOVER H.F.,THE NAZI STATE: WAR CRIMES AND WAR BIBLIOG
CRIMINALS. GERMANY CULTURE NAT/G SECT FORCES DIPLOM WAR
INT/TRADE EDU/PROP...INT/LAW BIOG HIST/WRIT CRIME
TIME/SEQ 20. PAGE 25 E0495

B45
REVES E.,THE ANATOMY OF PEACE. WOR-45 LAW CULTURE ACT/RES
NAT/G PLAN TEC/DEV EDU/PROP WAR NAT/LISM ATTIT CONCPT
ALL/VALS SOVEREIGN...POLICY HUM TIME/SEQ 20. NUC/PWR
PAGE 84 E1688 PEACE

B45
US LIBRARY OF CONGRESS,NETHERLANDS EAST INDIES. BIBLIOG/A
INDONESIA LAW CULTURE AGRI INDUS SCHOOL COLONIAL S/ASIA
HEALTH...GEOG JURID SOC 19/20 NETH/IND. PAGE 101 NAT/G
E2017

B46
GILLIN J.L.,SOCIAL PATHOLOGY. SOCIETY SECT CRIME SOC
ANOMIE DISPL ORD/FREE WEALTH...CRIMLGY PSY WORSHIP. ADJUST
PAGE 44 E0864 CULTURE
INGP/REL

B48
YAKOBSON S.,FIVE HUNDRED RUSSIAN WORKS FOR COLLEGE BIBLIOG
LIBRARIES (PAMPHLET). MOD/EUR USSR MARXISM SOCISM NAT/G
...ART/METH GEOG HUM JURID SOC 13/20. PAGE 108 CULTURE
E2162 COM

S48
ALEXANDER L.,"WAR CRIMES, THEIR SOCIAL- DRIVE
PSYCHOLOGICAL ASPECTS." EUR+WWI GERMANY LAW CULTURE WAR
ELITES KIN POL/PAR PUB/INST FORCES DOMIN EDU/PROP
COERCE CRIME ATTIT SUPEGO HEALTH MORAL PWR FASCISM
...PSY OBS TREND GEN/LAWS NAZI 20. PAGE 3 E0061

B49
HOLLERAN M.P.,CHURCH AND STATE IN GUATEMALA. SECT
GUATEMALA LAW STRUCT CATHISM...SOC SOC/INTEG 17/20 NAT/G
CHURCH/STA. PAGE 55 E1086 GP/REL
CULTURE

B49
MARITAIN J.,HUMAN RIGHTS: COMMENTS AND INT/ORG
INTERPRETATIONS. COM UNIV WOR+45 LAW CONSTN CULTURE CONCPT
SOCIETY ECO/DEV ECO/UNDEV SCHOOL DELIB/GP EDU/PROP
ATTIT PERCEPT ALL/VALS...HUM SOC TREND UNESCO 20.
PAGE 68 E1365

B49
SCHONS D.,BOOK CENSORSHIP IN NEW SPAIN (NEW WORLD CHRIST-17C
STUDIES, BOOK II). SPAIN LAW CULTURE INSPECT ADJUD EDU/PROP
CT/SYS SANCTION GP/REL ORD/FREE 14/17. PAGE 88 CONTROL
E1764 PRESS

B49
US DEPARTMENT OF STATE,SOVIET BIBLIOGRAPHY BIBLIOG/A
(PAMPHLET). CHINA/COM COM USSR LAW AGRI INT/ORG MARXISM
ECO/TAC EDU/PROP...POLICY GEOG 20. PAGE 99 E1994 CULTURE
DIPLOM

B50
BOHATTA H.,INTERNATIONALE BIBLIOGRAPHIE. WOR+45 LAW BIBLIOG
CULTURE PRESS. PAGE 13 E0260 DIPLOM
NAT/G
WRITING

B50
EMBREE J.F.,BIBLIOGRAPHY OF THE PEOPLES AND BIBLIOG/A
CULTURES OF MAINLAND SOUTHEAST ASIA. CAMBODIA LAOS CULTURE
THAILAND VIETNAM LAW...GEOG HUM SOC MYTH LING S/ASIA
CHARTS WORSHIP 20. PAGE 35 E0686

B50
MACIVER R.M.,GREAT EXPRESSIONS OF HUMAN RIGHTS. LAW UNIV
CONSTN INTELL SOCIETY R+D INT/ORG ATTIT CONCPT
DRIVE...JURID OBS HIST/WRIT GEN/LAWS. PAGE 67 E1340

B50
STONE J.,THE PROVINCE AND FUNCTION OF LAW. UNIV INT/ORG
WOR+45 WOR-45 CULTURE INTELL SOCIETY ECO/DEV LAW
ECO/UNDEV NAT/G LEGIT ROUTINE ATTIT PERCEPT PERSON
...JURID CONCPT GEN/LAWS GEN/METH 20. PAGE 94 E1877

C50
NUMELIN R.,"THE BEGINNINGS OF DIPLOMACY." INT/TRADE DIPLOM
WAR GP/REL PEACE STRANGE ATTIT...INT/LAW CONCPT KIN
BIBLIOG. PAGE 78 E1559 CULTURE
LAW

B51
HUXLEY J.,FREEDOM AND CULTURE. UNIV LAW SOCIETY R+D CULTURE
ACADEM SCHOOL CREATE SANCTION ATTIT KNOWL...HUM ORD/FREE
ANTHOL 20. PAGE 56 E1118 PHIL/SCI
IDEA/COMP

B52
ETTINGHAUSEN R.,SELECTED AND ANNOTATED BIBLIOGRAPHY BIBLIOG/A
OF BOOKS AND PERIODICALS IN WESTERN LANGUAGES ISLAM
DEALING WITH NEAR AND MIDDLE EAST. LAW CULTURE SECT MEDIT-7
...ART/METH GEOG SOC. PAGE 35 E0700

B52
FORSTER A.,THE TROUBLE MAKERS. USA+45 LAW CULTURE DISCRIM
SOCIETY STRUCT VOL/ASSN CROWD GP/REL MORAL...PSY SECT
SOC CONCPT 20 NEGRO JEWS. PAGE 39 E0771 RACE/REL

B53
PIERCE R.A.,RUSSIAN CENTRAL ASIA, 1867-1917: A BIBLIOG
SELECTED BIBLIOGRAPHY (PAMPHLET). USSR LAW CULTURE COLONIAL
NAT/G EDU/PROP WAR...GEOG SOC 19/20. PAGE 81 E1616 ADMIN
COM

B54
CARTER P.G.,STATISTICAL BULLETINS: AN ANNOTATED BIBLIOG/A
BIBLIOGRAPHY OF THE GENERAL STATISTICAL BULLETINS WOR+45
AND MAJOR POL SUBDIV OF WORLD. CULTURE AGRI FINAN NAT/G
INDUS LABOR TEC/DEV INT/TRADE CT/SYS WEALTH STAT
...CRIMLGY SOC 20. PAGE 20 E0400

B54
HOEBEL E.A.,THE LAW OF PRIMITIVE MAN: A STUDY IN LAW
COMPARATIVE LEGAL DYNAMICS. WOR-45...JURID SOC CULTURE
IDEA/COMP METH 20. PAGE 53 E1063 GP/COMP
SOCIETY

B54
SCHWARTZ B.,FRENCH ADMINISTRATIVE LAW AND THE JURID
COMMON-LAW WORLD. FRANCE CULTURE LOC/G NAT/G PROVS LAW
DELIB/GP EX/STRUC LEGIS PROB/SOLV CT/SYS EXEC METH/COMP
GOV/REL...IDEA/COMP ENGLSH/LAW. PAGE 89 E1786 ADJUD

B54
TOTOK W.,HANDBUCH DER BIBLIOGRAPHISCHEN BIBLIOG/A
NACHSCHLAGEWERKE. GERMANY LAW CULTURE ADMIN...SOC NAT/G
20. PAGE 97 E1936 DIPLOM
POLICY

B55
KHADDURI M.,WAR AND PEACE IN THE LAW OF ISLAM. ISLAM
CONSTN CULTURE SOCIETY STRATA NAT/G PROVS SECT JURID
FORCES TOP/EX CREATE DOMIN EDU/PROP ADJUD COERCE PEACE
ATTIT RIGID/FLEX ALL/VALS...CONCPT TIME/SEQ TOT/POP WAR
VAL/FREE. PAGE 61 E1209

B55
MID-EUROPEAN LAW PROJECT,CHURCH AND STATE BEHIND LAW
THE IRON CURTAIN. COM CZECHOSLVK HUNGARY POLAND MARXISM
USSR CULTURE SECT EDU/PROP GOV/REL CATHISM...CHARTS POLICY
ANTHOL BIBLIOG WORSHIP 20 CHURCH/STA. PAGE 73 E1455

B55
WRONG D.H.,AMERICAN AND CANADIAN VIEWPOINTS. CANADA DIPLOM
USA+45 CONSTN STRATA FAM SECT WORKER ECO/TAC ATTIT
EDU/PROP ADJUD MARRIAGE...IDEA/COMP 20. PAGE 108 NAT/COMP
E2161 CULTURE

B56
ALEXANDER F.,THE CRIMINAL, THE JUDGE, AND THE CRIME
PUBLIC. LAW CULTURE CONSULT LEGIT ADJUD SANCTION CRIMLGY
ORD/FREE 20. PAGE 3 E0060 PSY
ATTIT

B56
RECASENS SICHES S.,TRATADO GENERAL DE SOCIOLOGIA. SOC
CULTURE FAM NEIGH LEAD RACE/REL DISCRIM HABITAT STRATA
ORD/FREE...JURID LING T SOC/INTEG 20. PAGE 84 E1677 KIN
GP/REL

B56
SYKES G.M.,CRIME AND SOCIETY. LAW STRATA STRUCT CRIMLGY
ACT/RES ROUTINE ANOMIE WEALTH...POLICY SOC/INTEG CRIME
20. PAGE 95 E1903 CULTURE
INGP/REL

C56
TYLER P.,"IMMIGRATION AND THE UNITED STATES." CULTURE
USA+45 USA-45 LAW SECT INGP/REL RACE/REL NAT/LISM GP/REL
ATTIT...BIBLIOG SOC/INTEG 19/20. PAGE 97 E1949 DISCRIM

B57
CONOVER H.F.,NORTH AND NORTHEAST AFRICA; A SELECTED BIBLIOG/A
ANNOTATED LIST OF WRITINGS. ALGERIA MOROCCO SUDAN DIPLOM
UAR CULTURE INT/ORG PROB/SOLV ADJUD NAT/LISM PWR AFR
WEALTH...SOC 20 UN. PAGE 25 E0496 ECO/UNDEV

B58
CABLE G.W.,THE NEGRO QUESTION: A SELECTION OF RACE/REL
WRITINGS ON CIVIL RIGHTS IN THE SOUTH. USA+45 CULTURE
STRATA LOC/G POL/PAR GIVE EDU/PROP WRITING CT/SYS DISCRIM
SANCTION CRIME CHOOSE WORSHIP 20 NEGRO CIV/RIGHTS ORD/FREE
CONV/LEASE SOUTH/US. PAGE 18 E0355

B58
CLEMMER D.,THE PRISON COMMUNITY. CULTURE CONTROL PUB/INST
LEAD ROUTINE PERS/REL PERSON...SOC METH/CNCPT. CRIMLGY
PAGE 23 E0453 CLIENT
INGP/REL

B58
HALL J.,STUDIES IN JURISPRUDENCE AND CRIMINAL JURID

THEORY. USA-45 LAW CULTURE CREATE SUPEGO...CRIMLGY CRIME
PSY /20 PLATO. PAGE 49 E0983 CONCPT
CT/SYS

B58
KURL S.,ESTONIA: A SELECTED BIBLIOGRAPHY. USSR BIBLIOG
ESTONIA LAW INTELL SECT...ART/METH GEOG HUM SOC 20. CULTURE
PAGE 62 E1238 NAT/G

B59
GINSBURG M.,LAW AND OPINION IN ENGLAND. UK CULTURE JURID
KIN LABOR LEGIS EDU/PROP ADMIN CT/SYS CRIME OWN POLICY
HEALTH...ANTHOL 20 ENGLSH/LAW. PAGE 44 E0868 ECO/TAC

B59
HOBSBAWM E.J.,PRIMITIVE REBELS; STUDIES IN ARCHAIC SOCIETY
FORMS OF SOCIAL MOVEMENT IN THE 19TH AND 20TH CRIME
CENTURIES. ITALY SPAIN CULTURE VOL/ASSN RISK CROWD REV
GP/REL INGP/REL ISOLAT TOTALISM...PSY SOC 18/20. GUERRILLA
PAGE 53 E1058

S59
JENKS C.W.,"THE CHALLENGE OF UNIVERSALITY." FUT INT/ORG
UNIV CONSTN CULTURE CONSULT CREATE PLAN LEGIT ATTIT LAW
MORAL ORD/FREE RESPECT...MAJORIT JURID 20. PAGE 58 PEACE
E1155 INT/LAW

SUTTON F.X.,"REPRESENTATION AND THE NATURE OF NAT/G
POLITICAL SYSTEMS." UNIV WOR-45 CULTURE SOCIETY CONCPT
STRATA INT/ORG FORCES JUDGE DOMIN LEGIT EXEC REGION
REPRESENT ATTIT ORD/FREE RESPECT...SOC HIST/WRIT
TIME/SEQ. PAGE 95 E1896

EASTON D.,"POLITICAL ANTHROPOLOGY" IN BIENNIAL SOC
REVIEW OF ANTHROPOLOGY" UNIV LAW CULTURE ELITES BIBLIOG/A
SOCIETY CREATE...PSY CONCPT GP/COMP GEN/METH 20. NEW/IDEA
PAGE 34 E0671

B60
GIBNEY F.,THE OPERATORS. USA+45 LAW STRATA BIO/SOC CRIME
MORAL ORD/FREE SOC. PAGE 43 E0858 CULTURE
ANOMIE
CRIMLGY

B60
UNITED WORLD FEDERALISTS,UNITED WORLD FEDERALISTS; BIBLIOG/A
PANORAMA OF RECENT BOOKS, FILMS, AND JOURNALS ON DIPLOM
WORLD FEDERATION, THE UN, AND WORLD PEACE. CULTURE INT/ORG
ECO/UNDEV PROB/SOLV FOR/AID ARMS/CONT NUC/PWR PEACE
...INT/LAW PHIL/SCI 20 UN. PAGE 98 E1971

S60
SCHWELB E.,"INTERNATIONAL CONVENTIONS ON HUMAN INT/ORG
RIGHTS." FUT WOR+45 LAW CONSTN CULTURE SOCIETY HUM
STRUCT VOL/ASSN DELIB/GP PLAN ADJUD SUPEGO LOVE
MORAL...SOC CONCPT STAT RECORD HIST/WRIT TREND 20
UN. PAGE 89 E1790

S60
THOMPSON K.W.,"MORAL PURPOSE IN FOREIGN POLICY: MORAL
REALITIES AND ILLUSIONS." WOR+45 LAW CULTURE JURID
SOCIETY INT/ORG PLAN ADJUD ADMIN COERCE RIGID/FLEX DIPLOM
SUPEGO KNOWL ORD/FREE PWR...SOC TREND SOC/EXP
TOT/POP 20. PAGE 96 E1921

N60
RHODESIA-NYASA NATL ARCHIVES,A SELECT BIBLIOGRAPHY BIBLIOG
OF RECENT PUBLICATIONS CONCERNING THE FEDERATION OF ADMIN
RHODESIA AND NYASALAND (PAMPHLET). MALAWI RHODESIA ORD/FREE
LAW CULTURE STRUCT ECO/UNDEV LEGIS...GEOG 20. NAT/G
PAGE 84 E1689

B61
BEDFORD S.,THE FACES OF JUSTICE: A TRAVELLER'S CT/SYS
REPORT. AUSTRIA FRANCE GERMANY/W SWITZERLND UK UNIV ORD/FREE
WOR+45 WOR-45 CULTURE PARTIC GOV/REL MORAL...JURID PERSON
OBS GOV/COMP 20. PAGE 9 E0174 LAW

B61
KAPLAN M.A.,THE POLITICAL FOUNDATIONS OF INT/ORG
INTERNATIONAL LAW. WOR+45 WOR-45 CULTURE SOCIETY LAW
ECO/DEV DIPLOM PERCEPT...TECHNIC METH/CNCPT.
PAGE 59 E1184

B61
SMITH J.W.,RELIGIOUS PERSPECTIVES IN AMERICAN SECT
CULTURE. VOL. 2, RELIGION IN AMERICAN LIFE. USA+45 DOMIN
CULTURE NAT/G EDU/PROP ADJUD LOBBY ATTIT...ART/METH SOCIETY
ANTHOL 20 CHURCH/STA BIBLE. PAGE 92 E1845 GP/REL

L61
FELLMAN D.,"ACADEMIC FREEDOM IN AMERICAN LAW." LAW ACADEM
CONSTN NAT/G VOL/ASSN PLAN PERSON KNOWL NEW/LIB. ORD/FREE
PAGE 37 E0732 LEGIS

S61
MILLER E.,"LEGAL ASPECTS OF UN ACTION IN THE INT/ORG
CONGO." AFR CULTURE ADMIN PEACE DRIVE RIGID/FLEX LEGIT
ORD/FREE...WELF/ST JURID OBS UN CONGO 20. PAGE 73
E1458

B62
DAVIS F.J.,SOCIETY AND THE LAW. USA+45 CONSTN LAW
ACADEM FAM CONSULT ACT/RES GP/REL ORD/FREE SOC
ENGLSH/LAW 20. PAGE 29 E0572 CULTURE
STRUCT

B62
KIDDER F.E.,THESES ON PAN AMERICAN TOPICS. LAW BIBLIOG
CULTURE NAT/G SECT DIPLOM HEALTH...ART/METH GEOG CHRIST-17C
SOC 13/20. PAGE 61 E1213 L/A+17C
SOCIETY

B62
PAIKERT G.C.,THE GERMAN EXODUS. EUR+WWI GERMANY/W INGP/REL
LAW CULTURE SOCIETY STRUCT INDUS NAT/LISM RESPECT STRANGE
SOVEREIGN...CHARTS BIBLIOG SOC/INTEG 20 MIGRATION. GEOG
PAGE 79 E1591 GP/REL

L62
UNITED NATIONS,"CAPITAL PUNISHMENT." WOR+45 CULTURE LAW
NAT/G ROUTINE COERCE HEALTH PWR...POLICY SOC QU STAT
CHARTS VAL/FREE 20. PAGE 98 E1967

B63
CARTER G.M.,FIVE AFRICAN STATES: RESPONSES TO AFR
DIVERSITY. CONSTN CULTURE STRATA LEGIS PLAN ECO/TAC SOCIETY
DOMIN EDU/PROP CT/SYS EXEC CHOOSE ATTIT HEALTH
ORD/FREE PWR...TIME/SEQ TOT/POP VAL/FREE. PAGE 20
E0398

B63
CHOJNACKI S.,REGISTER ON CURRENT RESEARCH ON BIBLIOG
ETHIOPIA AND THE HORN OF AFRICA. ETHIOPIA LAW ACT/RES
CULTURE AGRI SECT EDU/PROP ADMIN...GEOG HEAL LING INTELL
20. PAGE 22 E0433 ACADEM

B63
EDDY J.P.,JUSTICE OF THE PEACE. UK LAW CONSTN CRIME
CULTURE 14/20 COMMON/LAW. PAGE 34 E0674 JURID
CT/SYS
ADJUD

B63
ELIAS T.O.,GOVERNMENT AND POLITICS IN AFRICA. AFR
CONSTN CULTURE SOCIETY NAT/G POL/PAR DIPLOM NAT/LISM
REPRESENT PERSON...SOC TREND BIBLIOG 4/20. PAGE 34 COLONIAL
E0681 LAW

B63
GEERTZ C.,OLD SOCIETIES AND NEW STATES: THE QUEST ECO/UNDEV
FOR MODERNITY IN ASIA AND AFRICA. AFR ASIA LAW TEC/DEV
CULTURE SECT EDU/PROP REV...GOV/COMP NAT/COMP 20. NAT/LISM
PAGE 42 E0842 SOVEREIGN

B63
HALL J.,COMPARATIVE LAW AND SOCIAL THEORY. WOR+45 LAW
CONSTN CULTURE DOMIN CT/SYS ORD/FREE...PLURIST SOC
JURID CONCPT NEW/IDEA GEN/LAWS VAL/FREE. PAGE 49
E0984

B63
MURPHY T.J.,CENSORSHIP: GOVERNMENT AND OBSCENITY. ORD/FREE
USA+45 CULTURE LEGIS JUDGE EDU/PROP CONTROL MORAL
INGP/REL RATIONAL POPULISM...CATH JURID 20. PAGE 75 LAW
E1507 CONSEN

L63
LISSITZYN O.J.,"INTERNATIONAL LAW IN A DIVIDED INT/ORG
WORLD." FUT WOR+45 CONSTN CULTURE ECO/DEV ECO/UNDEV LAW
DIST/IND NAT/G FORCES ECO/TAC LEGIT ADJUD ADMIN
COERCE ATTIT HEALTH MORAL ORD/FREE PWR RESPECT
WEALTH VAL/FREE. PAGE 65 E1306

L63
ROSE R.,"COMPARATIVE STUDIES IN POLITICAL FINANCE: FINAN
A SYMPOSIUM." ASIA EUR+WWI S/ASIA LAW CULTURE POL/PAR
DELIB/GP LEGIS ACT/RES ECO/TAC EDU/PROP CHOOSE
ATTIT RIGID/FLEX SUPEGO PWR SKILL WEALTH...STAT
ANTHOL VAL/FREE. PAGE 85 E1714

S63
MACWHINNEY E.,"LES CONCEPT SOVIETIQUE DE NAT/G
'COEXISTENCE PACIFIQUE' ET LES RAPPORTS JURIDIQUES CONCPT
ENTRE L'URSS ET LES ETATS OCIDENTAUX." COM FUT DIPLOM
WOR+45 LAW CULTURE INTELL POL/PAR ACT/RES BAL/PWR USSR
...INT/LAW 20. PAGE 67 E1346

B64

DRESSLER D.,READINGS IN CRIMINOLOGY AND PENOLOGY.   CRIMLGY
UNIV CULTURE PUB/INST FORCES ACT/RES PROB/SOLV   CRIME
ANOMIE BIO/SOC SUPEGO...GEOG PSY ANTHOL 20. PAGE 33   ADJUD
E0648   ADJUST

B64

FORBES A.H.,CURRENT RESEARCH IN BRITISH STUDIES. UK   BIBLIOG
CONSTN CULTURE POL/PAR SECT DIPLOM ADMIN...JURID   PERSON
BIOG WORSHIP 20. PAGE 39 E0769   NAT/G
                                                     PARL/PROC

B64

RAGHAVAN M.D.,INDIA IN CEYLONESE HISTORY, SOCIETY   DIPLOM
AND CULTURE. CEYLON INDIA S/ASIA LAW SOCIETY   CULTURE
INT/TRADE ATTIT...ART/METH JURID SOC LING 20.   SECT
PAGE 83 E1668   STRUCT

B64

UN PUB. INFORM. ORGAN.,EVERY MAN'S UNITED NATIONS.   INT/ORG
UNIV WOR+45 CONSTN CULTURE SOCIETY ECO/DEV   ROUTINE
ECO/UNDEV NAT/G ACT/RES PLAN ECO/TAC INT/TRADE
EDU/PROP LEGIT PEACE ATTIT ALL/VALS...POLICY HUM
INT/LAW CONCPT CHARTS UN TOT/POP 20. PAGE 97 E1954

B64

WRIGHT G.,RURAL REVOLUTION IN FRANCE: THE PEASANTRY   PWR
IN THE TWENTIETH CENTURY. EUR+WWI MOD/EUR LAW   STRATA
CULTURE AGRI POL/PAR DELIB/GP LEGIS ECO/TAC   FRANCE
EDU/PROP COERCE CHOOSE ATTIT RIGID/FLEX HEALTH   REV
...STAT CENSUS CHARTS VAL/FREE 20. PAGE 107 E2148

S64

GINSBURGS G.,"WARS OF NATIONAL LIBERATION - THE   COERCE
SOVIET THESIS." COM USSR WOR+45 WOR-45 LAW CULTURE   CONCPT
INT/ORG DIPLOM LEGIT COLONIAL GUERRILLA WAR   INT/LAW
NAT/LISM ATTIT PERSON MORAL PWR...JURID OBS TREND   REV
MARX/KARL 20. PAGE 44 E0869

S64

GREENBERG S.,"JUDAISM AND WORLD JUSTICE." MEDIT-7   SECT
WOR+45 LAW CULTURE SOCIETY INT/ORG NAT/G FORCES   JURID
EDU/PROP ATTIT DRIVE PERSON SUPEGO ALL/VALS   PEACE
...POLICY PSY CONCPT GEN/LAWS JEWS. PAGE 46 E0908

S64

KHAN M.Z.,"ISLAM AND INTERNATIONAL RELATIONS." FUT   ISLAM
WOR+45 LAW CULTURE SOCIETY NAT/G SECT DELIB/GP   INT/ORG
FORCES EDU/PROP ATTIT PERSON SUPEGO ALL/VALS   DIPLOM
...POLICY PSY CONCPT MYTH HIST/WRIT GEN/LAWS.
PAGE 61 E1211

B65

BLITZ L.F.,THE POLITICS AND ADMINISTRATION OF   NAT/G
NIGERIAN GOVERNMENT. NIGER CULTURE LOC/G LEGIS   GOV/REL
DIPLOM COLONIAL CT/SYS SOVEREIGN...GEOG SOC ANTHOL   POL/PAR
20. PAGE 13 E0245

B65

O'BRIEN W.V.,THE NEW NATIONS IN INTERNATIONAL LAW   INT/LAW
AND DIPLOMACY* THE YEAR BOOK OF WORLD POLITY*   CULTURE
VOLUME III. USA+45 ECO/UNDEV INT/ORG FORCES DIPLOM   SOVEREIGN
COLONIAL NEUTRAL REV NAT/LISM ATTIT RESPECT.   ANTHOL
PAGE 78 E1565

B66

BRAIBANTI R.,RESEARCH ON THE BUREAUCRACY OF   HABITAT
PAKISTAN. PAKISTAN LAW CULTURE INTELL ACADEM LOC/G   NAT/G
SECT PRESS CT/SYS...LING CHARTS 20 BUREAUCRCY.   ADMIN
PAGE 15 E0286   CONSTN

B66

DE TOCQUEVILLE A.DEMOCRACY IN AMERICA (1834-1840)   POPULISM
(2 VOLS. IN I; TRANS. BY G. LAWRENCE). FRANCE   USA-45
CULTURE STRATA POL/PAR CT/SYS REPRESENT FEDERAL   CONSTN
ORD/FREE SOVEREIGN...MAJORIT TREND GEN/LAWS 18/19.   NAT/COMP
PAGE 30 E0596

B66

DOUGLAS W.O.,THE BIBLE AND THE SCHOOLS. USA+45   SECT
CULTURE ADJUD INGP/REL AGE/C AGE/Y ATTIT KNOWL   NAT/G
WORSHIP 20 SUPREME/CT CHURCH/STA BIBLE CHRISTIAN.   SCHOOL
PAGE 32 E0644   GP/REL

B66

HOPKINS J.F.K.,ARABIC PERIODICAL LITERATURE, 1961.   BIBLIOG/A
ISLAM LAW CULTURE SECT...GEOG HEAL PHIL/SCI PSY SOC   NAT/LISM
20. PAGE 55 E1096   TEC/DEV
                                                     INDUS

B66

STEVENS R.E.,REFERENCE BOOKS IN THE SOCIAL SCIENCES   BIBLIOG/A
AND HUMANITIES. CULTURE PERF/ART SECT EDU/PROP   SOC
...JURID PSY SOC/WK STAT 20 MUSIC. PAGE 93 E1873   HUM
                                                     ART/METH

B66

STUMPF S.E.,MORALITY AND THE LAW. USA+45 LAW   JURID
CULTURE PROB/SOLV DOMIN ADJUD CONTROL ADJUST   MORAL
ALL/IDEOS MARXISM...INT/LAW 20 SUPREME/CT. PAGE 94   CT/SYS
E1890

B66

US DEPARTMENT OF STATE,RESEARCH ON AFRICA (EXTERNAL BIBLIOG/A
RESEARCH LIST NO 5-25). LAW CULTURE ECO/UNDEV   ASIA
POL/PAR DIPLOM EDU/PROP LEAD REGION MARXISM...GEOG   S/ASIA
LING WORSHIP 20. PAGE 100 E1996   NAT/G

B66

US DEPARTMENT OF STATE,RESEARCH ON THE USSR AND   BIBLIOG/A
EASTERN EUROPE (EXTERNAL RESEARCH LIST NO 1-25).   EUR+WWI
USSR LAW CULTURE SOCIETY NAT/G TEC/DEV DIPLOM   COM
EDU/PROP REGION...GEOG LING. PAGE 100 E1997   MARXISM

B66

US DEPARTMENT OF STATE,RESEARCH ON WESTERN EUROPE,   BIBLIOG/A
GREAT BRITAIN, AND CANADA (EXTERNAL RESEARCH LIST   EUR+WWI
NO 3-25). CANADA GERMANY/W UK LAW CULTURE NAT/G   DIPLOM
POL/PAR FORCES EDU/PROP REGION MARXISM...GEOG SOC
WORSHIP 20 CMN/WLTH. PAGE 100 E1998

B67

BOHANNAN P.,LAW AND WARFARE. CULTURE CT/SYS COERCE   METH/COMP
REV PEACE...JURID SOC CONCPT ANTHOL 20. PAGE 13   ADJUD
E0259   WAR
                                                     LAW

B67

MEYERS M.,SOURCES OF THE AMERICAN REPUBLIC; A   COLONIAL
DOCUMENTARY HISTORY OF POLITICS, SOCIETY, AND   REV
THOUGHT (VOL. I, REV. ED.). USA-45 CULTURE STRUCT   WAR
NAT/G LEGIS LEAD ATTIT...JURID SOC ANTHOL 17/19
PRESIDENT. PAGE 72 E1450

L67

SCHUBERT G.,"THE RHETORIC OF CONSTITUTIONAL   CONSTN
CHANGE." USA+45 LAW CULTURE CHIEF LEGIS ADJUD   METH/COMP
CT/SYS ARMS/CONT ADJUST...CHARTS SIMUL. PAGE 89   ORD/FREE
E1777

B68

GREGG R.W.,INTERNATIONAL ORGANIZATION IN THE   INT/ORG
WESTERN HEMISPHERE. L/A+17C USA+45 CULTURE PLAN   DIPLOM
DOMIN AGREE CONTROL DETER PWR...GEOG 20 OAS TREATY.   ECO/UNDEV
PAGE 46 E0913

B75

MAINE H.S.,LECTURES ON THE EARLY HISTORY OF   CULTURE
INSTITUTIONS. IRELAND UK CONSTN ELITES STRUCT FAM   LAW
KIN CHIEF LEGIS CT/SYS OWN SOVEREIGN...CONCPT 16   INGP/REL
BENTHAM/J BREHON ROMAN/LAW. PAGE 68 E1351

C93

PLAYFAIR R.L.,"A BIBLIOGRAPHY OF MOROCCO." MOROCCO   BIBLIOG
CULTURE AGRI FORCES DIPLOM WAR HEALTH...GEOG JURID   ISLAM
SOC CHARTS. PAGE 81 E1620   MEDIT-7

B97

JENKS E.J.,LAW AND POLITICS IN THE MIDDLE AGES.   LAW
CHRIST-17C CULTURE STRUCT KIN NAT/G SECT CT/SYS   SOCIETY
GP/REL...CLASSIF CHARTS IDEA/COMP BIBLIOG 8/16.   ADJUST
PAGE 58 E1162

B98

POLLOCK F.,THE HISTORY OF ENGLISH LAW BEFORE THE   LAW
TIME OF EDWARD I (2 VOLS, 2ND ED.). UK CULTURE   ADJUD
LOC/G LEGIS LICENSE AGREE CONTROL CT/SYS SANCTION   JURID
CRIME...TIME/SEQ 13 COMMON/LAW CANON/LAW. PAGE 81
E1626

B99

BROOKS S.,BRITAIN AND THE BOERS. AFR SOUTH/AFR UK   WAR
CULTURE INSPECT LEGIT...INT/LAW 19/20 BOER/WAR.   DIPLOM
PAGE 16 E0309   NAT/G

CULVER D.C. E0549,E0550,E0551

CUMMING J. E0552

CUMMINGS H. E0553

CUMMINS L. E0554

CUNNINGHAM W.B. E0555

CURLEY/JM....JAMES M. CURLEY

CURRIE D.P. E0556

CURRIER T.F. E0557

CURRY J.E. E0558

CURZON/GN....GEORGE NATHANIEL CURZON

CUSHMAN R.E. E0559

CYBERNETICS....SEE FEEDBACK, SIMUL, CONTROL

CYCLES....SEE TIME/SEQ

CYPRUS....SEE ALSO APPROPRIATE TIME/SPACE/CULTURE
INDEX

> WORLD PEACE FOUNDATION,"INTERNATIONAL   INT/ORG   L64
> ORGANIZATIONS: SUMMARY OF ACTIVITIES." INDIA   ROUTINE
> PAKISTAN TURKEY WOR+45 CONSTN CONSULT EX/STRUC
> ECO/TAC EDU/PROP LEGIT ORD/FREE...JURID SOC UN 20
> CYPRESS. PAGE 107 E2145

> BOWETT D.W.,UNITED NATIONS FORCES* A LEGAL STUDY.   OP/RES   B64
> CYPRUS ISRAEL KOREA LAW CONSTN ACT/RES CREATE   FORCES
> BUDGET CONTROL TASK PWR...INT/LAW IDEA/COMP UN   ARMS/CONT
> CONGO/LEOP SUEZ. PAGE 14 E0278

CZECHOSLVK....CZECHOSLOVAKIA; SEE ALSO COM

> MID-EUROPEAN LAW PROJECT,CHURCH AND STATE BEHIND   LAW   B55
> THE IRON CURTAIN. COM CZECHOSLVK HUNGARY POLAND   MARXISM
> USSR CULTURE SECT EDU/PROP GOV/REL CATHISM...CHARTS POLICY
> ANTHOL BIBLIOG WORSHIP 20 CHURCH/STA. PAGE 73 E1455

> BOHMER A.,LEGAL SOURCES AND BIBLIOGRAPHY OF   BIBLIOG   B59
> CZECHOSLOVAKIA. COM CZECHOSLVK PARL/PROC SANCTION   ADJUD
> CRIME MARXISM 20. PAGE 13 E0261   LAW
>   JURID

> PRYOR F.L.,THE COMMUNIST FOREIGN TRADE SYSTEM. COM   ATTIT   B63
> CZECHOSLVK GERMANY YUGOSLAVIA LAW ECO/DEV DIST/IND   ECO/TAC
> POL/PAR PLAN DOMIN TOTALISM DRIVE RIGID/FLEX WEALTH
> ...STAT STAND/INT CHARTS 20. PAGE 83 E1657

D

DAC....DEVELOPMENT ASSISTANCE COMMITTEE (PART OF OECD)

DAGGETT H.S. E0424

DAHL R.A. E0561

DAHOMEY....SEE ALSO AFR

DAKAR....DAKAR, SENEGAL

DALFEN C.M. E0562

DALLIN A. E0563

DANELSKI D.J. E0564

DANGERFIELD R. E0565,E0891

DANIEL C. E0566

DANIEL/Y....YULI DANIEL

DANTE....DANTE ALIGHIERI

> BORGESE G.A.,GOLIATH: THE MARCH OF FASCISM. GERMANY   POLICY   B37
> ITALY LAW POL/PAR SECT DIPLOM SOCISM...JURID MYTH   NAT/LISM
> 20 DANTE MACHIAVELL MUSSOLIN/B. PAGE 14 E0270   FASCISM
>   NAT/G

> ALIGHIERI D.,ON WORLD GOVERNMENT. ROMAN/EMP LAW   POLICY   B57
> SOCIETY INT/ORG NAT/G POL/PAR ADJUD WAR GP/REL   CONCPT
> PEACE WORSHIP 15 WORLDUNITY DANTE. PAGE 4 E0067   DIPLOM
>   SECT

DARBY W.E. E0567

DARWIN L. E0568

DARWIN/C....CHARLES DARWIN

DASH S. E0569

DATA ANALYSIS....SEE CON/ANAL, STAT, MATH, COMPUTER

DAVIDSON R. E0224

DAVIS A. E0570

DAVIS B.F. E0571

DAVIS F.J. E0572

DAVIS K. E0573

DAVIS K.C. E0574,E0575,E0576,E0577,E0578

DAVIS/JEFF....JEFFERSON DAVIS

DAVIS/W....WARREN DAVIS

> BORKIN J.,THE CORRUPT JUDGE. USA+45 CT/SYS ATTIT   ADJUD   B62
> SUPEGO MORAL RESPECT...BIBLIOG + SUPREME/CT   TRIBUTE
> MANTON/M DAVIS/W JOHNSN/ALB. PAGE 14 E0271   CRIME

DAY R.E. E0579

DE ARAGAO J.G. E0580

DE GRAZIA A. E0581,E0582,E0583

DE HUSZAR G.B. E0584,E0585

DE LAVALLE H. E0586

DE MARTENS G.F. E0587

DE MONTESQUIEU C. E0588

DE NOIA J. E0589,E0590,E0591,E0592,E0593

DE TOCQUEVILLE A. E0594,E0595

DE TOCQUEVILLE A E0596

DE VATTEL E. E0597

DE VICTORIA F. E0598

DE VISSCHER C. E0599

DEAN A.W. E0600

DEATH....DEATH

> DAVIS B.F.,THE DESPERATE AND THE DAMNED. USA+45 LAW   PUB/INST   B61
> DEATH ANOMIE...CRIMLGY 20 SAN/QUENTN. PAGE 29 E0571   SANCTION
>   CRIME

> BOULTON D.,OBJECTION OVERRULED. UK LAW POL/PAR   FORCES   B67
> DIPLOM ADJUD SANCTION DEATH WAR CIVMIL/REL 20.   SOCISM
> PAGE 14 E0273   SECT

> MANVELL R.,THE INCOMPARABLE CRIME. GERMANY ACT/RES   MURDER   B67
> DEATH...BIBLIOG 20 JEWS. PAGE 68 E1364   CRIME
>   WAR
>   HIST/WRIT

DEBATE....ORGANIZED COLLECTIVE ARGUMENT

> US SUPERINTENDENT OF DOCUMENTS,EDUCATION (PRICE   BIBLIOG/A   N
> LIST 31). USA+45 LAW FINAN LOC/G NAT/G DEBATE ADMIN   ACADEM
> LEAD RACE/REL FEDERAL HEALTH POLICY. PAGE 103 E2062   SCHOOL

> MEYER H.H.B.,LIST OF REFERENCES ON EMBARGOES   BIBLIOG   B17
> (PAMPHLET). USA-45 AGRI DIPLOM WRITING DEBATE   DIST/IND
> WEAPON...INT/LAW 18/20 CONGRESS. PAGE 72 E1447   ECO/TAC
>   INT/TRADE

> HALL A.B.,"DETERMINATION OF METHODS FOR   ADJUD   S26
> ASCERTAINING THE FACTORS THAT INFLUENCE JUDICIAL   DECISION
> DECISIONS IN CASES INVOLVING DUE PROCESS" LAW JUDGE   CONSTN
> DEBATE EFFICIENCY OPTIMAL UTIL...SOC CONCPT   JURID
> PROBABIL STAT SAMP. PAGE 49 E0981

> MACDONALD A.F.,ELEMENTS OF POLITICAL SCIENCE   LAW   B28
> RESEARCH. USA-45 ACADEM JUDGE EDU/PROP DEBATE ADJUD   FEDERAL
> EXEC...BIBLIOG METH T 20 CONGRESS. PAGE 67 E1338   DECISION
>   CT/SYS

> FLEMMING D.,THE UNITED STATES AND THE LEAGUE OF   INT/ORG   B32
> NATIONS, 1918-1920. FUT USA-45 NAT/G LEGIS TOP/EX   EDU/PROP
> DEBATE CHOOSE PEACE ATTIT SOVEREIGN...TIME/SEQ
> CON/ANAL CONGRESS LEAGUE/NAT 20 TREATY. PAGE 39
> E0764

B37
BUREAU OF NATIONAL AFFAIRS,LABOR RELATIONS
REFERENCE MANUAL VOL 1, 1935-1937. BARGAIN DEBATE
ROUTINE INGP/REL 20 NLRB. PAGE 17 E0335
LABOR
ADMIN
ADJUD
NAT/G

S46
CANTWELL F.V.,"PUBLIC OPINION AND THE LEGISLATIVE
PROCESS" USA+45 USA-45 NAT/G CT/SYS EXEC LEAD
DECISION. PAGE 19 E0374
CHARTS
DEBATE
LEGIS
ATTIT

B47
HOCKING W.E.,FREEDOM OF THE PRESS: A FRAMEWORK OF
PRINCIPLE. WOR-45 SOCIETY NAT/G PROB/SOLV DEBATE
LOBBY...JURID PSY 20 AMEND/I. PAGE 53 E1061
ORD/FREE
CONSTN
PRESS
LAW

S48
MILLER B.S.,"A LAW IS PASSED: THE ATOMIC ENERGY ACT
OF 1946." POL/PAR CHIEF CONFER DEBATE CONTROL
PARL/PROC ATTIT KNOWL...POLICY CONGRESS. PAGE 73
E1457
TEC/DEV
LEGIS
DECISION
LAW

B49
GROB F.,THE RELATIVITY OF WAR AND PEACE: A STUDY IN
LAW, HISTORY, AND POLITICS. WOR+45 WOR-45 LAW
DIPLOM DEBATE...CONCPT LING IDEA/COMP BIBLIOG
18/20. PAGE 48 E0944
WAR
PEACE
INT/LAW
STYLE

B53
GROSS B.M.,THE LEGISLATIVE STRUGGLE: A STUDY IN
SOCIAL COMBAT. STRUCT LOC/G POL/PAR JUDGE EDU/PROP
DEBATE ETIQUET ADMIN LOBBY CHOOSE GOV/REL INGP/REL
HEREDITY ALL/VALS...SOC PRESIDENT. PAGE 48 E0948
LEGIS
DECISION
PERSON
LEAD

B54
US SENATE COMM ON FOREIGN REL,REVIEW OF THE UNITED
NATIONS CHARTER: A COLLECTION OF DOCUMENTS. LEGIS
DIPLOM ADMIN ARMS/CONT WAR REPRESENT SOVEREIGN
...INT/LAW 20 UN. PAGE 101 E2029
BIBLIOG
CONSTN
INT/ORG
DEBATE

B55
PLISCHKE E.,AMERICAN FOREIGN RELATIONS: A
BIBLIOGRAPHY OF OFFICIAL SOURCES. USA+45 USA-45
INT/ORG FORCES PRESS WRITING DEBATE EXEC...POLICY
INT/LAW 18/20 CONGRESS. PAGE 81 E1621
BIBLIOG/A
DIPLOM
NAT/G

B58
GARDINER H.C.,CATHOLIC VIEWPOINT ON CENSORSHIP.
DEBATE COERCE GP/REL...JURID CONCPT 20. PAGE 42
E0835
WRITING
LOBBY
CATHISM
EDU/PROP

B58
STONE J.,AGGRESSION AND WORLD ORDER: A CRITIQUE OF
UNITED NATIONS THEORIES OF AGGRESSION. LAW CONSTN
DELIB/GP PROB/SOLV BAL/PWR DIPLOM DEBATE ADJUD
CRIME PWR...POLICY IDEA/COMP 20 UN SUEZ LEAGUE/NAT.
PAGE 94 E1879
ORD/FREE
INT/ORG
WAR
CONCPT

S58
RIKER W.H.,"THE PARADOX OF VOTING AND CONGRESSIONAL
RULES FOR VOTING ON AMENDMENTS." LAW DELIB/GP
EX/STRUC PROB/SOLV CONFER DEBATE EFFICIENCY ATTIT
HOUSE/REP CONGRESS SENATE. PAGE 85 E1700
PARL/PROC
DECISION
LEGIS
RATIONAL

C58
BRODEN T.F.,"CONGRESSIONAL COMMITTEE REPORTS: THEIR
ROLE AND HISTORY" USA-45 PARL/PROC ROLE. PAGE 15
E0303
LAW
DELIB/GP
LEGIS
DEBATE

B59
BECK C.,CONTEMPT OF CONGRESS: A STUDY OF THE
PROSECUTIONS INITIATED BY THE COMMITTEE ON UN-
AMERICAN ACTIVITIES. USA+45 CONSTN DEBATE EXEC.
PAGE 9 E0170
LEGIS
DELIB/GP
PWR
ADJUD

B62
BUREAU OF NATIONAL AFFAIRS,FEDERAL-STATE REGULATION
OF WELFARE FUNDS (REV. ED.). USA+45 LAW LEGIS
DEBATE AGE/O 20 CONGRESS. PAGE 17 E0337
WELF/ST
WEALTH
PLAN
SOC/WK

B62
GONNER R.,DAS KIRCHENPATRONATRECHT IM
GROSSHERZOGTUM BADEN. GERMANY LAW PROVS DEBATE
ATTIT CATHISM 14/19 PROTESTANT CHRISTIAN CHURCH/STA
BADEN. PAGE 44 E0882
JURID
SECT
NAT/G
GP/REL

B63
RAVENS J.P.,STAAT UND KATHOLISCHE KIRCHE IN
PREUSSENS POLNISCHEN TEILUNGSGEBIETEN. GERMANY
POLAND PRUSSIA PROVS DIPLOM EDU/PROP DEBATE
GP/REL
CATHISM
SECT

NAT/LISM...JURID 18 CHURCH/STA. PAGE 83 E1674 NAT/G

B64
ANASTAPLO G.,NOTES ON THE FIRST AMENDMENT TO THE
CONSTITUTION OF THE UNITED STATES (PART TWO).
USA+45 USA-45 NAT/G JUDGE DEBATE SUPEGO PWR
SOVEREIGN 18/20 SUPREME/CT CONGRESS AMEND/I. PAGE 5
E0088
ORD/FREE
CONSTN
CT/SYS
ATTIT

B64
BUREAU OF NAT'L AFFAIRS,THE CIVIL RIGHTS ACT OF
1964. USA+45 LOC/G NAT/G DELIB/GP CONFER DEBATE
DISCRIM...JURID 20 CONGRESS SUPREME/CT CIV/RIGHTS.
PAGE 17 E0333
LEGIS
RACE/REL
LAW
CONSTN

B64
DANELSKI D.J.,A SUPREME COURT JUSTICE IS APPOINTED.
CHIEF LEGIS CONFER DEBATE EXEC PERSON PWR...BIOG 20
CONGRESS PRESIDENT. PAGE 28 E0564
CHOOSE
JUDGE
DECISION

B64
DOOLIN D.J.,COMMUNIST CHINA: THE POLITICS OF
STUDENT OPPOSITION. CHINA/COM ELITES STRATA ACADEM
NAT/G WRITING CT/SYS LEAD PARTIC COERCE TOTALISM
20. PAGE 32 E0637
MARXISM
DEBATE
AGE/Y
PWR

B64
ENGEL S.,LAW, STATE, AND INTERNATIONAL LEGAL ORDER.
WOR+45 NAT/G ORD/FREE RELATISM...INT/LAW IDEA/COMP
ANTHOL 20 KELSEN/H. PAGE 35 E0690
JURID
OBJECTIVE
CONCPT
DEBATE

B64
GRASMUCK E.L.,COERCITIO STAAT UND KIRCHE IM
DONATISTENSTREIT. CHRIST-17C ROMAN/EMP LAW PROVS
DEBATE PERSON SOVEREIGN...JURID CONCPT 4/5
AUGUSTINE CHURCH/STA ROMAN/LAW. PAGE 45 E0898
GP/REL
NAT/G
SECT
COERCE

B64
KEEFE W.J.,THE AMERICAN LEGISLATIVE PROCESS:
CONGRESS AND THE STATES. USA+45 LAW POL/PAR
DELIB/GP DEBATE ADMIN LOBBY REPRESENT CONGRESS
PRESIDENT. PAGE 60 E1191
LEGIS
DECISION
PWR
PROVS

B64
MITCHELL B.,A BIOGRAPHY OF THE CONSTITUTION OF THE
UNITED STATES. USA+45 USA-45 PROVS CHIEF LEGIS
DEBATE ADJUD SUFF FEDERAL...SOC 18/20 SUPREME/CT
CONGRESS SENATE HOUSE/REP PRESIDENT. PAGE 73 E1472
CONSTN
LAW
JURID

B65
JENKS C.W.,SPACE LAW. DIPLOM DEBATE CONTROL
ORD/FREE TREATY 20 UN. PAGE 58 E1161
SPACE
INT/LAW
JURID
INT/ORG

B65
NJ LEGIS REAPPORT PLAN COMM,PUBLIC HEARING ON
REDISTRICTING AND REAPPORTIONMENT. USA+45 CONSTN
VOL/ASSN LEGIS DEBATE...POLICY GEOG CENSUS 20
NEW/JERSEY. PAGE 77 E1552
APPORT
REPRESENT
PROVS
JURID

B66
ANDERSON S.V.,CANADIAN OMBUDSMAN PROPOSALS. CANADA
LEGIS DEBATE PARL/PROC...MAJORIT JURID TIME/SEQ
IDEA/COMP 20 OMBUDSMAN PARLIAMENT. PAGE 5 E0092
NAT/G
CREATE
ADMIN
POL/PAR

B66
BAXTER M.G.,DANIEL WEBSTER & THE SUPREME COURT. LAW
NAT/G PROF/ORG DEBATE ADJUD LEAD FEDERAL PERSON.
PAGE 8 E0156
CONSTN
CT/SYS
JURID

B66
BURNS A.C.,PARLIAMENT AS AN EXPORT. WOR+45 CONSTN
BARGAIN DEBATE ROUTINE GOV/REL EFFICIENCY...ANTHOL
COMMONWLTH PARLIAMENT. PAGE 17 E0343
PARL/PROC
POL/PAR
CT/SYS
CHIEF

B67
JONES C.O.,EVERY SECOND YEAR: CONGRESSIONAL
BEHAVIOR AND THE TWO-YEAR TERM. LAW POL/PAR
PROB/SOLV DEBATE CHOOSE PERS/REL COST FEDERAL PWR
...CHARTS 20 CONGRESS SENATE HOUSE/REP. PAGE 59
E1172
EFFICIENCY
LEGIS
TIME/SEQ
NAT/G

S67
FLECHTHEIM O.K.,"BLOC FORMATION VS. DIALOGUE."
CONSTN ECO/DEV BAL/PWR PEACE ATTIT PWR COLD/WAR.
PAGE 38 E0761
FUT
CAP/ISM
MARXISM
DEBATE

S67
GOSSETT W.T.,"ELECTING THE PRESIDENT: NEW HOPE FOR
AN OLD IDEAL." FUT USA+45 USA-45 PROVS LEGIS
PROB/SOLV WRITING DEBATE ADJUD REPRESENT...MAJORIT
CONSTN
CHIEF
CHOOSE

DECISION 20 HOUSE/REP PRESIDENT. PAGE 45 E0892   NAT/G

CT/SYS

LARSEN P.B.,"THE UNITED STATES-ITALY AIR TRANSPORT INT/LAW
ARBITRATION: PROBLEMS OF TREATY INTERPRETATION AND   ADJUD
ENFORCEMENT." ITALY USA+45 AIR PROB/SOLV DIPLOM   INT/TRADE
DEBATE CONTROL CT/SYS...DECISION TREATY. PAGE 63   DIST/IND
E1257   S67

LLEWELLYN K.N.,"THE CONSTITUTION AS AN INSTITUTION"   CONSTN
(BMR)" USA-45 PROB/SOLV LOBBY REPRESENT...DECISION   LAW
JURID 18/20 SUPREME/CT. PAGE 66 E1313   CONCPT
                  CT/SYS
           L34

MACLEOD R.M.,"LAW, MEDICINE AND PUBLIC OPINION: THE   LAW
RESISTANCE TO COMPULSORY HEALTH LEGISLATION   HEALTH
1870-1907." UK CONSTN SECT DELIB/GP DEBATE   ATTIT
PARL/PROC GP/REL MORAL 19. PAGE 67 E1344   S67

MCLAUGHLIN A.C.,A CONSTITUTIONAL HISTORY OF THE   CONSTN
UNITED STATES. USA+45 USA-45 LOC/G NAT/G PROVS   DECISION
LEGIS JUDGE ADJUD...T 18/20. PAGE 71 E1422
           B35

DEBOLD R.C. E0601

HERRING E.P.,PUBLIC ADMINISTRATION AND THE PUBLIC   GP/REL
INTEREST. LABOR NAT/G PARTIC EFFICIENCY 20. PAGE 52   DECISION
E1033   PROB/SOLV
                  ADMIN
           B36

DEBS/E....EUGENE DEBS

DEBT....PUBLIC DEBT, INCLUDING NATIONAL DEBT; SEE ALSO
NAT/G

BEARDSLEY A.R.,LEGAL BIBLIOGRAPHY AND THE USE OF   BIBLIOG
LAW BOOKS. CONSTN CREATE PROB/SOLV...DECISION JURID   LAW
LAB/EXP. PAGE 9 E0166   METH
                  OP/RES
           B37

DECISION....DECISION-MAKING AND GAME THEORY; SEE ALSO GAME

FRANKFURTER F.,MR. JUSTICE HOLMES AND THE SUPREME   CREATE
COURT. USA-45 CONSTN SOCIETY FEDERAL OWN ATTIT   CT/SYS
ORD/FREE PWR...POLICY JURID 20 SUPREME/CT HOLMES/OW   DECISION
BILL/RIGHT. PAGE 40 E0790   LAW
           B38

AMERICAN JOURNAL OF INTERNATIONAL LAW. WOR+45   BIBLIOG/A
WOR-45 CONSTN INT/ORG NAT/G CT/SYS ARMS/CONT WAR   INT/LAW
...DECISION JURID NAT/COMP 20. PAGE 1 E0001   DIPLOM
                  ADJUD
              N

HAGUE PERMANENT CT INTL JUSTIC,WORLD COURT REPORTS: INT/ORG
COLLECTION OF THE JUDGEMENTS ORDERS AND OPINIONS   CT/SYS
VOLUME 3 1932-35. WOR-45 LAW DELIB/GP CONFER WAR   DIPLOM
PEACE ATTIT...DECISION ANTHOL 20 WORLD/CT CASEBOOK.   ADJUD
PAGE 49 E0976   B38

ADVANCED MANAGEMENT. INDUS EX/STRUC WORKER OP/RES   MGT
...DECISION BIBLIOG/A 20. PAGE 1 E0015   ADMIN
                  LABOR
                  GP/REL
           N

HART J.,AN INTRODUCTION TO ADMINISTRATIVE LAW, WITH   LAW
SELECTED CASES. USA-45 CONSTN SOCIETY NAT/G   ADMIN
EX/STRUC ADJUD CT/SYS LEAD CRIME ORD/FREE   LEGIS
...DECISION JURID 20 CASEBOOK. PAGE 50 E1002   PWR
           B40

GRIFFIN A.P.C.,A LIST OF BOOKS RELATING TO   BIBLIOG/A
RAILROADS IN THEIR RELATION TO THE GOVERNMENT AND   SERV/IND
THE PUBLIC (PAMPHLET). USA-45 LAW ECO/DEV NAT/G   ADJUD
TEC/DEV CAP/ISM LICENSE CENTRAL LAISSEZ...DECISION   ECO/TAC
19/20. PAGE 47 E0925   B04

WOLFERS A.,BRITAIN AND FRANCE BETWEEN TWO WORLD   DIPLOM
WARS. FRANCE UK INT/ORG NAT/G PLAN BARGAIN ECO/TAC   WAR
AGREE ISOLAT ALL/IDEOS...DECISION GEOG 20 TREATY   POLICY
VERSAILLES INTERVENT. PAGE 107 E2139   B40

GRIFFIN A.P.C.,LIST OF REFERENCES ON PRIMARY   BIBLIOG/A
ELECTIONS (PAMPHLET). USA-45 LAW LOC/G DELIB/GP   POL/PAR
LEGIS OP/RES TASK REPRESENT CONSEN...DECISION 19/20   CHOOSE
CONGRESS. PAGE 47 E0928   POPULISM
           B05

GILL N.N.,"PERMANENT ADVISORY COMMISSIONS IN THE   DELIB/GP
FEDERAL GOVERNMENT." CLIENT FINAN OP/RES EDU/PROP   NAT/G
PARTIC ROUTINE INGP/REL KNOWL SKILL...CLASSIF   DECISION
TREND. PAGE 43 E0860   S40

GRIFFIN A.P.C.,LIST OF REFERENCES ON INTERNATIONAL   BIBLIOG/A
ARBITRATION. FRANCE L/A+17C USA-45 WOR-45 DIPLOM   INT/ORG
CONFER COLONIAL ARMS/CONT BAL/PAY EQUILIB SOVEREIGN   INT/LAW
...DECISION 19/20 MEXIC/AMER. PAGE 47 E0932   DELIB/GP
           B08

CARR R.K.,THE SUPREME COURT AND JUDICIAL REVIEW.   CT/SYS
NAT/G CHIEF LEGIS OP/RES LEAD GOV/REL GP/REL ATTIT   CONSTN
...POLICY DECISION 18/20 SUPREME/CT PRESIDENT   JURID
CONGRESS. PAGE 20 E0394   PWR
           B42

SCHMIDHAUSER J.R.,JUDICIAL BEHAVIOR AND THE   JUDGE
SECTIONAL CRISIS OF 1837-1860. USA-45 ADJUD CT/SYS   POL/PAR
INGP/REL ATTIT HABITAT...DECISION PSY STAT CHARTS   PERS/COMP
SIMUL. PAGE 88 E1759   PERSON
           N13

HAGUE PERMANENT CT INTL JUSTIC,WORLD COURT REPORTS: INT/ORG
COLLECTION OF THE JUDGEMENTS ORDERS AND OPINIONS   CT/SYS
VOLUME 4 1936-42. WOR-45 CONFER PEACE ATTIT   DIPLOM
...DECISION JURID ANTHOL 20 WORLD/CT CASEBOOK.   ADJUD
PAGE 49 E0977   B43

POWELL T.R.,"THE LOGIC AND RHETORIC OF   CONSTN
CONSTITUTIONAL LAW" (BMR)" USA+45 USA-45 DELIB/GP   LAW
PROB/SOLV ADJUD CT/SYS...DECISION 20 SUPREME/CT   JURID
CON/INTERP. PAGE 82 E1642   LOG
           S18

FULLER G.H.,MILITARY GOVERNMENT: A LIST OF   BIBLIOG
REFERENCES (A PAMPHLET). ITALY UK USA-45 WOR-45 LAW   DIPLOM
FORCES DOMIN ADMIN ARMS/CONT ORD/FREE PWR   CIVMIL/REL
...DECISION 20 CHINJAP. PAGE 41 E0822   SOVEREIGN
           B44

CARDOZO B.N.,THE NATURE OF THE JUDICIAL PROCESS.   JURID
ROUTINE ORD/FREE...POLICY 20. PAGE 19 E0377   CT/SYS
                  LEAD
                  DECISION
           B21

CANTWELL F.V.,"PUBLIC OPINION AND THE LEGISLATIVE   CHARTS
PROCESS" USA+45 USA-45 NAT/G CT/SYS EXEC LEAD   DEBATE
DECISION. PAGE 19 E0374   LEGIS
                  ATTIT
           S46

HALL A.B.,"DETERMINATION OF METHODS FOR   ADJUD
ASCERTAINING THE FACTORS THAT INFLUENCE JUDICIAL   DECISION
DECISIONS IN CASES INVOLVING DUE PROCESS" LAW JUDGE   CONSTN
DEBATE EFFICIENCY OPTIMAL UTIL...SOC CONCPT   JURID
PROBABIL STAT SAMP. PAGE 49 E0981   S26

SLESSER H.,THE ADMINISTRATION OF THE LAW. UK CONSTN   LAW
EX/STRUC OP/RES PROB/SOLV CRIME ROLE...DECISION   CT/SYS
METH/COMP 20 CIVIL/LAW ENGLSH/LAW CIVIL/LAW.   ADJUD
PAGE 92 E1839   B48

MACDONALD A.F.,ELEMENTS OF POLITICAL SCIENCE   LAW
RESEARCH. USA-45 ACADEM JUDGE EDU/PROP DEBATE ADJUD   FEDERAL
EXEC...BIBLIOG METH T 20 CONGRESS. PAGE 67 E1338   DECISION
                  CT/SYS
           B28

MILLER B.S.,"A LAW IS PASSED: THE ATOMIC ENERGY ACT   TEC/DEV
OF 1946." POL/PAR CHIEF CONFER DEBATE CONTROL   LEGIS
PARL/PROC ATTIT KNOWL...POLICY CONGRESS. PAGE 73   DECISION
E1457   LAW
           S48

GREAT BRIT COMM MINISTERS PWR,REPORT. UK LAW CONSTN   EX/STRUC
CONSULT LEGIS PARL/PROC SANCTION SOVEREIGN   NAT/G
...DECISION JURID 20 PARLIAMENT. PAGE 45 E0902   PWR
                  CONTROL
           B32

BLODGETT R.H.,"COMPARATIVE ECONOMIC SYSTEMS (REV.   METH/COMP
ED.)" WOR-45 AGRI FINAN MARKET LABOR NAT/G PLAN   CONCPT
                  C49

LUNT D.C.,THE ROAD TO THE LAW. UK USA-45 LEGIS   ADJUD
EDU/PROP OWN ORD/FREE...DECISION TIME/SEQ NAT/COMP   LAW
16/20 AUSTRAL ENGLSH/LAW COMMON/LAW. PAGE 67 E1333   JURID
           B32

INT/TRADE PRICE...POLICY DECISION BIBLIOG 20.
PAGE 13 E0248

ROUTINE

B50

BAILEY S.K.,CONGRESS MAKES A LAW. USA+45 GP/REL
SOC. PAGE 7 E0136

DECISION
LEGIS
LAW
ECO/TAC

B50

MOCKFORD J.,SOUTH-WEST AFRICA AND THE INTERNATIONAL
COURT (PAMPHLET). AFR GERMANY SOUTH/AFR UK
ECO/UNDEV DIPLOM CONTROL DISCRIM...DECISION JURID
20 AFRICA/SW. PAGE 74 E1475

COLONIAL
SOVEREIGN
INT/LAW
DOMIN

S50

ROBINSON W.S.,"BIAS, PROBABILITY AND TRIAL BY JURY"
(BMR)" USA+45 USA-45 SOCIETY...SOC CONCPT. PAGE 85
E1707

REPRESENT
JURID
CT/SYS
DECISION

B51

FRIEDMANN W.,LAW AND SOCIAL CHANGE IN CONTEMPORARY
BRITAIN. UK LABOR LG/CO LEGIS JUDGE CT/SYS ORD/FREE
NEW/LIB...DECISION JURID TREND METH/COMP BIBLIOG 20
PARLIAMENT ENGLSH/LAW COMMON/LAW. PAGE 40 E0802

LAW
ADJUD
SOCIETY
CONSTN

B51

ROSSITER C.,THE SUPREME COURT AND THE COMMANDER IN
CHIEF. LAW CONSTN DELIB/GP EX/STRUC LEGIS TOP/EX
ADJUD CONTROL...DECISION SOC/EXP PRESIDENT. PAGE 86
E1724

CT/SYS
CHIEF
WAR
PWR

B53

GROSS B.M.,THE LEGISLATIVE STRUGGLE: A STUDY IN
SOCIAL COMBAT. STRUCT LOC/G POL/PAR JUDGE EDU/PROP
DEBATE ETIQUET ADMIN LOBBY CHOOSE GOV/REL INGP/REL
HEREDITY ALL/VALS...SOC PRESIDENT. PAGE 48 E0948

LEGIS
DECISION
PERSON
LEAD

B53

PADOVER S.K.,THE LIVING US CONSTITUTION. USA+45
USA-45 POL/PAR ADJUD...DECISION AUD/VIS IDEA/COMP
18/20 SUPREME/CT. PAGE 79 E1590

CONSTN
LEGIS
DELIB/GP
BIOG

B54

CAPLOW T.,THE SOCIOLOGY OF WORK. USA+45 USA-45
STRATA MARKET FAM GP/REL INGP/REL ALL/VALS
...DECISION STAT BIBLIOG SOC/INTEG 20. PAGE 19
E0375

LABOR
WORKER
INDUS
ROLE

B54

JAMES L.F.,THE SUPREME COURT IN AMERICAN LIFE.
USA+45 USA-45 CONSTN CRIME GP/REL INGP/REL RACE/REL
CONSEN FEDERAL PERSON ORD/FREE 18/20 SUPREME/CT
DEPRESSION CIV/RIGHTS CHURCH/STA FREE/SPEE. PAGE 58
E1147

ADJUD
CT/SYS
JURID
DECISION

B55

BRAUN K.,LABOR DISPUTES AND THEIR SETTLEMENT.
ECO/TAC ROUTINE TASK GP/REL...DECISION GEN/LAWS.
PAGE 15 E0288

INDUS
LABOR
BARGAIN
ADJUD

B55

CUSHMAN R.E.,LEADING CONSTITUTIONAL DECISIONS.
USA+45 USA-45 NAT/G EX/STRUC LEGIS JUDGE TAX
FEDERAL...DECISION 20 SUPREME/CT CASEBOOK. PAGE 28
E0559

CONSTN
PROB/SOLV
JURID
CT/SYS

B55

BETH L.P.,"THE CASE FOR JUDICIAL PROTECTION OF
CIVIL LIBERTIES" (BMR)" USA+45 CONSTN ELITES LEGIS
CONTROL...POLICY DECISION JURID 20 SUPREME/CT
CIVIL/LIB. PAGE 11 E0220

CT/SYS
JUDGE
ADJUD
ORD/FREE

B56

CARLSTON K.S.,LAW AND STRUCTURES OF SOCIAL ACTION.
LAW SOCIETY ECO/DEV DIPLOM CONTROL ATTIT...DECISION
CONCPT 20. PAGE 19 E0379

JURID
INT/LAW
INGP/REL
STRUCT

B56

ESTEP R.,AN AIR POWER BIBLIOGRAPHY. USA+45 TEC/DEV
BUDGET DIPLOM EDU/PROP DETER CIVMIL/REL...DECISION
INT/LAW 20. PAGE 35 E0698

BIBLIOG/A
FORCES
WEAPON
PLAN

B56

SOHN L.B.,CASES ON UNITED NATIONS LAW. STRUCT
DELIB/GP WAR PEACE ORD/FREE...DECISION ANTHOL 20
UN. PAGE 92 E1854

INT/ORG
INT/LAW
ADMIN
ADJUD

S56

ROSENBERG M.,"POWER AND DESEGREGATION." USA+45

PWR

STRATA MUNIC GP/REL. PAGE 85 E1715

DISCRIM
DECISION
LAW

B57

MEYER P.,ADMINISTRATIVE ORGANIZATION: A COMPARATIVE
STUDY OF THE ORGANIZATION OF PUBLIC ADMINISTRATION.
DENMARK FRANCE NORWAY SWEDEN UK USA+45 ELITES LOC/G
CONSULT LEGIS ADJUD CONTROL LEAD PWR SKILL
DECISION. PAGE 72 E1449

ADMIN
METH/COMP
NAT/G
CENTRAL

B57

SCHUBERT G.A.,THE PRESIDENCY IN THE COURTS. CONSTN
FORCES DIPLOM TARIFFS ADJUD CONTROL WAR...DECISION
MGT CHARTS 18/20 PRESIDENT CONGRESS SUPREME/CT.
PAGE 89 E1778

PWR
CT/SYS
LEGIT
CHIEF

B57

US COMMISSION GOVT SECURITY,RECOMMENDATIONS; AREA:
LEGISLATION. USA+45 USA-45 DELIB/GP PLAN TEC/DEV
CIVMIL/REL ORD/FREE...POLICY DECISION 20 PRIVACY.
PAGE 99 E1982

LEGIS
SANCTION
CRIME
CONTROL

B57

US SENATE COMM ON JUDICIARY,LIMITATION OF APPELLATE
JURISDICTION OF THE SUPREME COURT. USA+45 LAW NAT/G
DELIB/GP PLAN ADMIN CONTROL PWR...DECISION 20
CONGRESS SUPREME/CT. PAGE 102 E2041

CT/SYS
ADJUD
POLICY
GOV/REL

B57

US SENATE SPEC COMM POLIT ACT,REPORT OF SPECIAL
COMMITTEE TO INVESTIGATE POLITICAL ACTIVITIES,
LOBBYING, AND CAMPAIGN CONTRIBUTIONS. USA+45
BARGAIN CRIME ATTIT...DECISION 20 CONGRESS.
PAGE 103 E2061

LOBBY
LAW
ECO/TAC
PARL/PROC

B58

WESTIN A.F.,THE ANATOMY OF A CONSTITUTIONAL LAW
CASE. USA+45 LAW LEGIS ADMIN EXEC...DECISION MGT
SOC RECORD 20 SUPREME/CT. PAGE 105 E2113

CT/SYS
INDUS
ADJUD
CONSTN

L58

BEVAN W.,"JURY BEHAVIOR AS A FUNCTION OF THE
PRESTIGE OF THE FOREMAN AND THE NATURE OF HIS
LEADERSHIP" (BMR)" DELIB/GP DOMIN ADJUD LEAD
PERS/REL ATTIT...PSY STAT INT QU CHARTS SOC/EXP 20
JURY. PAGE 11 E0221

PERSON
EDU/PROP
DECISION
CT/SYS

S58

DAHL R.A.,"DECISION-MAKING IN A DEMOCRACY: THE
SUPREME COURT AS A NATIONAL POLICY-MAKER" (BMR)"
USA+45 USA-45 POL/PAR ADJUD GOV/REL PWR...POLICY
JURID 19/20 SUPREME/CT. PAGE 28 E0561

CT/SYS
CONSTN
DECISION
NAT/G

S58

FISHER F.M.,"THE MATHEMATICAL ANALYSIS OF SUPREME
COURT DECISIONS: THE USE AND ABUSE OF QUANTITATIVE
METHODS." USA+45 LAW EX/STRUC LEGIS JUDGE ROUTINE
ATTIT DECISION. PAGE 38 E0757

PROB/SOLV
CT/SYS
JURID
MATH

S58

RIKER W.H.,"THE PARADOX OF VOTING AND CONGRESSIONAL
RULES FOR VOTING ON AMENDMENTS." LAW DELIB/GP
EX/STRUC PROB/SOLV CONFER DEBATE EFFICIENCY ATTIT
HOUSE/REP CONGRESS SENATE. PAGE 85 E1700

PARL/PROC
DECISION
LEGIS
RATIONAL

S58

SCHUBERT G.A.,"THE STUDY OF JUDICIAL DECISION-
MAKING AS AN ASPECT OF POLITICAL BEHAVIOR." PLAN
ADJUD CT/SYS INGP/REL PERSON...PHIL/SCI SOC QUANT
STAT CHARTS IDEA/COMP SOC/EXP. PAGE 89 E1779

JUDGE
DECISION
CON/ANAL
GAME

B59

DESMITH S.A.,JUDICIAL REVIEW OF ADMINISTRATIVE
ACTION. UK LOC/G CONSULT DELIB/GP ADMIN PWR
...DECISION JURID 20 ENGLSH/LAW. PAGE 31 E0609

ADJUD
NAT/G
PROB/SOLV
CT/SYS

B59

SCHUBERT G.A.,QUANTITATIVE ANALYSIS OF JUDICIAL
BEHAVIOR. ADJUD LEAD CHOOSE INGP/REL MAJORITY ATTIT
...DECISION JURID CHARTS GAME SIMUL SUPREME/CT.
PAGE 89 E1780

JUDGE
CT/SYS
PERSON
QUANT

B59

SISSON C.H.,THE SPIRIT OF BRITISH ADMINISTRATION
AND SOME EUROPEAN COMPARISONS. FRANCE GERMANY/W
SWEDEN UK LAW EX/STRUC INGP/REL EFFICIENCY ORD/FREE
...DECISION 20. PAGE 91 E1835

GOV/COMP
ADMIN
ELITES
ATTIT

B59

SURRENCY E.C.,A GUIDE TO LEGAL RESEARCH. USA+45
ACADEM LEGIS ACT/RES ADMIN...DECISION METH/COMP
BIBLIOG METH. PAGE 94 E1894

NAT/G
PROVS
ADJUD
JURID

S59

DERGE D.R.,"THE LAWYER AS DECISION-MAKER IN THE
AMERICAN STATE LEGISLATURE." INTELL LOC/G POL/PAR
CHOOSE AGE HEREDITY PERSON CONSERVE...JURID STAT
CHARTS. PAGE 31 E0607

LEGIS
LAW
DECISION
LEAD

S59

MASON A.T.,"THE SUPREME COURT: TEMPLE AND FORUM"
(BMR)" USA+45 USA-45 CONSTN DELIB/GP RACE/REL
MAJORITY ORD/FREE...DECISION SOC/INTEG 19/20
SUPREME/CT WARRN/EARL CIV/RIGHTS. PAGE 69 E1377

CT/SYS
JURID
PWR
ATTIT

S59

MURPHY W.F.,"LOWER COURT CHECKS ON SUPREME COURT
POWER" (BMR)" USA+45 NAT/G PROVS SCHOOL GOV/REL
RACE/REL DISCRIM ATTIT...DECISION JURID 20
SUPREME/CT NEGRO. PAGE 75 E1508

CT/SYS
BAL/PWR
CONTROL
ADJUD

S59

PUGWASH CONFERENCE,"ON BIOLOGICAL AND CHEMICAL
WARFARE." WOR+45 SOCIETY PROC/MFG INT/ORG FORCES
EDU/PROP ADJUD RIGID/FLEX ORD/FREE PWR...DECISION
PSY NEW/IDEA MATH VAL/FREE 20. PAGE 83 E1661

ACT/RES
BIO/SOC
WAR
WEAPON

B60

PAUL A.M.,CONSERVATIVE CRISIS AND THE RULE OF LAW.
USA-45 LABOR WORKER ATTIT ORD/FREE CONSERVE LAISSEZ
...DECISION JURID 19 SUPREME/CT. PAGE 80 E1603

CONSTN
ADJUD
STRUCT
PROF/ORG

B60

PRICE D.,THE SECRETARY OF STATE. USA+45 CONSTN
ELITES INTELL CHIEF EX/STRUC TOP/EX LEGIT ATTIT PWR
SKILL...DECISION 20 CONGRESS. PAGE 82 E1650

CONSULT
DIPLOM
INT/LAW

B60

SCHMIDHAUSER J.R.,THE SUPREME COURT: ITS POLITICS,
PERSONALITIES, AND PROCEDURES. LAW DELIB/GP
EX/STRUC TOP/EX ADJUD CT/SYS CHOOSE RATIONAL PWR
SUPREME/CT. PAGE 88 E1760

JUDGE
JURID
DECISION

B60

SCHUBERT G.A.,CONSTITUTIONAL POLITICS: THE
POLITICAL BEHAVIOR OF SUPREME COURT JUSTICES AND
THE CONSTITUTIONAL POLICIES THEY MAKE. LAW ELITES
CHIEF DELIB/GP EX/STRUC LEGIS DISCRIM ORD/FREE PWR
...POLICY MAJORIT CHARTS SUPREME/CT CONGRESS.
PAGE 89 E1781

CONSTN
CT/SYS
JURID
DECISION

B60

WEBSTER J.A.,A GENERAL STUDY OF THE DEPARTMENT OF
DEFENSE INTERNAL SECURITY PROGRAM. USA+45 WORKER
TEC/DEV ADJUD CONTROL CT/SYS EXEC GOV/REL COST
...POLICY DECISION MGT 20 DEPT/DEFEN SUPREME/CT.
PAGE 105 E2105

ORD/FREE
PLAN
ADMIN
NAT/G

L60

DEAN A.W.,"SECOND GENEVA CONFERENCE OF THE LAW OF
THE SEA: THE FIGHT FOR FREEDOM OF THE SEAS." FUT
USA+45 USSR WOR+45 WOR-45 SEA CONSTN STRUCT PLAN
INT/TRADE ADJUD ADMIN ORD/FREE...DECISION RECORD
TREND GEN/LAWS 20 TREATY. PAGE 30 E0600

INT/ORG
JURID
INT/LAW

L60

MILLER A.S.,"THE MYTH OF NEUTRALITY IN
CONSTITUTIONAL ADJUDICATION." LAW...DECISION JURID
LING TREND IDEA/COMP. PAGE 73 E1456

ADJUD
CONSTN
MYTH
UTIL

S60

NAGEL S.S.,"USING SIMPLE CALCULATIONS TO PREDICT
JUDICIAL DECISIONS." ATTIT PERSON MATH. PAGE 76
E1517

JURID
LAW
DECISION
COMPUTER

S60

ROURKE F.E.,"ADMINISTRATIVE SECRECY: A
CONGRESSIONAL DILEMMA." DELIB/GP CT/SYS ATTIT
...MAJORIT DECISION JURID. PAGE 86 E1727

LEGIS
EXEC
ORD/FREE
POLICY

S60

ULMER S.S.,"THE ANALYSIS OF BEHAVIOR PATTERNS ON
THE UNITED STATES SUPREME COURT" USA+45 LAW CT/SYS
PERS/REL RACE/REL PERSON...DECISION PSY SOC TREND
METH/COMP METH 20 SUPREME/CT CIVIL/LIB. PAGE 97
E1951

ATTIT
ADJUD
PROF/ORG
INGP/REL

S60

WRIGHT Q.,"LEGAL ASPECTS OF THE U-2 INCIDENT." COM
USA+45 USSR STRUCT NAT/G FORCES PLAN TEC/DEV ADJUD
RIGID/FLEX MORAL ORD/FREE...DECISION INT/LAW JURID
PSY TREND GEN/LAWS COLD/WAR VAL/FREE 20 U-2.
PAGE 108 E2157

PWR
POLICY
SPACE

B61

AUERBACH C.A.,THE LEGAL PROCESS. USA+45 DELIB/GP
JUDGE CONFER ADJUD CONTROL...DECISION 20
SUPREME/CT. PAGE 6 E0116

JURID
ADMIN
LEGIS
CT/SYS

B61

BRENNAN D.G.,ARMS CONTROL, DISARMAMENT, AND
NATIONAL SECURITY. WOR+45 NAT/G FORCES CREATE
PROB/SOLV PARTIC WAR PEACE...DECISION INT/LAW
ANTHOL BIBLIOG 20. PAGE 15 E0291

ARMS/CONT
ORD/FREE
DIPLOM
POLICY

B61

FREUND P.A.,THE SUPREME COURT OF THE UNITED STATES:
ITS BUSINESS, PURPOSES, AND PERFORMANCE. CONSTN
CRIME CONSEN ORD/FREE...DECISION 20 SUPREME/CT
CIVIL/LIB. PAGE 40 E0797

CT/SYS
JURID
ADJUD
FEDERAL

B61

WASSERSTROM R.A.,THE JUDICIAL DECISION: TOWARD A
THEORY OF LEGAL JUSTIFICATION. ACT/RES RATIONAL
PERCEPT KNOWL OBJECTIVE...DECISION JURID. PAGE 105
E2102

JUDGE
LAW
ADJUD

B61

WESTIN A.F.,THE SUPREME COURT: VIEWS FROM INSIDE.
USA+45 NAT/G PROF/ORG PROVS DELIB/GP INGP/REL
DISCRIM ATTIT...POLICY DECISION JURID ANTHOL 20
SUPREME/CT CONGRESS CIVIL/LIB. PAGE 106 E2114

CT/SYS
LAW
ADJUD
GOV/REL

B61

WINTERS J.M.,STATE CONSTITUTIONAL LIMITATIONS ON
SOLUTIONS OF METROPOLITAN AREA PROBLEMS. CONSTN
LEGIS LEAD REPRESENT DECISION. PAGE 107 E2134

MUNIC
REGION
LOC/G
LAW

S61

SCHUBERT G.,"A PSYCHOMETRIC MODEL OF THE SUPREME
COURT." DELIB/GP ADJUD CHOOSE ATTIT...DECISION
JURID PSY QUANT STAT HYPO/EXP GEN/METH SUPREME/CT.
PAGE 88 E1771

JUDGE
CT/SYS
PERSON
SIMUL

B62

CARLSTON K.S.,LAW AND ORGANIZATION IN WORLD
SOCIETY. WOR+45 FINAN ECO/TAC DOMIN LEGIT CT/SYS
ROUTINE COERCE ORD/FREE PWR WEALTH...PLURIST
DECISION JURID MGT METH/CNCPT GEN/LAWS 20. PAGE 19
E0381

INT/ORG
LAW

B62

DIESING P.,REASON IN SOCIETY; FIVE TYPES OF
DECISIONS AND THEIR SOCIAL CONDITIONS. SOCIETY
STRUCT LABOR CREATE TEC/DEV BARGAIN ADJUD ROLE
...JURID BIBLIOG 20. PAGE 31 E0625

RATIONAL
METH/COMP
DECISION
CONCPT

B62

DONNELLY R.C.,CRIMINAL LAW: PROBLEMS FOR DECISION
IN THE PROMULGATION, INVOCATION AND ADMINISTRATION
OF A LAW OF CRIMES. USA+45 SANCTION BIO/SOC
...DECISION JURID BIBLIOG 20. PAGE 32 E0636

CRIME
LAW
ADJUD
PROB/SOLV

B62

FROMAN L.A. JR.,PEOPLE AND POLITICS: AN ANALYSIS OF
THE AMERICAN POLITICAL SYSTEM. USA+45 CHIEF
DELIB/GP EX/STRUC LEGIS TOP/EX CT/SYS LOBBY
PERS/REL PWR...POLICY DECISION. PAGE 41 E0813

POL/PAR
PROB/SOLV
GOV/REL

B62

GALENSON W.,TRADE UNIONS MONOGRAPH SERIES (A SERIES
OF NINE TEXTS). DELIB/GP LEAD PARTIC...DECISION
ORG/CHARTS. PAGE 42 E0827

LABOR
INGP/REL
CONSTN
REPRESENT

B62

HADWEN J.G.,HOW UNITED NATIONS DECISIONS ARE MADE.
WOR+45 LAW EDU/PROP LEGIT ADMIN PWR...DECISION
SELF/OBS GEN/LAWS UN 20. PAGE 49 E0972

INT/ORG
ROUTINE

B62

HIRSCHFIELD R.S.,THE CONSTITUTION AND THE COURT.
SCHOOL WAR RACE/REL EQUILIB ORD/FREE...POLICY
MAJORIT DECISION JURID 18/20 PRESIDENT COLD/WAR
CIVIL/LIB SUPREME/CT CONGRESS. PAGE 53 E1051

ADJUD
PWR
CONSTN
LAW

B62

KAUPER P.G.,CIVIL LIBERTIES AND THE CONSTITUTION.
USA+45 SECT EDU/PROP WRITING ADJUD SEX ORD/FREE 20
SUPREME/CT CIVIL/LIB CHURCH/STA. PAGE 60 E1188

LAW
CONSTN
CT/SYS
DECISION

B62

MARS D.,SUGGESTED LIBRARY IN PUBLIC ADMINISTRATION.
FINAN DELIB/GP EX/STRUC WORKER COMPUTER ADJUD
...DECISION PSY SOC METH/COMP 20. PAGE 68 E1368

BIBLIOG
ADMIN
METH
MGT

NATIONAL MUNICIPAL LEAGUE,COURT DECISIONS ON
LEGISLATIVE APPORTIONMENT (VOL. III). USA+45 JUDGE
ADJUD CONTROL ATTIT...DECISION JURID COURT/DIST
CASEBOOK. PAGE 76 E1528
B62
PROVS
CT/SYS
APPORT
LEGIS

PRESS C.,STATE MANUALS, BLUE BOOKS AND ELECTION
RESULTS. LAW LOC/G MUNIC LEGIS WRITING FEDERAL
SOVEREIGN...DECISION STAT CHARTS 20. PAGE 82 E1648
B62
BIBLIOG
PROVS
ADMIN
CHOOSE

WINTERS J.M.,INTERSTATE METROPOLITAN AREAS. CONSTN
LEAD CHOOSE PWR DECISION. PAGE 107 E2135
B62
MUNIC
LAW
REGION
GOV/REL

ERDMANN H.H.,"ADMINISTRATIVE LAW AND FARM
ECONOMICS." USA+45 LOC/G NAT/G PLAN PROB/SOLV LOBBY
...DECISION ANTHOL 20. PAGE 35 E0695
L62
AGRI
ADMIN
ADJUD
POLICY

N,"UNION INVESTMENT IN BUSINESS: A SOURCE OF UNION
CONFLICT OF INTEREST." LAW NAT/G LEGIS CONTROL
GP/REL INGP/REL DECISION. PAGE 76 E1515
L62
LABOR
POLICY
FINAN
LG/CO

SPAETH H.J.,"JUDICIAL POWER AS A VARIABLE
MOTIVATING SUPREME COURT BEHAVIOR." DELIB/GP ADJUD
RATIONAL ATTIT PERSON ORD/FREE...CLASSIF STAT
GEN/METH. PAGE 93 E1860
L62
JUDGE
DECISION
PERS/COMP
PSY

FINKELSTEIN L.S.,"THE UNITED NATIONS AND
ORGANIZATIONS FOR CONTROL OF ARMAMENT." FUT WOR+45
VOL/ASSN DELIB/GP TOP/EX CREATE EDU/PROP LEGIT
ADJUD NUC/PWR ATTIT RIGID/FLEX ORD/FREE...POLICY
DECISION CONCPT OBS TREND GEN/LAWS TOT/POP
COLD/WAR. PAGE 38 E0752
S62
INT/ORG
PWR
ARMS/CONT

SCHUBERT G.,"THE 1960 TERM OF THE SUPREME COURT: A
PSYCHOLOGICAL ANALYSIS." USA+45 LAW CT/SYS...STAT
SUPREME/CT. PAGE 88 E1772
S62
DECISION
LEGIS
JUDGE
EX/STRUC

CORLEY R.N.,THE LEGAL ENVIRONMENT OF BUSINESS.
CONSTN LEGIS TAX ADMIN CT/SYS DISCRIM ATTIT PWR
...TREND 18/20. PAGE 26 E0509
B63
NAT/G
INDUS
JURID
DECISION

FRAENKEL O.K.,THE SUPREME COURT AND CIVIL
LIBERTIES: HOW THE COURT HAS PROTECTED THE BILL OF
RIGHTS. NAT/G CT/SYS CHOOSE PERS/REL RACE/REL
DISCRIM PERSON...DECISION 20 SUPREME/CT CIVIL/LIB
BILL/RIGHT. PAGE 39 E0782
B63
ORD/FREE
CONSTN
ADJUD
JURID

JACOBS P.,STATE OF UNIONS. USA+45 STRATA TOP/EX
GP/REL RACE/REL DEMAND DISCRIM ATTIT PWR 20
CONGRESS NEGRO HOFFA/J. PAGE 57 E1145
B63
LABOR
ECO/TAC
BARGAIN
DECISION

MCDOUGAL M.S.,LAW AND PUBLIC ORDER IN SPACE. FUT
USA+45 ACT/RES TEC/DEV ADJUD...POLICY INT/LAW JURID
20. PAGE 70 E1410
B63
SPACE
ORD/FREE
DIPLOM
DECISION

NEWMAN E.S.,THE FREEDOM READER. USA+45 LEGIS TOP/EX
PLAN ADJUD CONTROL CT/SYS DISCRIM...DECISION ANTHOL
20 SUPREME/CT CIV/RIGHTS. PAGE 77 E1541
B63
RACE/REL
LAW
POLICY
ORD/FREE

PACHTER H.M.,COLLISION COURSE; THE CUBAN MISSILE
CRISIS AND COEXISTENCE. CUBA USA+45 DIPLOM
ARMS/CONT PEACE MARXISM...DECISION INT/LAW 20
COLD/WAR KHRUSH/N KENNEDY/JF CASTRO/F. PAGE 79
E1587
B63
WAR
BAL/PWR
NUC/PWR
DETER

PRITCHETT C.H.,THE ROOSEVELT COURT. USA-45 LAW
INGP/REL...CHARTS 20 SUPREME/CT. PAGE 82 E1653
B63
DECISION
PROB/SOLV
CT/SYS
JURID

SCHUMAN S.I.,LEGAL POSITIVISM: ITS SCOPE AND
B63
GEN/METH

LIMITATIONS. CONSTN NAT/G DIPLOM PARTIC UTOPIA
...POLICY DECISION PHIL/SCI CONCPT 20. PAGE 89
E1784
LAW
METH/COMP

US SENATE COMM ON JUDICIARY,ADMINISTERED PRICES.
USA+45 RATION ADJUD CONTROL LOBBY...POLICY 20
SENATE MONOPOLY. PAGE 102 E2047
B63
LG/CO
PRICE
ADMIN
DECISION

LOEVINGER L.,"JURIMETRICS* THE METHODOLOGY OF LEGAL
INQUIRY." COMPUTER CREATE PLAN TEC/DEV AUTOMAT
CT/SYS EFFICIENCY...DECISION PHIL/SCI NEW/IDEA
QUANT PREDICT. PAGE 66 E1318
L63
COMPUT/IR
JURID
GEN/METH
ADJUD

CLEVELAND H.,"CRISIS DIPLOMACY." USA+45 WOR+45 LAW
FORCES TASK NUC/PWR PWR 20. PAGE 23 E0454
S63
DECISION
DIPLOM
PROB/SOLV
POLICY

MENDELSON W.,"THE NEO-BEHAVIORAL APPROACH TO THE
JUDICIAL PROCESS: A CRITIQUE" ADJUD PERSON...SOC
RECORD IDEA/COMP. PAGE 72 E1438
S63
DECISION
JURID
JUDGE

NAGEL S.S.,"A CONCEPTUAL SCHEME OF THE JUDICIAL
PROCESS." ADJUD...DECISION NEW/IDEA AVERAGE MODAL
CHARTS. PAGE 76 E1518
S63
POLICY
LAW
JURID
DISCRIM

VINES K.N.,"THE ROLE OF THE CIRCUIT COURT OF
APPEALS IN THE FEDERAL JUDICIAL PROCESS: A CASE
STUDY." USA+45 STRATA JUDGE RESPECT...DECISION
JURID CHARTS GP/COMP. PAGE 104 E2078
S63
REGION
ADJUD
CT/SYS
RACE/REL

SCHUBERT G.,"JUDICIAL DECISION-MAKING." FORCES LEAD
ATTIT DRIVE...POLICY PSY STAT CHARTS ANTHOL BIBLIOG
20. PAGE 88 E1773
C63
ADJUD
DECISION
JUDGE
CT/SYS

BECKER T.L.,POLITICAL BEHAVIORALISM AND MODERN
JURISPRUDENCE* A WORKING THEORY AND STUDY IN
JUDICIAL DECISION-MAKING. CONSTN...JURID STAT
GEN/METH INDEX. PAGE 9 E0172
B64
JUDGE
LAW
DECISION
CT/SYS

BREVER E.H.,LEARNED HAND, JANUARY 27, 1872-AUGUST
18, 1961 (PAMPHLET). USA+45 USA-45 LAW CONSTN ADJUD
...DECISION BIOG 19/20. PAGE 15 E0295
B64
BIBLIOG/A
JUDGE
CT/SYS
JURID

DANELSKI D.J.,A SUPREME COURT JUSTICE IS APPOINTED.
CHIEF LEGIS CONFER DEBATE EXEC PERSON PWR...BIOG 20
CONGRESS PRESIDENT. PAGE 28 E0564
B64
CHOOSE
JUDGE
DECISION

ECONOMIDES C.P.,LE POUVOIR DE DECISION DES
ORGANISATIONS INTERNATIONALES EUROPEENNES. DIPLOM
DOMIN INGP/REL EFFICIENCY...INT/LAW JURID 20 NATO
OEEC EEC COUNCL/EUR EURATOM. PAGE 34 E0673
B64
INT/ORG
PWR
DECISION
GP/COMP

HOHFELD W.N.,FUNDAMENTAL LEGAL CONCEPTIONS.
PROB/SOLV OWN PWR...DECISION LING IDEA/COMP
GEN/METH. PAGE 54 E1069
B64
JURID
ADJUD
LAW
METH/CNCPT

KEEFE W.J.,THE AMERICAN LEGISLATIVE PROCESS:
CONGRESS AND THE STATES. USA+45 LAW POL/PAR
DELIB/GP DEBATE ADMIN LOBBY REPRESENT CONGRESS
PRESIDENT. PAGE 60 E1191
B64
LEGIS
DECISION
PWR
PROVS

MAKI J.M.,COURT AND CONSTITUTION IN JAPAN; SELECTED
SUPREME COURT DECISIONS, 1948-60. FAM LABOR GOV/REL
HABITAT ORD/FREE...DECISION JURID 20 CHINJAP
SUPREME/CT CIV/RIGHTS. PAGE 68 E1354
B64
CT/SYS
CONSTN
PROB/SOLV
LAW

NELSON D.H.,ADMINISTRATIVE AGENCIES OF THE USA:
THEIR DECISIONS AND AUTHORITY. USA+45 NAT/G CONTROL
CT/SYS REPRESENT...DECISION 20. PAGE 76 E1531
B64
ADMIN
EX/STRUC
ADJUD
LAW

ROBINSON R.D.,INTERNATIONAL BUSINESS POLICY. AFR
INDIA L/A+17C USA+45 ELITES AGRI FOR/AID COERCE
BAL/PAY...DECISION INT/LAW MGT 20. PAGE 85 E1706
B64
ECO/TAC
DIST/IND
COLONIAL

FINAN

B64

SCHUBERT G.A.,JUDICIAL BEHAVIOR: A READER IN THEORY ATTIT
AND RESEARCH. POL/PAR CT/SYS ROLE SUPEGO PWR   PERSON
...DECISION JURID REGRESS CHARTS SIMUL ANTHOL 20.   ADJUD
PAGE 89 E1782   ACT/RES

B64

SHAPIRO M.,LAW AND POLITICS IN THE SUPREME COURT: LEGIS
NEW APPROACHES TO POLITICAL JURISPRUDENCE. JUDGE   CT/SYS
PROB/SOLV LEGIT EXEC ROUTINE ATTIT ALL/VALS   LAW
...DECISION SOC. PAGE 90 E1811   JURID

B64

SHKLAR J.N.,LEGALISM. CREATE PROB/SOLV CT/SYS   MORAL
...POLICY CRIMLGY DECISION JURID METH/CNCPT.   LAW
PAGE 91 E1821   NEW/IDEA

L64

MAYO L.H.,"LEGAL-POLICY DECISION PROCESS: DECISION
ALTERNATIVE THINKING AND THE PREDICTIVE FUNCTION."   SIMUL
PROB/SOLV EFFICIENCY RATIONAL. PAGE 70 E1395   JURID
                                                      TEC/DEV

S64

PRITCHETT C.H.,"EQUAL PROTECTION AND THE URBAN   MUNIC
MAJORITY." POL/PAR LEAD CHOOSE GP/REL PWR...MAJORIT   LAW
DECISION. PAGE 83 E1655   REPRESENT
                                                      APPORT

C64

BECKER T.L.,"POLITICAL BEHAVIORALISM AND MODERN   DECISION
JURISPRUDENCE." LEGIS JUDGE OP/RES ADJUD CT/SYS   PROB/SOLV
ATTIT PWR...BIBLIOG 20. PAGE 9 E0173   JURID
                                                      GEN/LAWS

B65

CAMPBELL E.H.,SURVEYS, SUBDIVISIONS AND PLATTING,   CONSTN
AND BOUNDARIES: WASHINGTON STATE LAW AND JUDICIAL   PLAN
DECISIONS. USA+45 LAW LOC/G...DECISION JURID   GEOG
CON/ANAL BIBLIOG WASHINGT/G PARTITION WATER.   PROVS
PAGE 19 E0372

B65

CAVERS D.F.,THE CHOICE-OF-LAW PROCESS. PROB/SOLV   JURID
ADJUD CT/SYS CHOOSE RATIONAL...IDEA/COMP 16/20   DECISION
TREATY. PAGE 21 E0411   METH/COMP
                                                      ADMIN

B65

CONGRESSIONAL QUARTERLY SERV,REVOLUTION IN CIVIL   LAW
RIGHTS. USA+45 USA-45 LEGIS ADJUD CT/SYS CHOOSE   CONSTN
DISCRIM...DECISION CONGRESS SUPREME/CT. PAGE 25   RACE/REL
E0488   LOBBY

B65

FERRELL J.S.,CASES AND MATERIALS ON LOCAL   APPORT
APPORTIONMENT. CONSTN LEAD GP/REL...DECISION   LOC/G
GOV/COMP. PAGE 37 E0740   REPRESENT
                                                      LAW

B65

FRIEDMAN L.,SOUTHERN JUSTICE. USA+45 PUB/INST LEGIT   ADJUD
ADMIN CT/SYS DISCRIM...DECISION ANTHOL 20 NEGRO   LAW
SOUTH/US CIV/RIGHTS. PAGE 40 E0800   CONSTN
                                                      RACE/REL

B65

KRISLOV S.,THE SUPREME COURT IN THE POLITICAL   ADJUD
PROCESS. USA+45 LAW SOCIETY STRUCT WORKER ADMIN   DECISION
ROLE...JURID SOC 20 SUPREME/CT. PAGE 62 E1231   CT/SYS
                                                      CONSTN

B65

MURPHY W.F.,WIRETAPPING ON TRIAL: A CASE STUDY IN   JURID
THE JUDICIAL PROCESS. CONSTN ELITES CT/SYS CRIME   LAW
MORAL ORD/FREE...DECISION SUPREME/CT. PAGE 75 E1511   POLICY

B65

SCHUBERT G.,THE JUDICIAL MIND: THE ATTITUDES AND   CT/SYS
IDEOLOGIES OF SUPREME COURT JUSTICES 1946-1963.   JUDGE
USA+45 ELITES NAT/G CONTROL PERS/REL MAJORITY   ATTIT
CONSERVE...DECISION JURID MODAL STAT TREND GP/COMP   NEW/LIB
GAME. PAGE 88 E1774

B65

SCHUBERT G.,THE POLITICAL ROLE OF THE COURTS IN   CT/SYS
JUDICIAL POLICY MAKING. USA+45 CONSTN JUDGE   POLICY
FEEDBACK CHOOSE RACE/REL ORD/FREE...TRADIT PSY   DECISION
BIBLIOG/A 20 KENNEDY/JF SUPREME/CT. PAGE 89 E1776

B65

SMITH R.C.,THEY CLOSED THEIR SCHOOLS. USA+45 NEIGH   RACE/REL
ADJUD CROWD CONSEN WEALTH...DECISION OBS INT 20   DISCRIM
NEGRO VIRGINIA. PAGE 92 E1846   LOC/G

B65

UNIVERSAL REFERENCE SYSTEM,INTERNATIONAL AFFAIRS: BIBLIOG/A
VOLUME I IN THE POLITICAL SCIENCE, GOVERNMENT, AND   GEN/METH
PUBLIC POLICY SERIES...DECISION ECOMETRIC GEOG   COMPUT/IR
INT/LAW JURID MGT PHIL/SCI PSY SOC. PAGE 98 E1972   DIPLOM

B65

US LIBRARY OF CONGRESS,INTERNAL SECURITY AND   CONTROL
SUBVERSION. USA+45 ACADEM LOC/G NAT/G PROVS   ADJUD
...POLICY ANARCH DECISION 20 CIVIL/SERV SUBVERT   LAW
SEDITION. PAGE 101 E2020   PLAN

B65

WEIL G.L.,A HANDBOOK ON THE EUROPEAN ECONOMIC   INT/TRADE
COMMUNITY. BELGIUM EUR+WWI FRANCE GERMANY/W ITALY   INT/ORG
CONSTN ECO/DEV CREATE PARTIC GP/REL...DECISION MGT   TEC/DEV
CHARTS 20 EEC. PAGE 105 E2107   INT/LAW

S65

DIXON R.G.,"NEW CONSTITUTIONAL FORMS FOR   MUNIC
METROPOLIS: REAPPORTIONED COUNTY BOARDS; LOCAL   REGION
COUNCILS OF GOVERNMENT." LAW CONSTN LEAD APPORT   GOV/COMP
REPRESENT DECISION. PAGE 32 E0631   PLAN

B66

BEDI A.S.,FREEDOM OF EXPRESSION AND SECURITY;   METH
COMPARATIVE STUDY OF FUNCTIONS OF SUPREME COURTS IN   CT/SYS
UNITED STATES AND INDIA. INDIA USA+45 LAW CONSTN   ADJUD
PROB/SOLV...DECISION JURID BIBLIOG 20 SUPREME/CT   ORD/FREE
FREE/SPEE AMEND/I. PAGE 9 E0175

B66

CARMEN I.H.,MOVIES, CENSORSHIP, AND THE LAW. LOC/G   EDU/PROP
NAT/G ATTIT ORD/FREE...DECISION INT IDEA/COMP   LAW
BIBLIOG 20 SUPREME/CT FILM. PAGE 19 E0383   ART/METH
                                                      CONSTN

B66

FENN DH J.R.,BUSINESS DECISION MAKING AND   DECISION
GOVERNMENT POLICY. SERV/IND LEGIS LICENSE ADMIN   PLAN
CONTROL GP/REL INGP/REL 20 CASEBOOK. PAGE 37 E0736   NAT/G
                                                      LG/CO

B66

HANSON R.,THE POLITICAL THICKET. USA+45 MUNIC   APPORT
POL/PAR LEGIS EXEC LOBBY CHOOSE...MAJORIT DECISION.   LAW
PAGE 50 E0998   CONSTN
                                                      REPRESENT

B66

HOLDSWORTH W.S.,A HISTORY OF ENGLISH LAW; THE   BIOG
CENTURIES OF SETTLEMENT AND REFORM (VOL. XVI). UK   PERSON
LOC/G NAT/G EX/STRUC LEGIS CT/SYS LEAD ATTIT   PROF/ORG
...POLICY DECISION JURID IDEA/COMP 18 PARLIAMENT.   LAW
PAGE 54 E1083

B66

KEAY E.A.,THE NATIVE AND CUSTOMARY COURTS OF   AFR
NIGERIA. NIGERIA CONSTN ELITES NAT/G TOP/EX PARTIC   ADJUD
REGION...DECISION JURID 19/20. PAGE 60 E1190   LAW

B66

MAGRATH C.P.,YAZOO; LAW AND POLITICS IN THE NEW   CT/SYS
REPUBLIC: THE CASE OF FLETCHER V. PECK. USA-45 LAW   DECISION
...BIBLIOG 19 SUPREME/CT YAZOO. PAGE 67 E1348   CONSTN
                                                      LOBBY

B66

MENDELSON W.,JUSTICES BLACK AND FRANKFURTER: JURID
CONFLICT IN THE COURT (2ND ED.). NAT/G PROVS   ADJUD
PROB/SOLV BAL/PWR CONTROL FEDERAL ISOLAT ANOMIE   IDEA/COMP
ORD/FREE...DECISION 20 SUPREME/CT BLACK/HL   ROLE
FRANKFUR/F. PAGE 72 E1439

B66

TRESOLINI R.J.,CASES IN AMERICAN NATIONAL   NAT/G
GOVERNMENT AND POLITICS. LAW DIPLOM ADJUD LOBBY   LEGIS
FEDERAL ORD/FREE WEALTH...DECISION ANTHOL 20   CT/SYS
PRESIDENT. PAGE 97 E1940   POL/PAR

B67

COWLING M.,1867 DISRAELI, GLADSTONE, AND   PARL/PROC
REVOLUTION; THE PASSING OF THE SECOND REFORM BILL.   POL/PAR
UK LEGIS LEAD LOBBY GP/REL INGP/REL...DECISION   ATTIT
BIBLIOG 19 REFORMERS. PAGE 27 E0531   LAW

B67

ESTEY M.,THE UNIONS: STRUCTURE, DEVELOPMENT, AND   LABOR
MANAGEMENT. FUT USA+45 ADJUD CONTROL INGP/REL DRIVE   EX/STRUC
...DECISION T 20 AFL/CIO. PAGE 35 E0699   ADMIN
                                                      GOV/REL

B67

GREENE L.S.,AMERICAN GOVERNMENT POLICIES AND   POLICY

FUNCTIONS. USA+45 LAW AGRI DIST/IND LABOR MUNIC   NAT/G
BUDGET DIPLOM EDU/PROP ORD/FREE...BIBLIOG T 20.   ADMIN
PAGE 46 E0910   DECISION

B67
LEVY L.W.,JUDICIAL REVIEW AND THE SUPREME COURT.   ADJUD
USA+45 USA-45 NEUTRAL ATTIT ORD/FREE...POLICY   CONSTN
DECISION BIBLIOG 18/20 BILL/RIGHT SUPREME/CT.   LAW
PAGE 65 E1292   CT/SYS

B67
ROBINSON R.D., INTERNATIONAL MANAGEMENT. USA+45   INT/TRADE
FINAN R+D PLAN PRODUC...DECISION T. PAGE 67 E1336   MGT
                                                    INT/LAW
                                                    MARKET

B67
PADELFORD N.J.,THE DYNAMICS OF INTERNATIONAL   DIPLOM
POLITICS (2ND ED.). WOR+45 LAW INT/ORG FORCES   NAT/G
TEC/DEV REGION NAT/LISM PEACE ATTIT PWR ALL/IDEOS POLICY
UN COLD/WAR NATO TREATY. PAGE 79 E1589   DECISION

B67
VILE M.J.C.,CONSTITUTIONALISM AND THE SEPARATION OF CONSTN
POWERS. FRANCE UK USA+45 USA-45 NAT/G ADJUD CONTROL BAL/PWR
GOV/REL...POLICY DECISION JURID GEN/LAWS 15/20   CONCPT
MONTESQ. PAGE 104 E2076   LAW

L67
FRANCK T.M.,"SOME PSYCHOLOGICAL FACTORS IN   DIPLOM
INTERNATIONAL THIRD-PARTY DECISION-MAKING." UNIV   ADJUD
SOCIETY PROB/SOLV DISCRIM ATTIT HABITAT...DECISION PERSON
PSY. PAGE 40 E0786   CONSULT

L67
HOWARD A.E.D.,"MR. JUSTICE BLACK: THE NEGRO PROTEST ADJUD
MOVEMENT AND THE RULE OF LAW." USA+45 CONSTN CT/SYS JUDGE
CHOOSE GP/REL...DECISION JURID NEGRO SUPREME/CT.   LAW
PAGE 55 E1100   REPRESENT

S67
GOSSETT W.T.,"ELECTING THE PRESIDENT: NEW HOPE FOR CONSTN
AN OLD IDEAL." FUT USA+45 USA-45 PROVS LEGIS   CHIEF
PROB/SOLV WRITING DEBATE ADJUD REPRESENT...MAJORIT CHOOSE
DECISION 20 HOUSE/REP PRESIDENT. PAGE 45 E0892   NAT/G

S67
KIM R.C.C.,"THE SUPREME COURT: ORALLE WITHOUT   CT/SYS
TRUTH." USA+45 EDU/PROP RACE/REL ADJUST ALL/VALS   PROB/SOLV
ORD/FREE...DECISION WORSHIP SUPREME/CT. PAGE 61   ADJUD
E1214   REPRESENT

S67
LARSEN P.B.,"THE UNITED STATES-ITALY AIR TRANSPORT INT/LAW
ARBITRATION: PROBLEMS OF TREATY INTERPRETATION AND ADJUD
ENFORCEMENT." ITALY USA+45 AIR PROB/SOLV DIPLOM   INT/TRADE
DEBATE CONTROL CT/SYS...DECISION TREATY. PAGE 63   DIST/IND
E1257

S67
SHELDON C.H.,"PUBLIC OPINION AND HIGH COURTS: ATTIT
COMMUNIST PARTY CASES IN FOUR CONSTITUTIONAL   CT/SYS
SYSTEMS." CANADA GERMANY/W WOR+45 POL/PAR MARXISM   CONSTN
...METH/COMP NAT/COMP 20 AUSTRAL. PAGE 91 E1818   DECISION

S67
TRAYNOR R.J.,"WHO CAN BEST JUDGE THE JUDGES?"   CHOOSE
USA+45 PLAN PROB/SOLV ATTIT...DECISION JURID 20.   ADJUD
PAGE 97 E1938   REPRESENT
                                                    CT/SYS

B77
CADWALDER J.L.,DIGEST OF THE PUBLISHED OPINIONS OF BIBLIOG
THE ATTORNEYS-GENERAL, AND OF THE LEADING DECISIONS CT/SYS
OF THE FEDERAL COURTS (REV ED). USA-45 NAT/G JUDGE DECISION
PROB/SOLV DIPLOM ATTIT...POLICY INT/LAW ANTHOL 19. ADJUD
PAGE 18 E0356

DECISION-MAKING, DISIPLINE....SEE DECISION

DECISION-MAKING, INDIVIDUAL....SEE PROB/SOLV, PWR

DECISION-MAKING, PROCEDURAL....SEE PROB/SOLV

DECISION-MAKING, THEORY....SEE GAME

DECLAR/IND....DECLARATION OF INDEPENDENCE (U.S.)

B64
MINAR D.W.,IDEAS AND POLITICS: THE AMERICAN   CONSTN
EXPERIENCE. SECT CHIEF LEGIS CREATE ADJUD EXEC REV NAT/G
PWR...PHIL/SCI CONCPT IDEA/COMP 18/20 HAMILTON/A   FEDERAL
JEFFERSN/T DECLAR/IND JACKSON/A PRESIDENT. PAGE 73
E1464

DECOTTIGNIES R. E0602

DEENER D.R. E0603

DEEP/INT....DEPTH INTERVIEWS

DEEP/QU....DEPTH QUESTIONNAIRES

N19
BUREAU OF NAT'L AFFAIRS INC.,A CURRENT LOOK AT: DISCRIM
(1) THE NEGRO AND TITLE VII. (2) SEX AND TITLE VII SEX
(PAMPHLET). LAW LG/CO SML/CO RACE/REL...POLICY SOC WORKER
STAT DEEP/QU TREND CON/ANAL CHARTS 20 NEGRO   MGT
CIV/RIGHTS. PAGE 17 E0334

DEFENSE....SEE DETER, PLAN, FORCES, WAR, COERCE

DEFENSE DEPARTMENT....SEE DEPT/DEFEN

DEFINETT/B....BRUNO DEFINETTI

DEFLATION....DEFLATION

DEGAULLE/C....CHARLES DE GAULLE

B60
PICKLES D.,THE FIFTH FRENCH REPUBLIC. ALGERIA   CONSTN
FRANCE CHOOSE GOV/REL ATTIT CONSERVE...CHARTS 20   ADJUD
DEGAULLE/C. PAGE 80 E1615   NAT/G
                                                    EFFICIENCY

B61
LA PONCE J.A.,THE GOVERNMENT OF THE FIFTH REPUBLIC: PWR
FRENCH POLITICAL PARTIES AND THE CONSTITUTION.   POL/PAR
ALGERIA FRANCE LAW NAT/G DELIB/GP LEGIS ECO/TAC   CONSTN
MARXISM SOCISM...CHARTS BIBLIOG/A 20 DEGAULLE/C.   CHIEF
PAGE 62 E1243

DEITY....DEITY: GOD AND GODS

B16
PUFENDORF S.,LAW OF NATURE AND OF NATIONS   CONCPT
(ABRIDGED). UNIV LAW NAT/G DIPLOM AGREE WAR PERSON INT/LAW
ALL/VALS PWR...POLICY 18 DEITY NATURL/LAW. PAGE 83 SECT
E1659   MORAL

B66
US SENATE COMM ON JUDICIARY,SCHOOL PRAYER. USA+45   SCHOOL
LAW LOC/G SECT ADJUD WORSHIP 20 SENATE DEITY.   JURID
PAGE 103 E2058   NAT/G

DELANY V.T.H. E0604

DELAWARE....DELAWARE

DELEGACION NACIONAL DE PRENSA E0605

DELEGATION OF POWER....SEE EX/STRUC

DELIB/GP....CONFERENCES, COMMITTEES, BOARDS, CABINETS

N
INTERNATIONAL COMN JURISTS,AFRICAN CONFERENCE ON   CT/SYS
THE RULE OF LAW. AFR INT/ORG LEGIS DIPLOM CONFER   JURID
COLONIAL ORD/FREE...CONCPT METH/COMP 20. PAGE 57   DELIB/GP
E1131

N
UNITED NATIONS,OFFICIAL RECORDS OF THE UNITED   INT/ORG
NATIONS' GENERAL ASSEMBLY. WOR+45 BUDGET DIPLOM   DELIB/GP
ADMIN 20 UN. PAGE 98 E1964   INT/LAW
                                                    WRITING

N
UNITED NATIONS,YEARBOOK OF THE INTERNATIONAL LAW   BIBLIOG
COMMISSION....CON/ANAL 20 UN. PAGE 98 E1966   INT/ORG
                                                    INT/LAW
                                                    DELIB/GP

B03
GRIFFIN A.P.C.,LIST OF REFERENCES ON INDUSTRIAL   BIBLIOG/A
ARBITRATION (PAMPHLET). USA-45 STRATA VOL/ASSN   INDUS
DELIB/GP WORKER ADJUD GP/REL...MGT 19/20. PAGE 46   LABOR
E0921   BARGAIN

B03
GRIFFIN A.P.C.,SELECT LIST OF BOOKS ON LABOR   BIBLIOG/A
PARTICULARLY RELATING TO STRIKES. FRANCE GERMANY   GP/REL
MOD/EUR UK USA-45 LAW NAT/G DELIB/GP WORKER BARGAIN MGT
LICENSE PAY ADJUD 19/20. PAGE 46 E0924   LABOR

B05
GRIFFIN A.P.C.,LIST OF REFERENCES ON PRIMARY   BIBLIOG/A
ELECTIONS (PAMPHLET). USA-45 LAW LOC/G DELIB/GP   POL/PAR
LEGIS OP/RES TASK REPRESENT CONSEN...DECISION 19/20 CHOOSE
CONGRESS. PAGE 47 E0928   POPULISM

S05
PHILLIPS J.B.,"MODIFICATIONS OF THE JURY SYSTEM." JURID
PARTIC EFFICIENCY ATTIT PERCEPT...TREND 19 DELIB/GP
SUPREME/CT JURY. PAGE 80 E1612 PERS/REL
POLICY

B08
GRIFFIN A.P.C.,LIST OF REFERENCES ON INTERNATIONAL BIBLIOG/A
ARBITRATION. FRANCE L/A+17C USA+45 WOR+45 DIPLOM INT/ORG
CONFER COLONIAL ARMS/CONT BAL/PAY EQUILIB SOVEREIGN INT/LAW
...DECISION 19/20 MEXIC/AMER. PAGE 47 E0932 DELIB/GP

B10
COLORADO CIVIL SERVICE COMN,SECOND BIENNIAL REPORT PROVS
TO THE GOVERNOR, 1909-1910. USA+45 DELIB/GP LEGIS LOC/G
LICENSE PAY 20 COLORADO CIVIL/SERV. PAGE 24 E0477 ADMIN
WORKER

B18
YUKIO O.,THE VOICE OF JAPANESE DEMOCRACY, AN ESSAY CONSTN
ON CONSTITUTIONAL LOYALTY (TRANS BY J. E. BECKER). MAJORIT
ASIA POL/PAR DELIB/GP EX/STRUC RIGID/FLEX ORD/FREE CHOOSE
PWR...POLICY JURID METH/COMP 19/20 CHINJAP. NAT/G
PAGE 108 E2167

S18
POWELL T.R.,"THE LOGIC AND RHETORIC OF CONSTN
CONSTITUTIONAL LAW" (BMR)" USA+45 USA-45 DELIB/GP LAW
PROB/SOLV ADJUD CT/SYS...DECISION 20 SUPREME/CT JURID
CON/INTERP. PAGE 82 E1642 LOG

N19
ATOMIC INDUSTRIAL FORUM,COMMENTARY ON LEGISLATION NUC/PWR
TO PERMIT PRIVATE OWNERSHIP OF SPECIAL NUCLEAR MARKET
MATERIAL (PAMPHLET). USA+45 DELIB/GP LEGIS PLAN OWN INDUS
...POLICY 20 AEC CONGRESS. PAGE 6 E0111 LAW

N19
BAILEY S.D.,VETO IN THE SECURITY COUNCIL DELIB/GP
(PAMPHLET). COM USSR WOR+45 BAL/PWR PARL/PROC INT/ORG
ARMS/CONT PRIVIL PWR...INT/LAW TREND CHARTS 20 UN DIPLOM
SUEZ. PAGE 7 E0135

N19
GIBB A.D.,JUDICIAL CORRUPTION IN THE UNITED KINGDOM MORAL
(PAMPHLET). UK DELIB/GP CT/SYS CRIME PERSON SUPEGO ATTIT
17/20 SCOTLAND. PAGE 43 E0856 ADJUD

N19
MCCONNELL G.,THE STEEL SEIZURE OF 1952 (PAMPHLET). DELIB/GP
USA+45 FINAN INDUS PROC/MFG LG/CO EX/STRUC ADJUD LABOR
CONTROL GP/REL ORD/FREE PWR 20 TRUMAN/HS PRESIDENT PROB/SOLV
CONGRESS. PAGE 70 E1402 NAT/G

N19
MEZERIK AG,OUTER SPACE: UN, US, USSR (PAMPHLET). SPACE
USSR DELIB/GP FORCES DETER NUC/PWR SOVEREIGN CONTROL
...POLICY 20 UN TREATY. PAGE 73 E1453 DIPLOM
INT/ORG

N19
TAYLOR H.,WHY THE PENDING TREATY WITH COLOMBIA INT/LAW
SHOULD BE RATIFIED (PAMPHLET). PANAMA USA-45 DIPLOM
DELIB/GP INT/TRADE REV ORD/FREE...JURID TREATY
18/19 ROOSEVLT/T TAFT/WH COLOMB. PAGE 95 E1912

C20
BLACHLY F.F.,"THE GOVERNMENT AND ADMINISTRATION OF NAT/G
GERMANY." GERMANY CONSTN LOC/G PROVS DELIB/GP GOV/REL
EX/STRUC FORCES LEGIS TOP/EX CT/SYS...BIBLIOG/A ADMIN
19/20. PAGE 12 E0235 PHIL/SCI

B22
BRYCE J.,INTERNATIONAL RELATIONS. CHRIST-17C INT/ORG
EUR+WWI MOD/EUR CULTURE INTELL NAT/G DELIB/GP POLICY
CREATE BAL/PWR DIPLOM ATTIT DRIVE RIGID/FLEX
ALL/VALS...PLURIST JURID CONCPT TIME/SEQ GEN/LAWS
TOT/POP. PAGE 16 E0323

B22
FARRAND M.,THE FRAMING OF THE CONSTITUTION OF THE CONSTN
UNITED STATES (1913). USA-45 EX/STRUC PROB/SOLV DELIB/GP
PERSON. PAGE 36 E0721 LEGIS
CT/SYS

B23
ROBERT H.M.,PARLIAMENTARY LAW. POL/PAR LEGIS PARTIC PARL/PROC
CHOOSE REPRESENT GP/REL. PAGE 85 E1701 DELIB/GP
NAT/G
JURID

B26
INSTITUT INTERMEDIAIRE INTL,REPERTOIRE GENERAL DES BIBLIOG
TRAITES ET AUTRES ACTES DIPLOMATIQUES CONCLUS DIPLOM
DEPUIS 1895 JUSQU'EN 1920. MOD/EUR WOR-45 INT/ORG

VOL/ASSN DELIB/GP INT/TRADE WAR TREATY 19/20.
PAGE 56 E1125

B27
LAUTERPACHT H.,PRIVATE LAW SOURCES AND ANALOGIES OF INT/ORG
INTERNATIONAL LAW. WOR-45 NAT/G DELIB/GP LEGIT ADJUD
COERCE ATTIT ORD/FREE PWR SOVEREIGN...JURID CONCPT PEACE
HIST/WRIT TIME/SEQ GEN/METH LEAGUE/NAT 20. PAGE 63 INT/LAW
E1264

B27
RYAN J.A.,DECLINING LIVERTY AND OTHER ESSAYS. ORD/FREE
USA-45 SECT DELIB/GP ATTIT PWR SOCISM 20 LEGIS
SUPREME/CT. PAGE 87 E1740 JURID
NAT/G

B29
CAM H.M.,BIBLIOGRAPHY OF ENGLISH CONSTITUTIONAL BIBLIOG/A
HISTORY (PAMPHLET). UK LAW LOC/G NAT/G POL/PAR SECT CONSTN
DELIB/GP ADJUD ORD/FREE 19/20 PARLIAMENT. PAGE 19 ADMIN
E0369 PARL/PROC

B29
CONWELL-EVANS T.P.,THE LEAGUE COUNCIL IN ACTION. DELIB/GP
EUR+WWI TURKEY UK USSR WOR-45 INT/ORG FORCES JUDGE INT/LAW
ECO/TAC EDU/PROP LEGIT ROUTINE ARMS/CONT COERCE
ATTIT PWR...MAJORIT GEOG JURID CONCPT LEAGUE/NAT
TOT/POP VAL/FREE TUNIS 20. PAGE 25 E0498

B30
WRIGHT Q.,MANDATES UNDER THE LEAGUE OF NATIONS. INT/ORG
WOR-45 CONSTN ECO/DEV ECO/UNDEV NAT/G DELIB/GP LAW
TOP/EX LEGIT ALL/VALS...JURID CONCPT LEAGUE/NAT 20. INT/LAW
PAGE 107 E2151

B32
EAGLETON C.,INTERNATIONAL GOVERNMENT. BRAZIL FRANCE INT/ORG
GERMANY ITALY UK USSR WOR-45 DELIB/GP TOP/EX PLAN JURID
ECO/TAC EDU/PROP LEGIT ADJUD REGION ARMS/CONT DIPLOM
COERCE ATTIT PWR...GEOG MGT VAL/FREE LEAGUE/NAT 20. INT/LAW
PAGE 34 E0670

B33
DANGERFIELD R.,IN DEFENSE OF THE SENATE. USA-45 LEGIS
CONSTN NAT/G EX/STRUC TOP/EX ATTIT KNOWL DELIB/GP
...METH/CNCPT STAT TIME/SEQ TREND CON/ANAL CHARTS DIPLOM
CONGRESS 20 TREATY. PAGE 28 E0565

B33
REID H.D.,RECUEIL DES COURS; TOME 45: LES ORD/FREE
SERVITUDES INTERNATIONALES III. FRANCE CONSTN DIPLOM
DELIB/GP PRESS CONTROL REV WAR CHOOSE PEACE MORAL LAW
MARITIME TREATY. PAGE 84 E1680

B36
CHAMBERLAIN J.P.,LEGISLATIVE PROCESS: NATION AND CON/ANAL
STATE. LAW DELIB/GP ROUTINE. PAGE 21 E0414 PROVS
LEGIS
NAT/G

B38
HAGUE PERMANENT CT INTL JUSTIC,WORLD COURT REPORTS: INT/ORG
COLLECTION OF THE JUDGEMENTS ORDERS AND OPINIONS CT/SYS
VOLUME 3 1932-35. WOR-45 LAW DELIB/GP CONFER WAR DIPLOM
PEACE ATTIT...DECISION ANTHOL 20 WORLD/CT CASEBOOK. ADJUD
PAGE 49 E0976

B39
BENES E.,INTERNATIONAL SECURITY. GERMANY UK NAT/G EUR+WWI
DELIB/GP PLAN BAL/PWR ATTIT ORD/FREE PWR LEAGUE/NAT INT/ORG
20 TREATY. PAGE 10 E0186 WAR

B39
LAVES W.H.C.,INTERNATIONAL SECURITY. EUR+WWI ORD/FREE
GERMANY UK USA-45 LAW NAT/G DELIB/GP TOP/EX COERCE LEGIT
PWR...POLICY FASCIST CONCPT HIST/WRIT GEN/LAWS ARMS/CONT
LEAGUE/NAT NAZI 20. PAGE 63 E1267 BAL/PWR

B39
ZIMMERN A.,THE LEAGUE OF NATIONS AND THE RULE OF INT/ORG
LAW. WOR-45 STRUCT NAT/G DELIB/GP EX/STRUC BAL/PWR LAW
DOMIN LEGIT COERCE ORD/FREE PWR...POLICY RECORD DIPLOM
LEAGUE/NAT TOT/POP VAL/FREE 20 LEAGUE/NAT. PAGE 108
E2170

S40
GILL N.N.,"PERMANENT ADVISORY COMMISSIONS IN THE DELIB/GP
FEDERAL GOVERNMENT." CLIENT FINAN OP/RES EDU/PROP NAT/G
PARTIC ROUTINE INGP/REL KNOWL SKILL...CLASSIF DECISION
TREND. PAGE 43 E0860

B41
MCCLURE W.,INTERNATIONAL EXECUTIVE AGREEMENTS. TOP/EX
USA-45 WOR-45 INT/ORG NAT/G DELIB/GP ADJUD ROUTINE DIPLOM
ORD/FREE PWR...TIME/SEQ TREND CON/ANAL. PAGE 70
E1401

CROWE S.E.,THE BERLIN WEST AFRICA CONFERENCE, 1884-85. GERMANY ELITES MARKET INT/ORG DELIB/GP FORCES PROB/SOLV BAL/PWR CAP/ISM DOMIN COLONIAL ...INT/LAW 19. PAGE 28 E0548
B42
AFR
CONFER
INT/TRADE
DIPLOM

FULLER G.H.,DEFENSE FINANCING: A SUPPLEMENTARY LIST OF REFERENCES (PAMPHLET). CANADA UK USA-45 ECO/DEV NAT/G DELIB/GP BUDGET ADJUD ARMS/CONT WEAPON COST PEACE PWR 20 AUSTRAL CHINJAP CONGRESS. PAGE 41 E0821
B42
BIBLIOG/A
FINAN
FORCES
DIPLOM

KELSEN H.,LAW AND PEACE IN INTERNATIONAL RELATIONS. FUT WOR-45 NAT/G DELIB/GP DIPLOM LEGIT RIGID/FLEX ORD/FREE SOVEREIGN...JURID CONCPT TREND STERTYP GEN/LAWS LEAGUE/NAT 20. PAGE 60 E1197
B42
INT/ORG
ADJUD
PEACE
INT/LAW

CHENEY F.,CARTELS, COMBINES, AND TRUSTS: A SELECTED LIST OF REFERENCES. GERMANY UK USA-45 WOR-45 DELIB/GP OP/RES BARGAIN CAP/ISM ECO/TAC INT/TRADE LICENSE LEGIT CONFER PRICE 20. PAGE 22 E0428
B44
BIBLIOG/A
LG/CO
ECO/DEV
INDUS

RUDIN H.R.,ARMISTICE 1918. FRANCE GERMANY MOD/EUR UK USA-45 NAT/G CHIEF DELIB/GP FORCES BAL/PWR REPAR ARMS/CONT 20 WILSON/W TREATY. PAGE 86 E1732
B44
AGREE
WAR
PEACE
DIPLOM

TINGSTERN H.,PEACE AND SECURITY AFTER WW II. WOR-45 DELIB/GP TOP/EX LEGIT CT/SYS COERCE PEACE ATTIT PERCEPT...CONCPT LEAGUE/NAT 20. PAGE 96 E1927
B45
INT/ORG
ORD/FREE
WAR
INT/LAW

KEETON G.W.,MAKING INTERNATIONAL LAW WORK. FUT WOR-45 NAT/G DELIB/GP FORCES LEGIT COERCE PEACE ATTIT RIGID/FLEX ORD/FREE PWR...JURID CONCPT HIST/WRIT GEN/METH LEAGUE/NAT 20. PAGE 60 E1193
B46
INT/ORG
ADJUD
INT/LAW

JESSUP P.C.,A MODERN LAW OF NATIONS. FUT WOR+45 WOR-45 SOCIETY NAT/G DELIB/GP LEGIS BAL/PWR EDU/PROP LEGIT PWR...INT/LAW JURID TIME/SEQ LEAGUE/NAT 20. PAGE 58 E1166
B48
INT/ORG
ADJUD

JACKSON R.H.,INTERNATIONAL CONFERENCE ON MILITARY TRIALS. FRANCE GERMANY UK USA+45 USSR VOL/ASSN DELIB/GP REPAR ADJUD CT/SYS CRIME WAR 20 WAR/TRIAL. PAGE 57 E1141
B49
DIPLOM
INT/ORG
INT/LAW
CIVMIL/REL

MARITAIN J.,HUMAN RIGHTS: COMMENTS AND INTERPRETATIONS. COM UNIV WOR+45 LAW CONSTN CULTURE SOCIETY ECO/DEV ECO/UNDEV SCHOOL DELIB/GP EDU/PROP ATTIT PERCEPT ALL/VALS...HUM SOC TREND UNESCO 20. PAGE 68 E1365
B49
INT/ORG
CONCPT

COMM. STUDY ORGAN. PEACE,"A TEN YEAR RECORD, 1939-1949." FUT WOR+45 LAW R+D CONSULT DELIB/GP CREATE LEGIT ROUTINE ORD/FREE...TIME/SEQ UN 20. PAGE 24 E0480
L49
INT/ORG
CONSTN
PEACE

HURST J.W.,THE GROWTH OF AMERICAN LAW: THE LAW MAKERS. USA-45 LOC/G NAT/G DELIB/GP JUDGE ADJUD ADMIN ATTIT PWR...POLICY JURID BIBLIOG 18/20 CONGRESS SUPREME/CT ABA PRESIDENT. PAGE 56 E1115
B50
LAW
LEGIS
CONSTN
CT/SYS

JIMENEZ E.,VOTING AND HANDLING OF DISPUTES IN THE SECURITY COUNCIL. WOR+45 CONSTN INT/ORG DIPLOM LEGIT DETER CHOOSE MORAL ORD/FREE PWR...JURID TIME/SEQ COLD/WAR UN 20. PAGE 59 E1168
B50
DELIB/GP
ROUTINE

LAUTERPACHT H.,INTERNATIONAL LAW AND HUMAN RIGHTS. USA+45 CONSTN STRUCT INT/ORG ACT/RES EDU/PROP PEACE PERSON ALL/VALS...CONCPT CON/ANAL GEN/LAWS UN 20. PAGE 63 E1266
B50
DELIB/GP
LAW
INT/LAW

ROSS A.,CONSTITUTION OF THE UNITED NATIONS. CONSTN CONSULT DELIB/GP ECO/TAC...INT/LAW JURID 20 UN LEAGUE/NAT. PAGE 86 E1721
B50
PEACE
DIPLOM
ORD/FREE
INT/ORG

KEFAUVER E.,CRIME IN AMERICA. USA+45 USA-45 MUNIC NEIGH DELIB/GP TRIBUTE GAMBLE LOBBY SANCTION
B51
ELITES
CRIME

...AUD/VIS 20 CAPONE/AL MAFIA MIAMI CHICAGO DETROIT. PAGE 60 E1194
PWR
FORCES

ROSSITER C.,THE SUPREME COURT AND THE COMMANDER IN CHIEF. LAW CONSTN DELIB/GP EX/STRUC LEGIS TOP/EX ADJUD CONTROL...DECISION SOC/EXP PRESIDENT. PAGE 86 E1724
B51
CT/SYS
CHIEF
WAR
PWR

BENTHAM A.,HANDBOOK OF POLITICAL FALLACIES. FUT MOD/EUR LAW INTELL LOC/G MUNIC NAT/G DELIB/GP LEGIS CREATE EDU/PROP CT/SYS ATTIT RIGID/FLEX KNOWL PWR ...RELATIV PSY SOC CONCPT SELF/OBS TREND STERTYP TOT/POP. PAGE 10 E0189
B52
POL/PAR

GELLHORN W.,THE STATES AND SUBVERSION. USA+45 USA-45 LOC/G DELIB/GP LEGIS EDU/PROP LEGIT CT/SYS REGION PEACE ATTIT ORD/FREE SOCISM...INT CON/ANAL 20 CALIFORNIA MARYLAND ILLINOIS MICHIGAN NEW/YORK. PAGE 43 E0845
B52
PROVS
JURID

JACKSON E.,MEETING OF THE MINDS: A WAY TO PEACE THROUGH MEDIATION. WOR+45 INDUS INT/ORG NAT/G DELIB/GP DIPLOM EDU/PROP LEGIT ORD/FREE...NEW/IDEA SELF/OBS TIME/SEQ CHARTS GEN/LAWS TOT/POP 20 UN TREATY. PAGE 57 E1139
B52
LABOR
JUDGE

VANDENBOSCH A.,THE UN: BACKGROUND, ORGANIZATION, FUNCTIONS, ACTIVITIES. WOR+45 LAW CONSTN STRUCT INT/ORG CONSULT BAL/PWR EDU/PROP EXEC ALL/VALS ...POLICY CONCPT UN 20. PAGE 103 E2071
B52
DELIB/GP
TIME/SEQ
PEACE

WRIGHT Q.,"CONGRESS AND THE TREATY-MAKING POWER." USA+45 WOR+45 CONSTN INTELL NAT/G CHIEF CONSULT EX/STRUC LEGIS TOP/EX CREATE GOV/REL DISPL DRIVE RIGID/FLEX...TREND TOT/POP CONGRESS CONGRESS 20 TREATY. PAGE 108 E2154
L52
ROUTINE
DIPLOM
INT/LAW
DELIB/GP

DE GRAZIA A.,"GENERAL THEORY OF APPORTIONMENT" (BMR)" USA+45 USA-45 CONSTN ELITES DELIB/GP PARTIC REV CHOOSE...JURID 20. PAGE 29 E0582
S52
APPORT
LEGIS
PROVS
REPRESENT

STUART G.H.,"AMERICAN DIPLOMATIC AND CONSULAR PRACTICE (2ND ED.)" EUR+WWI MOD/EUR USA-45 DELIB/GP INT/TRADE ADJUD...BIBLIOG 20. PAGE 94 E1889
C52
DIPLOM
ADMIN
INT/ORG

PADOVER S.K.,THE LIVING US CONSTITUTION. USA+45 USA-45 POL/PAR ADJUD...DECISION AUD/VIS IDEA/COMP 18/20 SUPREME/CT. PAGE 79 E1590
B53
CONSTN
LEGIS
DELIB/GP
BIOG

SECKLER-HUDSON C.,BIBLIOGRAPHY ON PUBLIC ADMINISTRATION (4TH ED.). USA+45 LAW POL/PAR DELIB/GP BUDGET ADJUD LOBBY GOV/REL GP/REL ATTIT ...JURID 20. PAGE 90 E1800
B53
BIBLIOG/A
ADMIN
NAT/G
MGT

STOUT H.M.,BRITISH GOVERNMENT. UK FINAN LOC/G POL/PAR DELIB/GP DIPLOM ADMIN COLONIAL CHOOSE ORD/FREE...JURID BIBLIOG 20 COMMONWLTH. PAGE 94 E1883
B53
NAT/G
PARL/PROC
CONSTN
NEW/LIB

UNESCO,A REGISTER OF LEGAL DOCUMENTATION IN THE WORLD. WOR+45 WOR-45 NAT/G PROVS DELIB/GP LEGIS 13/20. PAGE 98 E1959
B53
BIBLIOG
CONSTN
LAW
JURID

US PRES CONF ADMIN PROCEDURE,REPORT (PAMPHLET). USA+45 CONFER ADJUD...METH/COMP 20 PRESIDENT. PAGE 101 E2024
N53
NAT/G
DELIB/GP
ADJUST
ADMIN

SCHWARTZ B.,FRENCH ADMINISTRATIVE LAW AND THE COMMON-LAW WORLD. FRANCE CULTURE LOC/G NAT/G PROVS DELIB/GP EX/STRUC LEGIS PROB/SOLV CT/SYS EXEC GOV/REL...IDEA/COMP ENGLSH/LAW. PAGE 89 E1786
B54
JURID
LAW
METH/COMP
ADJUD

BERNSTEIN M.H.,REGULATING BUSINESS BY INDEPENDENT COMMISSION. USA+45 USA-45 LG/CO CHIEF LEGIS PROB/SOLV ADJUD SANCTION GP/REL ATTIT...TIME/SEQ 19/20 MONOPOLY PRESIDENT CONGRESS. PAGE 11 E0214
B55
DELIB/GP
CONTROL
CONSULT

BURR R.N.,DOCUMENTS ON INTER-AMERICAN COOPERATION: BIBLIOG
VOL. I, 1810-1881; VOL. II, 1881-1948. DELIB/GP DIPLOM
BAL/PWR INT/TRADE REPRESENT NAT/LISM PEACE HABITAT INT/ORG
ORD/FREE PWR SOVEREIGN...INT/LAW 20 OAS. PAGE 18 L/A+17C
E0345
B55

CHOWDHURI R.N.,INTERNATIONAL MANDATES AND DELIB/GP
TRUSTEESHIP SYSTEMS. WOR+45 STRUCT ECO/UNDEV PLAN
INT/ORG LEGIS DOMIN EDU/PROP LEGIT ADJUD EXEC PWR SOVEREIGN
...CONCPT TIME/SEQ UN 20. PAGE 22 E0434
B55

WHEARE K.C.,GOVERNMENT BY COMMITTEE; AN ESSAY ON DELIB/GP
THE BRITISH CONSTITUTION. UK NAT/G LEGIS INSPECT CONSTN
CONFER ADJUD ADMIN CONTROL TASK EFFICIENCY ROLE LEAD
POPULISM 20. PAGE 106 E2116 GP/COMP
B55

CARR C.,"LEGISLATIVE CONTROL OF ADMINISTRATIVE EXEC
RULES AND REGULATIONS: PARLIAMENTARY SUPERVISION IN REPRESENT
BRITAIN." DELIB/GP CONTROL ROLE PWR PARLIAMENT. JURID
PAGE 20 E0392
S55

CORBETT P.E.,MORALS LAW, AND POWER IN INTERNATIONAL SUPEGO
RELATIONS. WOR+45 INT/ORG VOL/ASSN DELIB/GP CONCPT
CREATE BAL/PWR DIPLOM LEGIT ARMS/CONT MORAL...JURID POLICY
GEN/LAWS TOT/POP LEAGUE/NAT 20. PAGE 26 E0506 INT/LAW
B56

PERKINS D.,CHARLES EVANS HUGHES AND THE AMERICAN PERSON
DEMOCRATIC STATESMANSHIP. USA+45 USA-45 NAT/G BIOG
POL/PAR DELIB/GP JUDGE PLAN MORAL PWR...HIST/WRIT DIPLOM
LEAGUE/NAT 20. PAGE 80 E1609
B56

SOHN L.B.,BASIC DOCUMENTS OF THE UNITED NATIONS. DELIB/GP
WOR+45 LAW INT/ORG LEGIT EXEC ROUTINE CHOOSE PWR CONSTN
...JURID CONCPT GEN/LAWS ANTHOL UN TOT/POP OAS FAO
ILO 20. PAGE 92 E1853
B56

SOHN L.B.,CASES ON UNITED NATIONS LAW. STRUCT INT/ORG
DELIB/GP WAR PEACE ORD/FREE...DECISION ANTHOL 20 INT/LAW
UN. PAGE 92 E1854 ADMIN
ADJUD
B56

US HOUSE RULES COMM,HEARINGS BEFORE A SPECIAL ADMIN
SUBCOMMITTEE: ESTABLISHMENT OF A STANDING COMMITTEE DOMIN
ON ADMINISTRATIVE PROCEDURE. PRACTICE. USA+45 LAW DELIB/GP
EX/STRUC ADJUD CONTROL EXEC GOV/REL EFFICIENCY PWR NAT/G
...POLICY INT 20 CONGRESS. PAGE 100 E2009
B56

WIGGINS J.R.,FREEDOM OR SECRECY. USA+45 USA-45 ORD/FREE
DELIB/GP EX/STRUC FORCES ADJUD SANCTION KNOWL PWR PRESS
...AUD/VIS CONGRESS 20. PAGE 106 E2121 NAT/G
CONTROL
B56

ZINN C.J.,HOW OUR LAWS ARE MADE: BROCHURE HOUSE OF LEGIS
REPRESENTATIVES DOCUMENT 451. LAW CONSTN CHIEF DELIB/GP
EX/STRUC PROB/SOLV HOUSE/REP SENATE. PAGE 108 E2171 PARL/PROC
ROUTINE
B56

COMM. STUDY ORGAN. PEACE,STRENGTHENING THE UNITED INT/ORG
NATIONS. FUT USA+45 WOR+45 CONSTN NAT/G DELIB/GP ORD/FREE
FORCES LEGIS ECO/TAC LEGIT COERCE PEACE...JURID
CONCPT UN COLD/WAR 20. PAGE 24 E0482
B57

COOPER F.E.,THE LAWYER AND ADMINISTRATIVE AGENCIES. CONSULT
USA+45 CLIENT LAW PROB/SOLV CT/SYS PERSON ROLE. ADMIN
PAGE 25 E0500 ADJUD
DELIB/GP
B57

DIVINE R.A.,AMERICAN IMMIGRATION POLICY, 1924-52. GEOG
USA+45 USA-45 VOL/ASSN DELIB/GP ADJUD WAR ADJUST HABITAT
DISCRIM...POLICY JURID 20 DEPRESSION MIGRATION. LEGIS
PAGE 32 E0630 CONTROL
B57

HISS A.,IN THE COURT OF PUBLIC OPINION. USA+45 CRIME
DELIB/GP LEGIS LEGIT CT/SYS ATTIT 20 DEPT/STATE MARXISM
NIXON/RM HUAC HISS/ALGER. PAGE 53 E1053 BIOG
ADJUD
B57

JENKS C.W.,THE INTERNATIONAL PROTECTION OF TRADE LABOR
UNION FREEDOM. FUT WOR+45 WOR-45 VOL/ASSN DELIB/GP INT/ORG
CT/SYS REGION ROUTINE...JURID METH/CNCPT RECORD
B57

TIME/SEQ CHARTS ILO WORK OAS 20. PAGE 58 E1153

JENNINGS I.,PARLIAMENT. UK FINAN INDUS POL/PAR PARL/PROC
DELIB/GP EX/STRUC PLAN CONTROL...MAJORIT JURID TOP/EX
PARLIAMENT. PAGE 58 E1163 MGT
LEGIS
B57

US COMMISSION GOVT SECURITY,RECOMMENDATIONS; AREA: LEGIS
LEGISLATION. USA+45 USA-45 DELIB/GP PLAN TEC/DEV SANCTION
CIVMIL/REL ORD/FREE...POLICY DECISION 20 PRIVACY. CRIME
PAGE 99 E1982 CONTROL
B57

US SENATE COMM ON JUDICIARY,HEARING BEFORE LEGIS
SUBCOMMITTEE ON COMMITTEE OF JUDICIARY, UNITED CONSTN
STATES SENATE: S. J. RES. 3. USA+45 NAT/G CONSULT CONFER
DELIB/GP DIPLOM ADJUD LOBBY REPRESENT 20 CONGRESS AGREE
TREATY. PAGE 102 E2040
B57

US SENATE COMM ON JUDICIARY,LIMITATION OF APPELLATE CT/SYS
JURISDICTION OF THE SUPREME COURT. USA+45 LAW NAT/G ADJUD
DELIB/GP PLAN ADMIN CONTROL PWR...DECISION 20 POLICY
CONGRESS SUPREME/CT. PAGE 102 E2041 GOV/REL
B57

BUREAU OF NATIONAL AFFAIRS,THE MCCLELLAN COMMITTEE DELIB/GP
HEARINGS - 1957. USA+45 LEGIS CONTROL CRIME CONFER
...CHARTS 20 CONGRESS AFL/CIO MCCLELLN/J. PAGE 17 LABOR
E0336 MGT
B58

CHARLES R.,LA JUSTICE EN FRANCE. FRANCE LAW CONSTN JURID
DELIB/GP CRIME 20. PAGE 21 E0422 ADMIN
CT/SYS
ADJUD
B58

MARTIN L.J.,INTERNATIONAL PROPAGANDA: ITS LEGAL AND EDU/PROP
DIPLOMATIC CONTROL. UK USA+45 USSR CONSULT DELIB/GP DIPLOM
DOMIN CONTROL 20. PAGE 69 E1373 INT/LAW
ATTIT
B58

SHARMA M.P.,PUBLIC ADMINISTRATION IN THEORY AND MGT
PRACTICE. INDIA UK USA+45 USA-45 EX/STRUC ADJUD ADMIN
...POLICY CONCPT NAT/COMP 20. PAGE 90 E1813 DELIB/GP
JURID
B58

SPITZ D.,DEMOCRACY AND THE CHALLENGE OF POWER. FUT NAT/G
USA+45 USA-45 LAW SOCIETY STRUCT LOC/G POL/PAR PWR
PROVS DELIB/GP EX/STRUC LEGIS TOP/EX ACT/RES CREATE
DOMIN EDU/PROP LEGIT ADJUD ADMIN ATTIT DRIVE MORAL
ORD/FREE TOT/POP. PAGE 93 E1862
B58

STONE J.,AGGRESSION AND WORLD ORDER: A CRITIQUE OF ORD/FREE
UNITED NATIONS THEORIES OF AGGRESSION. LAW CONSTN INT/ORG
DELIB/GP PROB/SOLV BAL/PWR DIPLOM DEBATE ADJUD WAR
CRIME PWR...POLICY IDEA/COMP 20 UN SUEZ LEAGUE/NAT. CONCPT
PAGE 94 E1879
B58

STRONG C.F.,MODERN POLITICAL CONSTITUTIONS. LAW CONSTN
CHIEF DELIB/GP EX/STRUC LEGIS ADJUD CHOOSE FEDERAL IDEA/COMP
POPULISM...CONCPT BIBLIOG 20 UN. PAGE 94 E1887 NAT/G
B58

US CONGRESS,FREEDOM OF INFORMATION AND SECRECY IN CHIEF
GOVERNMENT (2 VOLS.). USA+45 DELIB/GP EX/STRUC PRIVIL
EDU/PROP PWR 20 CONGRESS PRESIDENT. PAGE 99 E1988 CONSTN
LAW
B58

WHITNEY S.N.,ANTITRUST POLICIES: AMERICAN INDUS
EXPERIENCE IN TWENTY INDUSTRIES. USA+45 USA-45 LAW CONTROL
DELIB/GP LEGIS ADJUD CT/SYS GOV/REL ATTIT...ANTHOL LG/CO
20 MONOPOLY CASEBOOK. PAGE 106 E2119 MARKET
B58

BEVAN W.,"JURY BEHAVIOR AS A FUNCTION OF THE PERSON
PRESTIGE OF THE FOREMAN AND THE NATURE OF HIS EDU/PROP
LEADERSHIP" (BMR)" DELIB/GP DOMIN ADJUD LEAD DECISION
PERS/REL ATTIT...PSY STAT INT QU CHARTS SOC/EXP 20 CT/SYS
JURY. PAGE 11 E0221
L58

INT. SOC. SCI. BULL.,"TECHNIQUES OF MEDIATION AND VOL/ASSN
CONCILIATION." EUR+WWI USA+45 SOCIETY INDUS INT/ORG DELIB/GP
LABOR NAT/G LEGIS DIPLOM EDU/PROP CHOOSE ATTIT INT/LAW
RIGID/FLEX...JURID CONCPT GEN/LAWS 20. PAGE 57
E1129
L58

S58
MCDOUGAL M.S.,"PERSPECTIVES FOR A LAW OF OUTER INT/ORG
SPACE." FUT WOR+45 AIR CONSULT DELIB/GP TEC/DEV SPACE
CT/SYS ORD/FREE...POLICY JURID 20 UN. PAGE 70 E1404 INT/LAW

S58
RIKER W.H.,"THE PARADOX OF VOTING AND CONGRESSIONAL PARL/PROC
RULES FOR VOTING ON AMENDMENTS." LAW DELIB/GP DECISION
EX/STRUC PROB/SOLV CONFER DEBATE EFFICIENCY ATTIT LEGIS
HOUSE/REP CONGRESS SENATE. PAGE 85 E1700 RATIONAL

C58
BRODEN T.F.,"CONGRESSIONAL COMMITTEE REPORTS: THEIR LAW
ROLE AND HISTORY" USA-45 PARL/PROC ROLE. PAGE 15 DELIB/GP
E0303 LEGIS
DEBATE

N58
US HOUSE COMM FOREIGN AFFAIRS,HEARINGS ON DRAFT LEGIS
LEGISLATION TO AMEND FURTHER THE MUTUAL SECURITY DELIB/GP
ACT OF 1954 (PAMPHLET). USA+45 CONSULT FORCES CONFER
BUDGET DIPLOM DETER COST ORD/FREE...JURID 20 WEAPON
DEPT/DEFEN UN DEPT/STATE. PAGE 100 E2002

B59
BECK C.,CONTEMPT OF CONGRESS: A STUDY OF THE LEGIS
PROSECUTIONS INITIATED BY THE COMMITTEE ON UN- DELIB/GP
AMERICAN ACTIVITIES. USA+45 CONSTN DEBATE EXEC. PWR
PAGE 9 E0170 ADJUD

B59
COMM. STUDY ORGAN. PEACE,ORGANIZING PEACE IN THE INT/ORG
NUCLEAR AGE. FUT CONSULT DELIB/GP DOMIN ADJUD ACT/RES
ROUTINE COERCE ORD/FREE...TECHNIC INT/LAW JURID NUC/PWR
NEW/IDEA UN COLD/WAR 20. PAGE 24 E0483

B59
DASH S.,THE EAVESDROPPERS. USA+45 DELIB/GP TEC/DEV CRIME
ORD/FREE...POLICY CRIMLGY JURID 20 PRIVACY. PAGE 29 CONTROL
E0569 ACT/RES
LAW

B59
DAVIS K.C.,ADMINISTRATIVE LAW TEXT. USA+45 NAT/G ADJUD
DELIB/GP EX/STRUC CONTROL ORD/FREE...T 20 ADMIN
SUPREME/CT. PAGE 29 E0577 JURID
CT/SYS

B59
DESMITH S.A.,JUDICIAL REVIEW OF ADMINISTRATIVE ADJUD
ACTION. UK LOC/G CONSULT DELIB/GP ADMIN PWR NAT/G
...DECISION JURID 20 ENGLSH/LAW. PAGE 31 E0609 PROB/SOLV
CT/SYS

B59
GINZBURG B.,REDEDICATION TO FREEDOM. DELIB/GP LEGIS JURID
ATTIT MARXISM 20 SUPREME/CT CON/INTERP HUAC AMEND/I ORD/FREE
FBI. PAGE 44 E0871 CONSTN
NAT/G

B59
GREENSPAN M.,THE MODERN LAW OF LAND WARFARE. WOR+45 ADJUD
INT/ORG NAT/G DELIB/GP FORCES ATTIT...POLICY PWR
HYPO/EXP STERTYP 20. PAGE 46 E0911 WAR

B59
HARVARD UNIVERSITY LAW SCHOOL,INTERNATIONAL NUC/PWR
PROBLEMS OF FINANCIAL PROTECTION AGAINST NUCLEAR ADJUD
RISK. WOR+45 NAT/G DELIB/GP PROB/SOLV DIPLOM INDUS
CONTROL ATTIT...POLICY INT/LAW MATH 20. PAGE 51 FINAN
E1009

B59
MOOS M.,THE CAMPUS AND THE STATE. LAW FINAN EDU/PROP
DELIB/GP LEGIS EXEC LOBBY GP/REL PWR...POLICY ACADEM
BIBLIOG. PAGE 74 E1489 PROVS
CONTROL

B59
REIFF H.,THE UNITED STATES AND THE TREATY LAW OF ADJUD
THE SEA. USA+45 USA-45 SEA SOCIETY INT/ORG CONSULT INT/LAW
DELIB/GP LEGIS DIPLOM LEGIT ATTIT ORD/FREE PWR
WEALTH...GEOG JURID TOT/POP 20 TREATY. PAGE 84
E1681

B59
SIMPSON J.L.,INTERNATIONAL ARBITRATION: LAW AND INT/LAW
PRACTICE. WOR+45 WOR-45 INT/ORG DELIB/GP ADJUD DIPLOM
PEACE MORAL ORD/FREE...METH 18/20. PAGE 91 E1829 CT/SYS
CONSULT

B59
US CONGRESS JT ATOM ENRGY COMM,SELECTED MATERIALS NAT/G
ON FEDERAL-STATE COOPERATION IN THE ATOMIC ENERGY NUC/PWR
FIELD. USA+45 LAW LOC/G PROVS CONSULT LEGIS ADJUD GOV/REL
...POLICY BIBLIOG 20 AEC. PAGE 99 E1991 DELIB/GP

B59
US SENATE COMM ON JUDICIARY,EXECUTIVE PRIVILEGE. CHIEF
USA+45 DELIB/GP CONTROL KNOWL PWR 20 CONGRESS PRIVIL
PRESIDENT. PAGE 102 E2042 CONSTN
LAW

B59
WILDNER H.,DIE TECHNIK DER DIPLOMATIE. TOP/EX ROLE DIPLOM
ORD/FREE...INT/LAW JURID IDEA/COMP NAT/COMP 20. POLICY
PAGE 106 E2122 DELIB/GP
NAT/G

L59
OBERER W.E.,"VOLUNTARY IMPARTIAL REVIEW OF LABOR: LABOR
SOME REFLECTIONS." DELIB/GP LEGIS PROB/SOLV ADJUD LAW
CONTROL COERCE PWR PLURISM POLICY. PAGE 78 E1570 PARTIC
INGP/REL

S59
MASON A.T.,"THE SUPREME COURT: TEMPLE AND FORUM" CT/SYS
(BMR)" USA+45 USA-45 CONSTN DELIB/GP RACE/REL JURID
MAJORITY ORD/FREE...DECISION SOC/INTEG 19/20 PWR
SUPREME/CT WARRN/EARL CIV/RIGHTS. PAGE 69 E1377 ATTIT

S59
POTTER P.B.,"OBSTACLES AND ALTERNATIVES TO INT/ORG
INTERNATIONAL LAW." WOR+45 NAT/G VOL/ASSN DELIB/GP LAW
BAL/PWR DOMIN ROUTINE...JURID VAL/FREE 20. PAGE 81 DIPLOM
E1632 INT/LAW

B60
CARPER E.T.,THE DEFENSE APPROPRIATIONS RIDER GOV/REL
(PAMPHLET). USA+45 CONSTN CHIEF DELIB/GP LEGIS ADJUD
BUDGET LOBBY CIVMIL/REL...POLICY 20 CONGRESS LAW
EISNHWR/DD DEPT/DEFEN PRESIDENT BOSTON. PAGE 20 CONTROL
E0390

B60
ENGEL J.,THE SECURITY OF THE FREE WORLD. USSR COM
WOR+45 STRATA STRUCT ECO/DEV ECO/UNDEV INT/ORG TREND
DELIB/GP FORCES DOMIN LEGIT ADJUD EXEC ARMS/CONT DIPLOM
COERCE...POLICY CONCPT NEW/IDEA TIME/SEQ GEN/LAWS
COLD/WAR WORK UN 20 NATO. PAGE 35 E0689

B60
FELLMAN D.,THE SUPREME COURT AND EDUCATION. ACADEM CT/SYS
NAT/G PROVS DELIB/GP ADJUD ORD/FREE...POLICY JURID SECT
WORSHIP 20 SUPREME/CT NEGRO CHURCH/STA. PAGE 37 RACE/REL
E0731 SCHOOL

B60
JENKS C.W.,HUMAN RIGHTS AND INTERNATIONAL LABOR CONCPT
STANDARDS. WOR+45 CONSTN LABOR VOL/ASSN DELIB/GP
ACT/RES EDU/PROP MORAL RESPECT...JURID SOC TREND
GEN/LAWS WORK ILO 20. PAGE 58 E1156

B60
JENNINGS R.,PROGRESS OF INTERNATIONAL LAW. FUT INT/ORG
WOR+45 WOR-45 SOCIETY NAT/G VOL/ASSN DELIB/GP LAW
DIPLOM EDU/PROP LEGIT COERCE ATTIT DRIVE MORAL INT/LAW
ORD/FREE...JURID CONCPT OBS TIME/SEQ TREND
GEN/LAWS. PAGE 58 E1164

B60
SCHMIDHAUSER J.R.,THE SUPREME COURT: ITS POLITICS, JUDGE
PERSONALITIES, AND PROCEDURES. LAW DELIB/GP JURID
EX/STRUC TOP/EX ADJUD CT/SYS CHOOSE RATIONAL PWR DECISION
SUPREME/CT. PAGE 88 E1760

B60
SCHUBERT G.,THE PUBLIC INTEREST. USA+45 CONSULT POLICY
PLAN PROB/SOLV ADJUD ADMIN GP/REL PWR ALL/IDEOS 20. DELIB/GP
PAGE 88 E1770 REPRESENT
POL/PAR

B60
SCHUBERT G.A.,CONSTITUTIONAL POLITICS: THE CONSTN
POLITICAL BEHAVIOR OF SUPREME COURT JUSTICES AND CT/SYS
THE CONSTITUTIONAL POLICIES THEY MAKE. LAW ELITES JURID
CHIEF DELIB/GP EX/STRUC LEGIS DISCRIM ORD/FREE PWR DECISION
...POLICY MAJORIT CHARTS SUPREME/CT CONGRESS.
PAGE 89 E1781

B60
US LIBRARY OF CONGRESS,INDEX TO LATIN AMERICAN BIBLIOG/A
LEGISLATION: 1950-1960 (2 VOLS.). NAT/G DELIB/GP LEGIS
ADMIN PARL/PROC 20. PAGE 101 E2019 L/A+17C
JURID

S60
ROURKE F.E.,"ADMINISTRATIVE SECRECY: A LEGIS
CONGRESSIONAL DILEMMA." DELIB/GP CT/SYS ATTIT EXEC
...MAJORIT DECISION JURID. PAGE 86 E1727 ORD/FREE
POLICY

S60

SCHWELB E.,"INTERNATIONAL CONVENTIONS ON HUMAN RIGHTS." FUT WOR+45 LAW CONSTN CULTURE SOCIETY STRUCT VOL/ASSN DELIB/GP PLAN ADJUD SUPEGO LOVE MORAL...SOC CONCPT STAT RECORD HIST/WRIT TREND 20 UN. PAGE 89 E1790
INT/ORG
HUM

B61

AUERBACH C.A.,THE LEGAL PROCESS. USA+45 DELIB/GP JUDGE CONFER ADJUD CONTROL...DECISION 20 SUPREME/CT. PAGE 6 E0116
JURID
ADMIN
LEGIS
CT/SYS

B61

AVERY M.W.,GOVERNMENT OF WASHINGTON STATE. USA+45 MUNIC DELIB/GP EX/STRUC LEGIS GIVE CT/SYS PARTIC REGION EFFICIENCY 20 WASHINGT/G GOVERNOR. PAGE 6 E0121
PROVS
LOC/G
ADMIN
GOV/REL

B61

HAGEN A.,STAAT UND KATHOLISCHE KIRCHE IN WURTTEMBERG IN DEN JAHREN 1848-1862 (2 VOLS.). GERMANY DELIB/GP EDU/PROP MARRIAGE CATHISM 19 CHURCH/STA. PAGE 49 E0975
SECT
PROVS
GP/REL
JURID

B61

LA PONCE J.A.,THE GOVERNMENT OF THE FIFTH REPUBLIC: FRENCH POLITICAL PARTIES AND THE CONSTITUTION. ALGERIA FRANCE LAW NAT/G DELIB/GP LEGIS ECO/TAC MARXISM SOCISM...CHARTS BIBLIOG/A 20 DEGAULLE/C. PAGE 62 E1243
PWR
POL/PAR
CONSTN
CHIEF

B61

MCDOUGAL M.S.,LAW AND MINIMUM WORLD PUBLIC ORDER. WOR+45 SOCIETY NAT/G DELIB/GP EDU/PROP LEGIT ADJUD COERCE ATTIT PERSON...JURID CONCPT RECORD TREND TOT/POP 20. PAGE 70 E1406
INT/ORG
ORD/FREE
INT/LAW

B61

NELSON H.L.,LIBEL IN NEWS OF CONGRESSIONAL INVESTIGATING COMMITTEES. USA+45 LAW PARL/PROC PRIVIL RESPECT HOUSE/REP. PAGE 76 E1532
DELIB/GP
LEGIS
LICENSE
PRESS

B61

POOLEY B.J.,PLANNING AND ZONING IN THE UNITED STATES. USA+45 MUNIC DELIB/GP ACT/RES PROB/SOLV TEC/DEV ADJUD ADMIN REGION 20 ZONING. PAGE 81 E1628
PLAN
LOC/G
PROVS
LAW

B61

ROBERTSON A.H.,THE LAW OF INTERNATIONAL INSTITUTIONS IN EUROPE. EUR+WWI MOD/EUR INT/ORG NAT/G VOL/ASSN DELIB/GP...JURID TIME/SEQ TOT/POP 20 TREATY. PAGE 85 E1704
RIGID/FLEX
ORD/FREE

B61

US CONGRESS,CONSTITUTIONAL RIGHTS OF THE MENTALLY ILL. USA+45 LAW PUB/INST DELIB/GP ADJUD ORD/FREE ...PSY QU 20 CONGRESS. PAGE 99 E1989
HEALTH
CONSTN
JURID
CONFER

B61

US HOUSE COMM ON JUDICIARY,LEGISLATION RELATING TO ORGANIZED CRIME. USA+45 DIST/IND DELIB/GP GAMBLE SANCTION HOUSE/REP. PAGE 100 E2004
LEGIS
CONTROL
CRIME
LAW

B61

WARD R.E.,JAPANESE POLITICAL SCIENCE: A GUIDE TO JAPANESE REFERENCE AND RESEARCH MATERIALS (2ND ED.). LAW CONSTN STRATA NAT/G POL/PAR DELIB/GP LEGIS ADMIN CHOOSE GP/REL...INT/LAW 19/20 CHINJAP. PAGE 105 E2099
BIBLIOG/A
PHIL/SCI

B61

WECHSLER H.,PRINCIPLES, POLITICS AND FUNDAMENTAL LAW: SELECTED ESSAYS. USA+45 USA-45 LAW SOCIETY NAT/G PROVS DELIB/GP EX/STRUC ACT/RES LEGIT PERSON KNOWL PWR...JURID 20 NUREMBERG. PAGE 105 E2106
CT/SYS
CONSTN
INT/LAW

B61

WESTIN A.F.,THE SUPREME COURT: VIEWS FROM INSIDE. USA+45 NAT/G PROF/ORG PROVS DELIB/GP INGP/REL DISCRIM ATTIT...POLICY DECISION JURID ANTHOL 20 SUPREME/CT CONGRESS CIVIL/LIB. PAGE 106 E2114
CT/SYS
LAW
ADJUD
GOV/REL

S61

ABLARD C.D.,"EX PARTE CONTACTS WITH FEDERAL ADMINISTRATIVE AGENCIES." USA+45 CLIENT NAT/G DELIB/GP ADMIN PWR 20. PAGE 2 E0044
EXEC
ADJUD
LOBBY
REPRESENT

S61

ALGER C.F.,"NON-RESOLUTION CONSEQUENCES OF THE UNITED NATIONS AND THEIR EFFECT ON INTERNATIONAL
INT/ORG
DRIVE

CONFLICT." WOR+45 CONSTN ECO/DEV NAT/G CONSULT DELIB/GP TOP/EX ACT/RES PLAN DIPLOM EDU/PROP ROUTINE ATTIT ALL/VALS...INT/LAW TOT/POP UN 20. PAGE 3 E0065
BAL/PWR

S61

SCHUBERT G.,"A PSYCHOMETRIC MODEL OF THE SUPREME COURT." DELIB/GP ADJUD CHOOSE ATTIT...DECISION JURID PSY QUANT STAT HYPO/EXP GEN/METH SUPREME/CT. PAGE 88 E1771
JUDGE
CT/SYS
PERSON
SIMUL

B62

FROMAN L.A. JR.,PEOPLE AND POLITICS: AN ANALYSIS OF THE AMERICAN POLITICAL SYSTEM. USA+45 CHIEF DELIB/GP EX/STRUC LEGIS TOP/EX CT/SYS LOBBY PERS/REL PWR...POLICY DECISION. PAGE 41 E0813
POL/PAR
PROB/SOLV
GOV/REL

B62

GALENSON W.,TRADE UNIONS MONOGRAPH SERIES (A SERIES OF NINE TEXTS). DELIB/GP LEAD PARTIC...DECISION ORG/CHARTS. PAGE 42 E0827
LABOR
INGP/REL
CONSTN
REPRESENT

B62

GANJI M.,INTERNATIONAL PROTECTION OF HUMAN RIGHTS. WOR+45 CONSTN INT/TRADE CT/SYS SANCTION CRIME WAR RACE/REL...CHARTS IDEA/COMP NAT/COMP BIBLIOG 20 TREATY NEGRO LEAGUE/NAT UN CIVIL/LIB. PAGE 42 E0831
ORD/FREE
DISCRIM
LEGIS
DELIB/GP

B62

GROGAN V.,ADMINISTRATIVE TRIBUNALS IN THE PUBLIC SERVICE. IRELAND UK NAT/G CONTROL CT/SYS...JURID GOV/COMP 20. PAGE 48 E0945
ADMIN
LAW
ADJUD
DELIB/GP

B62

HSUEH S.-S.,GOVERNMENT AND ADMINISTRATION OF HONG KONG. CHIEF DELIB/GP LEGIS CT/SYS REPRESENT GOV/REL 20 HONG/KONG CITY/MGT CIVIL/SERV GOVERNOR. PAGE 55 E1106
ADMIN
LOC/G
COLONIAL
EX/STRUC

B62

LAWSON R.,INTERNATIONAL REGIONAL ORGANIZATIONS. WOR+45 NAT/G VOL/ASSN CONSULT LEGIS EDU/PROP LEGIT ADMIN EXEC ROUTINE HEALTH PWR WEALTH...JURID EEC COLD/WAR 20 UN. PAGE 63 E1270
INT/ORG
DELIB/GP
REGION

B62

MARS D.,SUGGESTED LIBRARY IN PUBLIC ADMINISTRATION. FINAN DELIB/GP EX/STRUC WORKER COMPUTER ADJUD ...DECISION PSY SOC METH/COMP 20. PAGE 68 E1368
BIBLIOG
ADMIN
METH
MGT

B62

MCDOUGAL M.S.,THE PUBLIC ORDER OF THE OCEANS. WOR+45 WOR-45 SEA INT/ORG NAT/G CONSULT DELIB/GP DIPLOM LEGIT PEACE RIGID/FLEX...GEOG INT/LAW JURID RECORD TOT/POP 20 TREATY. PAGE 70 E1407
ADJUD
ORD/FREE

B62

MITCHELL G.E.,THE ANGRY BLACK SOUTH. USA+45 LAW CONSTN SCHOOL DELIB/GP EDU/PROP CONTROL SUFF ANOMIE DRIVE...ANTHOL 20 NEGRO CIV/RIGHTS SOUTH/US. PAGE 74 E1473
RACE/REL
DISCRIM
ADJUST
ORD/FREE

B62

NEW YORK STATE LEGISLATURE,REPORT AND DRAFT OF PROPOSED LEGISLATION ON COURT REORGANIZATION. LAW PROVS DELIB/GP CREATE ADJUD 20 NEW/YORK. PAGE 77 E1538
CT/SYS
JURID
MUNIC
LOC/G

B62

SOMMER T.,DEUTSCHLAND UND JAPAN ZWISCHEN DEN MACHTEN. GERMANY DELIB/GP BAL/PWR AGREE COERCE TOTALISM PWR 20 CHINJAP TREATY. PAGE 93 E1856
DIPLOM
WAR
ATTIT

B62

THOMPSON K.W.,AMERICAN DIPLOMACY AND EMERGENT PATTERNS. USA+45 USA-45 WOR+45 WOR-45 LAW DELIB/GP FORCES TOP/EX DIPLOM ATTIT DRIVE RIGID/FLEX ORD/FREE PWR SOVEREIGN...POLICY 20. PAGE 96 E1922
NAT/G
BAL/PWR

B62

US AIR FORCE,THE MILITARY JUSTICE SYSTEM (REV. ED.). USA+45 DELIB/GP...IDEA/COMP 20. PAGE 99 E1978
JURID
FORCES
ADJUD
ORD/FREE

B62

WOETZEL R.K.,THE NURENBERG TRIALS IN INTERNATIONAL LAW. CHRIST-17C MOD/EUR WOR+45 SOCIETY NAT/G DELIB/GP DOMIN LEGIT ROUTINE ATTIT DRIVE PERSON SUPEGO MORAL ORD/FREE...POLICY MAJORIT JURID PSY SOC SELF/OBS RECORD NAZI TOT/POP. PAGE 107 E2138
INT/ORG
ADJUD
WAR

L62

NIZARD L.,"CUBAN QUESTION AND SECURITY COUNCIL." INT/ORG
L/A+17C USA+45 ECO/UNDEV NAT/G POL/PAR DELIB/GP JURID
ECO/TAC PWR...RELATIV OBS TIME/SEQ TREND GEN/LAWS DIPLOM
UN 20 UN. PAGE 77 E1551 CUBA

L62

SPAETH H.J.,"JUDICIAL POWER AS A VARIABLE JUDGE
MOTIVATING SUPREME COURT BEHAVIOR." DELIB/GP ADJUD DECISION
RATIONAL ATTIT PERSON ORD/FREE...CLASSIF STAT PERS/COMP
GEN/METH. PAGE 93 E1860 PSY

L62

STEIN E.,"MR HAMMARSKJOLD, THE CHARTER LAW AND THE CONCPT
FUTURE ROLE OF THE UNITED NATIONS SECRETARY- BIOG
GENERAL." WOR+45 CONSTN INT/ORG DELIB/GP FORCES
TOP/EX BAL/PWR LEGIT RIGID/FLEX PWR
...POLICY JURID OBS STERTYP UN COLD/WAR 20
HAMMARSK/D. PAGE 93 E1869

S62

CRANE R.D.,"SOVIET ATTITUDE TOWARD INTERNATIONAL LAW
SPACE LAW." COM FUT USA+45 USSR AIR CONSTN DELIB/GP ATTIT
DOMIN PWR...JURID TREND TOT/POP 20. PAGE 27 E0543 INT/LAW
SPACE

S62

FENWICK C.G.,"ISSUES AT PUNTA DEL ESTE: NON- INT/ORG
INTERVENTION VS COLLECTIVE SECURITY." L/A+17C CUBA
USA+45 VOL/ASSN DELIB/GP ECO/TAC LEGIT ADJUD REGION
ORD/FREE OAS COLD/WAR 20. PAGE 37 E0738

S62

FINKELSTEIN L.S.,"THE UNITED NATIONS AND INT/ORG
ORGANIZATIONS FOR CONTROL OF ARMAMENT." FUT WOR+45 PWR
VOL/ASSN DELIB/GP TOP/EX CREATE EDU/PROP LEGIT ARMS/CONT
ADJUD NUC/PWR ATTIT RIGID/FLEX ORD/FREE...POLICY
DECISION CONCPT OBS TREND GEN/LAWS TOT/POP
COLD/WAR. PAGE 38 E0752

S62

MANGIN G.,"LES ACCORDS DE COOPERATION EN MATIERE DE INT/ORG
JUSTICE ENTRE LA FRANCE ET LES ETATS AFRICAINS ET LAW
MALGACHE." AFR ISLAM WOR+45 STRUCT ECO/UNDEV NAT/G FRANCE
DELIB/GP PERCEPT ALL/VALS...JURID MGT TIME/SEQ 20.
PAGE 68 E1356

S62

THOMPSON D.,"THE UNITED KINGDOM AND THE TREATY OF ADJUD
ROME." EUR+WWI INT/ORG NAT/G DELIB/GP LEGIS JURID
INT/TRADE RIGID/FLEX...CONCPT EEC PARLIAMENT
CMN/WLTH 20. PAGE 96 E1918

B63

ATTIA G.E.D.,LES FORCES ARMEES DES NATIONS UNIES EN FORCES
COREE ET AU MOYENORIENT. KOREA CONSTN NAT/G INT/LAW
DELIB/GP LEGIS PWR...IDEA/COMP NAT/COMP BIBLIOG UN
SUEZ. PAGE 6 E0114

B63

BADI J.,THE GOVERNMENT OF THE STATE OF ISRAEL: A NAT/G
CRITICAL ACCOUNT OF ITS PARLIAMENT, EXECUTIVE, AND CONSTN
JUDICIARY. ISRAEL ECO/DEV CHIEF DELIB/GP LEGIS EX/STRUC
DIPLOM CT/SYS INGP/REL PEACE ORD/FREE...BIBLIOG 20 POL/PAR
PARLIAMENT ARABS MIGRATION. PAGE 7 E0131

B63

BOWETT D.W.,THE LAW OF INTERNATIONAL INSTITUTIONS. INT/ORG
WOR+45 WOR-45 CONSTN DELIB/GP EX/STRUC JUDGE ADJUD
EDU/PROP LEGIT CT/SYS EXEC ROUTINE RIGID/FLEX DIPLOM
ORD/FREE PWR...JURID CONCPT ORG/CHARTS GEN/METH
LEAGUE/NAT OAS OEEC 20 UN. PAGE 14 E0277

B63

DILLIARD I.,ONE MAN'S STAND FOR FREEDOM: MR. CONSTN
JUSTICE BLACK AND THE BILL OF RIGHTS. USA+45 JURID
POL/PAR SECT DELIB/GP FORCES ADJUD CONTROL WAR JUDGE
DISCRIM MORAL...BIBLIOG 20 NEGRO SUPREME/CT ORD/FREE
BILL/RIGHT BLACK/HL. PAGE 32 E0628

B63

GINZBERG E.,DEMOCRATIC VALUES AND THE RIGHTS OF LABOR
MANAGEMENT. LAW CONSTN REPRESENT GP/REL ROLE PWR MGT
RESPECT POLICY. PAGE 44 E0870 DELIB/GP
ADJUD

B63

LEAGUE WOMEN VOTERS NEW YORK,APPORTIONMENT WORKSHOP APPORT
KIT. USA+45 VOL/ASSN DELIB/GP LEGIS ATTIT ORD/FREE REPRESENT
...METH/COMP 20 SUPREME/CT NEW/YORK. PAGE 64 E1275 PROVS
JURID

B63

LEGISLATIVE REFERENCE SERVICE,DIGEST OF PUBLIC BIBLIOG/A
GENERAL BILLS AND RESOLUTIONS. LAW COM/IND EDU/PROP LEGIS
GOV/REL INGP/REL KNOWL...JURID 20 CONGRESS. PAGE 64 DELIB/GP

E1280

NAT/G

B63

RICHARDS P.G.,PATRONAGE IN BRITISH GOVERNMENT. EX/STRUC
ELITES DELIB/GP TOP/EX PROB/SOLV CONTROL CT/SYS REPRESENT
EXEC PWR. PAGE 84 E1693 POL/PAR
ADMIN

B63

ROBERTSON A.H.,HUMAN RIGHTS IN EUROPE. CONSTN EUR+WWI
SOCIETY INT/ORG NAT/G VOL/ASSN DELIB/GP ACT/RES PERSON
PLAN ADJUD REGION ROUTINE ATTIT LOVE ORD/FREE
RESPECT...JURID SOC CONCPT SOC/EXP UN 20. PAGE 85
E1705

B63

US CONGRESS: SENATE,HEARINGS OF THE COMMITTEE ON LEGIS
THE JUDICIARY. USA+45 CONSTN NAT/G ADMIN GOV/REL 20 LAW
CONGRESS. PAGE 99 E1992 ORD/FREE
DELIB/GP

B63

US SENATE COMM ON JUDICIARY,US PERSONNEL SECURITY PLAN
PRACTICES. USA+45 DELIB/GP ADJUD ADMIN ORD/FREE NAT/G
...CHARTS 20 CONGRESS CIVIL/SERV. PAGE 102 E2049 CONTROL
WORKER

B63

US SENATE COMM ON JUDICIARY,CASTRO'S NETWORK IN THE PRESS
UNITED STATES. CUBA LAW DELIB/GP 20 SENATE MARXISM
CASTRO/F. PAGE 102 E2050 DIPLOM
INSPECT

B63

US SENATE COMM ON JUDICIARY,PACIFICA FOUNDATION. DELIB/GP
USA+45 LAW COM/IND 20 ODEGARD/P BINNS/JJ SCHINDLR/P EDU/PROP
HEALEY/D THOMAS/TK. PAGE 102 E2051 ORD/FREE
ATTIT

L63

ROSE R.,"COMPARATIVE STUDIES IN POLITICAL FINANCE: FINAN
A SYMPOSIUM." ASIA EUR+WWI S/ASIA LAW CULTURE POL/PAR
DELIB/GP LEGIS ACT/RES ECO/TAC EDU/PROP CHOOSE
ATTIT RIGID/FLEX SUPEGO PWR SKILL WEALTH...STAT
ANTHOL VAL/FREE. PAGE 85 E1714

S63

BECHHOEFER B.G.,"UNITED NATIONS PROCEDURES IN CASE INT/ORG
OF VIOLATIONS OF DISARMAMENT AGREEMENTS." COM DELIB/GP
USA+45 USSR LAW CONSTN NAT/G EX/STRUC FORCES LEGIS
BAL/PWR EDU/PROP CT/SYS ARMS/CONT ORD/FREE PWR
...POLICY STERTYP UN VAL/FREE 20. PAGE 9 E0169

S63

GARDNER R.N.,"COOPERATION IN OUTER SPACE." FUT USSR INT/ORG
WOR+45 AIR LAW COM/IND CONSULT DELIB/GP CREATE ACT/RES
KNOWL 20 TREATY. PAGE 42 E0837 PEACE
SPACE

S63

HARNETTY P.,"CANADA, SOUTH AFRICA AND THE AFR
COMMONWEALTH." CANADA SOUTH/AFR LAW INT/ORG ATTIT
VOL/ASSN DELIB/GP LEGIS TOP/EX ECO/TAC LEGIT DRIVE
MORAL...CONCPT CMN/WLTH 20. PAGE 50 E1000

S63

JOUGHIN L.,"ACADEMIC DUE PROCESS." DELIB/GP ADJUD ACADEM
ROUTINE ORD/FREE...POLICY MAJORIT TREND. PAGE 59 LAW
E1175 PROF/ORG
CLIENT

S63

LEPAWSKY A.,"INTERNATIONAL DEVELOPMENT OF RIVER INT/ORG
RESOURCES." CANADA EUR+WWI S/ASIA USA+45 SEA LEGIT DELIB/GP
ADJUD ORD/FREE PWR WEALTH...MGT TIME/SEQ VAL/FREE
MEXIC/AMER 20. PAGE 64 E1287

C63

ATTIA G.E.O.,"LES FORCES ARMEES DES NATIONS UNIES FORCES
EN COREE ET AU MOYENORIENT." KOREA CONSTN DELIB/GP NAT/G
LEGIS PWR...IDEA/COMP NAT/COMP BIBLIOG UN SUEZ. INT/LAW
PAGE 6 E0115

B64

AHLUWALIA K.,THE LEGAL STATUS, PRIVILEGES AND PRIVIL
IMMUNITIES OF SPECIALIZED AGENCIES OF UN AND DIPLOM
CERTAIN OTHER INTERNATIONAL ORGANIZATIONS. WOR+45 INT/ORG
LAW CONSULT DELIB/GP FORCES. PAGE 3 E0055 INT/LAW

B64

BENNETT H.A.,THE COMMISSION AND THE COMMON LAW: A ADJUD
STUDY IN ADMINISTRATIVE ADJUDICATION. LAW ADMIN DELIB/GP
CT/SYS LOBBY SANCTION GOV/REL 20 COMMON/LAW. DIST/IND
PAGE 10 E0188 POLICY

B64
BUREAU OF NAT'L AFFAIRS,THE CIVIL RIGHTS ACT OF 1964. USA+45 LOC/G NAT/G DELIB/GP CONFER DEBATE DISCRIM...JURID 20 CONGRESS SUPREME/CT CIV/RIGHTS. PAGE 17 E0333
LEGIS
RACE/REL
LAW
CONSTN

B64
COHEN M.,LAW AND POLITICS IN SPACE: SPECIFIC AND URGENT PROBLEMS IN THE LAW OF OUTER SPACE. CHINA/COM COM USA+45 USSR WOR+45 COM/IND INT/ORG NAT/G LEGIT NUC/PWR ATTIT BIO/SOC...JURID CONCPT CONGRESS 20 STALIN/J. PAGE 24 E0464
DELIB/GP
LAW
INT/LAW
SPACE

B64
EULAU H.,LAWYERS IN POLITICS: A STUDY IN PROFESSIONAL CONVERGENCE. USA+45 POL/PAR DELIB/GP GP/REL...QU 20. PAGE 35 E0701
PROF/ORG
JURID
LEGIS
ATTIT

B64
GRIFFITH W.E.,THE SINO-SOVIET RIFT. ASIA CHINA/COM COM CUBA USSR YUGOSLAVIA NAT/G POL/PAR VOL/ASSN DELIB/GP FORCES TOP/EX DIPLOM EDU/PROP DRIVE PERSON PWR...TREND 20 TREATY. PAGE 47 E0941
ATTIT
TIME/SEQ
BAL/PWR
SOCISM

B64
GROVES H.E.,THE CONSTITUTION OF MALAYSIA. MALAYSIA POL/PAR CHIEF CONSULT DELIB/GP CT/SYS PARL/PROC CHOOSE FEDERAL ORD/FREE 20. PAGE 48 E0953
CONSTN
NAT/G
LAW

B64
IKLE F.C.,HOW NATIONS NEGOTIATE. COM EUR+WWI USA+45 INTELL INT/ORG VOL/ASSN DELIB/GP ACT/RES CREATE DOMIN EDU/PROP ADJUD ROUTINE ATTIT PERSON ORD/FREE RESPECT SKILL...PSY SOC OBS VAL/FREE. PAGE 56 E1122
NAT/G
PWR
POLICY

B64
KAHNG T.J.,LAW, POLITICS, AND THE SECURITY COUNCIL* AN INQUIRY INTO THE HANDLING OF LEGAL QUESTIONS. LAW CONSTN NAT/G ACT/RES OP/RES CT/SYS TASK PWR ...INT/LAW BIBLIOG UN. PAGE 59 E1180
DELIB/GP
ADJUD
ROUTINE

B64
KEEFE W.J.,THE AMERICAN LEGISLATIVE PROCESS: CONGRESS AND THE STATES. USA+45 LAW POL/PAR DELIB/GP DEBATE ADMIN LOBBY REPRESENT CONGRESS PRESIDENT. PAGE 60 E1191
LEGIS
DECISION
PWR
PROVS

B64
NASA,PROCEEDINGS OF CONFERENCE ON THE LAW OF SPACE AND OF SATELLITE COMMUNICATIONS: CHICAGO 1963. FUT WOR+45 DELIB/GP PROB/SOLV TEC/DEV CONFER ADJUD NUC/PWR...POLICY IDEA/COMP 20 NASA. PAGE 76 E1522
SPACE
COM/IND
LAW
DIPLOM

B64
SCHWELB E.,HUMAN RIGHTS AND THE INTERNATIONAL COMMUNITY. WOR+45 WOR-45 NAT/G SECT DELIB/GP DIPLOM PEACE RESPECT TREATY 20 UN. PAGE 89 E1792
INT/ORG
ORD/FREE
INT/LAW

B64
THANT U.,TOWARD WORLD PEACE. DELIB/GP TEC/DEV EDU/PROP WAR SOVEREIGN...INT/LAW 20 UN MID/EAST. PAGE 96 E1915
DIPLOM
BIOG
PEACE
COERCE

B64
US AIR FORCE ACADEMY ASSEMBLY,OUTER SPACE: FINAL REPORT APRIL 1-4, 1964. FUT USA+45 WOR+45 LAW DELIB/GP CONFER ARMS/CONT WAR PEACE ATTIT MORAL ...ANTHOL 20 NASA. PAGE 99 E1979
SPACE
CIVMIL/REL
NUC/PWR
DIPLOM

B64
US HOUSE COMM ON JUDICIARY,CONGRESSIONAL REDISTRICTING. USA+45 PROVS DELIB/GP 20 CONGRESS. PAGE 100 E2005
APPORT
REPRESENT
LEGIS
LAW

B64
US HOUSE COMM ON JUDICIARY,IMMIGRATION HEARINGS. DELIB/GP STRANGE HABITAT...GEOG JURID 20 CONGRESS MIGRATION. PAGE 100 E2006
NAT/G
POLICY
DIPLOM
NAT/LISM

B64
WAY H.F. JR.,LIBERTY IN THE BALANCE - CURRENT ISSUES IN CIVIL LIBERTIES. USA+45 USA-45 DELIB/GP RACE/REL DISCRIM TOTALISM MARXISM SOCISM...CONCPT 20 CONGRESS SUPREME/CT CIVIL/LIB. PAGE 105 E2104
ORD/FREE
EDU/PROP
NAT/G
JURID

B64
WRIGHT G.,RURAL REVOLUTION IN FRANCE: THE PEASANTRY IN THE TWENTIETH CENTURY. EUR+WWI MOD/EUR LAW CULTURE AGRI POL/PAR DELIB/GP LEGIS ECO/TAC EDU/PROP COERCE CHOOSE ATTIT RIGID/FLEX HEALTH ...STAT CENSUS CHARTS VAL/FREE 20. PAGE 107 E2148
PWR
STRATA
FRANCE
REV

S64
CARNEGIE ENDOWMENT INT. PEACE,"LEGAL QUESTIONS (ISSUES BEFORE THE NINETEENTH GENERAL ASSEMBLY)." WOR+45 CONSTN NAT/G DELIB/GP ADJUD PEACE MORAL ORD/FREE...RECORD UN 20 TREATY. PAGE 20 E0386
INT/ORG
LAW
INT/LAW

S64
DERWINSKI E.J.,"THE COST OF THE INTERNATIONAL COFFEE AGREEMENT." L/A+17C USA+45 WOR+45 ECO/UNDEV NAT/G VOL/ASSN DELIB/GP DIPLOM ECO/TAC FOR/AID LEGIT ATTIT...TIME/SEQ CONGRESS 20 TREATY. PAGE 31 E0608
MARKET
DELIB/GP
INT/TRADE

S64
KHAN M.Z.,"ISLAM AND INTERNATIONAL RELATIONS." FUT WOR+45 LAW CULTURE SOCIETY NAT/G DELIB/GP FORCES EDU/PROP ATTIT PERSON SUPEGO ALL/VALS ...POLICY PSY CONCPT MYTH HIST/WRIT GEN/LAWS. PAGE 61 E1211
ISLAM
INT/ORG
DIPLOM

S64
SKUBISZEWSKI K.,"FORMS OF PARTICIPATION OF INTERNATIONAL ORGANIZATION IN THE LAW MAKING PROCESS." FUT WOR+45 NAT/G DELIB/GP DOMIN LEGIT KNOWL PWR...JURID TREND 20. PAGE 92 E1837
INT/ORG
LAW
INT/LAW

B65
ASSOCIATION BAR OF NYC,RADIO, TELEVISION, AND THE ADMINISTRATION OF JUSTICE: A DOCUMENTED SURVEY OF MATERIALS. USA+45 DELIB/GP FORCES PRESS ADJUD CONTROL CT/SYS CRIME...INT IDEA/COMP BIBLIOG. PAGE 6 E0109
AUD/VIS
ATTIT
ORD/FREE

B65
BELL J.,THE JOHNSON TREATMENT: HOW LYNDON JOHNSON TOOK OVER THE PRESIDENCY AND MADE IT HIS OWN. USA+45 DELIB/GP DIPLOM MURDER CHOOSE PERSON PWR...POLICY OBS INT TIME 20 JOHNSON/LB KENNEDY/JF PRESIDENT CONGRESS. PAGE 10 E0183
INGP/REL
TOP/EX
CONTROL
NAT/G

B65
BRIGGS H.W.,THE INTERNATIONAL LAW COMMISSION. LAW CONSTN LEGIS CREATE ADJUD CT/SYS ROUTINE TASK EFFICIENCY...CLASSIF OBS UN. PAGE 15 E0302
INT/LAW
DELIB/GP

B65
CALIFORNIA LEGISLATURE,COMMITTEE ON ELECTIONS AND REAPPORTIONMENT, FINAL REPORT. USA+45 LAW COMPUTER TEC/DEV CHOOSE JURID. PAGE 19 E0366
DELIB/GP
APPORT
LEGIS
ADJUD

B65
CHARNAY J.P.,LE SUFFRAGE POLITIQUE EN FRANCE; ELECTIONS PARLEMENTAIRES, ELECTION PRESIDENTIELLE, REFERENDUMS. FRANCE CONSTN CHIEF DELIB/GP ECO/TAC EDU/PROP CRIME INGP/REL MORAL ORD/FREE PWR CATHISM 20 PARLIAMENT PRESIDENT. PAGE 22 E0425
CHOOSE
SUFF
NAT/G
LEGIS

B65
CHRIMES S.B.,ENGLISH CONSTITUTIONAL HISTORY (3RD ED.). UK CHIEF CONSULT DELIB/GP LEGIS CT/SYS 15/20 COMMON/LAW PARLIAMENT. PAGE 22 E0435
CONSTN
BAL/PWR
NAT/G

B65
COHN H.J.,THE GOVERNMENT OF THE RHINE PALATINATE IN THE FIFTEENTH CENTURY. GERMANY FINAN LOC/G DELIB/GP LEGIS CT/SYS CHOOSE CATHISM 14/15 PALATINATE. PAGE 24 E0468
PROVS
JURID
GP/REL
ADMIN

B65
FLEMING R.W.,THE LABOR ARBITRATION PROCESS. USA+45 LAW BARGAIN ADJUD ROUTINE SANCTION COST...PREDICT CHARTS TIME 20. PAGE 38 E0763
GP/REL
LABOR
CONSULT
DELIB/GP

B65
FORGAC A.A.,NEW DIPLOMACY AND THE UNITED NATIONS. FRANCE GERMANY UK USSR INT/ORG DELIB/GP EX/STRUC PEACE...INT/LAW CONCPT UN. PAGE 39 E0770
DIPLOM
ETIQUET
NAT/G

B65
INST INTL DES CIVILISATION DIF,THE CONSTITUTIONS AND ADMINISTRATIVE INSTITUTIONS OF THE NEW STATES. AFR ISLAM S/ASIA NAT/G POL/PAR DELIB/GP EX/STRUC CONFER EFFICIENCY NAT/LISM...JURID SOC 20. PAGE 56 E1123
CONSTN
ADMIN
ADJUD
ECO/UNDEV

B65
MARTENS E.,DIE HANNOVERSCHE KIRCHENKOMMISSION. GERMANY LAW INT/ORG PROVS SECT CONFER GP/REL CATHISM 16/20. PAGE 69 E1371
JURID
DELIB/GP
CONSTN
PROF/ORG

B65
NWOGUGU E.I.,THE LEGAL PROBLEMS OF FOREIGN INVESTMENT IN DEVELOPING COUNTRIES. WOR+45 INT/ORG DELIB/GP LEGIS PROB/SOLV INT/TRADE TAX ADJUD
FOR/AID
FINAN
INT/LAW

SANCTION...BIBLIOG 20 TREATY. PAGE 78 E1561   ECO/UNDEV

ON CIVIL LIABILITY FOR NUCLEAR DAMAGE. FUT WOR+45   INT/ORG
ADJUD WAR COST PEACE SOVEREIGN...JURID 20. PAGE 57   DELIB/GP
E1135   NUC/PWR

                                                          B65
SHARMA S.A.,PARLIAMENTARY GOVERNMENT IN INDIA.   NAT/G
INDIA FINAN LOC/G PROVS DELIB/GP PLAN ADMIN CT/SYS   CONSTN
FEDERAL...JURID 20. PAGE 90 E1814   PARL/PROC
                                                          LEGIS

                                                          B66
O'NEILL C.E.,CHURCH AND STATE IN FRENCH COLONIAL   COLONIAL
LOUISIANA: POLICY AND POLITICS TO 1732. PROVS   NAT/G
VOL/ASSN DELIB/GP ADJUD ADMIN GP/REL ATTIT DRIVE   SECT
...POLICY BIBLIOG 17/18 LOUISIANA CHURCH/STA.   PWR
PAGE 78 E1568

                                                          B65
SWISHER C.B.,THE SUPREME COURT IN MODERN ROLE. COM   DELIB/GP
COM/IND NAT/G FORCES LEGIS LOBBY PARTIC RACE/REL 20   ATTIT
SUPREME/CT. PAGE 95 E1901   CT/SYS
                                                          ADJUD

                                                          B66
POLLACK R.S.,THE INDIVIDUAL'S RIGHTS AND   INT/LAW
INTERNATIONAL ORGANIZATION. LAW INT/ORG DELIB/GP   ORD/FREE
SUPEGO...JURID SOC/INTEG 20 TREATY UN. PAGE 81   DIPLOM
E1623   PERSON

                                                          B65
US SENATE COMM ON JUDICIARY,HEARINGS BEFORE   ROUTINE
SUBCOMMITTEE ON ADMINISTRATIVE PRACTICE AND   DELIB/GP
PROCEDURE ABOUT ADMINISTRATIVE PROCEDURE ACT 1965.   ADMIN
USA+45 LEGIS EDU/PROP ADJUD GOV/REL INGP/REL   NAT/G
EFFICIENCY...POLICY INT 20 CONGRESS. PAGE 103 E2055

                                                          B66
THOMPSON J.M.,RUSSIA, BOLSHEVISM, AND THE   DIPLOM
VERSAILLES PEACE. RUSSIA USSR INT/ORG NAT/G   PEACE
DELIB/GP AGREE REV WAR PWR 20 TREATY VERSAILLES   MARXISM
BOLSHEVISM. PAGE 96 E1919

                                                          L65
RUBIN A.P.,"UNITED STATES CONTEMPORARY PRACTICE   LAW
RELATING TO INTERNATIONAL LAW." USA+45 WOR+45   LEGIT
CONSTN INT/ORG NAT/G DELIB/GP EX/STRUC DIPLOM DOMIN   INT/LAW
CT/SYS ROUTINE ORD/FREE...CONCPT COLD/WAR 20.
PAGE 86 E1730

                                                          B66
WASHINGTON S.H.,BIBLIOGRAPHY: LABOR-MANAGEMENT   BIBLIOG
RELATIONS ACT, 1947 AS AMENDED BY LABOR-MANAGEMENT   LAW
REPORTING AND DISCLOSURE ACT, 1959. USA+45 CONSTN   LABOR
INDUS DELIB/GP LEGIS WORKER BARGAIN ECO/TAC ADJUD   MGT
GP/REL NEW/LIB...JURID CONGRESS. PAGE 105 E2100

                                                          S65
AMRAM P.W.,"REPORT ON THE TENTH SESSION OF THE   VOL/ASSN
HAGUE CONFERENCE ON PRIVATE INTERNATIONAL LAW."   DELIB/GP
USA+45 WOR+45 INT/ORG CREATE LEGIT ADJUD ALL/VALS   INT/LAW
...JURID CONCPT METH/CNCPT OBS GEN/METH 20. PAGE 4
E0085

                                                          S66
MATTHEWS D.G.,"ETHIOPIAN OUTLINE: A BIBLIOGRAPHIC   BIBLIOG
RESEARCH GUIDE." ETHIOPIA LAW STRUCT ECO/UNDEV AGRI   NAT/G
LABOR SECT CHIEF DELIB/GP EX/STRUC ADMIN...LING   DIPLOM
ORG/CHARTS 20. PAGE 69 E1384   POL/PAR

                                                          S65
BEVANS C.I.,"GHANA AND UNITED STATES - UNITED   NAT/G
KINGDOM AGREEMENTS." UK USA+45 LAW DELIB/GP   LEGIT
EX/STRUC ORD/FREE...JURID METH/CNCPT GEN/LAWS 20.   GHANA
PAGE 11 E0222   DIPLOM

                                                          C66
BLAISDELL D.C.,"INTERNATIONAL ORGANIZATION." FUT   BIBLIOG
WOR+45 ECO/DEV DELIB/GP FORCES EFFICIENCY PEACE   INT/ORG
ORD/FREE...INT/LAW 20 UN LEAGUE/NAT NATO. PAGE 12   DIPLOM
E0239   ARMS/CONT

                                                          S65
FOX A.B.,"NATO AND CONGRESS." CONSTN DELIB/GP   CONTROL
EX/STRUC FORCES TOP/EX BUDGET NUC/PWR GOV/REL   DIPLOM
...GP/COMP CONGRESS NATO TREATY. PAGE 39 E0779

                                                          N66
CONGRESSIONAL QUARTERLY SERV,HOUSING A NATION   HABITAT
(PAMPHLET). USA+45 LAW STRUCT DIST/IND DELIB/GP   NAT/G
...GEOG CHARTS 20 DEPT/HUD. PAGE 25 E0490   PLAN
                                                          MUNIC

                                                          S65
HAZARD J.N.,"CO-EXISTENCE LAW BOWS OUT." WOR+45 R+D   PROF/ORG
INT/ORG VOL/ASSN CONSULT DELIB/GP ACT/RES CREATE   ADJUD
PEACE KNOWL...JURID CONCPT COLD/WAR VAL/FREE 20.
PAGE 51 E1018

                                                          B67
MCBRIDE J.H.,THE TEST BAN TREATY: MILITARY,   ARMS/CONT
TECHNOLOGICAL, AND POLITICAL IMPLICATIONS. USA+45   DIPLOM
USSR DELIB/GP FORCES LEGIS TEC/DEV BAL/PWR TREATY.   NUC/PWR
PAGE 70 E1399

                                                          B66
AUERBACH J.S.,LABOR AND LIBERTY: THE LA FOLLETTE   DELIB/GP
COMMITTEE AND THE NEW DEAL. USA-45 LAW LEAD RESPECT   LABOR
SOCISM...BIBLIOG 20 CONGRESS BILL/RIGHT LAFOLLET/R   CONSTN
NEW/DEAL. PAGE 6 E0117   ORD/FREE

                                                          B67
US SENATE COMM ON FOREIGN REL,CONSULAR CONVENTION   LEGIS
WITH THE SOVIET UNION. USA+45 USSR DELIB/GP LEAD   LOBBY
REPRESENT ATTIT ORD/FREE CONGRESS TREATY. PAGE 101   DIPLOM
E2031

                                                          B66
CLARK G.,WORLD PEACE THROUGH WORLD LAW: TWO   INT/LAW
ALTERNATIVE PLANS. WOR+45 DELIB/GP FORCES TAX   PEACE
CONFER ADJUD SANCTION ARMS/CONT WAR CHOOSE PRIVIL   PLAN
20 UN COLD/WAR. PAGE 23 E0450   INT/ORG

                                                          B67
US SENATE COMM ON FOREIGN REL,INTER-AMERICAN   LAW
DEVELOPMENT BANK ACT AMENDMENT. L/A+17C USA+45   FINAN
DELIB/GP DIPLOM FOR/AID BAL/PAY...CHARTS SENATE.   INT/ORG
PAGE 102 E2034   ECO/UNDEV

                                                          B66
COUNCIL OF EUROPE,EUROPEAN CONVENTION ON HUMAN   ORD/FREE
RIGHTS - COLLECTED TEXTS (5TH ED.). EUR+WWI DIPLOM   DELIB/GP
ADJUD CT/SYS...INT/LAW 20 ECHR. PAGE 26 E0520   INT/ORG
                                                          JURID

                                                          B67
US SENATE COMM ON FOREIGN REL,FOREIGN ASSISTANCE   FOR/AID
ACT OF 1967. VIETNAM WOR+45 DELIB/GP CONFER CONTROL   LAW
WAR WEAPON BAL/PAY...CENSUS CHARTS SENATE. PAGE 102   DIPLOM
E2036   POLICY

                                                          B66
COUNCIL OF STATE GOVERNMENTS,THE HANDBOOK ON   CRIME
INTERSTATE CRIME CONTROL. USA+45 PUB/INST DELIB/GP   GOV/REL
AGREE AGE/Y 20 INTST/CRIM. PAGE 27 E0524   CONTROL
                                                          JURID

                                                          L67
BAADE H.W.,"THE ACQUIRED RIGHTS OF INTERNATIONAL   INT/ORG
PUBLIC SERVANTS: A CASE STUDY IN RECEPTION OF   WORKER
PUBLIC LAW." WOR+45 DELIB/GP DIPLOM ORD/FREE   ADJUD
...INT/LAW JURID UN. PAGE 7 E0125   LAW

                                                          B66
DOUMA J.,BIBLIOGRAPHY ON THE INTERNATIONAL COURT   BIBLIOG/A
INCLUDING THE PERMANENT COURT, 1918-1964. EUR+WWI   INT/ORG
WOR-45 DELIB/GP WAR PRIVIL...JURID NAT/COMP 20 UN   CT/SYS
LEAGUE/NAT. PAGE 33 E0645   DIPLOM

                                                          L67
CARMICHAEL D.M.,"FORTY YEARS OF WATER POLLUTION   HEALTH
CONTROL IN WISCONSIN: A CASE STUDY." LAW EXTR/IND   CONTROL
INDUS MUNIC DELIB/GP PLAN PROB/SOLV SANCTION   ADMIN
...CENSUS CHARTS 20 WISCONSIN. PAGE 20 E0384   ADJUD

                                                          B66
GHOSH P.K.,THE CONSTITUTION OF INDIA: HOW IT HAS   CONSTN
BEEN FRAMED. INDIA LOC/G DELIB/GP EX/STRUC   NAT/G
PROB/SOLV BUDGET INT/TRADE CT/SYS CHOOSE...LING 20.   LEGIS
PAGE 43 E0854   FEDERAL

                                                          L67
HITCHMAN J.M.,"THE PLATT AMENDMENT REVISITED: A   ATTIT
BIBLIOGRAPHICAL SURVEY." CUBA ACADEM DELIB/GP   DIPLOM
ORD/FREE...HIST/WRIT 20. PAGE 53 E1055   SOVEREIGN
                                                          INT/LAW

                                                          B66
HAYS P.R.,LABOR ARBITRATION: A DISSENTING VIEW.   GP/REL
USA+45 LAW DELIB/GP BARGAIN ADJUD...PREDICT 20.   LABOR
PAGE 51 E1016   CONSULT
                                                          CT/SYS

                                                          S67
"THE STATE OF ZONING ADMINISTRATION IN ILLINOIS: ADMIN
PROCEDURAL REQUIREMENTS OF JUDICIAL INTERVENTION."   CONTROL
USA+45 LAW CONSTN DELIB/GP ADJUD CT/SYS ORD/FREE   HABITAT
ILLINOIS. PAGE 2 E0038   PLAN

                                                          B66
INTL ATOMIC ENERGY AGENCY,INTERNATIONAL CONVENTIONS DIPLOM

S67

ALDRICH W.A.,"THE SUEZ CRISIS." UAR UK USA+45   DIPLOM
DELIB/GP FORCES BAL/PWR INT/TRADE CONFER CONTROL   INT/LAW
COERCE DETER 20. PAGE 3 E0058   COLONIAL

S67

BLUMSTEIN A.,"POLICE TECHNOLOGY." USA+45 DELIB/GP   TEC/DEV
COMPUTER EDU/PROP CRIME COMPUT/IR. PAGE 13 E0253   FORCES
                                                        CRIMLGY
                                                        ADJUD

S67

BRADLEY A.W.,"CONSTITUTION-MAKING IN UGANDA."   NAT/G
UGANDA LAW CHIEF DELIB/GP LEGIS ADMIN EXEC   CREATE
PARL/PROC RACE/REL ORD/FREE...GOV/COMP 20. PAGE 15   CONSTN
E0284   FEDERAL

S67

CUMMINS L.,"THE FORMULATION OF THE "PLATT"   DIPLOM
AMENDMENT." CUBA L/A+17C NAT/G DELIB/GP CONFER   INT/LAW
...POLICY 20. PAGE 28 E0554   LEGIS

S67

EDGEWORTH A.B. JR.,"CIVIL RIGHTS PLUS THREE YEARS: WORKER
BANKS AND THE ANTI-DISCRIMINATION LAW" USA+45   DISCRIM
SOCIETY DELIB/GP RACE/REL EFFICIENCY 20 NEGRO   FINAN
CIV/RIGHTS. PAGE 34 E0675   LAW

S67

GANZ G.,"THE CONTROL OF INDUSTRY BY ADMINISTRATIVE   INDUS
PROCESS." UK DELIB/GP WORKER 20. PAGE 42 E0832   LAW
                                                        ADMIN
                                                        CONTROL

S67

HILL D.G.,"HUMAN RIGHTS LEGISLATION IN ONTARIO."   DELIB/GP
CANADA R+D VOL/ASSN CONSULT INSPECT EDU/PROP ADJUD   ORD/FREE
AGREE TASK GP/REL INGP/REL DISCRIM 20 CIV/RIGHTS   LAW
ONTARIO CIVIL/LIB. PAGE 52 E1045   POLICY

S67

MACLEOD R.M.,"LAW, MEDICINE AND PUBLIC OPINION: THE   LAW
RESISTANCE TO COMPULSORY HEALTH LEGISLATION   HEALTH
1870-1907." UK CONSTN SECT DELIB/GP DEBATE   ATTIT
PARL/PROC GP/REL MORAL 19. PAGE 67 E1344

S67

WILLIG S.H.,"THE CONTROL OVER INTERSTATE   DIST/IND
DISTRIBUTION AND USE OF INVESTIGATIONAL DRUGS (IN   HEALTH
THE UNITED STATES)" USA+45 NAT/G INT/TRADE LICENSE.   CONTROL
PAGE 106 E2124   DELIB/GP

S67

WINES R.,"THE IMPERIAL CIRCLES, PRINCELY DIPLOMACY,   NAT/G
AND IMPERIAL REFORM* 1681-1714." MOD/EUR DELIB/GP   NAT/LISM
BAL/PWR CONFER ADJUD PARL/PROC PARTIC ATTIT PWR   CENTRAL
17/18. PAGE 106 E2132   REGION

S68

DUGARD J.,"THE REVOCATION OF THE MANDATE FOR SOUTH   AFR
WEST AFRICA." SOUTH/AFR WOR+45 STRATA NAT/G   INT/ORG
DELIB/GP DIPLOM ADJUD SANCTION CHOOSE RACE/REL   DISCRIM
...POLICY NAT/COMP 20 AFRICA/SW UN TRUST/TERR   COLONIAL
LEAGUE/NAT. PAGE 33 E0654

B70

BLACKSTONE W.,COMMENTARIES ON THE LAWS OF ENGLAND   LAW
(4 VOLS.) (4TH ED.). UK CHIEF DELIB/GP LEGIS WORKER   JURID
CT/SYS SANCTION CRIME OWN...CRIMLGY 18 ENGLSH/LAW.   ADJUD
PAGE 12 E0238   CONSTN

DEMAND....ECONOMIC DEMAND

B51

INSTITUTE DES RELATIONS INTL,LES ASPECTS   WEAPON
ECONOMIQUES DU REARMEMENT (ETUDE DE L'INSTITUT DES   DEMAND
RELATIONS INTERNATIONALES A BRUXELLES). BELGIUM UK   ECO/TAC
USA+45 EXTR/IND FINAN FORCES WORKER PROB/SOLV   INT/TRADE
DIPLOM PRICE...POLICY 20 TREATY. PAGE 57 E1127

B53

MAJUMDAR B.B.,PROBLEMS OF PUBLIC ADMINISTRATION IN   ECO/UNDEV
INDIA. INDIA INDUS PLAN BUDGET ADJUD CENTRAL DEMAND   GOV/REL
WEALTH...WELF/ST ANTHOL 20 CIVIL/SERV. PAGE 68   ADMIN
E1353   MUNIC

B60

CONANT M.,ANTITRUST IN THE MOTION PICTURE INDUSTRY: PRICE
ECONOMIC AND LEGAL ANALYSIS. USA+45 MARKET ADJUST   CONTROL
DEMAND BIBLIOG. PAGE 24 E0484   LAW
                                                        ART/METH

B63

JACOBS P.,STATE OF UNIONS. USA+45 STRATA TOP/EX   LABOR
GP/REL RACE/REL DEMAND DISCRIM ATTIT PWR 20   ECO/TAC
CONGRESS NEGRO HOFFA/J. PAGE 57 E1145   BARGAIN

DECISION

B65

HABERLER G.,A SURVEY OF INTERNATIONAL TRADE THEORY.   INT/TRADE
CANADA FRANCE GERMANY ECO/TAC TARIFFS AGREE COST   BAL/PAY
DEMAND WEALTH...ECOMETRIC 19/20 MONOPOLY TREATY.   DIPLOM
PAGE 49 E0968   POLICY

B67

CAVES R.,AMERICAN INDUSTRY: STRUCTURE, CONDUCT,   ECO/DEV
PERFORMANCE (2ND ED.). USA+45 MARKET NAT/G ADJUD   INDUS
CONTROL GP/REL DEMAND WEALTH 20. PAGE 21 E0412   POLICY
                                                        ECO/TAC

S67

SCHELLING T.C.,"ECONOMICS AND CRIMINAL ENTERPRISE."   CRIME
LAW FORCES BARGAIN ECO/TAC CONTROL GAMBLE ROUTINE   PROB/SOLV
ADJUST DEMAND INCOME PROFIT CRIMLGY. PAGE 87 E1756   CONCPT

DEMOCRACY....SEE MAJORIT, REPRESENT, CHOOSE, PWR
    POPULISM, NEW/LIB, ET AL.

DEMOCRAT....DEMOCRATIC PARTY (ALL NATIONS)

B62

SILVA R.C.,RUM, RELIGION, AND VOTES: 1928 RE-   POL/PAR
EXAMINED. USA-45 LAW SECT DISCRIM CATHISM...CORREL   CHOOSE
STAT 20 PRESIDENT SMITH/ALF DEMOCRAT. PAGE 91 E1827   GP/COMP
                                                        ATTIT

DEMOGRAPHY....SEE GEOG

DENMARK....SEE ALSO APPROPRIATE TIME/SPACE/CULTURE INDEX

B53

ORFIELD L.B.,THE GROWTH OF SCANDINAVIAN LAW.   JURID
DENMARK ICELAND NORWAY SWEDEN LAW DIPLOM...BIBLIOG   CT/SYS
9/20. PAGE 79 E1581   NAT/G

B57

MEYER P.,ADMINISTRATIVE ORGANIZATION: A COMPARATIVE   ADMIN
STUDY OF THE ORGANIZATION OF PUBLIC ADMINISTRATION.   METH/COMP
DENMARK FRANCE NORWAY SWEDEN UK USA+45 ELITES LOC/G   NAT/G
CONSULT LEGIS ADJUD CONTROL LEAD PWR SKILL   CENTRAL
DECISION. PAGE 72 E1449

B64

HALLER W.,DER SCHWEDISCHE JUSTITIEOMBUDSMAN.   JURID
DENMARK FINLAND NORWAY SWEDEN LEGIS ADJUD CONTROL   PARL/PROC
PERSON ORD/FREE...NAT/COMP 20 OMBUDSMAN. PAGE 50   ADMIN
E0986   CHIEF

B65

SMITH C.,THE OMBUDSMAN: A BIBLIOGRAPHY (PAMPHLET).   BIBLIOG
DENMARK SWEDEN USA+45 LAW LEGIS JUDGE GOV/REL   ADMIN
GP/REL...JURID 20. PAGE 92 E1841   CT/SYS
                                                        ADJUD

B66

AARON T.J.,THE CONTROL OF POLICE DISCRETION: THE   CONTROL
DANISH EXPERIENCE. DENMARK LAW CREATE ADMIN   FORCES
INGP/REL SUPEGO PWR 20 OMBUDSMAN. PAGE 2 E0042   REPRESENT
                                                        PROB/SOLV

DENNING A. E0606

DENVER....DENVER, COLORADO

DEPARTMENT HEADS...SEE EX/STRUC, TOP/EX

DEPORT....DEPORTATION

DEPRESSION....ECONOMIC DEPRESSION

B54

JAMES L.F.,THE SUPREME COURT IN AMERICAN LIFE.   ADJUD
USA+45 USA-45 CONSTN CRIME GP/REL INGP/REL RACE/REL   CT/SYS
CONSEN FEDERAL PERSON ORD/FREE 18/20 SUPREME/CT   JURID
DEPRESSION CIV/RIGHTS CHURCH/STA FREE/SPEE. PAGE 58   DECISION
E1147

B57

DIVINE R.A.,AMERICAN IMMIGRATION POLICY, 1924-52.   GEOG
USA+45 USA-45 VOL/ASSN DELIB/GP ADJUD WAR ADJUST   HABITAT
DISCRIM...POLICY JURID 20 DEPRESSION MIGRATION.   LEGIS
PAGE 32 E0630   CONTROL

B67

COHEN M.R.,LAW AND THE SOCIAL ORDER: ESSAYS IN   JURID
LEGAL PHILOSOPHY. USA-45 CONSULT WORKER ECO/TAC   LABOR
ATTIT WEALTH...POLICY WELF/ST SOC 20 NEW/DEAL   IDEA/COMP
DEPRESSION. PAGE 24 E0467

DEPT/AGRI....U.S. DEPARTMENT OF AGRICULTURE

DEPT/COM....U.S. DEPARTMENT OF COMMERCE

DEPT/DEFEN....U.S. DEPARTMENT OF DEFENSE

N58
US HOUSE COMM FOREIGN AFFAIRS,HEARINGS ON DRAFT   LEGIS
LEGISLATION TO AMEND FURTHER THE MUTUAL SECURITY   DELIB/GP
ACT OF 1954 (PAMPHLET). USA+45 CONSULT FORCES   CONFER
BUDGET DIPLOM DETER COST ORD/FREE...JURID 20   WEAPON
DEPT/DEFEN UN DEPT/STATE. PAGE 100 E2002

B60
CARPER E.T.,THE DEFENSE APPROPRIATIONS RIDER   GOV/REL
(PAMPHLET). USA+45 CONSTN CHIEF DELIB/GP LEGIS   ADJUD
BUDGET LOBBY CIVMIL/REL...POLICY 20 CONGRESS   LAW
EISNHWR/DD DEPT/DEFEN PRESIDENT BOSTON. PAGE 20   CONTROL
E0390

B60
WEBSTER J.A.,A GENERAL STUDY OF THE DEPARTMENT OF   ORD/FREE
DEFENSE INTERNAL SECURITY PROGRAM. USA+45 WORKER   PLAN
TEC/DEV ADJUD CONTROL CT/SYS EXEC GOV/REL COST   ADMIN
...POLICY DECISION MGT 20 DEPT/DEFEN SUPREME/CT.   NAT/G
PAGE 105 E2105

B62
INTERNAT CONGRESS OF JURISTS,EXECUTIVE ACTION AND   JURID
THE RULE OF RULE: REPORTION PROCEEDINGS OF INT'T   EXEC
CONGRESS OF JURISTS--RIO DE JANEIRO, BRAZIL. WOR+45   ORD/FREE
ACADEM CONSULT JUDGE EDU/PROP ADJUD CT/SYS INGP/REL   CONTROL
PERSON DEPT/DEFEN. PAGE 57 E1130

DEPT/HEW....U.S. DEPARTMENT OF HEALTH, EDUCATION,
    AND WELFARE

B67
ELDRIDGE W.B.,NARCOTICS AND THE LAW: A CRITIQUE OF   LAW
THE AMERICAN EXPERIMENT IN NARCOTIC DRUG CONTROL.   INSPECT
PUB/INST ACT/RES PLAN LICENSE GP/REL EFFICIENCY   BIO/SOC
ATTIT HEALTH...CRIMLGY HEAL STAT 20 ABA DEPT/HEW   JURID
NARCO/ACT. PAGE 34 E0679

DEPT/HUD....U.S. DEPARTMENT OF HOUSING AND URBAN DEVELOPMENT

N66
CONGRESSIONAL QUARTERLY SERV,HOUSING A NATION   HABITAT
(PAMPHLET). USA+45 LAW STRUCT DIST/IND DELIB/GP   NAT/G
...GEOG CHARTS 20 DEPT/HUD. PAGE 25 E0490   PLAN
    MUNIC

DEPT/INTER....U.S. DEPARTMENT OF THE INTERIOR

DEPT/JUST....U.S. DEPARTMENT OF JUSTICE

DEPT/LABOR....U.S. DEPARTMENT OF LABOR AND INDUSTRY

B55
BLOOM G.F.,ECONOMICS OF LABOR RELATIONS. USA+45 LAW   ECO/DEV
CONSULT WORKER CAP/ISM PAY ADJUD CONTROL EFFICIENCY   ECO/TAC
ORD/FREE...CHARTS 19/20 AFL/CIO NLRB DEPT/LABOR.   LABOR
PAGE 13 E0249   GOV/REL

DEPT/STATE....U.S. DEPARTMENT OF STATE

B51
PUSEY M.J.,CHARLES EVANS HUGHES (2 VOLS.). LAW   BIOG
CONSTN NAT/G POL/PAR DIPLOM LEGIT WAR CHOOSE   TOP/EX
PERS/REL DRIVE HEREDITY 19/20 DEPT/STATE LEAGUE/NAT   ADJUD
SUPREME/CT HUGHES/CE WWI. PAGE 83 E1663   PERSON

B57
HISS A.,IN THE COURT OF PUBLIC OPINION. USA+45   CRIME
DELIB/GP LEGIS LEGIT CT/SYS ATTIT 20 DEPT/STATE   MARXISM
NIXON/RM HUAC HISS/ALGER. PAGE 53 E1053   BIOG
    ADJUD

N58
US HOUSE COMM FOREIGN AFFAIRS,HEARINGS ON DRAFT   LEGIS
LEGISLATION TO AMEND FURTHER THE MUTUAL SECURITY   DELIB/GP
ACT OF 1954 (PAMPHLET). USA+45 CONSULT FORCES   CONFER
BUDGET DIPLOM DETER COST ORD/FREE...JURID 20   WEAPON
DEPT/DEFEN UN DEPT/STATE. PAGE 100 E2002

S67
WILSON G.D.,"CRIMINAL SANCTIONS AGAINST PASSPORT   LAW
AREA-RESTRICTION VIOLATIONS." USA+45 ADJUD CRIME   SANCTION
GOV/REL DEPT/STATE CONGRESS. PAGE 106 E2127   LICENSE
    POLICY

DEPT/TREAS....U.S. DEPARTMENT OF THE TREASURY

N19
ARNOW K.,SELF-INSURANCE IN THE TREASURY (PAMPHLET).   ADMIN
USA+45 LAW RIGID/FLEX...POLICY METH/COMP 20   PLAN
DEPT/TREAS. PAGE 5 E0104   EFFICIENCY
    NAT/G

DERGE D.R. E0607

DERWINSKI E.J. E0608

DESCARTE/R....RENE DESCARTES

DESEGREGATION....SEE NEGRO, SOUTH/US, RACE/REL, SOC/INTEG,
    CIV/RIGHTS, DISCRIM, MISCEGEN, ISOLAT, SCHOOL, STRANGE

DESMITH S.A. E0609

DESSALIN/J....JEAN-JACQUES DESSALINES

DESTALIN....DE-STALINIZATION

DETER....DETERRENCE; SEE ALSO PWR, PLAN

N19
MEZERIK A.G.,ATOM TESTS AND RADIATION HAZARDS   NUC/PWR
(PAMPHLET). WOR+45 INT/ORG DIPLOM DETER 20 UN   ARMS/CONT
TREATY. PAGE 73 E1452   CONFER
    HEALTH

N19
MEZERIK AG,OUTER SPACE: UN, US, USSR (PAMPHLET).   SPACE
USSR DELIB/GP FORCES DETER NUC/PWR SOVEREIGN   CONTROL
...POLICY 20 UN TREATY. PAGE 73 E1453   DIPLOM
    INT/ORG

B43
MICAUD C.A.,THE FRENCH RIGHT AND NAZI GERMANY   DIPLOM
1933-1939: A STUDY OF PUBLIC OPINION. GERMANY UK   AGREE
USSR POL/PAR ARMS/CONT DETER PEACE
RIGID/FLEX PWR MARXISM...FASCIST TREND 20
LEAGUE/NAT TREATY. PAGE 73 E1454

B49
KAFKA G.,FREIHEIT UND ANARCHIE. SECT COERCE DETER   CONCPT
WAR ATTIT...IDEA/COMP 20 NATO. PAGE 59 E1179   ORD/FREE
    JURID
    INT/ORG

B50
JIMENEZ E.,VOTING AND HANDLING OF DISPUTES IN THE   DELIB/GP
SECURITY COUNCIL. WOR+45 CONSTN INT/ORG DIPLOM   ROUTINE
LEGIT DETER CHOOSE MORAL ORD/FREE PWR...JURID
TIME/SEQ COLD/WAR UN 20. PAGE 59 E1168

L51
KELSEN H.,"RECENT TRENDS IN THE LAW OF THE UNITED   INT/ORG
NATIONS." KOREA WOR+45 CONSTN LEGIS DIPLOM LEGIT   LAW
DETER WAR RIGID/FLEX HEALTH ORD/FREE RESPECT   INT/LAW
...JURID CON/ANAL UN VAL/FREE 20 NATO. PAGE 60
E1199

B52
LIPPMANN W.,ISOLATION AND ALLIANCES: AN AMERICAN   DIPLOM
SPEAKS TO THE BRITISH. USA+45 USA-45 INT/ORG AGREE   SOVEREIGN
COERCE DETER WAR PEACE MORAL 20 TREATY INTERVENT.   COLONIAL
PAGE 65 E1301   ATTIT

B56
ESTEP R.,AN AIR POWER BIBLIOGRAPHY. USA+45 TEC/DEV   BIBLIOG/A
BUDGET DIPLOM EDU/PROP DETER CIVMIL/REL...DECISION   FORCES
INT/LAW 20. PAGE 35 E0698   WEAPON
    PLAN

B57
SINEY M.C.,THE ALLIED BLOCKADE OF GERMANY: DETER
1914-1916. EUR+WWI GERMANY MOD/EUR USA-45 DIPLOM   INT/TRADE
CONTROL NEUTRAL PWR 20. PAGE 91 E1832   INT/LAW
    WAR

N58
US HOUSE COMM FOREIGN AFFAIRS,HEARINGS ON DRAFT   LEGIS
LEGISLATION TO AMEND FURTHER THE MUTUAL SECURITY   DELIB/GP
ACT OF 1954 (PAMPHLET). USA+45 CONSULT FORCES   CONFER
BUDGET DIPLOM DETER COST ORD/FREE...JURID 20   WEAPON
DEPT/DEFEN UN DEPT/STATE. PAGE 100 E2002

S59
SOHN L.B.,"THE DEFINITION OF AGGRESSION." FUT LAW   INT/ORG
FORCES LEGIT ADJUD ROUTINE COERCE ORD/FREE PWR   CT/SYS
...MAJORIT JURID QUANT COLD/WAR 20. PAGE 92 E1855   DETER
    SOVEREIGN

B60
CLARK G.,WORLD PEACE THROUGH WORLD LAW. FUT WOR+45   INT/ORG
CONSULT FORCES ACT/RES CREATE PLAN ADMIN ROUTINE   LAW
ARMS/CONT DETER ATTIT PWR...JURID VAL/FREE UNESCO   PEACE
20 UN. PAGE 23 E0449   INT/LAW

S60
O'BRIEN W.,"THE ROLE OF FORCE IN THE INTERNATIONAL   INT/ORG
JURIDICAL ORDER." WOR+45 NAT/G FORCES DOMIN ADJUD   COERCE
ARMS/CONT DETER NUC/PWR WAR ATTIT PWR...CATH
INT/LAW JURID CONCPT TREND STERTYP GEN/LAWS 20.
PAGE 78 E1564

MACHOWSKI K.,"SELECTED PROBLEMS OF NATIONAL
SOVEREIGNTY WITH REFERENCE TO THE LAW OF OUTER
SPACE." FUT WOR+45 AIR LAW INTELL SOCIETY ECO/DEV
PLAN EDU/PROP DETER DRIVE PERCEPT SOVEREIGN
...POLICY INT/LAW OBS TREND TOT/POP 20. PAGE 67
E1339

S61
UNIV
ACT/RES
NUC/PWR
SPACE

FALK R.A.,"THE REALITY OF INTERNATIONAL LAW."
WOR+45 NAT/G LEGIT COERCE DETER WAR MORAL ORD/FREE
PWR SOVEREIGN...JURID CONCPT VAL/FREE COLD/WAR 20.
PAGE 36 E0714

S62
INT/ORG
ADJUD
NUC/PWR
INT/LAW

FALK R.A.,LAW, MORALITY, AND WAR IN THE
CONTEMPORARY WORLD. WOR+45 LAW INT/ORG EX/STRUC
FORCES EDU/PROP LEGIT DETER NUC/PWR MORAL ORD/FREE
...JURID TOT/POP 20. PAGE 36 E0715

B63
ADJUD
ARMS/CONT
PEACE
INT/LAW

PACHTER H.M.,COLLISION COURSE; THE CUBAN MISSILE
CRISIS AND COEXISTENCE. CUBA USA+45 DIPLOM
ARMS/CONT PEACE MARXISM...DECISION INT/LAW 20
COLD/WAR KHRUSH/N KENNEDY/JF CASTRO/F. PAGE 79
E1587

B63
WAR
BAL/PWR
NUC/PWR
DETER

MEYROWITZ H.,"LES JURISTES DEVANT L'ARME NUCLAIRE."
FUT WOR+45 INTELL SOCIETY BAL/PWR DETER WAR...JURID
CONCPT 20. PAGE 72 E1451

S63
ACT/RES
ADJUD
INT/LAW
NUC/PWR

FULBRIGHT J.W.,OLD MYTHS AND NEW REALITIES. USA+45
USSR LEGIS INT/TRADE DETER ATTIT...POLICY 20
COLD/WAR TREATY. PAGE 41 E0818

B64
DIPLOM
INT/ORG
ORD/FREE

HEKHUIS D.J.,INTERNATIONAL STABILITY: MILITARY,
ECONOMIC AND POLITICAL DIMENSIONS. FUT WOR+45 LAW
ECO/UNDEV INT/ORG NAT/G VOL/ASSN FORCES ACT/RES
BAL/PWR PWR WEALTH...STAT UN 20. PAGE 51 E1024

B64
TEC/DEV
DETER
REGION

BERKOWITZ M.,AMERICAN NATIONAL SECURITY: A READER
IN THEORY AND POLICY. USA+45 INT/ORG FORCES BAL/PWR
DIPLOM ECO/TAC DETER PWR...INT/LAW ANTHOL BIBLIOG
20 UN. PAGE 11 E0203

B65
ORD/FREE
WAR
ARMS/CONT
POLICY

BROWNLIE I.,"SOME LEGAL ASPECTS OF THE USE OF
NUCLEAR WEAPONS." UK NEUTRAL DETER UN TREATY.
PAGE 16 E0317

S65
LAW
NUC/PWR
WAR
INT/LAW

JACOBSON H.K.,DIPLOMATS, SCIENTISTS, AND
POLITICIANS* THE UNITED STATES AND THE NUCLEAR TEST
BAN NEGOTIATIONS. USA+45 USSR ACT/RES PLAN CONFER
DETER NUC/PWR CONSEN ORD/FREE...INT TREATY. PAGE 57
E1146

B66
DIPLOM
ARMS/CONT
TECHRACY
INT/ORG

SALTER L.M.,RESOLUTION OF INTERNATIONAL CONFLICT.
USA+45 INT/ORG SECT DIPLOM ECO/TAC FOR/AID DETER
NUC/PWR WAR 20. PAGE 87 E1743

B66
PROB/SOLV
PEACE
INT/LAW
POLICY

HOLSTI K.J.,INTERNATIONAL POLITICS* A FRAMEWORK FOR
ANALYSIS. WOR+45 WOR-45 NAT/G EDU/PROP DETER WAR
WEAPON PWR BIBLIOG. PAGE 55 E1090

B67
DIPLOM
BARGAIN
POLICY
INT/LAW

US DEPARTMENT OF STATE,TREATIES IN FORCE. USA+45
WOR+45 AGREE WAR PEACE 20 TREATY. PAGE 100 E1999

B67
BIBLIOG
DIPLOM
INT/ORG
DETER

ALDRICH W.A.,"THE SUEZ CRISIS." UAR UK USA+45
DELIB/GP FORCES BAL/PWR INT/TRADE CONFER CONTROL
COERCE DETER 20. PAGE 3 E0058

S67
DIPLOM
INT/LAW
COLONIAL

CHAMBLISS W.J.,"TYPES OF DEVIANCE AND THE
EFFECTIVENESS OF LEGAL SANCTIONS" SOCIETY PROB/SOLV
ADJUD CONTROL DETER. PAGE 21 E0417

S67
CRIME
SANCTION
EFFICIENCY
LAW

GREGG R.W.,INTERNATIONAL ORGANIZATION IN THE
WESTERN HEMISPHERE. L/A+17C USA+45 CULTURE PLAN

B68
INT/ORG
DIPLOM

DOMIN AGREE CONTROL DETER PWR...GEOG 20 OAS TREATY. ECO/UNDEV
PAGE 46 E0913

HULL R.H.,LAW AND VIETNAM. COM VIETNAM CONSTN
INT/ORG FORCES DIPLOM AGREE COERCE DETER WEAPON
PEACE ATTIT 20 UN TREATY. PAGE 56 E1113

B68
POLICY
LAW
WAR
INT/LAW

DETERRENCE....SEE DETER

DETROIT....DETROIT, MICHIGAN

KEFAUVER E.,CRIME IN AMERICA. USA+45 USA-45 MUNIC
NEIGH DELIB/GP TRIBUTE GAMBLE LOBBY SANCTION
...AUD/VIS 20 CAPONE/AL MAFIA MIAMI CHICAGO
DETROIT. PAGE 60 E1194

B51
ELITES
CRIME
PWR
FORCES

DETTER I. E0610

DEUTSCH E.P. E0611

DEUTSCHE BIBLIOTH FRANKF A M E0612

DEUTSCHE BUCHEREI E0613,E0614,E0615

DEUTSCHE GESELLS. VOELKERRECHT E0616

DEV/ASSIST....DEVELOPMENT AND ASSISTANCE COMMITTEE

DEVELOPMENT....SEE CREATE+ECO/UNDEV

DEVELOPMENT AND ASSISTANCE COMMITTEE....SEE DEV/ASSIST

DEVELOPMNT....HUMAN DEVELOPMENTAL CHANGE, PSYCHOLOGICAL
   AND PHYSIOLOGICAL

DEVIANT BEHAVIOR....SEE ANOMIE, CRIME

DEVLIN P. E0617

DEWEY J. E0618

DEWEY/JOHN....JOHN DEWEY

DEWEY/THOM....THOMAS DEWEY

DIAS R.W.M. E0619

DIAZ/P....PORFIRIO DIAZ

DICEY A. E0620

DICEY A.V. E0621

DICKINSON E. E0622

DICKINSON J. E0623

DICTIONARY....DICTIONARY

MCLAUGHLIN A.C.,CYCLOPEDIA OF AMERICAN GOVERNMENT
(3 VOLS.). LAW CONSTN POL/PAR ADMIN ROUTINE
...INT/LAW CONCPT BIBLIOG METH 20. PAGE 71 E1421

B14
USA+45
NAT/G
DICTIONARY

BOGEN J.I.,FINANCIAL HANDBOOK (4TH ED.). UNIV LAW
PLAN TAX RISK 20. PAGE 13 E0257

B64
FINAN
DICTIONARY

HOLT S.,THE DICTIONARY OF AMERICAN GOVERNMENT.
USA+45 LOC/G MUNIC PROVS LEGIS ADMIN JURID. PAGE 55
E1091

B64
DICTIONARY
INDEX
LAW
NAT/G

COLGNE A.B.,STATUTE MAKING (2ND ED.). LOC/G PROVS
CHOOSE MAJORITY...CHARTS DICTIONARY 20. PAGE 24
E0474

B65
LEGIS
LAW
CONSTN
NAT/G

HAENSCH G.,PAN-AFRICANISM IN ACTION: AN ACCOUNT OF
THE UAM TIC AND ALPHABETICAL IN GERMAN, ENGLISH,
FRENCH AND SPANISH. WOR+45 INT/ORG NAT/G ARMS/CONT
WAR...INT/LAW IDEA/COMP TREATY. PAGE 49 E0974

B65
DICTIONARY
DIPLOM
LING

MOSTECKY V.,SOVIET LEGAL BIBLIOGRAPHY. USSR LEGIS
PRESS WRITING CONFER ADJUD CT/SYS REV MARXISM
...INT/LAW JURID DICTIONARY 20. PAGE 75 E1503

B65
BIBLIOG/A
LAW
COM
CONSTN

COLEMAN-NORTON P.R.,ROMAN STATE AND CHRISTIAN CHURCH: A COLLECTION OF LEGAL DOCUMENTS TO A.D. 535 (3 VOLS.). CHRIST-17C ROMAN/EMP...ANTHOL DICTIONARY 6 CHRISTIAN CHURCH/STA. PAGE 24 E0473
GP/REL NAT/G SECT LAW
B66

KUNST H.,EVANGELISCHES STAATSLEXIKON. LAW CONSTN POL/PAR...PHIL/SCI CONCPT DICTIONARY. PAGE 62 E1232
JURID SECT SOC NAT/G
B66

DIDEROT/D....DENIS DIDEROT

DIEGUES M. E0624

DIEM....NGO DINH DIEM

DIESING P. E0625

DIETZE G. E0626

DILEY A.V. E0627

DILLIARD I. E0628

DILLON D.R. E0629

DIPLOM....DIPLOMACY

INTERNATIONAL COMN JURISTS,AFRICAN CONFERENCE ON THE RULE OF LAW. AFR INT/ORG LEGIS DIPLOM CONFER COLONIAL ORD/FREE...CONCPT METH/COMP 20. PAGE 57 E1131
CT/SYS JURID DELIB/GP
N

LIBRARY INTERNATIONAL REL,INTERNATIONAL INFORMATION SERVICE. WOR+45 CULTURE INT/ORG FORCES...GEOG HUM SOC. PAGE 65 E1295
BIBLIOG/A DIPLOM INT/TRADE INT/LAW
N

LONDON INSTITUTE WORLD AFFAIRS,THE YEAR BOOK OF WORLD AFFAIRS. FINAN BAL/PWR ARMS/CONT WAR ...INT/LAW BIBLIOG 20. PAGE 66 E1322
DIPLOM FOR/AID INT/ORG
N

TOSCANO M.,THE HISTORY OF TREATIES AND INTERNATIONAL POLITICS (REV. ED.). WOR-45 AGREE WAR ...BIOG 19/20 TREATY WWI. PAGE 97 E1935
DIPLOM INT/ORG
N

DEUTSCHE BIBLIOTH FRANKF A M,DEUTSCHE BIBLIOGRAPHIE. EUR+WWI GERMANY ECO/DEV FORCES DIPLOM LEAD...POLICY PHIL/SCI SOC 20. PAGE 31 E0612
BIBLIOG LAW ADMIN NAT/G
B

AMERICAN JOURNAL OF INTERNATIONAL LAW. WOR+45 WOR-45 CONSTN INT/ORG NAT/G CT/SYS ARMS/CONT WAR ...DECISION JURID NAT/COMP 20. PAGE 1 E0001
BIBLIOG/A INT/LAW DIPLOM ADJUD
N

AMERICAN POLITICAL SCIENCE REVIEW. USA+45 USA-45 WOR+45 WOR-45 INT/ORG ADMIN...INT/LAW PHIL/SCI CONCPT METH 20 UN. PAGE 1 E0002
BIBLIOG/A DIPLOM NAT/G GOV/COMP
N

ANNALS OF THE AMERICAN ACADEMY OF POLITICAL AND SOCIAL SCIENCE. AFR ASIA S/ASIA WOR+45 POL/PAR DIPLOM CRIME REV...SOC BIOG 20. PAGE 1 E0003
BIBLIOG/A NAT/G CULTURE ATTIT
N

BACKGROUND; JOURNAL OF INTERNATIONAL STUDIES ASSOCIATION. INT/ORG FORCES ACT/RES EDU/PROP COERCE NAT/LISM PEACE ATTIT...INT/LAW CONCPT 20. PAGE 1 E0004
BIBLIOG DIPLOM POLICY
N

CANADIAN GOVERNMENT PUBLICATIONS (1955-). CANADA AGRI FINAN LABOR FORCES INT/TRADE HEALTH...JURID 20 PARLIAMENT. PAGE 1 E0005
BIBLIOG/A NAT/G DIPLOM INT/ORG
N

INTERNATIONAL AFFAIRS. WOR+45 WOR-45 ECO/UNDEV INT/ORG NAT/G PROB/SOLV FOR/AID WAR...POLICY 20. PAGE 1 E0007
BIBLIOG/A DIPLOM INT/LAW INT/TRADE
N

INTERNATIONAL BOOK NEWS, 1928-1934. ECO/UNDEV FINAN INDUS LABOR INT/TRADE CONFER ADJUD COLONIAL...HEAL SOC/WK CHARTS 20 LEAGUE/NAT. PAGE 1 E0008
BIBLIOG DIPLOM INT/LAW INT/ORG
N

INTERNATIONAL STUDIES. ASIA S/ASIA WOR+45 ECO/UNDEV INT/ORG NAT/G LEAD ATTIT WEALTH...SOC 20. PAGE 1 E0009
BIBLIOG/A DIPLOM INT/LAW INT/TRADE
N

JOURNAL OF INTERNATIONAL AFFAIRS. WOR+45 ECO/UNDEV POL/PAR ECO/TAC WAR PEACE PERSON ALL/IDEOS ...INT/LAW TREND. PAGE 1 E0010
BIBLIOG DIPLOM INT/ORG NAT/G
N

JOURNAL OF POLITICS. USA+45 USA-45 CONSTN POL/PAR EX/STRUC LEGIS PROB/SOLV DIPLOM CT/SYS CHOOSE RACE/REL 20. PAGE 1 E0011
BIBLIOG/A NAT/G LAW LOC/G
N

MIDWEST JOURNAL OF POLITICAL SCIENCE. USA+45 CONSTN ECO/DEV LEGIS PROB/SOLV CT/SYS LEAD GOV/REL ATTIT POLICY. PAGE 1 E0012
BIBLIOG/A NAT/G DIPLOM POL/PAR
N

POLITICAL SCIENCE QUARTERLY. USA+45 USA-45 LAW CONSTN ECO/DEV INT/ORG LOC/G POL/PAR LEGIS LEAD NUC/PWR...CONCPT 20. PAGE 1 E0013
BIBLIOG/A NAT/G DIPLOM POLICY
N

TEXTBOOKS IN PRINT. WOR+45 WOR-45 LAW DIPLOM ALL/VALS ALL/IDEOS...SOC T 19/20. PAGE 1 E0014
BIBLIOG SCHOOL KNOWL
N

ARBITRATION JOURNAL. WOR+45 LAW INDUS JUDGE DIPLOM CT/SYS INGP/REL 20. PAGE 1 E0016
BIBLIOG MGT LABOR ADJUD
N

AUSTRALIAN PUBLIC AFFAIRS INFORMATION SERVICE. LAW ...HEAL HUM MGT SOC CON/ANAL 20 AUSTRAL. PAGE 1 E0017
BIBLIOG NAT/G CULTURE DIPLOM
N

BIBLIOGRAPHIE DER SOZIALWISSENSCHAFTEN. WOR-45 CONSTN SOCIETY ECO/DEV ECO/UNDEV DIPLOM LEAD WAR PEACE...PHIL/SCI SOC 19/20. PAGE 1 E0019
BIBLIOG LAW CONCPT NAT/G
N

DEUTSCHE BIBLIOGRAPHIE, HALBJAHRESVERZEICHNIS. WOR+45 LAW ADMIN PERSON. PAGE 1 E0020
BIBLIOG NAT/G DIPLOM
N

FOREIGN AFFAIRS. SPACE WOR+45 WOR-45 CULTURE ECO/UNDEV FINAN NAT/G TEC/DEV INT/TRADE ARMS/CONT NUC/PWR...POLICY 20 UN EURATOM ECSC EEC. PAGE 1 E0021
BIBLIOG DIPLOM INT/ORG INT/LAW
N

HANDBOOK OF LATIN AMERICAN STUDIES. LAW CULTURE ECO/UNDEV POL/PAR ADMIN LEAD...SOC 20. PAGE 1 E0022
BIBLIOG/A L/A+17C NAT/G DIPLOM
N

LATIN AMERICA IN PERIODICAL LITERATURE. LAW TEC/DEV DIPLOM RECEIVE EDU/PROP...GEOG HUM MGT 20. PAGE 2 E0024
BIBLIOG/A L/A+17C SOCIETY ECO/UNDEV
N

PUBLISHERS' CIRCULAR, THE OFFICIAL ORGAN OF THE PUBLISHERS' ASSOCIATION OF GREAT BRITAIN AND IRELAND. EUR+WWI MOD/EUR UK LAW PROB/SOLV DIPLOM COLONIAL ATTIT...HUM 19/20 CMN/WLTH. PAGE 2 E0025
BIBLIOG NAT/G WRITING LEAD
N

THE JAPAN SCIENCE REVIEW: LAW AND POLITICS: LIST OF BOOKS AND ARTICLES ON LAW AND POLITICS. CONSTN AGRI INDUS LABOR DIPLOM TAX ADMIN CRIME...INT/LAW SOC 20 CHINJAP. PAGE 2 E0027
BIBLIOG LAW S/ASIA PHIL/SCI
N

NEUE POLITISCHE LITERATUR; BERICHTE UBER DAS
BIBLIOG/A
N

INTERNATIONALE SCHRIFTTUM ZUR POLITIK. WOR+45 LAW   DIPLOM
CONSTN POL/PAR ADMIN LEAD GOV/REL...POLICY   NAT/G
IDEA/COMP. PAGE 2 E0028   NAT/COMP

AFRICAN BIBLIOGRAPHIC CENTER,A CURRENT BIBLIOGRAPHY BIBLIOG/A
ON AFRICAN AFFAIRS. LAW CULTURE ECO/UNDEV LABOR   AFR
SECT DIPLOM FOR/AID COLONIAL NAT/LISM...LING 20.   NAT/G
PAGE 3 E0053   REGION

                                                    N
AIR UNIVERSITY LIBRARY,INDEX TO MILITARY   BIBLIOG/A
PERIODICALS. FUT SPACE WOR+45 REGION ARMS/CONT   FORCES
NUC/PWR WAR PEACE INT/LAW. PAGE 3 E0056   NAT/G
                                                    DIPLOM

                                                    N
AMER COUNCIL OF LEARNED SOCIET,THE ACLS CONSTITUENT BIBLIOG/A
SOCIETY JOURNAL PROJECT. FUT USA+45 LAW NAT/G PLAN HUM
DIPLOM PHIL/SCI. PAGE 4 E0072   COMPUT/IR
                                                    COMPUTER

ASIA FOUNDATION,LIBRARY NOTES. LAW CONSTN CULTURE   BIBLIOG/A
SOCIETY ECO/UNDEV INT/ORG NAT/G COLONIAL LEAD   ASIA
REGION NAT/LISM ATTIT 20 UN. PAGE 6 E0107   S/ASIA
                                                    DIPLOM

                                                    N
ATLANTIC INSTITUTE,ATLANTIC STUDIES. COM EUR+WWI   BIBLIOG/A
USA+45 CULTURE STRUCT ECO/DEV FORCES LEAD ARMS/CONT DIPLOM
...INT/LAW JURID SOC. PAGE 6 E0110   POLICY
                                                    GOV/REL

                                                    N
CORNELL UNIVERSITY LIBRARY,SOUTHEAST ASIA   BIBLIOG
ACCESSIONS LIST. LAW SOCIETY STRUCT ECO/UNDEV   S/ASIA
POL/PAR TEC/DEV DIPLOM LEAD REGION. PAGE 26 E0510   NAT/G
                                                    CULTURE

                                                    N
DE MARTENS G.F.,RECUEIL GENERALE DE TRAITES ET   BIBLIOG
AUTRES ACTES RELATIFS AUX RAPPORTS DE DROIT   INT/LAW
INTERNATIONAL (41 VOLS.). EUR+WWI MOD/EUR USA-45   DIPLOM
...INDEX TREATY 18/20. PAGE 30 E0587

                                                    N
DEUTSCHE BUCHEREI,JAHRESVERZEICHNIS DES DEUTSCHEN   BIBLIOG
SCHRIFTUMS. AUSTRIA EUR+WWI GERMANY SWITZERLND LAW WRITING
LOC/G DIPLOM ADMIN...MGT SOC 19/20. PAGE 31 E0614   NAT/G

                                                    N
DEUTSCHE BUCHEREI,DEUTSCHES BUCHERVERZEICHNIS.   BIBLIOG
GERMANY LAW CULTURE POL/PAR ADMIN LEAD ATTIT PERSON NAT/G
...SOC 20. PAGE 31 E0615   DIPLOM
                                                    ECO/DEV

                                                    N
HARVARD UNIVERSITY LAW LIBRARY,CATALOG OF   BIBLIOG
INTERNATIONAL LAW AND RELATIONS. WOR+45 WOR-45   INT/LAW
INT/ORG NAT/G JUDGE DIPLOM INT/TRADE ADJUD CT/SYS   JURID
19/20. PAGE 51 E1007

                                                    N
MINISTERE DE L'EDUC NATIONALE,CATALOGUE DES THESES BIBLIOG
DE DOCTORAT SOUTENNES DEVANT LES UNIVERSITAIRES   ACADEM
FRANCAISES. FRANCE LAW DIPLOM ADMIN...HUM SOC 20.   KNOWL
PAGE 73 E1465   NAT/G

                                                    N
MINISTRY OF OVERSEAS DEVELOPME,TECHNICAL CO-   BIBLIOG
OPERATION -- A BIBLIOGRAPHY. UK LAW SOCIETY DIPLOM TEC/DEV
ECO/TAC FOR/AID...STAT 20 CMN/WLTH. PAGE 73 E1466   ECO/DEV
                                                    NAT/G

                                                    N
SOCIETE DES NATIONS,TRAITES INTERNATIONAUX ET ACTES BIBLIOG
LEGISLATIFS. WOR+45 INT/ORG NAT/G...INT/LAW JURID   DIPLOM
20 LEAGUE/NAT TREATY. PAGE 92 E1851   LEGIS
                                                    ADJUD

                                                    N
UNESCO,INTERNATIONAL BIBLIOGRAPHY OF POLITICAL   BIBLIOG
SCIENCE (VOLUMES 1-8). WOR+45 LAW NAT/G EX/STRUC   CONCPT
LEGIS PROB/SOLV DIPLOM ADMIN GOV/REL 20 UNESCO.   IDEA/COMP
PAGE 98 E1957

                                                    N
UNITED NATIONS,OFFICIAL RECORDS OF THE UNITED   INT/ORG
NATIONS' GENERAL ASSEMBLY. WOR+45 BUDGET DIPLOM   DELIB/GP
ADMIN 20 UN. PAGE 98 E1964   INT/LAW
                                                    WRITING

                                                    N
UNITED NATIONS,UNITED NATIONS PUBLICATIONS. WOR+45 BIBLIOG
ECO/UNDEV AGRI FINAN FORCES ADMIN LEAD WAR PEACE   INT/ORG

...POLICY INT/LAW 20 UN. PAGE 98 E1965   DIPLOM

                                                    N
US BUREAU OF THE CENSUS,BIBLIOGRAPHY OF SOCIAL   BIBLIOG/A
SCIENCE PERIODICALS AND MONOGRAPH SERIES. WOR+45   CULTURE
LAW DIPLOM EDU/PROP HEALTH...PSY SOC LING STAT.   NAT/G
PAGE 99 E1980   SOCIETY

                                                    B'
LALL A.S.,NEGOTIATING DISARMAMENT* THE EIGHTEEN   OBS
NATION DISARMAMENT CONFERENCE* THE FIRST TWO YEARS, ARMS/CONT
1962-1964. ASIA FRANCE INDIA USA+45 USSR PROB/SOLV DIPLOM
ADJUD NEUTRAL ATTIT...IDEA/COMP COLD/WAR. PAGE 62   OP/RES
E1246

                                                    B00
BERNARD M.,FOUR LECTURES ON SUBJECTS CONNECTED WITH LAW
DIPLOMACY. WOR-45 NAT/G VOL/ASSN RIGID/FLEX MORAL   ATTIT
PWR...JURID OBS GEN/LAWS GEN/METH 20 TREATY.   DIPLOM
PAGE 11 E0209

                                                    B00
DE TOCQUEVILLE A.,DEMOCRACY IN AMERICA (VOLUME   USA-45
ONE). LAW SOCIETY STRUCT NAT/G POL/PAR PROVS FORCES TREND
LEGIS TOP/EX DIPLOM LEGIT WAR PEACE ATTIT SOVEREIGN
...SELF/OBS TIME/SEQ CONGRESS 19. PAGE 30 E0594

                                                    B00
HOLLAND T.E.,STUDIES IN INTERNATIONAL LAW. TURKEY   INT/ORG
USSR WOR-45 CONSTN NAT/G DIPLOM DOMIN LEGIT COERCE LAW
WAR PEACE ORD/FREE PWR SOVEREIGN...JURID CHARTS 20 INT/LAW
PARLIAMENT SUEZ TREATY. PAGE 54 E1084

                                                    B00
LORIMER J.,THE INSTITUTES OF THE LAW OF NATIONS.   INT/ORG
WOR-45 CULTURE SOCIETY NAT/G VOL/ASSN DIPLOM LEGIT LAW
WAR PEACE DRIVE ORD/FREE SOVEREIGN...CONCPT RECORD INT/LAW
INT TREND HYPO/EXP GEN/METH TOT/POP VAL/FREE 20.
PAGE 66 E1327

                                                    B01
GRIFFIN A.P.C.,LIST OF BOOKS ON SAMOA (PAMPHLET).   BIBLIOG/A
GERMANY S/ASIA UK USA-45 WOR-45 ECO/UNDEV REGION   COLONIAL
ALL/VALS ORD/FREE ALL/IDEOS...GEOG INT/LAW 19 SAMOA DIPLOM
GUAM. PAGE 46 E0918

                                                    B03
CHANNING W.E.,DISCOURSES ON WAR (1820-1840). LAW   WAR
SECT DIPLOM INT/TRADE ALL/VALS. PAGE 21 E0418   PLAN
                                                    LOVE
                                                    ORD/FREE

                                                    B03
MOREL E.D.,THE BRITISH CASE IN FRENCH CONGO.   DIPLOM
CONGO/BRAZ FRANCE UK COERCE MORAL WEALTH...POLICY   INT/TRADE
INT/LAW 20 CONGO/LEOP. PAGE 74 E1490   COLONIAL
                                                    AFR

                                                    C05
DUNNING W.A.,"HISTORY OF POLITICAL THEORIES FROM   PHIL/SCI
LUTHER TO MONTESQUIEU." LAW NAT/G SECT DIPLOM REV   CONCPT
WAR ORD/FREE SOVEREIGN CONSERVE...TRADIT BIBLIOG   GEN/LAWS
16/18. PAGE 33 E0663

                                                    B06
FOSTER J.W.,THE PRACTICE OF DIPLOMACY AS   DIPLOM
ILLUSTRATED IN THE FOREIGN RELATIONS OF THE UNITED ROUTINE
STATES. MOD/EUR USA-45 NAT/G EX/STRUC ADMIN   PHIL/SCI
...POLICY INT/LAW BIBLIOG 19/20. PAGE 39 E0777

                                                    B08
GRIFFIN A.P.C.,LIST OF REFERENCES ON INTERNATIONAL BIBLIOG/A
ARBITRATION. FRANCE L/A+17C USA-45 WOR-45 DIPLOM   INT/ORG
CONFER COLONIAL ARMS/CONT BAL/PAY EQUILIB SOVEREIGN INT/LAW
...DECISION 19/20 MEXIC/AMER. PAGE 47 E0932   DELIB/GP

                                                    B11
REINSCH P.,PUBLIC INTERNATIONAL UNION. WOR-45 LAW   FUT
LABOR INT/TRADE LEGIT PERSON ALL/VALS...SOCIALIST   INT/ORG
CONCPT TIME/SEQ TREND GEN/LAWS 19/20. PAGE 84 E1683 DIPLOM

                                                    B13
BORCHARD E.M.,BIBLIOGRAPHY OF INTERNATIONAL LAW AND BIBLIOG
CONTINENTAL LAW. EUR+WWI MOD/EUR UK LAW INT/TRADE   INT/LAW
WAR PEACE...GOV/COMP NAT/COMP 19/20. PAGE 14 E0267 JURID
                                                    DIPLOM

                                                    B15
INTERNATIONAL LAW ASSOCIATION,A FORTY YEARS'   BIBLIOG
CATALOGUE OF THE BOOKS, PAMPHLETS AND PAPERS IN THE LAW
LIBRARY OF THE INTERNATIONAL LAW ASSOCIATION.   INT/LAW
INT/ORG DIPLOM ADJUD NEUTRAL...IDEA/COMP 19/20.
PAGE 57 E1134

                                                    B16
PUFENDORF S.,LAW OF NATURE AND OF NATIONS   CONCPT

(ABRIDGED). UNIV LAW NAT/G DIPLOM AGREE WAR PERSON ALL/VALS PWR...POLICY 18 DEITY NATURL/LAW. PAGE 83 E1659

INT/LAW
SECT
MORAL

B17
MEYER H.H.B.,LIST OF REFERENCES ON EMBARGOES (PAMPHLET). USA-45 AGRI DIPLOM WRITING DEBATE WEAPON...INT/LAW 18/20 CONGRESS. PAGE 72 E1447

BIBLIOG
DIST/IND
ECO/TAC
INT/TRADE

B19
LONDON SCHOOL ECONOMICS-POL,ANNUAL DIGEST OF PUBLIC INTERNATIONAL LAW CASES. INT/ORG MUNIC NAT/G PROVS ADMIN NEUTRAL WAR GOV/REL PRIVIL 20. PAGE 66 E1323

BIBLIOG/A
INT/LAW
ADJUD
DIPLOM

B19
VANDERPOL A.,LA DOCTRINE SCOLASTIQUE DU DROIT DE GUERRE. CHRIST-17C FORCES DIPLOM LEGIT SUPEGO MORAL ...BIOG AQUINAS/T SUAREZ/F CHRISTIAN. PAGE 103 E2072

WAR
SECT
INT/LAW

N19
BAILEY S.D.,VETO IN THE SECURITY COUNCIL (PAMPHLET). COM USSR WOR+45 BAL/PWR PARL/PROC ARMS/CONT PRIVIL PWR...INT/LAW TREND CHARTS 20 UN SUEZ. PAGE 7 E0135

DELIB/GP
INT/ORG
DIPLOM

N19
MEZERIK A.G.,ATOM TESTS AND RADIATION HAZARDS (PAMPHLET). WOR+45 INT/ORG DIPLOM DETER 20 UN TREATY. PAGE 73 E1452

NUC/PWR
ARMS/CONT
CONFER
HEALTH

N19
MEZERIK AG,OUTER SPACE: UN, US, USSR (PAMPHLET). USSR DELIB/GP FORCES DETER NUC/PWR SOVEREIGN ...POLICY 20 UN TREATY. PAGE 73 E1453

SPACE
CONTROL
DIPLOM
INT/ORG

N19
TAYLOR H.,WHY THE PENDING TREATY WITH COLOMBIA SHOULD BE RATIFIED (PAMPHLET). PANAMA USA-45 DELIB/GP INT/TRADE REV ORD/FREE...JURID TREATY 18/19 ROOSEVLT/T TAFT/WH COLOMB. PAGE 95 E1912

INT/LAW
DIPLOM

B20
DICKINSON E.,THE EQUALITY OF STATES IN INTERNATIONAL LAW. WOR-45 INT/ORG NAT/G DIPLOM EDU/PROP LEGIT PEACE ATTIT ALL/VALS...JURID TIME/SEQ LEAGUE/NAT. PAGE 31 E0622

LAW
CONCPT
SOVEREIGN

B20
MEYER H.H.B.,LIST OF REFERENCES ON THE TREATY-MAKING POWER. USA-45 CONTROL PWR...INT/LAW TIME/SEQ 18/20 TREATY. PAGE 72 E1448

BIBLIOG
DIPLOM
CONSTN

L21
HALDEMAN E.,"SERIALS OF AN INTERNATIONAL CHARACTER." WOR-45 DIPLOM...ART/METH GEOG HEAL HUM INT/LAW JURID PSY SOC. PAGE 49 E0978

BIBLIOG
PHIL/SCI

B22
BRYCE J.,INTERNATIONAL RELATIONS. CHRIST-17C EUR+WWI MOD/EUR CULTURE INTELL NAT/G DELIB/GP CREATE BAL/PWR DIPLOM ATTIT DRIVE RIGID/FLEX ALL/VALS...PLURIST JURID CONCPT TIME/SEQ GEN/LAWS TOT/POP. PAGE 16 E0323

INT/ORG
POLICY

B22
MYERS D.P.,MANUAL OF COLLECTIONS OF TREATIES AND OF COLLECTIONS RELATING TO TREATIES. MOD/EUR INT/ORG LEGIS WRITING ADMIN SOVEREIGN...INT/LAW 19/20. PAGE 75 E1514

BIBLIOG/A
DIPLOM
CONFER

B22
WRIGHT Q.,THE CONTROL OF AMERICAN FOREIGN RELATIONS. USA-45 WOR-45 CONSTN INT/ORG CONSULT LEGIS LEGIT ROUTINE ORD/FREE PWR...POLICY JURID CONCPT METH/CNCPT RECORD LEAGUE/NAT 20. PAGE 107 E2150

NAT/G
EXEC
DIPLOM

B23
HEADICAR B.M.,CATALOGUE OF THE BOOKS, PAMPHLETS, AND OTHER DOCUMENTS IN THE EDWARD FRY LIBRARY OF INTERNATIONAL LAW... UK INT/ORG 20. PAGE 51 E1019

BIBLIOG
INT/LAW
DIPLOM

S23
DEWEY J.,"ETHICS AND INTERNATIONAL RELATIONS." FUT WOR-45 SOCIETY INT/ORG VOL/ASSN DIPLOM LEGIT ORD/FREE...JURID CONCPT GEN/METH 20. PAGE 31 E0618

LAW
MORAL

B24
GENTILI A.,DE LEGATIONIBUS. CHRIST-17C NAT/G SECT CONSULT LEGIT...POLICY CATH JURID CONCPT MYTH. PAGE 43 E0848

DIPLOM
INT/LAW
INT/ORG

B24
HALL W.E.,A TREATISE ON INTERNATIONAL LAW. WOR-45 CONSTN INT/ORG NAT/G DIPLOM ORD/FREE LEAGUE/NAT 20 TREATY. PAGE 49 E0985

PWR
JURID
WAR
INT/LAW

B24
NAVILLE A.,LIBERTE, EGALITE, SOLIDARITE: ESSAIS D'ANALYSE. STRATA FAM VOL/ASSN INT/TRADE GP/REL MORAL MARXISM SOCISM...PSY TREATY. PAGE 76 E1529

ORD/FREE
SOC
IDEA/COMP
DIPLOM

C24
BARNES H.E.,"SOCIOLOGY AND POLITICAL THEORY: A CONSIDERATION OF THE SOCIOLOGICAL BASIS OF POLITICS." LAW CONSTN NAT/G DIPLOM DOMIN ROUTINE REV ORD/FREE SOVEREIGN...PHIL/SCI CLASSIF BIBLIOG 18/20. PAGE 8 E0151

CONCPT
STRUCT
SOC

B25
GODET M.,INDEX BIBLIOGRAPHICUS: INTERNATIONAL CATALOGUE OF SOURCES OF CURRENT BIBLIOGRAPHIC INFORMATION. EUR+WWI MOD/EUR SOCIETY SECT TAX ...JURID PHIL/SCI SOC MATH. PAGE 44 E0876

BIBLIOG/A
DIPLOM
EDU/PROP
LAW

L25
HUDSON M.,"THE PERMANENT COURT OF INTERNATIONAL JUSTICE AND THE QUESTION OF AMERICAN PARTICIPATION." WOR-45 LEGIT CT/SYS ORD/FREE ...JURID CONCPT TIME/SEQ GEN/LAWS VAL/FREE 20 ICJ. PAGE 56 E1108

INT/ORG
ADJUD
DIPLOM
INT/LAW

B26
INSTITUT INTERMEDIAIRE INTL,REPERTOIRE GENERAL DES TRAITES ET AUTRES ACTES DIPLOMATIQUES CONCLUS DEPUIS 1895 JUSQU'EN 1920. MOD/EUR WOR-45 INT/ORG VOL/ASSN DELIB/GP INT/TRADE WAR TREATY 19/20. PAGE 56 E1125

BIBLIOG
DIPLOM

B27
GOOCH G.P.,ENGLISH DEMOCRATIC IDEAS IN THE SEVENTEENTH CENTURY (2ND ED.). UK LAW SECT FORCES DIPLOM LEAD PARL/PROC REV ATTIT AUTHORIT...ANARCH CONCPT 17 PARLIAMENT CMN/WLTH REFORMERS. PAGE 45 E0885

IDEA/COMP
MAJORIT
EX/STRUC
CONSERVE

B28
BUTLER G.,THE DEVELOPMENT OF INTERNATIONAL LAW. WOR-45 SOCIETY NAT/G KNOWL ORD/FREE PWR...JURID CONCPT HIST/WRIT GEN/LAWS. PAGE 18 E0349

LAW
INT/LAW
DIPLOM
INT/ORG

B28
LAPRADELLE,ANNUAIRE DE LA VIE INTERNATIONALE: POLITIQUE, ECONOMIQUE, JURIDIQUE. INT/ORG CONFER ARMS/CONT 20. PAGE 63 E1255

BIBLIOG
DIPLOM
INT/LAW

B29
BUELL R.,INTERNATIONAL RELATIONS. WOR+45 WOR-45 CONSTN STRATA FORCES TOP/EX ADMIN ATTIT DRIVE SUPEGO MORAL ORD/FREE PWR SOVEREIGN...JURID SOC CONCPT 20. PAGE 17 E0326

INT/ORG
BAL/PWR
DIPLOM

B29
PRATT I.A.,MODERN EGYPT: A LIST OF REFERENCES TO MATERIAL IN THE NEW YORK PUBLIC LIBRARY. UAR ECO/UNDEV...GEOG JURID SOC LING 20. PAGE 82 E1647

BIBLIOG
ISLAM
DIPLOM
NAT/G

B29
STURZO L.,THE INTERNATIONAL COMMUNITY AND THE RIGHT OF WAR (TRANS. BY BARBARA BARCLAY CARTER). CULTURE CREATE PROB/SOLV DIPLOM ADJUD CONTROL PEACE PERSON ORD/FREE...INT/LAW IDEA/COMP PACIFIST 20 LEAGUE/NAT. PAGE 94 E1891

INT/ORG
PLAN
WAR
CONCPT

B30
BYNKERSHOEK C.,QUAESTIONUM JURIS PUBLICI LIBRI DUO. CHRIST-17C MOD/EUR CONSTN ELITES SOCIETY NAT/G PROVS EX/STRUC FORCES TOP/EX BAL/PWR DIPLOM ATTIT MORAL...TRADIT CONCPT. PAGE 18 E0352

INT/ORG
LAW
NAT/LISM
INT/LAW

B31
COLUMBIA UNIVERSITY,A BIBLIOGRAPHY OF THE FACULTY OF POLITICAL SCIENCE OF COLUMBIA UNIVERSITY, 1880-1930. USA-45 LAW NAT/G LEGIS DIPLOM LEAD WAR GOV/REL ATTIT...TIME/SEQ 19/20. PAGE 24 E0478

BIBLIOG
ACADEM
PHIL/SCI

B31
STOWELL E.C.,INTERNATIONAL LAW. FUT UNIV WOR-45 SOCIETY CONSULT EX/STRUC FORCES ACT/RES PLAN DIPLOM EDU/PROP LEGIT DISPL PWR SKILL...POLICY CONCPT OBS TREND TOT/POP 20. PAGE 94 E1885

INT/ORG
ROUTINE
INT/LAW

B32
EAGLETON C.,INTERNATIONAL GOVERNMENT. BRAZIL FRANCE INT/ORG
GERMANY ITALY UK USSR WOR-45 DELIB/GP TOP/EX PLAN JURID
ECO/TAC EDU/PROP LEGIT ADJUD REGION ARMS/CONT DIPLOM
COERCE ATTIT PWR...GEOG MGT VAL/FREE LEAGUE/NAT 20. INT/LAW
PAGE 34 E0670

B32
GREGORY W.,LIST OF THE SERIAL PUBLICATIONS OF BIBLIOG
FOREIGN GOVERNMENTS, 1815-1931. WOR-45 DIPLOM ADJUD NAT/G
...POLICY 20. PAGE 46 E0914 LAW
JURID

B33
AMERICAN FOREIGN LAW ASSN,BIOGRAPHICAL NOTES ON THE BIBLIOG/A
LAWS AND LEGAL LITERATURE OF URUGUAY AND CURACAO. LAW
URUGUAY CONSTN FINAN SECT FORCES JUDGE DIPLOM JURID
INT/TRADE ADJUD CT/SYS CRIME 20. PAGE 4 E0078 ADMIN

B33
DANGERFIELD R.,IN DEFENSE OF THE SENATE. USA-45 LEGIS
CONSTN NAT/G EX/STRUC TOP/EX ATTIT KNOWL DELIB/GP
...METH/CNCPT STAT TIME/SEQ TREND CON/ANAL CHARTS DIPLOM
CONGRESS 20 TREATY. PAGE 28 E0565

B33
GENTILI A.,DE JURE BELLI, LIBRI TRES (1612) (VOL. WAR
2). FORCES DIPLOM AGREE PEACE SOVEREIGN. PAGE 43 INT/LAW
E0849 MORAL
SUPEGO

B33
MATTHEWS M.A.,THE AMERICAN INSTITUTE OF BIBLIOG/A
INTERNATIONAL LAW AND THE CODIFICATION OF INT/LAW
INTERNATIONAL LAW (PAMPHLET). USA-45 CONSTN ADJUD L/A+17C
CT/SYS...JURID 20. PAGE 69 E1386 DIPLOM

B33
REID H.D.,RECUEIL DES COURS; TOME 45: LES ORD/FREE
SERVITUDES INTERNATIONALES III. FRANCE CONSTN DIPLOM
DELIB/GP PRESS CONTROL REV WAR CHOOSE PEACE MORAL LAW
MARITIME TREATY. PAGE 84 E1680

B34
US TARIFF COMMISSION,THE TARIFF; A BIBLIOGRAPHY: A BIBLIOG/A
SELECT LIST OF REFERENCES. USA-45 LAW DIPLOM TAX TARIFFS
ADMIN...POLICY TREATY 20. PAGE 103 E2064 ECO/TAC

B35
FOREIGN AFFAIRS BIBLIOGRAPHY: A SELECTED AND BIBLIOG/A
ANNOTATED LIST OF BOOKS ON INTERNATIONAL RELATIONS DIPLOM
1919-1962 (4 VOLS.). CONSTN FORCES COLONIAL INT/ORG
ARMS/CONT WAR NAT/LISM PEACE ATTIT DRIVE...POLICY
INT/LAW 20. PAGE 2 E0032

B35
BEMIS S.F.,GUIDE TO THE DIPLOMATIC HISTORY OF THE BIBLIOG/A
UNITED STATES, 1775-1921. NAT/G LEGIS TOP/EX DIPLOM
PROB/SOLV CAP/ISM INT/TRADE TARIFFS ADJUD USA-45
...CON/ANAL 18/20. PAGE 10 E0184

B35
BURCHFIELD L.,STUDENT'S GUIDE TO MATERIALS IN BIBLIOG
POLITICAL SCIENCE. FINAN INT/ORG NAT/G POL/PAR INDEX
DIPLOM PRESS ADMIN...BIOG 18/19. PAGE 17 E0328 LAW

B35
KENNEDY W.P.,THE LAW AND CUSTOM OF THE SOUTH CT/SYS
AFRICAN CONSTITUTION. AFR SOUTH/AFR KIN LOC/G PROVS CONSTN
DIPLOM ADJUD ADMIN EXEC 20. PAGE 60 E1203 JURID
PARL/PROC

B36
BRIERLY J.L.,THE LAW OF NATIONS (2ND ED.). WOR+45 DIPLOM
WOR-45 INT/ORG AGREE CONTROL COERCE WAR NAT/LISM INT/LAW
PEACE PWR 16/20 TREATY LEAGUE/NAT. PAGE 15 E0297 NAT/G

B36
HUDSON M.O.,INTERNATIONAL LEGISLATION: 1929-1931. INT/LAW
WOR-45 SEA AIR AGRI FINAN LABOR DIPLOM ECO/TAC PARL/PROC
REPAR CT/SYS ARMS/CONT WAR WEAPON...JURID 20 TREATY ADJUD
LEAGUE/NAT. PAGE 56 E1112 LAW

B36
MATTHEWS M.A.,DIPLOMACY: SELECT LIST ON DIPLOMACY, BIBLIOG/A
DIPLOMATIC AND CONSULAR PRACTICE, AND FOREIGN DIPLOM
OFFICE ORGANIZATION (PAMPHLET). EUR+WWI MOD/EUR NAT/G
USA-45 WOR-45...INT/LAW 20. PAGE 69 E1387

B36
MATTHEWS M.A.,INTERNATIONAL LAW: SELECT LIST OF BIBLIOG/A
WORKS IN ENGLISH ON PUBLIC INTERNATIONAL LAW: WITH INT/LAW
COLLECTIONS OF CASES AND OPINIONS. CHRIST-17C ATTIT
EUR+WWI MOD/EUR WOR-45 CONSTN ADJUD JURID. PAGE 69 DIPLOM
E1388

B36
RUSSEL F.M.,THEORIES OF INTERNATIONAL RELATIONS. PWR
EUR+WWI FUT MOD/EUR USA-45 INT/ORG DIPLOM...JURID POLICY
CONCPT. PAGE 86 E1735 BAL/PWR
SOVEREIGN

B37
BORGESE G.A.,GOLIATH: THE MARCH OF FASCISM. GERMANY POLICY
ITALY LAW POL/PAR SECT DIPLOM SOCISM...JURID MYTH NAT/LISM
20 DANTE MACHIAVELL MUSSOLIN/B. PAGE 14 E0270 FASCISM
NAT/G

B37
KETCHAM E.H.,PRELIMINARY SELECT BIBLIOGRAPHY OF BIBLIOG
INTERNATIONAL LAW (PAMPHLET). WOR-45 LAW INT/ORG DIPLOM
NAT/G PROB/SOLV CT/SYS NEUTRAL WAR 19/20. PAGE 60 ADJUD
E1207 INT/LAW

B37
THOMPSON J.W.,SECRET DIPLOMACY: A RECORD OF DIPLOM
ESPIONAGE AND DOUBLE-DEALING: 1500-1815. CHRIST-17C CRIME
MOD/EUR NAT/G WRITING RISK MORAL...ANTHOL BIBLIOG
16/19 ESPIONAGE. PAGE 96 E1920

B38
GRISWOLD A.W.,THE FAR EASTERN POLICY OF THE UNITED DIPLOM
STATES. ASIA S/ASIA USA-45 INT/ORG INT/TRADE WAR POLICY
NAT/LISM...BIBLIOG 19/20 LEAGUE/NAT ROOSEVLT/T CHIEF
ROOSEVLT/F WILSON/W TREATY. PAGE 47 E0943

B38
HAGUE PERMANENT CT INTL JUSTIC,WORLD COURT REPORTS: INT/ORG
COLLECTION OO THE JUDGEMENTS ORDERS AND OPINIONS CT/SYS
VOLUME 3 1932-35. WOR-45 LAW DELIB/GP CONFER WAR DIPLOM
PEACE ATTIT...DECISION ANTHOL 20 WORLD/CT CASEBOOK. ADJUD
PAGE 49 E0976

B38
HARPER S.N.,THE GOVERNMENT OF THE SOVIET UNION. COM MARXISM
USSR LAW CONSTN ECO/DEV PLAN TEC/DEV DIPLOM NAT/G
INT/TRADE ADMIN REV NAT/LISM...POLICY 20. PAGE 50 LEAD
E1001 POL/PAR

B38
HOLDSWORTH W.S.,A HISTORY OF ENGLISH LAW; THE LAW
CENTURIES OF SETTLEMENT AND REFORM (VOL. XI). UK COLONIAL
CONSTN NAT/G EX/STRUC DIPLOM ADJUD CT/SYS LEAD LEGIS
CRIME ATTIT...INT/LAW JURID 18 CMN/WLTH PARLIAMENT PARL/PROC
ENGLSH/LAW. PAGE 54 E1079

B38
LEAGUE OF NATIONS-SECRETARIAT,THE AIMS, METHODS ADJUD
AND ACTIVITY OF THE LEAGUE OF NATIONS. WOR+45 STRUCT
DIPLOM EDU/PROP LEGIT RIGID/FLEX ALL/VALS
...TIME/SEQ LEAGUE/NAT VAL/FREE 19/20. PAGE 64
E1273

B38
MCNAIR A.D.,THE LAW OF TREATIES: BRITISH PRACTICE AGREE
AND OPINIONS. UK CREATE DIPLOM LEGIT WRITING ADJUD LAW
WAR...INT/LAW JURID TREATY. PAGE 71 E1424 CT/SYS
NAT/G

B39
ZIMMERN A.,THE LEAGUE OF NATIONS AND THE RULE OF INT/ORG
LAW. WOR-45 STRUCT NAT/G DELIB/GP EX/STRUC BAL/PWR LAW
DOMIN LEGIT COERCE ORD/FREE PWR...POLICY RECORD DIPLOM
LEAGUE/NAT TOT/POP VAL/FREE 20 LEAGUE/NAT. PAGE 108
E2170

C39
SCOTT J.B.,"LAW, THE STATE, AND THE INTERNATIONAL LAW
COMMUNITY (2 VOLS.)" INTELL INT/ORG NAT/G SECT PHIL/SCI
INT/TRADE WAR...INT/LAW GEN/LAWS BIBLIOG. PAGE 90 DIPLOM
E1798 CONCPT

B40
CARR E.H.,THE TWENTY YEARS' CRISIS 1919-1939. FUT INT/ORG
WOR-45 BAL/PWR ECO/TAC LEGIT TOTALISM ATTIT DIPLOM
ALL/VALS...POLICY JURID CONCPT TIME/SEQ TREND PEACE
GEN/LAWS TOT/POP 20. PAGE 20 E0393

B40
CONOVER H.F.,FOREIGN RELATIONS OF THE UNITED BIBLIOG/A
STATES: A LIST OF RECENT BOOKS (PAMPHLET). ASIA USA-45
CANADA L/A+17C UK INT/ORG INT/TRADE TARIFFS NEUTRAL DIPLOM
WAR PEACE...INT/LAW CON/ANAL 20 CHINJAP. PAGE 25
E0492

B40
WOLFERS A.,BRITAIN AND FRANCE BETWEEN TWO WORLD DIPLOM
WARS. FRANCE UK INT/ORG NAT/G PLAN BARGAIN ECO/TAC WAR
AGREE ISOLAT ALL/IDEOS...DECISION GEOG 20 TREATY POLICY
VERSAILLES INTERVENT. PAGE 107 E2139

S40

FLORIN J.,"BOLSHEVIST AND NATIONAL SOCIALIST
DOCTRINES OF INTERNATIONAL LAW." EUR+WWI GERMANY
USSR R+D INT/ORG NAT/G DIPLOM DOMIN EDU/PROP SOCISM
...CONCPT TIME/SEQ 20. PAGE 39 E0768

LAW
ATTIT
TOTALISM
INT/LAW

B41

BIRDSALL P.,VERSAILLES TWENTY YEARS AFTER. MOD/EUR
POL/PAR CHIEF CONSULT FORCES LEGIS REPAR PEACE
ORD/FREE...BIBLIOG 20 PRESIDENT TREATY. PAGE 12
E0231

DIPLOM
NAT/LISM
WAR

B41

EVANS C.,AMERICAN BIBLIOGRAPHY... (12 VOLUMES).
USA-45 LAW DIPLOM ADMIN PERSON...HUM SOC 17/18.
PAGE 35 E0704

BIBLIOG
NAT/G
ALL/VALS
ALL/IDEOS

B41

MCCLURE W.,INTERNATIONAL EXECUTIVE AGREEMENTS.
USA-45 WOR-45 INT/ORG NAT/G DELIB/GP ADJUD ROUTINE
ORD/FREE PWR...TIME/SEQ TREND CON/ANAL. PAGE 70
E1401

TOP/EX
DIPLOM

B41

NIEMEYER G.,LAW WITHOUT FORCE: THE FUNCTION OF
POLITICS IN INTERNATIONAL LAW. PLAN INSPECT DIPLOM
REPAR LEGIT ADJUD WAR ORD/FREE...IDEA/COMP
METH/COMP GEN/LAWS 20. PAGE 77 E1549

COERCE
LAW
PWR
INT/LAW

L41

COMM. STUDY ORGAN. PEACE,"ORGANIZATION OF PEACE."
USA-45 WOR-45 STRATA NAT/G ACT/RES DIPLOM ECO/TAC
EDU/PROP ADJUD ATTIT ORD/FREE PWR...SOC CONCPT
ANTHOL LEAGUE/NAT 20. PAGE 24 E0479

INT/ORG
PLAN
PEACE

B42

CROWE S.E.,THE BERLIN WEST AFRICA CONFERENCE,
1884-85. GERMANY ELITES MARKET INT/ORG DELIB/GP
FORCES PROB/SOLV BAL/PWR CAP/ISM DOMIN COLONIAL
...INT/LAW 19. PAGE 28 E0548

AFR
CONFER
INT/TRADE
DIPLOM

B42

FEILCHENFELD E.H.,THE INTERNATIONAL ECONOMIC LAW OF
BELLIGERENT OCCUPATION. EUR+WWI MOD/EUR USA-45
INT/ORG DIPLOM ADJUD ARMS/CONT LEAGUE/NAT 20.
PAGE 37 E0726

ECO/TAC
INT/LAW
WAR

B42

FULLER G.H.,DEFENSE FINANCING: A SUPPLEMENTARY LIST
OF REFERENCES (PAMPHLET). CANADA UK USA-45 ECO/DEV
NAT/G DELIB/GP BUDGET ADJUD ARMS/CONT WEAPON COST
PEACE PWR 20 AUSTRAL CHINJAP CONGRESS. PAGE 41
E0821

BIBLIOG/A
FINAN
FORCES
DIPLOM

B42

KELSEN H.,LAW AND PEACE IN INTERNATIONAL RELATIONS.
FUT WOR-45 NAT/G DELIB/GP DIPLOM LEGIT RIGID/FLEX
ORD/FREE SOVEREIGN...JURID CONCPT TREND STERTYP
GEN/LAWS LEAGUE/NAT 20. PAGE 60 E1197

INT/ORG
ADJUD
PEACE
INT/LAW

B43

BEMIS S.F.,THE LATIN AMERICAN POLICY OF THE UNITED
STATES: AN HISTORICAL INTERPRETATION. INT/ORG AGREE
COLONIAL WAR PEACE ATTIT ORD/FREE...POLICY INT/LAW
CHARTS 18/20 MEXIC/AMER WILSON/W MONROE/DOC.
PAGE 10 E0185

DIPLOM
SOVEREIGN
USA-45
L/A+17C

B43

CONOVER H.F.,THE BALKANS: A SELECTED LIST OF
REFERENCES. ALBANIA BULGARIA ROMANIA YUGOSLAVIA
INT/ORG PROB/SOLV DIPLOM LEGIT CONFER ADJUD WAR
NAT/LISM PEACE PWR 20 LEAGUE/NAT. PAGE 25 E0493

BIBLIOG
EUR+WWI

B43

HAGUE PERMANENT CT INTL JUSTIC,WORLD COURT REPORTS:
COLLECTION OF THE JUDGEMENTS ORDERS AND OPINIONS
VOLUME 4 1936-42. WOR-45 CONFER PEACE ATTIT
...DECISION JURID ANTHOL 20 WORLD/CT CASEBOOK.
PAGE 49 E0977

INT/ORG
CT/SYS
DIPLOM
ADJUD

B43

MICAUD C.A.,THE FRENCH RIGHT AND NAZI GERMANY
1933-1939: A STUDY OF PUBLIC OPINION. GERMANY UK
USSR POL/PAR ARMS/CONT COERCE DETER PEACE
RIGID/FLEX PWR MARXISM...FASCIST TREND 20
LEAGUE/NAT TREATY. PAGE 73 E1454

DIPLOM
AGREE

C43

BENTHAM J.,"PRINCIPLES OF INTERNATIONAL LAW" IN J.
BOWRING, ED., THE WORKS OF JEREMY BENTHAM." UNIV
NAT/G PLAN PROB/SOLV DIPLOM CONTROL SANCTION MORAL
ORD/FREE PWR SOVEREIGN 19. PAGE 10 E0194

INT/LAW
JURID
WAR
PEACE

B44

ADLER M.J.,HOW TO THINK ABOUT WAR AND PEACE. WOR-45 INT/ORG

LAW SOCIETY EX/STRUC DIPLOM KNOWL ORD/FREE...POLICY CREATE
TREND GEN/LAWS 20. PAGE 3 E0049

ARMS/CONT
PEACE

B44

FULLER G.H.,MILITARY GOVERNMENT: A LIST OF
REFERENCES (A PAMPHLET). ITALY UK USA-45 WOR-45 LAW
FORCES DOMIN ADMIN ARMS/CONT ORD/FREE PWR
...DECISION 20 CHINJAP. PAGE 41 E0822

BIBLIOG
DIPLOM
CIVMIL/REL
SOVEREIGN

B44

FULLER G.H.,TURKEY: A SELECTED LIST OF REFERENCES.
ISLAM TURKEY CULTURE ECO/UNDEV AGRI DIPLOM NAT/LISM
CONSERVE...GEOG HUM INT/LAW SOC 7/20 MAPS. PAGE 42
E0824

BIBLIOG
ALL/VALS

B44

RUDIN H.R.,ARMISTICE 1918. FRANCE GERMANY MOD/EUR
UK USA-45 NAT/G CHIEF DELIB/GP FORCES BAL/PWR REPAR
ARMS/CONT 20 WILSON/W TREATY. PAGE 86 E1732

AGREE
WAR
PEACE
DIPLOM

B45

CONOVER H.F.,THE GOVERNMENTS OF THE MAJOR FOREIGN
POWERS: A BIBLIOGRAPHY. FRANCE GERMANY ITALY UK
USSR CONSTN LOC/G POL/PAR EX/STRUC FORCES ADMIN
CT/SYS CIVMIL/REL TOTALISM...POLICY 19/20. PAGE 25
E0494

BIBLIOG
NAT/G
DIPLOM

B45

CONOVER H.F.,THE NAZI STATE: WAR CRIMES AND WAR
CRIMINALS. GERMANY CULTURE NAT/G SECT FORCES DIPLOM
INT/TRADE EDU/PROP...INT/LAW BIOG HIST/WRIT
TIME/SEQ 20. PAGE 25 E0495

BIBLIOG
WAR
CRIME

B45

GALLOWAY E.,ABSTRACTS OF POSTWAR LITERATURE (VOL.
IV) JAN.-JULY, 1945 NOS. 901-1074. POLAND USA+45
USSR WOR+45 INDUS LABOR PLAN ECO/TAC INT/TRADE TAX
EDU/PROP ADMIN COLONIAL INT/LAW. PAGE 42 E0829

BIBLIOG/A
NUC/PWR
NAT/G
DIPLOM

B45

UNCIO CONFERENCE LIBRARY,SHORT TITLE CLASSIFIED
CATALOG. WOR-45 DOMIN COLONIAL WAR...SOC/WK 20
LEAGUE/NAT UN. PAGE 98 E1955

BIBLIOG
DIPLOM
INT/ORG
INT/LAW

B45

US DEPARTMENT OF STATE,PUBLICATIONS OF THE
DEPARTMENT OF STATE: A LIST CUMULATIVE FROM OCTOBER
1, 1929 (PAMPHLET). ASIA EUR+WWI ISLAM L/A+17C
USA-45 ADJUD...INT/LAW 20. PAGE 99 E1993

BIBLIOG
DIPLOM
INT/TRADE

B45

WEST R.,CONSCIENCE AND SOCIETY: A STUDY OF THE
PSYCHOLOGICAL PREREQUISITES OF LAW AND ORDER. FUT
UNIV LAW SOCIETY STRUCT DIPLOM WAR PERS/REL SUPEGO
...SOC 20. PAGE 105 E2112

COERCE
INT/LAW
ORD/FREE
PERSON

B45

WOOLBERT R.G.,FOREIGN AFFAIRS BIBLIOGRAPHY,
1932-1942. INT/ORG SECT INT/TRADE COLONIAL RACE/REL
NAT/LISM...GEOG INT/LAW GOV/COMP IDEA/COMP 20.
PAGE 107 E2144

BIBLIOG/A
DIPLOM
WAR

B46

GRIFFIN G.G.,A GUIDE TO MANUSCRIPTS RELATING TO
AMERICAN HISTORY IN BRITISH DEPOSITORIES. CANADA
IRELAND MOD/EUR UK USA-45 LAW DIPLOM ADMIN COLONIAL
WAR NAT/LISM SOVEREIGN...GEOG INT/LAW 15/19
CMN/WLTH. PAGE 47 E0936

BIBLIOG/A
ALL/VALS
NAT/G

B46

SCANLON H.L.,INTERNATIONAL LAW: A SELECTIVE LIST OF
WORKS IN ENGLISH ON PUBLIC INTERNATIONAL LAW (A
PAMPHLET). CHRIST-17C EUR+WWI MOD/EUR WOR-45 CT/SYS
...JURID 20. PAGE 87 E1749

BIBLIOG/A
INT/LAW
ADJUD
DIPLOM

C46

GOODRICH L.M.,"CHARTER OF THE UNITED NATIONS:
COMMENTARY AND DOCUMENTS." EX/STRUC ADMIN...INT/LAW
CON/ANAL BIBLIOG 20 UN. PAGE 45 E0890

CONSTN
INT/ORG
DIPLOM

B47

BORGESE G.,COMMON CAUSE. LAW CONSTN SOCIETY STRATA
ECO/DEV INT/ORG POL/PAR FORCES LEGIS TOP/EX CAP/ISM
DIPLOM ADMIN EXEC ATTIT PWR 20. PAGE 14 E0269

WOR+45
NAT/G
SOVEREIGN
REGION

B47

HILL M.,IMMUNITIES AND PRIVILEGES OF INTERNATIONAL
OFFICIALS. CANADA EUR+WWI NETHERLAND SWITZERLND LAW
LEGIS DIPLOM LEGIT RESPECT...TIME/SEQ LEAGUE/NAT UN
VAL/FREE 20. PAGE 52 E1046

INT/ORG
ADMIN

HIRSHBERG H.S.,SUBJECT GUIDE TO UNITED STATES
GOVERNMENT PUBLICATIONS. USA+45 USA-45 LAW ADMIN
...SOC 20. PAGE 53 E1052
B47 BIBLIOG NAT/G DIPLOM LOC/G

HYDE C.C.,INTERNATIONAL LAW, CHIEFLY AS INTERPRETED
AND APPLIED BY THE UNITED STATES (3 VOLS., 2ND REV.
ED.). USA-45 WOR+45 WOR-45 INT/ORG CT/SYS WAR
NAT/LISM PEACE ORD/FREE...JURID 19/20 TREATY.
PAGE 56 E1119
B47 INT/LAW DIPLOM NAT/G POLICY

INTERNATIONAL COURT OF JUSTICE,CHARTER OF THE
UNITED NATIONS, STATUTE AND RULES OF COURT AND
OTHER CONSTITUTIONAL DOCUMENTS. SWITZERLND LAW
ADJUD INGP/REL...JURID 20 ICJ UN. PAGE 57 E1133
B47 INT/LAW INT/ORG CT/SYS DIPLOM

FOX W.T.R.,UNITED STATES POLICY IN A TWO POWER
WORLD. COM USA+45 USSR FORCES DOMIN AGREE NEUTRAL
NUC/PWR ORD/FREE SOVEREIGN 20 COLD/WAR TREATY
EUROPE/W INTERVENT. PAGE 39 E0780
N47 DIPLOM FOR/AID POLICY

GRIFFITH E.S.,RESEARCH IN POLITICAL SCIENCE: THE
WORK OF PANELS OF RESEARCH COMMITTEE, APSA. WOR+45
WOR-45 COM/IND R+D FORCES ACT/RES WAR...GOV/COMP
ANTHOL 20. PAGE 47 E0939
B48 BIBLIOG PHIL/SCI DIPLOM JURID

HOLCOMBE A.N.,HUMAN RIGHTS IN THE MODERN WORLD.
WOR+45 LEGIS DIPLOM ADJUD PERSON...INT/LAW 20 UN
TREATY CIVIL/LIB BILL/RIGHT. PAGE 54 E1071
B48 ORD/FREE INT/ORG CONSTN LAW

KEIR D.L.,CASES IN CONSTITUTIONAL LAW. UK CHIEF
LEGIS DIPLOM TAX PARL/PROC CRIME GOV/REL...INT/LAW
JURID 17/20. PAGE 60 E1195
B48 CONSTN LAW ADJUD CT/SYS

LOGAN R.W.,THE AFRICAN MANDATES IN WORLD POLITICS.
EUR+WWI GERMANY ISLAM INT/ORG BARGAIN...POLICY
INT/LAW 20. PAGE 66 E1321
B48 WAR COLONIAL AFR DIPLOM

MORGENTHAL H.J.,POLITICS AMONG NATIONS: THE
STRUGGLE FOR POWER AND PEACE. FUT WOR+45 INT/ORG
OP/RES PROB/SOLV BAL/PWR CONTROL ATTIT MORAL
...INT/LAW BIBLIOG 20 COLD/WAR. PAGE 75 E1494
B48 DIPLOM PEACE PWR POLICY

NEUBURGER O.,GUIDE TO OFFICIAL PUBLICATIONS OF THE
OTHER AMERICAN REPUBLICS: VENEZUELA (VOL. XIX).
VENEZUELA FINAN LEGIS PLAN BUDGET DIPLOM CT/SYS
PARL/PROC 19/20. PAGE 77 E1535
B48 BIBLIOG/A NAT/G CONSTN LAW

STOKES W.S.,BIBLIOGRAPHY OF STANDARD AND CLASSICAL
WORKS IN THE FIELDS OF AMERICAN POLITICAL SCIENCE.
USA+45 USA-45 POL/PAR PROVS FORCES DIPLOM ADMIN
CT/SYS APPORT 20 CONGRESS PRESIDENT. PAGE 94 E1876
B48 BIBLIOG NAT/G LOC/G CONSTN

GROSS L.,"THE PEACE OF WESTPHALIA, 1648-1948."
WOR+45 WOR-45 CONSTN BAL/PWR FEDERAL 17/20 TREATY
WESTPHALIA. PAGE 48 E0949
S48 INT/LAW AGREE CONCPT DIPLOM

MORGENTHAU H.J.,"THE TWILIGHT OF INTERNATIONAL
MORALITY" (BMR)" WOR+45 WOR-45 BAL/PWR WAR NAT/LISM
PEACE...POLICY INT/LAW IDEA/COMP 15/20 TREATY
INTERVENT. PAGE 75 E1495
S48 MORAL DIPLOM NAT/G

GROB F.,THE RELATIVITY OF WAR AND PEACE: A STUDY IN
LAW, HISTORY, AND POLLTICS. WOR+45 WOR-45 LAW
DIPLOM DEBATE...CONCPT LING IDEA/COMP BIBLIOG
18/20. PAGE 48 E0944
B49 WAR PEACE INT/LAW STYLE

JACKSON R.H.,INTERNATIONAL CONFERENCE ON MILITARY
TRIALS. FRANCE GERMANY UK USA+45 USSR VOL/ASSN
DELIB/GP REPAR ADJUD CT/SYS CRIME WAR 20 WAR/TRIAL.
PAGE 57 E1141
B49 DIPLOM INT/ORG INT/LAW CIVMIL/REL

US DEPARTMENT OF STATE,SOVIET BIBLIOGRAPHY
(PAMPHLET). CHINA/COM COM USSR LAW AGRI INT/ORG
ECO/TAC EDU/PROP...POLICY GEOG 20. PAGE 99 E1994
B49 BIBLIOG/A MARXISM CULTURE DIPLOM

KIRK G.,"MATTERIALS FOR THE STUDY OF INTERNATIONAL
RELATIONS." FUT UNIV WOR+45 INTELL EDU/PROP ROUTINE
PEACE ATTIT...INT/LAW JURID CONCPT OBS. PAGE 61
E1219
S49 INT/ORG ACT/RES DIPLOM

BOHATTA H.,INTERNATIONALE BIBLIOGRAPHIE. WOR+45 LAW
CULTURE PRESS. PAGE 13 E0260
B50 BIBLIOG DIPLOM NAT/G WRITING

BROWN E.S.,MANUAL OF GOVERNMENT PUBLICATIONS.
WOR+45 WOR-45 CONSTN INT/ORG MUNIC PROVS DIPLOM
ADMIN 20. PAGE 16 E0313
B50 BIBLIOG/A NAT/G LAW

COUNCIL BRITISH NATIONAL BIB,BRITISH NATIONAL
BIBLIOGRAPHY. UK AGRI CONSTRUC PERF/ART POL/PAR
SECT CREATE INT/TRADE LEAD...HUM JURID PHIL/SCI 20.
PAGE 26 E0519
B50 BIBLIOG/A NAT/G DIPLOM

JIMENEZ E.,VOTING AND HANDLING OF DISPUTES IN THE
SECURITY COUNCIL. WOR+45 CONSTN INT/ORG DIPLOM
LEGIT DETER CHOOSE MORAL ORD/FREE PWR...JURID
TIME/SEQ COLD/WAR UN 20. PAGE 59 E1168
B50 DELIB/GP ROUTINE

MOCKFORD J.,SOUTH-WEST AFRICA AND THE INTERNATIONAL
COURT (PAMPHLET). AFR GERMANY SOUTH/AFR UK
ECO/UNDEV DIPLOM CONTROL DISCRIM...DECISION JURID
20 AFRICA/SW. PAGE 74 E1475
B50 COLONIAL SOVEREIGN INT/LAW DOMIN

MONPIED E.,BIBLIOGRAPHIE FEDERALISTE: OUVRAGES
CHOISIS (VOL. I, MIMEOGRAPHED PAPER). EUR+WWI
DIPLOM ADMIN REGION ATTIT PACIFISM SOCISM...INT/LAW
19/20. PAGE 74 E1486
B50 BIBLIOG/A FEDERAL CENTRAL INT/ORG

ROSS A.,CONSTITUTION OF THE UNITED NATIONS. CONSTN
CONSULT DELIB/GP ECO/TAC...INT/LAW JURID 20 UN
LEAGUE/NAT. PAGE 86 E1721
B50 PEACE DIPLOM ORD/FREE INT/ORG

NUMELIN R.,"THE BEGINNINGS OF DIPLOMACY." INT/TRADE
WAR GP/REL PEACE STRANGE ATTIT...INT/LAW CONCPT
BIBLIOG. PAGE 78 E1559
C50 DIPLOM KIN CULTURE LAW

MONPIED E.,FEDERALIST BIBLIOGRAPHY: ARTICLES AND
DOCUMENTS PUBLISHED IN BRITISH PERIODICALS
1945-1951 (MIMEOGRAPHED). EUR+WWI UK WOR+45 DIPLOM
REGION ATTIT SOCISM...INT/LAW 20. PAGE 74 E1487
N51 BIBLIOG/A INT/ORG FEDERAL CENTRAL

BISSAINTHE M.,DICTIONNAIRE DE BIBLIOGRAPHIE
HAITIENNE. HAITI ELITES AGRI LEGIS DIPLOM INT/TRADE
WRITING ORD/FREE CATHISM...ART/METH GEOG 19/20
NEGRO TREATY. PAGE 12 E0234
B51 BIBLIOG L/A+17C SOCIETY NAT/G

CORBETT P.E.,LAW AND SOCIETY IN THE RELATIONS OF
STATES. FUT WOR+45 WOR-45 CONTROL WAR PEACE PWR
...POLICY JURID 16/20 TREATY. PAGE 26 E0505
B51 INT/LAW DIPLOM INT/ORG

INSTITUTE DES RELATIONS INTL,LES ASPECTS
ECONOMIQUES DU REARMEMENT (ETUDE DE L'INSTITUT DES
RELATIONS INTERNATIONALES A BRUXELLES). BELGIUM UK
USA+45 EXTR/IND FINAN FORCES WORKER PROB/SOLV
DIPLOM PRICE...POLICY 20 TREATY. PAGE 57 E1127
B51 WEAPON DEMAND ECO/TAC INT/TRADE

PUSEY M.J.,CHARLES EVANS HUGHES (2 VOLS.). LAW
CONSTN NAT/G POL/PAR DIPLOM LEGIT WAR CHOOSE
PERS/REL DRIVE HEREDITY 19/20 DEPT/STATE LEAGUE/NAT
SUPREME/CT HUGHES/CE WWI. PAGE 83 E1663
B51 BIOG TOP/EX ADJUD PERSON

KELSEN H.,"RECENT TRENDS IN THE LAW OF THE UNITED
NATIONS." KOREA WOR+45 CONSTN LEGIS DIPLOM LEGIT
DETER WAR RIGID/FLEX HEALTH ORD/FREE RESPECT
...JURID CON/ANAL UN VAL/FREE 20 NATO. PAGE 60
E1199
L51 INT/ORG LAW INT/LAW

APPADORAI A.,THE SUBSTANCE OF POLITICS (6TH ED.).
EX/STRUC LEGIS DIPLOM CT/SYS CHOOSE FASCISM MARXISM
SOCISM...BIBLIOG T. PAGE 5 E0100
B52 PHIL/SCI NAT/G

BRIGGS H.W.,THE LAW OF NATIONS (2ND ED.). WOR+45 WOR-45 NAT/G LEGIS WAR...ANTHOL 20 TREATY. PAGE 15 E0301
B52 INT/LAW DIPLOM JURID

DILLON D.R.,LATIN AMERICA, 1935-1949; A SELECTED BIBLIOGRAPHY. LAW EDU/PROP...SOC 20. PAGE 32 E0629
B52 BIBLIOG L/A+17C NAT/G DIPLOM

DUNN F.S.,CURRENT RESEARCH IN INTERNATIONAL AFFAIRS. UK USA+45...POLICY TREATY. PAGE 33 E0660
B52 BIBLIOG/A DIPLOM INT/LAW

FERRELL R.H.,PEACE IN THEIR TIME. FRANCE UK USA-45 INT/ORG NAT/G FORCES CREATE AGREE ARMS/CONT COERCE WAR TREATY 20 WILSON/W LEAGUE/NAT BRIAND/A. PAGE 37 E0741
B52 PEACE DIPLOM

FLECHTHEIM O.K.,FUNDAMENTALS OF POLITICAL SCIENCE. WOR+45 WOR-45 LAW POL/PAR EX/STRUC LEGIS ADJUD ATTIT PWR...INT/LAW. PAGE 38 E0760
B52 NAT/G DIPLOM IDEA/COMP CONSTN

JACKSON E.,MEETING OF THE MINDS: A WAY TO PEACE THROUGH MEDIATION. WOR+45 INDUS INT/ORG NAT/G DELIB/GP DIPLOM EDU/PROP LEGIT ORD/FREE...NEW/IDEA SELF/OBS TIME/SEQ CHARTS GEN/LAWS TOT/POP 20 UN TREATY. PAGE 57 E1139
B52 LABOR JUDGE

LIPPMANN W.,ISOLATION AND ALLIANCES: AN AMERICAN SPEAKS TO THE BRITISH. USA+45 USA-45 INT/ORG AGREE COERCE DETER WAR PEACE MORAL 20 TREATY INTERVENT. PAGE 65 E1301
B52 DIPLOM SOVEREIGN COLONIAL ATTIT

THOM J.M.,GUIDE TO RESEARCH MATERIAL IN POLITICAL SCIENCE (PAMPHLET). ELITES LOC/G MUNIC NAT/G LEGIS DIPLOM ADJUD CIVMIL/REL GOV/REL PWR MGT. PAGE 96 E1916
B52 BIBLIOG/A KNOWL

UNESCO,THESES DE SCIENCES SOCIALES: CATALOGUE ANALYTIQUE INTERNATIONAL DE THESES INEDITES DE DOCTORAT, 1940-1950. INT/ORG DIPLOM EDU/PROP...GEOG INT/LAW MGT PSY SOC 20. PAGE 98 E1958
B52 BIBLIOG ACADEM WRITING

US DEPARTMENT OF STATE,RESEARCH ON EASTERN EUROPE (EXCLUDING USSR). EUR+WWI LAW ECO/DEV NAT/G PROB/SOLV DIPLOM ADMIN LEAD MARXISM...TREND 19/20. PAGE 100 E1995
B52 BIBLIOG R+D ACT/RES COM

WRIGHT Q.,"CONGRESS AND THE TREATY-MAKING POWER." USA+45 WOR+45 CONSTN INTELL NAT/G CHIEF CONSULT EX/STRUC LEGIS TOP/EX CREATE GOV/REL DISPL DRIVE RIGID/FLEX...TREND TOT/POP CONGRESS CONGRESS 20 TREATY. PAGE 108 E2154
L52 ROUTINE DIPLOM INT/LAW DELIB/GP

STUART G.H.,"AMERICAN DIPLOMATIC AND CONSULAR PRACTICE (2ND ED.)" EUR+WWI MOD/EUR USA-45 DELIB/GP INT/TRADE ADJUD...BIBLIOG 20. PAGE 94 E1889
C52 DIPLOM ADMIN INT/ORG

BRETTON H.L.,STRESEMANN AND THE REVISION OF VERSAILLES: A FIGHT FOR REASON. EUR+WWI GERMANY FORCES BUDGET ARMS/CONT WAR SUPEGO...BIBLIOG 20 TREATY VERSAILLES STRESEMN/G. PAGE 15 E0294
B53 POLICY DIPLOM BIOG

LANDHEER B.,FUNDAMENTALS OF PUBLIC INTERNATIONAL LAW (SELECTIVE BIBLIOGRAPHIES OF THE LIBRARY OF THE PEACE PALACE, VOL. I; PAMPH). INT/ORG OP/RES PEACE ...IDEA/COMP 20. PAGE 62 E1250
B53 BIBLIOG/A INT/LAW DIPLOM PHIL/SCI

OPPENHEIM L.,INTERNATIONAL LAW: A TREATISE (7TH ED., 2 VOLS.). LAW CONSTN PROB/SOLV INT/TRADE ADJUD AGREE NEUTRAL WAR ORD/FREE SOVEREIGN...BIBLIOG 20 LEAGUE/NAT UN ILO. PAGE 79 E1579
B53 INT/LAW INT/ORG DIPLOM

ORFIELD L.B.,THE GROWTH OF SCANDINAVIAN LAW. DENMARK ICELAND NORWAY SWEDEN LAW DIPLOM...BIBLIOG 9/20. PAGE 79 E1581
B53 JURID CT/SYS NAT/G

STOUT H.M.,BRITISH GOVERNMENT. UK FINAN LOC/G
B53 NAT/G

POL/PAR DELIB/GP DIPLOM ADMIN COLONIAL CHOOSE ORD/FREE...JURID BIBLIOG 20 COMMONWLTH. PAGE 94 E1883
PARL/PROC CONSTN NEW/LIB

BINANI G.D.,INDIA AT A GLANCE (REV. ED.). INDIA COM/IND FINAN INDUS LABOR PROVS SCHOOL PLAN DIPLOM INT/TRADE ADMIN...JURID 20. PAGE 12 E0229
B54 INDEX CON/ANAL NAT/G ECO/UNDEV

LANDHEER B.,RECOGNITION IN INTERNATIONAL LAW (SELECTIVE BIBLIOGRAPHIES OF THE LIBRARY OF THE PEACE PALACE, VOL. II; PAMPHLET). NAT/G LEGIT SANCTION 20. PAGE 63 E1251
B54 BIBLIOG/A INT/LAW INT/ORG DIPLOM

STONE J.,LEGAL CONTROLS OF INTERNATIONAL CONFLICT: A TREATISE ON THE DYNAMICS OF DISPUTES AND WAR LAW. WOR+45 WOR-45 NAT/G DIPLOM CT/SYS SOVEREIGN...JURID CONCPT METH/CNCPT GEN/LAWS TOT/POP VAL/FREE COLD/WAR LEAGUE/NAT 20. PAGE 94 E1878
B54 INT/ORG LAW WAR INT/LAW

TOTOK W.,HANDBUCH DER BIBLIOGRAPHISCHEN NACHSCHLAGEWERKE. GERMANY LAW CULTURE ADMIN...SOC 20. PAGE 97 E1936
B54 BIBLIOG/A NAT/G DIPLOM POLICY

US SENATE COMM ON FOREIGN REL,REVIEW OF THE UNITED NATIONS CHARTER: A COLLECTION OF DOCUMENTS. LEGIS DIPLOM ADMIN ARMS/CONT WAR REPRESENT SOVEREIGN ...INT/LAW 20 UN. PAGE 101 E2029
B54 BIBLIOG CONSTN INT/ORG DEBATE

WRIGHT Q.,PROBLEMS OF STABILITY AND PROGRESS IN INTERNATIONAL RELATIONSHIPS. FUT WOR+45 WOR-45 SOCIETY LEGIS CREATE TEC/DEV ECO/TAC EDU/PROP ADJUD WAR PEACE ORD/FREE PWR...KNO/TEST TREND GEN/LAWS 20. PAGE 108 E2155
B54 INT/ORG CONCPT DIPLOM

NICOLSON H.,"THE EVOLUTION OF DIPLOMATIC METHOD." CHRIST-17C EUR+WWI FRANCE FUT ITALY MEDIT-7 MOD/EUR USA+45 USA-45 LAW NAT/G CREATE EDU/PROP LEGIT PEACE ATTIT ORD/FREE RESPECT SOVEREIGN. PAGE 77 E1548
L54 RIGID/FLEX METH/CNCPT DIPLOM

BOWIE R.R.,"STUDIES IN FEDERALISM." AGRI FINAN LABOR EX/STRUC FORCES LEGIS DIPLOM INT/TRADE ADJUD ...BIBLIOG 20 EEC. PAGE 14 E0279
C54 FEDERAL EUR+WWI INT/ORG CONSTN

BURR R.N.,DOCUMENTS ON INTER-AMERICAN COOPERATION: VOL. I, 1810-1881; VOL. II, 1881-1948. DELIB/GP BAL/PWR INT/TRADE REPRESENT NAT/LISM PEACE HABITAT ORD/FREE PWR SOVEREIGN...INT/LAW 20 OAS. PAGE 18 E0345
B55 BIBLIOG DIPLOM INT/ORG L/A+17C

CRAIG J.,BIBLIOGRAPHY OF PUBLIC ADMINISTRATION IN AUSTRALIA. CONSTN FINAN EX/STRUC LEGIS PLAN DIPLOM RECEIVE ADJUD ROUTINE...HEAL 19/20 AUSTRAL PARLIAMENT. PAGE 27 E0540
B55 BIBLIOG GOV/REL ADMIN NAT/G

GRINDEL C.W.,CONCEPT OF FREEDOM. WOR+45 WOR-45 LAW LABOR NAT/G SECT EDU/PROP 20. PAGE 47 E0942
B55 ORD/FREE DIPLOM CONCPT GP/REL

HOGAN W.N.,INTERNATIONAL CONFLICT AND COLLECTIVE SECURITY: THE PRINCIPLE OF CONCERN IN INTERNATIONAL ORGANIZATION. CONSTN EX/STRUC BAL/PWR DIPLOM ADJUD CONTROL CENTRAL CONSEN PEACE...INT/LAW CONCPT METH/COMP 20 UN LEAGUE/NAT. PAGE 53 E1066
B55 INT/ORG WAR ORD/FREE FORCES

JAPAN MOMBUSHO DAIGAKU GAKIYUT,BIBLIOGRAPHY OF THE STUDIES ON LAW AND POLITICS (PAMPHLET). CONSTN INDUS LABOR DIPLOM TAX ADMIN...CRIMLGY INT/LAW 20 CHINJAP. PAGE 58 E1150
B55 BIBLIOG LAW PHIL/SCI

PLISCHKE E.,AMERICAN FOREIGN RELATIONS: A BIBLIOGRAPHY OF OFFICIAL SOURCES. USA+45 USA-45 INT/ORG FORCES PRESS WRITING DEBATE EXEC...POLICY INT/LAW 18/20 CONGRESS. PAGE 81 E1621
B55 BIBLIOG/A DIPLOM NAT/G

SVARLIEN O.,AN INTRODUCTION TO THE LAW OF NATIONS. SEA AIR INT/ORG NAT/G CHIEF ADMIN AGREE WAR PRIVIL ORD/FREE SOVEREIGN...BIBLIOG 16/20. PAGE 95 E1897
B55 INT/LAW DIPLOM

TROTIER A.H.,DOCTORAL DISSERTATIONS ACCEPTED BY
AMERICAN UNIVERSITIES 1954-55. SECT DIPLOM HEALTH
...ART/METH GEOG INT/LAW SOC LING CHARTS 20.
PAGE 97 E1943

B55
BIBLIOG
ACADEM
USA+45
WRITING

UN HEADQUARTERS LIBRARY,BIBLIOQRAPHIE DE LA CHARTE
DES NATIONS UNIES. CHINA/COM KOREA WOR+45 VOL/ASSN
CONFER ADMIN COERCE PEACE ATTIT ORD/FREE SOVEREIGN
...INT/LAW 20 UNESCO UN. PAGE 97 E1953

B55
BIBLIOG/A
INT/ORG
DIPLOM

WRONG D.H.,AMERICAN AND CANADIAN VIEWPOINTS. CANADA
USA+45 CONSTN STRATA FAM SECT WORKER ECO/TAC
EDU/PROP ADJUD MARRIAGE...IDEA/COMP 20. PAGE 108
E2161

B55
DIPLOM
ATTIT
NAT/COMP
CULTURE

CARLSTON K.S.,LAW AND STRUCTURES OF SOCIAL ACTION.
LAW SOCIETY ECO/DEV DIPLOM CONTROL ATTIT...DECISION
CONCPT 20. PAGE 19 E0379

B56
JURID
INT/LAW
INGP/REL
STRUCT

CORBETT P.E.,MORALS LAW, AND POWER IN INTERNATIONAL
RELATIONS. WOR+45 WOR-45 INT/ORG VOL/ASSN DELIB/GP
CREATE BAL/PWR DIPLOM LEGIT ARMS/CONT MORAL...JURID
GEN/LAWS TOT/POP LEAGUE/NAT 20. PAGE 26 E0506

B56
SUPEGO
CONCPT
POLICY
INT/LAW

ESTEP R.,AN AIR POWER BIBLIOGRAPHY. USA+45 TEC/DEV
BUDGET DIPLOM EDU/PROP DETER CIVMIL/REL...DECISION
INT/LAW 20. PAGE 35 E0698

B56
BIBLIOG/A
FORCES
WEAPON
PLAN

FIELD G.C.,POLITICAL THEORY. POL/PAR REPRESENT
MORAL SOVEREIGN...JURID IDEA/COMP. PAGE 38 E0745

B56
CONCPT
NAT/G
ORD/FREE
DIPLOM

PERKINS D.,CHARLES EVANS HUGHES AND THE AMERICAN
DEMOCRATIC STATESMANSHIP. USA+45 USA-45 NAT/G
POL/PAR DELIB/GP JUDGE PLAN MORAL PWR...HIST/WRIT
LEAGUE/NAT 20. PAGE 80 E1609

B56
PERSON
BIOG
DIPLOM

WEIS P.,NATIONALITY AND STATELESSNESS IN
INTERNATIONAL LAW. UK WOR+45 WOR-45 LAW CONSTN
NAT/G DIPLOM EDU/PROP LEGIT ROUTINE RIGID/FLEX
...JURID RECORD CMN/WLTH 20. PAGE 105 E2109

B56
INT/ORG
SOVEREIGN
INT/LAW

POTTER P.B.,"NEUTRALITY, 1955." WOR+45 WOR-45
INT/ORG NAT/G WAR ATTIT...POLICY IDEA/COMP 17/20
LEAGUE/NAT UN COLD/WAR. PAGE 81 E1631

S56
NEUTRAL
INT/LAW
DIPLOM
CONCPT

ALIGHIERI D.,ON WORLD GOVERNMENT. ROMAN/EMP LAW
SOCIETY INT/ORG NAT/G POL/PAR ADJUD WAR GP/REL
PEACE WORSHIP 15 WORLDUNITY DANTE. PAGE 4 E0067

B57
POLICY
CONCPT
DIPLOM
SECT

BYRNES R.F.,BIBLIOGRAPHY OF AMERICAN PUBLICATIONS
ON EAST CENTRAL EUROPE, 1945-1957 (VOL. XXII). SECT
DIPLOM EDU/PROP RACE/REL...ART/METH GEOG JURID SOC
LING 20 JEWS. PAGE 18 E0354

B57
BIBLIOG/A
COM
MARXISM
NAT/G

CONOVER H.F.,NORTH AND NORTHEAST AFRICA; A SELECTED
ANNOTATED LIST OF WRITINGS. ALGERIA MOROCCO SUDAN
UAR CULTURE INT/ORG PROB/SOLV ADJUD NAT/LISM PWR
WEALTH...SOC 20 UN. PAGE 25 E0496

B57
BIBLIOG/A
DIPLOM
AFR
ECO/UNDEV

DONALDSON A.G.,SOME COMPARATIVE ASPECTS OF IRISH
LAW. IRELAND NAT/G DIPLOM ADMIN CT/SYS LEAD ATTIT
SOVEREIGN...JURID BIBLIOG/A 12/20 CMN/WLTH. PAGE 32
E0635

B57
CONSTN
LAW
NAT/COMP
INT/LAW

FREUND G.,UNHOLY ALLIANCE. EUR+WWI GERMANY USSR
FORCES ECO/TAC CONTROL WAR PWR...TREND TREATY.
PAGE 40 E0796

B57
DIPLOM
PLAN
POLICY

INSTITUT DE DROIT INTL,TABLEAU GENERAL DES
RESOLUTIONS (1873-1956). LAW NEUTRAL CRIME WAR
MARRIAGE PEACE...JURID 19/20. PAGE 56 E1124

B57
INT/LAW
DIPLOM
ORD/FREE
ADJUD

PALMER N.D.,INTERNATIONAL RELATIONS. WOR+45 INT/ORG
NAT/G ECO/TAC EDU/PROP COLONIAL WAR PWR SOVEREIGN
...POLICY T 20 TREATY. PAGE 79 E1593

B57
DIPLOM
BAL/PWR
NAT/COMP

SCHLOCHAUER H.J.,OFFENTLICHES RECHT. GERMANY/W
FINAN EX/STRUC LEGIS DIPLOM FEDERAL ORD/FREE
...INT/LAW 20. PAGE 88 E1757

B57
CONSTN
JURID
ADMIN
CT/SYS

SCHUBERT G.A.,THE PRESIDENCY IN THE COURTS. CONSTN
FORCES DIPLOM TARIFFS ADJUD CONTROL WAR...DECISION
MGT CHARTS 18/20 PRESIDENT CONGRESS SUPREME/CT.
PAGE 89 E1778

B57
PWR
CT/SYS
LEGIT
CHIEF

SINEY M.C.,THE ALLIED BLOCKADE OF GERMANY:
1914-1916. EUR+WWI GERMANY MOD/EUR USA-45 DIPLOM
CONTROL NEUTRAL PWR 20. PAGE 91 E1832

B57
DETER
INT/TRADE
INT/LAW
WAR

US COMMISSION GOVT SECURITY,RECOMMENDATIONS; AREA:
IMMIGRANT PROGRAM. USA+45 LAW WORKER DIPLOM
EDU/PROP WRITING ADMIN PEACE ATTIT...CONCPT ANTHOL
20 MIGRATION SUBVERT. PAGE 99 E1981

B57
POLICY
CONTROL
PLAN
NAT/G

US SENATE COMM ON JUDICIARY,HEARING BEFORE
SUBCOMMITTEE ON COMMITTEE OF JUDICIARY, UNITED
STATES SENATE: S. J. RES. 3. USA+45 NAT/G CONSULT
DELIB/GP DIPLOM ADJUD LOBBY REPRESENT 20 CONGRESS
TREATY. PAGE 102 E2040

B57
LEGIS
CONSTN
CONFER
AGREE

BOWETT D.W.,SELF-DEFENSE IN INTERNATIONAL LAW.
EUR+WWI MOD/EUR WOR+45 WOR-45 SOCIETY INT/ORG
CONSULT DIPLOM LEGIT COERCE ATTIT ORD/FREE...JURID
20 UN. PAGE 14 E0276

B58
ADJUD
CONCPT
WAR
INT/LAW

BRIERLY J.L.,THE BASIS OF OBLIGATION IN
INTERNATIONAL LAW, AND OTHER PAPERS. WOR+45 WOR-45
LEGIS...JURID CONCPT NAT/COMP ANTHOL 20. PAGE 15
E0299

B58
INT/LAW
DIPLOM
ADJUD
SOVEREIGN

DEUTSCHE GESCHAFT VOLKERRECHT,DIE VOLKERRECHTLICHEN
DISSERTATIONEN AN DEN WESTDEUTSCHEN UNIVERSITATEN,
1945-1957. GERMANY/W NAT/G DIPLOM ADJUD CT/SYS
...POLICY 20. PAGE 31 E0616

B58
BIBLIOG
INT/LAW
ACADEM
JURID

DUCLOUX L.,FROM BLACKMAIL TO TREASON. FRANCE PLAN
DIPLOM EDU/PROP PRESS RUMOR NAT/LISM...CRIMLGY 20.
PAGE 33 E0653

B58
COERCE
CRIME
NAT/G
PWR

HUNT B.I.,BIPARTISANSHIP: A CASE STUDY OF THE
FOREIGN ASSISTANCE PROGRAM, 1947-56 (DOCTORAL
THESIS). USA+45 INT/ORG CONSULT LEGIS TEC/DEV
...BIBLIOG PRESIDENT TREATY NATO TRUMAN/HS
EISNHWR/DD CONGRESS. PAGE 56 E1114

B58
FOR/AID
POL/PAR
GP/REL
DIPLOM

MANSERGH N.,COMMONWEALTH PERSPECTIVES. GHANA UK LAW
VOL/ASSN CONFER HEALTH SOVEREIGN...GEOG CHARTS
ANTHOL 20 CMN/WLTH AUSTRAL. PAGE 68 E1363

B58
DIPLOM
COLONIAL
INT/ORG
INGP/REL

MARTIN L.J.,INTERNATIONAL PROPAGANDA: ITS LEGAL AND
DIPLOMATIC CONTROL. UK USA+45 USSR CONSULT DELIB/GP
DOMIN CONTROL 20. PAGE 69 E1373

B58
EDU/PROP
DIPLOM
INT/LAW
ATTIT

MASON H.L.,TOYNBEE'S APPROACH TO WORLD POLITICS.
AFR USA+45 USSR LAW WAR NAT/LISM ALL/IDEOS...HUM
BIBLIOG. PAGE 69 E1380

B58
DIPLOM
CONCPT
PHIL/SCI
SECT

MOSKOWITZ M.,HUMAN RIGHTS AND WORLD ORDER. INT/ORG
PLAN GP/REL NAT/LISM SOVEREIGN...CONCPT 20 UN
TREATY CIV/RIGHTS. PAGE 75 E1502

B58
DIPLOM
INT/LAW
ORD/FREE

SCHOEDER P.W.,THE AXIS ALLIANCE AND JAPANESE-
AMERICAN RELATIONS 1941. ASIA GERMANY UK USA-45
PEACE ATTIT...POLICY BIBLIOG 20 CHINJAP TREATY.
PAGE 88 E1763

B58
AGREE
DIPLOM
WAR

B58

SEYID MUHAMMAD V.A.,THE LEGAL FRAMEWORK OF WORLD TRADE. WOR+45 INT/ORG DIPLOM CONTROL...BIBLIOG 20 TREATY UN IMF GATT. PAGE 90 E1807
INT/LAW
VOL/ASSN
INT/TRADE
TARIFFS

B58

SOC OF COMP LEGIS AND INT LAW,THE LAW OF THE SEA... (PAMPHLET). WOR+45 NAT/G INT/TRADE ADJUD CONTROL NUC/PWR WAR PEACE ATTIT ORD/FREE...JURID CHARTS 20 UN TREATY RESOURCE/N. PAGE 92 E1850
INT/LAW
INT/ORG
DIPLOM
SEA

B58

STONE J.,AGGRESSION AND WORLD ORDER: A CRITIQUE OF UNITED NATIONS THEORIES OF AGGRESSION. LAW CONSTN DELIB/GP PROB/SOLV BAL/PWR DIPLOM DEBATE ADJUD CRIME PWR...POLICY IDEA/COMP 20 UN SUEZ LEAGUE/NAT. PAGE 94 E1879
ORD/FREE
INT/ORG
WAR
CONCPT

L58

INT. SOC. SCI. BULL.,"TECHNIQUES OF MEDIATION AND CONCILIATION." EUR+WWI USA+45 SOCIETY INDUS INT/ORG LABOR NAT/G LEGIS DIPLOM EDU/PROP CHOOSE ATTIT RIGID/FLEX...JURID CONCPT GEN/LAWS 20. PAGE 57 E1129
VOL/ASSN
DELIB/GP
INT/LAW

L58

UNESCO,"TECHNIQUES OF MEDIATION AND CONCILIATION." EUR+WWI USA+45 WOR+45 INDUS FACE/GP EX/STRUC EDU/PROP LEGIT PEACE ORD/FREE...INT/LAW TIME/SEQ LEAGUE/NAT 20. PAGE 98 E1961
INT/ORG
CONSULT
DIPLOM

C58

RAJAN M.S.,"UNITED NATIONS AND DOMESTIC JURISDICTION." WOR+45 WOR-45 PARL/PROC...IDEA/COMP BIBLIOG 20 UN. PAGE 83 E1670
INT/LAW
DIPLOM
CONSTN
INT/ORG

N58

US HOUSE COMM FOREIGN AFFAIRS,HEARINGS ON DRAFT LEGISLATION TO AMEND FURTHER THE MUTUAL SECURITY ACT OF 1954 (PAMPHLET). USA+45 CONSULT FORCES BUDGET DIPLOM DETER COST ORD/FREE...JURID 20 DEPT/DEFEN UN DEPT/STATE. PAGE 100 E2002
LEGIS
DELIB/GP
CONFER
WEAPON

B59

BROOKES E.H.,THE COMMONWEALTH TODAY. UK ROMAN/EMP INT/ORG RACE/REL NAT/LISM SOVEREIGN...TREND SOC/INTEG 20. PAGE 16 E0307
FEDERAL
DIPLOM
JURID
IDEA/COMP

B59

CORBETT P.E.,LAW IN DIPLOMACY. UK USA+45 USSR CONSTN SOCIETY INT/ORG JUDGE LEGIT ATTIT ORD/FREE TOT/POP LEAGUE/NAT 20. PAGE 26 E0507
NAT/G
ADJUD
JURID
DIPLOM

B59

GOMEZ ROBLES J.,A STATEMENT OF THE LAWS OF GUATEMALA IN MATTERS AFFECTING BUSINESS (2ND ED. REV., ENLARGED). GUATEMALA L/A+17C LAW FINAN FAM WORKER ACT/RES DIPLOM ADJUD ADMIN GP/REL 20 OAS. PAGE 44 E0881
JURID
NAT/G
INDUS
LEGIT

B59

HARVARD UNIVERSITY LAW SCHOOL,INTERNATIONAL PROBLEMS OF FINANCIAL PROTECTION AGAINST NUCLEAR RISK. WOR+45 NAT/G DELIB/GP PROB/SOLV DIPLOM CONTROL ATTIT...POLICY INT/LAW MATH 20. PAGE 51 E1009
NUC/PWR
ADJUD
INDUS
FINAN

B59

HOOK S.,POLITICAL POWER AND PERSONAL FREEDOM: CRITICAL STUDIES IN DEMOCRACY, COMMUNISM AND CIVIL RIGHTS. UNIV LAW SOCIETY DIPLOM TOTALISM MARXISM SOCISM...PHIL/SCI IDEA/COMP 20 CIV/RIGHTS. PAGE 55 E1094
ORD/FREE
PWR
WELF/ST
CHOOSE

B59

KIRCHHEIMER O.,GEGENWARTSPROBLEME DER ASYLGEWAHRUNG. DOMIN GP/REL ATTIT...NAT/COMP 20. PAGE 61 E1217
DIPLOM
INT/LAW
JURID
ORD/FREE

B59

MAYER A.J.,POLITICAL ORIGINS OF THE NEW DIPLOMACY, 1917-1918. EUR+WWI MOD/EUR USA-45 WAR PWR...POLICY INT/LAW BIBLIOG. PAGE 70 E1392
TREND
DIPLOM

B59

OKINSHEVICH L.A.,LATIN AMERICA IN SOVIET WRITINGS, 1945-1958: A BIBLIOGRAPHY. USSR LAW ECO/UNDEV LABOR DIPLOM EDU/PROP REV...GEOG SOC 20. PAGE 78 E1573
BIBLIOG
WRITING
COM
L/A+17C

B59

REIFF H.,THE UNITED STATES AND THE TREATY LAW OF THE SEA. USA+45 USA-45 SEA SOCIETY INT/ORG CONSULT DELIB/GP LEGIS DIPLOM LEGIT ATTIT ORD/FREE PWR WEALTH...GEOG JURID TOT/POP 20 TREATY. PAGE 84 E1681
ADJUD
INT/LAW

B59

SCHNEIDER J.,TREATY-MAKING POWER OF INTERNATIONAL ORGANIZATIONS. FUT WOR+45 WOR-45 LAW NAT/G JUDGE DIPLOM LEGIT CT/SYS ORD/FREE PWR...INT/LAW JURID GEN/LAWS TOT/POP UNESCO 20 TREATY. PAGE 88 E1762
INT/ORG
ROUTINE

B59

SIMPSON J.L.,INTERNATIONAL ARBITRATION: LAW AND PRACTICE. WOR+45 WOR-45 INT/ORG DELIB/GP ADJUD PEACE MORAL ORD/FREE...METH 18/20. PAGE 91 E1829
INT/LAW
DIPLOM
CT/SYS
CONSULT

B59

U OF MICHIGAN LAW SCHOOL,ATOMS AND THE LAW. USA+45 PROVS WORKER PROB/SOLV DIPLOM ADMIN GOV/REL ANTHOL. PAGE 97 E1950
NUC/PWR
NAT/G
CONTROL
LAW

B59

VITTACHIT,EMERGENCY '58. CEYLON UK STRUCT NAT/G FORCES ADJUD CRIME REV NAT/LISM 20. PAGE 104 E2081
RACE/REL
DISCRIM
DIPLOM
SOVEREIGN

B59

WILDNER H.,DIE TECHNIK DER DIPLOMATIE. TOP/EX ROLE ORD/FREE...INT/LAW JURID IDEA/COMP NAT/COMP 20. PAGE 106 E2122
DIPLOM
POLICY
DELIB/GP
NAT/G

B59

WOETZEL R.K.,DIE INTERNATIONALE KONTROLLE DER HOHEREN LUFTSCHICHTEN UND DES WELTRAUMS. INT/ORG NAT/G CONTROL SUPEGO...JURID CONCPT 20. PAGE 107 E2136
SPACE
INT/LAW
DIPLOM
SOVEREIGN

L59

MCDOUGAL M.S.,"THE IDENTIFICATION AND APPRAISAL OF DIVERSE SYSTEMS OF PUBLIC ORDER (BMR)" WOR+45 NAT/G CONSULT EDU/PROP POLICY. PAGE 70 E1405
INT/LAW
DIPLOM
ALL/IDEOS

S59

POTTER P.B.,"OBSTACLES AND ALTERNATIVES TO INTERNATIONAL LAW." WOR+45 NAT/G VOL/ASSN DELIB/GP BAL/PWR DOMIN ROUTINE...JURID VAL/FREE 20. PAGE 81 E1632
INT/ORG
LAW
DIPLOM
INT/LAW

B60

JUNZ A.J.,PRESENT TRENDS IN AMERICAN NATIONAL GOVERNMENT. LEGIS DIPLOM ADMIN CT/SYS ORD/FREE ...CONCPT ANTHOL 20 CONGRESS PRESIDENT SUPREME/CT. PAGE 2 E0040
POL/PAR
CHOOSE
CONSTN
NAT/G

B60

AMERICAN ASSOCIATION LAW LIB,INDEX TO FOREIGN LEGAL PERIODICALS. WOR+45 MUNIC...IDEA/COMP 20. PAGE 4 E0075
INDEX
LAW
JURID
DIPLOM

B60

BERTHOLD O.,KAISER, VOLK UND AVIGNON. GERMANY CHIEF LEGIT LEAD NAT/LISM CONSERVE 14 POPE CHRUCH/STA LUDWIG/BAV JOHN/XXII. PAGE 11 E0217
DIPLOM
CATHISM
JURID

B60

BYRD E.M. JR.,TREATIES AND EXECUTIVE AGREEMENTS IN THE UNITED STATES: THEIR SEPARATE ROLES AND LIMITATIONS. USA+45 USA-45 EX/STRUC TARIFFS CT/SYS GOV/REL FEDERAL...IDEA/COMP BIBLIOG SUPREME/CT SENATE CONGRESS. PAGE 18 E0353
CHIEF
INT/LAW
DIPLOM

B60

DUMON F.,LA COMMUNAUTE FRANCO-AFRO-MALGACHE: SES ORIGINES, SES INSTITUTIONS, SON EVOLUTION. FRANCE MADAGASCAR POL/PAR DIPLOM ADMIN ATTIT...TREND T 20. PAGE 33 E0657
JURID
INT/ORG
AFR
CONSTN

B60

ENGEL J.,THE SECURITY OF THE FREE WORLD. USSR WOR+45 STRATA STRUCT ECO/DEV ECO/UNDEV INT/ORG DELIB/GP FORCES DOMIN LEGIT ADJUD EXEC ARMS/CONT COERCE...POLICY CONCPT NEW/IDEA TIME/SEQ GEN/LAWS COLD/WAR WORK UN 20 NATO. PAGE 35 E0689
COM
TREND
DIPLOM

B60

FISCHER L.,THE SOVIETS IN WORLD AFFAIRS. CHINA/COM COM EUR+WWI USSR INT/ORG CONFER LEAD ARMS/CONT REV PWR...CHARTS 20 TREATY VERSAILLES. PAGE 38 E0755
DIPLOM
NAT/G
POLICY
MARXISM

B60
FLORES R.H.,CATALOGO DE TESIS DOCTORALES DE LAS FACULTADES DE LA UNIVERSIDAD DE EL SALVADOR. EL/SALVADR LAW DIPLOM ADMIN LEAD GOV/REL...SOC 19/20. PAGE 39 E0767
BIBLIOG
ACADEM
L/A+17C
NAT/G

B60
HEYSE T.,PROBLEMS FONCIERS ET REGIME DES TERRES (ASPECTS ECONOMIQUES, JURIDIQUES ET SOCIAUX). AFR CONGO/BRAZ INT/ORG DIPLOM SOVEREIGN...GEOG TREATY 20. PAGE 52 E1037
BIBLIOG
AGRI
ECO/UNDEV
LEGIS

B60
JENNINGS R.,PROGRESS OF INTERNATIONAL LAW. FUT WOR+45 WOR-45 SOCIETY NAT/G VOL/ASSN DELIB/GP DIPLOM EDU/PROP LEGIT COERCE ATTIT DRIVE MORAL ORD/FREE...JURID CONCPT OBS TIME/SEQ TREND GEN/LAWS. PAGE 58 E1164
INT/ORG
LAW
INT/LAW

B60
LEWIS P.R.,LITERATURE OF THE SOCIAL SCIENCES: AN INTRODUCTORY SURVEY AND GUIDE. UK LAW INDUS DIPLOM INT/TRADE ADMIN...MGT 19/20. PAGE 65 E1294
BIBLIOG/A
SOC

B60
MENDELSON W.,CAPITALISM, DEMOCRACY, AND THE SUPREME COURT. USA+45 USA-45 CONSTN DIPLOM GOV/REL ATTIT ORD/FREE LAISSEZ...POLICY CHARTS PERS/COMP 18/20 SUPREME/CT MARSHALL/J HOLMES/OW TANEY/RB FIELD/JJ. PAGE 72 E1437
JUDGE
CT/SYS
JURID
NAT/G

B60
PRICE D.,THE SECRETARY OF STATE. USA+45 CONSTN ELITES INTELL CHIEF EX/STRUC TOP/EX LEGIT ATTIT PWR SKILL...DECISION 20 CONGRESS. PAGE 82 E1650
CONSULT
DIPLOM
INT/LAW

B60
UNITED WORLD FEDERALISTS,UNITED WORLD FEDERALISTS; PANORAMA OF RECENT BOOKS, FILMS, AND JOURNALS ON WORLD FEDERATION, THE UN, AND WORLD PEACE. CULTURE ECO/UNDEV PROB/SOLV FOR/AID ARMS/CONT NUC/PWR ...INT/LAW PHIL/SCI 20 UN. PAGE 98 E1971
BIBLIOG/A
DIPLOM
INT/ORG
PEACE

L60
LAUTERPACHT E.,"THE SUEZ CANAL SETTLEMENT." FRANCE ISLAM ISRAEL UAR UK BAL/PWR DIPLOM LEGIT...JURID GEN/LAWS ANTHOL SUEZ VAL/FREE 20. PAGE 63 E1263
INT/ORG
LAW

S60
POTTER P.B.,"RELATIVE VALUES OF INTERNATIONAL RELATIONS, LAW, AND ORGANIZATIONS." WOR+45 NAT/G LEGIT ADJUD ORD/FREE...CONCPT TOT/POP COLD/WAR 20. PAGE 81 E1633
INT/ORG
LEGIS
DIPLOM
INT/LAW

S60
SANDERS R.,"NUCLEAR DYNAMITE: A NEW DIMENSION IN FOREIGN POLICY." FUT WOR+45 ECO/DEV CONSULT TEC/DEV PERCEPT...CONT/OBS TIME/SEQ TREND GEN/LAWS TOT/POP 20 TREATY. PAGE 87 E1745
INDUS
PWR
DIPLOM
NUC/PWR

S60
THOMPSON K.W.,"MORAL PURPOSE IN FOREIGN POLICY: REALITIES AND ILLUSIONS." WOR+45 WOR-45 LAW CULTURE SOCIETY INT/ORG PLAN ADJUD ADMIN COERCE RIGID/FLEX SUPEGO KNOWL ORD/FREE PWR...SOC TREND SOC/EXP TOT/POP 20. PAGE 96 E1921
MORAL
JURID
DIPLOM

B61
BAINS J.S.,STUDIES IN POLITICAL SCIENCE. INDIA WOR+45 WOR-45 CONSTN BAL/PWR ADJUD ADMIN PARL/PROC SOVEREIGN...SOC METH/COMP ANTHOL 17/20 UN. PAGE 7 E0137
DIPLOM
INT/LAW
NAT/G

B61
BRENNAN D.G.,ARMS CONTROL, DISARMAMENT, AND NATIONAL SECURITY. WOR+45 NAT/G FORCES CREATE PROB/SOLV PARTIC WAR PEACE...DECISION INT/LAW ANTHOL BIBLIOG 20. PAGE 15 E0291
ARMS/CONT
ORD/FREE
DIPLOM
POLICY

B61
BURDETTE F.L.,POLITICAL SCIENCE: A SELECTED BIBLIOGRAPHY OF BOOKS IN PRINT, WITH ANNOTATIONS (PAMPHLET). LAW LOC/G NAT/G POL/PAR PROVS DIPLOM EDU/PROP ADMIN CHOOSE ATTIT 20. PAGE 17 E0330
BIBLIOG/A
GOV/COMP
CONCPT
ROUTINE

B61
CARNELL F.,THE POLITICS OF THE NEW STATES: A SELECT ANNOTATED BIBLIOGRAPHY WITH SPECIAL REFERENCE TO THE COMMONWEALTH. CONSTN ELITES LABOR NAT/G POL/PAR EX/STRUC DIPLOM ADJUD ADMIN...GOV/COMP 20 COMMONWLTH. PAGE 20 E0387
BIBLIOG/A
AFR
ASIA
COLONIAL

B61
CONFERENCE ATLANTIC COMMUNITY,AN INTRODUCTORY BIBLIOGRAPHY. COM WOR+45 FORCES DIPLOM ECO/TAC WAR
BIBLIOG/A
CON/ANAL

...INT/LAW HIST/WRIT COLD/WAR NATO. PAGE 25 E0485
INT/ORG

B61
JENKS C.W.,INTERNATIONAL IMMUNITIES. PLAN EDU/PROP ADMIN PERCEPT...OLD/LIB JURID CONCPT TREND TOT/POP. PAGE 58 E1157
INT/ORG
DIPLOM

B61
KAPLAN M.A.,THE POLITICAL FOUNDATIONS OF INTERNATIONAL LAW. WOR+45 WOR-45 CULTURE SOCIETY ECO/DEV DIPLOM PERCEPT...TECHNIC METH/CNCPT. PAGE 59 E1184
INT/ORG
LAW

B61
LARSON A.,WHEN NATIONS DISAGREE. USA+45 WOR+45 INT/ORG ADJUD COERCE CRIME OWN SOVEREIGN...POLICY JURID 20. PAGE 63 E1258
INT/LAW
DIPLOM
WAR

B61
MECHAM J.L.,THE UNITED STATES AND INTER-AMERICAN SECURITY, 1889-1960. L/A+17C USA+45 USA-45 CONSTN FORCES INT/TRADE PEACE TOTALISM ATTIT...JURID 19/20 UN OAS. PAGE 72 E1432
DIPLOM
WAR
ORD/FREE
INT/ORG

B61
NEWMAN R.P.,RECOGNITION OF COMMUNIST CHINA? A STUDY IN ARGUMENT. CHINA/COM NAT/G PROB/SOLV RATIONAL ...INT/LAW LOG IDEA/COMP BIBLIOG 20. PAGE 77 E1544
MARXISM
ATTIT
DIPLOM
POLICY

B61
RIENOW R.,CONTEMPORARY INTERNATIONAL POLITICS. WOR+45 INT/ORG BAL/PWR EDU/PROP COLONIAL NEUTRAL REGION WAR PEACE...INT/LAW 20 COLD/WAR UN. PAGE 85 E1698
DIPLOM
PWR
POLICY
NAT/G

B61
SCOTT A.M.,POLITICS, USA; CASES ON THE AMERICAN DEMOCRATIC PROCESS. USA+45 CHIEF FORCES DIPLOM LOBBY CHOOSE RACE/REL FEDERAL ATTIT...JURID ANTHOL T 20 PRESIDENT CONGRESS CIVIL/LIB. PAGE 90 E1795
CT/SYS
CONSTN
NAT/G
PLAN

B61
WRIGHT Q.,THE ROLE OF INTERNATIONAL LAW IN THE ELIMINATION OF WAR. FUT WOR+45 WOR-45 NAT/G BAL/PWR DIPLOM DOMIN LEGIT PWR...POLICY INT/LAW JURID CONCPT TIME/SEQ TREND GEN/LAWS COLD/WAR 20. PAGE 108 E2158
INT/ORG
ADJUD
ARMS/CONT

L61
TAUBENFELD H.J.,"A TREATY FOR ANTARCTICA." FUT USA+45 INTELL INT/ORG LABOR 20 TREATY ANTARCTICA. PAGE 95 E1909
R+D
ACT/RES
DIPLOM

S61
ALGER C.F.,"NON-RESOLUTION CONSEQUENCES OF THE UNITED NATIONS AND THEIR EFFECT ON INTERNATIONAL CONFLICT." WOR+45 ECO/DEV NAT/G CONSULT DELIB/GP TOP/EX ACT/RES PLAN DIPLOM EDU/PROP ROUTINE ATTIT ALL/VALS...INT/LAW TOT/POP UN 20. PAGE 3 E0065
INT/ORG
DRIVE
BAL/PWR

S61
LIPSON L.,"AN ARGUMENT ON THE LEGALITY OF RECONNAISSANCE STATELLITES." COM USA+45 USSR WOR+45 AIR INTELL NAT/G CONSULT PLAN DIPLOM LEGIT ROUTINE ATTIT...INT/LAW JURID CONCPT METH/CNCPT TREND COLD/WAR 20. PAGE 65 E1302
INT/ORG
LAW
SPACE

S61
OLIVER C.T.,"THE AMERICAN LAW INSTITUTE'S DRAFT RESTATEMENT OF THE FOREIGN RELATIONS LAW OF THE UNITED STATES." FUT USA+45 SOCIETY CONSULT EDU/PROP. PAGE 78 E1574
KNOWL
JURID
DIPLOM

B62
ALEXANDROWICZ C.H.,WORLD ECONOMIC AGENCIES: LAW AND PRACTICE. WOR+45 DIST/IND FINAN LABOR CONSULT INT/TRADE TARIFFS REPRESENT HEALTH...JURID 20 UN GATT EEC OAS ECSC. PAGE 3 E0063
INT/LAW
INT/ORG
DIPLOM
ADJUD

B62
AMERICAN LAW INSTITUTE,FOREIGN RELATIONS LAW OF THE UNITED STATES: RESTATEMENT, SECOND. USA+45 NAT/G LEGIS ADJUD EXEC ROUTINE GOV/REL...INT/LAW JURID CONCPT 20 TREATY. PAGE 4 E0082
PROF/ORG
LAW
DIPLOM
ORD/FREE

B62
BIBLIOTHEQUE PALAIS DE LA PAIX,CATALOGUE OF THE PEACE PALACE LIBRARY, SUPPLEMENT 1937-1952 (7 VOLS.). WOR+45 WOR-45 INT/ORG NAT/G ADJUD WAR PEACE ...JURID 20. PAGE 12 E0225
BIBLIOG
INT/LAW
DIPLOM

B62
BISHOP W.W. JR.,INTERNATIONAL LAW: CASES AND MATERIALS. WOR+45 INT/ORG FORCES PROB/SOLV AGREE
INT/LAW
DIPLOM

WAR...JURID IDEA/COMP T 20 TREATY. PAGE 12 E0233 — CONCPT CT/SYS

E1787 — SPACE

B62

BLAUSTEIN A.P.,MANUAL ON FOREIGN LEGAL PERIODICALS AND THEIR INDEX. WOR+45 DIPLOM 20. PAGE 13 E0244 — BIBLIOG INDEX LAW JURID

B62

BOCHENSKI J.M.,HANDBOOK ON COMMUNISM. USSR WOR+45 LAW SOCIETY NAT/G POL/PAR SECT CRIME PERSON MARXISM ...SOC ANTHOL 20. PAGE 13 E0254 — COM DIPLOM POLICY CONCPT

B62

COLOMBOS C.J.,THE INTERNATIONAL LAW OF THE SEA. WOR+45 EXTR/IND DIPLOM INT/TRADE TARIFFS AGREE WAR ...TIME/SEQ 20 TREATY. PAGE 24 E0476 — INT/LAW SEA JURID ADJUD

B62

COSTA RICA UNIVERSIDAD BIBL,LISTA DE TESIS DE GRADO DE LA UNIVERSIDAD DE COSTA RICA. COSTA/RICA LAW LOC/G ADMIN LEAD...SOC 20. PAGE 26 E0518 — BIBLIOG/A NAT/G DIPLOM ECO/UNDEV

B62

DOUGLAS W.O.,DEMOCRACY'S MANIFESTO. COM USA+45 ECO/UNDEV INT/ORG FORCES PLAN NEUTRAL TASK MARXISM ...JURID 20 NATO SEATO. PAGE 32 E0642 — DIPLOM POLICY NAT/G ORD/FREE

B62

DUROSELLE J.B.,HISTOIRE DIPLOMATIQUE DE 1919 A NOS JOURS (3RD ED.). FRANCE INT/ORG CHIEF FORCES CONFER ARMS/CONT WAR PEACE ORD/FREE...T TREATY 20 COLD/WAR. PAGE 34 E0667 — DIPLOM WOR+45 WOR-45

B62

GYORGY A.,PROBLEMS IN INTERNATIONAL RELATIONS. COM CT/SYS NUC/PWR ALL/IDEOS 20 UN EEC ECSC. PAGE 49 E0966 — DIPLOM NEUTRAL BAL/PWR REV

B62

HENDERSON W.O.,THE GENESIS OF THE COMMON MARKET. EUR+WWI FRANCE MOD/EUR UK SEA COM/IND EXTR/IND COLONIAL DISCRIM...TIME/SEQ CHARTS BIBLIOG 18/20 EEC TREATY. PAGE 52 E1030 — ECO/DEV INT/TRADE DIPLOM

B62

JACOBINI H.B.,INTERNATIONAL LAW: A TEXT. DIPLOM ADJUD NEUTRAL WAR PEACE T. PAGE 57 E1143 — INT/LAW CT/SYS CONCPT

B62

JENKS C.W.,THE PROPER LAW OF INTERNATIONAL ORGANISATIONS. DIPLOM LEGIT AGREE CT/SYS SANCTION REPRESENT SOVEREIGN...GEN/LAWS 20 UN UNESCO ILO NATO OAS. PAGE 58 E1158 — LAW INT/ORG ADJUD INT/LAW

B62

KIDDER F.E.,THESES ON PAN AMERICAN TOPICS. LAW CULTURE NAT/G SECT DIPLOM HEALTH...ART/METH GEOG SOC 13/20. PAGE 61 E1213 — BIBLIOG CHRIST-17C L/A+17C SOCIETY

B62

MCDOUGAL M.S.,THE PUBLIC ORDER OF THE OCEANS. WOR+45 WOR-45 SEA INT/ORG NAT/G CONSULT DELIB/GP DIPLOM LEGIT PEACE RIGID/FLEX...GEOG INT/LAW JURID RECORD TOT/POP 20 TREATY. PAGE 70 E1407 — ADJUD ORD/FREE

B62

NORGAARD C.A.,THE POSITION OF THE INDIVIDUAL IN INTERNATIONAL LAW. INT/ORG SUPEGO ORD/FREE SOVEREIGN...CONCPT 20 UN. PAGE 78 E1556 — INT/LAW DIPLOM CRIME JURID

B62

OTTENBERG M.,THE FEDERAL INVESTIGATORS. USA+45 LAW COM/IND DIST/IND WORKER DIPLOM INT/TRADE CONTROL FEDERAL HEALTH ORD/FREE FBI CIA FTC SEC FDA. PAGE 79 E1585 — FORCES INSPECT NAT/G CRIME

B62

PERKINS D.,AMERICA'S QUEST FOR PEACE. USA+45 WOR+45 DIPLOM CONFER NAT/LISM ATTIT 20 UN TREATY. PAGE 80 E1610 — INT/LAW INT/ORG ARMS/CONT PEACE

B62

SCHWARTZ L.E.,INTERNATIONAL ORGANIZATIONS AND SPACE COOPERATION. VOL/ASSN CONSULT CREATE TEC/DEV SANCTION...POLICY INT/LAW PHIL/SCI 20 UN. PAGE 89 — INT/ORG DIPLOM R+D

B62

SHAW C.,LEGAL PROBLEMS IN INTERNATIONAL TRADE AND INVESTMENT. WOR+45 ECO/DEV ECO/UNDEV MARKET DIPLOM TAX INCOME ROLE...ANTHOL BIBLIOG 20 TREATY UN IMF GATT. PAGE 91 E1816 — INT/LAW INT/TRADE FINAN ECO/TAC

B62

SOMMER T.,DEUTSCHLAND UND JAPAN ZWISCHEN DEN MACHTEN. GERMANY DELIB/GP BAL/PWR AGREE COERCE TOTALISM PWR 20 CHINJAP TREATY. PAGE 93 E1856 — DIPLOM WAR ATTIT

B62

THOMPSON K.W.,AMERICAN DIPLOMACY AND EMERGENT PATTERNS. USA+45 USA-45 WOR+45 WOR-45 LAW DELIB/GP FORCES TOP/EX DIPLOM ATTIT DRIVE RIGID/FLEX ORD/FREE PWR SOVEREIGN...POLICY 20. PAGE 96 E1922 — NAT/G BAL/PWR

B62

US CONGRESS,COMMUNICATIONS SATELLITE LEGISLATION: HEARINGS BEFORE COMM ON AERON AND SPACE SCIENCES ON BILLS S2550 AND 2814. WOR+45 LAW VOL/ASSN PLAN DIPLOM CONTROL OWN PEACE...NEW/IDEA CONGRESS NASA. PAGE 99 E1990 — SPACE COM/IND ADJUD GOV/REL

B62

US SENATE COMM ON JUDICIARY,CONSTITUTIONAL RIGHTS OF MILITARY PERSONNEL. USA+45 USA-45 FORCES DIPLOM WAR CONGRESS. PAGE 102 E2046 — CONSTN ORD/FREE JURID CT/SYS

B62

WADSWORTH J.J.,THE PRICE OF PEACE. WOR+45 TEC/DEV CONTROL NUC/PWR PEACE ATTIT TREATY 20. PAGE 104 E2089 — DIPLOM INT/ORG ARMS/CONT POLICY

L62

GROSS L.,"IMMUNITIES AND PRIVILEGES OF DELIGATIONS TO THE UNITED NATIONS." USA+45 WOR+45 STRATA NAT/G VOL/ASSN CONSULT DIPLOM EDU/PROP ROUTINE RESPECT ...POLICY INT/LAW CONCPT UN 20. PAGE 48 E0950 — INT/ORG LAW ELITES

L62

NIZARD L.,"CUBAN QUESTION AND SECURITY COUNCIL." L/A+17C USA+45 ECO/UNDEV NAT/G POL/PAR DELIB/GP ECO/TAC PWR...RELATIV OBS TIME/SEQ TREND GEN/LAWS UN 20 UN. PAGE 77 E1551 — INT/ORG JURID DIPLOM CUBA

L62

PETKOFF D.K.,"RECOGNITION AND NON-RECOGNITION OF STATES AND GOVERNMENTS IN INTERNATIONAL LAW." ASIA COM USA+45 WOR+45 NAT/G ACT/RES DIPLOM DOMIN LEGIT COERCE ORD/FREE PWR...CONCPT GEN/LAWS 20. PAGE 80 E1611 — INT/ORG LAW INT/LAW

S62

BIERZANECK R.,"LA NON-RECONAISSANCE ET LE DROIT INTERNATIONAL CONTEMPORAIN." EUR+WWI FUT WOR+45 LAW ECO/DEV ATTIT RIGID/FLEX...CONCPT TIME/SEQ TOT/POP 20. PAGE 12 E0228 — EDU/PROP JURID DIPLOM INT/LAW

S62

LISSITZYN O.J.,"SOME LEGAL IMPLICATIONS OF THE U-2 AND RB-47 INCIDENTS." FUT USA+45 USSR WOR+45 AIR NAT/G DIPLOM LEGIT MORAL ORD/FREE SOVEREIGN...JURID GEN/LAWS GEN/METH COLD/WAR 20 U-2. PAGE 65 E1305 — LAW CONCPT SPACE INT/LAW

S62

MCWHINNEY E.,"CO-EXISTENCE, THE CUBA CRISIS, AND COLD WAR-INTERNATIONAL WAR." CUBA USA+45 USSR WOR+45 NAT/G TOP/EX BAL/PWR DIPLOM DOMIN LEGIT PEACE RIGID/FLEX ORD/FREE...STERTYP COLD/WAR 20. PAGE 71 E1427 — CONCPT INT/LAW

S62

SCHACHTER O.,"DAG HAMMARSKJOLD AND THE RELATION OF LAW TO POLITICS." FUT WOR+45 INT/ORG CONSULT PLAN TEC/DEV BAL/PWR DIPLOM LEGIT ATTIT PERCEPT ORD/FREE ...POLICY JURID CONCPT OBS TESTS STERTYP GEN/LAWS 20 HAMMARSK/D. PAGE 87 E1751 — ACT/RES ADJUD

S62

VIGNES D.,"L'AUTORITE DES TRAITES INTERNATIONAUX EN DROIT INTERNE." EUR+WWI UNIV LAW CONSTN INTELL NAT/G POL/PAR DIPLOM ATTIT PERCEPT ALL/VALS ...POLICY INT/LAW JURID CONCPT TIME/SEQ 20 TREATY. PAGE 104 E2075 — STRUCT LEGIT FRANCE

C62

BACON F.,"OF THE TRUE GREATNESS OF KINGDOMS AND ESTATES" (1612) IN F. BACON, ESSAYS." ELITES FORCES DOMIN EDU/PROP LEGIT...POLICY GEN/LAWS 16/17 TREATY. PAGE 7 E0129 — WAR PWR DIPLOM CONSTN

LILLICH R.B.,"INTERNATIONAL CLAIMS: THEIR
ADJUDICATION BY NATIONAL COMMISSIONS." WOR+45
WOR-45 NAT/G ADJUD...JURID BIBLIOG 18/20. PAGE 65
E1298

C62
INT/LAW
DIPLOM
PROB/SOLV

BADI J.,THE GOVERNMENT OF THE STATE OF ISRAEL: A
CRITICAL ACCOUNT OF ITS PARLIAMENT, EXECUTIVE, AND
JUDICIARY. ISRAEL ECO/DEV CHIEF DELIB/GP LEGIS
DIPLOM CT/SYS INGP/REL PEACE ORD/FREE...BIBLIOG 20
PARLIAMENT ARABS MIGRATION. PAGE 7 E0131

B63
NAT/G
CONSTN
EX/STRUC
POL/PAR

BOWETT D.W.,THE LAW OF INTERNATIONAL INSTITUTIONS.
WOR+45 WOR-45 CONSTN DELIB/GP EX/STRUC JUDGE
EDU/PROP LEGIT CT/SYS EXEC ROUTINE RIGID/FLEX
ORD/FREE PWR...JURID CONCPT ORG/CHARTS GEN/METH
LEAGUE/NAT OAS OEEC 20 UN. PAGE 14 E0277

B63
INT/ORG
ADJUD
DIPLOM

DECOTTIGNIES R.,LES NATIONALITES AFRICAINES. AFR
NAT/G PROB/SOLV DIPLOM COLONIAL ORD/FREE...CHARTS
GOV/COMP 20. PAGE 30 E0602

B63
NAT/LISM
JURID
LEGIS
LAW

DEENER D.R.,CANADA - UNITED STATES TREATY
RELATIONS. CANADA USA+45 USA-45 NAT/G FORCES PLAN
PROB/SOLV AGREE NUC/PWR...TREND 18/20 TREATY.
PAGE 30 E0603

B63
DIPLOM
INT/LAW
POLICY

DOUGLAS W.O.,THE ANATOMY OF LIBERTY: THE RIGHTS OF
MAN WITHOUT FORCE. WOR+45 ECO/DEV ECO/UNDEV LOC/G
FORCES GOV/REL...SOC/WK 20. PAGE 32 E0643

B63
PEACE
LAW
DIPLOM
ORD/FREE

DUNN F.S.,PEACE-MAKING AND THE SETTLEMENT WITH
JAPAN. ASIA USA+45 USA-45 FORCES BAL/PWR ECO/TAC
CONFER WAR PWR SOVEREIGN 20 CHINJAP COLD/WAR
TREATY. PAGE 33 E0661

B63
POLICY
PEACE
PLAN
DIPLOM

ELIAS T.O.,GOVERNMENT AND POLITICS IN AFRICA.
CONSTN CULTURE SOCIETY NAT/G POL/PAR DIPLOM
REPRESENT PERSON...SOC TREND BIBLIOG 4/20. PAGE 34
E0681

B63
AFR
NAT/LISM
COLONIAL
LAW

FAWCETT J.E.S.,THE BRITISH COMMONWEALTH IN
INTERNATIONAL LAW. LAW INT/ORG NAT/G VOL/ASSN
OP/RES DIPLOM ADJUD CENTRAL CONSEN...NET/THEORY
CMN/WLTH TREATY. PAGE 36 E0723

B63
INT/LAW
STRUCT
COLONIAL

HIGGINS R.,THE DEVELOPMENT OF INTERNATIONAL LAW
THROUGH THE POLITICAL ORGANS OF THE UNITED NATIONS.
WOR+45 FORCES DIPLOM AGREE COERCE ATTIT SOVEREIGN
...BIBLIOG 20 UN TREATY. PAGE 52 E1041

B63
INT/ORG
INT/LAW
TEC/DEV
JURID

JENKS C.W.,LAW, FREEDOM, AND WELFARE. WOR+45 GIVE
ADJUD WAR PEACE HABITAT ORD/FREE. PAGE 58 E1159

B63
INT/LAW
DIPLOM
SOVEREIGN
PROB/SOLV

LANOUE G.R.,A BIBLIOGRAPHY OF DOCTORAL
DISSERTATIONS ON POLITICS AND RELIGION. USA+45
USA-45 CONSTN PROVS DIPLOM CT/SYS MORAL...POLICY
JURID CONCPT 20. PAGE 63 E1252

B63
BIBLIOG
NAT/G
LOC/G
SECT

LYONS F.S.L.,INTERNATIONALISM IN EUROPE 1815-1914.
LAW AGRI COM/IND DIST/IND LABOR SECT INT/TRADE
TARIFFS...BIBLIOG 19/20. PAGE 67 E1335

B63
DIPLOM
MOD/EUR
INT/ORG

MCDOUGAL M.S.,LAW AND PUBLIC ORDER IN SPACE. FUT
USA+45 ACT/RES TEC/DEV ADJUD...POLICY INT/LAW JURID
20. PAGE 70 E1410

B63
SPACE
ORD/FREE
DIPLOM
DECISION

PACHTER H.M.,COLLISION COURSE; THE CUBAN MISSILE
CRISIS AND COEXISTENCE. CUBA USA+45 DIPLOM
ARMS/CONT PEACE MARXISM...DECISION INT/LAW 20
COLD/WAR KHRUSH/N KENNEDY/JF CASTRO/F. PAGE 79
E1587

B63
WAR
BAL/PWR
NUC/PWR
DETER

RAVENS J.P.,STAAT UND KATHOLISCHE KIRCHE IN
PREUSSENS POLNISCHEN TEILUNGSGEBIETEN. GERMANY
POLAND PRUSSIA PROVS DIPLOM EDU/PROP DEBATE

B63
GP/REL
CATHISM
SECT

NAT/LISM...JURID 18 CHURCH/STA. PAGE 83 E1674

NAT/G

SCHUMAN S.I.,LEGAL POSITIVISM: ITS SCOPE AND
LIMITATIONS. CONSTN NAT/G DIPLOM PARTIC UTOPIA
...POLICY DECISION PHIL/SCI CONCPT 20. PAGE 89
E1784

B63
GEN/METH
LAW
METH/COMP

US SENATE,DOCUMENTS ON INTERNATIONAL AS"ECTS OF
EXPLORATION AND USE OF OUTER SPACE, 1954-62: STAFF
REPORT FOR COMM AERON SPACE SCI. USA+45 USSR LEGIS
LEAD CIVMIL/REL PEACE...POLICY INT/LAW ANTHOL 20
CONGRESS NASA KHRUSH/N. PAGE 101 E2026

B63
SPACE
UTIL
GOV/REL
DIPLOM

US SENATE COMM ON JUDICIARY,CASTRO'S NETWORK IN THE
UNITED STATES. CUBA LAW DELIB/GP 20 SENATE
CASTRO/F. PAGE 102 E2050

B63
PRESS
MARXISM
DIPLOM
INSPECT

VAN SLYCK P.,PEACE: THE CONTROL OF NATIONAL POWER.
CUBA WOR+45 FINAN NAT/G FORCES PROB/SOLV TEC/DEV
BAL/PWR ADMIN CONTROL ORD/FREE...POLICY INT/LAW UN
COLD/WAR TREATY. PAGE 103 E2069

B63
ARMS/CONT
PEACE
INT/ORG
DIPLOM

CAHIER P.,"LE DROIT INTERNE DES ORGANISATIONS
INTERNATIONALES." UNIV CONSTN SOCIETY ECO/DEV R+D
NAT/G TOP/EX LEGIT ATTIT PERCEPT...TIME/SEQ 19/20.
PAGE 18 E0357

S63
INT/ORG
JURID
DIPLOM
INT/LAW

CLEVELAND H.,"CRISIS DIPLOMACY." USA+45 WOR+45 LAW
FORCES TASK NUC/PWR PWR 20. PAGE 23 E0454

S63
DECISION
DIPLOM
PROB/SOLV
POLICY

FRIEDMANN W.G.,"THE USES OF 'GENERAL PRINCIPLES' IN
THE DEVELOPMENT OF INTERNATIONAL LAW." WOR+45 NAT/G
DIPLOM INT/TRADE LEGIT ROUTINE RIGID/FLEX ORD/FREE
...JURID CONCPT STERTYP GEN/METH 20. PAGE 41 E0804

S63
LAW
INT/LAW
INT/ORG

GIRAUD E.,"L'INTERDICTION DU RECOURS A LA FORCE, LA
THEORIE ET LA PRATIQUE DES NATIONS UNIES." ALGERIA
COM CUBA HUNGARY WOR+45 ADJUD TOTALISM ATTIT
RIGID/FLEX PWR...POLICY JURID CONCPT UN 20 CONGO.
PAGE 44 E0872

S63
INT/ORG
FORCES
DIPLOM

MACWHINNEY E.,"LES CONCEPT SOVIETIQUE DE
'COEXISTENCE PACIFIQUE' ET LES RAPPORTS JURIDIQUES
ENTRE L'URSS ET LES ETATS OCIDENTAUX." COM FUT
WOR+45 LAW CULTURE INTELL POL/PAR ACT/RES BAL/PWR
...INT/LAW 20. PAGE 67 E1346

S63
NAT/G
CONCPT
DIPLOM
USSR

MODELSKI G.,"STUDY OF ALLIANCES." WOR+45 WOR-45
INT/ORG NAT/G FORCES LEGIT ADMIN CHOOSE ALL/VALS
PWR SKILL...INT/LAW CONCPT GEN/LAWS 20 TREATY.
PAGE 74 E1477

S63
VOL/ASSN
CON/ANAL
DIPLOM

AHLUWALIA K.,THE LEGAL STATUS, PRIVILEGES AND
IMMUNITIES OF SPECIALIZED AGENCIES OF UN AND
CERTAIN OTHER INTERNATIONAL ORGANIZATIONS. WOR+45
LAW CONSULT DELIB/GP FORCES. PAGE 3 E0055

B64
PRIVIL
DIPLOM
INT/ORG
INT/LAW

DIETZE G.,ESSAYS ON THE AMERICAN CONSTITUTION: A
COMMEMORATIVE VOLUME IN HONOR OF ALPHEUS T. MASON.
USA+45 USA-45 LAW INTELL...POLICY BIOG IDEA/COMP
ANTHOL SUPREME/CT. PAGE 32 E0626

B64
FEDERAL
CONSTN
DIPLOM
CT/SYS

DUBOIS J.,DANGER OVER PANAMA. FUT PANAMA SCHOOL
PROB/SOLV EDU/PROP MARXISM...POLICY 19/20 TREATY
INTERVENT CANAL/ZONE. PAGE 33 E0652

B64
DIPLOM
COERCE

ECONOMIDES C.P.,LE POUVOIR DE DECISION DES
ORGANISATIONS INTERNATIONALES EUROPEENNES. DIPLOM
DOMIN INGP/REL EFFICIENCY...INT/LAW JURID 20 NATO
OEEC EEC COUNCL/EUR EURATOM. PAGE 34 E0673

B64
INT/ORG
PWR
DECISION
GP/COMP

FORBES A.H.,CURRENT RESEARCH IN BRITISH STUDIES. UK
CONSTN CULTURE POL/PAR SECT DIPLOM ADMIN...JURID
BIOG WORSHIP 20. PAGE 39 E0769

B64
BIBLIOG
PERSON
NAT/G
PARL/PROC

FREUD A.,OF HUMAN SOVEREIGNTY. WOR+45 INDUS SECT

B64
NAT/LISM

ECO/TAC CRIME CHOOSE ATTIT MORAL MARXISM...POLICY
BIBLIOG 20. PAGE 40 E0794

DIPLOM
WAR
PEACE

B64

FRYDENSBERG P.,PEACE-KEEPING: EXPERIENCE AND
EVALUATION: THE OSLO PAPERS. NORWAY FORCES PLAN
CONTROL...INT/LAW 20 UN. PAGE 41 E0814

INT/ORG
DIPLOM
PEACE
COERCE

B64

FULBRIGHT J.W.,OLD MYTHS AND NEW REALITIES. USA+45
USSR LEGIS INT/TRADE DETER ATTIT...POLICY 20
COLD/WAR TREATY. PAGE 41 E0818

DIPLOM
INT/ORG
ORD/FREE

B64

GARDNER L.C.,ECONOMIC ASPECTS OF NEW DEAL
DIPLOMACY. USA-45 WOR-45 LAW ECO/DEV INT/ORG NAT/G
VOL/ASSN LEGIS TOP/EX EDU/PROP ORD/FREE PWR WEALTH
...POLICY TIME/SEQ VAL/FREE 20 ROOSEVLT/F. PAGE 42
E0836

ECO/TAC
DIPLOM

B64

GARDNER R.N.,IN PURSUIT OF WORLD ORDER* US FOREIGN
POLICY AND INTERNATIONAL ORGANIZATIONS. USA+45 USSR
ECO/UNDEV FORCES LEGIS DIPLOM FOR/AID INT/TRADE
PEACE...INT/LAW PREDICT UN. PAGE 42 E0839

OBS
INT/ORG
ALL/VALS

B64

GJUPANOVIC H.,LEGAL SOURCES AND BIBLIOGRAPHY OF
YUGOSLAVIA. COM YUGOSLAVIA LAW LEGIS DIPLOM ADMIN
PARL/PROC REGION CRIME CENTRAL 20. PAGE 44 E0873

BIBLIOG/A
JURID
CONSTN
ADJUD

B64

GRIFFITH W.E.,THE SINO-SOVIET RIFT. ASIA CHINA/COM
COM CUBA USSR YUGOSLAVIA NAT/G POL/PAR VOL/ASSN
DELIB/GP FORCES TOP/EX DIPLOM EDU/PROP DRIVE PERSON
PWR...TREND 20 TREATY. PAGE 47 E0941

ATTIT
TIME/SEQ
BAL/PWR
SOCISM

B64

GRZYBOWSKI K.,THE SOCIALIST COMMONWEALTH OF
NATIONS: ORGANIZATIONS AND INSTITUTIONS. FORCES
DIPLOM INT/TRADE ADJUD ADMIN LEAD WAR MARXISM
SOCISM...BIBLIOG 20 COMECON WARSAW/P. PAGE 48 E0956

INT/LAW
COM
REGION
INT/ORG

B64

JENKS C.W.,THE PROSPECTS OF INTERNATIONAL
ADJUDICATION. WOR+45 WOR-45 NAT/G DIPLOM CONTROL
PWR...POLICY JURID CONCPT METH/COMP 19/20 ICJ
LEAGUE/NAT UN TREATY. PAGE 58 E1160

INT/LAW
ADJUD
CT/SYS
INT/ORG

B64

KISER S.L.,AMERICANISM IN ACTION. USA+45 LAW PROVS
CAP/ISM DIPLOM RECEIVE CONTROL CT/SYS WAR FEDERAL
ATTIT WEALTH 20 SUPREME/CT. PAGE 61 E1221

OLD/LIB
FOR/AID
MARXISM
CONSTN

B64

LIGGETT E.,BRITISH POLITICAL ISSUES: VOLUME 1. UK
LAW CONSTN LOC/G NAT/G ADJUD 20. PAGE 65 E1296

POL/PAR
GOV/REL
CT/SYS
DIPLOM

B64

LOCKHART W.B.,CASES AND MATERIALS ON CONSTITUTIONAL
RIGHTS AND LIBERTIES. USA+45 FORCES LEGIS DIPLOM
PRESS CONTROL CRIME WAR PWR...AUD/VIS T WORSHIP 20
NEGRO. PAGE 66 E1317

ORD/FREE
CONSTN
NAT/G

B64

MCDOUGAL M.S.,STUDIES IN WORLD PUBLIC ORDER. SPACE
SEA INT/ORG CREATE AGREE NUC/PWR...POLICY PHIL/SCI
IDEA/COMP ANTHOL METH 20 UN. PAGE 71 E1411

INT/LAW
SOC
DIPLOM

B64

MCWHINNEY E.,"PEACEFUL COEXISTENCE" AND SOVIET-
WESTERN INTERNATIONAL LAW. USSR DIPLOM LEAD...JURID
20 COLD/WAR. PAGE 71 E1429

PEACE
IDEA/COMP
INT/LAW
ATTIT

B64

NASA,PROCEEDINGS OF CONFERENCE ON THE LAW OF SPACE
AND OF SATELLITE COMMUNICATIONS: CHICAGO 1963. FUT
WOR+45 DELIB/GP PROB/SOLV TEC/DEV CONFER ADJUD
NUC/PWR...POLICY IDEA/COMP 20 NASA. PAGE 76 E1522

SPACE
COM/IND
LAW
DIPLOM

B64

NICE R.W.,TREASURY OF LAW. WOR+45 WOR-45 SECT ADJUD
MORAL ORD/FREE...INT/LAW JURID PHIL/SCI ANTHOL.
PAGE 77 E1545

LAW
WRITING
PERS/REL
DIPLOM

B64

OSSENBECK F.J.,OPEN SPACE AND PEACE. CHINA/COM FUT
USA+45 USSR LAW PROB/SOLV TEC/DEV EDU/PROP NEUTRAL

SPACE
ORD/FREE

PEACE...AUD/VIS ANTHOL 20. PAGE 79 E1583

DIPLOM
CREATE

B64

RAGHAVAN M.D.,INDIA IN CEYLONESE HISTORY, SOCIETY
AND CULTURE. CEYLON INDIA S/ASIA LAW SOCIETY
INT/TRADE ATTIT...ART/METH JURID SOC LING 20.
PAGE 83 E1668

DIPLOM
CULTURE
SECT
STRUCT

B64

REGALA R.,WORLD PEACE THROUGH DIPLOMACY AND LAW.
S/ASIA WOR+45 ECO/UNDEV INT/ORG FORCES PLAN
PROB/SOLV FOR/AID NUC/PWR WAR...POLICY INT/LAW 20.
PAGE 84 E1679

DIPLOM
PEACE
ADJUD

B64

RICHARDSON I.L.,BIBLIOGRAFIA BRASILEIRA DE
ADMINISTRACAO PUBLICA E ASSUNTOS CORRELATOS. BRAZIL
CONSTN FINAN LOC/G NAT/G POL/PAR PLAN DIPLOM
RECEIVE ATTIT...METH 20. PAGE 84 E1694

BIBLIOG
MGT
ADMIN
LAW

B64

ROBERTS HL,FOREIGN AFFAIRS BIBLIOGRAPHY, 1952-1962.
ECO/DEV SECT PLAN FOR/AID INT/TRADE ARMS/CONT
NAT/LISM ATTIT...INT/LAW GOV/COMP IDEA/COMP 20.
PAGE 85 E1703

BIBLIOG/A
DIPLOM
INT/ORG
WAR

B64

RUSSELL R.B.,UNITED NATIONS EXPERIENCE WITH
MILITARY FORCES: POLITICAL AND LEGAL ASPECTS. AFR
KOREA WOR+45 LEGIS PROB/SOLV ADMIN CONTROL
EFFICIENCY PEACE...POLICY INT/LAW BIBLIOG UN.
PAGE 87 E1738

FORCES
DIPLOM
SANCTION
ORD/FREE

B64

SCHECHTER A.H.,INTERPRETATION OF AMBIGUOUS
DOCUMENTS BY INTERNATIONAL ADMINISTRATIVE
TRIBUNALS. WOR+45 EX/STRUC INT/TRADE CT/SYS
SOVEREIGN 20 UN ILO EURCT/JUST. PAGE 87 E1752

INT/LAW
DIPLOM
INT/ORG
ADJUD

B64

SCHWARTZ M.D.,CONFERENCE ON SPACE SCIENCE AND SPACE
LAW. FUT COM/IND NAT/G FORCES ACT/RES PLAN BUDGET
DIPLOM NUC/PWR WEAPON...POLICY ANTHOL 20. PAGE 89
E1788

SPACE
LAW
PEACE
TEC/DEV

B64

SCHWELB E.,HUMAN RIGHTS AND THE INTERNATIONAL
COMMUNITY. WOR+45 WOR-45 NAT/G SECT DELIB/GP DIPLOM
PEACE RESPECT TREATY 20 UN. PAGE 89 E1792

INT/ORG
ORD/FREE
INT/LAW

B64

STANGER R.J.,ESSAYS ON INTERVENTION. PLAN PROB/SOLV
BAL/PWR ADJUD COERCE WAR ROLE PWR...INT/LAW CONCPT
20 UN INTERVENT. PAGE 93 E1865

SOVEREIGN
DIPLOM
POLICY
LEGIT

B64

STRONG C.F.,HISTORY OF MODERN POLITICAL
CONSTITUTIONS. STRUCT INT/ORG NAT/G LEGIS TEC/DEV
DIPLOM INT/TRADE CT/SYS EXEC...METH/COMP T 12/20
UN. PAGE 94 E1888

CONSTN
CONCPT

B64

TAUBENFELD H.J.,SPACE AND SOCIETY. USA+45 LAW
FORCES CREATE TEC/DEV ADJUD CONTROL COST PEACE
...PREDICT ANTHOL 20. PAGE 95 E1911

SPACE
SOCIETY
ADJUST
DIPLOM

B64

THANT U.,TOWARD WORLD PEACE. DELIB/GP TEC/DEV
EDU/PROP WAR SOVEREIGN...INT/LAW 20 UN MID/EAST.
PAGE 96 E1915

DIPLOM
BIOG
PEACE
COERCE

B64

TONG T.,UNITED STATES DIPLOMACY IN CHINA,
1844-1860. ASIA USA-45 ECO/UNDEV ECO/TAC COERCE
GP/REL...INT/LAW 19 TREATY. PAGE 96 E1934

DIPLOM
INT/TRADE
COLONIAL

B64

US AIR FORCE ACADEMY ASSEMBLY,OUTER SPACE: FINAL
REPORT APRIL 1-4, 1964. FUT USA+45 WOR+45 LAW
DELIB/GP CONFER ARMS/CONT WAR PEACE ATTIT MORAL
...ANTHOL 20 NASA. PAGE 99 E1979

SPACE
CIVMIL/REL
NUC/PWR
DIPLOM

B64

US HOUSE COMM ON JUDICIARY,IMMIGRATION HEARINGS.
DELIB/GP STRANGE HABITAT...GEOG JURID 20 CONGRESS
MIGRATION. PAGE 100 E2006

NAT/G
POLICY
DIPLOM
NAT/LISM

B64

WILLIAMS S.P.,TOWARD A GENUINE WORLD SECURITY
SYSTEM (PAMPHLET). WOR+45 INT/ORG FORCES PLAN
NUC/PWR ORD/FREE...INT/LAW CONCPT UN PRESIDENT.

BIBLIOG/A
ARMS/CONT
DIPLOM

PAGE 106 E2123   PEACE

B64
WRIGHT Q.,A STUDY OF WAR. LAW NAT/G PROB/SOLV   WAR
BAL/PWR NAT/LISM PEACE ATTIT SOVEREIGN...CENSUS   CONCPT
SOC/INTEG. PAGE 108 E2159   DIPLOM
   CONTROL

S64
CRANE R.D.,"BASIC PRINCIPLES IN SOVIET SPACE LAW."   COM
FUT WOR+45 AIR INT/ORG DIPLOM DOMIN ARMS/CONT   LAW
COERCE NUC/PWR PEACE ATTIT DRIVE PWR...INT/LAW   USSR
METH/CNCPT NEW/IDEA OBS TREND GEN/LAWS VAL/FREE   SPACE
MARX/KARL 20. PAGE 27 E0544

S64
DERWINSKI E.J.,"THE COST OF THE INTERNATIONAL   MARKET
COFFEE AGREEMENT." L/A+17C USA+45 WOR+45 ECO/UNDEV   DELIB/GP
NAT/G VOL/ASSN LEGIS DIPLOM ECO/TAC FOR/AID LEGIT   INT/TRADE
ATTIT...TIME/SEQ CONGRESS 20 TREATY. PAGE 31 E0608

S64
GINSBURGS G.,"WARS OF NATIONAL LIBERATION - THE   COERCE
SOVIET THESIS." COM USSR WOR+45 WOR-45 LAW CULTURE   CONCPT
INT/ORG DIPLOM LEGIT COLONIAL GUERRILLA WAR   INT/LAW
NAT/LISM ATTIT PERSON MORAL PWR...JURID OBS TREND   REV
MARX/KARL 20. PAGE 44 E0869

S64
KARPOV P.V.,"PEACEFUL COEXISTENCE AND INTERNATIONAL   COM
LAW." WOR+45 LAW SOCIETY INT/ORG VOL/ASSN FORCES   ATTIT
CREATE CAP/ISM DIPLOM ADJUD NUC/PWR PEACE MORAL   INT/LAW
ORD/FREE PWR MARXISM...MARXIST JURID CONCPT OBS   USSR
TREND COLD/WAR MARX/KARL 20. PAGE 59 E1186

S64
KHAN M.Z.,"ISLAM AND INTERNATIONAL RELATIONS." FUT   ISLAM
WOR+45 LAW CULTURE SOCIETY NAT/G SECT DELIB/GP   INT/ORG
FORCES EDU/PROP ATTIT PERSON SUPEGO ALL/VALS   DIPLOM
...POLICY PSY CONCPT MYTH HIST/WRIT GEN/LAWS.
PAGE 61 E1211

S64
LIPSON L.,"PEACEFUL COEXISTENCE." COM USSR WOR+45   ATTIT
LAW INT/ORG DIPLOM LEGIT ADJUD ORD/FREE...CONCPT   JURID
OBS TREND GEN/LAWS VAL/FREE COLD/WAR 20. PAGE 65   INT/LAW
E1303   PEACE

S64
MAGGS P.B.,"SOVIET VIEWPOINT ON NUCLEAR WEAPONS IN   COM
INTERNATIONAL LAW." USSR WOR+45 INT/ORG FORCES   LAW
DIPLOM ARMS/CONT ATTIT ORD/FREE PWR...POLICY JURID   INT/LAW
CONCPT OBS TREND CON/ANAL GEN/LAWS VAL/FREE 20.   NUC/PWR
PAGE 67 E1347

S64
MCGHEE G.C.,"EAST-WEST RELATIONS TODAY." WOR+45   IDEA/COMP
PROB/SOLV BAL/PWR PEACE 20 COLD/WAR. PAGE 71 E1413   DIPLOM
   ADJUD

S64
SINGH N.,"THE CONTEMPORARY PRACTICE OF INDIA IN THE   LAW
FIELD OF INTERNATIONAL LAW." INDIA S/ASIA INT/ORG   ATTIT
NAT/G DOMIN EDU/PROP LEGIT KNOWL...CONCPT TOT/POP   DIPLOM
20. PAGE 91 E1833   INT/LAW

S64
TRISKA J.F.,"SOVIET TREATY LAW: A QUANTITATIVE   COM
ANALYSIS." WOR+45 LAW ECO/UNDEV AGRI COM/IND INDUS   ECO/TAC
CREATE TEC/DEV DIPLOM ATTIT PWR WEALTH...JURID SAMP   INT/LAW
TIME/SEQ TREND CHARTS VAL/FREE 20 TREATY. PAGE 97   USSR
E1942

B65
BELL J.,THE JOHNSON TREATMENT: HOW LYNDON JOHNSON   INGP/REL
TOOK OVER THE PRESIDENCY AND MADE IT HIS OWN.   TOP/EX
USA+45 DELIB/GP DIPLOM ADJUD MURDER CHOOSE PERSON   CONTROL
PWR...POLICY OBS INT TIME 20 JOHNSON/LB KENNEDY/JF   NAT/G
PRESIDENT CONGRESS. PAGE 10 E0183

B65
BERKOWITZ M.,AMERICAN NATIONAL SECURITY: A READER   ORD/FREE
IN THEORY AND POLICY. USA+45 INT/ORG FORCES BAL/PWR   WAR
DIPLOM ECO/TAC DETER PWR...INT/LAW ANTHOL BIBLIOG   ARMS/CONT
20 UN. PAGE 11 E0203   POLICY

B65
BLITZ L.F.,THE POLITICS AND ADMINISTRATION OF   NAT/G
NIGERIAN GOVERNMENT. NIGER CULTURE LOC/G LEGIS   GOV/REL
DIPLOM COLONIAL CT/SYS SOVEREIGN...GEOG SOC ANTHOL   POL/PAR
20. PAGE 13 E0245

B65
CONGRESSIONAL QUARTERLY SERV,POLITICS IN AMERICA,   CHOOSE
1945-1964: THE POLITICS AND ISSUES OF THE POSTWAR   REPRESENT
YEARS. USA+45 LAW FINAN CHIEF DIPLOM APPORT SUFF   POL/PAR

...POLICY STAT TREND CHARTS 20 CONGRESS PRESIDENT.   LEGIS
PAGE 25 E0489

B65
COWEN Z.,THE BRITISH COMMONWEALTH OF NATIONS IN A   JURID
CHANGING WORLD. UK ECO/UNDEV INT/ORG ECO/TAC   DIPLOM
INT/TRADE COLONIAL WAR GP/REL RACE/REL SOVEREIGN   PARL/PROC
SOC/INTEG 20 TREATY EEC COMMONWLTH. PAGE 27 E0530   NAT/LISM

B65
FORGAC A.A.,NEW DIPLOMACY AND THE UNITED NATIONS.   DIPLOM
FRANCE GERMANY UK USSR INT/ORG DELIB/GP EX/STRUC   ETIQUET
PEACE...INT/LAW CONCPT UN. PAGE 39 E0770   NAT/G

B65
HABERLER G.,A SURVEY OF INTERNATIONAL TRADE THEORY.   INT/TRADE
CANADA FRANCE GERMANY ECO/TAC TARIFFS AGREE COST   BAL/PAY
DEMAND WEALTH...ECOMETRIC 19/20 MONOPOLY TREATY.   DIPLOM
PAGE 49 E0968   POLICY

B65
HAEFELE E.T.,GOVERNMENT CONTROLS ON TRANSPORT. AFR   ECO/UNDEV
RHODESIA TANZANIA DIPLOM ECO/TAC TARIFFS PRICE   DIST/IND
ADJUD CONTROL REGION EFFICIENCY...POLICY 20 CONGO.   FINAN
PAGE 49 E0973   NAT/G

B65
HAENSCH G.,PAN-AFRICANISM IN ACTION: AN ACCOUNT OF   DICTIONARY
THE UAM TIC AND ALPHABETICAL IN GERMAN, ENGLISH,   DIPLOM
FRENCH AND SPANISH. WOR+45 INT/ORG NAT/G ARMS/CONT   LING
WAR...INT/LAW IDEA/COMP TREATY. PAGE 49 E0974

B65
JENKS C.W.,SPACE LAW. DIPLOM DEBATE CONTROL   SPACE
ORD/FREE TREATY 20 UN. PAGE 58 E1161   INT/LAW
   JURID
   INT/ORG

B65
JOHNSTON D.M.,THE INTERNATIONAL LAW OF FISHERIES: A   CONCPT
FRAMEWORK FOR POLICYORIENTED INQUIRIES. WOR+45   EXTR/IND
ACT/RES PLAN PROB/SOLV CONTROL SOVEREIGN. PAGE 59   JURID
E1171   DIPLOM

B65
LAFAVE W.R.,LAW AND SOVIET SOCIETY. EX/STRUC DIPLOM   JURID
DOMIN EDU/PROP PRESS ADMIN CRIME OWN MARXISM 20   CT/SYS
KHRUSH/N. PAGE 62 E1244   ADJUD
   GOV/REL

B65
LASLEY J.,THE WAR SYSTEM AND YOU. LAW FORCES   MORAL
ARMS/CONT NUC/PWR NAT/LISM ATTIT...MAJORIT   PERSON
IDEA/COMP UN WORSHIP. PAGE 63 E1261   DIPLOM
   WAR

B65
MILLIS W.,AN END TO ARMS. LAW INT/ORG FORCES   FUT
ACT/RES CREATE DIPLOM WAR...POLICY HUM NEW/IDEA   PWR
HYPO/EXP. PAGE 73 E1462   ARMS/CONT
   ORD/FREE

B65
MONCONDUIT F.,LA COMMISSION EUROPEENNE DES DROITS   INT/LAW
DE L'HOMME. DIPLOM AGREE GP/REL ORD/FREE PWR   INT/ORG
...BIBLIOG 20 TREATY. PAGE 74 E1483   ADJUD
   JURID

B65
MOODY M.,CATALOG OF INTERNATIONAL LAW AND RELATIONS   BIBLIOG
(20 VOLS.). WOR+45 INT/ORG NAT/G ADJUD ADMIN CT/SYS   INT/LAW
POLICY. PAGE 74 E1488   DIPLOM

B65
MORRIS R.B.,THE PEACEMAKERS; THE GREAT POWERS AND   SOVEREIGN
AMERICAN INDEPENDENCE. BAL/PWR CONFER COLONIAL   REV
NEUTRAL PEACE ORD/FREE TREATY 18 PRE/US/AM. PAGE 75   DIPLOM
E1499

B65
NEWBURY C.W.,BRITISH POLICY TOWARDS WEST AFRICA: DIPLOM
SELECT DOCUMENTS 1786-1874. AFR UK INT/TRADE DOMIN   POLICY
ADMIN COLONIAL CT/SYS COERCE ORD/FREE...BIBLIOG/A   NAT/G
18/19. PAGE 77 E1540   WRITING

B65
O'BRIEN W.V.,THE NEW NATIONS IN INTERNATIONAL LAW   INT/LAW
AND DIPLOMACY* THE YEAR BOOK OF WORLD POLITY*   CULTURE
VOLUME III. USA+45 ECO/UNDEV INT/ORG FORCES DIPLOM   SOVEREIGN
COLONIAL NEUTRAL REV NAT/LISM ATTIT RESPECT.   ANTHOL
PAGE 78 E1565

B65
O'CONNELL D.P.,INTERNATIONAL LAW (2 VOLS.). WOR+45   INT/LAW
WOR-45 ECO/DEV ECO/UNDEV INT/ORG NAT/G AGREE   DIPLOM
...POLICY JURID CONCPT NAT/COMP 20 TREATY. PAGE 78   CT/SYS

B65

PADELFORD N.,THE UNITED NATIONS IN THE BALANCE*   INT/ORG
ACCOMPLISHMENTS AND PROSPECTS. NAT/G VOL/ASSN   CONTROL
DIPLOM ADMIN COLONIAL CT/SYS REGION WAR ORD/FREE
...ANTHOL UN. PAGE 79 E1588

B65

PARRY C.,THE SOURCES AND EVIDENCES OF INTERNATIONAL   INT/LAW
LAW. WOR+45 WOR-45 DIPLOM AGREE SOVEREIGN...METH 20   ADJUD
TREATY UN LEAGUE/NAT. PAGE 80 E1599   INT/ORG
  CT/SYS

B65

PYLEE M.V.,CONSTITUTIONAL GOVERNMENT IN INDIA (2ND   CONSTN
REV. ED.). INDIA POL/PAR EX/STRUC DIPLOM COLONIAL   NAT/G
CT/SYS PARL/PROC PRIVIL...JURID 16/20. PAGE 83   PROVS
E1665   FEDERAL

B65

SEN B.,A DIPLOMAT'S HANDBOOK OF INTERNATIONAL LAW   DIPLOM
AND PRACTICE. WOR+45 NAT/G ADJUST. PAGE 90 E1803   INT/LAW
  TASK
  LAW

B65

THOMAS A.V.,NONINTERVENTION: THE LAW AND ITS IMPORT   INT/LAW
IN THE AMERICAS. L/A+17C USA+45 USA-45 WOR+45   PWR
DIPLOM ADJUD...JURID IDEA/COMP 20 UN INTERVENT.   COERCE
PAGE 96 E1917

B65

UNESCO,HANDBOOK OF INTERNATIONAL EXCHANGES. COM/IND   INDEX
R+D ACADEM PROF/ORG VOL/ASSN CREATE TEC/DEV   INT/ORG
EDU/PROP AGREE 20 TREATY. PAGE 98 E1963   DIPLOM
  PRESS

B65

UNIVERSAL REFERENCE SYSTEM,INTERNATIONAL AFFAIRS: BIBLIOG/A
VOLUME I IN THE POLITICAL SCIENCE, GOVERNMENT, AND   GEN/METH
PUBLIC POLICY SERIES....DECISION ECOMETRIC GEOG   COMPUT/IR
INT/LAW JURID MGT PHIL/SCI PSY SOC. PAGE 98 E1972   DIPLOM

B65

US SENATE,US INTERNATIONAL SPACE PROGRAMS, 1959-65:   SPACE
STAFF REPORT FOR COMM ON AERONAUTICAL AND SPACE   DIPLOM
SCIENCES. WOR+45 VOL/ASSN CIVMIL/REL 20 CONGRESS   PLAN
NASA TREATY. PAGE 101 E2027   GOV/REL

L65

RUBIN A.P.,"UNITED STATES CONTEMPORARY PRACTICE   LAW
RELATING TO INTERNATIONAL LAW." USA+45 WOR+45   LEGIT
CONSTN INT/ORG NAT/G DELIB/GP EX/STRUC DIPLOM DOMIN   INT/LAW
CT/SYS ROUTINE ORD/FREE...CONCPT COLD/WAR 20.
PAGE 86 E1730

S65

BEVANS C.I.,"GHANA AND UNITED STATES - UNITED   NAT/G
KINGDOM AGREEMENTS." UK USA+45 LAW DELIB/GP   LEGIT
EX/STRUC ORD/FREE...JURID METH/CNCPT GEN/LAWS 20.   GHANA
PAGE 11 E0222   DIPLOM

S65

FOX A.B.,"NATO AND CONGRESS." CONSTN DELIB/GP   CONTROL
EX/STRUC FORCES TOP/EX BUDGET NUC/PWR GOV/REL   DIPLOM
...GP/COMP CONGRESS NATO TREATY. PAGE 39 E0779

S65

FRIEDHEIM R.,"THE 'SATISFIED' AND 'DISSATISFIED'   INT/LAW
STATES NEGOTIATE INTERNATIONAL LAW* A CASE STUDY."   RECORD
DIPLOM CONFER ADJUD CONSEN PEACE ATTIT UN. PAGE 40
E0799

S65

MAC CHESNEY B.,"SOME COMMENTS ON THE 'QUARANTINE'   INT/ORG
OF CUBA." USA+45 WOR+45 NAT/G BAL/PWR DIPLOM LEGIT   LAW
ROUTINE ATTIT ORD/FREE...JURID METH/CNCPT 20.   CUBA
PAGE 67 E1337   USSR

S65

MERRITT R.L.,"SELECTED ARTICLES AND DOCUMENTS ON   BIBLIOG
INTERNATIONAL LAW AND RELATIONS." WOR+45 INT/ORG   DIPLOM
FORCES INT/TRADE. PAGE 72 E1443   INT/LAW
  GOV/REL

S65

PRABHAKAR P.,"SURVEY OF RESEARCH AND SOURCE   BIBLIOG
MATERIALS: THE SINO-INDIAN BORDER DISPUTE."   ASIA
CHINA/COM INDIA LAW NAT/G PLAN BAL/PWR WAR...POLICY   S/ASIA
20 COLD/WAR. PAGE 82 E1645   DIPLOM

S65

WRIGHT Q.,"THE ESCALATION OF INTERNATIONAL   WAR
CONFLICTS." WOR+45 WOR-45 FORCES DIPLOM RISK COST   PERCEPT
ATTIT ALL/VALS...INT/LAW QUANT STAT NAT/COMP.   PREDICT

C65

SEARA M.V.,"COSMIC INTERNATIONAL LAW." LAW ACADEM   SPACE
ACT/RES DIPLOM COLONIAL CONTROL NUC/PWR SOVEREIGN   INT/LAW
...GEN/LAWS BIBLIOG UN. PAGE 90 E1799   IDEA/COMP
  INT/ORG

B66

AMERICAN JOURNAL COMP LAW,THE AMERICAN JOURNAL OF   IDEA/COMP
COMPARATIVE LAW READER. EUR+WWI USA+45 USA-45 LAW   JURID
CONSTN LOC/G MUNIC NAT/G DIPLOM...ANTHOL 20   INT/LAW
SUPREME/CT EURCT/JUST. PAGE 4 E0081   CT/SYS

B66

ASAMOAH O.Y.,THE LEGAL SIGNIFICANCE OF THE   INT/LAW
DECLARATIONS OF THE GENERAL ASSEMBLY OF THE UNITED   INT/ORG
NATIONS. WOR+45 CREATE CONTROL...BIBLIOG 20 UN.   DIPLOM
PAGE 5 E0105

B66

BESTERMAN T.,A WORLD BIBLIOGRAPHY OF BIBLIOGRAPHIES   BIBLIOG/A
(4TH ED.). WOR+45 WOR-45 LAW INT/ORG ADMIN   DIPLOM
CON/ANAL. PAGE 11 E0219

B66

BROWNLIE I.,PRINCIPLES OF PUBLIC INTERNATIONAL LAW.   INT/LAW
WOR+45 WOR-45 LAW JUDGE REPAR ADJUD SOVEREIGN   DIPLOM
...JURID T. PAGE 16 E0319   INT/ORG

B66

BUTTERFIELD H.,DIPLOMATIC INVESTIGATIONS* ESSAYS IN   GEN/LAWS
THE THEORY OF INTERNATIONAL POLITICS. LAW INT/ORG   UK
FORCES BAL/PWR ARMS/CONT WAR ALL/VALS...HUM   DIPLOM
INT/LAW. PAGE 18 E0351

B66

CANFIELD L.H.,THE PRESIDENCY OF WOODROW WILSON: PERSON
PRELUDE TO A WORLD IN CRISIS. USA-45 ADJUD NEUTRAL   POLICY
WAR CHOOSE INGP/REL PEACE ORD/FREE 20 WILSON/W   DIPLOM
PRESIDENT TREATY LEAGUE/NAT. PAGE 19 E0373   GOV/REL

B66

COPLIN W.D.,THE FUNCTIONS OF INTERNATIONAL LAW.   INT/LAW
WOR+45 ECO/DEV ECO/UNDEV ADJUD COLONIAL WAR OWN   DIPLOM
SOVEREIGN...POLICY GEN/LAWS 20. PAGE 25 E0503   INT/ORG

B66

COUNCIL OF EUROPE,EUROPEAN CONVENTION ON HUMAN   ORD/FREE
RIGHTS - COLLECTED TEXTS (5TH ED.). EUR+WWI DIPLOM   DELIB/GP
ADJUD CT/SYS...INT/LAW 20 ECHR. PAGE 26 E0520   INT/ORG
  JURID

B66

DOUMA J.,BIBLIOGRAPHY ON THE INTERNATIONAL COURT   BIBLIOG/A
INCLUDING THE PERMANENT COURT, 1918-1964. WOR+45   INT/ORG
WOR-45 DELIB/GP WAR PRIVIL...JURID NAT/COMP 20 UN   CT/SYS
LEAGUE/NAT. PAGE 33 E0645   DIPLOM

B66

DYCK H.V.,WEIMAR GERMANY AND SOVIET RUSSIA   DIPLOM
1926-1933. EUR+WWI GERMANY UK USSR ECO/TAC   GOV/REL
INT/TRADE NEUTRAL WAR ATTIT 20 WEIMAR/REP TREATY.   POLICY
PAGE 34 E0669

B66

EDWARDS C.D.,TRADE REGULATIONS OVERSEAS. IRELAND   INT/TRADE
NEW/ZEALND SOUTH/AFR NAT/G CAP/ISM TARIFFS CONTROL   DIPLOM
...POLICY JURID 20 EEC CHINJAP. PAGE 34 E0676   INT/LAW
  ECO/TAC

B66

EPSTEIN F.T.,THE AMERICAN BIBLIOGRAPHY OF RUSSIAN   BIBLIOG
AND EAST EUROPEAN STUDIES FOR 1964. USSR LOC/G   COM
NAT/G POL/PAR FORCES ADMIN ARMS/CONT...JURID CONCPT   MARXISM
20 UN. PAGE 35 E0694   DIPLOM

B66

FALK R.A.,THE STRATEGY OF WORLD ORDER* 4 VOLUMES.   ORD/FREE
WOR+45 ECO/UNDEV ACADEM INT/ORG ACT/RES DIPLOM   GEN/LAWS
ARMS/CONT WAR...NET/THEORY SIMUL BIBLIOG UN.   ANTHOL
PAGE 36 E0719   INT/LAW

B66

HAUSNER G.,JUSTICE IN JERUSALEM. GERMANY ISRAEL   ADJUD
SOCIETY KIN DIPLOM LEGIT CT/SYS PARTIC MURDER   CRIME
MAJORITY ATTIT FASCISM...INT/LAW JURID 20 JEWS   RACE/REL
WAR/TRIAL. PAGE 51 E1013   COERCE

B66

HAY P.,FEDERALISM AND SUPRANATIONAL ORGANIZATIONS: SOVEREIGN
PATTERNS FOR NEW LEGAL STRUCTURES. EUR+WWI LAW   FEDERAL
NAT/G VOL/ASSN DIPLOM PWR...NAT/COMP TREATY EEC.   INT/ORG
PAGE 51 E1014   INT/LAW

B66

HOEVELER H.J.,INTERNATIONALE BEKAMPFUNG DES
VERBRECHENS. AUSTRIA SWITZERLND WOR+45 INT/ORG
CONTROL BIO/SOC...METH/COMP NAT/COMP 20 MAFIA
SCOT/YARD FBI. PAGE 53 E1064

CRIMLGY
CRIME
DIPLOM
INT/LAW

B66

HOYT E.C.,NATIONAL POLICY AND INTERNATIONAL LAW*
CASE STUDIES FROM AMERICAN CANAL POLICY* MONOGRAPH
NO. 1 -- 1966-1967. PANAMA UK ELITES BAL/PWR
EFFICIENCY...CLASSIF NAT/COMP SOC/EXP COLOMB
TREATY. PAGE 55 E1105

INT/LAW
USA-45
DIPLOM
PWR

B66

INTL ATOMIC ENERGY AGENCY,INTERNATIONAL CONVENTIONS
ON CIVIL LIABILITY FOR NUCLEAR DAMAGE. FUT WOR+45
ADJUD WAR COST PEACE SOVEREIGN...JURID 20. PAGE 57
E1135

DIPLOM
INT/ORG
DELIB/GP
NUC/PWR

B66

JACOBSON H.K.,DIPLOMATS, SCIENTISTS, AND
POLITICIANS* THE UNITED STATES AND THE NUCLEAR TEST
BAN NEGOTIATIONS. USA+45 USSR ACT/RES PLAN CONFER
DETER NUC/PWR CONSEN ORD/FREE...INT TREATY. PAGE 57
E1146

DIPLOM
ARMS/CONT
TECHRACY
INT/ORG

B66

LEE L.T.,VIENNA CONVENTION ON CONSULAR RELATIONS.
WOR+45 LAW INT/ORG CONFER GP/REL PRIVIL...INT/LAW
20 TREATY VIENNA/CNV. PAGE 64 E1277

AGREE
DIPLOM
ADMIN

B66

MCNAIR A.D.,THE LEGAL EFFECTS OF WAR. UK FINAN
DIPLOM ORD/FREE 20 ENGLSH/LAW. PAGE 71 E1425

JURID
WAR
INT/TRADE
LABOR

B66

NANTWI E.K.,THE ENFORCEMENT OF INTERNATIONAL
JUDICIAL DECISIONS AND ARBITAL AWARDS IN PUBLIC
INTERNATIONAL LAW. WOR+45 WOR-45 JUDGE PROB/SOLV
DIPLOM CT/SYS SUPEGO MORAL PWR RESPECT...METH/CNCPT
18/20 CASEBOOK. PAGE 76 E1520

INT/LAW
ADJUD
SOVEREIGN
INT/ORG

B66

OLSON W.C.,THE THEORY AND PRACTICE OF INTERNATIONAL
RELATIONS (2ND ED.). WOR+45 LEAD SUPEGO...INT/LAW
PHIL/SCI. PAGE 79 E1575

DIPLOM
NAT/G
INT/ORG
POLICY

B66

POLLACK R.S.,THE INDIVIDUAL'S RIGHTS AND
INTERNATIONAL ORGANIZATION. LAW INT/ORG DELIB/GP
SUPEGO...JURID SOC/INTEG 20 TREATY UN. PAGE 81
E1623

INT/LAW
ORD/FREE
DIPLOM
PERSON

B66

SALTER L.M.,RESOLUTION OF INTERNATIONAL CONFLICT.
USA+45 INT/ORG SECT DIPLOM ECO/TAC FOR/AID DETER
NUC/PWR WAR 20. PAGE 87 E1743

PROB/SOLV
PEACE
INT/LAW
POLICY

B66

THOMPSON J.M.,RUSSIA, BOLSHEVISM, AND THE
VERSAILLES PEACE. RUSSIA USSR INT/ORG NAT/G
DELIB/GP AGREE REV WAR PWR 20 TREATY VERSAILLES
BOLSHEVISM. PAGE 96 E1919

DIPLOM
PEACE
MARXISM

B66

TRESOLINI R.J.,CASES IN AMERICAN NATIONAL
GOVERNMENT AND POLITICS. LAW DIPLOM ADJUD LOBBY
FEDERAL ORD/FREE WEALTH...DECISION ANTHOL 20
PRESIDENT. PAGE 97 E1940

NAT/G
LEGIS
CT/SYS
POL/PAR

B66

UNITED NATIONS,INTERNATIONAL SPACE BIBLIOGRAPHY.
FUT INT/ORG TEC/DEV DIPLOM ARMS/CONT NUC/PWR
...JURID SOC UN. PAGE 98 E1969

BIBLIOG
SPACE
PEACE
R+D

B66

US DEPARTMENT OF STATE,RESEARCH ON AFRICA (EXTERNAL
RESEARCH LIST NO 5-25). LAW CULTURE ECO/UNDEV
POL/PAR DIPLOM EDU/PROP LEAD REGION MARXISM...GEOG
LING WORSHIP 20. PAGE 100 E1996

BIBLIOG/A
ASIA
S/ASIA
NAT/G

B66

US DEPARTMENT OF STATE,RESEARCH ON THE USSR AND
EASTERN EUROPE (EXTERNAL RESEARCH LIST NO 1-25).
USSR LAW CULTURE SOCIETY NAT/G TEC/DEV DIPLOM
EDU/PROP REGION...GEOG LING. PAGE 100 E1997

BIBLIOG/A
EUR+WWI
COM
MARXISM

B66

US DEPARTMENT OF STATE,RESEARCH ON WESTERN EUROPE,
GREAT BRITAIN, AND CANADA (EXTERNAL RESEARCH LIST
NO 3-25). CANADA GERMANY/W UK LAW CULTURE NAT/G

BIBLIOG/A
EUR+WWI
DIPLOM

B66

POL/PAR FORCES EDU/PROP REGION MARXISM...GEOG SOC
WORSHIP 20 CMN/WLTH. PAGE 100 E1998

B66

US SENATE COMM AERO SPACE SCI,SOVIET SPACE
PROGRAMS, 1962-65: GOALS AND PURPOSES,
ACHIEVEMENTS, PLANS, AND INTERNATIONAL
IMPLICATIONS. USA+45 USSR R+D FORCES PLAN EDU/PROP
PRESS ADJUD ARMS/CONT ATTIT MARXISM. PAGE 101 E2028

CONSULT
SPACE
FUT
DIPLOM

B66

US SENATE COMM ON FOREIGN REL,ASIAN DEVELOPMENT
BANK ACT. USA+45 LAW DIPLOM...CHARTS 20 BLACK/EUG
S/EASTASIA. PAGE 101 E2030

FOR/AID
FINAN
ECO/UNDEV
S/ASIA

B66

WAINHOUSE D.W.,INTERNATIONAL PEACE OBSERVATION: A
HISTORY AND FORECAST. INT/ORG PROB/SOLV BAL/PWR
AGREE ARMS/CONT COERCE NUC/PWR...PREDICT METH/COMP
20 UN LEAGUE/NAT OAS TREATY. PAGE 104 E2092

PEACE
DIPLOM

B66

WALL E.H.,THE COURT OF JUSTICE IN THE EUROPEAN
COMMUNITIES: JURISDICTION AND PROCEDURE. EUR+WWI
DIPLOM ADJUD ADMIN ROUTINE TASK...CONCPT LING 20.
PAGE 105 E2096

CT/SYS
INT/ORG
LAW
OP/RES

B66

WILSON G.,CASES AND MATERIALS ON CONSTITUTIONAL AND
ADMINISTRATIVE LAW. UK LAW NAT/G EX/STRUC LEGIS
BAL/PWR BUDGET DIPLOM ADJUD CONTROL CT/SYS GOV/REL
ORD/FREE 20 PARLIAMENT ENGLSH/LAW. PAGE 106 E2126

JURID
ADMIN
CONSTN
PWR

B66

YOUNG W.,EXISTING MECHANISMS OF ARMS CONTROL.
PROC/MFG OP/RES DIPLOM TASK CENTRAL...MGT TREATY.
PAGE 108 E2165

ARMS/CONT
ADMIN
NUC/PWR
ROUTINE

L66

HOLSTI K.J.,"RESOLVING INTERNATIONAL CONFLICTS* A
TAXONOMY OF BEHAVIOR AND SOME FIGURES ON
PROCEDURES." WOR+45 WOR-45 INT/ORG ADJUD EFFICIENCY
...STAT IDEA/COMP. PAGE 55 E1089

DIPLOM
PROB/SOLV
WAR
CLASSIF

S66

CHIU H.,"COMMUNIST CHINA'S ATTITUDE TOWARD
INTERNATIONAL LAW" CHINA/COM USSR LAW CONSTN DIPLOM
GP/REL 20 LENIN/VI. PAGE 22 E0431

INT/LAW
MARXISM
CONCPT
IDEA/COMP

S66

GREEN L.C.,"RHODESIAN OIL: BOOTLEGGERS OR PIRATES?"
AFR RHODESIA UK WOR+45 INT/ORG NAT/G DIPLOM LEGIT
COLONIAL SOVEREIGN 20 UN OAU. PAGE 46 E0907

INT/TRADE
SANCTION
INT/LAW
POLICY

S66

MATTHEWS D.G.,"ETHIOPIAN OUTLINE: A BIBLIOGRAPHIC
RESEARCH GUIDE." ETHIOPIA LAW STRUCT ECO/UNDEV AGRI
LABOR SECT CHIEF DELIB/GP EX/STRUC ADMIN...LING
ORG/CHARTS 20. PAGE 69 E1384

BIBLIOG
NAT/G
DIPLOM
POL/PAR

C66

BLAISDELL D.C.,"INTERNATIONAL ORGANIZATION." FUT
WOR+45 ECO/DEV DELIB/GP FORCES EFFICIENCY PEACE
ORD/FREE...INT/LAW 20 UN LEAGUE/NAT NATO. PAGE 12
E0239

BIBLIOG
INT/ORG
DIPLOM
ARMS/CONT

C66

ZAWODNY J.K.,"GUIDE TO THE STUDY OF INTERNATIONAL
RELATIONS." OP/RES PRESS...STAT INT 20. PAGE 108
E2169

BIBLIOG/A
DIPLOM
INT/LAW
INT/ORG

B67

BAILEY N.A.,LATIN AMERICA IN WORLD POLITICS. PWR
CONSERVE MARXISM...INT/LAW TREND BIBLIOG/A T OAS
COLD/WAR. PAGE 7 E0134

L/A+17C
DIPLOM
INT/ORG
ATTIT

B67

BOULTON D.,OBJECTION OVERRULED. UK LAW POL/PAR
DIPLOM ADJUD SANCTION DEATH WAR CIVMIL/REL 20.
PAGE 14 E0273

FORCES
SOCISM
SECT

B67

CAHIER P.,LE DROIT DIPLOMATIQUE CONTEMPORAIN.
INT/ORG CHIEF ADMIN...T 20. PAGE 18 E0358

INT/LAW
DIPLOM
JURID

B67

GARCIA ROBLES A.,THE DENUCLEARIZATION OF LATIN
AMERICA (TRANS. BY MARJORIE URQUIDI). LAW PLAN
DIPLOM...ANTHOL 20 TREATY UN. PAGE 42 E0833

NUC/PWR
ARMS/CONT
L/A+17C

INT/ORG

		B67
GREENE L.S.,AMERICAN GOVERNMENT POLICIES AND FUNCTIONS. USA+45 LAW AGRI DIST/IND LABOR MUNIC BUDGET DIPLOM EDU/PROP ORD/FREE...BIBLIOG T 20. PAGE 46 E0910	POLICY NAT/G ADMIN DECISION	
		B67
HOLCOMBE A.N.,A STRATEGY OF PEACE IN A CHANGING WORLD. USA+45 WOR+45 LAW NAT/G CREATE DIPLOM ARMS/CONT WAR...CHARTS 20 UN COLD/WAR. PAGE 54 E1072	PEACE PLAN INT/ORG INT/LAW	
		B67
HOLSTI K.J.,INTERNATIONAL POLITICS* A FRAMEWORK FOR ANALYSIS. WOR+45 WOR-45 NAT/G EDU/PROP DETER WAR WEAPON PWR BIBLIOG. PAGE 55 E1090	DIPLOM BARGAIN POLICY INT/LAW	
		B67
INTERNATIONAL CONCILIATION,ISSUES BEFORE THE 22ND GENERAL ASSEMBLY. WOR+45 ECO/UNDEV FINAN BAL/PWR BUDGET INT/TRADE STRANGE ORD/FREE...INT/LAW 20 UN COLD/WAR. PAGE 57 E1132	PROB/SOLV INT/ORG DIPLOM PEACE	
		B67
LAWYERS COMM AMER POLICY VIET,VIETNAM AND INTERNATIONAL LAW: AN ANALYSIS OF THE LEGALITY OF THE US MILITARY INVOLVEMENT. VIETNAM LAW INT/ORG COERCE WEAPON PEACE ORD/FREE 20 UN SEATO TREATY. PAGE 64 E1271	INT/LAW DIPLOM ADJUD WAR	
		B67
MARTIN L.W.,THE SEA IN MODERN STRATEGY. LAW ECO/TAC WAR. PAGE 69 E1374	ROLE PWR NUC/PWR DIPLOM	
		B67
MCBRIDE J.H.,THE TEST BAN TREATY: MILITARY, TECHNOLOGICAL, AND POLITICAL IMPLICATIONS. USA+45 USSR DELIB/GP FORCES LEGIS TEC/DEV BAL/PWR TREATY. PAGE 70 E1399	ARMS/CONT DIPLOM NUC/PWR	
		B67
MCDOUGAL M.S.,THE INTERPRETATION OF AGREEMENTS AND WORLD PUBLIC ORDER: PRINCIPLES OF CONTENT AND PROCEDURE. WOR+45 CONSTN PROB/SOLV TEC/DEV ...CON/ANAL TREATY. PAGE 71 E1412	INT/LAW STRUCT ECO/UNDEV DIPLOM	
		B67
PADELFORD N.J.,THE DYNAMICS OF INTERNATIONAL POLITICS (2ND ED.). WOR+45 LAW INT/ORG FORCES TEC/DEV REGION NAT/LISM PEACE ATTIT PWR ALL/IDEOS UN COLD/WAR NATO TREATY. PAGE 79 E1589	DIPLOM NAT/G POLICY DECISION	
		B67
PLANO J.C.,FORGING WORLD ORDER: THE POLITICS OF INTERNATIONAL ORGANIZATION. PROB/SOLV DIPLOM CONTROL CENTRAL RATIONAL ORD/FREE...INT/LAW CHARTS BIBLIOG 20 UN LEAGUE/NAT. PAGE 81 E1618	INT/ORG ADMIN JURID	
		B67
POGANY A.H.,POLITICAL SCIENCE AND INTERNATIONAL RELATIONS, BOOKS RECOMMENDED FOR AMERICAN CATHOLIC COLLEGE LIBRARIES. INT/ORG LOC/G NAT/G FORCES BAL/PWR ECO/TAC NUC/PWR...CATH INT/LAW TREATY 20. PAGE 81 E1622	BIBLIOG DIPLOM	
		B67
RAMUNDO B.A.,PEACEFUL COEXISTENCE: INTERNATIONAL LAW IN THE BUILDING OF COMMUNISM. USSR INT/ORG DIPLOM COLONIAL ARMS/CONT ROLE SOVEREIGN...POLICY METH/COMP NAT/COMP BIBLIOG. PAGE 83 E1673	INT/LAW PEACE MARXISM METH/CNCPT	
		B67
RUSSELL B.,WAR CRIMES IN VIETNAM. USA+45 VIETNAM FORCES DIPLOM WEAPON RACE/REL DISCRIM ISOLAT BIO/SOC 20 COLD/WAR RUSSELL/B. PAGE 87 E1736	WAR CRIME ATTIT POLICY	
		B67
SLATER J.,THE OAS AND UNITED STATES FOREIGN POLICY. KOREA L/A+17C USA+45 VOL/ASSN RISK COERCE PEACE ORD/FREE MARXISM...TREND 20 OAS. PAGE 92 E1838	INT/ORG DIPLOM ALL/IDEOS ADJUD	
		B67
UNITED NATIONS,UNITED NATIONS PUBLICATIONS: 1945-1966. WOR+45 COM/IND DIST/IND FINAN TEC/DEV ADMIN...POLICY INT/LAW MGT CHARTS 20 UN UNESCO. PAGE 98 E1970	BIBLIOG/A INT/ORG DIPLOM WRITING	
		B67
UNIVERSAL REFERENCE SYSTEM,BIBLIOGRAPHY OF	BIBLIOG/A	

BIBLIOGRAPHIES IN POLITICAL SCIENCE, GOVERNMENT, AND PUBLIC POLICY (VOLUME III). WOR+45 WOR-45 LAW ADMIN...SOC CON/ANAL COMPUT/IR GEN/METH. PAGE 98 E1973	NAT/G DIPLOM POLICY	
		B67
US DEPARTMENT OF STATE,TREATIES IN FORCE. USA+45 WOR+45 AGREE WAR PEACE 20 TREATY. PAGE 100 E1999	BIBLIOG DIPLOM INT/ORG DETER	
		B67
US SENATE COMM ON FOREIGN REL,CONSULAR CONVENTION WITH THE SOVIET UNION. USA+45 USSR DELIB/GP LEAD REPRESENT ATTIT ORD/FREE CONGRESS TREATY. PAGE 101 E2031	LEGIS LOBBY DIPLOM	
		B67
US SENATE COMM ON FOREIGN REL,TREATY ON OUTER SPACE. WOR+45 AIR FORCES PROB/SOLV NUC/PWR SENATE TREATY UN. PAGE 101 E2032	SPACE DIPLOM ARMS/CONT LAW	
		B67
US SENATE COMM ON FOREIGN REL,A SELECT CHRONOLOGY AND BACKGROUND DOCUMENTS RELATING TO THE MIDDLE EAST. ISRAEL UAR LAW INT/ORG FORCES PROB/SOLV CONFER CONSEN PEACE ATTIT...POLICY 20 UN SENATE TRUMAN/HS. PAGE 101 E2033	ISLAM TIME/SEQ DIPLOM	
		B67
US SENATE COMM ON FOREIGN REL,INTER-AMERICAN DEVELOPMENT BANK ACT AMENDMENT. L/A+17C USA+45 DELIB/GP DIPLOM FOR/AID BAL/PAY...CHARTS SENATE. PAGE 102 E2034	LAW FINAN INT/ORG ECO/UNDEV	
		B67
US SENATE COMM ON FOREIGN REL,UNITED STATES ARMAMENT AND DISARMAMENT PROBLEMS. USA+45 AIR BAL/PWR DIPLOM FOR/AID NUC/PWR ORD/FREE SENATE TREATY. PAGE 102 E2035	ARMS/CONT WEAPON FORCES PROB/SOLV	
		B67
US SENATE COMM ON FOREIGN REL,FOREIGN ASSISTANCE ACT OF 1967. VIETNAM WOR+45 DELIB/GP CONFER CONTROL WAR WEAPON BAL/PAY...CENSUS CHARTS SENATE. PAGE 102 E2036	FOR/AID LAW DIPLOM POLICY	
		B67
US SENATE COMM ON FOREIGN REL,USIA FOREIGN SERVICE PERSONNEL SYSTEM. USA+45 LAW CONSULT ADMIN 20 USIA. PAGE 102 E2038	DIPLOM EDU/PROP PRIVIL PROF/ORG	
		B67
WATT A.,THE EVOLUTION OF AUSTRALIAN FOREIGN POLICY 1938-65. ASIA S/ASIA USA+45 USA-45 INT/ORG NAT/G FORCES FOR/AID TREATY 20 AUSTRAL. PAGE 105 E2103	DIPLOM WAR	
		L67
BAADE H.W.,"THE ACQUIRED RIGHTS OF INTERNATIONAL PUBLIC SERVANTS; A CASE STUDY IN RECEPTION OF PUBLIC LAW." WOR+45 DELIB/GP DIPLOM ORD/FREE ...INT/LAW JURID UN. PAGE 7 E0125	INT/ORG WORKER ADJUD LAW	
		L67
FRANCK T.M.,"SOME PSYCHOLOGICAL FACTORS IN INTERNATIONAL THIRD-PARTY DECISION-MAKING." UNIV SOCIETY PROB/SOLV DISCRIM ATTIT HABITAT...DECISION PSY. PAGE 40 E0786	DIPLOM ADJUD PERSON CONSULT	
		L67
HITCHMAN J.M.,"THE PLATT AMENDMENT REVISITED: A BIBLIOGRAPHICAL SURVEY." CUBA ACADEM DELIB/GP ORD/FREE...HIST/WRIT 20. PAGE 53 E1055	ATTIT DIPLOM SOVEREIGN INT/LAW	
		L67
LISSITZYN O.J.,"TREATIES AND CHANGED CIRCUMSTANCES (REBUS SIC STANTIBUS)" WOR+45 CONSEN...JURID 20. PAGE 65 E1307	AGREE DIPLOM INT/LAW	
		S67
ALDRICH W.A.,"THE SUEZ CRISIS." UAR UK USA+45 DELIB/GP FORCES BAL/PWR INT/TRADE CONFER CONTROL COERCE DETER 20. PAGE 3 E0058	DIPLOM INT/LAW COLONIAL	
		S67
ALEXANDER B.,"GIBRALTAR" SPAIN UK CONSTN WORKER PROB/SOLV FOR/AID RECEIVE CONTROL 20. PAGE 3 E0059	DIPLOM INT/ORG ORD/FREE ECO/TAC	
		S67
BARTLETT J.L.,"AMERICAN BOND ISSUES IN THE EUROPEAN ECONOMIC COMMUNITY." EUR+WWI LUXEMBOURG USA+45	LAW ECO/TAC	

DIPLOM CONTROL BAL/PAY EEC. PAGE 8 E0153   FINAN
                                                           TAX

                                                           S67
BERRODIN E.F.,"AT THE BARGAINING TABLE." LABOR   PROVS
DIPLOM ECO/TAC ADMIN...MGT 20 MICHIGAN. PAGE 11   WORKER
E0216   LAW
                                                           BARGAIN

                                                           S67
CLOGGER T.J.,"THE BIG EAR." UK USA+45 USSR LAW   DIPLOM
LEGIS CRIME GP/REL INGP/REL ATTIT 20 FBI ESPIONAGE.   ORD/FREE
PAGE 23 E0458   COM/IND
                                                           INSPECT

                                                           S67
CUMMINS L.,"THE FORMULATION OF THE "PLATT"   DIPLOM
AMENDMENT." CUBA L/A+17C NAT/G DELIB/GP CONFER   INT/LAW
...POLICY 20. PAGE 28 E0554   LEGIS

                                                           S67
DALFEN C.M.,"THE WORLD COURT IN IDLE SPLENDOUR: THE   CT/SYS
BASIS OF STATES' ATTITUDES." WOR+45 LAW ADJUD   INT/ORG
COERCE...JURID 20 UN WORLD/CT. PAGE 28 E0562   INT/LAW
                                                           DIPLOM

                                                           S67
DEUTSCH E.P.,"A JUDICIAL PATH TO WORLD PEACE." FUT   INT/LAW
WOR+45 CONSTN PROB/SOLV DIPLOM LICENSE ADJUD   INT/ORG
SANCTION CHOOSE REPRESENT NAT/LISM SOVEREIGN 20   JURID
ICJ. PAGE 31 E0611   PEACE

                                                           S67
DOYLE S.E.,"COMMUNICATION SATELLITES* INTERNAL   TEC/DEV
ORGANIZATION FOR DEVELOPMENT AND CONTROL." USA+45   SPACE
R+D ACT/RES DIPLOM NAT/LISM...POLICY INT/LAW   COM/IND
PREDICT UN. PAGE 33 E0647   INT/ORG

                                                           S67
FABREGA J.,"ANTECEDENTES EXTRANJEROS EN LA   CONSTN
CONSTITUCION PANAMENA." CUBA L/A+17C PANAMA URUGUAY   JURID
EX/STRUC LEGIS DIPLOM ORD/FREE 19/20 COLOMB   NAT/G
MEXIC/AMER. PAGE 36 E0709   PARL/PROC

                                                           S67
HORVATH B.,"COMPARATIVE CONFLICTS LAW AND THE   INT/LAW
CONCEPT OF CHANGING LAW." UNIV RATIONAL...JURID   IDEA/COMP
LOG. PAGE 55 E1099   DIPLOM
                                                           CONCPT

                                                           S67
LARSEN P.B.,"THE UNITED STATES-ITALY AIR TRANSPORT   INT/LAW
ARBITRATION: PROBLEMS OF TREATY INTERPRETATION AND   ADJUD
ENFORCEMENT." ITALY USA+45 AIR PROB/SOLV DIPLOM   INT/TRADE
DEBATE CONTROL CT/SYS...DECISION TREATY. PAGE 63   DIST/IND
E1257

                                                           S67
MATTHEWS R.O.,"THE SUEZ CANAL DISPUTE* A CASE STUDY   PEACE
IN PEACEFUL SETTLEMENT." FRANCE ISRAEL UAR UK NAT/G   DIPLOM
CONTROL LEAD COERCE WAR NAT/LISM ROLE ORD/FREE PWR   ADJUD
...INT/LAW UN 20. PAGE 69 E1389

                                                           S67
MORENO F.J.,"THE SPANISH COLONIAL SYSTEM: A   COLONIAL
FUNCTIONAL APPROACH." SPAIN WOR-45 LAW CHIEF DIPLOM   CONTROL
ADJUD CIVMIL/REL AUTHORIT ROLE PWR...CONCPT 17/20.   NAT/G
PAGE 74 E1492   OP/RES

                                                           S67
READ J.S.,"CENSORED." UGANDA CONSTN INTELL SOCIETY   EDU/PROP
NAT/G DIPLOM PRESS WRITING ADJUD ADMIN COLONIAL   AFR
RISK...IDEA/COMP 20. PAGE 84 E1675   CREATE

                                                           S67
REILLY T.J.,"FREEZING AND CONFISCATION OF CUBAN   STRANGE
PROPERTY." CUBA USA+45 LAW DIPLOM LEGIT ADJUD   OWN
CONTROL. PAGE 84 E1682   ECO/TAC

                                                           S67
STEEL R.,"WHAT CAN THE UN DO?" RHODESIA ECO/UNDEV   INT/ORG
DIPLOM ECO/TAC SANCTION...INT/LAW UN. PAGE 93 E1866   BAL/PWR
                                                           PEACE
                                                           FOR/AID

                                                           S67
TOMASEK R.D.,"THE CHILEAN-BOLIVIAN LAUCA RIVER   INT/ORG
DISPUTE AND THE OAS." CHILE L/A+17C PROB/SOLV ADJUD   DIPLOM
CONTROL PEACE 20 BOLIV OAS. PAGE 96 E1930   GEOG
                                                           WAR

                                                           B68
GREGG R.W.,INTERNATIONAL ORGANIZATION IN THE   INT/ORG
WESTERN HEMISPHERE. L/A+17C USA+45 CULTURE PLAN   DIPLOM
DOMIN AGREE CONTROL DETER PWR...GEOG 20 OAS TREATY.   ECO/UNDEV
PAGE 46 E0913

                                                           B68
HULL R.H.,LAW AND VIETNAM. COM VIETNAM CONSTN   POLICY
INT/ORG FORCES DIPLOM AGREE COERCE DETER WEAPON   LAW
PEACE ATTIT 20 UN TREATY. PAGE 56 E1113   WAR
                                                           INT/LAW

                                                           L68
CHIU H.,"COMMUNIST CHINA'S ATTITUDE TOWARD THE   INT/LAW
UNITED NATIONS: A LEGAL ANALYSIS." CHINA/COM WOR+45   SOVEREIGN
LAW NAT/G DIPLOM CONFER ADJUD PARTIC ATTIT...POLICY   INT/ORG
TREND 20 UN. PAGE 22 E0432   REPRESENT

                                                           S68
DUGARD J.,"THE REVOCATION OF THE MANDATE FOR SOUTH   AFR
WEST AFRICA." SOUTH/AFR WOR+45 STRATA NAT/G   INT/ORG
DELIB/GP DIPLOM ADJUD SANCTION CHOOSE RACE/REL   DISCRIM
...POLICY NAT/COMP 20 AFRICA/SW UN TRUST/TERR   COLONIAL
LEAGUE/NAT. PAGE 33 E0654

                                                           B77
CADWALDER J.L.,DIGEST OF THE PUBLISHED OPINIONS OF   BIBLIOG
THE ATTORNEYS-GENERAL, AND OF THE LEADING DECISIONS   CT/SYS
OF THE FEDERAL COURTS (REV ED). USA-45 NAT/G JUDGE   DECISION
PROB/SOLV DIPLOM ATTIT...POLICY INT/LAW ANTHOL 19.   ADJUD
PAGE 18 E0356

                                                           B90
BURGESS J.W.,POLITICAL SCIENCE AND COMPARATIVE   CONSTN
CONSTITUTIONAL LAW. FRANCE GERMANY UK USA-45 LEGIS   LAW
DIPLOM ADJUD REPRESENT...CONCPT 19. PAGE 17 E0340   LOC/G
                                                           NAT/G

                                                           B91
SIDGWICK H.,THE ELEMENTS OF POLITICS. LOC/G NAT/G   POLICY
LEGIS DIPLOM ADJUD CONTROL EXEC PARL/PROC REPRESENT   LAW
GOV/REL SOVEREIGN ALL/IDEOS 19 MILL/JS BENTHAM/J.   CONCPT
PAGE 91 E1822

                                                           C93
PLAYFAIR R.L.,"A BIBLIOGRAPHY OF MOROCCO." MOROCCO   BIBLIOG
CULTURE AGRI FORCES DIPLOM WAR HEALTH...GEOG JURID   ISLAM
SOC CHARTS. PAGE 81 E1620   MEDIT-7

                                                           B96
DE VATTEL E.,THE LAW OF NATIONS. AGRI FINAN CHIEF   LAW
DIPLOM INT/TRADE AGREE OWN ALL/VALS MORAL ORD/FREE   CONCPT
SOVEREIGN...GEN/LAWS 18 NATURL/LAW WOLFF/C. PAGE 30   NAT/G
E0597   INT/LAW

                                                           B96
SMITH A.,LECTURES ON JUSTICE, POLICE, REVENUE AND   DIPLOM
ARMS (1763). UK LAW FAM FORCES TARIFFS AGREE COERCE   JURID
INCOME OWN WEALTH LAISSEZ...GEN/LAWS 17/18. PAGE 92   OLD/LIB
E1840   TAX

                                                           B97
US DEPARTMENT OF STATE,CATALOGUE OF WORKS RELATING   BIBLIOG/A
TO THE LAW OF NATIONS AND DIPLOMACY IN THE LIBRARY   DIPLOM
OF THE DEPARTMENT OF STATE (PAMPHLET). WOR-45 NAT/G   LAW
ADJUD CT/SYS...INT/LAW JURID 19. PAGE 100 E2000

                                                           B99
BROOKS S.,BRITAIN AND THE BOERS. AFR SOUTH/AFR UK   WAR
CULTURE INSPECT LEGIT...INT/LAW 19/20 BOER/WAR.   DIPLOM
PAGE 16 E0309   NAT/G

DIPLOMACY.....SEE DIPLOM

DIRECT/NAT.....DIRECTORY NATIONAL (IRELAND)

DIRECTORY NATIONAL (IRELAND).....SEE DIRECT/NAT

DIRKSEN/E.....EVERETT DIRKSEN

                                                           B62
CARPER E.T.,ILLINOIS GOES TO CONGRESS FOR ARMY   ADMIN
LAND. USA+45 LAW EXTR/IND PROVS REGION CIVMIL/REL   LOBBY
GOV/REL FEDERAL ATTIT 20 ILLINOIS SENATE CONGRESS   GEOG
DIRKSEN/E DOUGLAS/P. PAGE 20 E0391   LEGIS

DISARMAMENT.....SEE ARMS/CONT

DISCIPLINE.....SEE EDU/PROP, CONTROL

DISCRIM.....DISCRIMINATION; SEE ALSO GP/REL, RACE/REL,
  ISOLAT

                                                           NRE
MEYER C.S.,ELIZABETH I AND THE RELIGIOUS SETTLEMENT   GP/REL
OF 1559. UK ELITES CHIEF LEGIS DISCRIM CATHISM 16   SECT
CHURCH/STA ELIZABTH/I. PAGE 72 E1445   LAW
                                                           PARL/PROC

                                                           B02
GRIFFIN A.P.C.,A LIST OF BOOKS RELATING TO TRUSTS   BIBLIOG/A

(2ND REV. ED.) (PAMPHLET). FRANCE GERMANY UK USA-45   JURID
WOR-45 LAW ECO/DEV INDUS LG/CO NAT/G CAP/ISM   ECO/TAC
CENTRAL DISCRIM PWR LAISSEZ 19/20. PAGE 46 E0919   VOL/ASSN

                                          B03

FAGUET E.,LE LIBERALISME. FRANCE PRESS ADJUD ADMIN   ORD/FREE
DISCRIM CONSERVE SOCISM...TRADIT SOC LING WORSHIP   EDU/PROP
PARLIAMENT. PAGE 36 E0711   NAT/G
   LAW

                                          B06

GRIFFIN A.P.C.,SELECT LIST OF REFERENCES ON THE   BIBLIOG/A
NEGRO QUESTION (REV. ED.). USA-45 CONSTN SCHOOL   RACE/REL
SUFF ADJUST...JURID SOC/INTEG 19/20 NEGRO. PAGE 47   DISCRIM
E0930   ATTIT

                                          B18

PORTER K.H.,A HISTORY OF SUFFRAGE IN THE UNITED   SUFF
STATES. USA-45 LAW CONSTN LOC/G NAT/G POL/PAR WAR   REPRESENT
DISCRIM OWN ATTIT SEX 18/20 NEGRO FEMALE/SEX.   CHOOSE
PAGE 81 E1629   PARTIC

                                          B19

SMITH R.H.,JUSTICE AND THE POOR. LAW RECEIVE ADJUD   CT/SYS
CRIME GOV/REL COST...JURID SOC/WK CONCPT STAT   DISCRIM
CHARTS GP/COMP 20. PAGE 92 E1847   WEALTH

                                          N19

IN THE SHADOW OF FEAR; AMERICAN CIVIL LIBERTIES,   ORD/FREE
1948-49 (PAMPHLET). COM LAW LEGIS BAL/PWR EDU/PROP   CONSTN
CT/SYS RACE/REL DISCRIM MARXISM SOCISM 20 COLD/WAR   POLICY
CONGRESS ACLU CIV/RIGHTS ESPIONAGE. PAGE 2 E0030

                                          N19

AMERICAN CIVIL LIBERTIES UNION,"WE HOLD THESE   ORD/FREE
TRUTHS" FREEDOM. JUSTICE. EQUALITY: REPORT ON CIVIL   LAW
LIBERTIES (A PERIODICAL PAMPHLET COVERING 1951-53).   RACE/REL
USA+45 ACADEM NAT/G FORCES LEGIS COERCE CIVMIL/REL   CONSTN
GOV/REL DISCRIM PRIVIL MARXISM...OLD/LIB 20 ACLU UN
CIVIL/LIB. PAGE 4 E0076

                                          N19

BUREAU OF NAT'L AFFAIRS INC.,A CURRENT LOOK AT: DISCRIM
(1) THE NEGRO AND TITLE VII, (2) SEX AND TITLE VII   SEX
(PAMPHLET). LAW LG/CO SML/CO RACE/REL...POLICY SOC   WORKER
STAT DEEP/QU TREND CON/ANAL CHARTS 20 NEGRO   MGT
CIV/RIGHTS. PAGE 17 E0334

                                          N19

MISSISSIPPI ADVISORY COMMITTEE,REPORT ON   RACE/REL
MISSISSIPPI (PAMPHLET). USA+45 LAW PROVS FORCES   DISCRIM
ADJUD PWR...SOC/WK INT 20 MISSISSIPP NEGRO   COERCE
CIV/RIGHTS. PAGE 73 E1469   ORD/FREE

                                          B23

DE MONTESQUIEU C.,THE SPIRIT OF LAWS (2 VOLS.)   JURID
(TRANS. BY THOMAS NUGENT). FRANCE FINAN SECT   LAW
INT/TRADE TAX COERCE REV DISCRIM HABITAT ORD/FREE   CONCPT
19 ALEMBERT/J CIVIL/LAW. PAGE 30 E0588   GEN/LAWS

                                          B28

MAIR L.P.,THE PROTECTION OF MINORITIES. EUR+WWI   LAW
WOR-45 CONSTN INT/ORG NAT/G LEGIT CT/SYS GP/REL   SOVEREIGN
RACE/REL DISCRIM ORD/FREE RESPECT...JURID CONCPT
TIME/SEQ 20. PAGE 68 E1352

                                          S45

DAVIS A.,"CASTE, ECONOMY, AND VIOLENCE" (BMR)"   STRATA
USA-45 LAW SOCIETY STRUCT SECT SANCTION COERCE   RACE/REL
MARRIAGE SEX...PSY SOC SOC/INTEG 18/20 NEGRO   DISCRIM
MISCEGEN SOUTH/US. PAGE 29 E0570

                                          B49

DE HUSZAR G.B.,EQUALITY IN AMERICA: THE ISSUE OF   DISCRIM
MINORITY RIGHTS. USA+45 USA-45 LAW NEIGH SCHOOL   RACE/REL
LEGIS ACT/RES CHOOSE ATTIT RESPECT...ANTHOL 20   ORD/FREE
NEGRO. PAGE 29 E0585   PROB/SOLV

                                          B50

FRAGA IRIBARNE M.,RAZAS Y RACISMO IN NORTEAMERICA.   RACE/REL
USA+45 CONSTN STRATA NAT/G PROVS ATTIT...SOC CONCPT   JURID
19/20 NEGRO. PAGE 39 E0783   LAW
   DISCRIM

                                          B50

MOCKFORD J.,SOUTH-WEST AFRICA AND THE INTERNATIONAL   COLONIAL
COURT (PAMPHLET). AFR GERMANY SOUTH/AFR UK   SOVEREIGN
ECO/UNDEV DIPLOM CONTROL DISCRIM...DECISION JURID   INT/LAW
20 AFRICA/SW. PAGE 74 E1475   DOMIN

                                          B52

DU BOIS W.E.B.,IN BATTLE FOR PEACE. AFR USA+45   PEACE
COLONIAL CT/SYS PERS/REL PERSON ORD/FREE...JURID 20   RACE/REL
NEGRO CIVIL/LIB. PAGE 33 E0650   DISCRIM
   BIOG

                                          B52

FORSTER A.,THE TROUBLE MAKERS. USA+45 LAW CULTURE   DISCRIM
SOCIETY STRUCT VOL/ASSN CROWD GP/REL MORAL...PSY   SECT
SOC CONCPT 20 NEGRO JEWS. PAGE 39 E0771   RACE/REL
   ATTIT

                                          B52

WALTER P.A.F.,RACE AND CULTURE RELATIONS. FAM   RACE/REL
HEALTH WEALTH...POLICY CRIMLGY GEOG BIBLIOG T 20.   DISCRIM
PAGE 105 E2097   GP/REL
   CONCPT

                                          S55

CAHN E.,"A DANGEROUS MYTH IN THE SCHOOL SEGREGATION   JURID
CASES" (BMR)" USA+45 CONSTN PROVS ADJUD DISCRIM   SCHOOL
...POLICY MYTH SOC/INTEG 20 SUPREME/CT AMEND/XIV.   RACE/REL
PAGE 18 E0360

                                          B56

KUPER L.,PASSIVE RESISTANCE IN SOUTH AFRICA.   ORD/FREE
SOUTH/AFR LAW NAT/G POL/PAR VOL/ASSN DISCRIM   RACE/REL
...POLICY SOC AUD/VIS 20. PAGE 62 E1237   ATTIT

                                          B56

RECASENS SICHES S.,TRATADO GENERAL DE SOCIOLOGIA.   SOC
CULTURE FAM NEIGH LEAD RACE/REL DISCRIM HABITAT   STRATA
ORD/FREE...JURID LING T SOC/INTEG 20. PAGE 84 E1677   KIN
   GP/REL

                                          S56

ROSENBERG M.,"POWER AND DESEGREGATION." USA+45   PWR
STRATA MUNIC GP/REL. PAGE 85 E1715   DISCRIM
   DECISION
   LAW

                                          C56

TYLER P.,"IMMIGRATION AND THE UNITED STATES."   CULTURE
USA+45 USA-45 LAW SECT INGP/REL RACE/REL NAT/LISM   GP/REL
ATTIT...BIBLIOG SOC/INTEG 19/20. PAGE 97 E1949   DISCRIM

                                          B57

CLINARD M.B.,SOCIOLOGY OF DEVIANT BEHAVIOR. FAM   BIO/SOC
CONTROL MURDER DISCRIM PERSON...PSY SOC T SOC/INTEG   CRIME
20. PAGE 23 E0455   SEX
   ANOMIE

                                          B57

DIVINE R.A.,AMERICAN IMMIGRATION POLICY, 1924-52.   GEOG
USA+45 USA-45 VOL/ASSN DELIB/GP ADJUD WAR ADJUST   HABITAT
DISCRIM...POLICY JURID 20 DEPRESSION MIGRATION.   LEGIS
PAGE 32 E0630   CONTROL

                                          B57

ROWAN C.T.,GO SOUTH TO SORROW. USA+45 STRUCT NAT/G   RACE/REL
EDU/PROP LEAD COERCE ISOLAT DRIVE SUPEGO RESPECT   DISCRIM
...PREDICT 20 NEGRO SUPREME/CT SOUTH/US CIV/RIGHTS.   ANOMIE
PAGE 86 E1728   LAW

                                          B57

US SENATE COMM ON JUDICIARY,CIVIL RIGHTS - 1957.   INT
USA+45 LAW NAT/G CONFER GOV/REL RACE/REL ORD/FREE   LEGIS
PWR...JURID 20 SENATE CIV/RIGHTS. PAGE 102 E2039   DISCRIM
   PARL/PROC

                                          B58

CABLE G.W.,THE NEGRO QUESTION: A SELECTION OF   RACE/REL
WRITINGS ON CIVIL RIGHTS IN THE SOUTH. USA+45   CULTURE
STRATA LOC/G POL/PAR GIVE EDU/PROP WRITING CT/SYS   DISCRIM
SANCTION CRIME CHOOSE WORSHIP 20 NEGRO CIV/RIGHTS   ORD/FREE
CONV/LEASE SOUTH/US. PAGE 18 E0355

                                          B58

LAW COMMISSION OF INDIA,REFORM OF JUDICIAL   CT/SYS
ADMINISTRATION. INDIA TOP/EX ADMIN DISCRIM   ADJUD
EFFICIENCY...METH/COMP 20. PAGE 63 E1269   GOV/REL
   CONTROL

                                          B58

OGDEN F.D.,THE POLL TAX IN THE SOUTH. USA+45 USA-45   TAX
CONSTN ADJUD ADMIN PARTIC CRIME...TIME/SEQ GOV/COMP   CHOOSE
METH/COMP 18/20 SOUTH/US. PAGE 78 E1572   RACE/REL
   DISCRIM

                                          B59

HAYS B.,A SOUTHERN MODERATE SPEAKS. LAW PROVS   SECT
SCHOOL KNOWL...JURID SOC SELF/OBS BIOG 20 NEGRO   DISCRIM
SUPREME/CT. PAGE 51 E1015   CT/SYS
   RACE/REL

                                          B59

TOMPKINS D.C.,SUPREME COURT OF THE UNITED STATES: A   BIBLIOG/A
BIBLIOGRAPHY. LAW JUDGE ADJUD GOV/REL DISCRIM   CT/SYS
...JURID 18/20 SUPREME/CT NEGRO. PAGE 96 E1931   CONSTN
   NAT/G

VITTACHIT,EMERGENCY '58. CEYLON UK STRUCT NAT/G FORCES ADJUD CRIME REV NAT/LISM 20. PAGE 104 E2081
B59
RACE/REL
DISCRIM
DIPLOM
SOVEREIGN

VOSE C.E.,CAUCASIANS ONLY: THE SUPREME COURT, THE NAACP, AND THE RESTRICTIVE COVENANT CASES. USA+45 LAW CONSTN LOBBY...SOC 20 NAACP SUPREME/CT NEGRO. PAGE 104 E2086
B59
CT/SYS
RACE/REL
DISCRIM

DWYER R.J.,"THE ADMINISTRATIVE ROLE IN DESEGREGATION." USA+45 LAW PROB/SOLV LEAD RACE/REL ISOLAT STRANGE ROLE...POLICY SOC/INTEG MISSOURI NEGRO CIV/RIGHTS. PAGE 34 E0668
S59
ADMIN
SCHOOL
DISCRIM
ATTIT

MURPHY W.F.,"LOWER COURT CHECKS ON SUPREME COURT POWER" (BMR)" USA+45 NAT/G PROVS SCHOOL GOV/REL RACE/REL DISCRIM ATTIT...DECISION JURID 20 SUPREME/CT NEGRO. PAGE 75 E1508
S59
CT/SYS
BAL/PWR
CONTROL
ADJUD

CASTBERG F.,FREEDOM OF SPEECH IN THE WEST. FRANCE GERMANY USA+45 USA-45 LAW CONSTN CHIEF PRESS DISCRIM...CONCPT 18/20. PAGE 21 E0406
B60
ORD/FREE
SANCTION
ADJUD
NAT/COMP

GELLHORN W.,AMERICAN RIGHTS: THE CONSTITUTION IN ACTION. USA+45 USA-45 LEGIS ADJUD COERCE RACE/REL DISCRIM MARXISM 20 SUPREME/CT. PAGE 43 E0846
B60
ORD/FREE
JURID
CT/SYS
CONSTN

MOCTEZUMA A.P.,EL CONFLICTO RELIGIOSO DE 1926 (2ND ED.). L/A+17C LAW NAT/G LOBBY COERCE GP/REL ATTIT ...POLICY 20 MEXIC/AMER CHURCH/STA. PAGE 74 E1476
B60
SECT
ORD/FREE
DISCRIM
REV

SCHUBERT G.A.,CONSTITUTIONAL POLITICS: THE POLITICAL BEHAVIOR OF SUPREME COURT JUSTICES AND THE CONSTITUTIONAL POLICIES THEY MAKE. LAW ELITES CHIEF DELIB/GP EX/STRUC LEGIS DISCRIM ORD/FREE PWR ...POLICY MAJORIT CHARTS SUPREME/CT CONGRESS. PAGE 89 E1781
B60
CONSTN
CT/SYS
JURID
DECISION

COWEN D.V.,THE FOUNDATIONS OF FREEDOM. AFR SOUTH/AFR DOMIN LEGIT ADJUST DISCRIM TOTALISM ATTIT ORD/FREE...MAJORIT JURID SOC/INTEG WORSHIP 20 NEGRO. PAGE 27 E0529
B61
CONSTN
ELITES
RACE/REL

PRITCHETT C.H.,CONGRESS VERSUS THE SUPREME COURT, 1957-1960. PROB/SOLV DOMIN EXEC GP/REL DISCRIM PWR CONGRESS SUPREME/CT SUPREME/CT. PAGE 82 E1652
B61
LEGIS
JURID
LAW

US COMMISSION ON CIVIL RIGHTS,JUSTICE: BOOK 5, 1961 REPORT OF THE U.S. COMMISSION ON CIVIL RIGHTS. LOC/G NAT/G RACE/REL...JURID 20 NEGRO CIV/RIGHTS INDIAN/AM JURY INDIAN/AM. PAGE 99 E1983
B61
DISCRIM
LAW
FORCES

WESTIN A.F.,THE SUPREME COURT: VIEWS FROM INSIDE. USA+45 NAT/G PROF/ORG PROVS DELIB/GP INGP/REL DISCRIM ATTIT...POLICY DECISION JURID ANTHOL 20 SUPREME/CT CONGRESS CIVIL/LIB. PAGE 106 E2114
B61
CT/SYS
LAW
ADJUD
GOV/REL

BARLOW R.B.,CITIZENSHIP AND CONSCIENCE: STUDIES IN THEORY AND PRACTICE OF RELIGIOUS TOLERATION IN ENGLAND DURING EIGHTEENTH CENTURY. UK LAW VOL/ASSN EDU/PROP SANCTION REV GP/REL MAJORITY ATTIT ORD/FREE...BIBLIOG WORSHIP 18. PAGE 8 E0150
B62
SECT
LEGIS
DISCRIM

BERMAN D.M.,A BILL BECOMES A LAW: THE CIVIL RIGHTS ACT OF 1960. USA+45 LAW POL/PAR LOBBY RACE/REL KNOWL...CHARTS 20 CONGRESS NEGRO CIV/RIGHTS. PAGE 11 E0206
B62
DISCRIM
PARL/PROC
JURID
GOV/REL

BICKEL A.,THE LEAST DANGEROUS BRANCH. USA+45 USA-45 LAW CONSTN SCHOOL LEGIS ADJUD RACE/REL DISCRIM ORD/FREE ...JURID 18/20 SUPREME/CT CONGRESS MARSHALL/J HOLMES/OW FRANKFUR/F. PAGE 12 E0226
B62
LAW
NAT/G
CT/SYS

GANJI M.,INTERNATIONAL PROTECTION OF HUMAN RIGHTS. WOR+45 CONSTN INT/TRADE CT/SYS SANCTION CRIME WAR RACE/REL...CHARTS IDEA/COMP NAT/COMP BIBLIOG 20
B62
ORD/FREE
DISCRIM
LEGIS

TREATY NEGRO LEAGUE/NAT UN CIVIL/LIB. PAGE 42 E0831 DELIB/GP

HENDERSON W.O.,THE GENESIS OF THE COMMON MARKET. EUR+WWI FRANCE MOD/EUR UK SEA COM/IND EXTR/IND COLONIAL DISCRIM...TIME/SEQ CHARTS BIBLIOG 18/20 EEC TREATY. PAGE 52 E1030
B62
ECO/DEV
INT/TRADE
DIPLOM

MITCHELL G.E.,THE ANGRY BLACK SOUTH. USA+45 LAW CONSTN SCHOOL DELIB/GP EDU/PROP CONTROL SUFF ANOMIE DRIVE...ANTHOL 20 NEGRO CIV/RIGHTS SOUTH/US. PAGE 74 E1473
B62
RACE/REL
DISCRIM
ADJUST
ORD/FREE

SILVA R.C.,RUM, RELIGION, AND VOTES: 1928 RE-EXAMINED. USA-45 LAW SECT DISCRIM CATHISM...CORREL STAT 20 PRESIDENT SMITH/ALF DEMOCRAT. PAGE 91 E1827
B62
POL/PAR
CHOOSE
GP/COMP
ATTIT

US COMMISSION ON CIVIL RIGHTS,EQUAL PROTECTION OF THE LAWS IN NORTH CAROLINA. USA+45 LOC/G NAT/G CONSULT LEGIS WORKER PROB/SOLV ADJUD CHOOSE DISCRIM HEALTH 20 NEGRO NORTH/CAR CIV/RIGHTS. PAGE 99 E1984
B62
ORD/FREE
RESPECT
LAW
PROVS

US COMMISSION ON CIVIL RIGHTS,HEARINGS BEFORE UNITED STATES COMMISSION ON CIVIL RIGHTS. USA+45 ECO/DEV NAT/G CONSULT WORKER EDU/PROP ADJUD DISCRIM ISOLAT HABITAT HEALTH RESPECT 20 NEGRO CIV/RIGHTS. PAGE 99 E1985
B62
ORD/FREE
LAW
ADMIN
LEGIS

ABRAHAM H.J.,"THE JUDICIAL PROCESS." USA+45 USA-45 LAW NAT/G ADMIN CT/SYS INGP/REL RACE/REL DISCRIM ...JURID IDEA/COMP 19/20. PAGE 2 E0046
C62
BIBLIOG
CONSTN
JUDGE
ADJUD

BLACK C.L. JR.,THE OCCASIONS OF JUSTICE: ESSAYS MOSTLY ON LAW. USA+45 JUDGE RACE/REL DISCRIM ATTIT MORAL ORD/FREE 20 SUPREME/CT BLACK. PAGE 12 E0236
B63
JURID
CONSTN
CT/SYS
LAW

BLOCK E.B.,THE VINDICATORS. LAW FORCES CT/SYS DISCRIM 19/20. PAGE 13 E0247
B63
ATTIT
CRIME
ADJUD
CRIMLGY

CORLEY R.N.,THE LEGAL ENVIRONMENT OF BUSINESS. CONSTN LEGIS TAX ADMIN CT/SYS DISCRIM ATTIT PWR ...TREND 18/20. PAGE 26 E0509
B63
NAT/G
INDUS
JURID
DECISION

DAY R.E.,CIVIL RIGHTS USA: PUBLIC SCHOOLS, SOUTHERN STATES - NORTH CAROLINA, 1963. USA+45 LOC/G NEIGH LEGIS CREATE CT/SYS COERCE DISCRIM ATTIT...QU CHARTS 20 NORTH/CAR NEGRO KKK CIV/RIGHTS. PAGE 29 E0579
B63
EDU/PROP
ORD/FREE
RACE/REL
SANCTION

DE GRAZIA A.,APPORTIONMENT AND REPRESENTATIVE GOVERNMENT. CONSTN POL/PAR LEGIS PLAN ADJUD DISCRIM RATIONAL...CONCPT STAT PREDICT TREND IDEA/COMP. PAGE 29 E0583
B63
REPRESENT
APPORT
NAT/G
MUNIC

DILLIARD I.,ONE MAN'S STAND FOR FREEDOM: MR. JUSTICE BLACK AND THE BILL OF RIGHTS. USA+45 POL/PAR SECT DELIB/GP FORCES ADJUD CONTROL WAR DISCRIM MORAL...BIBLIOG 20 NEGRO SUPREME/CT BILL/RIGHT BLACK/HL. PAGE 32 E0628
B63
CONSTN
JURID
JUDGE
ORD/FREE

FRAENKEL O.K.,THE SUPREME COURT AND CIVIL LIBERTIES: HOW THE COURT HAS PROTECTED THE BILL OF RIGHTS. NAT/G CT/SYS CHOOSE PERS/REL RACE/REL DISCRIM PERSON...DECISION 20 SUPREME/CT CIVIL/LIB BILL/RIGHT. PAGE 39 E0782
B63
ORD/FREE
CONSTN
ADJUD
JURID

FRIEDRICH C.J.,MAN AND HIS GOVERNMENT: AN EMPIRICAL THEORY OF POLITICS. UNIV LOC/G NAT/G ADJUD REV INGP/REL DISCRIM PWR BIBLIOG. PAGE 41 E0810
B63
PERSON
ORD/FREE
PARTIC
CONTROL

HORRELL M.,LEGISLATION AND RACE RELATIONS (PAMPHLET). SOUTH/AFR SCHOOL TAX DOMIN CONTROL 20. PAGE 55 E1098
B63
LAW
RACE/REL
DISCRIM
PARTIC

B63

JACOBS P.,STATE OF UNIONS. USA+45 STRATA TOP/EX   LABOR
GP/REL RACE/REL DEMAND DISCRIM ATTIT PWR 20   ECO/TAC
CONGRESS NEGRO HOFFA/J. PAGE 57 E1145   BARGAIN
                                                     DECISION

B63

LEWIN J.,POLITICS AND LAW IN SOUTH AFRICA.   NAT/LISM
SOUTH/AFR UK POL/PAR BAL/PWR ECO/TAC COLONIAL   POLICY
CONTROL GP/REL DISCRIM PWR 20 NEGRO. PAGE 65 E1293   LAW
                                                     RACE/REL

B63

NEWMAN E.S.,THE FREEDOM READER. USA+45 LEGIS TOP/EX   RACE/REL
PLAN ADJUD CONTROL CT/SYS DISCRIM...DECISION ANTHOL   LAW
20 SUPREME/CT CIV/RIGHTS. PAGE 77 E1541   POLICY
                                                     ORD/FREE

B63

TUSSMAN J.,THE SUPREME COURT ON RACIAL   CT/SYS
DISCRIMINATION. USA+45 USA-45 NAT/G PROB/SOLV ADJUD   DISCRIM
RACE/REL ORD/FREE...JURID 20 SUPREME/CT CIV/RIGHTS.   ATTIT
PAGE 97 E1946   LAW

B63

US COMMISSION ON CIVIL RIGHTS,FREEDOM TO THE FREE.   RACE/REL
USA+45 USA-45 LAW VOL/ASSN CT/SYS ATTIT PWR...JURID   DISCRIM
BIBLIOG 17/20 SUPREME/CT NEGRO CIV/RIGHTS. PAGE 99   NAT/G
E1986   POLICY

B63

US COMN CIVIL RIGHTS,REPORT ON MISSISSIPPI. LAW   RACE/REL
LOC/G NAT/G LEGIS PLAN PROB/SOLV DISCRIM SOC/INTEG   CONSTN
20 MISSISSIPP NEGRO. PAGE 99 E1987   ORD/FREE
                                                     COERCE

S63

NAGEL S.S.,"A CONCEPTUAL SCHEME OF THE JUDICIAL   POLICY
PROCESS." ADJUD...DECISION NEW/IDEA AVERAGE MODAL   LAW
CHARTS. PAGE 76 E1518   JURID
                                                     DISCRIM

B64

BERWANGER E.H.,WESTERN ANTI-NEGRO SENTIMENT AND   RACE/REL
LAWS 1846-60: A FACTOR IN THE SLAVERY EXTENSION   REGION
CONTROVERSY (PAPER). USA-45 LAW CONSTN LEGIS ADJUD   DISCRIM
...BIBLIOG 19 NEGRO. PAGE 11 E0218   ORD/FREE

B64

BUREAU OF NAT'L AFFAIRS,THE CIVIL RIGHTS ACT OF   LEGIS
1964. USA+45 LOC/G NAT/G DELIB/GP CONFER DEBATE   RACE/REL
DISCRIM...JURID 20 CONGRESS SUPREME/CT CIV/RIGHTS.   LAW
PAGE 17 E0333   CONSTN

B64

BUREAU OF NATIONAL AFFAIRS,STATE FAIR EMPLOYMENT   PROVS
LAWS AND THEIR ADMINISTRATION. INDUS ADJUD PERS/REL   DISCRIM
RACE/REL ATTIT ORD/FREE WEALTH 20. PAGE 17 E0338   WORKER
                                                     JURID

B64

DORMAN M.,WE SHALL OVERCOME. USA+45 ELITES ACADEM   RACE/REL
FORCES TOP/EX MURDER...JURID 20 CIV/RIGHTS   LAW
MISSISSIPP EVERS/MED CLEMSON. PAGE 32 E0638   DISCRIM

B64

FACTS ON FILE, INC.,CIVIL RIGHTS 1960-63: THE NEGRO   DISCRIM
CAMPAIGN TO WIN EQUAL RIGHTS AND OPPORTUNITIES IN   PRESS
THE UNITED STATES. LAW CONSTN PARTIC SUFF 20 NEGRO   RACE/REL
CIV/RIGHTS MISSISSIPP. PAGE 36 E0710

B64

HOPKINSON T.,SOUTH AFRICA. SOUTH/AFR UK NAT/G   SOCIETY
POL/PAR LEGIS ECO/TAC PARL/PROC WAR...JURID AUD/VIS   RACE/REL
19/20. PAGE 55 E1097   DISCRIM

B64

OPPENHEIMER M.,A MANUAL FOR DIRECT ACTION. USA+45   PLAN
SCHOOL FORCES ADJUD CT/SYS SUFF RACE/REL DISCRIM   VOL/ASSN
...POLICY CHARTS 20. PAGE 79 E1580   JURID
                                                     LEAD

B64

SEGAL R.,SANCTIONS AGAINST SOUTH AFRICA. AFR   SANCTION
SOUTH/AFR NAT/G INT/TRADE RACE/REL PEACE PWR   DISCRIM
...INT/LAW ANTHOL 20 UN. PAGE 90 E1801   ECO/TAC
                                                     POLICY

B64

TENBROCK J.,EQUAL UNDER LAW. USA-45 CONSTN POL/PAR   LEGIS
EDU/PROP PARL/PROC ORD/FREE...BIBLIOG 19 AMEND/XIV.   LAW
PAGE 95 E1914   DISCRIM
                                                     DOMIN

B64

TODD A.,JUSTICE ON TRIAL: THE CASE OF LOUIS D.   PERSON
BRANDEIS. TOP/EX DISCRIM...JURID 20 WILSON/W   RACE/REL
CONGRESS SUPREME/CT BRANDEIS/L SENATE. PAGE 96   PERS/REL
E1929   NAT/G

B64

US SENATE COMM ON JUDICIARY,CIVIL RIGHTS - THE   INT
PRESIDENT'S PROGRAM. USA+45 LAW PROB/SOLV PRESS   LEGIS
ADJUD GOV/REL RACE/REL ORD/FREE PWR...JURID 20   DISCRIM
SUPREME/CT SENATE CIV/RIGHTS PRESIDENT. PAGE 102   PARL/PROC
E2053

B64

WAY H.F. JR.,LIBERTY IN THE BALANCE - CURRENT   ORD/FREE
ISSUES IN CIVIL LIBERTIES. USA+45 USA-45 DELIB/GP   EDU/PROP
RACE/REL DISCRIM TOTALISM MARXISM SOCISM...CONCPT   NAT/G
20 CONGRESS SUPREME/CT CIVIL/LIB. PAGE 105 E2104   JURID

S64

CARNEGIE ENDOWMENT INT. PEACE,"HUMAN RIGHTS (ISSUES   INT/ORG
BEFORE THE NINETEENTH GENERAL ASSEMBLY)." AFR   PERSON
WOR+45 LAW CONSTN NAT/G EDU/PROP GP/REL DISCRIM   RACE/REL
PEACE ATTIT MORAL ORD/FREE...INT/LAW PSY CONCPT
RECORD UN 20. PAGE 20 E0385

B65

MISSISSIPPI BLACK PAPER: (FIFTY-SEVEN NEGRO AND   COERCE
WHITE CITIZENS' TESTIMONY OF POLICE BRUTALITY...).   RACE/REL
USA+45 LAW SOCIETY CT/SYS SANCTION CRIME MORAL   DISCRIM
ORD/FREE RESPECT 20 NEGRO. PAGE 2 E0035   FORCES

B65

BEGGS D.W.,AMERICA'S SCHOOLS AND CHURCHES: PARTNERS   SECT
IN CONFLICT. USA+45 PROVS EDU/PROP ADJUD DISCRIM   GP/REL
ATTIT...IDEA/COMP ANTHOL BIBLIOG WORSHIP 20   SCHOOL
CHURCH/STA. PAGE 9 E0179   NAT/G

B65

CARTER R.L.,EQUALITY. LAW LABOR NEIGH SCHOOL   POLICY
RACE/REL 20 NEGRO. PAGE 20 E0402   DISCRIM
                                                     PLAN
                                                     CREATE

B65

CONGRESSIONAL QUARTERLY SERV,FEDERAL ROLE IN   ACADEM
EDUCATION (PAMPHLET). LAW SCHOOL PLAN TAX ADJUD   DISCRIM
...CHARTS SOC/INTEG 20 PRESIDENT. PAGE 25 E0487   RECEIVE
                                                     FEDERAL

B65

CONGRESSIONAL QUARTERLY SERV,REVOLUTION IN CIVIL   LAW
RIGHTS. USA+45 USA-45 LEGIS ADJUD CT/SYS CHOOSE   CONSTN
DISCRIM...DECISION CONGRESS SUPREME/CT. PAGE 25   RACE/REL
E0488   LOBBY

B65

EHLE J.,THE FREE MEN. USA+45 NAT/G PROVS FORCES   RACE/REL
JUDGE ADJUD ATTIT...POLICY SOC SOC/INTEG 20 NEGRO.   ORD/FREE
PAGE 34 E0677   DISCRIM

B65

FRIEDMAN L.,SOUTHERN JUSTICE. USA+45 PUB/INST LEGIT   ADJUD
ADMIN CT/SYS DISCRIM...DECISION ANTHOL 20 NEGRO   LAW
SOUTH/US CIV/RIGHTS. PAGE 40 E0800   CONSTN
                                                     RACE/REL

B65

GILLETTE W.,THE RIGHT TO VOTE: POLITICS AND THE   RACE/REL
PASSAGE OF THE FIFTEENTH AMENDMENT. USA-45 LAW LEAD   CONSTN
DISCRIM SEGREGAT CONGRESS. PAGE 44 E0863

B65

IANNIELLO L.,MILESTONES ALONG THE MARCH: TWELVE   RACE/REL
HISTORIC CIVIL RIGHTS DOCUMENTS--FROM WORLD WAR II   DISCRIM
TO SELMA. USA+45 LAW FORCES TOP/EX PARTIC SUFF...T   CONSTN
20 NEGRO CIV/RIGHTS TRUMAN/HS SUPREME/CT   NAT/G
KENNEDY/JF. PAGE 56 E1121

B65

KARIS T.,THE TREASON TRIAL IN SOUTH AFRICA: A GUIDE   BIBLIOG/A
TO THE MICROFILM RECORD OF THE TRIAL. SOUTH/AFR LAW   ADJUD
ELITES NAT/G LEGIT CT/SYS RACE/REL DISCRIM...SOC   CRIME
20. PAGE 59 E1185   AFR

B65

KING D.B.,LEGAL ASPECTS OF THE CIVIL RIGHTS   LAW
MOVEMENT. SERV/IND VOL/ASSN LEGIS EDU/PROP ADJUD   DISCRIM
PARTIC CHOOSE...JURID SEGREGAT WORK. PAGE 61 E1215   TREND

B65

ROSE A.M.,MINORITY PROBLEMS: A TEXTBOOK OF READINGS   RACE/REL
IN INTERGROUP RELATIONS. UNIV USA+45 LAW SCHOOL   DISCRIM
WORKER PROB/SOLV GP/REL PERSON...PSY ANTHOL WORSHIP   ISOLAT
20 NEGRO INDIAN/AM JEWS EUROPE. PAGE 85 E1713   ACT/RES

B65
SCHROEDER O.,DEFACTO SEGREGATION AND CIVIL RIGHTS.   ANTHOL
LAW PROVS SCHOOL WORKER ATTIT HABITAT HEALTH WEALTH   DISCRIM
...JURID CHARTS 19/20 NEGRO SUPREME/CT KKK. PAGE 88   RACE/REL
E1766   ORD/FREE

B65
SMITH R.C.,THEY CLOSED THEIR SCHOOLS. USA+45 NEIGH   RACE/REL
ADJUD CROWD CONSEN WEALTH...DECISION OBS INT 20   DISCRIM
NEGRO VIRGINIA. PAGE 92 E1846   LOC/G
                                                      SCHOOL

B65
STOREY R.G.,OUR UNALIENABLE RIGHTS. LAW SECT CT/SYS   CONSTN
SUFF DISCRIM 17/20 CIVIL/LIB ENGLSH/LAW. PAGE 94   JURID
E1882   ORD/FREE
                                                      LEGIS

B66
CAHN E.,CONFRONTING INJUSTICE. USA+45 PROB/SOLV TAX   ORD/FREE
EDU/PROP PRESS CT/SYS GP/REL DISCRIM BIO/SOC   CONSTN
...IDEA/COMP BIBLIOG WORSHIP 20 BILL/RIGHT. PAGE 18   ADJUD
E0362

B66
GILLMOR D.M.,FREE PRESS AND FAIR TRIAL. UK USA+45   ORD/FREE
CONSTN PROB/SOLV PRESS CONTROL CRIME DISCRIM   ADJUD
RESPECT...AUD/VIS 20 CIVIL/LIB. PAGE 44 E0865   ATTIT
                                                      EDU/PROP

B66
KUNSTLER W.M.,"DEEP IN MY HEART" USA+45 LAW   CT/SYS
PROF/ORG SECT LOBBY PARTIC CROWD DISCRIM ROLE   RACE/REL
...BIOG 20 KING/MAR/L NEGRO CIV/RIGHTS SOUTH/US.   ADJUD
PAGE 62 E1233   CONSULT

B66
MILLER E.W.,THE NEGRO IN AMERICA: A BIBLIOGRAPHY.   BIBLIOG
USA+45 LAW EDU/PROP REV GOV/REL GP/REL INGP/REL   DISCRIM
ADJUST HABITAT PERSON HEALTH ORD/FREE SOC/INTEG 20   RACE/REL
NEGRO. PAGE 73 E1459

B66
RUNCIMAN W.G.,RELATIVE DEPRIVATION AND SOCIAL   STRATA
JUSTICE: A STUDY OF ATTITUDES TO SOCIAL INEQUALITY   STRUCT
IN TWENTIETH-CENTURY ENGLAND. UK LAW POL/PAR PWR   DISCRIM
...CONCPT NEW/IDEA SAMP METH 19/20. PAGE 86 E1734   ATTIT

B66
SMITH E.A.,CHURCH-STATE RELATIONS IN ECUMENICAL   NAT/G
PERSPECTIVE. WOR+45 LAW MUNIC INGP/REL DISCRIM   SECT
ATTIT SUPEGO ORD/FREE CATHISM...PHIL/SCI IDEA/COMP   GP/REL
20 PROTESTANT ECUMENIC CHURCH/STA CHRISTIAN.   ADJUD
PAGE 92 E1843

B66
SWEET E.C.,CIVIL LIBERTIES IN AMERICA. LAW CONSTN   ADJUD
NAT/G PRESS CT/SYS DISCRIM ATTIT WORSHIP 20   ORD/FREE
CIVIL/LIB. PAGE 95 E1899   SUFF
                                                      COERCE

L66
KRENZ F.E.,"THE REFUGEE AS A SUBJECT OF   INT/LAW
INTERNATIONAL LAW." FUT LAW NAT/G CREATE ADJUD   DISCRIM
ISOLAT STRANGE...RECORD UN. PAGE 62 E1230   NEW/IDEA

B67
COX A.,CIVIL RIGHTS, THE CONSTITUTION, AND THE   LAW
COURTS. CONSTN EDU/PROP CRIME DISCRIM ATTIT...JURID   FEDERAL
20. PAGE 27 E0533   RACE/REL
                                                      PRESS

B67
GRAHAM H.D.,CRISIS IN PRINT: DESEGREGATION AND THE   PRESS
PRESS IN TENNESSEE. LAW SOCIETY MUNIC POL/PAR   PROVS
EDU/PROP LEAD REPRESENT DISCRIM ATTIT...IDEA/COMP   POLICY
BIBLIOG/A SOC/INTEG 20 TENNESSEE SUPREME/CT   RACE/REL
SOUTH/US. PAGE 45 E0896

B67
NARAIN I.,THE POLITICS OF RACIALISM. INDIA   DISCRIM
SOUTH/AFR LAW NAT/G RACE/REL ATTIT 20. PAGE 76   COLONIAL
E1521   HIST/WRIT

B67
RUSSELL B.,WAR CRIMES IN VIETNAM. USA+45 VIETNAM   WAR
FORCES DIPLOM WEAPON RACE/REL DISCRIM ISOLAT   CRIME
BIO/SOC 20 COLD/WAR RUSSELL/B. PAGE 87 E1736   ATTIT
                                                      POLICY

L67
FRANCK T.M.,"SOME PSYCHOLOGICAL FACTORS IN   DIPLOM
INTERNATIONAL THIRD-PARTY DECISION-MAKING." UNIV   ADJUD
SOCIETY PROB/SOLV DISCRIM ATTIT HABITAT...DECISION   PERSON
PSY. PAGE 40 E0786   CONSULT

L67
NAGEL S.S.,"DISPARITIES IN CRIMINAL PROCEDURE."   ADJUD
STRATA NAT/G PROVS EDU/PROP RACE/REL AGE HABITAT   DISCRIM
SEX...JURID CHARTS 20. PAGE 76 E1519   STRUCT
                                                      ACT/RES

S67
"THE FEDERAL AGRICULTURAL STABILIZATION PROGRAM AND   AGRI
THE NEGRO." LAW CONSTN PLAN REPRESENT DISCRIM   CONTROL
ORD/FREE 20 NEGRO CONGRESS. PAGE 2 E0039   NAT/G
                                                      RACE/REL

S67
EDGEWORTH A.B. JR.,"CIVIL RIGHTS PLUS THREE YEARS: WORKER
BANKS AND THE ANTI-DISCRIMINATION LAW" USA+45   DISCRIM
SOCIETY DELIB/GP RACE/REL EFFICIENCY 20 NEGRO   FINAN
CIV/RIGHTS. PAGE 34 E0675   LAW

S67
GRIFFIN H.C.,"PREJUDICIAL PUBLICITY: SEARCH FOR A   LAW
CIVIL REMEDY." EDU/PROP CONTROL DISCRIM...JURID 20.   SANCTION
PAGE 47 E0937   PRESS
                                                      ADJUD

S67
HILL D.G.,"HUMAN RIGHTS LEGISLATION IN ONTARIO."   DELIB/GP
CANADA R+D VOL/ASSN CONSULT INSPECT EDU/PROP ADJUD   ORD/FREE
AGREE TASK GP/REL INGP/REL DISCRIM 20 CIV/RIGHTS   LAW
ONTARIO CIVIL/LIB. PAGE 52 E1045   POLICY

S67
KETCHAM O.W.,"GUIDELINES FROM GAULT: REVOLUTIONARY   ADJUD
REQUIREMENTS AND REAPPRAISAL." LAW CONSTN CREATE   AGE/Y
LEGIT ROUTINE SANCTION CRIME DISCRIM PRIVIL ROLE   CT/SYS
...JURID NEW/IDEA 20 SUPREME/CT. PAGE 60 E1208

S67
MAYER M.,"THE IDEA OF JUSTICE AND THE POOR." USA+45   INCOME
CLIENT CONSULT RENT ADJUD DISCRIM KNOWL 20. PAGE 70   WEALTH
E1393   LAW
                                                      ORD/FREE

S67
SCOTT A.,"TWENTY-FIVE YEARS OF OPINION ON   ATTIT
INTEGRATION IN TEXAS." USA+45 USA-45 DISCRIM   ADJUST
...KNO/TEST TREND CHARTS 20 TEXAS. PAGE 89 E1794   RACE/REL
                                                      LAW

S67
VAUGHN W.P.,"SEPARATE AND UNEQUAL: THE CIVIL RIGHTS   LAW
ACT OF 1875 AND DEFEAT OF THE SCHOOL INTEGRATION   DISCRIM
CLAUSE." USA-45 LEGIS RACE/REL 19 CONGRESS.   EDU/PROP
PAGE 103 E2073   PARL/PROC

S68
DUGARD J.,"THE REVOCATION OF THE MANDATE FOR SOUTH   AFR
WEST AFRICA." SOUTH/AFR WOR+45 STRATA NAT/G   INT/ORG
DELIB/GP DIPLOM ADJUD SANCTION CHOOSE RACE/REL   DISCRIM
...POLICY NAT/COMP 20 AFRICA/SW UN TRUST/TERR   COLONIAL
LEAGUE/NAT. PAGE 33 E0654

L84
ELLMAKER E.G.,"REVELATION OF RIGHTS." JUDGE DISCRIM   ORD/FREE
SUPEGO...JURID PHIL/SCI CONCPT 17/18. PAGE 35 E0685   ADMIN
                                                      MORAL
                                                      NAT/G

DISCRIMINATION....SEE DISCRIM

DISEASE....SEE HEALTH

DISPL....DISPLACEMENT AND PROJECTION

B31
STOWELL E.C.,INTERNATIONAL LAW. FUT UNIV WOR-45   INT/ORG
SOCIETY CONSULT EX/STRUC FORCES ACT/RES PLAN DIPLOM   ROUTINE
EDU/PROP LEGIT DISPL PWR SKILL...POLICY CONCPT OBS   INT/LAW
TREND TOT/POP 20. PAGE 94 E1885

B39
WILSON G.G.,HANDBOOK OF INTERNATIONAL LAW. FUT UNIV   INT/ORG
USA-45 WOR-45 SOCIETY LEGIT ATTIT DISPL DRIVE   LAW
ALL/VALS...INT/LAW TIME/SEQ TREND. PAGE 106 E2128   CONCPT
                                                      WAR

B46
GILLIN J.L.,SOCIAL PATHOLOGY. SOCIETY SECT CRIME   SOC
ANOMIE DISPL ORD/FREE WEALTH...CRIMLGY PSY WORSHIP.   ADJUST
PAGE 44 E0864   CULTURE
                                                      INGP/REL

L52
WRIGHT Q.,"CONGRESS AND THE TREATY-MAKING POWER."   ROUTINE
USA+45 WOR+45 CONSTN INTELL NAT/G CHIEF CONSULT   DIPLOM
EX/STRUC LEGIS TOP/EX CREATE GOV/REL DISPL DRIVE   INT/LAW
RIGID/FLEX...TREND TOT/POP CONGRESS CONGRESS 20   DELIB/GP

TREATY. PAGE 108 E2154

B64

CLINARD M.B.,ANOMIE AND DEVIANT BEHAVIOR: A   PERSON
DISCUSSION AND CRITIQUE. SOCIETY FACE/GP CRIME   ANOMIE
STRANGE ATTIT BIO/SOC DISPL RIGID/FLEX HEALTH...PSY KIN
CONCPT BIBLIOG 20 MERTON/R. PAGE 23 E0456   NEIGH

DISPLACEMENT....SEE DISPL

DISPUTE, RESOLUTION OF....SEE ADJUD

DISRAELI/B....BENJAMIN DISRAELI

DIST/IND....DISTRIBUTIVE SYSTEM

B03

GRIFFIN A.P.C.,LISTS PUBLISHED 1902-03: GOVERNMENT   BIBLIOG
OWNERSHIP OF RAILROADS (PAMPHLET). USA-45 LAW NAT/G DIST/IND
RATION GOV/REL CENTRAL SOCISM...POLICY 19/20.   CONTROL
PAGE 46 E0922   ADJUD

B05

GRIFFIN A.P.C.,LIST OF BOOKS ON RAILROADS IN   BIBLIOG/A
FOREIGN COUNTRIES. MOD/EUR ECO/DEV NAT/G CONTROL   SERV/IND
SOCISM...JURID 19/20 RAILROAD. PAGE 47 E0927   ADMIN
                                                    DIST/IND

B17

MEYER H.H.B.,LIST OF REFERENCES ON EMBARGOES   BIBLIOG
(PAMPHLET). USA-45 AGRI DIPLOM WRITING DEBATE   DIST/IND
WEAPON...INT/LAW 18/20 CONGRESS. PAGE 72 E1447   ECO/TAC
                                                    INT/TRADE

S59

BELL D.,"THE RACKET RIDDEN LONGSHOREMEN" (BMR)"   CRIME
USA+45 SEA WORKER MURDER ROLE...SOC 20 NEWYORK/C.   LABOR
PAGE 9 E0182   DIST/IND
                                                    ELITES

N59

NATIONAL ASSN HOME BUILDERS,COMMUNITY FACILITIES: A BIBLIOG/A
LIST OF SELECTED REFERENCES (PAMPHLET). USA+45   PLAN
DIST/IND FINAN SERV/IND SCHOOL CREATE CONTROL   LOC/G
FEDERAL...JURID 20. PAGE 76 E1525   MUNIC

B61

FLINN M.W.,AN ECONOMIC AND SOCIAL HISTORY OF   SOCIETY
BRITAIN, 1066-1939. UK LAW STRATA STRUCT AGRI   SOC
DIST/IND INDUS WORKER INT/TRADE WAR...CENSUS 11/20.
PAGE 39 E0766

B61

US HOUSE COMM ON JUDICIARY,LEGISLATION RELATING TO   LEGIS
ORGANIZED CRIME. USA+45 DIST/IND DELIB/GP GAMBLE   CONTROL
SANCTION HOUSE/REP. PAGE 100 E2004   CRIME
                                                    LAW

B62

ALEXANDROWICZ C.H.,WORLD ECONOMIC AGENCIES: LAW AND INT/LAW
PRACTICE. WOR+45 DIST/IND FINAN LABOR CONSULT   INT/ORG
INT/TRADE TARIFFS REPRESENT HEALTH...JURID 20 UN   DIPLOM
GATT EEC OAS ECSC. PAGE 3 E0063   ADJUD

B62

OTTENBERG M.,THE FEDERAL INVESTIGATORS. USA+45 LAW   FORCES
COM/IND DIST/IND WORKER DIPLOM INT/TRADE CONTROL   INSPECT
FEDERAL HEALTH ORD/FREE FBI CIA FTC SEC FDA.   NAT/G
PAGE 79 E1585   CRIME

B63

HOWARD W.S.,AMERICAN SLAVERS AND THE FEDERAL LAW: DIST/IND
1837-1862. USA-45 NAT/G LEGIT COERCE RACE/REL   CRIMLGY
WEALTH...POLICY BIBLIOG/A 19. PAGE 55 E1102   LAW
                                                    EXEC

B63

LYONS F.S.L.,INTERNATIONALISM IN EUROPE 1815-1914.   DIPLOM
LAW AGRI COM/IND DIST/IND LABOR SECT INT/TRADE   MOD/EUR
TARIFFS...BIBLIOG 19/20. PAGE 67 E1335   INT/ORG

B63

PRYOR F.L.,THE COMMUNIST FOREIGN TRADE SYSTEM. COM   ATTIT
CZECHOSLVK GERMANY YUGOSLAVIA LAW ECO/DEV DIST/IND   ECO/TAC
POL/PAR PLAN DOMIN TOTALSM DRIVE RIGID/FLEX WEALTH
...STAT STAND/INT CHARTS 20. PAGE 83 E1657

L63

LISSITZYN O.J.,"INTERNATIONAL LAW IN A DIVIDED   INT/ORG
WORLD." FUT WOR+45 CONSTN CULTURE ECO/DEV ECO/UNDEV LAW
DIST/IND NAT/G FORCES ECO/TAC LEGIT ADJUD ADMIN
COERCE ATTIT HEALTH MORAL ORD/FREE PWR RESPECT
WEALTH VAL/FREE. PAGE 65 E1306

B64

BENNETT H.A.,THE COMMISSION AND THE COMMON LAW: A   ADJUD

STUDY IN ADMINISTRATIVE ADJUDICATION. LAW ADMIN   DELIB/GP
CT/SYS LOBBY SANCTION GOV/REL 20 COMMON/LAW.   DIST/IND
PAGE 10 E0188   POLICY

B64

FISK W.M.,ADMINISTRATIVE PROCEDURE IN A REGULATORY   SERV/IND
AGENCY: THE CAB AND THE NEW YORK-CHICAGO CASE   ECO/DEV
(PAMPHLET). USA+45 DIST/IND ADMIN CONTROL LOBBY   AIR
GP/REL ROLE ORD/FREE NEWYORK/C CHICAGO CAB. PAGE 38 JURID
E0758

B64

ROBINSON R.D.,INTERNATIONAL BUSINESS POLICY. AFR   ECO/TAC
INDIA L/A+17C USA+45 ELITES AGRI FOR/AID COERCE   DIST/IND
BAL/PAY...DECISION INT/LAW MGT 20. PAGE 85 E1706   COLONIAL
                                                    FINAN

B64

TELLADO A.,A STATEMENT OF THE LAWS OF THE DOMINICAN CONSTN
REPUBLIC IN MATTERS AFFECTING BUSINESS (3RD ED.).   LEGIS
DOMIN/REP AGRI DIST/IND EXTR/IND FINAN FAM WORKER   NAT/G
ECO/TAC TAX CT/SYS MARRIAGE OWN...BIBLIOG 20   INDUS
MIGRATION. PAGE 95 E1913

B65

HAEFELE E.T.,GOVERNMENT CONTROLS ON TRANSPORT. AFR   ECO/UNDEV
RHODESIA TANZANIA DIPLOM ECO/TAC TARIFFS PRICE   DIST/IND
ADJUD CONTROL REGION EFFICIENCY...POLICY 20 CONGO.   FINAN
PAGE 49 E0973   NAT/G

B65

LUGO-MARENCO J.J.,A STATEMENT OF THE LAWS OF   CONSTN
NICARAGUA IN MATTERS AFFECTING BUSINESS. NICARAGUA   NAT/G
AGRI DIST/IND EXTR/IND FINAN INDUS FAM WORKER   LEGIS
INT/TRADE TAX MARRIAGE OWN BIO/SOC 20 TREATY   JURID
RESOURCE/N MIGRATION. PAGE 67 E1332

B66

GREENE L.E.,GOVERNMENT IN TENNESSEE (2ND ED.).   PROVS
USA+45 DIST/IND INDUS POL/PAR EX/STRUC LEGIS PLAN   LOC/G
BUDGET GIVE CT/SYS...MGT T 20 TENNESSEE. PAGE 46   CONSTN
E0909   ADMIN

N66

CONGRESSIONAL QUARTERLY SERV,HOUSING A NATION   HABITAT
(PAMPHLET). USA+45 LAW STRUCT DIST/IND DELIB/GP   NAT/G
...GEOG CHARTS 20 DEPT/HUD. PAGE 25 E0490   PLAN
                                                    MUNIC

B67

GREENE L.S.,AMERICAN GOVERNMENT POLICIES AND   POLICY
FUNCTIONS. USA+45 LAW AGRI DIST/IND LABOR MUNIC   NAT/G
BUDGET DIPLOM EDU/PROP ORD/FREE...BIBLIOG T 20.   ADMIN
PAGE 46 E0910   DECISION

B67

UNITED NATIONS,UNITED NATIONS PUBLICATIONS: BIBLIOG/A
1945-1966. WOR+45 COM/IND DIST/IND FINAN TEC/DEV   INT/ORG
ADMIN...POLICY INT/LAW MGT CHARTS 20 UN UNESCO.   DIPLOM
PAGE 98 E1970   WRITING

S67

LARSEN P.B.,"THE UNITED STATES-ITALY AIR TRANSPORT   INT/LAW
ARBITRATION: PROBLEMS OF TREATY INTERPRETATION AND   ADJUD
ENFORCEMENT." ITALY USA+45 AIR PROB/SOLV DIPLOM   INT/TRADE
DEBATE CONTROL CT/SYS...DECISION TREATY. PAGE 63   DIST/IND
E1257

S67

WILLIG S.H.,"THE CONTROL OVER INTERSTATE   DIST/IND
DISTRIBUTION AND USE OF INVESTIGATIONAL DRUGS (IN   HEALTH
THE UNITED STATES)" USA+45 NAT/G INT/TRADE LICENSE. CONTROL
PAGE 106 E2124   DELIB/GP

DISTRIBUTIVE SYSTEM....SEE DIST/IND

DISTRICT COURTS....SEE COURT/DIST

DISTRICTING....SEE APPORT

DIVINE R.A. E0630

DIVORCE....DIVORCE

DIXON R.G. E0631

DIXON/YATE....DIXON-YATES BILL

DIZARD W.P. E0632

DOC/ANAL....CONVENTIONAL CONTENT ANALYSIS

DODD/TJ....SENATOR THOMAS J. DODD

DOLE C.F. E0633

DOMIN....DOMINATION THROUGH USE OF ESTABLISHED POWER

DARBY W.E.,INTERNATIONAL TRIBUNALS. WOR-45 NAT/G ECO/TAC DOMIN LEGIT CT/SYS COERCE ORD/FREE PWR SOVEREIGN JURID. PAGE 29 E0567
INT/ORG ADJUD PEACE INT/LAW
B00

GRIFFIN A.P.C.,LIST OF BOOKS RELATING TO THE THEORY OF COLONIZATION, GOVERNMENT OF DEPENDENCIES, PROTECTORATES, AND RELATED TOPICS. FRANCE GERMANY ITALY SPAIN UK USA-45 WOR-45 ECO/TAC ADMIN CONTROL REGION NAT/LISM ALL/VALS PWR...INT/LAW SOC 16/19. PAGE 46 E0917
BIBLIOG/A COLONIAL GOV/REL DOMIN
B00

HOLLAND T.E.,STUDIES IN INTERNATIONAL LAW. TURKEY USSR WOR-45 CONSTN NAT/G DIPLOM DOMIN LEGIT COERCE WAR PEACE ORD/FREE PWR SOVEREIGN...JURID CHARTS 20 PARLIAMENT SUEZ TREATY. PAGE 54 E1084
INT/ORG LAW INT/LAW
B00

BERKELEY G.,"DISCOURSE ON PASSIVE OBEDIENCE" (1712) THE WORKS... (VOL. IV)" UNIV DOMIN LEGIT CONTROL CRIME ADJUST CENTRAL MORAL ORD/FREE...POLICY WORSHIP. PAGE 10 E0202
INGP/REL SANCTION RESPECT GEN/LAWS
C01

VECCHIO G.D.,THE FORMAL BASES OF LAW (TRANS. BY J. LISLE). DOMIN LEGIT CONTROL COERCE UTIL MORAL PWR ...CONCPT TIME/SEQ 17/20 COMMON/LAW NATURL/LAW. PAGE 103 E2074
LAW JURID GEN/LAWS IDEA/COMP
B14

LIPPMAN W.,LIBERTY AND THE NEWS. USA+45 USA-45 LAW LEGIS DOMIN LEGIT ATTIT...POLICY SOC IDEA/COMP METH/COMP 19/20. PAGE 65 E1300
ORD/FREE PRESS COM/IND EDU/PROP
B20

BARNES H.E.,"SOCIOLOGY AND POLITICAL THEORY: A CONSIDERATION OF THE SOCIOLOGICAL BASIS OF POLITICS." LAW CONSTN NAT/G DIPLOM DOMIN ROUTINE REV ORD/FREE SOVEREIGN...PHIL/SCI CLASSIF BIBLIOG 18/20. PAGE 8 E0151
CONCPT STRUCT SOC
C24

FORTESCUE J.,THE GOVERNANCE OF ENGLAND (1471-76). UK LAW FINAN SECT LEGIS PROB/SOLV TAX DOMIN ADMIN GP/REL COST ORD/FREE PWR 14/15. PAGE 39 E0776
CONSERVE CONSTN CHIEF NAT/G
B26

DICKINSON J.,ADMINISTRATIVE JUSTICE AND THE SUPREMACY OF LAW IN THE UNITED STATES. USA-45 LAW INDUS DOMIN EDU/PROP CONTROL EXEC GP/REL ORD/FREE ...POLICY JURID 19/20. PAGE 31 E0623
CT/SYS ADJUD ADMIN NAT/G
B27

JOHN OF SALISBURY,THE STATESMAN'S BOOK (1159) (TRANS. BY J. DICKINSON). DOMIN GP/REL MORAL ORD/FREE PWR CONSERVE...CATH CONCPT 12. PAGE 59 E1169
NAT/G SECT CHIEF LAW
B27

LAUTERPACHT H.,THE FUNCTION OF LAW IN THE INTERNATIONAL COMMUNITY. WOR-45 NAT/G FORCES CREATE DOMIN LEGIT COERCE WAR PEACE ATTIT ORD/FREE PWR SOVEREIGN...JURID CONCPT METH/CNCPT TIME/SEQ GEN/LAWS GEN/METH LEAGUE/NAT TOT/POP VAL/FREE 20. PAGE 63 E1265
INT/ORG LAW INT/LAW
B33

EVANS I.L.,NATIVE POLICY IN SOUTHERN AFRICA. RHODESIA SOUTH/AFR UK STRUCT PARTIC RACE/REL ATTIT WEALTH SOC/INTEG AFRICA/SW. PAGE 35 E0705
AFR COLONIAL DOMIN LAW
B34

SCHULZ F.,PRINCIPLES OF ROMAN LAW. CONSTN FAM NAT/G DOMIN CONTROL CT/SYS CRIME ISOLAT ATTIT ORD/FREE PWR...JURID ROME/ANC ROMAN/LAW. PAGE 89 E1783
LAW LEGIS ADJUD CONCPT
B36

RUTHERFORD M.L.,THE INFLUENCE OF THE AMERICAN BAR ASSOCIATION ON PUBLIC OPINION AND LEGISLATION. USA+45 LAW CONSTN LABOR LEGIS DOMIN EDU/PROP LEGIT CT/SYS ROUTINE...TIME/SEQ 19/20 ABA. PAGE 87 E1739
ATTIT ADJUD PROF/ORG JURID
B37

LERNER M.,"CONSTITUTION AND COURT AS SYMBOLS" (BMR)" USA+45 USA-45 DOMIN PWR SOVEREIGN...PSY MYTH
CONSTN CT/SYS
L37

18/20 SUPREME/CT. PAGE 64 E1288
ATTIT EDU/PROP
B39

ZIMMERN A.,THE LEAGUE OF NATIONS AND THE RULE OF LAW. WOR-45 STRUCT NAT/G DELIB/GP EX/STRUC BAL/PWR DOMIN LEGIT COERCE ORD/FREE PWR...POLICY RECORD LEAGUE/NAT TOT/POP VAL/FREE 20 LEAGUE/NAT. PAGE 108 E2170
INT/ORG LAW DIPLOM
B39

HOBBES T.,A DIALOGUE BETWEEN A PHILOSOPHER AND A STUDENT OF THE COMMON LAWS OF ENGLAND (1667?). UK SECT DOMIN ADJUD CRIME INCOME OWN UTIL ORD/FREE PWR SOVEREIGN...JURID GEN/LAWS 17. PAGE 53 E1057
CT/SYS CHIEF SANCTION
B40

FLORIN J.,"BOLSHEVIST AND NATIONAL SOCIALIST DOCTRINES OF INTERNATIONAL LAW." EUR+WWI GERMANY USSR R+D INT/ORG NAT/G DIPLOM DOMIN EDU/PROP SOCISM ...CONCPT TIME/SEQ 20. PAGE 39 E0768
LAW ATTIT TOTALISM INT/LAW
S40

GERTH H.,"THE NAZI PARTY: ITS LEADERSHIP AND COMPOSITION" (BMR)" GERMANY ELITES STRATA STRUCT EX/STRUC FORCES ECO/TAC CT/SYS CHOOSE TOTALISM AGE/Y AUTHORIT PWR 20. PAGE 43 E0851
POL/PAR DOMIN LEAD ADMIN
S40

WRIGHT Q.,"FUNDAMENTAL PROBLEMS OF INTERNATIONAL ORGANIZATION." UNIV WOR-45 STRUCT FORCES ACT/RES CREATE DOMIN EDU/PROP LEGIT REGION NAT/LISM ORD/FREE PWR RESPECT SOVEREIGN...JURID SOC CONCPT METH/CNCPT TIME/SEQ 20. PAGE 107 E2152
INT/ORG ATTIT PEACE
S41

CROWE S.E.,THE BERLIN WEST AFRICA CONFERENCE, 1884-85. GERMANY ELITES MARKET INT/ORG DELIB/GP FORCES PROB/SOLV BAL/PWR CAP/ISM DOMIN COLONIAL ...INT/LAW 19. PAGE 28 E0548
AFR CONFER INT/TRADE DIPLOM
B42

SERENI A.P.,THE ITALIAN CONCEPTION OF INTERNATIONAL LAW. EUR+WWI MOD/EUR INT/ORG NAT/G DOMIN COERCE ORD/FREE FASCISM...OBS/ENVIR TREND 20. PAGE 90 E1804
LAW TIME/SEQ INT/LAW ITALY
B43

BRIERLY J.L.,THE OUTLOOK FOR INTERNATIONAL LAW. FUT WOR-45 CONSTN NAT/G VOL/ASSN FORCES ECO/TAC DOMIN LEGIT ADJUD ROUTINE PEACE ORD/FREE...INT/LAW JURID METH LEAGUE/NAT 20. PAGE 15 E0298
INT/ORG LAW
B44

DE HUSZAR G.B.,NEW PERSPECTIVES ON PEACE. UNIV CULTURE SOCIETY ECO/DEV ECO/UNDEV NAT/G FORCES CREATE ECO/TAC DOMIN ADJUD COERCE DRIVE ORD/FREE ...GEOG JURID PSY SOC CONCPT TOT/POP. PAGE 29 E0584
ATTIT MYTH PEACE WAR
B44

FULLER G.H.,MILITARY GOVERNMENT: A LIST OF REFERENCES (A PAMPHLET). ITALY UK USA-45 WOR-45 LAW FORCES DOMIN ADMIN ARMS/CONT ORD/FREE PWR ...DECISION 20 CHINJAP. PAGE 41 E0822
BIBLIOG DIPLOM CIVMIL/REL SOVEREIGN
B44

SUAREZ F.,A TREATISE ON LAWS AND GOD THE LAWGIVER (1612) IN SELECTIONS FROM THREE WORKS, VOL. II. FRANCE ITALY UK CULTURE NAT/G SECT CHIEF LEGIS DOMIN LEGIT CT/SYS ORD/FREE PWR WORSHIP 16/17. PAGE 94 E1892
LAW JURID GEN/LAWS CATH
B44

MASON J.B.,"THE JUDICIAL SYSTEM OF THE NAZI PARTY." GERMANY ELITES POL/PAR DOMIN CONTROL SANCTION TOTALISM...JURID 20 HITLER/A. PAGE 69 E1381
FASCISM CT/SYS ADJUD LAW
S44

HILL N.,CLAIMS TO TERRITORY IN INTERNATIONAL LAW AND RELATIONS. WOR-45 NAT/G DOMIN EDU/PROP LEGIT REGION ROUTINE ORD/FREE PWR WEALTH...GEOG INT/LAW JURID 20. PAGE 52 E1047
INT/ORG ADJUD SOVEREIGN
B45

UNCIO CONFERENCE LIBRARY,SHORT TITLE CLASSIFIED CATALOG. WOR-45 DOMIN COLONIAL WAR...SOC/WK 20 LEAGUE/NAT UN. PAGE 98 E1955
BIBLIOG DIPLOM INT/ORG INT/LAW
B45

GORDON D.L.,THE HIDDEN WEAPON: THE STORY OF ECONOMIC WARFARE. EUR+WWI USA-45 LAW FINAN INDUS NAT/G CONSULT FORCES PLAN DOMIN PWR WEALTH ...INT/LAW CONCPT OBS TOT/POP NAZI 20. PAGE 45 E0891
INT/ORG ECO/TAC INT/TRADE WAR
B47

FOX W.T.R.,UNITED STATES POLICY IN A TWO POWER WORLD. COM USA+45 USSR FORCES DOMIN AGREE NEUTRAL NUC/PWR ORD/FREE SOVEREIGN 20 COLD/WAR TREATY EUROPE/W INTERVENT. PAGE 39 E0780
N47 DIPLOM FOR/AID POLICY

MEIKLEJOHN A.,FREE SPEECH AND ITS RELATION TO SELF-GOVERNMENT. USA+45 USA-45 LAW DOMIN PRESS ORD/FREE 20 AMEND/I. PAGE 72 E1434
B48 LEGIS NAT/G CONSTN PRIVIL

ALEXANDER L.,"WAR CRIMES, THEIR SOCIAL-PSYCHOLOGICAL ASPECTS." EUR+WWI GERMANY LAW CULTURE ELITES KIN POL/PAR PUB/INST FORCES DOMIN EDU/PROP COERCE CRIME ATTIT SUPEGO HEALTH MORAL PWR FASCISM ...PSY OBS TREND GEN/LAWS NAZI 20. PAGE 3 E0061
S48 DRIVE WAR

BRUCKER H.,FREEDOM OF INFORMATION. USA-45 LAW LOC/G PRESS ECO/TAC DOMIN PWR...NEW/IDEA BIBLIOG 17/20. PAGE 16 E0320
B49 PRESS COM/IND ORD/FREE NAT/G

SUMMERS R.E.,FEDERAL INFORMATION CONTROLS IN PEACETIME. USA+45 COM/IND DOMIN INGP/REL ATTIT ORD/FREE 20. PAGE 94 E1893
B49 ADJUD CONTROL EDU/PROP PRESS

WORMUTH F.D.,THE ORIGINS OF MODERN CONSTITUTIONALISM. GREECE UK LEGIS CREATE TEC/DEV BAL/PWR DOMIN ADJUD REV WAR PWR...JURID ROMAN/REP CROMWELL/O. PAGE 107 E2146
B49 NAT/G CONSTN LAW

MARX C.M.,"ADMINISTRATIVE ETHICS AND THE RULE OF LAW." USA+45 ELITES ACT/RES DOMIN NEUTRAL ROUTINE INGP/REL ORD/FREE...JURID IDEA/COMP. PAGE 69 E1375
L49 ADMIN LAW

MOCKFORD J.,SOUTH-WEST AFRICA AND THE INTERNATIONAL COURT (PAMPHLET). AFR GERMANY SOUTH/AFR UK ECO/UNDEV DIPLOM CONTROL DISCRIM...DECISION JURID 20 AFRICA/SW. PAGE 74 E1475
B50 COLONIAL SOVEREIGN INT/LAW DOMIN

WADE E.C.S.,CONSTITUTIONAL LAW; AN OUTLINE OF THE LAW AND PRACTICE OF THE CONSTITUTION. UK LEGIS DOMIN ADMIN GP/REL 16/20 CMN/WLTH PARLIAMENT ENGLSH/LAW. PAGE 104 E2087
B50 CONSTN NAT/G PARL/PROC LAW

BIDDLE F.,THE FEAR OF FREEDOM. USA+45 LAW NAT/G PUB/INST PROB/SOLV DOMIN CONTROL SANCTION REV NAT/LISM 20. PAGE 12 E0227
B51 ANOMIE INGP/REL VOL/ASSN ORD/FREE

GUINS G.C.,"SOVIET LAW AND SOVIET SOCIETY." COM USSR STRATA FAM NAT/G WORKER DOMIN RACE/REL ...BIBLIOG 20. PAGE 48 E0960
C54 LAW STRUCT PLAN

CHENERY W.L.,FREEDOM OF THE PRESS. USA+45 USA-45 LAW NAT/G DOMIN EDU/PROP 17/20. PAGE 22 E0427
B55 ORD/FREE COM/IND PRESS CONSTN

CHOWDHURI R.N.,INTERNATIONAL MANDATES AND TRUSTEESHIP SYSTEMS. WOR+45 STRUCT ECO/UNDEV INT/ORG LEGIS DOMIN EDU/PROP LEGIT ADJUD EXEC PWR ...CONCPT TIME/SEQ UN 20. PAGE 22 E0434
B55 DELIB/GP PLAN SOVEREIGN

COMM. STUDY ORGAN. PEACE,REPORTS. WOR-45 ECO/DEV ECO/UNDEV VOL/ASSN CONSULT FORCES PLAN TEC/DEV DOMIN EDU/PROP NUC/PWR ATTIT PWR WEALTH...JURID STERTYP FAO ILO 20 UN. PAGE 24 E0481
B55 WOR+45 INT/ORG ARMS/CONT

KHADDURI M.,WAR AND PEACE IN THE LAW OF ISLAM. CONSTN CULTURE SOCIETY STRATA NAT/G PROVS SECT FORCES TOP/EX CREATE DOMIN EDU/PROP ADJUD COERCE ATTIT RIGID/FLEX ALL/VALS...CONCPT TIME/SEQ TOT/POP VAL/FREE. PAGE 61 E1209
B55 ISLAM JURID PEACE WAR

US HOUSE RULES COMM.HEARINGS BEFORE A SPECIAL SUBCOMMITTEE: ESTABLISHMENT OF A STANDING COMMITTEE ON ADMINISTRATIVE PROCEDURE, PRACTICE. USA+45 LAW EX/STRUC ADJUD CONTROL EXEC GOV/REL EFFICIENCY PWR
B56 ADMIN DOMIN DELIB/GP NAT/G

...POLICY INT 20 CONGRESS. PAGE 100 E2009

FALL B.B.,"THE VIET-MINH REGIME." VIETNAM LAW ECO/UNDEV POL/PAR FORCES DOMIN WAR ATTIT MARXISM ...BIOG PREDICT BIBLIOG/A 20. PAGE 36 E0720
C56 NAT/G ADMIN EX/STRUC LEAD

LONG H.A.,USURPERS - FOES OF FREE MAN. LAW NAT/G CHIEF LEGIS DOMIN ADJUD REPRESENT GOV/REL ORD/FREE LAISSEZ POPULISM...POLICY 18/20 SUPREME/CT ROOSEVLT/F CONGRESS CON/INTERP. PAGE 66 E1325
B57 CT/SYS CENTRAL FEDERAL CONSTN

NEUMANN F.,THE DEMOCRATIC AND THE AUTHORITARIAN STATE: ESSAYS IN POLITICAL AND LEGAL THEORY. USA+45 USA-45 CONTROL REV GOV/REL PEACE ALL/IDEOS ...INT/LAW CONCPT GEN/LAWS BIBLIOG 20. PAGE 77 E1536
B57 DOMIN NAT/G ORD/FREE POLICY

ROSENNE S.,THE INTERNATIONAL COURT OF JUSTICE. WOR+45 LAW DOMIN LEGIT PEACE PWR SOVEREIGN...JURID CONCPT RECORD TIME/SEQ CON/ANAL CHARTS UN TOT/POP VAL/FREE LEAGUE/NAT 20 ICJ. PAGE 86 E1716
B57 INT/ORG CT/SYS INT/LAW

WASSENBERGH H.A.,POST-WAR INTERNATIONAL CIVIL AVIATION POLICY AND THE LAW OF THE AIR. WOR+45 AIR INT/ORG DOMIN LEGIT PEACE ORD/FREE...POLICY JURID NEW/IDEA OBS TIME/SEQ TREND CHARTS 20 TREATY. PAGE 105 E2101
B57 COM/IND NAT/G INT/LAW

CAUGHEY J.W.,IN CLEAR AND PRESENT DANGER. USA+45 ADJUD COERCE ATTIT AUTHORIT...POLICY 20 COLD/WAR MCCARTHY/J. PAGE 21 E0408
B58 NAT/G CONTROL DOMIN ORD/FREE

MARTIN L.J.,INTERNATIONAL PROPAGANDA: ITS LEGAL AND DIPLOMATIC CONTROL. UK USA+45 USSR CONSULT DELIB/GP DOMIN CONTROL 20. PAGE 69 E1373
B58 EDU/PROP DIPLOM INT/LAW ATTIT

RUSSELL R.B.,A HISTORY OF THE UNITED NATIONS CHARTER: THE ROLE OF THE UNITED STATES. SOCIETY NAT/G CONSULT DOMIN LEGIT ATTIT ORD/FREE PWR ...POLICY JURID CONCPT UN LEAGUE/NAT. PAGE 87 E1737
B58 USA-45 INT/ORG CONSTN

SPITZ D.,DEMOCRACY AND THE CHALLANGE OF POWER. FUT USA+45 USA-45 LAW SOCIETY STRUCT LOC/G POL/PAR PROVS DELIB/GP EX/STRUC LEGIS TOP/EX ACT/RES CREATE DOMIN EDU/PROP LEGIT ADJUD ADMIN ATTIT DRIVE MORAL ORD/FREE TOT/POP. PAGE 93 E1862
B58 NAT/G PWR

BEVAN W.,"JURY BEHAVIOR AS A FUNCTION OF THE PRESTIGE OF THE FOREMAN AND THE NATURE OF HIS LEADERSHIP" (BMR)" DELIB/GP DOMIN ADJUD LEAD PERS/REL ATTIT...PSY STAT INT QU CHARTS SOC/EXP 20 JURY. PAGE 11 E0221
L58 PERSON EDU/PROP DECISION CT/SYS

COMM. STUDY ORGAN. PEACE,ORGANIZING PEACE IN THE NUCLEAR AGE. FUT CONSULT DELIB/GP DOMIN ADJUD ROUTINE COERCE ORD/FREE...TECHNIC INT/LAW JURID NEW/IDEA UN COLD/WAR 20. PAGE 24 E0483
B59 INT/ORG ACT/RES NUC/PWR

KIRCHHEIMER O.,GEGENWARTSPROBLEME DER ASYLGEWAHRUNG. DOMIN GP/REL ATTIT...NAT/COMP 20. PAGE 61 E1217
B59 DIPLOM INT/LAW JURID ORD/FREE

CARLSTON K.S.,"NATIONALIZATION: AN ANALYTIC APPROACH." WOR+45 INT/ORG ECO/TAC DOMIN LEGIT ADJUD COERCE ORD/FREE PWR WEALTH SOCISM...JURID CONCPT TREND STERTYP TOT/POP VAL/FREE 20. PAGE 19 E0380
S59 INDUS NAT/G NAT/LISM SOVEREIGN

POTTER P.B.,"OBSTACLES AND ALTERNATIVES TO INTERNATIONAL LAW." WOR+45 NAT/G VOL/ASSN DELIB/GP BAL/PWR DOMIN ROUTINE...JURID VAL/FREE 20. PAGE 81 E1632
S59 INT/ORG LAW DIPLOM INT/LAW

STONE J.,"CONFLICT MANAGEMENT THROUGH CONTEMPORARY INTERNATIONAL LAW AND ORGANIZATION." WOR+45 LAW NAT/G CREATE BAL/PWR DOMIN LEGIT ROUTINE COERCE ATTIT ORD/FREE PWR SOVEREIGN...JURID 20. PAGE 94 E1880
S59 INT/ORG INT/LAW

SUTTON F.X.,"REPRESENTATION AND THE NATURE OF POLITICAL SYSTEMS." UNIV WOR-45 CULTURE SOCIETY STRATA INT/ORG FORCES JUDGE DOMIN LEGIT EXEC REGION REPRESENT ATTIT ORD/FREE RESPECT...SOC HIST/WRIT TIME/SEQ. PAGE 95 E1896 — NAT/G CONCPT — S59

ENGEL J.,THE SECURITY OF THE FREE WORLD. USSR WOR+45 STRATA STRUCT ECO/DEV ECO/UNDEV INT/ORG DELIB/GP FORCES DOMIN LEGIT ADJUD/GP EXEC ARMS/CONT COERCE...POLICY CONCPT NEW/IDEA TIME/SEQ GEN/LAWS COLD/WAR WORK UN 20 NATO. PAGE 35 E0689 — COM TREND DIPLOM — B60

LA PONCE J.A.,THE PROTECTION OF MINORITIES. WOR+45 WOR-45 NAT/G POL/PAR SUFF...INT/LAW CLASSIF GP/COMP GOV/COMP BIBLIOG 17/20 CIVIL/LIB CIV/RIGHTS. PAGE 62 E1242 — INGP/REL DOMIN SOCIETY RACE/REL — B60

NICHOLS J.P.,"HAZARDS OF AMERICAN PRIVATE INVESTMENT IN UNDERDEVELOPED COUNTRIES." FUT L/A+17C USA+45 USA-45 EXTR/IND CONSULT BAL/PWR ECO/TAC DOMIN ADJUD ATTIT SOVEREIGN WEALTH ...HIST/WRIT TIME/SEQ TREND VAL/FREE 20. PAGE 77 E1546 — FINAN ECO/UNDEV CAP/ISM NAT/LISM — S60

O'BRIEN W.,"THE ROLE OF FORCE IN THE INTERNATIONAL JURIDICAL ORDER." WOR+45 NAT/G FORCES DOMIN ADJUD ARMS/CONT DETER NUC/PWR WAR ATTIT PWR...CATH INT/LAW JURID CONCPT TREND STERTYP GEN/LAWS 20. PAGE 78 E1564 — INT/ORG COERCE — S60

SCHACHTER O.,"THE ENFORCEMENT OF INTERNATIONAL JUDICIAL AND ARBITRAL DECISIONS." WOR+45 NAT/G ECO/TAC DOMIN LEGIT ROUTINE COERCE ATTIT DRIVE ALL/VALS PWR...METH/CNCPT TREND TOT/POP 20 UN. PAGE 87 E1750 — INT/ORG ADJUD INT/LAW — S60

MCCLEERY R.,"COMMUNICATION PATTERNS AS BASES OF SYSTEMS OF AUTHORITY AND POWER" IN THEORETICAL STUDIES IN SOCIAL ORGAN. OF PRISON-BMR. USA+45 SOCIETY STRUCT EDU/PROP ADMIN CONTROL COERCE CRIME GP/REL AUTHORIT...SOC 20. PAGE 70 E1400 — PERS/REL PUB/INST PWR DOMIN — C60

COWEN D.V.,THE FOUNDATIONS OF FREEDOM. AFR SOUTH/AFR DOMIN LEGIT ADJUST DISCRIM TOTALISM ATTIT ORD/FREE...MAJORIT JURID SOC/INTEG WORSHIP 20 NEGRO. PAGE 27 E0529 — CONSTN ELITES RACE/REL — B61

PRITCHETT C.H.,CONGRESS VERSUS THE SUPREME COURT, 1957-1960. PROB/SOLV DOMIN EXEC GP/REL DISCRIM PWR CONGRESS SUPREME/CT SUPREME/CT. PAGE 82 E1652 — LEGIS JURID LAW — B61

SMITH J.W.,RELIGIOUS PERSPECTIVES IN AMERICAN CULTURE, VOL. 2; RELIGION IN AMERICAN LIFE. USA+45 CULTURE NAT/G EDU/PROP ADJUD LOBBY ATTIT...ART/METH ANTHOL 20 CHURCH/STA BIBLE. PAGE 92 E1845 — SECT DOMIN SOCIETY GP/REL — B61

WRIGHT Q.,THE ROLE OF INTERNATIONAL LAW IN THE ELIMINATION OF WAR. FUT WOR+45 WOR-45 NAT/G BAL/PWR DIPLOM DOMIN LEGIT PWR...POLICY INT/LAW JURID CONCPT TIME/SEQ TREND GEN/LAWS COLD/WAR 20. PAGE 108 E2158 — INT/ORG ADJUD ARMS/CONT — B61

BEBR G.,JUDICIAL CONTROL OF THE EUROPEAN COMMUNITIES. EUR+WWI INT/ORG NAT/G DOMIN LEGIT PWR ...JURID CONCPT GEN/LAWS GEN/METH EEC 20. PAGE 9 E0168 — ADJUD VOL/ASSN INT/LAW — B62

CARLSTON K.S.,LAW AND ORGANIZATION IN WORLD SOCIETY. WOR+45 FINAN ECO/TAC DOMIN LEGIT CT/SYS ROUTINE COERCE ORD/FREE PWR WEALTH...PLURIST DECISION JURID MGT METH/CNCPT GEN/LAWS 20. PAGE 19 E0381 — INT/ORG LAW — B62

SWAYZE H.,POLITICAL CONTROL OF LITERATURE IN THE USSR, 1946-1959. USSR NAT/G CREATE LICENSE...JURID 20. PAGE 95 E1898 — MARXISM WRITING CONTROL DOMIN — B62

TRISKA J.F.,THE THEORY, LAW, AND POLICY OF SOVIET TREATIES. WOR+45 WOR-45 CONSTN INT/ORG NAT/G — COM LAW — B62

VOL/ASSN DOMIN LEGIT COERCE ATTIT PWR RESPECT ...POLICY JURID CONCPT OBS SAMP TIME/SEQ TREND GEN/LAWS 20. PAGE 97 E1941 — INT/LAW USSR

WOETZEL R.K.,THE NURENBERG TRIALS IN INTERNATIONAL LAW. CHRIST-17C MOD/EUR WOR+45 SOCIETY NAT/G DELIB/GP DOMIN LEGIT ROUTINE ATTIT DRIVE PERSON SUPEGO MORAL ORD/FREE...POLICY MAJORIT JURID PSY SOC SELF/OBS RECORD NAZI TOT/POP. PAGE 107 E2138 — INT/ORG ADJUD WAR — B62

PETKOFF D.K.,"RECOGNITION AND NON-RECOGNITION OF STATES AND GOVERNMENTS IN INTERNATIONAL LAW." ASIA COM USA+45 WOR+45 NAT/G ACT/RES DIPLOM DOMIN LEGIT COERCE ORD/FREE PWR...CONCPT GEN/LAWS 20. PAGE 80 E1611 — INT/ORG LAW INT/LAW — L62

CRANE R.D.,"SOVIET ATTITUDE TOWARD INTERNATIONAL SPACE LAW." COM FUT USA+45 USSR AIR CONSTN DELIB/GP DOMIN PWR...JURID TREND TOT/POP 20. PAGE 27 E0543 — LAW ATTIT INT/LAW SPACE — S62

MCWHINNEY E.,"CO-EXISTENCE, THE CUBA CRISIS, AND COLD WAR-INTERNATIONAL WAR." CUBA USA+45 USSR WOR+45 NAT/G TOP/EX BAL/PWR DIPLOM DOMIN LEGIT PEACE RIGID/FLEX ORD/FREE...STERTYP COLD/WAR 20. PAGE 71 E1427 — CONCPT INT/LAW — S62

BACON F.,"OF THE TRUE GREATNESS OF KINGDOMS AND ESTATES" (1612) IN F. BACON, ESSAYS." ELITES FORCES DOMIN EDU/PROP LEGIT...POLICY GEN/LAWS 16/17 TREATY. PAGE 7 E0129 — WAR PWR DIPLOM CONSTN — C62

CARTER G.M.,FIVE AFRICAN STATES: RESPONSES TO DIVERSITY. CONSTN CULTURE STRATA LEGIS PLAN ECO/TAC DOMIN EDU/PROP CT/SYS EXEC CHOOSE ATTIT HEALTH ORD/FREE PWR...TIME/SEQ TOT/POP VAL/FREE. PAGE 20 E0398 — AFR SOCIETY — B63

HALL J.,COMPARATIVE LAW AND SOCIAL THEORY. WOR+45 CONSTN CULTURE DOMIN CT/SYS ORD/FREE...PLURIST JURID CONCPT NEW/IDEA GEN/LAWS VAL/FREE. PAGE 49 E0984 — LAW SOC — B63

HORRELL M.,LEGISLATION AND RACE RELATIONS (PAMPHLET). SOUTH/AFR SCHOOL TAX DOMIN CONTROL 20. PAGE 55 E1098 — LAW RACE/REL DISCRIM PARTIC — B63

A BIBLIOGRAPHY OF DOCTORAL DISSERTATIONS UNDERTAKEN IN AMERICAN AND CANADIAN UNIVERSITIES ON RELIGION AND POLITICS. LAW CONSTN DOMIN LEGIT ADJUD GP/REL ...POLICY 20. PAGE 62 E1241 — BIBLIOG ACADEM SECT JURID — B63

PRYOR F.L.,THE COMMUNIST FOREIGN TRADE SYSTEM. COM CZECHOSLVK GERMANY YUGOSLAVIA LAW ECO/DEV DIST/IND POL/PAR PLAN DOMIN TOTALISM DRIVE RIGID/FLEX WEALTH ...STAT STAND/INT CHARTS 20. PAGE 83 E1657 — ATTIT ECO/TAC — B63

BRAUSCH G.E.,"AFRICAN ETHNOCRACIES: SOME SOCIOLOGICAL IMPLICATIONS OF CONSTITUTIONAL CHANGE IN EMERGENT TERRITORIES OF AFRICA." AFR CONSTN FACE/GP MUNIC NAT/G DOMIN ATTIT ALL/VALS ...HIST/WRIT GEN/LAWS VAL/FREE 20. PAGE 15 E0289 — LAW SOC ELITES — S63

DUBISSON M.,LA COUR INTERNATIONALE DE JUSTICE. FRANCE LAW CONSTN JUDGE DOMIN ADJUD...INT/LAW CLASSIF RECORD ORG/CHARTS UN. PAGE 33 E0651 — CT/SYS INT/ORG — B64

ECONOMIDES C.P.,LE POUVOIR DE DECISION DES ORGANISATIONS INTERNATIONALES EUROPEENNES. DIPLOM DOMIN INGP/REL EFFICIENCY...INT/LAW JURID 20 NATO OEEC EEC COUNCL/EUR EURATOM. PAGE 34 E0673 — INT/ORG PWR DECISION GP/COMP — B64

IKLE F.C.,HOW NATIONS NEGOTIATE. COM EUR+WWI USA+45 NAT/G INTELL INT/ORG VOL/ASSN DELIB/GP ACT/RES CREATE DOMIN EDU/PROP ADJUD ROUTINE ATTIT PERSON ORD/FREE RESPECT SKILL...PSY SOC OBS VAL/FREE. PAGE 56 E1122 — PWR POLICY — B64

LAPENNA I.,STATE AND LAW: SOVIET AND YUGOSLAV THEORY. USSR YUGOSLAVIA STRATA STRUCT NAT/G DOMIN COERCE MARXISM...GOV/COMP IDEA/COMP 20. PAGE 63 — JURID COM LAW — B64

E1253   SOVEREIGN

                                                              B64
TENBROCK J.,EQUAL UNDER LAW. USA-45 CONSTN POL/PAR   LEGIS
EDU/PROP PARL/PROC ORD/FREE...BIBLIOG 19 AMEND/XIV.   LAW
PAGE 95 E1914   DISCRIM
                                                     DOMIN

                                                              S64
CRANE R.D.,"BASIC PRINCIPLES IN SOVIET SPACE LAW."   COM
FUT WOR+45 AIR INT/ORG DIPLOM DOMIN ARMS/CONT   LAW
COERCE NUC/PWR PEACE ATTIT DRIVE PWR...INT/LAW   USSR
METH/CNCPT NEW/IDEA OBS TREND GEN/LAWS VAL/FREE   SPACE
MARX/KARL 20. PAGE 27 E0544

                                                              S64
GARDNER R.N.,"THE SOVIET UNION AND THE UNITED   COM
NATIONS." WOR+45 FINAN POL/PAR VOL/ASSN FORCES   INT/ORG
ECO/TAC DOMIN EDU/PROP LEGIT ADJUD ADMIN ARMS/CONT   USSR
COERCE ATTIT ALL/VALS...POLICY MAJORIT CONCPT OBS
TIME/SEQ TREND STERTYP UN. PAGE 42 E0838

                                                              S64
SINGH N.,"THE CONTEMPORARY PRACTICE OF INDIA IN THE   LAW
FIELD OF INTERNATIONAL LAW." INDIA S/ASIA INT/ORG   ATTIT
NAT/G DOMIN EDU/PROP LEGIT KNOWL...CONCPT TOT/POP   DIPLOM
20. PAGE 91 E1833   INT/LAW

                                                              S64
SKUBISZEWSKI K.,"FORMS OF PARTICIPATION OF   INT/ORG
INTERNATIONAL ORGANIZATION IN THE LAW MAKING   LAW
PROCESS." FUT WOR+45 NAT/G DELIB/GP DOMIN LEGIT   INT/LAW
KNOWL PWR...JURID TREND 20. PAGE 92 E1837

                                                              B65
BARKER L.J.,FREEDOM, COURTS, POLITICS: STUDIES IN   JURID
CIVIL LIBERTIES. USA+45 LEGIS CREATE DOMIN PRESS   CT/SYS
ADJUD LOBBY CRIME GP/REL RACE/REL MARXISM 20   ATTIT
CIVIL/LIB. PAGE 8 E0148   ORD/FREE

                                                              B65
LAFAVE W.R.,LAW AND SOVIET SOCIETY. EX/STRUC DIPLOM   JURID
DOMIN EDU/PROP PRESS ADMIN CRIME OWN MARXISM 20   CT/SYS
KHRUSH/N. PAGE 62 E1244   ADJUD
                                                     GOV/REL

                                                              B65
NEWBURY C.W.,BRITISH POLICY TOWARDS WEST AFRICA: DIPLOM
SELECT DOCUMENTS 1786-1874. AFR UK INT/TRADE DOMIN   POLICY
ADMIN COLONIAL CT/SYS COERCE ORD/FREE...BIBLIOG/A   NAT/G
18/19. PAGE 77 E1540   WRITING

                                                              B65
NORDEN A.,WAR AND NAZI CRIMINALS IN WEST GERMANY: FASCIST
STATE, ECONOMY, ADMINISTRATION, ARMY, JUSTICE,   WAR
SCIENCE. GERMANY GERMANY/W MOD/EUR ECO/DEV ACADEM   NAT/G
EX/STRUC FORCES DOMIN ADMIN CT/SYS...POLICY MAJORIT   TOP/EX
PACIFIST 20. PAGE 77 E1554

                                                              B65
SOPER T.,EVOLVING COMMONWEALTH. AFR CANADA INDIA   INT/ORG
IRELAND UK LAW CONSTN POL/PAR DOMIN CONTROL WAR PWR   COLONIAL
...AUD/VIS 18/20 COMMONWLTH OEEC. PAGE 93 E1857   VOL/ASSN

                                                              L65
RUBIN A.P.,"UNITED STATES CONTEMPORARY PRACTICE   LAW
RELATING TO INTERNATIONAL LAW." USA+45 WOR+45   LEGIT
CONSTN INT/ORG NAT/G DELIB/GP EX/STRUC DIPLOM DOMIN   INT/LAW
CT/SYS ROUTINE ORD/FREE...CONCPT COLD/WAR 20.
PAGE 86 E1730

                                                              S65
GROSS L.,"PROBLEMS OF INTERNATIONAL ADJUDICATION   LAW
AND COMPLIANCE WITH INTERNATIONAL LAW: SOME SIMPLE   METH/CNCPT
SOLUTIONS." WOR+45 SOCIETY NAT/G DOMIN LEGIT ADJUD   INT/LAW
CT/SYS RIGID/FLEX HEALTH PWR...JURID NEW/IDEA
COLD/WAR 20. PAGE 48 E0951

                                                              B66
DALLIN A.,POLITICS IN THE SOVIET UNION: 7 CASES.   MARXISM
COM USSR LAW POL/PAR CHIEF FORCES WRITING CONTROL   DOMIN
PARL/PROC CIVMIL/REL TOTALISM...ANTHOL 20 KHRUSH/N   ORD/FREE
STALIN/J CASEBOOK COM/PARTY. PAGE 28 E0563   GOV/REL

                                                              B66
STUMPF S.E.,MORALITY AND THE LAW. USA+45 LAW   JURID
CULTURE PROB/SOLV DOMIN ADJUD CONTROL ADJUST   MORAL
ALL/IDEOS MARXISM...INT/LAW 20 SUPREME/CT. PAGE 94   CT/SYS
E1890

                                                              L66
GREIG D.W.,"THE ADVISORY JURISDICTION OF THE   INT/LAW
INTERNATIONAL COURT AND THE SETTLEMENT OF DISPUTES   CT/SYS
BETWEEN STATES." ISRAEL KOREA FORCES BUDGET DOMIN
LEGIT ADJUD COST...RECORD UN CONGO/LEOP TREATY.
PAGE 46 E0915

                                                              S66
DETTER I.,"THE PROBLEM OF UNEQUAL TREATIES." CONSTN   SOVEREIGN
NAT/G LEGIS COLONIAL COERCE PWR...GEOG UN TIME   DOMIN
TREATY. PAGE 31 E0610   INT/LAW
                                                     ECO/UNDEV

                                                              B67
ASCH S.H.,POLICE AUTHORITY AND THE RIGHTS OF THE   FORCES
INDIVIDUAL. CONSTN DOMIN ADJUD CT/SYS...JURID 20.   OP/RES
PAGE 6 E0106   ORD/FREE

                                                              B67
BAKER L.,BACK TO BACK: THE DUEL BETWEEN FDR AND THE   CHIEF
SUPREME COURT. ELITES LEGIS CREATE DOMIN INGP/REL   CT/SYS
PERSON PWR NEW/LIB 20 ROOSEVLT/F SUPREME/CT SENATE.   PARL/PROC
PAGE 7 E0142   GOV/REL

                                                              B67
BROWN L.N.,FRENCH ADMINISTRATIVE LAW. FRANCE UK   EX/STRUC
CONSTN NAT/G LEGIS DOMIN CONTROL EXEC PARL/PROC PWR   LAW
...JURID METH/COMP GEN/METH. PAGE 16 E0314   IDEA/COMP
                                                     CT/SYS

                                                              S67
MIRONENKO Y.,"A NEW EXTENSION OF CRIMINAL LIABILITY   ADJUD
IN THE USSR." COM USSR DOMIN EDU/PROP 20. PAGE 73   SANCTION
E1467   CRIME
                                                     MARXISM

                                                              B68
GREGG R.W.,INTERNATIONAL ORGANIZATION IN THE   INT/ORG
WESTERN HEMISPHERE. L/A+17C USA+45 CULTURE PLAN   DIPLOM
DOMIN AGREE CONTROL DETER PWR...GEOG 20 OAS TREATY.   ECO/UNDEV
PAGE 46 E0913

                                                              B91
BENTHAM J.,A FRAGMENT ON GOVERNMENT (1776). CONSTN   SOVEREIGN
MUNIC NAT/G SECT AGREE HAPPINESS UTIL MORAL   LAW
ORD/FREE...JURID CONCPT. PAGE 10 E0198   DOMIN

                                                              B99
LILLY W.S.,FIRST PRINCIPLES IN POLITICS. UNIV LAW   NAT/G
LEGIS DOMIN ADJUD INGP/REL ORD/FREE SOVEREIGN   CONSTN
...JURID CONCPT 19 NATURL/LAW. PAGE 65 E1299   MORAL
                                                     POLICY

DOMIN/REP....DOMINICAN REPUBLIC; SEE ALSO L/A + 17C

                                                              B64
TELLADO A.,A STATEMENT OF THE LAWS OF THE DOMINICAN   CONSTN
REPUBLIC IN MATTERS AFFECTING BUSINESS (3RD ED.).   LEGIS
DOMIN/REP AGRI DIST/IND EXTR/IND FINAN FAM WORKER   NAT/G
ECO/TAC TAX CT/SYS MARRIAGE OWN...BIBLIOG 20   INDUS
MIGRATION. PAGE 95 E1913

                                                              B66
INSTITUTE COMP STUDY POL SYS,DOMINICAN REPUBLIC   SUFF
ELECTION FACT BOOK. DOMIN/REP LAW LEGIS REPRESENT   CHOOSE
...JURID CHARTS 20. PAGE 57 E1126   POL/PAR
                                                     NAT/G

DOMINATION....SEE DOMIN

DOMINICAN REPUBLIC....SEE DOMIN/REP

DOMINO....THE DOMINO THEORY

DOMKE M. E0634

DONALDSON A.G. E0635

DONNELLY R.C. E0636

DONNELLY/I....IGNATIUS DONNELLY

DOOLIN D.J. E0637

DORMAN M. E0638

DOROSH J.T. E0639

DOSTOYEV/F....FYODOR DOSTOYEVSKY

DOTSON L.O. E0686

DOUGLAS W.O. E0640,E0641,E0642,E0643,E0644

DOUGLAS/P....PAUL DOUGLAS

                                                              B62
CARPER E.T.,ILLINOIS GOES TO CONGRESS FOR ARMY   ADMIN
LAND. USA+45 LAW EXTR/IND PROVS REGION CIVMIL/REL   LOBBY
GOV/REL FEDERAL ATTIT 20 ILLINOIS SENATE CONGRESS   GEOG
DIRKSEN/E DOUGLAS/P. PAGE 20 E0391   LEGIS

DOUGLAS/WO....WILLIAM O. DOUGLAS

DOUMA J. E0645

DOYLE S.E. E0647

DRAPER/HAL....HAL DRAPER

DREAM....DREAMING

DRESSLER D. E0648

DREYFUS/A....ALFRED DREYFUS OR DREYFUS AFFAIR

DRINAN R.F. E0649

DRIVE....DRIVE AND MORALE

B00
LORIMER J.,THE INSTITUTES OF THE LAW OF NATIONS. INT/ORG
WOR-45 CULTURE SOCIETY NAT/G VOL/ASSN DIPLOM LEGIT LAW
WAR PEACE DRIVE ORD/FREE SOVEREIGN...CONCPT RECORD INT/LAW
INT TREND HYPO/EXP GEN/METH TOT/POP VAL/FREE 20.
PAGE 66 E1327

N19
CARPER E.T.,LOBBYING AND THE NATURAL GAS BILL LOBBY
(PAMPHLET). USA+45 SERV/IND BARGAIN PAY DRIVE ROLE ADJUD
WEALTH 20 CONGRESS SENATE EISNHWR/DD. PAGE 20 E0389 TRIBUTE
NAT/G

B22
BRYCE J.,INTERNATIONAL RELATIONS. CHRIST-17C INT/ORG
EUR+WWI MOD/EUR CULTURE INTELL NAT/G DELIB/GP POLICY
CREATE BAL/PWR DIPLOM ATTIT DRIVE RIGID/FLEX
ALL/VALS...PLURIST JURID CONCPT TIME/SEQ GEN/LAWS
TOT/POP. PAGE 16 E0323

B29
BUELL R.,INTERNATIONAL RELATIONS. WOR+45 WOR-45 INT/ORG
CONSTN STRATA FORCES TOP/EX ADMIN ATTIT DRIVE BAL/PWR
SUPEGO MORAL ORD/FREE PWR SOVEREIGN...JURID SOC DIPLOM
CONCPT 20. PAGE 17 E0326

B35
FOREIGN AFFAIRS BIBLIOGRAPHY: A SELECTED AND BIBLIOG/A
ANNOTATED LIST OF BOOKS ON INTERNATIONAL RELATIONS DIPLOM
1919-1962 (4 VOLS.). CONSTN FORCES COLONIAL INT/ORG
ARMS/CONT WAR NAT/LISM PEACE ATTIT DRIVE...POLICY
INT/LAW 20. PAGE 2 E0032

B39
TIMASHEFF N.S.,AN INTRODUCTION TO THE SOCIOLOGY OF SOC
LAW. CRIME ANOMIE ATTIT DRIVE ORD/FREE...JURID PSY BIBLIOG
CONCPT. PAGE 96 E1926 PWR

B39
WILSON G.G.,HANDBOOK OF INTERNATIONAL LAW. FUT UNIV INT/ORG
USA-45 WOR-45 SOCIETY LEGIT ATTIT DISPL DRIVE LAW
ALL/VALS...INT/LAW TIME/SEQ TREND. PAGE 106 E2128 CONCPT
WAR

B42
US LIBRARY OF CONGRESS,SOCIAL AND CULTURAL PROBLEMS BIBLIOG/A
IN WARTIME: APRIL 1941-MARCH 1942. WOR+45 CLIENT WAR
SECT EDU/PROP CRIME LEISURE RACE/REL STRANGE ATTIT SOC
DRIVE HEALTH...GEOG 20. PAGE 100 E2012 CULTURE

B43
US LIBRARY OF CONGRESS,SOCIAL AND CULTURAL PROBLEMS BIBLIOG/A
IN WARTIME: APRIL-DECEMBER (SUPPLEMENT 1). WOR-45 WAR
SECT EDU/PROP CRIME LEISURE CIVMIL/REL RACE/REL SOC
ATTIT DRIVE HEALTH...GEOG 20. PAGE 100 E2013 CULTURE

B43
US LIBRARY OF CONGRESS,SOCIAL AND CULTURAL PROBLEMS BIBLIOG/A
IN WARTIME: JANUARY-MAY 1943 (SUPPLEMENT 2). WOR-45 WAR
FAM SECT PLAN EDU/PROP CRIME LEISURE RACE/REL DRIVE SOC
HEALTH...GEOG 20 JEWS. PAGE 100 E2014 CULTURE

B44
DE HUSZAR G.B.,NEW PERSPECTIVES ON PEACE. UNIV ATTIT
CULTURE SOCIETY ECO/DEV ECO/UNDEV NAT/G FORCES MYTH
CREATE ECO/TAC DOMIN ADJUD COERCE DRIVE ORD/FREE PEACE
...GEOG JURID PSY SOC CONCPT TOT/POP. PAGE 29 E0584 WAR

S44
WRIGHT Q.,"CONSTITUTIONAL PROCEDURES OF THE US FOR TOP/EX
CARRYING OUT OBLIGATIONS FOR MILITARY SANCTIONS." FORCES
EUR+WWI FUT USA-45 WOR-45 CONSTN INTELL NAT/G INT/LAW
CONSULT EX/STRUC LEGIS ROUTINE DRIVE...POLICY JURID WAR
CONCPT OBS TREND TOT/POP 20. PAGE 108 E2153

S48
ALEXANDER L.,"WAR CRIMES, THEIR SOCIAL- DRIVE
PSYCHOLOGICAL ASPECTS." EUR+WWI GERMANY LAW CULTURE WAR
ELITES KIN POL/PAR PUB/INST FORCES DOMIN EDU/PROP
COERCE CRIME ATTIT SUPEGO HEALTH MORAL PWR FASCISM
...PSY OBS TREND GEN/LAWS NAZI 20. PAGE 3 E0061

B50
MACIVER R.M.,GREAT EXPRESSIONS OF HUMAN RIGHTS. LAW UNIV
CONSTN CULTURE INTELL SOCIETY R+D INT/ORG ATTIT CONCPT
DRIVE...JURID OBS HIST/WRIT GEN/LAWS. PAGE 67 E1340

B51
PUSEY M.J.,CHARLES EVANS HUGHES (2 VOLS.). LAW BIOG
CONSTN NAT/G POL/PAR DIPLOM LEGIT WAR CHOOSE TOP/EX
PERS/REL DRIVE HEREDITY 19/20 DEPT/STATE LEAGUE/NAT ADJUD
SUPREME/CT HUGHES/CE WWI. PAGE 83 E1663 PERSON

L52
WRIGHT Q.,"CONGRESS AND THE TREATY-MAKING POWER." ROUTINE
USA+45 WOR+45 CONSTN INTELL NAT/G CHIEF CONSULT DIPLOM
EX/STRUC LEGIS TOP/EX CREATE GOV/REL DISPL DRIVE INT/LAW
RIGID/FLEX...TREND TOT/POP CONGRESS CONGRESS 20 DELIB/GP
TREATY. PAGE 108 E2154

B55
CAVAN R.S.,CRIMINOLOGY (2ND ED.). USA+45 LAW FAM DRIVE
PUB/INST FORCES PLAN WAR AGE/Y PERSON ROLE SUPEGO CRIMLGY
...CHARTS 20 FBI. PAGE 21 E0409 CONTROL
METH/COMP

B56
DUNNILL F.,THE CIVIL SERVICE. UK LAW PLAN ADMIN PERSON
EFFICIENCY DRIVE NEW/LIB...STAT CHARTS 20 WORKER
PARLIAMENT CIVIL/SERV. PAGE 33 E0662 STRATA
SOC/WK

B57
BLOOMFIELD L.M.,EGYPT, ISRAEL AND THE GULF OF ISLAM
AQABA: IN INTERNATIONAL LAW. LAW NAT/G CONSULT INT/LAW
FORCES PLAN ECO/TAC ROUTINE COERCE ATTIT DRIVE UAR
PERCEPT PERSON RIGID/FLEX LOVE PWR WEALTH...GEOG
CONCPT MYTH TREND. PAGE 13 E0250

B57
ROWAN C.T.,GO SOUTH TO SORROW. USA+45 STRUCT NAT/G RACE/REL
EDU/PROP LEAD COERCE ISOLAT DRIVE SUPEGO RESPECT DISCRIM
...PREDICT 20 NEGRO SUPREME/CT SOUTH/US CIV/RIGHTS. ANOMIE
PAGE 86 E1728 LAW

B58
SPITZ D.,DEMOCRACY AND THE CHALLANGE OF POWER. FUT NAT/G
USA+45 USA-45 LAW SOCIETY STRUCT LOC/G POL/PAR PWR
PROVS DELIB/GP EX/STRUC LEGIS TOP/EX ACT/RES CREATE
DOMIN EDU/PROP LEGIT ADJUD ADMIN ATTIT DRIVE MORAL
ORD/FREE TOT/POP. PAGE 93 E1862

B59
ANDERSON J.N.D.,ISLAMIC LAW IN THE MODERN WORLD. ISLAM
FAM KIN SECT LEGIT ADJUD ATTIT DRIVE...TIME/SEQ JURID
TREND GEN/LAWS 20 MUSLIM. PAGE 5 E0089

B59
LAPIERE R.,THE FREUDIAN ETHIC. USA+45 FAM EDU/PROP PSY
CONTROL CRIME ADJUST AGE DRIVE PERCEPT PERSON SEX ORD/FREE
...SOC 20 FREUD/S. PAGE 63 E1254 SOCIETY

S59
CLOWARD R.A.,"ILLEGITIMATE MEANS, ANOMIE, AND ANOMIE
DEVIANT BEHAVIOR" STRUCT CRIME DRIVE PERSON...SOC CRIMLGY
CONCPT NEW/IDEA 20 DURKHEIM/E MERTON/R. PAGE 23 LEGIT
E0459 ADJUST

B60
BORGATTA E.F.,SOCIAL WORKERS' PERCEPTIONS OF SOC/WK
CLIENTS. SERV/IND ROUTINE PERS/REL DRIVE PERSON ATTIT
RESPECT...SOC PERS/COMP 20. PAGE 14 E0268 CLIENT
PROB/SOLV

B60
JENNINGS R.,PROGRESS OF INTERNATIONAL LAW. FUT INT/ORG
WOR+45 WOR-45 SOCIETY NAT/G VOL/ASSN DELIB/GP LAW
DIPLOM EDU/PROP LEGIT COERCE ATTIT DRIVE MORAL INT/LAW
ORD/FREE...JURID CONCPT OBS TIME/SEQ TREND
GEN/LAWS. PAGE 58 E1164

S60
SCHACHTER O.,"THE ENFORCEMENT OF INTERNATIONAL INT/ORG
JUDICIAL AND ARBITRAL DECISIONS." WOR+45 NAT/G ADJUD
ECO/TAC DOMIN LEGIT ROUTINE COERCE ATTIT DRIVE INT/LAW
ALL/VALS PWR...METH/CNCPT TREND TOT/POP 20 UN.
PAGE 87 E1750

B61
ANAND R.P.,COMPULSORY JURISDICTION OF INTERNATIONAL INT/ORG
COURT OF JUSTICE. FUT WOR+45 SOCIETY PLAN LEGIT COERCE

ADJUD ATTIT DRIVE PERSON ORD/FREE...JURID CONCPT INT/LAW
TREND 20 ICJ. PAGE 5 E0086

LEONI B.,FREEDOM AND THE LAW. WOR+45 SOCIETY ADJUD JURID
INGP/REL EFFICIENCY ATTIT DRIVE. PAGE 64 E1286 ORD/FREE
    B61
    LEGIS
    CONTROL

ALGER C.F.,"NON-RESOLUTION CONSEQUENCES OF THE INT/ORG
UNITED NATIONS AND THEIR EFFECT ON INTERNATIONAL DRIVE
CONFLICT." WOR+45 CONSTN ECO/DEV NAT/G CONSULT BAL/PWR
DELIB/GP TOP/EX ACT/RES PLAN DIPLOM EDU/PROP
ROUTINE ATTIT ALL/VALS...INT/LAW TOT/POP UN 20.
PAGE 3 E0065
    S61

MACHOWSKI K.,"SELECTED PROBLEMS OF NATIONAL UNIV
SOVEREIGNTY WITH REFERENCE TO THE LAW OF OUTER ACT/RES
SPACE." FUT WOR+45 AIR LAW INTELL SOCIETY ECO/DEV NUC/PWR
PLAN EDU/PROP DETER DRIVE PERCEPT SOVEREIGN SPACE
...POLICY INT/LAW OBS TREND TOT/POP 20. PAGE 67
E1339
    S61

MILLER E.,"LEGAL ASPECTS OF UN ACTION IN THE INT/ORG
CONGO." AFR CULTURE ADMIN PEACE DRIVE RIGID/FLEX LEGIT
ORD/FREE...WELF/ST JURID OBS UN CONGO 20. PAGE 73
E1458
    S61

MITCHELL G.E.,THE ANGRY BLACK SOUTH. USA+45 LAW RACE/REL
CONSTN SCHOOL DELIB/GP EDU/PROP CONTROL SUFF ANOMIE DISCRIM
DRIVE...ANTHOL 20 NEGRO CIV/RIGHTS SOUTH/US. ADJUST
PAGE 74 E1473 ORD/FREE
    B62

THOMPSON K.W.,AMERICAN DIPLOMACY AND EMERGENT NAT/G
PATTERNS. USA+45 WOR-45 WOR+45 LAW DELIB/GP BAL/PWR
FORCES TOP/EX DIPLOM ATTIT DRIVE RIGID/FLEX
ORD/FREE PWR SOVEREIGN...POLICY 20. PAGE 96 E1922
    B62

WOETZEL R.K.,THE NURENBERG TRIALS IN INTERNATIONAL INT/ORG
LAW. CHRIST-17C MOD/EUR WOR+45 SOCIETY NAT/G ADJUD
DELIB/GP DOMIN LEGIT ROUTINE ATTIT DRIVE PERSON WAR
SUPEGO MORAL ORD/FREE...POLICY MAJORIT JURID PSY
SOC SELF/OBS RECORD NAZI TOT/POP. PAGE 107 E2138
    B62

PRYOR F.L.,THE COMMUNIST FOREIGN TRADE SYSTEM. COM ATTIT
CZECHOSLVK GERMANY YUGOSLAVIA LAW ECO/DEV DIST/IND ECO/TAC
POL/PAR PLAN DOMIN TOTALISM DRIVE RIGID/FLEX WEALTH
...STAT STAND/INT CHARTS 20. PAGE 83 E1657
    B63

HARNETTY P.,"CANADA, SOUTH AFRICA AND THE AFR
COMMONWEALTH." CANADA SOUTH/AFR LAW INT/ORG ATTIT
VOL/ASSN DELIB/GP LEGIS TOP/EX ECO/TAC LEGIT DRIVE
MORAL...CONCPT CMN/WLTH 20. PAGE 50 E1000
    S63

RIGAUX F.,"LA SIGNIFICATION DES ACTES JUDICIARES A CONSULT
L'ETRANGER." EUR+WWI ITALY NETHERLAND LAW ACT/RES CT/SYS
DRIVE...JURID GEN/LAWS TOT/POP 20. PAGE 85 E1699 GERMANY
    S63

SCHUBERT G.,"JUDICIAL DECISION-MAKING." FORCES LEAD ADJUD
ATTIT DRIVE...POLICY PSY STAT CHARTS ANTHOL BIBLIOG DECISION
20. PAGE 88 E1773
    C63
    JUDGE
    CT/SYS

GRIFFITH W.E.,THE SINO-SOVIET RIFT. ASIA CHINA/COM ATTIT
COM CUBA USSR YUGOSLAVIA NAT/G POL/PAR VOL/ASSN TIME/SEQ
DELIB/GP FORCES TOP/EX DIPLOM EDU/PROP DRIVE PERSON BAL/PWR
PWR...TREND 20 TREATY. PAGE 47 E0941 SOCISM
    B64

CRANE R.D.,"BASIC PRINCIPLES IN SOVIET SPACE LAW." COM
FUT WOR+45 AIR INT/ORG DIPLOM DOMIN ARMS/CONT LAW
COERCE NUC/PWR PEACE ATTIT DRIVE PWR...INT/LAW USSR
METH/CNCPT NEW/IDEA OBS TREND GEN/LAWS VAL/FREE SPACE
MARX/KARL 20. PAGE 27 E0544
    S64

GREENBERG S.,"JUDAISM AND WORLD JUSTICE." MEDIT-7 SECT
WOR+45 LAW CULTURE SOCIETY INT/ORG NAT/G FORCES JURID
EDU/PROP ATTIT DRIVE PERSON SUPEGO ALL/VALS PEACE
...POLICY PSY CONCPT GEN/LAWS JEWS. PAGE 46 E0908
    S64

BROMBERG W.,CRIME AND THE MIND. LAW LEGIT ADJUD CRIMLGY
CRIME MURDER AGE/Y ANOMIE BIO/SOC DRIVE SEX PSY. SOC
PAGE 16 E0305 HEALTH
    B65

COERCE

HARTUNG F.E.,CRIME, LAW, AND SOCIETY. LAW PUB/INST PERCEPT
CRIME PERS/REL AGE/Y BIO/SOC PERSON ROLE SUPEGO CRIMLGY
...LING GP/COMP GEN/LAWS 20. PAGE 50 E1004 DRIVE
    B65
    CONTROL

SHARMA S.P.,"THE INDIA-CHINA BORDER DISPUTE: AN LAW
INDIAN PERSPECTIVE." ASIA CHINA/COM S/ASIA NAT/G ATTIT
LEGIT CT/SYS NAT/LISM DRIVE MORAL ORD/FREE PWR 20. SOVEREIGN
PAGE 91 E1815 INDIA
    L65

KHOURI F.J.,"THE JORDON RIVER CONTROVERSY." LAW ISLAM
SOCIETY ECO/UNDEV AGRI FINAN INDUS SECT FORCES INT/ORG
ACT/RES PLAN TEC/DEV ECO/TAC EDU/PROP COERCE ATTIT ISRAEL
DRIVE PERCEPT RIGID/FLEX ALL/VALS...GEOG SOC MYTH JORDAN
WORK. PAGE 61 E1212
    S65

O'NEILL C.E.,CHURCH AND STATE IN FRENCH COLONIAL COLONIAL
LOUISIANA: POLICY AND POLITICS TO 1732. PROVS NAT/G
VOL/ASSN DELIB/GP ADJUD ADMIN GP/REL ATTIT DRIVE SECT
...POLICY BIBLIOG 17/18 LOUISIANA CHURCH/STA. PWR
PAGE 78 E1568
    B66

GASS O.,"THE LITERATURE OF AMERICAN GOVERNMENT." NEW/LIB
CONSTN DRIVE ORD/FREE...JURID CONCPT METH/CNCPT CT/SYS
IDEA/COMP 20 WILSON/W BEARD/CA LINK/AS. PAGE 42 NAT/G
E0841
    S66

BERNSTEIN S.,ALTERNATIVES TO VIOLENCE: ALIENATED AGE/Y
YOUTH AND RIOTS, RACE AND POVERTY. MUNIC PUB/INST SOC/WK
SCHOOL INGP/REL RACE/REL UTOPIA DRIVE HABITAT ROLE NEIGH
WEALTH...INT 20. PAGE 11 E0215 CRIME
    B67

DEBOLD R.C.,LSD, MAN AND SOCIETY. USA+45 LAW HEALTH
SOCIETY SECT CONTROL SANCTION STRANGE ATTIT...HEAL DRIVE
CHARTS ANTHOL BIBLIOG. PAGE 30 E0601 PERSON
    B67
    BIO/SOC

ESTEY M.,THE UNIONS: STRUCTURE, DEVELOPMENT, AND LABOR
MANAGEMENT. FUT USA+45 ADJUD CONTROL INGP/REL DRIVE EX/STRUC
...DECISION T 20 AFL/CIO. PAGE 35 E0699 ADMIN
    B67
    GOV/REL

GIBSON G.H.,"LABOR PIRACY ON THE BRANDYWINE." ECO/TAC
USA-45 INDUS R+D VOL/ASSN CAP/ISM ADJUD DRIVE...PSY CREATE
19. PAGE 43 E0859 TEC/DEV
    S67
    WORKER

DRUG ADDICTION....SEE BIO/SOC, ANOMIE, CRIME

DU BOIS W.E.B. E0650

DUBCEK/A.....ALEXANDER DUBCEK

DUBISSON M. E0651

DUBOIS J. E0652

DUBOIS/J....JULES DUBOIS

DUBOIS/WEB....W.E.B. DUBOIS

DUCLOUX L. E0653

DUGARD J. E0654

DUGUIT L. E0655

DUGUIT/L....LEON DUGUIT

DUHRING/E....EUGEN DUHRING

DULLES/JF....JOHN FOSTER DULLES

DUMBAULD E. E0656

DUMON F. E0657,E0658

DUNHAM A. E0659

DUNN F.S. E0660,E0661

DUNNILL F. E0662

DUNNING W.A. E0663,E0664

DUPONT....DUPONT CORPORATION (E.I. DUPONT DE NEMOURS)

DUPRE C. E0666

DUPRE J.S. E0665

DUPRE L. E0666

DURKHEIM/E....EMIL DURKHEIM

CLOWARD R.A.,"ILLEGITIMATE MEANS, ANOMIE, AND   S59
DEVIANT BEHAVIOR" STRUCT CRIME DRIVE PERSON...SOC   ANOMIE
CONCPT NEW/IDEA 20 DURKHEIM/E MERTON/R. PAGE 23   CRIMLGY
E0459   LEGIT
                                                       ADJUST

DUROSELLE J.B. E0667

DUTY....SEE SUPEGO

DUVERGER/M....MAURICE DUVERGER

DWYER R.J. E0668

DYCK H.L. E0669 ————————————E————————————————————————

EACM....EAST AFRICAN COMMON MARKET

EAGLETON C. E0670

EAST AFRICA....SEE AFRICA/E

EAST GERMANY....SEE GERMANY/E

EASTERN EUROPE....SEE EUROPE/E

EASTON D. E0671

EATING....EATING, CUISINE

ECHR....EUROPEAN CONVENTION ON HUMAN RIGHTS

SCHWELB E.,"OPERATION OF THE EUROPEAN CONVENTION ON INT/ORG   S64
HUMAN RIGHTS," EUR+WWI LAW SOCIETY CREATE EDU/PROP   MORAL
ADJUD ADMIN PEACE ATTIT ORD/FREE PWR...POLICY
INT/LAW CONCPT OBS GEN/LAWS UN VAL/FREE ILO 20
ECHR. PAGE 89 E1791

                                                        B66
COUNCIL OF EUROPE,EUROPEAN CONVENTION ON HUMAN   ORD/FREE
RIGHTS - COLLECTED TEXTS (5TH ED.). EUR+WWI DIPLOM   DELIB/GP
ADJUD CT/SYS...INT/LAW 20 ECHR. PAGE 26 E0520   INT/ORG
                                                       JURID

ECO....ECONOMICS

ECO/DEV....ECONOMIC SYSTEM IN DEVELOPED COUNTRIES

ECO/TAC....ECONOMIC MEASURES

FULLER G.A.,DEMOBILIZATION: A SELECTED LIST OF   N
REFERENCES. USA+45 LAW AGRI LABOR WORKER ECO/TAC   BIBLIOG/A
RATION RECEIVE EDU/PROP ROUTINE ARMS/CONT ALL/VALS   INDUS
20. PAGE 41 E0819   FORCES
                                                       NAT/G

JOURNAL OF INTERNATIONAL AFFAIRS. WOR+45 ECO/UNDEV   N
POL/PAR ECO/TAC WAR PEACE PERSON ALL/IDEOS   BIBLIOG
...INT/LAW TREND. PAGE 1 E0010   DIPLOM
                                                       INT/ORG
                                                       NAT/G

MINISTRY OF OVERSEAS DEVELOPME,TECHNICAL CO-   N
OPERATION -- A BIBLIOGRAPHY. UK LAW SOCIETY DIPLOM   BIBLIOG
ECO/TAC FOR/AID...STAT 20 CMN/WLTH. PAGE 73 E1466   TEC/DEV
                                                       ECO/DEV
                                                       NAT/G

DARBY W.E.,INTERNATIONAL TRIBUNALS. WOR-45 NAT/G   B00
ECO/TAC DOMIN LEGIT CT/SYS COERCE ORD/FREE PWR   INT/ORG
SOVEREIGN JURID. PAGE 29 E0567   ADJUD
                                                       PEACE
                                                       INT/LAW

GRIFFIN A.P.C.,LIST OF BOOKS RELATING TO THE THEORY   BIBLIOG/A   B00
OF COLONIZATION, GOVERNMENT OF DEPENDENCIES,   COLONIAL
PROTECTORATES, AND RELATED TOPICS. FRANCE GERMANY   GOV/REL
ITALY SPAIN UK USA-45 WOR-45 ECO/TAC ADMIN CONTROL   DOMIN
REGION NAT/LISM ALL/VALS PWR...INT/LAW SOC 16/19.
PAGE 46 E0917

GRIFFIN A.P.C.,A LIST OF BOOKS RELATING TO TRUSTS   BIBLIOG/A   B02
(2ND REV. ED.) (PAMPHLET). FRANCE GERMANY UK USA-45   JURID

WOR-45 LAW ECO/DEV INDUS LG/CO NAT/G CAP/ISM   ECO/TAC
CENTRAL DISCRIM PWR LAISSEZ 19/20. PAGE 46 E0919   VOL/ASSN

                                                        B03
GRIFFIN A.P.C.,LISTS PUBLISHED 1902-03: LABOR   BIBLIOG/A
PARTICULARLY RELATING TO STRIKES (PAMPHLET). UK   LABOR
USA-45 FINAN WORKER PLAN BARGAIN CRIME GOV/REL   GP/REL
...POLICY 19/20 PARLIAMENT. PAGE 46 E0923   ECO/TAC

                                                        B04
BURKE E.,A LETTER TO THE SHERIFFS OF BRISTOL   LEGIS
(1777). USA-45 LAW ECO/TAC COLONIAL CT/SYS REV   ADJUD
GP/REL ORD/FREE...POLICY 18 PARLIAMENT BURKE/EDM.   CRIME
PAGE 17 E0341

                                                        B04
GRIFFIN A.P.C.,A LIST OF BOOKS RELATING TO   BIBLIOG/A
RAILROADS IN THEIR RELATION TO THE GOVERNMENT AND   SERV/IND
THE PUBLIC (PAMPHLET). USA-45 LAW ECO/DEV NAT/G   ADJUD
TEC/DEV CAP/ISM LICENSE CENTRAL LAISSEZ...DECISION   ECO/TAC
19/20. PAGE 47 E0925

                                                        B07
GRIFFIN A.P.C.,LIST OF MORE RECENT WORKS ON FEDERAL   BIBLIOG/A
CONTROL OF COMMERCE AND CORPORATIONS (PAMPHLET).   NAT/G
USA-45 LAW ECO/DEV FINAN LG/CO TARIFFS TAX LICENSE   JURID
CENTRAL ORD/FREE WEALTH LAISSEZ 19/20. PAGE 47   ECO/TAC
E0931

                                                        B09
HOLLAND T.E.,LETTERS UPON WAR AND NEUTRALITY.   LAW
WOR-45 NAT/G FORCES JUDGE ECO/TAC LEGIT CT/SYS   INT/LAW
NEUTRAL ROUTINE COERCE...JURID TIME/SEQ 20. PAGE 55   INT/ORG
E1085   WAR

                                                        B15
HOBSON J.A.,TOWARDS INTERNATIONAL GOVERNMENT.   FUT
MOD/EUR STRUCT ECO/TAC EDU/PROP ADJUD ALL/VALS   INT/ORG
...SOCIALIST CONCPT GEN/LAWS TOT/POP 20. PAGE 53   CENTRAL
E1059

                                                        B17
MEYER H.H.B.,LIST OF REFERENCES ON EMBARGOES   BIBLIOG
(PAMPHLET). USA-45 AGRI DIPLOM WRITING DEBATE   DIST/IND
WEAPON...INT/LAW 18/20 CONGRESS. PAGE 72 E1447   ECO/TAC
                                                      INT/TRADE

                                                        N19
BURRUS B.R.,INVESTIGATION AND DISCOVERY IN STATE   NAT/G
ANTITRUST (PAMPHLET). USA+45 USA-45 LEGIS ECO/TAC   PROVS
ADMIN CONTROL CT/SYS CRIME GOV/REL PWR...JURID   LAW
CHARTS 19/20 FTC MONOPOLY. PAGE 18 E0346   INSPECT

                                                        B20
COX H.,ECONOMIC LIBERTY. UNIV LAW INT/TRADE RATION   NAT/G
TARIFFS RACE/REL SOCISM POLICY. PAGE 27 E0535   ORD/FREE
                                                      ECO/TAC
                                                      PERSON

                                                        B22
SCHROEDER T.,FREE SPEECH BIBLIOGRAPHY. EUR+WWI   BIBLIOG/A
WOR-45 NAT/G SECT ECO/TAC WRITING ADJUD ATTIT   ORD/FREE
MARXISM SOCISM 16/20. PAGE 88 E1768   CONTROL
                                                      LAW

                                                        B28
CORBETT P.E.,CANADA AND WORLD POLITICS. LAW CULTURE   NAT/G
SOCIETY STRUCT MARKET INT/ORG FORCES ACT/RES PLAN   CANADA
ECO/TAC LEGIT ORD/FREE PWR RESPECT...SOC CONCPT
TIME/SEQ TREND CMN/WLTH 20 LEAGUE/NAT. PAGE 26
E0504

                                                        B28
YANG KUNG-SUN,THE BOOK OF LORD SHANG. LAW ECO/UNDEV   ASIA
LOC/G NAT/G NEIGH PLAN ECO/TAC LEGIT ATTIT SKILL   JURID
...CONCPT CON/ANAL WORK TOT/POP. PAGE 108 E2164

                                                        B29
CONWELL-EVANS T.P.,THE LEAGUE COUNCIL IN ACTION.   DELIB/GP
EUR+WWI TURKEY UK USSR WOR-45 INT/ORG FORCES JUDGE   INT/LAW
ECO/TAC EDU/PROP LEGIT ROUTINE ARMS/CONT COERCE
ATTIT PWR...MAJORIT GEOG JURID CONCPT LEAGUE/NAT
TOT/POP VAL/FREE TUNIS 20. PAGE 25 E0498

                                                        B29
LEITZ F.,DIE PUBLIZITAT DER AKTIENGESELLSCHAFT.   LG/CO
BELGIUM FRANCE GERMANY UK FINAN PRESS GP/REL PROFIT   JURID
KNOWL 20. PAGE 64 E1282   ECO/TAC
                                                      NAT/COMP

                                                        L29
DARWIN L.,"WHAT IS EUGENICS." USA-45 LAW SOCIETY   PLAN
FACE/GP FAM ACT/RES ECO/TAC HEALTH...HEAL TREND   BIO/SOC
STERYP 20. PAGE 29 E0568

B32
EAGLETON C.,INTERNATIONAL GOVERNMENT. BRAZIL FRANCE INT/ORG
GERMANY ITALY UK USSR WOR-45 DELIB/GP TOP/EX PLAN JURID
ECO/TAC EDU/PROP LEGIT ADJUD REGION ARMS/CONT DIPLOM
COERCE ATTIT PWR...GEOG MGT VAL/FREE LEAGUE/NAT 20. INT/LAW
PAGE 34 E0670

B34
US TARIFF COMMISSION,THE TARIFF; A BIBLIOGRAPHY: A BIBLIOG/A
SELECT LIST OF REFERENCES. USA-45 LAW DIPLOM TAX TARIFFS
ADMIN...POLICY TREATY 20. PAGE 103 E2064 ECO/TAC

B36
HUDSON M.O.,INTERNATIONAL LEGISLATION: 1929-1931. INT/LAW
WOR-45 SEA AIR AGRI FINAN LABOR DIPLOM ECO/TAC PARL/PROC
REPAR CT/SYS ARMS/CONT WAR WEAPON...JURID 20 TREATY ADJUD
LEAGUE/NAT. PAGE 56 E1112 LAW

B37
HAMILTON W.H.,THE POWER TO GOVERN. ECO/DEV FINAN LING
INDUS ECO/TAC INT/TRADE TARIFFS TAX CONTROL CT/SYS CONSTN
WAR COST PWR 18/20 SUPREME/CT. PAGE 50 E0991 NAT/G
POLICY

B40
CARR E.H.,THE TWENTY YEARS' CRISIS 1919-1939. FUT INT/ORG
WOR-45 BAL/PWR ECO/TAC LEGIT TOTALISM ATTIT DIPLOM
ALL/VALS...POLICY JURID CONCPT TIME/SEQ TREND PEACE
GEN/LAWS TOT/POP 20. PAGE 20 E0393

B40
WOLFERS A.,BRITAIN AND FRANCE BETWEEN TWO WORLD DIPLOM
WARS. FRANCE UK INT/ORG NAT/G PLAN BARGAIN ECO/TAC WAR
AGREE ISOLAT ALL/IDEOS...DECISION GEOG 20 TREATY POLICY
VERSAILLES INTERVENT. PAGE 107 E2139

S40
GERTH H.,"THE NAZI PARTY: ITS LEADERSHIP AND POL/PAR
COMPOSITION" (BMR)" GERMANY ELITES STRATA STRUCT DOMIN
EX/STRUC FORCES ECO/TAC CT/SYS CHOOSE TOTALISM LEAD
AGE/Y AUTHORIT PWR 20. PAGE 43 E0851 ADMIN

L41
COMM. STUDY ORGAN. PEACE,"ORGANIZATION OF PEACE." INT/ORG
USA-45 WOR-45 STRATA NAT/G ACT/RES DIPLOM ECO/TAC PLAN
EDU/PROP ADJUD ATTIT ORD/FREE PWR...SOC CONCPT PEACE
ANTHOL LEAGUE/NAT 20. PAGE 24 E0479

B42
FEILCHENFELD E.H.,THE INTERNATIONAL ECONOMIC LAW OF ECO/TAC
BELLIGERENT OCCUPATION. EUR+WWI MOD/EUR USA-45 INT/LAW
INT/ORG DIPLOM ADJUD ARMS/CONT LEAGUE/NAT 20. WAR
PAGE 37 E0726

B42
HAMBRO C.J.,HOW TO WIN THE PEACE. ECO/TAC EDU/PROP FUT
ADJUD PERSON ALL/VALS...SOCIALIST TREND GEN/LAWS INT/ORG
20. PAGE 50 E0987 PEACE

C43
BENTHAM J.,"THE RATIONALE OF REWARD" IN J. BOWRING, SANCTION
ED., THE WORKS OF JEREMY BENTHAM (VOL. 2)" LAW ECO/TAC
WORKER CREATE INSPECT PAY ROUTINE HAPPINESS PRODUC INCOME
SUPEGO WEALTH METH/CNCPT. PAGE 10 E0195 PWR

B44
BRIERLY J.L.,THE OUTLOOK FOR INTERNATIONAL LAW. FUT INT/ORG
WOR-45 CONSTN NAT/G VOL/ASSN FORCES ECO/TAC DOMIN LAW
LEGIT ADJUD ROUTINE PEACE ORD/FREE...INT/LAW JURID
METH LEAGUE/NAT 20. PAGE 15 E0298

B44
CHENEY F.,CARTELS, COMBINES, AND TRUSTS: A SELECTED BIBLIOG/A
LIST OF REFERENCES. GERMANY UK USA-45 WOR-45 LG/CO
DELIB/GP OP/RES BARGAIN CAP/ISM ECO/TAC INT/TRADE ECO/DEV
LICENSE LEGIT CONFER PRICE 20. PAGE 22 E0428 INDUS

B44
DE HUSZAR G.B.,NEW PERSPECTIVES ON PEACE. UNIV ATTIT
CULTURE SOCIETY ECO/DEV ECO/UNDEV NAT/G FORCES MYTH
CREATE ECO/TAC DOMIN ADJUD COERCE DRIVE ORD/FREE PEACE
...GEOG JURID PSY SOC CONCPT TOT/POP. PAGE 29 E0584 WAR

B45
GALLOWAY E.,ABSTRACTS OF POSTWAR LITERATURE (VOL. BIBLIOG/A
IV) JAN.-JULY, 1945 NOS. 901-1074. POLAND USA+45 NUC/PWR
USSR WOR+45 INDUS LABOR PLAN ECO/TAC INT/TRADE TAX NAT/G
EDU/PROP ADMIN COLONIAL INT/LAW. PAGE 42 E0829 DIPLOM

B47
ENKE S.,INTERNATIONAL ECONOMICS. UK USA+45 USSR INT/TRADE
INT/ORG BAL/PWR BARGAIN CAP/ISM BAL/PAY...NAT/COMP FINAN
20 TREATY. PAGE 35 E0691 TARIFFS
ECO/TAC

B47
GORDON D.L.,THE HIDDEN WEAPON: THE STORY OF INT/ORG
ECONOMIC WARFARE. EUR+WWI USA-45 LAW FINAN INDUS ECO/TAC
NAT/G CONSULT FORCES PLAN DOMIN PWR WEALTH INT/TRADE
...INT/LAW CONCPT OBS TOT/POP NAZI 20. PAGE 45 WAR
E0891

B47
TOWLE L.W.,INTERNATIONAL TRADE AND COMMERCIAL MARKET
POLICY. WOR+45 LAW ECO/DEV FINAN INDUS NAT/G INT/ORG
ECO/TAC WEALTH...TIME/SEQ ILO 20. PAGE 97 E1937 INT/TRADE

B49
BRUCKER H.,FREEDOM OF INFORMATION. USA+45 LAW LOC/G PRESS
ECO/TAC DOMIN PWR...NEW/IDEA BIBLIOG 17/20. PAGE 16 COM/IND
E0320 ORD/FREE
NAT/G

B49
US DEPARTMENT OF STATE,SOVIET BIBLIOGRAPHY BIBLIOG/A
(PAMPHLET). CHINA/COM COM USSR LAW AGRI INT/ORG MARXISM
ECO/TAC EDU/PROP...POLICY GEOG 20. PAGE 99 E1994 CULTURE
DIPLOM

B50
BAILEY S.K.,CONGRESS MAKES A LAW. USA+45 GP/REL DECISION
SOC. PAGE 7 E0136 LEGIS
LAW
ECO/TAC

B50
ROSS A.,CONSTITUTION OF THE UNITED NATIONS. CONSTN PEACE
CONSULT DELIB/GP ECO/TAC...INT/LAW JURID 20 UN DIPLOM
LEAGUE/NAT. PAGE 86 E1721 ORD/FREE
INT/ORG

B51
COOKE C.A.,CORPORATION TRUST AND COMPANY: AN ESSAY LG/CO
IN LEGAL HISTORY. UK STRUCT LEGIS CAP/ISM GP/REL FINAN
PROFIT 13/20 COMPNY/ACT. PAGE 25 E0499 ECO/TAC
JURID

B51
INSTITUTE DES RELATIONS INTL.LES ASPECTS WEAPON
ECONOMIQUES DU REARMEMENT (ETUDE DE L'INSTITUT DES DEMAND
RELATIONS INTERNATIONALES A BRUXELLES). BELGIUM UK ECO/TAC
USA+45 EXTR/IND FINAN FORCES WORKER PROB/SOLV INT/TRADE
DIPLOM PRICE...POLICY 20 TREATY. PAGE 57 E1127

B52
GELLER M.A.,ADVERTISING AT THE CROSSROADS: FEDERAL EDU/PROP
REGULATION VS. VOLUNTARY CONTROLS. USA+45 JUDGE NAT/G
ECO/TAC...POLICY JURID BIBLIOG 20 FTC. PAGE 43 CONSTN
E0843 COM/IND

B54
BATTEN T.R.,PROBLEMS OF AFRICAN DEVELOPMENT (2ND ECO/UNDEV
ED.). AFR LAW SOCIETY SCHOOL ECO/TAC TAX...GEOG AGRI
HEAL SOC 20. PAGE 8 E0154 LOC/G
PROB/SOLV

B54
SINCO,PHILIPPINE POLITICAL LAW: PRINCIPLES AND LAW
CONCEPTS (10TH ED.). PHILIPPINE LOC/G EX/STRUC CONSTN
BAL/PWR ECO/TAC TAX ADJUD ADMIN CONTROL CT/SYS SUFF LEGIS
ORD/FREE...T 20. PAGE 91 E1831

B54
WRIGHT Q.,PROBLEMS OF STABILITY AND PROGRESS IN INT/ORG
INTERNATIONAL RELATIONSHIPS. FUT WOR+45 WOR-45 CONCPT
SOCIETY LEGIS CREATE TEC/DEV ECO/TAC EDU/PROP ADJUD DIPLOM
WAR PEACE ORD/FREE PWR...KNO/TEST TREND GEN/LAWS
20. PAGE 108 E2155

B55
BLOOM G.F.,ECONOMICS OF LABOR RELATIONS. USA+45 LAW ECO/DEV
CONSULT WORKER CAP/ISM PAY ADJUD CONTROL EFFICIENCY ECO/TAC
ORD/FREE...CHARTS 19/20 AFL/CIO NLRB DEPT/LABOR. LABOR
PAGE 13 E0249 GOV/REL

B55
BRAUN K.,LABOR DISPUTES AND THEIR SETTLEMENT. INDUS
ECO/TAC ROUTINE TASK GP/REL...DECISION GEN/LAWS. LABOR
PAGE 15 E0288 BARGAIN
ADJUD

B55
WRONG D.H.,AMERICAN AND CANADIAN VIEWPOINTS. CANADA DIPLOM
USA+45 CONSTN STRATA FAM SECT WORKER ECO/TAC ATTIT
EDU/PROP ADJUD MARRIAGE...IDEA/COMP 20. PAGE 108 NAT/COMP
E2161 CULTURE

B56
NOTZ R.L.,FEDERAL GRANTS-IN-AID TO STATES: ANALYSIS GIVE
OF LAWS IN FORCE ON SEPTEMBER 10, 1956. USA+45 LAW NAT/G
SCHOOL PLAN ECO/TAC TAX RECEIVE...HEAL JURID 20. PROVS

GOV/REL

LG/CO

B57
BERLE A.A. JR.,ECONOMIC POWER AND FREE SOCIETY
(PAMPHLET). CLIENT CONSTN EX/STRUC ECO/TAC CONTROL
PARTIC PWR WEALTH MAJORIT. PAGE 11 E0205

LG/CO
CAP/ISM
INGP/REL
LEGIT

B57
BLOOMFIELD L.M.,EGYPT, ISRAEL AND THE GULF OF
AQABA: IN INTERNATIONAL LAW. LAW NAT/G CONSULT
FORCES PLAN ECO/TAC ROUTINE COERCE ATTIT DRIVE
PERCEPT PERSON RIGID/FLEX LOVE PWR WEALTH...GEOG
CONCPT MYTH TREND. PAGE 13 E0250

ISLAM
INT/LAW
UAR

B57
COMM. STUDY ORGAN. PEACE,STRENGTHENING THE UNITED
NATIONS. FUT USA+45 WOR+45 CONSTN NAT/G DELIB/GP
FORCES LEGIS ECO/TAC LEGIT COERCE PEACE...JURID
CONCPT UN COLD/WAR 20. PAGE 24 E0482

INT/ORG
ORD/FREE

B57
FREUND G.,UNHOLY ALLIANCE. EUR+WWI GERMANY USSR
FORCES ECO/TAC CONTROL WAR PWR...TREND TREATY.
PAGE 40 E0796

DIPLOM
PLAN
POLICY

B57
PALMER N.D.,INTERNATIONAL RELATIONS. WOR+45 INT/ORG
NAT/G ECO/TAC EDU/PROP COLONIAL WAR PWR SOVEREIGN
...POLICY T 20 TREATY. PAGE 79 E1593

DIPLOM
BAL/PWR
NAT/COMP

B57
US SENATE SPEC COMM POLIT ACT,REPORT OF SPECIAL
COMMITTEE TO INVESTIGATE POLITICAL ACTIVITIES,
LOBBYING, AND CAMPAIGN CONTRIBUTIONS. USA+45
BARGAIN CRIME ATTIT...DECISION 20 CONGRESS.
PAGE 103 E2061

LOBBY
LAW
ECO/TAC
PARL/PROC

B58
ATOMIC INDUSTRIAL FORUM,MANAGEMENT AND ATOMIC
ENERGY. WOR+45 SEA LAW MARKET NAT/G TEC/DEV INSPECT
INT/TRADE CONFER PEACE HEALTH...ANTHOL 20. PAGE 6
E0112

NUC/PWR
INDUS
MGT
ECO/TAC

B58
HOOD W.C.,FINANCING OF ECONOMIC ACTIVITY IN CANADA.
CANADA FUT VOL/ASSN WORKER ECO/TAC ADJUD ADMIN
...CHARTS 20. PAGE 55 E1093

BUDGET
FINAN
GP/REL
ECO/DEV

S58
STAAR R.F.,"ELECTIONS IN COMMUNIST POLAND." EUR+WWI COM
SOCIETY INT/ORG NAT/G POL/PAR LEGIS ACT/RES ECO/TAC CHOOSE
EDU/PROP ADJUD ADMIN ROUTINE COERCE TOTALISM ATTIT POLAND
ORD/FREE PWR 20. PAGE 93 E1864

B59
GINSBURG M.,LAW AND OPINION IN ENGLAND. UK CULTURE
KIN LABOR LEGIS EDU/PROP ADMIN CT/SYS CRIME OWN
HEALTH...ANTHOL 20 ENGLSH/LAW. PAGE 44 E0868

JURID
POLICY
ECO/TAC

S59
CARLSTON K.S.,"NATIONALIZATION: AN ANALYTIC
APPROACH." WOR+45 INT/ORG ECO/TAC DOMIN LEGIT ADJUD
COERCE ORD/FREE PWR WEALTH SOCISM...JURID CONCPT
TREND STERTYP TOT/POP VAL/FREE 20. PAGE 19 E0380

INDUS
NAT/G
NAT/LISM
SOVEREIGN

S59
CORY R.H. JR.,"INTERNATIONAL INSPECTION FROM
PROPOSALS TO REALIZATION." WOR+45 TEC/DEV ECO/TAC
ADJUD ORD/FREE PWR WEALTH...RECORD VAL/FREE 20.
PAGE 26 E0516

STRUCT
PSY
ARMS/CONT
NUC/PWR

S59
TIPTON J.B.,"PARTICIPATION OF THE UNITED STATES IN
THE INTERNATIONAL LABOR ORGANIZATION." USA+45 LAW
STRUCT ECO/DEV ECO/UNDEV INDUS TEC/DEV ECO/TAC
ADMIN PERCEPT ORD/FREE SKILL...STAT HIST/WRIT
GEN/METH ILO WORK 20. PAGE 96 E1928

LABOR
INT/ORG

B60
LASKIN B.,CANADIAN CONSTITUTIONAL LAW: TEXT AND
NOTES ON DISTRIBUTION OF LEGISLATIVE POWER (2ND
ED.). CANADA LOC/G ECO/TAC TAX CONTROL CT/SYS CRIME
FEDERAL PWR...JURID 20 PARLIAMENT. PAGE 63 E1259

CONSTN
NAT/G
LAW
LEGIS

B60
LENCZOWSKI G.,OIL AND STATE IN THE MIDDLE EAST. FUT
IRAN LAW ECO/UNDEV EXTR/IND NAT/G TOP/EX PLAN
TEC/DEV ECO/TAC LEGIT ADMIN COERCE ATTIT ALL/VALS
PWR...CHARTS 20. PAGE 64 E1283

ISLAM
INDUS
NAT/LISM

B60
MUTHESIUS V.,DAS GESPENST DER WIRTSCHAFTLICHEN
MACHT. GERMANY/W ECO/DEV FINAN MARKET TAX...JURID
20. PAGE 75 E1513

ECO/TAC
NAT/G
CONCPT

B60
STEIN E.,AMERICAN ENTERPRISE IN THE EUROPEAN COMMON MARKET
MARKET: A LEGAL PROFILE. EUR+WWI FUT USA+45 SOCIETY ADJUD
STRUCT ECO/DEV NAT/G VOL/ASSN CONSULT PLAN TEC/DEV INT/LAW
ECO/TAC INT/TRADE ADMIN ATTIT RIGID/FLEX PWR...MGT
NEW/IDEA STAT TREND COMPUT/IR SIMUL EEC 20. PAGE 93
E1867

L60
STEIN E.,"LEGAL REMEDIES OF ENTERPRISES IN THE
EUROPEAN ECONOMIC COMMUNITY." EUR+WWI FUT ECO/DEV
INDUS PLAN ECO/TAC ADMIN PWR...MGT MATH STAT TREND
CON/ANAL EEC 20. PAGE 93 E1868

MARKET
ADJUD

S60
NICHOLS J.P.,"HAZARDS OF AMERICAN PRIVATE
INVESTMENT IN UNDERDEVELOPED COUNTRIES." FUT
L/A+17C USA+45 USA-45 EXTR/IND CONSULT BAL/PWR
ECO/TAC DOMIN ADJUD ATTIT SOVEREIGN WEALTH
...HIST/WRIT TIME/SEQ TREND VAL/FREE 20. PAGE 77
E1546

FINAN
ECO/UNDEV
CAP/ISM
NAT/LISM

S60
SCHACHTER O.,"THE ENFORCEMENT OF INTERNATIONAL
JUDICIAL AND ARBITRAL DECISIONS." WOR+45 NAT/G
ECO/TAC DOMIN LEGIT ROUTINE COERCE ATTIT DRIVE
ALL/VALS PWR...METH/CNCPT TREND TOT/POP 20 UN.
PAGE 87 E1750

INT/ORG
ADJUD
INT/LAW

B61
ALFRED H.,PUBLIC OWNERSHIP IN THE USA: GOALS AND
PRIORITIES. LAW INDUS INT/TRADE ADJUD GOV/REL
EFFICIENCY PEACE SOCISM...POLICY ANTHOL 20 TVA.
PAGE 3 E0064

CONTROL
OWN
ECO/DEV
ECO/TAC

B61
CONFERENCE ATLANTIC COMMUNITY,AN INTRODUCTORY
BIBLIOGRAPHY. COM WOR+45 FORCES DIPLOM ECO/TAC WAR
...INT/LAW HIST/WRIT COLD/WAR NATO. PAGE 25 E0485

BIBLIOG/A
CON/ANAL
INT/ORG

B61
LA PONCE J.A.,THE GOVERNMENT OF THE FIFTH REPUBLIC:
FRENCH POLITICAL PARTIES AND THE CONSTITUTION.
ALGERIA FRANCE LAW NAT/G DELIB/GP LEGIS ECO/TAC
MARXISM SOCISM...CHARTS BIBLIOG/A 20 DEGAULLE/C.
PAGE 62 E1243

PWR
POL/PAR
CONSTN
CHIEF

N61
VINER J.,THE INTELLECTUAL HISTORY OF LAISSEZ FAIRE
(PAMPHLET). WOR+45 WOR-45 LAW INTELL...POLICY LING
LOG 19/20. PAGE 104 E2077

ATTIT
EDU/PROP
LAISSEZ
ECO/TAC

B62
CARLSTON K.S.,LAW AND ORGANIZATION IN WORLD
SOCIETY. WOR+45 FINAN ECO/TAC DOMIN LEGIT CT/SYS
ROUTINE COERCE ORD/FREE PWR WEALTH...PLURIST
DECISION JURID MGT METH/CNCPT GEN/LAWS 20. PAGE 19
E0381

INT/ORG
LAW

B62
FRIEDRICH C.J.,NOMOS V: THE PUBLIC INTEREST. UNIV
ECO/TAC ADJUD UTIL ATTIT...POLICY LING LOG GEN/LAWS
20. PAGE 41 E0808

METH/CNCPT
CONCPT
LAW
IDEA/COMP

B62
INTNTL COTTON ADVISORY COMMITT,GOVERNMENT
REGULATIONS ON COTTON, 1962 (PAMPHLET). WOR+45
RATION PRODUC...CHARTS 20. PAGE 57 E1136

ECO/TAC
LAW
CONTROL
AGRI

B62
SHAW C.,LEGAL PROBLEMS IN INTERNATIONAL TRADE AND
INVESTMENT. WOR+45 ECO/DEV ECO/UNDEV MARKET DIPLOM
TAX INCOME ROLE...ANTHOL BIBLIOG 20 TREATY UN IMF
GATT. PAGE 91 E1816

INT/LAW
INT/TRADE
FINAN
ECO/TAC

L62
NIZARD L.,"CUBAN QUESTION AND SECURITY COUNCIL."
L/A+17C USA+45 ECO/UNDEV NAT/G POL/PAR DELIB/GP
ECO/TAC PWR...RELATIV OBS TIME/SEQ TREND GEN/LAWS
UN 20 UN. PAGE 77 E1551

INT/ORG
JURID
DIPLOM
CUBA

S62
FENWICK C.G.,"ISSUES AT PUNTA DEL ESTE: NON-
INTERVENTION VS COLLECTIVE SECURITY." L/A+17C
USA+45 VOL/ASSN DELIB/GP ECO/TAC LEGIT ADJUD REGION
ORD/FREE OAS COLD/WAR 20. PAGE 37 E0738

INT/ORG
CUBA

S62
GANDOLFI A.,"REFLEXIONS SUR L'IMPOT DE CAPITATION
EN AFRIQUE NOIRE." GHANA SENEGAL LAW FINAN ACT/RES
TEC/DEV ECO/TAC WEALTH...MGT TREND 20. PAGE 42

AFR
CHOOSE

E0830

N62
US SENATE COMM ON JUDICIARY,LEGISLATION TO   LEAD
STRENGTHEN PENALTIES UNDER THE ANTITRUST LAWS   ADJUD
(PAMPHLET). USA+45 LG/CO CONFER CONTROL SANCTION   INDUS
ORD/FREE 20 SENATE MONOPOLY. PAGE 102 E2045   ECO/TAC

B63
BOWIE R.R.,GOVERNMENT REGULATION OF BUSINESS: CASES LAW
FROM THE NATIONAL REPORTER SYSTEM. USA+45 USA-45   CONTROL
NAT/G ECO/TAC ADJUD...ANTHOL 19/20 SUPREME/CT FTC   INDUS
FAIR/LABOR MONOPOLY. PAGE 14 E0280   CT/SYS

B63
CARTER G.M.,FIVE AFRICAN STATES: RESPONSES TO   AFR
DIVERSITY. CONSTN CULTURE STRATA LEGIS PLAN ECO/TAC SOCIETY
DOMIN EDU/PROP CT/SYS EXEC CHOOSE ATTIT HEALTH
ORD/FREE PWR...TIME/SEQ TOT/POP VAL/FREE. PAGE 20
E0398

B63
DUNN F.S.,PEACE-MAKING AND THE SETTLEMENT WITH   POLICY
JAPAN. ASIA USA+45 USA-45 FORCES BAL/PWR ECO/TAC   PEACE
CONFER WAR PWR SOVEREIGN 20 CHINJAP COLD/WAR   PLAN
TREATY. PAGE 33 E0661   DIPLOM

B63
JACOBS P.,STATE OF UNIONS. USA+45 STRATA TOP/EX   LABOR
GP/REL RACE/REL DEMAND DISCRIM ATTIT PWR 20   ECO/TAC
CONGRESS NEGRO HOFFA/J. PAGE 57 E1145   BARGAIN
                                                     DECISION

B63
LEWIN J.,POLITICS AND LAW IN SOUTH AFRICA.   NAT/LISM
SOUTH/AFR UK POL/PAR BAL/PWR ECO/TAC COLONIAL   POLICY
CONTROL GP/REL DISCRIM PWR 20 NEGRO. PAGE 65 E1293   LAW
                                                     RACE/REL

B63
PRYOR F.L.,THE COMMUNIST FOREIGN TRADE SYSTEM. COM   ATTIT
CZECHOSLVK GERMANY YUGOSLAVIA LAW ECO/DEV DIST/IND   ECO/TAC
POL/PAR PLAN DOMIN TOTALISM DRIVE RIGID/FLEX WEALTH
...STAT STAND/INT CHARTS 20. PAGE 83 E1657

L63
LISSITZYN O.J.,"INTERNATIONAL LAW IN A DIVIDED   INT/ORG
WORLD." FUT WOR+45 CONSTN CULTURE ECO/DEV ECO/UNDEV LAW
DIST/IND NAT/G FORCES ECO/TAC LEGIT ADJUD ADMIN
COERCE ATTIT HEALTH MORAL ORD/FREE PWR RESPECT
WEALTH VAL/FREE. PAGE 65 E1306

L63
MCDOUGAL M.S.,"THE ENJOYMENT AND ACQUISITION OF   PLAN
RESOURCES IN OUTER SPACE." CHRIST-17C FUT WOR+45   TREND
WOR-45 LAW EXTR/IND INT/ORG ACT/RES CREATE TEC/DEV
ECO/TAC LEGIT COERCE HEALTH KNOWL ORD/FREE PWR
WEALTH...JURID HIST/WRIT VAL/FREE. PAGE 70 E1408

L63
ROSE R.,"COMPARATIVE STUDIES IN POLITICAL FINANCE: FINAN
A SYMPOSIUM." ASIA EUR+WWI S/ASIA LAW CULTURE   POL/PAR
DELIB/GP LEGIS ACT/RES ECO/TAC EDU/PROP CHOOSE
ATTIT RIGID/FLEX SUPEGO PWR SKILL WEALTH...STAT
ANTHOL VAL/FREE. PAGE 85 E1714

S63
GERHARD H.,"COMMODITY TRADE STABILIZATION THROUGH   PLAN
INTERNATIONAL AGREEMENTS." WOR+45 ECO/DEV ECO/UNDEV ECO/TAC
NAT/G ROUTINE ORD/FREE...INT/LAW OBS TREND GEN/METH INT/TRADE
TOT/POP 20. PAGE 43 E0850

S63
HARNETTY P.,"CANADA, SOUTH AFRICA AND THE   AFR
COMMONWEALTH." CANADA SOUTH/AFR LAW INT/ORG   ATTIT
VOL/ASSN DELIB/GP LEGIS TOP/EX ECO/TAC LEGIT DRIVE
MORAL...CONCPT CMN/WLTH 20. PAGE 50 E1000

S63
WALKER H.,"THE INTERNATIONAL LAW OF COMMODITY   MARKET
AGREEMENTS." FUT WOR+45 ECO/DEV ECO/UNDEV FINAN   VOL/ASSN
INT/ORG NAT/G CONSULT CREATE PLAN ECO/TAC ATTIT   INT/LAW
PERCEPT...CONCPT GEN/LAWS TOT/POP GATT 20. PAGE 105 INT/TRADE
E2095

B64
FREUD A.,OF HUMAN SOVEREIGNTY. WOR+45 INDUS SECT   NAT/LISM
ECO/TAC CRIME CHOOSE ATTIT MORAL MARXISM...POLICY   DIPLOM
BIBLIOG 20. PAGE 40 E0794   WAR
                                                     PEACE

B64
GARDNER L.C.,ECONOMIC ASPECTS OF NEW DEAL   ECO/TAC
DIPLOMACY. USA-45 WOR-45 LAW ECO/DEV INT/ORG NAT/G   DIPLOM
VOL/ASSN LEGIS TOP/EX EDU/PROP ORD/FREE PWR WEALTH
...POLICY TIME/SEQ VAL/FREE 20 ROOSEVLT/F. PAGE 42

E0836

B64
HOPKINSON T.,SOUTH AFRICA. SOUTH/AFR UK NAT/G   SOCIETY
POL/PAR LEGIS ECO/TAC PARL/PROC WAR...JURID AUD/VIS RACE/REL
19/20. PAGE 55 E1097   DISCRIM

B64
ROBINSON R.D.,INTERNATIONAL BUSINESS POLICY. AFR   ECO/TAC
INDIA L/A+17C USA+45 ELITES AGRI FOR/AID COERCE   DIST/IND
BAL/PAY...DECISION INT/LAW MGT 20. PAGE 85 E1706   COLONIAL
                                                     FINAN

B64
SEGAL R.,SANCTIONS AGAINST SOUTH AFRICA. AFR   SANCTION
SOUTH/AFR NAT/G INT/TRADE RACE/REL PEACE PWR   DISCRIM
...INT/LAW ANTHOL 20 UN. PAGE 90 E1801   ECO/TAC
                                                     POLICY

B64
TELLADO A.,A STATEMENT OF THE LAWS OF THE DOMINICAN CONSTN
REPUBLIC IN MATTERS AFFECTING BUSINESS (3RD ED.).   LEGIS
DOMIN/REP AGRI DIST/IND EXTR/IND FINAN FAM WORKER   NAT/G
ECO/TAC TAX CT/SYS MARRIAGE OWN...BIBLIOG 20   INDUS
MIGRATION. PAGE 95 E1913

B64
TONG T.,UNITED STATES DIPLOMACY IN CHINA,   DIPLOM
1844-1860. ASIA USA-45 ECO/UNDEV ECO/TAC COERCE   INT/TRADE
GP/REL...INT/LAW 19 TREATY. PAGE 96 E1934   COLONIAL

B64
UN PUB. INFORM. ORGAN.,EVERY MAN'S UNITED NATIONS.   INT/ORG
UNIV WOR+45 CONSTN CULTURE SOCIETY ECO/DEV   ROUTINE
ECO/UNDEV NAT/G ACT/RES PLAN ECO/TAC INT/TRADE
EDU/PROP LEGIT PEACE ATTIT ALL/VALS...POLICY HUM
INT/LAW CONCPT CHARTS UN TOT/POP 20. PAGE 97 E1954

B64
US SENATE COMM ON JUDICIARY,HEARINGS BEFORE   ECO/DEV
SUBCOMMITTEE ON ANTITRUST AND MONOPOLY: ECONOMIC   CONTROL
CONCENTRATION VOLUMES 1-5 JULY 1964-SEPT 1966.   MARKET
USA+45 LAW FINAN ECO/TAC ADJUD COST EFFICIENCY   LG/CO
PRODUC...STAT CHARTS 20 CONGRESS MONOPOLY. PAGE 102
E2052

B64
WRIGHT G.,RURAL REVOLUTION IN FRANCE: THE PEASANTRY PWR
IN THE TWENTIETH CENTURY. EUR+WWI MOD/EUR LAW   STRATA
CULTURE AGRI POL/PAR DELIB/GP LEGIS ECO/TAC   FRANCE
EDU/PROP COERCE CHOOSE ATTIT RIGID/FLEX HEALTH   REV
...STAT CENSUS CHARTS VAL/FREE 20. PAGE 107 E2148

L64
WORLD PEACE FOUNDATION,"INTERNATIONAL   INT/ORG
ORGANIZATIONS: SUMMARY OF ACTIVITIES." INDIA   ROUTINE
PAKISTAN TURKEY WOR+45 CONSTN CONSULT EX/STRUC
ECO/TAC EDU/PROP LEGIT ORD/FREE...JURID SOC UN 20
CYPRESS. PAGE 107 E2145

S64
DERWINSKI E.J.,"THE COST OF THE INTERNATIONAL   MARKET
COFFEE AGREEMENT." L/A+17C USA+45 WOR+45 ECO/UNDEV   DELIB/GP
NAT/G VOL/ASSN LEGIS DIPLOM ECO/TAC FOR/AID LEGIT   INT/TRADE
ATTIT...TIME/SEQ CONGRESS 20 TREATY. PAGE 31 E0608

S64
GARDNER R.N.,"THE SOVIET UNION AND THE UNITED   COM
NATIONS." WOR+45 FINAN POL/PAR VOL/ASSN FORCES   INT/ORG
ECO/TAC DOMIN EDU/PROP LEGIT ADJUD ADMIN ARMS/CONT   USSR
COERCE ATTIT ALL/VALS...POLICY MAJORIT CONCPT OBS
TIME/SEQ TREND STERTYP UN. PAGE 42 E0838

S64
N.,"QUASI-LEGISLATIVE ARBITRATION AGREEMENTS." LAW   ADJUD
LG/CO ECO/TAC SANCTION ATTIT POLICY. PAGE 76 E1516   ADJUST
                                                     LABOR
                                                     GP/REL

S64
TRISKA J.F.,"SOVIET TREATY LAW: A QUANTITATIVE   COM
ANALYSIS." WOR+45 LAW ECO/UNDEV AGRI COM/IND INDUS   ECO/TAC
CREATE TEC/DEV DIPLOM ATTIT PWR WEALTH...JURID SAMP INT/LAW
TIME/SEQ TREND CHARTS VAL/FREE 20 TREATY. PAGE 97   USSR
E1942

B65
BERKOWITZ M.,AMERICAN NATIONAL SECURITY: A READER   ORD/FREE
IN THEORY AND POLICY. USA+45 INT/ORG FORCES BAL/PWR WAR
DIPLOM ECO/TAC DETER PWR...INT/LAW ANTHOL BIBLIOG   ARMS/CONT
20 UN. PAGE 11 E0203   POLICY

B65
CHARNAY J.P.,LE SUFFRAGE POLITIQUE EN FRANCE: CHOOSE
ELECTIONS PARLEMENTAIRES, ELECTION PRESIDENTIELLE,   SUFF
REFERENDUMS. FRANCE CONSTN CHIEF DELIB/GP ECO/TAC   NAT/G

EDU/PROP CRIME INGP/REL MORAL ORD/FREE PWR CATHISM LEGIS
20 PARLIAMENT PRESIDENT. PAGE 22 E0425

COWEN Z.,THE BRITISH COMMONWEALTH OF NATIONS IN A
CHANGING WORLD. UK ECO/UNDEV INT/ORG ECO/TAC
INT/TRADE COLONIAL WAR GP/REL RACE/REL SOVEREIGN
SOC/INTEG 20 TREATY EEC COMMONWLTH. PAGE 27 E0530
B65
JURID
DIPLOM
PARL/PROC
NAT/LISM

GAJENDRAGADKAR P.B.,LAW, LIBERTY AND SOCIAL
JUSTICE. INDIA CONSTN NAT/G SECT PLAN ECO/TAC PRESS
POPULISM...SOC METH/COMP 20 HINDU. PAGE 42 E0826
B65
ORD/FREE
LAW
ADJUD
JURID

HABERLER G.,A SURVEY OF INTERNATIONAL TRADE THEORY.
CANADA FRANCE GERMANY ECO/TAC TARIFFS AGREE COST
DEMAND WEALTH...ECOMETRIC 19/20 MONOPOLY TREATY.
PAGE 49 E0968
B65
INT/TRADE
BAL/PAY
DIPLOM
POLICY

HAEFELE E.T.,GOVERNMENT CONTROLS ON TRANSPORT. AFR
RHODESIA TANZANIA DIPLOM ECO/TAC TARIFFS PRICE
ADJUD CONTROL REGION EFFICIENCY...POLICY 20 CONGO.
PAGE 49 E0973
B65
ECO/UNDEV
DIST/IND
FINAN
NAT/G

HIGHSAW R.B.,CONFLICT AND CHANGE IN LOCAL
GOVERNMENT. USA+45 BUDGET ECO/TAC LEGIT ADJUD
ALABAMA. PAGE 52 E1044
B65
GOV/REL
PROB/SOLV
LOC/G
BAL/PWR

PROEHL P.O.,FOREIGN ENTERPRISE IN NIGERIA. NIGERIA
FINAN LABOR NAT/G TAX 20. PAGE 83 E1656
B65
ECO/UNDEV
ECO/TAC
JURID
CAP/ISM

ROSS P.,THE GOVERNMENT AS A SOURCE OF UNION POWER.
USA+45 LAW ECO/DEV PROB/SOLV ECO/TAC LEAD GP/REL
...MGT 20. PAGE 86 E1723
B65
LABOR
BARGAIN
POLICY
NAT/G

US OFFICE ECONOMIC OPPORTUNITY,CATALOG OF FEDERAL
PROGRAMS FOR INDIVIDUAL AND COMMUNITY IMPROVEMENT.
USA+45 GIVE RECEIVE ADMIN HEALTH KNOWL SKILL WEALTH
CHARTS. PAGE 101 E2021
B65
BIBLIOG
CLIENT
ECO/TAC
MUNIC

US SENATE COMM ON JUDICIARY,ANTITRUST EXEMPTIONS
FOR AGREEMENTS RELATING TO BALANCE OF PAYMENTS.
FINAN ECO/TAC CONTROL WEALTH...POLICY 20 CONGRESS.
PAGE 103 E2056
B65
BAL/PAY
ADJUD
MARKET
INT/TRADE

KHOURI F.J.,"THE JORDON RIVER CONTROVERSY." LAW
SOCIETY ECO/UNDEV AGRI FINAN INDUS SECT FORCES
ACT/RES PLAN TEC/DEV ECO/TAC EDU/PROP COERCE ATTIT
DRIVE PERCEPT RIGID/FLEX ALL/VALS...GEOG SOC MYTH
WORK. PAGE 61 E1212
S65
ISLAM
INT/ORG
ISRAEL
JORDAN

BEER U.,FRUCHTBARKEITSREGELUNG ALS KONSEQUENZ
VERANTWORTLICHER ELTERNSCHAFT. ASIA GERMANY/W INDIA
LAW ECO/DEV ECO/UNDEV TEC/DEV ECO/TAC BIO/SOC SEX
CATHISM...METH/COMP 20 CHINJAP BIRTH/CON. PAGE 9
E0178
B66
CONTROL
GEOG
FAM
SECT

DYCK H.V.,WEIMAR GERMANY AND SOVIET RUSSIA
1926-1933. EUR+WWI GERMANY UK USSR ECO/TAC
INT/TRADE NEUTRAL WAR ATTIT 20 WEIMAR/REP TREATY.
PAGE 34 E0669
B66
DIPLOM
GOV/REL
POLICY

EDWARDS C.D.,TRADE REGULATIONS OVERSEAS. IRELAND
NEW/ZEALND SOUTH/AFR NAT/G CAP/ISM TARIFFS CONTROL
...POLICY JURID 20 EEC CHINJAP. PAGE 34 E0676
B66
INT/TRADE
DIPLOM
INT/LAW
ECO/TAC

FRIEDMANN W.G.,INTERNATIONAL FINANCIAL AID. USA+45
ECO/DEV ECO/UNDEV NAT/G VOL/ASSN EX/STRUC PLAN RENT
GIVE BAL/PAY PWR...GEOG INT/LAW STAT TREND UN EEC
COMECON. PAGE 41 E0806
B66
INT/ORG
FOR/AID
TEC/DEV
ECO/TAC

SALTER L.M.,RESOLUTION OF INTERNATIONAL CONFLICT.
USA+45 INT/ORG SECT DIPLOM ECO/TAC FOR/AID DETER
NUC/PWR WAR 20. PAGE 87 E1743
B66
PROB/SOLV
PEACE
INT/LAW
POLICY

WASHINGTON S.H.,BIBLIOGRAPHY: LABOR-MANAGEMENT
RELATIONS ACT, 1947 AS AMENDED BY LABOR-MANAGEMENT
REPORTING AND DISCLOSURE ACT, 1959. USA+45 CONSTN
INDUS DELIB/GP LEGIS WORKER BARGAIN ECO/TAC ADJUD
GP/REL NEW/LIB...JURID CONGRESS. PAGE 105 E2100
B66
BIBLIOG
LAW
LABOR
MGT

BEAL E.F.,THE PRACTICE OF COLLECTIVE BARGAINING
(3RD ED.). USA+45 WOR+45 ECO/DEV INDUS LG/CO
PROF/ORG WORKER ECO/TAC GP/REL WEALTH...JURID
METH/CNCPT. PAGE 8 E0160
B67
BARGAIN
MGT
LABOR
ADJUD

CAVES R.,AMERICAN INDUSTRY: STRUCTURE, CONDUCT,
PERFORMANCE (2ND ED.). USA+45 MARKET NAT/G ADJUD
CONTROL GP/REL DEMAND WEALTH 20. PAGE 21 E0412
B67
ECO/DEV
INDUS
POLICY
ECO/TAC

COHEN M.R.,LAW AND THE SOCIAL ORDER: ESSAYS IN
LEGAL PHILOSOPHY. USA-45 CONSULT WORKER ECO/TAC
ATTIT WEALTH...POLICY WELF/ST SOC 20 NEW/DEAL
DEPRESSION. PAGE 24 E0467
B67
JURID
LABOR
IDEA/COMP

GABRIEL P.P.,THE INTERNATIONAL TRANSFER OF
CORPORATE SKILLS: MANAGEMENT CONTRACTS IN LESS
DEVELOPED COUNTRIES. CLIENT INDUS LG/CO PLAN
PROB/SOLV CAP/ISM ECO/TAC FOR/AID INT/TRADE RENT
ADMIN SKILL 20. PAGE 42 E0825
B67
ECO/UNDEV
AGREE
MGT
CONSULT

MARTIN L.W.,THE SEA IN MODERN STRATEGY. LAW ECO/TAC
WAR. PAGE 69 E1374
B67
ROLE
PWR
NUC/PWR
DIPLOM

POGANY A.H.,POLITICAL SCIENCE AND INTERNATIONAL
RELATIONS, BOOKS RECOMMENDED FOR AMERICAN CATHOLIC
COLLEGE LIBRARIES. INT/ORG LOC/G NAT/G FORCES
BAL/PWR ECO/TAC NUC/PWR...CATH INT/LAW TREATY 20.
PAGE 81 E1622
B67
BIBLIOG
DIPLOM

"A PROPOS DES INCITATIONS FINANCIERES AUX
GROUPEMENTS DES COMMUNES: ESSAI D'INTERPRETATION."
FRANCE NAT/G LEGIS ADMIN GOV/REL CENTRAL 20. PAGE 2
E0037
L67
LOC/G
ECO/TAC
APPORT
ADJUD

LENT G.E.,"TAX INCENTIVES FOR INVESTMENT IN
DEVELOPING COUNTRIES" WOR+45 LAW INDUS PLAN BUDGET
TARIFFS ADMIN...METH/COMP 20. PAGE 64 E1285
L67
ECO/UNDEV
TAX
FINAN
ECO/TAC

ALEXANDER B.,"GIBRALTAR" SPAIN UK CONSTN WORKER
PROB/SOLV FOR/AID RECEIVE CONTROL 20. PAGE 3 E0059
S67
DIPLOM
INT/ORG
ORD/FREE
ECO/TAC

ANDERSON W.,"THE PERILS OF 'SHARING'." USA+45
ECO/TAC RECEIVE LOBBY GOV/REL CENTRAL COST INCOME
...POLICY PLURIST CONGRESS. PAGE 5 E0095
S67
BUDGET
TAX
FEDERAL
LAW

BARTLETT J.L.,"AMERICAN BOND ISSUES IN THE EUROPEAN
ECONOMIC COMMUNITY." EUR+WWI LUXEMBOURG USA+45
DIPLOM CONTROL BAL/PAY EEC. PAGE 8 E0153
S67
LAW
ECO/TAC
FINAN
TAX

BERRODIN E.F.,"AT THE BARGAINING TABLE." LABOR
DIPLOM ECO/TAC ADMIN...MGT 20 MICHIGAN. PAGE 11
E0216
S67
PROVS
WORKER
LAW
BARGAIN

CREYKE G. JR.,"THE PAYMENT GAP IN FEDERAL
CONSTRUCTION CONTRACTS." USA+45 LAW FINAN ECO/TAC
CONTROL CT/SYS SUPREME/CT. PAGE 28 E0547
S67
CONSTRUC
PAY
COST
NAT/G

DANIEL C.,"FREEDOM, EQUITY, AND THE WAR ON
POVERTY." USA+45 WORKER ECO/TAC JURID. PAGE 29
E0566
S67
WEALTH
INCOME
SOCIETY
ORD/FREE

DOUTY H.M.," REFERENCE TO DEVELOPING COUNTRIES."
JAMAICA MALAYSIA UK WOR+45 LAW FINAN ACT/RES BUDGET
S67
TAX
ECO/UNDEV

CAP/ISM ECO/TAC TARIFFS RISK EFFICIENCY PROFIT ...CHARTS 20. PAGE 33 E0646 | NAT/G

S67

GIBSON G.H.,"LABOR PIRACY ON THE BRANDYWINE." USA-45 INDUS R+D VOL/ASSN CAP/ISM ADJUD DRIVE...PSY 19. PAGE 43 E0859 | ECO/TAC CREATE TEC/DEV WORKER

S67

HIRSCH W.Z.,"SOME ECONOMIC IMPLICATIONS OF CITY PLANNING." LAW PROB/SOLV RATION EFFICIENCY...METH 20. PAGE 53 E1050 | ECO/TAC JURID MUNIC PLAN

S67

REILLY T.J.,"FREEZING AND CONFISCATION OF CUBAN PROPERTY." CUBA USA+45 LAW DIPLOM LEGIT ADJUD CONTROL. PAGE 84 E1682 | STRANGE OWN ECO/TAC

S67

RICHARDSON J.J.,"THE MAKING OF THE RESTRICTIVE TRADE PRACTICES ACT 1956 A CASE STUDY OF THE POLICY PROCESS IN BRITAIN." UK FINAN MARKET LG/CO POL/PAR CONSULT PRESS ADJUD ADMIN AGREE LOBBY SANCTION ATTIT 20. PAGE 84 E1695 | LEGIS ECO/TAC POLICY INDUS

S67

SCHELLING T.C.,"ECONOMICS AND CRIMINAL ENTERPRISE." LAW FORCES BARGAIN ECO/TAC CONTROL GAMBLE ROUTINE ADJUST DEMAND INCOME PROFIT CRIMLGY. PAGE 87 E1756 | CRIME PROB/SOLV CONCPT

S67

STEEL R.,"WHAT CAN THE UN DO?" RHODESIA ECO/UNDEV DIPLOM ECO/TAC SANCTION...INT/LAW UN. PAGE 93 E1866 | INT/ORG BAL/PWR PEACE FOR/AID

N67

US SENATE COMM ON FOREIGN REL.SURVEY OF THE ALLIANCE FOR PROGRESS: FOREIGN TRADE POLICIES (PAMPHLET). L/A+17C LAW ECO/UNDEV ECO/TAC TARIFFS 20 GATT LAFTA UN. PAGE 102 E2037 | INT/TRADE REGION AGREE INT/ORG

B88

BENTHAM J.,DEFENCE OF USURY (1787). UK LAW NAT/G TEC/DEV ECO/TAC CONTROL ATTIT...CONCPT IDEA/COMP 18 SMITH/ADAM. PAGE 10 E0197 | TAX FINAN ECO/DEV POLICY

ECO/UNDEV....ECONOMIC SYSTEM IN DEVELOPING COUNTRIES

N

CONOVER H.F.,OFFICIAL PUBLICATIONS OF BRITISH EAST AFRICA (PAMPHLET). UK LAW ECO/UNDEV AGRI EXTR/IND SECT LEGIS BUDGET TAX...HEAL STAT 20. PAGE 25 E0491 | BIBLIOG/A AFR ADMIN COLONIAL

N

INTERNATIONAL AFFAIRS. WOR+45 WOR-45 ECO/UNDEV INT/ORG NAT/G PROB/SOLV FOR/AID WAR...POLICY 20. PAGE 1 E0007 | BIBLIOG/A DIPLOM INT/LAW INT/TRADE

N

INTERNATIONAL BOOK NEWS, 1928-1934. ECO/UNDEV FINAN INDUS LABOR INT/TRADE CONFER ADJUD COLONIAL...HEAL SOC/WK CHARTS 20 LEAGUE/NAT. PAGE 1 E0008 | BIBLIOG/A DIPLOM INT/LAW INT/ORG

N

INTERNATIONAL STUDIES. ASIA S/ASIA WOR+45 ECO/UNDEV INT/ORG NAT/G LEAD ATTIT WEALTH...SOC 20. PAGE 1 E0009 | BIBLIOG/A DIPLOM INT/LAW INT/TRADE

N

JOURNAL OF INTERNATIONAL AFFAIRS. WOR+45 ECO/UNDEV POL/PAR ECO/TAC WAR PEACE PERSON ALL/IDEOS ...INT/LAW TREND. PAGE 1 E0010 | BIBLIOG DIPLOM INT/ORG NAT/G

N

BIBLIOGRAPHIE DER SOZIALWISSENSCHAFTEN. WOR-45 CONSTN SOCIETY ECO/DEV ECO/UNDEV DIPLOM LEAD WAR PEACE...PHIL/SCI SOC 19/20. PAGE 1 E0019 | BIBLIOG LAW CONCPT NAT/G

N

FOREIGN AFFAIRS. SPACE WOR+45 WOR-45 CULTURE ECO/UNDEV FINAN NAT/G TEC/DEV INT/TRADE ARMS/CONT NUC/PWR...POLICY 20 UN EURATOM ECSC EEC. PAGE 1 E0021 | BIBLIOG DIPLOM INT/ORG INT/LAW

N

HANDBOOK OF LATIN AMERICAN STUDIES. LAW CULTURE | BIBLIOG/A

ECO/UNDEV POL/PAR ADMIN LEAD...SOC 20. PAGE 1 E0022 | L/A+17C NAT/G DIPLOM

N

LATIN AMERICA IN PERIODICAL LITERATURE. LAW TEC/DEV DIPLOM RECEIVE EDU/PROP...GEOG HUM MGT 20. PAGE 2 E0024 | BIBLIOG/A L/A+17C SOCIETY ECO/UNDEV

N

AFRICAN BIBLIOGRAPHIC CENTER.A CURRENT BIBLIOGRAPHY ON AFRICAN AFFAIRS. LAW CULTURE ECO/UNDEV LABOR SECT DIPLOM FOR/AID COLONIAL NAT/LISM...LING 20. PAGE 3 E0053 | BIBLIOG/A AFR NAT/G REGION

N

ASIA FOUNDATION.LIBRARY NOTES. LAW CONSTN CULTURE SOCIETY ECO/UNDEV INT/ORG NAT/G COLONIAL LEAD REGION NAT/LISM ATTIT 20 UN. PAGE 6 E0107 | BIBLIOG/A ASIA S/ASIA DIPLOM

N

CORNELL UNIVERSITY LIBRARY.SOUTHEAST ASIA ACCESSIONS LIST. LAW SOCIETY STRUCT ECO/UNDEV POL/PAR TEC/DEV DIPLOM LEAD REGION. PAGE 26 E0510 | BIBLIOG S/ASIA NAT/G CULTURE

N

UNITED NATIONS.UNITED NATIONS PUBLICATIONS. WOR+45 ECO/UNDEV AGRI FINAN FORCES ADMIN LEAD WAR PEACE ...POLICY INT/LAW 20 UN. PAGE 98 E1965 | BIBLIOG INT/ORG DIPLOM

B01

GRIFFIN A.P.C.,LIST OF BOOKS ON SAMOA (PAMPHLET). GERMANY S/ASIA UK USA-45 WOR-45 ECO/UNDEV REGION ALL/VALS ORD/FREE ALL/IDEOS...GEOG INT/LAW 19 SAMOA GUAM. PAGE 46 E0918 | BIBLIOG/A COLONIAL DIPLOM

B28

YANG KUNG-SUN.THE BOOK OF LORD SHANG. LAW ECO/UNDEV LOC/G NAT/G NEIGH PLAN ECO/TAC LEGIT ATTIT SKILL ...CONCPT CON/ANAL WORK TOT/POP. PAGE 108 E2164 | ASIA JURID

B29

PRATT I.A.,MODERN EGYPT: A LIST OF REFERENCES TO MATERIAL IN THE NEW YORK PUBLIC LIBRARY. UAR ECO/UNDEV...GEOG JURID SOC LING 20. PAGE 82 E1647 | BIBLIOG ISLAM DIPLOM NAT/G

B30

WRIGHT Q.,MANDATES UNDER THE LEAGUE OF NATIONS. WOR-45 CONSTN ECO/DEV ECO/UNDEV NAT/G DELIB/GP TOP/EX LEGIT ALL/VALS...JURID CONCPT LEAGUE/NAT 20. PAGE 107 E2151 | INT/ORG LAW INT/LAW

B44

DE HUSZAR G.B.,NEW PERSPECTIVES ON PEACE. UNIV CULTURE SOCIETY ECO/DEV ECO/UNDEV NAT/G FORCES CREATE ECO/TAC DOMIN ADJUD COERCE DRIVE ORD/FREE ...GEOG JURID PSY SOC CONCPT TOT/POP. PAGE 29 E0584 | ATTIT MYTH PEACE WAR

B44

FULLER G.H.,TURKEY: A SELECTED LIST OF REFERENCES. ISLAM TURKEY CULTURE ECO/UNDEV AGRI DIPLOM NAT/LISM CONSERVE...GEOG HUM INT/LAW SOC 7/20 MAPS. PAGE 42 E0824 | BIBLIOG/A ALL/VALS

B49

MARITAIN J.,HUMAN RIGHTS: COMMENTS AND INTERPRETATIONS. COM UNIV WOR+45 LAW CONSTN CULTURE SOCIETY ECO/DEV ECO/UNDEV SCHOOL DELIB/GP EDU/PROP ATTIT PERCEPT ALL/VALS...HUM SOC TREND UNESCO 20. PAGE 68 E1365 | INT/ORG CONCPT

B50

MOCKFORD J.,SOUTH-WEST AFRICA AND THE INTERNATIONAL COURT (PAMPHLET). AFR GERMANY SOUTH/AFR UK ECO/UNDEV DIPLOM CONTROL DISCRIM...DECISION JURID 20 AFRICA/SW. PAGE 74 E1475 | COLONIAL SOVEREIGN INT/LAW DOMIN

B50

STONE J.,THE PROVINCE AND FUNCTION OF LAW. UNIV WOR+45 WOR-45 CULTURE INTELL SOCIETY ECO/DEV ECO/UNDEV NAT/G LEGIT ROUTINE ATTIT PERCEPT PERSON ...JURID CONCPT GEN/LAWS GEN/METH 20. PAGE 94 E1877 | INT/ORG LAW

B52

PASCUAL R.R.,PARTYLESS DEMOCRACY. PHILIPPINE BARGAIN LOBBY CHOOSE EFFICIENCY ATTIT 20. PAGE 80 E1600 | POL/PAR ORD/FREE JURID ECO/UNDEV

B53

MAJUMDAR B.B.,PROBLEMS OF PUBLIC ADMINISTRATION IN INDIA. INDIA INDUS PLAN BUDGET ADJUD CENTRAL DEMAND | ECO/UNDEV GOV/REL

WEALTH...WELF/ST ANTHOL 20 CIVIL/SERV. PAGE 68   ADMIN
E1353   MUNIC

                                                    B54
BATTEN T.R.,PROBLEMS OF AFRICAN DEVELOPMENT (2ND   ECO/UNDEV
ED.). AFR LAW SOCIETY SCHOOL ECO/TAC TAX...GEOG   AGRI
HEAL SOC 20. PAGE 8 E0154   LOC/G
                                                    PROB/SOLV

                                                    B54
BINANI G.D.,INDIA AT A GLANCE (REV. ED.). INDIA   INDEX
COM/IND FINAN INDUS LABOR PROVS SCHOOL PLAN DIPLOM CON/ANAL
INT/TRADE ADMIN...JURID 20. PAGE 12 E0229   NAT/G
                                                    ECO/UNDEV

                                                    B55
CHOWDHURI R.N.,INTERNATIONAL MANDATES AND   DELIB/GP
TRUSTEESHIP SYSTEMS. WOR+45 STRUCT ECO/UNDEV   PLAN
INT/ORG LEGIS DOMIN EDU/PROP LEGIT ADJUD EXEC PWR   SOVEREIGN
...CONCPT TIME/SEQ UN 20. PAGE 22 E0434

                                                    B55
COMM. STUDY ORGAN. PEACE.REPORTS. WOR-45 ECO/DEV   WOR+45
ECO/UNDEV VOL/ASSN CONSULT FORCES PLAN TEC/DEV   INT/ORG
DOMIN EDU/PROP NUC/PWR ATTIT PWR WEALTH...JURID   ARMS/CONT
STERTYP FAO ILO 20 UN. PAGE 24 E0481

                                                    B55
SERRANO MOSCOSO E.,A STATEMENT OF THE LAWS OF   FINAN
ECUADOR IN MATTERS AFFECTING BUSINESS (2ND ED.).   ECO/UNDEV
ECUADOR INDUS LABOR LG/CO NAT/G LEGIS TAX CONTROL   LAW
MARRIAGE 20. PAGE 90 E1805   CONSTN

                                                    C56
FALL B.B.,"THE VIET-MINH REGIME." VIETNAM LAW   NAT/G
ECO/UNDEV POL/PAR FORCES DOMIN WAR ATTIT MARXISM   ADMIN
...BIOG PREDICT BIBLIOG/A 20. PAGE 36 E0720   EX/STRUC
                                                    LEAD

                                                    B57
CONOVER H.F.,NORTH AND NORTHEAST AFRICA; A SELECTED BIBLIOG/A
ANNOTATED LIST OF WRITINGS. ALGERIA MOROCCO SUDAN   DIPLOM
UAR CULTURE INT/ORG PROB/SOLV ADJUD NAT/LISM PWR   AFR
WEALTH...SOC 20 UN. PAGE 25 E0496   ECO/UNDEV

                                                    B59
MAYDA J.,ATOMIC ENERGY AND LAW. ECO/UNDEV FINAN   NUC/PWR
TEC/DEV FOR/AID EFFICIENCY PRODUC WEALTH...POLICY   L/A+17C
TECHNIC 20. PAGE 70 E1391   LAW
                                                    ADMIN

                                                    B59
OKINSHEVICH L.A.,LATIN AMERICA IN SOVIET WRITINGS, BIBLIOG
1945-1958: A BIBLIOGRAPHY. USSR LAW ECO/UNDEV LABOR WRITING
DIPLOM EDU/PROP REV...GEOG SOC 20. PAGE 78 E1573   COM
                                                    L/A+17C

                                                    S59
TIPTON J.B.,"PARTICIPATION OF THE UNITED STATES IN LABOR
THE INTERNATIONAL LABOR ORGANIZATION." USA+45 LAW   INT/ORG
STRUCT ECO/DEV ECO/UNDEV INDUS TEC/DEV ECO/TAC
ADMIN PERCEPT ORD/FREE SKILL...STAT HIST/WRIT
GEN/METH ILO WORK 20. PAGE 96 E1928

                                                    B60
ENGEL J.,THE SECURITY OF THE FREE WORLD. USSR   COM
WOR+45 STRATA STRUCT ECO/DEV ECO/UNDEV INT/ORG   TREND
DELIB/GP FORCES DOMIN LEGIT ADJUD EXEC ARMS/CONT   DIPLOM
COERCE...POLICY CONCPT NEW/IDEA TIME/SEQ GEN/LAWS
COLD/WAR WORK UN 20 NATO. PAGE 35 E0689

                                                    B60
GONZALEZ NAVARRO M.,LA COLONIZACION EN MEXICO,   ECO/UNDEV
1877-1910. AGRI NAT/G PLAN PROB/SOLV INCOME   GEOG
...POLICY JURID CENSUS 19/20 MEXIC/AMER MIGRATION. HABITAT
PAGE 44 E0883   COLONIAL

                                                    B60
HEYSE T.,PROBLEMS FONCIERS ET REGIME DES TERRES   BIBLIOG
(ASPECTS ECONOMIQUES, JURIDIQUES ET SOCIAUX). AFR   AGRI
CONGO/BRAZ INT/ORG DIPLOM SOVEREIGN...GEOG TREATY   ECO/UNDEV
20. PAGE 52 E1037   LEGIS

                                                    B60
LENCZOWSKI G.,OIL AND STATE IN THE MIDDLE EAST. FUT ISLAM
IRAN LAW ECO/UNDEV EXTR/IND NAT/G TOP/EX PLAN   INDUS
TEC/DEV ECO/TAC LEGIT ADMIN COERCE ATTIT ALL/VALS   NAT/LISM
PWR...CHARTS 20. PAGE 64 E1283

                                                    B60
UNITED WORLD FEDERALISTS,UNITED WORLD FEDERALISTS; BIBLIOG/A
PANORAMA OF RECENT BOOKS, FILMS, AND JOURNALS ON   DIPLOM
WORLD FEDERATION, THE UN, AND WORLD PEACE. CULTURE INT/ORG
ECO/UNDEV PROB/SOLV FOR/AID ARMS/CONT NUC/PWR   PEACE
...INT/LAW PHIL/SCI 20 UN. PAGE 98 E1971

                                                    S60
NICHOLS J.P.,"HAZARDS OF AMERICAN PRIVATE   FINAN
INVESTMENT IN UNDERDEVELOPED COUNTRIES." FUT   ECO/UNDEV
L/A+17C USA+45 USA-45 EXTR/IND CONSULT BAL/PWR   CAP/ISM
ECO/TAC DOMIN ADJUD ATTIT SOVEREIGN WEALTH   NAT/LISM
...HIST/WRIT TIME/SEQ TREND VAL/FREE 20. PAGE 77
E1546

                                                    N60
RHODESIA-NYASA NATL ARCHIVES,A SELECT BIBLIOGRAPHY BIBLIOG
OF RECENT PUBLICATIONS CONCERNING THE FEDERATION OF ADMIN
RHODESIA AND NYASALAND (PAMPHLET). MALAWI RHODESIA ORD/FREE
LAW CULTURE STRUCT ECO/UNDEV LEGIS...GEOG 20.   NAT/G
PAGE 84 E1689

                                                    B61
RUEDA B.,A STATEMENT OF THE LAWS OF COLOMBIA IN   FINAN
MATTERS AFFECTING BUSINESS (3RD ED.). INDUS FAM   ECO/UNDEV
LABOR LG/CO NAT/G LEGIS TAX CONTROL MARRIAGE 20   LAW
COLOMB. PAGE 86 E1733   CONSTN

                                                    B61
SYATAUW J.J.G.,SOME NEWLY ESTABLISHED ASIAN STATES INT/LAW
AND THE DEVELOPMENT OF INTERNATIONAL LAW. BURMA   ADJUST
CEYLON INDIA INDONESIA ECO/UNDEV COLONIAL NEUTRAL   SOCIETY
WAR PEACE SOVEREIGN...CHARTS 19/20. PAGE 95 E1902   S/ASIA

                                                    S61
CASTANEDA J.,"THE UNDERDEVELOPED NATIONS AND THE   INT/ORG
DEVELOPMENT OF INTERNATIONAL LAW." FUT UNIV LAW   ECO/UNDEV
ACT/RES FOR/AID LEGIT PERCEPT SKILL...JURID   PEACE
METH/CNCPT TIME/SEQ TOT/POP 20 UN. PAGE 21 E0405   INT/LAW

                                                    S61
HARVEY W.B.,"THE RULE OF LAW IN HISTORICAL   ACT/RES
PERSPECTIVE." USA+45 WOR+45 INTELL SOCIETY ECO/DEV LAW
ECO/UNDEV NAT/G EX/STRUC LEGIS TOP/EX LEGIT SKILL
...CONCPT HIST/WRIT TOT/POP. PAGE 51 E1010

                                                    B62
CARSON P.,MATERIALS FOR WEST AFRICAN HISTORY IN THE BIBLIOG/A
ARCHIVES OF BELGIUM AND HOLLAND. CLIENT INDUS   COLONIAL
INT/TRADE ADMIN 17/19. PAGE 20 E0397   AFR
                                                    ECO/UNDEV

                                                    B62
COSTA RICA UNIVERSIDAD BIBL,LISTA DE TESIS DE GRADO BIBLIOG/A
DE LA UNIVERSIDAD DE COSTA RICA. COSTA/RICA LAW   NAT/G
LOC/G ADMIN LEAD...SOC 20. PAGE 26 E0518   DIPLOM
                                                    ECO/UNDEV

                                                    B62
DOUGLAS W.O.,DEMOCRACY'S MANIFESTO. COM USA+45   DIPLOM
ECO/UNDEV INT/ORG FORCES PLAN NEUTRAL TASK MARXISM POLICY
...JURID 20 NATO SEATO. PAGE 32 E0642   NAT/G
                                                    ORD/FREE

                                                    B62
FATOUROS A.A.,GOVERNMENT GUARANTEES TO FOREIGN   NAT/G
INVESTORS. WOR+45 ECO/UNDEV INDUS WORKER ADJUD   FINAN
...NAT/COMP BIBLIOG TREATY. PAGE 36 E0722   INT/TRADE
                                                    ECO/DEV

                                                    B62
SHAW C.,LEGAL PROBLEMS IN INTERNATIONAL TRADE AND   INT/LAW
INVESTMENT. WOR+45 ECO/DEV ECO/UNDEV MARKET DIPLOM INT/TRADE
TAX INCOME ROLE...ANTHOL BIBLIOG 20 TREATY UN IMF   FINAN
GATT. PAGE 91 E1816   ECO/TAC

                                                    B62
UNECA LIBRARY,NEW ACQUISITIONS IN THE UNECA   BIBLIOG
LIBRARY. LAW NAT/G PLAN PROB/SOLV TEC/DEV ADMIN   AFR
REGION...GEOG SOC 20 UN. PAGE 98 E1956   ECO/UNDEV
                                                    INT/ORG

                                                    L62
MANGIN G.,"L'ORGANIZATION JUDICIAIRE DES ETATS   AFR
D'AFRIQUE ET DE MADAGASCAR." ISLAM WOR+45 STRATA   LEGIS
STRUCT ECO/UNDEV NAT/G LEGIT EXEC...JURID TIME/SEQ COLONIAL
TOT/POP 20 SUPREME/CT. PAGE 68 E1357   MADAGASCAR

                                                    L62
MURACCIOLE L.,"LA LOI FONDAMENTALE DE LA REPUBLIQUE AFR
DU CONGO." WOR+45 SOCIETY ECO/UNDEV INT/ORG NAT/G   CONSTN
LEGIS PLAN LEGIT ADJUD COLONIAL ROUTINE ATTIT
SOVEREIGN 20 CONGO. PAGE 75 E1504

                                                    L62
NIZARD L.,"CUBAN QUESTION AND SECURITY COUNCIL."   INT/ORG
L/A+17C USA+45 ECO/UNDEV NAT/G POL/PAR DELIB/GP   JURID
ECO/TAC PWR...RELATIV OBS TIME/SEQ TREND GEN/LAWS   DIPLOM
UN 20 UN. PAGE 77 E1551   CUBA

                                                    S62
MANGIN G.,"LES ACCORDS DE COOPERATION EN MATIERE DE INT/ORG
JUSTICE ENTRE LA FRANCE ET LES ETATS AFRICAINS ET   LAW

MALGACHE." AFR ISLAM WOR+45 STRUCT ECO/UNDEV NAT/G FRANCE
DELIB/GP PERCEPT ALL/VALS...JURID MGT TIME/SEQ 20.
PAGE 68 E1356

S62

MURACCIOLE L.,"LES MODIFICATIONS DE LA CONSTITUTION NAT/G
MALGACHE." AFR WOR+45 ECO/UNDEV LEGIT EXEC ALL/VALS STRUCT
...JURID 20. PAGE 75 E1505 SOVEREIGN
MADAGASCAR

B63

DOUGLAS W.O.,THE ANATOMY OF LIBERTY: THE RIGHTS OF PEACE
MAN WITHOUT FORCE. WOR+45 ECO/DEV ECO/UNDEV LOC/G LAW
FORCES GOV/REL...SOC/WK 20. PAGE 32 E0643 DIPLOM
ORD/FREE

B63

GEERTZ C.,OLD SOCIETIES AND NEW STATES: THE QUEST ECO/UNDEV
FOR MODERNITY IN ASIA AND AFRICA. AFR ASIA LAW TEC/DEV
CULTURE SECT EDU/PROP REV...GOV/COMP NAT/COMP 20. NAT/LISM
PAGE 42 E0842 SOVEREIGN

B63

HAUSMAN W.H.,MANAGING ECONOMIC DEVELOPMENT IN ECO/UNDEV
AFRICA. AFR USA+45 LAW FINAN WORKER TEC/DEV WEALTH PLAN
...ANTHOL 20. PAGE 51 E1012 FOR/AID
MGT

L63

LISSITZYN O.J.,"INTERNATIONAL LAW IN A DIVIDED INT/ORG
WORLD." FUT WOR+45 CONSTN CULTURE ECO/DEV ECO/UNDEV LAW
DIST/IND NAT/G FORCES ECO/TAC LEGIT ADJUD ADMIN
COERCE ATTIT HEALTH MORAL ORD/FREE PWR RESPECT
WEALTH VAL/FREE. PAGE 65 E1306

S63

GERHARD H.,"COMMODITY TRADE STABILIZATION THROUGH PLAN
INTERNATIONAL AGREEMENTS." WOR+45 ECO/DEV ECO/UNDEV ECO/TAC
NAT/G ROUTINE ORD/FREE...INT/LAW OBS TREND GEN/METH INT/TRADE
TOT/POP 20. PAGE 43 E0850

S63

WALKER H.,"THE INTERNATIONAL LAW OF COMMODITY MARKET
AGREEMENTS." FUT WOR+45 ECO/DEV ECO/UNDEV FINAN VOL/ASSN
INT/ORG NAT/G CONSULT CREATE PLAN ECO/TAC ATTIT INT/LAW
PERCEPT...CONCPT GEN/LAWS TOT/POP GATT 20. PAGE 105 INT/TRADE
E2095

B64

BERNSTEIN H.,A BOOKSHELF ON BRAZIL. BRAZIL ADMIN BIBLIOG/A
COLONIAL...HUM JURID SOC 20. PAGE 11 E0213 NAT/G
L/A+17C
ECO/UNDEV

B64

CURRIE D.P.,FEDERALISM AND THE NEW NATIONS OF FEDERAL
AFRICA. CANADA USA+45 INT/TRADE TAX GP/REL AFR
...NAT/COMP SOC/INTEG 20. PAGE 28 E0556 ECO/UNDEV
INT/LAW

B64

GARDNER R.N.,IN PURSUIT OF WORLD ORDER* US FOREIGN OBS
POLICY AND INTERNATIONAL ORGANIZATIONS. USA+45 USSR INT/ORG
ECO/UNDEV FORCES LEGIS DIPLOM FOR/AID INT/TRADE ALL/VALS
PEACE...INT/LAW PREDICT UN. PAGE 42 E0839

B64

GOODNOW H.F.,THE CIVIL SERVICE OF PAKISTAN: ADMIN
BUREAUCRACY IN A NEW NATION. INDIA PAKISTAN S/ASIA GOV/REL
ECO/UNDEV PROVS CHIEF PARTIC CHOOSE EFFICIENCY PWR LAW
...BIBLIOG 20. PAGE 45 E0889 NAT/G

B64

HEKHUIS D.J.,INTERNATIONAL STABILITY: MILITARY, TEC/DEV
ECONOMIC AND POLITICAL DIMENSIONS. FUT WOR+45 LAW DETER
ECO/UNDEV INT/ORG NAT/G VOL/ASSN FORCES ACT/RES REGION
BAL/PWR PWR WEALTH...STAT UN 20. PAGE 51 E1024

B64

REGALA R.,WORLD PEACE THROUGH DIPLOMACY AND LAW. DIPLOM
S/ASIA WOR+45 ECO/UNDEV INT/ORG FORCES PLAN PEACE
PROB/SOLV FOR/AID NUC/PWR WAR...POLICY INT/LAW 20. ADJUD
PAGE 84 E1679

B64

TONG T.,UNITED STATES DIPLOMACY IN CHINA, DIPLOM
1844-1860. ASIA USA-45 ECO/UNDEV ECO/TAC COERCE INT/TRADE
GP/REL...INT/LAW 19 TREATY. PAGE 96 E1934 COLONIAL

B64

UN PUB. INFORM. ORGAN.,EVERY MAN'S UNITED NATIONS. INT/ORG
UNIV WOR+45 CONSTN CULTURE SOCIETY ECO/DEV ROUTINE
ECO/UNDEV NAT/G ACT/RES PLAN ECO/TAC INT/TRADE
EDU/PROP LEGIT PEACE ATTIT ALL/VALS...POLICY HUM
INT/LAW CONCPT CHARTS UN TOT/POP 20. PAGE 97 E1954

L64

POUNDS N.J.G.,"THE POLITICS OF PARTITION." AFR ASIA NAT/G
COM EUR+WWI FUT ISLAM S/ASIA USA-45 LAW ECO/DEV NAT/LISM
ECO/UNDEV AGRI INDUS INT/ORG POL/PAR PROVS SECT
FORCES TOP/EX EDU/PROP LEGIT ATTIT MORAL ORD/FREE
PWR RESPECT WEALTH. PAGE 82 E1640

S64

DERWINSKI E.J.,"THE COST OF THE INTERNATIONAL MARKET
COFFEE AGREEMENT." L/A+17C USA+45 WOR+45 ECO/UNDEV DELIB/GP
NAT/G VOL/ASSN LEGIS DIPLOM ECO/TAC FOR/AID LEGIT INT/TRADE
ATTIT...TIME/SEQ CONGRESS 20 TREATY. PAGE 31 E0608

S64

TRISKA J.F.,"SOVIET TREATY LAW: A QUANTITATIVE COM
ANALYSIS." WOR+45 LAW ECO/UNDEV AGRI COM/IND INDUS ECO/TAC
CREATE TEC/DEV DIPLOM ATTIT PWR WEALTH...JURID SAMP INT/LAW
TIME/SEQ TREND CHARTS VAL/FREE 20 TREATY. PAGE 97 USSR
E1942

B65

AMERICAN UNIVERSITY IN CAIRO,GUIDE TO UAR BIBLIOG
GOVERNMENT PUBLICATIONS AT THE AUC LIBRARY NAT/G
(PAMPHLET). ISLAM UAR USA+45 ECO/UNDEV...SOC STAT LEGIS
20. PAGE 4 E0084 LAW

B65

BOVY L.,LE MOUVEMENT SYNDICAL OUEST AFRICAIN BIBLIOG
D'EXPRESSION FRANCAISE. AFR SECT...JURID SOC 20. SOCISM
PAGE 14 E0275 ECO/UNDEV
IDEA/COMP

B65

COWEN Z.,THE BRITISH COMMONWEALTH OF NATIONS IN A JURID
CHANGING WORLD. UK ECO/UNDEV INT/ORG ECO/TAC DIPLOM
INT/TRADE COLONIAL WAR GP/REL RACE/REL SOVEREIGN PARL/PROC
SOC/INTEG 20 TREATY EEC COMMONWLTH. PAGE 27 E0530 NAT/LISM

B65

HAEFELE E.T.,GOVERNMENT CONTROLS ON TRANSPORT. AFR ECO/UNDEV
RHODESIA TANZANIA DIPLOM ECO/TAC TARIFFS PRICE DIST/IND
ADJUD CONTROL REGION EFFICIENCY...POLICY 20 CONGO. FINAN
PAGE 49 E0973 NAT/G

B65

HIGGINS R.,CONFLICT OF INTERESTS* INTERNATIONAL LAW INT/LAW
IN A DIVIDED WORLD. ASIA USSR ECO/DEV ECO/UNDEV IDEA/COMP
SECT INT/TRADE COLD/WAR WORSHIP. PAGE 52 E1042 ADJUST

B65

INST INTL DES CIVILISATION DIF,THE CONSTITUTIONS CONSTN
AND ADMINISTRATIVE INSTITUTIONS OF THE NEW STATES. ADMIN
AFR ISLAM S/ASIA NAT/G POL/PAR DELIB/GP EX/STRUC ADJUD
CONFER EFFICIENCY NAT/LISM...JURID SOC 20. PAGE 56 ECO/UNDEV
E1123

B65

NWOGUGU E.I.,THE LEGAL PROBLEMS OF FOREIGN FOR/AID
INVESTMENT IN DEVELOPING COUNTRIES. WOR+45 INT/ORG FINAN
DELIB/GP LEGIS PROB/SOLV INT/TRADE TAX ADJUD INT/LAW
SANCTION...BIBLIOG 20 TREATY. PAGE 78 E1561 ECO/UNDEV

B65

O'BRIEN W.V.,THE NEW NATIONS IN INTERNATIONAL LAW INT/LAW
AND DIPLOMACY* THE YEAR BOOK OF WORLD POLITY* CULTURE
VOLUME III. USA+45 ECO/UNDEV INT/ORG FORCES DIPLOM SOVEREIGN
COLONIAL NEUTRAL REV NAT/LISM ATTIT RESPECT. ANTHOL
PAGE 78 E1565

B65

O'CONNELL D.P.,INTERNATIONAL LAW (2 VOLS.). WOR+45 INT/LAW
WOR-45 ECO/DEV ECO/UNDEV INT/ORG NAT/G AGREE DIPLOM
...POLICY JURID CONCPT NAT/COMP 20 TREATY. PAGE 78 CT/SYS
E1566

B65

PROEHL P.O.,FOREIGN ENTERPRISE IN NIGERIA. NIGERIA ECO/UNDEV
FINAN LABOR NAT/G TAX 20. PAGE 83 E1656 ECO/TAC
JURID
CAP/ISM

B65

VON RENESSE E.A.,UNVOLLENDETE DEMOKRATIEN. AFR ECO/UNDEV
ISLAM S/ASIA SOCIETY ACT/RES COLONIAL...JURID NAT/COMP
CHARTS BIBLIOG METH 13/20. PAGE 104 E2083 SOVEREIGN

S65

KHOURI F.J.,"THE JORDON RIVER CONTROVERSY." LAW ISLAM
SOCIETY ECO/UNDEV AGRI FINAN INDUS SECT FORCES INT/ORG
ACT/RES PLAN TEC/DEV ECO/TAC EDU/PROP COERCE ATTIT ISRAEL
DRIVE PERCEPT RIGID/FLEX ALL/VALS...GEOG SOC MYTH JORDAN
WORK. PAGE 61 E1212

B66

BEER U.,FRUCHTBARKEITSREGELUNG ALS KONSEQUENZ CONTROL
VERANTWORTLICHER ELTERNSCHAFT. ASIA GERMANY/W INDIA GEOG

LAW ECO/DEV ECO/UNDEV TEC/DEV ECO/TAC BIO/SOC SEX   FAM
CATHISM...METH/COMP 20 CHINJAP BIRTH/CON. PAGE 9   SECT
E0178

                                                          B66
COPLIN W.D.,THE FUNCTIONS OF INTERNATIONAL LAW.   INT/LAW
WOR+45 ECO/DEV ECO/UNDEV ADJUD COLONIAL WAR OWN   DIPLOM
SOVEREIGN...POLICY GEN/LAWS 20. PAGE 25 E0503   INT/ORG

                                                          B66
DIZARD W.P.,TELEVISION* A WORLD VIEW. WOR+45   COM/IND
ECO/UNDEV TEC/DEV LICENSE LITERACY...STAT OBS INT   ACT/RES
QU TREND AUD/VIS BIBLIOG. PAGE 32 E0632   EDU/PROP
                                                          CREATE

                                                          B66
FALK R.A.,THE STRATEGY OF WORLD ORDER* 4 VOLUMES.   ORD/FREE
WOR+45 ECO/UNDEV ACADEM INT/ORG ACT/RES DIPLOM   GEN/LAWS
ARMS/CONT WAR...NET/THEORY SIMUL BIBLIOG UN.   ANTHOL
PAGE 36 E0719   INT/LAW

                                                          B66
FRIEDMANN W.G.,INTERNATIONAL FINANCIAL AID. USA+45   INT/ORG
ECO/DEV ECO/UNDEV NAT/G VOL/ASSN EX/STRUC PLAN RENT   FOR/AID
GIVE BAL/PAY PWR...GEOG INT/LAW STAT TREND UN EEC   TEC/DEV
COMECON. PAGE 41 E0806   ECO/TAC

                                                          B66
US DEPARTMENT OF STATE,RESEARCH ON AFRICA (EXTERNAL   BIBLIOG/A
RESEARCH LIST NO 5-25). LAW CULTURE ECO/UNDEV   ASIA
POL/PAR DIPLOM EDU/PROP LEAD REGION MARXISM...GEOG   S/ASIA
LING WORSHIP 20. PAGE 100 E1996   NAT/G

                                                          B66
US SENATE COMM ON FOREIGN REL,ASIAN DEVELOPMENT   FOR/AID
BANK ACT. USA+45 LAW DIPLOM...CHARTS 20 BLACK/EUG   FINAN
S/EASTASIA. PAGE 101 E2030   ECO/UNDEV
                                                          S/ASIA

                                                          L66
HIGGINS R.,"THE INTERNATIONAL COURT AND SOUTH WEST   SOUTH/AFR
AFRICA* SOME IMPLICATIONS OF THE JUDGMENT." AFR LAW   COLONIAL
ECO/UNDEV JUDGE RACE/REL COST PWR...INT/LAW TREND   CT/SYS
UN TREATY. PAGE 52 E1043   ADJUD

                                                          S66
ANAND R.P.,"ATTITUDE OF THE ASIAN-AFRICAN STATES   INT/LAW
TOWARD CERTAIN PROBLEMS OF INTERNATIONAL LAW."   ATTIT
L/A+17C S/ASIA ECO/UNDEV CREATE CONFER ADJUD   ASIA
COLONIAL...RECORD GP/COMP UN. PAGE 5 E0087   AFR

                                                          S66
BROWNLIE I.,"NUCLEAR PROLIFERATION* SOME PROBLEMS   NUC/PWR
OF CONTROL." USA+45 USSR ECO/UNDEV INT/ORG FORCES   ARMS/CONT
TEC/DEV REGION CONSEN...RECORD TREATY. PAGE 16   VOL/ASSN
E0318   ORD/FREE

                                                          S66
DETTER I.,"THE PROBLEM OF UNEQUAL TREATIES." CONSTN   SOVEREIGN
NAT/G LEGIS COLONIAL COERCE PWR...GEOG UN TIME   DOMIN
TREATY. PAGE 31 E0610   INT/LAW
                                                          ECO/UNDEV

                                                          S66
MATTHEWS D.G.,"ETHIOPIAN OUTLINE: A BIBLIOGRAPHIC   BIBLIOG
RESEARCH GUIDE." ETHIOPIA LAW STRUCT ECO/UNDEV AGRI   NAT/G
LABOR SECT CHIEF DELIB/GP EX/STRUC ADMIN...LING   DIPLOM
ORG/CHARTS 20. PAGE 69 E1384   POL/PAR

                                                          B67
GABRIEL P.P.,THE INTERNATIONAL TRANSFER OF   ECO/UNDEV
CORPORATE SKILLS: MANAGEMENT CONTRACTS IN LESS   AGREE
DEVELOPED COUNTRIES. CLIENT INDUS LG/CO PLAN   MGT
PROB/SOLV CAP/ISM ECO/TAC FOR/AID INT/TRADE RENT   CONSULT
ADMIN SKILL 20. PAGE 42 E0825

                                                          B67
INTERNATIONAL CONCILIATION,ISSUES BEFORE THE 22ND   PROB/SOLV
GENERAL ASSEMBLY. WOR+45 ECO/UNDEV FINAN BAL/PWR   INT/ORG
BUDGET INT/TRADE STRANGE ORD/FREE...INT/LAW 20 UN   DIPLOM
COLD/WAR. PAGE 57 E1132   PEACE

                                                          B67
MCDOUGAL M.S.,THE INTERPRETATION OF AGREEMENTS AND   INT/LAW
WORLD PUBLIC ORDER: PRINCIPLES OF CONTENT AND   STRUCT
PROCEDURE. WOR+45 CONSTN PROB/SOLV TEC/DEV   ECO/UNDEV
...CON/ANAL TREATY. PAGE 71 E1412   DIPLOM

                                                          B67
US SENATE COMM ON FOREIGN REL,INTER-AMERICAN   LAW
DEVELOPMENT BANK ACT AMENDMENT. L/A+17C USA+45   FINAN
DELIB/GP DIPLOM FOR/AID BAL/PAY...CHARTS SENATE.   INT/ORG
PAGE 102 E2034   ECO/UNDEV

                                                          L67
LENT G.E.,"TAX INCENTIVES FOR INVESTMENT IN   ECO/UNDEV

DEVELOPING COUNTRIES" WOR+45 LAW INDUS PLAN BUDGET   TAX
TARIFFS ADMIN...METH/COMP 20. PAGE 64 E1285   FINAN
                                                          ECO/TAC

                                                          S67
DOUTY H.M.," REFERENCE TO DEVELOPING COUNTRIES."   TAX
JAMAICA MALAYSIA UK WOR+45 LAW FINAN ACT/RES BUDGET   ECO/UNDEV
CAP/ISM ECO/TAC TARIFFS RISK EFFICIENCY PROFIT   NAT/G
...CHARTS 20. PAGE 33 E0646

                                                          S67
STEEL R.,"WHAT CAN THE UN DO?" RHODESIA ECO/UNDEV   INT/ORG
DIPLOM ECO/TAC SANCTION...INT/LAW UN. PAGE 93 E1866   BAL/PWR
                                                          PEACE
                                                          FOR/AID

                                                          S67
WRAITH R.E.,"ADMINISTRATIVE CHANGE IN THE NEW   ADMIN
AFRICA." AFR LG/CO ADJUD INGP/REL PWR...RECORD   NAT/G
GP/COMP 20. PAGE 107 E2147   LOC/G
                                                          ECO/UNDEV

                                                          N67
US SENATE COMM ON FOREIGN REL,SURVEY OF THE   INT/TRADE
ALLIANCE FOR PROGRESS: FOREIGN TRADE POLICIES   REGION
(PAMPHLET). L/A+17C LAW ECO/UNDEV ECO/TAC TARIFFS   AGREE
20 GATT LAFTA UN. PAGE 102 E2037   INT/ORG

                                                          B68
GREGG R.W.,INTERNATIONAL ORGANIZATION IN THE   INT/ORG
WESTERN HEMISPHERE. L/A+17C USA+45 CULTURE PLAN   DIPLOM
DOMIN AGREE CONTROL DETER PWR...GEOG 20 OAS TREATY.   ECO/UNDEV
PAGE 46 E0913

ECOLE NATIONALE D'ADMIN E0672

ECOLOGY....SEE HABITAT

ECOMETRIC....MATHEMATICAL ECONOMICS, ECONOMETRICS

                                                          B65
HABERLER G.,A SURVEY OF INTERNATIONAL TRADE THEORY.   INT/TRADE
CANADA FRANCE GERMANY ECO/TAC TARIFFS AGREE COST   BAL/PAY
DEMAND WEALTH...ECOMETRIC 19/20 MONOPOLY TREATY.   DIPLOM
PAGE 49 E0968   POLICY

                                                          B65
UNIVERSAL REFERENCE SYSTEM,INTERNATIONAL AFFAIRS: BIBLIOG/A
VOLUME I IN THE POLITICAL SCIENCE, GOVERNMENT, AND   GEN/METH
PUBLIC POLICY SERIES....DECISION ECOMETRIC GEOG   COMPUT/IR
INT/LAW JURID MGT PHIL/SCI PSY SOC. PAGE 98 E1972   DIPLOM

ECONOMIC DATA....SEE ECO

ECONOMIC DETERMINISM....SEE GEN/LAWS

ECONOMIC WARFARE....SEE ECO/TAC

ECONOMICS....SEE ECO

ECONOMIDES C.P. E0673

ECOSOC....UNITED NATIONS ECONOMIC AND SOCIAL COUNCIL

ECSC....EUROPEAN COAL AND STEEL COMMUNITY; SEE ALSO VOL/ASSN,
     INT/ORG

                                                          N
FOREIGN AFFAIRS. SPACE WOR+45 WOR-45 CULTURE   BIBLIOG
ECO/UNDEV FINAN NAT/G TEC/DEV INT/TRADE ARMS/CONT   DIPLOM
NUC/PWR...POLICY 20 UN EURATOM ECSC EEC. PAGE 1   INT/ORG
E0021   INT/LAW

                                                          B62
ALEXANDROWICZ C.H.,WORLD ECONOMIC AGENCIES: LAW AND   INT/LAW
PRACTICE. WOR+45 DIST/IND FINAN LABOR CONSULT   INT/ORG
INT/TRADE TARIFFS REPRESENT HEALTH...JURID 20 UN   DIPLOM
GATT EEC OAS ECSC. PAGE 3 E0063   ADJUD

                                                          B62
GYORGY A.,PROBLEMS IN INTERNATIONAL RELATIONS. COM   DIPLOM
CT/SYS NUC/PWR ALL/IDEOS 20 UN EEC ECSC. PAGE 49   NEUTRAL
E0966   BAL/PWR
                                                          REV

                                                          C65
SCHEINGOLD S.A.,"THE RULE OF LAW IN EUROPEAN   INT/LAW
INTEGRATION: THE PATH OF THE SCHUMAN PLAN." EUR+WWI   CT/SYS
JUDGE ADJUD FEDERAL ATTIT PWR...RECORD INT BIBLIOG   REGION
EEC ECSC. PAGE 87 E1755   CENTRAL

ECUADOR....SEE ALSO L/A+17C

                                                          B47
CLAGETT H.L.,A GUIDE TO THE LAW AND LEGAL   BIBLIOG
LITERATURE OF ECUADOR. ECUADOR CONSTN LABOR LEGIS   JURID

JUDGE ADJUD ADMIN CIVMIL/REL...CRIMLGY INT/LAW
CON/ANAL 20. PAGE 22 E0443
LAW
L/A+17C

B47
DE NOIA J.,GUIDE TO OFFICIAL PUBLICATIONS OF OTHER
AMERICAN REPUBLICS: ECUADOR (VOL. IX). ECUADOR LAW
FINAN LEGIS BUDGET CT/SYS 19/20. PAGE 30 E0589
BIBLIOG/A
CONSTN
NAT/G
EDU/PROP

B55
SERRANO MOSCOSO E.,A STATEMENT OF THE LAWS OF
ECUADOR IN MATTERS AFFECTING BUSINESS (2ND ED.).
ECUADOR INDUS LABOR LG/CO NAT/G LEGIS TAX CONTROL
MARRIAGE 20. PAGE 90 E1805
FINAN
ECO/UNDEV
LAW
CONSTN

ECUMENIC....ECUMENICAL MOVEMENT OF CHURCHES

B66
SMITH E.A.,CHURCH-STATE RELATIONS IN ECUMENICAL
PERSPECTIVE. WOR+45 LAW MUNIC INGP/REL DISCRIM
ATTIT SUPEGO ORD/FREE CATHISM...PHIL/SCI IDEA/COMP
20 PROTESTANT ECUMENIC CHURCH/STA CHRISTIAN.
PAGE 92 E1843
NAT/G
SECT
GP/REL
ADJUD

EDDY J.P. E0674

EDEN/A....ANTHONY EDEN

EDER P.J. E0127

EDGEWORTH A.B. E0675

EDSEL....EDSEL (AUTOMOBILE)

EDU/PROP....EDUCATION, PROPAGANDA, PERSUASION

N
FULLER G.A.,DEMOBILIZATION: A SELECTED LIST OF
REFERENCES. USA+45 LAW AGRI LABOR WORKER ECO/TAC
RATION RECEIVE EDU/PROP ROUTINE ARMS/CONT ALL/VALS
20. PAGE 41 E0819
BIBLIOG/A
INDUS
FORCES
NAT/G

N
BACKGROUND; JOURNAL OF INTERNATIONAL STUDIES
ASSOCIATION. INT/ORG FORCES ACT/RES EDU/PROP COERCE
NAT/LISM PEACE ATTIT...INT/LAW CONCPT 20. PAGE 1
E0004
BIBLIOG
DIPLOM
POLICY

N
BIBLIOGRAPHIE DE LA PHILOSOPHIE. LAW CULTURE SECT
EDU/PROP MORAL...HUM METH/CNCPT 20. PAGE 1 E0018
BIBLIOG/A
PHIL/SCI
CONCPT
LOG

N
LATIN AMERICA IN PERIODICAL LITERATURE. LAW TEC/DEV
DIPLOM RECEIVE EDU/PROP...GEOG HUM MGT 20. PAGE 2
E0024
BIBLIOG/A
L/A+17C
SOCIETY
ECO/UNDEV

N
SOUTH AFRICA STATE LIBRARY,SOUTH AFRICAN NATIONAL
BIBLIOGRAPHY, SANB. SOUTH/AFR LAW NAT/G EDU/PROP
...MGT PSY SOC 20. PAGE 93 E1858
BIBLIOG
PRESS
WRITING

N
US BUREAU OF THE CENSUS,BIBLIOGRAPHY OF SOCIAL
SCIENCE PERIODICALS AND MONOGRAPH SERIES. WOR+45
LAW DIPLOM EDU/PROP HEALTH...PSY SOC LING STAT.
PAGE 99 E1980
BIBLIOG/A
CULTURE
NAT/G
SOCIETY

N
US SUPERINTENDENT OF DOCUMENTS,EDUCATION (PRICE
LIST 31). USA+45 LAW FINAN LOC/G NAT/G DEBATE ADMIN
LEAD RACE/REL FEDERAL HEALTH POLICY. PAGE 103 E2062
BIBLIOG/A
EDU/PROP
ACADEM
SCHOOL

B03
FAGUET E.,LE LIBERALISME. FRANCE PRESS ADJUD ADMIN
DISCRIM CONSERVE SOCISM...TRADIT SOC LING WORSHIP
PARLIAMENT. PAGE 36 E0711
ORD/FREE
EDU/PROP
NAT/G
LAW

B04
CRANDALL S.B.,TREATIES: THEIR MAKING AND
ENFORCEMENT. MOD/EUR USA-45 CONSTN INT/ORG NAT/G
LEGIS EDU/PROP LEGIT EXEC PEACE KNOWL MORAL...JURID
CONGRESS 19/20 TREATY. PAGE 27 E0541
LAW

B09
JUSTINIAN,THE DIGEST (DIGESTA CORPUS JURIS CIVILIS)
(2 VOLS.) (TRANS. BY C. H. MONRO). ROMAN/EMP LAW
FAM LOC/G LEGIS EDU/PROP CONTROL MARRIAGE OWN ROLE
CIVIL/LAW. PAGE 59 E1177
JURID
CT/SYS
NAT/G
STRATA

B12
FOUAD M.,LE REGIME DE LA PRESSE EN EGYPTE: THESE
POUR LE DOCTORAT. UAR LICENSE EDU/PROP ADMIN
SANCTION CRIME SUPEGO PWR...ART/METH JURID 19/20.
PAGE 39 E0778
ORD/FREE
LEGIS
CONTROL
PRESS

B15
HOBSON J.A.,TOWARDS INTERNATIONAL GOVERNMENT.
MOD/EUR STRUCT ECO/TAC EDU/PROP ADJUD ALL/VALS
...SOCIALIST CONCPT GEN/LAWS TOT/POP 20. PAGE 53
E1059
FUT
INT/ORG
CENTRAL

S17
ROOT E.,"THE EFFECT OF DEMOCRACY ON INTERNATIONAL
LAW." USA-45 WOR-45 INTELL SOCIETY INT/ORG NAT/G
CONSULT ACT/RES CREATE PLAN EDU/PROP PEACE SKILL
...CONCPT METH/CNCPT OBS 20. PAGE 85 E1712
LEGIS
JURID
INT/LAW

N19
IN THE SHADOW OF FEAR; AMERICAN CIVIL LIBERTIES,
1948-49 (PAMPHLET). COM LAW LEGIS BAL/PWR EDU/PROP
CT/SYS RACE/REL DISCRIM MARXISM SOCISM 20 COLD/WAR
CONGRESS ACLU CIV/RIGHTS ESPIONAGE. PAGE 2 E0030
ORD/FREE
CONSTN
POLICY

N19
THE REGIONAL DIRECTOR AND THE PRESS (PAMPHLET).
USA-45 COM/IND LOBBY ROLE 20 NLRB CINCINNATI
BILL/RIGHT. PAGE 2 E0031
PRESS
LABOR
ORD/FREE
EDU/PROP

N19
COUTROT A.,THE FIGHT OVER THE 1959 PRIVATE
EDUCATION LAW IN FRANCE (PAMPHLET). FRANCE NAT/G
SECT GIVE EDU/PROP GP/REL ATTIT RIGID/FLEX ORD/FREE
20 CHURCH/STA. PAGE 27 E0527
SCHOOL
PARL/PROC
CATHISM
LAW

N19
JANOWITZ M.,SOCIAL CONTROL OF ESCALATED RIOTS
(PAMPHLET). USA+45 USA-45 LAW SOCIETY MUNIC FORCES
PROB/SOLV EDU/PROP TV CRIME ATTIT...BIBLIOG 20
NEGRO CIV/RIGHTS. PAGE 58 E1148
CROWD
ORD/FREE
CONTROL
RACE/REL

B20
DICKINSON E.,THE EQUALITY OF STATES IN
INTERNATIONAL LAW. WOR-45 INT/ORG NAT/G DIPLOM
EDU/PROP LEGIT PEACE ATTIT ALL/VALS...JURID
TIME/SEQ LEAGUE/NAT. PAGE 31 E0622
LAW
CONCPT
SOVEREIGN

B20
LIPPMAN W.,LIBERTY AND THE NEWS. USA+45 USA-45 LAW
LEGIS DOMIN LEGIT ATTIT...POLICY SOC IDEA/COMP
METH/COMP 19/20. PAGE 65 E1300
ORD/FREE
PRESS
COM/IND
EDU/PROP

B25
GODET M.,INDEX BIBLIOGRAPHICUS: INTERNATIONAL
CATALOGUE OF SOURCES OF CURRENT BIBLIOGRAPHIC
INFORMATION. EUR+WWI MOD/EUR SOCIETY SECT TAX
...JURID PHIL/SCI SOC MATH. PAGE 44 E0876
BIBLIOG/A
DIPLOM
EDU/PROP
LAW

B27
DICKINSON J.,ADMINISTRATIVE JUSTICE AND THE
SUPREMACY OF LAW IN THE UNITED STATES. USA-45 LAW
INDUS DOMIN EDU/PROP CONTROL EXEC GP/REL ORD/FREE
...POLICY JURID 19/20. PAGE 31 E0623
CT/SYS
ADJUD
ADMIN
NAT/G

B28
MACDONALD A.F.,ELEMENTS OF POLITICAL SCIENCE
RESEARCH. USA-45 ACADEM JUDGE EDU/PROP DEBATE ADJUD
EXEC...BIBLIOG METH T 20 CONGRESS. PAGE 67 E1338
LAW
FEDERAL
DECISION
CT/SYS

L28
HUDSON M.,"THE TEACHING OF INTERNATIONAL LAW IN
AMERICA." USA-45 LAW CONSULT ACT/RES CREATE
EDU/PROP ATTIT RIGID/FLEX...JURID CONCPT RECORD
HIST/WRIT TREND GEN/LAWS 18/20. PAGE 56 E1109
PERCEPT
KNOWL
INT/LAW

B29
CONWELL-EVANS T.P.,THE LEAGUE COUNCIL IN ACTION.
EUR+WWI TURKEY UK USSR WOR-45 INT/ORG FORCES JUDGE
ECO/TAC EDU/PROP LEGIT ROUTINE ARMS/CONT COERCE
ATTIT PWR...MAJORIT GEOG JURID CONCPT LEAGUE/NAT
TOT/POP VAL/FREE TUNIS 20. PAGE 25 E0498
DELIB/GP
INT/LAW

B31
STOWELL E.C.,INTERNATIONAL LAW. FUT UNIV WOR-45
SOCIETY CONSULT EX/STRUC FORCES ACT/RES PLAN DIPLOM
EDU/PROP LEGIT DISPL PWR SKILL...POLICY CONCPT OBS
TREND TOT/POP 20. PAGE 94 E1885
INT/ORG
ROUTINE
INT/LAW

B32
EAGLETON C.,INTERNATIONAL GOVERNMENT. BRAZIL FRANCE
GERMANY ITALY UK USSR WOR-45 DELIB/GP TOP/EX PLAN
ECO/TAC EDU/PROP LEGIT ADJUD REGION ARMS/CONT
INT/ORG
JURID
DIPLOM

COERCE ATTIT PWR...GEOG MGT VAL/FREE LEAGUE/NAT 20. INT/LAW
PAGE 34 E0670

B32

FLEMMING D.,THE UNITED STATES AND THE LEAGUE OF INT/ORG
NATIONS, 1918-1920. FUT USA-45 NAT/G LEGIS TOP/EX EDU/PROP
DEBATE CHOOSE PEACE ATTIT SOVEREIGN...TIME/SEQ
CON/ANAL CONGRESS LEAGUE/NAT 20 TREATY. PAGE 39
E0764

B32

LUNT D.C.,THE ROAD TO THE LAW. UK USA-45 LEGIS ADJUD
EDU/PROP OWN ORD/FREE...DECISION TIME/SEQ NAT/COMP LAW
16/20 AUSTRAL ENGLSH/LAW COMMON/LAW. PAGE 67 E1333 JURID
CT/SYS

B32

MORLEY F.,THE SOCIETY OF NATIONS. EUR+WWI UNIV INT/ORG
WOR-45 LAW CONSTN ACT/RES PLAN EDU/PROP LEGIT CONCPT
ROUTINE...POLICY TIME/SEQ LEAGUE/NAT TOT/POP 20.
PAGE 75 E1496

B34

GONZALEZ PALENCIA A,ESTUDIO HISTORICO SOBRE LA LEGIT
CENSURA GUBERNATIVA EN ESPANA 1800-1833. NAT/G EDU/PROP
COERCE INGP/REL ATTIT AUTHORIT KNOWL...POLICY JURID PRESS
19. PAGE 44 E0884 CONTROL

B35

HUDSON M.,BY PACIFIC MEANS. WOR-45 EDU/PROP INT/ORG
ORD/FREE...CONCPT TIME/SEQ GEN/LAWS LEAGUE/NAT CT/SYS
TOT/POP 20 TREATY. PAGE 56 E1110 PEACE

B37

RUTHERFORD M.L.,THE INFLUENCE OF THE AMERICAN BAR ATTIT
ASSOCIATION ON PUBLIC OPINION AND LEGISLATION. ADJUD
USA+45 LAW CONSTN LABOR LEGIS DOMIN EDU/PROP LEGIT PROF/ORG
CT/SYS ROUTINE...TIME/SEQ 19/20 ABA. PAGE 87 E1739 JURID

L37

LERNER M.,"CONSTITUTION AND COURT AS SYMBOLS" CONSTN
(BMR)" USA+45 USA-45 DOMIN PWR SOVEREIGN...PSY MYTH CT/SYS
18/20 SUPREME/CT. PAGE 64 E1288 ATTIT
EDU/PROP

B38

LEAGUE OF NATIONS-SECRETARIAT..THE AIMS, METHODS ADJUD
AND ACTIVITY OF THE LEAGUE OF NATIONS. WOR+45 STRUCT
DIPLOM EDU/PROP LEGIT RIGID/FLEX ALL/VALS
...TIME/SEQ LEAGUE/NAT VAL/FREE 19/20. PAGE 64
E1273

S40

FLORIN J.,"BOLSHEVIST AND NATIONAL SOCIALIST LAW
DOCTRINES OF INTERNATIONAL LAW." EUR+WWI GERMANY ATTIT
USSR R+D INT/ORG NAT/G DIPLOM DOMIN EDU/PROP SOCISM TOTALISM
...CONCPT TIME/SEQ 20. PAGE 39 E0768 INT/LAW

S40

GILL N.N.,"PERMANENT ADVISORY COMMISSIONS IN THE DELIB/GP
FEDERAL GOVERNMENT." CLIENT FINAN OP/RES EDU/PROP NAT/G
PARTIC ROUTINE INGP/REL KNOWL SKILL...CLASSIF DECISION
TREND. PAGE 43 E0860

L41

COMM. STUDY ORGAN. PEACE,"ORGANIZATION OF PEACE." INT/ORG
USA-45 WOR-45 STRATA NAT/G ACT/RES DIPLOM ECO/TAC PLAN
EDU/PROP ADJUD ATTIT ORD/FREE PWR...SOC CONCPT PEACE
ANTHOL LEAGUE/NAT 20. PAGE 24 E0479

S41

WRIGHT Q.,"FUNDAMENTAL PROBLEMS OF INTERNATIONAL INT/ORG
ORGANIZATION." UNIV WOR-45 STRUCT FORCES ACT/RES ATTIT
CREATE DOMIN EDU/PROP LEGIT REGION NAT/LISM PEACE
ORD/FREE PWR RESPECT SOVEREIGN...JURID SOC CONCPT
METH/CNCPT TIME/SEQ 20. PAGE 107 E2152

B42

CRAIG A.,ABOVE ALL LIBERTIES. FRANCE UK USA-45 LAW ORD/FREE
CONSTN CULTURE INTELL NAT/G SECT JUDGE...IDEA/COMP MORAL
BIBLIOG 18/20. PAGE 27 E0536 WRITING
EDU/PROP

B42

HAMBRO C.J.,HOW TO WIN THE PEACE. ECO/TAC EDU/PROP FUT
ADJUD PERSON ALL/VALS...SOCIALIST TREND GEN/LAWS INT/ORG
20. PAGE 50 E0987 PEACE

B42

US LIBRARY OF CONGRESS,SOCIAL AND CULTURAL PROBLEMS BIBLIOG/A
IN WARTIME: APRIL 1941-MARCH 1942. WOR-45 CLIENT WAR
SECT EDU/PROP CRIME LEISURE RACE/REL STRANGE ATTIT SOC
DRIVE HEALTH...GEOG 20. PAGE 100 E2012 CULTURE

C42

CRAIG A.,"ABOVE ALL LIBERTIES." FRANCE UK LAW BIBLIOG/A

CULTURE INTELL SECT ORD/FREE 18/20. PAGE 27 E0537 EDU/PROP
WRITING
MORAL

B43

US LIBRARY OF CONGRESS,SOCIAL AND CULTURAL PROBLEMS BIBLIOG/A
IN WARTIME: APRIL-DECEMBER (SUPPLEMENT 1). WOR-45 WAR
SECT EDU/PROP CRIME LEISURE CIVMIL/REL RACE/REL SOC
ATTIT DRIVE HEALTH...GEOG 20. PAGE 100 E2013 CULTURE

B43

US LIBRARY OF CONGRESS,SOCIAL AND CULTURAL PROBLEMS BIBLIOG/A
IN WARTIME: JANUARY-MAY 1943 (SUPPLEMENT 2). WOR-45 WAR
FAM SECT PLAN EDU/PROP CRIME LEISURE RACE/REL DRIVE SOC
HEALTH...GEOG 20 JEWS. PAGE 100 E2014 CULTURE

B44

HUDSON M.,INTERNATIONAL TRIBUNALS PAST AND FUTURE. INT/ORG
FUT WOR-45 LAW EDU/PROP ADJUD ORD/FREE...CONCPT STRUCT
TIME/SEQ TREND GEN/LAWS TOT/POP VAL/FREE 18/20. INT/LAW
PAGE 56 E1111

B44

US LIBRARY OF CONGRESS,RUSSIA: A CHECK LIST BIBLIOG
PRELIMINARY TO A BASIC BIBLIOGRAPHY OF MATERIALS IN LAW
THE RUSSIAN LANGUAGE. COM USSR CULTURE EDU/PROP SECT
MARXISM...ART/METH HUM LING 19/20. PAGE 101 E2015

B45

CONOVER H.F.,THE NAZI STATE: WAR CRIMES AND WAR BIBLIOG
CRIMINALS. GERMANY CULTURE NAT/G SECT FORCES DIPLOM WAR
INT/TRADE EDU/PROP...INT/LAW BIOG HIST/WRIT CRIME
TIME/SEQ 20. PAGE 25 E0495

B45

GALLOWAY E.,ABSTRACTS OF POSTWAR LITERATURE (VOL. BIBLIOG/A
IV) JAN.-JULY, 1945 NOS. 901-1074. POLAND USA+45 NUC/PWR
USSR WOR+45 INDUS LABOR PLAN ECO/TAC INT/TRADE TAX NAT/G
EDU/PROP ADMIN COLONIAL INT/LAW. PAGE 42 E0829 DIPLOM

B45

HILL N.,CLAIMS TO TERRITORY IN INTERNATIONAL LAW INT/ORG
AND RELATIONS. WOR-45 NAT/G DOMIN EDU/PROP LEGIT ADJUD
REGION ROUTINE ORD/FREE PWR WEALTH...GEOG INT/LAW SOVEREIGN
JURID 20. PAGE 52 E1047

B45

REVES E.,THE ANATOMY OF PEACE. WOR-45 LAW CULTURE ACT/RES
NAT/G PLAN TEC/DEV EDU/PROP WAR NAT/LISM ATTIT CONCPT
ALL/VALS SOVEREIGN...POLICY HUM TIME/SEQ 20. NUC/PWR
PAGE 84 E1688 PEACE

B46

AMERICAN DOCUMENTATION INST,CATALOGUE OF AUXILIARY BIBLIOG
PUBLICATIONS IN MICROFILMS AND PHOTOPRINTS. USA-45 EDU/PROP
LAW AGRI CREATE TEC/DEV ADMIN...GEOG LING MATH 20. PSY
PAGE 4 E0077

B46

MANNHEIM H.,CRIMINAL JUSTICE AND SOCIAL ADJUD
RECONSTRUCTION. USA+45 EDU/PROP CRIME ANOMIE LAW
...JURID BIBLIOG 20. PAGE 68 E1361 STRUCT
ADJUST

L46

ERNST M.L.,"THE FIRST FREEDOM." USA-45 LAW R+D BIBLIOG
PRESS 20. PAGE 35 E0696 EDU/PROP
ORD/FREE
COM/IND

B47

DE NOIA J.,GUIDE TO OFFICIAL PUBLICATIONS OF OTHER BIBLIOG/A
AMERICAN REPUBLICS: ECUADOR (VOL. IX). ECUADOR LAW CONSTN
FINAN LEGIS BUDGET CT/SYS 19/20. PAGE 30 E0589 NAT/G
EDU/PROP

B47

DE NOIA J.,GUIDE TO OFFICIAL PUBLICATIONS OF THE BIBLIOG/A
OTHER AMERICAN REPUBLICS: EL SALVADOR. EL/SALVADR CONSTN
LAW LEGIS EDU/PROP CT/SYS 20. PAGE 30 E0590 NAT/G
ADMIN

B47

DE NOIA J.,GUIDE TO OFFICIAL PUBLICATIONS OF THE BIBLIOG/A
OTHER AMERICAN REPUBLICS: NICARAGUA (VOL. XIV). EDU/PROP
NICARAGUA LAW LEGIS ADMIN CT/SYS...JURID 19/20. NAT/G
PAGE 30 E0591 CONSTN

B47

DE NOIA J.,GUIDE TO OFFICIAL PUBLICATIONS OF THE BIBLIOG/A
OTHER AMERICAN REPUBLICS: PANAMA (VOL. XV). PANAMA CONSTN
LAW LEGIS EDU/PROP CT/SYS 20. PAGE 30 E0592 ADMIN
NAT/G

B47

NEUBURGER O.,GUIDE TO OFFICIAL PUBLICATIONS OF BIBLIOG/A

OTHER AMERICAN REPUBLICS: HONDURAS (VOL. XIII). HONDURAS LAW LEGIS ADMIN CT/SYS...JURID 19/20. PAGE 76 E1533
NAT/G
EDU/PROP
CONSTN

B47
NEUBURGER O.,GUIDE TO OFFICIAL PUBLICATIONS OF THE OTHER AMERICAN REPUBLICS: HAITI (VOL. XII). HAITI LAW FINAN LEGIS PRESS...JURID 20. PAGE 76 E1534
BIBLIOG/A
CONSTN
NAT/G
EDU/PROP

B48
DE NOIA J.,GUIDE TO OFFICIAL PUBLICATIONS OF OTHER AMERICAN REPUBLICS: PERU (VOL. XVII). PERU LAW LEGIS ADMIN CT/SYS...JURID 19/20. PAGE 30 E0593
BIBLIOG/A
CONSTN
NAT/G
EDU/PROP

B48
JESSUP P.C.,A MODERN LAW OF NATIONS. FUT WOR+45 WOR-45 SOCIETY NAT/G DELIB/GP LEGIS BAL/PWR EDU/PROP LEGIT PWR...INT/LAW JURID TIME/SEQ LEAGUE/NAT 20. PAGE 58 E1166
INT/ORG
ADJUD

S48
ALEXANDER L.,"WAR CRIMES, THEIR SOCIAL-PSYCHOLOGICAL ASPECTS." EUR+WWI GERMANY LAW CULTURE ELITES KIN POL/PAR PUB/INST FORCES DOMIN EDU/PROP COERCE CRIME ATTIT SUPEGO HEALTH MORAL PWR FASCISM ...PSY OBS TREND GEN/LAWS NAZI 20. PAGE 3 E0061
DRIVE
WAR

B49
BOYD A.M.,UNITED STATES GOVERNMENT PUBLICATIONS (3RD ED.). USA+45 EX/STRUC LEGIS ADMIN...JURID CHARTS 20. PAGE 14 E0281
BIBLIOG/A
PRESS
NAT/G
EDU/PROP

B49
MARITAIN J.,HUMAN RIGHTS: COMMENTS AND INTERPRETATIONS. COM UNIV WOR+45 LAW CONSTN CULTURE SOCIETY ECO/DEV ECO/UNDEV SCHOOL DELIB/GP EDU/PROP ATTIT PERCEPT ALL/VALS...HUM SOC TREND UNESCO 20. PAGE 68 E1365
INT/ORG
CONCPT

B49
SCHONS D.,BOOK CENSORSHIP IN NEW SPAIN (NEW WORLD STUDIES, BOOK II). SPAIN LAW CULTURE INSPECT ADJUD CT/SYS SANCTION GP/REL ORD/FREE 14/17. PAGE 88 E1764
CHRIST-17C
EDU/PROP
CONTROL
PRESS

B49
SUMMERS R.E.,FEDERAL INFORMATION CONTROLS IN PEACETIME. USA+45 COM/IND DOMIN INGP/REL ATTIT ORD/FREE 20. PAGE 94 E1893
ADJUD
CONTROL
EDU/PROP
PRESS

B49
US DEPARTMENT OF STATE,SOVIET BIBLIOGRAPHY (PAMPHLET). CHINA/COM COM USSR LAW AGRI INT/ORG ECO/TAC EDU/PROP...POLICY GEOG 20. PAGE 99 E1994
BIBLIOG/A
MARXISM
CULTURE
DIPLOM

B49
US LIBRARY OF CONGRESS,FREEDOM OF INFORMATION: SELECTIVE REPORT ON RECENT WRITINGS. USA+45 LAW CONSTN ELITES EDU/PROP PRESS LOBBY WAR TOTALISM ATTIT 20 UN UNESCO COLD/WAR. PAGE 101 E2018
BIBLIOG/A
ORD/FREE
LICENSE
COM/IND

S49
KIRK G.,"MATERIALS FOR THE STUDY OF INTERNATIONAL RELATIONS." FUT UNIV WOR+45 INTELL EDU/PROP ROUTINE PEACE ATTIT...INT/LAW JURID CONCPT OBS. PAGE 61 E1219
INT/ORG
ACT/RES
DIPLOM

B50
FRANK J.,COURTS ON TRIAL: MYTH AND REALITY IN AMERICAN JUSTICE. LAW CONSULT PROB/SOLV EDU/PROP ADJUD ROUTINE ROLE ORD/FREE...GEN/LAWS T 20. PAGE 40 E0788
JURID
CT/SYS
MYTH
CONSTN

B50
LAUTERPACHT H.,INTERNATIONAL LAW AND HUMAN RIGHTS. USA+45 CONSTN STRUCT INT/ORG ACT/RES EDU/PROP PEACE PERSON ALL/VALS...CONCPT CON/ANAL GEN/LAWS UN 20. PAGE 63 E1266
DELIB/GP
LAW
INT/LAW

S51
LEEK J.H.,"TREASON AND THE CONSTITUTION" (BMR)" USA+45 USA-45 EDU/PROP COLONIAL CT/SYS REV WAR ATTIT...TREND 18/20 SUPREME/CT CON/INTERP SMITH/ACT COMMON/LAW. PAGE 64 E1278
CONSTN
JURID
CRIME
NAT/G

B52
ANDREWS F.E.,CORPORATION GIVING. LAW TAX EDU/PROP ADMIN...POLICY STAT CHARTS. PAGE 5 E0096
LG/CO
GIVE
SML/CO
FINAN

B52
BENTHAM A.,HANDBOOK OF POLITICAL FALLACIES. FUT MOD/EUR LAW INTELL LOC/G MUNIC NAT/G DELIB/GP LEGIS CREATE EDU/PROP CT/SYS ATTIT RIGID/FLEX KNOWL PWR ...RELATIV PSY SOC CONCPT SELF/OBS TREND STERTYP TOT/POP. PAGE 10 E0189
POL/PAR

B52
DILLON D.R.,LATIN AMERICA, 1935-1949; A SELECTED BIBLIOGRAPHY. LAW EDU/PROP...SOC 20. PAGE 32 E0629
BIBLIOG
L/A+17C
NAT/G
DIPLOM

B52
GELLER M.A.,ADVERTISING AT THE CROSSROADS: FEDERAL REGULATION VS. VOLUNTARY CONTROLS. USA+45 JUDGE ECO/TAC...POLICY JURID BIBLIOG 20 FTC. PAGE 43 E0843
EDU/PROP
NAT/G
CONSTN
COM/IND

B52
GELLHORN W.,THE STATES AND SUBVERSION. USA+45 USA-45 LOC/G DELIB/GP LEGIS EDU/PROP LEGIT CT/SYS REGION PEACE ATTIT ORD/FREE SOCISM...INT CON/ANAL 20 CALIFORNIA MARYLAND ILLINOIS MICHIGAN NEW/YORK. PAGE 43 E0845
PROVS
JURID

B52
JACKSON E.,MEETING OF THE MINDS: A WAY TO PEACE THROUGH MEDIATION. WOR+45 INDUS INT/ORG NAT/G DELIB/GP DIPLOM EDU/PROP LEGIT ORD/FREE...NEW/IDEA SELF/OBS TIME/SEQ CHARTS GEN/LAWS TOT/POP 20 UN TREATY. PAGE 57 E1139
LABOR
JUDGE

B52
UNESCO,THESES DE SCIENCES SOCIALES: CATALOGUE ANALYTIQUE INTERNATIONAL DE THESES INEDITES DE DOCTORAT, 1940-1950. INT/ORG DIPLOM EDU/PROP...GEOG INT/LAW MGT PSY SOC 20. PAGE 98 E1958
BIBLIOG
ACADEM
WRITING

B52
VANDENBOSCH A.,THE UN: BACKGROUND, ORGANIZATION, FUNCTIONS, ACTIVITIES. WOR+45 LAW CONSTN STRUCT INT/ORG CONSULT BAL/PWR EDU/PROP EXEC ALL/VALS ...POLICY CONCPT UN 20. PAGE 103 E2071
DELIB/GP
TIME/SEQ
PEACE

B53
GROSS B.M.,THE LEGISLATIVE STRUGGLE: A STUDY IN SOCIAL COMBAT. STRUCT LOC/G POL/PAR JUDGE EDU/PROP DEBATE ETIQUET ADMIN LOBBY CHOOSE GOV/REL INGP/REL HEREDITY ALL/VALS...SOC PRESIDENT. PAGE 48 E0948
LEGIS
DECISION
PERSON
LEAD

B53
PIERCE R.A.,RUSSIAN CENTRAL ASIA, 1867-1917: A SELECTED BIBLIOGRAPHY (PAMPHLET). USSR LAW CULTURE NAT/G EDU/PROP WAR...GEOG SOC 19/20. PAGE 81 E1616
BIBLIOG
COLONIAL
ADMIN
COM

B54
O'NEILL J.M.,CATHOLICS IN CONTROVERSY. USA+45 NAT/G PROVS SCHOOL SECT EDU/PROP LEGIT CT/SYS SANCTION GP/REL 20 SUPREME/CT CHURCH/STA. PAGE 78 E1569
CATHISM
CONSTN
POLICY
LAW

B54
WRIGHT Q.,PROBLEMS OF STABILITY AND PROGRESS IN INTERNATIONAL RELATIONSHIPS. FUT WOR+45 WOR-45 SOCIETY LEGIS CREATE TEC/DEV ECO/TAC EDU/PROP ADJUD WAR PEACE ORD/FREE PWR...KNO/TEST TREND GEN/LAWS 20. PAGE 108 E2155
INT/ORG
CONCPT
DIPLOM

L54
NICOLSON H.,"THE EVOLUTION OF DIPLOMATIC METHOD." CHRIST-17C EUR+WWI FRANCE FUT ITALY MEDIT-7 MOD/EUR USA+45 USA-45 LAW NAT/G CREATE EDU/PROP LEGIT PEACE ATTIT ORD/FREE RESPECT SOVEREIGN. PAGE 77 E1548
RIGID/FLEX
METH/CNCPT
DIPLOM

B55
CHENERY W.L.,FREEDOM OF THE PRESS. USA+45 USA-45 LAW NAT/G DOMIN EDU/PROP 17/20. PAGE 22 E0427
ORD/FREE
COM/IND
PRESS
CONSTN

B55
CHOWDHURI R.N.,INTERNATIONAL MANDATES AND TRUSTEESHIP SYSTEMS. WOR+45 STRUCT ECO/UNDEV INT/ORG LEGIS DOMIN EDU/PROP LEGIT ADJUD EXEC PWR ...CONCPT TIME/SEQ UN 20. PAGE 22 E0434
DELIB/GP
PLAN
SOVEREIGN

B55
COMM. STUDY ORGAN. PEACE,REPORTS. WOR-45 ECO/DEV ECO/UNDEV VOL/ASSN CONSULT FORCES PLAN TEC/DEV DOMIN EDU/PROP NUC/PWR ATTIT PWR WEALTH...JURID STERTYP FAO ILO 20 UN. PAGE 24 E0481
WOR+45
INT/ORG
ARMS/CONT

B55
FLIESS P.J.,FREEDOM OF THE PRESS IN THE GERMAN
EDU/PROP

REPUBLIC, 1918-1933. GERMANY LAW CONSTN POL/PAR
LEGIS WRITING ADMIN COERCE MURDER MARXISM...POLICY
BIBLIOG 20 WEIMAR/REP. PAGE 39 E0765

ORD/FREE
JURID
PRESS

B55

GRINDEL C.W.,CONCEPT OF FREEDOM. WOR+45 WOR-45 LAW
LABOR NAT/G SECT EDU/PROP 20. PAGE 47 E0942

ORD/FREE
DIPLOM
CONCPT
GP/REL

B55

KHADDURI M.,WAR AND PEACE IN THE LAW OF ISLAM.
CONSTN CULTURE SOCIETY STRATA NAT/G PROVS SECT
FORCES TOP/EX CREATE DOMIN EDU/PROP ADJUD COERCE
ATTIT RIGID/FLEX ALL/VALS...CONCPT TIME/SEQ TOT/POP
VAL/FREE. PAGE 61 E1209

ISLAM
JURID
PEACE
WAR

B55

KHADDURI M.,LAW IN THE MIDDLE EAST. LAW CONSTN
ACADEM FAM EDU/PROP CT/SYS SANCTION CRIME...INT/LAW
GOV/COMP ANTHOL 6/20 MID/EAST. PAGE 61 E1210

ADJUD
JURID
ISLAM

B55

MID-EUROPEAN LAW PROJECT,CHURCH AND STATE BEHIND
THE IRON CURTAIN. COM CZECHOSLVK HUNGARY POLAND
USSR CULTURE SECT EDU/PROP GOV/REL CATHISM...CHARTS
ANTHOL BIBLIOG WORSHIP 20 CHURCH/STA. PAGE 73 E1455

LAW
MARXISM
POLICY

B55

PULLEN W.R.,A CHECK LIST OF LEGISLATIVE JOURNALS
ISSUED SINCE 1937 BY THE STATES OF THE UNITED
STATES OF AMERICA (PAMPHLET). USA+45 USA-45 LAW
WRITING ADJUD ADMIN...JURID 20. PAGE 83 E1662

BIBLIOG
PROVS
EDU/PROP
LEGIS

B55

WRONG D.H.,AMERICAN AND CANADIAN VIEWPOINTS. CANADA
USA+45 CONSTN STRATA FAM SECT WORKER ECO/TAC
EDU/PROP ADJUD MARRIAGE...IDEA/COMP 20. PAGE 108
E2161

DIPLOM
ATTIT
NAT/COMP
CULTURE

B55

ZABEL O.H.,GOD AND CAESAR IN NEBRASKA: A STUDY OF
LEGAL RELATIONSHIP OF CHURCH AND STATE, 1854-1954.
TAX GIVE ADMIN CONTROL GP/REL ROLE...GP/COMP 19/20
NEBRASKA. PAGE 108 E2168

SECT
PROVS
LAW
EDU/PROP

S55

WRIGHT Q.,"THE PEACEFUL ADJUSTMENT OF INTERNATIONAL
RELATIONS: PROBLEMS AND RESEARCH APPROACHES." UNIV
INTELL EDU/PROP ADJUD ROUTINE KNOWL SKILL...INT/LAW
JURID PHIL/SCI CLASSIF 20. PAGE 108 E2156

R+D
METH/CNCPT
PEACE

S56

ESTEP R.,AN AIR POWER BIBLIOGRAPHY. USA+45 TEC/DEV
BUDGET DIPLOM EDU/PROP DETER CIVMIL/REL...DECISION
INT/LAW 20. PAGE 35 E0698

BIBLIOG/A
FORCES
WEAPON
PLAN

B56

SCHROEDER T.,METHODS OF CONSTITUTIONAL
CONSTRUCTION. LAW...METH 20. PAGE 88 E1769

ORD/FREE
CONSTN
JURID
EDU/PROP

B56

US HOUSE WAYS MEANS COMMITTEE,TRAFFIC IN, AND
CONTROL OF NARCOTICS, BARBITURATES, AND
AMPHETAMINES. CHINA/COM USA+45 SOCIETY LEGIS
ACT/RES EDU/PROP CT/SYS SANCTION PROFIT HEALTH
...HEAL PSY STAT 20. PAGE 100 E2011

BIO/SOC
CONTROL
PROB/SOLV
CRIME

B56

WEIS P.,NATIONALITY AND STATELESSNESS IN
INTERNATIONAL LAW. UK WOR+45 WOR-45 LAW CONSTN
NAT/G DIPLOM EDU/PROP LEGIT ROUTINE RIGID/FLEX
...JURID RECORD CMN/WLTH 20. PAGE 105 E2109

INT/ORG
SOVEREIGN
INT/LAW

B57

BYRNES R.F.,BIBLIOGRAPHY OF AMERICAN PUBLICATIONS
ON EAST CENTRAL EUROPE, 1945-1957 (VOL. XXII). SECT
DIPLOM EDU/PROP RACE/REL...ART/METH GEOG JURID SOC
LING 20 JEWS. PAGE 18 E0354

BIBLIOG/A
COM
MARXISM
NAT/G

B57

COSSIO C.,LA POLITICA COMO CONCIENCIA; MEDITACION
SOBRE LA ARGENTINA DE 1955. WOR+45 LEGIS EDU/PROP
PARL/PROC PARTIC ATTIT PWR CATHISM 20 ARGEN
PERON/JUAN. PAGE 26 E0517

POL/PAR
REV
TOTALISM
JURID

B57

MILLS W.,INDIVIDUAL FREEDOM AND COMMON DEFENSE
(PAMPHLET). USA+45 USSR NAT/G EDU/PROP CRIME CHOOSE
20 COLD/WAR. PAGE 73 E1463

ORD/FREE
CONSTN
INGP/REL
FORCES

PALMER N.D.,INTERNATIONAL RELATIONS. WOR+45 INT/ORG
NAT/G ECO/TAC EDU/PROP COLONIAL WAR PWR SOVEREIGN
...POLICY T 20 TREATY. PAGE 79 E1593

B57

DIPLOM
BAL/PWR
NAT/COMP

ROWAN C.T.,GO SOUTH TO SORROW. USA+45 STRUCT NAT/G
EDU/PROP LEAD COERCE ISOLAT DRIVE SUPEGO RESPECT
...PREDICT 20 NEGRO SUPREME/CT SOUTH/US CIV/RIGHTS.
PAGE 86 E1728

B57

RACE/REL
DISCRIM
ANOMIE
LAW

US COMMISSION GOVT SECURITY,RECOMMENDATIONS; AREA:
IMMIGRANT PROGRAM. USA+45 LAW WORKER DIPLOM
EDU/PROP WRITING ADMIN PEACE ATTIT...CONCPT ANTHOL
20 MIGRATION SUBVERT. PAGE 99 E1981

B57

POLICY
CONTROL
PLAN
NAT/G

FRANKFURTER F.,"THE SUPREME COURT IN THE MIRROR OF
JUSTICES" (BMR)" USA+45 INTELL INSPECT
EFFICIENCY ROLE KNOWL MORAL 18/20 SUPREME/CT.
PAGE 40 E0792

S57

EDU/PROP
ADJUD
CT/SYS
PERSON

CABLE G.W.,THE NEGRO QUESTION: A SELECTION OF
WRITINGS ON CIVIL RIGHTS IN THE SOUTH. USA+45
STRATA LOC/G POL/PAR GIVE EDU/PROP WRITING CT/SYS
SANCTION CRIME CHOOSE WORSHIP 20 NEGRO CIV/RIGHTS
CONV/LEASE SOUTH/US. PAGE 18 E0355

B58

RACE/REL
CULTURE
DISCRIM
ORD/FREE

DOUGLAS W.O.,THE RIGHT OF THE PEOPLE. USA+45
EDU/PROP CONTROL REPRESENT PRIVIL...IDEA/COMP 20.
PAGE 32 E0641

B58

ORD/FREE
CONSTN
CT/SYS
CIVMIL/REL

DUCLOUX L.,FROM BLACKMAIL TO TREASON. FRANCE PLAN
DIPLOM EDU/PROP PRESS RUMOR NAT/LISM...CRIMLGY 20.
PAGE 33 E0653

B58

COERCE
CRIME
NAT/G
PWR

GARDINER H.C.,CATHOLIC VIEWPOINT ON CENSORSHIP.
DEBATE COERCE GP/REL...JURID CONCPT 20. PAGE 42
E0835

B58

WRITING
LOBBY
CATHISM
EDU/PROP

HENKIN L.,ARMS CONTROL AND INSPECTION IN AMERICAN
LAW. LAW CONSTN INT/ORG LOC/G MUNIC NAT/G PROVS
EDU/PROP LEGIT EXEC NUC/PWR KNOWL ORD/FREE...OBS
TOT/POP CONGRESS 20. PAGE 52 E1032

B58

USA+45
JURID
ARMS/CONT

HERRMANN K.,DAS STAATSDENKEN BEI LEIBNIZ. GP/REL
ATTIT ORD/FREE...CONCPT IDEA/COMP 17 LEIBNITZ/G
CHURCH/STA. PAGE 52 E1034

B58

NAT/G
JURID
SECT
EDU/PROP

MACKENZIE W.J.M.,FREE ELECTIONS: AN ELEMENTARY
TEXTBOOK. WOR+45 NAT/G POL/PAR LEGIS TOP/EX
EDU/PROP LEGIT CT/SYS ATTIT PWR...OBS CHARTS
STERTYP T CONGRESS PARLIAMENT 20. PAGE 67 E1342

B58

EX/STRUC
CHOOSE

MARTIN L.J.,INTERNATIONAL PROPAGANDA: ITS LEGAL AND
DIPLOMATIC CONTROL. UK USA+45 USSR CONSULT DELIB/GP
DOMIN CONTROL 20. PAGE 69 E1373

B58

EDU/PROP
DIPLOM
INT/LAW
ATTIT

MUSIKER R.,GUIDE TO SOUTH AFRICAN REFERENCE BOOKS.
SOUTH/AFR SOCIETY SECT EDU/PROP PRESS RACE/REL
...JURID SOC/WK 20. PAGE 75 E1512

B58

BIBLIOG/A
SOC
GEOG

ORTIZ R.P.,ANNUARIO BIBLIOGRAFICO COLOMBIANO,
1951-1956. LAW RECEIVE EDU/PROP ADMIN...LING STAT
20 COLOMB. PAGE 79 E1582

B58

BIBLIOG
SOC

SPITZ D.,DEMOCRACY AND THE CHALLANGE OF POWER. FUT
USA+45 USA-45 LAW SOCIETY STRUCT LOC/G POL/PAR
PROVS DELIB/GP EX/STRUC LEGIS TOP/EX ACT/RES CREATE
DOMIN EDU/PROP LEGIT ADJUD ADMIN ATTIT DRIVE MORAL
ORD/FREE TOT/POP. PAGE 93 E1862

B58

NAT/G
PWR

US CONGRESS,FREEDOM OF INFORMATION AND SECRECY IN
GOVERNMENT (2 VOLS.). USA+45 DELIB/GP EX/STRUC
EDU/PROP PWR 20 CONGRESS PRESIDENT. PAGE 99 E1988

B58

CHIEF
PRIVIL
CONSTN
LAW

BEVAN W.,"JURY BEHAVIOR AS A FUNCTION OF THE PRESTIGE OF THE FOREMAN AND THE NATURE OF HIS LEADERSHIP" (BMR)" DELIB/GP DOMIN ADJUD LEAD PERS/REL ATTIT...PSY STAT INT QU CHARTS SOC/EXP 20 JURY. PAGE 11 E0221
L58
PERSON
EDU/PROP
DECISION
CT/SYS

INT. SOC. SCI. BULL.,"TECHNIQUES OF MEDIATION AND CONCILIATION." EUR+WWI USA+45 SOCIETY INDUS INT/ORG LABOR NAT/G LEGIS DIPLOM EDU/PROP CHOOSE ATTIT RIGID/FLEX...JURID CONCPT GEN/LAWS 20. PAGE 57 E1129
L58
VOL/ASSN
DELIB/GP
INT/LAW

UNESCO.,"TECHNIQUES OF MEDIATION AND CONCILIATION." EUR+WWI USA+45 WOR+45 INDUS FACE/GP EX/STRUC EDU/PROP LEGIT PEACE ORD/FREE...INT/LAW TIME/SEQ LEAGUE/NAT 20. PAGE 98 E1961
L58
INT/ORG
CONSULT
DIPLOM

STAAR R.F.,"ELECTIONS IN COMMUNIST POLAND." EUR+WWI SOCIETY INT/ORG NAT/G POL/PAR LEGIS ACT/RES ECO/TAC EDU/PROP ADJUD ADMIN ROUTINE COERCE TOTALISM ATTIT ORD/FREE PWR 20. PAGE 93 E1864
S58
COM
CHOOSE
POLAND

BRIGGS A.,CHARTIST STUDIES. UK LAW NAT/G WORKER EDU/PROP COERCE SUFF GP/REL ATTIT...ANTHOL 19. PAGE 15 E0300
B59
INDUS
STRATA
LABOR
POLICY

CHRISTMAN H.M.,THE PUBLIC PAPERS OF CHIEF JUSTICE EARL WARREN. CONSTN POL/PAR EDU/PROP SANCTION HEALTH...TREND 20 SUPREME/CT WARRN/EARL. PAGE 22 E0436
B59
LAW
CT/SYS
PERSON
ADJUD

EPSTEIN F.T.,EAST GERMANY: A SELECTED BIBLIOGRAPHY (PAMPHLET). COM GERMANY/E LAW AGRI FINAN INDUS LABOR POL/PAR EDU/PROP ADMIN AGE/Y 20. PAGE 35 E0693
B59
BIBLIOG/A
INTELL
MARXISM
NAT/G

GINSBURG M.,LAW AND OPINION IN ENGLAND. UK CULTURE KIN LABOR LEGIS EDU/PROP ADMIN CT/SYS CRIME OWN HEALTH...ANTHOL 20 ENGLSH/LAW. PAGE 44 E0868
B59
JURID
POLICY
ECO/TAC

LAPIERE R.,THE FREUDIAN ETHIC. USA+45 FAM EDU/PROP CONTROL CRIME ADJUST AGE DRIVE PERCEPT PERSON SEX ...SOC 20 FREUD/S. PAGE 63 E1254
B59
PSY
ORD/FREE
SOCIETY

MOOS M.,THE CAMPUS AND THE STATE. LAW FINAN DELIB/GP LEGIS EXEC LOBBY GP/REL PWR...POLICY BIBLIOG. PAGE 74 E1489
B59
EDU/PROP
ACADEM
PROVS
CONTROL

MORRIS C.,THE GREAT LEGAL PHILOSOPHERS: SELECTED READINGS IN JURISPRUDENCE. UNIV INTELL SOCIETY EDU/PROP MAJORITY UTOPIA PERSON KNOWL...ANTHOL. PAGE 75 E1497
B59
JURID
ADJUD
PHIL/SCI
IDEA/COMP

OKINSHEVICH L.A.,LATIN AMERICA IN SOVIET WRITINGS, 1945-1958: A BIBLIOGRAPHY. USSR LAW ECO/UNDEV LABOR DIPLOM EDU/PROP REV...GEOG SOC 20. PAGE 78 E1573
B59
BIBLIOG
WRITING
COM
L/A+17C

MCDOUGAL M.S.,"THE IDENTIFICATION AND APPRAISAL OF DIVERSE SYSTEMS OF PUBLIC ORDER (BMR)" WOR+45 NAT/G CONSULT EDU/PROP POLICY. PAGE 70 E1405
L59
INT/LAW
DIPLOM
ALL/IDEOS

DOMKE M.,"THE SETTLEMENT OF DISPUTES IN INTERNATIONAL TRADE." USA+45 LAW STRATA STRUCT JUDGE EDU/PROP PWR...METH/CNCPT 20. PAGE 32 E0634
S59
CONSULT
LEGIT
INT/TRADE

MENDELSON W.,"JUDICIAL REVIEW AND PARTY POLITICS" (BMR)" UK USA+45 USA-45 NAT/G LEGIS PROB/SOLV EDU/PROP ADJUD EFFICIENCY...POLICY NAT/COMP 19/20 AUSTRAL SUPREME/CT. PAGE 72 E1436
S59
CT/SYS
POL/PAR
BAL/PWR
JURID

PUGWASH CONFERENCE."ON BIOLOGICAL AND CHEMICAL WARFARE." WOR+45 SOCIETY PROC/MFG INT/ORG FORCES EDU/PROP ADJUD RIGID/FLEX ORD/FREE PWR...DECISION PSY NEW/IDEA MATH VAL/FREE 20. PAGE 83 E1661
S59
ACT/RES
BIO/SOC
WAR
WEAPON

COLLINS I.,"THE GOVERNMENT AND THE NEWSPAPER PRESS
C59
PRESS

IN FRANCE, 1814-1881. FRANCE LAW ADMIN CT/SYS ...CON/ANAL BIBLIOG 19. PAGE 24 E0475
ORD/FREE
NAT/G
EDU/PROP

BAKER G.E.,THE POLITICS OF REAPPORTIONMENT IN WASHINGTON STATE. LAW POL/PAR CREATE EDU/PROP PARL/PROC CHOOSE INGP/REL...CHARTS METH/COMP 20 WASHINGT/G LEAGUE/WV. PAGE 7 E0139
B60
VOL/ASSN
APPORT
PROVS
LEGIS

JENKS C.W.,HUMAN RIGHTS AND INTERNATIONAL LABOR STANDARDS. WOR+45 CONSTN LABOR VOL/ASSN DELIB/GP ACT/RES EDU/PROP MORAL RESPECT...JURID SOC TREND GEN/LAWS WORK ILO 20. PAGE 58 E1156
B60
CONCPT

JENNINGS R.,PROGRESS OF INTERNATIONAL LAW. FUT WOR+45 WOR-45 SOCIETY NAT/G VOL/ASSN DELIB/GP DIPLOM EDU/PROP LEGIT COERCE ATTIT DRIVE MORAL ORD/FREE...JURID CONCPT OBS TIME/SEQ TREND GEN/LAWS. PAGE 58 E1164
B60
INT/ORG
LAW
INT/LAW

POWELL T.,THE SCHOOL BUS LAW: A CASE STUDY IN EDUCATION, RELIGION, AND POLITICS. USA+45 LAW NEIGH SECT LEGIS EDU/PROP ADJUD CT/SYS LOBBY CATHISM WORSHIP 20 CONNECTICT CHURCH/STA. PAGE 82 E1641
B60
JURID
SCHOOL

MACKINNON F.,"THE UNIVERSITY: COMMUNITY OR UTILITY?" CLIENT CONSTN INTELL FINAN NAT/G NEIGH EDU/PROP PARTIC REPRESENT ROLE. PAGE 67 E1343
S60
ACADEM
MGT
CONTROL
SERV/IND

RHYNE C.S.,"LAW AS AN INSTRUMENT FOR PEACE." FUT WOR+45 PLAN LEGIT ROUTINE ARMS/CONT NUC/PWR ATTIT ORD/FREE...JURID METH/CNCPT TREND CON/ANAL HYPO/EXP COLD/WAR 20. PAGE 84 E1690
S60
ADJUD
EDU/PROP
INT/LAW
PEACE

MCCLEERY R.,"COMMUNICATION PATTERNS AS BASES OF SYSTEMS OF AUTHORITY AND POWER" IN THEORETICAL STUDIES IN SOCIAL ORGAN. OF PRISON-BMR. USA+45 SOCIETY STRUCT EDU/PROP ADMIN CONTROL COERCE CRIME GP/REL AUTHORIT...SOC 20. PAGE 70 E1400
C60
PERS/REL
PUB/INST
PWR
DOMIN

BURDETTE F.L.,POLITICAL SCIENCE: A SELECTED BIBLIOGRAPHY OF BOOKS IN PRINT, WITH ANNOTATIONS (PAMPHLET). LAW LOC/G NAT/G POL/PAR PROVS DIPLOM EDU/PROP ADMIN CHOOSE ATTIT 20. PAGE 17 E0330
B61
BIBLIOG/A
GOV/COMP
CONCPT
ROUTINE

HAGEN A.,STAAT UND KATHOLISCHE KIRCHE IN WURTTEMBERG IN DEN JAHREN 1848-1862 (2 VOLS.). GERMANY DELIB/GP EDU/PROP MARRIAGE CATHISM 19 CHURCH/STA. PAGE 49 E0975
B61
SECT
PROVS
GP/REL
JURID

JENKS C.W.,INTERNATIONAL IMMUNITIES. PLAN EDU/PROP ADMIN PERCEPT...OLD/LIB JURID CONCPT TREND TOT/POP. PAGE 58 E1157
B61
INT/ORG
DIPLOM

MCDOUGAL M.S.,LAW AND MINIMUM WORLD PUBLIC ORDER. WOR+45 SOCIETY NAT/G DELIB/GP EDU/PROP LEGIT ADJUD COERCE ATTIT PERSON...JURID CONCPT RECORD TREND TOT/POP 20. PAGE 70 E1406
B61
INT/ORG
ORD/FREE
INT/LAW

RIENOW R.,CONTEMPORARY INTERNATIONAL POLITICS. WOR+45 INT/ORG BAL/PWR EDU/PROP COLONIAL NEUTRAL REGION WAR PEACE...INT/LAW 20 COLD/WAR UN. PAGE 85 E1698
B61
DIPLOM
PWR
POLICY
NAT/G

SMITH J.W.,RELIGIOUS PERSPECTIVES IN AMERICAN CULTURE, VOL. 2, RELIGION IN AMERICAN LIFE. USA+45 CULTURE NAT/G EDU/PROP ADJUD LOBBY ATTIT...ART/METH ANTHOL 20 CHURCH/STA BIBLE. PAGE 92 E1845
B61
SECT
DOMIN
SOCIETY
GP/REL

KAUPER P.G.,"CHURCH AND STATE: COOPERATIVE SEPARATISM." NAT/G LEGIS OP/RES TAX EDU/PROP GP/REL TREND. PAGE 59 E1187
L61
SECT
CONSTN
LAW
POLICY

ALGER C.F.,"NON-RESOLUTION CONSEQUENCES OF THE UNITED NATIONS AND THEIR EFFECT ON INTERNATIONAL CONFLICT." WOR+45 CONSTN ECO/DEV NAT/G CONSULT DELIB/GP TOP/EX ACT/RES PLAN DIPLOM EDU/PROP ROUTINE ATTIT ALL/VALS...INT/LAW TOT/POP UN 20. PAGE 3 E0065
S61
INT/ORG
DRIVE
BAL/PWR

S61

MACHOWSKI K.,"SELECTED PROBLEMS OF NATIONAL
SOVEREIGNTY WITH REFERENCE TO THE LAW OF OUTER
SPACE." FUT WOR+45 AIR LAW INTELL SOCIETY ECO/DEV
PLAN EDU/PROP DETER DRIVE PERCEPT SOVEREIGN
...POLICY INT/LAW OBS TREND TOT/POP 20. PAGE 67
E1339
UNIV
ACT/RES
NUC/PWR
SPACE

S61

OLIVER C.T.,"THE AMERICAN LAW INSTITUTE'S DRAFT
RESTATEMENT OF THE FOREIGN RELATIONS LAW OF THE
UNITED STATES." FUT USA+45 SOCIETY CONSULT
EDU/PROP. PAGE 78 E1574
KNOWL
JURID
DIPLOM

N61

DELEGACION NACIONAL DE PRENSA,FALANGE ESPANOL
TRADICIONALISTA Y DE LAS JUNTAS OFENSIVAS
NACIONALES SINDICALISTAS. IX CONSEJO NACIONAL
(PAMPHLET). LAW VOL/ASSN TOTALISM AUTHORIT ORD/FREE
FASCISM...ANTHOL 20 FRANCO/F FALANGIST. PAGE 31
E0605
EDU/PROP
FASCIST
CONFER
POL/PAR

N61

VINER J.,THE INTELLECTUAL HISTORY OF LAISSEZ FAIRE
(PAMPHLET). WOR+45 WOR-45 LAW INTELL...POLICY LING
LOG 19/20. PAGE 104 E2077
ATTIT
EDU/PROP
LAISSEZ
ECO/TAC

B62

AMER SOCIETY POL & LEGAL PHIL,THE PUBLIC INTEREST:
NOMOS V. LAW EDU/PROP...SOC METH/CNCPT ANTHOL.
PAGE 4 E0073
CONCPT
ATTIT
PWR
GEN/LAWS

B62

BARLOW R.B.,CITIZENSHIP AND CONSCIENCE: STUDIES IN
THEORY AND PRACTICE OF RELIGIOUS TOLERATION IN
ENGLAND DURING EIGHTEENTH CENTURY. UK LAW VOL/ASSN
EDU/PROP SANCTION REV GP/REL MAJORITY ATTIT
ORD/FREE...BIBLIOG WORSHIP 18. PAGE 8 E0150
SECT
LEGIS
DISCRIM

B62

BOCK E.A.,CASE STUDIES IN AMERICAN GOVERNMENT.
USA+45 ECO/DEV CHIEF EDU/PROP CT/SYS RACE/REL
ORD/FREE...JURID MGT PHIL/SCI PRESIDENT CASEBOOK.
PAGE 13 E0256
POLICY
LEGIS
IDEA/COMP
NAT/G

B62

EVAN W.M.,LAW AND SOCIOLOGY: EXPLORATORY ESSAYS.
CONSULT ACT/RES OP/RES PROB/SOLV EDU/PROP LEGIT
ADJUD CT/SYS GP/REL...PHIL/SCI ANTHOL SOC/INTEG 20.
PAGE 35 E0703
JURID
SOC
PROF/ORG

B62

GRZYBOWSKI K.,SOVIET LEGAL INSTITUTIONS. USA+45
USSR ECO/DEV NAT/G EDU/PROP CONTROL CT/SYS CRIME
OWN ATTIT PWR SOCISM...NAT/COMP 20. PAGE 48 E0955
ADJUD
LAW
JURID

B62

HADWEN J.G.,HOW UNITED NATIONS DECISIONS ARE MADE.
WOR+45 LAW EDU/PROP LEGIT ADMIN PWR...DECISION
SELF/OBS GEN/LAWS UN 20. PAGE 49 E0972
INT/ORG
ROUTINE

B62

INTERNAT CONGRESS OF JURISTS,EXECUTIVE ACTION AND
THE RULE OF RULE: REPORTION PROCEEDINGS OF INT'T
CONGRESS OF JURISTS,-RIO DE JANEIRO, BRAZIL. WOR+45
ACADEM CONSULT JUDGE EDU/PROP ADJUD CT/SYS INGP/REL
PERSON DEPT/DEFEN. PAGE 57 E1130
JURID
EXEC
ORD/FREE
CONTROL

B62

KAUPER P.G.,CIVIL LIBERTIES AND THE CONSTITUTION.
USA+45 SECT LAW EDU/PROP WRITING ADJUD SEX ORD/FREE 20
SUPREME/CT CIVIL/LIB CHURCH/STA. PAGE 60 E1188
LAW
CONSTN
CT/SYS
DECISION

B62

LAWSON R.,INTERNATIONAL REGIONAL ORGANIZATIONS.
WOR+45 NAT/G VOL/ASSN CONSULT LEGIS EDU/PROP LEGIT
ADMIN EXEC ROUTINE HEALTH PWR WEALTH...JURID EEC
COLD/WAR 20 UN. PAGE 63 E1270
INT/ORG
DELIB/GP
REGION

B62

MCGRATH J.J.,CHURCH AND STATE IN AMERICAN LAW:
CASES AND MATERIALS. USA+45 USA-45 LEGIS EDU/PROP
ADJUD CT/SYS PWR...ANTHOL 18/20 CHURCH/STA. PAGE 71
E1415
LAW
GOV/REL
SECT

B62

MITCHELL G.E.,THE ANGRY BLACK SOUTH. USA+45 LAW
CONSTN SCHOOL DELIB/GP EDU/PROP CONTROL SUFF ANOMIE
DRIVE...ANTHOL 20 NEGRO CIV/RIGHTS SOUTH/US.
PAGE 74 E1473
RACE/REL
DISCRIM
ADJUST
ORD/FREE

B62

ROSENNE S.,THE WORLD COURT: WHAT IT IS AND HOW IT
WORKS. WOR+45 WOR-45 LAW CONSTN JUDGE EDU/PROP
LEGIT ROUTINE CHOOSE PEACE ORD/FREE...JURID OBS
TIME/SEQ CHARTS UN TOT/POP VAL/FREE 20. PAGE 86
E1717
INT/ORG
ADJUD
INT/LAW

B62

US COMMISSION ON CIVIL RIGHTS,EQUAL PROTECTION OF
THE LAWS IN NORTH CAROLINA. USA+45 LOC/G NAT/G
CONSULT LEGIS WORKER PROB/SOLV EDU/PROP ADJUD
CHOOSE DISCRIM HEALTH 20 NEGRO NORTH/CAR
CIV/RIGHTS. PAGE 99 E1984
ORD/FREE
RESPECT
LAW
PROVS

B62

US COMMISSION ON CIVIL RIGHTS,HEARINGS BEFORE
UNITED STATES COMMISSION ON CIVIL RIGHTS. USA+45
ECO/DEV NAT/G CONSULT WORKER EDU/PROP ADJUD DISCRIM
ISOLAT HABITAT HEALTH RESPECT 20 NEGRO CIV/RIGHTS.
PAGE 99 E1985
ORD/FREE
LAW
ADMIN
LEGIS

L62

GROSS L.,"IMMUNITIES AND PRIVILEGES OF DELIGATIONS
TO THE UNITED NATIONS." USA+45 WOR+45 STRATA NAT/G
VOL/ASSN CONSULT DIPLOM EDU/PROP ROUTINE RESPECT
...POLICY INT/LAW CONCPT UN 20. PAGE 48 E0950
INT/ORG
LAW
ELITES

S62

BIERZANECK R.,"LA NON-RECONNAISSANCE ET LE DROIT
INTERNATIONAL CONTEMPORAIN." EUR+WWI FUT WOR+45 LAW
ECO/DEV ATTIT RIGID/FLEX...CONCPT TIME/SEQ TOT/POP
20. PAGE 12 E0228
EDU/PROP
JURID
DIPLOM
INT/LAW

S62

FINKELSTEIN L.S.,"THE UNITED NATIONS AND
ORGANIZATIONS FOR CONTROL OF ARMAMENT." FUT WOR+45
VOL/ASSN DELIB/GP TCP/EX CREATE EDU/PROP LEGIT
ADJUD NUC/PWR ATTIT RIGID/FLEX ORD/FREE...POLICY
DECISION CONCPT OBS TREND GEN/LAWS TOT/POP
COLD/WAR. PAGE 38 E0752
INT/ORG
PWR
ARMS/CONT

S62

JOHNSON O.H.,"THE ENGLISH TRADITION IN
INTERNATIONAL LAW." CHRIST-17C MOD/EUR EDU/PROP
LEGIT CT/SYS ORD/FREE...JURID CONCPT TIME/SEQ.
PAGE 59 E1170
LAW
INT/LAW
UK

C62

BACON F.,"OF THE TRUE GREATNESS OF KINGDOMS AND
ESTATES" (1612) IN F. BACON, ESSAYS." ELITES FORCES
DOMIN EDU/PROP LEGIT...POLICY GEN/LAWS 16/17
TREATY. PAGE 7 E0129
WAR
PWR
DIPLOM
CONSTN

B63

BOWETT D.W.,THE LAW OF INTERNATIONAL INSTITUTIONS.
WOR+45 WOR-45 CONSTN DELIB/GP EX/STRUC JUDGE
EDU/PROP LEGIT CT/SYS EXEC ROUTINE RIGID/FLEX
ORD/FREE PWR...JURID CONCPT ORG/CHARTS GEN/METH
LEAGUE/NAT OAS OEEC 20 UN. PAGE 14 E0277
INT/ORG
ADJUD
DIPLOM

B63

CARTER G.M.,FIVE AFRICAN STATES: RESPONSES TO
DIVERSITY. CONSTN CULTURE STRATA LEGIS PLAN ECO/TAC
DOMIN EDU/PROP CT/SYS EXEC CHOOSE ATTIT HEALTH
ORD/FREE PWR...TIME/SEQ TOT/POP VAL/FREE. PAGE 20
E0398
AFR
SOCIETY

B63

CHOJNACKI S.,REGISTER ON CURRENT RESEARCH ON
ETHIOPIA AND THE HORN OF AFRICA. ETHIOPIA LAW
CULTURE AGRI SECT EDU/PROP ADMIN...GEOG HEAL LING
20. PAGE 22 E0433
BIBLIOG
ACT/RES
INTELL
ACADEM

B63

CRAIG A.,SUPPRESSED BOOKS: A HISTORY OF THE
CONCEPTION OF LITERARY OBSCENITY. WOR+45 WOR-45
CREATE EDU/PROP LITERACY ATTIT...ART/METH PSY
CONCPT 20. PAGE 27 E0538
BIBLIOG/A
LAW
SEX
CONTROL

B63

DAY R.E.,CIVIL RIGHTS USA: PUBLIC SCHOOLS, SOUTHERN
STATES - NORTH CAROLINA, 1963. USA+45 LOC/G NEIGH
LEGIS CREATE CT/SYS COERCE DISCRIM ATTIT...QU
CHARTS 20 NORTH/CAR NEGRO KKK CIV/RIGHTS. PAGE 29
E0579
EDU/PROP
ORD/FREE
RACE/REL
SANCTION

B63

FALK R.A.,LAW, MORALITY, AND WAR IN THE
CONTEMPORARY WORLD. WOR+45 LAW INT/ORG EX/STRUC
FORCES EDU/PROP LEGIT DETER NUC/PWR MORAL ORD/FREE
...JURID TOT/POP 20. PAGE 36 E0715
ADJUD
ARMS/CONT
PEACE
INT/LAW

B63

GEERTZ C.,OLD SOCIETIES AND NEW STATES: THE QUEST
FOR MODERNITY IN ASIA AND AFRICA. AFR ASIA LAW
CULTURE SECT EDU/PROP REV...GOV/COMP NAT/COMP 20.
ECO/UNDEV
TEC/DEV
NAT/LISM

PAGE 42 E0842   SOVEREIGN

B63
GRANT D.R.,STATE AND LOCAL GOVERNMENT IN AMERICA.   PROVS
USA+45 FINAN LOC/G MUNIC EX/STRUC FORCES EDU/PROP   POL/PAR
ADMIN CHOOSE FEDERAL ATTIT...JURID 20. PAGE 45   LEGIS
E0897   CONSTN

B63
LEGISLATIVE REFERENCE SERVICE,DIGEST OF PUBLIC   BIBLIOG/A
GENERAL BILLS AND RESOLUTIONS. LAW COM/IND EDU/PROP   LEGIS
GOV/REL INGP/REL KNOWL...JURID 20 CONGRESS. PAGE 64   DELIB/GP
E1280   NAT/G

B63
MURPHY T.J.,CENSORSHIP: GOVERNMENT AND OBSCENITY.   ORD/FREE
USA+45 CULTURE LEGIS JUDGE EDU/PROP CONTROL   MORAL
INGP/REL RATIONAL POPULISM...CATH JURID 20. PAGE 75 LAW
E1507   CONSEN

B63
RAVENS J.P.,STAAT UND KATHOLISCHE KIRCHE IN   GP/REL
PREUSSENS POLNISCHEN TEILUNGSGEBIETEN. GERMANY   CATHISM
POLAND PRUSSIA PROVS DIPLOM EDU/PROP DEBATE   SECT
NAT/LISM...JURID 18 CHURCH/STA. PAGE 83 E1674   NAT/G

B63
STREET H.,FREEDOM: THE INDIVIDUAL AND THE LAW. UK   ORD/FREE
COM/IND EDU/PROP PRESS RUMOR TV PWR 20 CIVIL/LIB   NAT/G
FILM. PAGE 94 E1886   JURID
                                                         PARL/PROC

B63
US SENATE COMM ON JUDICIARY,PACIFICA FOUNDATION.   DELIB/GP
USA+45 LAW COM/IND 20 ODEGARD/P BINNS/JJ SCHINDLR/P   EDU/PROP
HEALEY/D THOMAS/TK. PAGE 102 E2051   ORD/FREE
                                                         ATTIT

L63
ROSE R.,"COMPARATIVE STUDIES IN POLITICAL FINANCE: FINAN
A SYMPOSIUM." ASIA EUR+WWI S/ASIA LAW CULTURE   POL/PAR
DELIB/GP LEGIS ACT/RES ECO/TAC EDU/PROP CHOOSE
ATTIT RIGID/FLEX SUPEGO PWR SKILL WEALTH...STAT
ANTHOL VAL/FREE. PAGE 85 E1714

S63
BECHHOEFER B.G.,"UNITED NATIONS PROCEDURES IN CASE   INT/ORG
OF VIOLATIONS OF DISARMAMENT AGREEMENTS." COM   DELIB/GP
USA+45 USSR LAW CONSTN NAT/G EX/STRUC FORCES LEGIS
BAL/PWR EDU/PROP CT/SYS ARMS/CONT ORD/FREE PWR
...POLICY STERTYP UN VAL/FREE 20. PAGE 9 E0169

N63
US PRES COMN REGIS AND VOTING,REPORT ON   CHOOSE
REGISTRATION AND VOTING (PAMPHLET). USA+45 POL/PAR   LAW
CHIEF EDU/PROP PARTIC REPRESENT ATTIT...PSY CHARTS   SUFF
20. PAGE 101 E2023   INSPECT

B64
DUBOIS J.,DANGER OVER PANAMA. FUT PANAMA SCHOOL   DIPLOM
PROB/SOLV EDU/PROP MARXISM...POLICY 19/20 TREATY   COERCE
INTERVENT CANAL/ZONE. PAGE 33 E0652

B64
FALK R.A.,THE ROLE OF DOMESTIC COURTS IN THE   LAW
INTERNATIONAL LEGAL ORDER. FUT WOR+45 INT/ORG NAT/G   INT/LAW
JUDGE EDU/PROP LEGIT CT/SYS...POLICY RELATIV JURID
CONCPT GEN/LAWS 20. PAGE 36 E0716

B64
FEINE H.E.,DIE BESETZUNG DER REICHSBISTUMER VOM   CHOOSE
WESTFALISCHEN FRIEDEN BIS ZUR SAKULARISATION.   SECT
GERMANY EDU/PROP GP/REL AGE 17/19. PAGE 37 E0727   JURID
                                                       PROVS

B64
FREISEN J.,STAAT UND KATHOLISCHE KIRCHE IN DEN   SECT
DEUTSCHEN BUNDESSTAATEN (2 VOLS.). GERMANY LAW FAM   CATHISM
NAT/G EDU/PROP GP/REL MARRIAGE WEALTH 19/20   JURID
CHURCH/STA. PAGE 40 E0793   PROVS

B64
GARDNER L.C.,ECONOMIC ASPECTS OF NEW DEAL   ECO/TAC
DIPLOMACY. USA-45 WOR+45 LAW ECO/DEV INT/ORG NAT/G   DIPLOM
VOL/ASSN LEGIS TOP/EX EDU/PROP ORD/FREE PWR WEALTH
...POLICY TIME/SEQ VAL/FREE 20 ROOSEVLT/F. PAGE 42
E0836

B64
GIANNELLA D.A.,RELIGION AND THE PUBLIC ORDER: AN   SECT
ANNUAL REVIEW OF CHURCH AND STATE, AND OF RELIGION,   NAT/G
LAW, AND SOCIETY. USA+45 LAW SOCIETY FAM POL/PAR   CONSTN
SCHOOL GIVE EDU/PROP GP/REL...JURID GEN/LAWS   ORD/FREE
BIBLIOG/A 20 CHURCH/STA BIRTH/CON CONSCN/OBJ
NATURL/LAW. PAGE 43 E0855

B64
GRIFFITH W.E.,THE SINO-SOVIET RIFT. ASIA CHINA/COM   ATTIT
COM CUBA USSR YUGOSLAVIA NAT/G POL/PAR VOL/ASSN   TIME/SEQ
DELIB/GP FORCES TOP/EX DIPLOM EDU/PROP DRIVE PERSON   BAL/PWR
PWR...TREND 20 TREATY. PAGE 47 E0941   SOCISM

B64
IKLE F.C.,HOW NATIONS NEGOTIATE. COM EUR+WWI USA+45   NAT/G
INTELL INT/ORG VOL/ASSN DELIB/GP ACT/RES CREATE   PWR
DOMIN EDU/PROP ADJUD ROUTINE ATTIT PERSON ORD/FREE   POLICY
RESPECT SKILL...PSY SOC OBS VAL/FREE. PAGE 56 E1122

B64
JACKSON R.M.,THE MACHINERY OF JUSTICE IN ENGLAND.   CT/SYS
UK EDU/PROP CONTROL COST ORD/FREE...MGT 20   ADJUD
ENGLSH/LAW. PAGE 57 E1142   JUDGE
                                                        JURID

B64
OSSENBECK F.J.,OPEN SPACE AND PEACE. CHINA/COM FUT   SPACE
USA+45 USSR LAW PROB/SOLV TEC/DEV EDU/PROP NEUTRAL   ORD/FREE
PEACE...AUD/VIS ANTHOL 20. PAGE 79 E1583   DIPLOM
                                                        CREATE

B64
SCHMEISER D.A.,CIVIL LIBERTIES IN CANADA. CANADA   ORD/FREE
LAW SECT PRESS RACE/REL NAT/LISM PRIVIL 20   CONSTN
COMMONWLTH PARLIAMENT CIVIL/LIB CHURCH/STA. PAGE 88   ADJUD
E1758   EDU/PROP

B64
TENBROCK J.,EQUAL UNDER LAW. USA-45 CONSTN POL/PAR   LEGIS
EDU/PROP PARL/PROC ORD/FREE...BIBLIOG 19 AMEND/XIV.   LAW
PAGE 95 E1914   DISCRIM
                                                        DOMIN

B64
THANT U.,TOWARD WORLD PEACE. DELIB/GP TEC/DEV   DIPLOM
EDU/PROP WAR SOVEREIGN...INT/LAW 20 UN MID/EAST.   BIOG
PAGE 96 E1915   PEACE
                                                        COERCE

B64
UN PUB. INFORM. ORGAN.,EVERY MAN'S UNITED NATIONS.   INT/ORG
UNIV WOR+45 CONSTN CULTURE SOCIETY ECO/DEV   ROUTINE
ECO/UNDEV NAT/G ACT/RES PLAN ECO/TAC INT/TRADE
EDU/PROP LEGIT PEACE ATTIT ALL/VALS...POLICY HUM
INT/LAW CONCPT CHARTS UN TOT/POP 20. PAGE 97 E1954

B64
WAY H.F. JR.,LIBERTY IN THE BALANCE - CURRENT   ORD/FREE
ISSUES IN CIVIL LIBERTIES. USA+45 USA-45 DELIB/GP   EDU/PROP
RACE/REL DISCRIM TOTALISM MARXISM SOCISM...CONCPT   NAT/G
20 CONGRESS SUPREME/CT CIVIL/LIB. PAGE 105 E2104   JURID

B64
WRIGHT G.,RURAL REVOLUTION IN FRANCE: THE PEASANTRY   PWR
IN THE TWENTIETH CENTURY. EUR+WWI MOD/EUR LAW   STRATA
CULTURE AGRI POL/PAR DELIB/GP LEGIS ECO/TAC   FRANCE
EDU/PROP COERCE CHOOSE ATTIT RIGID/FLEX HEALTH   REV
...STAT CENSUS CHARTS VAL/FREE 20. PAGE 107 E2148

L64
POUNDS N.J.G.,"THE POLITICS OF PARTITION." AFR ASIA   NAT/G
COM EUR+WWI FUT ISLAM S/ASIA USA-45 LAW ECO/DEV   NAT/LISM
ECO/UNDEV AGRI INDUS INT/ORG POL/PAR PROVS SECT
FORCES TOP/EX EDU/PROP LEGIT ATTIT MORAL ORD/FREE
PWR RESPECT WEALTH. PAGE 82 E1640

L64
WORLD PEACE FOUNDATION,"INTERNATIONAL   INT/ORG
ORGANIZATIONS: SUMMARY OF ACTIVITIES." INDIA   ROUTINE
PAKISTAN TURKEY WOR+45 CONSTN CONSULT EX/STRUC
ECO/TAC EDU/PROP LEGIT ORD/FREE...JURID SOC UN 20
CYPRESS. PAGE 107 E2145

S64
BALDWIN G.B.,"THE DEPENDENCE OF SCIENCE ON LAW AND   NAT/G
GOVERNMENT--THE INTERNATIONAL GEOPHYSICAL YEAR--A   KNOWL
CASE STUDY." WOR+45 LAW INT/ORG PROF/ORG LEGIS PLAN
EDU/PROP...TIME/SEQ VAL/FREE 20. PAGE 8 E0144

S64
CARNEGIE ENDOWMENT INT. PEACE,"HUMAN RIGHTS (ISSUES   INT/ORG
BEFORE THE NINETEENTH GENERAL ASSEMBLY)." AFR   PERSON
WOR+45 LAW CONSTN NAT/G EDU/PROP GP/REL DISCRIM   RACE/REL
PEACE ATTIT MORAL ORD/FREE...INT/LAW PSY CONCPT
RECORD UN 20. PAGE 20 E0385

S64
GARDNER R.N.,"THE SOVIET UNION AND THE UNITED   COM
NATIONS." WOR+45 FINAN POL/PAR VOL/ASSN FORCES   INT/ORG
ECO/TAC DOMIN EDU/PROP LEGIT ADJUD ADMIN ARMS/CONT   USSR
COERCE ATTIT ALL/VALS...POLICY MAJORIT CONCPT OBS
TIME/SEQ TREND STERTYP UN. PAGE 42 E0838

S64

GREENBERG S.,"JUDAISM AND WORLD JUSTICE." MEDIT-7 SECT
WOR+45 LAW CULTURE SOCIETY INT/ORG NAT/G FORCES JURID
EDU/PROP ATTIT DRIVE PERSON SUPEGO ALL/VALS PEACE
...POLICY PSY CONCPT GEN/LAWS JEWS. PAGE 46 E0908

S64

KHAN M.Z.,"ISLAM AND INTERNATIONAL RELATIONS." FUT ISLAM
WOR+45 LAW CULTURE SOCIETY NAT/G SECT DELIB/GP INT/ORG
FORCES EDU/PROP ATTIT PERSON SUPEGO ALL/VALS DIPLOM
...POLICY PSY CONCPT MYTH HIST/WRIT GEN/LAWS.
PAGE 61 E1211

S64

SCHWELB E.,"OPERATION OF THE EUROPEAN CONVENTION ON INT/ORG
HUMAN RIGHTS." EUR+WWI LAW SOCIETY CREATE EDU/PROP MORAL
ADJUD ADMIN PEACE ATTIT ORD/FREE PWR...POLICY
INT/LAW CONCPT OBS GEN/LAWS UN VAL/FREE ILO 20
ECHR. PAGE 89 E1791

S64

SINGH N.,"THE CONTEMPORARY PRACTICE OF INDIA IN THE LAW
FIELD OF INTERNATIONAL LAW." INDIA S/ASIA INT/ORG ATTIT
NAT/G DOMIN EDU/PROP LEGIT KNOWL...CONCPT TOT/POP DIPLOM
20. PAGE 91 E1833 INT/LAW

B65

AMERICAN ASSEMBLY COLUMBIA U,THE COURTS, THE CT/SYS
PUBLIC, AND THE LAW EXPLOSION. USA+45 ELITES PROVS ADJUD
EDU/PROP CRIME CHOOSE PERSON ORD/FREE PWR 20. NAT/G
PAGE 4 E0074

B65

BAR ASSOCIATION OF ST LOUIS,CONSTITUTIONAL FREEDOM ORD/FREE
AND THE LAW. USA+45 LAW LABOR LEGIS EDU/PROP CONSTN
...JURID CONCPT SUPREME/CT CIVIL/LIB CIV/RIGHTS. RACE/REL
PAGE 8 E0146 NAT/G

B65

BEGGS D.W.,AMERICA'S SCHOOLS AND CHURCHES: PARTNERS SECT
IN CONFLICT. USA+45 PROVS EDU/PROP ADJUD DISCRIM GP/REL
ATTIT...IDEA/COMP ANTHOL BIBLIOG WORSHIP 20 SCHOOL
CHURCH/STA. PAGE 9 E0179 NAT/G

B65

CHARLTON K.,EDUCATION IN RENAISSANCE ENGLAND. ITALY EDU/PROP
UK USA-45 WOR+45 LAW LOC/G NAT/G...IDEA/COMP 14/17 SCHOOL
HUMANISM. PAGE 21 E0423 ACADEM

B65

CHARNAY J.P.,LE SUFFRAGE POLITIQUE EN FRANCE: CHOOSE
ELECTIONS PARLEMENTAIRES, ELECTION PRESIDENTIELLE, SUFF
REFERENDUMS. FRANCE CONSTN CHIEF DELIB/GP ECO/TAC NAT/G
EDU/PROP CRIME INGP/REL MORAL ORD/FREE PWR CATHISM LEGIS
20 PARLIAMENT PRESIDENT. PAGE 22 E0425

B65

FISCHER F.C.,THE GOVERNMENT OF MICHIGAN. USA+45 PROVS
NAT/G PUB/INST EX/STRUC LEGIS BUDGET GIVE EDU/PROP LOC/G
CT/SYS CHOOSE GOV/REL...T MICHIGAN. PAGE 38 E0753 ADMIN
CONSTN

B65

GINSBERG M.,ON JUSTICE IN SOCIETY. LAW EDU/PROP ADJUD
LEGIT CT/SYS INGP/REL PRIVIL RATIONAL ATTIT MORAL ROLE
ORD/FREE...JURID 20. PAGE 44 E0867 CONCPT

B65

HOWE M.D.W.,THE GARDEN AND THE WILDERNESS. USA+45 CONSTN
LAW GIVE EDU/PROP LEGIT NAT/LISM ORD/FREE...POLICY SECT
JURID SUPREME/CT CHURCH/STA. PAGE 55 E1103 NAT/G
GP/REL

B65

HOWE R.,THE STORY OF SCOTLAND YARD: A HISTORY OF CRIMLGY
THE CID FROM THE EARLIEST TIMES TO THE PRESENT DAY. CRIME
UK MUNIC EDU/PROP 6/20 SCOT/YARD. PAGE 55 E1104 FORCES
ADMIN

B65

KING D.B.,LEGAL ASPECTS OF THE CIVIL RIGHTS LAW
MOVEMENT. SERV/IND VOL/ASSN LEGIS EDU/PROP ADJUD DISCRIM
PARTIC CHOOSE...JURID SEGREGAT WORK. PAGE 61 E1215 TREND

B65

LAFAVE W.R.,LAW AND SOVIET SOCIETY. EX/STRUC DIPLOM JURID
DOMIN EDU/PROP PRESS ADMIN CRIME OWN MARXISM 20 CT/SYS
KHRUSH/N. PAGE 62 E1244 ADJUD
GOV/REL

B65

UNESCO,HANDBOOK OF INTERNATIONAL EXCHANGES. COM/IND INDEX
R+D ACADEM PROF/ORG VOL/ASSN CREATE TEC/DEV INT/ORG
EDU/PROP AGREE 20 TREATY. PAGE 98 E1963 DIPLOM
PRESS

B65

US SENATE COMM ON JUDICIARY,HEARINGS BEFORE ROUTINE
SUBCOMMITTEE ON ADMINISTRATIVE PRACTICE AND DELIB/GP
PROCEDURE ABOUT ADMINISTRATIVE PROCEDURE ACT 1965. ADMIN
USA+45 LEGIS EDU/PROP ADJUD GOV/REL INGP/REL NAT/G
EFFICIENCY...POLICY INT 20 CONGRESS. PAGE 103 E2055

S65

KHOURI F.J.,"THE JORDON RIVER CONTROVERSY." LAW ISLAM
SOCIETY ECO/UNDEV AGRI FINAN INDUS SECT FORCES INT/ORG
ACT/RES PLAN TEC/DEV ECO/TAC EDU/PROP COERCE ATTIT ISRAEL
DRIVE PERCEPT RIGID/FLEX ALL/VALS...GEOG SOC MYTH JORDAN
WORK. PAGE 61 E1212

B66

AMERICAN JEWISH COMMITTEE,THE TYRANNY OF POVERTY BIBLIOG/A
(PAMPHLET). USA+45 LAW ECO/DEV LOC/G MUNIC NAT/G WEALTH
PUB/INST WORKER EDU/PROP CRIME...SOC/WK 20. PAGE 4 WELF/ST
E0080 PROB/SOLV

B66

BAHRO H.,DAS KINDSCHAFTSRECHT IN DER UNION DER JURID
SOZIALISTITSCHEN SOWJETREPUBLIKEN. USSR SECT AGE/C
EDU/PROP CONTROL PWR...SOC/WK 20. PAGE 7 E0133 PERS/REL
SUPEGO

B66

CAHN E.,CONFRONTING INJUSTICE. USA+45 PROB/SOLV TAX ORD/FREE
EDU/PROP PRESS CT/SYS GP/REL DISCRIM BIO/SOC CONSTN
...IDEA/COMP BIBLIOG WORSHIP 20 BILL/RIGHT. PAGE 18 ADJUD
E0362

B66

CARMEN I.H.,MOVIES, CENSORSHIP, AND THE LAW. LOC/G EDU/PROP
NAT/G ATTIT ORD/FREE...DECISION INT IDEA/COMP LAW
BIBLIOG 20 SUPREME/CT FILM. PAGE 19 E0383 ART/METH
CONSTN

B66

DIZARD W.P.,TELEVISION* A WORLD VIEW. WOR+45 COM/IND
ECO/UNDEV TEC/DEV LICENSE LITERACY...STAT OBS INT ACT/RES
QU TREND AUD/VIS BIBLIOG. PAGE 32 E0632 EDU/PROP
CREATE

B66

FELSHER H.,JUSTICE USA? USA+45 COM/IND JUDGE CT/SYS ADJUD
MORAL ORD/FREE...SAMP/SIZ HYPO/EXP. PAGE 37 E0735 EDU/PROP
LOBBY

B66

FINK M.,A SELECTIVE BIBLIOGRAPHY ON STATE BIBLIOG
CONSTITUTIONAL REVISION (PAMPHLET). USA+45 FINAN PROVS
EX/STRUC LEGIS EDU/PROP ADMIN CT/SYS APPORT CHOOSE LOC/G
GOV/REL 20. PAGE 38 E0751 CONSTN

B66

FISCHER H.,EINER IM VORDERGRUND: TARAS FASCISM
BORODAJKEWYCZ. AUSTRIA POL/PAR PROF/ORG EDU/PROP LAW
CT/SYS ORD/FREE 20 NAZI. PAGE 38 E0754 ATTIT
PRESS

B66

GILLMOR D.M.,FREE PRESS AND FAIR TRIAL. UK USA+45 ORD/FREE
CONSTN PROB/SOLV PRESS CONTROL CRIME DISCRIM ADJUD
RESPECT...AUD/VIS 20 CIVIL/LIB. PAGE 44 E0865 ATTIT
EDU/PROP

B66

HOLTZMAN A.,INTEREST GROUPS AND LOBBYING. USA+45 LOBBY
CHIEF ACT/RES ADJUD LEAD PARTIC CHOOSE...POLICY 20 NAT/G
CONGRESS. PAGE 55 E1092 EDU/PROP
GP/REL

B66

LEHMANN L.,LEGAL UND OPPORTUN - POLITISCHE JUSTIZ ORD/FREE
IN DER BUNDESREPUBLIK. GERMANY/W EDU/PROP ADJUD POL/PAR
CONTROL PARL/PROC COERCE TOTALISM ATTIT 20 JURID
COM/PARTY. PAGE 64 E1281 LEGIS

B66

LOFTON J.,JUSTICE AND THE PRESS. EDU/PROP GOV/REL PRESS
MORAL 20. PAGE 66 E1320 JURID
CT/SYS
ORD/FREE

B66

MILLER E.W.,THE NEGRO IN AMERICA: A BIBLIOGRAPHY. BIBLIOG
USA+45 LAW EDU/PROP REV GOV/REL GP/REL INGP/REL DISCRIM
ADJUST HABITAT PERSON HEALTH ORD/FREE SOC/INTEG 20 RACE/REL
NEGRO. PAGE 73 E1459

B66

MOSKOW M.H.,TEACHERS AND UNIONS. SCHOOL WORKER EDU/PROP
ADJUD LOBBY ATTIT ORD/FREE 20. PAGE 75 E1501 PROF/ORG
LABOR
BARGAIN

B66

SOBEL N.R.,THE NEW CONFESSION STANDARDS, MIRANDA V. JURID
ARIZONA. USA+45 USA-45 LAW PROF/ORG EDU/PROP 20   CT/SYS
SUPREME/CT. PAGE 92 E1849   ORD/FREE
                                                    ADJUD

B66

STEVENS R.E.,REFERENCE BOOKS IN THE SOCIAL SCIENCES BIBLIOG/A
AND HUMANITIES. CULTURE PERF/ART SECT EDU/PROP   SOC
...JURID PSY SOC/WK STAT 20 MUSIC. PAGE 93 E1873   HUM
                                                    ART/METH

B66

TIEDT S.W.,THE ROLE OF THE FEDERAL GOVERNMENT IN   NAT/G
EDUCATION. FUT USA+45 USA-45 CONSTN SECT BUDGET   EDU/PROP
CT/SYS GOV/REL 18/20 SUPREME/CT. PAGE 96 E1924   GIVE
                                                    SCHOOL

B66

US DEPARTMENT OF STATE,RESEARCH ON AFRICA (EXTERNAL BIBLIOG/A
RESEARCH LIST NO 5-25). LAW CULTURE ECO/UNDEV   ASIA
POL/PAR DIPLOM EDU/PROP LEAD REGION MARXISM...GEOG S/ASIA
LING WORSHIP 20. PAGE 100 E1996   NAT/G

B66

US DEPARTMENT OF STATE,RESEARCH ON THE USSR AND   BIBLIOG/A
EASTERN EUROPE (EXTERNAL RESEARCH LIST NO 1-25).   EUR+WWI
USSR LAW CULTURE SOCIETY NAT/G TEC/DEV DIPLOM   COM
EDU/PROP REGION...GEOG LING. PAGE 100 E1997   MARXISM

B66

US DEPARTMENT OF STATE,RESEARCH ON WESTERN EUROPE, BIBLIOG/A
GREAT BRITAIN, AND CANADA (EXTERNAL RESEARCH LIST   EUR+WWI
NO 3-25). CANADA GERMANY/W UK LAW CULTURE NAT/G   DIPLOM
POL/PAR FORCES EDU/PROP REGION MARXISM...GEOG SOC
WORSHIP 20 CMN/WLTH. PAGE 100 E1998

B66

US HOUSE UNAMER ACTIV COMM,HEARINGS ON BILLS TO   LAW
MAKE PUNISHABLE ASSISTANCE TO ENEMIES OF US IN TIME SANCTION
OF UNDECLARED WAR. USA+45 VIETNAM/N EDU/PROP   VOL/ASSN
CONTROL WAR MARXISM HOUSE/REP. PAGE 100 E2010   GIVE

B66

US PRES COMN CRIME IN DC,REPORT OF THE US   CRIME
PRESIDENT'S COMMISSION ON CRIME IN THE DISTRICT OF FORCES
COLUMBIA. LEGIS WORKER EDU/PROP ADJUD CONTROL   AGE/Y
CT/SYS GP/REL BIO/SOC HEALTH...CRIMLGY NEW/IDEA   SANCTION
STAT 20. PAGE 101 E2022

B66

US SENATE COMM AERO SPACE SCI,SOVIET SPACE   CONSULT
PROGRAMS, 1962-65; GOALS AND PURPOSES,   SPACE
ACHIEVEMENTS, PLANS, AND INTERNATIONAL   FUT
IMPLICATIONS. USA+45 USSR R+D FORCES PLAN EDU/PROP DIPLOM
PRESS ADJUD ARMS/CONT ATTIT MARXISM. PAGE 101 E2028

B66

US SENATE COMM ON JUDICIARY,HEARINGS ON FREE PRESS PRESS
AND FAIR TRIAL (2 VOLS). USA+45 CONSTN ELITES   LAW
LEGIS EDU/PROP CT/SYS LEAD CONGRESS. PAGE 103 E2057 CRIME
                                                    ORD/FREE

B67

BOLES D.E.,THE TWO SWORDS. USA+45 USA-45 LAW CONSTN SCHOOL
SOCIETY FINAN PRESS CT/SYS...HEAL JURID BIBLIOG   EDU/PROP
WORSHIP 20 SUPREME/CT CHURCH/STA. PAGE 13 E0263   ADJUD

B67

BONGER W.A.,CRIMINALITY AND ECONOMIC CONDITIONS.   PERSON
MOD/EUR STRUCT INDUS WORKER EDU/PROP CRIME HABITAT CRIMLGY
ALL/VALS...JURID SOC 20 REFORMERS. PAGE 14 E0265   IDEA/COMP
                                                    ANOMIE

B67

COX A.,CIVIL RIGHTS, THE CONSTITUTION, AND THE   LAW
COURTS. CONSTN EDU/PROP CRIME DISCRIM ATTIT...JURID FEDERAL
20. PAGE 27 E0533   RACE/REL
                                                    PRESS

B67

DIEGUES M.,SOCIAL SCIENCE IN LATIN AMERICA. L/A+17C METH
...JURID SOC ANTHOL 20. PAGE 31 E0624   ACADEM
                                                    EDU/PROP
                                                    ACT/RES

B67

GRAHAM H.D.,CRISIS IN PRINT: DESEGREGATION AND THE PRESS
PRESS IN TENNESSEE. LAW SOCIETY MUNIC POL/PAR   PROVS
EDU/PROP LEAD REPRESENT DISCRIM ATTIT...IDEA/COMP   POLICY
BIBLIOG/A SOC/INTEG 20 TENNESSEE SUPREME/CT   RACE/REL
SOUTH/US. PAGE 45 E0896

B67

GREENE L.S.,AMERICAN GOVERNMENT POLICIES AND   POLICY

FUNCTIONS. USA+45 LAW AGRI DIST/IND LABOR MUNIC   NAT/G
BUDGET DIPLOM EDU/PROP ORD/FREE...BIBLIOG T 20.   ADMIN
PAGE 46 E0910   DECISION

B67

HOLSTI K.J.,INTERNATIONAL POLITICS* A FRAMEWORK FOR DIPLOM
ANALYSIS. WOR+45 WOR-45 NAT/G EDU/PROP DETER WAR   BARGAIN
WEAPON PWR BIBLIOG. PAGE 55 E1090   POLICY
                                                    INT/LAW

B67

UNIVERSAL REFERENCE SYSTEM,CURRENT EVENTS AND   BIBLIOG/A
PROBLEMS OF MODERN SOCIETY (VOLUME V). WOR+45 LOC/G SOCIETY
MUNIC NAT/G PLAN EDU/PROP CRIME RACE/REL WEALTH   PROB/SOLV
...COMPUT/IR GEN/METH. PAGE 98 E1974   ATTIT

B67

US SENATE COMM ON FOREIGN REL,USIA FOREIGN SERVICE DIPLOM
PERSONNEL SYSTEM. USA+45 LAW CONSULT ADMIN 20 USIA. EDU/PROP
PAGE 102 E2038   PRIVIL
                                                    PROF/ORG

L67

BARRON J.A.,"ACCESS TO THE PRESS." USA+45 TEC/DEV   ORD/FREE
PRESS TV ADJUD AUD/VIS. PAGE 8 E0152   COM/IND
                                                    EDU/PROP
                                                    LAW

L67

NAGEL S.S.,"DISPARITIES IN CRIMINAL PROCEDURE."   ADJUD
STRATA NAT/G PROVS EDU/PROP RACE/REL AGE HABITAT   DISCRIM
SEX...JURID CHARTS 20. PAGE 76 E1519   STRUCT
                                                    ACT/RES

S67

BLUMSTEIN A.,"POLICE TECHNOLOGY." USA+45 DELIB/GP   TEC/DEV
COMPUTER EDU/PROP CRIME COMPUT/IR. PAGE 13 E0253   FORCES
                                                    CRIMLGY
                                                    ADJUD

S67

GRIFFIN H.C.,"PREJUDICIAL PUBLICITY: SEARCH FOR A   LAW
CIVIL REMEDY." EDU/PROP CONTROL DISCRIM...JURID 20. SANCTION
PAGE 47 E0937   PRESS
                                                    ADJUD

S67

HILL D.G.,"HUMAN RIGHTS LEGISLATION IN ONTARIO."   DELIB/GP
CANADA R+D VOL/ASSN CONSULT INSPECT EDU/PROP ADJUD ORD/FREE
AGREE TASK GP/REL INGP/REL DISCRIM 20 CIV/RIGHTS   LAW
ONTARIO CIVIL/LIB. PAGE 52 E1045   POLICY

S67

HUBERT C.J.,"PLANNED UNIT DEVELOPMENT" LAW VOL/ASSN PLAN
LEGIS EDU/PROP CT/SYS GOV/REL...NEW/IDEA 20   MUNIC
PLAN/UNIT. PAGE 56 E1107   HABITAT
                                                    ADJUD

S67

KIM R.C.C.,"THE SUPREME COURT: ORALLE WITHOUT   CT/SYS
TRUTH." USA+45 EDU/PROP RACE/REL ADJUST ALL/VALS   PROB/SOLV
ORD/FREE...DECISION WORSHIP SUPREME/CT. PAGE 61   ADJUD
E1214   REPRESENT

S67

MIRONENKO Y.,"A NEW EXTENSION OF CRIMINAL LIABILITY ADJUD
IN THE USSR." COM USSR DOMIN EDU/PROP 20. PAGE 73   SANCTION
E1467   CRIME
                                                    MARXISM

S67

MONEYPENNY P.,"UNIVERSITY PURPOSE, DISCIPLINE, AND ACADEM
DUE PROCESS." USA+45 EDU/PROP ADJUD LEISURE   AGE/Y
ORD/FREE. PAGE 74 E1484   CONTROL
                                                    ADMIN

S67

PEMBERTON J., JR.,"CONSTITUTIONAL PROBLEMS IN   LAW
RESTRAINT ON THE MEDIA." CONSTN PROB/SOLV EDU/PROP PRESS
CONFER CONTROL JURID. PAGE 80 E1608   ORD/FREE

S67

READ J.S.,"CENSORED." UGANDA CONSTN INTELL SOCIETY EDU/PROP
NAT/G DIPLOM PRESS WRITING ADJUD ADMIN COLONIAL   AFR
RISK...IDEA/COMP 20. PAGE 84 E1675   CREATE

S67

SHAFFER T.L.,"DIRECT RESTRAINT ON THE PRESS."   LAW
USA+45 EDU/PROP CONTROL...JURID NEW/IDEA ABA.   PRESS
PAGE 90 E1809   ORD/FREE
                                                    ADJUD

S67

VAUGHN W.P.,"SEPARATE AND UNEQUAL: THE CIVIL RIGHTS LAW
ACT OF 1875 AND DEFEAT OF THE SCHOOL INTEGRATION   DISCRIM
CLAUSE." USA-45 LEGIS RACE/REL 19 CONGRESS.   EDU/PROP

PAGE 103 E2073   PARL/PROC

SOC/INTEG 20 TREATY EEC COMMONWLTH. PAGE 27 E0530   NAT/LISM

S68
SHAPIRO J.P.,"SOVIET HISTORIOGRAPHY AND THE MOSCOW   HIST/WRIT
TRIALS: AFTER THIRTY YEARS." USSR NAT/G LEGIT PRESS   EDU/PROP
CONTROL LEAD ATTIT MARXISM...NEW/IDEA METH 20   SANCTION
TROTSKY/L STALIN/J KHRUSH/N. PAGE 90 E1810   ADJUD

EDUCATION....SEE EDU/PROP

EDUCATIONAL INSTITUTIONS....SEE ACADEM, SCHOOL

EDWARDS C.D. E0676

EDWARDS R.R. E0432

EEC....EUROPEAN ECONOMIC COMMUNITY; SEE ALSO VOL/ASSN,
    INT/ORG

N
FOREIGN AFFAIRS. SPACE WOR+45 WOR-45 CULTURE   BIBLIOG
ECO/UNDEV FINAN NAT/G TEC/DEV INT/TRADE ARMS/CONT   DIPLOM
NUC/PWR...POLICY 20 UN EURATOM ECSC EEC. PAGE 1   INT/ORG
E0021   INT/LAW

C54
BOWIE R.R.,"STUDIES IN FEDERALISM." AGRI FINAN   FEDERAL
LABOR EX/STRUC FORCES LEGIS DIPLOM INT/TRADE ADJUD   EUR+WWI
...BIBLIOG 20 EEC. PAGE 14 E0279   INT/ORG
                                                      CONSTN

B60
STEIN E.,AMERICAN ENTERPRISE IN THE EUROPEAN COMMON   MARKET
MARKET: A LEGAL PROFILE. EUR+WWI FUT USA+45 SOCIETY   ADJUD
STRUCT ECO/DEV NAT/G VOL/ASSN CONSULT PLAN TEC/DEV   INT/LAW
ECO/TAC INT/TRADE ADMIN ATTIT RIGID/FLEX PWR...MGT
NEW/IDEA STAT TREND COMPUT/IR SIMUL EEC 20. PAGE 93
E1867

L60
STEIN E.,"LEGAL REMEDIES OF ENTERPRISES IN THE   MARKET
EUROPEAN ECONOMIC COMMUNITY." EUR+WWI FUT ECO/DEV   ADJUD
INDUS PLAN ECO/TAC ADMIN PWR...MGT MATH STAT TREND
CON/ANAL EEC 20. PAGE 93 E1868

B62
ALEXANDROWICZ C.H.,WORLD ECONOMIC AGENCIES: LAW AND   INT/LAW
PRACTICE. WOR+45 DIST/IND FINAN LABOR CONSULT   INT/ORG
INT/TRADE TARIFFS REPRESENT HEALTH...JURID 20 UN   DIPLOM
GATT EEC OAS ECSC. PAGE 3 E0063   ADJUD

B62
BEBR G.,JUDICIAL CONTROL OF THE EUROPEAN   ADJUD
COMMUNITIES. EUR+WWI INT/ORG NAT/G DOMIN LEGIT PWR   VOL/ASSN
...JURID CONCPT GEN/LAWS GEN/METH EEC 20. PAGE 9   INT/LAW
E0168

B62
GYORGY A.,PROBLEMS IN INTERNATIONAL RELATIONS. COM   DIPLOM
CT/SYS NUC/PWR ALL/IDEOS 20 UN EEC ECSC. PAGE 49   NEUTRAL
E0966   BAL/PWR
                                                      REV

B62
HENDERSON W.O.,THE GENESIS OF THE COMMON MARKET.   ECO/DEV
EUR+WWI FRANCE MOD/EUR UK SEA COM/IND EXTR/IND   INT/TRADE
COLONIAL DISCRIM...TIME/SEQ CHARTS BIBLIOG 18/20   DIPLOM
EEC TREATY. PAGE 52 E1030

B62
LAWSON R.,INTERNATIONAL REGIONAL ORGANIZATIONS.   INT/ORG
WOR+45 NAT/G VOL/ASSN CONSULT LEGIS EDU/PROP LEGIT   DELIB/GP
ADMIN EXEC ROUTINE HEALTH PWR WEALTH...JURID EEC   REGION
COLD/WAR 20 UN. PAGE 63 E1270

S62
THOMPSON D.,"THE UNITED KINGDOM AND THE TREATY OF   ADJUD
ROME." EUR+WWI INT/ORG NAT/G DELIB/GP LEGIS   JURID
INT/TRADE RIGID/FLEX...CONCPT EEC PARLIAMENT
CMN/WLTH 20. PAGE 96 E1918

B64
ECONOMIDES C.P.,LE POUVOIR DE DECISION DES   INT/ORG
ORGANISATIONS INTERNATIONALES EUROPEENNES. DIPLOM   PWR
DOMIN INGP/REL EFFICIENCY...INT/LAW JURID 20 NATO   DECISION
OEEC EEC COUNCL/EUR EURATOM. PAGE 34 E0673   GP/COMP

B65
CARTER G.M.,POLITICS IN EUROPE. EUR+WWI FRANCE   GOV/COMP
GERMANY/W UK USSR LAW CONSTN POL/PAR VOL/ASSN PRESS   OP/RES
LOBBY PWR...ANTHOL SOC/INTEG EEC. PAGE 20 E0399   ECO/DEV

B65
COWEN Z.,THE BRITISH COMMONWEALTH OF NATIONS IN A   JURID
CHANGING WORLD. UK ECO/UNDEV INT/ORG ECO/TAC   DIPLOM
INT/TRADE COLONIAL WAR GP/REL RACE/REL SOVEREIGN   PARL/PROC

B65
WEIL G.L.,A HANDBOOK ON THE EUROPEAN ECONOMIC   INT/TRADE
COMMUNITY. BELGIUM EUR+WWI FRANCE GERMANY/W ITALY   INT/ORG
CONSTN ECO/DEV CREATE PARTIC GP/REL...DECISION MGT   TEC/DEV
CHARTS 20 EEC. PAGE 105 E2107   INT/LAW

C65
SCHEINGOLD S.A.,"THE RULE OF LAW IN EUROPEAN   INT/LAW
INTEGRATION: THE PATH OF THE SCHUMAN PLAN." EUR+WWI   CT/SYS
JUDGE ADJUD FEDERAL ATTIT PWR...RECORD INT BIBLIOG   REGION
EEC ECSC. PAGE 87 E1755   CENTRAL

B66
EDWARDS C.D.,TRADE REGULATIONS OVERSEAS. IRELAND   INT/TRADE
NEW/ZEALND SOUTH/AFR NAT/G CAP/ISM TARIFFS CONTROL   DIPLOM
...POLICY JURID 20 EEC CHINJAP. PAGE 34 E0676   INT/LAW
                                                      ECO/TAC

B66
FRIEDMANN W.G.,INTERNATIONAL FINANCIAL AID. USA+45   INT/ORG
ECO/DEV ECO/UNDEV NAT/G VOL/ASSN EX/STRUC PLAN RENT   FOR/AID
GIVE BAL/PAY PWR...GEOG INT/LAW STAT TREND UN EEC   TEC/DEV
COMECON. PAGE 41 E0806   ECO/TAC

B66
HAY P.,FEDERALISM AND SUPRANATIONAL ORGANIZATIONS: SOVEREIGN
PATTERNS FOR NEW LEGAL STRUCTURES. EUR+WWI LAW   FEDERAL
NAT/G VOL/ASSN DIPLOM PWR...NAT/COMP TREATY EEC.   INT/ORG
PAGE 51 E1014   INT/LAW

B67
LAFAVE W.R.,INTERNATIONAL TRADE, INVESTMENT, AND   INT/TRADE
ORGANIZATION. INDUS PROB/SOLV TARIFFS CONTROL   INT/LAW
...TREND ANTHOL BIBLIOG 20 EEC. PAGE 62 E1245   INT/ORG

L67
WAELBROECK M.,"THE APPLICATION OF EEC LAW BY   INT/LAW
NATIONAL COURTS." EUR+WWI INT/ORG CT/SYS...JURID   NAT/G
EEC TREATY. PAGE 104 E2090   LAW
                                                      PROB/SOLV

S67
BARTLETT J.L.,"AMERICAN BOND ISSUES IN THE EUROPEAN   LAW
ECONOMIC COMMUNITY." EUR+WWI LUXEMBOURG USA+45   ECO/TAC
DIPLOM CONTROL BAL/PAY EEC. PAGE 8 E0153   FINAN
                                                      TAX

EFFECTIVENESS....SEE EFFICIENCY, PRODUC

EFFICIENCY....EFFECTIVENESS

S05
PHILLIPS J.B.,"MODIFICATIONS OF THE JURY SYSTEM."   JURID
PARTIC EFFICIENCY ATTIT PERCEPT...TREND 19   DELIB/GP
SUPREME/CT JURY. PAGE 80 E1612   PERS/REL
                                                      POLICY

N19
ARNOW K.,SELF-INSURANCE IN THE TREASURY (PAMPHLET).   ADMIN
USA+45 LAW RIGID/FLEX...POLICY METH/COMP 20   PLAN
DEPT/TREAS. PAGE 5 E0104   EFFICIENCY
                                                      NAT/G

S26
HALL A.B.,"DETERMINATION OF METHODS FOR   ADJUD
ASCERTAINING THE FACTORS THAT INFLUENCE JUDICIAL   DECISION
DECISIONS IN CASES INVOLVING DUE PROCESS" LAW JUDGE CONSTN
DEBATE EFFICIENCY OPTIMAL UTIL...SOC CONCPT   JURID
PROBABIL STAT SAMP. PAGE 49 E0981

B36
HERRING E.P.,PUBLIC ADMINISTRATION AND THE PUBLIC   GP/REL
INTEREST. LABOR NAT/G PARTIC EFFICIENCY 20. PAGE 52 DECISION
E1033   PROB/SOLV
                                                     ADMIN

B38
CLARK J.P.,THE RISE OF A NEW FEDERALISM. LEGIS   FEDERAL
TARIFFS EFFICIENCY NAT/LISM UTIL...JURID SOC   PROVS
GEN/LAWS BIBLIOG 19/20. PAGE 23 E0451   NAT/G
                                                     GOV/REL

S47
FRANKFURTER F.,"SOME REFLECTIONS ON THE READING OF   JURID
STATUTES" USA+45 USA-45 PROB/SOLV CT/SYS TASK   LAW
EFFICIENCY...LING 20. PAGE 40 E0791   ADJUD
                                                     WRITING

B52
APPLEBY P.H.,MORALITY AND ADMINISTRATION IN   REPRESENT
DEMOCRATIC GOVERNMENT. USA+45 CLIENT NAT/G EXEC   LOBBY
EFFICIENCY 20. PAGE 5 E0102   ADMIN
                                                     EX/STRUC

PASCUAL R.R.,PARTYLESS DEMOCRACY. PHILIPPINE | B52 POL/PAR
BARGAIN LOBBY CHOOSE EFFICIENCY ATTIT 20. PAGE 80 | ORD/FREE
E1600 | JURID
| ECO/UNDEV

BLOOM G.F.,ECONOMICS OF LABOR RELATIONS. USA+45 LAW | B55 ECO/DEV
CONSULT WORKER CAP/ISM PAY ADJUD CONTROL EFFICIENCY | ECO/TAC
ORD/FREE...CHARTS 19/20 AFL/CIO NLRB DEPT/LABOR. | LABOR
PAGE 13 E0249 | GOV/REL

WHEARE K.C.,GOVERNMENT BY COMMITTEE; AN ESSAY ON | B55 DELIB/GP
THE BRITISH CONSTITUTION. UK NAT/G LEGIS INSPECT | CONSTN
CONFER ADJUD ADMIN CONTROL TASK EFFICIENCY ROLE | LEAD
POPULISM 20. PAGE 106 E2116 | GP/COMP

DUNNILL F.,THE CIVIL SERVICE. UK LAW PLAN ADMIN | B56 PERSON
EFFICIENCY DRIVE NEW/LIB...STAT CHARTS 20 | WORKER
PARLIAMENT CIVIL/SERV. PAGE 33 E0662 | STRATA
| SOC/WK

US HOUSE RULES COMM,HEARINGS BEFORE A SPECIAL | B56 ADMIN
SUBCOMMITTEE: ESTABLISHMENT OF A STANDING COMMITTEE | DOMIN
ON ADMINISTRATIVE PROCEDURE, PRACTICE. USA+45 LAW | DELIB/GP
EX/STRUC ADJUD CONTROL EXEC GOV/REL EFFICIENCY PWR | NAT/G
...POLICY INT 20 CONGRESS. PAGE 100 E2009 |

FRANKFURTER F.,"THE SUPREME COURT IN THE MIRROR OF | S57 EDU/PROP
JUSTICES" (BMR)" USA-45 INTELL INSPECT | ADJUD
EFFICIENCY ROLE KNOWL MORAL 18/20 SUPREME/CT. | CT/SYS
PAGE 40 E0792 | PERSON

AMERICAN SOCIETY PUBLIC ADMIN,STRENGTHENING | B58 ADMIN
MANAGEMENT FOR DEMOCRATIC GOVERNMENT. USA+45 ACADEM | NAT/G
EX/STRUC WORKER PLAN BUDGET CONFER CT/SYS | EXEC
EFFICIENCY ANTHOL. PAGE 4 E0083 | MGT

DEVLIN P.,THE CRIMINAL PROSECUTION IN ENGLAND. UK | B58 CRIME
NAT/G ADMIN ROUTINE EFFICIENCY...JURID SOC 20. | LAW
PAGE 31 E0617 | METH
| CT/SYS

LAW COMMISSION OF INDIA,REFORM OF JUDICIAL | B58 CT/SYS
ADMINISTRATION. INDIA TOP/EX ADMIN DISCRIM | ADJUD
EFFICIENCY...METH/COMP 20. PAGE 63 E1269 | GOV/REL
| CONTROL

RIKER W.H.,"THE PARADOX OF VOTING AND CONGRESSIONAL | S58 PARL/PROC
RULES FOR VOTING ON AMENDMENTS." LAW DELIB/GP | DECISION
EX/STRUC PROB/SOLV CONFER DEBATE EFFICIENCY ATTIT | LEGIS
HOUSE/REP CONGRESS SENATE. PAGE 85 E1700 | RATIONAL

ELLIOTT S.D.,IMPROVING OUR COURTS. LAW EX/STRUC | B59 CT/SYS
PLAN PROB/SOLV ADJUD ADMIN TASK CRIME EFFICIENCY | JURID
ORD/FREE 20. PAGE 34 E0684 | GOV/REL
| NAT/G

MAYDA J.,ATOMIC ENERGY AND LAW. ECO/UNDEV FINAN | B59 NUC/PWR
TEC/DEV FOR/AID EFFICIENCY PRODUC WEALTH...POLICY | L/A+17C
TECHNIC 20. PAGE 70 E1391 | LAW
| ADMIN

SISSON C.H.,THE SPIRIT OF BRITISH ADMINISTRATION | B59 GOV/COMP
AND SOME EUROPEAN COMPARISONS. FRANCE GERMANY/W | ADMIN
SWEDEN UK LAW EX/STRUC INGP/REL EFFICIENCY ORD/FREE | ELITES
...DECISION 20. PAGE 91 E1835 | ATTIT

US SENATE COMM ON POST OFFICE,TO PROVIDE FOR AN | B59 ADMIN
EFFECTIVE SYSTEM OF PERSONNEL ADMINISTRATION. | NAT/G
EFFICIENCY...MGT 20 CONGRESS CIVIL/SERV POSTAL/SYS | EX/STRUC
YARBROGH/R. PAGE 103 E2059 | LAW

WAGNER W.J.,THE FEDERAL STATES AND THEIR JUDICIARY. | B59 ADJUD
BRAZIL CANADA SWITZERLND USA+45 CONFER CT/SYS TASK | METH/COMP
EFFICIENCY FEDERAL PWR...JURID BIBLIOG 20 AUSTRAL | PROB/SOLV
MEXIC/AMER. PAGE 104 E2091 | NAT/G

MENDELSON W.,"JUDICIAL REVIEW AND PARTY POLITICS" | S59 CT/SYS
(BMR)" UK USA+45 USA-45 NAT/G LEGIS PROB/SOLV | POL/PAR
EDU/PROP ADJUD EFFICIENCY...POLICY NAT/COMP 19/20 | BAL/PWR
AUSTRAL SUPREME/CT. PAGE 72 E1436 | JURID

PICKLES D.,THE FIFTH FRENCH REPUBLIC. ALGERIA | B60 CONSTN
FRANCE CHOOSE GOV/REL ATTIT CONSERVE...CHARTS 20 | ADJUD
DEGAULLE/C. PAGE 80 E1615 | NAT/G
| EFFICIENCY

FUCHS R.F.,"FAIRNESS AND EFFECTIVENESS IN | L60 EFFICIENCY
ADMINISTRATIVE AGENCY ORGANIZATION AND PROCEDURES." | EX/STRUC
USA+45 ADJUD ADMIN REPRESENT. PAGE 41 E0816 | EXEC
| POLICY

ALFRED H.,PUBLIC OWNERSHIP IN THE USA: GOALS AND | B61 CONTROL
PRIORITIES. LAW INDUS INT/TRADE ADJUD GOV/REL | OWN
EFFICIENCY PEACE SOCISM...POLICY ANTHOL 20 TVA. | ECO/DEV
PAGE 3 E0064 | ECO/TAC

AVERY M.W.,GOVERNMENT OF WASHINGTON STATE. USA+45 | B61 PROVS
MUNIC DELIB/GP EX/STRUC LEGIS GIVE CT/SYS PARTIC | LOC/G
REGION EFFICIENCY 20 WASHINGT/G GOVERNOR. PAGE 6 | ADMIN
E0121 | GOV/REL

LEONI B.,FREEDOM AND THE LAW. WOR+45 SOCIETY ADJUD | B61 JURID
INGP/REL EFFICIENCY ATTIT DRIVE. PAGE 64 E1286 | ORD/FREE
| LEGIS
| CONTROL

LEAGUE WOMEN VOTERS MASSACHU,THE MERIT SYSTEM IN | N61 LOC/G
MASSACHUSETTS (PAMPHLET). USA+45 PROVS LEGIT PARTIC | LAW
CHOOSE REPRESENT GOV/REL EFFICIENCY...POLICY | SENIOR
GOV/COMP BIBLIOG 20 MASSACHU. PAGE 64 E1274 | PROF/ORG

DUPRE J.S.,SCIENCE AND THE NATION: POLICY AND | B62 R+D
POLITICS. USA+45 LAW ACADEM FORCES ADMIN CIVMIL/REL | INDUS
GOV/REL EFFICIENCY PEACE...TREND 20 SCI/ADVSRY. | TEC/DEV
PAGE 34 E0665 | NUC/PWR

MCWHINNEY E.,CONSTITUTIONALISM IN GERMANY AND THE | B62 CONSTN
FEDERAL CONSTITUTINAL COURT. GERMANY/W POL/PAR TV | CT/SYS
ADJUD CHOOSE EFFICIENCY ATTIT ORD/FREE MARXISM | CONTROL
...NEW/IDEA BIBLIOG 20. PAGE 71 E1428 | NAT/G

KLEIN F.J.,JUDICIAL ADMINISTRATION AND THE LEGAL | B63 BIBLIOG/A
PROFESSION. USA+45 ADMIN CONTROL EFFICIENCY | CT/SYS
...POLICY 20. PAGE 61 E1222 | ADJUD
| JUDGE

WOLL P.,ADMINISTRATIVE LAW: THE INFORMAL PROCESS. | B63 ADMIN
USA+45 NAT/G CONTROL EFFICIENCY 20. PAGE 107 E2141 | ADJUD
| REPRESENT
| EX/STRUC

LOEVINGER L.,"JURIMETRICS* THE METHODOLOGY OF LEGAL | L63 COMPUT/IR
INQUIRY." COMPUTER CREATE PLAN TEC/DEV AUTOMAT | JURID
CT/SYS EFFICIENCY...DECISION PHIL/SCI NEW/IDEA | GEN/METH
QUANT PREDICT. PAGE 66 E1318 | ADJUD

BROOKS T.R.,TOIL AND TROUBLE, A HISTORY OF AMERICAN | B64 INDUS
LABOR. WORKER BARGAIN CAP/ISM ADJUD AUTOMAT EXEC | LABOR
GP/REL RACE/REL EFFICIENCY INCOME PROFIT MARXISM | LEGIS
17/20 KENNEDY/JF AFL/CIO NEGRO. PAGE 16 E0310 |

ECONOMIDES C.P.,LE POUVOIR DE DECISION DES | B64 INT/ORG
ORGANISATIONS INTERNATIONALES EUROPEENNES. DIPLOM | PWR
DOMIN INGP/REL EFFICIENCY...INT/LAW JURID 20 NATO | DECISION
OEEC EEC COUNCL/EUR EURATOM. PAGE 34 E0673 | GP/COMP

GOODNOW H.F.,THE CIVIL SERVICE OF PAKISTAN: | B64 ADMIN
BUREAUCRACY IN A NEW NATION. INDIA PAKISTAN S/ASIA | GOV/REL
ECO/UNDEV PROVS CHIEF PARTIC CHOOSE EFFICIENCY PWR | LAW
...BIBLIOG 20. PAGE 45 E0889 | NAT/G

HAAR C.M.,LAW AND LAND: ANGLO-AMERICAN PLANNING | B64 LAW
PRACTICE. UK USA+45 NAT/G TEC/DEV BUDGET CT/SYS | PLAN
INGP/REL EFFICIENCY OWN...JURID 20. PAGE 49 E0967 | MUNIC
| NAT/COMP

RUSSELL R.B.,UNITED NATIONS EXPERIENCE WITH | B64 FORCES
MILITARY FORCES: POLITICAL AND LEGAL ASPECTS. AFR | DIPLOM
KOREA WOR+45 LEGIS PROB/SOLV ADMIN CONTROL | SANCTION
EFFICIENCY PEACE...POLICY INT/LAW BIBLIOG UN. | ORD/FREE

US SENATE COMM ON JUDICIARY,HEARINGS BEFORE
SUBCOMMITTEE ON ANTITRUST AND MONOPOLY: ECONOMIC
CONCENTRATION VOLUMES 1-5 JULY 1964-SEPT 1966.
USA+45 LAW FINAN ECO/TAC ADJUD COST EFFICIENCY
PRODUC...STAT CHARTS 20 CONGRESS MONOPOLY. PAGE 102
E2052
B64 ECO/DEV CONTROL MARKET LG/CO

MAYO L.H.,"LEGAL-POLICY DECISION PROCESS:
ALTERNATIVE THINKING AND THE PREDICTIVE FUNCTION."
PROB/SOLV EFFICIENCY RATIONAL. PAGE 70 E1395
L64 DECISION SIMUL JURID TEC/DEV

BRIGGS H.W.,THE INTERNATIONAL LAW COMMISSION. LAW
CONSTN LEGIS CREATE ADJUD CT/SYS ROUTINE TASK
EFFICIENCY...CLASSIF OBS UN. PAGE 15 E0302
B65 INT/LAW DELIB/GP

HAEFELE E.T.,GOVERNMENT CONTROLS ON TRANSPORT. AFR
RHODESIA TANZANIA DIPLOM ECO/TAC TARIFFS PRICE
ADJUD CONTROL REGION EFFICIENCY...POLICY 20 CONGO.
PAGE 49 E0973
B65 ECO/UNDEV DIST/IND FINAN NAT/G

INST INTL DES CIVILISATION DIF,THE CONSTITUTIONS
AND ADMINISTRATIVE INSTITUTIONS OF THE NEW STATES.
AFR ISLAM S/ASIA NAT/G POL/PAR DELIB/GP EX/STRUC
CONFER EFFICIENCY NAT/LISM...JURID SOC 20. PAGE 56
E1123
B65 CONSTN ADMIN ADJUD ECO/UNDEV

US SENATE COMM ON JUDICIARY,HEARINGS BEFORE
SUBCOMMITTEE ON ADMINISTRATIVE PRACTICE AND
PROCEDURE ABOUT ADMINISTRATIVE PROCEDURE ACT 1965.
USA+45 LEGIS EDU/PROP ADJUD GOV/REL INGP/REL
EFFICIENCY...POLICY INT 20 CONGRESS. PAGE 103 E2055
B65 ROUTINE DELIB/GP ADMIN NAT/G

HIBBS A.R.,"SPACE TECHNOLOGY* THE THREAT AND THE
PROMISE." FUT VOL/ASSN TEC/DEV NUC/PWR COST
EFFICIENCY UTIL UN TREATY. PAGE 52 E1038
S65 SPACE ARMS/CONT PREDICT

BEELEY A.L.,THE BAIL SYSTEM IN CHICAGO. LAW MUNIC
PUB/INST EFFICIENCY MORAL...CRIMLGY METH/CNCPT STAT
20 CHICAGO. PAGE 9 E0176
B66 JURID CT/SYS CRIME ADJUD

BRENNAN J.T.,THE COST OF THE AMERICAN JUDICIAL
SYSTEM. USA+45 PROF/ORG TV ADMIN EFFICIENCY.
PAGE 15 E0292
B66 COST CT/SYS ADJUD JURID

BURNS A.C.,PARLIAMENT AS AN EXPORT. WOR+45 CONSTN
BARGAIN DEBATE ROUTINE GOV/REL EFFICIENCY...ANTHOL
COMMONWLTH PARLIAMENT. PAGE 17 E0343
B66 PARL/PROC POL/PAR CT/SYS CHIEF

FRIED R.C.,COMPARATIVE POLITICAL INSTITUTIONS. USSR
EX/STRUC FORCES LEGIS JUDGE CONTROL REPRESENT
ALL/IDEOS 20 CONGRESS BUREAUCRCY. PAGE 40 E0798
B66 NAT/G PWR EFFICIENCY GOV/COMP

GARCON M.,LETTRE OUVERTE A LA JUSTICE. FRANCE NAT/G
PROB/SOLV PAY EFFICIENCY MORAL 20. PAGE 42 E0834
B66 ORD/FREE ADJUD CT/SYS

HOYT E.C.,NATIONAL POLICY AND INTERNATIONAL LAW*
CASE STUDIES FROM AMERICAN CANAL POLICY* MONOGRAPH
NO. 1 -- 1966-1967. PANAMA UK ELITES BAL/PWR
EFFICIENCY...CLASSIF NAT/COMP SOC/EXP COLOMB
TREATY. PAGE 55 E1105
B66 INT/LAW USA-45 DIPLOM PWR

OSTERMANN R.,A REPORT IN DEPTH ON CRIME IN AMERICA.
FUT USA+45 MUNIC PUB/INST TEC/DEV MURDER EFFICIENCY
ATTIT BIO/SOC...PSY 20. PAGE 79 E1584
B66 CRIME FORCES CONTROL LAW

HOLSTI K.J.,"RESOLVING INTERNATIONAL CONFLICTS* A
TAXONOMY OF BEHAVIOR AND SOME FIGURES ON
PROCEDURES." WOR+45 WOR-45 INT/ORG ADJUD EFFICIENCY
...STAT IDEA/COMP. PAGE 55 E1089
L66 DIPLOM PROB/SOLV WAR CLASSIF

LANDE G.R.,"THE EFFECT OF THE RESOLUTIONS OF THE
S66 LEGIS

UNITED NATIONS GENERAL ASSEMBLY." WOR+45 LAW
INT/ORG NAT/G CHOOSE ISOLAT ATTIT...CLASSIF
GEN/METH UN. PAGE 62 E1249
EFFICIENCY RESPECT

BLAISDELL D.C.,"INTERNATIONAL ORGANIZATION." FUT
WOR+45 ECO/DEV DELIB/GP FORCES EFFICIENCY PEACE
ORD/FREE...INT/LAW 20 UN LEAGUE/NAT NATO. PAGE 12
E0239
C66 BIBLIOG INT/ORG DIPLOM ARMS/CONT

ELDRIDGE W.B.,NARCOTICS AND THE LAW: A CRITIQUE OF
THE AMERICAN EXPERIMENT IN NARCOTIC DRUG CONTROL.
PUB/INST ACT/RES PLAN LICENSE GP/REL EFFICIENCY
ATTIT HEALTH...CRIMLGY HEAL STAT 20 ABA DEPT/HEW
NARCO/ACT. PAGE 34 E0679
B67 LAW INSPECT BIO/SOC JURID

HODGKINSON R.G.,THE ORIGINS OF THE NATIONAL HEALTH
SERVICE: THE MEDICAL SERVICES OF THE NEW POOR LAW,
1834-1871. UK INDUS MUNIC WORKER PROB/SOLV
EFFICIENCY ATTIT HEALTH WEALTH SOCISM...JURID
SOC/WK 19/20. PAGE 53 E1062
B67 HEAL NAT/G POLICY LAW

JONES C.O.,EVERY SECOND YEAR: CONGRESSIONAL
BEHAVIOR AND THE TWO-YEAR TERM. LAW POL/PAR
PROB/SOLV DEBATE CHOOSE PERS/REL COST FEDERAL PWR
...CHARTS 20 CONGRESS SENATE HOUSE/REP. PAGE 59
E1172
B67 EFFICIENCY LEGIS TIME/SEQ NAT/G

CHAMBERLAIN N.W.,"STRIKES IN CONTEMPORARY CONTEXT."
LAW INDUS NAT/G CHIEF CONFER COST ATTIT ORD/FREE
...POLICY MGT 20. PAGE 21 E0415
S67 LABOR BARGAIN EFFICIENCY PROB/SOLV

CHAMBLISS W.J.,"TYPES OF DEVIANCE AND THE
EFFECTIVENESS OF LEGAL SANCTIONS" SOCIETY PROB/SOLV
ADJUD CONTROL DETER. PAGE 21 E0417
S67 CRIME SANCTION EFFICIENCY LAW

DOUTY H.M.," REFERENCE TO DEVELOPING COUNTRIES."
JAMAICA MALAYSIA UK WOR+45 LAW FINAN ACT/RES BUDGET
CAP/ISM ECO/TAC TARIFFS RISK EFFICIENCY PROFIT
...CHARTS 20. PAGE 33 E0646
S67 TAX ECO/UNDEV NAT/G

EDGEWORTH A.B. JR.,"CIVIL RIGHTS PLUS THREE YEARS:
BANKS AND THE ANTI-DISCRIMINATION LAW" USA+45
SOCIETY DELIB/GP RACE/REL EFFICIENCY 20 NEGRO
CIV/RIGHTS. PAGE 34 E0675
S67 WORKER DISCRIM FINAN LAW

HIRSCH W.Z.,"SOME ECONOMIC IMPLICATIONS OF CITY
PLANNING." LAW PROB/SOLV RATION EFFICIENCY...METH
20. PAGE 53 E1050
S67 ECO/TAC JURID MUNIC PLAN

SEIDLER G.L.,"MARXIST LEGAL THOUGHT IN POLAND."
POLAND SOCIETY R+D LOC/G NAT/G ACT/RES ADJUD CT/SYS
SUPEGO PWR...SOC TREND 20 MARX/KARL. PAGE 90 E1802
S67 MARXISM LAW CONCPT EFFICIENCY

TYDINGS J.D.,"MODERNIZING THE ADMINISTRATION OF
JUSTICE." PLAN ADMIN ROUTINE EFFICIENCY...JURID
SIMUL. PAGE 97 E1948
S67 CT/SYS MGT COMPUTER CONSULT

EFTA....EUROPEAN FREE TRADE ASSOCIATION

EGYPT....SEE ALSO ISLAM, UAR

EGYPT/ANC....ANCIENT EGYPT

EHLE J. E0677

EHRLICH E. E0678

EIB....EUROPEAN INVESTMENT BANK

EICHMANN/A....ADOLF EICHMANN

SILVING H.,"IN RE EICHMANN: A DILEMMA OF LAW AND
MORALITY" WOR+45 INSPECT ADJUST MORAL...JURID 20
WAR/TRIAL EICHMANN/A NATURL/LAW. PAGE 91 E1828
L61 CT/SYS INT/LAW CONCPT

EINSTEIN/A....ALBERT EINSTEIN

EISNHWR/DD....PRESIDENT DWIGHT DAVID EISENHOWER

CARPER E.T.,LOBBYING AND THE NATURAL GAS BILL
(PAMPHLET). USA+45 SERV/IND BARGAIN PAY DRIVE ROLE
WEALTH 20 CONGRESS SENATE EISNHWR/DD. PAGE 20 E0389
N19
LOBBY
ADJUD
TRIBUTE
NAT/G

HUNT B.I.,BIPARTISANSHIP: A CASE STUDY OF THE
FOREIGN ASSISTANCE PROGRAM, 1947-56 (DOCTORAL
THESIS). USA+45 INT/ORG CONSULT LEGIS TEC/DEV
...BIBLIOG PRESIDENT TREATY NATO TRUMAN/HS
EISNHWR/DD CONGRESS. PAGE 56 E1114
B58
FOR/AID
POL/PAR
GP/REL
DIPLOM

CARPER E.T.,THE DEFENSE APPROPRIATIONS RIDER
(PAMPHLET). USA+45 CONSTN CHIEF DELIB/GP LEGIS
BUDGET LOBBY CIVMIL/REL...POLICY 20 CONGRESS
EISNHWR/DD DEPT/DEFEN PRESIDENT BOSTON. PAGE 20
E0390
B60
GOV/REL
ADJUD
LAW
CONTROL

ANDERSON J.W.,EISENHOWER, BROWNELL, AND THE
CONGRESS - THE TANGLED ORIGINS OF THE CIVIL RIGHTS
BILL OF 1956-1957. USA+45 POL/PAR LEGIS CREATE
PROB/SOLV LOBBY GOV/REL RIGID/FLEX...NEW/IDEA 20
EISNHWR/DD CONGRESS BROWNELL/H CIV/RIGHTS. PAGE 5
E0090
B64
LAW
CONSTN
POLICY
NAT/G

EL/SALVADR....EL SALVADOR; SEE ALSO L/A+17C

DE NOIA J.,GUIDE TO OFFICIAL PUBLICATIONS OF THE
OTHER AMERICAN REPUBLICS: EL SALVADOR. EL/SALVADR
LAW LEGIS EDU/PROP CT/SYS 20. PAGE 30 E0590
B47
BIBLIOG/A
CONSTN
NAT/G
ADMIN

FLORES R.H.,CATALOGO DE TESIS DOCTORALES DE LAS
FACULTADES DE LA UNIVERSIDAD DE EL SALVADOR.
EL/SALVADR LAW DIPLOM ADMIN LEAD GOV/REL...SOC
19/20. PAGE 39 E0767
B60
BIBLIOG
ACADEM
L/A+17C
NAT/G

ELDRIDGE W.B. E0679

ELECT/COLL....ELECTORAL COLLEGE

ELECTIONS....SEE CHOOSE

ELECTORAL COLLEGE....SEE ELECT/COLL

ELIAS T.O. E0680,E0681,E0682

ELITES....POWER-DOMINANT GROUPINGS OF A SOCIETY

MEYER C.S.,ELIZABETH I AND THE RELIGIOUS SETTLEMENT
OF 1559. UK ELITES CHIEF LEGIS DISCRIM CATHISM 16
CHURCH/STA ELIZABTH/I. PAGE 72 E1445
NRE
GP/REL
SECT
LAW
PARL/PROC

HOGARTY R.A.,NEW JERSEY FARMERS AND MIGRANT HOUSING
RULES (PAMPHLET). USA+45 LAW ELITES FACE/GP LABOR
PROF/ORG LOBBY PERS/REL RIGID/FLEX ROLE 20
NEW/JERSEY. PAGE 53 E1067
N19
AGRI
PROVS
WORKER
HEALTH

BYNKERSHOEK C.,QUAESTIONUM JURIS PUBLICI LIBRI DUO.
CHRIST-17C MOD/EUR CONSTN ELITES SOCIETY NAT/G
PROVS EX/STRUC FORCES TOP/EX BAL/PWR DIPLOM ATTIT
MORAL...TRADIT CONCPT. PAGE 18 E0352
B30
INT/ORG
LAW
NAT/LISM
INT/LAW

GREEN F.M.,CONSTITUTIONAL DEVELOPMENT IN THE SOUTH
ATLANTIC STATES, 1776-1860; A STUDY IN THE
EVOLUTION OF DEMOCRACY. USA-45 ELITES SOCIETY
STRATA ECO/DEV AGRI POL/PAR EX/STRUC LEGIS CT/SYS
REGION...BIBLIOG 18/19 MARYLAND VIRGINIA GEORGIA
NORTH/CAR SOUTH/CAR. PAGE 46 E0905
B30
CONSTN
PROVS
PLURISM
REPRESENT

GERTH H.,"THE NAZI PARTY: ITS LEADERSHIP AND
COMPOSITION" (BMR)" GERMANY ELITES STRATA STRUCT
EX/STRUC FORCES ECO/TAC CT/SYS CHOOSE TOTALISM
AGE/Y AUTHORIT PWR 20. PAGE 43 E0851
S40
POL/PAR
DOMIN
LEAD
ADMIN

CROWE S.E.,THE BERLIN WEST AFRICA CONFERENCE,
1884-85. GERMANY ELITES MARKET INT/ORG DELIB/GP
FORCES PROB/SOLV BAL/PWR CAP/ISM DOMIN COLONIAL
...INT/LAW 19. PAGE 28 E0548
B42
AFR
CONFER
INT/TRADE
DIPLOM

FORTESCU J.,IN PRAISE OF ENGLISH LAW (1464) (TRANS.
BY S.B. CHRIMES). UK ELITES CHIEF FORCES CT/SYS
COERCE CRIME GOV/REL ILLEGIT...JURID GOV/COMP
B42
LAW
CONSTN
LEGIS

GEN/LAWS 15. PAGE 39 E0774
ORD/FREE

BENTHAM J.,"ON THE LIBERTY OF THE PRESS, AND PUBLIC
DISCUSSION" IN J. BOWRING, ED., THE WORKS OF JEREMY
BENTHAM." SPAIN UK LAW ELITES NAT/G LEGIS INSPECT
LEGIT WRITING CONTROL PRIVIL TOTALISM AUTHORIT
...TRADIT 19 FREE/SPEE. PAGE 10 E0193
C43
ORD/FREE
PRESS
CONFER
CONSERVE

MASON J.B.,"THE JUDICIAL SYSTEM OF THE NAZI PARTY."
GERMANY ELITES POL/PAR DOMIN CONTROL SANCTION
TOTALISM...JURID 20 HITLER/A. PAGE 69 E1381
S44
FASCISM
CT/SYS
ADJUD
LAW

ALEXANDER L.,"WAR CRIMES, THEIR SOCIAL-
PSYCHOLOGICAL ASPECTS." EUR+WWI GERMANY LAW CULTURE
ELITES KIN POL/PAR PUB/INST FORCES DOMIN EDU/PROP
COERCE CRIME ATTIT SUPEGO HEALTH MORAL PWR FASCISM
...PSY OBS TREND GEN/LAWS NAZI 20. PAGE 3 E0061
S48
DRIVE
WAR

US LIBRARY OF CONGRESS,FREEDOM OF INFORMATION:
SELECTIVE REPORT ON RECENT WRITINGS. USA+45 LAW
CONSTN ELITES EDU/PROP PRESS LOBBY WAR TOTALISM
ATTIT 20 UN UNESCO COLD/WAR. PAGE 101 E2018
B49
BIBLIOG/A
ORD/FREE
LICENSE
COM/IND

MARX C.M.,"ADMINISTRATIVE ETHICS AND THE RULE OF
LAW." USA+45 ELITES ACT/RES DOMIN NEUTRAL ROUTINE
INGP/REL ORD/FREE...JURID IDEA/COMP. PAGE 69 E1375
L49
ADMIN
LAW

BROWN D.M.,"RECENT JAPANESE POLITICAL AND
HISTORICAL MATERIALS." ELITES CT/SYS CIVMIL/REL 20
CHINJAP. PAGE 16 E0312
S49
WAR
FORCES

BISSAINTHE M.,DICTIONNAIRE DE BIBLIOGRAPHIE
HAITIENNE. HAITI ELITES AGRI LEGIS DIPLOM INT/TRADE
WRITING ORD/FREE CATHISM...ART/METH GEOG 19/20
NEGRO TREATY. PAGE 12 E0234
B51
BIBLIOG
L/A+17C
SOCIETY
NAT/G

KEFAUVER E.,CRIME IN AMERICA. USA+45 USA-45 MUNIC
NEIGH DELIB/GP TRIBUTE GAMBLE LOBBY SANCTION
...AUD/VIS 20 CAPONE/AL MAFIA MIAMI CHICAGO
DETROIT. PAGE 60 E1194
B51
ELITES
CRIME
PWR
FORCES

THOM J.M.,GUIDE TO RESEARCH MATERIAL IN POLITICAL
SCIENCE (PAMPHLET). ELITES LOC/G MUNIC NAT/G LEGIS
DIPLOM ADJUD CIVMIL/REL GOV/REL PWR MGT. PAGE 96
E1916
B52
BIBLIOG/A
KNOWL

DE GRAZIA A.,"GENERAL THEORY OF APPORTIONMENT"
(BMR)" USA+45 USA-45 CONSTN ELITES DELIB/GP PARTIC
REV CHOOSE...JURID 20. PAGE 29 E0582
S52
APPORT
LEGIS
PROVS
REPRESENT

HAMSON C.J.,EXECUTIVE DISCRETION AND JUDICIAL
CONTROL; AN ASPECT OF THE FRENCH CONSEIL D'ETAT.
EUR+WWI FRANCE MOD/EUR UK NAT/G EX/STRUC PARTIC
CONSERVE...JURID BIBLIOG/A 18/20 SUPREME/CT.
PAGE 50 E0992
B54
ELITES
ADJUD
NAT/COMP

SMITH G.,A CONSTITUTIONAL AND LEGAL HISTORY OF
ENGLAND. UK ELITES NAT/G LEGIS ADJUD OWN HABITAT
POPULISM...JURID 20 ENGLSH/LAW. PAGE 92 E1844
B55
CONSTN
PARTIC
LAW
CT/SYS

BETH L.P.,"THE CASE FOR JUDICIAL PROTECTION OF
CIVIL LIBERTIES" (BMR)" USA+45 CONSTN ELITES LEGIS
CONTROL...POLICY DECISION JURID 20 SUPREME/CT
CIVIL/LIB. PAGE 11 E0220
B55
CT/SYS
JUDGE
ADJUD
ORD/FREE

MEYER P.,ADMINISTRATIVE ORGANIZATION: A COMPARATIVE
STUDY OF THE ORGANIZATION OF PUBLIC ADMINISTRATION.
DENMARK FRANCE NORWAY SWEDEN UK USA+45 ELITES LOC/G
CONSULT LEGIS ADJUD CONTROL LEAD PWR SKILL
DECISION. PAGE 72 E1449
B57
ADMIN
METH/COMP
NAT/G
CENTRAL

ABRAHAM H.J.,COURTS AND JUDGES: AN INTRODUCTION TO
THE JUDICIAL PROCESS. USA+45 CONSTN ELITES NAT/G
ORD/FREE PWR 19/20 SUPREME/CT. PAGE 2 E0045
B59
CT/SYS
PERSON
JURID
ADJUD

COLUMBIA U. BUREAU OF APPL SOC RES, ATTITUDES OF
B59
ATTIT

PROMINENT AMERICANS TOWARD "WORLD PEACE THROUGH WORLD LAW" (SUPRA-NATL ORGANIZATION FOR WAR PREVENTION). USA+45 USSR ELITES FORCES PLAN PROB/SOLV CONTROL WAR PWR...POLICY SOC QU IDEA/COMP 20 UN. PAGE 82 E1644   ACT/RES INT/LAW STAT

B59
SISSON C.H.,THE SPIRIT OF BRITISH ADMINISTRATION AND SOME EUROPEAN COMPARISONS. FRANCE GERMANY/W SWEDEN UK LAW EX/STRUC INGP/REL EFFICIENCY ORD/FREE ...DECISION 20. PAGE 91 E1835   GOV/COMP ADMIN ELITES ATTIT

S59
BELL D.,"THE RACKET RIDDEN LONGSHOREMEN" (BMR)" USA+45 SEA WORKER MURDER ROLE...SOC 20 NEWYORK/C. PAGE 9 E0182   CRIME LABOR DIST/IND ELITES

C59
EASTON D.,"POLITICAL ANTHROPOLOGY" IN BIENNIAL REVIEW OF ANTHROPOLOGY" UNIV LAW CULTURE ELITES SOCIETY CREATE...PSY CONCPT GP/COMP GEN/METH 20. PAGE 34 E0671   SOC BIBLIOG/A NEW/IDEA

B60
PINTO F.B.M.,ENRIQUECIMENTO ILICITO NO EXERCICIO DE CARGOS PUBLICOS. BRAZIL L/A+17C USA+45 ELITES TRIBUTE CONTROL INGP/REL ORD/FREE PWR...NAT/COMP 20. PAGE 81 E1617   ADMIN NAT/G CRIME LAW

B60
PRICE D.,THE SECRETARY OF STATE. USA+45 CONSTN ELITES INTELL CHIEF EX/STRUC TOP/EX LEGIT ATTIT PWR SKILL...DECISION 20 CONGRESS. PAGE 82 E1650   CONSULT DIPLOM INT/LAW

B60
SCHUBERT G.A.,CONSTITUTIONAL POLITICS: THE POLITICAL BEHAVIOR OF SUPREME COURT JUSTICES AND THE CONSTITUTIONAL POLICIES THEY MAKE. LAW ELITES CHIEF DELIB/GP EX/STRUC LEGIS DISCRIM ORD/FREE PWR ...POLICY MAJORIT CHARTS SUPREME/CT CONGRESS. PAGE 89 E1781   CONSTN CT/SYS JURID DECISION

B61
AYLMER G.,THE KING'S SERVANTS. UK ELITES CHIEF PAY CT/SYS WEALTH 17 CROMWELL/O CHARLES/I. PAGE 6 E0122   ADMIN ROUTINE EX/STRUC NAT/G

B61
CARNELL F.,THE POLITICS OF THE NEW STATES: A SELECT ANNOTATED BIBLIOGRAPHY WITH SPECIAL REFERENCE TO THE COMMONWEALTH. CONSTN ELITES LABOR NAT/G POL/PAR EX/STRUC DIPLOM ADJUD ADMIN...GOV/COMP 20 COMMONWLTH. PAGE 20 E0387   BIBLIOG/A AFR ASIA COLONIAL

B61
COWEN D.V.,THE FOUNDATIONS OF FREEDOM. AFR SOUTH/AFR DOMIN LEGIT ADJUST DISCRIM TOTALSM ATTIT ORD/FREE...MAJORIT JURID SOC/INTEG WORSHIP 20 NEGRO. PAGE 27 E0529   CONSTN ELITES RACE/REL

L62
GROSS L.,"IMMUNITIES AND PRIVILEGES OF DELIGATIONS TO THE UNITED NATIONS." USA+45 WOR+45 STRATA NAT/G VOL/ASSN CONSULT DIPLOM EDU/PROP ROUTINE RESPECT ...POLICY INT/LAW CONCPT UN 20. PAGE 48 E0950   INT/ORG LAW ELITES

C62
BACON F.,"OF THE TRUE GREATNESS OF KINGDOMS AND ESTATES" (1612) IN F. BACON, ESSAYS." ELITES FORCES DOMIN EDU/PROP LEGIT...POLICY GEN/LAWS 16/17 TREATY. PAGE 7 E0129   WAR PWR DIPLOM CONSTN

B63
RICHARDS P.G.,PATRONAGE IN BRITISH GOVERNMENT. ELITES DELIB/GP TOP/EX PROB/SOLV CONTROL CT/SYS EXEC PWR. PAGE 84 E1693   EX/STRUC REPRESENT POL/PAR ADMIN

B63
SARTORI G.,IL PARLAMENTO ITALIANO: 1946-1963. LAW CONSTN ELITES POL/PAR LOBBY PRIVIL ATTIT PERSON MORAL PWR SOC. PAGE 87 E1746   LEGIS PARL/PROC REPRESENT

S63
BRAUSCH G.E.,"AFRICAN ETHNOCRACIES: SOME SOCIOLOGICAL IMPLICATIONS OF CONSTITUTIONAL CHANGE IN EMERGENT TERRITORIES OF AFRICA." AFR CONSTN FACE/GP MUNIC NAT/G DOMIN ATTIT ALL/VALS ...HIST/WRIT GEN/LAWS VAL/FREE 20. PAGE 15 E0289   LAW SOC ELITES

B64
DOOLIN D.J.,COMMUNIST CHINA: THE POLITICS OF STUDENT OPPOSITION. CHINA/COM ELITES STRATA ACADEM NAT/G WRITING CT/SYS LEAD PARTIC COERCE TOTALSM   MARXISM DEBATE AGE/Y

20. PAGE 32 E0637   PWR

B64
DORMAN M.,WE SHALL OVERCOME. USA+45 ELITES ACADEM FORCES TOP/EX MURDER...JURID 20 CIV/RIGHTS MISSISSIPP EVERS/MED CLEMSON. PAGE 32 E0638   RACE/REL LAW DISCRIM

B64
ROBINSON R.D.,INTERNATIONAL BUSINESS POLICY. AFR INDIA L/A+17C USA+45 ELITES AGRI FOR/AID COERCE BAL/PAY...DECISION INT/LAW MGT 20. PAGE 85 E1706   ECO/TAC DIST/IND COLONIAL FINAN

B65
AMERICAN ASSEMBLY COLUMBIA U,THE COURTS, THE PUBLIC, AND THE LAW EXPLOSION. USA+45 ELITES PROVS EDU/PROP CRIME CHOOSE PERSON ORD/FREE PWR 20. PAGE 4 E0074   CT/SYS ADJUD NAT/G

B65
KARIS T.,THE TREASON TRIAL IN SOUTH AFRICA: A GUIDE TO THE MICROFILM RECORD OF THE TRIAL. SOUTH/AFR LAW ELITES NAT/G LEGIT CT/SYS RACE/REL DISCRIM...SOC 20. PAGE 59 E1185   BIBLIOG/A ADJUD CRIME AFR

B65
MURPHY W.F.,WIRETAPPING ON TRIAL: A CASE STUDY IN THE JUDICIAL PROCESS. CONSTN ELITES CT/SYS CRIME MORAL ORD/FREE...DECISION SUPREME/CT. PAGE 75 E1511   JURID LAW POLICY

B65
SCHUBERT G.,THE JUDICIAL MIND: THE ATTITUDES AND IDEOLOGIES OF SUPREME COURT JUSTICES 1946-1963. USA+45 ELITES NAT/G CONTROL PERS/REL MAJORITY CONSERVE...DECISION JURID MODAL STAT TREND GP/COMP GAME. PAGE 88 E1774   CT/SYS JUDGE ATTIT NEW/LIB

S65
ULMER S.S.,"TOWARD A THEORY OF SUBGROUP FORMATION IN THE UNITED STATES SUPREME COURT." USA+45 ROUTINE CHOOSE PWR...JURID STAT CON/ANAL SIMUL SUPREME/CT. PAGE 97 E1952   CT/SYS ADJUD ELITES INGP/REL

B66
HOYT E.C.,NATIONAL POLICY AND INTERNATIONAL LAW* CASE STUDIES FROM AMERICAN CANAL POLICY* MONOGRAPH NO. 1 -- 1966-1967. PANAMA UK ELITES BAL/PWR EFFICIENCY...CLASSIF NAT/COMP SOC/EXP COLOMB TREATY. PAGE 55 E1105   INT/LAW USA-45 DIPLOM PWR

B66
KEAY E.A.,THE NATIVE AND CUSTOMARY COURTS OF NIGERIA. NIGERIA CONSTN ELITES NAT/G TOP/EX PARTIC REGION...DECISION JURID 19/20. PAGE 60 E1190   AFR ADJUD LAW

B66
US SENATE COMM ON JUDICIARY,HEARINGS ON FREE PRESS AND FAIR TRIAL (2 VOLS.). USA+45 CONSTN ELITES LEGIS EDU/PROP CT/SYS LEAD CONGRESS. PAGE 103 E2057   PRESS LAW CRIME ORD/FREE

S66
SHKLAR J.,"SELECTED ARTICLES AND DOCUMENTS ON POLITICAL THEORY." ADJUD REV...JURID PHIL/SCI IDEA/COMP. PAGE 91 E1820   BIBLIOG ELITES PWR

B67
BAKER L.,BACK TO BACK: THE DUEL BETWEEN FDR AND THE SUPREME COURT. ELITES LEGIS CREATE DOMIN INGP/REL PERSON PWR NEW/LIB 20 ROOSEVLT/F SUPREME/CT SENATE. PAGE 7 E0142   CHIEF CT/SYS PARL/PROC GOV/REL

S67
BLAKEY G.R.,"ORGANIZED CRIME IN THE UNITED STATES." USA+45 USA-45 STRUCT LABOR NAT/G VOL/ASSN ADMIN PERS/REL PWR...CRIMLGY INT 17/20. PAGE 12 E0240   CRIME ELITES CONTROL

S67
GREY D.L.,"INTERVIEWING AT THE COURT." USA+45 ELITES COM/IND ACT/RES PRESS CT/SYS PERSON...SOC INT 20 SUPREME/CT. PAGE 46 E0916   JUDGE ATTIT PERS/COMP GP/COMP

B75
MAINE H.S.,LECTURES ON THE EARLY HISTORY OF INSTITUTIONS. IRELAND UK CONSTN ELITES STRUCT FAM KIN CHIEF LEGIS CT/SYS OWN SOVEREIGN...CONCPT 16 BENTHAM/J BREHON ROMAN/LAW. PAGE 68 E1351   CULTURE LAW INGP/REL

B90
GODWIN W.,POLITICAL JUSTICE. UK ELITES OWN KNOWL MORAL WEALTH...JURID 18/19. PAGE 44 E0877   ORD/FREE SOVEREIGN STRUCT CONCPT

ELIZABTH/I....ELIZABETH I OF ENGLAND

NRE

MEYER C.S.,ELIZABETH I AND THE RELIGIOUS SETTLEMENT GP/REL
OF 1559. UK ELITES CHIEF LEGIS DISCRIM CATHISM 16 SECT
CHURCH/STA ELIZABTH/I. PAGE 72 E1445 LAW
PARL/PROC

ELKIN/AP....A.P. ELKIN

ELLERT R.B. E0683

ELLIOTT S.D. E0684

ELLMAKER E.G. E0685

EMBREE J.F. E0686

EMDEN C.S. E0687

EMERGENCY....SEE DECISION

EMPLOYMENT....SEE WORKER

ENDACOTT G.B. E0688

ENG/CIV/WR....ENGLISH CIVIL WAR

ENGEL J. E0689

ENGEL S. E0690

ENGELENBURG F.V. E0309

ENGELS/F....FRIEDRICH ENGELS

ENGLAND....SEE UK. ALSO APPROPRIATE TIME/SPACE/CULTURE
INDEX

ENGLISH CIVIL WAR....SEE ENG/CIV/WR

ENGLSH/LAW....ENGLISH LAW

B05

DICEY A.V.,LECTURES ON THE RELATION BETWEEN LAW AND LAW
PUBLIC OPINION IN ENGLAND DURING THE NINETEENTH ADJUD
CENTURY. UK LEGIS CT/SYS...JURID 19 TORY/PARTY ATTIT
BENTHAM/J ENGLSH/LAW. PAGE 31 E0621 IDEA/COMP

B10

MCILWAIN C.H.,THE HIGH COURT OF PARLIAMENT AND ITS LAW
SUPREMACY B1910 1878 408. UK EX/STRUC PARL/PROC LEGIS
GOV/REL INGP/REL PRIVIL 12/20 PARLIAMENT CONSTN
ENGLSH/LAW. PAGE 71 E1416 NAT/G

B24

HOLDSWORTH W.S.,A HISTORY OF ENGLISH LAW; THE LAW
COMMON LAW AND ITS RIVALS (VOL. V). UK SEA EX/STRUC LEGIS
WRITING ADMIN...INT/LAW JURID CONCPT IDEA/COMP ADJUD
WORSHIP 16/17 PARLIAMENT ENGLSH/LAW COMMON/LAW. CT/SYS
PAGE 54 E1073

B24

HOLDSWORTH W.S.,A HISTORY OF ENGLISH LAW; THE LAW
COMMON LAW AND ITS RIVALS (VOL. VI). UK STRATA CONSTN
EX/STRUC ADJUD ADMIN CONTROL CT/SYS...JURID CONCPT LEGIS
GEN/LAWS 17 COMMONWLTH PARLIAMENT ENGLSH/LAW CHIEF
COMMON/LAW. PAGE 54 E1074

B24

HOLDSWORTH W.S.,A HISTORY OF ENGLISH LAW; THE LAW
COMMON LAW AND ITS RIVALS (VOL. IV). UK SEA AGRI LEGIS
CHIEF ADJUD CONTROL CRIME GOV/REL...INT/LAW JURID CT/SYS
NAT/COMP 16/17 PARLIAMENT COMMON/LAW CANON/LAW CONSTN
ENGLSH/LAW. PAGE 54 E1075

B32

LUNT D.C.,THE ROAD TO THE LAW. UK USA-45 LEGIS ADJUD
EDU/PROP OWN ORD/FREE...DECISION TIME/SEQ NAT/COMP LAW
16/20 AUSTRAL ENGLSH/LAW COMMON/LAW. PAGE 67 E1333 JURID
CT/SYS

B35

RAM J.,THE SCIENCE OF LEGAL JUDGMENT: A TREATISE... LAW
UK CONSTN NAT/G LEGIS CREATE PROB/SOLV AGREE CT/SYS JURID
...INT/LAW CONCPT 19 ENGLSH/LAW CANON/LAW CIVIL/LAW EX/STRUC
CTS/WESTM. PAGE 83 E1672 ADJUD

B38

HOLDSWORTH W.S.,A HISTORY OF ENGLISH LAW; THE LAW
CENTURIES OF SETTLEMENT AND REFORM (VOL. XII). UK PROF/ORG
CONSTN STRATA LEGIS JUDGE ADJUD CT/SYS ATTIT WRITING
...JURID CONCPT BIOG GEN/LAWS 18 ENGLSH/LAW IDEA/COMP
BLACKSTN/W COMMON/LAW. PAGE 54 E1078

B38

HOLDSWORTH W.S.,A HISTORY OF ENGLISH LAW; THE LAW
CENTURIES OF SETTLEMENT AND REFORM (VOL. XI). UK COLONIAL
CONSTN NAT/G EX/STRUC DIPLOM ADJUD CT/SYS LEAD LEGIS
CRIME ATTIT...INT/LAW JURID 18 CMN/WLTH PARLIAMENT PARL/PROC
ENGLSH/LAW. PAGE 54 E1079

B48

CORWIN E.S.,LIBERTY AGAINST GOVERNMENT. UK USA-45 JURID
ROMAN/EMP LAW CONSTN PERS/REL OWN ATTIT 1/20 ORD/FREE
ROMAN/LAW ENGLSH/LAW AMEND/XIV. PAGE 26 E0513 CONCPT

B48

SLESSER H.,THE ADMINISTRATION OF THE LAW. UK CONSTN LAW
EX/STRUC OP/RES PROB/SOLV CRIME ROLE...DECISION CT/SYS
METH/COMP 20 CIVIL/LAW ENGLSH/LAW CIVIL/LAW. ADJUD
PAGE 92 E1839

B49

DENNING A.,FREEDOM UNDER THE LAW. MOD/EUR UK LAW ORD/FREE
SOCIETY CHIEF EX/STRUC LEGIS ADJUD CT/SYS PERS/REL JURID
PERSON 17/20 ENGLSH/LAW. PAGE 31 E0606 NAT/G

B50

WADE E.C.S.,CONSTITUTIONAL LAW; AN OUTLINE OF THE CONSTN
LAW AND PRACTICE OF THE CONSTITUTION. UK LEGIS NAT/G
DOMIN ADMIN GP/REL 16/20 CMN/WLTH PARLIAMENT PARL/PROC
ENGLSH/LAW. PAGE 104 E2087 LAW

B51

FRIEDMANN W.,LAW AND SOCIAL CHANGE IN CONTEMPORARY LAW
BRITAIN. UK LABOR LG/CO LEGIS JUDGE CT/SYS ORD/FREE ADJUD
NEW/LIB...DECISION JURID TREND METH/COMP BIBLIOG 20 SOCIETY
PARLIAMENT ENGLSH/LAW COMMON/LAW. PAGE 40 E0802 CONSTN

B52

HOLDSWORTH W.S.,A HISTORY OF ENGLISH LAW; THE LAW
CENTURIES OF SETTLEMENT AND REFORM, 1701-1875 (VOL. CONSTN
XIII). UK POL/PAR PROF/ORG LEGIS JUDGE CT/SYS IDEA/COMP
ATTIT...JURID CONCPT BIOG GEN/LAWS 18/19 PARLIAMENT CT/SYS
REFORMERS ENGLSH/LAW COMMON/LAW. PAGE 54 E1080

B52

JENNINGS W.I.,CONSTITUTIONAL LAWS OF THE CONSTN
COMMONWEALTH. UK LAW CHIEF LEGIS TAX CT/SYS JURID
PARL/PROC GOV/REL...INT/LAW 18/20 COMMONWLTH ADJUD
ENGLSH/LAW COMMON/LAW. PAGE 58 E1165 COLONIAL

B54

SCHWARTZ B.,FRENCH ADMINISTRATIVE LAW AND THE JURID
COMMON-LAW WORLD. FRANCE CULTURE LOC/G NAT/G PROVS LAW
DELIB/GP EX/STRUC LEGIS PROB/SOLV CT/SYS EXEC METH/COMP
GOV/REL...IDEA/COMP ENGLSH/LAW. PAGE 89 E1786 ADJUD

B55

BEANEY W.M.,THE RIGHT TO COUNSEL IN AMERICAN ADJUD
COURTS. UK USA+45 USA-45 LAW NAT/G PROVS COLONIAL CONSTN
PERCEPT 18/20 SUPREME/CT AMEND/VI AMEND/XIV CT/SYS
ENGLSH/LAW. PAGE 8 E0163

B55

SMITH G.,A CONSTITUTIONAL AND LEGAL HISTORY OF CONSTN
ENGLAND. UK ELITES NAT/G LEGIS ADJUD OWN HABITAT PARTIC
POPULISM...JURID 20 ENGLSH/LAW. PAGE 92 E1844 LAW
CT/SYS

B58

ALLEN C.K.,ASPECTS OF JUSTICE. UK FAM COERCE CRIME JURID
MARRIAGE AGE/Y LOVE 20 ENGLSH/LAW. PAGE 4 E0068 MORAL
ORD/FREE

B58

ALLEN C.K.,LAW IN THE MAKING. LEGIS ATTIT ORD/FREE LAW
SOVEREIGN POPULISM...JURID IDEA/COMP NAT/COMP CREATE
GEN/LAWS 20 ENGLSH/LAW. PAGE 4 E0069 CONSTN
SOCIETY

B59

DESMITH S.A.,JUDICIAL REVIEW OF ADMINISTRATIVE ADJUD
ACTION. UK LOC/G CONSULT DELIB/GP ADMIN PWR NAT/G
...DECISION JURID 20 ENGLSH/LAW. PAGE 31 E0609 PROB/SOLV
CT/SYS

B59

GINSBURG M.,LAW AND OPINION IN ENGLAND. UK CULTURE JURID
KIN LABOR LEGIS EDU/PROP ADMIN CT/SYS CRIME OWN POLICY
HEALTH...ANTHOL 20 ENGLSH/LAW. PAGE 44 E0868 ECO/TAC

B59

SQUIBB G.D.,THE HIGH COURT OF CHIVALRY. UK NAT/G CT/SYS
FORCES ADJUD WAR 14/20 PARLIAMENT ENGLSH/LAW. PARL/PROC
PAGE 93 E1863 JURID

B60

DILEY A.V.,INTRODUCTION TO THE STUDY OF THE LAW OF CONSTN
THE CONSTITUTION. FRANCE UK USA+45 USA-45 CONSULT LAW

FORCES TAX ADMIN FEDERAL ORD/FREE SOVEREIGN ...IDEA/COMP 20 ENGLSH/LAW CON/INTERP PARLIAMENT. PAGE 32 E0627 — LEGIS GEN/LAWS

B60
HANBURY H.G.,ENGLISH COURTS OF LAW. UK EX/STRUC LEGIS CRIME ROLE 12/20 COMMON/LAW ENGLSH/LAW. PAGE 50 E0993 — JURID CT/SYS CONSTN GOV/REL

B62
DAVIS F.J.,SOCIETY AND THE LAW. USA+45 CONSTN ACADEM FAM CONSULT ACT/RES GP/REL ORD/FREE ENGLSH/LAW 20. PAGE 29 E0572 — LAW SOC CULTURE STRUCT

B63
ELIAS T.O.,THE NIGERIAN LEGAL SYSTEM. NIGERIA LAW FAM KIN SECT ADMIN NAT/LISM...JURID 18/20 ENGLSH/LAW COMMON/LAW. PAGE 34 E0682 — CT/SYS ADJUD COLONIAL PROF/ORG

B63
WADE H.W.R.,TOWARDS ADMINISTRATIVE JUSTICE. UK USA+45 CONSTN CONSULT PROB/SOLV CT/SYS PARL/PROC ...POLICY JURID METH/COMP 20 ENGLSH/LAW. PAGE 104 E2088 — ADJUD IDEA/COMP ADMIN

B64
HURST W.H.,JUSTICE HOLMES ON LEGAL HISTORY. USA-45 LAW SOCIETY NAT/G WRITING...POLICY PHIL/SCI SOC CONCPT 20 HOLMES/OW SUPREME/CT ENGLSH/LAW. PAGE 56 E1117 — ADJUD JURID BIOG

B64
JACKSON R.M.,THE MACHINERY OF JUSTICE IN ENGLAND. UK EDU/PROP CONTROL COST ORD/FREE...MGT 20 ENGLSH/LAW. PAGE 57 E1142 — CT/SYS ADJUD JUDGE JURID

B65
HOLDSWORTH W.S.,A HISTORY OF ENGLISH LAW; THE CENTURIES OF SETTLEMENT AND REFORM (VOL. XV). UK CONSTN SECT LEGIS JUDGE WRITING ADJUD CT/SYS CRIME OWN...JURID IDEA/COMP 18 PARLIAMENT ENGLSH/LAW COMMON/LAW. PAGE 54 E1082 — LAW INDUS PROF/ORG ATTIT

B65
STOREY R.G.,OUR UNALIENABLE RIGHTS. LAW SECT CT/SYS CONSTN SUFF DISCRIM 17/20 CIVIL/LIB ENGLSH/LAW. PAGE 94 E1882 — CONSTN JURID ORD/FREE LEGIS

B66
HOGUE A.R.,ORIGINS OF THE COMMON LAW. UK STRUCT AGRI CT/SYS SANCTION CONSERVE 12/14 ENGLSH/LAW COMMON/LAW. PAGE 54 E1068 — LAW SOCIETY CONSTN

B66
MCNAIR A.D.,THE LEGAL EFFECTS OF WAR. UK FINAN DIPLOM ORD/FREE 20 ENGLSH/LAW. PAGE 71 E1425 — JURID WAR INT/TRADE LABOR

B66
WILSON G.,CASES AND MATERIALS ON CONSTITUTIONAL AND ADMINISTRATIVE LAW. UK LAW NAT/G EX/STRUC LEGIS BAL/PWR BUDGET DIPLOM ADJUD CONTROL CT/SYS GOV/REL ORD/FREE 20 PARLIAMENT ENGLSH/LAW. PAGE 106 E2126 — JURID ADMIN CONSTN PWR

B70
BLACKSTONE W.,COMMENTARIES ON THE LAWS OF ENGLAND (4 VOLS.) (4TH ED.). UK CHIEF DELIB/GP LEGIS WORKER CT/SYS SANCTION CRIME OWN...CRIMLGY 18 ENGLSH/LAW. PAGE 12 E0238 — LAW JURID ADJUD CONSTN

ENKE S. E0691

ENLIGHTNMT....THE ENLIGHTENMENT

ENSOR R.C.K. E0692

ENTREPRENEURSHIP....SEE OWN, INDUS, CAP/ISM

ENVY....SEE WEALTH, LOVE, AND VALUES INDEX

EPIST....EPISTEMOLOGY, SOCIOLOGY OF KNOWLEDGE

S37
TIMASHEFF N.S.,"WHAT IS SOCIOLOGY OF LAW?" (BMR)" UNIV INTELL PWR...EPIST JURID PHIL/SCI IDEA/COMP. PAGE 96 E1925 — LAW SOC SOCIETY

S40
GURVITCH G.,"MAJOR PROBLEMS OF THE SOCIOLOGY OF LAW." CULTURE SANCTION KNOWL MORAL...POLICY EPIST — SOC LAW

JURID WORSHIP. PAGE 48 E0963 — PHIL/SCI

B42
GURVITCH G.,SOCIOLOGY OF LAW. CONSTN SOCIETY CREATE MORAL SOVEREIGN...POLICY EPIST JURID PHIL/SCI IDEA/COMP METH/COMP HOLMES/OW HOBBES/T. PAGE 48 E0964 — SOC LAW ADJUD

B54
BENTLEY A.F.,INQUIRY INTO INQUIRIES: ESSAYS IN SOCIAL THEORY. UNIV LEGIS ADJUD ADMIN LOBBY ...PHIL/SCI PSY NEW/IDEA LING METH 20. PAGE 10 E0200 — EPIST SOC CONCPT

EPISTEMOLOGY....SEE EPIST

EPSTEIN B. E0771

EPSTEIN F.T. E0693,E0694

EPTA....EXPANDED PROGRAM OF TECHNICAL ASSISTANCE

EQUILIB....EQUILIBRIUM; SEE ALSO BAL/PWR

B08
GRIFFIN A.P.C.,LIST OF REFERENCES ON INTERNATIONAL ARBITRATION. FRANCE L/A+17C USA-45 WOR-45 DIPLOM CONFER COLONIAL ARMS/CONT BAL/PAY EQUILIB SOVEREIGN ...DECISION 19/20 MEXIC/AMER. PAGE 47 E0932 — BIBLIOG/A INT/ORG INT/LAW DELIB/GP

C50
HOLCOMBE A.,"OUR MORE PERFECT UNION." USA+45 USA-45 POL/PAR JUDGE CT/SYS EQUILIB FEDERAL PWR...MAJORIT TREND BIBLIOG 18/20 CONGRESS PRESIDENT. PAGE 54 E1070 — CONSTN NAT/G ADMIN PLAN

B62
HIRSCHFIELD R.S.,THE CONSTITUTION AND THE COURT. SCHOOL WAR RACE/REL EQUILIB ORD/FREE...POLICY MAJORIT DECISION JURID 18/20 PRESIDENT COLD/WAR CIVIL/LIB SUPREME/CT CONGRESS. PAGE 53 E1051 — ADJUD PWR CONSTN LAW

C64
CORWIN E.S.,"AMERICAN CONSTITUTIONAL HISTORY." LAW NAT/G PROB/SOLV EQUILIB FEDERAL ATTIT PWR...JURID BIBLIOG 20. PAGE 26 E0515 — ANTHOL JUDGE ADJUD CT/SYS

ERDEMLI....ERDEMLI, TURKEY

ERDMANN H.H. E0695

ERNST M.L. E0696

ESMEIN A. E0697

ESPIONAGE....ESPIONAGE

N19
IN THE SHADOW OF FEAR; AMERICAN CIVIL LIBERTIES, 1948-49 (PAMPHLET). COM LAW LEGIS BAL/PWR EDU/PROP CT/SYS RACE/REL DISCRIM MARXISM SOCISM 20 COLD/WAR CONGRESS ACLU CIV/RIGHTS ESPIONAGE. PAGE 2 E0030 — ORD/FREE CONSTN POLICY

B37
THOMPSON J.W.,SECRET DIPLOMACY: A RECORD OF ESPIONAGE AND DOUBLE-DEALING: 1500-1815. CHRIST-17C MOD/EUR NAT/G WRITING RISK MORAL...ANTHOL BIBLIOG 16/19 ESPIONAGE. PAGE 96 E1920 — DIPLOM CRIME

B50
LOWENTHAL M.,THE FEDERAL BUREAU OF INVESTIGATION. USA+45 SOCIETY ADMIN TASK CRIME INGP/REL...CRIMLGY 20 FBI ESPIONAGE. PAGE 67 E1329 — FORCES NAT/G ATTIT LAW

S67
CLOGGER T.J.,"THE BIG EAR." UK USA+45 USSR LAW LEGIS CRIME GP/REL INGP/REL ATTIT 20 FBI ESPIONAGE. PAGE 23 E0458 — DIPLOM ORD/FREE COM/IND INSPECT

ESTEP R. E0698

ESTEY M. E0699

ESTIMATION....SEE COST

ESTONIA....SEE ALSO USSR

B58
KURL S.,ESTONIA: A SELECTED BIBLIOGRAPHY. USSR ESTONIA LAW INTELL SECT...ART/METH GEOG HUM SOC 20. PAGE 62 E1238 — BIBLIOG CULTURE NAT/G

GSOUSKI V.,LEGAL SOURCES AND BIBLIOGRAPHY OF THE
BALTIC STATES (ESTONIA, LATVIA, LITHUANIA). COM
ESTONIA LATVIA LITHUANIA NAT/G LEGIS CT/SYS
SANCTION CRIME 20. PAGE 48 E0957

B63
BIBLIOG
ADJUD
LAW
JURID

KLESMENT J.,LEGAL SOURCES AND BIBLIOGRAPHY OF THE
BALTIC STATES (ESTONIA, LATVIA, LITHUANIA). COM
ESTONIA LATVIA LITHUANIA LAW FINAN ADJUD CT/SYS
REGION CENTRAL MARXISM 19/20. PAGE 61 E1223

B63
BIBLIOG/A
JURID
CONSTN
ADMIN

ESTRANGEMENT....SEE STRANGE

ETHIC....PERSONAL ETHICS

ETHIOPIA....SEE ALSO AFR

CHOJNACKI S.,REGISTER ON CURRENT RESEARCH ON
ETHIOPIA AND THE HORN OF AFRICA. ETHIOPIA LAW
CULTURE AGRI SECT EDU/PROP ADMIN...GEOG HEAL LING
20. PAGE 22 E0433

B63
BIBLIOG
ACT/RES
INTELL
ACADEM

MATTHEWS D.G.,"ETHIOPIAN OUTLINE: A BIBLIOGRAPHIC
RESEARCH GUIDE." ETHIOPIA LAW STRUCT ECO/UNDEV AGRI
LABOR SECT CHIEF DELIB/GP EX/STRUC ADMIN...LING
ORG/CHARTS 20. PAGE 69 E1384

S66
BIBLIOG
NAT/G
DIPLOM
POL/PAR

ETHNICITY....SEE RACE/REL, CULTURE

ETHNOGRAPHY....SEE CULTURE

ETIQUET....ETIQUETTE, STYLING, FASHION, MANNERS

DE TOCQUEVILLE A.,DEMOCRACY IN AMERICA (4 VOLS.)
(TRANS. BY HENRY REEVE). CONSTN STRUCT LOC/G NAT/G
POL/PAR PROVS ETIQUET CT/SYS MAJORITY ATTIT 18/19.
PAGE 30 E0595

B35
POPULISM
MAJORIT
ORD/FREE
SOCIETY

LUCE R.,LEGISLATIVE PROBLEMS. CONSTN CHIEF JUDGE
BUDGET CONFER ETIQUET CONTROL MORAL PWR NEW/LIB
CONGRESS. PAGE 67 E1331

B35
TREND
ADMIN
LEGIS

GROSS B.M.,THE LEGISLATIVE STRUGGLE: A STUDY IN
SOCIAL COMBAT. STRUCT LOC/G POL/PAR JUDGE EDU/PROP
DEBATE ETIQUET ADMIN LOBBY CHOOSE GOV/REL INGP/REL
HEREDITY ALL/VALS...SOC PRESIDENT. PAGE 48 E0948

B53
LEGIS
DECISION
PERSON
LEAD

FORGAC A.A.,NEW DIPLOMACY AND THE UNITED NATIONS.
FRANCE GERMANY UK USSR INT/ORG DELIB/GP EX/STRUC
PEACE...INT/LAW CONCPT UN. PAGE 39 E0770

B65
DIPLOM
ETIQUET
NAT/G

ETTINGHAUSEN R. E0700

EUGENICS....SEE BIO/SOC+GEOG

EUGENIE....EMPRESS EUGENIE (FRANCE)

EULAU H. E0701

EUR+WWI....EUROPE SINCE WORLD WAR I

EURATOM....EUROPEAN ATOMIC ENERGY COMMUNITY

FOREIGN AFFAIRS. SPACE WOR+45 WOR-45 CULTURE
ECO/UNDEV FINAN NAT/G TEC/DEV INT/TRADE ARMS/CONT
NUC/PWR...POLICY 20 UN EURATOM ECSC EEC. PAGE 1
E0021

N
BIBLIOG
DIPLOM
INT/ORG
INT/LAW

ECONOMIDES C.P.,LE POUVOIR DE DECISION DES
ORGANISATIONS INTERNATIONALES EUROPEENNES. DIPLOM
DOMIN INGP/REL EFFICIENCY...INT/LAW JURID 20 NATO
OEEC EEC COUNCL/EUR EURATOM. PAGE 34 E0673

B64
INT/ORG
PWR
DECISION
GP/COMP

EYRAUD M.,"LA FRANCE FACE A UN EVENTUEL TRAITE DE
NON DISSEMINATION DES ARMES NUCLEAIRES." FRANCE
USA+45 EXTR/IND INDUS R+D INT/ORG ACT/RES TEC/DEV
AGREE PRODUC ATTIT 20 TREATY AEC EURATOM. PAGE 36
E0708

S67
NUC/PWR
ARMS/CONT
POLICY

EURCOALSTL....EUROPEAN COAL AND STEEL COMMUNITY; SEE ALSO
VOL/ASSN, INT/ORG

EURCT/JUST....EUROPEAN COURT OF JUSTICE

SCHECHTER A.H.,INTERPRETATION OF AMBIGUOUS
DOCUMENTS BY INTERNATIONAL ADMINISTRATIVE
TRIBUNALS. WOR+45 EX/STRUC INT/TRADE CT/SYS
SOVEREIGN 20 UN ILO EURCT/JUST. PAGE 87 E1752

B64
INT/LAW
DIPLOM
INT/ORG
ADJUD

AMERICAN JOURNAL COMP LAW,THE AMERICAN JOURNAL OF
COMPARATIVE LAW READER. EUR+WWI USA+45 USA-45 LAW
CONSTN LOC/G MUNIC NAT/G DIPLOM...ANTHOL 20
SUPREME/CT EURCT/JUST. PAGE 4 E0081

B66
IDEA/COMP
JURID
INT/LAW
CT/SYS

EUROPE....SEE MOD/EUR

POUND R.,ORGANIZATION OF THE COURTS (PAMPHLET).
MOD/EUR UK USA-45 ADJUD PWR...GOV/COMP 10/20
EUROPE. PAGE 82 E1635

N19
CT/SYS
JURID
STRUCT
ADMIN

MCILWAIN C.H.,CONSTITUTIONALISM: ANCIENT AND
MODERN. USA+45 ROMAN/EMP LAW CHIEF LEGIS CT/SYS
GP/REL ORD/FREE SOVEREIGN...POLICY TIME/SEQ
ROMAN/REP EUROPE. PAGE 71 E1419

B47
CONSTN
NAT/G
PARL/PROC
GOV/COMP

FRIEDMAN W.,THE PUBLIC CORPORATION: A COMPARATIVE
SYMPOSIUM (UNIVERSITY OF TORONTO SCHOOL OF LAW
COMPARATIVE LAW SERIES, VOL. I). SWEDEN USA+45
INDUS INT/ORG NAT/G REGION CENTRAL FEDERAL...POLICY
JURID IDEA/COMP NAT/COMP ANTHOL 20 COMMONWLTH
MONOPOLY EUROPE. PAGE 40 E0801

B54
LAW
SOCISM
LG/CO
OWN

ROSE A.M.,MINORITY PROBLEMS: A TEXTBOOK OF READINGS
IN INTERGROUP RELATIONS. UNIV USA+45 LAW SCHOOL
WORKER PROB/SOLV GP/REL PERSON...PSY ANTHOL WORSHIP
20 NEGRO INDIAN/AM JEWS EUROPE. PAGE 85 E1713

B65
RACE/REL
DISCRIM
ISOLAT
ACT/RES

FUCHS W.P.,STAAT UND KIRCHE IM WANDEL DER
JAHRHUNDERTE. EUR+WWI MOD/EUR UK REV...JURID CONCPT
4/20 EUROPE CHRISTIAN CHURCH/STA. PAGE 41 E0817

B66
SECT
NAT/G
ORD/FREE
GP/REL

EUROPE/E....EASTERN EUROPE (ALL EUROPEAN COMMUNIST NATIONS)

GSOVSKI V.,GOVERNMENT, LAW, AND COURTS IN THE
SOVIET UNION AND EASTERN EUROPE (2 VOLS.). COM USSR
AGRI INDUS WORKER CT/SYS CRIME...BIBLIOG 20
EUROPE/E. PAGE 48 E0958

B59
ADJUD
MARXISM
CONTROL
ORD/FREE

BOLGAR V.,"THE PUBLIC INTEREST: A JURISPRUDENTIAL
AND COMPARATIVE OVERVIEW OF SYMPOSIUM ON
FUNDAMENTAL CONCEPTS OF PUBLIC LAW" COM FRANCE
GERMANY SWITZERLND LAW ADJUD ADMIN AGREE LAISSEZ
...JURID GEN/LAWS 20 EUROPE/E. PAGE 14 E0264

L63
CONCPT
ORD/FREE
CONTROL
NAT/COMP

EUROPE/W....WESTERN EUROPE (NON-COMMUNIST EUROPE, EXCLUDING
GREECE, TURKEY, SCANDINAVIA, AND THE BRITISH ISLES)

FOX W.T.R.,UNITED STATES POLICY IN A TWO POWER
WORLD. COM USA+45 USSR FORCES DOMIN AGREE NEUTRAL
NUC/PWR ORD/FREE SOVEREIGN 20 COLD/WAR TREATY
EUROPE/W INTERVENT. PAGE 39 E0780

N47
DIPLOM
FOR/AID
POLICY

EUROPEAN ATOMIC ENERGY COMMUNITY....SEE EURATOM

EUROPEAN COAL AND STEEL COMMUNITY....SEE EURCOALSTL

EUROPEAN CONVENTION ON HUMAN RIGHTS....SEE ECHR

EUROPEAN COURT OF JUSTICE....SEE EURCT/JUST

EUROPEAN ECONOMIC COMMUNITY....SEE EEC

EUSDEN J.D. E0702

EVAN W.M. E0703

EVANS C. E0704

EVANS I.L. E0705

EVERETT C.W. E0191

EVERS/MED....MEDGAR EVERS

DORMAN M.,WE SHALL OVERCOME. USA+45 ELITES ACADEM   RACE/REL
FORCES TOP/EX MURDER...JURID 20 CIV/RIGHTS   LAW
MISSISSIPP EVERS/MED CLEMSON. PAGE 32 E0638   DISCRIM
                           B64

EWALD R.F. E0706

EX/IM/BANK....EXPORT-IMPORT BANK

EX/STRUC....EXECUTIVE ESTABLISHMENTS

                           N
JOURNAL OF POLITICS. USA+45 USA-45 CONSTN POL/PAR   BIBLIOG/A
EX/STRUC LEGIS PROB/SOLV DIPLOM CT/SYS CHOOSE   NAT/G
RACE/REL 20. PAGE 1 E0011   LAW
                           LOC/G

                           N
ADVANCED MANAGEMENT. INDUS EX/STRUC WORKER OP/RES   MGT
...DECISION BIBLIOG/A 20. PAGE 1 E0015   ADMIN
                           LABOR
                           GP/REL

                           N
UNESCO.INTERNATIONAL BIBLIOGRAPHY OF POLITICAL   BIBLIOG
SCIENCE (VOLUMES 1-8). WOR+45 LAW NAT/G EX/STRUC   CONCPT
LEGIS PROB/SOLV DIPLOM ADMIN GOV/REL 20 UNESCO.   IDEA/COMP
PAGE 98 E1957

US SUPERINTENDENT OF DOCUMENTS,POLITICAL SCIENCE: BIBLIOG/A
GOVERNMENT, CRIME, DISTRICT OF COLUMBIA (PRICE LIST   NAT/G
54). USA+45 LAW CONSTN EX/STRUC WORKER ADJUD ADMIN   CRIME
CT/SYS CHOOSE INGP/REL RACE/REL CONGRESS PRESIDENT.
PAGE 103 E2063
                           B03
GRIFFIN A.P.C.,LIST OF BOOKS ON THE CONSTITUTION OF   BIBLIOG/A
THE UNITED STATES (PAMPHLET). USA-45 NAT/G EX/STRUC   CONSTN
JUDGE TOP/EX CT/SYS 18/20 CONGRESS PRESIDENT   LAW
SUPREME/CT. PAGE 46 E0920   JURID

                           B05
GOODNOW F.J.,THE PRINCIPLES OF THE ADMINISTRATIVE   ADMIN
LAW OF THE UNITED STATES. USA-45 LAW STRUCT   NAT/G
EX/STRUC LEGIS BAL/PWR CONTROL GOV/REL PWR...JURID   PROVS
19/20 CIVIL/SERV. PAGE 45 E0887   LOC/G

                           B06
FOSTER J.W.,THE PRACTICE OF DIPLOMACY AS   DIPLOM
ILLUSTRATED IN THE FOREIGN RELATIONS OF THE UNITED   ROUTINE
STATES. MOD/EUR USA-45 NAT/G EX/STRUC ADMIN   PHIL/SCI
...POLICY INT/LAW BIBLIOG 19/20. PAGE 39 E0777

                           B10
MCILWAIN C.H.,THE HIGH COURT OF PARLIAMENT AND ITS   LAW
SUPREMACY B1910 1878 408. UK EX/STRUC PARL/PROC   LEGIS
GOV/REL INGP/REL PRIVIL 12/20 PARLIAMENT   CONSTN
ENGLSH/LAW. PAGE 71 E1416   NAT/G

                           B18
WILSON W.,THE STATE: ELEMENTS OF HISTORICAL AND   NAT/G
PRACTICAL POLITICS. FRANCE GERMANY ITALY UK USSR   JURID
CONSTN EX/STRUC LEGIS CT/SYS WAR PWR...POLICY   CONCPT
GOV/COMP 20. PAGE 106 E2131   NAT/COMP

                           B18
YUKIO O.,THE VOICE OF JAPANESE DEMOCRACY, AN ESSAY   CONSTN
ON CONSTITUTIONAL LOYALTY (TRANS BY J. E. BECKER).   MAJORIT
ASIA POL/PAR DELIB/GP EX/STRUC RIGID/FLEX ORD/FREE   CHOOSE
PWR...POLICY JURID METH/COMP 19/20 CHINJAP.   NAT/G
PAGE 108 E2167

                           N19
MCCONNELL G.,THE STEEL SEIZURE OF 1952 (PAMPHLET).   DELIB/GP
USA+45 FINAN INDUS PROC/MFG LG/CO EX/STRUC ADJUD   LABOR
CONTROL GP/REL ORD/FREE PWR 20 TRUMAN/HS PRESIDENT   PROB/SOLV
CONGRESS. PAGE 70 E1402   NAT/G

                           C20
BLACHLY F.F.,"THE GOVERNMENT AND ADMINISTRATION OF   NAT/G
GERMANY." GERMANY CONSTN LOC/G PROVS DELIB/GP   GOV/REL
EX/STRUC FORCES LEGIS TOP/EX CT/SYS...BIBLIOG/A   ADMIN
19/20. PAGE 12 E0235   PHIL/SCI

                           B21
BRYCE J.,MODERN DEMOCRACIES. FUT NEW/ZEALND USA-45   NAT/G
LAW CONSTN POL/PAR PROVS VOL/ASSN EX/STRUC LEGIS   TREND
LEGIT CT/SYS EXEC KNOWL CONGRESS AUSTRAL 20.
PAGE 16 E0322

                           B22
FARRAND M.,THE FRAMING OF THE CONSTITUTION OF THE   CONSTN
UNITED STATES (1913). USA-45 EX/STRUC PROB/SOLV   DELIB/GP

PERSON. PAGE 36 E0721   LEGIS
                           CT/SYS

                           B24
HOLDSWORTH W.S.,A HISTORY OF ENGLISH LAW; THE   LAW
COMMON LAW AND ITS RIVALS (VOL. V). UK SEA EX/STRUC   LEGIS
WRITING ADMIN...INT/LAW JURID CONCPT IDEA/COMP   ADJUD
WORSHIP 16/17 PARLIAMENT ENGLSH/LAW COMMON/LAW.   CT/SYS
PAGE 54 E1073

                           B24
HOLDSWORTH W.S.,A HISTORY OF ENGLISH LAW; THE   LAW
COMMON LAW AND ITS RIVALS (VOL. VI). UK STRATA   CONSTN
EX/STRUC ADJUD ADMIN CONTROL CT/SYS...JURID CONCPT   LEGIS
GEN/LAWS 17 COMMONWLTH PARLIAMENT ENGLSH/LAW   CHIEF
COMMON/LAW. PAGE 54 E1074

                           B27
GOOCH G.P.,ENGLISH DEMOCRATIC IDEAS IN THE   IDEA/COMP
SEVENTEENTH CENTURY (2ND ED.). UK LAW SECT FORCES   MAJORIT
DIPLOM LEAD PARL/PROC REV ATTIT AUTHORIT...ANARCH   EX/STRUC
CONCPT 17 PARLIAMENT CMN/WLTH REFORMERS. PAGE 45   CONSERVE
E0885

                           B28
FRANKFURTER F.,THE BUSINESS OF THE SUPREME COURT; A   CT/SYS
STUDY IN THE FEDERAL JUDICIAL SYSTEM. USA-45 CONSTN   ADJUD
EX/STRUC PROB/SOLV GP/REL ATTIT PWR...POLICY JURID   LAW
18/20 SUPREME/CT CONGRESS. PAGE 40 E0789   FEDERAL

                           B29
MOLEY R.,POLITICS AND CRIMINAL PROSECUTION. USA-45   PWR
POL/PAR EX/STRUC LEGIT CONTROL LEAD ROUTINE CHOOSE   CT/SYS
INGP/REL...JURID CHARTS 20. PAGE 74 E1481   CRIME
                           ADJUD

                           B30
BURLAMAQUI J.J.,PRINCIPLES OF NATURAL AND POLITIC   LAW
LAW (2 VOLS.) (1747-51). EX/STRUC LEGIS AGREE   NAT/G
CT/SYS CHOOSE ROLE SOVEREIGN 18 NATURL/LAW. PAGE 17   ORD/FREE
E0342   CONCPT

                           B30
BYNKERSHOEK C.,QUAESTIONUM JURIS PUBLICI LIBRI DUO.   INT/ORG
CHRIST-17C MOD/EUR CONSTN ELITES SOCIETY NAT/G   LAW
PROVS EX/STRUC FORCES TOP/EX BAL/PWR DIPLOM ATTIT   NAT/LISM
MORAL...TRADIT CONCPT. PAGE 18 E0352   INT/LAW

                           B30
GREEN F.M.,CONSTITUTIONAL DEVELOPMENT IN THE SOUTH   CONSTN
ATLANTIC STATES, 1776-1860; A STUDY IN THE   PROVS
EVOLUTION OF DEMOCRACY. USA-45 ELITES SOCIETY   PLURISM
STRATA ECO/DEV AGRI POL/PAR EX/STRUC LEGIS CT/SYS   REPRESENT
REGION...BIBLIOG 18/19 MARYLAND VIRGINIA GEORGIA
NORTH/CAR SOUTH/CAR. PAGE 46 E0905

                           B31
STOWELL E.C.,INTERNATIONAL LAW. FUT UNIV WOR-45   INT/ORG
SOCIETY CONSULT EX/STRUC FORCES ACT/RES PLAN DIPLOM   ROUTINE
EDU/PROP LEGIT DISPL PWR SKILL...POLICY CONCPT OBS   INT/LAW
TREND TOT/POP 20. PAGE 94 E1885

                           B32
GREAT BRIT COMM MINISTERS PWR,REPORT. UK LAW CONSTN   EX/STRUC
CONSULT LEGIS PARL/PROC SANCTION SOVEREIGN   NAT/G
...DECISION JURID 20 PARLIAMENT. PAGE 45 E0902   PWR
                           CONTROL

                           B33
DANGERFIELD R.,IN DEFENSE OF THE SENATE. USA-45   LEGIS
CONSTN NAT/G EX/STRUC TOP/EX ATTIT KNOWL   DELIB/GP
...METH/CNCPT STAT TIME/SEQ TREND CON/ANAL CHARTS   DIPLOM
CONGRESS 20 TREATY. PAGE 28 E0565

                           B33
ENSOR R.C.K.,COURTS AND JUDGES IN FRANCE, GERMANY,   CT/SYS
AND ENGLAND. FRANCE GERMANY UK LAW PROB/SOLV ADMIN   EX/STRUC
ROUTINE CRIME ROLE...METH/COMP 20 CIVIL/LAW.   ADJUD
PAGE 35 E0692   NAT/COMP

                           B33
HELLMAN F.S.,SELECTED LIST OF REFERENCES ON THE   BIBLIOG/A
CONSTITUTIONAL POWERS OF THE PRESIDENT INCLUDING   JURID
POWERS RECENTLY DELEGATED. USA-45 NAT/G EX/STRUC   LAW
TOP/EX CENTRAL FEDERAL PWR 20 PRESIDENT. PAGE 51   CONSTN
E1025

                           B35
RAM J.,THE SCIENCE OF LEGAL JUDGMENT: A TREATISE...   LAW
UK CONSTN NAT/G LEGIS CREATE PROB/SOLV AGREE CT/SYS   JURID
...INT/LAW CONCPT 19 ENGLSH/LAW CANON/LAW CIVIL/LAW   EX/STRUC
CTS/WESTM. PAGE 83 E1672   ADJUD

                           B36
GRAVES W.B.,AMERICAN STATE GOVERNMENT. CONSTN FINAN   NAT/G
EX/STRUC FORCES LEGIS BUDGET TAX CT/SYS REPRESENT   PROVS

GOV/REL...BIBLIOG/A 19/20. PAGE 45 E0900   ADMIN
                                                   FEDERAL

                                                      B38
FIELD G.L.,THE SYNDICAL AND CORPORATIVE   FASCISM
INSTITUTIONS OF ITALIAN FASCISM. ITALY CONSTN   INDUS
STRATA LABOR EX/STRUC TOP/EX ADJUD ADMIN LEAD   NAT/G
TOTALISM AUTHORIT...MGT 20 MUSSOLIN/B. PAGE 38   WORKER
E0746

                                                      B38
HELLMAN F.S.,THE SUPREME COURT ISSUE: SELECTED LIST BIBLIOG/A
OF REFERENCES. USA-45 NAT/G CHIEF EX/STRUC JUDGE   CONSTN
ATTIT...JURID 20 PRESIDENT ROOSEVLT/F SUPREME/CT. CT/SYS
PAGE 51 E1026   LAW

                                                      B38
HOLDSWORTH W.S.,A HISTORY OF ENGLISH LAW; THE   LAW
CENTURIES OF SETTLEMENT AND REFORM (VOL. X). INDIA LOC/G
UK CONSTN NAT/G COLONIAL CT/SYS   EX/STRUC
CHOOSE ORD/FREE PWR...JURID 18 PARLIAMENT   ADJUD
COMMONWLTH COMMON/LAW. PAGE 54 E1077

                                                      B38
HOLDSWORTH W.S.,A HISTORY OF ENGLISH LAW; THE   LAW
CENTURIES OF SETTLEMENT AND REFORM (VOL. XI). UK   COLONIAL
CONSTN NAT/G EX/STRUC DIPLOM ADJUD CT/SYS LEAD   LEGIS
CRIME ATTIT...INT/LAW JURID 18 CMN/WLTH PARLIAMENT PARL/PROC
ENGLSH/LAW. PAGE 54 E1079

                                                      B39
SIEYES E.J.,LES DISCOURS DE SIEYES DANS LES DEBATS CONSTN
CONSTITUTIONNELS DE L'AN III (2 ET 18 THERMIDOR). ADJUD
FRANCE LAW NAT/G PROB/SOLV BAL/PWR GOV/REL 18 JURY. LEGIS
PAGE 91 E1824   EX/STRUC

                                                      B39
ZIMMERN A.,THE LEAGUE OF NATIONS AND THE RULE OF   INT/ORG
LAW. WOR-45 STRUCT NAT/G DELIB/GP EX/STRUC BAL/PWR LAW
DOMIN LEGIT COERCE ORD/FREE PWR...POLICY RECORD   DIPLOM
LEAGUE/NAT TOT/POP VAL/FREE 20 LEAGUE/NAT. PAGE 108
E2170

                                                      B40
ANDERSON W.,FUNDAMENTALS OF AMERICAN GOVERNMENT.   NAT/G
USA-45 LAW POL/PAR CHIEF EX/STRUC BUDGET ADMIN   LOC/G
CT/SYS PARL/PROC CHOOSE FEDERAL...BIBLIOG 20.   GOV/REL
PAGE 5 E0093   CONSTN

                                                      B40
HART J.,AN INTRODUCTION TO ADMINISTRATIVE LAW, WITH LAW
SELECTED CASES. USA-45 CONSTN SOCIETY NAT/G   ADMIN
EX/STRUC ADJUD CT/SYS LEAD CRIME ORD/FREE   LEGIS
...DECISION JURID 20 CASEBOOK. PAGE 50 E1002   PWR

                                                      S40
GERTH H.,"THE NAZI PARTY: ITS LEADERSHIP AND   POL/PAR
COMPOSITION" (BMR)" GERMANY ELITES STRATA STRUCT   DOMIN
EX/STRUC FORCES ECO/TAC CT/SYS CHOOSE TOTALISM   LEAD
AGE/Y AUTHORIT PWR 20. PAGE 43 E0851   ADMIN

                                                      B41
GELLHORN W.,FEDERAL ADMINISTRATIVE PROCEEDINGS.   EX/STRUC
USA+45 CLIENT FACE/GP NAT/G LOBBY REPRESENT PWR 20. LAW
PAGE 43 E0844   ADJUD
                                                    POLICY

                                                      B44
ADLER M.J.,HOW TO THINK ABOUT WAR AND PEACE. WOR-45 INT/ORG
LAW SOCIETY EX/STRUC DIPLOM KNOWL ORD/FREE...POLICY CREATE
TREND GEN/LAWS 20. PAGE 3 E0049   ARMS/CONT
                                                    PEACE

                                                      B44
BEARD C.A.,AMERICAN GOVERNMENT AND POLITICS (REV. LEAD
ED.). CONSTN MUNIC POL/PAR PROVS EX/STRUC LEGIS   USA-45
TOP/EX CT/SYS GOV/REL...BIBLIOG T 18/20. PAGE 9   NAT/G
E0165   LOC/G

                                                      S44
WRIGHT Q.,"CONSTITUTIONAL PROCEDURES OF THE US FOR TOP/EX
CARRYING OUT OBLIGATIONS FOR MILITARY SANCTIONS." FORCES
EUR+WWI FUT USA-45 WOR-45 CONSTN INTELL NAT/G   INT/LAW
CONSULT EX/STRUC LEGIS ROUTINE DRIVE...POLICY JURID WAR
CONCPT OBS TREND TOT/POP 20. PAGE 108 E2153

                                                      B45
CONOVER H.F.,THE GOVERNMENTS OF THE MAJOR FOREIGN BIBLIOG
POWERS: A BIBLIOGRAPHY. FRANCE GERMANY ITALY UK   NAT/G
USSR CONSTN LOC/G POL/PAR EX/STRUC FORCES ADMIN   DIPLOM
CT/SYS CIVMIL/REL TOTALISM...POLICY 19/20. PAGE 25
E0494

                                                      B46
CORRY J.A.,DEMOCRATIC GOVERNMENT AND POLITICS.   NAT/G
WOR-45 EX/STRUC LOBBY TOTALISM...MAJORIT CONCPT   CONSTN

METH/COMP NAT/COMP 20. PAGE 26 E0511   POL/PAR
                                                   JURID

                                                      C46
GOODRICH L.M.,"CHARTER OF THE UNITED NATIONS: CONSTN
COMMENTARY AND DOCUMENTS." EX/STRUC ADMIN...INT/LAW INT/ORG
CON/ANAL BIBLIOG 20 UN. PAGE 45 E0890   DIPLOM

                                                      B48
BISHOP H.M.,BASIC ISSUES OF AMERICAN DEMOCRACY.   NAT/G
USA+45 USA-45 POL/PAR EX/STRUC LEGIS ADJUD FEDERAL PARL/PROC
...BIBLIOG 18/20. PAGE 12 E0232   CONSTN

                                                      B48
SLESSER H.,THE ADMINISTRATION OF THE LAW. UK CONSTN LAW
EX/STRUC OP/RES PROB/SOLV CRIME ROLE...DECISION   CT/SYS
METH/COMP 20 CIVIL/LAW ENGLSH/LAW CIVIL/LAW.   ADJUD
PAGE 92 E1839

                                                      C48
WALKER H.,"THE LEGISLATIVE PROCESS; LAWMAKING IN   PARL/PROC
THE UNITED STATES." NAT/G POL/PAR PROVS EX/STRUC   LEGIS
OP/RES PROB/SOLV LOBBY GOV/REL...CHARTS   LAW
BIBLIOG T 18/20 CONGRESS. PAGE 105 E2094   CONSTN

                                                      B49
BOYD A.M.,UNITED STATES GOVERNMENT PUBLICATIONS   BIBLIOG/A
(3RD ED.). USA+45 EX/STRUC LEGIS ADMIN...JURID   PRESS
CHARTS 20. PAGE 14 E0281   NAT/G
                                                   EDU/PROP

                                                      B49
DENNING A.,FREEDOM UNDER THE LAW. MOD/EUR UK LAW   ORD/FREE
SOCIETY CHIEF EX/STRUC LEGIS ADJUD CT/SYS PERS/REL JURID
PERSON 17/20 ENGLSH/LAW. PAGE 31 E0606   NAT/G

                                                      B51
ANDERSON W.,STATE AND LOCAL GOVERNMENT IN THE   LOC/G
UNITED STATES. USA+45 CONSTN POL/PAR EX/STRUC LEGIS MUNIC
BUDGET TAX ADJUD CT/SYS CHOOSE...CHARTS T 20.   PROVS
PAGE 5 E0094   GOV/REL

                                                      B51
DAVIS K.C.,ADMINISTRATIVE LAW. USA+45 USA-45 NAT/G ADMIN
PROB/SOLV BAL/PWR CONTROL ORD/FREE...POLICY 20   JURID
SUPREME/CT. PAGE 29 E0574   EX/STRUC
                                                   ADJUD

                                                      B51
ROSSITER C.,THE SUPREME COURT AND THE COMMANDER IN CT/SYS
CHIEF. LAW CONSTN DELIB/GP EX/STRUC LEGIS TOP/EX   CHIEF
ADJUD CONTROL...DECISION SOC/EXP PRESIDENT. PAGE 86 WAR
E1724   PWR

                                                      B52
APPADORAI A.,THE SUBSTANCE OF POLITICS (6TH ED.). PHIL/SCI
EX/STRUC LEGIS DIPLOM CT/SYS CHOOSE FASCISM MARXISM NAT/G
SOCISM...BIBLIOG T. PAGE 5 E0100

                                                      B52
APPLEBY P.H.,MORALITY AND ADMINISTRATION IN   REPRESENT
DEMOCRATIC GOVERNMENT. USA+45 CLIENT NAT/G EXEC   LOBBY
EFFICIENCY 20. PAGE 5 E0102   ADMIN
                                                   EX/STRUC

                                                      B52
COUNCIL STATE GOVERNMENTS,OCCUPATIONAL LICENSING IN PROF/ORG
THE STATES. USA+45 PROVS ADMIN EXEC LOBBY 20.   LICENSE
PAGE 27 E0526   REPRESENT
                                                   EX/STRUC

                                                      B52
FLECHTHEIM O.K.,FUNDAMENTALS OF POLITICAL SCIENCE. NAT/G
WOR+45 WOR-45 LAW POL/PAR EX/STRUC LEGIS ADJUD   DIPLOM
ATTIT PWR...INT/LAW. PAGE 38 E0760   IDEA/COMP
                                                   CONSTN

                                                      L52
WRIGHT Q.,"CONGRESS AND THE TREATY-MAKING POWER." ROUTINE
USA+45 WOR+45 CONSTN INTELL NAT/G CHIEF CONSULT   DIPLOM
EX/STRUC LEGIS TOP/EX CREATE GOV/REL DISPL DRIVE   INT/LAW
RIGID/FLEX...TREND TOT/POP CONGRESS CONGRESS 20   DELIB/GP
TREATY. PAGE 108 E2154

                                                      B54
HAMSON C.J.,EXECUTIVE DISCRETION AND JUDICIAL   ELITES
CONTROL; AN ASPECT OF THE FRENCH CONSEIL D'ETAT.   ADJUD
EUR+WWI FRANCE MOD/EUR UK NAT/G EX/STRUC PARTIC   NAT/COMP
CONSERVE...JURID BIBLIOG/A 18/20 SUPREME/CT.
PAGE 50 E0992

                                                      B54
SCHWARTZ B.,FRENCH ADMINISTRATIVE LAW AND THE   JURID
COMMON-LAW WORLD. FRANCE CULTURE LOC/G NAT/G PROVS LAW
DELIB/GP EX/STRUC LEGIS PROB/SOLV CT/SYS EXEC   METH/COMP
GOV/REL...IDEA/COMP ENGLSH/LAW. PAGE 89 E1786   ADJUD

SINCO,PHILIPPINE POLITICAL LAW: PRINCIPLES AND CONCEPTS (10TH ED.). PHILIPPINE LOC/G EX/STRUC BAL/PWR ECO/TAC TAX ADJUD ADMIN CONTROL CT/SYS SUFF ORD/FREE...T 20. PAGE 91 E1831
B54
LAW
CONSTN
LEGIS

COOPER L.,"ADMINISTRATIVE JUSTICE." UK ADMIN REPRESENT PWR...POLICY 20. PAGE 25 E0502
S54
LAW
ADJUD
CONTROL
EX/STRUC

BOWIE R.R.,"STUDIES IN FEDERALISM." AGRI FINAN LABOR EX/STRUC FORCES LEGIS DIPLOM INT/TRADE ADJUD ...BIBLIOG 20 EEC. PAGE 14 E0279
C54
FEDERAL
EUR+WWI
INT/ORG
CONSTN

CALDWELL L.K.,"THE GOVERNMENT AND ADMINISTRATION OF NEW YORK." LOC/G MUNIC POL/PAR SCHOOL CHIEF LEGIS PLAN TAX CT/SYS...MGT SOC/WK BIBLIOG 20 NEWYORK/C. PAGE 19 E0365
C54
PROVS
ADMIN
CONSTN
EX/STRUC

CRAIG J.,BIBLIOGRAPHY OF PUBLIC ADMINISTRATION IN AUSTRALIA. CONSTN FINAN EX/STRUC LEGIS PLAN DIPLOM RECEIVE ADJUD ROUTINE...HEAL 19/20 AUSTRAL PARLIAMENT. PAGE 27 E0540
B55
BIBLIOG
GOV/REL
ADMIN
NAT/G

CUSHMAN R.E.,LEADING CONSTITUTIONAL DECISIONS. USA+45 USA-45 NAT/G EX/STRUC LEGIS JUDGE TAX FEDERAL...DECISION 20 SUPREME/CT CASEBOOK. PAGE 28 E0559
B55
CONSTN
PROB/SOLV
JURID
CT/SYS

DE ARAGAO J.G.,LA JURIDICTION ADMINISTRATIVE AU BRESIL. BRAZIL ADJUD COLONIAL CT/SYS REV FEDERAL ORD/FREE...BIBLIOG 19/20. PAGE 29 E0580
B55
EX/STRUC
ADMIN
NAT/G

HOGAN W.N.,INTERNATIONAL CONFLICT AND COLLECTIVE SECURITY: THE PRINCIPLE OF CONCERN IN INTERNATIONAL ORGANIZATION. CONSTN EX/STRUC BAL/PWR DIPLOM ADJUD CONTROL CENTRAL CONSEN PEACE...INT/LAW CONCPT METH/COMP 20 UN LEAGUE/NAT. PAGE 53 E1066
B55
INT/ORG
WAR
ORD/FREE
FORCES

MAYERS L.,THE AMERICAN LEGAL SYSTEM. USA+45 USA-45 NAT/G EX/STRUC ADMIN CONTROL FEDERAL 20 SUPREME/CT. PAGE 70 E1394
B55
JURID
CT/SYS
LEGIS
ADJUD

MAZZINI J.,THE DUTIES OF MAN. MOD/EUR LAW SOCIETY FAM NAT/G POL/PAR SECT VOL/ASSN EX/STRUC ACT/RES CREATE REV PEACE ATTIT ALL/VALS...GEN/LAWS WORK 19. PAGE 70 E1396
B55
SUPEGO
CONCPT
NAT/LISM

PEASLEE A.J.,CONSTITUTIONS OF NATIONS. WOR+45 LAW NAT/G EX/STRUC LEGIS TOP/EX LEGIT CT/SYS ROUTINE CHOOSE ORD/FREE PWR SOVEREIGN...CHARTS TOT/POP. PAGE 80 E1605
B56
CONSTN
CON/ANAL

REDFORD E.S.,PUBLIC ADMINISTRATION AND POLICY FORMATION: STUDIES IN OIL, GAS, BANKING, RIVER DEVELOPMENT AND CORPORATE INVESTIGATIONS. USA+45 CLIENT NAT/G ADMIN LOBBY REPRESENT GOV/REL INGP/REL 20. PAGE 84 E1678
B56
EX/STRUC
PROB/SOLV
CONTROL
EXEC

US HOUSE RULES COMM,HEARINGS BEFORE A SPECIAL SUBCOMMITTEE: ESTABLISHMENT OF A STANDING COMMITTEE ON ADMINISTRATIVE PROCEDURE. PRACTICE. USA+45 LAW EX/STRUC ADJUD CONTROL EXEC GOV/REL EFFICIENCY PWR ...POLICY INT 20 CONGRESS. PAGE 100 E2009
B56
ADMIN
DOMIN
DELIB/GP
NAT/G

WIGGINS J.R.,FREEDOM OR SECRECY. USA+45 USA-45 DELIB/GP EX/STRUC FORCES ADJUD SANCTION KNOWL PWR ...AUD/VIS CONGRESS 20. PAGE 106 E2121
B56
ORD/FREE
PRESS
NAT/G
CONTROL

ZINN C.J.,HOW OUR LAWS ARE MADE: BROCHURE HOUSE OF REPRESENTATIVES DOCUMENT 451. LAW CONSTN CHIEF EX/STRUC PROB/SOLV HOUSE/REP SENATE. PAGE 108 E2171
B56
LEGIS
DELIB/GP
PARL/PROC
ROUTINE

NOBLEMAN E.E.,"THE DELEGATION OF PRESIDENTIAL FUNCTIONS: CONSTITUTIONAL AND LEGAL ASPECTS."
S56
CHIEF
REPRESENT

USA+45 CONSTN NAT/G CONTROL 20. PAGE 77 E1553
EX/STRUC
LAW

FALL B.B.,"THE VIET-MINH REGIME." VIETNAM LAW ECO/UNDEV POL/PAR FORCES DOMIN WAR ATTIT MARXISM ...BIOG PREDICT BIBLIOG/A 20. PAGE 36 E0720
C56
NAT/G
ADMIN
EX/STRUC
LEAD

BERLE A.A. JR.,ECONOMIC POWER AND FREE SOCIETY (PAMPHLET). CLIENT CONSTN EX/STRUC ECO/TAC CONTROL PARTIC PWR WEALTH MAJORIT. PAGE 11 E0205
B57
LG/CO
CAP/ISM
INGP/REL
LEGIT

JENNINGS I.,PARLIAMENT. UK FINAN INDUS POL/PAR DELIB/GP EX/STRUC PLAN CONTROL...MAJORIT JURID PARLIAMENT. PAGE 58 E1163
B57
PARL/PROC
TOP/EX
MGT
LEGIS

SCHLOCHAUER H.J.,OFFENTLICHES RECHT. GERMANY/W FINAN EX/STRUC LEGIS DIPLOM FEDERAL ORD/FREE ...INT/LAW 20. PAGE 88 E1757
B57
CONSTN
JURID
ADMIN
CT/SYS

AMERICAN SOCIETY PUBLIC ADMIN,STRENGTHENING MANAGEMENT FOR DEMOCRATIC GOVERNMENT. USA+45 ACADEM EX/STRUC WORKER PLAN BUDGET CONFER CT/SYS EFFICIENCY ANTHOL. PAGE 4 E0083
B58
ADMIN
NAT/G
EXEC
MGT

DAVIS K.C.,ADMINISTRATIVE LAW TREATISE (VOLS. I AND IV). NAT/G JUDGE PROB/SOLV ADJUD GP/REL 20 SUPREME/CT. PAGE 29 E0575
B58
ADMIN
JURID
CT/SYS
EX/STRUC

MACKENZIE W.J.M.,FREE ELECTIONS: AN ELEMENTARY TEXTBOOK. WOR+45 NAT/G POL/PAR LEGIS TOP/EX EDU/PROP LEGIT CT/SYS ATTIT PWR...OBS CHARTS STERTYP T CONGRESS PARLIAMENT 20. PAGE 67 E1342
B58
EX/STRUC
CHOOSE

MASON A.T.,THE SUPREME COURT FROM TAFT TO WARREN. EX/STRUC LEGIS ROLE 20 SUPREME/CT TAFT/WH HUGHES/CE STONE/HF. PAGE 69 E1376
B58
CT/SYS
JURID
ADJUD

SHARMA M.P.,PUBLIC ADMINISTRATION IN THEORY AND PRACTICE. INDIA UK USA+45 USA-45 EX/STRUC ADJUD ...POLICY CONCPT NAT/COMP 20. PAGE 90 E1813
B58
MGT
ADMIN
DELIB/GP
JURID

SPITZ D.,DEMOCRACY AND THE CHALLANGE OF POWER. FUT USA+45 USA-45 LAW SOCIETY STRUCT LOC/G POL/PAR PROVS DELIB/GP EX/STRUC LEGIS TOP/EX ACT/RES CREATE DOMIN EDU/PROP LEGIT ADJUD ADMIN ATTIT DRIVE MORAL ORD/FREE TOT/POP. PAGE 93 E1862
B58
NAT/G
PWR

STRONG C.F.,MODERN POLITICAL CONSTITUTIONS. LAW CHIEF DELIB/GP EX/STRUC LEGIS ADJUD CHOOSE FEDERAL POPULISM...CONCPT BIBLIOG 20 UN. PAGE 94 E1887
B58
CONSTN
IDEA/COMP
NAT/G

US CONGRESS,FREEDOM OF INFORMATION AND SECRECY IN GOVERNMENT (2 VOLS.). USA+45 DELIB/GP EX/STRUC EDU/PROP PWR 20 CONGRESS PRESIDENT. PAGE 99 E1988
B58
CHIEF
PRIVIL
CONSTN
LAW

US SENATE COMM POST OFFICE,TO PROVIDE AN EFFECTIVE SYSTEM OF PERSONNEL ADMINISTRATION. USA+45 NAT/G EX/STRUC PARL/PROC GOV/REL...JURID 20 SENATE CIVIL/SERV. PAGE 103 E2060
B58
INT
LEGIS
CONFER
ADMIN

UNESCO,"TECHNIQUES OF MEDIATION AND CONCILIATION." EUR+WWI USA+45 WOR+45 INDUS FACE/GP EX/STRUC EDU/PROP LEGIT PEACE ORD/FREE...INT/LAW TIME/SEQ LEAGUE/NAT 20. PAGE 98 E1961
L58
INT/ORG
CONSULT
DIPLOM

FISHER F.M.,"THE MATHEMATICAL ANALYSIS OF SUPREME COURT DECISIONS: THE USE AND ABUSE OF QUANTITATIVE METHODS." USA+45 LAW EX/STRUC LEGIS JUDGE ROUTINE ATTIT DECISION. PAGE 38 E0757
S58
PROB/SOLV
CT/SYS
JURID
MATH

RIKER W.H.,"THE PARADOX OF VOTING AND CONGRESSIONAL RULES FOR VOTING ON AMENDMENTS." LAW DELIB/GP EX/STRUC PROB/SOLV CONFER DEBATE EFFICIENCY ATTIT
S58
PARL/PROC
DECISION
LEGIS

HOUSE/REP CONGRESS SENATE. PAGE 85 E1700

RATIONAL

C58
FRIEDRICH C.J.,"AUTHORITY, REASON AND DISCRETION" AUTHORIT
IN C. FRIEDRICH'S AUTHORITY (BMR)" UNIV EX/STRUC CHOOSE
ADJUD ADMIN CONTROL INGP/REL ATTIT PERSON PWR. RATIONAL
PAGE 41 E0807 PERS/REL

B59
BROMWICH L.,UNION CONSTITUTIONS. CONSTN EX/STRUC LABOR
PRESS ADJUD CONTROL CHOOSE REPRESENT PWR SAMP. ROUTINE
PAGE 16 E0306 INGP/REL
RACE/REL

B59
DAVIS K.C.,ADMINISTRATIVE LAW TEXT. USA+45 NAT/G ADJUD
DELIB/GP EX/STRUC CONTROL ORD/FREE...T 20 ADMIN
SUPREME/CT. PAGE 29 E0577 JURID
CT/SYS

B59
ELLIOTT S.D.,IMPROVING OUR COURTS. LAW EX/STRUC CT/SYS
PLAN PROB/SOLV ADJUD ADMIN TASK CRIME EFFICIENCY JURID
ORD/FREE 20. PAGE 34 E0684 GOV/REL
NAT/G

B59
LOEWENSTEIN K.,VERFASSUNGSRECHT UND CONSTN
VERFASSUNGSPRAXIS DER VEREINIGTEN STAATEN. USA+45 POL/PAR
USA-45 COLONIAL CT/SYS GP/REL RACE/REL ORD/FREE EX/STRUC
...JURID 18/20 SUPREME/CT CONGRESS PRESIDENT NAT/G
BILL/RIGHT CIVIL/LIB. PAGE 66 E1319

B59
SISSON C.H.,THE SPIRIT OF BRITISH ADMINISTRATION GOV/COMP
AND SOME EUROPEAN COMPARISONS. FRANCE GERMANY/W ADMIN
SWEDEN UK EX/STRUC INGP/REL EFFICIENCY ORD/FREE ELITES
...DECISION 20. PAGE 91 E1835 ATTIT

B59
US SENATE COMM ON POST OFFICE,TO PROVIDE FOR AN ADMIN
EFFECTIVE SYSTEM OF PERSONNEL ADMINISTRATION. NAT/G
EFFICIENCY...MGT 20 CONGRESS CIVIL/SERV POSTAL/SYS EX/STRUC
YARBROGH/R. PAGE 103 E2059 LAW

L59
COX A.,"THE ROLE OF LAW IN PRESERVING UNION LABOR
DEMOCRACY." EX/STRUC LEGIS PARTIC ROUTINE CHOOSE REPRESENT
INGP/REL ORD/FREE. PAGE 27 E0532 LAW
MAJORIT

L59
HECTOR L.J.,"GOVERNMENT BY ANONYMITY: WHO WRITES ADJUD
OUR REGULATORY OPINIONS?" USA+45 NAT/G TOP/EX REPRESENT
CONTROL EXEC. PAGE 51 E1021 EX/STRUC
ADMIN

B60
BYRD E.M. JR.,TREATIES AND EXECUTIVE AGREEMENTS IN CHIEF
THE UNITED STATES: THEIR SEPARATE ROLES AND INT/LAW
LIMITATIONS. USA+45 USA-45 EX/STRUC TARIFFS CT/SYS DIPLOM
GOV/REL FEDERAL...IDEA/COMP BIBLIOG SUPREME/CT
SENATE CONGRESS. PAGE 18 E0353

B60
DAVIS K.C.,ADMINISTRATIVE LAW AND GOVERNMENT. ADMIN
USA+45 EX/STRUC PROB/SOLV ADJUD GP/REL PWR...POLICY JURID
20 SUPREME/CT. PAGE 29 E0578 CT/SYS
NAT/G

B60
HANBURY H.G.,ENGLISH COURTS OF LAW. UK EX/STRUC JURID
LEGIS CRIME ROLE 12/20 COMMON/LAW ENGLSH/LAW. CT/SYS
PAGE 50 E0993 CONSTN
GOV/REL

B60
PRICE D.,THE SECRETARY OF STATE. USA+45 CONSTN CONSULT
ELITES INTELL CHIEF EX/STRUC TOP/EX LEGIT ATTIT PWR DIPLOM
SKILL...DECISION 20 CONGRESS. PAGE 82 E1650 INT/LAW

B60
SCHMIDHAUSER J.R.,THE SUPREME COURT: ITS POLITICS, JUDGE
PERSONALITIES, AND PROCEDURES. LAW DELIB/GP JURID
EX/STRUC TOP/EX ADJUD CT/SYS CHOOSE RATIONAL PWR DECISION
SUPREME/CT. PAGE 88 E1760

B60
SCHUBERT G.A.,CONSTITUTIONAL POLITICS: THE CONSTN
POLITICAL BEHAVIOR OF SUPREME COURT JUSTICES AND CT/SYS
THE CONSTITUTIONAL POLICIES THEY MAKE. LAW ELITES JURID
CHIEF DELIB/GP EX/STRUC LEGIS DISCRIM ORD/FREE PWR DECISION
...POLICY MAJORIT CHARTS SUPREME/CT CONGRESS.
PAGE 89 E1781

L60
FUCHS R.F.,"FAIRNESS AND EFFECTIVENESS IN EFFICIENCY
ADMINISTRATIVE AGENCY ORGANIZATION AND PROCEDURES." EX/STRUC
USA+45 ADJUD ADMIN REPRESENT. PAGE 41 E0816 EXEC
POLICY

S60
MANN S.Z.,"POLICY FORMULATION IN THE EXECUTIVE EXEC
BRANCH: THE TAFT-HARTLEY EXPERIENCE." USA+45 LABOR GOV/REL
CHIEF INGP/REL 20 NLRB. PAGE 68 E1360 EX/STRUC
PROB/SOLV

B61
AVERY M.W.,GOVERNMENT OF WASHINGTON STATE. USA+45 PROVS
MUNIC DELIB/GP EX/STRUC LEGIS GIVE CT/SYS PARTIC LOC/G
REGION EFFICIENCY 20 WASHINGT/G GOVERNOR. PAGE 6 ADMIN
E0121 GOV/REL

B61
AYLMER G.,THE KING'S SERVANTS. UK ELITES CHIEF PAY ADMIN
CT/SYS WEALTH 17 CROMWELL/O CHARLES/I. PAGE 6 E0122 ROUTINE
EX/STRUC
NAT/G

B61
BARBASH J.,LABOR'S GRASS ROOTS. CONSTN NAT/G LABOR
EX/STRUC LEGIS WORKER LEAD...MAJORIT BIBLIOG. INGP/REL
PAGE 8 E0147 GP/REL
LAW

B61
CARNELL F.,THE POLITICS OF THE NEW STATES: A SELECT BIBLIOG/A
ANNOTATED BIBLIOGRAPHY WITH SPECIAL REFERENCE TO AFR
THE COMMONWEALTH. CONSTN ELITES LABOR NAT/G POL/PAR ASIA
EX/STRUC DIPLOM ADJUD ADMIN...GOV/COMP 20 COLONIAL
COMMONWLTH. PAGE 20 E0387

B61
MASSEL M.S.,THE REGULATORY PROCESS (JOURNAL ADJUD
REPRINT). NAT/G LOBBY REPRESENT GOV/REL 20. PAGE 69 EX/STRUC
E1382 EXEC

B61
TOMPKINS D.C.,CONFLICT OF INTEREST IN THE FEDERAL BIBLIOG
GOVERNMENT: A BIBLIOGRAPHY. USA+45 EX/STRUC LEGIS ROLE
ADJUD ADMIN CRIME CONGRESS PRESIDENT. PAGE 96 E1932 NAT/G
LAW

B61
WECHSLER H.,PRINCIPLES, POLITICS AND FUNDAMENTAL CT/SYS
LAW: SELECTED ESSAYS. USA+45 USA-45 LAW SOCIETY CONSTN
NAT/G PROVS DELIB/GP EX/STRUC ACT/RES LEGIT PERSON INT/LAW
KNOWL PWR...JURID 20 NUREMBERG. PAGE 105 E2106

L61
SAND P.T.,"AN HISTORICAL SURVEY OF INTERNATIONAL INT/ORG
AIR LAW SINCE 1944." USA+45 USA-45 WOR+45 WOR-45 LAW
SOCIETY ECO/DEV NAT/G CONSULT EX/STRUC ACT/RES PLAN INT/LAW
LEGIT ROUTINE...JURID CONCPT METH/CNCPT TREND 20. SPACE
PAGE 87 E1744

S61
BAER E.,"THE GENERAL ACCOUNTING OFFICE: THE FEDERAL ADJUD
GOVERNMENT'S AUDITOR." USA+45 NAT/G REPRESENT 20 EX/STRUC
GENACCOUNT. PAGE 7 E0132 EXEC
LAW

S61
HARVEY W.B.,"THE RULE OF LAW IN HISTORICAL ACT/RES
PERSPECTIVE." USA+45 WOR+45 INTELL SOCIETY ECO/DEV LAW
ECO/UNDEV NAT/G EX/STRUC LEGIS TOP/EX LEGIT SKILL
...CONCPT HIST/WRIT TOT/POP. PAGE 51 E1010

B62
FROMAN L.A. JR.,PEOPLE AND POLITICS: AN ANALYSIS OF POL/PAR
THE AMERICAN POLITICAL SYSTEM. USA+45 CHIEF PROB/SOLV
DELIB/GP EX/STRUC LEGIS TOP/EX CT/SYS LOBBY GOV/REL
PERS/REL PWR...POLICY DECISION. PAGE 41 E0813

B62
HSUEH S.-.S.,GOVERNMENT AND ADMINISTRATION OF HONG ADMIN
KONG. CHIEF DELIB/GP LEGIS CT/SYS REPRESENT GOV/REL LOC/G
20 HONG/KONG CITY/MGT CIVIL/SERV GOVERNOR. PAGE 55 COLONIAL
E1106 EX/STRUC

B62
MARS D.,SUGGESTED LIBRARY IN PUBLIC ADMINISTRATION. BIBLIOG
FINAN DELIB/GP EX/STRUC WORKER COMPUTER ADJUD ADMIN
...DECISION PSY SOC METH/COMP 20. PAGE 68 E1368 METH
MGT

B62
PHILLIPS O.H.,CONSTITUTIONAL AND ADMINISTRATIVE LAW JURID
(3RD ED.). UK INT/ORG LOC/G CHIEF EX/STRUC LEGIS ADMIN
BAL/PWR ADJUD COLONIAL CT/SYS PWR...CHARTS 20. CONSTN
PAGE 80 E1613 NAT/G

S62

SCHUBERT G.,"THE 1960 TERM OF THE SUPREME COURT: A
PSYCHOLOGICAL ANALYSIS." USA+45 LAW CT/SYS...STAT
SUPREME/CT. PAGE 88 E1772

DECISION
LEGIS
JUDGE
EX/STRUC

N62

US ADVISORY COMN INTERGOV REL,APPORTIONMENT OF
STATE LEGISLATURES (PAMPHLET). LAW CONSTN EX/STRUC
LEGIS LEAD MAJORITY. PAGE 99 E1977

MUNIC
PROVS
REPRESENT
APPORT

B63

ADRIAN C.R.,GOVERNING OVER FIFTY STATES AND THEIR
COMMUNITIES. USA+45 CONSTN FINAN MUNIC NAT/G
POL/PAR EX/STRUC LEGIS ADMIN CONTROL CT/SYS
...CHARTS 20. PAGE 3 E0052

PROVS
LOC/G
GOV/REL
GOV/COMP

B63

BADI J.,THE GOVERNMENT OF THE STATE OF ISRAEL: A
CRITICAL ACCOUNT OF ITS PARLIAMENT, EXECUTIVE, AND
JUDICIARY. ISRAEL ECO/DEV CHIEF DELIB/GP LEGIS
DIPLOM CT/SYS INGP/REL PEACE ORD/FREE...BIBLIOG 20
PARLIAMENT ARABS MIGRATION. PAGE 7 E0131

NAT/G
CONSTN
EX/STRUC
POL/PAR

B63

BOWETT D.W.,THE LAW OF INTERNATIONAL INSTITUTIONS.
WOR+45 WOR-45 CONSTN DELIB/GP EX/STRUC JUDGE
EDU/PROP LEGIT CT/SYS EXEC ROUTINE RIGID/FLEX
ORD/FREE PWR...JURID CONCPT ORG/CHARTS GEN/METH
LEAGUE/NAT OAS OEEC 20 UN. PAGE 14 E0277

INT/ORG
ADJUD
DIPLOM

B63

BURRUS B.R.,ADMINSTRATIVE LAW AND LOCAL GOVERNMENT.
USA+45 PROVS LEGIS LICENSE ADJUD ORD/FREE 20.
PAGE 18 E0347

EX/STRUC
LOC/G
JURID
CONSTN

B63

ECOLE NATIONALE D'ADMIN,BIBLIOGRAPHIE SELECTIVE
D'OUVRAGES DE LANGUE FRANCAISE TRAITANT DES
PROBLEMES GOUVERNEMENTAUX ET ADMINISTRATIFS. NAT/G
FORCES ACT/RES OP/RES PLAN PROB/SOLV BUDGET ADJUD
COLONIAL LEAD 20. PAGE 34 E0672

BIBLIOG
AFR
ADMIN
EX/STRUC

B63

FALK R.A.,LAW, MORALITY, AND WAR IN THE
CONTEMPORARY WORLD. WOR+45 LAW INT/ORG EX/STRUC
FORCES EDU/PROP LEGIT DETER NUC/PWR MORAL ORD/FREE
...JURID TOT/POP 20. PAGE 36 E0715

ADJUD
ARMS/CONT
PEACE
INT/LAW

B63

GARNER U.F.,ADMINISTRATIVE LAW. UK LAW LOC/G NAT/G
EX/STRUC LEGIS JUDGE BAL/PWR BUDGET ADJUD CONTROL
CT/SYS...BIBLIOG 20. PAGE 42 E0840

ADMIN
JURID
PWR
GOV/REL

B63

GOURNAY B.,PUBLIC ADMINISTRATION. FRANCE LAW CONSTN
AGRI FINAN LABOR SCHOOL EX/STRUC CHOOSE...MGT
METH/COMP 20. PAGE 45 E0894

BIBLIOG/A
ADMIN
NAT/G
LOC/G

B63

GRANT D.R.,STATE AND LOCAL GOVERNMENT IN AMERICA.
USA+45 FINAN LOC/G MUNIC EX/STRUC FORCES EDU/PROP
ADMIN CHOOSE FEDERAL ATTIT...JURID 20. PAGE 45
E0897

PROVS
POL/PAR
LEGIS
CONSTN

B63

GRIFFITH J.A.G.,PRINCIPLES OF ADMINISTRATIVE LAW
(3RD ED.). UK CONSTN EX/STRUC LEGIS ADJUD CONTROL
CT/SYS PWR...CHARTS 20. PAGE 47 E0940

JURID
ADMIN
NAT/G
BAL/PWR

B63

RICHARDS P.G.,PATRONAGE IN BRITISH GOVERNMENT.
ELITES DELIB/GP TOP/EX PROB/SOLV CONTROL CT/SYS
EXEC PWR. PAGE 84 E1693

EX/STRUC
REPRESENT
POL/PAR
ADMIN

B63

ROBERT J.,LA MONARCHIE MAROCAINE. MOROCCO LABOR
MUNIC POL/PAR EX/STRUC ORD/FREE PWR...JURID TREND T
20. PAGE 85 E1702

CHIEF
CONSERVE
ADMIN
CONSTN

B63

WOLL P.,ADMINISTRATIVE LAW: THE INFORMAL PROCESS.
USA+45 NAT/G CONTROL EFFICIENCY 20. PAGE 107 E2141

ADMIN
ADJUD
REPRESENT
EX/STRUC

S63

BECHHOEFER B.G.,"UNITED NATIONS PROCEDURES IN CASE

INT/ORG

OF VIOLATIONS OF DISARMAMENT AGREEMENTS." COM
USA+45 USSR LAW CONSTN NAT/G EX/STRUC FORCES LEGIS
BAL/PWR EDU/PROP CT/SYS ARMS/CONT ORD/FREE PWR
...POLICY STERTYP UN VAL/FREE 20. PAGE 9 E0169

DELIB/GP

B64

HOLDSWORTH W.S.,A HISTORY OF ENGLISH LAW: THE
CENTURIES OF DEVELOPMENT AND REFORM (VOL. XIV). UK
CONSTN LOC/G NAT/G POL/PAR CHIEF EX/STRUC ADJUD
COLONIAL ATTIT...INT/LAW JURID 18/19 TORY/PARTY
COMMONWLTH WHIG/PARTY COMMON/LAW. PAGE 54 E1081

LAW
LEGIS
LEAD
CT/SYS

B64

NELSON D.H.,ADMINISTRATIVE AGENCIES OF THE USA:
THEIR DECISIONS AND AUTHORITY. USA+45 NAT/G CONTROL
CT/SYS REPRESENT...DECISION 20. PAGE 76 E1531

ADMIN
EX/STRUC
ADJUD
LAW

B64

PRESS C.,A BIBLIOGRAPHIC INTRODUCTION TO AMERICAN
STATE GOVERNMENT AND POLITICS (PAMPHLET). USA+45
USA-45 EX/STRUC ADJUD INGP/REL FEDERAL ORD/FREE 20.
PAGE 82 E1649

BIBLIOG
LEGIS
LOC/G
POL/PAR

B64

SCHECHTER A.H.,INTERPRETATION OF AMBIGUOUS
DOCUMENTS BY INTERNATIONAL ADMINISTRATIVE
TRIBUNALS. WOR+45 EX/STRUC INT/TRADE CT/SYS
SOVEREIGN 20 UN ILO EURCT/JUST. PAGE 87 E1752

INT/LAW
DIPLOM
INT/ORG
ADJUD

B64

TOMPKINS D.C.,PRESIDENTIAL SUCCESSION. USA+45 CHIEF
ADJUD 20 PRESIDENT CONGRESS. PAGE 96 E1933

BIBLIOG/A
EX/STRUC
CONSTN
TOP/EX

L64

WORLD PEACE FOUNDATION,"INTERNATIONAL
ORGANIZATIONS: SUMMARY OF ACTIVITIES." INDIA
PAKISTAN TURKEY WOR+45 CONSTN CONSULT EX/STRUC
ECO/TAC EDU/PROP LEGIT ORD/FREE...JURID SOC UN 20
CYPRESS. PAGE 107 E2145

INT/ORG
ROUTINE

B65

BOCK E.,GOVERNMENT REGULATION OF BUSINESS. USA+45
LAW EX/STRUC LEGIS EXEC ORD/FREE PWR...ANTHOL
CONGRESS. PAGE 13 E0255

MGT
ADMIN
NAT/G
CONTROL

B65

BREITEL C.D.,THE LAWMAKERS. USA+45 EX/STRUC LEGIS
JUDGE ATTIT ORD/FREE JURID. PAGE 15 E0290

CT/SYS
ADJUD
FEDERAL
NAT/G

B65

FEERICK J.D.,FROM FAILING HANDS: THE STUDY OF
PRESIDENTIAL SUCCESSION. CONSTN NAT/G PROB/SOLV
LEAD PARL/PROC MURDER CHOOSE...NEW/IDEA BIBLIOG 20
KENNEDY/JF JOHNSON/LB PRESIDENT PRE/US/AM
VICE/PRES. PAGE 36 E0724

EX/STRUC
CHIEF
LAW
LEGIS

B65

FISCHER F.C.,THE GOVERNMENT OF MICHIGAN. USA+45
NAT/G PUB/INST EX/STRUC LEGIS BUDGET GIVE EDU/PROP
CT/SYS CHOOSE GOV/REL...T MICHIGAN. PAGE 38 E0753

PROVS
LOC/G
ADMIN
CONSTN

B65

FORGAC A.A.,NEW DIPLOMACY AND THE UNITED NATIONS.
FRANCE GERMANY UK USSR INT/ORG DELIB/GP EX/STRUC
PEACE...INT/LAW CONCPT UN. PAGE 39 E0770

DIPLOM
ETIQUET
NAT/G

B65

INST INTL DES CIVILISATION DIF,THE CONSTITUTIONS
AND ADMINISTRATIVE INSTITUTIONS OF THE NEW STATES.
AFR ISLAM S/ASIA NAT/G POL/PAR DELIB/GP EX/STRUC
CONFER EFFICIENCY NAT/LISM...JURID SOC 20. PAGE 56
E1123

CONSTN
ADMIN
ADJUD
ECO/UNDEV

B65

LAFAVE W.R.,LAW AND SOVIET SOCIETY. EX/STRUC DIPLOM
DOMIN EDU/PROP PRESS ADMIN CRIME OWN MARXISM 20
KHRUSH/N. PAGE 62 E1244

JURID
CT/SYS
ADJUD
GOV/REL

B65

NORDEN A.,WAR AND NAZI CRIMINALS IN WEST GERMANY:
STATE, ECONOMY, ADMINISTRATION, ARMY, JUSTICE,
SCIENCE. GERMANY GERMANY/W MOD/EUR ECO/DEV ACADEM
EX/STRUC FORCES DOMIN ADMIN CT/SYS...POLICY MAJORIT
PACIFIST 20. PAGE 77 E1554

FASCIST
WAR
NAT/G
TOP/EX

B65

PEASLEE A.J.,CONSTITUTIONS OF NATIONS* THIRD
REVISED EDITION (VOLUME I* AFRICA). LAW EX/STRUC

AFR
CHOOSE

LEGIS TOP/EX LEGIT CT/SYS ROUTINE ORD/FREE PWR   CONSTN
SOVEREIGN...CON/ANAL CHARTS. PAGE 80 E1606   NAT/G

                                                       B65
PYLEE M.V.,CONSTITUTIONAL GOVERNMENT IN INDIA (2ND   CONSTN
REV. ED.). INDIA POL/PAR EX/STRUC DIPLOM COLONIAL   NAT/G
CT/SYS PARL/PROC PRIVIL...JURID 16/20. PAGE 83   PROVS
E1665   FEDERAL
                                                       L65
RUBIN A.P.,"UNITED STATES CONTEMPORARY PRACTICE   LAW
RELATING TO INTERNATIONAL LAW." USA+45 WOR+45   LEGIT
CONSTN INT/ORG NAT/G DELIB/GP EX/STRUC DIPLOM DOMIN   INT/LAW
CT/SYS ROUTINE ORD/FREE...CONCPT COLD/WAR 20.
PAGE 86 E1730
                                                       S65
BEVANS C.I.,"GHANA AND UNITED STATES - UNITED   NAT/G
KINGDOM AGREEMENTS." UK USA+45 LAW DELIB/GP   LEGIT
EX/STRUC ORD/FREE...JURID METH/CNCPT GEN/LAWS 20.   GHANA
PAGE 11 E0222   DIPLOM
                                                       S65
FOX A.B.,"NATO AND CONGRESS." CONSTN DELIB/GP   CONTROL
EX/STRUC FORCES TOP/EX BUDGET NUC/PWR GOV/REL   DIPLOM
...GP/COMP CONGRESS NATO TREATY. PAGE 39 E0779
                                                       S65
LONG T.G.,"THE ADMINISTRATIVE PROCESS: AGONIZING   ADJUD
REAPPRAISAL IN THE FTC." NAT/G REPRESENT 20 FTC.   LOBBY
PAGE 66 E1326   ADMIN
                                                       EX/STRUC
                                                       B66
DAVIS K.,BUSINESS AND ITS ENVIRONMENT. LAW ECO/DEV   EX/STRUC
INDUS OP/RES ADMIN CONTROL ROUTINE GP/REL PROFIT   PROB/SOLV
POLICY. PAGE 29 E0573   CAP/ISM
                                                       EXEC
                                                       B66
FINK M.,A SELECTIVE BIBLIOGRAPHY ON STATE   BIBLIOG
CONSTITUTIONAL REVISION (PAMPHLET). USA+45 FINAN   PROVS
EX/STRUC LEGIS EDU/PROP ADMIN CT/SYS APPORT CHOOSE   LOC/G
GOV/REL 20. PAGE 38 E0751   CONSTN
                                                       B66
FRIED R.C.,COMPARATIVE POLITICAL INSTITUTIONS. USSR   NAT/G
EX/STRUC FORCES LEGIS JUDGE CONTROL REPRESENT   PWR
ALL/IDEOS 20 CONGRESS BUREAUCRCY. PAGE 40 E0798   EFFICIENCY
                                                       GOV/COMP
                                                       B66
FRIEDMANN W.G.,INTERNATIONAL FINANCIAL AID. USA+45   INT/ORG
ECO/DEV ECO/UNDEV NAT/G VOL/ASSN EX/STRUC PLAN RENT   FOR/AID
GIVE BAL/PAY PWR...GEOG INT/LAW STAT TREND UN EEC   TEC/DEV
COMECON. PAGE 41 E0806   ECO/TAC
                                                       B66
GHOSH P.K.,THE CONSTITUTION OF INDIA: HOW IT HAS   CONSTN
BEEN FRAMED. INDIA LOC/G DELIB/GP EX/STRUC   NAT/G
PROB/SOLV BUDGET INT/TRADE CT/SYS CHOOSE...LING 20.   LEGIS
PAGE 43 E0854   FEDERAL
                                                       B66
GREENE L.E.,GOVERNMENT IN TENNESSEE (2ND ED.).   PROVS
USA+45 DIST/IND INDUS POL/PAR EX/STRUC LEGIS PLAN   LOC/G
BUDGET GIVE CT/SYS...MGT T 20 TENNESSEE. PAGE 46   CONSTN
E0909   ADMIN
                                                       B66
HIDAYATULLAH M.,DEMOCRACY IN INDIA AND THE JUDICIAL   NAT/G
PROCESS. INDIA EX/STRUC LEGIS LEAD GOV/REL ATTIT   CT/SYS
ORD/FREE...MAJORIT CONCPT 20 NEHRU/J. PAGE 52 E1040   CONSTN
                                                       JURID
                                                       B66
HOLDSWORTH W.S.,A HISTORY OF ENGLISH LAW: THE   BIOG
CENTURIES OF SETTLEMENT AND REFORM (VOL. XVI). UK   PERSON
LOC/G NAT/G EX/STRUC LEGIS CT/SYS LEAD ATTIT   PROF/ORG
...POLICY DECISION JURID IDEA/COMP 18 PARLIAMENT.   LAW
PAGE 54 E1083
                                                       B66
WILSON G.,CASES AND MATERIALS ON CONSTITUTIONAL AND   JURID
ADMINISTRATIVE LAW. UK LAW NAT/G EX/STRUC LEGIS   ADMIN
BAL/PWR BUDGET DIPLOM ADJUD CONTROL CT/SYS GOV/REL   CONSTN
ORD/FREE 20 PARLIAMENT ENGLSH/LAW. PAGE 106 E2126   PWR
                                                       S66
MATTHEWS D.G.,"ETHIOPIAN OUTLINE: A BIBLIOGRAPHIC   BIBLIOG
RESEARCH GUIDE." ETHIOPIA LAW STRUCT ECO/UNDEV AGRI   NAT/G
LABOR SECT CHIEF DELIB/GP EX/STRUC ADMIN...LING   DIPLOM
ORG/CHARTS 20. PAGE 69 E1384   POL/PAR
                                                       B67
BROWN L.N.,FRENCH ADMINISTRATIVE LAW. FRANCE UK   EX/STRUC

CONSTN NAT/G LEGIS DOMIN CONTROL EXEC PARL/PROC PWR   LAW
...JURID METH/COMP GEN/METH. PAGE 16 E0314   IDEA/COMP
                                                       CT/SYS
                                                       B67
BUREAU GOVERNMENT RES AND SERV,COUNTY GOVERNMENT   BIBLIOG/A
REORGANIZATION - A SELECTED ANNOTATED BIBLIOGRAPHY   APPORT
(PAPER). USA+45 USA-45 LAW CONSTN MUNIC PROVS   LOC/G
EX/STRUC CREATE PLAN PROB/SOLV REPRESENT GOV/REL   ADMIN
20. PAGE 17 E0332
                                                       B67
ESTEY M.,THE UNIONS: STRUCTURE, DEVELOPMENT, AND   LABOR
MANAGEMENT. FUT USA+45 ADJUD CONTROL INGP/REL DRIVE   EX/STRUC
...DECISION T 20 AFL/CIO. PAGE 35 E0699   ADMIN
                                                       GOV/REL
                                                       B67
FINCHER F.,THE GOVERNMENT OF THE UNITED STATES.   NAT/G
USA+45 USA-45 POL/PAR CHIEF CT/SYS LOBBY GP/REL   EX/STRUC
INGP/REL...CONCPT CHARTS BIBLIOG T 18/20 PRESIDENT   LEGIS
CONGRESS SUPREME/CT. PAGE 38 E0749   OP/RES
                                                       B67
NIVEN R.,NIGERIA. NIGERIA CONSTN INDUS EX/STRUC   NAT/G
COLONIAL REV NAT/LISM...CHARTS 19/20. PAGE 77 E1550   REGION
                                                       CHOOSE
                                                       GP/REL
                                                       S67
FABREGA J.,"ANTECEDENTES EXTRANJEROS EN LA   CONSTN
CONSTITUCION PANAMENA." CUBA L/A+17C PANAMA URUGUAY   JURID
EX/STRUC LEGIS DIPLOM ORD/FREE 19/20 COLOMB   NAT/G
MEXIC/AMER. PAGE 36 E0709   PARL/PROC
                                                       S67
MITCHELL J.D.B.,"THE CONSTITUTIONAL IMPLICATIONS OF   CONSTN
JUDICIAL CONTROL OF THE ADMINISTRATION IN THE   CT/SYS
UNITED KINGDOM." UK LAW ADJUD ADMIN GOV/REL ROLE   CONTROL
...GP/COMP 20. PAGE 74 E1474   EX/STRUC
                                                       B87
ADAMS J.,A DEFENSE OF THE CONSTITUTIONS OF   CONSTN
GOVERNMENT OF THE UNITED STATES OF AMERICA. USA-45   BAL/PWR
STRATA CHIEF EX/STRUC LEGIS CT/SYS CONSERVE   PWR
POPULISM...CONCPT CON/ANAL GOV/COMP. PAGE 3 E0048   NAT/G
                                                       B92
COHN M.M.,AN INTRODUCTION TO THE STUDY OF THE   CONSTN
CONSTITUTION. USA+45 USA-45 SOCIETY NAT/G EX/STRUC   JURID
HABITAT...PSY CONCPT 18/20. PAGE 24 E0470   OLD/LIB
                                                       B96
ESMEIN A.,ELEMENTS DE DROIT CONSTITUTIONNEL. FRANCE   LAW
UK CHIEF EX/STRUC LEGIS ADJUD CT/SYS PARL/PROC REV   CONSTN
GOV/REL ORD/FREE...JURID METH/COMP 18/19. PAGE 35   NAT/G
E0697   CONCPT

EXEC....EXECUTIVE PROCESS

                                                       B00
MAINE H.S.,INTERNATIONAL LAW. MOD/EUR UNIV SOCIETY   INT/ORG
STRUCT ACT/RES EXEC WAR ATTIT PERSON ALL/VALS   LAW
...POLICY JURID CONCPT OBS TIME/SEQ TOT/POP.   PEACE
PAGE 68 E1349   INT/LAW
                                                       B04
CRANDALL S.B.,TREATIES: THEIR MAKING AND   LAW
ENFORCEMENT. MOD/EUR USA-45 CONSTN INT/ORG NAT/G
LEGIS EDU/PROP LEGIT EXEC PEACE KNOWL MORAL...JURID
CONGRESS 19/20 TREATY. PAGE 27 E0541
                                                       B08
WILSON W.,CONSTITUTIONAL GOVERNMENT IN THE UNITED   NAT/G
STATES. USA-45 LAW POL/PAR PROVS CHIEF LEGIS   GOV/REL
BAL/PWR ADJUD EXEC FEDERAL PWR 18/20 SUPREME/CT   CONSTN
HOUSE/REP SENATE. PAGE 106 E2130   PARL/PROC
                                                       B11
PHILLIPSON C.,THE INTERNATIONAL LAW AND CUSTOM OF   INT/ORG
ANCIENT GREECE AND ROME. MEDIT-7 UNIV INTELL   LAW
SOCIETY STRUCT NAT/G LEGIS EXEC PERSON...CONCPT OBS   INT/LAW
CON/ANAL ROM/EMP. PAGE 80 E1614
                                                       B16
ROOT E.,ADDRESSES ON INTERNATIONAL SUBJECTS.   INT/ORG
MOD/EUR UNIV USA-45 LAW SOCIETY EXEC ATTIT ALL/VALS   ACT/RES
...POLICY JURID CONCPT 20 CHINJAP. PAGE 85 E1711   PEACE
                                                       INT/LAW
                                                       B21
BRYCE J.,MODERN DEMOCRACIES. FUT NEW/ZEALND USA-45   NAT/G
LAW CONSTN POL/PAR PROVS VOL/ASSN EX/STRUC LEGIS   TREND
LEGIT CT/SYS EXEC KNOWL CONGRESS AUSTRAL 20.
PAGE 16 E0322

WRIGHT Q.,THE CONTROL OF AMERICAN FOREIGN RELATIONS. USA-45 WOR-45 CONSTN INT/ORG CONSULT LEGIS LEGIT ROUTINE ORD/FREE PWR...POLICY JURID CONCPT METH/CNCPT RECORD LEAGUE/NAT 20. PAGE 107 E2150
NAT/G EXEC DIPLOM
B22

DICKINSON J.,ADMINISTRATIVE JUSTICE AND THE SUPREMACY OF LAW IN THE UNITED STATES. USA-45 LAW INDUS DOMIN EDU/PROP CONTROL EXEC GP/REL ORD/FREE ...POLICY JURID 19/20. PAGE 31 E0623
CT/SYS ADJUD ADMIN NAT/G
B27

MACDONALD A.F.,ELEMENTS OF POLITICAL SCIENCE RESEARCH. USA-45 ACADEM JUDGE EDU/PROP DEBATE ADJUD EXEC...BIBLIOG METH T 20 CONGRESS. PAGE 67 E1338
LAW FEDERAL DECISION CT/SYS
B28

MASTERS R.D.,INTERNATIONAL LAW IN INTERNATIONAL COURTS. BELGIUM EUR+WWI FRANCE GERMANY MOD/EUR SWITZERLND WOR-45 SOCIETY STRATA STRUCT LEGIT EXEC ALL/VALS...JURID HIST/WRIT TIME/SEQ TREND GEN/LAWS 20. PAGE 69 E1383
INT/ORG LAW INT/LAW
B32

KENNEDY W.P.,THE LAW AND CUSTOM OF THE SOUTH AFRICAN CONSTITUTION. AFR SOUTH/AFR KIN LOC/G PROVS DIPLOM ADJUD ADMIN EXEC 20. PAGE 60 E1203
CT/SYS CONSTN JURID PARL/PROC
B35

CANTWELL F.V.,"PUBLIC OPINION AND THE LEGISLATIVE PROCESS" USA+45 USA-45 NAT/G CT/SYS EXEC LEAD DECISION. PAGE 19 E0374
CHARTS DEBATE LEGIS ATTIT
S46

BORGESE G.,COMMON CAUSE. LAW CONSTN SOCIETY STRATA ECO/DEV INT/ORG POL/PAR FORCES LEGIS TOP/EX CAP/ISM DIPLOM ADMIN EXEC ATTIT PWR 20. PAGE 14 E0269
WOR+45 NAT/G SOVEREIGN REGION
B47

APPLEBY P.H.,POLICY AND ADMINISTRATION. USA+45 NAT/G LOBBY PWR 20. PAGE 5 E0101
REPRESENT EXEC ADMIN CLIENT
B49

APPLEBY P.H.,MORALITY AND ADMINISTRATION IN DEMOCRATIC GOVERNMENT. USA+45 CLIENT NAT/G EXEC EFFICIENCY 20. PAGE 5 E0102
REPRESENT LOBBY ADMIN EX/STRUC
B52

COUNCIL STATE GOVERNMENTS,OCCUPATIONAL LICENSING IN THE STATES. USA+45 PROVS ADMIN EXEC LOBBY 20. PAGE 27 E0526
PROF/ORG LICENSE REPRESENT EX/STRUC
B52

VANDENBOSCH A.,THE UN: BACKGROUND, ORGANIZATION, FUNCTIONS, ACTIVITIES. WOR+45 LAW CONSTN STRUCT INT/ORG CONSULT BAL/PWR EDU/PROP EXEC ALL/VALS ...POLICY CONCPT UN 20. PAGE 103 E2071
DELIB/GP TIME/SEQ PEACE
B52

SCHWARTZ B.,FRENCH ADMINISTRATIVE LAW AND THE COMMON-LAW WORLD. FRANCE CULTURE LOC/G NAT/G PROVS DELIB/GP EX/STRUC LEGIS PROB/SOLV CT/SYS EXEC GOV/REL...IDEA/COMP ENGLSH/LAW. PAGE 89 E1786
JURID LAW METH/COMP ADJUD
B54

CHOWDHURI R.N.,INTERNATIONAL MANDATES AND TRUSTEESHIP SYSTEMS. WOR+45 STRUCT ECO/UNDEV INT/ORG LEGIS DOMIN EDU/PROP LEGIT ADJUD EXEC PWR ...CONCPT TIME/SEQ UN 20. PAGE 22 E0434
DELIB/GP PLAN SOVEREIGN
B55

PLISCHKE E.,AMERICAN FOREIGN RELATIONS: A BIBLIOGRAPHY OF OFFICIAL SOURCES. USA+45 USA-45 INT/ORG FORCES PRESS WRITING DEBATE EXEC...POLICY INT/LAW 18/20 CONGRESS. PAGE 81 E1621
BIBLIOG/A DIPLOM NAT/G
B55

CARR C.,"LEGISLATIVE CONTROL OF ADMINISTRATIVE RULES AND REGULATIONS: PARLIAMENTARY SUPERVISION IN
EXEC REPRESENT
S55

BRITAIN." DELIB/GP CONTROL ROLE PWR PARLIAMENT. PAGE 20 E0392
JURID

FRANCIS R.G.,SERVICE AND PROCEDURE IN BUREAUCRACY. EXEC LEAD ROUTINE...QU 20. PAGE 39 E0784
CLIENT ADMIN INGP/REL REPRESENT
B56

REDFORD E.S.,PUBLIC ADMINISTRATION AND POLICY FORMATION: STUDIES IN OIL, GAS, BANKING, RIVER DEVELOPMENT AND CORPORATE INVESTIGATIONS. USA+45 CLIENT NAT/G ADMIN LOBBY REPRESENT GOV/REL INGP/REL 20. PAGE 84 E1678
EX/STRUC PROB/SOLV CONTROL EXEC
B56

SOHN L.B.,BASIC DOCUMENTS OF THE UNITED NATIONS. WOR+45 LAW INT/ORG LEGIT EXEC ROUTINE CHOOSE PWR ...JURID CONCPT GEN/LAWS ANTHOL UN TOT/POP OAS FAO ILO 20. PAGE 92 E1853
DELIB/GP CONSTN
B56

US HOUSE RULES COMM,HEARINGS BEFORE A SPECIAL SUBCOMMITTEE: ESTABLISHMENT OF A STANDING COMMITTEE ON ADMINISTRATIVE PROCEDURE. PRACTICE. USA+45 LAW EX/STRUC ADJUD CONTROL EXEC GOV/REL EFFICIENCY PWR ...POLICY INT 20 CONGRESS. PAGE 100 E2009
ADMIN DOMIN DELIB/GP NAT/G
B56

CARRINGTON P.D.,"POLITICAL QUESTIONS: THE JUDICIAL CHECK ON THE EXECUTIVE." USA+45 LAW CHIEF 20. PAGE 20 E0395
ADJUD EXEC PWR REPRESENT
L56

AMERICAN SOCIETY PUBLIC ADMIN,STRENGTHENING MANAGEMENT FOR DEMOCRATIC GOVERNMENT. USA+45 ACADEM EX/STRUC WORKER PLAN BUDGET CONFER CT/SYS EFFICIENCY ANTHOL. PAGE 4 E0083
ADMIN NAT/G EXEC MGT
B58

HENKIN L.,ARMS CONTROL AND INSPECTION IN AMERICAN LAW. LAW CONSTN INT/ORG LOC/G MUNIC NAT/G PROVS EDU/PROP LEGIT EXEC NUC/PWR KNOWL ORD/FREE...OBS TOT/POP CONGRESS 20. PAGE 52 E1032
USA+45 JURID ARMS/CONT
B58

WESTIN A.F.,THE ANATOMY OF A CONSTITUTIONAL LAW CASE. USA+45 LAW LEGIS ADMIN EXEC...DECISION MGT SOC RECORD 20 SUPREME/CT. PAGE 105 E2113
CT/SYS INDUS ADJUD CONSTN
B58

BECK C.,CONTEMPT OF CONGRESS: A STUDY OF THE PROSECUTIONS INITIATED BY THE COMMITTEE ON UN-AMERICAN ACTIVITIES. USA+45 CONSTN DEBATE EXEC. PAGE 9 E0170
LEGIS DELIB/GP PWR ADJUD
B59

MOOS M.,THE CAMPUS AND THE STATE. LAW FINAN DELIB/GP LEGIS EXEC LOBBY GP/REL PWR...POLICY BIBLIOG. PAGE 74 E1489
EDU/PROP ACADEM PROVS CONTROL
B59

HECTOR L.J.,"GOVERNMENT BY ANONYMITY: WHO WRITES OUR REGULATORY OPINIONS?" USA+45 NAT/G TOP/EX CONTROL EXEC. PAGE 51 E1021
ADJUD REPRESENT EX/STRUC ADMIN
L59

SUTTON F.X.,"REPRESENTATION AND THE NATURE OF POLITICAL SYSTEMS." UNIV WOR-45 CULTURE SOCIETY STRATA INT/ORG FORCES JUDGE DOMIN LEGIT EXEC REGION REPRESENT ATTIT ORD/FREE RESPECT...SOC HIST/WRIT TIME/SEQ. PAGE 95 E1896
NAT/G CONCPT
S59

ADRIAN C.R.,STATE AND LOCAL GOVERNMENTS: A STUDY IN THE POLITICAL PROCESS. USA+45 LAW FINAN MUNIC POL/PAR LEGIS ADJUD EXEC CHOOSE REPRESENT. PAGE 3 E0051
LOC/G PROVS GOV/REL ATTIT
B60

AL3I F.,TRATADO DE LOS MODOS DE GESTION DE LAS CORPORACIONES LOCALES. SPAIN FINAN NAT/G BUDGET CONTROL EXEC ROUTINE GOV/REL ORD/FREE SOVEREIGN ...MGT 20. PAGE 3 E0057
LOC/G LAW ADMIN MUNIC
B60

ENGEL J.,THE SECURITY OF THE FREE WORLD. USSR WOR+45 STRATA STRUCT ECO/DEV ECO/UNDEV INT/ORG DELIB/GP FORCES DOMIN LEGIT ADJUD EXEC ARMS/CONT COERCE...POLICY CONCPT NEW/IDEA TIME/SEQ GEN/LAWS COLD/WAR WORK UN 20 NATO. PAGE 35 E0689
COM TREND DIPLOM
B60

WEBSTER J.A.,A GENERAL STUDY OF THE DEPARTMENT OF
DEFENSE INTERNAL SECURITY PROGRAM. USA+45 WORKER
TEC/DEV ADJUD CONTROL CT/SYS EXEC GOV/REL COST
...POLICY DECISION MGT 20 DEPT/DEFEN SUPREME/CT.
PAGE 105 E2105
B60
ORD/FREE
PLAN
ADMIN
NAT/G

FUCHS R.F.,"FAIRNESS AND EFFECTIVENESS IN
ADMINISTRATIVE AGENCY ORGANIZATION AND PROCEDURES."
USA+45 ADJUD ADMIN REPRESENT. PAGE 41 E0816
L60
EFFICIENCY
EX/STRUC
EXEC
POLICY

MANN S.Z.,"POLICY FORMULATION IN THE EXECUTIVE
BRANCH: THE TAFT-HARTLEY EXPERIENCE." USA+45 LABOR
CHIEF INGP/REL 20 NLRB. PAGE 68 E1360
S60
EXEC
GOV/REL
EX/STRUC
PROB/SOLV

MARSHALL G.,"POLICE RESPONSIBILITY." UK LOC/G ADJUD
ADMIN EXEC 20. PAGE 69 E1370
S60
CONTROL
REPRESENT
LAW
FORCES

ROURKE F.E.,"ADMINISTRATIVE SECRECY: A
CONGRESSIONAL DILEMMA." DELIB/GP CT/SYS ATTIT
...MAJORIT DECISION JURID. PAGE 86 E1727
S60
LEGIS
EXEC
ORD/FREE
POLICY

MASSEL M.S.,THE REGULATORY PROCESS (JOURNAL
REPRINT). NAT/G LOBBY REPRESENT GOV/REL 20. PAGE 69
E1382
B61
ADJUD
EX/STRUC
EXEC

PRITCHETT C.H.,CONGRESS VERSUS THE SUPREME COURT,
1957-1960. PROB/SOLV DOMIN EXEC GP/REL DISCRIM PWR
CONGRESS SUPREME/CT SUPREME/CT. PAGE 82 E1652
B61
LEGIS
JURID
LAW

ABLARD C.D.,"EX PARTE CONTACTS WITH FEDERAL
ADMINISTRATIVE AGENCIES." USA+45 CLIENT NAT/G
DELIB/GP ADMIN PWR 20. PAGE 2 E0044
S61
EXEC
ADJUD
LOBBY
REPRESENT

BAER E.,"THE GENERAL ACCOUNTING OFFICE: THE FEDERAL
GOVERNMENT'S AUDITOR." USA+45 NAT/G REPRESENT 20
GENACCOUNT. PAGE 7 E0132
S61
ADJUD
EX/STRUC
EXEC
LAW

AMERICAN LAW INSTITUTE,FOREIGN RELATIONS LAW OF THE
UNITED STATES: RESTATEMENT, SECOND. USA+45 NAT/G
LEGIS ADJUD EXEC ROUTINE GOV/REL...INT/LAW JURID
CONCPT 20 TREATY. PAGE 4 E0082
B62
PROF/ORG
LAW
DIPLOM
ORD/FREE

INTERNAT CONGRESS OF JURISTS,EXECUTIVE ACTION AND
THE RULE OF RULE: REPORTION PROCEEDINGS OF INT'T
CONGRESS OF JURISTS,-RIO DE JANEIRO, BRAZIL. WOR+45
ACADEM CONSULT JUDGE EDU/PROP ADJUD CT/SYS INGP/REL
PERSON DEPT/DEFEN. PAGE 57 E1130
B62
JURID
EXEC
ORD/FREE
CONTROL

LAWSON R.,INTERNATIONAL REGIONAL ORGANIZATIONS.
WOR+45 NAT/G VOL/ASSN CONSULT LEGIS EDU/PROP LEGIT
ADMIN EXEC ROUTINE HEALTH PWR WEALTH...JURID EEC
COLD/WAR 20 UN. PAGE 63 E1270
B62
INT/ORG
DELIB/GP
REGION

CAVERS D.F.,"ADMINISTRATIVE DECISION-MAKING IN
NUCLEAR FACILITIES LICENSING." USA+45 CLIENT ADMIN
EXEC 20 AEC. PAGE 21 E0410
L62
REPRESENT
LOBBY
PWR
CONTROL

CORET A.,"L'INDEPENDANCE DU SAMOA OCCIDENTAL."
S/ASIA LAW INT/ORG EXEC ALL/VALS SAMOA UN 20.
PAGE 26 E0508
L62
NAT/G
STRUCT
SOVEREIGN

MANGIN G.,"L'ORGANIZATION JUDICIAIRE DES ETATS
D'AFRIQUE ET DE MADAGASCAR." ISLAM WOR+45 STRATA
STRUCT ECO/UNDEV NAT/G LEGIT EXEC...JURID TIME/SEQ
TOT/POP 20 SUPREME/CT. PAGE 68 E1357
L62
AFR
LEGIS
COLONIAL
MADAGASCAR

MURACCIOLE L.,"LES MODIFICATIONS DE LA CONSTITUTION
MALGACHE." AFR WOR+45 ECO/UNDEV LEGIT EXEC ALL/VALS
...JURID 20. PAGE 75 E1505
S62
NAT/G
STRUCT
SOVEREIGN
MADAGASCAR

BOWETT D.W.,THE LAW OF INTERNATIONAL INSTITUTIONS.
WOR+45 WOR-45 CONSTN DELIB/GP EX/STRUC JUDGE
EDU/PROP LEGIT CT/SYS EXEC ROUTINE RIGID/FLEX
ORD/FREE PWR...JURID CONCPT ORG/CHARTS GEN/METH
LEAGUE/NAT OAS OEEC 20 UN. PAGE 14 E0277
B63
INT/ORG
ADJUD
DIPLOM

CARTER G.M.,FIVE AFRICAN STATES: RESPONSES TO
DIVERSITY. CONSTN CULTURE STRATA LEGIS PLAN ECO/TAC
DOMIN EDU/PROP CT/SYS EXEC CHOOSE ATTIT HEALTH
ORD/FREE PWR...TIME/SEQ TOT/POP VAL/FREE. PAGE 20
E0398
B63
AFR
SOCIETY

HOWARD W.S.,AMERICAN SLAVERS AND THE FEDERAL LAW:
1837-1862. USA-45 NAT/G LEGIT COERCE RACE/REL
WEALTH...POLICY BIBLIOG/A 19. PAGE 55 E1102
B63
DIST/IND
CRIMLGY
LAW
EXEC

RICHARDS P.G.,PATRONAGE IN BRITISH GOVERNMENT.
ELITES DELIB/GP TOP/EX PROB/SOLV CONTROL CT/SYS
EXEC PWR. PAGE 84 E1693
B63
EX/STRUC
REPRESENT
POL/PAR
ADMIN

HILLS R.J.,"THE REPRESENTATIVE FUNCTION: NEGLECTED
DIMENSION OF LEADERSHIP BEHAVIOR" USA+45 CLIENT
STRUCT SCHOOL PERS/REL...STAT QU SAMP LAB/EXP 20.
PAGE 53 E1048
S63
LEAD
ADMIN
EXEC
ACT/RES

BROOKS T.R.,TOIL AND TROUBLE, A HISTORY OF AMERICAN
LABOR. WORKER BARGAIN CAP/ISM ADJUD AUTOMAT EXEC
GP/REL RACE/REL EFFICIENCY INCOME PROFIT MARXISM
17/20 KENNEDY/JF AFL/CIO NEGRO. PAGE 16 E0310
B64
INDUS
LABOR
LEGIS

DANELSKI D.J.,A SUPREME COURT JUSTICE IS APPOINTED.
CHIEF LEGIS CONFER DEBATE EXEC PERSON PWR...BIOG 20
CONGRESS PRESIDENT. PAGE 28 E0564
B64
CHOOSE
JUDGE
DECISION

MINAR D.W.,IDEAS AND POLITICS: THE AMERICAN
EXPERIENCE. SECT CHIEF LEGIS CREATE ADJUD EXEC REV
PWR...PHIL/SCI CONCPT IDEA/COMP 18/20 HAMILTON/A
JEFFERSN/T DECLAR/IND JACKSON/A PRESIDENT. PAGE 73
E1464
B64
CONSTN
NAT/G
FEDERAL

MITAU G.T.,PROXIMATE SOLUTIONS: CASE PROBLEMS IN
STATE AND LOCAL GOVERNMENT. USA+45 CONSTN NAT/G
CHIEF LEGIS CT/SYS EXEC GOV/REL GP/REL PWR 20
CASEBOOK. PAGE 73 E1470
B64
PROVS
LOC/G
ADJUD

SHAPIRO M.,LAW AND POLITICS IN THE SUPREME COURT:
NEW APPROACHES TO POLITICAL JURISPRUDENCE. JUDGE
PROB/SOLV LEGIT EXEC ROUTINE ATTIT ALL/VALS
...DECISION SOC. PAGE 90 E1811
B64
LEGIS
CT/SYS
LAW
JURID

STRONG C.F.,HISTORY OF MODERN POLITICAL
CONSTITUTIONS. STRUCT INT/ORG NAT/G LEGIS TEC/DEV
DIPLOM INT/TRADE CT/SYS EXEC...METH/COMP T 12/20
UN. PAGE 94 E1888
B64
CONSTN
CONCPT

BERKS R.N.,"THE US AND WEAPONS CONTROL." WOR+45 LAW
INT/ORG NAT/G LEGIS EXEC COERCE PEACE ATTIT
RIGID/FLEX ALL/VALS PWR...POLICY TOT/POP 20.
PAGE 11 E0204
L64
USA+45
PLAN
ARMS/CONT

BOCK E.,GOVERNMENT REGULATION OF BUSINESS. USA+45
LAW EX/STRUC LEGIS EXEC ORD/FREE PWR...ANTHOL
CONGRESS. PAGE 13 E0255
B65
MGT
ADMIN
NAT/G
CONTROL

MCWHINNEY E.,JUDICIAL REVIEW IN THE ENGLISH-
SPEAKING WORLD (3RD ED.). CANADA UK WOR+45 LEGIS
CONTROL EXEC PARTIC...JURID 20 AUSTRAL. PAGE 71
E1431
B65
GOV/COMP
CT/SYS
ADJUD
CONSTN

VONGLAHN G.,LAW AMONG NATIONS: AN INTRODUCTION TO
PUBLIC INTERNATIONAL LAW. UNIV WOR+45 LAW INT/ORG
NAT/G LEGIT EXEC RIGID/FLEX...CONCPT TIME/SEQ
GEN/LAWS UN TOT/POP 20. PAGE 104 E2084
B65
CONSTN
JURID
INT/LAW

DAVIS K.,BUSINESS AND ITS ENVIRONMENT. LAW ECO/DEV
INDUS OP/RES ADMIN CONTROL ROUTINE GP/REL PROFIT
POLICY. PAGE 29 E0573
B66
EX/STRUC
PROB/SOLV
CAP/ISM

EXEC

B66
HANSON R.,THE POLITICAL THICKET. USA+45 MUNIC APPORT
POL/PAR LEGIS EXEC LOBBY CHOOSE...MAJORIT DECISION. LAW
PAGE 50 E0998 CONSTN
REPRESENT

S66
BURDETTE F.L.,"SELECTED ARTICLES AND DOCUMENTS ON BIBLIOG
AMERICAN GOVERNMENT AND POLITICS." LAW LOC/G MUNIC USA+45
NAT/G POL/PAR PROVS LEGIS BAL/PWR ADMIN EXEC JURID
REPRESENT MGT. PAGE 17 E0331 CONSTN

B67
BROWN L.N.,FRENCH ADMINISTRATIVE LAW. FRANCE UK EX/STRUC
CONSTN NAT/G LEGIS DOMIN CONTROL EXEC PARL/PROC PWR LAW
...JURID METH/COMP GEN/METH. PAGE 16 E0314 IDEA/COMP
CT/SYS

S67
ADOKO A.,"THE CONSTITUTION OF UGANDA." AFR UGANDA NAT/G
LOC/G CHIEF FORCES LEGIS ADJUD EXEC CHOOSE NAT/LISM CONSTN
...IDEA/COMP 20. PAGE 3 E0050 ORD/FREE
LAW

S67
BRADLEY A.W.,"CONSTITUTION-MAKING IN UGANDA." NAT/G
UGANDA LAW CHIEF DELIB/GP LEGIS ADMIN EXEC CREATE
PARL/PROC RACE/REL ORD/FREE...GOV/COMP 20. PAGE 15 CONSTN
E0284 FEDERAL

B91
SIDGWICK H.,THE ELEMENTS OF POLITICS. LOC/G NAT/G POLICY
LEGIS DIPLOM ADJUD CONTROL EXEC PARL/PROC REPRESENT LAW
GOV/REL SOVEREIGN ALL/IDEOS 19 MILL/JS BENTHAM/J. CONCPT
PAGE 91 E1822

EXECUTIVE....SEE TOP/EX

EXECUTIVE ESTABLISHMENTS....SEE EX/STRUC

EXECUTIVE PROCESS....SEE EXEC

EXHIBIT....DISPLAY

EXPECTATIONS....SEE PROBABIL, SUPEGO, PREDICT

EXPERIMENTATION....SEE EXPERIMENTATION INDEX, P. XIV

EXPOSTFACT....EX POST FACTO LAWS

EXPROPRIAT....EXPROPRIATION

B65
FALK R.A.,THE AFTERMATH OF SABBATINO: BACKGROUND SOVEREIGN
PAPERS AND PROCEEDINGS OF SEVENTH HAMMARSKJOLD CT/SYS
FORUM. USA+45 LAW ACT/RES ADJUD ROLE...BIBLIOG 20 INT/LAW
EXPROPRIAT SABBATINO HARLAN/JM. PAGE 36 E0718 OWN

EXTR/IND....EXTRACTIVE INDUSTRY (FISHING, LUMBERING, ETC.)

N
CONOVER H.F.,OFFICIAL PUBLICATIONS OF BRITISH EAST BIBLIOG/A
AFRICA (PAMPHLET). UK LAW ECO/UNDEV AGRI EXTR/IND AFR
SECT LEGIS BUDGET TAX...HEAL STAT 20. PAGE 25 E0491 ADMIN
COLONIAL

B51
INSTITUTE DES RELATIONS INTL,LES ASPECTS WEAPON
ECONOMIQUES DU REARMEMENT (ETUDE DE L'INSTITUT DES DEMAND
RELATIONS INTERNATIONALES A BRUXELLES). BELGIUM UK ECO/TAC
USA+45 EXTR/IND FINAN FORCES WORKER PROB/SOLV INT/TRADE
DIPLOM PRICE...POLICY 20 TREATY. PAGE 57 E1127

B58
MOSER J.J.,JOHANN JACOB MOSER'S GESAMMELTE UND ZU BIBLIOG
GEMEINNUTZIGEM GEBRAUCH EINGERICHTETE BIBLIOTHEK. EXTR/IND
GERMANY PROC/MFG INT/TRADE...POLICY JURID MGT 18. INDUS
PAGE 75 E1500

B60
LENCZOWSKI G.,OIL AND STATE IN THE MIDDLE EAST. FUT ISLAM
IRAN LAW ECO/UNDEV EXTR/IND NAT/G TOP/EX PLAN INDUS
TEC/DEV ECO/TAC LEGIT ADMIN COERCE ATTIT ALL/VALS NAT/LISM
PWR...CHARTS 20. PAGE 64 E1283

S60
NICHOLS J.P.,"HAZARDS OF AMERICAN PRIVATE FINAN
INVESTMENT IN UNDERDEVELOPED COUNTRIES." FUT ECO/UNDEV
L/A+17C USA+45 USA-45 EXTR/IND CONSULT BAL/PWR CAP/ISM
ECO/TAC DOMIN ADJUD ATTIT SOVEREIGN WEALTH NAT/LISM
...HIST/WRIT TIME/SEQ TREND VAL/FREE 20. PAGE 77
E1546

B62
CARPER E.T.,ILLINOIS GOES TO CONGRESS FOR ARMY ADMIN
LAND. USA+45 LAW EXTR/IND PROVS REGION CIVMIL/REL LOBBY
GOV/REL FEDERAL ATTIT 20 ILLINOIS SENATE CONGRESS GEOG
DIRKSEN/E DOUGLAS/P. PAGE 20 E0391 LEGIS

B62
COLOMBOS C.J.,THE INTERNATIONAL LAW OF THE SEA. INT/LAW
WOR+45 EXTR/IND DIPLOM INT/TRADE TARIFFS AGREE WAR SEA
...TIME/SEQ 20 TREATY. PAGE 24 E0476 JURID
ADJUD

B62
HENDERSON W.O.,THE GENESIS OF THE COMMON MARKET. ECO/DEV
EUR+WWI FRANCE MOD/EUR UK SEA COM/IND EXTR/IND INT/TRADE
COLONIAL DISCRIM...TIME/SEQ CHARTS BIBLIOG 18/20 DIPLOM
EEC TREATY. PAGE 52 E1030

L63
MCDOUGAL M.S.,"THE ENJOYMENT AND ACQUISITION OF PLAN
RESOURCES IN OUTER SPACE." CHRIST-17C FUT WOR+45 TREND
WOR-45 LAW EXTR/IND INT/ORG ACT/RES CREATE TEC/DEV
ECO/TAC LEGIT COERCE HEALTH KNOWL ORD/FREE PWR
WEALTH...JURID HIST/WRIT VAL/FREE. PAGE 70 E1408

B64
TELLADO A.,A STATEMENT OF THE LAWS OF THE DOMINICAN CONSTN
REPUBLIC IN MATTERS AFFECTING BUSINESS (3RD ED.). LEGIS
DOMIN/REP AGRI DIST/IND EXTR/IND FINAN FAM WORKER NAT/G
ECO/TAC TAX CT/SYS MARRIAGE OWN...BIBLIOG 20 INDUS
MIGRATION. PAGE 95 E1913

B65
JOHNSTON D.M.,THE INTERNATIONAL LAW OF FISHERIES: A CONCPT
FRAMEWORK FOR POLICYORIENTED INQUIRIES. WOR+45 EXTR/IND
ACT/RES PLAN PROB/SOLV CONTROL SOVEREIGN. PAGE 59 JURID
E1171 DIPLOM

B65
LUGO-MARENCO J.J.,A STATEMENT OF THE LAWS OF CONSTN
NICARAGUA IN MATTERS AFFECTING BUSINESS. NICARAGUA NAT/G
AGRI DIST/IND EXTR/IND FINAN INDUS FAM WORKER LEGIS
INT/TRADE TAX MARRIAGE OWN BIO/SOC 20 TREATY JURID
RESOURCE/N MIGRATION. PAGE 67 E1332

L67
CARMICHAEL D.M.,"FORTY YEARS OF WATER POLLUTION HEALTH
CONTROL IN WISCONSIN: A CASE STUDY." LAW EXTR/IND CONTROL
INDUS MUNIC DELIB/GP PLAN PROB/SOLV SANCTION ADMIN
...CENSUS CHARTS 20 WISCONSIN. PAGE 20 E0384 ADJUD

S67
EYRAUD M.,"LA FRANCE FACE A UN EVENTUEL TRAITE DE NUC/PWR
NON DISSEMINATION DES ARMES NUCLEAIRES." FRANCE ARMS/CONT
USA+45 EXTR/IND INDUS R+D INT/ORG ACT/RES TEC/DEV POLICY
AGREE PRODUC ATTIT 20 TREATY AEC EURATOM. PAGE 36
E0708

EXTRACTIVE INDUSTRY....SEE EXTR/IND

EYBERS G.W. E0707

EYRAUD M. E0708

F

FAA....U.S. FEDERAL AVIATION AGENCY

FABIAN....FABIANS: MEMBERS AND/OR SUPPORTERS OF FABIAN
SOCIETY

FABREGA J. E0709

FACE/GP....ACQUAINTANCE GROUP

N19
HOGARTY R.A.,NEW JERSEY FARMERS AND MIGRANT HOUSING AGRI
RULES (PAMPHLET). USA+45 LAW ELITES FACE/GP LABOR PROVS
PROF/ORG LOBBY PERS/REL RIGID/FLEX ROLE 20 WORKER
NEW/JERSEY. PAGE 53 E1067 HEALTH

B20
VINOGRADOFF P.,OUTLINES OF HISTORICAL JURISPRUDENCE JURID
(2 VOLS.). GREECE MEDIT-7 LAW CONSTN FACE/GP FAM METH
KIN MUNIC CRIME OWN...INT/LAW IDEA/COMP BIBLIOG.
PAGE 104 E2080

L29
DARWIN L.,"WHAT IS EUGENICS." USA-45 LAW SOCIETY PLAN
FACE/GP FAM ACT/RES ECO/TAC HEALTH...HEAL TREND BIO/SOC
STERTYP 20. PAGE 29 E0568

B41
GELLHORN W.,FEDERAL ADMINISTRATIVE PROCEEDINGS. EX/STRUC
USA+45 CLIENT FACE/GP NAT/G LOBBY REPRESENT PWR 20. LAW
PAGE 43 E0844 ADJUD
POLICY

L58
UNESCO.,"TECHNIQUES OF MEDIATION AND CONCILIATION." INT/ORG
EUR+WWI USA+45 WOR+45 INDUS FACE/GP EX/STRUC CONSULT
EDU/PROP LEGIT PEACE ORD/FREE...INT/LAW TIME/SEQ DIPLOM
LEAGUE/NAT 20. PAGE 98 E1961

S63
BRAUSCH G.E.,"AFRICAN ETHNOCRACIES: SOME LAW
SOCIOLOGICAL IMPLICATIONS OF CONSTITUTIONAL CHANGE SOC
IN EMERGENT TERRITORIES OF AFRICA." AFR CONSTN ELITES
FACE/GP MUNIC NAT/G DOMIN ATTIT ALL/VALS
...HIST/WRIT GEN/LAWS VAL/FREE 20. PAGE 15 E0289

B64
CLINARD M.B.,ANOMIE AND DEVIANT BEHAVIOR: A PERSON
DISCUSSION AND CRITIQUE. SOCIETY FACE/GP CRIME ANOMIE
STRANGE ATTIT BIO/SOC DISPL RIGID/FLEX HEALTH...PSY KIN
CONCPT BIBLIOG 20 MERTON/R. PAGE 23 E0456 NEIGH

S65
FALK R.A.,"INTERNATIONAL LEGAL ORDER." USA+45 ATTIT
INTELL FACE/GP INT/ORG LEGIT KNOWL...CONCPT GEN/LAWS
METH/CNCPT STYLE RECORD GEN/METH 20. PAGE 36 E0717 INT/LAW

FACTION....FACTION

FACTOR ANALYSIS....SEE CON/ANAL

FACTS ON FILE, INC. E0710

FAGUET E. E0711

FAIR/LABOR....FAIR LABOR STANDARD ACT

B63
BOWIE R.R.,GOVERNMENT REGULATION OF BUSINESS: CASES LAW
FROM THE NATIONAL REPORTER SYSTEM. USA+45 USA-45 CONTROL
NAT/G ECO/TAC ADJUD...ANTHOL 19/20 SUPREME/CT FTC INDUS
FAIR/LABOR MONOPOLY. PAGE 14 E0280 CT/SYS

FAIRCHILD H.P. E0712

FAIRLIE J.A. E0713

FAIRNESS, JUSTICE....SEE VALUES INDEX

FALANGE....FALANGE PARTY (SPAIN)

FALANGIST

N61
DELEGACION NACIONAL DE PRENSA,FALANGE ESPANOL EDU/PROP
TRADICIONALISTA Y DE LAS JUNTAS OFENSIVAS FASCIST
NACIONALES SINDICALISTAS. IX CONSEJO NACIONAL CONFER
(PAMPHLET). LAW VOL/ASSN TOTALISM AUTHORIT ORD/FREE POL/PAR
FASCISM...ANTHOL 20 FRANCO/F FALANGIST. PAGE 31
E0605

FALK R.A. E0714,E0715,E0716,E0717,E0718,E0719

FALKLAND/I....FALKLAND ISLANDS

FALL B.B. E0720

FAM....FAMILY

B00
MAINE H.S.,ANCIENT LAW. MEDIT-7 CULTURE SOCIETY KIN FAM
SECT LEGIS ROUTINE...JURID HIST/WRIT CON/ANAL LAW
TOT/POP VAL/FREE. PAGE 68 E1350

B09
JUSTINIAN,THE DIGEST (DIGESTA CORPUS JURIS CIVILIS) JURID
(2 VOLS.) (TRANS. BY C. H. MONRO). ROMAN/EMP LAW CT/SYS
FAM LOC/G LEGIS EDU/PROP CONTROL MARRIAGE OWN ROLE NAT/G
CIVIL/LAW. PAGE 59 E1177 STRATA

B20
VINOGRADOFF P.,OUTLINES OF HISTORICAL JURISPRUDENCE JURID
(2 VOLS.). GREECE MEDIT-7 LAW CONSTN FACE/GP FAM METH
KIN MUNIC CRIME OWN...INT/LAW IDEA/COMP BIBLIOG.
PAGE 104 E2080

B24
NAVILLE A.,LIBERTE, EGALITE, SOLIDARITE: ESSAIS ORD/FREE
D'ANALYSE. STRATA FAM VOL/ASSN INT/TRADE GP/REL SOC
MORAL MARXISM SOCISM...PSY TREATY. PAGE 76 E1529 IDEA/COMP
DIPLOM

L29
DARWIN L.,"WHAT IS EUGENICS." USA-45 LAW SOCIETY PLAN
FACE/GP FAM ACT/RES ECO/TAC HEALTH...HEAL TREND BIO/SOC
STERTYP 20. PAGE 29 E0568

B33
GILLETTE J.M.,CURRENT SOCIAL PROBLEMS. CONTROL GEOG
CRIME AGE/Y BIO/SOC...SOC 20. PAGE 43 E0861 HEALTH
RACE/REL
FAM

B36
SCHULZ F.,PRINCIPLES OF ROMAN LAW. CONSTN FAM NAT/G LAW
DOMIN CONTROL CT/SYS CRIME ISOLAT ATTIT ORD/FREE LEGIS
PWR...JURID ROME/ANC ROMAN/LAW. PAGE 89 E1783 ADJUD
CONCPT

B42
GILLETTE J.M.,PROBLEMS OF A CHANGING SOCIAL ORDER. BIO/SOC
USA+45 STRATA FAM CONTROL CRIME RACE/REL HEALTH ADJUST
WEALTH...GEOG GP/COMP. PAGE 43 E0862 ATTIT
SOC/WK

B42
HEGEL G.W.F.,PHILOSOPHY OF RIGHT. UNIV FAM SECT NAT/G
CHIEF AGREE WAR MARRIAGE OWN ORD/FREE...POLICY LAW
CONCPT. PAGE 51 E1023 RATIONAL

B43
US LIBRARY OF CONGRESS,SOCIAL AND CULTURAL PROBLEMS BIBLIOG/A
IN WARTIME: JANUARY-MAY 1943 (SUPPLEMENT 2). WOR+45 WAR
FAM SECT PLAN EDU/PROP CRIME LEISURE RACE/REL DRIVE SOC
HEALTH...GEOG 20 JEWS. PAGE 100 E2014 CULTURE

B52
BUCKLAND W.W.,ROMAN LAW AND COMMON LAW: A IDEA/COMP
COMPARISON IN OUTLINE (2ND REV. ED.). UK FAM LEGIT LAW
AGREE CT/SYS OWN...JURID ROMAN/REP ROMAN/LAW ADJUD
COMMON/LAW. PAGE 17 E0325 CONCPT

B52
WALTER P.A.F.,RACE AND CULTURE RELATIONS. FAM RACE/REL
HEALTH WEALTH...POLICY CRIMLGY GEOG BIBLIOG T 20. DISCRIM
PAGE 105 E2097 GP/REL
CONCPT

B54
CAPLOW T.,THE SOCIOLOGY OF WORK. USA+45 USA-45 LABOR
STRATA MARKET FAM GP/REL INGP/REL ALL/VALS WORKER
...DECISION STAT BIBLIOG SOC/INTEG 20. PAGE 19 INDUS
E0375 ROLE

C54
GUINS G.C.,"SOVIET LAW AND SOVIET SOCIETY." COM LAW
USSR STRATA FAM NAT/G WORKER DOMIN RACE/REL STRUCT
...BIBLIOG 20. PAGE 48 E0960 PLAN

B55
CAVAN R.S.,CRIMINOLOGY (2ND ED.). USA+45 LAW FAM DRIVE
PUB/INST FORCES PLAN WAR AGE/Y PERSON ROLE SUPEGO CRIMLGY
...CHARTS 20 FBI. PAGE 21 E0409 CONTROL
METH/COMP

B55
KHADDURI M.,LAW IN THE MIDDLE EAST. LAW CONSTN ADJUD
ACADEM FAM EDU/PROP CT/SYS SANCTION CRIME...INT/LAW JURID
GOV/COMP ANTHOL 6/20 MID/EAST. PAGE 61 E1210 ISLAM

B55
MAZZINI J.,THE DUTIES OF MAN. MOD/EUR LAW SOCIETY SUPEGO
FAM NAT/G POL/PAR SECT VOL/ASSN EX/STRUC ACT/RES CONCPT
CREATE REV PEACE ATTIT ALL/VALS...GEN/LAWS WORK 19. NAT/LISM
PAGE 70 E1396

B55
WRONG D.H.,AMERICAN AND CANADIAN VIEWPOINTS. CANADA DIPLOM
USA+45 CONSTN STRATA FAM SECT WORKER ECO/TAC ATTIT
EDU/PROP ADJUD MARRIAGE...IDEA/COMP 20. PAGE 108 NAT/COMP
E2161 CULTURE

B56
HOGAN J.D.,AMERICAN SOCIAL LEGISLATION. USA+45 FAM STRUCT
AGE/Y ATTIT...JURID CONCPT TREND. PAGE 53 E1065 RECEIVE
LEGIS
LABOR

B56
RECASENS SICHES S.,TRATADO GENERAL DE SOCIOLOGIA. SOC
CULTURE FAM NEIGH LEAD RACE/REL DISCRIM HABITAT STRATA
ORD/FREE...JURID LING T SOC/INTEG 20. PAGE 84 E1677 KIN
GP/REL

B57
CLINARD M.B.,SOCIOLOGY OF DEVIANT BEHAVIOR. FAM BIO/SOC
CONTROL MURDER DISCRIM PERSON...PSY SOC T SOC/INTEG CRIME
20. PAGE 23 E0455 SEX
ANOMIE

B58
ALLEN C.K.,ASPECTS OF JUSTICE. UK FAM COERCE CRIME JURID
MARRIAGE AGE/Y LOVE 20 ENGLSH/LAW. PAGE 4 E0068 MORAL

ORD/FREE

B58

BUGEDA LANZAS J.,A STATEMENT OF THE LAWS OF CUBA IN JURID
MATTERS AFFECTING BUSINESS (2ND ED. REV., NAT/G
ENLARGED). CUBA L/A+17C LAW FINAN FAM LEGIS ACT/RES INDUS
ADMIN GP/REL...BIBLIOG 20 OAS. PAGE 17 E0327 WORKER

B59

ANDERSON J.N.D.,ISLAMIC LAW IN THE MODERN WORLD. ISLAM
FAM KIN SECT LEGIT ADJUD ATTIT DRIVE...TIME/SEQ JURID
TREND GEN/LAWS 20 MUSLIM. PAGE 5 E0089

B59

GOMEZ ROBLES J.,A STATEMENT OF THE LAWS OF JURID
GUATEMALA IN MATTERS AFFECTING BUSINESS (2ND ED. NAT/G
REV., ENLARGED). GUATEMALA L/A+17C LAW FINAN FAM INDUS
WORKER ACT/RES DIPLOM ADJUD ADMIN GP/REL 20 OAS. LEGIT
PAGE 44 E0881

B59

KERREMANS-RAMIOULL,LE PROBLEME DE LA DELINQUENCE BIBLIOG
JUVENILE (2ND ED.). FAM PUB/INST SCHOOL FORCES CRIME
LEGIS MORAL...CRIMLGY SOC 20. PAGE 60 E1205 AGE/Y
SOC/WK

B59

LAPIERE R.,THE FREUDIAN ETHIC. USA+45 FAM EDU/PROP PSY
CONTROL CRIME ADJUST AGE DRIVE PERCEPT PERSON SEX ORD/FREE
...SOC 20 FREUD/S. PAGE 63 E1254 SOCIETY

B61

MERTON R.K.,CONTEMPORARY SOCIAL PROBLEMS: AN CRIME
INTRODUCTION TO THE SOCIOLOGY OF DEVIANT BEHAVIOR ANOMIE
AND SOCIAL DISORGANIZATION. FAM MUNIC FORCES WORKER STRANGE
PROB/SOLV INGP/REL RACE/REL ISOLAT...CRIMLGY GEOG SOC
PSY T 20 NEGRO. PAGE 72 E1444

B61

RUEDA B.,A STATEMENT OF THE LAWS OF COLOMBIA IN FINAN
MATTERS AFFECTING BUSINESS (3RD ED.). INDUS FAM ECO/UNDEV
LABOR LG/CO NAT/G LEGIS TAX CONTROL MARRIAGE 20 LAW
COLOMB. PAGE 86 E1733 CONSTN

B62

DAVIS F.J.,SOCIETY AND THE LAW. USA+45 CONSTN LAW
ACADEM FAM CONSULT ACT/RES GP/REL ORD/FREE SOC
ENGLSH/LAW 20. PAGE 29 E0572 CULTURE
STRUCT

B62

ROSENZWEIG F.,HEGEL UND DER STAAT. GERMANY SOCIETY JURID
FAM POL/PAR NAT/LISM...BIOG 19. PAGE 86 E1718 NAT/G
CONCPT
PHIL/SCI

B63

ELIAS T.O.,THE NIGERIAN LEGAL SYSTEM. NIGERIA LAW CT/SYS
FAM KIN SECT ADMIN NAT/LISM...JURID 18/20 ADJUD
ENGLSH/LAW COMMON/LAW. PAGE 34 E0682 COLONIAL
PROF/ORG

B64

FREISEN J.,STAAT UND KATHOLISCHE KIRCHE IN DEN SECT
DEUTSCHEN BUNDESSTAATEN (2 VOLS.). GERMANY LAW FAM CATHISM
NAT/G EDU/PROP GP/REL MARRIAGE WEALTH 19/20 JURID
CHURCH/STA. PAGE 40 E0793 PROVS

B64

GIANNELLA D.A.,RELIGION AND THE PUBLIC ORDER: AN SECT
ANNUAL REVIEW OF CHURCH AND STATE, AND OF RELIGION, NAT/G
LAW, AND SOCIETY. USA+45 LAW SOCIETY FAM POL/PAR CONSTN
SCHOOL GIVE EDU/PROP GP/REL...JURID GEN/LAWS ORD/FREE
BIBLIOG/A 20 CHURCH/STA BIRTH/CON CONSCN/OBJ
NATURL/LAW. PAGE 43 E0855

B64

MAKI J.M.,COURT AND CONSTITUTION IN JAPAN: SELECTED CT/SYS
SUPREME COURT DECISIONS, 1948-60. FAM LABOR GOV/REL CONSTN
HABITAT ORD/FREE...DECISION JURID 20 CHINJAP PROB/SOLV
SUPREME/CT CIV/RIGHTS. PAGE 68 E1354 LAW

B64

MAKI J.M.,COURT AND CONSTITUTION IN JAPAN: SELECTED CONSTN
SUPREME COURT DECISIONS, 1948-60. LAW AGRI FAM JURID
LEGIS BAL/PWR ADMIN CHOOSE...SOC ANTHOL CABINET 20 CT/SYS
CHINJAP CIVIL/LIB. PAGE 68 E1355 CRIME

B64

TELLADO A.,A STATEMENT OF THE LAWS OF THE DOMINICAN CONSTN
REPUBLIC IN MATTERS AFFECTING BUSINESS (3RD ED.). LEGIS
DOMIN/REP AGRI DIST/IND EXTR/IND FINAN FAM WORKER NAT/G
ECO/TAC TAX CT/SYS MARRIAGE OWN...BIBLIOG 20 INDUS
MIGRATION. PAGE 95 E1913

B65

GLUECK S.,ROSCOE POUND AND CRIMINAL JUSTICE. CT/SYS
SOCIETY FAM GOV/REL AGE/Y ATTIT ORD/FREE...CRIMLGY CRIME
BIOG ANTHOL SOC/INTEG 19/20. PAGE 44 E0875 LAW
ADJUD

B65

KUPER H.,AFRICAN LAW. LAW FAM KIN SECT JUDGE ADJUST AFR
NAT/LISM 17/20. PAGE 62 E1236 CT/SYS
ADJUD
COLONIAL

B65

LUGO-MARENCO J.J.,A STATEMENT OF THE LAWS OF CONSTN
NICARAGUA IN MATTERS AFFECTING BUSINESS. NICARAGUA NAT/G
AGRI DIST/IND EXTR/IND FINAN INDUS FAM WORKER LEGIS
INT/TRADE TAX MARRIAGE OWN BIO/SOC 20 TREATY JURID
RESOURCE/N MIGRATION. PAGE 67 E1332

B65

RENNER K.,MENSCH UND GESELLSCHAFT - GRUNDRISS EINER SOC
SOZIOLOGIE (2ND ED.). STRATA FAM LABOR PROF/ORG WAR STRUCT
...JURID CLASSIF 20. PAGE 84 E1685 NAT/G
SOCIETY

B66

BEER U.,FRUCHTBARKEITSREGELUNG ALS KONSEQUENZ CONTROL
VERANTWORTLICHER ELTERNSCHAFT. ASIA GERMANY/W INDIA GEOG
LAW ECO/DEV ECO/UNDEV TEC/DEV ECO/TAC BIO/SOC SEX FAM
CATHISM...METH/COMP 20 CHINJAP BIRTH/CON. PAGE 9 SECT
E0178

B66

SZLADITS C.,A BIBLIOGRAPHY ON FOREIGN AND BIBLIOG/A
COMPARATIVE LAW (SUPPLEMENT 1964). FINAN FAM LABOR CT/SYS
LG/CO LEGIS JUDGE ADMIN CRIME...CRIMLGY 20. PAGE 95 INT/LAW
E1905

B67

AMDS W.E.,DELINQUENCY PREVENTION: THEORY AND AGE/Y
PRACTICE. USA+45 SOCIETY FAM SCHOOL SECT FORCES CRIME
PROB/SOLV...HEAL JURID PREDICT ANTHOL. PAGE 4 E0071 PUB/INST
LAW

B67

LOBLE L.H.,DELINQUENCY CAN BE STOPPED. FAM PUB/INST AGE/Y
CT/SYS ADJUST ATTIT...NEW/IDEA METH/COMP 20. PROB/SOLV
PAGE 66 E1315 ADJUD
CRIME

L67

CICOUREL A.V.,"KINSHIP, MARRIAGE, AND DIVORCE IN SOC
COMPARATIVE FAMILY LAW." UNIV LAW FAM KIN GEN/METH. PHIL/SCI
PAGE 22 E0438 MARRIAGE
IDEA/COMP

S67

BOHANNAN P.,"INSTITUTIONS OF DIVORCE, FAMILY, AND FAM
THE LAW." WOR+45 LAW CONSULT...JURID SOC. PAGE 13 MARRIAGE
E0258 ADJUD
SOCIETY

S68

DUPRE L.,"TILL DEATH DO US PART?" UNIV FAM INSPECT MARRIAGE
LEGIT ADJUD SANCTION PERS/REL ANOMIE RIGID/FLEX SEX CATH
...JURID IDEA/COMP 20 CHURCH/STA BIBLE CANON/LAW LAW
CIVIL/LAW. PAGE 34 E0666

B75

MAINE H.S.,LECTURES ON THE EARLY HISTORY OF CULTURE
INSTITUTIONS. IRELAND UK CONSTN ELITES STRUCT FAM LAW
KIN CHIEF LEGIS CT/SYS OWN SOVEREIGN...CONCPT 16 INGP/REL
BENTHAM/J BREHON ROMAN/LAW. PAGE 68 E1351

B89

FICHTE J.G.,THE SCIENCE OF RIGHTS (TRANS. BY A.E. ORD/FREE
KROEGER). WOR+45 FAM MUNIC NAT/G PROVS ADJUD CRIME CONSTN
CHOOSE MARRIAGE SEX POPULISM 19 FICHTE/JG LAW
NATURL/LAW. PAGE 37 E0744 CONCPT

B96

SMITH A.,LECTURES ON JUSTICE, POLICE, REVENUE AND DIPLOM
ARMS (1763). UK LAW FAM FORCES TARIFFS AGREE COERCE JURID
INCOME OWN WEALTH LAISSEZ...GEN/LAWS 17/18. PAGE 92 OLD/LIB
E1840 TAX

FAMILY....SEE FAM

FAMINE....SEE AGRI, HEALTH

FANSHEL D. E0268

FAO....FOOD AND AGRICULTURE ORGANIZATION; SEE ALSO UN,
    INT/ORG

COMM. STUDY ORGAN. PEACE,REPORTS. WOR-45 ECO/DEV   WOR+45
ECO/UNDEV VOL/ASSN CONSULT FORCES PLAN TEC/DEV   INT/ORG
DOMIN EDU/PROP NUC/PWR ATTIT PWR WEALTH...JURID   ARMS/CONT
STERTYP FAO ILO 20 UN. PAGE 24 E0481   B55

SOHN L.B.,BASIC DOCUMENTS OF THE UNITED NATIONS.   DELIB/GP
WOR+45 LAW INT/ORG LEGIT EXEC ROUTINE CHOOSE PWR   CONSTN
...JURID CONCPT GEN/LAWS ANTHOL UN TOT/POP OAS FAO   B56
ILO 20. PAGE 92 E1853

FARM/BUR....FARM BUREAU

FARMING....SEE AGRI

FARRAND M. E0721

FASCISM....FASCISM; SEE ALSO TOTALISM, FASCIST

KONRAD F.,DIE PERSONLICHE FREIHEIT IM   ORD/FREE
NATIONALSOZIALISTISCHEN DEUTSCHEN REICHE. GERMANY   JURID
JUDGE ADJUD GP/REL FASCISM 20 CIVIL/LIB. PAGE 61   CONSTN
E1226   CONCPT
                                                        B36

BORGESE G.A.,GOLIATH: THE MARCH OF FASCISM. GERMANY   POLICY
ITALY LAW POL/PAR SECT DIPLOM SOCISM...JURID MYTH   NAT/LISM
20 DANTE MACHIAVELL MUSSOLIN/B. PAGE 14 E0270   FASCISM
                                                        NAT/G
                                                        B37

FIELD G.L.,THE SYNDICAL AND CORPORATIVE   FASCISM
INSTITUTIONS OF ITALIAN FASCISM. ITALY CONSTN   INDUS
STRATA LABOR EX/STRUC TOP/EX ADJUD ADMIN LEAD   NAT/G
TOTALISM AUTHORIT...MGT 20 MUSSOLIN/B. PAGE 38   WORKER
E0746   B38

SERENI A.P.,THE ITALIAN CONCEPTION OF INTERNATIONAL LAW LAW
LAW. EUR+WWI MOD/EUR INT/ORG NAT/G DOMIN COERCE   TIME/SEQ
ORD/FREE FASCISM...OBS/ENVIR TREND 20. PAGE 90   INT/LAW
E1804   ITALY
                                                        B43

MASON J.B.,"THE JUDICIAL SYSTEM OF THE NAZI PARTY."   FASCISM
GERMANY ELITES POL/PAR DOMIN CONTROL SANCTION   CT/SYS
TOTALISM...JURID 20 HITLER/A. PAGE 69 E1381   ADJUD
                                                        LAW
                                                        S44

ALEXANDER L.,"WAR CRIMES, THEIR SOCIAL-   DRIVE
PSYCHOLOGICAL ASPECTS." EUR+WWI GERMANY LAW CULTURE   WAR
ELITES KIN POL/PAR PUB/INST FORCES DOMIN EDU/PROP
COERCE CRIME ATTIT SUPEGO HEALTH MORAL PWR FASCISM
...PSY OBS TREND GEN/LAWS NAZI 20. PAGE 3 E0061   S48

APPADORAI A.,THE SUBSTANCE OF POLITICS (6TH ED.).   PHIL/SCI
EX/STRUC LEGIS DIPLOM CT/SYS CHOOSE FASCISM MARXISM   NAT/G
SOCISM...BIBLIOG T. PAGE 5 E0100   B52

SCHORN H.,DER RICHTER IM DRITTEN REICH; GESCHICHTE   ADJUD
UND DOKUMENTE. GERMANY NAT/G LEGIT CT/SYS INGP/REL   JUDGE
MORAL ORD/FREE RESPECT...JURID GP/COMP 20. PAGE 88   FASCISM
E1765   B59

DELEGACION NACIONAL DE PRENSA,FALANGE ESPANOL   EDU/PROP
TRADICIONALISTA Y DE LAS JUNTAS OFENSIVAS   FASCIST
NACIONALES SINDICALISTAS. IX CONSEJO NACIONAL   CONFER
(PAMPHLET). LAW VOL/ASSN TOTALISM AUTHORIT ORD/FREE   POL/PAR
FASCISM...ANTHOL 20 FRANCO/F FALANGIST. PAGE 31   N61
E0605

FISCHER H.,EINER IM VORDERGRUND: TARAS   FASCISM
BORODAJKEWYCZ. AUSTRIA POL/PAR PROF/ORG EDU/PROP   LAW
CT/SYS ORD/FREE 20 NAZI. PAGE 38 E0754   ATTIT
                                                        PRESS
                                                        B66

HAUSNER G.,JUSTICE IN JERUSALEM. GERMANY ISRAEL   ADJUD
SOCIETY KIN DIPLOM LEGIT CT/SYS PARTIC MURDER   CRIME
MAJORITY ATTIT FASCISM...INT/LAW JURID 20 JEWS   RACE/REL
WAR/TRIAL. PAGE 51 E1013   COERCE
                                                        B66

FASCIST....FASCIST

LAVES W.H.C.,INTERNATIONAL SECURITY. EUR+WWI   ORD/FREE
GERMANY UK USA-45 LAW NAT/G DELIB/GP TOP/EX COERCE   LEGIT
PWR...POLICY FASCIST CONCPT HIST/WRIT GEN/LAWS   ARMS/CONT
LEAGUE/NAT NAZI 20. PAGE 63 E1267   BAL/PWR
                                                        B39

MICAUD C.A.,THE FRENCH RIGHT AND NAZI GERMANY   DIPLOM
1933-1939: A STUDY OF PUBLIC OPINION. GERMANY UK   AGREE
USSR POL/PAR ARMS/CONT COERCE DETER PEACE
RIGID/FLEX PWR MARXISM...FASCIST TREND 20
LEAGUE/NAT TREATY. PAGE 73 E1454   B43

DELEGACION NACIONAL DE PRENSA,FALANGE ESPANOL   EDU/PROP
TRADICIONALISTA Y DE LAS JUNTAS OFENSIVAS   FASCIST
NACIONALES SINDICALISTAS. IX CONSEJO NACIONAL   CONFER
(PAMPHLET). LAW VOL/ASSN TOTALISM AUTHORIT ORD/FREE   POL/PAR
FASCISM...ANTHOL 20 FRANCO/F FALANGIST. PAGE 31   N61
E0605

NORDEN A.,WAR AND NAZI CRIMINALS IN WEST GERMANY: FASCIST
STATE, ECONOMY, ADMINISTRATION, ARMY, JUSTICE,   WAR
SCIENCE. GERMANY GERMANY/W MOD/EUR ECO/DEV ACADEM   NAT/G
EX/STRUC FORCES DOMIN ADMIN CT/SYS...POLICY MAJORIT   TOP/EX
PACIFIST 20. PAGE 77 E1554   B65

FASHION....SEE ETIQUET, MODAL

FATHER/DIV....FATHER DIVINE AND HIS FOLLOWERS

FATOUROS A.A. E0722

FAWCETT J.E.S. E0723

FBI....U.S. FEDERAL BUREAU OF INVESTIGATION

LOWENTHAL M.,THE FEDERAL BUREAU OF INVESTIGATION.   FORCES
USA+45 SOCIETY ADMIN TASK CRIME INGP/REL...CRIMLGY   NAT/G
20 FBI ESPIONAGE. PAGE 67 E1329   ATTIT
                                                        LAW
                                                        B50

CAVAN R.S.,CRIMINOLOGY (2ND ED.). USA+45 LAW FAM   DRIVE
PUB/INST FORCES PLAN WAR AGE/Y PERSON ROLE SUPEGO   CRIMLGY
...CHARTS 20 FBI. PAGE 21 E0409   CONTROL
                                                        METH/COMP
                                                        B55

GINZBURG B.,REDEDICATION TO FREEDOM. DELIB/GP LEGIS   JURID
ATTIT MARXISM 20 SUPREME/CT CON/INTERP HUAC AMEND/I   ORD/FREE
FBI. PAGE 44 E0871   CONSTN
                                                        NAT/G
                                                        B59

OTTENBERG M.,THE FEDERAL INVESTIGATORS. USA+45 LAW   FORCES
COM/IND DIST/IND WORKER DIPLOM INT/TRADE CONTROL   INSPECT
FEDERAL HEALTH ORD/FREE FBI CIA FTC SEC FDA.   NAT/G
PAGE 79 E1585   CRIME
                                                        B62

HOEVELER H.J.,INTERNATIONALE BEKAMPFUNG DES   CRIMLGY
VERBRECHENS. AUSTRIA SWITZERLND WOR+45 INT/ORG   CRIME
CONTROL BIO/SOC...METH/COMP NAT/COMP 20 MAFIA   DIPLOM
SCOT/YARD FBI. PAGE 53 E1064   INT/LAW
                                                        B66

CLOGGER T.J.,"THE BIG EAR." UK USA+45 USSR LAW   DIPLOM
LEGIS CRIME GP/REL INGP/REL ATTIT 20 FBI ESPIONAGE.   ORD/FREE
PAGE 23 E0458   COM/IND
                                                        INSPECT
                                                        S67

FCC....U.S. FEDERAL COMMUNICATIONS COMMISSION

FDA....U.S. FOOD AND DRUG ADMINISTRATION

OTTENBERG M.,THE FEDERAL INVESTIGATORS. USA+45 LAW   FORCES
COM/IND DIST/IND WORKER DIPLOM INT/TRADE CONTROL   INSPECT
FEDERAL HEALTH ORD/FREE FBI CIA FTC SEC FDA.   NAT/G
PAGE 79 E1585   CRIME
                                                        B62

FDR....FRANKLIN D. ROOSEVELT

FEARS....SEE ANOMIE

FECHNER/GT....GUSTAV THEODOR FECHNER

FED/OPNMKT....FEDERAL OPEN MARKET COMMITTEE

FED/RESERV....U.S. FEDERAL RESERVE SYSTEM (INCLUDES FEDERAL
    RESERVE BANK)

FEDERAL BUREAU OF INVESTIGATION....SEE FBI

FEDERAL COMMUNICATIONS COMMISSION....SEE FCC

FEDERAL COUNCIL FOR SCIENCE + TECHNOLOGY....SEE FEDSCI/TEC

FEDERAL HOUSING ADMINISTRATION...SEE FHA

FEDERAL RESERVE SYSTEM....SEE FED/RESERV

FEDERAL TRADE COMMISSION....SEE FTC

FEDERAL....FEDERALISM

INDEX TO LEGAL PERIODICALS. CANADA NEW/ZEALND UK BIBLIOG N
USA+45 USA-45 CONSTN LEGIS JUDGE ADJUD ADMIN INDEX
CONTROL CT/SYS FEDERAL...CRIMLGY INT/LAW 20 LAW
CMN/WLTH AUSTRAL. PAGE 1 E0006 JURID

US SUPERINTENDENT OF DOCUMENTS,EDUCATION (PRICE BIBLIOG/A N
LIST 31). USA+45 LAW FINAN LOC/G NAT/G DEBATE ADMIN EDU/PROP
LEAD RACE/REL FEDERAL HEALTH POLICY. PAGE 103 E2062 ACADEM
SCHOOL

WILSON W.,CONSTITUTIONAL GOVERNMENT IN THE UNITED NAT/G B08
STATES. USA-45 LAW POL/PAR PROVS CHIEF LEGIS GOV/REL
BAL/PWR ADJUD EXEC FEDERAL PWR 18/20 SUPREME/CT CONSTN
HOUSE/REP SENATE. PAGE 106 E2130 PARL/PROC

BRENNAN W.J. JR.,THE BILL OF RIGHTS AND THE STATES CONSTN N19
(PAMPHLET). USA+45 USA-45 LEGIS BAL/PWR ADJUD PROVS
CT/SYS FEDERAL PWR SOVEREIGN 18/20 SUPREME/CT GOV/REL
BILL/RIGHT. PAGE 15 E0293 ORD/FREE

FRANKFURTER F.,THE BUSINESS OF THE SUPREME COURT; A CT/SYS B28
STUDY IN THE FEDERAL JUDICIAL SYSTEM. USA-45 CONSTN ADJUD
EX/STRUC PROB/SOLV GP/REL ATTIT PWR...POLICY JURID LAW
18/20 SUPREME/CT CONGRESS. PAGE 40 E0789 FEDERAL

MACDONALD A.F.,ELEMENTS OF POLITICAL SCIENCE LAW B28
RESEARCH. USA-45 ACADEM JUDGE EDU/PROP DEBATE ADJUD FEDERAL
EXEC...BIBLIOG METH T 20 CONGRESS. PAGE 67 E1338 DECISION
CT/SYS

WILLOUGHBY W.W.,PRINCIPLES OF THE CONSTITUTIONAL CONSTN B30
LAW OF THE UNITED STATES. USA-45 ADJUD FEDERAL NAT/G
SOVEREIGN 18/20 COMMON/LAW. PAGE 106 E2125 CONCPT
JURID

HELLMAN F.S.,SELECTED LIST OF REFERENCES ON THE BIBLIOG/A B33
CONSTITUTIONAL POWERS OF THE PRESIDENT INCLUDING JURID
POWERS RECENTLY DELEGATED. USA-45 NAT/G EX/STRUC LAW
TOP/EX CENTRAL FEDERAL PWR 20 PRESIDENT. PAGE 51 CONSTN
E1025

GRAVES W.B.,AMERICAN STATE GOVERNMENT. CONSTN FINAN NAT/G B36
EX/STRUC FORCES LEGIS BUDGET TAX CT/SYS REPRESENT PROVS
GOV/REL...BIBLIOG/A 19/20. PAGE 45 E0900 ADMIN
FEDERAL

CLARK J.P.,THE RISE OF A NEW FEDERALISM. LEGIS FEDERAL B38
TARIFFS EFFICIENCY NAT/LISM UTIL...JURID SOC PROVS
GEN/LAWS BIBLIOG 19/20. PAGE 23 E0451 NAT/G
GOV/REL

FRANKFURTER F.,MR. JUSTICE HOLMES AND THE SUPREME CREATE B38
COURT. USA-45 CONSTN SOCIETY FEDERAL OWN ATTIT CT/SYS
ORD/FREE PWR...POLICY JURID 20 SUPREME/CT HOLMES/OW DECISION
BILL/RIGHT. PAGE 40 E0790 LAW

ANDERSON W.,FUNDAMENTALS OF AMERICAN GOVERNMENT. NAT/G B40
USA-45 LAW POL/PAR CHIEF EX/STRUC BUDGET ADMIN LOC/G
CT/SYS PARL/PROC CHOOSE FEDERAL...BIBLIOG 20. GOV/REL
PAGE 5 E0093 CONSTN

US LIBRARY OF CONGRESS,CONSTITUTIONAL AND STATUTORY CONSTN B45
PROVISIONS OF THE STATES (VOL. I). USA-45 CREATE FEDERAL
TAX CT/SYS CHOOSE SUFF INCOME PWR 20. PAGE 101 PROVS
E2016 JURID

BISHOP H.M.,BASIC ISSUES OF AMERICAN DEMOCRACY. NAT/G B48
USA+45 USA-45 POL/PAR EX/STRUC LEGIS ADJUD FEDERAL PARL/PROC
...BIBLIOG 18/20. PAGE 12 E0232 CONSTN

CORWIN E.S.,LIBERTY AGAINST GOVERNMENT: THE RISE, CONCPT B48
FLOWERING AND DECLINE OF A FAMOUS JURIDICAL ORD/FREE
CONCEPT. LEGIS ADJUD CT/SYS SANCTION GOV/REL JURID
FEDERAL CONSERVE NEW/LIB...OLD/LIB 18/20 ROMAN/LAW CONSTN
COMMON/LAW. PAGE 26 E0514

GROSS L.,"THE PEACE OF WESTPHALIA, 1648-1948." INT/LAW S48
WOR+45 WOR-45 CONSTN BAL/PWR FEDERAL 17/20 TREATY AGREE
WESTPHALIA. PAGE 48 E0949 CONCPT
DIPLOM

PRITCHETT C.H.,"THE PRESIDENT AND THE SUPREME GOV/REL S49
COURT." NAT/G CONTROL REPRESENT FEDERAL 20. PAGE 82 CT/SYS
E1651 CHIEF

MONPIED E.,BIBLIOGRAPHIE FEDERALISTE: OUVRAGES BIBLIOG/A B50
CHOISIS (VOL. I, MIMEOGRAPHED PAPER). EUR+WWI FEDERAL
DIPLOM ADMIN REGION ATTIT PACIFISM SOCISM...INT/LAW CENTRAL
19/20. PAGE 74 E1486 INT/ORG

HOLCOMBE A.,"OUR MORE PERFECT UNION." USA+45 USA-45 CONSTN C50
POL/PAR JUDGE CT/SYS EQUILIB FEDERAL PWR...MAJORIT NAT/G
TREND BIBLIOG 18/20 CONGRESS PRESIDENT. PAGE 54 ADMIN
E1070 PLAN

MONPIED E.,FEDERALIST BIBLIOGRAPHY: ARTICLES AND BIBLIOG/A N51
DOCUMENTS PUBLISHED IN BRITISH PERIODICALS INT/ORG
1945-1951 (MIMEOGRAPHED). EUR+WWI UK WOR+45 DIPLOM FEDERAL
REGION ATTIT SOCISM...INT/LAW 20. PAGE 74 E1487 CENTRAL

DE GRAZIA A.,POLITICAL ORGANIZATION. CONSTN LOC/G FEDERAL B52
MUNIC NAT/G CHIEF LEGIS TOP/EX ADJUD CT/SYS LAW
PERS/REL...INT/LAW MYTH UN. PAGE 29 E0581 ADMIN

CLAGETT H.L.,"THE ADMINISTRATION OF JUSTICE IN CT/SYS C52
LATIN AMERICA." L/A+17C ADMIN FEDERAL...JURID ADJUD
METH/COMP BIBLIOG 20. PAGE 23 E0448 JUDGE
CONSTN

BROGAN D.W.,POLITICS IN AMERICA. LAW POL/PAR CHIEF NAT/G B54
LEGIS LOBBY CHOOSE REPRESENT GP/REL RACE/REL CONSTN
FEDERAL MORAL...BIBLIOG 20 PRESIDENT CONGRESS. USA+45
PAGE 16 E0304

FRIEDMAN W.,THE PUBLIC CORPORATION: A COMPARATIVE LAW B54
SYMPOSIUM (UNIVERSITY OF TORONTO SCHOOL OF LAW SOCISM
COMPARATIVE LAW SERIES, VOL. I). SWEDEN USA+45 LG/CO
INDUS INT/ORG NAT/G REGION CENTRAL FEDERAL...POLICY OWN
JURID IDEA/COMP NAT/COMP ANTHOL 20 COMMONWLTH
MONOPOLY EUROPE. PAGE 40 E0801

JAMES L.F.,THE SUPREME COURT IN AMERICAN LIFE. ADJUD B54
USA+45 USA-45 CONSTN CRIME GP/REL INGP/REL RACE/REL CT/SYS
CONSEN FEDERAL PERSON ORD/FREE 18/20 SUPREME/CT JURID
DEPRESSION CIV/RIGHTS CHURCH/STA FREE/SPEE. PAGE 58 DECISION
E1147

HART J.,"ADMINISTRATION AND THE COURTS." USA+45 ADMIN S54
NAT/G REPRESENT 20. PAGE 50 E1003 GOV/REL
CT/SYS
FEDERAL

BOWIE R.R.,"STUDIES IN FEDERALISM." AGRI FINAN FEDERAL C54
LABOR EX/STRUC FORCES LEGIS DIPLOM INT/TRADE ADJUD EUR+WWI
...BIBLIOG 20 EEC. PAGE 14 E0279 INT/ORG
CONSTN

CUSHMAN R.E.,LEADING CONSTITUTIONAL DECISIONS. CONSTN B55
USA+45 USA-45 NAT/G EX/STRUC LEGIS JUDGE TAX PROB/SOLV
FEDERAL...DECISION 20 SUPREME/CT CASEBOOK. PAGE 28 JURID
E0559 CT/SYS

DE ARAGAO J.G.,LA JURIDICTION ADMINISTRATIVE AU EX/STRUC B55
BRESIL. BRAZIL ADJUD COLONIAL CT/SYS REV FEDERAL ADMIN
ORD/FREE...BIBLIOG 19/20. PAGE 29 E0580 NAT/G

MAYERS L.,THE AMERICAN LEGAL SYSTEM. USA+45 USA-45 JURID B55
NAT/G EX/STRUC ADMIN CONTROL FEDERAL 20 SUPREME/CT. CT/SYS
PAGE 70 E1394 LEGIS
ADJUD

B56

DOUGLAS W.O.,WE THE JUDGES. INDIA USA+45 USA-45 LAW   ADJUD
NAT/G SECT LEGIS PRESS CRIME FEDERAL ORD/FREE   CT/SYS
...POLICY GOV/COMP 19/20 WARRN/EARL MARSHALL/J   CONSTN
SUPREME/CT. PAGE 32 E0640   GOV/REL

B56

HURST J.W.,LAW AND THE CONDITIONS OF FREEDOM IN THE LAW
NINETEENTH CENTURY UNITED STATES. USA-45 CONSTN   ORD/FREE
STRUCT ADMIN GP/REL FEDERAL HABITAT...JURID 19.   POLICY
PAGE 56 E1116   NAT/G

S56

TANENHAUS J.,"THE SUPREME COURT AND PRESIDENTIAL   CT/SYS
POWER." USA+45 USA-45 NAT/G ADJUD GOV/REL FEDERAL   PWR
20 PRESIDENT. PAGE 95 E1907   CONTROL
                                                        CHIEF

B57

LONG H.A.,USURPERS - FOES OF FREE MAN. LAW NAT/G   CT/SYS
CHIEF LEGIS DOMIN ADJUD REPRESENT GOV/REL ORD/FREE   CENTRAL
LAISSEZ POPULISM...POLICY 18/20 SUPREME/CT   FEDERAL
ROOSEVLT/F CONGRESS CON/INTERP. PAGE 66 E1325   CONSTN

B57

SCHLOCHAUER H.J.,OFFENTLICHES RECHT. GERMANY/W   CONSTN
FINAN EX/STRUC LEGIS DIPLOM FEDERAL ORD/FREE   JURID
...INT/LAW 20. PAGE 88 E1757   ADMIN
                                                        CT/SYS

B58

BLOCH J.,STATES' RIGHTS: THE LAW OF THE LAND.   PROVS
USA+45 USA-45 LAW CONSTN LEGIS CONTROL CT/SYS   NAT/G
FEDERAL ORD/FREE...PREDICT 17/20 CONGRESS   BAL/PWR
SUPREME/CT. PAGE 13 E0246   CENTRAL

B58

DAVIS K.C.,ADMINISTRATIVE LAW: CASES, TEXT,   ADJUD
PROBLEMS. LAW LOC/G NAT/G TOP/EX PAY CONTROL   JURID
GOV/REL INGP/REL FEDERAL 20 SUPREME/CT. PAGE 29   CT/SYS
E0576   ADMIN

B58

O'BRIEN F.W.,JUSTICE REED AND THE FIRST AMENDMENT,   ADJUD
THE RELIGION CLAUSES. USA+45 USA-45 NAT/G PROVS   SECT
CONTROL FEDERAL...POLICY JURID TIME/SEQ 20   CT/SYS
SUPREME/CT CHRUCH/STA AMEND/I REED/STAN. PAGE 78
E1563

B58

STRONG C.F.,MODERN POLITICAL CONSTITUTIONS. LAW   CONSTN
CHIEF DELIB/GP EX/STRUC LEGIS ADJUD CHOOSE FEDERAL   IDEA/COMP
POPULISM...CONCPT BIBLIOG 20 UN. PAGE 94 E1887   NAT/G

B59

BROOKES E.H.,THE COMMONWEALTH TODAY. UK ROMAN/EMP   FEDERAL
INT/ORG RACE/REL NAT/LISM SOVEREIGN...TREND   DIPLOM
SOC/INTEG 20. PAGE 16 E0307   JURID
                                                      IDEA/COMP

B59

SCOTT F.R.,CIVIL LIBERTIES AND CANADIAN FEDERALISM.   ORD/FREE
CANADA LAW ADJUD CT/SYS GOV/REL 20 CIV/RIGHTS.   FEDERAL
PAGE 90 E1797   NAT/LISM
                                                      CONSTN

B59

WAGNER W.J.,THE FEDERAL STATES AND THEIR JUDICIARY.   ADJUD
BRAZIL CANADA SWITZERLND USA+45 CONFER CT/SYS TASK   METH/COMP
EFFICIENCY FEDERAL PWR...JURID BIBLIOG 20 AUSTRAL   PROB/SOLV
MEXIC/AMER. PAGE 104 E2091   NAT/G

N59

NATIONAL ASSN HOME BUILDERS,COMMUNITY FACILITIES: A   BIBLIOG/A
LIST OF SELECTED REFERENCES (PAMPHLET). USA+45   PLAN
DIST/IND FINAN SERV/IND SCHOOL CREATE CONTROL   LOC/G
FEDERAL...JURID 20. PAGE 76 E1525   MUNIC

B60

BYRD E.M. JR.,TREATIES AND EXECUTIVE AGREEMENTS IN   CHIEF
THE UNITED STATES: THEIR SEPARATE ROLES AND   INT/LAW
LIMITATIONS. USA+45 USA-45 EX/STRUC TARIFFS CT/SYS   DIPLOM
GOV/REL FEDERAL...IDEA/COMP BIBLIOG SUPREME/CT
SENATE CONGRESS. PAGE 18 E0353

B60

DILEY A.V.,INTRODUCTION TO THE STUDY OF THE LAW OF   CONSTN
THE CONSTITUTION. FRANCE UK USA+45 USA-45 CONSULT   LAW
FORCES TAX ADMIN FEDERAL ORD/FREE SOVEREIGN   LEGIS
...IDEA/COMP 20 ENGLSH/LAW CON/INTERP PARLIAMENT.   GEN/LAWS
PAGE 32 E0627

B60

LASKIN B.,CANADIAN CONSTITUTIONAL LAW: TEXT AND   CONSTN
NOTES ON DISTRIBUTION OF LEGISLATIVE POWER (2ND   NAT/G

ED.). CANADA LOC/G ECO/TAC TAX CONTROL CT/SYS CRIME   LAW
FEDERAL PWR...JURID 20 PARLIAMENT. PAGE 63 E1259   LEGIS

B60

RIENOW R.,INTRODUCTION TO GOVERNMENT (2ND ED.). UK   CONSTN
USA+45 USSR POL/PAR ADMIN REV CHOOSE SUFF FEDERAL   PARL/PROC
PWR...JURID GOV/COMP T 20. PAGE 85 E1697   REPRESENT
                                                      AUTHORIT

S60

BLACK H.,"THE BILL OF RIGHTS" (BMR)" USA+45 USA-45   CONSTN
LAW LEGIS CT/SYS FEDERAL PWR 18/20 CONGRESS   ORD/FREE
SUPREME/CT BILL/RIGHT CIV/RIGHTS. PAGE 12 E0237   NAT/G
                                                      JURID

B61

FREUND P.A.,THE SUPREME COURT OF THE UNITED STATES: CT/SYS
ITS BUSINESS, PURPOSES, AND PERFORMANCE. CONSTN   JURID
CRIME CONSEN ORD/FREE...DECISION 20 SUPREME/CT   ADJUD
CIVIL/LIB. PAGE 40 E0797   FEDERAL

B61

SCOTT A.M.,POLITICS, USA; CASES ON THE AMERICAN   CT/SYS
DEMOCRATIC PROCESS. USA+45 CHIEF FORCES DIPLOM   CONSTN
LOBBY CHOOSE RACE/REL FEDERAL ATTIT...JURID ANTHOL   NAT/G
T 20 PRESIDENT CONGRESS CIVIL/LIB. PAGE 90 E1795   PLAN

L61

GERWIG R.,"PUBLIC AUTHORITIES IN THE UNITED   LOC/G
STATES." LAW CONSTN PROVS TAX ADMIN FEDERAL.   MUNIC
PAGE 43 E0852   GOV/REL
                                                      PWR

B62

CARPER E.T.,ILLINOIS GOES TO CONGRESS FOR ARMY   ADMIN
LAND. USA+45 LAW EXTR/IND PROVS REGION CIVMIL/REL   LOBBY
GOV/REL FEDERAL ATTIT 20 ILLINOIS SENATE CONGRESS   GEOG
DIRKSEN/E DOUGLAS/P. PAGE 20 E0391   LEGIS

B62

MASON A.T.,THE SUPREME COURT: PALADIUM OF FREEDOM.   CONSTN
USA-45 NAT/G POL/PAR CHIEF LEGIS ADJUD PARL/PROC   CT/SYS
FEDERAL PWR...POLICY BIOG 18/20 SUPREME/CT   JURID
ROOSEVLT/F JEFFERSN/T MARSHALL/J HUGHES/CE. PAGE 69
E1378

B62

OTTENBERG M.,THE FEDERAL INVESTIGATORS. USA+45 LAW   FORCES
COM/IND DIST/IND WORKER DIPLOM INT/TRADE CONTROL   INSPECT
FEDERAL HEALTH ORD/FREE FBI CIA FTC SEC FDA.   NAT/G
PAGE 79 E1585   CRIME

B62

PRESS C.,STATE MANUALS, BLUE BOOKS AND ELECTION   BIBLIOG
RESULTS. LAW LOC/G MUNIC LEGIS WRITING FEDERAL   PROVS
SOVEREIGN...DECISION STAT CHARTS 20. PAGE 82 E1648   ADMIN
                                                      CHOOSE

B62

ROSTOW E.V.,THE SOVEREIGN PREROGATIVE: THE SUPREME   JURID
COURT AND THE QUEST FOR LAW. CONSTN CT/SYS FEDERAL   PROF/ORG
MORAL SOVEREIGN 20 SUPREME/CT. PAGE 86 E1726   ATTIT
                                                      ORD/FREE

N62

TWENTIETH CENTURY FUND,ONE MAN - ONE VOTE   APPORT
(PAMPHLET). USA+45 CONSTN CONFER CT/SYS REGION   LEGIS
CONSEN FEDERAL ROLE...CENSUS 20 CONGRESS. PAGE 97   REPRESENT
E1947   PROVS

B63

COUNCIL OF STATE GOVERNMENTS,INCREASED RIGHTS FOR   CT/SYS
DEFENDANTS IN STATE CRIMINAL PROSECUTIONS. USA+45   ADJUD
GOV/REL INGP/REL FEDERAL ORD/FREE...JURID 20   PROVS
SUPREME/CT. PAGE 26 E0522   CRIME

B63

GRANT D.R.,STATE AND LOCAL GOVERNMENT IN AMERICA.   PROVS
USA+45 FINAN LOC/G MUNIC EX/STRUC FORCES EDU/PROP   POL/PAR
ADMIN CHOOSE FEDERAL ATTIT...JURID 20. PAGE 45   LEGIS
E0897   CONSTN

B63

HYNEMAN C.S.,THE SUPREME COURT ON TRIAL. ADJUD LEAD   CT/SYS
GP/REL FEDERAL...IDEA/COMP 20 SUPREME/CT. PAGE 56   JURID
E1120   POLICY
                                                      NAT/G

B63

LIVELY E.,THE INVASION OF MISSISSIPPI. USA+45 LAW   RACE/REL
CONSTN NAT/G PROVS CT/SYS GOV/REL FEDERAL CONSERVE   CROWD
...TRADIT 20 MISSISSIPP NEGRO NAACP WARRN/EARL   COERCE
KENNEDY/JF. PAGE 66 E1309   MARXISM

B63

LIVINGSTON W.S.,FEDERALISM IN THE COMMONWEALTH - A   BIBLIOG

BIBLIOGRAPHICAL COMMENTARY. CANADA INDIA PAKISTAN
UK STRUCT LOC/G NAT/G POL/PAR...NAT/COMP 20
AUSTRAL. PAGE 66 E1310
JURID
FEDERAL
CONSTN

B63
SCHMIDHAUSER J.R.,CONSTITUTIONAL LAW IN THE
POLITICAL PROCESS. SOCIETY LEGIS ADJUD CT/SYS
FEDERAL...SOC TREND IDEA/COMP ANTHOL T SUPREME/CT
SENATE CONGRESS HOUSE/REP. PAGE 88 E1761
LAW
CONSTN
JURID

B64
CURRIE D.P.,FEDERALISM AND THE NEW NATIONS OF
AFRICA. CANADA USA+45 INT/TRADE TAX GP/REL
...NAT/COMP SOC/INTEG 20. PAGE 28 E0556
FEDERAL
AFR
ECO/UNDEV
INT/LAW

B64
DIETZE G.,ESSAYS ON THE AMERICAN CONSTITUTION: A
COMMEMORATIVE VOLUME IN HONOR OF ALPHEUS T. MASON.
USA+45 USA-45 LAW INTELL...POLICY BIOG IDEA/COMP
ANTHOL SUPREME/CT. PAGE 32 E0626
FEDERAL
CONSTN
DIPLOM
CT/SYS

B64
FRANCK T.M.,EAST AFRICAN UNITY THROUGH LAW. MALAWI
TANZANIA UGANDA UK ZAMBIA CONSTN INT/ORG NAT/G
ADMIN ROUTINE TASK NAT/LISM ATTIT SOVEREIGN
...RECORD IDEA/COMP NAT/COMP. PAGE 40 E0785
AFR
FEDERAL
REGION
INT/LAW

B64
GROVES H.E.,THE CONSTITUTION OF MALAYSIA. MALAYSIA
POL/PAR CHIEF CONSULT DELIB/GP CT/SYS PARL/PROC
CHOOSE FEDERAL ORD/FREE 20. PAGE 48 E0953
CONSTN
NAT/G
LAW

B64
KISER S.L.,AMERICANISM IN ACTION. USA+45 LAW PROVS
CAP/ISM DIPLOM RECEIVE CONTROL CT/SYS WAR FEDERAL
ATTIT WEALTH 20 SUPREME/CT. PAGE 61 E1221
OLD/LIB
FOR/AID
MARXISM
CONSTN

B64
MARSHALL B.,FEDERALISM AND CIVIL RIGHTS. USA+45
PROVS BAL/PWR CONTROL CT/SYS PARTIC SOVEREIGN
...JURID 20 NEGRO CIV/RIGHTS. PAGE 68 E1369
FEDERAL
ORD/FREE
CONSTN
FORCES

B64
MASON A.T.,AMERICAN CONSTITUTIONAL LAW:
INTRODUCTORY ESSAYS AND SELECTED CASES (3RD ED.).
LAW LEGIS TAX ADJUD GOV/REL FEDERAL ORD/FREE PWR
...TIME/SEQ BIBLIOG T 19/20 SUPREME/CT. PAGE 69
E1379
CONSTN
CT/SYS
JURID

B64
MINAR D.W.,IDEAS AND POLITICS: THE AMERICAN
EXPERIENCE. SECT CHIEF LEGIS CREATE ADJUD EXEC REV
PWR...PHIL/SCI CONCPT IDEA/COMP 18/20 HAMILTON/A
JEFFERSN/T DECLAR/IND JACKSON/A PRESIDENT. PAGE 73
E1464
CONSTN
NAT/G
FEDERAL

B64
MITCHELL B.,A BIOGRAPHY OF THE CONSTITUTION OF THE
UNITED STATES. USA+45 USA-45 PROVS CHIEF LEGIS
DEBATE ADJUD SUFF FEDERAL...SOC 18/20 SUPREME/CT
CONGRESS SENATE HOUSE/REP PRESIDENT. PAGE 73 E1472
CONSTN
LAW
JURID

B64
PRESS C.,A BIBLIOGRAPHIC INTRODUCTION TO AMERICAN
STATE GOVERNMENT AND POLITICS (PAMPHLET). USA+45
USA-45 EX/STRUC ADJUD INGP/REL FEDERAL ORD/FREE 20.
PAGE 82 E1649
BIBLIOG
LEGIS
LOC/G
POL/PAR

S64
BARKUN M.,"CONFLICT RESOLUTION THROUGH IMPLICIT
MEDIATION." UNIV BARGAIN CONSEN FEDERAL JURID.
PAGE 8 E0149
CONSULT
CENTRAL
INT/LAW
IDEA/COMP

C64
CORWIN E.S.,"AMERICAN CONSTITUTIONAL HISTORY." LAW
NAT/G PROB/SOLV EQUILIB FEDERAL ATTIT PWR...JURID
BIBLIOG 20. PAGE 26 E0515
ANTHOL
JUDGE
ADJUD
CT/SYS

B65
BREITEL C.D.,THE LAWMAKERS. USA+45 EX/STRUC LEGIS
JUDGE ATTIT ORD/FREE JURID. PAGE 15 E0290
CT/SYS
ADJUD
FEDERAL
NAT/G

B65
CONGRESSIONAL QUARTERLY SERV,FEDERAL ROLE IN
EDUCATION (PAMPHLET). LAW SCHOOL PLAN TAX ADJUD
...CHARTS SOC/INTEG 20 PRESIDENT. PAGE 25 E0487
ACADEM
DISCRIM
RECEIVE
FEDERAL

B65
COOPER F.E.,STATE ADMINISTRATIVE LAW (2 VOLS.). LAW
LEGIS PLAN TAX ADJUD CT/SYS FEDERAL PWR...CONCPT
20. PAGE 25 E0501
JURID
CONSTN
ADMIN
PROVS

B65
KEEFE W.J.,THE AMERICAN LEGISLATIVE PROCESS. USA+45
CONSTN POL/PAR CT/SYS REPRESENT FEDERAL ATTIT
PLURISM...MAJORIT 20 CONGRESS PRESIDENT. PAGE 60
E1192
LEGIS
NAT/G
CHIEF
GOV/REL

B65
MCKAY R.B.,REAPPORTIONMENT: THE LAW AND POLITICS OF
EQUAL REPRESENTATION. FUT USA+45 PROVS BAL/PWR
ADJUD CHOOSE REPRESENT GOV/REL FEDERAL...JURID
BIBLIOG 20 SUPREME/CT CONGRESS. PAGE 71 E1420
APPORT
MAJORIT
LEGIS
PWR

B65
PYLEE M.V.,CONSTITUTIONAL GOVERNMENT IN INDIA (2ND
REV. ED.). INDIA POL/PAR EX/STRUC DIPLOM COLONIAL
CT/SYS PARL/PROC PRIVIL...JURID 16/20. PAGE 83
E1665
CONSTN
NAT/G
PROVS
FEDERAL

B65
SHARMA S.A.,PARLIAMENTARY GOVERNMENT IN INDIA.
INDIA FINAN LOC/G PROVS DELIB/GP PLAN ADMIN CT/SYS
FEDERAL...JURID 20. PAGE 90 E1814
NAT/G
CONSTN
PARL/PROC
LEGIS

C65
SCHEINGOLD S.A.,"THE RULE OF LAW IN EUROPEAN
INTEGRATION: THE PATH OF THE SCHUMAN PLAN." EUR+WWI
JUDGE ADJUD FEDERAL ATTIT PWR...RECORD INT BIBLIOG
EEC ECSC. PAGE 87 E1755
INT/LAW
CT/SYS
REGION
CENTRAL

B66
BAXTER M.G.,DANIEL WEBSTER & THE SUPREME COURT. LAW
NAT/G PROF/ORG DEBATE ADJUD LEAD FEDERAL PERSON.
PAGE 8 E0156
CONSTN
CT/SYS
JURID

B66
DE TOCQUEVILLE A,DEMOCRACY IN AMERICA (1834-1840)
(2 VOLS. IN I; TRANS. BY G. LAWRENCE). FRANCE
CULTURE STRATA POL/PAR CT/SYS REPRESENT FEDERAL
ORD/FREE SOVEREIGN...MAJORIT TREND GEN/LAWS 18/19.
PAGE 30 E0596
POPULISM
USA-45
CONSTN
NAT/COMP

B66
GHOSH P.K.,THE CONSTITUTION OF INDIA: HOW IT HAS
BEEN FRAMED. INDIA LOC/G DELIB/GP EX/STRUC
PROB/SOLV BUDGET INT/TRADE CT/SYS CHOOSE...LING 20.
PAGE 43 E0854
CONSTN
NAT/G
LEGIS
FEDERAL

B66
HAY P.,FEDERALISM AND SUPRANATIONAL ORGANIZATIONS:
PATTERNS FOR NEW LEGAL STRUCTURES. EUR+WWI LAW
NAT/G VOL/ASSN DIPLOM PWR...NAT/COMP TREATY EEC.
PAGE 51 E1014
SOVEREIGN
FEDERAL
INT/ORG
INT/LAW

B66
MENDELSON W.,JUSTICES BLACK AND FRANKFURTER:
CONFLICT IN THE COURT (2ND ED.). NAT/G PROVS
PROB/SOLV BAL/PWR CONTROL FEDERAL ISOLAT ANOMIE
ORD/FREE...DECISION 20 SUPREME/CT BLACK/HL
FRANKFUR/F. PAGE 72 E1439
JURID
ADJUD
IDEA/COMP
ROLE

B66
TRESOLINI R.J.,CASES IN AMERICAN NATIONAL
GOVERNMENT AND POLITICS. LAW DIPLOM ADJUD LOBBY
FEDERAL ORD/FREE WEALTH...DECISION ANTHOL 20
PRESIDENT. PAGE 97 E1940
NAT/G
LEGIS
CT/SYS
POL/PAR

N66
BACHELDER G.L.,THE LITERATURE OF FEDERALISM: A
SELECTED BIBLIOGRAPHY (REV ED) (A PAMPHLET). USA+45
USA-45 WOR+45 WOR-45 LAW CONSTN PROVS ADMIN CT/SYS
GOV/REL ROLE...CONCPT 19/20. PAGE 7 E0126
BIBLIOG
FEDERAL
NAT/G
LOC/G

B67
COX A.,CIVIL RIGHTS, THE CONSTITUTION, AND THE
COURTS. CONSTN EDU/PROP CRIME DISCRIM ATTIT...JURID
20. PAGE 27 E0533
LAW
FEDERAL
RACE/REL
PRESS

B67
FESLER J.W.,THE FIFTY STATES AND THEIR LOCAL
GOVERNMENTS. FUT USA+45 POL/PAR LEGIS PROB/SOLV
ADMIN CT/SYS CHOOSE GOV/REL FEDERAL...POLICY CHARTS
20 SUPREME/CT. PAGE 37 E0743
PROVS
LOC/G

B67
JONES C.O.,EVERY SECOND YEAR: CONGRESSIONAL
BEHAVIOR AND THE TWO-YEAR TERM. LAW POL/PAR
PROB/SOLV DEBATE CHOOSE PERS/REL COST FEDERAL PWR
...CHARTS 20 CONGRESS SENATE HOUSE/REP. PAGE 59
EFFICIENCY
LEGIS
TIME/SEQ
NAT/G

E1172

                                                                                                                          B89
                                                                    FICHTE J.G.,THE SCIENCE OF RIGHTS (TRANS. BY A.E.   ORD/FREE
                                                        S67   KROEGER). WOR-45 FAM MUNIC NAT/G PROVS ADJUD CRIME   CONSTN
ANDERSON W.,"THE PERILS OF 'SHARING'." USA+45   BUDGET   CHOOSE MARRIAGE SEX POPULISM 19 FICHTE/JG   LAW
ECO/TAC RECEIVE LOBBY GOV/REL CENTRAL COST INCOME   TAX   NATURL/LAW. PAGE 37 E0744   CONCPT
...POLICY PLURIST CONGRESS. PAGE 5 E0095   FEDERAL
                                                      LAW   FICTIONS....SEE MYTH

                                                        S67   FIELD G.C. E0745
BRADLEY A.W.,"CONSTITUTION-MAKING IN UGANDA."   NAT/G
UGANDA LAW CHIEF DELIB/GP LEGIS ADMIN EXEC   CREATE   FIELD G.L. E0746,E0747
PARL/PROC RACE/REL ORD/FREE...GOV/COMP 20. PAGE 15   CONSTN
E0284   FEDERAL   FIELD/SJ....STEPHEN J. FIELD

                                                        S67   B60
MAYANJA A.,"THE GOVERNMENT'S PROPOSALS ON THE NEW   CONSTN   MENDELSON W.,CAPITALISM, DEMOCRACY, AND THE SUPREME JUDGE
CONSTITUTION." AFR UGANDA LAW CHIEF LEGIS ADJUD   CONFER   COURT. USA+45 USA-45 CONSTN DIPLOM GOV/REL ATTIT   CT/SYS
REPRESENT FEDERAL PWR 20. PAGE 69 E1390   ORD/FREE   ORD/FREE LAISSEZ...POLICY CHARTS PERS/COMP 18/20   JURID
                                                      NAT/G   SUPREME/CT MARSHALL/J HOLMES/OW TANEY/RB FIELD/JJ.   NAT/G
                                                                    PAGE 72 E1437
                                                        S68
BURGESS J.W.,"VON HOLST'S PUBLIC LAW OF THE UNITED   CONSTN
STATES" USA-45 LAW GOV/REL...GOV/COMP IDEA/COMP 19.   FEDERAL   FIGGIS J.N. E0748
PAGE 17 E0339   NAT/G
                                                      JURID   FILLMORE/M....PRESIDENT MILLARD FILLMORE

FEDERALIST....FEDERALIST PARTY (ALL NATIONS)   FILM....FILM AND CINEMA

                                                        B39   B63
BALDWIN L.D.,WHISKEY REBELS; THE STORY OF A   REV   STREET H.,FREEDOM: THE INDIVIDUAL AND THE LAW. UK   ORD/FREE
FRONTIER UPRISING. USA-45 LAW ADJUD LEAD COERCE PWR   POL/PAR   COM/IND EDU/PROP PRESS RUMOR TV PWR 20 CIVIL/LIB   NAT/G
...BIBLIOG/A 18 PENNSYLVAN FEDERALIST. PAGE 8 E0145   TAX   FILM. PAGE 94 E1886   JURID
                                                      TIME/SEQ   PARL/PROC

FEDSCI/TEC....FEDERAL COUNCIL FOR SCIENCE AND TECHNOLOGY   B66
                                                                    CARMEN I.H.,MOVIES, CENSORSHIP, AND THE LAW. LOC/G   EDU/PROP
FEEDBACK....FEEDBACK PHENOMENA   NAT/G ATTIT ORD/FREE...DECISION INT IDEA/COMP   LAW
                                                        B65   BIBLIOG 20 SUPREME/CT FILM. PAGE 19 E0383   ART/METH
SCHUBERT G.,THE POLITICAL ROLE OF THE COURTS IN   CT/SYS   CONSTN
JUDICIAL POLICY MAKING. USA+45 CONSTN JUDGE   POLICY
FEEDBACK RACE/REL ORD/FREE...TRADIT PSY   DECISION   FINAN....FINANCIAL SERVICE, BANKS, INSURANCE SYSTEMS,
BIBLIOG/A 20 KENNEDY/JF SUPREME/CT. PAGE 89 E1776   SECURITIES, EXCHANGES

FEERICK J.D. E0724   N
                                                                    LONDON INSTITUTE WORLD AFFAIRS,THE YEAR BOOK OF   DIPLOM
FEIFER G. E0725   WORLD AFFAIRS. FINAN BAL/PWR ARMS/CONT WAR   FOR/AID
                                                                    ...INT/LAW BIBLIOG 20. PAGE 66 E1322   INT/ORG
FEILCHENFELD E.H. E0726
                                                                                                                          N
FEINE H.E. E0727,E0728   CANADIAN GOVERNMENT PUBLICATIONS (1955-). CANADA   BIBLIOG/A
                                                                    AGRI FINAN LABOR FORCES INT/TRADE HEALTH...JURID 20 NAT/G
FEIS H. E0729   PARLIAMENT. PAGE 1 E0005   DIPLOM
                                                                                                                       INT/ORG
FELD B. E1894
                                                                                                                          N
FELICIANO F.P. E1406   INTERNATIONAL BOOK NEWS, 1928-1934. ECO/UNDEV FINAN BIBLIOG/A
                                                                    INDUS LABOR INT/TRADE CONFER ADJUD COLONIAL...HEAL DIPLOM
FELLMAN D. E0730,E0731,E0732,E0733   SOC/WK CHARTS 20 LEAGUE/NAT. PAGE 1 E0008   INT/LAW
                                                                                                                       INT/ORG
FELLMAN D. E0734
                                                                                                                          N
FELSHER H. E0735   FOREIGN AFFAIRS. SPACE WOR+45 WOR-45 CULTURE   BIBLIOG
                                                                    ECO/UNDEV FINAN NAT/G TEC/DEV INT/TRADE ARMS/CONT   DIPLOM
FEMALE/SEX....FEMALE SEX   NUC/PWR...POLICY 20 UN EURATOM ECSC EEC. PAGE 1   INT/ORG
                                                        B18   E0021   INT/LAW
PORTER K.H.,A HISTORY OF SUFFRAGE IN THE UNITED   SUFF
STATES. USA-45 LAW CONSTN LOC/G NAT/G POL/PAR WAR   REPRESENT   N
DISCRIM OWN ATTIT SEX 18/20 NEGRO FEMALE/SEX.   CHOOSE   CATHERINE R.,LA REVUE ADMINISTRATIVE. FRANCE LAW   ADMIN
PAGE 81 E1629   PARTIC   NAT/G LEGIS...JURID BIBLIOG/A 20. PAGE 21 E0407   MGT
                                                                                                                       FINAN
FENN DH J.R. E0736   METH/COMP

FENWICK C.G. E0737,E0738   N
                                                                    UNITED NATIONS,UNITED NATIONS PUBLICATIONS. WOR+45 BIBLIOG
FEPC....FAIR EMPLOYMENT PRACTICES COMMISSION   ECO/UNDEV AGRI FINAN FORCES ADMIN LEAD WAR PEACE   INT/ORG
                                                                    ...POLICY INT/LAW 20 UN. PAGE 98 E1965   DIPLOM
FERNEUIL T. E0739
                                                                                                                          N
FERRELL J.S. E0740   US SUPERINTENDENT OF DOCUMENTS,EDUCATION (PRICE   BIBLIOG/A
                                                                    LIST 31). USA+45 LAW FINAN LOC/G NAT/G DEBATE ADMIN EDU/PROP
FERRELL R.H. E0741   LEAD RACE/REL FEDERAL HEALTH POLICY. PAGE 103 E2062 ACADEM
                                                                                                                       SCHOOL
FERRY W.H. E0742

FESLER J.W. E0743   B03
                                                                    FORTESCUE G.K.,SUBJECT INDEX OF THE MODERN WORKS   BIBLIOG
FEUDALISM....FEUDALISM   ADDED TO THE LIBRARY OF THE BRITISH MUSEUM IN THE   INDEX
                                                                    YEARS 1881-1900 (3 VOLS.). UK LAW CONSTN LOC/G   WRITING
FHA....U.S. FEDERAL HOUSING ADMINISTRATION   NAT/G FORCES INT/TRADE COLONIAL 19. PAGE 39 E0775

FICHTE J.G. E0744   B03
                                                                    GRIFFIN A.P.C.,LISTS PUBLISHED 1902-03: LABOR   BIBLIOG/A
FICHTE/JG....JOHANN GOTTLIEB FICHTE   PARTICULARLY RELATING TO STRIKES (PAMPHLET). UK   LABOR
                                                                    USA-45 FINAN WORKER PLAN BARGAIN CRIME GOV/REL   GP/REL
                                                                    ...POLICY 19/20 PARLIAMENT. PAGE 46 E0923   ECO/TAC

GRIFFIN A.P.C.,LIST OF MORE RECENT WORKS ON FEDERAL
CONTROL OF COMMERCE AND CORPORATIONS (PAMPHLET).
USA-45 LAW ECO/DEV FINAN LG/CO TARIFFS TAX LICENSE
CENTRAL ORD/FREE WEALTH LAISSEZ 19/20. PAGE 47
E0931
B07
BIBLIOG/A
NAT/G
JURID
ECO/TAC

GRIFFIN A.P.C.,LIST OF WORKS RELATING TO GOVERNMENT
REGULATION OF INSURANCE UNITED STATES AND FOREIGN
COUNTRIES (2ND. ED.) (PAMPHLET). FRANCE GERMANY UK
USA-45 WOR-45 LG/CO LOC/G NAT/G LEGIS LICENSE ADJUD
LOBBY CENTRAL ORD/FREE 19/20. PAGE 47 E0933
B08
BIBLIOG/A
FINAN
LAW
CONTROL

POLLOCK F.,THE GENIUS OF THE COMMON LAW. CHRIST-17C
UK FINAN CHIEF ACT/RES ADMIN GP/REL ATTIT SOCISM
...ANARCH JURID. PAGE 81 E1624
B12
LAW
CULTURE
CREATE

SAWYER R.A.,A LIST OF WORKS ON COUNTY GOVERNMENT.
LAW FINAN MUNIC TOP/EX ROUTINE CRIME...CLASSIF
RECORD 19/20. PAGE 87 E1748
B15
BIBLIOG/A
LOC/G
GOV/REL
ADMIN

MCCONNELL G.,THE STEEL SEIZURE OF 1952 (PAMPHLET).
USA+45 FINAN INDUS PROC/MFG LG/CO EX/STRUC ADJUD
CONTROL GP/REL ORD/FREE PWR 20 TRUMAN/HS PRESIDENT
CONGRESS. PAGE 70 E1402
N19
DELIB/GP
LABOR
PROB/SOLV
NAT/G

DE MONTESQUIEU C.,THE SPIRIT OF LAWS (2 VOLS.)
(TRANS. BY THOMAS NUGENT). FRANCE FINAN SECT
INT/TRADE TAX COERCE REV DISCRIM HABITAT ORD/FREE
19 ALEMBERT/J CIVIL/LAW. PAGE 30 E0588
B23
JURID
LAW
CONCPT
GEN/LAWS

FORTESCUE J.,THE GOVERNANCE OF ENGLAND (1471-76).
UK LAW FINAN SECT LEGIS PROB/SOLV TAX DOMIN ADMIN
GP/REL COST ORD/FREE PWR 14/15. PAGE 39 E0776
B26
CONSERVE
CONSTN
CHIEF
NAT/G

LEITZ F.,DIE PUBLIZITAT DER AKTIENGESELLSCHAFT.
BELGIUM FRANCE GERMANY UK FINAN PRESS GP/REL PROFIT
KNOWL 20. PAGE 64 E1282
B29
LG/CO
JURID
ECO/TAC
NAT/COMP

BUCK A.E.,"PUBLIC BUDGETING." USA-45 FINAN LOC/G
NAT/G LEGIS BAL/PAY COST...JURID TREND BIBLIOG/A
20. PAGE 17 E0324
C29
BUDGET
ROUTINE
ADMIN

BORCHARD E.H.,GUIDE TO THE LAW AND LEGAL LITERATURE
OF FRANCE. FRANCE FINAN INDUS LABOR SECT LEGIS
ADMIN COLONIAL CRIME OWN...INT/LAW 20. PAGE 14
E0266
B31
BIBLIOG/A
LAW
CONSTN
METH

AMERICAN FOREIGN LAW ASSN.,BIOGRAPHICAL NOTES ON THE
LAWS AND LEGAL LITERATURE OF URUGUAY AND CURACAO.
URUGUAY CONSTN FINAN SECT FORCES JUDGE DIPLOM
INT/TRADE ADJUD CT/SYS CRIME 20. PAGE 4 E0078
B33
BIBLIOG/A
LAW
JURID
ADMIN

BURCHFIELD L.,STUDENT'S GUIDE TO MATERIALS IN
POLITICAL SCIENCE. FINAN INT/ORG NAT/G POL/PAR
DIPLOM PRESS ADMIN...BIOG 18/19. PAGE 17 E0328
B35
BIBLIOG
INDEX
LAW

GRAVES W.B.,AMERICAN STATE GOVERNMENT. CONSTN FINAN
EX/STRUC FORCES LEGIS BUDGET TAX CT/SYS REPRESENT
GOV/REL...BIBLIOG/A 19/20. PAGE 45 E0900
B36
NAT/G
PROVS
ADMIN
FEDERAL

HUDSON M.O.,INTERNATIONAL LEGISLATION: 1929-1931.
WOR+45 SEA AIR AGRI FINAN LABOR DIPLOM ECO/TAC
REPAR CT/SYS ARMS/CONT WAR WEAPON...JURID 20 TREATY
LEAGUE/NAT. PAGE 56 E1112
B36
INT/LAW
PARL/PROC
ADJUD
LAW

HAMILTON W.H.,THE POWER TO GOVERN. ECO/DEV FINAN
INDUS ECO/TAC INT/TRADE TARIFFS TAX CONTROL CT/SYS
WAR COST PWR 18/20 SUPREME/CT. PAGE 50 E0991
B37
LING
CONSTN
NAT/G
POLICY

GILL N.N.,"PERMANENT ADVISORY COMMISSIONS IN THE
FEDERAL GOVERNMENT." CLIENT FINAN OP/RES EDU/PROP
PARTIC ROUTINE INGP/REL KNOWL SKILL...CLASSIF
TREND. PAGE 43 E0860
S40
DELIB/GP
NAT/G
DECISION

FULLER G.H.,DEFENSE FINANCING: A SUPPLEMENTARY LIST
OF REFERENCES (PAMPHLET). CANADA UK USA-45 ECO/DEV
NAT/G DELIB/GP BUDGET ADJUD ARMS/CONT WEAPON COST
PEACE PWR 20 AUSTRAL CHINJAP CONGRESS. PAGE 41
E0821
B42
BIBLIOG/A
FINAN
FORCES
DIPLOM

BACKUS R.C.,A GUIDE TO THE LAW AND LEGAL LITERATURE
OF COLOMBIA. FINAN INDUS LABOR FORCES ADJUD ADMIN
COLONIAL CT/SYS CRIME...INT/LAW JURID 20 COLOMB.
PAGE 7 E0127
B43
BIBLIOG/A
LAW
CONSTN
L/A+17C

FULLER G.H.,RENEGOTIATION OF WAR CONTRACTS: A
SELECTED LIST OF REFERENCES (PAMPHLET). USA-45
ECO/DEV LG/CO NAT/G OP/RES PLAN BAL/PWR LEGIT
CONTROL...MGT 20. PAGE 42 E0823
B44
BIBLIOG
WAR
LAW
FINAN

GRIFFITH E.S.,"THE CHANGING PATTERN OF PUBLIC
POLICY FORMATION." MOD/EUR WOR+45 FINAN CHIEF
CONFER ADMIN LEAD CONSERVE SOCISM TECHRACY...SOC
CHARTS CONGRESS. PAGE 47 E0938
S44
LAW
POLICY
TEC/DEV

VANCE H.L.,GUIDE TO THE LAW AND LEGAL LITERATURE OF
MEXICO. LAW CONSTN FINAN LABOR FORCES ADJUD ADMIN
...CRIMLGY PHIL/SCI CON/ANAL 20 MEXIC/AMER.
PAGE 103 E2070
B45
BIBLIOG/A
INT/LAW
JURID
CT/SYS

CLAGETT H.L.,A GUIDE TO THE LAW AND LEGAL
LITERATURE OF URUGUAY. URUGUAY CONSTN COM/IND FINAN
LABOR MUNIC JUDGE PRESS ADMIN CT/SYS...INT/LAW
PHIL/SCI 20. PAGE 23 E0445
B47
BIBLIOG
LAW
JURID
L/A+17C

DE NOIA J.,GUIDE TO OFFICIAL PUBLICATIONS OF OTHER
AMERICAN REPUBLICS: ECUADOR (VOL. IX). ECUADOR LAW
FINAN LEGIS BUDGET CT/SYS 19/20. PAGE 30 E0589
B47
BIBLIOG/A
CONSTN
NAT/G
EDU/PROP

ENKE S.,INTERNATIONAL ECONOMICS. UK USA+45 USSR
INT/ORG BAL/PWR BARGAIN CAP/ISM BAL/PAY...NAT/COMP
20 TREATY. PAGE 35 E0691
B47
INT/TRADE
FINAN
TARIFFS
ECO/TAC

GORDON D.L.,THE HIDDEN WEAPON: THE STORY OF
ECONOMIC WARFARE. EUR+WWI USA-45 LAW FINAN INDUS
NAT/G CONSULT FORCES PLAN DOMIN PWR WEALTH
...INT/LAW CONCPT OBS TOT/POP NAZI 20. PAGE 45
E0891
B47
INT/ORG
ECO/TAC
INT/TRADE
WAR

NEUBURGER O.,GUIDE TO OFFICIAL PUBLICATIONS OF THE
OTHER AMERICAN REPUBLICS: HAITI (VOL. XII). HAITI
LAW FINAN LEGIS PRESS...JURID 20. PAGE 76 E1534
B47
BIBLIOG/A
CONSTN
NAT/G
EDU/PROP

TOWLE L.W.,INTERNATIONAL TRADE AND COMMERCIAL
POLICY. WOR+45 LAW ECO/DEV FINAN INDUS NAT/G
ECO/TAC WEALTH...TIME/SEQ ILO 20. PAGE 97 E1937
B47
MARKET
INT/ORG
INT/TRADE

NEUBURGER O.,GUIDE TO OFFICIAL PUBLICATIONS OF THE
OTHER AMERICAN REPUBLICS: VENEZUELA (VOL. XIX).
VENEZUELA FINAN LEGIS PLAN BUDGET DIPLOM CT/SYS
PARL/PROC 19/20. PAGE 77 E1535
B48
BIBLIOG/A
NAT/G
CONSTN
LAW

BLODGETT R.H.,"COMPARATIVE ECONOMIC SYSTEMS (REV.
ED.)" WOR-45 AGRI FINAN MARKET LABOR NAT/G PLAN
INT/TRADE PRICE...POLICY DECISION BIBLIOG 20.
PAGE 13 E0248
C49
METH/COMP
CONCPT
ROUTINE

GRAVES W.B.,PUBLIC ADMINISTRATION: A COMPREHENSIVE
BIBLIOGRAPHY ON PUBLIC ADMINISTRATION IN THE UNITED
STATES (PAMPHLET). USA+45 USA-45 LOC/G NAT/G LEGIS
ADJUD INGP/REL...MGT 20. PAGE 45 E0901
B50
BIBLIOG
FINAN
CONTROL
ADMIN

MERRIAM C.E.,THE AMERICAN PARTY SYSTEM; AN
INTRODUCTION TO THE STUDY OF POLITICAL PARTIES IN
THE UNITED STATES (4TH ED.). USA+45 USA-45 LAW
FINAN LOC/G NAT/G PROVS LEAD PARTIC CRIME ATTIT
18/20 NEGRO CONGRESS PRESIDENT. PAGE 72 E1442
B50
POL/PAR
CHOOSE
SUFF
REPRESENT

COOKE C.A.,CORPORATION TRUST AND COMPANY: AN ESSAY
IN LEGAL HISTORY. UK STRUCT LEGIS CAP/ISM GP/REL
PROFIT 13/20 COMPNY/ACT. PAGE 25 E0499
B51
LG/CO
FINAN
ECO/TAC

JURID

B51

INSTITUTE DES RELATIONS INTL,LES ASPECTS
ECONOMIQUES DU REARMEMENT (ETUDE DE L'INSTITUT DES
RELATIONS INTERNATIONALES A BRUXELLES). BELGIUM UK
USA+45 EXTR/IND FINAN FORCES WORKER PROB/SOLV
DIPLOM PRICE...POLICY 20 TREATY. PAGE 57 E1127
WEAPON
DEMAND
ECO/TAC
INT/TRADE

B52

ANDREWS F.E.,CORPORATION GIVING. LAW TAX EDU/PROP
ADMIN...POLICY STAT CHARTS. PAGE 5 E0096
LG/CO
GIVE
SML/CO
FINAN

B53

STOUT H.M.,BRITISH GOVERNMENT. UK FINAN LOC/G
POL/PAR DELIB/GP DIPLOM ADMIN COLONIAL CHOOSE
ORD/FREE...JURID BIBLIOG 20 COMMONWLTH. PAGE 94
E1883
NAT/G
PARL/PROC
CONSTN
NEW/LIB

B54

BINANI G.D.,INDIA AT A GLANCE (REV. ED.). INDIA
COM/IND FINAN INDUS LABOR PROVS SCHOOL PLAN DIPLOM
INT/TRADE ADMIN...JURID 20. PAGE 12 E0229
INDEX
CON/ANAL
NAT/G
ECO/UNDEV

B54

CARTER P.G.,STATISTICAL BULLETINS: AN ANNOTATED
BIBLIOGRAPHY OF THE GENERAL STATISTICAL BULLETINS
AND MAJOR POL SUBDIV OF WORLD. CULTURE AGRI FINAN
INDUS LABOR TEC/DEV INT/TRADE CT/SYS WEALTH
...CRIMLGY SOC 20. PAGE 20 E0400
BIBLIOG/A
WOR+45
NAT/G
STAT

C54

BOWIE R.R.,"STUDIES IN FEDERALISM." AGRI FINAN
LABOR EX/STRUC FORCES LEGIS DIPLOM INT/TRADE ADJUD
...BIBLIOG 20 EEC. PAGE 14 E0279
FEDERAL
EUR+WWI
INT/ORG
CONSTN

B55

CRAIG J.,BIBLIOGRAPHY OF PUBLIC ADMINISTRATION IN
AUSTRALIA. CONSTN FINAN EX/STRUC LEGIS PLAN DIPLOM
RECEIVE ADJUD ROUTINE...HEAL 19/20 AUSTRAL
PARLIAMENT. PAGE 27 E0540
BIBLIOG
GOV/REL
ADMIN
NAT/G

B55

SERRANO MOSCOSO E.,A STATEMENT OF THE LAWS OF
ECUADOR IN MATTERS AFFECTING BUSINESS (2ND ED.).
ECUADOR INDUS LABOR LG/CO NAT/G LEGIS TAX CONTROL
MARRIAGE 20. PAGE 90 E1805
FINAN
ECO/UNDEV
LAW
CONSTN

B57

JENNINGS I.,PARLIAMENT. UK FINAN INDUS POL/PAR
DELIB/GP EX/STRUC PLAN CONTROL...MAJORIT JURID
PARLIAMENT. PAGE 58 E1163
PARL/PROC
TOP/EX
MGT
LEGIS

B57

SCHLOCHAUER H.J.,OFFENTLICHES RECHT. GERMANY/W
FINAN EX/STRUC LEGIS DIPLOM FEDERAL ORD/FREE
...INT/LAW 20. PAGE 88 E1757
CONSTN
JURID
ADMIN
CT/SYS

B58

BUGEDA LANZAS J.,A STATEMENT OF THE LAWS OF CUBA IN
MATTERS AFFECTING BUSINESS (2ND ED. REV.,
ENLARGED). CUBA L/A+17C LAW FINAN FAM LEGIS ACT/RES
ADMIN GP/REL...BIBLIOG 20 OAS. PAGE 17 E0327
JURID
NAT/G
INDUS
WORKER

B58

HOOD W.C.,FINANCING OF ECONOMIC ACTIVITY IN CANADA.
CANADA FUT VOL/ASSN WORKER ECO/TAC ADJUD ADMIN
...CHARTS 20. PAGE 55 E1093
BUDGET
FINAN
GP/REL
ECO/DEV

B59

EPSTEIN F.T.,EAST GERMANY: A SELECTED BIBLIOGRAPHY
(PAMPHLET). COM GERMANY/E LAW AGRI FINAN INDUS
LABOR POL/PAR EDU/PROP ADMIN AGE/Y 20. PAGE 35
E0693
BIBLIOG/A
INTELL
MARXISM
NAT/G

B59

GOMEZ ROBLES J.,A STATEMENT OF THE LAWS OF
GUATEMALA IN MATTERS AFFECTING BUSINESS (2ND ED.
REV., ENLARGED). GUATEMALA L/A+17C LAW FINAN FAM
WORKER ACT/RES DIPLOM ADJUD ADMIN GP/REL 20 OAS.
PAGE 44 E0881
JURID
NAT/G
INDUS
LEGIT

B59

HARVARD UNIVERSITY LAW SCHOOL,INTERNATIONAL
PROBLEMS OF FINANCIAL PROTECTION AGAINST NUCLEAR
RISK. WOR+45 NAT/G DELIB/GP PROB/SOLV DIPLOM
CONTROL ATTIT...POLICY INT/LAW MATH 20. PAGE 51
E1009
NUC/PWR
ADJUD
INDUS
FINAN

B59

MAYDA J.,ATOMIC ENERGY AND LAW. ECO/UNDEV FINAN
TEC/DEV FOR/AID EFFICIENCY PRODUC WEALTH...POLICY
TECHNIC 20. PAGE 70 E1391
NUC/PWR
L/A+17C
LAW
ADMIN

B59

MOOS M.,THE CAMPUS AND THE STATE. LAW FINAN
DELIB/GP LEGIS EXEC LOBBY GP/REL PWR...POLICY
BIBLIOG. PAGE 74 E1489
EDU/PROP
ACADEM
PROVS
CONTROL

N59

NATIONAL ASSN HOME BUILDERS,COMMUNITY FACILITIES: A
LIST OF SELECTED REFERENCES (PAMPHLET). USA+45
DIST/IND FINAN SERV/IND SCHOOL CREATE CONTROL
FEDERAL...JURID 20. PAGE 76 E1525
BIBLIOG/A
PLAN
LOC/G
MUNIC

B60

ADRIAN C.R.,STATE AND LOCAL GOVERNMENTS: A STUDY IN
THE POLITICAL PROCESS. USA+45 LAW FINAN MUNIC
POL/PAR LEGIS ADJUD EXEC CHOOSE REPRESENT. PAGE 3
E0051
LOC/G
PROVS
GOV/REL
ATTIT

B60

ALBI F.,TRATADO DE LOS MODOS DE GESTION DE LAS
CORPORACIONES LOCALES. SPAIN FINAN NAT/G BUDGET
CONTROL EXEC ROUTINE GOV/REL ORD/FREE SOVEREIGN
...MGT 20. PAGE 3 E0057
LOC/G
LAW
ADMIN
MUNIC

B60

ATOMIC INDUSTRIAL FORUM,ATOMS FOR INDUSTRY: WORLD
FORUM. WOR+45 FINAN COST UTIL...JURID ANTHOL 20.
PAGE 6 E0113
NUC/PWR
INDUS
PLAN
PROB/SOLV

B60

CARTER R.F.,COMMUNITIES AND THEIR SCHOOLS. USA+45
LAW FINAN PROVS BUDGET TAX LEAD PARTIC CHOOSE...SOC
INT QU 20. PAGE 20 E0401
SCHOOL
ACT/RES
NEIGH
INGP/REL

B60

MUTHESIUS V.,DAS GESPENST DER WIRTSCHAFTLICHEN
MACHT. GERMANY/W ECO/DEV FINAN MARKET TAX...JURID
20. PAGE 75 E1513
ECO/TAC
NAT/G
CONCPT
LG/CO

B60

PRASAD B.,THE ORIGINS OF PROVINCIAL AUTONOMY. INDIA
UK FINAN LOC/G FORCES LEGIS CONTROL CT/SYS PWR
...JURID 19/20. PAGE 82 E1646
CENTRAL
PROVS
COLONIAL
NAT/G

S60

MACKINNON F.,"THE UNIVERSITY: COMMUNITY OR
UTILITY?" CLIENT CONSTN INTELL FINAN NAT/G NEIGH
EDU/PROP PARTIC REPRESENT ROLE. PAGE 67 E1343
ACADEM
MGT
CONTROL
SERV/IND

S60

NICHOLS J.P.,"HAZARDS OF AMERICAN PRIVATE
INVESTMENT IN UNDERDEVELOPED COUNTRIES." FUT
L/A+17C USA+45 USA-45 EXTR/IND CONSULT BAL/PWR
ECO/TAC DOMIN ADJUD ATTIT SOVEREIGN WEALTH
...HIST/WRIT TIME/SEQ TREND VAL/FREE 20. PAGE 77
E1546
FINAN
ECO/UNDEV
CAP/ISM
NAT/LISM

B61

BEASLEY K.E.,STATE SUPERVISION OF MUNICIPAL DEBT IN
KANSAS - A CASE STUDY. USA+45 USA-45 FINAN PROVS
BUDGET TAX ADJUD ADMIN CONTROL SUPEGO. PAGE 9 E0167
MUNIC
LOC/G
LEGIS
JURID

B61

NEW JERSEY LEGISLATURE-SENATE,PUBLIC HEARINGS
BEFORE COMMITTEE ON REVISION AND AMENDMENT OF LAWS
ON SENATE BILL NO. 8. USA+45 FINAN PROVS WORKER
ACT/RES PLAN BUDGET TAX CRIME...IDEA/COMP 20
NEW/JERSEY URBAN/RNWL. PAGE 77 E1537
LEGIS
MUNIC
INDUS
PROB/SOLV

B61

RUEDA B.,A STATEMENT OF THE LAWS OF COLOMBIA IN
MATTERS AFFECTING BUSINESS (3RD ED.). INDUS FAM
LABOR LG/CO NAT/G LEGIS TAX CONTROL MARRIAGE 20
COLOMB. PAGE 86 E1733
FINAN
ECO/UNDEV
LAW
CONSTN

S61

JACKSON E.,"THE FUTURE DEVELOPMENT OF THE UNITED
NATIONS: SOME SUGGESTIONS FOR RESEARCH." FUT LAW
CONSTN ECO/DEV FINAN PEACE WEALTH...WELF/ST CONCPT
UN 20. PAGE 57 E1140
INT/ORG
PWR

B62

ALEXANDROWICZ C.H.,WORLD ECONOMIC AGENCIES: LAW AND
PRACTICE. WOR+45 DIST/IND FINAN LABOR CONSULT
INT/LAW
INT/ORG

INT/TRADE TARIFFS REPRESENT HEALTH...JURID 20 JN
GATT EEC OAS ECSC. PAGE 3 E0063
`DIPLOM ADJUD`

B62
CARLSTON K.S.,LAW AND ORGANIZATION IN WORLD
SOCIETY. WOR+45 FINAN ECO/TAC DOMIN LEGIT CT/SYS
ROUTINE COERCE ORD/FREE PWR WEALTH...PLURIST
DECISION JURID MGT METH/CNCPT GEN/LAWS 20. PAGE 19
E0381
`INT/ORG LAW`

B62
DE LAVALLE H.,A STATEMENT OF THE LAWS OF PERU IN
MATTERS AFFECTING BUSINESS (3RD ED.). PERU WORKER
INT/TRADE INCOME ORD/FREE...INT/LAW 20. PAGE 30
E0586
`CONSTN JURID FINAN TAX`

B62
DELANY V.T.H.,THE ADMINISTRATION OF JUSTICE IN
IRELAND. IRELAND CONSTN FINAN JUDGE COLONIAL CRIME
...CRIMLGY 19/20. PAGE 30 E0604
`ADMIN JURID CT/SYS ADJUD`

B62
FATOUROS A.A.,GOVERNMENT GUARANTEES TO FOREIGN
INVESTORS. WOR+45 ECO/UNDEV INDUS WORKER ADJUD
...NAT/COMP BIBLIOG TREATY. PAGE 36 E0722
`NAT/G FINAN INT/TRADE ECO/DEV`

B62
MARS D.,SUGGESTED LIBRARY IN PUBLIC ADMINISTRATION.
FINAN DELIB/GP EX/STRUC WORKER COMPUTER ADJUD
...DECISION PSY SOC METH/COMP 20. PAGE 68 E1368
`BIBLIOG ADMIN METH MGT`

B62
SHAW C.,LEGAL PROBLEMS IN INTERNATIONAL TRADE AND
INVESTMENT. WOR+45 ECO/DEV ECO/UNDEV MARKET DIPLOM
TAX INCOME ROLE...ANTHOL BIBLIOG 20 TREATY UN IMF
GATT. PAGE 91 E1816
`INT/LAW INT/TRADE FINAN ECO/TAC`

L62
N.,"UNION INVESTMENT IN BUSINESS: A SOURCE OF UNION
CONFLICT OF INTEREST." LAW NAT/G LEGIS CONTROL
GP/REL INGP/REL DECISION. PAGE 76 E1515
`LABOR POLICY FINAN LG/CO`

S62
GANDOLFI A.,"REFLEXIONS SUR L'IMPOT DE CAPITATION
EN AFRIQUE NOIRE." GHANA SENEGAL LAW FINAN ACT/RES
TEC/DEV ECO/TAC WEALTH...MGT TREND 20. PAGE 42
E0830
`AFR CHOOSE`

B63
ADRIAN C.R.,GOVERNING OVER FIFTY STATES AND THEIR
COMMUNITIES. USA+45 CONSTN FINAN MUNIC NAT/G
POL/PAR EX/STRUC LEGIS ADMIN CONTROL CT/SYS
...CHARTS 20. PAGE 3 E0052
`PROVS LOC/G GOV/REL GOV/COMP`

B63
GOURNAY B.,PUBLIC ADMINISTRATION. FRANCE LAW CONSTN
AGRI FINAN LABOR SCHOOL EX/STRUC CHOOSE...MGT
METH/COMP 20. PAGE 45 E0894
`BIBLIOG/A ADMIN NAT/G LOC/G`

B63
GRANT D.R.,STATE AND LOCAL GOVERNMENT IN AMERICA.
USA+45 FINAN LOC/G MUNIC EX/STRUC FORCES EDU/PROP
ADMIN CHOOSE FEDERAL ATTIT...JURID 20. PAGE 45
E0897
`PROVS POL/PAR LEGIS CONSTN`

B63
HAUSMAN W.H.,MANAGING ECONOMIC DEVELOPMENT IN
AFRICA. AFR USA+45 LAW FINAN WORKER TEC/DEV WEALTH
...ANTHOL 20. PAGE 51 E1012
`ECO/UNDEV PLAN FOR/AID MGT`

B63
KLESMENT J.,LEGAL SOURCES AND BIBLIOGRAPHY OF THE
BALTIC STATES (ESTONIA, LATVIA, LITHUANIA). COM
ESTONIA LATVIA LITHUANIA LAW FINAN ADJUD CT/SYS
REGION CENTRAL MARXISM 19/20. PAGE 61 E1223
`BIBLIOG/A JURID CONSTN ADMIN`

B63
PALOTAI O.C.,PUBLICATIONS OF THE INSTITUTE OF
GOVERNMENT, 1930-1962. LAW PROVS SCHOOL WORKER
ACT/RES OP/RES CT/SYS GOV/REL...CRIMLGY SOC/WK.
PAGE 79 E1594
`BIBLIOG/A ADMIN LOC/G FINAN`

B63
ROYAL INSTITUTE PUBLIC ADMIN,BRITISH PUBLIC
ADMINISTRATION. UK LAW FINAN INDUS LOC/G POL/PAR
LEGIS LOBBY PARL/PROC CHOOSE JURID. PAGE 86 E1729
`BIBLIOG ADMIN MGT NAT/G`

B63
VAN SLYCK P.,PEACE: THE CONTROL OF NATIONAL POWER.
`ARMS/CONT`

CUBA WOR+45 FINAN NAT/G FORCES PROB/SOLV TEC/DEV
BAL/PWR ADMIN CONTROL ORD/FREE...POLICY INT/LAW UN
COLD/WAR TREATY. PAGE 103 E2069
`PEACE INT/ORG DIPLOM`

L63
ROSE R.,"COMPARATIVE STUDIES IN POLITICAL FINANCE:
A SYMPOSIUM." ASIA EUR+WWI S/ASIA LAW CULTURE
DELIB/GP LEGIS ACT/RES ECO/TAC EDU/PROP CHOOSE
ATTIT RIGID/FLEX SUPEGO PWR SKILL WEALTH...STAT
ANTHOL VAL/FREE. PAGE 85 E1714
`FINAN POL/PAR`

S63
WALKER H.,"THE INTERNATIONAL LAW OF COMMODITY
AGREEMENTS." FUT WOR+45 ECO/DEV ECO/UNDEV FINAN
INT/ORG NAT/G CONSULT CREATE PLAN ECO/TAC ATTIT
PERCEPT...CONCPT GEN/LAWS TOT/POP GATT 20. PAGE 105
E2095
`MARKET VOL/ASSN INT/LAW INT/TRADE`

B64
BOGEN J.I.,FINANCIAL HANDBOOK (4TH ED.). UNIV LAW
PLAN TAX RISK 20. PAGE 13 E0257
`FINAN DICTIONARY`

B64
GESELLSCHAFT RECHTSVERGLEICH,BIBLIOGRAPHIE DES
DEUTSCHEN RECHTS (BIBLIOGRAPHY OF GERMAN LAW,
TRANS. BY COURTLAND PETERSON). GERMANY FINAN INDUS
LABOR SECT FORCES CT/SYS PARL/PROC CRIME...INT/LAW
SOC NAT/COMP 20. PAGE 43 E0853
`BIBLIOG/A JURID CONSTN ADMIN`

B64
HEGEL G.W.,HEGEL'S POLITICAL WRITINGS (TRANS. BY
T.M. KNOX). GERMANY UK FINAN FORCES PARL/PROC
CHOOSE REPRESENT...BIOG 19. PAGE 51 E1022
`CONSTN LEGIS JURID`

B64
MITAU G.T.,INSOLUBLE PROBLEMS: CASE PROBLEMS ON THE
FUNCTIONS OF STATE AND LOCAL GOVERNMENT. USA+45 AIR
FINAN LABOR POL/PAR PROB/SOLV TAX RECEIVE CONTROL
GP/REL 20 CASEBOOK ZONING. PAGE 73 E1471
`ADJUD LOC/G PROVS`

B64
RICHARDSON I.L.,BIBLIOGRAFIA BRASILEIRA DE
ADMINISTRACAO PUBLICA E ASSUNTOS CORRELATOS. BRAZIL
CONSTN FINAN LOC/G NAT/G POL/PAR PLAN DIPLOM
RECEIVE ATTIT...METH 20. PAGE 84 E1694
`BIBLIOG MGT ADMIN LAW`

B64
ROBINSON R.D.,INTERNATIONAL BUSINESS POLICY. AFR
INDIA L/A+17C USA+45 ELITES AGRI FOR/AID COERCE
BAL/PAY...DECISION INT/LAW MGT 20. PAGE 85 E1706
`ECO/TAC DIST/IND COLONIAL FINAN`

B64
STOICOIU V.,LEGAL SOURCES AND BIBLIOGRAPHY OF
ROMANIA. COM ROMANIA LAW FINAN POL/PAR LEGIS JUDGE
ADJUD CT/SYS PARL/PROC MARXISM 20. PAGE 93 E1874
`BIBLIOG/A JURID CONSTN ADMIN`

B64
SZLADITS C.,BIBLIOGRAPHY ON FOREIGN AND COMPARATIVE
LAW: BOOKS AND ARTICLES IN ENGLISH (SUPPLEMENT
1962). FINAN INDUS JUDGE LICENSE ADMIN CT/SYS
PARL/PROC OWN...INT/LAW CLASSIF METH/COMP NAT/COMP
20. PAGE 95 E1904
`BIBLIOG/A JURID ADJUD LAW`

B64
TELLADO A.,A STATEMENT OF THE LAWS OF THE DOMINICAN
REPUBLIC IN MATTERS AFFECTING BUSINESS (3RD ED.).
DOMIN/REP AGRI DIST/IND EXTR/IND FINAN FAM WORKER
ECO/TAC TAX CT/SYS MARRIAGE OWN...BIBLIOG 20
MIGRATION. PAGE 95 E1913
`CONSTN LEGIS NAT/G INDUS`

B64
US SENATE COMM ON JUDICIARY,HEARINGS BEFORE
SUBCOMMITTEE ON ANTITRUST AND MONOPOLY: ECONOMIC
CONCENTRATION VOLUMES 1-5 JULY 1964-SEPT 1966.
USA+45 LAW FINAN ECO/TAC ADJUD COST EFFICIENCY
PRODUC...STAT CHARTS 20 CONGRESS MONOPOLY. PAGE 102
E2052
`ECO/DEV CONTROL MARKET LG/CO`

S64
GARDNER R.N.,"THE SOVIET UNION AND THE UNITED
NATIONS." WOR+45 FINAN POL/PAR VOL/ASSN FORCES
ECO/TAC DOMIN EDU/PROP LEGIT ADJUD ADMIN ARMS/CONT
COERCE ATTIT ALL/VALS...POLICY MAJORIT CONCPT OBS
TIME/SEQ TREND STERTYP UN. PAGE 42 E0838
`COM INT/ORG USSR`

B65
COHN H.J.,THE GOVERNMENT OF THE RHINE PALATINATE IN
THE FIFTEENTH CENTURY. GERMANY FINAN LOC/G DELIB/GP
LEGIS CT/SYS CHOOSE CATHISM 14/15 PALATINATE.
PAGE 24 E0468
`PROVS JURID GP/REL ADMIN`

B65
CONGRESSIONAL QUARTERLY SERV,POLITICS IN AMERICA,
1945-1964: THE POLITICS AND ISSUES OF THE POSTWAR
`CHOOSE REPRESENT`

YEARS. USA+45 LAW FINAN CHIEF DIPLOM APPORT SUFF   POL/PAR
...POLICY STAT TREND CHARTS 20 CONGRESS PRESIDENT.   LEGIS
PAGE 25 E0489

                                                              B65
HAEFELE E.T.,GOVERNMENT CONTROLS ON TRANSPORT. AFR   ECO/UNDEV
RHODESIA TANZANIA DIPLOM ECO/TAC TARIFFS PRICE   DIST/IND
ADJUD CONTROL REGION EFFICIENCY...POLICY 20 CONGO.   FINAN
PAGE 49 E0973   NAT/G

                                                              B65
LUGO-MARENCO J.J.,A STATEMENT OF THE LAWS OF   CONSTN
NICARAGUA IN MATTERS AFFECTING BUSINESS. NICARAGUA   NAT/G
AGRI DIST/IND EXTR/IND FINAN INDUS FAM WORKER   LEGIS
INT/TRADE TAX MARRIAGE OWN BIO/SOC 20 TREATY   JURID
RESOURCE/N MIGRATION. PAGE 67 E1332

                                                              B65
NWOGUGU E.I.,THE LEGAL PROBLEMS OF FOREIGN   FOR/AID
INVESTMENT IN DEVELOPING COUNTRIES. WOR+45 INT/ORG   FINAN
DELIB/GP LEGIS PROB/SOLV INT/TRADE TAX ADJUD   INT/LAW
SANCTION...BIBLIOG 20 TREATY. PAGE 78 E1561   ECO/UNDEV

                                                              B65
PROEHL P.O.,FOREIGN ENTERPRISE IN NIGERIA. NIGERIA   ECO/UNDEV
FINAN LABOR NAT/G TAX 20. PAGE 83 E1656   ECO/TAC
                                                        JURID
                                                        CAP/ISM

                                                              B65
SHARMA S.A.,PARLIAMENTARY GOVERNMENT IN INDIA.   NAT/G
INDIA FINAN LOC/G PROVS DELIB/GP PLAN ADMIN CT/SYS   CONSTN
FEDERAL...JURID 20. PAGE 90 E1814   PARL/PROC
                                                        LEGIS

US SENATE COMM ON JUDICIARY,ANTITRUST EXEMPTIONS   BAL/PAY
FOR AGREEMENTS RELATING TO BALANCE OF PAYMENTS.   ADJUD
FINAN ECO/TAC CONTROL WEALTH...POLICY 20 CONGRESS.   MARKET
PAGE 103 E2056   INT/TRADE

                                                              S65
KHOURI F.J.,"THE JORDON RIVER CONTROVERSY." LAW   ISLAM
SOCIETY ECO/UNDEV AGRI FINAN INDUS SECT FORCES   INT/ORG
ACT/RES PLAN TEC/DEV ECO/TAC EDU/PROP COERCE ATTIT   ISRAEL
DRIVE PERCEPT RIGID/FLEX ALL/VALS...GEOG SOC MYTH   JORDAN
WORK. PAGE 61 E1212

                                                              B66
FINK M.,A SELECTIVE BIBLIOGRAPHY ON STATE   BIBLIOG
CONSTITUTIONAL REVISION (PAMPHLET). USA+45 FINAN   PROVS
EX/STRUC LEGIS EDU/PROP ADMIN CT/SYS APPORT CHOOSE   LOC/G
GOV/REL 20. PAGE 38 E0751   CONSTN

                                                              B66
MCNAIR A.D.,THE LEGAL EFFECTS OF WAR. UK FINAN   JURID
DIPLOM ORD/FREE 20 ENGLSH/LAW. PAGE 71 E1425   WAR
                                                        INT/TRADE
                                                        LABOR

                                                              B66
PLATE H.,PARTEIFINANZIERUNG UND GRUNDESETZ. GERMANY   POL/PAR
NAT/G PLAN GIVE PAY INCOME WEALTH...JURID 20.   CONSTN
PAGE 81 E1619   FINAN

                                                              B66
SZLADITS C.,A BIBLIOGRAPHY ON FOREIGN AND   BIBLIOG/A
COMPARATIVE LAW (SUPPLEMENT 1964). FINAN FAM LABOR   CT/SYS
LG/CO LEGIS JUDGE ADMIN CRIME...CRIMLGY 20. PAGE 95   INT/LAW
E1905

                                                              B66
US HOUSE COMM ON JUDICIARY,CIVIL COMMITMENT AND   BIO/SOC
TREATMENT OF NARCOTIC ADDICTS. USA+45 SOCIETY FINAN   CRIME
LEGIS PROB/SOLV GIVE CT/SYS SANCTION HEALTH   IDEA/COMP
...POLICY HEAL 20. PAGE 100 E2008   CONTROL

                                                              B66
US SENATE COMM ON FOREIGN REL,ASIAN DEVELOPMENT   FOR/AID
BANK ACT. USA+45 LAW DIPLOM...CHARTS 20 BLACK/EUG   FINAN
S/EASTASIA. PAGE 101 E2030   ECO/UNDEV
                                                        S/ASIA

                                                              B67
BOLES D.E.,THE TWO SWORDS. USA+45 USA-45 LAW CONSTN   SCHOOL
SOCIETY FINAN PRESS CT/SYS...HEAL JURID BIBLIOG   EDU/PROP
WORSHIP 20 SUPREME/CT CHURCH/STA. PAGE 13 E0263   ADJUD

                                                              B67
INTERNATIONAL CONCILIATION,ISSUES BEFORE THE 22ND   PROB/SOLV
GENERAL ASSEMBLY. WOR+45 ECO/UNDEV FINAN BAL/PWR   INT/ORG
BUDGET INT/TRADE STRANGE ORD/FREE...INT/LAW 20 UN   DIPLOM
COLD/WAR. PAGE 57 E1132   PEACE

                                                              B67
KING W.L.,MELVILLE WESTON FULLER: CHIEF JUSTICE OF   BIOG

THE UNITED STATES, 1888-1910. USA-45 CONSTN FINAN   CT/SYS
LABOR TAX GOV/REL PERS/REL ATTIT PERSON PWR...JURID   LAW
BIBLIOG 19/20 SUPREME/CT FULLER/MW HOLMES/OW.   ADJUD
PAGE 61 E1216

                                                              B67
ROBINSON R.D., INTERNATIONAL MANAGEMENT. USA+45   INT/TRADE
FINAN R+D PLAN PRODUC...DECISION T. PAGE 67 E1336   MGT
                                                        INT/LAW
                                                        MARKET

                                                              B67
UNITED NATIONS,UNITED NATIONS PUBLICATIONS: BIBLIOG/A
1945-1966. WOR+45 COM/IND DIST/IND FINAN TEC/DEV   INT/ORG
ADMIN...POLICY INT/LAW MGT CHARTS 20 UN UNESCO.   DIPLOM
P4GE 98 E1970   WRITING

                                                              B67
US SENATE COMM ON FOREIGN REL,INTER-AMERICAN   LAW
DEVELOPMENT BANK ACT AMENDMENT. L/A+17C USA+45   FINAN
DELIB/GP DIPLOM FOR/AID BAL/PAY...CHARTS SENATE.   INT/ORG
PAGE 102 E2034   ECO/UNDEV

                                                              L67
LAMBERT J.D.,"CORPORATE POLITICAL SPENDING AND   USA+45
CAMPAIGN FINANCE." LAW CONSTN FINAN LABOR LG/CO   POL/PAR
LOC/G NAT/G VOL/ASSN TEC/DEV ADJUD ADMIN PARTIC.   CHOOSE
PAGE 62 E1247   COST

                                                              L67
LENT G.E.,"TAX INCENTIVES FOR INVESTMENT IN   ECO/UNDEV
DEVELOPING COUNTRIES" WOR+45 LAW INDUS PLAN BUDGET   TAX
TARIFFS ADMIN...METH/COMP 20. PAGE 64 E1285   FINAN
                                                        ECO/TAC

                                                              S67
BARTLETT J.L.,"AMERICAN BOND ISSUES IN THE EUROPEAN   LAW
ECONOMIC COMMUNITY." EUR+WWI LUXEMBOURG USA+45   ECO/TAC
DIPLOM CONTROL BAL/PAY EEC. PAGE 8 E0153   FINAN
                                                        TAX

                                                              S67
CREYKE G. JR.,"THE PAYMENT GAP IN FEDERAL   CONSTRUC
CONSTRUCTION CONTRACTS." USA+45 LAW FINAN ECO/TAC   PAY
CONTROL CT/SYS SUPREME/CT. PAGE 28 E0547   COST
                                                        NAT/G

                                                              S67
DOUTY H.M.," REFERENCE TO DEVELOPING COUNTRIES."   TAX
JAMAICA MALAYSIA UK WOR+45 LAW FINAN ACT/RES BUDGET   ECO/UNDEV
CAP/ISM ECO/TAC TARIFFS RISK EFFICIENCY PROFIT   NAT/G
...CHARTS 20. PAGE 33 E0646

                                                              S67
EDGEWORTH A.B. JR.,"CIVIL RIGHTS PLUS THREE YEARS: WORKER
BANKS AND THE ANTI-DISCRIMINATION LAW" USA+45   DISCRIM
SOCIETY DELIB/GP RACE/REL EFFICIENCY 20 NEGRO   FINAN
CIV/RIGHTS. PAGE 34 E0675   LAW

                                                              S67
LAY S.H.,"EXCLUSIVE GOVERNMENTAL LIABILITY FOR   NAT/G
SPACE ACCIDENTS." USA+45 LAW FINAN SERV/IND TEC/DEV   SUPEGO
ADJUD. PAGE 64 E1272   SPACE
                                                        PROB/SOLV

                                                              S67
RICHARDSON J.J.,"THE MAKING OF THE RESTRICTIVE   LEGIS
TRADE PRACTICES ACT 1956 A CASE STUDY OF THE POLICY   ECO/TAC
PROCESS IN BRITAIN." UK FINAN MARKET LG/CO POL/PAR   POLICY
CONSULT PRESS ADJUD ADMIN AGREE LOBBY SANCTION   INDUS
ATTIT 20. PAGE 84 E1695

                                                              B82
POLLOCK F.,ESSAYS IN JURISPRUDENCE AND ETHICS. UNIV   JURID
LAW FINAN MARKET WORKER INGP/REL MORAL...POLICY   CONCPT
GEN/LAWS. PAGE 81 E1625

                                                              B88
BENTHAM J.,DEFENCE OF USURY (1787). UK LAW NAT/G   TAX
TEC/DEV ECO/TAC CONTROL ATTIT...CONCPT IDEA/COMP 18   FINAN
SMITH/ADAM. PAGE 10 E0197   ECO/DEV
                                                        POLICY

                                                              B96
DE VATTEL E.,THE LAW OF NATIONS. AGRI FINAN CHIEF   LAW
DIPLOM INT/TRADE AGREE OWN ALL/VALS MORAL ORD/FREE   CONCPT
SOVEREIGN...GEN/LAWS 18 NATURL/LAW WOLFF/C. PAGE 30   NAT/G
E0597   INT/LAW

FINE R.I. E0750

FINE ARTS....SEE ART/METH

FINK M. E0751

FINKELSTEIN L.S. E0752

FINLAND....SEE ALSO APPROPRIATE TIME/SPACE/CULTURE INDEX

B64
HALLER W.,DER SCHWEDISCHE JUSTITIEOMBUDSMAN.   JURID
DENMARK FINLAND NORWAY SWEDEN LEGIS ADJUD CONTROL   PARL/PROC
PERSON ORD/FREE...NAT/COMP 20 OMBUDSMAN. PAGE 50   ADMIN
E0986   CHIEF

FIRM....SEE INDUS

FISCAL POLICY....SEE NAT/G, BUDGET

FISCHER F.C. E0753

FISCHER H. E0754

FISCHER L. E0755

FISCHER-GALATI S.A. E0756

FISHER F.M. E0757

FISHING INDUSTRY....SEE EXTR/IND

FISK W.M. E0758

FITCH R.E. E0759

FLANDERS....FLANDERS

FLECHTHEIM O.K. E0760,E0761

FLEISCHER B.M. E0762

FLEMING R.W. E0763

FLEMMING D. E0764

FLIESS P.J. E0765

FLINN M.W. E0766

FLORENCE....MEDIEVAL AND RENAISSANCE

FLORES R.H. E0767

FLORIDA....FLORIDA

FLORIN J. E0768

FLYNN/BOSS....BOSS FLYNN

FNMA....FEDERAL NATIONAL MORTGAGE ASSOCIATION

FOCH/F....FERDINAND FOCH

FOLKLORE....SEE MYTH

FONTANE/T....THEODORE FONTANE

FOOD....SEE AGRI

FOOD AND AGRICULTURAL ORGANIZATION....SEE FAO

FOOD AND DRUG ADMINISTRATION....SEE FDA

FOOD/PEACE....OFFICE OF FOOD FOR PEACE

FOR/AID....FOREIGN AID

N
LONDON INSTITUTE WORLD AFFAIRS,THE YEAR BOOK OF   DIPLOM
WORLD AFFAIRS. FINAN BAL/PWR ARMS/CONT WAR   FOR/AID
...INT/LAW BIBLIOG 20. PAGE 66 E1322   INT/ORG

N
INTERNATIONAL AFFAIRS. WOR+45 WOR-45 ECO/UNDEV   BIBLIOG/A
INT/ORG NAT/G PROB/SOLV FOR/AID WAR...POLICY 20.   DIPLOM
PAGE 1 E0007   INT/LAW
                                                             INT/TRADE

N
AFRICAN BIBLIOGRAPHIC CENTER,A CURRENT BIBLIOGRAPHY   BIBLIOG/A
ON AFRICAN AFFAIRS. LAW CULTURE ECO/UNDEV LABOR   AFR
SECT DIPLOM FOR/AID COLONIAL NAT/LISM...LING 20.   NAT/G
PAGE 3 E0053   REGION

N
MINISTRY OF OVERSEAS DEVELOPME,TECHNICAL CO-   BIBLIOG
OPERATION -- A BIBLIOGRAPHY. UK LAW SOCIETY DIPLOM   TEC/DEV
ECO/TAC FOR/AID...STAT 20 CMN/WLTH. PAGE 73 E1466   ECO/DEV
                                                             NAT/G

N47
FOX W.T.R.,UNITED STATES POLICY IN A TWO POWER   DIPLOM
WORLD. COM USA+45 USSR FORCES DOMIN AGREE NEUTRAL   FOR/AID
NUC/PWR ORD/FREE SOVEREIGN 20 COLD/WAR TREATY   POLICY
EUROPE/W INTERVENT. PAGE 39 E0780

B58
HUNT B.I.,BIPARTISANSHIP: A CASE STUDY OF THE   FOR/AID
FOREIGN ASSISTANCE PROGRAM, 1947-56 (DOCTORAL   POL/PAR
THESIS). USA+45 INT/ORG CONSULT LEGIS TEC/DEV   GP/REL
...BIBLIOG PRESIDENT TREATY NATO TRUMAN/HS   DIPLOM
EISNHWR/DD CONGRESS. PAGE 56 E1114

B59
MAYDA J.,ATOMIC ENERGY AND LAW. ECO/UNDEV FINAN   NUC/PWR
TEC/DEV FOR/AID EFFICIENCY PRODUC WEALTH...POLICY   L/A+17C
TECHNIC 20. PAGE 70 E1391   LAW
                                                             ADMIN

B60
UNITED WORLD FEDERALISTS,UNITED WORLD FEDERALISTS;   BIBLIOG/A
PANORAMA OF RECENT BOOKS, FILMS, AND JOURNALS ON   DIPLOM
WORLD FEDERATION, THE UN, AND WORLD PEACE. CULTURE   INT/ORG
ECO/UNDEV PROB/SOLV FOR/AID ARMS/CONT NUC/PWR   PEACE
...INT/LAW PHIL/SCI 20 UN. PAGE 98 E1971

S61
CASTANEDA J.,"THE UNDERDEVELOPED NATIONS AND THE   INT/ORG
DEVELOPMENT OF INTERNATIONAL LAW." FUT UNIV LAW   ECO/UNDEV
ACT/RES FOR/AID LEGIT PERCEPT SKILL...JURID   PEACE
METH/CNCPT TIME/SEQ TOT/POP 20 UN. PAGE 21 E0405   INT/LAW

B63
HAUSMAN W.H.,MANAGING ECONOMIC DEVELOPMENT IN   ECO/UNDEV
AFRICA. AFR USA+45 LAW FINAN WORKER TEC/DEV WEALTH   PLAN
...ANTHOL 20. PAGE 51 E1012   FOR/AID
                                                             MGT

B64
GARDNER R.N.,IN PURSUIT OF WORLD ORDER* US FOREIGN   OBS
POLICY AND INTERNATIONAL ORGANIZATIONS. USA+45 USSR   INT/ORG
ECO/UNDEV FORCES LEGIS DIPLOM FOR/AID INT/TRADE   ALL/VALS
PEACE...INT/LAW PREDICT UN. PAGE 42 E0839

B64
KISER S.L.,AMERICANISM IN ACTION. USA+45 LAW PROVS   OLD/LIB
CAP/ISM DIPLOM RECEIVE CONTROL CT/SYS WAR FEDERAL   FOR/AID
ATTIT WEALTH 20 SUPREME/CT. PAGE 61 E1221   MARXISM
                                                             CONSTN

B64
REGALA R.,WORLD PEACE THROUGH DIPLOMACY AND LAW.   DIPLOM
S/ASIA WOR+45 ECO/UNDEV INT/ORG FORCES PLAN   PEACE
PROB/SOLV FOR/AID NUC/PWR WAR...POLICY INT/LAW 20.   ADJUD
PAGE 84 E1679

B64
ROBERTS HL,FOREIGN AFFAIRS BIBLIOGRAPHY, 1952-1962.   BIBLIOG/A
ECO/DEV SECT PLAN FOR/AID INT/TRADE ARMS/CONT   DIPLOM
NAT/LISM ATTIT...INT/LAW GOV/COMP IDEA/COMP 20.   INT/ORG
PAGE 85 E1703   WAR

B64
ROBINSON R.D.,INTERNATIONAL BUSINESS POLICY. AFR   ECO/TAC
INDIA L/A+17C USA+45 ELITES AGRI FOR/AID COERCE   DIST/IND
BAL/PAY...DECISION INT/LAW MGT 20. PAGE 85 E1706   COLONIAL
                                                           FINAN

S64
DERWINSKI E.J.,"THE COST OF THE INTERNATIONAL   MARKET
COFFEE AGREEMENT." L/A+17C USA+45 WOR+45 ECO/UNDEV   DELIB/GP
NAT/G VOL/ASSN LEGIS DIPLOM ECO/TAC FOR/AID LEGIT   INT/TRADE
ATTIT...TIME/SEQ CONGRESS 20 TREATY. PAGE 31 E0608

B65
NWOGUGU E.I.,THE LEGAL PROBLEMS OF FOREIGN   FOR/AID
INVESTMENT IN DEVELOPING COUNTRIES. WOR+45 INT/ORG   FINAN
DELIB/GP LEGIS PROB/SOLV INT/TRADE TAX ADJUD   INT/LAW
SANCTION...BIBLIOG 20 TREATY. PAGE 78 E1561   ECO/UNDEV

B66
FRIEDMANN W.G.,INTERNATIONAL FINANCIAL AID. USA+45   INT/ORG
ECO/DEV ECO/UNDEV NAT/G VOL/ASSN EX/STRUC PLAN RENT   FOR/AID
GIVE BAL/PAY PWR...GEOG INT/LAW STAT TREND UN EEC   TEC/DEV
COMECON. PAGE 41 E0806   ECO/TAC

B66
SALTER L.M.,RESOLUTION OF INTERNATIONAL CONFLICT.   PROB/SOLV
USA+45 INT/ORG SECT DIPLOM ECO/TAC FOR/AID DETER   PEACE
NUC/PWR WAR 20. PAGE 87 E1743   INT/LAW

POLICY

DIPLOM

B66

US SENATE COMM ON FOREIGN REL,ASIAN DEVELOPMENT BANK ACT. USA+45 LAW DIPLOM...CHARTS 20 BLACK/EUG S/EASTASIA. PAGE 101 E2030
FOR/AID FINAN ECO/UNDEV S/ASIA

B67

GABRIEL P.P.,THE INTERNATIONAL TRANSFER OF CORPORATE SKILLS: MANAGEMENT CONTRACTS IN LESS DEVELOPED COUNTRIES. CLIENT INDUS LG/CO PLAN PROB/SOLV CAP/ISM ECO/TAC FOR/AID INT/TRADE RENT ADMIN SKILL 20. PAGE 42 E0825
ECO/UNDEV AGREE MGT CONSULT

B67

US SENATE COMM ON FOREIGN REL,INTER-AMERICAN DEVELOPMENT BANK ACT AMENDMENT. L/A+17C USA+45 DELIB/GP DIPLOM FOR/AID BAL/PAY...CHARTS SENATE. PAGE 102 E2034
LAW FINAN INT/ORG ECO/UNDEV

B67

US SENATE COMM ON FOREIGN REL,UNITED STATES ARMAMENT AND DISARMAMENT PROBLEMS. USA+45 AIR BAL/PWR DIPLOM FOR/AID NUC/PWR ORD/FREE SENATE TREATY. PAGE 102 E2035
ARMS/CONT WEAPON FORCES PROB/SOLV

B67

US SENATE COMM ON FOREIGN REL,FOREIGN ASSISTANCE ACT OF 1967. VIETNAM WOR+45 DELIB/GP CONFER CONTROL WAR WEAPON BAL/PAY...CENSUS CHARTS SENATE. PAGE 102 E2036
FOR/AID LAW DIPLOM POLICY

B67

WATT A.,THE EVOLUTION OF AUSTRALIAN FOREIGN POLICY 1938-65. ASIA S/ASIA USA+45 USA-45 INT/ORG NAT/G FORCES FOR/AID TREATY 20 AUSTRAL. PAGE 105 E2103
DIPLOM WAR

S67

ALEXANDER B.,"GIBRALTAR" SPAIN UK CONSTN WORKER PROB/SOLV FOR/AID RECEIVE CONTROL 20. PAGE 3 E0059
DIPLOM INT/ORG ORD/FREE ECO/TAC

S67

STEEL R.,"WHAT CAN THE UN DO?" RHODESIA ECO/UNDEV DIPLOM ECO/TAC SANCTION...INT/LAW UN. PAGE 93 E1866
INT/ORG BAL/PWR PEACE FOR/AID

FORBES A.H. E0769

FORCE AND VIOLENCE....SEE COERCE

FORCES....ARMED FORCES AND POLICE

N

FULLER G.A.,DEMOBILIZATION: A SELECTED LIST OF REFERENCES. USA+45 LAW AGRI LABOR WORKER ECO/TAC RATION RECEIVE EDU/PROP ROUTINE ARMS/CONT ALL/VALS 20. PAGE 41 E0819
BIBLIOG/A INDUS FORCES NAT/G

N

LIBRARY INTERNATIONAL REL,INTERNATIONAL INFORMATION SERVICE. WOR+45 CULTURE INT/ORG FORCES...GEOG HUM SOC. PAGE 65 E1295
BIBLIOG/A DIPLOM INT/TRADE INT/LAW

B

DEUTSCHE BIBLIOTH FRANKF A M,DEUTSCHE BIBLIOGRAPHIE. EUR+WWI GERMANY ECO/DEV FORCES DIPLOM LEAD...POLICY PHIL/SCI SOC 20. PAGE 31 E0612
BIBLIOG LAW ADMIN NAT/G

N

BACKGROUND; JOURNAL OF INTERNATIONAL STUDIES ASSOCIATION. INT/ORG FORCES ACT/RES EDU/PROP COERCE NAT/LISM PEACE ATTIT...INT/LAW CONCPT 20. PAGE 1 E0004
BIBLIOG DIPLOM POLICY

N

CANADIAN GOVERNMENT PUBLICATIONS (1955-). CANADA AGRI FINAN LABOR FORCES INT/TRADE HEALTH...JURID 20 PARLIAMENT. PAGE 1 E0005
BIBLIOG/A NAT/G DIPLOM INT/ORG

N

INTERNATIONAL BIBLIOGRAPHY ON CRIME AND DELINQUENCY. USA+45 LAW FORCES PROB/SOLV AGE/Y 20. PAGE 1 E0023
BIBLIOG/A CRIME ANOMIE CRIMLGY

N

AIR UNIVERSITY LIBRARY,INDEX TO MILITARY PERIODICALS. FUT SPACE WOR+45 REGION ARMS/CONT NUC/PWR WAR PEACE INT/LAW. PAGE 3 E0056
BIBLIOG/A FORCES NAT/G

N

ATLANTIC INSTITUTE,ATLANTIC STUDIES. COM EUR+WWI USA+45 CULTURE STRUCT ECO/DEV FORCES LEAD ARMS/CONT ...INT/LAW JURID SOC. PAGE 6 E0110
BIBLIOG/A DIPLOM POLICY GOV/REL

N

UNITED NATIONS,UNITED NATIONS PUBLICATIONS. WOR+45 ECO/UNDEV AGRI FINAN FORCES ADMIN LEAD WAR PEACE ...POLICY INT/LAW 20 UN. PAGE 98 E1965
BIBLIOG INT/ORG DIPLOM

B00

DE TOCQUEVILLE A.,DEMOCRACY IN AMERICA (VOLUME ONE). LAW SOCIETY STRUCT NAT/G POL/PAR PROVS FORCES LEGIS TOP/EX DIPLOM LEGIT WAR PEACE ATTIT SOVEREIGN ...SELF/OBS TIME/SEQ CONGRESS 19. PAGE 30 E0594
USA-45 TREND

B03

FORTESCUE G.K.,SUBJECT INDEX OF THE MODERN WORKS ADDED TO THE LIBRARY OF THE BRITISH MUSEUM IN THE YEARS 1881-1900 (3 VOLS.). UK LAW CONSTN FINAN NAT/G FORCES INT/TRADE COLONIAL 19. PAGE 39 E0775
BIBLIOG INDEX WRITING

B04

FREUND E.,THE POLICE POWER; PUBLIC POLICY AND CONSTITUTIONAL RIGHTS. USA-45 SOCIETY LOC/G NAT/G FORCES LEGIS ADJUD CT/SYS OWN PWR...JURID 18/19 SUPREME/CT. PAGE 40 E0795
CONSTN LAW ORD/FREE CONTROL

B09

HOLLAND T.E.,LETTERS UPON WAR AND NEUTRALITY. WOR-45 NAT/G FORCES JUDGE ECO/TAC LEGIT CT/SYS NEUTRAL ROUTINE COERCE...JURID TIME/SEQ 20. PAGE 55 E1085
LAW INT/LAW INT/ORG WAR

B14

CRAIG J.,ELEMENTS OF POLITICAL SCIENCE (3 VOLS.). CONSTN AGRI INDUS SCHOOL FORCES TAX CT/SYS SUFF MORAL WEALTH...CONCPT 19 CIVIL/LIB. PAGE 27 E0539
PHIL/SCI NAT/G ORD/FREE

B16

SCHROEDER T.,FREE SPEECH FOR RADICALS (REV. ED.). USA-45 CONSTN INDUS LOC/G FORCES SANCTION WAR ATTIT SEX...JURID REFORMERS 20 FREE/SPEE. PAGE 88 E1767
ORD/FREE CONTROL LAW PRESS

L16

WRIGHT Q.,"THE ENFORCEMENT OF INTERNATIONAL LAW THROUGH MUNICIPAL LAW IN THE US." USA-45 LOC/G NAT/G PUB/INST FORCES LEGIT CT/SYS PERCEPT ALL/VALS ...JURID 20. PAGE 107 E2149
INT/ORG LAW INT/LAW WAR

B19

VANDERPOL A.,LA DOCTRINE SCOLASTIQUE DU DROIT DE GUERRE. CHRIST-17C FORCES DIPLOM LEGIT SUPEGO MORAL ...BIOG AQUINAS/T SUAREZ/F CHRISTIAN. PAGE 103 E2072
WAR SECT INT/LAW

N19

AMERICAN CIVIL LIBERTIES UNION,"WE HOLD THESE TRUTHS" FREEDOM, JUSTICE, EQUALITY: REPORT ON CIVIL LIBERTIES (A PERIODICAL PAMPHLET COVERING 1951-53). USA+45 ACADEM NAT/G FORCES LEGIS COERCE CIVMIL/REL GOV/REL DISCRIM PRIVIL MARXISM...OLD/LIB 20 ACLU UN CIVIL/LIB. PAGE 4 E0076
ORD/FREE LAW RACE/REL CONSTN

N19

JANOWITZ M.,SOCIAL CONTROL OF ESCALATED RIOTS (PAMPHLET). USA+45 USA-45 LAW SOCIETY MUNIC FORCES PROB/SOLV EDU/PROP TV CRIME ATTIT...BIBLIOG 20 NEGRO CIV/RIGHTS. PAGE 58 E1148
CROWD ORD/FREE CONTROL RACE/REL

N19

MEZERIK AG,OUTER SPACE: UN, US, USSR (PAMPHLET). USSR DELIB/GP FORCES DETER NUC/PWR SOVEREIGN ...POLICY 20 UN TREATY. PAGE 73 E1453
SPACE CONTROL DIPLOM INT/ORG

N19

MISSISSIPPI ADVISORY COMMITTEE,REPORT ON MISSISSIPPI (PAMPHLET). USA+45 LAW PROVS FORCES ADJUD PWR...SOC/WK INT 20 MISSISSIPP NEGRO CIV/RIGHTS. PAGE 73 E1469
RACE/REL DISCRIM COERCE ORD/FREE

C20

BLACHLY F.F.,"THE GOVERNMENT AND ADMINISTRATION OF GERMANY." GERMANY CONSTN LOC/G PROVS DELIB/GP EX/STRUC FORCES LEGIS TOP/EX CT/SYS...BIBLIOG/A 19/20. PAGE 12 E0235
NAT/G GOV/REL ADMIN PHIL/SCI

B27

GOOCH G.P.,ENGLISH DEMOCRATIC IDEAS IN THE SEVENTEENTH CENTURY (2ND ED.). UK LAW SECT FORCES DIPLOM LEAD PARL/PROC REV ATTIT AUTHORIT...ANARCH
IDEA/COMP MAJORIT EX/STRUC

CONCPT 17 PARLIAMENT CMN/WLTH REFORMERS. PAGE 45   CONSERVE
E0885

B28
CORBETT P.E.,CANADA AND WORLD POLITICS. LAW CULTURE NAT/G
SOCIETY STRUCT MARKET INT/ORG FORCES ACT/RES PLAN   CANADA
ECO/TAC LEGIT ORD/FREE PWR RESPECT...SOC CONCPT
TIME/SEQ TREND CMN/WLTH 20 LEAGUE/NAT. PAGE 26
E0504

B29
BUELL R.,INTERNATIONAL RELATIONS. WOR+45 WOR-45   INT/ORG
CONSTN STRATA FORCES TOP/EX ADMIN ATTIT DRIVE   BAL/PWR
SUPEGO MORAL ORD/FREE PWR SOVEREIGN...JURID SOC   DIPLOM
CONCPT 20. PAGE 17 E0326

B29
CONWELL-EVANS T.P.,THE LEAGUE COUNCIL IN ACTION.   DELIB/GP
EUR+WWI TURKEY UK USSR WOR-45 INT/ORG FORCES JUDGE   INT/LAW
ECO/TAC EDU/PROP LEGIT ROUTINE ARMS/CONT COERCE
ATTIT PWR...MAJORIT GEOG JURID CONCPT LEAGUE/NAT
TOT/POP VAL/FREE TUNIS 20. PAGE 25 E0498

B30
BYNKERSHOEK C.,QUAESTIONUM JURIS PUBLICI LIBRI DUO. INT/ORG
CHRIST-17C MOD/EUR CONSTN ELITES SOCIETY NAT/G   LAW
PROVS EX/STRUC FORCES TOP/EX BAL/PWR DIPLOM ATTIT   NAT/LISM
MORAL...TRADIT CONCPT. PAGE 18 E0352   INT/LAW

B30
FAIRLIE J.A.,COUNTY GOVERNMENT AND ADMINISTRATION.   ADMIN
UK USA-45 NAT/G SCHOOL FORCES BUDGET TAX CT/SYS   GOV/REL
CHOOSE...JURID BIBLIOG 11/20. PAGE 36 E0713   LOC/G
                                                     MUNIC

B31
STOWELL E.C.,INTERNATIONAL LAW. FUT UNIV WOR-45   INT/ORG
SOCIETY CONSULT EX/STRUC FORCES ACT/RES PLAN DIPLOM ROUTINE
EDU/PROP LEGIT DISPL PWR SKILL...POLICY CONCPT OBS   INT/LAW
TREND TOT/POP 20. PAGE 94 E1885

B33
AMERICAN FOREIGN LAW ASSN,BIOGRAPHICAL NOTES ON THE BIBLIOG/A
LAWS AND LEGAL LITERATURE OF URUGUAY AND CURACAO.   LAW
URUGUAY CONSTN FINAN SECT FORCES JUDGE DIPLOM   JURID
INT/TRADE ADJUD CT/SYS CRIME 20. PAGE 4 E0078   ADMIN

B33
GENTILI A.,DE JURE BELLI, LIBRI TRES (1612) (VOL.   WAR
2). FORCES DIPLOM AGREE PEACE SOVEREIGN. PAGE 43   INT/LAW
E0849   MORAL
                                                     SUPEGO

B33
LAUTERPACHT H.,THE FUNCTION OF LAW IN THE   INT/ORG
INTERNATIONAL COMMUNITY. WOR-45 NAT/G FORCES CREATE LAW
DOMIN LEGIT COERCE WAR PEACE ATTIT ORD/FREE PWR   INT/LAW
SOVEREIGN...JURID CONCPT METH/CNCPT TIME/SEQ
GEN/LAWS GEN/METH LEAGUE/NAT TOT/POP VAL/FREE 20.
PAGE 63 E1265

B34
CLYDE W.M.,THE STRUGGLE FOR THE FREEDOM OF THE   PRESS
PRESS FROM CAXTON TO CROMWELL. UK LAW LOC/G SECT   ORD/FREE
FORCES LICENSE WRITING SANCTION REV ATTIT PWR   CONTROL
...POLICY 15/17 PARLIAMENT CROMWELL/O MILTON/J.
PAGE 23 E0460

B34
CULVER D.C.,BIBLIOGRAPHY OF CRIME AND CRIMINAL   BIBLIOG/A
JUSTICE, 1927-1931. LAW CULTURE PUB/INST PROB/SOLV   CRIMLGY
CT/SYS...PSY SOC STAT 20. PAGE 28 E0549   ADJUD
                                                     FORCES

B35
FOREIGN AFFAIRS BIBLIOGRAPHY: A SELECTED AND   BIBLIOG/A
ANNOTATED LIST OF BOOKS ON INTERNATIONAL RELATIONS   DIPLOM
1919-1962 (4 VOLS.). CONSTN FORCES COLONIAL   INT/ORG
ARMS/CONT WAR NAT/LISM PEACE ATTIT DRIVE...POLICY
INT/LAW 20. PAGE 2 E0032

B35
CUMMING J.,A CONTRIBUTION TOWARD A BIBLIOGRAPHY   BIBLIOG
DEALING WITH CRIME AND COGNATE SUBJECTS (3RD ED.).   CRIMLGY
UK LAW CULTURE PUB/INST ADJUD AGE BIO/SOC...PSY SOC FORCES
SOC/WK STAT METH/COMP 20. PAGE 28 E0552   CT/SYS

B36
GRAVES W.B.,AMERICAN STATE GOVERNMENT. CONSTN FINAN NAT/G
EX/STRUC FORCES LEGIS BUDGET TAX CT/SYS REPRESENT   PROVS
GOV/REL...BIBLIOG/A 19/20. PAGE 45 E0900   ADMIN
                                                     FEDERAL

B38
SAINT-PIERRE C.I.,SCHEME FOR LASTING PEACE (TRANS.   INT/ORG
BY H. BELLOT). INDUS NAT/G CHIEF FORCES INT/TRADE   PEACE

CT/SYS WAR PWR SOVEREIGN WEALTH...POLICY 18.   AGREE
PAGE 87 E1741   INT/LAW

B39
CULVER D.C.,BIBLIOGRAPHY OF CRIME AND CRIMINAL   BIBLIOG/A
JUSTICE, 1932-1937. USA-45 LAW CULTURE PUB/INST   CRIMLGY
PROB/SOLV CT/SYS...PSY SOC STAT 20. PAGE 28 E0551   ADJUD
                                                     FORCES

B40
BROWN A.D.,COMPULSORY MILITARY TRAINING: SELECT   BIBLIOG/A
LIST OF REFERENCES (PAMPHLET). USA-45 CONSTN   FORCES
VOL/ASSN COERCE 20. PAGE 16 E0311   JURID
                                                     ATTIT

S40
GERTH H.,"THE NAZI PARTY: ITS LEADERSHIP AND   POL/PAR
COMPOSITION" (BMR)" GERMANY ELITES STRATA STRUCT   DOMIN
EX/STRUC FORCES ECO/TAC CT/SYS CHOOSE TOTALISM   LEAD
AGE/Y AUTHORIT PWR 20. PAGE 43 E0851   ADMIN

B41
BIRDSALL P.,VERSAILLES TWENTY YEARS AFTER. MOD/EUR   DIPLOM
POL/PAR CHIEF CONSULT FORCES LEGIS REPAR PEACE   NAT/LISM
ORD/FREE...BIBLIOG 20 PRESIDENT TREATY. PAGE 12   WAR
E0231

S41
WRIGHT Q.,"FUNDAMENTAL PROBLEMS OF INTERNATIONAL   INT/ORG
ORGANIZATION." UNIV WOR-45 STRUCT FORCES ACT/RES   ATTIT
CREATE DOMIN EDU/PROP LEGIT REGION NAT/LISM   PEACE
ORD/FREE PWR RESPECT SOVEREIGN...JURID SOC CONCPT
METH/CNCPT TIME/SEQ 20. PAGE 107 E2152

B42
CROWE S.E.,THE BERLIN WEST AFRICA CONFERENCE,   AFR
1884-85. GERMANY ELITES MARKET INT/ORG DELIB/GP   CONFER
FORCES PROB/SOLV BAL/PWR CAP/ISM DOMIN COLONIAL   INT/TRADE
...INT/LAW 19. PAGE 28 E0548   DIPLOM

B42
FORTESCU J.,IN PRAISE OF ENGLISH LAW (1464) (TRANS. LAW
BY S.B. CHRIMES). UK ELITES CHIEF FORCES CT/SYS   CONSTN
COERCE CRIME GOV/REL ILLEGIT...JURID GOV/COMP   LEGIS
GEN/LAWS 15. PAGE 39 E0774   ORD/FREE

B42
FULLER G.H.,DEFENSE FINANCING: A SUPPLEMENTARY LIST BIBLIOG/A
OF REFERENCES (PAMPHLET). CANADA UK USA-45 ECO/DEV   FINAN
NAT/G DELIB/GP BUDGET ADJUD ARMS/CONT WEAPON COST   FORCES
PEACE PWR 20 AUSTRAL CHINJAP CONGRESS. PAGE 41   DIPLOM
E0821

B43
BACKUS R.C.,A GUIDE TO THE LAW AND LEGAL LITERATURE BIBLIOG/A
OF COLOMBIA. FINAN INDUS LABOR FORCES ADJUD ADMIN   LAW
COLONIAL CT/SYS CRIME...INT/LAW JURID 20 COLOMB.   CONSTN
PAGE 7 E0127   L/A+17C

B44
BRIERLY J.L.,THE OUTLOOK FOR INTERNATIONAL LAW. FUT INT/ORG
WOR-45 CONSTN NAT/G VOL/ASSN FORCES ECO/TAC DOMIN   LAW
LEGIT ADJUD ROUTINE PEACE ORD/FREE...INT/LAW JURID
METH LEAGUE/NAT 20. PAGE 15 E0298

B44
DE HUSZAR G.B.,NEW PERSPECTIVES ON PEACE. UNIV   ATTIT
CULTURE SOCIETY ECO/DEV ECO/UNDEV NAT/G FORCES   MYTH
CREATE ECO/TAC DOMIN ADJUD COERCE DRIVE ORD/FREE   PEACE
...GEOG JURID PSY SOC CONCPT TOT/POP. PAGE 29 E0584 WAR

B44
FULLER G.H.,MILITARY GOVERNMENT: A LIST OF   BIBLIOG
REFERENCES (A PAMPHLET). ITALY UK USA-45 WOR-45 LAW DIPLOM
FORCES DOMIN ADMIN ARMS/CONT ORD/FREE PWR   CIVMIL/REL
...DECISION 20 CHINJAP. PAGE 41 E0822   SOVEREIGN

B44
RUDIN H.R.,ARMISTICE 1918. FRANCE GERMANY MOD/EUR   AGREE
UK USA-45 NAT/G CHIEF DELIB/GP FORCES BAL/PWR REPAR WAR
ARMS/CONT 20 WILSON/W TREATY. PAGE 86 E1732   PEACE
                                                     DIPLOM

S44
WRIGHT Q.,"CONSTITUTIONAL PROCEDURES OF THE US FOR   TOP/EX
CARRYING OUT OBLIGATIONS FOR MILITARY SANCTIONS."   FORCES
EUR+WWI FUT USA-45 WOR-45 CONSTN INTELL NAT/G   INT/LAW
CONSULT EX/STRUC LEGIS ROUTINE DRIVE...POLICY JURID WAR
CONCPT OBS TREND TOT/POP 20. PAGE 108 E2153

B45
BEVERIDGE W.,THE PRICE OF PEACE. GERMANY UK WOR+45   INT/ORG
WOR-45 NAT/G FORCES CREATE LEGIT REGION WAR ATTIT   TREND
KNOWL ORD/FREE PWR...POLICY NEW/IDEA GEN/LAWS   PEACE
LEAGUE/NAT 20 TREATY. PAGE 12 E0223

CONOVER H.F.,THE GOVERNMENTS OF THE MAJOR FOREIGN
POWERS: A BIBLIOGRAPHY. FRANCE GERMANY ITALY UK
USSR CONSTN LOC/G POL/PAR EX/STRUC FORCES ADMIN
CT/SYS CIVMIL/REL TOTALISM...POLICY 19/20. PAGE 25
E0494
B45
BIBLIOG
NAT/G
DIPLOM

CONOVER H.F.,THE NAZI STATE: WAR CRIMES AND WAR
CRIMINALS. GERMANY CULTURE NAT/G SECT FORCES DIPLOM
INT/TRADE EDU/PROP...INT/LAW BIOG HIST/WRIT
TIME/SEQ 20. PAGE 25 E0495
B45
BIBLIOG
WAR
CRIME

VANCE H.L.,GUIDE TO THE LAW AND LEGAL LITERATURE OF
MEXICO. LAW CONSTN FINAN LABOR FORCES ADJUD ADMIN
...CRIMLGY PHIL/SCI CON/ANAL 20 MEXIC/AMER.
PAGE 103 E2070
B45
BIBLIOG/A
INT/LAW
JURID
CT/SYS

KEETON G.W.,MAKING INTERNATIONAL LAW WORK. FUT
WOR-45 NAT/G DELIB/GP FORCES LEGIT COERCE PEACE
ATTIT RIGID/FLEX ORD/FREE PWR...JURID CONCPT
HIST/WRIT GEN/METH LEAGUE/NAT 20. PAGE 60 E1193
B46
INT/ORG
ADJUD
INT/LAW

BORGESE G.,COMMON CAUSE. LAW CONSTN SOCIETY STRATA
ECO/DEV INT/ORG POL/PAR FORCES LEGIS TOP/EX CAP/ISM
DIPLOM ADMIN EXEC ATTIT PWR 20. PAGE 14 E0269
B47
WOR+45
NAT/G
SOVEREIGN
REGION

GORDON D.L.,THE HIDDEN WEAPON: THE STORY OF
ECONOMIC WARFARE. EUR+WWI USA-45 LAW FINAN INDUS
NAT/G CONSULT FORCES PLAN DOMIN PWR WEALTH
...INT/LAW CONCPT OBS TOT/POP NAZI 20. PAGE 45
E0891
B47
INT/ORG
ECO/TAC
INT/TRADE
WAR

FOX W.T.R.,UNITED STATES POLICY IN A TWO POWER
WORLD. COM USA+45 USSR FORCES DOMIN AGREE NEUTRAL
NUC/PWR ORD/FREE SOVEREIGN 20 COLD/WAR TREATY
EUROPE/W INTERVENT. PAGE 39 E0780
N47
DIPLOM
FOR/AID
POLICY

GRIFFITH E.S.,RESEARCH IN POLITICAL SCIENCE: THE
WORK OF PANELS OF RESEARCH COMMITTEE. APSA. WOR+45
WOR-45 COM/IND R+D FORCES ACT/RES WAR...GOV/COMP
ANTHOL 20. PAGE 47 E0939
B48
BIBLIOG
PHIL/SCI
DIPLOM
JURID

STOKES W.S.,BIBLIOGRAPHY OF STANDARD AND CLASSICAL
WORKS IN THE FIELDS OF AMERICAN POLITICAL SCIENCE.
USA+45 USA-45 POL/PAR PROVS FORCES DIPLOM ADMIN
CT/SYS APPORT 20 CONGRESS PRESIDENT. PAGE 94 E1876
B48
BIBLIOG
NAT/G
LOC/G
CONSTN

ALEXANDER L.,"WAR CRIMES, THEIR SOCIAL-
PSYCHOLOGICAL ASPECTS." EUR+WWI GERMANY LAW CULTURE
ELITES KIN POL/PAR PUB/INST FORCES DOMIN EDU/PROP
COERCE CRIME ATTIT SUPEGO HEALTH MORAL PWR FASCISM
...PSY OBS TREND GEN/LAWS NAZI 20. PAGE 3 E0061
S48
DRIVE
WAR

BROWN D.M.,"RECENT JAPANESE POLITICAL AND
HISTORICAL MATERIALS." ELITES CT/SYS CIVMIL/REL 20
CHINJAP. PAGE 16 E0312
S49
WAR
FORCES

BERMAN H.J.,JUSTICE IN RUSSIA; AN INTERPRETATION OF
SOVIET LAW. USSR LAW STRUCT LABOR FORCES AGREE
GP/REL ORD/FREE SOCISM...TIME/SEQ 20. PAGE 11 E0207
B50
JURID
ADJUD
MARXISM
COERCE

DOROSH J.T.,GUIDE TO SOVIET BIBLIOGRAPHIES. USSR
LAW AGRI SCHOOL SECT FORCES TEC/DEV...ART/METH GEOG
HUM SOC 20. PAGE 32 E0639
B50
BIBLIOG
METH
CON/ANAL

LOWENTHAL M.,THE FEDERAL BUREAU OF INVESTIGATION.
USA+45 SOCIETY ADMIN TASK CRIME INGP/REL...CRIMLGY
20 FBI ESPIONAGE. PAGE 67 E1329
B50
FORCES
NAT/G
ATTIT
LAW

INSTITUTE DES RELATIONS INTL,LES ASPECTS
ECONOMIQUES DU REARMEMENT (ETUDE DE L'INSTITUT DES
RELATIONS INTERNATIONALES A BRUXELLES). BELGIUM UK
USA+45 EXTR/IND FINAN FORCES WORKER PROB/SOLV
DIPLOM PRICE...POLICY 20 TREATY. PAGE 57 E1127
B51
WEAPON
DEMAND
ECO/TAC
INT/TRADE

KEFAUVER E.,CRIME IN AMERICA. USA+45 USA-45 MUNIC
NEIGH DELIB/GP TRIBUTE GAMBLE LOBBY SANCTION
...AUD/VIS 20 CAPONE/AL MAFIA MIAMI CHICAGO
B51
ELITES
CRIME
PWR

DETROIT. PAGE 60 E1194

FORCES

FERRELL R.H.,PEACE IN THEIR TIME. FRANCE UK USA-45
INT/ORG NAT/G FORCES CREATE AGREE ARMS/CONT COERCE
WAR TREATY 20 WILSON/W LEAGUE/NAT BRIAND/A. PAGE 37
E0741
B52
PEACE
DIPLOM

LANCASTER L.W.,"GOVERNMENT IN RURAL AMERICA."
USA+45 ECO/DEV AGRI SCHOOL FORCES LEGIS JUDGE
BUDGET TAX CT/SYS...CHARTS BIBLIOG. PAGE 62 E1248
C52
GOV/REL
LOC/G
MUNIC
ADMIN

BRETTON H.L.,STRESEMANN AND THE REVISION OF
VERSAILLES: A FIGHT FOR REASON. EUR+WWI GERMANY
FORCES BUDGET ARMS/CONT WAR SUPEGO...BIBLIOG 20
TREATY VERSAILLES STRESEMN/G. PAGE 15 E0294
B53
POLICY
DIPLOM
BIOG

BOWIE R.R.,"STUDIES IN FEDERALISM." AGRI FINAN
LABOR EX/STRUC FORCES LEGIS DIPLOM INT/TRADE ADJUD
...BIBLIOG 20 EEC. PAGE 14 E0279
C54
FEDERAL
EUR+WWI
INT/ORG
CONSTN

CAVAN R.S.,CRIMINOLOGY (2ND ED.). USA+45 LAW FAM
PUB/INST FORCES PLAN WAR AGE/Y PERSON ROLE SUPEGO
...CHARTS 20 FBI. PAGE 21 E0409
B55
DRIVE
CRIMLGY
CONTROL
METH/COMP

COMM. STUDY ORGAN. PEACE,REPORTS. WOR-45 ECO/DEV
ECO/UNDEV VOL/ASSN CONSULT FORCES PLAN TEC/DEV
DOMIN EDU/PROP NUC/PWR ATTIT PWR WEALTH...JURID
STERTYP FAO ILO 20 UN. PAGE 24 E0481
B55
WOR+45
INT/ORG
ARMS/CONT

HOGAN W.N.,INTERNATIONAL CONFLICT AND COLLECTIVE
SECURITY: THE PRINCIPLE OF CONCERN IN INTERNATIONAL
ORGANIZATION. CONSTN EX/STRUC BAL/PWR DIPLOM ADJUD
CONTROL CENTRAL CONSEN PEACE...INT/LAW CONCPT
METH/COMP 20 UN LEAGUE/NAT. PAGE 53 E1066
B55
INT/ORG
WAR
ORD/FREE
FORCES

KHADDURI M.,WAR AND PEACE IN THE LAW OF ISLAM.
CONSTN CULTURE SOCIETY STRATA NAT/G PROVS SECT
FORCES TOP/EX CREATE DOMIN EDU/PROP ADJUD COERCE
ATTIT RIGID/FLEX ALL/VALS...CONCPT TIME/SEQ TOT/POP
VAL/FREE. PAGE 61 E1209
B55
ISLAM
JURID
PEACE
WAR

PLISCHKE E.,AMERICAN FOREIGN RELATIONS: A
BIBLIOGRAPHY OF OFFICIAL SOURCES. USA+45 USA-45
INT/ORG FORCES PRESS WRITING DEBATE EXEC...POLICY
INT/LAW 18/20 CONGRESS. PAGE 81 E1621
B55
BIBLIOG/A
DIPLOM
NAT/G

BOTERO G.,THE REASON OF STATE AND THE GREATNESS OF
CITIES. SECT CHIEF FORCES PLAN LEAD WAR MORAL
...POLICY 16 MACHIAVELL TREATY. PAGE 14 E0272
B56
PHIL/SCI
NEW/IDEA
CONTROL

BROWNE D.G.,THE RISE OF SCOTLAND YARD: A HISTORY OF
THE METROPOLITAN POLICE. UK MUNIC CHIEF ADMIN CRIME
GP/REL 19/20. PAGE 16 E0316
B56
CRIMLGY
LEGIS
CONTROL
FORCES

ESTEP R.,AN AIR POWER BIBLIOGRAPHY. USA+45 TEC/DEV
BUDGET DIPLOM EDU/PROP DETER CIVMIL/REL...DECISION
INT/LAW 20. PAGE 35 E0698
B56
BIBLIOG/A
FORCES
WEAPON
PLAN

WIGGINS J.R.,FREEDOM OR SECRECY. USA+45 USA-45
DELIB/GP EX/STRUC FORCES ADJUD SANCTION KNOWL PWR
...AUD/VIS CONGRESS 20. PAGE 106 E2121
B56
ORD/FREE
PRESS
NAT/G
CONTROL

FALL B.B.,"THE VIET-MINH REGIME." VIETNAM LAW
ECO/UNDEV POL/PAR FORCES DOMIN WAR ATTIT MARXISM
...BIOG PREDICT BIBLIOG/A 20. PAGE 36 E0720
C56
NAT/G
ADMIN
EX/STRUC
LEAD

BLOOMFIELD L.M.,EGYPT, ISRAEL AND THE GULF OF
AQABA: IN INTERNATIONAL LAW. LAW NAT/G CONSULT
FORCES PLAN ECO/TAC ROUTINE COERCE ATTIT DRIVE
PERCEPT PERSON RIGID/FLEX LOVE PWR WEALTH...GEOG
CONCPT MYTH TREND. PAGE 13 E0250
B57
ISLAM
INT/LAW
UAR

COMM. STUDY ORGAN. PEACE,STRENGTHENING THE UNITED
B57
INT/ORG

NATIONS. FUT USA+45 WOR+45 CONSTN NAT/G DELIB/GP   ORD/FREE
FORCES LEGIS ECO/TAC LEGIT COERCE PEACE...JURID
CONCPT UN COLD/WAR 20. PAGE 24 E0482

                                                            B57
FREUND G.,UNHOLY ALLIANCE. EUR+WWI GERMANY USSR   DIPLOM
FORCES ECO/TAC CONTROL WAR PWR...TREND TREATY.   PLAN
PAGE 40 E0796   POLICY

                                                            B57
MILLS W.,INDIVIDUAL FREEDOM AND COMMON DEFENSE   ORD/FREE
(PAMPHLET). USA+45 USSR NAT/G EDU/PROP CRIME CHOOSE CONSTN
20 COLD/WAR. PAGE 73 E1463   INGP/REL
                                                    FORCES

                                                            B57
SCHUBERT G.A.,THE PRESIDENCY IN THE COURTS. CONSTN PWR
FORCES DIPLOM TARIFFS ADJUD CONTROL WAR...DECISION CT/SYS
MGT CHARTS 18/20 PRESIDENT CONGRESS SUPREME/CT.   LEGIT
PAGE 89 E1778   CHIEF

                                                            B58
JAPAN MINISTRY OF JUSTICE,CRIMINAL JUSTICE IN   CONSTN
JAPAN. LAW PROF/ORG PUB/INST FORCES CONTROL CT/SYS CRIME
PARL/PROC 20 CHINJAP. PAGE 58 E1149   JURID
                                                    ADMIN

                                                            N58
US HOUSE COMM FOREIGN AFFAIRS,HEARINGS ON DRAFT   LEGIS
LEGISLATION TO AMEND FURTHER THE MUTUAL SECURITY   DELIB/GP
ACT OF 1954 (PAMPHLET). USA+45 CONSULT FORCES   CONFER
BUDGET DIPLOM DETER COST ORD/FREE...JURID 20   WEAPON
DEPT/DEFEN UN DEPT/STATE. PAGE 100 E2002

                                                            B59
GREENSPAN M.,THE MODERN LAW OF LAND WARFARE. WOR+45 ADJUD
INT/ORG NAT/G DELIB/GP FORCES ATTIT...POLICY   PWR
HYPO/EXP STERTYP 20. PAGE 46 E0911   WAR

                                                            B59
KERREMANS-RAMIOULL,LE PROBLEME DE LA DELINQUENCE   BIBLIOG
JUVENILE (2ND ED.). FAM PUB/INST SCHOOL FORCES   CRIME
LEGIS MORAL...CRIMLGY SOC 20. PAGE 60 E1205   AGE/Y
                                                    SOC/WK

                                                            B59
COLUMBIA U. BUREAU OF APPL SOC RES, ATTITUDES OF   ATTIT
PROMINENT AMERICANS TOWARD "WORLD PEACE THROUGH   ACT/RES
WORLD LAW" (SUPRA-NATL ORGANIZATION FOR WAR   INT/LAW
PREVENTION). USA+45 USSR ELITES FORCES PLAN   STAT
PROB/SOLV CONTROL WAR PWR...POLICY SOC QU IDEA/COMP
20 UN. PAGE 82 E1644

                                                            B59
SQUIBB G.D.,THE HIGH COURT OF CHIVALRY. UK NAT/G   CT/SYS
FORCES ADJUD WAR 14/20 PARLIAMENT ENGLSH/LAW.   PARL/PROC
PAGE 93 E1863   JURID

                                                            B59
VITTACHIT,EMERGENCY '58. CEYLON UK STRUCT NAT/G   RACE/REL
FORCES ADJUD CRIME REV NAT/LISM 20. PAGE 104 E2081 DISCRIM
                                                    DIPLOM
                                                    SOVEREIGN

                                                            S59
PUGWASH CONFERENCE,"ON BIOLOGICAL AND CHEMICAL   ACT/RES
WARFARE." WOR+45 SOCIETY PROC/MFG INT/ORG FORCES   BIO/SOC
EDU/PROP ADJUD RIGID/FLEX ORD/FREE PWR...DECISION   WAR
PSY NEW/IDEA MATH VAL/FREE 20. PAGE 83 E1661   WEAPON

                                                            S59
SOHN L.B.,"THE DEFINITION OF AGGRESSION." FUT LAW   INT/ORG
FORCES LEGIT ADJUD ROUTINE COERCE ORD/FREE PWR   CT/SYS
...MAJORIT JURID QUANT COLD/WAR 20. PAGE 92 E1855   DETER
                                                    SOVEREIGN

                                                            S59
SUTTON F.X.,"REPRESENTATION AND THE NATURE OF   NAT/G
POLITICAL SYSTEMS." UNIV WOR-45 CULTURE SOCIETY   CONCPT
STRATA INT/ORG FORCES JUDGE DOMIN LEGIT EXEC REGION
REPRESENT ATTIT ORD/FREE RESPECT...SOC HIST/WRIT
TIME/SEQ. PAGE 95 E1896

                                                            B60
CLARK G.,WORLD PEACE THROUGH WORLD LAW. FUT WOR+45 INT/ORG
CONSULT FORCES ACT/RES CREATE PLAN ADMIN ROUTINE   LAW
ARMS/CONT DETER ATTIT PWR...JURID VAL/FREE UNESCO   PEACE
20 UN. PAGE 23 E0449   INT/LAW

                                                            B60
DILEY A.V.,INTRODUCTION TO THE STUDY OF THE LAW OF CONSTN
THE CONSTITUTION. FRANCE UK USA+45 USA-45 CONSULT   LAW
FORCES TAX ADMIN FEDERAL ORD/FREE SOVEREIGN   LEGIS
...IDEA/COMP 20 ENGLSH/LAW CON/INTERP PARLIAMENT.   GEN/LAWS
PAGE 32 E0627

                                                            B60
ENGEL J.,THE SECURITY OF THE FREE WORLD. USSR   COM
WOR+45 STRATA STRUCT ECO/DEV ECO/UNDEV INT/ORG   TREND
DELIB/GP FORCES DOMIN LEGIT ADJUD EXEC ARMS/CONT   DIPLOM
COERCE...POLICY CONCPT NEW/IDEA TIME/SEQ GEN/LAWS
COLD/WAR WORK UN 20 NATO. PAGE 35 E0689

                                                            B60
PRASAD B.,THE ORIGINS OF PROVINCIAL AUTONOMY. INDIA CENTRAL
UK FINAN LOC/G FORCES LEGIS CONTROL CT/SYS PWR   PROVS
...JURID 19/20. PAGE 82 E1646   COLONIAL
                                                    NAT/G

                                                            S60
MARSHALL G.,"POLICE RESPONSIBILITY." UK LOC/G ADJUD CONTROL
ADMIN EXEC 20. PAGE 69 E1370   REPRESENT
                                                    LAW
                                                    FORCES

                                                            S60
O'BRIEN W.,"THE ROLE OF FORCE IN THE INTERNATIONAL INT/ORG
JURIDICAL ORDER." WOR+45 NAT/G FORCES DOMIN ADJUD   COERCE
ARMS/CONT DETER NUC/PWR WAR ATTIT PWR...CATH
INT/LAW JURID CONCPT TREND STERTYP GEN/LAWS 20.
PAGE 78 E1564

                                                            S60
WRIGHT Q.,"LEGAL ASPECTS OF THE U-2 INCIDENT." COM PWR
USA+45 USSR STRUCT NAT/G FORCES PLAN TEC/DEV ADJUD POLICY
RIGID/FLEX MORAL ORD/FREE...DECISION INT/LAW JURID SPACE
PSY TREND GEN/LAWS COLD/WAR VAL/FREE 20 U-2.
PAGE 108 E2157

                                                            B61
BRENNAN D.G.,ARMS CONTROL, DISARMAMENT, AND   ARMS/CONT
NATIONAL SECURITY. WOR+45 NAT/G FORCES CREATE   ORD/FREE
PROB/SOLV PARTIC WAR PEACE...DECISION INT/LAW   DIPLOM
ANTHOL BIBLIOG 20. PAGE 15 E0291   POLICY

                                                            B61
CONFERENCE ATLANTIC COMMUNITY,AN INTRODUCTORY   BIBLIOG/A
BIBLIOGRAPHY. COM WOR+45 FORCES DIPLOM ECO/TAC WAR CON/ANAL
...INT/LAW HIST/WRIT COLD/WAR NATO. PAGE 25 E0485   INT/ORG

                                                            B61
GUIZOT F.P.G.,HISTORY OF THE ORIGIN OF   LEGIS
REPRESENTATIVE GOVERNMENT IN EUROPE. CHRIST-17C   REPRESENT
FRANCE MOD/EUR SPAIN UK LAW CHIEF FORCES POPULISM   CONSTN
...MAJORIT TIME/SEQ GOV/COMP NAT/COMP 4/19   NAT/G
PARLIAMENT. PAGE 48 E0961

                                                            B61
MECHAM J.L.,THE UNITED STATES AND INTER-AMERICAN   DIPLOM
SECURITY, 1889-1960. L/A+17C USA+45 USA-45 CONSTN   WAR
FORCES INT/TRADE PEACE TOTALISM ATTIT...JURID 19/20 ORD/FREE
UN OAS. PAGE 72 E1432   INT/ORG

                                                            B61
MERTON R.K.,CONTEMPORARY SOCIAL PROBLEMS: AN   CRIME
INTRODUCTION TO THE SOCIOLOGY OF DEVIANT BEHAVIOR   ANOMIE
AND SOCIAL DISORGANIZATION. FAM MUNIC FORCES WORKER STRANGE
PROB/SOLV INGP/REL RACE/REL ISOLAT...CRIMLGY GEOG   SOC
PSY T 20 NEGRO. PAGE 72 E1444

                                                            B61
SCOTT A.M.,POLITICS, USA; CASES ON THE AMERICAN   CT/SYS
DEMOCRATIC PROCESS. USA+45 CHIEF FORCES DIPLOM   CONSTN
LOBBY CHOOSE RACE/REL FEDERAL ATTIT...JURID ANTHOL NAT/G
T 20 PRESIDENT CONGRESS CIVIL/LIB. PAGE 90 E1795   PLAN

                                                            B61
US COMMISSION ON CIVIL RIGHTS,JUSTICE: BOOK 5, 1961 DISCRIM
REPORT OF THE U.S. COMMISSION ON CIVIL RIGHTS.   LAW
LOC/G NAT/G RACE/REL...JURID 20 NEGRO CIV/RIGHTS   FORCES
INDIAN/AM JURY INDIAN/AM. PAGE 99 E1983

                                                            S61
RICHSTEIN A.R.,"LEGAL RULES IN NUCLEAR WEAPONS   NUC/PWR
EMPLOYMENTS." FUT WOR+45 LAW SOCIETY FORCES PLAN   TEC/DEV
WEAPON RIGID/FLEX...HEAL CONCPT TREND VAL/FREE 20. MORAL
PAGE 85 E1696   ARMS/CONT

                                                            B62
BISHOP W.W. JR.,INTERNATIONAL LAW: CASES AND   INT/LAW
MATERIALS. WOR+45 INT/ORG FORCES PROB/SOLV AGREE   DIPLOM
WAR...JURID IDEA/COMP T 20 TREATY. PAGE 12 E0233   CONCPT
                                                    CT/SYS

                                                            B62
CURRY J.E.,RACE TENSIONS AND THE POLICE. LAW MUNIC FORCES
NEIGH TEC/DEV RUMOR CONTROL COERCE GP/REL ATTIT   RACE/REL
...SOC 20 NEGRO. PAGE 28 E0558   CROWD
                                                    ORD/FREE

                                                            B62
DOUGLAS W.O.,DEMOCRACY'S MANIFESTO. COM USA+45   DIPLOM

ECO/UNDEV INT/ORG FORCES PLAN NEUTRAL TASK MARXISM POLICY
...JURID 20 NATO SEATO. PAGE 32 E0642   NAT/G
                                                         ORD/FREE

                                                         B62
DUPRE J.S.,SCIENCE AND THE NATION: POLICY AND   R+D
POLITICS. USA+45 LAW ACADEM FORCES ADMIN CIVMIL/REL   INDUS
GOV/REL EFFICIENCY PEACE...TREND 20 SCI/ADVSRY.   TEC/DEV
PAGE 34 E0665   NUC/PWR

                                                         B62
DUROSELLE J.B.,HISTOIRE DIPLOMATIQUE DE 1919 A NOS   DIPLOM
JOURS (3RD ED.). FRANCE INT/ORG CHIEF FORCES CONFER   WOR+45
ARMS/CONT WAR PEACE ORD/FREE...T TREATY 20   WOR-45
COLD/WAR. PAGE 34 E0667

                                                         B62
OTTENBERG M.,THE FEDERAL INVESTIGATORS. USA+45 LAW   FORCES
COM/IND DIST/IND WORKER DIPLOM INT/TRADE CONTROL   INSPECT
FEDERAL HEALTH ORD/FREE FBI CIA FTC SEC FDA.   NAT/G
PAGE 79 E1585   CRIME

                                                         B62
SOWLE C.R.,POLICE POWER AND INDIVIDUAL FREEDOM: THE   FORCES
QUEST FOR BALANCE. CANADA EUR+WWI ISRAEL NORWAY   ORD/FREE
USA+45 LAW CONSTN SOCIETY CONTROL ROUTINE SANCTION   IDEA/COMP
GP/REL 20 CHINJAP. PAGE 93 E1859

                                                         B62
THOMPSON K.W.,AMERICAN DIPLOMACY AND EMERGENT   NAT/G
PATTERNS. USA-45 USA+45 WOR+45 WOR-45 LAW DELIB/GP   BAL/PWR
FORCES TOP/EX DIPLOM ATTIT DRIVE RIGID/FLEX
ORD/FREE PWR SOVEREIGN...POLICY 20. PAGE 96 E1922

                                                         B62
US AIR FORCE,THE MILITARY JUSTICE SYSTEM (REV.   JURID
ED.). USA+45 DELIB/GP...IDEA/COMP 20. PAGE 99 E1978   FORCES
                                                         ADJUD
                                                         ORD/FREE

                                                         B62
US SENATE COMM ON JUDICIARY,CONSTITUTIONAL RIGHTS   CONSTN
OF MILITARY PERSONNEL. USA+45 USA-45 FORCES DIPLOM   ORD/FREE
WAR CONGRESS. PAGE 102 E2046   JURID
                                                         CT/SYS

                                                         L62
STEIN E.,"MR HAMMARSKJOLD, THE CHARTER LAW AND THE   CONCPT
FUTURE ROLE OF THE UNITED NATIONS SECRETARY-   BIOG
GENERAL." WOR+45 CONSTN INT/ORG DELIB/GP FORCES
TOP/EX BAL/PWR LEGIT ROUTINE RIGID/FLEX PWR
...POLICY JURID OBS STERTYP UN COLD/WAR 20
HAMMARSK/D. PAGE 93 E1869

                                                         S62
CRANE R.D.,"LAW AND STRATEGY IN SPACE." FUT USA+45   CONCPT
WOR+45 AIR LAW INT/ORG NAT/G FORCES ACT/RES PLAN   SPACE
BAL/PWR LEGIT ARMS/CONT COERCE ORD/FREE...POLICY
INT/LAW JURID SOC/EXP 20 TREATY. PAGE 27 E0542

                                                         S62
GREENSPAN M.,"INTERNATIONAL LAW AND ITS PROTECTION   FORCES
FOR PARTICIPANTS IN UNCONVENTIONAL WARFARE." WOR+45   WAR
LAW INT/ORG NAT/G POL/PAR COERCE REV ORD/FREE   GUERRILLA
...INT/LAW TOT/POP 20. PAGE 46 E0912   WAR

                                                         C62
BACON F.,"OF THE TRUE GREATNESS OF KINGDOMS AND   WAR
ESTATES" (1612) IN F. BACON, ESSAYS." ELITES FORCES   PWR
DOMIN EDU/PROP LEGIT...POLICY GEN/LAWS 16/17   DIPLOM
TREATY. PAGE 7 E0129   CONSTN

                                                         B63
ATTIA G.E.D.,LES FORCES ARMEES DES NATIONS UNIES EN   FORCES
COREE ET AU MOYENORIENT. KOREA CONSTN NAT/G   INT/LAW
DELIB/GP LEGIS PWR...IDEA/COMP NAT/COMP BIBLIOG UN
SUEZ. PAGE 6 E0114

                                                         B63
BLOCK E.B.,THE VINDICATORS. LAW FORCES CT/SYS   ATTIT
DISCRIM 19/20. PAGE 13 E0247   CRIME
                                                         ADJUD
                                                         CRIMLGY

                                                         B63
DEENER D.R.,CANADA - UNITED STATES TREATY   DIPLOM
RELATIONS. CANADA USA+45 USA-45 NAT/G FORCES PLAN   INT/LAW
PROB/SOLV AGREE NUC/PWR...TREND 18/20 TREATY.   POLICY
PAGE 30 E0603

                                                         B63
DILLIARD I.,ONE MAN'S STAND FOR FREEDOM: MR.   CONSTN
JUSTICE BLACK AND THE BILL OF RIGHTS. USA+45   JURID
POL/PAR SECT DELIB/GP FORCES ADJUD CONTROL WAR   JUDGE
DISCRIM MORAL...BIBLIOG 20 NEGRO SUPREME/CT   ORD/FREE
BILL/RIGHT BLACK/HL. PAGE 32 E0628

                                                         B63
DOUGLAS W.O.,THE ANATOMY OF LIBERTY: THE RIGHTS OF   PEACE
MAN WITHOUT FORCE. WOR+45 ECO/DEV ECO/UNDEV LOC/G   LAW
FORCES GOV/REL...SOC/WK 20. PAGE 32 E0643   DIPLOM
                                                         ORD/FREE

                                                         B63
DUNN F.S.,PEACE-MAKING AND THE SETTLEMENT WITH   POLICY
JAPAN. ASIA USA+45 FORCES BAL/PWR ECO/TAC   PEACE
CONFER WAR PWR SOVEREIGN 20 CHINJAP COLD/WAR   PLAN
TREATY. PAGE 33 E0661   DIPLOM

                                                         B63
ECOLE NATIONALE D'ADMIN,BIBLIOGRAPHIE SELECTIVE   BIBLIOG
D'OUVRAGES DE LANGUE FRANCAISE TRAITANT DES   AFR
PROBLEMES GOUVERNEMENTAUX ET ADMINISTRATIFS. NAT/G   ADMIN
FORCES ACT/RES OP/RES PLAN PROB/SOLV BUDGET ADJUD   EX/STRUC
COLONIAL LEAD 20. PAGE 34 E0672

                                                         B63
ELLERT R.B.,NATO 'FAIR TRIAL' SAFEGUARDS: PRECURSOR   JURID
TO AN INTERNATIONAL BILL OF PROCEDURAL RIGHTS.   INT/LAW
WOR+45 FORCES CRIME CIVMIL/REL ATTIT ORD/FREE 20   INT/ORG
NATO. PAGE 34 E0683   CT/SYS

                                                         B63
FALK R.A.,LAW, MORALITY, AND WAR IN THE   ADJUD
CONTEMPORARY WORLD. WOR+45 LAW INT/ORG EX/STRUC   ARMS/CONT
FORCES EDU/PROP LEGIT DETER NUC/PWR MORAL ORD/FREE   PEACE
...JURID TOT/POP 20. PAGE 36 E0715   INT/LAW

                                                         B63
GRANT D.R.,STATE AND LOCAL GOVERNMENT IN AMERICA.   PROVS
USA+45 FINAN LOC/G MUNIC EX/STRUC FORCES EDU/PROP   POL/PAR
ADMIN CHOOSE FEDERAL ATTIT...JURID 20. PAGE 45   LEGIS
E0897   CONSTN

                                                         B63
HIGGINS R.,THE DEVELOPMENT OF INTERNATIONAL LAW   INT/ORG
THROUGH THE POLITICAL ORGANS OF THE UNITED NATIONS.   INT/LAW
WOR+45 FORCES DIPLOM AGREE COERCE ATTIT SOVEREIGN   TEC/DEV
...BIBLIOG 20 UN TREATY. PAGE 52 E1041   JURID

                                                         B63
LEVY L.W.,JEFFERSON AND CIVIL LIBERTIES: THE DARKER   BIOG
SIDE. USA-45 LAW INTELL ACADEM FORCES PRESS REV   ORD/FREE
INGP/REL PERSON 18/19 JEFFERSN/T CIVIL/LIB. PAGE 65   CONSTN
E1291   ATTIT

                                                         B63
ROSNER G.,THE UNITED NATIONS EMERGENCY FORCE.   INT/ORG
FRANCE ISRAEL UAR UK WOR+45 CREATE WAR PEACE   FORCES
ORD/FREE PWR...INT/LAW JURID HIST/WRIT TIME/SEQ UN.
PAGE 86 E1719

                                                         B63
VAN SLYCK P.,PEACE: THE CONTROL OF NATIONAL POWER.   ARMS/CONT
CUBA WOR+45 FINAN NAT/G FORCES PROB/SOLV TEC/DEV   PEACE
BAL/PWR ADMIN CONTROL ORD/FREE...POLICY INT/LAW UN   INT/ORG
COLD/WAR TREATY. PAGE 103 E2069   DIPLOM

                                                         L63
LISSITZYN O.J.,"INTERNATIONAL LAW IN A DIVIDED   INT/ORG
WORLD." FUT WOR+45 CONSTN CULTURE ECO/DEV ECO/UNDEV   LAW
DIST/IND NAT/G FORCES ECO/TAC LEGIT ADJUD COERCE
ATTIT HEALTH MORAL ORD/FREE PWR RESPECT
WEALTH VAL/FREE. PAGE 65 E1306

                                                         S63
BECHHOEFER B.G.,"UNITED NATIONS PROCEDURES IN CASE   INT/ORG
OF VIOLATIONS OF DISARMAMENT AGREEMENTS." COM   DELIB/GP
USA+45 USSR LAW CONSTN NAT/G EX/STRUC FORCES LEGIS
BAL/PWR EDU/PROP CT/SYS ARMS/CONT ORD/FREE PWR
...POLICY STERTYP UN VAL/FREE 20. PAGE 9 E0169

                                                         S63
CLEVELAND H.,"CRISIS DIPLOMACY." USA+45 WOR+45 LAW   DECISION
FORCES TASK NUC/PWR PWR 20. PAGE 23 E0454   DIPLOM
                                                         PROB/SOLV
                                                         POLICY

                                                         S63
GIRAUD E.,"L'INTERDICTION DU RECOURS A LA FORCE. LA   INT/ORG
THEORIE ET LA PRATIQUE DES NATIONS UNIES." ALGERIA   FORCES
COM CUBA HUNGARY WOR+45 ADJUD TOTALISM ATTIT   DIPLOM
RIGID/FLEX PWR...POLICY JURID CONCPT UN 20 CONGO.
PAGE 44 E0872

                                                         S63
MODELSKI G.,"STUDY OF ALLIANCES." WOR+45 WOR-45   VOL/ASSN
INT/ORG NAT/G FORCES LEGIT ADMIN CHOOSE ALL/VALS   CON/ANAL
PWR SKILL...INT/LAW CONCPT GEN/LAWS 20 TREATY.   DIPLOM
PAGE 74 E1477

C63

ATTIA G.E.O.,"LES FORCES ARMEES DES NATIONS UNIES   FORCES
EN COREE ET AU MOYENORIENT." KOREA CONSTN DELIB/GP   NAT/G
LEGIS PWR...IDEA/COMP NAT/COMP BIBLIOG UN SUEZ.   INT/LAW
PAGE 6 E0115

C63

SCHUBERT G.,"JUDICIAL DECISION-MAKING." FORCES LEAD   ADJUD
ATTIT DRIVE...POLICY PSY STAT CHARTS ANTHOL BIBLIOG   DECISION
20. PAGE 88 E1773   JUDGE
                                                       CT/SYS

B64

AHLUWALIA K.,THE LEGAL STATUS, PRIVILEGES AND   PRIVIL
IMMUNITIES OF SPECIALIZED AGENCIES OF UN AND   DIPLOM
CERTAIN OTHER INTERNATIONAL ORGANIZATIONS. WOR+45   INT/ORG
LAW CONSULT DELIB/GP FORCES. PAGE 3 E0055   INT/LAW

B64

BOWETT D.W.,UNITED NATIONS FORCES* A LEGAL STUDY.   OP/RES
CYPRUS ISRAEL KOREA LAW CONSTN ACT/RES CREATE   FORCES
BUDGET CONTROL TASK PWR...INT/LAW IDEA/COMP UN   ARMS/CONT
CONGO/LEOP SUEZ. PAGE 14 E0278

B64

DORMAN M.,WE SHALL OVERCOME. USA+45 ELITES ACADEM   RACE/REL
FORCES TOP/EX MURDER...JURID 20 CIV/RIGHTS   LAW
MISSISSIPP EVERS/MED CLEMSON. PAGE 32 E0638   DISCRIM

B64

DRESSLER D.,READINGS IN CRIMINOLOGY AND PENOLOGY.   CRIMLGY
UNIV CULTURE PUB/INST FORCES ACT/RES PROB/SOLV   CRIME
ANOMIE BIO/SOC SUPEGO...GEOG PSY ANTHOL 20. PAGE 33   ADJUD
E0648   ADJUST

B64

FRYDENSBERG P.,PEACE-KEEPING: EXPERIENCE AND   INT/ORG
EVALUATION: THE OSLO PAPERS. NORWAY FORCES PLAN   DIPLOM
CONTROL...INT/LAW 20 UN. PAGE 41 E0814   PEACE
                                                       COERCE

B64

GARDNER R.N.,IN PURSUIT OF WORLD ORDER* US FOREIGN   OBS
POLICY AND INTERNATIONAL ORGANIZATIONS. USA+45 USSR   INT/ORG
ECO/UNDEV FORCES LEGIS DIPLOM FOR/AID INT/TRADE   ALL/VALS
PEACE...INT/LAW PREDICT UN. PAGE 42 E0839

B64

GESELLSCHAFT RECHTSVERGLEICH,BIBLIOGRAPHIE DES   BIBLIOG/A
DEUTSCHEN RECHTS (BIBLIOGRAPHY OF GERMAN LAW,   JURID
TRANS. BY COURTLAND PETERSON). GERMANY FINAN INDUS   CONSTN
LABOR SECT FORCES CT/SYS PARL/PROC CRIME...INT/LAW   ADMIN
SOC NAT/COMP 20. PAGE 43 E0853

B64

GRIFFITH W.E.,THE SINO-SOVIET RIFT. ASIA CHINA/COM   ATTIT
COM CUBA USSR YUGOSLAVIA NAT/G POL/PAR VOL/ASSN   TIME/SEQ
DELIB/GP FORCES TOP/EX DIPLOM EDU/PROP DRIVE PERSON   BAL/PWR
PWR...TREND 20 TREATY. PAGE 47 E0941   SOCISM

B64

GRZYBOWSKI K.,THE SOCIALIST COMMONWEALTH OF   INT/LAW
NATIONS: ORGANIZATIONS AND INSTITUTIONS. FORCES   COM
DIPLOM INT/TRADE ADJUD ADMIN LEAD WAR MARXISM   REGION
SOCISM...BIBLIOG 20 COMECON WARSAW/P. PAGE 48 E0956   INT/ORG

B64

HEGEL G.W.,HEGEL'S POLITICAL WRITINGS (TRANS. BY   CONSTN
T.M. KNOX). GERMANY UK FINAN FORCES PARL/PROC   LEGIS
CHOOSE REPRESENT...BIOG 19. PAGE 51 E1022   JURID

B64

HEKHUIS D.J.,INTERNATIONAL STABILITY: MILITARY,   TEC/DEV
ECONOMIC AND POLITICAL DIMENSIONS. FUT WOR+45 LAW   DETER
ECO/UNDEV INT/ORG NAT/G VOL/ASSN FORCES ACT/RES   REGION
BAL/PWR PWR WEALTH...STAT UN 20. PAGE 51 E1024

B64

LOCKHART W.B.,CASES AND MATERIALS ON CONSTITUTIONAL   ORD/FREE
RIGHTS AND LIBERTIES. USA+45 FORCES LEGIS DIPLOM   CONSTN
PRESS CONTROL CRIME WAR PWR...AUD/VIS T WORSHIP 20   NAT/G
NEGRO. PAGE 66 E1317

B64

MARSHALL B.,FEDERALISM AND CIVIL RIGHTS. USA+45   FEDERAL
PROVS BAL/PWR CONTROL CT/SYS PARTIC SOVEREIGN   ORD/FREE
...JURID 20 NEGRO CIV/RIGHTS. PAGE 68 E1369   CONSTN
                                                       FORCES

B64

NEWMAN E.S.,POLICE, THE LAW, AND PERSONAL FREEDOM.   JURID
USA+45 CONSTN JUDGE CT/SYS CRIME PERS/REL RESPECT   FORCES
...CRIMLGY 20. PAGE 77 E1542   ORD/FREE
                                                       ADJUD

B64

NEWMAN E.S.,CIVIL LIBERTY AND CIVIL RIGHTS. USA+45   ORD/FREE
USA-45 CONSTN PROVS FORCES LEGIS CT/SYS RACE/REL   LAW
ATTIT...MAJORIT JURID WORSHIP 20 SUPREME/CT NEGRO   CONTROL
CIV/RIGHTS CHURCH/STA. PAGE 77 E1543   NAT/G

B64

OPPENHEIMER M.,A MANUAL FOR DIRECT ACTION. USA+45   PLAN
SCHOOL FORCES ADJUD CT/SYS SUFF RACE/REL DISCRIM   VOL/ASSN
...POLICY CHARTS 20. PAGE 79 E1580   JURID
                                                       LEAD

B64

REGALA R.,WORLD PEACE THROUGH DIPLOMACY AND LAW.   DIPLOM
S/ASIA WOR+45 ECO/UNDEV INT/ORG FORCES PLAN   PEACE
PROB/SOLV FOR/AID NUC/PWR WAR...POLICY INT/LAW 20.   ADJUD
PAGE 84 E1679

B64

RUSSELL R.B.,UNITED NATIONS EXPERIENCE WITH   FORCES
MILITARY FORCES: POLITICAL AND LEGAL ASPECTS. AFR   DIPLOM
KOREA WOR+45 LEGIS PROB/SOLV ADMIN CONTROL   SANCTION
EFFICIENCY PEACE...POLICY INT/LAW BIBLIOG UN.   ORD/FREE
PAGE 87 E1738

B64

SCHWARTZ M.D.,CONFERENCE ON SPACE SCIENCE AND SPACE   SPACE
LAW. FUT COM/IND NAT/G FORCES ACT/RES PLAN BUDGET   LAW
DIPLOM NUC/PWR WEAPON...POLICY ANTHOL 20. PAGE 89   PEACE
E1788   TEC/DEV

B64

TAUBENFELD H.J.,SPACE AND SOCIETY. USA+45 LAW   SPACE
FORCES CREATE TEC/DEV ADJUD CONTROL COST PEACE   SOCIETY
...PREDICT ANTHOL 20. PAGE 95 E1911   ADJUST
                                                       DIPLOM

B64

WILLIAMS S.P.,TOWARD A GENUINE WORLD SECURITY   BIBLIOG/A
SYSTEM (PAMPHLET). WOR+45 INT/ORG FORCES PLAN   ARMS/CONT
NUC/PWR ORD/FREE...INT/LAW CONCPT UN PRESIDENT.   DIPLOM
PAGE 106 E2123   PEACE

L64

POUNDS N.J.G.,"THE POLITICS OF PARTITION." AFR ASIA   NAT/G
COM EUR+WWI FUT ISLAM S/ASIA USA-45 LAW ECO/DEV   NAT/LISM
ECO/UNDEV AGRI INDUS INT/ORG POL/PAR PROVS SECT
FORCES TOP/EX EDU/PROP LEGIT ATTIT MORAL ORD/FREE
PWR RESPECT WEALTH. PAGE 82 E1640

S64

GARDNER R.N.,"THE SOVIET UNION AND THE UNITED   COM
NATIONS." WOR+45 FINAN POL/PAR VOL/ASSN FORCES   INT/ORG
ECO/TAC DOMIN EDU/PROP LEGIT ADJUD ADMIN ARMS/CONT   USSR
COERCE ATTIT ALL/VALS...POLICY MAJORIT CONCPT OBS
TIME/SEQ TREND STERTYP UN. PAGE 42 E0838

S64

GREENBERG S.,"JUDAISM AND WORLD JUSTICE." MEDIT-7   SECT
WOR+45 LAW CULTURE SOCIETY INT/ORG NAT/G FORCES   JURID
EDU/PROP ATTIT DRIVE PERSON SUPEGO ALL/VALS   PEACE
...POLICY PSY CONCPT GEN/LAWS JEWS. PAGE 46 E0908

S64

KARPOV P.V.,"PEACEFUL COEXISTENCE AND INTERNATIONAL   COM
LAW." WOR+45 LAW SOCIETY INT/ORG VOL/ASSN FORCES   ATTIT
CREATE CAP/ISM DIPLOM ADJUD NUC/PWR PEACE MORAL   INT/LAW
ORD/FREE PWR MARXISM...MARXIST JURID CONCPT OBS   USSR
TREND COLD/WAR MARX/KARL 20. PAGE 59 E1186

S64

KHAN M.Z.,"ISLAM AND INTERNATIONAL RELATIONS." FUT   ISLAM
WOR+45 LAW CULTURE SOCIETY NAT/G SECT DELIB/GP   INT/ORG
FORCES EDU/PROP ATTIT PERSON SUPEGO ALL/VALS   DIPLOM
...POLICY PSY CONCPT MYTH HIST/WRIT GEN/LAWS.
PAGE 61 E1211

S64

MAGGS P.B.,"SOVIET VIEWPOINT ON NUCLEAR WEAPONS IN   COM
INTERNATIONAL LAW." USSR WOR+45 INT/ORG FORCES   LAW
DIPLOM ARMS/CONT ATTIT ORD/FREE PWR...POLICY JURID   INT/LAW
CONCPT OBS TREND CON/ANAL GEN/LAWS VAL/FREE 20.   NUC/PWR
PAGE 67 E1347

B65

MISSISSIPPI BLACK PAPER: (FIFTY-SEVEN NEGRO AND   COERCE
WHITE CITIZENS' TESTIMONY OF POLICE BRUTALITY...).   RACE/REL
USA+45 LAW SOCIETY CT/SYS SANCTION CRIME MORAL   DISCRIM
ORD/FREE RESPECT 20 NEGRO. PAGE 2 E0035   FORCES

B65

ASSOCIATION BAR OF NYC,RADIO, TELEVISION, AND THE   AUD/VIS
ADMINISTRATION OF JUSTICE: A DOCUMENTED SURVEY OF   ATTIT
MATERIALS. USA+45 DELIB/GP FORCES PRESS ADJUD   ORD/FREE
CONTROL CT/SYS CRIME...INT IDEA/COMP BIBLIOG.
PAGE 6 E0109

BERKOWITZ M.,AMERICAN NATIONAL SECURITY: A READER IN THEORY AND POLICY. USA+45 INT/ORG FORCES BAL/PWR DIPLOM ECO/TAC DETER PWR...INT/LAW ANTHOL BIBLIOG 20 UN. PAGE 11 E0203
ORD/FREE WAR ARMS/CONT POLICY
B65

EHLE J.,THE FREE MEN. USA+45 NAT/G PROVS FORCES JUDGE ADJUD ATTIT...POLICY SOC SOC/INTEG 20 NEGRO. PAGE 34 E0677
RACE/REL ORD/FREE DISCRIM
B65

HOWE R.,THE STORY OF SCOTLAND YARD: A HISTORY OF THE CID FROM THE EARLIEST TIMES TO THE PRESENT DAY. UK MUNIC EDU/PROP 6/20 SCOT/YARD. PAGE 55 E1104
CRIMLGY CRIME FORCES ADMIN
B65

IANNIELLO L.,MILESTONES ALONG THE MARCH: TWELVE HISTORIC CIVIL RIGHTS DOCUMENTS--FROM WORLD WAR II TO SELMA. USA+45 LAW FORCES TOP/EX PARTIC SUFF...T 20 NEGRO CIV/RIGHTS TRUMAN/HS SUPREME/CT KENNEDY/JF. PAGE 56 E1121
RACE/REL DISCRIM CONSTN NAT/G
B65

KAMISAR Y.,CRIMINAL JUSTICE IN OUR TIME. USA+45 FORCES JUDGE PROB/SOLV COERCE MORAL 20 CIVIL/LIB CIV/RIGHTS. PAGE 59 E1182
ORD/FREE CRIME CT/SYS LAW
B65

LASLEY J.,THE WAR SYSTEM AND YOU. LAW FORCES ARMS/CONT NUC/PWR NAT/LISM ATTIT...MAJORIT IDEA/COMP UN WORSHIP. PAGE 63 E1261
MORAL PERSON DIPLOM WAR
B65

MILLIS W.,AN END TO ARMS. LAW INT/ORG FORCES ACT/RES CREATE DIPLOM WAR...POLICY HUM NEW/IDEA HYPO/EXP. PAGE 73 E1462
FUT PWR ARMS/CONT ORD/FREE
B65

NORDEN A.,WAR AND NAZI CRIMINALS IN WEST GERMANY: STATE, ECONOMY, ADMINISTRATION, ARMY, JUSTICE, SCIENCE. GERMANY GERMANY/W MOD/EUR ECO/DEV ACADEM EX/STRUC FORCES DOMIN ADMIN CT/SYS...POLICY MAJORIT PACIFIST 20. PAGE 77 E1554
FASCIST WAR NAT/G TOP/EX
B65

O'BRIEN W.V.,THE NEW NATIONS IN INTERNATIONAL LAW AND DIPLOMACY* THE YEAR BOOK OF WORLD POLITY* VOLUME III. USA+45 ECO/UNDEV INT/ORG FORCES DIPLOM COLONIAL NEUTRAL REV NAT/LISM ATTIT RESPECT. PAGE 78 E1565
INT/LAW CULTURE SOVEREIGN ANTHOL
B65

SWISHER C.B.,THE SUPREME COURT IN MODERN ROLE. COM COM/IND NAT/G FORCES LEGIS LOBBY PARTIC RACE/REL 20 SUPREME/CT. PAGE 95 E1901
DELIB/GP CT/SYS ADJUD
B65

FOX A.B.,"NATO AND CONGRESS." CONSTN DELIB/GP EX/STRUC FORCES TOP/EX BUDGET NUC/PWR GOV/REL ...GP/COMP CONGRESS NATO TREATY. PAGE 39 E0779
CONTROL DIPLOM
S65

KHOURI F.J.,"THE JORDON RIVER CONTROVERSY." LAW SOCIETY ECO/UNDEV AGRI FINAN INDUS SECT FORCES ACT/RES PLAN TEC/DEV ECO/TAC EDU/PROP COERCE ATTIT DRIVE PERCEPT RIGID/FLEX ALL/VALS...GEOG SOC MYTH WORK. PAGE 61 E1212
ISLAM INT/ORG ISRAEL JORDAN
S65

LUSKY L.,"FOUR PROBLEMS IN LAWMAKING FOR PEACE." FORCES LEGIS CREATE ADJUD COERCE WAR MAJORITY PEACE PWR. PAGE 67 E1334
ORD/FREE INT/LAW UTOPIA RECORD
S65

MERRITT R.L.,"SELECTED ARTICLES AND DOCUMENTS ON INTERNATIONAL LAW AND RELATIONS." WOR+45 INT/ORG FORCES INT/TRADE. PAGE 72 E1443
BIBLIOG DIPLOM INT/LAW GOV/REL
S65

WRIGHT Q.,"THE ESCALATION OF INTERNATIONAL CONFLICTS." WOR+45 WOR-45 FORCES DIPLOM RISK COST ATTIT ALL/VALS...INT/LAW QUANT STAT NAT/COMP. PAGE 108 E2160
WAR PERCEPT PREDICT MATH
S65

AARON T.J.,THE CONTROL OF POLICE DISCRETION: THE DANISH EXPERIENCE. DENMARK LAW CREATE ADMIN
CONTROL FORCES
B66

INGP/REL SUPEGO PWR 20 OMBUDSMAN. PAGE 2 E0042
REPRESENT PROB/SOLV
B66

BUTTERFIELD H.,DIPLOMATIC INVESTIGATIONS* ESSAYS IN THE THEORY OF INTERNATIONAL POLITICS. LAW INT/ORG FORCES BAL/PWR ARMS/CONT WAR ALL/VALS...HUM INT/LAW. PAGE 18 E0351
GEN/LAWS UK DIPLOM
B66

CLARK G.,WORLD PEACE THROUGH WORLD LAW; TWO ALTERNATIVE PLANS. WOR+45 DELIB/GP FORCES TAX CONFER ADJUD SANCTION ARMS/CONT WAR CHOOSE PRIVIL 20 UN COLD/WAR. PAGE 23 E0450
INT/LAW PEACE PLAN INT/ORG
B66

DALLIN A.,POLITICS IN THE SOVIET UNION: 7 CASES. COM USSR LAW POL/PAR CHIEF FORCES WRITING CONTROL PARL/PROC CIVMIL/REL TOTALISM...ANTHOL 20 KHRUSH/N STALIN/J CASEBOOK COM/PARTY. PAGE 28 E0563
MARXISM DOMIN ORD/FREE GOV/REL
B66

EPSTEIN F.T.,THE AMERICAN BIBLIOGRAPHY OF RUSSIAN AND EAST EUROPEAN STUDIES FOR 1964. USSR LOC/G NAT/G POL/PAR FORCES ADMIN ARMS/CONT...JURID CONCPT 20 UN. PAGE 35 E0694
BIBLIOG COM MARXISM DIPLOM
B66

FRIED R.C.,COMPARATIVE POLITICAL INSTITUTIONS. USSR EX/STRUC FORCES LEGIS JUDGE CONTROL REPRESENT ALL/IDEOS 20 CONGRESS BUREAUCRCY. PAGE 40 E0798
NAT/G PWR EFFICIENCY GOV/COMP
B66

OBERMANN E.,VERTEIDIGUNG PER FREIHEIT. GERMANY/W WOR+45 INT/ORG COERCE NUC/PWR WEAPON MARXISM 20 UN NATO WARSAW/P TREATY. PAGE 78 E1571
FORCES ORD/FREE WAR PEACE
B66

OSTERMANN R.,A REPORT IN DEPTH ON CRIME IN AMERICA. FUT USA+45 MUNIC PUB/INST TEC/DEV MURDER EFFICIENCY ATTIT BIO/SOC...PSY 20. PAGE 79 E1584
CRIME FORCES CONTROL LAW
B66

SKOLNICK J.H.,JUSTICE WITHOUT TRIAL: LAW ENFORCEMENT IN DEMOCRATIC SOCIETY. USA+45 LAW TRIBUTE RACE/REL BIO/SOC PERSON...PSY SOC 20 NEGRO BUREAUCRCY PROSTITUTN. PAGE 92 E1836
FORCES CRIMLGY CRIME
B66

US DEPARTMENT OF STATE,RESEARCH ON WESTERN EUROPE, GREAT BRITAIN, AND CANADA (EXTERNAL RESEARCH LIST NO 3-25). CANADA GERMANY/W UK LAW CULTURE NAT/G POL/PAR FORCES EDU/PROP REGION MARXISM...GEOG SOC WORSHIP 20 CMN/WLTH. PAGE 100 E1998
BIBLIOG/A EUR+WWI DIPLOM
B66

US PRES COMN CRIME IN DC,REPORT OF THE US PRESIDENT'S COMMISSION ON CRIME IN THE DISTRICT OF COLUMBIA. LEGIS WORKER EDU/PROP ADJUD CONTROL CT/SYS GP/REL BIO/SOC HEALTH...CRIMLGY NEW/IDEA STAT 20. PAGE 101 E2022
CRIME FORCES AGE/Y SANCTION
B66

US SENATE COMM AERO SPACE SCI,SOVIET SPACE PROGRAMS, 1962-65; GOALS AND PURPOSES, ACHIEVEMENTS, PLANS, AND INTERNATIONAL IMPLICATIONS. USA+45 USSR R+D FORCES PLAN EDU/PROP PRESS ADJUD ARMS/CONT ATTIT MARXISM. PAGE 101 E2028
CONSULT SPACE FUT DIPLOM
B66

GREIG D.W.,"THE ADVISORY JURISDICTION OF THE INTERNATIONAL COURT AND THE SETTLEMENT OF DISPUTES BETWEEN STATES." ISRAEL KOREA FORCES BUDGET DOMIN LEGIT ADJUD COST...RECORD UN CONGO/LEOP TREATY. PAGE 46 E0915
INT/LAW CT/SYS
L66

BROWNLIE I.,"NUCLEAR PROLIFERATION* SOME PROBLEMS OF CONTROL." USA+45 USSR ECO/UNDEV INT/ORG FORCES TEC/DEV REGION CONSEN...RECORD TREATY. PAGE 16 E0318
NUC/PWR ARMS/CONT VOL/ASSN ORD/FREE
S66

FINE R.I.,"PEACE-KEEPING COSTS AND ARTICLE 19 OF THE UN CHARTER* AN INVITATION TO RESPONSIBILITY." INT/ORG NAT/G ADJUD CT/SYS CHOOSE CONSEN...RECORD IDEA/COMP UN. PAGE 38 E0750
FORCES COST CONSTN
S66

BLAISDELL D.C.,"INTERNATIONAL ORGANIZATION." FUT WOR+45 ECO/DEV DELIB/GP FORCES EFFICIENCY PEACE ORD/FREE...INT/LAW 20 UN LEAGUE/NAT NATO. PAGE 12 E0239
BIBLIOG INT/ORG DIPLOM ARMS/CONT
C66

AMDS W.E.,DELINQUENCY PREVENTION: THEORY AND PRACTICE. USA+45 SOCIETY FAM SCHOOL SECT FORCES PROB/SOLV...HEAL JURID PREDICT ANTHOL. PAGE 4 E0071
AGE/Y CRIME PUB/INST LAW
B67

ASCH S.H.,POLICE AUTHORITY AND THE RIGHTS OF THE INDIVIDUAL. CONSTN DOMIN ADJUD CT/SYS...JURID 20. PAGE 6 E0106
FORCES OP/RES ORD/FREE
B67

BOULTON D.,OBJECTION OVERRULED. UK LAW POL/PAR DIPLOM ADJUD SANCTION DEATH WAR CIVMIL/REL 20. PAGE 14 E0273
FORCES SOCISM SECT
B67

HEWITT W.H.,ADMINISTRATION OF CRIMINAL JUSTICE IN NEW YORK. LAW PROB/SOLV ADJUD ADMIN...CRIMLGY CHARTS T 20 NEW/YORK. PAGE 52 E1035
CRIME ROLE CT/SYS FORCES
B67

LENG S.C.,JUSTICE IN COMMUNIST CHINA: A SURVEY OF THE JUDICIAL SYSTEM OF THE CHINESE PEOPLE'S REPUBLIC. CHINA/COM LAW CONSTN LOC/G NAT/G PROF/ORG CONSULT FORCES ADMIN CRIME ORD/FREE...BIBLIOG 20 MAO. PAGE 64 E1284
CT/SYS ADJUD JURID MARXISM
B67

MCBRIDE J.H.,THE TEST BAN TREATY: MILITARY, TECHNOLOGICAL, AND POLITICAL IMPLICATIONS. USA+45 USSR DELIB/GP FORCES LEGIS TEC/DEV BAL/PWR TREATY. PAGE 70 E1399
ARMS/CONT DIPLOM NUC/PWR
B67

PADELFORD N.J.,THE DYNAMICS OF INTERNATIONAL POLITICS (2ND ED.). WOR+45 LAW INT/ORG FORCES TEC/DEV REGION NAT/LISM PEACE ATTIT PWR ALL/IDEOS UN COLD/WAR NATO TREATY. PAGE 79 E1589
DIPLOM NAT/G POLICY DECISION
B67

POGANY A.H.,POLITICAL SCIENCE AND INTERNATIONAL RELATIONS, BOOKS RECOMMENDED FOR AMERICAN CATHOLIC COLLEGE LIBRARIES. INT/ORG LOC/G NAT/G FORCES BAL/PWR ECO/TAC NUC/PWR...CATH INT/LAW TREATY 20. PAGE 81 E1622
BIBLIOG DIPLOM
B67

RUSSELL B.,WAR CRIMES IN VIETNAM. USA+45 VIETNAM FORCES DIPLOM WEAPON RACE/REL DISCRIM ISOLAT BIO/SOC 20 COLD/WAR RUSSELL/B. PAGE 87 E1736
WAR CRIME ATTIT POLICY
B67

US SENATE COMM ON FOREIGN REL,TREATY ON OUTER SPACE. WOR+45 AIR FORCES PROB/SOLV NUC/PWR SENATE TREATY UN. PAGE 101 E2032
SPACE DIPLOM ARMS/CONT LAW
B67

US SENATE COMM ON FOREIGN REL,A SELECT CHRONOLOGY AND BACKGROUND DOCUMENTS RELATING TO THE MIDDLE EAST. ISRAEL UAR LAW INT/ORG FORCES PROB/SOLV CONFER CONSEN PEACE ATTIT...POLICY 20 UN SENATE TRUMAN/HS. PAGE 101 E2033
ISLAM TIME/SEQ DIPLOM
B67

US SENATE COMM ON FOREIGN REL,UNITED STATES ARMAMENT AND DISARMAMENT PROBLEMS. USA+45 AIR BAL/PWR DIPLOM FOR/AID NUC/PWR ORD/FREE SENATE TREATY. PAGE 102 E2035
ARMS/CONT WEAPON FORCES PROB/SOLV
B67

WATT A.,THE EVOLUTION OF AUSTRALIAN FOREIGN POLICY 1938-65. ASIA S/ASIA USA+45 USA-45 INT/ORG NAT/G FORCES FOR/AID TREATY 20 AUSTRAL. PAGE 105 E2103
DIPLOM WAR
B67

LEGAULT A.,"ORGANISATION ET CONDUITE DES OPERATIONS DE MAINTIEN DE LA PAIX." FORCES ACT/RES ADJUD AGREE CONTROL NEUTRAL TASK PRIVIL ORD/FREE 20 UN. PAGE 64 E1279
INT/ORG PEACE WAR INT/LAW
L67

ADOKO A.,"THE CONSTITUTION OF UGANDA." AFR UGANDA LOC/G CHIEF FORCES LEGIS ADJUD EXEC CHOOSE NAT/LISM ...IDEA/COMP 20. PAGE 3 E0050
NAT/G CONSTN ORD/FREE LAW
S67

ALDRICH W.A.,"THE SUEZ CRISIS." UAR UK USA+45 DELIB/GP FORCES BAL/PWR INT/TRADE CONFER CONTROL COERCE DETER 20. PAGE 3 E0058
DIPLOM INT/LAW COLONIAL
S67

BLUMSTEIN A.,"POLICE TECHNOLOGY." USA+45 DELIB/GP COMPUTER EDU/PROP CRIME COMPUT/IR. PAGE 13 E0253
TEC/DEV FORCES CRIMLGY ADJUD
S67

MC REYNOLDS D.,"THE RESISTANCE." USA+45 LAW ADJUD SANCTION INGP/REL PEACE 20. PAGE 70 E1398
ATTIT WAR LEGIT FORCES
S67

RAI H.,"DISTRICT MAGISTRATE AND POLICE SUPERINTENDENT IN INDIA: THE CONTROVERSY OF DUAL CONTROL" INDIA LAW PROVS ADMIN PWR 19/20. PAGE 83 E1669
STRUCT CONTROL ROLE FORCES
S67

SCHELLING T.C.,"ECONOMICS AND CRIMINAL ENTERPRISE." LAW FORCES BARGAIN ECO/TAC CONTROL GAMBLE ROUTINE ADJUST DEMAND INCOME PROFIT CRIMLGY. PAGE 87 E1756
CRIME PROB/SOLV CONCPT
S67

HULL R.H.,LAW AND VIETNAM. COM VIETNAM CONSTN INT/ORG FORCES DIPLOM AGREE COERCE DETER WEAPON PEACE ATTIT 20 UN TREATY. PAGE 56 E1113
POLICY LAW WAR INT/LAW
B68

PLAYFAIR R.L.,"A BIBLIOGRAPHY OF MOROCCO." MOROCCO CULTURE AGRI FORCES DIPLOM WAR HEALTH...GEOG JURID SOC CHARTS. PAGE 81 E1620
BIBLIOG ISLAM MEDIT-7
C93

SMITH A.,LECTURES ON JUSTICE, POLICE, REVENUE AND ARMS (1763). UK LAW FAM FORCES TARIFFS AGREE COERCE INCOME OWN WEALTH LAISSEZ...GEN/LAWS 17/18. PAGE 92 E1840
DIPLOM JURID OLD/LIB TAX
B96

FORD FOUNDATION....SEE FORD/FOUND

FORD/FOUND....FORD FOUNDATION

FOREIGN AID....SEE FOR/AID

FOREIGN TRADE....SEE INT/TRADE

FOREIGNREL....UNITED STATES SENATE COMMITTEE ON FOREIGN RELATIONS

FORGAC A.A. E0770

FORGN/SERV....FOREIGN SERVICE

FORMOSA....FORMOSA, PRE-1949; SEE ALSO ASIA

FORSTER A. E0771

FORTE W.E. E0772

FORTES A.B. E0773

FORTESCU J. E0774

FORTESCUE G.K. E0775

FORTESCUE J. E0776

FORTRAN....FORTRAN - COMPUTER LANGUAGE

FOSTER H.H. E0572

FOSTER J.W. E0777

FOSTER/G....G. FOSTER

FOUAD M. E0778

FOURIER/FM....FRANCOIS MARIE CHARLES FOURIER

FOX A.B. E0779

FOX H. E1829

FOX W.T.R. E0780

FOX/CJ....CHARLES J. FOX

FOX/INDIAN....FOX INDIANS

FPC....U.S. FEDERAL POWER COMMISSION

FRAENKEL H. E1364

FRAENKEL O.K. E0781,E0782

FRAGA IRIBARNE M. E0783

FRANCE....SEE ALSO APPROPRIATE TIME/SPACE/CULTURE INDEX

N
CATHERINE R.,LA REVUE ADMINISTRATIVE. FRANCE LAW   ADMIN
NAT/G LEGIS...JURID BIBLIOG/A 20. PAGE 21 E0407   MGT
                                                    FINAN
                                                    METH/COMP

N
MINISTERE DE L'EDUC NATIONALE,CATALOGUE DES THESES   BIBLIOG
DE DOCTORAT SOUTENNES DEVANT LES UNIVERSITAIRES   ACADEM
FRANCAISES. FRANCE LAW DIPLOM ADMIN...HUM SOC 20.   KNOWL
PAGE 73 E1465   NAT/G

B*
LALL A.S.,NEGOTIATING DISARMAMENT* THE EIGHTEEN   OBS
NATION DISARMAMENT CONFERENCE* THE FIRST TWO YEARS, ARMS/CONT
1962-1964. ASIA FRANCE INDIA USA+45 USSR PROB/SOLV   DIPLOM
ADJUD NEUTRAL ATTIT...IDEA/COMP COLD/WAR. PAGE 62   OP/RES
E1246

B00
GRIFFIN A.P.C.,LIST OF BOOKS RELATING TO THE THEORY BIBLIOG/A
OF COLONIZATION, GOVERNMENT OF DEPENDENCIES,   COLONIAL
PROTECTORATES, AND RELATED TOPICS. FRANCE GERMANY   GOV/REL
ITALY SPAIN UK USA-45 WOR-45 ECO/TAC ADMIN CONTROL   DOMIN
REGION NAT/LISM ALL/VALS PWR...INT/LAW SOC 16/19.
PAGE 46 E0917

L00
HISTORICUS,"LETTERS AND SOME QUESTIONS OF   WEALTH
INTERNATIONAL LAW." FRANCE NETHERLAND UK USA-45   JURID
WOR-45 LAW NAT/G COERCE...SOC CONCPT GEN/LAWS   WAR
TOT/POP 19 CIVIL/WAR. PAGE 53 E1054   INT/LAW

B02
GRIFFIN A.P.C.,A LIST OF BOOKS RELATING TO TRUSTS   BIBLIOG/A
(2ND REV. ED.) (PAMPHLET). FRANCE GERMANY UK USA-45 JURID
WOR-45 LAW ECO/DEV INDUS LG/CO NAT/G CAP/ISM   ECO/TAC
CENTRAL DISCRIM PWR LAISSEZ 19/20. PAGE 46 E0919   VOL/ASSN

B03
FAGUET E.,LE LIBERALISME. FRANCE PRESS ADJUD ADMIN   ORD/FREE
DISCRIM CONSERVE SOCISM...TRADIT SOC LING WORSHIP   EDU/PROP
PARLIAMENT. PAGE 36 E0711   NAT/G
                                                    LAW

B03
GRIFFIN A.P.C.,SELECT LIST OF BOOKS ON LABOR   BIBLIOG/A
PARTICULARLY RELATING TO STRIKES. FRANCE GERMANY   GP/REL
MOD/EUR UK USA-45 LAW NAT/G DELIB/GP WORKER BARGAIN MGT
LICENSE PAY ADJUD 19/20. PAGE 46 E0924   LABOR

B03
MOREL E.D.,THE BRITISH CASE IN FRENCH CONGO.   DIPLOM
CONGO/BRAZ FRANCE UK COERCE MORAL WEALTH...POLICY   INT/TRADE
INT/LAW 20 CONGO/LEOP. PAGE 74 E1490   COLONIAL
                                                    AFR

B06
GRIFFIN A.P.C.,LIST OF BOOKS RELATING TO CHILD   BIBLIOG/A
LABOR (PAMPHLET). BELGIUM FRANCE GERMANY MOD/EUR UK LABOR
USA-45 ECO/DEV INDUS WORKER CAP/ISM PAY ROUTINE   AGE/C
ALL/IDEOS...MGT SOC 19/20. PAGE 47 E0929

B08
GRIFFIN A.P.C.,LIST OF REFERENCES ON INTERNATIONAL   BIBLIOG/A
ARBITRATION. FRANCE L/A+17C USA-45 WOR-45 DIPLOM   INT/ORG
CONFER COLONIAL ARMS/CONT BAL/PAY EQUILIB SOVEREIGN INT/LAW
...DECISION 19/20 MEXIC/AMER. PAGE 47 E0932   DELIB/GP

B08
GRIFFIN A.P.C.,LIST OF WORKS RELATING TO GOVERNMENT BIBLIOG/A
REGULATION OF INSURANCE UNITED STATES AND FOREIGN   FINAN
COUNTRIES (2ND. ED.) (PAMPHLET). FRANCE GERMANY UK   LAW
USA-45 WOR-45 LG/CO LOC/G NAT/G LEGIS LICENSE ADJUD CONTROL
LOBBY CENTRAL ORD/FREE 19/20. PAGE 47 E0933

B09
LOBINGIER C.S.,THE PEOPLE'S LAW OR POPULAR   CONSTN
PARTICIPATION IN LAW-MAKING. FRANCE SWITZERLND UK   LAW
LOC/G NAT/G PROVS LEGIS SUFF MAJORITY PWR POPULISM   PARTIC
...GOV/COMP BIBLIOG 19. PAGE 66 E1314

B16
CARLYLE A.J.,BIBLIOGRAPHY OF POLITICAL THEORY   BIBLIOG/A
(PAMPHLET). FRANCE GERMANY UK USA-45...JURID 9/19.   CONCPT
PAGE 19 E0382   PHIL/SCI

B18
WILSON W.,THE STATE: ELEMENTS OF HISTORICAL AND   NAT/G
PRACTICAL POLITICS. FRANCE GERMANY ITALY UK USSR   JURID

CONSTN EX/STRUC LEGIS CT/SYS WAR PWR...POLICY   CONCPT
GOV/COMP 20. PAGE 106 E2131   NAT/COMP

N19
COUTROT A.,THE FIGHT OVER THE 1959 PRIVATE   SCHOOL
EDUCATION LAW IN FRANCE (PAMPHLET). FRANCE NAT/G   PARL/PROC
SECT GIVE EDU/PROP GP/REL ATTIT RIGID/FLEX ORD/FREE CATHISM
20 CHURCH/STA. PAGE 27 E0527   LAW

B23
DE MONTESQUIEU C.,THE SPIRIT OF LAWS (2 VOLS.)   JURID
(TRANS. BY THOMAS NUGENT). FRANCE FINAN SECT   LAW
INT/TRADE TAX COERCE REV DISCRIM HABITAT ORD/FREE   CONCPT
19 ALEMBERT/J CIVIL/LAW. PAGE 30 E0588   GEN/LAWS

B29
LEITZ F.,DIE PUBLIZITAT DER AKTIENGESELLSCHAFT.   LG/CO
BELGIUM FRANCE GERMANY UK FINAN PRESS GP/REL PROFIT JURID
KNOWL 20. PAGE 64 E1282   ECO/TAC
                                                    NAT/COMP

B31
BORCHARD E.H.,GUIDE TO THE LAW AND LEGAL LITERATURE BIBLIOG/A
OF FRANCE. FRANCE FINAN INDUS LABOR SECT LEGIS   LAW
ADMIN COLONIAL CRIME OWN...INT/LAW 20. PAGE 14   CONSTN
E0266   METH

B32
EAGLETON C.,INTERNATIONAL GOVERNMENT. BRAZIL FRANCE INT/ORG
GERMANY ITALY UK USSR WOR-45 DELIB/GP TOP/EX PLAN   JURID
ECO/TAC EDU/PROP LEGIT ADJUD REGION ARMS/CONT   DIPLOM
COERCE ATTIT PWR...GEOG MGT VAL/FREE LEAGUE/NAT 20. INT/LAW
PAGE 34 E0670

B32
MASTERS R.D.,INTERNATIONAL LAW IN INTERNATIONAL   INT/ORG
COURTS. BELGIUM EUR+WWI FRANCE GERMANY MOD/EUR   LAW
SWITZERLND WOR-45 SOCIETY STRATA STRUCT LEGIT EXEC   INT/LAW
ALL/VALS...JURID HIST/WRIT TIME/SEQ TREND GEN/LAWS
20. PAGE 69 E1383

B33
ENSOR R.C.K.,COURTS AND JUDGES IN FRANCE, GERMANY,   CT/SYS
AND ENGLAND. FRANCE GERMANY UK LAW PROB/SOLV ADMIN   EX/STRUC
ROUTINE CRIME ROLE...METH/COMP 20 CIVIL/LAW.   ADJUD
PAGE 35 E0692   NAT/COMP

B33
REID H.D.,RECUEIL DES COURS: TOME 45: LES   ORD/FREE
SERVITUDES INTERNATIONALES III. FRANCE CONSTN   DIPLOM
DELIB/GP PRESS CONTROL REV WAR CHOOSE PEACE MORAL   LAW
MARITIME TREATY. PAGE 84 E1680

B39
SIEYES E.J.,LES DISCOURS DE SIEYES DANS LES DEBATS   CONSTN
CONSTITUTIONNELS DE L'AN III (2 ET 18 THERMIDOR).   ADJUD
FRANCE LAW NAT/G PROB/SOLV BAL/PWR GOV/REL 18 JURY. LEGIS
PAGE 91 E1824   EX/STRUC

B40
WOLFERS A.,BRITAIN AND FRANCE BETWEEN TWO WORLD   DIPLOM
WARS. FRANCE UK INT/ORG NAT/G PLAN BARGAIN ECO/TAC   WAR
AGREE ISOLAT ALL/IDEOS...DECISION GEOG 20 TREATY   POLICY
VERSAILLES INTERVENT. PAGE 107 E2139

B42
CRAIG A.,ABOVE ALL LIBERTIES. FRANCE UK USA-45 LAW   ORD/FREE
CONSTN CULTURE INTELL NAT/G SECT JUDGE...IDEA/COMP   MORAL
BIBLIOG 18/20. PAGE 27 E0536   WRITING
                                                    EDU/PROP

C42
CRAIG A.,"ABOVE ALL LIBERTIES." FRANCE UK LAW   BIBLIOG/A
CULTURE INTELL SECT ORD/FREE 18/20. PAGE 27 E0537   EDU/PROP
                                                    WRITING
                                                    MORAL

B44
RUDIN H.R.,ARMISTICE 1918. FRANCE GERMANY MOD/EUR   AGREE
UK USA-45 NAT/G CHIEF DELIB/GP FORCES BAL/PWR REPAR WAR
ARMS/CONT 20 WILSON/W TREATY. PAGE 86 E1732   PEACE
                                                    DIPLOM

B44
SUAREZ F.,A TREATISE ON LAWS AND GOD THE LAWGIVER   LAW
(1612) IN SELECTIONS FROM THREE WORKS. VOL. II.   JURID
FRANCE ITALY UK CULTURE NAT/G SECT CHIEF LEGIS   GEN/LAWS
DOMIN LEGIT CT/SYS ORD/FREE PWR WORSHIP 16/17.   CATH
PAGE 94 E1892

B45
CONOVER H.F.,THE GOVERNMENTS OF THE MAJOR FOREIGN   BIBLIOG
POWERS: A BIBLIOGRAPHY. FRANCE GERMANY ITALY UK   NAT/G
USSR CONSTN LOC/G POL/PAR EX/STRUC FORCES ADMIN   DIPLOM
CT/SYS CIVMIL/REL TOTALISM...POLICY 19/20. PAGE 25
E0494

JACKSON R.H.,INTERNATIONAL CONFERENCE ON MILITARY DIPLOM B49
TRIALS. FRANCE GERMANY UK USA+45 USSR VOL/ASSN INT/ORG
DELIB/GP REPAR ADJUD CT/SYS CRIME WAR 20 WAR/TRIAL. INT/LAW
PAGE 57 E1141 CIVMIL/REL

WALINE M.,LE CONTROLE JURIDICTIONNEL DE JURID B49
L'ADMINISTRATION. BELGIUM FRANCE UAR JUDGE BAL/PWR ADMIN
ADJUD CONTROL CT/SYS...GP/COMP 20. PAGE 104 E2093 PWR
ORD/FREE

FERRELL R.H.,PEACE IN THEIR TIME. FRANCE UK USA-45 PEACE B52
INT/ORG NAT/G FORCES CREATE AGREE ARMS/CONT COERCE DIPLOM
WAR TREATY 20 WILSON/W LEAGUE/NAT BRIAND/A. PAGE 37
E0741

HAMSON C.J.,EXECUTIVE DISCRETION AND JUDICIAL ELITES B54
CONTROL; AN ASPECT OF THE FRENCH CONSEIL D'ETAT. ADJUD
EUR+WWI FRANCE MOD/EUR UK NAT/G EX/STRUC PARTIC NAT/COMP
CONSERVE...JURID BIBLIOG/A 18/20 SUPREME/CT.
PAGE 50 E0992

SCHWARTZ B.,FRENCH ADMINISTRATIVE LAW AND THE JURID B54
COMMON-LAW WORLD. FRANCE CULTURE LOC/G NAT/G PROVS LAW
DELIB/GP EX/STRUC LEGIS PROB/SOLV CT/SYS EXEC METH/COMP
GOV/REL...IDEA/COMP ENGLSH/LAW. PAGE 89 E1786 ADJUD

NICOLSON H.,"THE EVOLUTION OF DIPLOMATIC METHOD." RIGID/FLEX L54
CHRIST-17C EUR+WWI FRANCE FUT ITALY MEDIT-7 MOD/EUR METH/CNCPT
USA+45 USA-45 LAW NAT/G CREATE EDU/PROP LEGIT PEACE DIPLOM
ATTIT ORD/FREE RESPECT SOVEREIGN. PAGE 77 E1548

CHARMATZ J.P.,COMPARATIVE STUDIES IN COMMUNITY MARRIAGE B55
PROPERTY LAW. FRANCE USA+45...JURID GOV/COMP ANTHOL LAW
20. PAGE 22 E0424 OWN
MUNIC

MEYER P.,ADMINISTRATIVE ORGANIZATION: A COMPARATIVE ADMIN B57
STUDY OF THE ORGANIZATION OF PUBLIC ADMINISTRATION. METH/COMP
DENMARK FRANCE NORWAY SWEDEN UK USA+45 ELITES LOC/G NAT/G
CONSULT LEGIS ADJUD CONTROL LEAD PWR SKILL CENTRAL
DECISION. PAGE 72 E1449

CHARLES R.,LA JUSTICE EN FRANCE. FRANCE LAW CONSTN JURID B58
DELIB/GP CRIME 20. PAGE 21 E0422 ADMIN
CT/SYS
ADJUD

DUCLOUX L.,FROM BLACKMAIL TO TREASON. FRANCE PLAN COERCE B58
DIPLOM EDU/PROP PRESS RUMOR NAT/LISM...CRIMLGY 20. CRIME
PAGE 33 E0653 NAT/G
PWR

SISSON C.H.,THE SPIRIT OF BRITISH ADMINISTRATION GOV/COMP B59
AND SOME EUROPEAN COMPARISONS. FRANCE GERMANY/W ADMIN
SWEDEN UK LAW EX/STRUC INGP/REL EFFICIENCY ORD/FREE ELITES
...DECISION 20. PAGE 91 E1835 ATTIT

CHAPMAN B.,"THE FRENCH CONSEIL D'ETAT." FRANCE ADMIN S59
NAT/G CONSULT OP/RES PROB/SOLV PWR...OBS 20. LAW
PAGE 21 E0421 CT/SYS
LEGIS

COLLINS I.,"THE GOVERNMENT AND THE NEWSPAPER PRESS PRESS C59
IN FRANCE, 1814-1881. FRANCE LAW ADMIN CT/SYS ORD/FREE
...CON/ANAL BIBLIOG 19. PAGE 24 E0475 NAT/G
EDU/PROP

CASTBERG F.,FREEDOM OF SPEECH IN THE WEST. FRANCE ORD/FREE B60
GERMANY USA+45 USA-45 LAW CONSTN CHIEF PRESS SANCTION
DISCRIM...CONCPT 18/20. PAGE 21 E0406 ADJUD
NAT/COMP

DILEY A.V.,INTRODUCTION TO THE STUDY OF THE LAW OF CONSTN B60
THE CONSTITUTION. FRANCE UK USA+45 USA-45 CONSULT LAW
FORCES TAX ADMIN FEDERAL ORD/FREE SOVEREIGN LEGIS
...IDEA/COMP 20 ENGLSH/LAW CON/INTERP PARLIAMENT. GEN/LAWS
PAGE 32 E0627

DUMON F.,LA COMMUNAUTE FRANCO-AFRO-MALGACHE: SES JURID B60

ORIGINES, SES INSTITUTIONS, SON EVOLUTION. FRANCE INT/ORG
MADAGASCAR POL/PAR DIPLOM ADMIN ATTIT...TREND T 20. AFR
PAGE 33 E0657 CONSTN

PICKLES D.,THE FIFTH FRENCH REPUBLIC. ALGERIA CONSTN B60
FRANCE CHOOSE GOV/REL ATTIT CONSERVE...CHARTS 20 ADJUD
DEGAULLE/C. PAGE 80 E1615 NAT/G
EFFICIENCY

LAUTERPACHT E.,"THE SUEZ CANAL SETTLEMENT." FRANCE INT/ORG L60
ISLAM ISRAEL UAR UK BAL/PWR DIPLOM LEGIT...JURID LAW
GEN/LAWS ANTHOL SUEZ VAL/FREE 20. PAGE 63 E1263

BEDFORD S.,THE FACES OF JUSTICE: A TRAVELLER'S CT/SYS B61
REPORT. AUSTRIA FRANCE GERMANY/W SWITZERLND UK UNIV ORD/FREE
WOR+45 WOR-45 CULTURE PARTIC GOV/REL MORAL...JURID PERSON
OBS GOV/COMP 20. PAGE 9 E0174 LAW

GUIZOT F.P.G.,HISTORY OF THE ORIGIN OF LEGIS B61
REPRESENTATIVE GOVERNMENT IN EUROPE. CHRIST-17C REPRESENT
FRANCE MOD/EUR SPAIN UK LAW CHIEF FORCES POPULISM CONSTN
...MAJORIT TIME/SEQ GOV/COMP NAT/COMP 4/19 NAT/G
PARLIAMENT. PAGE 48 E0961

LA PONCE J.A.,THE GOVERNMENT OF THE FIFTH REPUBLIC: PWR B61
FRENCH POLITICAL PARTIES AND THE CONSTITUTION. POL/PAR
ALGERIA FRANCE LAW NAT/G DELIB/GP LEGIS ECO/TAC CONSTN
MARXISM SOCISM...CHARTS BIBLIOG/A 20 DEGAULLE/C. CHIEF
PAGE 62 E1243

DUROSELLE J.B.,HISTOIRE DIPLOMATIQUE DE 1919 A NOS DIPLOM B62
JOURS (3RD ED.). FRANCE INT/ORG CHIEF FORCES CONFER WOR+45
ARMS/CONT WAR PEACE ORD/FREE...T TREATY 20 WOR-45
COLD/WAR. PAGE 34 E0667

HENDERSON W.O.,THE GENESIS OF THE COMMON MARKET. ECO/DEV B62
EUR+WWI FRANCE MOD/EUR UK SEA COM/IND EXTR/IND INT/TRADE
COLONIAL DISCRIM...TIME/SEQ CHARTS BIBLIOG 18/20 DIPLOM
EEC TREATY. PAGE 52 E1030

MANGIN G.,"LES ACCORDS DE COOPERATION EN MATIERE DE INT/ORG S62
JUSTICE ENTRE LA FRANCE ET LES ETATS AFRICAINS ET LAW
MALGACHE." AFR ISLAM WOR+45 STRUCT ECO/UNDEV NAT/G FRANCE
DELIB/GP PERCEPT ALL/VALS...JURID MGT TIME/SEQ 20.
PAGE 68 E1356

VIGNES D.,"L'AUTORITE DES TRAITES INTERNATIONAUX EN STRUCT S62
DROIT INTERNE." EUR+WWI UNIV LAW CONSTN INTELL LEGIT
NAT/G POL/PAR DIPLOM ATTIT PERCEPT ALL/VALS FRANCE
...POLICY INT/LAW JURID CONCPT TIME/SEQ 20 TREATY.
PAGE 104 E2075

GOURNAY B.,PUBLIC ADMINISTRATION. FRANCE LAW CONSTN BIBLIOG/A B63
AGRI FINAN LABOR SCHOOL EX/STRUC CHOOSE...MGT ADMIN
METH/COMP 20. PAGE 45 E0894 NAT/G
LOC/G

ROSNER G.,THE UNITED NATIONS EMERGENCY FORCE. INT/ORG B63
FRANCE ISRAEL UAR UK WOR+45 CREATE WAR PEACE FORCES
ORD/FREE PWR...INT/LAW JURID HIST/WRIT TIME/SEQ UN.
PAGE 86 E1719

BOLGAR V.,"THE PUBLIC INTEREST: A JURISPRUDENTIAL CONCPT L63
AND COMPARATIVE OVERVIEW OF SYMPOSIUM ON ORD/FREE
FUNDAMENTAL CONCEPTS OF PUBLIC LAW" COM FRANCE CONTROL
GERMANY SWITZERLND LAW ADJUD ADMIN AGREE LAISSEZ NAT/COMP
...JURID GEN/LAWS 20 EUROPE/E. PAGE 14 E0264

BOUVIER-AJAM M.,MANUEL TECHNIQUE ET PRATIQUE DU MUNIC B64
MAIRE ET DES ELUS ET AGENTS COMMUNAUX. FRANCE LOC/G ADMIN
BUDGET CHOOSE GP/REL SUPEGO...JURID BIBLIOG 20 CHIEF
MAYOR COMMUNES. PAGE 14 E0274 NEIGH

DUBISSON M.,LA COUR INTERNATIONALE DE JUSTICE. CT/SYS B64
FRANCE LAW CONSTN JUDGE DOMIN ADJUD...INT/LAW INT/ORG
CLASSIF RECORD ORG/CHARTS UN. PAGE 33 E0651

WRIGHT G.,RURAL REVOLUTION IN FRANCE: THE PEASANTRY PWR B64
IN THE TWENTIETH CENTURY. EUR+WWI MOD/EUR LAW STRATA
CULTURE AGRI POL/PAR DELIB/GP LEGIS ECO/TAC FRANCE
EDU/PROP COERCE CHOOSE ATTIT RIGID/FLEX HEALTH REV

...STAT CENSUS CHARTS VAL/FREE 20. PAGE 107 E2148

                                                                    B65
CARTER G.M.,POLITICS IN EUROPE. EUR+WWI FRANCE   GOV/COMP
GERMANY/W UK USSR LAW CONSTN POL/PAR VOL/ASSN PRESS   OP/RES
LOBBY PWR...ANTHOL SOC/INTEG EEC. PAGE 20 E0399   ECO/DEV

                                                                    B65
CHARNAY J.P.,LE SUFFRAGE POLITIQUE EN FRANCE;   CHOOSE
ELECTIONS PARLEMENTAIRES, ELECTION PRESIDENTIELLE,   SUFF
REFERENDUMS. FRANCE CONSTN CHIEF DELIB/GP ECO/TAC   NAT/G
EDU/PROP CRIME INGP/REL MORAL ORD/FREE PWR CATHISM   LEGIS
20 PARLIAMENT PRESIDENT. PAGE 22 E0425

                                                                    B65
FORGAC A.A.,NEW DIPLOMACY AND THE UNITED NATIONS.   DIPLOM
FRANCE GERMANY UK USSR INT/ORG DELIB/GP EX/STRUC   ETIQUET
PEACE...INT/LAW CONCPT UN. PAGE 39 E0770   NAT/G

                                                                    B65
HABERLER G.,A SURVEY OF INTERNATIONAL TRADE THEORY.   INT/TRADE
CANADA FRANCE GERMANY ECO/TAC TARIFFS AGREE COST   BAL/PAY
DEMAND WEALTH...ECOMETRIC 19/20 MONOPOLY TREATY.   DIPLOM
PAGE 49 E0968   POLICY

                                                                    B65
ISORNI J.,LES CAS DE CONSCIENCE DE L'AVOCAT.   SUPEGO
FRANCE LAW ACT/RES CT/SYS PARTIC ROLE MORAL 20.   JURID
PAGE 57 E1138   CRIME

                                                                    B65
WEIL G.L.,A HANDBOOK ON THE EUROPEAN ECONOMIC   INT/TRADE
COMMUNITY. BELGIUM EUR+WWI FRANCE GERMANY/W ITALY   BAL/PAY
CONSTN ECO/DEV CREATE PARTIC GP/REL...DECISION MGT   TEC/DEV
CHARTS 20 EEC. PAGE 105 E2107   INT/LAW

                                                                    B66
DE TOCQUEVILLE A.DEMOCRACY IN AMERICA (1834-1840)   POPULISM
(2 VOLS. IN I; TRANS. BY G. LAWRENCE). FRANCE   USA-45
CULTURE STRATA POL/PAR CT/SYS REPRESENT FEDERAL   CONSTN
ORD/FREE SOVEREIGN...MAJORIT TREND GEN/LAWS 18/19.   NAT/COMP
PAGE 30 E0596

                                                                    B66
GARCON M.,LETTRE OUVERTE A LA JUSTICE. FRANCE NAT/G   ORD/FREE
PROB/SOLV PAY EFFICIENCY MORAL 20. PAGE 42 E0834   ADJUD
                                                        CT/SYS

                                                                    B67
BROWN L.N.,FRENCH ADMINISTRATIVE LAW. FRANCE UK   EX/STRUC
CONSTN NAT/G LEGIS DOMIN CONTROL EXEC PARL/PROC PWR   LAW
...JURID METH/COMP GEN/METH. PAGE 16 E0314   IDEA/COMP
                                                        CT/SYS

                                                                    B67
VILE M.J.C.,CONSTITUTIONALISM AND THE SEPARATION OF   CONSTN
POWERS. FRANCE UK USA+45 USA-45 NAT/G ADJUD CONTROL   BAL/PWR
GOV/REL...POLICY DECISION JURID GEN/LAWS 15/20   CONCPT
MONTESQ. PAGE 104 E2076   LAW

                                                                    L67
"A PROPOS DES INCITATIONS FINANCIERES AUX   LOC/G
GROUPEMENTS DES COMMUNES: ESSAI D'INTERPRETATION."   ECO/TAC
FRANCE NAT/G LEGIS ADMIN GOV/REL CENTRAL 20. PAGE 2   APPORT
E0037   ADJUD

                                                                    S67
EYRAUD M.,"LA FRANCE FACE A UN EVENTUEL TRAITE DE   NUC/PWR
NON DISSEMINATION DES ARMES NUCLEAIRES." FRANCE   ARMS/CONT
USA+45 EXTR/IND INDUS R+D INT/ORG ACT/RES TEC/DEV   POLICY
AGREE PRODUC ATTIT 20 TREATY AEC EURATOM. PAGE 36
E0708

                                                                    S67
MATTHEWS R.O.,"THE SUEZ CANAL DISPUTE* A CASE STUDY   PEACE
IN PEACEFUL SETTLEMENT." FRANCE ISRAEL UAR UK NAT/G   DIPLOM
CONTROL LEAD COERCE WAR NAT/LISM ROLE ORD/FREE PWR   ADJUD
...INT/LAW UN 20. PAGE 69 E1389

                                                                    L86
GOODNOW F.J.,"AN EXECUTIVE AND THE COURTS: JUDICIAL   CT/SYS
REMEDIES AGAINST ADMINISTRATIVE ACTION" FRANCE UK   GOV/REL
USA-45 WOR-45 LAW CONSTN SANCTION ORD/FREE 19.   ADMIN
PAGE 45 E0888   ADJUD

                                                                    B89
FERNEUIL T.,LES PRINCIPES DE 1789 ET LA SCIENCE   CONSTN
SOCIALE. FRANCE NAT/G REV ATTIT...CONCPT TREND   POLICY
IDEA/COMP 18/19. PAGE 37 E0739   LAW

                                                                    B90
BURGESS J.W.,POLITICAL SCIENCE AND COMPARATIVE   CONSTN
CONSTITUTIONAL LAW. FRANCE GERMANY UK USA+45 LEGIS   LAW
DIPLOM ADJUD REPRESENT...CONCPT 19. PAGE 17 E0340   LOC/G
                                                        NAT/G

                                                                    B96
ESMEIN A.,ELEMENTS DE DROIT CONSTITUTIONNEL. FRANCE   LAW
UK CHIEF EX/STRUC LEGIS ADJUD CT/SYS PARL/PROC REV   CONSTN
GOV/REL ORD/FREE...JURID METH/COMP 18/19. PAGE 35   NAT/G
E0697   CONCPT

FRANCHISE....FRANCHISE

FRANCIS R.G. E0784

FRANCK T.M. E0785,E0786

FRANCO/F....FRANCISCO FRANCO

                                                                    N61
DELEGACION NACIONAL DE PRENSA,FALANGE ESPANOL   EDU/PROP
TRADICIONALISTA Y DE LAS JUNTAS OFENSIVAS   FASCIST
NACIONALES SINDICALISTAS. IX CONSEJO NACIONAL   CONFER
(PAMPHLET). LAW VOL/ASSN TOTALISM AUTHORIT ORD/FREE   POL/PAR
FASCISM...ANTHOL 20 FRANCO/F FALANGIST. PAGE 31
E0605

FRANK J. E0787,E0788

FRANK/PARL....FRANKFURT PARLIAMENT

FRANKFUR/F....FELIX FRANKFURTER

                                                                    B61
JACOBS C.E.,JUSTICE FRANKFURTER AND CIVIL   BIOG
LIBERTIES. USA+45 USA-45 LAW NAT/G PROB/SOLV PRESS   CONSTN
PERS/REL...JURID WORSHIP 20 SUPREME/CT FRANKFUR/F   ADJUD
CIVIL/LIB. PAGE 57 E1144   ORD/FREE

                                                                    B62
BICKEL A.,THE LEAST DANGEROUS BRANCH. USA+45 USA-45   LAW
CONSTN SCHOOL LEGIS ADJUD RACE/REL DISCRIM ORD/FREE   NAT/G
...JURID 18/20 SUPREME/CT CONGRESS MARSHALL/J   CT/SYS
HOLMES/OW FRANKFUR/F. PAGE 12 E0226

                                                                    B66
MENDELSON W.,JUSTICES BLACK AND FRANKFURTER: JURID
CONFLICT IN THE COURT (2ND ED.). NAT/G PROVS   ADJUD
PROB/SOLV BAL/PWR CONTROL FEDERAL ISOLAT ANOMIE   IDEA/COMP
ORD/FREE...DECISION 20 SUPREME/CT BLACK/HL   ROLE
FRANKFUR/F. PAGE 72 E1439

FRANKFURT PARLIAMENT....SEE FRANK/PARL

FRANKFURTER F. E0789,E0790,E0791,E0792

FRANKLIN/B....BENJAMIN FRANKLIN

FRASER A.C. E0202

FREDERICK....FREDERICK THE GREAT

FREDRKSBRG....FREDERICKSBURG, VIRGINIA

FREE/SOIL....FREE-SOIL DEBATE (U.S.)

FREE/SPEE....FREE SPEECH MOVEMENT; SEE ALSO AMEND/I

                                                                    B16
SCHROEDER T.,FREE SPEECH FOR RADICALS (REV. ED.).   ORD/FREE
USA-45 CONSTN INDUS LOC/G FORCES SANCTION WAR ATTIT   CONTROL
SEX...JURID REFORMERS 20 FREE/SPEE. PAGE 88 E1767   LAW
                                                        PRESS

                                                                    B41
CHAFEE Z. JR.,FREE SPEECH IN THE UNITED STATES.   ORD/FREE
USA-45 ADJUD CONTROL CRIME WAR...BIBLIOG 20   CONSTN
FREE/SPEE AMEND/I SUPREME/CT. PAGE 21 E0413   ATTIT
                                                        JURID

                                                                    C43
BENTHAM J.,"ON THE LIBERTY OF THE PRESS, AND PUBLIC   ORD/FREE
DISCUSSION" IN J. BOWRING, ED., THE WORKS OF JEREMY   PRESS
BENTHAM." SPAIN UK LAW ELITES NAT/G LEGIS INSPECT   CONFER
LEGIT WRITING CONTROL PRIVIL TOTALISM AUTHORIT   CONSERVE
...TRADIT 19 FREE/SPEE. PAGE 10 E0193

                                                                    B54
JAMES L.F.,THE SUPREME COURT IN AMERICAN LIFE.   ADJUD
USA+45 USA-45 CONSTN CRIME GP/REL INGP/REL RACE/REL   CT/SYS
CONSEN FEDERAL PERSON ORD/FREE 18/20 SUPREME/CT   JURID
DEPRESSION CIV/RIGHTS CHURCH/STA FREE/SPEE. PAGE 58   DECISION
E1147

                                                                    B59
FELLMANN D.,THE LIMITS OF FREEDOM. USA+45 USA-45   CONCPT
NAT/G SECT ROLE ORD/FREE WORSHIP 18/20 FREE/SPEE.   JURID

PAGE 37 E0734   CONSTN

FTC....FEDERAL TRADE COMMISSION

KAUPER P.G.,RELIGION AND THE CONSTITUTION. USA+45 CONSTN
USA-45 LAW NAT/G SCHOOL SECT GP/REL ATTIT...BIBLIOG JURID
WORSHIP 18/20 SUPREME/CT FREE/SPEE CHURCH/STA. ORD/FREE
PAGE 60 E1189
                                     B64

PARKER D.,CIVIL LIBERTIES CASE STUDIES AND THE LAW. ORD/FREE
SECT ADJUD...CONCPT WORSHIP 20 SUPREME/CT JURID
CIV/RIGHTS FREE/SPEE. PAGE 80 E1598 CONSTN
                                  JUDGE
                                   B65

BEDI A.S.,FREEDOM OF EXPRESSION AND SECURITY; METH
COMPARATIVE STUDY OF FUNCTIONS OF SUPREME COURTS IN CT/SYS
UNITED STATES AND INDIA. INDIA USA+45 LAW CONSTN ADJUD
PROB/SOLV...DECISION JURID BIBLIOG 20 SUPREME/CT ORD/FREE
FREE/SPEE AMEND/I. PAGE 9 E0175
                                   B66

CAMPBELL E.,PARLIAMENTARY PRIVILEGE IN AUSTRALIA. LEGIS
UK LAW CONSTN COLONIAL ROLE ORD/FREE SOVEREIGN PARL/PROC
18/20 COMMONWLTH AUSTRAL FREE/SPEE PARLIAMENT. JURID
PAGE 19 E0370 PRIVIL
                                   B66

SHAPIRO M.,FREEDOM OF SPEECH: THE SUPREME COURT AND CT/SYS
JUDICIAL REVIEW. USA+45 LEGIS...CHARTS 20 ORD/FREE
SUPREME/CT FREE/SPEE. PAGE 90 E1812 CONSTN
                                   JURID
                                   B66

FREEDOM....SEE ORD/FREE

FREEDOM/HS....FREEDOM HOUSE

FREISEN J. E0793

FRELIMO....MOZAMBIQUE LIBERATION FRONT

FRENCH/CAN....FRENCH CANADA

FREUD A. E0794

FREUD/S....SIGMUND FREUD

LAPIERE R.,THE FREUDIAN ETHIC. USA+45 FAM EDU/PROP PSY
CONTROL CRIME ADJUST AGE DRIVE PERCEPT PERSON SEX ORD/FREE
...SOC 20 FREUD/S. PAGE 63 E1254 SOCIETY
                                   B59

FREUND E. E0795

FREUND G. E0796

FREUND P.A. E0797

FRIED R.C. E0798

FRIEDHEIM R. E0799

FRIEDMAN L. E0800

FRIEDMANN W. E0801,E0802

FRIEDMANN W.G. E0803,E0804,E0805,E0806

FRIEDRICH C.J. E0279,E0807,E0808,E0809,E0810

FRIENDLY A. E0811

FRIENDSHIP....SEE LOVE

FRNCO/PRUS....FRANCO-PRUSSIAN WAR

FROEBEL J. E0812

FROMAN L.A. E0813

FROMM/E....ERICH FROMM

FRONTIER....FRONTIER

FROST R.T. E1940

FRUSTRATION....SEE BIO/SOC, ANOMIE, DRIVE

FRYDENSBERG P. E0814

FRYE R.J. E0815

BURRUS B.R.,INVESTIGATION AND DISCOVERY IN STATE NAT/G
ANTITRUST (PAMPHLET). USA+45 USA-45 LEGIS ECO/TAC PROVS
ADMIN CONTROL CT/SYS CRIME GOV/REL PWR...JURID LAW
CHARTS 19/20 FTC MONOPOLY. PAGE 18 E0346 INSPECT
                                   N19

GELLER M.A.,ADVERTISING AT THE CROSSROADS: FEDERAL EDU/PROP
REGULATION VS. VOLUNTARY CONTROLS. USA+45 JUDGE NAT/G
ECO/TAC...POLICY JURID BIBLIOG 20 FTC. PAGE 43 CONSTN
E0843 COM/IND
                                   B52

OTTENBERG M.,THE FEDERAL INVESTIGATORS. USA+45 LAW FORCES
COM/IND DIST/IND WORKER DIPLOM INT/TRADE CONTROL INSPECT
FEDERAL HEALTH ORD/FREE FBI CIA FTC SEC FDA. NAT/G
PAGE 79 E1585 CRIME
                                   B62

BOWIE R.R.,GOVERNMENT REGULATION OF BUSINESS: CASES LAW
FROM THE NATIONAL REPORTER SYSTEM. USA+45 USA-45 CONTROL
NAT/G ECO/TAC ADJUD...ANTHOL 19/20 SUPREME/CT FTC INDUS
FAIR/LABOR MONOPOLY. PAGE 14 E0280 CT/SYS
                                   B63

FORTE W.E.,"THE FOOD AND DRUG ADMINISTRATION, THE CONTROL
FEDERAL TRADE COMMISSION AND THE DECEPTIVE HEALTH
PACKAGING." ROUTINE...JURID 20 FTC. PAGE 39 E0772 ADJUD
                                   INDUS
                                   L65

LONG T.G.,"THE ADMINISTRATIVE PROCESS: AGONIZING ADJUD
REAPPRAISAL IN THE FTC." NAT/G REPRESENT 20 FTC. LOBBY
PAGE 66 E1326 ADMIN
                                   EX/STRUC
                                   S65

FUCHS R.F. E0816

FUCHS W.P. E0817

FULBRGHT/J....J. WILLIAM FULBRIGHT

FULBRIGHT J.W. E0818

FULLER G.A. E0819

FULLER G.H. E0820,E0821,E0822,E0823,E0824

FULLER/MW....MELVILLE WESTON FULLER

KING W.L.,MELVILLE WESTON FULLER: CHIEF JUSTICE OF BIOG
THE UNITED STATES, 1888-1910. USA-45 CONSTN FINAN CT/SYS
LABOR TAX GOV/REL PERS/REL ATTIT PERSON PWR...JURID LAW
BIBLIOG 19/20 SUPREME/CT FULLER/MW HOLMES/OW. ADJUD
PAGE 61 E1216
                                   B67

FUNCTIONAL ANALYSIS....SEE OP/RES

FUNCTIONALISM (THEORY)....SEE GEN/LAWS

FURNIVAL/J....J.S. FURNIVALL

FUT....FUTURE (PAST AND PRESENT ATTEMPTS TO DEPICT IT)

AIR UNIVERSITY LIBRARY,INDEX TO MILITARY BIBLIOG/A
PERIODICALS. FUT SPACE WOR+45 REGION ARMS/CONT FORCES
NUC/PWR WAR PEACE INT/LAW. PAGE 3 E0056 NAT/G
                                   DIPLOM
                                   N

AMER COUNCIL OF LEARNED SOCIET,THE ACLS CONSTITUENT BIBLIOG/A
SOCIETY JOURNAL PROJECT. FUT USA+45 LAW NAT/G PLAN HUM
DIPLOM PHIL/SCI. PAGE 4 E0072 COMPUT/IR
                                   COMPUTER
                                   N

REINSCH P.,PUBLIC INTERNATIONAL UNION. WOR-45 LAW FUT
LABOR INT/TRADE LEGIT PERSON ALL/VALS...SOCIALIST INT/ORG
CONCPT TIME/SEQ TREND GEN/LAWS 19/20. PAGE 84 E1683 DIPLOM
                                   B11

ADAMS B.,THE THEORY OF SOCIAL REVOLUTIONS. FUT CAP/ISM
USA-45 GP/REL PEACE...NEW/IDEA 20. PAGE 3 E0047 REV
                                   SOCIETY
                                   CT/SYS
                                   B13

HOBSON J.A.,TOWARDS INTERNATIONAL GOVERNMENT. FUT
MOD/EUR STRUCT ECO/TAC EDU/PROP ADJUD ALL/VALS INT/ORG
...SOCIALIST CONCPT GEN/LAWS TOT/POP 20. PAGE 53 CENTRAL
E1059
                                   B15

BRYCE J.,MODERN DEMOCRACIES. FUT NEW/ZEALND USA-45 | NAT/G | B21
LAW CONSTN POL/PAR PROVS VOL/ASSN EX/STRUC LEGIS | TREND
LEGIT CT/SYS EXEC KNOWL CONGRESS AUSTRAL 20.
PAGE 16 E0322

HOLMES O.W. JR.,THE COMMON LAW. FUT WOR-45 CULTURE | ADJUD | B23
SOCIETY CREATE LEGIT ROUTINE ATTIT ALL/VALS...JURID | CON/ANAL
METH/CNCPT TIME/SEQ GEN/LAWS TOT/POP VAL/FREE.
PAGE 55 E1087

DEWEY J.,"ETHICS AND INTERNATIONAL RELATIONS." FUT | LAW | S23
WOR-45 SOCIETY INT/ORG VOL/ASSN DIPLOM LEGIT | MORAL
ORD/FREE...JURID CONCPT GEN/METH 20. PAGE 31 E0618

STOWELL E.C.,INTERNATIONAL LAW. FUT UNIV WOR-45 | INT/ORG | B31
SOCIETY CONSULT EX/STRUC FORCES ACT/RES PLAN DIPLOM | ROUTINE
EDU/PROP LEGIT DISPL PWR SKILL...POLICY CONCPT OBS | INT/LAW
TREND TOT/POP 20. PAGE 94 E1885

FLEMMING D.,THE UNITED STATES AND THE LEAGUE OF | INT/ORG | B32
NATIONS, 1918-1920. FUT USA-45 NAT/G LEGIS TOP/EX | EDU/PROP
DEBATE CHOOSE PEACE ATTIT SOVEREIGN...TIME/SEQ
CON/ANAL CONGRESS LEAGUE/NAT 20 TREATY. PAGE 39
E0764

RUSSEL F.M.,THEORIES OF INTERNATIONAL RELATIONS. | PWR | B36
EUR+WWI FUT MOD/EUR USA-45 INT/ORG DIPLOM...JURID | POLICY
CONCPT. PAGE 86 E1735 | BAL/PWR
| SOVEREIGN

WILSON G.G.,HANDBOOK OF INTERNATIONAL LAW. FUT UNIV | INT/ORG | B39
USA-45 WOR-45 SOCIETY LEGIT ATTIT DISPL DRIVE | LAW
ALL/VALS...INT/LAW TIME/SEQ TREND. PAGE 106 E2128 | CONCPT
| WAR

CARR E.H.,THE TWENTY YEARS' CRISIS 1919-1939. FUT | INT/ORG | B40
WOR-45 BAL/PWR ECO/TAC LEGIT TOTALISM ATTIT | DIPLOM
ALL/VALS...POLICY JURID CONCPT TIME/SEQ TREND | PEACE
GEN/LAWS TOT/POP 20. PAGE 20 E0393

HAMBRO C.J.,HOW TO WIN THE PEACE. ECO/TAC EDU/PROP | FUT | B42
ADJUD PERSON ALL/VALS...SOCIALIST TREND GEN/LAWS | INT/ORG
20. PAGE 50 E0987 | PEACE

KELSEN H.,LAW AND PEACE IN INTERNATIONAL RELATIONS. | INT/ORG | B42
FUT WOR-45 NAT/G DELIB/GP DIPLOM LEGIT RIGID/FLEX | ADJUD
ORD/FREE SOVEREIGN...JURID CONCPT TREND STERTYP | PEACE
GEN/LAWS LEAGUE/NAT 20. PAGE 60 E1197 | INT/LAW

BRIERLY J.L.,THE OUTLOOK FOR INTERNATIONAL LAW. FUT | INT/ORG | B44
WOR-45 CONSTN NAT/G VOL/ASSN FORCES ECO/TAC DOMIN | LAW
LEGIT ADJUD ROUTINE PEACE ORD/FREE...INT/LAW JURID
METH LEAGUE/NAT 20. PAGE 15 E0298

HUDSON M.,INTERNATIONAL TRIBUNALS PAST AND FUTURE. | INT/ORG | B44
FUT WOR-45 LAW EDU/PROP ADJUD ORD/FREE...CONCPT | STRUCT
TIME/SEQ TREND GEN/LAWS TOT/POP VAL/FREE 18/20. | INT/LAW
PAGE 56 E1111

WRIGHT Q.,"CONSTITUTIONAL PROCEDURES OF THE US FOR | TOP/EX | S44
CARRYING OUT OBLIGATIONS FOR MILITARY SANCTIONS." | FORCES
EUR+WWI FUT USA-45 WOR-45 CONSTN INTELL NAT/G | INT/LAW
CONSULT EX/STRUC LEGIS ROUTINE DRIVE...POLICY JURID | WAR
CONCPT OBS TREND TOT/POP 20. PAGE 108 E2153

WEST R.,CONSCIENCE AND SOCIETY: A STUDY OF THE | COERCE | B45
PSYCHOLOGICAL PREREQUISITES OF LAW AND ORDER. FUT | INT/LAW
UNIV LAW SOCIETY STRUCT DIPLOM WAR PERS/REL SUPEGO | ORD/FREE
...SOC 20. PAGE 105 E2112 | PERSON

KEETON G.W.,MAKING INTERNATIONAL LAW WORK. FUT | INT/ORG | B46
WOR-45 NAT/G DELIB/GP FORCES LEGIT COERCE PEACE | ADJUD
ATTIT RIGID/FLEX ORD/FREE PWR...JURID CONCPT | INT/LAW
HIST/WRIT GEN/METH LEAGUE/NAT 20. PAGE 60 E1193

JESSUP P.C.,A MODERN LAW OF NATIONS. FUT WOR+45 | INT/ORG | B48
WOR-45 SOCIETY NAT/G DELIB/GP LEGIS BAL/PWR | ADJUD
EDU/PROP LEGIT PWR...INT/LAW JURID TIME/SEQ
LEAGUE/NAT 20. PAGE 58 E1166

MORGENTHAL H.J.,POLITICS AMONG NATIONS: THE | DIPLOM | B48
STRUGGLE FOR POWER AND PEACE. FUT WOR+45 INT/ORG | PEACE
OP/RES PROB/SOLV BAL/PWR CONTROL ATTIT MORAL | PWR
...INT/LAW BIBLIOG 20 COLD/WAR. PAGE 75 E1494 | POLICY

COMM. STUDY ORGAN. PEACE,"A TEN YEAR RECORD, | INT/ORG | L49
1939-1949." FUT WOR-45 LAW R+D CONSULT DELIB/GP | CONSTN
CREATE LEGIT ROUTINE ORD/FREE...TIME/SEQ UN 20. | PEACE
PAGE 24 E0480

KIRK G.,"MATERIALS FOR THE STUDY OF INTERNATIONAL | INT/ORG | S49
RELATIONS." FUT UNIV WOR-45 INTELL EDU/PROP ROUTINE | ACT/RES
PEACE ATTIT...INT/LAW JURID CONCPT OBS. PAGE 61 | DIPLOM
E1219

SOHN L.B.,CASES AND OTHER MATERIALS ON WORLD LAW. | CT/SYS | B50
FUT WOR+45 LAW INT/ORG...INT/LAW JURID METH/CNCPT | CONSTN
20 UN. PAGE 92 E1852

CORBETT P.E.,LAW AND SOCIETY IN THE RELATIONS OF | INT/LAW | B51
STATES. FUT WOR+45 WOR-45 CONTROL WAR PEACE PWR | DIPLOM
...POLICY JURID 16/20 TREATY. PAGE 26 E0505 | INT/ORG

MANGONE G.,"THE IDEA AND PRACTICE OF WORLD | INT/ORG | L51
GOVERNMENT." FUT WOR+45 ECO/DEV LEGIS CREATE | SOCIETY
LEGIT ROUTINE ATTIT MORAL PWR WEALTH...CONCPT | INT/LAW
GEN/LAWS 20. PAGE 68 E1358

BENTHAM A.,HANDBOOK OF POLITICAL FALLACIES. FUT | POL/PAR | B52
MOD/EUR LAW INTELL LOC/G MUNIC NAT/G DELIB/GP LEGIS
CREATE EDU/PROP CT/SYS ATTIT RIGID/FLEX KNOWL PWR
...RELATIV PSY SOC CONCPT SELF/OBS TREND STERTYP
TOT/POP. PAGE 10 E0189

MCDOUGAL M.S.,"THE COMPARATIVE STUDY OF LAW FOR | PLAN | S52
POLICY PURPOSES." FUT NAT/G POL/PAR CONSULT ADJUD | JURID
PWR SOVEREIGN...METH/CNCPT IDEA/COMP SIMUL 20. | NAT/LISM
PAGE 70 E1403

WRIGHT Q.,PROBLEMS OF STABILITY AND PROGRESS IN | INT/ORG | B54
INTERNATIONAL RELATIONSHIPS. FUT WOR+45 WOR-45 | CONCPT
SOCIETY LEGIS CREATE TEC/DEV ECO/TAC EDU/PROP ADJUD | DIPLOM
WAR PEACE ORD/FREE PWR...KNO/TEST TREND GEN/LAWS
20. PAGE 108 E2155

NICOLSON H.,"THE EVOLUTION OF DIPLOMATIC METHOD." | RIGID/FLEX | L54
CHRIST-17C EUR+WWI FRANCE FUT ITALY MEDIT-7 MOD/EUR | METH/CNCPT
USA+45 USA-45 LAW NAT/G CREATE EDU/PROP LEGIT PEACE | DIPLOM
ATTIT ORD/FREE RESPECT SOVEREIGN. PAGE 77 E1548

JESSUP P.C.,TRANSNATIONAL LAW. FUT WOR+45 JUDGE | LAW | B56
CREATE ADJUD ORD/FREE...CONCPT VAL/FREE 20. PAGE 59 | JURID
E1167 | INT/LAW

COMM. STUDY ORGAN. PEACE,STRENGTHENING THE UNITED | INT/ORG | B57
NATIONS. FUT USA+45 WOR+45 CONSTN NAT/G DELIB/GP | ORD/FREE
FORCES LEGIS ECO/TAC LEGIT COERCE PEACE...JURID
CONCPT UN COLD/WAR 20. PAGE 24 E0482

JENKS C.W.,THE INTERNATIONAL PROTECTION OF TRADE | LABOR | B57
UNION FREEDOM. FUT WOR+45 WOR-45 VOL/ASSN DELIB/GP | INT/ORG
CT/SYS REGION ROUTINE...JURID METH/CNCPT RECORD
TIME/SEQ CHARTS ILO WORK OAS 20. PAGE 58 E1153

LEVONTIN A.V.,THE MYTH OF INTERNATIONAL SECURITY: A | INT/ORG | B57
JURIDICAL AND CRITICAL ANALYSIS. FUT WOR+45 WOR-45 | INT/LAW
LAW NAT/G VOL/ASSN ACT/RES BAL/PWR ATTIT ORD/FREE | SOVEREIGN
...JURID METH/CNCPT TIME/SEQ TREND STERTYP 20. | MYTH
PAGE 64 E1289

HOOD W.C.,FINANCING OF ECONOMIC ACTIVITY IN CANADA. | BUDGET | B58
CANADA FUT VOL/ASSN WORKER ECO/TAC ADJUD ADMIN | FINAN
...CHARTS 20. PAGE 55 E1093 | GP/REL
| ECO/DEV

SPITZ D.,DEMOCRACY AND THE CHALLANGE OF POWER. FUT | NAT/G | B58
USA+45 USA-45 LAW SOCIETY STRUCT LOC/G POL/PAR | PWR
PROVS DELIB/GP EX/STRUC LEGIS TOP/EX ACT/RES CREATE
DOMIN EDU/PROP LEGIT ADJUD ADMIN ATTIT DRIVE MORAL
ORD/FREE TOT/POP. PAGE 93 E1862

MCDOUGAL M.S.,"PERSPECTIVES FOR A LAW OF OUTER
SPACE." FUT WOR+45 AIR CONSULT DELIB/GP TEC/DEV
CT/SYS ORD/FREE...POLICY JURID 20 UN. PAGE 70 E1404
INT/ORG
SPACE
INT/LAW
S58

COMM. STUDY ORGAN. PEACE,ORGANIZING PEACE IN THE
NUCLEAR AGE. FUT CONSULT DELIB/GP DOMIN ADJUD
ROUTINE COERCE ORD/FREE...TECHNIC INT/LAW JURID
NEW/IDEA UN COLD/WAR 20. PAGE 24 E0483
INT/ORG
ACT/RES
NUC/PWR
B59

FRIEDMANN W.G.,LAW IN A CHANGING SOCIETY. FUT
WOR+45 WOR-45 LAW SOCIETY STRUCT INT/TRADE LEGIT
ATTIT BIO/SOC HEALTH ORD/FREE SOVEREIGN...CONCPT
GEN/LAWS ILO 20. PAGE 41 E0803
SOC
JURID
B59

SCHNEIDER J.,TREATY-MAKING POWER OF INTERNATIONAL
ORGANIZATIONS. FUT WOR+45 WOR-45 LAW NAT/G JUDGE
DIPLOM LEGIT CT/SYS ORD/FREE PWR...INT/LAW JURID
GEN/LAWS TOT/POP UNESCO 20 TREATY. PAGE 88 E1762
INT/ORG
ROUTINE
B59

SPIRO H.J.,GOVERNMENT BY CONSTITUTIONS: THE
POLITICAL SYSTEMS OF DEMOCRACY. CANADA EUR+WWI FUT
USA+45 WOR+45 WOR-45 LEGIS TOP/EX LEGIT ADMIN
CT/SYS ORD/FREE PWR...TREND TOT/POP VAL/FREE 20.
PAGE 93 E1861
NAT/G
CONSTN
B59

JENKS C.W.,"THE CHALLENGE OF UNIVERSALITY." FUT
UNIV CONSTN CULTURE CONSULT CREATE PLAN LEGIT ATTIT
MORAL ORD/FREE RESPECT...MAJORIT JURID 20. PAGE 58
E1155
INT/ORG
LAW
PEACE
INT/LAW
S59

SOHN L.B.,"THE DEFINITION OF AGGRESSION." FUT LAW
FORCES LEGIT ADJUD ROUTINE COERCE ORD/FREE PWR
...MAJORIT JURID QUANT COLD/WAR 20. PAGE 92 E1855
INT/ORG
CT/SYS
DETER
SOVEREIGN
S59

CLARK G.,WORLD PEACE THROUGH WORLD LAW. FUT WOR+45
CONSULT FORCES ACT/RES CREATE PLAN ADMIN ROUTINE
ARMS/CONT DETER ATTIT PWR...JURID VAL/FREE UNESCO
20 UN. PAGE 23 E0449
INT/ORG
LAW
PEACE
INT/LAW
B60

GOLDSEN J.M.,INTERNATIONAL POLITICAL IMPLICATIONS
OF ACTIVITIES IN OUTER SPACE. FUT USA+45 WOR+45 AIR
LAW ACT/RES LEGIT ATTIT KNOWL ORD/FREE PWR...CONCPT
20. PAGE 44 E0879
R+D
SPACE
B60

JENNINGS R.,PROGRESS OF INTERNATIONAL LAW. FUT
WOR+45 WOR-45 SOCIETY NAT/G VOL/ASSN DELIB/GP
DIPLOM EDU/PROP LEGIT COERCE ATTIT DRIVE MORAL
ORD/FREE...JURID CONCPT OBS TIME/SEQ TREND
GEN/LAWS. PAGE 58 E1164
INT/ORG
LAW
INT/LAW
B60

LENCZOWSKI G.,OIL AND STATE IN THE MIDDLE EAST. FUT
IRAN LAW ECO/UNDEV EXTR/IND NAT/G TOP/EX PLAN
TEC/DEV ECO/TAC LEGIT ADMIN COERCE ATTIT ALL/VALS
PWR...CHARTS 20. PAGE 64 E1283
ISLAM
INDUS
NAT/LISM
B60

STEIN E.,AMERICAN ENTERPRISE IN THE EUROPEAN COMMON
MARKET: A LEGAL PROFILE. EUR+WWI FUT USA+45 SOCIETY
STRUCT ECO/DEV NAT/G VOL/ASSN CONSULT PLAN TEC/DEV
ECO/TAC INT/TRADE ADMIN ATTIT RIGID/FLEX PWR...MGT
NEW/IDEA STAT TREND COMPUT/IR SIMUL EEC 20. PAGE 93
E1867
MARKET
ADJUD
INT/LAW
B60

WOETZEL R.K.,THE INTERNATIONAL CONTROL OF AIRSPACE
AND OUTERSPACE. FUT WOR+45 AIR CONSTN STRUCT
CONSULT PLAN TEC/DEV ADJUD RIGID/FLEX KNOWL
ORD/FREE PWR...TECHNIC GEOG MGT NEW/IDEA TREND
COMPUT/IR VAL/FREE 20 TREATY. PAGE 107 E2137
INT/ORG
JURID
SPACE
INT/LAW
B60

DEAN A.W.,"SECOND GENEVA CONFERENCE OF THE LAW OF
THE SEA: THE FIGHT FOR FREEDOM OF THE SEAS." FUT
USA+45 USSR WOR+45 WOR-45 SEA CONSTN STRUCT PLAN
INT/TRADE ADJUD ADMIN ORD/FREE...DECISION RECORD
TREND GEN/LAWS 20 TREATY. PAGE 30 E0600
INT/ORG
JURID
INT/LAW
L60

STEIN E.,"LEGAL REMEDIES OF ENTERPRISES IN THE
EUROPEAN ECONOMIC COMMUNITY." EUR+WWI FUT ECO/DEV
INDUS PLAN ECO/TAC ADMIN PWR...MGT MATH STAT TREND
CON/ANAL EEC 20. PAGE 93 E1868
MARKET
ADJUD
L60

NICHOLS J.P.,"HAZARDS OF AMERICAN PRIVATE
INVESTMENT IN UNDERDEVELOPED COUNTRIES." FUT
L/A+17C USA+45 USA-45 EXTR/IND CONSULT BAL/PWR
ECO/TAC DOMIN ADJUD ATTIT SOVEREIGN WEALTH
...HIST/WRIT TIME/SEQ TREND VAL/FREE 20. PAGE 77
E1546
FINAN
ECO/UNDEV
CAP/ISM
NAT/LISM
S60

RHYNE C.S.,"LAW AS AN INSTRUMENT FOR PEACE." FUT
WOR+45 PLAN LEGIT ROUTINE ARMS/CONT NUC/PWR ATTIT
ORD/FREE...JURID METH/CNCPT TREND CON/ANAL HYPO/EXP
COLD/WAR 20. PAGE 84 E1690
ADJUD
EDU/PROP
INT/LAW
PEACE
S60

SANDERS R.,"NUCLEAR DYNAMITE: A NEW DIMENSION IN
FOREIGN POLICY." FUT WOR+45 ECO/DEV CONSULT TEC/DEV
PERCEPT...CONT/OBS TIME/SEQ GEN/LAWS TOT/POP
20 TREATY. PAGE 87 E1745
INDUS
PWR
DIPLOM
NUC/PWR
S60

SCHWELB E.,"INTERNATIONAL CONVENTIONS ON HUMAN
RIGHTS." FUT WOR+45 LAW CONSTN CULTURE SOCIETY
STRUCT VOL/ASSN DELIB/GP PLAN ADJUD SUPEGO LOVE
MORAL...SOC CONCPT STAT RECORD HIST/WRIT TREND 20
UN. PAGE 89 E1790
INT/ORG
HUM
S60

ANAND R.P.,COMPULSORY JURISDICTION OF INTERNATIONAL
COURT OF JUSTICE. FUT WOR+45 SOCIETY PLAN LEGIT
ADJUD ATTIT DRIVE PERSON ORD/FREE...JURID CONCPT
TREND 20 ICJ. PAGE 5 E0086
INT/ORG
COERCE
INT/LAW
B61

CASSINELLI C.W.,THE POLITICS OF FREEDOM. FUT UNIV
LAW POL/PAR CHOOSE ORD/FREE...POLICY CONCPT MYTH
BIBLIOG. PAGE 21 E0404
MAJORIT
NAT/G
PARL/PROC
PARTIC
B61

WRIGHT Q.,THE ROLE OF INTERNATIONAL LAW IN THE
ELIMINATION OF WAR. FUT WOR+45 WOR-45 NAT/G BAL/PWR
DIPLOM DOMIN LEGIT PWR...POLICY INT/LAW JURID
CONCPT TIME/SEQ TREND GEN/LAWS COLD/WAR 20.
PAGE 108 E2158
INT/ORG
ADJUD
ARMS/CONT
B61

TAUBENFELD H.J.,"A TREATY FOR ANTARCTICA." FUT
USA+45 INTELL INT/ORG LABOR 20 TREATY ANTARCTICA.
PAGE 95 E1909
R+D
ACT/RES
DIPLOM
L61

TAUBENFELD H.J.,"A REGIME FOR OUTER SPACE." FUT
UNIV R+D ACT/RES PLAN BAL/PWR LEGIT ARMS/CONT
ORD/FREE...POLICY JURID TREND UN TOT/POP 20
COLD/WAR. PAGE 95 E1910
INT/ORG
ADJUD
SPACE
L61

CASTANEDA J.,"THE UNDERDEVELOPED NATIONS AND THE
DEVELOPMENT OF INTERNATIONAL LAW." FUT UNIV LAW
ACT/RES FOR/AID LEGIT PERCEPT SKILL...JURID
METH/CNCPT TIME/SEQ TOT/POP 20 UN. PAGE 21 E0405
INT/ORG
ECO/UNDEV
PEACE
INT/LAW
S61

JACKSON E.,"THE FUTURE DEVELOPMENT OF THE UNITED
NATIONS: SOME SUGGESTIONS FOR RESEARCH." FUT LAW
CONSTN ECO/DEV FINAN PEACE WEALTH...WELF/ST CONCPT
UN 20. PAGE 57 E1140
INT/ORG
PWR
S61

MACHOWSKI K.,"SELECTED PROBLEMS OF NATIONAL
SOVEREIGNTY WITH REFERENCE TO THE LAW OF OUTER
SPACE." FUT WOR+45 AIR LAW INTELL SOCIETY ECO/DEV
PLAN EDU/PROP DETER DRIVE PERCEPT SOVEREIGN
...POLICY INT/LAW OBS TREND TOT/POP 20. PAGE 67
E1339
UNIV
ACT/RES
NUC/PWR
SPACE
S61

OLIVER C.T.,"THE AMERICAN LAW INSTITUTE'S DRAFT
RESTATEMENT OF THE FOREIGN RELATIONS LAW OF THE
UNITED STATES." FUT USA+45 SOCIETY CONSULT
EDU/PROP. PAGE 78 E1574
KNOWL
JURID
DIPLOM
S61

RICHSTEIN A.R.,"LEGAL RULES IN NUCLEAR WEAPONS
EMPLOYMENTS." FUT WOR+45 LAW SOCIETY FORCES PLAN
WEAPON RIGID/FLEX...HEAL CONCPT TREND VAL/FREE 20.
PAGE 85 E1696
NUC/PWR
TEC/DEV
MORAL
ARMS/CONT
S61

BIERZANECK R.,"LA NON-RECONAISSANCE ET LE DROIT
INTERNATIONAL CONTEMPORAIN." EUR+WWI FUT WOR+45 LAW
ECO/DEV ATTIT RIGID/FLEX...CONCPT TIME/SEQ TOT/POP
20. PAGE 12 E0228
EDU/PROP
JURID
DIPLOM
INT/LAW
S62

CRANE R.D.,"LAW AND STRATEGY IN SPACE." FUT USA+45 WOR+45 AIR LAW INT/ORG NAT/G FORCES ACT/RES PLAN BAL/PWR LEGIT ARMS/CONT COERCE ORD/FREE...POLICY INT/LAW JURID SOC/EXP 20 TREATY. PAGE 27 E0542
CONCPT SPACE
S62

CRANE R.D.,"SOVIET ATTITUDE TOWARD INTERNATIONAL SPACE LAW." COM FUT USA+45 USSR AIR CONSTN DELIB/GP DOMIN PWR...JURID TREND TOT/POP 20. PAGE 27 E0543
LAW ATTIT INT/LAW SPACE
S62

FINKELSTEIN L.S.,"THE UNITED NATIONS AND ORGANIZATIONS FOR CONTROL OF ARMAMENT." FUT WOR+45 VOL/ASSN DELIB/GP TOP/EX CREATE EDU/PROP LEGIT ADJUD NUC/PWR ATTIT RIGID/FLEX ORD/FREE...POLICY DECISION CONCPT OBS TREND GEN/LAWS TOT/POP COLD/WAR. PAGE 38 E0752
INT/ORG PWR ARMS/CONT
S62

LISSITZYN O.J.,"SOME LEGAL IMPLICATIONS OF THE U-2 AND RB-47 INCIDENTS." FUT USA+45 USSR WOR+45 AIR NAT/G DIPLOM LEGIT MORAL ORD/FREE SOVEREIGN...JURID GEN/LAWS GEN/METH COLD/WAR 20 U-2. PAGE 65 E1305
LAW CONCPT SPACE INT/LAW
S62

SCHACHTER O.,"DAG HAMMARSKJOLD AND THE RELATION OF LAW TO POLITICS." FUT WOR+45 INT/ORG CONSULT PLAN TEC/DEV BAL/PWR DIPLOM LEGIT ATTIT PERCEPT ORD/FREE ...POLICY JURID CONCPT OBS TESTS STERTYP GEN/LAWS 20 HAMMARSK/D. PAGE 87 E1751
ACT/RES ADJUD
S62

HACKER A.,CONGRESSIONAL DISTRICTING: THE ISSUE OF EQUAL REPRESENTATION. FUT CT/SYS GEOG. PAGE 49 E0970
LEGIS REPRESENT APPORT
B63

HALEY A.G.,SPACE LAW AND GOVERNMENT. FUT USA+45 WOR+45 LEGIS ACT/RES CREATE ATTIT RIGID/FLEX ORD/FREE PWR SOVEREIGN...POLICY JURID CONCPT CHARTS VAL/FREE 20. PAGE 49 E0980
INT/ORG LAW SPACE
B63

MCDOUGAL M.S.,LAW AND PUBLIC ORDER IN SPACE. FUT USA+45 ACT/RES TEC/DEV ADJUD...POLICY INT/LAW JURID 20. PAGE 70 E1410
SPACE ORD/FREE DIPLOM DECISION
B63

LISSITZYN O.J.,"INTERNATIONAL LAW IN A DIVIDED WORLD." FUT WOR+45 CONSTN CULTURE ECO/DEV ECO/UNDEV DIST/IND NAT/G FORCES ECO/TAC LEGIT ADJUD ADMIN COERCE ATTIT HEALTH MORAL ORD/FREE PWR RESPECT WEALTH VAL/FREE. PAGE 65 E1306
INT/ORG LAW
L63

MCDOUGAL M.S.,"THE ENJOYMENT AND ACQUISITION OF RESOURCES IN OUTER SPACE." CHRIST-17C FUT WOR+45 WOR-45 LAW EXTR/IND INT/ORG ACT/RES CREATE TEC/DEV ECO/TAC LEGIT COERCE HEALTH KNOWL ORD/FREE PWR WEALTH...JURID HIST/WRIT VAL/FREE. PAGE 70 E1408
PLAN TREND
L63

GARDNER R.N.,"COOPERATION IN OUTER SPACE." FUT USSR WOR+45 AIR LAW COM/IND CONSULT DELIB/GP CREATE KNOWL 20 TREATY. PAGE 42 E0837
INT/ORG ACT/RES PEACE SPACE
S63

MACWHINNEY E.,"LES CONCEPT SOVIETIQUE DE 'COEXISTENCE PACIFIQUE' ET LES RAPPORTS JURIDIQUES ENTRE L'URSS ET LES ETATS OCIDENTAUX." COM FUT WOR+45 LAW CULTURE INTELL POL/PAR ACT/RES BAL/PWR ...INT/LAW 20. PAGE 67 E1346
NAT/G CONCPT DIPLOM USSR
S63

MEYROWITZ H.,"LES JURISTES DEVANT L'ARME NUCLAIRE." FUT WOR+45 INTELL SOCIETY BAL/PWR DETER WAR...JURID CONCPT 20. PAGE 72 E1451
ACT/RES ADJUD INT/LAW NUC/PWR
S63

WALKER H.,"THE INTERNATIONAL LAW OF COMMODITY AGREEMENTS." FUT WOR+45 ECO/DEV ECO/UNDEV FINAN INT/ORG NAT/G CONSULT CREATE PLAN ECO/TAC ATTIT PERCEPT...CONCPT GEN/LAWS TOT/POP GATT 20. PAGE 105 E2095
MARKET VOL/ASSN INT/LAW INT/TRADE
S63

DUBOIS J.,DANGER OVER PANAMA. FUT PANAMA SCHOOL PROB/SOLV EDU/PROP MARXISM...POLICY 19/20 TREATY INTERVENT CANAL/ZONE. PAGE 33 E0652
DIPLOM COERCE
B64

FALK R.A.,THE ROLE OF DOMESTIC COURTS IN THE INTERNATIONAL LEGAL ORDER. FUT WOR+45 INT/ORG NAT/G JUDGE EDU/PROP LEGIT CT/SYS...POLICY RELATIV JURID CONCPT GEN/LAWS 20. PAGE 36 E0716
LAW INT/LAW
B64

HEKHUIS D.J.,INTERNATIONAL STABILITY: MILITARY, ECONOMIC AND POLITICAL DIMENSIONS. FUT WOR+45 LAW ECO/UNDEV INT/ORG NAT/G VOL/ASSN FORCES ACT/RES BAL/PWR PWR WEALTH...STAT UN 20. PAGE 51 E1024
TEC/DEV DETER REGION
B64

NASA,PROCEEDINGS OF CONFERENCE ON THE LAW OF SPACE AND OF SATELLITE COMMUNICATIONS: CHICAGO 1963. FUT WOR+45 DELIB/GP PROB/SOLV TEC/DEV CONFER ADJUD NUC/PWR...POLICY IDEA/COMP 20 NASA. PAGE 76 E1522
SPACE COM/IND LAW DIPLOM
B64

OSSENBECK F.J.,OPEN SPACE AND PEACE. CHINA/COM FUT USA+45 USSR LAW PROB/SOLV TEC/DEV EDU/PROP NEUTRAL PEACE...AUD/VIS ANTHOL 20. PAGE 79 E1583
SPACE ORD/FREE DIPLOM CREATE
B64

SCHWARTZ M.D.,CONFERENCE ON SPACE SCIENCE AND SPACE LAW. FUT COM/IND NAT/G FORCES ACT/RES PLAN BUDGET DIPLOM NUC/PWR WEAPON...POLICY ANTHOL 20. PAGE 89 E1788
SPACE LAW PEACE TEC/DEV
B64

US AIR FORCE ACADEMY ASSEMBLY.OUTER SPACE: FINAL REPORT APRIL 1-4, 1964. FUT USA+45 WOR+45 LAW DELIB/GP CONFER ARMS/CONT WAR PEACE ATTIT MORAL ...ANTHOL 20 NASA. PAGE 99 E1979
SPACE CIVMIL/REL NUC/PWR DIPLOM
B64

POUNDS N.J.G.,"THE POLITICS OF PARTITION." AFR ASIA COM EUR+WWI FUT ISLAM S/ASIA USA-45 LAW ECO/DEV ECO/UNDEV AGRI INDUS INT/ORG POL/PAR PROVS SECT FORCES TOP/EX EDU/PROP LEGIT ATTIT MORAL ORD/FREE PWR RESPECT WEALTH. PAGE 82 E1640
NAT/G NAT/LISM
L64

CRANE R.D.,"BASIC PRINCIPLES IN SOVIET SPACE LAW." FUT WOR+45 AIR INT/ORG DIPLOM DOMIN ARMS/CONT COERCE NUC/PWR PEACE ATTIT DRIVE PWR...INT/LAW METH/CNCPT NEW/IDEA OBS TREND GEN/LAWS VAL/FREE MARX/KARL 20. PAGE 27 E0544
COM LAW USSR SPACE
S64

HICKEY D.,"THE PHILOSOPHICAL ARGUMENT FOR WORLD GOVERNMENT." WOR+45 SOCIETY ACT/RES PLAN LEGIT ADJUD PEACE PERCEPT PERSON ORD/FREE...HUM JURID PHIL/SCI METH/CNCPT CON/ANAL STERTYP GEN/LAWS TOT/POP 20. PAGE 52 E1039
FUT INT/ORG
S64

KHAN M.Z.,"ISLAM AND INTERNATIONAL RELATIONS." FUT WOR+45 LAW CULTURE SOCIETY NAT/G SECT DELIB/GP FORCES EDU/PROP ATTIT PERSON SUPEGO ALL/VALS ...POLICY PSY CONCPT MYTH HIST/WRIT GEN/LAWS. PAGE 61 E1211
ISLAM INT/ORG DIPLOM
S64

KUNZ J.,"THE CHANGING SCIENCE OF INTERNATIONAL LAW." FUT WOR+45 WOR-45 INT/ORG LEGIT ORD/FREE ...JURID TIME/SEQ GEN/LAWS 20. PAGE 62 E1235
ADJUD CONCPT INT/LAW
S64

SKUBISZEWSKI K.,"FORMS OF PARTICIPATION OF INTERNATIONAL ORGANIZATION IN THE LAW MAKING PROCESS." FUT WOR+45 NAT/G DELIB/GP DOMIN LEGIT KNOWL PWR...JURID TREND 20. PAGE 92 E1837
INT/ORG LAW INT/LAW
S64

MCKAY R.B.,REAPPORTIONMENT: THE LAW AND POLITICS OF EQUAL REPRESENTATION. FUT USA+45 PROVS BAL/PWR ADJUD CHOOSE REPRESENT GOV/REL FEDERAL...JURID BIBLIOG 20 SUPREME/CT CONGRESS. PAGE 71 E1420
APPORT MAJORIT LEGIS PWR
B65

MILLIS W.,AN END TO ARMS. LAW INT/ORG FORCES ACT/RES CREATE DIPLOM WAR...POLICY HUM NEW/IDEA HYPO/EXP. PAGE 73 E1462
FUT PWR ARMS/CONT ORD/FREE
B65

RADZINOWICZ L.,THE NEED FOR CRIMINOLOGY AND A PROPOSAL FOR AN INSTITUTE OF CRIMINOLOGY. FUT UK USA+45 SOCIETY ACT/RES PROB/SOLV CRIME...PSY SOC BIBLIOG 20. PAGE 83 E1666
CRIMLGY PROF/ORG ACADEM CONTROL
B65

HIBBS A.R.,"SPACE TECHNOLOGY* THE THREAT AND THE PROMISE." FUT VOL/ASSN TEC/DEV NUC/PWR COST
SPACE ARMS/CONT
S65

EFFICIENCY UTIL UN TREATY. PAGE 52 E1038   PREDICT

                                                  S65
MARTIN A.,"PROLIFERATION." FUT WOR+45 PROB/SOLV   RECORD
REGION ADJUST...PREDICT NAT/COMP UN TREATY. PAGE 69 NUC/PWR
E1372   ARMS/CONT
                                                  VOL/ASSN

                                                  B66
INTL ATOMIC ENERGY AGENCY,INTERNATIONAL CONVENTIONS DIPLOM
ON CIVIL LIABILITY FOR NUCLEAR DAMAGE. FUT WOR+45 INT/ORG
ADJUD WAR COST PEACE SOVEREIGN...JURID 20. PAGE 57 DELIB/GP
E1135   NUC/PWR

                                                  B66
OSTERMANN R.,A REPORT IN DEPTH ON CRIME IN AMERICA. CRIME
FUT USA+45 MUNIC PUB/INST TEC/DEV MURDER EFFICIENCY FORCES
ATTIT BIO/SOC...PSY 20. PAGE 79 E1584   CONTROL
                                                  LAW

                                                  B66
TIEDT S.W.,THE ROLE OF THE FEDERAL GOVERNMENT IN NAT/G
EDUCATION. FUT USA+45 USA-45 CONSTN SECT BUDGET   EDU/PROP
CT/SYS GOV/REL 18/20 SUPREME/CT. PAGE 96 E1924   GIVE
                                                  SCHOOL

                                                  B66
UNITED NATIONS,INTERNATIONAL SPACE BIBLIOGRAPHY. BIBLIOG
FUT INT/ORG TEC/DEV DIPLOM ARMS/CONT NUC/PWR   SPACE
...JURID SOC UN. PAGE 98 E1969   PEACE
                                                  R+D

                                                  B66
US SENATE COMM AERO SPACE SCI,SOVIET SPACE   CONSULT
PROGRAMS, 1962-65; GOALS AND PURPOSES,   SPACE
ACHIEVEMENTS, PLANS, AND INTERNATIONAL   FUT
IMPLICATIONS. USA+45 USSR R+D FORCES PLAN EDU/PROP DIPLOM
PRESS ADJUD ARMS/CONT ATTIT MARXISM. PAGE 101 E2028

                                                  L66
KRENZ F.E.,"THE REFUGEE AS A SUBJECT OF   INT/LAW
INTERNATIONAL LAW." FUT LAW NAT/G CREATE ADJUD   DISCRIM
ISOLAT STRANGE...RECORD UN. PAGE 62 E1230   NEW/IDEA

                                                  C66
BLAISDELL D.C.,"INTERNATIONAL ORGANIZATION." FUT BIBLIOG
WOR+45 ECO/DEV DELIB/GP FORCES EFFICIENCY PEACE   INT/ORG
ORD/FREE...INT/LAW 20 UN LEAGUE/NAT NATO. PAGE 12 DIPLOM
E0239   ARMS/CONT

                                                  B67
ESTEY M.,THE UNIONS: STRUCTURE, DEVELOPMENT, AND LABOR
MANAGEMENT. FUT USA+45 ADJUD CONTROL INGP/REL DRIVE EX/STRUC
...DECISION T 20 AFL/CIO. PAGE 35 E0699   ADMIN
                                                  GOV/REL

                                                  B67
FESLER J.W.,THE FIFTY STATES AND THEIR LOCAL   PROVS
GOVERNMENTS. FUT USA+45 POL/PAR LEGIS PROB/SOLV   LOC/G
ADMIN CT/SYS CHOOSE GOV/REL FEDERAL...POLICY CHARTS
20 SUPREME/CT. PAGE 37 E0743

                                                  B67
UNIVERSAL REFERENCE SYSTEM,PUBLIC POLICY AND THE BIBLIOG/A
MANAGEMENT OF SCIENCE (VOLUME IX). FUT SPACE WOR+45 POLICY
LAW NAT/G TEC/DEV CONTROL NUC/PWR GOV/REL   MGT
...COMPUT/IR GEN/METH. PAGE 99 E1975   PHIL/SCI

                                                  S67
DEUTSCH E.P.,"A JUDICIAL PATH TO WORLD PEACE." FUT INT/LAW
WOR+45 CONSTN PROB/SOLV DIPLOM LICENSE ADJUD   INT/ORG
SANCTION CHOOSE REPRESENT NAT/LISM SOVEREIGN 20   JURID
ICJ. PAGE 31 E0611   PEACE

                                                  S67
FLECHTHEIM O.K.,"BLOC FORMATION VS. DIALOGUE."   FUT
CONSTN ECO/DEV BAL/PWR PEACE ATTIT PWR COLD/WAR. CAP/ISM
PAGE 38 E0761   MARXISM
                                                  DEBATE

                                                  S67
GLASER D.,"NATIONAL GOALS AND INDICATORS FOR THE CRIME
REDUCTION OF CRIME AND DELINQUENCY." FUT USA+45   CRIMLGY
NAT/G...CON/ANAL METH 20. PAGE 44 E0874   LAW
                                                  STAT

                                                  S67
GOSSETT W.T.,"ELECTING THE PRESIDENT: NEW HOPE FOR CONSTN
AN OLD IDEAL." FUT USA+45 USA-45 PROVS LEGIS   CHIEF
PROB/SOLV WRITING DEBATE ADJUD REPRESENT...MAJORIT CHOOSE
DECISION 20 HOUSE/REP PRESIDENT. PAGE 45 E0892   NAT/G

FUTURE....SEE FUT

——————————————————— G ———————————————————

GABON....SEE ALSO AFR

GABRIEL P.P. E0825

GAJENDRAGADKAR P.B. E0826

GALBRAITH, JOHN KENNETH....SEE GALBRTH/JK

GALBRTH/JK....JOHN KENNETH GALBRAITH

GALENSON W. E0827

GALLAGHER J.F. E0828

GALLOWAY E. E0829

GAMBIA....SEE ALSO AFR

GAMBLE....SPECULATION ON AN UNCERTAIN EVENT

                                                  B51
KEFAUVER E.,CRIME IN AMERICA. USA+45 USA-45 MUNIC ELITES
NEIGH DELIB/GP TRIBUTE GAMBLE LOBBY SANCTION   CRIME
...AUD/VIS 20 CAPONE/AL MAFIA MIAMI CHICAGO   PWR
DETROIT. PAGE 60 E1194   FORCES

                                                  B61
US HOUSE COMM ON JUDICIARY,LEGISLATION RELATING TO LEGIS
ORGANIZED CRIME. USA+45 DIST/IND DELIB/GP GAMBLE CONTROL
SANCTION HOUSE/REP. PAGE 100 E2004   CRIME
                                                  LAW

                                                  S67
SCHELLING T.C.,"ECONOMICS AND CRIMINAL ENTERPRISE." CRIME
LAW FORCES BARGAIN ECO/TAC CONTROL GAMBLE ROUTINE PROB/SOLV
ADJUST DEMAND INCOME PROFIT CRIMLGY. PAGE 87 E1756 CONCPT

GAMBLING....SEE RISK, GAMBLE

GAME....GAME THEORY AND DECISION THEORY IN MODELS

                                                  S58
SCHUBERT G.A.,"THE STUDY OF JUDICIAL DECISION-   JUDGE
MAKING AS AN ASPECT OF POLITICAL BEHAVIOR." PLAN DECISION
ADJUD CT/SYS INGP/REL PERSON...PHIL/SCI SOC QUANT CON/ANAL
STAT CHARTS IDEA/COMP SOC/EXP. PAGE 89 E1779   GAME

                                                  B59
SCHUBERT G.A.,QUANTITATIVE ANALYSIS OF JUDICIAL   JUDGE
BEHAVIOR. ADJUD LEAD CHOOSE INGP/REL MAJORITY ATTIT CT/SYS
...DECISION JURID CHARTS GAME SIMUL SUPREME/CT.   PERSON
PAGE 89 E1780   QUANT

                                                  B65
SCHUBERT G.,THE JUDICIAL MIND: THE ATTITUDES AND CT/SYS
IDEOLOGIES OF SUPREME COURT JUSTICES 1946-1963.   JUDGE
USA+45 ELITES NAT/G CONTROL PERS/REL MAJORITY   ATTIT
CONSERVE...DECISION JURID MODAL STAT TREND GP/COMP NEW/LIB
GAME. PAGE 88 E1774

                                                  S66
EWALD R.F.,"ONE OF MANY POSSIBLE GAMES." ACADEM   SIMUL
INT/ORG ARMS/CONT...INT/LAW GAME. PAGE 36 E0706   HYPO/EXP
                                                  PROG/TEAC
                                                  RECORD

GANDHI/I....MME. INDIRA GANDHI

GANDHI/M....MAHATMA GANDHI

GANDOLFI A. E0830

GANJI M. E0831

GANZ G. E0832

GAO....THE EMPIRE OF GAO

GARCIA ROBLES A. E0833

GARCON M. E0834

GARDINER H.C. E0835

GARDNER L.C. E0836

GARDNER R.N. E0837,E0838,E0839

GARFIELD/J....PRESIDENT JAMES A. GARFIELD

GARIBALD/G....GUISEPPE GARIBALDI

GARNER J.F. E0314

GARNER U.F. E0840

GARRISON L.K. E0116

GARY....GARY, INDIANA

GAS/NATURL....GAS, NATURAL

GASS O. E0841

GATT....GENERAL AGREEMENT ON TARIFFS AND TRADE; SEE ALSO
VOL/ASSN, INT/ORG

B58
SEYID MUHAMMAD V.A.,THE LEGAL FRAMEWORK OF WORLD INT/LAW
TRADE. WOR+45 INT/ORG DIPLOM CONTROL...BIBLIOG 20 VOL/ASSN
TREATY UN IMF GATT. PAGE 90 E1807 INT/TRADE
TARIFFS

B62
ALEXANDROWICZ C.H.,WORLD ECONOMIC AGENCIES: LAW AND INT/LAW
PRACTICE. WOR+45 DIST/IND FINAN LABOR CONSULT INT/ORG
INT/TRADE TARIFFS REPRESENT HEALTH...JURID 20 UN DIPLOM
GATT EEC OAS ECSC. PAGE 3 E0063 ADJUD

B62
SHAW C.,LEGAL PROBLEMS IN INTERNATIONAL TRADE AND INT/LAW
INVESTMENT. WOR+45 ECO/DEV ECO/UNDEV MARKET DIPLOM INT/TRADE
TAX INCOME ROLE...ANTHOL BIBLIOG 20 TREATY UN IMF FINAN
GATT. PAGE 91 E1816 ECO/TAC

S63
WALKER H.,"THE INTERNATIONAL LAW OF COMMODITY MARKET
AGREEMENTS." FUT WOR+45 ECO/DEV ECO/UNDEV FINAN VOL/ASSN
INT/ORG NAT/G CONSULT CREATE PLAN ECO/TAC ATTIT INT/LAW
PERCEPT...CONCPT GEN/LAWS TOT/POP GATT 20. PAGE 105 INT/TRADE
E2095

N67
US SENATE COMM ON FOREIGN REL,SURVEY OF THE INT/TRADE
ALLIANCE FOR PROGRESS: FOREIGN TRADE POLICIES REGION
(PAMPHLET). L/A+17C LAW ECO/UNDEV ECO/TAC TARIFFS AGREE
20 GATT LAFTA UN. PAGE 102 E2037 INT/ORG

GEARY....GEARY ACT

GEERTZ C. E0842

GELLER M.A. E0843

GELLHORN W. E0844,E0845,E0846,E0847

GEN/DYNMCS....GENERAL DYNAMICS CORPORATION

GEN/ELCTRC....GENERAL ELECTRIC CO.

GEN/LAWS....SYSTEMS AND APPROACHES BASED ON SUBSTANTIVE
RELATIONS

GEN/METH....SYSTEMS BASED ON METHODOLGY

GEN/MOTORS....GENERAL MOTORS CORPORATION

GENACCOUNT....GENERAL ACCOUNTING OFFICE

S61
BAER E.,"THE GENERAL ACCOUNTING OFFICE: THE FEDERAL ADJUD
GOVERNMENT'S AUDITOR." USA+45 NAT/G REPRESENT 20 EX/STRUC
GENACCOUNT. PAGE 7 E0132 EXEC
LAW

GENERAL ACCOUNTING OFFICE....SEE GENACCOUNT

GENERAL AGREEMENT ON TARIFFS AND TRADE....SEE GATT

GENERAL AND COMPLETE DISARMAMENT....SEE ARMS/CONT

GENERAL ASSEMBLY....SEE UN+LEGIS

GENERAL DYNAMICS CORPORATION....SEE GEN/DYNMCS

GENERAL ELECTRIC COMPANY....SEE GEN/ELCTRC

GENERAL MOTORS CORPORATION....SEE GEN/MOTORS

GENEVA/CON....GENEVA CONFERENCES (ANY OR ALL)

GENTILI A. E0848,E0849

GEOG....DEMOGRAPHY AND GEOGRAPHY

N
LIBRARY INTERNATIONAL REL,INTERNATIONAL INFORMATION BIBLIOG/A
SERVICE. WOR+45 CULTURE INT/ORG FORCES...GEOG HUM DIPLOM
SOC. PAGE 65 E1295 INT/TRADE
INT/LAW

N
LATIN AMERICA IN PERIODICAL LITERATURE. LAW TEC/DEV BIBLIOG/A
DIPLOM RECEIVE EDU/PROP...GEOG HUM MGT 20. PAGE 2 L/A+17C

E0024 SOCIETY
ECO/UNDEV

B01
GRIFFIN A.P.C.,LIST OF BOOKS ON SAMOA (PAMPHLET). BIBLIOG/A
GERMANY S/ASIA UK USA-45 WOR-45 ECO/UNDEV REGION COLONIAL
ALL/VALS ORD/FREE ALL/IDEOS...GEOG INT/LAW 19 SAMOA DIPLOM
GUAM. PAGE 46 E0918

B10
MENDELSSOHN S.,MENDELSSOHN'S SOUTH AFRICA BIBLIOG/A
BIBLIOGRAPHY (VOL. I). SOUTH/AFR RACE/REL...GEOG CULTURE
JURID 19/20. PAGE 72 E1440

L21
HALDEMAN E.,"SERIALS OF AN INTERNATIONAL BIBLIOG
CHARACTER." WOR-45 DIPLOM...ART/METH GEOG HEAL HUM PHIL/SCI
INT/LAW JURID PSY SOC. PAGE 49 E0978

B29
CONWELL-EVANS T.P.,THE LEAGUE COUNCIL IN ACTION. DELIB/GP
EUR+WWI TURKEY UK USSR WOR-45 INT/ORG FORCES JUDGE INT/LAW
ECO/TAC EDU/PROP LEGIT ROUTINE ARMS/CONT COERCE
ATTIT PWR...MAJORIT GEOG JURID CONCPT LEAGUE/NAT
TOT/POP VAL/FREE TUNIS 20. PAGE 25 E0498

B29
PRATT I.A.,MODERN EGYPT: A LIST OF REFERENCES TO BIBLIOG
MATERIAL IN THE NEW YORK PUBLIC LIBRARY. UAR ISLAM
ECO/UNDEV...GEOG JURID SOC LING 20. PAGE 82 E1647 DIPLOM
NAT/G

B32
EAGLETON C.,INTERNATIONAL GOVERNMENT. BRAZIL FRANCE INT/ORG
GERMANY ITALY UK USSR WOR-45 DELIB/GP TOP/EX PLAN JURID
ECO/TAC EDU/PROP LEGIT ADJUD REGION ARMS/CONT DIPLOM
COERCE ATTIT PWR...GEOG MGT VAL/FREE LEAGUE/NAT 20. INT/LAW
PAGE 34 E0670

B33
GILLETTE J.M.,CURRENT SOCIAL PROBLEMS. CONTROL GEOG
CRIME AGE/Y BIO/SOC...SOC 20. PAGE 43 E0861 HEALTH
RACE/REL
FAM

S35
MCMAHON A.H.,"INTERNATIONAL BOUNDARIES." WOR-45 GEOG
INT/ORG NAT/G LEGIT SKILL...CHARTS GEN/LAWS 20. VOL/ASSN
PAGE 71 E1423 INT/LAW

B36
CULVER D.C.,METHODOLOGY OF SOCIAL SCIENCE RESEARCH: BIBLIOG/A
A BIBLIOGRAPHY. LAW CULTURE...CRIMLGY GEOG STAT OBS METH
INT QU HIST/WRIT CHARTS 20. PAGE 28 E0550 SOC

B37
BADEN A.L.,IMMIGRATION AND ITS RESTRICTION IN THE BIBLIOG
US (PAMPHLET). USA-45 NAT/G LEGIS...GEOG 20 STRANGE
CONGRESS. PAGE 7 E0130 CONTROL
LAW

B40
WOLFERS A.,BRITAIN AND FRANCE BETWEEN TWO WORLD DIPLOM
WARS. FRANCE UK INT/ORG NAT/G PLAN BARGAIN ECO/TAC WAR
AGREE ISOLAT ALL/IDEOS...DECISION GEOG 20 TREATY POLICY
VERSAILLES INTERVENT. PAGE 107 E2139

B42
BLANCHARD L.R.,MARTINIQUE: A SELECTED LIST OF BIBLIOG/A
REFERENCES (PAMPHLET). WEST/IND AGRI LOC/G SCHOOL SOCIETY
...ART/METH GEOG JURID CHARTS 20. PAGE 12 E0241 CULTURE
COLONIAL

B42
GILLETTE J.M.,PROBLEMS OF A CHANGING SOCIAL ORDER. BIO/SOC
USA+45 STRATA FAM CONTROL CRIME RACE/REL HEALTH ADJUST
WEALTH...GEOG GP/COMP. PAGE 43 E0862 ATTIT
SOC/WK

B42
US LIBRARY OF CONGRESS,SOCIAL AND CULTURAL PROBLEMS BIBLIOG/A
IN WARTIME: APRIL 1941-MARCH 1942. WOR-45 CLIENT WAR
SECT EDU/PROP CRIME LEISURE RACE/REL STRANGE ATTIT SOC
DRIVE HEALTH...GEOG 20. PAGE 100 E2012 CULTURE

B43
US LIBRARY OF CONGRESS,SOCIAL AND CULTURAL PROBLEMS BIBLIOG/A
IN WARTIME: APRIL-DECEMBER (SUPPLEMENT 1). WOR-45 WAR
SECT EDU/PROP CRIME LEISURE CIVMIL/REL RACE/REL SOC
ATTIT DRIVE HEALTH...GEOG 20. PAGE 100 E2013 CULTURE

B43
US LIBRARY OF CONGRESS,SOCIAL AND CULTURAL PROBLEMS BIBLIOG/A
IN WARTIME: JANUARY-MAY 1943 (SUPPLEMENT 2). WOR-45 WAR
FAM SECT PLAN EDU/PROP CRIME LEISURE RACE/REL DRIVE SOC
HEALTH...GEOG 20 JEWS. PAGE 100 E2014 CULTURE

B44

DE HUSZAR G.B.,NEW PERSPECTIVES ON PEACE. UNIV
CULTURE SOCIETY ECO/DEV ECO/UNDEV NAT/G FORCES
CREATE ECO/TAC DOMIN ADJUD COERCE DRIVE ORD/FREE
...GEOG JURID PSY SOC CONCPT TOT/POP. PAGE 29 E0584

ATTIT
MYTH
PEACE
WAR

B44

FULLER G.H.,TURKEY: A SELECTED LIST OF REFERENCES.
ISLAM TURKEY CULTURE ECO/UNDEV AGRI DIPLOM NAT/LISM
CONSERVE...GEOG HUM INT/LAW SOC 7/20 MAPS. PAGE 42
E0824

BIBLIOG/A
ALL/VALS

B45

HILL N.,CLAIMS TO TERRITORY IN INTERNATIONAL LAW
AND RELATIONS. WOR-45 NAT/G DOMIN EDU/PROP LEGIT
REGION ROUTINE ORD/FREE PWR WEALTH...GEOG INT/LAW
JURID 20. PAGE 52 E1047

INT/ORG
ADJUD
SOVEREIGN

B45

US LIBRARY OF CONGRESS,NETHERLANDS EAST INDIES.
INDONESIA LAW CULTURE AGRI INDUS SCHOOL COLONIAL
HEALTH...GEOG JURID SOC 19/20 NETH/IND. PAGE 101
E2017

BIBLIOG/A
S/ASIA
NAT/G

B45

WOOLBERT R.G.,FOREIGN AFFAIRS BIBLIOGRAPHY,
1932-1942. INT/ORG SECT INT/TRADE COLONIAL RACE/REL
NAT/LISM...GEOG INT/LAW GOV/COMP IDEA/COMP 20.
PAGE 107 E2144

BIBLIOG/A
DIPLOM
WAR

B46

AMERICAN DOCUMENTATION INST,CATALOGUE OF AUXILIARY
PUBLICATIONS IN MICROFILMS AND PHOTOPRINTS. USA-45
LAW AGRI CREATE TEC/DEV ADMIN...GEOG LING MATH 20.
PAGE 4 E0077

BIBLIOG
EDU/PROP
PSY

B46

GRIFFIN G.G.,A GUIDE TO MANUSCRIPTS RELATING TO
AMERICAN HISTORY IN BRITISH DEPOSITORIES. CANADA
IRELAND MOD/EUR UK USA-45 LAW DIPLOM ADMIN COLONIAL
WAR NAT/LISM SOVEREIGN...GEOG INT/LAW 15/19
CMN/WLTH. PAGE 47 E0936

BIBLIOG/A
ALL/VALS
NAT/G

S47

ANGELL R.C.,"THE SOCIAL INTEGRATION OF AMERICAN
CITIES OF MORE THAN 1000,000 POPULATION" (BMR)"
USA+45 SOCIETY CRIME ADJUST WEALTH...GEOG SOC
CONCPT INDICATOR SAMP CHARTS SOC/INTEG 20. PAGE 5
E0098

MUNIC
CENSUS
GP/REL

B48

YAKOBSON S.,FIVE HUNDRED RUSSIAN WORKS FOR COLLEGE
LIBRARIES (PAMPHLET). MOD/EUR USSR MARXISM SOCISM
...ART/METH GEOG HUM JURID SOC 13/20. PAGE 108
E2162

BIBLIOG
NAT/G
CULTURE
COM

B49

US DEPARTMENT OF STATE,SOVIET BIBLIOGRAPHY
(PAMPHLET). CHINA/COM COM USSR LAW AGRI INT/ORG
ECO/TAC EDU/PROP...POLICY GEOG 20. PAGE 99 E1994

BIBLIOG/A
MARXISM
CULTURE
DIPLOM

B50

DOROSH J.T.,GUIDE TO SOVIET BIBLIOGRAPHIES. USSR
LAW AGRI SCHOOL SECT FORCES TEC/DEV...ART/METH GEOG
HUM SOC 20. PAGE 32 E0639

BIBLIOG
METH
CON/ANAL

B50

EMBREE J.F.,BIBLIOGRAPHY OF THE PEOPLES AND
CULTURES OF MAINLAND SOUTHEAST ASIA. CAMBODIA LAOS
THAILAND VIETNAM LAW...GEOG HUM SOC MYTH LING
CHARTS WORSHIP 20. PAGE 35 E0686

BIBLIOG/A
CULTURE
S/ASIA

B51

BISSAINTHE M.,DICTIONNAIRE DE BIBLIOGRAPHIE
HAITIENNE. HAITI ELITES AGRI LEGIS DIPLOM INT/TRADE
WRITING ORD/FREE CATHISM...ART/METH GEOG 19/20
NEGRO TREATY. PAGE 12 E0234

BIBLIOG
L/A+17C
SOCIETY
NAT/G

B52

ETTINGHAUSEN R.,SELECTED AND ANNOTATED BIBLIOGRAPHY
OF BOOKS AND PERIODICALS IN WESTERN LANGUAGES
DEALING WITH NEAR AND MIDDLE EAST. LAW CULTURE SECT
...ART/METH GEOG SOC. PAGE 35 E0700

BIBLIOG/A
ISLAM
MEDIT-7

B52

UNESCO,THESES DE SCIENCES SOCIALES: CATALOGUE
ANALYTIQUE INTERNATIONAL DE THESES INEDITES DE
DOCTORAT, 1940-1950. INT/ORG DIPLOM EDU/PROP...GEOG
INT/LAW MGT PSY SOC 20. PAGE 98 E1958

BIBLIOG
ACADEM
WRITING

B52

WALTER P.A.F.,RACE AND CULTURE RELATIONS. FAM
HEALTH WEALTH...POLICY CRIMLGY GEOG BIBLIOG T 20.
PAGE 105 E2097

RACE/REL
DISCRIM
GP/REL

B53

PIERCE R.A.,RUSSIAN CENTRAL ASIA, 1867-1917: A
SELECTED BIBLIOGRAPHY (PAMPHLET). USSR LAW CULTURE
NAT/G EDU/PROP WAR...GEOG SOC 19/20. PAGE 81 E1616

BIBLIOG
COLONIAL
ADMIN
COM

B54

BATTEN T.R.,PROBLEMS OF AFRICAN DEVELOPMENT (2ND
ED.). AFR LAW SOCIETY SCHOOL ECO/TAC TAX...GEOG
HEAL SOC 20. PAGE 8 E0154

ECO/UNDEV
AGRI
LOC/G
PROB/SOLV

B55

TROTIER A.H.,DOCTORAL DISSERTATIONS ACCEPTED BY
AMERICAN UNIVERSITIES 1954-55. SECT DIPLOM HEALTH
...ART/METH GEOG INT/LAW SOC LING CHARTS 20.
PAGE 97 E1943

BIBLIOG
ACADEM
USA+45
WRITING

B57

BLOOMFIELD L.M.,EGYPT, ISRAEL AND THE GULF OF
AQABA: IN INTERNATIONAL LAW. LAW NAT/G CONSULT
FORCES PLAN ECO/TAC ROUTINE COERCE ATTIT DRIVE
PERCEPT PERSON RIGID/FLEX LOVE PWR WEALTH...GEOG
CONCPT MYTH TREND. PAGE 13 E0250

ISLAM
INT/LAW
UAR

B57

BYRNES R.F.,BIBLIOGRAPHY OF AMERICAN PUBLICATIONS
ON EAST CENTRAL EUROPE, 1945-1957 (VOL. XXII). SECT
DIPLOM EDU/PROP RACE/REL...ART/METH GEOG JURID SOC
LING 20 JEWS. PAGE 18 E0354

BIBLIOG/A
COM
MARXISM
NAT/G

B57

DIVINE R.A.,AMERICAN IMMIGRATION POLICY, 1924-52.
USA+45 USA-45 VOL/ASSN DELIB/GP ADJUD WAR ADJUST
DISCRIM...POLICY JURID 20 DEPRESSION MIGRATION.
PAGE 32 E0630

GEOG
HABITAT
LEGIS
CONTROL

B58

KURL S.,ESTONIA: A SELECTED BIBLIOGRAPHY. USSR
ESTONIA LAW INTELL SECT...ART/METH GEOG HUM SOC 20.
PAGE 62 E1238

BIBLIOG
CULTURE
NAT/G

B58

MANSERGH N.,COMMONWEALTH PERSPECTIVES. GHANA UK LAW
VOL/ASSN CONFER HEALTH SOVEREIGN...GEOG CHARTS
ANTHOL 20 CMN/WLTH AUSTRAL. PAGE 68 E1363

DIPLOM
COLONIAL
INT/ORG
INGP/REL

B58

MUSIKER R.,GUIDE TO SOUTH AFRICAN REFERENCE BOOKS.
SOUTH/AFR SOCIETY SECT EDU/PROP PRESS RACE/REL
...JURID SOC/WK 20. PAGE 75 E1512

BIBLIOG/A
SOC
GEOG

B59

OKINSHEVICH L.A.,LATIN AMERICA IN SOVIET WRITINGS,
1945-1958: A BIBLIOGRAPHY. USSR LAW ECO/UNDEV LABOR
DIPLOM EDU/PROP REV...GEOG SOC 20. PAGE 78 E1573

BIBLIOG
WRITING
COM
L/A+17C

B59

REIFF H.,THE UNITED STATES AND THE TREATY LAW OF
THE SEA. USA+45 USA-45 SEA SOCIETY INT/ORG CONSULT
DELIB/GP LEGIS DIPLOM LEGIT ATTIT ORD/FREE PWR
WEALTH...GEOG JURID TOT/POP 20 TREATY. PAGE 84
E1681

ADJUD
INT/LAW

B60

GONZALEZ NAVARRO M.,LA COLONIZACION EN MEXICO,
1877-1910. AGRI NAT/G PLAN PROB/SOLV INCOME
...POLICY JURID CENSUS 19/20 MEXIC/AMER MIGRATION.
PAGE 44 E0883

ECO/UNDEV
GEOG
HABITAT
COLONIAL

B60

HEYSE T.,PROBLEMS FONCIERS ET REGIME DES TERRES
(ASPECTS ECONOMIQUES, JURIDIQUES ET SOCIAUX). AFR
CONGO/BRAZ INT/ORG DIPLOM SOVEREIGN...GEOG TREATY
20. PAGE 52 E1037

BIBLIOG
AGRI
ECO/UNDEV
LEGIS

B60

WOETZEL R.K.,THE INTERNATIONAL CONTROL OF AIRSPACE
AND OUTERSPACE. FUT WOR+45 AIR CONSTN STRUCT
CONSULT PLAN TEC/DEV ADJUD RIGID/FLEX KNOWL
ORD/FREE PWR...TECHNIC GEOG MGT NEW/IDEA TREND
COMPUT/IR VAL/FREE 20 TREATY. PAGE 107 E2137

INT/ORG
JURID
SPACE
INT/LAW

N60

RHODESIA-NYASA NATL ARCHIVES,A SELECT BIBLIOGRAPHY
OF RECENT PUBLICATIONS CONCERNING THE FEDERATION OF
RHODESIA AND NYASALAND (PAMPHLET). MALAWI RHODESIA
LAW CULTURE STRUCT ECO/UNDEV LEGIS...GEOG 20.
PAGE 84 E1689

BIBLIOG
ADMIN
ORD/FREE
NAT/G

B61

MERTON R.K.,CONTEMPORARY SOCIAL PROBLEMS: AN

CRIME

INTRODUCTION TO THE SOCIOLOGY OF DEVIANT BEHAVIOR
AND SOCIAL DISORGANIZATION. FAM MUNIC FORCES WORKER
PROB/SOLV INGP/REL RACE/REL ISOLAT...CRIMLGY GEOG
PSY T 20 NEGRO. PAGE 72 E1444
ANOMIE
STRANGE
SOC

B62
CARPER E.T.,ILLINOIS GOES TO CONGRESS FOR ARMY
LAND. USA+45 LAW EXTR/IND PROVS REGION CIVMIL/REL
GOV/REL FEDERAL ATTIT 20 ILLINOIS SENATE CONGRESS
DIRKSEN/E DOUGLAS/P. PAGE 20 E0391
ADMIN
LOBBY
GEOG
LEGIS

B62
KIDDER F.E.,THESES ON PAN AMERICAN TOPICS. LAW
CULTURE NAT/G SECT DIPLOM HEALTH...ART/METH GEOG
SOC 13/20. PAGE 61 E1213
BIBLIOG
CHRIST-17C
L/A+17C
SOCIETY

B62
MCDOUGAL M.S.,THE PUBLIC ORDER OF THE OCEANS.
WOR+45 WOR-45 SEA INT/ORG NAT/G CONSULT DELIB/GP
DIPLOM LEGIT PEACE RIGID/FLEX...GEOG INT/LAW JURID
RECORD TOT/POP 20 TREATY. PAGE 70 E1407
ADJUD
ORD/FREE

B62
PAIKERT G.C.,THE GERMAN EXODUS. EUR+WWI GERMANY/W
LAW CULTURE SOCIETY STRUCT INDUS NAT/LISM RESPECT
SOVEREIGN...CHARTS BIBLIOG SOC/INTEG 20 MIGRATION.
PAGE 79 E1591
INGP/REL
STRANGE
GEOG
GP/REL

B62
UNECA LIBRARY,NEW ACQUISITIONS IN THE UNECA
LIBRARY. LAW NAT/G PLAN PROB/SOLV TEC/DEV ADMIN
REGION...GEOG SOC 20 UN. PAGE 98 E1956
BIBLIOG
AFR
ECO/UNDEV
INT/ORG

B63
CHOJNACKI S.,REGISTER ON CURRENT RESEARCH ON
ETHIOPIA AND THE HORN OF AFRICA. ETHIOPIA LAW
CULTURE AGRI SECT EDU/PROP ADMIN...GEOG HEAL LING
20. PAGE 22 E0433
BIBLIOG
ACT/RES
INTELL
ACADEM

B63
FISCHER-GALATI S.A.,RUMANIA; A BIBLIOGRAPHIC GUIDE
(PAMPHLET). ROMANIA INTELL ECO/DEV LABOR SECT
WEALTH...GEOG SOC/WK LING 20. PAGE 38 E0756
BIBLIOG/A
NAT/G
COM
LAW

B63
HACKER A.,CONGRESSIONAL DISTRICTING: THE ISSUE OF
EQUAL REPRESENTATION. FUT CT/SYS GEOG. PAGE 49
E0970
LEGIS
REPRESENT
APPORT

S63
WEISSBERG G.,"MAPS AS EVIDENCE IN INTERNATIONAL
BOUNDARY DISPUTES: A REAPPRAISAL." CHINA/COM
EUR+WWI INDIA MOD/EUR S/ASIA INT/ORG NAT/G LEGIT
PERCEPT...JURID CHARTS 20. PAGE 105 E2110
LAW
GEOG
SOVEREIGN

B64
DRESSLER D.,READINGS IN CRIMINOLOGY AND PENOLOGY.
UNIV CULTURE PUB/INST FORCES ACT/RES PROB/SOLV
ANOMIE BIO/SOC SUPEGO...GEOG PSY ANTHOL 20. PAGE 33
E0648
CRIMLGY
CRIME
ADJUD
ADJUST

B64
US HOUSE COMM ON JUDICIARY,IMMIGRATION HEARINGS.
DELIB/GP STRANGE HABITAT...GEOG JURID 20 CONGRESS
MIGRATION. PAGE 100 E2006
NAT/G
POLICY
DIPLOM
NAT/LISM

B65
BLITZ L.F.,THE POLITICS AND ADMINISTRATION OF
NIGERIAN GOVERNMENT. NIGER CULTURE LOC/G LEGIS
DIPLOM COLONIAL CT/SYS SOVEREIGN...GEOG SOC ANTHOL
20. PAGE 13 E0245
NAT/G
GOV/REL
POL/PAR

B65
CAMPBELL E.H.,SURVEYS, SUBDIVISIONS AND PLATTING,
AND BOUNDARIES: WASHINGTON STATE LAW AND JUDICIAL
DECISIONS. USA+45 LAW LOC/G...DECISION JURID
CON/ANAL BIBLIOG WASHINGT/G PARTITION WATER.
PAGE 19 E0372
CONSTN
PLAN
GEOG
PROVS

B65
NJ LEGIS REAPPORT PLAN COMM,PUBLIC HEARING ON
REDISTRICTING AND REAPPORTIONMENT. USA+45 CONSTN
VOL/ASSN LEGIS DEBATE...POLICY GEOG CENSUS 20
NEW/JERSEY. PAGE 77 E1552
APPORT
REPRESENT
PROVS
JURID

B65
UNESCO,INTERNATIONAL ORGANIZATIONS IN THE SOCIAL
SCIENCES(REV. ED.). LAW ADMIN ATTIT...CRIMLGY GEOG
INT/LAW PSY SOC STAT 20 UNESCO. PAGE 98 E1962
INT/ORG
R+D
PROF/ORG
ACT/RES

B65
UNIVERSAL REFERENCE SYSTEM,INTERNATIONAL AFFAIRS:
VOLUME I IN THE POLITICAL SCIENCE, GOVERNMENT, AND
PUBLIC POLICY SERIES....DECISION ECOMETRIC GEOG
INT/LAW JURID MGT PHIL/SCI PSY SOC. PAGE 98 E1972
BIBLIOG/A
GEN/METH
COMPUT/IR
DIPLOM

B65
VON GLAHN G.,LAW AMONG NATIONS: AN INTRODUCTION TO
PUBLIC INTERNATIONAL LAW. WOR+45 WOR-45 INT/ORG
NAT/G CREATE ADJUD WAR...GEOG CLASSIF TREND
BIBLIOG. PAGE 104 E2082
ACADEM
INT/LAW
GEN/LAWS
LAW

S65
KHOURI F.J.,"THE JORDON RIVER CONTROVERSY." LAW
SOCIETY ECO/UNDEV AGRI FINAN INDUS SECT FORCES
ACT/RES PLAN TEC/DEV ECO/TAC EDU/PROP COERCE ATTIT
DRIVE PERCEPT RIGID/FLEX ALL/VALS...GEOG SOC MYTH
WORK. PAGE 61 E1212
ISLAM
INT/ORG
ISRAEL
JORDAN

B66
BEER U.,FRUCHTBARKEITSREGELUNG ALS KONSEQUENZ
VERANTWORTLICHER ELTERNSCHAFT. ASIA GERMANY/W INDIA
LAW ECO/DEV ECO/UNDEV TEC/DEV ECO/TAC BIO/SOC SEX
CATHISM...METH/COMP 20 CHINJAP BIRTH/CON. PAGE 9
E0178
CONTROL
GEOG
FAM
SECT

B66
FRIEDMANN W.G.,INTERNATIONAL FINANCIAL AID. USA+45
ECO/DEV ECO/UNDEV NAT/G VOL/ASSN EX/STRUC PLAN RENT
GIVE BAL/PAY PWR...GEOG INT/LAW STAT TREND UN EEC
COMECON. PAGE 41 E0806
INT/ORG
FOR/AID
TEC/DEV
ECO/TAC

B66
HOPKINS J.F.K.,"ARABIC PERIODICAL LITERATURE, 1961."
ISLAM LAW CULTURE SECT...GEOG HEAL PHIL/SCI PSY SOC
20. PAGE 55 E1096
BIBLIOG/A
NAT/LISM
TEC/DEV
INDUS

B66
US DEPARTMENT OF STATE,RESEARCH ON AFRICA (EXTERNAL
RESEARCH LIST NO 5-25). LAW CULTURE ECO/UNDEV
POL/PAR DIPLOM EDU/PROP LEAD REGION MARXISM...GEOG
LING WORSHIP 20. PAGE 100 E1996
BIBLIOG/A
ASIA
S/ASIA
NAT/G

B66
US DEPARTMENT OF STATE,RESEARCH ON THE USSR AND
EASTERN EUROPE (EXTERNAL RESEARCH LIST NO 1-25).
USSR LAW CULTURE SOCIETY NAT/G TEC/DEV DIPLOM
EDU/PROP REGION...GEOG LING. PAGE 100 E1997
BIBLIOG/A
EUR+WWI
COM
MARXISM

B66
US DEPARTMENT OF STATE,RESEARCH ON WESTERN EUROPE,
GREAT BRITAIN, AND CANADA (EXTERNAL RESEARCH LIST
NO 3-25). CANADA GERMANY/W UK LAW CULTURE NAT/G
POL/PAR FORCES EDU/PROP REGION MARXISM...GEOG SOC
WORSHIP 20 CMN/WLTH. PAGE 100 E1998
BIBLIOG/A
EUR+WWI
DIPLOM

S66
DETTER I.,"THE PROBLEM OF UNEQUAL TREATIES." CONSTN
NAT/G LEGIS COLONIAL COERCE PWR...GEOG UN TIME
TREATY. PAGE 31 E0610
SOVEREIGN
DOMIN
INT/LAW
ECO/UNDEV

S66
SHEEHY E.P.,"SELECTED REFERENCE BOOKS OF
1965-1966." AGRI PERF/ART PRESS...GEOG HUM JURID
SOC LING WORSHIP. PAGE 91 E1817
BIBLIOG/A
INDEX
CLASSIF

N66
CONGRESSIONAL QUARTERLY SERV,HOUSING A NATION
(PAMPHLET). USA+45 LAW STRUCT DIST/IND DELIB/GP
...GEOG CHARTS 20 DEPT/HUD. PAGE 25 E0490
HABITAT
NAT/G
PLAN
MUNIC

S67
TOMASEK R.D.,"THE CHILEAN-BOLIVIAN LAUCA RIVER
DISPUTE AND THE OAS." CHILE L/A+17C PROB/SOLV ADJUD
CONTROL PEACE 20 BOLIV OAS. PAGE 96 E1930
INT/ORG
DIPLOM
GEOG
WAR

B68
GREGG R.W.,INTERNATIONAL ORGANIZATION IN THE
WESTERN HEMISPHERE. L/A+17C USA+45 CULTURE PLAN
DOMIN AGREE CONTROL DETER PWR...GEOG 20 OAS TREATY.
PAGE 46 E0913
INT/ORG
DIPLOM
ECO/UNDEV

C93
PLAYFAIR R.L.,"A BIBLIOGRAPHY OF MOROCCO." MOROCCO
CULTURE AGRI FORCES DIPLOM WAR HEALTH...GEOG JURID
SOC CHARTS. PAGE 81 E1620
BIBLIOG
ISLAM
MEDIT-7

GEOGRAPHY....SEE GEOG

GEOPOLITIC....GEOPOLITICS

GEOPOLITICS....SEE GEOG, GEOPOLITIC

GEORGE/DL....DAVID LLOYD GEORGE

GEORGE/III....GEORGE THE THIRD OF ENGLAND

GEORGIA....GEORGIA

B30
GREEN F.M.,CONSTITUTIONAL DEVELOPMENT IN THE SOUTH CONSTN
ATLANTIC STATES, 1776-1860; A STUDY IN THE PROVS
EVOLUTION OF DEMOCRACY. USA-45 ELITES SOCIETY PLURISM
STRATA ECO/DEV AGRI POL/PAR EX/STRUC LEGIS CT/SYS REPRESENT
REGION...BIBLIOG 18/19 MARYLAND VIRGINIA GEORGIA
NORTH/CAR SOUTH/CAR. PAGE 46 E0905

GER/CONFED....GERMAN CONFEDERATION

GERHARD H. E0850

GERMAN CONFEDERATION....SEE GER/CONFED

GERMAN/AM....GERMAN-AMERICANS

GERMANS/PA....GERMANS IN PENNSYLVANIA

GERMANY....GERMANY IN GENERAL; SEE ALSO APPROPRIATE TIME/
SPACE/CULTURE INDEX

B
DEUTSCHE BIBLIOTH FRANKF A M,DEUTSCHE BIBLIOG
BIBLIOGRAPHIE. EUR+WWI GERMANY ECO/DEV FORCES LAW
DIPLOM LEAD...POLICY PHIL/SCI SOC 20. PAGE 31 E0612 ADMIN
NAT/G

N
DEUTSCHE BUCHEREI,JAHRESVERZEICHNIS DER DEUTSCHEN BIBLIOG
HOCHSCHULSCHRIFTEN. EUR+WWI GERMANY LAW ADMIN WRITING
PERSON...MGT SOC 19/20. PAGE 31 E0613 ACADEM
INTELL

N
DEUTSCHE BUCHEREI,JAHRESVERZEICHNIS DES DEUTSCHEN BIBLIOG
SCHRIFTUMS. AUSTRIA EUR+WWI GERMANY SWITZERLND LAW WRITING
LOC/G DIPLOM ADMIN...MGT SOC 19/20. PAGE 31 E0614 NAT/G

N
DEUTSCHE BUCHEREI,DEUTSCHES BUCHERVERZEICHNIS. BIBLIOG
GERMANY LAW CULTURE POL/PAR ADMIN LEAD ATTIT PERSON NAT/G
...SOC 20. PAGE 31 E0615 DIPLOM
ECO/DEV

B00
GRIFFIN A.P.C.,LIST OF BOOKS RELATING TO THE THEORY BIBLIOG/A
OF COLONIZATION, GOVERNMENT OF DEPENDENCIES, COLONIAL
PROTECTORATES, AND RELATED TOPICS. FRANCE GERMANY GOV/REL
ITALY SPAIN UK USA-45 WOR-45 ECO/TAC ADMIN CONTROL DOMIN
REGION NAT/LISM ALL/VALS PWR...INT/LAW SOC 16/19.
PAGE 46 E0917

B01
GRIFFIN A.P.C.,LIST OF BOOKS ON SAMOA (PAMPHLET). BIBLIOG/A
GERMANY S/ASIA UK USA-45 WOR-45 ECO/UNDEV REGION COLONIAL
ALL/VALS ORD/FREE ALL/IDEOS...GEOG INT/LAW 19 SAMOA DIPLOM
GUAM. PAGE 46 E0918

B02
GRIFFIN A.P.C.,A LIST OF BOOKS RELATING TO TRUSTS BIBLIOG/A
(2ND REV. ED.) (PAMPHLET). FRANCE GERMANY UK USA-45 JURID
WOR-45 LAW ECO/DEV INDUS LG/CO NAT/G CAP/ISM ECO/TAC
CENTRAL DISCRIM PWR LAISSEZ 19/20. PAGE 46 E0919 VOL/ASSN

B03
GRIFFIN A.P.C.,SELECT LIST OF BOOKS ON LABOR BIBLIOG/A
PARTICULARLY RELATING TO STRIKES. FRANCE GERMANY GP/REL
MOD/EUR UK USA-45 LAW NAT/G DELIB/GP WORKER BARGAIN MGT
LICENSE PAY ADJUD 19/20. PAGE 46 E0924 LABOR

B06
GRIFFIN A.P.C.,LIST OF BOOKS RELATING TO CHILD BIBLIOG/A
LABOR (PAMPHLET). BELGIUM FRANCE GERMANY MOD/EUR UK LAW
USA-45 ECO/DEV INDUS WORKER CAP/ISM PAY ROUTINE LABOR
ALL/IDEOS...MGT SOC 19/20. PAGE 47 E0929 AGE/C

B08
GRIFFIN A.P.C.,LIST OF WORKS RELATING TO GOVERNMENT BIBLIOG/A
REGULATION OF INSURANCE UNITED STATES AND FOREIGN FINAN
COUNTRIES (2ND. ED.) (PAMPHLET). FRANCE GERMANY UK LAW
USA-45 WOR-45 LG/CO LOC/G NAT/G LEGIS LICENSE ADJUD CONTROL
LOBBY CENTRAL ORD/FREE 19/20. PAGE 47 E0933

B16
CARLYLE A.J.,BIBLIOGRAPHY OF POLITICAL THEORY BIBLIOG/A
(PAMPHLET). FRANCE GERMANY UK USA-45...JURID 9/19. CONCPT
PAGE 19 E0382 PHIL/SCI

B18
WILSON W.,THE STATE: ELEMENTS OF HISTORICAL AND NAT/G

PRACTICAL POLITICS. FRANCE GERMANY ITALY UK USSR JURID
CONSTN EX/STRUC LEGIS CT/SYS WAR PWR...POLICY CONCPT
GOV/COMP 20. PAGE 106 E2131 NAT/COMP

C20
BLACHLY F.F.,"THE GOVERNMENT AND ADMINISTRATION OF NAT/G
GERMANY." GERMANY CONSTN LOC/G PROVS DELIB/GP GOV/REL
EX/STRUC FORCES LEGIS TOP/EX CT/SYS...BIBLIOG/A ADMIN
19/20. PAGE 12 E0235 PHIL/SCI

B29
LEITZ F.,DIE PUBLIZITAT DER AKTIENGESELLSCHAFT. LG/CO
BELGIUM FRANCE GERMANY UK FINAN PRESS GP/REL PROFIT JURID
KNOWL 20. PAGE 64 E1282 ECO/TAC
NAT/COMP

B32
EAGLETON C.,INTERNATIONAL GOVERNMENT. BRAZIL FRANCE INT/ORG
GERMANY ITALY USSR WOR-45 DELIB/GP TOP/EX GP PLAN JURID
ECO/TAC EDU/PROP LEGIT ADJUD REGION ARMS/CONT DIPLOM
COERCE ATTIT PWR...GEOG MGT VAL/FREE LEAGUE/NAT 20. INT/LAW
PAGE 34 E0670

B32
MASTERS R.D.,INTERNATIONAL LAW IN INTERNATIONAL INT/ORG
COURTS. BELGIUM EUR+WWI FRANCE GERMANY MOD/EUR LAW
SWITZERLND WOR-45 SOCIETY STRATA STRUCT LEGIT EXEC INT/LAW
ALL/VALS...JURID HIST/WRIT TIME/SEQ TREND GEN/LAWS
20. PAGE 69 E1383

B33
ENSOR R.C.K.,COURTS AND JUDGES IN FRANCE, GERMANY, CT/SYS
AND ENGLAND. FRANCE GERMANY UK LAW PROB/SOLV ADMIN EX/STRUC
ROUTINE CRIME ROLE...METH/COMP 20 CIVIL/LAW. ADJUD
PAGE 35 E0692 NAT/COMP

B36
KONRAD F.,DIE PERSONLICHE FREIHEIT IM ORD/FREE
NATIONALSOZIALISTISCHEN DEUTSCHEN REICHE. GERMANY JURID
JUDGE ADJUD GP/REL FASCISM 20 CIVIL/LIB. PAGE 61 CONSTN
E1226 CONCPT

B37
BORGESE G.A.,GOLIATH: THE MARCH OF FASCISM. GERMANY POLICY
ITALY LAW POL/PAR SECT DIPLOM SOCISM...JURID MYTH NAT/LISM
20 DANTE MACHIAVELL MUSSOLIN/B. PAGE 14 E0270 FASCISM
NAT/G

B39
BENES E.,INTERNATIONAL SECURITY. GERMANY UK NAT/G EUR+WWI
DELIB/GP PLAN BAL/PWR ATTIT ORD/FREE PWR LEAGUE/NAT INT/ORG
20 TREATY. PAGE 10 E0186 WAR

B39
LAVES W.H.C.,INTERNATIONAL SECURITY. EUR+WWI ORD/FREE
GERMANY UK USA-45 LAW NAT/G DELIB/GP TOP/EX COERCE LEGIT
PWR...POLICY FASCIST CONCPT HIST/WRIT GEN/LAWS ARMS/CONT
LEAGUE/NAT NAZI 20. PAGE 63 E1267 BAL/PWR

S40
FLORIN J.,"BOLSHEVIST AND NATIONAL SOCIALIST LAW
DOCTRINES OF INTERNATIONAL LAW." EUR+WWI GERMANY ATTIT
USSR R+D INT/ORG NAT/G DIPLOM DOMIN EDU/PROP SOCISM TOTALISM
...CONCPT TIME/SEQ 20. PAGE 39 E0768 INT/LAW

S40
GERTH H.,"THE NAZI PARTY: ITS LEADERSHIP AND POL/PAR
COMPOSITION" (BMR)" GERMANY ELITES STRATA STRUCT DOMIN
EX/STRUC FORCES ECO/TAC CT/SYS CHOOSE TOTALISM LEAD
AGE/Y AUTHORIT PWR 20. PAGE 43 E0851 ADMIN

B42
CROWE S.E.,THE BERLIN WEST AFRICA CONFERENCE, AFR
1884-85. GERMANY ELITES MARKET INT/ORG DELIB/GP CONFER
FORCES PROB/SOLV BAL/PWR CAP/ISM DOMIN COLONIAL INT/TRADE
...INT/LAW 19. PAGE 28 E0548 DIPLOM

B43
MICAUD C.A.,THE FRENCH RIGHT AND NAZI GERMANY DIPLOM
1933-1939: A STUDY OF PUBLIC OPINION. GERMANY UK AGREE
USSR POL/PAR ARMS/CONT COERCE DETER PEACE
RIGID/FLEX PWR MARXISM...FASCIST TREND 20
LEAGUE/NAT TREATY. PAGE 73 E1454

B44
CHENEY F.,CARTELS, COMBINES, AND TRUSTS: A SELECTED BIBLIOG/A
LIST OF REFERENCES. GERMANY UK USA-45 WOR-45 LG/CO
DELIB/GP OP/RES BARGAIN CAP/ISM ECO/TAC INT/TRADE ECO/DEV
LICENSE LEGIT CONFER PRICE 20. PAGE 22 E0428 INDUS

B44
RUDIN H.R.,ARMISTICE 1918. FRANCE GERMANY MOD/EUR AGREE
UK USA-45 NAT/G CHIEF DELIB/GP FORCES BAL/PWR REPAR WAR
ARMS/CONT 20 WILSON/W TREATY. PAGE 86 E1732 PEACE
DIPLOM

MASON J.B.,"THE JUDICIAL SYSTEM OF THE NAZI PARTY." FASCISM
GERMANY ELITES POL/PAR DOMIN CONTROL SANCTION   CT/SYS
TOTALISM...JURID 20 HITLER/A. PAGE 69 E1381   ADJUD
                                                     LAW
                                                S44

BEVERIDGE W.,THE PRICE OF PEACE. GERMANY UK WOR+45 INT/ORG
WOR-45 NAT/G FORCES CREATE LEGIT REGION WAR ATTIT   TREND
KNOWL ORD/FREE PWR...POLICY NEW/IDEA GEN/LAWS   PEACE
LEAGUE/NAT 20 TREATY. PAGE 12 E0223
                                                B45

CONOVER H.F.,THE GOVERNMENTS OF THE MAJOR FOREIGN   BIBLIOG
POWERS: A BIBLIOGRAPHY. FRANCE GERMANY ITALY UK   NAT/G
USSR CONSTN LOC/G POL/PAR EX/STRUC FORCES ADMIN   DIPLOM
CT/SYS CIVMIL/REL TOTALISM...POLICY 19/20. PAGE 25
E0494
                                                B45

CONOVER H.F.,THE NAZI STATE: WAR CRIMES AND WAR   BIBLIOG
CRIMINALS. GERMANY CULTURE NAT/G SECT FORCES DIPLOM WAR
INT/TRADE EDU/PROP...INT/LAW BIOG HIST/WRIT   CRIME
TIME/SEQ 20. PAGE 25 E0495
                                                B45

LOGAN R.W.,THE AFRICAN MANDATES IN WORLD POLITICS. WAR
EUR+WWI GERMANY ISLAM INT/ORG BARGAIN...POLICY   COLONIAL
INT/LAW 20. PAGE 66 E1321   AFR
                                                     DIPLOM
                                                B48

ALEXANDER L.,"WAR CRIMES, THEIR SOCIAL-   DRIVE
PSYCHOLOGICAL ASPECTS." EUR+WWI GERMANY LAW CULTURE WAR
ELITES KIN POL/PAR PUB/INST FORCES DOMIN EDU/PROP
COERCE CRIME ATTIT SUPEGO HEALTH MORAL PWR FASCISM
...PSY OBS TREND GEN/LAWS NAZI 20. PAGE 3 E0061
                                                S48

JACKSON R.H.,INTERNATIONAL CONFERENCE ON MILITARY   DIPLOM
TRIALS. FRANCE GERMANY UK USA+45 USSR VOL/ASSN   INT/ORG
DELIB/GP REPAR ADJUD CT/SYS CRIME WAR 20 WAR/TRIAL. INT/LAW
PAGE 57 E1141   CIVMIL/REL
                                                B49

MOCKFORD J.,SOUTH-WEST AFRICA AND THE INTERNATIONAL COLONIAL
COURT (PAMPHLET). AFR GERMANY SOUTH/AFR UK   SOVEREIGN
ECO/UNDEV DIPLOM CONTROL DISCRIM...DECISION JURID   INT/LAW
20 AFRICA/SW. PAGE 74 E1475   DOMIN
                                                B50

BRETTON H.L.,STRESEMANN AND THE REVISION OF   POLICY
VERSAILLES: A FIGHT FOR REASON. EUR+WWI GERMANY   DIPLOM
FORCES BUDGET ARMS/CONT WAR SUPEGO...BIBLIOG 20   BIOG
TREATY VERSAILLES STRESEMN/G. PAGE 15 E0294
                                                B53

TOTOK W.,HANDBUCH DER BIBLIOGRAPHISCHEN   BIBLIOG/A
NACHSCHLAGEWERKE. GERMANY LAW CULTURE ADMIN...SOC   NAT/G
20. PAGE 97 E1936   DIPLOM
                                                     POLICY
                                                B54

BENTON W.E.,NUREMBERG: GERMAN VIEWS OF THE WAR   CRIME
TRIALS. EUR+WWI GERMANY VOL/ASSN LEAD PARTIC COERCE WAR
INGP/REL RACE/REL TOTALISM SUPEGO ORD/FREE...ANTHOL LAW
NUREMBERG. PAGE 10 E0201   JURID
                                                B55

FLIESS P.J.,FREEDOM OF THE PRESS IN THE GERMAN   EDU/PROP
REPUBLIC, 1918-1933. GERMANY LAW CONSTN POL/PAR   ORD/FREE
LEGIS WRITING ADMIN COERCE MURDER MARXISM...POLICY   JURID
BIBLIOG 20 WEIMAR/REP. PAGE 39 E0765   PRESS
                                                B55

FREUND G.,UNHOLY ALLIANCE. EUR+WWI GERMANY USSR   DIPLOM
FORCES ECO/TAC CONTROL WAR PWR...TREND TREATY.   PLAN
PAGE 40 E0796   POLICY
                                                B57

SINEY M.C.,THE ALLIED BLOCKADE OF GERMANY: DETER
1914-1916. EUR+WWI GERMANY MOD/EUR USA-45 DIPLOM   INT/TRADE
CONTROL NEUTRAL PWR 20. PAGE 91 E1832   INT/LAW
                                                     WAR
                                                B57

MOSER J.J.,JOHANN JACOB MOSER'S GESAMMELTE UND ZU   BIBLIOG
GEMEINNUTZIGEM GEBRAUCH EINGERICHTETE BIBLIOTHEK.   EXTR/IND
GERMANY PROC/MFG INT/TRADE...POLICY JURID MGT 18.   INDUS
PAGE 75 E1500
                                                B58

SCHOEDER P.W.,THE AXIS ALLIANCE AND JAPANESE-   AGREE
AMERICAN RELATIONS 1941. ASIA GERMANY UK USA-45   DIPLOM
PEACE ATTIT...POLICY BIBLIOG 20 CHINJAP TREATY.   WAR
PAGE 88 E1763
                                                B58

KNIERIEM A.,THE NUREMBERG TRIALS. EUR+WWI GERMANY   INT/LAW
VOL/ASSN LEAD COERCE WAR INGP/REL TOTALISM SUPEGO   CRIME
ORD/FREE...CONCPT METH/COMP. PAGE 61 E1225   PARTIC
                                                     JURID
                                                B59

SCHORN H.,DER RICHTER IM DRITTEN REICH; GESCHICHTE ADJUD
UND DOKUMENTE. GERMANY NAT/G LEGIT CT/SYS INGP/REL   JUDGE
MORAL ORD/FREE RESPECT...JURID GP/COMP 20. PAGE 88   FASCISM
E1765
                                                B59

BERTHOLD O.,KAISER, VOLK UND AVIGNON. GERMANY CHIEF DIPLOM
LEGIT LEAD NAT/LISM CONSERVE 14 POPE CHRUCH/STA   CATHISM
LUDWIG/BAV JOHN/XXII. PAGE 11 E0217   JURID
                                                B60

CASTBERG F.,FREEDOM OF SPEECH IN THE WEST. FRANCE   ORD/FREE
GERMANY USA-45 LAW CONSTN CHIEF PRESS   SANCTION
DISCRIM...CONCPT 18/20. PAGE 21 E0406   ADJUD
                                                     NAT/COMP
                                                B60

HAGEN A.,STAAT UND KATHOLISCHE KIRCHE IN   SECT
WURTTEMBERG IN DEN JAHREN 1848-1862 (2 VOLS.).   PROVS
GERMANY DELIB/GP EDU/PROP MARRIAGE CATHISM 19   GP/REL
CHURCH/STA. PAGE 49 E0975   JURID
                                                B61

GONNER R.,DAS KIRCHENPATRONATRECHT IM   JURID
GROSSHERZOGTUM BADEN. GERMANY LAW PROVS DEBATE   SECT
ATTIT CATHISM 14/19 PROTESTANT CHRISTIAN CHURCH/STA NAT/G
BADEN. PAGE 44 E0882   GP/REL
                                                B62

HEYDECKER J.J.,THE NUREMBERG TRIAL: HISTORY OF NAZI LAW
GERMANY AS REVEALED THROUGH THE TESTIMONY AT   CRIME
NUREMBERG. EUR+WWI GERMANY VOL/ASSN LEAD COERCE   PARTIC
CROWD INGP/REL RACE/REL SUPEGO ORD/FREE...CONCPT 20 TOTALISM
NAZI ANTI/SEMIT NUREMBERG JEWS. PAGE 52 E1036
                                                B62

ROSENZWEIG F.,HEGEL UND DER STAAT. GERMANY SOCIETY JURID
FAM POL/PAR NAT/LISM...BIOG 19. PAGE 86 E1718   NAT/G
                                                     CONCPT
                                                     PHIL/SCI
                                                B62

SOMMER T.,DEUTSCHLAND UND JAPAN ZWISCHEN DEN   DIPLOM
MACHTEN. GERMANY DELIB/GP BAL/PWR AGREE COERCE   WAR
TOTALISM PWR 20 CHINJAP TREATY. PAGE 93 E1856   ATTIT
                                                B62

PRYOR F.L.,THE COMMUNIST FOREIGN TRADE SYSTEM. COM ATTIT
CZECHOSLVK GERMANY YUGOSLAVIA LAW ECO/DEV DIST/IND   ECO/TAC
POL/PAR PLAN DOMIN TOTALISM DRIVE RIGID/FLEX WEALTH
...STAT STAND/INT CHARTS 20. PAGE 83 E1657
                                                B63

RAVENS J.P.,STAAT UND KATHOLISCHE KIRCHE IN   GP/REL
PREUSSENS POLNISCHEN TEILUNGSGEBIETEN. GERMANY   CATHISM
POLAND PRUSSIA PROVS DIPLOM EDU/PROP DEBATE   SECT
NAT/LISM...JURID 18 CHURCH/STA. PAGE 83 E1674   NAT/G
                                                B63

REITZEL A.M.,DAS MAINZER KRONUNGSRECHT UND DIE   CHIEF
POLITISCHE PROBLEMATIK. GERMANY MUNIC LEGIT CATHISM JURID
12/13. PAGE 84 E1684   CHOOSE
                                                     SECT
                                                B63

BOLGAR V.,"THE PUBLIC INTEREST: A JURISPRUDENTIAL   CONCPT
AND COMPARATIVE OVERVIEW OF SYMPOSIUM ON   ORD/FREE
FUNDAMENTAL CONCEPTS OF PUBLIC LAW" COM FRANCE   CONTROL
GERMANY SWITZERLND LAW ADJUD ADMIN AGREE LAISSEZ   NAT/COMP
...JURID GEN/LAWS 20 EUROPE/E. PAGE 14 E0264
                                                L63

RIGAUX F.,"LA SIGNIFICATION DES ACTES JUDICIARES A CONSULT
L'ETRANGER." EUR+WWI ITALY NETHERLAND LAW ACT/RES   CT/SYS
DRIVE...JURID GEN/LAWS TOT/POP 20. PAGE 85 E1699   GERMANY
                                                S63

FEINE H.E.,DIE BESETZUNG DER REICHSBISTUMER VOM   CHOOSE
WESTFALISCHEN FRIEDEN BIS ZUR SAKULARISATION.   SECT
GERMANY EDU/PROP GP/REL AGE 17/19. PAGE 37 E0727   JURID
                                                     PROVS
                                                B64

FREISEN J.,STAAT UND KATHOLISCHE KIRCHE IN DEN   SECT
DEUTSCHEN BUNDESSTAATEN (2 VOLS.). GERMANY LAW FAM   CATHISM
NAT/G EDU/PROP GP/REL MARRIAGE WEALTH 19/20   JURID
CHURCH/STA. PAGE 40 E0793   PROVS
                                                B64

GESELLSCHAFT RECHTSVERGLEICH,BIBLIOGRAPHIE DES
DEUTSCHEN RECHTS (BIBLIOGRAPHY OF GERMAN LAW,
TRANS. BY COURTLAND PETERSON). GERMANY FINAN INDUS
LABOR SECT FORCES CT/SYS PARL/PROC CRIME...INT/LAW
SOC NAT/COMP 20. PAGE 43 E0853
B64
BIBLIOG/A
JURID
CONSTN
ADMIN

HEGEL G.W.,HEGEL'S POLITICAL WRITINGS (TRANS. BY
T.M. KNOX). GERMANY UK FINAN FORCES PARL/PROC
CHOOSE REPRESENT...BIOG 19. PAGE 51 E1022
B64
CONSTN
LEGIS
JURID

COHN H.J.,THE GOVERNMENT OF THE RHINE PALATINATE IN
THE FIFTEENTH CENTURY. GERMANY FINAN LOC/G DELIB/GP
LEGIS CT/SYS CHOOSE CATHISM 14/15 PALATINATE.
PAGE 24 E0468
B65
PROVS
JURID
GP/REL
ADMIN

FORGAC A.A.,NEW DIPLOMACY AND THE UNITED NATIONS.
FRANCE GERMANY UK USSR INT/ORG DELIB/GP EX/STRUC
PEACE...INT/LAW CONCPT UN. PAGE 39 E0770
B65
DIPLOM
ETIQUET
NAT/G

HABERLER G.,A SURVEY OF INTERNATIONAL TRADE THEORY.
CANADA FRANCE GERMANY ECO/TAC TARIFFS AGREE COST
DEMAND WEALTH...ECOMETRIC 19/20 MONOPOLY TREATY.
PAGE 49 E0968
B65
INT/TRADE
BAL/PAY
DIPLOM
POLICY

MARTENS E.,DIE HANNOVERSCHE KIRCHENKOMMISSION.
GERMANY LAW INT/ORG PROVS SECT CONFER GP/REL
CATHISM 16/20. PAGE 69 E1371
B65
JURID
DELIB/GP
CONSTN
PROF/ORG

MOELLER R.,LUDWIG DER BAYER UND DIE KURIE IM KAMPF
UM DAS REICH. GERMANY LAW SECT LEGIT LEAD GP/REL
CATHISM CONSERVE 14 LUDWIG/BAV POPE CHURCH/STA.
PAGE 74 E1478
B65
JURID
CHIEF
CHOOSE
NAT/LISM

NORDEN A.,WAR AND NAZI CRIMINALS IN WEST GERMANY:
STATE, ECONOMY, ADMINISTRATION, ARMY, JUSTICE,
SCIENCE. GERMANY GERMANY/W MOD/EUR ECO/DEV ACADEM
EX/STRUC FORCES DOMIN ADMIN CT/SYS...POLICY MAJORIT
PACIFIST 20. PAGE 77 E1554
B65
FASCIST
WAR
NAT/G
TOP/EX

DYCK H.V.,WEIMAR GERMANY AND SOVIET RUSSIA
1926-1933. EUR+WWI GERMANY UK USSR ECO/TAC
INT/TRADE NEUTRAL WAR ATTIT 20 WEIMAR/REP TREATY.
PAGE 34 E0669
B66
DIPLOM
GOV/REL
POLICY

HAUSNER G.,JUSTICE IN JERUSALEM. GERMANY ISRAEL
SOCIETY KIN DIPLOM LEGIT CT/SYS PARTIC MURDER
MAJORITY ATTIT FASCISM...INT/LAW JURID 20 JEWS
WAR/TRIAL. PAGE 51 E1013
B66
ADJUD
CRIME
RACE/REL
COERCE

PLATE H.,PARTEIFINANZIERUNG UND GRUNDESETZ. GERMANY
NAT/G PLAN GIVE PAY INCOME WEALTH...JURID 20.
PAGE 81 E1619
B66
POL/PAR
CONSTN
FINAN

MANVELL R.,THE INCOMPARABLE CRIME. GERMANY ACT/RES
DEATH...BIBLIOG 20 JEWS. PAGE 68 E1364
B67
MURDER
CRIME
WAR
HIST/WRIT

COHN K.,"CRIMES AGAINST HUMANITY." GERMANY INT/ORG
SANCTION ATTIT ORD/FREE...MARXIST CRIMLGY 20 UN.
PAGE 24 E0469
S67
WAR
INT/LAW
CRIME
ADJUD

BURGESS J.W.,POLITICAL SCIENCE AND COMPARATIVE
CONSTITUTIONAL LAW. FRANCE GERMANY UK USA-45 LEGIS
DIPLOM ADJUD REPRESENT...CONCPT 19. PAGE 17 E0340
B90
CONSTN
LAW
LOC/G
NAT/G

GERMANY/E....EAST GERMANY; SEE ALSO COM

EPSTEIN F.T.,EAST GERMANY: A SELECTED BIBLIOGRAPHY
(PAMPHLET). COM GERMANY/E LAW AGRI FINAN INDUS
LABOR POL/PAR EDU/PROP ADMIN AGE/Y 20. PAGE 35
E0693
B59
BIBLIOG/A
INTELL
MARXISM
NAT/G

GERMANY/W....WEST GERMANY

HINDERLING A.,DIE REFORMATORISCHE
VERWALTUNGSGERICHTSBARKEIT. GERMANY/W PROB/SOLV
B57
ADMIN
CT/SYS

ADJUD SUPEGO PWR...CONCPT 20. PAGE 53 E1049
JURID
CONTROL

SCHLOCHAUER H.J.,OFFENTLICHES RECHT. GERMANY/W
FINAN EX/STRUC LEGIS DIPLOM FEDERAL ORD/FREE
...INT/LAW 20. PAGE 88 E1757
B57
CONSTN
JURID
ADMIN
CT/SYS

DEUTSCHE GESCHAFT VOLKERRECHT,DIE VOLKERRECHTLICHEN
DISSERTATIONEN AN DEN WESTDEUTSCHEN UNIVERSITATEN,
1945-1957. GERMANY/W NAT/G DIPLOM ADJUD CT/SYS
...POLICY 20. PAGE 31 E0616
B58
BIBLIOG
INT/LAW
ACADEM
JURID

SISSON C.H.,THE SPIRIT OF BRITISH ADMINISTRATION
AND SOME EUROPEAN COMPARISONS. FRANCE GERMANY/W
SWEDEN UK LAW EX/STRUC INGP/REL EFFICIENCY ORD/FREE
...DECISION 20. PAGE 91 E1835
B59
GOV/COMP
ADMIN
ELITES
ATTIT

MUTHESIUS V.,DAS GESPENST DER WIRTSCHAFTLICHEN
MACHT. GERMANY/W ECO/DEV FINAN MARKET TAX...JURID
20. PAGE 75 E1513
B60
ECO/TAC
NAT/G
CONCPT
LG/CO

BEDFORD S.,THE FACES OF JUSTICE: A TRAVELLER'S
REPORT. AUSTRIA FRANCE GERMANY/W SWITZERLND UK UNIV
WOR+45 WOR-45 CULTURE PARTIC GOV/REL MORAL...JURID
OBS GOV/COMP 20. PAGE 9 E0174
B61
CT/SYS
ORD/FREE
PERSON
LAW

MCWHINNEY E.,CONSTITUTIONALISM IN GERMANY AND THE
FEDERAL CONSTITUTINAL COURT. GERMANY/W POL/PAR TV
ADJUD CHOOSE EFFICIENCY ATTIT ORD/FREE MARXISM
...NEW/IDEA BIBLIOG 20. PAGE 71 E1428
B62
CONSTN
CT/SYS
CONTROL
NAT/G

PAIKERT G.C.,THE GERMAN EXODUS. EUR+WWI GERMANY/W
LAW CULTURE SOCIETY STRUCT INDUS NAT/LISM RESPECT
SOVEREIGN...CHARTS BIBLIOG SOC/INTEG 20 MIGRATION.
PAGE 79 E1591
B62
INGP/REL
STRANGE
GEOG
GP/REL

HENKE W.,DAS RECHT DER POLITISCHEN PARTEIEN.
GERMANY/W LAW CT/SYS GP/REL SUPEGO 20. PAGE 52
E1031
B64
POL/PAR
JURID
CONSTN
NAT/G

CARTER G.M.,POLITICS IN EUROPE. EUR+WWI FRANCE
GERMANY/W UK USSR LAW CONSTN POL/PAR VOL/ASSN PRESS
LOBBY PWR...ANTHOL SOC/INTEG EEC. PAGE 20 E0399
B65
GOV/COMP
OP/RES
ECO/DEV

NORDEN A.,WAR AND NAZI CRIMINALS IN WEST GERMANY:
STATE, ECONOMY, ADMINISTRATION, ARMY, JUSTICE,
SCIENCE. GERMANY GERMANY/W MOD/EUR ECO/DEV ACADEM
EX/STRUC FORCES DOMIN ADMIN CT/SYS...POLICY MAJORIT
PACIFIST 20. PAGE 77 E1554
B65
FASCIST
WAR
NAT/G
TOP/EX

WEIL G.L.,A HANDBOOK ON THE EUROPEAN ECONOMIC
COMMUNITY. BELGIUM EUR+WWI FRANCE GERMANY/W ITALY
CONSTN ECO/DEV CREATE PARTIC GP/REL...DECISION MGT
CHARTS 20 EEC. PAGE 105 E2107
B65
INT/TRADE
INT/ORG
TEC/DEV
INT/LAW

BEER U.,FRUCHTBARKEITSREGELUNG ALS KONSEQUENZ
VERANTWORTLICHER ELTERNSCHAFT. ASIA GERMANY/W INDIA
LAW ECO/DEV ECO/UNDEV TEC/DEV ECO/TAC BIO/SOC SEX
CATHISM...METH/COMP 20 CHINJAP BIRTH/CON. PAGE 9
E0178
B66
CONTROL
GEOG
FAM
SECT

LEHMANN L.,LEGAL UND OPPORTUN - POLITISCHE JUSTIZ
IN DER BUNDESREPUBLIK. GERMANY/W EDU/PROP ADJUD
CONTROL PARL/PROC COERCE TOTALISM ATTIT 20
COM/PARTY. PAGE 64 E1281
B66
ORD/FREE
POL/PAR
JURID
LEGIS

OBERMANN E.,VERTEIDIGUNG PER FREIHEIT. GERMANY/W
WOR+45 INT/ORG COERCE NUC/PWR WEAPON MARXISM 20 UN
NATO WARSAW/P TREATY. PAGE 78 E1571
B66
FORCES
ORD/FREE
WAR
PEACE

US DEPARTMENT OF STATE,RESEARCH ON WESTERN EUROPE,
GREAT BRITAIN, AND CANADA (EXTERNAL RESEARCH LIST
NO 3-25). CANADA GERMANY/W UK LAW CULTURE NAT/G
POL/PAR FORCES EDU/PROP REGION MARXISM...GEOG SOC
WORSHIP 20 CMN/WLTH. PAGE 100 E1998
B66
BIBLIOG/A
EUR+WWI
DIPLOM

S67
SHELDON C.H.,"PUBLIC OPINION AND HIGH COURTS: ATTIT
COMMUNIST PARTY CASES IN FOUR CONSTITUTIONAL CT/SYS
SYSTEMS." CANADA GERMANY/W WOR+45 POL/PAR MARXISM CONSTN
...METH/COMP NAT/COMP 20 AUSTRAL. PAGE 91 E1818 DECISION

GERTH H. E0851

GERWIG R. E0852

GESELLSCHAFT RECHTSVERGLEICH E0853

GETTYSBURG....BATTLE OF GETTYSBURG

GHANA.....SEE ALSO AFR

B58
MANSERGH N.,COMMONWEALTH PERSPECTIVES. GHANA UK LAW DIPLOM
VOL/ASSN CONFER HEALTH SOVEREIGN...GEOG CHARTS COLONIAL
ANTHOL 20 CMN/WLTH AUSTRAL. PAGE 68 E1363 INT/ORG
INGP/REL

S62
GANDOLFI A.,"REFLEXIONS SUR L'IMPOT DE CAPITATION AFR
EN AFRIQUE NOIRE." GHANA SENEGAL LAW FINAN ACT/RES CHOOSE
TEC/DEV ECO/TAC WEALTH...MGT TREND 20. PAGE 42
E0830

S65
BEVANS C.I.,"GHANA AND UNITED STATES - UNITED NAT/G
KINGDOM AGREEMENTS." UK USA+45 LAW DELIB/GP LEGIT
EX/STRUC ORD/FREE...JURID METH/CNCPT GEN/LAWS 20. GHANA
PAGE 11 E0222 DIPLOM

B66
HARVEY W.B.,LAW AND SOCIAL CHANGE IN GHANA. AFR JURID
GHANA CONSULT CONTROL CT/SYS INGP/REL 20. PAGE 51 CONSTN
E1011 LEAD
ORD/FREE

GHOSH P.K. E0854

GIANNELLA D.A. E0855

GIBB A.D. E0856

GIBBON/EDW....EDWARD GIBBON

GIBBS C.R. E0857

GIBBS H.P. E0966

GIBNEY F. E0858

GIBRALTAR....SEE UK

GIBSON G.H. E0859

GILL N.N. E0860

GILLETTE J.M. E0861,E0862

GILLETTE W. E0863

GILLIN J.L. E0864

GILLMOR D.M. E0865

GILMORE M.P. E0866

GINSBERG M. E0867, E0868

GINSBURGS G. E0869

GINZBERG E. E0870

GINZBURG B. E0871

GIRAUD E. E0872

GIVE....GIVING, PHILANTHROPY

N19
COUTROT A.,THE FIGHT OVER THE 1959 PRIVATE SCHOOL
EDUCATION LAW IN FRANCE (PAMPHLET). FRANCE NAT/G PARL/PROC
SECT GIVE EDU/PROP GP/REL ATTIT RIGID/FLEX ORD/FREE CATHISM
20 CHURCH/STA. PAGE 27 E0527 LAW

B52
ANDREWS F.E.,CORPORATION GIVING. LAW TAX EDU/PROP LG/CO
ADMIN...POLICY STAT CHARTS. PAGE 5 E0096 GIVE
SML/CO
FINAN

B55
ZABEL O.H.,GOD AND CAESAR IN NEBRASKA: A STUDY OF SECT
LEGAL RELATIONSHIP OF CHURCH AND STATE. 1854-1954. PROVS
TAX GIVE ADMIN CONTROL GP/REL ROLE...GP/COMP 19/20 LAW
NEBRASKA. PAGE 108 E2168 EDU/PROP

B56
NOTZ R.L.,FEDERAL GRANTS-IN-AID TO STATES: ANALYSIS GIVE
OF LAWS IN FORCE ON SEPTEMBER 10, 1956. USA+45 LAW NAT/G
SCHOOL PLAN ECO/TAC TAX RECEIVE...HEAL JURID 20. PROVS
PAGE 78 E1558 GOV/REL

B58
CABLE G.W.,THE NEGRO QUESTION: A SELECTION OF RACE/REL
WRITINGS ON CIVIL RIGHTS IN THE SOUTH. USA+45 CULTURE
STRATA LOC/G POL/PAR GIVE EDU/PROP WRITING CT/SYS DISCRIM
SANCTION CRIME CHOOSE WORSHIP 20 NEGRO CIV/RIGHTS ORD/FREE
CONV/LEASE SOUTH/US. PAGE 18 E0355

B61
AVERY M.W.,GOVERNMENT OF WASHINGTON STATE. USA+45 PROVS
MUNIC DELIB/GP EX/STRUC LEGIS GIVE CT/SYS PARTIC LOC/G
REGION EFFICIENCY 20 WASHINGT/G GOVERNOR. PAGE 6 ADMIN
E0121 GOV/REL

B62
MCGRATH J.J.,CHURCH AND STATE IN AMERICAN LAW. LAW SECT
PROVS SCHOOL TAX GIVE CT/SYS GP/REL...POLICY ANTHOL ADJUD
18/20 SUPREME/CT CHURCH/STA CASEBOOK. PAGE 71 E1414 CONSTN
NAT/G

B63
DRINAN R.F.,RELIGION, THE COURTS, AND PUBLIC SECT
POLICY. USA+45 CONSTN BUDGET TAX GIVE ADJUD CT/SYS
SANCTION GP/REL PRIVIL 20 CHURCH/STA. PAGE 33 E0649 POLICY
SCHOOL

B63
JENKS C.W.,LAW, FREEDOM, AND WELFARE. WOR+45 GIVE INT/LAW
ADJUD WAR PEACE HABITAT ORD/FREE. PAGE 58 E1159 DIPLOM
SOVEREIGN
PROB/SOLV

B64
GIANNELLA D.A.,RELIGION AND THE PUBLIC ORDER: AN SECT
ANNUAL REVIEW OF CHURCH AND STATE, AND OF RELIGION, NAT/G
LAW, AND SOCIETY. USA+45 LAW SOCIETY FAM POL/PAR CONSTN
SCHOOL GIVE EDU/PROP GP/REL...JURID GEN/LAWS ORD/FREE
BIBLIOG/A 20 CHURCH/STA BIRTH/CON CONSCN/OBJ
NATURL/LAW. PAGE 43 E0855

B65
FISCHER F.C.,THE GOVERNMENT OF MICHIGAN. USA+45 PROVS
NAT/G PUB/INST EX/STRUC LEGIS BUDGET GIVE EDU/PROP LOC/G
CT/SYS CHOOSE GOV/REL...T MICHIGAN. PAGE 38 E0753 ADMIN
CONSTN

B65
HOWE M.D.W.,THE GARDEN AND THE WILDERNESS. USA+45 CONSTN
LAW GIVE EDU/PROP LEGIT NAT/LISM ORD/FREE...POLICY SECT
JURID SUPREME/CT CHURCH/STA. PAGE 55 E1103 NAT/G
GP/REL

B65
US OFFICE ECONOMIC OPPORTUNITY,CATALOG OF FEDERAL BIBLIOG
PROGRAMS FOR INDIVIDUAL AND COMMUNITY IMPROVEMENT. CLIENT
USA+45 GIVE RECEIVE ADMIN HEALTH KNOWL SKILL WEALTH ECO/TAC
CHARTS. PAGE 101 E2021 MUNIC

B66
FRIEDMANN W.G.,INTERNATIONAL FINANCIAL AID. USA+45 INT/ORG
ECO/DEV ECO/UNDEV NAT/G VOL/ASSN EX/STRUC PLAN RENT FOR/AID
GIVE BAL/PAY PWR...GEOG INT/LAW STAT TREND UN EEC TEC/DEV
COMECON. PAGE 41 E0806 ECO/TAC

B66
GREENE L.E.,GOVERNMENT IN TENNESSEE (2ND ED.). PROVS
USA+45 DIST/IND INDUS POL/PAR EX/STRUC LEGIS PLAN LOC/G
BUDGET GIVE CT/SYS...MGT T 20 TENNESSEE. PAGE 46 CONSTN
E0909 ADMIN

B66
PLATE H.,PARTEIFINANZIERUNG UND GRUNDESETZ. GERMANY POL/PAR
NAT/G PLAN GIVE PAY INCOME WEALTH...JURID 20. CONSTN
PAGE 81 E1619 FINAN

B66
TIEDT S.W.,THE ROLE OF THE FEDERAL GOVERNMENT IN NAT/G
EDUCATION. FUT USA+45 USA-45 CONSTN SECT BUDGET EDU/PROP
CT/SYS GOV/REL 18/20 SUPREME/CT. PAGE 96 E1924 GIVE
SCHOOL

B66
US HOUSE COMM ON JUDICIARY,CIVIL COMMITMENT AND BIO/SOC
TREATMENT OF NARCOTIC ADDICTS. USA+45 SOCIETY FINAN CRIME
LEGIS PROB/SOLV GIVE CT/SYS SANCTION HEALTH IDEA/COMP

...POLICY HEAL 20. PAGE 100 E2008   CONTROL

                                                     B66
US HOUSE UNAMER ACTIV COMM,HEARINGS ON BILLS TO   LAW
MAKE PUNISHABLE ASSISTANCE TO ENEMIES OF US IN TIME SANCTION
OF UNDECLARED WAR. USA+45 VIETNAM/N EDU/PROP   VOL/ASSN
CONTROL WAR MARXISM HOUSE/REP. PAGE 100 E2010   GIVE

GJUPANOVIC H. E0873

GLADSTON/W....WILLIAM GLADSTONE

GLASER D. E0874

GLUECK S. E0875

GMP/REG....GOOD MANUFACTURING PRACTICE REGULATIONS

GOD AND GODS....SEE DEITY

GODET M. E0876

GODWIN W. E0877

GOEBBELS/J....JOSEPH GOEBBELS

GOETHE/J....JOHANN WOLFGANG VON GOETHE

GOLD....GOLD

GOLD/COAST....GOLD COAST (PRE-GHANA)

GOLD/STAND....GOLD STANDARD

GOLDFARB R.L. E0811

GOLDMAN/E....ERIC GOLDMAN

GOLDSEN J.M. E0879

GOLDSTEIN J. E0636

GOLDWATR/B....BARRY GOLDWATER

GOLDWIN R.A. E0880

GOMEZ ROBLES J. E0881

GOMILLN/CG....C.G. GOMILLION

                                                     B62
TAPER B.,GOMILLION VERSUS LIGHTFOOT: THE TUSKEGEE   APPORT
GERRYMANDER CASE. USA+45 LAW CONSTN LOC/G MUNIC   REPRESENT
CT/SYS 20 NEGRO CIV/RIGHTS GOMILLN/CG LIGHTFT/PM   RACE/REL
TUSKEGEE. PAGE 95 E1908   ADJUD

GONNER R. E0882

GONZALEZ NAVARRO M. E0883

GONZALEZ PALENCIA A E0884

GOOCH G.P. E0885

GOOD MANUFACTURING PRACTICE REGULATIONS....SEE GMP/REG

GOODE W.J. E0886

GOODHART A.L. E1082,E1083

GOODNOW F.J. E0887,E0888

GOODNOW H.F. E0889

GOODRICH L. E1588

GOODRICH L.M. E0890

GORDON D.L. E0891

GORDON/K....K. GORDON

GORDON/W....WILLIAM GORDON

GOROKHOFF C.J. E1573

GOSNELL H.F. E1442

GOSSETT W.T. E0892

GOTLIEB A. E0893

GOURNAY B. E0894

GOV/COMP....COMPARISON OF GOVERNMENTS

                                                     N
AMERICAN POLITICAL SCIENCE REVIEW. USA+45 USA-45   BIBLIOG/A
WOR+45 WOR-45 INT/ORG ADMIN...INT/LAW PHIL/SCI   DIPLOM
CONCPT METH 20 UN. PAGE 1 E0002   NAT/G
                                                     GOV/COMP

                                                     B09
LOBINGIER C.S.,THE PEOPLE'S LAW OR POPULAR   CONSTN
PARTICIPATION IN LAW-MAKING. FRANCE SWITZERLND UK   LAW
LOC/G NAT/G PROVS LEGIS SUFF MAJORITY PWR POPULISM   PARTIC
...GOV/COMP BIBLIOG 19. PAGE 66 E1314

                                                     B13
BORCHARD E.M.,BIBLIOGRAPHY OF INTERNATIONAL LAW AND BIBLIOG
CONTINENTAL LAW. EUR+WWI MOD/EUR UK LAW INT/TRADE   INT/LAW
WAR PEACE...GOV/COMP NAT/COMP 19/20. PAGE 14 E0267   JURID
                                                     DIPLOM

                                                     B18
WILSON W.,THE STATE: ELEMENTS OF HISTORICAL AND   NAT/G
PRACTICAL POLITICS. FRANCE GERMANY ITALY UK USSR   JURID
CONSTN EX/STRUC LEGIS CT/SYS WAR PWR...POLICY   CONCPT
GOV/COMP 20. PAGE 106 E2131   NAT/COMP

                                                     N19
POUND R.,ORGANIZATION OF THE COURTS (PAMPHLET).   CT/SYS
MOD/EUR UK USA-45 ADJUD PWR...GOV/COMP 10/20   JURID
EUROPE. PAGE 82 E1635   STRUCT
                                                     ADMIN

                                                     B39
MCILWAIN C.H.,CONSTITUTIONALISM AND THE CHANGING   CONSTN
WORLD. UK USA-45 LEGIS PRIVIL AUTHORIT SOVEREIGN   POLICY
...GOV/COMP 15/20 MAGNA/CART HOUSE/CMNS. PAGE 71   JURID
E1417

                                                     B42
FORTESCU J.,IN PRAISE OF ENGLISH LAW (1464) (TRANS. LAW
BY S.B. CHRIMES). UK ELITES CHIEF FORCES CT/SYS   CONSTN
COERCE CRIME GOV/REL ILLEGIT...JURID GOV/COMP   LEGIS
GEN/LAWS 15. PAGE 39 E0774   ORD/FREE

                                                     B45
WOOLBERT R.G.,FOREIGN AFFAIRS BIBLIOGRAPHY,   BIBLIOG/A
1932-1942. INT/ORG SECT INT/TRADE COLONIAL RACE/REL DIPLOM
NAT/LISM...GEOG INT/LAW GOV/COMP IDEA/COMP 20.   WAR
PAGE 107 E2144

                                                     B47
MCILWAIN C.H.,CONSTITUTIONALISM: ANCIENT AND   CONSTN
MODERN. USA+45 ROMAN/EMP LAW CHIEF LEGIS CT/SYS   NAT/G
GP/REL ORD/FREE SOVEREIGN...POLICY TIME/SEQ   PARL/PROC
ROMAN/REP EUROPE. PAGE 71 E1419   GOV/COMP

                                                     B48
GRIFFITH E.S.,RESEARCH IN POLITICAL SCIENCE: THE   BIBLIOG
WORK OF PANELS OF RESEARCH COMMITTEE. APSA. WOR+45   PHIL/SCI
WOR-45 COM/IND R+D FORCES ACT/RES WAR...GOV/COMP   DIPLOM
ANTHOL 20. PAGE 47 E0939   JURID

                                                     B55
CHARMATZ J.P.,COMPARATIVE STUDIES IN COMMUNITY   MARRIAGE
PROPERTY LAW. FRANCE USA+45...JURID GOV/COMP ANTHOL LAW
20. PAGE 22 E0424   OWN
                                                     MUNIC

                                                     B55
KHADDURI M.,LAW IN THE MIDDLE EAST. LAW CONSTN   ADJUD
ACADEM FAM EDU/PROP CT/SYS SANCTION CRIME...INT/LAW JURID
GOV/COMP ANTHOL 6/20 MID/EAST. PAGE 61 E1210   ISLAM

                                                     B56
DOUGLAS W.O.,WE THE JUDGES. INDIA USA+45 USA-45 LAW ADJUD
NAT/G SECT LEGIS CRIME PRESS FEDERAL ORD/FREE   CT/SYS
...POLICY GOV/COMP 19/20 WARRN/EARL MARSHALL/J   CONSTN
SUPREME/CT. PAGE 32 E0640   GOV/REL

                                                     B58
OGDEN F.D.,THE POLL TAX IN THE SOUTH. USA+45 USA-45 TAX
CONSTN ADJUD ADMIN PARTIC CRIME...TIME/SEQ GOV/COMP CHOOSE
METH/COMP 18/20 SOUTH/US. PAGE 78 E1572   RACE/REL
                                                     DISCRIM

                                                     B59
SISSON C.H.,THE SPIRIT OF BRITISH ADMINISTRATION   GOV/COMP
AND SOME EUROPEAN COMPARISONS. FRANCE GERMANY/W   ADMIN
SWEDEN UK LAW EX/STRUC INGP/REL EFFICIENCY ORD/FREE ELITES
...DECISION 20. PAGE 91 E1835   ATTIT

                                                     B60
LA PONCE J.A.,THE PROTECTION OF MINORITIES. WOR+45   INGP/REL
WOR-45 NAT/G POL/PAR SUFF...INT/LAW CLASSIF GP/COMP DOMIN
GOV/COMP BIBLIOG 17/20 CIVIL/LIB CIV/RIGHTS.   SOCIETY
PAGE 62 E1242   RACE/REL

B60
RIENOW R.,INTRODUCTION TO GOVERNMENT (2ND ED.). UK   CONSTN
USA+45 USSR POL/PAR ADMIN REV CHOOSE SUFF FEDERAL   PARL/PROC
PWR...JURID GOV/COMP T 20. PAGE 85 E1697   REPRESENT
                                                        AUTHORIT

B61
BEDFORD S.,THE FACES OF JUSTICE: A TRAVELLER'S   CT/SYS
REPORT. AUSTRIA FRANCE GERMANY/W SWITZERLND UK UNIV   ORD/FREE
WOR+45 WOR-45 CULTURE PARTIC GOV/REL MORAL...JURID   PERSON
OBS GOV/COMP 20. PAGE 9 E0174   LAW

B61
BURDETTE F.L.,POLITICAL SCIENCE: A SELECTED   BIBLIOG/A
BIBLIOGRAPHY OF BOOKS IN PRINT, WITH ANNOTATIONS   GOV/COMP
(PAMPHLET). LAW LOC/G NAT/G POL/PAR PROVS DIPLOM   CONCPT
EDU/PROP ADMIN CHOOSE ATTIT 20. PAGE 17 E0330   ROUTINE

B61
CARNELL F.,THE POLITICS OF THE NEW STATES: A SELECT   BIBLIOG/A
ANNOTATED BIBLIOGRAPHY WITH SPECIAL REFERENCE TO   AFR
THE COMMONWEALTH. CONSTN ELITES LABOR NAT/G POL/PAR   ASIA
EX/STRUC DIPLOM ADJUD ADMIN...GOV/COMP 20   COLONIAL
COMMONWLTH. PAGE 20 E0387

B61
GUIZOT F.P.G.,HISTORY OF THE ORIGIN OF   LEGIS
REPRESENTATIVE GOVERNMENT IN EUROPE. CHRIST-17C   REPRESENT
FRANCE MOD/EUR SPAIN UK LAW CHIEF FORCES POPULISM   CONSTN
...MAJORIT TIME/SEQ GOV/COMP NAT/COMP 4/19   NAT/G
PARLIAMENT. PAGE 48 E0961

B61
ROCHE J.P.,COURTS AND RIGHTS: THE AMERICAN   JURID
JUDICIARY IN ACTION (2ND ED.). UK USA+45 USA-45   CT/SYS
STRUCT TEC/DEV SANCTION PERS/REL RACE/REL ORD/FREE   NAT/G
...METH/CNCPT GOV/COMP METH/COMP T 13/20. PAGE 85   PROVS
E1710

N61
LEAGUE WOMEN VOTERS MASSACHU.THE MERIT SYSTEM IN   LOC/G
MASSACHUSETTS (PAMPHLET). USA+45 PROVS LEGIT PARTIC   LAW
CHOOSE REPRESENT GOV/REL EFFICIENCY...POLICY   SENIOR
GOV/COMP BIBLIOG 20 MASSACHU. PAGE 64 E1274   PROF/ORG

B62
BOYD W.J.,PATTERNS OF APPORTIONMENT (PAMPHLET). LAW   MUNIC
CONSTN CHOOSE GOV/COMP. PAGE 14 E0282   PROVS
                                                        REPRESENT
                                                        APPORT

B62
GROGAN V.,ADMINISTRATIVE TRIBUNALS IN THE PUBLIC   ADMIN
SERVICE. IRELAND UK NAT/G CONTROL CT/SYS...JURID   LAW
GOV/COMP 20. PAGE 48 E0945   ADJUD
                                                        DELIB/GP

B63
ADRIAN C.R.,GOVERNING OVER FIFTY STATES AND THEIR   PROVS
COMMUNITIES. USA+45 CONSTN FINAN MUNIC NAT/G   LOC/G
POL/PAR EX/STRUC LEGIS ADMIN CONTROL CT/SYS   GOV/REL
...CHARTS 20. PAGE 3 E0052   GOV/COMP

B63
DECOTTIGNIES R.,LES NATIONALITES AFRICAINES. AFR   NAT/LISM
NAT/G PROB/SOLV DIPLOM COLONIAL ORD/FREE...CHARTS   JURID
GOV/COMP 20. PAGE 30 E0602   LEGIS
                                                        LAW

B63
GEERTZ C.,OLD SOCIETIES AND NEW STATES: THE QUEST   ECO/UNDEV
FOR MODERNITY IN ASIA AND AFRICA. AFR ASIA LAW   TEC/DEV
CULTURE SECT EDU/PROP REV...GOV/COMP NAT/COMP 20.   NAT/LISM
PAGE 42 E0842   SOVEREIGN

B64
LAPENNA I.,STATE AND LAW: SOVIET AND YUGOSLAV   JURID
THEORY. USSR YUGOSLAVIA STRATA STRUCT NAT/G DOMIN   COM
COERCE MARXISM...GOV/COMP IDEA/COMP 20. PAGE 63   LAW
E1253   SOVEREIGN

B64
LEDERMAN W.R.,THE COURTS AND THE CANDIAN   CONSTN
CONSTITUTION. CANADA PARL/PROC...POLICY JURID   CT/SYS
GOV/COMP ANTHOL 19/20 SUPREME/CT PARLIAMENT.   LEGIS
PAGE 64 E1276   LAW

B64
ROBERTS HL.FOREIGN AFFAIRS BIBLIOGRAPHY, 1952-1962.   BIBLIOG/A
ECO/DEV SECT PLAN FOR/AID INT/TRADE ARMS/CONT   DIPLOM
NAT/LISM ATTIT...INT/LAW GOV/COMP IDEA/COMP 20.   INT/ORG
PAGE 85 E1703   WAR

B65
CARTER G.M.,POLITICS IN EUROPE. EUR+WWI FRANCE   GOV/COMP
GERMANY/W UK USSR LAW CONSTN POL/PAR VOL/ASSN PRESS   OP/RES

LOBBY PWR...ANTHOL SOC/INTEG EEC. PAGE 20 E0399   ECO/DEV

B65
FERRELL J.S.,CASES AND MATERIALS ON LOCAL   APPORT
APPORTIONMENT. CONSTN LEAD GP/REL...DECISION   LOC/G
GOV/COMP. PAGE 37 E0740   REPRESENT
                                                        LAW

B65
MCWHINNEY E.,JUDICIAL REVIEW IN THE ENGLISH-   GOV/COMP
SPEAKING WORLD (3RD ED.). CANADA UK WOR+45 LEGIS   CT/SYS
CONTROL EXEC PARTIC...JURID 20 AUSTRAL. PAGE 71   ADJUD
E1431   CONSTN

B65
SCHUBERT G.,REAPPORTIONMENT. LAW MUNIC POL/PAR PWR   REPRESENT
GOV/COMP. PAGE 88 E1775   LOC/G
                                                        APPORT
                                                        LEGIS

L65
WEINSTEIN J.B.,"THE EFFECT OF THE FEDERAL   MUNIC
REAPPORTIONMENT DECISIONS ON COUNTIES AND OTHER   LOC/G
FORMS OF GOVERNMENT." LAW CONSTN LEGIS CHOOSE   APPORT
GOV/COMP. PAGE 105 E2108   REPRESENT

S65
DIXON R.G.,"NEW CONSTITUTIONAL FORMS FOR   MUNIC
METROPOLIS: REAPPORTIONED COUNTY BOARDS; LOCAL   REGION
COUNCILS OF GOVERNMENT." LAW CONSTN LEAD APPORT   GOV/COMP
REPRESENT DECISION. PAGE 32 E0631   PLAN

B66
FRIED R.C.,COMPARATIVE POLITICAL INSTITUTIONS. USSR   NAT/G
EX/STRUC FORCES LEGIS JUDGE CONTROL REPRESENT   PWR
ALL/IDEOS 20 CONGRESS BUREAUCRCY. PAGE 40 E0798   EFFICIENCY
                                                        GOV/COMP

L66
SEYLER W.C.,"DOCTORAL DISSERTATIONS IN POLITICAL   BIBLIOG
SCIENCE IN UNIVERSITIES OF THE UNITED STATES AND   LAW
CANADA." INT/ORG LOC/G ADMIN...INT/LAW MGT   NAT/G
GOV/COMP. PAGE 90 E1808

S67
BRADLEY A.W.,"CONSTITUTION-MAKING IN UGANDA."   NAT/G
UGANDA LAW CHIEF DELIB/GP LEGIS ADMIN EXEC   CREATE
PARL/PROC RACE/REL ORD/FREE...GOV/COMP 20. PAGE 15   CONSTN
E0284   FEDERAL

S68
BURGESS J.W.,"VON HOLST'S PUBLIC LAW OF THE UNITED   CONSTN
STATES" USA-45 LAW GOV/REL...GOV/COMP IDEA/COMP 19.   FEDERAL
PAGE 17 E0339   NAT/G
                                                        JURID

B87
ADAMS J.,A DEFENSE OF THE CONSTITUTIONS OF   CONSTN
GOVERNMENT OF THE UNITED STATES OF AMERICA. USA-45   BAL/PWR
STRATA CHIEF EX/STRUC LEGIS CT/SYS CONSERVE   PWR
POPULISM...CONCPT CON/ANAL GOV/COMP. PAGE 3 E0048   NAT/G

GOV/REL....RELATIONS BETWEEN GOVERNMENTS

N
MIDWEST JOURNAL OF POLITICAL SCIENCE. USA+45 CONSTN   BIBLIOG/A
ECO/DEV LEGIS PROB/SOLV CT/SYS LEAD GOV/REL ATTIT   NAT/G
POLICY. PAGE 1 E0012   DIPLOM
                                                        POL/PAR

N
NEUE POLITISCHE LITERATUR; BERICHTE UBER DAS   BIBLIOG/A
INTERNATIONALE SCHRIFTTUM ZUR POLITIK. WOR+45 LAW   DIPLOM
CONSTN POL/PAR ADMIN LEAD GOV/REL...POLICY   NAT/G
IDEA/COMP. PAGE 2 E0028   NAT/COMP

N
PERSONNEL. USA+45 LAW LABOR LG/CO WORKER CREATE   BIBLIOG/A
GOV/REL PERS/REL ATTIT WEALTH. PAGE 2 E0029   ADMIN
                                                        MGT
                                                        GP/REL

N
ATLANTIC INSTITUTE.ATLANTIC STUDIES. COM EUR+WWI   BIBLIOG/A
USA+45 CULTURE STRUCT ECO/DEV FORCES LEAD ARMS/CONT   DIPLOM
...INT/LAW JURID SOC. PAGE 6 E0110   POLICY
                                                        GOV/REL

N
NEW YORK STATE LIBRARY.CHECKLIST OF OFFICIAL   BIBLIOG
PUBLICATIONS OF THE STATE OF NEW YORK. USA+45   PROVS
USA-45 LAW PROB/SOLV LEAD ATTIT 19/20. PAGE 77   WRITING
E1539   GOV/REL

N
UNESCO.INTERNATIONAL BIBLIOGRAPHY OF POLITICAL   BIBLIOG

SCIENCE (VOLUMES 1-8). WOR+45 LAW NAT/G EX/STRUC   CONCPT
LEGIS PROB/SOLV DIPLOM ADMIN GOV/REL 20 UNESCO.   IDEA/COMP
PAGE 98 E1957

                                                          B00
GRIFFIN A.P.C.,LIST OF BOOKS RELATING TO THE THEORY   BIBLIOG/A
OF COLONIZATION, GOVERNMENT OF DEPENDENCIES,   COLONIAL
PROTECTORATES, AND RELATED TOPICS. FRANCE GERMANY   GOV/REL
ITALY SPAIN UK USA-45 WOR-45 ECO/TAC ADMIN CONTROL   DOMIN
REGION NAT/LISM ALL/VALS PWR...INT/LAW SOC 16/19.
PAGE 46 E0917

                                                          B03
GRIFFIN A.P.C.,LISTS PUBLISHED 1902-03: GOVERNMENT   BIBLIOG
OWNERSHIP OF RAILROADS (PAMPHLET). USA-45 LAW NAT/G   DIST/IND
RATION GOV/REL CENTRAL SOCISM...POLICY 19/20.   CONTROL
PAGE 46 E0922   ADJUD

                                                          B03
GRIFFIN A.P.C.,LISTS PUBLISHED 1902-03: LABOR   BIBLIOG/A
PARTICULARLY RELATING TO STRIKES (PAMPHLET). UK   LABOR
USA-45 FINAN WORKER PLAN BARGAIN CRIME GOV/REL   GP/REL
...POLICY 19/20 PARLIAMENT. PAGE 46 E0923   ECO/TAC

                                                          B05
GOODNOW F.J.,THE PRINCIPLES OF THE ADMINISTRATIVE   ADMIN
LAW OF THE UNITED STATES. USA-45 LAW STRUCT   NAT/G
EX/STRUC LEGIS BAL/PWR CONTROL GOV/REL PWR...JURID   PROVS
19/20 CIVIL/SERV. PAGE 45 E0887   LOC/G

                                                          B08
WILSON W.,CONSTITUTIONAL GOVERNMENT IN THE UNITED   NAT/G
STATES. USA-45 LAW POL/PAR PROVS CHIEF LEGIS   GOV/REL
BAL/PWR ADJUD EXEC FEDERAL PWR 18/20 SUPREME/CT   CONSTN
HOUSE/REP SENATE. PAGE 106 E2130   PARL/PROC

                                                          B10
MCILWAIN C.H.,THE HIGH COURT OF PARLIAMENT AND ITS   LAW
SUPREMACY B1910 1878 408. UK EX/STRUC PARL/PROC   LEGIS
GOV/REL INGP/REL PRIVIL 12/20 PARLIAMENT   CONSTN
ENGLSH/LAW. PAGE 71 E1416   NAT/G

                                                          B12
BEARD C.A.,THE SUPREME COURT AND THE CONSTITUTION.   CONSTN
LAW NAT/G PROVS LEGIS GOV/REL ATTIT POPULISM   CT/SYS
SUPREME/CT. PAGE 9 E0164   ADJUD
                                                        CONTROL

                                                          B15
SAWYER R.A.,A LIST OF WORKS ON COUNTY GOVERNMENT.   BIBLIOG/A
LAW FINAN MUNIC TOP/EX ROUTINE CRIME...CLASSIF   LOC/G
RECORD 19/20. PAGE 87 E1748   GOV/REL
                                                        ADMIN

                                                          B19
LONDON SCHOOL ECONOMICS-POL,ANNUAL DIGEST OF PUBLIC   BIBLIOG/A
INTERNATIONAL LAW CASES. INT/ORG MUNIC NAT/G PROVS   INT/LAW
ADMIN NEUTRAL WAR GOV/REL PRIVIL 20. PAGE 66 E1323   ADJUD
                                                        DIPLOM

                                                          B19
SMITH R.H.,JUSTICE AND THE POOR. LAW RECEIVE ADJUD   CT/SYS
CRIME GOV/REL COST...JURID SOC/WK CONCPT STAT   DISCRIM
CHARTS GP/COMP 20. PAGE 92 E1847   WEALTH

                                                          N19
AMERICAN CIVIL LIBERTIES UNION,"WE HOLD THESE   ORD/FREE
TRUTHS" FREEDOM, JUSTICE, EQUALITY: REPORT ON CIVIL   LAW
LIBERTIES (A PERIODICAL PAMPHLET COVERING 1951-53).   RACE/REL
USA+45 ACADEM NAT/G FORCES LEGIS COERCE CIVMIL/REL   CONSTN
GOV/REL DISCRIM PRIVIL MARXISM...OLD/LIB 20 ACLU UN
CIVIL/LIB. PAGE 4 E0076

                                                          N19
BRENNAN W.J. JR.,THE BILL OF RIGHTS AND THE STATES   CONSTN
(PAMPHLET). USA+45 USA-45 LEGIS BAL/PWR ADJUD   PROVS
CT/SYS FEDERAL PWR SOVEREIGN 18/20 SUPREME/CT   GOV/REL
BILL/RIGHT. PAGE 15 E0293   ORD/FREE

                                                          N19
BURRUS B.R.,INVESTIGATION AND DISCOVERY IN STATE   NAT/G
ANTITRUST (PAMPHLET). USA+45 USA-45 LEGIS ECO/TAC   PROVS
ADMIN CONTROL CT/SYS CRIME GOV/REL PWR...JURID   LAW
CHARTS 19/20 FTC MONOPOLY. PAGE 18 E0346   INSPECT

                                                          C20
BLACHLY F.F.,"THE GOVERNMENT AND ADMINISTRATION OF   NAT/G
GERMANY." GERMANY CONSTN LOC/G PROVS DELIB/GP   GOV/REL
EX/STRUC FORCES LEGIS TOP/EX CT/SYS...BIBLIOG/A   ADMIN
19/20. PAGE 12 E0235   PHIL/SCI

                                                          B24
HOLDSWORTH W.S.,A HISTORY OF ENGLISH LAW; THE   LAW
COMMON LAW AND ITS RIVALS (VOL. IV). UK SEA AGRI   LEGIS
CHIEF ADJUD CONTROL CRIME GOV/REL...INT/LAW JURID   CT/SYS
NAT/COMP 16/17 PARLIAMENT COMMON/LAW CANON/LAW   CONSTN

ENGLSH/LAW. PAGE 54 E1075

                                                          B30
FAIRLIE J.A.,COUNTY GOVERNMENT AND ADMINISTRATION.   ADMIN
UK USA-45 NAT/G SCHOOL FORCES BUDGET TAX CT/SYS   GOV/REL
CHOOSE...JURID BIBLIOG 11/20. PAGE 36 E0713   LOC/G
                                                        MUNIC

                                                          B31
COLUMBIA UNIVERSITY,A BIBLIOGRAPHY OF THE FACULTY   BIBLIOG
OF POLITICAL SCIENCE OF COLUMBIA UNIVERSITY,   ACADEM
1880-1930. USA-45 LAW NAT/G LEGIS DIPLOM LEAD WAR   PHIL/SCI
GOV/REL ATTIT...TIME/SEQ 19/20. PAGE 24 E0478

                                                          B36
GRAVES W.B.,AMERICAN STATE GOVERNMENT. CONSTN FINAN   NAT/G
EX/STRUC FORCES LEGIS BUDGET TAX CT/SYS REPRESENT   PROVS
GOV/REL...BIBLIOG/A 19/20. PAGE 45 E0900   ADMIN
                                                        FEDERAL

                                                          B38
CLARK J.P.,THE RISE OF A NEW FEDERALISM. LEGIS   FEDERAL
TARIFFS EFFICIENCY NAT/LISM UTIL...JURID SOC   PROVS
GEN/LAWS BIBLIOG 19/20. PAGE 23 E0451   NAT/G
                                                        GOV/REL

                                                          B39
SIEYES E.J.,LES DISCOURS DE SIEYES DANS LES DEBATS   CONSTN
CONSTITUTIONNELS DE L'AN III (2 ET 18 THERMIDOR).   ADJUD
FRANCE LAW NAT/G PROB/SOLV BAL/PWR GOV/REL 18 JURY.   LEGIS
PAGE 91 E1824   EX/STRUC

                                                          B40
ANDERSON W.,FUNDAMENTALS OF AMERICAN GOVERNMENT.   NAT/G
USA-45 LAW POL/PAR CHIEF EX/STRUC BUDGET ADMIN   LOC/G
CT/SYS PARL/PROC CHOOSE FEDERAL...BIBLIOG 20.   GOV/REL
PAGE 5 E0093   CONSTN

                                                          B40
FULLER G.H.,A SELECTED LIST OF RECENT REFERENCES ON   BIBLIOG/A
THE CONSTITUTION OF THE UNITED STATES (PAMPHLET).   CONSTN
CULTURE NAT/G LEGIS CONFER ADJUD GOV/REL CONSEN   LAW
POPULISM...JURID CONCPT 18/20 CONGRESS. PAGE 41   USA-45
E0820

                                                          B41
GILMORE M.P.,ARGUMENT FROM ROMAN LAW IN POLITICAL   JURID
THOUGHT, 1200-1600. INTELL LICENSE CONTROL CT/SYS   LAW
GOV/REL PRIVIL PWR...IDEA/COMP BIBLIOG 13/16.   CONCPT
PAGE 44 E0866   NAT/G

                                                          B42
CARR R.K.,THE SUPREME COURT AND JUDICIAL REVIEW.   CT/SYS
NAT/G CHIEF LEGIS OP/RES LEAD GOV/REL GP/REL ATTIT   CONSTN
...POLICY DECISION 18/20 SUPREME/CT PRESIDENT   JURID
CONGRESS. PAGE 20 E0394   PWR

                                                          B42
FORTESCU J.,IN PRAISE OF ENGLISH LAW (1464) (TRANS.   LAW
BY S.B. CHRIMES). UK ELITES CHIEF FORCES CT/SYS   CONSTN
COERCE CRIME GOV/REL ILLEGIT...JURID GOV/COMP   LEGIS
GEN/LAWS 15. PAGE 39 E0774   ORD/FREE

                                                          B44
BEARD C.A.,AMERICAN GOVERNMENT AND POLITICS (REV.   LEAD
ED.). CONSTN MUNIC POL/PAR PROVS EX/STRUC LEGIS   USA-45
TOP/EX CT/SYS GOV/REL...BIBLIOG T 18/20. PAGE 9   NAT/G
E0165   LOC/G

                                                          B47
HARGRETT L.,A BIBLIOGRAPHY OF THE CONSTITUTIONS AND   BIBLIOG/A
LAWS OF THE AMERICAN INDIANS. USA-45 LOC/G GOV/REL   CONSTN
GP/REL 19/20 INDIAN/AM. PAGE 50 E0999   LAW
                                                        NAT/G

                                                          B47
KONVITZ M.R.,THE CONSTITUTION AND CIVIL RIGHTS.   CONSTN
USA-45 NAT/G ADJUD GP/REL RACE/REL POPULISM   LAW
...MAJORIT 19/20 SUPREME/CT CIV/RIGHTS. PAGE 61   GOV/REL
E1227   ORD/FREE

                                                          B48
CORWIN E.S.,LIBERTY AGAINST GOVERNMENT: THE RISE,   CONCPT
FLOWERING AND DECLINE OF A FAMOUS JURIDICAL   ORD/FREE
CONCEPT. LEGIS ADJUD CT/SYS SANCTION GOV/REL   JURID
FEDERAL CONSERVE NEW/LIB...OLD/LIB 18/20 ROMAN/LAW   CONSTN
COMMON/LAW. PAGE 26 E0514

                                                          B48
KEIR D.L.,CASES IN CONSTITUTIONAL LAW. UK CHIEF   CONSTN
LEGIS DIPLOM TAX PARL/PROC CRIME GOV/REL...INT/LAW   LAW
JURID 17/20. PAGE 60 E1195   ADJUD
                                                        CT/SYS

                                                          C48
WALKER H.,"THE LEGISLATIVE PROCESS; LAWMAKING IN   PARL/PROC

THE UNITED STATES." NAT/G POL/PAR PROVS EX/STRUC OP/RES PROB/SOLV CT/SYS LOBBY GOV/REL...CHARTS BIBLIOG T 18/20 CONGRESS. PAGE 105 E2094
`LEGIS LAW CONSTN`

S49
PRITCHETT C.H.,"THE PRESIDENT AND THE SUPREME COURT." NAT/G CONTROL REPRESENT FEDERAL 20. PAGE 82 E1651
`GOV/REL CT/SYS CHIEF`

B51
ANDERSON W.,STATE AND LOCAL GOVERNMENT IN THE UNITED STATES. USA+45 CONSTN POL/PAR EX/STRUC LEGIS BUDGET TAX ADJUD CT/SYS CHOOSE...CHARTS T 20. PAGE 5 E0094
`LOC/G MUNIC PROVS GOV/REL`

B51
WOOD V.,DUE PROCESS OF LAW 1932-1949: SUPREME COURT'S USE OF A CONSTITUTIONAL TOOL. USA+45 USA-45 SOCIETY TAX CRIME...POLICY CHARTS 20 SUPREME/CT. PAGE 107 E2143
`CONSTN TREND ADJUD GOV/REL`

B52
JENNINGS W.I.,CONSTITUTIONAL LAWS OF THE COMMONWEALTH. UK LAW CHIEF LEGIS TAX CT/SYS PARL/PROC GOV/REL...INT/LAW 18/20 COMMONWLTH ENGLSH/LAW. PAGE 58 E1165
`CONSTN JURID ADJUD COLONIAL`

B52
THOM J.M.,GUIDE TO RESEARCH MATERIAL IN POLITICAL SCIENCE (PAMPHLET). ELITES LOC/G MUNIC NAT/G LEGIS DIPLOM ADJUD CIVMIL/REL GOV/REL PWR MGT. PAGE 96 E1916
`BIBLIOG/A KNOWL`

L52
WRIGHT Q.,"CONGRESS AND THE TREATY-MAKING POWER." USA+45 WOR+45 CONSTN INTELL NAT/G CHIEF CONSULT EX/STRUC LEGIS TOP/EX CREATE GOV/REL DISPL DRIVE RIGID/FLEX...TREND TOT/POP CONGRESS CONGRESS 20 TREATY. PAGE 108 E2154
`ROUTINE DIPLOM INT/LAW DELIB/GP`

C52
LANCASTER L.W.,"GOVERNMENT IN RURAL AMERICA." USA+45 ECO/DEV AGRI SCHOOL FORCES LEGIS JUDGE BUDGET TAX CT/SYS...CHARTS BIBLIOG. PAGE 62 E1248
`GOV/REL LOC/G MUNIC ADMIN`

B53
GROSS B.M.,THE LEGISLATIVE STRUGGLE: A STUDY IN SOCIAL COMBAT. STRUCT LOC/G POL/PAR JUDGE EDU/PROP DEBATE ETIQUET ADMIN LOBBY CHOOSE GOV/REL INGP/REL HEREDITY ALL/VALS...SOC PRESIDENT. PAGE 48 E0948
`LEGIS DECISION PERSON LEAD`

B53
MAJUMDAR B.B.,PROBLEMS OF PUBLIC ADMINISTRATION IN INDIA. INDIA INDUS PLAN BUDGET ADJUD CENTRAL DEMAND WEALTH...WELF/ST ANTHOL 20 CIVIL/SERV. PAGE 68 E1353
`ECO/UNDEV GOV/REL ADMIN MUNIC`

B53
SECKLER-HUDSON C.,BIBLIOGRAPHY ON PUBLIC ADMINISTRATION (4TH ED.). USA+45 LAW POL/PAR DELIB/GP BUDGET ADJUD LOBBY GOV/REL GP/REL ATTIT ...JURID 20. PAGE 90 E1800
`BIBLIOG/A ADMIN NAT/G MGT`

B54
SCHWARTZ B.,FRENCH ADMINISTRATIVE LAW AND THE COMMON-LAW WORLD. FRANCE CULTURE LOC/G NAT/G PROVS DELIB/GP EX/STRUC LEGIS PROB/SOLV CT/SYS EXEC GOV/REL...IDEA/COMP ENGLSH/LAW. PAGE 89 E1786
`JURID LAW METH/COMP ADJUD`

S54
HART J.,"ADMINISTRATION AND THE COURTS." USA+45 NAT/G REPRESENT 20. PAGE 50 E1003
`ADMIN GOV/REL CT/SYS FEDERAL`

B55
BLOOM G.F.,ECONOMICS OF LABOR RELATIONS. USA+45 LAW CONSULT WORKER CAP/ISM PAY ADJUD CONTROL EFFICIENCY ORD/FREE...CHARTS 19/20 AFL/CIO NLRB DEPT/LABOR. PAGE 13 E0249
`ECO/DEV ECO/TAC LABOR GOV/REL`

B55
CRAIG J.,BIBLIOGRAPHY OF PUBLIC ADMINISTRATION IN AUSTRALIA. CONSTN FINAN EX/STRUC LEGIS PLAN DIPLOM RECEIVE ADJUD ROUTINE...HEAL 19/20 AUSTRAL PARLIAMENT. PAGE 27 E0540
`BIBLIOG GOV/REL ADMIN NAT/G`

B55
GUAITA A.,BIBLIOGRAFIA ESPANOLA DE DERECHO ADMINISTRATIVO (PAMPHLET). SPAIN LOC/G MUNIC NAT/G PROVS JUDGE BAL/PWR GOV/REL OWN...JURID 18/19. PAGE 48 E0959
`BIBLIOG ADMIN CONSTN PWR`

B55
MID-EUROPEAN LAW PROJECT,CHURCH AND STATE BEHIND
`LAW`

THE IRON CURTAIN. COM CZECHOSLVK HUNGARY POLAND USSR CULTURE SECT EDU/PROP GOV/REL CATHISM...CHARTS ANTHOL BIBLIOG WORSHIP 20 CHURCH/STA. PAGE 73 E1455
`MARXISM POLICY`

B56
DOUGLAS W.O.,WE THE JUDGES. INDIA USA+45 USA-45 LAW NAT/G SECT LEGIS PRESS CRIME FEDERAL ORD/FREE ...POLICY GOV/COMP 19/20 WARRN/EARL MARSHALL/J SUPREME/CT. PAGE 32 E0640
`ADJUD CT/SYS CONSTN GOV/REL`

B56
NOTZ R.L.,FEDERAL GRANTS-IN-AID TO STATES: ANALYSIS OF LAWS IN FORCE ON SEPTEMBER 10, 1956. USA+45 LAW SCHOOL PLAN ECO/TAC TAX RECEIVE...HEAL JURID 20. PAGE 78 E1558
`GIVE NAT/G PROVS GOV/REL`

B56
REDFORD E.S.,PUBLIC ADMINISTRATION AND POLICY FORMATION: STUDIES IN OIL, GAS, BANKING, RIVER DEVELOPMENT AND CORPORATE INVESTIGATIONS. USA+45 CLIENT NAT/G ADMIN LOBBY REPRESENT GOV/REL INGP/REL 20. PAGE 84 E1678
`EX/STRUC PROB/SOLV CONTROL EXEC`

B56
US HOUSE RULES COMM,HEARINGS BEFORE A SPECIAL SUBCOMMITTEE: ESTABLISHMENT OF A STANDING COMMITTEE ON ADMINISTRATIVE PROCEDURE. PRACTICE. USA+45 LAW EX/STRUC ADJUD CONTROL EXEC GOV/REL EFFICIENCY PWR ...POLICY INT 20 CONGRESS. PAGE 100 E2009
`ADMIN DOMIN DELIB/GP NAT/G`

S56
TANENHAUS J.,"THE SUPREME COURT AND PRESIDENTIAL POWER." USA+45 USA-45 NAT/G ADJUD GOV/REL FEDERAL 20 PRESIDENT. PAGE 95 E1907
`CT/SYS PWR CONTROL CHIEF`

B57
CHICAGO U LAW SCHOOL,CONFERENCE ON JUDICIAL ADMINISTRATION. LOC/G MUNIC NAT/G PROVS...ANTHOL 20. PAGE 22 E0429
`CT/SYS ADJUD ADMIN GOV/REL`

B57
LONG H.A.,USURPERS - FOES OF FREE MAN. LAW NAT/G CHIEF LEGIS DOMIN ADJUD REPRESENT GOV/REL ORD/FREE LAISSEZ POPULISM...POLICY 18/20 SUPREME/CT ROOSEVLT/F CONGRESS CON/INTERP. PAGE 66 E1325
`CT/SYS CENTRAL FEDERAL CONSTN`

B57
NEUMANN F.,THE DEMOCRATIC AND THE AUTHORITARIAN STATE: ESSAYS IN POLITICAL AND LEGAL THEORY. USA+45 USA-45 CONTROL REV GOV/REL PEACE ALL/IDEOS ...INT/LAW CONCPT GEN/LAWS BIBLIOG 20. PAGE 77 E1536
`DOMIN NAT/G ORD/FREE POLICY`

B57
US SENATE COMM ON JUDICIARY,CIVIL RIGHTS - 1957. USA+45 LAW NAT/G CONFER GOV/REL RACE/REL ORD/FREE PWR...JURID 20 SENATE CIV/RIGHTS. PAGE 102 E2039
`INT LEGIS DISCRIM PARL/PROC`

B57
US SENATE COMM ON JUDICIARY,LIMITATION OF APPELLATE JURISDICTION OF THE SUPREME COURT. USA+45 LAW NAT/G DELIB/GP PLAN ADMIN CONTROL PWR...DECISION 20 CONGRESS SUPREME/CT. PAGE 102 E2041
`CT/SYS ADJUD POLICY GOV/REL`

B58
DAVIS K.C.,ADMINISTRATIVE LAW; CASES, TEXT, PROBLEMS. LAW LOC/G NAT/G TOP/EX PAY CONTROL GOV/REL INGP/REL FEDERAL 20 SUPREME/CT. PAGE 29 E0576
`ADJUD JURID CT/SYS ADMIN`

B58
KAPLAN H.E.,THE LAW OF CIVIL SERVICE. USA+45 LAW POL/PAR CT/SYS CRIME GOV/REL...POLICY JURID 20. PAGE 59 E1183
`ADJUD NAT/G ADMIN CONSTN`

B58
LAW COMMISSION OF INDIA,REFORM OF JUDICIAL ADMINISTRATION. INDIA TOP/EX ADMIN DISCRIM EFFICIENCY...METH/COMP 20. PAGE 63 E1269
`CT/SYS ADJUD GOV/REL CONTROL`

B58
US SENATE COMM POST OFFICE,TO PROVIDE AN EFFECTIVE SYSTEM OF PERSONNEL ADMINISTRATION. USA+45 NAT/G EX/STRUC PARL/PROC GOV/REL...JURID 20 SENATE CIVIL/SERV. PAGE 103 E2060
`INT LEGIS CONFER ADMIN`

B58
WHITNEY S.N.,ANTITRUST POLICIES: AMERICAN EXPERIENCE IN TWENTY INDUSTRIES. USA+45 USA-45 LAW DELIB/GP LEGIS ADJUD CT/SYS GOV/REL ATTIT...ANTHOL 20 MONOPOLY CASEBOOK. PAGE 106 E2119
`INDUS CONTROL LG/CO MARKET`

DAHL R.A.,"DECISION-MAKING IN A DEMOCRACY: THE
SUPREME COURT AS A NATIONAL POLICY-MAKER" (BMR)"
USA+45 USA-45 POL/PAR ADJUD GOV/REL PWR...POLICY
JURID 19/20 SUPREME/CT. PAGE 28 E0561

S58
CT/SYS
CONSTN
DECISION
NAT/G

ELLIOTT S.D.,IMPROVING OUR COURTS. LAW EX/STRUC
PLAN PROB/SOLV ADJUD ADMIN TASK CRIME EFFICIENCY
ORD/FREE 20. PAGE 34 E0684

B59
CT/SYS
JURID
GOV/REL
NAT/G

SCOTT F.R.,CIVIL LIBERTIES AND CANADIAN FEDERALISM.
CANADA LAW ADJUD CT/SYS GOV/REL 20 CIV/RIGHTS.
PAGE 90 E1797

B59
ORD/FREE
FEDERAL
NAT/LISM
CONSTN

TOMPKINS D.C.,SUPREME COURT OF THE UNITED STATES: A
BIBLIOGRAPHY. LAW JUDGE ADJUD GOV/REL DISCRIM
...JURID 18/20 SUPREME/CT NEGRO. PAGE 96 E1931

B59
BIBLIOG/A
CT/SYS
CONSTN
NAT/G

U OF MICHIGAN LAW SCHOOL,ATOMS AND THE LAW. USA+45
PROVS WORKER PROB/SOLV DIPLOM ADMIN GOV/REL ANTHOL.
PAGE 97 E1950

B59
NUC/PWR
NAT/G
CONTROL
LAW

US CONGRESS JT ATOM ENRGY COMM,SELECTED MATERIALS
ON FEDERAL-STATE COOPERATION IN THE ATOMIC ENERGY
FIELD. USA+45 LAW LOC/G PROVS CONSULT LEGIS ADJUD
...POLICY BIBLIOG 20 AEC. PAGE 99 E1991

B59
NAT/G
NUC/PWR
GOV/REL
DELIB/GP

MURPHY W.F.,"LOWER COURT CHECKS ON SUPREME COURT
POWER" (BMR)" USA+45 NAT/G PROVS SCHOOL GOV/REL
RACE/REL DISCRIM ATTIT...DECISION JURID 20
SUPREME/CT NEGRO. PAGE 75 E1508

S59
CT/SYS
BAL/PWR
CONTROL
ADJUD

SCHEEHAN D.,"PUBLIC AND PRIVATE GROUPS AS
IDENTIFIED IN THE FIELD OF TRADE REGULATIONS."
USA+45 ADMIN REPRESENT GOV/REL. PAGE 87 E1753

S59
LAW
CONTROL
ADJUD
LOBBY

ADRIAN C.R.,STATE AND LOCAL GOVERNMENTS: A STUDY IN
THE POLITICAL PROCESS. USA+45 LAW FINAN MUNIC
POL/PAR LEGIS ADJUD EXEC CHOOSE REPRESENT. PAGE 3
E0051

B60
LOC/G
PROVS
GOV/REL
ATTIT

ALBI F.,TRATADO DE LOS MODOS DE GESTION DE LAS
CORPORACIONES LOCALES. SPAIN FINAN NAT/G BUDGET
CONTROL EXEC ROUTINE GOV/REL ORD/FREE SOVEREIGN
...MGT 20. PAGE 3 E0057

B60
LOC/G
LAW
ADMIN
MUNIC

BYRD E.M. JR.,TREATIES AND EXECUTIVE AGREEMENTS IN
THE UNITED STATES: THEIR SEPARATE ROLES AND
LIMITATIONS. USA+45 USA-45 EX/STRUC TARIFFS CT/SYS
GOV/REL FEDERAL...IDEA/COMP BIBLIOG SUPREME/CT
SENATE CONGRESS. PAGE 18 E0353

B60
CHIEF
INT/LAW
DIPLOM

CARPER E.T.,THE DEFENSE APPROPRIATIONS RIDER
(PAMPHLET). USA+45 CONSTN CHIEF DELIB/GP LEGIS
BUDGET LOBBY CIVMIL/REL...POLICY 20 CONGRESS
EISNHWR/DD DEPT/DEFEN PRESIDENT BOSTON. PAGE 20
E0390

B60
GOV/REL
ADJUD
LAW
CONTROL

FLORES R.H.,CATALOGO DE TESIS DOCTORALES DE LAS
FACULTADES DE LA UNIVERSIDAD DE EL SALVADOR.
EL/SALVADR LAW DIPLOM ADMIN LEAD GOV/REL...SOC
19/20. PAGE 39 E0767

B60
BIBLIOG
ACADEM
L/A+17C
NAT/G

HANBURY H.G.,ENGLISH COURTS OF LAW. UK EX/STRUC
LEGIS CRIME ROLE 12/20 COMMON/LAW ENGLSH/LAW.
PAGE 50 E0993

B60
JURID
CT/SYS
CONSTN
GOV/REL

MENDELSON W.,CAPITALISM, DEMOCRACY, AND THE SUPREME
COURT. USA+45 USA-45 CONSTN DIPLOM GOV/REL ATTIT
ORD/FREE LAISSEZ...POLICY CHARTS PERS/COMP 18/20
SUPREME/CT MARSHALL/J HOLMES/OW TANEY/RB FIELD/JJ.
PAGE 72 E1437

B60
JUDGE
CT/SYS
JURID
NAT/G

PICKLES D.,THE FIFTH FRENCH REPUBLIC. ALGERIA

B60
CONSTN

FRANCE CHOOSE GOV/REL ATTIT CONSERVE...CHARTS 20
DEGAULLE/C. PAGE 80 E1615

ADJUD
NAT/G
EFFICIENCY

SCHEIBER H.N.,THE WILSON ADMINISTRATION AND CIVIL
LIBERTIES 1917-1921. LAW GOV/REL ATTIT 20 WILSON/W
CIVIL/LIB. PAGE 87 E1754

B60
ORD/FREE
WAR
NAT/G
CONTROL

US SENATE COMM ON JUDICIARY,FEDERAL ADMINISTRATIVE
PROCEDURE. USA+45 CONSTN NAT/G PROB/SOLV CONFER
GOV/REL...JURID INT 20 SENATE. PAGE 102 E2043

B60
PARL/PROC
LEGIS
ADMIN
LAW

US SENATE COMM ON JUDICIARY,ADMINISTRATIVE
PROCEDURE LEGISLATION. USA+45 CONSTN NAT/G
PROB/SOLV CONFER ROUTINE GOV/REL...INT 20 SENATE.
PAGE 102 E2044

B60
PARL/PROC
LEGIS
ADMIN
JURID

WEBSTER J.A.,A GENERAL STUDY OF THE DEPARTMENT OF
DEFENSE INTERNAL SECURITY PROGRAM. USA+45 WORKER
TEC/DEV ADJUD CONTROL CT/SYS EXEC GOV/REL COST
...POLICY DECISION MGT 20 DEPT/DEFEN SUPREME/CT.
PAGE 105 E2105

B60
ORD/FREE
PLAN
ADMIN
NAT/G

MANN S.Z.,"POLICY FORMULATION IN THE EXECUTIVE
BRANCH: THE TAFT-HARTLEY EXPERIENCE." USA+45 LABOR
CHIEF INGP/REL 20 NLRB. PAGE 68 E1360

S60
EXEC
GOV/REL
EX/STRUC
PROB/SOLV

ALFRED H.,PUBLIC OWNERSHIP IN THE USA: GOALS AND
PRIORITIES. LAW INDUS INT/TRADE ADJUD GOV/REL
EFFICIENCY PEACE SOCISM...POLICY ANTHOL 20 TVA.
PAGE 3 E0064

B61
CONTROL
OWN
ECO/DEV
ECO/TAC

AVERY M.W.,GOVERNMENT OF WASHINGTON STATE. USA+45
MUNIC DELIB/GP EX/STRUC LEGIS GIVE CT/SYS PARTIC
REGION EFFICIENCY 20 WASHINGT/G GOVERNOR. PAGE 6
E0121

B61
PROVS
LOC/G
ADMIN
GOV/REL

BEDFORD S.,THE FACES OF JUSTICE: A TRAVELLER'S
REPORT. AUSTRIA FRANCE GERMANY/W SWITZERLND UK UNIV
WOR+45 WOR-45 CULTURE PARTIC GOV/REL MORAL...JURID
OBS GOV/COMP 20. PAGE 9 E0174

B61
CT/SYS
ORD/FREE
PERSON
LAW

MASSEL M.S.,THE REGULATORY PROCESS (JOURNAL
REPRINT). NAT/G LOBBY REPRESENT GOV/REL 20. PAGE 69
E1382

B61
ADJUD
EX/STRUC
EXEC

WESTIN A.F.,THE SUPREME COURT: VIEWS FROM INSIDE.
USA+45 NAT/G PROF/ORG PROVS DELIB/GP INGP/REL
DISCRIM ATTIT...POLICY DECISION JURID ANTHOL 20
SUPREME/CT CONGRESS CIVIL/LIB. PAGE 106 E2114

B61
CT/SYS
LAW
ADJUD
GOV/REL

GERWIG R.,"PUBLIC AUTHORITIES IN THE UNITED
STATES." LAW CONSTN PROVS TAX ADMIN FEDERAL.
PAGE 43 E0852

L61
LOC/G
MUNIC
GOV/REL
PWR

LEAGUE WOMEN VOTERS MASSACHU,THE MERIT SYSTEM IN
MASSACHUSETTS (PAMPHLET). USA+45 PROVS LEGIT PARTIC
CHOOSE REPRESENT GOV/REL EFFICIENCY...POLICY
GOV/COMP BIBLIOG 20 MASSACHU. PAGE 64 E1274

N61
LOC/G
LAW
SENIOR
PROF/ORG

AMERICAN LAW INSTITUTE,FOREIGN RELATIONS LAW OF THE
UNITED STATES: RESTATEMENT, SECOND. USA+45 NAT/G
LEGIS ADJUD EXEC ROUTINE GOV/REL...INT/LAW JURID
CONCPT 20 TREATY. PAGE 4 E0082

B62
PROF/ORG
LAW
DIPLOM
ORD/FREE

BERMAN D.M.,A BILL BECOMES A LAW: THE CIVIL RIGHTS
ACT OF 1960. USA+45 LAW POL/PAR LOBBY RACE/REL
KNOWL...CHARTS 20 CONGRESS NEGRO CIV/RIGHTS.
PAGE 11 E0206

B62
DISCRIM
PARL/PROC
JURID
GOV/REL

CARPER E.T.,ILLINOIS GOES TO CONGRESS FOR ARMY
LAND. USA+45 LAW EXTR/IND PROVS REGION CIVMIL/REL
GOV/REL FEDERAL ATTIT 20 ILLINOIS SENATE CONGRESS
DIRKSEN/E DOUGLAS/P. PAGE 20 E0391

B62
ADMIN
LOBBY
GEOG
LEGIS

DUPRE J.S.,SCIENCE AND THE NATION: POLICY AND

B62
R+D

POLITICS. USA+45 LAW ACADEM FORCES ADMIN CIVMIL/REL INDUS
GOV/REL EFFICIENCY PEACE...TREND 20 SCI/ADVSRY. TEC/DEV
PAGE 34 E0665 NUC/PWR

B62
FROMAN L.A. JR.,PEOPLE AND POLITICS: AN ANALYSIS OF POL/PAR
THE AMERICAN POLITICAL SYSTEM. USA+45 CHIEF PROB/SOLV
DELIB/GP EX/STRUC LEGIS TOP/EX CT/SYS LOBBY GOV/REL
PERS/REL PWR...POLICY DECISION. PAGE 41 E0813

B62
HSUEH S.-.S.,GOVERNMENT AND ADMINISTRATION OF HONG ADMIN
KONG. CHIEF DELIB/GP LEGIS CT/SYS REPRESENT GOV/REL LOC/G
20 HONG/KONG CITY/MGT CIVIL/SERV GOVERNOR. PAGE 55 COLONIAL
E1106 EX/STRUC

B62
INSTITUTE JUDICIAL ADMIN,JUDGES: THEIR TEMPORARY NAT/G
APPOINTMENT, ASSIGNMENT AND TRANSFER: SURVEY OF FED LOC/G
AND STATE CONSTN'S STATUTES, ROLES OF CT. USA+45 JUDGE
CONSTN PROVS CT/SYS GOV/REL PWR JURID. PAGE 57 ADMIN
E1128

B62
MCGRATH J.J.,CHURCH AND STATE IN AMERICAN LAW: LAW
CASES AND MATERIALS. USA+45 USA-45 LEGIS EDU/PROP GOV/REL
ADJUD CT/SYS PWR...ANTHOL 18/20 CHURCH/STA. PAGE 71 SECT
E1415

B62
MURPHY W.F.,CONGRESS AND THE COURT. USA+45 LAW LEGIS
LOBBY GP/REL RACE/REL ATTIT PWR...JURID INT BIBLIOG CT/SYS
CONGRESS SUPREME/CT WARRN/EARL. PAGE 75 E1509 GOV/REL
ADJUD

B62
US CONGRESS,COMMUNICATIONS SATELLITE LEGISLATION: SPACE
HEARINGS BEFORE COMM ON AERON AND SPACE SCIENCES ON COM/IND
BILLS S2550 AND 2814. WOR+45 LAW VOL/ASSN PLAN ADJUD
DIPLOM CONTROL OWN PEACE...NEW/IDEA CONGRESS NASA. GOV/REL
PAGE 99 E1990

B62
WINTERS J.M.,INTERSTATE METROPOLITAN AREAS. CONSTN MUNIC
LEAD CHOOSE PWR DECISION. PAGE 107 E2135 LAW
REGION
GOV/REL

C62
VAN DER SPRENKEL S.,"LEGAL INSTITUTIONS IN MANCHU LAW
CHINA." ASIA STRUCT CT/SYS ROUTINE GOV/REL GP/REL JURID
...CONCPT BIBLIOG 17/20. PAGE 103 E2068 ADMIN
ADJUD

B63
ADRIAN C.R.,GOVERNING OVER FIFTY STATES AND THEIR PROVS
COMMUNITIES. USA+45 CONSTN FINAN MUNIC NAT/G LOC/G
POL/PAR EX/STRUC LEGIS ADMIN CONTROL CT/SYS GOV/REL
...CHARTS 20. PAGE 3 E0052 GOV/COMP

B63
COUNCIL OF STATE GOVERNMENTS,INCREASED RIGHTS FOR CT/SYS
DEFENDANTS IN STATE CRIMINAL PROSECUTIONS. USA+45 ADJUD
GOV/REL INGP/REL FEDERAL ORD/FREE...JURID 20 PROVS
SUPREME/CT. PAGE 26 E0522 CRIME

B63
DOUGLAS W.O.,THE ANATOMY OF LIBERTY: THE RIGHTS OF PEACE
MAN WITHOUT FORCE. WOR+45 ECO/DEV ECO/UNDEV LOC/G LAW
FORCES GOV/REL...SOC/WK 20. PAGE 32 E0643 DIPLOM
ORD/FREE

B63
GARNER U.F.,ADMINISTRATIVE LAW. UK LAW LOC/G NAT/G ADMIN
EX/STRUC LEGIS JUDGE BAL/PWR BUDGET ADJUD CONTROL JURID
CT/SYS...BIBLIOG 20. PAGE 42 E0840 PWR
GOV/REL

B63
LEGISLATIVE REFERENCE SERVICE,DIGEST OF PUBLIC BIBLIOG/A
GENERAL BILLS AND RESOLUTIONS. LAW COM/IND EDU/PROP LEGIS
GOV/REL INGP/REL KNOWL...JURID 20 CONGRESS. PAGE 64 DELIB/GP
E1280 NAT/G

B63
LIVELY E.,THE INVASION OF MISSISSIPPI. USA+45 LAW RACE/REL
CONSTN NAT/G PROVS CT/SYS GOV/REL FEDERAL CONSERVE CROWD
...TRADIT 20 MISSISSIPP NEGRO NAACP WARRN/EARL COERCE
KENNEDY/JF. PAGE 66 E1309 MARXISM

B63
PALOTAI O.C.,PUBLICATIONS OF THE INSTITUTE OF BIBLIOG/A
GOVERNMENT, 1930-1962. LAW PROVS SCHOOL WORKER ADMIN
ACT/RES OP/RES CT/SYS GOV/REL...CRIMLGY SOC/WK. LOC/G
PAGE 79 E1594 FINAN

B63
PRITCHETT C.H.,THE THIRD BRANCH OF GOVERNMENT. JURID
USA+45 USA-45 CONSTN SOCIETY INDUS SECT LEGIS JUDGE NAT/G
PROB/SOLV GOV/REL 20 SUPREME/CT CHURCH/STA. PAGE 82 ADJUD
E1654 CT/SYS

B63
US CONGRESS: SENATE,HEARINGS OF THE COMMITTEE ON LEGIS
THE JUDICIARY. USA+45 CONSTN NAT/G ADMIN GOV/REL 20 LAW
CONGRESS. PAGE 99 E1992 ORD/FREE
DELIB/GP

B63
US SENATE,DOCUMENTS ON INTERNATIONAL ASPECTS OF SPACE
EXPLORATION AND USE OF OUTER SPACE, 1954-62: STAFF UTIL
REPORT FOR COMM AERON SPACE SCI. USA+45 USSR LEGIS GOV/REL
LEAD CIVMIL/REL PEACE...POLICY INT/LAW ANTHOL 20 DIPLOM
CONGRESS NASA KHRUSH/N. PAGE 101 E2026

B63
US SENATE COMM ON JUDICIARY,ADMINISTRATIVE PARL/PROC
CONFERENCE OF THE UNITED STATES. USA+45 CONSTN JURID
NAT/G PROB/SOLV CONFER GOV/REL...INT 20 SENATE. ADMIN
PAGE 102 E2048 LEGIS

B63
VINES K.N.,STUDIES IN JUDICIAL POLITICS: TULANE CT/SYS
STUDIES IN POLITICAL SCIENCE (VOL. 8). POL/PAR GOV/REL
JUDGE ADJUD SANCTION CRIME CHOOSE PWR...JURID STAT PROVS
TIME/SEQ CHARTS. PAGE 104 E2079

B64
ANDERSON J.W.,EISENHOWER, BROWNELL, AND THE LAW
CONGRESS - THE TANGLED ORIGINS OF THE CIVIL RIGHTS CONSTN
BILL OF 1956-1957. USA+45 POL/PAR LEGIS CREATE POLICY
PROB/SOLV LOBBY GOV/REL RIGID/FLEX...NEW/IDEA 20 NAT/G
EISNHWR/DD CONGRESS BROWNELL/H CIV/RIGHTS. PAGE 5
E0090

B64
BENNETT H.A.,THE COMMISSION AND THE COMMON LAW: A ADJUD
STUDY IN ADMINISTRATIVE ADJUDICATION. LAW ADMIN DELIB/GP
CT/SYS LOBBY SANCTION GOV/REL 20 COMMON/LAW. DIST/IND
PAGE 10 E0188 POLICY

B64
DUMON F.,LE BRESIL; SES INSTITUTIONS POLITIQUES ET CONSTN
JUDICIARIES. BRAZIL POL/PAR CHIEF LEGIS ORD/FREE JURID
19/20. PAGE 33 E0658 CT/SYS
GOV/REL

B64
GOODNOW H.F.,THE CIVIL SERVICE OF PAKISTAN: ADMIN
BUREAUCRACY IN A NEW NATION. INDIA PAKISTAN S/ASIA GOV/REL
ECO/UNDEV PROVS CHIEF PARTIC CHOOSE EFFICIENCY PWR LAW
...BIBLIOG 20. PAGE 45 E0889 NAT/G

B64
HANSON R.,FAIR REPRESENTATION COMES TO MARYLAND APPORT
(PAMPHLET). BAL/PWR CT/SYS CHOOSE GOV/REL 20 REPRESENT
MARYLAND SUPREME/CT. PAGE 50 E0997 PROVS
LEGIS

B64
IRION F.C.,APPORTIONMENT OF THE NEW MEXICO APPORT
LEGISLATURE. NAT/G LEGIS PRESS CT/SYS ATTIT REPRESENT
...POLICY TIME/SEQ 19/20 SUPREME/CT. PAGE 57 E1137 GOV/REL
PROVS

B64
KOREA (REPUBLIC) SUPREME COURT,KOREAN LEGAL SYSTEM. JURID
KOREA/S WOR+45 LAW LEAD ROUTINE GOV/REL ORD/FREE 20 CT/SYS
SUPREME/CT. PAGE 61 E1229 CONSTN
CRIME

B64
LIGGETT E.,BRITISH POLITICAL ISSUES: VOLUME 1. UK POL/PAR
LAW CONSTN LOC/G NAT/G ADJUD 20. PAGE 65 E1296 GOV/REL
CT/SYS
DIPLOM

B64
MAKI J.M.,COURT AND CONSTITUTION IN JAPAN; SELECTED CT/SYS
SUPREME COURT DECISIONS, 1948-60. FAM LABOR GOV/REL CONSTN
HABITAT ORD/FREE...DECISION JURID 20 CHINJAP PROB/SOLV
SUPREME/CT CIV/RIGHTS. PAGE 68 E1354 LAW

B64
MARNELL W.H.,THE FIRST AMENDMENT: THE HISTORY OF CONSTN
RELIGIOUS FREEDOM IN AMERICA. WOR+45 WOR-45 PROVS SECT
CREATE CT/SYS...POLICY BIBLIOG/A WORSHIP 16/20. ORD/FREE
PAGE 68 E1367 GOV/REL

B64
MASON A.T.,AMERICAN CONSTITUTIONAL LAW: CONSTN
INTRODUCTORY ESSAYS AND SELECTED CASES (3RD ED.). CT/SYS

LAW LEGIS TAX ADJUD GOV/REL FEDERAL ORD/FREE PWR   JURID
...TIME/SEQ BIBLIOG T 19/20 SUPREME/CT. PAGE 69
E1379

B64
MITAU G.T.,PROXIMATE SOLUTIONS: CASE PROBLEMS IN   PROVS
STATE AND LOCAL GOVERNMENT. USA+45 CONSTN NAT/G   LOC/G
CHIEF LEGIS CT/SYS EXEC GOV/REL GP/REL PWR 20   ADJUD
CASEBOOK. PAGE 73 E1470

US SENATE COMM ON JUDICIARY,CIVIL RIGHTS - THE   INT
PRESIDENT'S PROGRAM. USA+45 LAW PROB/SOLV PRESS   LEGIS
ADJUD GOV/REL RACE/REL ORD/FREE PWR...JURID 20   DISCRIM
SUPREME/CT SENATE CIV/RIGHTS PRESIDENT. PAGE 102   PARL/PROC
E2053

B64
US SENATE COMM ON JUDICIARY,ADMINISTRATIVE   PARL/PROC
PROCEDURE ACT. USA+45 CONSTN NAT/G PROB/SOLV CONFER   LEGIS
GOV/REL PWR...INT 20 SENATE. PAGE 102 E2054   JURID
                                                      ADMIN

B65
BLITZ L.F.,THE POLITICS AND ADMINISTRATION OF   NAT/G
NIGERIAN GOVERNMENT. NIGER CULTURE LOC/G LEGIS   GOV/REL
DIPLOM COLONIAL CT/SYS SOVEREIGN...GEOG SOC ANTHOL   POL/PAR
20. PAGE 13 E0245

B65
FISCHER F.C.,THE GOVERNMENT OF MICHIGAN. USA+45   PROVS
NAT/G PUB/INST EX/STRUC LEGIS BUDGET GIVE EDU/PROP   LOC/G
CT/SYS CHOOSE GOV/REL...T MICHIGAN. PAGE 38 E0753   ADMIN
                                                      CONSTN

B65
FRYE R.J.,HOUSING AND URBAN RENEWAL IN ALABAMA.   MUNIC
USA+45 NEIGH LEGIS BUDGET ADJUD ADMIN PARTIC...MGT   PROB/SOLV
20 ALABAMA URBAN/RNWL. PAGE 41 E0815   PLAN
                                                      GOV/REL

B65
GLUECK S.,ROSCOE POUND AND CRIMINAL JUSTICE.   CT/SYS
SOCIETY FAM GOV/REL AGE/Y ATTIT ORD/FREE...CRIMLGY   CRIME
BIOG ANTHOL SOC/INTEG 19/20. PAGE 44 E0875   LAW
                                                      ADJUD

B65
HIGHSAW R.B.,CONFLICT AND CHANGE IN LOCAL   GOV/REL
GOVERNMENT. USA+45 BUDGET ECO/TAC LEGIT ADJUD   PROB/SOLV
ALABAMA. PAGE 52 E1044   LOC/G
                                                      BAL/PWR

B65
KEEFE W.J.,THE AMERICAN LEGISLATIVE PROCESS. USA+45   LEGIS
CONSTN POL/PAR CT/SYS REPRESENT FEDERAL ATTIT   NAT/G
PLURISM...MAJORIT 20 CONGRESS PRESIDENT. PAGE 60   CHIEF
E1192   GOV/REL

B65
LAFAVE W.R.,LAW AND SOVIET SOCIETY. EX/STRUC DIPLOM   JURID
DOMIN EDU/PROP PRESS ADMIN CRIME OWN MARXISM 20   CT/SYS
KHRUSH/N. PAGE 62 E1244   ADJUD
                                                      GOV/REL

B65
MCKAY R.B.,REAPPORTIONMENT: THE LAW AND POLITICS OF   APPORT
EQUAL REPRESENTATION. FUT USA+45 PROVS BAL/PWR   MAJORIT
ADJUD CHOOSE REPRESENT GOV/REL FEDERAL...JURID   LEGIS
BIBLIOG 20 SUPREME/CT CONGRESS. PAGE 71 E1420   PWR

B65
SMITH C.,THE OMBUDSMAN: A BIBLIOGRAPHY (PAMPHLET).   BIBLIOG
DENMARK SWEDEN USA+45 LAW LEGIS JUDGE GOV/REL   ADMIN
GP/REL...JURID 20. PAGE 92 E1841   CT/SYS
                                                      ADJUD

B65
SNOW J.H.,REAPPORTIONMENT. LAW CONSTN NAT/G GOV/REL   APPORT
ORD/FREE...JURID 20 SUPREME/CT CONNECTICT. PAGE 92   ADJUD
E1848   LEGIS
                                                      PROVS

B65
US SENATE,US INTERNATIONAL SPACE PROGRAMS, 1959-65:   SPACE
STAFF REPORT FOR COMM ON AERONAUTICAL AND SPACE   DIPLOM
SCIENCES. WOR+45 VOL/ASSN CIVMIL/REL 20 CONGRESS   PLAN
NASA TREATY. PAGE 101 E2027   GOV/REL

B65
US SENATE COMM ON JUDICIARY,HEARINGS BEFORE   ROUTINE
SUBCOMMITTEE ON ADMINISTRATIVE PRACTICE AND   DELIB/GP
PROCEDURE ABOUT ADMINISTRATIVE PROCEDURE ACT 1965.   ADMIN
USA+45 LEGIS EDU/PROP ADJUD GOV/REL INGP/REL   NAT/G
EFFICIENCY...POLICY INT 20 CONGRESS. PAGE 103 E2055

S65
FOX A.B.,"NATO AND CONGRESS." CONSTN DELIB/GP   CONTROL
EX/STRUC FORCES TOP/EX BUDGET NUC/PWR GOV/REL   DIPLOM
...GP/COMP CONGRESS NATO TREATY. PAGE 39 E0779

S65
MERRITT R.L.,"SELECTED ARTICLES AND DOCUMENTS ON   BIBLIOG
INTERNATIONAL LAW AND RELATIONS." WOR+45 INT/ORG   DIPLOM
FORCES INT/TRADE. PAGE 72 E1443   INT/LAW
                                                      GOV/REL

B66
BURNS A.C.,PARLIAMENT AS AN EXPORT. WOR+45 CONSTN   PARL/PROC
BARGAIN DEBATE ROUTINE GOV/REL EFFICIENCY...ANTHOL   POL/PAR
COMMONWLTH PARLIAMENT. PAGE 17 E0343   CT/SYS
                                                      CHIEF

B66
CALIFORNIA STATE LIBRARY,REAPPORTIONMENT, A   BIBLIOG
SELECTIVE BIBLIOGRAPHY. USA+45 LEGIS CT/SYS   APPORT
REPRESENT GOV/REL. PAGE 19 E0367   NAT/G
                                                      PROVS

B66
CANFIELD L.H.,THE PRESIDENCY OF WOODROW WILSON: PERSON
PRELUDE TO A WORLD IN CRISIS. USA+45 ADJUD NEUTRAL   POLICY
WAR CHOOSE INGP/REL PEACE ORD/FREE 20 WILSON/W   DIPLOM
PRESIDENT TREATY LEAGUE/NAT. PAGE 19 E0373   GOV/REL

B66
COUNCIL OF STATE GOVERNMENTS,THE HANDBOOK ON   CRIME
INTERSTATE CRIME CONTROL. USA+45 PUB/INST DELIB/GP   GOV/REL
AGREE AGE/Y 20 INTST/CRIM. PAGE 27 E0524   CONTROL
                                                      JURID

B66
DALLIN A.,POLITICS IN THE SOVIET UNION: 7 CASES.   MARXISM
COM USSR LAW POL/PAR CHIEF FORCES WRITING CONTROL   DOMIN
PARL/PROC CIVMIL/REL TOTALISM...ANTHOL 20 KHRUSH/N   ORD/FREE
STALIN/J CASEBOOK COM/PARTY. PAGE 28 E0563   GOV/REL

B66
DYCK H.V.,WEIMAR GERMANY AND SOVIET RUSSIA   DIPLOM
1926-1933. EUR+WWI GERMANY UK USSR ECO/TAC   GOV/REL
INT/TRADE NEUTRAL WAR ATTIT 20 WEIMAR/REP TREATY.   POLICY
PAGE 34 E0669

B66
FINK M.,A SELECTIVE BIBLIOGRAPHY ON STATE   BIBLIOG
CONSTITUTIONAL REVISION (PAMPHLET). USA+45 FINAN   PROVS
EX/STRUC LEGIS EDU/PROP ADMIN CT/SYS APPORT CHOOSE   LOC/G
GOV/REL 20. PAGE 38 E0751   CONSTN

B66
HIDAYATULLAH M.,DEMOCRACY IN INDIA AND THE JUDICIAL   NAT/G
PROCESS. INDIA EX/STRUC LEGIS LEAD GOV/REL ATTIT   CT/SYS
ORD/FREE...MAJORIT CONCPT 20 NEHRU/J. PAGE 52 E1040   CONSTN
                                                      JURID

B66
LOFTON J.,JUSTICE AND THE PRESS. EDU/PROP GOV/REL   PRESS
MORAL 20. PAGE 66 E1320   JURID
                                                      CT/SYS
                                                      ORD/FREE

B66
MILLER E.W.,THE NEGRO IN AMERICA: A BIBLIOGRAPHY.   BIBLIOG
USA+45 LAW EDU/PROP REV GOV/REL GP/REL INGP/REL   DISCRIM
ADJUST HABITAT PERSON HEALTH ORD/FREE SOC/INTEG 20   RACE/REL
NEGRO. PAGE 73 E1459

B66
TIEDT S.W.,THE ROLE OF THE FEDERAL GOVERNMENT IN   NAT/G
EDUCATION. FUT USA+45 USA-45 CONSTN SECT BUDGET   EDU/PROP
CT/SYS GOV/REL 18/20 SUPREME/CT. PAGE 96 E1924   GIVE
                                                      SCHOOL

B66
WILSON G.,CASES AND MATERIALS ON CONSTITUTIONAL AND   JURID
ADMINISTRATIVE LAW. UK LAW NAT/G EX/STRUC LEGIS   ADMIN
BAL/PWR BUDGET DIPLOM ADJUD CONTROL CT/SYS GOV/REL   CONSTN
ORD/FREE 20 PARLIAMENT ENGLSH/LAW. PAGE 106 E2126   PWR

S66
MATTHEWS D.G.,"PRELUDE-COUP D'ETAT-MILITARY   BIBLIOG
GOVERNMENT: A BIBLIOGRAPHICAL AND RESEARCH GUIDE TO   NAT/G
NIGERIAN POL AND GOVT, JAN, 1965-66." AFR NIGER LAW   ADMIN
CONSTN POL/PAR LEGIS CIVMIL/REL GOV/REL...STAT 20.   CHOOSE
PAGE 69 E1385

N66
BACHELDER G.L.,THE LITERATURE OF FEDERALISM: A   BIBLIOG
SELECTED BIBLIOGRAPHY (REV ED) (A PAMPHLET). USA+45   FEDERAL
USA-45 WOR+45 WOR-45 LAW CONSTN PROVS ADMIN CT/SYS   NAT/G
GOV/REL ROLE...CONCPT 19/20. PAGE 7 E0126   LOC/G

CONSTN

B67
BAKER L.,BACK TO BACK: THE DUEL BETWEEN FDR AND THE CHIEF
SUPREME COURT. ELITES LEGIS CREATE DOMIN INGP/REL CT/SYS
PERSON PWR NEW/LIB 20 ROOSEVLT/F SUPREME/CT SENATE. PARL/PROC
PAGE 7 E0142   GOV/REL

B67
BIBBY J.,ON CAPITOL HILL. POL/PAR LOBBY PARL/PROC CONFER
GOV/REL PERS/REL...JURID PHIL/SCI OBS INT BIBLIOG LEGIS
20 CONGRESS PRESIDENT. PAGE 12 E0224   CREATE
LEAD

B67
BUREAU GOVERNMENT RES AND SERV,COUNTY GOVERNMENT BIBLIOG/A
REORGANIZATION - A SELECTED ANNOTATED BIBLIOGRAPHY APPORT
(PAPER). USA+45 USA-45 LAW CONSTN MUNIC PROVS LOC/G
EX/STRUC CREATE PLAN PROB/SOLV REPRESENT GOV/REL ADMIN
20. PAGE 17 E0332

B67
ESTEY M.,THE UNIONS: STRUCTURE, DEVELOPMENT, AND LABOR
MANAGEMENT. FUT USA+45 ADJUD CONTROL INGP/REL DRIVE EX/STRUC
...DECISION T 20 AFL/CIO. PAGE 35 E0699   ADMIN
GOV/REL

B67
FESLER J.W.,THE FIFTY STATES AND THEIR LOCAL PROVS
GOVERNMENTS. FUT USA+45 POL/PAR LEGIS PROB/SOLV LOC/G
ADMIN CT/SYS CHOOSE GOV/REL FEDERAL...POLICY CHARTS
20 SUPREME/CT. PAGE 37 E0743

B67
KING W.L.,MELVILLE WESTON FULLER: CHIEF JUSTICE OF BIOG
THE UNITED STATES, 1888-1910. USA+45 CONSTN FINAN CT/SYS
LABOR TAX GOV/REL PERS/REL ATTIT PERSON PWR...JURID LAW
BIBLIOG 19/20 SUPREME/CT FULLER/MW HOLMES/OW. ADJUD
PAGE 61 E1216

B67
UNIVERSAL REFERENCE SYSTEM,PUBLIC POLICY AND THE BIBLIOG/A
MANAGEMENT OF SCIENCE (VOLUME IX). FUT SPACE WOR+45 POLICY
LAW NAT/G TEC/DEV CONTROL NUC/PWR GOV/REL MGT
...COMPUT/IR GEN/METH. PAGE 99 E1975   PHIL/SCI

B67
VILE M.J.C.,CONSTITUTIONALISM AND THE SEPARATION OF CONSTN
POWERS. FRANCE UK USA-45 NAT/G ADJUD CONTROL BAL/PWR
GOV/REL...POLICY DECISION JURID GEN/LAWS 15/20 CONCPT
MONTESQ. PAGE 104 E2076   LAW

L67
"A PROPOS DES INCITATIONS FINANCIERES AUX LOC/G
GROUPEMENTS DES COMMUNES: ESSAI D'INTERPRETATION." ECO/TAC
FRANCE NAT/G LEGIS ADMIN GOV/REL CENTRAL 20. PAGE 2 APPORT
E0037   ADJUD

S67
ANDERSON W.,"THE PERILS OF 'SHARING'." USA+45 BUDGET
ECO/TAC RECEIVE LOBBY GOV/REL CENTRAL COST INCOME TAX
...POLICY PLURIST CONGRESS. PAGE 5 E0095   FEDERAL
LAW

S67
HUBERT C.J.,"PLANNED UNIT DEVELOPMENT" LAW VOL/ASSN PLAN
LEGIS EDU/PROP CT/SYS GOV/REL...NEW/IDEA 20 MUNIC
PLAN/UNIT. PAGE 56 E1107   HABITAT
ADJUD

S67
MITCHELL J.D.B.,"THE CONSTITUTIONAL IMPLICATIONS OF CONSTN
JUDICIAL CONTROL OF THE ADMINISTRATION IN THE CT/SYS
UNITED KINGDOM." UK LAW ADJUD ADMIN GOV/REL ROLE CONTROL
...GP/COMP 20. PAGE 74 E1474   EX/STRUC

S67
WILSON G.D.,"CRIMINAL SANCTIONS AGAINST PASSPORT LAW
AREA-RESTRICTION VIOLATIONS." USA+45 ADJUD CRIME SANCTION
GOV/REL DEPT/STATE CONGRESS. PAGE 106 E2127   LICENSE
POLICY

S68
BURGESS J.W.,"VON HOLST'S PUBLIC LAW OF THE UNITED CONSTN
STATES" USA-45 LAW GOV/REL...GOV/COMP IDEA/COMP 19. FEDERAL
PAGE 17 E0339   NAT/G
JURID

L86
GOODNOW F.J.,"AN EXECUTIVE AND THE COURTS: JUDICIAL CT/SYS
REMEDIES AGAINST ADMINISTRATIVE ACTION" FRANCE UK GOV/REL
USA-45 WOR-45 LAW CONSTN SANCTION ORD/FREE 19. ADMIN
PAGE 45 E0888   ADJUD

L86
WHITRIDGE L.I.,"LEGISLATIVE INQUESTS" USA-45 ADJUD CT/SYS
GOV/REL SOVEREIGN 19/20 CONGRESS. PAGE 106 E2120 LEGIS
JURID

B91
SIDGWICK H.,THE ELEMENTS OF POLITICS. LOC/G NAT/G POLICY
LEGIS DIPLOM ADJUD CONTROL EXEC PARL/PROC REPRESENT LAW
GOV/REL SOVEREIGN ALL/IDEOS 19 MILL/JS BENTHAM/J. CONCPT
PAGE 91 E1822

B96
ESMEIN A.,ELEMENTS DE DROIT CONSTITUTIONNEL. FRANCE LAW
UK CHIEF EX/STRUC LEGIS ADJUD CT/SYS PARL/PROC REV CONSTN
GOV/REL ORD/FREE...JURID METH/COMP 18/19. PAGE 35 NAT/G
E0697   CONCPT

GOVERNMENT....SEE NAT/G, LOC/G, PROVS

GOVERNOR....GOVERNOR; SEE ALSO PROVS, CHIEF, LEAD

B61
AVERY M.W.,GOVERNMENT OF WASHINGTON STATE. USA+45 PROVS
MUNIC DELIB/GP EX/STRUC LEGIS GIVE CT/SYS PARTIC LOC/G
REGION EFFICIENCY 20 WASHINGT/G GOVERNOR. PAGE 6 ADMIN
E0121   GOV/REL

B62
HSUEH S.-.S.,GOVERNMENT AND ADMINISTRATION OF HONG ADMIN
KONG. CHIEF DELIB/GP LEGIS CT/SYS REPRESENT GOV/REL LOC/G
20 HONG/KONG CITY/MGT CIVIL/SERV GOVERNOR. PAGE 55 COLONIAL
E1106   EX/STRUC

GP/COMP....COMPARISON OF GROUPS

B19
SMITH R.H.,JUSTICE AND THE POOR. LAW RECEIVE ADJUD CT/SYS
CRIME GOV/REL COST...JURID SOC/WK CONCPT STAT DISCRIM
CHARTS GP/COMP 20. PAGE 92 E1847   WEALTH

B36
EHRLICH E.,FUNDAMENTAL PRINCIPLES OF THE SOCIOLOGY LAW
OF LAW (TRANS. BY WALTER L. MOLL). UNIV SOCIETY JURID
ADJUD CT/SYS...POLICY GP/COMP GEN/LAWS GEN/METH. SOC
PAGE 34 E0678   CONCPT

B42
GILLETTE J.M.,PROBLEMS OF A CHANGING SOCIAL ORDER. BIO/SOC
USA+45 STRATA FAM CONTROL CRIME RACE/REL HEALTH ADJUST
WEALTH...GEOG GP/COMP. PAGE 43 E0862   ATTIT
SOC/WK

B49
WALINE M.,LE CONTROLE JURIDICTIONNEL DE JURID
L'ADMINISTRATION. BELGIUM FRANCE UAR JUDGE BAL/PWR ADMIN
ADJUD CONTROL CT/SYS...GP/COMP 20. PAGE 104 E2093 PWR
ORD/FREE

B54
HOEBEL E.A.,THE LAW OF PRIMITIVE MAN: A STUDY IN LAW
COMPARATIVE LEGAL DYNAMICS. WOR-45...JURID SOC CULTURE
IDEA/COMP METH 20. PAGE 53 E1063   GP/COMP
SOCIETY

B55
WHEARE K.C.,GOVERNMENT BY COMMITTEE; AN ESSAY ON DELIB/GP
THE BRITISH CONSTITUTION. UK NAT/G LEGIS INSPECT CONSTN
CONFER ADJUD ADMIN CONTROL TASK EFFICIENCY ROLE LEAD
POPULISM 20. PAGE 106 E2116   GP/COMP

B55
ZABEL O.H.,GOD AND CAESAR IN NEBRASKA: A STUDY OF SECT
LEGAL RELATIONSHIP OF CHURCH AND STATE, 1854-1954. PROVS
TAX GIVE ADMIN CONTROL GP/REL ROLE...GP/COMP 19/20 LAW
NEBRASKA. PAGE 108 E2168   EDU/PROP

S57
GOODE W.J.,"COMMUNITY WITHIN A COMMUNITY: THE PROF/ORG
PROFESSIONS." STRATA STRUCT SANCTION INGP/REL...SOC NEIGH
GP/COMP. PAGE 45 E0886   CLIENT
CONTROL

B59
SCHORN H.,DER RICHTER IM DRITTEN REICH; GESCHICHTE ADJUD
UND DOKUMENTE. GERMANY NAT/G LEGIT CT/SYS INGP/REL JUDGE
MORAL ORD/FREE RESPECT...JURID GP/COMP 20. PAGE 88 FASCISM
E1765

C59
EASTON D.,"POLITICAL ANTHROPOLOGY" IN BIENNIAL SOC
REVIEW OF ANTHROPOLOGY" UNIV LAW CULTURE ELITES BIBLIOG/A
SOCIETY CREATE...PSY CONCPT GP/COMP GEN/METH 20. NEW/IDEA
PAGE 34 E0671

B60
LA PONCE J.A.,THE PROTECTION OF MINORITIES. WOR+45 INGP/REL
WOR-45 NAT/G POL/PAR SUFF...INT/LAW CLASSIF GP/COMP DOMIN
GOV/COMP BIBLIOG 17/20 CIVIL/LIB CIV/RIGHTS. SOCIETY
PAGE 62 E1242   RACE/REL

SILVA R.C.,RUM, RELIGION, AND VOTES: 1928 RE-   B62
EXAMINED. USA-45 LAW SECT DISCRIM CATHISM...CORREL   POL/PAR
STAT 20 PRESIDENT SMITH/ALF DEMOCRAT. PAGE 91 E1827   CHOOSE
                                                           GP/COMP
                                                           ATTIT

VINES K.N.,"THE ROLE OF THE CIRCUIT COURT OF   S63
APPEALS IN THE FEDERAL JUDICIAL PROCESS: A CASE   REGION
STUDY." USA+45 STRATA JUDGE RESPECT...DECISION   ADJUD
JURID CHARTS GP/COMP. PAGE 104 E2078   CT/SYS
                                                           RACE/REL

ECONOMIDES C.P.,LE POUVOIR DE DECISION DES   B64
ORGANISATIONS INTERNATIONALES EUROPEENNES. DIPLOM   INT/ORG
DOMIN INGP/REL EFFICIENCY...INT/LAW JURID 20 NATO   PWR
OEEC EEC COUNCL/EUR EURATOM. PAGE 34 E0673   DECISION
                                                           GP/COMP

HARTUNG F.E.,CRIME, LAW, AND SOCIETY. LAW PUB/INST   B65
CRIME PERS/REL AGE/Y BIO/SOC PERSON ROLE SUPEGO   PERCEPT
...LING GP/COMP GEN/LAWS 20. PAGE 50 E1004   CRIMLGY
                                                           DRIVE
                                                           CONTROL

SCHUBERT G.,THE JUDICIAL MIND: THE ATTITUDES AND   B65
IDEOLOGIES OF SUPREME COURT JUSTICES 1946-1963.   CT/SYS
USA+45 ELITES NAT/G CONSTN PERS/REL MAJORITY   JUDGE
CONSERVE...DECISION JURID MODAL STAT TREND GP/COMP   ATTIT
GAME. PAGE 88 E1774   NEW/LIB

FOX A.B.,"NATO AND CONGRESS." CONSTN DELIB/GP   S65
EX/STRUC FORCES TOP/EX BUDGET NUC/PWR GOV/REL   CONTROL
...GP/COMP CONGRESS NATO TREATY. PAGE 39 E0779   DIPLOM

ANAND R.P.,"ATTITUDE OF THE ASIAN-AFRICAN STATES   S66
TOWARD CERTAIN PROBLEMS OF INTERNATIONAL LAW."   INT/LAW
L/A+17C S/ASIA ECO/UNDEV CREATE CONFER ADJUD   ATTIT
COLONIAL...RECORD GP/COMP UN. PAGE 5 E0087   ASIA
                                                           AFR

GREY D.L.,"INTERVIEWING AT THE COURT." USA+45   S67
ELITES COM/IND ACT/RES PRESS CT/SYS PERSON...SOC   JUDGE
INT 20 SUPREME/CT. PAGE 46 E0916   ATTIT
                                                           PERS/COMP
                                                           GP/COMP

MITCHELL J.D.B.,"THE CONSTITUTIONAL IMPLICATIONS OF   S67
JUDICIAL CONTROL OF THE ADMINISTRATION IN THE   CONSTN
UNITED KINGDOM." UK LAW ADJUD ADMIN GOV/REL ROLE   CT/SYS
...GP/COMP 20. PAGE 74 E1474   CONTROL
                                                           EX/STRUC

POSPISIL L.,"LEGAL LEVELS AND MULTIPLICITY OF LEGAL   S67
SYSTEMS IN HUMAN SOCIETIES." WOR+45 CENTRAL PWR   LAW
...SOC CHARTS GP/COMP GEN/LAWS. PAGE 81 E1630   STRATA
                                                           JURID
                                                           STRUCT

WRAITH R.E.,"ADMINISTRATIVE CHANGE IN THE NEW   S67
AFRICA." AFR LG/CO ADJUD INGP/REL PWR...RECORD   ADMIN
GP/COMP 20. PAGE 107 E2147   NAT/G
                                                           LOC/G
                                                           ECO/UNDEV

GP/REL....RELATIONS AMONG GROUPS

ADVANCED MANAGEMENT. INDUS EX/STRUC WORKER OP/RES   N
...DECISION BIBLIOG/A 20. PAGE 1 E0015   MGT
                                                           ADMIN
                                                           LABOR
                                                           GP/REL

PERSONNEL. USA+45 LAW LABOR LG/CO WORKER CREATE   N
GOV/REL PERS/REL ATTIT WEALTH. PAGE 2 E0029   BIBLIOG/A
                                                           ADMIN
                                                           MGT
                                                           GP/REL

MEYER C.S.,ELIZABETH I AND THE RELIGIOUS SETTLEMENT   NRE
OF 1559. UK ELITES CHIEF LEGIS DISCRIM CATHISM 16   GP/REL
CHURCH/STA ELIZABTH/I. PAGE 72 E1445   SECT
                                                           LAW
                                                           PARL/PROC

GRIFFIN A.P.C.,LIST OF REFERENCES ON INDUSTRIAL   B03
ARBITRATION (PAMPHLET). USA-45 STRATA VOL/ASSN   BIBLIOG/A
DELIB/GP WORKER ADJUD GP/REL...MGT 19/20. PAGE 46   INDUS
E0921   LABOR
                                                           BARGAIN

GRIFFIN A.P.C.,LISTS PUBLISHED 1902-03: LABOR   B03
PARTICULARLY RELATING TO STRIKES (PAMPHLET). UK   BIBLIOG/A
                                                           LABOR

USA-45 FINAN WORKER PLAN BARGAIN CRIME GOV/REL   GP/REL
...POLICY 19/20 PARLIAMENT. PAGE 46 E0923   ECO/TAC

GRIFFIN A.P.C.,SELECT LIST OF BOOKS ON LABOR   B03
PARTICULARLY RELATING TO STRIKES. FRANCE GERMANY   BIBLIOG/A
MOD/EUR UK USA-45 LAW NAT/G DELIB/GP WORKER BARGAIN   GP/REL
LICENSE PAY ADJUD 19/20. PAGE 46 E0924   MGT
                                                           LABOR

BURKE E.,A LETTER TO THE SHERIFFS OF BRISTOL   B04
(1777). USA-45 LAW ECO/TAC COLONIAL CT/SYS REV   LEGIS
GP/REL ORD/FREE...POLICY 18 PARLIAMENT BURKE/EDM.   ADJUD
PAGE 17 E0341   CRIME

POLLOCK F.,THE GENIUS OF THE COMMON LAW. CHRIST-17C   B12
UK FINAN CHIEF ACT/RES ADMIN GP/REL ATTIT SOCISM   LAW
...ANARCH JURID. PAGE 81 E1624   CULTURE
                                                           CREATE

ADAMS B.,THE THEORY OF SOCIAL REVOLUTIONS. FUT   B13
USA-45 GP/REL PEACE...NEW/IDEA 20. PAGE 3 E0047   CAP/ISM
                                                           REV
                                                           SOCIETY
                                                           CT/SYS

BREWER D.J.,THE MOVEMENT OF COERCION (PAMPHLET).   N18
CONSTN INDUS ADJUD COERCE OWN WEALTH...OLD/LIB   GP/REL
JURID 19 SUPREME/CT. PAGE 15 E0296   LABOR
                                                           LG/CO
                                                           LAW

COUTROT A.,THE FIGHT OVER THE 1959 PRIVATE   N19
EDUCATION LAW IN FRANCE (PAMPHLET). FRANCE NAT/G   SCHOOL
SECT GIVE EDU/PROP GP/REL ATTIT RIGID/FLEX ORD/FREE   PARL/PROC
20 CHURCH/STA. PAGE 27 E0527   CATHISM
                                                           LAW

MCCONNELL G.,THE STEEL SEIZURE OF 1952 (PAMPHLET).   N19
USA+45 FINAN INDUS PROC/MFG LG/CO EX/STRUC ADJUD   DELIB/GP
CONTROL GP/REL ORD/FREE PWR 20 TRUMAN/HS PRESIDENT   LABOR
CONGRESS. PAGE 70 E1402   PROB/SOLV
                                                           NAT/G

ROBERT H.M.,PARLIAMENTARY LAW. POL/PAR LEGIS PARTIC   B23
CHOOSE REPRESENT GP/REL. PAGE 85 E1701   PARL/PROC
                                                           DELIB/GP
                                                           NAT/G
                                                           JURID

NAVILLE A.,LIBERTE, EGALITE, SOLIDARITE: ESSAIS   B24
D'ANALYSE. STRATA FAM VOL/ASSN INT/TRADE GP/REL   ORD/FREE
MORAL MARXISM SOCISM...PSY TREATY. PAGE 76 E1529   SOC
                                                           IDEA/COMP
                                                           DIPLOM

FORTESCUE J.,THE GOVERNANCE OF ENGLAND (1471-76).   B26
UK LAW FINAN SECT LEGIS PROB/SOLV TAX DOMIN ADMIN   CONSERVE
GP/REL COST ORD/FREE PWR 14/15. PAGE 39 E0776   CONSTN
                                                           CHIEF
                                                           NAT/G

DICKINSON J.,ADMINISTRATIVE JUSTICE AND THE   B27
SUPREMACY OF LAW IN THE UNITED STATES. USA-45 LAW   CT/SYS
INDUS DOMIN EDU/PROP CONTROL EXEC GP/REL ORD/FREE   ADJUD
...POLICY JURID 19/20. PAGE 31 E0623   ADMIN
                                                           NAT/G

JOHN OF SALISBURY,THE STATESMAN'S BOOK (1159)   B27
(TRANS. BY J. DICKINSON). DOMIN GP/REL MORAL   NAT/G
ORD/FREE PWR CONSERVE...CATH CONCPT 12. PAGE 59   SECT
E1169   CHIEF
                                                           LAW

FRANKFURTER F.,THE BUSINESS OF THE SUPREME COURT; A   B28
STUDY IN THE FEDERAL JUDICIAL SYSTEM. USA-45 CONSTN   CT/SYS
EX/STRUC PROB/SOLV GP/REL ATTIT PWR...POLICY JURID   ADJUD
18/20 SUPREME/CT CONGRESS. PAGE 40 E0789   LAW
                                                           FEDERAL

MAIR L.P.,THE PROTECTION OF MINORITIES. EUR+WWI   B28
WOR-45 CONSTN INT/ORG NAT/G LEGIT CT/SYS GP/REL   LAW
RACE/REL DISCRIM ORD/FREE RESPECT...JURID CONCPT   SOVEREIGN
TIME/SEQ 20. PAGE 68 E1352

LEITZ F.,DIE PUBLIZITAT DER AKTIENGESELLSCHAFT.   B29
BELGIUM FRANCE GERMANY UK FINAN PRESS GP/REL PROFIT   LG/CO
KNOWL 20. PAGE 64 E1282   JURID
                                                           ECO/TAC
                                                           NAT/COMP

LLEWELLYN K.N.,"A REALISTIC JURISPRUDENCE - THE   L30
NEXT STEP." PROB/SOLV ADJUD GP/REL PERS/REL   LAW
IDEA/COMP. PAGE 66 E1312   CONCPT
                                                           JURID

	GEN/LAWS

HERRING E.P.,PUBLIC ADMINISTRATION AND THE PUBLIC
INTEREST. LABOR NAT/G PARTIC EFFICIENCY 20. PAGE 52
E1033

B36
GP/REL
DECISION
PROB/SOLV
ADMIN

KONRAD F.,DIE PERSONLICHE FREIHEIT IM
NATIONALSOZIALISTISCHEN DEUTSCHEN REICHE. GERMANY
JUDGE ADJUD GP/REL FASCISM 20 CIVIL/LIB. PAGE 61
E1226

B36
ORD/FREE
JURID
CONSTN
CONCPT

CARR R.K.,THE SUPREME COURT AND JUDICIAL REVIEW.
NAT/G CHIEF LEGIS LEAD GOV/REL GP/REL ATTIT
...POLICY DECISION 18/20 SUPREME/CT PRESIDENT
CONGRESS. PAGE 20 E0394

B42
CT/SYS
CONSTN
JURID
PWR

HARGRETT L.,A BIBLIOGRAPHY OF THE CONSTITUTIONS AND
LAWS OF THE AMERICAN INDIANS. USA-45 LOC/G GOV/REL
GP/REL 19/20 INDIAN/AM. PAGE 50 E0999

B47
BIBLIOG/A
CONSTN
LAW
NAT/G

KONVITZ M.R.,THE CONSTITUTION AND CIVIL RIGHTS.
USA-45 NAT/G ADJUD GP/REL RACE/REL POPULISM
...MAJORIT 19/20 SUPREME/CT CIV/RIGHTS. PAGE 61
E1227

B47
CONSTN
LAW
GOV/REL
ORD/FREE

MCILWAIN C.H.,CONSTITUTIONALISM: ANCIENT AND
MODERN. USA+45 ROMAN/EMP LAW CHIEF LEGIS CT/SYS
GP/REL ORD/FREE SOVEREIGN...POLICY TIME/SEQ
ROMAN/REP EUROPE. PAGE 71 E1419

B47
CONSTN
NAT/G
PARL/PROC
GOV/COMP

ANGELL R.C.,"THE SOCIAL INTEGRATION OF AMERICAN
CITIES OF MORE THAN 1000,000 POPULATION" (BMR)"
USA+45 SOCIETY CRIME ADJUST WEALTH...GEOG SOC
CONCPT INDICATOR SAMP CHARTS SOC/INTEG 20. PAGE 5
E0098

S47
MUNIC
CENSUS
GP/REL

HOLLERAN M.P.,CHURCH AND STATE IN GUATEMALA.
GUATEMALA LAW STRUCT CATHISM...SOC SOC/INTEG 17/20
CHURCH/STA. PAGE 55 E1086

B49
SECT
NAT/G
GP/REL
CULTURE

SCHONS D.,BOOK CENSORSHIP IN NEW SPAIN (NEW WORLD
STUDIES, BOOK II). SPAIN LAW CULTURE INSPECT ADJUD
CT/SYS SANCTION GP/REL ORD/FREE 14/17. PAGE 88
E1764

B49
CHRIST-17C
EDU/PROP
CONTROL
PRESS

THOREAU H.D.,CIVIL DISOBEDIENCE (1849). USA-45 LAW
CONSTN TAX COERCE REPRESENT GP/REL SUPEGO...MAJORIT
CONCPT 19. PAGE 96 E1923

B49
GEN/LAWS
ORD/FREE
POLICY

BAILEY S.K.,CONGRESS MAKES A LAW. USA+45 GP/REL
SOC. PAGE 7 E0136

B50
DECISION
LEGIS
LAW
ECO/TAC

BERMAN H.J.,JUSTICE IN RUSSIA; AN INTERPRETATION OF
SOVIET LAW. USSR LAW STRUCT LABOR FORCES AGREE
GP/REL ORD/FREE SOCISM...TIME/SEQ 20. PAGE 11 E0207

B50
JURID
ADJUD
MARXISM
COERCE

WADE E.C.S.,CONSTITUTIONAL LAW; AN OUTLINE OF THE
LAW AND PRACTICE OF THE CONSTITUTION. UK LEGIS
DOMIN ADMIN GP/REL 16/20 CMN/WLTH PARLIAMENT
ENGLSH/LAW. PAGE 104 E2087

B50
CONSTN
NAT/G
PARL/PROC
LAW

NUMELIN R.,"THE BEGINNINGS OF DIPLOMACY." INT/TRADE
WAR GP/REL PEACE STRANGE ATTIT...INT/LAW CONCPT
BIBLIOG. PAGE 78 E1559

C50
DIPLOM
KIN
CULTURE
LAW

COOKE C.A.,CORPORATION TRUST AND COMPANY: AN ESSAY
IN LEGAL HISTORY. UK STRUCT LEGIS CAP/ISM GP/REL
PROFIT 13/20 COMPNY/ACT. PAGE 25 E0499

B51
LG/CO
FINAN
ECO/TAC
JURID

CAHILL F.V.,JUDICIAL LEGISLATION: A STUDY IN
AMERICAN LEGAL THEORY. USA+45 USA-45 LAW NAT/G
GP/REL...POLICY PHIL/SCI SOC 20 HOLMES/OW. PAGE 18

B52
JURID
ADJUD
LEGIS

E0359

CONTROL

FORSTER A.,THE TROUBLE MAKERS. USA+45 LAW CULTURE
SOCIETY STRUCT VOL/ASSN CROWD GP/REL MORAL...PSY
SOC CONCPT 20 NEGRO JEWS. PAGE 39 E0771

B52
DISCRIM
SECT
RACE/REL
ATTIT

WALTER P.A.F.,RACE AND CULTURE RELATIONS. FAM
HEALTH WEALTH...POLICY CRIMLGY GEOG BIBLIOG T 20.
PAGE 105 E2097

B52
RACE/REL
DISCRIM
GP/REL
CONCPT

SECKLER-HUDSON C.,BIBLIOGRAPHY ON PUBLIC
ADMINISTRATION (4TH ED.). USA+45 LAW POL/PAR
DELIB/GP BUDGET ADJUD LOBBY GOV/REL GP/REL ATTIT
...JURID 20. PAGE 90 E1800

B53
BIBLIOG/A
ADMIN
NAT/G
MGT

BROGAN D.W.,POLITICS IN AMERICA. LAW POL/PAR CHIEF
LEGIS LOBBY CHOOSE REPRESENT GP/REL RACE/REL
FEDERAL MORAL...BIBLIOG 20 PRESIDENT CONGRESS.
PAGE 16 E0304

B54
NAT/G
CONSTN
USA+45

CAPLOW T.,THE SOCIOLOGY OF WORK. USA+45 USA-45
STRATA MARKET FAM GP/REL INGP/REL ALL/VALS
...DECISION STAT BIBLIOG SOC/INTEG 20. PAGE 19
E0375

B54
LABOR
WORKER
INDUS
ROLE

JAMES L.F.,THE SUPREME COURT IN AMERICAN LIFE.
USA+45 USA-45 CONSTN CRIME GP/REL INGP/REL RACE/REL
CONSEN FEDERAL PERSON ORD/FREE 18/20 SUPREME/CT
DEPRESSION CIV/RIGHTS CHURCH/STA FREE/SPEE. PAGE 58
E1147

B54
ADJUD
CT/SYS
JURID
DECISION

O'NEILL J.M.,CATHOLICS IN CONTROVERSY. USA+45 NAT/G
PROVS SCHOOL SECT EDU/PROP LEGIT CT/SYS SANCTION
GP/REL 20 SUPREME/CT CHURCH/STA. PAGE 78 E1569

B54
CATHISM
CONSTN
POLICY
LAW

BERNSTEIN M.H.,REGULATING BUSINESS BY INDEPENDENT
COMMISSION. USA+45 USA-45 LG/CO CHIEF LEGIS
PROB/SOLV ADJUD SANCTION GP/REL ATTIT...TIME/SEQ
19/20 MONOPOLY PRESIDENT CONGRESS. PAGE 11 E0214

B55
DELIB/GP
CONTROL
CONSULT

BRAUN K.,LABOR DISPUTES AND THEIR SETTLEMENT.
ECO/TAC ROUTINE TASK GP/REL...DECISION GEN/LAWS.
PAGE 15 E0288

B55
INDUS
LABOR
BARGAIN
ADJUD

GRINDEL C.W.,CONCEPT OF FREEDOM. WOR+45 WOR-45 LAW
LABOR NAT/G SECT EDU/PROP 20. PAGE 47 E0942

B55
ORD/FREE
DIPLOM
CONCPT
GP/REL

LARROWE C.P.,SHAPE-UP AND HIRING HALL. TRIBUTE
ADJUD CONTROL SANCTION COERCE CRIME GP/REL PWR
...CHARTS 20 AFL/CIO NEWYORK/C SEATTLE. PAGE 63
E1256

B55
LABOR
INDUS
WORKER
NAT/G

ZABEL O.H.,GOD AND CAESAR IN NEBRASKA: A STUDY OF
LEGAL RELATIONSHIP OF CHURCH AND STATE, 1854-1954.
TAX GIVE ADMIN CONTROL GP/REL ROLE...GP/COMP 19/20
NEBRASKA. PAGE 108 E2168

B55
SECT
PROVS
LAW
EDU/PROP

BROWNE D.G.,THE RISE OF SCOTLAND YARD: A HISTORY OF
THE METROPOLITAN POLICE. UK MUNIC CHIEF ADMIN CRIME
GP/REL 19/20. PAGE 16 E0316

B56
CRIMLGY
LEGIS
CONTROL
FORCES

HURST J.W.,LAW AND THE CONDITIONS OF FREEDOM IN THE
NINETEENTH CENTURY UNITED STATES. USA-45 CONSTN
STRUCT ADMIN GP/REL FEDERAL HABITAT...JURID 19.
PAGE 56 E1116

B56
LAW
ORD/FREE
POLICY
NAT/G

RECASENS SICHES S.,TRATADO GENERAL DE SOCIOLOGIA.
CULTURE FAM NEIGH LEAD RACE/REL DISCRIM HABITAT
ORD/FREE...JURID LING T SOC/INTEG 20. PAGE 84 E1677

B56
SOC
STRATA
KIN
GP/REL

ROSENBERG M.,"POWER AND DESEGREGATION." USA+45
STRATA MUNIC GP/REL. PAGE 85 E1715

S56
PWR
DISCRIM

DECISION
LAW

C56
TYLER P.,"IMMIGRATION AND THE UNITED STATES."   CULTURE
USA+45 USA-45 LAW SECT INGP/REL RACE/REL NAT/LISM   GP/REL
ATTIT...BIBLIOG SOC/INTEG 19/20. PAGE 97 E1949   DISCRIM

B57
ALIGHIERI D.,ON WORLD GOVERNMENT. ROMAN/EMP LAW   POLICY
SOCIETY INT/ORG NAT/G POL/PAR ADJUD WAR GP/REL   CONCPT
PEACE WORSHIP 15 WORLDUNITY DANTE. PAGE 4 E0067   DIPLOM
                                                       SECT

B58
BUGEDA LANZAS J.,A STATEMENT OF THE LAWS OF CUBA IN   JURID
MATTERS AFFECTING BUSINESS (2ND ED. REV.,   NAT/G
ENLARGED). CUBA L/A+17C LAW FINAN FAM LEGIS ACT/RES   INDUS
ADMIN GP/REL...BIBLIOG 20 OAS. PAGE 17 E0327   WORKER

B58
CUNNINGHAM W.B.,COMPULSORY CONCILIATION AND   POLICY
COLLECTIVE BARGAINING. CANADA NAT/G LEGIS ADJUD   BARGAIN
CT/SYS GP/REL...MGT 20 NEW/BRUNS STRIKE CASEBOOK.   LABOR
PAGE 28 E0555   INDUS

B58
DAVIS K.C.,ADMINISTRATIVE LAW TREATISE (VOLS. I AND   ADMIN
IV). NAT/G JUDGE PROB/SOLV ADJUD GP/REL 20   JURID
SUPREME/CT. PAGE 29 E0575   CT/SYS
                                                       EX/STRUC

B58
EUSDEN J.D.,PURITANS, LAWYERS, AND POLITICS IN   GP/REL
EARLY SEVENTEENTH-CENTURY ENGLAND. UK CT/SYS   SECT
PARL/PROC RATIONAL PWR SOVEREIGN...IDEA/COMP   NAT/G
BIBLIOG 17 PURITAN COMMON/LAW. PAGE 35 E0702   LAW

B58
GARDINER H.C.,CATHOLIC VIEWPOINT ON CENSORSHIP.   WRITING
DEBATE COERCE GP/REL...JURID CONCPT 20. PAGE 42   LOBBY
E0835   CATHISM
                                                       EDU/PROP

B58
HERRMANN K.,DAS STAATSDENKEN BEI LEIBNIZ. GP/REL   NAT/G
ATTIT ORD/FREE...CONCPT IDEA/COMP 17 LEIBNITZ/G   JURID
CHURCH/STA. PAGE 52 E1034   SECT
                                                       EDU/PROP

B58
HOOD W.C.,FINANCING OF ECONOMIC ACTIVITY IN CANADA.   BUDGET
CANADA FUT VOL/ASSN WORKER ECO/TAC ADJUD ADMIN   FINAN
...CHARTS 20. PAGE 55 E1093   GP/REL
                                                       ECO/DEV

B58
HUNT B.I.,BIPARTISANSHIP: A CASE STUDY OF THE   FOR/AID
FOREIGN ASSISTANCE PROGRAM, 1947-56 (DOCTORAL   POL/PAR
THESIS). USA+45 INT/ORG CONSULT LEGIS TEC/DEV   GP/REL
...BIBLIOG PRESIDENT TREATY NATO TRUMAN/HS   DIPLOM
EISNHWR/DD CONGRESS. PAGE 56 E1114

B58
MOEN N.W.,THE GOVERNMENT OF SCOTLAND 1603 - 1625.   CHIEF
UK JUDGE ADMIN GP/REL PWR 17 SCOTLAND COMMON/LAW.   JURID
PAGE 74 E1479   CONTROL
                                                       PARL/PROC

B58
MOSKOWITZ M.,HUMAN RIGHTS AND WORLD ORDER. INT/ORG   DIPLOM
PLAN GP/REL NAT/LISM SOVEREIGN...CONCPT 20 UN   INT/LAW
TREATY CIV/RIGHTS. PAGE 75 E1502   ORD/FREE

B58
WOOD J.E.,CHURCH AND STATE IN SCRIPTURE HISTORY AND   GP/REL
CONSTITUTIONAL LAW. LAW CONSTN SOCIETY PROVS   SECT
VOL/ASSN BAL/PWR COLONIAL CT/SYS ATTIT...BIBLIOG 20   NAT/G
SUPREME/CT CHURCH/STA BIBLE. PAGE 107 E2142   ADJUD

B59
BRIGGS A.,CHARTIST STUDIES. UK LAW NAT/G WORKER   INDUS
EDU/PROP COERCE SUFF GP/REL ATTIT...ANTHOL 19.   STRATA
PAGE 15 E0300   LABOR
                                                       POLICY

B59
GOMEZ ROBLES J.,A STATEMENT OF THE LAWS OF   JURID
GUATEMALA IN MATTERS AFFECTING BUSINESS (2ND ED.   NAT/G
REV. ENLARGED). GUATEMALA L/A+17C LAW FINAN FAM   INDUS
WORKER ACT/RES DIPLOM ADJUD ADMIN GP/REL 20 OAS.   LEGIT
PAGE 44 E0881

B59
HOBSBAWM E.J.,PRIMITIVE REBELS: STUDIES IN ARCHAIC   SOCIETY
FORMS OF SOCIAL MOVEMENT IN THE 19TH AND 20TH   CRIME

CENTURIES. ITALY SPAIN CULTURE VOL/ASSN RISK CROWD   REV
GP/REL INGP/REL ISOLAT TOTALISM...PSY SOC 18/20.   GUERRILLA
PAGE 53 E1058

B59
KIRCHHEIMER O.,GEGENWARTSPROBLEME DER   DIPLOM
ASYLGEWAHRUNG. DOMIN GP/REL ATTIT...NAT/COMP 20.   INT/LAW
PAGE 61 E1217   JURID
                                                       ORD/FREE

B59
LOEWENSTEIN K.,VERFASSUNGSRECHT UND   CONSTN
VERFASSUNGSPRAXIS DER VEREINIGTEN STAATEN. USA+45   POL/PAR
USA-45 COLONIAL CT/SYS GP/REL RACE/REL ORD/FREE   EX/STRUC
...JURID 18/20 SUPREME/CT CONGRESS PRESIDENT   NAT/G
BILL/RIGHT CIVIL/LIB. PAGE 66 E1319

B59
MOOS M.,THE CAMPUS AND THE STATE. LAW FINAN   EDU/PROP
DELIB/GP LEGIS EXEC LOBBY GP/REL PWR...POLICY   ACADEM
BIBLIOG. PAGE 74 E1489   PROVS
                                                       CONTROL

B60
BLANSHARD P.,GOD AND MAN IN WASHINGTON. USA+45   NAT/G
CHIEF LEGIS LEGIT CT/SYS PRIVIL ATTIT ORD/FREE   SECT
...POLICY CONCPT 20 SUPREME/CT CONGRESS PRESIDENT   GP/REL
CHURCH/STA. PAGE 12 E0242   POL/PAR

B60
DAVIS K.C.,ADMINISTRATIVE LAW AND GOVERNMENT.   ADMIN
USA+45 EX/STRUC PROB/SOLV ADJUD GP/REL PWR...POLICY   JURID
20 SUPREME/CT. PAGE 29 E0578   CT/SYS
                                                       NAT/G

B60
MOCTEZUMA A.P.,EL CONFLICTO RELIGIOSO DE 1926 (2ND   SECT
ED.). L/A+17C LAW NAT/G LOBBY COERCE GP/REL ATTIT   ORD/FREE
...POLICY 20 MEXIC/AMER CHURCH/STA. PAGE 74 E1476   DISCRIM
                                                       REV

B60
SCHUBERT G.,THE PUBLIC INTEREST. USA+45 CONSULT   POLICY
PLAN PROB/SOLV ADJUD ADMIN GP/REL PWR ALL/IDEOS 20.   DELIB/GP
PAGE 88 E1770   REPRESENT
                                                       POL/PAR

C60
MCCLEERY R.,"COMMUNICATION PATTERNS AS BASES OF   PERS/REL
SYSTEMS OF AUTHORITY AND POWER" IN THEORETICAL   PUB/INST
STUDIES IN SOCIAL ORGAN. OF PRISON-BMR. USA+45   PWR
SOCIETY STRUCT EDU/PROP ADMIN CONTROL COERCE CRIME   DOMIN
GP/REL AUTHORIT...SOC 20. PAGE 70 E1400

B61
BARBASH J.,LABOR'S GRASS ROOTS. CONSTN NAT/G   LABOR
EX/STRUC LEGIS WORKER LEAD...MAJORIT BIBLIOG.   INGP/REL
PAGE 8 E0147   GP/REL
                                                       LAW

B61
CARROTHERS A.W.R.,LABOR ARBITRATION IN CANADA.   LABOR
CANADA LAW NAT/G CONSULT LEGIS WORKER ADJUD ADMIN   MGT
CT/SYS 20. PAGE 20 E0396   GP/REL
                                                       BARGAIN

B61
HAGEN A.,STAAT UND KATHOLISCHE KIRCHE IN   SECT
WURTTEMBERG IN DEN JAHREN 1848-1862 (2 VOLS.).   PROVS
GERMANY DELIB/GP EDU/PROP MARRIAGE CATHISM 19   GP/REL
CHURCH/STA. PAGE 49 E0975   JURID

B61
KURLAND P.B.,RELIGION AND THE LAW. USA+45 USA-45   SECT
CONSTN PROVS CHIEF ADJUD SANCTION PRIVIL CATHISM   NAT/G
...POLICY 17/20 SUPREME/CT PRESIDENT CHURCH/STA.   CT/SYS
PAGE 62 E1239   GP/REL

B61
MURPHY E.F.,WATER PURITY: A STUDY IN LEGAL CONTROL   SEA
OF NATURAL RESOURCES. LOC/G ACT/RES PLAN TEC/DEV   LAW
LOBBY GP/REL COST ATTIT HEALTH ORD/FREE...HEAL   PROVS
JURID 20 WISCONSIN WATER. PAGE 75 E1506   CONTROL

B61
PRITCHETT C.H.,CONGRESS VERSUS THE SUPREME COURT,   LEGIS
1957-1960. PROB/SOLV DOMIN EXEC GP/REL DISCRIM PWR   JURID
CONGRESS SUPREME/CT. PAGE 82 E1652   LAW

B61
SMITH J.W.,RELIGIOUS PERSPECTIVES IN AMERICAN   SECT
CULTURE. VOL. 2. RELIGION IN AMERICAN LIFE. USA+45   DOMIN
CULTURE NAT/G EDU/PROP ADJUD LOBBY ATTIT...ART/METH   SOCIETY
ANTHOL 20 CHURCH/STA BIBLE. PAGE 92 E1845   GP/REL

WARD R.E.,JAPANESE POLITICAL SCIENCE: A GUIDE TO JAPANESE REFERENCE AND RESEARCH MATERIALS (2ND ED.). LAW CONSTN STRATA NAT/G POL/PAR DELIB/GP LEGIS ADMIN CHOOSE GP/REL...INT/LAW 19/20 CHINJAP. PAGE 105 E2099
B61 BIBLIOG/A PHIL/SCI

KAUPER P.G.,"CHURCH AND STATE: COOPERATIVE SEPARATISM." NAT/G LEGIS OP/RES TAX EDU/PROP GP/REL TREND. PAGE 59 E1187
L61 SECT CONSTN LAW POLICY

BARLOW R.B.,CITIZENSHIP AND CONSCIENCE: STUDIES IN THEORY AND PRACTICE OF RELIGIOUS TOLERATION IN ENGLAND DURING EIGHTEENTH CENTURY. UK LAW VOL/ASSN EDU/PROP SANCTION REV GP/REL MAJORITY ATTIT ORD/FREE...BIBLIOG WORSHIP 18. PAGE 8 E0150
B62 SECT LEGIS DISCRIM

BRANDT R.B.,SOCIAL JUSTICE. UNIV LAW GP/REL PWR ALL/IDEOS...POLICY SOC ANTHOL 20. PAGE 15 E0287
B62 ORD/FREE CONSTN CONCPT

CURRY J.E.,RACE TENSIONS AND THE POLICE. LAW MUNIC NEIGH TEC/DEV RUMOR CONTROL COERCE GP/REL ATTIT ...SOC 20 NEGRO. PAGE 28 E0558
B62 FORCES RACE/REL CROWD ORD/FREE

DAVIS F.J.,SOCIETY AND THE LAW. USA+45 CONSTN ACADEM FAM CONSULT ACT/RES GP/REL ORD/FREE ENGLSH/LAW 20. PAGE 29 E0572
B62 LAW SOC CULTURE STRUCT

EVAN W.M.,LAW AND SOCIOLOGY: EXPLORATORY ESSAYS. CONSULT ACT/RES OP/RES PROB/SOLV EDU/PROP LEGIT ADJUD CT/SYS GP/REL...PHIL/SCI ANTHOL SOC/INTEG 20. PAGE 35 E0703
B62 JURID SOC PROF/ORG

GONNER R.,DAS KIRCHENPATRONATRECHT IM GROSSHERZOGTUM BADEN. GERMANY LAW PROVS DEBATE ATTIT CATHSM 14/19 PROTESTANT CHRISTIAN CHURCH/STA BADEN. PAGE 44 E0882
B62 JURID SECT NAT/REL GP/REL

LEVY H.V.,LIBERDADE E JUSTICA SOCIAL (2ND ED.). BRAZIL COM L/A+17C USSR INT/ORG PARTIC GP/REL WEALTH 20 UN COM/PARTY. PAGE 65 E1290
B62 ORD/FREE MARXISM CAP/ISM LAW

LITTLEFIELD N.,METROPOLITAN AREA PROBLEMS AND MUNICIPAL HOME RULE. USA+45 PROVS ADMIN CONTROL GP/REL PWR. PAGE 65 E1308
B62 LOC/G SOVEREIGN JURID LEGIS

MCGRATH J.J.,CHURCH AND STATE IN AMERICAN LAW. LAW PROVS SCHOOL TAX GIVE CT/SYS GP/REL...POLICY ANTHOL 18/20 SUPREME/CT CHURCH/STA CASEBOOK. PAGE 71 E1414
B62 SECT ADJUD CONSTN NAT/G

MURPHY W.F.,CONGRESS AND THE COURT. USA+45 LAW LOBBY GP/REL RACE/REL ATTIT PWR...JURID INT BIBLIOG CONGRESS SUPREME/CT WARRN/EARL. PAGE 75 E1509
B62 LEGIS CT/SYS GOV/REL ADJUD

PAIKERT G.C.,THE GERMAN EXODUS. EUR+WWI GERMANY/W LAW CULTURE SOCIETY STRUCT INDUS NAT/LISM RESPECT SOVEREIGN...CHARTS BIBLIOG SOC/INTEG 20 MIGRATION. PAGE 79 E1591
B62 INGP/REL STRANGE GEOG GP/REL

RICE C.E.,FREEDOM OF ASSOCIATION. USA+45 USA-45 POL/PAR LOBBY GP/REL...JURID BIBLIOG 18/20 SUPREME/CT PRE/US/AM. PAGE 84 E1691
B62 LAW NAT/G CONSTN

SOWLE C.R.,POLICE POWER AND INDIVIDUAL FREEDOM: THE QUEST FOR BALANCE. CANADA EUR+WWI ISRAEL NORWAY USA+45 LAW CONSTN SOCIETY CONTROL ROUTINE SANCTION GP/REL 20 CHINJAP. PAGE 93 E1859
B62 FORCES ORD/FREE IDEA/COMP

N.,"UNION INVESTMENT IN BUSINESS: A SOURCE OF UNION CONFLICT OF INTEREST." LAW NAT/G LEGIS CONTROL GP/REL INGP/REL DECISION. PAGE 76 E1515
L62 LABOR POLICY FINAN LG/CO

VAN DER SPRENKEL S.,"LEGAL INSTITUTIONS IN MANCHU CHINA." ASIA STRUCT CT/SYS ROUTINE GOV/REL GP/REL ...CONCPT BIBLIOG 17/20. PAGE 103 E2068
C62 LAW JURID ADMIN ADJUD

DRINAN R.F.,RELIGION, THE COURTS, AND PUBLIC POLICY. USA+45 CONSTN BUDGET TAX GIVE ADJUD SANCTION GP/REL PRIVIL 20 CHURCH/STA. PAGE 33 E0649
B63 SECT CT/SYS POLICY SCHOOL

GALLAGHER J.F.,SUPERVISORIAL DISTRICTING IN CALIFORNIA COUNTIES: 1960-1963 (PAMPHLET). USA+45 ADJUD ADMIN PARTIC CHOOSE GP/REL...CENSUS 20 CALIFORNIA. PAGE 42 E0828
B63 APPORT REGION REPRESENT LOC/G

GINZBERG E.,DEMOCRATIC VALUES AND THE RIGHTS OF MANAGEMENT. LAW CONSTN REPRESENT GP/REL ROLE PWR RESPECT POLICY. PAGE 44 E0870
B63 LABOR MGT DELIB/GP ADJUD

HYNEMAN C.S.,THE SUPREME COURT ON TRIAL. ADJUD LEAD GP/REL FEDERAL...IDEA/COMP 20 SUPREME/CT. PAGE 56 E1120
B63 CT/SYS JURID POLICY NAT/G

JACOBS P.,STATE OF UNIONS. USA+45 STRATA TOP/EX GP/REL RACE/REL DEMAND DISCRIM ATTIT PWR 20 CONGRESS NEGRO HOFFA/J. PAGE 57 E1145
B63 LABOR ECO/TAC BARGAIN DECISION

A BIBLIOGRAPHY OF DOCTORAL DISSERTATIONS UNDERTAKEN IN AMERICAN AND CANADIAN UNIVERSITIES ON RELIGION AND POLITICS. LAW CONSTN DOMIN LEGIT ADJUD GP/REL ...POLICY 20. PAGE 62 E1241
B63 BIBLIOG ACADEM SECT JURID

LEWIN J.,POLITICS AND LAW IN SOUTH AFRICA. SOUTH/AFR UK POL/PAR BAL/PWR ECO/TAC COLONIAL CONTROL GP/REL DISCRIM PWR 20 NEGRO. PAGE 65 E1293
B63 NAT/LISM POLICY LAW RACE/REL

LOWRY C.W.,TO PRAY OR NOT TO PRAY. ADJUD SANCTION GP/REL ORD/FREE PWR CATHSM WORSHIP 20 SUPREME/CT CHRISTIAN CHRUCH/STA. PAGE 67 E1330
B63 SECT CT/SYS CONSTN PRIVIL

MOLLARD P.T.,LE REGIME JURIDIQUE DE LA PRESSE AU MAROC. MOROCCO CONTROL CRIME GP/REL ORD/FREE 20. PAGE 74 E1482
B63 PRESS LAW LEAD LEGIT

OTTOSON H.W.,LAND USE POLICY AND PROBLEMS IN THE UNITED STATES. USA+45 USA-45 LAW AGRI INDUS NAT/G GP/REL...CHARTS ANTHOL 19/20 HOMEST/ACT. PAGE 79 E1586
B63 PROB/SOLV UTIL HABITAT POLICY

RAVENS J.P.,STAAT UND KATHOLISCHE KIRCHE IN PREUSSENS POLNISCHEN TEILUNGSGEBIETEN. GERMANY POLAND PRUSSIA PROVS DIPLOM EDU/PROP DEBATE NAT/LISM...JURID 18 CHURCH/STA. PAGE 83 E1674
B63 GP/REL CATHSM SECT NAT/G

SMITH E.A.,CHURCH AND STATE IN YOUR COMMUNITY. USA+45 PROVS SCHOOL ACT/RES CT/SYS PARTIC ATTIT MORAL ORD/FREE CATHSM 20 PROTESTANT CHURCH/STA. PAGE 92 E1842
B63 GP/REL SECT NAT/G NEIGH

YOUNGER R.D.,THE PEOPLE'S PANEL: THE GRAND JURY IN THE UNITED STATES, 1634-1941. USA-45 LAW LEGIT CONTROL TASK GP/REL ROLE...TREND 17/20 GRAND/JURY. PAGE 108 E2166
B63 CT/SYS JURID CONSTN LOC/G

BLOUSTEIN E.J.,NUCLEAR ENERGY, PUBLIC POLICY, AND THE LAW. USA+45 NAT/G ADJUD ADMIN GP/REL OWN PEACE ATTIT HEALTH...ANTHOL 20. PAGE 13 E0251
B64 TEC/DEV LAW POLICY NUC/PWR

BOUVIER-AJAM M.,MANUEL TECHNIQUE ET PRATIQUE DU MAIRE ET DES ELUS ET AGENTS COMMUNAUX. FRANCE LOC/G BUDGET CHOOSE GP/REL SUPEGO...JURID BIBLIOG 20 MAYOR COMMUNES. PAGE 14 E0274
B64 MUNIC ADMIN CHIEF NEIGH

BROOKS T.R.,TOIL AND TROUBLE, A HISTORY OF AMERICAN INDUS
LABOR. WORKER BARGAIN CAP/ISM ADJUD AUTOMAT EXEC LABOR
GP/REL RACE/REL EFFICIENCY INCOME PROFIT MARXISM LEGIS
17/20 KENNEDY/JF AFL/CIO NEGRO. PAGE 16 E0310
B64

CURRIE D.P.,FEDERALISM AND THE NEW NATIONS OF FEDERAL
AFRICA. CANADA USA+45 INT/TRADE TAX GP/REL AFR
...NAT/COMP SOC/INTEG 20. PAGE 28 E0556 ECO/UNDEV
INT/LAW
B64

EULAU H.,LAWYERS IN POLITICS: A STUDY IN PROF/ORG
PROFESSIONAL CONVERGENCE. USA+45 POL/PAR DELIB/GP JURID
GP/REL...QU 20. PAGE 35 E0701 LEGIS
ATTIT
B64

FEINE H.E.,DIE BESETZUNG DER REICHSBISTUMER VOM CHOOSE
WESTFALISCHEN FRIEDEN BIS ZUR SAKULARISATION. SECT
GERMANY EDU/PROP GP/REL AGE 17/19. PAGE 37 E0727 JURID
PROVS
B64

FISK W.M.,ADMINISTRATIVE PROCEDURE IN A REGULATORY SERV/IND
AGENCY: THE CAB AND THE NEW YORK-CHICAGO CASE ECO/DEV
(PAMPHLET). USA+45 DIST/IND ADMIN CONTROL LOBBY AIR
GP/REL ROLE ORD/FREE NEWYORK/C CHICAGO CAB. PAGE 38 JURID
E0758
B64

FREISEN J.,STAAT UND KATHOLISCHE KIRCHE IN DEN SECT
DEUTSCHEN BUNDESSTAATEN (2 VOLS.). GERMANY LAW FAM CATHISM
NAT/G EDU/PROP GP/REL MARRIAGE WEALTH 19/20 JURID
CHURCH/STA. PAGE 40 E0793 PROVS
B64

GIANNELLA D.A.,RELIGION AND THE PUBLIC ORDER: AN SECT
ANNUAL REVIEW OF CHURCH AND STATE, AND OF RELIGION, NAT/G
LAW, AND SOCIETY. USA+45 LAW SOCIETY FAM POL/PAR CONSTN
SCHOOL GIVE EDU/PROP GP/REL...JURID GEN/LAWS ORD/FREE
BIBLIOG/A 20 CHURCH/STA BIRTH/CON CONSCN/OBJ
NATURL/LAW. PAGE 43 E0855
B64

GRASMUCK E.L.,COERCITIO STAAT UND KIRCHE IM GP/REL
DONATISTENSTREIT. CHRIST-17C ROMAN/EMP LAW PROVS NAT/G
DEBATE PERSON SOVEREIGN...JURID CONCPT 4/5 SECT
AUGUSTINE CHURCH/STA ROMAN/LAW. PAGE 45 E0898 COERCE
B64

HENKE W.,DAS RECHT DER POLITISCHEN PARTEIEN. POL/PAR
GERMANY/W LAW CT/SYS GP/REL SUPEGO 20. PAGE 52 JURID
E1031 CONSTN
NAT/G
B64

KAUPER P.G.,RELIGION AND THE CONSTITUTION. USA+45 CONSTN
USA-45 LAW SCHOOL SECT GP/REL ATTIT...BIBLIOG JURID
WORSHIP 18/20 SUPREME/CT FREE/SPEE CHURCH/STA. ORD/FREE
PAGE 60 E1189
B64

MITAU G.T.,PROXIMATE SOLUTIONS: CASE PROBLEMS IN PROVS
STATE AND LOCAL GOVERNMENT. USA+45 CONSTN NAT/G LOC/G
CHIEF LEGIS CT/SYS EXEC GOV/REL GP/REL PWR 20 ADJUD
CASEBOOK. PAGE 73 E1470
B64

MITAU G.T.,INSOLUBLE PROBLEMS: CASE PROBLEMS ON THE ADJUD
FUNCTIONS OF STATE AND LOCAL GOVERNMENT. USA+45 AIR LOC/G
FINAN LABOR POL/PAR PROB/SOLV TAX RECEIVE CONTROL PROVS
GP/REL 20 CASEBOOK ZONING. PAGE 73 E1471
B64

TONG T.,UNITED STATES DIPLOMACY IN CHINA, DIPLOM
1844-1860. ASIA USA-45 ECO/UNDEV ECO/TAC COERCE INT/TRADE
GP/REL...INT/LAW 19 TREATY. PAGE 96 E1934 COLONIAL
B64

CARNEGIE ENDOWMENT INT. PEACE,"HUMAN RIGHTS (ISSUES INT/ORG
BEFORE THE NINETEENTH GENERAL ASSEMBLY)." AFR PERSON
WOR+45 LAW CONSTN NAT/G EDU/PROP GP/REL DISCRIM RACE/REL
PEACE ATTIT MORAL ORD/FREE...INT/LAW PSY CONCPT
RECORD UN 20. PAGE 20 E0385
S64

N.,"QUASI-LEGISLATIVE ARBITRATION AGREEMENTS." LAW ADJUD
LG/CO ECO/TAC SANCTION ATTIT POLICY. PAGE 76 E1516 ADJUST
LABOR
GP/REL
S64

PRITCHETT C.H.,"EQUAL PROTECTION AND THE URBAN MUNIC
MAJORITY." POL/PAR LEAD CHOOSE GP/REL PWR...MAJORIT LAW
S64

DECISION. PAGE 83 E1655 REPRESENT
APPORT
B65

ANTIEU C.J.,RELIGION UNDER THE STATE CONSTITUTIONS. SECT
USA+45 LAW SCHOOL TAX SANCTION PRIVIL ORD/FREE CONSTN
...JURID 20 SUPREME/CT CHURCH/STA. PAGE 5 E0099 PROVS
GP/REL
B65

BARKER L.J.,FREEDOM, COURTS, POLITICS: STUDIES IN JURID
CIVIL LIBERTIES. USA+45 LEGIS CREATE DOMIN PRESS CT/SYS
ADJUD LOBBY CRIME GP/REL RACE/REL MARXISM 20 ATTIT
CIVIL/LIB. PAGE 8 E0148 ORD/FREE
B65

BEGGS D.W.,AMERICA'S SCHOOLS AND CHURCHES: PARTNERS SECT
IN CONFLICT. USA+45 PROVS EDU/PROP ADJUD DISCRIM GP/REL
ATTIT...IDEA/COMP ANTHOL BIBLIOG WORSHIP 20 SCHOOL
CHURCH/STA. PAGE 9 E0179 NAT/G
B65

COHN H.J.,THE GOVERNMENT OF THE RHINE PALATINATE IN PROVS
THE FIFTEENTH CENTURY. GERMANY FINAN LOC/G DELIB/GP JURID
LEGIS CT/SYS CHOOSE CATHISM 14/15 PALATINATE. GP/REL
PAGE 24 E0468 ADMIN
B65

CONRING E.,KIRCHE UND STAAT NACH DER LEHRE DER SECT
NIEDERLANDISCHEN CALVINISTEN IN DER ERSTEN HALFTE JURID
DES 17. JAHRHUNDERTS. NETHERLAND GP/REL...CONCPT 17 NAT/G
CHURCH/STA. PAGE 25 E0497 ORD/FREE
B65

COWEN Z.,THE BRITISH COMMONWEALTH OF NATIONS IN A JURID
CHANGING WORLD. UK ECO/UNDEV INT/ORG ECO/TAC DIPLOM
INT/TRADE COLONIAL WAR GP/REL RACE/REL SOVEREIGN PARL/PROC
SOC/INTEG 20 TREATY EEC COMMONWLTH. PAGE 27 E0530 NAT/LISM
B65

FELLMAN D.,RELIGION IN AMERICAN PUBLIC LAW. USA+45 SECT
USA-45 NAT/G PROVS ADJUD SANCTION GP/REL PRIVIL CONSTN
ORD/FREE...JURID TIME/SEQ 18/20 SUPREME/CT LAW
CHURCH/STA. PAGE 37 E0733 POLICY
B65

FERRELL J.S.,CASES AND MATERIALS ON LOCAL APPORT
APPORTIONMENT. CONSTN LEAD GP/REL...DECISION LOC/G
GOV/COMP. PAGE 37 E0740 REPRESENT
LAW
B65

FLEMING R.W.,THE LABOR ARBITRATION PROCESS. USA+45 GP/REL
LAW BARGAIN ADJUD ROUTINE SANCTION COST...PREDICT LABOR
CHARTS TIME 20. PAGE 38 E0763 CONSULT
DELIB/GP
B65

HOWE M.D.W.,THE GARDEN AND THE WILDERNESS. USA+45 CONSTN
LAW GIVE EDU/PROP LEGIT NAT/LISM ORD/FREE...POLICY SECT
JURID SUPREME/CT CHURCH/STA. PAGE 55 E1103 NAT/G
GP/REL
B65

KAAS L.,DIE GEISTLICHE GERICHTSBARKEIT DER JURID
KATHOLISCHEN KIRCHE IN PREUSSEN (2 VOLS.). PRUSSIA CATHISM
CONSTN NAT/G PROVS SECT ADJUD ADMIN ATTIT 16/20. GP/REL
PAGE 59 E1178 CT/SYS
B65

MARTENS E.,DIE HANNOVERSCHE KIRCHENKOMMISSION. JURID
GERMANY LAW INT/ORG PROVS SECT CONFER GP/REL DELIB/GP
CATHISM 16/20. PAGE 69 E1371 CONSTN
PROF/ORG
B65

MOELLER R.,LUDWIG DER BAYER UND DIE KURIE IM KAMPF JURID
UM DAS REICH. GERMANY LAW SECT LEGIT LEAD GP/REL CHIEF
CATHISM CONSERVE 14 LUDWIG/BAV POPE CHURCH/STA. CHOOSE
PAGE 74 E1478 NAT/LISM
B65

MONCONDUIT F.,LA COMMISSION EUROPEENNE DES DROITS INT/LAW
DE L'HOMME. DIPLOM AGREE GP/REL ORD/FREE PWR INT/ORG
...BIBLIOG 20 TREATY. PAGE 74 E1483 ADJUD
JURID
B65

ROSE A.M.,MINORITY PROBLEMS: A TEXTBOOK OF READINGS RACE/REL
IN INTERGROUP RELATIONS. UNIV USA+45 LAW SCHOOL DISCRIM
WORKER PROB/SOLV GP/REL PERSON...PSY ANTHOL WORSHIP ISOLAT
20 NEGRO INDIAN/AM JEWS EUROPE. PAGE 85 E1713 ACT/RES
B65

ROSS P.,THE GOVERNMENT AS A SOURCE OF UNION POWER. LABOR
USA+45 LAW ECO/DEV PROB/SOLV ECO/TAC LEAD GP/REL BARGAIN

...MGT 20. PAGE 86 E1723 | POLICY NAT/G

B65

SMITH C.,THE OMBUDSMAN: A BIBLIOGRAPHY (PAMPHLET). DENMARK SWEDEN USA+45 LAW LEGIS JUDGE GOV/REL GP/REL...JURID 20. PAGE 92 E1841 | BIBLIOG ADMIN CT/SYS ADJUD

B65

US HOUSE COMM ON JUDICIARY,IMMIGRATION AND NATIONALITY. LAW...POLICY 20. PAGE 100 E2007 | GP/REL NAT/LISM NAT/G JURID

B65

WEIL G.L.,A HANDBOOK ON THE EUROPEAN ECONOMIC COMMUNITY. BELGIUM EUR+WWI FRANCE GERMANY/W ITALY CONSTN ECO/DEV CREATE PARTIC GP/REL...DECISION MGT CHARTS 20 EEC. PAGE 105 E2107 | INT/TRADE INT/ORG TEC/DEV INT/LAW

B65

WILSON J.F.,CHURCH AND STATE IN AMERICAN HISTORY. USA+45 USA-45 ADJUD CT/SYS ORD/FREE SOVEREIGN ...ANTHOL BIBLIOG/A 17/20 CHURCH/STA. PAGE 106 E2129 | SECT NAT/G GP/REL CONTROL

B66

AMERICAN JEWISH COMMITTEE,GROUP RELATIONS IN THE UNITED STATES: PROBLEMS AND PERSPECTIVES: A SELECTED, ANNOTATED BIBLIOGRAPHY (PAMPHLET). LAW CONSTN STRATA SCHOOL SECT PROB/SOLV ATTIT...POLICY WELF/ST SOC/WK 20. PAGE 4 E0079 | BIBLIOG/A USA+45 STRUCT GP/REL

B66

CAHN E.,CONFRONTING INJUSTICE. USA+45 PROB/SOLV TAX EDU/PROP PRESS CT/SYS GP/REL DISCRIM BIO/SOC ...IDEA/COMP BIBLIOG WORSHIP 20 BILL/RIGHT. PAGE 18 E0362 | ORD/FREE CONSTN ADJUD

B66

COLEMAN-NORTON P.R.,ROMAN STATE AND CHRISTIAN CHURCH: A COLLECTION OF LEGAL DOCUMENTS TO A.D. 535 (3 VOLS.). CHRIST-17C ROMAN/EMP...ANTHOL DICTIONARY 6 CHRISTIAN CHURCH/STA. PAGE 24 E0473 | GP/REL NAT/G SECT LAW

B66

DAVIS K.,BUSINESS AND ITS ENVIRONMENT. LAW ECO/DEV INDUS OP/RES ADMIN CONTROL ROUTINE GP/REL PROFIT POLICY. PAGE 29 E0573 | EX/STRUC PROB/SOLV CAP/ISM EXEC

B66

DOUGLAS W.O.,THE BIBLE AND THE SCHOOLS. USA+45 CULTURE ADJUD INGP/REL AGE/C AGE/Y ATTIT KNOWL WORSHIP 20 SUPREME/CT CHURCH/STA BIBLE CHRISTIAN. PAGE 32 E0644 | SECT NAT/G SCHOOL GP/REL

B66

FEINE H.E.,REICH UND KIRCHE. CHRIST-17C MOD/EUR ROMAN/EMP LAW CHOOSE ATTIT 10/19 CHURCH/STA ROMAN/LAW. PAGE 37 E0728 | JURID SECT NAT/G GP/REL

B66

FENN DH J.R.,BUSINESS DECISION MAKING AND GOVERNMENT POLICY. SERV/IND LEGIS LICENSE ADMIN CONTROL GP/REL INGP/REL 20 CASEBOOK. PAGE 37 E0736 | DECISION PLAN NAT/G LG/CO

B66

FUCHS W.P.,STAAT UND KIRCHE IM WANDEL DER JAHRHUNDERTE. EUR+WWI MOD/EUR UK REV...JURID CONCPT 4/20 EUROPE CHRISTIAN CHURCH/STA. PAGE 41 E0817 | SECT NAT/G ORD/FREE GP/REL

B66

GOLDWIN R.A.,APPORTIONMENT AND REPRESENTATION. MUNIC CT/SYS GP/REL ORD/FREE...POLICY ANTHOL 20 SUPREME/CT. PAGE 44 E0880 | APPORT REPRESENT LEGIS CONSTN

B66

HAYS P.R.,LABOR ARBITRATION: A DISSENTING VIEW. USA+45 LAW DELIB/GP BARGAIN ADJUD...PREDICT 20. PAGE 51 E1016 | GP/REL LABOR CONSULT CT/SYS

B66

HOLTZMAN A.,INTEREST GROUPS AND LOBBYING. USA+45 CHIEF ACT/RES ADJUD LEAD PARTIC CHOOSE...POLICY 20 CONGRESS. PAGE 55 E1092 | LOBBY NAT/G EDU/PROP GP/REL

B66

LEE L.T.,VIENNA CONVENTION ON CONSULAR RELATIONS. | AGREE

WOR+45 LAW INT/ORG CONFER GP/REL PRIVIL...INT/LAW 20 TREATY VIENNA/CNV. PAGE 64 E1277 | DIPLOM ADMIN

B66

MC CONNELL J.P.,LAW AND BUSINESS: PATTERNS AND ISSUES IN COMMERCIAL LAW. USA+45 USA-45 LOC/G WORKER LICENSE CRIME REPRESENT GP/REL 20. PAGE 70 E1397 | ECO/DEV JURID ADJUD MGT

B66

MILLER E.W.,THE NEGRO IN AMERICA: A BIBLIOGRAPHY. USA+45 LAW EDU/PROP REV GOV/REL GP/REL INGP/REL ADJUST HABITAT PERSON HEALTH ORD/FREE SOC/INTEG 20 NEGRO. PAGE 73 E1459 | BIBLIOG DISCRIM RACE/REL

B66

O'NEILL C.E.,CHURCH AND STATE IN FRENCH COLONIAL LOUISIANA: POLICY AND POLITICS TO 1732. PROVS VOL/ASSN DELIB/GP ADJUD ADMIN GP/REL ATTIT DRIVE ...POLICY BIBLIOG 17/18 LOUISIANA CHURCH/STA. PAGE 78 E1568 | COLONIAL NAT/G SECT PWR

B66

SMITH E.A.,CHURCH-STATE RELATIONS IN ECUMENICAL PERSPECTIVE. WOR+45 LAW MUNIC INGP/REL DISCRIM ATTIT SUPEGO ORD/FREE CATHISM...PHIL/SCI IDEA/COMP 20 PROTESTANT ECUMENIC CHURCH/STA CHRISTIAN. PAGE 92 E1843 | NAT/G SECT GP/REL ADJUD

B66

US PRES COMN CRIME IN DC,REPORT OF THE US PRESIDENT'S COMMISSION ON CRIME IN THE DISTRICT OF COLUMBIA. LEGIS WORKER EDU/PROP ADJUD CONTROL CT/SYS GP/REL BIO/SOC HEALTH...CRIMLGY NEW/IDEA STAT 20. PAGE 101 E2022 | CRIME FORCES AGE/Y SANCTION

B66

WASHINGTON S.H.,BIBLIOGRAPHY: LABOR-MANAGEMENT RELATIONS ACT, 1947 AS AMENDED BY LABOR-MANAGEMENT REPORTING AND DISCLOSURE ACT, 1959. USA+45 CONSTN INDUS DELIB/GP LEGIS WORKER BARGAIN ECO/TAC ADJUD GP/REL NEW/LIB...JURID CONGRESS. PAGE 105 E2100 | BIBLIOG LAW LABOR MGT

S66

CHIU H.,"COMMUNIST CHINA'S ATTITUDE TOWARD INTERNATIONAL LAW" CHINA/COM USSR LAW CONSTN DIPLOM GP/REL 20 LENIN/VI. PAGE 22 E0431 | INT/LAW MARXISM CONCPT IDEA/COMP

B67

BAKKE E.W.,UNIONS, MANAGEMENT AND THE PUBLIC* READINGS AND TEXT. WORKER LOBBY...POLICY JURID ANTHOL T. PAGE 7 E0143 | LABOR INDUS ADJUD GP/REL

B67

BEAL E.F.,THE PRACTICE OF COLLECTIVE BARGAINING (3RD ED.). USA+45 WOR+45 ECO/DEV INDUS LG/CO PROF/ORG WORKER ECO/TAC GP/REL WEALTH...JURID METH/CNCPT. PAGE 8 E0160 | BARGAIN MGT LABOR ADJUD

B67

CAVES R.,AMERICAN INDUSTRY: STRUCTURE, CONDUCT, PERFORMANCE (2ND ED.). USA+45 MARKET NAT/G ADJUD CONTROL GP/REL DEMAND WEALTH 20. PAGE 21 E0412 | ECO/DEV INDUS POLICY ECO/TAC

B67

COWLING M.,1867 DISRAELI, GLADSTONE, AND REVOLUTION: THE PASSING OF THE SECOND REFORM BILL. UK LEGIS LEAD LOBBY GP/REL INGP/REL...DECISION BIBLIOG 19 REFORMERS. PAGE 27 E0531 | PARL/PROC POL/PAR ATTIT LAW

B67

ELDRIDGE W.B.,NARCOTICS AND THE LAW: A CRITIQUE OF THE AMERICAN EXPERIMENT IN NARCOTIC DRUG CONTROL. PUB/INST ACT/RES PLAN LICENSE GP/REL EFFICIENCY ATTIT HEALTH...CRIMLGY HEAL STAT 20 ABA DEPT/HEW NARCO/ACT. PAGE 34 E0679 | LAW INSPECT BIO/SOC JURID

B67

FINCHER F.,THE GOVERNMENT OF THE UNITED STATES. USA+45 USA-45 POL/PAR CHIEF CT/SYS LOBBY GP/REL INGP/REL...CONCPT CHARTS BIBLIOG T 18/20 PRESIDENT CONGRESS SUPREME/CT. PAGE 38 E0749 | NAT/G EX/STRUC LEGIS OP/RES

B67

NIVEN R.,NIGERIA. NIGERIA CONSTN INDUS EX/STRUC COLONIAL REV NAT/LISM...CHARTS 19/20. PAGE 77 E1550 | NAT/G REGION CHOOSE GP/REL

B67

RAE D.,THE POLITICAL CONSEQUENCES OF ELECTORAL LAWS. EUR+WWI ICELAND ISRAEL NEW/ZEALND UK USA+45 ADJUD APPORT GP/REL MAJORITY...MATH STAT CENSUS | POL/PAR CHOOSE NAT/COMP

CHARTS BIBLIOG 20 AUSTRAL. PAGE 83 E1667   REPRESENT

L67
BLUMBERG A.S.,"THE PRACTICE OF LAW AS CONFIDENCE   CT/SYS
GAME; ORGANIZATIONAL COOPTATION OF A PROFESSION."   ADJUD
USA+45 CLIENT SOCIETY CONSULT ROLE JURID. PAGE 13   GP/REL
E0252   ADMIN

L67
HOWARD A.E.D.,"MR. JUSTICE BLACK: THE NEGRO PROTEST ADJUD
MOVEMENT AND THE RULE OF LAW." USA+45 CONSTN CT/SYS JUDGE
CHOOSE GP/REL...DECISION JURID NEGRO SUPREME/CT.   LAW
PAGE 55 E1100   REPRESENT

S67
CLOGGER T.J.,"THE BIG EAR." UK USA+45 USSR LAW   DIPLOM
LEGIS CRIME GP/REL INGP/REL ATTIT 20 FBI ESPIONAGE. ORD/FREE
PAGE 23 E0458   COM/IND
                                                     INSPECT

S67
HILL D.G.,"HUMAN RIGHTS LEGISLATION IN ONTARIO."   DELIB/GP
CANADA R+D VOL/ASSN CONSULT INSPECT EDU/PROP ADJUD   ORD/FREE
AGREE TASK GP/REL INGP/REL DISCRIM 20 CIV/RIGHTS   LAW
ONTARIO CIVIL/LIB. PAGE 52 E1045   POLICY

S67
MACLEOD R.M.,"LAW, MEDICINE AND PUBLIC OPINION: THE LAW
RESISTANCE TO COMPULSORY HEALTH LEGISLATION   HEALTH
1870-1907." UK CONSTN SECT DELIB/GP DEBATE   ATTIT
PARL/PROC GP/REL MORAL 19. PAGE 67 E1344

B97
JENKS E.J.,LAW AND POLITICS IN THE MIDDLE AGES.   LAW
CHRIST-17C CULTURE STRUCT KIN NAT/G SECT CT/SYS   SOCIETY
GP/REL...CLASSIF CHARTS IDEA/COMP BIBLIOG 8/16.   ADJUST
PAGE 58 E1162

GRACIA-MORA M.R. E0895

GRAFT....SEE TRIBUTE

GRAHAM H.D. E0896

GRAND/JURY....GRAND JURIES

B63
YOUNGER R.D.,THE PEOPLE'S PANEL: THE GRAND JURY IN   CT/SYS
THE UNITED STATES, 1634-1941. USA-45 LAW LEGIT   JURID
CONTROL TASK GP/REL ROLE...TREND 17/20 GRAND/JURY.   CONSTN
PAGE 108 E2166   LOC/G

GRANGE....GRANGE AND GRANGERS

GRANT D.R. E0897

GRANT/US....PRESIDENT ULYSSES S. GRANT

GRANTS....SEE GIVE+FOR/AID

GRASMUCK E.L. E0898

GRAVEN J. E0899

GRAVES W.B. E0900,E0901

GREAT BRITAIN....SEE UK

GREAT BRIT COMM MINISTERS PWR E0902

GREAT/SOC....GREAT SOCIETY

GRECO/ROMN....GRECO-ROMAN CIVILIZATION

GREECE....MODERN GREECE

B20
VINOGRADOFF P.,OUTLINES OF HISTORICAL JURISPRUDENCE JURID
(2 VOLS.). GREECE MEDIT-7 LAW CONSTN FACE/GP FAM   METH
KIN MUNIC CRIME OWN...INT/LAW IDEA/COMP BIBLIOG.
PAGE 104 E2080

B49
WORMUTH F.D.,THE ORIGINS OF MODERN   NAT/G
CONSTITUTIONALISM. GREECE UK LEGIS CREATE TEC/DEV   CONSTN
BAL/PWR DOMIN ADJUD REV WAR PWR...JURID ROMAN/REP   LAW
CROMWELL/O. PAGE 107 E2146

GREECE/ANC....ANCIENT GREECE

GREEK ORTHODOX CATHOLIC....SEE ORTHO/GK

GREELY A.W. E0904

GREEN F.M. E0905

GREEN L.C. E0906,E0907

GREEN/TH....T.H. GREEN

GREENBACK....GREENBACK PARTY

GREENBERG S. E0908

GREENE L.E. E0909

GREENE L.S. E0910

GREENSPAN M. E0911,E0912

GREENWICH VILLAGE....SEE GRNWCH/VIL

GREENWICH....GREENWICH, ENGLAND

GREGG R.W. E0913

GREGORY W. E0914

GREIG D.W. E0915

GRENADA....GRENADA (WEST INDIES)

GRENVILLES....GRENVILLES - ENGLISH FAMILY; SEE ALSO UK

GRESHAM-YANG TREATY....SEE GRESHMYANG

GRESHAM'S LAW....SEE GRESHM/LAW

GRESHM/LAW....GRESHAM'S LAW

GRESHMYANG....GRESHAM-YANG TREATY

GRESSMAN E. E1872

GREY D.L. E0916

GRIFFIN A.P.C. E0917,E0918,E0919,E0920,E0921,E0922,E0923,E0924 ,
    E0925,E0926,E0927,E0928,E0929,E0930,E0931,E0932,E0933 ,
    E0934,E0935

GRIFFIN G.G. E0184,E0936

GRIFFIN H.C. E0937

GRIFFITH E.S. E0938,E0939

GRIFFITH J.A.G. E0940

GRIFFITH W.E. E0941

GRINDEL C.W. E0942

GRISWOLD A.W. E0943

GRNWCH/VIL....GREENWICH VILLAGE

GROB F. E0944

GROGAN V. E0945

GRONING J. E0946,E0947

GROSS B.M. E0948

GROSS L. E0949,E0950,E0951

GROSS NATIONAL PRODUCT....WEALTH+PRODUC

GROTIUS H. E0952

GROUP RELATIONS....SEE GP/REL

GROVES H.E. E0953

GROWTH....SEE CREATE+ECO/UNDEV

GRUNDMANN S. E1232

GRUNEWALD D. E0736,E0954

GRZYBOWSKI K. E0955,E0956,E0958

GSOVSKI V. E0957,E0958,E1823

GUAITA A. E0959

GUAM....GUAM

B01
GRIFFIN A.P.C.,LIST OF BOOKS ON SAMOA (PAMPHLET).   BIBLIOG/A
GERMANY S/ASIA UK USA-45 WOR-45 ECO/UNDEV REGION   COLONIAL
ALL/VALS ORD/FREE ALL/IDEOS...GEOG INT/LAW 19 SAMOA DIPLOM
GUAM. PAGE 46 E0918

B59
COUNCIL OF STATE GOVERNORS,AMERICAN LEGISLATURES: LEGIS
STRUCTURE AND PROCEDURES. SUMMARY AND TABULATIONS   CHARTS
OF A 1959 SURVEY. PUERT/RICO USA+45 PAY ADJUD ADMIN PROVS
APPORT...IDEA/COMP 20 GUAM VIRGIN/ISL. PAGE 27   REPRESENT
E0525

GUATEMALA....SEE ALSO L/A+17C

N
VALENZUELE G.,BIBLIOGRAFIA GUATEMALTECA, Y CATALOG   BIBLIOG/A
GENERAL DE LIBROS, FOLLETOS, PERIODICOS, REVISTAS,   L/A+17C
ETC. (10 VOLS.). GUATEMALA LAW...ART/METH 17/20.
PAGE 103 E2066

B49
HOLLERAN M.P.,CHURCH AND STATE IN GUATEMALA.   SECT
GUATEMALA LAW STRUCT CATHISM...SOC SOC/INTEG 17/20   NAT/G
CHURCH/STA. PAGE 55 E1086   GP/REL
                                                     CULTURE

B59
GOMEZ ROBLES J.,A STATEMENT OF THE LAWS OF   JURID
GUATEMALA IN MATTERS AFFECTING BUSINESS (2ND ED.   NAT/G
REV., ENLARGED). GUATEMALA L/A+17C LAW FINAN FAM   INDUS
WORKER ACT/RES DIPLOM ADJUD ADMIN GP/REL 20 OAS.   LEGIT
PAGE 44 E0881

GUEMES/M....MARTIN GUEMES

GUERRILLA....GUERRILLA WARFARE

B59
HOBSBAWM E.J.,PRIMITIVE REBELS; STUDIES IN ARCHAIC   SOCIETY
FORMS OF SOCIAL MOVEMENT IN THE 19TH AND 20TH   CRIME
CENTURIES. ITALY SPAIN CULTURE VOL/ASSN RISK CROWD   REV
GP/REL INGP/REL ISOLAT TOTALISM...PSY SOC 18/20.   GUERRILLA
PAGE 53 E1058

S62
GREENSPAN M.,"INTERNATIONAL LAW AND ITS PROTECTION   FORCES
FOR PARTICIPANTS IN UNCONVENTIONAL WARFARE." WOR+45 JURID
LAW INT/ORG NAT/G POL/PAR COERCE REV ORD/FREE   GUERRILLA
...INT/LAW TOT/POP 20. PAGE 46 E0912   WAR

S64
GINSBURGS G.,"WARS OF NATIONAL LIBERATION - THE   COERCE
SOVIET THESIS." COM USSR WOR+45 WOR-45 LAW CULTURE   CONCPT
INT/ORG DIPLOM LEGIT COLONIAL GUERRILLA WAR   INT/LAW
NAT/LISM ATTIT PERSON MORAL PWR...JURID OBS TREND   REV
MARX/KARL 20. PAGE 44 E0869

GUEVARA/E....ERNESTO GUEVARA

GUIANA/BR....BRITISH GUIANA; SEE ALSO GUYANA

GUIANA/FR....FRENCH GUIANA

GUILDS....SEE PROF/ORG

GUINEA....SEE ALSO AFR

GUINS G.C. E0960

GUIZOT F.P.G. E0961

GUJARAT....GUJARAT (STATE OF INDIA)

GUMPLOWICZ L. E0962

GURVITCH G. E0963,E0964

GUTTMAN/L....LOUIS GUTTMAN (AND GUTTMAN SCALE)

GUTTMANN A. E0965

GUYANA....GUYANA; SEE ALSO GUIANA/BR. L/A+17C

GYORGY A. E0966
                        ——— H ———
HAAR C.M. E0967

HABERLER G. E0968

HABERMAS J. E0969

HABITAT....ECOLOGY

N13
SCHMIDHAUSER J.R.,JUDICIAL BEHAVIOR AND THE   JUDGE

SECTIONAL CRISIS OF 1837-1860. USA-45 ADJUD CT/SYS   POL/PAR
INGP/REL ATTIT HABITAT...DECISION PSY STAT CHARTS   PERS/COMP
SIMUL. PAGE 88 E1759   PERSON

B23
DE MONTESQUIEU C.,THE SPIRIT OF LAWS (2 VOLS.)   JURID
(TRANS. BY THOMAS NUGENT). FRANCE FINAN SECT   LAW
INT/TRADE TAX COERCE REV DISCRIM HABITAT ORD/FREE   CONCPT
19 ALEMBERT/J CIVIL/LAW. PAGE 30 E0588   GEN/LAWS

B55
BURR R.N.,DOCUMENTS ON INTER-AMERICAN COOPERATION: BIBLIOG
VOL. I, 1810-1881; VOL. II, 1881-1948. DELIB/GP   DIPLOM
BAL/PWR INT/TRADE REPRESENT NAT/LISM PEACE HABITAT   INT/ORG
ORD/FREE PWR SOVEREIGN...INT/LAW 20 OAS. PAGE 18   L/A+17C
E0345

B55
SMITH G.,A CONSTITUTIONAL AND LEGAL HISTORY OF   CONSTN
ENGLAND. UK ELITES NAT/G LEGIS ADJUD OWN HABITAT   PARTIC
POPULISM...JURID 20 ENGLSH/LAW. PAGE 92 E1844   LAW
                                                     CT/SYS

B56
HURST J.W.,LAW AND THE CONDITIONS OF FREEDOM IN THE LAW
NINETEENTH CENTURY UNITED STATES. USA-45 CONSTN   ORD/FREE
STRUCT ADMIN GP/REL FEDERAL HABITAT...JURID 19.   POLICY
PAGE 56 E1116   NAT/G

B56
RECASENS SICHES S.,TRATADO GENERAL DE SOCIOLOGIA.   SOC
CULTURE FAM NEIGH LEAD RACE/REL DISCRIM HABITAT   STRATA
ORD/FREE...JURID LING T SOC/INTEG 20. PAGE 84 E1677 KIN
                                                     GP/REL

B57
DIVINE R.A.,AMERICAN IMMIGRATION POLICY, 1924-52.   GEOG
USA+45 USA-45 VOL/ASSN DELIB/GP ADJUD WAR ADJUST   HABITAT
DISCRIM...POLICY JURID 20 DEPRESSION MIGRATION.   LEGIS
PAGE 32 E0630   CONTROL

B60
GONZALEZ NAVARRO M.,LA COLONIZACION EN MEXICO,   ECO/UNDEV
1877-1910. AGRI NAT/G PLAN PROB/SOLV INCOME   GEOG
...POLICY JURID CENSUS 19/20 MEXIC/AMER MIGRATION.   HABITAT
PAGE 44 E0883   COLONIAL

B62
STERN A.C.,AIR POLLUTION (2 VOLS.). LAW INDUS   AIR
PROB/SOLV TEC/DEV INSPECT RISK BIO/SOC HABITAT   OP/RES
...OBS/ENVIR TESTS SAMP 20 POLLUTION. PAGE 93 E1871 CONTROL
                                                     HEALTH

B62
US COMMISSION ON CIVIL RIGHTS,HEARINGS BEFORE   ORD/FREE
UNITED STATES COMMISSION ON CIVIL RIGHTS. USA+45   LAW
ECO/DEV NAT/G CONSULT WORKER EDU/PROP ADJUD DISCRIM ADMIN
ISOLAT HABITAT HEALTH RESPECT 20 NEGRO CIV/RIGHTS.   LEGIS
PAGE 99 E1985

B63
JENKS C.W.,LAW, FREEDOM, AND WELFARE. WOR+45 GIVE   INT/LAW
ADJUD WAR PEACE HABITAT ORD/FREE. PAGE 58 E1159   DIPLOM
                                                     SOVEREIGN
                                                     PROB/SOLV

B63
OTTOSON H.W.,LAND USE POLICY AND PROBLEMS IN THE   PROB/SOLV
UNITED STATES. USA+45 USA-45 LAW AGRI INDUS NAT/G   UTIL
GP/REL...CHARTS ANTHOL 19/20 HOMEST/ACT. PAGE 79   HABITAT
E1586   POLICY

B64
MAKI J.M.,COURT AND CONSTITUTION IN JAPAN; SELECTED CT/SYS
SUPREME COURT DECISIONS, 1948-60. FAM LABOR GOV/REL CONSTN
HABITAT ORD/FREE...DECISION JURID 20 CHINJAP   PROB/SOLV
SUPREME/CT CIV/RIGHTS. PAGE 68 E1354   LAW

B64
US HOUSE COMM ON JUDICIARY,IMMIGRATION HEARINGS.   NAT/G
DELIB/GP STRANGE HABITAT...GEOG JURID 20 CONGRESS   POLICY
MIGRATION. PAGE 100 E2006   DIPLOM
                                                     NAT/LISM

B65
SCHROEDER O.,DEFACTO SEGREGATION AND CIVIL RIGHTS.   ANTHOL
LAW PROVS SCHOOL WORKER ATTIT HABITAT HEALTH WEALTH DISCRIM
...JURID CHARTS 19/20 NEGRO SUPREME/CT KKK. PAGE 88 RACE/REL
E1766   ORD/FREE

B66
BRAIBANTI R.,RESEARCH ON THE BUREAUCRACY OF   HABITAT
PAKISTAN. PAKISTAN LAW CULTURE INTELL ACADEM LOC/G   NAT/G
SECT PRESS CT/SYS...LING CHARTS 20 BUREAUCRCY.   ADMIN
PAGE 15 E0286   CONSTN

B66
MACIVER R.M.,THE PREVENTION AND CONTROL OF   AGE/Y
DELINQUENCY. USA+45 STRATA PUB/INST ANOMIE ATTIT   PLAN
HABITAT PERSON HEALTH...CRIMLGY PSY SOC METH.   ADJUST
PAGE 67 E1341   CRIME

B66
MILLER E.W.,THE NEGRO IN AMERICA: A BIBLIOGRAPHY.   BIBLIOG
USA+45 LAW EDU/PROP REV GOV/REL GP/REL INGP/REL   DISCRIM
ADJUST HABITAT PERSON HEALTH ORD/FREE SOC/INTEG 20   RACE/REL
NEGRO. PAGE 73 E1459

N66
CONGRESSIONAL QUARTERLY SERV,HOUSING A NATION   HABITAT
(PAMPHLET). USA+45 LAW STRUCT DIST/IND DELIB/GP   NAT/G
...GEOG CHARTS 20 DEPT/HUD. PAGE 25 E0490   PLAN
                                                    MUNIC

B67
BERNSTEIN S.,ALTERNATIVES TO VIOLENCE: ALIENATED   AGE/Y
YOUTH AND RIOTS, RACE AND POVERTY. MUNIC PUB/INST   SOC/WK
SCHOOL INGP/REL RACE/REL UTOPIA DRIVE HABITAT ROLE   NEIGH
WEALTH...INT 20. PAGE 11 E0215   CRIME

B67
BONGER W.A.,CRIMINALITY AND ECONOMIC CONDITIONS.   PERSON
MOD/EUR STRUCT INDUS WORKER EDU/PROP CRIME HABITAT   CRIMLGY
ALL/VALS...JURID SOC 20 REFORMERS. PAGE 14 E0265   IDEA/COMP
                                                    ANOMIE

L67
FRANCK T.M.,"SOME PSYCHOLOGICAL FACTORS IN   DIPLOM
INTERNATIONAL THIRD-PARTY DECISION-MAKING." UNIV   ADJUD
SOCIETY PROB/SOLV DISCRIM ATTIT HABITAT...DECISION   PERSON
PSY. PAGE 40 E0786   CONSULT

L67
NAGEL S.S.,"DISPARITIES IN CRIMINAL PROCEDURE."   ADJUD
STRATA NAT/G PROVS EDU/PROP RACE/REL AGE HABITAT   DISCRIM
SEX...JURID CHARTS 20. PAGE 76 E1519   STRUCT
                                                    ACT/RES

S67
"THE STATE OF ZONING ADMINISTRATION IN ILLINOIS: ADMIN
PROCEDURAL REQUIREMENTS OF JUDICIAL INTERVENTION."   CONTROL
USA+45 LAW CONSTN DELIB/GP ADJUD CT/SYS ORD/FREE   HABITAT
ILLINOIS. PAGE 2 E0038   PLAN

S67
HUBERT C.J.,"PLANNED UNIT DEVELOPMENT" LAW VOL/ASSN PLAN
LEGIS EDU/PROP CT/SYS GOV/REL...NEW/IDEA 20   MUNIC
PLAN/UNIT. PAGE 56 E1107   HABITAT
                                                    ADJUD

B92
COHN M.M.,AN INTRODUCTION TO THE STUDY OF THE   CONSTN
CONSTITUTION. USA+45 USA-45 SOCIETY NAT/G EX/STRUC   JURID
HABITAT...PSY CONCPT 18/20. PAGE 24 E0470   OLD/LIB

HACKER A. E0970

HADDOW A. E0971

HADWEN J.G. E0972

HAEFELE E.T. E0973

HAENSCH G. E0974

HAGEN A. E0975

HAGUE PERMANENT CT INTL JUSTIC E0976,E0977

HAGUE/F....FRANK HAGUE

HAITI....SEE ALSO L/A+17C

B47
NEUBURGER O.,GUIDE TO OFFICIAL PUBLICATIONS OF THE   BIBLIOG/A
OTHER AMERICAN REPUBLICS: HAITI (VOL. XII). HAITI   CONSTN
LAW FINAN LEGIS PRESS...JURID 20. PAGE 76 E1534   NAT/G
                                                    EDU/PROP

B51
BISSAINTHE M.,DICTIONNAIRE DE BIBLIOGRAPHIE   BIBLIOG
HAITIENNE. HAITI ELITES AGRI LEGIS DIPLOM INT/TRADE L/A+17C
WRITING ORD/FREE CATHISM...ART/METH GEOG 19/20   SOCIETY
NEGRO TREATY. PAGE 12 E0234   NAT/G

HAKLUYT/R....RICHARD HAKLUYT

HALDEMAN E. E0978

HALEY A.G. E0979,E0980

HALL A.B. E0981

HALL J. E0982,E0983,E0984

HALL W.E. E0985

HALLECK/C....CHARLES HALLECK

HALLER W. E0986

HAMBRO C.J. E0987

HAMBRO E. E0890

HAMBURG....HAMBURG, GERMANY

HAMILTON H.D. E0988,E0989,E0990

HAMILTON W.H. E0991

HAMILTON/A....ALEXANDER HAMILTON

B64
MINAR D.W.,IDEAS AND POLITICS: THE AMERICAN   CONSTN
EXPERIENCE. SECT CHIEF LEGIS CREATE ADJUD EXEC REV   NAT/G
PWR...PHIL/SCI CONCPT IDEA/COMP 18/20 HAMILTON/A   FEDERAL
JEFFERSN/T DECLAR/IND JACKSON/A PRESIDENT. PAGE 73
E1464

HAMMARSK/D....DAG HAMMARSKJOLD

L62
STEIN E.,"MR HAMMARSKJOLD, THE CHARTER LAW AND THE   CONCPT
FUTURE ROLE OF THE UNITED NATIONS SECRETARY-   BIOG
GENERAL." WOR+45 CONSTN INT/ORG DELIB/GP FORCES
TOP/EX BAL/PWR LEGIT RIGID/FLEX PWR
...POLICY JURID OBS STERTYP UN COLD/WAR 20
HAMMARSK/D. PAGE 93 E1869

S62
SCHACHTER O.,"DAG HAMMARSKJOLD AND THE RELATION OF   ACT/RES
LAW TO POLITICS." FUT WOR+45 INT/ORG CONSULT PLAN   ADJUD
TEC/DEV BAL/PWR DIPLOM LEGIT ATTIT PERCEPT ORD/FREE
...POLICY JURID CONCPT OBS TESTS STERTYP GEN/LAWS
20 HAMMARSK/D. PAGE 87 E1751

HAMMARSKJOLD, DAG....SEE HAMMARSK/D

HAMSON C.J. E0992

HANBURY H.G. E0993,E1082,E1083

HAND L. E0994

HANNA J.L. E0995

HANNA W.J. E0995

HANNA/MARK....MARK HANNA

HANSON L. E0996

HANSON R. E0997,E0998

HAPPINESS.... HAPPINESS AS A CONDITION (UNHAPPINESS)

B28
BENTHAM J.,A COMMENT OF THE COMMENTARIES (1765-69). LAW
MUNIC SECT ADJUD AGREE CT/SYS CONSEN HAPPINESS   CONCPT
ORD/FREE 18. PAGE 10 E0191   IDEA/COMP

C43
BENTHAM J.,"THE RATIONALE OF REWARD" IN J. BOWRING, SANCTION
ED., THE WORKS OF JEREMY BENTHAM (VOL. 2)" LAW   ECO/TAC
WORKER CREATE INSPECT PAY ROUTINE HAPPINESS PRODUC   INCOME
SUPEGO WEALTH METH/CNCPT. PAGE 10 E0195   PWR

B65
ANDRUS H.L.,LIBERALISM, CONSERVATISM, MORMONISM.   SECT
USA+45 PLAN ADJUD CONTROL HAPPINESS ORD/FREE   UTOPIA
CONSERVE NEW/LIB WORSHIP 20. PAGE 5 E0097   MORAL

B91
BENTHAM J.,A FRAGMENT ON GOVERNMENT (1776). CONSTN   SOVEREIGN
MUNIC NAT/G SECT AGREE HAPPINESS UTIL MORAL   LAW
ORD/FREE...JURID CONCPT. PAGE 10 E0198   DOMIN

HAPSBURG....HAPSBURG MONARCHY

HAPTHEKER....HAPTHEKER THEORY

HARDING/WG....PRESIDENT WARREN G. HARDING

HARGIS/BJ....BILLY JAMES HARGIS

HARGRETT L. E0999

HARLAN/JM....JOHN MARSHALL HARLAN

PROB/SOLV

FALK R.A.,THE AFTERMATH OF SABBATINO: BACKGROUND PAPERS AND PROCEEDINGS OF SEVENTH HAMMARSKJOLD FORUM. USA+45 LAW ACT/RES ADJUD ROLE...BIBLIOG 20 EXPROPRIAT SABBATINO HARLAN/JM. PAGE 36 E0718
B65
SOVEREIGN
CT/SYS
INT/LAW
OWN

HARLEM....HARLEM

HARMAN M. E1943

HARNETTY P. E1000

HARPER S.N. E1001

HARRIMAN/A....AVERILL HARRIMAN

HARRISN/WH....PRESIDENT WILLIAM HENRY HARRISON

HARRISON/B....PRESIDENT BENJAMIN HARRISON

HART A.B. E1421

HART J. E1002,E1003

HARTUNG F.E. E1004

HARVARD LAW SCHOOL LIBRARY E1005,E1006

HARVARD UNIVERSITY LAW LIBRARY E1007,E1008

HARVARD UNIVERSITY LAW SCHOOL E1009

HARVARD/U....HARVARD UNIVERSITY

HARVEY W.B. E1010,E1011

HATCHER/R....RICHARD HATCHER

HATRED....SEE LOVE

HAUSMAN W.H. E1012

HAUSNER G. E1013

HAWAII....HAWAII
HAWVER C. E0374
HAY P. E1014,E1245,E1868

HAYEK/V....VON HAYEK

HAYES/RB....PRESIDENT RUTHERFORD B. HAYES

HAYS B. E1015

HAYS P.R. E1016

HAZARD J.N. E1017,E1018

HEAD/START....THE "HEAD START" PROGRAM

HEADICAR B.M. E1019

HEAL....HEALTH SCIENCES

N
CONOVER H.F.,OFFICIAL PUBLICATIONS OF BRITISH EAST AFRICA (PAMPHLET). UK LAW ECO/UNDEV AGRI EXTR/IND SECT LEGIS BUDGET TAX...HEAL STAT 20. PAGE 25 E0491
BIBLIOG/A
AFR
ADMIN
COLONIAL

N
INTERNATIONAL BOOK NEWS, 1928-1934. ECO/UNDEV FINAN INDUS LABOR INT/TRADE CONFER ADJUD COLONIAL...HEAL SOC/WK CHARTS 20 LEAGUE/NAT. PAGE 1 E0008
BIBLIOG/A
DIPLOM
INT/LAW
INT/ORG

N
AUSTRALIAN PUBLIC AFFAIRS INFORMATION SERVICE. LAW ...HEAL HUM MGT SOC CON/ANAL 20 AUSTRAL. PAGE 1 E0017
BIBLIOG
NAT/G
CULTURE
DIPLOM

L21
HALDEMAN E.,"SERIALS OF AN INTERNATIONAL CHARACTER." WOR-45 DIPLOM...ART/METH GEOG HEAL HUM INT/LAW JURID PSY SOC. PAGE 49 E0978
BIBLIOG
PHIL/SCI

L29
DARWIN L.,"WHAT IS EUGENICS." USA-45 LAW SOCIETY FACE/GP FAM ACT/RES ECO/TAC HEALTH...HEAL TREND STERTYP 20. PAGE 29 E0568
PLAN
BIO/SOC

B54
BATTEN T.R.,PROBLEMS OF AFRICAN DEVELOPMENT (2ND ED.). AFR LAW SOCIETY SCHOOL ECO/TAC TAX...GEOG HEAL SOC 20. PAGE 8 E0154
ECO/UNDEV
AGRI
LOC/G

B55
CRAIG J.,BIBLIOGRAPHY OF PUBLIC ADMINISTRATION IN AUSTRALIA. CONSTN FINAN EX/STRUC LEGIS PLAN DIPLOM RECEIVE ADJUD ROUTINE...HEAL 19/20 AUSTRAL PARLIAMENT. PAGE 27 E0540
BIBLIOG
GOV/REL
ADMIN
NAT/G

B56
NOTZ R.L.,FEDERAL GRANTS-IN-AID TO STATES: ANALYSIS OF LAWS IN FORCE ON SEPTEMBER 10, 1956. USA+45 LAW SCHOOL PLAN ECO/TAC TAX RECEIVE...HEAL JURID 20. PAGE 78 E1558
GIVE
NAT/G
PROVS
GOV/REL

B56
US HOUSE WAYS MEANS COMMITTEE,TRAFFIC IN, AND CONTROL OF NARCOTICS, BARBITURATES, AND AMPHETAMINES. CHINA/COM USA+45 SOCIETY LEGIS ACT/RES EDU/PROP CT/SYS SANCTION PROFIT HEALTH ...HEAL PSY STAT 20. PAGE 100 E2011
BIO/SOC
CONTROL
PROB/SOLV
CRIME

B59
COUNCIL OF STATE GOVERNMENTS,STATE GOVERNMENT: AN ANNOTATED BIBLIOGRAPHY (PAMPHLET). USA+45 LAW AGRI INDUS WORKER PLAN TAX ADJUST AGE/Y ORD/FREE...HEAL MGT 20. PAGE 26 E0521
BIBLIOG/A
PROVS
LOC/G
ADMIN

B61
MURPHY E.F.,WATER PURITY: A STUDY IN LEGAL CONTROL OF NATURAL RESOURCES. LOC/G ACT/RES PLAN TEC/DEV LOBBY GP/REL COST ATTIT HEALTH ORD/FREE...HEAL JURID 20 WISCONSIN WATER. PAGE 75 E1506
SEA
LAW
PROVS
CONTROL

S61
RICHSTEIN A.R.,"LEGAL RULES IN NUCLEAR WEAPONS EMPLOYMENTS." FUT WOR+45 LAW SOCIETY FORCES PLAN WEAPON RIGID/FLEX...HEAL CONCPT TREND VAL/FREE 20. PAGE 85 E1696
NUC/PWR
TEC/DEV
MORAL
ARMS/CONT

B63
CHOJNACKI S.,REGISTER ON CURRENT RESEARCH ON ETHIOPIA AND THE HORN OF AFRICA. ETHIOPIA LAW CULTURE AGRI SECT EDU/PROP ADMIN...GEOG HEAL LING 20. PAGE 22 E0433
BIBLIOG
ACT/RES
INTELL
ACADEM

B66
HOPKINS J.F.K.,ARABIC PERIODICAL LITERATURE, 1961. ISLAM LAW CULTURE SECT...GEOG HEAL PHIL/SCI PSY SOC 20. PAGE 55 E1096
BIBLIOG/A
NAT/LISM
TEC/DEV
INDUS

B66
US HOUSE COMM ON JUDICIARY,CIVIL COMMITMENT AND TREATMENT OF NARCOTIC ADDICTS. USA+45 SOCIETY FINAN LEGIS PROB/SOLV GIVE CT/SYS SANCTION HEALTH ...POLICY HEAL 20. PAGE 100 E2008
BIO/SOC
CRIME
IDEA/COMP
CONTROL

B67
AMDS W.E.,DELINQUENCY PREVENTION: THEORY AND PRACTICE. USA+45 SOCIETY FAM SCHOOL SECT FORCES PROB/SOLV...HEAL JURID PREDICT ANTHOL. PAGE 4 E0071
AGE/Y
CRIME
PUB/INST
LAW

B67
BOLES D.E.,THE TWO SWORDS. USA+45 USA-45 LAW CONSTN SOCIETY FINAN PRESS CT/SYS...HEAL JURID BIBLIOG WORSHIP 20 SUPREME/CT CHURCH/STA. PAGE 13 E0263
SCHOOL
EDU/PROP
ADJUD

B67
DEBOLD R.C.,LSD, MAN AND SOCIETY. USA+45 LAW SOCIETY SECT CONTROL SANCTION STRANGE ATTIT...HEAL CHARTS ANTHOL BIBLIOG. PAGE 30 E0601
HEALTH
DRIVE
PERSON
BIO/SOC

B67
ELDRIDGE W.B.,NARCOTICS AND THE LAW: A CRITIQUE OF THE AMERICAN EXPERIMENT IN NARCOTIC DRUG CONTROL. PUB/INST ACT/RES PLAN LICENSE GP/REL EFFICIENCY ATTIT HEALTH...CRIMLGY HEAL STAT 20 ABA DEPT/HEW NARCO/ACT. PAGE 34 E0679
LAW
INSPECT
BIO/SOC
JURID

B67
HODGKINSON R.G.,THE ORIGINS OF THE NATIONAL HEALTH SERVICE: THE MEDICAL SERVICES OF THE NEW POOR LAW, 1834-1871. UK INDUS MUNIC WORKER PROB/SOLV EFFICIENCY ATTIT HEALTH WEALTH SOCISM...JURID SOC/WK 19/20. PAGE 53 E1062
HEAL
NAT/G
POLICY
LAW

HEALEY/D....DOROTHY HEALEY

B63
US SENATE COMM ON JUDICIARY,PACIFICA FOUNDATION. USA+45 LAW COM/IND 20 ODEGARD/P BINNS/JJ SCHINDLR/P HEALEY/D THOMAS/TK. PAGE 102 E2051
DELIB/GP
EDU/PROP
ORD/FREE
ATTIT

N

CANADIAN GOVERNMENT PUBLICATIONS (1955-). CANADA BIBLIOG/A
AGRI FINAN LABOR FORCES INT/TRADE HEALTH...JURID 20 NAT/G
PARLIAMENT. PAGE 1 E0005   DIPLOM
                                                       INT/ORG

N

US BUREAU OF THE CENSUS,BIBLIOGRAPHY OF SOCIAL   BIBLIOG/A
SCIENCE PERIODICALS AND MONOGRAPH SERIES. WOR+45   CULTURE
LAW DIPLOM EDU/PROP HEALTH...PSY SOC LING STAT.   NAT/G
PAGE 99 E1980   SOCIETY

N

US SUPERINTENDENT OF DOCUMENTS,EDUCATION (PRICE   BIBLIOG/A
LIST 31). USA+45 LAW FINAN LOC/G NAT/G DEBATE ADMIN   EDU/PROP
LEAD RACE/REL FEDERAL HEALTH POLICY. PAGE 103 E2062   ACADEM
                                                       SCHOOL

N19

HOGARTY R.A.,NEW JERSEY FARMERS AND MIGRANT HOUSING   AGRI
RULES (PAMPHLET). USA+45 LAW ELITES FACE/GP LABOR   PROVS
PROF/ORG LOBBY PERS/REL RIGID/FLEX ROLE 20   WORKER
NEW/JERSEY. PAGE 53 E1067   HEALTH

N19

MEZERIK A.G.,ATOM TESTS AND RADIATION HAZARDS   NUC/PWR
(PAMPHLET). WOR+45 INT/ORG DIPLOM DETER 20 UN   ARMS/CONT
TREATY. PAGE 73 E1452   CONFER
                                                       HEALTH

B29

BURNS C.D.,POLITICAL IDEALS. WOR-45 LAW CULTURE   CONCPT
SOCIETY INT/ORG HEALTH MORAL...POLICY TOT/POP 20.   GEN/LAWS
PAGE 18 E0344

L29

DARWIN L.,"WHAT IS EUGENICS." USA-45 LAW SOCIETY   PLAN
FACE/GP FAM ACT/RES ECO/TAC HEALTH...HEAL TREND   BIO/SOC
STERTYP 20. PAGE 29 E0568

B33

GILLETTE J.M.,CURRENT SOCIAL PROBLEMS. CONTROL   GEOG
CRIME AGE/Y BIO/SOC...SOC 20. PAGE 43 E0861   HEALTH
                                                       RACE/REL
                                                       FAM

B42

GILLETTE J.M.,PROBLEMS OF A CHANGING SOCIAL ORDER.   BIO/SOC
USA+45 STRATA FAM CONTROL CRIME RACE/REL HEALTH   ADJUST
WEALTH...GEOG GP/COMP. PAGE 43 E0862   ATTIT
                                                       SOC/WK

B42

US LIBRARY OF CONGRESS,SOCIAL AND CULTURAL PROBLEMS   BIBLIOG/A
IN WARTIME: APRIL 1941-MARCH 1942. WOR-45 CLIENT   WAR
SECT EDU/PROP CRIME LEISURE RACE/REL STRANGE ATTIT   SOC
DRIVE HEALTH...GEOG 20. PAGE 100 E2012   CULTURE

B43

US LIBRARY OF CONGRESS,SOCIAL AND CULTURAL PROBLEMS   BIBLIOG/A
IN WARTIME: APRIL-DECEMBER (SUPPLEMENT 1). WOR-45   WAR
SECT EDU/PROP CRIME LEISURE CIVMIL/REL RACE/REL   SOC
ATTIT DRIVE HEALTH...GEOG 20. PAGE 100 E2013   CULTURE

B43

US LIBRARY OF CONGRESS,SOCIAL AND CULTURAL PROBLEMS   BIBLIOG/A
IN WARTIME: JANUARY-MAY 1943 (SUPPLEMENT 2). WOR-45   WAR
FAM SECT PLAN EDU/PROP CRIME LEISURE RACE/REL DRIVE   SOC
HEALTH...GEOG 20 JEWS. PAGE 100 E2014   CULTURE

B45

US LIBRARY OF CONGRESS,NETHERLANDS EAST INDIES.   BIBLIOG/A
INDONESIA LAW CULTURE AGRI INDUS SCHOOL COLONIAL   S/ASIA
HEALTH...GEOG JURID SOC 19/20 NETH/IND. PAGE 101   NAT/G
E2017

S48

ALEXANDER L.,"WAR CRIMES, THEIR SOCIAL-   DRIVE
PSYCHOLOGICAL ASPECTS." EUR+WWI GERMANY LAW CULTURE   WAR
ELITES KIN POL/PAR PUB/INST FORCES DOMIN EDU/PROP
COERCE CRIME ATTIT SUPEGO HEALTH MORAL PWR FASCISM
...PSY OBS TREND GEN/LAWS NAZI 20. PAGE 3 E0061

L51

KELSEN H.,"RECENT TRENDS IN THE LAW OF THE UNITED   INT/ORG
NATIONS." KOREA WOR+45 CONSTN LEGIS DIPLOM LEGIT   LAW
DETER WAR RIGID/FLEX HEALTH ORD/FREE RESPECT   INT/LAW
...JURID CON/ANAL UN VAL/FREE 20 NATO. PAGE 60
E1199

B52

WALTER P.A.F.,RACE AND CULTURE RELATIONS. FAM   RACE/REL
HEALTH WEALTH...POLICY CRIMLGY GEOG BIBLIOG T 20.   DISCRIM
PAGE 105 E2097   GP/REL

B55

TROTIER A.H.,DOCTORAL DISSERTATIONS ACCEPTED BY   BIBLIOG
AMERICAN UNIVERSITIES 1954-55. SECT DIPLOM HEALTH   ACADEM
...ART/METH GEOG INT/LAW SOC LING CHARTS 20.   USA+45
PAGE 97 E1943   WRITING

B56

US HOUSE WAYS MEANS COMMITTEE,TRAFFIC IN, AND   BIO/SOC
CONTROL OF NARCOTICS, BARBITURATES, AND   CONTROL
AMPHETAMINES. CHINA/COM USA+45 SOCIETY LEGIS   PROB/SOLV
ACT/RES EDU/PROP CT/SYS SANCTION PROFIT HEALTH   CRIME
...HEAL PSY STAT 20. PAGE 100 E2011

B58

ATOMIC INDUSTRIAL FORUM,MANAGEMENT AND ATOMIC   NUC/PWR
ENERGY. WOR+45 SEA LAW MARKET NAT/G TEC/DEV INSPECT   INDUS
INT/TRADE CONFER PEACE HEALTH...ANTHOL 20. PAGE 6   MGT
E0112   ECO/TAC

B58

MANSERGH N.,COMMONWEALTH PERSPECTIVES. GHANA UK LAW   DIPLOM
VOL/ASSN CONFER HEALTH SOVEREIGN...GEOG CHARTS   COLONIAL
ANTHOL 20 CMN/WLTH AUSTRAL. PAGE 68 E1363   INT/ORG
                                                       INGP/REL

B59

CHRISTMAN H.M.,THE PUBLIC PAPERS OF CHIEF JUSTICE   LAW
EARL WARREN. CONSTN POL/PAR EDU/PROP SANCTION   CT/SYS
HEALTH...TREND 20 SUPREME/CT WARRN/EARL. PAGE 22   PERSON
E0436   ADJUD

B59

FRIEDMANN W.G.,LAW IN A CHANGING SOCIETY. FUT   SOC
WOR+45 WOR-45 LAW SOCIETY STRUCT INT/TRADE LEGIT   JURID
ATTIT BIO/SOC HEALTH ORD/FREE SOVEREIGN...CONCPT
GEN/LAWS ILO 20. PAGE 41 E0803

B59

GINSBURG M.,LAW AND OPINION IN ENGLAND. UK CULTURE   JURID
KIN LABOR LEGIS EDU/PROP ADMIN CT/SYS CRIME OWN   POLICY
HEALTH...ANTHOL 20 ENGLSH/LAW. PAGE 44 E0868   ECO/TAC

B61

MURPHY E.F.,WATER PURITY: A STUDY IN LEGAL CONTROL   SEA
OF NATURAL RESOURCES. LOC/G ACT/RES PLAN TEC/DEV   LAW
LOBBY GP/REL COST ATTIT HEALTH ORD/FREE...HEAL   PROVS
JURID 20 WISCONSIN WATER. PAGE 75 E1506   CONTROL

B61

US CONGRESS,CONSTITUTIONAL RIGHTS OF THE MENTALLY   HEALTH
ILL. USA+45 LAW PUB/INST DELIB/GP ADJUD ORD/FREE   CONSTN
...PSY QU 20 CONGRESS. PAGE 99 E1989   JURID
                                                       CONFER

B62

ALEXANDROWICZ C.H.,WORLD ECONOMIC AGENCIES: LAW AND   INT/LAW
PRACTICE. WOR+45 DIST/IND FINAN LABOR CONSULT   INT/ORG
INT/TRADE TARIFFS REPRESENT HEALTH...JURID 20 UN   DIPLOM
GATT EEC OAS ECSC. PAGE 3 E0063   ADJUD

B62

ASSOCIATION BAR OF NYC,REPORT ON ADMISSION   PUB/INST
PROCEDURES TO NEW YORK STATE MENTAL HOSPITALS. LAW   HEALTH
CONSTN INGP/REL RESPECT...PSY OBS RECORD. PAGE 6   CLIENT
E0108   ROUTINE

B62

KIDDER F.E.,THESES ON PAN AMERICAN TOPICS. LAW   BIBLIOG
CULTURE NAT/G SECT DIPLOM HEALTH...ART/METH GEOG   CHRIST-17C
SOC 13/20. PAGE 61 E1213   L/A+17C
                                                       SOCIETY

B62

LAWSON R.,INTERNATIONAL REGIONAL ORGANIZATIONS.   INT/ORG
WOR+45 NAT/G VOL/ASSN CONSULT LEGIS EDU/PROP LEGIT   DELIB/GP
ADMIN EXEC ROUTINE HEALTH PWR WEALTH...JURID EEC   REGION
COLD/WAR 20 UN. PAGE 63 E1270

B62

OTTENBERG M.,THE FEDERAL INVESTIGATORS. USA+45 LAW   FORCES
COM/IND DIST/IND WORKER DIPLOM INT/TRADE CONTROL   INSPECT
FEDERAL HEALTH ORD/FREE FBI CIA FTC SEC FDA.   NAT/G
PAGE 79 E1585   CRIME

B62

STERN A.C.,AIR POLLUTION (2 VOLS.). LAW INDUS   AIR
PROB/SOLV TEC/DEV INSPECT RISK BIO/SOC HABITAT   OP/RES
...OBS/ENVIR TESTS SAMP 20 POLLUTION. PAGE 93 E1871   CONTROL
                                                       HEALTH

B62

US COMMISSION ON CIVIL RIGHTS,EQUAL PROTECTION OF   ORD/FREE
THE LAWS IN NORTH CAROLINA. USA+45 LOC/G NAT/G   RESPECT
CONSULT LEGIS WORKER PROB/SOLV EDU/PROP ADJUD   LAW

CHOOSE DISCRIM HEALTH 20 NEGRO NORTH/CAR   PROVS
CIV/RIGHTS. PAGE 99 E1984

                                                                                                              B62
US COMMISSION ON CIVIL RIGHTS,HEARINGS BEFORE   ORD/FREE
UNITED STATES COMMISSION ON CIVIL RIGHTS. USA+45 LAW
ECO/DEV NAT/G CONSULT WORKER EDU/PROP ADJUD DISCRIM ADMIN
ISOLAT HABITAT HEALTH RESPECT 20 NEGRO CIV/RIGHTS. LEGIS
PAGE 99 E1985

                                                                                                              L62
UNITED NATIONS,"CAPITAL PUNISHMENT." WOR+45 CULTURE LAW
NAT/G ROUTINE COERCE HEALTH PWR...POLICY SOC QU   STAT
CHARTS VAL/FREE 20. PAGE 98 E1967

                                                                                                              B63
CARTER G.M.,FIVE AFRICAN STATES: RESPONSES TO   AFR
DIVERSITY. CONSTN CULTURE STRATA LEGIS PLAN ECO/TAC SOCIETY
DOMIN EDU/PROP CT/SYS EXEC CHOOSE ATTIT HEALTH
ORD/FREE PWR...TIME/SEQ TOT/POP VAL/FREE. PAGE 20
E0398

                                                                                                              L63
LISSITZYN O.J.,"INTERNATIONAL LAW IN A DIVIDED   INT/ORG
WORLD." FUT WOR+45 CONSTN CULTURE ECO/DEV ECO/UNDEV LAW
DIST/IND NAT/G FORCES ECO/TAC LEGIT ADJUD ADMIN
COERCE ATTIT HEALTH MORAL ORD/FREE PWR RESPECT
WEALTH VAL/FREE. PAGE 65 E1306

                                                                                                              L63
MCDOUGAL M.S.,"THE ENJOYMENT AND ACQUISITION OF   PLAN
RESOURCES IN OUTER SPACE." CHRIST-17C FUT WOR+45 TREND
WOR-45 LAW EXTR/IND INT/ORG ACT/RES CREATE TEC/DEV
ECO/TAC LEGIT COERCE HEALTH KNOWL ORD/FREE PWR
WEALTH...JURID HIST/WRIT VAL/FREE. PAGE 70 E1408

                                                                                                              B64
BLOUSTEIN E.J.,NUCLEAR ENERGY, PUBLIC POLICY, AND TEC/DEV
THE LAW. USA+45 NAT/G ADJUD ADMIN GP/REL OWN PEACE LAW
ATTIT HEALTH...ANTHOL 20. PAGE 13 E0251   POLICY
                                                  NUC/PWR

                                                                                                              B64
CLINARD M.B.,ANOMIE AND DEVIANT BEHAVIOR: A   PERSON
DISCUSSION AND CRITIQUE. SOCIETY FACE/GP CRIME   ANOMIE
STRANGE ATTIT BIO/SOC DISPL RIGID/FLEX HEALTH...PSY KIN
CONCPT BIBLIOG 20 MERTON/R. PAGE 23 E0456   NEIGH

                                                                                                              B64
WRIGHT G.,RURAL REVOLUTION IN FRANCE: THE PEASANTRY PWR
IN THE TWENTIETH CENTURY. EUR+WWI MOD/EUR LAW   STRATA
CULTURE AGRI POL/PAR DELIB/GP LEGIS ECO/TAC   FRANCE
EDU/PROP COERCE CHOOSE ATTIT RIGID/FLEX HEALTH   REV
...STAT CENSUS CHARTS VAL/FREE 20. PAGE 107 E2148

                                                                                                              B65
BROMBERG W.,CRIME AND THE MIND. LAW LEGIT ADJUD   CRIMLGY
CRIME MURDER AGE/Y ANOMIE BIO/SOC DRIVE SEX PSY. SOC
PAGE 16 E0305   HEALTH
                                                  COERCE

                                                                                                              B65
SCHROEDER O.,DEFACTO SEGREGATION AND CIVIL RIGHTS. ANTHOL
LAW PROVS SCHOOL WORKER ATTIT HABITAT HEALTH WEALTH DISCRIM
...JURID CHARTS 19/20 NEGRO SUPREME/CT KKK. PAGE 88 RACE/REL
E1766   ORD/FREE

                                                                                                              B65
US OFFICE ECONOMIC OPPORTUNITY,CATALOG OF FEDERAL BIBLIOG
PROGRAMS FOR INDIVIDUAL AND COMMUNITY IMPROVEMENT. CLIENT
USA+45 GIVE RECEIVE ADMIN HEALTH KNOWL SKILL WEALTH ECO/TAC
CHARTS. PAGE 101 E2021   MUNIC

                                                                                                              L65
FORTE W.E.,"THE FOOD AND DRUG ADMINISTRATION, THE CONTROL
FEDERAL TRADE COMMISSION AND THE DECEPTIVE   HEALTH
PACKAGING." ROUTINE...JURID 20 FTC. PAGE 39 E0772 ADJUD
                                                  INDUS

                                                                                                              S65
GROSS L.,"PROBLEMS OF INTERNATIONAL ADJUDICATION LAW
AND COMPLIANCE WITH INTERNATIONAL LAW: SOME SIMPLE METH/CNCPT
SOLUTIONS." WOR+45 SOCIETY NAT/G DOMIN LEGIT ADJUD INT/LAW
CT/SYS RIGID/FLEX HEALTH PWR...JURID NEW/IDEA
COLD/WAR 20. PAGE 48 E0951

                                                                                                              B66
MACIVER R.M.,THE PREVENTION AND CONTROL OF   AGE/Y
DELINQUENCY. USA+45 STRATA PUB/INST ANOMIE ATTIT PLAN
HABITAT PERSON HEALTH...CRIMLGY PSY SOC METH.   ADJUST
PAGE 67 E1341   CRIME

                                                                                                              B66
MILLER E.W.,THE NEGRO IN AMERICA: A BIBLIOGRAPHY. BIBLIOG
USA+45 LAW EDU/PROP REV GOV/REL GP/REL INGP/REL   DISCRIM
ADJUST HABITAT PERSON HEALTH ORD/FREE SOC/INTEG 20 RACE/REL

NEGRO. PAGE 73 E1459

                                                                                                              B66
US HOUSE COMM ON JUDICIARY,CIVIL COMMITMENT AND   BIO/SOC
TREATMENT OF NARCOTIC ADDICTS. USA+45 SOCIETY FINAN CRIME
LEGIS PROB/SOLV GIVE CT/SYS SANCTION HEALTH   IDEA/COMP
...POLICY HEAL 20. PAGE 100 E2008   CONTROL

                                                                                                              B66
US PRES COMN CRIME IN DC,REPORT OF THE US   CRIME
PRESIDENT'S COMMISSION ON CRIME IN THE DISTRICT OF FORCES
COLUMBIA. LEGIS WORKER EDU/PROP ADJUD CONTROL   AGE/Y
CT/SYS GP/REL BIO/SOC HEALTH...CRIMLGY NEW/IDEA   SANCTION
STAT 20. PAGE 101 E2022

                                                                                                              B67
DEBOLD R.C.,LSD, MAN AND SOCIETY. USA+45 LAW   HEALTH
SOCIETY SECT CONTROL SANCTION STRANGE ATTIT...HEAL DRIVE
CHARTS ANTHOL BIBLIOG. PAGE 30 E0601   PERSON
                                                  BIO/SOC

                                                                                                              B67
ELDRIDGE W.B.,NARCOTICS AND THE LAW: A CRITIQUE OF LAW
THE AMERICAN EXPERIMENT IN NARCOTIC DRUG CONTROL. INSPECT
PUB/INST ACT/RES PLAN LICENSE GP/REL EFFICIENCY   BIO/SOC
ATTIT HEALTH...CRIMLGY HEAL STAT 20 ABA DEPT/HEW JURID
NARCO/ACT. PAGE 34 E0679

                                                                                                              B67
HODGKINSON R.G.,THE ORIGINS OF THE NATIONAL HEALTH HEAL
SERVICE: THE MEDICAL SERVICES OF THE NEW POOR LAW, NAT/G
1834-1871. UK INDUS MUNIC WORKER PROB/SOLV   POLICY
EFFICIENCY ATTIT HEALTH WEALTH SOCISM...JURID   LAW
SOC/WK 19/20. PAGE 53 E1062

                                                                                                              L67
CARMICHAEL D.M.,"FORTY YEARS OF WATER POLLUTION   HEALTH
CONTROL IN WISCONSIN: A CASE STUDY." LAW EXTR/IND CONTROL
INDUS MUNIC DELIB/GP PLAN PROB/SOLV SANCTION   ADMIN
...CENSUS CHARTS 20 WISCONSIN. PAGE 20 E0384   ADJUD

                                                                                                              S67
MACLEOD R.M.,"LAW, MEDICINE AND PUBLIC OPINION: THE LAW
RESISTANCE TO COMPULSORY HEALTH LEGISLATION   HEALTH
1870-1907." UK CONSTN SECT DELIB/GP DEBATE   ATTIT
PARL/PROC GP/REL MORAL 19. PAGE 67 E1344

                                                                                                              S67
WILLIG S.H.,"THE CONTROL OVER INTERSTATE   DIST/IND
DISTRIBUTION AND USE OF INVESTIGATIONAL DRUGS (IN HEALTH
THE UNITED STATES)" USA+45 NAT/G INT/TRADE LICENSE. CONTROL
PAGE 106 E2124   DELIB/GP

                                                                                                              C93
PLAYFAIR R.L.,"A BIBLIOGRAPHY OF MOROCCO." MOROCCO BIBLIOG
CULTURE AGRI FORCES DIPLOM WAR HEALTH...GEOG JURID ISLAM
SOC CHARTS. PAGE 81 E1620   MEDIT-7

HEAP D. E1020

HECTOR L.J. E1021

HEGEL G.W.F. E1022,E1023

HEGEL/G....GEORG WILHELM FRIEDRICH HEGEL

                                                                                                              L11
POUND R.,"THE SCOPE AND PURPOSE OF SOCIOLOGICAL   JURID
JURISPRUDENCE."...GEN/LAWS 20 KANT/I HEGEL/GWF.   IDEA/COMP
PAGE 81 E1634   METH/COMP
                                                  SOC

                                                                                                              B63
HABERMAS J.,THEORIE UND PRAXIS. RATIONAL PERSON   JURID
...PHIL/SCI ANTHOL 19/20 HEGEL/GWF MARX/KARL BLOCH REV
LOWITH. PAGE 49 E0969   GEN/LAWS
                                                  MARXISM

HEIDENHEIMER A. E1714

HEILBRNR/R....ROBERT HEILBRONER

HEINRICH W. E0979

HEKHUIS D.J. E1024

HELLMAN F.S. E0311,E1025,E1026

HENDEL S. E0232

HENDERSON D.F. E1028,E1029

HENDERSON W.O. E1030

HENKE W. E1031

HENKIN L. E1032

HERDER/J....JOHANN GOTTFRIED VON HERDER

HEREDITY....GENETIC INFLUENCES ON PERSONALITY DEVELOPMENT
    AND SOCIAL GROWTH

B47
LOCKE J.,TWO TREATISES OF GOVERNMENT (1690). UK LAW CONCPT
SOCIETY LEGIS LEGIT AGREE REV OWN HEREDITY MORAL ORD/FREE
CONSERVE...POLICY MAJORIT 17 WILLIAM/3 NATURL/LAW. NAT/G
PAGE 66 E1316 CONSEN

B51
PUSEY M.J.,CHARLES EVANS HUGHES (2 VOLS.). LAW BIOG
CONSTN NAT/G POL/PAR DIPLOM LEGIT WAR CHOOSE TOP/EX
PERS/REL DRIVE HEREDITY 19/20 DEPT/STATE LEAGUE/NAT ADJUD
SUPREME/CT HUGHES/CE WWI. PAGE 83 E1663 PERSON

B53
GROSS B.M.,THE LEGISLATIVE STRUGGLE: A STUDY IN LEGIS
SOCIAL COMBAT. STRUCT LOC/G POL/PAR JUDGE EDU/PROP DECISION
DEBATE ETIQUET ADMIN LOBBY CHOOSE GOV/REL INGP/REL PERSON
HEREDITY ALL/VALS...SOC PRESIDENT. PAGE 48 E0948 LEAD

S59
DERGE D.R.,"THE LAWYER AS DECISION-MAKER IN THE LEGIS
AMERICAN STATE LEGISLATURE." INTELL LOC/G POL/PAR LAW
CHOOSE AGE HEREDITY PERSON CONSERVE...JURID STAT DECISION
CHARTS. PAGE 31 E0607 LEAD

HERESY....HERESY

HERRING E.P. E1033

HERRMANN K. E1034

HERZ J.H. E0768

HEWITT W.H. E1035

HEYDECKER J.J. E1036

HEYSE T. E1037

HIBBS A.R. E1038

HICKEY D. E1039

HIDAYATULLAH M. E1040

HIESTAND/F....FRED J. HIESTAND

HIGGINS R. E1041,E1042,E1043

HIGGINS/G....GODFREY HIGGINS

HIGHSAW R.B. E1044

HIGHWAY PLANNING AND DEVELOPMENT....SEE HIGHWAY

HIGHWAY....HIGHWAY PLANNING AND DEVELOPMENT

HILL D.G. E1045

HILL M. E1046

HILL N. E1047

HILLS R.J. E1048

HINDERLING A. E1049

HINDU....HINDUISM AND HINDU PEOPLE

B65
GAJENDRAGADKAR P.B.,LAW, LIBERTY AND SOCIAL ORD/FREE
JUSTICE. INDIA CONSTN NAT/G SECT PLAN ECO/TAC PRESS LAW
POPULISM...SOC METH/COMP 20 HINDU. PAGE 42 E0826 ADJUD
JURID

HIROSHIMA....SEE WAR, NUC/PWR, PLAN, PROB/SOLV, CONSULT

HIRSCH W.Z. E1050

HIRSCHFIELD R.S. E1051

HIRSHBERG A. E0571

HIRSHBERG H.S. E1052

HISS A. E1053

HISS/ALGER....ALGER HISS

B57
HISS A.,IN THE COURT OF PUBLIC OPINION. USA+45 CRIME
DELIB/GP LEGIS LEGIT CT/SYS ATTIT 20 DEPT/STATE MARXISM
NIXON/RM HUAC HISS/ALGER. PAGE 53 E1053 BIOG
ADJUD

HIST....HISTORY, INCLUDING CURRENT EVENTS

HIST/WRIT....HISTORIOGRAPHY

B00
MAINE H.S.,ANCIENT LAW. MEDIT-7 CULTURE SOCIETY KIN FAM
SECT LEGIS LEGIT ROUTINE...JURID HIST/WRIT CON/ANAL LAW
TOT/POP VAL/FREE. PAGE 68 E1350

B27
LAUTERPACHT H.,PRIVATE LAW SOURCES AND ANALOGIES OF INT/ORG
INTERNATIONAL LAW. WOR-45 NAT/G DELIB/GP LEGIT ADJUD
COERCE ATTIT ORD/FREE PWR SOVEREIGN...JURID CONCPT PEACE
HIST/WRIT TIME/SEQ GEN/METH LEAGUE/NAT 20. PAGE 63 INT/LAW
E1264

B28
BUTLER G.,THE DEVELOPMENT OF INTERNATIONAL LAW. LAW
WOR-45 SOCIETY NAT/G KNOWL ORD/FREE PWR...JURID INT/LAW
CONCPT HIST/WRIT GEN/LAWS. PAGE 18 E0349 DIPLOM
INT/ORG

B28
HOLDSWORTH W.S.,THE HISTORIANS OF ANGLO-AMERICAN HIST/WRIT
LAW. UK USA-45 INTELL LEGIS RESPECT...BIOG NAT/COMP LAW
17/20 COMMON/LAW. PAGE 54 E1076 JURID

L28
HUDSON M.,"THE TEACHING OF INTERNATIONAL LAW IN PERCEPT
AMERICA." USA-45 LAW CONSULT ACT/RES CREATE KNOWL
EDU/PROP ATTIT RIGID/FLEX...JURID CONCPT RECORD INT/LAW
HIST/WRIT TREND GEN/LAWS 18/20. PAGE 56 E1109

B32
MASTERS R.D.,INTERNATIONAL LAW IN INTERNATIONAL INT/ORG
COURTS. BELGIUM EUR+WWI FRANCE GERMANY MOD/EUR LAW
SWITZERLND WOR-45 SOCIETY STRATA STRUCT LEGIT EXEC INT/LAW
ALL/VALS...JURID HIST/WRIT TIME/SEQ TREND GEN/LAWS
20. PAGE 69 E1383

B36
CULVER D.C.,METHODOLOGY OF SOCIAL SCIENCE RESEARCH: BIBLIOG/A
A BIBLIOGRAPHY. LAW CULTURE...CRIMLGY GEOG STAT OBS METH
INT QU HIST/WRIT CHARTS 20. PAGE 28 E0550 SOC

B39
LAVES W.H.C.,INTERNATIONAL SECURITY. EUR+WWI ORD/FREE
GERMANY UK USA-45 LAW NAT/G DELIB/GP TOP/EX COERCE LEGIT
PWR...POLICY FASCIST CONCPT HIST/WRIT GEN/LAWS ARMS/CONT
LEAGUE/NAT NAZI 20. PAGE 63 E1267 BAL/PWR

B45
CONOVER H.F.,THE NAZI STATE: WAR CRIMES AND WAR BIBLIOG
CRIMINALS. GERMANY CULTURE NAT/G SECT FORCES DIPLOM WAR
INT/TRADE EDU/PROP...INT/LAW BIOG HIST/WRIT CRIME
TIME/SEQ 20. PAGE 25 E0495

B46
KEETON G.W.,MAKING INTERNATIONAL LAW WORK. FUT INT/ORG
WOR-45 NAT/G DELIB/GP FORCES LEGIT COERCE PEACE ADJUD
ATTIT RIGID/FLEX ORD/FREE PWR...JURID CONCPT INT/LAW
HIST/WRIT GEN/METH LEAGUE/NAT 20. PAGE 60 E1193

B50
MACIVER R.M.,GREAT EXPRESSIONS OF HUMAN RIGHTS. LAW UNIV
CONSTN CULTURE INTELL SOCIETY R+D INT/ORG ATTIT CONCPT
DRIVE...JURID OBS HIST/WRIT GEN/LAWS. PAGE 67 E1340

B54
NUSSBAUM D.,A CONCISE HISTORY OF THE LAW OF INT/ORG
NATIONS. CHRIST-17C EUR+WWI ISLAM MEDIT-7 LAW
MOD/EUR S/ASIA UNIV WOR+45 WOR-45 SOCIETY STRUCT PEACE
EXEC ATTIT ALL/VALS...CONCPT HIST/WRIT TIME/SEQ. INT/LAW
PAGE 78 E1560

B56
PERKINS D.,CHARLES EVANS HUGHES AND THE AMERICAN PERSON
DEMOCRATIC STATESMANSHIP. USA+45 USA-45 NAT/G BIOG
POL/PAR DELIB/GP JUDGE PLAN MORAL PWR...HIST/WRIT DIPLOM
LEAGUE/NAT 20. PAGE 80 E1609

S59
SUTTON F.X.,"REPRESENTATION AND THE NATURE OF NAT/G
POLITICAL SYSTEMS." UNIV WOR-45 CULTURE SOCIETY CONCPT
STRATA INT/ORG FORCES JUDGE DOMIN LEGIT EXEC REGION
REPRESENT ATTIT ORD/FREE RESPECT...SOC HIST/WRIT
TIME/SEQ. PAGE 95 E1896

S59
TIPTON J.B.,"PARTICIPATION OF THE UNITED STATES IN   LABOR
THE INTERNATIONAL LABOR ORGANIZATION." USA+45 LAW   INT/ORG
STRUCT ECO/DEV ECO/UNDEV INDUS TEC/DEV ECO/TAC
ADMIN PERCEPT ORD/FREE SKILL...STAT HIST/WRIT
GEN/METH ILO WORK 20. PAGE 96 E1928

S60
NICHOLS J.P.,"HAZARDS OF AMERICAN PRIVATE   FINAN
INVESTMENT IN UNDERDEVELOPED COUNTRIES." FUT   ECO/UNDEV
L/A+17C USA+45 USA-45 EXTR/IND CONSULT BAL/PWR   CAP/ISM
ECO/TAC DOMIN ADJUD ATTIT SOVEREIGN WEALTH   NAT/LISM
...HIST/WRIT TIME/SEQ TREND VAL/FREE 20. PAGE 77
E1546

S60
SCHWELB E.,"INTERNATIONAL CONVENTIONS ON HUMAN   INT/ORG
RIGHTS." FUT WOR+45 LAW CONSTN CULTURE SOCIETY   HUM
STRUCT VOL/ASSN DELIB/GP PLAN ADJUD SUPEGO LOVE
MORAL...SOC CONCPT STAT RECORD HIST/WRIT TREND 20
UN. PAGE 89 E1790

B61
CONFERENCE ATLANTIC COMMUNITY,AN INTRODUCTORY   BIBLIOG/A
BIBLIOGRAPHY. COM WOR+45 FORCES DIPLOM ECO/TAC WAR   CON/ANAL
...INT/LAW HIST/WRIT COLD/WAR NATO. PAGE 25 E0485   INT/ORG

S61
HARVEY W.B.,"THE RULE OF LAW IN HISTORICAL   ACT/RES
PERSPECTIVE." USA+45 WOR+45 INTELL SOCIETY ECO/DEV   LAW
ECO/UNDEV NAT/G EX/STRUC LEGIS TOP/EX LEGIT SKILL
...CONCPT HIST/WRIT TOT/POP. PAGE 51 E1010

B63
ROSNER G.,THE UNITED NATIONS EMERGENCY FORCE.   INT/ORG
FRANCE ISRAEL UAR UK WOR+45 CREATE WAR PEACE   FORCES
ORD/FREE PWR...INT/LAW JURID HIST/WRIT TIME/SEQ UN.
PAGE 86 E1719

L63
MCDOUGAL M.S.,"THE ENJOYMENT AND ACQUISITION OF   PLAN
RESOURCES IN OUTER SPACE." CHRIST-17C FUT WOR+45   TREND
WOR-45 LAW EXTR/IND INT/ORG ACT/RES CREATE TEC/DEV
ECO/TAC LEGIT COERCE HEALTH KNOWL ORD/FREE PWR
WEALTH...JURID HIST/WRIT VAL/FREE. PAGE 70 E1408

S63
BRAUSCH G.E.,"AFRICAN ETHNOCRACIES: SOME   LAW
SOCIOLOGICAL IMPLICATIONS OF CONSTITUTIONAL CHANGE   SOC
IN EMERGENT TERRITORIES OF AFRICA." AFR CONSTN   ELITES
FACE/GP MUNIC NAT/G DOMIN ATTIT ALL/VALS
...HIST/WRIT GEN/LAWS VAL/FREE 20. PAGE 15 E0289

S64
KHAN M.Z.,"ISLAM AND INTERNATIONAL RELATIONS." FUT   ISLAM
WOR+45 LAW CULTURE SOCIETY NAT/G SECT DELIB/GP   INT/ORG
FORCES EDU/PROP ATTIT PERSON SUPEGO ALL/VALS   DIPLOM
...POLICY PSY CONCPT MYTH HIST/WRIT GEN/LAWS.
PAGE 61 E1211

S64
PARADIES F.,"SOBRE LA HISTORIA DE LA LOGICA Y DE LA   ADJUD
LOGICA JURIDICA." LEGIT KNOWL...JURID METH/CNCPT
HIST/WRIT 20. PAGE 80 E1597

L66
YALEM R.J.,"THE STUDY OF INTERNATIONAL   VOL/ASSN
ORGANIZATION, 1920-1965* A SURVEY OF THE   INT/ORG
LITERATURE." WOR+45 WOR-45 REGION...INT/LAW CLASSIF   BIBLIOG/A
RECORD HIST/WRIT CON/ANAL IDEA/COMP UN. PAGE 108
E2163

B67
MANVELL R.,THE INCOMPARABLE CRIME. GERMANY ACT/RES   MURDER
DEATH...BIBLIOG 20 JEWS. PAGE 68 E1364   CRIME
                                                        WAR
                                                        HIST/WRIT

B67
NARAIN I.,THE POLITICS OF RACIALISM. INDIA   DISCRIM
SOUTH/AFR LAW NAT/G RACE/REL ATTIT 20. PAGE 76   COLONIAL
E1521   HIST/WRIT

L67
HITCHMAN J.M.,"THE PLATT AMENDMENT REVISITED: A   ATTIT
BIBLIOGRAPHICAL SURVEY." CUBA ACADEM DELIB/GP   DIPLOM
ORD/FREE...HIST/WRIT 20. PAGE 53 E1055   SOVEREIGN
                                                        INT/LAW

S68
SHAPIRO J.P.,"SOVIET HISTORIOGRAPHY AND THE MOSCOW   HIST/WRIT
TRIALS: AFTER THIRTY YEARS." USSR NAT/G LEGIT PRESS   EDU/PROP
CONTROL LEAD ATTIT MARXISM...NEW/IDEA METH 20   SANCTION
TROTSKY/L STALIN/J KHRUSH/N. PAGE 90 E1810   ADJUD

HISTORICUS E1054

HITCHMAN J.M. E1055

HITLER/A....ADOLF HITLER

S44
MASON J.B.,"THE JUDICIAL SYSTEM OF THE NAZI PARTY."   FASCISM
GERMANY ELITES POL/PAR DOMIN CONTROL SANCTION   CT/SYS
TOTALISM...JURID 20 HITLER/A. PAGE 69 E1381   ADJUD
                                                        LAW

HO/CHI/MIN....HO CHI MINH

HOBBES T. E1056,E1057

HOBBES/T....THOMAS HOBBES

B42
GURVITCH G.,SOCIOLOGY OF LAW. CONSTN SOCIETY CREATE   SOC
MORAL SOVEREIGN...POLICY EPIST JURID PHIL/SCI   LAW
IDEA/COMP METH/COMP HOLMES/OW HOBBES/T. PAGE 48   ADJUD
E0964

B64
GUMPLOWICZ L.,RECHTSSTAAT UND SOZIALISMUS. STRATA   JURID
ORD/FREE SOVEREIGN MARXISM...IDEA/COMP 16/20 KANT/I   NAT/G
HOBBES/T. PAGE 48 E0962   SOCISM
                                                        CONCPT

HOBSBAWM E.J. E1058

HOBSON J.A. E1059

HOCKING W.E. E1060,E1061

HODES F. E0260

HODGKINSON R.G. E1062

HOEBEL E.A. E1063

HOEVELER H.J. E1064

HOFFA/J....JAMES HOFFA

B63
JACOBS P.,STATE OF UNIONS. USA+45 STRATA TOP/EX   LABOR
GP/REL RACE/REL DEMAND DISCRIM ATTIT PWR 20   ECO/TAC
CONGRESS NEGRO HOFFA/J. PAGE 57 E1145   BARGAIN
                                                        DECISION

HOGAN J.D. E1065

HOGAN W.N. E1066,E2071

HOGARTY R.A. E1067

HOGUE A.R. E1068

HOHFELD W.N. E1069

HOLCOMBE A. E1070

HOLCOMBE A.N. E1071,E1072

HOLDSWORTH W.S. E1073,E1074,E1075,E1076,E1077,E1078,E1079,E1080
     E1081,E1082,E1083

HOLIFLD/C....CHET HOLIFIELD

HOLLAND T.E. E1084,E1085

HOLLAND....SEE NETHERLAND

HOLLERAN M.P. E1086

HOLMES O.W. E1087,E1088

HOLMES/OW....OLIVER WENDELL HOLMES

B38
FRANKFURTER F.,MR. JUSTICE HOLMES AND THE SUPREME   CREATE
COURT. USA-45 CONSTN SOCIETY FEDERAL OWN ATTIT   CT/SYS
ORD/FREE PWR...POLICY JURID 20 SUPREME/CT HOLMES/OW   DECISION
BILL/RIGHT. PAGE 40 E0790   LAW

B42
GURVITCH G.,SOCIOLOGY OF LAW. CONSTN SOCIETY CREATE   SOC
MORAL SOVEREIGN...POLICY EPIST JURID PHIL/SCI   LAW
IDEA/COMP METH/COMP HOLMES/OW HOBBES/T. PAGE 48   ADJUD
E0964

B49
FRANK J.,LAW AND THE MODERN MIND. UNIV LAW CT/SYS   JURID
RATIONAL ATTIT...CONCPT 20 HOLMES/OW JURY. PAGE 40   ADJUD
E0787   IDEA/COMP
                                                        MYTH

B52
CAHILL F.V.,JUDICIAL LEGISLATION: A STUDY IN   JURID
AMERICAN LEGAL THEORY. USA+45 USA-45 LAW NAT/G   ADJUD
GP/REL...POLICY PHIL/SCI SOC 20 HOLMES/OW. PAGE 18   LEGIS
E0359   CONTROL

B60
MENDELSON W.,CAPITALISM, DEMOCRACY, AND THE SUPREME   JUDGE
COURT. USA+45 USA-45 CONSTN DIPLOM GOV/REL ATTIT   CT/SYS
ORD/FREE LAISSEZ...POLICY CHARTS PERS/COMP 18/20   JURID
SUPREME/CT MARSHALL/J HOLMES/OW TANEY/RB FIELD/JJ.   NAT/G
PAGE 72 E1437

B62
BICKEL A.,THE LEAST DANGEROUS BRANCH. USA+45 USA-45   LAW
CONSTN SCHOOL LEGIS ADJUD RACE/REL DISCRIM ORD/FREE   NAT/G
...JURID 18/20 SUPREME/CT CONGRESS MARSHALL/J   CT/SYS
HOLMES/OW FRANKFUR/F. PAGE 12 E0226

B64
HURST W.H.,JUSTICE HOLMES ON LEGAL HISTORY. USA-45   ADJUD
LAW SOCIETY NAT/G WRITING...POLICY PHIL/SCI SOC   JURID
CONCPT 20 HOLMES/OW SUPREME/CT ENGLSH/LAW. PAGE 56   BIOG
E1117

B66
HOLMES O.W.,JUSTICE HOLMES, EX CATHEDRA. USA+45   BIOG
USA-45 LAW INTELL ADMIN ATTIT...BIBLIOG 20   PERSON
SUPREME/CT HOLMES/OW. PAGE 55 E1088   CT/SYS
                                                      ADJUD

B67
KING W.L.,MELVILLE WESTON FULLER: CHIEF JUSTICE OF   BIOG
THE UNITED STATES, 1888-1910. USA-45 CONSTN FINAN   CT/SYS
LABOR TAX GOV/REL PERS/REL ATTIT PERSON PWR...JURID   LAW
BIBLIOG 19/20 SUPREME/CT FULLER/MW HOLMES/OW.   ADJUD
PAGE 61 E1216

HOLMES/OWJ....OLIVER WENDELL HOLMES, JR.

HOLSTI K.J. E1089,E1090

HOLSTI/KJ....K.J. HOLSTI

HOLT S. E1091

HOLTZMAN A. E1092

HOMEOSTASIS....SEE FEEDBACK

HOMER....HOMER

HOMEST/ACT....HOMESTEAD ACT OF 1862

B63
OTTOSON H.W.,LAND USE POLICY AND PROBLEMS IN THE   PROB/SOLV
UNITED STATES. USA+45 USA-45 LAW AGRI INDUS NAT/G   UTIL
GP/REL...CHARTS ANTHOL 19/20 HOMEST/ACT. PAGE 79   HABITAT
E1586   POLICY

HOMESTEAD ACT OF 1862....SEE HOMEST/ACT

HOMICIDE....SEE MURDER

HOMOSEXUAL....HOMOSEXUALITY; SEE ALSO BIO/SOC, CRIME, SEX

HONDURAS....SEE ALSO L/A+17C

N19
PAN AMERICAN UNION,INFORME DE LA MISION DE   CHOOSE
ASISTENCIA TECNICA DE LA OEA A LA REPUBLICA DE   SUFF
HONDURAS EN MATERIA ELECTORAL (PAMPHLET). HONDURAS   POL/PAR
CONSTN ORD/FREE...JURID OBS 20 OAS. PAGE 80 E1595   NAT/G

B47
NEUBURGER O.,GUIDE TO OFFICIAL PUBLICATIONS OF   BIBLIOG/A
OTHER AMERICAN REPUBLICS: HONDURAS (VOL. XIII).   NAT/G
HONDURAS LAW LEGIS ADMIN CT/SYS...JURID 19/20.   EDU/PROP
PAGE 76 E1533   CONSTN

HONG/KONG....HONG KONG

B62
HSUEH S.-.S.,GOVERNMENT AND ADMINISTRATION OF HONG   ADMIN
KONG. CHIEF DELIB/GP LEGIS CT/SYS REPRESENT GOV/REL   LOC/G
20 HONG/KONG CITY/MGT CIVIL/SERV GOVERNOR. PAGE 55   COLONIAL
E1106   EX/STRUC

B64
ENDACOTT G.B.,GOVERNMENT AND PEOPLE IN HONG KONG   CONSTN
1841-1962: A CONSTITUTIONAL HISTORY. UK LEGIS ADJUD   COLONIAL
REPRESENT ATTIT 19/20 HONG/KONG. PAGE 35 E0688   CONTROL
                                                      ADMIN

HOOD W.C. E1093

HOOK S. E1094,E1095

HOOVER/H....HERBERT HOOVER

HOPI....HOPI INDIANS

HOPKINS J.F.K. E1096

HOPKINS/H....HARRY HOPKINS

HOPKINSON T. E1097

HORRELL M. E1098

HORVATH B. E1099

HOSPITALS....SEE PUB/INST

HOUSE OF REPRESENTATIVES....SEE HOUSE/REP

HOUSE RULES COMMITTEE....SEE HOUSE/REP

HOUSE UNAMERICAN ACTIVITIES COMMITTEE....SEE HUAC

HOUSE/CMNS....HOUSE OF COMMONS (ALL NATIONS)

B39
MCILWAIN C.H.,CONSTITUTIONALISM AND THE CHANGING   CONSTN
WORLD. UK USA-45 LEGIS PRIVIL AUTHORIT SOVEREIGN   POLICY
...GOV/COMP 15/20 MAGNA/CART HOUSE/CMNS. PAGE 71   JURID
E1417

HOUSE/LORD....HOUSE OF LORDS (ALL NATIONS)

HOUSE/REP....HOUSE OF REPRESENTATIVES (ALL NATIONS); SEE
          ALSO CONGRESS, LEGIS

B08
WILSON W.,CONSTITUTIONAL GOVERNMENT IN THE UNITED   NAT/G
STATES. USA-45 LAW POL/PAR PROVS CHIEF LEGIS   GOV/REL
BAL/PWR ADJUD EXEC FEDERAL PWR 18/20 SUPREME/CT   CONSTN
HOUSE/REP SENATE. PAGE 106 E2130   PARL/PROC

B56
ZINN C.J.,HOW OUR LAWS ARE MADE: BROCHURE HOUSE OF   LEGIS
REPRESENTATIVES DOCUMENT 451. LAW CONSTN CHIEF   DELIB/GP
EX/STRUC PROB/SOLV HOUSE/REP SENATE. PAGE 108 E2171   PARL/PROC
                                                      ROUTINE

S58
RIKER W.H.,"THE PARADOX OF VOTING AND CONGRESSIONAL   PARL/PROC
RULES FOR VOTING ON AMENDMENTS." LAW DELIB/GP   DECISION
EX/STRUC PROB/SOLV CONFER DEBATE EFFICIENCY ATTIT   LEGIS
HOUSE/REP CONGRESS SENATE. PAGE 85 E1700   RATIONAL

B60
US HOUSE COMM ON JUDICIARY,ESTABLISHMENT OF   APPORT
CONGRESSIONAL DISTRICTS. USA+45 PROB/SOLV 20   REPRESENT
CONGRESS HOUSE/REP. PAGE 100 E2003   LEGIS
                                                      LAW

B61
NELSON H.L.,LIBEL IN NEWS OF CONGRESSIONAL   DELIB/GP
INVESTIGATING COMMITTEES. USA+45 LAW PARL/PROC   LEGIS
PRIVIL RESPECT HOUSE/REP. PAGE 76 E1532   LICENSE
                                                      PRESS

B61
US HOUSE COMM ON JUDICIARY,LEGISLATION RELATING TO   LEGIS
ORGANIZED CRIME. USA+45 DIST/IND DELIB/GP GAMBLE   CONTROL
SANCTION HOUSE/REP. PAGE 100 E2004   CRIME
                                                      LAW

B63
SCHMIDHAUSER J.R.,CONSTITUTIONAL LAW IN THE   LAW
POLITICAL PROCESS. SOCIETY LEGIS ADJUD CT/SYS   CONSTN
FEDERAL...SOC TREND IDEA/COMP ANTHOL T SUPREME/CT   JURID
SENATE CONGRESS HOUSE/REP. PAGE 88 E1761

B64
MITCHELL B.,A BIOGRAPHY OF THE CONSTITUTION OF THE   CONSTN
UNITED STATES. USA+45 USA-45 PROVS CHIEF LEGIS   LAW
DEBATE ADJUD SUFF FEDERAL...SOC 18/20 SUPREME/CT   JURID
CONGRESS SENATE HOUSE/REP PRESIDENT. PAGE 73 E1472

B66
US HOUSE UNAMER ACTIV COMM,HEARINGS ON BILLS TO   LAW
MAKE PUNISHABLE ASSISTANCE TO ENEMIES OF US IN TIME   SANCTION
OF UNDECLARED WAR. USA+45 VIETNAM/N EDU/PROP   VOL/ASSN
CONTROL WAR MARXISM HOUSE/REP. PAGE 100 E2010   GIVE

JONES C.O.,EVERY SECOND YEAR: CONGRESSIONAL
BEHAVIOR AND THE TWO-YEAR TERM. LAW POL/PAR
PROB/SOLV DEBATE CHOOSE PERS/REL COST FEDERAL PWR
...CHARTS 20 CONGRESS SENATE HOUSE/REP. PAGE 59
E1172
B67 EFFICIENCY LEGIS TIME/SEQ NAT/G

GOSSETT W.T.,"ELECTING THE PRESIDENT: NEW HOPE FOR
AN OLD IDEAL." FUT USA+45 USA-45 PROVS LEGIS
PROB/SOLV WRITING DEBATE ADJUD REPRESENT...MAJORIT
DECISION 20 HOUSE/REP PRESIDENT. PAGE 45 E0892
S67 CONSTN CHIEF CHOOSE NAT/G

HOUSTON....HOUSTON, TEXAS

HOWARD A.E.D. E1100

HOWARD C.G. E1101

HOWARD W.S. E1102

HOWE M. E0533

HOWE M.D.W. E1103

HOWE R. E1104

HOWELL R.F. E1456

HOYT E.C. E1105

HS/SCIASTR....HOUSE COMMITTEE ON SCIENCE AND ASTRONAUTICS

HSU F.L.K. E0054

HSUEH S.-.S. E1106

HU/FENG....HU FENG

HUAC....HOUSE UNAMERICAN ACTIVITIES COMMITTEE

HISS A.,IN THE COURT OF PUBLIC OPINION. USA+45
DELIB/GP LEGIS LEGIT CT/SYS ATTIT 20 DEPT/STATE
NIXON/RM HUAC HISS/ALGER. PAGE 53 E1053
B57 CRIME MARXISM BIOG ADJUD

GINZBURG B.,REDEDICATION TO FREEDOM. DELIB/GP LEGIS
ATTIT MARXISM 20 SUPREME/CT CON/INTERP HUAC AMEND/I
FBI. PAGE 44 E0871
B59 JURID ORD/FREE CONSTN NAT/G

HUBERT C.J. E1107

HUCKLEBERRY K. E0258

HUDSON M. E1108,E1109,E1110,E1111

HUDSON M.O. E1112

HUGHES/CE....CHARLES EVANS HUGHES

PUSEY M.J.,CHARLES EVANS HUGHES (2 VOLS.). LAW
CONSTN NAT/G POL/PAR DIPLOM LEGIT WAR CHOOSE
PERS/REL DRIVE HEREDITY 19/20 DEPT/STATE LEAGUE/NAT
SUPREME/CT HUGHES/CE WWI. PAGE 83 E1663
B51 BIOG TOP/EX ADJUD PERSON

MASON A.T.,THE SUPREME COURT FROM TAFT TO WARREN.
EX/STRUC LEGIS ROLE 20 SUPREME/CT TAFT/WH HUGHES/CE
STONE/HF. PAGE 69 E1376
B58 CT/SYS JURID ADJUD

MASON A.T.,THE SUPREME COURT: PALADIUM OF FREEDOM.
USA-45 NAT/G POL/PAR CHIEF LEGIS ADJUD PARL/PROC
FEDERAL PWR...POLICY BIOG 18/20 SUPREME/CT
ROOSEVLT/F JEFFERSN/T MARSHALL/J HUGHES/CE. PAGE 69
E1378
B62 CONSTN CT/SYS JURID

HUKS....HUKS (PHILIPPINES)

HULL R.H. E1113

HUM....METHODS OF HUMANITIES, LITERARY ANALYSIS

LIBRARY INTERNATIONAL REL,INTERNATIONAL INFORMATION
SERVICE. WOR+45 CULTURE INT/ORG FORCES...GEOG HUM
SOC. PAGE 65 E1295
N BIBLIOG/A DIPLOM INT/TRADE INT/LAW

AUSTRALIAN PUBLIC AFFAIRS INFORMATION SERVICE. LAW
...HEAL HUM MGT SOC CON/ANAL 20 AUSTRAL. PAGE 1
N BIBLIOG NAT/G

E0017
CULTURE DIPLOM

BIBLIOGRAPHIE DE LA PHILOSOPHIE. LAW CULTURE SECT
EDU/PROP MORAL...HUM METH/CNCPT 20. PAGE 1 E0018
N BIBLIOG/A PHIL/SCI CONCPT LOG

LATIN AMERICA IN PERIODICAL LITERATURE. LAW TEC/DEV
DIPLOM RECEIVE EDU/PROP...GEOG HUM MGT 20. PAGE 2
E0024
N BIBLIOG/A L/A+17C SOCIETY ECO/UNDEV

PUBLISHERS' CIRCULAR, THE OFFICIAL ORGAN OF THE
PUBLISHERS' ASSOCIATION OF GREAT BRITAIN AND
IRELAND. EUR+WWI MOD/EUR UK LAW PROB/SOLV DIPLOM
COLONIAL ATTIT...HUM 19/20 CMN/WLTH. PAGE 2 E0025
N BIBLIOG/A NAT/G WRITING LEAD

AMER COUNCIL OF LEARNED SOCIET,THE ACLS CONSTITUENT
SOCIETY JOURNAL PROJECT. FUT USA+45 LAW NAT/G PLAN
DIPLOM PHIL/SCI. PAGE 4 E0072
N BIBLIOG/A HUM COMPUT/IR COMPUTER

MINISTERE DE L'EDUC NATIONALE,CATALOGUE DES THESES
DE DOCTORAT SOUTENNES DEVANT LES UNIVERSITAIRES
FRANCAISES. FRANCE LAW DIPLOM ADMIN...HUM SOC 20.
PAGE 73 E1465
N BIBLIOG ACADEM KNOWL NAT/G

HALDEMAN E.,"SERIALS OF AN INTERNATIONAL
CHARACTER." WOR-45 DIPLOM...ART/METH GEOG HEAL HUM
INT/LAW JURID PSY SOC. PAGE 49 E0978
L21 BIBLIOG PHIL/SCI

EVANS C.,AMERICAN BIBLIOGRAPHY... (12 VOLUMES).
USA-45 LAW DIPLOM ADMIN PERSON...HUM SOC 17/18.
PAGE 35 E0704
B41 BIBLIOG NAT/G ALL/VALS ALL/IDEOS

FULLER G.H.,TURKEY: A SELECTED LIST OF REFERENCES.
ISLAM TURKEY CULTURE ECO/UNDEV AGRI DIPLOM NAT/LISM
CONSERVE...GEOG HUM INT/LAW SOC 7/20 MAPS. PAGE 42
E0824
B44 BIBLIOG/A ALL/VALS

US LIBRARY OF CONGRESS,RUSSIA: A CHECK LIST
PRELIMINARY TO A BASIC BIBLIOGRAPHY OF MATERIALS IN
THE RUSSIAN LANGUAGE. COM USSR CULTURE EDU/PROP
MARXISM...ART/METH HUM LING 19/20. PAGE 101 E2015
B44 BIBLIOG LAW SECT

REVES E.,THE ANATOMY OF PEACE. WOR-45 LAW CULTURE
NAT/G PLAN TEC/DEV EDU/PROP WAR NAT/LISM ATTIT
ALL/VALS SOVEREIGN...POLICY HUM TIME/SEQ 20.
PAGE 84 E1688
B45 ACT/RES CONCPT NUC/PWR PEACE

YAKOBSON S.,FIVE HUNDRED RUSSIAN WORKS FOR COLLEGE
LIBRARIES (PAMPHLET). MOD/EUR USSR MARXISM SOCISM
...ART/METH GEOG HUM JURID SOC 13/20. PAGE 108
E2162
B48 BIBLIOG NAT/G CULTURE COM

MARITAIN J.,HUMAN RIGHTS: COMMENTS AND
INTERPRETATIONS. COM UNIV WOR+45 LAW CONSTN CULTURE
SOCIETY ECO/DEV ECO/UNDEV SCHOOL DELIB/GP EDU/PROP
ATTIT PERCEPT ALL/VALS...HUM SOC TREND UNESCO 20.
PAGE 68 E1365
B49 INT/ORG CONCPT

COUNCIL BRITISH NATIONAL BIB,BRITISH NATIONAL
BIBLIOGRAPHY. UK AGRI CONSTRUC PERF/ART POL/PAR
SECT CREATE INT/TRADE LEAD...HUM JURID PHIL/SCI 20.
PAGE 26 E0519
B50 BIBLIOG/A NAT/G TEC/DEV DIPLOM

DOROSH J.T.,GUIDE TO SOVIET BIBLIOGRAPHIES. USSR
LAW AGRI SCHOOL SECT FORCES TEC/DEV...ART/METH GEOG
HUM SOC 20. PAGE 32 E0639
B50 BIBLIOG METH CON/ANAL

EMBREE J.F.,BIBLIOGRAPHY OF THE PEOPLES AND
CULTURES OF MAINLAND SOUTHEAST ASIA. CAMBODIA LAOS
THAILAND VIETNAM LAW...GEOG HUM SOC MYTH LING
CHARTS WORSHIP 20. PAGE 35 E0686
B50 BIBLIOG/A CULTURE S/ASIA

HUXLEY J.,FREEDOM AND CULTURE. UNIV LAW SOCIETY R+D
ACADEM SCHOOL CREATE SANCTION ATTIT KNOWL...HUM
ANTHOL 20. PAGE 56 E1118
B51 CULTURE ORD/FREE PHIL/SCI

IDEA/COMP

B53
CURRIER T.F.,A BIBLIOGRAPHY OF OLIVER WENDELL
HOLMES. USA-45...BIOG 19/20. PAGE 28 E0557
BIBLIOG/A
HUM
JURID
JUDGE

B58
KURL S.,ESTONIA: A SELECTED BIBLIOGRAPHY. USSR
ESTONIA LAW INTELL SECT...ART/METH GEOG HUM SOC 20.
PAGE 62 E1238
BIBLIOG
CULTURE
NAT/G

B58
MASON H.L.,TOYNBEE'S APPROACH TO WORLD POLITICS.
AFR USA+45 USSR LAW WAR NAT/LISM ALL/IDEOS...HUM
BIBLIOG. PAGE 69 E1380
DIPLOM
CONCPT
PHIL/SCI
SECT

S60
SCHWELB E.,"INTERNATIONAL CONVENTIONS ON HUMAN
RIGHTS." FUT WOR+45 LAW CONSTN CULTURE SOCIETY
STRUCT VOL/ASSN DELIB/GP PLAN ADJUD SUPEGO LOVE
MORAL...SOC CONCPT STAT RECORD HIST/WRIT TREND 20
UN. PAGE 89 E1790
INT/ORG
HUM

B64
BERNSTEIN H.,A BOOKSHELF ON BRAZIL. BRAZIL ADMIN
COLONIAL...HUM JURID SOC 20. PAGE 11 E0213
BIBLIOG/A
NAT/G
L/A+17C
ECO/UNDEV

B64
UN PUB. INFORM. ORGAN.,EVERY MAN'S UNITED NATIONS.
UNIV WOR+45 CONSTN CULTURE SOCIETY ECO/DEV
ECO/UNDEV NAT/G ACT/RES PLAN ECO/TAC INT/TRADE
EDU/PROP LEGIT PEACE ATTIT ALL/VALS...POLICY HUM
INT/LAW CONCPT CHARTS UN TOT/POP 20. PAGE 97 E1954
INT/ORG
ROUTINE

S64
HICKEY D.,"THE PHILOSOPHICAL ARGUMENT FOR WORLD
GOVERNMENT." WOR+45 SOCIETY ACT/RES PLAN LEGIT
ADJUD PEACE PERCEPT PERSON ORD/FREE...HUM JURID
PHIL/SCI METH/CNCPT CON/ANAL STERTYP GEN/LAWS
TOT/POP 20. PAGE 52 E1039
FUT
INT/ORG

B65
MILLIS W.,AN END TO ARMS. LAW INT/ORG FORCES
ACT/RES CREATE DIPLOM WAR...POLICY HUM NEW/IDEA
HYPO/EXP. PAGE 73 E1462
FUT
PWR
ARMS/CONT
ORD/FREE

S65
MCWHINNEY E.,"CHANGING INTERNATIONAL LAW METHOD AND
OBJECTIVES IN THE ERA OF THE SOVIET-WESTERN
DETENTE." COM USA+45 NAT/G BAL/PWR CT/SYS ATTIT
ORD/FREE...HUM JURID NEW/IDEA COLD/WAR VAL/FREE 20.
PAGE 71 E1430
LAW
TREND

B66
BUTTERFIELD H.,DIPLOMATIC INVESTIGATIONS* ESSAYS IN
THE THEORY OF INTERNATIONAL POLITICS. LAW INT/ORG
FORCES BAL/PWR ARMS/CONT WAR ALL/VALS...HUM
INT/LAW. PAGE 18 E0351
GEN/LAWS
UK
DIPLOM

B66
STEVENS R.E.,REFERENCE BOOKS IN THE SOCIAL SCIENCES
AND HUMANITIES. CULTURE PERF/ART SECT EDU/PROP
...JURID PSY SOC/WK STAT 20 MUSIC. PAGE 93 E1873
BIBLIOG/A
SOC
HUM
ART/METH

S66
SHEEHY E.P.,"SELECTED REFERENCE BOOKS OF
1965-1966." AGRI PERF/ART PRESS...GEOG HUM JURID
SOC LING WORSHIP. PAGE 91 E1817
BIBLIOG/A
INDEX
CLASSIF

HUM/RIGHTS....HUMAN RIGHTS, DECLARATIONS OF HUMAN RIGHTS,
AND HUMAN RIGHTS COMMISSIONS (OFFICIAL ORGANIZATIONS)

HUMAN NATURE....SEE PERSON

HUMAN RELATIONS....SEE RELATIONS INDEX

HUMAN RIGHTS, DECLARATIONS OF HUMAN RIGHTS, AND HUMAN
RIGHTS COMMISSIONS (OFFICIAL ORGANIZATIONS)....SEE
HUM/RIGHTS

HUMANISM....HUMANISM AND HUMANISTS

B65
CHARLTON K.,EDUCATION IN RENAISSANCE ENGLAND. ITALY
UK USA-45 WOR-45 LAW LOC/G NAT/G...IDEA/COMP 14/17
HUMANISM. PAGE 21 E0423
EDU/PROP
SCHOOL
ACADEM

HUMANITARIANISM....SEE HUMANISM

HUMANITIES....SEE HUM

HUME/D....DAVID HUME

HUMPHREY/H....HUBERT HORATIO HUMPHREY

HUNGARY....SEE ALSO COM

B55
MID-EUROPEAN LAW PROJECT,CHURCH AND STATE BEHIND
THE IRON CURTAIN. COM CZECHOSLVK HUNGARY POLAND
USSR CULTURE SECT EDU/PROP GOV/REL CATHISM...CHARTS
ANTHOL BIBLIOG WORSHIP 20 CHURCH/STA. PAGE 73 E1455
LAW
MARXISM
POLICY

B56
KALNOKI BEDO A.,LEGAL SOURCES AND BIBLIOGRAPHY OF
HUNGARY. COM HUNGARY CONSTN LEGIS JUDGE CT/SYS
SANCTION CRIME 16/20. PAGE 59 E1181
BIBLIOG
ADJUD
LAW
JURID

S63
GIRAUD E.,"L'INTERDICTION DU RECOURS A LA FORCE, LA
THEORIE ET LA PRATIQUE DES NATIONS UNIES." ALGERIA
COM CUBA HUNGARY WOR+45 ADJUD TOTALISM ATTIT
RIGID/FLEX PWR...POLICY JURID CONCPT UN 20 CONGO.
PAGE 44 E0872
INT/ORG
FORCES
DIPLOM

HUNT B.I. E1114

HUNTNGTN/S....SAMUEL P. HUNTINGTON

HUNTON/P....PHILIP HUNTON

HURLEY/PJ....PATRICK J. HURLEY

HURST J.W. E1115,E1116

HURST W.H. E1117

HUSSEIN....KING HUSSEIN I, KING OF JORDAN

HUSSEY R.D. E0345

HUTCHINS/R....ROBERT HUTCHINS

HUXLEY J. E1118

HYDE C.C. E1119

HYNEMAN C.S. E1120

HYPO/EXP....INTELLECTUAL CONSTRUCTS

B00
LORIMER J.,THE INSTITUTES OF THE LAW OF NATIONS.
WOR-45 CULTURE SOCIETY NAT/G VOL/ASSN DIPLOM LEGIT
WAR PEACE DRIVE ORD/FREE SOVEREIGN...CONCPT RECORD
INT TREND HYPO/EXP GEN/METH TOT/POP VAL/FREE 20.
PAGE 66 E1327
INT/ORG
LAW
INT/LAW

B59
GREENSPAN M.,THE MODERN LAW OF LAND WARFARE. WOR+45
INT/ORG NAT/G DELIB/GP FORCES ATTIT...POLICY
HYPO/EXP STERTYP 20. PAGE 46 E0911
ADJUD
PWR
WAR

S60
RHYNE C.S.,"LAW AS AN INSTRUMENT FOR PEACE." FUT
WOR+45 PLAN LEGIT ROUTINE ARMS/CONT NUC/PWR ATTIT
ORD/FREE...JURID METH/CNCPT TREND CON/ANAL HYPO/EXP
COLD/WAR 20. PAGE 84 E1690
ADJUD
EDU/PROP
INT/LAW
PEACE

S61
SCHUBERT G.,"A PSYCHOMETRIC MODEL OF THE SUPREME
COURT." DELIB/GP ADJUD CHOOSE ATTIT...DECISION
JURID PSY QUANT STAT HYPO/EXP GEN/METH SUPREME/CT.
PAGE 88 E1771
JUDGE
CT/SYS
PERSON
SIMUL

B65
MILLIS W.,AN END TO ARMS. LAW INT/ORG FORCES
ACT/RES CREATE DIPLOM WAR...POLICY HUM NEW/IDEA
HYPO/EXP. PAGE 73 E1462
FUT
PWR
ARMS/CONT
ORD/FREE

B66
FELSHER H.,JUSTICE USA? USA+45 COM/IND JUDGE CT/SYS
MORAL ORD/FREE...SAMP/SIZ HYPO/EXP. PAGE 37 E0735
ADJUD
EDU/PROP
LOBBY

S66
EWALD R.F.,"ONE OF MANY POSSIBLE GAMES." ACADEM
INT/ORG ARMS/CONT...INT/LAW GAME. PAGE 36 E0706
SIMUL
HYPO/EXP
PROG/TEAC
RECORD

HYPOTHETICAL EXPERIMENTS....SEE HYPO/EXP

IADB....INTER-ASIAN DEVELOPMENT BANK

IAEA....INTERNATIONAL ATOMIC ENERGY AGENCY

IANNI F.A. E1065

IANNIELLO L. E1121

IBO....IBO TRIBE

IBRD....INTERNATIONAL BANK FOR RECONSTRUCTION AND
DEVELOPMENT

ICA....INTERNATIONAL COOPERATION ADMINISTRATION

ICC....U.S. INTERSTATE COMMERCE COMMISSION

ICELAND....ICELAND

B01
BRYCE J.,STUDIES IN HISTORY AND JURISPRUDENCE (2   IDEA/COMP
VOLS.). ICELAND SOUTH/AFR UK LAW PROB/SOLV   CONSTN
SOVEREIGN...PHIL/SCI NAT/COMP ROME/ANC ROMAN/LAW.   JURID
PAGE 16 E0321

B53
ORFIELD L.B.,THE GROWTH OF SCANDINAVIAN LAW.   JURID
DENMARK ICELAND NORWAY SWEDEN LAW DIPLOM...BIBLIOG   CT/SYS
9/20. PAGE 79 E1581   NAT/G

B67
RAE D.,THE POLITICAL CONSEQUENCES OF ELECTORAL   POL/PAR
LAWS. EUR+WWI ICELAND ISRAEL NEW/ZEALND UK USA+45   CHOOSE
ADJUD APPORT GP/REL MAJORITY...MATH STAT CENSUS   NAT/COMP
CHARTS BIBLIOG 20 AUSTRAL. PAGE 83 E1667   REPRESENT

ICJ....INTERNATIONAL COURT OF JUSTICE; SEE ALSO WORLD/CT

L25
HUDSON M.,"THE PERMANENT COURT OF INTERNATIONAL   INT/ORG
JUSTICE AND THE QUESTION OF AMERICAN   ADJUD
PARTICIPATION." WOR-45 LEGIT CT/SYS ORD/FREE   DIPLOM
...JURID CONCPT TIME/SEQ GEN/LAWS VAL/FREE 20 ICJ.   INT/LAW
PAGE 56 E1108

B47
INTERNATIONAL COURT OF JUSTICE,CHARTER OF THE   INT/LAW
UNITED NATIONS, STATUTE AND RULES OF COURT AND   INT/ORG
OTHER CONSTITUTIONAL DOCUMENTS. SWITZERLND LAW   CT/SYS
ADJUD INGP/REL...JURID 20 ICJ UN. PAGE 57 E1133   DIPLOM

L51
LISSITZYN O.J.,"THE INTERNATIONAL COURT OF   ADJUD
JUSTICE." WOR+45 INT/ORG LEGIT ORD/FREE...CONCPT   JURID
TIME/SEQ TREND GEN/LAWS VAL/FREE 20 ICJ. PAGE 65   INT/LAW
E1304

B57
ROSENNE S.,THE INTERNATIONAL COURT OF JUSTICE.   INT/ORG
WOR+45 LAW DOMIN LEGIT PEACE PWR SOVEREIGN...JURID   CT/SYS
CONCPT RECORD TIME/SEQ CON/ANAL CHARTS UN TOT/POP   INT/LAW
VAL/FREE LEAGUE/NAT 20 ICJ. PAGE 86 E1716

B61
ANAND R.P.,COMPULSORY JURISDICTION OF INTERNATIONAL INT/ORG
COURT OF JUSTICE. FUT WOR+45 SOCIETY PLAN LEGIT   COERCE
ADJUD ATTIT DRIVE PERSON ORD/FREE...JURID CONCPT   INT/LAW
TREND 20 ICJ. PAGE 5 E0086

B64
JENKS C.W.,THE PROSPECTS OF INTERNATIONAL   INT/LAW
ADJUDICATION. WOR+45 NAT/G DIPLOM CONTROL   ADJUD
PWR...POLICY JURID CONCPT METH/COMP 19/20 ICJ   CT/SYS
LEAGUE/NAT UN TREATY. PAGE 58 E1160   INT/ORG

S67
DEUTSCH E.P.,"A JUDICIAL PATH TO WORLD PEACE." FUT   INT/LAW
WOR+45 CONSTN PROB/SOLV DIPLOM LICENSE ADJUD   INT/ORG
SANCTION CHOOSE REPRESENT NAT/LISM SOVEREIGN 20   JURID
ICJ. PAGE 31 E0611   PEACE

ICSU....INTERNATIONAL COUNCIL OF SCIENTIFIC UNIONS

IDA....INTERNATIONAL DEVELOPMENT ASSOCIATION

IDAHO....IDAHO

IDEA/COMP....COMPARISON OF IDEAS

N
NEUE POLITISCHE LITERATUR; BERICHTE UBER DAS   BIBLIOG/A
INTERNATIONALE SCHRIFTTUM ZUR POLITIK. WOR+45 LAW   DIPLOM

CONSTN POL/PAR ADMIN LEAD GOV/REL...POLICY   NAT/G
IDEA/COMP. PAGE 2 E0028   NAT/COMP

N
UNESCO,INTERNATIONAL BIBLIOGRAPHY OF POLITICAL   BIBLIOG
SCIENCE (VOLUMES 1-8). WOR+45 LAW NAT/G EX/STRUC   CONCPT
LEGIS PROB/SOLV DIPLOM ADMIN GOV/REL 20 UNESCO.   IDEA/COMP
PAGE 98 E1957

B'
LALL A.S.,NEGOTIATING DISARMAMENT* THE EIGHTEEN   OBS
NATION DISARMAMENT CONFERENCE* THE FIRST TWO YEARS,   ARMS/CONT
1962-1964. ASIA FRANCE INDIA USA+45 USSR PROB/SOLV   DIPLOM
ADJUD NEUTRAL ATTIT...IDEA/COMP COLD/WAR. PAGE 62   OP/RES
E1246

B01
BRYCE J.,STUDIES IN HISTORY AND JURISPRUDENCE (2   IDEA/COMP
VOLS.). ICELAND SOUTH/AFR UK LAW PROB/SOLV   CONSTN
SOVEREIGN...PHIL/SCI NAT/COMP ROME/ANC ROMAN/LAW.   JURID
PAGE 16 E0321

B05
DICEY A.V.,LECTURES ON THE RELATION BETWEEN LAW AND LAW
PUBLIC OPINION IN ENGLAND DURING THE NINETEENTH   ADJUD
CENTURY. UK LEGIS CT/SYS...JURID 19 TORY/PARTY   ATTIT
BENTHAM/J ENGLSH/LAW. PAGE 31 E0621   IDEA/COMP

L11
POUND R.,"THE SCOPE AND PURPOSE OF SOCIOLOGICAL   JURID
JURISPRUDENCE."...GEN/LAWS 20 KANT/I HEGEL/GWF.   IDEA/COMP
PAGE 81 E1634   METH/COMP
    SOC

B14
VECCHIO G.D.,THE FORMAL BASES OF LAW (TRANS. BY J.   LAW
LISLE). DOMIN LEGIT CONTROL COERCE UTIL MORAL PWR   JURID
...CONCPT TIME/SEQ 17/20 COMMON/LAW NATURL/LAW.   GEN/LAWS
PAGE 103 E2074   IDEA/COMP

B15
INTERNATIONAL LAW ASSOCIATION,A FORTY YEARS'   BIBLIOG
CATALOGUE OF THE BOOKS, PAMPHLETS AND PAPERS IN THE LAW
LIBRARY OF THE INTERNATIONAL LAW ASSOCIATION.   INT/LAW
INT/ORG DIPLOM ADJUD NEUTRAL...IDEA/COMP 19/20.
PAGE 57 E1134

B20
LIPPMAN W.,LIBERTY AND THE NEWS. USA+45 USA-45 LAW   ORD/FREE
LEGIS DOMIN LEGIT ATTIT...POLICY SOC IDEA/COMP   PRESS
METH/COMP 19/20. PAGE 65 E1300   COM/IND
    EDU/PROP

B20
VINOGRADOFF P.,OUTLINES OF HISTORICAL JURISPRUDENCE JURID
(2 VOLS.). GREECE MEDIT-7 LAW CONSTN FACE/GP FAM   METH
KIN MUNIC CRIME OWN...INT/LAW IDEA/COMP BIBLIOG.
PAGE 104 E2080

C20
DUNNING W.A.,"A HISTORY OF POLITICAL THINKERS FROM   IDEA/COMP
ROUSSEAU TO SPENCER." NAT/G REV NAT/LISM UTIL   PHIL/SCI
CONSERVE MARXISM POPULISM...JURID BIBLIOG 18/19.   CONCPT
PAGE 33 E0664   GEN/LAWS

B23
POUND R.,INTERPRETATIONS OF LEGAL HISTORY. CULTURE   LAW
...PHIL/SCI NEW/IDEA CLASSIF SIMUL GEN/LAWS 19/20.   IDEA/COMP
PAGE 82 E1636   JURID

B24
HOLDSWORTH W.S.,A HISTORY OF ENGLISH LAW; THE   LAW
COMMON LAW AND ITS RIVALS (VOL. V). UK SEA EX/STRUC LEGIS
WRITING ADMIN...INT/LAW JURID CONCPT IDEA/COMP   ADJUD
WORSHIP 16/17 PARLIAMENT ENGLSH/LAW COMMON/LAW.   CT/SYS
PAGE 54 E1073

B24
NAVILLE A.,LIBERTE, EGALITE, SOLIDARITE: ESSAIS   ORD/FREE
D'ANALYSE. STRATA FAM VOL/ASSN INT/TRADE GP/REL   SOC
MORAL MARXISM SOCISM...PSY TREATY. PAGE 76 E1529   IDEA/COMP
    DIPLOM

B27
GOOCH G.P.,ENGLISH DEMOCRATIC IDEAS IN THE   IDEA/COMP
SEVENTEENTH CENTURY (2ND ED.). UK LAW SECT FORCES   MAJORIT
DIPLOM LEAD PARL/PROC REV ATTIT AUTHORIT...ANARCH   EX/STRUC
CONCPT 17 PARLIAMENT CMN/WLTH REFORMERS. PAGE 45   CONSERVE
E0885

B28
BENTHAM J.,A COMMENT OF THE COMMENTARIES (1765-69). LAW
MUNIC SECT ADJUD AGREE CT/SYS CONSEN HAPPINESS   CONCPT
ORD/FREE 18. PAGE 10 E0191   IDEA/COMP

B29
STURZO L.,THE INTERNATIONAL COMMUNITY AND THE RIGHT INT/ORG
OF WAR (TRANS. BY BARBARA BARCLAY CARTER). CULTURE PLAN
CREATE PROB/SOLV DIPLOM ADJUD CONTROL PEACE PERSON WAR
ORD/FREE...INT/LAW IDEA/COMP PACIFIST 20 CONCPT
LEAGUE/NAT. PAGE 94 E1891

L30
LLEWELLYN K.N.,"A REALISTIC JURISPRUDENCE - THE LAW
NEXT STEP." PROB/SOLV ADJUD GP/REL PERS/REL CONCPT
IDEA/COMP. PAGE 66 E1312 JURID
GEN/LAWS

B35
ROBSON W.A.,CIVILISATION AND THE GROWTH OF LAW. LAW
UNIV CONSTN SOCIETY LEGIS ADJUD ATTIT PERCEPT MORAL IDEA/COMP
ALL/IDEOS...CONCPT WORSHIP 20. PAGE 85 E1708 SOC

S37
TIMASHEFF N.S.,"WHAT IS SOCIOLOGY OF LAW?" (BMR)" LAW
UNIV INTELL PWR...EPIST JURID PHIL/SCI IDEA/COMP. SOC
PAGE 96 E1925 SOCIETY

B38
HOLDSWORTH W.S.,A HISTORY OF ENGLISH LAW; THE LAW
CENTURIES OF SETTLEMENT AND REFORM (VOL. XII). UK PROF/ORG
CONSTN STRATA LEGIS JUDGE ADJUD CT/SYS ATTIT WRITING
...JURID CONCPT BIOG GEN/LAWS 18 ENGLSH/LAW IDEA/COMP
BLACKSTN/W COMMON/LAW. PAGE 54 E1078

B38
POUND R.,THE FORMATIVE ERA OF AMERICAN LAW. CULTURE CONSTN
NAT/G PROVS LEGIS ADJUD CT/SYS PERSON SOVEREIGN LAW
...POLICY IDEA/COMP GEN/LAWS 18/19. PAGE 82 E1637 CREATE
JURID

B41
GILMORE M.P.,ARGUMENT FROM ROMAN LAW IN POLITICAL JURID
THOUGHT, 1200-1600. INTELL LICENSE CONTROL CT/SYS LAW
GOV/REL PRIVIL PWR...IDEA/COMP BIBLIOG 13/16. CONCPT
PAGE 44 E0866 NAT/G

B41
NIEMEYER G.,LAW WITHOUT FORCE: THE FUNCTION OF COERCE
POLITICS IN INTERNATIONAL LAW. PLAN INSPECT DIPLOM LAW
REPAR LEGIT ADJUD WAR ORD/FREE...IDEA/COMP PWR
METH/COMP GEN/LAWS 20. PAGE 77 E1549 INT/LAW

B42
CRAIG A.,ABOVE ALL LIBERTIES. FRANCE UK USA-45 LAW ORD/FREE
CONSTN CULTURE INTELL NAT/G SECT JUDGE...IDEA/COMP MORAL
BIBLIOG 18/20. PAGE 27 E0536 WRITING
EDU/PROP

B42
GURVITCH G.,SOCIOLOGY OF LAW. CONSTN SOCIETY CREATE SOC
MORAL SOVEREIGN...POLICY EPIST JURID PHIL/SCI LAW
IDEA/COMP METH/COMP HOLMES/OW HOBBES/T. PAGE 48 ADJUD
E0964

B45
WOOLBERT R.G.,FOREIGN AFFAIRS BIBLIOGRAPHY, BIBLIOG/A
1932-1942. INT/ORG SECT INT/TRADE COLONIAL RACE/REL DIPLOM
NAT/LISM...GEOG INT/LAW GOV/COMP IDEA/COMP 20. WAR
PAGE 107 E2144

B46
ROSS A.,TOWARDS A REALISTIC JURISPRUDENCE: A LAW
CRITICISM OF THE DUALISM IN LAW (TRANS. BY ANNIE I. CONCPT
FAUSBOLL). PLAN ADJUD CT/SYS ATTIT RIGID/FLEX IDEA/COMP
POPULISM...JURID PHIL/SCI LOG METH/COMP GEN/LAWS 20
SCANDINAV. PAGE 86 E1720

S48
BRADEN G.D.,"THE SEARCH FOR OBJECTIVITY IN CONSTN
CONSTITUTIONAL LAW" (BMR)" USA+45 USA-45 LAW NAT/G CT/SYS
CONTROL ORD/FREE PWR OBJECTIVE...JURID 20 IDEA/COMP
SUPREME/CT. PAGE 15 E0283 POLICY

S48
MORGENTHAU H.J.,"THE TWILIGHT OF INTERNATIONAL MORAL
MORALITY" (BMR)" WOR+45 WOR-45 BAL/PWR WAR NAT/LISM DIPLOM
PEACE...POLICY INT/LAW IDEA/COMP 15/20 TREATY NAT/G
INTERVENT. PAGE 75 E1495

B49
FRANK J.,LAW AND THE MODERN MIND. UNIV LAW CT/SYS JURID
RATIONAL ATTIT...CONCPT 20 HOLMES/OW JURY. PAGE 40 ADJUD
E0787 IDEA/COMP
MYTH

B49
GROB F.,THE RELATIVITY OF WAR AND PEACE: A STUDY IN WAR
LAW, HISTORY, AND POLITICS. WOR+45 WOR-45 LAW PEACE
DIPLOM DEBATE...CONCPT LING IDEA/COMP BIBLIOG INT/LAW
18/20. PAGE 48 E0944 STYLE

B49
KAFKA G.,FREIHEIT UND ANARCHIE. SECT COERCE DETER CONCPT
WAR ATTIT...IDEA/COMP 20 NATO. PAGE 59 E1179 ORD/FREE
JURID
INT/ORG

L49
MARX C.M.,"ADMINISTRATIVE ETHICS AND THE RULE OF ADMIN
LAW." USA+45 ELITES ACT/RES DOMIN NEUTRAL ROUTINE LAW
INGP/REL ORD/FREE...JURID IDEA/COMP. PAGE 69 E1375

B51
HUXLEY J.,FREEDOM AND CULTURE. UNIV LAW SOCIETY R+D CULTURE
ACADEM SCHOOL CREATE SANCTION ATTIT KNOWL...HUM ORD/FREE
ANTHOL 20. PAGE 56 E1118 PHIL/SCI
IDEA/COMP

B52
BUCKLAND W.W.,ROMAN LAW AND COMMON LAW; A IDEA/COMP
COMPARISON IN OUTLINE (2ND REV. ED.). UK FAM LEGIT LAW
AGREE CT/SYS OWN...JURID ROMAN/REP ROMAN/LAW ADJUD
COMMON/LAW. PAGE 17 E0325 CONCPT

B52
FLECHTHEIM O.K.,FUNDAMENTALS OF POLITICAL SCIENCE. NAT/G
WOR+45 WOR-45 LAW POL/PAR EX/STRUC LEGIS ADJUD DIPLOM
ATTIT PWR...INT/LAW. PAGE 38 E0760 IDEA/COMP
CONSTN

B52
HOLDSWORTH W.S.,A HISTORY OF ENGLISH LAW; THE LAW
CENTURIES OF SETTLEMENT AND REFORM, 1701-1875 (VOL. CONSTN
XIII). UK POL/PAR PROF/ORG LEGIS JUDGE ADJUD IDEA/COMP
ATTIT...JURID CONCPT BIOG GEN/LAWS 18/19 PARLIAMENT CT/SYS
REFORMERS ENGLSH/LAW COMMON/LAW. PAGE 54 E1080

S52
MCDOUGAL M.S.,"THE COMPARATIVE STUDY OF LAW FOR PLAN
POLICY PURPOSES." FUT NAT/G POL/PAR CONSULT ADJUD JURID
PWR SOVEREIGN...METH/CNCPT IDEA/COMP SIMUL 20. NAT/LISM
PAGE 70 E1403

B53
KIRK R.,THE CONSERVATIVE MIND. POL/PAR ORD/FREE CONSERVE
...JURID CONCPT 18/20. PAGE 61 E1220 PERSON
PHIL/SCI
IDEA/COMP

B53
LANDHEER B.,FUNDAMENTALS OF PUBLIC INTERNATIONAL BIBLIOG/A
LAW (SELECTIVE BIBLIOGRAPHIES OF THE LIBRARY OF THE INT/LAW
PEACE PALACE, VOL. I; PAMPH). INT/ORG OP/RES PEACE DIPLOM
...IDEA/COMP 20. PAGE 62 E1250 PHIL/SCI

B53
MARKE J.J.,A CATALOGUE OF THE LAW COLLECTION AT NEW BIBLIOG/A
YORK UNIVERSITY, WITH SELECTED ANNOTATIONS. ACADEM LAW
ADJUD CT/SYS...CONCPT BIOG 20. PAGE 68 E1366 PHIL/SCI
IDEA/COMP

B53
PADOVER S.K.,THE LIVING US CONSTITUTION. USA+45 CONSTN
USA-45 POL/PAR ADJUD...DECISION AUD/VIS IDEA/COMP LEGIS
18/20 SUPREME/CT. PAGE 79 E1590 DELIB/GP
BIOG

B54
FRIEDMAN W.,THE PUBLIC CORPORATION: A COMPARATIVE LAW
SYMPOSIUM (UNIVERSITY OF TORONTO SCHOOL OF LAW SOCISM
COMPARATIVE LAW SERIES, VOL. I). SWEDEN USA+45 LG/CO
INDUS INT/ORG NAT/G REGION CENTRAL FEDERAL...POLICY OWN
JURID IDEA/COMP NAT/COMP ANTHOL 20 COMMONWLTH
MONOPOLY EUROPE. PAGE 40 E0801

B54
HOEBEL E.A.,THE LAW OF PRIMITIVE MAN: A STUDY IN LAW
COMPARATIVE LEGAL DYNAMICS. WOR-45...JURID SOC CULTURE
IDEA/COMP METH 20. PAGE 53 E1063 GP/COMP
SOCIETY

B54
SCHWARTZ B.,FRENCH ADMINISTRATIVE LAW AND THE JURID
COMMON-LAW WORLD. FRANCE CULTURE LOC/G NAT/G PROVS LAW
DELIB/GP EX/STRUC LEGIS PROB/SOLV CT/SYS EXEC METH/COMP
GOV/REL...IDEA/COMP ENGLSH/LAW. PAGE 89 E1786 ADJUD

B55
WRONG D.H.,AMERICAN AND CANADIAN VIEWPOINTS. CANADA DIPLOM
USA+45 CONSTN STRATA FAM SECT WORKER ECO/TAC ATTIT
EDU/PROP ADJUD MARRIAGE...IDEA/COMP 20. PAGE 108 NAT/COMP
E2161 CULTURE

B56
FIELD G.C.,POLITICAL THEORY. POL/PAR REPRESENT CONCPT
MORAL SOVEREIGN...JURID IDEA/COMP. PAGE 38 E0745 NAT/G

POTTER P.B.,"NEUTRALITY, 1955." WOR+45 WOR-45
INT/ORG NAT/G WAR ATTIT...POLICY IDEA/COMP 17/20
LEAGUE/NAT UN COLD/WAR. PAGE 81 E1631

S56
NEUTRAL
INT/LAW
DIPLOM
CONCPT

UNESCO,A REGISTER OF LEGAL DOCUMENTATION IN THE
WORLD (2ND ED.). CT/SYS...JURID IDEA/COMP METH/COMP
NAT/COMP 20. PAGE 98 E1960

B57
BIBLIOG
LAW
INT/LAW
CONSTN

ALLEN C.K.,LAW IN THE MAKING. LEGIS ATTIT ORD/FREE
SOVEREIGN POPULISM...JURID IDEA/COMP NAT/COMP
GEN/LAWS 20 ENGLSH/LAW. PAGE 4 E0069

B58
LAW
CREATE
CONSTN
SOCIETY

DOUGLAS W.O.,THE RIGHT OF THE PEOPLE. USA+45
EDU/PROP CONTROL REPRESENT PRIVIL...IDEA/COMP 20.
PAGE 32 E0641

B58
ORD/FREE
CONSTN
CT/SYS
CIVMIL/REL

EUSDEN J.D.,PURITANS, LAWYERS, AND POLITICS IN
EARLY SEVENTEENTH-CENTURY ENGLAND. UK CT/SYS
PARL/PROC RATIONAL PWR SOVEREIGN...IDEA/COMP
BIBLIOG 17 PURITAN COMMON/LAW. PAGE 35 E0702

B58
GP/REL
SECT
NAT/G
LAW

HERRMANN K.,DAS STAATSDENKEN BEI LEIBNIZ. GP/REL
ATTIT ORD/FREE...CONCPT IDEA/COMP 17 LEIBNITZ/G
CHURCH/STA. PAGE 52 E1034

B58
NAT/G
JURID
SECT
EDU/PROP

STONE J.,AGGRESSION AND WORLD ORDER: A CRITIQUE OF
UNITED NATIONS THEORIES OF AGGRESSION. LAW CONSTN
DELIB/GP PROB/SOLV BAL/PWR DIPLOM DEBATE ADJUD
CRIME PWR...POLICY IDEA/COMP 20 UN SUEZ LEAGUE/NAT.
PAGE 94 E1879

B58
ORD/FREE
INT/ORG
WAR
CONCPT

STRONG C.F.,MODERN POLITICAL CONSTITUTIONS. LAW
CHIEF DELIB/GP EX/STRUC LEGIS ADJUD CHOOSE FEDERAL
POPULISM...CONCPT BIBLIOG 20 UN. PAGE 94 E1887

B58
CONSTN
IDEA/COMP
NAT/G

ROCHE J.P.,"POLITICAL SCIENCE AND SCIENCE FICTION"
(BMR)" WOR+45 INTELL OP/RES ADJUD...JURID SOC
IDEA/COMP 20. PAGE 85 E1709

S58
QUANT
RATIONAL
MATH
METH

SCHUBERT G.A.,"THE STUDY OF JUDICIAL DECISION-
MAKING AS AN ASPECT OF POLITICAL BEHAVIOR." PLAN
ADJUD CT/SYS INGP/REL PERSON...PHIL/SCI SOC QUANT
STAT CHARTS IDEA/COMP SOC/EXP. PAGE 89 E1779

S58
JUDGE
DECISION
CON/ANAL
GAME

RAJAN M.S.,"UNITED NATIONS AND DOMESTIC
JURISDICTION." WOR+45 WOR-45 PARL/PROC...IDEA/COMP
BIBLIOG 20 UN. PAGE 83 E1670

C58
INT/LAW
DIPLOM
CONSTN
INT/ORG

BROOKES E.H.,THE COMMONWEALTH TODAY. UK ROMAN/EMP
INT/ORG RACE/REL NAT/LISM SOVEREIGN...TREND
SOC/INTEG 20. PAGE 16 E0307

B59
FEDERAL
DIPLOM
JURID
IDEA/COMP

COUNCIL OF STATE GOVERNORS,AMERICAN LEGISLATURES:
STRUCTURE AND PROCEDURES. SUMMARY AND TABULATIONS
OF A 1959 SURVEY. PUERT/RICO USA+45 PAY ADJUD ADMIN
APPORT...IDEA/COMP 20 GUAM VIRGIN/ISL. PAGE 27
E0525

B59
LEGIS
CHARTS
PROVS
REPRESENT

HOOK S.,POLITICAL POWER AND PERSONAL FREEDOM:
CRITICAL STUDIES IN DEMOCRACY, COMMUNISM AND CIVIL
RIGHTS. UNIV LAW SOCIETY DIPLOM TOTALISM MARXISM
SOCISM...PHIL/SCI IDEA/COMP 20 CIV/RIGHTS. PAGE 55
E1094

B59
ORD/FREE
PWR
WELF/ST
CHOOSE

MORRIS C.,THE GREAT LEGAL PHILOSOPHERS: SELECTED
READINGS IN JURISPRUDENCE. UNIV INTELL SOCIETY
EDU/PROP MAJORITY UTOPIA PERSON KNOWL...ANTHOL.
PAGE 75 E1497

B59
JURID
ADJUD
PHIL/SCI
IDEA/COMP

COLUMBIA U. BUREAU OF APPL SOC RES, ATTITUDES OF
PROMINENT AMERICANS TOWARD "WORLD PEACE THROUGH
WORLD LAW" (SUPRA-NATL ORGANIZATION FOR WAR
PREVENTION). USA+45 USSR ELITES FORCES PLAN
PROB/SOLV CONTROL WAR PWR...POLICY SOC QU IDEA/COMP
20 UN. PAGE 82 E1644

B59
ATTIT
ACT/RES
INT/LAW
STAT

ROSS A.,ON LAW AND JUSTICE. USA+45 RATIONAL
...IDEA/COMP GEN/LAWS 20 SCANDINAV NATURL/LAW.
PAGE 86 E1722

B59
JURID
PHIL/SCI
LAW
CONCPT

VAN CAENEGEM R.C.,ROYAL WRITS IN ENGLAND FROM THE
CONQUEST TO GLANVILL. UK JUDGE...TREND IDEA/COMP
11/12 COMMON/LAW. PAGE 103 E2067

B59
JURID
CHIEF
ADJUD
CT/SYS

WILDNER H.,DIE TECHNIK DER DIPLOMATIE. TOP/EX ROLE
ORD/FREE...INT/LAW JURID IDEA/COMP NAT/COMP 20.
PAGE 106 E2122

B59
DIPLOM
POLICY
DELIB/GP
NAT/G

AMERICAN ASSOCIATION LAW LIB,INDEX TO FOREIGN LEGAL
PERIODICALS. WOR+45 MUNIC...IDEA/COMP 20. PAGE 4
E0075

B60
INDEX
LAW
JURID
DIPLOM

BYRD E.M. JR.,TREATIES AND EXECUTIVE AGREEMENTS IN
THE UNITED STATES: THEIR SEPARATE ROLES AND
LIMITATIONS. USA+45 USA-45 EX/STRUC TARIFFS CT/SYS
GOV/REL FEDERAL...IDEA/COMP BIBLIOG SUPREME/CT
SENATE CONGRESS. PAGE 18 E0353

B60
CHIEF
INT/LAW
DIPLOM

DILEY A.V.,INTRODUCTION TO THE STUDY OF THE LAW OF
THE CONSTITUTION. FRANCE UK USA+45 USA-45 CONSULT
FORCES TAX ADMIN FEDERAL ORD/FREE SOVEREIGN
...IDEA/COMP 20 ENGLSH/LAW CON/INTERP PARLIAMENT.
PAGE 32 E0627

B60
CONSTN
LAW
LEGIS
GEN/LAWS

MILLER A.S.,"THE MYTH OF NEUTRALITY IN
CONSTITUTIONAL ADJUDICATION." LAW...DECISION JURID
LING TREND IDEA/COMP. PAGE 73 E1456

L60
ADJUD
CONSTN
MYTH
UTIL

CHILDS M.W.,THE EROSION OF INDIVIDUAL LIBERTIES.
NAT/G LEGIS ATTIT...JURID SOC CONCPT IDEA/COMP 20
SUPREME/CT AMEND/I. PAGE 22 E0430

B61
ADJUD
CT/SYS
ORD/FREE
CONSTN

JUSTICE,THE CITIZEN AND THE ADMINISTRATION: THE
REDRESS OF GRIEVANCES (PAMPHLET). EUR+WWI UK LAW
CONSTN STRATA NAT/G CT/SYS PARTIC COERCE...NEW/IDEA
IDEA/COMP 20 OMBUDSMAN. PAGE 59 E1176

B61
INGP/REL
CONSULT
ADJUD
REPRESENT

NEW JERSEY LEGISLATURE-SENATE,PUBLIC HEARINGS
BEFORE COMMITTEE ON REVISION AND AMENDMENT OF LAWS
ON SENATE BILL NO. 8. USA+45 FINAN PROVS WORKER
ACT/RES PLAN BUDGET TAX CRIME...IDEA/COMP 20
NEW/JERSEY URBAN/RNWL. PAGE 77 E1537

B61
LEGIS
MUNIC
INDUS
PROB/SOLV

NEWMAN R.P.,RECOGNITION OF COMMUNIST CHINA? A STUDY
IN ARGUMENT. CHINA/COM NAT/G PROB/SOLV RATIONAL
...INT/LAW LOG IDEA/COMP BIBLIOG 20. PAGE 77 E1544

B61
MARXISM
ATTIT
DIPLOM
POLICY

LASSWELL H.D.,"THE INTERPLAY OF ECONOMIC, POLITICAL
AND SOCIAL CRITERIA IN LEGAL POLICY." LAW LOVE
MORAL PWR RESPECT WEALTH...SOC IDEA/COMP. PAGE 63
E1262

S61
JURID
POLICY

BISHOP W.W. JR.,INTERNATIONAL LAW: CASES AND
MATERIALS. WOR+45 INT/ORG FORCES PROB/SOLV AGREE
WAR...JURID IDEA/COMP T 20 TREATY. PAGE 12 E0233

B62
INT/LAW
DIPLOM
CONCPT
CT/SYS

BOCK E.A.,CASE STUDIES IN AMERICAN GOVERNMENT.
USA+45 ECO/DEV CHIEF EDU/PROP CT/SYS RACE/REL
ORD/FREE...JURID MGT PHIL/SCI PRESIDENT CASEBOOK.
PAGE 13 E0256

B62
POLICY
LEGIS
IDEA/COMP
NAT/G

CRANSTON M.,WHAT ARE HUMAN RIGHTS? UNIV WOR+45 LAW B62
INT/ORG MORAL...POLICY CONCPT METH/CNCPT GEN/LAWS ORD/FREE
20. PAGE 28 E0545 JURID
IDEA/COMP

FRIEDRICH C.J.,NOMOS V: THE PUBLIC INTEREST. UNIV METH/CNCPT B62
ECO/TAC ADJUD UTIL ATTIT...POLICY LING LOG GEN/LAWS CONCPT
20. PAGE 41 E0808 LAW
IDEA/COMP

GANJI M.,INTERNATIONAL PROTECTION OF HUMAN RIGHTS. ORD/FREE B62
WOR+45 CONSTN INT/TRADE CT/SYS SANCTION CRIME WAR DISCRIM
RACE/REL...CHARTS IDEA/COMP NAT/COMP BIBLIOG 20 LEGIS
TREATY NEGRO LEAGUE/NAT UN CIVIL/LIB. PAGE 42 E0831 DELIB/GP

HOOK S.,THE PARADOXES OF FREEDOM. UNIV CONSTN CONCPT B62
INTELL LEGIS CONTROL REV CHOOSE SUPEGO...POLICY MAJORIT
JURID IDEA/COMP 19/20 CIV/RIGHTS. PAGE 55 E1095 ORD/FREE
ALL/VALS

SOWLE C.R.,POLICE POWER AND INDIVIDUAL FREEDOM: THE FORCES B62
QUEST FOR BALANCE. CANADA EUR+WWI ISRAEL NORWAY ORD/FREE
USA+45 LAW CONSTN SOCIETY CONTROL ROUTINE SANCTION IDEA/COMP
GP/REL 20 CHINJAP. PAGE 93 E1859

US AIR FORCE,THE MILITARY JUSTICE SYSTEM (REV. JURID B62
ED.). USA+45 DELIB/GP...IDEA/COMP 20. PAGE 99 E1978 FORCES
ADJUD
ORD/FREE

ABRAHAM H.J.,"THE JUDICIAL PROCESS." USA+45 USA-45 BIBLIOG C62
LAW NAT/G ADMIN CT/SYS INGP/REL RACE/REL DISCRIM CONSTN
...JURID IDEA/COMP 19/20. PAGE 2 E0046 JUDGE
ADJUD

ATTIA G.E.D.,LES FORCES ARMEES DES NATIONS UNIES EN FORCES B63
COREE ET AU MOYENORIENT. KOREA CONSTN NAT/G INT/LAW
DELIB/GP LEGIS PWR...IDEA/COMP NAT/COMP BIBLIOG UN
SUEZ. PAGE 6 E0114

BROOKES E.H.,POWER, LAW, RIGHT, AND LOVE: A STUDY PWR B63
IN POLITICAL VALUES. SOUTH/AFR NAT/G PERSON ORD/FREE
...CONCPT IDEA/COMP 20. PAGE 16 E0308 JURID
LOVE

CAHN E.,THE GREAT RIGHTS. USA+45 NAT/G PROVS CONSTN B63
CIVMIL/REL...IDEA/COMP ANTHOL BIBLIOG 18/20 LAW
MADISON/J BILL/RIGHT CIV/RIGHTS WARRN/EARL ORD/FREE
BLACK/HL. PAGE 18 E0361 INGP/REL

DE GRAZIA A.,APPORTIONMENT AND REPRESENTATIVE REPRESENT B63
GOVERNMENT. CONSTN POL/PAR LEGIS PLAN ADJUD DISCRIM APPORT
RATIONAL...CONCPT STAT PREDICT TREND IDEA/COMP. NAT/G
PAGE 29 E0583 MUNIC

HYNEMAN C.S.,THE SUPREME COURT ON TRIAL. ADJUD LEAD CT/SYS B63
GP/REL FEDERAL...IDEA/COMP 20 SUPREME/CT. PAGE 56 JURID
E1120 POLICY
NAT/G

SCHMIDHAUSER J.R.,CONSTITUTIONAL LAW IN THE LAW B63
POLITICAL PROCESS. SOCIETY LEGIS ADJUD CT/SYS CONSTN
FEDERAL...SOC TREND IDEA/COMP ANTHOL T SUPREME/CT JURID
SENATE CONGRESS HOUSE/REP. PAGE 88 E1761

WADE H.W.R.,TOWARDS ADMINISTRATIVE JUSTICE. UK ADJUD B63
USA+45 CONSTN CONSULT PROB/SOLV CT/SYS PARL/PROC IDEA/COMP
...POLICY JURID METH/COMP 20 ENGLSH/LAW. PAGE 104 ADMIN
E2088

MENDELSON W.,"THE NEO-BEHAVIORAL APPROACH TO THE DECISION S63
JUDICIAL PROCESS: A CRITIQUE" ADJUD PERSON...SOC JURID
RECORD IDEA/COMP. PAGE 72 E1438 JUDGE

ATTIA G.E.O.,"LES FORCES ARMEES DES NATIONS UNIES FORCES C63
EN COREE ET AU MOYENORIENT." KOREA CONSTN DELIB/GP NAT/G
LEGIS PWR...IDEA/COMP NAT/COMP BIBLIOG UN SUEZ. INT/LAW
PAGE 6 E0115

BOWETT D.W.,UNITED NATIONS FORCES* A LEGAL STUDY. OP/RES B64
CYPRUS ISRAEL KOREA LAW CONSTN ACT/RES CREATE FORCES
BUDGET CONTROL TASK PWR...INT/LAW IDEA/COMP UN ARMS/CONT
CONGO/LEOP SUEZ. PAGE 14 E0278

COHEN M.L.,SELECTED BIBLIOGRAPHY OF FOREIGN AND BIBLIOG/A B64
INTERNATIONAL LAW....IDEA/COMP METH/COMP 20. JURID
PAGE 24 E0466 LAW
INT/LAW

DIETZE G.,ESSAYS ON THE AMERICAN CONSTITUTION: A FEDERAL B64
COMMEMORATIVE VOLUME IN HONOR OF ALPHEUS T. MASON. CONSTN
USA+45 USA-45 LAW INTELL...POLICY BIOG IDEA/COMP DIPLOM
ANTHOL SUPREME/CT. PAGE 32 E0626 CT/SYS

ENGEL S.,LAW, STATE, AND INTERNATIONAL LEGAL ORDER. JURID B64
WOR+45 NAT/G ORD/FREE RELATISM...INT/LAW IDEA/COMP OBJECTIVE
ANTHOL 20 KELSEN/H. PAGE 35 E0690 CONCPT
DEBATE

FRANCK T.M.,EAST AFRICAN UNITY THROUGH LAW. MALAWI AFR B64
TANZANIA UGANDA UK ZAMBIA CONSTN INT/ORG NAT/G FEDERAL
ADMIN ROUTINE TASK NAT/LISM ATTIT SOVEREIGN REGION
...RECORD IDEA/COMP NAT/COMP. PAGE 40 E0785 INT/LAW

GUMPLOWICZ L.,RECHTSSTAAT UND SOZIALISMUS. STRATA JURID B64
ORD/FREE SOVEREIGN MARXISM...IDEA/COMP 16/20 KANT/I NAT/G
HOBBES/T. PAGE 48 E0962 SOCISM
CONCPT

HOHFELD W.N.,FUNDAMENTAL LEGAL CONCEPTIONS. JURID B64
PROB/SOLV OWN PWR...DECISION LING IDEA/COMP ADJUD
GEN/METH. PAGE 54 E1069 LAW
METH/CNCPT

LAPENNA I.,STATE AND LAW: SOVIET AND YUGOSLAV JURID B64
THEORY. USSR YUGOSLAVIA STRATA STRUCT NAT/G DOMIN COM
COERCE MARXISM...GOV/COMP IDEA/COMP 20. PAGE 63 LAW
E1253 SOVEREIGN

MCDOUGAL M.S.,STUDIES IN WORLD PUBLIC ORDER. SPACE INT/LAW B64
SEA INT/ORG CREATE AGREE NUC/PWR...POLICY PHIL/SCI SOC
IDEA/COMP ANTHOL METH 20 UN. PAGE 71 E1411 DIPLOM

MCWHINNEY E.,"PEACEFUL COEXISTENCE" AND SOVIET- PEACE B64
WESTERN INTERNATIONAL LAW. USSR DIPLOM LEAD...JURID IDEA/COMP
20 COLD/WAR. PAGE 71 E1429 INT/LAW
ATTIT

MINAR D.W.,IDEAS AND POLITICS: THE AMERICAN CONSTN B64
EXPERIENCE. SECT CHIEF LEGIS CREATE ADJUD EXEC REV NAT/G
PWR...PHIL/SCI CONCPT IDEA/COMP 18/20 HAMILTON/A FEDERAL
JEFFERSN/T DECLAR/IND JACKSON/A PRESIDENT. PAGE 73
E1464

NASA,PROCEEDINGS OF CONFERENCE ON THE LAW OF SPACE SPACE B64
AND OF SATELLITE COMMUNICATIONS: CHICAGO 1963. FUT COM/IND
WOR+45 DELIB/GP PROB/SOLV TEC/DEV CONFER ADJUD LAW
NUC/PWR...POLICY IDEA/COMP 20 NASA. PAGE 76 E1522 DIPLOM

ROBERTS HL,FOREIGN AFFAIRS BIBLIOGRAPHY, 1952-1962. BIBLIOG/A B64
ECO/DEV SECT PLAN FOR/AID INT/TRADE ARMS/CONT DIPLOM
NAT/LISM ATTIT...INT/LAW GOV/COMP IDEA/COMP 20. INT/ORG
PAGE 85 E1703 WAR

BARKUN M.,"CONFLICT RESOLUTION THROUGH IMPLICIT CONSULT S64
MEDIATION." UNIV BARGAIN CONSEN FEDERAL JURID. CENTRAL
PAGE 8 E0149 INT/LAW
IDEA/COMP

MCGHEE G.C.,"EAST-WEST RELATIONS TODAY." WOR+45 IDEA/COMP S64
PROB/SOLV BAL/PWR PEACE 20 COLD/WAR. PAGE 71 E1413 DIPLOM
ADJUD

ASSOCIATION BAR OF NYC,RADIO, TELEVISION, AND THE AUD/VIS B65
ADMINISTRATION OF JUSTICE: A DOCUMENTED SURVEY OF ATTIT
MATERIALS. USA+45 DELIB/GP FORCES PRESS ADJUD ORD/FREE
CONTROL CT/SYS CRIME...INT IDEA/COMP BIBLIOG.
PAGE 6 E0109

BEGGS D.W.,AMERICA'S SCHOOLS AND CHURCHES: PARTNERS SECT
IN CONFLICT. USA+45 PROVS EDU/PROP ADJUD DISCRIM GP/REL
ATTIT...IDEA/COMP ANTHOL BIBLIOG WORSHIP 20 SCHOOL
CHURCH/STA. PAGE 9 E0179 NAT/G
B65

BOVY L.,LE MOUVEMENT SYNDICAL OUEST AFRICAIN BIBLIOG
D'EXPRESSION FRANCAISE. AFR SECT...JURID SOC 20. SOCISM
PAGE 14 E0275 ECO/UNDEV
IDEA/COMP
B65

CAVERS D.F.,THE CHOICE-OF-LAW PROCESS. PROB/SOLV JURID
ADJUD CT/SYS CHOOSE RATIONAL...IDEA/COMP 16/20 DECISION
TREATY. PAGE 21 E0411 METH/COMP
ADMIN
B65

CHARLTON K.,EDUCATION IN RENAISSANCE ENGLAND. ITALY EDU/PROP
UK USA+45 WOR+45 LAW LOC/G NAT/G...IDEA/COMP 14/17 SCHOOL
HUMANISM. PAGE 21 E0423 ACADEM
B65

GOTLIEB A.,DISARMAMENT AND INTERNATIONAL LAW* A INT/LAW
STUDY OF THE ROLE OF LAW IN THE DISARMAMENT INT/ORG
PROCESS. USA+45 USSR PROB/SOLV CONFER ADMIN ROUTINE ARMS/CONT
NUC/PWR ORD/FREE SOVEREIGN UN TREATY. PAGE 45 E0893 IDEA/COMP
B65

HAENSCH G.,PAN-AFRICANISM IN ACTION: AN ACCOUNT OF DICTIONARY
THE UAM TIC AND ALPHABETICAL IN GERMAN, ENGLISH, DIPLOM
FRENCH AND SPANISH. WOR+45 INT/ORG NAT/G ARMS/CONT LING
WAR...INT/LAW IDEA/COMP TREATY. PAGE 49 E0974
B65

HIGGINS R.,CONFLICT OF INTERESTS* INTERNATIONAL LAW INT/LAW
IN A DIVIDED WORLD. ASIA USSR ECO/DEV ECO/UNDEV IDEA/COMP
SECT INT/TRADE COLD/WAR WORSHIP. PAGE 52 E1042 ADJUST
B65

HOLDSWORTH W.S.,A HISTORY OF ENGLISH LAW; THE LAW
CENTURIES OF SETTLEMENT AND REFORM (VOL. XV). UK INDUS
CONSTN SECT LEGIS JUDGE WRITING ADJUD CT/SYS CRIME PROF/ORG
OWN...JURID IDEA/COMP 18 PARLIAMENT ENGLSH/LAW ATTIT
COMMON/LAW. PAGE 54 E1082
B65

LASLEY J.,THE WAR SYSTEM AND YOU. LAW FORCES MORAL
ARMS/CONT NUC/PWR NAT/LISM ATTIT...MAJORIT PERSON
IDEA/COMP UN WORSHIP. PAGE 63 E1261 DIPLOM
WAR
B65

MEIKLEJOHN D.,FREEDOM AND THE PUBLIC: PUBLIC AND NAT/G
PRIVATE MORALITY IN AMERICA. USA+45 USA-45...POLICY CONCPT
JURID IDEA/COMP. PAGE 72 E1435 ORD/FREE
B65

STONE J.,HUMAN LAW AND HUMAN JUSTICE. JUDGE...SOC CONCPT
MYTH IDEA/COMP. PAGE 94 E1881 SANCTION
JURID
B65

THOMAS A.V.,NONINTERVENTION: THE LAW AND ITS IMPORT INT/LAW
IN THE AMERICAS. L/A+17C USA+45 USA-45 WOR+45 PWR
DIPLOM ADJUD...JURID IDEA/COMP 20 UN INTERVENT. COERCE
PAGE 96 E1917
B65

WHITEMAN M.M.,DIGEST OF INTERNATIONAL LAW* VOLUME INT/LAW
5, DEPARTMENT OF STATE PUBLICATION 7873. USA+45 NAT/G
WOR+45 OP/RES...CONCPT CLASSIF RECORD IDEA/COMP. NAT/COMP
PAGE 106 E2118
C65

SEARA M.V.,"COSMIC INTERNATIONAL LAW." LAW ACADEM SPACE
ACT/RES DIPLOM COLONIAL CONTROL NUC/PWR SOVEREIGN INT/LAW
...GEN/LAWS BIBLIOG UN. PAGE 90 E1799 IDEA/COMP
INT/ORG
B66

AMERICAN JOURNAL COMP LAW,THE AMERICAN JOURNAL OF IDEA/COMP
COMPARATIVE LAW READER. EUR+WWI USA+45 USA-45 LAW JURID
CONSTN LOC/G MUNIC NAT/G DIPLOM...ANTHOL 20 INT/LAW
SUPREME/CT EURCT/JUST. PAGE 4 E0081 CT/SYS
B66

ANDERSON S.V.,CANADIAN OMBUDSMAN PROPOSALS. CANADA NAT/G
LEGIS DEBATE PARL/PROC...MAJORIT JURID TIME/SEQ CREATE
IDEA/COMP 20 OMBUDSMAN PARLIAMENT. PAGE 5 E0092 ADMIN
POL/PAR
B66

CAHN E.,CONFRONTING INJUSTICE. USA+45 PROB/SOLV TAX ORD/FREE
EDU/PROP PRESS CT/SYS GP/REL DISCRIM BIO/SOC CONSTN

...IDEA/COMP BIBLIOG WORSHIP 20 BILL/RIGHT. PAGE 18 ADJUD
E0362
B66

CARMEN I.H.,MOVIES, CENSORSHIP, AND THE LAW. LOC/G EDU/PROP
NAT/G ATTIT ORD/FREE...DECISION INT IDEA/COMP LAW
BIBLIOG 20 SUPREME/CT FILM. PAGE 19 E0383 ART/METH
CONSTN
B66

HOLDSWORTH W.S.,A HISTORY OF ENGLISH LAW; THE BIOG
CENTURIES OF SETTLEMENT AND REFORM (VOL. XVI). UK PERSON
LOC/G NAT/G EX/STRUC LEGIS CT/SYS LEAD ATTIT PROF/ORG
...POLICY DECISION JURID IDEA/COMP 18 PARLIAMENT. LAW
PAGE 54 E1083
B66

MENDELSON W.,JUSTICES BLACK AND FRANKFURTER: JURID
CONFLICT IN THE COURT (2ND ED.). NAT/G PROVS ADJUD
PROB/SOLV BAL/PWR CONTROL FEDERAL ISOLAT ANOMIE IDEA/COMP
ORD/FREE...DECISION 20 SUPREME/CT BLACK/HL ROLE
FRANKFUR/F. PAGE 72 E1439
B66

SMITH E.A.,CHURCH-STATE RELATIONS IN ECUMENICAL NAT/G
PERSPECTIVE. WOR+45 LAW MUNIC INGP/REL DISCRIM SECT
ATTIT SUPEGO ORD/FREE CATHISM...PHIL/SCI IDEA/COMP GP/REL
20 PROTESTANT ECUMENIC CHURCH/STA CHRISTIAN. ADJUD
PAGE 92 E1843
B66

US HOUSE COMM ON JUDICIARY,CIVIL COMMITMENT AND BIO/SOC
TREATMENT OF NARCOTIC ADDICTS. USA+45 SOCIETY FINAN CRIME
LEGIS PROB/SOLV GIVE CT/SYS SANCTION HEALTH IDEA/COMP
...POLICY HEAL 20. PAGE 100 E2008 CONTROL
L66

HOLSTI K.J.,"RESOLVING INTERNATIONAL CONFLICTS* A DIPLOM
TAXONOMY OF BEHAVIOR AND SOME FIGURES ON PROB/SOLV
PROCEDURES." WOR+45 WOR-45 INT/ORG ADJUD EFFICIENCY WAR
...STAT IDEA/COMP. PAGE 55 E1089 CLASSIF
L66

YALEM R.J.,"THE STUDY OF INTERNATIONAL VOL/ASSN
ORGANIZATION, 1920-1965* A SURVEY OF THE INT/ORG
LITERATURE." WOR+45 WOR-45 REGION...INT/LAW CLASSIF BIBLIOG/A
RECORD HIST/WRIT CON/ANAL IDEA/COMP UN. PAGE 108
E2163
S66

CHIU H.,"COMMUNIST CHINA'S ATTITUDE TOWARD INT/LAW
INTERNATIONAL LAW" CHINA/COM USSR LAW CONSTN DIPLOM MARXISM
GP/REL 20 LENIN/VI. PAGE 22 E0431 CONCPT
IDEA/COMP
S66

FINE R.I.,"PEACE-KEEPING COSTS AND ARTICLE 19 OF FORCES
THE UN CHARTER* AN INVITATION TO RESPONSIBILITY." COST
INT/ORG NAT/G ADJUD CT/SYS CHOOSE CONSEN...RECORD CONSTN
IDEA/COMP UN. PAGE 38 E0750
S66

GASS O.,"THE LITERATURE OF AMERICAN GOVERNMENT." NEW/LIB
CONSTN DRIVE ORD/FREE...JURID CONCPT METH/CNCPT CT/SYS
IDEA/COMP 20 WILSON/W BEARD/CA LINK/AS. PAGE 42 NAT/G
E0841
S66

SHKLAR J.,"SELECTED ARTICLES AND DOCUMENTS ON BIBLIOG
POLITICAL THEORY." ADJUD REV...JURID PHIL/SCI ELITES
IDEA/COMP. PAGE 91 E1820 PWR
B67

BONGER W.A.,CRIMINALITY AND ECONOMIC CONDITIONS. PERSON
MOD/EUR STRUCT INDUS WORKER EDU/PROP CRIME HABITAT CRIMLGY
ALL/VALS...JURID SOC 20 REFORMERS. PAGE 14 E0265 IDEA/COMP
ANOMIE
B67

BROWN L.N.,FRENCH ADMINISTRATIVE LAW. FRANCE UK EX/STRUC
CONSTN NAT/G LEGIS DOMIN CONTROL EXEC PARL/PROC PWR LAW
...JURID METH/COMP GEN/METH. PAGE 16 E0314 IDEA/COMP
CT/SYS
B67

COHEN M.R.,LAW AND THE SOCIAL ORDER: ESSAYS IN JURID
LEGAL PHILOSOPHY. USA-45 CONSULT WORKER ECO/TAC LABOR
ATTIT WEALTH...POLICY WELF/ST SOC 20 NEW/DEAL IDEA/COMP
DEPRESSION. PAGE 24 E0467
B67

GRAHAM H.D.,CRISIS IN PRINT: DESEGREGATION AND THE PRESS
PRESS IN TENNESSEE. LAW SOCIETY MUNIC POL/PAR PROVS
EDU/PROP LEAD REPRESENT DISCRIM ATTIT...IDEA/COMP POLICY
BIBLIOG/A SOC/INTEG 20 TENNESSEE SUPREME/CT RACE/REL
SOUTH/US. PAGE 45 E0896

BERNHARD R.C.,"COMPETITION IN LAW AND ECONOMICS." MARKET
LAW PLAN PRICE CONTROL PRODUC PROFIT...METH/CNCPT POLICY
IDEA/COMP GEN/LAWS 20. PAGE 11 E0210 NAT/G
    L67 CT/SYS

CICOUREL A.V.,"KINSHIP, MARRIAGE, AND DIVORCE IN SOC
COMPARATIVE FAMILY LAW." UNIV LAW FAM KIN GEN/METH. PHIL/SCI
PAGE 22 E0438 MARRIAGE
    L67 IDEA/COMP

ADOKO A.,"THE CONSTITUTION OF UGANDA." AFR UGANDA NAT/G
LOC/G CHIEF FORCES LEGIS ADJUD EXEC CHOOSE NAT/LISM CONSTN
...IDEA/COMP 20. PAGE 3 E0050 ORD/FREE
    S67 LAW

HORVATH B.,"COMPARATIVE CONFLICTS LAW AND THE INT/LAW
CONCEPT OF CHANGING LAW." UNIV RATIONAL...JURID IDEA/COMP
LOG. PAGE 55 E1099 DIPLOM
    S67 CONCPT

READ J.S.,"CENSORED." UGANDA CONSTN INTELL SOCIETY EDU/PROP
NAT/G DIPLOM PRESS WRITING ADJUD ADMIN COLONIAL AFR
RISK...IDEA/COMP 20. PAGE 84 E1675 CREATE
    S67

RUCKER B.W.,"WHAT SOLUTIONS DO PEOPLE ENDORSE IN CONCPT
FREE PRESS-FAIR TRIAL DILEMMA?" LAW NAT/G CT/SYS PRESS
ATTIT...NET/THEORY SAMP CHARTS IDEA/COMP METH 20. ADJUD
PAGE 86 E1731 ORD/FREE
    S67

BURGESS J.W.,"VON HOLST'S PUBLIC LAW OF THE UNITED CONSTN
STATES" USA-45 LAW GOV/REL...GOV/COMP IDEA/COMP 19. FEDERAL
PAGE 17 E0339 NAT/G
    S68 JURID

DUPRE L.,"TILL DEATH DO US PART?" UNIV FAM INSPECT MARRIAGE
LEGIT ADJUD SANCTION PERS/REL ANOMIE RIGID/FLEX SEX CATH
...JURID IDEA/COMP 20 CHURCH/STA BIBLE CANON/LAW LAW
CIVIL/LAW. PAGE 34 E0666
    S68

BENTHAM J.,DEFENCE OF USURY (1787). UK LAW NAT/G TAX
TEC/DEV ECO/TAC CONTROL ATTIT...CONCPT IDEA/COMP 18 FINAN
SMITH/ADAM. PAGE 10 E0197 ECO/DEV
    B88 POLICY

FERNEUIL T.,LES PRINCIPES DE 1789 ET LA SCIENCE CONSTN
SOCIALE. FRANCE NAT/G REV ATTIT...CONCPT TREND POLICY
IDEA/COMP 18/19. PAGE 37 E0739 LAW
    B89

JENKS E.J.,LAW AND POLITICS IN THE MIDDLE AGES. LAW
CHRIST-17C CULTURE STRUCT KIN NAT/G SECT CT/SYS SOCIETY
GP/REL...CLASSIF CHARTS IDEA/COMP BIBLIOG 8/16. ADJUST
PAGE 58 E1162
    B97

IDEOLOGY....SEE ATTIT, STERTYP, ALSO IDEOLOGICAL TOPIC
    INDEX, P. XIII

IFC....INTERNATIONAL FINANCE CORPORATION

IGNORANCE....SEE KNOWL

IGY....INTERNATIONAL GEOPHYSICAL YEAR

IKLE F.C. E1122

ILLEGIT....BASTARDY

FORTESCU J.,IN PRAISE OF ENGLISH LAW (1464) (TRANS. LAW
BY S.B. CHRIMES). UK ELITES CHIEF FORCES CT/SYS CONSTN
COERCE CRIME GOV/REL ILLEGIT...JURID GOV/COMP LEGIS
GEN/LAWS 15. PAGE 39 E0774 ORD/FREE
    B42

ILLEGITIMACY....SEE ILLEGIT

ILLINOIS....ILLINOIS

GELLHORN W.,THE STATES AND SUBVERSION. USA+45 PROVS
USA-45 LOC/G DELIB/GP LEGIS EDU/PROP LEGIT CT/SYS JURID
REGION PEACE ATTIT ORD/FREE SOCISM...INT CON/ANAL
20 CALIFORNIA MARYLAND ILLINOIS MICHIGAN NEW/YORK.
PAGE 43 E0845
    B52

CARPER E.T.,ILLINOIS GOES TO CONGRESS FOR ARMY ADMIN
LAND. USA+45 LAW EXTR/IND PROVS REGION CIVMIL/REL LOBBY
GOV/REL FEDERAL ATTIT 20 ILLINOIS SENATE CONGRESS GEOG
DIRKSEN/E DOUGLAS/P. PAGE 20 E0391 LEGIS
    B62

"THE STATE OF ZONING ADMINISTRATION IN ILLINOIS: ADMIN
PROCEDURAL REQUIREMENTS OF JUDICIAL INTERVENTION." CONTROL
USA+45 LAW CONSTN DELIB/GP ADJUD CT/SYS ORD/FREE HABITAT
ILLINOIS. PAGE 2 E0038 PLAN
    S67

ILO....INTERNATIONAL LABOR ORGANIZATION; SEE ALSO INT/ORG

FEIS H.,"RESEARCH ACTIVITIES OF THE LEAGUE OF CONSULT
NATIONS." EUR+WWI WOR-45 R+D INT/ORG CT/SYS KNOWL
ARMS/CONT WEALTH...OBS RECORD LEAGUE/NAT ILO 20. PEACE
PAGE 37 E0729
    L29

TOWLE L.W.,INTERNATIONAL TRADE AND COMMERCIAL MARKET
POLICY. WOR+45 LAW ECO/DEV FINAN INDUS NAT/G INT/ORG
ECO/TAC WEALTH...TIME/SEQ ILO 20. PAGE 97 E1937 INT/TRADE
    B47

OPPENHEIM L.,INTERNATIONAL LAW: A TREATISE (7TH INT/LAW
ED., 2 VOLS.). LAW CONSTN PROB/SOLV INT/TRADE ADJUD INT/ORG
AGREE NEUTRAL WAR ORD/FREE SOVEREIGN...BIBLIOG 20 DIPLOM
LEAGUE/NAT UN ILO. PAGE 79 E1579
    B53

COMM. STUDY ORGAN. PEACE,REPORTS. WOR-45 ECO/DEV WOR+45
ECO/UNDEV VOL/ASSN CONSULT FORCES PLAN TEC/DEV INT/ORG
DOMIN EDU/PROP NUC/PWR ATTIT PWR WEALTH...JURID ARMS/CONT
STERTYP FAO ILO 20 UN. PAGE 24 E0481
    B55

SOHN L.B.,BASIC DOCUMENTS OF THE UNITED NATIONS. DELIB/GP
WOR+45 LAW INT/ORG LEGIT EXEC ROUTINE CHOOSE PWR CONSTN
...JURID CONCPT GEN/LAWS ANTHOL UN TOT/POP OAS FAO
ILO 20. PAGE 92 E1853
    B56

JENKS C.W.,THE INTERNATIONAL PROTECTION OF TRADE LABOR
UNION FREEDOM. FUT WOR+45 WOR-45 VOL/ASSN DELIB/GP INT/ORG
CT/SYS REGION ROUTINE...JURID METH/CNCPT RECORD
TIME/SEQ CHARTS ILO WORK OAS 20. PAGE 58 E1153
    B57

FRIEDMANN W.G.,LAW IN A CHANGING SOCIETY. FUT SOC
WOR+45 WOR-45 LAW SOCIETY STRUCT INT/TRADE LEGIT JURID
ATTIT BIO/SOC HEALTH ORD/FREE SOVEREIGN...CONCPT
GEN/LAWS ILO 20. PAGE 41 E0803
    B59

TIPTON J.B.,"PARTICIPATION OF THE UNITED STATES IN LABOR
THE INTERNATIONAL LABOR ORGANIZATION." USA+45 LAW INT/ORG
STRUCT ECO/DEV ECO/UNDEV INDUS TEC/DEV ECO/TAC
ADMIN PERCEPT ORD/FREE SKILL...STAT HIST/WRIT
GEN/METH ILO WORK 20. PAGE 96 E1928
    S59

JENKS C.W.,HUMAN RIGHTS AND INTERNATIONAL LABOR CONCPT
STANDARDS. WOR+45 CONSTN LABOR VOL/ASSN DELIB/GP
ACT/RES EDU/PROP MORAL RESPECT...JURID SOC TREND
GEN/LAWS WORK ILO 20. PAGE 58 E1156
    B60

JENKS C.W.,THE PROPER LAW OF INTERNATIONAL LAW
ORGANISATIONS. DIPLOM LEGIT AGREE CT/SYS SANCTION INT/ORG
REPRESENT SOVEREIGN...GEN/LAWS 20 UN UNESCO ILO ADJUD
NATO OAS. PAGE 58 E1158 INT/LAW
    B62

SCHECHTER A.H.,INTERPRETATION OF AMBIGUOUS INT/LAW
DOCUMENTS BY INTERNATIONAL ADMINISTRATIVE DIPLOM
TRIBUNALS. WOR+45 EX/STRUC INT/TRADE CT/SYS INT/ORG
SOVEREIGN 20 UN ILO EURCT/JUST. PAGE 87 E1752 ADJUD
    B64

SCHWELB E.,"OPERATION OF THE EUROPEAN CONVENTION ON INT/ORG
HUMAN RIGHTS." EUR+WWI LAW INT/ORG CREATE EDU/PROP MORAL
ADJUD ADMIN PEACE ATTIT ORD/FREE PWR...POLICY
INT/LAW CONCPT OBS GEN/LAWS UN VAL/FREE ILO 20
ECHR. PAGE 89 E1791
    S64

IMF....INTERNATIONAL MONETARY FUND

SEYID MUHAMMAD V.A.,THE LEGAL FRAMEWORK OF WORLD INT/LAW
TRADE. WOR+45 INT/ORG DIPLOM CONTROL...BIBLIOG 20 VOL/ASSN
TREATY UN IMF GATT. PAGE 90 E1807 INT/TRADE
    B58 TARIFFS

SHAW C.,LEGAL PROBLEMS IN INTERNATIONAL TRADE AND INVESTMENT. WOR+45 ECO/DEV ECO/UNDEV MARKET DIPLOM TAX INCOME ROLE...ANTHOL BIBLIOG 20 TREATY UN IMF GATT. PAGE 91 E1816
B62
INT/LAW
INT/TRADE
FINAN
ECO/TAC

IMITATION....SEE CONSEN, CREATE

IMMUNITY....SEE PRIVIL

IMPERIALISM....SEE COLONIAL, SOVEREIGN, DOMIN

IMPERSONALITY....SEE STRANGE

INAUGURATE....INAUGURATIONS AND CORONATIONS

INBAU F.E. E1182

INCOME....SEE ALSO FINAN, WEALTH

HOBBES T.,A DIALOGUE BETWEEN A PHILOSOPHER AND A STUDENT OF THE COMMON LAWS OF ENGLAND (1667?). UK SECT DOMIN ADJUD CRIME INCOME OWN UTIL ORD/FREE PWR SOVEREIGN...JURID GEN/LAWS 17. PAGE 53 E1057
B40
CT/SYS
CHIEF
SANCTION

BENTHAM J.,"THE RATIONALE OF REWARD" IN J. BOWRING, ED., THE WORKS OF JEREMY BENTHAM (VOL. 2)" LAW WORKER CREATE INSPECT PAY ROUTINE HAPPINESS PRODUC SUPEGO WEALTH METH/CNCPT. PAGE 10 E0195
C43
SANCTION
ECO/TAC
INCOME
PWR

US LIBRARY OF CONGRESS,CONSTITUTIONAL AND STATUTORY PROVISIONS OF THE STATES (VOL. I). USA-45 CREATE TAX CT/SYS CHOOSE SUFF INCOME PWR 20. PAGE 101 E2016
B45
CONSTN
FEDERAL
PROVS
JURID

GONZALEZ NAVARRO M.,LA COLONIZACION EN MEXICO, 1877-1910. AGRI NAT/G PLAN PROB/SOLV INCOME ...POLICY JURID CENSUS 19/20 MEXIC/AMER MIGRATION. PAGE 44 E0883
B60
ECO/UNDEV
GEOG
HABITAT
COLONIAL

DE LAVALLE H.,A STATEMENT OF THE LAWS OF PERU IN MATTERS AFFECTING BUSINESS (3RD ED.). PERU WORKER INT/TRADE INCOME ORD/FREE...INT/LAW 20. PAGE 30 E0586
B62
CONSTN
JURID
FINAN
TAX

SHAW C.,LEGAL PROBLEMS IN INTERNATIONAL TRADE AND INVESTMENT. WOR+45 ECO/DEV ECO/UNDEV MARKET DIPLOM TAX INCOME ROLE...ANTHOL BIBLIOG 20 TREATY UN IMF GATT. PAGE 91 E1816
B62
INT/LAW
INT/TRADE
FINAN
ECO/TAC

BROOKS T.R.,TOIL AND TROUBLE, A HISTORY OF AMERICAN LABOR. WORKER BARGAIN CAP/ISM ADJUD AUTOMAT EXEC GP/REL RACE/REL EFFICIENCY INCOME PROFIT MARXISM 17/20 KENNEDY/JF AFL/CIO NEGRO. PAGE 16 E0310
B64
INDUS
LABOR
LEGIS

FLEISCHER B.M.,THE ECONOMICS OF DELINQUENCY. UNIV WORKER STRANGE ANOMIE...STAT CHARTS 20. PAGE 38 E0762
B66
STRATA
INCOME
AGE/Y
CRIME

PLATE H.,PARTEIFINANZIERUNG UND GRUNDESETZ. GERMANY NAT/G PLAN GIVE PAY INCOME WEALTH...JURID 20. PAGE 81 E1619
B66
POL/PAR
CONSTN
FINAN

BRAGER G.A.,COMMUNITY ACTION AGAINST POVERTY. USA+45 LAW STRATA INGP/REL INCOME NEW/LIB...POLICY WELF/ST ANTHOL. PAGE 15 E0285
B67
NEIGH
WEALTH
SOC/WK
CREATE

ANDERSON W.,"THE PERILS OF 'SHARING'". USA+45 ECO/TAC RECEIVE LOBBY GOV/REL CENTRAL COST INCOME ...POLICY PLURIST CONGRESS. PAGE 5 E0095
S67
BUDGET
TAX
FEDERAL
LAW

DANIEL C.,"FREEDOM, EQUITY, AND THE WAR ON POVERTY." USA+45 WORKER ECO/TAC JURID. PAGE 29 E0566
S67
WEALTH
INCOME
SOCIETY
ORD/FREE

MAYER M.,"THE IDEA OF JUSTICE AND THE POOR." USA+45 CLIENT CONSULT RENT ADJUD DISCRIM KNOWL 20. PAGE 70
S67
INCOME
WEALTH

E1393
LAW
ORD/FREE

SCHELLING T.C.,"ECONOMICS AND CRIMINAL ENTERPRISE." LAW FORCES BARGAIN ECO/TAC CONTROL GAMBLE ROUTINE ADJUST DEMAND INCOME PROFIT CRIMLGY. PAGE 87 E1756
S67
CRIME
PROB/SOLV
CONCPT

SMITH A.,LECTURES ON JUSTICE, POLICE, REVENUE AND ARMS (1763). UK LAW FAM FORCES TARIFFS AGREE COERCE INCOME OWN WEALTH LAISSEZ...GEN/LAWS 17/18. PAGE 92 E1840
B96
DIPLOM
JURID
OLD/LIB
TAX

INCOMPETENCE....SEE SKILL

IND/WRK/AF....INDUSTRIAL AND WORKERS' COMMERCIAL UNION OF AFRICA

INDEX....INDEX SYSTEM

INDEX TO LEGAL PERIODICALS. CANADA NEW/ZEALND UK USA+45 USA-45 CONSTN LEGIS JUDGE ADJUD ADMIN CONTROL CT/SYS FEDERAL...CRIMLGY INT/LAW 20 CMN/WLTH AUSTRAL. PAGE 1 E0006
N
BIBLIOG
INDEX
LAW
JURID

DE MARTENS G.F.,RECUEIL GENERALE DE TRAITES ET AUTRES ACTES RELATIFS AUX RAPPORTS DE DROIT INTERNATIONAL (41 VOLS.). EUR+WWI MOD/EUR USA+45 ...INDEX TREATY 18/20. PAGE 30 E0587
N
BIBLIOG
INT/LAW
DIPLOM

FORTESCUE G.K.,SUBJECT INDEX OF THE MODERN WORKS ADDED TO THE LIBRARY OF THE BRITISH MUSEUM IN THE YEARS 1881-1900 (3 VOLS.). UK LAW CONSTN FINAN NAT/G FORCES INT/TRADE COLONIAL 19. PAGE 39 E0775
B03
BIBLIOG
INDEX
WRITING

BURCHFIELD L.,STUDENT'S GUIDE TO MATERIALS IN POLITICAL SCIENCE. FINAN INT/ORG NAT/G POL/PAR DIPLOM PRESS ADMIN...BIOG 18/19. PAGE 17 E0328
B35
BIBLIOG
INDEX
LAW

BECKER O.,MASTER RESEARCH GUIDE. USA+45 USA-45 PRESS...JURID INDEX 20. PAGE 9 E0171
B51
BIBLIOG
LAW
ADJUD
CT/SYS

BINANI G.D.,INDIA AT A GLANCE (REV. ED.). INDIA COM/IND FINAN INDUS LABOR PROVS SCHOOL PLAN DIPLOM INT/TRADE ADMIN...JURID 20. PAGE 12 E0229
B54
INDEX
CON/ANAL
NAT/G
ECO/UNDEV

AMERICAN ASSOCIATION LAW LIB,INDEX TO FOREIGN LEGAL PERIODICALS. WOR+45 MUNIC...IDEA/COMP 20. PAGE 4 E0075
B60
INDEX
LAW
JURID
DIPLOM

BLAUSTEIN A.P.,MANUAL ON FOREIGN LEGAL PERIODICALS AND THEIR INDEX. WOR+45 DIPLOM 20. PAGE 13 E0244
B62
BIBLIOG
INDEX
LAW
JURID

BECKER T.L.,POLITICAL BEHAVIORALISM AND MODERN JURISPRUDENCE* A WORKING THEORY AND STUDY IN JUDICIAL DECISION-MAKING. CONSTN...JURID STAT GEN/METH INDEX. PAGE 9 E0172
B64
JUDGE
LAW
DECISION
CT/SYS

HOLT S.,THE DICTIONARY OF AMERICAN GOVERNMENT. USA+45 LOC/G MUNIC PROVS LEGIS ADMIN JURID. PAGE 55 E1091
B64
DICTIONARY
INDEX
LAW
NAT/G

UNESCO,HANDBOOK OF INTERNATIONAL EXCHANGES. COM/IND R+D ACADEM PROF/ORG VOL/ASSN CREATE TEC/DEV EDU/PROP AGREE 20 TREATY. PAGE 98 E1963
B65
INDEX
INT/ORG
DIPLOM
PRESS

SHEEHY E.P.,"SELECTED REFERENCE BOOKS OF 1965-1966." AGRI PERF/ART PRESS...GEOG HUM JURID SOC LING WORSHIP. PAGE 91 E1817
S66
BIBLIOG/A
INDEX
CLASSIF

INDIA....SEE ALSO S/ASIA

LALL A.S.,NEGOTIATING DISARMAMENT* THE EIGHTEEN NATION DISARMAMENT CONFERENCE* THE FIRST TWO YEARS.
B'
OBS
ARMS/CONT

1962-1964. ASIA FRANCE INDIA USA+45 USSR PROB/SOLV DIPLOM
ADJUD NEUTRAL ATTIT...IDEA/COMP COLD/WAR. PAGE 62 OP/RES
E1246

B38
HOLDSWORTH W.S.,A HISTORY OF ENGLISH LAW; THE LAW
CENTURIES OF SETTLEMENT AND REFORM (VOL. X). INDIA LOC/G
UK CONSTN NAT/G CHIEF LEGIS ADMIN COLONIAL CT/SYS EX/STRUC
CHOOSE ORD/FREE PWR...JURID 18 PARLIAMENT ADJUD
COMMONWLTH COMMON/LAW. PAGE 54 E1077

B53
MAJUMDAR B.B.,PROBLEMS OF PUBLIC ADMINISTRATION IN ECO/UNDEV
INDIA. INDIA INDUS PLAN BUDGET ADJUD CENTRAL DEMAND GOV/REL
WEALTH...WELF/ST ANTHOL 20 CIVIL/SERV. PAGE 68 ADMIN
E1353 MUNIC

B54
BINANI G.D.,INDIA AT A GLANCE (REV. ED.). INDIA INDEX
COM/IND FINAN INDUS LABOR PROVS SCHOOL PLAN DIPLOM CON/ANAL
INT/TRADE ADMIN...JURID 20. PAGE 12 E0229 NAT/G
ECO/UNDEV

B56
DOUGLAS W.O.,WE THE JUDGES. INDIA USA+45 USA-45 LAW ADJUD
NAT/G SECT LEGIS PRESS CRIME FEDERAL ORD/FREE CT/SYS
...POLICY GOV/COMP 19/20 WARRN/EARL MARSHALL/J CONSTN
SUPREME/CT. PAGE 32 E0640 GOV/REL

B58
ALEXANDROWICZ,A BIBLIOGRAPHY OF INDIAN LAW. INDIA BIBLIOG
S/ASIA CONSTN CT/SYS...INT/LAW 19/20. PAGE 3 E0062 LAW
ADJUD
JURID

B58
LAW COMMISSION OF INDIA,REFORM OF JUDICIAL CT/SYS
ADMINISTRATION. INDIA TOP/EX ADMIN DISCRIM ADJUD
EFFICIENCY...METH/COMP 20. PAGE 63 E1269 GOV/REL
CONTROL

B58
SHARMA M.P.,PUBLIC ADMINISTRATION IN THEORY AND MGT
PRACTICE. INDIA UK USA+45 USA-45 EX/STRUC ADJUD ADMIN
...POLICY CONCPT NAT/COMP 20. PAGE 90 E1813 DELIB/GP
JURID

B60
BAYLEY D.H.,VIOLENT AGITATION AND THE DEMOCRATIC COERCE
PROCESS IN INDIA. INDIA LAW POL/PAR 20. PAGE 8 CROWD
E0159 CONSTN
PROB/SOLV

B60
PRASAD B.,THE ORIGINS OF PROVINCIAL AUTONOMY. INDIA CENTRAL
UK FINAN LOC/G FORCES LEGIS CONTROL CT/SYS PWR PROVS
...JURID 19/20. PAGE 82 E1646 COLONIAL
NAT/G

B61
BAINS J.S.,STUDIES IN POLITICAL SCIENCE. INDIA DIPLOM
WOR+45 WOR-45 CONSTN BAL/PWR ADJUD ADMIN PARL/PROC INT/LAW
SOVEREIGN...SOC METH/COMP ANTHOL 17/20 UN. PAGE 7 NAT/G
E0137

B61
SYATAUW J.J.G.,SOME NEWLY ESTABLISHED ASIAN STATES INT/LAW
AND THE DEVELOPMENT OF INTERNATIONAL LAW. BURMA ADJUST
CEYLON INDIA INDONESIA ECO/UNDEV COLONIAL NEUTRAL SOCIETY
WAR PEACE SOVEREIGN...CHARTS 19/20. PAGE 95 E1902 S/ASIA

B63
LIVINGSTON W.S.,FEDERALISM IN THE COMMONWEALTH - A BIBLIOG
BIBLIOGRAPHICAL COMMENTARY. CANADA INDIA PAKISTAN JURID
UK STRUCT LOC/G NAT/G POL/PAR...NAT/COMP 20 FEDERAL
AUSTRAL. PAGE 66 E1310 CONSTN

B63
PATRA A.C.,THE ADMINISTRATION OF JUSTICE UNDER THE ADMIN
EAST INDIA COMPANY IN BENGAL, BIHAR AND ORISSA. JURID
INDIA UK LG/CO CAP/ISM INT/TRADE ADJUD COLONIAL CONCPT
CONTROL CT/SYS...POLICY 20. PAGE 80 E1602

S63
WEISSBERG G.,"MAPS AS EVIDENCE IN INTERNATIONAL LAW
BOUNDARY DISPUTES: A REAPPRAISAL." CHINA/COM GEOG
EUR+WWI INDIA MOD/EUR S/ASIA INT/ORG NAT/G LEGIT SOVEREIGN
PERCEPT...JURID CHARTS 20. PAGE 105 E2110

B64
GOODNOW H.F.,THE CIVIL SERVICE OF PAKISTAN: ADMIN
BUREAUCRACY IN A NEW NATION. INDIA PAKISTAN S/ASIA GOV/REL
ECO/UNDEV PROVS CHIEF PARTIC CHOOSE EFFICIENCY PWR LAW
...BIBLIOG 20. PAGE 45 E0889 NAT/G

B64
RAGHAVAN M.D.,INDIA IN CEYLONESE HISTORY, SOCIETY DIPLOM
AND CULTURE. CEYLON INDIA S/ASIA LAW SOCIETY CULTURE
INT/TRADE ATTIT...ART/METH JURID SOC LING 20. SECT
PAGE 83 E1668 STRUCT

B64
ROBINSON R.D.,INTERNATIONAL BUSINESS POLICY. AFR ECO/TAC
INDIA L/A+17C USA+45 ELITES AGRI FOR/AID COERCE DIST/IND
BAL/PAY...DECISION INT/LAW MGT 20. PAGE 85 E1706 COLONIAL
FINAN

L64
WORLD PEACE FOUNDATION,"INTERNATIONAL INT/ORG
ORGANIZATIONS: SUMMARY OF ACTIVITIES." INDIA ROUTINE
PAKISTAN TURKEY WOR+45 CONSTN CONSULT EX/STRUC
ECO/TAC EDU/PROP LEGIT ORD/FREE...JURID SOC UN 20
CYPRESS. PAGE 107 E2145

S64
SINGH N.,"THE CONTEMPORARY PRACTICE OF INDIA IN THE LAW
FIELD OF INTERNATIONAL LAW." INDIA S/ASIA INT/ORG ATTIT
NAT/G DOMIN EDU/PROP LEGIT KNOWL...CONCPT TOT/POP DIPLOM
20. PAGE 91 E1833 INT/LAW

B65
GAJENDRAGADKAR P.B.,LAW, LIBERTY AND SOCIAL ORD/FREE
JUSTICE. INDIA CONSTN NAT/G SECT PLAN ECO/TAC PRESS LAW
POPULISM...SOC METH/COMP 20 HINDU. PAGE 42 E0826 ADJUD
JURID

B65
PYLEE M.V.,CONSTITUTIONAL GOVERNMENT IN INDIA (2ND CONSTN
REV. ED.). INDIA POL/PAR EX/STRUC DIPLOM COLONIAL NAT/G
CT/SYS PARL/PROC PRIVIL...JURID 16/20. PAGE 83 PROVS
E1665 FEDERAL

B65
SHARMA S.A.,PARLIAMENTARY GOVERNMENT IN INDIA. NAT/G
INDIA FINAN LOC/G PROVS DELIB/GP PLAN ADMIN CT/SYS CONSTN
FEDERAL...JURID 20. PAGE 90 E1814 PARL/PROC
LEGIS

B65
SOPER T.,EVOLVING COMMONWEALTH. AFR CANADA INDIA INT/ORG
IRELAND UK LAW CONSTN POL/PAR DOMIN CONTROL WAR PWR COLONIAL
...AUD/VIS 18/20 COMMONWLTH OEEC. PAGE 93 E1857 VOL/ASSN

L65
SHARMA S.P.,"THE INDIA-CHINA BORDER DISPUTE: AN LAW
INDIAN PERSPECTIVE." ASIA CHINA/COM S/ASIA NAT/G ATTIT
LEGIT CT/SYS NAT/LISM DRIVE MORAL ORD/FREE PWR 20. SOVEREIGN
PAGE 91 E1815 INDIA

S65
PRABHAKAR P.,"SURVEY OF RESEARCH AND SOURCE BIBLIOG
MATERIALS; THE SINO-INDIAN BORDER DISPUTE." ASIA
CHINA/COM INDIA LAW NAT/G PLAN BAL/PWR WAR...POLICY S/ASIA
20 COLD/WAR. PAGE 82 E1645 DIPLOM

B66
BEDI A.S.,FREEDOM OF EXPRESSION AND SECURITY; METH
COMPARATIVE STUDY OF FUNCTIONS OF SUPREME COURTS IN CT/SYS
UNITED STATES AND INDIA. INDIA USA+45 LAW CONSTN ADJUD
PROB/SOLV...DECISION JURID BIBLIOG 20 SUPREME/CT ORD/FREE
FREE/SPEE AMEND/I. PAGE 9 E0175

B66
BEER U.,FRUCHTBARKEITSREGELUNG ALS KONSEQUENZ CONTROL
VERANTWORTLICHER ELTERNSCHAFT. ASIA GERMANY/W INDIA GEOG
LAW ECO/DEV ECO/UNDEV TEC/DEV ECO/TAC BIO/SOC SEX FAM
CATHISM...METH/COMP 20 CHINJAP BIRTH/CON. PAGE 9 SECT
E0178

B66
GHOSH P.K.,THE CONSTITUTION OF INDIA: HOW IT HAS CONSTN
BEEN FRAMED. INDIA LOC/G DELIB/GP EX/STRUC NAT/G
PROB/SOLV BUDGET INT/TRADE CT/SYS CHOOSE...LING 20. LEGIS
PAGE 43 E0854 FEDERAL

B66
HIDAYATULLAH M.,DEMOCRACY IN INDIA AND THE JUDICIAL NAT/G
PROCESS. INDIA EX/STRUC LEGIS LEAD GOV/REL ATTIT CT/SYS
ORD/FREE...MAJORIT CONCPT 20 NEHRU/J. PAGE 52 E1040 CONSTN
JURID

B67
NARAIN I.,THE POLITICS OF RACIALISM. INDIA DISCRIM
SOUTH/AFR LAW NAT/G RACE/REL ATTIT 20. PAGE 76 COLONIAL
E1521 HIST/WRIT

S67
RAI H.,"DISTRICT MAGISTRATE AND POLICE STRUCT
SUPERINTENDENT IN INDIA: THE CONTROVERSY OF DUAL CONTROL
CONTROL" INDIA LAW PROVS ADMIN PWR 19/20. PAGE 83 ROLE
E1669 FORCES

INDIAN/AM....AMERICAN INDIANS

B17
DE VICTORIA F.,DE INDIS ET DE JURE BELLI (1557) IN   WAR
F. DE VICTORIA, DE INDIS ET DE JURE BELLI   INT/LAW
REFLECTIONES. UNIV NAT/G SECT CHIEF PARTIC COERCE   OWN
PEACE MORAL...POLICY 16 INDIAN/AM CHRISTIAN
CONSCN/OBJ. PAGE 30 E0598

B47
HARGRETT L.,A BIBLIOGRAPHY OF THE CONSTITUTIONS AND   BIBLIOG/A
LAWS OF THE AMERICAN INDIANS. USA-45 LOC/G GOV/REL   CONSTN
GP/REL 19/20 INDIAN/AM. PAGE 50 E0999   LAW
                                                         NAT/G

B61
US COMMISSION ON CIVIL RIGHTS,JUSTICE: BOOK 5, 1961   DISCRIM
REPORT OF THE U.S. COMMISSION ON CIVIL RIGHTS.   LAW
LOC/G NAT/G RACE/REL...JURID 20 NEGRO CIV/RIGHTS   FORCES
INDIAN/AM JURY INDIAN/AM. PAGE 99 E1983

B61
US COMMISSION ON CIVIL RIGHTS,JUSTICE: BOOK 5, 1961   DISCRIM
REPORT OF THE U.S. COMMISSION ON CIVIL RIGHTS.   LAW
LOC/G NAT/G RACE/REL...JURID 20 NEGRO CIV/RIGHTS   FORCES
INDIAN/AM JURY INDIAN/AM. PAGE 99 E1983

B65
ROSE A.M.,MINORITY PROBLEMS: A TEXTBOOK OF READINGS   RACE/REL
IN INTERGROUP RELATIONS. UNIV USA+45 LAW SCHOOL   DISCRIM
WORKER PROB/SOLV GP/REL PERSON...PSY ANTHOL WORSHIP   ISOLAT
20 NEGRO INDIAN/AM JEWS EUROPE. PAGE 85 E1713   ACT/RES

INDIANA....INDIANA

INDICATOR....NUMERICAL INDICES AND INDICATORS

S47
ANGELL R.C.,"THE SOCIAL INTEGRATION OF AMERICAN   MUNIC
CITIES OF MORE THAN 1000,000 POPULATION" (BMR)"   CENSUS
USA+45 SOCIETY CRIME ADJUST WEALTH...GEOG SOC   GP/REL
CONCPT INDICATOR SAMP CHARTS SOC/INTEG 20. PAGE 5
E0098

INDIVIDUAL....SEE PERSON

INDOCTRINATION....SEE EDU/PROP

INDONESIA....SEE ALSO S/ASIA

B45
US LIBRARY OF CONGRESS,NETHERLANDS EAST INDIES.   BIBLIOG/A
INDONESIA LAW CULTURE AGRI INDUS SCHOOL COLONIAL   S/ASIA
HEALTH...GEOG JURID SOC 19/20 NETH/IND. PAGE 101   NAT/G
E2017

B61
SYATAUW J.J.G.,SOME NEWLY ESTABLISHED ASIAN STATES   INT/LAW
AND THE DEVELOPMENT OF INTERNATIONAL LAW. BURMA   ADJUST
CEYLON INDIA INDONESIA ECO/UNDEV COLONIAL NEUTRAL   SOCIETY
WAR PEACE SOVEREIGN...CHARTS 19/20. PAGE 95 E1902   S/ASIA

INDUS....ALL OR MOST INDUSTRY; SEE ALSO SPECIFIC
  INDUSTRIES, INSTITUTIONAL INDEX, PART C, P. XII

N
FULLER G.A.,DEMOBILIZATION: A SELECTED LIST OF   BIBLIOG/A
REFERENCES. USA+45 LAW AGRI LABOR WORKER ECO/TAC   INDUS
RATION RECEIVE EDU/PROP ROUTINE ARMS/CONT ALL/VALS   FORCES
20. PAGE 41 E0819   NAT/G

N
INTERNATIONAL BOOK NEWS, 1928-1934. ECO/UNDEV FINAN   BIBLIOG/A
INDUS LABOR INT/TRADE CONFER ADJUD COLONIAL...HEAL   DIPLOM
SOC/WK CHARTS 20 LEAGUE/NAT. PAGE 1 E0008   INT/LAW
                                                         INT/ORG

N
ADVANCED MANAGEMENT. INDUS EX/STRUC WORKER OP/RES   MGT
...DECISION BIBLIOG/A 20. PAGE 1 E0015   ADMIN
                                                         LABOR
                                                         GP/REL

N
ARBITRATION JOURNAL. WOR+45 LAW INDUS JUDGE DIPLOM   BIBLIOG
CT/SYS INGP/REL 20. PAGE 1 E0016   MGT
                                                         LABOR
                                                         ADJUD

N
THE JAPAN SCIENCE REVIEW: LAW AND POLITICS: LIST OF   BIBLIOG
BOOKS AND ARTICLES ON LAW AND POLITICS. CONSTN AGRI   LAW
INDUS LABOR DIPLOM TAX ADMIN CRIME...INT/LAW SOC 20   S/ASIA
CHINJAP. PAGE 2 E0027   PHIL/SCI

B02
GRIFFIN A.P.C.,A LIST OF BOOKS RELATING TO TRUSTS   BIBLIOG/A
(2ND REV. ED.) (PAMPHLET). FRANCE GERMANY UK USA-45   JURID
WOR-45 LAW ECO/DEV INDUS LG/CO NAT/G CAP/ISM   ECO/TAC
CENTRAL DISCRIM PWR LAISSEZ 19/20. PAGE 46 E0919   VOL/ASSN

B03
GRIFFIN A.P.C.,LIST OF REFERENCES ON INDUSTRIAL   BIBLIOG/A
ARBITRATION (PAMPHLET). USA-45 STRATA VOL/ASSN   INDUS
DELIB/GP WORKER ADJUD GP/REL...MGT 19/20. PAGE 46   LABOR
E0921   BARGAIN

B06
GRIFFIN A.P.C.,LIST OF BOOKS RELATING TO CHILD   BIBLIOG/A
LABOR (PAMPHLET). BELGIUM FRANCE GERMANY MOD/EUR UK   LAW
USA-45 ECO/DEV INDUS WORKER CAP/ISM PAY ROUTINE   LABOR
ALL/IDEOS...MGT SOC 19/20. PAGE 47 E0929   AGE/C

B14
CRAIG J.,ELEMENTS OF POLITICAL SCIENCE (3 VOLS.).   PHIL/SCI
CONSTN AGRI INDUS SCHOOL FORCES TAX CT/SYS SUFF   NAT/G
MORAL WEALTH...CONCPT 19 CIVIL/LIB. PAGE 27 E0539   ORD/FREE

B16
SCHROEDER T.,FREE SPEECH FOR RADICALS (REV. ED.).   ORD/FREE
USA-45 CONSTN INDUS LOC/G FORCES SANCTION WAR ATTIT   CONTROL
SEX...JURID REFORMERS 20 FREE/SPEE. PAGE 88 E1767   LAW
                                                         PRESS

N18
BREWER D.J.,THE MOVEMENT OF COERCION (PAMPHLET).   GP/REL
CONSTN INDUS ADJUD COERCE OWN WEALTH...OLD/LIB   LABOR
JURID 19 SUPREME/CT. PAGE 15 E0296   LG/CO
                                                         LAW

N19
ATOMIC INDUSTRIAL FORUM,COMMENTARY ON LEGISLATION   NUC/PWR
TO PERMIT PRIVATE OWNERSHIP OF SPECIAL NUCLEAR   MARKET
MATERIAL (PAMPHLET). USA+45 DELIB/GP LEGIS PLAN OWN   INDUS
...POLICY 20 AEC CONGRESS. PAGE 6 E0111   LAW

N19
MCCONNELL G.,THE STEEL SEIZURE OF 1952 (PAMPHLET).   DELIB/GP
USA+45 FINAN INDUS PROC/MFG LG/CO EX/STRUC ADJUD   LABOR
CONTROL GP/REL ORD/FREE PWR 20 TRUMAN/HS PRESIDENT   PROB/SOLV
CONGRESS. PAGE 70 E1402   NAT/G

B27
DICKINSON J.,ADMINISTRATIVE JUSTICE AND THE   CT/SYS
SUPREMACY OF LAW IN THE UNITED STATES. USA-45 LAW   ADJUD
INDUS DOMIN EDU/PROP CONTROL EXEC GP/REL ORD/FREE   ADMIN
...POLICY JURID 19/20. PAGE 31 E0623   NAT/G

B31
BORCHARD E.H.,GUIDE TO THE LAW AND LEGAL LITERATURE   BIBLIOG/A
OF FRANCE. FRANCE FINAN INDUS LABOR SECT LEGIS   LAW
ADMIN COLONIAL CRIME OWN...INT/LAW 20. PAGE 14   CONSTN
E0266   METH

B35
NORDSKOG J.E.,SOCIAL REFORM IN NORWAY. NORWAY INDUS   LABOR
NAT/G POL/PAR LEGIS ADJUD...SOC BIBLIOG SOC/INTEG   ADJUST
20. PAGE 78 E1555

S36
CORWIN E.S.,"THE CONSTITUTION AS INSTRUMENT AND AS   CONSTN
SYMBOL." USA-45 ECO/DEV INDUS CAP/ISM SANCTION   LAW
RIGID/FLEX ORD/FREE LAISSEZ OBJECTIVE 20 CONGRESS   ADJUD
SUPREME/CT. PAGE 26 E0512   PWR

B37
HAMILTON W.H.,THE POWER TO GOVERN. ECO/DEV FINAN   LING
INDUS ECO/TAC INT/TRADE TARIFFS TAX CONTROL CT/SYS   CONSTN
WAR COST PWR 18/20 SUPREME/CT. PAGE 50 E0991   NAT/G
                                                         POLICY

B38
FIELD G.L.,THE SYNDICAL AND CORPORATIVE   FASCISM
INSTITUTIONS OF ITALIAN FASCISM. ITALY CONSTN   INDUS
STRATA LABOR EX/STRUC TOP/EX ADJUD ADMIN LEAD   NAT/G
TOTALISM AUTHORIT...MGT 20 MUSSOLIN/B. PAGE 38   WORKER
E0746

B38
SAINT-PIERRE C.I.,SCHEME FOR LASTING PEACE (TRANS.   INT/ORG
BY H. BELLOT). INDUS NAT/G CHIEF FORCES INT/TRADE   PEACE
CT/SYS WAR PWR SOVEREIGN WEALTH...POLICY 18.   AGREE
PAGE 87 E1741   INT/LAW

B43
BACKUS R.C.,A GUIDE TO THE LAW AND LEGAL LITERATURE   BIBLIOG/A
OF COLOMBIA. FINAN INDUS LABOR FORCES ADJUD ADMIN   LAW
COLONIAL CT/SYS CRIME...INT/LAW JURID 20 COLOMB.   CONSTN
PAGE 7 E0127   L/A+17C

CHENEY F.,CARTELS, COMBINES, AND TRUSTS: A SELECTED
LIST OF REFERENCES. GERMANY UK USA-45 WOR-45
DELIB/GP OP/RES BARGAIN CAP/ISM ECO/TAC INT/TRADE
LICENSE LEGIT CONFER PRICE 20. PAGE 22 E0428
B44
BIBLIOG/A
LG/CO
ECO/DEV
INDUS

GALLOWAY E.,ABSTRACTS OF POSTWAR LITERATURE (VOL.
IV) JAN.-JULY, 1945 NOS. 901-1074. POLAND USA+45
USSR WOR+45 INDUS LABOR PLAN ECO/TAC INT/TRADE TAX
EDU/PROP ADMIN COLONIAL INT/LAW. PAGE 42 E0829
B45
BIBLIOG/A
NUC/PWR
NAT/G
DIPLOM

US LIBRARY OF CONGRESS,NETHERLANDS EAST INDIES.
INDONESIA LAW CULTURE AGRI INDUS SCHOOL COLONIAL
HEALTH...GEOG JURID SOC 19/20 NETH/IND. PAGE 101
E2017
B45
BIBLIOG/A
S/ASIA
NAT/G

GORDON D.L.,THE HIDDEN WEAPON: THE STORY OF
ECONOMIC WARFARE. EUR+WWI USA-45 LAW FINAN INDUS
NAT/G CONSULT FORCES PLAN DOMIN PWR WEALTH
...INT/LAW CONCPT OBS TOT/POP NAZI 20. PAGE 45
E0891
B47
INT/ORG
ECO/TAC
INT/TRADE
WAR

TOWLE L.W.,INTERNATIONAL TRADE AND COMMERCIAL
POLICY. WOR+45 LAW ECO/DEV FINAN INDUS NAT/G
ECO/TAC WEALTH...TIME/SEQ ILO 20. PAGE 97 E1937
B47
MARKET
INT/ORG
INT/TRADE

JACKSON E.,MEETING OF THE MINDS: A WAY TO PEACE
THROUGH MEDIATION. WOR+45 INDUS INT/ORG NAT/G
DELIB/GP DIPLOM EDU/PROP LEGIT ORD/FREE...NEW/IDEA
SELF/OBS TIME/SEQ CHARTS GEN/LAWS TOT/POP 20 UN
TREATY. PAGE 57 E1139
B52
LABOR
JUDGE

MAJUMDAR B.B.,PROBLEMS OF PUBLIC ADMINISTRATION IN
INDIA. INDIA INDUS PLAN BUDGET ADJUD CENTRAL DEMAND
WEALTH...WELF/ST ANTHOL 20 CIVIL/SERV. PAGE 68
E1353
B53
ECO/UNDEV
GOV/REL
ADMIN
MUNIC

BINANI G.D.,INDIA AT A GLANCE (REV. ED.). INDIA
COM/IND FINAN INDUS LABOR PROVS SCHOOL PLAN DIPLOM
INT/TRADE ADMIN...JURID 20. PAGE 12 E0229
B54
INDEX
CON/ANAL
NAT/G
ECO/UNDEV

CAPLOW T.,THE SOCIOLOGY OF WORK. USA+45 USA-45
STRATA MARKET FAM GP/REL INGP/REL ALL/VALS
...DECISION STAT BIBLIOG SOC/INTEG 20. PAGE 19
E0375
B54
LABOR
WORKER
INDUS
ROLE

CARTER P.G.,STATISTICAL BULLETINS: AN ANNOTATED
BIBLIOGRAPHY OF THE GENERAL STATISTICAL BULLETINS
AND MAJOR POL SUBDIV OF WORLD. CULTURE AGRI FINAN
INDUS LABOR TEC/DEV INT/TRADE CT/SYS WEALTH
...CRIMLGY SOC 20. PAGE 20 E0400
B54
BIBLIOG/A
WOR+45
NAT/G
STAT

FRIEDMAN W.,THE PUBLIC CORPORATION: A COMPARATIVE
SYMPOSIUM (UNIVERSITY OF TORONTO SCHOOL OF LAW
COMPARATIVE LAW SERIES, VOL. I). SWEDEN USA+45
INDUS INT/ORG NAT/G REGION CENTRAL FEDERAL...POLICY
JURID IDEA/COMP NAT/COMP ANTHOL 20 COMMONWLTH
MONOPOLY EUROPE. PAGE 40 E0801
B54
LAW
SOCISM
LG/CO
OWN

BRAUN K.,LABOR DISPUTES AND THEIR SETTLEMENT.
ECO/TAC ROUTINE TASK GP/REL...DECISION GEN/LAWS.
PAGE 15 E0288
B55
INDUS
LABOR
BARGAIN
ADJUD

JAPAN MOMBUSHO DAIGAKU GAKIYUT,BIBLIOGRAPHY OF THE
STUDIES ON LAW AND POLITICS (PAMPHLET). CONSTN
INDUS LABOR DIPLOM TAX ADMIN...CRIMLGY INT/LAW 20
CHINJAP. PAGE 58 E1150
B55
BIBLIOG
LAW
PHIL/SCI

LARROWE C.P.,SHAPE-UP AND HIRING HALL. TRIBUTE
ADJUD CONTROL SANCTION COERCE CRIME GP/REL PWR
...CHARTS 20 AFL/CIO NEWYORK/C SEATTLE. PAGE 63
E1256
B55
LABOR
INDUS
WORKER
NAT/G

SERRANO MOSCOSO E.,A STATEMENT OF THE LAWS OF
ECUADOR IN MATTERS AFFECTING BUSINESS (2ND ED.).
ECUADOR INDUS LABOR LG/CO NAT/G LEGIS TAX CONTROL
MARRIAGE 20. PAGE 90 E1805
B55
FINAN
ECO/UNDEV
LAW
CONSTN

JENNINGS I.,PARLIAMENT. UK FINAN INDUS POL/PAR
B57
PARL/PROC

DELIB/GP EX/STRUC PLAN CONTROL...MAJORIT JURID
PARLIAMENT. PAGE 58 E1163
TOP/EX
MGT
LEGIS

ATOMIC INDUSTRIAL FORUM,MANAGEMENT AND ATOMIC
ENERGY. WOR+45 SEA LAW MARKET NAT/G TEC/DEV INSPECT
INT/TRADE CONFER PEACE HEALTH...ANTHOL 20. PAGE 6
E0112
B58
NUC/PWR
INDUS
MGT
ECO/TAC

BUGEDA LANZAS J.,A STATEMENT OF THE LAWS OF CUBA IN
MATTERS AFFECTING BUSINESS (2ND ED. REV.,
ENLARGED). CUBA L/A+17C LAW FINAN FAM LEGIS ACT/RES
ADMIN GP/REL...BIBLIOG 20 OAS. PAGE 17 E0327
B58
JURID
NAT/G
INDUS
WORKER

CUNNINGHAM W.B.,COMPULSORY CONCILIATION AND
COLLECTIVE BARGAINING. CANADA NAT/G LEGIS ADJUD
CT/SYS GP/REL...MGT 20 NEW/BRUNS STRIKE CASEBOOK.
PAGE 28 E0555
B58
POLICY
BARGAIN
LABOR
INDUS

MOSER J.J.,JOHANN JACOB MOSER'S GESAMMELTE UND ZU
GEMEINNUTZIGEM GEBRAUCH EINGERICHTETE BIBLIOTHEK.
GERMANY PROC/MFG INT/TRADE...POLICY JURID MGT 18.
PAGE 75 E1500
B58
BIBLIOG
EXTR/IND
INDUS

WESTIN A.F.,THE ANATOMY OF A CONSTITUTIONAL LAW
CASE. USA+45 LAW LEGIS ADMIN EXEC...DECISION MGT
SOC RECORD 20 SUPREME/CT. PAGE 105 E2113
B58
CT/SYS
INDUS
ADJUD
CONSTN

WHITNEY S.N.,ANTITRUST POLICIES: AMERICAN
EXPERIENCE IN TWENTY INDUSTRIES. USA+45 USA-45 LAW
DELIB/GP LEGIS ADJUD CT/SYS GOV/REL ATTIT...ANTHOL
20 MONOPOLY CASEBOOK. PAGE 106 E2119
B58
INDUS
CONTROL
LG/CO
MARKET

INT. SOC. SCI. BULL.,"TECHNIQUES OF MEDIATION AND
CONCILIATION." EUR+WWI USA+45 SOCIETY INDUS INT/ORG
LABOR NAT/G LEGIS DIPLOM EDU/PROP CHOOSE ATTIT
RIGID/FLEX...JURID CONCPT GEN/LAWS 20. PAGE 57
E1129
L58
VOL/ASSN
DELIB/GP
INT/LAW

UNESCO,"TECHNIQUES OF MEDIATION AND CONCILIATION."
EUR+WWI USA+45 WOR+45 INDUS FACE/GP EX/STRUC
EDU/PROP LEGIT PEACE ORD/FREE...INT/LAW TIME/SEQ
LEAGUE/NAT 20. PAGE 98 E1961
L58
INT/ORG
CONSULT
DIPLOM

BRIGGS A.,CHARTIST STUDIES. UK LAW NAT/G WORKER
EDU/PROP COERCE SUFF GP/REL ATTIT...ANTHOL 19.
PAGE 15 E0300
B59
INDUS
STRATA
LABOR
POLICY

COUNCIL OF STATE GOVERNMENTS,STATE GOVERNMENT: AN
ANNOTATED BIBLIOGRAPHY (PAMPHLET). USA+45 LAW AGRI
INDUS WORKER PLAN TAX ADJUST AGE/Y ORD/FREE...HEAL
MGT 20. PAGE 26 E0521
B59
BIBLIOG/A
PROVS
LOC/G
ADMIN

EPSTEIN F.T.,EAST GERMANY: A SELECTED BIBLIOGRAPHY
(PAMPHLET). COM GERMANY/E LAW AGRI FINAN INDUS
LABOR POL/PAR EDU/PROP ADMIN AGE/Y 20. PAGE 35
E0693
B59
BIBLIOG/A
INTELL
MARXISM
NAT/G

GOMEZ ROBLES J.,A STATEMENT OF THE LAWS OF
GUATEMALA IN MATTERS AFFECTING BUSINESS (2ND ED.
REV., ENLARGED). GUATEMALA L/A+17C LAW FINAN FAM
WORKER ACT/RES DIPLOM ADJUD ADMIN GP/REL 20 OAS.
PAGE 44 E0881
B59
JURID
NAT/G
INDUS
LEGIT

GSOVSKI V.,GOVERNMENT, LAW, AND COURTS IN THE
SOVIET UNION AND EASTERN EUROPE (2 VOLS.). COM USSR
AGRI INDUS WORKER CT/SYS CRIME...BIBLIOG 20
EUROPE/E. PAGE 48 E0958
B59
ADJUD
MARXISM
CONTROL
ORD/FREE

HARVARD UNIVERSITY LAW SCHOOL,INTERNATIONAL
PROBLEMS OF FINANCIAL PROTECTION AGAINST NUCLEAR
RISK. WOR+45 NAT/G DELIB/GP PROB/SOLV DIPLOM
CONTROL ATTIT...POLICY INT/LAW MATH 20. PAGE 51
E1009
B59
NUC/PWR
ADJUD
INDUS
FINAN

CARLSTON K.S.,"NATIONALIZATION: AN ANALYTIC
APPROACH." WOR+45 INT/ORG ECO/TAC DOMIN LEGIT ADJUD
COERCE ORD/FREE PWR WEALTH SOCISM...JURID CONCPT
TREND STERTYP TOT/POP VAL/FREE 20. PAGE 19 E0380
S59
INDUS
NAT/G
NAT/LISM
SOVEREIGN

S59
TIPTON J.B.,"PARTICIPATION OF THE UNITED STATES IN   LABOR
THE INTERNATIONAL LABOR ORGANIZATION." USA+45 LAW   INT/ORG
STRUCT ECO/DEV ECO/UNDEV INDUS TEC/DEV ECO/TAC
ADMIN PERCEPT ORD/FREE SKILL...STAT HIST/WRIT
GEN/METH ILO WORK 20. PAGE 96 E1928

B60
ATOMIC INDUSTRIAL FORUM,ATOMS FOR INDUSTRY: WORLD   NUC/PWR
FORUM. WOR+45 FINAN COST UTIL...JURID ANTHOL 20.   INDUS
PAGE 6 E0113   PLAN
                                                       PROB/SOLV

B60
LENCZOWSKI G.,OIL AND STATE IN THE MIDDLE EAST. FUT   ISLAM
IRAN LAW ECO/UNDEV EXTR/IND NAT/G TOP/EX PLAN   INDUS
TEC/DEV ECO/TAC LEGIT ADMIN COERCE ATTIT ALL/VALS   NAT/LISM
PWR...CHARTS 20. PAGE 64 E1283

B60
LEWIS P.R.,LITERATURE OF THE SOCIAL SCIENCES: AN   BIBLIOG/A
INTRODUCTORY SURVEY AND GUIDE. UK LAW INDUS DIPLOM   SOC
INT/TRADE ADMIN...MGT 19/20. PAGE 65 E1294

L60
STEIN E.,"LEGAL REMEDIES OF ENTERPRISES IN THE   MARKET
EUROPEAN ECONOMIC COMMUNITY." EUR+45 FUT ECO/DEV   ADJUD
INDUS PLAN ECO/TAC ADMIN PWR...MGT MATH STAT TREND
CON/ANAL EEC 20. PAGE 93 E1868

S60
SANDERS R.,"NUCLEAR DYNAMITE: A NEW DIMENSION IN   INDUS
FOREIGN POLICY." FUT WOR+45 ECO/DEV CONSULT TEC/DEV   PWR
PERCEPT...CONT/OBS TIME/SEQ TREND GEN/LAWS TOT/POP   DIPLOM
20 TREATY. PAGE 87 E1745   NUC/PWR

B61
ALFRED H.,PUBLIC OWNERSHIP IN THE USA: GOALS AND   CONTROL
PRIORITIES. LAW INDUS INT/TRADE ADJUD GOV/REL   OWN
EFFICIENCY PEACE SOCISM...POLICY ANTHOL 20 TVA.   ECO/DEV
PAGE 3 E0064   ECO/TAC

B61
FLINN M.W.,AN ECONOMIC AND SOCIAL HISTORY OF   SOCIETY
BRITAIN, 1066-1939. UK LAW STRATA STRUCT AGRI   SOC
DIST/IND INDUS WORKER INT/TRADE WAR...CENSUS 11/20.
PAGE 39 E0766

B61
NEW JERSEY LEGISLATURE-SENATE,PUBLIC HEARINGS   LEGIS
BEFORE COMMITTEE ON REVISION AND AMENDMENT OF LAWS   MUNIC
ON SENATE BILL NO. 8. USA+45 FINAN PROVS WORKER   INDUS
ACT/RES PLAN BUDGET TAX CRIME...IDEA/COMP 20   PROB/SOLV
NEW/JERSEY URBAN/RNWL. PAGE 77 E1537

B61
RUEDA B.,A STATEMENT OF THE LAWS OF COLOMBIA IN   FINAN
MATTERS AFFECTING BUSINESS (3RD ED.). INDUS FAM   ECO/UNDEV
LABOR LG/CO NAT/G LEGIS TAX CONTROL MARRIAGE 20   LAW
COLOMB. PAGE 86 E1733   CONSTN

B62
CARSON P.,MATERIALS FOR WEST AFRICAN HISTORY IN THE   BIBLIOG/A
ARCHIVES OF BELGIUM AND HOLLAND. CLIENT INDUS   COLONIAL
INT/TRADE ADMIN 17/19. PAGE 20 E0397   AFR
                                                       ECO/UNDEV

B62
DUPRE J.S.,SCIENCE AND THE NATION: POLICY AND   R+D
POLITICS. USA+45 LAW ACADEM FORCES ADMIN CIVMIL/REL   INDUS
GOV/REL EFFICIENCY PEACE...TREND 20 SCI/ADVSRY.   TEC/DEV
PAGE 34 E0665   NUC/PWR

B62
FATOUROS A.A.,GOVERNMENT GUARANTEES TO FOREIGN   NAT/G
INVESTORS. WOR+45 ECO/UNDEV INDUS WORKER ADJUD   FINAN
...NAT/COMP BIBLIOG TREATY. PAGE 36 E0722   INT/TRADE
                                                       ECO/DEV

B62
PAIKERT G.C.,THE GERMAN EXODUS. EUR+WWI GERMANY/W   INGP/REL
LAW CULTURE SOCIETY STRUCT INDUS NAT/LISM RESPECT   STRANGE
SOVEREIGN...CHARTS BIBLIOG SOC/INTEG 20 MIGRATION.   GEOG
PAGE 79 E1591   GP/REL

B62
STERN A.C.,AIR POLLUTION (2 VOLS.). LAW INDUS   AIR
PROB/SOLV TEC/DEV INSPECT RISK BIO/SOC HABITAT   OP/RES
...OBS/ENVIR TESTS SAMP 20 POLLUTION. PAGE 93 E1871   CONTROL
                                                       HEALTH

N62
US SENATE COMM ON JUDICIARY,LEGISLATION TO   LEAD
STRENGTHEN PENALTIES UNDER THE ANTITRUST LAWS   ADJUD
(PAMPHLET). USA+45 LG/CO CONFER CONTROL SANCTION   INDUS

ORD/FREE 20 SENATE MONOPOLY. PAGE 102 E2045   ECO/TAC

B63
BOWIE R.R.,GOVERNMENT REGULATION OF BUSINESS: CASES   LAW
FROM THE NATIONAL REPORTER SYSTEM. USA+45 USA-45   CONTROL
NAT/G ECO/TAC ADJUD...ANTHOL 19/20 SUPREME/CT FTC   INDUS
FAIR/LABOR MONOPOLY. PAGE 14 E0280   CT/SYS

B63
CORLEY R.N.,THE LEGAL ENVIRONMENT OF BUSINESS.   NAT/G
CONSTN LEGIS TAX ADMIN CT/SYS DISCRIM ATTIT PWR   INDUS
...TREND 18/20. PAGE 26 E0509   JURID
                                                       DECISION

B63
OTTOSON H.W.,LAND USE POLICY AND PROBLEMS IN THE   PROB/SOLV
UNITED STATES. USA+45 USA-45 LAW AGRI INDUS NAT/G   UTIL
GP/REL...CHARTS ANTHOL 19/20 HOMEST/ACT. PAGE 79   HABITAT
E1586   POLICY

B63
PRITCHETT C.H.,THE THIRD BRANCH OF GOVERNMENT.   JURID
USA+45 CONSTN SOCIETY INDUS SECT LEGIS JUDGE   NAT/G
PROB/SOLV GOV/REL 20 SUPREME/CT CHURCH/STA. PAGE 82   ADJUD
E1654   CT/SYS

B63
ROYAL INSTITUTE PUBLIC ADMIN,BRITISH PUBLIC   BIBLIOG
ADMINISTRATION. UK LAW FINAN INDUS LOC/G POL/PAR   ADMIN
LEGIS LOBBY PARL/PROC CHOOSE JURID. PAGE 86 E1729   MGT
                                                       NAT/G

B64
BROOKS T.R.,TOIL AND TROUBLE, A HISTORY OF AMERICAN   INDUS
LABOR. WORKER BARGAIN CAP/ISM ADJUD AUTOMAT EXEC   LABOR
GP/REL RACE/REL EFFICIENCY INCOME PROFIT MARXISM   LEGIS
17/20 KENNEDY/JF AFL/CIO NEGRO. PAGE 16 E0310

B64
BUREAU OF NATIONAL AFFAIRS,STATE FAIR EMPLOYMENT   PROVS
LAWS AND THEIR ADMINISTRATION. INDUS ADJUD PERS/REL   DISCRIM
RACE/REL ATTIT ORD/FREE WEALTH 20. PAGE 17 E0338   WORKER
                                                       JURID

B64
FREUD A.,OF HUMAN SOVEREIGNTY. WOR+45 INDUS SECT   NAT/LISM
ECO/TAC CRIME CHOOSE ATTIT MORAL MARXISM...POLICY   DIPLOM
BIBLIOG 20. PAGE 40 E0794   WAR
                                                       PEACE

B64
GESELLSCHAFT RECHTSVERGLEICH,BIBLIOGRAPHIE DES   BIBLIOG/A
DEUTSCHEN RECHTS (BIBLIOGRAPHY OF GERMAN LAW,   JURID
TRANS. BY COURTLAND PETERSON). GERMANY FINAN INDUS   CONSTN
LABOR SECT FORCES CT/SYS PARL/PROC CRIME...INT/LAW   ADMIN
SOC NAT/COMP 20. PAGE 43 E0853

B64
SZLADITS C.,BIBLIOGRAPHY ON FOREIGN AND COMPARATIVE   BIBLIOG/A
LAW: BOOKS AND ARTICLES IN ENGLISH (SUPPLEMENT   JURID
1962). FINAN INDUS JUDGE LICENSE ADMIN CT/SYS   ADJUD
PARL/PROC OWN...INT/LAW CLASSIF METH/COMP NAT/COMP   LAW
20. PAGE 95 E1904

B64
TELLADO A.,A STATEMENT OF THE LAWS OF THE DOMINICAN   CONSTN
REPUBLIC IN MATTERS AFFECTING BUSINESS (3RD ED.).   LEGIS
DOMIN/REP AGRI DIST/IND EXTR/IND FINAN FAM WORKER   NAT/G
ECO/TAC TAX CT/SYS MARRIAGE OWN...BIBLIOG 20   INDUS
MIGRATION. PAGE 95 E1913

L64
POUNDS N.J.G.,"THE POLITICS OF PARTITION." AFR ASIA   NAT/G
COM EUR+WWI FUT ISLAM S/ASIA USA-45 LAW ECO/DEV   NAT/LISM
ECO/UNDEV AGRI INDUS INT/ORG POL/PAR PROVS SECT
FORCES TOP/EX EDU/PROP LEGIT ATTIT MORAL ORD/FREE
PWR RESPECT WEALTH. PAGE 82 E1640

S64
TRISKA J.F.,"SOVIET TREATY LAW: A QUANTITATIVE   COM
ANALYSIS." WOR+45 LAW ECO/UNDEV AGRI COM/IND INDUS   ECO/TAC
CREATE TEC/DEV DIPLOM ATTIT PWR WEALTH...JURID SAMP   INT/LAW
TIME/SEQ TREND CHARTS VAL/FREE 20 TREATY. PAGE 97   USSR
E1942

B65
HOLDSWORTH W.S.,A HISTORY OF ENGLISH LAW; THE   LAW
CENTURIES OF SETTLEMENT AND REFORM (VOL. XV). UK   INDUS
CONSTN SECT LEGIS JUDGE WRITING ADJUD CT/SYS CRIME   PROF/ORG
OWN...JURID IDEA/COMP 18 PARLIAMENT ENGLSH/LAW   ATTIT
COMMON/LAW. PAGE 54 E1082

B65
LUGO-MARENCO J.J.,A STATEMENT OF THE LAWS OF   CONSTN
NICARAGUA IN MATTERS AFFECTING BUSINESS. NICARAGUA   NAT/G
AGRI DIST/IND EXTR/IND FINAN INDUS FAM WORKER   LEGIS

INT/TRADE TAX MARRIAGE OWN BIO/SOC 20 TREATY   JURID
RESOURCE/N MIGRATION. PAGE 67 E1332

L65

FORTE W.E.,"THE FOOD AND DRUG ADMINISTRATION, THE   CONTROL
FEDERAL TRADE COMMISSION AND THE DECEPTIVE   HEALTH
PACKAGING." ROUTINE...JURID 20 FTC. PAGE 39 E0772   ADJUD
                                                        INDUS

S65

KHOURI F.J.,"THE JORDON RIVER CONTROVERSY." LAW   ISLAM
SOCIETY ECO/UNDEV AGRI FINAN INDUS SECT FORCES   INT/ORG
ACT/RES PLAN TEC/DEV ECO/TAC EDU/PROP COERCE ATTIT   ISRAEL
DRIVE PERCEPT RIGID/FLEX ALL/VALS...GEOG, SOC MYTH   JORDAN
WORK. PAGE 61 E1212

B66

DAVIS K.,BUSINESS AND ITS ENVIRONMENT. LAW ECO/DEV   EX/STRUC
INDUS OP/RES ADMIN CONTROL ROUTINE GP/REL PROFIT   PROB/SOLV
POLICY. PAGE 29 E0573   CAP/ISM
                                                        EXEC

B66

GREENE L.E.,GOVERNMENT IN TENNESSEE (2ND ED.).   PROVS
USA+45 DIST/IND INDUS POL/PAR EX/STRUC LEGIS PLAN   LOC/G
BUDGET GIVE CT/SYS...MGT T 20 TENNESSEE. PAGE 46   CONSTN
E0909   ADMIN

B66

HOPKINS J.F.K.,ARABIC PERIODICAL LITERATURE, 1961.   BIBLIOG/A
ISLAM LAW CULTURE SECT...GEOG HEAL PHIL/SCI PSY SOC   NAT/LISM
20. PAGE 55 E1096   TEC/DEV
                                                        INDUS

B66

WASHINGTON S.H.,BIBLIOGRAPHY: LABOR-MANAGEMENT   BIBLIOG
RELATIONS ACT, 1947 AS AMENDED BY LABOR-MANAGEMENT   LAW
REPORTING AND DISCLOSURE ACT, 1959. USA+45 CONSTN   LABOR
INDUS DELIB/GP LEGIS WORKER BARGAIN ECO/TAC ADJUD   MGT
GP/REL NEW/LIB...JURID CONGRESS. PAGE 105 E2100

B67

BAKKE E.W.,UNIONS, MANAGEMENT AND THE PUBLIC*   LABOR
READINGS AND TEXT. WORKER LOBBY...POLICY JURID   INDUS
ANTHOL T. PAGE 7 E0143   ADJUD
                                                        GP/REL

B67

BEAL E.F.,THE PRACTICE OF COLLECTIVE BARGAINING   BARGAIN
(3RD ED.). USA+45 WOR+45 ECO/DEV INDUS LG/CO   MGT
PROF/ORG WORKER ECO/TAC GP/REL WEALTH...JURID   LABOR
METH/CNCPT. PAGE 8 E0160   ADJUD

B67

BONGER W.A.,CRIMINALITY AND ECONOMIC CONDITIONS.   PERSON
MOD/EUR STRUCT INDUS WORKER EDU/PROP CRIME HABITAT   CRIMLGY
ALL/VALS...JURID SOC 20 REFORMERS. PAGE 14 E0265   IDEA/COMP
                                                        ANOMIE

B67

CAVES R.,AMERICAN INDUSTRY: STRUCTURE, CONDUCT,   ECO/DEV
PERFORMANCE (2ND ED.). USA+45 MARKET NAT/G ADJUD   INDUS
CONTROL GP/REL DEMAND WEALTH 20. PAGE 21 E0412   POLICY
                                                        ECO/TAC

B67

GABRIEL P.P.,THE INTERNATIONAL TRANSFER OF   ECO/UNDEV
CORPORATE SKILLS: MANAGEMENT CONTRACTS IN LESS   AGREE
DEVELOPED COUNTRIES. CLIENT INDUS LG/CO PLAN   MGT
PROB/SOLV CAP/ISM ECO/TAC FOR/AID INT/TRADE RENT   CONSULT
ADMIN SKILL 20. PAGE 42 E0825

B67

HODGKINSON R.G.,THE ORIGINS OF THE NATIONAL HEALTH   HEAL
SERVICE: THE MEDICAL SERVICES OF THE NEW POOR LAW,   NAT/G
1834-1871. UK INDUS MUNIC WORKER PROB/SOLV   POLICY
EFFICIENCY ATTIT HEALTH WEALTH SOCISM...JURID   LAW
SOC/WK 19/20. PAGE 53 E1062

B67

LAFAVE W.R.,INTERNATIONAL TRADE, INVESTMENT, AND   INT/TRADE
ORGANIZATION. INDUS PROB/SOLV TARIFFS CONTROL   INT/LAW
...TREND ANTHOL BIBLIOG 20 EEC. PAGE 62 E1245   INT/ORG

B67

LONG E.V.,THE INTRUDERS: THE INVASION OF PRIVACY BY   LAW
GOVERNMENT AND INDUSTRY. USA+45 COM/IND INDUS LEGIS   PARTIC
TASK PERS/REL...JURID 20 CONGRESS. PAGE 66 E1324   NAT/G

B67

NIVEN R.,NIGERIA. NIGERIA CONSTN INDUS EX/STRUC   NAT/G
COLONIAL REV NAT/LISM...CHARTS 19/20. PAGE 77 E1550   REGION
                                                        CHOOSE
                                                        GP/REL

L67

CARMICHAEL D.M.,"FORTY YEARS OF WATER POLLUTION   HEALTH
CONTROL IN WISCONSIN: A CASE STUDY." LAW EXTR/IND   CONTROL
INDUS MUNIC DELIB/GP PLAN PROB/SOLV SANCTION   ADMIN
...CENSUS CHARTS 20 WISCONSIN. PAGE 20 E0384   ADJUD

L67

LENT G.E.,"TAX INCENTIVES FOR INVESTMENT IN   ECO/UNDEV
DEVELOPING COUNTRIES" WOR+45 LAW INDUS PLAN BUDGET   TAX
TARIFFS ADMIN...METH/COMP 20. PAGE 64 E1285   FINAN
                                                        ECO/TAC

S67

CHAMBERLAIN N.W.,"STRIKES IN CONTEMPORARY CONTEXT."   LABOR
LAW INDUS NAT/G CHIEF CONFER COST ATTIT ORD/FREE   BARGAIN
...POLICY MGT 20. PAGE 21 E0415   EFFICIENCY
                                                        PROB/SOLV

S67

EYRAUD M.,"LA FRANCE FACE A UN EVENTUEL TRAITE DE   NUC/PWR
NON DISSEMINATION DES ARMES NUCLEAIRES." FRANCE   ARMS/CONT
USA+45 EXTR/IND INDUS R+D INT/ORG ACT/RES TEC/DEV   POLICY
AGREE PRODUC ATTIT 20 TREATY AEC EURATOM. PAGE 36
E0708

S67

GANZ G.,"THE CONTROL OF INDUSTRY BY ADMINISTRATIVE   INDUS
PROCESS." UK DELIB/GP WORKER 20. PAGE 42 E0832   LAW
                                                        ADMIN
                                                        CONTROL

S67

GIBSON G.H.,"LABOR PIRACY ON THE BRANDYWINE."   ECO/TAC
USA-45 INDUS R+D VOL/ASSN CAP/ISM ADJUD DRIVE...PSY   CREATE
19. PAGE 43 E0859   TEC/DEV
                                                        WORKER

S67

RICHARDSON J.J.,"THE MAKING OF THE RESTRICTIVE   LEGIS
TRADE PRACTICES ACT 1956 A CASE STUDY OF THE POLICY   ECO/TAC
PROCESS IN BRITAIN." UK FINAN MARKET LG/CO POL/PAR   POLICY
CONSULT PRESS ADJUD ADMIN AGREE LOBBY SANCTION   INDUS
ATTIT 20. PAGE 84 E1695

INDUS/REV....INDUSTRIAL REVOLUTION

INDUSTRIAL RELATIONS....SEE LABOR, MGT, INDUS

INDUSTRIALIZATION....SEE ECO/DEV, ECO/UNDEV

INDUSTRY....SEE INDUS

INDUSTRY, COMMUNICATION....SEE COM/IND

INDUSTRY, CONSTRUCTION....SEE CONSTRUC

INDUSTRY, EXTRACTIVE....SEE EXTR/IND

INDUSTRY, MANUFACTURING....SEE PROC/MFG

INDUSTRY, PROCESSING....SEE PROC/MFG

INDUSTRY, SERVICE....SEE SERV/IND

INDUSTRY, TRANSPORTATION....SEE DIST/IND

INDUSTRY, WAREHOUSING....SEE DIST/IND

INFLATION....INFLATION

INFLUENCING....SEE MORE SPECIFIC FORMS, E.G., DOMIN, PWR,
     WEALTH, EDU/PROP, SKILL, CHANGE, LOBBY

INGP/REL....INTRAGROUP RELATIONS

N

ARBITRATION JOURNAL. WOR+45 LAW INDUS JUDGE DIPLOM   BIBLIOG
CT/SYS INGP/REL 20. PAGE 1 E0016   MGT
                                                        LABOR
                                                        ADJUD

N

CANON LAW ABSTRACTS. LEGIT CONFER CT/SYS INGP/REL   BIBLIOG/A
MARRIAGE ATTIT MORAL WORSHIP 20. PAGE 2 E0026   CATHISM
                                                        SECT
                                                        LAW

N

US SUPERINTENDENT OF DOCUMENTS,POLITICAL SCIENCE: BIBLIOG/A
GOVERNMENT, CRIME, DISTRICT OF COLUMBIA (PRICE LIST   NAT/G
54). USA+45 LAW CONSTN EX/STRUC WORKER ADJUD ADMIN   CRIME
CT/SYS CHOOSE INGP/REL RACE/REL CONGRESS PRESIDENT.
PAGE 103 E2063

C01
BERKELEY G.,"DISCOURSE ON PASSIVE OBEDIENCE" (1712)   INGP/REL
THE WORKS... (VOL. IV)" UNIV DOMIN LEGIT CONTROL   SANCTION
CRIME ADJUST CENTRAL MORAL ORD/FREE...POLICY   RESPECT
WORSHIP. PAGE 10 E0202   GEN/LAWS

B10
MCILWAIN C.H.,THE HIGH COURT OF PARLIAMENT AND ITS   LAW
SUPREMACY B1910 1878 408. UK EX/STRUC PARL/PROC   LEGIS
GOV/REL INGP/REL PRIVIL 12/20 PARLIAMENT   CONSTN
ENGLSH/LAW. PAGE 71 E1416   NAT/G

N13
SCHMIDHAUSER J.R.,JUDICIAL BEHAVIOR AND THE   JUDGE
SECTIONAL CRISIS OF 1837-1860. USA-45 ADJUD CT/SYS   POL/PAR
INGP/REL ATTIT HABITAT...DECISION PSY STAT CHARTS   PERS/COMP
SIMUL. PAGE 88 E1759   PERSON

B29
MOLEY R.,POLITICS AND CRIMINAL PROSECUTION. USA-45   PWR
POL/PAR EX/STRUC LEGIT CONTROL LEAD ROUTINE CHOOSE   CT/SYS
INGP/REL...JURID CHARTS 20. PAGE 74 E1481   CRIME
                                                       ADJUD

B34
GONZALEZ PALENCIA A.ESTUDIO HISTORICO SOBRE LA   LEGIT
CENSURA GUBERNATIVA EN ESPANA 1800-1833. NAT/G   EDU/PROP
COERCE INGP/REL ATTIT AUTHORIT KNOWL...POLICY JURID   PRESS
19. PAGE 44 E0884   CONTROL

B37
BUREAU OF NATIONAL AFFAIRS.LABOR RELATIONS   LABOR
REFERENCE MANUAL VOL 1, 1935-1937. BARGAIN DEBATE   ADMIN
ROUTINE INGP/REL 20 NLRB. PAGE 17 E0335   ADJUD
                                                       NAT/G

S40
GILL N.N.,"PERMANENT ADVISORY COMMISSIONS IN THE   DELIB/GP
FEDERAL GOVERNMENT." CLIENT FINAN OP/RES EDU/PROP   NAT/G
PARTIC ROUTINE INGP/REL KNOWL SKILL...CLASSIF   DECISION
TREND. PAGE 43 E0860

B46
GILLIN J.L.,SOCIAL PATHOLOGY. SOCIETY SECT CRIME   SOC
ANOMIE DISPL ORD/FREE WEALTH...CRIMLGY PSY WORSHIP.   ADJUST
PAGE 44 E0864   CULTURE
                                                       INGP/REL

B46
PATON G.W.,A TEXT-BOOK OF JURISPRUDENCE. CREATE   LAW
INSPECT LEGIT CT/SYS ROUTINE CRIME INGP/REL PRIVIL   ADJUD
...CONCPT BIBLIOG 20. PAGE 80 E1601   JURID
                                                       T

B47
INTERNATIONAL COURT OF JUSTICE,CHARTER OF THE   INT/LAW
UNITED NATIONS, STATUTE AND RULES OF COURT AND   INT/ORG
OTHER CONSTITUTIONAL DOCUMENTS. SWITZERLND LAW   CT/SYS
ADJUD INGP/REL...JURID 20 ICJ UN. PAGE 57 E1133   DIPLOM

B49
SUMMERS R.E.,FEDERAL INFORMATION CONTROLS IN   ADJUD
PEACETIME. USA+45 COM/IND DOMIN INGP/REL ATTIT   CONTROL
ORD/FREE 20. PAGE 94 E1893   EDU/PROP
                                                       PRESS

L49
MARX C.M.,"ADMINISTRATIVE ETHICS AND THE RULE OF   ADMIN
LAW." USA+45 ELITES ACT/RES DOMIN NEUTRAL ROUTINE   LAW
INGP/REL ORD/FREE...JURID IDEA/COMP. PAGE 69 E1375

B50
GRAVES W.B.,PUBLIC ADMINISTRATION: A COMPREHENSIVE   BIBLIOG
BIBLIOGRAPHY ON PUBLIC ADMINISTRATION IN THE UNITED   FINAN
STATES (PAMPHLET). USA+45 USA-45 LOC/G NAT/G LEGIS   CONTROL
ADJUD INGP/REL...MGT 20. PAGE 45 E0901   ADMIN

B50
LOWENTHAL M.,THE FEDERAL BUREAU OF INVESTIGATION.   FORCES
USA+45 SOCIETY ADMIN TASK CRIME INGP/REL...CRIMLGY   NAT/G
20 FBI ESPIONAGE. PAGE 67 E1329   ATTIT
                                                       LAW

B51
BIDDLE F.,THE FEAR OF FREEDOM. USA+45 LAW NAT/G   ANOMIE
PUB/INST PROB/SOLV DOMIN CONTROL SANCTION REV   INGP/REL
NAT/LISM 20. PAGE 12 E0227   VOL/ASSN
                                                       ORD/FREE

B53
GROSS B.M.,THE LEGISLATIVE STRUGGLE: A STUDY IN   LEGIS
SOCIAL COMBAT. STRUCT LOC/G POL/PAR JUDGE EDU/PROP   DECISION
DEBATE ETIQUET ADMIN LOBBY CHOOSE GOV/REL INGP/REL   PERSON
HEREDITY ALL/VALS...SOC PRESIDENT. PAGE 48 E0948   LEAD

B54
CAPLOW T.,THE SOCIOLOGY OF WORK. USA+45 USA-45   LABOR
STRATA MARKET FAM GP/REL INGP/REL ALL/VALS   WORKER
...DECISION STAT BIBLIOG SOC/INTEG 20. PAGE 19   INDUS
E0375   ROLE

B54
ELIAS T.O.,GROUNDWORK OF NIGERIAN LAW. AFR LEAD   JURID
CRIME INGP/REL ORD/FREE 17/20. PAGE 34 E0680   CT/SYS
                                                       CONSTN
                                                       CONSULT

B54
JAMES L.F.,THE SUPREME COURT IN AMERICAN LIFE.   ADJUD
USA+45 USA-45 CONSTN CRIME GP/REL INGP/REL RACE/REL   CT/SYS
CONSEN FEDERAL PERSON ORD/FREE 18/20 SUPREME/CT   JURID
DEPRESSION CIV/RIGHTS CHURCH/STA FREE/SPEE. PAGE 58   DECISION
E1147

B55
BENTON W.E.,NUREMBERG: GERMAN VIEWS OF THE WAR   CRIME
TRIALS. EUR+WWI GERMANY VOL/ASSN LEAD PARTIC COERCE   WAR
INGP/REL RACE/REL TOTALISM SUPEGO ORD/FREE...ANTHOL   LAW
NUREMBERG. PAGE 10 E0201   JURID

B56
CARLSTON K.S.,LAW AND STRUCTURES OF SOCIAL ACTION.   JURID
LAW SOCIETY ECO/DEV DIPLOM CONTROL ATTIT...DECISION   INT/LAW
CONCPT 20. PAGE 19 E0379   INGP/REL
                                                       STRUCT

B56
FRANCIS R.G.,SERVICE AND PROCEDURE IN BUREAUCRACY.   CLIENT
EXEC LEAD ROUTINE...QU 20. PAGE 39 E0784   ADMIN
                                                       INGP/REL
                                                       REPRESENT

B56
REDFORD E.S.,PUBLIC ADMINISTRATION AND POLICY   EX/STRUC
FORMATION: STUDIES IN OIL, GAS, BANKING, RIVER   PROB/SOLV
DEVELOPMENT AND CORPORATE INVESTIGATIONS. USA+45   CONTROL
CLIENT NAT/G ADMIN LOBBY REPRESENT GOV/REL INGP/REL   EXEC
20. PAGE 84 E1678

B56
SUTHERLAND A.E.,THE LAW AND ONE MAN AMONG MANY.   JURID
USA+45 INTELL ADJUD CT/SYS 20. PAGE 95 E1895   INGP/REL
                                                       ORD/FREE
                                                       CONCPT

B56
SYKES G.M.,CRIME AND SOCIETY. LAW STRATA STRUCT   CRIMLGY
ACT/RES ROUTINE ANOMIE WEALTH...POLICY SOC/INTEG   CRIME
20. PAGE 95 E1903   CULTURE
                                                       INGP/REL

C56
TYLER P.,"IMMIGRATION AND THE UNITED STATES."   CULTURE
USA+45 USA-45 LAW SECT INGP/REL RACE/REL NAT/LISM   GP/REL
ATTIT...BIBLIOG SOC/INTEG 19/20. PAGE 97 E1949   DISCRIM

B57
BERLE A.A. JR.,ECONOMIC POWER AND FREE SOCIETY   LG/CO
(PAMPHLET). CLIENT CONSTN EX/STRUC ECO/TAC CONTROL   CAP/ISM
PARTIC PWR WEALTH MAJORIT. PAGE 11 E0205   INGP/REL
                                                       LEGIT

B57
MILLS W.,INDIVIDUAL FREEDOM AND COMMON DEFENSE   ORD/FREE
(PAMPHLET). USA+45 USSR NAT/G EDU/PROP CRIME CHOOSE   CONSTN
20 COLD/WAR. PAGE 73 E1463   INGP/REL
                                                       FORCES

S57
GOODE W.J.,"COMMUNITY WITHIN A COMMUNITY: THE   PROF/ORG
PROFESSIONS." STRATA STRUCT SANCTION INGP/REL...SOC   NEIGH
GP/COMP. PAGE 45 E0886   CLIENT
                                                       CONTROL

B58
CHAMBERLIN E.H.,LABOR UNIONS AND PUBLIC POLICY.   LABOR
PLAN BARGAIN SANCTION INGP/REL JURID. PAGE 21 E0416   WEALTH
                                                       PWR
                                                       NAT/G

B58
CLEMMER D.,THE PRISON COMMUNITY. CULTURE CONTROL   PUB/INST
LEAD ROUTINE PERS/REL PERSON...SOC METH/CNCPT.   CRIMLGY
PAGE 23 E0453   CLIENT
                                                       INGP/REL

B58
DAVIS K.C.,ADMINISTRATIVE LAW: CASES, TEXT,   ADJUD
PROBLEMS. LAW LOC/G NAT/G TOP/EX PAY CONTROL   JURID
GOV/REL INGP/REL FEDERAL 20 SUPREME/CT. PAGE 29   CT/SYS
E0576   ADMIN

MANSERGH N.,COMMONWEALTH PERSPECTIVES. GHANA UK LAW DIPLOM
VOL/ASSN CONFER HEALTH SOVEREIGN...GEOG CHARTS COLONIAL
ANTHOL 20 CMN/WLTH AUSTRAL. PAGE 68 E1363 INT/ORG
INGP/REL
B58

CRESSEY D.R.,"ACHIEVEMENT OF AN UNSTATED PUB/INST
ORGANIZATIONAL GOAL: AN OBSERVATION ON PRISONS." CLIENT
OP/RES PROB/SOLV PERS/REL ANOMIE ATTIT ROLE RESPECT NEIGH
CRIMLGY. PAGE 28 E0546 INGP/REL
S58

SCHUBERT G.A.,"THE STUDY OF JUDICIAL DECISION- JUDGE
MAKING AS AN ASPECT OF POLITICAL BEHAVIOR." PLAN DECISION
ADJUD CT/SYS INGP/REL PERSON...PHIL/SCI SOC QUANT CON/ANAL
STAT CHARTS IDEA/COMP SOC/EXP. PAGE 89 E1779 GAME
S58

FRIEDRICH C.J.,"AUTHORITY, REASON AND DISCRETION" AUTHORIT
IN C. FRIEDRICH'S AUTHORITY (BMR)" UNIV EX/STRUC CHOOSE
ADJUD ADMIN CONTROL INGP/REL ATTIT PERSON PWR. RATIONAL
PAGE 41 E0807 PERS/REL
C58

BROMWICH L.,UNION CONSTITUTIONS. CONSTN EX/STRUC LABOR
PRESS ADJUD CONTROL CHOOSE REPRESENT PWR SAMP. ROUTINE
PAGE 16 E0306 INGP/REL
RACE/REL
B59

HOBSBAWM E.J.,PRIMITIVE REBELS; STUDIES IN ARCHAIC SOCIETY
FORMS OF SOCIAL MOVEMENT IN THE 19TH AND 20TH CRIME
CENTURIES. ITALY SPAIN CULTURE VOL/ASSN RISK CROWD REV
GP/REL INGP/REL ISOLAT TOTALISM...PSY SOC 18/20. GUERRILLA
PAGE 53 E1058
B59

KNIERIEM A.,THE NUREMBERG TRIALS. EUR+WWI GERMANY INT/LAW
VOL/ASSN LEAD COERCE WAR INGP/REL TOTALISM SUPEGO CRIME
ORD/FREE...CONCPT METH/COMP. PAGE 61 E1225 PARTIC
JURID
B59

PANHUYS H.F.,THE ROLE OF NATIONALITY IN INT/LAW
INTERNATIONAL LAW. ADJUD CRIME WAR STRANGE...JURID NAT/LISM
TREND. PAGE 80 E1596 INGP/REL
B59

SCHORN H.,DER RICHTER IM DRITTEN REICH; GESCHICHTE ADJUD
UND DOKUMENTE. GERMANY NAT/G LEGIT CT/SYS INGP/REL JUDGE
MORAL ORD/FREE RESPECT...JURID GP/COMP 20. PAGE 88 FASCISM
E1765
B59

SCHUBERT G.A.,QUANTITATIVE ANALYSIS OF JUDICIAL JUDGE
BEHAVIOR. ADJUD LEAD CHOOSE INGP/REL MAJORITY ATTIT CT/SYS
...DECISION JURID CHARTS GAME SIMUL SUPREME/CT. PERSON
PAGE 89 E1780 QUANT
B59

SISSON C.H.,THE SPIRIT OF BRITISH ADMINISTRATION GOV/COMP
AND SOME EUROPEAN COMPARISONS. FRANCE GERMANY/W ADMIN
SWEDEN UK LAW EX/STRUC INGP/REL EFFICIENCY ORD/FREE ELITES
...DECISION 20. PAGE 91 E1835 ATTIT

COWAN T.A.,"A SYMPOSIUM ON GROUP INTERESTS AND THE ADJUD
LAW" USA+45 LAW MARKET LABOR PLAN INT/TRADE TAX PWR
RACE/REL RIGID/FLEX...JURID ANTHOL 20. PAGE 27 INGP/REL
E0528 CREATE
L59

COX A.,"THE ROLE OF LAW IN PRESERVING UNION LABOR
DEMOCRACY." EX/STRUC LEGIS PARTIC ROUTINE CHOOSE REPRESENT
INGP/REL ORD/FREE. PAGE 27 E0532 LAW
MAJORIT
L59

OBERER W.E.,"VOLUNTARY IMPARTIAL REVIEW OF LABOR: LABOR
SOME REFLECTIONS." DELIB/GP LEGIS PROB/SOLV ADJUD LAW
CONTROL COERCE PWR PLURISM POLICY. PAGE 78 E1570 PARTIC
INGP/REL
L59

BAKER G.E.,THE POLITICS OF REAPPORTIONMENT IN VOL/ASSN
WASHINGTON STATE. LAW POL/PAR CREATE EDU/PROP APPORT
PARL/PROC CHOOSE INGP/REL...CHARTS METH/COMP 20 PROVS
WASHINGT/G LEAGUE/WV. PAGE 7 E0139 LEGIS
B60

CARTER R.F.,COMMUNITIES AND THEIR SCHOOLS. USA+45 SCHOOL
LAW FINAN PROVS BUDGET TAX LEAD PARTIC CHOOSE...SOC ACT/RES
INT QU 20. PAGE 20 E0401 NEIGH
INGP/REL
B60

LA PONCE J.A.,THE PROTECTION OF MINORITIES. WOR+45 INGP/REL
WOR-45 NAT/G POL/PAR SUFF...INT/LAW CLASSIF GP/COMP DOMIN
GOV/COMP BIBLIOG 17/20 CIVIL/LIB CIV/RIGHTS. SOCIETY
PAGE 62 E1242 RACE/REL
B60

PINTO F.B.M.,ENRIQUECIMENTO ILICITO NO EXERCICIO DE ADMIN
CARGOS PUBLICOS. BRAZIL L/A+17C USA+45 ELITES NAT/G
TRIBUTE CONTROL INGP/REL ORD/FREE PWR...NAT/COMP CRIME
20. PAGE 81 E1617 LAW
B60

MANN S.Z.,"POLICY FORMULATION IN THE EXECUTIVE EXEC
BRANCH: THE TAFT-HARTLEY EXPERIENCE." USA+45 LABOR GOV/REL
CHIEF INGP/REL 20 NLRB. PAGE 68 E1360 EX/STRUC
PROB/SOLV
S60

ULMER S.S.,"THE ANALYSIS OF BEHAVIOR PATTERNS ON ATTIT
THE UNITED STATES SUPREME COURT" USA+45 LAW CT/SYS ADJUD
PERS/REL RACE/REL PERSON...DECISION PSY SOC TREND PROF/ORG
METH/COMP METH 20 SUPREME/CT CIVIL/LIB. PAGE 97 INGP/REL
E1951
S60

BARBASH J.,LABOR'S GRASS ROOTS. CONSTN NAT/G LABOR
EX/STRUC LEGIS WORKER LEAD...MAJORIT BIBLIOG. INGP/REL
PAGE 8 E0147 GP/REL
LAW
B61

BENNETT G.,THE KENYATTA ELECTION: KENYA 1960-1961. CHOOSE
AFR INGP/REL RACE/REL CONSEN ATTIT 20 KENYATTA. POL/PAR
PAGE 10 E0187 LAW
SUFF
B61

JUSTICE,THE CITIZEN AND THE ADMINISTRATION: THE INGP/REL
REDRESS OF GRIEVANCES (PAMPHLET). EUR+WWI UK LAW CONSULT
CONSTN STRATA NAT/G CT/SYS PARTIC COERCE...NEW/IDEA ADJUD
IDEA/COMP 20 OMBUDSMAN. PAGE 59 E1176 REPRESENT
B61

LEONI B.,FREEDOM AND THE LAW. WOR+45 SOCIETY ADJUD JURID
INGP/REL EFFICIENCY ATTIT DRIVE. PAGE 64 E1286 ORD/FREE
LEGIS
CONTROL
B61

MERTON R.K.,CONTEMPORARY SOCIAL PROBLEMS: AN CRIME
INTRODUCTION TO THE SOCIOLOGY OF DEVIANT BEHAVIOR ANOMIE
AND SOCIAL DISORGANIZATION. FAM MUNIC FORCES WORKER STRANGE
PROB/SOLV INGP/REL RACE/REL ISOLAT...CRIMLGY GEOG SOC
PSY T 20 NEGRO. PAGE 72 E1444
B61

UTLEY T.E.,OCCASION FOR OMBUDSMAN. UK CREATE PROB/SOLV
CONTROL 20 OMBUDSMAN. PAGE 103 E2065 INGP/REL
REPRESENT
ADJUD
B61

WESTIN A.F.,THE SUPREME COURT: VIEWS FROM INSIDE. CT/SYS
USA+45 NAT/G PROF/ORG PROVS DELIB/GP INGP/REL LAW
DISCRIM ATTIT...POLICY DECISION JURID ANTHOL 20 ADJUD
SUPREME/CT CONGRESS CIVIL/LIB. PAGE 106 E2114 GOV/REL
B61

AGNEW P.C.,"INTRODUCING CHANGE IN A MENTAL ORD/FREE
HOSPITAL." CLIENT WORKER PROB/SOLV INGP/REL PUB/INST
PERS/REL ADJUST. PAGE 3 E0054 PSY
ADMIN
S61

ASSOCIATION BAR OF NYC,REPORT ON ADMISSION PUB/INST
PROCEDURES TO NEW YORK STATE MENTAL HOSPITALS. LAW HEALTH
CONSTN INGP/REL RESPECT...PSY OBS RECORD. PAGE 6 CLIENT
E0108 ROUTINE
B62

GALENSON W.,TRADE UNIONS MONOGRAPH SERIES (A SERIES LABOR
OF NINE TEXTS). DELIB/GP LEAD PARTIC...DECISION INGP/REL
ORG/CHARTS. PAGE 42 E0827 CONSTN
REPRESENT
B62

HEYDECKER J.J.,THE NUREMBERG TRIAL: HISTORY OF NAZI LAW
GERMANY AS REVEALED THROUGH THE TESTIMONY AT CRIME
NUREMBERG. EUR+WWI GERMANY VOL/ASSN LEAD COERCE PARTIC
CROWD INGP/REL RACE/REL SUPEGO ORD/FREE...CONCPT 20 TOTALISM
NAZI ANTI/SEMIT NUREMBERG JEWS. PAGE 52 E1036
B62

INTERNAT CONGRESS OF JURISTS,EXECUTIVE ACTION AND JURID
B62

THE RULE OF RULE: REPORTION *PROCEEDINGS OF INT'T*
CONGRESS OF JURISTS.--RIO DE JANEIRO, BRAZIL. WOR+45
ACADEM CONSULT JUDGE EDU/PROP ADJUD CT/SYS INGP/REL
PERSON DEPT/DEFEN. PAGE 57 E1130

EXEC
ORD/FREE
CONTROL

B62

PAIKERT G.C.,THE GERMAN EXODUS. EUR+WWI GERMANY/W
LAW CULTURE SOCIETY STRUCT INDUS NAT/LISM RESPECT
SOVEREIGN...CHARTS BIBLIOG SOC/INTEG 20 MIGRATION.
PAGE 79 E1591

INGP/REL
STRANGE
GEOG
GP/REL

L62

N.,"UNION INVESTMENT IN BUSINESS: A SOURCE OF UNION
CONFLICT OF INTEREST." LAW NAT/G LEGIS CONTROL
GP/REL INGP/REL DECISION. PAGE 76 E1515

LABOR
POLICY
FINAN
LG/CO

C62

ABRAHAM H.J.,"THE JUDICIAL PROCESS." USA+45 USA-45
LAW NAT/G ADMIN CT/SYS INGP/REL RACE/REL DISCRIM
...JURID IDEA/COMP 19/20. PAGE 2 E0046

BIBLIOG
CONSTN
JUDGE
ADJUD

B63

BADI J.,THE GOVERNMENT OF THE STATE OF ISRAEL: A
CRITICAL ACCOUNT OF ITS PARLIAMENT, EXECUTIVE, AND
JUDICIARY. ISRAEL ECO/DEV CHIEF DELIB/GP LEGIS
DIPLOM CT/SYS INGP/REL PEACE ORD/FREE...BIBLIOG 20
PARLIAMENT ARABS MIGRATION. PAGE 7 E0131

NAT/G
CONSTN
EX/STRUC
POL/PAR

B63

CAHN E.,THE GREAT RIGHTS. USA+45 NAT/G PROVS
CIVMIL/REL...IDEA/COMP ANTHOL BIBLIOG 18/20
MADISON/J BILL/RIGHT CIV/RIGHTS WARRN/EARL
BLACK/HL. PAGE 18 E0361

CONSTN
LAW
ORD/FREE
INGP/REL

B63

COUNCIL OF STATE GOVERNMENTS.INCREASED RIGHTS FOR
DEFENDANTS IN STATE CRIMINAL PROSECUTIONS. USA+45
GOV/REL INGP/REL FEDERAL ORD/FREE...JURID 20
SUPREME/CT. PAGE 26 E0522

CT/SYS
ADJUD
PROVS
CRIME

B63

FRIEDRICH C.J.,MAN AND HIS GOVERNMENT: AN EMPIRICAL
THEORY OF POLITICS. UNIV LOC/G NAT/G ADJUD REV
INGP/REL DISCRIM PWR BIBLIOG. PAGE 41 E0810

PERSON
ORD/FREE
PARTIC
CONTROL

B63

LEGISLATIVE REFERENCE SERVICE.DIGEST OF PUBLIC
GENERAL BILLS AND RESOLUTIONS. LAW COM/IND EDU/PROP
GOV/REL INGP/REL KNOWL...JURID 20 CONGRESS. PAGE 64
E1280

BIBLIOG/A
LEGIS
DELIB/GP
NAT/G

B63

LEVY L.W.,JEFFERSON AND CIVIL LIBERTIES: THE DARKER
SIDE. USA-45 LAW INTELL ACADEM FORCES PRESS REV
INGP/REL PERSON 18/19 JEFFERSN/T CIVIL/LIB. PAGE 65
E1291

BIOG
ORD/FREE
CONSTN
ATTIT

B63

MURPHY T.J.,CENSORSHIP: GOVERNMENT AND OBSCENITY.
USA+45 CULTURE LEGIS JUDGE EDU/PROP CONTROL
INGP/REL RATIONAL POPULISM...CATH JURID 20. PAGE 75
E1507

ORD/FREE
MORAL
LAW
CONSEN

B63

PRITCHETT C.H.,THE ROOSEVELT COURT. USA-45 LAW
INGP/REL...CHARTS 20 SUPREME/CT. PAGE 82 E1653

DECISION
PROB/SOLV
CT/SYS
JURID

B63

REALE M.,PLURALISMO E LIBERDADE. STRUCT ADJUST
ATTIT 20 CIVIL/LIB. PAGE 84 E1676

CONCPT
ORD/FREE
JURID
INGP/REL

B64

CHEIN I.,THE ROAD TO H; NARCOTICS, DELINQUENCY, AND
SOCIAL POLICY. USA+45 NEIGH CRIME INGP/REL ATTIT
PERSON...SOC/WK 20 NEWYORK/C. PAGE 22 E0426

BIO/SOC
AGE/Y
POLICY
ANOMIE

B64

ECONOMIDES C.P.,LE POUVOIR DE DECISION DES
ORGANISATIONS INTERNATIONALES EUROPEENNES. DIPLOM
DOMIN INGP/REL EFFICIENCY...INT/LAW JURID 20 NATO
OEEC EEC COUNCL/EUR EURATOM. PAGE 34 E0673

INT/ORG
PWR
DECISION
GP/COMP

B64

HAAR C.M.,LAW AND LAND: ANGLO-AMERICAN PLANNING
PRACTICE. UK USA+45 NAT/G TEC/DEV BUDGET CT/SYS
INGP/REL EFFICIENCY OWN...JURID 20. PAGE 49 E0967

LAW
PLAN
MUNIC
NAT/COMP

B64

PRESS C.,A BIBLIOGRAPHIC INTRODUCTION TO AMERICAN
STATE GOVERNMENT AND POLITICS (PAMPHLET). USA+45
USA-45 EX/STRUC ADJUD INGP/REL FEDERAL ORD/FREE 20.
PAGE 82 E1649

BIBLIOG
LEGIS
LOC/G
POL/PAR

S64

BAKER H.R.,"INMATE SELF-GOVERNMENT." ACT/RES CREATE
CONTROL PARTIC ATTIT RIGID/FLEX QU. PAGE 7 E0141

PUB/INST
CRIME
INGP/REL
REPRESENT

B65

BELL J.,THE JOHNSON TREATMENT: HOW LYNDON JOHNSON
TOOK OVER THE PRESIDENCY AND MADE IT HIS OWN.
USA+45 DELIB/GP DIPLOM ADJUD MURDER CHOOSE PERSON
PWR...POLICY OBS INT TIME 20 JOHNSON/LB KENNEDY/JF
PRESIDENT CONGRESS. PAGE 10 E0183

INGP/REL
TOP/EX
CONTROL
NAT/G

B65

CHARNAY J.P.,LE SUFFRAGE POLITIQUE EN FRANCE;
ELECTIONS PARLEMENTAIRES, ELECTION PRESIDENTIELLE,
REFERENDUMS. FRANCE CONSTN CHIEF DELIB/GP ECO/TAC
EDU/PROP CRIME INGP/REL MORAL ORD/FREE PWR CATHISM
20 PARLIAMENT PRESIDENT. PAGE 22 E0425

CHOOSE
SUFF
NAT/G
LEGIS

B65

GINSBERG M.,ON JUSTICE IN SOCIETY. LAW EDU/PROP
LEGIT CT/SYS INGP/REL PRIVIL RATIONAL ATTIT MORAL
ORD/FREE...JURID 20. PAGE 44 E0867

ADJUD
ROLE
CONCPT

B65

US SENATE COMM ON JUDICIARY.HEARINGS BEFORE
SUBCOMMITTEE ON ADMINISTRATIVE PRACTICE AND
PROCEDURE ABOUT ADMINISTRATIVE PROCEDURE ACT 1965.
USA+45 LEGIS EDU/PROP ADJUD GOV/REL INGP/REL
EFFICIENCY...POLICY INT 20 CONGRESS. PAGE 103 E2055

ROUTINE
DELIB/GP
ADMIN
NAT/G

S65

ULMER S.S.,"TOWARD A THEORY OF SUBGROUP FORMATION
IN THE UNITED STATES SUPREME COURT." USA+45 ROUTINE
CHOOSE PWR...JURID STAT CON/ANAL SIMUL SUPREME/CT.
PAGE 97 E1952

CT/SYS
ADJUD
ELITES
INGP/REL

B66

AARON T.J.,THE CONTROL OF POLICE DISCRETION: THE
DANISH EXPERIENCE. DENMARK LAW CREATE ADMIN
INGP/REL SUPEGO PWR 20 OMBUDSMAN. PAGE 2 E0042

CONTROL
FORCES
REPRESENT
PROB/SOLV

B66

CANFIELD L.H.,THE PRESIDENCY OF WOODROW WILSON:
PRELUDE TO A WORLD IN CRISIS. USA-45 ADJUD NEUTRAL
WAR CHOOSE INGP/REL PEACE ORD/FREE 20 WILSON/W
PRESIDENT TREATY LEAGUE/NAT. PAGE 19 E0373

PERSON
POLICY
DIPLOM
GOV/REL

B66

DOUGLAS W.O.,THE BIBLE AND THE SCHOOLS. USA+45
CULTURE ADJUD INGP/REL AGE/C AGE/Y ATTIT KNOWL
WORSHIP 20 SUPREME/CT CHURCH/STA BIBLE CHRISTIAN.
PAGE 32 E0644

SECT
NAT/G
SCHOOL
GP/REL

B66

FENN DH J.R.,BUSINESS DECISION MAKING AND
GOVERNMENT POLICY. SERV/IND LEGIS LICENSE ADMIN
CONTROL GP/REL INGP/REL 20 CASEBOOK. PAGE 37 E0736

DECISION
PLAN
NAT/G
LG/CO

B66

HARVEY W.B.,LAW AND SOCIAL CHANGE IN GHANA. AFR
GHANA CONSULT CONTROL CT/SYS INGP/REL 20. PAGE 51
E1011

JURID
CONSTN
LEAD
ORD/FREE

B66

MILLER E.W.,THE NEGRO IN AMERICA: A BIBLIOGRAPHY.
USA+45 LAW EDU/PROP REV GOV/REL GP/REL INGP/REL
ADJUST HABITAT PERSON HEALTH ORD/FREE SOC/INTEG 20
NEGRO. PAGE 73 E1459

BIBLIOG
DISCRIM
RACE/REL

B66

SMITH E.A.,CHURCH-STATE RELATIONS IN ECUMENICAL
PERSPECTIVE. WOR+45 LAW MUNIC INGP/REL DISCRIM
ATTIT SUPEGO ORD/FREE CATHISM...PHIL/SCI IDEA/COMP
20 PROTESTANT ECUMENIC CHURCH/STA CHRISTIAN.
PAGE 92 E1843

NAT/G
SECT
GP/REL
ADJUD

B67

BAKER L.,BACK TO BACK: THE DUEL BETWEEN FDR AND THE
SUPREME COURT. ELITES LEGIS CREATE DOMIN INGP/REL
PERSON PWR NEW/LIB 20 ROOSEVLT/F SUPREME/CT SENATE.
PAGE 7 E0142

CHIEF
CT/SYS
PARL/PROC
GOV/REL

B67

BERNSTEIN S.,ALTERNATIVES TO VIOLENCE: ALIENATED
YOUTH AND RIOTS, RACE AND POVERTY. MUNIC PUB/INST

AGE/Y
SOC/WK

SCHOOL INGP/REL RACE/REL UTOPIA DRIVE HABITAT ROLE NEIGH
WEALTH...INT 20. PAGE 11 E0215 CRIME

B67
BRAGER G.A.,COMMUNITY ACTION AGAINST POVERTY. NEIGH
USA+45 LAW STRATA INGP/REL INCOME NEW/LIB...POLICY WEALTH
WELF/ST ANTHOL. PAGE 15 E0285 SOC/WK
CREATE

B67
COWLING M.,1867 DISRAELI, GLADSTONE, AND PARL/PROC
REVOLUTION; THE PASSING OF THE SECOND REFORM BILL. POL/PAR
UK LEGIS LEAD LOBBY GP/REL INGP/REL...DECISION ATTIT
BIBLIOG 19 REFORMERS. PAGE 27 E0531 LAW

B67
ESTEY M.,THE UNIONS: STRUCTURE, DEVELOPMENT, AND LABOR
MANAGEMENT. FUT USA+45 ADJUD CONTROL INGP/REL DRIVE EX/STRUC
...DECISION T 20 AFL/CIO. PAGE 35 E0699 ADMIN
GOV/REL

B67
FINCHER F.,THE GOVERNMENT OF THE UNITED STATES. NAT/G
USA+45 USA-45 POL/PAR CHIEF CT/SYS LOBBY GP/REL EX/STRUC
INGP/REL...CONCPT CHARTS BIBLIOG T 18/20 PRESIDENT LEGIS
CONGRESS SUPREME/CT. PAGE 38 E0749 OP/RES

B67
GELLHORN W.,OMBUDSMEN AND OTHERS: CITIZENS' NAT/COMP
PROTECTORS IN NINE COUNTRIES. WOR+45 LAW CONSTN REPRESENT
LEGIS INSPECT ADJUD ADMIN CONTROL CT/SYS CHOOSE INGP/REL
PERS/REL...STAT CHARTS 20. PAGE 43 E0847 PROB/SOLV

S67
CLOGGER T.J.,"THE BIG EAR." UK USA+45 USSR LAW DIPLOM
LEGIS CRIME GP/REL INGP/REL ATTIT 20 FBI ESPIONAGE. ORD/FREE
PAGE 23 E0458 COM/IND
INSPECT

S67
HILL D.G.,"HUMAN RIGHTS LEGISLATION IN ONTARIO." DELIB/GP
CANADA R+D VOL/ASSN CONSULT INSPECT EDU/PROP ADJUD ORD/FREE
AGREE TASK GP/REL INGP/REL DISCRIM 20 CIV/RIGHTS LAW
ONTARIO CIVIL/LIB. PAGE 52 E1045 POLICY

S67
KENNEDY R.F.,"TOWARD A NATION WHERE THE LAW IS CRIMLGY
KING." PLAN CT/SYS CRIME INGP/REL...JURID SOC. ADJUST
PAGE 60 E1202 LAW
PUB/INST

S67
MC REYNOLDS D.,"THE RESISTANCE." USA+45 LAW ADJUD ATTIT
SANCTION INGP/REL PEACE 20. PAGE 70 E1398 WAR
LEGIT
FORCES

S67
WRAITH R.E.,"ADMINISTRATIVE CHANGE IN THE NEW ADMIN
AFRICA." AFR LG/CO ADJUD INGP/REL PWR...RECORD NAT/G
GP/COMP 20. PAGE 107 E2147 LOC/G
ECO/UNDEV

B73
AUSTIN J.,LECTURES ON JURISPRUDENCE OR THE LAW
PHILOSOPHY OF POSITIVE LAW (VOL. II) (4TH ED., ADJUD
REV.). UK CONSTN STRUCT PROB/SOLV LEGIT CT/SYS JURID
SANCTION CRIME INGP/REL OWN SUPEGO ORD/FREE...T 19. METH/CNCPT
PAGE 6 E0120

B75
MAINE H.S.,LECTURES ON THE EARLY HISTORY OF CULTURE
INSTITUTIONS. IRELAND UK CONSTN ELITES STRUCT FAM LAW
KIN CHIEF LEGIS CT/SYS OWN SOVEREIGN...CONCPT 16 INGP/REL
BENTHAM/J BREHON ROMAN/LAW. PAGE 68 E1351

B82
POLLOCK F.,ESSAYS IN JURISPRUDENCE AND ETHICS. UNIV JURID
LAW FINAN MARKET WORKER INGP/REL MORAL...POLICY CONCPT
GEN/LAWS. PAGE 81 E1625

B99
LILLY W.S.,FIRST PRINCIPLES IN POLITICS. UNIV LAW NAT/G
LEGIS DOMIN ADJUD INGP/REL ORD/FREE SOVEREIGN CONSTN
...JURID CONCPT 19 NATURL/LAW. PAGE 65 E1299 MORAL
POLICY

INNIS/H....HAROLD ADAMS INNIS

INNOVATION....SEE CREATE

INONU/I....ISMET INONU

INSPECT....EXAMINING FOR QUALITY, OUTPUT, LEGALITY

N19
BURRUS B.R.,INVESTIGATION AND DISCOVERY IN STATE NAT/G
ANTITRUST (PAMPHLET). USA+45 USA-45 LEGIS ECO/TAC PROVS
ADMIN CONTROL CT/SYS CRIME GOV/REL PWR...JURID LAW
CHARTS 19/20 FTC MONOPOLY. PAGE 18 E0346 INSPECT

B40
MCILWAIN C.H.,CONSTITUTIONALISM, ANCIENT AND CONSTN
MODERN. CHRIST-17C MOD/EUR NAT/G CHIEF PROB/SOLV GEN/LAWS
INSPECT AUTHORIT ORD/FREE PWR...TIME/SEQ ROMAN/REP. LAW
PAGE 71 E1418

B41
NIEMEYER G.,LAW WITHOUT FORCE: THE FUNCTION OF COERCE
POLITICS IN INTERNATIONAL LAW. PLAN INSPECT DIPLOM LAW
REPAR LEGIT ADJUD WAR ORD/FREE...IDEA/COMP PWR
METH/COMP GEN/LAWS 20. PAGE 77 E1549 INT/LAW

C43
BENTHAM J.,"ON THE LIBERTY OF THE PRESS, AND PUBLIC ORD/FREE
DISCUSSION" IN J. BOWRING, ED., THE WORKS OF JEREMY PRESS
BENTHAM." SPAIN UK LAW ELITES NAT/G LEGIS INSPECT CONFER
LEGIT WRITING CONTROL PRIVIL TOTALISM AUTHORIT CONSERVE
...TRADIT 19 FREE/SPEE. PAGE 10 E0193

C43
BENTHAM J.,"THE RATIONALE OF REWARD" IN J. BOWRING, SANCTION
ED., THE WORKS OF JEREMY BENTHAM (VOL. 2)" LAW ECO/TAC
WORKER CREATE INSPECT PAY ROUTINE HAPPINESS PRODUC INCOME
SUPEGO WEALTH METH/CNCPT. PAGE 10 E0195 PWR

B46
PATON G.W.,A TEXT-BOOK OF JURISPRUDENCE. CREATE LAW
INSPECT LEGIT CT/SYS ROUTINE CRIME INGP/REL PRIVIL ADJUD
...CONCPT BIBLIOG 20. PAGE 80 E1601 JURID
T

B49
SCHONS D.,BOOK CENSORSHIP IN NEW SPAIN (NEW WORLD CHRIST-17C
STUDIES, BOOK II). SPAIN LAW CULTURE INSPECT ADJUD EDU/PROP
CT/SYS SANCTION GP/REL ORD/FREE 14/17. PAGE 88 CONTROL
E1764 PRESS

B50
BURDETTE F.L.,LOBBYISTS IN ACTION (PAMPHLET). LOBBY
CONSULT TEC/DEV INSPECT BARGAIN PARL/PROC SANCTION ATTIT
20 CONGRESS. PAGE 17 E0329 POLICY
LAW

B55
WHEARE K.C.,GOVERNMENT BY COMMITTEE; AN ESSAY ON DELIB/GP
THE BRITISH CONSTITUTION. UK NAT/G LEGIS INSPECT CONSTN
CONFER ADJUD ADMIN CONTROL TASK EFFICIENCY ROLE LEAD
POPULISM 20. PAGE 106 E2116 GP/COMP

S57
FRANKFURTER F.,"THE SUPREME COURT IN THE MIRROR OF EDU/PROP
JUSTICES" (BMR)" USA+45 USA-45 INTELL INSPECT ADJUD
EFFICIENCY ROLE KNOWL MORAL 18/20 SUPREME/CT. CT/SYS
PAGE 40 E0792 PERSON

B58
ATOMIC INDUSTRIAL FORUM,MANAGEMENT AND ATOMIC NUC/PWR
ENERGY. WOR+45 SEA LAW MARKET NAT/G TEC/DEV INSPECT INDUS
INT/TRADE CONFER PEACE HEALTH...ANTHOL 20. PAGE 6 MGT
E0112 ECO/TAC

L61
SILVING H.,"IN RE EICHMANN: A DILEMMA OF LAW AND CT/SYS
MORALITY" WOR+45 INSPECT ADJUST MORAL...JURID 20 INT/LAW
WAR/TRIAL EICHMANN/A NATURL/LAW. PAGE 91 E1828 CONCPT

B62
OTTENBERG M.,THE FEDERAL INVESTIGATORS. USA+45 LAW FORCES
COM/IND DIST/IND WORKER DIPLOM INT/TRADE CONTROL INSPECT
FEDERAL HEALTH ORD/FREE FBI CIA FTC SEC FDA. NAT/G
PAGE 79 E1585 CRIME

B62
STERN A.C.,AIR POLLUTION (2 VOLS.). LAW INDUS AIR
PROB/SOLV TEC/DEV INSPECT RISK BIO/SOC HABITAT OP/RES
...OBS/ENVIR TESTS SAMP 20 POLLUTION. PAGE 93 E1871 CONTROL
HEALTH

B63
US SENATE COMM ON JUDICIARY,CASTRO'S NETWORK IN THE PRESS
UNITED STATES. CUBA LAW DELIB/GP 20 SENATE MARXISM
CASTRO/F. PAGE 102 E2050 DIPLOM
INSPECT

N63
US PRES COMN REGIS AND VOTING,REPORT ON CHOOSE
REGISTRATION AND VOTING (PAMPHLET). USA+45 POL/PAR LAW
CHIEF EDU/PROP PARTIC REPRESENT ATTIT...PSY CHARTS SUFF
20. PAGE 101 E2023 INSPECT

B67

ELDRIDGE W.B.,NARCOTICS AND THE LAW: A CRITIQUE OF
THE AMERICAN EXPERIMENT IN NARCOTIC DRUG CONTROL.
PUB/INST ACT/RES PLAN LICENSE GP/REL EFFICIENCY
ATTIT HEALTH...CRIMLGY HEAL STAT 20 ABA DEPT/HEW
NARCO/ACT. PAGE 34 E0679
LAW
INSPECT
BIO/SOC
JURID

B67

GELLHORN W.,OMBUDSMEN AND OTHERS: CITIZENS'
PROTECTORS IN NINE COUNTRIES. WOR+45 LAW CONSTN
LEGIS INSPECT ADJUD ADMIN CONTROL CT/SYS CHOOSE
PERS/REL...STAT CHARTS 20. PAGE 43 E0847
NAT/COMP
REPRESENT
INGP/REL
PROB/SOLV

S67

CLOGGER T.J.,"THE BIG EAR." UK USA+45 USSR LAW
LEGIS CRIME GP/REL INGP/REL ATTIT 20 FBI ESPIONAGE.
PAGE 23 E0458
DIPLOM
ORD/FREE
COM/IND
INSPECT

S67

HILL D.G.,"HUMAN RIGHTS LEGISLATION IN ONTARIO."
CANADA R+D VOL/ASSN CONSULT INSPECT EDU/PROP ADJUD
AGREE TASK GP/REL INGP/REL DISCRIM 20 CIV/RIGHTS
ONTARIO CIVIL/LIB. PAGE 52 E1045
DELIB/GP
ORD/FREE
LAW
POLICY

S68

DUPRE L.,"TILL DEATH DO US PART?" UNIV FAM INSPECT
LEGIT ADJUD SANCTION PERS/REL ANOMIE RIGID/FLEX SEX
...JURID IDEA/COMP 20 CHURCH/STA BIBLE CANON/LAW
CIVIL/LAW. PAGE 34 E0666
MARRIAGE
CATH
LAW

B99

BROOKS S.,BRITAIN AND THE BOERS. AFR SOUTH/AFR UK
CULTURE INSPECT LEGIT...INT/LAW 19/20 BOER/WAR.
PAGE 16 E0309
WAR
DIPLOM
NAT/G

INST INTL DES CIVILISATION DIF E1123

INSTITUT DE DROIT INTL E1124

INSTITUT INTERMEDIAIRE INTL E1125

INSTITUTE COMP STUDY POL SYS E1126

INSTITUTE DES RELATIONS INTL E1127

INSTITUTE JUDICIAL ADMIN E1128

INSTITUTION, EDUCATIONAL....SEE SCHOOL, ACADEM

INSTITUTION, MENTAL....SEE PUB/INST

INSTITUTION, RELIGIOUS....SEE SECT

INSTITUTIONS....SEE DESCRIPTORS IN INSTITUTIONAL INDEX
    (TOPICAL INDEX, NO. 2)

INSURANCE....SEE FINAN, SERV/IND

INSURRECTION....SEE REV

INT....INTERVIEW; SEE ALSO INTERVIEWS INDEX, P. XIV

B00

LORIMER J.,THE INSTITUTES OF THE LAW OF NATIONS.
WOR-45 CULTURE SOCIETY NAT/G VOL/ASSN DIPLOM LEGIT
WAR PEACE DRIVE ORD/FREE SOVEREIGN...CONCPT RECORD
INT TREND HYPO/EXP GEN/METH TOT/POP VAL/FREE 20.
PAGE 66 E1327
INT/ORG
LAW
INT/LAW

N19

MISSISSIPPI ADVISORY COMMITTEE,REPORT ON
MISSISSIPPI (PAMPHLET). USA+45 LAW PROVS FORCES
ADJUD PWR...SOC/WK INT 20 MISSISSIPP NEGRO
CIV/RIGHTS. PAGE 73 E1469
RACE/REL
DISCRIM
COERCE
ORD/FREE

B36

CULVER D.C.,METHODOLOGY OF SOCIAL SCIENCE RESEARCH:
A BIBLIOGRAPHY. LAW CULTURE...CRIMLGY GEOG STAT OBS
INT QU HIST/WRIT CHARTS 20. PAGE 28 E0550
BIBLIOG/A
METH
SOC

S38

CLEMMER D.,"LEADERSHIP PHENOMENA IN A PRISON
COMMUNITY." NEIGH PLAN CHOOSE PERSON ROLE...OBS
INT. PAGE 23 E0452
PUB/INST
CRIMLGY
LEAD
CLIENT

S51

COHEN M.B.,"PERSONALITY AS A FACTOR IN
ADMINISTRATIVE DECISIONS." ADJUD PERS/REL ANOMIE
SUPEGO...OBS SELF/OBS INT. PAGE 24 E0465
PERSON
ADMIN
PROB/SOLV
PSY

B52

GELLHORN W.,THE STATES AND SUBVERSION. USA+45
USA-45 LOC/G DELIB/GP LEGIS EDU/PROP LEGIT CT/SYS
PROVS
JURID

REGION PEACE ATTIT ORD/FREE SOCISM...INT CON/ANAL
20 CALIFORNIA MARYLAND ILLINOIS MICHIGAN NEW/YORK.
PAGE 43 E0845

B56

US HOUSE RULES COMM,HEARINGS BEFORE A SPECIAL
SUBCOMMITTEE: ESTABLISHMENT OF A STANDING COMMITTEE
ON ADMINISTRATIVE PROCEDURE, PRACTICE. USA+45 LAW
EX/STRUC ADJUD CONTROL EXEC GOV/REL EFFICIENCY PWR
...POLICY INT 20 CONGRESS. PAGE 100 E2009
ADMIN
DOMIN
DELIB/GP
NAT/G

B57

US SENATE COMM ON JUDICIARY,CIVIL RIGHTS - 1957.
USA+45 LAW NAT/G CONFER GOV/REL RACE/REL ORD/FREE
PWR...JURID 20 SENATE CIV/RIGHTS. PAGE 102 E2039
INT
LEGIS
DISCRIM
PARL/PROC

B58

US SENATE COMM POST OFFICE,TO PROVIDE AN EFFECTIVE
SYSTEM OF PERSONNEL ADMINISTRATION. USA+45 NAT/G
EX/STRUC PARL/PROC GOV/REL...JURID 20 SENATE
CIVIL/SERV. PAGE 103 E2060
INT
LEGIS
CONFER
ADMIN

L58

BEVAN W.,"JURY BEHAVIOR AS A FUNCTION OF THE
PRESTIGE OF THE FOREMAN AND THE NATURE OF HIS
LEADERSHIP" (BMR)" DELIB/GP DOMIN ADJUD LEAD
PERS/REL ATTIT...PSY STAT INT QU CHARTS SOC/EXP 20
JURY. PAGE 11 E0221
PERSON
EDU/PROP
DECISION
CT/SYS

B60

CARTER R.F.,COMMUNITIES AND THEIR SCHOOLS. USA+45
LAW FINAN PROVS BUDGET TAX LEAD PARTIC CHOOSE...SOC
INT QU 20. PAGE 20 E0401
SCHOOL
ACT/RES
NEIGH
INGP/REL

B60

US SENATE COMM ON JUDICIARY,FEDERAL ADMINISTRATIVE
PROCEDURE. USA+45 CONSTN NAT/G PROB/SOLV CONFER
GOV/REL...JURID INT 20 SENATE. PAGE 102 E2043
PARL/PROC
LEGIS
ADMIN
LAW

B60

US SENATE COMM ON JUDICIARY,ADMINISTRATIVE
PROCEDURE LEGISLATION. USA+45 CONSTN NAT/G
PROB/SOLV CONFER ROUTINE GOV/REL...INT 20 SENATE.
PAGE 102 E2044
PARL/PROC
LEGIS
ADMIN
JURID

B62

MURPHY W.F.,CONGRESS AND THE COURT. USA+45 LAW
LOBBY GP/REL RACE/REL ATTIT PWR...JURID INT BIBLIOG
CONGRESS SUPREME/CT WARRN/EARL. PAGE 75 E1509
LEGIS
CT/SYS
GOV/REL
ADJUD

B63

US SENATE COMM ON JUDICIARY,ADMINISTRATIVE
CONFERENCE OF THE UNITED STATES. USA+45 CONSTN
NAT/G PROB/SOLV CONFER GOV/REL...INT 20 SENATE.
PAGE 102 E2048
PARL/PROC
JURID
ADMIN
LEGIS

B64

US SENATE COMM ON JUDICIARY,CIVIL RIGHTS - THE
PRESIDENT'S PROGRAM. USA+45 LAW PROB/SOLV PRESS
ADJUD GOV/REL RACE/REL ORD/FREE PWR...JURID 20
SUPREME/CT SENATE CIV/RIGHTS PRESIDENT. PAGE 102
E2053
INT
LEGIS
DISCRIM
PARL/PROC

B64

US SENATE COMM ON JUDICIARY,ADMINISTRATIVE
PROCEDURE ACT. USA+45 CONSTN NAT/G PROB/SOLV CONFER
GOV/REL PWR...INT 20 SENATE. PAGE 102 E2054
PARL/PROC
LEGIS
JURID
ADMIN

B65

ASSOCIATION BAR OF NYC,RADIO, TELEVISION, AND THE
ADMINISTRATION OF JUSTICE: A DOCUMENTED SURVEY OF
MATERIALS. USA+45 DELIB/GP FORCES PRESS ADJUD
CONTROL CT/SYS CRIME...INT IDEA/COMP BIBLIOG.
PAGE 6 E0109
AUD/VIS
ATTIT
ORD/FREE

B65

BELL J.,THE JOHNSON TREATMENT: HOW LYNDON JOHNSON
TOOK OVER THE PRESIDENCY AND MADE IT HIS OWN.
USA+45 DELIB/GP DIPLOM ADJUD MURDER CHOOSE PERSON
PWR...POLICY OBS INT TIME 20 JOHNSON/LB KENNEDY/JF
PRESIDENT CONGRESS. PAGE 10 E0183
INGP/REL
TOP/EX
CONTROL
NAT/G

B65

SMITH R.C.,THEY CLOSED THEIR SCHOOLS. USA+45 NEIGH
ADJUD CROWD CONSEN WEALTH...DECISION OBS INT 20
NEGRO VIRGINIA. PAGE 92 E1846
RACE/REL
DISCRIM
LOC/G
SCHOOL

B65

US SENATE COMM ON JUDICIARY,HEARINGS BEFORE
SUBCOMMITTEE ON ADMINISTRATIVE PRACTICE AND
ROUTINE
DELIB/GP

PROCEDURE ABOUT ADMINISTRATIVE PROCEDURE ACT 1965. ADMIN
USA+45 LEGIS EDU/PROP ADJUD GOV/REL INGP/REL   NAT/G
EFFICIENCY...POLICY INT 20 CONGRESS. PAGE 103 E2055

                                                   C65
SCHEINGOLD S.A.,"THE RULE OF LAW IN EUROPEAN   INT/LAW
INTEGRATION: THE PATH OF THE SCHUMAN PLAN." EUR+WWI CT/SYS
JUDGE ADJUD FEDERAL ATTIT PWR...RECORD INT BIBLIOG REGION
EEC ECSC. PAGE 87 E1755   CENTRAL

                                                   B66
CARLIN J.E.,LAWYER'S ETHICS. CLIENT STRUCT CONSULT ATTIT
PERS/REL PWR...JURID OBS CHARTS 20. PAGE 19 E0378   PROF/ORG
                                                    INT

                                                   B66
CARMEN I.H.,MOVIES, CENSORSHIP, AND THE LAW. LOC/G EDU/PROP
NAT/G ATTIT ORD/FREE...DECISION INT IDEA/COMP   LAW
BIBLIOG 20 SUPREME/CT FILM. PAGE 19 E0383   ART/METH
                                                    CONSTN

                                                   B66
DIZARD W.P.,TELEVISION* A WORLD VIEW. WOR+45   COM/IND
ECO/UNDEV TEC/DEV LICENSE LITERACY...STAT OBS INT   ACT/RES
QU TREND AUD/VIS BIBLIOG. PAGE 32 E0632   EDU/PROP
                                                    CREATE

                                                   B66
JACOBSON H.K.,DIPLOMATS, SCIENTISTS, AND   DIPLOM
POLITICIANS* THE UNITED STATES AND THE NUCLEAR TEST ARMS/CONT
BAN NEGOTIATIONS. USA+45 USSR ACT/RES PLAN CONFER   TECHRACY
DETER NUC/PWR CONSEN ORD/FREE...INT TREATY. PAGE 57 INT/ORG
E1146

                                                   C66
ZAWODNY J.K.,"GUIDE TO THE STUDY OF INTERNATIONAL   BIBLIOG/A
RELATIONS." OP/RES PRESS...STAT INT 20. PAGE 108   DIPLOM
E2169   INT/LAW
                                                    INT/ORG

                                                   B67
BERNSTEIN S.,ALTERNATIVES TO VIOLENCE: ALIENATED   AGE/Y
YOUTH AND RIOTS, RACE AND POVERTY. MUNIC PUB/INST   SOC/WK
SCHOOL INGP/REL RACE/REL UTOPIA DRIVE HABITAT ROLE   NEIGH
WEALTH...INT 20. PAGE 11 E0215   CRIME

                                                   B67
BIBBY J.,ON CAPITOL HILL. POL/PAR LOBBY PARL/PROC   CONFER
GOV/REL PERS/REL...JURID PHIL/SCI OBS INT BIBLIOG   LEGIS
20 CONGRESS PRESIDENT. PAGE 12 E0224   CREATE
                                                    LEAD

                                                   S67
BLAKEY G.R.,"ORGANIZED CRIME IN THE UNITED STATES." CRIME
USA+45 USA-45 STRUCT LABOR NAT/G VOL/ASSN ADMIN   ELITES
PERS/REL PWR...CRIMLGY INT 17/20. PAGE 12 E0240   CONTROL

                                                   S67
GREY D.L.,"INTERVIEWING AT THE COURT." USA+45   JUDGE
ELITES COM/IND ACT/RES PRESS CT/SYS PERSON...SOC   ATTIT
INT 20 SUPREME/CT. PAGE 46 E0916   PERS/COMP
                                                    GP/COMP

INT. SOC. SCI. BULL. E1129

INT/AM/DEV....INTER-AMERICAN DEVELOPMENT BANK

INT/AVIATN....INTERNATIONAL CIVIL AVIATION ORGANIZATION

INT/LAW....INTERNATIONAL LAW

                                                        N
LIBRARY INTERNATIONAL REL,INTERNATIONAL INFORMATION BIBLIOG/A
SERVICE. WOR+45 CULTURE INT/ORG FORCES...GEOG HUM   DIPLOM
SOC. PAGE 65 E1295   INT/TRADE
                                                    INT/LAW

                                                        N
LONDON INSTITUTE WORLD AFFAIRS,THE YEAR BOOK OF   DIPLOM
WORLD AFFAIRS. FINAN BAL/PWR ARMS/CONT WAR   FOR/AID
...INT/LAW BIBLIOG 20. PAGE 66 E1322   INT/ORG

                                                        N
AMERICAN JOURNAL OF INTERNATIONAL LAW. WOR+45   BIBLIOG/A
WOR-45 CONSTN INT/ORG NAT/G CT/SYS ARMS/CONT WAR   INT/LAW
...DECISION JURID NAT/COMP 20. PAGE 1 E0001   DIPLOM
                                                    ADJUD

                                                        N
AMERICAN POLITICAL SCIENCE REVIEW. USA+45 USA-45   BIBLIOG/A
WOR+45 WOR-45 INT/ORG ADMIN...INT/LAW PHIL/SCI   DIPLOM
CONCPT METH 20 UN. PAGE 1 E0002   NAT/G
                                                    GOV/COMP

                                                        N
BACKGROUND; JOURNAL OF INTERNATIONAL STUDIES   BIBLIOG

ASSOCIATION. INT/ORG FORCES ACT/RES EDU/PROP COERCE DIPLOM
NAT/LISM PEACE ATTIT...INT/LAW CONCPT 20. PAGE 1   POLICY
E0004

                                                        N
INDEX TO LEGAL PERIODICALS. CANADA NEW/ZEALND UK   BIBLIOG
USA+45 USA-45 CONSTN LEGIS JUDGE ADJUD ADMIN   INDEX
CONTROL CT/SYS FEDERAL...CRIMLGY INT/LAW 20   LAW
CMN/WLTH AUSTRAL. PAGE 1 E0006   JURID

                                                        N
INTERNATIONAL AFFAIRS. WOR+45 WOR-45 ECO/UNDEV   BIBLIOG/A
INT/ORG NAT/G PROB/SOLV FOR/AID WAR...POLICY 20.   DIPLOM
PAGE 1 E0007   INT/LAW
                                                    INT/TRADE

                                                        N
INTERNATIONAL BOOK NEWS. 1928-1934. ECO/UNDEV FINAN BIBLIOG/A
INDUS LABOR INT/TRADE CONFER ADJUD COLONIAL...HEAL   DIPLOM
SOC/WK CHARTS 20 LEAGUE/NAT. PAGE 1 E0008   INT/LAW
                                                    INT/ORG

                                                        N
INTERNATIONAL STUDIES. ASIA S/ASIA WOR+45 ECO/UNDEV BIBLIOG/A
INT/ORG NAT/G LEAD ATTIT WEALTH...SOC 20. PAGE 1   DIPLOM
E0009   INT/LAW
                                                    INT/TRADE

                                                        N
JOURNAL OF INTERNATIONAL AFFAIRS. WOR+45 ECO/UNDEV BIBLIOG
POL/PAR ECO/TAC WAR PEACE PERSON ALL/IDEOS   DIPLOM
...INT/LAW TREND. PAGE 1 E0010   INT/ORG
                                                    NAT/G

                                                        N
FOREIGN AFFAIRS. SPACE WOR+45 WOR-45 CULTURE   BIBLIOG
ECO/UNDEV FINAN NAT/G TEC/DEV INT/TRADE ARMS/CONT   DIPLOM
NUC/PWR...POLICY 20 UN EURATOM ECSC EEC. PAGE 1   INT/ORG
E0021   INT/LAW

                                                        N
THE JAPAN SCIENCE REVIEW: LAW AND POLITICS: LIST OF BIBLIOG
BOOKS AND ARTICLES ON LAW AND POLITICS. CONSTN AGRI LAW
INDUS LABOR DIPLOM TAX ADMIN CRIME...INT/LAW SOC 20 S/ASIA
CHINJAP. PAGE 2 E0027   PHIL/SCI

                                                        N
AIR UNIVERSITY LIBRARY,INDEX TO MILITARY   BIBLIOG/A
PERIODICALS. FUT SPACE WOR+45 REGION ARMS/CONT   FORCES
NUC/PWR WAR PEACE INT/LAW. PAGE 3 E0056   NAT/G
                                                    DIPLOM

                                                        N
ATLANTIC INSTITUTE,ATLANTIC STUDIES. COM EUR+WWI   BIBLIOG/A
USA+45 CULTURE STRUCT ECO/DEV FORCES LEAD ARMS/CONT DIPLOM
...INT/LAW JURID SOC. PAGE 6 E0110   POLICY
                                                    GOV/REL

                                                        N
DE MARTENS G.F.,RECUEIL GENERALE DE TRAITES ET   BIBLIOG
AUTRES ACTES RELATIFS AUX RAPPORTS DE DROIT   INT/LAW
INTERNATIONAL (41 VOLS.). EUR+WWI MOD/EUR USA-45   DIPLOM
...INDEX TREATY 18/20. PAGE 30 E0587

                                                        N
HARVARD LAW SCHOOL LIBRARY,ANNUAL LEGAL   BIBLIOG
BIBLIOGRAPHY. USA+45 CONSTN LEGIS ADJUD CT/SYS   JURID
...POLICY 20. PAGE 50 E1005   LAW
                                                    INT/LAW

                                                        N
HARVARD UNIVERSITY LAW LIBRARY,CATALOG OF   BIBLIOG
INTERNATIONAL LAW AND RELATIONS. WOR+45 WOR-45   INT/LAW
INT/ORG NAT/G JUDGE DIPLOM INT/TRADE ADJUD CT/SYS   JURID
19/20. PAGE 51 E1007

                                                        N
SOCIETE DES NATIONS,TRAITES INTERNATIONAUX ET ACTES BIBLIOG
LEGISLATIFS. WOR-45 INT/ORG NAT/G...INT/LAW JURID   DIPLOM
20 LEAGUE/NAT TREATY. PAGE 92 E1851   LEGIS
                                                    ADJUD

                                                        N
TURNER R.K.,BIBLIOGRAPHY ON WORLD ORGANIZATION.   BIBLIOG/A
INT/TRADE CT/SYS ARMS/CONT WEALTH...INT/LAW 20.   INT/ORG
PAGE 97 E1944   PEACE
                                                    WAR

                                                        N
UNITED NATIONS,OFFICIAL RECORDS OF THE UNITED   INT/ORG
NATIONS' GENERAL ASSEMBLY. WOR+45 BUDGET DIPLOM   DELIB/GP
ADMIN 20 UN. PAGE 98 E1964   INT/LAW
                                                    WRITING

                                                        N
UNITED NATIONS,UNITED NATIONS PUBLICATIONS. WOR+45 BIBLIOG

ECO/UNDEV AGRI FINAN FORCES ADMIN LEAD WAR PEACE   INT/ORG
...POLICY INT/LAW 20 UN. PAGE 98 E1965   DIPLOM

                                                        N
UNITED NATIONS.YEARBOOK OF THE INTERNATIONAL LAW   BIBLIOG
COMMISSION....CON/ANAL 20 UN. PAGE 98 E1966   INT/ORG
                                                      INT/LAW
                                                      DELIB/GP

                                                        B00
DARBY W.E..INTERNATIONAL TRIBUNALS. WOR-45 NAT/G   INT/ORG
ECO/TAC DOMIN LEGIT CT/SYS COERCE ORD/FREE PWR   ADJUD
SOVEREIGN JURID. PAGE 29 E0567   PEACE
                                                      INT/LAW

                                                        B00
GRIFFIN A.P.C..LIST OF BOOKS RELATING TO THE THEORY   BIBLIOG/A
OF COLONIZATION, GOVERNMENT OF DEPENDENCIES,   COLONIAL
PROTECTORATES, AND RELATED TOPICS. FRANCE GERMANY   GOV/REL
ITALY SPAIN UK USA-45 WOR-45 ECO/TAC ADMIN CONTROL   DOMIN
REGION NAT/LISM ALL/VALS PWR...INT/LAW SOC 16/19.
PAGE 46 E0917

                                                        B00
GROTIUS H..DE JURE BELLI AC PACIS. CHRIST-17C UNIV   JURID
LAW SOCIETY PROVS LEGIT PEACE PERCEPT MORAL PWR   INT/LAW
...CONCPT CON/ANAL GEN/LAWS. PAGE 48 E0952   WAR

                                                        B00
HOLLAND T.E..STUDIES IN INTERNATIONAL LAW. TURKEY   INT/ORG
USSR WOR-45 CONSTN NAT/G DIPLOM DOMIN LEGIT COERCE   LAW
WAR PEACE ORD/FREE PWR SOVEREIGN...JURID CHARTS 20   INT/LAW
PARLIAMENT SUEZ TREATY. PAGE 54 E1084

                                                        B00
LORIMER J..THE INSTITUTES OF THE LAW OF NATIONS.   INT/ORG
WOR-45 CULTURE SOCIETY NAT/G VOL/ASSN DIPLOM LEGIT   LAW
WAR PEACE DRIVE ORD/FREE SOVEREIGN...CONCPT RECORD   INT/LAW
INT TREND HYPO/EXP GEN/METH TOT/POP VAL/FREE 20.
PAGE 66 E1327

                                                        B00
MAINE H.S..INTERNATIONAL LAW. MOD/EUR UNIV SOCIETY   INT/ORG
STRUCT ACT/RES EXEC WAR ATTIT PERSON ALL/VALS   LAW
...POLICY JURID CONCPT OBS TIME/SEQ TOT/POP.   PEACE
PAGE 68 E1349   INT/LAW

                                                        L00
HISTORICUS."LETTERS AND SOME QUESTIONS OF   WEALTH
INTERNATIONAL LAW." FRANCE NETHERLAND UK USA-45   JURID
WOR-45 LAW NAT/G COERCE...SOC CONCPT GEN/LAWS   WAR
TOT/POP 19 CIVIL/WAR. PAGE 53 E1054   INT/LAW

                                                        B01
GRIFFIN A.P.C..LIST OF BOOKS ON SAMOA (PAMPHLET).   BIBLIOG/A
GERMANY S/ASIA UK USA-45 WOR-45 ECO/UNDEV REGION   COLONIAL
ALL/VALS ORD/FREE ALL/IDEOS...GEOG INT/LAW 19 SAMOA   DIPLOM
GUAM. PAGE 46 E0918

                                                        B03
MOREL E.D..THE BRITISH CASE IN FRENCH CONGO.   DIPLOM
CONGO/BRAZ FRANCE UK COERCE MORAL WEALTH...POLICY   INT/TRADE
INT/LAW 20 CONGO/LEOP. PAGE 74 E1490   COLONIAL
                                                      AFR

                                                        B06
FOSTER J.W..THE PRACTICE OF DIPLOMACY AS   DIPLOM
ILLUSTRATED IN THE FOREIGN RELATIONS OF THE UNITED   ROUTINE
STATES. MOD/EUR USA-45 NAT/G EX/STRUC ADMIN   PHIL/SCI
...POLICY INT/LAW BIBLIOG 19/20. PAGE 39 E0777

                                                        B08
GRIFFIN A.P.C..LIST OF REFERENCES ON INTERNATIONAL   BIBLIOG/A
ARBITRATION. FRANCE L/A+17C USA-45 WOR-45 DIPLOM   INT/ORG
CONFER COLONIAL ARMS/CONT BAL/PAY EQUILIB SOVEREIGN   INT/LAW
...DECISION 19/20 MEXIC/AMER. PAGE 47 E0932   DELIB/GP

                                                        B09
HOLLAND T.E..LETTERS UPON WAR AND NEUTRALITY.   LAW
WOR-45 NAT/G FORCES JUDGE ECO/TAC LEGIT CT/SYS   INT/LAW
NEUTRAL ROUTINE COERCE...JURID TIME/SEQ 20. PAGE 55   INT/ORG
E1085   WAR

                                                        B11
PHILLIPSON C..THE INTERNATIONAL LAW AND CUSTOM OF   INT/ORG
ANCIENT GREECE AND ROME. MEDIT-7 UNIV INTELL   LAW
SOCIETY STRUCT NAT/G LEGIS EXEC PERSON...CONCPT OBS   INT/LAW
CON/ANAL ROM/EMP. PAGE 80 E1614

                                                        B13
BORCHARD E.M..BIBLIOGRAPHY OF INTERNATIONAL LAW AND   BIBLIOG
CONTINENTAL LAW. EUR+WWI MOD/EUR UK LAW INT/TRADE   INT/LAW
WAR PEACE...GOV/COMP NAT/COMP 19/20. PAGE 14 E0267   JURID
                                                      DIPLOM

                                                        B13
BUTLER N.M..THE INTERNATIONAL MIND. WOR-45 INT/ORG   ADJUD
LEGIT PWR...JURID CONCPT 20. PAGE 18 E0350   ORD/FREE
                                                      INT/LAW

                                                        B14
MCLAUGHLIN A.C..CYCLOPEDIA OF AMERICAN GOVERNMENT   USA+45
(3 VOLS.). LAW CONSTN POL/PAR ADMIN ROUTINE   NAT/G
...INT/LAW CONCPT BIBLIOG METH 20. PAGE 71 E1421   DICTIONARY

                                                        B15
INTERNATIONAL LAW ASSOCIATION,A FORTY YEARS'   BIBLIOG
CATALOGUE OF THE BOOKS, PAMPHLETS AND PAPERS IN THE   LAW
LIBRARY OF THE INTERNATIONAL LAW ASSOCIATION.   INT/LAW
INT/ORG DIPLOM ADJUD NEUTRAL...IDEA/COMP 19/20.
PAGE 57 E1134

                                                        B16
PUFENDORF S..LAW OF NATURE AND OF NATIONS   CONCPT
(ABRIDGED). UNIV LAW NAT/G DIPLOM AGREE WAR PERSON   INT/LAW
ALL/VALS PWR...POLICY 18 DEITY NATURL/LAW. PAGE 83   SECT
E1659   MORAL

                                                        B16
ROOT E..ADDRESSES ON INTERNATIONAL SUBJECTS.   INT/ORG
MOD/EUR UNIV USA-45 LAW SOCIETY EXEC ATTIT ALL/VALS   ACT/RES
...POLICY JURID CONCPT 20 CHINJAP. PAGE 85 E1711   PEACE
                                                      INT/LAW

                                                        L16
WRIGHT Q.."THE ENFORCEMENT OF INTERNATIONAL LAW   INT/ORG
THROUGH MUNICIPAL LAW IN THE US." USA-45 LOC/G   LAW
NAT/G PUB/INST FORCES LEGIT CT/SYS PERCEPT ALL/VALS   INT/LAW
...JURID 20. PAGE 107 E2149   WAR

                                                        B17
DE VICTORIA F..DE INDIS ET DE JURE BELLI (1557) IN   WAR
F. DE VICTORIA, DE INDIS ET DE JURE BELLI   INT/LAW
REFLECTIONES. UNIV NAT/G SECT CHIEF PARTIC COERCE   OWN
PEACE MORAL...POLICY 16 INDIAN/AM CHRISTIAN
CONSCN/OBJ. PAGE 30 E0598

                                                        B17
MEYER H.H.B..LIST OF REFERENCES ON EMBARGOES   BIBLIOG
(PAMPHLET). USA-45 AGRI DIPLOM WRITING DEBATE   DIST/IND
WEAPON...INT/LAW 18/20 CONGRESS. PAGE 72 E1447   ECO/TAC
                                                      INT/TRADE

                                                        S17
ROOT E.."THE EFFECT OF DEMOCRACY ON INTERNATIONAL   LEGIS
LAW." USA-45 WOR-45 INTELL SOCIETY INT/ORG NAT/G   JURID
CONSULT ACT/RES CREATE PLAN EDU/PROP PEACE SKILL   INT/LAW
...CONCPT METH/CNCPT OBS 20. PAGE 85 E1712

                                                        B19
LONDON SCHOOL ECONOMICS-POL,ANNUAL DIGEST OF PUBLIC   BIBLIOG/A
INTERNATIONAL LAW CASES. INT/ORG MUNIC NAT/G PROVS   INT/LAW
ADMIN NEUTRAL WAR GOV/REL PRIVIL 20. PAGE 66 E1323   ADJUD
                                                      DIPLOM

                                                        B19
VANDERPOL A..LA DOCTRINE SCOLASTIQUE DU DROIT DE   WAR
GUERRE. CHRIST-17C FORCES DIPLOM LEGIT SUPEGO MORAL   SECT
...BIOG AQUINAS/T SUAREZ/F CHRISTIAN. PAGE 103   INT/LAW
E2072

                                                        N19
BAILEY S.D..VETO IN THE SECURITY COUNCIL   DELIB/GP
(PAMPHLET). COM USSR WOR+45 BAL/PWR PARL/PROC   INT/ORG
ARMS/CONT PRIVIL PWR...INT/LAW TREND CHARTS 20 UN   DIPLOM
SUEZ. PAGE 7 E0135

                                                        N19
TAYLOR H..WHY THE PENDING TREATY WITH COLOMBIA   INT/LAW
SHOULD BE RATIFIED (PAMPHLET). PANAMA USA-45   DIPLOM
DELIB/GP INT/TRADE REV ORD/FREE...JURID TREATY
18/19 ROOSEVLT/T TAFT/WH COLOMB. PAGE 95 E1912

                                                        B20
MEYER H.H.B..LIST OF REFERENCES ON THE TREATY-   BIBLIOG
MAKING POWER. USA-45 CONTROL PWR...INT/LAW TIME/SEQ   DIPLOM
18/20 TREATY. PAGE 72 E1448   CONSTN

                                                        B20
VINOGRADOFF P..OUTLINES OF HISTORICAL JURISPRUDENCE   JURID
(2 VOLS.). GREECE MEDIT-7 LAW CONSTN FACE/GP FAM   METH
KIN MUNIC CRIME OWN...INT/LAW IDEA/COMP BIBLIOG.
PAGE 104 E2080

                                                        B21
OPPENHEIM L..THE FUTURE OF INTERNATIONAL LAW.   INT/ORG
EUR+WWI MOD/EUR LAW LEGIS JUDGE LEGIT ORD/FREE   CT/SYS
...JURID TIME/SEQ GEN/LAWS 20. PAGE 79 E1578   INT/LAW

                                                        L21
HALDEMAN E.."SERIALS OF AN INTERNATIONAL   BIBLIOG

CHARACTER." WOR-45 DIPLOM...ART/METH GEOG HEAL HUM PHIL/SCI INT/LAW JURID PSY SOC. PAGE 49 E0978

B22
MYERS D.P.,MANUAL OF COLLECTIONS OF TREATIES AND OF BIBLIOG/A COLLECTIONS RELATING TO TREATIES. MOD/EUR INT/ORG LAW LEGIS WRITING ADMIN SOVEREIGN...INT/LAW 19/20. DIPLOM PAGE 75 E1514 CONFER

B23
HEADICAR B.M.,CATALOGUE OF THE BOOKS, PAMPHLETS, BIBLIOG AND OTHER DOCUMENTS IN THE EDWARD FRY LIBRARY OF INT/LAW INTERNATIONAL LAW... UK INT/ORG 20. PAGE 51 E1019 DIPLOM

B24
GENTILI A.,DE LEGATIONIBUS. CHRIST-17C NAT/G SECT DIPLOM CONSULT LEGIT...POLICY CATH JURID CONCPT MYTH. INT/LAW PAGE 43 E0848 INT/ORG LAW

B24
HALL W.E.,A TREATISE ON INTERNATIONAL LAW. WOR-45 PWR CONSTN INT/ORG NAT/G DIPLOM ORD/FREE LEAGUE/NAT 20 JURID TREATY. PAGE 49 E0985 WAR INT/LAW

B24
HOLDSWORTH W.S.,A HISTORY OF ENGLISH LAW; THE LAW COMMON LAW AND ITS RIVALS (VOL. V). UK SEA EX/STRUC LEGIS WRITING ADMIN...INT/LAW JURID CONCPT IDEA/COMP ADJUD WORSHIP 16/17 PARLIAMENT ENGLSH/LAW COMMON/LAW. CT/SYS PAGE 54 E1073

B24
HOLDSWORTH W.S.,A HISTORY OF ENGLISH LAW; THE LAW COMMON LAW AND ITS RIVALS (VOL. IV). UK SEA AGRI LEGIS CHIEF ADJUD CONTROL CRIME GOV/REL...INT/LAW JURID CT/SYS NAT/COMP 16/17 PARLIAMENT COMMON/LAW CANON/LAW CONSTN ENGLSH/LAW. PAGE 54 E1075

L25
HUDSON M.,"THE PERMANENT COURT OF INTERNATIONAL INT/ORG JUSTICE AND THE QUESTION OF AMERICAN ADJUD PARTICIPATION." WOR-45 LEGIT CT/SYS ORD/FREE DIPLOM ...JURID CONCPT TIME/SEQ GEN/LAWS VAL/FREE 20 ICJ. INT/LAW PAGE 56 E1108

B27
LAUTERPACHT H.,PRIVATE LAW SOURCES AND ANALOGIES OF INT/ORG INTERNATIONAL LAW. WOR-45 NAT/G DELIB/GP LEGIT ADJUD COERCE ATTIT ORD/FREE PWR SOVEREIGN...JURID CONCPT PEACE HIST/WRIT TIME/SEQ GEN/METH LEAGUE/NAT 20. PAGE 63 INT/LAW E1264

B28
BUTLER G.,THE DEVELOPMENT OF INTERNATIONAL LAW. LAW WOR-45 SOCIETY NAT/G KNOWL ORD/FREE PWR...JURID INT/LAW CONCPT HIST/WRIT GEN/LAWS. PAGE 18 E0349 DIPLOM INT/ORG

B28
LAPRADELLE,ANNUAIRE DE LA VIE INTERNATIONALE: BIBLIOG POLITIQUE, ECONOMIQUE, JURIDIQUE. INT/ORG CONFER DIPLOM ARMS/CONT 20. PAGE 63 E1255 INT/LAW

L28
HUDSON M.,"THE TEACHING OF INTERNATIONAL LAW IN PERCEPT AMERICA." USA-45 LAW CONSULT ACT/RES CREATE KNOWL EDU/PROP ATTIT RIGID/FLEX...JURID CONCPT RECORD INT/LAW HIST/WRIT TREND GEN/LAWS 18/20. PAGE 56 E1109

B29
CONWELL-EVANS T.P.,THE LEAGUE COUNCIL IN ACTION. DELIB/GP EUR+WWI TURKEY UK USSR WOR-45 INT/ORG FORCES JUDGE INT/LAW ECO/TAC EDU/PROP LEGIT ROUTINE ARMS/CONT COERCE ATTIT PWR...MAJORIT GEOG JURID CONCPT LEAGUE/NAT TOT/POP VAL/FREE TUNIS 20. PAGE 25 E0498

B29
STURZO L.,THE INTERNATIONAL COMMUNITY AND THE RIGHT INT/ORG OF WAR (TRANS. BY BARBARA BARCLAY CARTER). CULTURE PLAN CREATE PROB/SOLV DIPLOM ADJUD CONTROL PEACE PERSON WAR ORD/FREE...INT/LAW IDEA/COMP PACIFIST 20 CONCPT LEAGUE/NAT. PAGE 94 E1891

B30
BYNKERSHOEK C.,QUAESTIONUM JURIS PUBLICI LIBRI DUO. INT/ORG CHRIST-17C MOD/EUR CONSTN ELITES SOCIETY NAT/G LAW PROVS EX/STRUC FORCES TOP/EX BAL/PWR DIPLOM ATTIT NAT/LISM MORAL...TRADIT CONCPT. PAGE 18 E0352 INT/LAW

B30
WRIGHT Q.,MANDATES UNDER THE LEAGUE OF NATIONS. INT/ORG WOR-45 CONSTN ECO/DEV ECO/UNDEV NAT/G DELIB/GP LAW TOP/EX LEGIT ALL/VALS...JURID CONCPT LEAGUE/NAT 20. INT/LAW PAGE 107 E2151

B31
BORCHARD E.H.,GUIDE TO THE LAW AND LEGAL LITERATURE BIBLIOG/A OF FRANCE. FRANCE FINAN INDUS LABOR SECT LEGIS LAW ADMIN COLONIAL CRIME OWN...INT/LAW 20. PAGE 14 CONSTN E0266 METH

B31
STOWELL E.C.,INTERNATIONAL LAW. FUT UNIV WOR-45 INT/ORG SOCIETY CONSULT EX/STRUC FORCES ACT/RES PLAN DIPLOM ROUTINE EDU/PROP LEGIT DISPL PWR SKILL...POLICY CONCPT OBS INT/LAW TREND TOT/POP 20. PAGE 94 E1885

B32
EAGLETON C.,INTERNATIONAL GOVERNMENT. BRAZIL FRANCE INT/ORG GERMANY ITALY UK USSR WOR-45 DELIB/GP TOP/EX PLAN JURID ECO/TAC EDU/PROP LEGIT ADJUD REGION ARMS/CONT DIPLOM COERCE ATTIT PWR...GEOG MGT VAL/FREE LEAGUE/NAT 20. INT/LAW PAGE 34 E0670

B32
MASTERS R.D.,INTERNATIONAL LAW IN INTERNATIONAL INT/ORG COURTS. BELGIUM EUR+WWI FRANCE GERMANY MOD/EUR LAW SWITZERLND WOR-45 SOCIETY STRATA STRUCT LEGIT EXEC INT/LAW ALL/VALS...JURID HIST/WRIT TIME/SEQ TREND GEN/LAWS 20. PAGE 69 E1383

B33
GENTILI A.,DE JURE BELLI, LIBRI TRES (1612) (VOL. WAR 2). FORCES DIPLOM AGREE PEACE SOVEREIGN. PAGE 43 INT/LAW E0849 MORAL SUPEGO

B33
LAUTERPACHT H.,THE FUNCTION OF LAW IN THE INT/ORG INTERNATIONAL COMMUNITY. WOR-45 NAT/G FORCES CREATE LAW DOMIN LEGIT COERCE WAR PEACE ATTIT ORD/FREE PWR INT/LAW SOVEREIGN...JURID CONCPT METH/CNCPT TIME/SEQ GEN/LAWS GEN/METH LEAGUE/NAT TOT/POP VAL/FREE 20. PAGE 63 E1265

B33
MATTHEWS M.A.,THE AMERICAN INSTITUTE OF BIBLIOG/A INTERNATIONAL LAW AND THE CODIFICATION OF INT/LAW INTERNATIONAL LAW (PAMPHLET). USA-45 CONSTN ADJUD L/A+17C CT/SYS...JURID 20. PAGE 69 E1386 DIPLOM

B34
WOLFF C.,JUS GENTIUM METHODO SCIENTIFICA NAT/G PERTRACTATUM. MOD/EUR INT/ORG VOL/ASSN LEGIT PEACE LAW ATTIT...JURID 20. PAGE 107 E2140 INT/LAW WAR

B35
FOREIGN AFFAIRS BIBLIOGRAPHY: A SELECTED AND BIBLIOG/A ANNOTATED LIST OF BOOKS ON INTERNATIONAL RELATIONS DIPLOM 1919-1962 (4 VOLS.). CONSTN FORCES COLONIAL INT/ORG ARMS/CONT WAR NAT/LISM PEACE ATTIT DRIVE...POLICY INT/LAW 20. PAGE 2 E0032

B35
RAM J.,THE SCIENCE OF LEGAL JUDGMENT: A TREATISE... LAW UK CONSTN NAT/G LEGIS CREATE PROB/SOLV AGREE CT/SYS JURID ...INT/LAW CONCPT 19 ENGLSH/LAW CANON/LAW CIVIL/LAW EX/STRUC CTS/WESTM. PAGE 83 E1672 ADJUD

S35
MCMAHON A.H.,"INTERNATIONAL BOUNDARIES." WOR-45 GEOG INT/ORG NAT/G LEGIT SKILL...CHARTS GEN/LAWS 20. VOL/ASSN PAGE 71 E1423 INT/LAW

B36
BRIERLY J.L.,THE LAW OF NATIONS (2ND ED.). WOR+45 DIPLOM WOR-45 INT/ORG AGREE CONTROL COERCE WAR NAT/LISM INT/LAW PEACE PWR 16/20 TREATY LEAGUE/NAT. PAGE 15 E0297 NAT/G

B36
HUDSON M.O.,INTERNATIONAL LEGISLATION: 1929-1931. INT/LAW WOR-45 SEA AIR AGRI FINAN LABOR DIPLOM ECO/TAC PARL/PROC REPAR CT/SYS ARMS/CONT WAR WEAPON...JURID 20 TREATY ADJUD LEAGUE/NAT. PAGE 56 E1112 LAW

B36
MATTHEWS M.A.,DIPLOMACY: SELECT LIST ON DIPLOMACY, BIBLIOG/A DIPLOMATIC AND CONSULAR PRACTICE, AND FOREIGN DIPLOM OFFICE ORGANIZATION (PAMPHLET). EUR+WWI MOD/EUR NAT/G USA-45 WOR-45...INT/LAW 20. PAGE 69 E1387

B36
MATTHEWS M.A.,INTERNATIONAL LAW: SELECT LIST OF BIBLIOG/A WORKS IN ENGLISH ON PUBLIC INTERNATIONAL LAW: WITH INT/LAW COLLECTIONS OF CASES AND OPINIONS. CHRIST-17C ATTIT EUR+WWI MOD/EUR WOR-45 CONSTN ADJUD JURID. PAGE 69 DIPLOM E1388

KETCHAM E.H.,PRELIMINARY SELECT BIBLIOGRAPHY OF INTERNATIONAL LAW (PAMPHLET). WOR-45 LAW INT/ORG NAT/G PROB/SOLV CT/SYS NEUTRAL WAR 19/20. PAGE 60 E1207
B37
BIBLIOG
DIPLOM
ADJUD
INT/LAW

HOLDSWORTH W.S.,A HISTORY OF ENGLISH LAW; THE CENTURIES OF SETTLEMENT AND REFORM (VOL. XI). UK CONSTN NAT/G EX/STRUC DIPLOM ADJUD CT/SYS LEAD CRIME ATTIT...INT/LAW JURID 18 CMN/WLTH PARLIAMENT ENGLSH/LAW. PAGE 54 E1079
B38
LAW
COLONIAL
LEGIS
PARL/PROC

MCNAIR A.D.,THE LAW OF TREATIES: BRITISH PRACTICE AND OPINIONS. UK CREATE DIPLOM LEGIT WRITING ADJUD WAR...INT/LAW JURID TREATY. PAGE 71 E1424
B38
AGREE
LAW
CT/SYS
NAT/G

SAINT-PIERRE C.I.,SCHEME FOR LASTING PEACE (TRANS. BY H. BELLOT). INDUS NAT/G CHIEF FORCES INT/TRADE CT/SYS WAR PWR SOVEREIGN WEALTH...POLICY 18. PAGE 87 E1741
B38
INT/ORG
PEACE
AGREE
INT/LAW

WILSON G.G.,HANDBOOK OF INTERNATIONAL LAW. FUT UNIV USA-45 WOR-45 SOCIETY LEGIT ATTIT DISPL DRIVE ALL/VALS...INT/LAW TIME/SEQ TREND. PAGE 106 E2128
B39
INT/ORG
LAW
CONCPT
WAR

HADDOW A.,"POLITICAL SCIENCE IN AMERICAN COLLEGES AND UNIVERSITIES 1636-1900." CONSTN MORAL...POLICY INT/LAW CON/ANAL BIBLIOG T 17/20. PAGE 49 E0971
C39
USA-45
LAW
ACADEM
KNOWL

SCOTT J.B.,"LAW, THE STATE, AND THE INTERNATIONAL COMMUNITY (2 VOLS.)" INTELL INT/ORG NAT/G SECT INT/TRADE WAR...INT/LAW GEN/LAWS BIBLIOG. PAGE 90 E1798
C39
LAW
PHIL/SCI
DIPLOM
CONCPT

CONOVER H.F.,FOREIGN RELATIONS OF THE UNITED STATES: A LIST OF RECENT BOOKS (PAMPHLET). ASIA CANADA L/A+17C UK INT/ORG INT/TRADE TARIFFS NEUTRAL WAR PEACE...INT/LAW CON/ANAL 20 CHINJAP. PAGE 25 E0492
B40
BIBLIOG/A
USA-45
DIPLOM

FLORIN J.,"BOLSHEVIST AND NATIONAL SOCIALIST DOCTRINES OF INTERNATIONAL LAW." EUR+WWI GERMANY USSR R+D INT/ORG NAT/G DIPLOM DOMIN EDU/PROP SOCISM ...CONCPT TIME/SEQ 20. PAGE 39 E0768
S40
LAW
ATTIT
TOTALISM
INT/LAW

NIEMEYER G.,LAW WITHOUT FORCE: THE FUNCTION OF POLITICS IN INTERNATIONAL LAW. PLAN INSPECT DIPLOM REPAR LEGIT ADJUD WAR ORD/FREE...IDEA/COMP METH/COMP GEN/LAWS 20. PAGE 77 E1549
B41
COERCE
LAW
PWR
INT/LAW

CROWE S.E.,THE BERLIN WEST AFRICA CONFERENCE, 1884-85. GERMANY ELITES MARKET INT/ORG DELIB/GP FORCES PROB/SOLV BAL/PWR CAP/ISM DOMIN COLONIAL ...INT/LAW 19. PAGE 28 E0548
B42
AFR
CONFER
INT/TRADE
DIPLOM

FEILCHENFELD E.H.,THE INTERNATIONAL ECONOMIC LAW OF BELLIGERENT OCCUPATION. EUR+WWI MOD/EUR USA-45 INT/ORG DIPLOM ADJUD ARMS/CONT LEAGUE/NAT 20. PAGE 37 E0726
B42
ECO/TAC
INT/LAW
WAR

KELSEN H.,LAW AND PEACE IN INTERNATIONAL RELATIONS. INT/ORG FUT WOR-45 NAT/G DELIB/GP DIPLOM LEGIT RIGID/FLEX ORD/FREE SOVEREIGN...JURID CONCPT TREND STERTYP GEN/LAWS LEAGUE/NAT 20. PAGE 60 E1197
B42
INT/ORG
ADJUD
PEACE
INT/LAW

BACKUS R.C.,A GUIDE TO THE LAW AND LEGAL LITERATURE OF COLOMBIA. FINAN INDUS LABOR FORCES ADJUD ADMIN COLONIAL CT/SYS CRIME...INT/LAW JURID 20 COLOMB. PAGE 7 E0127
B43
BIBLIOG/A
LAW
CONSTN
L/A+17C

BEMIS S.F.,THE LATIN AMERICAN POLICY OF THE UNITED STATES: AN HISTORICAL INTERPRETATION. INT/ORG AGREE COLONIAL WAR PEACE ATTIT ORD/FREE...POLICY INT/LAW CHARTS 18/20 MEXIC/AMER WILSON/W MONROE/DOC. PAGE 10 E0185
B43
DIPLOM
SOVEREIGN
USA-45
L/A+17C

CLAGETT H.L.,A GUIDE TO THE LAW AND LEGAL LITERATURE OF PARAGUAY. PARAGUAY CONSTN COM/IND
B43
BIBLIOG
JURID

LABOR MUNIC JUDGE ADMIN CT/SYS...CRIMLGY INT/LAW CON/ANAL 20. PAGE 22 E0439
LAW
L/A+17C

SERENI A.P.,THE ITALIAN CONCEPTION OF INTERNATIONAL LAW. EUR+WWI MOD/EUR INT/ORG NAT/G DOMIN COERCE ORD/FREE FASCISM...OBS/ENVIR TREND 20. PAGE 90 E1804
B43
LAW
TIME/SEQ
INT/LAW
ITALY

BENTHAM J.,"PRINCIPLES OF INTERNATIONAL LAW" IN J. BOWRING, ED., THE WORKS OF JEREMY BENTHAM." UNIV NAT/G PLAN PROB/SOLV DIPLOM CONTROL SANCTION MORAL ORD/FREE PWR SOVEREIGN 19. PAGE 10 E0194
C43
INT/LAW
JURID
WAR
PEACE

BRIERLY J.L.,THE OUTLOOK FOR INTERNATIONAL LAW. FUT WOR-45 CONSTN NAT/G VOL/ASSN FORCES ECO/TAC DOMIN LEGIT ADJUD ROUTINE PEACE ORD/FREE...INT/LAW JURID METH LEAGUE/NAT 20. PAGE 15 E0298
B44
INT/ORG
LAW

FULLER G.H.,TURKEY: A SELECTED LIST OF REFERENCES. ISLAM TURKEY CULTURE ECO/UNDEV AGRI DIPLOM NAT/LISM CONSERVE...GEOG HUM INT/LAW SOC 7/20 MAPS. PAGE 42 E0824
B44
BIBLIOG/A
ALL/VALS

HUDSON M.,INTERNATIONAL TRIBUNALS PAST AND FUTURE. FUT WOR-45 LAW EDU/PROP ADJUD ORD/FREE...CONCPT TIME/SEQ TREND GEN/LAWS TOT/POP VAL/FREE 18/20. PAGE 56 E1111
B44
INT/ORG
STRUCT
INT/LAW

PUTTKAMMER E.W.,WAR AND THE LAW. UNIV USA-45 CONSTN CULTURE SOCIETY NAT/G POL/PAR ROUTINE ALL/VALS ...JURID CONCPT OBS WORK VAL/FREE 20. PAGE 83 E1664
B44
INT/ORG
LAW
WAR
INT/LAW

WRIGHT Q.,"CONSTITUTIONAL PROCEDURES OF THE US FOR CARRYING OUT OBLIGATIONS FOR MILITARY SANCTIONS." EUR+WWI FUT USA-45 WOR-45 CONSTN INTELL NAT/G CONSULT EX/STRUC LEGIS ROUTINE DRIVE...POLICY JURID CONCPT OBS TREND TOT/POP 20. PAGE 108 E2153
S44
TOP/EX
FORCES
INT/LAW
WAR

CLAGETT H.L.,A GUIDE TO THE LAW AND LEGAL LITERATURE OF THE MEXICAN STATES. CONSTN LEGIS JUDGE ADJUD ADMIN...INT/LAW CON/ANAL 20 MEXIC/AMER. PAGE 22 E0440
B45
BIBLIOG
JURID
L/A+17C
LAW

CONOVER H.F.,THE NAZI STATE: WAR CRIMES AND WAR CRIMINALS. GERMANY CULTURE NAT/G SECT FORCES DIPLOM INT/TRADE EDU/PROP...INT/LAW BIOG HIST/WRIT TIME/SEQ 20. PAGE 25 E0495
B45
BIBLIOG
WAR
CRIME

GALLOWAY E.,ABSTRACTS OF POSTWAR LITERATURE (VOL. IV) JAN.-JULY, 1945 NOS. 901-1074. POLAND USA+45 USSR WOR+45 INDUS LABOR PLAN ECO/TAC INT/TRADE TAX EDU/PROP ADMIN COLONIAL INT/LAW. PAGE 42 E0829
B45
BIBLIOG/A
NUC/PWR
NAT/G
DIPLOM

HILL N.,CLAIMS TO TERRITORY IN INTERNATIONAL LAW AND RELATIONS. WOR-45 NAT/G DOMIN EDU/PROP LEGIT REGION ROUTINE ORD/FREE PWR WEALTH...GEOG INT/LAW JURID 20. PAGE 52 E1047
B45
INT/ORG
ADJUD
SOVEREIGN

TINGSTERN H.,PEACE AND SECURITY AFTER WW II. WOR-45 DELIB/GP TOP/EX LEGIT CT/SYS COERCE PEACE ATTIT PERCEPT...CONCPT LEAGUE/NAT 20. PAGE 96 E1927
B45
INT/ORG
ORD/FREE
WAR
INT/LAW

UNCIO CONFERENCE LIBRARY,SHORT TITLE CLASSIFIED CATALOG. WOR-45 DOMIN COLONIAL WAR...SOC/WK 20 LEAGUE/NAT UN. PAGE 98 E1955
B45
BIBLIOG
DIPLOM
INT/ORG
INT/LAW

US DEPARTMENT OF STATE,PUBLICATIONS OF THE DEPARTMENT OF STATE: A LIST CUMULATIVE FROM OCTOBER 1, 1929 (PAMPHLET). ASIA EUR+WWI ISLAM L/A+17C USA-45 ADJUD...INT/LAW 20. PAGE 99 E1993
B45
BIBLIOG
DIPLOM
INT/TRADE

VANCE H.L.,GUIDE TO THE LAW AND LEGAL LITERATURE OF MEXICO. LAW CONSTN FINAN LABOR FORCES ADJUD ADMIN ...CRIMLGY PHIL/SCI CON/ANAL 20 MEXIC/AMER. PAGE 103 E2070
B45
BIBLIOG/A
INT/LAW
JURID
CT/SYS

WEST R.,CONSCIENCE AND SOCIETY: A STUDY OF THE
B45
COERCE

PSYCHOLOGICAL PREREQUISITES OF LAW AND ORDER. FUT INT/LAW
UNIV LAW SOCIETY STRUCT DIPLOM WAR PERS/REL SUPEGO ORD/FREE
...SOC 20. PAGE 105 E2112   PERSON

B45
WOOLBERT R.G.,FOREIGN AFFAIRS BIBLIOGRAPHY,   BIBLIOG/A
1932-1942. INT/ORG SECT INT/TRADE COLONIAL RACE/REL DIPLOM
NAT/LISM...GEOG INT/LAW GOV/COMP IDEA/COMP 20.   WAR
PAGE 107 E2144

B46
GRIFFIN G.G.,A GUIDE TO MANUSCRIPTS RELATING TO   BIBLIOG/A
AMERICAN HISTORY IN BRITISH DEPOSITORIES. CANADA   ALL/VALS
IRELAND MOD/EUR UK USA-45 LAW DIPLOM ADMIN COLONIAL NAT/G
WAR NAT/LISM SOVEREIGN...GEOG INT/LAW 15/19
CMN/WLTH. PAGE 47 E0936

B46
KEETON G.W.,MAKING INTERNATIONAL LAW WORK. FUT   INT/ORG
WOR-45 NAT/G DELIB/GP FORCES LEGIT COERCE PEACE   ADJUD
ATTIT RIGID/FLEX ORD/FREE PWR...JURID CONCPT   INT/LAW
HIST/WRIT GEN/METH LEAGUE/NAT 20. PAGE 60 E1193

B46
SCANLON H.L.,INTERNATIONAL LAW: A SELECTIVE LIST OF BIBLIOG/A
WORKS IN ENGLISH ON PUBLIC INTERNATIONAL LAW (A   INT/LAW
PAMPHLET). CHRIST-17C EUR+WWI MOD/EUR WOR-45 CT/SYS ADJUD
...JURID 20. PAGE 87 E1749   DIPLOM

C46
GOODRICH L.M.,"CHARTER OF THE UNITED NATIONS: CONSTN
COMMENTARY AND DOCUMENTS." EX/STRUC ADMIN...INT/LAW INT/ORG
CON/ANAL BIBLIOG 20 UN. PAGE 45 E0890   DIPLOM

B47
CLAGETT H.L.,A GUIDE TO THE LAW AND LEGAL   BIBLIOG/A
LITERATURE OF BOLIVIA. L/A+17C CONSTN LABOR LEGIS   JURID
ADMIN...CRIMLGY INT/LAW PHIL/SCI 16/20 BOLIV.   LAW
PAGE 22 E0441   CT/SYS

B47
CLAGETT H.L.,A GUIDE TO THE LAW AND LEGAL   BIBLIOG
LITERATURE OF CHILE, 1917-1946. CHILE CONSTN LABOR L/A+17C
JUDGE ADJUD ADMIN...CRIMLGY INT/LAW JURID CON/ANAL LAW
20. PAGE 22 E0442   LEGIS

B47
CLAGETT H.L.,A GUIDE TO THE LAW AND LEGAL   BIBLIOG
LITERATURE OF ECUADOR. ECUADOR CONSTN LABOR LEGIS   JURID
JUDGE ADJUD ADMIN CIVMIL/REL...CRIMLGY INT/LAW   LAW
CON/ANAL 20. PAGE 22 E0443   L/A+17C

B47
CLAGETT H.L.,A GUIDE TO THE LAW AND LEGAL   BIBLIOG
LITERATURE OF PERU. PERU CONSTN COM/IND LABOR MUNIC L/A+17C
JUDGE ADMIN CT/SYS...CRIMLGY INT/LAW JURID 20.   PHIL/SCI
PAGE 23 E0444   LAW

B47
CLAGETT H.L.,A GUIDE TO THE LAW AND LEGAL   BIBLIOG
LITERATURE OF URUGUAY. URUGUAY CONSTN COM/IND FINAN LAW
LABOR MUNIC JUDGE PRESS ADMIN CT/SYS...INT/LAW   JURID
PHIL/SCI 20. PAGE 23 E0445   L/A+17C

B47
CLAGETT H.L.,A GUIDE TO THE LAW AND LEGAL   BIBLIOG
LITERATURE OF VENEZUELA. VENEZUELA CONSTN LABOR   L/A+17C
LEGIS JUDGE ADJUD ADMIN CIVMIL/REL...CRIMLGY JURID INT/LAW
CON/ANAL 20. PAGE 23 E0446   LAW

B47
GORDON D.L.,THE HIDDEN WEAPON: THE STORY OF   INT/ORG
ECONOMIC WARFARE. EUR+WWI USA-45 LAW FINAN INDUS   ECO/TAC
NAT/G CONSULT FORCES PLAN DOMIN PWR WEALTH   INT/TRADE
...INT/LAW CONCPT OBS TOT/POP NAZI 20. PAGE 45   WAR
E0891

B47
HYDE C.C.,INTERNATIONAL LAW, CHIEFLY AS INTERPRETED INT/LAW
AND APPLIED BY THE UNITED STATES (3 VOLS., 2ND REV. DIPLOM
ED.). USA-45 WOR+45 WOR-45 INT/ORG CT/SYS WAR   NAT/G
NAT/LISM PEACE ORD/FREE...JURID 19/20 TREATY.   POLICY
PAGE 56 E1119

B47
INTERNATIONAL COURT OF JUSTICE,CHARTER OF THE   INT/LAW
UNITED NATIONS, STATUTE AND RULES OF COURT AND   INT/ORG
OTHER CONSTITUTIONAL DOCUMENTS. SWITZERLND LAW   CT/SYS
ADJUD INGP/REL...JURID 20 ICJ UN. PAGE 57 E1133   DIPLOM

B48
CLAGETT H.L.,A GUIDE TO THE LAW AND LEGAL   BIBLIOG
LITERATURE OF ARGENTINA, 1917-1946. CONSTN LABOR   L/A+17C
JUDGE ADJUD ADMIN...CRIMLGY INT/LAW JURID CON/ANAL LAW
20 ARGEN. PAGE 23 E0447   LEGIS

B48
FENWICK C.G.,INTERNATIONAL LAW. WOR+45 WOR-45   INT/ORG
CONSTN NAT/G LEGIT CT/SYS REGION...CONCPT   JURID
LEAGUE/NAT UN 20. PAGE 37 E0737   INT/LAW

B48
HOLCOMBE A.N.,HUMAN RIGHTS IN THE MODERN WORLD.   ORD/FREE
WOR+45 LEGIS DIPLOM ADJUD PERSON...INT/LAW 20 UN   INT/ORG
TREATY CIVIL/LIB BILL/RIGHT. PAGE 54 E1071   CONSTN
                                                    LAW

B48
JESSUP P.C.,A MODERN LAW OF NATIONS. FUT WOR+45   INT/ORG
WOR-45 SOCIETY NAT/G DELIB/GP LEGIS BAL/PWR   ADJUD
EDU/PROP LEGIT PWR...INT/LAW JURID TIME/SEQ
LEAGUE/NAT 20. PAGE 58 E1166

B48
KEIR D.L.,CASES IN CONSTITUTIONAL LAW. UK CHIEF   CONSTN
LEGIS DIPLOM TAX PARL/PROC CRIME GOV/REL...INT/LAW LAW
JURID 17/20. PAGE 60 E1195   ADJUD
                                                    CT/SYS

B48
LOGAN R.W.,THE AFRICAN MANDATES IN WORLD POLITICS. WAR
EUR+WWI GERMANY ISLAM INT/ORG BARGAIN...POLICY   COLONIAL
INT/LAW 20. PAGE 66 E1321   AFR
                                                    DIPLOM

B48
MORGENTHAL H.J.,POLITICS AMONG NATIONS: THE   DIPLOM
STRUGGLE FOR POWER AND PEACE. FUT WOR+45 INT/ORG   PEACE
OP/RES PROB/SOLV BAL/PWR CONTROL ATTIT MORAL   PWR
...INT/LAW BIBLIOG 20 COLD/WAR. PAGE 75 E1494   POLICY

S48
GROSS L.,"THE PEACE OF WESTPHALIA, 1648-1948."   INT/LAW
WOR+45 WOR-45 CONSTN BAL/PWR FEDERAL 17/20 TREATY   AGREE
WESTPHALIA. PAGE 48 E0949   CONCPT
                                                    DIPLOM

S48
MORGENTHAU H.J.,"THE TWILIGHT OF INTERNATIONAL   MORAL
MORALITY" (BMR)" WOR+45 WOR-45 BAL/PWR WAR NAT/LISM DIPLOM
PEACE...POLICY INT/LAW IDEA/COMP 15/20 TREATY   NAT/G
INTERVENT. PAGE 75 E1495

B49
GROB F.,THE RELATIVITY OF WAR AND PEACE: A STUDY IN WAR
LAW, HISTORY, AND POLITICS. WOR+45 WOR-45 LAW   PEACE
DIPLOM DEBATE...CONCPT LING IDEA/COMP BIBLIOG   INT/LAW
18/20. PAGE 48 E0944   STYLE

B49
JACKSON R.H.,INTERNATIONAL CONFERENCE ON MILITARY   DIPLOM
TRIALS. FRANCE GERMANY UK USA+45 USSR VOL/ASSN   INT/ORG
DELIB/GP REPAR ADJUD CT/SYS CRIME WAR 20 WAR/TRIAL. INT/LAW
PAGE 57 E1141   CIVMIL/REL

S49
KIRK G.,"MATTERIALS FOR THE STUDY OF INTERNATIONAL INT/ORG
RELATIONS." FUT UNIV WOR+45 INTELL EDU/PROP ROUTINE ACT/RES
PEACE ATTIT...INT/LAW JURID CONCPT OBS. PAGE 61   DIPLOM
E1219

B50
LAUTERPACHT H.,INTERNATIONAL LAW AND HUMAN RIGHTS. DELIB/GP
USA+45 CONSTN STRUCT INT/ORG ACT/RES EDU/PROP PEACE LAW
PERSON ALL/VALS...CONCPT CON/ANAL GEN/LAWS UN 20.   INT/LAW
PAGE 63 E1266

B50
MOCKFORD J.,SOUTH-WEST AFRICA AND THE INTERNATIONAL COLONIAL
COURT (PAMPHLET). AFR GERMANY SOUTH/AFR UK   SOVEREIGN
ECO/UNDEV DIPLOM CONTROL DISCRIM...DECISION JURID   INT/LAW
20 AFRICA/SW. PAGE 74 E1475   DOMIN

B50
MONPIED E.,BIBLIOGRAPHIE FEDERALISTE: OUVRAGES   BIBLIOG/A
CHOISIS (VOL. I, MIMEOGRAPHED PAPER). EUR+WWI   FEDERAL
DIPLOM ADMIN REGION ATTIT PACIFISM SOCISM...INT/LAW CENTRAL
19/20. PAGE 74 E1486   INT/ORG

B50
ROSS A.,CONSTITUTION OF THE UNITED NATIONS. CONSTN PEACE
CONSULT DELIB/GP ECO/TAC...INT/LAW JURID 20 UN   DIPLOM
LEAGUE/NAT. PAGE 86 E1721   ORD/FREE
                                                    INT/ORG

B50
SOHN L.B.,CASES AND OTHER MATERIALS ON WORLD LAW.   CT/SYS
FUT WOR+45 LAW INT/ORG...INT/LAW JURID METH/CNCPT   CONSTN
20 UN. PAGE 92 E1852

C50
NUMELIN R.,"THE BEGINNINGS OF DIPLOMACY." INT/TRADE DIPLOM

WAR GP/REL PEACE STRANGE ATTIT...INT/LAW CONCPT
BIBLIOG. PAGE 78 E1559
KIN
CULTURE
LAW

N51
MONPIED E.,FEDERALIST BIBLIOGRAPHY: ARTICLES AND
DOCUMENTS PUBLISHED IN BRITISH PERIODICALS
1945-1951 (MIMEOGRAPHED). EUR+WWI UK WOR+45 DIPLOM
REGION ATTIT SOCISM...INT/LAW 20. PAGE 74 E1487
BIBLIOG/A
INT/ORG
FEDERAL
CENTRAL

B51
CORBETT P.E.,LAW AND SOCIETY IN THE RELATIONS OF
STATES. FUT WOR+45 WOR-45 CONTROL WAR PEACE PWR
...POLICY JURID 16/20 TREATY. PAGE 26 E0505
INT/LAW
DIPLOM
INT/ORG

B51
KELSEN H.,THE LAW OF THE UNITED NATIONS. WOR+45
STRUCT RIGID/FLEX ORD/FREE...INT/LAW JURID CONCPT
CON/ANAL GEN/METH UN TOT/POP VAL/FREE 20. PAGE 60
E1198
INT/ORG
ADJUD

L51
KELSEN H.,"RECENT TRENDS IN THE LAW OF THE UNITED
NATIONS." KOREA WOR+45 CONSTN LEGIS DIPLOM LEGIT
DETER WAR RIGID/FLEX HEALTH ORD/FREE RESPECT
...JURID CON/ANAL UN VAL/FREE 20 NATO. PAGE 60
E1199
INT/ORG
LAW
INT/LAW

L51
LISSITZYN O.J.,"THE INTERNATIONAL COURT OF
JUSTICE." WOR+45 INT/ORG LEGIT ORD/FREE...CONCPT
TIME/SEQ TREND GEN/LAWS VAL/FREE 20 ICJ. PAGE 65
E1304
ADJUD
JURID
INT/LAW

L51
MANGONE G.,"THE IDEA AND PRACTICE OF WORLD
GOVERNMENT." FUT WOR+45 WOR-45 ECO/DEV LEGIS CREATE
LEGIT ROUTINE ATTIT MORAL PWR WEALTH...CONCPT
GEN/LAWS 20. PAGE 68 E1358
INT/ORG
SOCIETY
INT/LAW

B52
BRIGGS H.W.,THE LAW OF NATIONS (2ND ED.). WOR+45
WOR-45 NAT/G LEGIS WAR...ANTHOL 20 TREATY. PAGE 15
E0301
INT/LAW
DIPLOM
JURID

B52
DE GRAZIA A.,POLITICAL ORGANIZATION. CONSTN LOC/G
MUNIC NAT/G CHIEF LEGIS TOP/EX ADJUD CT/SYS
PERS/REL...INT/LAW MYTH UN. PAGE 29 E0581
FEDERAL
LAW
ADMIN

B52
DUNN F.S.,CURRENT RESEARCH IN INTERNATIONAL
AFFAIRS. UK USA+45...POLICY TREATY. PAGE 33 E0660
BIBLIOG/A
DIPLOM
INT/LAW

B52
FLECHTHEIM O.K.,FUNDAMENTALS OF POLITICAL SCIENCE.
WOR+45 WOR-45 LAW POL/PAR EX/STRUC LEGIS ADJUD
ATTIT PWR...INT/LAW. PAGE 38 E0760
NAT/G
DIPLOM
IDEA/COMP
CONSTN

B52
JENNINGS W.I.,CONSTITUTIONAL LAWS OF THE
COMMONWEALTH. UK LAW CHIEF LEGIS TAX CT/SYS
PARL/PROC GOV/REL...INT/LAW 18/20 COMMONWLTH
ENGLSH/LAW COMMON/LAW. PAGE 58 E1165
CONSTN
JURID
ADJUD
COLONIAL

B52
KELSEN H.,PRINCIPLES OF INTERNATIONAL LAW. WOR+45
WOR-45 INT/ORG ORD/FREE...JURID GEN/LAWS TOT/POP
20. PAGE 60 E1200
ADJUD
CONSTN
INT/LAW

B52
UNESCO,THESES DE SCIENCES SOCIALES: CATALOGUE
ANALYTIQUE INTERNATIONAL DE THESES INEDITES DE
DOCTORAT, 1940-1950. INT/ORG DIPLOM EDU/PROP...GEOG
INT/LAW MGT PSY SOC 20. PAGE 98 E1958
BIBLIOG
ACADEM
WRITING

L52
WRIGHT Q.,"CONGRESS AND THE TREATY-MAKING POWER."
USA+45 WOR+45 CONSTN INTELL NAT/G CHIEF CONSULT
EX/STRUC LEGIS TOP/EX CREATE GOV/REL DISPL DRIVE
RIGID/FLEX...TREND TOT/POP CONGRESS CONGRESS 20
TREATY. PAGE 108 E2154
ROUTINE
DIPLOM
INT/LAW
DELIB/GP

B53
LANDHEER B.,FUNDAMENTALS OF PUBLIC INTERNATIONAL
LAW (SELECTIVE BIBLIOGRAPHIES OF THE LIBRARY OF THE
PEACE PALACE, VOL. I; PAMPH). INT/ORG OP/RES PEACE
...IDEA/COMP 20. PAGE 62 E1250
BIBLIOG/A
INT/LAW
DIPLOM
PHIL/SCI

B53
OPPENHEIM L.,INTERNATIONAL LAW: A TREATISE (7TH
ED., 2 VOLS.). LAW CONSTN PROB/SOLV INT/TRADE ADJUD
AGREE NEUTRAL WAR ORD/FREE SOVEREIGN...BIBLIOG 20
LEAGUE/NAT UN ILO. PAGE 79 E1579
INT/LAW
INT/ORG
DIPLOM

B54
LANDHEER B.,RECOGNITION IN INTERNATIONAL LAW
(SELECTIVE BIBLIOGRAPHIES OF THE LIBRARY OF THE
PEACE PALACE, VOL. II; PAMPHLET). NAT/G LEGIT
SANCTION 20. PAGE 63 E1251
BIBLIOG/A
INT/LAW
INT/ORG
DIPLOM

B54
MANGONE G.,A SHORT HISTORY OF INTERNATIONAL
ORGANIZATION. MOD/EUR USA+45 USA-45 WOR+45 WOR-45
LAW LEGIS CREATE LEGIT ROUTINE RIGID/FLEX PWR
...JURID CONCPT OBS TIME/SEQ STERTYP GEN/LAWS UN
TOT/POP VAL/FREE 18/20. PAGE 68 E1359
INT/ORG
INT/LAW

B54
NUSSBAUM D.,A CONCISE HISTORY OF THE LAW OF
NATIONS. ASIA CHRIST-17C EUR+WWI ISLAM MEDIT-7
MOD/EUR S/ASIA UNIV WOR+45 WOR-45 SOCIETY STRUCT
EXEC ATTIT ALL/VALS...CONCPT HIST/WRIT TIME/SEQ.
PAGE 78 E1560
INT/ORG
LAW
PEACE
INT/LAW

B54
STONE J.,LEGAL CONTROLS OF INTERNATIONAL CONFLICT:
A TREATISE ON THE DYNAMICS OF DISPUTES AND WAR LAW.
WOR+45 WOR-45 NAT/G DIPLOM CT/SYS SOVEREIGN...JURID
CONCPT METH/CNCPT GEN/LAWS TOT/POP VAL/FREE
COLD/WAR LEAGUE/NAT 20. PAGE 94 E1878
INT/ORG
LAW
WAR
INT/LAW

B54
US SENATE COMM ON FOREIGN REL,REVIEW OF THE UNITED
NATIONS CHARTER: A COLLECTION OF DOCUMENTS. LEGIS
DIPLOM ADMIN ARMS/CONT WAR REPRESENT SOVEREIGN
...INT/LAW 20 UN. PAGE 101 E2029
BIBLIOG
CONSTN
INT/ORG
DEBATE

B55
BURR R.N.,DOCUMENTS ON INTER-AMERICAN COOPERATION:
VOL. I, 1810-1881; VOL. II, 1881-1948. DELIB/GP
BAL/PWR INT/TRADE REPRESENT NAT/LISM PEACE HABITAT
ORD/FREE PWR SOVEREIGN...INT/LAW 20 OAS. PAGE 18
E0345
BIBLIOG
DIPLOM
INT/ORG
L/A+17C

B55
HOGAN W.N.,INTERNATIONAL CONFLICT AND COLLECTIVE
SECURITY: THE PRINCIPLE OF CONCERN IN INTERNATIONAL
ORGANIZATION. CONSTN EX/STRUC BAL/PWR DIPLOM ADJUD
CONTROL CENTRAL CONSEN PEACE...INT/LAW CONCPT
METH/COMP 20 UN LEAGUE/NAT. PAGE 53 E1066
INT/ORG
WAR
ORD/FREE
FORCES

B55
JAPAN MOMBUSHO DAIGAKU GAKIYUT,BIBLIOGRAPHY OF THE
STUDIES ON LAW AND POLITICS (PAMPHLET). CONSTN
INDUS LABOR DIPLOM TAX ADMIN...CRIMLGY INT/LAW 20
CHINJAP. PAGE 58 E1150
BIBLIOG
LAW
PHIL/SCI

B55
KHADDURI M.,LAW IN THE MIDDLE EAST. LAW CONSTN
ACADEM FAM EDU/PROP CT/SYS SANCTION CRIME...INT/LAW
GOV/COMP ANTHOL 6/20 MID/EAST. PAGE 61 E1210
ADJUD
JURID
ISLAM

B55
PLISCHKE E.,AMERICAN FOREIGN RELATIONS: A
BIBLIOGRAPHY OF OFFICIAL SOURCES. USA+45 USA-45
INT/ORG FORCES PRESS WRITING DEBATE EXEC...POLICY
INT/LAW 18/20 CONGRESS. PAGE 81 E1621
BIBLIOG/A
DIPLOM
NAT/G

B55
SVARLIEN O.,AN INTRODUCTION TO THE LAW OF NATIONS.
SEA AIR INT/ORG NAT/G CHIEF ADMIN AGREE WAR PRIVIL
ORD/FREE SOVEREIGN...BIBLIOG 16/20. PAGE 95 E1897
INT/LAW
DIPLOM

B55
TROTIER A.H.,DOCTORAL DISSERTATIONS ACCEPTED BY
AMERICAN UNIVERSITIES 1954-55. SECT DIPLOM HEALTH
...ART/METH GEOG INT/LAW SOC LING CHARTS 20.
PAGE 97 E1943
BIBLIOG
ACADEM
USA+45
WRITING

B55
UN HEADQUARTERS LIBRARY,BIBLIOGRAPHIE DE LA CHARTE
DES NATIONS UNIES. CHINA/COM KOREA WOR+45 VOL/ASSN
CONFER ADMIN COERCE PEACE ATTIT ORD/FREE SOVEREIGN
...INT/LAW 20 UNESCO UN. PAGE 97 E1953
BIBLIOG/A
INT/ORG
DIPLOM

S55
WRIGHT Q.,"THE PEACEFUL ADJUSTMENT OF INTERNATIONAL
RELATIONS: PROBLEMS AND RESEARCH APPROACHES." UNIV
INTELL EDU/PROP ADJUD ROUTINE KNOWL SKILL...INT/LAW
JURID PHIL/SCI CLASSIF 20. PAGE 108 E2156
R+D
METH/CNCPT
PEACE

B56
CARLSTON K.S.,LAW AND STRUCTURES OF SOCIAL ACTION.
LAW SOCIETY ECO/DEV DIPLOM CONTROL ATTIT...DECISION
CONCPT 20. PAGE 19 E0379
JURID
INT/LAW
INGP/REL
STRUCT

B56
CORBETT P.E.,MORALS LAW, AND POWER IN INTERNATIONAL
SUPEGO

RELATIONS. WOR+45 WOR-45 INT/ORG VOL/ASSN DELIB/GP CONCPT
CREATE BAL/PWR DIPLOM LEGIT ARMS/CONT MORAL...JURID POLICY
GEN/LAWS TOT/POP LEAGUE/NAT 20. PAGE 26 E0506   INT/LAW

                                                    B56
ESTEP R.,AN AIR POWER BIBLIOGRAPHY. USA+45 TEC/DEV BIBLIOG/A
BUDGET DIPLOM EDU/PROP DETER CIVMIL/REL...DECISION   FORCES
INT/LAW 20. PAGE 35 E0698   WEAPON
                                                    PLAN

                                                    B56
JESSUP P.C.,TRANSNATIONAL LAW. FUT WOR+45 JUDGE   LAW
CREATE ADJUD ORD/FREE...CONCPT VAL/FREE 20. PAGE 59 JURID
E1167   INT/LAW

                                                    B56
SIPKOV I.,LEGAL SOURCES AND BIBLIOGRAPHY OF   BIBLIOG
BULGARIA. BULGARIA COM LEGIS WRITING ADJUD CT/SYS   LAW
...INT/LAW TREATY 20. PAGE 91 E1834   TOTALISM
                                                    MARXISM

                                                    B56
SOHN L.B.,CASES ON UNITED NATIONS LAW. STRUCT   INT/ORG
DELIB/GP WAR PEACE ORD/FREE...DECISION ANTHOL 20   INT/LAW
UN. PAGE 92 E1854   ADMIN
                                                    ADJUD

WEIS P.,NATIONALITY AND STATELESSNESS IN   INT/ORG
INTERNATIONAL LAW. UK WOR+45 WOR-45 LAW CONSTN   SOVEREIGN
NAT/G DIPLOM EDU/PROP LEGIT ROUTINE RIGID/FLEX   INT/LAW
...JURID RECORD CMN/WLTH 20. PAGE 105 E2109

                                                    S56
POTTER P.B.,"NEUTRALITY, 1955." WOR+45 WOR-45   NEUTRAL
INT/ORG NAT/G WAR ATTIT...POLICY IDEA/COMP 17/20   INT/LAW
LEAGUE/NAT UN COLD/WAR. PAGE 81 E1631   DIPLOM
                                                    CONCPT

                                                    B57
BLOOMFIELD L.M.,EGYPT, ISRAEL AND THE GULF OF   ISLAM
AQABA: IN INTERNATIONAL LAW. WOR+45 NAT/G CONSULT   INT/LAW
FORCES PLAN ECO/TAC ROUTINE COERCE ATTIT DRIVE   UAR
PERCEPT PERSON RIGID/FLEX LOVE PWR WEALTH...GEOG
CONCPT MYTH TREND. PAGE 13 E0250

                                                    B57
DE VISSCHER C.,THEORY AND REALITY IN PUBLIC   INT/ORG
INTERNATIONAL LAW. WOR+45 WOR-45 SOCIETY NAT/G   LAW
CT/SYS ATTIT MORAL ORD/FREE PWR...JURID CONCPT   INT/LAW
METH/CNCPT TIME/SEQ GEN/LAWS LEAGUE/NAT TOT/POP
VAL/FREE COLD/WAR. PAGE 30 E0599

                                                    B57
DONALDSON A.G.,SOME COMPARATIVE ASPECTS OF IRISH   CONSTN
LAW. IRELAND NAT/G DIPLOM ADMIN CT/SYS LEAD ATTIT   LAW
SOVEREIGN...JURID BIBLIOG/A 12/20 CMN/WLTH. PAGE 32 NAT/COMP
E0635   INT/LAW

                                                    B57
INSTITUT DE DROIT INTL,TABLEAU GENERAL DES   INT/LAW
RESOLUTIONS (1873-1956). LAW NEUTRAL CRIME WAR   DIPLOM
MARRIAGE PEACE...JURID 19/20. PAGE 56 E1124   ORD/FREE
                                                    ADJUD

                                                    B57
LEVONTIN A.V.,THE MYTH OF INTERNATIONAL SECURITY: A INT/ORG
JURIDICAL AND CRITICAL ANALYSIS. FUT WOR+45 WOR-45 INT/LAW
LAW NAT/G VOL/ASSN ACT/RES BAL/PWR ATTIT ORD/FREE   SOVEREIGN
...JURID METH/CNCPT TIME/SEQ TREND STERTYP 20.   MYTH
PAGE 64 E1289

                                                    B57
NEUMANN F.,THE DEMOCRATIC AND THE AUTHORITARIAN   DOMIN
STATE: ESSAYS IN POLITICAL AND LEGAL THEORY. USA+45 NAT/G
USA-45 CONTROL REV GOV/REL PEACE ALL/IDEOS   ORD/FREE
...INT/LAW CONCPT GEN/LAWS BIBLIOG 20. PAGE 77   POLICY
E1536

                                                    B57
ROSENNE S.,THE INTERNATIONAL COURT OF JUSTICE.   INT/ORG
WOR+45 LAW DOMIN LEGIT PEACE PWR SOVEREIGN...JURID   CT/SYS
CONCPT RECORD TIME/SEQ CON/ANAL CHARTS UN TOT/POP   INT/LAW
VAL/FREE LEAGUE/NAT 20 ICJ. PAGE 86 E1716

                                                    B57
SCHLOCHAUER H.J.,OFFENTLICHES RECHT. GERMANY/W   CONSTN
FINAN EX/STRUC LEGIS DIPLOM FEDERAL ORD/FREE   JURID
...INT/LAW 20. PAGE 88 E1757   ADMIN
                                                    CT/SYS

                                                    B57
SINEY M.C.,THE ALLIED BLOCKADE OF GERMANY: DETER
1914-1916. EUR+WWI GERMANY MOD/EUR USA-45 DIPLOM   INT/TRADE
CONTROL NEUTRAL PWR 20. PAGE 91 E1832   INT/LAW
                                                    WAR

                                                    B57
UNESCO,A REGISTER OF LEGAL DOCUMENTATION IN THE   BIBLIOG
WORLD (2ND ED.). CT/SYS...JURID IDEA/COMP METH/COMP LAW
NAT/COMP 20. PAGE 98 E1960   INT/LAW
                                                    CONSTN

                                                    B57
WASSENBERGH H.A.,POST-WAR INTERNATIONAL CIVIL   COM/IND
AVIATION POLICY AND THE LAW OF THE AIR. WOR+45 AIR NAT/G
INT/ORG DOMIN LEGIT PEACE ORD/FREE...POLICY JURID   INT/LAW
NEW/IDEA OBS TIME/SEQ TREND CHARTS 20 TREATY.
PAGE 105 E2101

                                                    B58
ALEXANDROWICZ,A BIBLIOGRAPHY OF INDIAN LAW. INDIA   BIBLIOG
S/ASIA CONSTN CT/SYS...INT/LAW 19/20. PAGE 3 E0062   LAW
                                                    ADJUD
                                                    JURID

                                                    B58
BOWETT D.W.,SELF-DEFENSE IN INTERNATIONAL LAW.   ADJUD
EUR+WWI MOD/EUR WOR+45 WOR-45 SOCIETY INT/ORG   CONCPT
CONSULT DIPLOM LEGIT COERCE ATTIT ORD/FREE...JURID   WAR
20 UN. PAGE 14 E0276   INT/LAW

                                                    B58
BRIERLY J.L.,THE BASIS OF OBLIGATION IN   INT/LAW
INTERNATIONAL LAW, AND OTHER PAPERS. WOR+45 WOR-45 DIPLOM
LEGIS...JURID CONCPT NAT/COMP ANTHOL 20. PAGE 15   ADJUD
E0299   SOVEREIGN

                                                    B58
DEUTSCHE GESCHAFT VOLKERRECHT,DIE VOLKERRECHTLICHEN BIBLIOG
DISSERTATIONEN AN DEN WESTDEUTSCHEN UNIVERSITATEN, INT/LAW
1945-1957. GERMANY/W NAT/G DIPLOM ADJUD CT/SYS   ACADEM
...POLICY 20. PAGE 31 E0616   JURID

                                                    B58
MARTIN L.J.,INTERNATIONAL PROPAGANDA: ITS LEGAL AND EDU/PROP
DIPLOMATIC CONTROL. UK USA+45 USSR CONSULT DELIB/GP DIPLOM
DOMIN CONTROL 20. PAGE 69 E1373   INT/LAW
                                                    ATTIT

                                                    B58
MOSKOWITZ M.,HUMAN RIGHTS AND WORLD ORDER. INT/ORG DIPLOM
PLAN GP/REL NAT/LISM SOVEREIGN...CONCPT 20 UN   INT/LAW
TREATY CIV/RIGHTS. PAGE 75 E1502   ORD/FREE

                                                    B58
SEYID MUHAMMAD V.A.,THE LEGAL FRAMEWORK OF WORLD   INT/LAW
TRADE. WOR+45 INT/ORG DIPLOM CONTROL...BIBLIOG 20   VOL/ASSN
TREATY UN IMF GATT. PAGE 90 E1807   INT/TRADE
                                                    TARIFFS

                                                    B58
SOC OF COMP LEGIS AND INT LAW,THE LAW OF THE SEA... INT/LAW
(PAMPHLET). WOR+45 NAT/G INT/TRADE ADJUD CONTROL   INT/ORG
NUC/PWR WAR PEACE ATTIT ORD/FREE...JURID CHARTS 20   DIPLOM
UN TREATY RESOURCE/N. PAGE 92 E1850   SEA

                                                    L58
INT. SOC. SCI. BULL.,"TECHNIQUES OF MEDIATION AND   VOL/ASSN
CONCILIATION." EUR+WWI USA+45 SOCIETY INDUS INT/ORG DELIB/GP
LABOR NAT/G LEGIS DIPLOM EDU/PROP CHOOSE ATTIT   INT/LAW
RIGID/FLEX...JURID CONCPT GEN/LAWS 20. PAGE 57
E1129

                                                    L58
UNESCO,"TECHNIQUES OF MEDIATION AND CONCILIATION." INT/ORG
EUR+WWI USA+45 WOR+45 INDUS FACE/GP EX/STRUC   CONSULT
EDU/PROP LEGIT PEACE ORD/FREE...INT/LAW TIME/SEQ   DIPLOM
LEAGUE/NAT 20. PAGE 98 E1961

                                                    S58
MCDOUGAL M.S.,"PERSPECTIVES FOR A LAW OF OUTER   INT/ORG
SPACE." FUT WOR+45 AIR CONSULT DELIB/GP TEC/DEV   SPACE
CT/SYS ORD/FREE...POLICY JURID 20 UN. PAGE 70 E1404 INT/LAW

                                                    C58
RAJAN M.S.,"UNITED NATIONS AND DOMESTIC   INT/LAW
JURISDICTION." WOR+45 WOR-45 PARL/PROC...IDEA/COMP   DIPLOM
BIBLIOG 20 UN. PAGE 83 E1670   CONSTN
                                                    INT/ORG

                                                    B59
COMM. STUDY ORGAN. PEACE,ORGANIZING PEACE IN THE   INT/ORG
NUCLEAR AGE. FUT CONSULT DELIB/GP DOMIN ADJUD   ACT/RES
ROUTINE COERCE ORD/FREE...TECHNIC INT/LAW JURID   NUC/PWR
NEW/IDEA UN COLD/WAR 20. PAGE 24 E0483

                                                    B59
HARVARD UNIVERSITY LAW SCHOOL,INTERNATIONAL   NUC/PWR
PROBLEMS OF FINANCIAL PROTECTION AGAINST NUCLEAR   ADJUD
RISK. WOR+45 NAT/G DELIB/GP PROB/SOLV DIPLOM   INDUS
CONTROL ATTIT...POLICY INT/LAW MATH 20. PAGE 51   FINAN

E1009

KIRCHHEIMER O.,GEGENWARTSPROBLEME DER
ASYLGEWAHRUNG. DOMIN GP/REL ATTIT...NAT/COMP 20.
PAGE 61 E1217
DIPLOM
INT/LAW
JURID
ORD/FREE
B59

KNIERIEM A.,THE NUREMBERG TRIALS. EUR+WWI GERMANY
VOL/ASSN LEAD COERCE WAR INGP/REL TOTALSM SUPEGO
ORD/FREE...CONCPT METH/COMP. PAGE 61 E1225
INT/LAW
CRIME
PARTIC
JURID
B59

MAYER A.J.,POLITICAL ORIGINS OF THE NEW DIPLOMACY.
1917-1918. EUR+WWI MOD/EUR USA-45 WAR PWR...POLICY
INT/LAW BIBLIOG. PAGE 70 E1392
TREND
DIPLOM
B59

PANHUYS H.F.,THE ROLE OF NATIONALITY IN
INTERNATIONAL LAW. ADJUD CRIME WAR STRANGE...JURID
TREND. PAGE 80 E1596
INT/LAW
NAT/LISM
INGP/REL
B59

COLUMBIA U. BUREAU OF APPL SOC RES, ATTITUDES OF
PROMINENT AMERICANS TOWARD "WORLD PEACE THROUGH
WORLD LAW" (SUPRA-NATL ORGANIZATION FOR WAR
PREVENTION). USA+45 USSR ELITES FORCES PLAN
PROB/SOLV CONTROL WAR PWR...POLICY SOC QU IDEA/COMP
20 UN. PAGE 82 E1644
ATTIT
ACT/RES
INT/LAW
STAT
B59

REIFF H.,THE UNITED STATES AND THE TREATY LAW OF
THE SEA. USA+45 USA-45 SEA SOCIETY INT/ORG CONSULT
DELIB/GP LEGIS DIPLOM LEGIT ATTIT ORD/FREE PWR
WEALTH...GEOG JURID TOT/POP 20 TREATY. PAGE 84
E1681
ADJUD
INT/LAW
B59

SCHNEIDER J.,TREATY-MAKING POWER OF INTERNATIONAL
ORGANIZATIONS. FUT WOR+45 WOR-45 LAW NAT/G JUDGE
DIPLOM LEGIT CT/SYS ORD/FREE PWR...INT/LAW JURID
GEN/LAWS TOT/POP UNESCO 20 TREATY. PAGE 88 E1762
INT/ORG
ROUTINE
B59

SIMPSON J.L.,INTERNATIONAL ARBITRATION: LAW AND
PRACTICE. WOR+45 WOR-45 INT/ORG DELIB/GP ADJUD
PEACE MORAL ORD/FREE...METH 18/20. PAGE 91 E1829
INT/LAW
DIPLOM
CT/SYS
CONSULT
B59

WILDNER H.,DIE TECHNIK DER DIPLOMATIE. TOP/EX ROLE
ORD/FREE...INT/LAW JURID IDEA/COMP NAT/COMP 20.
PAGE 106 E2122
DIPLOM
POLICY
DELIB/GP
NAT/G
B59

WOETZEL R.K.,DIE INTERNATIONALE KONTROLLE DER
HOHEREN LUFTSCHICHTEN UND DES WELTRAUMS. INT/ORG
NAT/G CONTROL SUPEGO...JURID CONCPT 20. PAGE 107
E2136
SPACE
INT/LAW
DIPLOM
SOVEREIGN
B59

MCDOUGAL M.S.,"THE IDENTIFICATION AND APPRAISAL OF
DIVERSE SYSTEMS OF PUBLIC ORDER (BMR)" WOR+45 NAT/G
CONSULT EDU/PROP POLICY. PAGE 70 E1405
INT/LAW
DIPLOM
ALL/IDEOS
L59

JENKS C.W.,"THE CHALLENGE OF UNIVERSALITY." FUT
UNIV CONSTN CULTURE CONSULT CREATE PLAN LEGIT ATTIT
MORAL ORD/FREE RESPECT...MAJORIT JURID 20. PAGE 58
E1155
INT/ORG
LAW
PEACE
INT/LAW
S59

POTTER P.B.,"OBSTACLES AND ALTERNATIVES TO
INTERNATIONAL LAW." WOR+45 NAT/G VOL/ASSN DELIB/GP
BAL/PWR DOMIN ROUTINE...JURID VAL/FREE 20. PAGE 81
E1632
INT/ORG
LAW
DIPLOM
INT/LAW
S59

STONE J.,"CONFLICT MANAGEMENT THROUGH CONTEMPORARY
INTERNATIONAL LAW AND ORGANIZATION." WOR+45 LAW
NAT/G CREATE BAL/PWR DOMIN LEGIT ROUTINE COERCE
ATTIT ORD/FREE PWR SOVEREIGN...JURID 20. PAGE 94
E1880
INT/ORG
INT/LAW
S59

BYRD E.M. JR.,TREATIES AND EXECUTIVE AGREEMENTS IN
THE UNITED STATES: THEIR SEPARATE ROLES AND
LIMITATIONS. USA+45 USA-45 EX/STRUC TARIFFS CT/SYS
GOV/REL FEDERAL...IDEA/COMP BIBLIOG SUPREME/CT
SENATE CONGRESS. PAGE 18 E0353
CHIEF
INT/LAW
DIPLOM
B60

CLARK G.,WORLD PEACE THROUGH WORLD LAW. FUT WOR+45
INT/ORG
B60

CONSULT FORCES ACT/RES CREATE PLAN ADMIN ROUTINE
ARMS/CONT DETER ATTIT PWR...JURID VAL/FREE UNESCO
20 UN. PAGE 23 E0449
LAW
PEACE
INT/LAW

HARVARD LAW SCHOOL LIBRARY,CURRENT LEGAL
BIBLIOGRAPHY. USA+45 CONSTN LEGIS ADJUD CT/SYS
POLICY. PAGE 51 E1006
BIBLIOG
JURID
LAW
INT/LAW
B60

JENNINGS R.,PROGRESS OF INTERNATIONAL LAW. FUT
WOR+45 WOR-45 SOCIETY NAT/G VOL/ASSN DELIB/GP
DIPLOM EDU/PROP LEGIT COERCE ATTIT DRIVE MORAL
ORD/FREE...JURID CONCPT OBS TIME/SEQ TREND
GEN/LAWS. PAGE 58 E1164
INT/ORG
LAW
INT/LAW
B60

LA PONCE J.A.,THE PROTECTION OF MINORITIES. WOR+45
WOR-45 POL/PAR SUFF...INT/LAW CLASSIF GP/COMP
GOV/COMP BIBLIOG 17/20 CIVIL/LIB CIV/RIGHTS.
PAGE 62 E1242
INGP/REL
DOMIN
SOCIETY
RACE/REL
B60

PRICE D.,THE SECRETARY OF STATE. USA+45 CONSTN
ELITES INTELL CHIEF EX/STRUC TOP/EX LEGIT ATTIT PWR
SKILL...DECISION 20 CONGRESS. PAGE 82 E1650
CONSULT
DIPLOM
INT/LAW
B60

STEIN E.,AMERICAN ENTERPRISE IN THE EUROPEAN COMMON
MARKET: A LEGAL PROFILE. EUR+WWI FUT USA+45 SOCIETY
STRUCT ECO/DEV NAT/G VOL/ASSN CONSULT PLAN TEC/DEV
ECO/TAC INT/TRADE ADMIN ATTIT RIGID/FLEX PWR...MGT
NEW/IDEA STAT TREND COMPUT/IR SIMUL EEC 20. PAGE 93
E1867
MARKET
ADJUD
INT/LAW
B60

UNITED WORLD FEDERALISTS,UNITED WORLD FEDERALISTS;
PANORAMA OF RECENT BOOKS, FILMS, AND JOURNALS ON
WORLD FEDERATION. THE UN, AND WORLD PEACE. CULTURE
ECO/UNDEV PROB/SOLV FOR/AID ARMS/CONT NUC/PWR
...INT/LAW PHIL/SCI 20 UN. PAGE 98 E1971
BIBLIOG/A
DIPLOM
INT/ORG
PEACE
B60

WOETZEL R.K.,THE INTERNATIONAL CONTROL OF AIRSPACE
AND OUTERSPACE. FUT WOR+45 AIR CONSTN STRUCT
CONSULT PLAN TEC/DEV ADJUD RIGID/FLEX KNOWL
ORD/FREE PWR...TECHNIC GEOG MGT NEW/IDEA TREND
COMPUT/IR VAL/FREE 20 TREATY. PAGE 107 E2137
INT/ORG
JURID
SPACE
INT/LAW
B60

DEAN A.W.,"SECOND GENEVA CONFERENCE OF THE LAW OF
THE SEA: THE FIGHT FOR FREEDOM OF THE SEAS." FUT
USA+45 USSR WOR+45 WOR-45 SEA CONSTN STRUCT PLAN
INT/TRADE ADJUD ADMIN ORD/FREE...DECISION RECORD
TREND GEN/LAWS 20 TREATY. PAGE 30 E0600
INT/ORG
JURID
INT/LAW
L60

KUNZ J.,"SANCTIONS IN INTERNATIONAL LAW." WOR+45
WOR-45 LEGIT ARMS/CONT COERCE PEACE ATTIT
...METH/CNCPT TIME/SEQ TREND 20. PAGE 62 E1234
INT/ORG
ADJUD
INT/LAW
L60

GRACIA-MORA M.R.,"INTERNATIONAL RESPONSIBILITY FOR
SUBVERSIVE ACTIVITIES AND HOSTILE PROPAGANDA BY
PRIVATE PERSONS AGAINST." COM EUR+WWI L/A+17C UK
USA+45 USSR WOR-45 CONSTN NAT/G LEGIT ADJUD REV
PEACE TOTALSM ORD/FREE...INT/LAW 20. PAGE 45 E0895
INT/ORG
JURID
SOVEREIGN
S60

O'BRIEN W.,"THE ROLE OF FORCE IN THE INTERNATIONAL
JURIDICAL ORDER." WOR+45 NAT/G FORCES DOMIN ADJUD
ARMS/CONT DETER NUC/PWR WAR ATTIT PWR...CATH
INT/LAW JURID CONCPT TREND STERTYP GEN/LAWS 20.
PAGE 78 E1564
INT/ORG
COERCE
S60

POTTER P.B.,"RELATIVE VALUES OF INTERNATIONAL
RELATIONS, LAW, AND ORGANIZATIONS." WOR+45 NAT/G
LEGIT ADJUD ORD/FREE...CONCPT TOT/POP COLD/WAR 20.
PAGE 81 E1633
INT/ORG
LEGIS
DIPLOM
INT/LAW
S60

RHYNE C.S.,"LAW AS AN INSTRUMENT FOR PEACE." FUT
WOR+45 PLAN LEGIT ADJUD ARMS/CONT NUC/PWR ATTIT
ORD/FREE...JURID METH/CNCPT TREND CON/ANAL HYPO/EXP
COLD/WAR 20. PAGE 84 E1690
ADJUD
EDU/PROP
INT/LAW
PEACE
S60

SCHACHTER O.,"THE ENFORCEMENT OF INTERNATIONAL
JUDICIAL AND ARBITRAL DECISIONS." WOR+45 NAT/G
ECO/TAC DOMIN LEGIT ROUTINE COERCE ATTIT DRIVE
ALL/VALS PWR...METH/CNCPT TREND TOT/POP 20 UN.
PAGE 87 E1750
INT/ORG
ADJUD
INT/LAW
S60

WRIGHT Q.,"LEGAL ASPECTS OF THE U-2 INCIDENT." COM
USA+45 USSR STRUCT NAT/G FORCES PLAN TEC/DEV ADJUD
RIGID/FLEX MORAL ORD/FREE...DECISION INT/LAW JURID
PSY TREND GEN/LAWS COLD/WAR VAL/FREE 20 U-2.
PAGE 108 E2157

S60
PWR
POLICY
SPACE

ANAND R.P.,COMPULSORY JURISDICTION OF INTERNATIONAL
COURT OF JUSTICE. FUT WOR+45 SOCIETY PLAN LEGIT
ADJUD ATTIT DRIVE PERSON ORD/FREE...JURID CONCPT
TREND 20 ICJ. PAGE 5 E0086

B61
INT/ORG
COERCE
INT/LAW

BAINS J.S.,STUDIES IN POLITICAL SCIENCE. INDIA
WOR+45 WOR-45 CONSTN BAL/PWR ADJUD ADMIN PARL/PROC
SOVEREIGN...SOC METH/COMP ANTHOL 17/20 UN. PAGE 7
E0137

B61
DIPLOM
INT/LAW
NAT/G

BRENNAN D.G.,ARMS CONTROL, DISARMAMENT, AND
NATIONAL SECURITY. WOR+45 NAT/G FORCES CREATE
PROB/SOLV PARTIC WAR PEACE...DECISION INT/LAW
ANTHOL BIBLIOG 20. PAGE 15 E0291

B61
ARMS/CONT
ORD/FREE
DIPLOM
POLICY

CONFERENCE ATLANTIC COMMUNITY,AN INTRODUCTORY
BIBLIOGRAPHY. COM WOR+45 FORCES DIPLOM ECO/TAC WAR
...INT/LAW HIST/WRIT COLD/WAR NATO. PAGE 25 E0485

B61
BIBLIOG/A
CON/ANAL
INT/ORG

LARSON A.,WHEN NATIONS DISAGREE. USA+45 WOR+45
INT/ORG ADJUD COERCE CRIME OWN SOVEREIGN...POLICY
JURID 20. PAGE 63 E1258

B61
INT/LAW
DIPLOM
WAR

MCDOUGAL M.S.,LAW AND MINIMUM WORLD PUBLIC ORDER.
WOR+45 SOCIETY NAT/G DELIB/GP EDU/PROP LEGIT ADJUD
COERCE ATTIT PERSON...JURID CONCPT RECORD TREND
TOT/POP 20. PAGE 70 E1406

B61
INT/ORG
ORD/FREE
INT/LAW

NEWMAN R.P.,RECOGNITION OF COMMUNIST CHINA? A STUDY
IN ARGUMENT. CHINA/COM NAT/G PROB/SOLV RATIONAL
...INT/LAW LOG IDEA/COMP BIBLIOG 20. PAGE 77 E1544

B61
MARXISM
ATTIT
DIPLOM
POLICY

RIENOW R.,CONTEMPORARY INTERNATIONAL POLITICS.
WOR+45 INT/ORG BAL/PWR EDU/PROP COLONIAL NEUTRAL
REGION WAR PEACE...INT/LAW 20 COLD/WAR UN. PAGE 85
E1698

B61
DIPLOM
PWR
POLICY
NAT/G

SYATAUW J.J.G.,SOME NEWLY ESTABLISHED ASIAN STATES
AND THE DEVELOPMENT OF INTERNATIONAL LAW. BURMA
CEYLON INDIA INDONESIA ECO/UNDEV COLONIAL NEUTRAL
WAR PEACE SOVEREIGN...CHARTS 19/20. PAGE 95 E1902

B61
INT/LAW
ADJUST
SOCIETY
S/ASIA

WARD R.E.,JAPANESE POLITICAL SCIENCE: A GUIDE TO
JAPANESE REFERENCE AND RESEARCH MATERIALS (2ND
ED.). LAW CONSTN STRATA NAT/G POL/PAR DELIB/GP
LEGIS ADMIN CHOOSE GP/REL...INT/LAW 19/20 CHINJAP.
PAGE 105 E2099

B61
BIBLIOG/A
PHIL/SCI

WECHSLER H.,PRINCIPLES, POLITICS AND FUNDAMENTAL
LAW: SELECTED ESSAYS. USA+45 USA-45 LAW SOCIETY
NAT/G PROVS DELIB/GP EX/STRUC ACT/RES LEGIT PERSON
KNOWL PWR...JURID 20 NUREMBERG. PAGE 105 E2106

B61
CT/SYS
CONSTN
INT/LAW

WRIGHT Q.,THE ROLE OF INTERNATIONAL LAW IN THE
ELIMINATION OF WAR. FUT WOR+45 WOR-45 NAT/G BAL/PWR
DIPLOM DOMIN LEGIT PWR...POLICY INT/LAW JURID
CONCPT TIME/SEQ TREND GEN/LAWS COLD/WAR 20.
PAGE 108 E2158

B61
INT/ORG
ADJUD
ARMS/CONT

SAND P.T.,"AN HISTORICAL SURVEY OF INTERNATIONAL
AIR LAW SINCE 1944." USA+45 USA-45 WOR+45 WOR-45
SOCIETY ECO/DEV NAT/G CONSULT EX/STRUC ACT/RES PLAN
LEGIT ROUTINE...JURID CONCPT METH/CNCPT TREND 20.
PAGE 87 E1744

L61
INT/ORG
LAW
INT/LAW
SPACE

SILVING H.,"IN RE EICHMANN: A DILEMMA OF LAW AND
MORALITY" WOR+45 INSPECT ADJUST MORAL...JURID 20
WAR/TRIAL EICHMANN/A NATURL/LAW. PAGE 91 E1828

L61
CT/SYS
INT/LAW
CONCPT

ALGER C.F.,"NON-RESOLUTION CONSEQUENCES OF THE
UNITED NATIONS AND THEIR EFFECT ON INTERNATIONAL
CONFLICT." WOR+45 CONSTN ECO/DEV NAT/G CONSULT
DELIB/GP TOP/EX ACT/RES PLAN DIPLOM EDU/PROP

S61
INT/ORG
DRIVE
BAL/PWR

ROUTINE ATTIT ALL/VALS...INT/LAW TOT/POP UN 20.
PAGE 3 E0065

CASTANEDA J.,"THE UNDERDEVELOPED NATIONS AND THE
DEVELOPMENT OF INTERNATIONAL LAW." FUT UNIV LAW
ACT/RES FOR/AID LEGIT PERCEPT SKILL...JURID
METH/CNCPT TIME/SEQ TOT/POP 20 UN. PAGE 21 E0405

S61
INT/ORG
ECO/UNDEV
PEACE
INT/LAW

LIPSON L.,"AN ARGUMENT ON THE LEGALITY OF
RECONNAISSANCE SATELLITES." COM USA+45 USSR WOR+45
AIR INTELL NAT/G CONSULT PLAN DIPLOM LEGIT ROUTINE
ATTIT...INT/LAW JURID CONCPT METH/CNCPT TREND
COLD/WAR 20. PAGE 65 E1302

S61
INT/ORG
LAW
SPACE

MACHOWSKI K.,"SELECTED PROBLEMS OF NATIONAL
SOVEREIGNTY WITH REFERENCE TO THE LAW OF OUTER
SPACE." FUT WOR+45 AIR LAW INTELL SOCIETY ECO/DEV
PLAN EDU/PROP DETER DRIVE PERCEPT SOVEREIGN
...POLICY INT/LAW OBS TREND TOT/POP 20. PAGE 67
E1339

S61
UNIV
ACT/RES
NUC/PWR
SPACE

ALEXANDROWICZ C.H.,WORLD ECONOMIC AGENCIES: LAW AND
PRACTICE. WOR+45 DIST/IND FINAN LABOR CONSULT
INT/TRADE TARIFFS REPRESENT HEALTH...JURID 20 UN
GATT EEC OAS ECSC. PAGE 3 E0063

B62
INT/LAW
INT/ORG
DIPLOM
ADJUD

AMERICAN LAW INSTITUTE,FOREIGN RELATIONS LAW OF THE
UNITED STATES: RESTATEMENT, SECOND. USA+45 NAT/G
LEGIS ADJUD EXEC ROUTINE GOV/REL...INT/LAW JURID
CONCPT 20 TREATY. PAGE 4 E0082

B62
PROF/ORG
LAW
DIPLOM
ORD/FREE

BEBR G.,JUDICIAL CONTROL OF THE EUROPEAN
COMMUNITIES. EUR+WWI INT/ORG NAT/G DOMIN LEGIT PWR
...JURID CONCPT GEN/LAWS GEN/METH EEC 20. PAGE 9
E0168

B62
ADJUD
VOL/ASSN
INT/LAW

BIBLIOTHEQUE PALAIS DE LA PAIX,CATALOGUE OF THE
PEACE PALACE LIBRARY, SUPPLEMENT 1937-1952 (7
VOLS.). WOR+45 WOR-45 INT/ORG NAT/G ADJUD WAR PEACE
...JURID 20. PAGE 12 E0225

B62
BIBLIOG
INT/LAW
DIPLOM

BISHOP W.W. JR.,INTERNATIONAL LAW: CASES AND
MATERIALS. WOR+45 INT/ORG FORCES PROB/SOLV AGREE
WAR...JURID IDEA/COMP T 20 TREATY. PAGE 12 E0233

B62
INT/LAW
DIPLOM
CONCPT
CT/SYS

COLOMBOS C.J.,THE INTERNATIONAL LAW OF THE SEA.
WOR+45 EXTR/IND DIPLOM INT/TRADE TARIFFS AGREE WAR
...TIME/SEQ 20 TREATY. PAGE 24 E0476

B62
INT/LAW
SEA
JURID
ADJUD

DE LAVALLE H.,A STATEMENT OF THE LAWS OF PERU IN
MATTERS AFFECTING BUSINESS (3RD ED.). PERU WORKER
INT/TRADE INCOME ORD/FREE...INT/LAW 20. PAGE 30
E0586

B62
CONSTN
JURID
FINAN
TAX

JACOBINI H.B.,INTERNATIONAL LAW: A TEXT. DIPLOM
ADJUD NEUTRAL WAR PEACE T. PAGE 57 E1143

B62
INT/LAW
CT/SYS
CONCPT

JENKS C.W.,THE PROPER LAW OF INTERNATIONAL
ORGANISATIONS. DIPLOM LEGIT AGREE CT/SYS SANCTION
REPRESENT SOVEREIGN...GEN/LAWS 20 UN UNESCO ILO
NATO OAS. PAGE 58 E1158

B62
LAW
INT/ORG
ADJUD
INT/LAW

LILLICH R.B.,INTERNATIONAL CLAIMS: THEIR
ADJUDICATION BY NATIONAL COMMISSIONS. WOR+45 WOR-45
INT/ORG LEGIT CT/SYS TOT/POP 20. PAGE 65 E1297

B62
ADJUD
JURID
INT/LAW

MCDOUGAL M.S.,THE PUBLIC ORDER OF THE OCEANS.
WOR+45 WOR-45 SEA INT/ORG NAT/G CONSULT DELIB/GP
DIPLOM LEGIT PEACE RIGID/FLEX...GEOG INT/LAW JURID
RECORD TOT/POP 20 TREATY. PAGE 70 E1407

B62
ADJUD
ORD/FREE

NORGAARD C.A.,THE POSITION OF THE INDIVIDUAL IN
INTERNATIONAL LAW. INT/ORG SUPEGO ORD/FREE
SOVEREIGN...CONCPT 20 UN. PAGE 78 E1556

B62
INT/LAW
DIPLOM
CRIME
JURID

PERKINS D.,AMERICA'S QUEST FOR PEACE. USA+45 WOR+45

B62
INT/LAW

DIPLOM CONFER NAT/LISM ATTIT 20 UN TREATY. PAGE 80
E1610
    INT/ORG
    ARMS/CONT
    PEACE

    B62

ROSENNE S.,THE WORLD COURT: WHAT IT IS AND HOW IT
WORKS. WOR+45 WOR-45 LAW CONSTN JUDGE EDU/PROP
LEGIT ROUTINE CHOOSE PEACE ORD/FREE...JURID OBS
TIME/SEQ CHARTS UN TOT/POP VAL/FREE 20. PAGE 86
E1717
    INT/ORG
    ADJUD
    INT/LAW

    B62

SCHWARTZ L.E.,INTERNATIONAL ORGANIZATIONS AND SPACE
COOPERATION. VOL/ASSN CONSULT CREATE TEC/DEV
SANCTION...POLICY INT/LAW PHIL/SCI 20 UN. PAGE 89
E1787
    INT/ORG
    DIPLOM
    R+D
    SPACE

    B62

SCHWARZENBERGER G.,THE FRONTIERS OF INTERNATIONAL
LAW. WOR+45 WOR-45 NAT/G LEGIT CT/SYS ROUTINE MORAL
ORD/FREE PWR...JURID SOC GEN/METH 20 COLD/WAR.
PAGE 89 E1789
    INT/ORG
    LAW
    INT/LAW

    B62

SHAW C.,LEGAL PROBLEMS IN INTERNATIONAL TRADE AND
INVESTMENT. WOR+45 ECO/DEV ECO/UNDEV MARKET DIPLOM
TAX INCOME ROLE...ANTHOL BIBLIOG 20 TREATY UN IMF
GATT. PAGE 91 E1816
    INT/LAW
    INT/TRADE
    FINAN
    ECO/TAC

    B62

TRISKA J.F.,THE THEORY, LAW, AND POLICY OF SOVIET
TREATIES. WOR+45 WOR-45 CONSTN INT/ORG NAT/G
VOL/ASSN DOMIN LEGIT COERCE ATTIT PWR RESPECT
...POLICY JURID CONCPT OBS SAMP TIME/SEQ TREND
GEN/LAWS 20. PAGE 97 E1941
    COM
    LAW
    INT/LAW
    USSR

    L62

GROSS L.,"IMMUNITIES AND PRIVILEGES OF DELIGATIONS
TO THE UNITED NATIONS." USA+45 WOR+45 STRATA NAT/G
VOL/ASSN CONSULT DIPLOM EDU/PROP ROUTINE RESPECT
...POLICY INT/LAW CONCPT UN 20. PAGE 48 E0950
    INT/ORG
    LAW
    ELITES

    L62

PETKOFF D.K.,"RECOGNITION AND NON-RECOGNITION OF
STATES AND GOVERNMENTS IN INTERNATIONAL LAW." ASIA
COM USA+45 WOR+45 NAT/G ACT/RES DIPLOM DOMIN LEGIT
COERCE ORD/FREE PWR...CONCPT GEN/LAWS 20. PAGE 80
E1611
    INT/ORG
    LAW
    INT/LAW

    L62

SCHWERIN K.,"LAW LIBRARIES AND FOREIGN LAW
COLLECTION IN THE USA." USA+45 USA-45...INT/LAW
STAT 20. PAGE 89 E1793
    BIBLIOG
    LAW
    ACADEM
    ADMIN

    S62

BIERZANECK R.,"LA NON-RECONAISSANCE ET LE DROIT
INTERNATIONAL CONTEMPORAIN." EUR+WWI FUT WOR+45 LAW
ECO/DEV ATTIT RIGID/FLEX...CONCPT TIME/SEQ TOT/POP
20. PAGE 12 E0228
    EDU/PROP
    JURID
    DIPLOM
    INT/LAW

    S62

CRANE R.D.,"LAW AND STRATEGY IN SPACE." FUT USA+45
WOR+45 AIR LAW INT/ORG NAT/G FORCES ACT/RES PLAN
BAL/PWR LEGIT ARMS/CONT COERCE ORD/FREE...POLICY
INT/LAW JURID SOC/EXP 20 TREATY. PAGE 27 E0542
    CONCPT
    SPACE

    S62

CRANE R.D.,"SOVIET ATTITUDE TOWARD INTERNATIONAL
SPACE LAW." COM FUT USA+45 USSR AIR CONSTN DELIB/GP
DOMIN PWR...JURID TREND TOT/POP 20. PAGE 27 E0543
    LAW
    ATTIT
    INT/LAW
    SPACE

    S62

FALK R.A.,"THE REALITY OF INTERNATIONAL LAW."
WOR+45 NAT/G LEGIT COERCE DETER WAR MORAL ORD/FREE
PWR SOVEREIGN...JURID CONCPT VAL/FREE COLD/WAR 20.
PAGE 36 E0714
    INT/ORG
    ADJUD
    NUC/PWR
    INT/LAW

    S62

GRAVEN J.,"LE MOUVEAU DROIT PENAL INTERNATIONAL."
UNIV STRUCT LEGIS ACT/RES CRIME ATTIT PERCEPT
PERSON...JURID CONCPT 20. PAGE 45 E0899
    CT/SYS
    PUB/INST
    INT/ORG
    INT/LAW

    S62

GREEN L.C.,"POLITICAL OFFENSES, WAR CRIMES AND
EXTRADITION." WOR+45 YUGOSLAVIA INT/ORG LEGIT
ROUTINE WAR ORD/FREE SOVEREIGN...JURID NAZI 20
INTERPOL. PAGE 46 E0906
    LAW
    CONCPT
    INT/LAW

    S62

GREENSPAN M.,"INTERNATIONAL LAW AND ITS PROTECTION
FOR PARTICIPANTS IN UNCONVENTIONAL WARFARE." WOR+45
LAW INT/ORG NAT/G POL/PAR COERCE REV ORD/FREE
...INT/LAW TOT/POP 20. PAGE 46 E0912
    FORCES
    JURID
    GUERRILLA
    WAR

    S62

JOHNSON O.H.,"THE ENGLISH TRADITION IN
INTERNATIONAL LAW." CHRIST-17C MOD/EUR EDU/PROP
LEGIT CT/SYS ORD/FREE...JURID CONCPT TIME/SEQ.
PAGE 59 E1170
    LAW
    INT/LAW
    UK

    S62

LISSITZYN O.J.,"SOME LEGAL IMPLICATIONS OF THE U-2
AND RB-47 INCIDENTS." FUT USA+45 USSR WOR+45 AIR
NAT/G DIPLOM LEGIT MORAL ORD/FREE SOVEREIGN...JURID
GEN/LAWS GEN/METH COLD/WAR 20 U-2. PAGE 65 E1305
    LAW
    CONCPT
    SPACE
    INT/LAW

    S62

MCWHINNEY E.,"CO-EXISTENCE, THE CUBA CRISIS, AND
COLD WAR-INTERNATIONAL WAR." CUBA USA+45 USSR
WOR+45 NAT/G TOP/EX BAL/PWR DIPLOM DOMIN LEGIT
PEACE RIGID/FLEX ORD/FREE...STERTYP COLD/WAR 20.
PAGE 71 E1427
    CONCPT
    INT/LAW

    S62

MONNIER J.P.,"LA SUCCESSION D'ETATS EN MATIERE DE
RESPONSABILITE INTERNATIONALE." UNIV CONSTN INTELL
SOCIETY ADJUD ROUTINE PERCEPT SUPEGO...GEN/LAWS
TOT/POP 20. PAGE 74 E1485
    NAT/G
    JURID
    INT/LAW

    S62

VIGNES D.,"L'AUTORITE DES TRAITES INTERNATIONAUX EN
DROIT INTERNE." EUR+WWI UNIV LAW CONSTN INTELL
NAT/G POL/PAR DIPLOM ATTIT PERCEPT ALL/VALS
...POLICY INT/LAW JURID CONCPT TIME/SEQ 20 TREATY.
PAGE 104 E2075
    STRUCT
    LEGIT
    FRANCE

    C62

LILLICH R.B.,"INTERNATIONAL CLAIMS: THEIR
ADJUDICATION BY NATIONAL COMMISSIONS." WOR+45
WOR-45 NAT/G ADJUD...JURID BIBLIOG 18/20. PAGE 65
E1298
    INT/LAW
    DIPLOM
    PROB/SOLV

    B63

ATTIA G.E.D.,LES FORCES ARMEES DES NATIONS UNIES EN
COREE ET AU MOYENORIENT. KOREA CONSTN NAT/G
DELIB/GP LEGIS PWR...IDEA/COMP NAT/COMP BIBLIOG UN
SUEZ. PAGE 6 E0114
    FORCES
    INT/LAW

    B63

DEENER D.R.,CANADA - UNITED STATES TREATY
RELATIONS. CANADA USA+45 USA-45 NAT/G FORCES PLAN
PROB/SOLV AGREE NUC/PWR...TREND 18/20 TREATY.
PAGE 30 E0603
    DIPLOM
    INT/LAW
    POLICY

    B63

ELLERT R.B.,NATO 'FAIR TRIAL' SAFEGUARDS: PRECURSOR
TO AN INTERNATIONAL BILL OF PROCEDURAL RIGHTS.
WOR+45 FORCES CRIME CIVMIL/REL ATTIT ORD/FREE 20
NATO. PAGE 34 E0683
    JURID
    INT/LAW
    INT/ORG
    CT/SYS

    B63

FALK R.A.,LAW, MORALITY, AND WAR IN THE
CONTEMPORARY WORLD. WOR+45 LAW INT/ORG EX/STRUC
FORCES EDU/PROP LEGIT DETER NUC/PWR MORAL ORD/FREE
...JURID TOT/POP 20. PAGE 36 E0715
    ADJUD
    ARMS/CONT
    PEACE
    INT/LAW

    B63

FAWCETT J.E.S.,THE BRITISH COMMONWEALTH IN
INTERNATIONAL LAW. LAW INT/ORG NAT/G VOL/ASSN
OP/RES DIPLOM ADJUD CENTRAL CONSEN...NET/THEORY
CMN/WLTH TREATY. PAGE 36 E0723
    INT/LAW
    STRUCT
    COLONIAL

    B63

HIGGINS R.,THE DEVELOPMENT OF INTERNATIONAL LAW
THROUGH THE POLITICAL ORGANS OF THE UNITED NATIONS.
WOR+45 FORCES DIPLOM AGREE COERCE ATTIT SOVEREIGN
...BIBLIOG 20 UN TREATY. PAGE 52 E1041
    INT/ORG
    INT/LAW
    TEC/DEV
    JURID

    B63

JENKS C.W.,LAW, FREEDOM, AND WELFARE. WOR+45 GIVE
ADJUD WAR PEACE HABITAT ORD/FREE. PAGE 58 E1159
    INT/LAW
    DIPLOM
    SOVEREIGN
    PROB/SOLV

    B63

LIVNEH E.,ISRAEL LEGAL BIBLIOGRAPHY IN EUROPEAN
LANGUAGES. ISRAEL LOC/G JUDGE TAX...INT/LAW 20.
PAGE 66 E1311
    BIBLIOG
    LAW
    NAT/G
    CONSTN

    B63

MCDOUGAL M.S.,LAW AND PUBLIC ORDER IN SPACE. FUT
USA+45 ACT/RES TEC/DEV ADJUD...POLICY INT/LAW JURID
20. PAGE 70 E1410
    SPACE
    ORD/FREE
    DIPLOM
    DECISION

    B63

PACHTER H.M.,COLLISION COURSE: THE CUBAN MISSILE
CRISIS AND COEXISTENCE. CUBA USA+45 DIPLOM
    WAR
    BAL/PWR

ARMS/CONT PEACE MARXISM...DECISION INT/LAW 20
COLD/WAR KHRUSH/N KENNEDY/JF CASTRO/F. PAGE 79
E1587

NUC/PWR
DETER

B63
ROSNER G.,THE UNITED NATIONS EMERGENCY FORCE.
FRANCE ISRAEL UAR UK WOR+45 CREATE WAR PEACE
ORD/FREE PWR...INT/LAW JURID HIST/WRIT TIME/SEQ UN.
PAGE 86 E1719

INT/ORG
FORCES

B63
US SENATE,DOCUMENTS ON INTERNATIONAL AS"ECTS OF
EXPLORATION AND USE OF OUTER SPACE, 1954-62: STAFF
REPORT FOR COMM AERON SPACE SCI. USA+45 USSR LEGIS
LEAD CIVMIL/REL PEACE...POLICY INT/LAW ANTHOL 20
CONGRESS NASA KHRUSH/N. PAGE 101 E2026

SPACE
UTIL
GOV/REL
DIPLOM

B63
VAN SLYCK P.,PEACE: THE CONTROL OF NATIONAL POWER.
CUBA WOR+45 FINAN NAT/G FORCES PROB/SOLV TEC/DEV
BAL/PWR ADMIN CONTROL ORD/FREE...POLICY INT/LAW UN
COLD/WAR TREATY. PAGE 103 E2069

ARMS/CONT
PEACE
INT/ORG
DIPLOM

S63
CAHIER P.,"LE DROIT INTERNE DES ORGANISATIONS
INTERNATIONALES." UNIV CONSTN SOCIETY ECO/DEV R+D
NAT/G TOP/EX LEGIT ATTIT PERCEPT...TIME/SEQ 19/20.
PAGE 18 E0357

INT/ORG
JURID
DIPLOM
INT/LAW

S63
FRIEDMANN W.G.,"THE USES OF 'GENERAL PRINCIPLES' IN
THE DEVELOPMENT OF INTERNATIONAL LAW." WOR+45 NAT/G
DIPLOM INT/TRADE LEGIT ROUTINE RIGID/FLEX ORD/FREE
...JURID CONCPT STERTYP GEN/METH 20. PAGE 41 E0804

LAW
INT/LAW
INT/ORG

S63
GERHARD H.,"COMMODITY TRADE STABILIZATION THROUGH
INTERNATIONAL AGREEMENTS." WOR+45 ECO/DEV ECO/UNDEV
NAT/G ROUTINE ORD/FREE...INT/LAW OBS TREND GEN/METH
TOT/POP 20. PAGE 43 E0850

PLAN
ECO/TAC
INT/TRADE

S63
MACWHINNEY E.,"LES CONCEPT SOVIETIQUE DE
'COEXISTENCE PACIFIQUE' ET LES RAPPORTS JURIDIQUES
ENTRE L'URSS ET LES ETATS OCIDENTAUX." COM FUT
WOR+45 LAW CULTURE INTELL POL/PAR ACT/RES BAL/PWR
...INT/LAW 20. PAGE 67 E1346

NAT/G
CONCPT
DIPLOM
USSR

S63
MEYROWITZ H.,"LES JURISTES DEVANT L'ARME NUCLAIRE."
FUT WOR+45 INTELL SOCIETY BAL/PWR DETER WAR...JURID
CONCPT 20. PAGE 72 E1451

ACT/RES
ADJUD
INT/LAW
NUC/PWR

S63
MODELSKI G.,"STUDY OF ALLIANCES." WOR+45 WOR-45
INT/ORG NAT/G FORCES LEGIT ADMIN CHOOSE ALL/VALS
PWR SKILL...INT/LAW CONCPT GEN/LAWS 20 TREATY.
PAGE 74 E1477

VOL/ASSN
CON/ANAL
DIPLOM

S63
TALLON D.,"L'ETUDE DU DROIT COMPARE COMME MOYEN DE
RECHERCHER LES MATIERES SUSCEPTIBLES D'UNIFICATION
INTERNATIONALE." WOR+45 LAW SOCIETY VOL/ASSN
CONSULT LEGIT CT/SYS RIGID/FLEX KNOWL 20. PAGE 95
E1906

INT/ORG
JURID
INT/LAW

S63
WALKER H.,"THE INTERNATIONAL LAW OF COMMODITY
AGREEMENTS." FUT WOR+45 ECO/DEV ECO/UNDEV FINAN
INT/ORG NAT/G CONSULT CREATE PLAN ECO/TAC ATTIT
PERCEPT...CONCPT GEN/LAWS TOT/POP GATT 20. PAGE 105
E2095

MARKET
VOL/ASSN
INT/LAW
INT/TRADE

S63
WENGLER W.,"LES CONFLITS DE LOIS ET LE PRINCIPE
D'EGALITE." UNIV LAW SOCIETY ACT/RES LEGIT ATTIT
PERCEPT 20. PAGE 105 E2111

JURID
CONCPT
INT/LAW

C63
ATTIA G.E.O.,"LES FORCES ARMEES DES NATIONS UNIES
EN COREE ET AU MOYENORIENT." KOREA CONSTN DELIB/GP
LEGIS PWR...IDEA/COMP NAT/COMP BIBLIOG UN SUEZ.
PAGE 6 E0115

FORCES
NAT/G
INT/LAW

B64
AHLUWALIA K.,THE LEGAL STATUS, PRIVILEGES AND
IMMUNITIES OF SPECIALIZED AGENCIES OF UN AND
CERTAIN OTHER INTERNATIONAL ORGANIZATIONS. WOR+45
LAW CONSULT DELIB/GP FORCES. PAGE 3 E0055

PRIVIL
DIPLOM
INT/ORG
INT/LAW

B64
BOWETT D.W.,UNITED NATIONS FORCES* A LEGAL STUDY.
CYPRUS ISRAEL KOREA LAW CONSTN ACT/RES CREATE
BUDGET CONTROL TASK PWR...INT/LAW IDEA/COMP UN
CONGO/LEOP SUEZ. PAGE 14 E0278

OP/RES
FORCES
ARMS/CONT

B64
COHEN M.,LAW AND POLITICS IN SPACE: SPECIFIC AND
URGENT PROBLEMS IN THE LAW OF OUTER SPACE.
CHINA/COM COM USA+45 USSR WOR+45 COM/IND INT/ORG
NAT/G LEGIT NUC/PWR ATTIT BIO/SOC...JURID CONCPT
CONGRESS 20 STALIN/J. PAGE 24 E0464

DELIB/GP
LAW
INT/LAW
SPACE

B64
COHEN M.L.,SELECTED BIBLIOGRAPHY OF FOREIGN AND
INTERNATIONAL LAW....IDEA/COMP METH/COMP 20.
PAGE 24 E0466

BIBLIOG/A
JURID
LAW
INT/LAW

B64
CURRIE D.P.,FEDERALISM AND THE NEW NATIONS OF
AFRICA. CANADA USA+45 INT/TRADE TAX GP/REL
...NAT/COMP SOC/INTEG 20. PAGE 28 E0556

FEDERAL
AFR
ECO/UNDEV
INT/LAW

B64
DIAS R.W.M.,A BIBLIOGRAPHY OF JURISPRUDENCE (2ND
ED.). VOL/ASSN LEGIS ADJUD CT/SYS OWN...INT/LAW
18/20. PAGE 31 E0619

BIBLIOG/A
JURID
LAW
CONCPT

B64
DUBISSON M.,LA COUR INTERNATIONALE DE JUSTICE.
FRANCE LAW CONSTN JUDGE DOMIN ADJUD...INT/LAW
CLASSIF RECORD ORG/CHARTS UN. PAGE 33 E0651

CT/SYS
INT/ORG

B64
ECONOMIDES C.P.,LE POUVOIR DE DECISION DES
ORGANISATIONS INTERNATIONALES EUROPEENNES. DIPLOM
DOMIN INGP/REL EFFICIENCY...INT/LAW JURID 20 NATO
OEEC EEC COUNCL/EUR EURATOM. PAGE 34 E0673

INT/ORG
PWR
DECISION
GP/COMP

B64
ENGEL S.,LAW, STATE, AND INTERNATIONAL LEGAL ORDER.
WOR+45 NAT/G ORD/FREE RELATISM...INT/LAW IDEA/COMP
ANTHOL 20 KELSEN/H. PAGE 35 E0690

JURID
OBJECTIVE
CONCPT
DEBATE

B64
FALK R.A.,THE ROLE OF DOMESTIC COURTS IN THE
INTERNATIONAL LEGAL ORDER. FUT WOR+45 INT/ORG NAT/G
JUDGE EDU/PROP LEGIT CT/SYS...POLICY RELATIV JURID
CONCPT GEN/LAWS 20. PAGE 36 E0716

LAW
INT/LAW

B64
FRANCK T.M.,EAST AFRICAN UNITY THROUGH LAW. MALAWI
TANZANIA UGANDA UK ZAMBIA CONSTN INT/ORG NAT/G
ADMIN ROUTINE TASK NAT/LISM ATTIT SOVEREIGN
...RECORD IDEA/COMP NAT/COMP. PAGE 40 E0785

AFR
FEDERAL
REGION
INT/LAW

B64
FRIEDMANN W.G.,THE CHANGING STRUCTURE OF
INTERNATIONAL LAW. WOR+45 INT/ORG NAT/G PROVS LEGIT
ORD/FREE PWR...JURID CONCPT GEN/LAWS TOT/POP UN 20.
PAGE 41 E0805

ADJUD
TREND
INT/LAW

B64
FRYDENSBERG P.,PEACE-KEEPING: EXPERIENCE AND
EVALUATION: THE OSLO PAPERS. NORWAY FORCES PLAN
CONTROL...INT/LAW 20 UN. PAGE 41 E0814

INT/ORG
DIPLOM
PEACE
COERCE

B64
GARDNER R.N.,IN PURSUIT OF WORLD ORDER* US FOREIGN
POLICY AND INTERNATIONAL ORGANIZATIONS. USA+45 USSR
ECO/UNDEV FORCES LEGIS DIPLOM FOR/AID INT/TRADE
PEACE...INT/LAW PREDICT UN. PAGE 42 E0839

OBS
INT/ORG
ALL/VALS

B64
GESELLSCHAFT RECHTSVERGLEICH,BIBLIOGRAPHIE DES
DEUTSCHEN RECHTS (BIBLIOGRAPHY OF GERMAN LAW,
TRANS. BY COURTLAND PETERSON). GERMANY FINAN INDUS
LABOR SECT FORCES CT/SYS PARL/PROC CRIME...INT/LAW
SOC NAT/COMP 20. PAGE 43 E0853

BIBLIOG/A
JURID
CONSTN
ADMIN

B64
GRZYBOWSKI K.,THE SOCIALIST COMMONWEALTH OF
NATIONS: ORGANIZATIONS AND INSTITUTIONS. FORCES
DIPLOM INT/TRADE ADJUD ADMIN LEAD WAR MARXISM
SOCISM...BIBLIOG 20 COMECON WARSAW/P. PAGE 48 E0956

INT/LAW
COM
REGION
INT/ORG

B64
HOLDSWORTH W.S.,A HISTORY OF ENGLISH LAW; THE
CENTURIES OF DEVELOPMENT AND REFORM (VOL. XIV). UK
CONSTN LOC/G NAT/G POL/PAR CHIEF EX/STRUC ADJUD
COLONIAL ATTIT...INT/LAW JURID 18/19 TORY/PARTY
COMMONWLTH WHIG/PARTY COMMON/LAW. PAGE 54 E1081

LAW
LEGIS
LEAD
CT/SYS

B64
JENKS C.W.,THE PROSPECTS OF INTERNATIONAL
ADJUDICATION. WOR+45 WOR-45 NAT/G DIPLOM CONTROL

INT/LAW
ADJUD

PWR...POLICY JURID CONCPT METH/COMP 19/20 ICJ   CT/SYS
LEAGUE/NAT UN TREATY. PAGE 58 E1160   INT/ORG

                                                         B64
KAHNG T.J.,LAW, POLITICS, AND THE SECURITY COUNCIL*   DELIB/GP
AN INQUIRY INTO THE HANDLING OF LEGAL QUESTIONS.   ADJUD
LAW CONSTN NAT/G ACT/RES OP/RES CT/SYS TASK PWR   ROUTINE
...INT/LAW BIBLIOG UN. PAGE 59 E1180

                                                         B64
MCDOUGAL M.S.,STUDIES IN WORLD PUBLIC ORDER. SPACE   INT/LAW
SEA INT/ORG CREATE AGREE NUC/PWR...POLICY PHIL/SCI   SOC
IDEA/COMP ANTHOL METH 20 UN. PAGE 71 E1411   DIPLOM

                                                         B64
MCWHINNEY E.,"PEACEFUL COEXISTENCE" AND SOVIET-   PEACE
WESTERN INTERNATIONAL LAW. USSR DIPLOM LEAD...JURID   IDEA/COMP
20 COLD/WAR. PAGE 71 E1429   INT/LAW
                                                       ATTIT

                                                         B64
NICE R.W.,TREASURY OF LAW. WOR+45 WOR-45 SECT ADJUD   LAW
MORAL ORD/FREE...INT/LAW JURID PHIL/SCI ANTHOL.   WRITING
PAGE 77 E1545   PERS/REL
                                                       DIPLOM

                                                         B64
REGALA R.,WORLD PEACE THROUGH DIPLOMACY AND LAW.   DIPLOM
S/ASIA WOR+45 ECO/UNDEV INT/ORG FORCES PLAN   PEACE
PROB/SOLV FOR/AID NUC/PWR WAR...POLICY INT/LAW 20.   ADJUD
PAGE 84 E1679

                                                         B64
ROBERTS HL,FOREIGN AFFAIRS BIBLIOGRAPHY, 1952-1962.   BIBLIOG/A
ECO/DEV SECT PLAN FOR/AID INT/TRADE ARMS/CONT   DIPLOM
NAT/LISM ATTIT...INT/LAW GOV/COMP IDEA/COMP 20.   INT/ORG
PAGE 85 E1703   WAR

                                                         B64
ROBINSON R.D.,INTERNATIONAL BUSINESS POLICY. AFR   ECO/TAC
INDIA L/A+17C USA+45 ELITES AGRI FOR/AID COERCE   DIST/IND
BAL/PAY...DECISION INT/LAW MGT 20. PAGE 85 E1706   COLONIAL
                                                       FINAN

                                                         B64
RUSSELL R.B.,UNITED NATIONS EXPERIENCE WITH   FORCES
MILITARY FORCES: POLITICAL AND LEGAL ASPECTS. AFR   DIPLOM
KOREA WOR+45 LEGIS PROB/SOLV ADMIN CONTROL   SANCTION
EFFICIENCY PEACE...POLICY INT/LAW BIBLIOG UN.   ORD/FREE
PAGE 87 E1738

                                                         B64
SCHECHTER A.H.,INTERPRETATION OF AMBIGUOUS   INT/LAW
DOCUMENTS BY INTERNATIONAL ADMINISTRATIVE   DIPLOM
TRIBUNALS. WOR+45 EX/STRUC INT/TRADE CT/SYS   INT/ORG
SOVEREIGN 20 UN ILO EURCT/JUST. PAGE 87 E1752   ADJUD

                                                         B64
SCHWELB E.,HUMAN RIGHTS AND THE INTERNATIONAL   INT/ORG
COMMUNITY. WOR+45 WOR-45 NAT/G SECT DELIB/GP DIPLOM   ORD/FREE
PEACE RESPECT TREATY 20 UN. PAGE 89 E1792   INT/LAW

                                                         B64
SEGAL R.,SANCTIONS AGAINST SOUTH AFRICA. AFR   SANCTION
SOUTH/AFR NAT/G INT/TRADE RACE/REL PEACE PWR   DISCRIM
...INT/LAW ANTHOL 20 UN. PAGE 90 E1801   ECO/TAC
                                                       POLICY

                                                         B64
STANGER R.J.,ESSAYS ON INTERVENTION. PLAN PROB/SOLV   SOVEREIGN
BAL/PWR ADJUD COERCE WAR ROLE PWR...INT/LAW CONCPT   DIPLOM
20 UN INTERVENT. PAGE 93 E1865   POLICY
                                                       LEGIT

                                                         B64
SZLADITS C.,BIBLIOGRAPHY ON FOREIGN AND COMPARATIVE   BIBLIOG/A
LAW: BOOKS AND ARTICLES IN ENGLISH (SUPPLEMENT   JURID
1962). FINAN INDUS JUDGE LICENSE ADMIN CT/SYS   ADJUD
PARL/PROC OWN...INT/LAW CLASSIF METH/COMP NAT/COMP   LAW
20. PAGE 95 E1904

                                                         B64
THANT U.,TOWARD WORLD PEACE. DELIB/GP TEC/DEV   DIPLOM
EDU/PROP WAR SOVEREIGN...INT/LAW 20 UN MID/EAST.   BIOG
PAGE 96 E1915   PEACE
                                                       COERCE

                                                         B64
TONG T.,UNITED STATES DIPLOMACY IN CHINA,   DIPLOM
1844-1860. ASIA USA-45 ECO/UNDEV ECO/TAC COERCE   INT/TRADE
GP/REL...INT/LAW 19 TREATY. PAGE 96 E1934   COLONIAL

                                                         B64
UN PUB. INFORM. ORGAN.,EVERY MAN'S UNITED NATIONS.   INT/ORG
UNIV WOR+45 CONSTN CULTURE SOCIETY ECO/DEV   ROUTINE
ECO/UNDEV NAT/G ACT/RES PLAN ECO/TAC INT/TRADE

EDU/PROP LEGIT PEACE ATTIT ALL/VALS...POLICY HUM
INT/LAW CONCPT CHARTS UN TOT/POP 20. PAGE 97 E1954

                                                         B64
WILLIAMS S.P.,TOWARD A GENUINE WORLD SECURITY   BIBLIOG/A
SYSTEM (PAMPHLET). WOR+45 INT/ORG FORCES PLAN   ARMS/CONT
NUC/PWR ORD/FREE...INT/LAW CONCPT UN PRESIDENT.   DIPLOM
PAGE 106 E2123   PEACE

                                                         S64
BARKUN M.,"CONFLICT RESOLUTION THROUGH IMPLICIT   CONSULT
MEDIATION." UNIV BARGAIN CONSEN FEDERAL JURID.   CENTRAL
PAGE 8 E0149   INT/LAW
                                                       IDEA/COMP

                                                         S64
CARNEGIE ENDOWMENT INT. PEACE,"HUMAN RIGHTS (ISSUES   INT/ORG
BEFORE THE NINETEENTH GENERAL ASSEMBLY)." AFR   PERSON
WOR+45 LAW CONSTN NAT/G EDU/PROP GP/REL DISCRIM   RACE/REL
PEACE ATTIT MORAL ORD/FREE...INT/LAW PSY CONCPT
RECORD UN 20. PAGE 20 E0385

                                                         S64
CARNEGIE ENDOWMENT INT. PEACE,"LEGAL QUESTIONS   INT/ORG
(ISSUES BEFORE THE NINETEENTH GENERAL ASSEMBLY)."   LAW
WOR+45 CONSTN NAT/G DELIB/GP ADJUD PEACE MORAL   INT/LAW
ORD/FREE...RECORD UN 20 TREATY. PAGE 20 E0386

                                                         S64
COHEN M.,"BASIC PRINCIPLES OF INTERNATIONAL LAW."   INT/ORG
UNIV WOR+45 WOR-45 BAL/PWR LEGIT ADJUD WAR ATTIT   INT/LAW
MORAL ORD/FREE...JURID CONCPT MYTH TOT/POP 20.
PAGE 23 E0463

                                                         S64
CRANE R.D.,"BASIC PRINCIPLES IN SOVIET SPACE LAW."   COM
FUT WOR+45 AIR INT/ORG DIPLOM DOMIN ARMS/CONT   LAW
COERCE NUC/PWR PEACE ATTIT DRIVE PWR...INT/LAW   USSR
METH/CNCPT NEW/IDEA OBS TREND GEN/LAWS VAL/FREE   SPACE
MARX/KARL 20. PAGE 27 E0544

                                                         S64
GINSBURGS G.,"WARS OF NATIONAL LIBERATION - THE   COERCE
SOVIET THESIS." COM USSR WOR+45 WOR-45 LAW CULTURE   CONCPT
INT/ORG DIPLOM LEGIT COLONIAL GUERRILLA WAR   INT/LAW
NAT/LISM ATTIT PERSON MORAL PWR...JURID OBS TREND   REV
MARX/KARL 20. PAGE 44 E0869

                                                         S64
KARPOV P.V.,"PEACEFUL COEXISTENCE AND INTERNATIONAL   COM
LAW." WOR+45 LAW SOCIETY INT/ORG VOL/ASSN FORCES   ATTIT
CREATE CAP/ISM DIPLOM ADJUD NUC/PWR PEACE MORAL   INT/LAW
ORD/FREE PWR MARXISM...MARXIST JURID CONCPT OBS   USSR
TREND COLD/WAR MARX/KARL 20. PAGE 59 E1186

                                                         S64
KUNZ J.,"THE CHANGING SCIENCE OF INTERNATIONAL   ADJUD
LAW." FUT WOR+45 WOR-45 INT/ORG LEGIT ORD/FREE   CONCPT
...JURID TIME/SEQ GEN/LAWS 20. PAGE 62 E1235   INT/LAW

                                                         S64
LIPSON L.,"PEACEFUL COEXISTENCE." COM USSR WOR+45   ATTIT
LAW INT/ORG DIPLOM LEGIT ADJUD ORD/FREE...CONCPT   JURID
OBS TREND GEN/LAWS VAL/FREE COLD/WAR 20. PAGE 65   INT/LAW
E1303   PEACE

                                                         S64
MAGGS P.B.,"SOVIET VIEWPOINT ON NUCLEAR WEAPONS IN   COM
INTERNATIONAL LAW." USSR WOR+45 INT/ORG FORCES   LAW
DIPLOM ARMS/CONT ATTIT ORD/FREE PWR...POLICY JURID   INT/LAW
CONCPT OBS TREND CON/ANAL GEN/LAWS VAL/FREE 20.   NUC/PWR
PAGE 67 E1347

                                                         S64
SCHWELB E.,"OPERATION OF THE EUROPEAN CONVENTION ON   INT/ORG
HUMAN RIGHTS." EUR+WWI LAW SOCIETY CREATE EDU/PROP   MORAL
ADJUD ADMIN PEACE ATTIT ORD/FREE PWR...POLICY
INT/LAW CONCPT OBS GEN/LAWS UN VAL/FREE ILO 20
ECHR. PAGE 89 E1791

                                                         S64
SINGH N.,"THE CONTEMPORARY PRACTICE OF INDIA IN THE   LAW
FIELD OF INTERNATIONAL LAW." INDIA S/ASIA INT/ORG   ATTIT
NAT/G DOMIN EDU/PROP LEGIT KNOWL...CONCPT TOT/POP   DIPLOM
20. PAGE 91 E1833   INT/LAW

                                                         S64
SKUBISZEWSKI K.,"FORMS OF PARTICIPATION OF   INT/ORG
INTERNATIONAL ORGANIZATION IN THE LAW MAKING   LAW
PROCESS." FUT WOR+45 NAT/G DELIB/GP DOMIN LEGIT   INT/LAW
KNOWL PWR...JURID TREND 20. PAGE 92 E1837

                                                         S64
TRISKA J.F.,"SOVIET TREATY LAW: A QUANTITATIVE   COM
ANALYSIS." WOR+45 LAW ECO/UNDEV AGRI COM/IND INDUS   ECO/TAC
CREATE TEC/DEV DIPLOM ATTIT PWR WEALTH...JURID SAMP   INT/LAW

TIME/SEQ TREND CHARTS VAL/FREE 20 TREATY. PAGE 97
E1942

USSR

B65
BAADE H.,THE SOVIET IMPACT ON INTERNATIONAL LAW.
INT/ORG INT/TRADE LEGIT COLONIAL ARMS/CONT REV WAR
...CON/ANAL ANTHOL TREATY. PAGE 6 E0124

INT/LAW
USSR
CREATE
ORD/FREE

B65
BERKOWITZ M.,AMERICAN NATIONAL SECURITY: A READER
IN THEORY AND POLICY. USA+45 INT/ORG FORCES BAL/PWR
DIPLOM ECO/TAC DETER PWR...INT/LAW ANTHOL BIBLIOG
20 UN. PAGE 11 E0203

ORD/FREE
WAR
ARMS/CONT
POLICY

B65
BRIGGS H.W.,THE INTERNATIONAL LAW COMMISSION. LAW
CONSTN LEGIS CREATE ADJUD CT/SYS ROUTINE TASK
EFFICIENCY...CLASSIF OBS UN. PAGE 15 E0302

INT/LAW
DELIB/GP

B65
FALK R.A.,THE AFTERMATH OF SABBATINO: BACKGROUND
PAPERS AND PROCEEDINGS OF SEVENTH HAMMARSKJOLD
FORUM. USA+45 LAW ACT/RES ADJUD ROLE...BIBLIOG 20
EXPROPRIAT SABBATINO HARLAN/JM. PAGE 36 E0718

SOVEREIGN
CT/SYS
INT/LAW
OWN

B65
FORGAC A.A.,NEW DIPLOMACY AND THE UNITED NATIONS.
FRANCE GERMANY UK USSR INT/ORG DELIB/GP EX/STRUC
PEACE...INT/LAW CONCPT UN. PAGE 39 E0770

DIPLOM
ETIQUET
NAT/G

B65
GOTLIEB A.,DISARMAMENT AND INTERNATIONAL LAW* A
STUDY OF THE ROLE OF LAW IN THE DISARMAMENT
PROCESS. USA+45 USSR PROB/SOLV CONFER ADMIN ROUTINE
NUC/PWR ORD/FREE SOVEREIGN UN TREATY. PAGE 45 E0893

INT/LAW
INT/ORG
ARMS/CONT
IDEA/COMP

B65
HAENSCH G.,PAN-AFRICANISM IN ACTION: AN ACCOUNT OF
THE UAM TIC AND ALPHABETICAL IN GERMAN, ENGLISH,
FRENCH AND SPANISH. WOR+45 INT/ORG NAT/G ARMS/CONT
WAR...INT/LAW IDEA/COMP TREATY. PAGE 49 E0974

DICTIONARY
DIPLOM
LING

B65
HIGGINS R.,CONFLICT OF INTERESTS* INTERNATIONAL LAW
IN A DIVIDED WORLD. ASIA USSR ECO/DEV ECO/UNDEV
SECT INT/TRADE COLD/WAR WORSHIP. PAGE 52 E1042

INT/LAW
IDEA/COMP
ADJUST

B65
JENKS C.W.,SPACE LAW. DIPLOM DEBATE CONTROL
ORD/FREE TREATY 20 UN. PAGE 58 E1161

SPACE
INT/LAW
JURID
INT/ORG

B65
MONCONDUIT F.,LA COMMISSION EUROPEENNE DES DROITS
DE L'HOMME. DIPLOM AGREE GP/REL ORD/FREE PWR
...BIBLIOG 20 TREATY. PAGE 74 E1483

INT/LAW
INT/ORG
ADJUD
JURID

B65
MOODY M.,CATALOG OF INTERNATIONAL LAW AND RELATIONS
(20 VOLS.). WOR+45 INT/ORG NAT/G ADJUD ADMIN CT/SYS
POLICY. PAGE 74 E1488

BIBLIOG
INT/LAW
DIPLOM

B65
MOSTECKY V.,SOVIET LEGAL BIBLIOGRAPHY. USSR LEGIS
PRESS WRITING CONFER ADJUD CT/SYS REV MARXISM
...INT/LAW JURID DICTIONARY 20. PAGE 75 E1503

BIBLIOG/A
LAW
COM
CONSTN

B65
NEGLEY G.,POLITICAL AUTHORITY AND MORAL JUDGMENT.
INTELL SOCIETY LEGIS SANCTION UTOPIA SOVEREIGN
MARXISM...INT/LAW LOG 20. PAGE 76 E1530

MORAL
PWR
CONTROL

B65
NWOGUGU E.I.,THE LEGAL PROBLEMS OF FOREIGN
INVESTMENT IN DEVELOPING COUNTRIES. WOR+45 INT/ORG
DELIB/GP LEGIS PROB/SOLV INT/TRADE TAX ADJUD
SANCTION...BIBLIOG 20 TREATY. PAGE 78 E1561

FOR/AID
FINAN
INT/LAW
ECO/UNDEV

B65
O'BRIEN W.V.,THE NEW NATIONS IN INTERNATIONAL LAW
AND DIPLOMACY* THE YEAR BOOK OF WORLD POLITY*
VOLUME III. USA+45 ECO/UNDEV INT/ORG FORCES DIPLOM
COLONIAL NEUTRAL REV NAT/LISM ATTIT RESPECT.
PAGE 78 E1565

INT/LAW
CULTURE
SOVEREIGN
ANTHOL

B65
O'CONNELL D.P.,INTERNATIONAL LAW (2 VOLS.). WOR+45
WOR-45 ECO/DEV ECO/UNDEV INT/ORG NAT/G AGREE
...POLICY JURID CONCPT NAT/COMP 20 TREATY. PAGE 78
E1566

INT/LAW
DIPLOM
CT/SYS

B65
PARRY C.,THE SOURCES AND EVIDENCES OF INTERNATIONAL
LAW. WOR+45 WOR-45 DIPLOM AGREE SOVEREIGN...METH 20
TREATY UN LEAGUE/NAT. PAGE 80 E1599

INT/LAW
ADJUD
INT/ORG
CT/SYS

B65
SEN B.,A DIPLOMAT'S HANDBOOK OF INTERNATIONAL LAW
AND PRACTICE. WOR+45 NAT/G ADJUST. PAGE 90 E1803

DIPLOM
INT/LAW
TASK
LAW

B65
THOMAS A.V.,NONINTERVENTION: THE LAW AND ITS IMPORT
IN THE AMERICAS. L/A+17C USA+45 WOR+45
DIPLOM ADJUD...JURID IDEA/COMP 20 UN INTERVENT.
PAGE 96 E1917

INT/LAW
PWR
COERCE

B65
UNESCO,INTERNATIONAL ORGANIZATIONS IN THE SOCIAL
SCIENCES(REV. ED.). LAW ADMIN ATTIT...CRIMLGY GEOG
INT/LAW PSY SOC STAT 20 UNESCO. PAGE 98 E1962

INT/ORG
R+D
PROF/ORG
ACT/RES

B65
UNIVERSAL REFERENCE SYSTEM,INTERNATIONAL AFFAIRS:
VOLUME I IN THE POLITICAL SCIENCE, GOVERNMENT, AND
PUBLIC POLICY SERIES....DECISION ECOMETRIC GEOG
INT/LAW JURID MGT PHIL/SCI PSY SOC. PAGE 98 E1972

BIBLIOG/A
GEN/METH
COMPUT/IR
DIPLOM

B65
VON GLAHN G.,LAW AMONG NATIONS: AN INTRODUCTION TO
PUBLIC INTERNATIONAL LAW. WOR+45 WOR-45 INT/ORG
NAT/G CREATE ADJUD WAR...GEOG CLASSIF TREND
BIBLIOG. PAGE 104 E2082

ACADEM
INT/LAW
GEN/LAWS
LAW

B65
VONGLAHN G.,LAW AMONG NATIONS: AN INTRODUCTION TO
PUBLIC INTERNATIONAL LAW. UNIV WOR+45 LAW INT/ORG
NAT/G LEGIT EXEC RIGID/FLEX...CONCPT TIME/SEQ
GEN/LAWS UN TOT/POP 20. PAGE 104 E2084

CONSTN
JURID
INT/LAW

B65
WEIL G.L.,A HANDBOOK ON THE EUROPEAN ECONOMIC
COMMUNITY. BELGIUM EUR+WWI FRANCE GERMANY/W ITALY
CONSTN ECO/DEV CREATE PARTIC GP/REL...DECISION MGT
CHARTS 20 EEC. PAGE 105 E2107

INT/TRADE
INT/ORG
TEC/DEV
INT/LAW

B65
WHITE G.M.,THE USE OF EXPERTS BY INTERNATIONAL
TRIBUNALS. WOR+45 WOR-45 INT/ORG NAT/G PAY ADJUD
COST...OBS BIBLIOG 20. PAGE 106 E2117

INT/LAW
ROUTINE
CONSULT
CT/SYS

B65
WHITEMAN M.M.,DIGEST OF INTERNATIONAL LAW* VOLUME
5, DEPARTMENT OF STATE PUBLICATION 7873. USA+45
WOR+45 OP/RES...CONCPT CLASSIF RECORD IDEA/COMP.
PAGE 106 E2118

INT/LAW
NAT/G
NAT/COMP

L65
RUBIN A.P.,"UNITED STATES CONTEMPORARY PRACTICE
RELATING TO INTERNATIONAL LAW." USA+45 WOR+45
CONSTN INT/ORG NAT/G DELIB/GP EX/STRUC DIPLOM DOMIN
CT/SYS ROUTINE ORD/FREE...CONCPT COLD/WAR 20.
PAGE 86 E1730

LAW
LEGIT
INT/LAW

S65
AMRAM P.W.,"REPORT ON THE TENTH SESSION OF THE
HAGUE CONFERENCE ON PRIVATE INTERNATIONAL LAW."
USA+45 WOR+45 INT/ORG CREATE LEGIT ADJUD ALL/VALS
...JURID CONCPT METH/CNCPT OBS GEN/METH 20. PAGE 4
E0085

VOL/ASSN
DELIB/GP
INT/LAW

S65
BROWNLIE I.,"SOME LEGAL ASPECTS OF THE USE OF
NUCLEAR WEAPONS." UK NEUTRAL DETER UN TREATY.
PAGE 16 E0317

LAW
NUC/PWR
WAR
INT/LAW

S65
FALK R.A.,"INTERNATIONAL LEGAL ORDER." USA+45
INTELL FACE/GP INT/ORG LEGIT KNOWL...CONCPT
METH/CNCPT STYLE RECORD GEN/METH 20. PAGE 36 E0717

ATTIT
GEN/LAWS
INT/LAW

S65
FRIEDHEIM R.,"THE 'SATISFIED' AND 'DISSATISFIED'
STATES NEGOTIATE INTERNATIONAL LAW* A CASE STUDY."
DIPLOM CONFER ADJUD CONSEN PEACE ATTIT UN. PAGE 40
E0799

INT/LAW
RECORD

S65
GROSS L.,"PROBLEMS OF INTERNATIONAL ADJUDICATION
AND COMPLIANCE WITH INTERNATIONAL LAW: SOME SIMPLE
SOLUTIONS." WOR+45 SOCIETY NAT/G DOMIN LEGIT ADJUD
CT/SYS RIGID/FLEX HEALTH PWR...JURID NEW/IDEA

LAW
METH/CNCPT
INT/LAW

COLD/WAR 20. PAGE 48 E0951

S65
LUSKY L.,"FOUR PROBLEMS IN LAWMAKING FOR PEACE."   ORD/FREE
FORCES LEGIS CREATE ADJUD COERCE WAR MAJORITY PEACE INT/LAW
PWR. PAGE 67 E1334   UTOPIA
                                                     RECORD

S65
MERRITT R.L.,"SELECTED ARTICLES AND DOCUMENTS ON   BIBLIOG
INTERNATIONAL LAW AND RELATIONS." WOR+45 INT/ORG   DIPLOM
FORCES INT/TRADE. PAGE 72 E1443   INT/LAW
                                                     GOV/REL

S65
STEIN E.,"TOWARD SUPREMACY OF TREATY-CONSTITUTION   ADJUD
BY JUDICIAL FIAT: ON THE MARGIN OF THE COSTA CASE." CONSTN
EUR+WWI ITALY WOR+45 INT/ORG NAT/G LEGIT REGION   SOVEREIGN
NAT/LISM PWR...JURID CONCPT TREND TOT/POP VAL/FREE   INT/LAW
20. PAGE 93 E1870

S65
WRIGHT Q.,"THE ESCALATION OF INTERNATIONAL   WAR
CONFLICTS." WOR+45 WOR-45 FORCES DIPLOM RISK COST   PERCEPT
ATTIT ALL/VALS...INT/LAW QUANT STAT NAT/COMP.   PREDICT
PAGE 108 E2160   MATH

C65
SCHEINGOLD S.A.,"THE RULE OF LAW IN EUROPEAN   INT/LAW
INTEGRATION: THE PATH OF THE SCHUMAN PLAN." EUR+WWI CT/SYS
JUDGE ADJUD FEDERAL ATTIT PWR...RECORD INT BIBLIOG   REGION
EEC ECSC. PAGE 87 E1755   CENTRAL

C65
SEARA M.V.,"COSMIC INTERNATIONAL LAW." LAW ACADEM   SPACE
ACT/RES DIPLOM COLONIAL CONTROL NUC/PWR SOVEREIGN   INT/LAW
...GEN/LAWS BIBLIOG UN. PAGE 90 E1799   IDEA/COMP
                                                     INT/ORG

B66
AMERICAN JOURNAL COMP LAW,THE AMERICAN JOURNAL OF   IDEA/COMP
COMPARATIVE LAW READER. EUR+WWI USA+45 USA-45 LAW   JURID
CONSTN LOC/G MUNIC NAT/G DIPLOM...ANTHOL 20   INT/LAW
SUPREME/CT EURCT/JUST. PAGE 4 E0081   CT/SYS

B66
ASAMOAH O.Y.,THE LEGAL SIGNIFICANCE OF THE   INT/LAW
DECLARATIONS OF THE GENERAL ASSEMBLY OF THE UNITED   INT/ORG
NATIONS. WOR+45 CREATE CONTROL...BIBLIOG 20 UN.   DIPLOM
PAGE 5 E0105

B66
BROWNLIE I.,PRINCIPLES OF PUBLIC INTERNATIONAL LAW. INT/LAW
WOR+45 WOR-45 LAW JUDGE REPAR ADJUD SOVEREIGN   DIPLOM
...JURID T. PAGE 16 E0319   INT/ORG

B66
BUTTERFIELD H.,DIPLOMATIC INVESTIGATIONS* ESSAYS IN GEN/LAWS
THE THEORY OF INTERNATIONAL POLITICS. LAW INT/ORG   UK
FORCES BAL/PWR ARMS/CONT WAR ALL/VALS...HUM   DIPLOM
INT/LAW. PAGE 18 E0351

B66
CLARK G.,WORLD PEACE THROUGH WORLD LAW; TWO   INT/LAW
ALTERNATIVE PLANS. WOR+45 DELIB/GP FORCES TAX   PEACE
CONFER ADJUD SANCTION ARMS/CONT WAR CHOOSE PRIVIL   PLAN
20 UN COLD/WAR. PAGE 23 E0450   INT/ORG

B66
COPLIN W.D.,THE FUNCTIONS OF INTERNATIONAL LAW.   INT/LAW
WOR+45 ECO/DEV ECO/UNDEV ADJUD COLONIAL WAR OWN   DIPLOM
SOVEREIGN...POLICY GEN/LAWS 20. PAGE 25 E0503   INT/ORG

B66
COUNCIL OF EUROPE,EUROPEAN CONVENTION ON HUMAN   ORD/FREE
RIGHTS - COLLECTED TEXTS (5TH ED.). EUR+WWI DIPLOM   DELIB/GP
ADJUD CT/SYS...INT/LAW 20 ECHR. PAGE 26 E0520   INT/ORG
                                                     JURID

B66
EDWARDS C.D.,TRADE REGULATIONS OVERSEAS. IRELAND   INT/TRADE
NEW/ZEALND SOUTH/AFR NAT/G CAP/ISM TARIFFS CONTROL   DIPLOM
...POLICY JURID 20 EEC CHINJAP. PAGE 34 E0676   INT/LAW
                                                     ECO/TAC

B66
FALK R.A.,THE STRATEGY OF WORLD ORDER* 4 VOLUMES.   ORD/FREE
WOR+45 ECO/DEV ECO/UNDEV ACADEM INT/ORG ACT/RES DIPLOM GEN/LAWS
ARMS/CONT WAR...NET/THEORY SIMUL BIBLIOG UN.   ANTHOL
PAGE 36 E0719   INT/LAW

B66
FRIEDMANN W.G.,INTERNATIONAL FINANCIAL AID. USA+45   INT/ORG
ECO/DEV ECO/UNDEV NAT/G VOL/ASSN EX/STRUC PLAN RENT FOR/AID
GIVE BAL/PAY PWR...GEOG INT/LAW STAT TREND UN EEC   TEC/DEV
COMECON. PAGE 41 E0806   ECO/TAC

B66
HAUSNER G.,JUSTICE IN JERUSALEM. GERMANY ISRAEL   ADJUD
SOCIETY KIN DIPLOM LEGIT CT/SYS PARTIC MURDER   CRIME
MAJORITY ATTIT FASCISM...INT/LAW JURID 20 JEWS   RACE/REL
WAR/TRIAL. PAGE 51 E1013   COERCE

B66
HAY P.,FEDERALISM AND SUPRANATIONAL ORGANIZATIONS: SOVEREIGN
PATTERNS FOR NEW LEGAL STRUCTURES. EUR+WWI LAW   FEDERAL
NAT/G VOL/ASSN DIPLOM PWR...NAT/COMP TREATY EEC.   INT/ORG
PAGE 51 E1014   INT/LAW

B66
HOEVELER H.J.,INTERNATIONALE BEKAMPFUNG DES   CRIMLGY
VERBRECHENS. AUSTRIA SWITZERLND WOR+45 INT/ORG   CRIME
CONTROL BIO/SOC...METH/COMP NAT/COMP 20 MAFIA   DIPLOM
SCOT/YARD FBI. PAGE 53 E1064   INT/LAW

B66
HOYT E.C.,NATIONAL POLICY AND INTERNATIONAL LAW*   INT/LAW
CASE STUDIES FROM AMERICAN CANAL POLICY* MONOGRAPH   USA-45
NO. 1 -- 1966-1967. PANAMA UK ELITES BAL/PWR   DIPLOM
EFFICIENCY...CLASSIF NAT/COMP SOC/EXP COLOMB   PWR
TREATY. PAGE 55 E1105

B66
LEE L.T.,VIENNA CONVENTION ON CONSULAR RELATIONS.   AGREE
WOR+45 LAW INT/ORG CONFER GP/REL PRIVIL...INT/LAW   DIPLOM
20 TREATY VIENNA/CNV. PAGE 64 E1277   ADMIN

B66
MERILLAT H.C.L.,LEGAL ADVISERS AND INTERNATIONAL   INT/ORG
ORGANIZATIONS. LAW NAT/G CONSULT OP/RES ADJUD   INT/LAW
SANCTION TASK CONSEN ORG/CHARTS. PAGE 72 E1441   CREATE
                                                     OBS

B66
NANTWI E.K.,THE ENFORCEMENT OF INTERNATIONAL   INT/LAW
JUDICIAL DECISIONS AND ARBITAL AWARDS IN PUBLIC   ADJUD
INTERNATIONAL LAW. WOR+45 WOR-45 JUDGE PROB/SOLV   SOVEREIGN
DIPLOM CT/SYS SUPEGO MORAL PWR RESPECT...METH/CNCPT INT/ORG
18/20 CASEBOOK. PAGE 76 E1520

B66
OLSON W.C.,THE THEORY AND PRACTICE OF INTERNATIONAL DIPLOM
RELATIONS (2ND ED.). WOR+45 LEAD SUPEGO...INT/LAW   NAT/G
PHIL/SCI. PAGE 79 E1575   INT/ORG
                                                     POLICY

B66
POLLACK R.S.,THE INDIVIDUAL'S RIGHTS AND   INT/LAW
INTERNATIONAL ORGANIZATION. LAW INT/ORG DELIB/GP   ORD/FREE
SUPEGO...JURID SOC/INTEG 20 TREATY UN. PAGE 81   DIPLOM
E1623   PERSON

B66
SALTER L.M.,RESOLUTION OF INTERNATIONAL CONFLICT.   PROB/SOLV
USA+45 INT/ORG SECT DIPLOM ECO/TAC FOR/AID DETER   PEACE
NUC/PWR WAR 20. PAGE 87 E1743   INT/LAW
                                                     POLICY

B66
STUMPF S.E.,MORALITY AND THE LAW. USA+45 LAW   JURID
CULTURE PROB/SOLV DOMIN ADJUD CONTROL ADJUST   MORAL
ALL/IDEOS MARXISM...INT/LAW 20 SUPREME/CT. PAGE 94   CT/SYS
E1890

B66
SZLADITS C.,A BIBLIOGRAPHY ON FOREIGN AND   BIBLIOG/A
COMPARATIVE LAW (SUPPLEMENT 1964). FINAN FAM LABOR   CT/SYS
LG/CO LEGIS JUDGE ADMIN CRIME...CRIMLGY 20. PAGE 95 INT/LAW
E1905

L66
GREIG D.W.,"THE ADVISORY JURISDICTION OF THE   INT/LAW
INTERNATIONAL COURT AND THE SETTLEMENT OF DISPUTES   CT/SYS
BETWEEN STATES." ISRAEL KOREA FORCES BUDGET DOMIN
LEGIT ADJUD COST...RECORD UN CONGO/LEOP TREATY.
PAGE 46 E0915

L66
HIGGINS R.,"THE INTERNATIONAL COURT AND SOUTH WEST   SOUTH/AFR
AFRICA* SOME IMPLICATIONS OF THE JUDGMENT." AFR LAW COLONIAL
ECO/UNDEV JUDGE RACE/REL COST PWR...INT/LAW TREND   CT/SYS
UN TREATY. PAGE 52 E1043   ADJUD

L66
KRENZ F.E.,"THE REFUGEE AS A SUBJECT OF   INT/LAW
INTERNATIONAL LAW." FUT LAW NAT/G CREATE ADJUD   DISCRIM
ISOLAT STRANGE...RECORD UN. PAGE 62 E1230   NEW/IDEA

L66
SEYLER W.C.,"DOCTORAL DISSERTATIONS IN POLITICAL   BIBLIOG
SCIENCE IN UNIVERSITIES OF THE UNITED STATES AND   LAW
CANADA." INT/ORG LOC/G ADMIN...INT/LAW MGT   NAT/G

L66
YALEM R.J.,"THE STUDY OF INTERNATIONAL
ORGANIZATION, 1920-1965* A SURVEY OF THE
LITERATURE." WOR+45 WOR-45 REGION...INT/LAW CLASSIF
RECORD HIST/WRIT CON/ANAL IDEA/COMP UN. PAGE 108
E2163

VOL/ASSN
INT/ORG
BIBLIOG/A

S66
ANAND R.P.,"ATTITUDE OF THE ASIAN-AFRICAN STATES
TOWARD CERTAIN PROBLEMS OF INTERNATIONAL LAW."
L/A+17C S/ASIA ECO/UNDEV CREATE CONFER ADJUD
COLONIAL...RECORD GP/COMP UN. PAGE 5 E0087

INT/LAW
ATTIT
ASIA
AFR

S66
CHIU H.,"COMMUNIST CHINA'S ATTITUDE TOWARD
INTERNATIONAL LAW" CHINA/COM USSR LAW CONSTN DIPLOM
GP/REL 20 LENIN/VI. PAGE 22 E0431

INT/LAW
MARXISM
CONCPT
IDEA/COMP

S66
DETTER I.,"THE PROBLEM OF UNEQUAL TREATIES." CONSTN
NAT/G LEGIS COLONIAL COERCE PWR...GEOG UN TIME
TREATY. PAGE 31 E0610

SOVEREIGN
DOMIN
INT/LAW
ECO/UNDEV

S66
EWALD R.F.,"ONE OF MANY POSSIBLE GAMES." ACADEM
INT/ORG ARMS/CONT...INT/LAW GAME. PAGE 36 E0706

SIMUL
HYPO/EXP
PROG/TEAC
RECORD

S66
GREEN L.C.,"RHODESIAN OIL: BOOTLEGGERS OR PIRATES?"
AFR RHODESIA UK WOR+45 INT/ORG NAT/G DIPLOM LEGIT
COLONIAL SOVEREIGN 20 UN OAU. PAGE 46 E0907

INT/TRADE
SANCTION
INT/LAW
POLICY

C66
BLAISDELL D.C.,"INTERNATIONAL ORGANIZATION." FUT
WOR+45 ECO/DEV DELIB/GP FORCES EFFICIENCY PEACE
ORD/FREE...INT/LAW 20 UN LEAGUE/NAT NATO. PAGE 12
E0239

BIBLIOG
INT/ORG
DIPLOM
ARMS/CONT

C66
ZAWODNY J.K.,"GUIDE TO THE STUDY OF INTERNATIONAL
RELATIONS." OP/RES PRESS...STAT INT 20. PAGE 108
E2169

BIBLIOG/A
DIPLOM
INT/LAW
INT/ORG

B67
BAILEY N.A.,LATIN AMERICA IN WORLD POLITICS. PWR
CONSERVE MARXISM...INT/LAW TREND BIBLIOG/A T OAS
COLD/WAR. PAGE 7 E0134

L/A+17C
DIPLOM
INT/ORG
ATTIT

B67
CAHIER P.,LE DROIT DIPLOMATIQUE CONTEMPORAIN.
INT/ORG CHIEF ADMIN...T 20. PAGE 18 E0358

INT/LAW
DIPLOM
JURID

B67
HOLCOMBE A.N.,A STRATEGY OF PEACE IN A CHANGING
WORLD. USA+45 WOR+45 LAW NAT/G CREATE DIPLOM
ARMS/CONT WAR...CHARTS 20 UN COLD/WAR. PAGE 54
E1072

PEACE
PLAN
INT/ORG
INT/LAW

B67
HOLSTI K.J.,INTERNATIONAL POLITICS* A FRAMEWORK FOR
ANALYSIS. WOR+45 WOR-45 NAT/G EDU/PROP DETER WAR
WEAPON PWR BIBLIOG. PAGE 55 E1090

DIPLOM
BARGAIN
POLICY
INT/LAW

B67
INTERNATIONAL CONCILIATION,ISSUES BEFORE THE 22ND
GENERAL ASSEMBLY. WOR+45 ECO/UNDEV FINAN BAL/PWR
BUDGET INT/TRADE STRANGE ORD/FREE...INT/LAW 20 UN
COLD/WAR. PAGE 57 E1132

PROB/SOLV
INT/ORG
DIPLOM
PEACE

B67
LAFAVE W.R.,INTERNATIONAL TRADE, INVESTMENT, AND
ORGANIZATION. INDUS PROB/SOLV TARIFFS CONTROL
...TREND ANTHOL BIBLIOG 20 EEC. PAGE 62 E1245

INT/TRADE
INT/LAW
INT/ORG

B67
LAWYERS COMM AMER POLICY VIET,VIETNAM AND
INTERNATIONAL LAW: AN ANALYSIS OF THE LEGALITY OF
THE US MILITARY INVOLVEMENT. VIETNAM LAW INT/ORG
COERCE WEAPON PEACE ORD/FREE 20 UN SEATO TREATY.
PAGE 64 E1271

INT/LAW
DIPLOM
ADJUD
WAR

B67
ROBINSON R.D., INTERNATIONAL MANAGEMENT. USA+45
FINAN R+D PLAN PRODUC...DECISION T. PAGE 67 E1336

INT/TRADE
MGT
INT/LAW

B67
MCDOUGAL M.S.,THE INTERPRETATION OF AGREEMENTS AND
WORLD PUBLIC ORDER: PRINCIPLES OF CONTENT AND
PROCEDURE. WOR+45 CONSTN PROB/SOLV TEC/DEV
...CON/ANAL TREATY. PAGE 71 E1412

INT/LAW
STRUCT
ECO/UNDEV
DIPLOM

B67
PLANO J.C.,FORGING WORLD ORDER: THE POLITICS OF
INTERNATIONAL ORGANIZATION. PROB/SOLV DIPLOM
CONTROL CENTRAL RATIONAL ORD/FREE...INT/LAW CHARTS
BIBLIOG 20 UN LEAGUE/NAT. PAGE 81 E1618

INT/ORG
ADMIN
JURID

B67
POGANY A.H.,POLITICAL SCIENCE AND INTERNATIONAL
RELATIONS, BOOKS RECOMMENDED FOR AMERICAN CATHOLIC
COLLEGE LIBRARIES. INT/ORG LOC/G NAT/G FORCES
BAL/PWR ECO/TAC NUC/PWR...CATH INT/LAW TREATY 20.
PAGE 81 E1622

BIBLIOG
DIPLOM

B67
RAMUNDO B.A.,PEACEFUL COEXISTENCE: INTERNATIONAL
LAW IN THE BUILDING OF COMMUNISM. USSR INT/ORG
DIPLOM COLONIAL ARMS/CONT ROLE SOVEREIGN...POLICY
METH/COMP NAT/COMP BIBLIOG. PAGE 83 E1673

INT/LAW
PEACE
MARXISM
METH/CNCPT

B67
UNITED NATIONS,UNITED NATIONS PUBLICATIONS:
1945-1966. WOR+45 COM/IND DIST/IND FINAN TEC/DEV
ADMIN...POLICY INT/LAW MGT CHARTS 20 UN UNESCO.
PAGE 98 E1970

BIBLIOG/A
INT/ORG
DIPLOM
WRITING

B67
UNIVERSAL REFERENCE SYSTEM,LAW, JURISPRUDENCE, AND
JUDICIAL PROCESS (VOLUME VII). WOR+45 WOR-45 CONSTN
NAT/G LEGIS JUDGE CT/SYS...INT/LAW COMPUT/IR
GEN/METH METH. PAGE 99 E1976

BIBLIOG/A
LAW
JURID
ADJUD

L67
"FOCUS ON WORLD LAW." WOR+45 NAT/G CT/SYS PEACE
...BIBLIOG 20 UN. PAGE 2 E0036

INT/LAW
INT/ORG
PROB/SOLV
CONCPT

L67
BAADE H.W.,"THE ACQUIRED RIGHTS OF INTERNATIONAL
PUBLIC SERVANTS; A CASE STUDY IN RECEPTION OF
PUBLIC LAW." WOR+45 DELIB/GP DIPLOM ORD/FREE
...INT/LAW JURID UN. PAGE 7 E0125

INT/ORG
WORKER
ADJUD
LAW

L67
HITCHMAN J.M.,"THE PLATT AMENDMENT REVISITED: A
BIBLIOGRAPHICAL SURVEY." CUBA ACADEM DELIB/GP
ORD/FREE...HIST/WRIT 20. PAGE 53 E1055

ATTIT
DIPLOM
SOVEREIGN
INT/LAW

L67
LEGAULT A.,"ORGANISATION ET CONDUITE DES OPERATIONS
DE MAINTIEN DE LA PAIX." FORCES ACT/RES ADJUD AGREE
CONTROL NEUTRAL TASK PRIVIL ORD/FREE 20 UN. PAGE 64
E1279

INT/ORG
PEACE
WAR
INT/LAW

L67
LISSITZYN O.J.,"TREATIES AND CHANGED CIRCUMSTANCES
(REBUS SIC STANTIBUS)" WOR+45 CONSEN...JURID 20.
PAGE 65 E1307

AGREE
DIPLOM
INT/LAW

L67
WAELBROECK M.,"THE APPLICATION OF EEC LAW BY
NATIONAL COURTS." EUR+WWI INT/ORG CT/SYS...JURID
EEC TREATY. PAGE 104 E2090

INT/LAW
NAT/G
LAW
PROB/SOLV

S67
ALDRICH W.A.,"THE SUEZ CRISIS." UAR UK USA+45
DELIB/GP FORCES BAL/PWR INT/TRADE CONFER CONTROL
COERCE DETER 20. PAGE 3 E0058

DIPLOM
INT/LAW
COLONIAL

S67
COHN K.,"CRIMES AGAINST HUMANITY." GERMANY INT/ORG
SANCTION ATTIT ORD/FREE...MARXIST CRIMLGY 20 UN.
PAGE 24 E0469

WAR
INT/LAW
CRIME
ADJUD

S67
CUMMINS L.,"THE FORMULATION OF THE "PLATT"
AMENDMENT." CUBA L/A+17C NAT/G DELIB/GP CONFER
...POLICY 20. PAGE 28 E0554

DIPLOM
INT/LAW
LEGIS

S67
DALFEN C.M.,"THE WORLD COURT IN IDLE SPLENDOUR: THE
BASIS OF STATES' ATTITUDES." WOR+45 LAW ADJUD
COERCE...JURID 20 UN WORLD/CT. PAGE 28 E0562

CT/SYS
INT/ORG
INT/LAW
DIPLOM

DEUTSCH E.P.,"A JUDICIAL PATH TO WORLD PEACE." FUT   INT/LAW
WOR+45 CONSTN PROB/SOLV DIPLOM LICENSE ADJUD   INT/ORG
SANCTION CHOOSE REPRESENT NAT/LISM SOVEREIGN 20   JURID
ICJ. PAGE 31 E0611   PEACE
                                                     S67

DOYLE S.E.,"COMMUNICATION SATELLITES* INTERNAL   TEC/DEV
ORGANIZATION FOR DEVELOPMENT AND CONTROL." USA+45   SPACE
R+D ACT/RES DIPLOM NAT/LISM...POLICY INT/LAW   COM/IND
PREDICT UN. PAGE 33 E0647   INT/ORG
                                                     S67

HORVATH B.,"COMPARATIVE CONFLICTS LAW AND THE   INT/LAW
CONCEPT OF CHANGING LAW." UNIV RATIONAL...JURID   IDEA/COMP
LOG. PAGE 55 E1099   DIPLOM
                                                     CONCPT
                                                     S67

LARSEN P.B.,"THE UNITED STATES-ITALY AIR TRANSPORT   INT/LAW
ARBITRATION: PROBLEMS OF TREATY INTERPRETATION AND   ADJUD
ENFORCEMENT." ITALY USA+45 AIR PROB/SOLV DIPLOM   INT/TRADE
DEBATE CONTROL CT/SYS...DECISION TREATY. PAGE 63   DIST/IND
E1257
                                                     S67

MATTHEWS R.O.,"THE SUEZ CANAL DISPUTE* A CASE STUDY   PEACE
IN PEACEFUL SETTLEMENT." FRANCE ISRAEL UAR UK NAT/G DIPLOM
CONTROL LEAD COERCE WAR NAT/LISM ROLE ORD/FREE PWR   ADJUD
...INT/LAW UN 20. PAGE 69 E1389
                                                     S67

STEEL R.,"WHAT CAN THE UN DO?" RHODESIA ECO/UNDEV   INT/ORG
DIPLOM ECO/TAC SANCTION...INT/LAW UN. PAGE 93 E1866 BAL/PWR
                                                     PEACE
                                                     FOR/AID
                                                     B68

HULL R.H.,LAW AND VIETNAM. COM VIETNAM CONSTN   POLICY
INT/ORG FORCES DIPLOM AGREE COERCE DETER WEAPON   LAW
PEACE ATTIT 20 UN TREATY. PAGE 56 E1113   WAR
                                                     INT/LAW
                                                     L68

CHIU H.,"COMMUNIST CHINA'S ATTITUDE TOWARD THE   INT/LAW
UNITED NATIONS: A LEGAL ANALYSIS." CHINA/COM WOR+45 SOVEREIGN
LAW NAT/G DIPLOM CONFER ADJUD PARTIC ATTIT...POLICY INT/ORG
TREND 20 UN. PAGE 22 E0432   REPRESENT
                                                     B77

CADWALDER J.L.,DIGEST OF THE PUBLISHED OPINIONS OF   BIBLIOG
THE ATTORNEYS-GENERAL, AND OF THE LEADING DECISIONS CT/SYS
OF THE FEDERAL COURTS (REV ED). USA-45 NAT/G JUDGE   DECISION
PROB/SOLV DIPLOM ATTIT...POLICY INT/LAW ANTHOL 19.   ADJUD
PAGE 18 E0356
                                                     B91

DOLE C.F.,THE AMERICAN CITIZEN. USA-45 LAW PARTIC   NAT/G
ATTIT...INT/LAW 19. PAGE 32 E0633   MORAL
                                                     NAT/LISM
                                                     MAJORITY
                                                     B96

DE VATTEL E.,THE LAW OF NATIONS. AGRI FINAN CHIEF   LAW
DIPLOM INT/TRADE AGREE OWN ALL/VALS MORAL ORD/FREE   CONCPT
SOVEREIGN...GEN/LAWS 18 NATURL/LAW WOLFF/C. PAGE 30 NAT/G
E0597   INT/LAW
                                                     B97

US DEPARTMENT OF STATE,CATALOGUE OF WORKS RELATING   BIBLIOG/A
TO THE LAW OF NATIONS AND DIPLOMACY IN THE LIBRARY   DIPLOM
OF THE DEPARTMENT OF STATE (PAMPHLET). WOR-45 NAT/G LAW
ADJUD CT/SYS...INT/LAW JURID 19. PAGE 100 E2000
                                                     B99

BROOKS S.,BRITAIN AND THE BOERS. AFR SOUTH/AFR UK   WAR
CULTURE INSPECT LEGIT...INT/LAW 19/20 BOER/WAR.   DIPLOM
PAGE 16 E0309   NAT/G

INT/ORG....INTERNATIONAL ORGANIZATIONS; SEE ALSO VOL/ASSN
    AND APPROPRIATE ORGANIZATION

                                                     N
INTERNATIONAL COMN JURISTS,AFRICAN CONFERENCE ON   CT/SYS
THE RULE OF LAW. AFR INT/ORG LEGIS DIPLOM CONFER   JURID
COLONIAL ORD/FREE...CONCPT METH/COMP 20. PAGE 57   DELIB/GP
E1131
                                                     N
LIBRARY INTERNATIONAL REL,INTERNATIONAL INFORMATION BIBLIOG/A
SERVICE. WOR+45 CULTURE INT/ORG FORCES...GEOG HUM   DIPLOM
SOC. PAGE 65 E1295   INT/TRADE
                                                     INT/LAW
                                                     N
LONDON INSTITUTE WORLD AFFAIRS,THE YEAR BOOK OF   DIPLOM

WORLD AFFAIRS. FINAN BAL/PWR ARMS/CONT WAR   FOR/AID
...INT/LAW BIBLIOG 20. PAGE 66 E1322   INT/ORG

                                                     N
TOSCANO M.,THE HISTORY OF TREATIES AND   DIPLOM
INTERNATIONAL POLITICS (REV. ED.). WOR-45 AGREE WAR INT/ORG
...BIOG 19/20 TREATY WWI. PAGE 97 E1935

                                                     N
AMERICAN JOURNAL OF INTERNATIONAL LAW. WOR+45   BIBLIOG/A
WOR-45 CONSTN INT/ORG NAT/G CT/SYS ARMS/CONT WAR   INT/LAW
...DECISION JURID NAT/COMP 20. PAGE 1 E0001   DIPLOM
                                                     ADJUD

                                                     N
AMERICAN POLITICAL SCIENCE REVIEW. USA+45 USA-45   BIBLIOG/A
WOR+45 WOR-45 INT/ORG ADMIN...INT/LAW PHIL/SCI   DIPLOM
CONCPT METH 20 UN. PAGE 1 E0002   NAT/G
                                                     GOV/COMP

                                                     N
BACKGROUND; JOURNAL OF INTERNATIONAL STUDIES   BIBLIOG
ASSOCIATION. INT/ORG FORCES ACT/RES EDU/PROP COERCE DIPLOM
NAT/LISM PEACE ATTIT...INT/LAW CONCPT 20. PAGE 1   POLICY
E0004

                                                     N
CANADIAN GOVERNMENT PUBLICATIONS (1955-). CANADA   BIBLIOG/A
AGRI FINAN LABOR FORCES INT/TRADE HEALTH...JURID 20 NAT/G
PARLIAMENT. PAGE 1 E0005   DIPLOM
                                                     INT/ORG

                                                     N
INTERNATIONAL AFFAIRS. WOR+45 WOR-45 ECO/UNDEV   BIBLIOG/A
INT/ORG NAT/G PROB/SOLV FOR/AID WAR...POLICY 20.   DIPLOM
PAGE 1 E0007   INT/LAW
                                                     INT/TRADE

                                                     N
INTERNATIONAL BOOK NEWS, 1928-1934. ECO/UNDEV FINAN BIBLIOG/A
INDUS LABOR INT/TRADE CONFER ADJUD COLONIAL...HEAL   DIPLOM
SOC/WK CHARTS 20 LEAGUE/NAT. PAGE 1 E0008   INT/LAW
                                                     INT/ORG

                                                     N
INTERNATIONAL STUDIES. ASIA S/ASIA WOR+45 ECO/UNDEV BIBLIOG/A
INT/ORG NAT/G LEAD ATTIT WEALTH...SOC 20. PAGE 1   DIPLOM
E0009   INT/LAW
                                                     INT/TRADE

                                                     N
JOURNAL OF INTERNATIONAL AFFAIRS. WOR+45 ECO/UNDEV   BIBLIOG
POL/PAR ECO/TAC WAR PEACE PERSON ALL/IDEOS   DIPLOM
...INT/LAW TREND. PAGE 1 E0010   INT/ORG
                                                     NAT/G

                                                     N
POLITICAL SCIENCE QUARTERLY. USA+45 USA-45 LAW   BIBLIOG/A
CONSTN ECO/DEV INT/ORG LOC/G POL/PAR LEGIS LEAD   NAT/G
NUC/PWR...CONCPT 20. PAGE 1 E0013   DIPLOM
                                                     POLICY

                                                     N
FOREIGN AFFAIRS. SPACE WOR+45 WOR-45 CULTURE   BIBLIOG
ECO/UNDEV FINAN NAT/G TEC/DEV INT/TRADE ARMS/CONT   DIPLOM
NUC/PWR...POLICY 20 UN EURATOM ECSC EEC. PAGE 1   INT/ORG
E0021   INT/LAW

                                                     N
ASIA FOUNDATION,LIBRARY NOTES. LAW CONSTN CULTURE   BIBLIOG/A
SOCIETY ECO/UNDEV INT/ORG NAT/G COLONIAL LEAD   ASIA
REGION NAT/LISM ATTIT 20 UN. PAGE 6 E0107   S/ASIA
                                                     DIPLOM

                                                     N
HARVARD UNIVERSITY LAW LIBRARY,CATALOG OF   BIBLIOG
INTERNATIONAL LAW AND RELATIONS. WOR+45 WOR-45   INT/LAW
INT/ORG NAT/G JUDGE DIPLOM INT/TRADE ADJUD CT/SYS   JURID
19/20. PAGE 51 E1007

                                                     N
SOCIETE DES NATIONS,TRAITES INTERNATIONAUX ET ACTES BIBLIOG
LEGISLATIFS. WOR-45 INT/ORG NAT/G...INT/LAW JURID   DIPLOM
20 LEAGUE/NAT TREATY. PAGE 92 E1851   LEGIS
                                                     ADJUD

                                                     N
TURNER R.K.,BIBLIOGRAPHY ON WORLD ORGANIZATION.   BIBLIOG/A
INT/TRADE CT/SYS ARMS/CONT WEALTH...INT/LAW 20.   INT/ORG
PAGE 97 E1944   PEACE
                                                     WAR

                                                     N
UNITED NATIONS,OFFICIAL RECORDS OF THE UNITED   INT/ORG
NATIONS' GENERAL ASSEMBLY. WOR+45 BUDGET DIPLOM   DELIB/GP
ADMIN 20 UN. PAGE 98 E1964   INT/LAW

WRITING

N

UNITED NATIONS,UNITED NATIONS PUBLICATIONS. WOR+45   BIBLIOG
ECO/UNDEV AGRI FINAN FORCES ADMIN LEAD WAR PEACE   INT/ORG
...POLICY INT/LAW 20 UN. PAGE 98 E1965   DIPLOM

N

UNITED NATIONS,YEARBOOK OF THE INTERNATIONAL LAW   BIBLIOG
COMMISSION....CON/ANAL 20 UN. PAGE 98 E1966   INT/ORG
                                                         INT/LAW
                                                         DELIB/GP

B00

DARBY W.E.,INTERNATIONAL TRIBUNALS. WOR-45 NAT/G   INT/ORG
ECO/TAC DOMIN LEGIT CT/SYS COERCE ORD/FREE PWR   ADJUD
SOVEREIGN JURID. PAGE 29 E0567   PEACE
                                                         INT/LAW

B00

HOLLAND T.E.,STUDIES IN INTERNATIONAL LAW. TURKEY   INT/ORG
USSR WOR-45 CONSTN NAT/G DIPLOM DOMIN LEGIT COERCE   LAW
WAR PEACE ORD/FREE PWR SOVEREIGN...JURID CHARTS 20   INT/LAW
PARLIAMENT SUEZ TREATY. PAGE 54 E1084

B00

LORIMER J.,THE INSTITUTES OF THE LAW OF NATIONS.   INT/ORG
WOR-45 CULTURE SOCIETY NAT/G VOL/ASSN DIPLOM LEGIT   LAW
WAR PEACE DRIVE ORD/FREE SOVEREIGN...CONCPT RECORD   INT/LAW
INT TREND HYPO/EXP GEN/METH TOT/POP VAL/FREE 20.
PAGE 66 E1327

B00

MAINE H.S.,INTERNATIONAL LAW. MOD/EUR UNIV SOCIETY   INT/ORG
STRUCT ACT/RES EXEC WAR ATTIT PERSON ALL/VALS   LAW
...POLICY JURID CONCPT OBS TIME/SEQ TOT/POP.   PEACE
PAGE 68 E1349   INT/LAW

B04

CRANDALL S.B.,TREATIES: THEIR MAKING AND   LAW
ENFORCEMENT. MOD/EUR USA-45 CONSTN INT/ORG NAT/G
LEGIS EDU/PROP LEGIT EXEC PEACE KNOWL MORAL...JURID
CONGRESS 19/20 TREATY. PAGE 27 E0541

B08

GRIFFIN A.P.C.,LIST OF REFERENCES ON INTERNATIONAL   BIBLIOG/A
ARBITRATION. FRANCE L/A+17C USA-45 WOR-45 DIPLOM   INT/ORG
CONFER COLONIAL ARMS/CONT BAL/PAY EQUILIB SOVEREIGN   INT/LAW
...DECISION 19/20 MEXIC/AMER. PAGE 47 E0932   DELIB/GP

B09

HOLLAND T.E.,LETTERS UPON WAR AND NEUTRALITY.   LAW
WOR-45 NAT/G FORCES JUDGE ECO/TAC LEGIT CT/SYS   INT/LAW
NEUTRAL ROUTINE COERCE...JURID TIME/SEQ 20. PAGE 55   INT/ORG
E1085   WAR

B11

PHILLIPSON C.,THE INTERNATIONAL LAW AND CUSTOM OF   INT/ORG
ANCIENT GREECE AND ROME. MEDIT-7 UNIV INTELL   LAW
SOCIETY STRUCT NAT/G LEGIS EXEC PERSON...CONCPT OBS   INT/LAW
CON/ANAL ROM/EMP. PAGE 80 E1614

B11

REINSCH P.,PUBLIC INTERNATIONAL UNION. WOR-45 LAW   FUT
LABOR INT/TRADE LEGIT PERSON ALL/VALS...SOCIALIST   INT/ORG
CONCPT TIME/SEQ TREND GEN/LAWS 19/20. PAGE 84 E1683   DIPLOM

B13

BUTLER N.M.,THE INTERNATIONAL MIND. WOR-45 INT/ORG   ADJUD
LEGIT PWR...JURID CONCPT 20. PAGE 18 E0350   ORD/FREE
                                                         INT/LAW

B15

HOBSON J.A.,TOWARDS INTERNATIONAL GOVERNMENT.   FUT
MOD/EUR STRUCT ECO/TAC EDU/PROP ADJUD ALL/VALS   INT/ORG
...SOCIALIST CONCPT GEN/LAWS TOT/POP 20. PAGE 53   CENTRAL
E1059

B15

INTERNATIONAL LAW ASSOCIATION,A FORTY YEARS'   BIBLIOG
CATALOGUE OF THE BOOKS, PAMPHLETS AND PAPERS IN THE   LAW
LIBRARY OF THE INTERNATIONAL LAW ASSOCIATION.   INT/LAW
INT/ORG DIPLOM ADJUD NEUTRAL...IDEA/COMP 19/20.
PAGE 57 E1134

B16

ROOT E.,ADDRESSES ON INTERNATIONAL SUBJECTS.   INT/ORG
MOD/EUR UNIV USA-45 LAW SOCIETY EXEC ATTIT ALL/VALS   ACT/RES
...POLICY JURID CONCPT 20 CHINJAP. PAGE 85 E1711   PEACE
                                                         INT/LAW

L16

WRIGHT Q.,"THE ENFORCEMENT OF INTERNATIONAL LAW   INT/ORG
THROUGH MUNICIPAL LAW IN THE US." USA-45 LOC/G   LAW
NAT/G PUB/INST FORCES LEGIT CT/SYS PERCEPT ALL/VALS   INT/LAW
...JURID 20. PAGE 107 E2149   WAR

S17

ROOT E.,"THE EFFECT OF DEMOCRACY ON INTERNATIONAL   LEGIS
LAW." USA-45 WOR-45 INTELL SOCIETY INT/ORG NAT/G   JURID
CONSULT ACT/RES CREATE PLAN EDU/PROP PEACE SKILL   INT/LAW
...CONCPT METH/CNCPT OBS 20. PAGE 85 E1712

B19

LONDON SCHOOL ECONOMICS-POL,ANNUAL DIGEST OF PUBLIC   BIBLIOG/A
INTERNATIONAL LAW CASES. INT/ORG MUNIC NAT/G PROVS   INT/LAW
ADMIN NEUTRAL WAR GOV/REL PRIVIL 20. PAGE 66 E1323   ADJUD
                                                         DIPLOM

N19

BAILEY S.D.,VETO IN THE SECURITY COUNCIL   DELIB/GP
(PAMPHLET). COM USSR WOR+45 PARL/PROC   INT/ORG
ARMS/CONT PRIVIL PWR...INT/LAW TREND CHARTS 20 UN   DIPLOM
SUEZ. PAGE 7 E0135

N19

MEZERIK A.G.,ATOM TESTS AND RADIATION HAZARDS   NUC/PWR
(PAMPHLET). WOR+45 INT/ORG DIPLOM DETER 20 UN   ARMS/CONT
TREATY. PAGE 73 E1452   CONFER
                                                         HEALTH

N19

MEZERIK AG,OUTER SPACE: UN, US, USSR (PAMPHLET).   SPACE
USSR DELIB/GP FORCES DETER NUC/PWR SOVEREIGN   CONTROL
...POLICY 20 UN TREATY. PAGE 73 E1453   DIPLOM
                                                         INT/ORG

B20

DICKINSON E.,THE EQUALITY OF STATES IN   LAW
INTERNATIONAL LAW. WOR-45 INT/ORG NAT/G DIPLOM   CONCPT
EDU/PROP LEGIT PEACE ATTIT ALL/VALS...JURID   SOVEREIGN
TIME/SEQ LEAGUE/NAT. PAGE 31 E0622

B21

OPPENHEIM L.,THE FUTURE OF INTERNATIONAL LAW.   INT/ORG
EUR+WWI MOD/EUR LAW LEGIS JUDGE LEGIT ORD/FREE   CT/SYS
...JURID TIME/SEQ GEN/LAWS 20. PAGE 79 E1578   INT/LAW

B21

STOWELL E.C.,INTERVENTION IN INTERNATIONAL LAW.   BAL/PWR
UNIV LAW SOCIETY INT/ORG ACT/RES PLAN LEGIT ROUTINE   SOVEREIGN
WAR...JURID OBS GEN/LAWS 20. PAGE 94 E1884

B22

BRYCE J.,INTERNATIONAL RELATIONS. CHRIST-17C   INT/ORG
EUR+WWI MOD/EUR CULTURE INTELL NAT/G DELIB/GP   POLICY
CREATE BAL/PWR DIPLOM ATTIT DRIVE RIGID/FLEX
ALL/VALS...PLURIST JURID CONCPT TIME/SEQ GEN/LAWS
TOT/POP. PAGE 16 E0323

B22

MYERS D.P.,MANUAL OF COLLECTIONS OF TREATIES AND OF   BIBLIOG/A
COLLECTIONS RELATING TO TREATIES. MOD/EUR INT/ORG   DIPLOM
LEGIS WRITING ADMIN SOVEREIGN...INT/LAW 19/20.   CONFER
PAGE 75 E1514

B22

WRIGHT Q.,THE CONTROL OF AMERICAN FOREIGN   NAT/G
RELATIONS. USA-45 WOR-45 CONSTN INT/ORG CONSULT   EXEC
LEGIS LEGIT ROUTINE ORD/FREE PWR...POLICY JURID   DIPLOM
CONCPT METH/CNCPT RECORD LEAGUE/NAT 20. PAGE 107
E2150

B23

HEADICAR B.M.,CATALOGUE OF THE BOOKS, PAMPHLETS,   BIBLIOG
AND OTHER DOCUMENTS IN THE EDWARD FRY LIBRARY OF   INT/LAW
INTERNATIONAL LAW... UK INT/ORG 20. PAGE 51 E1019   DIPLOM

S23

DEWEY J.,"ETHICS AND INTERNATIONAL RELATIONS." FUT   LAW
WOR-45 SOCIETY INT/ORG VOL/ASSN DIPLOM LEGIT   MORAL
ORD/FREE...JURID CONCPT GEN/METH 20. PAGE 31 E0618

B24

GENTILI A.,DE LEGATIONIBUS. CHRIST-17C NAT/G SECT   DIPLOM
CONSULT LEGIT...POLICY CATH JURID CONCPT MYTH.   INT/LAW
PAGE 43 E0848   INT/ORG
                                                         LAW

B24

HALL W.E.,A TREATISE ON INTERNATIONAL LAW. WOR-45   PWR
CONSTN INT/ORG NAT/G DIPLOM ORD/FREE LEAGUE/NAT 20   JURID
TREATY. PAGE 49 E0985   WAR
                                                         INT/LAW

L25

HUDSON M.,"THE PERMANENT COURT OF INTERNATIONAL   INT/ORG
JUSTICE AND THE QUESTION OF AMERICAN   ADJUD
PARTICIPATION." WOR-45 LEGIT CT/SYS ORD/FREE   DIPLOM
...JURID CONCPT TIME/SEQ GEN/LAWS VAL/FREE 20 ICJ.   INT/LAW
PAGE 56 E1108

B26

INSTITUT INTERMEDIAIRE INTL.REPERTOIRE GENERAL DES   BIBLIOG
TRAITES ET AUTRES ACTES DIPLOMATIQUES CONCLUS   DIPLOM
DEPUIS 1895 JUSQU'EN 1920. MOD/EUR WOR-45 INT/ORG
VOL/ASSN DELIB/GP INT/TRADE WAR TREATY 19/20.
PAGE 56 E1125

B27

LAUTERPACHT H.,PRIVATE LAW SOURCES AND ANALOGIES OF   INT/ORG
INTERNATIONAL LAW. WOR-45 NAT/G DELIB/GP LEGIT   ADJUD
COERCE ATTIT ORD/FREE PWR SOVEREIGN...JURID CONCPT   PEACE
HIST/WRIT TIME/SEQ GEN/METH LEAGUE/NAT 20. PAGE 63   INT/LAW
E1264

B28

BUTLER G.,THE DEVELOPMENT OF INTERNATIONAL LAW.   LAW
WOR-45 SOCIETY NAT/G KNOWL ORD/FREE PWR...JURID   INT/LAW
CONCPT HIST/WRIT GEN/LAWS. PAGE 18 E0349   DIPLOM
                                                      INT/ORG

B28

CORBETT P.E.,CANADA AND WORLD POLITICS. LAW CULTURE   NAT/G
SOCIETY STRUCT MARKET INT/ORG FORCES ACT/RES PLAN   CANADA
ECO/TAC LEGIT ORD/FREE PWR RESPECT...SOC CONCPT
TIME/SEQ TREND CMN/WLTH 20 LEAGUE/NAT. PAGE 26
E0504

B28

LAPRADELLE,ANNUAIRE DE LA VIE INTERNATIONALE: BIBLIOG
POLITIQUE, ECONOMIQUE, JURIDIQUE. INT/ORG CONFER   DIPLOM
ARMS/CONT 20. PAGE 63 E1255   INT/LAW

B28

MAIR L.P.,THE PROTECTION OF MINORITIES. EUR+WWI   LAW
WOR-45 INT/ORG NAT/G LEGIT CT/SYS GP/REL   SOVEREIGN
RACE/REL DISCRIM ORD/FREE RESPECT...JURID CONCPT
TIME/SEQ 20. PAGE 68 E1352

B29

BUELL R.,INTERNATIONAL RELATIONS. WOR+45 WOR-45   INT/ORG
CONSTN STRATA FORCES TOP/EX ADMIN ATTIT DRIVE   BAL/PWR
SUPEGO MORAL ORD/FREE PWR SOVEREIGN...JURID SOC   DIPLOM
CONCPT 20. PAGE 17 E0326

B29

BURNS C.D.,POLITICAL IDEALS. WOR-45 LAW CULTURE   CONCPT
SOCIETY INT/ORG HEALTH MORAL...POLICY TOT/POP 20.   GEN/LAWS
PAGE 18 E0344

B29

CONWELL-EVANS T.P.,THE LEAGUE COUNCIL IN ACTION.   DELIB/GP
EUR+WWI TURKEY UK USSR WOR-45 INT/ORG FORCES JUDGE   INT/LAW
ECO/TAC EDU/PROP LEGIT ROUTINE ARMS/CONT COERCE
ATTIT PWR...MAJORIT GEOG JURID CONCPT LEAGUE/NAT
TOT/POP VAL/FREE TUNIS 20. PAGE 25 E0498

B29

STURZO L.,THE INTERNATIONAL COMMUNITY AND THE RIGHT   INT/ORG
OF WAR (TRANS. BY BARBARA BARCLAY CARTER). CULTURE   PLAN
CREATE PROB/SOLV DIPLOM ADJUD CONTROL PEACE PERSON   WAR
ORD/FREE...INT/LAW IDEA/COMP PACIFIST 20   CONCPT
LEAGUE/NAT. PAGE 94 E1891

L29

FEIS H.,"RESEARCH ACTIVITIES OF THE LEAGUE OF   CONSULT
NATIONS." EUR+WWI WOR-45 R+D INT/ORG CT/SYS   KNOWL
ARMS/CONT WEALTH...OBS RECORD LEAGUE/NAT ILO 20.   PEACE
PAGE 37 E0729

B30

BYNKERSHOEK C.,QUAESTIONUM JURIS PUBLICI LIBRI DUO.   INT/ORG
CHRIST-17C MOD/EUR CONSTN ELITES SOCIETY NAT/G   LAW
PROVS EX/STRUC FORCES TOP/EX BAL/PWR DIPLOM ATTIT   NAT/LISM
MORAL...TRADIT CONCPT. PAGE 18 E0352   INT/LAW

B30

WRIGHT Q.,MANDATES UNDER THE LEAGUE OF NATIONS.   INT/ORG
WOR-45 CONSTN ECO/DEV ECO/UNDEV NAT/G DELIB/GP   LAW
TOP/EX LEGIT ALL/VALS...JURID CONCPT LEAGUE/NAT 20.   INT/LAW
PAGE 107 E2151

B31

STOWELL E.C.,INTERNATIONAL LAW. FUT UNIV WOR-45   INT/ORG
SOCIETY CONSULT EX/STRUC FORCES ACT/RES PLAN DIPLOM   ROUTINE
EDU/PROP LEGIT DISPL PWR SKILL...POLICY CONCPT OBS   INT/LAW
TREND TOT/POP 20. PAGE 94 E1885

B32

EAGLETON C.,INTERNATIONAL GOVERNMENT. BRAZIL FRANCE   INT/ORG
GERMANY ITALY UK USSR WOR-45 DELIB/GP TOP/EX PLAN   JURID
ECO/TAC EDU/PROP LEGIT ADJUD REGION ARMS/CONT   DIPLOM
COERCE ATTIT PWR...GEOG MGT VAL/FREE LEAGUE/NAT 20.   INT/LAW
PAGE 34 E0670

B32

FLEMMING D.,THE UNITED STATES AND THE LEAGUE OF   INT/ORG

EDU/PROP

NATIONS, 1918-1920. FUT USA-45 NAT/G LEGIS TOP/EX
DEBATE CHOOSE PEACE ATTIT SOVEREIGN...TIME/SEQ
CON/ANAL CONGRESS LEAGUE/NAT 20 TREATY. PAGE 39
E0764

B32

MASTERS R.D.,INTERNATIONAL LAW IN INTERNATIONAL   INT/ORG
COURTS. BELGIUM EUR+WWI FRANCE GERMANY MOD/EUR   LAW
SWITZERLND WOR-45 SOCIETY STRATA STRUCT LEGIT EXEC   INT/LAW
ALL/VALS...JURID HIST/WRIT TIME/SEQ TREND GEN/LAWS
20. PAGE 69 E1383

B32

MORLEY F.,THE SOCIETY OF NATIONS. EUR+WWI UNIV   INT/ORG
WOR-45 LAW CONSTN ACT/RES PLAN EDU/PROP LEGIT   CONCPT
ROUTINE...POLICY TIME/SEQ LEAGUE/NAT TOT/POP 20.
PAGE 75 E1496

B33

LAUTERPACHT H.,THE FUNCTION OF LAW IN THE   INT/ORG
INTERNATIONAL COMMUNITY. WOR-45 NAT/G FORCES CREATE   LAW
DOMIN LEGIT COERCE WAR PEACE ATTIT ORD/FREE PWR   INT/LAW
SOVEREIGN...JURID CONCPT METH/CNCPT TIME/SEQ
GEN/LAWS GEN/METH LEAGUE/NAT TOT/POP VAL/FREE 20.
PAGE 63 E1265

B34

WOLFF C.,JUS GENTIUM METHODO SCIENTIFICA   NAT/G
PERTRACTATUM. MOD/EUR INT/ORG VOL/ASSN LEGIT PEACE   LAW
ATTIT...JURID 20. PAGE 107 E2140   INT/LAW
                                                      WAR

B35

FOREIGN AFFAIRS BIBLIOGRAPHY: A SELECTED AND   BIBLIOG/A
ANNOTATED LIST OF BOOKS ON INTERNATIONAL RELATIONS   DIPLOM
1919-1962 (4 VOLS.). CONSTN FORCES COLONIAL   INT/ORG
ARMS/CONT WAR NAT/LISM PEACE ATTIT DRIVE...POLICY
INT/LAW 20. PAGE 2 E0032

B35

BURCHFIELD L.,STUDENT'S GUIDE TO MATERIALS IN   BIBLIOG
POLITICAL SCIENCE. FINAN INT/ORG NAT/G POL/PAR   INDEX
DIPLOM PRESS ADMIN...BIOG 18/19. PAGE 17 E0328   LAW

B35

HUDSON M.,BY PACIFIC MEANS. WOR-45 EDU/PROP   INT/ORG
ORD/FREE...CONCPT TIME/SEQ GEN/LAWS LEAGUE/NAT   CT/SYS
TOT/POP 20 TREATY. PAGE 56 E1110   PEACE

S35

MCMAHON A.H.,"INTERNATIONAL BOUNDARIES." WOR-45   GEOG
INT/ORG NAT/G LEGIT SKILL...CHARTS GEN/LAWS 20.   VOL/ASSN
PAGE 71 E1423   INT/LAW

B36

BRIERLY J.L.,THE LAW OF NATIONS (2ND ED.). WOR+45   DIPLOM
WOR-45 INT/ORG AGREE CONTROL COERCE WAR NAT/LISM   INT/LAW
PEACE PWR 16/20 TREATY LEAGUE/NAT. PAGE 15 E0297   NAT/G

B36

RUSSEL F.M.,THEORIES OF INTERNATIONAL RELATIONS.   PWR
EUR+WWI FUT MOD/EUR USA-45 INT/ORG DIPLOM...JURID   POLICY
CONCPT. PAGE 86 E1735   BAL/PWR
                                                      SOVEREIGN

B37

KETCHAM E.H.,PRELIMINARY SELECT BIBLIOGRAPHY OF   BIBLIOG
INTERNATIONAL LAW (PAMPHLET). WOR-45 LAW INT/ORG   DIPLOM
NAT/G PROB/SOLV CT/SYS NEUTRAL WAR 19/20. PAGE 60   ADJUD
E1207   INT/LAW

B37

SCHUSTER E.,GUIDE TO LAW AND LEGAL LITERATURE OF   BIBLIOG/A
CENTRAL AMERICAN REPUBLICS. L/A+17C INT/ORG ADJUD   REGION
SANCTION CRIME...JURID 19/20. PAGE 89 E1785   CT/SYS
                                                      LAW

B38

GRISWOLD A.W.,THE FAR EASTERN POLICY OF THE UNITED   DIPLOM
STATES. ASIA S/ASIA USA-45 INT/ORG INT/TRADE WAR   POLICY
NAT/LISM...BIBLIOG 19/20 LEAGUE/NAT ROOSEVLT/T   CHIEF
ROOSEVLT/F WILSON/W TREATY. PAGE 47 E0943

B38

HAGUE PERMANENT CT INTL JUSTIC,WORLD COURT REPORTS: INT/ORG
COLLECTION OF THE JUDGEMENTS ORDERS AND OPINIONS   CT/SYS
VOLUME 3 1932-35. WOR-45 LAW DELIB/GP CONFER WAR   DIPLOM
PEACE ATTIT...DECISION ANTHOL 20 WORLD/CT CASEBOOK.   ADJUD
PAGE 49 E0976

B38

SAINT-PIERRE C.I.,SCHEME FOR LASTING PEACE (TRANS.   INT/ORG
BY H. BELLOT). INDUS NAT/G CHIEF FORCES INT/TRADE   PEACE
CT/SYS WAR PWR SOVEREIGN WEALTH...POLICY 18.   AGREE
PAGE 87 E1741   INT/LAW

BENES E.,INTERNATIONAL SECURITY. GERMANY UK NAT/G | EUR+WWI | B39
DELIB/GP PLAN BAL/PWR ATTIT ORD/FREE PWR LEAGUE/NAT | INT/ORG
20 TREATY. PAGE 10 E0186 | WAR

WILSON G.G.,HANDBOOK OF INTERNATIONAL LAW. FUT UNIV | INT/ORG | B39
USA-45 WOR-45 SOCIETY LEGIT ATTIT DISPL DRIVE | LAW
ALL/VALS...INT/LAW TIME/SEQ TREND. PAGE 106 E2128 | CONCPT
| WAR

ZIMMERN A.,THE LEAGUE OF NATIONS AND THE RULE OF | INT/ORG | B39
LAW. WOR-45 STRUCT NAT/G DELIB/GP EX/STRUC BAL/PWR | LAW
DOMIN LEGIT COERCE ORD/FREE PWR...POLICY RECORD | DIPLOM
LEAGUE/NAT TOT/POP VAL/FREE 20 LEAGUE/NAT. PAGE 108
E2170

SCOTT J.B.,"LAW, THE STATE, AND THE INTERNATIONAL | LAW | C39
COMMUNITY (2 VOLS.)" INTELL INT/ORG NAT/G SECT | PHIL/SCI
INT/TRADE WAR...INT/LAW GEN/LAWS BIBLIOG. PAGE 90 | DIPLOM
E1798 | CONCPT

CARR E.H.,THE TWENTY YEARS' CRISIS 1919-1939. FUT | INT/ORG | B40
WOR-45 BAL/PWR ECO/TAC LEGIT TOTALISM ATTIT | DIPLOM
ALL/VALS...POLICY JURID CONCPT TIME/SEQ TREND | PEACE
GEN/LAWS TOT/POP 20. PAGE 20 E0393

CONOVER H.F.,FOREIGN RELATIONS OF THE UNITED | BIBLIOG/A | B40
STATES: A LIST OF RECENT BOOKS (PAMPHLET). ASIA | USA-45
CANADA L/A+17C UK INT/ORG INT/TRADE TARIFFS NEUTRAL | DIPLOM
WAR PEACE...INT/LAW CON/ANAL 20 CHINJAP. PAGE 25
E0492

WOLFERS A.,BRITAIN AND FRANCE BETWEEN TWO WORLD | DIPLOM | B40
WARS. FRANCE UK INT/ORG NAT/G PLAN BARGAIN ECO/TAC | WAR
AGREE ISOLAT ALL/IDEOS...DECISION GEOG 20 TREATY | POLICY
VERSAILLES INTERVENT. PAGE 107 E2139

FLORIN J.,"BOLSHEVIST AND NATIONAL SOCIALIST | LAW | S40
DOCTRINES OF INTERNATIONAL LAW." EUR+WWI GERMANY | ATTIT
USSR R+D INT/ORG NAT/G DIPLOM DOMIN EDU/PROP SOCISM | TOTALISM
...CONCPT TIME/SEQ 20. PAGE 39 E0768 | INT/LAW

MCCLURE W.,INTERNATIONAL EXECUTIVE AGREEMENTS. | TOP/EX | B41
USA-45 WOR-45 INT/ORG NAT/G DELIB/GP ADJUD ROUTINE | DIPLOM
ORD/FREE PWR...TIME/SEQ TREND CON/ANAL. PAGE 70
E1401

COMM. STUDY ORGAN. PEACE,"ORGANIZATION OF PEACE." | INT/ORG | L41
USA-45 WOR-45 STRATA NAT/G ACT/RES DIPLOM ECO/TAC | PLAN
EDU/PROP ADJUD ATTIT ORD/FREE PWR...SOC CONCPT | PEACE
ANTHOL LEAGUE/NAT 20. PAGE 24 E0479

WRIGHT Q.,"FUNDAMENTAL PROBLEMS OF INTERNATIONAL | INT/ORG | S41
ORGANIZATION." UNIV WOR-45 STRUCT FORCES ACT/RES | ATTIT
CREATE DOMIN EDU/PROP LEGIT REGION NAT/LISM | PEACE
ORD/FREE PWR RESPECT SOVEREIGN...JURID SOC CONCPT
METH/CNCPT TIME/SEQ 20. PAGE 107 E2152

CROWE S.E.,THE BERLIN WEST AFRICA CONFERENCE, | AFR | B42
1884-85. GERMANY ELITES MARKET INT/ORG DELIB/GP | CONFER
FORCES PROB/SOLV BAL/PWR CAP/ISM DOMIN COLONIAL | INT/TRADE
...INT/LAW 19. PAGE 28 E0548 | DIPLOM

FEILCHENFELD E.H.,THE INTERNATIONAL ECONOMIC LAW OF | ECO/TAC | B42
BELLIGERENT OCCUPATION. EUR+WWI MOD/EUR USA-45 | INT/LAW
INT/ORG DIPLOM ADJUD ARMS/CONT LEAGUE/NAT 20. | WAR
PAGE 37 E0726

HAMBRO C.J.,HOW TO WIN THE PEACE. ECO/TAC EDU/PROP | FUT | B42
ADJUD PERSON ALL/VALS...SOCIALIST TREND GEN/LAWS | INT/ORG
20. PAGE 50 E0987 | PEACE

KELSEN H.,LAW AND PEACE IN INTERNATIONAL RELATIONS. | INT/ORG | B42
FUT WOR-45 NAT/G DELIB/GP DIPLOM LEGIT RIGID/FLEX | ADJUD
ORD/FREE SOVEREIGN...JURID CONCPT TREND STERTYP | PEACE
GEN/LAWS LEAGUE/NAT 20. PAGE 60 E1197 | INT/LAW

BEMIS S.F.,THE LATIN AMERICAN POLICY OF THE UNITED | DIPLOM | B43
STATES: AN HISTORICAL INTERPRETATION. INT/ORG AGREE | SOVEREIGN
COLONIAL WAR PEACE ATTIT ORD/FREE...POLICY INT/LAW | USA-45
CHARTS 18/20 MEXIC/AMER WILSON/W MONROE/DOC. | L/A+17C

PAGE 10 E0185

CONOVER H.F.,THE BALKANS: A SELECTED LIST OF | BIBLIOG | B43
REFERENCES. ALBANIA BULGARIA ROMANIA YUGOSLAVIA | EUR+WWI
INT/ORG PROB/SOLV DIPLOM LEGIT CONFER ADJUD WAR
NAT/LISM PEACE PWR 20 LEAGUE/NAT. PAGE 25 E0493

HAGUE PERMANENT CT INTL JUSTIC,WORLD COURT REPORTS: | INT/ORG | B43
COLLECTION OF THE JUDGEMENTS ORDERS AND OPINIONS | CT/SYS
VOLUME 4 1936-42. WOR-45 CONFER PEACE ATTIT | DIPLOM
...DECISION JURID ANTHOL 20 WORLD/CT CASEBOOK. | ADJUD
PAGE 49 E0977

SERENI A.P.,THE ITALIAN CONCEPTION OF INTERNATIONAL | LAW | B43
LAW. EUR+WWI MOD/EUR INT/ORG NAT/G DOMIN COERCE | TIME/SEQ
ORD/FREE FASCISM...OBS/ENVIR TREND 20. PAGE 90 | INT/LAW
E1804 | ITALY

ADLER M.J.,HOW TO THINK ABOUT WAR AND PEACE. WOR-45 | INT/ORG | B44
LAW SOCIETY EX/STRUC DIPLOM KNOWL ORD/FREE...POLICY | CREATE
TREND GEN/LAWS 20. PAGE 3 E0049 | ARMS/CONT
| PEACE

BRIERLY J.L.,THE OUTLOOK FOR INTERNATIONAL LAW. FUT | INT/ORG | B44
WOR-45 CONSTN NAT/G ASSN FORCES ECO/TAC DOMIN | LAW
LEGIT ADJUD ROUTINE PEACE ORD/FREE...INT/LAW JURID
METH LEAGUE/NAT 20. PAGE 15 E0298

HUDSON M.,INTERNATIONAL TRIBUNALS PAST AND FUTURE. | INT/ORG | B44
FUT WOR-45 LAW EDU/PROP ADJUD ORD/FREE...CONCPT | STRUCT
TIME/SEQ TREND GEN/LAWS TOT/POP VAL/FREE 18/20. | INT/LAW
PAGE 56 E1111

PUTTKAMMER E.W.,WAR AND THE LAW. UNIV USA-45 CONSTN | INT/ORG | B44
CULTURE SOCIETY NAT/G POL/PAR ROUTINE ALL/VALS | LAW
...JURID CONCPT OBS WORK VAL/FREE 20. PAGE 83 E1664 | WAR
| INT/LAW

BEVERIDGE W.,THE PRICE OF PEACE. GERMANY UK WOR+45 | INT/ORG | B45
WOR-45 NAT/G FORCES CREATE LEGIT REGION WAR ATTIT | TREND
KNOWL ORD/FREE PWR...POLICY NEW/IDEA GEN/LAWS | PEACE
LEAGUE/NAT 20 TREATY. PAGE 12 E0223

HILL N.,CLAIMS TO TERRITORY IN INTERNATIONAL LAW | INT/ORG | B45
AND RELATIONS. WOR-45 NAT/G DOMIN EDU/PROP LEGIT | ADJUD
REGION ROUTINE ORD/FREE PWR WEALTH...GEOG INT/LAW | SOVEREIGN
JURID 20. PAGE 52 E1047

TINGSTERN H.,PEACE AND SECURITY AFTER WW II. WOR-45 | INT/ORG | B45
DELIB/GP TOP/EX LEGIT CT/SYS COERCE PEACE ATTIT | ORD/FREE
PERCEPT...CONCPT LEAGUE/NAT 20. PAGE 96 E1927 | WAR
| INT/LAW

UNCIO CONFERENCE LIBRARY,SHORT TITLE CLASSIFIED | BIBLIOG | B45
CATALOG. WOR-45 DOMIN COLONIAL WAR...SOC/WK 20 | DIPLOM
LEAGUE/NAT UN. PAGE 98 E1955 | INT/ORG
| INT/LAW

WOOLBERT R.G.,FOREIGN AFFAIRS BIBLIOGRAPHY, | BIBLIOG/A | B45
1932-1942. INT/ORG SECT INT/TRADE COLONIAL RACE/REL | DIPLOM
NAT/LISM...GEOG INT/LAW GOV/COMP IDEA/COMP 20. | WAR
PAGE 107 E2144

KEETON G.W.,MAKING INTERNATIONAL LAW WORK. FUT | INT/ORG | B46
WOR-45 NAT/G DELIB/GP FORCES LEGIT COERCE PEACE | ADJUD
ATTIT RIGID/FLEX ORD/FREE PWR...JURID CONCPT | INT/LAW
HIST/WRIT GEN/METH LEAGUE/NAT 20. PAGE 60 E1193

GOODRICH L.M.,"CHARTER OF THE UNITED NATIONS: | CONSTN | C46
COMMENTARY AND DOCUMENTS." EX/STRUC ADMIN...INT/LAW | INT/ORG
CON/ANAL BIBLIOG 20 UN. PAGE 45 E0890 | DIPLOM

BORGESE G.,COMMON CAUSE. LAW CONSTN SOCIETY STRATA | WOR+45 | B47
ECO/DEV INT/ORG POL/PAR FORCES LEGIS TOP/EX CAP/ISM | NAT/G
DIPLOM ADMIN EXEC ATTIT PWR 20. PAGE 14 E0269 | SOVEREIGN
| REGION

ENKE S.,INTERNATIONAL ECONOMICS. UK USA+45 USSR | INT/TRADE | B47
INT/ORG BAL/PWR BARGAIN CAP/ISM BAL/PAY...NAT/COMP | FINAN
20 TREATY. PAGE 35 E0691 | TARIFFS

ECO/TAC

B47

GORDON D.L.,THE HIDDEN WEAPON: THE STORY OF   INT/ORG
ECONOMIC WARFARE. EUR+WWI USA-45 LAW FINAN INDUS   ECO/TAC
NAT/G CONSULT FORCES PLAN DOMIN PWR WEALTH   INT/TRADE
...INT/LAW CONCPT OBS TOT/POP NAZI 20. PAGE 45   WAR
E0891

B47

HILL M.,IMMUNITIES AND PRIVILEGES OF INTERNATIONAL   INT/ORG
OFFICIALS. CANADA EUR+WWI NETHERLAND SWITZERLND LAW   ADMIN
LEGIS DIPLOM LEGIT RESPECT...TIME/SEQ LEAGUE/NAT UN
VAL/FREE 20. PAGE 52 E1046

B47

HYDE C.C.,INTERNATIONAL LAW, CHIEFLY AS INTERPRETED   INT/LAW
AND APPLIED BY THE UNITED STATES (3 VOLS., 2ND REV.   DIPLOM
ED.). USA-45 WOR+45 WOR-45 INT/ORG CT/SYS WAR   NAT/G
NAT/LISM PEACE ORD/FREE...JURID 19/20 TREATY.   POLICY
PAGE 56 E1119

B47

INTERNATIONAL COURT OF JUSTICE,CHARTER OF THE   INT/LAW
UNITED NATIONS, STATUTE AND RULES OF COURT AND   INT/ORG
OTHER CONSTITUTIONAL DOCUMENTS. SWITZERLND LAW   CT/SYS
ADJUD INGP/REL...JURID 20 ICJ UN. PAGE 57 E1133   DIPLOM

B47

TOWLE L.W.,INTERNATIONAL TRADE AND COMMERCIAL   MARKET
POLICY. WOR+45 LAW ECO/DEV FINAN INDUS NAT/G   INT/ORG
ECO/TAC WEALTH...TIME/SEQ ILO 20. PAGE 97 E1937   INT/TRADE

B48

FENWICK C.G.,INTERNATIONAL LAW. WOR+45 WOR-45   INT/ORG
CONSTN NAT/G LEGIT CT/SYS REGION...CONCPT   JURID
LEAGUE/NAT UN 20. PAGE 37 E0737   INT/LAW

B48

HOLCOMBE A.N.,HUMAN RIGHTS IN THE MODERN WORLD.   ORD/FREE
WOR+45 LEGIS DIPLOM ADJUD PERSON...INT/LAW 20 UN   INT/ORG
TREATY CIVIL/LIB BILL/RIGHT. PAGE 54 E1071   CONSTN
LAW

B48

JESSUP P.C.,A MODERN LAW OF NATIONS. FUT WOR+45   INT/ORG
WOR-45 SOCIETY NAT/G DELIB/GP LEGIS BAL/PWR   ADJUD
EDU/PROP LEGIT PWR...INT/LAW JURID TIME/SEQ
LEAGUE/NAT 20. PAGE 58 E1166

B48

LOGAN R.W.,THE AFRICAN MANDATES IN WORLD POLITICS.   WAR
EUR+WWI GERMANY ISLAM INT/ORG BARGAIN...POLICY   COLONIAL
INT/LAW 20. PAGE 66 E1321   AFR
DIPLOM

B48

MORGENTHAL H.J.,POLITICS AMONG NATIONS: THE   DIPLOM
STRUGGLE FOR POWER AND PEACE. FUT WOR+45 INT/ORG   PEACE
OP/RES PROB/SOLV BAL/PWR CONTROL ATTIT MORAL   PWR
...INT/LAW BIBLIOG 20 COLD/WAR. PAGE 75 E1494   POLICY

B49

JACKSON R.H.,INTERNATIONAL CONFERENCE ON MILITARY   DIPLOM
TRIALS. FRANCE GERMANY UK USA+45 USSR VOL/ASSN   INT/ORG
DELIB/GP REPAR ADJUD CT/SYS CRIME WAR 20 WAR/TRIAL.   INT/LAW
PAGE 57 E1141   CIVMIL/REL

B49

KAFKA G.,FREIHEIT UND ANARCHIE. SECT COERCE DETER   CONCPT
WAR ATTIT...IDEA/COMP 20 NATO. PAGE 59 E1179   ORD/FREE
JURID
INT/ORG

B49

MARITAIN J.,HUMAN RIGHTS: COMMENTS AND   INT/ORG
INTERPRETATIONS. COM UNIV WOR+45 LAW CONSTN CULTURE   CONCPT
SOCIETY ECO/DEV ECO/UNDEV SCHOOL DELIB/GP EDU/PROP
ATTIT PERCEPT ALL/VALS...HUM SOC TREND UNESCO 20.
PAGE 68 E1365

B49

US DEPARTMENT OF STATE,SOVIET BIBLIOGRAPHY   BIBLIOG/A
(PAMPHLET). CHINA/COM COM USSR LAW AGRI INT/ORG   MARXISM
ECO/TAC EDU/PROP...POLICY GEOG 20. PAGE 99 E1994   CULTURE
DIPLOM

L49

COMM. STUDY ORGAN. PEACE,"A TEN YEAR RECORD,   INT/ORG
1939-1949." FUT WOR+45 LAW R+D CONSULT DELIB/GP   CONSTN
CREATE LEGIT ROUTINE ORD/FREE...TIME/SEQ UN 20.   PEACE
PAGE 24 E0480

S49

KIRK G.,"MATERIALS FOR THE STUDY OF INTERNATIONAL   INT/ORG.
RELATIONS." FUT UNIV WOR+45 INTELL EDU/PROP ROUTINE   ACT/RES

PEACE ATTIT...INT/LAW JURID CONCPT OBS. PAGE 61   DIPLOM
E1219

B50

BROWN E.S.,MANUAL OF GOVERNMENT PUBLICATIONS.   BIBLIOG/A
WOR+45 WOR-45 CONSTN INT/ORG MUNIC PROVS DIPLOM   NAT/G
ADMIN 20. PAGE 16 E0313   LAW

B50

JIMENEZ E.,VOTING AND HANDLING OF DISPUTES IN THE   DELIB/GP
SECURITY COUNCIL. WOR+45 CONSTN INT/ORG DIPLOM   ROUTINE
LEGIT DETER CHOOSE MORAL ORD/FREE PWR...JURID
TIME/SEQ COLD/WAR UN 20. PAGE 59 E1168

B50

LAUTERPACHT H.,INTERNATIONAL LAW AND HUMAN RIGHTS.   DELIB/GP
USA+45 CONSTN STRUCT INT/ORG ACT/RES EDU/PROP PEACE   LAW
PERSON ALL/VALS...CONCPT CON/ANAL GEN/LAWS UN 20.   INT/LAW
PAGE 63 E1266

B50

MACIVER R.M.,GREAT EXPRESSIONS OF HUMAN RIGHTS. LAW   UNIV
CONSTN CULTURE INTELL SOCIETY R+D INT/ORG ATTIT   CONCPT
DRIVE...JURID OBS HIST/WRIT GEN/LAWS. PAGE 67 E1340

B50

MONPIED E.,BIBLIOGRAPHIE FEDERALISTE: OUVRAGES   BIBLIOG/A
CHOISIS (VOL. I, MIMEOGRAPHED PAPER). EUR+WWI   FEDERAL
DIPLOM ADMIN REGION ATTIT PACIFISM SOCISM...INT/LAW   CENTRAL
19/20. PAGE 74 E1486   INT/ORG

B50

ROSS A.,CONSTITUTION OF THE UNITED NATIONS. CONSTN   PEACE
CONSULT DELIB/GP ECO/TAC...INT/LAW JURID 20 UN   DIPLOM
LEAGUE/NAT. PAGE 86 E1721   ORD/FREE
INT/ORG

B50

SOHN L.B.,CASES AND OTHER MATERIALS ON WORLD LAW.   CT/SYS
FUT WOR+45 LAW INT/ORG...INT/LAW JURID METH/CNCPT   CONSTN
20 UN. PAGE 92 E1852

B50

STONE J.,THE PROVINCE AND FUNCTION OF LAW. UNIV   INT/ORG
WOR+45 CULTURE INTELL SOCIETY ECO/DEV   LAW
ECO/UNDEV NAT/G LEGIT ROUTINE ATTIT PERCEPT PERSON
...JURID CONCPT GEN/LAWS GEN/METH 20. PAGE 94 E1877

N51

MONPIED E.,FEDERALIST BIBLIOGRAPHY: ARTICLES AND   BIBLIOG/A
DOCUMENTS PUBLISHED IN BRITISH PERIODICALS   INT/ORG
1945-1951 (MIMEOGRAPHED). EUR+WWI UK WOR+45 DIPLOM   FEDERAL
REGION ATTIT SOCISM...INT/LAW 20. PAGE 74 E1487   CENTRAL

B51

CORBETT P.E.,LAW AND SOCIETY IN THE RELATIONS OF   INT/LAW
STATES. FUT WOR+45 WOR-45 CONTROL WAR PEACE PWR   DIPLOM
...POLICY JURID 16/20 TREATY. PAGE 26 E0505   INT/ORG

B51

KELSEN H.,THE LAW OF THE UNITED NATIONS. WOR+45   INT/ORG
STRUCT RIGID/FLEX ORD/FREE...INT/LAW JURID CONCPT   ADJUD
CON/ANAL GEN/METH UN TOT/POP VAL/FREE 20. PAGE 60
E1198

L51

KELSEN H.,"RECENT TRENDS IN THE LAW OF THE UNITED   INT/ORG
NATIONS." KOREA WOR+45 CONSTN LEGIS DIPLOM LEGIT   LAW
DETER WAR RIGID/FLEX HEALTH ORD/FREE RESPECT   INT/LAW
...JURID CON/ANAL UN VAL/FREE 20 NATO. PAGE 60
E1199

L51

LISSITZYN O.J.,"THE INTERNATIONAL COURT OF   ADJUD
JUSTICE." WOR+45 INT/ORG LEGIT ORD/FREE...CONCPT   JURID
TIME/SEQ TREND GEN/LAWS VAL/FREE 20 ICJ. PAGE 65   INT/LAW
E1304

L51

MANGONE G.,"THE IDEA AND PRACTICE OF WORLD   INT/ORG
GOVERNMENT." FUT WOR+45 WOR-45 ECO/DEV LEGIS CREATE   SOCIETY
LEGIT ROUTINE ATTIT MORAL PWR WEALTH...CONCPT   INT/LAW
GEN/LAWS 20. PAGE 68 E1358

B52

FERRELL R.H.,PEACE IN THEIR TIME. FRANCE UK USA-45   PEACE
INT/ORG NAT/G FORCES CREATE AGREE ARMS/CONT COERCE   DIPLOM
WAR TREATY 20 WILSON/W LEAGUE/NAT BRIAND/A. PAGE 37
E0741

B52

JACKSON E.,MEETING OF THE MINDS: A WAY TO PEACE   LABOR
THROUGH MEDIATION. WOR+45 INDUS INT/ORG NAT/G   JUDGE
DELIB/GP DIPLOM EDU/PROP LEGIT ORD/FREE...NEW/IDEA
SELF/OBS TIME/SEQ CHARTS GEN/LAWS TOT/POP 20 UN
TREATY. PAGE 57 E1139

KELSEN H.,PRINCIPLES OF INTERNATIONAL LAW. WOR+45 **B52** ADJUD
WOR-45 INT/ORG ORD/FREE...JURID GEN/LAWS TOT/POP CONSTN
20. PAGE 60 E1200 INT/LAW

LIPPMANN W.,ISOLATION AND ALLIANCES: AN AMERICAN **B52** DIPLOM
SPEAKS TO THE BRITISH. USA+45 USA-45 INT/ORG AGREE SOVEREIGN
COERCE DETER WAR PEACE MORAL 20 TREATY INTERVENT. COLONIAL
PAGE 65 E1301 ATTIT

UNESCO,THESES DE SCIENCES SOCIALES: CATALOGUE **B52** BIBLIOG
ANALYTIQUE INTERNATIONAL DE THESES INEDITES DE ACADEM
DOCTORAT, 1940-1950. INT/ORG DIPLOM EDU/PROP...GEOG WRITING
INT/LAW MGT PSY SOC 20. PAGE 98 E1958

VANDENBOSCH A.,THE UN: BACKGROUND, ORGANIZATION, **B52** DELIB/GP
FUNCTIONS, ACTIVITIES. WOR+45 LAW CONSTN STRUCT TIME/SEQ
INT/ORG CONSULT BAL/PWR EDU/PROP EXEC ALL/VALS PEACE
...POLICY CONCPT UN 20. PAGE 103 E2071

STUART G.H.,"AMERICAN DIPLOMATIC AND CONSULAR **C52** DIPLOM
PRACTICE (2ND ED.)" EUR+WWI MOD/EUR USA-45 DELIB/GP ADMIN
INT/TRADE ADJUD...BIBLIOG 20. PAGE 94 E1889 INT/ORG

LANDHEER B.,FUNDAMENTALS OF PUBLIC INTERNATIONAL **B53** BIBLIOG/A
LAW (SELECTIVE BIBLIOGRAPHIES OF THE LIBRARY OF THE INT/LAW
PEACE PALACE, VOL. I; PAMPH). INT/ORG OP/RES PEACE DIPLOM
...IDEA/COMP 20. PAGE 62 E1250 PHIL/SCI

OPPENHEIM L.,INTERNATIONAL LAW: A TREATISE (7TH **B53** INT/LAW
ED., 2 VOLS.). LAW CONSTN PROB/SOLV INT/TRADE ADJUD INT/ORG
AGREE NEUTRAL WAR ORD/FREE SOVEREIGN...BIBLIOG 20 DIPLOM
LEAGUE/NAT UN ILO. PAGE 79 E1579

FRIEDMAN W.,THE PUBLIC CORPORATION: A COMPARATIVE **B54** LAW
SYMPOSIUM (UNIVERSITY OF TORONTO SCHOOL OF LAW SOCISM
COMPARATIVE LAW SERIES, VOL. I). SWEDEN USA+45 LG/CO
INDUS INT/ORG NAT/G REGION CENTRAL FEDERAL...POLICY OWN
JURID IDEA/COMP NAT/COMP ANTHOL 20 COMMONWLTH
MONOPOLY EUROPE. PAGE 40 E0801

LANDHEER B.,RECOGNITION IN INTERNATIONAL LAW **B54** BIBLIOG/A
(SELECTIVE BIBLIOGRAPHIES OF THE LIBRARY OF THE INT/LAW
PEACE PALACE, VOL. II; PAMPHLET). NAT/G LEGIT INT/ORG
SANCTION 20. PAGE 63 E1251 DIPLOM

MANGONE G.,A SHORT HISTORY OF INTERNATIONAL **B54** INT/ORG
ORGANIZATION. MOD/EUR USA+45 USA-45 WOR+45 WOR-45 INT/LAW
LAW LEGIS CREATE LEGIT ROUTINE RIGID/FLEX PWR
...JURID CONCPT OBS TIME/SEQ STERTYP GEN/LAWS UN
TOT/POP VAL/FREE 18/20. PAGE 68 E1359

NUSSBAUM D.,A CONCISE HISTORY OF THE LAW OF **B54** INT/ORG
NATIONS. ASIA CHRIST-17C EUR+WWI ISLAM MEDIT-7 LAW
MOD/EUR S/ASIA UNIV WOR+45 WOR-45 SOCIETY STRUCT PEACE
EXEC ATTIT ALL/VALS...CONCPT HIST/WRIT TIME/SEQ. INT/LAW
PAGE 78 E1560

STONE J.,LEGAL CONTROLS OF INTERNATIONAL CONFLICT: **B54** INT/ORG
A TREATISE ON THE DYNAMICS OF DISPUTES AND WAR LAW. LAW
WOR+45 WOR-45 NAT/G DIPLOM CT/SYS SOVEREIGN...JURID WAR
CONCPT METH/CNCPT GEN/LAWS TOT/POP VAL/FREE INT/LAW
COLD/WAR LEAGUE/NAT 20. PAGE 94 E1878

US SENATE COMM ON FOREIGN REL,REVIEW OF THE UNITED **B54** BIBLIOG
NATIONS CHARTER: A COLLECTION OF DOCUMENTS. LEGIS CONSTN
DIPLOM ADMIN ARMS/CONT WAR REPRESENT SOVEREIGN INT/ORG
...INT/LAW 20 UN. PAGE 101 E2029 DEBATE

WRIGHT Q.,PROBLEMS OF STABILITY AND PROGRESS IN **B54** INT/ORG
INTERNATIONAL RELATIONSHIPS. FUT WOR+45 WOR-45 CONCPT
SOCIETY LEGIS CREATE TEC/DEV ECO/TAC EDU/PROP ADJUD DIPLOM
WAR PEACE ORD/FREE PWR...KNO/TEST TREND GEN/LAWS
20. PAGE 108 E2155

BOWIE R.R.,"STUDIES IN FEDERALISM." AGRI FINAN **C54** FEDERAL
LABOR EX/STRUC FORCES LEGIS DIPLOM INT/TRADE ADJUD EUR+WWI
...BIBLIOG 20 EEC. PAGE 14 E0279 INT/ORG
CONSTN

BURR R.N.,DOCUMENTS ON INTER-AMERICAN COOPERATION: **B55** BIBLIOG
VOL. I, 1810-1881; VOL. II, 1881-1948. DELIB/GP DIPLOM
BAL/PWR INT/TRADE REPRESENT NAT/LISM PEACE HABITAT INT/ORG
ORD/FREE PWR SOVEREIGN...INT/LAW 20 OAS. PAGE 18 L/A+17C
E0345

CHOWDHURI R.N.,INTERNATIONAL MANDATES AND **B55** DELIB/GP
TRUSTEESHIP SYSTEMS. WOR+45 STRUCT ECO/UNDEV PLAN
INT/ORG LEGIS DOMIN EDU/PROP LEGIT ADJUD EXEC PWR SOVEREIGN
...CONCPT TIME/SEQ UN 20. PAGE 22 E0434

COMM. STUDY ORGAN. PEACE,REPORTS. WOR-45 ECO/DEV **B55** WOR+45
ECO/UNDEV VOL/ASSN CONSULT FORCES PLAN TEC/DEV INT/ORG
DOMIN EDU/PROP NUC/PWR ATTIT PWR WEALTH...JURID ARMS/CONT
STERTYP FAO ILO 20 UN. PAGE 24 E0481

HOGAN W.N.,INTERNATIONAL CONFLICT AND COLLECTIVE **B55** INT/ORG
SECURITY: THE PRINCIPLE OF CONCERN IN INTERNATIONAL WAR
ORGANIZATION. CONSTN EX/STRUC BAL/PWR DIPLOM ADJUD ORD/FREE
CONTROL CENTRAL CONSEN PEACE...INT/LAW CONCPT FORCES
METH/COMP 20 UN LEAGUE/NAT. PAGE 53 E1066

PLISCHKE E.,AMERICAN FOREIGN RELATIONS: A **B55** BIBLIOG/A
BIBLIOGRAPHY OF OFFICIAL SOURCES. USA+45 USA-45 DIPLOM
INT/ORG FORCES PRESS WRITING DEBATE EXEC...POLICY NAT/G
INT/LAW 18/20 CONGRESS. PAGE 81 E1621

SVARLIEN O.,AN INTRODUCTION TO THE LAW OF NATIONS. **B55** INT/LAW
SEA AIR INT/ORG NAT/G CHIEF ADMIN AGREE WAR PRIVIL DIPLOM
ORD/FREE SOVEREIGN...BIBLIOG 16/20. PAGE 95 E1897

UN HEADQUARTERS LIBRARY,BIBLIOGRAPHIE DE LA CHARTE **B55** BIBLIOG/A
DES NATIONS UNIES. CHINA/COM KOREA WOR+45 VOL/ASSN INT/ORG
CONFER ADMIN COERCE PEACE ATTIT ORD/FREE SOVEREIGN DIPLOM
...INT/LAW 20 UNESCO UN. PAGE 97 E1953

CORBETT P.E.,MORALS LAW, AND POWER IN INTERNATIONAL **B56** SUPEGO
RELATIONS. WOR+45 WOR-45 INT/ORG VOL/ASSN DELIB/GP CONCPT
CREATE BAL/PWR DIPLOM LEGIT ARMS/CONT MORAL...JURID POLICY
GEN/LAWS TOT/POP LEAGUE/NAT 20. PAGE 26 E0506 INT/LAW

SOHN L.B.,BASIC DOCUMENTS OF THE UNITED NATIONS. **B56** DELIB/GP
WOR+45 LAW INT/ORG LEGIT EXEC ROUTINE CHOOSE PWR CONSTN
...JURID CONCPT GEN/LAWS ANTHOL UN TOT/POP OAS FAO
ILO 20. PAGE 92 E1853

SOHN L.B.,CASES ON UNITED NATIONS LAW. STRUCT **B56** INT/ORG
DELIB/GP WAR PEACE ORD/FREE...DECISION ANTHOL 20 INT/LAW
UN. PAGE 92 E1854 ADMIN
ADJUD

WEIS P.,NATIONALITY AND STATELESSNESS IN **B56** INT/ORG
INTERNATIONAL LAW. UK WOR+45 WOR-45 LAW CONSTN SOVEREIGN
NAT/G DIPLOM EDU/PROP LEGIT ROUTINE RIGID/FLEX INT/LAW
...JURID RECORD CMN/WLTH 20. PAGE 105 E2109

POTTER P.B.,"NEUTRALITY, 1955." WOR+45 WOR-45 **S56** NEUTRAL
INT/ORG NAT/G WAR ATTIT...POLICY IDEA/COMP 17/20 INT/LAW
LEAGUE/NAT UN COLD/WAR. PAGE 81 E1631 DIPLOM
CONCPT

ALIGHIERI D.,ON WORLD GOVERNMENT. ROMAN/EMP LAW **B57** POLICY
SOCIETY INT/ORG NAT/G POL/PAR ADJUD WAR GP/REL CONCPT
PEACE WORSHIP 15 WORLDUNITY DANTE. PAGE 4 E0067 DIPLOM
SECT

COMM. STUDY ORGAN. PEACE,STRENGTHENING THE UNITED **B57** INT/ORG
NATIONS. FUT USA+45 WOR+45 CONSTN NAT/G DELIB/GP ORD/FREE
FORCES LEGIS ECO/TAC LEGIT COERCE PEACE...JURID
CONCPT UN COLD/WAR 20. PAGE 24 E0482

CONOVER H.F.,NORTH AND NORTHEAST AFRICA; A SELECTED **B57** BIBLIOG/A
ANNOTATED LIST OF WRITINGS. ALGERIA MOROCCO SUDAN DIPLOM
UAR CULTURE INT/ORG PROB/SOLV ADJUD NAT/LISM PWR AFR
WEALTH...SOC 20 UN. PAGE 25 E0496 ECO/UNDEV

DE VISSCHER C.,THEORY AND REALITY IN PUBLIC **B57** INT/ORG
INTERNATIONAL LAW. WOR+45 WOR-45 SOCIETY NAT/G LAW
CT/SYS ATTIT MORAL ORD/FREE PWR...JURID CONCPT INT/LAW
METH/CNCPT TIME/SEQ GEN/LAWS LEAGUE/NAT TOT/POP

VAL/FREE COLD/WAR. PAGE 30 E0599

B57
JENKS C.W.,THE INTERNATIONAL PROTECTION OF TRADE   LABOR
UNION FREEDOM. FUT WOR+45 WOR-45 VOL/ASSN DELIB/GP   INT/ORG
CT/SYS REGION ROUTINE...JURID METH/CNCPT RECORD
TIME/SEQ CHARTS ILO WORK OAS 20. PAGE 58 E1153

B57
LEVONTIN A.V.,THE MYTH OF INTERNATIONAL SECURITY: A   INT/ORG
JURIDICAL AND CRITICAL ANALYSIS. FUT WOR+45 WOR-45   INT/LAW
LAW NAT/G VOL/ASSN ACT/RES BAL/PWR ATTIT ORD/FREE   SOVEREIGN
...JURID METH/CNCPT TIME/SEQ TREND STERTYP 20.   MYTH
PAGE 64 E1289

B57
PALMER N.D.,INTERNATIONAL RELATIONS. WOR+45 INT/ORG   DIPLOM
NAT/G ECO/TAC EDU/PROP COLONIAL WAR PWR SOVEREIGN   BAL/PWR
...POLICY T 20 TREATY. PAGE 79 E1593   NAT/COMP

B57
ROSENNE S.,THE INTERNATIONAL COURT OF JUSTICE.   INT/ORG
WOR+45 LAW DOMIN LEGIT PEACE PWR SOVEREIGN...JURID   CT/SYS
CONCPT RECORD TIME/SEQ CON/ANAL CHARTS UN TOT/POP   INT/LAW
VAL/FREE LEAGUE/NAT 20 ICJ. PAGE 86 E1716

B57
WASSENBERGH H.A.,POST-WAR INTERNATIONAL CIVIL   COM/IND
AVIATION POLICY AND THE LAW OF THE AIR. WOR+45 AIR   NAT/G
INT/ORG DOMIN LEGIT PEACE ORD/FREE...POLICY JURID   INT/LAW
NEW/IDEA OBS TIME/SEQ TREND CHARTS 20 TREATY.
PAGE 105 E2101

B58
BOWETT D.W.,SELF-DEFENSE IN INTERNATIONAL LAW.   ADJUD
EUR+WWI MOD/EUR WOR+45 WOR-45 SOCIETY INT/ORG   CONCPT
CONSULT DIPLOM LEGIT COERCE ATTIT ORD/FREE...JURID   WAR
20 UN. PAGE 14 E0276   INT/LAW

B58
HENKIN L.,ARMS CONTROL AND INSPECTION IN AMERICAN   USA+45
LAW. LAW CONSTN INT/ORG LOC/G MUNIC NAT/G PROVS   JURID
EDU/PROP LEGIT EXEC NUC/PWR KNOWL ORD/FREE...OBS   ARMS/CONT
TOT/POP CONGRESS 20. PAGE 52 E1032

B58
HUNT B.I.,BIPARTISANSHIP: A CASE STUDY OF THE   FOR/AID
FOREIGN ASSISTANCE PROGRAM, 1947-56 (DOCTORAL   POL/PAR
THESIS). USA+45 INT/ORG CONSULT LEGIS TEC/DEV   GP/REL
...BIBLIOG PRESIDENT TREATY NATO TRUMAN/HS   DIPLOM
EISNHWR/DD CONGRESS. PAGE 56 E1114

B58
JENKS C.W.,THE COMMON LAW OF MANKIND. EUR+WWI   JURID
MOD/EUR SPACE WOR+45 INT/ORG BAL/PWR ARMS/CONT   SOVEREIGN
COERCE SUPEGO MORAL...TREND 20. PAGE 58 E1154

B58
MANSERGH N.,COMMONWEALTH PERSPECTIVES. GHANA UK LAW   DIPLOM
VOL/ASSN CONFER HEALTH SOVEREIGN...GEOG CHARTS   COLONIAL
ANTHOL 20 CMN/WLTH AUSTRAL. PAGE 68 E1363   INT/ORG
  INGP/REL

B58
MOSKOWITZ M.,HUMAN RIGHTS AND WORLD ORDER. INT/ORG   DIPLOM
PLAN GP/REL NAT/LISM SOVEREIGN...CONCPT 20 UN   INT/LAW
TREATY CIV/RIGHTS. PAGE 75 E1502   ORD/FREE

B58
RUSSELL R.B.,A HISTORY OF THE UNITED NATIONS   USA-45
CHARTER: THE ROLE OF THE UNITED STATES. SOCIETY   INT/ORG
NAT/G CONSULT DOMIN LEGIT ATTIT ORD/FREE PWR   CONSTN
...POLICY JURID CONCPT UN LEAGUE/NAT. PAGE 87 E1737

B58
SEYID MUHAMMAD V.A.,THE LEGAL FRAMEWORK OF WORLD   INT/LAW
TRADE. WOR+45 INT/ORG DIPLOM CONTROL...BIBLIOG 20   VOL/ASSN
TREATY UN IMF GATT. PAGE 90 E1807   INT/TRADE
  TARIFFS

B58
SOC OF COMP LEGIS AND INT LAW,THE LAW OF THE SEA...   INT/LAW
(PAMPHLET). WOR+45 NAT/G INT/TRADE ADJUD CONTROL   INT/ORG
NUC/PWR WAR PEACE ATTIT ORD/FREE...JURID CHARTS 20   DIPLOM
UN TREATY RESOURCE/N. PAGE 92 E1850   SEA

B58
STONE J.,AGGRESSION AND WORLD ORDER: A CRITIQUE OF   ORD/FREE
UNITED NATIONS THEORIES OF AGGRESSION. LAW CONSTN   INT/ORG
DELIB/GP PROB/SOLV BAL/PWR DIPLOM DEBATE ADJUD   WAR
CRIME PWR...POLICY IDEA/COMP 20 UN SUEZ LEAGUE/NAT.   CONCPT
PAGE 94 E1879

L58
INT. SOC. SCI. BULL.,"TECHNIQUES OF MEDIATION AND   VOL/ASSN
CONCILIATION." EUR+WWI USA+45 SOCIETY INDUS INT/ORG   DELIB/GP

LABOR NAT/G LEGIS DIPLOM EDU/PROP CHOOSE ATTIT   INT/LAW
RIGID/FLEX...JURID CONCPT GEN/LAWS 20. PAGE 57
E1129

L58
UNESCO,"TECHNIQUES OF MEDIATION AND CONCILIATION."   INT/ORG
EUR+WWI WOR+45 INDUS FACE/GP EX/STRUC   CONSULT
EDU/PROP LEGIT PEACE ORD/FREE...INT/LAW TIME/SEQ   DIPLOM
LEAGUE/NAT 20. PAGE 98 E1961

S58
MCDOUGAL M.S.,"PERSPECTIVES FOR A LAW OF OUTER   INT/ORG
SPACE." FUT WOR+45 AIR CONSULT DELIB/GP TEC/DEV   SPACE
CT/SYS ORD/FREE...POLICY JURID 20 UN. PAGE 70 E1404   INT/LAW

S58
STAAR R.F.,"ELECTIONS IN COMMUNIST POLAND." EUR+WWI   COM
SOCIETY INT/ORG NAT/G POL/PAR LEGIS ACT/RES ECO/TAC   CHOOSE
EDU/PROP ADJUD ADMIN ROUTINE COERCE TOTALISM ATTIT   POLAND
ORD/FREE PWR 20. PAGE 93 E1864

C58
RAJAN M.S.,"UNITED NATIONS AND DOMESTIC   INT/LAW
JURISDICTION." WOR+45 WOR-45 PARL/PROC...IDEA/COMP   DIPLOM
BIBLIOG 20 UN. PAGE 83 E1670   CONSTN
  INT/ORG

B59
BROOKES E.H.,THE COMMONWEALTH TODAY. UK ROMAN/EMP   FEDERAL
INT/ORG RACE/REL NAT/LISM SOVEREIGN...TREND   DIPLOM
SOC/INTEG 20. PAGE 16 E0307   JURID
  IDEA/COMP

B59
COMM. STUDY ORGAN. PEACE,ORGANIZING PEACE IN THE   INT/ORG
NUCLEAR AGE. FUT CONSULT DELIB/GP DOMIN ADJUD   ACT/RES
ROUTINE COERCE ORD/FREE...TECHNIC INT/LAW JURID   NUC/PWR
NEW/IDEA UN COLD/WAR 20. PAGE 24 E0483

B59
CORBETT P.E.,LAW IN DIPLOMACY. UK USA+45 USSR   NAT/G
CONSTN SOCIETY INT/ORG JUDGE LEGIT ATTIT ORD/FREE   ADJUD
TOT/POP LEAGUE/NAT 20. PAGE 26 E0507   JURID
  DIPLOM

B59
GREENSPAN M.,THE MODERN LAW OF LAND WARFARE. WOR+45   ADJUD
INT/ORG NAT/G DELIB/GP FORCES ATTIT...POLICY   PWR
HYPO/EXP STERTYP 20. PAGE 46 E0911   WAR

B59
HALEY A.G.,FIRST COLLOQUIUM ON THE LAW OF OUTER   SPACE
SPACE. WOR+45 INT/ORG ACT/RES PLAN BAL/PWR CONFER   LAW
ATTIT PWR...POLICY JURID CHARTS ANTHOL 20. PAGE 49   SOVEREIGN
E0979   CONTROL

B59
REIFF H.,THE UNITED STATES AND THE TREATY LAW OF   ADJUD
THE SEA. USA+45 USA-45 SEA SOCIETY INT/ORG CONSULT   INT/LAW
DELIB/GP LEGIS DIPLOM LEGIT ATTIT ORD/FREE PWR
WEALTH...GEOG JURID TOT/POP 20 TREATY. PAGE 84
E1681

B59
SCHNEIDER J.,TREATY-MAKING POWER OF INTERNATIONAL   INT/ORG
ORGANIZATIONS. FUT WOR+45 WOR-45 LAW NAT/G JUDGE   ROUTINE
DIPLOM LEGIT CT/SYS ORD/FREE PWR...INT/LAW JURID
GEN/LAWS TOT/POP UNESCO 20 TREATY. PAGE 88 E1762

B59
SIMPSON J.L.,INTERNATIONAL ARBITRATION: LAW AND   INT/LAW
PRACTICE. WOR+45 WOR-45 INT/ORG DELIB/GP ADJUD   DIPLOM
PEACE MORAL ORD/FREE...METH 18/20. PAGE 91 E1829   CT/SYS
  CONSULT

B59
WOETZEL R.K.,DIE INTERNATIONALE KONTROLLE DER   SPACE
HOHEREN LUFTSCHICHTEN UND DES WELTRAUMS. INT/ORG   INT/LAW
NAT/G CONTROL SUPEGO...JURID CONCPT 20. PAGE 107   DIPLOM
E2136   SOVEREIGN

S59
CARLSTON K.S.,"NATIONALIZATION: AN ANALYTIC   INDUS
APPROACH." WOR+45 INT/ORG ECO/TAC DOMIN LEGIT ADJUD   NAT/G
COERCE ORD/FREE PWR WEALTH SOCISM...JURID CONCPT   NAT/LISM
TREND STERTYP TOT/POP VAL/FREE 20. PAGE 19 E0380   SOVEREIGN

S59
JENKS C.W.,"THE CHALLENGE OF UNIVERSALITY." FUT   INT/ORG
UNIV CONSTN CULTURE CONSULT CREATE PLAN LEGIT ATTIT   LAW
MORAL ORD/FREE RESPECT...MAJORIT JURID 20. PAGE 58   PEACE
E1155   INT/LAW

S59
POTTER P.B.,"OBSTACLES AND ALTERNATIVES TO   INT/ORG
INTERNATIONAL LAW." WOR+45 NAT/G VOL/ASSN DELIB/GP   LAW

BAL/PWR DOMIN ROUTINE...JURID VAL/FREE 20. PAGE 81
E1632

DIPLOM
INT/LAW

S59

PUGWASH CONFERENCE,"ON BIOLOGICAL AND CHEMICAL
WARFARE." WOR+45 SOCIETY PROC/MFG INT/ORG FORCES
EDU/PROP ADJUD RIGID/FLEX ORD/FREE PWR...DECISION
PSY NEW/IDEA MATH VAL/FREE 20. PAGE 83 E1661

ACT/RES
BIO/SOC
WAR
WEAPON

S59

SOHN L.B.,"THE DEFINITION OF AGGRESSION." FUT LAW
FORCES LEGIT ADJUD ROUTINE COERCE ORD/FREE PWR
...MAJORIT JURID QUANT COLD/WAR 20. PAGE 92 E1855

INT/ORG
CT/SYS
DETER
SOVEREIGN

S59

STONE J.,"CONFLICT MANAGEMENT THROUGH CONTEMPORARY
INTERNATIONAL LAW." WOR+45 LAW
NAT/G CREATE BAL/PWR DOMIN LEGIT ROUTINE COERCE
ATTIT ORD/FREE PWR SOVEREIGN...JURID 20. PAGE 94
E1880

INT/ORG
INT/LAW

S59

SUTTON F.X.,"REPRESENTATION AND THE NATURE OF
POLITICAL SYSTEMS." UNIV WOR-45 CULTURE SOCIETY
STRATA INT/ORG FORCES JUDGE DOMIN LEGIT EXEC REGION
REPRESENT ATTIT ORD/FREE RESPECT...SOC HIST/WRIT
TIME/SEQ. PAGE 95 E1896

NAT/G
CONCPT

S59

TIPTON J.B.,"PARTICIPATION OF THE UNITED STATES IN
THE INTERNATIONAL LABOR ORGANIZATION." WOR+45 LAW
STRUCT ECO/DEV ECO/UNDEV INDUS TEC/DEV ECO/TAC
ADMIN PERCEPT ORD/FREE SKILL...STAT HIST/WRIT
GEN/METH ILO WORK 20. PAGE 96 E1928

LABOR
INT/ORG

B60

CLARK G.,WORLD PEACE THROUGH WORLD LAW. FUT WOR+45
CONSULT FORCES ACT/RES CREATE PLAN ADMIN ROUTINE
ARMS/CONT DETER ATTIT PWR...JURID VAL/FREE UNESCO
20 UN. PAGE 23 E0449

INT/ORG
LAW
PEACE
INT/LAW

B60

DUMON F.,LA COMMUNAUTE FRANCO-AFRO-MALGACHE: SES
ORIGINES, SES INSTITUTIONS, SON EVOLUTION. FRANCE
MADAGASCAR POL/PAR DIPLOM ADMIN ATTIT...TREND T 20.
PAGE 33 E0657

JURID
INT/ORG
AFR
CONSTN

B60

ENGEL J.,THE SECURITY OF THE FREE WORLD. USSR
WOR+45 STRATA STRUCT ECO/DEV ECO/UNDEV INT/ORG
DELIB/GP FORCES DOMIN LEGIT ADJUD EXEC ARMS/CONT
COERCE...POLICY CONCPT NEW/IDEA TIME/SEQ GEN/LAWS
COLD/WAR WORK UN 20 NATO. PAGE 35 E0689

COM
TREND
DIPLOM

B60

FISCHER L.,THE SOVIETS IN WORLD AFFAIRS. CHINA/COM
COM EUR+WWI USSR INT/ORG CONFER LEAD ARMS/CONT REV
PWR...CHARTS 20 TREATY VERSAILLES. PAGE 38 E0755

DIPLOM
NAT/G
POLICY
MARXISM

B60

HEYSE T.,PROBLEMS FONCIERS ET REGIME DES TERRES
(ASPECTS ECONOMIQUES, JURIDIQUES ET SOCIAUX). AFR
CONGO/BRAZ INT/ORG DIPLOM SOVEREIGN...GEOG TREATY
20. PAGE 52 E1037

BIBLIOG
AGRI
ECO/UNDEV
LEGIS

B60

JENNINGS R.,PROGRESS OF INTERNATIONAL LAW. FUT
WOR+45 WOR-45 SOCIETY NAT/G VOL/ASSN DELIB/GP
DIPLOM EDU/PROP LEGIT COERCE ATTIT DRIVE MORAL
ORD/FREE...JURID CONCPT OBS TIME/SEQ TREND
GEN/LAWS. PAGE 58 E1164

INT/ORG
LAW
INT/LAW

B60

UNITED WORLD FEDERALISTS,UNITED WORLD FEDERALISTS;
PANORAMA OF RECENT BOOKS, FILMS, AND JOURNALS ON
WORLD FEDERATION, THE UN, AND WORLD PEACE. CULTURE
ECO/UNDEV PROB/SOLV FOR/AID ARMS/CONT NUC/PWR
...INT/LAW PHIL/SCI 20 UN. PAGE 98 E1971

BIBLIOG/A
DIPLOM
INT/ORG
PEACE

B60

WOETZEL R.K.,THE INTERNATIONAL CONTROL OF AIRSPACE
AND OUTERSPACE. FUT WOR+45 AIR CONSTN STRUCT
CONSULT PLAN TEC/DEV ADJUD RIGID/FLEX KNOWL
ORD/FREE PWR...TECHNIC GEOG MGT NEW/IDEA TREND
COMPUT/IR VAL/FREE 20 TREATY. PAGE 107 E2137

INT/ORG
JURID
SPACE
INT/LAW

L60

DEAN A.W.,"SECOND GENEVA CONFERENCE OF THE LAW OF
THE SEA: THE FIGHT FOR FREEDOM OF THE SEAS." FUT
USA+45 USSR WOR+45 WOR-45 SEA CONSTN STRUCT PLAN
INT/TRADE ADJUD ADMIN ORD/FREE...DECISION RECORD
TREND GEN/LAWS 20 TREATY. PAGE 30 E0600

INT/ORG
JURID
INT/LAW

L60

KUNZ J.,"SANCTIONS IN INTERNATIONAL LAW." WOR+45
WOR-45 LEGIT ARMS/CONT COERCE PEACE ATTIT
...METH/CNCPT TIME/SEQ TREND 20. PAGE 62 E1234

INT/ORG
ADJUD
INT/LAW

L60

LAUTERPACHT E.,"THE SUEZ CANAL SETTLEMENT." FRANCE
ISLAM ISRAEL UAR UK BAL/PWR DIPLOM LEGIT...JURID
GEN/LAWS ANTHOL SUEZ VAL/FREE 20. PAGE 63 E1263

INT/ORG
LAW

S60

GRACIA-MORA M.R.,"INTERNATIONAL RESPONSIBILITY FOR
SUBVERSIVE ACTIVITIES AND HOSTILE PROPAGANDA BY
PRIVATE PERSONS AGAINST." COM EUR+WWI L/A+17C UK
USA+45 USSR WOR-45 CONSTN NAT/G LEGIT ADJUD REV
PEACE TOTALISM ORD/FREE...INT/LAW 20. PAGE 45 E0895

INT/ORG
JURID
SOVEREIGN

S60

O'BRIEN W.,"THE ROLE OF FORCE IN THE INTERNATIONAL
JURIDICAL ORDER." WOR+45 NAT/G FORCES DOMIN ADJUD
ARMS/CONT DETER NUC/PWR WAR ATTIT PWR...CATH
INT/LAW JURID CONCPT TREND STERTYP GEN/LAWS 20.
PAGE 78 E1564

INT/ORG
COERCE

S60

POTTER P.B.,"RELATIVE VALUES OF INTERNATIONAL
RELATIONS, LAW, AND ORGANIZATIONS." WOR+45 NAT/G
LEGIT ADJUD ORD/FREE...CONCPT TOT/POP COLD/WAR 20.
PAGE 81 E1633

INT/ORG
LEGIS
DIPLOM
INT/LAW

S60

SCHACHTER O.,"THE ENFORCEMENT OF INTERNATIONAL
JUDICIAL AND ARBITRAL DECISIONS." WOR+45 NAT/G
ECO/TAC DOMIN LEGIT ROUTINE COERCE ATTIT DRIVE
ALL/VALS PWR...METH/CNCPT TREND TOT/POP 20 UN.
PAGE 87 E1750

INT/ORG
ADJUD
INT/LAW

S60

SCHWELB E.,"INTERNATIONAL CONVENTIONS ON HUMAN
RIGHTS." FUT WOR+45 LAW CONSTN CULTURE SOCIETY
STRUCT VOL/ASSN DELIB/GP PLAN ADJUD SUPEGO LOVE
MORAL...SOC CONCPT STAT RECORD HIST/WRIT TREND 20
UN. PAGE 89 E1790

INT/ORG
HUM

S60

THOMPSON K.W.,"MORAL PURPOSE IN FOREIGN POLICY:
REALITIES AND ILLUSIONS." WOR+45 WOR-45 LAW CULTURE
SOCIETY INT/ORG PLAN ADJUD ADMIN COERCE RIGID/FLEX
SUPEGO KNOWL ORD/FREE PWR...SOC TREND SOC/EXP
TOT/POP 20. PAGE 96 E1921

MORAL
JURID
DIPLOM

B61

ANAND R.P.,COMPULSORY JURISDICTION OF INTERNATIONAL
COURT OF JUSTICE. FUT WOR+45 SOCIETY PLAN LEGIT
ADJUD ATTIT DRIVE PERSON ORD/FREE...JURID CONCPT
TREND 20 ICJ. PAGE 5 E0086

INT/ORG
COERCE
INT/LAW

B61

CONFERENCE ATLANTIC COMMUNITY,AN INTRODUCTORY
BIBLIOGRAPHY. COM WOR+45 FORCES DIPLOM ECO/TAC WAR
...INT/LAW HIST/WRIT COLD/WAR NATO. PAGE 25 E0485

BIBLIOG/A
CON/ANAL
INT/ORG

B61

JENKS C.W.,INTERNATIONAL IMMUNITIES. PLAN EDU/PROP
ADMIN PERCEPT...OLD/LIB JURID CONCPT TREND TOT/POP.
PAGE 58 E1157

INT/ORG
DIPLOM

B61

KAPLAN M.A.,THE POLITICAL FOUNDATIONS OF
INTERNATIONAL LAW. WOR+45 WOR-45 CULTURE SOCIETY
ECO/DEV DIPLOM PERCEPT...TECHNIC METH/CNCPT.
PAGE 59 E1184

INT/ORG
LAW

B61

LARSON A.,WHEN NATIONS DISAGREE. USA+45 WOR+45
INT/ORG ADJUD COERCE CRIME OWN SOVEREIGN...POLICY
JURID 20. PAGE 63 E1258

INT/LAW
DIPLOM
WAR

B61

MCDOUGAL M.S.,LAW AND MINIMUM WORLD PUBLIC ORDER.
WOR+45 SOCIETY NAT/G DELIB/GP EDU/PROP LEGIT ADJUD
COERCE ATTIT PERSON...JURID CONCPT RECORD TREND
TOT/POP 20. PAGE 70 E1406

INT/ORG
ORD/FREE
INT/LAW

B61

MECHAM J.L.,THE UNITED STATES AND INTER-AMERICAN
SECURITY, 1889-1960. L/A+17C USA+45 USA-45 CONSTN
FORCES INT/TRADE PEACE TOTALISM ATTIT...JURID 19/20
UN OAS. PAGE 72 E1432

DIPLOM
WAR
ORD/FREE
INT/LAW

B61

RIENOW R.,CONTEMPORARY INTERNATIONAL POLITICS.
WOR+45 INT/ORG BAL/PWR EDU/PROP COLONIAL NEUTRAL
REGION WAR PEACE...INT/LAW 20 COLD/WAR UN. PAGE 85
E1698

DIPLOM
PWR
POLICY
NAT/G

B61
ROBERTSON A.H.,THE LAW OF INTERNATIONAL RIGID/FLEX
INSTITUTIONS IN EUROPE. EUR+WWI MOD/EUR INT/ORG ORD/FREE
NAT/G VOL/ASSN DELIB/GP...JURID TIME/SEQ TOT/POP 20
TREATY. PAGE 85 E1704

B61
WRIGHT Q.,THE ROLE OF INTERNATIONAL LAW IN THE INT/ORG
ELIMINATION OF WAR. FUT WOR+45 WOR-45 NAT/G BAL/PWR ADJUD
DIPLOM DOMIN LEGIT PWR...POLICY INT/LAW JURID ARMS/CONT
CONCPT TIME/SEQ TREND GEN/LAWS COLD/WAR 20.
PAGE 108 E2158

L61
SAND P.T.,"AN HISTORICAL SURVEY OF INTERNATIONAL INT/ORG
AIR LAW SINCE 1944." USA+45 USA-45 WOR+45 WOR-45 LAW
SOCIETY ECO/DEV NAT/G CONSULT EX/STRUC ACT/RES PLAN INT/LAW
LEGIT ROUTINE...JURID CONCPT METH/CNCPT TREND 20. SPACE
PAGE 87 E1744

L61
TAUBENFELD H.J.,"A TREATY FOR ANTARCTICA." FUT R+D
USA+45 INTELL INT/ORG LABOR 20 TREATY ANTARCTICA. ACT/RES
PAGE 95 E1909 DIPLOM

L61
TAUBENFELD H.J.,"A REGIME FOR OUTER SPACE." FUT INT/ORG
UNIV R+D ACT/RES PLAN BAL/PWR LEGIT ARMS/CONT ADJUD
ORD/FREE...POLICY JURID TREND UN TOT/POP 20 SPACE
COLD/WAR. PAGE 95 E1910

S61
ALGER C.F.,"NON-RESOLUTION CONSEQUENCES OF THE INT/ORG
UNITED NATIONS AND THEIR EFFECT ON INTERNATIONAL DRIVE
CONFLICT." WOR+45 CONSTN ECO/DEV NAT/G CONSULT BAL/PWR
DELIB/GP TOP/EX ACT/RES PLAN DIPLOM EDU/PROP
ROUTINE ATTIT ALL/VALS...INT/LAW TOT/POP UN 20.
PAGE 3 E0065

S61
CASTANEDA J.,"THE UNDERDEVELOPED NATIONS AND THE INT/ORG
DEVELOPMENT OF INTERNATIONAL LAW." FUT UNIV LAW ECO/UNDEV
ACT/RES FOR/AID LEGIT PERCEPT SKILL...JURID PEACE
METH/CNCPT TIME/SEQ TOT/POP 20 UN. PAGE 21 E0405 INT/LAW

S61
JACKSON E.,"THE FUTURE DEVELOPMENT OF THE UNITED INT/ORG
NATIONS: SOME SUGGESTIONS FOR RESEARCH." FUT LAW PWR
CONSTN ECO/DEV FINAN PEACE WEALTH...WELF/ST CONCPT
UN 20. PAGE 57 E1140

S61
LIPSON L.,"AN ARGUMENT ON THE LEGALITY OF INT/ORG
RECONNAISSANCE STATELLITES." COM USA+45 USSR WOR+45 LAW
AIR INTELL NAT/G CONSULT PLAN DIPLOM LEGIT ROUTINE SPACE
ATTIT...INT/LAW JURID CONCPT METH/CNCPT TREND
COLD/WAR 20. PAGE 65 E1302

S61
MILLER E.,"LEGAL ASPECTS OF UN ACTION IN THE INT/ORG
CONGO." AFR CULTURE ADMIN PEACE DRIVE RIGID/FLEX LEGIT
ORD/FREE...WELF/ST JURID OBS UN CONGO 20. PAGE 73
E1458

B62
ALEXANDROWICZ C.H.,WORLD ECONOMIC AGENCIES: LAW AND INT/LAW
PRACTICE. WOR+45 DIST/IND FINAN LABOR CONSULT INT/ORG
INT/TRADE TARIFFS REPRESENT HEALTH...JURID 20 UN DIPLOM
GATT EEC OAS ECSC. PAGE 3 E0063 ADJUD

B62
BEBR G.,JUDICIAL CONTROL OF THE EUROPEAN ADJUD
COMMUNITIES. EUR+WWI INT/ORG NAT/G DOMIN LEGIT PWR VOL/ASSN
...JURID CONCPT GEN/LAWS GEN/METH EEC 20. PAGE 9 INT/LAW
E0168

B62
BIBLIOTHEQUE PALAIS DE LA PAIX,CATALOGUE OF THE BIBLIOG
PEACE PALACE LIBRARY, SUPPLEMENT 1937-1952 (7 INT/LAW
VOLS.). WOR+45 WOR-45 INT/ORG NAT/G ADJUD WAR PEACE DIPLOM
...JURID 20. PAGE 12 E0225

B62
BISHOP W.W. JR.,INTERNATIONAL LAW: CASES AND INT/LAW
MATERIALS. WOR+45 INT/ORG FORCES PROB/SOLV AGREE DIPLOM
WAR...JURID IDEA/COMP T 20 TREATY. PAGE 12 E0233 CONCPT
CT/SYS

B62
CARLSTON K.S.,LAW AND ORGANIZATION IN WORLD INT/ORG
SOCIETY. WOR+45 FINAN ECO/TAC DOMIN LEGIT CT/SYS LAW
ROUTINE COERCE ORD/FREE PWR WEALTH...PLURIST
DECISION JURID MGT METH/CNCPT GEN/LAWS 20. PAGE 19
E0381

B62
CRANSTON M.,WHAT ARE HUMAN RIGHTS? UNIV WOR+45 LAW
INT/ORG MORAL...POLICY CONCPT METH/CNCPT GEN/LAWS ORD/FREE
20. PAGE 28 E0545 JURID
IDEA/COMP

B62
DOUGLAS W.O.,DEMOCRACY'S MANIFESTO. COM USA+45 DIPLOM
ECO/UNDEV INT/ORG FORCES PLAN NEUTRAL TASK MARXISM POLICY
...JURID 20 NATO SEATO. PAGE 32 E0642 NAT/G
ORD/FREE

B62
DUROSELLE J.B.,HISTOIRE DIPLOMATIQUE DE 1919 A NOS DIPLOM
JOURS (3RD ED.). FRANCE INT/ORG CHIEF FORCES CONFER WOR+45
ARMS/CONT WAR PEACE ORD/FREE...T TREATY 20 WOR-45
COLD/WAR. PAGE 34 E0667

B62
HADWEN J.G.,HOW UNITED NATIONS DECISIONS ARE MADE. INT/ORG
WOR+45 LAW EDU/PROP LEGIT ADMIN PWR...DECISION ROUTINE
SELF/OBS GEN/LAWS UN 20. PAGE 49 E0972

B62
JENKS C.W.,THE PROPER LAW OF INTERNATIONAL LAW
ORGANISATIONS. DIPLOM LEGIT AGREE CT/SYS SANCTION INT/ORG
REPRESENT SOVEREIGN...GEN/LAWS 20 UN UNESCO ILO ADJUD
NATO OAS. PAGE 58 E1158 INT/LAW

B62
LAWSON R.,INTERNATIONAL REGIONAL ORGANIZATIONS. INT/ORG
WOR+45 NAT/G VOL/ASSN CONSULT LEGIS EDU/PROP LEGIT DELIB/GP
ADMIN EXEC ROUTINE HEALTH PWR WEALTH...JURID EEC REGION
COLD/WAR 20 UN. PAGE 63 E1270

B62
LEVY H.V.,LIBERDADE E JUSTICA SOCIAL (2ND ED.). ORD/FREE
BRAZIL COM L/A+17C USSR INT/ORG PARTIC GP/REL MARXISM
WEALTH 20 UN COM/PARTY. PAGE 65 E1290 CAP/ISM
LAW

B62
LILLICH R.B.,INTERNATIONAL CLAIMS: THEIR ADJUD
ADJUDICATION BY NATIONAL COMMISSIONS. WOR+45 WOR-45 JURID
INT/ORG LEGIT CT/SYS TOT/POP 20. PAGE 65 E1297 INT/LAW

B62
MCDOUGAL M.S.,THE PUBLIC ORDER OF THE OCEANS. ADJUD
WOR+45 WOR-45 SEA INT/ORG NAT/G CONSULT DELIB/GP ORD/FREE
DIPLOM LEGIT PEACE RIGID/FLEX...GEOG INT/LAW JURID
RECORD TOT/POP 20 TREATY. PAGE 70 E1407

B62
NORGAARD C.A.,THE POSITION OF THE INDIVIDUAL IN INT/LAW
INTERNATIONAL LAW. INT/ORG SUPEGO ORD/FREE DIPLOM
SOVEREIGN...CONCPT 20 UN. PAGE 78 E1556 CRIME
JURID

B62
PERKINS D.,AMERICA'S QUEST FOR PEACE. USA+45 WOR+45 INT/LAW
DIPLOM CONFER NAT/LISM ATTIT 20 UN TREATY. PAGE 80 INT/ORG
E1610 ARMS/CONT
PEACE

B62
PHILLIPS O.H.,CONSTITUTIONAL AND ADMINISTRATIVE LAW JURID
(3RD ED.). UK INT/ORG LOC/G CHIEF EX/STRUC LEGIS ADMIN
BAL/PWR ADJUD COLONIAL CT/SYS PWR...CHARTS 20. CONSTN
PAGE 80 E1613 NAT/G

B62
ROSENNE S.,THE WORLD COURT: WHAT IT IS AND HOW IT INT/ORG
WORKS. WOR+45 WOR-45 LAW CONSTN JUDGE EDU/PROP ADJUD
LEGIT ROUTINE CHOOSE PEACE ORD/FREE...JURID OBS INT/LAW
TIME/SEQ CHARTS UN TOT/POP VAL/FREE 20. PAGE 86
E1717

B62
SCHWARTZ L.E.,INTERNATIONAL ORGANIZATIONS AND SPACE INT/ORG
COOPERATION. VOL/ASSN CONSULT CREATE TEC/DEV DIPLOM
SANCTION...POLICY INT/LAW PHIL/SCI 20 UN. PAGE 89 R+D
E1787 SPACE

B62
SCHWARZENBERGER G.,THE FRONTIERS OF INTERNATIONAL INT/ORG
LAW. WOR+45 WOR-45 NAT/G LEGIT CT/SYS ROUTINE MORAL LAW
ORD/FREE PWR...JURID SOC GEN/METH 20 COLD/WAR. INT/LAW
PAGE 89 E1789

B62
TRISKA J.F.,THE THEORY, LAW, AND POLICY OF SOVIET COM
TREATIES. WOR+45 WOR-45 CONSTN INT/ORG NAT/G LAW
VOL/ASSN DOMIN LEGIT COERCE ATTIT PWR RESPECT INT/LAW
...POLICY JURID CONCPT OBS SAMP TIME/SEQ TREND USSR
GEN/LAWS 20. PAGE 97 E1941

UNECA LIBRARY,NEW ACQUISITIONS IN THE UNECA
LIBRARY. LAW NAT/G PLAN PROB/SOLV TEC/DEV ADMIN
REGION...GEOG SOC 20 UN. PAGE 98 E1956

B62
BIBLIOG
AFR
ECO/UNDEV
INT/ORG

WADSWORTH J.J.,THE PRICE OF PEACE. WOR+45 TEC/DEV
CONTROL NUC/PWR PEACE ATTIT TREATY 20. PAGE 104
E2089

B62
DIPLOM
INT/ORG
ARMS/CONT
POLICY

WOETZEL R.K.,THE NURENBERG TRIALS IN INTERNATIONAL
LAW. CHRIST-17C MOD/EUR WOR+45 SOCIETY NAT/G
DELIB/GP DOMIN LEGIT ROUTINE ATTIT DRIVE PERSON
SUPEGO MORAL ORD/FREE...POLICY MAJORIT JURID PSY
SOC SELF/OBS RECORD NAZI TOT/POP. PAGE 107 E2138

B62
INT/ORG
ADJUD
WAR

CORET A.,"L'INDEPENDANCE DU SAMOA OCCIDENTAL."
S/ASIA LAW INT/ORG EXEC ALL/VALS SAMOA UN 20.
PAGE 26 E0508

L62
NAT/G
STRUCT
SOVEREIGN

GROSS L.,"IMMUNITIES AND PRIVILEGES OF DELIGATIONS
TO THE UNITED NATIONS." USA+45 WOR+45 STRATA NAT/G
VOL/ASSN CONSULT DIPLOM EDU/PROP ROUTINE RESPECT
...POLICY INT/LAW CONCPT UN 20. PAGE 48 E0950

L62
INT/ORG
LAW
ELITES

MURACCIOLE L.,"LA LOI FONDAMENTALE DE LA REPUBLIQUE
DU CONGO." WOR+45 SOCIETY ECO/UNDEV INT/ORG NAT/G
LEGIS PLAN LEGIT ADJUD COLONIAL ROUTINE ATTIT
SOVEREIGN 20 CONGO. PAGE 75 E1504

L62
AFR
CONSTN

NIZARD L.,"CUBAN QUESTION AND SECURITY COUNCIL."
L/A+17C USA+45 ECO/UNDEV NAT/G POL/PAR DELIB/GP
ECO/TAC PWR...RELATIV OBS TIME/SEQ TREND GEN/LAWS
UN 20 UN. PAGE 77 E1551

L62
INT/ORG
JURID
DIPLOM
CUBA

PETKOFF D.K.,"RECOGNITION AND NON-RECOGNITION OF
STATES AND GOVERNMENTS IN INTERNATIONAL LAW." ASIA
COM USA+45 WOR+45 NAT/G ACT/RES DIPLOM DOMIN LEGIT
COERCE ORD/FREE PWR...CONCPT GEN/LAWS 20. PAGE 80
E1611

L62
INT/ORG
LAW
INT/LAW

STEIN E.,"MR HAMMARSKJOLD, THE CHARTER LAW AND THE
FUTURE ROLE OF THE UNITED NATIONS SECRETARY-
GENERAL." WOR+45 CONSTN INT/ORG DELIB/GP FORCES
TOP/EX BAL/PWR LEGIT ROUTINE RIGID/FLEX PWR
...POLICY JURID OBS STERTYP UN COLD/WAR 20
HAMMARSK/D. PAGE 93 E1869

L62
CONCPT
BIOG

CRANE R.D.,"LAW AND STRATEGY IN SPACE." FUT USA+45
WOR+45 AIR LAW INT/ORG NAT/G FORCES ACT/RES PLAN
BAL/PWR LEGIT ARMS/CONT COERCE ORD/FREE...POLICY
INT/LAW JURID SOC/EXP 20 TREATY. PAGE 27 E0542

S62
CONCPT
SPACE

FALK R.A.,"THE REALITY OF INTERNATIONAL LAW."
WOR+45 NAT/G LEGIT COERCE DETER WAR MORAL ORD/FREE
PWR SOVEREIGN...JURID CONCPT VAL/FREE COLD/WAR 20.
PAGE 36 E0714

S62
INT/ORG
ADJUD
NUC/PWR
INT/LAW

FENWICK C.G.,"ISSUES AT PUNTA DEL ESTE: NON-
INTERVENTION VS COLLECTIVE SECURITY." L/A+17C
USA+45 VOL/ASSN DELIB/GP ECO/TAC LEGIT ADJUD REGION
ORD/FREE OAS COLD/WAR 20. PAGE 37 E0738

S62
INT/ORG
CUBA

FINKELSTEIN L.S.,"THE UNITED NATIONS AND
ORGANIZATIONS FOR CONTROL OF ARMAMENT." FUT WOR+45
VOL/ASSN DELIB/GP TOP/EX CREATE EDU/PROP LEGIT
ADJUD NUC/PWR ATTIT RIGID/FLEX ORD/FREE...POLICY
DECISION CONCPT OBS TREND GEN/LAWS TOT/POP
COLD/WAR. PAGE 38 E0752

S62
INT/ORG
PWR
ARMS/CONT

GRAVEN J.,"LE MOUVEAU DROIT PENAL INTERNATIONAL."
UNIV STRUCT LEGIS ACT/RES CRIME ATTIT PERCEPT
PERSON...JURID CONCPT 20. PAGE 45 E0899

S62
CT/SYS
PUB/INST
INT/ORG
INT/LAW

GREEN L.C.,"POLITICAL OFFENSES, WAR CRIMES AND
EXTRADITION." WOR+45 YUGOSLAVIA INT/ORG LEGIT
ROUTINE WAR ORD/FREE SOVEREIGN...JURID NAZI 20
INTERPOL. PAGE 46 E0906

S62
LAW
CONCPT
INT/LAW

GREENSPAN M.,"INTERNATIONAL LAW AND ITS PROTECTION
FOR PARTICIPANTS IN UNCONVENTIONAL WARFARE." WOR+45
LAW INT/ORG NAT/G POL/PAR COERCE REV ORD/FREE
...INT/LAW TOT/POP 20. PAGE 46 E0912

S62
FORCES
JURID
GUERRILLA
WAR

MANGIN G.,"LES ACCORDS DE COOPERATION EN MATIERE DE
JUSTICE ENTRE LA FRANCE ET LES ETATS AFRICAINS ET
MALGACHE." AFR ISLAM WOR+45 STRUCT ECO/UNDEV NAT/G
DELIB/GP PERCEPT ALL/VALS...JURID MGT TIME/SEQ 20.
PAGE 68 E1356

S62
INT/ORG
LAW
FRANCE

SCHACHTER O.,"DAG HAMMARSKJOLD AND THE RELATION OF
LAW TO POLITICS." FUT WOR+45 INT/ORG CONSULT PLAN
TEC/DEV BAL/PWR DIPLOM LEGIT ATTIT PERCEPT ORD/FREE
...POLICY JURID CONCPT OBS TESTS STERTYP GEN/LAWS
20 HAMMARSK/D. PAGE 87 E1751

S62
ACT/RES
ADJUD

THOMPSON D.,"THE UNITED KINGDOM AND THE TREATY OF
ROME." EUR+WWI INT/ORG NAT/G DELIB/GP LEGIS
INT/TRADE RIGID/FLEX...CONCPT EEC PARLIAMENT
CMN/WLTH 20. PAGE 96 E1918

S62
ADJUD
JURID

BOWETT D.W.,THE LAW OF INTERNATIONAL INSTITUTIONS.
WOR+45 CONSTN DELIB/GP EX/STRUC JUDGE
EDU/PROP LEGIT CT/SYS EXEC ROUTINE RIGID/FLEX
ORD/FREE PWR...JURID CONCPT ORG/CHARTS GEN/METH
LEAGUE/NAT OAS OEEC 20 UN. PAGE 14 E0277

B63
INT/ORG
ADJUD
DIPLOM

ELLERT R.B.,NATO 'FAIR TRIAL' SAFEGUARDS: PRECURSOR
TO AN INTERNATIONAL BILL OF PROCEDURAL RIGHTS.
WOR+45 FORCES CRIME CIVMIL/REL ATTIT ORD/FREE 20
NATO. PAGE 34 E0683

B63
JURID
INT/LAW
INT/ORG
CT/SYS

FALK R.A.,LAW, MORALITY, AND WAR IN THE
CONTEMPORARY WORLD. WOR+45 INT/ORG EX/STRUC
FORCES EDU/PROP LEGIT DETER NUC/PWR MORAL ORD/FREE
...JURID TOT/POP 20. PAGE 36 E0715

B63
ADJUD
ARMS/CONT
PEACE
INT/LAW

FAWCETT J.E.S.,THE BRITISH COMMONWEALTH IN
INTERNATIONAL LAW. LAW INT/ORG NAT/G VOL/ASSN
OP/RES DIPLOM ADJUD CENTRAL CONSEN...NET/THEORY
CMN/WLTH TREATY. PAGE 36 E0723

B63
INT/LAW
STRUCT
COLONIAL

HALEY A.G.,SPACE LAW AND GOVERNMENT. FUT USA+45
WOR+45 LEGIS ACT/RES CREATE ATTIT RIGID/FLEX
ORD/FREE PWR SOVEREIGN...POLICY JURID CONCPT CHARTS
VAL/FREE 20. PAGE 49 E0980

B63
INT/ORG
LAW
SPACE

HIGGINS R.,THE DEVELOPMENT OF INTERNATIONAL LAW
THROUGH THE POLITICAL ORGANS OF THE UNITED NATIONS.
WOR+45 FORCES DIPLOM AGREE COERCE ATTIT SOVEREIGN
...BIBLIOG 20 UN TREATY. PAGE 52 E1041

B63
INT/ORG
INT/LAW
TEC/DEV
JURID

LYONS F.S.L.,INTERNATIONALISM IN EUROPE 1815-1914.
LAW AGRI COM/IND DIST/IND LABOR SECT INT/TRADE
TARIFFS...BIBLIOG 19/20. PAGE 67 E1335

B63
DIPLOM
MOD/EUR
INT/ORG

ROBERTSON A.H.,HUMAN RIGHTS IN EUROPE. CONSTN
SOCIETY INT/ORG NAT/G VOL/ASSN DELIB/GP ACT/RES
PLAN ADJUD REGION ROUTINE ATTIT LOVE ORD/FREE
RESPECT...JURID SOC CONCPT SOC/EXP UN 20. PAGE 85
E1705

B63
EUR+WWI
PERSON

ROSNER G.,THE UNITED NATIONS EMERGENCY FORCE.
FRANCE ISRAEL UAR UK WOR+45 CREATE WAR PEACE
ORD/FREE PWR...INT/LAW JURID HIST/WRIT TIME/SEQ UN.
PAGE 86 E1719

B63
INT/ORG
FORCES

VAN SLYCK P.,PEACE: THE CONTROL OF NATIONAL POWER.
CUBA WOR+45 FINAN NAT/G FORCES PROB/SOLV TEC/DEV
BAL/PWR ADMIN CONTROL ORD/FREE...POLICY INT/LAW UN
COLD/WAR TREATY. PAGE 103 E2069

B63
ARMS/CONT
PEACE
INT/ORG
DIPLOM

LISSITZYN O.J.,"INTERNATIONAL LAW IN A DIVIDED
WORLD." FUT WOR+45 CONSTN CULTURE ECO/DEV ECO/UNDEV
DIST/IND NAT/G FORCES ECO/TAC LEGIT ADJUD ADMIN
COERCE ATTIT HEALTH MORAL ORD/FREE PWR RESPECT
WEALTH VAL/FREE. PAGE 65 E1306

L63
INT/ORG
LAW

MCDOUGAL M.S.,"THE ENJOYMENT AND ACQUISITION OF

L63
PLAN

RESOURCES IN OUTER SPACE." CHRIST-17C FUT WOR+45   TREND
WOR-45 LAW EXTR/IND INT/ORG ACT/RES CREATE TEC/DEV
ECO/TAC LEGIT COERCE HEALTH KNOWL ORD/FREE PWR
WEALTH...JURID HIST/WRIT VAL/FREE. PAGE 70 E1408

          S63
ALGER C.F.,"HYPOTHESES ON RELATIONSHIPS BETWEEN THE INT/ORG
ORGANIZATION OF INTERNATIONAL SOCIETY AND   LAW
INTERNATIONAL ORDER." WOR+45 WOR-45 ORD/FREE PWR
...JURID GEN/LAWS VAL/FREE 20. PAGE 3 E0066

          S63
BECHHOEFER B.G.,"UNITED NATIONS PROCEDURES IN CASE INT/ORG
OF VIOLATIONS OF DISARMAMENT AGREEMENTS." COM   DELIB/GP
USA+45 USSR LAW CONSTN NAT/G EX/STRUC FORCES LEGIS
BAL/PWR EDU/PROP CT/SYS ARMS/CONT ORD/FREE PWR
...POLICY STERTYP UN VAL/FREE 20. PAGE 9 E0169

          S63
BOHN L.,"WHOSE NUCLEAR TEST: NON-PHYSICAL   ADJUD
INSPECTION AND TEST BAN." WOR+45 R+D INT/ORG   ARMS/CONT
VOL/ASSN ORD/FREE...GEN/LAWS GEN/METH COLD/WAR 20. TEC/DEV
PAGE 13 E0262   NUC/PWR

          S63
CAHIER P.,"LE DROIT INTERNE DES ORGANISATIONS   INT/ORG
INTERNATIONALES." UNIV CONSTN SOCIETY ECO/DEV R+D JURID
NAT/G TOP/EX LEGIT ATTIT PERCEPT...TIME/SEQ 19/20. DIPLOM
PAGE 18 E0357   INT/LAW

          S63
FRIEDMANN W.G.,"THE USES OF 'GENERAL PRINCIPLES' IN LAW
THE DEVELOPMENT OF INTERNATIONAL LAW." WOR+45 NAT/G INT/LAW
DIPLOM INT/TRADE LEGIT ROUTINE RIGID/FLEX ORD/FREE INT/ORG
...JURID CONCPT STERTYP GEN/METH 20. PAGE 41 E0804

          S63
GARDNER R.N.,"COOPERATION IN OUTER SPACE." FUT USSR INT/ORG
WOR+45 AIR LAW COM/IND CONSULT DELIB/GP CREATE   ACT/RES
KNOWL 20 TREATY. PAGE 42 E0837   PEACE
                                           SPACE

          S63
GIRAUD E.,"L'INTERDICTION DU RECOURS A LA FORCE, LA INT/ORG
THEORIE ET LA PRATIQUE DES NATIONS UNIES." ALGERIA FORCES
COM CUBA HUNGARY WOR+45 ADJUD TOTALSM ATTIT   DIPLOM
RIGID/FLEX PWR...POLICY JURID CONCPT UN 20 CONGO.
PAGE 44 E0872

          S63
HARNETTY P.,"CANADA, SOUTH AFRICA AND THE   AFR
COMMONWEALTH." CANADA SOUTH/AFR LAW INT/ORG   ATTIT
VOL/ASSN DELIB/GP LEGIS TOP/EX ECO/TAC LEGIT DRIVE
MORAL...CONCPT CMN/WLTH 20. PAGE 50 E1000

          S63
LEPAWSKY A.,"INTERNATIONAL DEVELOPMENT OF RIVER   INT/ORG
RESOURCES." CANADA EUR+WWI S/ASIA USA+45 SEA LEGIT DELIB/GP
ADJUD ORD/FREE PWR WEALTH...MGT TIME/SEQ VAL/FREE
MEXIC/AMER 20. PAGE 64 E1287

          S63
MCDOUGAL M.S.,"THE SOVIET-CUBAN QUARANTINE AND   ORD/FREE
SELF-DEFENSE." CUBA USA+45 USSR WOR+45 INT/ORG   LEGIT
NAT/G BAL/PWR NUC/PWR ATTIT...JURID CONCPT. PAGE 70 SOVEREIGN
E1409

          S63
MODELSKI G.,"STUDY OF ALLIANCES." WOR+45 WOR-45   VOL/ASSN
INT/ORG NAT/G FORCES LEGIT ADMIN CHOOSE ALL/VALS   CON/ANAL
PWR SKILL...INT/LAW CONCPT GEN/LAWS 20 TREATY.   DIPLOM
PAGE 74 E1477

          S63
TALLON D.,"L'ETUDE DU DROIT COMPARE COMME MOYEN DE INT/ORG
RECHERCHER LES MATIERES SUSCEPTIBLES D'UNIFICATION JURID
INTERNATIONALE." WOR+45 LAW SOCIETY VOL/ASSN   INT/LAW
CONSULT LEGIT CT/SYS RIGID/FLEX KNOWL 20. PAGE 95
E1906

          S63
WALKER H.,"THE INTERNATIONAL LAW OF COMMODITY   MARKET
AGREEMENTS." FUT WOR+45 ECO/DEV ECO/UNDEV FINAN   VOL/ASSN
INT/ORG NAT/G CONSULT CREATE PLAN ECO/TAC ATTIT   INT/LAW
PERCEPT...CONCPT GEN/LAWS TOT/POP GATT 20. PAGE 105 INT/TRADE
E2095

          S63
WEISSBERG G.,"MAPS AS EVIDENCE IN INTERNATIONAL   LAW
BOUNDARY DISPUTES: A REAPPRAISAL." CHINA/COM   GEOG
EUR+WWI INDIA MOD/EUR S/ASIA INT/ORG NAT/G LEGIT   SOVEREIGN
PERCEPT...JURID CHARTS 20. PAGE 105 E2110

          B64
AHLUWALIA K.,THE LEGAL STATUS, PRIVILEGES AND   PRIVIL
IMMUNITIES OF SPECIALIZED AGENCIES OF UN AND   DIPLOM

CERTAIN OTHER INTERNATIONAL ORGANIZATIONS. WOR+45 INT/ORG
LAW CONSULT DELIB/GP FORCES. PAGE 3 E0055   INT/LAW

          B64
COHEN M.,LAW AND POLITICS IN SPACE: SPECIFIC AND   DELIB/GP
URGENT PROBLEMS IN THE LAW OF OUTER SPACE.   LAW
CHINA/COM COM USA+45 USSR WOR+45 COM/IND INT/ORG   INT/LAW
NAT/G LEGIT NUC/PWR ATTIT BIO/SOC...JURID CONCPT   SPACE
CONGRESS 20 STALIN/J. PAGE 24 E0464

          B64
DUBISSON M.,LA COUR INTERNATIONALE DE JUSTICE.   CT/SYS
FRANCE LAW CONSTN JUDGE DOMIN ADJUD...INT/LAW   INT/ORG
CLASSIF RECORD ORG/CHARTS UN. PAGE 33 E0651

          B64
ECONOMIDES C.P.,LE POUVOIR DE DECISION DES   INT/ORG
ORGANISATIONS INTERNATIONALES EUROPEENNES. DIPLOM PWR
DOMIN INGP/REL EFFICIENCY...INT/LAW JURID 20 NATO DECISION
OEEC EEC COUNCL/EUR EURATOM. PAGE 34 E0673   GP/COMP

          B64
FALK R.A.,THE ROLE OF DOMESTIC COURTS IN THE   LAW
INTERNATIONAL LEGAL ORDER. FUT WOR+45 INT/ORG NAT/G INT/LAW
JUDGE EDU/PROP LEGIT CT/SYS...POLICY RELATIV JURID
CONCPT GEN/LAWS 20. PAGE 36 E0716

          B64
FRANCK T.M.,EAST AFRICAN UNITY THROUGH LAW. MALAWI AFR
TANZANIA UGANDA UK ZAMBIA CONSTN INT/ORG NAT/G   FEDERAL
ADMIN ROUTINE TASK NAT/LISM ATTIT SOVEREIGN   REGION
...RECORD IDEA/COMP NAT/COMP. PAGE 40 E0785   INT/LAW

          B64
FRIEDMANN W.G.,THE CHANGING STRUCTURE OF   ADJUD
INTERNATIONAL LAW. WOR+45 INT/ORG NAT/G PROVS LEGIT TREND
ORD/FREE PWR...JURID CONCPT GEN/LAWS TOT/POP UN 20. INT/LAW
PAGE 41 E0805

          B64
FRYDENSBERG P.,PEACE-KEEPING: EXPERIENCE AND   INT/ORG
EVALUATION: THE OSLO PAPERS. NORWAY FORCES PLAN   DIPLOM
CONTROL...INT/LAW 20 UN. PAGE 41 E0814   PEACE
                                           COERCE

          B64
FULBRIGHT J.W.,OLD MYTHS AND NEW REALITIES. USA+45 DIPLOM
USSR LEGIS INT/TRADE DETER ATTIT...POLICY 20   INT/ORG
COLD/WAR TREATY. PAGE 41 E0818   ORD/FREE

          B64
GARDNER L.C.,ECONOMIC ASPECTS OF NEW DEAL   ECO/TAC
DIPLOMACY. USA-45 WOR+45 LAW ECO/DEV INT/ORG NAT/G DIPLOM
VOL/ASSN LEGIS TOP/EX EDU/PROP ORD/FREE PWR WEALTH
...POLICY TIME/SEQ VAL/FREE 20 ROOSEVLT/F. PAGE 42
E0836

          B64
GARDNER R.N.,IN PURSUIT OF WORLD ORDER* US FOREIGN OBS
POLICY AND INTERNATIONAL ORGANIZATIONS. USA+45 USSR INT/ORG
ECO/UNDEV FORCES LEGIS DIPLOM FOR/AID INT/TRADE   ALL/VALS
PEACE...INT/LAW PREDICT UN. PAGE 42 E0839

          B64
GRZYBOWSKI K.,THE SOCIALIST COMMONWEALTH OF   INT/LAW
NATIONS: ORGANIZATIONS AND INSTITUTIONS. FORCES   COM
DIPLOM INT/TRADE ADJUD ADMIN LEAD WAR MARXISM   REGION
SOCISM...BIBLIOG 20 COMECON WARSAW/P. PAGE 48 E0956 INT/ORG

          B64
HEKHUIS D.J.,INTERNATIONAL STABILITY: MILITARY,   TEC/DEV
ECONOMIC AND POLITICAL DIMENSIONS. FUT WOR+45 LAW DETER
ECO/UNDEV INT/ORG NAT/G VOL/ASSN FORCES ACT/RES   REGION
BAL/PWR PWR WEALTH...STAT UN 20. PAGE 51 E1024

          B64
IKLE F.C.,HOW NATIONS NEGOTIATE. COM EUR+WWI USA+45 NAT/G
INTELL INT/ORG VOL/ASSN DELIB/GP ACT/RES CREATE   PWR
DOMIN EDU/PROP ADJUD ROUTINE ATTIT PERSON ORD/FREE POLICY
RESPECT SKILL...PSY SOC OBS VAL/FREE. PAGE 56 E1122

          B64
JENKS C.W.,THE PROSPECTS OF INTERNATIONAL   INT/LAW
ADJUDICATION. WOR+45 WOR-45 NAT/G DIPLOM CONTROL   ADJUD
PWR...POLICY JURID CONCPT METH/COMP 19/20 ICJ   CT/SYS
LEAGUE/NAT UN TREATY. PAGE 58 E1160   INT/ORG

          B64
MCDOUGAL M.S.,STUDIES IN WORLD PUBLIC ORDER. SPACE INT/LAW
SEA INT/ORG CREATE AGREE NUC/PWR...POLICY PHIL/SCI SOC
IDEA/COMP ANTHOL METH 20 UN. PAGE 71 E1411   DIPLOM

          B64
REGALA R.,WORLD PEACE THROUGH DIPLOMACY AND LAW.   DIPLOM
S/ASIA WOR+45 ECO/UNDEV INT/ORG FORCES PLAN   PEACE
PROB/SOLV FOR/AID NUC/PWR WAR...POLICY INT/LAW 20. ADJUD

ROBERTS HL,FOREIGN AFFAIRS BIBLIOGRAPHY, 1952-1962. BIBLIOG/A
ECO/DEV SECT PLAN FOR/AID INT/TRADE ARMS/CONT DIPLOM
NAT/LISM ATTIT...INT/LAW GOV/COMP IDEA/COMP 20. INT/ORG
PAGE 85 E1703 WAR

SCHECHTER A.H.,INTERPRETATION OF AMBIGUOUS INT/LAW
DOCUMENTS BY INTERNATIONAL ADMINISTRATIVE DIPLOM
TRIBUNALS. WOR+45 EX/STRUC INT/TRADE CT/SYS INT/ORG
SOVEREIGN 20 UN ILO EURCT/JUST. PAGE 87 E1752 ADJUD

SCHWELB E.,HUMAN RIGHTS AND THE INTERNATIONAL INT/ORG
COMMUNITY. WOR+45 WOR-45 NAT/G SECT DELIB/GP DIPLOM ORD/FREE
PEACE RESPECT TREATY 20 UN. PAGE 89 E1792 INT/LAW

STRONG C.F.,HISTORY OF MODERN POLITICAL CONSTN
CONSTITUTIONS. STRUCT INT/ORG NAT/G LEGIS TEC/DEV CONCPT
DIPLOM INT/TRADE CT/SYS EXEC...METH/COMP T 12/20
UN. PAGE 94 E1888

UN PUB. INFORM. ORGAN.,EVERY MAN'S UNITED NATIONS. INT/ORG
UNIV WOR+45 CONSTN CULTURE SOCIETY ECO/DEV ROUTINE
ECO/UNDEV NAT/G ACT/RES PLAN ECO/TAC INT/TRADE
EDU/PROP LEGIT PEACE ATTIT ALL/VALS...POLICY HUM
INT/LAW CONCPT CHARTS UN TOT/POP 20. PAGE 97 E1954

WILLIAMS S.P.,TOWARD A GENUINE WORLD SECURITY BIBLIOG/A
SYSTEM (PAMPHLET). WOR+45 INT/ORG FORCES PLAN ARMS/CONT
NUC/PWR ORD/FREE...INT/LAW CONCPT UN PRESIDENT. DIPLOM
PAGE 106 E2123 PEACE

BERKS R.N.,"THE US AND WEAPONS CONTROL." WOR+45 LAW USA+45
INT/ORG NAT/G LEGIS EXEC COERCE PEACE ATTIT PLAN
RIGID/FLEX ALL/VALS PWR...POLICY TOT/POP 20. ARMS/CONT
PAGE 11 E0204

POUNDS N.J.G.,"THE POLITICS OF PARTITION." AFR ASIA NAT/G
COM EUR+WWI FUT ISLAM S/ASIA USA-45 LAW ECO/DEV NAT/LISM
ECO/UNDEV AGRI INDUS INT/ORG POL/PAR PROVS SECT
FORCES TOP/EX EDU/PROP LEGIT ATTIT MORAL ORD/FREE
PWR RESPECT WEALTH. PAGE 82 E1640

WORLD PEACE FOUNDATION.,"INTERNATIONAL INT/ORG
ORGANIZATIONS: SUMMARY OF ACTIVITIES." INDIA ROUTINE
PAKISTAN TURKEY WOR+45 CONSTN CONSULT EX/STRUC
ECO/TAC EDU/PROP LEGIT ORD/FREE...JURID SOC UN 20
CYPRESS. PAGE 107 E2145

BALDWIN G.B.,"THE DEPENDENCE OF SCIENCE ON LAW AND NAT/G
GOVERNMENT--THE INTERNATIONAL GEOPHYSICAL YEAR--A KNOWL
CASE STUDY." WOR+45 LAW INT/ORG PROF/ORG LEGIS PLAN
EDU/PROP...TIME/SEQ VAL/FREE 20. PAGE 8 E0144

CARNEGIE ENDOWMENT INT. PEACE.,"HUMAN RIGHTS (ISSUES INT/ORG
BEFORE THE NINETEENTH GENERAL ASSEMBLY)." AFR PERSON
WOR+45 LAW CONSTN NAT/G EDU/PROP GP/REL DISCRIM RACE/REL
PEACE ATTIT MORAL ORD/FREE...INT/LAW PSY CONCPT
RECORD UN 20. PAGE 20 E0385

CARNEGIE ENDOWMENT INT. PEACE.,"LEGAL QUESTIONS INT/ORG
(ISSUES BEFORE THE NINETEENTH GENERAL ASSEMBLY)." LAW
WOR+45 CONSTN NAT/G DELIB/GP ADJUD PEACE MORAL INT/LAW
ORD/FREE...RECORD UN 20 TREATY. PAGE 20 E0386

COHEN M.,"BASIC PRINCIPLES OF INTERNATIONAL LAW." INT/ORG
UNIV WOR+45 WOR-45 BAL/PWR LEGIT ADJUD WAR ATTIT INT/LAW
MORAL ORD/FREE PWR...JURID CONCPT MYTH TOT/POP 20.
PAGE 23 E0463

CRANE R.D.,"BASIC PRINCIPLES IN SOVIET SPACE LAW." COM
FUT WOR+45 AIR INT/ORG DIPLOM DOMIN ARMS/CONT LAW
COERCE NUC/PWR PEACE ATTIT DRIVE PWR...INT/LAW USSR
METH/CNCPT NEW/IDEA OBS TREND GEN/LAWS VAL/FREE SPACE
MARX/KARL 20. PAGE 27 E0544

GARDNER R.N.,"THE SOVIET UNION AND THE UNITED COM
NATIONS." WOR+45 FINAN POL/PAR VOL/ASSN FORCES INT/ORG
ECO/TAC DOMIN EDU/PROP LEGIT ADJUD ADMIN ARMS/CONT USSR
COERCE ATTIT ALL/VALS...POLICY MAJORIT CONCPT OBS
TIME/SEQ TREND STERTYP UN. PAGE 42 E0838

GINSBURGS G.,"WARS OF NATIONAL LIBERATION - THE COERCE
SOVIET THESIS." COM USSR WOR+45 WOR-45 LAW CULTURE CONCPT
INT/ORG DIPLOM LEGIT COLONIAL GUERRILLA WAR INT/LAW
NAT/LISM ATTIT PERSON MORAL PWR...JURID OBS TREND REV
MARX/KARL 20. PAGE 44 E0869

GREENBERG S.,"JUDAISM AND WORLD JUSTICE." MEDIT-7 SECT
WOR+45 LAW CULTURE SOCIETY INT/ORG NAT/G FORCES JURID
EDU/PROP ATTIT DRIVE PERSON SUPEGO ALL/VALS PEACE
...POLICY PSY CONCPT GEN/LAWS JEWS. PAGE 46 E0908

HICKEY D.,"THE PHILOSOPHICAL ARGUMENT FOR WORLD FUT
GOVERNMENT." WOR+45 SOCIETY ACT/RES PLAN LEGIT INT/ORG
ADJUD PEACE PERCEPT PERSON ORD/FREE...HUM JURID
PHIL/SCI METH/CNCPT CON/ANAL STERTYP GEN/LAWS
TOT/POP 20. PAGE 52 E1039

KARPOV P.V.,"PEACEFUL COEXISTENCE AND INTERNATIONAL COM
LAW." WOR+45 LAW SOCIETY INT/ORG VOL/ASSN FORCES ATTIT
CREATE CAP/ISM DIPLOM ADJUD NUC/PWR PEACE MORAL INT/LAW
ORD/FREE PWR MARXISM...MARXIST JURID CONCPT OBS USSR
TREND COLD/WAR MARX/KARL 20. PAGE 59 E1186

KHAN M.Z.,"ISLAM AND INTERNATIONAL RELATIONS." FUT ISLAM
WOR+45 LAW CULTURE SOCIETY NAT/G SECT DELIB/GP INT/ORG
FORCES EDU/PROP ATTIT PERSON SUPEGO ALL/VALS DIPLOM
...POLICY PSY CONCPT MYTH HIST/WRIT GEN/LAWS.
PAGE 61 E1211

KUNZ J.,"THE CHANGING SCIENCE OF INTERNATIONAL ADJUD
LAW." FUT WOR+45 WOR-45 INT/ORG LEGIT ORD/FREE CONCPT
...JURID TIME/SEQ GEN/LAWS 20. PAGE 62 E1235 INT/LAW

LIPSON L.,"PEACEFUL COEXISTENCE." COM USSR WOR+45 ATTIT
LAW INT/ORG DIPLOM LEGIT ADJUD ORD/FREE...CONCPT JURID
OBS TREND GEN/LAWS VAL/FREE COLD/WAR 20. PAGE 65 INT/LAW
E1303 PEACE

MAGGS P.B.,"SOVIET VIEWPOINT ON NUCLEAR WEAPONS IN COM
INTERNATIONAL LAW." USSR WOR+45 INT/ORG FORCES LAW
DIPLOM ARMS/CONT ATTIT ORD/FREE PWR...POLICY JURID INT/LAW
CONCPT CON/ANAL GEN/LAWS VAL/FREE 20. NUC/PWR
PAGE 67 E1347

SCHWELB E.,"OPERATION OF THE EUROPEAN CONVENTION ON INT/ORG
HUMAN RIGHTS." EUR+WWI LAW SOCIETY CREATE EDU/PROP MORAL
ADJUD ADMIN PEACE ATTIT ORD/FREE PWR...POLICY
INT/LAW CONCPT OBS GEN/LAWS UN VAL/FREE ILO 20
ECHR. PAGE 89 E1791

SINGH N.,"THE CONTEMPORARY PRACTICE OF INDIA IN THE LAW
FIELD OF INTERNATIONAL LAW." INDIA S/ASIA INT/ORG ATTIT
NAT/G DOMIN EDU/PROP LEGIT KNOWL...CONCPT TOT/POP DIPLOM
20. PAGE 91 E1833 INT/LAW

SKUBISZEWSKI K.,"FORMS OF PARTICIPATION OF INT/ORG
INTERNATIONAL ORGANIZATION IN THE LAW MAKING LAW
PROCESS." FUT WOR+45 NAT/G DELIB/GP DOMIN LEGIT INT/LAW
KNOWL PWR...JURID TREND 20. PAGE 92 E1837

BAADE H.,THE SOVIET IMPACT ON INTERNATIONAL LAW. INT/LAW
INT/ORG INT/TRADE LEGIT COLONIAL ARMS/CONT REV WAR USSR
...CON/ANAL ANTHOL TREATY. PAGE 6 E0124 CREATE
ORD/FREE

BERKOWITZ M.,AMERICAN NATIONAL SECURITY: A READER ORD/FREE
IN THEORY AND POLICY. USA+45 INT/ORG FORCES BAL/PWR WAR
DIPLOM ECO/TAC DETER PWR...INT/LAW ANTHOL BIBLIOG ARMS/CONT
20 UN. PAGE 11 E0203 POLICY

COWEN Z.,THE BRITISH COMMONWEALTH OF NATIONS IN A JURID
CHANGING WORLD. UK ECO/UNDEV INT/ORG ECO/TAC DIPLOM
INT/TRADE COLONIAL WAR GP/REL RACE/REL SOVEREIGN PARL/PROC
SOC/INTEG 20 TREATY EEC COMMONWLTH. PAGE 27 E0530 NAT/LISM

FORGAC A.A.,NEW DIPLOMACY AND THE UNITED NATIONS. DIPLOM
FRANCE GERMANY UK USSR INT/ORG DELIB/GP EX/STRUC ETIQUET
PEACE...INT/LAW CONCPT UN. PAGE 39 E0770 NAT/G

GOTLIEB A.,DISARMAMENT AND INTERNATIONAL LAW* A
STUDY OF THE ROLE OF LAW IN THE DISARMAMENT
PROCESS. USA+45 USSR PROB/SOLV CONFER ADMIN ROUTINE
NUC/PWR ORD/FREE SOVEREIGN UN TREATY. PAGE 45 E0893
B65 INT/LAW INT/ORG ARMS/CONT IDEA/COMP

HAENSCH G.,PAN-AFRICANISM IN ACTION: AN ACCOUNT OF
THE UAM TIC AND ALPHABETICAL IN GERMAN, ENGLISH,
FRENCH AND SPANISH. WOR+45 INT/ORG NAT/G ARMS/CONT
WAR...INT/LAW IDEA/COMP TREATY. PAGE 49 E0974
B65 DICTIONARY DIPLOM LING

JENKS C.W.,SPACE LAW. DIPLOM DEBATE CONTROL
ORD/FREE TREATY 20 UN. PAGE 58 E1161
B65 SPACE INT/LAW JURID INT/ORG

MARTENS E.,DIE HANNOVERSCHE KIRCHENKOMMISSION.
GERMANY LAW INT/ORG PROVS SECT CONFER GP/REL
CATHISM 16/20. PAGE 69 E1371
B65 JURID DELIB/GP CONSTN PROF/ORG

MILLIS W.,AN END TO ARMS. LAW INT/ORG FORCES
ACT/RES CREATE DIPLOM WAR...POLICY HUM NEW/IDEA
HYPO/EXP. PAGE 73 E1462
B65 FUT PWR ARMS/CONT ORD/FREE

MONCONDUIT F.,LA COMMISSION EUROPEENNE DES DROITS
DE L'HOMME. DIPLOM AGREE GP/REL ORD/FREE PWR
...BIBLIOG 20 TREATY. PAGE 74 E1483
B65 INT/LAW INT/ORG ADJUD JURID

MOODY M.,CATALOG OF INTERNATIONAL LAW AND RELATIONS
(20 VOLS.). WOR+45 INT/ORG NAT/G ADJUD ADMIN CT/SYS
POLICY. PAGE 74 E1488
B65 BIBLIOG INT/LAW DIPLOM

NWOGUGU E.I.,THE LEGAL PROBLEMS OF FOREIGN
INVESTMENT IN DEVELOPING COUNTRIES. WOR+45 INT/ORG
DELIB/GP LEGIS PROB/SOLV INT/TRADE TAX ADJUD
SANCTION...BIBLIOG 20 TREATY. PAGE 78 E1561
B65 FOR/AID FINAN INT/LAW ECO/UNDEV

O'BRIEN W.V.,THE NEW NATIONS IN INTERNATIONAL LAW
AND DIPLOMACY* THE YEAR BOOK OF WORLD POLITY*
VOLUME III. USA+45 ECO/UNDEV INT/ORG FORCES DIPLOM
COLONIAL NEUTRAL REV NAT/LISM ATTIT RESPECT.
PAGE 78 E1565
B65 INT/LAW CULTURE SOVEREIGN ANTHOL

O'CONNELL D.P.,INTERNATIONAL LAW (2 VOLS.). WOR+45
WOR-45 ECO/DEV ECO/UNDEV INT/ORG NAT/G AGREE
...POLICY JURID CONCPT NAT/COMP 20 TREATY. PAGE 78
E1566
B65 INT/LAW DIPLOM CT/SYS

PADELFORD N.,THE UNITED NATIONS IN THE BALANCE*
ACCOMPLISHMENTS AND PROSPECTS. NAT/G VOL/ASSN
DIPLOM ADMIN COLONIAL CT/SYS REGION WAR ORD/FREE
...ANTHOL UN. PAGE 79 E1588
B65 INT/ORG CONTROL

PARRY C.,THE SOURCES AND EVIDENCES OF INTERNATIONAL
LAW. WOR+45 WOR-45 DIPLOM AGREE SOVEREIGN...METH 20
TREATY UN LEAGUE/NAT. PAGE 80 E1599
B65 INT/LAW ADJUD INT/ORG CT/SYS

SOPER T.,EVOLVING COMMONWEALTH. AFR CANADA INDIA
IRELAND UK LAW CONSTN POL/PAR DOMIN CONTROL WAR PWR
...AUD/VIS 18/20 COMMONWLTH OEEC. PAGE 93 E1857
B65 INT/ORG COLONIAL VOL/ASSN

UNESCO,INTERNATIONAL ORGANIZATIONS IN THE SOCIAL
SCIENCES(REV. ED.). LAW ADMIN ATTIT...CRIMLGY GEOG
INT/LAW PSY SOC STAT 20 UNESCO. PAGE 98 E1962
B65 INT/ORG R+D PROF/ORG ACT/RES

UNESCO,HANDBOOK OF INTERNATIONAL EXCHANGES. COM/IND
R+D ACADEM PROF/ORG VOL/ASSN CREATE TEC/DEV
EDU/PROP AGREE 20 TREATY. PAGE 98 E1963
B65 INDEX INT/ORG DIPLOM PRESS

VON GLAHN G.,LAW AMONG NATIONS: AN INTRODUCTION TO
PUBLIC INTERNATIONAL LAW. WOR+45 WOR-45 INT/ORG
NAT/G CREATE ADJUD WAR...GEOG CLASSIF TREND
BIBLIOG. PAGE 104 E2082
B65 ACADEM INT/LAW GEN/LAWS LAW

VONGLAHN G.,LAW AMONG NATIONS: AN INTRODUCTION TO
PUBLIC INTERNATIONAL LAW. UNIV WOR+45 LAW INT/ORG
NAT/G LEGIT EXEC RIGID/FLEX...CONCPT TIME/SEQ
GEN/LAWS UN TOT/POP 20. PAGE 104 E2084
B65 CONSTN JURID INT/LAW

WEIL G.L.,A HANDBOOK ON THE EUROPEAN ECONOMIC
COMMUNITY. BELGIUM EUR+WWI FRANCE GERMANY/W ITALY
CONSTN ECO/DEV CREATE PARTIC GP/REL...DECISION MGT
CHARTS 20 EEC. PAGE 105 E2107
B65 INT/TRADE INT/ORG TEC/DEV INT/LAW

WHITE G.M.,THE USE OF EXPERTS BY INTERNATIONAL
TRIBUNALS. WOR+45 WOR-45 INT/ORG NAT/G PAY ADJUD
COST...OBS BIBLIOG 20. PAGE 106 E2117
B65 INT/LAW ROUTINE CONSULT CT/SYS

RUBIN A.P.,"UNITED STATES CONTEMPORARY PRACTICE
RELATING TO INTERNATIONAL LAW." USA+45 WOR+45
CONSTN INT/ORG NAT/G DELIB/GP EX/STRUC DIPLOM DOMIN
CT/SYS ROUTINE ORD/FREE...CONCPT COLD/WAR 20.
PAGE 86 E1730
L65 LAW LEGIT INT/LAW

AMRAM P.W.,"REPORT ON THE TENTH SESSION OF THE
HAGUE CONFERENCE ON PRIVATE INTERNATIONAL LAW."
USA+45 WOR+45 INT/ORG CREATE LEGIT ADJUD ALL/VALS
...JURID CONCPT METH/CNCPT OBS GEN/METH 20. PAGE 4
E0085
S65 VOL/ASSN DELIB/GP INT/LAW

FALK R.A.,"INTERNATIONAL LEGAL ORDER." USA+45
INTELL FACE/GP INT/ORG LEGIT KNOWL...CONCPT
METH/CNCPT STYLE RECORD GEN/METH 20. PAGE 36 E0717
S65 ATTIT GEN/LAWS INT/LAW

HAZARD J.N.,"CO-EXISTENCE LAW BOWS OUT." WOR+45 R+D
INT/ORG VOL/ASSN CONSULT DELIB/GP ACT/RES CREATE
PEACE KNOWL...JURID CONCPT COLD/WAR VAL/FREE 20.
PAGE 51 E1018
S65 PROF/ORG ADJUD

KHOURI F.J.,"THE JORDON RIVER CONTROVERSY." LAW
SOCIETY ECO/UNDEV AGRI FINAN INDUS SECT FORCES
ACT/RES PLAN TEC/DEV ECO/TAC EDU/PROP COERCE ATTIT
DRIVE PERCEPT RIGID/FLEX ALL/VALS...GEOG SOC MYTH
WORK. PAGE 61 E1212
S65 ISLAM INT/ORG ISRAEL JORDAN

MAC CHESNEY B.,"SOME COMMENTS ON THE 'QUARANTINE'
OF CUBA." USA+45 WOR+45 NAT/G BAL/PWR DIPLOM LEGIT
ROUTINE ATTIT ORD/FREE...JURID METH/CNCPT 20.
PAGE 67 E1337
S65 INT/ORG LAW CUBA USSR

MERRITT R.L.,"SELECTED ARTICLES AND DOCUMENTS ON
INTERNATIONAL LAW AND RELATIONS." WOR+45 INT/ORG
FORCES INT/TRADE. PAGE 72 E1443
S65 BIBLIOG DIPLOM INT/LAW GOV/REL

STEIN E.,"TOWARD SUPREMACY OF TREATY-CONSTITUTION
BY JUDICIAL FIAT: ON THE MARGIN OF THE COSTA CASE."
EUR+WWI ITALY WOR+45 INT/ORG NAT/G LEGIT REGION
NAT/LISM PWR...JURID CONCPT TREND TOT/POP VAL/FREE
20. PAGE 93 E1870
S65 ADJUD CONSTN SOVEREIGN INT/LAW

SEARA M.V.,"COSMIC INTERNATIONAL LAW." LAW ACADEM
ACT/RES DIPLOM COLONIAL CONTROL NUC/PWR SOVEREIGN
...GEN/LAWS BIBLIOG UN. PAGE 90 E1799
C65 SPACE INT/LAW IDEA/COMP INT/ORG

ASAMOAH O.Y.,THE LEGAL SIGNIFICANCE OF THE
DECLARATIONS OF THE GENERAL ASSEMBLY OF THE UNITED
NATIONS. WOR+45 CREATE CONTROL...BIBLIOG 20 UN.
PAGE 5 E0105
B66 INT/LAW INT/ORG DIPLOM

BESTERMAN T.,A WORLD BIBLIOGRAPHY OF BIBLIOGRAPHIES
(4TH ED.). WOR+45 WOR-45 LAW INT/ORG ADMIN
CON/ANAL. PAGE 11 E0219
B66 BIBLIOG/A DIPLOM

BROWNLIE I.,PRINCIPLES OF PUBLIC INTERNATIONAL LAW.
WOR+45 WOR-45 LAW JUDGE REPAR ADJUD SOVEREIGN
...JURID T. PAGE 16 E0319
B66 INT/LAW DIPLOM INT/ORG

BUTTERFIELD H.,DIPLOMATIC INVESTIGATIONS* ESSAYS IN
THE THEORY OF INTERNATIONAL POLITICS. LAW INT/ORG
FORCES BAL/PWR ARMS/CONT WAR ALL/VALS...HUM
INT/LAW. PAGE 18 E0351
B66 GEN/LAWS UK DIPLOM

B66
CLARK G.,WORLD PEACE THROUGH WORLD LAW: TWO   INT/LAW
ALTERNATIVE PLANS. WOR+45 DELIB/GP FORCES TAX   PEACE
CONFER ADJUD SANCTION ARMS/CONT WAR CHOOSE PRIVIL   PLAN
20 UN COLD/WAR. PAGE 23 E0450   INT/ORG

B66
COPLIN W.D.,THE FUNCTIONS OF INTERNATIONAL LAW.   INT/LAW
WOR+45 ECO/DEV ECO/UNDEV ADJUD COLONIAL WAR OWN   DIPLOM
SOVEREIGN...POLICY GEN/LAWS 20. PAGE 25 E0503   INT/ORG

B66
COUNCIL OF EUROPE,EUROPEAN CONVENTION ON HUMAN   ORD/FREE
RIGHTS - COLLECTED TEXTS (5TH ED.). EUR+WWI DIPLOM   DELIB/GP
ADJUD CT/SYS...INT/LAW 20 ECHR. PAGE 26 E0520   INT/ORG
                                                       JURID

B66
DOUMA J.,BIBLIOGRAPHY ON THE INTERNATIONAL COURT   BIBLIOG/A
INCLUDING THE PERMANENT COURT, 1918-1964. WOR+45   INT/ORG
WOR-45 DELIB/GP WAR PRIVIL...JURID NAT/COMP 20 UN   CT/SYS
LEAGUE/NAT. PAGE 33 E0645   DIPLOM

B66
FALK R.A.,THE STRATEGY OF WORLD ORDER* 4 VOLUMES.   ORD/FREE
WOR+45 ECO/UNDEV ACADEM INT/ORG ACT/RES DIPLOM   GEN/LAWS
ARMS/CONT WAR...NET/THEORY SIMUL BIBLIOG UN.   ANTHOL
PAGE 36 E0719   INT/LAW

B66
FRIEDMANN W.G.,INTERNATIONAL FINANCIAL AID. USA+45   INT/ORG
ECO/DEV ECO/UNDEV NAT/G VOL/ASSN EX/STRUC PLAN RENT   FOR/AID
GIVE BAL/PAY PWR...GEOG INT/LAW STAT TREND UN EEC   TEC/DEV
COMECON. PAGE 41 E0806   ECO/TAC

B66
HAY P.,FEDERALISM AND SUPRANATIONAL ORGANIZATIONS: SOVEREIGN
PATTERNS FOR NEW LEGAL STRUCTURES. EUR+WWI LAW   FEDERAL
NAT/G VOL/ASSN DIPLOM PWR...NAT/COMP TREATY EEC.   INT/ORG
PAGE 51 E1014   INT/LAW

B66
HOEVELER H.J.,INTERNATIONALE BEKAMPFUNG DES   CRIMLGY
VERBRECHENS. AUSTRIA SWITZERLND WOR+45 INT/ORG   CRIME
CONTROL BIO/SOC...METH/COMP NAT/COMP 20 MAFIA   DIPLOM
SCOT/YARD FBI. PAGE 53 E1064   INT/LAW

B66
INTL ATOMIC ENERGY AGENCY,INTERNATIONAL CONVENTIONS   DIPLOM
ON CIVIL LIABILITY FOR NUCLEAR DAMAGE. FUT WOR+45   INT/ORG
ADJUD WAR COST PEACE SOVEREIGN...JURID 20. PAGE 57   DELIB/GP
E1135   NUC/PWR

B66
JACOBSON H.K.,DIPLOMATS, SCIENTISTS, AND   DIPLOM
POLITICIANS* THE UNITED STATES AND THE NUCLEAR TEST   ARMS/CONT
BAN NEGOTIATIONS. USA+45 USSR ACT/RES PLAN CONFER   TECHRACY
DETER NUC/PWR CONSEN ORD/FREE...INT TREATY. PAGE 57   INT/ORG
E1146

B66
LEE L.T.,VIENNA CONVENTION ON CONSULAR RELATIONS.   AGREE
WOR+45 LAW INT/ORG CONFER GP/REL PRIVIL...INT/LAW   DIPLOM
20 TREATY VIENNA/CNV. PAGE 64 E1277   ADMIN

B66
MERILLAT H.C.L.,LEGAL ADVISERS AND INTERNATIONAL   INT/ORG
ORGANIZATIONS. LAW NAT/G CONSULT OP/RES ADJUD   INT/LAW
SANCTION TASK CONSEN ORG/CHARTS. PAGE 72 E1441   CREATE
                                                       OBS

B66
NANTWI E.K.,THE ENFORCEMENT OF INTERNATIONAL   INT/LAW
JUDICIAL DECISIONS AND ARBITAL AWARDS IN PUBLIC   ADJUD
INTERNATIONAL LAW. WOR+45 WOR-45 JUDGE PROB/SOLV   SOVEREIGN
DIPLOM CT/SYS SUPEGO MORAL PWR RESPECT...METH/CNCPT   INT/ORG
18/20 CASEBOOK. PAGE 76 E1520

B66
OBERMANN E.,VERTEIDIGUNG PER FREIHEIT. GERMANY/W   FORCES
WOR+45 INT/ORG COERCE NUC/PWR WEAPON MARXISM 20 UN   ORD/FREE
NATO WARSAW/P TREATY. PAGE 78 E1571   WAR
                                                       PEACE

B66
OLSON W.C.,THE THEORY AND PRACTICE OF INTERNATIONAL   DIPLOM
RELATIONS (2ND ED.). WOR+45 LEAD SUPEGO...INT/LAW   NAT/G
PHIL/SCI. PAGE 79 E1575   INT/ORG
                                                       POLICY

B66
POLLACK R.S.,THE INDIVIDUAL'S RIGHTS AND   INT/LAW
INTERNATIONAL ORGANIZATION. LAW INT/ORG DELIB/GP   ORD/FREE
SUPEGO...JURID SOC/INTEG 20 TREATY UN. PAGE 81   DIPLOM
E1623   PERSON

B66
SALTER L.M.,RESOLUTION OF INTERNATIONAL CONFLICT.   PROB/SOLV
USA+45 INT/ORG SECT DIPLOM ECO/TAC FOR/AID DETER   PEACE
NUC/PWR WAR 20. PAGE 87 E1743   INT/LAW
                                                       POLICY

B66
THOMPSON J.M.,RUSSIA, BOLSHEVISM, AND THE   DIPLOM
VERSAILLES PEACE. RUSSIA USSR INT/ORG NAT/G   PEACE
DELIB/GP AGREE REV WAR PWR 20 TREATY VERSAILLES   MARXISM
BOLSHEVISM. PAGE 96 E1919

B66
UNITED NATIONS,INTERNATIONAL SPACE BIBLIOGRAPHY.   BIBLIOG
FUT INT/ORG TEC/DEV DIPLOM ARMS/CONT NUC/PWR   SPACE
...JURID SOC UN. PAGE 98 E1969   PEACE
                                                       R+D

B66
WAINHOUSE D.W.,INTERNATIONAL PEACE OBSERVATION: A   PEACE
HISTORY AND FORECAST. INT/ORG PROB/SOLV BAL/PWR   DIPLOM
AGREE ARMS/CONT COERCE NUC/PWR...PREDICT METH/COMP
20 UN LEAGUE/NAT OAS TREATY. PAGE 104 E2092

B66
WALL E.H.,THE COURT OF JUSTICE IN THE EUROPEAN   CT/SYS
COMMUNITIES: JURISDICTION AND PROCEDURE. EUR+WWI   INT/ORG
DIPLOM ADJUD ADMIN ROUTINE TASK...CONCPT LING 20.   LAW
PAGE 105 E2096   OP/RES

L66
HOLSTI K.J.,"RESOLVING INTERNATIONAL CONFLICTS* A   DIPLOM
TAXONOMY OF BEHAVIOR AND SOME FIGURES ON   PROB/SOLV
PROCEDURES." WOR+45 WOR-45 INT/ORG ADJUD EFFICIENCY   WAR
...STAT IDEA/COMP. PAGE 55 E1089   CLASSIF

L66
SEYLER W.C.,"DOCTORAL DISSERTATIONS IN POLITICAL   BIBLIOG
SCIENCE IN UNIVERSITIES OF THE UNITED STATES AND   LAW
CANADA." INT/ORG LOC/G ADMIN...INT/LAW MGT   NAT/G
GOV/COMP. PAGE 90 E1808

L66
YALEM R.J.,"THE STUDY OF INTERNATIONAL   VOL/ASSN
ORGANIZATION, 1920-1965* A SURVEY OF THE   INT/ORG
LITERATURE." WOR+45 WOR-45 REGION...INT/LAW CLASSIF   BIBLIOG/A
RECORD HIST/WRIT CON/ANAL IDEA/COMP UN. PAGE 108
E2163

S66
BROWNLIE I.,"NUCLEAR PROLIFERATION* SOME PROBLEMS   NUC/PWR
OF CONTROL." USA+45 USSR ECO/UNDEV INT/ORG FORCES   ARMS/CONT
TEC/DEV REGION CONSEN...RECORD TREATY. PAGE 16   VOL/ASSN
E0318   ORD/FREE

S66
EWALD R.F.,"ONE OF MANY POSSIBLE GAMES." ACADEM   SIMUL
INT/ORG ARMS/CONT...INT/LAW GAME. PAGE 36 E0706   HYPO/EXP
                                                       PROG/TEAC
                                                       RECORD

S66
FINE R.I.,"PEACE-KEEPING COSTS AND ARTICLE 19 OF   FORCES
THE UN CHARTER* AN INVITATION TO RESPONSIBILITY."   COST
INT/ORG NAT/G ADJUD CT/SYS CHOOSE CONSEN...RECORD   CONSTN
IDEA/COMP UN. PAGE 38 E0750

S66
GREEN L.C.,"RHODESIAN OIL: BOOTLEGGERS OR PIRATES?"   INT/TRADE
AFR RHODESIA UK WOR+45 INT/ORG NAT/G DIPLOM LEGIT   SANCTION
COLONIAL SOVEREIGN 20 UN OAU. PAGE 46 E0907   INT/LAW
                                                       POLICY

S66
LANDE G.R.,"THE EFFECT OF THE RESOLUTIONS OF THE   LEGIS
UNITED NATIONS GENERAL ASSEMBLY." WOR+45 LAW   EFFICIENCY
INT/ORG NAT/G CHOOSE ISOLAT ATTIT...CLASSIF   RESPECT
GEN/METH UN. PAGE 62 E1249

C66
BLAISDELL D.C.,"INTERNATIONAL ORGANIZATION." FUT   BIBLIOG
WOR+45 ECO/DEV DELIB/GP FORCES EFFICIENCY PEACE   INT/ORG
ORD/FREE...INT/LAW 20 UN LEAGUE/NAT NATO. PAGE 12   DIPLOM
E0239   ARMS/CONT

C66
ZAWODNY J.K.,"GUIDE TO THE STUDY OF INTERNATIONAL   BIBLIOG/A
RELATIONS." OP/RES PRESS...STAT INT 20. PAGE 108   DIPLOM
E2169   INT/LAW
                                                       INT/ORG

L/A+17C
BAILEY N.A.,LATIN AMERICA IN WORLD POLITICS. PWR   L/A+17C
CONSERVE MARXISM...INT/LAW TREND BIBLIOG/A T OAS   DIPLOM
COLD/WAR. PAGE 7 E0134   INT/ORG

ATTIT

FORCES FOR/AID TREATY 20 AUSTRAL. PAGE 105 E2103

CAHIER P.,LE DROIT DIPLOMATIQUE CONTEMPORAIN.
INT/ORG CHIEF ADMIN...T 20. PAGE 18 E0358
B67
INT/LAW
DIPLOM
JURID

"FOCUS ON WORLD LAW." WOR+45 NAT/G CT/SYS PEACE
...BIBLIOG 20 UN. PAGE 2 E0036
L67
INT/LAW
INT/ORG
PROB/SOLV
CONCPT

GARCIA ROBLES A.,THE DENUCLEARIZATION OF LATIN
AMERICA (TRANS. BY MARJORIE URQUIDI). LAW PLAN
DIPLOM...ANTHOL 20 TREATY UN. PAGE 42 E0833
B67
NUC/PWR
ARMS/CONT
L/A+17C
INT/ORG

BAADE H.W.,"THE ACQUIRED RIGHTS OF INTERNATIONAL
PUBLIC SERVANTS: A CASE STUDY IN RECEPTION OF
PUBLIC LAW." WOR+45 DELIB/GP DIPLOM ORD/FREE
...INT/LAW JURID UN. PAGE 7 E0125
L67
INT/ORG
WORKER
ADJUD
LAW

HOLCOMBE A.N.,A STRATEGY OF PEACE IN A CHANGING
WORLD. USA+45 WOR+45 LAW NAT/G CREATE DIPLOM
ARMS/CONT WAR...CHARTS 20 UN COLD/WAR. PAGE 54
E1072
B67
PEACE
PLAN
INT/ORG
INT/LAW

LEGAULT A.,"ORGANISATION ET CONDUITE DES OPERATIONS
DE MAINTIEN DE LA PAIX." FORCES ACT/RES ADJUD AGREE
CONTROL NEUTRAL TASK PRIVIL ORD/FREE 20 UN. PAGE 64
E1279
L67
INT/ORG
PEACE
WAR
INT/LAW

INTERNATIONAL CONCILIATION,ISSUES BEFORE THE 22ND
GENERAL ASSEMBLY. WOR+45 ECO/UNDEV FINAN BAL/PWR
BUDGET INT/TRADE STRANGE ORD/FREE...INT/LAW 20 UN
COLD/WAR. PAGE 57 E1132
B67
PROB/SOLV
INT/ORG
DIPLOM
PEACE

WAELBROECK M.,"THE APPLICATION OF EEC LAW BY
NATIONAL COURTS." EUR+WWI INT/ORG CT/SYS...JURID
EEC TREATY. PAGE 104 E2090
L67
INT/LAW
NAT/G
LAW
PROB/SOLV

LAFAVE W.R.,INTERNATIONAL TRADE, INVESTMENT, AND
ORGANIZATION. INDUS PROB/SOLV TARIFFS CONTROL
...TREND ANTHOL BIBLIOG 20 EEC. PAGE 62 E1245
B67
INT/TRADE
INT/LAW
INT/ORG

ALEXANDER B.,"GIBRALTAR" SPAIN UK CONSTN WORKER
PROB/SOLV FOR/AID RECEIVE CONTROL 20. PAGE 3 E0059
S67
DIPLOM
INT/ORG
ORD/FREE
ECO/TAC

LAWYERS COMM AMER POLICY VIET,VIETNAM AND
INTERNATIONAL LAW: AN ANALYSIS OF THE LEGALITY OF
THE US MILITARY INVOLVEMENT. VIETNAM LAW INT/ORG
COERCE WEAPON PEACE ORD/FREE 20 UN SEATO TREATY.
PAGE 64 E1271
B67
INT/LAW
DIPLOM
ADJUD
WAR

COHN K.,"CRIMES AGAINST HUMANITY." GERMANY INT/ORG
SANCTION ATTIT ORD/FREE...MARXIST CRIMLGY 20 UN.
PAGE 24 E0469
S67
WAR
INT/LAW
CRIME
ADJUD

PADELFORD N.J.,THE DYNAMICS OF INTERNATIONAL
POLITICS (2ND ED.). WOR+45 LAW INT/ORG FORCES
TEC/DEV REGION NAT/LISM PEACE ATTIT PWR ALL/IDEOS
UN COLD/WAR NATO TREATY. PAGE 79 E1589
B67
DIPLOM
NAT/G
POLICY
DECISION

DALFEN C.M.,"THE WORLD COURT IN IDLE SPLENDOUR: THE
BASIS OF STATES' ATTITUDES." WOR+45 LAW ADJUD
COERCE...JURID 20 UN WORLD/CT. PAGE 28 E0562
S67
CT/SYS
INT/ORG
INT/LAW
DIPLOM

PLANO J.C.,FORGING WORLD ORDER: THE POLITICS OF
INTERNATIONAL ORGANIZATION. PROB/SOLV DIPLOM
CONTROL CENTRAL RATIONAL ORD/FREE...INT/LAW CHARTS
BIBLIOG 20 UN LEAGUE/NAT. PAGE 81 E1618
B67
INT/ORG
ADMIN
JURID

DEUTSCH E.P.,"A JUDICIAL PATH TO WORLD PEACE." FUT
WOR+45 CONSTN PROB/SOLV DIPLOM LICENSE ADJUD
SANCTION CHOOSE REPRESENT NAT/LISM SOVEREIGN 20
ICJ. PAGE 31 E0611
S67
INT/LAW
INT/ORG
JURID
PEACE

POGANY A.H.,POLITICAL SCIENCE AND INTERNATIONAL
RELATIONS. BOOKS RECOMMENDED FOR AMERICAN CATHOLIC
COLLEGE LIBRARIES. INT/ORG LOC/G NAT/G FORCES
BAL/PWR ECO/TAC NUC/PWR...CATH INT/LAW TREATY 20.
PAGE 81 E1622
B67
BIBLIOG
DIPLOM

DOYLE S.E.,"COMMUNICATION SATELLITES* INTERNAL
ORGANIZATION FOR DEVELOPMENT AND CONTROL." USA+45
R+D ACT/RES DIPLOM NAT/LISM...POLICY INT/LAW
PREDICT UN. PAGE 33 E0647
S67
TEC/DEV
SPACE
COM/IND
INT/ORG

RAMUNDO B.A.,PEACEFUL COEXISTENCE: INTERNATIONAL
LAW IN THE BUILDING OF COMMUNISM. USSR INT/ORG
DIPLOM COLONIAL ARMS/CONT ROLE SOVEREIGN...POLICY
METH/COMP NAT/COMP BIBLIOG. PAGE 83 E1673
B67
INT/LAW
PEACE
MARXISM
METH/CNCPT

EYRAUD M.,"LA FRANCE FACE A UN EVENTUEL TRAITE DE
NON DISSEMINATION DES ARMES NUCLEAIRES." FRANCE
USA+45 EXTR/IND INDUS R+D INT/ORG ACT/RES TEC/DEV
AGREE PRODUC ATTIT 20 TREATY AEC EURATOM. PAGE 36
E0708
S67
NUC/PWR
ARMS/CONT
POLICY

SLATER J.,THE OAS AND UNITED STATES FOREIGN POLICY.
KOREA L/A+17C USA+45 VOL/ASSN RISK COERCE PEACE
ORD/FREE MARXISM...TREND 20 OAS. PAGE 92 E1838
B67
INT/ORG
DIPLOM
ALL/IDEOS
ADJUD

STEEL R.,"WHAT CAN THE UN DO?" RHODESIA ECO/UNDEV
DIPLOM ECO/TAC SANCTION...INT/LAW UN. PAGE 93 E1866
S67
INT/ORG
BAL/PWR
PEACE
FOR/AID

UNITED NATIONS,UNITED NATIONS PUBLICATIONS:
1945-1966. WOR+45 COM/IND DIST/IND FINAN TEC/DEV
ADMIN...POLICY INT/LAW MGT CHARTS 20 UN UNESCO.
PAGE 98 E1970
B67
BIBLIOG/A
INT/ORG
DIPLOM
WRITING

TOMASEK R.D.,"THE CHILEAN-BOLIVIAN LAUCA RIVER
DISPUTE AND THE OAS." CHILE L/A+17C PROB/SOLV ADJUD
CONTROL PEACE 20 BOLIV OAS. PAGE 96 E1930
S67
INT/ORG
DIPLOM
GEOG
WAR

US DEPARTMENT OF STATE,TREATIES IN FORCE. USA+45
WOR+45 AGREE WAR PEACE 20 TREATY. PAGE 100 E1999
B67
BIBLIOG
DIPLOM
INT/ORG
DETER

US SENATE COMM ON FOREIGN REL,SURVEY OF THE
ALLIANCE FOR PROGRESS: FOREIGN TRADE POLICIES
(PAMPHLET). L/A+17C LAW ECO/UNDEV ECO/TAC TARIFFS
20 GATT LAFTA UN. PAGE 102 E2037
N67
INT/TRADE
REGION
AGREE
INT/ORG

US SENATE COMM ON FOREIGN REL,A SELECT CHRONOLOGY
AND BACKGROUND DOCUMENTS RELATING TO THE MIDDLE
EAST. ISRAEL UAR LAW INT/ORG FORCES PROB/SOLV
CONFER CONSEN PEACE ATTIT...POLICY 20 UN SENATE
TRUMAN/HS. PAGE 101 E2033
B67
ISLAM
TIME/SEQ
DIPLOM

GREGG R.W.,INTERNATIONAL ORGANIZATION IN THE
WESTERN HEMISPHERE. L/A+17C USA+45 CULTURE PLAN
DOMIN AGREE CONTROL DETER PWR...GEOG 20 OAS TREATY.
PAGE 46 E0913
B68
INT/ORG
DIPLOM
ECO/UNDEV

US SENATE COMM ON FOREIGN REL,INTER-AMERICAN
DEVELOPMENT BANK ACT AMENDMENT. L/A+17C USA+45
DELIB/GP DIPLOM FOR/AID BAL/PAY...CHARTS SENATE.
PAGE 102 E2034
B67
LAW
FINAN
INT/ORG
ECO/UNDEV

HULL R.H.,LAW AND VIETNAM. COM VIETNAM CONSTN
INT/ORG FORCES DIPLOM AGREE COERCE DETER WEAPON
PEACE ATTIT 20 UN TREATY. PAGE 56 E1113
B68
POLICY
LAW
WAR
INT/LAW

WATT A.,THE EVOLUTION OF AUSTRALIAN FOREIGN POLICY
1938-65. ASIA S/ASIA USA+45 USA-45 INT/ORG NAT/G
B67
DIPLOM
WAR

CHIU H.,"COMMUNIST CHINA'S ATTITUDE TOWARD THE
UNITED NATIONS: A LEGAL ANALYSIS." CHINA/COM WOR+45
L68
INT/LAW
SOVEREIGN

LAW NAT/G DIPLOM CONFER ADJUD PARTIC ATTIT...POLICY INT/ORG
TREND 20 UN. PAGE 22 E0432   REPRESENT

S68
DUGARD J.,"THE REVOCATION OF THE MANDATE FOR SOUTH   AFR
WEST AFRICA." SOUTH/AFR WOR+45 STRATA NAT/G   INT/ORG
DELIB/GP DIPLOM ADJUD SANCTION CHOOSE RACE/REL   DISCRIM
...POLICY NAT/COMP 20 AFRICA/SW UN TRUST/TERR   COLONIAL
LEAGUE/NAT. PAGE 33 E0654

INT/REL....INTERNATIONAL RELATIONS

INT/TRADE....INTERNATIONAL TRADE

N
LIBRARY INTERNATIONAL REL,INTERNATIONAL INFORMATION   BIBLIOG/A
SERVICE. WOR+45 CULTURE INT/ORG FORCES...GEOG HUM   DIPLOM
SOC. PAGE 65 E1295   INT/TRADE
                                                      INT/LAW

N
CANADIAN GOVERNMENT PUBLICATIONS (1955-). CANADA   BIBLIOG/A
AGRI FINAN LABOR FORCES INT/TRADE HEALTH...JURID 20   NAT/G
PARLIAMENT. PAGE 1 E0005   DIPLOM
                                                      INT/ORG

N
INTERNATIONAL AFFAIRS. WOR+45 WOR-45 ECO/UNDEV   BIBLIOG/A
INT/ORG NAT/G PROB/SOLV FOR/AID WAR...POLICY 20.   DIPLOM
PAGE 1 E0007   INT/LAW
                                                      INT/TRADE

N
INTERNATIONAL BOOK NEWS, 1928-1934. ECO/UNDEV FINAN   BIBLIOG/A
INDUS LABOR INT/TRADE CONFER ADJUD COLONIAL...HEAL   DIPLOM
SOC/WK CHARTS 20 LEAGUE/NAT. PAGE 1 E0008   INT/LAW
                                                      INT/ORG

N
INTERNATIONAL STUDIES. ASIA S/ASIA WOR+45 ECO/UNDEV   BIBLIOG/A
INT/ORG NAT/G LEAD ATTIT WEALTH...SOC 20. PAGE 1   DIPLOM
E0009   INT/LAW
                                                      INT/TRADE

N
FOREIGN AFFAIRS. SPACE WOR+45 WOR-45 CULTURE   BIBLIOG
ECO/UNDEV FINAN NAT/G TEC/DEV INT/TRADE ARMS/CONT   DIPLOM
NUC/PWR...POLICY 20 UN EURATOM ECSC EEC. PAGE 1   INT/ORG
E0021   INT/LAW

N
HARVARD UNIVERSITY LAW LIBRARY,CATALOG OF   BIBLIOG
INTERNATIONAL LAW AND RELATIONS. WOR+45 WOR-45   INT/LAW
INT/ORG NAT/G JUDGE DIPLOM INT/TRADE ADJUD CT/SYS   JURID
19/20. PAGE 51 E1007

N
TURNER R.K.,BIBLIOGRAPHY ON WORLD ORGANIZATION.   BIBLIOG/A
INT/TRADE CT/SYS ARMS/CONT WEALTH...INT/LAW 20.   INT/ORG
PAGE 97 E1944   PEACE
                                                      WAR

B03
CHANNING W.E.,DISCOURSES ON WAR (1820-1840). LAW   WAR
SECT DIPLOM INT/TRADE ALL/VALS. PAGE 21 E0418   PLAN
                                                      LOVE
                                                      ORD/FREE

B03
FORTESCUE G.K.,SUBJECT INDEX OF THE MODERN WORKS   BIBLIOG
ADDED TO THE LIBRARY OF THE BRITISH MUSEUM IN THE   INDEX
YEARS 1881-1900 (3 VOLS.). UK LAW CONSTN FINAN   WRITING
NAT/G FORCES INT/TRADE COLONIAL 19. PAGE 39 E0775

B03
MOREL E.D.,THE BRITISH CASE IN FRENCH CONGO.   DIPLOM
CONGO/BRAZ FRANCE UK COERCE MORAL WEALTH...POLICY   INT/TRADE
INT/LAW 20 CONGO/LEOP. PAGE 74 E1490   COLONIAL
                                                      AFR

B11
REINSCH P.,PUBLIC INTERNATIONAL UNION. WOR-45 LAW   FUT
LABOR INT/TRADE LEGIT PERSON ALL/VALS...SOCIALIST   INT/ORG
CONCPT TIME/SEQ TREND GEN/LAWS 19/20. PAGE 84 E1683   DIPLOM

B13
BORCHARD E.M.,BIBLIOGRAPHY OF INTERNATIONAL LAW AND   BIBLIOG
CONTINENTAL LAW. EUR+WWI MOD/EUR UK LAW INT/TRADE   INT/LAW
WAR PEACE...GOV/COMP NAT/COMP 19/20. PAGE 14 E0267   JURID
                                                      DIPLOM

B17
MEYER H.H.B.,LIST OF REFERENCES ON EMBARGOES   BIBLIOG
(PAMPHLET). USA-45 AGRI DIPLOM WRITING DEBATE   DIST/IND
WEAPON...INT/LAW 18/20 CONGRESS. PAGE 72 E1447   ECO/TAC
                                                      INT/TRADE

N19
TAYLOR H.,WHY THE PENDING TREATY WITH COLOMBIA   INT/LAW
SHOULD BE RATIFIED (PAMPHLET). PANAMA USA-45   DIPLOM
DELIB/GP INT/TRADE REV ORD/FREE...JURID TREATY
18/19 ROOSEVLT/T TAFT/WH COLOMB. PAGE 95 E1912

B20
COX H.,ECONOMIC LIBERTY. UNIV LAW INT/TRADE RATION   NAT/G
TARIFFS RACE/REL SOCISM POLICY. PAGE 27 E0535   ORD/FREE
                                                      ECO/TAC
                                                      PERSON

B23
DE MONTESQUIEU C.,THE SPIRIT OF LAWS (2 VOLS.)   JURID
(TRANS. BY THOMAS NUGENT). FRANCE FINAN SECT   LAW
INT/TRADE TAX COERCE REV DISCRIM HABITAT ORD/FREE   CONCPT
19 ALEMBERT/J CIVIL/LAW. PAGE 30 E0588   GEN/LAWS

B24
NAVILLE A.,LIBERTE, EGALITE, SOLIDARITE: ESSAIS   ORD/FREE
D'ANALYSE. STRATA FAM VOL/ASSN INT/TRADE GP/REL   SOC
MORAL MARXISM SOCISM...PSY TREATY. PAGE 76 E1529   IDEA/COMP
                                                      DIPLOM

B26
INSTITUT INTERMEDIAIRE INTL,REPERTOIRE GENERAL DES   BIBLIOG
TRAITES ET AUTRES ACTES DIPLOMATIQUES CONCLUS   DIPLOM
DEPUIS 1895 JUSQU'EN 1920. MOD/EUR WOR-45 INT/ORG
VOL/ASSN DELIB/GP INT/TRADE WAR TREATY 19/20.
PAGE 56 E1125

B33
AMERICAN FOREIGN LAW ASSN,BIOGRAPHICAL NOTES ON THE   BIBLIOG/A
LAWS AND LEGAL LITERATURE OF URUGUAY AND CURACAO.   LAW
URUGUAY CONSTN FINAN SECT FORCES JUDGE DIPLOM   JURID
INT/TRADE ADJUD CT/SYS CRIME 20. PAGE 4 E0078   ADMIN

B35
BEMIS S.F.,GUIDE TO THE DIPLOMATIC HISTORY OF THE   BIBLIOG/A
UNITED STATES, 17751921. NAT/G LEGIS TOP/EX   DIPLOM
PROB/SOLV CAP/ISM INT/TRADE TARIFFS ADJUD   USA-45
...CON/ANAL 18/20. PAGE 10 E0184

B37
HAMILTON W.H.,THE POWER TO GOVERN. ECO/DEV FINAN   LING
INDUS ECO/TAC INT/TRADE TARIFFS TAX CONTROL CT/SYS   CONSTN
WAR COST PWR 18/20 SUPREME/CT. PAGE 50 E0991   NAT/G
                                                      POLICY

B38
GRISWOLD A.W.,THE FAR EASTERN POLICY OF THE UNITED   DIPLOM
STATES. ASIA S/ASIA USA-45 INT/ORG INT/TRADE WAR   POLICY
NAT/LISM...BIBLIOG 19/20 LEAGUE/NAT ROOSEVLT/T   CHIEF
ROOSEVLT/F WILSON/W TREATY. PAGE 47 E0943

B38
HARPER S.N.,THE GOVERNMENT OF THE SOVIET UNION. COM   MARXISM
USSR LAW CONSTN ECO/DEV PLAN TEC/DEV DIPLOM   NAT/G
INT/TRADE ADMIN REV NAT/LISM...POLICY 20. PAGE 50   LEAD
E1001   POL/PAR

B38
SAINT-PIERRE C.I.,SCHEME FOR LASTING PEACE (TRANS.   INT/ORG
BY H. BELLOT). INDUS NAT/G CHIEF FORCES INT/TRADE   PEACE
CT/SYS WAR PWR SOVEREIGN WEALTH...POLICY 18.   AGREE
PAGE 87 E1741   INT/LAW

C39
SCOTT J.B.,"LAW, THESTATE, AND THE INTERNATIONAL   LAW
COMMUNITY (2 VOLS.)" INTELL INT/ORG NAT/G SECT   PHIL/SCI
INT/TRADE WAR...INT/LAW GEN/LAWS BIBLIOG. PAGE 90   DIPLOM
E1798   CONCPT

B40
CONOVER H.F.,FOREIGN RELATIONS OF THE UNITED   BIBLIOG/A
STATES: A LIST OF RECENT BOOKS (PAMPHLET). ASIA   USA-45
CANADA L/A+17C UK INT/ORG INT/TRADE TARIFFS NEUTRAL   DIPLOM
WAR PEACE...INT/LAW CON/ANAL 20 CHINJAP. PAGE 25
E0492

B42
CROWE S.E.,THE BERLIN WEST AFRICA CONFERENCE,   AFR
1884-85. GERMANY ELITES MARKET INT/ORG DELIB/GP   CONFER
FORCES PROB/SOLV BAL/PWR CAP/ISM DOMIN COLONIAL   INT/TRADE
...INT/LAW 19. PAGE 28 E0548   DIPLOM

B44
CHENEY F.,CARTELS, COMBINES, AND TRUSTS: A SELECTED   BIBLIOG/A
LIST OF REFERENCES. GERMANY UK USA-45 WOR-45   LG/CO
DELIB/GP OP/RES BARGAIN CAP/ISM ECO/TAC INT/TRADE   ECO/DEV
LICENSE LEGIT CONFER PRICE 20. PAGE 22 E0428   INDUS

B45
CONOVER H.F.,THE NAZI STATE: WAR CRIMES AND WAR   BIBLIOG
CRIMINALS. GERMANY CULTURE NAT/G SECT FORCES DIPLOM   WAR

INT/TRADE EDU/PROP...INT/LAW BIOG HIST/WRIT
TIME/SEQ 20. PAGE 25 E0495

CRIME

B45
GALLOWAY E.,ABSTRACTS OF POSTWAR LITERATURE (VOL.
IV) JAN.-JULY, 1945 NOS. 901-1074. POLAND USA+45
USSR WOR+45 INDUS LABOR PLAN ECO/TAC INT/TRADE TAX
EDU/PROP ADMIN COLONIAL INT/LAW. PAGE 42 E0829

BIBLIOG/A
NUC/PWR
NAT/G
DIPLOM

B45
US DEPARTMENT OF STATE,PUBLICATIONS OF THE
DEPARTMENT OF STATE: A LIST CUMULATIVE FROM OCTOBER
1, 1929 (PAMPHLET). ASIA EUR+WWI ISLAM L/A+17C
USA-45 ADJUD...INT/LAW 20. PAGE 99 E1993

BIBLIOG
DIPLOM
INT/TRADE

B45
WOOLBERT R.G.,FOREIGN AFFAIRS BIBLIOGRAPHY,
1932-1942. INT/ORG SECT INT/TRADE COLONIAL RACE/REL
NAT/LISM...GEOG INT/LAW GOV/COMP IDEA/COMP 20.
PAGE 107 E2144

BIBLIOG/A
DIPLOM
WAR

B47
ENKE S.,INTERNATIONAL ECONOMICS. UK USA+45 USSR
INT/ORG BAL/PWR BARGAIN CAP/ISM BAL/PAY...NAT/COMP
20 TREATY. PAGE 35 E0691

INT/TRADE
FINAN
TARIFFS
ECO/TAC

B47
GORDON D.L.,THE HIDDEN WEAPON: THE STORY OF
ECONOMIC WARFARE. EUR+WWI USA-45 LAW FINAN INDUS
NAT/G CONSULT FORCES PLAN DOMIN PWR WEALTH
...INT/LAW CONCPT OBS TOT/POP NAZI 20. PAGE 45
E0891

INT/ORG
ECO/TAC
INT/TRADE
WAR

B47
TOWLE L.W.,INTERNATIONAL TRADE AND COMMERCIAL
POLICY. WOR+45 LAW ECO/DEV FINAN INDUS NAT/G
ECO/TAC WEALTH...TIME/SEQ ILO 20. PAGE 97 E1937

MARKET
INT/ORG
INT/TRADE

C49
BLODGETT R.H.,"COMPARATIVE ECONOMIC SYSTEMS (REV.
ED.)" WOR-45 AGRI FINAN MARKET LABOR NAT/G PLAN
INT/TRADE PRICE...POLICY DECISION BIBLIOG 20.
PAGE 13 E0248

METH/COMP
CONCPT
ROUTINE

B50
COUNCIL BRITISH NATIONAL BIB,BRITISH NATIONAL
BIBLIOGRAPHY. UK AGRI CONSTRUC PERF/ART POL/PAR
SECT CREATE INT/TRADE LEAD...HUM JURID PHIL/SCI 20.
PAGE 26 E0519

BIBLIOG/A
NAT/G
TEC/DEV
DIPLOM

C50
NUMELIN R.,"THE BEGINNINGS OF DIPLOMACY." INT/TRADE
WAR GP/REL PEACE STRANGE ATTIT...INT/LAW CONCPT
BIBLIOG. PAGE 78 E1559

DIPLOM
KIN
CULTURE
LAW

B51
BISSAINTHE M.,DICTIONNAIRE DE BIBLIOGRAPHIE
HAITIENNE. HAITI ELITES AGRI LEGIS DIPLOM INT/TRADE
WRITING ORD/FREE CATHISM...ART/METH GEOG 19/20.
NEGRO TREATY. PAGE 12 E0234

BIBLIOG
L/A+17C
SOCIETY
NAT/G

B51
INSTITUTE DES RELATIONS INTL,LES ASPECTS
ECONOMIQUES DU REARMEMENT (ETUDE DE L'INSTITUT DES
RELATIONS INTERNATIONALES A BRUXELLES). BELGIUM UK
USA+45 EXTR/IND FINAN FORCES WORKER PROB/SOLV
DIPLOM PRICE...POLICY 20 TREATY. PAGE 57 E1127

WEAPON
DEMAND
ECO/TAC
INT/TRADE

C52
STUART G.H.,"AMERICAN DIPLOMATIC AND CONSULAR
PRACTICE (2ND ED.)" EUR+WWI MOD/EUR USA-45 DELIB/GP
INT/TRADE ADJUD...BIBLIOG 20. PAGE 94 E1889

DIPLOM
ADMIN
INT/ORG

B53
OPPENHEIM L.,INTERNATIONAL LAW: A TREATISE (7TH
ED., 2 VOLS.). LAW CONSTN PROB/SOLV INT/TRADE ADJUD
AGREE NEUTRAL WAR ORD/FREE SOVEREIGN...BIBLIOG 20
LEAGUE/NAT UN ILO. PAGE 79 E1579

INT/LAW
INT/ORG
DIPLOM

B54
BINANI G.D.,INDIA AT A GLANCE (REV. ED.). INDIA
COM/IND FINAN INDUS LABOR PROVS SCHOOL PLAN DIPLOM
INT/TRADE ADMIN...JURID 20. PAGE 12 E0229

INDEX
CON/ANAL
NAT/G
ECO/UNDEV

B54
CARTER P.G.,STATISTICAL BULLETINS: AN ANNOTATED
BIBLIOGRAPHY OF THE GENERAL STATISTICAL BULLETINS
AND MAJOR POL SUBDIV OF WORLD. CULTURE AGRI FINAN
INDUS LABOR TEC/DEV INT/TRADE CT/SYS WEALTH
...CRIMLGY SOC 20. PAGE 20 E0400

BIBLIOG/A
WOR+45
NAT/G
STAT

C54
BOWIE R.R.,"STUDIES IN FEDERALISM." AGRI FINAN

FEDERAL

LABOR EX/STRUC FORCES LEGIS DIPLOM INT/TRADE ADJUD
...BIBLIOG 20 EEC. PAGE 14 E0279

EUR+WWI
INT/ORG
CONSTN

B55
BURR R.N.,DOCUMENTS ON INTER-AMERICAN COOPERATION:
VOL. I: 1810-1881; VOL. II: 1881-1948. DELIB/GP
BAL/PWR INT/TRADE REPRESENT NAT/LISM PEACE HABITAT
ORD/FREE PWR SOVEREIGN...INT/LAW 20 OAS. PAGE 18
E0345

BIBLIOG
DIPLOM
INT/ORG
L/A+17C

B57
SINEY M.C.,THE ALLIED BLOCKADE OF GERMANY:
1914-1916. EUR+WWI GERMANY MOD/EUR USA-45 DIPLOM
CONTROL NEUTRAL PWR 20. PAGE 91 E1832

DETER
INT/TRADE
INT/LAW
WAR

B58
ATOMIC INDUSTRIAL FORUM,MANAGEMENT AND ATOMIC
ENERGY. WOR+45 SEA LAW MARKET NAT/G TEC/DEV INSPECT
INT/TRADE CONFER PEACE HEALTH...ANTHOL 20. PAGE 6
E0112

NUC/PWR
INDUS
MGT
ECO/TAC

B58
MOSER J.J.,JOHANN JACOB MOSER'S GESAMMELTE UND ZU
GEMEINNUTZIGEM GEBRAUCH EINGERICHTETE BIBLIOTHEK.
GERMANY PROC/MFG INT/TRADE...POLICY JURID MGT 18.
PAGE 75 E1500

BIBLIOG
EXTR/IND
INDUS

B58
SEYID MUHAMMAD V.A.,THE LEGAL FRAMEWORK OF WORLD
TRADE. WOR+45 INT/ORG DIPLOM CONTROL...BIBLIOG 20
TREATY UN IMF GATT. PAGE 90 E1807

INT/LAW
VOL/ASSN
INT/TRADE
TARIFFS

B58
SOC OF COMP LEGIS AND INT LAW,THE LAW OF THE SEA...
(PAMPHLET). WOR+45 NAT/G INT/TRADE ADJUD CONTROL
NUC/PWR WAR PEACE ATTIT ORD/FREE...JURID CHARTS 20
UN TREATY RESOURCE/N. PAGE 92 E1850

INT/LAW
INT/ORG
DIPLOM
SEA

B59
FERRY W.H.,THE CORPORATION AND THE ECONOMY. CLIENT
LAW CONSTN LABOR NAT/G PLAN INT/TRADE PARTIC CONSEN
ORD/FREE PWR POLICY. PAGE 37 E0742

LG/CO
CONTROL
REPRESENT

B59
FRIEDMANN W.G.,LAW IN A CHANGING SOCIETY. FUT
WOR+45 WOR-45 LAW SOCIETY STRUCT INT/TRADE LEGIT
ATTIT BIO/SOC HEALTH ORD/FREE SOVEREIGN...CONCPT
GEN/LAWS ILO 20. PAGE 41 E0803

SOC
JURID

L59
COWAN T.A.,"A SYMPOSIUM ON GROUP INTERESTS AND THE
LAW" USA+45 LAW MARKET LABOR PLAN INT/TRADE TAX
RACE/REL RIGID/FLEX...JURID ANTHOL 20. PAGE 27
E0528

ADJUD
PWR
INGP/REL
CREATE

S59
DOMKE M.,"THE SETTLEMENT OF DISPUTES IN
INTERNATIONAL TRADE." USA+45 LAW STRATA STRUCT
JUDGE EDU/PROP PWR...METH/CNCPT 20. PAGE 32 E0634

CONSULT
LEGIT
INT/TRADE

B60
LEWIS P.R.,LITERATURE OF THE SOCIAL SCIENCES: AN
INTRODUCTORY SURVEY AND GUIDE. UK LAW INDUS DIPLOM
INT/TRADE ADMIN...MGT 19/20. PAGE 65 E1294

BIBLIOG/A
SOC

B60
STEIN E.,AMERICAN ENTERPRISE IN THE EUROPEAN COMMON
MARKET: A LEGAL PROFILE. EUR+WWI FUT USA+45 SOCIETY
STRUCT ECO/DEV NAT/G VOL/ASSN CONSULT PLAN TEC/DEV
ECO/TAC INT/TRADE ADMIN ATTIT RIGID/FLEX PWR...MGT
NEW/IDEA STAT TREND COMPUT/IR SIMUL EEC 20. PAGE 93
E1867

MARKET
ADJUD
INT/LAW

L60
DEAN A.W.,"SECOND GENEVA CONFERENCE OF THE LAW OF
THE SEA: THE FIGHT FOR FREEDOM OF THE SEAS." FUT
USA+45 USSR WOR+45 WOR-45 SEA CONSTN STRUCT PLAN
INT/TRADE ADJUD ADMIN ORD/FREE...DECISION RECORD
TREND GEN/LAWS 20 TREATY. PAGE 30 E0600

INT/ORG
JURID
INT/LAW

B61
ALFRED H.,PUBLIC OWNERSHIP IN THE USA: GOALS AND
PRIORITIES. LAW INDUS INT/TRADE ADJUD GOV/REL
EFFICIENCY PEACE SOCISM...POLICY ANTHOL 20 TVA.
PAGE 3 E0064

CONTROL
OWN
ECO/DEV
ECO/TAC

B61
FLINN M.W.,AN ECONOMIC AND SOCIAL HISTORY OF
BRITAIN, 1066-1939. UK LAW STRATA STRUCT AGRI
DIST/IND INDUS WORKER INT/TRADE WAR...CENSUS 11/20.
PAGE 39 E0766

SOCIETY
SOC

MECHAM J.L.,THE UNITED STATES AND INTER-AMERICAN
SECURITY, 1889-1960. L/A+17C USA+45 USA-45 CONSTN
FORCES INT/TRADE PEACE TOTALISM ATTIT...JURID 19/20
UN OAS. PAGE 72 E1432
B61
DIPLOM
WAR
ORD/FREE
INT/ORG

ALEXANDROWICZ C.H.,WORLD ECONOMIC AGENCIES: LAW AND
PRACTICE. WOR+45 DIST/IND FINAN LABOR CONSULT
INT/TRADE TARIFFS REPRESENT HEALTH...JURID 20 UN
GATT EEC OAS ECSC. PAGE 3 E0063
B62
INT/LAW
INT/ORG
DIPLOM
ADJUD

CARSON P.,MATERIALS FOR WEST AFRICAN HISTORY IN THE
ARCHIVES OF BELGIUM AND HOLLAND. CLIENT INDUS
INT/TRADE ADMIN 17/19. PAGE 20 E0397
B62
BIBLIOG/A
COLONIAL
AFR
ECO/UNDEV

COLOMBOS C.J.,THE INTERNATIONAL LAW OF THE SEA.
WOR+45 EXTR/IND DIPLOM INT/TRADE TARIFFS AGREE WAR
...TIME/SEQ 20 TREATY. PAGE 24 E0476
B62
INT/LAW
SEA
JURID
ADJUD

DE LAVALLE H.,A STATEMENT OF THE LAWS OF PERU IN
MATTERS AFFECTING BUSINESS (3RD ED.). PERU WORKER
INT/TRADE INCOME ORD/FREE...INT/LAW 20. PAGE 30
E0586
B62
CONSTN
JURID
FINAN
TAX

FATOUROS A.A.,GOVERNMENT GUARANTEES TO FOREIGN
INVESTORS. WOR+45 ECO/UNDEV INDUS WORKER ADJUD
...NAT/COMP BIBLIOG TREATY. PAGE 36 E0722
B62
NAT/G
FINAN
INT/TRADE
ECO/DEV

GANJI M.,INTERNATIONAL PROTECTION OF HUMAN RIGHTS.
WOR+45 CONSTN INT/TRADE CT/SYS SANCTION CRIME WAR
RACE/REL...CHARTS IDEA/COMP NAT/COMP BIBLIOG 20
TREATY NEGRO LEAGUE/NAT UN CIVIL/LIB. PAGE 42 E0831
B62
ORD/FREE
DISCRIM
LEGIS
DELIB/GP

HENDERSON W.O.,THE GENESIS OF THE COMMON MARKET.
EUR+WWI FRANCE MOD/EUR UK SEA COM/IND EXTR/IND
COLONIAL DISCRIM...TIME/SEQ CHARTS BIBLIOG 18/20
EEC TREATY. PAGE 52 E1030
B62
ECO/DEV
INT/TRADE
DIPLOM

OTTENBERG M.,THE FEDERAL INVESTIGATORS. USA+45 LAW
COM/IND DIST/IND WORKER DIPLOM INT/TRADE CONTROL
FEDERAL HEALTH ORD/FREE FBI CIA FTC SEC FDA.
PAGE 79 E1585
B62
FORCES
INSPECT
NAT/G
CRIME

SHAW C.,LEGAL PROBLEMS IN INTERNATIONAL TRADE AND
INVESTMENT. WOR+45 ECO/DEV ECO/UNDEV MARKET DIPLOM
TAX INCOME ROLE...ANTHOL BIBLIOG 20 TREATY UN IMF
GATT. PAGE 91 E1816
B62
INT/LAW
INT/TRADE
FINAN
ECO/TAC

THOMPSON D.,"THE UNITED KINGDOM AND THE TREATY OF
ROME." EUR+WWI INT/ORG NAT/G DELIB/GP LEGIS
INT/TRADE RIGID/FLEX...CONCPT EEC PARLIAMENT
CMN/WLTH 20. PAGE 96 E1918
S62
ADJUD
JURID

LYONS F.S.L.,INTERNATIONALISM IN EUROPE 1815-1914.
LAW AGRI COM/IND DIST/IND LABOR SECT INT/TRADE
TARIFFS...BIBLIOG 19/20. PAGE 67 E1335
B63
DIPLOM
MOD/EUR
INT/ORG

PATRA A.C.,THE ADMINISTRATION OF JUSTICE UNDER THE
EAST INDIA COMPANY IN BENGAL, BIHAR AND ORISSA.
INDIA UK LG/CO CAP/ISM INT/TRADE ADJUD COLONIAL
CONTROL CT/SYS...POLICY 20. PAGE 80 E1602
B63
ADMIN
JURID
CONCPT

FRIEDMANN W.G.,"THE USES OF 'GENERAL PRINCIPLES' IN
THE DEVELOPMENT OF INTERNATIONAL LAW." WOR+45 NAT/G
DIPLOM INT/TRADE LEGIT ROUTINE RIGID/FLEX ORD/FREE
...JURID CONCPT STERTYP GEN/METH 20. PAGE 41 E0804
S63
LAW
INT/LAW
INT/ORG

GERHARD H.,"COMMODITY TRADE STABILIZATION THROUGH
INTERNATIONAL AGREEMENTS." WOR+45 ECO/DEV ECO/UNDEV
NAT/G ROUTINE ORD/FREE...INT/LAW OBS TREND GEN/METH
TOT/POP 20. PAGE 43 E0850
S63
PLAN
ECO/TAC
INT/TRADE

WALKER H.,"THE INTERNATIONAL LAW OF COMMODITY
AGREEMENTS." FUT WOR+45 ECO/DEV ECO/UNDEV FINAN
INT/ORG NAT/G CONSULT CREATE PLAN ECO/TAC ATTIT
PERCEPT...CONCPT GEN/LAWS TOT/POP GATT 20. PAGE 105
E2095
S63
MARKET
VOL/ASSN
INT/LAW
INT/TRADE

CURRIE D.P.,FEDERALISM AND THE NEW NATIONS OF
AFRICA. CANADA USA+45 INT/TRADE TAX GP/REL
...NAT/COMP SOC/INTEG 20. PAGE 28 E0556
B64
FEDERAL
AFR
ECO/UNDEV
INT/LAW

FULBRIGHT J.W.,OLD MYTHS AND NEW REALITIES. USA+45
USSR LEGIS INT/TRADE DETER ATTIT...POLICY 20
COLD/WAR TREATY. PAGE 41 E0818
B64
DIPLOM
INT/ORG
ORD/FREE

GARDNER R.N.,IN PURSUIT OF WORLD ORDER* US FOREIGN
POLICY AND INTERNATIONAL ORGANIZATIONS. USA+45 USSR
ECO/UNDEV FORCES LEGIS DIPLOM FOR/AID INT/TRADE
PEACE...INT/LAW PREDICT UN. PAGE 42 E0839
B64
OBS
INT/ORG
ALL/VALS

GRZYBOWSKI K.,THE SOCIALIST COMMONWEALTH OF
NATIONS: ORGANIZATIONS AND INSTITUTIONS. FORCES
DIPLOM INT/TRADE ADJUD ADMIN LEAD WAR MARXISM
SOCISM...BIBLIOG 20 COMECON WARSAW/P. PAGE 48 E0956
B64
INT/LAW
COM
REGION
INT/ORG

RAGHAVAN M.D.,INDIA IN CEYLONESE HISTORY, SOCIETY
AND CULTURE. CEYLON INDIA S/ASIA LAW SOCIETY
INT/TRADE ATTIT...ART/METH JURID SOC LING 20.
PAGE 83 E1668
B64
DIPLOM
CULTURE
SECT
STRUCT

ROBERTS HL,FOREIGN AFFAIRS BIBLIOGRAPHY, 1952-1962.
ECO/DEV SECT PLAN FOR/AID INT/TRADE ARMS/CONT
NAT/LISM ATTIT...INT/LAW GOV/COMP IDEA/COMP 20.
PAGE 85 E1703
B64
BIBLIOG/A
DIPLOM
INT/ORG
WAR

SCHECHTER A.H.,INTERPRETATION OF AMBIGUOUS
DOCUMENTS BY INTERNATIONAL ADMINISTRATIVE
TRIBUNALS. WOR+45 EX/STRUC INT/TRADE CT/SYS
SOVEREIGN 20 UN ILO EURCT/JUST. PAGE 87 E1752
B64
INT/LAW
DIPLOM
INT/ORG
ADJUD

SEGAL R.,SANCTIONS AGAINST SOUTH AFRICA. AFR
SOUTH/AFR NAT/G INT/TRADE RACE/REL PEACE PWR
...INT/LAW ANTHOL 20 UN. PAGE 90 E1801
B64
SANCTION
DISCRIM
ECO/TAC
POLICY

STRONG C.F.,HISTORY OF MODERN POLITICAL
CONSTITUTIONS. STRUCT INT/ORG NAT/G LEGIS TEC/DEV
DIPLOM INT/TRADE CT/SYS EXEC...METH/COMP T 12/20
UN. PAGE 94 E1888
B64
CONSTN
CONCPT

TONG T.,UNITED STATES DIPLOMACY IN CHINA,
1844-1860. ASIA USA-45 ECO/UNDEV ECO/TAC COERCE
GP/REL...INT/LAW 19 TREATY. PAGE 96 E1934
B64
DIPLOM
INT/TRADE
COLONIAL

UN PUB. INFORM. ORGAN.,EVERY MAN'S UNITED NATIONS.
UNIV WOR+45 CONSTN CULTURE SOCIETY ECO/DEV
ECO/UNDEV NAT/G ACT/RES PLAN ECO/TAC INT/TRADE
EDU/PROP LEGIT PEACE ATTIT ALL/VALS...POLICY HUM
INT/LAW CONCPT CHARTS UN TOT/POP 20. PAGE 97 E1954
B64
INT/ORG
ROUTINE

DERWINSKI E.J.,"THE COST OF THE INTERNATIONAL
COFFEE AGREEMENT." L/A+17C USA+45 WOR+45 ECO/UNDEV
NAT/G VOL/ASSN LEGIS DIPLOM ECO/TAC FOR/AID LEGIT
ATTIT...TIME/SEQ CONGRESS 20 TREATY. PAGE 31 E0608
S64
MARKET
DELIB/GP
INT/TRADE

BAADE H.,THE SOVIET IMPACT ON INTERNATIONAL LAW.
INT/ORG INT/TRADE LEGIT COLONIAL ARMS/CONT REV WAR
...CON/ANAL ANTHOL TREATY. PAGE 6 E0124
B65
INT/LAW
USSR
CREATE
ORD/FREE

COWEN Z.,THE BRITISH COMMONWEALTH OF NATIONS IN A
CHANGING WORLD. UK ECO/UNDEV INT/ORG ECO/TAC
INT/TRADE COLONIAL WAR GP/REL RACE/REL SOVEREIGN
SOC/INTEG 20 TREATY EEC COMMONWLTH. PAGE 27 E0530
B65
JURID
DIPLOM
PARL/PROC
NAT/LISM

HABERLER G.,A SURVEY OF INTERNATIONAL TRADE THEORY.
CANADA FRANCE GERMANY ECO/TAC TARIFFS AGREE COST
DEMAND WEALTH...ECOMETRIC 19/20 MONOPOLY TREATY.
PAGE 49 E0968
B65
INT/TRADE
BAL/PAY
DIPLOM
POLICY

HIGGINS R.,CONFLICT OF INTERESTS* INTERNATIONAL LAW
IN A DIVIDED WORLD. ASIA USSR ECO/DEV ECO/UNDEV
SECT INT/TRADE COLD/WAR WORSHIP. PAGE 52 E1042
B65
INT/LAW
IDEA/COMP
ADJUST

LUGO-MARENCO J.J.,A STATEMENT OF THE LAWS OF
B65
CONSTN

NICARAGUA IN MATTERS AFFECTING BUSINESS. NICARAGUA AGRI DIST/IND EXTR/IND FINAN INDUS FAM WORKER INT/TRADE TAX MARRIAGE OWN BIO/SOC 20 TREATY RESOURCE/N MIGRATION. PAGE 67 E1332
NAT/G
LEGIS
JURID

B65
NEWBURY C.W.,BRITISH POLICY TOWARDS WEST AFRICA: SELECT DOCUMENTS 1786-1874. AFR UK INT/TRADE DOMIN ADMIN COLONIAL CT/SYS COERCE ORD/FREE...BIBLIOG/A 18/19. PAGE 77 E1540
DIPLOM
POLICY
NAT/G
WRITING

B65
NWOGUGU E.I.,THE LEGAL PROBLEMS OF FOREIGN INVESTMENT IN DEVELOPING COUNTRIES. WOR+45 INT/ORG DELIB/GP LEGIS PROB/SOLV INT/TRADE TAX ADJUD SANCTION...BIBLIOG 20 TREATY. PAGE 78 E1561
FOR/AID
FINAN
INT/LAW
ECO/UNDEV

B65
US SENATE COMM ON JUDICIARY,ANTITRUST EXEMPTIONS FOR AGREEMENTS RELATING TO BALANCE OF PAYMENTS. FINAN ECO/TAC CONTROL WEALTH...POLICY 20 CONGRESS. PAGE 103 E2056
BAL/PAY
ADJUD
MARKET
INT/TRADE

B65
WEIL G.L.,A HANDBOOK ON THE EUROPEAN ECONOMIC COMMUNITY. BELGIUM EUR+WWI FRANCE GERMANY/W ITALY CONSTN ECO/DEV CREATE PARTIC GP/REL...DECISION MGT CHARTS 20 EEC. PAGE 105 E2107
INT/TRADE
INT/ORG
TEC/DEV
INT/LAW

S65
MERRITT R.L.,"SELECTED ARTICLES AND DOCUMENTS ON INTERNATIONAL LAW AND RELATIONS." WOR+45 INT/ORG FORCES INT/TRADE. PAGE 72 E1443
BIBLIOG
DIPLOM
INT/LAW
GOV/REL

B66
DYCK H.V.,WEIMAR GERMANY AND SOVIET RUSSIA 1926-1933. EUR+WWI GERMANY UK USSR ECO/TAC INT/TRADE NEUTRAL WAR ATTIT 20 WEIMAR/REP TREATY. PAGE 34 E0669
DIPLOM
GOV/REL
POLICY

B66
EDWARDS C.D.,TRADE REGULATIONS OVERSEAS. IRELAND NEW/ZEALND SOUTH/AFR NAT/G CAP/ISM TARIFFS CONTROL ...POLICY JURID 20 EEC CHINJAP. PAGE 34 E0676
INT/TRADE
DIPLOM
INT/LAW
ECO/TAC

B66
GHOSH P.K.,THE CONSTITUTION OF INDIA: HOW IT HAS BEEN FRAMED. INDIA LOC/G DELIB/GP EX/STRUC PROB/SOLV BUDGET INT/TRADE CT/SYS CHOOSE...LING 20. PAGE 43 E0854
CONSTN
NAT/G
LEGIS
FEDERAL

B66
GRUNEWALD D.,PUBLIC POLICY AND THE MODERN COOPERATION: SELECTED READINGS. USA+45 LAW MARKET VOL/ASSN CAP/ISM INT/TRADE CENTRAL OWN...SOC ANTHOL 20. PAGE 48 E0954
LG/CO
POLICY
NAT/G
CONTROL

B66
MCNAIR A.D.,THE LEGAL EFFECTS OF WAR. UK FINAN DIPLOM ORD/FREE 20 ENGLSH/LAW. PAGE 71 E1425
JURID
WAR
INT/TRADE
LABOR

S66
GREEN L.C.,"RHODESIAN OIL: BOOTLEGGERS OR PIRATES?" AFR RHODESIA UK WOR+45 INT/ORG NAT/G DIPLOM LEGIT COLONIAL SOVEREIGN 20 UN OAU. PAGE 46 E0907
INT/TRADE
SANCTION
INT/LAW
POLICY

B67
GABRIEL P.P.,THE INTERNATIONAL TRANSFER OF CORPORATE SKILLS: MANAGEMENT CONTRACTS IN LESS DEVELOPED COUNTRIES. CLIENT INDUS LG/CO PLAN PROB/SOLV CAP/ISM ECO/TAC FOR/AID INT/TRADE RENT ADMIN SKILL 20. PAGE 42 E0825
ECO/UNDEV
AGREE
MGT
CONSULT

B67
INTERNATIONAL CONCILIATION,ISSUES BEFORE THE 22ND GENERAL ASSEMBLY. WOR+45 ECO/UNDEV FINAN BAL/PWR BUDGET INT/TRADE STRANGE ORD/FREE...INT/LAW 20 UN COLD/WAR. PAGE 57 E1132
PROB/SOLV
INT/ORG
DIPLOM
PEACE

B67
LAFAVE W.R.,INTERNATIONAL TRADE, INVESTMENT, AND ORGANIZATION. INDUS PROB/SOLV TARIFFS CONTROL ...TREND ANTHOL BIBLIOG 20 EEC. PAGE 62 E1245
INT/TRADE
INT/LAW
INT/ORG

B67
ROBINSON R.D., INTERNATIONAL MANAGEMENT. USA+45 FINAN R+D PLAN PRODUC...DECISION T. PAGE 67 E1336
INT/TRADE
MGT
INT/LAW
MARKET

S67
ALDRICH W.A.,"THE SUEZ CRISIS." UAR UK USA+45 DELIB/GP FORCES BAL/PWR INT/TRADE CONFER CONTROL COERCE DETER 20. PAGE 3 E0058
DIPLOM
INT/LAW
COLONIAL

S67
LARSEN P.B.,"THE UNITED STATES-ITALY AIR TRANSPORT ARBITRATION: PROBLEMS OF TREATY INTERPRETATION AND ENFORCEMENT." ITALY USA+45 AIR PROB/SOLV DIPLOM DEBATE CONTROL CT/SYS...DECISION TREATY. PAGE 63 E1257
INT/LAW
ADJUD
INT/TRADE
DIST/IND

S67
WILLIG S.H.,"THE CONTROL OVER INTERSTATE DISTRIBUTION AND USE OF INVESTIGATIONAL DRUGS (IN THE UNITED STATES)" USA+45 NAT/G INT/TRADE LICENSE. PAGE 106 E2124
DIST/IND
HEALTH
CONTROL
DELIB/GP

N67
US SENATE COMM ON FOREIGN REL,SURVEY OF THE ALLIANCE FOR PROGRESS: FOREIGN TRADE POLICIES (PAMPHLET). L/A+17C LAW ECO/UNDEV ECO/TAC TARIFFS 20 GATT LAFTA UN. PAGE 102 E2037
INT/TRADE
REGION
AGREE
INT/ORG

B96
DE VATTEL E.,THE LAW OF NATIONS. AGRI FINAN CHIEF DIPLOM INT/TRADE AGREE OWN ALL/VALS MORAL ORD/FREE SOVEREIGN...GEN/LAWS 18 NATURL/LAW WOLFF/C. PAGE 30 E0597
LAW
CONCPT
NAT/G
INT/LAW

INTEGRATION....SEE NEGRO, SOUTH/US, RACE/REL, SOC/INTEG, CIV/RIGHTS, DISCRIM, ISOLAT, SCHOOL, STRANGE

INTEGRATION, POLITICAL+ECONOMIC....SEE REGION+INT/ORG+ VOL/ASSN+CENTRAL

INTELL....INTELLIGENTSIA

N
DEUTSCHE BUCHEREI,JAHRESVERZEICHNIS DER DEUTSCHEN HOCHSCHULSCHRIFTEN. EUR+WWI GERMANY LAW ADMIN PERSON...MGT SOC 19/20. PAGE 31 E0613
BIBLIOG
WRITING
ACADEM
INTELL

B05
DICEY A.,LAW AND PUBLIC OPINION IN ENGLAND. LAW CULTURE INTELL SOCIETY NAT/G SECT JUDGE LEGIT CHOOSE RIGID/FLEX KNOWL...OLD/LIB CONCPT STERTYP GEN/LAWS 20. PAGE 31 E0620
ATTIT
UK

B11
PHILLIPSON C.,THE INTERNATIONAL LAW AND CUSTOM OF ANCIENT GREECE AND ROME. MEDIT-7 UNIV INTELL SOCIETY STRUCT NAT/G LEGIS EXEC PERSON...CONCPT OBS CON/ANAL ROM/EMP. PAGE 80 E1614
INT/ORG
LAW
INT/LAW

S17
ROOT E.,"THE EFFECT OF DEMOCRACY ON INTERNATIONAL LAW." USA-45 WOR-45 INTELL SOCIETY INT/ORG NAT/G CONSULT ACT/RES CREATE PLAN EDU/PROP PEACE SKILL ...CONCPT METH/CNCPT OBS 20. PAGE 85 E1712
LEGIS
JURID
INT/LAW

B22
BRYCE J.,INTERNATIONAL RELATIONS. CHRIST-17C EUR+WWI MOD/EUR CULTURE INTELL NAT/G DELIB/GP CREATE BAL/PWR DIPLOM ATTIT DRIVE RIGID/FLEX ALL/VALS...PLURIST JURID CONCPT TIME/SEQ GEN/LAWS TOT/POP. PAGE 16 E0323
INT/ORG
POLICY

B26
HOCKING W.E.,PRESENT STATUS OF THE PHILOSOPHY OF LAW AND OF RIGHTS. UNIV CULTURE INTELL SOCIETY NAT/G CREATE LEGIT SANCTION ALL/VALS SOC/INTEG 18/20. PAGE 53 E1060
JURID
PHIL/SCI
ORD/FREE

B28
HOLDSWORTH W.S.,THE HISTORIANS OF ANGLO-AMERICAN LAW. UK USA-45 INTELL LEGIS RESPECT...BIOG NAT/COMP 17/20 COMMON/LAW. PAGE 54 E1076
HIST/WRIT
LAW
JURID

S37
TIMASHEFF N.S.,"WHAT IS SOCIOLOGY OF LAW?" (BMR)" UNIV INTELL PWR...EPIST JURID PHIL/SCI IDEA/COMP. PAGE 96 E1925
LAW
SOC
SOCIETY

C39
SCOTT J.B.,"LAW, THESTATE, AND THE INTERNATIONAL COMMUNITY (2 VOLS.)" INTELL INT/ORG NAT/G SECT INT/TRADE WAR...INT/LAW GEN/LAWS BIBLIOG. PAGE 90 E1798
LAW
PHIL/SCI
DIPLOM
CONCPT

B41
GILMORE M.P.,ARGUMENT FROM ROMAN LAW IN POLITICAL THOUGHT, 1200-1600. INTELL LICENSE CONTROL CT/SYS GOV/REL PRIVIL PWR...IDEA/COMP BIBLIOG 13/16. PAGE 44 E0866
JURID
LAW
CONCPT
NAT/G

CRAIG A.,ABOVE ALL LIBERTIES. FRANCE UK USA-45 LAW   B42
CONSTN CULTURE INTELL NAT/G SECT JUDGE...IDEA/COMP   ORD/FREE
BIBLIOG 18/20. PAGE 27 E0536   MORAL
                                               WRITING
                                               EDU/PROP

CRAIG A.,"ABOVE ALL LIBERTIES." FRANCE UK LAW   C42
CULTURE INTELL SECT ORD/FREE 18/20. PAGE 27 E0537   BIBLIOG/A
                                               EDU/PROP
                                               WRITING
                                               MORAL

WRIGHT Q.,"CONSTITUTIONAL PROCEDURES OF THE US FOR   TOP/EX
CARRYING OUT OBLIGATIONS FOR MILITARY SANCTIONS."   FORCES
EUR+WWI FUT USA-45 WOR+45 CONSTN INTELL NAT/G   INT/LAW
CONSULT EX/STRUC LEGIS ROUTINE DRIVE...POLICY JURID   WAR
CONCPT OBS TREND TOT/POP 20. PAGE 108 E2153   S44

KIRK G.,"MATERIALS FOR THE STUDY OF INTERNATIONAL   INT/ORG
RELATIONS." FUT UNIV WOR+45 INTELL EDU/PROP ROUTINE   ACT/RES
PEACE ATTIT...INT/LAW JURID CONCPT OBS. PAGE 61   DIPLOM
E1219   S49

MACIVER R.M.,GREAT EXPRESSIONS OF HUMAN RIGHTS. LAW   UNIV
CONSTN CULTURE INTELL SOCIETY R+D INT/ORG ATTIT   CONCPT
DRIVE...JURID OBS HIST/WRIT GEN/LAWS. PAGE 67 E1340   B50

STONE J.,THE PROVINCE AND FUNCTION OF LAW. UNIV   INT/ORG
WOR+45 WOR-45 CULTURE INTELL SOCIETY ECO/DEV   LAW
ECO/UNDEV NAT/G LEGIT ROUTINE ATTIT PERCEPT PERSON
...JURID CONCPT GEN/LAWS GEN/METH 20. PAGE 94 E1877   B50

BENTHAM A.,HANDBOOK OF POLITICAL FALLACIES. FUT   POL/PAR
MOD/EUR LAW INTELL LOC/G MUNIC NAT/G DELIB/GP LEGIS
CREATE EDU/PROP CT/SYS ATTIT RIGID/FLEX KNOWL PWR
...RELATIV PSY SOC CONCPT SELF/OBS TREND STERTYP
TOT/POP. PAGE 10 E0189   B52

WRIGHT Q.,"CONGRESS AND THE TREATY-MAKING POWER."   ROUTINE
USA+45 WOR+45 CONSTN INTELL NAT/G CHIEF CONSULT   DIPLOM
EX/STRUC LEGIS TOP/EX CREATE GOV/REL DISPL DRIVE   INT/LAW
RIGID/FLEX...TREND TOT/POP CONGRESS CONGRESS 20   DELIB/GP
TREATY. PAGE 108 E2154   L52

WRIGHT Q.,"THE PEACEFUL ADJUSTMENT OF INTERNATIONAL   R+D
RELATIONS: PROBLEMS AND RESEARCH APPROACHES." UNIV   METH/CNCPT
INTELL EDU/PROP ADJUD ROUTINE KNOWL SKILL...INT/LAW   PEACE
JURID PHIL/SCI CLASSIF 20. PAGE 108 E2156   S55

SUTHERLAND A.E.,THE LAW AND ONE MAN AMONG MANY.   JURID
USA+45 INTELL ADJUD CT/SYS 20. PAGE 95 E1895   INGP/REL
                                               ORD/FREE
                                               CONCPT

BERNS W.,FREEDOM, VIRTUE AND THE FIRST AMENDMENT.   JURID
USA+45 USA-45 CONSTN INTELL JUDGE ADJUD RIGID/FLEX   ORD/FREE
MORAL...CONCPT 20 AMEND/I. PAGE 11 E0211   CT/SYS
                                               LAW

FRANKFURTER F.,"THE SUPREME COURT IN THE MIRROR OF   EDU/PROP
JUSTICES" (BMR)" USA+45 USA-45 INTELL INSPECT   ADJUD
EFFICIENCY ROLE KNOWL MORAL 18/20 SUPREME/CT.   CT/SYS
PAGE 40 E0792   PERSON

KURL S.,ESTONIA: A SELECTED BIBLIOGRAPHY. USSR   BIBLIOG
ESTONIA LAW INTELL SECT...ART/METH GEOG HUM SOC 20.   CULTURE
PAGE 62 E1238   NAT/G

ROCHE J.P.,"POLITICAL SCIENCE AND SCIENCE FICTION"   QUANT
(BMR)" WOR+45 INTELL OP/RES ADJUD...JURID SOC   RATIONAL
IDEA/COMP 20. PAGE 85 E1709   MATH
                                               METH

EPSTEIN F.T.,EAST GERMANY: A SELECTED BIBLIOGRAPHY   BIBLIOG/A
(PAMPHLET). COM GERMANY/E LAW AGRI FINAN INDUS   INTELL
LABOR POL/PAR EDU/PROP ADMIN AGE/Y 20. PAGE 35   MARXISM
E0693   NAT/G

MORRIS C.,THE GREAT LEGAL PHILOSOPHERS: SELECTED   JURID
READINGS IN JURISPRUDENCE. UNIV INTELL SOCIETY   ADJUD
EDU/PROP MAJORITY UTOPIA PERSON KNOWL...ANTHOL.   PHIL/SCI

DERGE D.R.,"THE LAWYER AS DECISION-MAKER IN THE   LEGIS
AMERICAN STATE LEGISLATURE." INTELL LOC/G POL/PAR   LAW
CHOOSE AGE HEREDITY PERSON CONSERVE...JURID STAT   DECISION
CHARTS. PAGE 31 E0607   LEAD

PRICE D.,THE SECRETARY OF STATE. USA+45 CONSTN   CONSULT
ELITES INTELL CHIEF EX/STRUC TOP/EX LEGIT ATTIT PWR   DIPLOM
SKILL...DECISION 20 CONGRESS. PAGE 82 E1650   INT/LAW

MACKINNON F.,"THE UNIVERSITY: COMMUNITY OR   ACADEM
UTILITY?" CLIENT CONSTN INTELL FINAN NAT/G NEIGH   MGT
EDU/PROP PARTIC REPRESENT ROLE. PAGE 67 E1343   CONTROL
                                               SERV/IND

TAUBENFELD H.J.,"A TREATY FOR ANTARCTICA." FUT   R+D
USA+45 INTELL INT/ORG LABOR 20 TREATY ANTARCTICA.   ACT/RES
PAGE 95 E1909   DIPLOM

HARVEY W.B.,"THE RULE OF LAW IN HISTORICAL   ACT/RES
PERSPECTIVE." USA+45 WOR+45 INTELL SOCIETY ECO/DEV   LAW
ECO/UNDEV NAT/G EX/STRUC LEGIS TOP/EX LEGIT SKILL
...CONCPT HIST/WRIT TOT/POP. PAGE 51 E1010   S61

LIPSON L.,"AN ARGUMENT ON THE LEGALITY OF   INT/ORG
RECONNAISSANCE STATELLITES." COM USA+45 USSR WOR+45   LAW
AIR INTELL NAT/G CONSULT PLAN DIPLOM LEGIT ROUTINE   SPACE
ATTIT...INT/LAW JURID CONCPT METH/CNCPT TREND
COLD/WAR 20. PAGE 65 E1302   S61

MACHOWSKI K.,"SELECTED PROBLEMS OF NATIONAL   UNIV
SOVEREIGNTY WITH REFERENCE TO THE LAW OF OUTER   ACT/RES
SPACE." FUT WOR+45 AIR LAW INTELL SOCIETY ECO/DEV   NUC/PWR
PLAN EDU/PROP DETER DRIVE PERCEPT SOVEREIGN   SPACE
...POLICY INT/LAW OBS TREND TOT/POP 20. PAGE 67
E1339   N61

VINER J.,THE INTELLECTUAL HISTORY OF LAISSEZ FAIRE   ATTIT
(PAMPHLET). WOR+45 WOR-45 LAW INTELL...POLICY LING   EDU/PROP
LOG 19/20. PAGE 104 E2077   LAISSEZ
                                               ECO/TAC

HOOK S.,THE PARADOXES OF FREEDOM. UNIV CONSTN   CONCPT
INTELL LEGIS CONTROL REV CHOOSE SUPEGO...POLICY   MAJORIT
JURID IDEA/COMP 19/20 CIV/RIGHTS. PAGE 55 E1095   ORD/FREE
                                               ALL/VALS

MONNIER J.P.,"LA SUCCESSION D'ETATS EN MATIERE DE   NAT/G
RESPONSABILITE INTERNATIONALE." UNIV CONSTN INTELL   JURID
SOCIETY ADJUD ROUTINE PERCEPT SUPEGO...GEN/LAWS   INT/LAW
TOT/POP 20. PAGE 74 E1485   S62

VIGNES D.,"L'AUTORITE DES TRAITES INTERNATIONAUX EN   STRUCT
DROIT INTERNE." EUR+WWI UNIV LAW CONSTN INTELL   LEGIT
NAT/G POL/PAR DIPLOM ATTIT PERCEPT ALL/VALS   FRANCE
...POLICY INT/LAW JURID CONCPT TIME/SEQ 20 TREATY.
PAGE 104 E2075

CHOJNACKI S.,REGISTER ON CURRENT RESEARCH ON   BIBLIOG
ETHIOPIA AND THE HORN OF AFRICA. ETHIOPIA LAW   ACT/RES
CULTURE AGRI SECT EDU/PROP ADMIN...GEOG HEAL LING   INTELL
20. PAGE 22 E0433   ACADEM

FISCHER-GALATI S.A.,RUMANIA; A BIBLIOGRAPHIC GUIDE   BIBLIOG/A
(PAMPHLET). ROMANIA INTELL ECO/DEV LABOR SECT   NAT/G
WEALTH...GEOG SOC/WK LING 20. PAGE 38 E0756   COM
                                               LAW

LEVY L.W.,JEFFERSON AND CIVIL LIBERTIES: THE DARKER   BIOG
SIDE. USA-45 LAW INTELL ACADEM FORCES PRESS REV   ORD/FREE
INGP/REL PERSON 18/19 JEFFERSN/T CIVIL/LIB. PAGE 65   CONSTN
E1291   ATTIT

MACWHINNEY E.,"LES CONCEPT SOVIETIQUE DE   NAT/G
'COEXISTENCE PACIFIQUE' ET LES RAPPORTS JURIDIQUES   CONCPT
ENTRE L'URSS ET LES ETATS OCIDENTAUX." COM FUT   DIPLOM
WOR+45 LAW CULTURE INTELL POL/PAR ACT/RES BAL/PWR   USSR
...INT/LAW 20. PAGE 67 E1346

                                                      S63
MEYROWITZ H.,"LES JURISTES DEVANT L'ARME NUCLEAIRE."   ACT/RES
FUT WOR+45 INTELL SOCIETY BAL/PWR DETER WAR...JURID   ADJUD
CONCPT 20. PAGE 72 E1451   INT/LAW
                                                       NUC/PWR

                                                      B64
DIETZE G.,ESSAYS ON THE AMERICAN CONSTITUTION: A   FEDERAL
COMMEMORATIVE VOLUME IN HONOR OF ALPHEUS T. MASON.   CONSTN
USA+45 USA-45 LAW INTELL...POLICY BIOG IDEA/COMP   DIPLOM
ANTHOL SUPREME/CT. PAGE 32 E0626   CT/SYS

                                                      B64
IKLE F.C.,HOW NATIONS NEGOTIATE. COM EUR+WWI USA+45   NAT/G
INTELL INT/ORG VOL/ASSN DELIB/GP ACT/RES CREATE   POLICY
DOMIN EDU/PROP ADJUD ROUTINE ATTIT PERSON ORD/FREE
RESPECT SKILL...PSY SOC OBS VAL/FREE. PAGE 56 E1122

                                                      B65
NEGLEY G.,POLITICAL AUTHORITY AND MORAL JUDGMENT.   MORAL
INTELL SOCIETY LEGIS SANCTION UTOPIA SOVEREIGN   PWR
MARXISM...INT/LAW LOG 20. PAGE 76 E1530   CONTROL

                                                      S65
FALK R.A.,"INTERNATIONAL LEGAL ORDER." USA+45   ATTIT
INTELL FACE/GP INT/ORG LEGIT KNOWL...CONCPT   GEN/LAWS
METH/CNCPT STYLE RECORD GEN/METH 20. PAGE 36 E0717   INT/LAW

                                                      B66
BRAIBANTI R.,RESEARCH ON THE BUREAUCRACY OF   HABITAT
PAKISTAN. PAKISTAN LAW CULTURE INTELL ACADEM LOC/G   NAT/G
SECT PRESS CT/SYS...LING CHARTS 20 BUREAUCRCY.   ADMIN
PAGE 15 E0286   CONSTN

                                                      B66
HOLMES O.W.,JUSTICE HOLMES, EX CATHEDRA. USA+45   BIOG
USA-45 LAW INTELL ADMIN ATTIT...BIBLIOG 20   PERSON
SUPREME/CT HOLMES/OW. PAGE 55 E1088   CT/SYS
                                                       ADJUD

                                                      S67
READ J.S.,"CENSORED." UGANDA CONSTN INTELL SOCIETY   EDU/PROP
NAT/G DIPLOM PRESS WRITING ADJUD ADMIN COLONIAL   AFR
RISK...IDEA/COMP 20. PAGE 84 E1675   CREATE

INTELLIGENCE, MILITARY....SEE ACT/RES+FORCES+KNOWL

INTELLIGENTSIA....SEE INTELL

INTEREST....INTEREST

INTER-AMERICAN DEVELOPMENT BANK....SEE INT/AM/DEV

INTER-ASIAN DEVELOPMENT BANK....SEE IADB

INTERNAL REVENUE SERVICE....SEE IRS

INTERNAL WARFARE....SEE REV

INTERNAT CONGRESS OF JURISTS E1130

INTERNATIONAL COMN JURISTS E1131

INTERNATIONAL CONCILIATION E1132

INTERNATIONAL COURT OF JUSTICE E1133

INTERNATIONAL LAW ASSOCIATION E1134

INTERNATIONAL ATOMIC ENERGY AGENCY....SEE IAEA

INTERNATIONAL BANK FOR RECONSTRUCT. AND DEV....SEE IBRD

INTERNATIONAL CIVIL AVIATION ORGANIZATION....SEE INT/AVIATN

INTERNATIONAL COOPERATION ADMINISTRATION....SEE ICA

INTERNATIONAL COUNCIL OF SCIENTIFIC UNIONS....SEE ICSU

INTERNATIONAL COURT OF JUSTICE....SEE ICJ

INTERNATIONAL DEVELOPMENT ASSOCIATION....SEE INTL/DEV

INTERNATIONAL ECONOMIC ASSOCIATION....SEE INTL/ECON

INTERNATIONAL FINANCE CORPORATION....SEE INTL/FINAN

INTERNATIONAL GEOPHYSICAL YEAR....SEE IGY

INTERNATIONAL INTEGRATION....SEE INT/ORG, INT/REL

INTERNATIONAL LABOR ORGANIZATION....SEE ILO

INTERNATIONAL LAW....SEE INT/LAW

INTERNATIONAL MONETARY FUND....SEE IMF

INTERNATIONAL ORGANIZATIONS....SEE INT/ORG

INTERNATIONAL RELATIONS....SEE INT/REL

INTERNATIONAL SYSTEMS....SEE NET/THEORY+INT/REL+WOR+45

INTERNATIONAL TELECOMMUNICATIONS UNION....SEE ITU

INTERNATIONAL TRADE....SEE INT/TRADE

INTERNATIONAL WORKERS OF THE WORLD....SEE IWW

INTERPOL ....INTERNATIONAL CRIMINAL POLICE ORGANIZATION

                                                      S62
GREEN L.C.,"POLITICAL OFFENSES, WAR CRIMES AND   LAW
EXTRADITION." WOR+45 YUGOSLAVIA INT/ORG LEGIT   CONCPT
ROUTINE WAR ORD/FREE SOVEREIGN...JURID NAZI 20   INT/LAW
INTERPOL. PAGE 46 E0906

INTERSTATE COMMERCE COMMISSION....SEE ICC

INTERSTATE COMMISSION ON CRIME....SEE INTST/CRIM

INTERVENT....INTERVENTIONISM (MILITARY, POLITICAL, AND/OR
    ECONOMIC INTERFERENCE BY A SOVEREIGN STATE OR AN
    INTERNATIONAL AGENCY IN THE AFFAIRS OF ANOTHER
    SOVEREIGN STATE)

                                                      B40
WOLFERS A.,BRITAIN AND FRANCE BETWEEN TWO WORLD   DIPLOM
WARS. FRANCE UK INT/ORG NAT/G PLAN BARGAIN ECO/TAC   WAR
AGREE ISOLAT ALL/IDEOS...DECISION GEOG 20 TREATY   POLICY
VERSAILLES INTERVENT. PAGE 107 E2139

                                                      N47
FOX W.T.R.,UNITED STATES POLICY IN A TWO POWER   DIPLOM
WORLD. COM USA+45 USSR FORCES DOMIN AGREE NEUTRAL   FOR/AID
NUC/PWR ORD/FREE SOVEREIGN 20 COLD/WAR TREATY   POLICY
EUROPE/W INTERVENT. PAGE 39 E0780

                                                      S48
MORGENTHAU H.J.,"THE TWILIGHT OF INTERNATIONAL   MORAL
MORALITY" (BMR)" WOR+45 WOR-45 BAL/PWR WAR NAT/LISM   DIPLOM
PEACE...POLICY INT/LAW IDEA/COMP 15/20 TREATY   NAT/G
INTERVENT. PAGE 75 E1495

                                                      B52
LIPPMANN W.,ISOLATION AND ALLIANCES: AN AMERICAN   DIPLOM
SPEAKS TO THE BRITISH. USA+45 USA-45 INT/ORG AGREE   SOVEREIGN
COERCE DETER WAR PEACE MORAL 20 TREATY INTERVENT.   COLONIAL
PAGE 65 E1301   ATTIT

                                                      B64
DUBOIS J.,DANGER OVER PANAMA. FUT PANAMA SCHOOL   DIPLOM
PROB/SOLV EDU/PROP MARXISM...POLICY 19/20 TREATY   COERCE
INTERVENT CANAL/ZONE. PAGE 33 E0652

                                                      B64
STANGER R.J.,ESSAYS ON INTERVENTION. PLAN PROB/SOLV   SOVEREIGN
BAL/PWR ADJUD COERCE WAR ROLE PWR...INT/LAW CONCPT   DIPLOM
20 UN INTERVENT. PAGE 93 E1865   POLICY
                                                       LEGIT

                                                      B65
THOMAS A.V.,NONINTERVENTION: THE LAW AND ITS IMPORT   INT/LAW
IN THE AMERICAS. L/A+17C USA+45 USA-45 WOR+45   PWR
DIPLOM ADJUD...JURID IDEA/COMP 20 UN INTERVENT.   COERCE
PAGE 96 E1917

INTERVIEWING....SEE INT, REC/INT

INTERVIEWS....SEE INTERVIEWS INDEX, P. XIV

INTGOV/REL....ADVISORY COMMISSION ON INTERGOVERNMENTAL
    RELATIONS

INTL ATOMIC ENERGY AGENCY E1135

INTL/DEV....INTERNATIONAL DEVELOPMENT ASSOCIATION

INTL/ECON....INTERNATIONAL ECONOMIC ASSOCIATION

INTL/FINAN....INTERNATIONAL FINANCE CORPORATION

INTNTL COTTON ADVISORY COMMITT E1136

INTRAGROUP RELATIONS....SEE INGP/REL

INTRVN/ECO....INTERVENTION (ECONOMIC) - PHILOSOPHY OF
    GOVERNMENTAL INTERFERENCE IN DOMESTIC ECONOMIC AFFAIRS

INTST/CRIM....U.S. INTERSTATE COMMISSION ON CRIME

                                                      B66
COUNCIL OF STATE GOVERNMENTS,THE HANDBOOK ON   CRIME

INTERSTATE CRIME CONTROL. USA+45 PUB/INST DELIB/GP   GOV/REL
AGREE AGE/Y 20 INTST/CRIM. PAGE 27 E0524   CONTROL
                                                   JURID

INVENTION....SEE CREATE

INVESTMENT....SEE FINAN

IOWA.....IOWA

IRAN.....SEE ALSO ISLAM

                                                   B60
LENCZOWSKI G.,OIL AND STATE IN THE MIDDLE EAST. FUT ISLAM
IRAN LAW ECO/UNDEV EXTR/IND NAT/G TOP/EX PLAN   INDUS
TEC/DEV ECO/TAC LEGIT ADMIN COERCE ATTIT ALL/VALS   NAT/LISM
PWR...CHARTS 20. PAGE 64 E1283

IRAQ.....SEE ALSO ISLAM

IRELAND.....SEE ALSO UK

                                                   B46
GRIFFIN G.G.,A GUIDE TO MANUSCRIPTS RELATING TO   BIBLIOG/A
AMERICAN HISTORY IN BRITISH DEPOSITORIES. CANADA   ALL/VALS
IRELAND MOD/EUR UK USA-45 LAW DIPLOM ADMIN COLONIAL NAT/G
WAR NAT/LISM SOVEREIGN...GEOG INT/LAW 15/19
CMN/WLTH. PAGE 47 E0936

                                                   B57
DONALDSON A.G.,SOME COMPARATIVE ASPECTS OF IRISH   CONSTN
LAW. IRELAND NAT/G DIPLOM ADMIN CT/SYS LEAD ATTIT   LAW
SOVEREIGN...JURID BIBLIOG/A 12/20 CMN/WLTH. PAGE 32 NAT/COMP
E0635   INT/LAW

                                                   B62
DELANY V.T.H.,THE ADMINISTRATION OF JUSTICE IN   ADMIN
IRELAND. IRELAND CONSTN FINAN JUDGE COLONIAL CRIME JURID
...CRIMLGY 19/20. PAGE 30 E0604   CT/SYS
                                                   ADJUD

                                                   B62
GROGAN V.,ADMINISTRATIVE TRIBUNALS IN THE PUBLIC   ADMIN
SERVICE. IRELAND UK NAT/G CONTROL CT/SYS...JURID   LAW
GOV/COMP 20. PAGE 48 E0945   ADJUD
                                                   DELIB/GP

                                                   B65
SOPER T.,EVOLVING COMMONWEALTH. AFR CANADA INDIA   INT/ORG
IRELAND UK LAW CONSTN POL/PAR DOMIN CONTROL WAR PWR COLONIAL
...AUD/VIS 18/20 COMMONWLTH OEEC. PAGE 93 E1857   VOL/ASSN

                                                   B66
EDWARDS C.D.,TRADE REGULATIONS OVERSEAS. IRELAND   INT/TRADE
NEW/ZEALND SOUTH/AFR NAT/G CAP/ISM TARIFFS CONTROL DIPLOM
...POLICY JURID 20 EEC CHINJAP. PAGE 34 E0676   INT/LAW
                                                   ECO/TAC

                                                   S67
O'HIGGINS P.,"A BIBLIOGRAPHY OF PERIODICAL   BIBLIOG
LITERATURE RELATING TO IRISH LAW." IRELAND...JURID LAW
20. PAGE 78 E1567   ADJUD

                                                   B75
MAINE H.S.,LECTURES ON THE EARLY HISTORY OF   CULTURE
INSTITUTIONS. IRELAND UK CONSTN ELITES STRUCT FAM   LAW
KIN CHIEF LEGIS CT/SYS OWN SOVEREIGN...CONCPT 16   INGP/REL
BENTHAM/J BREHON ROMAN/LAW. PAGE 68 E1351

IRGUN.....IRGUN - PALESTINE REVOLUTIONARY ORGANIZATION

IRION F.C. E1137

IRISH/AMER.....IRISH AMERICANS

IRS.....U.S. INTERNAL REVENUE SERVICE

ISLAM.....ISLAMIC WORLD; SEE ALSO APPROPRIATE NATIONS

                                                   B29
PRATT I.A.,MODERN EGYPT: A LIST OF REFERENCES TO   BIBLIOG
MATERIAL IN THE NEW YORK PUBLIC LIBRARY. UAR   ISLAM
ECO/UNDEV...GEOG JURID SOC LING 20. PAGE 82 E1647   DIPLOM
                                                   NAT/G

                                                   B44
FULLER G.H.,TURKEY: A SELECTED LIST OF REFERENCES. BIBLIOG/A
ISLAM TURKEY CULTURE ECO/UNDEV AGRI DIPLOM NAT/LISM ALL/VALS
CONSERVE...GEOG HUM INT/LAW SOC 7/20 MAPS. PAGE 42
E0824

                                                   B45
US DEPARTMENT OF STATE,PUBLICATIONS OF THE   BIBLIOG
DEPARTMENT OF STATE: A LIST CUMULATIVE FROM OCTOBER DIPLOM
1, 1929 (PAMPHLET). ASIA EUR+WWI ISLAM L/A+17C   INT/TRADE
USA-45 ADJUD...INT/LAW 20. PAGE 99 E1993

                                                   B48
LOGAN R.W.,THE AFRICAN MANDATES IN WORLD POLITICS. WAR
EUR+WWI GERMANY ISLAM INT/ORG BARGAIN...POLICY   COLONIAL
INT/LAW 20. PAGE 66 E1321   AFR
                                                   DIPLOM

                                                   B52
ETTINGHAUSEN R.,SELECTED AND ANNOTATED BIBLIOGRAPHY BIBLIOG/A
OF BOOKS AND PERIODICALS IN WESTERN LANGUAGES   ISLAM
DEALING WITH NEAR AND MIDDLE EAST. LAW CULTURE SECT MEDIT-7
...ART/METH GEOG SOC. PAGE 35 E0700

                                                   B54
NUSSBAUM D.,A CONCISE HISTORY OF THE LAW OF   INT/ORG
NATIONS. ASIA CHRIST-17C EUR+WWI ISLAM MEDIT-7   LAW
MOD/EUR S/ASIA UNIV WOR+45 WOR-45 SOCIETY STRUCT   PEACE
EXEC ATTIT ALL/VALS...CONCPT HIST/WRIT TIME/SEQ.   INT/LAW
PAGE 78 E1560

                                                   B55
KHADDURI M.,WAR AND PEACE IN THE LAW OF ISLAM.   ISLAM
CONSTN CULTURE SOCIETY STRATA NAT/G PROVS SECT   JURID
FORCES TOP/EX CREATE DOMIN EDU/PROP ADJUD COERCE   PEACE
ATTIT RIGID/FLEX ALL/VALS...CONCPT TIME/SEQ TOT/POP WAR
VAL/FREE. PAGE 61 E1209

                                                   B55
KHADDURI M.,LAW IN THE MIDDLE EAST. LAW CONSTN   ADJUD
ACADEM FAM EDU/PROP CT/SYS SANCTION CRIME...INT/LAW JURID
GOV/COMP ANTHOL 6/20 MID/EAST. PAGE 61 E1210   ISLAM

                                                   B57
BLOOMFIELD L.M.,EGYPT, ISRAEL AND THE GULF OF   ISLAM
AQABA: IN INTERNATIONAL LAW. LAW NAT/G CONSULT   INT/LAW
FORCES PLAN ECO/TAC ROUTINE COERCE ATTIT DRIVE   UAR
PERCEPT PERSON RIGID/FLEX LOVE PWR WEALTH...GEOG
CONCPT MYTH TREND. PAGE 13 E0250

                                                   B59
ANDERSON J.N.D.,ISLAMIC LAW IN THE MODERN WORLD.   ISLAM
FAM KIN SECT LEGIT ADJUD ATTIT DRIVE...TIME/SEQ   JURID
TREND GEN/LAWS 20 MUSLIM. PAGE 5 E0089

                                                   B60
LENCZOWSKI G.,OIL AND STATE IN THE MIDDLE EAST. FUT ISLAM
IRAN LAW ECO/UNDEV EXTR/IND NAT/G TOP/EX PLAN   INDUS
TEC/DEV ECO/TAC LEGIT ADMIN COERCE ATTIT ALL/VALS   NAT/LISM
PWR...CHARTS 20. PAGE 64 E1283

                                                   L60
LAUTERPACHT E.,"THE SUEZ CANAL SETTLEMENT." FRANCE INT/ORG
ISLAM ISRAEL UAR UK BAL/PWR DIPLOM LEGIT...JURID   LAW
GEN/LAWS ANTHOL SUEZ VAL/FREE 20. PAGE 63 E1263

                                                   L62
MANGIN G.,"L'ORGANIZATION JUDICIAIRE DES ETATS   AFR
D'AFRIQUE ET DE MADAGASCAR." ISLAM WOR+45 STRATA   LEGIS
STRUCT ECO/UNDEV NAT/G LEGIT EXEC...JURID TIME/SEQ COLONIAL
TOT/POP 20 SUPREME/CT. PAGE 68 E1357   MADAGASCAR

                                                   S62
MANGIN G.,"LES ACCORDS DE COOPERATION EN MATIERE DE INT/ORG
JUSTICE ENTRE LA FRANCE ET LES ETATS AFRICAINS ET   LAW
MALGACHE." AFR ISLAM WOR+45 STRUCT ECO/UNDEV NAT/G FRANCE
DELIB/GP PERCEPT ALL/VALS...JURID MGT TIME/SEQ 20.
PAGE 68 E1356

                                                   L64
POUNDS N.J.G.,"THE POLITICS OF PARTITION." AFR ASIA NAT/G
COM EUR+WWI FUT ISLAM S/ASIA USA-45 LAW ECO/DEV   NAT/LISM
ECO/UNDEV AGRI INDUS INT/ORG POL/PAR PROVS SECT
FORCES TOP/EX EDU/PROP LEGIT ATTIT MORAL ORD/FREE
PWR RESPECT WEALTH. PAGE 82 E1640

                                                   S64
KHAN M.Z.,"ISLAM AND INTERNATIONAL RELATIONS." FUT ISLAM
WOR+45 LAW CULTURE SOCIETY NAT/G SECT DELIB/GP   INT/ORG
FORCES EDU/PROP ATTIT PERSON SUPEGO ALL/VALS   DIPLOM
...POLICY PSY CONCPT MYTH HIST/WRIT GEN/LAWS.
PAGE 61 E1211

                                                   B65
AMERICAN UNIVERSITY IN CAIRO,GUIDE TO UAR   BIBLIOG
GOVERNMENT PUBLICATIONS AT THE AUC LIBRARY   NAT/G
(PAMPHLET). ISLAM UAR USA+45 ECO/UNDEV...SOC STAT   LEGIS
20. PAGE 4 E0084   LAW

                                                   B65
INST INTL DES CIVILISATION DIF,THE CONSTITUTIONS   CONSTN
AND ADMINISTRATIVE INSTITUTIONS OF THE NEW STATES. ADMIN
AFR ISLAM S/ASIA NAT/G POL/PAR DELIB/GP EX/STRUC   ADJUD
CONFER EFFICIENCY NAT/LISM...JURID SOC 20. PAGE 56 ECO/UNDEV
E1123

VON RENESSE E.A.,UNVOLLENDETE DEMOKRATIEN. AFR | ECO/UNDEV | B65
ISLAM S/ASIA SOCIETY ACT/RES COLONIAL...JURID | NAT/COMP
CHARTS BIBLIOG METH 13/20. PAGE 104 E2083 | SOVEREIGN

KHOURI F.J.,"THE JORDON RIVER CONTROVERSY." LAW | ISLAM | S65
SOCIETY ECO/UNDEV AGRI FINAN INDUS SECT FORCES | INT/ORG
ACT/RES PLAN TEC/DEV ECO/TAC EDU/PROP COERCE ATTIT | ISRAEL
DRIVE PERCEPT RIGID/FLEX ALL/VALS...GEOG SOC MYTH | JORDAN
WORK. PAGE 61 E1212

HOPKINS J.F.K.,ARABIC PERIODICAL LITERATURE, 1961. | BIBLIOG/A | B66
ISLAM LAW CULTURE SECT...GEOG HEAL PHIL/SCI PSY SOC | NAT/LISM
20. PAGE 55 E1096 | TEC/DEV
| INDUS

KERR M.H.,ISLAMIC REFORM: THE POLITICAL AND LEGAL | LAW | B66
THEORIES OF MUHAMMAD 'ABDUH AND RASHID RIDA. NAT/G | CONCPT
SECT LEAD SOVEREIGN CONSERVE...JURID BIBLIOG | ISLAM
WORSHIP 20. PAGE 60 E1204

US SENATE COMM ON FOREIGN REL,A SELECT CHRONOLOGY | ISLAM | B67
AND BACKGROUND DOCUMENTS RELATING TO THE MIDDLE | TIME/SEQ
EAST. ISRAEL UAR LAW INT/ORG FORCES PROB/SOLV | DIPLOM
CONFER CONSEN PEACE ATTIT...POLICY 20 UN SENATE
TRUMAN/HS. PAGE 101 E2033

PLAYFAIR R.L.,"A BIBLIOGRAPHY OF MOROCCO." MOROCCO | BIBLIOG | C93
CULTURE AGRI FORCES DIPLOM WAR HEALTH...GEOG JURID | ISLAM
SOC CHARTS. PAGE 81 E1620 | MEDIT-7

ISOLAT.....ISOLATION AND COMMUNITY, CONDITIONS OF HIGH
    GROUP SEGREGATION

SCHULZ F.,PRINCIPLES OF ROMAN LAW. CONSTN FAM NAT/G | LAW | B36
DOMIN CONTROL CT/SYS CRIME ISOLAT ATTIT ORD/FREE | LEGIS
PWR...JURID ROME/ANC ROMAN/LAW. PAGE 89 E1783 | ADJUD
| CONCPT

WOLFERS A.,BRITAIN AND FRANCE BETWEEN TWO WORLD | DIPLOM | B40
WARS. FRANCE UK INT/ORG NAT/G PLAN BARGAIN ECO/TAC | WAR
AGREE ISOLAT ALL/IDEOS...DECISION GEOG 20 TREATY | POLICY
VERSAILLES INTERVENT. PAGE 107 E2139

ROWAN C.T.,GO SOUTH TO SORROW. USA+45 STRUCT NAT/G | RACE/REL | B57
EDU/PROP LEAD COERCE ISOLAT DRIVE SUPEGO RESPECT | DISCRIM
...PREDICT 20 NEGRO SUPREME/CT SOUTH/US CIV/RIGHTS. | ANOMIE
PAGE 86 E1728 | LAW

HOBSBAWM E.J.,PRIMITIVE REBELS; STUDIES IN ARCHAIC | SOCIETY | B59
FORMS OF SOCIAL MOVEMENT IN THE 19TH AND 20TH | CRIME
CENTURIES. ITALY SPAIN CULTURE VOL/ASSN RISK CROWD | REV
GP/REL INGP/REL ISOLAT TOTALISM...PSY SOC 18/20. | GUERRILLA
PAGE 53 E1058

DWYER R.J.,"THE ADMINISTRATIVE ROLE IN | ADMIN | S59
DESEGREGATION." USA+45 LAW PROB/SOLV LEAD RACE/REL | SCHOOL
ISOLAT STRANGE ROLE...POLICY SOC/INTEG MISSOURI | DISCRIM
NEGRO CIV/RIGHTS. PAGE 34 E0668 | ATTIT

MERTON R.K.,CONTEMPORARY SOCIAL PROBLEMS: AN | CRIME | B61
INTRODUCTION TO THE SOCIOLOGY OF DEVIANT BEHAVIOR | ANOMIE
AND SOCIAL DISORGANIZATION. FAM MUNIC FORCES WORKER | STRANGE
PROB/SOLV INGP/REL RACE/REL ISOLAT...CRIMLGY GEOG | SOC
PSY T 20 NEGRO. PAGE 72 E1444

US COMMISSION ON CIVIL RIGHTS,HEARINGS BEFORE | ORD/FREE | B62
UNITED STATES COMMISSION ON CIVIL RIGHTS. USA+45 | LAW
ECO/DEV NAT/G CONSULT WORKER EDU/PROP ADJUD DISCRIM | ADMIN
ISOLAT HABITAT HEALTH RESPECT 20 NEGRO CIV/RIGHTS. | LEGIS
PAGE 99 E1985

ROSE A.M.,MINORITY PROBLEMS: A TEXTBOOK OF READINGS | RACE/REL | B65
IN INTERGROUP RELATIONS. UNIV USA+45 LAW SCHOOL | DISCRIM
WORKER PROB/SOLV GP/REL PERSON...PSY ANTHOL WORSHIP | ISOLAT
20 NEGRO INDIAN/AM JEWS EUROPE. PAGE 85 E1713 | ACT/RES

MENDELSON W.,JUSTICES BLACK AND FRANKFURTER: | JURID | B66
CONFLICT IN THE COURT (2ND ED.). NAT/G PROVS | ADJUD
PROB/SOLV BAL/PWR CONTROL FEDERAL ISOLAT ANOMIE | IDEA/COMP
ORD/FREE...DECISION 20 SUPREME/CT BLACK/HL | ROLE
FRANKFUR/F. PAGE 72 E1439

KRENZ F.E.,"THE REFUGEE AS A SUBJECT OF | INT/LAW | L66
INTERNATIONAL LAW." FUT LAW NAT/G CREATE ADJUD | DISCRIM
ISOLAT STRANGE...RECORD UN. PAGE 62 E1230 | NEW/IDEA

LANDE G.R.,"THE EFFECT OF THE RESOLUTIONS OF THE | LEGIS | S66
UNITED NATIONS GENERAL ASSEMBLY." WOR+45 LAW | EFFICIENCY
INT/ORG NAT/G CHOOSE ISOLAT ATTIT...CLASSIF | RESPECT
GEN/METH UN. PAGE 62 E1249

RUSSELL B.,WAR CRIMES IN VIETNAM. USA+45 VIETNAM | WAR | B67
FORCES DIPLOM WEAPON RACE/REL DISCRIM ISOLAT | CRIME
BIO/SOC 20 COLD/WAR RUSSELL/B. PAGE 87 E1736 | ATTIT
| POLICY

ISOLATION.....SEE ISOLAT

ISORNI J. E1138

ISRAEL.....SEE ALSO JEWS, ISLAM

LAUTERPACHT E.,"THE SUEZ CANAL SETTLEMENT." FRANCE | INT/ORG | L60
ISLAM ISRAEL UAR UK BAL/PWR DIPLOM LEGIT...JURID | LAW
GEN/LAWS ANTHOL SUEZ VAL/FREE 20. PAGE 63 E1263

SOWLE C.R.,POLICE POWER AND INDIVIDUAL FREEDOM: THE | FORCES | B62
QUEST FOR BALANCE. CANADA EUR+WWI ISRAEL NORWAY | ORD/FREE
USA+45 LAW CONSTN SOCIETY CONTROL ROUTINE SANCTION | IDEA/COMP
GP/REL 20 CHINJAP. PAGE 93 E1859

BADI J.,THE GOVERNMENT OF THE STATE OF ISRAEL: A | NAT/G | B63
CRITICAL ACCOUNT OF ITS PARLIAMENT, EXECUTIVE, AND | CONSTN
JUDICIARY. ISRAEL ECO/DEV CHIEF DELIB/GP LEGIS | EX/STRUC
DIPLOM CT/SYS INGP/REL PEACE ORD/FREE...BIBLIOG 20 | POL/PAR
PARLIAMENT ARABS MIGRATION. PAGE 7 E0131

LIVNEH E.,ISRAEL LEGAL BIBLIOGRAPHY IN EUROPEAN | BIBLIOG | B63
LANGUAGES. ISRAEL LOC/G JUDGE TAX...INT/LAW 20. | LAW
PAGE 66 E1311 | NAT/G
| CONSTN

ROSNER G.,THE UNITED NATIONS EMERGENCY FORCE. | INT/ORG | B63
FRANCE ISRAEL UAR UK WOR+45 CREATE WAR PEACE | FORCES
ORD/FREE PWR...INT/LAW JURID HIST/WRIT TIME/SEQ UN.
PAGE 86 E1719

BOWETT D.W.,UNITED NATIONS FORCES* A LEGAL STUDY. | OP/RES | B64
CYPRUS ISRAEL KOREA LAW CONSTN ACT/RES CREATE | FORCES
BUDGET CONTROL TASK PWR...INT/LAW IDEA/COMP UN | ARMS/CONT
CONGO/LEOP SUEZ. PAGE 14 E0278

KHOURI F.J.,"THE JORDON RIVER CONTROVERSY." LAW | ISLAM | S65
SOCIETY ECO/UNDEV AGRI FINAN INDUS SECT FORCES | INT/ORG
ACT/RES PLAN TEC/DEV ECO/TAC EDU/PROP COERCE ATTIT | ISRAEL
DRIVE PERCEPT RIGID/FLEX ALL/VALS...GEOG SOC MYTH | JORDAN
WORK. PAGE 61 E1212

HAUSNER G.,JUSTICE IN JERUSALEM. GERMANY ISRAEL | ADJUD | B66
SOCIETY KIN DIPLOM LEGIT CT/SYS PARTIC MURDER | CRIME
MAJORITY ATTIT FASCISM...INT/LAW JURID 20 JEWS | RACE/REL
WAR/TRIAL. PAGE 51 E1013 | COERCE

GREIG D.W.,"THE ADVISORY JURISDICTION OF THE | INT/LAW | L66
INTERNATIONAL COURT AND THE SETTLEMENT OF DISPUTES | CT/SYS
BETWEEN STATES." ISRAEL KOREA FORCES BUDGET DOMIN
LEGIT ADJUD COST...RECORD UN CONGO/LEOP TREATY.
PAGE 46 E0915

RAE D.,THE POLITICAL CONSEQUENCES OF ELECTORAL | POL/PAR | B67
LAWS. EUR+WWI ICELAND ISRAEL NEW/ZEALND UK USA+45 | CHOOSE
ADJUD APPORT GP/REL MAJORITY...MATH STAT CENSUS | NAT/COMP
CHARTS BIBLIOG 20 AUSTRAL. PAGE 83 E1667 | REPRESENT

US SENATE COMM ON FOREIGN REL,A SELECT CHRONOLOGY | ISLAM | B67
AND BACKGROUND DOCUMENTS RELATING TO THE MIDDLE | TIME/SEQ
EAST. ISRAEL UAR LAW INT/ORG FORCES PROB/SOLV | DIPLOM
CONFER CONSEN PEACE ATTIT...POLICY 20 UN SENATE
TRUMAN/HS. PAGE 101 E2033

MATTHEWS R.O.,"THE SUEZ CANAL DISPUTE* A CASE STUDY | PEACE | S67
IN PEACEFUL SETTLEMENT." FRANCE ISRAEL UAR UK NAT/G | DIPLOM

CONTROL LEAD COERCE WAR NAT/LISM ROLE ORD/FREE PWR   ADJUD
...INT/LAW UN 20. PAGE 69 E1389

ISSUES (CURRENT SUBJECTS OF DISCOURSE)....SEE CONCPT, POLICY

ITAL/AMER....ITALIAN-AMERICANS

ITALY....SEE ALSO APPROPRIATE TIME/SPACE/CULTURE INDEX

B00
GRIFFIN A.P.C.,LIST OF BOOKS RELATING TO THE THEORY   BIBLIOG/A
OF COLONIZATION, GOVERNMENT OF DEPENDENCIES,   COLONIAL
PROTECTORATES, AND RELATED TOPICS. FRANCE GERMANY   GOV/REL
ITALY SPAIN UK USA-45 WOR-45 ECO/TAC ADMIN CONTROL   DOMIN
REGION NAT/LISM ALL/VALS PWR...INT/LAW SOC 16/19.
PAGE 46 E0917

B18
WILSON W.,THE STATE: ELEMENTS OF HISTORICAL AND   NAT/G
PRACTICAL POLITICS. FRANCE GERMANY ITALY UK USSR   JURID
CONSTN EX/STRUC LEGIS CT/SYS WAR PWR...POLICY   CONCPT
GOV/COMP 20. PAGE 106 E2131   NAT/COMP

B32
EAGLETON C.,INTERNATIONAL GOVERNMENT. BRAZIL FRANCE   INT/ORG
GERMANY ITALY UK USSR WOR-45 DELIB/GP TOP/EX PLAN   JURID
ECO/TAC EDU/PROP LEGIT ADJUD REGION ARMS/CONT   DIPLOM
COERCE ATTIT PWR...GEOG MGT VAL/FREE LEAGUE/NAT 20.   INT/LAW
PAGE 34 E0670

B37
BORGESE G.A.,GOLIATH: THE MARCH OF FASCISM. GERMANY   POLICY
ITALY LAW POL/PAR SECT DIPLOM SOCISM...JURID MYTH   NAT/LISM
20 DANTE MACHIAVELL MUSSOLIN/B. PAGE 14 E0270   FASCISM
                                                       NAT/G

B38
FIELD G.L.,THE SYNDICAL AND CORPORATIVE   FASCISM
INSTITUTIONS OF ITALIAN FASCISM. ITALY CONSTN   INDUS
STRATA LABOR EX/STRUC TOP/EX ADJUD ADMIN LEAD   NAT/G
TOTALISM AUTHORIT...MGT 20 MUSSOLIN/B. PAGE 38   WORKER
E0746

B43
SERENI A.P.,THE ITALIAN CONCEPTION OF INTERNATIONAL   LAW
LAW. EUR+WWI MOD/EUR INT/ORG NAT/G DOMIN COERCE   TIME/SEQ
ORD/FREE FASCISM...OBS/ENVIR TREND 20. PAGE 90   INT/LAW
E1804   ITALY

B44
FULLER G.H.,MILITARY GOVERNMENT: A LIST OF   BIBLIOG
REFERENCES (A PAMPHLET). ITALY UK USA-45 WOR-45 LAW   DIPLOM
FORCES DOMIN ADMIN ARMS/CONT ORD/FREE PWR   CIVMIL/REL
...DECISION 20 CHINJAP. PAGE 41 E0822   SOVEREIGN

B44
SUAREZ F.,A TREATISE ON LAWS AND GOD THE LAWGIVER   LAW
(1612) IN SELECTIONS FROM THREE WORKS, VOL. II.   JURID
FRANCE ITALY UK CULTURE NAT/G SECT CHIEF LEGIS   GEN/LAWS
DOMIN LEGIT CT/SYS ORD/FREE PWR WORSHIP 16/17.   CATH
PAGE 94 E1892

B45
CONOVER H.F.,THE GOVERNMENTS OF THE MAJOR FOREIGN   BIBLIOG
POWERS: A BIBLIOGRAPHY. FRANCE GERMANY ITALY UK   NAT/G
USSR CONSTN LOC/G POL/PAR EX/STRUC FORCES ADMIN   DIPLOM
CT/SYS CIVMIL/REL TOTALISM...POLICY 19/20. PAGE 25
E0494

L54
NICOLSON H.,"THE EVOLUTION OF DIPLOMATIC METHOD."   RIGID/FLEX
CHRIST-17C EUR+WWI FRANCE FUT ITALY MEDIT-7 MOD/EUR   METH/CNCPT
USA+45 USA-45 LAW NAT/G CREATE EDU/PROP LEGIT PEACE   DIPLOM
ATTIT ORD/FREE RESPECT SOVEREIGN. PAGE 77 E1548

B59
HOBSBAWM E.J.,PRIMITIVE REBELS; STUDIES IN ARCHAIC   SOCIETY
FORMS OF SOCIAL MOVEMENT IN THE 19TH AND 20TH   CRIME
CENTURIES. ITALY SPAIN CULTURE VOL/ASSN RISK CROWD   REV
GP/REL INGP/REL ISOLAT TOTALISM...PSY SOC 18/20.   GUERRILLA
PAGE 53 E1058

S63
RIGAUX F.,"LA SIGNIFICATION DES ACTES JUDICIARES A   CONSULT
L'ETRANGER." EUR+WWI ITALY NETHERLAND LAW ACT/RES   CT/SYS
DRIVE...JURID GEN/LAWS TOT/POP 20. PAGE 85 E1699   GERMANY

B65
CHARLTON K.,EDUCATION IN RENAISSANCE ENGLAND. ITALY   EDU/PROP
UK USA-45 WOR-45 LAW LOC/G NAT/G...IDEA/COMP 14/17   SCHOOL
HUMANISM. PAGE 21 E0423   ACADEM

B65
WEIL G.L.,A HANDBOOK ON THE EUROPEAN ECONOMIC   INT/TRADE
COMMUNITY. BELGIUM EUR+WWI FRANCE GERMANY/W ITALY   INT/ORG
CONSTN ECO/DEV CREATE PARTIC GP/REL...DECISION MGT   TEC/DEV

CHARTS 20 EEC. PAGE 105 E2107   INT/LAW

S65
STEIN E.,"TOWARD SUPREMACY OF TREATY-CONSTITUTION   ADJUD
BY JUDICIAL FIAT: ON THE MARGIN OF THE COSTA CASE."   CONSTN
EUR+WWI ITALY WOR+45 INT/ORG NAT/G LEGIT REGION   SOVEREIGN
NAT/LISM PWR...JURID CONCPT TREND TOT/POP VAL/FREE   INT/LAW
20. PAGE 93 E1870

S67
LARSEN P.B.,"THE UNITED STATES-ITALY AIR TRANSPORT   INT/LAW
ARBITRATION: PROBLEMS OF TREATY INTERPRETATION AND   ADJUD
ENFORCEMENT." ITALY USA+45 AIR PROB/SOLV DIPLOM   INT/TRADE
DEBATE CONTROL CT/SYS...DECISION TREATY. PAGE 63   DIST/IND
E1257

ITO....INTERNATIONAL TRADE ORGANIZATION

ITU....INTERNATIONAL TELECOMMUNICATIONS UNION

IVORY COAST....SEE IVORY/CST

IVORY/CST....IVORY COAST; SEE ALSO AFR

IWW....INTERNATIONAL WORKERS OF THE WORLD

— J —

JACKSON E. E1139,E1140

JACKSON R.H. E1141

JACKSON R.M. E1142

JACKSON/A....PRESIDENT ANDREW JACKSON

B64
MINAR D.W.,IDEAS AND POLITICS: THE AMERICAN   CONSTN
EXPERIENCE. SECT CHIEF LEGIS CREATE ADJUD EXEC REV   NAT/G
PWR...PHIL/SCI CONCPT IDEA/COMP 18/20 HAMILTON/A   FEDERAL
JEFFERSN/T DECLAR/IND JACKSON/A PRESIDENT. PAGE 73
E1464

JACKSON/RH....R.H. JACKSON

JACOB H. E2079

JACOBINI H.B. E1143

JACOBINISM....JACOBINISM: FRENCH DEMOCRATIC REVOLUTIONARY
     DOCTRINE, 1789

JACOBS C.E. E1144

JACOBS P. E1145

JACOBSON H.K. E1146

JAFFA/HU....H.U. JAFFA

JAKARTA....JAKARTA, INDONESIA

JAMAICA....SEE ALSO L/A+17C

S67
DOUTY H.M.," REFERENCE TO DEVELOPING COUNTRIES."   TAX
JAMAICA MALAYSIA UK WOR+45 LAW FINAN ACT/RES BUDGET   ECO/UNDEV
CAP/ISM ECO/TAC TARIFFS RISK EFFICIENCY PROFIT   NAT/G
...CHARTS 20. PAGE 33 E0646

JAMES L.F. E1147

JAMISON A.L. E1845

JANET/P....PIERRE JANET

JANOWITZ M. E1148

JAPAN....SEE ALSO ASIA

JAPAN MINISTRY OF JUSTICE E1149

JAPAN MOMBUSHO DAIGAKU GAKIYUT E1150

JAPANESE AMERICANS....SEE NISEI

JARMO....JARMO, A PRE- OR EARLY HISTORIC SOCIETY

JAROSLAV J. E0261

JASPERS/K....KARL JASPERS

JAT....A POLITICAL SYSTEM OF INDIA

JAURES/JL....JEAN LEON JAURES (FRENCH SOCIALIST 1859-1914)

JAVA....JAVA, INDONESIA; SEE ALSO INDONESIA

JEFFERSN/T....PRESIDENT THOMAS JEFFERSON

C44
JEFFERSON T.."DEMOCRACY" (1816) IN BASIC WRITINGS." POPULISM
USA-45 LOC/G NAT/G TAX CT/SYS CHOOSE ORD/FREE   MAJORIT
...GEN/LAWS 18/19 JEFFERSN/T. PAGE 58 E1151   REPRESENT
                                                      CONSTN

B62
MASON A.T..THE SUPREME COURT: PALADIUM OF FREEDOM.   CONSTN
USA-45 NAT/G POL/PAR CHIEF LEGIS ADJUD PARL/PROC   CT/SYS
FEDERAL PWR...POLICY BIOG 18/20 SUPREME/CT   JURID
ROOSEVLT/F JEFFERSN/T MARSHALL/J HUGHES/CE. PAGE 69
E1378

B63
LEVY L.W..JEFFERSON AND CIVIL LIBERTIES: THE DARKER   BIOG
SIDE. USA-45 LAW INTELL ACADEM FORCES PRESS REV   ORD/FREE
INGP/REL PERSON 18/19 JEFFERSN/T CIVIL/LIB. PAGE 65   CONSTN
E1291   ATTIT

B64
MINAR D.W..IDEAS AND POLITICS: THE AMERICAN   CONSTN
EXPERIENCE. SECT CHIEF LEGIS CREATE ADJUD EXEC REV   NAT/G
PWR...PHIL/SCI CONCPT IDEA/COMP 18/20 HAMILTON/A   FEDERAL
JEFFERSN/T DECLAR/IND JACKSON/A PRESIDENT. PAGE 73
E1464

JEFFERSON T. E1151

JEHOVA/WIT....JEHOVAH'S WITNESSES

JENCKS/C....C. JENCKS

JENKINS W.S. E1152

JENKS C.W. E1153,E1154,E1155,E1156,E1157,E1158,E1159,E1160 ,
   E1161

JENKS E.J. E1162

JENNINGS R. E1164

JENNINGS W.I. E1163,E1165

JESSUP P.C. E1166,E1167

JEWS....JEWS, JUDAISM

B43
US LIBRARY OF CONGRESS,SOCIAL AND CULTURAL PROBLEMS   BIBLIOG/A
IN WARTIME: JANUARY-MAY 1943 (SUPPLEMENT 2). WOR-45   WAR
FAM SECT PLAN EDU/PROP CRIME LEISURE RACE/REL DRIVE   SOC
HEALTH...GEOG 20 JEWS. PAGE 100 E2014   CULTURE

B52
FORSTER A..THE TROUBLE MAKERS. USA+45 LAW CULTURE   DISCRIM
SOCIETY STRUCT VOL/ASSN CROWD GP/REL MORAL...PSY   SECT
SOC CONCPT 20 NEGRO JEWS. PAGE 39 E0771   RACE/REL
                                                      ATTIT

B57
BYRNES R.F.,BIBLIOGRAPHY OF AMERICAN PUBLICATIONS   BIBLIOG/A
ON EAST CENTRAL EUROPE, 1945-1957 (VOL. XXII). SECT   COM
DIPLOM EDU/PROP RACE/REL...ART/METH GEOG JURID SOC   MARXISM
LING 20 JEWS. PAGE 18 E0354   NAT/G

B62
HEYDECKER J.J..THE NUREMBERG TRIAL: HISTORY OF NAZI   LAW
GERMANY AS REVEALED THROUGH THE TESTIMONY AT   CRIME
NUREMBERG. EUR+WWI GERMANY VOL/ASSN LEAD COERCE   PARTIC
CROWD INGP/REL RACE/REL SUPEGO ORD/FREE...CONCPT 20   TOTALISM
NAZI ANTI/SEMIT NUREMBERG JEWS. PAGE 52 E1036

S64
GREENBERG S.."JUDAISM AND WORLD JUSTICE." MEDIT-7   SECT
WOR+45 LAW CULTURE SOCIETY INT/ORG NAT/G FORCES   JURID
EDU/PROP ATTIT DRIVE PERSON SUPEGO ALL/VALS   PEACE
...POLICY PSY CONCPT GEN/LAWS JEWS. PAGE 46 E0908

B65
ROSE A.M..MINORITY PROBLEMS: A TEXTBOOK OF READINGS   RACE/REL
IN INTERGROUP RELATIONS. UNIV USA+45 LAW SCHOOL   DISCRIM
WORKER PROB/SOLV GP/REL PERSON...PSY ANTHOL WORSHIP   ISOLAT
20 NEGRO INDIAN/AM JEWS EUROPE. PAGE 85 E1713   ACT/RES

B66
HAUSNER G..JUSTICE IN JERUSALEM. GERMANY ISRAEL   ADJUD
SOCIETY KIN DIPLOM LEGIT CT/SYS PARTIC MURDER   CRIME
MAJORITY ATTIT FASCISM...INT/LAW JURID 20 JEWS   RACE/REL
WAR/TRIAL. PAGE 51 E1013   COERCE

B67
MANVELL R..THE INCOMPARABLE CRIME. GERMANY ACT/RES   MURDER

DEATH...BIBLIOG 20 JEWS. PAGE 68 E1364   CRIME
                                                     WAR
                                                     HIST/WRIT

JIMENEZ E. E1168

JOHN BIRCH SOCIETY....SEE BIRCH/SOC

JOHN OF SALISBURY E1169

JOHN/XXII....POPE JOHN XXII

B60
BERTHOLD O..KAISER, VOLK UND AVIGNON. GERMANY CHIEF DIPLOM
LEGIT LEAD NAT/LISM CONSERVE 14 POPE CHRUCH/STA   CATHISM
LUDWIG/BAV JOHN/XXII. PAGE 11 E0217   JURID

JOHN/XXIII....POPE JOHN XXIII

JOHNSN/ALB....ALBERT JOHNSON

B62
BORKIN J..THE CORRUPT JUDGE. USA+45 CT/SYS ATTIT   ADJUD
SUPEGO MORAL RESPECT...BIBLIOG + SUPREME/CT   TRIBUTE
MANTON/M DAVIS/W JOHNSN/ALB. PAGE 14 E0271   CRIME

JOHNSN/AND....PRESIDENT ANDREW JOHNSON

JOHNSN/LB....PRESIDENT LYNDON BAINES JOHNSON

JOHNSON O.H. E1170

JOHNSON/D....D. JOHNSON

JOHNSON/LB....LYNDON BAINES JOHNSON

B65
BELL J..THE JOHNSON TREATMENT: HOW LYNDON JOHNSON   INGP/REL
TOOK OVER THE PRESIDENCY AND MADE IT HIS OWN.   TOP/EX
USA+45 DELIB/GP DIPLOM ADJUD MURDER CHOOSE PERSON   CONTROL
PWR...POLICY OBS INT TIME 20 JOHNSON/LB KENNEDY/JF   NAT/G
PRESIDENT CONGRESS. PAGE 10 E0183

B65
FEERICK J.D..FROM FAILING HANDS: THE STUDY OF   EX/STRUC
PRESIDENTIAL SUCCESSION. CONSTN NAT/G PROB/SOLV   CHIEF
LEAD PARL/PROC MURDER CHOOSE...NEW/IDEA BIBLIOG 20   LAW
KENNEDY/JF JOHNSON/LB PRESIDENT PRE/US/AM   LEGIS
VICE/PRES. PAGE 36 E0724

JOHNSTN/GD....GEORGE D. JOHNSTON

JOHNSTON D.M. E1171

JONES C.O. E1172

JONES E.M. E1395

JONESVILLE....JONESVILLE: LOCATION OF W.L. WARNER'S
   "DEMOCRACY IN JONESVILLE"

JORDAN E. E1173

JORDAN....SEE ALSO ISLAM

S65
KHOURI F.J.."THE JORDON RIVER CONTROVERSY." LAW   ISLAM
SOCIETY ECO/UNDEV AGRI FINAN INDUS SECT FORCES   INT/ORG
ACT/RES PLAN TEC/DEV ECO/TAC EDU/PROP COERCE ATTIT   ISRAEL
DRIVE PERCEPT RIGID/FLEX ALL/VALS...GEOG SOC MYTH   JORDAN
WORK. PAGE 61 E1212

JOSEPH H. E1174

JOUGHIN L. E1175

JOURNALISM....SEE PRESS

JUDGE....JUDGES; SEE ALSO ADJUD

N
INDEX TO LEGAL PERIODICALS. CANADA NEW/ZEALND UK   BIBLIOG
USA+45 USA-45 CONSTN LEGIS JUDGE ADJUD ADMIN   INDEX
CONTROL CT/SYS FEDERAL...CRIMLGY INT/LAW 20   LAW
CMN/WLTH AUSTRAL. PAGE 1 E0006   JURID

N
ARBITRATION JOURNAL. WOR+45 LAW INDUS JUDGE DIPLOM   BIBLIOG
CT/SYS INGP/REL 20. PAGE 1 E0016   MGT
                                                     LABOR
                                                     ADJUD

N
HARVARD UNIVERSITY LAW LIBRARY,CATALOG OF   BIBLIOG
INTERNATIONAL LAW AND RELATIONS. WOR+45 WOR-45   INT/LAW
INT/ORG NAT/G JUDGE DIPLOM INT/TRADE ADJUD CT/SYS   JURID

B03

GRIFFIN A.P.C.,LIST OF BOOKS ON THE CONSTITUTION OF BIBLIOG/A
THE UNITED STATES (PAMPHLET). USA-45 NAT/G EX/STRUC CONSTN
JUDGE TOP/EX CT/SYS 18/20 CONGRESS PRESIDENT LAW
SUPREME/CT. PAGE 46 E0920 JURID

B05

DICEY A..LAW AND PUBLIC OPINION IN ENGLAND. LAW ATTIT
CULTURE INTELL SOCIETY NAT/G SECT JUDGE LEGIT UK
CHOOSE RIGID/FLEX KNOWL...OLD/LIB CONCPT STERTYP
GEN/LAWS 20. PAGE 31 E0620

B07

BENTHAM J..AN INTRODUCTION TO THE PRINCIPLES OF LAW
MORALS AND LEGISLATION. UNIV CONSTN CULTURE SOCIETY GEN/LAWS
NAT/G CONSULT LEGIS JUDGE ADJUD CT/SYS...JURID
CONCPT NEW/IDEA. PAGE 10 E0190

B09

HARVARD UNIVERSITY LAW LIBRARY,CATALOGUE OF THE BIBLIOG/A
LIBRARY OF THE LAW SCHOOL OF HARVARD UNIVERSITY (3 LAW
VOLS.). UK USA-45 LEGIS JUDGE ADJUD CT/SYS...JURID ADMIN
CHARTS 14/20. PAGE 51 E1008

B09

HOLLAND T.E.,LETTERS UPON WAR AND NEUTRALITY. LAW
WOR-45 NAT/G FORCES JUDGE ECO/TAC LEGIT CT/SYS INT/LAW
NEUTRAL ROUTINE COERCE...JURID TIME/SEQ 20. PAGE 55 INT/ORG
E1085 WAR

N13

SCHMIDHAUSER J.R.,JUDICIAL BEHAVIOR AND THE JUDGE
SECTIONAL CRISIS OF 1837-1860. USA-45 ADJUD CT/SYS POL/PAR
INGP/REL ATTIT HABITAT...DECISION PSY STAT CHARTS PERS/COMP
SIMUL. PAGE 88 E1759 PERSON

B21

OPPENHEIM L..THE FUTURE OF INTERNATIONAL LAW. INT/ORG
EUR+WWI MOD/EUR LAW LEGIS JUDGE LEGIT ORD/FREE CT/SYS
...JURID TIME/SEQ GEN/LAWS 20. PAGE 79 E1578 INT/LAW

B25

WINFIELD P.H.,THE CHIEF SOURCES OF ENGLISH LEGAL BIBLIOG/A
HISTORY. UK CONSTN JUDGE ADJUD CT/SYS 13/18. JURID
PAGE 107 E2133 LAW

S26

HALL A.B.,"DETERMINATION OF METHODS FOR ADJUD
ASCERTAINING THE FACTORS THAT INFLUENCE JUDICIAL DECISION
DECISIONS IN CASES INVOLVING DUE PROCESS" LAW JUDGE CONSTN
DEBATE EFFICIENCY OPTIMAL UTIL...SOC CONCPT JURID
PROBABIL STAT SAMP. PAGE 49 E0981

B28

MACDONALD A.F.,ELEMENTS OF POLITICAL SCIENCE LAW
RESEARCH. USA-45 ACADEM JUDGE EDU/PROP DEBATE ADJUD FEDERAL
EXEC...BIBLIOG METH T 20 CONGRESS. PAGE 67 E1338 DECISION
CT/SYS

B28

NORTON T.J.,LOSING LIBERTY JUDICIALLY. PROVS LEGIS NAT/G
BAL/PWR CT/SYS...JURID 18/20 SUPREME/CT CIV/RIGHTS ORD/FREE
CONGRESS. PAGE 78 E1557 CONSTN
JUDGE

B29

CONWELL-EVANS T.P.,THE LEAGUE COUNCIL IN ACTION. DELIB/GP
EUR+WWI TURKEY UK USSR WOR-45 INT/ORG FORCES JUDGE INT/LAW
ECO/TAC EDU/PROP LEGIT ROUTINE ARMS/CONT COERCE
ATTIT PWR...MAJORIT GEOG JURID CONCPT LEAGUE/NAT
TOT/POP VAL/FREE TUNIS 20. PAGE 25 E0498

B33

AMERICAN FOREIGN LAW ASSN,BIOGRAPHICAL NOTES ON THE BIBLIOG/A
LAWS AND LEGAL LITERATURE OF URUGUAY AND CURACAO. LAW
URUGUAY CONSTN FINAN SECT FORCES JUDGE DIPLOM JURID
INT/TRADE ADJUD CT/SYS CRIME 20. PAGE 4 E0078 ADMIN

B35

LUCE R.,LEGISLATIVE PROBLEMS. CONSTN CHIEF JUDGE TREND
BUDGET CONFER ETIQUET CONTROL MORAL PWR NEW/LIB ADMIN
CONGRESS. PAGE 67 E1331 LEGIS

B35

MCLAUGHLIN A.C.,A CONSTITUTIONAL HISTORY OF THE CONSTN
UNITED STATES. USA+45 USA-45 LOC/G NAT/G PROVS DECISION
LEGIS JUDGE ADJUD...T 18/20. PAGE 71 E1422

B36

KONRAD F..DIE PERSONLICHE FREIHEIT IM ORD/FREE
NATIONALSOZIALISTISCHEN DEUTSCHEN REICHE. GERMANY JURID
JUDGE ADJUD GP/REL FASCISM 20 CIVIL/LIB. PAGE 61 CONSTN
E1226 CONCPT

B38

HELLMAN F.S.,THE SUPREME COURT ISSUE: SELECTED LIST BIBLIOG/A
OF REFERENCES. USA-45 NAT/G CHIEF EX/STRUC JUDGE CONSTN
ATTIT...JURID 20 PRESIDENT ROOSEVLT/F SUPREME/CT. CT/SYS
PAGE 51 E1026 LAW

B38

HOLDSWORTH W.S.,A HISTORY OF ENGLISH LAW: THE LAW
CENTURIES OF SETTLEMENT AND REFORM (VOL. XII). UK PROF/ORG
CONSTN STRATA LEGIS JUDGE ADJUD CT/SYS ATTIT WRITING
...JURID CONCPT BIOG GEN/LAWS 18 ENGLSH/LAW IDEA/COMP
BLACKSTN/W COMMON/LAW. PAGE 54 E1078

B42

CRAIG A.,ABOVE ALL LIBERTIES. FRANCE UK USA-45 LAW ORD/FREE
CONSTN CULTURE INTELL NAT/G SECT JUDGE...IDEA/COMP MORAL
BIBLIOG 18/20. PAGE 27 E0536 WRITING
EDU/PROP

B42

SETARO F.C.,A BIBLIOGRAPHY OF THE WRITINGS OF BIBLIOG
ROSCOE POUND. USA-45 CT/SYS 20. PAGE 90 E1806 LAW
ATTIT
JUDGE

B43

CLAGETT H.L.,A GUIDE TO THE LAW AND LEGAL BIBLIOG
LITERATURE OF PARAGUAY. PARAGUAY CONSTN COM/IND JURID
LABOR MUNIC JUDGE ADMIN CT/SYS...CRIMLGY INT/LAW LAW
CON/ANAL 20. PAGE 22 E0439 L/A+17C

B45

CLAGETT H.L.,A GUIDE TO THE LAW AND LEGAL BIBLIOG
LITERATURE OF THE MEXICAN STATES. CONSTN LEGIS JURID
JUDGE ADJUD ADMIN...INT/LAW CON/ANAL 20 MEXIC/AMER. L/A+17C
PAGE 22 E0440 LAW

B47

CLAGETT H.L.,A GUIDE TO THE LAW AND LEGAL BIBLIOG
LITERATURE OF CHILE, 1917-1946. CHILE CONSTN LABOR L/A+17C
JUDGE ADJUD ADMIN...CRIMLGY INT/LAW JURID CON/ANAL LAW
20. PAGE 22 E0442 LEGIS

B47

CLAGETT H.L.,A GUIDE TO THE LAW AND LEGAL BIBLIOG
LITERATURE OF ECUADOR. ECUADOR CONSTN LABOR LEGIS JURID
JUDGE ADJUD ADMIN CIVMIL/REL...CRIMLGY INT/LAW LAW
CON/ANAL 20. PAGE 22 E0443 L/A+17C

B47

CLAGETT H.L.,A GUIDE TO THE LAW AND LEGAL BIBLIOG
LITERATURE OF PERU. PERU CONSTN COM/IND LABOR MUNIC L/A+17C
JUDGE ADMIN CT/SYS...CRIMLGY INT/LAW JURID 20. PHIL/SCI
PAGE 23 E0444 LAW

B47

CLAGETT H.L.,A GUIDE TO THE LAW AND LEGAL BIBLIOG
LITERATURE OF URUGUAY. URUGUAY CONSTN COM/IND FINAN LAW
LABOR MUNIC JUDGE PRESS ADMIN CT/SYS...INT/LAW JURID
PHIL/SCI 20. PAGE 23 E0445 L/A+17C

B47

CLAGETT H.L.,A GUIDE TO THE LAW AND LEGAL BIBLIOG
LITERATURE OF VENEZUELA. VENEZUELA CONSTN LABOR L/A+17C
LEGIS JUDGE ADJUD ADMIN CIVMIL/REL...CRIMLGY JURID INT/LAW
CON/ANAL 20. PAGE 23 E0446 LAW

B48

CLAGETT H.L.,A GUIDE TO THE LAW AND LEGAL BIBLIOG
LITERATURE OF ARGENTINA, 1917-1946. CONSTN LABOR L/A+17C
JUDGE ADJUD ADMIN...CRIMLGY INT/LAW JURID CON/ANAL LAW
20 ARGEN. PAGE 23 E0447 LEGIS

B49

WALINE M..LE CONTROLE JURIDICTIONNEL DE JURID
L'ADMINISTRATION. BELGIUM FRANCE UAR JUDGE BAL/PWR ADMIN
ADJUD CONTROL CT/SYS...GP/COMP 20. PAGE 104 E2093 PWR
ORD/FREE

B50

HURST J.W.,THE GROWTH OF AMERICAN LAW: THE LAW LAW
MAKERS. USA+45 LOC/G NAT/G DELIB/GP JUDGE ADJUD LEGIS
ADMIN ATTIT PWR...POLICY JURID BIBLIOG 18/20 CONSTN
CONGRESS SUPREME/CT ABA PRESIDENT. PAGE 56 E1115 CT/SYS

C50

HOLCOMBE A.,"OUR MORE PERFECT UNION." USA+45 USA-45 CONSTN
POL/PAR JUDGE CT/SYS EQUILIB FEDERAL PWR...MAJORIT NAT/G
TREND BIBLIOG 18/20 CONGRESS PRESIDENT. PAGE 54 ADMIN
E1070 PLAN

B51

FRIEDMANN W.,LAW AND SOCIAL CHANGE IN CONTEMPORARY LAW
BRITAIN. UK LABOR LG/CO LEGIS JUDGE CT/SYS ORD/FREE ADJUD
NEW/LIB...DECISION JURID TREND METH/COMP BIBLIOG 20 SOCIETY
PARLIAMENT ENGLSH/LAW COMMON/LAW. PAGE 40 E0802 CONSTN

GELLER M.A.,ADVERTISING AT THE CROSSROADS: FEDERAL REGULATION VS. VOLUNTARY CONTROLS. USA+45 JUDGE ECO/TAC...POLICY JURID BIBLIOG 20 FTC. PAGE 43 E0843
B52
EDU/PROP
NAT/G
CONSTN
COM/IND

HOLDSWORTH W.S.,A HISTORY OF ENGLISH LAW; THE CENTURIES OF SETTLEMENT AND REFORM, 1701-1875 (VOL. XIII). UK POL/PAR PROF/ORG LEGIS JUDGE WRITING ATTIT...JURID CONCPT BIOG GEN/LAWS 18/19 PARLIAMENT REFORMERS ENGLSH/LAW COMMON/LAW. PAGE 54 E1080
B52
LAW
CONSTN
IDEA/COMP
CT/SYS

JACKSON E.,MEETING OF THE MINDS: A WAY TO PEACE THROUGH MEDIATION. WOR+45 INDUS INT/ORG NAT/G DELIB/GP DIPLOM EDU/PROP LEGIT ORD/FREE...NEW/IDEA SELF/OBS TIME/SEQ CHARTS GEN/LAWS TOT/POP 20 UN TREATY. PAGE 57 E1139
B52
LABOR
JUDGE

MORRIS R.B.,FAIR TRIAL. USA-45 JUDGE ORD/FREE ...JURID 20. PAGE 75 E1498
B52
ADJUD
CT/SYS
CRIME
LAW

CLAGETT H.L.,"THE ADMINISTRATION OF JUSTICE IN LATIN AMERICA." L/A+17C ADMIN FEDERAL...JURID METH/COMP BIBLIOG 20. PAGE 23 E0448
C52
CT/SYS
ADJUD
JUDGE
CONSTN

LANCASTER L.W.,"GOVERNMENT IN RURAL AMERICA." USA+45 ECO/DEV AGRI SCHOOL FORCES LEGIS JUDGE BUDGET TAX CT/SYS...CHARTS BIBLIOG. PAGE 62 E1248
C52
GOV/REL
LOC/G
MUNIC
ADMIN

CURRIER T.F.,A BIBLIOGRAPHY OF OLIVER WENDELL HOLMES. USA-45...BIOG 19/20. PAGE 28 E0557
B53
BIBLIOG/A
HUM
JURID
JUDGE

GROSS B.M.,THE LEGISLATIVE STRUGGLE: A STUDY IN SOCIAL COMBAT. STRUCT LOC/G POL/PAR JUDGE EDU/PROP DEBATE ETIQUET ADMIN LOBBY CHOOSE GOV/REL INGP/REL HEREDITY ALL/VALS...SOC PRESIDENT. PAGE 48 E0948
B53
LEGIS
DECISION
PERSON
LEAD

CUSHMAN R.E.,LEADING CONSTITUTIONAL DECISIONS. USA+45 USA-45 NAT/G EX/STRUC LEGIS JUDGE TAX FEDERAL...DECISION 20 SUPREME/CT CASEBOOK. PAGE 28 E0559
B55
CONSTN
PROB/SOLV
JURID
CT/SYS

GUAITA A.,BIBLIOGRAFIA ESPANOLA DE DERECHO ADMINISTRATIVO (PAMPHLET). SPAIN LOC/G MUNIC NAT/G PROVS JUDGE BAL/PWR GOV/REL OWN...JURID 18/19. PAGE 48 E0959
B55
BIBLIOG
ADMIN
CONSTN
PWR

SWEET AND MAXWELL,A LEGAL BIBLIOGRAPHY OF THE BRITISH COMMONWEALTH OF NATIONS (2ND ED. 7 VOLS.). UK LOC/G MUNIC JUDGE ADJUD CRIME OWN...JURID 14/20 CMN/WLTH. PAGE 95 E1900
B55
BIBLIOG/A
LAW
CONSTN
CT/SYS

BETH L.P.,"THE CASE FOR JUDICIAL PROTECTION OF CIVIL LIBERTIES" (BMR)" USA+45 CONSTN ELITES LEGIS CONTROL...POLICY DECISION JURID 20 SUPREME/CT CIVIL/LIB. PAGE 11 E0220
S55
CT/SYS
JUDGE
ADJUD
ORD/FREE

CALLISON I.P.,COURTS OF INJUSTICE. USA+45 PROF/ORG ADJUD CRIME PERSON MORAL PWR RESPECT SKILL 20. PAGE 19 E0368
B56
CT/SYS
JUDGE
JURID

JESSUP P.C.,TRANSNATIONAL LAW. FUT WOR+45 JUDGE CREATE ADJUD ORD/FREE...CONCPT VAL/FREE 20. PAGE 59 E1167
B56
LAW
JURID
INT/LAW

KALNOKI BEDO A.,LEGAL SOURCES AND BIBLIOGRAPHY OF HUNGARY. COM HUNGARY CONSTN LEGIS JUDGE CT/SYS SANCTION CRIME 16/20. PAGE 59 E1181
B56
BIBLIOG
ADJUD
LAW
JURID

PERKINS D.,CHARLES EVANS HUGHES AND THE AMERICAN DEMOCRATIC STATESMANSHIP. USA+45 USA-45 NAT/G POL/PAR DELIB/GP JUDGE PLAN MORAL PWR...HIST/WRIT LEAGUE/NAT 20. PAGE 80 E1609
B56
PERSON
BIOG
DIPLOM

AUMANN F.R.,"THE ISTRUMENTALITIES OF JUSTICE: THEIR FORMS, FUNCTIONS, AND LIMITATIONS." WOR+45 WOR-45 JUDGE PROB/SOLV ROUTINE ATTIT...BIBLIOG 20. PAGE 6 E0118
C56
JURID
ADMIN
CT/SYS
ADJUD

BERNS W.,FREEDOM, VIRTUE AND THE FIRST AMENDMENT. USA+45 USA-45 CONSTN INTELL JUDGE ADJUD RIGID/FLEX MORAL...CONCPT 20 AMEND/I. PAGE 11 E0211
B57
JURID
ORD/FREE
CT/SYS
LAW

MORELAND C.C.,EQUAL JUSTICE UNDER LAW. USA+45 USA-45 PROF/ORG PROVS JUDGE...POLICY JURID. PAGE 74 E1491
B57
CONSTN
ADJUD
CT/SYS
ORD/FREE

DAVIS K.C.,ADMINISTRATIVE LAW TREATISE (VOLS. I AND IV). NAT/G JUDGE PROB/SOLV ADJUD GP/REL 20 SUPREME/CT. PAGE 29 E0575
B58
ADMIN
JURID
CT/SYS
EX/STRUC

MOEN N.W.,THE GOVERNMENT OF SCOTLAND 1603 - 1625. UK JUDGE ADMIN GP/REL PWR 17 SCOTLAND COMMON/LAW. PAGE 74 E1479
B58
CHIEF
JURID
CONTROL
PARL/PROC

FISHER F.M.,"THE MATHEMATICAL ANALYSIS OF SUPREME COURT DECISIONS: THE USE AND ABUSE OF QUANTITATIVE METHODS." USA+45 LAW EX/STRUC LEGIS JUDGE ROUTINE ATTIT DECISION. PAGE 38 E0757
S58
PROB/SOLV
CT/SYS
JURID
MATH

SCHUBERT G.A.,"THE STUDY OF JUDICIAL DECISION-MAKING AS AN ASPECT OF POLITICAL BEHAVIOR." PLAN ADJUD CT/SYS INGP/REL PERSON...PHIL/SCI SOC QUANT STAT CHARTS IDEA/COMP SOC/EXP. PAGE 89 E1779
S58
JUDGE
DECISION
CON/ANAL
GAME

CORBETT P.E.,LAW IN DIPLOMACY. UK USA+45 USSR CONSTN SOCIETY INT/ORG JUDGE LEGIT ATTIT ORD/FREE TOT/POP LEAGUE/NAT 20. PAGE 26 E0507
B59
NAT/G
ADJUD
JURID
DIPLOM

PAULSEN M.G.,LEGAL INSTITUTIONS TODAY AND TOMORROW. UK USA+45 NAT/G PROF/ORG PROVS ADMIN PARL/PROC ORD/FREE NAT/COMP. PAGE 80 E1604
B59
JURID
ADJUD
JUDGE
LEGIS

SCHNEIDER J.,TREATY-MAKING POWER OF INTERNATIONAL ORGANIZATIONS. FUT WOR+45 WOR-45 LAW NAT/G JUDGE DIPLOM LEGIT CT/SYS ORD/FREE PWR...INT/LAW JURID GEN/LAWS TOT/POP UNESCO 20 TREATY. PAGE 88 E1762
B59
INT/ORG
ROUTINE

SCHORN H.,DER RICHTER IM DRITTEN REICH; GESCHICHTE UND DOKUMENTE. GERMANY NAT/G LEGIT CT/SYS INGP/REL MORAL ORD/FREE RESPECT...JURID GP/COMP 20. PAGE 88 E1765
B59
ADJUD
JUDGE
FASCISM

SCHUBERT G.A.,QUANTITATIVE ANALYSIS OF JUDICIAL BEHAVIOR. ADJUD LEAD CHOOSE INGP/REL MAJORITY ATTIT ...DECISION JURID CHARTS GAME SIMUL SUPREME/CT. PAGE 89 E1780
B59
JUDGE
CT/SYS
PERSON
QUANT

TOMPKINS D.C.,SUPREME COURT OF THE UNITED STATES: A BIBLIOGRAPHY. LAW JUDGE ADJUD GOV/REL DISCRIM ...JURID 18/20 SUPREME/CT NEGRO. PAGE 96 E1931
B59
BIBLIOG/A
CT/SYS
CONSTN
NAT/G

VAN CAENEGEM R.C.,ROYAL WRITS IN ENGLAND FROM THE CONQUEST TO GLANVILL. UK JUDGE...TREND IDEA/COMP 11/12 COMMON/LAW. PAGE 103 E2067
B59
JURID
CHIEF
ADJUD
CT/SYS

DOMKE M.,"THE SETTLEMENT OF DISPUTES IN INTERNATIONAL TRADE." USA+45 LAW STRATA STRUCT JUDGE EDU/PROP PWR...METH/CNCPT 20. PAGE 32 E0634
S59
CONSULT
LEGIT
INT/TRADE

SUTTON F.X.,"REPRESENTATION AND THE NATURE OF POLITICAL SYSTEMS." UNIV WOR-45 CULTURE SOCIETY STRATA INT/ORG FORCES JUDGE DOMIN LEGIT EXEC REGION REPRESENT ATTIT ORD/FREE RESPECT...SOC HIST/WRIT TIME/SEQ. PAGE 95 E1896
S59
NAT/G
CONCPT

B60
MENDELSON W.,CAPITALISM, DEMOCRACY, AND THE SUPREME   JUDGE
COURT. USA+45 USA-45 CONSTN DIPLOM GOV/REL ATTIT   CT/SYS
ORD/FREE LAISSEZ...POLICY CHARTS PERS/COMP 18/20   JURID
SUPREME/CT MARSHALL/J HOLMES/OW TANEY/RB FIELD/JJ.   NAT/G
PAGE 72 E1437

B60
SCHMIDHAUSER J.R.,THE SUPREME COURT: ITS POLITICS,   JUDGE
PERSONALITIES, AND PROCEDURES. LAW DELIB/GP   JURID
EX/STRUC TOP/EX ADJUD CT/SYS CHOOSE RATIONAL PWR   DECISION
SUPREME/CT. PAGE 88 E1760

B61
AUERBACH C.A.,THE LEGAL PROCESS. USA+45 DELIB/GP   JURID
JUDGE CONFER ADJUD CONTROL...DECISION 20   ADMIN
SUPREME/CT. PAGE 6 E0116   LEGIS
                                                       CT/SYS

B61
BAYITCH S.A.,LATIN AMERICA: A BIBLIOGRAPHICAL   BIBLIOG
GUIDE. LAW CONSTN LEGIS JUDGE ADJUD CT/SYS 20.   L/A+17C
PAGE 8 E0158   NAT/G
                                                       JURID

B61
WASSERSTROM R.A.,THE JUDICIAL DECISION: TOWARD A   JUDGE
THEORY OF LEGAL JUSTIFICATION. ACT/RES RATIONAL   LAW
PERCEPT KNOWL OBJECTIVE...DECISION JURID. PAGE 105   ADJUD
E2102

S61
SCHUBERT G.,"A PSYCHOMETRIC MODEL OF THE SUPREME   JUDGE
COURT." DELIB/GP ADJUD CHOOSE ATTIT...DECISION   CT/SYS
JURID PSY QUANT STAT HYPO/EXP GEN/METH SUPREME/CT.   PERSON
PAGE 88 E1771   SIMUL

B62
ALLOTT A.N.,JUDICIAL AND LEGAL SYSTEMS IN AFRICA.   CT/SYS
LAW CONSTN JUDGE CONTROL...METH/CNCPT CLASSIF   AFR
CHARTS 20 COMMON/LAW. PAGE 4 E0070   JURID
                                                       COLONIAL

B62
DELANY V.T.H.,THE ADMINISTRATION OF JUSTICE IN   ADMIN
IRELAND. IRELAND CONSTN FINAN JUDGE COLONIAL CRIME   JURID
...CRIMLGY 19/20. PAGE 30 E0604   CT/SYS
                                                       ADJUD

B62
INSTITUTE JUDICIAL ADMIN,JUDGES: THEIR TEMPORARY   NAT/G
APPOINTMENT, ASSIGNMENT AND TRANSFER: SURVEY OF FED   LOC/G
AND STATE CONSTN'S STATUTES, ROLES OF CT. USA+45   JUDGE
CONSTN PROVS CT/SYS GOV/REL PWR JURID. PAGE 57   ADMIN
E1128

B62
INTERNAT CONGRESS OF JURISTS,EXECUTIVE ACTION AND   JURID
THE RULE OF RULE: REPORTION PROCEEDINGS OF INT'T   EXEC
CONGRESS OF JURISTS,-RIO DE JANEIRO, BRAZIL. WOR+45   ORD/FREE
ACADEM CONSULT JUDGE EDU/PROP ADJUD CT/SYS INGP/REL   CONTROL
PERSON DEPT/DEFEN. PAGE 57 E1130

B62
MILLER P.,THE LEGAL MIND IN AMERICA. PROF/ORG JUDGE   JURID
ADJUD CT/SYS 18/19 SUPREME/CT. PAGE 73 E1461   CONSTN
                                                       NAT/G
                                                       CONCPT

B62
NATIONAL MUNICIPAL LEAGUE,COURT DECISIONS ON   PROVS
LEGISLATIVE APPORTIONMENT (VOL. III). USA+45 JUDGE   CT/SYS
ADJUD CONTROL ATTIT...DECISION JURID COURT/DIST   APPORT
CASEBOOK. PAGE 76 E1528   LEGIS

B62
ROSENNE S.,THE WORLD COURT: WHAT IT IS AND HOW IT   INT/ORG
WORKS. WOR+45 WOR-45 LAW CONSTN JUDGE EDU/PROP   ADJUD
LEGIT ROUTINE CHOOSE PEACE ORD/FREE...JURID OBS   INT/LAW
TIME/SEQ CHARTS UN TOT/POP VAL/FREE 20. PAGE 86
E1717

B62
SIGLIANO R E.,THE COURTS. USA+45 USA-45 LAW CONSTN   ADJUD
NAT/G ROUTINE CHOOSE 18/20 SUPREME/CT. PAGE 91   PROB/SOLV
E1825   CT/SYS
                                                       JUDGE

L62
SPAETH H.J.,"JUDICIAL POWER AS A VARIABLE   JUDGE
MOTIVATING SUPREME COURT BEHAVIOR." DELIB/GP ADJUD   DECISION
RATIONAL ATTIT PERSON ORD/FREE...CLASSIF STAT   PERS/COMP
GEN/METH. PAGE 93 E1860   PSY

S62
SCHUBERT G.,"THE 1960 TERM OF THE SUPREME COURT: A   DECISION
PSYCHOLOGICAL ANALYSIS." USA+45 LAW CT/SYS...STAT   LEGIS
SUPREME/CT. PAGE 88 E1772   JUDGE
                                                       EX/STRUC

C62
ABRAHAM H.J.,"THE JUDICIAL PROCESS." USA+45 USA-45   BIBLIOG
LAW NAT/G ADMIN CT/SYS INGP/REL RACE/REL DISCRIM   CONSTN
...JURID IDEA/COMP 19/20. PAGE 2 E0046   JUDGE
                                                       ADJUD

B63
BLACK C.L. JR.,THE OCCASIONS OF JUSTICE: ESSAYS   JURID
MOSTLY ON LAW. USA+45 JUDGE RACE/REL DISCRIM ATTIT   CONSTN
MORAL ORD/FREE 20 SUPREME/CT BLACK. PAGE 12 E0236   CT/SYS
                                                       LAW

B63
BOWETT D.W.,THE LAW OF INTERNATIONAL INSTITUTIONS.   INT/ORG
WOR+45 WOR-45 CONSTN DELIB/GP EX/STRUC JUDGE   ADJUD
EDU/PROP LEGIT CT/SYS EXEC ROUTINE RIGID/FLEX   DIPLOM
ORD/FREE PWR...JURID CONCPT ORG/CHARTS GEN/METH
LEAGUE/NAT OAS OEEC 20 UN. PAGE 14 E0277

B63
DILLIARD I.,ONE MAN'S STAND FOR FREEDOM: MR.   CONSTN
JUSTICE BLACK AND THE BILL OF RIGHTS. USA+45   JURID
POL/PAR SECT DELIB/GP FORCES ADJUD CONTROL WAR   JUDGE
DISCRIM MORAL...BIBLIOG 20 NEGRO SUPREME/CT   ORD/FREE
BILL/RIGHT BLACK/HL. PAGE 32 E0628

B63
GARNER U.F.,ADMINISTRATIVE LAW. UK LAW LOC/G NAT/G   ADMIN
EX/STRUC LEGIS JUDGE BAL/PWR BUDGET ADJUD CONTROL   JURID
CT/SYS...BIBLIOG 20. PAGE 42 E0840   PWR
                                                       GOV/REL

B63
KLEIN F.J.,JUDICIAL ADMINISTRATION AND THE LEGAL   BIBLIOG/A
PROFESSION. USA+45 ADMIN CONTROL EFFICIENCY   CT/SYS
...POLICY 20. PAGE 61 E1222   ADJUD
                                                       JUDGE

B63
LIVNEH E.,ISRAEL LEGAL BIBLIOGRAPHY IN EUROPEAN   BIBLIOG
LANGUAGES. ISRAEL LOC/G JUDGE TAX...INT/LAW 20.   LAW
PAGE 66 E1311   NAT/G
                                                       CONSTN

B63
MURPHY T.J.,CENSORSHIP: GOVERNMENT AND OBSCENITY.   ORD/FREE
USA+45 CULTURE LEGIS JUDGE EDU/PROP CONTROL   MORAL
INGP/REL RATIONAL POPULISM...CATH JURID 20. PAGE 75   LAW
E1507   CONSEN

B63
PRITCHETT C.H.,THE THIRD BRANCH OF GOVERNMENT.   JURID
USA+45 USA-45 CONSTN SOCIETY INDUS SECT LEGIS JUDGE   NAT/G
PROB/SOLV GOV/REL 20 SUPREME/CT CHURCH/STA. PAGE 82   ADJUD
E1654   CT/SYS

B63
VINES K.N.,STUDIES IN JUDICIAL POLITICS: TULANE   CT/SYS
STUDIES IN POLITICAL SCIENCE (VOL. 8). POL/PAR   GOV/REL
JUDGE ADJUD SANCTION CRIME CHOOSE PWR...JURID STAT   PROVS
TIME/SEQ CHARTS. PAGE 104 E2079

S63
MENDELSON W.,"THE NEO-BEHAVIORAL APPROACH TO THE   DECISION
JUDICIAL PROCESS: A CRITIQUE" ADJUD PERSON...SOC   JURID
RECORD IDEA/COMP. PAGE 72 E1438   JUDGE

S63
VINES K.N.,"THE ROLE OF THE CIRCUIT COURT OF   REGION
APPEALS IN THE FEDERAL JUDICIAL PROCESS: A CASE   ADJUD
STUDY." USA+45 STRATA JUDGE RESPECT...DECISION   CT/SYS
JURID CHARTS GP/COMP. PAGE 104 E2078   RACE/REL

C63
SCHUBERT G.,"JUDICIAL DECISION-MAKING." FORCES LEAD   ADJUD
ATTIT DRIVE...POLICY PSY STAT CHARTS ANTHOL BIBLIOG   DECISION
20. PAGE 88 E1773   JUDGE
                                                       CT/SYS

B64
ANASTAPLO G.,NOTES ON THE FIRST AMENDMENT TO THE   ORD/FREE
CONSTITUTION OF THE UNITED STATES (PART TWO).   CONSTN
USA+45 USA-45 NAT/G JUDGE DEBATE SUPEGO PWR   CT/SYS
SOVEREIGN 18/20 SUPREME/CT CONGRESS AMEND/I. PAGE 5   ATTIT
E0088

B64
BECKER T.L.,POLITICAL BEHAVIORALISM AND MODERN   JUDGE
JURISPRUDENCE* A WORKING THEORY AND STUDY IN   LAW
JUDICIAL DECISION-MAKING. CONSTN...JURID STAT   DECISION

GEN/METH INDEX. PAGE 9 E0172   CT/SYS

B64
BREVER E.H.,LEARNED HAND, JANUARY 27, 1872-AUGUST   BIBLIOG/A
18, 1961 (PAMPHLET). USA+45 USA-45 LAW CONSTN ADJUD JUDGE
...DECISION BIOG 19/20. PAGE 15 E0295   CT/SYS
                                                     JURID

B64
CHAPIN B.,THE AMERICAN LAW OF TREASON. USA-45 LAW   LEGIS
NAT/G JUDGE CRIME REV...BIBLIOG 18. PAGE 21 E0419   JURID
                                                     CONSTN
                                                     POLICY

B64
DANELSKI D.J.,A SUPREME COURT JUSTICE IS APPOINTED. CHOOSE
CHIEF LEGIS CONFER DEBATE EXEC PERSON PWR...BIOG 20   JUDGE
CONGRESS PRESIDENT. PAGE 28 E0564   DECISION

B64
DUBISSON M.,LA COUR INTERNATIONALE DE JUSTICE.   CT/SYS
FRANCE LAW CONSTN JUDGE DOMIN ADJUD...INT/LAW   INT/ORG
CLASSIF RECORD ORG/CHARTS UN. PAGE 33 E0651

B64
FALK R.A.,THE ROLE OF DOMESTIC COURTS IN THE   LAW
INTERNATIONAL LEGAL ORDER. FUT WOR+45 INT/ORG NAT/G INT/LAW
JUDGE EDU/PROP LEGIT CT/SYS...POLICY RELATIV JURID
CONCPT GEN/LAWS 20. PAGE 36 E0716

B64
JACKSON R.M.,THE MACHINERY OF JUSTICE IN ENGLAND.   CT/SYS
UK EDU/PROP CONTROL COST ORD/FREE...MGT 20   ADJUD
ENGLSH/LAW. PAGE 57 E1142   JUDGE
                                                     JURID

B64
MURPHY W.F.,ELEMENTS OF JUDICIAL STRATEGY. CONSTN   CT/SYS
JUDGE PERS/REL PERSON 19/20 SUPREME/CT. PAGE 75   ADJUD
E1510   JURID

B64
NEWMAN E.S.,POLICE, THE LAW, AND PERSONAL FREEDOM.   JURID
USA+45 CONSTN JUDGE CT/SYS CRIME PERS/REL RESPECT   FORCES
...CRIMLGY 20. PAGE 77 E1542   ORD/FREE
                                                     ADJUD

B64
SHAPIRO M.,LAW AND POLITICS IN THE SUPREME COURT: LEGIS
NEW APPROACHES TO POLITICAL JURISPRUDENCE. JUDGE   CT/SYS
PROB/SOLV LEGIT EXEC ROUTINE ATTIT ALL/VALS   LAW
...DECISION SOC. PAGE 90 E1811   JURID

B64
STOICOIU V.,LEGAL SOURCES AND BIBLIOGRAPHY OF   BIBLIOG/A
ROMANIA. COM ROMANIA LAW FINAN POL/PAR LEGIS JUDGE   JURID
ADJUD CT/SYS PARL/PROC MARXISM 20. PAGE 93 E1874   CONSTN
                                                     ADMIN

B64
SZLADITS C.,BIBLIOGRAPHY ON FOREIGN AND COMPARATIVE BIBLIOG/A
LAW: BOOKS AND ARTICLES IN ENGLISH (SUPPLEMENT   JURID
1962). FINAN INDUS JUDGE LICENSE ADMIN CT/SYS   ADJUD
PARL/PROC OWN...INT/LAW CLASSIF METH/COMP NAT/COMP   LAW
20. PAGE 95 E1904

C64
BECKER T.L.,"POLITICAL BEHAVIORALISM AND MODERN   DECISION
JURISPRUDENCE." LEGIS JUDGE OP/RES ADJUD CT/SYS   PROB/SOLV
ATTIT PWR...BIBLIOG 20. PAGE 9 E0173   JURID
                                                     GEN/LAWS

C64
CORWIN E.S.,"AMERICAN CONSTITUTIONAL HISTORY." LAW   ANTHOL
NAT/G PROB/SOLV EQUILIB FEDERAL ATTIT PWR...JURID   JUDGE
BIBLIOG 20. PAGE 26 E0515   ADJUD
                                                     CT/SYS

B65
BREITEL C.D.,THE LAWMAKERS. USA+45 EX/STRUC LEGIS   CT/SYS
JUDGE ATTIT ORD/FREE JURID. PAGE 15 E0290   ADJUD
                                                     FEDERAL
                                                     NAT/G

B65
EHLE J.,THE FREE MEN. USA+45 NAT/G PROVS FORCES   RACE/REL
JUDGE ADJUD ATTIT...POLICY SOC SOC/INTEG 20 NEGRO.   ORD/FREE
PAGE 34 E0677   DISCRIM

B65
HOLDSWORTH W.S.,A HISTORY OF ENGLISH LAW; THE   LAW
CENTURIES OF SETTLEMENT AND REFORM (VOL. XV). UK   INDUS
CONSTN SECT LEGIS JUDGE WRITING ADJUD CT/SYS CRIME   PROF/ORG
OWN...JURID IDEA/COMP 18 PARLIAMENT ENGLSH/LAW   ATTIT
COMMON/LAW. PAGE 54 E1082

B65
KAMISAR Y.,CRIMINAL JUSTICE IN OUR TIME. USA+45   ORD/FREE
FORCES JUDGE PROB/SOLV COERCE MORAL 20 CIVIL/LIB   CRIME
CIV/RIGHTS. PAGE 59 E1182   CT/SYS
                                                     LAW

B65
KUPER H.,AFRICAN LAW. LAW FAM KIN SECT JUDGE ADJUST AFR
NAT/LISM 17/20. PAGE 62 E1236   CT/SYS
                                                     ADJUD
                                                     COLONIAL

B65
MILLER H.H.,THE CASE FOR LIBERTY. USA-45 LAW JUDGE   COLONIAL
CT/SYS...AUD/VIS 18 PRE/US/AM CASEBOOK. PAGE 73   JURID
E1460   PROB/SOLV

B65
PARKER D.,CIVIL LIBERTIES CASE STUDIES AND THE LAW. ORD/FREE
SECT ADJUD...CONCPT WORSHIP 20 SUPREME/CT   JURID
CIV/RIGHTS FREE/SPEE. PAGE 80 E1598   CONSTN
                                                     JUDGE

B65
SCHUBERT G.,THE JUDICIAL MIND: THE ATTITUDES AND   CT/SYS
IDEOLOGIES OF SUPREME COURT JUSTICES 1946-1963.   JUDGE
USA+45 ELITES NAT/G CONTROL PERS/REL MAJORITY   ATTIT
CONSERVE...DECISION JURID MODAL STAT TREND GP/COMP   NEW/LIB
GAME. PAGE 88 E1774

B65
SCHUBERT G.,THE POLITICAL ROLE OF THE COURTS IN   CT/SYS
JUDICIAL POLICY MAKING. USA+45 CONSTN JUDGE   POLICY
FEEDBACK CHOOSE RACE/REL ORD/FREE...TRADIT PSY   DECISION
BIBLIOG/A 20 KENNEDY/JF SUPREME/CT. PAGE 89 E1776

B65
SMITH C.,THE OMBUDSMAN: A BIBLIOGRAPHY (PAMPHLET).   BIBLIOG
DENMARK SWEDEN USA+45 LAW LEGIS JUDGE GOV/REL   ADMIN
GP/REL...JURID 20. PAGE 92 E1841   CT/SYS
                                                     ADJUD

B65
STONE J.,HUMAN LAW AND HUMAN JUSTICE. JUDGE...SOC   CONCPT
MYTH IDEA/COMP. PAGE 94 E1881   SANCTION
                                                     JURID

C65
SCHEINGOLD S.A.,"THE RULE OF LAW IN EUROPEAN   INT/LAW
INTEGRATION: THE PATH OF THE SCHUMAN PLAN." EUR+WWI CT/SYS
JUDGE ADJUD FEDERAL ATTIT PWR...RECORD INT BIBLIOG   REGION
EEC ECSC. PAGE 87 E1755   CENTRAL

B66
ARCHER P.,FREEDOM AT STAKE. UK LAW NAT/G LEGIS   ORD/FREE
JUDGE CRIME MORAL...CONCPT 20 CIVIL/LIB. PAGE 5   NAT/COMP
E0103   POLICY

B66
BROWNLIE I.,PRINCIPLES OF PUBLIC INTERNATIONAL LAW. INT/LAW
WOR+45 WOR-45 LAW JUDGE REPAR ADJUD SOVEREIGN   DIPLOM
...JURID T. PAGE 16 E0319   INT/ORG

B66
FELSHER H.,JUSTICE USA? USA+45 COM/IND JUDGE CT/SYS ADJUD
MORAL ORD/FREE...SAMP/SIZ HYPO/EXP. PAGE 37 E0735   EDU/PROP
                                                     LOBBY

B66
FRIED R.C.,COMPARATIVE POLITICAL INSTITUTIONS. USSR NAT/G
EX/STRUC FORCES LEGIS JUDGE CONTROL REPRESENT   PWR
ALL/IDEOS 20 CONGRESS BUREAUCRCY. PAGE 40 E0798   EFFICIENCY
                                                     GOV/COMP

B66
NANTWI E.K.,THE ENFORCEMENT OF INTERNATIONAL   INT/LAW
JUDICIAL DECISIONS AND ARBITAL AWARDS IN PUBLIC   ADJUD
INTERNATIONAL LAW. WOR+45 WOR-45 JUDGE PROB/SOLV   SOVEREIGN
DIPLOM CT/SYS SUPEGO MORAL PWR RESPECT...METH/CNCPT INT/ORG
18/20 CASEBOOK. PAGE 76 E1520

B66
SZLADITS C.,A BIBLIOGRAPHY ON FOREIGN AND   BIBLIOG/A
COMPARATIVE LAW (SUPPLEMENT 1964). FINAN FAM LABOR   CT/SYS
LG/CO LEGIS JUDGE ADMIN CRIME...CRIMLGY 20. PAGE 95 INT/LAW
E1905

L66
HIGGINS R.,"THE INTERNATIONAL COURT AND SOUTH WEST   SOUTH/AFR
AFRICA* SOME IMPLICATIONS OF THE JUDGMENT." AFR LAW COLONIAL
ECO/UNDEV JUDGE RACE/REL COST PWR...INT/LAW TREND   CT/SYS
UN TREATY. PAGE 52 E1043   ADJUD

B67
UNIVERSAL REFERENCE SYSTEM,LAW, JURISPRUDENCE, AND   BIBLIOG/A
JUDICIAL PROCESS (VOLUME VII). WOR+45 WOR-45 CONSTN LAW
E1905

NAT/G LEGIS JUDGE CT/SYS...INT/LAW COMPUT/IR GEN/METH METH. PAGE 99 E1976 — JURID ADJUD

L67

HOWARD A.E.D.,"MR. JUSTICE BLACK: THE NEGRO PROTEST MOVEMENT AND THE RULE OF LAW." USA+45 CONSTN CT/SYS CHOOSE GP/REL...DECISION JURID NEGRO SUPREME/CT. PAGE 55 E1100 — ADJUD JUDGE LAW REPRESENT

S67

GREY D.L.,"INTERVIEWING AT THE COURT." USA+45 ELITES COM/IND ACT/RES PRESS CT/SYS PERSON...SOC INT 20 SUPREME/CT. PAGE 46 E0916 — JUDGE ATTIT PERS/COMP GP/COMP

B77

CADWALDER J.L.,DIGEST OF THE PUBLISHED OPINIONS OF THE ATTORNEYS-GENERAL, AND OF THE LEADING DECISIONS OF THE FEDERAL COURTS (REV ED). USA-45 NAT/G JUDGE PROB/SOLV DIPLOM ATTIT...POLICY INT/LAW ANTHOL 19. PAGE 18 E0356 — BIBLIOG CT/SYS DECISION ADJUD

L84

ELLMAKER E.G.,"REVELATION OF RIGHTS." JUDGE DISCRIM SUPEGO...JURID PHIL/SCI CONCPT 17/18. PAGE 35 E0685 — ORD/FREE ADMIN MORAL NAT/G

JUDICIAL PROCESS....SEE ADJUD

JUGOSLAVIA....SEE YUGOSLAVIA

JUNKER ....JUNKER: REACTIONARY PRUSSIAN ARISTOCRACY

JURID....LAW

N

INTERNATIONAL COMN JURISTS,AFRICAN CONFERENCE ON THE RULE OF LAW. AFR INT/ORG LEGIS DIPLOM CONFER COLONIAL ORD/FREE...CONCPT METH/COMP 20. PAGE 57 E1131 — CT/SYS JURID DELIB/GP

N

KEITT L.,AN ANNOTATED BIBLIOGRAPHY OF BIBLIOGRAPHIES OF STATUTORY MATERIALS OF THE UNITED STATES. CHRIST-17C USA-45 LEGIS ADJUD COLONIAL CT/SYS...JURID 16/20. PAGE 60 E1196 — BIBLIOG/A LAW CONSTN PROVS

N

AMERICAN JOURNAL OF INTERNATIONAL LAW. WOR+45 WOR-45 CONSTN INT/ORG NAT/G CT/SYS ARMS/CONT WAR ...DECISION JURID NAT/COMP 20. PAGE 1 E0001 — BIBLIOG/A INT/LAW DIPLOM ADJUD

N

CANADIAN GOVERNMENT PUBLICATIONS (1955-). CANADA AGRI FINAN LABOR FORCES INT/TRADE HEALTH...JURID 20 PARLIAMENT. PAGE 1 E0005 — BIBLIOG/A NAT/G DIPLOM INT/ORG

N

INDEX TO LEGAL PERIODICALS. CANADA NEW/ZEALND UK USA+45 USA-45 CONSTN LEGIS JUDGE ADJUD ADMIN CONTROL CT/SYS FEDERAL...CRIMLGY INT/LAW 20 CMN/WLTH AUSTRAL. PAGE 1 E0006 — BIBLIOG INDEX LAW JURID

N

ATLANTIC INSTITUTE,ATLANTIC STUDIES. COM EUR+WWI USA+45 CULTURE STRUCT ECO/DEV FORCES LEAD ARMS/CONT ...INT/LAW JURID SOC. PAGE 6 E0110 — BIBLIOG/A DIPLOM POLICY GOV/REL

N

CATHERINE R.,LA REVUE ADMINISTRATIVE. FRANCE LAW NAT/G LEGIS...JURID BIBLIOG/A 20. PAGE 21 E0407 — ADMIN MGT FINAN METH/COMP

N

HARVARD LAW SCHOOL LIBRARY,ANNUAL LEGAL BIBLIOGRAPHY. USA+45 CONSTN LEGIS ADJUD CT/SYS ...POLICY 20. PAGE 50 E1005 — BIBLIOG JURID LAW INT/LAW

N

HARVARD UNIVERSITY LAW LIBRARY,CATALOG OF INTERNATIONAL LAW AND RELATIONS. WOR+45 WOR-45 INT/ORG NAT/G JUDGE DIPLOM INT/TRADE ADJUD CT/SYS 19/20. PAGE 51 E1007 — BIBLIOG INT/LAW JURID

N

SOCIETE DES NATIONS,TRAITES INTERNATIONAUX ET ACTES LEGISLATIFS. WOR-45 INT/ORG NAT/G...INT/LAW JURID 20 LEAGUE/NAT TREATY. PAGE 92 E1851 — BIBLIOG DIPLOM LEGIS ADJUD

B00

BATY T.,INTERNATIONAL LAW IN SOUTH AFRICA. AFR SOUTH/AFR LAW CONFER 19/20. PAGE 8 E0155 — JURID WAR SOVEREIGN COLONIAL

B00

BERNARD M.,FOUR LECTURES ON SUBJECTS CONNECTED WITH DIPLOMACY. WOR-45 NAT/G VOL/ASSN RIGID/FLEX MORAL PWR...JURID OBS GEN/LAWS GEN/METH 20 TREATY. PAGE 11 E0209 — LAW ATTIT DIPLOM

B00

DARBY W.E.,INTERNATIONAL TRIBUNALS. WOR-45 NAT/G ECO/TAC DOMIN LEGIT CT/SYS COERCE ORD/FREE PWR SOVEREIGN JURID. PAGE 29 E0567 — INT/ORG ADJUD PEACE INT/LAW

B00

GROTIUS H.,DE JURE BELLI AC PACIS. CHRIST-17C UNIV LAW SOCIETY PROVS LEGIT PEACE PERCEPT MORAL PWR ...CONCPT CON/ANAL GEN/LAWS. PAGE 48 E0952 — JURID INT/LAW WAR

B00

HOLLAND T.E.,STUDIES IN INTERNATIONAL LAW. TURKEY USSR WOR-45 CONSTN NAT/G DIPLOM DOMIN LEGIT COERCE WAR PEACE ORD/FREE PWR SOVEREIGN...JURID CHARTS 20 PARLIAMENT SUEZ TREATY. PAGE 54 E1084 — INT/ORG LAW INT/LAW

B00

MAINE H.S.,INTERNATIONAL LAW. MOD/EUR UNIV SOCIETY STRUCT ACT/RES EXEC WAR ATTIT PERSON ALL/VALS ...POLICY JURID CONCPT OBS TIME/SEQ TOT/POP. PAGE 68 E1349 — INT/ORG LAW PEACE INT/LAW

B00

MAINE H.S.,ANCIENT LAW. MEDIT-7 CULTURE SOCIETY KIN SECT LEGIS LEGIT ROUTINE...JURID HIST/WRIT CON/ANAL TOT/POP VAL/FREE. PAGE 68 E1350 — FAM LAW

L00

HISTORICUS,"LETTERS AND SOME QUESTIONS OF INTERNATIONAL LAW." FRANCE NETHERLAND UK USA-45 WOR-45 LAW NAT/G COERCE...SOC CONCPT GEN/LAWS TOT/POP 19 CIVIL/WAR. PAGE 53 E1054 — WEALTH JURID WAR INT/LAW

B01

BRYCE J.,STUDIES IN HISTORY AND JURISPRUDENCE (2 VOLS.). ICELAND SOUTH/AFR UK LAW PROB/SOLV SOVEREIGN...PHIL/SCI NAT/COMP ROME/ANC ROMAN/LAW. PAGE 16 E0321 — IDEA/COMP CONSTN JURID

B01

GRONING J.,BIBLIOTHECA JURIS GENTIUM COMMUNIS, QUA PRAECIPUORUM, ASIAE, AFRICAE, ET AMERICAE, POPULORUM DE JURIS NATURAE... AFR ASIA S/ASIA USA-45 16/17. PAGE 48 E0946 — BIBLIOG JURID LAW NAT/G

B02

GRIFFIN A.P.C.,A LIST OF BOOKS RELATING TO TRUSTS (2ND REV. ED.) (PAMPHLET). FRANCE GERMANY UK USA-45 WOR-45 LAW ECO/DEV INDUS LG/CO NAT/G CAP/ISM CENTRAL DISCRIM PWR LAISSEZ 19/20. PAGE 46 E0919 — BIBLIOG/A JURID ECO/TAC VOL/ASSN

B03

GRIFFIN A.P.C.,LIST OF BOOKS ON THE CONSTITUTION OF THE UNITED STATES (PAMPHLET). USA-45 NAT/G EX/STRUC JUDGE TOP/EX CT/SYS 18/20 CONGRESS PRESIDENT SUPREME/CT. PAGE 46 E0920 — BIBLIOG/A CONSTN LAW JURID

B03

GRONING J.,BIBLIOTHECA JURIS GENTIUM EXOTICA. AFR ASIA S/ASIA USA-45 16/17. PAGE 48 E0947 — BIBLIOG JURID NAT/G LAW

B04

CRANDALL S.B.,TREATIES: THEIR MAKING AND ENFORCEMENT. MOD/EUR USA-45 INT/ORG NAT/G LEGIS EDU/PROP LEGIT EXEC PEACE KNOWL MORAL...JURID CONGRESS 19/20 TREATY. PAGE 27 E0541 — LAW

B04

FREUND E.,THE POLICE POWER; PUBLIC POLICY AND CONSTITUTIONAL RIGHTS. USA-45 SOCIETY LOC/G NAT/G FORCES LEGIS ADJUD CT/SYS OWN PWR...JURID 18/19 SUPREME/CT. PAGE 40 E0795 — CONSTN LAW ORD/FREE CONTROL

B04

GRIFFIN A.P.C.,REFERENCES ON CHINESE IMMIGRATIONS (PAMPHLET). USA-45 KIN NAT/LISM ATTIT...SOC 19/20. PAGE 47 E0926 — BIBLIOG/A STRANGE JURID RACE/REL

B05

DICEY A.V.,LECTURES ON THE RELATION BETWEEN LAW AND — LAW

PUBLIC OPINION IN ENGLAND DURING THE NINETEENTH
CENTURY. UK LEGIS CT/SYS...JURID 19 TORY/PARTY
BENTHAM/J ENGLSH/LAW. PAGE 31 E0621
ADJUD
ATTIT
IDEA/COMP

B05
GOODNOW F.J..THE PRINCIPLES OF THE ADMINISTRATIVE
LAW OF THE UNITED STATES. USA-45 LAW STRUCT
EX/STRUC LEGIS BAL/PWR CONTROL GOV/REL PWR...JURID
19/20 CIVIL/SERV. PAGE 45 E0887
ADMIN
NAT/G
PROVS
LOC/G

B05
GRIFFIN A.P.C..LIST OF BOOKS ON RAILROADS IN
FOREIGN COUNTRIES. MOD/EUR ECO/DEV NAT/G CONTROL
SOCISM...JURID 19/20 RAILROAD. PAGE 47 E0927
BIBLIOG/A
SERV/IND
ADMIN
DIST/IND

S05
PHILLIPS J.B.."MODIFICATIONS OF THE JURY SYSTEM."
PARTIC EFFICIENCY ATTIT PERCEPT...TREND 19
SUPREME/CT JURY. PAGE 80 E1612
JURID
DELIB/GP
PERS/REL
POLICY

B06
GRIFFIN A.P.C..SELECT LIST OF REFERENCES ON THE
NEGRO QUESTION (REV. ED.). USA-45 CONSTN SCHOOL
SUFF ADJUST...JURID SOC/INTEG 19/20 NEGRO. PAGE 47
E0930
BIBLIOG/A
RACE/REL
DISCRIM
ATTIT

B07
BENTHAM J..AN INTRODUCTION TO THE PRINCIPLES OF
MORALS AND LEGISLATION. UNIV CONSTN CULTURE SOCIETY
NAT/G CONSULT LEGIS JUDGE ADJUD CT/SYS...JURID
CONCPT NEW/IDEA. PAGE 10 E0190
LAW
GEN/LAWS

B07
GRIFFIN A.P.C..LIST OF MORE RECENT WORKS ON FEDERAL
CONTROL OF COMMERCE AND CORPORATIONS (PAMPHLET).
USA-45 LAW ECO/DEV FINAN LG/CO TARIFFS TAX LICENSE
CENTRAL ORD/FREE WEALTH LAISSEZ 19/20. PAGE 47
E0931
BIBLIOG/A
NAT/G
JURID
ECO/TAC

B08
GRIFFIN A.P.C..REFERENCES ON CORRUPT PRACTICES IN
ELECTIONS (PAMPHLET). USA-45 LAW CONSTN TRIBUTE
CRIME REPRESENT...JURID 19/20. PAGE 47 E0934
BIBLIOG/A
CHOOSE
SUFF
APPORT

B09
HARVARD UNIVERSITY LAW LIBRARY.CATALOGUE OF THE
LIBRARY OF THE LAW SCHOOL OF HARVARD UNIVERSITY (3
VOLS.). UK USA-45 LEGIS JUDGE ADJUD CT/SYS...JURID
CHARTS 14/20. PAGE 51 E1008
BIBLIOG/A
LAW
ADMIN

B09
HOLLAND T.E..LETTERS UPON WAR AND NEUTRALITY.
WOR-45 NAT/G FORCES JUDGE ECO/TAC LEGIT CT/SYS
NEUTRAL ROUTINE COERCE...JURID TIME/SEQ 20. PAGE 55
E1085
LAW
INT/LAW
INT/ORG
WAR

B09
JUSTINIAN.THE DIGEST (DIGESTA CORPUS JURIS CIVILIS)
(2 VOLS.) (TRANS. BY C. H. MONRO). ROMAN/EMP LAW
FAM LOC/G LEGIS EDU/PROP CONTROL MARRIAGE OWN ROLE
CIVIL/LAW. PAGE 59 E1177
JURID
CT/SYS
NAT/G
STRATA

B10
MENDELSSOHN S..MENDELSSOHN'S SOUTH AFRICA
BIBLIOGRAPHY (VOL. I). SOUTH/AFR RACE/REL...GEOG
JURID 19/20. PAGE 72 E1440
BIBLIOG/A
CULTURE

L11
POUND R.."THE SCOPE AND PURPOSE OF SOCIOLOGICAL
JURISPRUDENCE."...GEN/LAWS 20 KANT/I HEGEL/GWF.
PAGE 81 E1634
JURID
IDEA/COMP
METH/COMP
SOC

B12
FOUAD M..LE REGIME DE LA PRESSE EN EGYPTE: THESE
POUR LE DOCTORAT. UAR LICENSE EDU/PROP ADMIN
SANCTION CRIME SUPEGO PWR...ART/METH JURID 19/20.
PAGE 39 E0778
ORD/FREE
LEGIS
CONTROL
PRESS

B12
GRIFFIN A.P.C..SELECT LIST OF REFERENCES ON
IMPEACHMENT (REV. ED.) (PAMPHLET). USA-45 LAW PROVS
ADJUD ATTIT...JURID 19/20 NEGRO. PAGE 47 E0935
BIBLIOG/A
CONSTN
NAT/G
LEGIS

B12
POLLOCK F..THE GENIUS OF THE COMMON LAW. CHRIST-17C
UK FINAN CHIEF ACT/RES ADMIN GP/REL ATTIT SOCISM
...ANARCH JURID. PAGE 81 E1624
LAW
CULTURE
CREATE

B13
BORCHARD E.M..BIBLIOGRAPHY OF INTERNATIONAL LAW AND
CONTINENTAL LAW. EUR+WWI MOD/EUR UK LAW INT/TRADE
BIBLIOG
INT/LAW

WAR PEACE...GOV/COMP NAT/COMP 19/20. PAGE 14 E0267
JURID
DIPLOM

B13
BUTLER N.M..THE INTERNATIONAL MIND. WOR-45 INT/ORG
LEGIT PWR...JURID CONCPT 20. PAGE 18 E0350
ADJUD
ORD/FREE
INT/LAW

B14
VECCHIO G.D..THE FORMAL BASES OF LAW (TRANS. BY J.
LISLE). DOMIN LEGIT CONTROL COERCE UTIL MORAL PWR
...CONCPT TIME/SEQ 17/20 COMMON/LAW NATURL/LAW.
PAGE 103 E2074
LAW
JURID
GEN/LAWS
IDEA/COMP

B16
CARLYLE A.J..BIBLIOGRAPHY OF POLITICAL THEORY
(PAMPHLET). FRANCE GERMANY UK USA-45...JURID 9/19.
PAGE 19 E0382
BIBLIOG/A
CONCPT
PHIL/SCI

B16
ROOT E..ADDRESSES ON INTERNATIONAL SUBJECTS.
MOD/EUR UNIV USA-45 LAW SOCIETY EXEC ATTIT ALL/VALS
...POLICY JURID CONCPT 20 CHINJAP. PAGE 85 E1711
INT/ORG
ACT/RES
PEACE
INT/LAW

B16
SALMOND J.W..JURISPRUDENCE. UK LOC/G NAT/G LEGIS
PROB/SOLV LICENSE LEGIT CRIME PERS/REL OWN ORD/FREE
...T 20. PAGE 87 E1742
LAW
CT/SYS
JURID
ADJUD

B16
SCHROEDER T..FREE SPEECH FOR RADICALS (REV. ED.).
USA-45 CONSTN INDUS LOC/G FORCES SANCTION WAR ATTIT
SEX...JURID REFORMERS 20 FREE/SPEE. PAGE 88 E1767
ORD/FREE
CONTROL
LAW
PRESS

L16
WRIGHT Q.."THE ENFORCEMENT OF INTERNATIONAL LAW
THROUGH MUNICIPAL LAW IN THE US." USA-45 LOC/G
NAT/G PUB/INST FORCES LEGIT CT/SYS PERCEPT ALL/VALS
...JURID 20. PAGE 107 E2149
INT/ORG
LAW
INT/LAW
WAR

S17
ROOT E.."THE EFFECT OF DEMOCRACY ON INTERNATIONAL
LAW." USA-45 WOR-45 INTELL SOCIETY INT/ORG NAT/G
CONSULT ACT/RES CREATE PLAN EDU/PROP PEACE SKILL
...CONCPT METH/CNCPT OBS 20. PAGE 85 E1712
LEGIS
JURID
INT/LAW

B18
EYBERS G.W..SELECT CONSTITUTIONAL DOCUMENTS
ILLUSTRATING SOUTH AFRICAN HISTORY 1795-1910.
SOUTH/AFR LOC/G LEGIS CT/SYS...JURID ANTHOL 18/20
NATAL CAPE/HOPE ORANGE/STA. PAGE 36 E0707
CONSTN
LAW
NAT/G
COLONIAL

B18
WILSON W..THE STATE: ELEMENTS OF HISTORICAL AND
PRACTICAL POLITICS. FRANCE GERMANY ITALY UK USSR
CONSTN EX/STRUC LEGIS CT/SYS WAR PWR...POLICY
GOV/COMP 20. PAGE 106 E2131
NAT/G
JURID
CONCPT
NAT/COMP

B18
YUKIO O..THE VOICE OF JAPANESE DEMOCRACY, AN ESSAY
ON CONSTITUTIONAL LOYALTY (TRANS BY J. E. BECKER).
ASIA POL/PAR DELIB/GP EX/STRUC RIGID/FLEX ORD/FREE
PWR...POLICY JURID METH/COMP 19/20 CHINJAP.
PAGE 108 E2167
CONSTN
MAJORIT
CHOOSE
NAT/G

S18
POWELL T.R.."THE LOGIC AND RHETORIC OF
CONSTITUTIONAL LAW (BMR)" USA+45 USA-45 DELIB/GP
PROB/SOLV ADJUD CT/SYS...DECISION 20 SUPREME/CT
CON/INTERP. PAGE 82 E1642
CONSTN
LAW
JURID
LOG

N18
BREWER D.J..THE MOVEMENT OF COERCION (PAMPHLET).
CONSTN INDUS ADJUD COERCE OWN WEALTH...OLD/LIB
JURID 19 SUPREME/CT. PAGE 15 E0296
GP/REL
LABOR
LG/CO
LAW

B19
SMITH R.H..JUSTICE AND THE POOR. LAW RECEIVE ADJUD
CRIME GOV/REL COST...JURID SOC/WK CONCPT STAT
CHARTS GP/COMP 20. PAGE 92 E1847
CT/SYS
DISCRIM
WEALTH

N19
BURRUS B.R..INVESTIGATION AND DISCOVERY IN STATE
ANTITRUST (PAMPHLET). USA+45 USA-45 LEGIS ECO/TAC
ADMIN CONTROL CT/SYS CRIME GOV/REL PWR...JURID
CHARTS 19/20 FTC MONOPOLY. PAGE 18 E0346
NAT/G
PROVS
LAW
INSPECT

N19
PAN AMERICAN UNION.INFORME DE LA MISION DE
ASISTENCIA TECNICA DE LA OEA A LA REPUBLICA DE
HONDURAS EN MATERIA ELECTORAL (PAMPHLET). HONDURAS
CONSTN ORD/FREE...JURID OBS 20 OAS. PAGE 80 E1595
CHOOSE
SUFF
POL/PAR
NAT/G

POUND R.,ORGANIZATION OF THE COURTS (PAMPHLET). CT/SYS
MOD/EUR UK USA-45 ADJUD PWR...GOV/COMP 10/20 JURID
EUROPE. PAGE 82 E1635   STRUCT
                                                                                          ADMIN
N19

RALSTON A.,A FRESH LOOK AT LEGISLATIVE APPORT
APPORTIONMENT IN NEW JERSEY (PAMPHLET). USA+45 REPRESENT
CONSTN LEGIS OBJECTIVE...MATH METH 20 NEW/JERSEY. PROVS
PAGE 83 E1671   JURID
N19

TAYLOR H.,WHY THE PENDING TREATY WITH COLOMBIA INT/LAW
SHOULD BE RATIFIED (PAMPHLET). PANAMA USA-45 DIPLOM
DELIB/GP INT/TRADE REV ORD/FREE...JURID TREATY
18/19 ROOSEVLT/T TAFT/WH COLOMB. PAGE 95 E1912
N19

DICKINSON E.,THE EQUALITY OF STATES IN LAW
INTERNATIONAL LAW. WOR-45 INT/ORG NAT/G DIPLOM CONCPT
EDU/PROP LEGIT PEACE ATTIT ALL/VALS...JURID SOVEREIGN
TIME/SEQ LEAGUE/NAT. PAGE 31 E0622
B20

VINOGRADOFF P.,OUTLINES OF HISTORICAL JURISPRUDENCE JURID
(2 VOLS.). GREECE MEDIT-7 LAW CONSTN FACE/GP FAM METH
KIN MUNIC CRIME OWN...INT/LAW IDEA/COMP BIBLIOG.
PAGE 104 E2080
B20

DUNNING W.A.,"A HISTORY OF POLITICAL THINKERS FROM IDEA/COMP
ROUSSEAU TO SPENCER." NAT/G REV NAT/LISM UTIL PHIL/SCI
CONSERVE MARXISM POPULISM...JURID BIBLIOG 18/19. CONCPT
PAGE 33 E0664   GEN/LAWS
C20

CARDOZO B.N.,THE NATURE OF THE JUDICIAL PROCESS. JURID
ROUTINE ORD/FREE...POLICY 20. PAGE 19 E0377 CT/SYS
                                                                                          LEAD
                                                                                          DECISION
B21

OPPENHEIM L.,THE FUTURE OF INTERNATIONAL LAW. INT/ORG
EUR+WWI MOD/EUR LAW LEGIS JUDGE LEGIT ORD/FREE CT/SYS
...JURID TIME/SEQ GEN/LAWS 20. PAGE 79 E1578 INT/LAW
B21

STOWELL E.C.,INTERVENTION IN INTERNATIONAL LAW. BAL/PWR
UNIV LAW SOCIETY INT/ORG ACT/RES PLAN LEGIT ROUTINE SOVEREIGN
WAR...JURID OBS GEN/LAWS 20. PAGE 94 E1884
B21

HALDEMAN E.,"SERIALS OF AN INTERNATIONAL BIBLIOG
CHARACTER." WOR-45 DIPLOM...ART/METH GEOG HEAL HUM PHIL/SCI
INT/LAW JURID PSY SOC. PAGE 49 E0978
L21

BRYCE J.,INTERNATIONAL RELATIONS. CHRIST-17C INT/ORG
EUR+WWI MOD/EUR CULTURE INTELL NAT/G DELIB/GP POLICY
CREATE BAL/PWR DIPLOM ATTIT DRIVE RIGID/FLEX
ALL/VALS...PLURIST JURID CONCPT TIME/SEQ GEN/LAWS
TOT/POP. PAGE 16 E0323
B22

WRIGHT Q.,THE CONTROL OF AMERICAN FOREIGN NAT/G
RELATIONS. USA-45 WOR-45 CONSTN INT/ORG CONSULT EXEC
LEGIS LEGIT ROUTINE ORD/FREE PWR...POLICY JURID DIPLOM
CONCPT METH/CNCPT RECORD LEAGUE/NAT 20. PAGE 107
E2150
B22

DE MONTESQUIEU C.,THE SPIRIT OF LAWS (2 VOLS.) JURID
(TRANS. BY THOMAS NUGENT). FRANCE FINAN SECT LAW
INT/TRADE TAX COERCE REV DISCRIM HABITAT ORD/FREE CONCPT
19 ALEMBERT/J CIVIL/LAW. PAGE 30 E0588 GEN/LAWS
B23

HOLMES O.W. JR.,THE COMMON LAW. FUT WOR-45 CULTURE ADJUD
SOCIETY CREATE LEGIT ROUTINE ATTIT ALL/VALS...JURID CON/ANAL
METH/CNCPT TIME/SEQ GEN/LAWS TOT/POP VAL/FREE.
PAGE 55 E1087
B23

POUND R.,INTERPRETATIONS OF LEGAL HISTORY. CULTURE LAW
...PHIL/SCI NEW/IDEA CLASSIF SIMUL GEN/LAWS 19/20. IDEA/COMP
PAGE 82 E1636   JURID
B23

ROBERT H.M.,PARLIAMENTARY LAW. POL/PAR LEGIS PARTIC PARL/PROC
CHOOSE REPRESENT GP/REL. PAGE 85 E1701 DELIB/GP
                                                                                          NAT/G
                                                                                          JURID
B23

DEWEY J.,"ETHICS AND INTERNATIONAL RELATIONS." FUT LAW
WOR-45 SOCIETY INT/ORG VOL/ASSN DIPLOM LEGIT MORAL
ORD/FREE...JURID CONCPT GEN/METH 20. PAGE 31 E0618
S23

CARDOZO B.,THE GROWTH OF THE LAW. USA-45 CULTURE LAW
...JURID 20. PAGE 19 E0376 ADJUD
                                                                                          CT/SYS
B24

GENTILI A.,DE LEGATIONIBUS. CHRIST-17C NAT/G SECT DIPLOM
CONSULT LEGIT...POLICY CATH JURID CONCPT MYTH. INT/LAW
PAGE 43 E0848   INT/ORG
                                                                                          LAW
B24

HALL W.E.,A TREATISE ON INTERNATIONAL LAW. WOR-45 PWR
CONSTN INT/ORG NAT/G DIPLOM ORD/FREE LEAGUE/NAT 20 JURID
TREATY. PAGE 49 E0985 WAR
                                                                                          INT/LAW
B24

HOLDSWORTH W.S.,A HISTORY OF ENGLISH LAW; THE LAW
COMMON LAW AND ITS RIVALS (VOL. V). UK SEA EX/STRUC LEGIS
WRITING ADMIN...INT/LAW JURID CONCPT IDEA/COMP ADJUD
WORSHIP 16/17 PARLIAMENT ENGLSH/LAW COMMON/LAW. CT/SYS
PAGE 54 E1073
B24

HOLDSWORTH W.S.,A HISTORY OF ENGLISH LAW; THE LAW
COMMON LAW AND ITS RIVALS (VOL. VI). UK STRATA CONSTN
EX/STRUC ADJUD ADMIN CONTROL CT/SYS...JURID CONCPT LEGIS
GEN/LAWS 17 COMMONWLTH PARLIAMENT ENGLSH/LAW CHIEF
COMMON/LAW. PAGE 54 E1074
B24

HOLDSWORTH W.S.,A HISTORY OF ENGLISH LAW; THE LAW
COMMON LAW AND ITS RIVALS (VOL. IV). UK SEA AGRI LEGIS
CHIEF ADJUD CONTROL CRIME GOV/REL...INT/LAW JURID CT/SYS
NAT/COMP 16/17 PARLIAMENT COMMON/LAW CANON/LAW CONSTN
ENGLSH/LAW. PAGE 54 E1075
B24

SHERMAN C.P.,"ROMAN LAW IN THE MODERN WORLD (2ND LAW
ED.) (3 VOLS.)" MEDIT-7...JURID BIBLIOG. PAGE 91 ADJUD
E1819   OWN
                                                                                          CONSTN
C24

GODET M.,INDEX BIBLIOGRAPHICUS: INTERNATIONAL BIBLIOG/A
CATALOGUE OF SOURCES OF CURRENT BIBLIOGRAPHIC DIPLOM
INFORMATION. EUR+WWI MOD/EUR SOCIETY SECT TAX EDU/PROP
...JURID PHIL/SCI SOC MATH. PAGE 44 E0876 LAW
B25

WINFIELD P.H.,THE CHIEF SOURCES OF ENGLISH LEGAL BIBLIOG/A
HISTORY. UK CONSTN JUDGE ADJUD CT/SYS 13/18. JURID
PAGE 107 E2133 LAW
B25

HUDSON M.,"THE PERMANENT COURT OF INTERNATIONAL INT/ORG
JUSTICE AND THE QUESTION OF AMERICAN ADJUD
PARTICIPATION." WOR-45 LEGIT CT/SYS ORD/FREE DIPLOM
...JURID CONCPT TIME/SEQ GEN/LAWS VAL/FREE 20 ICJ. INT/LAW
PAGE 56 E1108
L25

BEALE J.H.,A BIBLIOGRAPHY OF EARLY ENGLISH LAW BIBLIOG/A
BOOKS. MOD/EUR UK PRESS ADJUD CT/SYS ATTIT...CHARTS JURID
10/16. PAGE 8 E0161 LAW
B26

HOCKING W.E.,PRESENT STATUS OF THE PHILOSOPHY OF JURID
LAW AND OF RIGHTS. UNIV CULTURE INTELL SOCIETY PHIL/SCI
NAT/G CREATE LEGIT SANCTION ALL/VALS SOC/INTEG ORD/FREE
18/20. PAGE 53 E1060
B26

HALL A.B.,"DETERMINATION OF METHODS FOR ADJUD
ASCERTAINING THE FACTORS THAT INFLUENCE JUDICIAL DECISION
DECISIONS IN CASES INVOLVING DUE PROCESS" LAW JUDGE CONSTN
DEBATE EFFICIENCY OPTIMAL UTIL...SOC CONCPT JURID
PROBABIL STAT SAMP. PAGE 49 E0981
S26

DICKINSON J.,ADMINISTRATIVE JUSTICE AND THE CT/SYS
SUPREMACY OF LAW IN THE UNITED STATES. USA-45 LAW ADJUD
INDUS DOMIN EDU/PROP CONTROL EXEC GP/REL ORD/FREE ADMIN
...POLICY JURID 19/20. PAGE 31 E0623 NAT/G
B27

LAUTERPACHT H.,PRIVATE LAW SOURCES AND ANALOGIES OF INT/ORG
INTERNATIONAL LAW. WOR-45 NAT/G DELIB/GP LEGIT ADJUD
COERCE ATTIT ORD/FREE PWR SOVEREIGN...JURID CONCPT PEACE
HIST/WRIT TIME/SEQ GEN/METH LEAGUE/NAT 20. PAGE 63 INT/LAW
B27

E1264

B27
RYAN J.A..DECLINING LIVERTY AND OTHER ESSAYS. ORD/FREE
USA-45 SECT DELIB/GP ATTIT PWR SOCISM 20 LEGIS
SUPREME/CT. PAGE 87 E1740 JURID
NAT/G

B28
BUTLER G..THE DEVELOPMENT OF INTERNATIONAL LAW. LAW
WOR-45 SOCIETY NAT/G KNOWL ORD/FREE PWR...JURID INT/LAW
CONCPT HIST/WRIT GEN/LAWS. PAGE 18 E0349 DIPLOM
INT/ORG

B28
FRANKFURTER F..THE BUSINESS OF THE SUPREME COURT; A CT/SYS
STUDY IN THE FEDERAL JUDICIAL SYSTEM. USA-45 CONSTN ADJUD
EX/STRUC PROB/SOLV GP/REL ATTIT PWR...POLICY JURID LAW
18/20 SUPREME/CT CONGRESS. PAGE 40 E0789 FEDERAL

B28
HOLDSWORTH W.S..THE HISTORIANS OF ANGLO-AMERICAN HIST/WRIT
LAW. UK USA-45 INTELL LEGIS RESPECT...BIOG NAT/COMP LAW
17/20 COMMON/LAW. PAGE 54 E1076 JURID

B28
MAIR L.P..THE PROTECTION OF MINORITIES. EUR+WWI LAW
WOR-45 CONSTN INT/ORG NAT/G LEGIT CT/SYS GP/REL SOVEREIGN
RACE/REL DISCRIM ORD/FREE RESPECT...JURID CONCPT
TIME/SEQ 20. PAGE 68 E1352

B28
NORTON T.J..LOSING LIBERTY JUDICIALLY. PROVS LEGIS NAT/G
BAL/PWR CT/SYS...JURID 18/20 SUPREME/CT CIV/RIGHTS ORD/FREE
CONGRESS. PAGE 78 E1557 CONSTN
JUDGE

B28
YANG KUNG-SUN.THE BOOK OF LORD SHANG. LAW ECO/UNDEV ASIA
LOC/G NAT/G NEIGH PLAN ECO/TAC LEGIT ATTIT SKILL JURID
...CONCPT CON/ANAL WORK TOT/POP. PAGE 108 E2164

L28
HUDSON M.."THE TEACHING OF INTERNATIONAL LAW IN PERCEPT
AMERICA." USA-45 LAW CONSULT ACT/RES CREATE KNOWL
EDU/PROP ATTIT RIGID/FLEX...JURID CONCPT RECORD INT/LAW
HIST/WRIT TREND GEN/LAWS 18/20. PAGE 56 E1109

B29
BUELL R..INTERNATIONAL RELATIONS. WOR+45 WOR-45 INT/ORG
CONSTN STRATA FORCES TOP/EX ADMIN ATTIT DRIVE BAL/PWR
SUPEGO MORAL ORD/FREE PWR SOVEREIGN...JURID SOC DIPLOM
CONCPT 20. PAGE 17 E0326

B29
CONWELL-EVANS T.P..THE LEAGUE COUNCIL IN ACTION. DELIB/GP
EUR+WWI TURKEY UK USSR WOR-45 INT/ORG FORCES JUDGE INT/LAW
ECO/TAC EDU/PROP LEGIT ROUTINE ARMS/CONT COERCE
ATTIT PWR...MAJORIT GEOG JURID CONCPT LEAGUE/NAT
TOT/POP VAL/FREE TUNIS 20. PAGE 25 E0498

B29
LEITZ F..DIE PUBLIZITAT DER AKTIENGESELLSCHAFT. LG/CO
BELGIUM FRANCE GERMANY UK FINAN PRESS GP/REL PROFIT JURID
KNOWL 20. PAGE 64 E1282 ECO/TAC
NAT/COMP

B29
MOLEY R..POLITICS AND CRIMINAL PROSECUTION. USA-45 PWR
POL/PAR EX/STRUC LEGIT CONTROL LEAD ROUTINE CHOOSE CT/SYS
INGP/REL...JURID CHARTS 20. PAGE 74 E1481 CRIME
ADJUD

B29
PRATT I.A..MODERN EGYPT: A LIST OF REFERENCES TO BIBLIOG
MATERIAL IN THE NEW YORK PUBLIC LIBRARY. UAR ISLAM
ECO/UNDEV...GEOG JURID SOC LING 20. PAGE 82 E1647 DIPLOM
NAT/G

C29
BUCK A.E.."PUBLIC BUDGETING." USA-45 FINAN LOC/G BUDGET
NAT/G LEGIS BAL/PAY COST...JURID TREND BIBLIOG/A ROUTINE
20. PAGE 17 E0324 ADMIN

B30
BENTHAM J..THE RATIONALE OF PUNISHMENT. UK LAW CRIME
LOC/G NAT/G LEGIS CONTROL...JURID GEN/LAWS SANCTION
COURT/SYS 19. PAGE 10 E0192 COERCE
ORD/FREE

B30
FAIRLIE J.A..COUNTY GOVERNMENT AND ADMINISTRATION. ADMIN
UK USA-45 NAT/G SCHOOL FORCES BUDGET TAX CT/SYS GOV/REL
CHOOSE...JURID BIBLIOG 11/20. PAGE 36 E0713 LOC/G
MUNIC

B30
JORDAN E..THEORY OF LEGISLATION: AN ESSAY ON THE LEGIS
DYNAMICS OF PUBLIC MIND. NAT/G CREATE REPRESENT CONCPT
MAJORITY ATTIT GEN/LAWS. PAGE 59 E1173 JURID
CT/SYS

B30
WILLOUGHBY W.W..PRINCIPLES OF THE CONSTITUTIONAL CONSTN
LAW OF THE UNITED STATES. USA-45 ADJUD FEDERAL NAT/G
SOVEREIGN 18/20 COMMON/LAW. PAGE 106 E2125 CONCPT
JURID

B30
WRIGHT Q..MANDATES UNDER THE LEAGUE OF NATIONS. INT/ORG
WOR-45 CONSTN ECO/DEV ECO/UNDEV NAT/G DELIB/GP LAW
TOP/EX LEGIT ALL/VALS...JURID CONCPT LEAGUE/NAT 20. INT/LAW
PAGE 107 E2151

L30
LLEWELLYN K.N.."A REALISTIC JURISPRUDENCE - THE LAW
NEXT STEP." PROB/SOLV ADJUD GP/REL PERS/REL CONCPT
IDEA/COMP. PAGE 66 E1312 JURID
GEN/LAWS

B32
EAGLETON C..INTERNATIONAL GOVERNMENT. BRAZIL FRANCE INT/ORG
GERMANY ITALY UK USSR WOR-45 DELIB/GP TOP/EX PLAN JURID
ECO/TAC EDU/PROP LEGIT ADJUD REGION ARMS/CONT DIPLOM
COERCE ATTIT PWR...GEOG MGT VAL/FREE LEAGUE/NAT 20. INT/LAW
PAGE 34 E0670

B32
GREAT BRIT COMM MINISTERS PWR.REPORT. UK LAW CONSTN EX/STRUC
CONSULT LEGIS PARL/PROC SANCTION SOVEREIGN NAT/G
...DECISION JURID 20 PARLIAMENT. PAGE 45 E0902 PWR
CONTROL

B32
GREGORY W..LIST OF THE SERIAL PUBLICATIONS OF BIBLIOG
FOREIGN GOVERNMENTS, 1815-1931. WOR-45 DIPLOM ADJUD NAT/G
...POLICY 20. PAGE 46 E0914 LAW
JURID

B32
LUNT D.C..THE ROAD TO THE LAW. UK USA-45 LEGIS ADJUD
EDU/PROP OWN ORD/FREE...DECISION TIME/SEQ NAT/COMP LAW
16/20 AUSTRAL ENGLSH/LAW COMMON/LAW. PAGE 67 E1333 JURID
CT/SYS

B32
MASTERS R.D..INTERNATIONAL LAW IN INTERNATIONAL INT/ORG
COURTS. BELGIUM EUR+WWI FRANCE GERMANY MOD/EUR LAW
SWITZERLND WOR-45 SOCIETY STRATA STRUCT LEGIT EXEC INT/LAW
ALL/VALS...JURID HIST/WRIT TIME/SEQ TREND GEN/LAWS
20. PAGE 69 E1383

B33
AMERICAN FOREIGN LAW ASSN.BIOGRAPHICAL NOTES ON THE BIBLIOG/A
LAWS AND LEGAL LITERATURE OF URUGUAY AND CURACAO. LAW
URUGUAY CONSTN FINAN SECT FORCES JUDGE DIPLOM JURID
INT/TRADE ADJUD CT/SYS CRIME 20. PAGE 4 E0078 ADMIN

B33
HELLMAN F.S..SELECTED LIST OF REFERENCES ON THE BIBLIOG/A
CONSTITUTIONAL POWERS OF THE PRESIDENT INCLUDING JURID
POWERS RECENTLY DELEGATED. USA-45 NAT/G EX/STRUC LAW
TOP/EX CENTRAL FEDERAL PWR 20 PRESIDENT. PAGE 51 CONSTN
E1025

B33
LAUTERPACHT H..THE FUNCTION OF LAW IN THE INT/ORG
INTERNATIONAL COMMUNITY. WOR-45 NAT/G FORCES CREATE LAW
DOMIN LEGIT COERCE WAR PEACE ATTIT ORD/FREE PWR INT/LAW
SOVEREIGN...JURID CONCPT METH/CNCPT TIME/SEQ
GEN/LAWS GEN/METH LEAGUE/NAT TOT/POP VAL/FREE 20.
PAGE 63 E1265

B33
MATTHEWS M.A..THE AMERICAN INSTITUTE OF BIBLIOG/A
INTERNATIONAL LAW AND THE CODIFICATION OF INT/LAW
INTERNATIONAL LAW (PAMPHLET). USA-45 CONSTN ADJUD L/A+17C
CT/SYS...JURID 20. PAGE 69 E1386 DIPLOM

B34
CUMMINGS H..LIBERTY UNDER LAW AND ADMINISTRATION. ORD/FREE
MOD/EUR USA-45 ADMIN ATTIT...JURID PHIL/SCI. LAW
PAGE 28 E0553 NAT/G
SOCIETY

B34
GONZALEZ PALENCIA A.ESTUDIO HISTORICO SOBRE LA LEGIT
CENSURA GUBERNATIVA EN ESPANA 1800-1833. NAT/G EDU/PROP
COERCE INGP/REL ATTIT AUTHORIT KNOWL...POLICY JURID PRESS
19. PAGE 44 E0884 CONTROL

B34

WOLFF C.,JUS GENTIUM METHODO SCIENTIFICA   NAT/G
PERTRACTATUM. MOD/EUR INT/ORG VOL/ASSN LEGIT PEACE   LAW
ATTIT...JURID 20. PAGE 107 E2140   INT/LAW
                                                           WAR

L34

LLEWELLYN K.N.,"THE CONSTITUTION AS AN INSTITUTION"   CONSTN
(BMR)" USA-45 PROB/SOLV LOBBY REPRESENT...DECISION   LAW
JURID 18/20 SUPREME/CT. PAGE 66 E1313   CONCPT
                                                           CT/SYS

B35

KENNEDY W.P.,THE LAW AND CUSTOM OF THE SOUTH   CT/SYS
AFRICAN CONSTITUTION. AFR SOUTH/AFR KIN LOC/G PROVS   CONSTN
DIPLOM ADJUD ADMIN EXEC 20. PAGE 60 E1203   JURID
                                                          PARL/PROC

B35

RAM J.,THE SCIENCE OF LEGAL JUDGMENT: A TREATISE...   LAW
UK CONSTN NAT/G LEGIS CREATE PROB/SOLV AGREE CT/SYS   JURID
...INT/LAW CONCPT 19 ENGLSH/LAW CANON/LAW CIVIL/LAW   EX/STRUC
CTS/WESTM. PAGE 83 E1672   ADJUD

B36

EHRLICH E.,FUNDAMENTAL PRINCIPLES OF THE SOCIOLOGY   LAW
OF LAW (TRANS. BY WALTER L. MOLL). UNIV SOCIETY   JURID
ADJUD CT/SYS...POLICY GP/COMP GEN/LAWS GEN/METH.   SOC
PAGE 34 E0678   CONCPT

B36

HANSON L.,GOVERNMENT AND THE PRESS 1695-1763. UK   LAW
LOC/G LEGIS LICENSE CONTROL SANCTION CRIME ATTIT   JURID
ORD/FREE 17/18 PARLIAMENT AMEND/I. PAGE 50 E0996   PRESS
                                                           POLICY

B36

HUDSON M.O.,INTERNATIONAL LEGISLATION: 1929-1931.   INT/LAW
WOR-45 SEA AIR AGRI FINAN LABOR DIPLOM ECO/TAC   PARL/PROC
REPAR CT/SYS ARMS/CONT WAR WEAPON...JURID 20 TREATY   ADJUD
LEAGUE/NAT. PAGE 56 E1112   LAW

B36

KONRAD F.,DIE PERSONLICHE FREIHEIT IM   ORD/FREE
NATIONALSOZIALISTISCHEN DEUTSCHEN REICHE. GERMANY   JURID
JUDGE ADJUD GP/REL FASCISM 20 CIVIL/LIB. PAGE 61   CONSTN
E1226   CONCPT

B36

MATTHEWS M.A.,INTERNATIONAL LAW: SELECT LIST OF   BIBLIOG/A
WORKS IN ENGLISH ON PUBLIC INTERNATIONAL LAW: WITH   INT/LAW
COLLECTIONS OF CASES AND OPINIONS. CHRIST-17C   ATTIT
EUR+WWI MOD/EUR WOR-45 CONSTN ADJUD JURID. PAGE 69   DIPLOM
E1388

B36

RUSSEL F.M.,THEORIES OF INTERNATIONAL RELATIONS.   PWR
EUR+WWI FUT MOD/EUR USA-45 INT/ORG DIPLOM...JURID   POLICY
CONCPT. PAGE 86 E1735   BAL/PWR
                                                          SOVEREIGN

B36

SCHULZ F.,PRINCIPLES OF ROMAN LAW. CONSTN FAM NAT/G   LAW
DOMIN CONTROL CT/SYS CRIME ISOLAT ATTIT ORD/FREE   LEGIS
PWR...JURID ROME/ANC ROMAN/LAW. PAGE 89 E1783   ADJUD
                                                          CONCPT

B37

BEARDSLEY A.R.,LEGAL BIBLIOGRAPHY AND THE USE OF   BIBLIOG
LAW BOOKS. CONSTN CREATE PROB/SOLV...DECISION JURID   LAW
LAB/EXP. PAGE 9 E0166   METH
                                                          OP/RES

B37

BORGESE G.A.,GOLIATH: THE MARCH OF FASCISM. GERMANY   POLICY
ITALY LAW POL/PAR SECT DIPLOM SOCISM...JURID MYTH   NAT/LISM
20 DANTE MACHIAVELL MUSSOLIN/B. PAGE 14 E0270   FASCISM
                                                          NAT/G

B37

RUTHERFORD M.L.,THE INFLUENCE OF THE AMERICAN BAR   ATTIT
ASSOCIATION ON PUBLIC OPINION AND LEGISLATION.   ADJUD
USA+45 LAW CONSTN LABOR LEGIS DOMIN EDU/PROP LEGIT   PROF/ORG
CT/SYS ROUTINE...TIME/SEQ 19/20 ABA. PAGE 87 E1739   JURID

B37

SCHUSTER E.,GUIDE TO LAW AND LEGAL LITERATURE OF   BIBLIOG/A
CENTRAL AMERICAN REPUBLICS. L/A+17C INT/ORG ADJUD   REGION
SANCTION CRIME...JURID 19/20. PAGE 89 E1785   CT/SYS
                                                          LAW

S37

TIMASHEFF N.S.,"WHAT IS SOCIOLOGY OF LAW?" (BMR)"   LAW
UNIV INTELL PWR...EPIST JURID PHIL/SCI IDEA/COMP.   SOC
PAGE 96 E1925   SOCIETY

B38

CLARK J.P.,THE RISE OF A NEW FEDERALISM. LEGIS   FEDERAL
TARIFFS EFFICIENCY NAT/LISM UTIL...JURID SOC   PROVS
GEN/LAWS BIBLIOG 19/20. PAGE 23 E0451   NAT/G
                                                          GOV/REL

B38

FRANKFURTER F.,MR. JUSTICE HOLMES AND THE SUPREME   CREATE
COURT. USA-45 CONSTN SOCIETY FEDERAL OWN ATTIT   CT/SYS
ORD/FREE PWR...POLICY JURID 20 SUPREME/CT HOLMES/OW   DECISION
BILL/RIGHT. PAGE 40 E0790   LAW

B38

HELLMAN F.S.,THE SUPREME COURT ISSUE: SELECTED LIST   BIBLIOG/A
OF REFERENCES. USA-45 NAT/G CHIEF EX/STRUC JUDGE   CONSTN
ATTIT...JURID 20 PRESIDENT ROOSEVLT/F SUPREME/CT.   CT/SYS
PAGE 51 E1026   LAW

B38

HOLDSWORTH W.S.,A HISTORY OF ENGLISH LAW; THE   LAW
CENTURIES OF SETTLEMENT AND REFORM (VOL. X). INDIA   LOC/G
UK CONSTN NAT/G CHIEF LEGIS ADMIN COLONIAL CT/SYS   EX/STRUC
CHOOSE ORD/FREE PWR...JURID 18 PARLIAMENT   ADJUD
COMMONWLTH COMMON/LAW. PAGE 54 E1077

B38

HOLDSWORTH W.S.,A HISTORY OF ENGLISH LAW; THE   LAW
CENTURIES OF SETTLEMENT AND REFORM (VOL. XII). UK   PROF/ORG
CONSTN STRATA LEGIS JUDGE ADJUD CT/SYS ATTIT   WRITING
...JURID CONCPT BIOG GEN/LAWS 18 ENGLSH/LAW   IDEA/COMP
BLACKSTN/W COMMON/LAW. PAGE 54 E1078

B38

HOLDSWORTH W.S.,A HISTORY OF ENGLISH LAW; THE   LAW
CENTURIES OF SETTLEMENT AND REFORM (VOL. XI). UK   COLONIAL
CONSTN NAT/G EX/STRUC DIPLOM ADJUD CT/SYS LEAD   LEGIS
CRIME ATTIT...INT/LAW JURID 18 CMN/WLTH PARLIAMENT   PARL/PROC
ENGLSH/LAW. PAGE 54 E1079

B38

MCNAIR A.D.,THE LAW OF TREATIES: BRITISH PRACTICE   AGREE
AND OPINIONS. UK CREATE DIPLOM LEGIT WRITING ADJUD   LAW
WAR...INT/LAW JURID TREATY. PAGE 71 E1424   CT/SYS
                                                          NAT/G

B38

POUND R.,THE FORMATIVE ERA OF AMERICAN LAW. CULTURE   CONSTN
NAT/G PROVS LEGIS ADJUD CT/SYS PERSON SOVEREIGN   LAW
...POLICY IDEA/COMP GEN/LAWS 18/19. PAGE 82 E1637   CREATE
                                                          JURID

B39

MCILWAIN C.H.,CONSTITUTIONALISM AND THE CHANGING   CONSTN
WORLD. UK USA-45 LEGIS PRIVIL AUTHORIT SOVEREIGN   POLICY
...GOV/COMP 15/20 MAGNA/CART HOUSE/CMNS. PAGE 71   JURID
E1417

B39

TIMASHEFF N.S.,AN INTRODUCTION TO THE SOCIOLOGY OF   SOC
LAW. CRIME ANOMIE ATTIT DRIVE ORD/FREE...JURID PSY   BIBLIOG
CONCPT. PAGE 96 E1926   PWR

B40

BROWN A.D.,COMPULSORY MILITARY TRAINING: SELECT   BIBLIOG/A
LIST OF REFERENCES (PAMPHLET). USA-45 CONSTN   FORCES
VOL/ASSN COERCE 20. PAGE 16 E0311   JURID
                                                          ATTIT

B40

CARR E.H.,THE TWENTY YEARS' CRISIS 1919-1939. FUT   INT/ORG
WOR-45 BAL/PWR ECO/TAC LEGIT TOTALISM ATTIT   DIPLOM
ALL/VALS...POLICY JURID CONCPT TIME/SEQ TREND   PEACE
GEN/LAWS TOT/POP 20. PAGE 20 E0393

B40

FULLER G.H.,A SELECTED LIST OF RECENT REFERENCES ON   BIBLIOG/A
THE CONSTITUTION OF THE UNITED STATES (PAMPHLET).   CONSTN
CULTURE NAT/G LEGIS CONFER ADJUD GOV/REL CONSEN   LAW
POPULISM...JURID CONCPT 18/20 CONGRESS. PAGE 41   USA-45
E0820

B40

HART J.,AN INTRODUCTION TO ADMINISTRATIVE LAW, WITH   LAW
SELECTED CASES. USA-45 CONSTN SOCIETY NAT/G   ADMIN
EX/STRUC ADJUD CT/SYS LEAD CRIME ORD/FREE   LEGIS
...DECISION JURID 20 CASEBOOK. PAGE 50 E1002   PWR

B40

HOBBES T.,A DIALOGUE BETWEEN A PHILOSOPHER AND A   CT/SYS
STUDENT OF THE COMMON LAWS OF ENGLAND (1667?). UK   CHIEF
SECT DOMIN ADJUD CRIME INCOME OWN UTIL ORD/FREE PWR   SANCTION
SOVEREIGN...JURID GEN/LAWS 17. PAGE 53 E1057   LAW

S40

GURVITCH G.,"MAJOR PROBLEMS OF THE SOCIOLOGY OF   SOC
LAW." CULTURE SANCTION KNOWL MORAL...POLICY EPIST   LAW

JURID WORSHIP. PAGE 48 E0963   PHIL/SCI

CHAFEE Z. JR.,FREE SPEECH IN THE UNITED STATES.   ORD/FREE
USA-45 ADJUD CONTROL CRIME WAR...BIBLIOG 20   CONSTN
FREE/SPEE AMEND/I SUPREME/CT. PAGE 21 E0413   ATTIT
                                                   JURID

GILMORE M.P.,ARGUMENT FROM ROMAN LAW IN POLITICAL JURID
THOUGHT, 1200-1600. INTELL LICENSE CONTROL CT/SYS LAW
GOV/REL PRIVIL PWR...IDEA/COMP BIBLIOG 13/16.   CONCPT
PAGE 44 E0866   NAT/G

WRIGHT Q.,"FUNDAMENTAL PROBLEMS OF INTERNATIONAL   INT/ORG
ORGANIZATION." UNIV WOR-45 STRUCT FORCES ACT/RES   ATTIT
CREATE DOMIN EDU/PROP LEGIT REGION NAT/LISM   PEACE
ORD/FREE PWR RESPECT SOVEREIGN...JURID SOC CONCPT
METH/CNCPT TIME/SEQ 20. PAGE 107 E2152

BLANCHARD L.R.,MARTINIQUE: A SELECTED LIST OF   BIBLIOG/A
REFERENCES (PAMPHLET). WEST/IND AGRI LOC/G SCHOOL   SOCIETY
...ART/METH GEOG JURID CHARTS 20. PAGE 12 E0241   CULTURE
                                                   COLONIAL

CARR R.K.,THE SUPREME COURT AND JUDICIAL REVIEW.   CT/SYS
NAT/G CHIEF LEGIS OP/RES LEAD GOV/REL GP/REL ATTIT CONSTN
...POLICY DECISION 18/20 SUPREME/CT PRESIDENT   JURID
CONGRESS. PAGE 20 E0394   PWR

FORTESCU J.,IN PRAISE OF ENGLISH LAW (1464) (TRANS. LAW
BY S.B. CHRIMES). UK ELITES CHIEF FORCES CT/SYS   CONSTN
COERCE CRIME GOV/REL ILLEGIT...JURID GOV/COMP   LEGIS
GEN/LAWS 15. PAGE 39 E0774   ORD/FREE

GURVITCH G.,SOCIOLOGY OF LAW. CONSTN SOCIETY CREATE SOC
MORAL SOVEREIGN...POLICY EPIST JURID PHIL/SCI   LAW
IDEA/COMP METH/COMP HOLMES/OW HOBBES/T. PAGE 48   ADJUD
E0964

KELSEN H.,LAW AND PEACE IN INTERNATIONAL RELATIONS. INT/ORG
FUT WOR-45 NAT/G DELIB/GP FORCES LEGIT RIGID/FLEX   ADJUD
ORD/FREE SOVEREIGN...JURID CONCPT TREND STERTYP   PEACE
GEN/LAWS LEAGUE/NAT 20. PAGE 60 E1197   INT/LAW

ANDERSON R.B.,SUPPLEMENT TO BEALE'S BIBLIOGRAPHY OF BIBLIOG/A
EARLY ENGLISH LAW BOOKS. MOD/EUR UK CONSTN PRESS   JURID
ADJUD...CHARTS 10/15. PAGE 5 E0091   CT/SYS
                                                   LAW

BACKUS R.C.,A GUIDE TO THE LAW AND LEGAL LITERATURE BIBLIOG/A
OF COLOMBIA. FINAN INDUS LABOR FORCES ADJUD ADMIN   LAW
COLONIAL CT/SYS CRIME...INT/LAW JURID 20 COLOMB.   CONSTN
PAGE 7 E0127   L/A+17C

CLAGETT H.L.,A GUIDE TO THE LAW AND LEGAL   BIBLIOG
LITERATURE OF PARAGUAY. PARAGUAY CONSTN COM/IND   JURID
LABOR MUNIC JUDGE ADMIN CT/SYS...CRIMLGY INT/LAW   LAW
CON/ANAL 20. PAGE 22 E0439   L/A+17C

HAGUE PERMANENT CT INTL JUSTIC,WORLD COURT REPORTS: INT/ORG
COLLECTION OF THE JUDGEMENTS ORDERS AND OPINIONS   CT/SYS
VOLUME 4 1936-42. WOR-45 CONFER PEACE ATTIT   DIPLOM
...DECISION JURID ANTHOL 20 WORLD/CT CASEBOOK.   ADJUD
PAGE 49 E0977

BENTHAM J.,"PRINCIPLES OF INTERNATIONAL LAW" IN J. INT/LAW
BOWRING, ED., THE WORKS OF JEREMY BENTHAM." UNIV   JURID
NAT/G PLAN PROB/SOLV DIPLOM CONTROL SANCTION MORAL WAR
ORD/FREE PWR SOVEREIGN 19. PAGE 10 E0194   PEACE

BRIERLY J.L.,THE OUTLOOK FOR INTERNATIONAL LAW. FUT INT/ORG
WOR-45 CONSTN NAT/G VOL/ASSN FORCES ECO/TAC DOMIN   LAW
LEGIT ADJUD ROUTINE PEACE ORD/FREE...INT/LAW JURID
METH LEAGUE/NAT 20. PAGE 15 E0298

DE HUSZAR G.B.,NEW PERSPECTIVES ON PEACE. UNIV   ATTIT
CULTURE SOCIETY ECO/DEV ECO/UNDEV NAT/G FORCES   MYTH
CREATE ECO/TAC DOMIN ADJUD COERCE DRIVE ORD/FREE   PEACE
...GEOG JURID PSY SOC CONCPT TOT/POP. PAGE 29 E0584 WAR

FRAENKEL O.K.,OUR CIVIL LIBERTIES. USA-45...JURID CONSTN

CONCPT 18/20 BILL/RIGHT. PAGE 39 E0781   LAW
                                                  ATTIT

PUTTKAMMER E.W.,WAR AND THE LAW. UNIV USA-45 CONSTN INT/ORG
CULTURE SOCIETY NAT/G POL/PAR ROUTINE ALL/VALS   LAW
...JURID CONCPT OBS WORK VAL/FREE 20. PAGE 83 E1664 WAR
                                                  INT/LAW

SUAREZ F.,A TREATISE ON LAWS AND GOD THE LAWGIVER LAW
(1612) IN SELECTIONS FROM THREE WORKS, VOL. II.   JURID
FRANCE ITALY UK CULTURE NAT/G SECT CHIEF LEGIS   GEN/LAWS
DOMIN LEGIT CT/SYS ORD/FREE PWR WORSHIP 16/17.   CATH
PAGE 94 E1892

MASON J.B.,"THE JUDICIAL SYSTEM OF THE NAZI PARTY." FASCISM
GERMANY ELITES POL/PAR DOMIN CONTROL SANCTION   CT/SYS
TOTALISM...JURID 20 HITLER/A. PAGE 69 E1381   ADJUD
                                                  LAW

WRIGHT Q.,"CONSTITUTIONAL PROCEDURES OF THE US FOR TOP/EX
CARRYING OUT OBLIGATIONS FOR MILITARY SANCTIONS." FORCES
EUR+WWI FUT USA-45 WOR-45 CONSTN INTELL NAT/G   INT/LAW
CONSULT EX/STRUC LEGIS ROUTINE DRIVE...POLICY JURID WAR
CONCPT OBS TREND TOT/POP 20. PAGE 108 E2153

CLAGETT H.L.,A GUIDE TO THE LAW AND LEGAL   BIBLIOG
LITERATURE OF THE MEXICAN STATES. CONSTN LEGIS   JURID
JUDGE ADJUD ADMIN...INT/LAW CON/ANAL 20 MEXIC/AMER. L/A+17C
PAGE 22 E0440   LAW

HILL N.,CLAIMS TO TERRITORY IN INTERNATIONAL LAW   INT/ORG
AND RELATIONS. WOR-45 NAT/G DOMIN EDU/PROP LEGIT   ADJUD
REGION ROUTINE ORD/FREE PWR WEALTH...GEOG INT/LAW SOVEREIGN
JURID 20. PAGE 52 E1047

US LIBRARY OF CONGRESS,CONSTITUTIONAL AND STATUTORY CONSTN
PROVISIONS OF THE STATES (VOL. I). USA-45 CREATE   FEDERAL
TAX CT/SYS CHOOSE SUFF INCOME PWR 20. PAGE 101   PROVS
E2016   JURID

US LIBRARY OF CONGRESS,NETHERLANDS EAST INDIES.   BIBLIOG/A
INDONESIA LAW CULTURE AGRI INDUS SCHOOL COLONIAL   S/ASIA
HEALTH...GEOG JURID SOC 19/20 NETH/IND. PAGE 101   NAT/G
E2017

VANCE H.L.,GUIDE TO THE LAW AND LEGAL LITERATURE OF BIBLIOG/A
MEXICO. LAW CONSTN FINAN LABOR FORCES ADJUD ADMIN INT/LAW
...CRIMLGY PHIL/SCI CON/ANAL 20 MEXIC/AMER.   JURID
PAGE 103 E2070   CT/SYS

CORRY J.A.,DEMOCRATIC GOVERNMENT AND POLITICS.   NAT/G
WOR-45 EX/STRUC LOBBY TOTALISM...MAJORIT CONCPT   CONSTN
METH/COMP NAT/COMP 20. PAGE 26 E0511   POL/PAR
                                                  JURID

KEETON G.W.,MAKING INTERNATIONAL LAW WORK. FUT   INT/ORG
WOR-45 NAT/G DELIB/GP FORCES LEGIT COERCE PEACE   ADJUD
ATTIT RIGID/FLEX ORD/FREE PWR...JURID CONCPT   INT/LAW
HIST/WRIT GEN/METH LEAGUE/NAT 20. PAGE 60 E1193

MANNHEIM H.,CRIMINAL JUSTICE AND SOCIAL   ADJUD
RECONSTRUCTION. USA+45 EDU/PROP CRIME ANOMIE   LAW
...JURID BIBLIOG 20. PAGE 68 E1361   STRUCT
                                                  ADJUST

PATON G.W.,A TEXT-BOOK OF JURISPRUDENCE. CREATE   LAW
INSPECT LEGIT CT/SYS ROUTINE CRIME INGP/REL PRIVIL ADJUD
...CONCPT BIBLIOG 20. PAGE 80 E1601   JURID
                                                  T

ROSS A.,TOWARDS A REALISTIC JURISPRUDENCE: A   LAW
CRITICISM OF THE DUALISM IN LAW (TRANS. BY ANNIE I. CONCPT
FAUSBOLL). PLAN ADJUD CT/SYS ATTIT RIGID/FLEX   IDEA/COMP
POPULISM...JURID PHIL/SCI LOG METH/COMP GEN/LAWS 20
SCANDINAV. PAGE 86 E1720

SCANLON H.L.,INTERNATIONAL LAW: A SELECTIVE LIST OF BIBLIOG/A
WORKS IN ENGLISH ON PUBLIC INTERNATIONAL LAW (A   INT/LAW
PAMPHLET). CHRIST-17C EUR+WWI MOD/EUR WOR-45 CT/SYS ADJUD
...JURID 20. PAGE 87 E1749   DIPLOM

Column markers (right side): B41, B41, S41, B42, B42, B42, B42, B42, B43, B43, B43, B43, C43, B44, B44, B44
Column markers (right-hand column): B44, B44, S44, S44, B45, B45, B45, B45, B45, B46, B46, B46, B46, B46, B46

CLAGETT H.L.,A GUIDE TO THE LAW AND LEGAL LITERATURE OF BOLIVIA. L/A+17C CONSTN LABOR LEGIS ADMIN...CRIMLGY INT/LAW PHIL/SCI 16/20 BOLIV. PAGE 22 E0441
B47 BIBLIOG/A JURID LAW CT/SYS

CLAGETT H.L.,A GUIDE TO THE LAW AND LEGAL LITERATURE OF CHILE, 1917-1946. CHILE CONSTN LABOR JUDGE ADJUD ADMIN...CRIMLGY INT/LAW JURID CON/ANAL 20. PAGE 22 E0442
B47 BIBLIOG L/A+17C LAW LEGIS

CLAGETT H.L.,A GUIDE TO THE LAW AND LEGAL LITERATURE OF ECUADOR. ECUADOR CONSTN LABOR LEGIS JUDGE ADJUD ADMIN CIVMIL/REL...CRIMLGY INT/LAW CON/ANAL 20. PAGE 22 E0443
B47 BIBLIOG JURID LAW L/A+17C

CLAGETT H.L.,A GUIDE TO THE LAW AND LEGAL LITERATURE OF PERU. PERU CONSTN COM/IND LABOR MUNIC JUDGE ADMIN CT/SYS...CRIMLGY INT/LAW JURID 20. PAGE 23 E0444
B47 BIBLIOG L/A+17C PHIL/SCI LAW

CLAGETT H.L.,A GUIDE TO THE LAW AND LEGAL LITERATURE OF URUGUAY. URUGUAY CONSTN COM/IND FINAN LABOR MUNIC JUDGE PRESS ADMIN CT/SYS...INT/LAW PHIL/SCI 20. PAGE 23 E0445
B47 BIBLIOG LAW JURID L/A+17C

CLAGETT H.L.,A GUIDE TO THE LAW AND LEGAL LITERATURE OF VENEZUELA. VENEZUELA CONSTN LABOR LEGIS JUDGE ADJUD ADMIN CIVMIL/REL...CRIMLGY JURID CON/ANAL 20. PAGE 23 E0446
B47 BIBLIOG L/A+17C INT/LAW LAW

DE NOIA J.,GUIDE TO OFFICIAL PUBLICATIONS OF THE OTHER AMERICAN REPUBLICS: NICARAGUA (VOL. XIV). NICARAGUA LAW LEGIS ADMIN CT/SYS...JURID 19/20. PAGE 30 E0591
B47 BIBLIOG/A EDU/PROP NAT/G CONSTN

HOCKING W.E.,FREEDOM OF THE PRESS: A FRAMEWORK OF PRINCIPLE. WOR-45 SOCIETY NAT/G PROB/SOLV DEBATE LOBBY...JURID PSY 20 AMEND/I. PAGE 53 E1061
B47 ORD/FREE CONSTN PRESS LAW

HYDE C.C.,INTERNATIONAL LAW, CHIEFLY AS INTERPRETED AND APPLIED BY THE UNITED STATES (3 VOLS., 2ND REV. ED.). USA-45 WOR+45 WOR-45 INT/ORG CT/SYS WAR NAT/LISM PEACE ORD/FREE...JURID 19/20 TREATY. PAGE 56 E1119
B47 INT/LAW DIPLOM NAT/G POLICY

INTERNATIONAL COURT OF JUSTICE,CHARTER OF THE UNITED NATIONS, STATUTE AND RULES OF COURT AND OTHER CONSTITUTIONAL DOCUMENTS. SWITZERLND LAW ADJUD INGP/REL...JURID 20 ICJ UN. PAGE 57 E1133
B47 INT/LAW INT/ORG CT/SYS DIPLOM

NEUBURGER O.,GUIDE TO OFFICIAL PUBLICATIONS OF OTHER AMERICAN REPUBLICS: HONDURAS (VOL. XIII). HONDURAS LAW LEGIS ADMIN CT/SYS...JURID 19/20. PAGE 76 E1533
B47 BIBLIOG/A NAT/G EDU/PROP CONSTN

NEUBURGER O.,GUIDE TO OFFICIAL PUBLICATIONS OF THE OTHER AMERICAN REPUBLICS: HAITI (VOL. XII). HAITI LAW FINAN LEGIS PRESS...JURID 20. PAGE 76 E1534
B47 BIBLIOG/A CONSTN NAT/G EDU/PROP

FRANKFURTER F.,"SOME REFLECTIONS ON THE READING OF STATUTES" USA+45 USA-45 PROB/SOLV CT/SYS TASK EFFICIENCY...LING 20. PAGE 40 E0791
S47 JURID LAW ADJUD WRITING

CLAGETT H.L.,A GUIDE TO THE LAW AND LEGAL LITERATURE OF ARGENTINA, 1917-1946. CONSTN LABOR JUDGE ADJUD ADMIN...CRIMLGY INT/LAW JURID CON/ANAL 20 ARGEN. PAGE 23 E0447
B48 BIBLIOG L/A+17C LAW LEGIS

CORWIN E.S.,LIBERTY AGAINST GOVERNMENT. UK USA-45 ROMAN/EMP LAW CONSTN PERS/REL OWN ATTIT 1/20 ROMAN/LAW ENGLSH/LAW AMEND/XIV. PAGE 26 E0513
B48 JURID ORD/FREE CONCPT

CORWIN E.S.,LIBERTY AGAINST GOVERNMENT: THE RISE, FLOWERING AND DECLINE OF A FAMOUS JURIDICAL CONCEPT. LEGIS ADJUD CT/SYS SANCTION GOV/REL FEDERAL CONSERVE NEW/LIB...OLD/LIB 18/20 ROMAN/LAW COMMON/LAW. PAGE 26 E0514
B48 CONCPT ORD/FREE JURID CONSTN

DE NOIA J.,GUIDE TO OFFICIAL PUBLICATIONS OF OTHER AMERICAN REPUBLICS: PERU (VOL. XVII). PERU LAW LEGIS ADMIN CT/SYS...JURID 19/20. PAGE 30 E0593
B48 BIBLIOG/A CONSTN NAT/G EDU/PROP

FENWICK C.G.,INTERNATIONAL LAW. WOR+45 WOR-45 CONSTN NAT/G LEGIT CT/SYS REGION...CONCPT LEAGUE/NAT UN 20. PAGE 37 E0737
B48 INT/ORG JURID INT/LAW

GRIFFITH E.S.,RESEARCH IN POLITICAL SCIENCE: THE WORK OF PANELS OF RESEARCH COMMITTEE, APSA. WOR+45 WOR-45 COM/IND R+D FORCES ACT/RES WAR...GOV/COMP ANTHOL 20. PAGE 47 E0939
B48 BIBLIOG PHIL/SCI DIPLOM JURID

JESSUP P.C.,A MODERN LAW OF NATIONS. FUT WOR+45 WOR-45 SOCIETY NAT/G DELIB/GP LEGIS BAL/PWR EDU/PROP LEGIT PWR...INT/LAW JURID TIME/SEQ LEAGUE/NAT 20. PAGE 58 E1166
B48 INT/ORG ADJUD

KEIR D.L.,CASES IN CONSTITUTIONAL LAW. UK CHIEF LEGIS DIPLOM TAX PARL/PROC CRIME GOV/REL...INT/LAW JURID 17/20. PAGE 60 E1195
B48 CONSTN LAW ADJUD CT/SYS

YAKOBSON S.,FIVE HUNDRED RUSSIAN WORKS FOR COLLEGE LIBRARIES (PAMPHLET). MOD/EUR USSR MARXISM SOCISM ...ART/METH GEOG HUM JURID SOC 13/20. PAGE 108 E2162
B48 BIBLIOG NAT/G CULTURE COM

BRADEN G.D.,"THE SEARCH FOR OBJECTIVITY IN CONSTITUTIONAL LAW" (BMR)" USA+45 USA-45 LAW NAT/G CONTROL ORD/FREE PWR OBJECTIVE...JURID 20 SUPREME/CT. PAGE 15 E0283
S48 CONSTN CT/SYS IDEA/COMP POLICY

BOYD A.M.,UNITED STATES GOVERNMENT PUBLICATIONS (3RD ED.). USA+45 EX/STRUC LEGIS ADMIN...JURID CHARTS 20. PAGE 14 E0281
B49 BIBLIOG/A PRESS NAT/G EDU/PROP

DENNING A.,FREEDOM UNDER THE LAW. MOD/EUR UK LAW SOCIETY CHIEF EX/STRUC LEGIS ADJUD CT/SYS PERS/REL PERSON 17/20 ENGLSH/LAW. PAGE 31 E0606
B49 ORD/FREE JURID NAT/G

FRANK J.,LAW AND THE MODERN MIND. UNIV LAW CT/SYS RATIONAL ATTIT...CONCPT 20 HOLMES/OW JURY. PAGE 40 E0787
B49 JURID ADJUD IDEA/COMP MYTH

KAFKA G.,FREIHEIT UND ANARCHIE. SECT COERCE DETER WAR ATTIT...IDEA/COMP 20 NATO. PAGE 59 E1179
B49 CONCPT ORD/FREE JURID INT/ORG

WALINE M.,LE CONTROLE JURIDICTIONNEL DE L'ADMINISTRATION. BELGIUM FRANCE UAR JUDGE BAL/PWR ADJUD CONTROL CT/SYS...GP/COMP 20. PAGE 104 E2093
B49 JURID ADMIN PWR ORD/FREE

WORMUTH F.D.,THE ORIGINS OF MODERN CONSTITUTIONALISM. GREECE UK LEGIS CREATE TEC/DEV BAL/PWR DOMIN ADJUD REV WAR PWR...JURID ROMAN/REP CROMWELL/O. PAGE 107 E2146
B49 NAT/G CONSTN LAW

MARX C.M.,"ADMINISTRATIVE ETHICS AND THE RULE OF LAW." USA+45 ELITES ACT/RES DOMIN NEUTRAL ROUTINE INGP/REL ORD/FREE...JURID IDEA/COMP. PAGE 69 E1375
L49 ADMIN LAW

FIELD G.L.,"LAW AS AN OBJECTIVE POLITICAL CONCEPT" (BMR)" UNIV SOCIETY RATIONAL JURID. PAGE 38 E0747
S49 LAW CONCPT METH/CNCPT SANCTION

KIRK G.,"MATERIALS FOR THE STUDY OF INTERNATIONAL RELATIONS." FUT UNIV WOR+45 INTELL EDU/PROP ROUTINE PEACE ATTIT...INT/LAW JURID CONCPT OBS. PAGE 61 E1219
S49 INT/ORG ACT/RES DIPLOM

BERMAN H.J.,JUSTICE IN RUSSIA; AN INTERPRETATION OF
B50 JURID

SOVIET LAW. USSR LAW STRUCT LABOR FORCES AGREE GP/REL ORD/FREE SOCISM...TIME/SEQ 20. PAGE 11 E0207
ADJUD
MARXISM
COERCE

B50
COUNCIL BRITISH NATIONAL BIB,BRITISH NATIONAL BIBLIOGRAPHY. UK AGRI CONSTRUC PERF/ART POL/PAR SECT CREATE INT/TRADE LEAD...HUM JURID PHIL/SCI 20. PAGE 26 E0519
BIBLIOG/A
NAT/G
TEC/DEV
DIPLOM

B50
FRAGA IRIBARNE M.,RAZAS Y RACISMO IN NORTEAMERICA. USA+45 CONSTN STRATA NAT/G PROVS ATTIT...SOC CONCPT 19/20 NEGRO. PAGE 39 E0783
RACE/REL
JURID
LAW
DISCRIM

B50
FRANK J.,COURTS ON TRIAL: MYTH AND REALITY IN AMERICAN JUSTICE. LAW CONSULT PROB/SOLV EDU/PROP ADJUD ROUTINE ROLE ORD/FREE...GEN/LAWS T 20. PAGE 40 E0788
JURID
CT/SYS
MYTH
CONSTN

B50
HURST J.W.,THE GROWTH OF AMERICAN LAW; THE LAW MAKERS. USA-45 LOC/G NAT/G DELIB/GP JUDGE ADJUD ADMIN ATTIT PWR...POLICY JURID BIBLIOG 18/20 CONGRESS SUPREME/CT ABA PRESIDENT. PAGE 56 E1115
LAW
LEGIS
CONSTN
CT/SYS

B50
JIMENEZ E.,VOTING AND HANDLING OF DISPUTES IN THE SECURITY COUNCIL. WOR+45 CONSTN INT/ORG DIPLOM LEGIT DETER CHOOSE MORAL ORD/FREE PWR...JURID TIME/SEQ COLD/WAR UN 20. PAGE 59 E1168
DELIB/GP
ROUTINE

B50
MACIVER R.M.,GREAT EXPRESSIONS OF HUMAN RIGHTS. LAW CONSTN CULTURE INTELL SOCIETY R+D INT/ORG ATTIT DRIVE...JURID OBS HIST/WRIT GEN/LAWS. PAGE 67 E1340
UNIV
CONCPT

B50
MOCKFORD J.,SOUTH-WEST AFRICA AND THE INTERNATIONAL COURT (PAMPHLET). AFR GERMANY SOUTH/AFR UK ECO/UNDEV DIPLOM CONTROL DISCRIM...DECISION JURID 20 AFRICA/SW. PAGE 74 E1475
COLONIAL
SOVEREIGN
INT/LAW
DOMIN

B50
ROSS A.,CONSTITUTION OF THE UNITED NATIONS. CONSTN CONSULT DELIB/GP ECO/TAC...INT/LAW JURID 20 UN LEAGUE/NAT. PAGE 86 E1721
PEACE
DIPLOM
ORD/FREE
INT/ORG

B50
SOHN L.B.,CASES AND OTHER MATERIALS ON WORLD LAW. FUT WOR+45 LAW INT/ORG...INT/LAW JURID METH/CNCPT 20 UN. PAGE 92 E1852
CT/SYS
CONSTN

B50
STONE J.,THE PROVINCE AND FUNCTION OF LAW. UNIV WOR+45 WOR-45 CULTURE INTELL SOCIETY ECO/DEV ECO/UNDEV NAT/G LEGIT ROUTINE ATTIT PERCEPT PERSON ...JURID CONCPT GEN/LAWS GEN/METH 20. PAGE 94 E1877
INT/ORG
LAW

S50
ROBINSON W.S.,"BIAS, PROBABILITY AND TRIAL BY JURY" (BMR)" USA+45 USA-45 SOCIETY...SOC CONCPT. PAGE 85 E1707
REPRESENT
JURID
CT/SYS
DECISION

B51
BECKER O.,MASTER RESEARCH GUIDE. USA+45 USA-45 PRESS...JURID INDEX 20. PAGE 9 E0171
BIBLIOG
LAW
ADJUD
CT/SYS

B51
COOKE C.A.,CORPORATION TRUST AND COMPANY: AN ESSAY IN LEGAL HISTORY. UK STRUCT LEGIS CAP/ISM GP/REL PROFIT 13/20 COMPNY/ACT. PAGE 25 E0499
LG/CO
FINAN
ECO/TAC
JURID

B51
CORBETT P.E.,LAW AND SOCIETY IN THE RELATIONS OF STATES. FUT WOR+45 WOR-45 CONTROL WAR PEACE PWR ...POLICY JURID 16/20 TREATY. PAGE 26 E0505
INT/LAW
DIPLOM
INT/ORG

B51
DAVIS K.C.,ADMINISTRATIVE LAW. USA+45 USA-45 NAT/G PROB/SOLV BAL/PWR CONTROL ORD/FREE...POLICY 20 SUPREME/CT. PAGE 29 E0574
ADMIN
JURID
EX/STRUC
ADJUD

B51
FITCH R.E.,THE LIMITS OF LIBERTY. COERCE...JURID GEN/LAWS. PAGE 38 E0759
ORD/FREE
CONCPT
PWR

B51
FRIEDMANN W.,LAW AND SOCIAL CHANGE IN CONTEMPORARY BRITAIN. UK LABOR LG/CO LEGIS JUDGE CT/SYS ORD/FREE NEW/LIB...DECISION JURID TREND METH/COMP BIBLIOG 20 PARLIAMENT ENGLSH/LAW COMMON/LAW. PAGE 40 E0802
LAW
ADJUD
SOCIETY
CONSTN

B51
GIBBS C.R.,CONSTITUTIONAL AND STATUTORY PROVISIONS OF THE STATES (VOL. IX). USA+45 LICENSE ADJUD LEAD 20. PAGE 43 E0857
PROVS
CONSTN
JURID
LOBBY

B51
KELSEN H.,THE LAW OF THE UNITED NATIONS. WOR+45 STRUCT RIGID/FLEX ORD/FREE...INT/LAW JURID CONCPT CON/ANAL GEN/METH UN TOT/POP VAL/FREE 20. PAGE 60 E1198
INT/ORG
ADJUD

L51
KELSEN H.,"RECENT TRENDS IN THE LAW OF THE UNITED NATIONS." KOREA WOR+45 CONSTN LEGIS DIPLOM LEGIT DETER WAR RIGID/FLEX HEALTH ORD/FREE RESPECT ...JURID CON/ANAL UN VAL/FREE 20 NATO. PAGE 60 E1199
INT/ORG
LAW
INT/LAW

L51
LISSITZYN O.J.,"THE INTERNATIONAL COURT OF JUSTICE." WOR+45 INT/ORG LEGIT ORD/FREE...CONCPT TIME/SEQ TREND GEN/LAWS VAL/FREE 20 ICJ. PAGE 65 E1304
ADJUD
JURID
INT/LAW

S51
LEEK J.H.,"TREASON AND THE CONSTITUTION" (BMR)" USA+45 USA-45 EDU/PROP COLONIAL CT/SYS REV WAR ATTIT...TREND 18/20 SUPREME/CT CON/INTERP SMITH/ACT COMMON/LAW. PAGE 64 E1278
CONSTN
JURID
CRIME
NAT/G

B52
BRIGGS H.W.,THE LAW OF NATIONS (2ND ED.). WOR+45 WOR-45 NAT/G LEGIS WAR...ANTHOL 20 TREATY. PAGE 15 E0301
INT/LAW
DIPLOM
JURID

B52
BUCKLAND W.W.,ROMAN LAW AND COMMON LAW; A COMPARISON IN OUTLINE (2ND REV. ED.). UK FAM LEGIT AGREE CT/SYS OWN...JURID ROMAN/REP ROMAN/LAW COMMON/LAW. PAGE 17 E0325
IDEA/COMP
LAW
ADJUD
CONCPT

B52
CAHILL F.V.,JUDICIAL LEGISLATION: A STUDY IN AMERICAN LEGAL THEORY. USA+45 USA-45 LAW NAT/G GP/REL...POLICY PHIL/SCI SOC 20 HOLMES/OW. PAGE 18 E0359
JURID
ADJUD
LEGIS
CONTROL

B52
DU BOIS W.E.B.,IN BATTLE FOR PEACE. AFR USA+45 COLONIAL CT/SYS PERS/REL PERSON ORD/FREE...JURID 20 NEGRO CIVIL/LIB. PAGE 33 E0650
PEACE
RACE/REL
DISCRIM
BIOG

B52
GELLER M.A.,ADVERTISING AT THE CROSSROADS: FEDERAL REGULATION VS. VOLUNTARY CONTROLS. USA+45 JUDGE ECO/TAC...POLICY JURID BIBLIOG 20 FTC. PAGE 43 E0843
EDU/PROP
NAT/G
CONSTN
COM/IND

B52
GELLHORN W.,THE STATES AND SUBVERSION. USA+45 USA-45 LOC/G DELIB/GP LEGIS EDU/PROP LEGIT CT/SYS REGION PEACE ATTIT ORD/FREE SOCISM...INT CON/ANAL 20 CALIFORNIA MARYLAND ILLINOIS MICHIGAN NEW/YORK. PAGE 43 E0845
PROVS
JURID

B52
HOLDSWORTH W.S.,A HISTORY OF ENGLISH LAW; THE CENTURIES OF SETTLEMENT AND REFORM, 1701-1875 (VOL. XIII). UK POL/PAR PROF/ORG LEGIS JUDGE WRITING ATTIT...JURID CONCPT BIOG GEN/LAWS 18/19 PARLIAMENT REFORMERS ENGLSH/LAW COMMON/LAW. PAGE 54 E1080
LAW
CONSTN
IDEA/COMP
CT/SYS

B52
JENNINGS W.I.,CONSTITUTIONAL LAWS OF THE COMMONWEALTH. UK LAW CHIEF LEGIS TAX CT/SYS PARL/PROC GOV/REL...INT/LAW 18/20 COMMONWLTH ENGLSH/LAW COMMON/LAW. PAGE 58 E1165
CONSTN
JURID
ADJUD
COLONIAL

B52
KELSEN H.,PRINCIPLES OF INTERNATIONAL LAW. WOR+45 WOR-45 INT/ORG ORD/FREE...JURID GEN/LAWS TOT/POP 20. PAGE 60 E1200
ADJUD
CONSTN
INT/LAW

B52
MORRIS R.B.,FAIR TRIAL. USA-45 JUDGE ORD/FREE ...JURID 20. PAGE 75 E1498
ADJUD
CT/SYS
CRIME
LAW

MONOPOLY EUROPE. PAGE 40 E0801

B52
PASCUAL R.R.,PARTYLESS DEMOCRACY. PHILIPPINE   POL/PAR
BARGAIN LOBBY CHOOSE EFFICIENCY ATTIT 20. PAGE 80   ORD/FREE
E1600   JURID
                                                       ECO/UNDEV

L52
ROSTOW E.V.,"THE DEMOCRATIC CHARACTER OF JUDICIAL   CONSTN
REVIEW" (BMR)" USA+45 LAW NAT/G LEGIS TASK...JURID   PROB/SOLV
20 SUPREME/CT. PAGE 86 E1725   ADJUD
                                                       CT/SYS

S52
DE GRAZIA A.,"GENERAL THEORY OF APPORTIONMENT"   APPORT
(BMR)" USA+45 USA-45 CONSTN ELITES DELIB/GP PARTIC   LEGIS
REV CHOOSE...JURID 20. PAGE 29 E0582   PROVS
                                                       REPRESENT

S52
MCDOUGAL M.S.,"THE COMPARATIVE STUDY OF LAW FOR   PLAN
POLICY PURPOSES." FUT NAT/G POL/PAR CONSULT ADJUD   JURID
PWR SOVEREIGN...METH/CNCPT IDEA/COMP SIMUL 20.   NAT/LISM
PAGE 70 E1403

C52
CLAGETT H.L.,"THE ADMINISTRATION OF JUSTICE IN   CT/SYS
LATIN AMERICA." L/A+17C ADMIN FEDERAL...JURID   ADJUD
METH/COMP BIBLIOG 20. PAGE 23 E0448   JUDGE
                                                       CONSTN

B53
COKE E.,INSTITUTES OF THE LAWS OF ENGLAND   JURID
(1628-1658). UK LAW ADJUD PERS/REL ORD/FREE   OWN
...CRIMLGY 11/17. PAGE 24 E0471   CT/SYS
                                                       CONSTN

B53
CURRIER T.F.,A BIBLIOGRAPHY OF OLIVER WENDELL   BIBLIOG/A
HOLMES. USA-45...BIOG 19/20. PAGE 28 E0557   HUM
                                                       JURID
                                                       JUDGE

B53
KIRK R.,THE CONSERVATIVE MIND. POL/PAR ORD/FREE   CONSERVE
...JURID CONCPT 18/20. PAGE 61 E1220   PERSON
                                                       PHIL/SCI
                                                       IDEA/COMP

B53
ORFIELD L.B.,THE GROWTH OF SCANDINAVIAN LAW.   JURID
DENMARK ICELAND NORWAY SWEDEN LAW DIPLOM...BIBLIOG   CT/SYS
9/20. PAGE 79 E1581   NAT/G

B53
SECKLER-HUDSON C.,BIBLIOGRAPHY ON PUBLIC   BIBLIOG/A
ADMINISTRATION (4TH ED.). USA+45 LAW POL/PAR   ADMIN
DELIB/GP BUDGET ADJUD LOBBY GOV/REL GP/REL ATTIT   NAT/G
...JURID 20. PAGE 90 E1800   MGT

B53
STOUT H.M.,BRITISH GOVERNMENT. UK FINAN LOC/G   NAT/G
POL/PAR DELIB/GP DIPLOM ADMIN COLONIAL CHOOSE   PARL/PROC
ORD/FREE...JURID BIBLIOG 20 COMMONWLTH. PAGE 94   CONSTN
E1883   NEW/LIB

B53
UNESCO,A REGISTER OF LEGAL DOCUMENTATION IN THE   BIBLIOG
WORLD. WOR+45 WOR-45 NAT/G PROVS DELIB/GP LEGIS   CONSTN
13/20. PAGE 98 E1959   LAW
                                                       JURID

B54
AUSTIN J.,THE PROVINCE OF JURISPRUDENCE DETERMINED   CONCPT
AND THE USES OF THE STUDY OF JURISPRUDENCE. MORAL   LAW
...CLASSIF LING STYLE 19. PAGE 6 E0119   JURID
                                                       GEN/LAWS

B54
BINANI G.D.,INDIA AT A GLANCE (REV. ED.). INDIA   INDEX
COM/IND FINAN INDUS LABOR PROVS SCHOOL PLAN DIPLOM   CON/ANAL
INT/TRADE ADMIN...JURID 20. PAGE 12 E0229   NAT/G
                                                       ECO/UNDEV

B54
ELIAS T.O.,GROUNDWORK OF NIGERIAN LAW. AFR LEAD   JURID
CRIME INGP/REL ORD/FREE 17/20. PAGE 34 E0680   CT/SYS
                                                       CONSTN
                                                       CONSULT

B54
FRIEDMAN W.,THE PUBLIC CORPORATION: A COMPARATIVE   LAW
SYMPOSIUM (UNIVERSITY OF TORONTO SCHOOL OF LAW   SOCISM
COMPARATIVE LAW SERIES, VOL. I). SWEDEN USA+45   LG/CO
INDUS INT/ORG NAT/G REGION CENTRAL FEDERAL...POLICY   OWN
JURID IDEA/COMP NAT/COMP ANTHOL 20 COMMONWLTH

B54
HAMSON C.J.,EXECUTIVE DISCRETION AND JUDICIAL   ELITES
CONTROL; AN ASPECT OF THE FRENCH CONSEIL D'ETAT.   ADJUD
EUR+WWI FRANCE MOD/EUR UK NAT/G EX/STRUC PARTIC   NAT/COMP
CONSERVE...JURID BIBLIOG/A 18/20 SUPREME/CT.
PAGE 50 E0992

B54
HOEBEL E.A.,THE LAW OF PRIMITIVE MAN: A STUDY IN   LAW
COMPARATIVE LEGAL DYNAMICS. WOR-45...JURID SOC   CULTURE
IDEA/COMP METH 20. PAGE 53 E1063   GP/COMP
                                                       SOCIETY

B54
JAMES L.F.,THE SUPREME COURT IN AMERICAN LIFE.   ADJUD
USA+45 USA-45 CONSTN CRIME GP/REL INGP/REL RACE/REL   CT/SYS
CONSEN FEDERAL PERSON ORD/FREE 18/20 SUPREME/CT   JURID
DEPRESSION CIV/RIGHTS CHURCH/STA FREE/SPEE. PAGE 58   DECISION
E1147

B54
MANGONE G.,A SHORT HISTORY OF INTERNATIONAL   INT/ORG
ORGANIZATION. MOD/EUR USA+45 USA-45 WOR+45 WOR-45   INT/LAW
LAW LEGIS CREATE LEGIT ROUTINE RIGID/FLEX PWR
...JURID CONCPT OBS TIME/SEQ STERTYP GEN/LAWS UN
TOT/POP VAL/FREE 18/20. PAGE 68 E1359

B54
SCHWARTZ B.,FRENCH ADMINISTRATIVE LAW AND THE   JURID
COMMON-LAW WORLD. FRANCE CULTURE LOC/G NAT/G PROVS   LAW
DELIB/GP EX/STRUC LEGIS PROB/SOLV CT/SYS EXEC   METH/COMP
GOV/REL...IDEA/COMP ENGLSH/LAW. PAGE 89 E1786   ADJUD

B54
STONE J.,LEGAL CONTROLS OF INTERNATIONAL CONFLICT: INT/ORG
A TREATISE ON THE DYNAMICS OF DISPUTES AND WAR LAW.   LAW
WOR+45 WOR-45 NAT/G DIPLOM CT/SYS SOVEREIGN...JURID   WAR
CONCPT METH/CNCPT GEN/LAWS TOT/POP VAL/FREE   INT/LAW
COLD/WAR LEAGUE/NAT 20. PAGE 94 E1878

B55
BENTON W.E.,NUREMBERG: GERMAN VIEWS OF THE WAR   CRIME
TRIALS. EUR+WWI GERMANY VOL/ASSN LEAD PARTIC COERCE   WAR
INGP/REL RACE/REL TOTALISM SUPEGO ORD/FREE...ANTHOL   LAW
NUREMBERG. PAGE 10 E0201   JURID

B55
CHARMATZ J.P.,COMPARATIVE STUDIES IN COMMUNITY   MARRIAGE
PROPERTY LAW. FRANCE USA+45...JURID GOV/COMP ANTHOL   LAW
20. PAGE 22 E0424   OWN
                                                       MUNIC

B55
COMM. STUDY ORGAN. PEACE,REPORTS. WOR-45 ECO/DEV   WOR+45
ECO/UNDEV VOL/ASSN CONSULT FORCES PLAN TEC/DEV   INT/ORG
DOMIN EDU/PROP NUC/PWR ATTIT PWR WEALTH...JURID   ARMS/CONT
STERTYP FAO ILO 20 UN. PAGE 24 E0481

B55
CUSHMAN R.E.,LEADING CONSTITUTIONAL DECISIONS.   CONSTN
USA+45 USA-45 NAT/G EX/STRUC LEGIS JUDGE TAX   PROB/SOLV
FEDERAL...DECISION 20 SUPREME/CT CASEBOOK. PAGE 28   JURID
E0559   CT/SYS

B55
FLIESS P.J.,FREEDOM OF THE PRESS IN THE GERMAN   EDU/PROP
REPUBLIC. 1918-1933. GERMANY LAW CONSTN POL/PAR   ORD/FREE
LEGIS WRITING ADMIN COERCE MURDER MARXISM...POLICY   JURID
BIBLIOG 20 WEIMAR/REP. PAGE 39 E0765   PRESS

B55
GUAITA A.,BIBLIOGRAFIA ESPANOLA DE DERECHO   BIBLIOG
ADMINISTRATIVO (PAMPHLET). SPAIN LOC/G MUNIC NAT/G   ADMIN
PROVS JUDGE BAL/PWR GOV/REL OWN...JURID 18/19.   CONSTN
PAGE 48 E0959   PWR

B55
KHADDURI M.,WAR AND PEACE IN THE LAW OF ISLAM.   ISLAM
CONSTN CULTURE SOCIETY STRATA NAT/G PROVS SECT   JURID
FORCES TOP/EX CREATE DOMIN EDU/PROP ADJUD COERCE   PEACE
ATTIT RIGID/FLEX ALL/VALS...CONCPT TIME/SEQ TOT/POP   WAR
VAL/FREE. PAGE 61 E1209

B55
KHADDURI M.,LAW IN THE MIDDLE EAST. LAW CONSTN   ADJUD
ACADEM FAM EDU/PROP CT/SYS SANCTION CRIME...INT/LAW   JURID
GOV/COMP ANTHOL 6/20 MID/EAST. PAGE 61 E1210   ISLAM

B55
MAYERS L.,THE AMERICAN LEGAL SYSTEM. USA+45 USA-45   JURID
NAT/G EX/STRUC ADMIN CONTROL FEDERAL 20 SUPREME/CT.   CT/SYS
PAGE 70 E1394   LEGIS
                                                       ADJUD

B55

MOHL R.V.,DIE GESCHICHTE UND LITERATUR DER
STAATSWISSENSCHAFTEN (3 VOLS.). LAW NAT/G...JURID
METH/COMP METH. PAGE 74 E1480

PHIL/SCI
MOD/EUR

B55

PULLEN W.R.,A CHECK LIST OF LEGISLATIVE JOURNALS
ISSUED SINCE 1937 BY THE STATES OF THE UNITED
STATES OF AMERICA (PAMPHLET). USA+45 USA-45 LAW
WRITING ADJUD ADMIN...JURID 20. PAGE 83 E1662

BIBLIOG
PROVS
EDU/PROP
LEGIS

B55

SMITH G.,A CONSTITUTIONAL AND LEGAL HISTORY OF
ENGLAND. UK ELITES NAT/G LEGIS ADJUD OWN HABITAT
POPULISM...JURID 20 ENGLSH/LAW. PAGE 92 E1844

CONSTN
PARTIC
LAW
CT/SYS

B55

SWEET AND MAXWELL,A LEGAL BIBLIOGRAPHY OF THE
BRITISH COMMONWEALTH OF NATIONS (2ND ED. 7 VOLS.).
UK LOC/G MUNIC JUDGE ADJUD CRIME OWN...JURID 14/20
CMN/WLTH. PAGE 95 E1900

BIBLIOG/A
LAW
CONSTN
CT/SYS

S55

BETH L.P.,"THE CASE FOR JUDICIAL PROTECTION OF
CIVIL LIBERTIES" (BMR)" USA+45 CONSTN ELITES LEGIS
CONTROL...POLICY DECISION JURID 20 SUPREME/CT
CIVIL/LIB. PAGE 11 E0220

CT/SYS
JUDGE
ADJUD
ORD/FREE

S55

CAHN E.,"A DANGEROUS MYTH IN THE SCHOOL SEGREGATION
CASES" (BMR)" USA+45 CONSTN PROVS ADJUD DISCRIM
...POLICY MYTH SOC/INTEG 20 SUPREME/CT AMEND/XIV.
PAGE 18 E0360

JURID
SCHOOL
RACE/REL

S55

CARR C.,"LEGISLATIVE CONTROL OF ADMINISTRATIVE
RULES AND REGULATIONS: PARLIAMENTARY SUPERVISION IN
BRITAIN." DELIB/GP CONTROL ROLE PWR PARLIAMENT.
PAGE 20 E0392

EXEC
REPRESENT
JURID

S55

WRIGHT Q.,"THE PEACEFUL ADJUSTMENT OF INTERNATIONAL
RELATIONS: PROBLEMS AND RESEARCH APPROACHES." UNIV
INTELL EDU/PROP ADJUD ROUTINE KNOWL SKILL...INT/LAW
JURID PHIL/SCI CLASSIF 20. PAGE 108 E2156

R+D
METH/CNCPT
PEACE

B56

CALLISON I.P.,COURTS OF INJUSTICE. USA+45 PROF/ORG
ADJUD CRIME PERSON MORAL PWR RESPECT SKILL 20.
PAGE 19 E0368

CT/SYS
JUDGE
JURID

B56

CARLSTON K.S.,LAW AND STRUCTURES OF SOCIAL ACTION.
LAW SOCIETY ECO/DEV DIPLOM CONTROL ATTIT...DECISION
CONCPT 20. PAGE 19 E0379

JURID
INT/LAW
INGP/REL
STRUCT

B56

CORBETT P.E.,MORALS LAW, AND POWER IN INTERNATIONAL
RELATIONS. WOR+45 WOR-45 INT/ORG VOL/ASSN DELIB/GP
CREATE BAL/PWR DIPLOM LEGIT ARMS/CONT MORAL...JURID
GEN/LAWS TOT/POP LEAGUE/NAT 20. PAGE 26 E0506

SUPEGO
CONCPT
POLICY
INT/LAW

B56

FIELD G.C.,POLITICAL THEORY. POL/PAR REPRESENT
MORAL SOVEREIGN...JURID IDEA/COMP. PAGE 38 E0745

CONCPT
NAT/G
ORD/FREE
DIPLOM

B56

HOGAN J.D.,AMERICAN SOCIAL LEGISLATION. USA+45 FAM
AGE/Y ATTIT...JURID CONCPT TREND. PAGE 53 E1065

STRUCT
RECEIVE
LEGIS
LABOR

B56

HURST J.W.,LAW AND THE CONDITIONS OF FREEDOM IN THE
NINETEENTH CENTURY UNITED STATES. USA-45 CONSTN
STRUCT ADMIN GP/REL FEDERAL HABITAT...JURID 19.
PAGE 56 E1116

LAW
ORD/FREE
POLICY
NAT/G

B56

JESSUP P.C.,TRANSNATIONAL LAW. FUT WOR+45 JUDGE
CREATE ADJUD ORD/FREE...CONCPT VAL/FREE 20. PAGE 59
E1167

LAW
JURID
INT/LAW

B56

KALNOKI BEDO A.,LEGAL SOURCES AND BIBLIOGRAPHY OF
HUNGARY. COM HUNGARY CONSTN LEGIS JUDGE CT/SYS
SANCTION CRIME 16/20. PAGE 59 E1181

BIBLIOG
ADJUD
LAW
JURID

B56

LASLETT P.,PHILOSOPHY, POLITICS AND SOCIETY. UNIV
CRIME SOVEREIGN...JURID PHIL/SCI ANTHOL PLATO

CONSTN
ATTIT

NATURL/LAW. PAGE o3 E1260

CONCPT
GEN/LAWS

B56

NOTZ R.L.,FEDERAL GRANTS-IN-AID TO STATES: ANALYSIS
OF LAWS IN FORCE ON SEPTEMBER 10, 1956. USA+45 LAW
SCHOOL PLAN ECO/TAC TAX RECEIVE...HEAL JURID 20.
PAGE 78 E1558

GIVE
NAT/G
PROVS
GOV/REL

B56

RECASENS SICHES S.,TRATADO GENERAL DE SOCIOLOGIA.
CULTURE FAM NEIGH LEAD RACE/REL DISCRIM HABITAT
ORD/FREE...JURID LING T SOC/INTEG 20. PAGE 84 E1677

SOC
STRATA
KIN
GP/REL

B56

SCHROEDER T.,METHODS OF CONSTITUTIONAL
CONSTRUCTION. LAW...METH 20. PAGE 88 E1769

ORD/FREE
CONSTN
JURID
EDU/PROP

B56

SOHN L.B.,BASIC DOCUMENTS OF THE UNITED NATIONS.
WOR+45 LAW INT/ORG LEGIT EXEC ROUTINE CHOOSE PWR
...JURID CONCPT GEN/LAWS ANTHOL UN TOT/POP OAS FAO
ILO 20. PAGE 92 E1853

DELIB/GP
CONSTN

B56

SUTHERLAND A.E.,THE LAW AND ONE MAN AMONG MANY.
USA+45 INTELL ADJUD CT/SYS 20. PAGE 95 E1895

JURID
INGP/REL
ORD/FREE
CONCPT

B56

WEIS P.,NATIONALITY AND STATELESSNESS IN
INTERNATIONAL LAW. UK WOR+45 WOR-45 LAW CONSTN
NAT/G DIPLOM EDU/PROP LEGIT ROUTINE RIGID/FLEX
...JURID RECORD CMN/WLTH 20. PAGE 105 E2109

INT/ORG
SOVEREIGN
INT/LAW

C56

AUMANN F.R.,"THE ISTRUMENTALITIES OF JUSTICE: THEIR
FORMS, FUNCTIONS, AND LIMITATIONS." WOR+45 WOR-45
JUDGE PROB/SOLV ROUTINE ATTIT...BIBLIOG 20. PAGE 6
E0118

JURID
ADMIN
CT/SYS
ADJUD

B57

BAYITCH S.A.,A GUIDE TO INTERAMERICAN LEGAL
STUDIES: A SELECTIVE BIBLIOGRAPHY OF WORKS IN
ENGLISH. NAT/G LEGIS ADJUD CT/SYS CONGRESS 20.
PAGE 8 E0157

BIBLIOG
L/A+17C
LAW
JURID

B57

BERNS W.,FREEDOM, VIRTUE AND THE FIRST AMENDMENT.
USA+45 USA-45 CONSTN INTELL JUDGE ADJUD RIGID/FLEX
MORAL...CONCPT 20 AMEND/I. PAGE 11 E0211

JURID
ORD/FREE
CT/SYS
LAW

B57

BERNS W.,FREEDOM, VIRTUE, AND THE FIRST AMENDMENT.
USA-45 LAW CONSTN PROB/SOLV NEW/LIB...JURID 20
SUPREME/CT AMEND/I. PAGE 11 E0212

ADJUD
CT/SYS
ORD/FREE

B57

BYRNES R.F.,BIBLIOGRAPHY OF AMERICAN PUBLICATIONS
ON EAST CENTRAL EUROPE, 1945-1957 (VOL. XXII). SECT
DIPLOM EDU/PROP RACE/REL...ART/METH GEOG JURID SOC
LING 20 JEWS. PAGE 18 E0354

BIBLIOG/A
COM
MARXISM
NAT/G

B57

COMM. STUDY ORGAN. PEACE,STRENGTHENING THE UNITED
NATIONS. FUT USA+45 WOR+45 CONSTN NAT/G DELIB/GP
FORCES LEGIS ECO/TAC LEGIT COERCE PEACE...JURID
CONCPT UN COLD/WAR 20. PAGE 24 E0482

INT/ORG
ORD/FREE

B57

COSSIO C.,LA POLITICA COMO CONCIENCIA; MEDITACION
SOBRE LA ARGENTINA DE 1955. WOR+45 LEGIS EDU/PROP
PARL/PROC PARTIC ATTIT PWR CATHISM 20 ARGEN
PERON/JUAN. PAGE 26 E0517

POL/PAR
REV
TOTALISM
JURID

B57

DE VISSCHER C.,THEORY AND REALITY IN PUBLIC
INTERNATIONAL LAW. WOR+45 WOR-45 SOCIETY NAT/G
CT/SYS ATTIT MORAL ORD/FREE PWR...JURID CONCPT
METH/CNCPT TIME/SEQ GEN/LAWS LEAGUE/NAT TOT/POP
VAL/FREE COLD/WAR. PAGE 30 E0599

INT/ORG
LAW
INT/LAW

B57

DIVINE R.A.,AMERICAN IMMIGRATION POLICY, 1924-52.
USA+45 USA-45 VOL/ASSN DELIB/GP ADJUD WAR ADJUST
DISCRIM...POLICY JURID 20 DEPRESSION MIGRATION.
PAGE 32 E0630

GEOG
HABITAT
LEGIS
CONTROL

B57

DONALDSON A.G.,SOME COMPARATIVE ASPECTS OF IRISH
LAW. IRELAND NAT/G DIPLOM ADMIN CT/SYS LEAD ATTIT

CONSTN
LAW

SOVEREIGN...JURID BIBLIOG/A 12/20 CMN/WLTH. PAGE 32 NAT/COMP
E0635   INT/LAW

                                                     B57
DUMBAULD E.,THE BILL OF RIGHTS AND WHAT IT MEANS   CONSTN
TODAY. USA+45 USA-45 CT/SYS...JURID STYLE TIME/SEQ   LAW
BIBLIOG 18/20 BILL/RIGHT. PAGE 33 E0656   ADJUD
                                                     ORD/FREE

                                                     B57
FAIRCHILD H.P.,THE ANATOMY OF FREEDOM. USA+45   ORD/FREE
ACADEM SCHOOL SECT CAP/ISM PRESS CHOOSE SOCISM.   CONCPT
PAGE 36 E0712   NAT/G
                                                     JURID

                                                     B57
HINDERLING A.,DIE REFORMATORISCHE   ADMIN
VERWALTUNGSGERICHTSBARKEIT. GERMANY/W PROB/SOLV   CT/SYS
ADJUD SUPEGO PWR...CONCPT 20. PAGE 53 E1049   JURID
                                                     CONTROL

                                                     B57
INSTITUT DE DROIT INTL,TABLEAU GENERAL DES   INT/LAW
RESOLUTIONS (1873-1956). LAW NEUTRAL CRIME WAR   DIPLOM
MARRIAGE PEACE...JURID 19/20. PAGE 56 E1124   ORD/FREE
                                                     ADJUD

                                                     B57
JENKS C.W.,THE INTERNATIONAL PROTECTION OF TRADE   LABOR
UNION FREEDOM. FUT WOR+45 WOR-45 VOL/ASSN DELIB/GP   INT/ORG
CT/SYS REGION ROUTINE...JURID METH/CNCPT RECORD
TIME/SEQ CHARTS ILO WORK OAS 20. PAGE 58 E1153

                                                     B57
JENNINGS I.,PARLIAMENT. UK FINAN INDUS POL/PAR   PARL/PROC
DELIB/GP EX/STRUC PLAN CONTROL...MAJORIT JURID   TOP/EX
PARLIAMENT. PAGE 58 E1163   MGT
                                                     LEGIS

                                                     B57
KELSEN H.,WHAT IS JUSTICE. WOR+45 WOR-45...CONCPT   JURID
BIBLE. PAGE 60 E1201   ORD/FREE
                                                     OBJECTIVE
                                                     PHIL/SCI

                                                     B57
LEVONTIN A.V.,THE MYTH OF INTERNATIONAL SECURITY: A INT/ORG
JURIDICAL AND CRITICAL ANALYSIS. FUT WOR+45 WOR-45   INT/LAW
LAW NAT/G VOL/ASSN ACT/RES BAL/PWR ATTIT ORD/FREE   SOVEREIGN
...JURID METH/CNCPT TIME/SEQ TREND STERTYP 20.   MYTH
PAGE 64 E1289

                                                     B57
MORELAND C.C.,EQUAL JUSTICE UNDER LAW. USA+45   CONSTN
USA-45 PROF/ORG PROVS JUDGE...POLICY JURID. PAGE 74 ADJUD
E1491   CT/SYS
                                                     ORD/FREE

                                                     B57
POUND R.,THE DEVELOPMENT OF CONSTITUTIONAL   LAW
GUARANTEES OF LIBERTY. UK USA-45 CHIEF COLONIAL REV CONSTN
...JURID CONCPT 15/20. PAGE 82 E1638   ORD/FREE
                                                     ATTIT

                                                     B57
ROSENNE S.,THE INTERNATIONAL COURT OF JUSTICE.   INT/ORG
WOR+45 LAW DOMIN LEGIT PEACE PWR SOVEREIGN...JURID   CT/SYS
CONCPT RECORD TIME/SEQ CON/ANAL CHARTS UN TOT/POP   INT/LAW
VAL/FREE LEAGUE/NAT 20 ICJ. PAGE 86 E1716

                                                     B57
SCHLOCHAUER H.J.,OFFENTLICHES RECHT. GERMANY/W   CONSTN
FINAN EX/STRUC LEGIS DIPLOM FEDERAL ORD/FREE   JURID
...INT/LAW 20. PAGE 88 E1757   ADMIN
                                                     CT/SYS

                                                     B57
SINCLAIR T.C.,THE POLITICS OF JUDICIAL REVIEW   JURID
1937-1957. USA+45 USA-45 NAT/G 20 SUPREME/CT   ATTIT
CIVIL/LIB. PAGE 91 E1830   ORD/FREE
                                                     RACE/REL

                                                     B57
UNESCO,A REGISTER OF LEGAL DOCUMENTATION IN THE   BIBLIOG
WORLD (2ND ED.). CT/SYS...JURID IDEA/COMP METH/COMP LAW
NAT/COMP 20. PAGE 98 E1960   INT/LAW
                                                     CONSTN

                                                     B57
US SENATE COMM ON JUDICIARY,CIVIL RIGHTS - 1957.   INT
USA+45 LAW NAT/G CONFER GOV/REL RACE/REL ORD/FREE   LEGIS
PWR...JURID 20 SENATE CIV/RIGHTS. PAGE 102 E2039   DISCRIM
                                                     PARL/PROC

                                                     B57
WASSENBERGH H.A.,POST-WAR INTERNATIONAL CIVIL   COM/IND

AVIATION POLICY AND THE LAW OF THE AIR. WOR+45 AIR   NAT/G
INT/ORG DOMIN LEGIT PEACE ORD/FREE...POLICY JURID   INT/LAW
NEW/IDEA OBS TIME/SEQ TREND CHARTS 20 TREATY.
PAGE 105 E2101

                                                     B58
ALEXANDROWICZ,A BIBLIOGRAPHY OF INDIAN LAW. INDIA   BIBLIOG
S/ASIA CONSTN CT/SYS...INT/LAW 19/20. PAGE 3 E0062   LAW
                                                     ADJUD
                                                     JURID

                                                     B58
ALLEN C.K.,ASPECTS OF JUSTICE. UK FAM COERCE CRIME   JURID
MARRIAGE AGE/Y LOVE 20 ENGLSH/LAW. PAGE 4 E0068   MORAL
                                                     ORD/FREE

                                                     B58
ALLEN C.K.,LAW IN THE MAKING. LEGIS ATTIT ORD/FREE   LAW
SOVEREIGN POPULISM...JURID IDEA/COMP NAT/COMP   CREATE
GEN/LAWS 20 ENGLSH/LAW. PAGE 4 E0069   CONSTN
                                                     SOCIETY

                                                     B58
BOWETT D.W.,SELF-DEFENSE IN INTERNATIONAL LAW.   ADJUD
EUR+WWI MOD/EUR WOR+45 WOR-45 SOCIETY INT/ORG   CONCPT
CONSULT DIPLOM LEGIT COERCE ATTIT ORD/FREE...JURID   WAR
20 UN. PAGE 14 E0276   INT/LAW

                                                     B58
BRIERLY J.L.,THE BASIS OF OBLIGATION IN   INT/LAW
INTERNATIONAL LAW, AND OTHER PAPERS. WOR+45 WOR-45   DIPLOM
LEGIS...JURID CONCPT NAT/COMP ANTHOL 20. PAGE 15   ADJUD
E0299   SOVEREIGN

                                                     B58
BUGEDA LANZAS J.,A STATEMENT OF THE LAWS OF CUBA IN JURID
MATTERS AFFECTING BUSINESS (2ND ED. REV.,   NAT/G
ENLARGED). CUBA L/A+17C LAW FINAN FAM LEGIS ACT/RES INDUS
ADMIN GP/REL...BIBLIOG 20 OAS. PAGE 17 E0327   WORKER

                                                     B58
CARPENTER W.S.,FOUNDATIONS OF MODERN JURISPRUDENCE. LAW
UNIV PROB/SOLV ADJUD CT/SYS CRIME ATTIT...CONCPT   JURID
18/20. PAGE 20 E0388

                                                     B58
CHAMBERLIN E.H.,LABOR UNIONS AND PUBLIC POLICY.   LABOR
PLAN BARGAIN SANCTION INGP/REL JURID. PAGE 21 E0416 WEALTH
                                                     PWR
                                                     NAT/G

                                                     B58
CHARLES R.,LA JUSTICE EN FRANCE. FRANCE LAW CONSTN   JURID
DELIB/GP CRIME 20. PAGE 21 E0422   ADMIN
                                                     CT/SYS
                                                     ADJUD

                                                     B58
DAVIS K.C.,ADMINISTRATIVE LAW TREATISE (VOLS. I AND ADMIN
IV). NAT/G JUDGE PROB/SOLV ADJUD GP/REL 20   JURID
SUPREME/CT. PAGE 29 E0575   CT/SYS
                                                     EX/STRUC

                                                     B58
DAVIS K.C.,ADMINISTRATIVE LAW; CASES, TEXT,   ADJUD
PROBLEMS. LAW LOC/G NAT/G TOP/EX PAY CONTROL   JURID
GOV/REL INGP/REL FEDERAL 20 SUPREME/CT. PAGE 29   CT/SYS
E0576   ADMIN

                                                     B58
DEUTSCHE GESCHAFT VOLKERRECHT,DIE VOLKERRECHTLICHEN BIBLIOG
DISSERTATIONEN AN DEN WESTDEUTSCHEN UNIVERSITATEN,   INT/LAW
1945-1957. GERMANY/W NAT/G DIPLOM ADJUD CT/SYS   ACADEM
...POLICY 20. PAGE 31 E0616   JURID

                                                     B58
DEVLIN P.,THE CRIMINAL PROSECUTION IN ENGLAND. UK   CRIME
NAT/G ADMIN ROUTINE EFFICIENCY...JURID SOC 20.   LAW
PAGE 31 E0617   METH
                                                     CT/SYS

                                                     B58
GARDINER H.C.,CATHOLIC VIEWPOINT ON CENSORSHIP.   WRITING
DEBATE COERCE GP/REL...JURID CONCPT 20. PAGE 42   LOBBY
E0835   CATHISM
                                                     EDU/PROP

                                                     B58
HALL J.,STUDIES IN JURISPRUDENCE AND CRIMINAL   JURID
THEORY. USA-45 LAW CULTURE CREATE SUPEGO...CRIMLGY   CRIME
PSY /20 PLATO. PAGE 49 E0983   CONCPT
                                                     CT/SYS

                                                     B58
HAND L.,THE BILL OF RIGHTS. USA+45 USA-45 CHIEF   CONSTN
LEGIS BAL/PWR ROLE PWR 18/20 SUPREME/CT CONGRESS   JURID

AMEND/V PRESIDENT AMEND/XIV. PAGE 50 E0994
ORD/FREE
CT/SYS

B58

HENKIN L.,ARMS CONTROL AND INSPECTION IN AMERICAN
LAW. LAW CONSTN INT/ORG LOC/G MUNIC NAT/G PROVS
EDU/PROP LEGIT EXEC NUC/PWR KNOWL ORD/FREE...OBS
TOT/POP CONGRESS 20. PAGE 52 E1032
USA+45
JURID
ARMS/CONT

B58

HERRMANN K.,DAS STAATSDENKEN BEI LEIBNIZ. GP/REL
ATTIT ORD/FREE...CONCPT IDEA/COMP 17 LEIBNITZ/G
CHURCH/STA. PAGE 52 E1034
NAT/G
JURID
SECT
EDU/PROP

B58

JAPAN MINISTRY OF JUSTICE,CRIMINAL JUSTICE IN
JAPAN. LAW PROF/ORG PUB/INST FORCES CONTROL CT/SYS
PARL/PROC 20 CHINJAP. PAGE 58 E1149
CONSTN
CRIME
JURID
ADMIN

B58

JENKS C.W.,THE COMMON LAW OF MANKIND. EUR+WWI
MOD/EUR SPACE WOR+45 INT/ORG BAL/PWR ARMS/CONT
COERCE SUPEGO MORAL...TREND 20. PAGE 58 E1154
JURID
SOVEREIGN

B58

KAPLAN H.E.,THE LAW OF CIVIL SERVICE. USA+45 LAW
POL/PAR CT/SYS CRIME GOV/REL...POLICY JURID 20.
PAGE 59 E1183
ADJUD
NAT/G
ADMIN
CONSTN

B58

MASON A.T.,THE SUPREME COURT FROM TAFT TO WARREN.
EX/STRUC LEGIS ROLE 20 SUPREME/CT TAFT/WH HUGHES/CE
STONE/HF. PAGE 69 E1376
CT/SYS
JURID
ADJUD

B58

MOEN N.W.,THE GOVERNMENT OF SCOTLAND 1603 - 1625.
UK JUDGE ADMIN GP/REL PWR 17 SCOTLAND COMMON/LAW.
PAGE 74 E1479
CHIEF
JURID
CONTROL
PARL/PROC

B58

MOSER J.J.,JOHANN JACOB MOSER'S GESAMMELTE UND ZU
GEMEINNUTZIGEM GEBRAUCH EINGERICHTETE BIBLIOTHEK.
GERMANY PROC/MFG INT/TRADE...POLICY JURID MGT 18.
PAGE 75 E1500
BIBLIOG
EXTR/IND
INDUS

B58

MUSIKER R.,GUIDE TO SOUTH AFRICAN REFERENCE BOOKS.
SOUTH/AFR SOCIETY SECT EDU/PROP PRESS RACE/REL
...JURID SOC/WK 20. PAGE 75 E1512
BIBLIOG/A
SOC
GEOG

B58

O'BRIEN F.W.,JUSTICE REED AND THE FIRST AMENDMENT,
THE RELIGION CLAUSES. USA+45 USA-45 NAT/G PROVS
CONTROL FEDERAL...POLICY JURID TIME/SEQ 20
SUPREME/CT CHRUCH/STA AMEND/I REED/STAN. PAGE 78
E1563
ADJUD
SECT
CT/SYS

B58

PALMER E.E.,CIVIL LIBERTIES. USA+45 ADJUD CT/SYS
PARTIC OWN LAISSEZ POPULISM...JURID CONCPT ANTHOL
20 SUPREME/CT CIVIL/LIB. PAGE 79 E1592
ORD/FREE
CONSTN
RACE/REL
LAW

B58

POUND R.,JUSTICE ACCORDING TO LAW. LAW SOCIETY
CT/SYS 20. PAGE 82 E1639
CONCPT
JURID
ADJUD
ADMIN

B58

RUSSELL R.B.,A HISTORY OF THE UNITED NATIONS
CHARTER: THE ROLE OF THE UNITED STATES. SOCIETY
NAT/G CONSULT DOMIN LEGIT ATTIT ORD/FREE PWR
...POLICY JURID CONCPT UN LEAGUE/NAT. PAGE 87 E1737
USA-45
INT/ORG
CONSTN

B58

SHARMA M.P.,PUBLIC ADMINISTRATION IN THEORY AND
PRACTICE. INDIA UK USA+45 USA-45 EX/STRUC ADJUD
...POLICY CONCPT NAT/COMP 20. PAGE 90 E1813
MGT
ADMIN
DELIB/GP
JURID

B58

SOC OF COMP LEGIS AND INT LAW,THE LAW OF THE SEA...
(PAMPHLET). WOR+45 NAT/G INT/TRADE ADJUD CONTROL
NUC/PWR WAR PEACE ATTIT ORD/FREE...JURID CHARTS 20
UN TREATY RESOURCE/N. PAGE 92 E1850
INT/LAW
INT/ORG
DIPLOM
SEA

B58

US SENATE COMM POST OFFICE,TO PROVIDE AN EFFECTIVE
SYSTEM OF PERSONNEL ADMINISTRATION. USA+45 NAT/G
EX/STRUC PARL/PROC GOV/REL...JURID 20 SENATE
CIVIL/SERV. PAGE 103 E2060
INT
LEGIS
CONFER
ADMIN

L58

INT. SOC. SCI. BULL.,"TECHNIQUES OF MEDIATION AND
CONCILIATION." EUR+WWI USA+45 SOCIETY INDUS INT/ORG
LABOR NAT/G LEGIS DIPLOM EDU/PROP CHOOSE ATTIT
RIGID/FLEX...JURID CONCPT GEN/LAWS 20. PAGE 57
E1129
VOL/ASSN
DELIB/GP
INT/LAW

S58

DAHL R.A.,"DECISION-MAKING IN A DEMOCRACY: THE
SUPREME COURT AS A NATIONAL POLICY-MAKER" (BMR)"
USA+45 USA-45 POL/PAR ADJUD GOV/REL PWR...POLICY
JURID 19/20 SUPREME/CT. PAGE 28 E0561
CT/SYS
CONSTN
DECISION
NAT/G

S58

FISHER F.M.,"THE MATHEMATICAL ANALYSIS OF SUPREME
COURT DECISIONS: THE USE AND ABUSE OF QUANTITATIVE
METHODS." USA+45 LAW EX/STRUC LEGIS JUDGE ROUTINE
ATTIT DECISION. PAGE 38 E0757
PROB/SOLV
CT/SYS
JURID
MATH

S58

MCDOUGAL M.S.,"PERSPECTIVES FOR A LAW OF OUTER
SPACE." FUT WOR+45 AIR CONSULT DELIB/GP TEC/DEV
CT/SYS ORD/FREE...POLICY JURID 20 UN. PAGE 70 E1404
INT/ORG
SPACE
INT/LAW

S58

ROCHE J.P.,"POLITICAL SCIENCE AND SCIENCE FICTION"
(BMR)" WOR+45 INTELL OP/RES ADJUD...JURID SOC
IDEA/COMP 20. PAGE 85 E1709
QUANT
RATIONAL
MATH
METH

N58

US HOUSE COMM FOREIGN AFFAIRS,HEARINGS ON DRAFT
LEGISLATION TO AMEND FURTHER THE MUTUAL SECURITY
ACT OF 1954 (PAMPHLET). USA+45 CONSULT FORCES
BUDGET DIPLOM DETER COST ORD/FREE...JURID 20
DEPT/DEFEN UN DEPT/STATE. PAGE 100 E2002
LEGIS
DELIB/GP
CONFER
WEAPON

B59

ABRAHAM H.J.,COURTS AND JUDGES: AN INTRODUCTION TO
THE JUDICIAL PROCESS. USA+45 CONSTN ELITES NAT/G
ORD/FREE PWR 19/20 SUPREME/CT. PAGE 2 E0045
CT/SYS
PERSON
JURID
ADJUD

B59

ANDERSON J.N.D.,ISLAMIC LAW IN THE MODERN WORLD.
FAM KIN SECT LEGIT ADJUD ATTIT DRIVE...TIME/SEQ
TREND GEN/LAWS 20 MUSLIM. PAGE 5 E0089
ISLAM
JURID

B59

BOHMER A.,LEGAL SOURCES AND BIBLIOGRAPHY OF
CZECHOSLOVAKIA. COM CZECHOSLVK PARL/PROC SANCTION
CRIME MARXISM 20. PAGE 13 E0261
BIBLIOG
ADJUD
LAW
JURID

B59

BROOKES E.H.,THE COMMONWEALTH TODAY. UK ROMAN/EMP
INT/ORG RACE/REL NAT/LISM SOVEREIGN...TREND
SOC/INTEG 20. PAGE 16 E0307
FEDERAL
DIPLOM
JURID
IDEA/COMP

B59

COMM. STUDY ORGAN. PEACE,ORGANIZING PEACE IN THE
NUCLEAR AGE. FUT CONSULT DELIB/GP DOMIN ADJUD
ROUTINE COERCE ORD/FREE...TECHNIC INT/LAW JURID
NEW/IDEA UN COLD/WAR 20. PAGE 24 E0483
INT/ORG
ACT/RES
NUC/PWR

B59

CORBETT P.E.,LAW IN DIPLOMACY. UK USA+45 USSR
CONSTN SOCIETY INT/ORG JUDGE LEGIT ATTIT ORD/FREE
TOT/POP LEAGUE/NAT 20. PAGE 26 E0507
NAT/G
ADJUD
JURID
DIPLOM

B59

DASH S.,THE EAVESDROPPERS. USA+45 DELIB/GP TEC/DEV
ORD/FREE...POLICY CRIMLGY JURID 20 PRIVACY. PAGE 29
E0569
CRIME
CONTROL
ACT/RES
LAW

B59

DAVIS K.C.,ADMINISTRATIVE LAW TEXT. USA+45 NAT/G
DELIB/GP EX/STRUC CONTROL ORD/FREE...T 20
SUPREME/CT. PAGE 29 E0577
ADJUD
ADMIN
JURID
CT/SYS

B59

DESMITH S.A.,JUDICIAL REVIEW OF ADMINISTRATIVE
ACTION. UK LOC/G CONSULT DELIB/GP ADMIN PWR
...DECISION JURID 20 ENGLSH/LAW. PAGE 31 E0609
ADJUD
NAT/G
PROB/SOLV
CT/SYS

B59

ELLIOTT S.D.,IMPROVING OUR COURTS. LAW EX/STRUC
PLAN PROB/SOLV ADJUD ADMIN TASK CRIME EFFICIENCY
ORD/FREE 20. PAGE 34 E0684
CT/SYS
JURID
GOV/REL
NAT/G

B59

FELLMANN D., THE LIMITS OF FREEDOM. USA+45 USA-45   CONCPT
NAT/G SECT ROLE ORD/FREE WORSHIP 18/20 FREE/SPEE.   JURID
PAGE 37 E0734   CONSTN

B59

FRIEDMANN W.G., LAW IN A CHANGING SOCIETY. FUT   SOC
WOR+45 WOR-45 LAW SOCIETY STRUCT INT/TRADE LEGIT   JURID
ATTIT BIO/SOC HEALTH ORD/FREE SOVEREIGN...CONCPT
GEN/LAWS ILO 20. PAGE 41 E0803

B59

GINSBURG M., LAW AND OPINION IN ENGLAND. UK CULTURE JURID
KIN LABOR LEGIS EDU/PROP ADMIN CT/SYS CRIME OWN   POLICY
HEALTH...ANTHOL 20 ENGLSH/LAW. PAGE 44 E0868   ECO/TAC

B59

GINZBURG B., REDEDICATION TO FREEDOM. DELIB/GP LEGIS JURID
ATTIT MARXISM 20 SUPREME/CT CON/INTERP HUAC AMEND/I   ORD/FREE
FBI. PAGE 44 E0871   CONSTN
                                                     NAT/G

B59

GOMEZ ROBLES J., A STATEMENT OF THE LAWS OF   JURID
GUATEMALA IN MATTERS AFFECTING BUSINESS (2ND ED.   NAT/G
REV., ENLARGED). GUATEMALA L/A+17C LAW FINAN FAM   INDUS
WORKER ACT/RES DIPLOM ADJUD ADMIN GP/REL 20 OAS.   LEGIT
PAGE 44 E0881

B59

HALEY A.G., FIRST COLLOQUIUM ON THE LAW OF OUTER   SPACE
SPACE. WOR+45 INT/ORG ACT/RES PLAN BAL/PWR CONFER   LAW
ATTIT PWR...POLICY JURID CHARTS ANTHOL 20. PAGE 49   SOVEREIGN
E0979   CONTROL

B59

HAYS B., A SOUTHERN MODERATE SPEAKS. LAW PROVS   SECT
SCHOOL KNOWL...JURID SOC SELF/OBS BIOG 20 NEGRO   DISCRIM
SUPREME/CT. PAGE 51 E1015   CT/SYS
                                                     RACE/REL

B59

KIRCHHEIMER O., GEGENWARTSPROBLEME DER   DIPLOM
ASYLGEWAHRUNG. DOMIN GP/REL ATTIT...NAT/COMP 20.   INT/LAW
PAGE 61 E1217   JURID
                                                     ORD/FREE

B59

KNIERIEM A., THE NUREMBERG TRIALS. EUR+WWI GERMANY   INT/LAW
VOL/ASSN LEAD COERCE WAR INGP/REL TOTALISM SUPEGO   CRIME
ORD/FREE...CONCPT METH/COMP. PAGE 61 E1225   PARTIC
                                                     JURID

B59

LOEWENSTEIN K., VERFASSUNGSRECHT UND   CONSTN
VERFASSUNGSPRAXIS DER VEREINIGTEN STAATEN. USA+45   POL/PAR
USA-45 COLONIAL CT/SYS GP/REL RACE/REL ORD/FREE   EX/STRUC
...JURID 18/20 SUPREME/CT CONGRESS PRESIDENT   NAT/G
BILL/RIGHT CIVIL/LIB. PAGE 66 E1319

B59

MORRIS C., THE GREAT LEGAL PHILOSOPHERS: SELECTED   JURID
READINGS IN JURISPRUDENCE. UNIV INTELL SOCIETY   ADJUD
EDU/PROP MAJORITY UTOPIA PERSON KNOWL...ANTHOL.   PHIL/SCI
PAGE 75 E1497   IDEA/COMP

B59

PANHUYS H.F., THE ROLE OF NATIONALITY IN   INT/LAW
INTERNATIONAL LAW. ADJUD CRIME WAR STRANGE...JURID   NAT/LISM
TREND. PAGE 80 E1596   INGP/REL

B59

PAULSEN M.G., LEGAL INSTITUTIONS TODAY AND TOMORROW. JURID
UK USA+45 NAT/G PROF/ORG PROVS ADMIN PARL/PROC   ADJUD
ORD/FREE NAT/COMP. PAGE 80 E1604   JUDGE
                                                     LEGIS

B59

REIFF H., THE UNITED STATES AND THE TREATY LAW OF   ADJUD
THE SEA. USA+45 USA-45 SEA SOCIETY INT/ORG CONSULT   INT/LAW
DELIB/GP LEGIS DIPLOM LEGIT ATTIT ORD/FREE PWR
WEALTH...GEOG JURID TOT/POP 20 TREATY. PAGE 84
E1681

B59

ROSS A., ON LAW AND JUSTICE. USA+45 RATIONAL   JURID
...IDEA/COMP GEN/LAWS 20 SCANDINAV NATURL/LAW.   PHIL/SCI
PAGE 86 E1722   LAW
                                                     CONCPT

B59

SCHNEIDER J., TREATY-MAKING POWER OF INTERNATIONAL   INT/ORG
ORGANIZATIONS. FUT WOR+45 WOR-45 LAW NAT/G JUDGE   ROUTINE
DIPLOM LEGIT CT/SYS ORD/FREE PWR...INT/LAW JURID
GEN/LAWS TOT/POP UNESCO 20 TREATY. PAGE 88 E1762

B59

SCHORN H., DER RICHTER IM DRITTEN REICH; GESCHICHTE ADJUD
UND DOKUMENTE. GERMANY NAT/G LEGIT CT/SYS INGP/REL   JUDGE
MORAL ORD/FREE RESPECT...JURID GP/COMP 20. PAGE 88   FASCISM
E1765

B59

SCHUBERT G.A., QUANTITATIVE ANALYSIS OF JUDICIAL   JUDGE
BEHAVIOR. ADJUD LEAD CHOOSE INGP/REL MAJORITY ATTIT CT/SYS
...DECISION JURID CHARTS GAME SIMUL SUPREME/CT.   PERSON
PAGE 89 E1780   QUANT

B59

SQUIBB G.D., THE HIGH COURT OF CHIVALRY. UK NAT/G   CT/SYS
FORCES ADJUD WAR 14/20 PARLIAMENT ENGLSH/LAW.   PARL/PROC
PAGE 93 E1863   JURID

B59

SURRENCY E.C., A GUIDE TO LEGAL RESEARCH. USA+45   NAT/G
ACADEM LEGIS ACT/RES ADMIN...DECISION METH/COMP   PROVS
BIBLIOG METH. PAGE 94 E1894   ADJUD
                                                     JURID

B59

TOMPKINS D.C., SUPREME COURT OF THE UNITED STATES: A BIBLIOG/A
BIBLIOGRAPHY. LAW JUDGE ADJUD GOV/REL DISCRIM   CT/SYS
...JURID 18/20 SUPREME/CT NEGRO. PAGE 96 E1931   CONSTN
                                                     NAT/G

B59

VAN CAENEGEM R.C., ROYAL WRITS IN ENGLAND FROM THE   JURID
CONQUEST TO GLANVILL. UK JUDGE...TREND IDEA/COMP   CHIEF
11/12 COMMON/LAW. PAGE 103 E2067   ADJUD
                                                     CT/SYS

B59

WAGNER W.J., THE FEDERAL STATES AND THEIR JUDICIARY. ADJUD
BRAZIL CANADA SWITZERLND USA+45 CONFER CT/SYS TASK   METH/COMP
EFFICIENCY FEDERAL PWR...JURID BIBLIOG 20 AUSTRAL   PROB/SOLV
MEXIC/AMER. PAGE 104 E2091   NAT/G

B59

WILDNER H., DIE TECHNIK DER DIPLOMATIE. TOP/EX ROLE DIPLOM
ORD/FREE...INT/LAW JURID IDEA/COMP NAT/COMP 20.   POLICY
PAGE 106 E2122   DELIB/GP
                                                     NAT/G

B59

WOETZEL R.K., DIE INTERNATIONALE KONTROLLE DER   SPACE
HOHEREN LUFTSCHICHTEN UND DES WELTRAUMS. INT/ORG   INT/LAW
NAT/G CONTROL SUPEGO...JURID CONCPT 20. PAGE 107   DIPLOM
E2136   SOVEREIGN

L59

COWAN T.A., "A SYMPOSIUM ON GROUP INTERESTS AND THE ADJUD
LAW" USA+45 LAW MARKET LABOR PLAN INT/TRADE TAX   PWR
RACE/REL RIGID/FLEX...JURID ANTHOL 20. PAGE 27   INGP/REL
E0528   CREATE

S59

CARLSTON K.S., "NATIONALIZATION: AN ANALYTIC   INDUS
APPROACH." WOR+45 INT/ORG ECO/TAC DOMIN LEGIT ADJUD NAT/G
COERCE ORD/FREE PWR WEALTH SOCISM...JURID CONCPT   NAT/LISM
TREND STERTYP TOT/POP VAL/FREE 20. PAGE 19 E0380   SOVEREIGN

S59

DERGE D.R., "THE LAWYER AS DECISION-MAKER IN THE   LEGIS
AMERICAN STATE LEGISLATURE." INTELL LOC/G POL/PAR   LAW
CHOOSE AGE HEREDITY PERSON CONSERVE...JURID STAT   DECISION
CHARTS. PAGE 31 E0607   LEAD

S59

JENKS C.W., "THE CHALLENGE OF UNIVERSALITY." FUT   INT/ORG
UNIV CONSTN CULTURE CONSULT CREATE PLAN LEGIT ATTIT LAW
MORAL ORD/FREE RESPECT...MAJORIT JURID 20. PAGE 58   PEACE
E1155   INT/LAW

S59

MASON A.T., "THE SUPREME COURT: TEMPLE AND FORUM"   CT/SYS
(BMR)" USA+45 USA-45 CONSTN DELIB/GP RACE/REL   JURID
MAJORITY ORD/FREE...DECISION SOC/INTEG 19/20   PWR
SUPREME/CT WARRN/EARL CIV/RIGHTS. PAGE 69 E1377   ATTIT

S59

MENDELSON W., "JUDICIAL REVIEW AND PARTY POLITICS"   CT/SYS
(BMR)" UK USA+45 USA-45 NAT/G LEGIS PROB/SOLV   POL/PAR
EDU/PROP ADJUD EFFICIENCY...POLICY NAT/COMP 19/20   BAL/PWR
AUSTRAL SUPREME/CT. PAGE 72 E1436   JURID

S59

MURPHY W.F., "LOWER COURT CHECKS ON SUPREME COURT   CT/SYS
POWER" (BMR)" USA+45 NAT/G PROVS SCHOOL GOV/REL   BAL/PWR
RACE/REL DISCRIM ATTIT...DECISION JURID 20   CONTROL
SUPREME/CT NEGRO. PAGE 75 E1508   ADJUD

POTTER P.B.,"OBSTACLES AND ALTERNATIVES TO INTERNATIONAL LAW." WOR+45 NAT/G VOL/ASSN DELIB/GP BAL/PWR DOMIN ROUTINE...JURID VAL/FREE 20. PAGE 81 E1632
S59
INT/ORG
LAW
DIPLOM
INT/LAW

SOHN L.B.,"THE DEFINITION OF AGGRESSION." FUT LAW FORCES LEGIT ADJUD ROUTINE COERCE ORD/FREE PWR ...MAJORIT JURID QUANT COLD/WAR 20. PAGE 92 E1855
S59
INT/ORG
CT/SYS
DETER
SOVEREIGN

STONE J.,"CONFLICT MANAGEMENT THROUGH CONTEMPORARY INTERNATIONAL LAW AND ORGANIZATION." WOR+45 LAW NAT/G CREATE BAL/PWR DOMIN LEGIT ROUTINE COERCE ATTIT ORD/FREE PWR SOVEREIGN...JURID 20. PAGE 94 E1880
S59
INT/ORG
INT/LAW

NATIONAL ASSN HOME BUILDERS,COMMUNITY FACILITIES: A LIST OF SELECTED REFERENCES (PAMPHLET). USA+45 DIST/IND FINAN SERV/IND SCHOOL CREATE CONTROL FEDERAL...JURID 20. PAGE 76 E1525
N59
BIBLIOG/A
PLAN
LOC/G
MUNIC

AMERICAN ASSOCIATION LAW LIB,INDEX TO FOREIGN LEGAL PERIODICALS. WOR+45 MUNIC...IDEA/COMP 20. PAGE 4 E0075
B60
INDEX
LAW
JURID
DIPLOM

ATOMIC INDUSTRIAL FORUM,ATOMS FOR INDUSTRY: WORLD FORUM. WOR+45 FINAN COST UTIL...JURID ANTHOL 20. PAGE 6 E0113
B60
NUC/PWR
INDUS
PLAN
PROB/SOLV

BAKER G.E.,STATE CONSTITUTIONS - REAPPORTIONMENT. USA+45 USA-45 CONSTN CHOOSE ATTIT ORD/FREE...JURID 20. PAGE 7 E0138
B60
APPORT
REPRESENT
PROVS
LEGIS

BEEM H.D.,AN INTRODUCTION TO LEGAL BIBLIOGRAPHY FOT THE NON-PROFESSIONAL STUDENT. LOC/G NAT/G TAX 20. PAGE 9 E0177
B60
BIBLIOG/A
JURID
METH
ADJUD

BERTHOLD O.,KAISER, VOLK UND AVIGNON. GERMANY CHIEF LEGIT LEAD NAT/LISM CONSERVE 14 POPE CHRUCH/STA LUDWIG/BAV JOHN/XXII. PAGE 11 E0217
B60
DIPLOM
CATHISM
JURID

CLARK G.,WORLD PEACE THROUGH WORLD LAW. FUT WOR+45 CONSULT FORCES ACT/RES CREATE PLAN ADMIN ROUTINE ARMS/CONT DETER ATTIT PWR...JURID VAL/FREE UNESCO 20 UN. PAGE 23 E0449
B60
INT/ORG
LAW
PEACE
INT/LAW

DAVIS K.C.,ADMINISTRATIVE LAW AND GOVERNMENT. USA+45 EX/STRUC PROB/SOLV ADJUD GP/REL PWR...POLICY 20 SUPREME/CT. PAGE 29 E0578
B60
ADMIN
JURID
CT/SYS
NAT/G

DUMON F.,LA COMMUNAUTE FRANCO-AFRO-MALGACHE: SES ORIGINES, SES INSTITUTIONS, SON EVOLUTION. FRANCE MADAGASCAR POL/PAR DIPLOM ADMIN ATTIT...TREND T 20. PAGE 33 E0657
B60
JURID
INT/ORG
AFR
CONSTN

FELLMAN D.,THE SUPREME COURT AND EDUCATION. ACADEM NAT/G PROVS DELIB/GP ADJUD ORD/FREE...POLICY JURID WORSHIP 20 SUPREME/CT NEGRO CHURCH/STA. PAGE 37 E0731
B60
CT/SYS
SECT
RACE/REL
SCHOOL

GELLHORN W.,AMERICAN RIGHTS: THE CONSTITUTION IN ACTION. USA+45 USA-45 LEGIS ADJUD COERCE RACE/REL DISCRIM MARXISM 20 SUPREME/CT. PAGE 43 E0846
B60
ORD/FREE
JURID
CT/SYS
CONSTN

GONZALEZ NAVARRO M.,LA COLONIZACION EN MEXICO, 1877-1910. AGRI NAT/G PLAN PROB/SOLV INCOME ...POLICY JURID CENSUS 19/20 MEXIC/AMER MIGRATION. PAGE 44 E0883
B60
ECO/UNDEV
GEOG
HABITAT
COLONIAL

HANBURY H.G.,ENGLISH COURTS OF LAW. UK EX/STRUC LEGIS CRIME ROLE 12/20 COMMON/LAW ENGLSH/LAW. PAGE 50 E0993
B60
JURID
CT/SYS
CONSTN
GOV/REL

HARVARD LAW SCHOOL LIBRARY,CURRENT LEGAL BIBLIOGRAPHY. USA+45 CONSTN LEGIS ADJUD CT/SYS POLICY. PAGE 51 E1006
B60
BIBLIOG
JURID
LAW
INT/LAW

HEAP D.,AN OUTLINE OF PLANNING LAW (3RD ED.). UK LAW PROB/SOLV ADMIN CONTROL 20. PAGE 51 E1020
B60
MUNIC
PLAN
JURID
LOC/G

JENKS C.W.,HUMAN RIGHTS AND INTERNATIONAL LABOR STANDARDS. WOR+45 CONSTN LABOR VOL/ASSN DELIB/GP ACT/RES EDU/PROP MORAL RESPECT...JURID SOC TREND GEN/LAWS WORK ILO 20. PAGE 58 E1156
B60
CONCPT

JENNINGS R.,PROGRESS OF INTERNATIONAL LAW. FUT WOR+45 SOCIETY NAT/G VOL/ASSN DELIB/GP DIPLOM EDU/PROP LEGIT COERCE ATTIT DRIVE MORAL ORD/FREE...JURID CONCPT OBS TIME/SEQ TREND GEN/LAWS. PAGE 58 E1164
B60
INT/ORG
LAW
INT/LAW

LASKIN B.,CANADIAN CONSTITUTIONAL LAW: TEXT AND NOTES ON DISTRIBUTION OF LEGISLATIVE POWER (2ND ED.). CANADA LOC/G ECO/TAC TAX CONTROL CT/SYS CRIME FEDERAL PWR...JURID 20 PARLIAMENT. PAGE 63 E1259
B60
CONSTN
NAT/G
LAW
LEGIS

MENDELSON W.,CAPITALISM, DEMOCRACY, AND THE SUPREME COURT. USA+45 USA-45 CONSTN DIPLOM GOV/REL ATTIT ORD/FREE LAISSEZ...POLICY CHARTS PERS/COMP 18/20 SUPREME/CT MARSHALL/J HOLMES/OW TANEY/RB FIELD/JJ. PAGE 72 E1437
B60
JUDGE
CT/SYS
JURID
NAT/G

MUTHESIUS V.,DAS GESPENST DER WIRTSCHAFTLICHEN MACHT. GERMANY/W ECO/DEV FINAN MARKET TAX...JURID 20. PAGE 75 E1513
B60
ECO/TAC
NAT/G
CONCPT
LG/CO

PAUL A.M.,CONSERVATIVE CRISIS AND THE RULE OF LAW. USA-45 LABOR WORKER ATTIT ORD/FREE CONSERVE LAISSEZ ...DECISION JURID 19 SUPREME/CT. PAGE 80 E1603
B60
CONSTN
ADJUD
STRUCT
PROF/ORG

POWELL T.,THE SCHOOL BUS LAW: A CASE STUDY IN EDUCATION, RELIGION, AND POLITICS. USA+45 LAW NEIGH SECT LEGIS EDU/PROP ADJUD CT/SYS LOBBY CATHISM WORSHIP 20 CONNECTICT CHURCH/STA. PAGE 82 E1641
B60
JURID
SCHOOL

PRASAD B.,THE ORIGINS OF PROVINCIAL AUTONOMY. INDIA UK FINAN LOC/G FORCES LEGIS CONTROL CT/SYS PWR ...JURID 19/20. PAGE 82 E1646
B60
CENTRAL
PROVS
COLONIAL
NAT/G

RIENOW R.,INTRODUCTION TO GOVERNMENT (2ND ED.). UK USA+45 USSR POL/PAR ADMIN REV CHOOSE SUFF FEDERAL PWR...JURID GOV/COMP T 20. PAGE 85 E1697
B60
CONSTN
PARL/PROC
REPRESENT
AUTHORIT

SCHMIDHAUSER J.R.,THE SUPREME COURT: ITS POLITICS, PERSONALITIES, AND PROCEDURES. LAW DELIB/GP EX/STRUC TOP/EX ADJUD CT/SYS CHOOSE RATIONAL PWR SUPREME/CT. PAGE 88 E1760
B60
JUDGE
JURID
DECISION

SCHUBERT G.A.,CONSTITUTIONAL POLITICS: THE POLITICAL BEHAVIOR OF SUPREME COURT JUSTICES AND THE CONSTITUTIONAL POLICIES THEY MAKE. LAW ELITES CHIEF DELIB/GP EX/STRUC LEGIS DISCRIM ORD/FREE PWR ...POLICY MAJORIT CHARTS SUPREME/CT CONGRESS. PAGE 89 E1781
B60
CONSTN
CT/SYS
JURID
DECISION

US LIBRARY OF CONGRESS,INDEX TO LATIN AMERICAN LEGISLATION: 1950-1960 (2 VOLS.). NAT/G DELIB/GP ADMIN PARL/PROC 20. PAGE 101 E2019
B60
BIBLIOG/A
LEGIS
L/A+17C
JURID

US SENATE COMM ON JUDICIARY,FEDERAL ADMINISTRATIVE PROCEDURE. USA+45 CONSTN NAT/G PROB/SOLV CONFER GOV/REL...JURID INT 20 SENATE. PAGE 102 E2043
B60
PARL/PROC
LEGIS
ADMIN
LAW

US SENATE COMM ON JUDICIARY,ADMINISTRATIVE
B60
PARL/PROC

PROCEDURE LEGISLATION. USA+45 CONSTN NAT/G   LEGIS
PROB/SOLV CONFER ROUTINE GOV/REL...INT 20 SENATE.   ADMIN
PAGE 102 E2044   JURID

                                                     B60
WOETZEL R.K.,THE INTERNATIONAL CONTROL OF AIRSPACE   INT/ORG
AND OUTERSPACE. FUT WOR+45 AIR CONSTN STRUCT   JURID
CONSULT PLAN TEC/DEV ADJUD RIGID/FLEX KNOWL   SPACE
ORD/FREE PWR...TECHNIC GEOG MGT NEW/IDEA TREND   INT/LAW
COMPUT/IR VAL/FREE 20 TREATY. PAGE 107 E2137

                                                     L60
DEAN A.W.,"SECOND GENEVA CONFERENCE OF THE LAW OF   INT/ORG
THE SEA: THE FIGHT FOR FREEDOM OF THE SEAS." FUT   JURID
USA+45 USSR WOR+45 WOR-45 SEA CONSTN STRUCT PLAN   INT/LAW
INT/TRADE ADJUD ADMIN ORD/FREE...DECISION RECORD
TREND GEN/LAWS 20 TREATY. PAGE 30 E0600

                                                     L60
LAUTERPACHT E.,"THE SUEZ CANAL SETTLEMENT." FRANCE   INT/ORG
ISLAM ISRAEL UAR UK BAL/PWR DIPLOM LEGIT...JURID   LAW
GEN/LAWS ANTHOL SUEZ VAL/FREE 20. PAGE 63 E1263

                                                     L60
MILLER A.S.,"THE MYTH OF NEUTRALITY IN   ADJUD
CONSTITUTIONAL ADJUDICATION." LAW...DECISION JURID   CONSTN
LING TREND IDEA/COMP. PAGE 73 E1456   MYTH
                                                     UTIL

                                                     S60
BLACK H.,"THE BILL OF RIGHTS" (BMR)" USA+45 USA-45   CONSTN
LAW LEGIS CT/SYS FEDERAL PWR 18/20 CONGRESS   ORD/FREE
SUPREME/CT BILL/RIGHT CIV/RIGHTS. PAGE 12 E0237   NAT/G
                                                     JURID

                                                     S60
GRACIA-MORA M.R.,"INTERNATIONAL RESPONSIBILITY FOR   INT/ORG
SUBVERSIVE ACTIVITIES AND HOSTILE PROPAGANDA BY   JURID
PRIVATE PERSONS AGAINST." COM EUR+WWI L/A+17C UK   SOVEREIGN
USA+45 USSR WOR-45 CONSTN NAT/G LEGIT ADJUD REV
PEACE TOTALISM ORD/FREE...INT/LAW 20. PAGE 45 E0895

                                                     S60
NAGEL S.S.,"USING SIMPLE CALCULATIONS TO PREDICT   JURID
JUDICIAL DECISIONS." ATTIT PERSON MATH. PAGE 76   LAW
E1517   DECISION
                                                     COMPUTER

                                                     S60
O'BRIEN W.,"THE ROLE OF FORCE IN THE INTERNATIONAL   INT/ORG
JURIDICAL ORDER." WOR+45 NAT/G FORCES DOMIN ADJUD   COERCE
ARMS/CONT DETER NUC/PWR WAR ATTIT PWR...CATH
INT/LAW JURID CONCPT TREND STERTYP GEN/LAWS 20.
PAGE 78 E1564

                                                     S60
RHYNE C.S.,"LAW AS AN INSTRUMENT FOR PEACE." FUT   ADJUD
WOR+45 PLAN LEGIT ROUTINE ARMS/CONT NUC/PWR ATTIT   EDU/PROP
ORD/FREE...JURID METH/CNCPT TREND CON/ANAL HYPO/EXP INT/LAW
COLD/WAR 20. PAGE 84 E1690   PEACE

                                                     S60
ROURKE F.E.,"ADMINISTRATIVE SECRECY: A   LEGIS
CONGRESSIONAL DILEMMA." DELIB/GP CT/SYS ATTIT   EXEC
...MAJORIT DECISION JURID. PAGE 86 E1727   ORD/FREE
                                                     POLICY

                                                     S60
THOMPSON K.W.,"MORAL PURPOSE IN FOREIGN POLICY: MORAL
REALITIES AND ILLUSIONS." WOR+45 WOR-45 LAW CULTURE JURID
SOCIETY INT/ORG PLAN ADJUD ADMIN COERCE RIGID/FLEX   DIPLOM
SUPEGO KNOWL ORD/FREE PWR...SOC TREND SOC/EXP
TOT/POP 20. PAGE 96 E1921

                                                     S60
WRIGHT Q.,"LEGAL ASPECTS OF THE U-2 INCIDENT." COM   PWR
USA+45 USSR STRUCT NAT/G FORCES PLAN TEC/DEV ADJUD   POLICY
RIGID/FLEX MORAL ORD/FREE...DECISION INT/LAW JURID   SPACE
PSY TREND GEN/LAWS COLD/WAR VAL/FREE 20 U-2.
PAGE 108 E2157

                                                     C60
HAZARD J.N.,"SETTLING DISPUTES IN SOVIET SOCIETY: ADJUD
THE FORMATIVE YEARS OF LEGAL INSTITUTIONS." USSR   LAW
NAT/G PROF/ORG PROB/SOLV CONTROL CT/SYS ROUTINE REV COM
CENTRAL...JURID BIBLIOG 20. PAGE 51 E1017   POLICY

                                                     B61
ANAND R.P.,COMPULSORY JURISDICTION OF INTERNATIONAL INT/ORG
COURT OF JUSTICE. FUT WOR+45 SOCIETY PLAN LEGIT   COERCE
ADJUD ATTIT DRIVE PERSON ORD/FREE...JURID CONCPT   INT/LAW
TREND 20 ICJ. PAGE 5 E0086

                                                     B61
AUERBACH C.A.,THE LEGAL PROCESS. USA+45 DELIB/GP   JURID
JUDGE CONFER ADJUD CONTROL...DECISION 20   ADMIN

SUPREME/CT. PAGE 6 E0116   LEGIS
                                                     CT/SYS

                                                     B61
BAYITCH S.A.,LATIN AMERICA: A BIBLIOGRAPHICAL   BIBLIOG
GUIDE. LAW CONSTN LEGIS JUDGE ADJUD CT/SYS 20.   L/A+17C
PAGE 8 E0158   NAT/G
                                                     JURID

                                                     B61
BEASLEY K.E.,STATE SUPERVISION OF MUNICIPAL DEBT IN MUNIC
KANSAS - A CASE STUDY. USA+45 USA-45 FINAN PROVS   LOC/G
BUDGET TAX ADJUD ADMIN CONTROL SUPEGO. PAGE 9 E0167 LEGIS
                                                     JURID

                                                     B61
BEDFORD S.,THE FACES OF JUSTICE: A TRAVELLER'S   CT/SYS
REPORT. AUSTRIA FRANCE GERMANY/W SWITZERLND UK UNIV ORD/FREE
WOR+45 WOR-45 CULTURE PARTIC GOV/REL MORAL...JURID   PERSON
OBS GOV/COMP 20. PAGE 9 E0174   LAW

                                                     B61
CHILDS M.W.,THE EROSION OF INDIVIDUAL LIBERTIES.   ADJUD
NAT/G LEGIS ATTIT...JURID SOC CONCPT IDEA/COMP 20   CT/SYS
SUPREME/CT AMEND/I. PAGE 22 E0430   ORD/FREE
                                                     CONSTN

                                                     B61
COWEN D.V.,THE FOUNDATIONS OF FREEDOM. AFR   CONSTN
SOUTH/AFR DOMIN LEGIT ADJUST DISCRIM TOTALSM ATTIT   ELITES
ORD/FREE...MAJORIT JURID SOC/INTEG WORSHIP 20   RACE/REL
NEGRO. PAGE 27 E0529

                                                     B61
FREUND P.A.,THE SUPREME COURT OF THE UNITED STATES: CT/SYS
ITS BUSINESS, PURPOSES, AND PERFORMANCE. CONSTN   JURID
CRIME CONSEN ORD/FREE...DECISION 20 SUPREME/CT   ADJUD
CIVIL/LIB. PAGE 40 E0797   FEDERAL

                                                     B61
FROEBEL J.,THEORIE DER POLITIK, ALS ERGEBNIS EINER   JURID
ERNEUERTEN PRUEFUNG DEMOKRATISCHER LEHRMEINUNGEN.   ORD/FREE
WOR-45 SOCIETY POL/PAR SECT REV REPRESENT PWR   NAT/G
SOVEREIGN...MAJORIT 19. PAGE 41 E0812

                                                     B61
HAGEN A.,STAAT UND KATHOLISCHE KIRCHE IN   SECT
WURTTEMBERG IN DEN JAHREN 1848-1862 (2 VOLS.).   PROVS
GERMANY DELIB/GP EDU/PROP MARRIAGE CATHISM 19   GP/REL
CHURCH/STA. PAGE 49 E0975   JURID

                                                     B61
JACOBS C.E.,JUSTICE FRANKFURTER AND CIVIL   BIOG
LIBERTIES. USA+45 USA-45 LAW NAT/G PROB/SOLV PRESS   CONSTN
PERS/REL...JURID WORSHIP 20 SUPREME/CT FRANKFUR/F   ADJUD
CIVIL/LIB. PAGE 57 E1144   ORD/FREE

                                                     B61
JENKS C.W.,INTERNATIONAL IMMUNITIES. PLAN EDU/PROP   INT/ORG
ADMIN PERCEPT...OLD/LIB JURID CONCPT TREND TOT/POP. DIPLOM
PAGE 58 E1157

                                                     B61
LARSON A.,WHEN NATIONS DISAGREE. USA+45 WOR+45   INT/LAW
INT/ORG ADJUD COERCE CRIME OWN SOVEREIGN...POLICY   DIPLOM
JURID 20. PAGE 63 E1258   WAR

                                                     B61
LEONI B.,FREEDOM AND THE LAW. WOR+45 SOCIETY ADJUD   JURID
INGP/REL EFFICIENCY ATTIT DRIVE. PAGE 64 E1286   ORD/FREE
                                                     LEGIS
                                                     CONTROL

                                                     B61
MCDOUGAL M.S.,LAW AND MINIMUM WORLD PUBLIC ORDER.   INT/ORG
WOR+45 SOCIETY NAT/G DELIB/GP EDU/PROP LEGIT ADJUD   ORD/FREE
COERCE ATTIT PERSON...JURID CONCPT RECORD TREND   INT/LAW
TOT/POP 20. PAGE 70 E1406

                                                     B61
MECHAM J.L.,THE UNITED STATES AND INTER-AMERICAN   DIPLOM
SECURITY, 1889-1960. L/A+17C USA+45 USA-45 CONSTN   WAR
FORCES INT/TRADE PEACE TOTALSM ATTIT...JURID 19/20   ORD/FREE
UN OAS. PAGE 72 E1432   INT/ORG

                                                     B61
MURPHY E.F.,WATER PURITY: A STUDY IN LEGAL CONTROL   SEA
OF NATURAL RESOURCES. LOC/G ACT/RES PLAN TEC/DEV   LAW
LOBBY GP/REL COST ATTIT HEALTH ORD/FREE...HEAL   PROVS
JURID 20 WISCONSIN WATER. PAGE 75 E1506   CONTROL

                                                     B61
PRITCHETT C.H.,CONGRESS VERSUS THE SUPREME COURT,   LEGIS
1957-1960. PROB/SOLV DOMIN EXEC GP/REL DISCRIM PWR   JURID
CONGRESS SUPREME/CT SUPREME/CT. PAGE 82 E1652   LAW

B61
ROBERTSON A.H.,THE LAW OF INTERNATIONAL   RIGID/FLEX
INSTITUTIONS IN EUROPE. EUR+WWI MOD/EUR INT/ORG   ORD/FREE
NAT/G VOL/ASSN DELIB/GP...JURID TIME/SEQ TOT/POP 20
TREATY. PAGE 85 E1704

B61
ROCHE J.P.,COURTS AND RIGHTS: THE AMERICAN   JURID
JUDICIARY IN ACTION (2ND ED.). UK USA+45 USA-45   CT/SYS
STRUCT TEC/DEV SANCTION PERS/REL RACE/REL ORD/FREE   NAT/G
...METH/CNCPT GOV/COMP METH/COMP T 13/20. PAGE 85   PROVS
E1710

B61
SCOTT A.M.,POLITICS, USA: CASES ON THE AMERICAN   CT/SYS
DEMOCRATIC PROCESS. USA+45 CHIEF FORCES DIPLOM   CONSTN
LOBBY CHOOSE RACE/REL FEDERAL ATTIT...JURID ANTHOL   NAT/G
T 20 PRESIDENT CONGRESS CIVIL/LIB. PAGE 90 E1795   PLAN

B61
US COMMISSION ON CIVIL RIGHTS,JUSTICE: BOOK 5, 1961   DISCRIM
REPORT OF THE U.S. COMMISSION ON CIVIL RIGHTS.   LAW
LOC/G NAT/G RACE/REL...JURID 20 NEGRO CIV/RIGHTS   FORCES
INDIAN/AM JURY INDIAN/AM. PAGE 99 E1983

B61
US CONGRESS,CONSTITUTIONAL RIGHTS OF THE MENTALLY   HEALTH
ILL. USA+45 LAW PUB/INST DELIB/GP ADJUD ORD/FREE   CONSTN
...PSY QU 20 CONGRESS. PAGE 99 E1989   JURID
                                                       CONFER

B61
WASSERSTROM R.A.,THE JUDICIAL DECISION: TOWARD A   JUDGE
THEORY OF LEGAL JUSTIFICATION. ACT/RES RATIONAL   LAW
PERCEPT KNOWL OBJECTIVE...DECISION JURID. PAGE 105   ADJUD
E2102

B61
WECHSLER H.,PRINCIPLES, POLITICS AND FUNDAMENTAL   CT/SYS
LAW: SELECTED ESSAYS. USA+45 USA-45 LAW SOCIETY   CONSTN
NAT/G PROVS DELIB/GP EX/STRUC ACT/RES LEGIT PERSON   INT/LAW
KNOWL PWR...JURID 20 NUREMBERG. PAGE 105 E2106

B61
WESTIN A.F.,THE SUPREME COURT: VIEWS FROM INSIDE.   CT/SYS
USA+45 NAT/G PROF/ORG PROVS DELIB/GP INGP/REL   LAW
DISCRIM ATTIT...POLICY DECISION JURID ANTHOL 20   ADJUD
SUPREME/CT CONGRESS CIVIL/LIB. PAGE 106 E2114   GOV/REL

B61
WRIGHT Q.,THE ROLE OF INTERNATIONAL LAW IN THE   INT/ORG
ELIMINATION OF WAR. FUT WOR+45 WOR-45 NAT/G BAL/PWR   LAW
DIPLOM DOMIN LEGIT PWR...POLICY INT/LAW JURID   ARMS/CONT
CONCPT TIME/SEQ TREND GEN/LAWS COLD/WAR 20.
PAGE 108 E2158

L61
SAND P.T.,"AN HISTORICAL SURVEY OF INTERNATIONAL   INT/ORG
AIR LAW SINCE 1944." USA+45 USA-45 WOR+45 WOR-45   LAW
SOCIETY ECO/DEV NAT/G CONSULT EX/STRUC ACT/RES PLAN   INT/LAW
LEGIT ROUTINE...JURID CONCPT METH/CNCPT TREND 20.   SPACE
PAGE 87 E1744

L61
SILVING H.,"IN RE EICHMANN: A DILEMMA OF LAW AND   CT/SYS
MORALITY" WOR+45 INSPECT ADJUST MORAL...JURID 20   INT/LAW
WAR/TRIAL EICHMANN/A NATURL/LAW. PAGE 91 E1828   CONCPT

L61
TAUBENFELD H.J.,"A REGIME FOR OUTER SPACE." FUT   INT/ORG
UNIV R+D ACT/RES PLAN BAL/PWR LEGIT ARMS/CONT   ADJUD
ORD/FREE...POLICY JURID TREND UN TOT/POP 20   SPACE
COLD/WAR. PAGE 95 E1910

S61
CASTANEDA J.,"THE UNDERDEVELOPED NATIONS AND THE   INT/ORG
DEVELOPMENT OF INTERNATIONAL LAW." FUT UNIV LAW   ECO/UNDEV
ACT/RES FOR/AID LEGIT PERCEPT SKILL...JURID   PEACE
METH/CNCPT TIME/SEQ TOT/POP 20 UN. PAGE 21 E0405   INT/LAW

S61
LASSWELL H.D.,"THE INTERPLAY OF ECONOMIC, POLITICAL   JURID
AND SOCIAL CRITERIA IN LEGAL POLICY." LAW LOVE   POLICY
MORAL PWR RESPECT WEALTH...SOC IDEA/COMP. PAGE 63
E1262

S61
LIPSON L.,"AN ARGUMENT ON THE LEGALITY OF   INT/ORG
RECONNAISSANCE STATELLITES." COM USA+45 USSR WOR+45   LAW
AIR INTELL NAT/G CONSULT PLAN DIPLOM LEGIT ROUTINE   SPACE
ATTIT...INT/LAW JURID CONCPT METH/CNCPT TREND
COLD/WAR 20. PAGE 65 E1302

S61
MILLER E.,"LEGAL ASPECTS OF UN ACTION IN THE   INT/ORG
CONGO." AFR CULTURE ADMIN PEACE DRIVE RIGID/FLEX   LEGIT

ORD/FREE...WELF/ST JURID OBS UN CONGO 20. PAGE 73
E1458

S61
OLIVER C.T.,"THE AMERICAN LAW INSTITUTE'S DRAFT   KNOWL
RESTATEMENT OF THE FOREIGN RELATIONS LAW OF THE   JURID
UNITED STATES." FUT USA+45 SOCIETY CONSULT   DIPLOM
EDU/PROP. PAGE 78 E1574

S61
SCHUBERT G.,"A PSYCHOMETRIC MODEL OF THE SUPREME   JUDGE
COURT." DELIB/GP ADJUD CHOOSE ATTIT...DECISION   CT/SYS
JURID PSY QUANT STAT HYPO/EXP GEN/METH SUPREME/CT.   PERSON
PAGE 88 E1771   SIMUL

B62
ALEXANDROWICZ C.H.,WORLD ECONOMIC AGENCIES: LAW AND   INT/LAW
PRACTICE. WOR+45 DIST/IND FINAN LABOR CONSULT   INT/ORG
INT/TRADE TARIFFS REPRESENT HEALTH...JURID 20 UN   DIPLOM
GATT EEC OAS ECSC. PAGE 3 E0063   ADJUD

B62
ALLOTT A.N.,JUDICIAL AND LEGAL SYSTEMS IN AFRICA.   CT/SYS
LAW CONSTN JUDGE CONTROL...METH/CNCPT CLASSIF   AFR
CHARTS 20 COMMON/LAW. PAGE 4 E0070   JURID
                                                       COLONIAL

B62
AMERICAN LAW INSTITUTE,FOREIGN RELATIONS LAW OF THE   PROF/ORG
UNITED STATES: RESTATEMENT, SECOND. USA+45 NAT/G   LAW
LEGIS ADJUD EXEC ROUTINE GOV/REL...INT/LAW JURID   DIPLOM
CONCPT 20 TREATY. PAGE 4 E0082   ORD/FREE

B62
BEBR G.,JUDICIAL CONTROL OF THE EUROPEAN   ADJUD
COMMUNITIES. EUR+WWI INT/ORG NAT/G DOMIN LEGIT PWR   VOL/ASSN
...JURID CONCPT GEN/LAWS GEN/METH EEC 20. PAGE 9   INT/LAW
E0168

B62
BERMAN D.M.,A BILL BECOMES A LAW: THE CIVIL RIGHTS   DISCRIM
ACT OF 1960. USA+45 LAW POL/PAR LOBBY RACE/REL   PARL/PROC
KNOWL...CHARTS 20 CONGRESS NEGRO CIV/RIGHTS.   JURID
PAGE 11 E0206   GOV/REL

B62
BIBLIOTHEQUE PALAIS DE LA PAIX,CATALOGUE OF THE   BIBLIOG
PEACE PALACE LIBRARY, SUPPLEMENT 1937-1952 (7   INT/LAW
VOLS.). WOR+45 WOR-45 INT/ORG NAT/G ADJUD WAR PEACE   DIPLOM
...JURID 20. PAGE 12 E0225

B62
BICKEL A.,THE LEAST DANGEROUS BRANCH. USA+45 USA-45   LAW
CONSTN SCHOOL LEGIS ADJUD RACE/REL DISCRIM ORD/FREE   NAT/G
...JURID 18/20 SUPREME/CT CONGRESS MARSHALL/J   CT/SYS
HOLMES/OW FRANKFUR/F. PAGE 12 E0226

B62
BISHOP W.W. JR.,INTERNATIONAL LAW: CASES AND   INT/LAW
MATERIALS. WOR+45 INT/ORG FORCES PROB/SOLV AGREE   DIPLOM
WAR...JURID IDEA/COMP T 20 TREATY. PAGE 12 E0233   CONCPT
                                                       CT/SYS

B62
BLAUSTEIN A.P.,MANUAL ON FOREIGN LEGAL PERIODICALS   BIBLIOG
AND THEIR INDEX. WOR+45 DIPLOM 20. PAGE 13 E0244   INDEX
                                                       LAW
                                                       JURID

B62
BOCK E.A.,CASE STUDIES IN AMERICAN GOVERNMENT.   POLICY
USA+45 ECO/DEV CHIEF EDU/PROP CT/SYS RACE/REL   LEGIS
ORD/FREE...JURID MGT PHIL/SCI PRESIDENT CASEBOOK.   IDEA/COMP
PAGE 13 E0256   NAT/G

B62
CARLSTON K.S.,LAW AND ORGANIZATION IN WORLD   INT/ORG
SOCIETY. WOR+45 FINAN ECO/TAC DOMIN LEGIT CT/SYS   LAW
ROUTINE COERCE ORD/FREE PWR WEALTH...PLURIST
DECISION JURID MGT METH/CNCPT GEN/LAWS 20. PAGE 19
E0381

B62
COLOMBOS C.J.,THE INTERNATIONAL LAW OF THE SEA.   INT/LAW
WOR+45 EXTR/IND DIPLOM INT/TRADE TARIFFS AGREE WAR   SEA
...TIME/SEQ 20 TREATY. PAGE 24 E0476   JURID
                                                       ADJUD

B62
CRANSTON M.,WHAT ARE HUMAN RIGHTS? UNIV WOR+45   LAW
INT/ORG MORAL...POLICY CONCPT METH/CNCPT GEN/LAWS   ORD/FREE
20. PAGE 28 E0545   JURID
                                                       IDEA/COMP

B62
DE LAVALLE H.,A STATEMENT OF THE LAWS OF PERU IN   CONSTN

MATTERS AFFECTING BUSINESS (3RD ED.). PERU WORKER
INT/TRADE INCOME ORD/FREE...INT/LAW 20. PAGE 30
E0586
JURID
FINAN
TAX

B62
DELANY V.T.H.,THE ADMINISTRATION OF JUSTICE IN
IRELAND. IRELAND CONSTN FINAN JUDGE COLONIAL CRIME
...CRIMLGY 19/20. PAGE 30 E0604
ADMIN
JURID
CT/SYS
ADJUD

B62
DIESING P.,REASON IN SOCIETY: FIVE TYPES OF
DECISIONS AND THEIR SOCIAL CONDITIONS. SOCIETY
STRUCT LABOR CREATE TEC/DEV BARGAIN ADJUD ROLE
...JURID BIBLIOG 20. PAGE 31 E0625
RATIONAL
METH/COMP
DECISION
CONCPT

B62
DONNELLY R.C.,CRIMINAL LAW: PROBLEMS FOR DECISION
IN THE PROMULGATION, INVOCATION AND ADMINISTRATION
OF A LAW OF CRIMES. USA+45 SANCTION BIO/SOC
...DECISION JURID BIBLIOG 20. PAGE 32 E0636
CRIME
LAW
ADJUD
PROB/SOLV

B62
DOUGLAS W.O.,DEMOCRACY'S MANIFESTO. COM USA+45
ECO/UNDEV INT/ORG FORCES PLAN NEUTRAL TASK MARXISM
...JURID 20 NATO SEATO. PAGE 32 E0642
DIPLOM
POLICY
NAT/G
ORD/FREE

B62
EVAN W.M.,LAW AND SOCIOLOGY: EXPLORATORY ESSAYS.
CONSULT ACT/RES OP/RES PROB/SOLV EDU/PROP LEGIT
ADJUD CT/SYS GP/REL...PHIL/SCI ANTHOL SOC/INTEG 20.
PAGE 35 E0703
JURID
SOC
PROF/ORG

B62
GONNER R.,DAS KIRCHENPATRONATRECHT IM
GROSSHERZOGTUM BADEN. GERMANY LAW PROVS DEBATE
ATTIT CATHISM 14/19 PROTESTANT CHRISTIAN CHURCH/STA
BADEN. PAGE 44 E0882
JURID
SECT
NAT/G
GP/REL

B62
GROGAN V.,ADMINISTRATIVE TRIBUNALS IN THE PUBLIC
SERVICE. IRELAND UK NAT/G CONTROL CT/SYS...JURID
GOV/COMP 20. PAGE 48 E0945
ADMIN
LAW
ADJUD
DELIB/GP

B62
GRZYBOWSKI K.,SOVIET LEGAL INSTITUTIONS. USA+45
USSR ECO/DEV NAT/G EDU/PROP CONTROL CT/SYS CRIME
OWN ATTIT PWR SOCISM...NAT/COMP 20. PAGE 48 E0955
ADJUD
LAW
JURID

B62
HIRSCHFIELD R.S.,THE CONSTITUTION AND THE COURT.
SCHOOL WAR RACE/REL EQUILIB ORD/FREE...POLICY
MAJORIT DECISION JURID 18/20 PRESIDENT COLD/WAR
CIVIL/LIB SUPREME/CT CONGRESS. PAGE 53 E1051
ADJUD
PWR
CONSTN
LAW

B62
HOOK S.,THE PARADOXES OF FREEDOM. UNIV CONSTN
INTELL LEGIS CONTROL REV CHOOSE SUPEGO...POLICY
JURID IDEA/COMP 19/20 CIV/RIGHTS. PAGE 55 E1095
CONCPT
MAJORIT
ORD/FREE
ALL/VALS

B62
INSTITUTE JUDICIAL ADMIN,JUDGES: THEIR TEMPORARY
APPOINTMENT, ASSIGNMENT AND TRANSFER: SURVEY OF FED
AND STATE CONSTN'S STATUTES, ROLES OF CT. USA+45
CONSTN PROVS CT/SYS GOV/REL PWR JURID. PAGE 57
E1128
NAT/G
LOC/G
JUDGE
ADMIN

B62
INTERNAT CONGRESS OF JURISTS,EXECUTIVE ACTION AND
THE RULE OF RULE: REPORTION PROCEEDINGS OF INT'T
CONGRESS OF JURISTS,-RIO DE JANEIRO, BRAZIL. WOR+45
ACADEM CONSULT JUDGE EDU/PROP ADJUD CT/SYS INGP/REL
PERSON DEPT/DEFEN. PAGE 57 E1130
JURID
EXEC
ORD/FREE
CONTROL

B62
LAWSON R.,INTERNATIONAL REGIONAL ORGANIZATIONS.
WOR+45 NAT/G VOL/ASSN CONSULT LEGIS EDU/PROP LEGIT
ADMIN EXEC ROUTINE HEALTH PWR WEALTH...JURID EEC
COLD/WAR 20 UN. PAGE 63 E1270
INT/ORG
DELIB/GP
REGION

B62
LILLICH R.B.,INTERNATIONAL CLAIMS: THEIR
ADJUDICATION BY NATIONAL COMMISSIONS. WOR+45 WOR-45
INT/ORG LEGIT CT/SYS TOT/POP 20. PAGE 65 E1297
ADJUD
JURID
INT/LAW

B62
LITTLEFIELD N.,METROPOLITAN AREA PROBLEMS AND
MUNICIPAL HOME RULE. USA+45 PROVS ADMIN CONTROL
GP/REL PWR. PAGE 65 E1308
LOC/G
SOVEREIGN
JURID
LEGIS

B62
MASON A.T.,THE SUPREME COURT: PALADIUM OF FREEDOM.   CONSTN

USA-45 NAT/G POL/PAR CHIEF LEGIS ADJUD PARL/PROC
FEDERAL PWR...POLICY BIOG 18/20 SUPREME/CT
ROOSEVLT/F JEFFERSN/T MARSHALL/J HUGHES/CE. PAGE 69
E1378
CT/SYS
JURID

B62
MCDOUGAL M.S.,THE PUBLIC ORDER OF THE OCEANS.
WOR+45 WOR-45 SEA INT/ORG NAT/G CONSULT DELIB/GP
DIPLOM LEGIT PEACE RIGID/FLEX...GEOG INT/LAW JURID
RECORD TOT/POP 20 TREATY. PAGE 70 E1407
ADJUD
ORD/FREE

B62
MILLER P.,THE LEGAL MIND IN AMERICA. PROF/ORG JUDGE
ADJUD CT/SYS 18/19 SUPREME/CT. PAGE 73 E1461
JURID
CONSTN
NAT/G
CONCPT

B62
MURPHY W.F.,CONGRESS AND THE COURT. USA+45 LAW
LOBBY GP/REL RACE/REL ATTIT PWR...JURID INT BIBLIOG
CONGRESS SUPREME/CT WARRN/EARL. PAGE 75 E1509
LEGIS
CT/SYS
GOV/REL
ADJUD

B62
NATIONAL MUNICIPAL LEAGUE,COURT DECISIONS ON
LEGISLATIVE APPORTIONMENT (VOL. III). USA+45 JUDGE
ADJUD CONTROL ATTIT...DECISION JURID COURT/DIST
CASEBOOK. PAGE 76 E1528
PROVS
CT/SYS
APPORT
LEGIS

B62
NEW YORK STATE LEGISLATURE,REPORT AND DRAFT OF
PROPOSED LEGISLATION ON COURT REORGANIZATION. LAW
PROVS DELIB/GP CREATE ADJUD 20 NEW/YORK. PAGE 77
E1538
CT/SYS
JURID
MUNIC
LOC/G

B62
NORGAARD C.A.,THE POSITION OF THE INDIVIDUAL IN
INTERNATIONAL LAW. INT/ORG SUPEGO ORD/FREE
SOVEREIGN...CONCPT 20 UN. PAGE 78 E1556
INT/LAW
DIPLOM
CRIME
JURID

B62
PHILLIPS O.H.,CONSTITUTIONAL AND ADMINISTRATIVE LAW
(3RD ED.). UK INT/ORG LOC/G CHIEF EX/STRUC LEGIS
BAL/PWR ADJUD COLONIAL CT/SYS PWR...CHARTS 20.
PAGE 80 E1613
JURID
ADMIN
CONSTN
NAT/G

B62
RICE C.E.,FREEDOM OF ASSOCIATION. USA+45 USA-45
POL/PAR LOBBY GP/REL...JURID BIBLIOG 18/20
SUPREME/CT PRE/US/AM. PAGE 84 E1691
LAW
NAT/G
CONSTN

B62
ROSENNE S.,THE WORLD COURT: WHAT IT IS AND HOW IT
WORKS. WOR+45 WOR-45 LAW CONSTN JUDGE EDU/PROP
LEGIT ROUTINE CHOOSE PEACE ORD/FREE...JURID OBS
TIME/SEQ CHARTS UN TOT/POP VAL/FREE 20. PAGE 86
E1717
INT/ORG
ADJUD
INT/LAW

B62
ROSENZWEIG F.,HEGEL UND DER STAAT. GERMANY SOCIETY
FAM POL/PAR NAT/LISM...BIOG 19. PAGE 86 E1718
JURID
NAT/G
CONCPT
PHIL/SCI

B62
ROSTOW E.V.,THE SOVEREIGN PREROGATIVE: THE SUPREME
COURT AND THE QUEST FOR LAW. CONSTN CT/SYS FEDERAL
MORAL SOVEREIGN 20 SUPREME/CT. PAGE 86 E1726
JURID
PROF/ORG
ATTIT
ORD/FREE

B62
SCHWARZENBERGER G.,THE FRONTIERS OF INTERNATIONAL
LAW. WOR+45 WOR-45 NAT/G LEGIT CT/SYS ROUTINE MORAL
ORD/FREE PWR...JURID SOC GEN/METH 20 COLD/WAR.
PAGE 89 E1789
INT/ORG
LAW
INT/LAW

B62
STERN R.L.,SUPREME COURT PRACTICE. USA+45 USA-45
OP/RES...STYLE METH 20 SUPREME/CT. PAGE 93 E1872
CT/SYS
ADJUD
JURID
ROUTINE

B62
SWAYZE H.,POLITICAL CONTROL OF LITERATURE IN THE
USSR, 1946-1959. USSR NAT/G CREATE LICENSE...JURID
20. PAGE 95 E1898
MARXISM
WRITING
CONTROL
DOMIN

B62
TRISKA J.F.,THE THEORY, LAW, AND POLICY OF SOVIET
TREATIES. WOR+45 WOR-45 CONSTN INT/ORG NAT/G
VOL/ASSN DOMIN LEGIT COERCE ATTIT PWR RESPECT
...POLICY JURID CONCPT OBS SAMP TIME/SEQ TREND
GEN/LAWS 20. PAGE 97 E1941
COM
LAW
INT/LAW
USSR

B62

TUSSMAN J.,THE SUPREME COURT ON CHURCH AND STATE.   CT/SYS
USA+45 USA-45 SANCTION PRIVIL...POLICY JURID 19/20   SECT
SUPREME/CT CHURCH/STA. PAGE 97 E1945   ADJUD

B62

US AIR FORCE,THE MILITARY JUSTICE SYSTEM (REV.   JURID
ED.). USA+45 DELIB/GP...IDEA/COMP 20. PAGE 99 E1978   FORCES
                                                           ADJUD
                                                           ORD/FREE

B62

US SENATE COMM ON JUDICIARY,CONSTITUTIONAL RIGHTS   CONSTN
OF MILITARY PERSONNEL. USA+45 USA-45 FORCES DIPLOM   ORD/FREE
WAR CONGRESS. PAGE 102 E2046   JURID
                                                           CT/SYS

B62

WOETZEL R.K.,THE NURENBERG TRIALS IN INTERNATIONAL   INT/ORG
LAW. CHRIST-17C MOD/EUR WOR+45 SOCIETY NAT/G   ADJUD
DELIB/GP DOMIN LEGIT ROUTINE ATTIT DRIVE PERSON   WAR
SUPEGO MORAL ORD/FREE...POLICY MAJORIT JURID PSY
SOC SELF/OBS RECORD NAZI TOT/POP. PAGE 107 E2138

L62

MANGIN G.,"L'ORGANIZATION JUDICIAIRE DES ETATS   AFR
D'AFRIQUE ET DE MADAGASCAR." ISLAM WOR+45 STRATA   LEGIS
STRUCT ECO/UNDEV NAT/G LEGIT EXEC...JURID TIME/SEQ   COLONIAL
TOT/POP 20 SUPREME/CT. PAGE 68 E1357   MADAGASCAR

L62

NIZARD L.,"CUBAN QUESTION AND SECURITY COUNCIL."   INT/ORG
L/A+17C USA+45 ECO/UNDEV NAT/G POL/PAR DELIB/GP   JURID
ECO/TAC PWR...RELATIV OBS TIME/SEQ TREND GEN/LAWS   DIPLOM
UN 20 UN. PAGE 77 E1551   CUBA

L62

STEIN E.,"MR HAMMARSKJOLD, THE CHARTER LAW AND THE   CONCPT
FUTURE ROLE OF THE UNITED NATIONS SECRETARY-   BIOG
GENERAL." WOR+45 CONSTN INT/ORG DELIB/GP FORCES
TOP/EX BAL/PWR LEGIT ROUTINE RIGID/FLEX PWR
...POLICY JURID OBS STERTYP UN COLD/WAR 20
HAMMARSK/D. PAGE 93 E1869

S62

BIERZANECK R.,"LA NON-RECONNAISSANCE ET LE DROIT   EDU/PROP
INTERNATIONAL CONTEMPORAIN." EUR+WWI FUT WOR+45 LAW   JURID
ECO/DEV ATTIT RIGID/FLEX...CONCPT TIME/SEQ TOT/POP   DIPLOM
20. PAGE 12 E0228   INT/LAW

S62

CRANE R.D.,"LAW AND STRATEGY IN SPACE." FUT USA+45   CONCPT
WOR+45 AIR LAW INT/ORG NAT/G FORCES ACT/RES PLAN   SPACE
BAL/PWR LEGIT ARMS/CONT COERCE ORD/FREE...POLICY
INT/LAW JURID SOC/EXP 20 TREATY. PAGE 27 E0542

S62

CRANE R.D.,"SOVIET ATTITUDE TOWARD INTERNATIONAL   LAW
SPACE LAW." COM FUT USA+45 USSR AIR CONSTN DELIB/GP   ATTIT
DOMIN PWR...JURID TREND TOT/POP 20. PAGE 27 E0543   INT/LAW
                                                           SPACE

S62

FALK R.A.,"THE REALITY OF INTERNATIONAL LAW."   INT/ORG
WOR+45 NAT/G LEGIT COERCE DETER WAR MORAL ORD/FREE   ADJUD
PWR SOVEREIGN...JURID CONCPT VAL/FREE COLD/WAR 20.   NUC/PWR
PAGE 36 E0714   INT/LAW

S62

GRAVEN J.,"LE MOUVEAU DROIT PENAL INTERNATIONAL."   CT/SYS
UNIV STRUCT LEGIS ACT/RES CRIME ATTIT PERCEPT   PUB/INST
PERSON...JURID CONCPT 20. PAGE 45 E0899   INT/ORG
                                                           INT/LAW

S62

GREEN L.C.,"POLITICAL OFFENSES, WAR CRIMES AND   LAW
EXTRADITION." WOR+45 YUGOSLAVIA INT/ORG LEGIT   CONCPT
ROUTINE WAR ORD/FREE SOVEREIGN...JURID NAZI 20   INT/LAW
INTERPOL. PAGE 46 E0906

S62

GREENSPAN M.,"INTERNATIONAL LAW AND ITS PROTECTION   FORCES
FOR PARTICIPANTS IN UNCONVENTIONAL WARFARE." WOR+45   JURID
LAW INT/ORG NAT/G POL/PAR COERCE REV ORD/FREE   GUERRILLA
...INT/LAW TOT/POP 20. PAGE 46 E0912   WAR

S62

JOHNSON O.H.,"THE ENGLISH TRADITION IN   LAW
INTERNATIONAL LAW." CHRIST-17C MOD/EUR EDU/PROP   INT/LAW
LEGIT CT/SYS ORD/FREE...JURID CONCPT TIME/SEQ.   UK
PAGE 59 E1170

S62

LISSITZYN O.J.,"SOME LEGAL IMPLICATIONS OF THE U-2   LAW
AND RB-47 INCIDENTS." FUT USA+45 USSR WOR+45 AIR   CONCPT
NAT/G DIPLOM LEGIT MORAL ORD/FREE SOVEREIGN...JURID   SPACE

GEN/LAWS GEN/METH COLD/WAR 20 U-2. PAGE 65 E1305   INT/LAW

S62

MANGIN G.,"LES ACCORDS DE COOPERATION EN MATIERE DE   INT/ORG
JUSTICE ENTRE LA FRANCE ET LES ETATS AFRICAINS ET   LAW
MALGACHE." AFR ISLAM WOR+45 STRUCT ECO/UNDEV NAT/G   FRANCE
DELIB/GP PERCEPT ALL/VALS...JURID MGT TIME/SEQ 20.
PAGE 68 E1356

S62

MONNIER J.P.,"LA SUCCESSION D'ETATS EN MATIERE DE   NAT/G
RESPONSABILITE INTERNATIONALE." UNIV CONSTN INTELL   JURID
SOCIETY ADJUD ROUTINE PERCEPT SUPEGO...GEN/LAWS   INT/LAW
TOT/POP 20. PAGE 74 E1485

S62

MURACCIOLE L.,"LES MODIFICATIONS DE LA CONSTITUTION   NAT/G
MALGACHE." AFR WOR+45 ECO/UNDEV LEGIT EXEC ALL/VALS   STRUCT
...JURID 20. PAGE 75 E1505   SOVEREIGN
                                                           MADAGASCAR

S62

SCHACHTER O.,"DAG HAMMARSKJOLD AND THE RELATION OF   ACT/RES
LAW TO POLITICS." FUT WOR+45 INT/ORG CONSULT PLAN   ADJUD
TEC/DEV BAL/PWR DIPLOM LEGIT ATTIT PERCEPT ORD/FREE
...POLICY JURID CONCPT OBS TESTS STERTYP GEN/LAWS
20 HAMMARSK/D. PAGE 87 E1751

S62

THOMPSON D.,"THE UNITED KINGDOM AND THE TREATY OF   ADJUD
ROME." EUR+WWI INT/ORG NAT/G DELIB/GP LEGIS   JURID
INT/TRADE RIGID/FLEX...CONCPT EEC PARLIAMENT
CMN/WLTH 20. PAGE 96 E1918

S62

VIGNES D.,"L'AUTORITE DES TRAITES INTERNATIONAUX EN   STRUCT
DROIT INTERNE." EUR+WWI UNIV LAW CONSTN INTELL   LEGIT
NAT/G POL/PAR DIPLOM ATTIT PERCEPT ALL/VALS   FRANCE
...POLICY INT/LAW JURID CONCPT TIME/SEQ 20 TREATY.
PAGE 104 E2075

C62

ABRAHAM H.J.,"THE JUDICIAL PROCESS." USA+45 USA-45   BIBLIOG
LAW NAT/G ADMIN CT/SYS INGP/REL RACE/REL DISCRIM   CONSTN
...JURID IDEA/COMP 19/20. PAGE 2 E0046   JUDGE
                                                           ADJUD

C62

BACON F.,"OF JUDICATURE" (1612) IN F. BACON,   CT/SYS
ESSAYS." ADJUD ADMIN SANCTION CRIME PWR...JURID   LEGIS
GEN/LAWS. PAGE 7 E0128   LAW

C62

LILLICH R.B.,"INTERNATIONAL CLAIMS: THEIR   INT/LAW
ADJUDICATION BY NATIONAL COMMISSIONS." WOR+45   DIPLOM
WOR-45 NAT/G ADJUD...JURID BIBLIOG 18/20. PAGE 65   PROB/SOLV
E1298

C62

VAN DER SPRENKEL S.,"LEGAL INSTITUTIONS IN MANCHU   LAW
CHINA." ASIA STRUCT CT/SYS ROUTINE GOV/REL GP/REL   JURID
...CONCPT BIBLIOG 17/20. PAGE 103 E2068   ADMIN
                                                           ADJUD

B63

BLACK C.L. JR.,THE OCCASIONS OF JUSTICE: ESSAYS   JURID
MOSTLY ON LAW. USA+45 JUDGE RACE/REL DISCRIM ATTIT   CONSTN
MORAL ORD/FREE 20 SUPREME/CT BLACK. PAGE 12 E0236   CT/SYS
                                                          LAW

B63

BOWETT D.W.,THE LAW OF INTERNATIONAL INSTITUTIONS.   INT/ORG
WOR+45 WOR-45 CONSTN DELIB/GP EX/STRUC JUDGE   ADJUD
EDU/PROP LEGIT CT/SYS EXEC ROUTINE RIGID/FLEX   DIPLOM
ORD/FREE PWR...JURID CONCPT ORG/CHARTS GEN/METH
LEAGUE/NAT OAS OEEC 20 UN. PAGE 14 E0277

B63

BROOKES E.H.,POWER, LAW, RIGHT, AND LOVE: A STUDY   PWR
IN POLITICAL VALUES. SOUTH/AFR NAT/G PERSON   ORD/FREE
...CONCPT IDEA/COMP 20. PAGE 16 E0308   JURID
                                                          LOVE

B63

BROWN R.M.,THE SOUTH CAROLINA REGULATORS. USA-45   ORD/FREE
LEGIS LEGIT ADJUD COLONIAL CONTROL WAR...BIBLIOG/A   JURID
18 CHARLESTON SOUTH/CAR. PAGE 16 E0315   PWR
                                                         PROVS

B63

BURRUS B.R.,ADMINSTRATIVE LAW AND LOCAL GOVERNMENT.   EX/STRUC
USA+45 PROVS LEGIS LICENSE ADJUD ORD/FREE 20.   LOC/G
PAGE 18 E0347   JURID
                                                        CONSTN

CORLEY R.N.,THE LEGAL ENVIRONMENT OF BUSINESS. B63 NAT/G
CONSTN LEGIS TAX ADMIN CT/SYS DISCRIM ATTIT PWR   INDUS
...TREND 18/20. PAGE 26 E0509   JURID
                                                      DECISION

COUNCIL OF STATE GOVERNMENTS,INCREASED RIGHTS FOR B63 CT/SYS
DEFENDANTS IN STATE CRIMINAL PROSECUTIONS. USA+45   ADJUD
GOV/REL INGP/REL FEDERAL ORD/FREE...JURID 20   PROVS
SUPREME/CT. PAGE 26 E0522   CRIME

DECOTTIGNIES R.,LES NATIONALITES AFRICAINES. AFR B63 NAT/LISM
NAT/G PROB/SOLV DIPLOM COLONIAL ORD/FREE...CHARTS   JURID
GOV/COMP 20. PAGE 30 E0602   LEGIS
                                                      LAW

DILLIARD I.,ONE MAN'S STAND FOR FREEDOM: MR. B63 CONSTN
JUSTICE BLACK AND THE BILL OF RIGHTS. USA+45   JURID
POL/PAR SECT DELIB/GP FORCES ADJUD CONTROL WAR   JUDGE
DISCRIM MORAL...BIBLIOG 20 NEGRO SUPREME/CT   ORD/FREE
BILL/RIGHT BLACK/HL. PAGE 32 E0628

DUNHAM A.,MR. JUSTICE. ADJUD PWR...JURID ANTHOL B63 BIOG
18/20 SUPREME/CT. PAGE 33 E0659   PERSON
                                                      LAW
                                                      CT/SYS

EDDY J.P.,JUSTICE OF THE PEACE. UK LAW CONSTN B63 CRIME
CULTURE 14/20 COMMON/LAW. PAGE 34 E0674   JURID
                                                      CT/SYS
                                                      ADJUD

ELIAS T.O.,THE NIGERIAN LEGAL SYSTEM. NIGERIA LAW B63 CT/SYS
FAM KIN SECT ADMIN NAT/LISM...JURID 18/20   ADJUD
ENGLSH/LAW COMMON/LAW. PAGE 34 E0682   COLONIAL
                                                      PROF/ORG

ELLERT R.B.,NATO 'FAIR TRIAL' SAFEGUARDS: PRECURSOR B63 JURID
TO AN INTERNATIONAL BILL OF PROCEDURAL RIGHTS.   INT/LAW
WOR+45 FORCES CRIME CIVMIL/REL ATTIT ORD/FREE 20   INT/ORG
NATO. PAGE 34 E0683   CT/SYS

FALK R.A.,LAW, MORALITY, AND WAR IN THE B63 ADJUD
CONTEMPORARY WORLD. WOR+45 LAW INT/ORG EX/STRUC   ARMS/CONT
FORCES EDU/PROP LEGIT DETER NUC/PWR MORAL ORD/FREE   PEACE
...JURID TOT/POP 20. PAGE 36 E0715   INT/LAW

FORTES A.B.,HISTORIA ADMINISTRATIVA, JUDICIARIA E B63 PROVS
ECLESIASTICA DO RIO GRANDE DO SUL. BRAZIL L/A+17C   ADMIN
LOC/G SECT COLONIAL CT/SYS ORD/FREE CATHISM 16/20.   JURID
PAGE 39 E0773

FRAENKEL O.K.,THE SUPREME COURT AND CIVIL B63 ORD/FREE
LIBERTIES: HOW THE COURT HAS PROTECTED THE BILL OF   CONSTN
RIGHTS. NAT/G CT/SYS CHOOSE PERS/REL RACE/REL   ADJUD
DISCRIM PERSON...DECISION 20 SUPREME/CT CIVIL/LIB   JURID
BILL/RIGHT. PAGE 39 E0782

FRIEDRICH C.J.,JUSTICE: NOMOS VI. UNIV LAW SANCTION B63 LEGIT
CRIME...CONCPT ANTHOL MARX/KARL LOCKE/JOHN   ADJUD
AQUINAS/T. PAGE 41 E0809   ORD/FREE
                                                      JURID

GARNER U.F.,ADMINISTRATIVE LAW. UK LAW LOC/G NAT/G B63 ADMIN
EX/STRUC LEGIS JUDGE BAL/PWR BUDGET ADJUD CONTROL   JURID
CT/SYS...BIBLIOG 20. PAGE 42 E0840   PWR
                                                      GOV/REL

GRANT D.R.,STATE AND LOCAL GOVERNMENT IN AMERICA. B63 PROVS
USA+45 FINAN LOC/G MUNIC EX/STRUC FORCES EDU/PROP   POL/PAR
ADMIN CHOOSE FEDERAL ATTIT...JURID 20. PAGE 45   LEGIS
E0897   CONSTN

GRIFFITH J.A.G.,PRINCIPLES OF ADMINISTRATIVE LAW B63 JURID
(3RD ED.). UK CONSTN EX/STRUC LEGIS ADJUD CONTROL   ADMIN
CT/SYS PWR...CHARTS 20. PAGE 47 E0940   NAT/G
                                                      BAL/PWR

GSOUSKI V.,LEGAL SOURCES AND BIBLIOGRAPHY OF THE B63 BIBLIOG
BALTIC STATES (ESTONIA, LATVIA, LITHUANIA). COM   ADJUD
ESTONIA LATVIA LITHUANIA NAT/G LEGIS CT/SYS   LAW

SANCTION CRIME 20. PAGE 48 E0957   JURID

HABERMAS J.,THEORIE UND PRAXIS. RATIONAL PERSON B63 JURID
...PHIL/SCI ANTHOL 19/20 HEGEL/GWF MARX/KARL BLOCH   REV
LOWITH. PAGE 49 E0969   GEN/LAWS
                                                      MARXISM

HALEY A.G.,SPACE LAW AND GOVERNMENT. FUT USA+45 B63 INT/ORG
WOR+45 LEGIS ACT/RES CREATE ATTIT RIGID/FLEX   LAW
ORD/FREE PWR SOVEREIGN...POLICY JURID CONCPT CHARTS   SPACE
VAL/FREE 20. PAGE 49 E0980

HALL J.,COMPARATIVE LAW AND SOCIAL THEORY. WOR+45 B63 LAW
CONSTN CULTURE DOMIN CT/SYS ORD/FREE...PLURIST   SOC
JURID CONCPT NEW/IDEA GEN/LAWS VAL/FREE. PAGE 49
E0984

HIGGINS R.,THE DEVELOPMENT OF INTERNATIONAL LAW B63 INT/ORG
THROUGH THE POLITICAL ORGANS OF THE UNITED NATIONS.   INT/LAW
WOR+45 FORCES DIPLOM AGREE COERCE ATTIT SOVEREIGN   TEC/DEV
...BIBLIOG 20 UN TREATY. PAGE 52 E1041   JURID

HYNEMAN C.S.,THE SUPREME COURT ON TRIAL. ADJUD LEAD B63 CT/SYS
GP/REL FEDERAL...IDEA/COMP 20 SUPREME/CT. PAGE 56   JURID
E1120   POLICY
                                                      NAT/G

KLESMENT J.,LEGAL SOURCES AND BIBLIOGRAPHY OF THE B63 BIBLIOG/A
BALTIC STATES (ESTONIA, LATVIA, LITHUANIA). COM   JURID
ESTONIA LATVIA LITHUANIA LAW FINAN ADJUD CT/SYS   CONSTN
REGION CENTRAL MARXISM 19/20. PAGE 61 E1223   ADMIN

A BIBLIOGRAPHY OF DOCTORAL DISSERTATIONS UNDERTAKEN B63 BIBLIOG
IN AMERICAN AND CANADIAN UNIVERSITIES ON RELIGION   ACADEM
AND POLITICS. LAW CONSTN DOMIN LEGIT ADJUD GP/REL   SECT
...POLICY 20. PAGE 62 E1241   JURID

LANOUE G.R.,A BIBLIOGRAPHY OF DOCTORAL B63 BIBLIOG
DISSERTATIONS ON POLITICS AND RELIGION. USA+45   NAT/G
USA-45 CONSTN PROVS DIPLOM CT/SYS MORAL...POLICY   LOC/G
JURID CONCPT 20. PAGE 63 E1252   SECT

LAVROFF D.-.G.,LES LIBERTES PUBLIQUES EN UNION B63 ORD/FREE
SOVIETIQUE (REV. ED.). USSR NAT/G WORKER SANCTION   LAW
CRIME MARXISM NEW/LIB...JURID BIBLIOG WORSHIP 20.   ATTIT
PAGE 63 E1268   COM

LEAGUE WOMEN VOTERS NEW YORK,APPORTIONMENT WORKSHOP B63 APPORT
KIT. USA+45 VOL/ASSN DELIB/GP LEGIS ATTIT ORD/FREE   REPRESENT
...METH/COMP 20 SUPREME/CT NEW/YORK. PAGE 64 E1275   PROVS
                                                      JURID

LEGISLATIVE REFERENCE SERVICE,DIGEST OF PUBLIC B63 BIBLIOG/A
GENERAL BILLS AND RESOLUTIONS. LAW COM/IND EDU/PROP   LEGIS
GOV/REL INGP/REL KNOWL...JURID 20 CONGRESS. PAGE 64   DELIB/GP
E1280   NAT/G

LIVINGSTON W.S.,FEDERALISM IN THE COMMONWEALTH - A B63 BIBLIOG
BIBLIOGRAPHICAL COMMENTARY. CANADA INDIA PAKISTAN   JURID
UK STRUCT LOC/G NAT/G POL/PAR...NAT/COMP 20   FEDERAL
AUSTRAL. PAGE 66 E1310   CONSTN

MCDOUGAL M.S.,LAW AND PUBLIC ORDER IN SPACE. FUT B63 SPACE
USA+45 ACT/RES TEC/DEV ADJUD...POLICY INT/LAW JURID   ORD/FREE
20. PAGE 70 E1410   DIPLOM
                                                      DECISION

MURPHY T.J.,CENSORSHIP: GOVERNMENT AND OBSCENITY. B63 ORD/FREE
USA+45 CULTURE LEGIS JUDGE EDU/PROP CONTROL   MORAL
INGP/REL RATIONAL POPULISM...CATH JURID 20. PAGE 75   LAW
E1507   CONSEN

PATRA A.C.,THE ADMINISTRATION OF JUSTICE UNDER THE B63 ADMIN
EAST INDIA COMPANY IN BENGAL, BIHAR AND ORISSA.   JURID
INDIA UK LG/CO CAP/ISM INT/TRADE ADJUD COLONIAL   CONCPT
CONTROL CT/SYS...POLICY 20. PAGE 80 E1602

PRITCHETT C.H.,THE ROOSEVELT COURT. USA-45 LAW B63 DECISION
INGP/REL...CHARTS 20 SUPREME/CT. PAGE 82 E1653   PROB/SOLV
                                                      CT/SYS

JURID

...POLICY JURID METH/COMP 20 ENGLSH/LAW. PAGE 104   ADMIN
E2088

B63

PRITCHETT C.H.,THE THIRD BRANCH OF GOVERNMENT.   JURID
USA+45 USA-45 CONSTN SOCIETY INDUS SECT LEGIS JUDGE   NAT/G
PROB/SOLV GOV/REL 20 SUPREME/CT CHURCH/STA. PAGE 82   ADJUD
E1654   CT/SYS

B63

YOUNGER R.D.,THE PEOPLE'S PANEL: THE GRAND JURY IN   CT/SYS
THE UNITED STATES, 1634-1941. USA-45 LAW LEGIT   JURID
CONTROL TASK GP/REL ROLE...TREND 17/20 GRAND/JURY.   CONSTN
PAGE 108 E2166   LOC/G

B63

RAVENS J.P.,STAAT UND KATHOLISCHE KIRCHE IN   GP/REL
PREUSSENS POLNISCHEN TEILUNGSGEBIETEN. GERMANY   CATHISM
POLAND PRUSSIA PROVS DIPLOM EDU/PROP DEBATE   SECT
NAT/LISM...JURID 18 CHURCH/STA. PAGE 83 E1674   NAT/G

L63

BOLGAR V.,"THE PUBLIC INTEREST: A JURISPRUDENTIAL   CONCPT
AND COMPARATIVE OVERVIEW OF SYMPOSIUM ON   ORD/FREE
FUNDAMENTAL CONCEPTS OF PUBLIC LAW" COM FRANCE   CONTROL
GERMANY SWITZERLND LAW ADJUD ADMIN AGREE LAISSEZ   NAT/COMP
...JURID GEN/LAWS 20 EUROPE/E. PAGE 14 E0264

B63

REALE M.,PLURALISMO E LIBERDADE. STRUCT ADJUST   CONCPT
ATTIT 20 CIVIL/LIB. PAGE 84 E1676   ORD/FREE
                                                        JURID
                                                        INGP/REL

L63

LOEVINGER L.,"JURIMETRICS* THE METHODOLOGY OF LEGAL   COMPUT/IR
INQUIRY." COMPUTER CREATE PLAN TEC/DEV AUTOMAT   JURID
CT/SYS EFFICIENCY...DECISION PHIL/SCI NEW/IDEA   GEN/METH
QUANT PREDICT. PAGE 66 E1318   ADJUD

B63

REITZEL A.M.,DAS MAINZER KRONUNGSRECHT UND DIE   CHIEF
POLITISCHE PROBLEMATIK. GERMANY MUNIC LEGIT CATHISM   JURID
12/13. PAGE 84 E1684   CHOOSE
                                                        SECT

L63

MCDOUGAL M.S.,"THE ENJOYMENT AND ACQUISITION OF   PLAN
RESOURCES IN OUTER SPACE." CHRIST-17C FUT WOR+45   TREND
WOR-45 LAW EXTR/IND INT/ORG ACT/RES CREATE TEC/DEV
ECO/TAC LEGIT COERCE HEALTH KNOWL ORD/FREE PWR
WEALTH...JURID HIST/WRIT VAL/FREE. PAGE 70 E1408

B63

REOCK E.C. JR.,POPULATION INEQUALITY AMONG COUNTIES   APPORT
IN THE NEW JERSEY LEGISLATURE 1791-1962. PROVS   REPRESENT
ORD/FREE...CENSUS CHARTS 18/20 NEW/JERSEY. PAGE 84   LEGIS
E1687   JURID

S63

ALGER C.F.,"HYPOTHESES ON RELATIONSHIPS BETWEEN THE   INT/ORG
ORGANIZATION OF INTERNATIONAL SOCIETY AND   LAW
INTERNATIONAL ORDER." WOR+45 WOR-45 ORD/FREE PWR
...JURID GEN/LAWS VAL/FREE 20. PAGE 3 E0066

B63

ROBERT J.,LA MONARCHIE MAROCAINE. MOROCCO LABOR   CHIEF
MUNIC POL/PAR EX/STRUC ORD/FREE PWR...JURID TREND T   CONSERVE
20. PAGE 85 E1702   ADMIN
                                                        CONSTN

S63

BERMAN H.J.,"THE DILEMMA OF SOVIET LAW REFORM."   COM
NAT/G POL/PAR CT/SYS ALL/VALS ORD/FREE PWR...POLICY   LAW
JURID VAL/FREE 20. PAGE 11 E0208   USSR

B63

ROBERTSON A.H.,HUMAN RIGHTS IN EUROPE. CONSTN   EUR+WWI
SOCIETY INT/ORG NAT/G VOL/ASSN DELIB/GP ACT/RES   PERSON
PLAN ADJUD REGION ROUTINE ATTIT LOVE ORD/FREE
RESPECT...JURID SOC CONCPT SOC/EXP UN 20. PAGE 85
E1705

S63

CAHIER P.,"LE DROIT INTERNE DES ORGANISATIONS   INT/ORG
INTERNATIONALES." UNIV CONSTN SOCIETY ECO/DEV R+D   JURID
NAT/G TOP/EX LEGIT ATTIT PERCEPT...TIME/SEQ 19/20.   DIPLOM
PAGE 18 E0357   INT/LAW

B63

ROSNER G.,THE UNITED NATIONS EMERGENCY FORCE.   INT/ORG
FRANCE ISRAEL UAR UK WOR+45 CREATE WAR PEACE   FORCES
ORD/FREE PWR...INT/LAW JURID HIST/WRIT TIME/SEQ UN.
PAGE 86 E1719

S63

FRIEDMANN W.G.,"THE USES OF 'GENERAL PRINCIPLES' IN   LAW
THE DEVELOPMENT OF INTERNATIONAL LAW." WOR+45 NAT/G   INT/LAW
DIPLOM INT/TRADE LEGIT ROUTINE RIGID/FLEX ORD/FREE   INT/ORG
...JURID CONCPT STERTYP GEN/METH 20. PAGE 41 E0804

B63

ROYAL INSTITUTE PUBLIC ADMIN,BRITISH PUBLIC   BIBLIOG
ADMINISTRATION. UK LAW FINAN INDUS LOC/G POL/PAR   ADMIN
LEGIS LOBBY PARL/PROC CHOOSE JURID. PAGE 86 E1729   MGT
                                                        NAT/G

S63

GIRAUD E.,"L'INTERDICTION DU RECOURS A LA FORCE. LA   INT/ORG
THEORIE ET LA PRATIQUE DES NATIONS UNIES." ALGERIA   FORCES
COM CUBA HUNGARY WOR+45 ADJUD TOTALISM ATTIT   DIPLOM
RIGID/FLEX PWR...POLICY JURID CONCPT UN 20 CONGO.
PAGE 44 E0872

B63

SCHMIDHAUSER J.R.,CONSTITUTIONAL LAW IN THE   LAW
POLITICAL PROCESS. SOCIETY LEGIS ADJUD CT/SYS   CONSTN
FEDERAL...SOC TREND IDEA/COMP ANTHOL T SUPREME/CT   JURID
SENATE CONGRESS HOUSE/REP. PAGE 88 E1761

S63

MCDOUGAL M.S.,"THE SOVIET-CUBAN QUARANTINE AND   ORD/FREE
SELF-DEFENSE." CUBA USA+45 USSR WOR+45 INT/ORG   LEGIT
NAT/G BAL/PWR NUC/PWR ATTIT...JURID CONCPT. PAGE 70   SOVEREIGN
E1409

B63

STREET H.,FREEDOM: THE INDIVIDUAL AND THE LAW. UK   ORD/FREE
COM/IND EDU/PROP PRESS RUMOR TV PWR 20 CIVIL/LIB   NAT/G
FILM. PAGE 94 E1886   JURID
                                                        PARL/PROC

S63

MENDELSON W.,"THE NEO-BEHAVIORAL APPROACH TO THE   DECISION
JUDICIAL PROCESS: A CRITIQUE" ADJUD PERSON...SOC   JURID
RECORD IDEA/COMP. PAGE 72 E1438   JUDGE

B63

TUSSMAN J.,THE SUPREME COURT ON RACIAL   CT/SYS
DISCRIMINATION. USA+45 USA-45 NAT/G PROB/SOLV ADJUD   DISCRIM
RACE/REL ORD/FREE...JURID 20 SUPREME/CT CIV/RIGHTS.   ATTIT
PAGE 97 E1946   LAW

S63

MEYROWITZ H.,"LES JURISTES DEVANT L'ARME NUCLEAIRE."   ACT/RES
FUT WOR+45 INTELL SOCIETY BAL/PWR DETER WAR...JURID   ADJUD
CONCPT 20. PAGE 72 E1451   INT/LAW
                                                        NUC/PWR

B63

US COMMISSION ON CIVIL RIGHTS,FREEDOM TO THE FREE.   RACE/REL
USA+45 USA-45 LAW VOL/ASSN CT/SYS ATTIT PWR...JURID   DISCRIM
BIBLIOG 17/20 SUPREME/CT NEGRO CIV/RIGHTS. PAGE 99   NAT/G
E1986   POLICY

S63

NAGEL S.S.,"A CONCEPTUAL SCHEME OF THE JUDICIAL   POLICY
PROCESS." ADJUD...DECISION NEW/IDEA AVERAGE MODAL   LAW
CHARTS. PAGE 76 E1518   JURID
                                                        DISCRIM

B63

US SENATE COMM ON JUDICIARY,ADMINISTRATIVE   PARL/PROC
CONFERENCE OF THE UNITED STATES. USA+45 CONSTN   JURID
NAT/G PROB/SOLV CONFER GOV/REL...INT 20 SENATE.   ADMIN
PAGE 102 E2048   LEGIS

S63

RIGAUX F.,"LA SIGNIFICATION DES ACTES JUDICIARES A   CONSULT
L'ETRANGER." EUR+WWI ITALY NETHERLAND LAW ACT/RES   CT/SYS
DRIVE...JURID GEN/LAWS TOT/POP 20. PAGE 85 E1699   GERMANY

B63

VINES K.N.,STUDIES IN JUDICIAL POLITICS: TULANE   CT/SYS
STUDIES IN POLITICAL SCIENCE (VOL. 8). POL/PAR   GOV/REL
JUDGE ADJUD SANCTION CRIME CHOOSE PWR...JURID STAT   PROVS
TIME/SEQ CHARTS. PAGE 104 E2079

S63

TALLON D.,"L'ETUDE DU DROIT COMPARE COMME MOYEN DE   INT/ORG
RECHERCHER LES MATIERES SUSCEPTIBLES D'UNIFICATION   JURID
INTERNATIONALE." WOR+45 LAW SOCIETY VOL/ASSN   INT/LAW
CONSULT LEGIT CT/SYS RIGID/FLEX KNOWL 20. PAGE 95
E1906

B63

WADE H.W.R.,TOWARDS ADMINISTRATIVE JUSTICE. UK   ADJUD
USA+45 CONSTN CONSULT PROB/SOLV CT/SYS PARL/PROC   IDEA/COMP

S63

VINES K.N.,"THE ROLE OF THE CIRCUIT COURT OF   REGION

APPEALS IN THE FEDERAL JUDICIAL PROCESS: A CASE
STUDY." USA+45 STRATA JUDGE RESPECT...DECISION
JURID CHARTS GP/COMP. PAGE 104 E2078
ADJUD
CT/SYS
RACE/REL

S63

WEISSBERG G.,"MAPS AS EVIDENCE IN INTERNATIONAL
BOUNDARY DISPUTES: A REAPPRAISAL." CHINA/COM
EUR+WWI INDIA MOD/EUR S/ASIA INT/ORG NAT/G LEGIT
PERCEPT...JURID CHARTS 20. PAGE 105 E2110
LAW
GEOG
SOVEREIGN

S63

WENGLER W.,"LES CONFLITS DE LOIS ET LE PRINCIPE
D'EGALITE." UNIV LAW SOCIETY ACT/RES LEGIT ATTIT
PERCEPT 20. PAGE 105 E2111
JURID
CONCPT
INT/LAW

B64

BECKER T.L.,POLITICAL BEHAVIORALISM AND MODERN
JURISPRUDENCE* A WORKING THEORY AND STUDY IN
JUDICIAL DECISION-MAKING. CONSTN...JURID STAT
GEN/METH INDEX. PAGE 9 E0172
JUDGE
LAW
DECISION
CT/SYS

B64

BERNSTEIN H.,A BOOKSHELF ON BRAZIL. BRAZIL ADMIN
COLONIAL...HUM JURID SOC 20. PAGE 11 E0213
BIBLIOG/A
NAT/G
L/A+17C
ECO/UNDEV

B64

BOUVIER-AJAM M.,MANUEL TECHNIQUE ET PRATIQUE DU
MAIRE ET DES ELUS ET AGENTS COMMUNAUX. FRANCE LOC/G
BUDGET CHOOSE GP/REL SUPEGO...JURID BIBLIOG 20
MAYOR COMMUNES. PAGE 14 E0274
MUNIC
ADMIN
CHIEF
NEIGH

B64

BREVER E.H.,LEARNED HAND, JANUARY 27, 1872-AUGUST
18, 1961 (PAMPHLET). USA+45 USA-45 LAW CONSTN ADJUD
...DECISION BIOG 19/20. PAGE 15 E0295
BIBLIOG/A
JUDGE
CT/SYS
JURID

B64

BUREAU OF NAT'L AFFAIRS,THE CIVIL RIGHTS ACT OF
1964. USA+45 LOC/G NAT/G DELIB/GP CONFER DEBATE
DISCRIM...JURID 20 CONGRESS SUPREME/CT CIV/RIGHTS.
PAGE 17 E0333
LEGIS
RACE/REL
LAW
CONSTN

B64

BUREAU OF NATIONAL AFFAIRS,STATE FAIR EMPLOYMENT
LAWS AND THEIR ADMINISTRATION. INDUS ADJUD PERS/REL
RACE/REL ATTIT ORD/FREE WEALTH 20. PAGE 17 E0338
PROVS
DISCRIM
WORKER
JURID

B64

CHAPIN B.,THE AMERICAN LAW OF TREASON. USA-45 LAW
NAT/G JUDGE CRIME REV...BIBLIOG 18. PAGE 21 E0419
LEGIS
JURID
CONSTN
POLICY

B64

COHEN M.,LAW AND POLITICS IN SPACE: SPECIFIC AND
URGENT PROBLEMS IN THE LAW OF OUTER SPACE.
CHINA/COM COM USA+45 USSR WOR+45 COM/IND INT/ORG
NAT/G LEGIT NUC/PWR ATTIT BIO/SOC...JURID CONCPT
CONGRESS 20 STALIN/J. PAGE 24 E0464
DELIB/GP
LAW
INT/LAW
SPACE

B64

COHEN M.L.,SELECTED BIBLIOGRAPHY OF FOREIGN AND
INTERNATIONAL LAW....IDEA/COMP METH/COMP 20.
PAGE 24 E0466
BIBLIOG/A
JURID
LAW
INT/LAW

B64

DIAS R.W.M.,A BIBLIOGRAPHY OF JURISPRUDENCE (2ND
ED.). VOL/ASSN LEGIS ADJUD CT/SYS OWN...INT/LAW
18/20. PAGE 31 E0619
BIBLIOG/A
JURID
LAW
CONCPT

B64

DORMAN M.,WE SHALL OVERCOME. USA+45 ELITES ACADEM
FORCES TOP/EX MURDER...JURID 20 CIV/RIGHTS
MISSISSIPP EVERS/MED CLEMSON. PAGE 32 E0638
RACE/REL
LAW
DISCRIM

B64

DUMON F.,LE BRESIL; SES INSTITUTIONS POLITIQUES ET
JUDICIARIES. BRAZIL POL/PAR CHIEF LEGIS ORD/FREE
19/20. PAGE 33 E0658
CONSTN
JURID
CT/SYS
GOV/REL

B64

ECONOMIDES C.P.,LE POUVOIR DE DECISION DES
ORGANISATIONS INTERNATIONALES EUROPEENNES. DIPLOM
DOMIN INGP/REL EFFICIENCY...INT/LAW JURID 20 NATO
OEEC EEC COUNCL/EUR EURATOM. PAGE 34 E0673
INT/ORG
PWR
DECISION
GP/COMP

B64

ENGEL S.,LAW, STATE, AND INTERNATIONAL LEGAL ORDER.
WOR+45 NAT/G ORD/FREE RELATISM...INT/LAW IDEA/COMP
JURID
OBJECTIVE

ANTHOL 20 KELSEN/H. PAGE 35 E0690
CONCPT
DEBATE

B64

EULAU H.,LAWYERS IN POLITICS: A STUDY IN
PROFESSIONAL CONVERGENCE. USA+45 POL/PAR DELIB/GP
GP/REL...QU 20. PAGE 35 E0701
PROF/ORG
JURID
LEGIS
ATTIT

B64

FALK R.A.,THE ROLE OF DOMESTIC COURTS IN THE
INTERNATIONAL LEGAL ORDER. FUT WOR+45 INT/ORG NAT/G
JUDGE EDU/PROP LEGIT CT/SYS...POLICY RELATIV JURID
CONCPT GEN/LAWS 20. PAGE 36 E0716
LAW
INT/LAW

B64

FEIFER G.,JUSTICE IN MOSCOW. USSR LAW CRIME
...RECORD 20. PAGE 37 E0725
ADJUD
JURID
CT/SYS
MARXISM

B64

FEINE H.E.,DIE BESETZUNG DER REICHSBISTUMER VOM
WESTFALISCHEN FRIEDEN BIS ZUR SAKULARISATION.
GERMANY EDU/PROP GP/REL AGE 17/19. PAGE 37 E0727
CHOOSE
SECT
JURID
PROVS

B64

FISK W.M.,ADMINISTRATIVE PROCEDURE IN A REGULATORY
AGENCY: THE CAB AND THE NEW YORK-CHICAGO CASE
(PAMPHLET). USA+45 DIST/IND ADMIN CONTROL LOBBY
GP/REL ROLE ORD/FREE NEWYORK/C CHICAGO CAB. PAGE 38
E0758
SERV/IND
ECO/DEV
AIR
JURID

B64

FORBES A.H.,CURRENT RESEARCH IN BRITISH STUDIES. UK
CONSTN CULTURE POL/PAR SECT DIPLOM ADMIN...JURID
BIOG WORSHIP 20. PAGE 39 E0769
BIBLIOG
PERSON
NAT/G
PARL/PROC

B64

FREISEN J.,STAAT UND KATHOLISCHE KIRCHE IN DEN
DEUTSCHEN BUNDESSTAATEN (2 VOLS.). GERMANY LAW FAM
NAT/G EDU/PROP GP/REL MARRIAGE WEALTH 19/20
CHURCH/STA. PAGE 40 E0793
SECT
CATHISM
JURID
PROVS

B64

FRIEDMANN W.G.,THE CHANGING STRUCTURE OF
INTERNATIONAL LAW. WOR+45 INT/ORG NAT/G PROVS LEGIT
ORD/FREE PWR...JURID CONCPT GEN/LAWS TOT/POP UN 20.
PAGE 41 E0805
ADJUD
TREND
INT/LAW

B64

GESELLSCHAFT RECHTSVERGLEICH,BIBLIOGRAPHIE DES
DEUTSCHEN RECHTS (BIBLIOGRAPHY OF GERMAN LAW,
TRANS. BY COURTLAND PETERSON). GERMANY FINAN INDUS
LABOR SECT FORCES CT/SYS PARL/PROC CRIME...INT/LAW
SOC NAT/COMP 20. PAGE 43 E0853
BIBLIOG/A
JURID
CONSTN
ADMIN

B64

GIANNELLA D.A.,RELIGION AND THE PUBLIC ORDER: AN
ANNUAL REVIEW OF CHURCH AND STATE, AND OF RELIGION,
LAW, AND SOCIETY. USA+45 LAW SOCIETY FAM POL/PAR
SCHOOL GIVE EDU/PROP GP/REL...JURID GEN/LAWS
BIBLIOG/A 20 CHURCH/STA BIRTH/CON CONSCN/OBJ
NATURL/LAW. PAGE 43 E0855
SECT
NAT/G
CONSTN
ORD/FREE

B64

GJUPANOVIC H.,LEGAL SOURCES AND BIBLIOGRAPHY OF
YUGOSLAVIA. COM YUGOSLAVIA LAW LEGIS DIPLOM ADMIN
PARL/PROC REGION CRIME CENTRAL 20. PAGE 44 E0873
BIBLIOG/A
JURID
CONSTN
ADJUD

B64

GRASMUCK E.L.,COERCITIO STAAT UND KIRCHE IM
DONATISTENSTREIT. CHRIST-17C ROMAN/EMP LAW PROVS
DEBATE PERSON SOVEREIGN...JURID CONCPT 4/5
AUGUSTINE CHURCH/STA ROMAN/LAW. PAGE 45 E0898
GP/REL
NAT/G
SECT
COERCE

B64

GUMPLOWICZ L.,RECHTSSTAAT UND SOZIALISMUS. STRATA
ORD/FREE SOVEREIGN MARXISM...IDEA/COMP 16/20 KANT/I
HOBBES/T. PAGE 48 E0962
JURID
NAT/G
SOCISM
CONCPT

B64

HAAR C.M.,LAW AND LAND: ANGLO-AMERICAN PLANNING
PRACTICE. UK USA+45 NAT/G TEC/DEV BUDGET CT/SYS
INGP/REL EFFICIENCY OWN...JURID 20. PAGE 49 E0967
LAW
PLAN
MUNIC
NAT/COMP

B64

HALLER W.,DER SCHWEDISCHE JUSTITIEOMBUDSMAN.
DENMARK FINLAND NORWAY SWEDEN LEGIS ADJUD CONTROL
PERSON ORD/FREE...NAT/COMP 20 OMBUDSMAN. PAGE 50
E0986
JURID
PARL/PROC
ADMIN
CHIEF

B64

HEGEL G.W.,HEGEL'S POLITICAL WRITINGS (TRANS. BY   CONSTN
T.M. KNOX). GERMANY UK FINAN FORCES PARL/PROC   LEGIS
CHOOSE REPRESENT...BIOG 19. PAGE 51 E1022   JURID

B64

HENKE W.,DAS RECHT DER POLITISCHEN PARTEIEN.   POL/PAR
GERMANY/W LAW CT/SYS GP/REL SUPEGO 20. PAGE 52   JURID
E1031   CONSTN
                                                        NAT/G

B64

HOHFELD W.N.,FUNDAMENTAL LEGAL CONCEPTIONS.   JURID
PROB/SOLV OWN PWR...DECISION LING IDEA/COMP   ADJUD
GEN/METH. PAGE 54 E1069   LAW
                                                        METH/CNCPT

B64

HOLDSWORTH W.S.,A HISTORY OF ENGLISH LAW; THE   LAW
CENTURIES OF DEVELOPMENT AND REFORM (VOL. XIV). UK   LEGIS
CONSTN LOC/G NAT/G POL/PAR CHIEF EX/STRUC ADJUD   LEAD
COLONIAL ATTIT...INT/LAW JURID 18/19 TORY/PARTY   CT/SYS
COMMONWLTH WHIG/PARTY COMMON/LAW. PAGE 54 E1081

B64

HOLT S.,THE DICTIONARY OF AMERICAN GOVERNMENT.   DICTIONARY
USA+45 LOC/G MUNIC PROVS LEGIS ADMIN JURID. PAGE 55   INDEX
E1091   LAW
                                                        NAT/G

B64

HOPKINSON T.,SOUTH AFRICA. SOUTH/AFR UK NAT/G   SOCIETY
POL/PAR LEGIS ECO/TAC PARL/PROC WAR...JURID AUD/VIS   RACE/REL
19/20. PAGE 55 E1097   DISCRIM

B64

HURST W.H.,JUSTICE HOLMES ON LEGAL HISTORY. USA-45   ADJUD
LAW SOCIETY NAT/G WRITING...POLICY PHIL/SCI SOC   JURID
CONCPT 20 HOLMES/OW SUPREME/CT ENGLSH/LAW. PAGE 56   BIOG
E1117

B64

JACKSON R.M.,THE MACHINERY OF JUSTICE IN ENGLAND.   CT/SYS
UK EDU/PROP CONTROL COST ORD/FREE...MGT 20   ADJUD
ENGLSH/LAW. PAGE 57 E1142   JUDGE
                                                        JURID

B64

JENKS C.W.,THE PROSPECTS OF INTERNATIONAL   INT/LAW
ADJUDICATION. WOR+45 WOR-45 NAT/G DIPLOM CONTROL   ADJUD
PWR...POLICY JURID CONCPT METH/COMP 19/20 ICJ   CT/SYS
LEAGUE/NAT UN TREATY. PAGE 58 E1160   INT/ORG

B64

KAUPER P.G.,RELIGION AND THE CONSTITUTION. USA+45   CONSTN
USA-45 LAW NAT/G SCHOOL SECT GP/REL ATTIT...BIBLIOG   JURID
WORSHIP 18/20 SUPREME/CT FREE/SPEE CHURCH/STA.   ORD/FREE
PAGE 60 E1189

B64

KOREA (REPUBLIC) SUPREME COURT,KOREAN LEGAL SYSTEM.   JURID
KOREA/S WOR+45 LAW LEAD ROUTINE GOV/REL ORD/FREE 20   CT/SYS
SUPREME/CT. PAGE 61 E1229   CONSTN
                                                        CRIME

B64

LAPENNA I.,STATE AND LAW: SOVIET AND YUGOSLAV   JURID
THEORY. USSR YUGOSLAVIA STRATA STRUCT NAT/G DOMIN   COM
COERCE MARXISM...GOV/COMP IDEA/COMP 20. PAGE 63   LAW
E1253   SOVEREIGN

B64

LEDERMAN W.R.,THE COURTS AND THE CANDIAN   CONSTN
CONSTITUTION. CANADA PARL/PROC...POLICY JURID   CT/SYS
GOV/COMP ANTHOL 19/20 SUPREME/CT PARLIAMENT.   LEGIS
PAGE 64 E1276   LAW

B64

MAKI J.M.,COURT AND CONSTITUTION IN JAPAN; SELECTED CT/SYS
SUPREME COURT DECISIONS, 1948-60. FAM LABOR GOV/REL   CONSTN
HABITAT ORD/FREE...DECISION JURID 20 CHINJAP   PROB/SOLV
SUPREME/CT CIV/RIGHTS. PAGE 68 E1354   LAW

B64

MAKI J.M.,COURT AND CONSTITUTION IN JAPAN: SELECTED CONSTN
SUPREME COURT DECISIONS, 1948-60. LAW AGRI FAM   JURID
LEGIS BAL/PWR ADMIN CHOOSE...SOC ANTHOL CABINET 20   CT/SYS
CHINJAP CIVIL/LIB. PAGE 68 E1355   CRIME

B64

MANNING B.,FEDERAL CONFLICT OF INTEREST LAW. USA+45 LAW
NAT/G PWR 20. PAGE 68 E1362   CONTROL
                                                        ADMIN
                                                        JURID

B64

MARSHALL B.,FEDERALISM AND CIVIL RIGHTS. USA+45   FEDERAL
PROVS BAL/PWR CONTROL CT/SYS PARTIC SOVEREIGN   ORD/FREE
...JURID 20 NEGRO CIV/RIGHTS. PAGE 68 E1369   CONSTN
                                                        FORCES

B64

MASON A.T.,AMERICAN CONSTITUTIONAL LAW: CONSTN
INTRODUCTORY ESSAYS AND SELECTED CASES (3RD ED.).   CT/SYS
LAW LEGIS TAX ADJUD GOV/REL FEDERAL ORD/FREE PWR   JURID
...TIME/SEQ BIBLIOG T 19/20 SUPREME/CT. PAGE 69
E1379

B64

MCWHINNEY E.,"PEACEFUL COEXISTENCE" AND SOVIET-   PEACE
WESTERN INTERNATIONAL LAW. USSR DIPLOM LEAD...JURID   IDEA/COMP
20 COLD/WAR. PAGE 71 E1429   INT/LAW
                                                        ATTIT

B64

MITCHELL B.,A BIOGRAPHY OF THE CONSTITUTION OF THE   CONSTN
UNITED STATES. USA+45 USA-45 PROVS CHIEF LEGIS   LAW
DEBATE ADJUD SUFF FEDERAL...SOC 18/20 SUPREME/CT   JURID
CONGRESS SENATE HOUSE/REP PRESIDENT. PAGE 73 E1472

B64

MURPHY W.F.,ELEMENTS OF JUDICIAL STRATEGY. CONSTN   CT/SYS
JUDGE PERS/REL PERSON 19/20 SUPREME/CT. PAGE 75   ADJUD
E1510   JURID

B64

NATIONAL BOOK LEAGUE,THE COMMONWEALTH IN BOOKS: AN   BIBLIOG/A
ANNOTATED LIST. CANADA UK LOC/G SECT ADMIN...SOC   JURID
BIOG 20 CMN/WLTH. PAGE 76 E1526   NAT/G

B64

NEWMAN E.S.,POLICE, THE LAW, AND PERSONAL FREEDOM.   JURID
USA+45 CONSTN JUDGE CT/SYS CRIME PERS/REL RESPECT   FORCES
...CRIMLGY 20. PAGE 77 E1542   ORD/FREE
                                                        ADJUD

B64

NEWMAN E.S.,CIVIL LIBERTY AND CIVIL RIGHTS. USA+45   ORD/FREE
USA-45 CONSTN PROVS FORCES LEGIS CT/SYS RACE/REL   LAW
ATTIT...MAJORIT JURID WORSHIP 20 SUPREME/CT NEGRO   CONTROL
CIV/RIGHTS CHURCH/STA. PAGE 77 E1543   NAT/G

B64

NICE R.W.,TREASURY OF LAW. WOR+45 WOR-45 SECT ADJUD LAW
MORAL ORD/FREE...INT/LAW JURID PHIL/SCI ANTHOL.   WRITING
PAGE 77 E1545   PERS/REL
                                                        DIPLOM

B64

OPPENHEIMER M.,A MANUAL FOR DIRECT ACTION. USA+45   PLAN
SCHOOL FORCES ADJUD CT/SYS SUFF RACE/REL DISCRIM   VOL/ASSN
...POLICY CHARTS 20. PAGE 79 E1580   JURID
                                                        LEAD

B64

A CHECK LIST OF THE SPECIAL AND STANDING COMMITTEES BIBLIOG
OF THE AMERICAN BAR ASSOCIATION (VOL. II). USA+45   LAW
LEGIS PRESS CONFER...JURID CON/ANAL. PAGE 80 E1607   VOL/ASSN

B64

RAGHAVAN M.D.,INDIA IN CEYLONESE HISTORY, SOCIETY   DIPLOM
AND CULTURE. CEYLON INDIA S/ASIA LAW SOCIETY   CULTURE
INT/TRADE ATTIT...ART/METH JURID SOC LING 20.   SECT
PAGE 83 E1668   STRUCT

B64

RICE C.E.,THE SUPREME COURT AND PUBLIC PRAYER.   JURID
CONSTN SCHOOL SECT PROB/SOLV TAX ATTIT WORSHIP   POLICY
18/20 SUPREME/CT CHURCH/STA. PAGE 84 E1692   NAT/G

B64

SARTORIUS R.E.,THE JUSTIFICATION OF THE JUDICIAL   LAW
DECISION (DISSERTATION). PROB/SOLV LEGIT...JURID   PHIL/SCI
GEN/LAWS BIBLIOG 20. PAGE 87 E1747   CT/SYS
                                                        ADJUD

B64

SCHUBERT G.A.,JUDICIAL BEHAVIOR: A READER IN THEORY ATTIT
AND RESEARCH. POL/PAR CT/SYS ROLE SUPEGO PWR   PERSON
...DECISION JURID REGRESS CHARTS SIMUL ANTHOL 20.   ADJUD
PAGE 89 E1782   ACT/RES

B64

SHAPIRO M.,LAW AND POLITICS IN THE SUPREME COURT: LEGIS
NEW APPROACHES TO POLITICAL JURISPRUDENCE. JUDGE   CT/SYS
PROB/SOLV LEGIT EXEC ROUTINE ATTIT ALL/VALS   LAW
...DECISION SOC. PAGE 90 E1811   JURID

B64

SHKLAR J.N.,LEGALISM. CREATE PROB/SOLV CT/SYS   MORAL
...POLICY CRIMLGY DECISION JURID METH/CNCPT.   LAW

PAGE 91 E1821   NEW/IDEA

SIEKANOWICZ P.,LEGAL SOURCES AND BIBLIOGRAPHY OF   B64
POLAND. COM POLAND CONSTN NAT/G PARL/PROC SANCTION   BIBLIOG
CRIME MARXISM 16/20. PAGE 91 E1823   ADJUD
                                                     LAW
                                                     JURID

                                                     B64
STOICOIU V.,LEGAL SOURCES AND BIBLIOGRAPHY OF   BIBLIOG/A
ROMANIA. COM ROMANIA LAW FINAN POL/PAR LEGIS JUDGE   JURID
ADJUD CT/SYS PARL/PROC MARXISM 20. PAGE 93 E1874   CONSTN
                                                     ADMIN

                                                     B64
SZLADITS C.,BIBLIOGRAPHY ON FOREIGN AND COMPARATIVE BIBLIOG/A
LAW: BOOKS AND ARTICLES IN ENGLISH (SUPPLEMENT   JURID
1962). FINAN INDUS JUDGE LICENSE ADMIN CT/SYS   ADJUD
PARL/PROC OWN...INT/LAW CLASSIF METH/COMP NAT/COMP   LAW
20. PAGE 95 E1904

                                                     B64
TODD A.,JUSTICE ON TRIAL: THE CASE OF LOUIS D.   PERSON
BRANDEIS. TOP/EX DISCRIM...JURID 20 WILSON/W   RACE/REL
CONGRESS SUPREME/CT BRANDEIS/L SENATE. PAGE 96   PERS/REL
E1929   NAT/G

                                                     B64
US HOUSE COMM ON JUDICIARY,IMMIGRATION HEARINGS.   NAT/G
DELIB/GP STRANGE HABITAT...GEOG JURID 20 CONGRESS   POLICY
MIGRATION. PAGE 100 E2006   DIPLOM
                                                     NAT/LISM

                                                     B64
US SENATE COMM ON JUDICIARY,CIVIL RIGHTS - THE   INT
PRESIDENT'S PROGRAM. USA+45 LAW PROB/SOLV PRESS   LEGIS
ADJUD GOV/REL RACE/REL ORD/FREE PWR...JURID 20   DISCRIM
SUPREME/CT SENATE CIV/RIGHTS PRESIDENT. PAGE 102   PARL/PROC
E2053

                                                     B64
US SENATE COMM ON JUDICIARY,ADMINISTRATIVE   PARL/PROC
PROCEDURE ACT. USA+45 CONSTN NAT/G PROB/SOLV CONFER LEGIS
GOV/REL PWR...INT 20 SENATE. PAGE 102 E2054   JURID
                                                     ADMIN

                                                     B64
WAY H.F. JR.,LIBERTY IN THE BALANCE - CURRENT   ORD/FREE
ISSUES IN CIVIL LIBERTIES. USA+45 USA-45 DELIB/GP   EDU/PROP
RACE/REL DISCRIM TOTALISM MARXISM SOCISM...CONCPT   NAT/G
20 CONGRESS SUPREME/CT CIVIL/LIB. PAGE 105 E2104   JURID

MAYO L.H.,"LEGAL-POLICY DECISION PROCESS: L64
ALTERNATIVE THINKING AND THE PREDICTIVE FUNCTION."   DECISION
PROB/SOLV EFFICIENCY RATIONAL. PAGE 70 E1395   SIMUL
                                                     JURID
                                                     TEC/DEV

WORLD PEACE FOUNDATION.,"INTERNATIONAL   L64
ORGANIZATIONS: SUMMARY OF ACTIVITIES." INDIA   INT/ORG
PAKISTAN TURKEY WOR+45 CONSTN CONSULT EX/STRUC   ROUTINE
ECO/TAC EDU/PROP LEGIT ORD/FREE...JURID SOC UN 20
CYPRESS. PAGE 107 E2145

BARKUN M.,"CONFLICT RESOLUTION THROUGH IMPLICIT   S64
MEDIATION." UNIV BARGAIN CONSEN FEDERAL JURID.   CONSULT
PAGE 8 E0149   CENTRAL
                                                     INT/LAW
                                                     IDEA/COMP

                                                     S64
COHEN M.,"BASIC PRINCIPLES OF INTERNATIONAL LAW."   INT/ORG
UNIV WOR+45 WOR-45 BAL/PWR LEGIT ADJUD WAR ATTIT   INT/LAW
MORAL ORD/FREE PWR...JURID CONCPT MYTH TOT/POP 20.
PAGE 23 E0463

                                                     S64
GINSBURGS G.,"WARS OF NATIONAL LIBERATION - THE   COERCE
SOVIET THESIS." COM USSR WOR+45 WOR-45 LAW CULTURE   CONCPT
INT/ORG DIPLOM LEGIT COLONIAL GUERRILLA WAR   INT/LAW
NAT/LISM ATTIT PERSON MORAL PWR...JURID OBS TREND   REV
MARX/KARL 20. PAGE 44 E0869

                                                     S64
GREENBERG S.,"JUDAISM AND WORLD JUSTICE." MEDIT-7   SECT
WOR+45 LAW CULTURE SOCIETY INT/ORG NAT/G FORCES   JURID
EDU/PROP ATTIT DRIVE PERSON SUPEGO ALL/VALS   PEACE
...POLICY PSY CONCPT GEN/LAWS JEWS. PAGE 46 E0908

                                                     S64
HICKEY D.,"THE PHILOSOPHICAL ARGUMENT FOR WORLD   FUT
GOVERNMENT." WOR+45 SOCIETY ACT/RES PLAN LEGIT   INT/ORG
ADJUD PEACE PERCEPT PERSON ORD/FREE...HUM JURID
PHIL/SCI METH/CNCPT CON/ANAL STERTYP GEN/LAWS
TOT/POP 20. PAGE 52 E1039

KARPOV P.V.,"PEACEFUL COEXISTENCE AND INTERNATIONAL COM   S64
LAW." WOR+45 LAW SOCIETY INT/ORG VOL/ASSN FORCES   ATTIT
CREATE CAP/ISM DIPLOM ADJUD NUC/PWR PEACE MORAL   INT/LAW
ORD/FREE PWR MARXISM...MARXIST JURID CONCPT OBS   USSR
TREND COLD/WAR MARX/KARL 20. PAGE 59 E1186

                                                             S64
KUNZ J.,"THE CHANGING SCIENCE OF INTERNATIONAL   ADJUD
LAW." FUT WOR+45 WOR-45 INT/ORG LEGIT ORD/FREE   CONCPT
...JURID TIME/SEQ GEN/LAWS 20. PAGE 62 E1235   INT/LAW

                                                             S64
LIPSON L.,"PEACEFUL COEXISTENCE." COM USSR WOR+45   ATTIT
LAW INT/ORG DIPLOM LEGIT ADJUD ORD/FREE...CONCPT   JURID
OBS TREND GEN/LAWS VAL/FREE COLD/WAR 20. PAGE 65   INT/LAW
E1303   PEACE

MAGGS P.B.,"SOVIET VIEWPOINT ON NUCLEAR WEAPONS IN   COM   S64
INTERNATIONAL LAW." USSR WOR+45 INT/ORG FORCES   LAW
DIPLOM ARMS/CONT ATTIT ORD/FREE PWR...POLICY JURID   INT/LAW
CONCPT OBS TREND CON/ANAL GEN/LAWS VAL/FREE 20.   NUC/PWR
PAGE 67 E1347

PARADIES F.,"SOBRE LA HISTORIA DE LA LOGICA Y DE LA ADJUD   S64
LOGICA JURIDICA." LEGIT KNOWL...JURID METH/CNCPT
HIST/WRIT 20. PAGE 80 E1597

                                                             S64
SKUBISZEWSKI K.,"FORMS OF PARTICIPATION OF   INT/ORG
INTERNATIONAL ORGANIZATION IN THE LAW MAKING   LAW
PROCESS." FUT WOR+45 NAT/G DELIB/GP DOMIN LEGIT   INT/LAW
KNOWL PWR...JURID TREND 20. PAGE 92 E1837

                                                             S64
TRISKA J.F.,"SOVIET TREATY LAW: A QUANTITATIVE   COM
ANALYSIS." WOR+45 LAW ECO/UNDEV AGRI COM/IND INDUS   ECO/TAC
CREATE TEC/DEV DIPLOM ATTIT PWR WEALTH...JURID SAMP INT/LAW
TIME/SEQ TREND CHARTS VAL/FREE 20 TREATY. PAGE 97   USSR
E1942

BECKER T.L.,"POLITICAL BEHAVIORALISM AND MODERN   DECISION C64
JURISPRUDENCE." LEGIS JUDGE OP/RES ADJUD CT/SYS   PROB/SOLV
ATTIT PWR...BIBLIOG 20. PAGE 9 E0173   JURID
                                                     GEN/LAWS

                                                             C64
CORWIN E.S.,"AMERICAN CONSTITUTIONAL HISTORY." LAW   ANTHOL
NAT/G PROB/SOLV EQUILIB FEDERAL ATTIT PWR...JURID   JUDGE
BIBLIOG 20. PAGE 26 E0515   ADJUD
                                                     CT/SYS

                                                             B65
ANTIEU C.J.,RELIGION UNDER THE STATE CONSTITUTIONS. SECT
USA+45 LAW SCHOOL TAX SANCTION PRIVIL ORD/FREE   CONSTN
...JURID 20 SUPREME/CT CHURCH/STA. PAGE 5 E0099   PROVS
                                                     GP/REL

                                                             B65
BAR ASSOCIATION OF ST LOUIS,CONSTITUTIONAL FREEDOM   ORD/FREE
AND THE LAW. USA+45 LAW LABOR LEGIS EDU/PROP   CONSTN
...JURID CONCPT SUPREME/CT CIVIL/LIB CIV/RIGHTS.   RACE/REL
PAGE 8 E0146   NAT/G

                                                             B65
BARKER L.J.,FREEDOM, COURTS, POLITICS: STUDIES IN   JURID
CIVIL LIBERTIES. USA+45 LEGIS CREATE DOMIN PRESS   CT/SYS
ADJUD LOBBY CRIME GP/REL RACE/REL MARXISM 20   ATTIT
CIVIL/LIB. PAGE 8 E0148   ORD/FREE

                                                             B65
BOVY L.,LE MOUVEMENT SYNDICAL OUEST AFRICAIN   BIBLIOG
D'EXPRESSION FRANCAISE. AFR SECT...JURID SOC 20.   SOCISM
PAGE 14 E0275   ECO/UNDEV
                                                     IDEA/COMP

                                                             B65
BREITEL C.D.,THE LAWMAKERS. USA+45 EX/STRUC LEGIS   CT/SYS
JUDGE ATTIT ORD/FREE JURID. PAGE 15 E0290   ADJUD
                                                     FEDERAL
                                                     NAT/G

                                                             B65
CALIFORNIA LEGISLATURE,COMMITTEE ON ELECTIONS AND   DELIB/GP
REAPPORTIONMENT, FINAL REPORT. USA+45 LAW COMPUTER   APPORT
TEC/DEV CHOOSE JURID. PAGE 19 E0366   LEGIS
                                                     ADJUD

                                                             B65
CAMPBELL E.H.,SURVEYS, SUBDIVISIONS AND PLATTING,   CONSTN
AND BOUNDARIES: WASHINGTON STATE LAW AND JUDICIAL   PLAN
DECISIONS. USA+45 LAW LOC/G...DECISION JURID   GEOG

CON/ANAL BIBLIOG WASHINGT/G PARTITION WATER.   PROVS
PAGE 19 E0372

                                                                      B65
CAVERS D.F..THE CHOICE-OF-LAW PROCESS. PROB/SOLV   JURID
ADJUD CT/SYS CHOOSE RATIONAL...IDEA/COMP 16/20   DECISION
TREATY. PAGE 21 E0411   METH/COMP
                                                       ADMIN

                                                                      B65
CHROUST A.H..THE RISE OF THE LEGAL PROFESSION IN   JURID
AMERICA (3 VOLS.). STRATA STRUCT POL/PAR PROF/ORG   USA-45
COLONIAL LEAD REV SKILL...SOC 17/20. PAGE 22 E0437   CT/SYS
                                                       LAW

                                                                      B65
COHN H.J..THE GOVERNMENT OF THE RHINE PALATINATE IN   PROVS
THE FIFTEENTH CENTURY. GERMANY FINAN LOC/G DELIB/GP   JURID
LEGIS CT/SYS CHOOSE CATHISM 14/15 PALATINATE.   GP/REL
PAGE 24 E0468   ADMIN

                                                                      B65
CONRING E..KIRCHE UND STAAT NACH DER LEHRE DER   SECT
NIEDERLANDISCHEN CALVINISTEN IN DER ERSTEN HALFTE   JURID
DES 17. JAHRHUNDERTS. NETHERLAND GP/REL...CONCPT 17   NAT/G
CHURCH/STA. PAGE 25 E0497   ORD/FREE

                                                                      B65
COOPER F.E..STATE ADMINISTRATIVE LAW (2 VOLS.). LAW   JURID
LEGIS PLAN TAX ADJUD CT/SYS FEDERAL PWR...CONCPT   CONSTN
20. PAGE 25 E0501   ADMIN
                                                       PROVS

                                                                      B65
COWEN Z..THE BRITISH COMMONWEALTH OF NATIONS IN A   JURID
CHANGING WORLD. UK ECO/UNDEV INT/ORG ECO/TAC   DIPLOM
INT/TRADE COLONIAL WAR GP/REL RACE/REL SOVEREIGN   PARL/PROC
SOC/INTEG 20 TREATY EEC COMMONWLTH. PAGE 27 E0530   NAT/LISM

                                                                      B65
FELLMAN D..RELIGION IN AMERICAN PUBLIC LAW. USA+45   SECT
USA-45 NAT/G PROVS ADJUD SANCTION GP/REL PRIVIL   CONSTN
ORD/FREE...JURID TIME/SEQ 18/20 SUPREME/CT   LAW
CHURCH/STA. PAGE 37 E0733   POLICY

                                                                      B65
GAJENDRAGADKAR P.B..LAW, LIBERTY AND SOCIAL   ORD/FREE
JUSTICE. INDIA CONSTN NAT/G SECT PLAN ECO/TAC PRESS   LAW
POPULISM...SOC METH/COMP 20 HINDU. PAGE 42 E0826   ADJUD
                                                       JURID

                                                                      B65
GINSBERG M..ON JUSTICE IN SOCIETY. LAW EDU/PROP   ADJUD
LEGIT CT/SYS INGP/REL PRIVIL RATIONAL ATTIT MORAL   ROLE
ORD/FREE...JURID 20. PAGE 44 E0867   CONCPT

                                                                      B65
HOLDSWORTH W.S..A HISTORY OF ENGLISH LAW; THE   LAW
CENTURIES OF SETTLEMENT AND REFORM (VOL. XV). UK   INDUS
CONSTN SECT LEGIS JUDGE WRITING ADJUD CT/SYS CRIME   PROF/ORG
OWN...JURID IDEA/COMP 18 PARLIAMENT ENGLSH/LAW   ATTIT
COMMON/LAW. PAGE 54 E1082

                                                                      B65
HOWARD C.G..LAW: ITS NATURE, FUNCTIONS, AND LIMITS.   LAW
USA+45 CONSTN LEGIS CREATE SANCTION ORD/FREE   JURID
...BIBLIOG 20. PAGE 55 E1101   CONTROL
                                                       SOCIETY

                                                                      B65
HOWE M.D.W..THE GARDEN AND THE WILDERNESS. USA+45   CONSTN
LAW GIVE EDU/PROP LEGIT NAT/LISM ORD/FREE...POLICY   SECT
JURID SUPREME/CT CHURCH/STA. PAGE 55 E1103   NAT/G
                                                       GP/REL

                                                                      B65
INST INTL DES CIVILISATION DIF,THE CONSTITUTIONS   CONSTN
AND ADMINISTRATIVE INSTITUTIONS OF THE NEW STATES.   ADMIN
AFR ISLAM S/ASIA NAT/G POL/PAR DELIB/GP EX/STRUC   ADJUD
CONFER EFFICIENCY NAT/LISM...JURID SOC 20. PAGE 56   ECO/UNDEV
E1123

                                                                      B65
ISORNI J..LES CAS DE CONSCIENCE DE L'AVOCAT.   SUPEGO
FRANCE LAW ACT/RES CT/SYS PARTIC ROLE MORAL 20.   JURID
PAGE 57 E1138   CRIME

                                                                      B65
JENKS C.W..SPACE LAW. DIPLOM DEBATE CONTROL   SPACE
ORD/FREE TREATY 20 UN. PAGE 58 E1161   INT/LAW
                                                       JURID
                                                       INT/ORG

                                                                      B65
JOHNSTON D.M..THE INTERNATIONAL LAW OF FISHERIES: A   CONCPT
FRAMEWORK FOR POLICYORIENTED INQUIRIES. WOR+45   EXTR/IND

ACT/RES PLAN PROB/SOLV CONTROL SOVEREIGN. PAGE 59   JURID
E1171   DIPLOM

                                                                      B65
KAAS L..DIE GEISTLICHE GERICHTSBARKEIT DER   JURID
KATHOLISCHEN KIRCHE IN PREUSSEN (2 VOLS.). PRUSSIA   CATHISM
CONSTN NAT/G PROVS SECT ADJUD ADMIN ATTIT 16/20.   GP/REL
PAGE 59 E1178   CT/SYS

                                                                      B65
KING D.B..LEGAL ASPECTS OF THE CIVIL RIGHTS   LAW
MOVEMENT. SERV/IND VOL/ASSN LEGIS EDU/PROP ADJUD   DISCRIM
PARTIC CHOOSE...JURID SEGREGAT WORK. PAGE 61 E1215   TREND

                                                                      B65
KRISLOV S..THE SUPREME COURT IN THE POLITICAL   ADJUD
PROCESS. USA+45 LAW SOCIETY STRUCT WORKER ADMIN   DECISION
ROLE...JURID SOC 20 SUPREME/CT. PAGE 62 E1231   CT/SYS
                                                       CONSTN

                                                                      B65
LAFAVE W.R..LAW AND SOVIET SOCIETY. EX/STRUC DIPLOM   JURID
DOMIN EDU/PROP PRESS ADMIN CRIME OWN MARXISM 20   CT/SYS
KHRUSH/N. PAGE 62 E1244   ADJUD
                                                       GOV/REL

                                                                      B65
LUGO-MARENCO J.J..A STATEMENT OF THE LAWS OF   CONSTN
NICARAGUA IN MATTERS AFFECTING BUSINESS. NICARAGUA   NAT/G
AGRI DIST/IND EXTR/IND FINAN INDUS FAM WORKER   LEGIS
INT/TRADE TAX MARRIAGE OWN BIO/SOC 20 TREATY   JURID
RESOURCE/N MIGRATION. PAGE 67 E1332

                                                                      B65
MARTENS E..DIE HANNOVERSCHE KIRCHENKOMMISSION.   JURID
GERMANY LAW INT/ORG PROVS SECT CONFER GP/REL   DELIB/GP
CATHISM 16/20. PAGE 69 E1371   CONSTN
                                                       PROF/ORG

                                                                      B65
MCKAY R.B..REAPPORTIONMENT: THE LAW AND POLITICS OF   APPORT
EQUAL REPRESENTATION. FUT USA+45 PROVS BAL/PWR   MAJORIT
ADJUD CHOOSE REPRESENT GOV/REL FEDERAL...JURID   LEGIS
BIBLIOG 20 SUPREME/CT CONGRESS. PAGE 71 E1420   PWR

                                                                      B65
MCWHINNEY E..JUDICIAL REVIEW IN THE ENGLISH-   GOV/COMP
SPEAKING WORLD (3RD ED.). CANADA UK WOR+45 LEGIS   CT/SYS
CONTROL EXEC PARTIC...JURID 20 AUSTRAL. PAGE 71   ADJUD
E1431   CONSTN

                                                                      B65
MEIKLEJOHN D..FREEDOM AND THE PUBLIC: PUBLIC AND   NAT/G
PRIVATE MORALITY IN AMERICA. USA+45 USA-45...POLICY   CONCPT
JURID IDEA/COMP. PAGE 72 E1435   ORD/FREE

                                                                      B65
MILLER H.H..THE CASE FOR LIBERTY. USA-45 LAW JUDGE   COLONIAL
CT/SYS...AUD/VIS 18 PRE/US/AM CASEBOOK. PAGE 73   JURID
E1460   PROB/SOLV

                                                                      B65
MOELLER R..LUDWIG DER BAYER UND DIE KURIE IM KAMPF   JURID
UM DAS REICH. GERMANY LAW SECT LEGIT LEAD GP/REL   CHIEF
CATHISM CONSERVE 14 LUDWIG/BAV POPE CHURCH/STA.   CHOOSE
PAGE 74 E1478   NAT/LISM

                                                                      B65
MONCONDUIT F..LA COMMISSION EUROPEENNE DES DROITS   INT/LAW
DE L'HOMME. DIPLOM AGREE GP/REL ORD/FREE PWR   INT/ORG
...BIBLIOG 20 TREATY. PAGE 74 E1483   ADJUD
                                                       JURID

                                                                      B65
MOSTECKY V..SOVIET LEGAL BIBLIOGRAPHY. USSR LEGIS   BIBLIOG/A
PRESS WRITING CONFER ADJUD CT/SYS REV MARXISM   LAW
...INT/LAW JURID DICTIONARY 20. PAGE 75 E1503   COM
                                                       CONSTN

                                                                      B65
MURPHY W.F..WIRETAPPING ON TRIAL: A CASE STUDY IN   JURID
THE JUDICIAL PROCESS. CONSTN ELITES CT/SYS CRIME   LAW
MORAL ORD/FREE...DECISION SUPREME/CT. PAGE 75 E1511   POLICY

                                                                      B65
NJ LEGIS REAPPORT PLAN COMM,PUBLIC HEARING ON   APPORT
REDISTRICTING AND REAPPORTIONMENT. USA+45 CONSTN   REPRESENT
VOL/ASSN LEGIS DEBATE...POLICY GEOG CENSUS 20   PROVS
NEW/JERSEY. PAGE 77 E1552   JURID

                                                                      B65
O'CONNELL D.P..INTERNATIONAL LAW (2 VOLS.). WOR+45   INT/LAW
WOR-45 ECO/DEV ECO/UNDEV INT/ORG NAT/G AGREE   DIPLOM
...POLICY JURID CONCPT NAT/COMP 20 TREATY. PAGE 78   CT/SYS
E1566

B65

PARKER D.,CIVIL LIBERTIES CASE STUDIES AND THE LAW. ORD/FREE
SECT ADJUD...CONCPT WORSHIP 20 SUPREME/CT   JURID
CIV/RIGHTS FREE/SPEE. PAGE 80 E1598   CONSTN
                                                           JUDGE

B65

PROEHL P.O.,FOREIGN ENTERPRISE IN NIGERIA. NIGERIA ECO/UNDEV
FINAN LABOR NAT/G TAX 20. PAGE 83 E1656   ECO/TAC
                                                  JURID
                                                  CAP/ISM

B65

PYLEE M.V.,CONSTITUTIONAL GOVERNMENT IN INDIA (2ND CONSTN
REV. ED.). INDIA POL/PAR EX/STRUC DIPLOM COLONIAL NAT/G
CT/SYS PARL/PROC PRIVIL...JURID 16/20. PAGE 83   PROVS
E1665   FEDERAL

B65

RENNER K.,MENSCH UND GESELLSCHAFT - GRUNDRISS EINER SOC
SOZIOLOGIE (2ND ED.). STRATA FAM LABOR PROF/ORG WAR STRUCT
...JURID CLASSIF 20. PAGE 84 E1685   NAT/G
                                                    SOCIETY

B65

SCHROEDER O.,DEFACTO SEGREGATION AND CIVIL RIGHTS. ANTHOL
LAW PROVS SCHOOL WORKER ATTIT HABITAT HEALTH WEALTH DISCRIM
...JURID CHARTS 19/20 NEGRO SUPREME/CT KKK. PAGE 88 RACE/REL
E1766   ORD/FREE

B65

SCHUBERT G.,THE JUDICIAL MIND: THE ATTITUDES AND   CT/SYS
IDEOLOGIES OF SUPREME COURT JUSTICES 1946-1963.   JUDGE
USA+45 ELITES NAT/G CONTROL PERS/REL MAJORITY   ATTIT
CONSERVE...DECISION JURID MODAL STAT TREND GP/COMP NEW/LIB
GAME. PAGE 88 E1774

B65

SHARMA S.A.,PARLIAMENTARY GOVERNMENT IN INDIA.   NAT/G
INDIA FINAN LOC/G PROVS DELIB/GP PLAN ADMIN CT/SYS CONSTN
FEDERAL...JURID 20. PAGE 90 E1814   PARL/PROC
                                                    LEGIS

B65

SMITH C.,THE OMBUDSMAN: A BIBLIOGRAPHY (PAMPHLET). BIBLIOG
DENMARK SWEDEN USA+45 LAW LEGIS JUDGE GOV/REL   ADMIN
GP/REL...JURID 20. PAGE 92 E1841   CT/SYS
                                                    ADJUD

B65

SNOW J.H.,REAPPORTIONMENT. LAW CONSTN NAT/G GOV/REL APPORT
ORD/FREE...JURID 20 SUPREME/CT CONNECTICT. PAGE 92 ADJUD
E1848   LEGIS
                                                    PROVS

B65

STONE J.,HUMAN LAW AND HUMAN JUSTICE. JUDGE...SOC CONCPT
MYTH IDEA/COMP. PAGE 94 E1881   SANCTION
                                                    JURID

B65

STOREY R.G.,OUR UNALIENABLE RIGHTS. LAW SECT CT/SYS CONSTN
SUFF DISCRIM 17/20 CIVIL/LIB ENGLSH/LAW. PAGE 94   JURID
E1882   ORD/FREE
                                                    LEGIS

B65

THOMAS A.V.,NONINTERVENTION: THE LAW AND ITS IMPORT INT/LAW
IN THE AMERICAS. L/A+17C USA+45 USA-45 WOR+45   PWR
DIPLOM ADJUD...JURID IDEA/COMP 20 UN INTERVENT.   COERCE
PAGE 96 E1917

B65

TRESOLINI R.J.,AMERICAN CONSTITUTIONAL LAW. USA+45 CONSTN
USA-45 NAT/G ADJUD ORD/FREE PWR...POLICY BIOG 20   CT/SYS
SUPREME/CT CASEBOOK. PAGE 97 E1939   JURID
                                                    LAW

B65

UNIVERSAL REFERENCE SYSTEM,INTERNATIONAL AFFAIRS: BIBLIOG/A
VOLUME I IN THE POLITICAL SCIENCE, GOVERNMENT, AND GEN/METH
PUBLIC POLICY SERIES....DECISION ECOMETRIC GEOG   COMPUT/IR
INT/LAW JURID MGT PHIL/SCI PSY SOC. PAGE 98 E1972 DIPLOM

B65

US HOUSE COMM ON JUDICIARY,IMMIGRATION AND   GP/REL
NATIONALITY. LAW...POLICY 20. PAGE 100 E2007   NAT/LISM
                                                    NAT/G
                                                    JURID

B65

VON RENESSE E.A.,UNVOLLENDETE DEMOKRATIEN. AFR   ECO/UNDEV
ISLAM S/ASIA SOCIETY ACT/RES COLONIAL...JURID   NAT/COMP
CHARTS BIBLIOG METH 13/20. PAGE 104 E2083   SOVEREIGN

B65

VONGLAHN G.,LAW AMONG NATIONS: AN INTRODUCTION TO CONSTN
PUBLIC INTERNATIONAL LAW. UNIV WOR+45 LAW INT/ORG JURID
NAT/G LEGIT EXEC RIGID/FLEX...CONCPT TIME/SEQ   INT/LAW
GEN/LAWS UN TOT/POP 20. PAGE 104 E2084

L65

FORTE W.E.,"THE FOOD AND DRUG ADMINISTRATION, THE CONTROL
FEDERAL TRADE COMMISSION AND THE DECEPTIVE   HEALTH
PACKAGING." ROUTINE...JURID 20 FTC. PAGE 39 E0772 ADJUD
                                                    INDUS

S65

AMRAM P.W.,"REPORT ON THE TENTH SESSION OF THE   VOL/ASSN
HAGUE CONFERENCE ON PRIVATE INTERNATIONAL LAW."   DELIB/GP
USA+45 WOR+45 INT/ORG CREATE LEGIT ADJUD ALL/VALS INT/LAW
...JURID CONCPT METH/CNCPT OBS GEN/METH 20. PAGE 4
E0085

S65

BEVANS C.I.,"GHANA AND UNITED STATES - UNITED   NAT/G
KINGDOM AGREEMENTS." UK USA+45 LAW DELIB/GP   LEGIT
EX/STRUC ORD/FREE...JURID METH/CNCPT GEN/LAWS 20. GHANA
PAGE 11 E0222   DIPLOM

S65

GROSS L.,"PROBLEMS OF INTERNATIONAL ADJUDICATION   LAW
AND COMPLIANCE WITH INTERNATIONAL LAW: SOME SIMPLE METH/CNCPT
SOLUTIONS." WOR+45 SOCIETY NAT/G DOMIN LEGIT ADJUD INT/LAW
CT/SYS RIGID/FLEX HEALTH PWR...JURID NEW/IDEA
COLD/WAR 20. PAGE 48 E0951

S65

HAZARD J.N.,"CO-EXISTENCE LAW BOWS OUT." WOR+45 R+D PROF/ORG
INT/ORG VOL/ASSN CONSULT DELIB/GP ACT/RES CREATE   ADJUD
PEACE KNOWL...JURID CONCPT COLD/WAR VAL/FREE 20.
PAGE 51 E1018

S65

MAC CHESNEY B.,"SOME COMMENTS ON THE 'QUARANTINE' INT/ORG
OF CUBA." USA+45 WOR+45 NAT/G BAL/PWR DIPLOM LEGIT LAW
ROUTINE ATTIT ORD/FREE...JURID METH/CNCPT 20.   CUBA
PAGE 67 E1337   USSR

S65

MCWHINNEY E.,"CHANGING INTERNATIONAL LAW METHOD AND LAW
OBJECTIVES IN THE ERA OF THE SOVIET-WESTERN   TREND
DETENTE." COM USA+45 NAT/G BAL/PWR CT/SYS ATTIT
ORD/FREE...HUM JURID NEW/IDEA COLD/WAR VAL/FREE 20.
PAGE 71 E1430

S65

STEIN E.,"TOWARD SUPREMACY OF TREATY-CONSTITUTION ADJUD
BY JUDICIAL FIAT: ON THE MARGIN OF THE COSTA CASE." CONSTN
EUR+WWI ITALY WOR+45 INT/ORG NAT/G LEGIT REGION   SOVEREIGN
NAT/LISM PWR...JURID CONCPT TREND TOT/POP VAL/FREE INT/LAW
20. PAGE 93 E1870

S65

ULMER S.S.,"TOWARD A THEORY OF SUBGROUP FORMATION CT/SYS
IN THE UNITED STATES SUPREME COURT." USA+45 ROUTINE ADJUD
CHOOSE PWR...JURID STAT CON/ANAL SIMUL SUPREME/CT. ELITES
PAGE 97 E1952   INGP/REL

B66

AMERICAN JOURNAL COMP LAW,THE AMERICAN JOURNAL OF IDEA/COMP
COMPARATIVE LAW READER. EUR+WWI USA+45 USA-45 LAW JURID
CONSTN LOC/G MUNIC NAT/G DIPLOM...ANTHOL 20   INT/LAW
SUPREME/CT EURCT/JUST. PAGE 4 E0081   CT/SYS

B66

ANDERSON S.V.,CANADIAN OMBUDSMAN PROPOSALS. CANADA NAT/G
LEGIS DEBATE PARL/PROC...MAJORIT JURID TIME/SEQ   CREATE
IDEA/COMP 20 OMBUDSMAN PARLIAMENT. PAGE 5 E0092   ADMIN
                                                    POL/PAR

B66

BAHRO H.,DAS KINDSCHAFTSRECHT IN DER UNION DER   JURID
SOZIALISTITSCHEN SOWJETREPUBLIKEN. USSR SECT   AGE/C
EDU/PROP CONTROL PWR...SOC/WK 20. PAGE 7 E0133   PERS/REL
                                                    SUPEGO

B66

BAXTER M.G.,DANIEL WEBSTER & THE SUPREME COURT. LAW CONSTN
NAT/G PROF/ORG DEBATE ADJUD LEAD FEDERAL PERSON.   CT/SYS
PAGE 8 E0156   JURID

B66

BEDI A.S.,FREEDOM OF EXPRESSION AND SECURITY;   METH
COMPARATIVE STUDY OF FUNCTIONS OF SUPREME COURTS IN CT/SYS
UNITED STATES AND INDIA. INDIA USA+45 LAW CONSTN   ADJUD
PROB/SOLV...DECISION JURID BIBLIOG 20 SUPREME/CT   ORD/FREE
FREE/SPEE AMEND/I. PAGE 9 E0175

B66

BEELEY A.L.,THE BAIL SYSTEM IN CHICAGO. LAW MUNIC JURID

PUB/INST EFFICIENCY MORAL...CRIMLGY METH/CNCPT STAT CT/SYS
20 CHICAGO. PAGE 9 E0176   CRIME
                                                          ADJUD

                                                          B66
BRENNAN J.T.,THE COST OF THE AMERICAN JUDICIAL   COST
SYSTEM. USA+45 PROF/ORG TV ADMIN EFFICIENCY.   CT/SYS
PAGE 15 E0292   ADJUD
                                                          JURID

                                                          B66
BROWNLIE I.,PRINCIPLES OF PUBLIC INTERNATIONAL LAW.   INT/LAW
WOR+45 WOR-45 LAW JUDGE REPAR ADJUD SOVEREIGN   DIPLOM
...JURID T. PAGE 16 E0319   INT/ORG

                                                          B66
CAMPBELL E.,PARLIAMENTARY PRIVILEGE IN AUSTRALIA.   LEGIS
UK LAW CONSTN COLONIAL ROLE ORD/FREE SOVEREIGN   PARL/PROC
18/20 COMMONWLTH AUSTRAL FREE/SPEE PARLIAMENT.   JURID
PAGE 19 E0370   PRIVIL

                                                          B66
CARLIN J.E.,LAWYER'S ETHICS. CLIENT STRUCT CONSULT   ATTIT
PERS/REL PWR...JURID OBS CHARTS 20. PAGE 19 E0378   PROF/ORG
                                                          INT

                                                          B66
COUNCIL OF EUROPE,EUROPEAN CONVENTION ON HUMAN   ORD/FREE
RIGHTS - COLLECTED TEXTS (5TH ED.). EUR+WWI DIPLOM   DELIB/GP
ADJUD CT/SYS...INT/LAW 20 ECHR. PAGE 26 E0520   INT/ORG
                                                          JURID

                                                          B66
COUNCIL OF STATE GOVERNMENTS,THE HANDBOOK ON   CRIME
INTERSTATE CRIME CONTROL. USA+45 PUB/INST DELIB/GP   GOV/REL
AGREE AGE/Y 20 INTST/CRIM. PAGE 27 E0524   CONTROL
                                                          JURID

                                                          B66
DOUMA J.,BIBLIOGRAPHY ON THE INTERNATIONAL COURT   BIBLIOG/A
INCLUDING THE PERMANENT COURT, 1918-1964. WOR+45   INT/ORG
WOR-45 DELIB/GP WAR PRIVIL...JURID NAT/COMP 20 UN   CT/SYS
LEAGUE/NAT. PAGE 33 E0645   DIPLOM

                                                          B66
EDWARDS C.D.,TRADE REGULATIONS OVERSEAS. IRELAND   INT/TRADE
NEW/ZEALND SOUTH/AFR NAT/G CAP/ISM TARIFFS CONTROL   DIPLOM
...POLICY JURID 20 EEC CHINJAP. PAGE 34 E0676   INT/LAW
                                                          ECO/TAC

                                                          B66
EPSTEIN F.T.,THE AMERICAN BIBLIOGRAPHY OF RUSSIAN   BIBLIOG
AND EAST EUROPEAN STUDIES FOR 1964. USSR LOC/G   COM
NAT/G POL/PAR FORCES ADMIN ARMS/CONT...JURID CONCPT   MARXISM
20 UN. PAGE 35 E0694   DIPLOM

                                                          B66
FEINE H.E.,REICH UND KIRCHE. CHRIST-17C MOD/EUR   JURID
ROMAN/EMP LAW CHOOSE ATTIT 10/19 CHURCH/STA   SECT
ROMAN/LAW. PAGE 37 E0728   NAT/G
                                                          GP/REL

                                                          B66
FUCHS W.P.,STAAT UND KIRCHE IM WANDEL DER   SECT
JAHRHUNDERTE. EUR+WWI MOD/EUR UK REV...JURID CONCPT   NAT/G
4/20 EUROPE CHRISTIAN CHURCH/STA. PAGE 41 E0817   ORD/FREE
                                                          GP/REL

                                                          B66
HARVEY W.B.,LAW AND SOCIAL CHANGE IN GHANA. AFR   JURID
GHANA CONSULT CONTROL CT/SYS INGP/REL 20. PAGE 51   CONSTN
E1011   LEAD
                                                          ORD/FREE

                                                          B66
HAUSNER G.,JUSTICE IN JERUSALEM. GERMANY ISRAEL   ADJUD
SOCIETY KIN DIPLOM LEGIT CT/SYS PARTIC MURDER   CRIME
MAJORITY ATTIT FASCISM...INT/LAW JURID 20 JEWS   RACE/REL
WAR/TRIAL. PAGE 51 E1013   COERCE

                                                          B66
HIDAYATULLAH M.,DEMOCRACY IN INDIA AND THE JUDICIAL   NAT/G
PROCESS. INDIA EX/STRUC LEGIS LEAD GOV/REL ATTIT   CT/SYS
ORD/FREE...MAJORIT CONCPT 20 NEHRU/J. PAGE 52 E1040   CONSTN
                                                          JURID

                                                          B66
HOLDSWORTH W.S.,A HISTORY OF ENGLISH LAW; THE   BIOG
CENTURIES OF SETTLEMENT AND REFORM (VOL. XVI). UK   PERSON
LOC/G NAT/G EX/STRUC LEGIS CT/SYS LEAD ATTIT   PROF/ORG
...POLICY DECISION JURID IDEA/COMP 18 PARLIAMENT.   LAW
PAGE 54 E1083

                                                          B66
INSTITUTE COMP STUDY POL SYS,DOMINICAN REPUBLIC   SUFF
ELECTION FACT BOOK. DOMIN/REP LAW LEGIS REPRESENT   CHOOSE

...JURID CHARTS 20. PAGE 57 E1126   POL/PAR
                                                          NAT/G

                                                          B66
INTL ATOMIC ENERGY AGENCY,INTERNATIONAL CONVENTIONS   DIPLOM
ON CIVIL LIABILITY FOR NUCLEAR DAMAGE. FUT WOR+45   INT/ORG
ADJUD WAR COST PEACE SOVEREIGN...JURID 20. PAGE 57   DELIB/GP
E1135   NUC/PWR

                                                          B66
KEAY E.A.,THE NATIVE AND CUSTOMARY COURTS OF   AFR
NIGERIA. NIGERIA CONSTN ELITES NAT/G TOP/EX PARTIC   ADJUD
REGION...DECISION JURID 19/20. PAGE 60 E1190   LAW

                                                          B66
KERR M.H.,ISLAMIC REFORM: THE POLITICAL AND LEGAL   LAW
THEORIES OF MUHAMMAD 'ABDUH AND RASHID RIDA. NAT/G   CONCPT
SECT LEAD SOVEREIGN CONSERVE...JURID BIBLIOG   ISLAM
WORSHIP 20. PAGE 60 E1204

                                                          B66
KUNST H.,EVANGELISCHES STAATSLEXIKON. LAW CONSTN   JURID
POL/PAR...PHIL/SCI CONCPT DICTIONARY. PAGE 62 E1232   SECT
                                                          SOC
                                                          NAT/G

                                                          B66
KURLAND P.B.,THE SUPREME COURT REVIEW. USA+45   JURID
USA-45 LAW LABOR SUFF...ANTHOL 20 SUPREME/CT.   PROB/SOLV
PAGE 62 E1240   ADJUD
                                                          NAT/G

                                                          B66
LEHMANN L.,LEGAL UND OPPORTUN - POLITISCHE JUSTIZ   ORD/FREE
IN DER BUNDESREPUBLIK. GERMANY/W EDU/PROP ADJUD   POL/PAR
CONTROL PARL/PROC COERCE TOTALISM ATTIT 20   JURID
COM/PARTY. PAGE 64 E1281   LEGIS

                                                          B66
LOFTON J.,JUSTICE AND THE PRESS. EDU/PROP GOV/REL   PRESS
MORAL 20. PAGE 66 E1320   JURID
                                                          CT/SYS
                                                          ORD/FREE

                                                          B66
MC CONNELL J.P.,LAW AND BUSINESS: PATTERNS AND   ECO/DEV
ISSUES IN COMMERCIAL LAW. USA+45 USA-45 LOC/G   JURID
WORKER LICENSE CRIME REPRESENT GP/REL 20. PAGE 70   ADJUD
E1397   MGT

                                                          B66
MCNAIR A.D.,THE LEGAL EFFECTS OF WAR. UK FINAN   JURID
DIPLOM ORD/FREE 20 ENGLSH/LAW. PAGE 71 E1425   WAR
                                                          INT/TRADE
                                                          LABOR

                                                          B66
MEDER A.E. JR.,LEGISLATIVE APPORTIONMENT. USA+45   APPORT
BAL/PWR REPRESENT ORD/FREE PWR...JURID 20   LEGIS
SUPREME/CT. PAGE 72 E1433   MATH
                                                          POLICY

                                                          B66
MENDELSON W.,JUSTICES BLACK AND FRANKFURTER: JURID
CONFLICT IN THE COURT (2ND ED.). NAT/G PROVS   ADJUD
PROB/SOLV BAL/PWR CONTROL FEDERAL ISOLAT ANOMIE   IDEA/COMP
ORD/FREE...DECISION 20 SUPREME/CT BLACK/HL   ROLE
FRANKFUR/F. PAGE 72 E1439

                                                          B66
PLATE H.,PARTEIFINANZIERUNG UND GRUNDESETZ. GERMANY   POL/PAR
NAT/G PLAN GIVE PAY INCOME WEALTH...JURID 20.   CONSTN
PAGE 81 E1619   FINAN

                                                          B66
POLLACK R.S.,THE INDIVIDUAL'S RIGHTS AND   INT/LAW
INTERNATIONAL ORGANIZATION. LAW INT/ORG DELIB/GP   ORD/FREE
SUPEGO...JURID SOC/INTEG 20 TREATY UN. PAGE 81   DIPLOM
E1623   PERSON

                                                          B66
SHAPIRO M.,FREEDOM OF SPEECH: THE SUPREME COURT AND   CT/SYS
JUDICIAL REVIEW. USA+45 LEGIS...CHARTS 20   ORD/FREE
SUPREME/CT FREE/SPEE. PAGE 90 E1812   CONSTN
                                                          JURID

                                                          B66
SOBEL N.R.,THE NEW CONFESSION STANDARDS, MIRANDA V.   JURID
ARIZONA. USA+45 USA-45 LAW PROF/ORG EDU/PROP 20   CT/SYS
SUPREME/CT. PAGE 92 E1849   ORD/FREE
                                                          ADJUD

                                                          B66
STEVENS R.E.,REFERENCE BOOKS IN THE SOCIAL SCIENCES   BIBLIOG/A
AND HUMANITIES. CULTURE PERF/ART SECT EDU/PROP   SOC
...JURID PSY SOC/WK STAT 20 MUSIC. PAGE 93 E1873   HUM

ART/METH

B66
STUMPF S.E.,MORALITY AND THE LAW. USA+45 LAW   JURID
CULTURE PROB/SOLV DOMIN ADJUD CONTROL ADJUST   MORAL
ALL/IDEOS MARXISM...INT/LAW 20 SUPREME/CT. PAGE 94   CT/SYS
E1890

B66
UNITED NATIONS,INTERNATIONAL SPACE BIBLIOGRAPHY.   BIBLIOG
FUT INT/ORG TEC/DEV DIPLOM ARMS/CONT NUC/PWR   SPACE
...JURID SOC UN. PAGE 98 E1969   PEACE
R+D

B66
US SENATE COMM ON JUDICIARY,SCHOOL PRAYER. USA+45   SCHOOL
LAW LOC/G SECT ADJUD WORSHIP 20 SENATE DEITY.   JURID
PAGE 103 E2058   NAT/G

B66
WASHINGTON S.H.,BIBLIOGRAPHY: LABOR-MANAGEMENT   BIBLIOG
RELATIONS ACT, 1947 AS AMENDED BY LABOR-MANAGEMENT   LAW
REPORTING AND DISCLOSURE ACT, 1959. USA+45 CONSTN   LABOR
INDUS DELIB/GP LEGIS WORKER BARGAIN ECO/TAC ADJUD   MGT
GP/REL NEW/LIB...JURID CONGRESS. PAGE 105 E2100

B66
WILSON G.,CASES AND MATERIALS ON CONSTITUTIONAL AND   JURID
ADMINISTRATIVE LAW. UK LAW NAT/G EX/STRUC LEGIS   ADMIN
BAL/PWR BUDGET DIPLOM ADJUD CONTROL CT/SYS GOV/REL   CONSTN
ORD/FREE 20 PARLIAMENT ENGLSH/LAW. PAGE 106 E2126   PWR

S66
BURDETTE F.L.,"SELECTED ARTICLES AND DOCUMENTS ON   BIBLIOG
AMERICAN GOVERNMENT AND POLITICS." LAW LOC/G MUNIC   USA+45
NAT/G POL/PAR PROVS LEGIS BAL/PWR ADMIN EXEC   JURID
REPRESENT MGT. PAGE 17 E0331   CONSTN

S66
GASS O.,"THE LITERATURE OF AMERICAN GOVERNMENT."   NEW/LIB
CONSTN DRIVE ORD/FREE...JURID CONCPT METH/CNCPT   CT/SYS
IDEA/COMP 20 WILSON/W BEARD/CA LINK/AS. PAGE 42   NAT/G
E0841

S66
NYC BAR ASSOCIATION RECORD,"PAPERBACKS FOR THE   BIBLIOG
BAR." USA+45 LEGIS ADJUD CT/SYS. PAGE 78 E1562   JURID
LAW
WRITING

S66
POLSBY N.W.,"BOOKS IN THE FIELD: POLITICAL   BIBLIOG/A
SCIENCE." LAW CONSTN LOC/G NAT/G LEGIS ADJUD PWR 20   ATTIT
SUPREME/CT. PAGE 81 E1627   ADMIN
JURID

S66
SHEEHY E.P.,"SELECTED REFERENCE BOOKS OF   BIBLIOG/A
1965-1966." AGRI PERF/ART PRESS...GEOG HUM JURID   INDEX
SOC LING WORSHIP. PAGE 91 E1817   CLASSIF

S66
SHKLAR J.,"SELECTED ARTICLES AND DOCUMENTS ON   BIBLIOG
POLITICAL THEORY." ADJUD REV...JURID PHIL/SCI   ELITES
IDEA/COMP. PAGE 91 E1820   PWR

B67
AMDS W.E.,DELINQUENCY PREVENTION: THEORY AND   AGE/Y
PRACTICE. USA+45 SOCIETY FAM SCHOOL SECT FORCES   CRIME
PROB/SOLV...HEAL JURID PREDICT ANTHOL. PAGE 4 E0071   PUB/INST
LAW

B67
ASCH S.H.,POLICE AUTHORITY AND THE RIGHTS OF THE   FORCES
INDIVIDUAL. CONSTN DOMIN ADJUD CT/SYS...JURID 20.   OP/RES
PAGE 6 E0106   ORD/FREE

B67
BAKKE E.W.,UNIONS, MANAGEMENT AND THE PUBLIC*   LABOR
READINGS AND TEXT. WORKER LOBBY...POLICY JURID   INDUS
ANTHOL T. PAGE 7 E0143   ADJUD
GP/REL

B67
BEAL E.F.,THE PRACTICE OF COLLECTIVE BARGAINING   BARGAIN
(3RD ED.). USA+45 WOR+45 ECO/DEV INDUS LG/CO   MGT
PROF/ORG WORKER ECO/TAC GP/REL WEALTH...JURID   LABOR
METH/CNCPT. PAGE 8 E0160   ADJUD

B67
BIBBY J.,ON CAPITOL HILL. POL/PAR LOBBY PARL/PROC   CONFER
GOV/REL PERS/REL...JURID PHIL/SCI OBS INT BIBLIOG   LEGIS
20 CONGRESS PRESIDENT. PAGE 12 E0224   CREATE
LEAD

B67
BOHANNAN P.,LAW AND WARFARE. CULTURE CT/SYS COERCE   METH/COMP
REV PEACE...JURID SOC CONCPT ANTHOL 20. PAGE 13   ADJUD
E0259   WAR
LAW

B67
BOLES D.E.,THE TWO SWORDS. USA+45 USA-45 LAW CONSTN   SCHOOL
SOCIETY FINAN PRESS CT/SYS...HEAL JURID BIBLIOG   EDU/PROP
WORSHIP 20 SUPREME/CT CHURCH/STA. PAGE 13 E0263   ADJUD

B67
BONGER W.A.,CRIMINALITY AND ECONOMIC CONDITIONS.   PERSON
MOD/EUR STRUCT INDUS WORKER EDU/PROP CRIME HABITAT   CRIMLGY
ALL/VALS...JURID SOC 20 REFORMERS. PAGE 14 E0265   IDEA/COMP
ANOMIE

B67
BROWN L.N.,FRENCH ADMINISTRATIVE LAW. FRANCE UK   EX/STRUC
CONSTN NAT/G LEGIS DOMIN CONTROL EXEC PARL/PROC PWR   LAW
...JURID METH/COMP GEN/METH. PAGE 16 E0314   IDEA/COMP
CT/SYS

B67
CAHIER P.,LE DROIT DIPLOMATIQUE CONTEMPORAIN.   INT/LAW
INT/ORG CHIEF ADMIN...T 20. PAGE 18 E0358   DIPLOM
JURID

B67
COHEN M.R.,LAW AND THE SOCIAL ORDER: ESSAYS IN   JURID
LEGAL PHILOSOPHY. USA-45 CONSULT WORKER ECO/TAC   LABOR
ATTIT WEALTH...POLICY WELF/ST SOC 20 NEW/DEAL   IDEA/COMP
DEPRESSION. PAGE 24 E0467

B67
COX A.,CIVIL RIGHTS, THE CONSTITUTION, AND THE   LAW
COURTS. CONSTN EDU/PROP CRIME DISCRIM ATTIT...JURID   FEDERAL
20. PAGE 27 E0533   RACE/REL
PRESS

B67
DIEGUES M.,SOCIAL SCIENCE IN LATIN AMERICA. L/A+17C   METH
...JURID SOC ANTHOL 20. PAGE 31 E0624   ACADEM
EDU/PROP
ACT/RES

B67
ELDRIDGE W.B.,NARCOTICS AND THE LAW: A CRITIQUE OF   LAW
THE AMERICAN EXPERIMENT IN NARCOTIC DRUG CONTROL.   INSPECT
PUB/INST ACT/RES PLAN LICENSE GP/REL EFFICIENCY   BIO/SOC
ATTIT HEALTH...CRIMLGY HEAL STAT 20 ABA DEPT/HEW   JURID
NARCO/ACT. PAGE 34 E0679

B67
HODGKINSON R.G.,THE ORIGINS OF THE NATIONAL HEALTH   HEAL
SERVICE: THE MEDICAL SERVICES OF THE NEW POOR LAW,   NAT/G
1834-1871. UK INDUS MUNIC WORKER PROB/SOLV   POLICY
EFFICIENCY ATTIT HEALTH WEALTH SOCISM...JURID   LAW
SOC/WK 19/20. PAGE 53 E1062

B67
KING W.L.,MELVILLE WESTON FULLER: CHIEF JUSTICE OF   BIOG
THE UNITED STATES, 1888-1910. USA-45 CONSTN FINAN   CT/SYS
LABOR TAX GOV/REL PERS/REL ATTIT PERSON PWR...JURID   LAW
BIBLIOG 19/20 SUPREME/CT FULLER/MW HOLMES/OW.   ADJUD
PAGE 61 E1216

B67
LENG S.C.,JUSTICE IN COMMUNIST CHINA: A SURVEY OF   CT/SYS
THE JUDICIAL SYSTEM OF THE CHINESE PEOPLE'S   ADJUD
REPUBLIC. CHINA/COM LAW CONSTN LOC/G NAT/G PROF/ORG   JURID
CONSULT FORCES ADMIN CRIME ORD/FREE...BIBLIOG 20   MARXISM
MAO. PAGE 64 E1284

B67
LONG E.V.,THE INTRUDERS: THE INVASION OF PRIVACY BY   LAW
GOVERNMENT AND INDUSTRY. USA+45 COM/IND INDUS LEGIS   PARTIC
TASK PERS/REL...JURID 20 CONGRESS. PAGE 66 E1324   NAT/G

B67
MEYERS M.,SOURCES OF THE AMERICAN REPUBLIC: A   COLONIAL
DOCUMENTARY HISTORY OF POLITICS, SOCIETY, AND   REV
THOUGHT (VOL. I, REV. ED.). USA-45 CULTURE STRUCT   WAR
NAT/G LEGIS LEAD ATTIT...JURID SOC ANTHOL 17/19
PRESIDENT. PAGE 72 E1450

B67
PLANO J.C.,FORGING WORLD ORDER: THE POLITICS OF   INT/ORG
INTERNATIONAL ORGANIZATION. PROB/SOLV DIPLOM   ADMIN
CONTROL CENTRAL RATIONAL ORD/FREE...INT/LAW CHARTS   JURID
BIBLIOG 20 UN LEAGUE/NAT. PAGE 81 E1618

B67
UNIVERSAL REFERENCE SYSTEM,LAW, JURISPRUDENCE, AND   BIBLIOG/A
JUDICIAL PROCESS (VOLUME VII). WOR+45 WOR-45 CONSTN   LAW
NAT/G LEGIS JUDGE CT/SYS...INT/LAW COMPUT/IR   JURID

GEN/METH METH. PAGE 99 E1976
ADJUD

B67
US PRES TASK FORCE ADMIN JUS,TASK FORCE REPORT: THE CT/SYS
COURTS. USA+45 CONSULT CONFER...JURID CHARTS. ADJUD
PAGE 101 E2025 ROUTINE
ADMIN

B67
VILE M.J.C.,CONSTITUTIONALISM AND THE SEPARATION OF CONSTN
POWERS. FRANCE UK USA+45 USA-45 NAT/G ADJUD CONTROL BAL/PWR
GOV/REL...POLICY DECISION JURID GEN/LAWS 15/20 CONCPT
MONTESQ. PAGE 104 E2076 LAW

L67
BAADE H.W.,"THE ACQUIRED RIGHTS OF INTERNATIONAL INT/ORG
PUBLIC SERVANTS; A CASE STUDY IN RECEPTION OF WORKER
PUBLIC LAW." WOR+45 DELIB/GP DIPLOM ORD/FREE ADJUD
...INT/LAW JURID UN. PAGE 7 E0125 LAW

L67
BLUMBERG A.S.,"THE PRACTICE OF LAW AS CONFIDENCE CT/SYS
GAME; ORGANIZATIONAL COOPTATION OF A PROFESSION." ADJUD
USA+45 CLIENT SOCIETY CONSULT ROLE JURID. PAGE 13 GP/REL
E0252 ADMIN

L67
HOWARD A.E.D.,"MR. JUSTICE BLACK: THE NEGRO PROTEST ADJUD
MOVEMENT AND THE RULE OF LAW." USA+45 CONSTN CT/SYS JUDGE
CHOOSE GP/REL...DECISION JURID NEGRO SUPREME/CT. LAW
PAGE 55 E1100 REPRESENT

L67
LISSITZYN O.J.,"TREATIES AND CHANGED CIRCUMSTANCES AGREE
(REBUS SIC STANTIBUS)" WOR+45 CONSEN...JURID 20. DIPLOM
PAGE 65 E1307 INT/LAW

L67
NAGEL S.S.,"DISPARITIES IN CRIMINAL PROCEDURE." ADJUD
STRATA NAT/G PROVS EDU/PROP RACE/REL AGE HABITAT DISCRIM
SEX...JURID CHARTS 20. PAGE 76 E1519 STRUCT
ACT/RES

L67
WAELBROECK M.,"THE APPLICATION OF EEC LAW BY INT/LAW
NATIONAL COURTS." EUR+WWI INT/ORG CT/SYS...JURID NAT/G
EEC TREATY. PAGE 104 E2090 LAW
PROB/SOLV

S67
BOHANNAN P.,"INSTITUTIONS OF DIVORCE, FAMILY, AND FAM
THE LAW." WOR+45 LAW CONSULT...JURID SOC. PAGE 13 MARRIAGE
E0258 ADJUD
SOCIETY

S67
CARTER R.M.,"SOME FACTORS IN SENTENCING POLICY." ADJUD
LAW PUB/INST CRIME PERS/REL...POLICY JURID SOC CT/SYS
TREND CON/ANAL CHARTS SOC/EXP 20. PAGE 20 E0403 ADMIN

S67
DALFEN C.M.,"THE WORLD COURT IN IDLE SPLENDOUR: THE CT/SYS
BASIS OF STATES' ATTITUDES." WOR+45 LAW ADJUD INT/ORG
COERCE...JURID 20 UN WORLD/CT. PAGE 28 E0562 INT/LAW
DIPLOM

S67
DANIEL C.,"FREEDOM, EQUITY, AND THE WAR ON WEALTH
POVERTY." USA+45 WORKER ECO/TAC JURID. PAGE 29 INCOME
E0566 SOCIETY
ORD/FREE

S67
DEUTSCH E.P.,"A JUDICIAL PATH TO WORLD PEACE." FUT INT/LAW
WOR+45 CONSTN PROB/SOLV DIPLOM LICENSE ADJUD INT/ORG
SANCTION CHOOSE REPRESENT NAT/LISM SOVEREIGN 20 JURID
ICJ. PAGE 31 E0611 PEACE

S67
FABREGA J.,"ANTECEDENTES EXTRANJEROS EN LA CONSTN
CONSTITUCION PANAMENA." CUBA L/A+17C PANAMA URUGUAY JURID
EX/STRUC LEGIS DIPLOM ORD/FREE 19/20 COLOMB NAT/G
MEXIC/AMER. PAGE 36 E0709 PARL/PROC

S67
GRIFFIN H.C.,"PREJUDICIAL PUBLICITY: SEARCH FOR A LAW
CIVIL REMEDY." EDU/PROP CONTROL DISCRIM...JURID 20. SANCTION
PAGE 47 E0937 PRESS
ADJUD

S67
HIRSCH W.Z.,"SOME ECONOMIC IMPLICATIONS OF CITY ECO/TAC
PLANNING." LAW PROB/SOLV RATION EFFICIENCY...METH JURID
20. PAGE 53 E1050 MUNIC
PLAN

S67
HORVATH B.,"COMPARATIVE CONFLICTS LAW AND THE INT/LAW
CONCEPT OF CHANGING LAW." UNIV RATIONAL...JURID IDEA/COMP
LOG. PAGE 55 E1099 DIPLOM
CONCPT

S67
KENNEDY R.F.,"TOWARD A NATION WHERE THE LAW IS CRIMLGY
KING." PLAN CT/SYS CRIME INGP/REL...JURID SOC. ADJUST
PAGE 60 E1202 LAW
PUB/INST

S67
KETCHAM O.W.,"GUIDELINES FROM GAULT: REVOLUTIONARY ADJUD
REQUIREMENTS AND REAPPRAISAL." LAW CONSTN CREATE AGE/Y
LEGIT ROUTINE SANCTION CRIME DISCRIM PRIVIL ROLE CT/SYS
...JURID NEW/IDEA 20 SUPREME/CT. PAGE 60 E1208

S67
O'HIGGINS P.,"A BIBLIOGRAPHY OF PERIODICAL BIBLIOG
LITERATURE RELATING TO IRISH LAW." IRELAND...JURID LAW
20. PAGE 78 E1567 ADJUD

S67
PEMBERTON J., JR.,"CONSTITUTIONAL PROBLEMS IN LAW
RESTRAINT ON THE MEDIA." CONSTN PROB/SOLV EDU/PROP PRESS
CONFER CONTROL JURID. PAGE 80 E1608 ORD/FREE

S67
POSPISIL L.,"LEGAL LEVELS AND MULTIPLICITY OF LEGAL LAW
SYSTEMS IN HUMAN SOCIETIES." WOR+45 CENTRAL PWR STRATA
...SOC CHARTS GP/COMP GEN/LAWS. PAGE 81 E1630 JURID
STRUCT

S67
SHAFFER T.L.,"DIRECT RESTRAINT ON THE PRESS." LAW
USA+45 EDU/PROP CONTROL...JURID NEW/IDEA ABA. PRESS
PAGE 90 E1809 ORD/FREE
ADJUD

S67
TRAYNOR R.J.,"WHO CAN BEST JUDGE THE JUDGES?" CHOOSE
USA+45 PLAN PROB/SOLV ATTIT...DECISION JURID 20. ADJUD
PAGE 97 E1938 REPRESENT
CT/SYS

S67
TYDINGS J.D.,"MODERNIZING THE ADMINISTRATION OF CT/SYS
JUSTICE." PLAN ADMIN ROUTINE EFFICIENCY...JURID MGT
SIMUL. PAGE 97 E1948 COMPUTER
CONSULT

S68
BURGESS J.W.,"VON HOLST'S PUBLIC LAW OF THE UNITED CONSTN
STATES" USA-45 LAW GOV/REL...GOV/COMP IDEA/COMP 19. FEDERAL
PAGE 17 E0339 NAT/G
JURID

S68
DUPRE L.,"TILL DEATH DO US PART?" UNIV FAM INSPECT MARRIAGE
LEGIT ADJUD SANCTION PERS/REL ANOMIE RIGID/FLEX SEX CATH
...JURID IDEA/COMP 20 CHURCH/STA BIBLE CANON/LAW LAW
CIVIL/LAW. PAGE 34 E0666

B70
BLACKSTONE W.,COMMENTARIES ON THE LAWS OF ENGLAND LAW
(4 VOLS.) (4TH ED.). UK CHIEF DELIB/GP LEGIS WORKER JURID
CT/SYS SANCTION CRIME OWN...CRIMLGY 18 ENGLSH/LAW. ADJUD
PAGE 12 E0238 CONSTN

B73
AUSTIN J.,LECTURES ON JURISPRUDENCE OR THE LAW
PHILOSOPHY OF POSITIVE LAW (VOL. II) (4TH ED., ADJUD
REV.). UK CONSTN STRUCT PROB/SOLV LEGIT CT/SYS JURID
SANCTION CRIME INGP/REL OWN SUPEGO ORD/FREE...T 19. METH/CNCPT
PAGE 6 E0120

B82
POLLOCK F.,ESSAYS IN JURISPRUDENCE AND ETHICS. UNIV JURID
LAW FINAN MARKET WORKER INGP/REL MORAL...POLICY CONCPT
GEN/LAWS. PAGE 81 E1625

L84
ELLMAKER E.G.,"REVELATION OF RIGHTS." JUDGE DISCRIM ORD/FREE
SUPEGO...JURID PHIL/SCI CONCPT 17/18. PAGE 35 E0685 ADMIN
MORAL
NAT/G

L86
WHITRIDGE L.I.,"LEGISLATIVE INQUESTS" USA-45 ADJUD CT/SYS
GOV/REL SOVEREIGN 19/20 CONGRESS. PAGE 106 E2120 LEGIS
JURID
CONSTN

B90
GODWIN W.,POLITICAL JUSTICE. UK ELITES OWN KNOWL ORD/FREE

MORAL WEALTH...JURID 18/19. PAGE 44 E0877   SOVEREIGN
                                                            STRUCT
                                                            CONCPT

                                                    B91
BENTHAM J.,A FRAGMENT ON GOVERNMENT (1776). CONSTN   SOVEREIGN
MUNIC NAT/G SECT AGREE HAPPINESS UTIL MORAL   LAW
ORD/FREE...JURID CONCPT. PAGE 10 E0198   DOMIN

                                                    B92
COHN M.M.,AN INTRODUCTION TO THE STUDY OF THE   CONSTN
CONSTITUTION. USA+45 USA-45 SOCIETY NAT/G EX/STRUC   JURID
HABITAT...PSY CONCPT 18/20. PAGE 24 E0470   OLD/LIB

                                                    C93
PLAYFAIR R.L.,"A BIBLIOGRAPHY OF MOROCCO." MOROCCO   BIBLIOG
CULTURE AGRI FORCES DIPLOM WAR HEALTH...GEOG JURID   ISLAM
SOC CHARTS. PAGE 81 E1620   MEDIT-7

                                                    B96
ESMEIN A.,ELEMENTS DE DROIT CONSTITUTIONNEL. FRANCE   LAW
UK CHIEF EX/STRUC LEGIS ADJUD CT/SYS PARL/PROC REV   CONSTN
GOV/REL ORD/FREE...JURID METH/COMP 18/19. PAGE 35   NAT/G
E0697   CONCPT

                                                    B96
SMITH A.,LECTURES ON JUSTICE, POLICE, REVENUE AND   DIPLOM
ARMS (1763). UK LAW FAM FORCES TARIFFS AGREE COERCE   JURID
INCOME OWN WEALTH LAISSEZ...GEN/LAWS 17/18. PAGE 92   OLD/LIB
E1840   TAX

                                                    B97
US DEPARTMENT OF STATE,CATALOGUE OF WORKS RELATING   BIBLIOG/A
TO THE LAW OF NATIONS AND DIPLOMACY IN THE LIBRARY   DIPLOM
OF THE DEPARTMENT OF STATE (PAMPHLET). WOR-45 NAT/G   LAW
ADJUD CT/SYS...INT/LAW JURID 19. PAGE 100 E2000

                                                    B98
POLLOCK F.,THE HISTORY OF ENGLISH LAW BEFORE THE   LAW
TIME OF EDWARD I (2 VOLS, 2ND ED.). UK CULTURE   ADJUD
LOC/G LEGIS LICENSE AGREE CONTROL CT/SYS SANCTION   JURID
CRIME...TIME/SEQ 13 COMMON/LAW CANON/LAW. PAGE 81
E1626

                                                    B99
LILLY W.S.,FIRST PRINCIPLES IN POLITICS. UNIV LAW   NAT/G
LEGIS DOMIN ADJUD INGP/REL ORD/FREE SOVEREIGN   CONSTN
...JURID CONCPT 19 NATURL/LAW. PAGE 65 E1299   MORAL
                                                         POLICY

JURISPRUDENCE....SEE LAW

JURY....JURIES AND JURY BEHAVIOR; SEE ALSO DELIB/GP, ADJUD

                                                    S05
PHILLIPS J.B.,"MODIFICATIONS OF THE JURY SYSTEM."   JURID
PARTIC EFFICIENCY ATTIT PERCEPT...TREND 19   DELIB/GP
SUPREME/CT JURY. PAGE 80 E1612   PERS/REL
                                                        POLICY

                                                    B39
SIEYES E.J.,LES DISCOURS DE SIEYES DANS LES DEBATS   CONSTN
CONSTITUTIONNELS DE L'AN III (2 ET 18 THERMIDOR).   ADJUD
FRANCE LAW NAT/G PROB/SOLV BAL/PWR GOV/REL 18 JURY.   LEGIS
PAGE 91 E1824   EX/STRUC

                                                    B49
FRANK J.,LAW AND THE MODERN MIND. UNIV LAW CT/SYS   JURID
RATIONAL ATTIT...CONCPT 20 HOLMES/OW JURY. PAGE 40   ADJUD
E0787   IDEA/COMP
                                                         MYTH

                                                    L58
BEVAN W.,"JURY BEHAVIOR AS A FUNCTION OF THE   PERSON
PRESTIGE OF THE FOREMAN AND THE NATURE OF HIS   EDU/PROP
LEADERSHIP" (BMR)" DELIB/GP DOMIN ADJUD LEAD   DECISION
PERS/REL ATTIT...PSY STAT INT QU CHARTS SOC/EXP 20   CT/SYS
JURY. PAGE 11 E0221

                                                    B61
US COMMISSION ON CIVIL RIGHTS,JUSTICE: BOOK 5, 1961   DISCRIM
REPORT OF THE U.S. COMMISSION ON CIVIL RIGHTS.   LAW
LOC/G NAT/G RACE/REL...JURID 20 NEGRO CIV/RIGHTS   FORCES
INDIAN/AM JURY INDIAN/AM. PAGE 99 E1983

JUSTICE E1176

JUSTICE DEPARTMENT....SEE DEPT/JUST

JUSTINIAN E1177

─────────────────────────────── K ───────────────────────────────

KAAŠ L. E1178

KADALIE/C....CLEMENTS KADALIE

KAFKA G. E1179

KAHNG T.J. E1180

KAISR/ALUM....KAISER ALUMINUM

KALMANOFF G. E0806

KALNOKI BEDO A. E1181

KAMCHATKA....KAMCHATKA, U.S.S.R.

KAMISAR Y. E1182,E1317

KANSAS....KANSAS

KANT/I....IMMANUEL KANT

                                                    L11
    POUND R.,"THE SCOPE AND PURPOSE OF SOCIOLOGICAL   JURID
    JURISPRUDENCE."...GEN/LAWS 20 KANT/I HEGEL/GWF.   IDEA/COMP
    PAGE 81 E1634   METH/COMP
                                                         SOC

                                                    B64
    GUMPLOWICZ L.,RECHTSSTAAT UND SOZIALISMUS. STRATA   JURID
    ORD/FREE SOVEREIGN MARXISM...IDEA/COMP 16/20 KANT/I   NAT/G
    HOBBES/T. PAGE 48 E0962   SOCISM
                                                         CONCPT

KAPINGAMAR....KAPINGAMARANGI

KAPLAN H.E. E1183

KAPLAN M.A. E1184

KARIS T. E1185

KARPOV P.V. E1186

KASHMIR....SEE ALSO S/ASIA

KATANGA....SEE ALSO AFR

KATZ R.N. E0736

KATZENBACH N. E1184

KAUFMANN J. E0972

KAUNDA/K....KENNETH KAUNDA, PRESIDENT OF ZAMBIA

KAUPER P.G. E1187,E1188,E1189

KEAY E.A. E1190

KEEFE W.J. E1191,E1192

KEETON G.W. E1193

KEFAUVER E. E1194

KEFAUVER/E....ESTES KEFAUVER

KEIR D.L. E1195

KEITA/M....MOBIDO KEITA

KEITT L. E1196

KEL/BRIAND....KELLOGG BRIAND PEACE PACT

KELLOG BRIAND PEACE PACT....SEE KEL/BRIAND

KELSEN H. E1197,E1198,E1199,E1200,E1201

KELSEN/H....HANS KELSEN

                                                    B64
    ENGEL S.,LAW, STATE, AND INTERNATIONAL LEGAL ORDER.   JURID
    WOR+45 NAT/G ORD/FREE RELATISM...INT/LAW IDEA/COMP   OBJECTIVE
    ANTHOL 20 KELSEN/H. PAGE 35 E0690   CONCPT
                                                         DEBATE

KENNAN/G....GEORGE KENNAN

KENNEDY R.F. E1202

KENNEDY W.P. E1203

KENNEDY/JF....PRESIDENT JOHN F. KENNEDY

                                                    B63
    LIVELY E.,THE INVASION OF MISSISSIPPI. USA+45 LAW   RACE/REL
    CONSTN NAT/G PROVS CT/SYS GOV/REL FEDERAL CONSERVE   CROWD
    ...TRADIT 20 MISSISSIPP NEGRO NAACP WARRN/EARL   COERCE
    KENNEDY/JF. PAGE 66 E1309   MARXISM

B63
PACHTER H.M.,COLLISION COURSE; THE CUBAN MISSILE   WAR
CRISIS AND COEXISTENCE. CUBA USA+45 DIPLOM   BAL/PWR
ARMS/CONT PEACE MARXISM...DECISION INT/LAW 20   NUC/PWR
COLD/WAR KHRUSH/N KENNEDY/JF CASTRO/F. PAGE 79   DETER
E1587

B64
BROOKS T.R.,TOIL AND TROUBLE, A HISTORY OF AMERICAN   INDUS
LABOR. WORKER BARGAIN CAP/ISM ADJUD AUTOMAT EXEC   LABOR
GP/REL RACE/REL EFFICIENCY INCOME PROFIT MARXISM   LEGIS
17/20 KENNEDY/JF AFL/CIO NEGRO. PAGE 16 E0310

B65
BELL J.,THE JOHNSON TREATMENT: HOW LYNDON JOHNSON   INGP/REL
TOOK OVER THE PRESIDENCY AND MADE IT HIS OWN.   TOP/EX
USA+45 DELIB/GP DIPLOM ADJUD MURDER CHOOSE PERSON   CONTROL
PWR...POLICY OBS INT TIME 20 JOHNSON/LB KENNEDY/JF   NAT/G
PRESIDENT CONGRESS. PAGE 10 E0183

B65
FEERICK J.D.,FROM FAILING HANDS: THE STUDY OF   EX/STRUC
PRESIDENTIAL SUCCESSION. CONSTN NAT/G PROB/SOLV   CHIEF
LEAD PARL/PROC MURDER CHOOSE...NEW/IDEA BIBLIOG 20   LAW
KENNEDY/JF JOHNSON/LB PRESIDENT PRE/US/AM   LEGIS
VICE/PRES. PAGE 36 E0724

B65
IANNIELLO L.,MILESTONES ALONG THE MARCH: TWELVE   RACE/REL
HISTORIC CIVIL RIGHTS DOCUMENTS--FROM WORLD WAR II   DISCRIM
TO SELMA. USA+45 LAW FORCES TOP/EX PARTIC SUFF...T   CONSTN
20 NEGRO CIV/RIGHTS TRUMAN/HS SUPREME/CT   NAT/G
KENNEDY/JF. PAGE 56 E1121

B65
SCHUBERT G.,THE POLITICAL ROLE OF THE COURTS IN   CT/SYS
JUDICIAL POLICY MAKING. USA+45 CONSTN JUDGE   POLICY
FEEDBACK CHOOSE RACE/REL ORD/FREE...TRADIT PSY   DECISION
BIBLIOG/A 20 KENNEDY/JF SUPREME/CT. PAGE 89 E1776

KENNEDY/RF....ROBERT F. KENNEDY

KENTUCKY....KENTUCKY

B52
COLEMAN J.W. JR.,DEATH AT THE COURT-HOUSE. CONTROL   CROWD
COERCE 20 KENTUCKY. PAGE 24 E0472   ORD/FREE
                                                       CRIME
                                                       CT/SYS

KENYA....KENYA

KENYATTA....JOMO KENYATTA

B61
BENNETT G.,THE KENYATTA ELECTION: KENYA 1960-1961.   CHOOSE
AFR INGP/REL RACE/REL CONSEN ATTIT 20 KENYATTA.   POL/PAR
PAGE 10 E0187   LAW
                                                       SUFF

KENYON D. E0402

KERN A. E1450

KERR C. E0143

KERR M.H. E1204

KERREMANS-RAMIOULL E1205

KETCHAM E.H. E1207

KETCHAM O.W. E1208

KEYNES/G....GEOFFREY KEYNES

KEYNES/JM....JOHN MAYNARD KEYNES

KHADDURI M. E1209,E1210

KHAN M.Z. E1211

KHASAS....KHASAS (ANCIENT COMMUNITY)

KHOURI F.J. E1212

KHRUSH/N....NIKITA KHRUSHCHEV

B63
PACHTER H.M.,COLLISION COURSE; THE CUBAN MISSILE   WAR
CRISIS AND COEXISTENCE. CUBA USA+45 DIPLOM   BAL/PWR
ARMS/CONT PEACE MARXISM...DECISION INT/LAW 20   NUC/PWR
COLD/WAR KHRUSH/N KENNEDY/JF CASTRO/F. PAGE 79   DETER
E1587

B63
US SENATE,DOCUMENTS ON INTERNATIONAL AS"ECTS OF   SPACE
EXPLORATION AND USE OF OUTER SPACE, 1954-62: STAFF   UTIL
REPORT FOR COMM AERON SPACE SCI. USA+45 USSR LEGIS   GOV/REL
LEAD CIVMIL/REL PEACE...POLICY INT/LAW ANTHOL 20   DIPLOM
CONGRESS NASA KHRUSH/N. PAGE 101 E2026

B65
LAFAVE W.R.,LAW AND SOVIET SOCIETY. EX/STRUC DIPLOM   JURID
DOMIN EDU/PROP PRESS ADMIN CRIME OWN MARXISM 20   CT/SYS
KHRUSH/N. PAGE 62 E1244   ADJUD
                                                       GOV/REL

B66
DALLIN A.,POLITICS IN THE SOVIET UNION: 7 CASES.   MARXISM
COM USSR LAW POL/PAR CHIEF FORCES WRITING CONTROL   DOMIN
PARL/PROC CIVMIL/REL TOTALISM...ANTHOL 20 KHRUSH/N   ORD/FREE
STALIN/J CASEBOOK COM/PARTY. PAGE 28 E0563   GOV/REL

S68
SHAPIRO J.P.,"SOVIET HISTORIOGRAPHY AND THE MOSCOW   HIST/WRIT
TRIALS: AFTER THIRTY YEARS." USSR NAT/G LEGIT PRESS   EDU/PROP
CONTROL LEAD ATTIT MARXISM...NEW/IDEA METH 20   SANCTION
TROTSKY/L STALIN/J KHRUSH/N. PAGE 90 E1810   ADJUD

KIDDER F.E. E1213

KIERKE/S....SOREN KIERKEGAARD

KIM R.C.C. E1214

KIM/IL-SON....IL-SON KIM

KIN....KINSHIP (EXCEPT NUCLEAR FAMILY)

B00
MAINE H.S.,ANCIENT LAW. MEDIT-7 CULTURE SOCIETY KIN   FAM
SECT LEGIS LEGIT ROUTINE...JURID HIST/WRIT CON/ANAL   LAW
TOT/POP VAL/FREE. PAGE 68 E1350

B04
GRIFFIN A.P.C.,REFERENCES ON CHINESE IMMIGRATIONS   BIBLIOG/A
(PAMPHLET). USA-45 KIN NAT/LISM ATTIT...SOC 19/20.   STRANGE
PAGE 47 E0926   JURID
                                                       RACE/REL

B20
VINOGRADOFF P.,OUTLINES OF HISTORICAL JURISPRUDENCE   JURID
(2 VOLS.). GREECE MEDIT-7 LAW CONSTN FACE/GP FAM   METH
KIN MUNIC CRIME OWN...INT/LAW IDEA/COMP BIBLIOG.
PAGE 104 E2080

B35
KENNEDY W.P.,THE LAW AND CUSTOM OF THE SOUTH   CT/SYS
AFRICAN CONSTITUTION. AFR SOUTH/AFR KIN LOC/G PROVS   CONSTN
DIPLOM ADJUD ADMIN EXEC 20. PAGE 60 E1203   JURID
                                                       PARL/PROC

S48
ALEXANDER L.,"WAR CRIMES, THEIR SOCIAL-   DRIVE
PSYCHOLOGICAL ASPECTS." EUR+WWI GERMANY LAW CULTURE   WAR
ELITES KIN POL/PAR PUB/INST FORCES DOMIN EDU/PROP
COERCE CRIME ATTIT SUPEGO HEALTH MORAL PWR FASCISM
...PSY OBS TREND GEN/LAWS NAZI 20. PAGE 3 E0061

C50
NUMELIN R.,"THE BEGINNINGS OF DIPLOMACY." INT/TRADE   DIPLOM
WAR GP/REL PEACE STRANGE ATTIT...INT/LAW CONCPT   KIN
BIBLIOG. PAGE 78 E1559   CULTURE
                                                       LAW

B56
RECASENS SICHES S.,TRATADO GENERAL DE SOCIOLOGIA.   SOC
CULTURE FAM NEIGH LEAD RACE/REL DISCRIM HABITAT   STRATA
ORD/FREE...JURID LING T SOC/INTEG 20. PAGE 84 E1677   KIN
                                                       GP/REL

B59
ANDERSON J.N.D.,ISLAMIC LAW IN THE MODERN WORLD.   ISLAM
FAM KIN SECT LEGIT ADJUD ATTIT DRIVE...TIME/SEQ   JURID
TREND GEN/LAWS 20 MUSLIM. PAGE 5 E0089

B59
GINSBURG M.,LAW AND OPINION IN ENGLAND. UK CULTURE   JURID
KIN LABOR LEGIS EDU/PROP ADMIN CT/SYS CRIME OWN   POLICY
HEALTH...ANTHOL 20 ENGLSH/LAW. PAGE 44 E0868   ECO/TAC

B63
ELIAS T.O.,THE NIGERIAN LEGAL SYSTEM. NIGERIA LAW   CT/SYS
FAM KIN SECT ADMIN NAT/LISM...JURID 18/20   ADJUD
ENGLSH/LAW COMMON/LAW. PAGE 34 E0682   COLONIAL
                                                       PROF/ORG

B64
CLINARD M.B.,ANOMIE AND DEVIANT BEHAVIOR: A   PERSON
DISCUSSION AND CRITIQUE. SOCIETY FACE/GP CRIME   ANOMIE

STRANGE ATTIT BIO/SOC DISPL RIGID/FLEX HEALTH...PSY KIN
CONCPT BIBLIOG 20 MERTON/R. PAGE 23 E0456   NEIGH

B65
KUPER H.,AFRICAN LAW. LAW FAM KIN SECT JUDGE ADJUST AFR
NAT/LISM 17/20. PAGE 62 E1236   CT/SYS
                                                    ADJUD
                                                    COLONIAL

B66
HAUSNER G.,JUSTICE IN JERUSALEM. GERMANY ISRAEL   ADJUD
SOCIETY KIN DIPLOM LEGIT CT/SYS PARTIC MURDER   CRIME
MAJORITY ATTIT FASCISM...INT/LAW JURID 20 JEWS   RACE/REL
WAR/TRIAL. PAGE 51 E1013   COERCE

L67
CICOUREL A.V.,"KINSHIP, MARRIAGE, AND DIVORCE IN   SOC
COMPARATIVE FAMILY LAW." UNIV LAW FAM KIN GEN/METH. PHIL/SCI
PAGE 22 E0438   MARRIAGE
                                                    IDEA/COMP

B75
MAINE H.S.,LECTURES ON THE EARLY HISTORY OF   CULTURE
INSTITUTIONS. IRELAND UK CONSTN ELITES STRUCT FAM   LAW
KIN CHIEF LEGIS CT/SYS OWN SOVEREIGN...CONCPT 16   INGP/REL
BENTHAM/J BREHON ROMAN/LAW. PAGE 68 E1351

B97
JENKS E.J.,LAW AND POLITICS IN THE MIDDLE AGES.   LAW
CHRIST-17C CULTURE STRUCT KIN NAT/G SECT CT/SYS   SOCIETY
GP/REL...CLASSIF CHARTS IDEA/COMP BIBLIOG 8/16.   ADJUST
PAGE 58 E1162

KING D.B. E1215

KING G.D. E0558

KING W.L. E1216

KING....KING AND KINGSHIP; SEE ALSO CHIEF, CONSERVE, TRADIT

KING/MAR/L....REVEREND MARTIN LUTHER KING

B66
KUNSTLER W.M.,"DEEP IN MY HEART" USA+45 LAW   CT/SYS
PROF/ORG SECT LOBBY PARTIC CROWD DISCRIM ROLE   RACE/REL
...BIOG 20 KING/MAR/L NEGRO CIV/RIGHTS SOUTH/US.   ADJUD
PAGE 62 E1233   CONSULT

KINSEY/A....ALFRED KINSEY

KIPLING/R....RUDYARD KIPLING

KIRCHHEIMER O. E1217

KIRK G. E1219

KIRK R. E1220

KIRK/GRAY....GRAYSON KIRK

KISER S.L. E1221

KKK....KU KLUX KLAN

B63
DAY R.E.,CIVIL RIGHTS USA: PUBLIC SCHOOLS, SOUTHERN EDU/PROP
STATES - NORTH CAROLINA, 1963. USA+45 LOC/G NEIGH   ORD/FREE
LEGIS CREATE CT/SYS COERCE DISCRIM ATTIT...QU   RACE/REL
CHARTS 20 NORTH/CAR NEGRO KKK CIV/RIGHTS. PAGE 29   SANCTION
E0579

B65
SCHROEDER O.,DEFACTO SEGREGATION AND CIVIL RIGHTS.   ANTHOL
LAW PROVS SCHOOL WORKER ATTIT HABITAT HEALTH WEALTH DISCRIM
...JURID CHARTS 19/20 NEGRO SUPREME/CT KKK. PAGE 88 RACE/REL
E1766   ORD/FREE

KLEIN F.J. E1222

KLESMENT J. E0957,E1223

KLUCKHN/C....CLYDE KLUCKHOHN

KNEIER C.M. E0713,E1224

KNIERIEM A. E1225

KNO/TEST....TESTS FOR FACTUAL KNOWLEDGE

B54
WRIGHT Q.,PROBLEMS OF STABILITY AND PROGRESS IN   INT/ORG
INTERNATIONAL RELATIONSHIPS. FUT WOR+45 WOR-45   CONCPT
SOCIETY LEGIS CREATE TEC/DEV ECO/TAC EDU/PROP ADJUD DIPLOM

WAR PEACE ORD/FREE PWR...KNO/TEST TREND GEN/LAWS
20. PAGE 108 E2155

S67
SCOTT A.,"TWENTY-FIVE YEARS OF OPINION ON   ATTIT
INTEGRATION IN TEXAS." USA+45 USA-45 DISCRIM   ADJUST
...KNO/TEST TREND CHARTS 20 TEXAS. PAGE 89 E1794   RACE/REL
                                                    LAW

KNOWL....ENLIGHTENMENT, KNOWLEDGE

N
TEXTBOOKS IN PRINT. WOR+45 WOR-45 LAW DIPLOM   BIBLIOG
ALL/VALS ALL/IDEOS...SOC T 19/20. PAGE 1 E0014   SCHOOL
                                                    KNOWL

N
MINISTERE DE L'EDUC NATIONALE,CATALOGUE DES THESES   BIBLIOG
DE DOCTORAT SOUTENNES DEVANT LES UNIVERSITAIRES   ACADEM
FRANCAISES. FRANCE LAW DIPLOM ADMIN...HUM SOC 20.   KNOWL
PAGE 73 E1465   NAT/G

B04
CRANDALL S.B.,TREATIES: THEIR MAKING AND   LAW
ENFORCEMENT. MOD/EUR USA-45 CONSTN INT/ORG NAT/G
LEGIS EDU/PROP LEGIT EXEC PEACE KNOWL...JURID
CONGRESS 19/20 TREATY. PAGE 27 E0541

B05
DICEY A.,LAW AND PUBLIC OPINION IN ENGLAND. LAW   ATTIT
CULTURE INTELL SOCIETY NAT/G SECT JUDGE LEGIT   UK
CHOOSE RIGID/FLEX KNOWL...OLD/LIB CONCPT STERTYP
GEN/LAWS 20. PAGE 31 E0620

B21
BRYCE J.,MODERN DEMOCRACIES. FUT NEW/ZEALND USA-45   NAT/G
LAW CONSTN POL/PAR PROVS VOL/ASSN EX/STRUC LEGIS   TREND
LEGIT CT/SYS EXEC KNOWL CONGRESS AUSTRAL 20.
PAGE 16 E0322

B28
BUTLER G.,THE DEVELOPMENT OF INTERNATIONAL LAW.   LAW
WOR-45 SOCIETY NAT/G KNOWL ORD/FREE PWR...JURID   INT/LAW
CONCPT HIST/WRIT GEN/LAWS. PAGE 18 E0349   DIPLOM
                                                    INT/ORG

L28
HUDSON M.,"THE TEACHING OF INTERNATIONAL LAW IN   PERCEPT
AMERICA." USA-45 LAW CONSULT ACT/RES CREATE   KNOWL
EDU/PROP ATTIT RIGID/FLEX...JURID CONCPT RECORD   INT/LAW
HIST/WRIT TREND GEN/LAWS 18/20. PAGE 56 E1109

B29
LEITZ F.,DIE PUBLIZITAT DER AKTIENGESELLSCHAFT.   LG/CO
BELGIUM FRANCE GERMANY UK FINAN PRESS GP/REL PROFIT JURID
KNOWL 20. PAGE 64 E1282   ECO/TAC
                                                    NAT/COMP

L29
FEIS H.,"RESEARCH ACTIVITIES OF THE LEAGUE OF   CONSULT
NATIONS." EUR+WWI WOR-45 R+D INT/ORG CT/SYS   KNOWL
ARMS/CONT WEALTH...OBS RECORD LEAGUE/NAT ILO 20.   PEACE
PAGE 37 E0729

B33
DANGERFIELD R.,IN DEFENSE OF THE SENATE. USA-45   LEGIS
CONSTN NAT/G EX/STRUC TOP/EX ATTIT KNOWL   DELIB/GP
...METH/CNCPT STAT TIME/SEQ TREND CON/ANAL CHARTS   DIPLOM
CONGRESS 20 TREATY. PAGE 28 E0565

B34
GONZALEZ PALENCIA A,ESTUDIO HISTORICO SOBRE LA   LEGIT
CENSURA GUBERNATIVA EN ESPANA 1800-1833. NAT/G   EDU/PROP
COERCE INGP/REL ATTIT AUTHORIT KNOWL...POLICY JURID PRESS
19. PAGE 44 E0884   CONTROL

C39
HADDOW A.,"POLITICAL SCIENCE IN AMERICAN COLLEGES   USA-45
AND UNIVERSITIES 1636-1900." CONSTN MORAL...POLICY   LAW
INT/LAW CON/ANAL BIBLIOG T 17/20. PAGE 49 E0971   ACADEM
                                                    KNOWL

S40
GILL N.N.,"PERMANENT ADVISORY COMMISSIONS IN THE   DELIB/GP
FEDERAL GOVERNMENT." CLIENT FINAN OP/RES EDU/PROP   NAT/G
PARTIC ROUTINE INGP/REL KNOWL SKILL...CLASSIF   DECISION
TREND. PAGE 43 E0860

S40
GURVITCH G.,"MAJOR PROBLEMS OF THE SOCIOLOGY OF   SOC
LAW." CULTURE SANCTION KNOWL MORAL...POLICY EPIST   LAW
JURID WORSHIP. PAGE 48 E0963   PHIL/SCI

B44
ADLER M.J.,HOW TO THINK ABOUT WAR AND PEACE. WOR-45 INT/ORG
LAW SOCIETY EX/STRUC DIPLOM KNOWL ORD/FREE...POLICY CREATE

TREND GEN/LAWS 20. PAGE 3 E0049   ARMS/CONT
                                                         PEACE

                                                              B45
BEVERIDGE W.,THE PRICE OF PEACE. GERMANY UK WOR+45   INT/ORG
WOR-45 NAT/G FORCES CREATE LEGIT REGION WAR ATTIT   TREND
KNOWL ORD/FREE PWR...POLICY NEW/IDEA GEN/LAWS   PEACE
LEAGUE/NAT 20 TREATY. PAGE 12 E0223

                                                              S48
MILLER B.S.,"A LAW IS PASSED: THE ATOMIC ENERGY ACT   TEC/DEV
OF 1946." POL/PAR CHIEF CONFER DEBATE CONTROL   LEGIS
PARL/PROC ATTIT KNOWL...POLICY CONGRESS. PAGE 73   DECISION
E1457   LAW

                                                              B51
HUXLEY J.,FREEDOM AND CULTURE. UNIV LAW SOCIETY R+D   CULTURE
ACADEM SCHOOL CREATE SANCTION ATTIT KNOWL...HUM   ORD/FREE
ANTHOL 20. PAGE 56 E1118   PHIL/SCI
                                                        IDEA/COMP

                                                              B52
BENTHAM A.,HANDBOOK OF POLITICAL FALLACIES. FUT   POL/PAR
MOD/EUR LAW INTELL LOC/G MUNIC NAT/G DELIB/GP LEGIS
CREATE EDU/PROP CT/SYS ATTIT RIGID/FLEX KNOWL PWR
...RELATIV PSY SOC CONCPT SELF/OBS TREND STERTYP
TOT/POP. PAGE 10 E0189

                                                              B52
THOM J.M.,GUIDE TO RESEARCH MATERIAL IN POLITICAL   BIBLIOG/A
SCIENCE (PAMPHLET). ELITES LOC/G MUNIC NAT/G LEGIS   KNOWL
DIPLOM ADJUD CIVMIL/REL GOV/REL PWR MGT. PAGE 96
E1916

                                                              B53
CALDWELL L.K.,RESEARCH METHODS IN PUBLIC   BIBLIOG/A
ADMINISTRATION; AN OUTLINE OF TOPICS AND READINGS   METH/COMP
(PAMPHLET). LAW ACT/RES COMPUTER KNOWL...SOC STAT   ADMIN
GEN/METH 20. PAGE 18 E0364   OP/RES

                                                              S55
WRIGHT Q.,"THE PEACEFUL ADJUSTMENT OF INTERNATIONAL   R+D
RELATIONS: PROBLEMS AND RESEARCH APPROACHES." UNIV   METH/CNCPT
INTELL EDU/PROP ADJUD ROUTINE KNOWL SKILL...INT/LAW   PEACE
JURID PHIL/SCI CLASSIF 20. PAGE 108 E2156

                                                              B56
WIGGINS J.R.,FREEDOM OR SECRECY. USA+45 USA-45   ORD/FREE
DELIB/GP EX/STRUC FORCES ADJUD SANCTION KNOWL PWR   PRESS
...AUD/VIS CONGRESS 20. PAGE 106 E2121   NAT/G
                                                       CONTROL

                                                              S57
FRANKFURTER F.,"THE SUPREME COURT IN THE MIRROR OF   EDU/PROP
JUSTICES" (BMR)" USA+45 USA-45 INTELL INSPECT   ADJUD
EFFICIENCY ROLE KNOWL MORAL 18/20 SUPREME/CT.   CT/SYS
PAGE 40 E0792   PERSON

                                                              B58
HENKIN L.,ARMS CONTROL AND INSPECTION IN AMERICAN   USA+45
LAW. LAW CONSTN INT/ORG LOC/G MUNIC NAT/G PROVS   JURID
EDU/PROP LEGIT EXEC NUC/PWR KNOWL ORD/FREE...OBS   ARMS/CONT
TOT/POP CONGRESS 20. PAGE 52 E1032

                                                              B59
HAYS B.,A SOUTHERN MODERATE SPEAKS. LAW PROVS   SECT
SCHOOL KNOWL...JURID SOC SELF/OBS BIOG 20 NEGRO   DISCRIM
SUPREME/CT. PAGE 51 E1015   CT/SYS
                                                       RACE/REL

                                                              B59
MORRIS C.,THE GREAT LEGAL PHILOSOPHERS: SELECTED   JURID
READINGS IN JURISPRUDENCE. UNIV INTELL SOCIETY   ADJUD
EDU/PROP MAJORITY UTOPIA PERSON KNOWL...ANTHOL.   PHIL/SCI
PAGE 75 E1497   IDEA/COMP

                                                              B59
US SENATE COMM ON JUDICIARY,EXECUTIVE PRIVILEGE.   CHIEF
USA+45 DELIB/GP CONTROL KNOWL PWR 20 CONGRESS   PRIVIL
PRESIDENT. PAGE 102 E2042   CONSTN
                                                       LAW

                                                              B60
GOLDSEN J.M.,INTERNATIONAL POLITICAL IMPLICATIONS   R+D
OF ACTIVITIES IN OUTER SPACE. FUT USA+45 WOR+45 AIR   SPACE
LAW ACT/RES LEGIT ATTIT KNOWL ORD/FREE PWR...CONCPT
20. PAGE 44 E0879

                                                              B60
WOETZEL R.K.,THE INTERNATIONAL CONTROL OF AIRSPACE   INT/ORG
AND OUTERSPACE. FUT WOR+45 AIR CONSTN STRUCT   JURID
CONSULT PLAN TEC/DEV ADJUD RIGID/FLEX KNOWL   SPACE
ORD/FREE PWR...TECHNIC GEOG MGT NEW/IDEA TREND   INT/LAW
COMPUT/IR VAL/FREE 20 TREATY. PAGE 107 E2137

                                                              S60
THOMPSON K.W.,"MORAL PURPOSE IN FOREIGN POLICY: MORAL
REALITIES AND ILLUSIONS." WOR+45 WOR-45 LAW CULTURE   JURID
SOCIETY INT/ORG PLAN ADJUD ADMIN COERCE RIGID/FLEX   DIPLOM
SUPEGO KNOWL ORD/FREE PWR...SOC TREND SOC/EXP
TOT/POP 20. PAGE 96 E1921

                                                              B61
WASSERSTROM R.A.,THE JUDICIAL DECISION: TOWARD A   JUDGE
THEORY OF LEGAL JUSTIFICATION. ACT/RES RATIONAL   LAW
PERCEPT KNOWL OBJECTIVE...DECISION JURID. PAGE 105   ADJUD
E2102

                                                              B61
WECHSLER H.,PRINCIPLES, POLITICS AND FUNDAMENTAL   CT/SYS
LAW: SELECTED ESSAYS. USA+45 USA-45 LAW SOCIETY   CONSTN
NAT/G PROVS DELIB/GP EX/STRUC ACT/RES LEGIT PERSON   INT/LAW
KNOWL PWR...JURID 20 NUREMBERG. PAGE 105 E2106

                                                              L61
FELLMAN D.,"ACADEMIC FREEDOM IN AMERICAN LAW." LAW   ACADEM
CONSTN NAT/G VOL/ASSN PLAN PERSON KNOWL NEW/LIB.   ORD/FREE
PAGE 37 E0732   LEGIS
                                                       CULTURE

                                                              S61
OLIVER C.T.,"THE AMERICAN LAW INSTITUTE'S DRAFT   KNOWL
RESTATEMENT OF THE FOREIGN RELATIONS LAW OF THE   JURID
UNITED STATES." FUT USA+45 SOCIETY CONSULT   DIPLOM
EDU/PROP. PAGE 78 E1574

                                                              B62
BERMAN D.M.,A BILL BECOMES A LAW: THE CIVIL RIGHTS   DISCRIM
ACT OF 1960. USA+45 LAW POL/PAR LOBBY RACE/REL   PARL/PROC
KNOWL...CHARTS 20 CONGRESS NEGRO CIV/RIGHTS.   JURID
PAGE 11 E0206   GOV/REL

                                                              B63
LEGISLATIVE REFERENCE SERVICE,DIGEST OF PUBLIC   BIBLIOG/A
GENERAL BILLS AND RESOLUTIONS. LAW COM/IND EDU/PROP   LEGIS
GOV/REL INGP/REL KNOWL...JURID 20 CONGRESS. PAGE 64   DELIB/GP
E1280   NAT/G

                                                              L63
MCDOUGAL M.S.,"THE ENJOYMENT AND ACQUISITION OF   PLAN
RESOURCES IN OUTER SPACE." CHRIST-17C FUT WOR+45   TREND
WOR-45 LAW EXTR/IND INT/ORG ACT/RES CREATE TEC/DEV
ECO/TAC LEGIT COERCE HEALTH KNOWL ORD/FREE PWR
WEALTH...JURID HIST/WRIT VAL/FREE. PAGE 70 E1408

                                                              S63
GARDNER R.N.,"COOPERATION IN OUTER SPACE." FUT USSR   INT/ORG
WOR+45 AIR LAW COM/IND CONSULT DELIB/GP CREATE   ACT/RES
KNOWL 20 TREATY. PAGE 42 E0837   PEACE
                                                       SPACE

                                                              S63
TALLON D.,"L'ETUDE DU DROIT COMPARE COMME MOYEN DE   INT/ORG
RECHERCHER LES MATIERES SUSCEPTIBLES D'UNIFICATION   JURID
INTERNATIONALE." WOR+45 LAW SOCIETY VOL/ASSN   INT/LAW
CONSULT LEGIT CT/SYS RIGID/FLEX KNOWL 20. PAGE 95
E1906

                                                              S64
BALDWIN G.B.,"THE DEPENDENCE OF SCIENCE ON LAW AND   NAT/G
GOVERNMENT--THE INTERNATIONAL GEOPHYSICAL YEAR--A   KNOWL
CASE STUDY." WOR+45 LAW INT/ORG PROF/ORG LEGIS PLAN
EDU/PROP...TIME/SEQ VAL/FREE 20. PAGE 8 E0144

                                                              S64
PARADIES F.,"SOBRE LA HISTORIA DE LA LOGICA Y DE LA   ADJUD
LOGICA JURIDICA." LEGIT KNOWL...JURID METH/CNCPT
HIST/WRIT 20. PAGE 80 E1597

                                                              S64
SINGH N.,"THE CONTEMPORARY PRACTICE OF INDIA IN THE   LAW
FIELD OF INTERNATIONAL LAW." INDIA S/ASIA INT/ORG   ATTIT
NAT/G DOMIN EDU/PROP LEGIT KNOWL...CONCPT TOT/POP   DIPLOM
20. PAGE 91 E1833   INT/LAW

                                                              S64
SKUBISZEWSKI K.,"FORMS OF PARTICIPATION OF   INT/ORG
INTERNATIONAL ORGANIZATION IN THE LAW MAKING   LAW
PROCESS." FUT WOR+45 NAT/G DELIB/GP DOMIN LEGIT   INT/LAW
KNOWL PWR...JURID TREND 20. PAGE 92 E1837

                                                              B65
US OFFICE ECONOMIC OPPORTUNITY,CATALOG OF FEDERAL   BIBLIOG
PROGRAMS FOR INDIVIDUAL AND COMMUNITY IMPROVEMENT.   CLIENT
USA+45 GIVE RECEIVE ADMIN HEALTH KNOWL SKILL WEALTH   ECO/TAC
CHARTS. PAGE 101 E2021   MUNIC

                                                              S65
FALK R.A.,"INTERNATIONAL LEGAL ORDER." USA+45   ATTIT
INTELL FACE/GP INT/ORG LEGIT KNOWL...CONCPT   GEN/LAWS
METH/CNCPT STYLE RECORD GEN/METH 20. PAGE 36 E0717   INT/LAW

STATES: AN HISTORICAL INTERPRETATION. INT/ORG AGREE SOVEREIGN
COLONIAL WAR PEACE ATTIT ORD/FREE...POLICY INT/LAW USA-45
CHARTS 18/20 MEXIC/AMER WILSON/W MONROE/DOC. L/A+17C
PAGE 10 E0185

B43
CLAGETT H.L.,A GUIDE TO THE LAW AND LEGAL BIBLIOG
LITERATURE OF PARAGUAY. PARAGUAY CONSTN COM/IND JURID
LABOR MUNIC JUDGE ADMIN CT/SYS...CRIMLGY INT/LAW LAW
CON/ANAL 20. PAGE 22 E0439 L/A+17C

B45
CLAGETT H.L.,A GUIDE TO THE LAW AND LEGAL BIBLIOG
LITERATURE OF THE MEXICAN STATES. CONSTN LEGIS JURID
JUDGE ADJUD ADMIN...INT/LAW CON/ANAL 20 MEXIC/AMER. L/A+17C
PAGE 22 E0440 LAW

B45
US DEPARTMENT OF STATE,PUBLICATIONS OF THE BIBLIOG
DEPARTMENT OF STATE: A LIST CUMULATIVE FROM OCTOBER DIPLOM
1, 1929 (PAMPHLET). ASIA EUR+WWI ISLAM L/A+17C INT/TRADE
USA-45 ADJUD...INT/LAW 20. PAGE 99 E1993

B47
CLAGETT H.L.,A GUIDE TO THE LAW AND LEGAL BIBLIOG/A
LITERATURE OF BOLIVIA. L/A+17C CONSTN LABOR LEGIS JURID
ADMIN...CRIMLGY INT/LAW PHIL/SCI 16/20 BOLIV. LAW
PAGE 22 E0441 CT/SYS

B47
CLAGETT H.L.,A GUIDE TO THE LAW AND LEGAL BIBLIOG
LITERATURE OF CHILE, 1917-1946. CHILE CONSTN LABOR L/A+17C
JUDGE ADJUD ADMIN...CRIMLGY INT/LAW JURID CON/ANAL LAW
20. PAGE 22 E0442 LEGIS

B47
CLAGETT H.L.,A GUIDE TO THE LAW AND LEGAL BIBLIOG
LITERATURE OF ECUADOR. ECUADOR CONSTN LABOR LEGIS JURID
JUDGE ADJUD ADMIN CIVMIL/REL...CRIMLGY INT/LAW LAW
CON/ANAL 20. PAGE 22 E0443 L/A+17C

B47
CLAGETT H.L.,A GUIDE TO THE LAW AND LEGAL BIBLIOG
LITERATURE OF PERU. PERU CONSTN COM/IND LABOR MUNIC L/A+17C
JUDGE ADMIN CT/SYS...CRIMLGY INT/LAW JURID 20. PHIL/SCI
PAGE 23 E0444 LAW

B47
CLAGETT H.L.,A GUIDE TO THE LAW AND LEGAL BIBLIOG
LITERATURE OF URUGUAY. URUGUAY CONSTN COM/IND FINAN LAW
LABOR MUNIC JUDGE PRESS ADMIN CT/SYS...INT/LAW JURID
PHIL/SCI 20. PAGE 23 E0445 L/A+17C

B47
CLAGETT H.L.,A GUIDE TO THE LAW AND LEGAL BIBLIOG
LITERATURE OF VENEZUELA. VENEZUELA CONSTN LABOR L/A+17C
LEGIS JUDGE ADJUD ADMIN CIVMIL/REL...CRIMLGY JURID INT/LAW
CON/ANAL 20. PAGE 23 E0446 LAW

B48
CLAGETT H.L.,A GUIDE TO THE LAW AND LEGAL BIBLIOG
LITERATURE OF ARGENTINA, 1917-1946. CONSTN LABOR L/A+17C
JUDGE ADJUD ADMIN...CRIMLGY INT/LAW JURID CON/ANAL LAW
20 ARGEN. PAGE 23 E0447 LEGIS

B51
BISSAINTHE M.,DICTIONNAIRE DE BIBLIOGRAPHIE BIBLIOG
HAITIENNE. HAITI ELITES AGRI LEGIS DIPLOM INT/TRADE L/A+17C
WRITING ORD/FREE CATHISM...ART/METH GEOG 19/20 SOCIETY
NEGRO TREATY. PAGE 12 E0234 NAT/G

B52
DILLON D.R.,LATIN AMERICA, 1935-1949; A SELECTED BIBLIOG
BIBLIOGRAPHY. LAW EDU/PROP...SOC 20. PAGE 32 E0629 L/A+17C
NAT/G
DIPLOM

C52
CLAGETT H.L.,"THE ADMINISTRATION OF JUSTICE IN CT/SYS
LATIN AMERICA." L/A+17C ADMIN FEDERAL...JURID ADJUD
METH/COMP BIBLIOG 20. PAGE 23 E0448 JUDGE
CONSTN

B55
BURR R.N.,DOCUMENTS ON INTER-AMERICAN COOPERATION: BIBLIOG
VOL. I, 1810-1881; VOL. II, 1881-1948. DELIB/GP DIPLOM
BAL/PWR INT/TRADE REPRESENT NAT/LISM PEACE HABITAT INT/ORG
ORD/FREE PWR SOVEREIGN...INT/LAW 20 OAS. PAGE 18 L/A+17C
E0345

B57
BAYITCH S.A.,A GUIDE TO INTERAMERICAN LEGAL BIBLIOG
STUDIES: A SELECTIVE BIBLIOGRAPHY OF WORKS IN L/A+17C
ENGLISH. NAT/G LEGIS ADJUD CT/SYS CONGRESS 20. LAW
PAGE 8 E0157 JURID

B58
BUGEDA LANZAS J.,A STATEMENT OF THE LAWS OF CUBA IN JURID
MATTERS AFFECTING BUSINESS (2ND ED. REV., NAT/G
ENLARGED). CUBA L/A+17C LAW FINAN FAM LEGIS ACT/RES INDUS
ADMIN GP/REL...BIBLIOG 20 OAS. PAGE 17 E0327 WORKER

B59
GOMEZ ROBLES J.,A STATEMENT OF THE LAWS OF JURID
GUATEMALA IN MATTERS AFFECTING BUSINESS (2ND ED. NAT/G
REV., ENLARGED). GUATEMALA L/A+17C LAW FINAN FAM INDUS
WORKER ACT/RES DIPLOM ADJUD ADMIN GP/REL 20 OAS. LEGIT
PAGE 44 E0881

B59
MAYDA J.,ATOMIC ENERGY AND LAW. ECO/UNDEV FINAN NUC/PWR
TEC/DEV FOR/AID EFFICIENCY PRODUC WEALTH...POLICY L/A+17C
TECHNIC 20. PAGE 70 E1391 LAW
ADMIN

B59
OKINSHEVICH L.A.,LATIN AMERICA IN SOVIET WRITINGS, BIBLIOG
1945-1958: A BIBLIOGRAPHY. USSR LAW ECO/UNDEV LABOR WRITING
DIPLOM EDU/PROP REV...GEOG SOC 20. PAGE 78 E1573 COM
L/A+17C

B60
FLORES R.H.,CATALOGO DE TESIS DOCTORALES DE LAS BIBLIOG
FACULTADES DE LA UNIVERSIDAD DE EL SALVADOR. ACADEM
EL/SALVADR LAW DIPLOM ADMIN LEAD GOV/REL...SOC L/A+17C
19/20. PAGE 39 E0767 NAT/G

B60
MOCTEZUMA A.P.,EL CONFLICTO RELIGIOSO DE 1926 (2ND SECT
ED.). L/A+17C LAW NAT/G LOBBY COERCE GP/REL ATTIT ORD/FREE
...POLICY 20 MEXIC/AMER CHURCH/STA. PAGE 74 E1476 DISCRIM
REV

B60
PINTO F.B.M.,ENRIQUECIMENTO ILICITO NO EXERCICIO DE ADMIN
CARGOS PUBLICOS. BRAZIL L/A+17C USA+45 ELITES NAT/G
TRIBUTE CONTROL INGP/REL ORD/FREE PWR...NAT/COMP CRIME
20. PAGE 81 E1617 LAW

B60
US LIBRARY OF CONGRESS,INDEX TO LATIN AMERICAN BIBLIOG/A
LEGISLATION: 1950-1960 (2 VOLS.). NAT/G DELIB/GP LEGIS
ADMIN PARL/PROC 20. PAGE 101 E2019 L/A+17C
JURID

S60
GRACIA-MORA M.R.,"INTERNATIONAL RESPONSIBILITY FOR INT/ORG
SUBVERSIVE ACTIVITIES AND HOSTILE PROPAGANDA BY JURID
PRIVATE PERSONS AGAINST." COM EUR+WWI L/A+17C UK SOVEREIGN
USA+45 USSR WOR-45 CONSTN NAT/G LEGIT ADJUD REV
PEACE TOTALISM ORD/FREE...INT/LAW 20. PAGE 45 E0895

S60
NICHOLS J.P.,"HAZARDS OF AMERICAN PRIVATE FINAN
INVESTMENT IN UNDERDEVELOPED COUNTRIES." FUT ECO/UNDEV
L/A+17C USA+45 USA-45 EXTR/IND CONSULT BAL/PWR CAP/ISM
ECO/TAC DOMIN ADJUD ATTIT SOVEREIGN WEALTH NAT/LISM
...HIST/WRIT TIME/SEQ TREND VAL/FREE 20. PAGE 77
E1546

B61
BAYITCH S.A.,LATIN AMERICA: A BIBLIOGRAPHICAL BIBLIOG
GUIDE. LAW CONSTN LEGIS JUDGE ADJUD CT/SYS 20. L/A+17C
PAGE 8 E0158 NAT/G
JURID

B61
MECHAM J.L.,THE UNITED STATES AND INTER-AMERICAN DIPLOM
SECURITY, 1889-1960. L/A+17C USA+45 USA-45 CONSTN WAR
FORCES INT/TRADE PEACE TOTALISM ATTIT...JURID 19/20 ORD/FREE
UN OAS. PAGE 72 E1432 INT/ORG

B62
KIDDER F.E.,THESES ON PAN AMERICAN TOPICS. LAW BIBLIOG
CULTURE NAT/G SECT DIPLOM HEALTH...ART/METH GEOG CHRIST-17C
SOC 13/20. PAGE 61 E1213 L/A+17C
SOCIETY

B62
LEVY H.V.,LIBERDADE E JUSTICA SOCIAL (2ND ED.). ORD/FREE
BRAZIL COM L/A+17C USSR INT/ORG PARTIC GP/REL MARXISM
WEALTH 20 UN COM/PARTY. PAGE 65 E1290 CAP/ISM
LAW

L62
NIZARD L.,"CUBAN QUESTION AND SECURITY COUNCIL." INT/ORG
L/A+17C USA+45 ECO/UNDEV NAT/G POL/PAR DELIB/GP JURID
ECO/TAC PWR...RELATIV OBS TIME/SEQ TREND GEN/LAWS DIPLOM
UN 20 UN. PAGE 77 E1551 CUBA

S62
FENWICK C.G.,"ISSUES AT PUNTA DEL ESTE: NON- INT/ORG

INTERVENTION VS COLLECTIVE SECURITY." L/A+17C   CUBA
USA+45 VOL/ASSN DELIB/GP ECO/TAC LEGIT ADJUD REGION
ORD/FREE OAS COLD/WAR 20. PAGE 37 E0738

B63
FORTES A.B.,HISTORIA ADMINISTRATIVA, JUDICIARIA E   PROVS
ECLESIASTICA DO RIO GRANDE DO SUL. BRAZIL L/A+17C   ADMIN
LOC/G SECT COLONIAL CT/SYS ORD/FREE CATHISM 16/20.   JURID
PAGE 39 E0773

B64
BERNSTEIN H.,A BOOKSHELF ON BRAZIL. BRAZIL ADMIN   BIBLIOG/A
COLONIAL...HUM JURID SOC 20. PAGE 11 E0213   NAT/G
                                                      L/A+17C
                                                      ECO/UNDEV

B64
ROBINSON R.D.,INTERNATIONAL BUSINESS POLICY. AFR   ECO/TAC
INDIA L/A+17C USA+45 ELITES AGRI FOR/AID COERCE   DIST/IND
BAL/PAY...DECISION INT/LAW MGT 20. PAGE 85 E1706   COLONIAL
                                                      FINAN

S64
DERWINSKI E.J.,"THE COST OF THE INTERNATIONAL   MARKET
COFFEE AGREEMENT." L/A+17C USA+45 WOR+45 ECO/UNDEV   DELIB/GP
NAT/G VOL/ASSN LEGIS DIPLOM ECO/TAC FOR/AID LEGIT   INT/TRADE
ATTIT...TIME/SEQ CONGRESS 20 TREATY. PAGE 31 E0608

B65
THOMAS A.V.,NONINTERVENTION: THE LAW AND ITS IMPORT   INT/LAW
IN THE AMERICAS. L/A+17C USA+45 USA-45 WOR+45   PWR
DIPLOM ADJUD...JURID IDEA/COMP 20 UN INTERVENT.   COERCE
PAGE 96 E1917

S66
ANAND R.P.,"ATTITUDE OF THE ASIAN-AFRICAN STATES   INT/LAW
TOWARD CERTAIN PROBLEMS OF INTERNATIONAL LAW."   ATTIT
L/A+17C S/ASIA ECO/UNDEV CREATE CONFER ADJUD   ASIA
COLONIAL...RECORD GP/COMP UN. PAGE 5 E0087   AFR

B67
BAILEY N.A.,LATIN AMERICA IN WORLD POLITICS. PWR   L/A+17C
CONSERVE MARXISM...INT/LAW TREND BIBLIOG/A T OAS   DIPLOM
COLD/WAR. PAGE 7 E0134   INT/ORG
                                                      ATTIT

B67
DIEGUES M.,SOCIAL SCIENCE IN LATIN AMERICA. L/A+17C   METH
...JURID SOC ANTHOL 20. PAGE 31 E0624   ACADEM
                                                      EDU/PROP
                                                      ACT/RES

B67
GARCIA ROBLES A.,THE DENUCLEARIZATION OF LATIN   NUC/PWR
AMERICA (TRANS. BY MARJORIE URQUIDI). LAW PLAN   ARMS/CONT
DIPLOM...ANTHOL 20 TREATY UN. PAGE 42 E0833   L/A+17C
                                                      INT/ORG

B67
SLATER J.,THE OAS AND UNITED STATES FOREIGN POLICY.   INT/ORG
KOREA L/A+17C USA+45 VOL/ASSN RISK COERCE PEACE   DIPLOM
ORD/FREE MARXISM...TREND 20 OAS. PAGE 92 E1838   ALL/IDEOS
                                                      ADJUD

B67
US SENATE COMM ON FOREIGN REL,INTER-AMERICAN   LAW
DEVELOPMENT BANK ACT AMENDMENT. L/A+17C USA+45   FINAN
DELIB/GP DIPLOM FOR/AID BAL/PAY...CHARTS SENATE.   INT/ORG
PAGE 102 E2034   ECO/UNDEV

S67
CUMMINS L.,"THE FORMULATION OF THE "PLATT"   DIPLOM
AMENDMENT." CUBA L/A+17C NAT/G DELIB/GP CONFER   INT/LAW
...POLICY 20. PAGE 28 E0554   LEGIS

S67
FABREGA J.,"ANTECEDENTES EXTRANJEROS EN LA   CONSTN
CONSTITUCION PANAMENA." CUBA L/A+17C PANAMA URUGUAY   JURID
EX/STRUC LEGIS DIPLOM ORD/FREE 19/20 COLOMB   NAT/G
MEXIC/AMER. PAGE 36 E0709   PARL/PROC

S67
TOMASEK R.D.,"THE CHILEAN-BOLIVIAN LAUCA RIVER   INT/ORG
DISPUTE AND THE OAS." CHILE L/A+17C PROB/SOLV ADJUD   DIPLOM
CONTROL PEACE 20 BOLIV OAS. PAGE 96 E1930   GEOG
                                                      WAR

N67
US SENATE COMM ON FOREIGN REL,SURVEY OF THE   INT/TRADE
ALLIANCE FOR PROGRESS: FOREIGN TRADE POLICIES   REGION
(PAMPHLET). L/A+17C LAW ECO/UNDEV ECO/TAC TARIFFS   AGREE
20 GATT LAFTA UN. PAGE 102 E2037   INT/ORG

B68
GREGG R.W.,INTERNATIONAL ORGANIZATION IN THE   INT/ORG
WESTERN HEMISPHERE. L/A+17C USA+45 CULTURE PLAN   DIPLOM

DOMIN AGREE CONTROL DETER PWR...GEOG 20 OAS TREATY. ECO/UNDEV
PAGE 46 E0913

LA PONCE J.A. E1242,E1243

LAB/EXP....LABORATORY EXPERIMENTS

B37
BEARDSLEY A.R.,LEGAL BIBLIOGRAPHY AND THE USE OF   BIBLIOG
LAW BOOKS. CONSTN CREATE PROB/SOLV...DECISION JURID   LAW
LAB/EXP. PAGE 9 E0166   METH
                                                      OP/RES

S63
HILLS R.J.,"THE REPRESENTATIVE FUNCTION: NEGLECTED   LEAD
DIMENSION OF LEADERSHIP BEHAVIOR" USA+45 CLIENT   ADMIN
STRUCT SCHOOL PERS/REL...STAT QU SAMP LAB/EXP 20.   EXEC
PAGE 53 E1048   ACT/RES

LABOR FORCE....SEE WORKER

LABOR RELATIONS....SEE LABOR, ALSO RELATIONS INDEX

LABOR UNIONS....SEE LABOR

LABOR....LABOR UNIONS (BUT NOT GUILDS)

N
FULLER G.A.,DEMOBILIZATION: A SELECTED LIST OF   BIBLIOG/A
REFERENCES. USA+45 LAW AGRI LABOR WORKER ECO/TAC   INDUS
RATION RECEIVE EDU/PROP ROUTINE ARMS/CONT ALL/VALS   FORCES
20. PAGE 41 E0819   NAT/G

N
CANADIAN GOVERNMENT PUBLICATIONS (1955-). CANADA   BIBLIOG/A
AGRI FINAN LABOR FORCES INT/TRADE HEALTH...JURID 20   NAT/G
PARLIAMENT. PAGE 1 E0005   DIPLOM
                                                      INT/ORG

N
INTERNATIONAL BOOK NEWS, 1928-1934. ECO/UNDEV FINAN   BIBLIOG/A
INDUS LABOR INT/TRADE CONFER ADJUD COLONIAL...HEAL   DIPLOM
SOC/WK CHARTS 20 LEAGUE/NAT. PAGE 1 E0008   INT/LAW
                                                      INT/ORG

N
ADVANCED MANAGEMENT. INDUS EX/STRUC WORKER OP/RES   MGT
...DECISION BIBLIOG/A 20. PAGE 1 E0015   ADMIN
                                                      LABOR
                                                      GP/REL

N
ARBITRATION JOURNAL. WOR+45 LAW INDUS JUDGE DIPLOM   BIBLIOG
CT/SYS INGP/REL 20. PAGE 1 E0016   MGT
                                                      LABOR
                                                      ADJUD

N
THE JAPAN SCIENCE REVIEW: LAW AND POLITICS: LIST OF   BIBLIOG
BOOKS AND ARTICLES ON LAW AND POLITICS. CONSTN AGRI   LAW
INDUS LABOR DIPLOM TAX ADMIN CRIME...INT/LAW SOC 20   S/ASIA
CHINJAP. PAGE 2 E0027   PHIL/SCI

N
PERSONNEL. USA+45 LAW LABOR LG/CO WORKER CREATE   BIBLIOG/A
GOV/REL PERS/REL ATTIT WEALTH. PAGE 2 E0029   ADMIN
                                                      MGT
                                                      GP/REL

N
AFRICAN BIBLIOGRAPHIC CENTER,A CURRENT BIBLIOGRAPHY   BIBLIOG/A
ON AFRICAN AFFAIRS. LAW CULTURE ECO/UNDEV LABOR   AFR
SECT DIPLOM FOR/AID COLONIAL NAT/LISM...LING 20.   NAT/G
PAGE 3 E0053   REGION

B03
GRIFFIN A.P.C.,LIST OF REFERENCES ON INDUSTRIAL   BIBLIOG/A
ARBITRATION (PAMPHLET). USA-45 STRATA VOL/ASSN   INDUS
DELIB/GP WORKER ADJUD GP/REL...MGT 19/20. PAGE 46   LABOR
E0921   BARGAIN

B03
GRIFFIN A.P.C.,LISTS PUBLISHED 1902-03: LABOR   BIBLIOG/A
PARTICULARLY RELATING TO STRIKES (PAMPHLET). UK   LABOR
USA-45 FINAN WORKER PLAN BARGAIN CRIME GOV/REL   GP/REL
...POLICY 19/20 PARLIAMENT. PAGE 46 E0923   ECO/TAC

B03
GRIFFIN A.P.C.,SELECT LIST OF BOOKS ON LABOR   BIBLIOG/A
PARTICULARLY RELATING TO STRIKES. FRANCE GERMANY   GP/REL
MOD/EUR UK USA-45 LAW NAT/G DELIB/GP WORKER BARGAIN   MGT
LICENSE PAY ADJUD 19/20. PAGE 46 E0924   LABOR

B06
GRIFFIN A.P.C.,LIST OF BOOKS RELATING TO CHILD   BIBLIOG/A
LABOR (PAMPHLET). BELGIUM FRANCE GERMANY MOD/EUR UK   LAW

USA-45 ECO/DEV INDUS WORKER CAP/ISM PAY ROUTINE   LABOR
ALL/IDEOS...MGT SOC 19/20. PAGE 47 E0929   AGE/C

B11
REINSCH P.,PUBLIC INTERNATIONAL UNION. WOR-45 LAW   FUT
LABOR INT/TRADE LEGIT PERSON ALL/VALS...SOCIALIST   INT/ORG
CONCPT TIME/SEQ TREND GEN/LAWS 19/20. PAGE 84 E1683   DIPLOM

N18
BREWER D.J.,THE MOVEMENT OF COERCION (PAMPHLET).   GP/REL
CONSTN INDUS ADJUD COERCE OWN WEALTH...OLD/LIB   LABOR
JURID 19 SUPREME/CT. PAGE 15 E0296   LG/CO
  LAW

N19
THE REGIONAL DIRECTOR AND THE PRESS (PAMPHLET).   PRESS
USA-45 COM/IND LOBBY ROLE 20 NLRB CINCINNATI   LABOR
BILL/RIGHT. PAGE 2 E0031   ORD/FREE
  EDU/PROP

N19
HOGARTY R.A.,NEW JERSEY FARMERS AND MIGRANT HOUSING AGRI
RULES (PAMPHLET). USA+45 LAW ELITES FACE/GP LABOR   PROVS
PROF/ORG LOBBY PERS/REL RIGID/FLEX ROLE 20   WORKER
NEW/JERSEY. PAGE 53 E1067   HEALTH

N19
MCCONNELL G.,THE STEEL SEIZURE OF 1952 (PAMPHLET).   DELIB/GP
USA+45 FINAN INDUS PROC/MFG LG/CO EX/STRUC ADJUD   LABOR
CONTROL GP/REL ORD/FREE PWR 20 TRUMAN/HS PRESIDENT   PROB/SOLV
CONGRESS. PAGE 70 E1402   NAT/G

B31
BORCHARD E.H.,GUIDE TO THE LAW AND LEGAL LITERATURE BIBLIOG/A
OF FRANCE. FRANCE FINAN INDUS LABOR SECT LEGIS   LAW
ADMIN COLONIAL CRIME OWN...INT/LAW 20. PAGE 14   CONSTN
E0266   METH

B35
NORDSKOG J.E.,SOCIAL REFORM IN NORWAY. NORWAY INDUS LABOR
NAT/G POL/PAR LEGIS ADJUD...SOC BIBLIOG SOC/INTEG   ADJUST
20. PAGE 78 E1555

B36
HERRING E.P.,PUBLIC ADMINISTRATION AND THE PUBLIC   GP/REL
INTEREST. LABOR NAT/G PARTIC EFFICIENCY 20. PAGE 52 DECISION
E1033   PROB/SOLV
  ADMIN

B36
HUDSON M.O.,INTERNATIONAL LEGISLATION: 1929-1931.   INT/LAW
WOR-45 SEA AIR AGRI FINAN LABOR DIPLOM ECO/TAC   PARL/PROC
REPAR CT/SYS ARMS/CONT WAR WEAPON...JURID 20 TREATY ADJUD
LEAGUE/NAT. PAGE 56 E1112   LAW

B37
BUREAU OF NATIONAL AFFAIRS,LABOR RELATIONS   LABOR
REFERENCE MANUAL VOL 1, 1935-1937. BARGAIN DEBATE   ADMIN
ROUTINE INGP/REL 20 NLRB. PAGE 17 E0335   ADJUD
  NAT/G

B37
RUTHERFORD M.L.,THE INFLUENCE OF THE AMERICAN BAR   ATTIT
ASSOCIATION ON PUBLIC OPINION AND LEGISLATION.   ADJUD
USA+45 LAW CONSTN LABOR LEGIS DOMIN EDU/PROP LEGIT   PROF/ORG
CT/SYS ROUTINE...TIME/SEQ 19/20 ABA. PAGE 87 E1739   JURID

B38
FIELD G.L.,THE SYNDICAL AND CORPORATIVE   FASCISM
INSTITUTIONS OF ITALIAN FASCISM. ITALY CONSTN   INDUS
STRATA LABOR EX/STRUC TOP/EX ADJUD ADMIN LEAD   NAT/G
TOTALISM AUTHORIT...MGT 20 MUSSOLINI/B. PAGE 38   WORKER
E0746

B43
BACKUS R.C.,A GUIDE TO THE LAW AND LEGAL LITERATURE BIBLIOG/A
OF COLOMBIA. FINAN INDUS LABOR FORCES ADJUD ADMIN   LAW
COLONIAL CT/SYS CRIME...INT/LAW JURID 20 COLOMB.   CONSTN
PAGE 7 E0127   L/A+17C

B43
CLAGETT H.L.,A GUIDE TO THE LAW AND LEGAL   BIBLIOG
LITERATURE OF PARAGUAY. PARAGUAY CONSTN COM/IND   JURID
LABOR MUNIC JUDGE ADMIN CT/SYS...CRIMLGY INT/LAW   LAW
CON/ANAL 20. PAGE 22 E0439   L/A+17C

B45
GALLOWAY E.,ABSTRACTS OF POSTWAR LITERATURE (VOL.   BIBLIOG/A
IV) JAN.-JULY, 1945 NOS. 901-1074. POLAND USA+45   NUC/PWR
USSR WOR+45 INDUS LABOR PLAN ECO/TAC INT/TRADE TAX   NAT/G
EDU/PROP ADMIN COLONIAL INT/LAW. PAGE 42 E0829   DIPLOM

B45
VANCE H.L.,GUIDE TO THE LAW AND LEGAL LITERATURE OF BIBLIOG/A
MEXICO. LAW CONSTN FINAN LABOR FORCES ADJUD ADMIN   INT/LAW
...CRIMLGY PHIL/SCI CON/ANAL 20 MEXIC/AMER.   JURID

PAGE 103 E2070   CT/SYS

B47
CLAGETT H.L.,A GUIDE TO THE LAW AND LEGAL   BIBLIOG/A
LITERATURE OF BOLIVIA. L/A+17C CONSTN LABOR LEGIS   JURID
ADMIN...CRIMLGY INT/LAW PHIL/SCI 16/20 BOLIV.   LAW
PAGE 22 E0441   CT/SYS

B47
CLAGETT H.L.,A GUIDE TO THE LAW AND LEGAL   BIBLIOG
LITERATURE OF CHILE, 1917-1946. CHILE CONSTN LABOR L/A+17C
JUDGE ADJUD ADMIN...CRIMLGY INT/LAW JURID CON/ANAL   LAW
20. PAGE 22 E0442   LEGIS

B47
CLAGETT H.L.,A GUIDE TO THE LAW AND LEGAL   BIBLIOG
LITERATURE OF ECUADOR. ECUADOR CONSTN LABOR LEGIS   JURID
JUDGE ADJUD ADMIN CIVMIL/REL...CRIMLGY INT/LAW   LAW
CON/ANAL 20. PAGE 22 E0443   L/A+17C

B47
CLAGETT H.L.,A GUIDE TO THE LAW AND LEGAL   BIBLIOG
LITERATURE OF PERU. PERU CONSTN COM/IND LABOR MUNIC L/A+17C
JUDGE ADMIN CT/SYS...CRIMLGY INT/LAW JURID 20.   PHIL/SCI
PAGE 23 E0444   LAW

B47
CLAGETT H.L.,A GUIDE TO THE LAW AND LEGAL   BIBLIOG
LITERATURE OF URUGUAY. URUGUAY CONSTN COM/IND FINAN LAW
LABOR MUNIC JUDGE PRESS ADMIN CT/SYS...INT/LAW   JURID
PHIL/SCI 20. PAGE 23 E0445   L/A+17C

B47
CLAGETT H.L.,A GUIDE TO THE LAW AND LEGAL   BIBLIOG
LITERATURE OF VENEZUELA. VENEZUELA CONSTN LABOR   L/A+17C
LEGIS JUDGE ADJUD ADMIN CIVMIL/REL...CRIMLGY JURID   INT/LAW
CON/ANAL 20. PAGE 23 E0446   LAW

B48
CLAGETT H.L.,A GUIDE TO THE LAW AND LEGAL   BIBLIOG
LITERATURE OF ARGENTINA, 1917-1946. CONSTN LABOR   L/A+17C
JUDGE ADJUD ADMIN...CRIMLGY INT/LAW JURID CON/ANAL   LAW
20 ARGEN. PAGE 23 E0447   LEGIS

C49
BLODGETT R.H.,"COMPARATIVE ECONOMIC SYSTEMS (REV.   METH/COMP
ED.)" WOR-45 AGRI FINAN MARKET LABOR NAT/G PLAN   CONCPT
INT/TRADE PRICE...POLICY DECISION BIBLIOG 20.   ROUTINE
PAGE 13 E0248

B50
BERMAN H.J.,JUSTICE IN RUSSIA; AN INTERPRETATION OF JURID
SOVIET LAW. USSR LAW STRUCT LABOR FORCES AGREE   ADJUD
GP/REL ORD/FREE SOCISM...TIME/SEQ 20. PAGE 11 E0207 MARXISM
  COERCE

B51
FRIEDMANN W.,LAW AND SOCIAL CHANGE IN CONTEMPORARY   LAW
BRITAIN. UK LABOR LG/CO LEGIS JUDGE CT/SYS ORD/FREE ADJUD
NEW/LIB...DECISION JURID TREND METH/COMP BIBLIOG 20 SOCIETY
PARLIAMENT ENGLSH/LAW COMMON/LAW. PAGE 40 E0802   CONSTN

B52
JACKSON E.,MEETING OF THE MINDS: A WAY TO PEACE   LABOR
THROUGH MEDIATION. WOR+45 INDUS INT/ORG NAT/G   JUDGE
DELIB/GP DIPLOM EDU/PROP LEGIT ORD/FREE...NEW/IDEA
SELF/OBS TIME/SEQ CHARTS GEN/LAWS TOT/POP 20 UN
TREATY. PAGE 57 E1139

B54
BINANI G.D.,INDIA AT A GLANCE (REV. ED.). INDIA   INDEX
COM/IND FINAN INDUS LABOR PROVS SCHOOL PLAN DIPLOM   CON/ANAL
INT/TRADE ADMIN...JURID 20. PAGE 12 E0229   NAT/G
  ECO/UNDEV

B54
CAPLOW T.,THE SOCIOLOGY OF WORK. USA+45 USA-45   LABOR
STRATA MARKET FAM GP/REL INGP/REL ALL/VALS   WORKER
...DECISION STAT BIBLIOG SOC/INTEG 20. PAGE 19   INDUS
E0375   ROLE

B54
CARTER P.G.,STATISTICAL BULLETINS: AN ANNOTATED   BIBLIOG/A
BIBLIOGRAPHY OF THE GENERAL STATISTICAL BULLETINS   WOR+45
AND MAJOR POL SUBDIV OF WORLD. CULTURE AGRI FINAN   NAT/G
INDUS LABOR TEC/DEV INT/TRADE CT/SYS WEALTH   STAT
...CRIMLGY SOC 20. PAGE 20 E0400

C54
BOWIE R.R.,"STUDIES IN FEDERALISM." AGRI FINAN   FEDERAL
LABOR EX/STRUC FORCES LEGIS DIPLOM INT/TRADE ADJUD   EUR+WWI
...BIBLIOG 20 EEC. PAGE 14 E0279   INT/ORG
  CONSTN

B55
BLOOM G.F.,ECONOMICS OF LABOR RELATIONS. USA+45 LAW ECO/DEV

CONSULT WORKER CAP/ISM PAY ADJUD CONTROL EFFICIENCY ECO/TAC
ORD/FREE...CHARTS 19/20 AFL/CIO NLRB DEPT/LABOR. LABOR
PAGE 13 E0249 GOV/REL

B55

BRAUN K.,LABOR DISPUTES AND THEIR SETTLEMENT. INDUS
ECO/TAC ROUTINE TASK GP/REL...DECISION GEN/LAWS. LABOR
PAGE 15 E0288 BARGAIN
ADJUD

B55

GRINDEL C.W.,CONCEPT OF FREEDOM. WOR+45 WOR-45 LAW ORD/FREE
LABOR NAT/G SECT EDU/PROP 20. PAGE 47 E0942 DIPLOM
CONCPT
GP/REL

B55

JAPAN MOMBUSHO DAIGAKU GAKIYUT,BIBLIOGRAPHY OF THE BIBLIOG
STUDIES ON LAW AND POLITICS (PAMPHLET). CONSTN LAW
INDUS LABOR DIPLOM TAX ADMIN...CRIMLGY INT/LAW 20 PHIL/SCI
CHINJAP. PAGE 58 E1150

B55

LARROWE C.P.,SHAPE-UP AND HIRING HALL. TRIBUTE LABOR
ADJUD CONTROL SANCTION COERCE CRIME GP/REL PWR INDUS
...CHARTS 20 AFL/CIO NEWYORK/C SEATTLE. PAGE 63 WORKER
E1256 NAT/G

B55

SERRANO MOSCOSO E.,A STATEMENT OF THE LAWS OF FINAN
ECUADOR IN MATTERS AFFECTING BUSINESS (2ND ED.). ECO/UNDEV
ECUADOR INDUS LABOR LG/CO NAT/G LEGIS TAX CONTROL LAW
MARRIAGE 20. PAGE 90 E1805 CONSTN

B56

HOGAN J.D.,AMERICAN SOCIAL LEGISLATION. USA+45 FAM STRUCT
AGE/Y ATTIT...JURID CONCPT TREND. PAGE 53 E1065 RECEIVE
LEGIS
LABOR

B57

JENKS C.W.,THE INTERNATIONAL PROTECTION OF TRADE LABOR
UNION FREEDOM. FUT WOR+45 WOR-45 VOL/ASSN DELIB/GP INT/ORG
CT/SYS REGION ROUTINE...JURID METH/CNCPT RECORD
TIME/SEQ CHARTS ILO WORK OAS 20. PAGE 58 E1153

B58

BUREAU OF NATIONAL AFFAIRS,THE MCCLELLAN COMMITTEE DELIB/GP
HEARINGS - 1957. USA+45 LEGIS CONTROL CRIME CONFER
...CHARTS 20 CONGRESS AFL/CIO MCCLELLN/J. PAGE 17 LABOR
E0336 MGT

B58

CHAMBERLIN E.H.,LABOR UNIONS AND PUBLIC POLICY. LABOR
PLAN BARGAIN SANCTION INGP/REL JURID. PAGE 21 E0416 WEALTH
PWR
NAT/G

B58

CUNNINGHAM W.B.,COMPULSORY CONCILIATION AND POLICY
COLLECTIVE BARGAINING. CANADA NAT/G LEGIS ADJUD BARGAIN
CT/SYS GP/REL...MGT 20 NEW/BRUNS STRIKE CASEBOOK. LABOR
PAGE 28 E0555 INDUS

L58

INT. SOC. SCI. BULL.,"TECHNIQUES OF MEDIATION AND VOL/ASSN
CONCILIATION." EUR+WWI USA+45 SOCIETY INDUS INT/ORG DELIB/GP
LABOR NAT/G LEGIS DIPLOM EDU/PROP CHOOSE ATTIT INT/LAW
RIGID/FLEX...JURID CONCPT GEN/LAWS 20. PAGE 57
E1129

B59

BRIGGS A.,CHARTIST STUDIES. UK LAW NAT/G WORKER INDUS
EDU/PROP COERCE SUFF GP/REL ATTIT...ANTHOL 19. STRATA
PAGE 15 E0300 LABOR
POLICY

B59

BROMWICH L.,UNION CONSTITUTIONS. CONSTN EX/STRUC LABOR
PRESS ADJUD CONTROL CHOOSE REPRESENT PWR SAMP. ROUTINE
PAGE 16 E0306 INGP/REL
RACE/REL

B59

EPSTEIN F.T.,EAST GERMANY: A SELECTED BIBLIOGRAPHY BIBLIOG/A
(PAMPHLET). COM GERMANY/E LAW AGRI FINAN INDUS INTELL
LABOR POL/PAR EDU/PROP ADMIN AGE/Y 20. PAGE 35 MARXISM
E0693 NAT/G

B59

FERRY W.H.,THE CORPORATION AND THE ECONOMY. CLIENT LG/CO
LAW CONSTN LABOR NAT/G PLAN INT/TRADE PARTIC CONSEN CONTROL
ORD/FREE PWR POLICY. PAGE 37 E0742 REPRESENT

B59

GINSBURG M.,LAW AND OPINION IN ENGLAND. UK CULTURE JURID

KIN LABOR LEGIS EDU/PROP ADMIN CT/SYS CRIME OWN POLICY
HEALTH...ANTHOL 20 ENGLSH/LAW. PAGE 44 E0868 ECO/TAC

B59

OKINSHEVICH L.A.,LATIN AMERICA IN SOVIET WRITINGS, BIBLIOG
1945-1958: A BIBLIOGRAPHY. USSR LAW ECO/UNDEV LABOR WRITING
DIPLOM EDU/PROP REV...GEOG SOC 20. PAGE 78 E1573 COM
L/A+17C

L59

COWAN T.A.,"A SYMPOSIUM ON GROUP INTERESTS AND THE ADJUD
LAW" USA+45 LAW MARKET LABOR PLAN INT/TRADE TAX PWR
RACE/REL RIGID/FLEX...JURID ANTHOL 20. PAGE 27 INGP/REL
E0528 CREATE

L59

COX A.,"THE ROLE OF LAW IN PRESERVING UNION LABOR
DEMOCRACY." EX/STRUC LEGIS PARTIC ROUTINE CHOOSE REPRESENT
INGP/REL ORD/FREE. PAGE 27 E0532 LAW
MAJORIT

L59

OBERER W.E.,"VOLUNTARY IMPARTIAL REVIEW OF LABOR: LABOR
SOME REFLECTIONS." DELIB/GP LEGIS PROB/SOLV ADJUD LAW
CONTROL COERCE PWR PLURISM POLICY. PAGE 78 E1570 PARTIC
INGP/REL

S59

BELL D.,"THE RACKET RIDDEN LONGSHOREMEN" (BMR)" CRIME
USA+45 SEA WORKER MURDER ROLE...SOC 20 NEWYORK/C. LABOR
PAGE 9 E0182 DIST/IND
ELITES

S59

TIPTON J.B.,"PARTICIPATION OF THE UNITED STATES IN LABOR
THE INTERNATIONAL LABOR ORGANIZATION." USA+45 LAW INT/ORG
STRUCT ECO/DEV ECO/UNDEV INDUS TEC/DEV ECO/TAC
ADMIN PERCEPT ORD/FREE SKILL...STAT HIST/WRIT
GEN/METH ILO WORK 20. PAGE 96 E1928

B60

JENKS C.W.,HUMAN RIGHTS AND INTERNATIONAL LABOR CONCPT
STANDARDS. WOR+45 CONSTN LABOR VOL/ASSN DELIB/GP
ACT/RES EDU/PROP MORAL RESPECT...JURID SOC TREND
GEN/LAWS WORK ILO 20. PAGE 58 E1156

B60

PAUL A.M.,CONSERVATIVE CRISIS AND THE RULE OF LAW. CONSTN
USA-45 LABOR WORKER ATTIT ORD/FREE CONSERVE LAISSEZ ADJUD
...DECISION JURID 19 SUPREME/CT. PAGE 80 E1603 STRUCT
PROF/ORG

S60

MANN S.Z.,"POLICY FORMULATION IN THE EXECUTIVE EXEC
BRANCH: THE TAFT-HARTLEY EXPERIENCE." USA+45 LABOR GOV/REL
CHIEF INGP/REL 20 NLRB. PAGE 68 E1360 EX/STRUC
PROB/SOLV

B61

BARBASH J.,LABOR'S GRASS ROOTS. CONSTN NAT/G LABOR
EX/STRUC LEGIS WORKER LEAD...MAJORIT BIBLIOG. INGP/REL
PAGE 8 E0147 GP/REL
LAW

B61

CARNELL F.,THE POLITICS OF THE NEW STATES: A SELECT BIBLIOG/A
ANNOTATED BIBLIOGRAPHY WITH SPECIAL REFERENCE TO AFR
THE COMMONWEALTH. CONSTN ELITES LABOR NAT/G POL/PAR ASIA
EX/STRUC DIPLOM ADJUD ADMIN...GOV/COMP 20 COLONIAL
COMMONWLTH. PAGE 20 E0387

B61

CARROTHERS A.W.R.,LABOR ARBITRATION IN CANADA. LABOR
CANADA LAW NAT/G CONSULT LEGIS WORKER ADJUD ADMIN MGT
CT/SYS 20. PAGE 20 E0396 GP/REL
BARGAIN

B61

RUEDA B.,A STATEMENT OF THE LAWS OF COLOMBIA IN FINAN
MATTERS AFFECTING BUSINESS (3RD ED.). INDUS FAM ECO/UNDEV
LABOR LG/CO NAT/G LEGIS TAX CONTROL MARRIAGE 20 LAW
COLOMB. PAGE 86 E1733 CONSTN

L61

TAUBENFELD H.J.,"A TREATY FOR ANTARCTICA." FUT R+D
USA+45 INTELL INT/ORG LABOR 20 TREATY ANTARCTICA. ACT/RES
PAGE 95 E1909 DIPLOM

B62

ALEXANDROWICZ C.H.,WORLD ECONOMIC AGENCIES: LAW AND INT/LAW
PRACTICE. WOR+45 DIST/IND FINAN LABOR CONSULT INT/ORG
INT/TRADE TARIFFS REPRESENT HEALTH...JURID 20 UN DIPLOM
GATT EEC OAS ECSC. PAGE 3 E0063 ADJUD

B62

DIESING P.,REASON IN SOCIETY; FIVE TYPES OF RATIONAL

DECISIONS AND THEIR SOCIAL CONDITIONS. SOCIETY STRUCT LABOR CREATE TEC/DEV BARGAIN ADJUD ROLE ...JURID BIBLIOG 20. PAGE 31 E0625
METH/COMP
DECISION
CONCPT

B62

GALENSON W.,TRADE UNIONS MONOGRAPH SERIES (A SERIES OF NINE TEXTS). DELIB/GP LEAD PARTIC...DECISION ORG/CHARTS. PAGE 42 E0827
LABOR
INGP/REL
CONSTN
REPRESENT

L62

N,"UNION INVESTMENT IN BUSINESS: A SOURCE OF UNION CONFLICT OF INTEREST." LAW NAT/G LEGIS CONTROL GP/REL INGP/REL DECISION. PAGE 76 E1515
LABOR
POLICY
FINAN
LG/CO

B63

FISCHER-GALATI S.A.,RUMANIA; A BIBLIOGRAPHIC GUIDE (PAMPHLET). ROMANIA INTELL ECO/DEV LABOR SECT WEALTH...GEOG SOC/WK LING 20. PAGE 38 E0756
BIBLIOG/A
NAT/G
COM
LAW

B63

GINZBERG E.,DEMOCRATIC VALUES AND THE RIGHTS OF MANAGEMENT. LAW CONSTN REPRESENT GP/REL ROLE PWR RESPECT POLICY. PAGE 44 E0870
LABOR
MGT
DELIB/GP
ADJUD

B63

GOURNAY B.,PUBLIC ADMINISTRATION. FRANCE LAW CONSTN AGRI FINAN LABOR SCHOOL EX/STRUC CHOOSE...MGT METH/COMP 20. PAGE 45 E0894
BIBLIOG/A
ADMIN
NAT/G
LOC/G

B63

JACOBS P.,STATE OF UNIONS. USA+45 STRATA TOP/EX GP/REL RACE/REL DEMAND DISCRIM ATTIT PWR 20 CONGRESS NEGRO HOFFA/J. PAGE 57 E1145
LABOR
ECO/TAC
BARGAIN
DECISION

B63

LYONS F.S.L.,INTERNATIONALISM IN EUROPE 1815-1914. LAW AGRI COM/IND DIST/IND LABOR SECT INT/TRADE TARIFFS...BIBLIOG 19/20. PAGE 67 E1335
DIPLOM
MOD/EUR
INT/ORG

B63

ROBERT J.,LA MONARCHIE MAROCAINE. MOROCCO LABOR MUNIC POL/PAR EX/STRUC ORD/FREE PWR...JURID TREND T 20. PAGE 85 E1702
CHIEF
CONSERVE
ADMIN
CONSTN

B64

BROOKS T.R.,TOIL AND TROUBLE, A HISTORY OF AMERICAN LABOR. WORKER BARGAIN CAP/ISM ADJUD AUTOMAT EXEC GP/REL RACE/REL EFFICIENCY INCOME PROFIT MARXISM 17/20 KENNEDY/JF AFL/CIO NEGRO. PAGE 16 E0310
INDUS
LABOR
LEGIS

B64

GESELLSCHAFT RECHTSVERGLEICH,BIBLIOGRAPHIE DES DEUTSCHEN RECHTS (BIBLIOGRAPHY OF GERMAN LAW, TRANS. BY COURTLAND PETERSON). GERMANY FINAN INDUS LABOR SECT FORCES CT/SYS PARL/PROC CRIME...INT/LAW SOC NAT/COMP 20. PAGE 43 E0853
BIBLIOG/A
JURID
CONSTN
ADMIN

B64

MAKI J.M.,COURT AND CONSTITUTION IN JAPAN; SELECTED SUPREME COURT DECISIONS, 1948-60. FAM LABOR GOV/REL HABITAT ORD/FREE...DECISION JURID 20 CHINJAP SUPREME/CT CIV/RIGHTS. PAGE 68 E1354
CT/SYS
CONSTN
PROB/SOLV
LAW

B64

MITAU G.T.,INSOLUBLE PROBLEMS: CASE PROBLEMS ON THE FUNCTIONS OF STATE AND LOCAL GOVERNMENT. USA+45 AIR FINAN LABOR POL/PAR PROB/SOLV TAX RECEIVE CONTROL GP/REL 20 CASEBOOK ZONING. PAGE 73 E1471
ADJUD
LOC/G
PROVS

S64

N,"QUASI-LEGISLATIVE ARBITRATION AGREEMENTS." LAW LG/CO ECO/TAC SANCTION ATTIT POLICY. PAGE 76 E1516
ADJUD
ADJUST
LABOR
GP/REL

B65

BAR ASSOCIATION OF ST LOUIS,CONSTITUTIONAL FREEDOM AND THE LAW. USA+45 LAW LABOR LEGIS EDU/PROP ...JURID CONCPT SUPREME/CT CIVIL/LIB CIV/RIGHTS. PAGE 8 E0146
ORD/FREE
CONSTN
RACE/REL
NAT/G

B65

CARTER R.L.,EQUALITY. LAW LABOR NEIGH SCHOOL RACE/REL 20 NEGRO. PAGE 20 E0402
POLICY
DISCRIM
PLAN
CREATE

B65

FLEMING R.W.,THE LABOR ARBITRATION PROCESS. USA+45
GP/REL

LAW BARGAIN ADJUD ROUTINE SANCTION COST...PREDICT CHARTS TIME 20. PAGE 38 E0763
LABOR
CONSULT
DELIB/GP

B65

PROEHL P.O.,FOREIGN ENTERPRISE IN NIGERIA. NIGERIA FINAN LABOR NAT/G TAX 20. PAGE 83 E1656
ECO/UNDEV
ECO/TAC
JURID
CAP/ISM

B65

RENNER K.,MENSCH UND GESELLSCHAFT - GRUNDRISS EINER SOZIOLOGIE (2ND ED.). STRATA FAM LABOR PROF/ORG WAR ...JURID CLASSIF 20. PAGE 84 E1685
SOC
STRUCT
NAT/G
SOCIETY

B65

ROSS P.,THE GOVERNMENT AS A SOURCE OF UNION POWER. USA+45 LAW ECO/DEV PROB/SOLV ECO/TAC LEAD GP/REL ...MGT 20. PAGE 86 E1723
LABOR
BARGAIN
POLICY
NAT/G

B66

AUERBACH J.S.,LABOR AND LIBERTY; THE LA FOLLETTE COMMITTEE AND THE NEW DEAL. USA-45 LAW LEAD RESPECT SOCISM...BIBLIOG 20 CONGRESS BILL/RIGHT LAFOLLET/R NEW/DEAL. PAGE 6 E0117
DELIB/GP
LABOR
CONSTN
ORD/FREE

B66

HAYS P.R.,LABOR ARBITRATION: A DISSENTING VIEW. USA+45 LAW DELIB/GP BARGAIN ADJUD...PREDICT 20. PAGE 51 E1016
GP/REL
LABOR
CONSULT
CT/SYS

B66

KURLAND P.B.,THE SUPREME COURT REVIEW. USA+45 USA-45 LAW LABOR SUFF...ANTHOL 20 SUPREME/CT. PAGE 62 E1240
JURID
PROB/SOLV
ADJUD
NAT/G

B66

MCNAIR A.D.,THE LEGAL EFFECTS OF WAR. UK FINAN DIPLOM ORD/FREE 20 ENGLSH/LAW. PAGE 71 E1425
JURID
WAR
INT/TRADE
LABOR

B66

MOSKOW M.H.,TEACHERS AND UNIONS. SCHOOL WORKER ADJUD LOBBY ATTIT ORD/FREE 20. PAGE 75 E1501
EDU/PROP
PROF/ORG
LABOR
BARGAIN

B66

SZLADITS C.,A BIBLIOGRAPHY ON FOREIGN AND COMPARATIVE LAW (SUPPLEMENT 1964). FINAN FAM LABOR LG/CO LEGIS JUDGE ADMIN CRIME...CRIMLGY 20. PAGE 95 E1905
BIBLIOG/A
CT/SYS
INT/LAW

B66

WASHINGTON S.H.,BIBLIOGRAPHY: LABOR-MANAGEMENT RELATIONS ACT, 1947 AS AMENDED BY LABOR-MANAGEMENT REPORTING AND DISCLOSURE ACT, 1959. USA+45 CONSTN INDUS DELIB/GP LEGIS WORKER BARGAIN ECO/TAC ADJUD GP/REL NEW/LIB...JURID CONGRESS. PAGE 105 E2100
BIBLIOG
LAW
LABOR
MGT

S66

MATTHEWS D.G.,"ETHIOPIAN OUTLINE: A BIBLIOGRAPHIC RESEARCH GUIDE." ETHIOPIA LAW STRUCT ECO/UNDEV AGRI LABOR SECT CHIEF DELIB/GP EX/STRUC ADMIN...LING ORG/CHARTS 20. PAGE 69 E1384
BIBLIOG
NAT/G
DIPLOM
POL/PAR

B67

BAKKE E.W.,UNIONS, MANAGEMENT AND THE PUBLIC* READINGS AND TEXT. WORKER LOBBY...POLICY JURID ANTHOL T. PAGE 7 E0143
LABOR
INDUS
ADJUD
GP/REL

B67

BEAL E.F.,THE PRACTICE OF COLLECTIVE BARGAINING (3RD ED.). USA+45 WOR+45 ECO/DEV INDUS LG/CO PROF/ORG WORKER ECO/TAC GP/REL WEALTH...JURID METH/CNCPT. PAGE 8 E0160
BARGAIN
MGT
LABOR
ADJUD

B67

COHEN M.R.,LAW AND THE SOCIAL ORDER: ESSAYS IN LEGAL PHILOSOPHY. USA-45 CONSULT WORKER ECO/TAC ATTIT WEALTH...POLICY WELF/ST SOC 20 NEW/DEAL DEPRESSION. PAGE 24 E0467
JURID
LABOR
IDEA/COMP

B67

ESTEY M.,THE UNIONS: STRUCTURE, DEVELOPMENT, AND MANAGEMENT. FUT USA+45 ADJUD CONTROL INGP/REL DRIVE ...DECISION T 20 AFL/CIO. PAGE 35 E0699
LABOR
EX/STRUC
ADMIN
GOV/REL

GREENE L.S.,AMERICAN GOVERNMENT POLICIES AND   POLICY   B67
FUNCTIONS. USA+45 LAW AGRI DIST/IND LABOR MUNIC   NAT/G
BUDGET DIPLOM EDU/PROP ORD/FREE...BIBLIOG T 20.   ADMIN
PAGE 46 E0910   DECISION

KING W.L.,MELVILLE WESTON FULLER: CHIEF JUSTICE OF   BIOG   B67
THE UNITED STATES, 1888-1910. USA-45 CONSTN FINAN   CT/SYS
LABOR TAX GOV/REL PERS/REL ATTIT PERSON PWR...JURID   LAW
BIBLIOG 19/20 SUPREME/CT FULLER/MW HOLMES/OW.   ADJUD
PAGE 61 E1216

LAMBERT J.D.,"CORPORATE POLITICAL SPENDING AND   USA+45   L67
CAMPAIGN FINANCE." LAW CONSTN FINAN LABOR LG/CO   POL/PAR
LOC/G NAT/G VOL/ASSN TEC/DEV ADJUD ADMIN PARTIC.   CHOOSE
PAGE 62 E1247   COST

BERRODIN E.F.,"AT THE BARGAINING TABLE." LABOR   PROVS   S67
DIPLOM ECO/TAC ADMIN...MGT 20 MICHIGAN. PAGE 11   WORKER
E0216   LAW
                                                      BARGAIN

BLAKEY G.R.,"ORGANIZED CRIME IN THE UNITED STATES."   CRIME   S67
USA+45 USA-45 STRUCT LABOR NAT/G VOL/ASSN ADMIN   ELITES
PERS/REL PWR...CRIMLGY INT 17/20. PAGE 12 E0240   CONTROL

CHAMBERLAIN N.W.,"STRIKES IN CONTEMPORARY CONTEXT."   LABOR   S67
LAW INDUS NAT/G CHIEF CONFER COST ATTIT ORD/FREE   BARGAIN
...POLICY MGT 20. PAGE 21 E0415   EFFICIENCY
                                                      PROB/SOLV

LABOR/PAR....LABOR PARTY (ALL NATIONS)

LABORATORY EXPERIMENTS....SEE LAB/EXP

LAFAVE W.R. E1244,E1245

LAFOLLET/R....ROBERT M. LAFOLLETTE,JR.

AUERBACH J.S.,LABOR AND LIBERTY; THE LA FOLLETTE   DELIB/GP   B66
COMMITTEE AND THE NEW DEAL. USA-45 LAW LEAD RESPECT   LABOR
SOCISM...BIBLIOG 20 CONGRESS BILL/RIGHT LAFOLLET/R   CONSTN
NEW/DEAL. PAGE 6 E0117   ORD/FREE

LAFTA....LATIN AMERICAN FREE TRADE ASSOCIATION; SEE ALSO
   INT/ORG, VOL/ASSN, INT/TRADE

US SENATE COMM ON FOREIGN REL,SURVEY OF THE   INT/TRADE   N67
ALLIANCE FOR PROGRESS: FOREIGN TRADE POLICIES   REGION
(PAMPHLET). L/A+17C LAW ECO/UNDEV ECO/TAC TARIFFS   AGREE
20 GATT LAFTA UN. PAGE 102 E2037   INT/ORG

LAGUARD/F....FIORELLO LAGUARDIA

LAISSEZ....LAISSEZ-FAIRE-ISM; SEE ALSO OLD/LIB

GRIFFIN A.P.C.,A LIST OF BOOKS RELATING TO TRUSTS   BIBLIOG/A   B02
(2ND REV. ED.) (PAMPHLET). FRANCE GERMANY UK USA-45   JURID
WOR-45 LAW ECO/DEV INDUS LG/CO NAT/G CAP/ISM   ECO/TAC
CENTRAL DISCRIM PWR LAISSEZ 19/20. PAGE 46 E0919   VOL/ASSN

GRIFFIN A.P.C.,A LIST OF BOOKS RELATING TO   BIBLIOG/A   B04
RAILROADS IN THEIR RELATION TO THE GOVERNMENT AND   SERV/IND
THE PUBLIC (PAMPHLET). USA-45 LAW ECO/DEV NAT/G   ADJUD
TEC/DEV CAP/ISM LICENSE CENTRAL LAISSEZ...DECISION   ECO/TAC
19/20. PAGE 47 E0925

GRIFFIN A.P.C.,LIST OF MORE RECENT WORKS ON FEDERAL   BIBLIOG/A   B07
CONTROL OF COMMERCE AND CORPORATIONS (PAMPHLET).   NAT/G
USA-45 LAW ECO/DEV FINAN LG/CO TARIFFS TAX LICENSE   JURID
CENTRAL ORD/FREE WEALTH LAISSEZ 19/20. PAGE 47   ECO/TAC
E0931

CORWIN E.S.,"THE CONSTITUTION AS INSTRUMENT AND AS   CONSTN   S36
SYMBOL." USA-45 ECO/DEV INDUS CAP/ISM SANCTION   LAW
RIGID/FLEX ORD/FREE LAISSEZ OBJECTIVE 20 CONGRESS   ADJUD
SUPREME/CT. PAGE 26 E0512   PWR

LONG H.A.,USURPERS - FOES OF FREE MAN. LAW NAT/G   CT/SYS   B57
CHIEF LEGIS DOMIN ADJUD REPRESENT GOV/REL ORD/FREE   CENTRAL
LAISSEZ POPULISM...POLICY 18/20 SUPREME/CT   FEDERAL
ROOSEVLT/F CONGRESS CON/INTERP. PAGE 66 E1325   CONSTN

PALMER E.E.,CIVIL LIBERTIES. USA+45 ADJUD CT/SYS   ORD/FREE   B58
PARTIC OWN LAISSEZ POPULISM...JURID CONCPT ANTHOL   CONSTN
20 SUPREME/CT CIVIL/LIB. PAGE 79 E1592   RACE/REL
                                                      LAW

MENDELSON W.,CAPITALISM, DEMOCRACY, AND THE SUPREME   JUDGE   B60
COURT. USA+45 USA-45 CONSTN DIPLOM GOV/REL ATTIT   CT/SYS
ORD/FREE LAISSEZ...POLICY CHARTS PERS/COMP 18/20   JURID
SUPREME/CT MARSHALL/J HOLMES/OW TANEY/RB FIELD/JJ.   NAT/G
PAGE 72 E1437

PAUL A.M.,CONSERVATIVE CRISIS AND THE RULE OF LAW.   CONSTN   B60
USA-45 LABOR WORKER ATTIT ORD/FREE CONSERVE LAISSEZ   ADJUD
...DECISION JURID 19 SUPREME/CT. PAGE 80 E1603   STRUCT
                                                      PROF/ORG

VINER J.,THE INTELLECTUAL HISTORY OF LAISSEZ FAIRE   ATTIT   N61
(PAMPHLET). WOR+45 WOR-45 LAW INTELL...POLICY LING   EDU/PROP
LOG 19/20. PAGE 104 E2077   LAISSEZ
                                                      ECO/TAC

BOLGAR V.,"THE PUBLIC INTEREST: A JURISPRUDENTIAL   CONCPT   L63
AND COMPARATIVE OVERVIEW OF SYMPOSIUM ON   ORD/FREE
FUNDAMENTAL CONCEPTS OF PUBLIC LAW" COM FRANCE   CONTROL
GERMANY SWITZERLND LAW ADJUD ADMIN AGREE LAISSEZ   NAT/COMP
...JURID GEN/LAWS 20 EUROPE/E. PAGE 14 E0264

SMITH A.,LECTURES ON JUSTICE, POLICE, REVENUE AND   DIPLOM   B96
ARMS (1763). UK LAW FAM FORCES TARIFFS AGREE COERCE   JURID
INCOME OWN WEALTH LAISSEZ...GEN/LAWS 17/18. PAGE 92   OLD/LIB
E1840   TAX

LAKEWOOD....LAKEWOOD, CALIFORNIA

LAKEY G. E1580

LAKOFF/SA....SANFORD A. LAKOFF
LAKOFF S.A. E0665
LALL A.S. E1246

LAMBERT J.D. E1247

LANCASTER L.W. E1248

LAND REFORM....SEE AGRI + CREATE

LAND/LEAG....LAND LEAGUE (IRELAND)

LAND/VALUE....LAND VALUE TAX

LANDE G.R. E1249

LANDHEER B. E1250,E1251

LANDIS J.M. E0789

LANDRAT....COUNTY CHIEF EXECUTIVE (GERMANY)

LANDRM/GRF....LANDRUM-GRIFFIN ACT

LANDRUM-GRIFFIN ACT....SEE LANDRM/GRF

LANGLEY....LANGLEY-PORTER NEUROPSYCHIATRIC INSTITUTE

LANGUAGE....SEE LING, ALSO LOGIC, MATHEMATICS, AND
   LANGUAGE INDEX, P. XIV

LANGUEDOC....LANGUEDOC, SOUTHERN FRANCE

LANOUE G.R. E1252

LAO/TZU....LAO TZU

LAOS....SEE ALSO S/ASIA

EMBREE J.F.,BIBLIOGRAPHY OF THE PEOPLES AND   BIBLIOG/A   B50
CULTURES OF MAINLAND SOUTHEAST ASIA. CAMBODIA LAOS   CULTURE
THAILAND VIETNAM LAW...GEOG HUM SOC MYTH LING   S/ASIA
CHARTS WORSHIP 20. PAGE 35 E0686

LAPENNA I. E1253

LAPIERE R. E1254

LAPRADELLE E1255

LARCENCY

HALL J.,THEFT, LAW, AND SOCIETY. SOCIETY PROB/SOLV ...CRIMLGY SOC CONCPT TREND METH/COMP 18/20 LARCENCY. PAGE 49 E0982
B35
CRIME
LAW
ADJUD
ADJUST

LARROWE C.P. E1256

LARSEN P.B. E1257

LARSON A. E1258

LARTEH....LARTEH, GHANA

LASKI/H....HAROLD LASKI

LASKIN B. E1259

LASLETT P. E1260

LASLEY J. E1261

LASSALLE/F....FERDINAND LASSALLE

LASSWELL H.D. E1262,E1405,E1408,E1410,E1412

LASSWELL/H....HAROLD D. LASSWELL

LATIN AMERICA....SEE L/A+17C

LATIN AMERICAN FREE TRADE ASSOCIATION....SEE LAFTA

LATVIA....SEE ALSO USSR

GSOUSKI V.,LEGAL SOURCES AND BIBLIOGRAPHY OF THE BALTIC STATES (ESTONIA, LATVIA, LITHUANIA). COM ESTONIA LATVIA LITHUANIA NAT/G LEGIS CT/SYS SANCTION CRIME 20. PAGE 48 E0957
B63
BIBLIOG
ADJUD
LAW
JURID

KLESMENT J.,LEGAL SOURCES AND BIBLIOGRAPHY OF THE BALTIC STATES (ESTONIA, LATVIA, LITHUANIA). COM ESTONIA LATVIA LITHUANIA LAW FINAN ADJUD CT/SYS REGION CENTRAL MARXISM 19/20. PAGE 61 E1223
B63
BIBLIOG/A
JURID
CONSTN
ADMIN

LAURIER/W....SIR WILFRED LAURIER

LAUTERPACHT E. E1263

LAUTERPACHT H. E1264,E1265,E1266,E1579

LAVES W.H.C. E1267

LAVROFF D-G. E1268

LAW....LAW, ETHICAL DIRECTIVES IN A COMMUNITY; SEE ALSO JURID

CONOVER H.F.,OFFICIAL PUBLICATIONS OF BRITISH EAST AFRICA (PAMPHLET). UK LAW ECO/UNDEV AGRI EXTR/IND SECT LEGIS BUDGET TAX...HEAL STAT 20. PAGE 25 E0491
N
BIBLIOG/A
AFR
ADMIN
COLONIAL

FULLER G.A.,DEMOBILIZATION: A SELECTED LIST OF REFERENCES. USA+45 LAW AGRI LABOR WORKER ECO/TAC RATION RECEIVE EDU/PROP ROUTINE ARMS/CONT ALL/VALS 20. PAGE 41 E0819
N
BIBLIOG/A
INDUS
FORCES
NAT/G

KEITT L.,AN ANNOTATED BIBLIOGRAPHY OF BIBLIOGRAPHIES OF STATUTORY MATERIALS OF THE UNITED STATES. CHRIST-17C USA+45 LEGIS ADJUD COLONIAL CT/SYS...JURID 16/20. PAGE 60 E1196
N
BIBLIOG/A
LAW
CONSTN
PROVS

VALENZUELE G.,BIBLIOGRAFIA GUATEMALTECA, Y CATALOG GENERAL DE LIBROS, FOLLETOS, PERIODICOS, REVISTAS, ETC. (10 VOLS.). GUATEMALA LAW...ART/METH 17/20. PAGE 103 E2066
N
BIBLIOG/A
L/A+17C

DEUTSCHE BIBLIOTH FRANKF A M,DEUTSCHE BIBLIOGRAPHIE. EUR+WWI GERMANY ECO/DEV FORCES DIPLOM LEAD...POLICY PHIL/SCI SOC 20. PAGE 31 E0612
B
BIBLIOG
LAW
ADMIN
NAT/G

INDEX TO LEGAL PERIODICALS. CANADA NEW/ZEALND UK USA+45 USA-45 CONSTN LEGIS JUDGE ADJUD ADMIN CONTROL CT/SYS FEDERAL...CRIMLGY INT/LAW 20 CMN/WLTH AUSTRAL. PAGE 1 E0006
N
BIBLIOG
INDEX
LAW
JURID

JOURNAL OF POLITICS. USA+45 USA-45 CONSTN POL/PAR EX/STRUC LEGIS PROB/SOLV DIPLOM CT/SYS CHOOSE RACE/REL 20. PAGE 1 E0011
N
BIBLIOG/A
NAT/G
LAW
LOC/G

POLITICAL SCIENCE QUARTERLY. USA+45 USA-45 LAW CONSTN ECO/DEV INT/ORG LOC/G POL/PAR LEGIS LEAD NUC/PWR...CONCPT 20. PAGE 1 E0013
N
BIBLIOG/A
NAT/G
DIPLOM
POLICY

TEXTBOOKS IN PRINT. WOR+45 WOR-45 LAW DIPLOM ALL/VALS ALL/IDEOS...SOC T 19/20. PAGE 1 E0014
N
BIBLIOG
SCHOOL
KNOWL

ARBITRATION JOURNAL. WOR+45 LAW INDUS JUDGE DIPLOM CT/SYS INGP/REL 20. PAGE 1 E0016
N
BIBLIOG
MGT
LABOR
ADJUD

AUSTRALIAN PUBLIC AFFAIRS INFORMATION SERVICE. LAW ...HEAL HUM MGT SOC CON/ANAL 20 AUSTRAL. PAGE 1 E0017
N
BIBLIOG
NAT/G
CULTURE
DIPLOM

BIBLIOGRAPHIE DE LA PHILOSOPHIE. LAW CULTURE SECT EDU/PROP MORAL...HUM METH/CNCPT 20. PAGE 1 E0018
N
BIBLIOG/A
PHIL/SCI
CONCPT
LOG

BIBLIOGRAPHIE DER SOZIALWISSENSCHAFTEN. WOR-45 CONSTN SOCIETY ECO/DEV ECO/UNDEV DIPLOM LEAD WAR PEACE...PHIL/SCI SOC 19/20. PAGE 1 E0019
N
BIBLIOG
LAW
CONCPT
NAT/G

DEUTSCHE BIBLIOGRAPHIE, HALBJAHRESVERZEICHNIS. WOR+45 LAW ADMIN PERSON. PAGE 1 E0020
N
BIBLIOG
NAT/G
DIPLOM

HANDBOOK OF LATIN AMERICAN STUDIES. LAW CULTURE ECO/UNDEV POL/PAR ADMIN LEAD...SOC 20. PAGE 1 E0022
N
BIBLIOG/A
L/A+17C
NAT/G
DIPLOM

INTERNATIONAL BIBLIOGRAPHY ON CRIME AND DELINQUENCY. USA+45 LAW FORCES PROB/SOLV AGE/Y 20. PAGE 1 E0023
N
BIBLIOG/A
CRIME
ANOMIE
CRIMLGY

LATIN AMERICA IN PERIODICAL LITERATURE. LAW TEC/DEV DIPLOM RECEIVE EDU/PROP...GEOG HUM MGT 20. PAGE 2 E0024
N
BIBLIOG/A
L/A+17C
SOCIETY
ECO/UNDEV

PUBLISHERS' CIRCULAR, THE OFFICIAL ORGAN OF THE PUBLISHERS' ASSOCIATION OF GREAT BRITAIN AND IRELAND. EUR+WWI MOD/EUR UK LAW PROB/SOLV DIPLOM COLONIAL ATTIT...HUM 19/20 CMN/WLTH. PAGE 2 E0025
N
BIBLIOG
NAT/G
WRITING
LEAD

CANON LAW ABSTRACTS. LEGIT CONFER CT/SYS INGP/REL MARRIAGE ATTIT MORAL WORSHIP 20. PAGE 2 E0026
N
BIBLIOG/A
CATHISM
SECT
LAW

THE JAPAN SCIENCE REVIEW: LAW AND POLITICS: LIST OF BOOKS AND ARTICLES ON LAW AND POLITICS. CONSTN AGRI LAW INDUS LABOR DIPLOM TAX ADMIN CRIME...INT/LAW SOC 20 CHINJAP. PAGE 2 E0027
N
BIBLIOG
LAW
S/ASIA
PHIL/SCI

NEUE POLITISCHE LITERATUR; BERICHTE UBER DAS INTERNATIONALE SCHRIFTTUM ZUR POLITIK. WOR+45 LAW CONSTN POL/PAR ADMIN LEAD GOV/REL...POLICY IDEA/COMP. PAGE 2 E0028
N
BIBLIOG/A
DIPLOM
NAT/G
NAT/COMP

PERSONNEL. USA+45 LAW LABOR LG/CO WORKER CREATE GOV/REL PERS/REL ATTIT WEALTH. PAGE 2 E0029
N
BIBLIOG/A
ADMIN
MGT
GP/REL

AFRICAN BIBLIOGRAPHIC CENTER,A CURRENT BIBLIOGRAPHY ON AFRICAN AFFAIRS. LAW CULTURE ECO/UNDEV LABOR SECT DIPLOM FOR/AID COLONIAL NAT/LISM...LING 20. PAGE 3 E0053
N
BIBLIOG/A
AFR
NAT/G
REGION

AMER COUNCIL OF LEARNED SOCIET,THE ACLS CONSTITUENT SOCIETY JOURNAL PROJECT. FUT USA+45 LAW NAT/G PLAN DIPLOM PHIL/SCI. PAGE 4 E0072
N
BIBLIOG/A
HUM
COMPUT/IR
COMPUTER

ASIA FOUNDATION,LIBRARY NOTES. LAW CONSTN CULTURE SOCIETY ECO/UNDEV INT/ORG NAT/G COLONIAL LEAD REGION NAT/LISM ATTIT 20 UN. PAGE 6 E0107
N
BIBLIOG/A
ASIA
S/ASIA
DIPLOM

CATHERINE R.,LA REVUE ADMINISTRATIVE. FRANCE LAW NAT/G LEGIS...JURID BIBLIOG/A 20. PAGE 21 E0407
N
ADMIN
MGT
FINAN
METH/COMP

CORNELL UNIVERSITY LIBRARY,SOUTHEAST ASIA ACCESSIONS LIST. LAW SOCIETY STRUCT ECO/UNDEV POL/PAR TEC/DEV DIPLOM LEAD REGION. PAGE 26 E0510
N
BIBLIOG
S/ASIA
NAT/G
CULTURE

DEUTSCHE BUCHEREI,JAHRESVERZEICHNIS DER DEUTSCHEN HOCHSCHULSCHRIFTEN. EUR+WWI GERMANY LAW ADMIN PERSON...MGT SOC 19/20. PAGE 31 E0613
N
BIBLIOG
WRITING
ACADEM
INTELL

DEUTSCHE BUCHEREI,JAHRESVERZEICHNIS DES DEUTSCHEN SCHRIFTUMS. AUSTRIA EUR+WWI GERMANY SWITZERLND LAW LOC/G DIPLOM ADMIN...MGT SOC 19/20. PAGE 31 E0614
N
BIBLIOG
WRITING
NAT/G

DEUTSCHE BUCHEREI,DEUTSCHES BUCHERVERZEICHNIS. GERMANY LAW CULTURE POL/PAR ADMIN LEAD ATTIT PERSON ...SOC 20. PAGE 31 E0615
N
BIBLIOG
NAT/G
DIPLOM
ECO/DEV

HARVARD LAW SCHOOL LIBRARY,ANNUAL LEGAL BIBLIOGRAPHY. USA+45 CONSTN LEGIS ADJUD CT/SYS ...POLICY 20. PAGE 50 E1005
N
BIBLIOG
JURID
LAW
INT/LAW

MINISTERE DE L'EDUC NATIONALE,CATALOGUE DES THESES DE DOCTORAT SOUTENNES DEVANT LES UNIVERSITAIRES FRANCAISES. FRANCE LAW DIPLOM ADMIN...HUM SOC 20. PAGE 73 E1465
N
BIBLIOG
ACADEM
KNOWL
NAT/G

MINISTRY OF OVERSEAS DEVELOPME,TECHNICAL CO-OPERATION -- A BIBLIOGRAPHY. UK LAW SOCIETY DIPLOM ECO/TAC FOR/AID...STAT 20 CMN/WLTH. PAGE 73 E1466
N
BIBLIOG
TEC/DEV
ECO/DEV
NAT/G

NEW YORK STATE LIBRARY,CHECKLIST OF OFFICIAL PUBLICATIONS OF THE STATE OF NEW YORK. USA+45 USA-45 LAW PROB/SOLV LEAD ATTIT 19/20. PAGE 77 E1539
N
BIBLIOG
PROVS
WRITING
GOV/REL

PUBLISHERS' CIRCULAR LIMITED,THE ENGLISH CATALOGUE OF BOOKS. UK WOR+45 WOR-45 LAW CULTURE LOC/G NAT/G ADMIN LEAD...MGT 19/20. PAGE 83 E1658
N
BIBLIOG
ALL/VALS
ALL/IDEOS
SOCIETY

SOUTH AFRICA STATE LIBRARY,SOUTH AFRICAN NATIONAL BIBLIOGRAPHY, SANB. SOUTH/AFR LAW NAT/G EDU/PROP ...MGT PSY SOC 20. PAGE 93 E1858
N
BIBLIOG
PRESS
WRITING

UNESCO,INTERNATIONAL BIBLIOGRAPHY OF POLITICAL SCIENCE (VOLUMES 1-8). WOR+45 LAW NAT/G EX/STRUC LEGIS PROB/SOLV DIPLOM ADMIN GOV/REL 20 UNESCO. PAGE 98 E1957
N
BIBLIOG
CONCPT
IDEA/COMP

US BUREAU OF THE CENSUS,BIBLIOGRAPHY OF SOCIAL SCIENCE PERIODICALS AND MONOGRAPH SERIES. WOR+45 LAW DIPLOM EDU/PROP HEALTH...PSY SOC LING STAT. PAGE 99 E1980
N
BIBLIOG/A
CULTURE
NAT/G
SOCIETY

US SUPERINTENDENT OF DOCUMENTS,EDUCATION (PRICE
N
BIBLIOG/A

LIST 31). USA+45 LAW FINAN LOC/G NAT/G DEBATE ADMIN LEAD RACE/REL FEDERAL HEALTH POLICY. PAGE 103 E2062
N
EDU/PROP
ACADEM
SCHOOL

US SUPERINTENDENT OF DOCUMENTS,POLITICAL SCIENCE: GOVERNMENT, CRIME, DISTRICT OF COLUMBIA (PRICE LIST 54). USA+45 LAW CONSTN EX/STRUC WORKER ADJUD ADMIN CT/SYS CHOOSE INGP/REL RACE/REL CONGRESS PRESIDENT. PAGE 103 E2063
N
BIBLIOG/A
NAT/G
CRIME

MEYER C.S.,ELIZABETH I AND THE RELIGIOUS SETTLEMENT OF 1559. UK ELITES CHIEF LEGIS DISCRIM CATHISM 16 CHURCH/STA ELIZABTH/I. PAGE 72 E1445
NRE
GP/REL
SECT
LAW
PARL/PROC

BATY T.,INTERNATIONAL LAW IN SOUTH AFRICA. AFR SOUTH/AFR LAW CONFER 19/20. PAGE 8 E0155
B00
JURID
WAR
SOVEREIGN
COLONIAL

BERNARD M.,FOUR LECTURES ON SUBJECTS CONNECTED WITH DIPLOMACY. WOR-45 NAT/G VOL/ASSN RIGID/FLEX MORAL PWR...JURID OBS GEN/LAWS GEN/METH 20 TREATY. PAGE 11 E0209
B00
LAW
ATTIT
DIPLOM

DE TOCQUEVILLE A.,DEMOCRACY IN AMERICA (VOLUME ONE). LAW SOCIETY STRUCT NAT/G POL/PAR PROVS FORCES LEGIS TOP/EX DIPLOM LEGIT WAR PEACE ATTIT SOVEREIGN ...SELF/OBS TIME/SEQ CONGRESS 19. PAGE 30 E0594
B00
USA-45
TREND

GREELY A.W.,PUBLIC DOCUMENTS OF THE FIRST FOURTEEN CONGRESSES, 1789-1817. USA-45 LEAD REPRESENT ATTIT 18/19 CONGRESS. PAGE 45 E0904
B00
BIBLIOG/A
NAT/G
LAW
LEGIS

GROTIUS H.,DE JURE BELLI AC PACIS. CHRIST-17C UNIV LAW SOCIETY PROVS LEGIT PEACE PERCEPT MORAL PWR ...CONCPT CON/ANAL GEN/LAWS. PAGE 48 E0952
B00
JURID
INT/LAW
WAR

HOLLAND T.E.,STUDIES IN INTERNATIONAL LAW. TURKEY USSR WOR-45 CONSTN NAT/G DIPLOM DOMIN LEGIT COERCE WAR PEACE ORD/FREE PWR SOVEREIGN...JURID CHARTS 20 PARLIAMENT SUEZ TREATY. PAGE 54 E1084
B00
INT/ORG
LAW
INT/LAW

LORIMER J.,THE INSTITUTES OF THE LAW OF NATIONS. WOR-45 CULTURE SOCIETY NAT/G VOL/ASSN DIPLOM LEGIT WAR PEACE DRIVE ORD/FREE SOVEREIGN...CONCPT RECORD INT TREND HYPO/EXP GEN/METH TOT/POP VAL/FREE 20. PAGE 66 E1327
B00
INT/ORG
LAW
INT/LAW

MAINE H.S.,INTERNATIONAL LAW. MOD/EUR UNIV SOCIETY STRUCT ACT/RES EXEC WAR ATTIT PERSON ALL/VALS ...POLICY JURID CONCPT OBS TIME/SEQ TOT/POP. PAGE 68 E1349
B00
INT/ORG
LAW
PEACE
INT/LAW

MAINE H.S.,ANCIENT LAW. MEDIT-7 CULTURE SOCIETY KIN SECT LEGIS LEGIT ROUTINE...JURID HIST/WRIT CON/ANAL TOT/POP VAL/FREE. PAGE 68 E1350
B00
FAM
LAW

HISTORICUS,"LETTERS AND SOME QUESTIONS OF INTERNATIONAL LAW." FRANCE NETHERLAND UK USA-45 WOR-45 LAW NAT/G COERCE...SOC CONCPT GEN/LAWS TOT/POP 19 CIVIL/WAR. PAGE 53 E1054
L00
WEALTH
JURID
WAR
INT/LAW

BRYCE J.,STUDIES IN HISTORY AND JURISPRUDENCE (2 VOLS.). ICELAND SOUTH/AFR UK LAW PROB/SOLV SOVEREIGN...PHIL/SCI NAT/COMP ROME/ANC ROMAN/LAW. PAGE 16 E0321
B01
IDEA/COMP
CONSTN
JURID

GRONING J.,BIBLIOTHECA JURIS GENTIUM COMMUNIS, QUA PRAECIPUORUM, ASIAE, AFRICAE, ET AMERICAE, POPULORUM DE JURIS NATURAE... AFR ASIA S/ASIA USA-45 16/17. PAGE 48 E0946
B01
BIBLIOG
JURID
LAW
NAT/G

GRIFFIN A.P.C.,A LIST OF BOOKS RELATING TO TRUSTS (2ND REV. ED.) (PAMPHLET). FRANCE GERMANY UK USA-45 WOR-45 LAW ECO/DEV INDUS LG/CO NAT/G CAP/ISM CENTRAL DISCRIM PWR LAISSEZ 19/20. PAGE 46 E0919
B02
BIBLIOG/A
JURID
ECO/TAC
VOL/ASSN

CHANNING W.E.,DISCOURSES ON WAR (1820-1840). LAW
B03
WAR

SECT DIPLOM INT/TRADE ALL/VALS. PAGE 21 E0418
    PLAN
    LOVE
    ORD/FREE

B03
FAGUET E.,LE LIBERALISME. FRANCE PRESS ADJUD ADMIN
DISCRIM CONSERVE SOCISM...TRADIT SOC LING WORSHIP
PARLIAMENT. PAGE 36 E0711
    ORD/FREE
    EDU/PROP
    NAT/G
    LAW

B03
FORTESCUE G.K.,SUBJECT INDEX OF THE MODERN WORKS
ADDED TO THE LIBRARY OF THE BRITISH MUSEUM IN THE
YEARS 1881-1900 (3 VOLS.). UK LAW CONSTN FINAN
NAT/G FORCES INT/TRADE COLONIAL 19. PAGE 39 E0775
    BIBLIOG
    INDEX
    WRITING

B03
GRIFFIN A.P.C.,LIST OF BOOKS ON THE CONSTITUTION OF
THE UNITED STATES (PAMPHLET). USA-45 NAT/G EX/STRUC
JUDGE TOP/EX CT/SYS 18/20 CONGRESS PRESIDENT
SUPREME/CT. PAGE 46 E0920
    BIBLIOG/A
    CONSTN
    LAW
    JURID

B03
GRIFFIN A.P.C.,LISTS PUBLISHED 1902-03: GOVERNMENT
OWNERSHIP OF RAILROADS (PAMPHLET). USA-45 LAW NAT/G
RATION GOV/REL CENTRAL SOCISM...POLICY 19/20.
PAGE 46 E0922
    BIBLIOG
    DIST/IND
    CONTROL
    ADJUD

B03
GRIFFIN A.P.C.,SELECT LIST OF BOOKS ON LABOR
PARTICULARLY RELATING TO STRIKES. FRANCE GERMANY
MOD/EUR UK USA-45 LAW NAT/G DELIB/GP WORKER BARGAIN
LICENSE PAY ADJUD 19/20. PAGE 46 E0924
    BIBLIOG/A
    GP/REL
    MGT
    LABOR

B03
GRONING J.,BIBLIOTHECA JURIS GENTIUM EXOTICA. AFR
ASIA S/ASIA USA-45 16/17. PAGE 48 E0947
    BIBLIOG
    JURID
    NAT/G
    LAW

B04
BURKE E.,A LETTER TO THE SHERIFFS OF BRISTOL
(1777). USA-45 LAW ECO/TAC COLONIAL CT/SYS REV
GP/REL ORD/FREE...POLICY 18 PARLIAMENT BURKE/EDM.
PAGE 17 E0341
    LEGIS
    ADJUD
    CRIME

B04
CRANDALL S.B.,TREATIES: THEIR MAKING AND
ENFORCEMENT. MOD/EUR USA-45 CONSTN INT/ORG NAT/G
LEGIS EDU/PROP LEGIT EXEC PEACE KNOWL MORAL...JURID
CONGRESS 19/20 TREATY. PAGE 27 E0541
    LAW

B04
FREUND E.,THE POLICE POWER: PUBLIC POLICY AND
CONSTITUTIONAL RIGHTS. USA-45 SOCIETY LOC/G NAT/G
FORCES LEGIS ADJUD CT/SYS OWN PWR...JURID 18/19
SUPREME/CT. PAGE 40 E0795
    CONSTN
    LAW
    ORD/FREE
    CONTROL

B04
GRIFFIN A.P.C.,A LIST OF BOOKS RELATING TO
RAILROADS IN THEIR RELATION TO THE GOVERNMENT AND
THE PUBLIC (PAMPHLET). USA-45 LAW ECO/DEV NAT/G
TEC/DEV CAP/ISM LICENSE CENTRAL LAISSEZ...DECISION
19/20. PAGE 47 E0925
    BIBLIOG/A
    SERV/IND
    ADJUD
    ECO/TAC

B05
DICEY A.,LAW AND PUBLIC OPINION IN ENGLAND. LAW
CULTURE INTELL SOCIETY NAT/G SECT JUDGE LEGIT
CHOOSE RIGID/FLEX KNOWL...OLD/LIB CONCPT STERTYP
GEN/LAWS 20. PAGE 31 E0620
    ATTIT
    UK

B05
DICEY A.V.,LECTURES ON THE RELATION BETWEEN LAW AND
PUBLIC OPINION IN ENGLAND DURING THE NINETEENTH
CENTURY. UK LEGIS CT/SYS...JURID 19 TORY/PARTY
BENTHAM/J ENGLSH/LAW. PAGE 31 E0621
    LAW
    ADJUD
    ATTIT
    IDEA/COMP

B05
GOODNOW F.J.,THE PRINCIPLES OF THE ADMINISTRATIVE
LAW OF THE UNITED STATES. USA-45 LAW STRUCT
EX/STRUC LEGIS BAL/PWR CONTROL GOV/REL PWR...JURID
19/20 CIVIL/SERV. PAGE 45 E0887
    ADMIN
    NAT/G
    PROVS
    LOC/G

B05
GRIFFIN A.P.C.,LIST OF REFERENCES ON PRIMARY
ELECTIONS (PAMPHLET). USA-45 LAW LOC/G DELIB/GP
LEGIS OP/RES TASK REPRESENT CONSEN...DECISION 19/20
CONGRESS. PAGE 47 E0928
    BIBLIOG/A
    POL/PAR
    CHOOSE
    POPULISM

C05
DUNNING W.A.,"HISTORY OF POLITICAL THEORIES FROM
LUTHER TO MONTESQUIEU." LAW NAT/G SECT DIPLOM REV
WAR ORD/FREE SOVEREIGN CONSERVE...TRADIT BIBLIOG
16/18. PAGE 33 E0663
    PHIL/SCI
    CONCPT
    GEN/LAWS

B06
GRIFFIN A.P.C.,LIST OF BOOKS RELATING TO CHILD
LABOR (PAMPHLET). BELGIUM FRANCE GERMANY MOD/EUR UK
USA-45 ECO/DEV INDUS WORKER CAP/ISM PAY ROUTINE
ALL/IDEOS...MGT SOC 19/20. PAGE 47 E0929
    BIBLIOG/A
    LAW
    LABOR
    AGE/C

B07
BENTHAM J.,AN INTRODUCTION TO THE PRINCIPLES OF
MORALS AND LEGISLATION. UNIV CONSTN CULTURE SOCIETY
NAT/G CONSULT LEGIS JUDGE ADJUD CT/SYS...JURID
CONCPT NEW/IDEA. PAGE 10 E0190
    LAW
    GEN/LAWS

B07
GRIFFIN A.P.C.,LIST OF MORE RECENT WORKS ON FEDERAL
CONTROL OF COMMERCE AND CORPORATIONS (PAMPHLET).
USA-45 LAW ECO/DEV FINAN LG/CO TARIFFS TAX LICENSE
CENTRAL ORD/FREE WEALTH LAISSEZ 19/20. PAGE 47
E0931
    BIBLIOG/A
    NAT/G
    JURID
    ECO/TAC

B08
GRIFFIN A.P.C.,LIST OF WORKS RELATING TO GOVERNMENT
REGULATION OF INSURANCE UNITED STATES AND FOREIGN
COUNTRIES (2ND. ED.) (PAMPHLET). FRANCE GERMANY UK
USA-45 WOR-45 LG/CO LOC/G NAT/G LEGIS LICENSE ADJUD
LOBBY CENTRAL ORD/FREE 19/20. PAGE 47 E0933
    BIBLIOG/A
    FINAN
    LAW
    CONTROL

B08
GRIFFIN A.P.C.,REFERENCES ON CORRUPT PRACTICES IN
ELECTIONS (PAMPHLET). USA-45 LAW CONSTN TRIBUTE
CRIME REPRESENT...JURID 19/20. PAGE 47 E0934
    BIBLIOG/A
    CHOOSE
    SUFF
    APPORT

B08
WILSON W.,CONSTITUTIONAL GOVERNMENT IN THE UNITED
STATES. USA-45 LAW POL/PAR PROVS CHIEF LEGIS
BAL/PWR ADJUD EXEC FEDERAL PWR 18/20 SUPREME/CT
HOUSE/REP SENATE. PAGE 106 E2130
    NAT/G
    GOV/REL
    CONSTN
    PARL/PROC

B09
HARVARD UNIVERSITY LAW LIBRARY,CATALOGUE OF THE
LIBRARY OF THE LAW SCHOOL OF HARVARD UNIVERSITY (3
VOLS.). UK USA-45 LEGIS JUDGE ADJUD CT/SYS...JURID
CHARTS 14/20. PAGE 51 E1008
    BIBLIOG/A
    LAW
    ADMIN

B09
HOLLAND T.E.,LETTERS UPON WAR AND NEUTRALITY.
WOR-45 NAT/G FORCES JUDGE ECO/TAC LEGIT CT/SYS
NEUTRAL ROUTINE COERCE...JURID TIME/SEQ 20. PAGE 55
E1085
    LAW
    INT/LAW
    INT/ORG
    WAR

B09
JUSTINIAN,THE DIGEST (DIGESTA CORPUS JURIS CIVILIS)
(2 VOLS.) (TRANS. BY C. H. MONRO). ROMAN/EMP LAW
FAM LOC/G LEGIS EDU/PROP CONTROL MARRIAGE OWN ROLE
CIVIL/LAW. PAGE 59 E1177
    JURID
    CT/SYS
    NAT/G
    STRATA

B09
LOBINGIER C.S.,THE PEOPLE'S LAW OR POPULAR
PARTICIPATION IN LAW-MAKING. FRANCE SWITZERLND UK
LOC/G NAT/G PROVS LEGIS SUFF MAJORITY PWR POPULISM
...GOV/COMP BIBLIOG 19. PAGE 66 E1314
    CONSTN
    LAW
    PARTIC

B10
MCILWAIN C.H.,THE HIGH COURT OF PARLIAMENT AND ITS
SUPREMACY B1910 1878 408. UK EX/STRUC PARL/PROC
GOV/REL INGP/REL PRIVIL 12/20 PARLIAMENT
ENGLSH/LAW. PAGE 71 E1416
    LAW
    LEGIS
    CONSTN
    NAT/G

B11
PHILLIPSON C.,THE INTERNATIONAL LAW AND CUSTOM OF
ANCIENT GREECE AND ROME. MEDIT-7 UNIV INTELL
SOCIETY STRUCT NAT/G LEGIS EXEC PERSON...CONCPT OBS
CON/ANAL ROM/EMP. PAGE 80 E1614
    INT/ORG
    LAW
    INT/LAW

B11
REINSCH P.,PUBLIC INTERNATIONAL UNION. WOR-45 LAW
LABOR INT/TRADE LEGIT PERSON ALL/VALS...SOCIALIST
CONCPT TIME/SEQ TREND GEN/LAWS 19/20. PAGE 84 E1683
    FUT
    INT/ORG
    DIPLOM

B12
BEARD C.A.,THE SUPREME COURT AND THE CONSTITUTION.
LAW NAT/G PROVS LEGIS GOV/REL ATTIT POPULISM
SUPREME/CT. PAGE 9 E0164
    CONSTN
    CT/SYS
    ADJUD
    CONTROL

B12
GRIFFIN A.P.C.,SELECT LIST OF REFERENCES ON
IMPEACHMENT (REV. ED.) (PAMPHLET). USA-45 LAW PROVS
ADJUD ATTIT...JURID 19/20 NEGRO. PAGE 47 E0935
    BIBLIOG/A
    CONSTN
    NAT/G
    LEGIS

B12
MEYER H.H.B.,SELECT LIST OF REFERENCES ON THE
INITIATIVE, REFERENDUM, AND RECALL. MOD/EUR USA-45
LAW LOC/G MUNIC REPRESENT POPULISM 20 CONGRESS.
PAGE 72 E1446
    BIBLIOG/A
    NAT/G
    LEGIS
    CHOOSE

B12

POLLOCK F.,THE GENIUS OF THE COMMON LAW. CHRIST-17C LAW
UK FINAN CHIEF ACT/RES ADMIN GP/REL ATTIT SOCISM CULTURE
...ANARCH JURID. PAGE 81 E1624 CREATE

B13

BORCHARD E.M.,BIBLIOGRAPHY OF INTERNATIONAL LAW AND BIBLIOG
CONTINENTAL LAW. EUR+WWI MOD/EUR UK LAW INT/TRADE INT/LAW
WAR PEACE...GOV/COMP NAT/COMP 19/20. PAGE 14 E0267 JURID
DIPLOM

B14

FIGGIS J.N.,CHURCHES IN THE MODERN STATE (2ND ED.). SECT
LAW CHIEF BAL/PWR PWR...CONCPT CHURCH/STA POPE. NAT/G
PAGE 38 E0748 SOCIETY
ORD/FREE

B14

MCLAUGHLIN A.C.,CYCLOPEDIA OF AMERICAN GOVERNMENT USA+45
(3 VOLS.). LAW CONSTN POL/PAR ADMIN ROUTINE NAT/G
...INT/LAW CONCPT BIBLIOG METH 20. PAGE 71 E1421 DICTIONARY

B14

VECCHIO G.D.,THE FORMAL BASES OF LAW (TRANS. BY J. LAW
LISLE). DOMIN LEGIT CONTROL COERCE UTIL MORAL PWR JURID
...CONCPT TIME/SEQ 17/20 COMMON/LAW NATURL/LAW. GEN/LAWS
PAGE 103 E2074 IDEA/COMP

B15

INTERNATIONAL LAW ASSOCIATION,A FORTY YEARS' BIBLIOG
CATALOGUE OF THE BOOKS, PAMPHLETS AND PAPERS IN THE LAW
LIBRARY OF THE INTERNATIONAL LAW ASSOCIATION. INT/LAW
INT/ORG DIPLOM ADJUD NEUTRAL...IDEA/COMP 19/20.
PAGE 57 E1134

B15

SAWYER R.A.,A LIST OF WORKS ON COUNTY GOVERNMENT. BIBLIOG/A
LAW FINAN MUNIC TOP/EX ROUTINE CRIME...CLASSIF LOC/G
RECORD 19/20. PAGE 87 E1748 GOV/REL
ADMIN

B16

PUFENDORF S.,LAW OF NATURE AND OF NATIONS CONCPT
(ABRIDGED). UNIV LAW NAT/G DIPLOM AGREE WAR PERSON INT/LAW
ALL/VALS PWR...POLICY 18 DEITY NATURL/LAW. PAGE 83 SECT
E1659 MORAL

B16

ROOT E.,ADDRESSES ON INTERNATIONAL SUBJECTS. INT/ORG
MOD/EUR UNIV USA-45 LAW SOCIETY EXEC ATTIT ALL/VALS ACT/RES
...POLICY JURID CONCPT 20 CHINJAP. PAGE 85 E1711 PEACE
INT/LAW

B16

SALMOND J.W.,JURISPRUDENCE. UK LOC/G NAT/G LEGIS LAW
PROB/SOLV LICENSE LEGIT CRIME PERS/REL OWN ORD/FREE CT/SYS
...T 20. PAGE 87 E1742 JURID
ADJUD

B16

SCHROEDER T.,FREE SPEECH FOR RADICALS (REV. ED.). ORD/FREE
USA-45 CONSTN INDUS LOC/G FORCES SANCTION WAR ATTIT CONTROL
SEX...JURID REFORMERS 20 FREE/SPEE. PAGE 88 E1767 LAW
PRESS

L16

WRIGHT Q.,"THE ENFORCEMENT OF INTERNATIONAL LAW INT/ORG
THROUGH MUNICIPAL LAW IN THE US." USA-45 LOC/G LAW
NAT/G PUB/INST FORCES LEGIT CT/SYS PERCEPT ALL/VALS INT/LAW
...JURID 20. PAGE 107 E2149 WAR

B18

EYBERS G.W.,SELECT CONSTITUTIONAL DOCUMENTS CONSTN
ILLUSTRATING SOUTH AFRICAN HISTORY 1795-1910. LAW
SOUTH/AFR LOC/G LEGIS CT/SYS...JURID ANTHOL 18/20 NAT/G
NATAL CAPE/HOPE ORANGE/STA. PAGE 36 E0707 COLONIAL

B18

PORTER K.H.,A HISTORY OF SUFFRAGE IN THE UNITED SUFF
STATES. USA-45 LAW CONSTN LOC/G NAT/G POL/PAR WAR REPRESENT
DISCRIM OWN ATTIT SEX 18/20 NEGRO FEMALE/SEX. CHOOSE
PAGE 81 E1629 PARTIC

S18

POWELL T.R.,"THE LOGIC AND RHETORIC OF CONSTN
CONSTITUTIONAL LAW" (BMR)" USA-45 USA-45 DELIB/GP LAW
PROB/SOLV ADJUD CT/SYS...DECISION 20 SUPREME/CT JURID
CON/INTERP. PAGE 82 E1642 LOG

N18

BREWER D.J.,THE MOVEMENT OF COERCION (PAMPHLET). GP/REL
CONSTN INDUS ADJUD COERCE OWN WEALTH...OLD/LIB LABOR
JURID 19 SUPREME/CT. PAGE 15 E0296 LG/CO
LAW

B19

DUGUIT L.,LAW IN THE MODERN STATE (TRANS. BY FRIDA GEN/LAWS
AND HAROLD LASKI). CONSTN SOCIETY STRUCT MORAL CONCPT
ORD/FREE SOVEREIGN 20. PAGE 33 E0655 NAT/G
LAW

B19

SMITH R.H.,JUSTICE AND THE POOR. LAW RECEIVE ADJUD CT/SYS
CRIME GOV/REL COST...JURID SOC/WK CONCPT STAT DISCRIM
CHARTS GP/COMP 20. PAGE 92 E1847 WEALTH

N19

IN THE SHADOW OF FEAR; AMERICAN CIVIL LIBERTIES, ORD/FREE
1948-49 (PAMPHLET). COM LAW LEGIS BAL/PWR EDU/PROP CONSTN
CT/SYS RACE/REL DISCRIM MARXISM SOCISM 20 COLD/WAR POLICY
CONGRESS ACLU CIV/RIGHTS ESPIONAGE. PAGE 2 E0030

N19

AMERICAN CIVIL LIBERTIES UNION,"WE HOLD THESE ORD/FREE
TRUTHS" FREEDOM, JUSTICE, EQUALITY: REPORT ON CIVIL LAW
LIBERTIES (A PERIODICAL PAMPHLET COVERING 1951-53) RACE/REL
USA+45 ACADEM NAT/G FORCES LEGIS COERCE CIVMIL/REL CONSTN
GOV/REL DISCRIM PRIVIL MARXISM...OLD/LIB 20 ACLU UN
CIV/LIB. PAGE 4 E0076

N19

ARNOW K.,SELF-INSURANCE IN THE TREASURY (PAMPHLET). ADMIN
USA+45 LAW RIGID/FLEX...POLICY METH/COMP 20 PLAN
DEPT/TREAS. PAGE 5 E0104 EFFICIENCY
NAT/G

N19

ATOMIC INDUSTRIAL FORUM,COMMENTARY ON LEGISLATION NUC/PWR
TO PERMIT PRIVATE OWNERSHIP OF SPECIAL NUCLEAR MARKET
MATERIAL (PAMPHLET). USA+45 DELIB/GP LEGIS PLAN OWN INDUS
...POLICY 20 AEC CONGRESS. PAGE 6 E0111 LAW

N19

BUREAU OF NAT'L AFFAIRS INC.,A CURRENT LOOK AT: DISCRIM
(1) THE NEGRO AND TITLE VII, (2) SEX AND TITLE VII SEX
(PAMPHLET). LAW LG/CO SML/CO RACE/REL...POLICY SOC WORKER
STAT DEEP/QU TREND CON/ANAL CHARTS 20 NEGRO MGT
CIV/RIGHTS. PAGE 17 E0334

N19

BURRUS B.R.,INVESTIGATION AND DISCOVERY IN STATE NAT/G
ANTITRUST (PAMPHLET). USA+45 USA-45 LEGIS ECO/TAC PROVS
ADMIN CONTROL CT/SYS CRIME GOV/REL PWR...JURID LAW
CHARTS 19/20 FTC MONOPOLY. PAGE 18 E0346 INSPECT

N19

COUTROT A.,THE FIGHT OVER THE 1959 PRIVATE SCHOOL
EDUCATION LAW IN FRANCE (PAMPHLET). FRANCE NAT/G PARL/PROC
SECT GIVE EDU/PROP GP/REL ATTIT RIGID/FLEX ORD/FREE CATHISM
20 CHURCH/STA. PAGE 27 E0527 LAW

N19

HOGARTY R.A.,NEW JERSEY FARMERS AND MIGRANT HOUSING AGRI
RULES (PAMPHLET). USA+45 LAW ELITES FACE/GP LABOR PROVS
PROF/ORG LOBBY PERS/REL RIGID/FLEX ROLE 20 WORKER
NEW/JERSEY. PAGE 53 E1067 HEALTH

N19

JANOWITZ M.,SOCIAL CONTROL OF ESCALATED RIOTS CROWD
(PAMPHLET). USA+45 USA-45 LAW SOCIETY MUNIC FORCES ORD/FREE
PROB/SOLV EDU/PROP TV CRIME ATTIT...BIBLIOG 20 CONTROL
NEGRO CIV/RIGHTS. PAGE 58 E1148 RACE/REL

N19

MISSISSIPPI ADVISORY COMMITTEE,REPORT ON RACE/REL
MISSISSIPPI (PAMPHLET). USA+45 LAW PROVS FORCES DISCRIM
ADJUD PWR...SOC/WK INT 20 MISSISSIPP NEGRO COERCE
CIV/RIGHTS. PAGE 73 E1469 ORD/FREE

N19

OPERATIONS AND POLICY RESEARCH,URUGUAY: ELECTION POL/PAR
FACTBOOK: NOVEMBER 27, 1966 (PAMPHLET). URUGUAY LAW CHOOSE
NAT/G LEAD REPRESENT...STAT BIOG CHARTS 20. PAGE 79 PLAN
E1576 ATTIT

B20

COX H.,ECONOMIC LIBERTY. UNIV LAW INT/TRADE RATION NAT/G
TARIFFS RACE/REL SOCISM POLICY. PAGE 27 E0535 ORD/FREE
ECO/TAC
PERSON

B20

DICKINSON E.,THE EQUALITY OF STATES IN LAW
INTERNATIONAL LAW. WOR-45 INT/ORG NAT/G DIPLOM CONCPT
EDU/PROP LEGIT PEACE ATTIT ALL/VALS...JURID SOVEREIGN
TIME/SEQ LEAGUE/NAT. PAGE 31 E0622

B20

LIPPMAN W.,LIBERTY AND THE NEWS. USA+45 USA-45 LAW ORD/FREE
LEGIS DOMIN LEGIT ATTIT...POLICY SOC IDEA/COMP PRESS
METH/COMP 19/20. PAGE 65 E1300 COM/IND

EDU/PROP

B20

VINOGRADOFF P.,OUTLINES OF HISTORICAL JURISPRUDENCE JURID
(2 VOLS.). GREECE MEDIT-7 LAW CONSTN FACE/GP FAM METH
KIN MUNIC CRIME OWN...INT/LAW IDEA/COMP BIBLIOG.
PAGE 104 E2080

B21

BRYCE J.,MODERN DEMOCRACIES. FUT NEW/ZEALND USA-45 NAT/G
LAW CONSTN POL/PAR PROVS VOL/ASSN EX/STRUC LEGIS TREND
LEGIT CT/SYS EXEC KNOWL CONGRESS AUSTRAL 20.
PAGE 16 E0322

B21

OPPENHEIM L.,THE FUTURE OF INTERNATIONAL LAW. INT/ORG
EUR+WWI MOD/EUR LAW LEGIS JUDGE LEGIT ORD/FREE CT/SYS
...JURID TIME/SEQ GEN/LAWS 20. PAGE 79 E1578 INT/LAW

B21

STOWELL E.C.,INTERVENTION IN INTERNATIONAL LAW. BAL/PWR
UNIV LAW SOCIETY INT/ORG ACT/RES PLAN LEGIT ROUTINE SOVEREIGN
WAR...JURID OBS GEN/LAWS 20. PAGE 94 E1884

B22

SCHROEDER T.,FREE SPEECH BIBLIOGRAPHY. EUR+WWI BIBLIOG/A
WOR-45 NAT/G SECT ECO/TAC WRITING ADJUD ATTIT ORD/FREE
MARXISM SOCISM 16/20. PAGE 88 E1768 CONTROL
LAW

B23

DE MONTESQUIEU C.,THE SPIRIT OF LAWS (2 VOLS.) JURID
(TRANS. BY THOMAS NUGENT). FRANCE FINAN SECT LAW
INT/TRADE TAX COERCE REV DISCRIM HABITAT ORD/FREE CONCPT
19 ALEMBERT/J CIVIL/LAW. PAGE 30 E0588 GEN/LAWS

B23

POUND R.,INTERPRETATIONS OF LEGAL HISTORY. CULTURE LAW
...PHIL/SCI NEW/IDEA CLASSIF SIMUL GEN/LAWS 19/20. IDEA/COMP
PAGE 82 E1636 JURID

S23

DEWEY J.,"ETHICS AND INTERNATIONAL RELATIONS." FUT LAW
WOR-45 SOCIETY INT/ORG VOL/ASSN DIPLOM LEGIT MORAL
ORD/FREE...JURID CONCPT GEN/METH 20. PAGE 31 E0618

B24

CARDOZO B.,THE GROWTH OF THE LAW. USA-45 CULTURE LAW
...JURID 20. PAGE 19 E0376 ADJUD
CT/SYS

B24

GENTILI A.,DE LEGATIONIBUS. CHRIST-17C NAT/G SECT DIPLOM
CONSULT LEGIT...POLICY CATH JURID CONCPT MYTH. INT/LAW
PAGE 43 E0848 INT/ORG
LAW

B24

HOLDSWORTH W.S.,A HISTORY OF ENGLISH LAW; THE LAW
COMMON LAW AND ITS RIVALS (VOL. V). UK SEA EX/STRUC LEGIS
WRITING ADMIN...INT/LAW JURID CONCPT IDEA/COMP ADJUD
WORSHIP 16/17 PARLIAMENT ENGLSH/LAW COMMON/LAW. CT/SYS
PAGE 54 E1073

B24

HOLDSWORTH W.S.,A HISTORY OF ENGLISH LAW; THE LAW
COMMON LAW AND ITS RIVALS (VOL. VI). UK STRATA CONSTN
EX/STRUC ADJUD ADMIN CONTROL CT/SYS...JURID CONCPT LEGIS
GEN/LAWS 17 COMMONWLTH PARLIAMENT ENGLSH/LAW CHIEF
COMMON/LAW. PAGE 54 E1074

B24

HOLDSWORTH W.S.,A HISTORY OF ENGLISH LAW; THE LAW
COMMON LAW AND ITS RIVALS (VOL. IV). UK SEA AGRI LEGIS
CHIEF ADJUD CONTROL CRIME GOV/REL...INT/LAW JURID CT/SYS
NAT/COMP 16/17 PARLIAMENT COMMON/LAW CANON/LAW CONSTN
ENGLSH/LAW. PAGE 54 E1075

C24

BARNES H.E.,"SOCIOLOGY AND POLITICAL THEORY: A CONCPT
CONSIDERATION OF THE SOCIOLOGICAL BASIS OF STRUCT
POLITICS." LAW CONSTN NAT/G DIPLOM DOMIN ROUTINE SOC
REV ORD/FREE SOVEREIGN...PHIL/SCI CLASSIF BIBLIOG
18/20. PAGE 8 E0151

C24

SHERMAN C.P.,"ROMAN LAW IN THE MODERN WORLD (2ND LAW
ED.) (3 VOLS.)" MEDIT-7...JURID BIBLIOG. PAGE 91 ADJUD
E1819 OWN
CONSTN

B25

GODET M.,INDEX BIBLIOGRAPHICUS: INTERNATIONAL BIBLIOG/A
CATALOGUE OF SOURCES OF CURRENT BIBLIOGRAPHIC DIPLOM
INFORMATION. EUR+WWI MOD/EUR SOCIETY SECT TAX EDU/PROP
...JURID PHIL/SCI SOC MATH. PAGE 44 E0876 LAW

B25

WINFIELD P.H.,THE CHIEF SOURCES OF ENGLISH LEGAL BIBLIOG/A
HISTORY. UK CONSTN JUDGE ADJUD CT/SYS 13/18. JURID
PAGE 107 E2133 LAW

B26

BEALE J.H.,A BIBLIOGRAPHY OF EARLY ENGLISH LAW BIBLIOG/A
BOOKS. MOD/EUR UK PRESS ADJUD CT/SYS ATTIT...CHARTS JURID
10/16. PAGE 8 E0161 LAW

B26

FORTESCUE J.,THE GOVERNANCE OF ENGLAND (1471-76). CONSERVE
UK LAW FINAN SECT LEGIS PROB/SOLV TAX DOMIN ADMIN CONSTN
GP/REL COST ORD/FREE PWR 14/15. PAGE 39 E0776 CHIEF
NAT/G

S26

HALL A.B.,"DETERMINATION OF METHODS FOR ADJUD
ASCERTAINING THE FACTORS THAT INFLUENCE JUDICIAL DECISION
DECISIONS IN CASES INVOLVING DUE PROCESS" LAW JUDGE CONSTN
DEBATE EFFICIENCY OPTIMAL UTIL...SOC CONCPT JURID
PROBABIL STAT SAMP. PAGE 49 E0981

B27

DICKINSON J.,ADMINISTRATIVE JUSTICE AND THE CT/SYS
SUPREMACY OF LAW IN THE UNITED STATES. USA-45 LAW ADJUD
INDUS DOMIN EDU/PROP CONTROL EXEC GP/REL ORD/FREE ADMIN
...POLICY JURID 19/20. PAGE 31 E0623 NAT/G

B27

GOOCH G.P.,ENGLISH DEMOCRATIC IDEAS IN THE IDEA/COMP
SEVENTEENTH CENTURY (2ND ED.). UK LAW SECT FORCES MAJORIT
DIPLOM LEAD PARL/PROC REV ATTIT AUTHORIT...ANARCH EX/STRUC
CONCPT 17 PARLIAMENT CMN/WLTH REFORMERS. PAGE 45 CONSERVE
E0885

B27

JOHN OF SALISBURY,THE STATESMAN'S BOOK (1159) NAT/G
(TRANS. BY J. DICKINSON). DOMIN GP/REL MORAL SECT
ORD/FREE PWR CONSERVE...CATH CONCPT 12. PAGE 59 CHIEF
E1169 LAW

B28

BENTHAM J.,A COMMENT OF THE COMMENTARIES (1765-69). LAW
MUNIC SECT ADJUD AGREE CT/SYS CONSEN HAPPINESS CONCPT
ORD/FREE 18. PAGE 10 E0191 IDEA/COMP

B28

BUTLER G.,THE DEVELOPMENT OF INTERNATIONAL LAW. LAW
WOR-45 SOCIETY NAT/G KNOWL ORD/FREE PWR...JURID INT/LAW
CONCPT HIST/WRIT GEN/LAWS. PAGE 18 E0349 DIPLOM
INT/ORG

B28

CORBETT P.E.,CANADA AND WORLD POLITICS. LAW CULTURE NAT/G
SOCIETY STRUCT MARKET INT/ORG FORCES ACT/RES PLAN CANADA
ECO/TAC LEGIT ORD/FREE PWR RESPECT...SOC CONCPT
TIME/SEQ TREND CMN/WLTH 20 LEAGUE/NAT. PAGE 26
E0504

B28

FRANKFURTER F.,THE BUSINESS OF THE SUPREME COURT; A CT/SYS
STUDY IN THE FEDERAL JUDICIAL SYSTEM. USA-45 CONSTN ADJUD
EX/STRUC PROB/SOLV GP/REL ATTIT PWR...POLICY JURID LAW
18/20 SUPREME/CT CONGRESS. PAGE 40 E0789 FEDERAL

B28

HOBBES T.,THE ELEMENTS OF LAW, NATURAL AND POLITIC PERSON
(1650). STRATA NAT/G SECT CHIEF AGREE ATTIT LAW
ALL/VALS MORAL ORD/FREE POPULISM...POLICY CONCPT. SOVEREIGN
PAGE 53 E1056 CONSERVE

B28

HOLDSWORTH W.S.,THE HISTORIANS OF ANGLO-AMERICAN HIST/WRIT
LAW. UK USA-45 INTELL LEGIS RESPECT...BIOG NAT/COMP LAW
17/20 COMMON/LAW. PAGE 54 E1076 JURID

B28

MACDONALD A.F.,ELEMENTS OF POLITICAL SCIENCE LAW
RESEARCH. USA-45 ACADEM JUDGE EDU/PROP DEBATE ADJUD FEDERAL
EXEC...BIBLIOG METH T 20 CONGRESS. PAGE 67 E1338 DECISION
CT/SYS

B28

MAIR L.P.,THE PROTECTION OF MINORITIES. EUR+WWI LAW
WOR-45 CONSTN INT/ORG NAT/G LEGIT CT/SYS GP/REL SOVEREIGN
RACE/REL DISCRIM ORD/FREE RESPECT...JURID CONCPT
TIME/SEQ 20. PAGE 68 E1352

B28

YANG KUNG-SUN,THE BOOK OF LORD SHANG. LAW ECO/UNDEV ASIA
LOC/G NAT/G NEIGH PLAN ECO/TAC LEGIT ATTIT SKILL JURID
...CONCPT CON/ANAL WORK TOT/POP. PAGE 108 E2164

L28

HUDSON M.,"THE TEACHING OF INTERNATIONAL LAW IN AMERICA." USA-45 LAW CONSULT ACT/RES CREATE EDU/PROP ATTIT RIGID/FLEX...JURID CONCPT RECORD HIST/WRIT TREND GEN/LAWS 18/20. PAGE 56 E1109

PERCEPT
KNOWL
INT/LAW

B29

BURNS C.D.,POLITICAL IDEALS. WOR-45 LAW CULTURE SOCIETY INT/ORG HEALTH MORAL...POLICY TOT/POP 20. PAGE 18 E0344

CONCPT
GEN/LAWS

B29

CAM H.M.,BIBLIOGRAPHY OF ENGLISH CONSTITUTIONAL HISTORY (PAMPHLET). UK LAW LOC/G NAT/G POL/PAR SECT DELIB/GP ADJUD ORD/FREE 19/20 PARLIAMENT. PAGE 19 E0369

BIBLIOG/A
CONSTN
ADMIN
PARL/PROC

L29

DARWIN L.,"WHAT IS EUGENICS." USA-45 LAW SOCIETY FACE/GP FAM ACT/RES ECO/TAC HEALTH...HEAL TREND STERTYP 20. PAGE 29 E0568

PLAN
BIO/SOC

B30

BENTHAM J.,THE RATIONALE OF PUNISHMENT. UK LAW LOC/G NAT/G LEGIS CONTROL...JURID GEN/LAWS COURT/SYS 19. PAGE 10 E0192

CRIME
SANCTION
COERCE
ORD/FREE

B30

BIRD F.L.,THE RECALL OF PUBLIC OFFICERS; A STUDY OF THE OPERATION OF RECALL IN CALIFORNIA. LOC/G MUNIC POL/PAR PROVS PROB/SOLV ADJUD PARTIC...CHARTS METH/COMP 20 CALIFORNIA RECALL. PAGE 12 E0230

REPRESENT
SANCTION
CHOOSE
LAW

B30

BURLAMAQUI J.J.,PRINCIPLES OF NATURAL AND POLITIC LAW (2 VOLS.) (1747-51). EX/STRUC LEGIS AGREE CT/SYS CHOOSE ROLE SOVEREIGN 18 NATURL/LAW. PAGE 17 E0342

LAW
NAT/G
ORD/FREE
CONCPT

B30

BYNKERSHOEK C.,QUAESTIONUM JURIS PUBLICI LIBRI DUO. CHRIST-17C MOD/EUR CONSTN ELITES SOCIETY NAT/G PROVS EX/STRUC FORCES TOP/EX BAL/PWR DIPLOM ATTIT MORAL...TRADIT CONCPT. PAGE 18 E0352

INT/ORG
LAW
NAT/LISM
INT/LAW

B30

WRIGHT Q.,MANDATES UNDER THE LEAGUE OF NATIONS. WOR-45 CONSTN ECO/DEV ECO/UNDEV NAT/G DELIB/GP TOP/EX LEGIT ALL/VALS...JURID CONCPT LEAGUE/NAT 20. PAGE 107 E2151

INT/ORG
LAW
INT/LAW

L30

LLEWELLYN K.N.,"A REALISTIC JURISPRUDENCE - THE NEXT STEP." PROB/SOLV ADJUD GP/REL PERS/REL IDEA/COMP. PAGE 66 E1312

LAW
CONCPT
JURID
GEN/LAWS

B31

BORCHARD E.H.,GUIDE TO THE LAW AND LEGAL LITERATURE OF FRANCE. FRANCE FINAN INDUS LABOR SECT LEGIS ADMIN COLONIAL CRIME OWN...INT/LAW 20. PAGE 14 E0266

BIBLIOG/A
LAW
CONSTN
METH

B31

COLUMBIA UNIVERSITY,A BIBLIOGRAPHY OF THE FACULTY OF POLITICAL SCIENCE OF COLUMBIA UNIVERSITY, 1880-1930. USA-45 LAW NAT/G LEGIS DIPLOM LEAD WAR GOV/REL ATTIT...TIME/SEQ 19/20. PAGE 24 E0478

BIBLIOG
ACADEM
PHIL/SCI

B32

GREAT BRIT COMM MINISTERS PWR,REPORT. UK LAW CONSTN CONSULT LEGIS PARL/PROC SANCTION SOVEREIGN ...DECISION JURID 20 PARLIAMENT. PAGE 45 E0902

EX/STRUC
NAT/G
PWR
CONTROL

B32

GREGORY W.,LIST OF THE SERIAL PUBLICATIONS OF FOREIGN GOVERNMENTS, 1815-1931. WOR-45 DIPLOM ADJUD ...POLICY 20. PAGE 46 E0914

BIBLIOG
NAT/G
LAW
JURID

B32

LUNT D.C.,THE ROAD TO THE LAW. UK USA-45 LEGIS EDU/PROP OWN ORD/FREE...DECISION TIME/SEQ NAT/COMP 16/20 AUSTRAL ENGLSH/LAW COMMON/LAW. PAGE 67 E1333

ADJUD
LAW
JURID
CT/SYS

B32

MASTERS R.D.,INTERNATIONAL LAW IN INTERNATIONAL COURTS. BELGIUM EUR+WWI FRANCE GERMANY MOD/EUR SWITZERLND WOR-45 SOCIETY STRATA STRUCT LEGIT EXEC ALL/VALS...JURID HIST/WRIT TIME/SEQ TREND GEN/LAWS 20. PAGE 69 E1383

INT/ORG
LAW
INT/LAW

B32

MORLEY F.,THE SOCIETY OF NATIONS. EUR+WWI UNIV WOR-45 LAW CONSTN ACT/RES PLAN EDU/PROP LEGIT ROUTINE...POLICY TIME/SEQ LEAGUE/NAT TOT/POP 20. PAGE 75 E1496

INT/ORG
CONCPT

B33

AMERICAN FOREIGN LAW ASSN,BIOGRAPHICAL NOTES ON THE LAWS AND LEGAL LITERATURE OF URUGUAY AND CURACAO. URUGUAY CONSTN FINAN SECT FORCES JUDGE DIPLOM INT/TRADE ADJUD CT/SYS CRIME 20. PAGE 4 E0078

BIBLIOG/A
LAW
JURID
ADMIN

B33

ENSOR R.C.K.,COURTS AND JUDGES IN FRANCE, GERMANY, AND ENGLAND. FRANCE GERMANY UK LAW PROB/SOLV ADMIN ROUTINE CRIME ROLE...METH/COMP 20 CIVIL/LAW. PAGE 35 E0692

CT/SYS
EX/STRUC
ADJUD
NAT/COMP

B33

HELLMAN F.S.,SELECTED LIST OF REFERENCES ON THE CONSTITUTIONAL POWERS OF THE PRESIDENT INCLUDING POWERS RECENTLY DELEGATED. USA-45 NAT/G EX/STRUC TOP/EX CENTRAL FEDERAL PWR 20 PRESIDENT. PAGE 51 E1025

BIBLIOG/A
JURID
LAW
CONSTN

B33

LAUTERPACHT H.,THE FUNCTION OF LAW IN THE INTERNATIONAL COMMUNITY. WOR-45 NAT/G FORCES CREATE DOMIN LEGIT COERCE WAR PEACE ATTIT ORD/FREE PWR SOVEREIGN...JURID CONCPT METH/CNCPT TIME/SEQ GEN/LAWS GEN/METH LEAGUE/NAT TOT/POP VAL/FREE 20. PAGE 63 E1265

INT/ORG
LAW
INT/LAW

B33

REID H.D.,RECUEIL DES COURS; TOME 45: LES SERVITUDES INTERNATIONALES III. FRANCE CONSTN DELIB/GP PRESS CONTROL REV WAR CHOOSE PEACE MORAL MARITIME TREATY. PAGE 84 E1680

ORD/FREE
DIPLOM
LAW

B34

CLYDE W.M.,THE STRUGGLE FOR THE FREEDOM OF THE PRESS FROM CAXTON TO CROMWELL. UK LAW LOC/G SECT FORCES LICENSE WRITING SANCTION REV ATTIT PWR ...POLICY 15/17 PARLIAMENT CROMWELL/O MILTON/J. PAGE 23 E0460

PRESS
ORD/FREE
CONTROL

B34

CULVER D.C.,BIBLIOGRAPHY OF CRIME AND CRIMINAL JUSTICE, 1927-1931. LAW CULTURE PUB/INST PROB/SOLV CT/SYS...PSY SOC STAT 20. PAGE 28 E0549

BIBLIOG/A
CRIMLGY
ADJUD
FORCES

B34

CUMMINGS H.,LIBERTY UNDER LAW AND ADMINISTRATION. MOD/EUR USA-45 ADMIN ATTIT...JURID PHIL/SCI. PAGE 28 E0553

ORD/FREE
LAW
NAT/G
SOCIETY

B34

EVANS I.L.,NATIVE POLICY IN SOUTHERN AFRICA. RHODESIA SOUTH/AFR UK STRUCT PARTIC RACE/REL ATTIT WEALTH SOC/INTEG AFRICA/SW. PAGE 35 E0705

AFR
COLONIAL
DOMIN
LAW

B34

US TARIFF COMMISSION,THE TARIFF; A BIBLIOGRAPHY: A SELECT LIST OF REFERENCES. USA-45 LAW DIPLOM TAX ADMIN...POLICY TREATY 20. PAGE 103 E2064

BIBLIOG/A
TARIFFS
ECO/TAC

B34

WOLFF C.,JUS GENTIUM METHODO SCIENTIFICA PERTRACTATUM. MOD/EUR INT/ORG VOL/ASSN LEGIT PEACE ATTIT...JURID 20. PAGE 107 E2140

NAT/G
LAW
INT/LAW
WAR

L34

LLEWELLYN K.N.,"THE CONSTITUTION AS AN INSTITUTION" (BMR)" USA-45 PROB/SOLV LOBBY REPRESENT...DECISION JURID 18/20 SUPREME/CT. PAGE 66 E1313

CONSTN
LAW
CONCPT
CT/SYS

B35

BURCHFIELD L.,STUDENT'S GUIDE TO MATERIALS IN POLITICAL SCIENCE. FINAN INT/ORG NAT/G POL/PAR DIPLOM PRESS ADMIN...BIOG 18/19. PAGE 17 E0328

BIBLIOG
INDEX
LAW

B35

CUMMING J.,A CONTRIBUTION TOWARD A BIBLIOGRAPHY DEALING WITH CRIME AND COGNATE SUBJECTS (3RD ED.). UK LAW CULTURE PUB/INST ADJUD AGE BIO/SOC...PSY SOC SOC/WK STAT METH/COMP 20. PAGE 28 E0552

BIBLIOG
CRIMLGY
FORCES
CT/SYS

B35

HALL J.,THEFT, LAW, AND SOCIETY. SOCIETY PROB/SOLV ...CRIMLGY SOC CONCPT TREND METH/COMP 18/20 LARCENCY. PAGE 49 E0982

CRIME
LAW
ADJUD

ADJUST

B35

RAM J.,THE SCIENCE OF LEGAL JUDGMENT: A TREATISE... LAW
UK CONSTN NAT/G LEGIS CREATE PROB/SOLV AGREE CT/SYS JURID
...INT/LAW CONCPT 19 ENGLSH/LAW CANON/LAW CIVIL/LAW EX/STRUC
CTS/WESTM. PAGE 83 E1672 ADJUD

B35

ROBSON W.A.,CIVILISATION AND THE GROWTH OF LAW. LAW
UNIV CONSTN SOCIETY LEGIS ADJUD ATTIT PERCEPT MORAL IDEA/COMP
ALL/IDEOS...CONCPT WORSHIP 20. PAGE 85 E1708 SOC

B36

CHAMBERLAIN J.P.,LEGISLATIVE PROCESS: NATION AND CON/ANAL
STATE. LAW DELIB/GP ROUTINE. PAGE 21 E0414 PROVS
LEGIS
NAT/G

B36

CULVER D.C.,METHODOLOGY OF SOCIAL SCIENCE RESEARCH: BIBLIOG/A
A BIBLIOGRAPHY. LAW CULTURE...CRIMLGY GEOG STAT OBS METH
INT QU HIST/WRIT CHARTS 20. PAGE 28 E0550 SOC

B36

EHRLICH E.,FUNDAMENTAL PRINCIPLES OF THE SOCIOLOGY LAW
OF LAW (TRANS. BY WALTER L. MOLL). UNIV SOCIETY JURID
ADJUD CT/SYS...POLICY GP/COMP GEN/LAWS GEN/METH. SOC
PAGE 34 E0678 CONCPT

B36

HANSON L.,GOVERNMENT AND THE PRESS 1695-1763. UK LAW
LOC/G LEGIS LICENSE CONTROL SANCTION CRIME ATTIT JURID
ORD/FREE 17/18 PARLIAMENT AMEND/I. PAGE 50 E0996 PRESS
POLICY

B36

HUDSON M.O.,INTERNATIONAL LEGISLATION: 1929-1931. INT/LAW
WOR-45 SEA AIR AGRI FINAN LABOR DIPLOM ECO/TAC PARL/PROC
REPAR CT/SYS ARMS/CONT WAR WEAPON...JURID 20 TREATY ADJUD
LEAGUE/NAT. PAGE 56 E1112 LAW

B36

SCHULZ F.,PRINCIPLES OF ROMAN LAW. CONSTN FAM NAT/G LAW
DOMIN CONTROL CT/SYS CRIME ISOLAT ATTIT ORD/FREE LEGIS
PWR...JURID ROME/ANC ROMAN/LAW. PAGE 89 E1783 ADJUD
CONCPT

S36

CORWIN E.S.,"THE CONSTITUTION AS INSTRUMENT AND AS CONSTN
SYMBOL." USA-45 ECO/DEV INDUS CAP/ISM SANCTION LAW
RIGID/FLEX ORD/FREE LAISSEZ OBJECTIVE 20 CONGRESS ADJUD
SUPREME/CT. PAGE 26 E0512 PWR

B37

BADEN A.L.,IMMIGRATION AND ITS RESTRICTION IN THE BIBLIOG
US (PAMPHLET). USA-45 NAT/G LEGIS...GEOG 20 STRANGE
CONGRESS. PAGE 7 E0130 CONTROL
LAW

B37

BEARDSLEY A.R.,LEGAL BIBLIOGRAPHY AND THE USE OF BIBLIOG
LAW BOOKS. CONSTN CREATE PROB/SOLV...DECISION JURID LAW
LAB/EXP. PAGE 9 E0166 METH
OP/RES

B37

BORGESE G.A.,GOLIATH: THE MARCH OF FASCISM. GERMANY POLICY
ITALY LAW POL/PAR SECT DIPLOM SOCISM...JURID MYTH NAT/LISM
20 DANTE MACHIAVELL MUSSOLIN/B. PAGE 14 E0270 FASCISM
NAT/G

B37

KETCHAM E.H.,PRELIMINARY SELECT BIBLIOGRAPHY OF BIBLIOG
INTERNATIONAL LAW (PAMPHLET). WOR-45 LAW INT/ORG DIPLOM
NAT/G PROB/SOLV CT/SYS NEUTRAL WAR 19/20. PAGE 60 ADJUD
E1207 INT/LAW

B37

RUTHERFORD M.L.,THE INFLUENCE OF THE AMERICAN BAR ATTIT
ASSOCIATION ON PUBLIC OPINION AND LEGISLATION. ADJUD
USA+45 LAW CONSTN LABOR LEGIS DOMIN EDU/PROP LEGIT PROF/ORG
CT/SYS ROUTINE...TIME/SEQ 19/20 ABA. PAGE 87 E1739 JURID

B37

SCHUSTER E.,GUIDE TO LAW AND LEGAL LITERATURE OF BIBLIOG/A
CENTRAL AMERICAN REPUBLICS. L/A+17C INT/ORG ADJUD REGION
SANCTION CRIME...JURID 19/20. PAGE 89 E1785 CT/SYS
LAW

S37

TIMASHEFF N.S.,"WHAT IS SOCIOLOGY OF LAW?" (BMR)" LAW
UNIV INTELL PWR...EPIST JURID PHIL/SCI IDEA/COMP. SOC
PAGE 96 E1925 SOCIETY

B38

FRANKFURTER F.,MR. JUSTICE HOLMES AND THE SUPREME CREATE
COURT. USA-45 CONSTN SOCIETY FEDERAL OWN ATTIT CT/SYS
ORD/FREE PWR...POLICY JURID 20 SUPREME/CT HOLMES/OW DECISION
BILL/RIGHT. PAGE 40 E0790 LAW

B38

HAGUE PERMANENT CT INTL JUSTIC,WORLD COURT REPORTS: INT/ORG
COLLECTION OF THE JUDGEMENTS ORDERS AND OPINIONS CT/SYS
VOLUME 3 1932-35. WOR-45 LAW DELIB/GP CONFER WAR DIPLOM
PEACE ATTIT...DECISION ANTHOL 20 WORLD/CT CASEBOOK. ADJUD
PAGE 49 E0976

B38

HARPER S.N.,THE GOVERNMENT OF THE SOVIET UNION. COM MARXISM
USSR LAW CONSTN ECO/DEV PLAN TEC/DEV DIPLOM NAT/G
INT/TRADE ADMIN REV NAT/LISM...POLICY 20. PAGE 50 LEAD
E1001 POL/PAR

B38

HELLMAN F.S.,THE SUPREME COURT ISSUE: SELECTED LIST BIBLIOG/A
OF REFERENCES. USA-45 NAT/G CHIEF EX/STRUC JUDGE CONSTN
ATTIT...JURID 20 PRESIDENT ROOSEVLT/F SUPREME/CT. CT/SYS
PAGE 51 E1026 LAW

B38

HOLDSWORTH W.S.,A HISTORY OF ENGLISH LAW; THE LAW
CENTURIES OF SETTLEMENT AND REFORM (VOL. X). INDIA LOC/G
UK CONSTN NAT/G CHIEF LEGIS ADMIN COLONIAL CT/SYS EX/STRUC
CHOOSE ORD/FREE PWR...JURID 18 PARLIAMENT ADJUD
COMMONWLTH COMMON/LAW. PAGE 54 E1077

B38

HOLDSWORTH W.S.,A HISTORY OF ENGLISH LAW; THE LAW
CENTURIES OF SETTLEMENT AND REFORM (VOL. XII). UK PROF/ORG
CONSTN STRATA LEGIS JUDGE ADJUD CT/SYS ATTIT WRITING
...JURID CONCPT BIOG GEN/LAWS 18 ENGLSH/LAW IDEA/COMP
BLACKSTN/W COMMON/LAW. PAGE 54 E1078

B38

HOLDSWORTH W.S.,A HISTORY OF ENGLISH LAW; THE LAW
CENTURIES OF SETTLEMENT AND REFORM (VOL. XI). UK COLONIAL
CONSTN NAT/G EX/STRUC DIPLOM ADJUD CT/SYS LEAD LEGIS
CRIME ATTIT...INT/LAW JURID 18 CMN/WLTH PARLIAMENT PARL/PROC
ENGLSH/LAW. PAGE 54 E1079

B38

MCNAIR A.D.,THE LAW OF TREATIES: BRITISH PRACTICE AGREE
AND OPINIONS. UK CREATE DIPLOM LEGIT WRITING ADJUD LAW
WAR...INT/LAW JURID TREATY. PAGE 71 E1424 CT/SYS
NAT/G

B38

POUND R.,THE FORMATIVE ERA OF AMERICAN LAW. CULTURE CONSTN
NAT/G PROVS LEGIS ADJUD CT/SYS PERSON SOVEREIGN LAW
...POLICY IDEA/COMP GEN/LAWS 18/19. PAGE 82 E1637 CREATE
JURID

B39

BALDWIN L.D.,WHISKEY REBELS; THE STORY OF A REV
FRONTIER UPRISING. USA-45 LAW ADJUD LEAD COERCE PWR POL/PAR
...BIBLIOG/A 18 PENNSYLVAN FEDERALIST. PAGE 8 E0145 TAX
TIME/SEQ

B39

CULVER D.C.,BIBLIOGRAPHY OF CRIME AND CRIMINAL BIBLIOG/A
JUSTICE. 1932-1937. USA-45 LAW CULTURE PUB/INST CRIMLGY
PROB/SOLV CT/SYS...PSY SOC STAT 20. PAGE 28 E0551 ADJUD
FORCES

B39

LAVES W.H.C.,INTERNATIONAL SECURITY. EUR+WWI ORD/FREE
GERMANY UK USA-45 LAW NAT/G DELIB/GP TOP/EX COERCE LEGIT
PWR...POLICY FASCIST CONCPT HIST/WRIT GEN/LAWS ARMS/CONT
LEAGUE/NAT NAZI 20. PAGE 63 E1267 BAL/PWR

B39

SIEYES E.J.,LES DISCOURS DE SIEYES DANS LES DEBATS CONSTN
CONSTITUTIONNELS DE L'AN III (2 ET 18 THERMIDOR). ADJUD
FRANCE LAW NAT/G PROB/SOLV BAL/PWR GOV/REL 18 JURY. LEGIS
PAGE 91 E1824 EX/STRUC

B39

WILSON G.G.,HANDBOOK OF INTERNATIONAL LAW. FUT UNIV INT/ORG
USA-45 WOR-45 SOCIETY LEGIT ATTIT DISPL DRIVE LAW
ALL/VALS...INT/LAW TIME/SEQ TREND. PAGE 106 E2128 CONCPT
WAR

B39

ZIMMERN A.,THE LEAGUE OF NATIONS AND THE RULE OF INT/ORG
LAW. WOR-45 STRUCT NAT/G DELIB/GP EX/STRUC BAL/PWR LAW
DOMIN LEGIT COERCE ORD/FREE PWR...POLICY RECORD DIPLOM
LEAGUE/NAT TOT/POP VAL/FREE 20 LEAGUE/NAT. PAGE 108
E2170

HADDOW A.,"POLITICAL SCIENCE IN AMERICAN COLLEGES AND UNIVERSITIES 1636-1900." CONSTN MORAL...POLICY INT/LAW CON/ANAL BIBLIOG T 17/20. PAGE 49 E0971

C39
USA-45
LAW
ACADEM
KNOWL

SCOTT J.B.,"LAW, THE STATE, AND THE INTERNATIONAL COMMUNITY (2 VOLS.)" INTELL INT/ORG NAT/G SECT INT/TRADE WAR...INT/LAW GEN/LAWS BIBLIOG. PAGE 90 E1798

C39
LAW
PHIL/SCI
DIPLOM
CONCPT

ANDERSON W.,FUNDAMENTALS OF AMERICAN GOVERNMENT. USA-45 LAW POL/PAR CHIEF EX/STRUC BUDGET ADMIN CT/SYS PARL/PROC CHOOSE FEDERAL...BIBLIOG 20. PAGE 5 E0093

B40
NAT/G
LOC/G
GOV/REL
CONSTN

FULLER G.H.,A SELECTED LIST OF RECENT REFERENCES ON THE CONSTITUTION OF THE UNITED STATES (PAMPHLET). CULTURE NAT/G LEGIS CONFER ADJUD GOV/REL CONSEN POPULISM...JURID CONCPT 18/20 CONGRESS. PAGE 41 E0820

B40
BIBLIOG/A
CONSTN
LAW
USA-45

HART J.,AN INTRODUCTION TO ADMINISTRATIVE LAW, WITH SELECTED CASES. USA-45 CONSTN SOCIETY NAT/G EX/STRUC ADJUD CT/SYS LEAD CRIME ORD/FREE ...DECISION JURID 20 CASEBOOK. PAGE 50 E1002

B40
LAW
ADMIN
LEGIS
PWR

MCILWAIN C.H.,CONSTITUTIONALISM, ANCIENT AND MODERN. CHRIST-17C MOD/EUR NAT/G CHIEF PROB/SOLV INSPECT AUTHORIT ORD/FREE PWR...TIME/SEQ ROMAN/REP. PAGE 71 E1418

B40
CONSTN
GEN/LAWS
LAW

FLORIN J.,"BOLSHEVIST AND NATIONAL SOCIALIST DOCTRINES OF INTERNATIONAL LAW." EUR+WWI GERMANY USSR R+D INT/ORG NAT/G DIPLOM DOMIN EDU/PROP SOCISM ...CONCPT TIME/SEQ 20. PAGE 39 E0768

S40
LAW
ATTIT
TOTALISM
INT/LAW

GURVITCH G.,"MAJOR PROBLEMS OF THE SOCIOLOGY OF LAW." CULTURE SANCTION KNOWL MORAL...POLICY EPIST JURID WORSHIP. PAGE 48 E0963

S40
SOC
LAW
PHIL/SCI

COUNTY GOVERNMENT IN THE UNITED STATES: A LIST OF RECENT REFERENCES (PAMPHLET). USA-45 LAW PUB/INST PLAN BUDGET CT/SYS CENTRAL 20. PAGE 52 E1027

N40
BIBLIOG/A
LOC/G
ADMIN
MUNIC

EVANS C.,AMERICAN BIBLIOGRAPHY... (12 VOLUMES). USA-45 LAW DIPLOM ADMIN PERSON...HUM SOC 17/18. PAGE 35 E0704

B41
BIBLIOG
NAT/G
ALL/VALS
ALL/IDEOS

GELLHORN W.,FEDERAL ADMINISTRATIVE PROCEEDINGS. USA+45 CLIENT FACE/GP NAT/G LOBBY REPRESENT PWR 20. PAGE 43 E0844

B41
EX/STRUC
LAW
ADJUD
POLICY

GILMORE M.P.,ARGUMENT FROM ROMAN LAW IN POLITICAL THOUGHT, 1200-1600. INTELL LICENSE CONTROL CT/SYS GOV/REL PRIVIL PWR...IDEA/COMP BIBLIOG 13/16. PAGE 44 E0866

B41
JURID
LAW
CONCPT
NAT/G

NIEMEYER G.,LAW WITHOUT FORCE: THE FUNCTION OF POLITICS IN INTERNATIONAL LAW. PLAN INSPECT DIPLOM REPAR LEGIT ADJUD WAR ORD/FREE...IDEA/COMP METH/COMP GEN/LAWS 20. PAGE 77 E1549

B41
COERCE
LAW
PWR
INT/LAW

CRAIG A.,ABOVE ALL LIBERTIES. FRANCE UK USA-45 LAW CONSTN CULTURE INTELL NAT/G SECT JUDGE...IDEA/COMP BIBLIOG 18/20. PAGE 27 E0536

B42
ORD/FREE
MORAL
WRITING
EDU/PROP

FORTESCU J.,IN PRAISE OF ENGLISH LAW (1464) (TRANS. BY S.B. CHRIMES). UK ELITES CHIEF FORCES CT/SYS COERCE CRIME GOV/REL ILLEGIT...JURID GOV/COMP GEN/LAWS 15. PAGE 39 E0774

B42
LAW
CONSTN
LEGIS
ORD/FREE

GURVITCH G.,SOCIOLOGY OF LAW. CONSTN SOCIETY CREATE MORAL SOVEREIGN...POLICY EPIST JURID PHIL/SCI IDEA/COMP METH/COMP HOLMES/OW HOBBES/T. PAGE 48 E0964

B42
SOC
LAW
ADJUD

HEGEL G.W.F.,PHILOSOPHY OF RIGHT. UNIV FAM SECT CHIEF AGREE WAR MARRIAGE OWN ORD/FREE...POLICY CONCPT. PAGE 51 E1023

B42
NAT/G
LAW
RATIONAL

SETARO F.C.,A BIBLIOGRAPHY OF THE WRITINGS OF ROSCOE POUND. USA-45 CT/SYS 20. PAGE 90 E1806

B42
BIBLIOG
LAW
ATTIT
JUDGE

CRAIG A.,"ABOVE ALL LIBERTIES." FRANCE UK LAW CULTURE INTELL SECT ORD/FREE 18/20. PAGE 27 E0537

C42
BIBLIOG/A
EDU/PROP
WRITING
MORAL

ANDERSON R.B.,SUPPLEMENT TO BEALE'S BIBLIOGRAPHY OF EARLY ENGLISH LAW BOOKS. MOD/EUR UK CONSTN PRESS ADJUD...CHARTS 10/15. PAGE 5 E0091

B43
BIBLIOG/A
JURID
CT/SYS
LAW

BACKUS R.C.,A GUIDE TO THE LAW AND LEGAL LITERATURE OF COLOMBIA. FINAN INDUS LABOR FORCES ADJUD ADMIN COLONIAL CT/SYS CRIME...INT/LAW JURID 20 COLOMB. PAGE 7 E0127

B43
BIBLIOG/A
LAW
CONSTN
L/A+17C

CLAGETT H.L.,A GUIDE TO THE LAW AND LEGAL LITERATURE OF PARAGUAY. PARAGUAY CONSTN COM/IND LABOR MUNIC JUDGE ADMIN CT/SYS...CRIMLGY INT/LAW CON/ANAL 20. PAGE 22 E0439

B43
BIBLIOG
JURID
LAW
L/A+17C

SERENI A.P.,THE ITALIAN CONCEPTION OF INTERNATIONAL LAW. EUR+WWI MOD/EUR INT/ORG NAT/G DOMIN COERCE ORD/FREE FASCISM...OBS/ENVIR TREND 20. PAGE 90 E1804

B43
LAW
TIME/SEQ
INT/LAW
ITALY

BENTHAM J.,"ON THE LIBERTY OF THE PRESS, AND PUBLIC DISCUSSION" IN J. BOWRING, ED., THE WORKS OF JEREMY BENTHAM." SPAIN UK LAW ELITES NAT/G LEGIS INSPECT LEGIT WRITING CONTROL PRIVIL TOTALISM AUTHORIT ...TRADIT 19 FREE/SPEE. PAGE 10 E0193

C43
ORD/FREE
PRESS
CONFER
CONSERVE

BENTHAM J.,"THE RATIONALE OF REWARD" IN J. BOWRING, ED., THE WORKS OF JEREMY BENTHAM (VOL. 2)" LAW WORKER CREATE INSPECT PAY ROUTINE HAPPINESS PRODUC SUPEGO WEALTH METH/CNCPT. PAGE 10 E0195

C43
SANCTION
ECO/TAC
INCOME
PWR

ADLER M.J.,HOW TO THINK ABOUT WAR AND PEACE. WOR-45 LAW SOCIETY EX/STRUC DIPLOM KNOWL ORD/FREE...POLICY TREND GEN/LAWS 20. PAGE 3 E0049

B44
INT/ORG
CREATE
ARMS/CONT
PEACE

BRIERLY J.L.,THE OUTLOOK FOR INTERNATIONAL LAW. FUT WOR-45 CONSTN NAT/G VOL/ASSN FORCES ECO/TAC DOMIN LEGIT ADJUD ROUTINE PEACE ORD/FREE...INT/LAW JURID METH LEAGUE/NAT 20. PAGE 15 E0298

B44
INT/ORG
LAW

FRAENKEL O.K.,OUR CIVIL LIBERTIES. USA-45...JURID CONCPT 18/20 BILL/RIGHT. PAGE 39 E0781

B44
CONSTN
LAW
ATTIT

FULLER G.H.,MILITARY GOVERNMENT: A LIST OF REFERENCES (A PAMPHLET). ITALY UK USA-45 WOR-45 LAW FORCES DOMIN ADMIN ARMS/CONT ORD/FREE PWR ...DECISION 20 CHINJAP. PAGE 41 E0822

B44
BIBLIOG
DIPLOM
CIVMIL/REL
SOVEREIGN

FULLER G.H.,RENEGOTIATION OF WAR CONTRACTS: A SELECTED LIST OF REFERENCES (PAMPHLET). USA-45 ECO/DEV LG/CO NAT/G OP/RES PLAN BAL/PWR LEGIT CONTROL...MGT 20. PAGE 42 E0823

B44
BIBLIOG
WAR
LAW
FINAN

HUDSON M.,INTERNATIONAL TRIBUNALS PAST AND FUTURE. FUT WOR-45 LAW EDU/PROP ADJUD ORD/FREE...CONCPT TIME/SEQ TREND GEN/LAWS TOT/POP VAL/FREE 18/20. PAGE 56 E1111

B44
INT/ORG
STRUCT
INT/LAW

PUTTKAMMER E.W.,WAR AND THE LAW. UNIV USA-45 CONSTN CULTURE SOCIETY NAT/G POL/PAR ROUTINE ALL/VALS ...JURID CONCPT OBS WORK VAL/FREE 20. PAGE 83 E1664

B44
INT/ORG
LAW
WAR
INT/LAW

B44
SUAREZ F.,A TREATISE ON LAWS AND GOD THE LAWGIVER   LAW
(1612) IN SELECTIONS FROM THREE WORKS, VOL. II.   JURID
FRANCE ITALY UK CULTURE NAT/G SECT CHIEF LEGIS   GEN/LAWS
DOMIN LEGIT CT/SYS ORD/FREE PWR WORSHIP 16/17.   CATH
PAGE 94 E1892

B44
US LIBRARY OF CONGRESS,RUSSIA: A CHECK LIST   BIBLIOG
PRELIMINARY TO A BASIC BIBLIOGRAPHY OF MATERIALS IN LAW
THE RUSSIAN LANGUAGE. COM USSR CULTURE EDU/PROP   SECT
MARXISM...ART/METH HUM LING 19/20. PAGE 101 E2015

S44
GRIFFITH E.S.,"THE CHANGING PATTERN OF PUBLIC   LAW
POLICY FORMATION." MOD/EUR WOR+45 FINAN CHIEF   POLICY
CONFER ADMIN LEAD CONSERVE SOCISM TECHRACY...SOC   TEC/DEV
CHARTS CONGRESS. PAGE 47 E0938

S44
MASON J.B.,"THE JUDICIAL SYSTEM OF THE NAZI PARTY." FASCISM
GERMANY ELITES POL/PAR DOMIN CONTROL SANCTION   CT/SYS
TOTALISM...JURID 20 HITLER/A. PAGE 69 E1381   ADJUD
                                                     LAW

B45
CLAGETT H.L.,A GUIDE TO THE LAW AND LEGAL   BIBLIOG
LITERATURE OF THE MEXICAN STATES. CONSTN LEGIS   JURID
JUDGE ADJUD ADMIN...INT/LAW CON/ANAL 20 MEXIC/AMER. L/A+17C
PAGE 22 E0440   LAW

B45
REVES E.,THE ANATOMY OF PEACE. WOR-45 LAW CULTURE   ACT/RES
NAT/G PLAN TEC/DEV EDU/PROP WAR NAT/LISM ATTIT   CONCPT
ALL/VALS SOVEREIGN...POLICY HUM TIME/SEQ 20.   NUC/PWR
PAGE 84 E1688   PEACE

B45
US LIBRARY OF CONGRESS,NETHERLANDS EAST INDIES.   BIBLIOG/A
INDONESIA LAW CULTURE AGRI INDUS SCHOOL COLONIAL   S/ASIA
HEALTH...GEOG JURID SOC 19/20 NETH/IND. PAGE 101   NAT/G
E2017

B45
VANCE H.L.,GUIDE TO THE LAW AND LEGAL LITERATURE OF BIBLIOG/A
MEXICO. LAW CONSTN FINAN LABOR FORCES ADJUD ADMIN   INT/LAW
...CRIMLGY PHIL/SCI CON/ANAL 20 MEXIC/AMER.   JURID
PAGE 103 E2070   CT/SYS

B45
WEST R.,CONSCIENCE AND SOCIETY: A STUDY OF THE   COERCE
PSYCHOLOGICAL PREREQUISITES OF LAW AND ORDER. FUT   INT/LAW
UNIV LAW SOCIETY STRUCT DIPLOM WAR PERS/REL SUPEGO   ORD/FREE
...SOC 20. PAGE 105 E2112   PERSON

S45
DAVIS A.,"CASTE, ECONOMY, AND VIOLENCE" (BMR)"   STRATA
USA-45 LAW SOCIETY STRUCT SECT SANCTION COERCE   RACE/REL
MARRIAGE SEX...PSY SOC SOC/INTEG 18/20 NEGRO   DISCRIM
MISCEGEN SOUTH/US. PAGE 29 E0570

B46
AMERICAN DOCUMENTATION INST,CATALOGUE OF AUXILIARY   BIBLIOG
PUBLICATIONS IN MICROFILMS AND PHOTOPRINTS. USA-45   EDU/PROP
LAW AGRI CREATE TEC/DEV ADMIN...GEOG LING MATH 20.   PSY
PAGE 4 E0077

B46
GRIFFIN G.G.,A GUIDE TO MANUSCRIPTS RELATING TO   BIBLIOG/A
AMERICAN HISTORY IN BRITISH DEPOSITORIES. CANADA   ALL/VALS
IRELAND MOD/EUR UK USA-45 LAW DIPLOM ADMIN COLONIAL NAT/G
WAR NAT/LISM SOVEREIGN...GEOG INT/LAW 15/19
CMN/WLTH. PAGE 47 E0936

B46
MANNHEIM H.,CRIMINAL JUSTICE AND SOCIAL   ADJUD
RECONSTRUCTION. USA+45 EDU/PROP CRIME ANOMIE   LAW
...JURID BIBLIOG 20. PAGE 68 E1361   STRUCT
                                                     ADJUST

B46
PATON G.W.,A TEXT-BOOK OF JURISPRUDENCE. CREATE   LAW
INSPECT LEGIT CT/SYS ROUTINE CRIME INGP/REL PRIVIL   ADJUD
...CONCPT BIBLIOG 20. PAGE 80 E1601   JURID
                                                     T

B46
ROSS A.,TOWARDS A REALISTIC JURISPRUDENCE: A   LAW
CRITICISM OF THE DUALISM IN LAW (TRANS. BY ANNIE I. CONCPT
FAUSBOLL). PLAN ADJUD CT/SYS ATTIT RIGID/FLEX   IDEA/COMP
POPULISM...JURID PHIL/SCI LOG METH/COMP GEN/LAWS 20
SCANDINAV. PAGE 86 E1720

L46
ERNST M.L.,"THE FIRST FREEDOM." USA-45 LAW R+D   BIBLIOG
PRESS 20. PAGE 35 E0696   EDU/PROP

ORD/FREE
COM/IND

B47
BORGESE G.,COMMON CAUSE. LAW CONSTN SOCIETY STRATA   WOR+45
ECO/DEV INT/ORG POL/PAR FORCES LEGIS TOP/EX CAP/ISM NAT/G
DIPLOM ADMIN EXEC ATTIT PWR 20. PAGE 14 E0269   SOVEREIGN
                                                     REGION

B47
CLAGETT H.L.,A GUIDE TO THE LAW AND LEGAL   BIBLIOG/A
LITERATURE OF BOLIVIA. L/A+17C CONSTN LABOR LEGIS   JURID
ADMIN...CRIMLGY INT/LAW PHIL/SCI 16/20 BOLIV.   LAW
PAGE 22 E0441   CT/SYS

B47
CLAGETT H.L.,A GUIDE TO THE LAW AND LEGAL   BIBLIOG
LITERATURE OF CHILE, 1917-1946. CHILE CONSTN LABOR   L/A+17C
JUDGE ADJUD ADMIN...CRIMLGY INT/LAW JURID CON/ANAL   LAW
20. PAGE 22 E0442   LEGIS

B47
CLAGETT H.L.,A GUIDE TO THE LAW AND LEGAL   BIBLIOG
LITERATURE OF ECUADOR. ECUADOR CONSTN LABOR LEGIS   JURID
JUDGE ADJUD ADMIN CIVMIL/REL...CRIMLGY INT/LAW   LAW
CON/ANAL 20. PAGE 22 E0443   L/A+17C

B47
CLAGETT H.L.,A GUIDE TO THE LAW AND LEGAL   BIBLIOG
LITERATURE OF PERU. PERU CONSTN COM/IND LABOR MUNIC L/A+17C
JUDGE ADMIN CT/SYS...CRIMLGY INT/LAW JURID 20.   PHIL/SCI
PAGE 23 E0444   LAW

B47
CLAGETT H.L.,A GUIDE TO THE LAW AND LEGAL   BIBLIOG
LITERATURE OF URUGUAY. URUGUAY CONSTN COM/IND FINAN LAW
LABOR MUNIC JUDGE PRESS ADMIN CT/SYS...INT/LAW   JURID
PHIL/SCI 20. PAGE 23 E0445   L/A+17C

B47
CLAGETT H.L.,A GUIDE TO THE LAW AND LEGAL   BIBLIOG
LITERATURE OF VENEZUELA. VENEZUELA CONSTN LABOR   L/A+17C
LEGIS JUDGE ADJUD ADMIN CIVMIL/REL...CRIMLGY JURID   INT/LAW
CON/ANAL 20. PAGE 23 E0446   LAW

B47
DE NOIA J.,GUIDE TO OFFICIAL PUBLICATIONS OF OTHER   BIBLIOG/A
AMERICAN REPUBLICS: ECUADOR (VOL. IX). ECUADOR LAW   CONSTN
FINAN LEGIS BUDGET CT/SYS 19/20. PAGE 30 E0589   NAT/G
                                                     EDU/PROP

B47
DE NOIA J.,GUIDE TO OFFICIAL PUBLICATIONS OF THE   BIBLIOG/A
OTHER AMERICAN REPUBLICS: EL SALVADOR. EL/SALVADR   CONSTN
LAW LEGIS EDU/PROP CT/SYS 20. PAGE 30 E0590   NAT/G
                                                     ADMIN

B47
DE NOIA J.,GUIDE TO OFFICIAL PUBLICATIONS OF THE   BIBLIOG/A
OTHER AMERICAN REPUBLICS: NICARAGUA (VOL. XIV).   EDU/PROP
NICARAGUA LAW LEGIS ADMIN CT/SYS...JURID 19/20.   NAT/G
PAGE 30 E0591   CONSTN

B47
DE NOIA J.,GUIDE TO OFFICIAL PUBLICATIONS OF THE   BIBLIOG/A
OTHER AMERICAN REPUBLICS: PANAMA (VOL. XV). PANAMA   CONSTN
LAW LEGIS EDU/PROP CT/SYS 20. PAGE 30 E0592   ADMIN
                                                     NAT/G

B47
GORDON D.L.,THE HIDDEN WEAPON: THE STORY OF   INT/ORG
ECONOMIC WARFARE. EUR+WWI USA-45 LAW FINAN INDUS   ECO/TAC
NAT/G CONSULT FORCES PLAN DOMIN PWR WEALTH   INT/TRADE
...INT/LAW CONCPT OBS TOT/POP NAZI 20. PAGE 45   WAR
E0891

B47
HARGRETT L.,A BIBLIOGRAPHY OF THE CONSTITUTIONS AND BIBLIOG/A
LAWS OF THE AMERICAN INDIANS. USA-45 LOC/G GOV/REL   CONSTN
GP/REL 19/20 INDIAN/AM. PAGE 50 E0999   LAW
                                                     NAT/G

B47
HILL M.,IMMUNITIES AND PRIVILEGES OF INTERNATIONAL   INT/ORG
OFFICIALS. CANADA EUR+WWI NETHERLAND SWITZERLND LAW ADMIN
LEGIS DIPLOM LEGIT RESPECT...TIME/SEQ LEAGUE/NAT UN
VAL/FREE 20. PAGE 52 E1046

B47
HIRSHBERG H.S.,SUBJECT GUIDE TO UNITED STATES   BIBLIOG
GOVERNMENT PUBLICATIONS. USA+45 USA-45 LAW ADMIN   NAT/G
...SOC 20. PAGE 53 E1052   DIPLOM
                                                     LOC/G

B47
HOCKING W.E.,FREEDOM OF THE PRESS: A FRAMEWORK OF   ORD/FREE

PRINCIPLE. WOR-45 SOCIETY NAT/G PROB/SOLV DEBATE   CONSTN
LOBBY...JURID PSY 20 AMEND/I. PAGE 53 E1061   PRESS
                                                         LAW

                                                         B47
INTERNATIONAL COURT OF JUSTICE,CHARTER OF THE   INT/LAW
UNITED NATIONS, STATUTE AND RULES OF COURT AND   INT/ORG
OTHER CONSTITUTIONAL DOCUMENTS. SWITZERLND LAW   CT/SYS
ADJUD INGP/REL...JURID 20 ICJ UN. PAGE 57 E1133   DIPLOM

                                                         B47
KONVITZ M.R.,THE CONSTITUTION AND CIVIL RIGHTS.   CONSTN
USA-45 NAT/G ADJUD GP/REL RACE/REL POPULISM   LAW
...MAJORIT 19/20 SUPREME/CT CIV/RIGHTS. PAGE 61   GOV/REL
E1227   ORD/FREE

                                                         B47
LOCKE J.,TWO TREATISES OF GOVERNMENT (1690). UK LAW   CONCPT
SOCIETY LEGIS LEGIT AGREE REV OWN HEREDITY MORAL   ORD/FREE
CONSERVE...POLICY MAJORIT 17 WILLIAM/3 NATURL/LAW.   NAT/G
PAGE 66 E1316   CONSEN

                                                         B47
MCILWAIN C.H.,CONSTITUTIONALISM: ANCIENT AND   CONSTN
MODERN. USA+45 ROMAN/EMP LAW CHIEF LEGIS CT/SYS   NAT/G
GP/REL ORD/FREE SOVEREIGN...POLICY TIME/SEQ   PARL/PROC
ROMAN/REP EUROPE. PAGE 71 E1419   GOV/COMP

                                                         B47
NEUBURGER O.,GUIDE TO OFFICIAL PUBLICATIONS OF   BIBLIOG/A
OTHER AMERICAN REPUBLICS: HONDURAS (VOL. XIII).   NAT/G
HONDURAS LAW LEGIS ADMIN CT/SYS...JURID 19/20.   EDU/PROP
PAGE 76 E1533   CONSTN

                                                         B47
NEUBURGER O.,GUIDE TO OFFICIAL PUBLICATIONS OF THE   BIBLIOG/A
OTHER AMERICAN REPUBLICS: HAITI (VOL. XII). HAITI   CONSTN
LAW FINAN LEGIS PRESS...JURID 20. PAGE 76 E1534   NAT/G
                                                         EDU/PROP

                                                         B47
TOWLE L.W.,INTERNATIONAL TRADE AND COMMERCIAL   MARKET
POLICY. WOR+45 LAW ECO/DEV FINAN INDUS NAT/G   INT/ORG
ECO/TAC WEALTH...TIME/SEQ ILO 20. PAGE 97 E1937   INT/TRADE

                                                         S47
FRANKFURTER F.,"SOME REFLECTIONS ON THE READING OF   JURID
STATUTES" USA+45 USA-45 PROB/SOLV CT/SYS TASK   LAW
EFFICIENCY...LING 20. PAGE 40 E0791   ADJUD
                                                         WRITING

                                                         B48
CLAGETT H.L.,A GUIDE TO THE LAW AND LEGAL   BIBLIOG
LITERATURE OF ARGENTINA, 1917-1946. CONSTN LABOR   L/A+17C
JUDGE ADJUD ADMIN...CRIMLGY INT/LAW JURID CON/ANAL   LAW
20 ARGEN. PAGE 23 E0447   LEGIS

                                                         B48
CORWIN E.S.,LIBERTY AGAINST GOVERNMENT. UK USA-45   JURID
ROMAN/EMP LAW CONSTN PERS/REL OWN ATTIT 1/20   ORD/FREE
ROMAN/LAW ENGLSH/LAW AMEND/XIV. PAGE 26 E0513   CONCPT

                                                         B48
DE NOIA J.,GUIDE TO OFFICIAL PUBLICATIONS OF OTHER   BIBLIOG/A
AMERICAN REPUBLICS: PERU (VOL. XVII). PERU LAW   CONSTN
LEGIS ADMIN CT/SYS...JURID 19/20. PAGE 30 E0593   NAT/G
                                                         EDU/PROP

                                                         B48
HOLCOMBE A.N.,HUMAN RIGHTS IN THE MODERN WORLD.   ORD/FREE
WOR+45 LEGIS DIPLOM ADJUD PERSON...INT/LAW 20 UN   INT/ORG
TREATY CIVIL/LIB BILL/RIGHT. PAGE 54 E1071   CONSTN
                                                         LAW

                                                         B48
KEIR D.L.,CASES IN CONSTITUTIONAL LAW. UK CHIEF   CONSTN
LEGIS DIPLOM TAX PARL/PROC CRIME GOV/REL...INT/LAW   LAW
JURID 17/20. PAGE 60 E1195   ADJUD
                                                         CT/SYS

                                                         B48
MEIKLEJOHN A.,FREE SPEECH AND ITS RELATION TO SELF-   LEGIS
GOVERNMENT. USA+45 USA-45 LAW DOMIN PRESS ORD/FREE   NAT/G
20 AMEND/I. PAGE 72 E1434   CONSTN
                                                         PRIVIL

                                                         B48
NEUBURGER O.,GUIDE TO OFFICIAL PUBLICATIONS OF THE   BIBLIOG/A
OTHER AMERICAN REPUBLICS: VENEZUELA (VOL. XIX).   NAT/G
VENEZUELA FINAN LEGIS PLAN BUDGET DIPLOM CT/SYS   CONSTN
PARL/PROC 19/20. PAGE 77 E1535   LAW

                                                         B48
SLESSER H.,THE ADMINISTRATION OF THE LAW. UK CONSTN   LAW
EX/STRUC OP/RES PROB/SOLV CRIME ROLE...DECISION   CT/SYS
METH/COMP 20 CIVIL/LAW ENGLSH/LAW CIVIL/LAW.   ADJUD

PAGE 92 E1839

                                                         S48
ALEXANDER L.,"WAR CRIMES, THEIR SOCIAL-   DRIVE
PSYCHOLOGICAL ASPECTS." EUR+WWI GERMANY LAW CULTURE   WAR
ELITES KIN POL/PAR PUB/INST FORCES DOMIN EDU/PROP
COERCE CRIME ATTIT SUPEGO HEALTH MORAL PWR FASCISM
...PSY OBS TREND GEN/LAWS NAZI 20. PAGE 3 E0061

                                                         S48
BRADEN G.D.,"THE SEARCH FOR OBJECTIVITY IN   CONSTN
CONSTITUTIONAL LAW" (BMR)" USA+45 USA-45 LAW NAT/G   CT/SYS
CONTROL ORD/FREE PWR OBJECTIVE...JURID 20   IDEA/COMP
SUPREME/CT. PAGE 15 E0283   POLICY

                                                         S48
MILLER B.S.,"A LAW IS PASSED: THE ATOMIC ENERGY ACT   TEC/DEV
OF 1946." POL/PAR CHIEF CONFER DEBATE CONTROL   LEGIS
PARL/PROC ATTIT KNOWL...POLICY CONGRESS. PAGE 73   DECISION
E1457   LAW

                                                         C48
WALKER H.,"THE LEGISLATIVE PROCESS; LAWMAKING IN   PARL/PROC
THE UNITED STATES." NAT/G POL/PAR PROVS EX/STRUC   LEGIS
OP/RES PROB/SOLV CT/SYS LOBBY GOV/REL...CHARTS   LAW
BIBLIOG T 18/20 CONGRESS. PAGE 105 E2094   CONSTN

                                                         B49
BRUCKER H.,FREEDOM OF INFORMATION. USA-45 LAW LOC/G   PRESS
ECO/TAC DOMIN PWR...NEW/IDEA BIBLIOG 17/20. PAGE 16   COM/IND
E0320   ORD/FREE
                                                         NAT/G

                                                         B49
DE HUSZAR G.B.,EQUALITY IN AMERICA: THE ISSUE OF   DISCRIM
MINORITY RIGHTS. USA+45 USA-45 LAW NEIGH SCHOOL   RACE/REL
LEGIS ACT/RES CHOOSE ATTIT RESPECT...ANTHOL 20   ORD/FREE
NEGRO. PAGE 29 E0585   PROB/SOLV

                                                         B49
DENNING A.,FREEDOM UNDER THE LAW. MOD/EUR UK LAW   ORD/FREE
SOCIETY CHIEF EX/STRUC LEGIS ADJUD CT/SYS PERS/REL   JURID
PERSON 17/20 ENGLSH/LAW. PAGE 31 E0606   NAT/G

                                                         B49
FRANK J.,LAW AND THE MODERN MIND. UNIV LAW CT/SYS   JURID
RATIONAL ATTIT...CONCPT 20 HOLMES/OW JURY. PAGE 40   ADJUD
E0787   IDEA/COMP
                                                         MYTH

                                                         B49
GROB F.,THE RELATIVITY OF WAR AND PEACE: A STUDY IN   WAR
LAW, HISTORY, AND POLITICS. WOR+45 WOR-45 LAW   PEACE
DIPLOM DEBATE...CONCPT LING IDEA/COMP BIBLIOG   INT/LAW
18/20. PAGE 48 E0944   STYLE

                                                         B49
HOLLERAN M.P.,CHURCH AND STATE IN GUATEMALA.   SECT
GUATEMALA LAW STRUCT CATHISM...SOC SOC/INTEG 17/20   NAT/G
CHURCH/STA. PAGE 55 E1086   GP/REL
                                                         CULTURE

                                                         B49
MARITAIN J.,HUMAN RIGHTS: COMMENTS AND   INT/ORG
INTERPRETATIONS. COM UNIV WOR+45 LAW CONSTN CULTURE   CONCPT
SOCIETY ECO/DEV ECO/UNDEV SCHOOL DELIB/GP EDU/PROP
ATTIT PERCEPT ALL/VALS...HUM SOC TREND UNESCO 20.
PAGE 68 E1365

                                                         B49
SCHONS D.,BOOK CENSORSHIP IN NEW SPAIN (NEW WORLD   CHRIST-17C
STUDIES, BOOK II). SPAIN LAW CULTURE INSPECT ADJUD   EDU/PROP
CT/SYS SANCTION GP/REL ORD/FREE 14/17. PAGE 88   CONTROL
E1764   PRESS

                                                         B49
THOREAU H.D.,CIVIL DISOBEDIENCE (1849). USA-45 LAW   GEN/LAWS
CONSTN TAX COERCE REPRESENT GP/REL SUPEGO...MAJORIT   ORD/FREE
CONCPT 19. PAGE 96 E1923   POLICY

                                                         B49
US DEPARTMENT OF STATE,SOVIET BIBLIOGRAPHY   BIBLIOG/A
(PAMPHLET). CHINA/COM COM USSR LAW AGRI INT/ORG   MARXISM
ECO/TAC EDU/PROP...POLICY GEOG 20. PAGE 99 E1994   CULTURE
                                                         DIPLOM

                                                         B49
US LIBRARY OF CONGRESS,FREEDOM OF INFORMATION: BIBLIOG/A
SELECTIVE REPORT ON RECENT WRITINGS. USA+45 LAW   ORD/FREE
CONSTN ELITES EDU/PROP PRESS LOBBY WAR TOTALISM   LICENSE
ATTIT 20 UN UNESCO COLD/WAR. PAGE 101 E2018   COM/IND

                                                         B49
WORMUTH F.D.,THE ORIGINS OF MODERN   NAT/G
CONSTITUTIONALISM. GREECE UK LEGIS CREATE TEC/DEV   CONSTN
BAL/PWR DOMIN ADJUD REV WAR PWR...JURID ROMAN/REP   LAW

CROMWELL/O. PAGE 107 E2146

L49

COMM. STUDY ORGAN. PEACE."A TEN YEAR RECORD. 1939-1949." FUT WOR+45 LAW R+D CONSULT DELIB/GP CREATE LEGIT ROUTINE ORD/FREE...TIME/SEQ UN 20. PAGE 24 E0480

INT/ORG
CONSTN
PEACE

L49

MARX C.M.,"ADMINISTRATIVE ETHICS AND THE RULE OF LAW." USA+45 ELITES ACT/RES DOMIN NEUTRAL ROUTINE INGP/REL ORD/FREE...JURID IDEA/COMP. PAGE 69 E1375

ADMIN
LAW

S49

FIELD G.L.,"LAW AS AN OBJECTIVE POLITICAL CONCEPT" (BMR)" UNIV SOCIETY RATIONAL JURID. PAGE 38 E0747

LAW
CONCPT
METH/CNCPT
SANCTION

B50

BAILEY S.K.,CONGRESS MAKES A LAW. USA+45 GP/REL SOC. PAGE 7 E0136

DECISION
LEGIS
LAW
ECO/TAC

B50

BERMAN H.J.,JUSTICE IN RUSSIA; AN INTERPRETATION OF SOVIET LAW. USSR LAW STRUCT LABOR FORCES AGREE GP/REL ORD/FREE SOCISM...TIME/SEQ 20. PAGE 11 E0207

JURID
ADJUD
MARXISM
COERCE

B50

BOHATTA H.,INTERNATIONALE BIBLIOGRAPHIE. WOR+45 LAW CULTURE PRESS. PAGE 13 E0260

BIBLIOG
DIPLOM
NAT/G
WRITING

B50

BROWN E.S.,MANUAL OF GOVERNMENT PUBLICATIONS. WOR+45 WOR-45 CONSTN INT/ORG MUNIC PROVS DIPLOM ADMIN 20. PAGE 16 E0313

BIBLIOG/A
NAT/G
LAW

B50

BURDETTE F.L.,LOBBYISTS IN ACTION (PAMPHLET). CONSULT TEC/DEV INSPECT BARGAIN PARL/PROC SANCTION 20 CONGRESS. PAGE 17 E0329

LOBBY
ATTIT
POLICY
LAW

B50

DOROSH J.T.,GUIDE TO SOVIET BIBLIOGRAPHIES. USSR LAW AGRI SCHOOL SECT FORCES TEC/DEV...ART/METH GEOG HUM SOC 20. PAGE 32 E0639

BIBLIOG
METH
CON/ANAL

B50

EMBREE J.F.,BIBLIOGRAPHY OF THE PEOPLES AND CULTURES OF MAINLAND SOUTHEAST ASIA. CAMBODIA LAOS THAILAND VIETNAM LAW...GEOG HUM SOC MYTH LING CHARTS WORSHIP 20. PAGE 35 E0686

BIBLIOG/A
CULTURE
S/ASIA

B50

FRAGA IRIBARNE M.,RAZAS Y RACISMO IN NORTEAMERICA. USA+45 CONSTN STRATA NAT/G PROVS ATTIT...SOC CONCPT 19/20 NEGRO. PAGE 39 E0783

RACE/REL
JURID
LAW
DISCRIM

B50

FRANK J.,COURTS ON TRIAL: MYTH AND REALITY IN AMERICAN JUSTICE. LAW CONSULT PROB/SOLV EDU/PROP ADJUD ROUTINE ROLE ORD/FREE...GEN/LAWS T 20. PAGE 40 E0788

JURID
CT/SYS
MYTH
CONSTN

B50

HURST J.W.,THE GROWTH OF AMERICAN LAW; THE LAW MAKERS. USA-45 LOC/G NAT/G DELIB/GP JUDGE ADJUD ADMIN ATTIT PWR...POLICY JURID BIBLIOG 18/20 CONGRESS SUPREME/CT ABA PRESIDENT. PAGE 56 E1115

LAW
LEGIS
CONSTN
CT/SYS

B50

LAUTERPACHT H.,INTERNATIONAL LAW AND HUMAN RIGHTS. USA+45 CONSTN STRUCT INT/ORG ACT/RES EDU/PROP PEACE PERSON ALL/VALS...CONCPT CON/ANAL GEN/LAWS UN 20. PAGE 63 E1266

DELIB/GP
LAW
INT/LAW

B50

LOWENTHAL M.,THE FEDERAL BUREAU OF INVESTIGATION. USA+45 SOCIETY ADMIN TASK CRIME INGP/REL...CRIMLGY 20 FBI ESPIONAGE. PAGE 67 E1329

FORCES
NAT/G
ATTIT
LAW

B50

MACIVER R.M.,GREAT EXPRESSIONS OF HUMAN RIGHTS. LAW CONSTN CULTURE INTELL SOCIETY R+D INT/ORG ATTIT DRIVE...JURID OBS HIST/WRIT GEN/LAWS. PAGE 67 E1340

UNIV
CONCPT

B50

MERRIAM C.E.,THE AMERICAN PARTY SYSTEM; AN

POL/PAR

CHOOSE
SUFF
REPRESENT

INTRODUCTION TO THE STUDY OF POLITICAL PARTIES IN THE UNITED STATES (4TH ED.). USA+45 USA-45 LAW FINAN LOC/G NAT/G PROVS LEAD PARTIC CRIME ATTIT 18/20 NEGRO CONGRESS PRESIDENT. PAGE 72 E1442

B50

SOHN L.B.,CASES AND OTHER MATERIALS ON WORLD LAW. FUT WOR+45 LAW INT/ORG...INT/LAW JURID METH/CNCPT 20 UN. PAGE 92 E1852

CT/SYS
CONSTN

B50

STONE J.,THE PROVINCE AND FUNCTION OF LAW. UNIV WOR+45 WOR-45 CULTURE INTELL SOCIETY ECO/DEV ECO/UNDEV NAT/G LEGIT ROUTINE ATTIT PERCEPT PERSON ...JURID CONCPT GEN/LAWS GEN/METH 20. PAGE 94 E1877

INT/ORG
LAW

B50

US FEDERAL BUREAU INVESTIGAT,BIBLIOGRAPHY OF CRIME AND KINDRED SUBJECTS (PAPER). USA+45 PROB/SOLV TREND. PAGE 100 E2001

BIBLIOG/A
CRIME
LAW
CRIMLGY

B50

WADE E.C.S.,CONSTITUTIONAL LAW; AN OUTLINE OF THE LAW AND PRACTICE OF THE CONSTITUTION. UK LEGIS DOMIN ADMIN GP/REL 16/20 CMN/WLTH PARLIAMENT ENGLSH/LAW. PAGE 104 E2087

CONSTN
NAT/G
PARL/PROC
LAW

B50

WARD R.E.,A GUIDE TO JAPANESE REFERENCE AND RESEARCH MATERIALS IN THE FIELD OF POLITICAL SCIENCE. LAW CONSTN LOC/G PRESS ADMIN...SOC CON/ANAL METH 19/20 CHINJAP. PAGE 105 E2098

BIBLIOG/A
ASIA
NAT/G

C50

NUMELIN R.,"THE BEGINNINGS OF DIPLOMACY." INT/TRADE WAR GP/REL PEACE STRANGE ATTIT...INT/LAW CONCPT BIBLIOG. PAGE 78 E1559

DIPLOM
KIN
CULTURE
LAW

B51

BECKER O.,MASTER RESEARCH GUIDE. USA+45 USA-45 PRESS...JURID INDEX 20. PAGE 9 E0171

BIBLIOG
LAW
ADJUD
CT/SYS

B51

BIDDLE F.,THE FEAR OF FREEDOM. USA+45 LAW NAT/G PUB/INST PROB/SOLV DOMIN CONTROL SANCTION REV NAT/LISM 20. PAGE 12 E0227

ANOMIE
INGP/REL
VOL/ASSN
ORD/FREE

B51

CAMPBELL E.H.,UNITED STATES CITIZENSHIP AND QUALIFICATIONS FOR VOTING IN WASHINGTON. USA+45 NAT/G PROVS...CHARTS BIBLIOG 20 WASHINGT/G. PAGE 19 E0371

LAW
CONSTN
SUFF
CHOOSE

B51

FRIEDMANN W.,LAW AND SOCIAL CHANGE IN CONTEMPORARY BRITAIN. UK LABOR LG/CO LEGIS JUDGE CT/SYS ORD/FREE NEW/LIB...DECISION JURID TREND METH/COMP BIBLIOG 20 PARLIAMENT ENGLSH/LAW COMMON/LAW. PAGE 40 E0802

LAW
ADJUD
SOCIETY
CONSTN

B51

HUXLEY J.,FREEDOM AND CULTURE. UNIV LAW SOCIETY R+D ACADEM SCHOOL CREATE SANCTION ATTIT KNOWL...HUM ANTHOL 20. PAGE 56 E1118

CULTURE
ORD/FREE
PHIL/SCI
IDEA/COMP

B51

PUSEY M.J.,CHARLES EVANS HUGHES (2 VOLS.). LAW CONSTN NAT/G POL/PAR DIPLOM LEGIT WAR CHOOSE PERS/REL DRIVE HEREDITY 19/20 DEPT/STATE LEAGUE/NAT SUPREME/CT HUGHES/CE WWI. PAGE 83 E1663

BIOG
TOP/EX
ADJUD
PERSON

B51

ROSSITER C.,THE SUPREME COURT AND THE COMMANDER IN CHIEF. LAW CONSTN DELIB/GP EX/STRUC LEGIS TOP/EX ADJUD CONTROL...DECISION SOC/EXP PRESIDENT. PAGE 86 E1724

CT/SYS
CHIEF
WAR
PWR

B51

WHEARE K.C.,MODERN CONSTITUTIONS (HOME UNIVERSITY LIBRARY). UNIV LAW NAT/G LEGIS...CONCPT TREND BIBLIOG. PAGE 106 E2115

CONSTN
CLASSIF
PWR
CREATE

L51

KELSEN H.,"RECENT TRENDS IN THE LAW OF THE UNITED NATIONS." KOREA WOR+45 CONSTN LEGIS DIPLOM LEGIT DETER WAR RIGID/FLEX HEALTH ORD/FREE RESPECT ...JURID CON/ANAL UN VAL/FREE 20 NATO. PAGE 60 E1199

INT/ORG
LAW
INT/LAW

B52

ANDREWS F.E.,CORPORATION GIVING. LAW TAX EDU/PROP   LG/CO
ADMIN...POLICY STAT CHARTS. PAGE 5 E0096   GIVE
                                                     SML/CO
                                                     FINAN

B52

BENTHAM A.,HANDBOOK OF POLITICAL FALLACIES. FUT   POL/PAR
MOD/EUR LAW INTELL LOC/G MUNIC NAT/G DELIB/GP LEGIS
CREATE EDU/PROP CT/SYS ATTIT RIGID/FLEX KNOWL PWR
...RELATIV PSY SOC CONCPT SELF/OBS TREND STERTYP
TOT/POP. PAGE 10 E0189

B52

BUCKLAND W.W.,ROMAN LAW AND COMMON LAW; A   IDEA/COMP
COMPARISON IN OUTLINE (2ND REV. ED.). UK FAM LEGIT   LAW
AGREE CT/SYS OWN...JURID ROMAN/REP ROMAN/LAW   ADJUD
COMMON/LAW. PAGE 17 E0325   CONCPT

B52

CAHILL F.V.,JUDICIAL LEGISLATION: A STUDY IN   JURID
AMERICAN LEGAL THEORY. USA+45 USA-45 LAW NAT/G   ADJUD
GP/REL...POLICY PHIL/SCI SOC 20 HOLMES/OW. PAGE 18   LEGIS
E0359   CONTROL

B52

DE GRAZIA A.,POLITICAL ORGANIZATION. CONSTN LOC/G   FEDERAL
MUNIC NAT/G CHIEF LEGIS TOP/EX ADJUD CT/SYS   LAW
PERS/REL...INT/LAW MYTH UN. PAGE 29 E0581   ADMIN

B52

DILLON D.R.,LATIN AMERICA, 1935-1949; A SELECTED   BIBLIOG
BIBLIOGRAPHY. LAW EDU/PROP...SOC 20. PAGE 32 E0629   L/A+17C
                                                     NAT/G
                                                     DIPLOM

B52

ETTINGHAUSEN R.,SELECTED AND ANNOTATED BIBLIOGRAPHY   BIBLIOG/A
OF BOOKS AND PERIODICALS IN WESTERN LANGUAGES   ISLAM
DEALING WITH NEAR AND MIDDLE EAST. LAW CULTURE SECT   MEDIT-7
...ART/METH GEOG SOC. PAGE 35 E0700

B52

FLECHTHEIM O.K.,FUNDAMENTALS OF POLITICAL SCIENCE.   NAT/G
WOR+45 WOR-45 LAW POL/PAR EX/STRUC LEGIS ADJUD   DIPLOM
ATTIT PWR...INT/LAW. PAGE 38 E0760   IDEA/COMP
                                                     CONSTN

B52

FORSTER A.,THE TROUBLE MAKERS. USA+45 LAW CULTURE   DISCRIM
SOCIETY STRUCT VOL/ASSN CROWD GP/REL MORAL...PSY   SECT
SOC CONCPT 20 NEGRO JEWS. PAGE 39 E0771   RACE/REL
                                                     ATTIT

B52

HOLDSWORTH W.S.,A HISTORY OF ENGLISH LAW; THE   LAW
CENTURIES OF SETTLEMENT AND REFORM, 1701-1875 (VOL.   CONSTN
XIII). UK POL/PAR PROF/ORG LEGIS JUDGE WRITING   IDEA/COMP
ATTIT...JURID CONCPT BIOG GEN/LAWS 18/19 PARLIAMENT   CT/SYS
REFORMERS ENGLSH/LAW COMMON/LAW. PAGE 54 E1080

B52

JENNINGS W.I.,CONSTITUTIONAL LAWS OF THE   CONSTN
COMMONWEALTH. UK LAW CHIEF LEGIS TAX CT/SYS   JURID
PARL/PROC GOV/REL...INT/LAW 18/20 COMMONWLTH   ADJUD
ENGLSH/LAW COMMON/LAW. PAGE 58 E1165   COLONIAL

B52

MORRIS R.B.,FAIR TRIAL. USA-45 JUDGE ORD/FREE   ADJUD
...JURID 20. PAGE 75 E1498   CT/SYS
                                                     CRIME
                                                     LAW

B52

US DEPARTMENT OF STATE,RESEARCH ON EASTERN EUROPE   BIBLIOG
(EXCLUDING USSR). EUR+WWI LAW ECO/DEV NAT/G   R+D
PROB/SOLV DIPLOM ADMIN LEAD MARXISM...TREND 19/20.   ACT/RES
PAGE 100 E1995   COM

B52

VANDENBOSCH A.,THE UN: BACKGROUND, ORGANIZATION,   DELIB/GP
FUNCTIONS, ACTIVITIES. WOR+45 LAW CONSTN STRUCT   TIME/SEQ
INT/ORG CONSULT BAL/PWR EDU/PROP EXEC ALL/VALS   PEACE
...POLICY CONCPT UN 20. PAGE 103 E2071

L52

ROSTOW E.V.,"THE DEMOCRATIC CHARACTER OF JUDICIAL   CONSTN
REVIEW" (BMR)" USA+45 LAW NAT/G LEGIS TASK...JURID   PROB/SOLV
20 SUPREME/CT. PAGE 86 E1725   ADJUD
                                                     CT/SYS

B53

AYMARD A.,HISTOIRE GENERALE DES CIVILISATIONS (7   BIBLIOG/A
VOLS.). WOR+45 WOR-45 LAW SECT CREATE ATTIT   SOC
...ART/METH WORSHIP. PAGE 6 E0123

B53

BUTLER D.E.,THE ELECTORAL SYSTEM IN BRITAIN,   CHOOSE
1918-1951. UK LAW POL/PAR SUFF...STAT BIBLIOG 20   LEGIS
PARLIAMENT. PAGE 18 E0348   REPRESENT
                                                     PARTIC

B53

CALDWELL L.K.,RESEARCH METHODS IN PUBLIC   BIBLIOG/A
ADMINISTRATION; AN OUTLINE OF TOPICS AND READINGS   METH/COMP
(PAMPHLET). LAW ACT/RES COMPUTER KNOWL...SOC STAT   ADMIN
GEN/METH 20. PAGE 18 E0364   OP/RES

B53

COKE E.,INSTITUTES OF THE LAWS OF ENGLAND   JURID
(1628-1658). UK LAW ADJUD PERS/REL ORD/FREE   OWN
...CRIMLGY 11/17. PAGE 24 E0471   CT/SYS
                                                     CONSTN

B53

MARKE J.J.,A CATALOGUE OF THE LAW COLLECTION AT NEW   BIBLIOG/A
YORK UNIVERSITY, WITH SELECTED ANNOTATIONS. ACADEM   LAW
ADJUD CT/SYS...CONCPT BIOG 20. PAGE 68 E1366   PHIL/SCI
                                                     IDEA/COMP

B53

OPPENHEIM L.,INTERNATIONAL LAW: A TREATISE (7TH   INT/LAW
ED., 2 VOLS.). LAW CONSTN PROB/SOLV INT/TRADE ADJUD   INT/ORG
AGREE NEUTRAL WAR ORD/FREE SOVEREIGN...BIBLIOG 20   DIPLOM
LEAGUE/NAT UN ILO. PAGE 79 E1579

B53

ORFIELD L.B.,THE GROWTH OF SCANDINAVIAN LAW.   JURID
DENMARK ICELAND NORWAY SWEDEN LAW DIPLOM...BIBLIOG   CT/SYS
9/20. PAGE 79 E1581   NAT/G

B53

PIERCE R.A.,RUSSIAN CENTRAL ASIA, 1867-1917: A   BIBLIOG
SELECTED BIBLIOGRAPHY (PAMPHLET). USSR LAW CULTURE   COLONIAL
NAT/G EDU/PROP WAR...GEOG SOC 19/20. PAGE 81 E1616   ADMIN
                                                     COM

B53

SECKLER-HUDSON C.,BIBLIOGRAPHY ON PUBLIC   BIBLIOG/A
ADMINISTRATION (4TH ED.). USA+45 LAW POL/PAR   ADMIN
DELIB/GP BUDGET ADJUD LOBBY GOV/REL GP/REL ATTIT   NAT/G
...JURID 20. PAGE 90 E1800   MGT

B53

UNESCO,A REGISTER OF LEGAL DOCUMENTATION IN THE   BIBLIOG
WORLD. WOR+45 WOR-45 NAT/G PROVS DELIB/GP LEGIS   CONSTN
13/20. PAGE 98 E1959   LAW
                                                     JURID

B54

AUSTIN J.,THE PROVINCE OF JURISPRUDENCE DETERMINED   CONCPT
AND THE USES OF THE STUDY OF JURISPRUDENCE. MORAL   LAW
...CLASSIF LING STYLE 19. PAGE 6 E0119   JURID
                                                     GEN/LAWS

B54

BATTEN T.R.,PROBLEMS OF AFRICAN DEVELOPMENT (2ND   ECO/UNDEV
ED.). AFR LAW SOCIETY SCHOOL ECO/TAC TAX...GEOG   AGRI
HEAL SOC 20. PAGE 8 E0154   LOC/G
                                                     PROB/SOLV

B54

BROGAN D.W.,POLITICS IN AMERICA. LAW POL/PAR CHIEF   NAT/G
LEGIS LOBBY CHOOSE REPRESENT GP/REL RACE/REL   CONSTN
FEDERAL MORAL...BIBLIOG 20 PRESIDENT CONGRESS.   USA+45
PAGE 16 E0304

B54

FRIEDMAN W.,THE PUBLIC CORPORATION: A COMPARATIVE   LAW
SYMPOSIUM (UNIVERSITY OF TORONTO SCHOOL OF LAW   SOCISM
COMPARATIVE LAW SERIES, VOL. I). SWEDEN USA+45   LG/CO
INDUS INT/ORG NAT/G REGION CENTRAL FEDERAL...POLICY   OWN
JURID IDEA/COMP NAT/COMP ANTHOL 20 COMMONWLTH
MONOPOLY EUROPE. PAGE 40 E0801

B54

HOEBEL E.A.,THE LAW OF PRIMITIVE MAN: A STUDY IN   LAW
COMPARATIVE LEGAL DYNAMICS. WOR-45...JURID SOC   CULTURE
IDEA/COMP METH 20. PAGE 53 E1063   GP/COMP
                                                     SOCIETY

B54

MANGONE G.,A SHORT HISTORY OF INTERNATIONAL   INT/ORG
ORGANIZATION. MOD/EUR USA+45 USA-45 WOR+45 WOR-45   INT/LAW
LAW LEGIS CREATE LEGIT ROUTINE RIGID/FLEX PWR
...JURID CONCPT OBS TIME/SEQ STERTYP GEN/LAWS UN
TOT/POP VAL/FREE 18/20. PAGE 68 E1359

B54

NUSSBAUM D.,A CONCISE HISTORY OF THE LAW OF   INT/ORG
NATIONS. ASIA CHRIST-17C EUR+WWI ISLAM MEDIT-7   LAW
MOD/EUR S/ASIA UNIV WOR+45 WOR-45 SOCIETY STRUCT   PEACE

EXEC ATTIT ALL/VALS...CONCPT HIST/WRIT TIME/SEQ.   INT/LAW
PAGE 78 E1560

                                                B54
O'NEILL J.M.,CATHOLICS IN CONTROVERSY. USA+45 NAT/G   CATHISM
PROVS SCHOOL SECT EDU/PROP LEGIT CT/SYS SANCTION   CONSTN
GP/REL 20 SUPREME/CT CHURCH/STA. PAGE 78 E1569   POLICY
                                                     LAW

                                                B54
SCHWARTZ B.,FRENCH ADMINISTRATIVE LAW AND THE   JURID
COMMON-LAW WORLD. FRANCE CULTURE LOC/G NAT/G PROVS   LAW
DELIB/GP EX/STRUC LEGIS PROB/SOLV CT/SYS EXEC   METH/COMP
GOV/REL...IDEA/COMP ENGLSH/LAW. PAGE 89 E1786   ADJUD

                                                B54
SINCO,PHILIPPINE POLITICAL LAW: PRINCIPLES AND   LAW
CONCEPTS (10TH ED.). PHILIPPINE LOC/G EX/STRUC   CONSTN
BAL/PWR ECO/TAC TAX ADJUD ADMIN CONTROL CT/SYS SUFF LEGIS
ORD/FREE...T 20. PAGE 91 E1831

                                                B54
STONE J.,LEGAL CONTROLS OF INTERNATIONAL CONFLICT: INT/ORG
A TREATISE ON THE DYNAMICS OF DISPUTES AND WAR LAW. LAW
WOR+45 WOR-45 NAT/G DIPLOM CT/SYS SOVEREIGN...JURID   WAR
CONCPT METH/CNCPT GEN/LAWS TOT/POP VAL/FREE   INT/LAW
COLD/WAR LEAGUE/NAT 20. PAGE 94 E1878

                                                B54
TOTOK W.,HANDBUCH DER BIBLIOGRAPHISCHEN   BIBLIOG/A
NACHSCHLAGEWERKE. GERMANY LAW CULTURE ADMIN...SOC   NAT/G
20. PAGE 97 E1936   DIPLOM
                                                     POLICY

                                                L54
NICOLSON H.,"THE EVOLUTION OF DIPLOMATIC METHOD."   RIGID/FLEX
CHRIST-17C EUR+WWI FRANCE FUT ITALY MEDIT-7 MOD/EUR METH/CNCPT
USA+45 USA-45 LAW NAT/G CREATE EDU/PROP LEGIT PEACE DIPLOM
ATTIT ORD/FREE RESPECT SOVEREIGN. PAGE 77 E1548

                                                S54
COOPER L.,"ADMINISTRATIVE JUSTICE." UK ADMIN   LAW
REPRESENT PWR...POLICY 20. PAGE 25 E0502   ADJUD
                                                     CONTROL
                                                     EX/STRUC

                                                C54
GUINS G.C.,"SOVIET LAW AND SOVIET SOCIETY." COM   LAW
USSR STRATA FAM NAT/G WORKER DOMIN RACE/REL   STRUCT
...BIBLIOG 20. PAGE 48 E0960   PLAN

                                                B55
BEANEY W.M.,THE RIGHT TO COUNSEL IN AMERICAN   ADJUD
COURTS. UK USA+45 USA-45 LAW NAT/G PROVS COLONIAL   CONSTN
PERCEPT 18/20 SUPREME/CT AMEND/VI AMEND/XIV   CT/SYS
ENGLSH/LAW. PAGE 8 E0163

                                                B55
BEISEL A.R.,CONTROL OVER ILLEGAL ENFORCEMENT OF THE ORD/FREE
CRIMINAL LAW: ROLE OF THE SUPREME COURT. CONSTN   LAW
ROUTINE MORAL PWR...SOC 20 SUPREME/CT. PAGE 9 E0180 CRIME

                                                B55
BENTON W.E.,NUREMBERG: GERMAN VIEWS OF THE WAR   CRIME
TRIALS. EUR+WWI GERMANY VOL/ASSN LEAD PARTIC COERCE WAR
INGP/REL RACE/REL TOTALISM SUPEGO ORD/FREE...ANTHOL LAW
NUREMBERG. PAGE 10 E0201   JURID

                                                B55
BLOOM G.F.,ECONOMICS OF LABOR RELATIONS. USA+45 LAW ECO/DEV
CONSULT WORKER CAP/ISM PAY ADJUD CONTROL EFFICIENCY ECO/TAC
ORD/FREE...CHARTS 19/20 AFL/CIO NLRB DEPT/LABOR.   LABOR
PAGE 13 E0249   GOV/REL

                                                B55
CAVAN R.S.,CRIMINOLOGY (2ND ED.). USA+45 LAW FAM   DRIVE
PUB/INST FORCES PLAN WAR AGE/Y PERSON ROLE SUPEGO   CRIMLGY
...CHARTS 20 FBI. PAGE 21 E0409   CONTROL
                                                     METH/COMP

                                                B55
CHARMATZ J.P.,COMPARATIVE STUDIES IN COMMUNITY   MARRIAGE
PROPERTY LAW. FRANCE USA+45...JURID GOV/COMP ANTHOL LAW
20. PAGE 22 E0424   OWN
                                                     MUNIC

                                                B55
CHENERY W.L.,FREEDOM OF THE PRESS. USA+45 USA-45   ORD/FREE
LAW NAT/G DOMIN EDU/PROP 17/20. PAGE 22 E0427   COM/IND
                                                     PRESS
                                                     CONSTN

                                                B55
FLIESS P.J.,FREEDOM OF THE PRESS IN THE GERMAN   EDU/PROP
REPUBLIC, 1918-1933. GERMANY LAW CONSTN POL/PAR   ORD/FREE
LEGIS WRITING ADMIN COERCE MURDER MARXISM...POLICY   JURID

BIBLIOG 20 WEIMAR/REP. PAGE 39 E0765   PRESS

                                                B55
GRINDEL C.W.,CONCEPT OF FREEDOM. WOR+45 WOR-45 LAW   ORD/FREE
LABOR NAT/G SECT EDU/PROP 20. PAGE 47 E0942   DIPLOM
                                                     CONCPT
                                                     GP/REL

                                                B55
JAPAN MOMBUSHO DAIGAKU GAKIYUT,BIBLIOGRAPHY OF THE   BIBLIOG
STUDIES ON LAW AND POLITICS (PAMPHLET). CONSTN   LAW
INDUS LABOR DIPLOM TAX ADMIN...CRIMLGY INT/LAW 20   PHIL/SCI
CHINJAP. PAGE 58 E1150

                                                B55
KHADDURI M.,LAW IN THE MIDDLE EAST. LAW CONSTN   ADJUD
ACADEM FAM EDU/PROP CT/SYS SANCTION CRIME...INT/LAW JURID
GOV/COMP ANTHOL 6/20 MID/EAST. PAGE 61 E1210   ISLAM

                                                B55
MAZZINI J.,THE DUTIES OF MAN. MOD/EUR LAW SOCIETY   SUPEGO
FAM NAT/G POL/PAR SECT VOL/ASSN EX/STRUC ACT/RES   CONCPT
CREATE REV PEACE ATTIT ALL/VALS...GEN/LAWS WORK 19. NAT/LISM
PAGE 70 E1396

                                                B55
MID-EUROPEAN LAW PROJECT,CHURCH AND STATE BEHIND   LAW
THE IRON CURTAIN. COM CZECHOSLVK HUNGARY POLAND   MARXISM
USSR CULTURE SECT EDU/PROP GOV/REL CATHISM...CHARTS POLICY
ANTHOL BIBLIOG WORSHIP 20 CHURCH/STA. PAGE 73 E1455

                                                B55
MOHL R.V.,DIE GESCHICHTE UND LITERATUR DER   PHIL/SCI
STAATSWISSENSCHAFTEN (3 VOLS.). LAW NAT/G...JURID   MOD/EUR
METH/COMP METH. PAGE 74 E1480

                                                B55
PULLEN W.R.,A CHECK LIST OF LEGISLATIVE JOURNALS   BIBLIOG
ISSUED SINCE 1937 BY THE STATES OF THE UNITED   PROVS
STATES OF AMERICA (PAMPHLET). USA+45 USA-45 LAW   EDU/PROP
WRITING ADJUD ADMIN...JURID 20. PAGE 83 E1662   LEGIS

                                                B55
SERRANO MOSCOSO E.,A STATEMENT OF THE LAWS OF   FINAN
ECUADOR IN MATTERS AFFECTING BUSINESS (2ND ED.).   ECO/UNDEV
ECUADOR INDUS LABOR LG/CO NAT/G LEGIS TAX CONTROL   LAW
MARRIAGE 20. PAGE 90 E1805   CONSTN

                                                B55
SMITH G.,A CONSTITUTIONAL AND LEGAL HISTORY OF   CONSTN
ENGLAND. UK ELITES NAT/G LEGIS ADJUD OWN HABITAT   PARTIC
POPULISM...JURID 20 ENGLSH/LAW. PAGE 92 E1844   LAW
                                                     CT/SYS

                                                B55
SWEET AND MAXWELL,A LEGAL BIBLIOGRAPHY OF THE   BIBLIOG/A
BRITISH COMMONWEALTH OF NATIONS (2ND ED. 7 VOLS.).   LAW
UK LOC/G MUNIC JUDGE ADJUD CRIME OWN...JURID 14/20   CONSTN
CMN/WLTH. PAGE 95 E1900   CT/SYS

                                                B55
ZABEL O.H.,GOD AND CAESAR IN NEBRASKA: A STUDY OF   SECT
LEGAL RELATIONSHIP OF CHURCH AND STATE, 1854-1954.   PROVS
TAX GIVE ADMIN CONTROL GP/REL ROLE...GP/COMP 19/20   LAW
NEBRASKA. PAGE 108 E2168   EDU/PROP

                                                B56
ALEXANDER F.,THE CRIMINAL, THE JUDGE, AND THE   CRIME
PUBLIC. LAW CULTURE CONSULT LEGIT ADJUD SANCTION   CRIMLGY
ORD/FREE 20. PAGE 3 E0060   PSY
                                                     ATTIT

                                                B56
CARLSTON K.S.,LAW AND STRUCTURES OF SOCIAL ACTION.   JURID
LAW SOCIETY ECO/DEV DIPLOM CONTROL ATTIT...DECISION INT/LAW
CONCPT 20. PAGE 19 E0379   INGP/REL
                                                     STRUCT

                                                B56
COHEN A.,THE SUTHERLAND PAPERS. USA+45 USA-45 LAW   CRIMLGY
CONTROL CRIME AGE/Y...TREND ANTHOL BIBLIOG 20.   PHIL/SCI
PAGE 23 E0461   ACT/RES
                                                     METH

                                                B56
DOUGLAS W.O.,WE THE JUDGES. INDIA USA+45 USA-45 LAW ADJUD
NAT/G SECT LEGIS PRESS CRIME FEDERAL ORD/FREE   CT/SYS
...POLICY GOV/COMP 19/20 WARRN/EARL MARSHALL/J   CONSTN
SUPREME/CT. PAGE 32 E0640   GOV/REL

                                                B56
DUNNILL F.,THE CIVIL SERVICE. UK LAW PLAN ADMIN   PERSON
EFFICIENCY DRIVE NEW/LIB...STAT CHARTS 20   WORKER
PARLIAMENT CIVIL/SERV. PAGE 33 E0662   STRATA
                                                     SOC/WK

B56

EMDEN C.S.,THE PEOPLE AND THE CONSTITUTION (2ND ED.). UK LEGIS POPULISM 17/20 PARLIAMENT. PAGE 35 E0687

CONSTN
PARL/PROC
NAT/G
LAW

B56

HURST J.W.,LAW AND THE CONDITIONS OF FREEDOM IN THE NINETEENTH CENTURY UNITED STATES. USA+45 LAW CONSTN STRUCT ADMIN GP/REL FEDERAL HABITAT...JURID 19. PAGE 56 E1116

LAW
ORD/FREE
POLICY
NAT/G

B56

JESSUP P.C.,TRANSNATIONAL LAW. FUT WOR+45 JUDGE CREATE ADJUD ORD/FREE...CONCPT VAL/FREE 20. PAGE 59 E1167

LAW
JURID
INT/LAW

B56

KALNOKI BEDO A.,LEGAL SOURCES AND BIBLIOGRAPHY OF HUNGARY. COM HUNGARY CONSTN LEGIS JUDGE CT/SYS SANCTION CRIME 16/20. PAGE 59 E1181

BIBLIOG
ADJUD
LAW
JURID

B56

KUPER L.,PASSIVE RESISTANCE IN SOUTH AFRICA. SOUTH/AFR LAW NAT/G POL/PAR VOL/ASSN DISCRIM ...POLICY SOC AUD/VIS 20. PAGE 62 E1237

ORD/FREE
RACE/REL
ATTIT

B56

NOTZ R.L.,FEDERAL GRANTS-IN-AID TO STATES: ANALYSIS OF LAWS IN FORCE ON SEPTEMBER 10, 1956. USA+45 LAW SCHOOL PLAN ECO/TAC TAX RECEIVE...HEAL JURID 20. PAGE 78 E1558

GIVE
NAT/G
PROVS
GOV/REL

B56

PEASLEE A.J.,CONSTITUTIONS OF NATIONS. WOR+45 LAW NAT/G EX/STRUC LEGIS TOP/EX LEGIT CT/SYS ROUTINE CHOOSE ORD/FREE PWR SOVEREIGN...CHARTS TOT/POP. PAGE 80 E1605

CONSTN
CON/ANAL

B56

SCHROEDER T.,METHODS OF CONSTITUTIONAL CONSTRUCTION. LAW...METH 20. PAGE 88 E1769

ORD/FREE
CONSTN
JURID
EDU/PROP

B56

SIPKOV I.,LEGAL SOURCES AND BIBLIOGRAPHY OF BULGARIA. BULGARIA COM LEGIS WRITING ADJUD CT/SYS ...INT/LAW TREATY 20. PAGE 91 E1834

BIBLIOG
LAW
TOTALISM
MARXISM

B56

SOHN L.B.,BASIC DOCUMENTS OF THE UNITED NATIONS. WOR+45 LAW INT/ORG LEGIT EXEC ROUTINE CHOOSE PWR ...JURID CONCPT GEN/LAWS ANTHOL UN TOT/POP OAS FAO ILO 20. PAGE 92 E1853

DELIB/GP
CONSTN

B56

SYKES G.M.,CRIME AND SOCIETY. LAW STRATA STRUCT ACT/RES ROUTINE ANOMIE WEALTH...POLICY SOC/INTEG 20. PAGE 95 E1903

CRIMLGY
CRIME
CULTURE
INGP/REL

B56

US HOUSE RULES COMM,HEARINGS BEFORE A SPECIAL SUBCOMMITTEE: ESTABLISHMENT OF A STANDING COMMITTEE ON ADMINISTRATIVE PROCEDURE, PRACTICE. USA+45 LAW EX/STRUC ADJUD CONTROL EXEC GOV/REL EFFICIENCY PWR ...POLICY INT 20 CONGRESS. PAGE 100 E2009

ADMIN
DOMIN
DELIB/GP
NAT/G

B56

WEIS P.,NATIONALITY AND STATELESSNESS IN INTERNATIONAL LAW. UK WOR+45 WOR-45 LAW CONSTN NAT/G DIPLOM EDU/PROP LEGIT ROUTINE RIGID/FLEX ...JURID RECORD CMN/WLTH 20. PAGE 105 E2109

INT/ORG
SOVEREIGN
INT/LAW

B56

ZINN C.J.,HOW OUR LAWS ARE MADE: BROCHURE HOUSE OF REPRESENTATIVES DOCUMENT 451. LAW CONSTN CHIEF EX/STRUC PROB/SOLV HOUSE/REP SENATE. PAGE 108 E2171

LEGIS
DELIB/GP
PARL/PROC
ROUTINE

L56

CARRINGTON P.D.,"POLITICAL QUESTIONS: THE JUDICIAL CHECK ON THE EXECUTIVE." USA+45 LAW CHIEF 20. PAGE 20 E0395

ADJUD
EXEC
PWR
REPRESENT

S56

NOBLEMAN E.E.,"THE DELEGATION OF PRESIDENTIAL FUNCTIONS: CONSTITUTIONAL AND LEGAL ASPECTS." USA+45 CONSTN NAT/G CONTROL 20. PAGE 77 E1553

CHIEF
REPRESENT
EX/STRUC
LAW

S56

ROSENBERG M.,"POWER AND DESEGREGATION." USA+45 STRATA MUNIC GP/REL. PAGE 85 E1715

PWR
DISCRIM
DECISION
LAW

C56

FALL B.B.,"THE VIET-MINH REGIME." VIETNAM LAW ECO/UNDEV POL/PAR FORCES DOMIN WAR ATTIT MARXISM ...BIOG PREDICT BIBLIOG/A 20. PAGE 36 E0720

NAT/G
ADMIN
EX/STRUC
LEAD

C56

TYLER P.,"IMMIGRATION AND THE UNITED STATES." USA+45 USA-45 LAW SECT INGP/REL RACE/REL NAT/LISM ATTIT...BIBLIOG SOC/INTEG 19/20. PAGE 97 E1949

CULTURE
GP/REL
DISCRIM

B57

ALIGHIERI D.,ON WORLD GOVERNMENT. ROMAN/EMP LAW SOCIETY INT/ORG NAT/G POL/PAR ADJUD WAR GP/REL PEACE WORSHIP 15 WORLDUNITY DANTE. PAGE 4 E0067

POLICY
CONCPT
DIPLOM
SECT

B57

BAYITCH S.A.,A GUIDE TO INTERAMERICAN LEGAL STUDIES: A SELECTIVE BIBLIOGRAPHY OF WORKS IN ENGLISH. NAT/G LEGIS ADJUD CT/SYS CONGRESS 20. PAGE 8 E0157

BIBLIOG
L/A+17C
LAW
JURID

B57

BERNS W.,FREEDOM, VIRTUE AND THE FIRST AMENDMENT. USA+45 USA-45 CONSTN INTELL JUDGE ADJUD RIGID/FLEX MORAL...CONCPT 20 AMEND/I. PAGE 11 E0211

JURID
ORD/FREE
CT/SYS
LAW

B57

BERNS W.,FREEDOM, VIRTUE, AND THE FIRST AMENDMENT. USA-45 LAW CONSTN PROB/SOLV NEW/LIB...JURID 20 SUPREME/CT AMEND/I. PAGE 11 E0212

ADJUD
CT/SYS
ORD/FREE

B57

BLOOMFIELD L.M.,EGYPT, ISRAEL AND THE GULF OF AQABA: IN INTERNATIONAL LAW. LAW NAT/G CONSULT FORCES PLAN ECO/TAC ROUTINE COERCE ATTIT DRIVE PERCEPT PERSON RIGID/FLEX LOVE PWR WEALTH...GEOG CONCPT MYTH TREND. PAGE 13 E0250

ISLAM
INT/LAW
UAR

B57

COOPER F.E.,THE LAWYER AND ADMINISTRATIVE AGENCIES. USA+45 CLIENT LAW PROB/SOLV CT/SYS PERSON ROLE. PAGE 25 E0500

CONSULT
ADMIN
ADJUD
DELIB/GP

B57

DE VISSCHER C.,THEORY AND REALITY IN PUBLIC INTERNATIONAL LAW. WOR+45 WOR-45 SOCIETY NAT/G CT/SYS ATTIT MORAL ORD/FREE PWR...JURID CONCPT METH/CNCPT TIME/SEQ GEN/LAWS LEAGUE/NAT TOT/POP VAL/FREE COLD/WAR. PAGE 30 E0599

INT/ORG
LAW
INT/LAW

B57

DONALDSON A.G.,SOME COMPARATIVE ASPECTS OF IRISH LAW. IRELAND NAT/G DIPLOM ADMIN CT/SYS LEAD ATTIT SOVEREIGN...JURID BIBLIOG/A 12/20 CMN/WLTH. PAGE 32 E0635

CONSTN
LAW
NAT/COMP
INT/LAW

B57

DUMBAULD E.,THE BILL OF RIGHTS AND WHAT IT MEANS TODAY. USA+45 USA-45 CT/SYS...JURID STYLE TIME/SEQ BIBLIOG 18/20 BILL/RIGHT. PAGE 33 E0656

CONSTN
LAW
ADJUD
ORD/FREE

B57

INSTITUT DE DROIT INTL,TABLEAU GENERAL DES RESOLUTIONS (1873-1956). LAW NEUTRAL CRIME WAR MARRIAGE PEACE...JURID 19/20. PAGE 56 E1124

INT/LAW
DIPLOM
ORD/FREE
ADJUD

B57

LEVONTIN A.V.,THE MYTH OF INTERNATIONAL SECURITY: A JURIDICAL AND CRITICAL ANALYSIS. FUT WOR+45 WOR-45 LAW NAT/G VOL/ASSN ACT/RES BAL/PWR ATTIT ORD/FREE ...JURID METH/CNCPT TIME/SEQ TREND STERTYP 20. PAGE 64 E1289

INT/ORG
INT/LAW
SOVEREIGN
MYTH

B57

LONG H.A.,USURPERS - FOES OF FREE MAN. LAW NAT/G CHIEF LEGIS DOMIN ADJUD REPRESENT GOV/REL ORD/FREE LAISSEZ POPULISM...POLICY 18/20 SUPREME/CT ROOSEVLT/F CONGRESS CON/INTERP. PAGE 66 E1325

CT/SYS
CENTRAL
FEDERAL
CONSTN

B57

POUND R.,THE DEVELOPMENT OF CONSTITUTIONAL GUARANTEES OF LIBERTY. UK USA-45 CHIEF COLONIAL REV ...JURID CONCPT 15/20. PAGE 82 E1638

LAW
CONSTN
ORD/FREE
ATTIT

ROSENNE S.,THE INTERNATIONAL COURT OF JUSTICE. INT/ORG B57
WOR+45 LAW DOMIN LEGIT PEACE PWR SOVEREIGN...JURID CT/SYS
CONCPT RECORD TIME/SEQ CON/ANAL CHARTS UN TOT/POP INT/LAW
VAL/FREE LEAGUE/NAT 20 ICJ. PAGE 86 E1716

ROWAN C.T.,GO SOUTH TO SORROW. USA+45 STRUCT NAT/G RACE/REL B57
EDU/PROP LEAD COERCE ISOLAT DRIVE SUPEGO RESPECT DISCRIM
...PREDICT 20 NEGRO SUPREME/CT SOUTH/US CIV/RIGHTS. ANOMIE
PAGE 86 E1728   LAW

UNESCO,A REGISTER OF LEGAL DOCUMENTATION IN THE BIBLIOG B57
WORLD (2ND ED.). CT/SYS...JURID IDEA/COMP METH/COMP LAW
NAT/COMP 20. PAGE 98 E1960   INT/LAW
                                                    CONSTN

US COMMISSION GOVT SECURITY,RECOMMENDATIONS; AREA: POLICY B57
IMMIGRANT PROGRAM. USA+45 LAW WORKER DIPLOM CONTROL
EDU/PROP WRITING ADMIN PEACE ATTIT...CONCPT ANTHOL PLAN
20 MIGRATION SUBVERT. PAGE 99 E1981   NAT/G

US SENATE COMM ON JUDICIARY,CIVIL RIGHTS - 1957. INT B57
USA+45 LAW NAT/G CONFER GOV/REL RACE/REL ORD/FREE LEGIS
PWR...JURID 20 SENATE CIV/RIGHTS. PAGE 102 E2039 DISCRIM
                                                    PARL/PROC

US SENATE COMM ON JUDICIARY,LIMITATION OF APPELLATE CT/SYS B57
JURISDICTION OF THE SUPREME COURT. USA+45 LAW NAT/G ADJUD
DELIB/GP PLAN ADMIN CONTROL PWR...DECISION 20 POLICY
CONGRESS SUPREME/CT. PAGE 102 E2041   GOV/REL

US SENATE SPEC COMM POLIT ACT,REPORT OF SPECIAL LOBBY B57
COMMITTEE TO INVESTIGATE POLITICAL ACTIVITIES, LAW
LOBBYING, AND CAMPAIGN CONTRIBUTIONS. USA+45 ECO/TAC
BARGAIN CRIME ATTIT...DECISION 20 CONGRESS. PARL/PROC
PAGE 103 E2061

KNEIER C.M.,"MISLEADING THE VOTERS." CONSTN LEAD MUNIC S57
CHOOSE PERS/REL. PAGE 61 E1224   REPRESENT
                                                    LAW
                                                    ATTIT

ALEXANDROWICZ,A BIBLIOGRAPHY OF INDIAN LAW. INDIA BIBLIOG B58
S/ASIA CONSTN CT/SYS...INT/LAW 19/20. PAGE 3 E0062 LAW
                                                    ADJUD
                                                    JURID

ALLEN C.K.,LAW IN THE MAKING. LEGIS ATTIT ORD/FREE LAW B58
SOVEREIGN POPULISM...JURID IDEA/COMP NAT/COMP CREATE
GEN/LAWS 20 ENGLSH/LAW. PAGE 4 E0069   CONSTN
                                                    SOCIETY

ATOMIC INDUSTRIAL FORUM,MANAGEMENT AND ATOMIC NUC/PWR B58
ENERGY. WOR+45 SEA LAW MARKET NAT/G TEC/DEV INSPECT INDUS
INT/TRADE CONFER PEACE HEALTH...ANTHOL 20. PAGE 6 MGT
E0112   ECO/TAC

BLOCH J.,STATES' RIGHTS: THE LAW OF THE LAND. PROVS B58
USA+45 USA-45 LAW CONSTN LEGIS CONTROL CT/SYS NAT/G
FEDERAL ORD/FREE...PREDICT 17/20 CONGRESS BAL/PWR
SUPREME/CT. PAGE 13 E0246   CENTRAL

BUGEDA LANZAS J.,A STATEMENT OF THE LAWS OF CUBA IN JURID B58
MATTERS AFFECTING BUSINESS (2ND ED. REV., NAT/G
ENLARGED). CUBA L/A+17C LAW FINAN FAM LEGIS ACT/RES INDUS
ADMIN GP/REL...BIBLIOG 20 OAS. PAGE 17 E0327 WORKER

CARPENTER W.S.,FOUNDATIONS OF MODERN JURISPRUDENCE. LAW B58
UNIV PROB/SOLV ADJUD CT/SYS CRIME ATTIT...CONCPT JURID
18/20. PAGE 20 E0388

CHARLES R.,LA JUSTICE EN FRANCE. FRANCE LAW CONSTN JURID B58
DELIB/GP CRIME 20. PAGE 21 E0422   ADMIN
                                                    CT/SYS
                                                    ADJUD

DAVIS K.C.,ADMINISTRATIVE LAW; CASES, TEXT, ADJUD B58
PROBLEMS. LAW LOC/G NAT/G TOP/EX PAY CONTROL JURID
GOV/REL INGP/REL FEDERAL 20 SUPREME/CT. PAGE 29 CT/SYS
E0576   ADMIN

DEVLIN P.,THE CRIMINAL PROSECUTION IN ENGLAND. UK CRIME B58
NAT/G ADMIN ROUTINE EFFICIENCY...JURID SOC 20. LAW
PAGE 31 E0617   METH
                                                    CT/SYS

EUSDEN J.D.,PURITANS, LAWYERS, AND POLITICS IN GP/REL B58
EARLY SEVENTEENTH-CENTURY ENGLAND. UK CT/SYS SECT
PARL/PROC RATIONAL PWR SOVEREIGN...IDEA/COMP NAT/G
BIBLIOG 17 PURITAN COMMON/LAW. PAGE 35 E0702 LAW

FELLMAN D.,THE DEFENDANT'S RIGHTS. USA+45 NAT/G CONSTN B58
CONSULT CT/SYS SUPEGO ORD/FREE...BIBLIOG SUPREME/CT LAW
CIVIL/SERV. PAGE 37 E0730   CRIME
                                                    ADJUD

HALL J.,STUDIES IN JURISPRUDENCE AND CRIMINAL JURID B58
THEORY. USA-45 LAW CULTURE CREATE SUPEGO...CRIMLGY CRIME
PSY /20 PLATO. PAGE 49 E0983   CONCPT
                                                    CT/SYS

HENKIN L.,ARMS CONTROL AND INSPECTION IN AMERICAN USA+45 B58
LAW. LAW CONSTN INT/ORG LOC/G MUNIC NAT/G PROVS JURID
EDU/PROP LEGIT EXEC NUC/PWR KNOWL ORD/FREE...OBS ARMS/CONT
TOT/POP CONGRESS 20. PAGE 52 E1032

JAPAN MINISTRY OF JUSTICE,CRIMINAL JUSTICE IN CONSTN B58
JAPAN. LAW PROF/ORG PUB/INST FORCES CONTROL CT/SYS CRIME
PARL/PROC 20 CHINJAP. PAGE 58 E1149   JURID
                                                    ADMIN

KAPLAN H.E.,THE LAW OF CIVIL SERVICE. USA+45 LAW ADJUD B58
POL/PAR CT/SYS CRIME GOV/REL...POLICY JURID 20. NAT/G
PAGE 59 E1183   ADMIN
                                                    CONSTN

KURL S.,ESTONIA: A SELECTED BIBLIOGRAPHY. USSR BIBLIOG B58
ESTONIA LAW INTELL SECT...ART/METH GEOG HUM SOC 20. CULTURE
PAGE 62 E1238   NAT/G

MANSERGH N.,COMMONWEALTH PERSPECTIVES. GHANA UK LAW DIPLOM B58
VOL/ASSN CONFER HEALTH SOVEREIGN...GEOG CHARTS COLONIAL
ANTHOL 20 CMN/WLTH AUSTRAL. PAGE 68 E1363 INT/ORG
                                                    INGP/REL

MASON H.L.,TOYNBEE'S APPROACH TO WORLD POLITICS. DIPLOM B58
AFR USA+45 USSR LAW WAR NAT/LISM ALL/IDEOS...HUM CONCPT
BIBLIOG. PAGE 69 E1380   PHIL/SCI
                                                    SECT

ORTIZ R.P.,ANNUARIO BIBLIOGRAFICO COLOMBIANO, BIBLIOG B58
1951-1956. LAW RECEIVE EDU/PROP ADMIN...LING STAT SOC
20 COLOMB. PAGE 79 E1582

PALMER E.E.,CIVIL LIBERTIES. USA+45 ADJUD CT/SYS ORD/FREE B58
PARTIC OWN LAISSEZ POPULISM...JURID CONCPT ANTHOL CONSTN
20 SUPREME/CT CIVIL/LIB. PAGE 79 E1592   RACE/REL
                                                    LAW

POUND R.,JUSTICE ACCORDING TO LAW. LAW SOCIETY CONCPT B58
CT/SYS 20. PAGE 82 E1639   JURID
                                                    ADJUD
                                                    ADMIN

SPITZ D.,DEMOCRACY AND THE CHALLANGE OF POWER. FUT NAT/G B58
USA+45 USA-45 LAW SOCIETY STRUCT LOC/G POL/PAR PWR
PROVS DELIB/GP EX/STRUC LEGIS TOP/EX ACT/RES CREATE
DOMIN EDU/PROP LEGIT ADJUD ADMIN ATTIT DRIVE MORAL
ORD/FREE TOT/POP. PAGE 93 E1862

STONE J.,AGGRESSION AND WORLD ORDER: A CRITIQUE OF ORD/FREE B58
UNITED NATIONS THEORIES OF AGGRESSION. LAW CONSTN INT/ORG
DELIB/GP PROB/SOLV BAL/PWR DIPLOM DEBATE ADJUD WAR
CRIME PWR...POLICY IDEA/COMP 20 UN SUEZ LEAGUE/NAT. CONCPT
PAGE 94 E1879

STRONG C.F.,MODERN POLITICAL CONSTITUTIONS. LAW CONSTN B58
CHIEF DELIB/GP EX/STRUC LEGIS ADJUD CHOOSE FEDERAL IDEA/COMP
POPULISM...CONCPT BIBLIOG 20 UN. PAGE 94 E1887 NAT/G

US CONGRESS,FREEDOM OF INFORMATION AND SECRECY IN
GOVERNMENT (2 VOLS.). USA+45 DELIB/GP EX/STRUC
EDU/PROP PWR 20 CONGRESS PRESIDENT. PAGE 99 E1988
B58
CHIEF
PRIVIL
CONSTN
LAW

WESTIN A.F.,THE ANATOMY OF A CONSTITUTIONAL LAW
CASE. USA+45 LAW LEGIS ADMIN EXEC...DECISION MGT
SOC RECORD 20 SUPREME/CT. PAGE 105 E2113
B58
CT/SYS
INDUS
ADJUD
CONSTN

WHITNEY S.N.,ANTITRUST POLICIES: AMERICAN
EXPERIENCE IN TWENTY INDUSTRIES. USA+45 USA-45 LAW
DELIB/GP LEGIS ADJUD CT/SYS GOV/REL ATTIT...ANTHOL
20 MONOPOLY CASEBOOK. PAGE 106 E2119
B58
INDUS
CONTROL
LG/CO
MARKET

WOOD J.E.,CHURCH AND STATE IN SCRIPTURE HISTORY AND
CONSTITUTIONAL LAW. LAW CONSTN SOCIETY PROVS
VOL/ASSN BAL/PWR COLONIAL CT/SYS ATTIT...BIBLIOG 20
SUPREME/CT CHURCH/STA BIBLE. PAGE 107 E2142
B58
GP/REL
SECT
NAT/G
ADJUD

FISHER F.M.,"THE MATHEMATICAL ANALYSIS OF SUPREME
COURT DECISIONS: THE USE AND ABUSE OF QUANTITATIVE
METHODS." USA+45 LAW EX/STRUC LEGIS JUDGE ROUTINE
ATTIT DECISION. PAGE 38 E0757
S58
PROB/SOLV
CT/SYS
JURID
MATH

RIKER W.H.,"THE PARADOX OF VOTING AND CONGRESSIONAL
RULES FOR VOTING ON AMENDMENTS." LAW DELIB/GP
EX/STRUC PROB/SOLV CONFER DEBATE EFFICIENCY ATTIT
HOUSE/REP CONGRESS SENATE. PAGE 85 E1700
S58
PARL/PROC
DECISION
LEGIS
RATIONAL

BRODEN T.F.,"CONGRESSIONAL COMMITTEE REPORTS: THEIR
ROLE AND HISTORY" USA-45 PARL/PROC ROLE. PAGE 15
E0303
C58
LAW
DELIB/GP
LEGIS
DEBATE

BOHMER A.,LEGAL SOURCES AND BIBLIOGRAPHY OF
CZECHOSLOVAKIA. COM CZECHOSLVK PARL/PROC SANCTION
CRIME MARXISM 20. PAGE 13 E0261
B59
BIBLIOG
ADJUD
LAW
JURID

BRIGGS A.,CHARTIST STUDIES. UK LAW NAT/G WORKER
EDU/PROP COERCE SUFF GP/REL ATTIT...ANTHOL 19.
PAGE 15 E0300
B59
INDUS
STRATA
LABOR
POLICY

CHRISTMAN H.M.,THE PUBLIC PAPERS OF CHIEF JUSTICE
EARL WARREN. CONSTN POL/PAR EDU/PROP SANCTION
HEALTH...TREND 20 SUPREME/CT WARRN/EARL. PAGE 22
E0436
B59
LAW
CT/SYS
PERSON
ADJUD

COUNCIL OF STATE GOVERNMENTS,STATE GOVERNMENT: AN
ANNOTATED BIBLIOGRAPHY (PAMPHLET). USA+45 LAW AGRI
INDUS WORKER PLAN TAX ADJUST AGE/Y ORD/FREE...HEAL
MGT 20. PAGE 26 E0521
B59
BIBLIOG/A
PROVS
LOC/G
ADMIN

DASH S.,THE EAVESDROPPERS. USA+45 DELIB/GP TEC/DEV
ORD/FREE...POLICY CRIMLGY JURID 20 PRIVACY. PAGE 29
E0569
B59
CRIME
CONTROL
ACT/RES
LAW

ELLIOTT S.D.,IMPROVING OUR COURTS. LAW EX/STRUC
PLAN PROB/SOLV ADJUD ADMIN TASK CRIME EFFICIENCY
ORD/FREE 20. PAGE 34 E0684
B59
CT/SYS
JURID
GOV/REL
NAT/G

EPSTEIN F.T.,EAST GERMANY: A SELECTED BIBLIOGRAPHY
(PAMPHLET). COM GERMANY/E LAW AGRI FINAN INDUS
LABOR POL/PAR EDU/PROP ADMIN AGE/Y 20. PAGE 35
E0693
B59
BIBLIOG/A
INTELL
MARXISM
NAT/G

FERRY W.H.,THE CORPORATION AND THE ECONOMY. CLIENT
LAW CONSTN LABOR NAT/G PLAN INT/TRADE PARTIC CONSEN
ORD/FREE PWR POLICY. PAGE 37 E0742
B59
LG/CO
CONTROL
REPRESENT

FRIEDMANN W.G.,LAW IN A CHANGING SOCIETY. FUT
WOR+45 WOR-45 LAW SOCIETY STRUCT INT/TRADE LEGIT
ATTIT BIO/SOC HEALTH ORD/FREE SOVEREIGN...CONCPT
GEN/LAWS ILO 20. PAGE 41 E0803
B59
SOC
JURID

GOMEZ ROBLES J.,A STATEMENT OF THE LAWS OF
GUATEMALA IN MATTERS AFFECTING BUSINESS (2ND ED.
REV., ENLARGED). GUATEMALA L/A+17C LAW FINAN FAM
WORKER ACT/RES DIPLOM ADJUD ADMIN GP/REL 20 OAS.
PAGE 44 E0881
B59
JURID
NAT/G
INDUS
LEGIT

HALEY A.G.,FIRST COLLOQUIUM ON THE LAW OF OUTER
SPACE. WOR+45 INT/ORG ACT/RES PLAN BAL/PWR CONFER
ATTIT PWR...POLICY JURID CHARTS ANTHOL 20. PAGE 49
E0979
B59
SPACE
LAW
SOVEREIGN
CONTROL

HAYS B.,A SOUTHERN MODERATE SPEAKS. LAW PROVS
SCHOOL KNOWL...JURID SOC SELF/OBS BIOG 20 NEGRO
SUPREME/CT. PAGE 51 E1015
B59
SECT
DISCRIM
CT/SYS
RACE/REL

HOOK S.,POLITICAL POWER AND PERSONAL FREEDOM:
CRITICAL STUDIES IN DEMOCRACY, COMMUNISM AND CIVIL
RIGHTS. UNIV LAW SOCIETY DIPLOM TOTALISM MARXISM
SOCISM...PHIL/SCI IDEA/COMP 20 CIV/RIGHTS. PAGE 55
E1094
B59
ORD/FREE
PWR
WELF/ST
CHOOSE

MAYDA J.,ATOMIC ENERGY AND LAW. ECO/UNDEV FINAN
TEC/DEV FOR/AID EFFICIENCY PRODUC WEALTH...POLICY
TECHNIC 20. PAGE 70 E1391
B59
NUC/PWR
L/A+17C
LAW
ADMIN

MOOS M.,THE CAMPUS AND THE STATE. LAW FINAN
DELIB/GP LEGIS EXEC LOBBY GP/REL PWR...POLICY
BIBLIOG. PAGE 74 E1489
B59
EDU/PROP
ACADEM
PROVS
CONTROL

NICHOLS R.F.,RELIGION AND AMERICAN DEMOCRACY.
USA+45 USA-45 LAW CHOOSE SUFF MORAL ORD/FREE
POPULISM...POLICY BIBLIOG 16/20 PRE/US/AM
CHRISTIAN. PAGE 77 E1547
B59
NAT/G
SECT
CONSTN
CONCPT

OKINSHEVICH L.A.,LATIN AMERICA IN SOVIET WRITINGS,
1945-1958: A BIBLIOGRAPHY. USSR LAW ECO/UNDEV LABOR
DIPLOM EDU/PROP REV...GEOG SOC 20. PAGE 78 E1573
B59
BIBLIOG
WRITING
COM
L/A+17C

ROSS A.,ON LAW AND JUSTICE. USA+45 RATIONAL
...IDEA/COMP GEN/LAWS 20 SCANDINAV NATURL/LAW.
PAGE 86 E1722
B59
JURID
PHIL/SCI
LAW
CONCPT

SCHNEIDER J.,TREATY-MAKING POWER OF INTERNATIONAL
ORGANIZATIONS. FUT WOR+45 WOR-45 LAW NAT/G JUDGE
DIPLOM LEGIT CT/SYS ORD/FREE PWR...INT/LAW JURID
GEN/LAWS TOT/POP UNESCO 20 TREATY. PAGE 88 E1762
B59
INT/ORG
ROUTINE

SCOTT F.R.,CIVIL LIBERTIES AND CANADIAN FEDERALISM.
CANADA LAW ADJUD CT/SYS GOV/REL 20 CIV/RIGHTS.
PAGE 90 E1797
B59
ORD/FREE
FEDERAL
NAT/LISM
CONSTN

SISSON C.H.,THE SPIRIT OF BRITISH ADMINISTRATION
AND SOME EUROPEAN COMPARISONS. FRANCE GERMANY/W
SWEDEN UK LAW EX/STRUC INGP/REL EFFICIENCY ORD/FREE
...DECISION 20. PAGE 91 E1835
B59
GOV/COMP
ADMIN
ELITES
ATTIT

TOMPKINS D.C.,SUPREME COURT OF THE UNITED STATES: A
BIBLIOGRAPHY. LAW JUDGE ADJUD GOV/REL DISCRIM
...JURID 18/20 SUPREME/CT NEGRO. PAGE 96 E1931
B59
BIBLIOG/A
CT/SYS
CONSTN
NAT/G

U OF MICHIGAN LAW SCHOOL,ATOMS AND THE LAW. USA+45
PROVS WORKER PROB/SOLV DIPLOM ADMIN GOV/REL ANTHOL.
PAGE 97 E1950
B59
NUC/PWR
NAT/G
CONTROL
LAW

US CONGRESS JT ATOM ENRGY COMM,SELECTED MATERIALS
ON FEDERAL-STATE COOPERATION IN THE ATOMIC ENERGY
FIELD. USA+45 LAW LOC/G PROVS CONSULT LEGIS ADJUD
...POLICY BIBLIOG 20 AEC. PAGE 99 E1991
B59
NAT/G
NUC/PWR
GOV/REL
DELIB/GP

US SENATE COMM ON JUDICIARY,EXECUTIVE PRIVILEGE.
USA+45 DELIB/GP CONTROL KNOWL PWR 20 CONGRESS
PRESIDENT. PAGE 102 E2042
B59
CHIEF
PRIVIL
CONSTN

LAW

ADMIN PERCEPT ORD/FREE SKILL...STAT HIST/WRIT
GEN/METH ILO WORK 20. PAGE 96 E1928

B59

US SENATE COMM ON POST OFFICE,TO PROVIDE FOR AN
EFFECTIVE SYSTEM OF PERSONNEL ADMINISTRATION.
EFFICIENCY...MGT 20 CONGRESS CIVIL/SERV POSTAL/SYS
YARBROGH/R. PAGE 103 E2059
ADMIN
NAT/G
EX/STRUC
LAW

C59

COLLINS I.,"THE GOVERNMENT AND THE NEWSPAPER PRESS
IN FRANCE, 1814-1881. FRANCE LAW ADMIN CT/SYS
...CON/ANAL BIBLIOG 19. PAGE 24 E0475
PRESS
ORD/FREE
NAT/G
EDU/PROP

B59

VOSE C.E.,CAUCASIANS ONLY: THE SUPREME COURT, THE
NAACP, AND THE RESTRICTIVE COVENANT CASES. USA+45
LAW CONSTN LOBBY...SOC 20 NAACP SUPREME/CT NEGRO.
PAGE 104 E2086
CT/SYS
RACE/REL
DISCRIM

C59

EASTON D.,"POLITICAL ANTHROPOLOGY" IN BIENNIAL
REVIEW OF ANTHROPOLOGY" UNIV LAW CULTURE ELITES
SOCIETY CREATE...PSY CONCPT GP/COMP GEN/METH 20.
PAGE 34 E0671
SOC
BIBLIOG/A
NEW/IDEA

L59

COWAN T.A.,"A SYMPOSIUM ON GROUP INTERESTS AND THE
LAW" USA+45 LAW MARKET LABOR PLAN INT/TRADE TAX
RACE/REL RIGID/FLEX...JURID ANTHOL 20. PAGE 27
E0528
ADJUD
PWR
INGP/REL
CREATE

B60

ADRIAN C.R.,STATE AND LOCAL GOVERNMENTS: A STUDY IN
THE POLITICAL PROCESS. USA+45 LAW FINAN MUNIC
POL/PAR LEGIS ADJUD EXEC CHOOSE REPRESENT. PAGE 3
E0051
LOC/G
PROVS
GOV/REL
ATTIT

L59

COX A.,"THE ROLE OF LAW IN PRESERVING UNION
DEMOCRACY." EX/STRUC LEGIS PARTIC ROUTINE CHOOSE
INGP/REL ORD/FREE. PAGE 27 E0532
LABOR
REPRESENT
LAW
MAJORIT

B60

ALBI F.,TRATADO DE LOS MODOS DE GESTION DE LAS
CORPORACIONES LOCALES. SPAIN FINAN NAT/G BUDGET
CONTROL EXEC ROUTINE GOV/REL ORD/FREE SOVEREIGN
...MGT 20. PAGE 3 E0057
LOC/G
LAW
ADMIN
MUNIC

L59

OBERER W.E.,"VOLUNTARY IMPARTIAL REVIEW OF LABOR:
SOME REFLECTIONS." DELIB/GP LEGIS PROB/SOLV ADJUD
CONTROL COERCE PWR PLURISM POLICY. PAGE 78 E1570
LABOR
LAW
PARTIC
INGP/REL

B60

AMERICAN ASSOCIATION LAW LIB,INDEX TO FOREIGN LEGAL
PERIODICALS. WOR+45 MUNIC...IDEA/COMP 20. PAGE 4
E0075
INDEX
LAW
JURID
DIPLOM

S59

BEANEY W.B.,"CIVIL LIBERTIES AND STATUTORY
CONSTRUCTION"(BMR)" USA+45 LEGIS BAL/PWR 20
SUPREME/CT. PAGE 8 E0162
CT/SYS
ORD/FREE
ADJUD
LAW

B60

BAKER G.E.,THE POLITICS OF REAPPORTIONMENT IN
WASHINGTON STATE. LAW POL/PAR CREATE EDU/PROP
PARL/PROC CHOOSE INGP/REL...CHARTS METH/COMP 20
WASHINGT/G LEAGUE/WV. PAGE 7 E0139
VOL/ASSN
APPORT
PROVS
LEGIS

S59

CHAPMAN B.,"THE FRENCH CONSEIL D'ETAT." FRANCE
NAT/G CONSULT OP/RES PROB/SOLV PWR...OBS 20.
PAGE 21 E0421
ADMIN
LAW
CT/SYS
LEGIS

B60

BAYLEY D.H.,VIOLENT AGITATION AND THE DEMOCRATIC
PROCESS IN INDIA. INDIA LAW POL/PAR 20. PAGE 8
E0159
COERCE
CROWD
CONSTN
PROB/SOLV

S59

DERGE D.R.,"THE LAWYER AS DECISION-MAKER IN THE
AMERICAN STATE LEGISLATURE." INTELL LOC/G POL/PAR
CHOOSE AGE HEREDITY PERSON CONSERVE...JURID STAT
CHARTS. PAGE 31 E0607
LEGIS
LAW
DECISION
LEAD

B60

CARPER E.T.,THE DEFENSE APPROPRIATIONS RIDER
(PAMPHLET). USA+45 CONSTN CHIEF DELIB/GP LEGIS
BUDGET LOBBY CIVMIL/REL...POLICY 20 CONGRESS
EISNHWR/DD DEPT/DEFEN PRESIDENT BOSTON. PAGE 20
E0390
GOV/REL
ADJUD
LAW
CONTROL

S59

DOMKE M.,"THE SETTLEMENT OF DISPUTES IN
INTERNATIONAL TRADE." USA+45 LAW STRATA STRUCT
JUDGE EDU/PROP PWR...METH/CNCPT 20. PAGE 32 E0634
CONSULT
LEGIT
INT/TRADE

B60

CARTER R.F.,COMMUNITIES AND THEIR SCHOOLS. USA+45
LAW FINAN PROVS BUDGET TAX LEAD PARTIC CHOOSE...SOC
INT QU 20. PAGE 20 E0401
SCHOOL
ACT/RES
NEIGH
INGP/REL

S59

DWYER R.J.,"THE ADMINISTRATIVE ROLE IN
DESEGREGATION." USA+45 LAW PROB/SOLV LEAD RACE/REL
ISOLAT STRANGE ROLE...POLICY SOC/INTEG MISSOURI
NEGRO CIV/RIGHTS. PAGE 34 E0668
ADMIN
SCHOOL
DISCRIM
ATTIT

B60

CASTBERG F.,FREEDOM OF SPEECH IN THE WEST. FRANCE
GERMANY USA+45 USA-45 LAW CONSTN CHIEF PRESS
DISCRIM...CONCPT 18/20. PAGE 21 E0406
ORD/FREE
SANCTION
ADJUD
NAT/COMP

S59

JENKS C.W.,"THE CHALLENGE OF UNIVERSALITY." FUT
UNIV CONSTN CULTURE CONSULT CREATE PLAN LEGIT ATTIT
MORAL ORD/FREE RESPECT...MAJORIT JURID 20. PAGE 58
E1155
INT/ORG
LAW
PEACE
INT/LAW

B60

CLARK G.,WORLD PEACE THROUGH WORLD LAW. FUT WOR+45
CONSULT FORCES ACT/RES CREATE PLAN ADMIN ROUTINE
ARMS/CONT DETER ATTIT PWR...JURID VAL/FREE UNESCO
20 UN. PAGE 23 E0449
INT/ORG
LAW
PEACE
INT/LAW

S59

POTTER P.B.,"OBSTACLES AND ALTERNATIVES TO
INTERNATIONAL LAW." WOR+45 NAT/G VOL/ASSN DELIB/GP
BAL/PWR DOMIN ROUTINE...JURID VAL/FREE 20. PAGE 81
E1632
INT/ORG
LAW
DIPLOM
INT/LAW

B60

CONANT M.,ANTITRUST IN THE MOTION PICTURE INDUSTRY:
ECONOMIC AND LEGAL ANALYSIS. USA+45 MARKET ADJUST
DEMAND BIBLIOG. PAGE 24 E0484
PRICE
CONTROL
LAW
ART/METH

S59

SCHEEHAN D.,"PUBLIC AND PRIVATE GROUPS AS
IDENTIFIED IN THE FIELD OF TRADE REGULATIONS."
USA+45 ADMIN REPRESENT GOV/REL. PAGE 87 E1753
LAW
CONTROL
ADJUD
LOBBY

B60

DILEY A.V.,INTRODUCTION TO THE STUDY OF THE LAW OF
THE CONSTITUTION. FRANCE UK USA+45 USA-45 CONSULT
FORCES TAX ADMIN FEDERAL ORD/FREE SOVEREIGN
...IDEA/COMP 20 ENGLSH/LAW CON/INTERP PARLIAMENT.
PAGE 32 E0627
CONSTN
LAW
LEGIS
GEN/LAWS

S59

SOHN L.B.,"THE DEFINITION OF AGGRESSION." FUT LAW
FORCES LEGIT ADJUD ROUTINE COERCE ORD/FREE PWR
...MAJORIT JURID QUANT COLD/WAR 20. PAGE 92 E1855
INT/ORG
CT/SYS
DETER
SOVEREIGN

B60

FLORES R.H.,CATALOGO DE TESIS DOCTORALES DE LAS
FACULTADES DE LA UNIVERSIDAD DE EL SALVADOR.
EL/SALVADR LAW DIPLOM ADMIN LEAD GOV/REL...SOC
19/20. PAGE 39 E0767
BIBLIOG
ACADEM
L/A+17C
NAT/G

S59

STONE J.,"CONFLICT MANAGEMENT THROUGH CONTEMPORARY
INTERNATIONAL LAW AND ORGANIZATION." WOR+45 LAW
NAT/G CREATE BAL/PWR DOMIN LEGIT ROUTINE COERCE
ATTIT ORD/FREE PWR SOVEREIGN...JURID 20. PAGE 94
E1880
INT/ORG
INT/LAW

B60

GIBNEY F.,THE OPERATORS. USA+45 LAW STRATA BIO/SOC
MORAL ORD/FREE SOC. PAGE 43 E0858
CRIME
CULTURE
ANOMIE
CRIMLGY

S59

TIPTON J.B.,"PARTICIPATION OF THE UNITED STATES IN
THE INTERNATIONAL LABOR ORGANIZATION." USA+45 LAW
STRUCT ECO/DEV ECO/UNDEV INDUS TEC/DEV ECO/TAC
LABOR
INT/ORG

GOLDSEN J.M.,INTERNATIONAL POLITICAL IMPLICATIONS   R+D
OF ACTIVITIES IN OUTER SPACE. FUT USA+45 WOR+45 AIR SPACE
LAW ACT/RES LEGIT ATTIT KNOWL ORD/FREE PWR...CONCPT
20. PAGE 44 E0879
B60

HARVARD LAW SCHOOL LIBRARY,CURRENT LEGAL   BIBLIOG
BIBLIOGRAPHY. USA+45 CONSTN LEGIS ADJUD CT/SYS   JURID
POLICY. PAGE 51 E1006   LAW
                                                     INT/LAW
B60

HEAP D.,AN OUTLINE OF PLANNING LAW (3RD ED.). UK   MUNIC
LAW PROB/SOLV ADMIN CONTROL 20. PAGE 51 E1020   PLAN
                                                     JURID
                                                     LOC/G
B60

JENNINGS R.,PROGRESS OF INTERNATIONAL LAW. FUT   INT/ORG
WOR+45 WOR-45 SOCIETY NAT/G VOL/ASSN DELIB/GP   LAW
DIPLOM EDU/PROP LEGIT COERCE ATTIT DRIVE MORAL   INT/LAW
ORD/FREE...JURID CONCPT OBS TIME/SEQ TREND
GEN/LAWS. PAGE 58 E1164
B60

LASKIN B.,CANADIAN CONSTITUTIONAL LAW: TEXT AND   CONSTN
NOTES ON DISTRIBUTION OF LEGISLATIVE POWER (2ND   NAT/G
ED.). CANADA LOC/G ECO/TAC TAX CONTROL CT/SYS CRIME LAW
FEDERAL PWR...JURID 20 PARLIAMENT. PAGE 63 E1259   LEGIS
B60

LENCZOWSKI G.,OIL AND STATE IN THE MIDDLE EAST. FUT ISLAM
IRAN LAW ECO/UNDEV EXTR/IND NAT/G TOP/EX PLAN   INDUS
TEC/DEV ECO/TAC LEGIT ADMIN COERCE ATTIT ALL/VALS   NAT/LISM
PWR...CHARTS 20. PAGE 64 E1283
B60

LEWIS P.R.,LITERATURE OF THE SOCIAL SCIENCES: AN   BIBLIOG/A
INTRODUCTORY SURVEY AND GUIDE. UK LAW INDUS DIPLOM   SOC
INT/TRADE ADMIN...MGT 19/20. PAGE 65 E1294
B60

MOCTEZUMA A.P.,EL CONFLICTO RELIGIOSO DE 1926 (2ND   SECT
ED.). L/A+17C LAW NAT/G LOBBY COERCE GP/REL ATTIT   ORD/FREE
...POLICY 20 MEXIC/AMER CHURCH/STA. PAGE 74 E1476   DISCRIM
                                                     REV
B60

PINTO F.B.M.,ENRIQUECIMENTO ILICITO NO EXERCICIO DE ADMIN
CARGOS PUBLICOS. BRAZIL L/A+17C USA+45 ELITES   NAT/G
TRIBUTE CONTROL INGP/REL ORD/FREE PWR...NAT/COMP   CRIME
20. PAGE 81 E1617   LAW
B60

POWELL T.,THE SCHOOL BUS LAW: A CASE STUDY IN   JURID
EDUCATION, RELIGION, AND POLITICS. USA+45 LAW NEIGH SCHOOL
SECT LEGIS EDU/PROP ADJUD CT/SYS LOBBY CATHISM
WORSHIP 20 CONNECTICT CHURCH/STA. PAGE 82 E1641
B60

SCHEIBER H.N.,THE WILSON ADMINISTRATION AND CIVIL   ORD/FREE
LIBERTIES 1917-1921. LAW GOV/REL ATTIT 20 WILSON/W   WAR
CIVIL/LIB. PAGE 87 E1754   NAT/G
                                                     CONTROL
B60

SCHMIDHAUSER J.R.,THE SUPREME COURT: ITS POLITICS,   JUDGE
PERSONALITIES, AND PROCEDURES. LAW DELIB/GP   JURID
EX/STRUC TOP/EX ADJUD CT/SYS CHOOSE RATIONAL PWR   DECISION
SUPREME/CT. PAGE 88 E1760
B60

SCHUBERT G.A.,CONSTITUTIONAL POLITICS: THE   CONSTN
POLITICAL BEHAVIOR OF SUPREME COURT JUSTICES AND   CT/SYS
THE CONSTITUTIONAL POLICIES THEY MAKE. LAW ELITES   JURID
CHIEF DELIB/GP EX/STRUC LEGIS DISCRIM ORD/FREE PWR   DECISION
...POLICY MAJORIT CHARTS SUPREME/CT CONGRESS.
PAGE 89 E1781
B60

US HOUSE COMM ON JUDICIARY,ESTABLISHMENT OF   APPORT
CONGRESSIONAL DISTRICTS. USA+45 PROB/SOLV 20   REPRESENT
CONGRESS HOUSE/REP. PAGE 100 E2003   LEGIS
                                                     LAW
B60

US SENATE COMM ON JUDICIARY,FEDERAL ADMINISTRATIVE   PARL/PROC
PROCEDURE. USA+45 CONSTN NAT/G PROB/SOLV CONFER   LEGIS
GOV/REL...JURID INT 20 SENATE. PAGE 102 E2043   ADMIN
                                                     LAW
L60

LAUTERPACHT E.,"THE SUEZ CANAL SETTLEMENT." FRANCE   INT/ORG
ISLAM ISRAEL UAR UK BAL/PWR DIPLOM LEGIT...JURID   LAW
GEN/LAWS ANTHOL SUEZ VAL/FREE 20. PAGE 63 E1263

L60

MILLER A.S.,"THE MYTH OF NEUTRALITY IN   ADJUD
CONSTITUTIONAL ADJUDICATION." LAW...DECISION JURID   CONSTN
LING TREND IDEA/COMP. PAGE 73 E1456   MYTH
                                                     UTIL
S60

BLACK H.,"THE BILL OF RIGHTS" (BMR)" USA+45 USA-45   CONSTN
LAW LEGIS CT/SYS FEDERAL PWR 18/20 CONGRESS   ORD/FREE
SUPREME/CT BILL/RIGHT CIV/RIGHTS. PAGE 12 E0237   NAT/G
                                                     JURID
S60

MARSHALL G.,"POLICE RESPONSIBILITY." UK LOC/G ADJUD CONTROL
ADMIN EXEC 20. PAGE 69 E1370   REPRESENT
                                                     LAW
                                                     FORCES
S60

NAGEL S.S.,"USING SIMPLE CALCULATIONS TO PREDICT   JURID
JUDICIAL DECISIONS." ATTIT PERSON MATH. PAGE 76   LAW
E1517   DECISION
                                                     COMPUTER
S60

SCHWELB E.,"INTERNATIONAL CONVENTIONS ON HUMAN   INT/ORG
RIGHTS." FUT WOR+45 LAW CONSTN CULTURE SOCIETY   HUM
STRUCT VOL/ASSN DELIB/GP PLAN ADJUD SUPEGO LOVE
MORAL...SOC CONCPT STAT RECORD HIST/WRIT TREND 20
UN. PAGE 89 E1790
S60

THOMPSON K.W.,"MORAL PURPOSE IN FOREIGN POLICY: MORAL
REALITIES AND ILLUSIONS." WOR+45 WOR-45 LAW CULTURE JURID
SOCIETY INT/ORG PLAN ADJUD ADMIN COERCE RIGID/FLEX   DIPLOM
SUPEGO KNOWL ORD/FREE PWR...SOC TREND SOC/EXP
TOT/POP 20. PAGE 96 E1921
S60

ULMER S.S.,"THE ANALYSIS OF BEHAVIOR PATTERNS ON   ATTIT
THE UNITED STATES SUPREME COURT" USA+45 LAW CT/SYS   ADJUD
PERS/REL RACE/REL PERSON...DECISION PSY SOC TREND   PROF/ORG
METH/COMP METH 20 SUPREME/CT CIVIL/LIB. PAGE 97   INGP/REL
E1951
C60

HAZARD J.N.,"SETTLING DISPUTES IN SOVIET SOCIETY: ADJUD
THE FORMATIVE YEARS OF LEGAL INSTITUTIONS." USSR   LAW
NAT/G PROF/ORG PROB/SOLV CONTROL CT/SYS ROUTINE REV COM
CENTRAL...JURID BIBLIOG 20. PAGE 51 E1017   POLICY
N60

RHODESIA-NYASA NATL ARCHIVES,A SELECT BIBLIOGRAPHY   BIBLIOG
OF RECENT PUBLICATIONS CONCERNING THE FEDERATION OF ADMIN
RHODESIA AND NYASALAND (PAMPHLET). MALAWI RHODESIA   ORD/FREE
LAW CULTURE STRUCT ECO/UNDEV LEGIS...GEOG 20.   NAT/G
PAGE 84 E1689
B61

ALFRED H.,PUBLIC OWNERSHIP IN THE USA: GOALS AND   CONTROL
PRIORITIES. LAW INDUS INT/TRADE ADJUD GOV/REL   OWN
EFFICIENCY PEACE SOCISM...POLICY ANTHOL 20 TVA.   ECO/DEV
PAGE 3 E0064   ECO/TAC
B61

BARBASH J.,LABOR'S GRASS ROOTS. CONSTN NAT/G   LABOR
EX/STRUC LEGIS WORKER LEAD...MAJORIT BIBLIOG.   INGP/REL
PAGE 8 E0147   GP/REL
                                                     LAW
B61

BAYITCH S.A.,LATIN AMERICA: A BIBLIOGRAPHICAL   BIBLIOG
GUIDE. LAW CONSTN LEGIS JUDGE ADJUD CT/SYS 20.   L/A+17C
PAGE 8 E0158   NAT/G
                                                     JURID
B61

BEDFORD S.,THE FACES OF JUSTICE: A TRAVELLER'S   CT/SYS
REPORT. AUSTRIA FRANCE GERMANY/W SWITZERLND UK UNIV ORD/FREE
WOR+45 WOR-45 CULTURE PARTIC GOV/REL MORAL...JURID   PERSON
OBS GOV/COMP 20. PAGE 9 E0174   LAW
B61

BENNETT G.,THE KENYATTA ELECTION: KENYA 1960-1961.   CHOOSE
AFR INGP/REL RACE/REL CONSEN ATTIT 20 KENYATTA.   POL/PAR
PAGE 10 E0187   LAW
                                                     SUFF
B61

BURDETTE F.L.,POLITICAL SCIENCE: A SELECTED   BIBLIOG/A
BIBLIOGRAPHY OF BOOKS IN PRINT, WITH ANNOTATIONS   GOV/COMP
(PAMPHLET). LAW LOC/G NAT/G POL/PAR PROVS DIPLOM   CONCPT
EDU/PROP ADMIN CHOOSE ATTIT 20. PAGE 17 E0330   ROUTINE

CARROTHERS A.W.R.,LABOR ARBITRATION IN CANADA. LABOR
CANADA LAW NAT/G CONSULT LEGIS WORKER ADJUD ADMIN MGT
CT/SYS 20. PAGE 20 E0396 GP/REL
BARGAIN
B61

CASSINELLI C.W.,THE POLITICS OF FREEDOM. FUT UNIV MAJORIT
LAW POL/PAR CHOOSE ORD/FREE...POLICY CONCPT MYTH NAT/G
BIBLIOG. PAGE 21 E0404 PARL/PROC
PARTIC
B61

DAVIS B.F.,THE DESPERATE AND THE DAMNED. USA+45 LAW PUB/INST
DEATH ANOMIE...CRIMLGY 20 SAN/QUENTN. PAGE 29 E0571 SANCTION
CRIME
B61

FLINN M.W.,AN ECONOMIC AND SOCIAL HISTORY OF SOCIETY
BRITAIN, 1066-1939. UK LAW STRATA STRUCT AGRI SOC
DIST/IND INDUS WORKER INT/TRADE WAR...CENSUS 11/20.
PAGE 39 E0766
B61

GUIZOT F.P.G.,HISTORY OF THE ORIGIN OF LEGIS
REPRESENTATIVE GOVERNMENT IN EUROPE. CHRIST-17C REPRESENT
FRANCE MOD/EUR SPAIN UK LAW CHIEF FORCES POPULISM CONSTN
...MAJORIT TIME/SEQ GOV/COMP NAT/COMP 4/19 NAT/G
PARLIAMENT. PAGE 48 E0961
B61

JACOBS C.E.,JUSTICE FRANKFURTER AND CIVIL BIOG
LIBERTIES. USA+45 USA-45 LAW NAT/G PROB/SOLV PRESS CONSTN
PERS/REL...JURID WORSHIP 20 SUPREME/CT FRANKFUR/F ADJUD
CIVIL/LIB. PAGE 57 E1144 ORD/FREE
B61

JUSTICE,THE CITIZEN AND THE ADMINISTRATION: THE INGP/REL
REDRESS OF GRIEVANCES (PAMPHLET). EUR+WWI UK LAW CONSULT
CONSTN STRATA NAT/G CT/SYS PARTIC COERCE...NEW/IDEA ADJUD
IDEA/COMP 20 OMBUDSMAN. PAGE 59 E1176 REPRESENT
B61

KAPLAN M.A.,THE POLITICAL FOUNDATIONS OF INT/ORG
INTERNATIONAL LAW. WOR+45 WOR-45 CULTURE SOCIETY LAW
ECO/DEV DIPLOM PERCEPT...TECHNIC METH/CNCPT.
PAGE 59 E1184
B61

LA PONCE J.A.,THE GOVERNMENT OF THE FIFTH REPUBLIC: PWR
FRENCH POLITICAL PARTIES AND THE CONSTITUTION. POL/PAR
ALGERIA FRANCE LAW NAT/G DELIB/GP LEGIS ECO/TAC CONSTN
MARXISM SOCISM...CHARTS BIBLIOG/A 20 DEGAULLE/C. CHIEF
PAGE 62 E1243
B61

MURPHY E.F.,WATER PURITY: A STUDY IN LEGAL CONTROL SEA
OF NATURAL RESOURCES. LOC/G ACT/RES PLAN TEC/DEV LAW
LOBBY GP/REL COST ATTIT HEALTH ORD/FREE...HEAL PROVS
JURID 20 WISCONSIN WATER. PAGE 75 E1506 CONTROL
B61

NELSON H.L.,LIBEL IN NEWS OF CONGRESSIONAL DELIB/GP
INVESTIGATING COMMITTEES. USA+45 LAW PARL/PROC LEGIS
PRIVIL RESPECT HOUSE/REP. PAGE 76 E1532 LICENSE
PRESS
B61

POOLEY B.J.,PLANNING AND ZONING IN THE UNITED PLAN
STATES. USA+45 MUNIC DELIB/GP ACT/RES PROB/SOLV LOC/G
TEC/DEV ADJUD ADMIN REGION 20 ZONING. PAGE 81 E1628 PROVS
LAW
B61

PRITCHETT C.H.,CONGRESS VERSUS THE SUPREME COURT, LEGIS
1957-1960. PROB/SOLV DOMIN EXEC GP/REL DISCRIM PWR JURID
CONGRESS SUPREME/CT SUPREME/CT. PAGE 82 E1652 LAW
B61

PUGET H.,ESSAI DE BIBLIOGRAPHIE DES PRINCIPAUX BIBLIOG
OUVRAGES DE DROIT PUBLIC... QUI ONT PARU HORS DE MGT
FRANCE DE 1945 A 1958. EUR+WWI USA+45 CONSTN LOC/G ADMIN
...METH 20. PAGE 83 E1660 LAW
B61

RUEDA B.,A STATEMENT OF THE LAWS OF COLOMBIA IN FINAN
MATTERS AFFECTING BUSINESS (3RD ED.). INDUS FAM ECO/UNDEV
LABOR LG/CO NAT/G LEGIS TAX CONTROL MARRIAGE 20 LAW
COLOMB. PAGE 86 E1733 CONSTN
B61

TOMPKINS D.C.,CONFLICT OF INTEREST IN THE FEDERAL BIBLIOG
GOVERNMENT: A BIBLIOGRAPHY. USA+45 EX/STRUC LEGIS ROLE
ADJUD ADMIN CRIME CONGRESS PRESIDENT. PAGE 96 E1932 NAT/G
LAW

US COMMISSION ON CIVIL RIGHTS,JUSTICE: BOOK 5, 1961 DISCRIM
REPORT OF THE U.S. COMMISSION ON CIVIL RIGHTS. LAW
LOC/G NAT/G RACE/REL...JURID 20 NEGRO CIV/RIGHTS FORCES
INDIAN/AM JURY INDIAN/AM. PAGE 99 E1983
B61

US CONGRESS,CONSTITUTIONAL RIGHTS OF THE MENTALLY HEALTH
ILL. USA+45 LAW PUB/INST DELIB/GP ADJUD ORD/FREE CONSTN
...PSY QU 20 CONGRESS. PAGE 99 E1989 JURID
CONFER
B61

US HOUSE COMM ON JUDICIARY,LEGISLATION RELATING TO LEGIS
ORGANIZED CRIME. USA+45 DIST/IND DELIB/GP GAMBLE CONTROL
SANCTION HOUSE/REP. PAGE 100 E2004 CRIME
LAW
B61

WARD R.E.,JAPANESE POLITICAL SCIENCE: A GUIDE TO BIBLIOG/A
JAPANESE REFERENCE AND RESEARCH MATERIALS (2ND PHIL/SCI
ED.). LAW CONSTN STRATA NAT/G POL/PAR DELIB/GP
LEGIS ADMIN CHOOSE GP/REL...INT/LAW 19/20 CHINJAP.
PAGE 105 E2099
B61

WASSERSTROM R.A.,THE JUDICIAL DECISION: TOWARD A JUDGE
THEORY OF LEGAL JUSTIFICATION. ACT/RES RATIONAL LAW
PERCEPT KNOWL OBJECTIVE...DECISION JURID. PAGE 105 ADJUD
E2102
B61

WECHSLER H.,PRINCIPLES, POLITICS AND FUNDAMENTAL CT/SYS
LAW: SELECTED ESSAYS. USA+45 USA-45 LAW SOCIETY CONSTN
NAT/G PROVS DELIB/GP EX/STRUC ACT/RES LEGIT PERSON INT/LAW
KNOWL PWR...JURID 20 NUREMBERG. PAGE 105 E2106
B61

WESTIN A.F.,THE SUPREME COURT: VIEWS FROM INSIDE. CT/SYS
USA+45 NAT/G PROF/ORG PROVS DELIB/GP INGP/REL LAW
DISCRIM ATTIT...POLICY DECISION JURID ANTHOL 20 ADJUD
SUPREME/CT CONGRESS CIVIL/LIB. PAGE 106 E2114 GOV/REL
B61

WINTERS J.M.,STATE CONSTITUTIONAL LIMITATIONS ON MUNIC
SOLUTIONS OF METROPOLITAN AREA PROBLEMS. CONSTN REGION
LEGIS LEAD REPRESENT DECISION. PAGE 107 E2134 LOC/G
LAW
B61

FELLMAN D.,"ACADEMIC FREEDOM IN AMERICAN LAW." LAW ACADEM
CONSTN NAT/G VOL/ASSN PLAN PERSON KNOWL NEW/LIB. ORD/FREE
PAGE 37 E0732 LEGIS
CULTURE
L61

GERWIG R.,"PUBLIC AUTHORITIES IN THE UNITED LOC/G
STATES." LAW CONSTN PROVS TAX ADMIN FEDERAL. MUNIC
PAGE 43 E0852 GOV/REL
PWR
L61

KAUPER P.G.,"CHURCH AND STATE: COOPERATIVE SECT
SEPARATISM." NAT/G LEGIS OP/RES TAX EDU/PROP GP/REL CONSTN
TREND. PAGE 59 E1187 LAW
POLICY
L61

MCNAMEE B.J.,"CONFLICT OF INTEREST: STATE LAW
GOVERNMENT EMPLOYEES." USA+45 PROVS 20. PAGE 71 REPRESENT
E1426 ADMIN
CONTROL
L61

SAND P.T.,"AN HISTORICAL SURVEY OF INTERNATIONAL INT/ORG
AIR LAW SINCE 1944." USA+45 USA-45 WOR+45 WOR-45 LAW
SOCIETY ECO/DEV NAT/G CONSULT EX/STRUC ACT/RES PLAN INT/LAW
LEGIT ROUTINE...JURID CONCPT METH/CNCPT TREND 20. SPACE
PAGE 87 E1744
L61

BAER E.,"THE GENERAL ACCOUNTING OFFICE: THE FEDERAL ADJUD
GOVERNMENT'S AUDITOR." USA+45 NAT/G REPRESENT 20 EX/STRUC
GENACCOUNT. PAGE 7 E0132 EXEC
LAW
S61

CASTANEDA J.,"THE UNDERDEVELOPED NATIONS AND THE INT/ORG
DEVELOPMENT OF INTERNATIONAL LAW." FUT UNIV LAW ECO/UNDEV
ACT/RES FOR/AID LEGIT PERCEPT SKILL...JURID PEACE
METH/CNCPT TIME/SEQ TOT/POP 20 UN. PAGE 21 E0405 INT/LAW
S61

HARVEY W.B.,"THE RULE OF LAW IN HISTORICAL ACT/RES
PERSPECTIVE." USA+45 WOR+45 INTELL SOCIETY ECO/DEV LAW
ECO/UNDEV NAT/G EX/STRUC LEGIS TOP/EX LEGIT SKILL

...CONCPT HIST/WRIT TOT/POP. PAGE 51 E1010

HOLMES/OW FRANKFUR/F. PAGE 12 E0226

S61
JACKSON E.,"THE FUTURE DEVELOPMENT OF THE UNITED NATIONS: SOME SUGGESTIONS FOR RESEARCH." FUT LAW CONSTN ECO/DEV FINAN PEACE WEALTH...WELF/ST CONCPT UN 20. PAGE 57 E1140
INT/ORG
PWR

S61
LASSWELL H.D.,"THE INTERPLAY OF ECONOMIC, POLITICAL AND SOCIAL CRITERIA IN LEGAL POLICY." LAW LOVE MORAL PWR RESPECT WEALTH...SOC IDEA/COMP. PAGE 63 E1262
JURID
POLICY

S61
LIPSON L.,"AN ARGUMENT ON THE LEGALITY OF RECONNAISSANCE STATELLITES." COM USA+45 USSR WOR+45 AIR INTELL NAT/G CONSULT PLAN DIPLOM LEGIT ROUTINE ATTIT...INT/LAW JURID CONCPT METH/CNCPT TREND COLD/WAR 20. PAGE 65 E1302
INT/ORG
LAW
SPACE

S61
MACHOWSKI K.,"SELECTED PROBLEMS OF NATIONAL SOVEREIGNTY WITH REFERENCE TO THE LAW OF OUTER SPACE." FUT WOR+45 AIR LAW INTELL SOCIETY ECO/DEV PLAN EDU/PROP DETER DRIVE PERCEPT SOVEREIGN ...POLICY INT/LAW OBS TREND TOT/POP 20. PAGE 67 E1339
UNIV
ACT/RES
NUC/PWR
SPACE

S61
RICHSTEIN A.R.,"LEGAL RULES IN NUCLEAR WEAPONS EMPLOYMENTS." FUT WOR+45 LAW SOCIETY FORCES PLAN WEAPON RIGID/FLEX...HEAL CONCPT TREND VAL/FREE 20. PAGE 85 E1696
NUC/PWR
TEC/DEV
MORAL
ARMS/CONT

N61
DELEGACION NACIONAL DE PRENSA,FALANGE ESPANOL TRADICIONALISTA Y DE LAS JUNTAS OFENSIVAS NACIONALES SINDICALISTAS. IX CONSEJO NACIONAL (PAMPHLET). LAW VOL/ASSN TOTALISM AUTHORIT ORD/FREE FASCISM...ANTHOL 20 FRANCO/F FALANGIST. PAGE 31 E0605
EDU/PROP
FASCIST
CONFER
POL/PAR

N61
LEAGUE WOMEN VOTERS MASSACHU,THE MERIT SYSTEM IN MASSACHUSETTS (PAMPHLET). USA+45 PROVS LEGIT PARTIC CHOOSE REPRESENT GOV/REL EFFICIENCY...POLICY GOV/COMP BIBLIOG 20 MASSACHU. PAGE 64 E1274
LOC/G
LAW
SENIOR
PROF/ORG

N61
VINER J.,THE INTELLECTUAL HISTORY OF LAISSEZ FAIRE (PAMPHLET). WOR+45 WOR-45 LAW INTELL...POLICY LING LOG 19/20. PAGE 104 E2077
ATTIT
EDU/PROP
LAISSEZ
ECO/TAC

B62
ALLOTT A.N.,JUDICIAL AND LEGAL SYSTEMS IN AFRICA. LAW CONSTN JUDGE CONTROL...METH/CNCPT CLASSIF CHARTS 20 COMMON/LAW. PAGE 4 E0070
CT/SYS
AFR
JURID
COLONIAL

B62
AMER SOCIETY POL & LEGAL PHIL,THE PUBLIC INTEREST: NOMOS V. LAW EDU/PROP...SOC METH/CNCPT ANTHOL. PAGE 4 E0073
CONCPT
ATTIT
PWR
GEN/LAWS

B62
AMERICAN LAW INSTITUTE,FOREIGN RELATIONS LAW OF THE UNITED STATES: RESTATEMENT, SECOND. USA+45 NAT/G LEGIS ADJUD EXEC ROUTINE GOV/REL...INT/LAW JURID CONCPT 20 TREATY. PAGE 4 E0082
PROF/ORG
LAW
DIPLOM
ORD/FREE

B62
ASSOCIATION BAR OF NYC,REPORT ON ADMISSION PROCEDURES TO NEW YORK STATE MENTAL HOSPITALS. LAW CONSTN INGP/REL RESPECT...PSY OBS RECORD. PAGE 6 E0108
PUB/INST
HEALTH
CLIENT
ROUTINE

B62
BARLOW R.B.,CITIZENSHIP AND CONSCIENCE: STUDIES IN THEORY AND PRACTICE OF RELIGIOUS TOLERATION IN ENGLAND DURING EIGHTEENTH CENTURY. UK LAW VOL/ASSN EDU/PROP SANCTION REV GP/REL MAJORITY ATTIT ORD/FREE...BIBLIOG WORSHIP 18. PAGE 8 E0150
SECT
LEGIS
DISCRIM

B62
BERMAN D.M.,A BILL BECOMES A LAW: THE CIVIL RIGHTS ACT OF 1960. USA+45 LAW POL/PAR LOBBY RACE/REL KNOWL...CHARTS 20 CONGRESS NEGRO CIV/RIGHTS. PAGE 11 E0206
DISCRIM
PARL/PROC
JURID
GOV/REL

B62
BICKEL A.,THE LEAST DANGEROUS BRANCH. USA+45 USA-45 CONSTN SCHOOL LEGIS ADJUD RACE/REL DISCRIM ORD/FREE ...JURID 18/20 SUPREME/CT CONGRESS MARSHALL/J
LAW
NAT/G
CT/SYS

B62
BLAUSTEIN A.P.,MANUAL ON FOREIGN LEGAL PERIODICALS AND THEIR INDEX. WOR+45 DIPLOM 20. PAGE 13 E0244
BIBLIOG
INDEX
LAW
JURID

B62
BOCHENSKI J.M.,HANDBOOK ON COMMUNISM. USSR WOR+45 LAW SOCIETY NAT/G POL/PAR SECT CRIME PERSON MARXISM ...SOC ANTHOL 20. PAGE 13 E0254
COM
DIPLOM
POLICY
CONCPT

B62
BOYD W.J.,PATTERNS OF APPORTIONMENT (PAMPHLET). LAW CONSTN CHOOSE GOV/COMP. PAGE 14 E0282
MUNIC
PROVS
REPRESENT
APPORT

B62
BRANDT R.B.,SOCIAL JUSTICE. UNIV LAW GP/REL PWR ALL/IDEOS...POLICY SOC ANTHOL 20. PAGE 15 E0287
ORD/FREE
CONSTN
CONCPT

B62
BUREAU OF NATIONAL AFFAIRS,FEDERAL-STATE REGULATION OF WELFARE FUNDS (REV. ED.). USA+45 LAW LEGIS DEBATE AGE/O 20 CONGRESS. PAGE 17 E0337
WELF/ST
WEALTH
PLAN
SOC/WK

B62
CARLSTON K.S.,LAW AND ORGANIZATION IN WORLD SOCIETY. WOR+45 FINAN ECO/TAC DOMIN LEGIT CT/SYS ROUTINE COERCE ORD/FREE PWR WEALTH...PLURIST DECISION JURID MGT METH/CNCPT GEN/LAWS 20. PAGE 19 E0381
INT/ORG
LAW

B62
CARPER E.T.,ILLINOIS GOES TO CONGRESS FOR ARMY LAND. USA+45 LAW EXTR/IND PROVS REGION CIVMIL/REL GOV/REL FEDERAL ATTIT 20 ILLINOIS SENATE CONGRESS DIRKSEN/E DOUGLAS/P. PAGE 20 E0391
ADMIN
LOBBY
GEOG
LEGIS

B62
COSTA RICA UNIVERSIDAD BIBL,LISTA DE TESIS DE GRADO DE LA UNIVERSIDAD DE COSTA RICA. COSTA/RICA LAW LOC/G ADMIN LEAD...SOC 20. PAGE 26 E0518
BIBLIOG/A
NAT/G
DIPLOM
ECO/UNDEV

B62
CRANSTON M.,WHAT ARE HUMAN RIGHTS? UNIV WOR+45 INT/ORG MORAL...POLICY CONCPT METH/CNCPT GEN/LAWS 20. PAGE 28 E0545
LAW
ORD/FREE
JURID
IDEA/COMP

B62
CURRY J.E.,RACE TENSIONS AND THE POLICE. LAW MUNIC NEIGH TEC/DEV RUMOR CONTROL COERCE GP/REL ATTIT ...SOC 20 NEGRO. PAGE 28 E0558
FORCES
RACE/REL
CROWD
ORD/FREE

B62
DAVIS F.J.,SOCIETY AND THE LAW. USA+45 CONSTN ACADEM FAM CONSULT ACT/RES GP/REL ORD/FREE ENGLSH/LAW 20. PAGE 29 E0572
LAW
SOC
CULTURE
STRUCT

B62
DONNELLY R.C.,CRIMINAL LAW: PROBLEMS FOR DECISION IN THE PROMULGATION, INVOCATION AND ADMINISTRATION OF A LAW OF CRIMES. USA+45 SANCTION BIO/SOC ...DECISION JURID BIBLIOG 20. PAGE 32 E0636
CRIME
LAW
ADJUD
PROB/SOLV

B62
DUPRE J.S.,SCIENCE AND THE NATION: POLICY AND POLITICS. USA+45 LAW ACADEM FORCES ADMIN CIVMIL/REL GOV/REL EFFICIENCY PEACE...TREND 20 SCI/ADVSRY. PAGE 34 E0665
R+D
INDUS
TEC/DEV
NUC/PWR

B62
FRIEDRICH C.J.,NOMOS V: THE PUBLIC INTEREST. UNIV ECO/TAC ADJUD UTIL ATTIT...POLICY LING LOG GEN/LAWS 20. PAGE 41 E0808
METH/CNCPT
CONCPT
LAW
IDEA/COMP

B62
GONNER R.,DAS KIRCHENPATRONATRECHT IM GROSSHERZOGTUM BADEN. GERMANY LAW PROVS DEBATE ATTIT CATHISM 14/19 PROTESTANT CHRISTIAN CHURCH/STA BADEN. PAGE 44 E0882
JURID
SECT
NAT/G
GP/REL

B62
GROGAN V.,ADMINISTRATIVE TRIBUNALS IN THE PUBLIC SERVICE. IRELAND UK NAT/G CONTROL CT/SYS...JURID GOV/COMP 20. PAGE 48 E0945
ADMIN
LAW
ADJUD

DELIB/GP

B62

GRZYBOWSKI K.,SOVIET LEGAL INSTITUTIONS. USA+45   ADJUD
USSR ECO/DEV NAT/G EDU/PROP CONTROL CT/SYS CRIME   LAW
OWN ATTIT PWR SOCISM...NAT/COMP 20. PAGE 48 E0955   JURID

B62

HADWEN J.G.,HOW UNITED NATIONS DECISIONS ARE MADE.   INT/ORG
WOR+45 LAW EDU/PROP LEGIT ADMIN PWR...DECISION   ROUTINE
SELF/OBS GEN/LAWS UN 20. PAGE 49 E0972

B62

HEYDECKER J.J.,THE NUREMBERG TRIAL: HISTORY OF NAZI   LAW
GERMANY AS REVEALED THROUGH THE TESTIMONY AT   CRIME
NUREMBERG. EUR+WWI GERMANY VOL/ASSN LEAD COERCE   PARTIC
CROWD INGP/REL RACE/REL SUPEGO ORD/FREE...CONCPT 20   TOTALISM
NAZI ANTI/SEMIT NUREMBERG JEWS. PAGE 52 E1036

B62

HIRSCHFIELD R.S.,THE CONSTITUTION AND THE COURT.   ADJUD
SCHOOL WAR RACE/REL EQUILIB ORD/FREE...POLICY   PWR
MAJORIT DECISION JURID 18/20 PRESIDENT COLD/WAR   CONSTN
CIVIL/LIB SUPREME/CT CONGRESS. PAGE 53 E1051   LAW

B62

INTNTL COTTON ADVISORY COMMITT.GOVERNMENT   ECO/TAC
REGULATIONS ON COTTON, 1962 (PAMPHLET). WOR+45   LAW
RATION PRODUC...CHARTS 20. PAGE 57 E1136   CONTROL
AGRI

B62

JENKS C.W.,THE PROPER LAW OF INTERNATIONAL   LAW
ORGANISATIONS. DIPLOM LEGIT AGREE CT/SYS SANCTION   INT/ORG
REPRESENT SOVEREIGN...GEN/LAWS 20 UN UNESCO ILO   ADJUD
NATO OAS. PAGE 58 E1158   INT/LAW

B62

KAUPER P.G.,CIVIL LIBERTIES AND THE CONSTITUTION.   LAW
USA+45 SECT EDU/PROP WRITING ADJUD SEX ORD/FREE 20   CONSTN
SUPREME/CT CIVIL/LIB CHURCH/STA. PAGE 60 E1188   CT/SYS
DECISION

B62

KIDDER F.E.,THESES ON PAN AMERICAN TOPICS. LAW   BIBLIOG
CULTURE NAT/G SECT DIPLOM HEALTH...ART/METH GEOG   CHRIST-17C
SOC 13/20. PAGE 61 E1213   L/A+17C
SOCIETY

B62

LEVY H.V.,LIBERDADE E JUSTICA SOCIAL (2ND ED.).   ORD/FREE
BRAZIL COM L/A+17C USSR INT/ORG PARTIC GP/REL   MARXISM
WEALTH 20 UN COM/PARTY. PAGE 65 E1290   CAP/ISM
LAW

B62

MCGRATH J.J.,CHURCH AND STATE IN AMERICAN LAW. LAW   SECT
PROVS SCHOOL TAX GIVE CT/SYS GP/REL...POLICY ANTHOL   ADJUD
18/20 SUPREME/CT CHURCH/STA CASEBOOK. PAGE 71 E1414   CONSTN
NAT/G

B62

MCGRATH J.J.,CHURCH AND STATE IN AMERICAN LAW: LAW
CASES AND MATERIALS. USA+45 USA-45 LEGIS EDU/PROP   GOV/REL
ADJUD CT/SYS PWR...ANTHOL 18/20 CHURCH/STA. PAGE 71   SECT
E1415

B62

MITCHELL G.E.,THE ANGRY BLACK SOUTH. USA+45 LAW   RACE/REL
CONSTN SCHOOL DELIB/GP EDU/PROP CONTROL SUFF ANOMIE   DISCRIM
DRIVE...ANTHOL 20 NEGRO CIV/RIGHTS SOUTH/US.   ADJUST
PAGE 74 E1473   ORD/FREE

B62

MURPHY W.F.,CONGRESS AND THE COURT. USA+45 LAW   LEGIS
LOBBY GP/REL RACE/REL ATTIT PWR...JURID INT BIBLIOG   CT/SYS
CONGRESS SUPREME/CT WARRN/EARL. PAGE 75 E1509   GOV/REL
ADJUD

B62

NEW YORK STATE LEGISLATURE,REPORT AND DRAFT OF   CT/SYS
PROPOSED LEGISLATION ON COURT REORGANIZATION. LAW   JURID
PROVS DELIB/GP CREATE ADJUD 20 NEW/YORK. PAGE 77   MUNIC
E1538   LOC/G

B62

OTTENBERG M.,THE FEDERAL INVESTIGATORS. USA+45 LAW   FORCES
COM/IND DIST/IND WORKER DIPLOM INT/TRADE CONTROL   INSPECT
FEDERAL HEALTH ORD/FREE FBI CIA FTC SEC FDA.   NAT/G
PAGE 79 E1585   CRIME

B62

PAIKERT G.C.,THE GERMAN EXODUS. EUR+WWI GERMANY/W   INGP/REL
LAW CULTURE SOCIETY STRUCT INDUS NAT/LISM RESPECT   STRANGE
SOVEREIGN...CHARTS BIBLIOG SOC/INTEG 20 MIGRATION.   GEOG
PAGE 79 E1591   GP/REL

B62

PRESS C.,STATE MANUALS, BLUE BOOKS AND ELECTION   BIBLIOG
RESULTS. LAW LOC/G MUNIC LEGIS WRITING FEDERAL   PROVS
SOVEREIGN...DECISION STAT CHARTS 20. PAGE 82 E1648   ADMIN
CHOOSE

B62

RICE C.E.,FREEDOM OF ASSOCIATION. USA+45 USA-45   LAW
POL/PAR LOBBY GP/REL...JURID BIBLIOG 18/20   NAT/G
SUPREME/CT PRE/US/AM. PAGE 84 E1691   CONSTN

B62

ROSENNE S.,THE WORLD COURT: WHAT IT IS AND HOW IT   INT/ORG
WORKS. WOR+45 WOR-45 LAW CONSTN JUDGE EDU/PROP   ADJUD
LEGIT ROUTINE CHOOSE PEACE ORD/FREE...JURID OBS   INT/LAW
TIME/SEQ CHARTS UN TOT/POP VAL/FREE 20. PAGE 86
E1717

B62

SCHWARZENBERGER G.,THE FRONTIERS OF INTERNATIONAL   INT/ORG
LAW. WOR+45 WOR-45 NAT/G LEGIT CT/SYS ROUTINE MORAL   LAW
ORD/FREE PWR...JURID SOC GEN/METH 20 COLD/WAR.   INT/LAW
PAGE 89 E1789

B62

SIGLIANO R E.,THE COURTS. USA+45 USA-45 LAW CONSTN   ADJUD
NAT/G ROUTINE CHOOSE 18/20 SUPREME/CT. PAGE 91   PROB/SOLV
E1825   CT/SYS
JUDGE

B62

SILVA R.C.,RUM, RELIGION, AND VOTES: 1928 RE-   POL/PAR
EXAMINED. USA-45 LAW SECT DISCRIM CATHISM...CORREL   CHOOSE
STAT 20 PRESIDENT SMITH/ALF DEMOCRAT. PAGE 91 E1827   GP/COMP
ATTIT

B62

SOWLE C.R.,POLICE POWER AND INDIVIDUAL FREEDOM: THE   FORCES
QUEST FOR BALANCE. CANADA EUR+WWI ISRAEL NORWAY   ORD/FREE
USA+45 LAW CONSTN SOCIETY CONTROL ROUTINE SANCTION   IDEA/COMP
GP/REL 20 CHINJAP. PAGE 93 E1859

B62

STERN A.C.,AIR POLLUTION (2 VOLS.). LAW INDUS   AIR
PROB/SOLV TEC/DEV INSPECT RISK BIO/SOC HABITAT   OP/RES
...OBS/ENVIR TESTS SAMP 20 POLLUTION. PAGE 93 E1871   CONTROL
HEALTH

B62

TAPER B.,GOMILLION VERSUS LIGHTFOOT: THE TUSKEGEE   APPORT
GERRYMANDER CASE. USA+45 LAW CONSTN LOC/G MUNIC   REPRESENT
CT/SYS 20 NEGRO CIV/RIGHTS GOMILLN/CG LIGHTFT/PM   RACE/REL
TUSKEGEE. PAGE 95 E1908   ADJUD

B62

THOMPSON K.W.,AMERICAN DIPLOMACY AND EMERGENT   NAT/G
PATTERNS. USA+45 USA-45 WOR+45 WOR-45 LAW DELIB/GP   BAL/PWR
FORCES TOP/EX DIPLOM ATTIT DRIVE RIGID/FLEX
ORD/FREE PWR SOVEREIGN...POLICY 20. PAGE 96 E1922

B62

TRISKA J.F.,THE THEORY, LAW, AND POLICY OF SOVIET   COM
TREATIES. WOR+45 WOR-45 CONSTN INT/ORG NAT/G   LAW
VOL/ASSN DOMIN LEGIT COERCE ATTIT PWR RESPECT   INT/LAW
...POLICY JURID CONCPT OBS SAMP TIME/SEQ TREND   USSR
GEN/LAWS 20. PAGE 97 E1941

B62

UNECA LIBRARY,NEW ACQUISITIONS IN THE UNECA   BIBLIOG
LIBRARY. LAW NAT/G PLAN PROB/SOLV TEC/DEV ADMIN   AFR
REGION...GEOG SOC 20 UN. PAGE 98 E1956   ECO/UNDEV
INT/ORG

B62

US COMMISSION ON CIVIL RIGHTS,EQUAL PROTECTION OF   ORD/FREE
THE LAWS IN NORTH CAROLINA. USA+45 LOC/G NAT/G   RESPECT
CONSULT LEGIS WORKER PROB/SOLV EDU/PROP ADJUD   LAW
CHOOSE DISCRIM HEALTH 20 NEGRO NORTH/CAR   PROVS
CIV/RIGHTS. PAGE 99 E1984

B62

US COMMISSION ON CIVIL RIGHTS,HEARINGS BEFORE   ORD/FREE
UNITED STATES COMMISSION ON CIVIL RIGHTS. USA+45   LAW
ECO/DEV NAT/G CONSULT WORKER EDU/PROP ADJUD DISCRIM   ADMIN
ISOLAT HABITAT HEALTH RESPECT 20 NEGRO CIV/RIGHTS.   LEGIS
PAGE 99 E1985

B62

US CONGRESS,COMMUNICATIONS SATELLITE LEGISLATION: SPACE
HEARINGS BEFORE COMM ON AERON AND SPACE SCIENCES ON   COM/IND
BILLS S2550 AND 2814. WOR+45 LAW VOL/ASSN PLAN   ADJUD
DIPLOM CONTROL OWN PEACE...NEW/IDEA CONGRESS NASA.   GOV/REL
PAGE 99 E1990

WINTERS J.M.,"INTERSTATE METROPOLITAN AREAS. CONSTN LEAD CHOOSE PWR DECISION. PAGE 107 E2135
MUNIC LAW REGION GOV/REL
B62

"AMERICAN BEHAVIORAL SCIENTIST." USSR LAW NAT/G ...SOC 20 UN. PAGE 2 E0034
BIBLIOG AFR R+D
L62

CORET A.,"L'INDEPENDANCE DU SAMOA OCCIDENTAL." S/ASIA LAW INT/ORG EXEC ALL/VALS SAMOA UN 20. PAGE 26 E0508
NAT/G STRUCT SOVEREIGN
L62

GROSS L.,"IMMUNITIES AND PRIVILEGES OF DELIGATIONS TO THE UNITED NATIONS." USA+45 WOR+45 STRATA NAT/G VOL/ASSN CONSULT DIPLOM EDU/PROP ROUTINE RESPECT ...POLICY INT/LAW CONCPT UN 20. PAGE 48 E0950
INT/ORG LAW ELITES
L62

N.,"UNION INVESTMENT IN BUSINESS: A SOURCE OF UNION CONFLICT OF INTEREST." LAW NAT/G LEGIS CONTROL GP/REL INGP/REL DECISION. PAGE 76 E1515
LABOR POLICY FINAN LG/CO
L62

PETKOFF D.K.,"RECOGNITION AND NON-RECOGNITION OF STATES AND GOVERNMENTS IN INTERNATIONAL LAW." ASIA COM USA+45 WOR+45 NAT/G ACT/RES DIPLOM DOMIN LEGIT COERCE ORD/FREE PWR...CONCPT GEN/LAWS 20. PAGE 80 E1611
INT/ORG LAW INT/LAW
L62

SCHWERIN K.,"LAW LIBRARIES AND FOREIGN LAW COLLECTION IN THE USA." USA+45 USA-45...INT/LAW STAT 20. PAGE 89 E1793
BIBLIOG LAW ACADEM ADMIN
L62

UNITED NATIONS,"CAPITAL PUNISHMENT." WOR+45 CULTURE NAT/G ROUTINE COERCE HEALTH PWR...POLICY SOC QU CHARTS VAL/FREE 20. PAGE 98 E1967
LAW STAT
L62

BIERZANECK R.,"LA NON-RECONAISSANCE ET LE DROIT INTERNATIONAL CONTEMPORAIN." EUR+WWI FUT WOR+45 LAW ECO/DEV ATTIT RIGID/FLEX...CONCPT TIME/SEQ TOT/POP 20. PAGE 12 E0228
EDU/PROP JURID DIPLOM INT/LAW
S62

CRANE R.D.,"LAW AND STRATEGY IN SPACE." FUT USA+45 WOR+45 AIR LAW INT/ORG NAT/G FORCES ACT/RES PLAN BAL/PWR LEGIT ARMS/CONT COERCE ORD/FREE...POLICY INT/LAW JURID SOC/EXP 20 TREATY. PAGE 27 E0542
CONCPT SPACE
S62

CRANE R.D.,"SOVIET ATTITUDE TOWARD INTERNATIONAL SPACE LAW." COM FUT USA+45 USSR AIR CONSTN DELIB/GP DOMIN PWR...JURID TREND TOT/POP 20. PAGE 27 E0543
LAW ATTIT INT/LAW SPACE
S62

GANDOLFI A.,"REFLEXIONS SUR L'IMPOT DE CAPITATION EN AFRIQUE NOIRE." GHANA SENEGAL LAW FINAN ACT/RES TEC/DEV ECO/TAC WEALTH...MGT TREND 20. PAGE 42 E0830
AFR CHOOSE
S62

GREEN L.C.,"POLITICAL OFFENSES, WAR CRIMES AND EXTRADITION." WOR+45 YUGOSLAVIA INT/ORG LEGIT ROUTINE WAR ORD/FREE SOVEREIGN...JURID NAZI 20 INTERPOL. PAGE 46 E0906
LAW CONCPT INT/LAW
S62

GREENSPAN M.,"INTERNATIONAL LAW AND ITS PROTECTION FOR PARTICIPANTS IN UNCONVENTIONAL WARFARE." WOR+45 LAW INT/ORG NAT/G POL/PAR COERCE REV ORD/FREE ...INT/LAW TOT/POP 20. PAGE 46 E0912
FORCES JURID GUERRILLA WAR
S62

JOHNSON O.H.,"THE ENGLISH TRADITION IN INTERNATIONAL LAW." CHRIST-17C MOD/EUR EDU/PROP LEGIT CT/SYS ORD/FREE...JURID CONCPT TIME/SEQ. PAGE 59 E1170
LAW INT/LAW UK
S62

LISSITZYN O.J.,"SOME LEGAL IMPLICATIONS OF THE U-2 AND RB-47 INCIDENTS." FUT USA+45 WOR+45 AIR NAT/G DIPLOM LEGIT MORAL ORD/FREE SOVEREIGN...JURID GEN/LAWS GEN/METH COLD/WAR 20 U-2. PAGE 65 E1305
LAW CONCPT SPACE INT/LAW
S62

MANGIN G.,"LES ACCORDS DE COOPERATION EN MATIERE DE
INT/ORG
S62

JUSTICE ENTRE LA FRANCE ET LES ETATS AFRICAINS ET MALGACHE." AFR ISLAM WOR+45 STRUCT ECO/UNDEV NAT/G DELIB/GP PERCEPT ALL/VALS...JURID MGT TIME/SEQ 20. PAGE 68 E1356
LAW FRANCE

SCHUBERT G.,"THE 1960 TERM OF THE SUPREME COURT: A PSYCHOLOGICAL ANALYSIS." USA+45 LAW CT/SYS...STAT SUPREME/CT. PAGE 88 E1772
DECISION LEGIS JUDGE EX/STRUC
S62

SILVA R.C.,"LEGISLATIVE REPESENTATION - WITH SPECIAL REFERENCE TO NEW YORK." LAW CONSTN LOC/G NAT/G PROVS. PAGE 91 E1826
MUNIC LEGIS REPRESENT APPORT
S62

VIGNES D.,"L'AUTORITE DES TRAITES INTERNATIONAUX EN DROIT INTERNE." EUR+WWI UNIV LAW CONSTN INTELL NAT/G POL/PAR DIPLOM ATTIT PERCEPT ALL/VALS ...POLICY INT/LAW JURID CONCPT TIME/SEQ 20 TREATY. PAGE 104 E2075
STRUCT LEGIT FRANCE
S62

ABRAHAM H.J.,"THE JUDICIAL PROCESS." USA+45 USA-45 LAW NAT/G ADMIN CT/SYS INGP/REL RACE/REL DISCRIM ...JURID IDEA/COMP 19/20. PAGE 2 E0046
BIBLIOG CONSTN JUDGE ADJUD
C62

BACON F.,"OF JUDICATURE" (1612) IN F. BACON, ESSAYS." ADJUD ADMIN SANCTION CRIME PWR...JURID GEN/LAWS. PAGE 7 E0128
CT/SYS LEGIS LAW
C62

MORGAN G.G.,"SOVIET ADMINISTRATIVE LEGALITY: THE ROLE OF THE ATTORNEY GENERAL'S OFFICE." COM USSR CONTROL ROUTINE...CONCPT BIBLIOG 18/20. PAGE 74 E1493
LAW CONSTN LEGIS ADMIN
C62

VAN DER SPRENKEL S.,"LEGAL INSTITUTIONS IN MANCHU CHINA." ASIA STRUCT CT/SYS ROUTINE GOV/REL GP/REL ...CONCPT BIBLIOG 17/20. PAGE 103 E2068
LAW JURID ADMIN ADJUD
C62

US ADVISORY COMN INTERGOV REL,APPORTIONMENT OF STATE LEGISLATURES (PAMPHLET). LAW CONSTN EX/STRUC LEGIS LEAD MAJORITY. PAGE 99 E1977
MUNIC PROVS REPRESENT APPORT
N62

BLACK C.L. JR.,THE OCCASIONS OF JUSTICE: ESSAYS MOSTLY ON LAW. USA+45 JUDGE RACE/REL DISCRIM ATTIT MORAL ORD/FREE 20 SUPREME/CT BLACK. PAGE 12 E0236
JURID CONSTN CT/SYS LAW
B63

BLOCK E.B.,THE VINDICATORS. LAW FORCES CT/SYS DISCRIM 19/20. PAGE 13 E0247
ATTIT CRIME ADJUD CRIMLGY
B63

BOWIE R.R.,GOVERNMENT REGULATION OF BUSINESS: CASES FROM THE NATIONAL REPORTER SYSTEM. USA+45 USA-45 NAT/G ECO/TAC ADJUD...ANTHOL 19/20 SUPREME/CT FTC FAIR/LABOR MONOPOLY. PAGE 14 E0280
LAW CONTROL INDUS CT/SYS
B63

CAHN E.,THE GREAT RIGHTS. USA+45 NAT/G PROVS CIVMIL/REL...IDEA/COMP ANTHOL BIBLIOG 18/20 MADISON/J BILL/RIGHT CIV/RIGHTS WARRN/EARL BLACK/HL. PAGE 18 E0361
CONSTN LAW ORD/FREE INGP/REL
B63

CHOJNACKI S.,REGISTER ON CURRENT RESEARCH ON ETHIOPIA AND THE HORN OF AFRICA. ETHIOPIA LAW CULTURE AGRI SECT EDU/PROP ADMIN...GEOG HEAL LING 20. PAGE 22 E0433
BIBLIOG ACT/RES INTELL ACADEM
B63

CRAIG A.,SUPPRESSED BOOKS: A HISTORY OF THE CONCEPTION OF LITERARY OBSCENITY. WOR+45 WOR-45 CREATE EDU/PROP LITERACY ATTIT...ART/METH PSY CONCPT 20. PAGE 27 E0538
BIBLIOG/A LAW SEX CONTROL
B63

DECOTTIGNIES R.,LES NATIONALITES AFRICAINES. AFR NAT/G PROB/SOLV DIPLOM COLONIAL ORD/FREE...CHARTS GOV/COMP 20. PAGE 30 E0602
NAT/LISM JURID LEGIS LAW
B63

DOUGLAS W.O.,THE ANATOMY OF LIBERTY: THE RIGHTS OF
MAN WITHOUT FORCE. WOR+45 ECO/DEV ECO/UNDEV LOC/G
FORCES GOV/REL...SOC/WK 20. PAGE 32 E0643
PEACE
LAW
DIPLOM
ORD/FREE
B63

DUNHAM A.,MR. JUSTICE. ADJUD PWR...JURID ANTHOL
18/20 SUPREME/CT. PAGE 33 E0659
BIOG
PERSON
LAW
CT/SYS
B63

EDDY J.P.,JUSTICE OF THE PEACE. UK LAW CONSTN
CULTURE 14/20 COMMON/LAW. PAGE 34 E0674
CRIME
JURID
CT/SYS
ADJUD
B63

ELIAS T.O.,GOVERNMENT AND POLITICS IN AFRICA.
CONSTN CULTURE SOCIETY NAT/G POL/PAR DIPLOM
REPRESENT PERSON...SOC TREND BIBLIOG 4/20. PAGE 34
E0681
AFR
NAT/LISM
COLONIAL
LAW
B63

ELIAS T.O.,THE NIGERIAN LEGAL SYSTEM. NIGERIA LAW
FAM KIN SECT ADMIN NAT/LISM...JURID 18/20
ENGLSH/LAW COMMON/LAW. PAGE 34 E0682
CT/SYS
ADJUD
COLONIAL
PROF/ORG
B63

FALK R.A.,LAW, MORALITY, AND WAR IN THE
CONTEMPORARY WORLD. WOR+45 LAW INT/ORG EX/STRUC
FORCES EDU/PROP LEGIT DETER NUC/PWR MORAL ORD/FREE
...JURID TOT/POP 20. PAGE 36 E0715
ADJUD
ARMS/CONT
PEACE
INT/LAW
B63

FAWCETT J.E.S.,THE BRITISH COMMONWEALTH IN
INTERNATIONAL LAW. LAW INT/ORG NAT/G VOL/ASSN
OP/RES DIPLOM ADJUD CENTRAL CONSEN...NET/THEORY
CMN/WLTH TREATY. PAGE 36 E0723
INT/LAW
STRUCT
COLONIAL
B63

FISCHER-GALATI S.A.,RUMANIA: A BIBLIOGRAPHIC GUIDE
(PAMPHLET). ROMANIA INTELL ECO/DEV LABOR SECT
WEALTH...GEOG SOC/WK LING 20. PAGE 38 E0756
BIBLIOG/A
NAT/G
COM
LAW
B63

FRIEDRICH C.J.,JUSTICE: NOMOS VI. UNIV LAW SANCTION
CRIME...CONCPT ANTHOL MARX/KARL LOCKE/JOHN
AQUINAS/T. PAGE 41 E0809
LEGIT
ADJUD
ORD/FREE
JURID
B63

GARNER U.F.,ADMINISTRATIVE LAW. UK LAW LOC/G NAT/G
EX/STRUC LEGIS JUDGE BAL/PWR BUDGET ADJUD CONTROL
CT/SYS...BIBLIOG 20. PAGE 42 E0840
ADMIN
JURID
PWR
GOV/REL
B63

GEERTZ C.,OLD SOCIETIES AND NEW STATES: THE QUEST
FOR MODERNITY IN ASIA AND AFRICA. AFR ASIA LAW
CULTURE SECT EDU/PROP REV...GOV/COMP NAT/COMP 20.
PAGE 42 E0842
ECO/UNDEV
TEC/DEV
NAT/LISM
SOVEREIGN
B63

GINZBERG E.,DEMOCRATIC VALUES AND THE RIGHTS OF
MANAGEMENT. LAW CONSTN REPRESENT GP/REL ROLE PWR
RESPECT POLICY. PAGE 44 E0870
LABOR
MGT
DELIB/GP
ADJUD
B63

GOURNAY B.,PUBLIC ADMINISTRATION. FRANCE LAW CONSTN
AGRI FINAN LABOR SCHOOL EX/STRUC CHOOSE...MGT
METH/COMP 20. PAGE 45 E0894
BIBLIOG/A
ADMIN
NAT/G
LOC/G
B63

GSOUSKI V.,LEGAL SOURCES AND BIBLIOGRAPHY OF THE
BALTIC STATES (ESTONIA, LATVIA, LITHUANIA). COM
ESTONIA LATVIA LITHUANIA NAT/G LEGIS CT/SYS
SANCTION CRIME 20. PAGE 48 E0957
BIBLIOG
ADJUD
LAW
JURID
B63

HALEY A.G.,SPACE LAW AND GOVERNMENT. FUT USA+45
WOR+45 LEGIS ACT/RES CREATE ATTIT RIGID/FLEX
ORD/FREE PWR SOVEREIGN...POLICY JURID CONCPT CHARTS
VAL/FREE 20. PAGE 49 E0980
INT/ORG
LAW
SPACE
B63

HALL J.,COMPARATIVE LAW AND SOCIAL THEORY. WOR+45
CONSTN CULTURE DOMIN CT/SYS ORD/FREE...PLURIST
JURID CONCPT NEW/IDEA GEN/LAWS VAL/FREE. PAGE 49
E0984
LAW
SOC
B63

HAUSMAN W.H.,MANAGING ECONOMIC DEVELOPMENT IN
AFRICA. AFR USA+45 LAW FINAN WORKER TEC/DEV WEALTH
...ANTHOL 20. PAGE 51 E1012
ECO/UNDEV
PLAN
FOR/AID
MGT
B63

HORRELL M.,LEGISLATION AND RACE RELATIONS
(PAMPHLET). SOUTH/AFR SCHOOL TAX DOMIN CONTROL 20.
PAGE 55 E1098
LAW
RACE/REL
DISCRIM
PARTIC
B63

HOWARD W.S.,AMERICAN SLAVERS AND THE FEDERAL LAW:
1837-1862. USA-45 NAT/G LEGIT COERCE RACE/REL
WEALTH...POLICY BIBLIOG/A 19. PAGE 55 E1102
DIST/IND
CRIMLGY
LAW
EXEC
B63

JOSEPH H.,IF THIS BE TREASON. SOUTH/AFR 20. PAGE 59
E1174
AFR
LAW
CT/SYS
CRIME
B63

KLESMENT J.,LEGAL SOURCES AND BIBLIOGRAPHY OF THE
BALTIC STATES (ESTONIA, LATVIA, LITHUANIA). COM
ESTONIA LATVIA LITHUANIA LAW FINAN ADJUD CT/SYS
REGION CENTRAL MARXISM 19/20. PAGE 61 E1223
BIBLIOG/A
JURID
CONSTN
ADMIN
B63

A BIBLIOGRAPHY OF DOCTORAL DISSERTATIONS UNDERTAKEN
IN AMERICAN AND CANADIAN UNIVERSITIES ON RELIGION
AND POLITICS. LAW CONSTN DOMIN LEGIT ADJUD GP/REL
...POLICY 20. PAGE 62 E1241
BIBLIOG
ACADEM
SECT
JURID
B63

LAVROFF D.-.G.,LES LIBERTES PUBLIQUES EN UNION
SOVIETIQUE (REV. ED.). USSR NAT/G WORKER SANCTION
CRIME MARXISM NEW/LIB...JURID BIBLIOG WORSHIP 20.
PAGE 63 E1268
ORD/FREE
LAW
ATTIT
COM
B63

LEGISLATIVE REFERENCE SERVICE.DIGEST OF PUBLIC
GENERAL BILLS AND RESOLUTIONS. LAW COM/IND EDU/PROP
GOV/REL INGP/REL KNOWL...JURID 20 CONGRESS. PAGE 64
E1280
BIBLIOG/A
LEGIS
DELIB/GP
NAT/G
B63

LEVY L.W.,JEFFERSON AND CIVIL LIBERTIES: THE DARKER
SIDE. USA-45 LAW INTELL ACADEM FORCES PRESS REV
INGP/REL PERSON 18/19 JEFFERSN/T CIVIL/LIB. PAGE 65
E1291
BIOG
ORD/FREE
CONSTN
ATTIT
B63

LEWIN J.,POLITICS AND LAW IN SOUTH AFRICA.
SOUTH/AFR UK POL/PAR BAL/PWR ECO/TAC COLONIAL
CONTROL GP/REL DISCRIM PWR 20 NEGRO. PAGE 65 E1293
NAT/LISM
POLICY
LAW
RACE/REL
B63

LIVELY E.,THE INVASION OF MISSISSIPPI. USA+45 LAW
CONSTN NAT/G PROVS CT/SYS GOV/REL FEDERAL CONSERVE
...TRADIT 20 MISSISSIPP NEGRO NAACP WARRN/EARL
KENNEDY/JF. PAGE 66 E1309
RACE/REL
CROWD
COERCE
MARXISM
B63

LIVNEH E.,ISRAEL LEGAL BIBLIOGRAPHY IN EUROPEAN
LANGUAGES. ISRAEL LOC/G JUDGE TAX...INT/LAW 20.
PAGE 66 E1311
BIBLIOG
LAW
NAT/G
CONSTN
B63

LYONS F.S.L.,INTERNATIONALISM IN EUROPE 1815-1914.
LAW AGRI COM/IND DIST/IND LABOR SECT INT/TRADE
TARIFFS...BIBLIOG 19/20. PAGE 67 E1335
DIPLOM
MOD/EUR
INT/ORG
B63

MOLLARD P.T.,LE REGIME JURIDIQUE DE LA PRESSE AU
MAROC. MOROCCO CONTROL CRIME GP/REL ORD/FREE 20.
PAGE 74 E1482
PRESS
LAW
LEAD
LEGIT
B63

MURPHY T.J.,CENSORSHIP: GOVERNMENT AND OBSCENITY.
USA+45 CULTURE LEGIS JUDGE EDU/PROP CONTROL
INGP/REL RATIONAL POPULISM...CATH JURID 20. PAGE 75
E1507
ORD/FREE
MORAL
LAW
CONSEN
B63

NATIONAL CIVIC REVIEW.REAPPORTIONMENT: A YEAR IN
REVIEW (PAMPHLET). USA+45 LAW CT/SYS CHOOSE
ORD/FREE PWR...ANTHOL 20 CONGRESS. PAGE 76 E1527
APPORT
REPRESENT
LEGIS
CONSTN
B63

NEWMAN E.S.,THE FREEDOM READER. USA+45 LEGIS TOP/EX RACE/REL
PLAN ADJUD CONTROL CT/SYS DISCRIM...DECISION ANTHOL   LAW
20 SUPREME/CT CIV/RIGHTS. PAGE 77 E1541   POLICY
                                                     ORD/FREE
                                          B63

OTTOSON H.W.,LAND USE POLICY AND PROBLEMS IN THE   PROB/SOLV
UNITED STATES. USA+45 USA-45 LAW AGRI INDUS NAT/G   UTIL
GP/REL...CHARTS ANTHOL 19/20 HOMEST/ACT. PAGE 79   HABITAT
E1586   POLICY
                                          B63

PALOTAI O.C.,PUBLICATIONS OF THE INSTITUTE OF   BIBLIOG/A
GOVERNMENT, 1930-1962. LAW PROVS SCHOOL WORKER   ADMIN
ACT/RES OP/RES CT/SYS GOV/REL...CRIMLGY SOC/WK.   LOC/G
PAGE 79 E1594   FINAN
                                          B63

PRITCHETT C.H.,THE ROOSEVELT COURT. USA+45 LAW   DECISION
INGP/REL...CHARTS 20 SUPREME/CT. PAGE 82 E1653   PROB/SOLV
                                                     CT/SYS
                                                     JURID
                                          B63

PRYOR F.L.,THE COMMUNIST FOREIGN TRADE SYSTEM. COM   ATTIT
CZECHOSLVK GERMANY YUGOSLAVIA LAW ECO/DEV DIST/IND   ECO/TAC
POL/PAR PLAN DOMIN TOTALISM DRIVE RIGID/FLEX WEALTH
...STAT STAND/INT CHARTS 20. PAGE 83 E1657
                                          B63

ROYAL INSTITUTE PUBLIC ADMIN,BRITISH PUBLIC   BIBLIOG
ADMINISTRATION. UK LAW FINAN INDUS LOC/G POL/PAR   ADMIN
LEGIS LOBBY PARL/PROC CHOOSE JURID. PAGE 86 E1729   MGT
                                                     NAT/G
                                          B63

SARTORI G.,IL PARLAMENTO ITALIANO: 1946-1963. LAW   LEGIS
CONSTN ELITES POL/PAR LOBBY PRIVIL ATTIT PERSON   PARL/PROC
MORAL PWR SOC. PAGE 87 E1746   REPRESENT
                                          B63

SCHMIDHAUSER J.R.,CONSTITUTIONAL LAW IN THE   LAW
POLITICAL PROCESS. SOCIETY LEGIS ADJUD CT/SYS   CONSTN
FEDERAL...SOC TREND IDEA/COMP ANTHOL T SUPREME/CT   JURID
SENATE CONGRESS HOUSE/REP. PAGE 88 E1761
                                          B63

SCHUMAN S.I.,LEGAL POSITIVISM: ITS SCOPE AND   GEN/METH
LIMITATIONS. CONSTN NAT/G DIPLOM PARTIC UTOPIA   LAW
...POLICY DECISION PHIL/SCI CONCPT 20. PAGE 89   METH/COMP
E1784
                                          B63

TUSSMAN J.,THE SUPREME COURT ON RACIAL   CT/SYS
DISCRIMINATION. USA+45 USA-45 NAT/G PROB/SOLV ADJUD   DISCRIM
RACE/REL ORD/FREE...JURID 20 SUPREME/CT CIV/RIGHTS.   ATTIT
PAGE 97 E1946   LAW
                                          B63

US COMMISSION ON CIVIL RIGHTS,FREEDOM TO THE FREE.   RACE/REL
USA+45 USA-45 LAW VOL/ASSN CT/SYS ATTIT PWR...JURID   DISCRIM
BIBLIOG 17/20 SUPREME/CT NEGRO CIV/RIGHTS. PAGE 99   NAT/G
E1986   POLICY
                                          B63

US COMN CIVIL RIGHTS,REPORT ON MISSISSIPPI. LAW   RACE/REL
LOC/G NAT/G LEGIS PLAN PROB/SOLV DISCRIM SOC/INTEG   CONSTN
20 MISSISSIPP NEGRO. PAGE 99 E1987   ORD/FREE
                                                     COERCE
                                          B63

US CONGRESS: SENATE,HEARINGS OF THE COMMITTEE ON   LEGIS
THE JUDICIARY. USA+45 CONSTN NAT/G ADMIN GOV/REL 20   LAW
CONGRESS. PAGE 99 E1992   ORD/FREE
                                                     DELIB/GP
                                          B63

US SENATE COMM ON JUDICIARY,CASTRO'S NETWORK IN THE   PRESS
UNITED STATES. CUBA LAW DELIB/GP 20 SENATE   MARXISM
CASTRO/F. PAGE 102 E2050   DIPLOM
                                                     INSPECT
                                          B63

US SENATE COMM ON JUDICIARY,PACIFICA FOUNDATION.   DELIB/GP
USA+45 LAW COM/IND 20 ODEGARD/P BINNS/JJ SCHINDLR/P   EDU/PROP
HEALEY/D THOMAS/TK. PAGE 102 E2051   ORD/FREE
                                                     ATTIT
                                          B63

YOUNGER R.D.,THE PEOPLE'S PANEL: THE GRAND JURY IN   CT/SYS
THE UNITED STATES, 1634-1941. USA-45 LAW LEGIT   JURID
CONTROL TASK GP/REL ROLE...TREND 17/20 GRAND/JURY.   CONSTN
PAGE 108 E2166   LOC/G

                                          L63

BOLGAR V.,"THE PUBLIC INTEREST: A JURISPRUDENTIAL   CONCPT
AND COMPARATIVE OVERVIEW OF SYMPOSIUM ON   ORD/FREE
FUNDAMENTAL CONCEPTS OF PUBLIC LAW" COM FRANCE   CONTROL
GERMANY SWITZERLND LAW ADJUD ADMIN AGREE LAISSEZ   NAT/COMP
...JURID GEN/LAWS 20 EUROPE/E. PAGE 14 E0264
                                          L63

LISSITZYN O.J.,"INTERNATIONAL LAW IN A DIVIDED   INT/ORG
WORLD." FUT WOR+45 CONSTN CULTURE ECO/DEV ECO/UNDEV   LAW
DIST/IND NAT/G FORCES ECO/TAC LEGIT ADJUD ADMIN
COERCE ATTIT HEALTH MORAL ORD/FREE PWR RESPECT
WEALTH VAL/FREE. PAGE 65 E1306
                                          L63

MCDOUGAL M.S.,"THE ENJOYMENT AND ACQUISITION OF   PLAN
RESOURCES IN OUTER SPACE." CHRIST-17C FUT WOR+45   TREND
WOR-45 LAW EXTR/IND INT/ORG ACT/RES CREATE TEC/DEV
ECO/TAC LEGIT COERCE HEALTH KNOWL ORD/FREE PWR
WEALTH...JURID HIST/WRIT VAL/FREE. PAGE 70 E1408
                                          L63

ROSE R.,"COMPARATIVE STUDIES IN POLITICAL FINANCE: FINAN
A SYMPOSIUM." ASIA EUR+WWI S/ASIA LAW CULTURE   POL/PAR
DELIB/GP LEGIS ACT/RES ECO/TAC EDU/PROP CHOOSE
ATTIT RIGID/FLEX SUPEGO PWR SKILL WEALTH...STAT
ANTHOL VAL/FREE. PAGE 85 E1714
                                          S63

ALGER C.F.,"HYPOTHESES ON RELATIONSHIPS BETWEEN THE   INT/ORG
ORGANIZATION OF INTERNATIONAL SOCIETY AND   LAW
INTERNATIONAL ORDER." WOR+45 WOR-45 ORD/FREE PWR
...JURID GEN/LAWS VAL/FREE 20. PAGE 3 E0066
                                          S63

BECHHOEFER B.G.,"UNITED NATIONS PROCEDURES IN CASE   INT/ORG
OF VIOLATIONS OF DISARMAMENT AGREEMENTS." COM   DELIB/GP
USA+45 USSR LAW CONSTN NAT/G EX/STRUC FORCES LEGIS
BAL/PWR EDU/PROP CT/SYS ARMS/CONT ORD/FREE PWR
...POLICY STERTYP UN VAL/FREE 20. PAGE 9 E0169
                                          S63

BERMAN H.J.,"THE DILEMMA OF SOVIET LAW REFORM."   COM
NAT/G POL/PAR CT/SYS ALL/VALS ORD/FREE PWR...POLICY   LAW
JURID VAL/FREE 20. PAGE 11 E0208   USSR
                                          S63

BRAUSCH G.E.,"AFRICAN ETHNOCRACIES: SOME   LAW
SOCIOLOGICAL IMPLICATIONS OF CONSTITUTIONAL CHANGE   SOC
IN EMERGENT TERRITORIES OF AFRICA." AFR CONSTN   ELITES
FACE/GP MUNIC NAT/G DOMIN ATTIT ALL/VALS
...HIST/WRIT GEN/LAWS VAL/FREE 20. PAGE 15 E0289
                                          S63

CLEVELAND H.,"CRISIS DIPLOMACY." USA+45 WOR+45 LAW   DECISION
FORCES TASK NUC/PWR PWR 20. PAGE 23 E0454   DIPLOM
                                                     PROB/SOLV
                                                     POLICY
                                          S63

FRIEDMANN W.G.,"THE USES OF 'GENERAL PRINCIPLES' IN   LAW
THE DEVELOPMENT OF INTERNATIONAL LAW." WOR+45 NAT/G   INT/LAW
DIPLOM INT/TRADE LEGIT ROUTINE RIGID/FLEX ORD/FREE   INT/ORG
...JURID CONCPT STERTYP GEN/METH 20. PAGE 41 E0804
                                          S63

GARDNER R.N.,"COOPERATION IN OUTER SPACE." FUT USSR   INT/ORG
WOR+45 AIR LAW COM/IND CONSULT DELIB/GP CREATE   ACT/RES
KNOWL 20 TREATY. PAGE 42 E0837   PEACE
                                                     SPACE
                                          S63

HARNETTY P.,"CANADA, SOUTH AFRICA AND THE   AFR
COMMONWEALTH." CANADA SOUTH/AFR LAW INT/ORG   ATTIT
VOL/ASSN DELIB/GP LEGIS TOP/EX ECO/TAC LEGIT DRIVE
MORAL...CONCPT CMN/WLTH 20. PAGE 50 E1000
                                          S63

JOUGHIN L.,"ACADEMIC DUE PROCESS." DELIB/GP ADJUD   ACADEM
ROUTINE ORD/FREE...POLICY MAJORIT TREND. PAGE 59   LAW
E1175   PROF/ORG
                                                     CLIENT
                                          S63

MACWHINNEY E.,"LES CONCEPT SOVIETIQUE DE   NAT/G
'COEXISTENCE PACIFIQUE' ET LES RAPPORTS JURIDIQUES   CONCPT
ENTRE L'URSS ET LES ETATS OCIDENTAUX." COM FUT   DIPLOM
WOR+45 LAW CULTURE INTELL POL/PAR ACT/RES BAL/PWR   USSR
...INT/LAW 20. PAGE 67 E1346
                                          S63

NAGEL S.S.,"A CONCEPTUAL SCHEME OF THE JUDICIAL   POLICY
PROCESS." ADJUD...DECISION NEW/IDEA AVERAGE MODAL   LAW
CHARTS. PAGE 76 E1518   JURID
                                                     DISCRIM

RIGAUX F.,"LA SIGNIFICATION DES ACTES JUDICIARES A
L'ETRANGER." EUR+WWI ITALY NETHERLAND LAW ACT/RES
DRIVE...JURID GEN/LAWS TOT/POP 20. PAGE 85 E1699

S63
CONSULT
CT/SYS
GERMANY

TALLON D.,"L'ETUDE DU DROIT COMPARE COMME MOYEN DE
RECHERCHER LES MATIERES SUSCEPTIBLES D'UNIFICATION
INTERNATIONALE." WOR+45 LAW SOCIETY VOL/ASSN
CONSULT LEGIT CT/SYS RIGID/FLEX KNOWL 20. PAGE 95
E1906

S63
INT/ORG
JURID
INT/LAW

WEISSBERG G.,"MAPS AS EVIDENCE IN INTERNATIONAL
BOUNDARY DISPUTES: A REAPPRAISAL." CHINA/COM
EUR+WWI INDIA MOD/EUR S/ASIA INT/ORG NAT/G LEGIT
PERCEPT...JURID CHARTS 20. PAGE 105 E2110

S63
LAW
GEOG
SOVEREIGN

WENGLER W.,"LES CONFLITS DE LOIS ET LE PRINCIPE
D'EGALITE." UNIV LAW SOCIETY ACT/RES LEGIT ATTIT
PERCEPT 20. PAGE 105 E2111

S63
JURID
CONCPT
INT/LAW

US PRES COMN REGIS AND VOTING,REPORT ON
REGISTRATION AND VOTING (PAMPHLET). USA+45 POL/PAR
CHIEF EDU/PROP PARTIC REPRESENT ATTIT...PSY CHARTS
20. PAGE 101 E2023

N63
CHOOSE
LAW
SUFF
INSPECT

AHLUWALIA K.,THE LEGAL STATUS, PRIVILEGES AND
IMMUNITIES OF SPECIALIZED AGENCIES OF UN AND
CERTAIN OTHER INTERNATIONAL ORGANIZATIONS. WOR+45
LAW CONSULT DELIB/GP FORCES. PAGE 3 E0055

B64
PRIVIL
DIPLOM
INT/ORG
INT/LAW

ANDERSON J.W.,EISENHOWER, BROWNELL, AND THE
CONGRESS - THE TANGLED ORIGINS OF THE CIVIL RIGHTS
BILL OF 1956-1957. USA+45 POL/PAR LEGIS CREATE
PROB/SOLV LOBBY GOV/REL RIGID/FLEX...NEW/IDEA 20
EISNHWR/DD CONGRESS BROWNELL/H CIV/RIGHTS. PAGE 5
E0090

B64
LAW
CONSTN
POLICY
NAT/G

BECKER T.L.,POLITICAL BEHAVIORALISM AND MODERN
JURISPRUDENCE* A WORKING THEORY AND STUDY IN
JUDICIAL DECISION-MAKING. CONSTN...JURID STAT
GEN/METH INDEX. PAGE 9 E0172

B64
JUDGE
LAW
DECISION
CT/SYS

BENNETT H.A.,THE COMMISSION AND THE COMMON LAW: A
STUDY IN ADMINISTRATIVE ADJUDICATION. LAW ADMIN
CT/SYS LOBBY SANCTION GOV/REL 20 COMMON/LAW.
PAGE 10 E0188

B64
ADJUD
DELIB/GP
DIST/IND
POLICY

BERWANGER E.H.,WESTERN ANTI-NEGRO SENTIMENT AND
LAWS 1846-60: A FACTOR IN THE SLAVERY EXTENSION
CONTROVERSY (PAPER). USA-45 LAW CONSTN LEGIS ADJUD
...BIBLIOG 19 NEGRO. PAGE 11 E0218

B64
RACE/REL
REGION
DISCRIM
ORD/FREE

BLOUSTEIN E.J.,NUCLEAR ENERGY, PUBLIC POLICY, AND
THE LAW. USA+45 NAT/G ADJUD ADMIN GP/REL OWN PEACE
ATTIT HEALTH...ANTHOL 20. PAGE 13 E0251

B64
TEC/DEV
LAW
POLICY
NUC/PWR

BOGEN J.I.,FINANCIAL HANDBOOK (4TH ED.). UNIV LAW
PLAN TAX RISK 20. PAGE 13 E0257

B64
FINAN
DICTIONARY

BOWETT D.W.,UNITED NATIONS FORCES* A LEGAL STUDY.
CYPRUS ISRAEL KOREA LAW CONSTN ACT/RES CREATE
BUDGET CONTROL TASK PWR...INT/LAW IDEA/COMP UN
CONGO/LEOP SUEZ. PAGE 14 E0278

B64
OP/RES
FORCES
ARMS/CONT

BREVER E.H.,LEARNED HAND, JANUARY 27, 1872-AUGUST
18, 1961 (PAMPHLET). USA+45 USA-45 LAW CONSTN ADJUD
...DECISION BIOG 19/20. PAGE 15 E0295

B64
BIBLIOG/A
JUDGE
CT/SYS
JURID

BUREAU OF NAT'L AFFAIRS,THE CIVIL RIGHTS ACT OF
1964. USA+45 LOC/G NAT/G DELIB/GP CONFER DEBATE
DISCRIM...JURID 20 CONGRESS SUPREME/CT CIV/RIGHTS.
PAGE 17 E0333

B64
LEGIS
RACE/REL
LAW
CONSTN

CHAPIN B.,THE AMERICAN LAW OF TREASON. USA-45 LAW
NAT/G JUDGE CRIME REV...BIBLIOG 18. PAGE 21 E0419

B64
LEGIS
JURID
CONSTN
POLICY

COHEN M.,LAW AND POLITICS IN SPACE: SPECIFIC AND
URGENT PROBLEMS IN THE LAW OF OUTER SPACE.
CHINA/COM COM USA+45 USSR WOR+45 COM/IND INT/ORG
NAT/G LEGIT NUC/PWR ATTIT BIO/SOC...JURID CONCPT
CONGRESS 20 STALIN/J. PAGE 24 E0464

B64
DELIB/GP
LAW
INT/LAW
SPACE

COHEN M.L.,SELECTED BIBLIOGRAPHY OF FOREIGN AND
INTERNATIONAL LAW....IDEA/COMP METH/COMP 20.
PAGE 24 E0466

B64
BIBLIOG/A
JURID
LAW
INT/LAW

DIAS R.W.M.,A BIBLIOGRAPHY OF JURISPRUDENCE (2ND
ED.). VOL/ASSN LEGIS ADJUD CT/SYS OWN...INT/LAW
18/20. PAGE 31 E0619

B64
BIBLIOG/A
JURID
LAW
CONCPT

DIETZE G.,ESSAYS ON THE AMERICAN CONSTITUTION: A
COMMEMORATIVE VOLUME IN HONOR OF ALPHEUS T. MASON.
USA+45 USA-45 LAW INTELL...POLICY BIOG IDEA/COMP
ANTHOL SUPREME/CT. PAGE 32 E0626

B64
FEDERAL
CONSTN
DIPLOM
CT/SYS

DORMAN M.,WE SHALL OVERCOME. USA+45 ELITES ACADEM
FORCES TOP/EX MURDER...JURID 20 CIV/RIGHTS
MISSISSIPP EVERS/MED CLEMSON. PAGE 32 E0638

B64
RACE/REL
LAW
DISCRIM

DUBISSON M.,LA COUR INTERNATIONALE DE JUSTICE.
FRANCE LAW CONSTN JUDGE DOMIN ADJUD...INT/LAW
CLASSIF RECORD ORG/CHARTS UN. PAGE 33 E0651

B64
CT/SYS
INT/ORG

FACTS ON FILE, INC.,CIVIL RIGHTS 1960-63: THE NEGRO
CAMPAIGN TO WIN EQUAL RIGHTS AND OPPORTUNITIES IN
THE UNITED STATES. LAW CONSTN PARTIC SUFF 20 NEGRO
CIV/RIGHTS MISSISSIPP. PAGE 36 E0710

B64
DISCRIM
PRESS
RACE/REL

FALK R.A.,THE ROLE OF DOMESTIC COURTS IN THE
INTERNATIONAL LEGAL ORDER. FUT WOR+45 INT/ORG NAT/G
JUDGE EDU/PROP LEGIT CT/SYS...POLICY RELATIV JURID
CONCPT GEN/LAWS 20. PAGE 36 E0716

B64
LAW
INT/LAW

FEIFER G.,JUSTICE IN MOSCOW. USSR LAW CRIME
...RECORD 20. PAGE 37 E0725

B64
ADJUD
JURID
CT/SYS
MARXISM

FREISEN J.,STAAT UND KATHOLISCHE KIRCHE IN DEN
DEUTSCHEN BUNDESSTAATEN (2 VOLS.). GERMANY LAW FAM
NAT/G EDU/PROP GP/REL MARRIAGE WEALTH 19/20
CHURCH/STA. PAGE 40 E0793

B64
SECT
CATHISM
JURID
PROVS

GARDNER L.C.,ECONOMIC ASPECTS OF NEW DEAL
DIPLOMACY. USA-45 WOR-45 LAW ECO/DEV INT/ORG NAT/G
VOL/ASSN LEGIS TOP/EX EDU/PROP ORD/FREE PWR WEALTH
...POLICY TIME/SEQ VAL/FREE 20 ROOSEVLT/F. PAGE 42
E0836

B64
ECO/TAC
DIPLOM

GIANNELLA D.A.,RELIGION AND THE PUBLIC ORDER: AN
ANNUAL REVIEW OF CHURCH AND STATE, AND OF RELIGION,
LAW, AND SOCIETY. USA+45 LAW SOCIETY FAM POL/PAR
SCHOOL GIVE EDU/PROP GP/REL...JURID GEN/LAWS
BIBLIOG/A 20 CHURCH/STA BIRTH/CON CONSCN/OBJ
NATURL/LAW. PAGE 43 E0855

B64
SECT
NAT/G
CONSTN
ORD/FREE

GJUPANOVIC H.,LEGAL SOURCES AND BIBLIOGRAPHY OF
YUGOSLAVIA. COM YUGOSLAVIA LAW LEGIS DIPLOM ADMIN
PARL/PROC REGION CRIME CENTRAL 20. PAGE 44 E0873

B64
BIBLIOG/A
JURID
CONSTN
ADJUD

GOODNOW H.F.,THE CIVIL SERVICE OF PAKISTAN:
BUREAUCRACY IN A NEW NATION. INDIA PAKISTAN S/ASIA
ECO/UNDEV PROVS CHIEF PARTIC CHOOSE EFFICIENCY PWR
...BIBLIOG 20. PAGE 45 E0889

B64
ADMIN
GOV/REL
LAW
NAT/G

GRASMUCK E.L.,COERCITIO STAAT UND KIRCHE IM
DONATISTENSTREIT. CHRIST-17C ROMAN/EMP LAW PROVS
DEBATE PERSON SOVEREIGN...JURID CONCPT 4/5
AUGUSTINE CHURCH/STA ROMAN/LAW. PAGE 45 E0898

B64
GP/REL
NAT/G
SECT
COERCE

GROVES H.E.,THE CONSTITUTION OF MALAYSIA. MALAYSIA
POL/PAR CHIEF CONSULT DELIB/GP CT/SYS PARL/PROC
CHOOSE FEDERAL ORD/FREE 20. PAGE 48 E0953

B64
CONSTN
NAT/G
LAW

GUTTMANN A., COMMUNISM, THE COURTS, AND THE   MARXISM   B64
CONSTITUTION. USA+45 CT/SYS ORD/FREE...ANTHOL 20   POL/PAR
COM/PARTY CIV/RIGHTS. PAGE 48 E0965   CONSTN
    LAW

HAAR C.M., LAW AND LAND: ANGLO-AMERICAN PLANNING   LAW   B64
PRACTICE. UK USA+45 NAT/G TEC/DEV BUDGET CT/SYS   PLAN
INGP/REL EFFICIENCY OWN...JURID 20. PAGE 49 E0967   MUNIC
    NAT/COMP

HAMILTON H.D., LEGISLATIVE APPORTIONMENT; KEY TO   APPORT   B64
POWER. USA+45 LAW CONSTN PROVS LOBBY CHOOSE ATTIT   CT/SYS
SUPREME/CT. PAGE 50 E0988   LEAD
    REPRESENT

HANNA W.J., POLITICS IN BLACK AFRICA: A SELECTIVE   BIBLIOG   B64
BIBLIOGRAPHY OF RELEVANT PERIODICAL LITERATURE. AFR   NAT/LISM
LAW LOC/G MUNIC NAT/G POL/PAR LOBBY CHOOSE RACE/REL   COLONIAL
SOVEREIGN 20. PAGE 50 E0995

HEKHUIS D.J., INTERNATIONAL STABILITY: MILITARY,   TEC/DEV   B64
ECONOMIC AND POLITICAL DIMENSIONS. FUT WOR+45 LAW   DETER
ECO/UNDEV INT/ORG NAT/G VOL/ASSN FORCES ACT/RES   REGION
BAL/PWR PWR WEALTH...STAT UN 20. PAGE 51 E1024

HENDERSON D.F., CONCILIATION AND JAPANESE LAW (VOL.   CONCPT   B64
II). LAW SOCIETY...BIBLIOG 17/20 CHINJAP. PAGE 52   CT/SYS
E1028   ADJUD
    POLICY

HENDERSON D.F., CONCILIATION AND JAPANESE LAW (VOL.   CT/SYS   B64
I). LAW SOCIETY 17/19 CHINJAP. PAGE 52 E1029   CONCPT
    ADJUD
    POLICY

HENKE W., DAS RECHT DER POLITISCHEN PARTEIEN.   POL/PAR   B64
GERMANY/W LAW CT/SYS GP/REL SUPEGO 20. PAGE 52   JURID
E1031   CONSTN
    NAT/G

HOHFELD W.N., FUNDAMENTAL LEGAL CONCEPTIONS.   JURID   B64
PROB/SOLV OWN PWR...DECISION LING IDEA/COMP   ADJUD
GEN/METH. PAGE 54 E1069   LAW
    METH/CNCPT

HOLDSWORTH W.S., A HISTORY OF ENGLISH LAW; THE   LAW   B64
CENTURIES OF DEVELOPMENT AND REFORM (VOL. XIV). UK   LEGIS
CONSTN LOC/G NAT/G POL/PAR CHIEF EX/STRUC ADJUD   LEAD
COLONIAL ATTIT...INT/LAW JURID 18/19 TORY/PARTY   CT/SYS
COMMONWLTH WHIG/PARTY COMMON/LAW. PAGE 54 E1081

HOLT S., THE DICTIONARY OF AMERICAN GOVERNMENT.   DICTIONARY   B64
USA+45 LOC/G MUNIC PROVS LEGIS ADMIN JURID. PAGE 55   INDEX
E1091   LAW
    NAT/G

HURST W.H., JUSTICE HOLMES ON LEGAL HISTORY. USA-45   ADJUD   B64
LAW SOCIETY NAT/G WRITING...POLICY PHIL/SCI SOC   JURID
CONCPT 20 HOLMES/OW SUPREME/CT ENGLSH/LAW. PAGE 56   BIOG
E1117

KAHNG T.J., LAW, POLITICS, AND THE SECURITY COUNCIL*   DELIB/GP   B64
AN INQUIRY INTO THE HANDLING OF LEGAL QUESTIONS.   ADJUD
LAW CONSTN NAT/G ACT/RES OP/RES CT/SYS TASK PWR   ROUTINE
...INT/LAW BIBLIOG UN. PAGE 59 E1180

KAUPER P.G., RELIGION AND THE CONSTITUTION. USA+45   CONSTN   B64
USA-45 LAW NAT/G SCHOOL SECT GP/REL ATTIT...BIBLIOG   JURID
WORSHIP 18/20 SUPREME/CT FREE/SPEE CHURCH/STA.   ORD/FREE
PAGE 60 E1189

KEEFE W.J., THE AMERICAN LEGISLATIVE PROCESS: LEGIS   B64
CONGRESS AND THE STATES. USA+45 LAW POL/PAR   DECISION
DELIB/GP DEBATE ADMIN LOBBY REPRESENT CONGRESS   PWR
PRESIDENT. PAGE 60 E1191   PROVS

KISER S.L., AMERICANISM IN ACTION. USA+45 LAW PROVS   OLD/LIB   B64
CAP/ISM DIPLOM RECEIVE CONTROL CT/SYS WAR FEDERAL   FOR/AID
ATTIT WEALTH 20 SUPREME/CT. PAGE 61 E1221   MARXISM

KOREA (REPUBLIC) SUPREME COURT, KOREAN LEGAL SYSTEM.   JURID   B64
KOREA/S WOR+45 LAW LEAD ROUTINE GOV/REL ORD/FREE 20   CT/SYS
SUPREME/CT. PAGE 61 E1229   CONSTN
    CRIME

LAPENNA I., STATE AND LAW: SOVIET AND YUGOSLAV   JURID   B64
THEORY. USSR YUGOSLAVIA STRATA STRUCT NAT/G DOMIN   COM
COERCE MARXISM...GOV/COMP IDEA/COMP 20. PAGE 63   LAW
E1253   SOVEREIGN

LEDERMAN W.R., THE COURTS AND THE CANDIAN   CONSTN   B64
CONSTITUTION. CANADA PARL/PROC...POLICY JURID   CT/SYS
GOV/COMP ANTHOL 19/20 SUPREME/CT PARLIAMENT.   LEGIS
PAGE 64 E1276   LAW

LIGGETT E., BRITISH POLITICAL ISSUES: VOLUME 1. UK   POL/PAR   B64
LAW CONSTN LOC/G NAT/G ADJUD 20. PAGE 65 E1296   GOV/REL
    CT/SYS
    DIPLOM

MAKI J.M., COURT AND CONSTITUTION IN JAPAN; SELECTED   CT/SYS   B64
SUPREME COURT DECISIONS, 1948-60. FAM LABOR GOV/REL   CONSTN
HABITAT ORD/FREE...DECISION JURID 20 CHINJAP   PROB/SOLV
SUPREME/CT CIV/RIGHTS. PAGE 68 E1354   LAW

MAKI J.M., COURT AND CONSTITUTION IN JAPAN: SELECTED   CONSTN   B64
SUPREME COURT DECISIONS, 1948-60. LAW AGRI FAM   JURID
LEGIS BAL/PWR ADMIN CHOOSE...SOC ANTHOL CABINET 20   CT/SYS
CHINJAP CIVIL/LIB. PAGE 68 E1355   CRIME

MANNING B., FEDERAL CONFLICT OF INTEREST LAW. USA+45   LAW   B64
NAT/G PWR 20. PAGE 68 E1362   CONTROL
    ADMIN
    JURID

MASON A.T., AMERICAN CONSTITUTIONAL LAW: CONSTN   B64
INTRODUCTORY ESSAYS AND SELECTED CASES (3RD ED.).   CT/SYS
LAW LEGIS TAX ADJUD GOV/REL FEDERAL ORD/FREE PWR   JURID
...TIME/SEQ BIBLIOG T 19/20 SUPREME/CT. PAGE 69
E1379

MITCHELL B., A BIOGRAPHY OF THE CONSTITUTION OF THE   CONSTN   B64
UNITED STATES. USA+45 USA-45 PROVS CHIEF LEGIS   LAW
DEBATE ADJUD SUFF FEDERAL...SOC 18/20 SUPREME/CT   JURID
CONGRESS SENATE HOUSE/REP PRESIDENT. PAGE 73 E1472

NASA, PROCEEDINGS OF CONFERENCE ON THE LAW OF SPACE   SPACE   B64
AND OF SATELLITE COMMUNICATIONS: CHICAGO 1963. FUT   COM/IND
WOR+45 DELIB/GP PROB/SOLV TEC/DEV CONFER ADJUD   LAW
NUC/PWR...POLICY IDEA/COMP 20 NASA. PAGE 76 E1522   DIPLOM

NELSON D.H., ADMINISTRATIVE AGENCIES OF THE USA: ADMIN   B64
THEIR DECISIONS AND AUTHORITY. USA+45 NAT/G CONTROL   EX/STRUC
CT/SYS REPRESENT...DECISION 20. PAGE 76 E1531   ADJUD
    LAW

NEWMAN E.S., CIVIL LIBERTY AND CIVIL RIGHTS. USA+45   ORD/FREE   B64
USA-45 CONSTN PROVS FORCES LEGIS CT/SYS RACE/REL   LAW
ATTIT...MAJORIT JURID WORSHIP 20 SUPREME/CT NEGRO   CONTROL
CIV/RIGHTS CHURCH/STA. PAGE 77 E1543   NAT/G

NICE R.W., TREASURY OF LAW. WOR+45 WOR-45 SECT ADJUD   LAW   B64
MORAL ORD/FREE...INT/LAW JURID PHIL/SCI ANTHOL.   WRITING
PAGE 77 E1545   PERS/REL
    DIPLOM

OSSENBECK F.J., OPEN SPACE AND PEACE. CHINA/COM FUT   SPACE   B64
USA+45 USSR LAW PROB/SOLV TEC/DEV EDU/PROP NEUTRAL   ORD/FREE
PEACE...AUD/VIS ANTHOL 20. PAGE 79 E1583   DIPLOM
    CREATE

A CHECK LIST OF THE SPECIAL AND STANDING COMMITTEES   BIBLIOG   B64
OF THE AMERICAN BAR ASSOCIATION (VOL. II). USA+45   LAW
LEGIS PRESS CONFER...JURID CON/ANAL. PAGE 80 E1607   VOL/ASSN

RAGHAVAN M.D., INDIA IN CEYLONESE HISTORY, SOCIETY   DIPLOM   B64
AND CULTURE. CEYLON INDIA S/ASIA LAW SOCIETY   CULTURE
INT/TRADE ATTIT...ART/METH JURID SOC LING 20.   SECT

PAGE 83 E1668   STRUCT

B64

RICHARDSON I.L.,BIBLIOGRAFIA BRASILEIRA DE   BIBLIOG
ADMINISTRACAO PUBLICA E ASSUNTOS CORRELATOS. BRAZIL MGT
CONSTN FINAN LOC/G NAT/G POL/PAR PLAN DIPLOM   ADMIN
RECEIVE ATTIT...METH 20. PAGE 84 E1694   LAW

B64

SARTORIUS R.E.,THE JUSTIFICATION OF THE JUDICIAL   LAW
DECISION (DISSERTATION). PROB/SOLV LEGIT...JURID   PHIL/SCI
GEN/LAWS BIBLIOG 20. PAGE 87 E1747   CT/SYS
                                                   ADJUD

B64

SCHMEISER D.A.,CIVIL LIBERTIES IN CANADA. CANADA   ORD/FREE
LAW SECT PRESS RACE/REL NAT/LISM PRIVIL 20   CONSTN
COMMONWLTH PARLIAMENT CIVIL/LIB CHURCH/STA. PAGE 88 ADJUD
E1758   EDU/PROP

B64

SCHWARTZ M.D.,CONFERENCE ON SPACE SCIENCE AND SPACE SPACE
LAW. FUT COM/IND NAT/G FORCES ACT/RES PLAN BUDGET LAW
DIPLOM NUC/PWR WEAPON...POLICY ANTHOL 20. PAGE 89 PEACE
E1788   TEC/DEV

B64

SHAPIRO M.,LAW AND POLITICS IN THE SUPREME COURT: LEGIS
NEW APPROACHES TO POLITICAL JURISPRUDENCE. JUDGE   CT/SYS
PROB/SOLV LEGIT EXEC ROUTINE ATTIT ALL/VALS   LAW
...DECISION SOC. PAGE 90 E1811   JURID

B64

SHKLAR J.N.,LEGALISM. CREATE PROB/SOLV CT/SYS   MORAL
...POLICY CRIMLGY DECISION JURID METH/CNCPT.   LAW
PAGE 91 E1821   NEW/IDEA

B64

SIEKANOWICZ P.,LEGAL SOURCES AND BIBLIOGRAPHY OF   BIBLIOG
POLAND. COM POLAND CONSTN NAT/G PARL/PROC SANCTION ADJUD
CRIME MARXISM 16/20. PAGE 91 E1823   LAW
                                                   JURID

B64

STOICOIU V.,LEGAL SOURCES AND BIBLIOGRAPHY OF   BIBLIOG/A
ROMANIA. COM ROMANIA LAW FINAN POL/PAR LEGIS JUDGE JURID
ADJUD CT/SYS PARL/PROC MARXISM 20. PAGE 93 E1874   CONSTN
                                                   ADMIN

B64

SZLADITS C.,BIBLIOGRAPHY ON FOREIGN AND COMPARATIVE BIBLIOG/A
LAW: BOOKS AND ARTICLES IN ENGLISH (SUPPLEMENT   JURID
1962). FINAN INDUS JUDGE LICENSE ADMIN CT/SYS   ADJUD
PARL/PROC OWN...INT/LAW CLASSIF METH/COMP NAT/COMP LAW
20. PAGE 95 E1904

B64

TAUBENFELD H.J.,SPACE AND SOCIETY. USA+45 LAW   SPACE
FORCES CREATE TEC/DEV ADJUD CONTROL COST PEACE   SOCIETY
...PREDICT ANTHOL 20. PAGE 95 E1911   ADJUST
                                                   DIPLOM

B64

TENBROCK J.,EQUAL UNDER LAW. USA-45 CONSTN POL/PAR LEGIS
EDU/PROP PARL/PROC ORD/FREE...BIBLIOG 19 AMEND/XIV. LAW
PAGE 95 E1914   DISCRIM
                                                   DOMIN

B64

US AIR FORCE ACADEMY ASSEMBLY,OUTER SPACE: FINAL   SPACE
REPORT APRIL 1-4, 1964. FUT USA+45 WOR+45 LAW   CIVMIL/REL
DELIB/GP CONFER ARMS/CONT WAR PEACE ATTIT MORAL   NUC/PWR
...ANTHOL 20 NASA. PAGE 99 E1979   DIPLOM

B64

US HOUSE COMM ON JUDICIARY,CONGRESSIONAL   APPORT
REDISTRICTING. USA+45 PROVS DELIB/GP 20 CONGRESS. REPRESENT
PAGE 100 E2005   LEGIS
                                                   LAW

B64

US SENATE COMM ON JUDICIARY,HEARINGS BEFORE   ECO/DEV
SUBCOMMITTEE ON ANTITRUST AND MONOPOLY: ECONOMIC   CONTROL
CONCENTRATION VOLUMES 1-5 JULY 1964-SEPT 1966.   MARKET
USA+45 LAW FINAN ECO/TAC ADJUD COST EFFICIENCY   LG/CO
PRODUC...STAT CHARTS 20 CONGRESS MONOPOLY. PAGE 102
E2052

B64

US SENATE COMM ON JUDICIARY,CIVIL RIGHTS - THE   INT
PRESIDENT'S PROGRAM. USA+45 LAW PROB/SOLV PRESS   LEGIS
ADJUD GOV/REL RACE/REL ORD/FREE PWR...JURID 20   DISCRIM
SUPREME/CT SENATE CIV/RIGHTS PRESIDENT. PAGE 102   PARL/PROC
E2053

B64

WRIGHT G.,RURAL REVOLUTION IN FRANCE: THE PEASANTRY PWR
IN THE TWENTIETH CENTURY. EUR+WWI MOD/EUR LAW   STRATA
CULTURE AGRI POL/PAR DELIB/GP LEGIS ECO/TAC   FRANCE
EDU/PROP COERCE CHOOSE ATTIT RIGID/FLEX HEALTH   REV
...STAT CENSUS CHARTS VAL/FREE 20. PAGE 107 E2148

B64

WRIGHT Q.,A STUDY OF WAR. LAW NAT/G PROB/SOLV   WAR
BAL/PWR NAT/LISM PEACE ATTIT SOVEREIGN...CENSUS   CONCPT
SOC/INTEG. PAGE 108 E2159   DIPLOM
                                                   CONTROL

L64

BERKS R.N.,"THE US AND WEAPONS CONTROL." WOR+45 LAW USA+45
INT/ORG NAT/G LEGIS EXEC COERCE PEACE ATTIT   PLAN
RIGID/FLEX ALL/VALS PWR...POLICY TOT/POP 20.   ARMS/CONT
PAGE 11 E0204

L64

POUNDS N.J.G.,"THE POLITICS OF PARTITION." AFR ASIA NAT/G
COM EUR+WWI FUT ISLAM S/ASIA USA-45 LAW ECO/DEV   NAT/LISM
ECO/UNDEV AGRI INDUS INT/ORG POL/PAR PROVS SECT
FORCES TOP/EX EDU/PROP LEGIT ATTIT MORAL ORD/FREE
PWR RESPECT WEALTH. PAGE 82 E1640

S64

BALDWIN G.B.,"THE DEPENDENCE OF SCIENCE ON LAW AND NAT/G
GOVERNMENT--THE INTERNATIONAL GEOPHYSICAL YEAR--A KNOWL
CASE STUDY." WOR+45 LAW INT/ORG PROF/ORG LEGIS PLAN
EDU/PROP...TIME/SEQ VAL/FREE 20. PAGE 8 E0144

S64

CARNEGIE ENDOWMENT INT. PEACE,"HUMAN RIGHTS (ISSUES INT/ORG
BEFORE THE NINETEENTH GENERAL ASSEMBLY)." AFR   PERSON
WOR+45 LAW CONSTN NAT/G EDU/PROP GP/REL DISCRIM   RACE/REL
PEACE ATTIT MORAL ORD/FREE...INT/LAW PSY CONCPT
RECORD UN 20. PAGE 20 E0385

S64

CARNEGIE ENDOWMENT INT. PEACE,"LEGAL QUESTIONS   INT/ORG
(ISSUES BEFORE THE NINETEENTH GENERAL ASSEMBLY)." LAW
WOR+45 CONSTN NAT/G DELIB/GP ADJUD PEACE MORAL   INT/LAW
ORD/FREE...RECORD UN 20 TREATY. PAGE 20 E0386

S64

CRANE R.D.,"BASIC PRINCIPLES IN SOVIET SPACE LAW." COM
FUT WOR+45 AIR INT/ORG DIPLOM DOMIN ARMS/CONT   LAW
COERCE NUC/PWR PEACE ATTIT DRIVE PWR...INT/LAW   USSR
METH/CNCPT NEW/IDEA OBS TREND GEN/LAWS VAL/FREE   SPACE
MARX/KARL 20. PAGE 27 E0544

S64

GINSBURGS G.,"WARS OF NATIONAL LIBERATION - THE   COERCE
SOVIET THESIS." COM USSR WOR+45 WOR-45 LAW CULTURE CONCPT
INT/ORG DIPLOM LEGIT COLONIAL GUERRILLA WAR   INT/LAW
NAT/LISM ATTIT PERSON MORAL PWR...JURID OBS TREND REV
MARX/KARL 20. PAGE 44 E0869

S64

GREENBERG S.,"JUDAISM AND WORLD JUSTICE." MEDIT-7 SECT
WOR+45 LAW CULTURE SOCIETY INT/ORG NAT/G FORCES   JURID
EDU/PROP ATTIT DRIVE PERSON SUPEGO ALL/VALS   PEACE
...POLICY PSY CONCPT GEN/LAWS JEWS. PAGE 46 E0908

S64

KARPOV P.V.,"PEACEFUL COEXISTENCE AND INTERNATIONAL COM
LAW." WOR+45 LAW SOCIETY INT/ORG VOL/ASSN FORCES   ATTIT
CREATE CAP/ISM DIPLOM ADJUD NUC/PWR PEACE MORAL   INT/LAW
ORD/FREE PWR MARXISM...MARXIST JURID CONCPT OBS   USSR
TREND COLD/WAR MARX/KARL 20. PAGE 59 E1186

S64

KHAN M.Z.,"ISLAM AND INTERNATIONAL RELATIONS." FUT ISLAM
WOR+45 LAW CULTURE SOCIETY NAT/G SECT DELIB/GP   INT/ORG
FORCES EDU/PROP ATTIT PERSON SUPEGO ALL/VALS   DIPLOM
...POLICY PSY CONCPT MYTH HIST/WRIT GEN/LAWS.
PAGE 61 E1211

S64

LIPSON L.,"PEACEFUL COEXISTENCE." COM USSR WOR+45 ATTIT
LAW INT/ORG DIPLOM LEGIT ADJUD ORD/FREE...CONCPT   JURID
OBS TREND GEN/LAWS VAL/FREE COLD/WAR 20. PAGE 65   INT/LAW
E1303   PEACE

S64

MAGGS P.B.,"SOVIET VIEWPOINT ON NUCLEAR WEAPONS IN COM
INTERNATIONAL LAW." USSR WOR+45 INT/ORG FORCES   LAW
DIPLOM ARMS/CONT ATTIT ORD/FREE PWR...POLICY JURID INT/LAW
CONCPT OBS TREND CON/ANAL GEN/LAWS VAL/FREE 20.   NUC/PWR
PAGE 67 E1347

S64

N."QUASI-LEGISLATIVE ARBITRATION AGREEMENTS." LAW ADJUD
LG/CO ECO/TAC SANCTION ATTIT POLICY. PAGE 76 E1516 ADJUST
                                                   LABOR

GP/REL

S64
PRITCHETT C.H.,"EQUAL PROTECTION AND THE URBAN   MUNIC
MAJORITY." POL/PAR LEAD CHOOSE GP/REL PWR...MAJORIT   LAW
DECISION. PAGE 83 E1655   REPRESENT
                                                     APPORT

S64
SCHWELB E.,"OPERATION OF THE EUROPEAN CONVENTION ON   INT/ORG
HUMAN RIGHTS." EUR+WWI LAW SOCIETY CREATE EDU/PROP   MORAL
ADJUD ADMIN PEACE ATTIT ORD/FREE PWR...POLICY
INT/LAW CONCPT OBS GEN/LAWS UN VAL/FREE ILO 20
ECHR. PAGE 89 E1791

S64
SINGH N.,"THE CONTEMPORARY PRACTICE OF INDIA IN THE   LAW
FIELD OF INTERNATIONAL LAW." INDIA S/ASIA INT/ORG   ATTIT
NAT/G DOMIN EDU/PROP LEGIT KNOWL...CONCPT TOT/POP   DIPLOM
20. PAGE 91 E1833   INT/LAW

S64
SKUBISZEWSKI K.,"FORMS OF PARTICIPATION OF   INT/ORG
INTERNATIONAL ORGANIZATION IN THE LAW MAKING   LAW
PROCESS." FUT WOR+45 NAT/G DELIB/GP DOMIN LEGIT   INT/LAW
KNOWL PWR...JURID TREND 20. PAGE 92 E1837

S64
TRISKA J.F.,"SOVIET TREATY LAW: A QUANTITATIVE   COM
ANALYSIS." WOR+45 LAW ECO/UNDEV AGRI COM/IND INDUS   ECO/TAC
CREATE TEC/DEV DIPLOM ATTIT PWR WEALTH...JURID SAMP   INT/LAW
TIME/SEQ TREND CHARTS VAL/FREE 20 TREATY. PAGE 97   USSR
E1942

C64
CORWIN E.S.,"AMERICAN CONSTITUTIONAL HISTORY." LAW   ANTHOL
NAT/G PROB/SOLV EQUILIB FEDERAL ATTIT PWR...JURID   JUDGE
BIBLIOG 20. PAGE 26 E0515   ADJUD
                                                     CT/SYS

B65
MISSISSIPPI BLACK PAPER: (FIFTY-SEVEN NEGRO AND   COERCE
WHITE CITIZENS' TESTIMONY OF POLICE BRUTALITY...).   RACE/REL
USA+45 LAW SOCIETY CT/SYS SANCTION CRIME MORAL   DISCRIM
ORD/FREE RESPECT 20 NEGRO. PAGE 2 E0035   FORCES

B65
AMERICAN UNIVERSITY IN CAIRO,GUIDE TO UAR   BIBLIOG
GOVERNMENT PUBLICATIONS AT THE AUC LIBRARY   NAT/G
(PAMPHLET). ISLAM UAR USA+45 ECO/UNDEV...SOC STAT   LEGIS
20. PAGE 4 E0084   LAW

B65
ANTIEU C.J.,RELIGION UNDER THE STATE CONSTITUTIONS.   SECT
USA+45 LAW SCHOOL TAX SANCTION PRIVIL ORD/FREE   CONSTN
...JURID 20 SUPREME/CT CHURCH/STA. PAGE 5 E0099   PROVS
                                                     GP/REL

B65
BAR ASSOCIATION OF ST LOUIS,CONSTITUTIONAL FREEDOM   ORD/FREE
AND THE LAW. USA+45 LAW LABOR LEGIS EDU/PROP   CONSTN
...JURID CONCPT SUPREME/CT CIVIL/LIB CIV/RIGHTS.   RACE/REL
PAGE 8 E0146   NAT/G

B65
BOCK E.,GOVERNMENT REGULATION OF BUSINESS. USA+45   MGT
LAW EX/STRUC LEGIS EXEC ORD/FREE PWR...ANTHOL   ADMIN
CONGRESS. PAGE 13 E0255   NAT/G
                                                     CONTROL

B65
BRIGGS H.W.,THE INTERNATIONAL LAW COMMISSION. LAW   INT/LAW
CONSTN LEGIS CREATE ADJUD CT/SYS ROUTINE TASK   DELIB/GP
EFFICIENCY...CLASSIF OBS UN. PAGE 15 E0302

B65
BROMBERG W.,CRIME AND THE MIND. LAW LEGIT ADJUD   CRIMLGY
CRIME MURDER AGE/Y ANOMIE BIO/SOC DRIVE SEX PSY.   SOC
PAGE 16 E0305   HEALTH
                                                     COERCE

B65
CALIFORNIA LEGISLATURE,COMMITTEE ON ELECTIONS AND   DELIB/GP
REAPPORTIONMENT, FINAL REPORT. USA+45 LAW COMPUTER   APPORT
TEC/DEV CHOOSE JURID. PAGE 19 E0366   LEGIS
                                                     ADJUD

B65
CAMPBELL E.H.,SURVEYS, SUBDIVISIONS AND PLATTING,   CONSTN
AND BOUNDARIES: WASHINGTON STATE LAW AND JUDICIAL   PLAN
DECISIONS. USA+45 LAW LOC/G...DECISION JURID   GEOG
CON/ANAL BIBLIOG WASHINGT/G PARTITION WATER.   PROVS
PAGE 19 E0372

B65
CARTER G.M.,POLITICS IN EUROPE. EUR+WWI FRANCE   GOV/COMP

GERMANY/W UK USSR LAW CONSTN POL/PAR VOL/ASSN PRESS   OP/RES
LOBBY PWR...ANTHOL SOC/INTEG EEC. PAGE 20 E0399   ECO/DEV

B65
CARTER R.L.,EQUALITY. LAW LABOR NEIGH SCHOOL   POLICY
RACE/REL 20 NEGRO. PAGE 20 E0402   DISCRIM
                                                     PLAN
                                                     CREATE

B65
CHARLTON K.,EDUCATION IN RENAISSANCE ENGLAND. ITALY   EDU/PROP
UK USA-45 WOR-45 LAW LOC/G NAT/G...IDEA/COMP 14/17   SCHOOL
HUMANISM. PAGE 21 E0423   ACADEM

B65
CHROUST A.H.,THE RISE OF THE LEGAL PROFESSION IN   JURID
AMERICA (3 VOLS.). STRATA STRUCT POL/PAR PROF/ORG   USA-45
COLONIAL LEAD REV SKILL...SOC 17/20. PAGE 22 E0437   CT/SYS
                                                     LAW

B65
COLGNE A.B.,STATUTE MAKING (2ND ED.). LOC/G PROVS   LEGIS
CHOOSE MAJORITY...CHARTS DICTIONARY 20. PAGE 24   LAW
E0474   CONSTN
                                                     NAT/G

B65
CONGRESSIONAL QUARTERLY SERV,FEDERAL ROLE IN   ACADEM
EDUCATION (PAMPHLET). LAW SCHOOL PLAN TAX ADJUD   DISCRIM
...CHARTS SOC/INTEG 20 PRESIDENT. PAGE 25 E0487   RECEIVE
                                                     FEDERAL

B65
CONGRESSIONAL QUARTERLY SERV,REVOLUTION IN CIVIL   LAW
RIGHTS. USA+45 USA-45 LEGIS ADJUD CT/SYS CHOOSE   CONSTN
DISCRIM...DECISION CONGRESS SUPREME/CT. PAGE 25   RACE/REL
E0488   LOBBY

B65
CONGRESSIONAL QUARTERLY SERV,POLITICS IN AMERICA,   CHOOSE
1945-1964: THE POLITICS AND ISSUES OF THE POSTWAR   REPRESENT
YEARS. USA+45 LAW FINAN CHIEF DIPLOM APPORT SUFF   POL/PAR
...POLICY STAT TREND CHARTS 20 CONGRESS PRESIDENT.   LEGIS
PAGE 25 E0489

B65
COOPER F.E.,STATE ADMINISTRATIVE LAW (2 VOLS.). LAW   JURID
LEGIS PLAN TAX ADJUD CT/SYS FEDERAL PWR...CONCPT   CONSTN
20. PAGE 25 E0501   ADMIN
                                                     PROVS

B65
FALK R.A.,THE AFTERMATH OF SABBATINO: BACKGROUND   SOVEREIGN
PAPERS AND PROCEEDINGS OF SEVENTH HAMMARSKJOLD   CT/SYS
FORUM. USA+45 LAW ACT/RES ADJUD ROLE...BIBLIOG 20   INT/LAW
EXPROPRIAT SABBATINO HARLAN/JM. PAGE 36 E0718   OWN

B65
FEERICK J.D.,FROM FAILING HANDS: THE STUDY OF   EX/STRUC
PRESIDENTIAL SUCCESSION. CONSTN NAT/G PROB/SOLV   CHIEF
LEAD PARL/PROC MURDER CHOOSE...NEW/IDEA BIBLIOG 20   LAW
KENNEDY/JF JOHNSON/LB PRESIDENT PRE/US/AM   LEGIS
VICE/PRES. PAGE 36 E0724

B65
FELLMAN D.,RELIGION IN AMERICAN PUBLIC LAW. USA+45   SECT
USA-45 NAT/G PROVS ADJUD SANCTION GP/REL PRIVIL   CONSTN
ORD/FREE...JURID TIME/SEQ 18/20 SUPREME/CT   LAW
CHURCH/STA. PAGE 37 E0733   POLICY

B65
FERRELL J.S.,CASES AND MATERIALS ON LOCAL   APPORT
APPORTIONMENT. CONSTN LEAD GP/REL...DECISION   LOC/G
GOV/COMP. PAGE 37 E0740   REPRESENT
                                                     LAW

B65
FLEMING R.W.,THE LABOR ARBITRATION PROCESS. USA+45   GP/REL
LAW BARGAIN ADJUD ROUTINE SANCTION COST...PREDICT   LABOR
CHARTS TIME 20. PAGE 38 E0763   CONSULT
                                                     DELIB/GP

B65
FRIEDMAN L.,SOUTHERN JUSTICE. USA+45 PUB/INST LEGIT   ADJUD
ADMIN CT/SYS DISCRIM...DECISION ANTHOL 20 NEGRO   LAW
SOUTH/US CIV/RIGHTS. PAGE 40 E0800   CONSTN
                                                     RACE/REL

B65
GAJENDRAGADKAR P.B.,LAW, LIBERTY AND SOCIAL   ORD/FREE
JUSTICE. INDIA CONSTN NAT/G SECT PLAN ECO/TAC PRESS   LAW
POPULISM...SOC METH/COMP 20 HINDU. PAGE 42 E0826   ADJUD
                                                     JURID

B65
GILLETTE W.,THE RIGHT TO VOTE: POLITICS AND THE   RACE/REL

PASSAGE OF THE FIFTEENTH AMENDMENT. USA-45 LAW LEAD CONSTN
DISCRIM SEGREGAT CONGRESS. PAGE 44 E0863

B65
GINSBERG M.,ON JUSTICE IN SOCIETY. LAW EDU/PROP   ADJUD
LEGIT CT/SYS INGP/REL PRIVIL RATIONAL ATTIT MORAL   ROLE
ORD/FREE...JURID 20. PAGE 44 E0867   CONCPT

B65
GLUECK S.,ROSCOE POUND AND CRIMINAL JUSTICE.   CT/SYS
SOCIETY FAM GOV/REL AGE/Y ATTIT ORD/FREE...CRIMLGY   CRIME
BIOG ANTHOL SOC/INTEG 19/20. PAGE 44 E0875   LAW
                                                      ADJUD

B65
HARTUNG F.E.,CRIME, LAW, AND SOCIETY. LAW PUB/INST   PERCEPT
CRIME PERS/REL AGE/Y BIO/SOC PERSON ROLE SUPEGO   CRIMLGY
...LING GP/COMP GEN/LAWS 20. PAGE 50 E1004   DRIVE
                                                      CONTROL

B65
HOLDSWORTH W.S.,A HISTORY OF ENGLISH LAW; THE   LAW
CENTURIES OF SETTLEMENT AND REFORM (VOL. XV). UK   INDUS
CONSTN SECT LEGIS JUDGE WRITING ADJUD CT/SYS CRIME   PROF/ORG
OWN...JURID IDEA/COMP 18 PARLIAMENT ENGLSH/LAW   ATTIT
COMMON/LAW. PAGE 54 E1082

B65
HOWARD C.G.,LAW: ITS NATURE, FUNCTIONS, AND LIMITS.   LAW
USA+45 CONSTN LEGIS CREATE SANCTION ORD/FREE   JURID
...BIBLIOG 20. PAGE 55 E1101   CONTROL
                                                      SOCIETY

B65
HOWE M.D.W.,THE GARDEN AND THE WILDERNESS. USA+45   CONSTN
LAW GIVE EDU/PROP LEGIT NAT/LISM ORD/FREE...POLICY   SECT
JURID SUPREME/CT CHURCH/STA. PAGE 55 E1103   NAT/G
                                                      GP/REL

B65
IANNIELLO L.,MILESTONES ALONG THE MARCH: TWELVE   RACE/REL
HISTORIC CIVIL RIGHTS DOCUMENTS--FROM WORLD WAR II   DISCRIM
TO SELMA. USA+45 LAW FORCES TOP/EX PARTIC SUFF...T   CONSTN
20 NEGRO CIV/RIGHTS TRUMAN/HS SUPREME/CT   NAT/G
KENNEDY/JF. PAGE 56 E1121

B65
ISORNI J.,LES CAS DE CONSCIENCE DE L'AVOCAT.   SUPEGO
FRANCE LAW ACT/RES CT/SYS PARTIC ROLE MORAL 20.   JURID
PAGE 57 E1138   CRIME

B65
KAMISAR Y.,CRIMINAL JUSTICE IN OUR TIME. USA+45   ORD/FREE
FORCES JUDGE PROB/SOLV COERCE MORAL 20 CIVIL/LIB   CRIME
CIV/RIGHTS. PAGE 59 E1182   CT/SYS
                                                      LAW

B65
KARIS T.,THE TREASON TRIAL IN SOUTH AFRICA: A GUIDE   BIBLIOG/A
TO THE MICROFILM RECORD OF THE TRIAL. SOUTH/AFR LAW   ADJUD
ELITES NAT/G LEGIT CT/SYS RACE/REL DISCRIM...SOC   CRIME
20. PAGE 59 E1185   AFR

B65
KING D.B.,LEGAL ASPECTS OF THE CIVIL RIGHTS   LAW
MOVEMENT. SERV/IND VOL/ASSN LEGIS EDU/PROP ADJUD   DISCRIM
PARTIC CHOOSE...JURID SEGREGAT WORK. PAGE 61 E1215   TREND

B65
KRISLOV S.,THE SUPREME COURT IN THE POLITICAL   ADJUD
PROCESS. USA+45 LAW SOCIETY STRUCT WORKER ADMIN   DECISION
ROLE...JURID SOC 20 SUPREME/CT. PAGE 62 E1231   CT/SYS
                                                      CONSTN

B65
KUPER H.,AFRICAN LAW. LAW FAM KIN SECT JUDGE ADJUST   AFR
NAT/LISM 17/20. PAGE 62 E1236   CT/SYS
                                                      ADJUD
                                                      COLONIAL

B65
LASLEY J.,THE WAR SYSTEM AND YOU. LAW FORCES   MORAL
ARMS/CONT NUC/PWR NAT/LISM ATTIT...MAJORIT   PERSON
IDEA/COMP UN WORSHIP. PAGE 63 E1261   DIPLOM
                                                      WAR

B65
MARTENS E.,DIE HANNOVERSCHE KIRCHENKOMMISSION.   JURID
GERMANY LAW INT/ORG PROVS SECT CONFER GP/REL   DELIB/GP
CATHISM 16/20. PAGE 69 E1371   CONSTN
                                                      PROF/ORG

B65
MILLER H.H.,THE CASE FOR LIBERTY. USA-45 LAW JUDGE   COLONIAL
CT/SYS...AUD/VIS 18 PRE/US/AM CASEBOOK. PAGE 73   JURID
E1460   PROB/SOLV

B65
MILLIS W.,AN END TO ARMS. LAW INT/ORG FORCES   FUT
ACT/RES CREATE DIPLOM WAR...POLICY HUM NEW/IDEA   PWR
HYPO/EXP. PAGE 73 E1462   ARMS/CONT
                                                      ORD/FREE

B65
MISHKIN P.J.,ON LAW IN COURTS. USA+45 LEGIS CREATE   LAW
ROLE 20. PAGE 73 E1468   CT/SYS
                                                      ADJUD
                                                      CONSTN

B65
MOELLER R.,LUDWIG DER BAYER UND DIE KURIE IM KAMPF   JURID
UM DAS REICH. GERMANY LAW SECT LEGIT LEAD GP/REL   CHIEF
CATHISM CONSERVE 14 LUDWIG/BAV POPE CHURCH/STA.   CHOOSE
PAGE 74 E1478   NAT/LISM

B65
MOSTECKY V.,SOVIET LEGAL BIBLIOGRAPHY. USSR LEGIS   BIBLIOG/A
PRESS WRITING CONFER ADJUD CT/SYS REV MARXISM   LAW
...INT/LAW JURID DICTIONARY 20. PAGE 75 E1503   COM
                                                      CONSTN

B65
MURPHY W.F.,WIRETAPPING ON TRIAL: A CASE STUDY IN   JURID
THE JUDICIAL PROCESS. CONSTN ELITES CT/SYS CRIME   LAW
MORAL ORD/FREE...DECISION SUPREME/CT. PAGE 75 E1511 POLICY

B65
PEASLEE A.J.,CONSTITUTIONS OF NATIONS* THIRD   AFR
REVISED EDITION (VOLUME I* AFRICA). LAW EX/STRUC   CHOOSE
LEGIS TOP/EX LEGIT CT/SYS ROUTINE ORD/FREE PWR   CONSTN
SOVEREIGN...CON/ANAL CHARTS. PAGE 80 E1606   NAT/G

B65
ROSE A.M.,MINORITY PROBLEMS: A TEXTBOOK OF READINGS RACE/REL
IN INTERGROUP RELATIONS. UNIV USA+45 LAW SCHOOL   DISCRIM
WORKER PROB/SOLV GP/REL PERSON...PSY ANTHOL WORSHIP   ISOLAT
20 NEGRO INDIAN/AM JEWS EUROPE. PAGE 85 E1713   ACT/RES

B65
ROSS P.,THE GOVERNMENT AS A SOURCE OF UNION POWER.   LABOR
USA+45 LAW ECO/DEV PROB/SOLV ECO/TAC LEAD GP/REL   BARGAIN
...MGT 20. PAGE 86 E1723   POLICY
                                                      NAT/G

B65
SCHROEDER O.,DEFACTO SEGREGATION AND CIVIL RIGHTS.   ANTHOL
LAW PROVS SCHOOL WORKER ATTIT HABITAT HEALTH WEALTH   DISCRIM
...JURID CHARTS 19/20 NEGRO SUPREME/CT KKK. PAGE 88 RACE/REL
E1766   ORD/FREE

B65
SCHUBERT G.,REAPPORTIONMENT. LAW MUNIC POL/PAR PWR   REPRESENT
GOV/COMP. PAGE 88 E1775   LOC/G
                                                      APPORT
                                                      LEGIS

B65
SEN B.,A DIPLOMAT'S HANDBOOK OF INTERNATIONAL LAW   DIPLOM
AND PRACTICE. WOR+45 NAT/G ADJUST. PAGE 90 E1803   INT/LAW
                                                      TASK
                                                      LAW

B65
SMITH C.,THE OMBUDSMAN: A BIBLIOGRAPHY (PAMPHLET).   BIBLIOG
DENMARK SWEDEN USA+45 LAW LEGIS JUDGE GOV/REL   ADMIN
GP/REL...JURID 20. PAGE 92 E1841   CT/SYS
                                                      ADJUD

B65
SNOW J.H.,REAPPORTIONMENT. LAW CONSTN NAT/G GOV/REL   APPORT
ORD/FREE...JURID 20 SUPREME/CT CONNECTICT. PAGE 92   ADJUD
E1848   LEGIS
                                                      PROVS

B65
SOPER T.,EVOLVING COMMONWEALTH. AFR CANADA INDIA   INT/ORG
IRELAND UK LAW CONSTN POL/PAR DOMIN CONTROL WAR PWR   COLONIAL
...AUD/VIS 18/20 COMMONWLTH OEEC. PAGE 93 E1857   VOL/ASSN

B65
STOREY R.G.,OUR UNALIENABLE RIGHTS. LAW SECT CT/SYS   CONSTN
SUFF DISCRIM 17/20 CIVIL/LIB ENGLSH/LAW. PAGE 94   JURID
E1882   ORD/FREE
                                                      LEGIS

B65
TRESOLINI R.J.,AMERICAN CONSTITUTIONAL LAW. USA+45   CONSTN
USA-45 NAT/G ADJUD ORD/FREE PWR...POLICY BIOG 20   CT/SYS
SUPREME/CT CASEBOOK. PAGE 97 E1939   JURID
                                                      LAW

UNESCO,INTERNATIONAL ORGANIZATIONS IN THE SOCIAL SCIENCES(REV. ED.). LAW ADMIN ATTIT...CRIMLGY GEOG INT/LAW PSY SOC STAT 20 UNESCO. PAGE 98 E1962
B65
INT/ORG R+D PROF/ORG ACT/RES

US HOUSE COMM ON JUDICIARY,IMMIGRATION AND NATIONALITY. LAW...POLICY 20. PAGE 100 E2007
B65
GP/REL NAT/LISM NAT/G JURID

US LIBRARY OF CONGRESS,INTERNAL SECURITY AND SUBVERSION. USA+45 ACADEM LOC/G NAT/G PROVS ...POLICY ANARCH DECISION 20 CIVIL/SERV SUBVERT SEDITION. PAGE 101 E2020
B65
CONTROL ADJUD LAW PLAN

VON GLAHN G.,LAW AMONG NATIONS: AN INTRODUCTION TO PUBLIC INTERNATIONAL LAW. WOR+45 WOR-45 INT/ORG NAT/G CREATE ADJUD WAR...GEOG CLASSIF TREND BIBLIOG. PAGE 104 E2082
B65
ACADEM INT/LAW GEN/LAWS LAW

VONGLAHN G.,LAW AMONG NATIONS: AN INTRODUCTION TO PUBLIC INTERNATIONAL LAW. UNIV WOR+45 LAW INT/ORG NAT/G LEGIT EXEC RIGID/FLEX...CONCPT TIME/SEQ GEN/LAWS UN TOT/POP 20. PAGE 104 E2084
B65
CONSTN JURID INT/LAW

RUBIN A.P.,"UNITED STATES CONTEMPORARY PRACTICE RELATING TO INTERNATIONAL LAW." USA+45 WOR+45 CONSTN INT/ORG NAT/G DELIB/GP EX/STRUC DIPLOM DOMIN CT/SYS ROUTINE ORD/FREE...CONCPT COLD/WAR 20. PAGE 86 E1730
L65
LAW LEGIT INT/LAW

SHARMA S.P.,"THE INDIA-CHINA BORDER DISPUTE: AN INDIAN PERSPECTIVE." ASIA CHINA/COM S/ASIA NAT/G LEGIT CT/SYS NAT/LISM DRIVE MORAL ORD/FREE PWR 20. PAGE 91 E1815
L65
LAW ATTIT SOVEREIGN INDIA

WEINSTEIN J.B.,"THE EFFECT OF THE FEDERAL REAPPORTIONMENT DECISIONS ON COUNTIES AND OTHER FORMS OF GOVERNMENT." LAW CONSTN LEGIS CHOOSE GOV/COMP. PAGE 105 E2108
L65
MUNIC LOC/G APPORT REPRESENT

BEVANS C.I.,"GHANA AND UNITED STATES - UNITED KINGDOM AGREEMENTS." UK USA+45 LAW DELIB/GP EX/STRUC ORD/FREE...JURID METH/CNCPT GEN/LAWS 20. PAGE 11 E0222
S65
NAT/G LEGIT GHANA DIPLOM

BROWNLIE I.,"SOME LEGAL ASPECTS OF THE USE OF NUCLEAR WEAPONS." UK NEUTRAL DETER UN TREATY. PAGE 16 E0317
S65
LAW NUC/PWR WAR INT/LAW

DIXON R.G.,"NEW CONSTITUTIONAL FORMS FOR METROPOLIS: REAPPORTIONED COUNTY BOARDS; LOCAL COUNCILS OF GOVERNMENT." LAW CONSTN LEAD APPORT REPRESENT DECISION. PAGE 32 E0631
S65
MUNIC REGION GOV/COMP PLAN

GROSS L.,"PROBLEMS OF INTERNATIONAL ADJUDICATION AND COMPLIANCE WITH INTERNATIONAL LAW: SOME SIMPLE SOLUTIONS." WOR+45 SOCIETY NAT/G DOMIN LEGIT ADJUD CT/SYS RIGID/FLEX HEALTH PWR...JURID NEW/IDEA COLD/WAR 20. PAGE 48 E0951
S65
LAW METH/CNCPT INT/LAW

KHOURI F.J.,"THE JORDON RIVER CONTROVERSY." LAW SOCIETY ECO/UNDEV AGRI FINAN INDUS SECT FORCES ACT/RES PLAN TEC/DEV ECO/TAC EDU/PROP COERCE ATTIT DRIVE PERCEPT RIGID/FLEX ALL/VALS...GEOG SOC MYTH WORK. PAGE 61 E1212
S65
ISLAM INT/ORG ISRAEL JORDAN

MAC CHESNEY B.,"SOME COMMENTS ON THE 'QUARANTINE' OF CUBA." USA+45 WOR+45 NAT/G BAL/PWR DIPLOM LEGIT ROUTINE ATTIT ORD/FREE...JURID METH/CNCPT 20. PAGE 67 E1337
S65
INT/ORG LAW CUBA USSR

MCWHINNEY E.,"CHANGING INTERNATIONAL LAW METHOD AND OBJECTIVES IN THE ERA OF THE SOVIET-WESTERN DETENTE." COM USA+45 NAT/G BAL/PWR CT/SYS ATTIT ORD/FREE...HUM JURID NEW/IDEA COLD/WAR VAL/FREE 20. PAGE 71 E1430
S65
LAW TREND

PRABHAKAR P.,"SURVEY OF RESEARCH AND SOURCE
S65
BIBLIOG

MATERIALS; THE SINO-INDIAN BORDER DISPUTE." CHINA/COM INDIA LAW NAT/G PLAN BAL/PWR WAR...POLICY 20 COLD/WAR. PAGE 82 E1645
ASIA S/ASIA DIPLOM

SEARA M.V.,"COSMIC INTERNATIONAL LAW." LAW ACADEM ACT/RES DIPLOM COLONIAL CONTROL NUC/PWR SOVEREIGN ...GEN/LAWS BIBLIOG UN. PAGE 90 E1799
C65
SPACE INT/LAW IDEA/COMP INT/ORG

AARON T.J.,THE CONTROL OF POLICE DISCRETION: THE DANISH EXPERIENCE. DENMARK LAW CREATE ADMIN INGP/REL SUPEGO PWR 20 OMBUDSMAN. PAGE 2 E0042
B66
CONTROL FORCES REPRESENT PROB/SOLV

AMERICAN JEWISH COMMITTEE,GROUP RELATIONS IN THE UNITED STATES: PROBLEMS AND PERSPECTIVES: A SELECTED, ANNOTATED BIBLIOGRAPHY (PAMPHLET). LAW CONSTN STRATA SCHOOL SECT PROB/SOLV ATTIT...POLICY WELF/ST SOC/WK 20. PAGE 4 E0079
B66
BIBLIOG/A USA+45 STRUCT GP/REL

AMERICAN JEWISH COMMITTEE,THE TYRANNY OF POVERTY (PAMPHLET). USA+45 LAW ECO/DEV LOC/G MUNIC NAT/G PUB/INST WORKER EDU/PROP CRIME...SOC/WK 20. PAGE 4 E0080
B66
BIBLIOG/A WEALTH WELF/ST PROB/SOLV

AMERICAN JOURNAL COMP LAW,THE AMERICAN JOURNAL OF COMPARATIVE LAW READER. EUR+WWI USA+45 USA-45 LAW CONSTN LOC/G MUNIC NAT/G DIPLOM...ANTHOL 20 SUPREME/CT EURCT/JUST. PAGE 4 E0081
B66
IDEA/COMP JURID INT/LAW CT/SYS

ARCHER P.,FREEDOM AT STAKE. UK LAW NAT/G LEGIS JUDGE CRIME MORAL...CONCPT 20 CIVIL/LIB. PAGE 5 E0103
B66
ORD/FREE NAT/COMP POLICY

AUERBACH J.S.,LABOR AND LIBERTY; THE LA FOLLETTE COMMITTEE AND THE NEW DEAL. USA-45 LAW LEAD RESPECT SOCISM...BIBLIOG 20 CONGRESS BILL/RIGHT LAFOLLET/R NEW/DEAL. PAGE 6 E0117
B66
DELIB/GP LABOR CONSTN ORD/FREE

BAXTER M.G.,DANIEL WEBSTER & THE SUPREME COURT. LAW NAT/G PROF/ORG DEBATE ADJUD LEAD FEDERAL PERSON. PAGE 8 E0156
B66
CONSTN CT/SYS JURID

BEDI A.S.,FREEDOM OF EXPRESSION AND SECURITY; COMPARATIVE STUDY OF FUNCTIONS OF SUPREME COURTS IN UNITED STATES AND INDIA. INDIA USA+45 LAW CONSTN PROB/SOLV...DECISION JURID BIBLIOG 20 SUPREME/CT FREE/SPEE AMEND/I. PAGE 9 E0175
B66
METH CT/SYS ADJUD ORD/FREE

BEELEY A.L.,THE BAIL SYSTEM IN CHICAGO. LAW MUNIC PUB/INST EFFICIENCY MORAL...CRIMLGY METH/CNCPT STAT 20 CHICAGO. PAGE 9 E0176
B66
JURID CT/SYS CRIME ADJUD

BEER U.,FRUCHTBARKEITSREGELUNG ALS KONSEQUENZ VERANTWORTLICHER ELTERNSCHAFT. ASIA GERMANY/W INDIA LAW ECO/DEV ECO/UNDEV TEC/DEV ECO/TAC BIO/SOC SEX CATHISM...METH/COMP 20 CHINJAP BIRTH/CON. PAGE 9 E0178
B66
CONTROL GEOG FAM SECT

BESTERMAN T.,A WORLD BIBLIOGRAPHY OF BIBLIOGRAPHIES (4TH ED.). WOR+45 WOR-45 LAW INT/ORG ADMIN CON/ANAL. PAGE 11 E0219
B66
BIBLIOG/A DIPLOM

BRAIBANTI R.,RESEARCH ON THE BUREAUCRACY OF PAKISTAN. PAKISTAN LAW CULTURE INTELL ACADEM LOC/G SECT PRESS CT/SYS...LING CHARTS 20 BUREAUCRCY. PAGE 15 E0286
B66
HABITAT NAT/G ADMIN CONSTN

BROWNLIE I.,PRINCIPLES OF PUBLIC INTERNATIONAL LAW. WOR+45 WOR-45 LAW JUDGE REPAR ADJUD SOVEREIGN ...JURID T. PAGE 16 E0319
B66
INT/LAW DIPLOM INT/ORG

BUTTERFIELD H.,DIPLOMATIC INVESTIGATIONS* ESSAYS IN THE THEORY OF INTERNATIONAL POLITICS. LAW INT/ORG FORCES BAL/PWR ARMS/CONT WAR ALL/VALS...HUM INT/LAW. PAGE 18 E0351
B66
GEN/LAWS UK DIPLOM

CAMPBELL E.,PARLIAMENTARY PRIVILEGE IN AUSTRALIA. UK LAW CONSTN COLONIAL ROLE ORD/FREE SOVEREIGN
B66
LEGIS PARL/PROC

18/20 COMMONWLTH AUSTRAL FREE/SPEE PARLIAMENT.   JURID
PAGE 19 E0370   PRIVIL

                                                        B66
CARMEN I.H.,MOVIES, CENSORSHIP, AND THE LAW. LOC/G   EDU/PROP
NAT/G ATTIT ORD/FREE...DECISION INT IDEA/COMP   LAW
BIBLIOG 20 SUPREME/CT FILM. PAGE 19 E0383   ART/METH
                                                        CONSTN

                                                        B66
COLEMAN-NORTON P.R.,ROMAN STATE AND CHRISTIAN   GP/REL
CHURCH: A COLLECTION OF LEGAL DOCUMENTS TO A.D. 535   NAT/G
(3 VOLS.). CHRIST-17C ROMAN/EMP...ANTHOL DICTIONARY   SECT
6 CHRISTIAN CHURCH/STA. PAGE 24 E0473   LAW

                                                        B66
DALLIN A.,POLITICS IN THE SOVIET UNION: 7 CASES.   MARXISM
COM USSR LAW POL/PAR CHIEF FORCES WRITING CONTROL   DOMIN
PARL/PROC CIVMIL/REL TOTALISM...ANTHOL 20 KHRUSH/N   ORD/FREE
STALIN/J CASEBOOK COM/PARTY. PAGE 28 E0563   GOV/REL

                                                        B66
DAVIS K.,BUSINESS AND ITS ENVIRONMENT. LAW ECO/DEV   EX/STRUC
INDUS OP/RES ADMIN CONTROL ROUTINE GP/REL PROFIT   PROB/SOLV
POLICY. PAGE 29 E0573   CAP/ISM
                                                        EXEC

                                                        B66
FEINE H.E.,REICH UND KIRCHE. CHRIST-17C MOD/EUR   JURID
ROMAN/EMP LAW CHOOSE ATTIT 10/19 CHURCH/STA   SECT
ROMAN/LAW. PAGE 37 E0728   NAT/G
                                                        GP/REL

                                                        B66
FISCHER H.,EINER IM VORDERGRUND: TARAS   FASCISM
BORODAJKEWYCZ. AUSTRIA POL/PAR PROF/ORG EDU/PROP   LAW
CT/SYS ORD/FREE 20 NAZI. PAGE 38 E0754   ATTIT
                                                        PRESS

                                                        B66
GRUNEWALD D.,PUBLIC POLICY AND THE MODERN   LG/CO
COOPERATION: SELECTED READINGS. USA+45 LAW MARKET   POLICY
VOL/ASSN CAP/ISM INT/TRADE CENTRAL OWN...SOC ANTHOL   NAT/G
20. PAGE 48 E0954   CONTROL

                                                        B66
HANSON R.,THE POLITICAL THICKET. USA+45 MUNIC   APPORT
POL/PAR LEGIS EXEC LOBBY CHOOSE...MAJORIT DECISION.   LAW
PAGE 50 E0998   CONSTN
                                                        REPRESENT

                                                        B66
HAY P.,FEDERALISM AND SUPRANATIONAL ORGANIZATIONS: SOVEREIGN
PATTERNS FOR NEW LEGAL STRUCTURES. EUR+WWI LAW   FEDERAL
NAT/G VOL/ASSN DIPLOM PWR...NAT/COMP TREATY EEC.   INT/ORG
PAGE 51 E1014   INT/LAW

                                                        B66
HAYS P.R.,LABOR ARBITRATION: A DISSENTING VIEW.   GP/REL
USA+45 LAW DELIB/GP BARGAIN ADJUD...PREDICT 20.   LABOR
PAGE 51 E1016   CONSULT
                                                        CT/SYS

                                                        B66
HOGUE A.R.,ORIGINS OF THE COMMON LAW. UK STRUCT   LAW
AGRI CT/SYS SANCTION CONSERVE 12/14 ENGLSH/LAW   SOCIETY
COMMON/LAW. PAGE 54 E1068   CONSTN

                                                        B66
HOLDSWORTH W.S.,A HISTORY OF ENGLISH LAW; THE   BIOG
CENTURIES OF SETTLEMENT AND REFORM (VOL. XVI). UK   PERSON
LOC/G NAT/G EX/STRUC LEGIS LEAD ATTIT   PROF/ORG
...POLICY DECISION JURID IDEA/COMP 18 PARLIAMENT.   LAW
PAGE 54 E1083

                                                        B66
HOLMES O.W.,JUSTICE HOLMES, EX CATHEDRA. USA+45   BIOG
USA-45 LAW INTELL ADMIN ATTIT...BIBLIOG 20   PERSON
SUPREME/CT HOLMES/OW. PAGE 55 E1088   CT/SYS
                                                        ADJUD

                                                        B66
HOPKINS J.F.K.,ARABIC PERIODICAL LITERATURE, 1961.   BIBLIOG/A
ISLAM LAW CULTURE SECT...GEOG HEAL PHIL/SCI PSY SOC   NAT/LISM
20. PAGE 55 E1096   TEC/DEV
                                                        INDUS

                                                        B66
INSTITUTE COMP STUDY POL SYS,DOMINICAN REPUBLIC   SUFF
ELECTION FACT BOOK. DOMIN/REP LAW LEGIS REPRESENT   CHOOSE
...JURID CHARTS 20. PAGE 57 E1126   POL/PAR
                                                        NAT/G

                                                        B66
KEAY E.A.,THE NATIVE AND CUSTOMARY COURTS OF   AFR
NIGERIA. NIGERIA CONSTN ELITES NAT/G TOP/EX PARTIC   ADJUD

REGION...DECISION JURID 19/20. PAGE 60 E1190   LAW

                                                        B66
KERR M.H.,ISLAMIC REFORM: THE POLITICAL AND LEGAL   LAW
THEORIES OF MUHAMMAD 'ABDUH AND RASHID RIDA. NAT/G   CONCPT
SECT LEAD SOVEREIGN CONSERVE...JURID BIBLIOG   ISLAM
WORSHIP 20. PAGE 60 E1204

                                                        B66
KUNST H.,EVANGELISCHES STAATSLEXIKON. LAW CONSTN   JURID
POL/PAR...PHIL/SCI CONCPT DICTIONARY. PAGE 62 E1232   SECT
                                                        SOC
                                                        NAT/G

                                                        B66
KUNSTLER W.M.,"DEEP IN MY HEART" USA+45 LAW   CT/SYS
PROF/ORG SECT LOBBY PARTIC CROWD DISCRIM ROLE   RACE/REL
...BIOG 20 KING/MAR/L NEGRO CIV/RIGHTS SOUTH/US.   ADJUD
PAGE 62 E1233   CONSULT

                                                        B66
KURLAND P.B.,THE SUPREME COURT REVIEW. USA+45   JURID
USA-45 LAW LABOR SUFF...ANTHOL 20 SUPREME/CT.   PROB/SOLV
PAGE 62 E1240   ADJUD
                                                        NAT/G

                                                        B66
LEE L.T.,VIENNA CONVENTION ON CONSULAR RELATIONS.   AGREE
WOR+45 LAW INT/ORG CONFER GP/REL PRIVIL...INT/LAW   DIPLOM
20 TREATY VIENNA/CNV. PAGE 64 E1277   ADMIN

                                                        B66
MAGRATH C.P.,YAZOO; LAW AND POLITICS IN THE NEW   CT/SYS
REPUBLIC: THE CASE OF FLETCHER V. PECK. USA-45 LAW   DECISION
...BIBLIOG 19 SUPREME/CT YAZOO. PAGE 67 E1348   CONSTN
                                                        LOBBY

                                                        B66
MERILLAT H.C.L.,LEGAL ADVISERS AND INTERNATIONAL   INT/ORG
ORGANIZATIONS. LAW NAT/G CONSULT OP/RES ADJUD   INT/LAW
SANCTION TASK CONSEN ORG/CHARTS. PAGE 72 E1441   CREATE
                                                        OBS

                                                        B66
MILLER E.W.,THE NEGRO IN AMERICA: A BIBLIOGRAPHY.   BIBLIOG
USA+45 LAW EDU/PROP REV GOV/REL GP/REL INGP/REL   DISCRIM
ADJUST HABITAT PERSON HEALTH ORD/FREE SOC/INTEG 20   RACE/REL
NEGRO. PAGE 73 E1459

                                                        B66
OSTERMANN R.,A REPORT IN DEPTH ON CRIME IN AMERICA.   CRIME
FUT USA+45 MUNIC PUB/INST TEC/DEV MURDER EFFICIENCY   FORCES
ATTIT BIO/SOC...PSY 20. PAGE 79 E1584   CONTROL
                                                        LAW

                                                        B66
POLLACK R.S.,THE INDIVIDUAL'S RIGHTS AND   INT/LAW
INTERNATIONAL ORGANIZATION. LAW INT/ORG DELIB/GP   ORD/FREE
SUPEGO...JURID SOC/INTEG 20 TREATY UN. PAGE 81   DIPLOM
E1623   PERSON

                                                        B66
RUNCIMAN W.G.,RELATIVE DEPRIVATION AND SOCIAL   STRATA
JUSTICE: A STUDY OF ATTITUDES TO SOCIAL INEQUALITY   STRUCT
IN TWENTIETH-CENTURY ENGLAND. UK LAW POL/PAR PWR   DISCRIM
...CONCPT NEW/IDEA SAMP METH 19/20. PAGE 86 E1734   ATTIT

                                                        B66
SKOLNICK J.H.,JUSTICE WITHOUT TRIAL: LAW   FORCES
ENFORCEMENT IN DEMOCRATIC SOCIETY. USA+45 LAW   CRIMLGY
TRIBUTE RACE/REL BIO/SOC PERSON...PSY SOC 20 NEGRO   CRIME
BUREAUCRCY PROSTITUTN. PAGE 92 E1836

                                                        B66
SMITH E.A.,CHURCH-STATE RELATIONS IN ECUMENICAL   NAT/G
PERSPECTIVE. WOR+45 LAW MUNIC INGP/REL DISCRIM   SECT
ATTIT SUPEGO ORD/FREE CATHISM...PHIL/SCI IDEA/COMP   GP/REL
20 PROTESTANT ECUMENIC CHURCH/STA CHRISTIAN.   ADJUD
PAGE 92 E1843

                                                        B66
SOBEL N.R.,THE NEW CONFESSION STANDARDS, MIRANDA V.   JURID
ARIZONA. USA+45 USA-45 LAW PROF/ORG EDU/PROP 20   CT/SYS
SUPREME/CT. PAGE 92 E1849   ORD/FREE
                                                        ADJUD

                                                        B66
STUMPF S.E.,MORALITY AND THE LAW. USA+45 LAW   JURID
CULTURE PROB/SOLV DOMIN ADJUD CONTROL ADJUST   MORAL
ALL/IDEOS MARXISM...INT/LAW 20 SUPREME/CT. PAGE 94   CT/SYS
E1890

                                                        B66
SWEET E.C.,CIVIL LIBERTIES IN AMERICA. LAW CONSTN   ADJUD
NAT/G PRESS CT/SYS DISCRIM ATTIT WORSHIP 20   ORD/FREE
CIVIL/LIB. PAGE 95 E1899   SUFF

COERCE

IDEA/COMP

B66
TRESOLINI R.J.,CASES IN AMERICAN NATIONAL   NAT/G
GOVERNMENT AND POLITICS. LAW DIPLOM ADJUD LOBBY LEGIS
FEDERAL ORD/FREE WEALTH...DECISION ANTHOL 20   CT/SYS
PRESIDENT. PAGE 97 E1940   POL/PAR

B66
US DEPARTMENT OF STATE,RESEARCH ON AFRICA (EXTERNAL BIBLIOG/A
RESEARCH LIST NO 5-25). LAW CULTURE ECO/UNDEV   ASIA
POL/PAR DIPLOM EDU/PROP LEAD REGION MARXISM...GEOG   S/ASIA
LING WORSHIP 20. PAGE 100 E1996   NAT/G

B66
US DEPARTMENT OF STATE,RESEARCH ON THE USSR AND   BIBLIOG/A
EASTERN EUROPE (EXTERNAL RESEARCH LIST NO 1-25). EUR+WWI
USSR LAW CULTURE SOCIETY NAT/G TEC/DEV DIPLOM   COM
EDU/PROP REGION...GEOG LING. PAGE 100 E1997   MARXISM

B66
US DEPARTMENT OF STATE,RESEARCH ON WESTERN EUROPE, BIBLIOG/A
GREAT BRITAIN, AND CANADA (EXTERNAL RESEARCH LIST   EUR+WWI
NO 3-25). CANADA GERMANY/W UK LAW CULTURE NAT/G   DIPLOM
POL/PAR FORCES EDU/PROP REGION MARXISM...GEOG SOC
WORSHIP 20 CMN/WLTH. PAGE 100 E1998

B66
US HOUSE UNAMER ACTIV COMM,HEARINGS ON BILLS TO   LAW
MAKE PUNISHABLE ASSISTANCE TO ENEMIES OF US IN TIME SANCTION
OF UNDECLARED WAR. USA+45 VIETNAM/N EDU/PROP   VOL/ASSN
CONTROL WAR MARXISM HOUSE/REP. PAGE 100 E2010   GIVE

B66
US SENATE COMM ON FOREIGN REL,ASIAN DEVELOPMENT   FOR/AID
BANK ACT. USA+45 LAW DIPLOM...CHARTS 20 BLACK/EUG FINAN
S/EASTASIA. PAGE 101 E2030   ECO/UNDEV
                                                   S/ASIA

B66
US SENATE COMM ON JUDICIARY,HEARINGS ON FREE PRESS PRESS
AND FAIR TRIAL (2 VOLS.). USA+45 CONSTN ELITES   LAW
LEGIS EDU/PROP CT/SYS LEAD CONGRESS. PAGE 103 E2057 CRIME
                                                   ORD/FREE

B66
US SENATE COMM ON JUDICIARY,SCHOOL PRAYER. USA+45 SCHOOL
LAW LOC/G SECT ADJUD WORSHIP 20 SENATE DEITY.   JURID
PAGE 103 E2058   NAT/G

B66
WALL E.H.,THE COURT OF JUSTICE IN THE EUROPEAN   CT/SYS
COMMUNITIES: JURISDICTION AND PROCEDURE. EUR+WWI   INT/ORG
DIPLOM ADJUD ADMIN ROUTINE TASK...CONCPT LING 20. LAW
PAGE 105 E2096   OP/RES

B66
WASHINGTON S.H.,BIBLIOGRAPHY: LABOR-MANAGEMENT   BIBLIOG
RELATIONS ACT, 1947 AS AMENDED BY LABOR-MANAGEMENT LAW
REPORTING AND DISCLOSURE ACT, 1959. USA+45 CONSTN LABOR
INDUS DELIB/GP LEGIS WORKER BARGAIN ECO/TAC ADJUD MGT
GP/REL NEW/LIB...JURID CONGRESS. PAGE 105 E2100

B66
WILSON G.,CASES AND MATERIALS ON CONSTITUTIONAL AND JURID
ADMINISTRATIVE LAW. UK LAW NAT/G EX/STRUC LEGIS   ADMIN
BAL/PWR BUDGET DIPLOM ADJUD CONTROL CT/SYS GOV/REL   CONSTN
ORD/FREE 20 PARLIAMENT ENGLSH/LAW. PAGE 106 E2126   PWR

L66
HIGGINS R.,"THE INTERNATIONAL COURT AND SOUTH WEST SOUTH/AFR
AFRICA* SOME IMPLICATIONS OF THE JUDGMENT." AFR LAW COLONIAL
ECO/UNDEV JUDGE RACE/REL COST PWR...INT/LAW TREND   CT/SYS
UN TREATY. PAGE 52 E1043   ADJUD

L66
KRENZ F.E.,"THE REFUGEE AS A SUBJECT OF   INT/LAW
INTERNATIONAL LAW." FUT LAW NAT/G CREATE ADJUD   DISCRIM
ISOLAT STRANGE...RECORD UN. PAGE 62 E1230   NEW/IDEA

L66
SEYLER W.C.,"DOCTORAL DISSERTATIONS IN POLITICAL   BIBLIOG
SCIENCE IN UNIVERSITIES OF THE UNITED STATES AND   LAW
CANADA." INT/LAW LOC/G ADMIN...INT/LAW MGT   NAT/G
GOV/COMP. PAGE 90 E1808

S66
BURDETTE F.L.,"SELECTED ARTICLES AND DOCUMENTS ON BIBLIOG
AMERICAN GOVERNMENT AND POLITICS." LAW LOC/G MUNIC USA+45
NAT/G POL/PAR PROVS LEGIS BAL/PWR ADMIN EXEC   JURID
REPRESENT MGT. PAGE 17 E0331   CONSTN

S66
CHIU H.,"COMMUNIST CHINA'S ATTITUDE TOWARD   INT/LAW
INTERNATIONAL LAW" CHINA/COM USSR LAW CONSTN DIPLOM MARXISM
GP/REL 20 LENIN/VI. PAGE 22 E0431   CONCPT

S66
LANDE G.R.,"THE EFFECT OF THE RESOLUTIONS OF THE   LEGIS
UNITED NATIONS GENERAL ASSEMBLY." WOR+45 LAW   EFFICIENCY
INT/ORG NAT/G CHOOSE ISOLAT ATTIT...CLASSIF   RESPECT
GEN/METH UN. PAGE 62 E1249

S66
MATTHEWS D.G.,"ETHIOPIAN OUTLINE: A BIBLIOGRAPHIC BIBLIOG
RESEARCH GUIDE." ETHIOPIA LAW STRUCT ECO/UNDEV AGRI NAT/G
LABOR SECT CHIEF DELIB/GP EX/STRUC ADMIN...LING   DIPLOM
ORG/CHARTS 20. PAGE 69 E1384   POL/PAR

S66
MATTHEWS D.G.,"PRELUDE-COUP D'ETAT-MILITARY   BIBLIOG
GOVERNMENT: A BIBLIOGRAPHICAL AND RESEARCH GUIDE TO NAT/G
NIGERIAN POL AND GOVT, JAN. 1965-66." AFR NIGER LAW ADMIN
CONSTN POL/PAR LEGIS CIVMIL/REL GOV/REL...STAT 20. CHOOSE
PAGE 69 E1385

S66
NYC BAR ASSOCIATION RECORD,"PAPERBACKS FOR THE   BIBLIOG
BAR." USA+45 LEGIS ADJUD CT/SYS. PAGE 78 E1562   JURID
                                                   LAW
                                                   WRITING

S66
POLSBY N.W.,"BOOKS IN THE FIELD: POLITICAL   BIBLIOG/A
SCIENCE." LAW CONSTN LOC/G NAT/G LEGIS ADJUD PWR 20 ATTIT
SUPREME/CT. PAGE 81 E1627   ADMIN
                                                   JURID

N66
BACHELDER G.L.,THE LITERATURE OF FEDERALISM: A   BIBLIOG
SELECTED BIBLIOGRAPHY (REV ED) (A PAMPHLET). USA+45 FEDERAL
USA-45 WOR+45 WOR-45 LAW CONSTN PROVS ADMIN CT/SYS NAT/G
GOV/REL ROLE...CONCPT 19/20. PAGE 7 E0126   LOC/G

N66
CONGRESSIONAL QUARTERLY SERV,HOUSING A NATION   HABITAT
(PAMPHLET). USA+45 LAW STRUCT DIST/IND DELIB/GP   NAT/G
...GEOG CHARTS 20 DEPT/HUD. PAGE 25 E0490   PLAN
                                                   MUNIC

B67
AMDS W.E.,DELINQUENCY PREVENTION: THEORY AND   AGE/Y
PRACTICE. USA+45 SOCIETY FAM SCHOOL SECT FORCES   CRIME
PROB/SOLV...HEAL JURID PREDICT ANTHOL. PAGE 4 E0071 PUB/INST
                                                   LAW

B67
BOHANNAN P.,LAW AND WARFARE. CULTURE CT/SYS COERCE METH/COMP
REV PEACE...JURID SOC CONCPT ANTHOL 20. PAGE 13   ADJUD
E0259   WAR
                                                   LAW

B67
BOLES D.E.,THE TWO SWORDS. USA+45 USA-45 LAW CONSTN SCHOOL
SOCIETY FINAN PRESS CT/SYS...HEAL JURID BIBLIOG   EDU/PROP
WORSHIP 20 SUPREME/CT CHURCH/STA. PAGE 13 E0263   ADJUD

B67
BOULTON D.,OBJECTION OVERRULED. UK LAW POL/PAR   FORCES
DIPLOM ADJUD SANCTION DEATH WAR CIVMIL/REL 20.   SOCISM
PAGE 14 E0273   SECT

B67
BRAGER G.A.,COMMUNITY ACTION AGAINST POVERTY.   NEIGH
USA+45 LAW STRATA INGP/REL INCOME NEW/LIB...POLICY WEALTH
WELF/ST ANTHOL. PAGE 15 E0285   SOC/WK
                                                   CREATE

B67
BROWN L.N.,FRENCH ADMINISTRATIVE LAW. FRANCE UK   EX/STRUC
CONSTN NAT/G LEGIS DOMIN CONTROL EXEC PARL/PROC PWR LAW
...JURID METH/COMP GEN/METH. PAGE 16 E0314   IDEA/COMP
                                                   CT/SYS

B67
BUREAU GOVERNMENT RES AND SERV,COUNTY GOVERNMENT   BIBLIOG/A
REORGANIZATION - A SELECTED ANNOTATED BIBLIOGRAPHY APPORT
(PAPER). USA+45 USA-45 LAW CONSTN MUNIC PROVS   LOC/G
EX/STRUC CREATE PLAN PROB/SOLV REPRESENT GOV/REL   ADMIN
20. PAGE 17 E0332

B67
CHAPIN F.S. JR.,SELECTED REFERENCES ON URBAN   BIBLIOG
PLANNING METHODS AND TECHNIQUES. USA+45 LAW ECO/DEV NEIGH
LOC/G NAT/G SCHOOL CONSULT CREATE PROB/SOLV TEC/DEV MUNIC
SOC/WK. PAGE 21 E0420   PLAN

B67
CLINARD M.B.,CRIMINAL BEHAVIOR SYSTEMS: A TYPOLOGY. BIBLIOG
WOR+45 LAW SOCIETY STRUCT R+D AGE/Y ATTIT WEALTH   CRIME
...CLASSIF CHARTS METH/COMP METH. PAGE 23 E0457   CRIMLGY

PERSON

B67
COWLING M.,1867 DISRAELI, GLADSTONE, AND   PARL/PROC
REVOLUTION; THE PASSING OF THE SECOND REFORM BILL. POL/PAR
UK LEGIS LEAD LOBBY GP/REL INGP/REL...DECISION   ATTIT
BIBLIOG 19 REFORMERS. PAGE 27 E0531   LAW

B67
COX A.,CIVIL RIGHTS, THE CONSTITUTION, AND THE   LAW
COURTS. CONSTN EDU/PROP CRIME DISCRIM ATTIT...JURID FEDERAL
20. PAGE 27 E0533   RACE/REL
                                                    PRESS

B67
DEBOLD R.C.,LSD, MAN AND SOCIETY. USA+45 LAW   HEALTH
SOCIETY SECT CONTROL SANCTION STRANGE ATTIT...HEAL DRIVE
CHARTS ANTHOL BIBLIOG. PAGE 30 E0601   PERSON
                                                    BIO/SOC

B67
ELDRIDGE W.B.,NARCOTICS AND THE LAW: A CRITIQUE OF LAW
THE AMERICAN EXPERIMENT IN NARCOTIC DRUG CONTROL.   INSPECT
PUB/INST ACT/RES PLAN LICENSE GP/REL EFFICIENCY   BIO/SOC
ATTIT HEALTH...CRIMLGY HEAL STAT 20 ABA DEPT/HEW   JURID
NARCO/ACT. PAGE 34 E0679

B67
FRIENDLY A.,CRIME AND PUBLICITY. TV CT/SYS SUPEGO   PRESS
20. PAGE 41 E0811   CRIME
                                                    ROLE
                                                    LAW

B67
GARCIA ROBLES A.,THE DENUCLEARIZATION OF LATIN   NUC/PWR
AMERICA (TRANS. BY MARJORIE URQUIDI). LAW PLAN   ARMS/CONT
DIPLOM...ANTHOL 20 TREATY UN. PAGE 42 E0833   L/A+17C
                                                    INT/ORG

B67
GELLHORN W.,OMBUDSMEN AND OTHERS: CITIZENS'   NAT/COMP
PROTECTORS IN NINE COUNTRIES. WOR+45 LAW CONSTN   REPRESENT
LEGIS INSPECT ADJUD ADMIN CONTROL CT/SYS CHOOSE   INGP/REL
PERS/REL...STAT CHARTS 20. PAGE 43 E0847   PROB/SOLV

B67
GRAHAM H.D.,CRISIS IN PRINT: DESEGREGATION AND THE PRESS
PRESS IN TENNESSEE. LAW SOCIETY MUNIC POL/PAR   PROVS
EDU/PROP LEAD REPRESENT DISCRIM ATTIT...IDEA/COMP   POLICY
BIBLIOG/A SOC/INTEG 20 TENNESSEE SUPREME/CT   RACE/REL
SOUTH/US. PAGE 45 E0896

B67
GREENE L.S.,AMERICAN GOVERNMENT POLICIES AND   POLICY
FUNCTIONS. USA+45 LAW AGRI DIST/IND LABOR MUNIC   NAT/G
BUDGET DIPLOM EDU/PROP ORD/FREE...BIBLIOG T 20.   ADMIN
PAGE 46 E0910   DECISION

B67
HEWITT W.H.,ADMINISTRATION OF CRIMINAL JUSTICE IN   CRIME
NEW YORK. LAW PROB/SOLV ADJUD ADMIN...CRIMLGY   ROLE
CHARTS T 20 NEW/YORK. PAGE 52 E1035   CT/SYS
                                                    FORCES

B67
HODGKINSON R.G.,THE ORIGINS OF THE NATIONAL HEALTH HEAL
SERVICE: THE MEDICAL SERVICES OF THE NEW POOR LAW, NAT/G
1834-1871. UK INDUS MUNIC WORKER PROB/SOLV   POLICY
EFFICIENCY ATTIT HEALTH WEALTH SOCISM...JURID   LAW
SOC/WK 19/20. PAGE 53 E1062

B67
HOLCOMBE A.N.,A STRATEGY OF PEACE IN A CHANGING   PEACE
WORLD. USA+45 WOR+45 LAW NAT/G CREATE DIPLOM   PLAN
ARMS/CONT WAR...CHARTS 20 UN COLD/WAR. PAGE 54   INT/ORG
E1072   INT/LAW

B67
JONES C.O.,EVERY SECOND YEAR: CONGRESSIONAL   EFFICIENCY
BEHAVIOR AND THE TWO-YEAR TERM. LAW POL/PAR   LEGIS
PROB/SOLV DEBATE CHOOSE PERS/REL COST FEDERAL PWR   TIME/SEQ
...CHARTS 20 CONGRESS SENATE HOUSE/REP. PAGE 59   NAT/G
E1172

B67
KING W.L.,MELVILLE WESTON FULLER: CHIEF JUSTICE OF BIOG
THE UNITED STATES, 1888-1910. USA-45 CONSTN FINAN   CT/SYS
LABOR TAX GOV/REL PERS/REL ATTIT PERSON PWR...JURID LAW
BIBLIOG 19/20 SUPREME/CT FULLER/MW HOLMES/OW.   ADJUD
PAGE 61 E1216

B67
LAWYERS COMM AMER POLICY VIET,VIETNAM AND   INT/LAW
INTERNATIONAL LAW: AN ANALYSIS OF THE LEGALITY OF   DIPLOM
THE US MILITARY INVOLVEMENT. VIETNAM LAW INT/ORG   ADJUD
COERCE WEAPON PEACE ORD/FREE 20 UN SEATO TREATY.   WAR

B67
LENG S.C.,JUSTICE IN COMMUNIST CHINA: A SURVEY OF   CT/SYS
THE JUDICIAL SYSTEM OF THE CHINESE PEOPLE'S   ADJUD
REPUBLIC. CHINA/COM LAW CONSTN LOC/G NAT/G PROF/ORG JURID
CONSULT FORCES ADMIN CRIME ORD/FREE...BIBLIOG 20   MARXISM
MAO. PAGE 64 E1284

B67
LEVY L.W.,JUDICIAL REVIEW AND THE SUPREME COURT.   ADJUD
USA+45 USA-45 NEUTRAL ATTIT ORD/FREE...POLICY   CONSTN
DECISION BIBLIOG 18/20 BILL/RIGHT SUPREME/CT.   LAW
PAGE 65 E1292   CT/SYS

B67
LONG E.V.,THE INTRUDERS: THE INVASION OF PRIVACY BY LAW
GOVERNMENT AND INDUSTRY. USA+45 COM/IND INDUS LEGIS PARTIC
TASK PERS/REL...JURID 20 CONGRESS. PAGE 66 E1324   NAT/G

B67
MARTIN L.W.,THE SEA IN MODERN STRATEGY. LAW ECO/TAC ROLE
WAR. PAGE 69 E1374   PWR
                                                    NUC/PWR
                                                    DIPLOM

B67
NARAIN I.,THE POLITICS OF RACIALISM. INDIA   DISCRIM
SOUTH/AFR LAW NAT/G RACE/REL ATTIT 20. PAGE 76   COLONIAL
E1521   HIST/WRIT

B67
OPERATIONS AND POLICY RESEARCH,NICARAGUA: ELECTION POL/PAR
FACTBOOK: FEBRUARY 5, 1967 (PAMPHLET). NICARAGUA   CHOOSE
LAW NAT/G LEAD REPRESENT...STAT BIOG CHARTS 20.   PLAN
PAGE 79 E1577   ATTIT

B67
PADELFORD N.J.,THE DYNAMICS OF INTERNATIONAL   DIPLOM
POLITICS (2ND ED.). WOR+45 LAW INT/ORG FORCES   NAT/G
TEC/DEV REGION NAT/LISM PEACE ATTIT PWR ALL/IDEOS   POLICY
UN COLD/WAR NATO TREATY. PAGE 79 E1589   DECISION

B67
UNIVERSAL REFERENCE SYSTEM,BIBLIOGRAPHY OF   BIBLIOG/A
BIBLIOGRAPHIES IN POLITICAL SCIENCE, GOVERNMENT,   NAT/G
AND PUBLIC POLICY (VOLUME III). WOR+45 WOR-45 LAW   DIPLOM
ADMIN...SOC CON/ANAL COMPUT/IR GEN/METH. PAGE 98   POLICY
E1973

B67
UNIVERSAL REFERENCE SYSTEM,PUBLIC POLICY AND THE   BIBLIOG/A
MANAGEMENT OF SCIENCE (VOLUME IX). FUT TEC/DEV   POLICY
LAW NAT/G TEC/DEV CONTROL NUC/PWR GOV/REL   MGT
...COMPUT/IR GEN/METH. PAGE 99 E1975   PHIL/SCI

B67
UNIVERSAL REFERENCE SYSTEM,LAW, JURISPRUDENCE, AND BIBLIOG/A
JUDICIAL PROCESS (VOLUME VII). WOR+45 WOR-45 CONSTN LAW
NAT/G LEGIS JUDGE CT/SYS...INT/LAW COMPUT/IR   JURID
GEN/METH METH. PAGE 99 E1976   ADJUD

B67
US SENATE COMM ON FOREIGN REL,TREATY ON OUTER   SPACE
SPACE. WOR+45 AIR FORCES PROB/SOLV NUC/PWR SENATE   DIPLOM
TREATY UN. PAGE 101 E2032   ARMS/CONT
                                                    LAW

B67
US SENATE COMM ON FOREIGN REL,A SELECT CHRONOLOGY   ISLAM
AND BACKGROUND DOCUMENTS RELATING TO THE MIDDLE   TIME/SEQ
EAST. ISRAEL UAR LAW INT/ORG FORCES PROB/SOLV   DIPLOM
CONFER CONSEN PEACE ATTIT...POLICY 20 UN SENATE
TRUMAN/HS. PAGE 101 E2033

B67
US SENATE COMM ON FOREIGN REL,INTER-AMERICAN   LAW
DEVELOPMENT BANK ACT AMENDMENT. L/A+17C USA+45   FINAN
DELIB/GP DIPLOM FOR/AID BAL/PAY...CHARTS SENATE.   INT/ORG
PAGE 102 E2034   ECO/UNDEV

B67
US SENATE COMM ON FOREIGN REL,FOREIGN ASSISTANCE   FOR/AID
ACT OF 1967. VIETNAM WOR+45 DELIB/GP CONFER CONTROL LAW
WAR WEAPON BAL/PAY...CENSUS CHARTS SENATE. PAGE 102 DIPLOM
E2036   POLICY

B67
US SENATE COMM ON FOREIGN REL,USIA FOREIGN SERVICE DIPLOM
PERSONNEL SYSTEM. USA+45 LAW CONSULT ADMIN 20 USIA. EDU/PROP
PAGE 102 E2038   PRIVIL
                                                    PROF/ORG

B67
VILE M.J.C.,CONSTITUTIONALISM AND THE SEPARATION OF CONSTN
POWERS. FRANCE UK USA+45 USA-45 NAT/G ADJUD CONTROL BAL/PWR

GOV/REL...POLICY DECISION JURID GEN/LAWS 15/20   CONCPT
MONTESQ. PAGE 104 E2076   LAW

E0216   LAW
                                                        BARGAIN

                                                        L67
BAADE H.W.,"THE ACQUIRED RIGHTS OF INTERNATIONAL   INT/ORG
PUBLIC SERVANTS; A CASE STUDY IN RECEPTION OF   WORKER
PUBLIC LAW." WOR+45 DELIB/GP DIPLOM ORD/FREE   ADJUD
...INT/LAW JURID UN. PAGE 7 E0125   LAW

                                                        S67
BOHANNAN P.,"INSTITUTIONS OF DIVORCE, FAMILY, AND   FAM
THE LAW." WOR+45 LAW CONSULT...JURID SOC. PAGE 13   MARRIAGE
E0258   ADJUD
                                                        SOCIETY

                                                        L67
BARRON J.A.,"ACCESS TO THE PRESS." USA+45 TEC/DEV   ORD/FREE
PRESS TV ADJUD AUD/VIS. PAGE 8 E0152   COM/IND
                                                        EDU/PROP
                                                        LAW

                                                        S67
BRADLEY A.W.,"CONSTITUTION-MAKING IN UGANDA."   NAT/G
UGANDA LAW CHIEF DELIB/GP LEGIS ADMIN EXEC   CREATE
PARL/PROC RACE/REL ORD/FREE...GOV/COMP 20. PAGE 15   CONSTN
E0284   FEDERAL

                                                        L67
BERNHARD R.C.,"COMPETITION IN LAW AND ECONOMICS."   MARKET
LAW PLAN PRICE CONTROL PRODUC PROFIT...METH/CNCPT   POLICY
IDEA/COMP GEN/LAWS 20. PAGE 11 E0210   NAT/G
                                                        CT/SYS

                                                        S67
CARTER R.M.,"SOME FACTORS IN SENTENCING POLICY."   ADJUD
LAW PUB/INST CRIME PERS/REL...POLICY JURID SOC   CT/SYS
TREND CON/ANAL CHARTS SOC/EXP 20. PAGE 20 E0403   ADMIN

                                                        L67
CARMICHAEL D.M.,"FORTY YEARS OF WATER POLLUTION   HEALTH
CONTROL IN WISCONSIN: A CASE STUDY." LAW EXTR/IND   CONTROL
INDUS MUNIC DELIB/GP PLAN PROB/SOLV SANCTION   ADMIN
...CENSUS CHARTS 20 WISCONSIN. PAGE 20 E0384   ADJUD

                                                        S67
CHAMBERLAIN N.W.,"STRIKES IN CONTEMPORARY CONTEXT."   LABOR
LAW INDUS NAT/G CHIEF CONFER COST ATTIT ORD/FREE   BARGAIN
...POLICY MGT 20. PAGE 21 E0415   EFFICIENCY
                                                        PROB/SOLV

                                                        L67
CICOUREL A.V.,"KINSHIP, MARRIAGE, AND DIVORCE IN   SOC
COMPARATIVE FAMILY LAW." UNIV LAW FAM KIN GEN/METH.   PHIL/SCI
PAGE 22 E0438   MARRIAGE
                                                        IDEA/COMP

                                                        S67
CHAMBLISS W.J.,"TYPES OF DEVIANCE AND THE   CRIME
EFFECTIVENESS OF LEGAL SANCTIONS" SOCIETY PROB/SOLV   SANCTION
ADJUD CONTROL DETER. PAGE 21 E0417   EFFICIENCY
                                                        LAW

                                                        L67
HOWARD A.E.D.,"MR. JUSTICE BLACK: THE NEGRO PROTEST   ADJUD
MOVEMENT AND THE RULE OF LAW." USA+45 CONSTN CT/SYS   JUDGE
CHOOSE GP/REL...DECISION JURID NEGRO SUPREME/CT.   LAW
PAGE 55 E1100   REPRESENT

                                                        S67
CLOGGER T.J.,"THE BIG EAR." UK USA+45 USSR LAW   DIPLOM
LEGIS CRIME GP/REL INGP/REL ATTIT 20 FBI ESPIONAGE.   ORD/FREE
PAGE 23 E0458   COM/IND
                                                        INSPECT

                                                        L67
LAMBERT J.D.,"CORPORATE POLITICAL SPENDING AND   USA+45
CAMPAIGN FINANCE." LAW CONSTN FINAN LABOR LG/CO   POL/PAR
LOC/G NAT/G VOL/ASSN TEC/DEV ADJUD ADMIN PARTIC.   CHOOSE
PAGE 62 E1247   COST

                                                        S67
CREYKE G. JR.,"THE PAYMENT GAP IN FEDERAL   CONSTRUC
CONSTRUCTION CONTRACTS." USA+45 LAW FINAN ECO/TAC   PAY
CONTROL CT/SYS SUPREME/CT. PAGE 28 E0547   COST
                                                        NAT/G

                                                        L67
LENT G.E.,"TAX INCENTIVES FOR INVESTMENT IN   ECO/UNDEV
DEVELOPING COUNTRIES" WOR+45 LAW INDUS PLAN BUDGET   TAX
TARIFFS ADMIN...METH/COMP 20. PAGE 64 E1285   FINAN
                                                        ECO/TAC

                                                        S67
DALFEN C.M.,"THE WORLD COURT IN IDLE SPLENDOUR: THE   CT/SYS
BASIS OF STATES' ATTITUDES." WOR+45 LAW ADJUD   INT/ORG
COERCE...JURID 20 UN WORLD/CT. PAGE 28 E0562   INT/LAW
                                                        DIPLOM

                                                        L67
SCHUBERT G.,"THE RHETORIC OF CONSTITUTIONAL   CONSTN
CHANGE." USA+45 LAW CULTURE CHIEF LEGIS ADJUD   METH/COMP
CT/SYS ARMS/CONT ADJUST...CHARTS SIMUL. PAGE 89   ORD/FREE
E1777

                                                        S67
DOUTY H.M.," REFERENCE TO DEVELOPING COUNTRIES."   TAX
JAMAICA MALAYSIA UK WOR+45 LAW FINAN ACT/RES BUDGET   ECO/UNDEV
CAP/ISM ECO/TAC TARIFFS RISK EFFICIENCY PROFIT   NAT/G
...CHARTS 20. PAGE 33 E0646

                                                        L67
WAELBROECK M.,"THE APPLICATION OF EEC LAW BY   INT/LAW
NATIONAL COURTS." EUR+WWI INT/ORG CT/SYS...JURID   NAT/G
EEC TREATY. PAGE 104 E2090   LAW
                                                        PROB/SOLV

                                                        S67
EDGEWORTH A.B. JR.,"CIVIL RIGHTS PLUS THREE YEARS: WORKER
BANKS AND THE ANTI-DISCRIMINATION LAW" USA+45   DISCRIM
SOCIETY DELIB/GP RACE/REL EFFICIENCY 20 NEGRO   FINAN
CIV/RIGHTS. PAGE 34 E0675   LAW

                                                        S67
"THE STATE OF ZONING ADMINISTRATION IN ILLINOIS: ADMIN
PROCEDURAL REQUIREMENTS OF JUDICIAL INTERVENTION."   CONTROL
USA+45 LAW CONSTN DELIB/GP ADJUD CT/SYS ORD/FREE   HABITAT
ILLINOIS. PAGE 2 E0038   PLAN

                                                        S67
GANZ G.,"THE CONTROL OF INDUSTRY BY ADMINISTRATIVE   INDUS
PROCESS." UK DELIB/GP WORKER 20. PAGE 42 E0832   LAW
                                                        ADMIN
                                                        CONTROL

                                                        S67
"THE FEDERAL AGRICULTURAL STABILIZATION PROGRAM AND   AGRI
THE NEGRO." LAW CONSTN PLAN REPRESENT DISCRIM   CONTROL
ORD/FREE 20 NEGRO CONGRESS. PAGE 2 E0039   NAT/G
                                                        RACE/REL

                                                        S67
GLASER D.,"NATIONAL GOALS AND INDICATORS FOR THE   CRIME
REDUCTION OF CRIME AND DELINQUENCY." FUT USA+45   CRIMLGY
NAT/G...CON/ANAL METH 20. PAGE 44 E0874   LAW
                                                        STAT

                                                        S67
ADOKO A.,"THE CONSTITUTION OF UGANDA." AFR UGANDA   NAT/G
LOC/G CHIEF FORCES LEGIS ADJUD EXEC CHOOSE NAT/LISM   CONSTN
...IDEA/COMP 20. PAGE 3 E0050   ORD/FREE
                                                        LAW

                                                        S67
GRIFFIN H.C.,"PREJUDICIAL PUBLICITY: SEARCH FOR A   LAW
CIVIL REMEDY." EDU/PROP CONTROL DISCRIM...JURID 20.   SANCTION
PAGE 47 E0937   PRESS
                                                        ADJUD

                                                        S67
ANDERSON W.,"THE PERILS OF 'SHARING'." USA+45   BUDGET
ECO/TAC RECEIVE LOBBY GOV/REL CENTRAL COST INCOME   TAX
...POLICY PLURIST CONGRESS. PAGE 5 E0095   FEDERAL
                                                        LAW

                                                        S67
HAMILTON H.D.,"LEGISLATIVE CONSTITUENCIES: SINGLE-   LEGIS
MEMBER DISTRICTS, MULTI-MEMBER DISTRICTS, AND   REPRESENT
FLOTERAL DISTRICTS." USA+45 LAW POL/PAR ADJUD   APPORT
RACE/REL...CHARTS METH/COMP 20. PAGE 50 E0990   PLAN

                                                        S67
BARTLETT J.L.,"AMERICAN BOND ISSUES IN THE EUROPEAN   LAW
ECONOMIC COMMUNITY." EUR+WWI LUXEMBOURG USA+45   ECO/TAC
DIPLOM CONTROL BAL/PAY EEC. PAGE 8 E0153   FINAN
                                                        TAX

                                                        S67
HILL D.G.,"HUMAN RIGHTS LEGISLATION IN ONTARIO."   DELIB/GP
CANADA R+D VOL/ASSN CONSULT INSPECT EDU/PROP ADJUD   ORD/FREE
AGREE TASK GP/REL INGP/REL DISCRIM 20 CIV/RIGHTS   LAW
ONTARIO CIVIL/LIB. PAGE 52 E1045   POLICY

                                                        S67
BERRODIN E.F.,"AT THE BARGAINING TABLE." LABOR   PROVS
DIPLOM ECO/TAC ADMIN...MGT 20 MICHIGAN. PAGE 11   WORKER

                                                        S67
HIRSCH W.Z.,"SOME ECONOMIC IMPLICATIONS OF CITY   ECO/TAC
PLANNING." LAW PROB/SOLV RATION EFFICIENCY...METH   JURID
20. PAGE 53 E1050   MUNIC

PLAN

S67
HUBERT C.J.,"PLANNED UNIT DEVELOPMENT" LAW VOL/ASSN PLAN
LEGIS EDU/PROP CT/SYS GOV/REL...NEW/IDEA 20 MUNIC
PLAN/UNIT. PAGE 56 E1107 HABITAT
ADJUD

S67
KENNEDY R.F.,"TOWARD A NATION WHERE THE LAW IS CRIMLGY
KING." PLAN CT/SYS CRIME INGP/REL...JURID SOC. ADJUST
PAGE 60 E1202 LAW
PUB/INST

S67
KETCHAM O.W.,"GUIDELINES FROM GAULT: REVOLUTIONARY ADJUD
REQUIREMENTS AND REAPPRAISAL." LAW CONSTN CREATE AGE/Y
LEGIT ROUTINE SANCTION CRIME DISCRIM PRIVIL ROLE CT/SYS
...JURID NEW/IDEA 20 SUPREME/CT. PAGE 60 E1208

S67
KONVITZ M.R.,"CIVIL LIBERTIES." USA+45 R+D...METH LAW
20. PAGE 61 E1228 MORAL
ORD/FREE
NAT/G

S67
LAY S.H.,"EXCLUSIVE GOVERNMENTAL LIABILITY FOR NAT/G
SPACE ACCIDENTS." USA+45 LAW FINAN SERV/IND TEC/DEV SUPEGO
ADJUD. PAGE 64 E1272 SPACE
PROB/SOLV

S67
MACLEOD R.M.,"LAW, MEDICINE AND PUBLIC OPINION: THE LAW
RESISTANCE TO COMPULSORY HEALTH LEGISLATION HEALTH
1870-1907." UK CONSTN SECT DELIB/GP DEBATE ATTIT
PARL/PROC GP/REL MORAL 19. PAGE 67 E1344

S67
MAYANJA A.,"THE GOVERNMENT'S PROPOSALS ON THE NEW CONSTN
CONSTITUTION." AFR UGANDA LAW CHIEF LEGIS ADJUD CONFER
REPRESENT FEDERAL PWR 20. PAGE 69 E1390 ORD/FREE
NAT/G

S67
MAYER M.,"THE IDEA OF JUSTICE AND THE POOR." USA+45 INCOME
CLIENT CONSULT RENT ADJUD DISCRIM KNOWL 20. PAGE 70 WEALTH
E1393 LAW
ORD/FREE

S67
MC REYNOLDS D.,"THE RESISTANCE." USA+45 LAW ADJUD ATTIT
SANCTION INGP/REL PEACE 20. PAGE 70 E1398 WAR
LEGIT
FORCES

S67
MITCHELL J.D.B.,"THE CONSTITUTIONAL IMPLICATIONS OF CONSTN
JUDICIAL CONTROL OF THE ADMINISTRATION IN THE CT/SYS
UNITED KINGDOM." UK LAW ADJUD ADMIN GOV/REL ROLE CONTROL
...GP/COMP 20. PAGE 74 E1474 EX/STRUC

S67
MORENO F.J.,"THE SPANISH COLONIAL SYSTEM: A COLONIAL
FUNCTIONAL APPROACH." SPAIN WOR-45 LAW CHIEF DIPLOM CONTROL
ADJUD CIVMIL/REL AUTHORIT ROLE PWR...CONCPT 17/20. NAT/G
PAGE 74 E1492 OP/RES

S67
O'HIGGINS P.,"A BIBLIOGRAPHY OF PERIODICAL BIBLIOG
LITERATURE RELATING TO IRISH LAW." IRELAND...JURID LAW
20. PAGE 78 E1567 ADJUD

S67
PEMBERTON J., JR.,"CONSTITUTIONAL PROBLEMS IN LAW
RESTRAINT ON THE MEDIA." CONSTN PROB/SOLV EDU/PROP PRESS
CONFER CONTROL JURID. PAGE 80 E1608 ORD/FREE

S67
POSPISIL L.,"LEGAL LEVELS AND MULTIPLICITY OF LEGAL LAW
SYSTEMS IN HUMAN SOCIETIES." WOR+45 CENTRAL PWR STRATA
...SOC CHARTS GP/COMP GEN/LAWS. PAGE 81 E1630 JURID
STRUCT

S67
RAI H.,"DISTRICT MAGISTRATE AND POLICE STRUCT
SUPERINTENDENT IN INDIA: THE CONTROVERSY OF DUAL CONTROL
CONTROL" INDIA LAW PROVS ADMIN PWR 19/20. PAGE 83 ROLE
E1669 FORCES

S67
REILLY T.J.,"FREEZING AND CONFISCATION OF CUBAN STRANGE
PROPERTY." CUBA USA+45 LAW DIPLOM LEGIT ADJUD OWN
CONTROL. PAGE 84 E1682 ECO/TAC

S67
RUCKER B.W.,"WHAT SOLUTIONS DO PEOPLE ENDORSE IN CONCPT
FREE PRESS-FAIR TRIAL DILEMMA?" LAW NAT/G CT/SYS PRESS
ATTIT...NET/THEORY SAMP CHARTS IDEA/COMP METH 20. ADJUD
PAGE 86 E1731 ORD/FREE

S67
SCHELLING T.C.,"ECONOMICS AND CRIMINAL ENTERPRISE." CRIME
LAW FORCES BARGAIN ECO/TAC CONTROL GAMBLE ROUTINE PROB/SOLV
ADJUST DEMAND INCOME PROFIT CRIMLGY. PAGE 87 E1756 CONCPT

S67
SCOTT A.,"TWENTY-FIVE YEARS OF OPINION ON ATTIT
INTEGRATION IN TEXAS." USA+45 USA-45 DISCRIM ADJUST
...KNO/TEST TREND CHARTS 20 TEXAS. PAGE 89 E1794 RACE/REL
LAW

S67
SEIDLER G.L.,"MARXIST LEGAL THOUGHT IN POLAND." MARXISM
POLAND SOCIETY R+D LOC/G NAT/G ACT/RES ADJUD CT/SYS LAW
SUPEGO PWR...SOC TREND 20 MARX/KARL. PAGE 90 E1802 CONCPT
EFFICIENCY

S67
SHAFFER T.L.,"DIRECT RESTRAINT ON THE PRESS." LAW
USA+45 EDU/PROP CONTROL...JURID NEW/IDEA ABA. PRESS
PAGE 90 E1809 ORD/FREE
ADJUD

S67
VAUGHN W.P.,"SEPARATE AND UNEQUAL: THE CIVIL RIGHTS LAW
ACT OF 1875 AND DEFEAT OF THE SCHOOL INTEGRATION DISCRIM
CLAUSE." USA-45 LEGIS RACE/REL 19 CONGRESS. EDU/PROP
PAGE 103 E2073 PARL/PROC

S67
WILSON G.D.,"CRIMINAL SANCTIONS AGAINST PASSPORT LAW
AREA-RESTRICTION VIOLATIONS." USA+45 ADJUD CRIME SANCTION
GOV/REL DEPT/STATE CONGRESS. PAGE 106 E2127 LICENSE
POLICY

N67
US SENATE COMM ON FOREIGN REL,SURVEY OF THE INT/TRADE
ALLIANCE FOR PROGRESS: FOREIGN TRADE POLICIES REGION
(PAMPHLET). L/A+17C LAW ECO/UNDEV ECO/TAC TARIFFS AGREE
20 GATT LAFTA UN. PAGE 102 E2037 INT/ORG

B68
HULL R.H.,LAW AND VIETNAM. COM VIETNAM CONSTN POLICY
INT/ORG FORCES DIPLOM AGREE COERCE DETER WEAPON LAW
PEACE ATTIT 20 UN TREATY. PAGE 56 E1113 WAR
INT/LAW

L68
CHIU H.,"COMMUNIST CHINA'S ATTITUDE TOWARD THE INT/LAW
UNITED NATIONS: A LEGAL ANALYSIS." CHINA/COM WOR+45 SOVEREIGN
LAW NAT/G DIPLOM CONFER ADJUD PARTIC ATTIT...POLICY INT/ORG
TREND 20 UN. PAGE 22 E0432 REPRESENT

S68
BURGESS J.W.,"VON HOLST'S PUBLIC LAW OF THE UNITED CONSTN
STATES" USA-45 LAW GOV/REL...GOV/COMP IDEA/COMP 19. FEDERAL
PAGE 17 E0339 NAT/G
JURID

S68
DUPRE L.,"TILL DEATH DO US PART?" UNIV FAM INSPECT MARRIAGE
LEGIT ADJUD SANCTION PERS/REL ANOMIE RIGID/FLEX SEX CATH
...JURID IDEA/COMP 20 CHURCH/STA BIBLE CANON/LAW LAW
CIVIL/LAW. PAGE 34 E0666

B70
BLACKSTONE W.,COMMENTARIES ON THE LAWS OF ENGLAND LAW
(4 VOLS.) (4TH ED.). UK CHIEF DELIB/GP LEGIS WORKER JURID
CT/SYS SANCTION CRIME OWN...CRIMLGY 18 ENGLSH/LAW. ADJUD
PAGE 12 E0238 CONSTN

B73
AUSTIN J.,LECTURES ON JURISPRUDENCE OR THE LAW
PHILOSOPHY OF POSITIVE LAW (VOL. II) (4TH ED., ADJUD
REV.). UK CONSTN STRUCT PROB/SOLV LEGIT CT/SYS JURID
SANCTION CRIME INGP/REL OWN SUPEGO ORD/FREE...T 19. METH/CNCPT
PAGE 6 E0120

B75
MAINE H.S.,LECTURES ON THE EARLY HISTORY OF CULTURE
INSTITUTIONS. IRELAND UK CONSTN ELITES STRUCT FAM LAW
KIN CHIEF LEGIS CT/SYS OWN SOVEREIGN...CONCPT 16 INGP/REL
BENTHAM/J BREHON ROMAN/LAW. PAGE 68 E1351

B76
BENTHAM J.,THE THEORY OF LEGISLATION. UK CREATE LEGIS
CRIME ATTIT ORD/FREE...CONCPT 18 REFORMERS. PAGE 10 LAW
E0196 CRIMLGY
UTIL

POLLOCK F.,ESSAYS IN JURISPRUDENCE AND ETHICS. UNIV LAW FINAN MARKET WORKER INGP/REL MORAL...POLICY GEN/LAWS. PAGE 81 E1625
B82
JURID
CONCPT

GOODNOW F.J.,"AN EXECUTIVE AND THE COURTS: JUDICIAL REMEDIES AGAINST ADMINISTRATIVE ACTION" FRANCE UK USA-45 WOR-45 LAW CONSTN SANCTION ORD/FREE 19. PAGE 45 E0888
L86
CT/SYS
GOV/REL
ADMIN
ADJUD

BENTHAM J.,DEFENCE OF USURY (1787). UK LAW NAT/G TEC/DEV ECO/TAC CONTROL ATTIT...CONCPT IDEA/COMP 18 SMITH/ADAM. PAGE 10 E0197
B88
TAX
FINAN
ECO/DEV
POLICY

FERNEUIL T.,LES PRINCIPES DE 1789 ET LA SCIENCE SOCIALE. FRANCE NAT/G REV ATTIT...CONCPT TREND IDEA/COMP 18/19. PAGE 37 E0739
B89
CONSTN
POLICY
LAW

FICHTE J.G.,THE SCIENCE OF RIGHTS (TRANS. BY A.E. KROEGER). WOR-45 FAM MUNIC NAT/G PROVS ADJUD CRIME CHOOSE MARRIAGE SEX POPULISM 19 FICHTE/JG NATURL/LAW. PAGE 37 E0744
B89
ORD/FREE
CONSTN
LAW
CONCPT

BURGESS J.W.,POLITICAL SCIENCE AND COMPARATIVE CONSTITUTIONAL LAW. FRANCE GERMANY UK USA-45 LEGIS DIPLOM ADJUD REPRESENT...CONCPT 19. PAGE 17 E0340
B90
CONSTN
LAW
LOC/G
NAT/G

BENTHAM J.,A FRAGMENT ON GOVERNMENT (1776). CONSTN MUNIC NAT/G SECT AGREE HAPPINESS UTIL MORAL ORD/FREE...JURID CONCPT. PAGE 10 E0198
B91
SOVEREIGN
LAW
DOMIN

DOLE C.F.,THE AMERICAN CITIZEN. USA-45 LAW PARTIC ATTIT...INT/LAW 19. PAGE 32 E0633
B91
NAT/G
MORAL
NAT/LISM
MAJORITY

SIDGWICK H.,THE ELEMENTS OF POLITICS. LOC/G NAT/G LEGIS DIPLOM ADJUD CONTROL EXEC PARL/PROC REPRESENT GOV/REL SOVEREIGN ALL/IDEOS 19 MILL/JS BENTHAM/J. PAGE 91 E1822
B91
POLICY
LAW
CONCPT

DE VATTEL E.,THE LAW OF NATIONS. AGRI FINAN CHIEF DIPLOM INT/TRADE AGREE OWN ALL/VALS MORAL ORD/FREE SOVEREIGN...GEN/LAWS 18 NATURL/LAW WOLFF/C. PAGE 30 E0597
B96
LAW
CONCPT
NAT/G
INT/LAW

ESMEIN A.,ELEMENTS DE DROIT CONSTITUTIONNEL. FRANCE UK CHIEF EX/STRUC LEGIS ADJUD CT/SYS PARL/PROC REV GOV/REL ORD/FREE...JURID METH/COMP 18/19. PAGE 35 E0697
B96
LAW
CONSTN
NAT/G
CONCPT

SMITH A.,LECTURES ON JUSTICE, POLICE, REVENUE AND ARMS (1763). UK LAW FAM FORCES TARIFFS AGREE COERCE INCOME OWN WEALTH LAISSEZ...GEN/LAWS 17/18. PAGE 92 E1840
B96
DIPLOM
JURID
OLD/LIB
TAX

JENKS E.J.,LAW AND POLITICS IN THE MIDDLE AGES. CHRIST-17C CULTURE STRUC KIN NAT/G SECT CT/SYS GP/REL...CLASSIF CHARTS IDEA/COMP BIBLIOG 8/16. PAGE 58 E1162
B97
LAW
SOCIETY
ADJUST

US DEPARTMENT OF STATE,CATALOGUE OF WORKS RELATING TO THE LAW OF NATIONS AND DIPLOMACY IN THE LIBRARY OF THE DEPARTMENT OF STATE (PAMPHLET). WOR-45 NAT/G LAW ADJUD CT/SYS...INT/LAW JURID 19. PAGE 100 E2000
B97
BIBLIOG/A
DIPLOM
LAW

POLLOCK F.,THE HISTORY OF ENGLISH LAW BEFORE THE TIME OF EDWARD I (2 VOLS, 2ND ED.). UK CULTURE LOC/G LEGIS LICENSE AGREE CONTROL CT/SYS SANCTION CRIME...TIME/SEQ 13 COMMON/LAW CANON/LAW. PAGE 81 E1626
B98
LAW
ADJUD
JURID

LILLY W.S.,FIRST PRINCIPLES IN POLITICS. UNIV LAW LEGIS DOMIN ADJUD INGP/REL ORD/FREE SOVEREIGN ...JURID CONCPT 19 NATURL/LAW. PAGE 65 E1299
B99
NAT/G
CONSTN
MORAL
POLICY

LAW COMMISSION OF INDIA E1269

LAW/ETHIC....ETHICS OF LAW AND COURT PROCESSES

LAWRENC/TE....THOMAS EDWARD LAWRENCE

LAWSON F.H. E1195

LAWSON R. E1270

LAWYERS COMM AMER POLICY VIET E1271

LAY S.H. E1272

LAZRSFLD/P....PAUL LAZARSFELD (AND LAZARSFELD SCALE)

LEAD....LEADING, CONTRIBUTING MORE THAN AVERAGE

DEUTSCHE BIBLIOTH FRANKF A M,DEUTSCHE BIBLIOGRAPHIE. EUR+WWI GERMANY ECO/DEV FORCES DIPLOM LEAD...POLICY PHIL/SCI SOC 20. PAGE 31 E0612
B
BIBLIOG
LAW
ADMIN
NAT/G

INTERNATIONAL STUDIES. ASIA S/ASIA WOR+45 ECO/UNDEV INT/ORG NAT/G LEAD ATTIT WEALTH...SOC 20. PAGE 1 E0009
N
BIBLIOG/A
DIPLOM
INT/LAW
INT/TRADE

MIDWEST JOURNAL OF POLITICAL SCIENCE. USA+45 CONSTN ECO/DEV LEGIS PROB/SOLV CT/SYS LEAD GOV/REL ATTIT POLICY. PAGE 1 E0012
N
BIBLIOG/A
NAT/G
DIPLOM
POL/PAR

POLITICAL SCIENCE QUARTERLY. USA+45 USA-45 LAW CONSTN ECO/DEV INT/ORG LOC/G POL/PAR LEGIS LEAD NUC/PWR...CONCPT 20. PAGE 1 E0013
N
BIBLIOG/A
NAT/G
DIPLOM
POLICY

BIBLIOGRAPHIE DER SOZIALWISSENSCHAFTEN. WOR-45 CONSTN SOCIETY ECO/DEV ECO/UNDEV DIPLOM LEAD WAR PEACE...PHIL/SCI SOC 19/20. PAGE 1 E0019
N
BIBLIOG
LAW
CONCPT
NAT/G

HANDBOOK OF LATIN AMERICAN STUDIES. LAW CULTURE ECO/UNDEV POL/PAR ADMIN LEAD...SOC 20. PAGE 1 E0022
N
BIBLIOG/A
L/A+17C
NAT/G
DIPLOM

PUBLISHERS' CIRCULAR, THE OFFICIAL ORGAN OF THE PUBLISHERS' ASSOCIATION OF GREAT BRITAIN AND IRELAND. EUR+WWI MOD/EUR UK LAW PROB/SOLV DIPLOM COLONIAL ATTIT...HUM 19/20 CMN/WLTH. PAGE 2 E0025
N
BIBLIOG
NAT/G
WRITING
LEAD

NEUE POLITISCHE LITERATUR; BERICHTE UBER DAS INTERNATIONALE SCHRIFTTUM ZUR POLITIK. WOR+45 LAW CONSTN POL/PAR ADMIN LEAD GOV/REL...POLICY IDEA/COMP. PAGE 2 E0028
N
BIBLIOG/A
DIPLOM
NAT/G
NAT/COMP

ASIA FOUNDATION,LIBRARY NOTES. LAW CONSTN CULTURE SOCIETY ECO/UNDEV INT/ORG NAT/G COLONIAL LEAD REGION NAT/LISM ATTIT 20 UN. PAGE 6 E0107
N
BIBLIOG/A
ASIA
S/ASIA
DIPLOM

ATLANTIC INSTITUTE,ATLANTIC STUDIES. COM EUR+WWI USA+45 CULTURE STRUC ECO/DEV FORCES LEAD ARMS/CONT ...INT/LAW JURID SOC. PAGE 6 E0110
N
BIBLIOG/A
DIPLOM
POLICY
GOV/REL

CORNELL UNIVERSITY LIBRARY,SOUTHEAST ASIA ACCESSIONS LIST. LAW SOCIETY STRUC ECO/UNDEV POL/PAR TEC/DEV DIPLOM LEAD REGION. PAGE 26 E0510
N
BIBLIOG
S/ASIA
NAT/G
CULTURE

DEUTSCHE BUCHEREI,DEUTSCHES BUCHERVERZEICHNIS. GERMANY LAW CULTURE POL/PAR ADMIN LEAD ATTIT PERSON ...SOC 20. PAGE 31 E0615
N
BIBLIOG
NAT/G
DIPLOM
ECO/DEV

NEW YORK STATE LIBRARY,CHECKLIST OF OFFICIAL PUBLICATIONS OF THE STATE OF NEW YORK. USA+45 USA-45 LAW PROB/SOLV LEAD ATTIT 19/20. PAGE 77 E1539
N
BIBLIOG
PROVS
WRITING
GOV/REL

PUBLISHERS' CIRCULAR LIMITED,THE ENGLISH CATALOGUE
N
BIBLIOG

OF BOOKS. UK WOR+45 WOR-45 LAW CULTURE LOC/G NAT/G ADMIN LEAD...MGT 19/20. PAGE 83 E1658
ALL/VALS ALL/IDEOS SOCIETY

N
UNITED NATIONS,UNITED NATIONS PUBLICATIONS. WOR+45 ECO/UNDEV AGRI FINAN FORCES ADMIN LEAD WAR PEACE ...POLICY INT/LAW 20 UN. PAGE 98 E1965
BIBLIOG INT/ORG DIPLOM

N
US SUPERINTENDENT OF DOCUMENTS,EDUCATION (PRICE LIST 31). USA+45 LAW FINAN LOC/G NAT/G DEBATE ADMIN LEAD RACE/REL FEDERAL HEALTH POLICY. PAGE 103 E2062
BIBLIOG/A EDU/PROP ACADEM SCHOOL

B00
GREELY A.W.,PUBLIC DOCUMENTS OF THE FIRST FOURTEEN CONGRESSES, 1789-1817. USA-45 LEAD REPRESENT ATTIT 18/19 CONGRESS. PAGE 45 E0904
BIBLIOG/A NAT/G LAW LEGIS

N19
OPERATIONS AND POLICY RESEARCH,URUGUAY: ELECTION FACTBOOK: NOVEMBER 27, 1966 (PAMPHLET). URUGUAY LAW NAT/G LEAD REPRESENT...STAT BIOG CHARTS 20. PAGE 79 E1576
POL/PAR CHOOSE PLAN ATTIT

B21
CARDOZO B.N.,THE NATURE OF THE JUDICIAL PROCESS. ROUTINE ORD/FREE...POLICY 20. PAGE 19 E0377
JURID CT/SYS LEAD DECISION

B27
GOOCH G.P.,ENGLISH DEMOCRATIC IDEAS IN THE SEVENTEENTH CENTURY (2ND ED). UK LAW SECT FORCES DIPLOM LEAD PARL/PROC REV ATTIT AUTHORIT...ANARCH CONCPT 17 PARLIAMENT CMN/WLTH REFORMERS. PAGE 45 E0885
IDEA/COMP MAJORIT EX/STRUC CONSERVE

B29
MOLEY R.,POLITICS AND CRIMINAL PROSECUTION. USA-45 POL/PAR EX/STRUC LEGIT CONTROL LEAD ROUTINE CHOOSE INGP/REL...JURID CHARTS 20. PAGE 74 E1481
PWR CT/SYS CRIME ADJUD

B31
COLUMBIA UNIVERSITY,A BIBLIOGRAPHY OF THE FACULTY OF POLITICAL SCIENCE OF COLUMBIA UNIVERSITY, 1880-1930. USA-45 LAW NAT/G LEGIS DIPLOM LEAD WAR GOV/REL ATTIT...TIME/SEQ 19/20. PAGE 24 E0478
BIBLIOG ACADEM PHIL/SCI

B38
FIELD G.L.,THE SYNDICAL AND CORPORATIVE INSTITUTIONS OF ITALIAN FASCISM. ITALY CONSTN STRATA LABOR EX/STRUC TOP/EX ADJUD ADMIN LEAD TOTALISM AUTHORIT...MGT 20 MUSSOLIN/B. PAGE 38 E0746
FASCISM INDUS NAT/G WORKER

B38
HARPER S.N.,THE GOVERNMENT OF THE SOVIET UNION. COM USSR LAW CONSTN ECO/DEV PLAN TEC/DEV DIPLOM INT/TRADE ADMIN REV NAT/LISM...POLICY 20. PAGE 50 E1001
MARXISM NAT/G LEAD POL/PAR

B38
HOLDSWORTH W.S.,A HISTORY OF ENGLISH LAW; THE CENTURIES OF SETTLEMENT AND REFORM (VOL. XI). UK CONSTN NAT/G EX/STRUC DIPLOM ADJUD CT/SYS LEAD CRIME ATTIT...INT/LAW JURID 18 CMN/WLTH PARLIAMENT ENGLSH/LAW. PAGE 54 E1079
LAW COLONIAL LEGIS PARL/PROC

S38
CLEMMER D.,"LEADERSHIP PHENOMENA IN A PRISON COMMUNITY." NEIGH PLAN CHOOSE PERSON ROLE...OBS INT. PAGE 23 E0452
PUB/INST CRIMLGY LEAD CLIENT

B39
BALDWIN L.D.,WHISKEY REBELS; THE STORY OF A FRONTIER UPRISING. USA-45 LAW ADJUD LEAD COERCE PWR ...BIBLIOG/A 18 PENNSYLVAN FEDERALIST. PAGE 8 E0145
REV POL/PAR TAX TIME/SEQ

B40
HART J.,AN INTRODUCTION TO ADMINISTRATIVE LAW, WITH SELECTED CASES. USA-45 CONSTN SOCIETY NAT/G EX/STRUC ADJUD CT/SYS LEAD CRIME ORD/FREE ...DECISION JURID 20 CASEBOOK. PAGE 50 E1002
LAW ADMIN LEGIS PWR

S40
GERTH H.,"THE NAZI PARTY: ITS LEADERSHIP AND COMPOSITION" (BMR). GERMANY ELITES STRATA STRUCT EX/STRUC FORCES ECO/TAC CT/SYS CHOOSE TOTALISM AGE/Y AUTHORIT PWR 20. PAGE 43 E0851
POL/PAR DOMIN LEAD ADMIN

B42
CARR R.K.,THE SUPREME COURT AND JUDICIAL REVIEW. NAT/G CHIEF LEGIS OP/RES LEAD GOV/REL GP/REL ATTIT ...POLICY DECISION 18/20 SUPREME/CT PRESIDENT CONGRESS. PAGE 20 E0394
CT/SYS CONSTN JURID PWR

B44
BEARD C.A.,AMERICAN GOVERNMENT AND POLITICS (REV. ED). CONSTN MUNIC POL/PAR PROVS EX/STRUC LEGIS TOP/EX CT/SYS GOV/REL...BIBLIOG T 18/20. PAGE 9 E0165
LEAD USA+45 NAT/G LOC/G

S44
GRIFFITH E.S.,"THE CHANGING PATTERN OF PUBLIC POLICY FORMATION." MOD/EUR WOR+45 FINAN CHIEF CONFER ADMIN LEAD CONSERVE SOCISM TECHRACY...SOC CHARTS CONGRESS. PAGE 47 E0938
LAW POLICY TEC/DEV

S46
CANTWELL F.V.,"PUBLIC OPINION AND THE LEGISLATIVE PROCESS" USA+45 USA-45 NAT/G CT/SYS EXEC LEAD DECISION. PAGE 19 E0374
CHARTS DEBATE LEGIS ATTIT

B50
COUNCIL BRITISH NATIONAL BIB,BRITISH NATIONAL BIBLIOGRAPHY. UK AGRI CONSTRUC PERF/ART POL/PAR SECT CREATE INT/TRADE LEAD...HUM JURID PHIL/SCI 20. PAGE 26 E0519
BIBLIOG/A NAT/G TEC/DEV DIPLOM

B50
MERRIAM C.E.,THE AMERICAN PARTY SYSTEM; AN INTRODUCTION TO THE STUDY OF POLITICAL PARTIES IN THE UNITED STATES (4TH ED). USA+45 USA-45 LAW FINAN LOC/G NAT/G PROVS LEAD PARTIC CRIME ATTIT 18/20 NEGRO CONGRESS PRESIDENT. PAGE 72 E1442
POL/PAR CHOOSE SUFF REPRESENT

B51
GIBBS C.R.,CONSTITUTIONAL AND STATUTORY PROVISIONS OF THE STATES (VOL. IX). USA+45 LICENSE ADJUD LEAD 20. PAGE 43 E0857
PROVS CONSTN JURID LOBBY

B52
US DEPARTMENT OF STATE,RESEARCH ON EASTERN EUROPE (EXCLUDING USSR). EUR+WWI LAW ECO/DEV NAT/G PROB/SOLV DIPLOM ADMIN LEAD MARXISM...TREND 19/20. PAGE 100 E1995
BIBLIOG R+D ACT/RES COM

B53
GROSS B.M.,THE LEGISLATIVE STRUGGLE: A STUDY IN SOCIAL COMBAT. STRUCT LOC/G POL/PAR JUDGE EDU/PROP DEBATE ETIQUET ADMIN LOBBY CHOOSE GOV/REL INGP/REL HEREDITY ALL/VALS...SOC PRESIDENT. PAGE 48 E0948
LEGIS DECISION PERSON LEAD

B54
ELIAS T.O.,GROUNDWORK OF NIGERIAN LAW. AFR LEAD CRIME INGP/REL ORD/FREE 17/20. PAGE 34 E0680
JURID CT/SYS CONSTN CONSULT

B55
BENTON W.E.,NUREMBERG: GERMAN VIEWS OF THE WAR TRIALS. EUR+WWI GERMANY VOL/ASSN LEAD PARTIC COERCE INGP/REL RACE/REL TOTALISM SUPEGO ORD/FREE...ANTHOL NUREMBERG. PAGE 10 E0201
CRIME WAR LAW JURID

B55
WHEARE K.C.,GOVERNMENT BY COMMITTEE; AN ESSAY ON THE BRITISH CONSTITUTION. UK NAT/G LEGIS INSPECT CONFER ADJUD ADMIN CONTROL TASK EFFICIENCY ROLE POPULISM 20. PAGE 106 E2116
DELIB/GP CONSTN LEAD GP/COMP

B56
BOTERO G.,THE REASON OF STATE AND THE GREATNESS OF CITIES. SECT CHIEF FORCES PLAN LEAD WAR MORAL ...POLICY 16 MACHIAVELL TREATY. PAGE 14 E0272
PHIL/SCI NEW/IDEA CONTROL

B56
FRANCIS R.G.,SERVICE AND PROCEDURE IN BUREAUCRACY. EXEC LEAD ROUTINE...QU 20. PAGE 39 E0784
CLIENT ADMIN INGP/REL REPRESENT

B56
RECASENS SICHES S.,TRATADO GENERAL DE SOCIOLOGIA. CULTURE FAM NEIGH LEAD RACE/REL DISCRIM HABITAT ORD/FREE...JURID LING T SOC/INTEG 20. PAGE 84 E1677
SOC STRATA KIN GP/REL

C56
FALL B.B.,"THE VIET-MINH REGIME." VIETNAM LAW ECO/UNDEV POL/PAR FORCES DOMIN WAR ATTIT MARXISM ...BIOG PREDICT BIBLIOG/A 20. PAGE 36 E0720
NAT/G ADMIN EX/STRUC LEAD

DONALDSON A.G.,SOME COMPARATIVE ASPECTS OF IRISH
LAW. IRELAND NAT/G DIPLOM ADMIN CT/SYS LEAD ATTIT
SOVEREIGN...JURID BIBLIOG/A 12/20 CMN/WLTH. PAGE 32
E0635
CONSTN
LAW
NAT/COMP
INT/LAW
B57

MEYER P.,ADMINISTRATIVE ORGANIZATION: A COMPARATIVE
STUDY OF THE ORGANIZATION OF PUBLIC ADMINISTRATION.
DENMARK FRANCE NORWAY SWEDEN UK USA+45 ELITES LOC/G
CONSULT LEGIS ADJUD CONTROL LEAD PWR SKILL
DECISION. PAGE 72 E1449
ADMIN
METH/COMP
NAT/G
CENTRAL
B57

ROWAN C.T.,GO SOUTH TO SORROW. USA+45 STRUCT NAT/G
EDU/PROP LEAD COERCE ISOLAT DRIVE SUPEGO RESPECT
...PREDICT 20 NEGRO SUPREME/CT SOUTH/US CIV/RIGHTS.
PAGE 86 E1728
RACE/REL
DISCRIM
ANOMIE
LAW
B57

KNEIER C.M.,"MISLEADING THE VOTERS." CONSTN LEAD
CHOOSE PERS/REL. PAGE 61 E1224
MUNIC
REPRESENT
LAW
ATTIT
S57

CLEMMER D.,THE PRISON COMMUNITY. CULTURE CONTROL
LEAD ROUTINE PERS/REL PERSON...SOC METH/CNCPT.
PAGE 23 E0453
PUB/INST
CRIMLGY
CLIENT
INGP/REL
B58

BEVAN W.,"JURY BEHAVIOR AS A FUNCTION OF THE
PRESTIGE OF THE FOREMAN AND THE NATURE OF HIS
LEADERSHIP" (BMR)" DELIB/GP DOMIN ADJUD LEAD
PERS/REL ATTIT...PSY STAT INT QU CHARTS SOC/EXP 20
JURY. PAGE 11 E0221
PERSON
EDU/PROP
DECISION
CT/SYS
L58

KNIERIEM A.,THE NUREMBERG TRIALS. EUR+WWI GERMANY
VOL/ASSN LEAD COERCE WAR INGP/REL TOTALISM SUPEGO
ORD/FREE...CONCPT METH/COMP. PAGE 61 E1225
INT/LAW
CRIME
PARTIC
JURID
B59

SCHUBERT G.A.,QUANTITATIVE ANALYSIS OF JUDICIAL
BEHAVIOR. ADJUD LEAD CHOOSE INGP/REL MAJORITY ATTIT
...DECISION JURID CHARTS GAME SIMUL SUPREME/CT.
PAGE 89 E1780
JUDGE
CT/SYS
PERSON
QUANT
B59

DERGE D.R.,"THE LAWYER AS DECISION-MAKER IN THE
AMERICAN STATE LEGISLATURE." INTELL LOC/G POL/PAR
CHOOSE AGE HEREDITY PERSON CONSERVE...JURID STAT
CHARTS. PAGE 31 E0607
LEGIS
LAW
DECISION
LEAD
S59

DWYER R.J.,"THE ADMINISTRATIVE ROLE IN
DESEGREGATION." USA+45 LAW PROB/SOLV LEAD RACE/REL
ISOLAT STRANGE ROLE...POLICY SOC/INTEG MISSOURI
NEGRO CIV/RIGHTS. PAGE 34 E0668
ADMIN
SCHOOL
DISCRIM
ATTIT
S59

BERTHOLD O.,KAISER, VOLK UND AVIGNON. GERMANY CHIEF
LEGIT LEAD NAT/LISM CONSERVE 14 POPE CHRUCH/STA
LUDWIG/BAV JOHN/XXII. PAGE 11 E0217
DIPLOM
CATHISM
JURID
B60

CARTER R.F.,COMMUNITIES AND THEIR SCHOOLS. USA+45
LAW FINAN PROVS BUDGET TAX LEAD PARTIC CHOOSE...SOC
INT QU 20. PAGE 20 E0401
SCHOOL
ACT/RES
NEIGH
INGP/REL
B60

FISCHER L.,THE SOVIETS IN WORLD AFFAIRS. CHINA/COM
COM EUR+WWI USSR INT/ORG CONFER LEAD ARMS/CONT REV
PWR...CHARTS 20 TREATY VERSAILLES. PAGE 38 E0755
DIPLOM
NAT/G
POLICY
MARXISM
B60

FLORES R.H.,CATALOGO DE TESIS DOCTORALES DE LAS
FACULTADES DE LA UNIVERSIDAD DE EL SALVADOR.
EL/SALVADR LAW DIPLOM ADMIN LEAD GOV/REL...SOC
19/20. PAGE 39 E0767
BIBLIOG
ACADEM
L/A+17C
NAT/G
B60

BARBASH J.,LABOR'S GRASS ROOTS. CONSTN NAT/G
EX/STRUC LEGIS WORKER LEAD...MAJORIT BIBLIOG.
PAGE 8 E0147
LABOR
INGP/REL
GP/REL
LAW
B61

WINTERS J.M.,STATE CONSTITUTIONAL LIMITATIONS ON
SOLUTIONS OF METROPOLITAN AREA PROBLEMS. CONSTN
LEGIS LEAD REPRESENT DECISION. PAGE 107 E2134
MUNIC
REGION
LOC/G
LAW
B61

COSTA RICA UNIVERSIDAD BIBL,LISTA DE TESIS DE GRADO
DE LA UNIVERSIDAD DE COSTA RICA. COSTA/RICA LAW
LOC/G ADMIN LEAD...SOC 20. PAGE 26 E0518
BIBLIOG/A
NAT/G
DIPLOM
ECO/UNDEV
B62

GALENSON W.,TRADE UNIONS MONOGRAPH SERIES (A SERIES
OF NINE TEXTS). DELIB/GP LEAD PARTIC...DECISION
ORG/CHARTS. PAGE 42 E0827
LABOR
INGP/REL
CONSTN
REPRESENT
B62

HEYDECKER J.J.,THE NUREMBERG TRIAL: HISTORY OF NAZI
GERMANY AS REVEALED THROUGH THE TESTIMONY AT
NUREMBERG. EUR+WWI GERMANY VOL/ASSN LEAD COERCE
CROWD INGP/REL RACE/REL SUPEGO ORD/FREE...CONCPT 20
NAZI ANTI/SEMIT NUREMBERG JEWS. PAGE 52 E1036
LAW
CRIME
PARTIC
TOTALISM
B62

WINTERS J.M.,INTERSTATE METROPOLITAN AREAS. CONSTN
LEAD CHOOSE PWR DECISION. PAGE 107 E2135
MUNIC
LAW
REGION
GOV/REL
B62

US ADVISORY COMN INTERGOV REL,APPORTIONMENT OF
STATE LEGISLATURES (PAMPHLET). LAW CONSTN EX/STRUC
LEGIS LEAD MAJORITY. PAGE 99 E1977
MUNIC
PROVS
REPRESENT
APPORT
N62

US SENATE COMM ON JUDICIARY,LEGISLATION TO
STRENGTHEN PENALTIES UNDER THE ANTITRUST LAWS
(PAMPHLET). USA+45 LG/CO CONFER CONTROL SANCTION
ORD/FREE 20 SENATE MONOPOLY. PAGE 102 E2045
LEAD
ADJUD
INDUS
ECO/TAC
N62

ECOLE NATIONALE D'ADMIN,BIBLIOGRAPHIE SELECTIVE
D'OUVRAGES DE LANGUE FRANCAISE TRAITANT DES
PROBLEMES GOUVERNEMENTAUX ET ADMINISTRATIFS. NAT/G
FORCES ACT/RES OP/RES PLAN PROB/SOLV BUDGET ADJUD
COLONIAL LEAD 20. PAGE 34 E0672
BIBLIOG
AFR
ADMIN
EX/STRUC
B63

HYNEMAN C.S.,THE SUPREME COURT ON TRIAL. ADJUD LEAD
GP/REL FEDERAL...IDEA/COMP 20 SUPREME/CT. PAGE 56
E1120
CT/SYS
JURID
POLICY
NAT/G
B63

MOLLARD P.T.,LE REGIME JURIDIQUE DE LA PRESSE AU
MAROC. MOROCCO CONTROL CRIME GP/REL ORD/FREE 20.
PAGE 74 E1482
PRESS
LAW
LEAD
LEGIT
B63

US SENATE,DOCUMENTS ON INTERNATIONAL AS"ECTS OF
EXPLORATION AND USE OF OUTER SPACE, 1954-62: STAFF
REPORT FOR COMM AERON SPACE SCI. USA+45 USSR LEGIS
LEAD CIVMIL/REL PEACE...POLICY INT/LAW ANTHOL 20
CONGRESS NASA KHRUSH/N. PAGE 101 E2026
SPACE
UTIL
GOV/REL
DIPLOM
B63

HILLS R.J.,"THE REPRESENTATIVE FUNCTION: NEGLECTED
DIMENSION OF LEADERSHIP BEHAVIOR" USA+45 CLIENT
STRUCT SCHOOL PERS/REL...STAT QU SAMP LAB/EXP 20.
PAGE 53 E1048
LEAD
ADMIN
EXEC
ACT/RES
S63

SCHUBERT G.,"JUDICIAL DECISION-MAKING." FORCES LEAD
ATTIT DRIVE...POLICY PSY STAT CHARTS ANTHOL BIBLIOG
20. PAGE 88 E1773
ADJUD
DECISION
JUDGE
CT/SYS
C63

DOOLIN D.J.,COMMUNIST CHINA: THE POLITICS OF
STUDENT OPPOSITION. CHINA/COM ELITES STRATA ACADEM
NAT/G WRITING CT/SYS LEAD PARTIC COERCE TOTALISM
20. PAGE 32 E0637
MARXISM
DEBATE
AGE/Y
PWR
B64

GRZYBOWSKI K.,THE SOCIALIST COMMONWEALTH OF
NATIONS: ORGANIZATIONS AND INSTITUTIONS. FORCES
DIPLOM INT/TRADE ADJUD ADMIN LEAD WAR MARXISM
SOCISM...BIBLIOG 20 COMECON WARSAW/P. PAGE 48 E0956
INT/LAW
COM
REGION
INT/ORG
B64

HAMILTON H.D.,LEGISLATIVE APPORTIONMENT; KEY TO
POWER. USA+45 LAW CONSTN PROVS LOBBY CHOOSE ATTIT
SUPREME/CT. PAGE 50 E0988
APPORT
CT/SYS
LEAD
REPRESENT
B64

HOLDSWORTH W.S.,A HISTORY OF ENGLISH LAW; THE
LAW
B64

CENTURIES OF DEVELOPMENT AND REFORM (VOL. XIV). UK   LEGIS
CONSTN LOC/G NAT/G POL/PAR CHIEF EX/STRUC ADJUD   LEAD
COLONIAL ATTIT...INT/LAW JURID 18/19 TORY/PARTY   CT/SYS
COMMONWLTH WHIG/PARTY COMMON/LAW. PAGE 54 E1081

B64

KOREA (REPUBLIC) SUPREME COURT,KOREAN LEGAL SYSTEM.   JURID
KOREA/S WOR+45 LAW LEAD ROUTINE GOV/REL ORD/FREE 20   CT/SYS
SUPREME/CT. PAGE 61 E1229   CONSTN
   CRIME

B64

MCWHINNEY E.,"PEACEFUL COEXISTENCE" AND SOVIET-   PEACE
WESTERN INTERNATIONAL LAW. USSR DIPLOM LEAD...JURID   IDEA/COMP
20 COLD/WAR. PAGE 71 E1429   INT/LAW
   ATTIT

B64

OPPENHEIMER M.,A MANUAL FOR DIRECT ACTION. USA+45   PLAN
SCHOOL FORCES ADJUD CT/SYS SUFF RACE/REL DISCRIM   VOL/ASSN
...POLICY CHARTS 20. PAGE 79 E1580   JURID
   LEAD

S64

PRITCHETT C.H.,"EQUAL PROTECTION AND THE URBAN   MUNIC
MAJORITY." POL/PAR LEAD CHOOSE GP/REL PWR...MAJORIT   LAW
DECISION. PAGE 83 E1655   REPRESENT
   APPORT

B65

CHROUST A.H.,THE RISE OF THE LEGAL PROFESSION IN   JURID
AMERICA (3 VOLS.). STRATA STRUCT POL/PAR PROF/ORG   USA-45
COLONIAL LEAD REV SKILL...SOC 17/20. PAGE 22 E0437   CT/SYS
   LAW

B65

FEERICK J.D.,FROM FAILING HANDS: THE STUDY OF   EX/STRUC
PRESIDENTIAL SUCCESSION. CONSTN NAT/G PROB/SOLV   CHIEF
LEAD PARL/PROC MURDER CHOOSE...NEW/IDEA BIBLIOG 20   LAW
KENNEDY/JF JOHNSON/LB PRESIDENT PRE/US/AM   LEGIS
VICE/PRES. PAGE 36 E0724

B65

FERRELL J.S.,CASES AND MATERIALS ON LOCAL   APPORT
APPORTIONMENT. CONSTN LEAD GP/REL...DECISION   LOC/G
GOV/COMP. PAGE 37 E0740   REPRESENT
   LAW

B65

GILLETTE W.,THE RIGHT TO VOTE: POLITICS AND THE   RACE/REL
PASSAGE OF THE FIFTEENTH AMENDMENT. USA-45 LAW LEAD   CONSTN
DISCRIM SEGREGAT CONGRESS. PAGE 44 E0863

B65

MOELLER R.,LUDWIG DER BAYER UND DIE KURIE IM KAMPF   JURID
UM DAS REICH. GERMANY LAW SECT LEGIT LEAD GP/REL   CHIEF
CATHISM CONSERVE 14 LUDWIG/BAV POPE CHURCH/STA.   CHOOSE
PAGE 74 E1478   NAT/LISM

B65

ROSS P.,THE GOVERNMENT AS A SOURCE OF UNION POWER.   LABOR
USA+45 LAW ECO/DEV PROB/SOLV ECO/TAC LEAD GP/REL   BARGAIN
...MGT 20. PAGE 86 E1723   POLICY
   NAT/G

S65

DIXON R.G.,"NEW CONSTITUTIONAL FORMS FOR   MUNIC
METROPOLIS: REAPPORTIONED COUNTY BOARDS; LOCAL   REGION
COUNCILS OF GOVERNMENT." LAW CONSTN LEAD APPORT   GOV/COMP
REPRESENT DECISION. PAGE 32 E0631   PLAN

B66

AUERBACH J.S.,LABOR AND LIBERTY; THE LA FOLLETTE   DELIB/GP
COMMITTEE AND THE NEW DEAL. USA-45 LAW LEAD RESPECT   LABOR
SOCISM...BIBLIOG 20 CONGRESS BILL/RIGHT LAFOLLET/R   CONSTN
NEW/DEAL. PAGE 6 E0117   ORD/FREE

B66

BAXTER M.G.,DANIEL WEBSTER & THE SUPREME COURT. LAW   CONSTN
NAT/G PROF/ORG DEBATE ADJUD LEAD FEDERAL PERSON.   CT/SYS
PAGE 8 E0156   JURID

B66

HARVEY W.B.,LAW AND SOCIAL CHANGE IN GHANA. AFR   JURID
GHANA CONSULT CONTROL CT/SYS INGP/REL 20. PAGE 51   CONSTN
E1011   LEAD
   ORD/FREE

B66

HIDAYATULLAH M.,DEMOCRACY IN INDIA AND THE JUDICIAL   NAT/G
PROCESS. INDIA EX/STRUC LEGIS LEAD GOV/REL ATTIT   CT/SYS
ORD/FREE...MAJORIT CONCPT 20 NEHRU/J. PAGE 52 E1040   CONSTN
   JURID

B66

HOLDSWORTH W.S.,A HISTORY OF ENGLISH LAW; THE   BIOG

CENTURIES OF SETTLEMENT AND REFORM (VOL. XVI). UK   PERSON
LOC/G NAT/G EX/STRUC LEGIS CT/SYS LEAD ATTIT   PROF/ORG
...POLICY DECISION JURID IDEA/COMP 18 PARLIAMENT.   LAW
PAGE 54 E1083

B66

HOLTZMAN A.,INTEREST GROUPS AND LOBBYING. USA+45   LOBBY
CHIEF ACT/RES ADJUD LEAD PARTIC CHOOSE...POLICY 20   NAT/G
CONGRESS. PAGE 55 E1092   EDU/PROP
   GP/REL

B66

KERR M.H.,ISLAMIC REFORM: THE POLITICAL AND LEGAL   LAW
THEORIES OF MUHAMMAD 'ABDUH AND RASHID RIDA. NAT/G   CONCPT
SECT LEAD SOVEREIGN CONSERVE...JURID BIBLIOG   ISLAM
WORSHIP 20. PAGE 60 E1204

B66

MACMULLEN R.,ENEMIES OF THE ROMAN EMPIRE: TREASON,   CRIME
UNREST, AND ALIENATION IN THE EMPIRE. ROMAN/EMP   ADJUD
MUNIC CONTROL LEAD ATTIT PERSON MYSTISM...PHIL/SCI   MORAL
BIBLIOG. PAGE 67 E1345   SOCIETY

B66

OLSON W.C.,THE THEORY AND PRACTICE OF INTERNATIONAL   DIPLOM
RELATIONS (2ND ED.). WOR+45 LEAD SUPEGO...INT/LAW   NAT/G
PHIL/SCI. PAGE 79 E1575   INT/ORG
   POLICY

B66

US DEPARTMENT OF STATE,RESEARCH ON AFRICA (EXTERNAL   BIBLIOG/A
RESEARCH LIST NO 5-25). LAW CULTURE ECO/UNDEV   ASIA
POL/PAR DIPLOM EDU/PROP LEAD REGION MARXISM...GEOG   S/ASIA
LING WORSHIP 20. PAGE 100 E1996   NAT/G

B66

US SENATE COMM ON JUDICIARY,HEARINGS ON FREE PRESS   PRESS
AND FAIR TRIAL (2 VOLS.). USA+45 CONSTN ELITES   LAW
LEGIS EDU/PROP CT/SYS LEAD CONGRESS. PAGE 103 E2057   CRIME
   ORD/FREE

B67

BIBBY J.,ON CAPITOL HILL. POL/PAR LOBBY PARL/PROC   CONFER
GOV/REL PERS/REL...JURID PHIL/SCI OBS INT BIBLIOG   LEGIS
20 CONGRESS PRESIDENT. PAGE 12 E0224   CREATE
   LEAD

B67

COWLING M.,1867 DISRAELI, GLADSTONE, AND   PARL/PROC
REVOLUTION; THE PASSING OF THE SECOND REFORM BILL.   POL/PAR
UK LEGIS LEAD LOBBY GP/REL INGP/REL...DECISION   ATTIT
BIBLIOG 19 REFORMERS. PAGE 27 E0531   LAW

B67

GRAHAM H.D.,CRISIS IN PRINT: DESEGREGATION AND THE   PRESS
PRESS IN TENNESSEE. LAW SOCIETY MUNIC POL/PAR   PROVS
EDU/PROP LEAD REPRESENT DISCRIM ATTIT...IDEA/COMP   POLICY
BIBLIOG/A SOC/INTEG 20 TENNESSEE SUPREME/CT   RACE/REL
SOUTH/US. PAGE 45 E0896

B67

MEYERS M.,SOURCES OF THE AMERICAN REPUBLIC; A   COLONIAL
DOCUMENTARY HISTORY OF POLITICS, SOCIETY, AND   REV
THOUGHT (VOL. I, REV. ED.). USA-45 CULTURE STRUCT   WAR
NAT/G LEGIS LEAD ATTIT...JURID SOC ANTHOL 17/19
PRESIDENT. PAGE 72 E1450

B67

OPERATIONS AND POLICY RESEARCH,NICARAGUA: ELECTION   POL/PAR
FACTBOOK: FEBRUARY 5, 1967 (PAMPHLET). NICARAGUA   CHOOSE
LAW NAT/G LEAD REPRESENT...STAT BIOG CHARTS 20.   PLAN
PAGE 79 E1577   ATTIT

B67

US SENATE COMM ON FOREIGN REL,CONSULAR CONVENTION   LEGIS
WITH THE SOVIET UNION. USA+45 USSR DELIB/GP LEAD   LOBBY
REPRESENT ATTIT ORD/FREE CONGRESS TREATY. PAGE 101   DIPLOM
E2031

S67

MATTHEWS R.O.,"THE SUEZ CANAL DISPUTE* A CASE STUDY   PEACE
IN PEACEFUL SETTLEMENT." FRANCE ISRAEL UAR UK NAT/G   DIPLOM
CONTROL LEAD COERCE WAR NAT/LISM ROLE ORD/FREE PWR   ADJUD
...INT/LAW UN 20. PAGE 69 E1389

S68

SHAPIRO J.P.,"SOVIET HISTORIOGRAPHY AND THE MOSCOW   HIST/WRIT
TRIALS: AFTER THIRTY YEARS." USSR NAT/G LEGIT PRESS   EDU/PROP
CONTROL LEAD ATTIT MARXISM...NEW/IDEA METH 20   SANCTION
TROTSKY/L STALIN/J KHRUSH/N. PAGE 90 E1810   ADJUD

LEADING....SEE LEAD

LEAF R.C. E0601

LEAGUE OF WOMEN VOTERS....SEE LEAGUE/WV

LEAGUE OF NATIONS-SECRETARIAT. E1273

LEAGUE WOMEN VOTERS MASSACHU E1274

LEAGUE WOMEN VOTERS NEW YORK E1275

LEAGUE/NAT....LEAGUE OF NATIONS; SEE ALSO INT/ORG

                                                                                      N
INTERNATIONAL BOOK NEWS, 1928-1934. ECO/UNDEV FINAN   BIBLIOG/A
INDUS LABOR INT/TRADE CONFER ADJUD COLONIAL...HEAL   DIPLOM
SOC/WK CHARTS 20 LEAGUE/NAT. PAGE 1 E0008   INT/LAW
                                                       INT/ORG

                                                                                      N
SOCIETE DES NATIONS,TRAITES INTERNATIONAUX ET ACTES   BIBLIOG
LEGISLATIFS. WOR-45 INT/ORG NAT/G...INT/LAW JURID   DIPLOM
20 LEAGUE/NAT TREATY. PAGE 92 E1851   LEGIS
                                                       ADJUD

                                                         B20
DICKINSON E.,THE EQUALITY OF STATES IN   LAW
INTERNATIONAL LAW. WOR-45 INT/ORG NAT/G DIPLOM   CONCPT
EDU/PROP LEGIT PEACE ATTIT ALL/VALS...JURID   SOVEREIGN
TIME/SEQ LEAGUE/NAT. PAGE 31 E0622

                                                         B22
WRIGHT Q.,THE CONTROL OF AMERICAN FOREIGN   NAT/G
RELATIONS. USA-45 WOR-45 CONSTN INT/ORG CONSULT   EXEC
LEGIS LEGIT ROUTINE ORD/FREE PWR...POLICY JURID   DIPLOM
CONCPT METH/CNCPT RECORD LEAGUE/NAT 20. PAGE 107
E2150

                                                         B24
HALL W.E.,A TREATISE ON INTERNATIONAL LAW. WOR-45   PWR
CONSTN INT/ORG NAT/G DIPLOM ORD/FREE LEAGUE/NAT 20   JURID
TREATY. PAGE 49 E0985   WAR
                                                       INT/LAW

                                                         B27
LAUTERPACHT H.,PRIVATE LAW SOURCES AND ANALOGIES OF   INT/ORG
INTERNATIONAL LAW. WOR-45 NAT/G DELIB/GP LEGIT   ADJUD
COERCE ATTIT ORD/FREE PWR SOVEREIGN...JURID CONCPT   PEACE
HIST/WRIT TIME/SEQ GEN/METH LEAGUE/NAT 20. PAGE 63   INT/LAW
E1264

                                                         B28
CORBETT P.E.,CANADA AND WORLD POLITICS. LAW CULTURE   NAT/G
SOCIETY STRUCT MARKET INT/ORG FORCES ACT/RES PLAN   CANADA
ECO/TAC LEGIT ORD/FREE PWR RESPECT...SOC CONCPT
TIME/SEQ TREND CMN/WLTH 20 LEAGUE/NAT. PAGE 26
E0504

                                                         B29
CONWELL-EVANS T.P.,THE LEAGUE COUNCIL IN ACTION.   DELIB/GP
EUR+WWI TURKEY UK USSR WOR-45 INT/ORG FORCES JUDGE   INT/LAW
ECO/TAC EDU/PROP LEGIT ROUTINE ARMS/CONT COERCE
ATTIT PWR...MAJORIT GEOG JURID CONCPT LEAGUE/NAT
TOT/POP VAL/FREE TUNIS 20. PAGE 25 E0498

                                                         B29
STURZO L.,THE INTERNATIONAL COMMUNITY AND THE RIGHT   INT/ORG
OF WAR (TRANS. BY BARBARA BARCLAY CARTER). CULTURE   PLAN
CREATE PROB/SOLV DIPLOM ADJUD CONTROL PEACE PERSON   WAR
ORD/FREE...INT/LAW IDEA/COMP PACIFIST 20   CONCPT
LEAGUE/NAT. PAGE 94 E1891

                                                         L29
FEIS H.,"RESEARCH ACTIVITIES OF THE LEAGUE OF   CONSULT
NATIONS." EUR+WWI WOR-45 R+D INT/ORG CT/SYS   KNOWL
ARMS/CONT WEALTH...OBS RECORD LEAGUE/NAT ILO 20.   PEACE
PAGE 37 E0729

                                                         B30
WRIGHT Q.,MANDATES UNDER THE LEAGUE OF NATIONS.   INT/ORG
WOR-45 CONSTN ECO/DEV ECO/UNDEV NAT/G DELIB/GP   LAW
TOP/EX LEGIT ALL/VALS...JURID CONCPT LEAGUE/NAT 20.   INT/LAW
PAGE 107 E2151

                                                         B32
EAGLETON C.,INTERNATIONAL GOVERNMENT. BRAZIL FRANCE   INT/ORG
GERMANY ITALY UK USSR WOR-45 DELIB/GP TOP/EX PLAN   JURID
ECO/TAC EDU/PROP LEGIT ADJUD REGION ARMS/CONT   DIPLOM
COERCE ATTIT PWR...GEOG MGT VAL/FREE LEAGUE/NAT 20.   INT/LAW
PAGE 34 E0670

                                                         B32
FLEMMING D.,THE UNITED STATES AND THE LEAGUE OF   INT/ORG
NATIONS, 1918-1920. FUT USA-45 NAT/G LEGIS TOP/EX   EDU/PROP
DEBATE CHOOSE PEACE ATTIT SOVEREIGN...TIME/SEQ
CON/ANAL CONGRESS LEAGUE/NAT 20 TREATY. PAGE 39
E0764

                                                         B32
MORLEY F.,THE SOCIETY OF NATIONS. EUR+WWI UNIV   INT/ORG
WOR-45 LAW CONSTN ACT/RES PLAN EDU/PROP LEGIT   CONCPT
ROUTINE...POLICY TIME/SEQ LEAGUE/NAT TOT/POP 20.
PAGE 75 E1496

                                                         B33
LAUTERPACHT H.,THE FUNCTION OF LAW IN THE   INT/ORG
INTERNATIONAL COMMUNITY. WOR-45 NAT/G FORCES CREATE   LAW
DOMIN LEGIT COERCE WAR PEACE ATTIT ORD/FREE PWR   INT/LAW
SOVEREIGN...JURID CONCPT METH/CNCPT TIME/SEQ
GEN/LAWS GEN/METH LEAGUE/NAT TOT/POP VAL/FREE 20.
PAGE 63 E1265

                                                         B35
HUDSON M.,BY PACIFIC MEANS. WOR-45 EDU/PROP   INT/ORG
ORD/FREE...CONCPT TIME/SEQ GEN/LAWS LEAGUE/NAT   CT/SYS
TOT/POP 20 TREATY. PAGE 56 E1110   PEACE

                                                         B36
BRIERLY J.L.,THE LAW OF NATIONS (2ND ED.). WOR+45   DIPLOM
WOR-45 INT/ORG AGREE CONTROL COERCE WAR NAT/LISM   INT/LAW
PEACE PWR 16/20 TREATY LEAGUE/NAT. PAGE 15 E0297   NAT/G

                                                         B36
HUDSON M.O.,INTERNATIONAL LEGISLATION: 1929-1931.   INT/LAW
WOR-45 SEA AIR AGRI FINAN LABOR DIPLOM ECO/TAC   PARL/PROC
REPAR CT/SYS ARMS/CONT WAR WEAPON...JURID 20 TREATY   ADJUD
LEAGUE/NAT. PAGE 56 E1112   LAW

                                                         B38
GRISWOLD A.W.,THE FAR EASTERN POLICY OF THE UNITED   DIPLOM
STATES. ASIA S/ASIA USA-45 INT/ORG INT/TRADE WAR   POLICY
NAT/LISM...BIBLIOG 19/20 LEAGUE/NAT ROOSEVLT/T   CHIEF
ROOSEVLT/F WILSON/W TREATY. PAGE 47 E0943

                                                         B38
LEAGUE OF NATIONS-SECRETARIAT.,THE AIMS, METHODS   ADJUD
AND ACTIVITY OF THE LEAGUE OF NATIONS. WOR+45   STRUCT
DIPLOM EDU/PROP LEGIT RIGID/FLEX ALL/VALS
...TIME/SEQ LEAGUE/NAT VAL/FREE 19/20. PAGE 64
E1273

                                                         B39
BENES E.,INTERNATIONAL SECURITY. GERMANY UK NAT/G   EUR+WWI
DELIB/GP PLAN BAL/PWR ATTIT ORD/FREE PWR LEAGUE/NAT   INT/ORG
20 TREATY. PAGE 10 E0186   WAR

                                                         B39
LAVES W.H.C.,INTERNATIONAL SECURITY. EUR+WWI   ORD/FREE
GERMANY UK USA-45 LAW NAT/G DELIB/GP TOP/EX COERCE   LEGIT
PWR...POLICY FASCIST CONCPT HIST/WRIT GEN/LAWS   ARMS/CONT
LEAGUE/NAT NAZI 20. PAGE 63 E1267   BAL/PWR

                                                         B39
ZIMMERN A.,THE LEAGUE OF NATIONS AND THE RULE OF   INT/ORG
LAW. WOR-45 STRUCT NAT/G DELIB/GP EX/STRUC BAL/PWR   LAW
DOMIN LEGIT COERCE ORD/FREE PWR...POLICY RECORD   DIPLOM
LEAGUE/NAT TOT/POP VAL/FREE 20 LEAGUE/NAT. PAGE 108
E2170

                                                         B39
ZIMMERN A.,THE LEAGUE OF NATIONS AND THE RULE OF   INT/ORG
LAW. WOR-45 STRUCT NAT/G DELIB/GP EX/STRUC BAL/PWR   LAW
DOMIN LEGIT COERCE ORD/FREE PWR...POLICY RECORD   DIPLOM
LEAGUE/NAT TOT/POP VAL/FREE 20 LEAGUE/NAT. PAGE 108
E2170

                                                         L41
COMM. STUDY ORGAN. PEACE,"ORGANIZATION OF PEACE."   INT/ORG
USA-45 WOR-45 STRATA NAT/G ACT/RES DIPLOM ECO/TAC   PLAN
EDU/PROP ADJUD ATTIT ORD/FREE PWR...SOC CONCPT   PEACE
ANTHOL LEAGUE/NAT 20. PAGE 24 E0479

                                                         B42
FEILCHENFELD E.H.,THE INTERNATIONAL ECONOMIC LAW OF   ECO/TAC
BELLIGERENT OCCUPATION. EUR+WWI MOD/EUR USA-45   INT/LAW
INT/ORG DIPLOM ADJUD ARMS/CONT LEAGUE/NAT 20.   WAR
PAGE 37 E0726

                                                         B42
KELSEN H.,LAW AND PEACE IN INTERNATIONAL RELATIONS.   INT/ORG
FUT WOR-45 NAT/G DELIB/GP DIPLOM LEGIT RIGID/FLEX   ADJUD
ORD/FREE SOVEREIGN...JURID CONCPT TREND STERTYP   PEACE
GEN/LAWS LEAGUE/NAT 20. PAGE 60 E1197   INT/LAW

                                                         B43
CONOVER H.F.,THE BALKANS: A SELECTED LIST OF   BIBLIOG
REFERENCES. ALBANIA BULGARIA ROMANIA YUGOSLAVIA   EUR+WWI
INT/ORG PROB/SOLV DIPLOM LEGIT CONFER ADJUD WAR
NAT/LISM PEACE PWR 20 LEAGUE/NAT. PAGE 25 E0493

                                                         B43
MICAUD C.A.,THE FRENCH RIGHT AND NAZI GERMANY   DIPLOM
1933-1939: A STUDY OF PUBLIC OPINION. GERMANY UK   AGREE
USSR POL/PAR ARMS/CONT COERCE DETER PEACE

RIGID/FLEX PWR MARXISM...FASCIST TREND 20
LEAGUE/NAT TREATY. PAGE 73 E1454

B44
BRIERLY J.L.,THE OUTLOOK FOR INTERNATIONAL LAW. FUT   INT/ORG
WOR-45 CONSTN NAT/G VOL/ASSN FORCES ECO/TAC DOMIN   LAW
LEGIT ADJUD ROUTINE PEACE ORD/FREE...INT/LAW JURID
METH LEAGUE/NAT 20. PAGE 15 E0298

B45
BEVERIDGE W.,THE PRICE OF PEACE. GERMANY UK WOR+45   INT/ORG
WOR-45 NAT/G FORCES CREATE LEGIT REGION WAR ATTIT   TREND
KNOWL ORD/FREE PWR...POLICY NEW/IDEA GEN/LAWS   PEACE
LEAGUE/NAT 20 TREATY. PAGE 12 E0223

B45
TINGSTERN H.,PEACE AND SECURITY AFTER WW II. WOR-45   INT/ORG
DELIB/GP TOP/EX LEGIT CT/SYS COERCE PEACE ATTIT   ORD/FREE
PERCEPT...CONCPT LEAGUE/NAT 20. PAGE 96 E1927   WAR
                                                       INT/LAW

B45
UNCIO CONFERENCE LIBRARY,SHORT TITLE CLASSIFIED   BIBLIOG
CATALOG. WOR-45 DOMIN COLONIAL WAR...SOC/WK 20   DIPLOM
LEAGUE/NAT UN. PAGE 98 E1955   INT/ORG
                                                       INT/LAW

B46
KEETON G.W.,MAKING INTERNATIONAL LAW WORK. FUT   INT/ORG
WOR-45 NAT/G DELIB/GP FORCES LEGIT COERCE PEACE   ADJUD
ATTIT RIGID/FLEX ORD/FREE PWR...JURID CONCPT   INT/LAW
HIST/WRIT GEN/METH LEAGUE/NAT 20. PAGE 60 E1193

B47
HILL M.,IMMUNITIES AND PRIVILEGES OF INTERNATIONAL   INT/ORG
OFFICIALS. CANADA EUR+WWI NETHERLAND SWITZERLND LAW   ADMIN
LEGIS DIPLOM LEGIT RESPECT...TIME/SEQ LEAGUE/NAT UN
VAL/FREE 20. PAGE 52 E1046

B48
FENWICK C.G.,INTERNATIONAL LAW. WOR+45 WOR-45   INT/ORG
CONSTN NAT/G LEGIT CT/SYS REGION...CONCPT   JURID
LEAGUE/NAT UN 20. PAGE 37 E0737   INT/LAW

B48
JESSUP P.C.,A MODERN LAW OF NATIONS. FUT WOR+45   INT/ORG
WOR-45 SOCIETY NAT/G DELIB/GP LEGIS BAL/PWR   ADJUD
EDU/PROP LEGIT PWR...INT/LAW JURID TIME/SEQ
LEAGUE/NAT 20. PAGE 58 E1166

B50
ROSS A.,CONSTITUTION OF THE UNITED NATIONS. CONSTN   PEACE
CONSULT DELIB/GP ECO/TAC...INT/LAW JURID 20 UN   DIPLOM
LEAGUE/NAT. PAGE 86 E1721   ORD/FREE
                                                       INT/ORG

B51
PUSEY M.J.,CHARLES EVANS HUGHES (2 VOLS.). LAW   BIOG
CONSTN NAT/G POL/PAR DIPLOM LEGIT WAR CHOOSE   TOP/EX
PERS/REL DRIVE HEREDITY 19/20 DEPT/STATE LEAGUE/NAT   ADJUD
SUPREME/CT HUGHES/CE WWI. PAGE 83 E1663   PERSON

B52
FERRELL R.H.,PEACE IN THEIR TIME. FRANCE UK USA-45   PEACE
INT/ORG NAT/G FORCES CREATE AGREE ARMS/CONT COERCE   DIPLOM
WAR TREATY 20 WILSON/W LEAGUE/NAT BRIAND/A. PAGE 37
E0741

B53
OPPENHEIM L.,INTERNATIONAL LAW: A TREATISE (7TH   INT/LAW
ED., 2 VOLS.). LAW CONSTN PROB/SOLV INT/TRADE ADJUD   INT/ORG
AGREE NEUTRAL WAR ORD/FREE SOVEREIGN...BIBLIOG 20   DIPLOM
LEAGUE/NAT UN ILO. PAGE 79 E1579

B54
STONE J.,LEGAL CONTROLS OF INTERNATIONAL CONFLICT: INT/ORG
A TREATISE ON THE DYNAMICS OF DISPUTES AND WAR LAW.   LAW
WOR+45 WOR-45 NAT/G DIPLOM CT/SYS SOVEREIGN...JURID   WAR
CONCPT METH/CNCPT GEN/LAWS TOT/POP VAL/FREE   INT/LAW
COLD/WAR LEAGUE/NAT 20. PAGE 94 E1878

B55
HOGAN W.N.,INTERNATIONAL CONFLICT AND COLLECTIVE   INT/ORG
SECURITY: THE PRINCIPLE OF CONCERN IN INTERNATIONAL   WAR
ORGANIZATION. CONSTN EX/STRUC BAL/PWR DIPLOM ADJUD   ORD/FREE
CONTROL CENTRAL CONSEN PEACE...INT/LAW CONCPT   FORCES
METH/COMP 20 UN LEAGUE/NAT. PAGE 53 E1066

B56
CORBETT P.E.,MORALS LAW, AND POWER IN INTERNATIONAL   SUPEGO
RELATIONS. WOR+45 WOR-45 INT/ORG VOL/ASSN DELIB/GP   CONCPT
CREATE BAL/PWR DIPLOM LEGIT ARMS/CONT MORAL...JURID   POLICY
GEN/LAWS TOT/POP LEAGUE/NAT 20. PAGE 26 E0506   INT/LAW

B56
PERKINS D.,CHARLES EVANS HUGHES AND THE AMERICAN   PERSON

DEMOCRATIC STATESMANSHIP. USA+45 USA-45 NAT/G   BIOG
POL/PAR DELIB/GP JUDGE PLAN MORAL PWR...HIST/WRIT   DIPLOM
LEAGUE/NAT 20. PAGE 80 E1609

S56
POTTER P.B.,"NEUTRALITY, 1955." WOR+45 WOR-45   NEUTRAL
INT/ORG NAT/G WAR ATTIT...POLICY IDEA/COMP 17/20   INT/LAW
LEAGUE/NAT UN COLD/WAR. PAGE 81 E1631   DIPLOM
                                                       CONCPT

B57
DE VISSCHER C.,THEORY AND REALITY IN PUBLIC   INT/ORG
INTERNATIONAL LAW. WOR+45 WOR-45 SOCIETY NAT/G   LAW
CT/SYS ATTIT MORAL ORD/FREE PWR...JURID CONCPT   INT/LAW
METH/CNCPT TIME/SEQ GEN/LAWS LEAGUE/NAT TOT/POP
VAL/FREE COLD/WAR. PAGE 30 E0599

B57
ROSENNE S.,THE INTERNATIONAL COURT OF JUSTICE.   INT/ORG
WOR+45 LAW DOMIN LEGIT PEACE PWR SOVEREIGN...JURID   CT/SYS
CONCPT RECORD TIME/SEQ CON/ANAL CHARTS UN TOT/POP   INT/LAW
VAL/FREE LEAGUE/NAT 20 ICJ. PAGE 86 E1716

B58
RUSSELL R.B.,A HISTORY OF THE UNITED NATIONS   USA-45
CHARTER: THE ROLE OF THE UNITED STATES. SOCIETY   INT/ORG
NAT/G CONSULT DOMIN LEGIT ATTIT ORD/FREE PWR   CONSTN
...POLICY JURID CONCPT UN LEAGUE/NAT. PAGE 87 E1737

B58
STONE J.,AGGRESSION AND WORLD ORDER: A CRITIQUE OF   ORD/FREE
UNITED NATIONS THEORIES OF AGGRESSION. LAW CONSTN   INT/ORG
DELIB/GP PROB/SOLV BAL/PWR DIPLOM DEBATE ADJUD   WAR
CRIME PWR...POLICY IDEA/COMP 20 UN SUEZ LEAGUE/NAT.   CONCPT
PAGE 94 E1879

L58
UNESCO.,"TECHNIQUES OF MEDIATION AND CONCILIATION."   INT/ORG
EUR+WWI USA+45 WOR+45 INDUS FACE/GP EX/STRUC   CONSULT
EDU/PROP LEGIT PEACE ORD/FREE...INT/LAW TIME/SEQ   DIPLOM
LEAGUE/NAT 20. PAGE 98 E1961

B59
CORBETT P.E.,LAW IN DIPLOMACY. UK USA+45 USSR   NAT/G
CONSTN SOCIETY INT/ORG JUDGE LEGIT ATTIT ORD/FREE   ADJUD
TOT/POP LEAGUE/NAT 20. PAGE 26 E0507   JURID
                                                       DIPLOM

B62
GANJI M.,INTERNATIONAL PROTECTION OF HUMAN RIGHTS.   ORD/FREE
WOR+45 CONSTN INT/TRADE CT/SYS SANCTION CRIME WAR   DISCRIM
RACE/REL...CHARTS IDEA/COMP NAT/COMP BIBLIOG 20   LEGIS
TREATY NEGRO LEAGUE/NAT UN CIVIL/LIB. PAGE 42 E0831   DELIB/GP

B63
BOWETT D.W.,THE LAW OF INTERNATIONAL INSTITUTIONS.   INT/ORG
WOR+45 WOR-45 CONSTN DELIB/GP EX/STRUC JUDGE   ADJUD
EDU/PROP LEGIT CT/SYS EXEC ROUTINE RIGID/FLEX   DIPLOM
ORD/FREE PWR...JURID CONCPT ORG/CHARTS GEN/METH
LEAGUE/NAT OAS OEEC 20 UN. PAGE 14 E0277

B64
JENKS C.W.,THE PROSPECTS OF INTERNATIONAL   INT/LAW
ADJUDICATION. WOR+45 WOR-45 NAT/G DIPLOM CONTROL   ADJUD
PWR...POLICY JURID CONCPT METH/COMP 19/20 ICJ   CT/SYS
LEAGUE/NAT UN TREATY. PAGE 58 E1160   INT/ORG

B65
PARRY C.,THE SOURCES AND EVIDENCES OF INTERNATIONAL   INT/LAW
LAW. WOR+45 WOR-45 DIPLOM AGREE SOVEREIGN...METH 20   ADJUD
TREATY UN LEAGUE/NAT. PAGE 80 E1599   INT/ORG
                                                       CT/SYS

B66
CANFIELD L.H.,THE PRESIDENCY OF WOODROW WILSON: PERSON
PRELUDE TO A WORLD IN CRISIS. USA-45 ADJUD NEUTRAL   POLICY
WAR CHOOSE INGP/REL PEACE ORD/FREE 20 WILSON/W   DIPLOM
PRESIDENT TREATY LEAGUE/NAT. PAGE 19 E0373   GOV/REL

B66
DOUMA J.,BIBLIOGRAPHY ON THE INTERNATIONAL COURT   BIBLIOG/A
INCLUDING THE PERMANENT COURT, 1918-1964. WOR+45   INT/ORG
WOR-45 DELIB/GP WAR PRIVIL...JURID NAT/COMP 20 UN   CT/SYS
LEAGUE/NAT. PAGE 33 E0645   DIPLOM

B66
WAINHOUSE D.W.,INTERNATIONAL PEACE OBSERVATION: A   PEACE
HISTORY AND FORECAST. INT/ORG PROB/SOLV BAL/PWR   DIPLOM
AGREE ARMS/CONT COERCE NUC/PWR...PREDICT METH/COMP
20 UN LEAGUE/NAT OAS TREATY. PAGE 104 E2092

C66
BLAISDELL D.C.,"INTERNATIONAL ORGANIZATION." FUT   BIBLIOG
WOR+45 ECO/DEV DELIB/GP FORCES EFFICIENCY PEACE   INT/ORG
ORD/FREE...INT/LAW 20 UN LEAGUE/NAT NATO. PAGE 12   DIPLOM
E0239   ARMS/CONT

B67
PLANO J.C.,FORGING WORLD ORDER: THE POLITICS OF   INT/ORG
INTERNATIONAL ORGANIZATION. PROB/SOLV DIPLOM   ADMIN
CONTROL CENTRAL RATIONAL ORD/FREE...INT/LAW CHARTS   JURID
BIBLIOG 20 UN LEAGUE/NAT. PAGE 81 E1618

S68
DUGARD J.,"THE REVOCATION OF THE MANDATE FOR SOUTH   AFR
WEST AFRICA." SOUTH/AFR WOR+45 STRATA NAT/G   INT/ORG
DELIB/GP DIPLOM ADJUD SANCTION CHOOSE RACE/REL   DISCRIM
...POLICY NAT/COMP 20 AFRICA/SW UN TRUST/TERR   COLONIAL
LEAGUE/NAT. PAGE 33 E0654

LEAGUE/WV....LEAGUE OF WOMEN VOTERS

B60
BAKER G.E.,THE POLITICS OF REAPPORTIONMENT IN   VOL/ASSN
WASHINGTON STATE. LAW POL/PAR CREATE EDU/PROP   APPORT
PARL/PROC CHOOSE INGP/REL...CHARTS METH/COMP 20   PROVS
WASHINGT/G LEAGUE/WV. PAGE 7 E0139   LEGIS

LEARNING....SEE PERCEPT

LEASE....SEE RENT

LEBANON....SEE ALSO ISLAM

LEDERMAN W.R. E1276

LEDYARD/J....JOHN LEDYARD

LEE L.T. E1277

LEE/IVY....IVY LEE

LEEB J. E1036

LEEK J.H. E1278

LEEVILLE....LEEVILLE, TEXAS

LEGAL SYSTEM....SEE LAW

LEGAL PERMIT....SEE LICENSE

LEGAULT A. E1279

LEGION/DCY....LEGION OF DECENCY

LEGIS....LEGISLATURES; SEE ALSO PARLIAMENT, CONGRESS

N
CONOVER H.F.,OFFICIAL PUBLICATIONS OF BRITISH EAST   BIBLIOG/A
AFRICA (PAMPHLET). UK LAW ECO/UNDEV AGRI EXTR/IND   AFR
SECT LEGIS BUDGET TAX...HEAL STAT 20. PAGE 25 E0491   ADMIN
                                                        COLONIAL

N
INTERNATIONAL COMN JURISTS,AFRICAN CONFERENCE ON   CT/SYS
THE RULE OF LAW. AFR INT/ORG LEGIS DIPLOM CONFER   JURID
COLONIAL ORD/FREE...CONCPT METH/COMP 20. PAGE 57   DELIB/GP
E1131

N
KEITT L.,AN ANNOTATED BIBLIOGRAPHY OF   BIBLIOG/A
BIBLIOGRAPHIES OF STATUTORY MATERIALS OF THE UNITED   LAW
STATES. CHRIST-17C USA+45 LEGIS ADJUD COLONIAL   CONSTN
CT/SYS...JURID 16/20. PAGE 60 E1196   PROVS

N
INDEX TO LEGAL PERIODICALS. CANADA NEW/ZEALND UK   BIBLIOG
USA+45 USA-45 CONSTN LEGIS JUDGE ADJUD ADMIN   INDEX
CONTROL CT/SYS FEDERAL...CRIMLGY INT/LAW 20   LAW
CMN/WLTH AUSTRAL. PAGE 1 E0006   JURID

N
JOURNAL OF POLITICS. USA+45 USA-45 CONSTN POL/PAR   BIBLIOG/A
EX/STRUC LEGIS PROB/SOLV DIPLOM CT/SYS CHOOSE   NAT/G
RACE/REL 20. PAGE 1 E0011   LAW
                                                        LOC/G

N
MIDWEST JOURNAL OF POLITICAL SCIENCE. USA+45 CONSTN   BIBLIOG/A
ECO/DEV LEGIS PROB/SOLV CT/SYS LEAD GOV/REL ATTIT   NAT/G
POLICY. PAGE 1 E0012   DIPLOM
                                                        POL/PAR

N
POLITICAL SCIENCE QUARTERLY. USA+45 USA-45 LAW   BIBLIOG/A
CONSTN ECO/DEV INT/ORG LOC/G POL/PAR LEGIS LEAD   NAT/G
NUC/PWR...CONCPT 20. PAGE 1 E0013   DIPLOM
                                                        POLICY

N
CATHERINE R.,LA REVUE ADMINISTRATIVE. FRANCE LAW   ADMIN
NAT/G LEGIS...JURID BIBLIOG/A 20. PAGE 21 E0407   MGT
                                                        FINAN
                                                        METH/COMP

N
HARVARD LAW SCHOOL LIBRARY,ANNUAL LEGAL   BIBLIOG
BIBLIOGRAPHY. USA+45 CONSTN LEGIS ADJUD CT/SYS   JURID
...POLICY 20. PAGE 50 E1005   LAW
                                                        INT/LAW

N
SOCIETE DES NATIONS,TRAITES INTERNATIONAUX ET ACTES   BIBLIOG
LEGISLATIFS. WOR-45 INT/ORG NAT/G...INT/LAW JURID   DIPLOM
20 LEAGUE/NAT TREATY. PAGE 92 E1851   LEGIS
                                                        ADJUD

N
UNESCO,INTERNATIONAL BIBLIOGRAPHY OF POLITICAL   BIBLIOG
SCIENCE (VOLUMES 1-8). WOR+45 LAW NAT/G EX/STRUC   CONCPT
LEGIS PROB/SOLV DIPLOM ADMIN GOV/REL 20 UNESCO.   IDEA/COMP
PAGE 98 E1957

NRE
MEYER C.S.,ELIZABETH I AND THE RELIGIOUS SETTLEMENT   GP/REL
OF 1559. UK ELITES CHIEF LEGIS DISCRIM CATHISM 16   SECT
CHURCH/STA ELIZABTH/I. PAGE 72 E1445   LAW
                                                        PARL/PROC

B00
DE TOCQUEVILLE A.,DEMOCRACY IN AMERICA (VOLUME   USA-45
ONE). LAW SOCIETY STRUCT NAT/G POL/PAR PROVS FORCES   TREND
LEGIS TOP/EX DIPLOM LEGIT WAR PEACE ATTIT SOVEREIGN
...SELF/OBS TIME/SEQ CONGRESS 19. PAGE 30 E0594

B00
GREELY A.W.,PUBLIC DOCUMENTS OF THE FIRST FOURTEEN   BIBLIOG/A
CONGRESSES, 1789-1817. USA-45 LEAD REPRESENT ATTIT   NAT/G
18/19 CONGRESS. PAGE 45 E0904   LAW
                                                        LEGIS

B00
MAINE H.S.,ANCIENT LAW. MEDIT-7 CULTURE SOCIETY KIN   FAM
SECT LEGIS LEGIT ROUTINE...JURID HIST/WRIT CON/ANAL   LAW
TOT/POP VAL/FREE. PAGE 68 E1350

B04
BURKE E.,A LETTER TO THE SHERIFFS OF BRISTOL   LEGIS
(1777). USA-45 LAW ECO/TAC COLONIAL CT/SYS REV   ADJUD
GP/REL ORD/FREE...POLICY 18 PARLIAMENT BURKE/EDM.   CRIME
PAGE 17 E0341

B04
CRANDALL S.B.,TREATIES: THEIR MAKING AND   LAW
ENFORCEMENT. MOD/EUR USA+45 CONSTN INT/ORG NAT/G
LEGIS EDU/PROP LEGIT EXEC PEACE KNOWL MORAL...JURID
CONGRESS 19/20 TREATY. PAGE 27 E0541

B04
FREUND E.,THE POLICE POWER; PUBLIC POLICY AND   CONSTN
CONSTITUTIONAL RIGHTS. USA+45 SOCIETY LOC/G NAT/G   LAW
FORCES LEGIS ADJUD CT/SYS OWN PWR...JURID 18/19   ORD/FREE
SUPREME/CT. PAGE 40 E0795   CONTROL

B05
DICEY A.V.,LECTURES ON THE RELATION BETWEEN LAW AND   LAW
PUBLIC OPINION IN ENGLAND DURING THE NINETEENTH   ADJUD
CENTURY. UK LEGIS CT/SYS...JURID 19 TORY/PARTY   ATTIT
BENTHAM/J ENGLSH/LAW. PAGE 31 E0621   IDEA/COMP

B05
GOODNOW F.J.,THE PRINCIPLES OF THE ADMINISTRATIVE   ADMIN
LAW OF THE UNITED STATES. USA+45 LAW STRUCT   NAT/G
EX/STRUC LEGIS BAL/PWR CONTROL GOV/REL PWR...JURID   PROVS
19/20 CIVIL/SERV. PAGE 45 E0887   LOC/G

B05
GRIFFIN A.P.C.,LIST OF REFERENCES ON PRIMARY   BIBLIOG/A
ELECTIONS (PAMPHLET). USA-45 LAW LOC/G DELIB/GP   POL/PAR
LEGIS OP/RES TASK REPRESENT CONSEN...DECISION 19/20   CHOOSE
CONGRESS. PAGE 47 E0928   POPULISM

B07
BENTHAM J.,AN INTRODUCTION TO THE PRINCIPLES OF   LAW
MORALS AND LEGISLATION. UNIV CONSTN CULTURE SOCIETY   GEN/LAWS
NAT/G CONSULT LEGIS JUDGE ADJUD CT/SYS...JURID
CONCPT NEW/IDEA. PAGE 10 E0190

B08
GRIFFIN A.P.C.,LIST OF WORKS RELATING TO GOVERNMENT   BIBLIOG/A
REGULATION OF INSURANCE UNITED STATES AND FOREIGN   FINAN
COUNTRIES (2ND. ED.) (PAMPHLET). FRANCE GERMANY UK   LAW
USA-45 WOR-45 LG/CO LOC/G NAT/G LEGIS LICENSE   CONTROL
LOBBY CENTRAL ORD/FREE 19/20. PAGE 47 E0933

B08
WILSON W.,CONSTITUTIONAL GOVERNMENT IN THE UNITED NAT/G
STATES. USA-45 LAW POL/PAR PROVS CHIEF LEGIS GOV/REL
BAL/PWR ADJUD EXEC FEDERAL PWR 18/20 SUPREME/CT CONSTN
HOUSE/REP SENATE. PAGE 106 E2130 PARL/PROC

B09
HARVARD UNIVERSITY LAW LIBRARY,CATALOGUE OF THE BIBLIOG/A
LIBRARY OF THE LAW SCHOOL OF HARVARD UNIVERSITY (3 LAW
VOLS.). UK USA-45 LEGIS JUDGE ADJUD CT/SYS...JURID ADMIN
CHARTS 14/20. PAGE 51 E1008

B09
JUSTINIAN,THE DIGEST (DIGESTA CORPUS JURIS CIVILIS) JURID
(2 VOLS.) (TRANS. BY C. H. MONRO). ROMAN/EMP LAW CT/SYS
FAM LOC/G LEGIS EDU/PROP CONTROL MARRIAGE OWN ROLE NAT/G
CIVIL/LAW. PAGE 59 E1177 STRATA

B09
LOBINGIER C.S.,THE PEOPLE'S LAW OR POPULAR CONSTN
PARTICIPATION IN LAW-MAKING. FRANCE SWITZERLND UK LAW
LOC/G NAT/G PROVS LEGIS SUFF MAJORITY PWR POPULISM PARTIC
...GOV/COMP BIBLIOG 19. PAGE 66 E1314

B10
COLORADO CIVIL SERVICE COMN,SECOND BIENNIAL REPORT PROVS
TO THE GOVERNOR, 1909-1910. USA+45 DELIB/GP LEGIS LOC/G
LICENSE PAY 20 COLORADO CIVIL/SERV. PAGE 24 E0477 ADMIN
WORKER

B10
MCILWAIN C.H.,THE HIGH COURT OF PARLIAMENT AND ITS LAW
SUPREMACY B1910 1878 408. UK EX/STRUC PARL/PROC LEGIS
GOV/REL INGP/REL PRIVIL 12/20 PARLIAMENT CONSTN
ENGLSH/LAW. PAGE 71 E1416 NAT/G

B11
PHILLIPSON C.,THE INTERNATIONAL LAW AND CUSTOM OF INT/ORG
ANCIENT GREECE AND ROME. MEDIT-7 UNIV INTELL LAW
SOCIETY STRUCT NAT/G LEGIS EXEC PERSON...CONCPT OBS INT/LAW
CON/ANAL ROM/EMP. PAGE 80 E1614

B12
BEARD C.A.,THE SUPREME COURT AND THE CONSTITUTION. CONSTN
LAW NAT/G PROVS LEGIS GOV/REL ATTIT POPULISM CT/SYS
SUPREME/CT. PAGE 9 E0164 ADJUD
CONTROL

B12
FOUAD M.,LE REGIME DE LA PRESSE EN EGYPTE: THESE ORD/FREE
POUR LE DOCTORAT. UAR LICENSE EDU/PROP ADMIN LEGIS
SANCTION CRIME SUPEGO PWR...ART/METH JURID 19/20. CONTROL
PAGE 39 E0778 PRESS

B12
GRIFFIN A.P.C.,SELECT LIST OF REFERENCES ON BIBLIOG/A
IMPEACHMENT (REV. ED.) (PAMPHLET). USA-45 LAW PROVS CONSTN
ADJUD ATTIT...JURID 19/20 NEGRO. PAGE 47 E0935 NAT/G
LEGIS

B12
MEYER H.H.B.,SELECT LIST OF REFERENCES ON THE BIBLIOG/A
INITIATIVE, REFERENDUM, AND RECALL. MOD/EUR USA-45 NAT/G
LAW LOC/G MUNIC REPRESENT POPULISM 20 CONGRESS. LEGIS
PAGE 72 E1446 CHOOSE

B16
SALMOND J.W.,JURISPRUDENCE. UK LOC/G NAT/G LEGIS LAW
PROB/SOLV LICENSE LEGIT CRIME PERS/REL OWN ORD/FREE CT/SYS
...T 20. PAGE 87 E1742 JURID
ADJUD

S17
ROOT E.,"THE EFFECT OF DEMOCRACY ON INTERNATIONAL LEGIS
LAW." USA-45 WOR-45 INTELL SOCIETY INT/ORG NAT/G JURID
CONSULT ACT/RES CREATE PLAN EDU/PROP PEACE SKILL INT/LAW
...CONCPT METH/CNCPT OBS 20. PAGE 85 E1712

B18
EYBERS G.W.,SELECT CONSTITUTIONAL DOCUMENTS CONSTN
ILLUSTRATING SOUTH AFRICAN HISTORY 1795-1910. LAW
SOUTH/AFR LOC/G LEGIS CT/SYS...JURID ANTHOL 18/20 NAT/G
NATAL CAPE/HOPE ORANGE/STA. PAGE 36 E0707 COLONIAL

B18
WILSON W.,THE STATE: ELEMENTS OF HISTORICAL AND NAT/G
PRACTICAL POLITICS. FRANCE GERMANY ITALY UK USSR JURID
CONSTN EX/STRUC LEGIS CT/SYS WAR PWR...POLICY CONCPT
GOV/COMP 20. PAGE 106 E2131 NAT/COMP

N19
IN THE SHADOW OF FEAR; AMERICAN CIVIL LIBERTIES, ORD/FREE
1948-49 (PAMPHLET). COM LAW LEGIS BAL/PWR EDU/PROP CONSTN
CT/SYS RACE/REL DISCRIM MARXISM SOCISM 20 COLD/WAR POLICY
CONGRESS ACLU CIV/RIGHTS ESPIONAGE. PAGE 2 E0030

N19
AMERICAN CIVIL LIBERTIES UNION,"WE HOLD THESE ORD/FREE
TRUTHS" FREEDOM, JUSTICE, EQUALITY: REPORT ON CIVIL LAW
LIBERTIES (A PERIODICAL PAMPHLET COVERING 1951-53). RACE/REL
USA+45 ACADEM NAT/G FORCES LEGIS COERCE CIVMIL/REL CONSTN
GOV/REL DISCRIM PRIVIL MARXISM...OLD/LIB 20 ACLU UN
CIVIL/LIB. PAGE 4 E0076

N19
ATOMIC INDUSTRIAL FORUM,COMMENTARY ON LEGISLATION NUC/PWR
TO PERMIT PRIVATE OWNERSHIP OF SPECIAL NUCLEAR MARKET
MATERIAL (PAMPHLET). USA+45 DELIB/GP LEGIS PLAN OWN INDUS
...POLICY 20 AEC CONGRESS. PAGE 6 E0111 LAW

N19
BRENNAN W.J. JR.,THE BILL OF RIGHTS AND THE STATES CONSTN
(PAMPHLET). USA+45 USA-45 LEGIS BAL/PWR ADJUD PROVS
CT/SYS FEDERAL PWR SOVEREIGN 18/20 SUPREME/CT GOV/REL
BILL/RIGHT. PAGE 15 E0293 ORD/FREE

N19
BURRUS B.R.,INVESTIGATION AND DISCOVERY IN STATE NAT/G
ANTITRUST (PAMPHLET). USA+45 USA-45 LEGIS ECO/TAC PROVS
ADMIN CONTROL CT/SYS CRIME GOV/REL PWR...JURID LAW
CHARTS 19/20 FTC MONOPOLY. PAGE 18 E0346 INSPECT

N19
RALSTON A.,A FRESH LOOK AT LEGISLATIVE APPORT
APPORTIONMENT IN NEW JERSEY (PAMPHLET). USA+45 REPRESENT
CONSTN LEGIS OBJECTIVE...MATH METH 20 NEW/JERSEY. PROVS
PAGE 83 E1671 JURID

B20
LIPPMAN W.,LIBERTY AND THE NEWS. USA+45 USA-45 LAW ORD/FREE
LEGIS DOMIN LEGIT ATTIT...POLICY SOC IDEA/COMP PRESS
METH/COMP 19/20. PAGE 65 E1300 COM/IND
EDU/PROP

C20
BLACHLY F.F.,"THE GOVERNMENT AND ADMINISTRATION OF NAT/G
GERMANY." GERMANY CONSTN LOC/G PROVS DELIB/GP GOV/REL
EX/STRUC FORCES LEGIS TOP/EX CT/SYS...BIBLIOG/A ADMIN
19/20. PAGE 12 E0235 PHIL/SCI

B21
BRYCE J.,MODERN DEMOCRACIES. FUT NEW/ZEALND USA-45 NAT/G
LAW CONSTN POL/PAR PROVS VOL/ASSN EX/STRUC LEGIS TREND
LEGIT CT/SYS EXEC KNOWL CONGRESS AUSTRAL 20.
PAGE 16 E0322

B21
OPPENHEIM L.,THE FUTURE OF INTERNATIONAL LAW. INT/ORG
EUR+WWI MOD/EUR LAW LEGIS JUDGE LEGIT ORD/FREE CT/SYS
...JURID TIME/SEQ GEN/LAWS 20. PAGE 79 E1578 INT/LAW

B22
FARRAND M.,THE FRAMING OF THE CONSTITUTION OF THE CONSTN
UNITED STATES (1913). USA-45 EX/STRUC PROB/SOLV DELIB/GP
PERSON. PAGE 36 E0721 LEGIS
CT/SYS

B22
MYERS D.P.,MANUAL OF COLLECTIONS OF TREATIES AND OF BIBLIOG/A
COLLECTIONS RELATING TO TREATIES. MOD/EUR INT/ORG DIPLOM
LEGIS WRITING ADMIN SOVEREIGN...INT/LAW 19/20. CONFER
PAGE 75 E1514

B22
WRIGHT Q.,THE CONTROL OF AMERICAN FOREIGN NAT/G
RELATIONS. USA-45 WOR-45 CONSTN INT/ORG CONSULT EXEC
LEGIS LEGIT ROUTINE ORD/FREE PWR...POLICY JURID DIPLOM
CONCPT METH/CNCPT RECORD LEAGUE/NAT 20. PAGE 107
E2150

B23
ROBERT H.M.,PARLIAMENTARY LAW. POL/PAR LEGIS PARTIC PARL/PROC
CHOOSE REPRESENT GP/REL. PAGE 85 E1701 DELIB/GP
NAT/G
JURID

B24
HOLDSWORTH W.S.,A HISTORY OF ENGLISH LAW; THE LAW
COMMON LAW AND ITS RIVALS (VOL. V). UK SEA EX/STRUC LEGIS
WRITING ADMIN...INT/LAW JURID CONCPT IDEA/COMP ADJUD
WORSHIP 16/17 PARLIAMENT ENGLSH/LAW COMMON/LAW. CT/SYS
PAGE 54 E1073

B24
HOLDSWORTH W.S.,A HISTORY OF ENGLISH LAW; THE LAW
COMMON LAW AND ITS RIVALS (VOL. VI). UK STRATA CONSTN
EX/STRUC ADJUD ADMIN CONTROL CT/SYS...JURID CONCPT LEGIS
GEN/LAWS 17 COMMONWLTH PARLIAMENT ENGLSH/LAW CHIEF
COMMON/LAW. PAGE 54 E1074

B24
HOLDSWORTH W.S.,A HISTORY OF ENGLISH LAW; THE LAW

COMMON LAW AND ITS RIVALS (VOL. IV). UK SEA AGRI   LEGIS
CHIEF ADJUD CONTROL CRIME GOV/REL...INT/LAW JURID   CT/SYS
NAT/COMP 16/17 PARLIAMENT COMMON/LAW CANON/LAW   CONSTN
ENGLSH/LAW. PAGE 54 E1075

                                                       B26
FORTESCUE J.,THE GOVERNANCE OF ENGLAND (1471-76).   CONSERVE
UK LAW FINAN SECT LEGIS PROB/SOLV TAX DOMIN ADMIN   CONSTN
GP/REL COST ORD/FREE PWR 14/15. PAGE 39 E0776   CHIEF
                                                       NAT/G

                                                       B27
RYAN J.A.,DECLINING LIVERTY AND OTHER ESSAYS.   ORD/FREE
USA-45 SECT DELIB/GP ATTIT PWR SOCISM 20   LEGIS
SUPREME/CT. PAGE 87 E1740   JURID
                                                       NAT/G

                                                       B28
HOLDSWORTH W.S.,THE HISTORIANS OF ANGLO-AMERICAN   HIST/WRIT
LAW. UK USA-45 INTELL LEGIS RESPECT...BIOG NAT/COMP   LAW
17/20 COMMON/LAW. PAGE 54 E1076   JURID

                                                       B28
NORTON T.J.,LOSING LIBERTY JUDICIALLY. PROVS LEGIS   NAT/G
BAL/PWR CT/SYS...JURID 18/20 SUPREME/CT CIV/RIGHTS   ORD/FREE
CONGRESS. PAGE 78 E1557   CONSTN
                                                       JUDGE

                                                       C29
BUCK A.E.,"PUBLIC BUDGETING." USA-45 FINAN LOC/G   BUDGET
NAT/G LEGIS BAL/PAY COST...JURID TREND BIBLIOG/A   ROUTINE
20. PAGE 17 E0324   ADMIN

                                                       B30
BENTHAM J.,THE RATIONALE OF PUNISHMENT. UK LAW   CRIME
LOC/G NAT/G LEGIS CONTROL...JURID GEN/LAWS   SANCTION
COURT/SYS 19. PAGE 10 E0192   COERCE
                                                       ORD/FREE

                                                       B30
BURLAMAQUI J.J.,PRINCIPLES OF NATURAL AND POLITIC   LAW
LAW (2 VOLS.) (1747-51). EX/STRUC LEGIS AGREE   NAT/G
CT/SYS CHOOSE ROLE SOVEREIGN 18 NATURL/LAW. PAGE 17   ORD/FREE
E0342   CONCPT

                                                       B30
GREEN F.M.,CONSTITUTIONAL DEVELOPMENT IN THE SOUTH   CONSTN
ATLANTIC STATES, 1776-1860; A STUDY IN THE   PROVS
EVOLUTION OF DEMOCRACY. USA-45 ELITES SOCIETY   PLURISM
STRATA ECO/DEV AGRI POL/PAR EX/STRUC LEGIS CT/SYS   REPRESENT
REGION...BIBLIOG 18/19 MARYLAND VIRGINIA GEORGIA
NORTH/CAR SOUTH/CAR. PAGE 46 E0905

                                                       B30
JORDAN E.,THEORY OF LEGISLATION: AN ESSAY ON THE   LEGIS
DYNAMICS OF PUBLIC MIND. NAT/G CREATE REPRESENT   CONCPT
MAJORITY ATTIT GEN/LAWS. PAGE 59 E1173   JURID
                                                       CT/SYS

                                                       B31
BORCHARD E.H.,GUIDE TO THE LAW AND LEGAL LITERATURE   BIBLIOG/A
OF FRANCE. FRANCE FINAN INDUS LABOR SECT LEGIS   LAW
ADMIN COLONIAL CRIME OWN...INT/LAW 20. PAGE 14   CONSTN
E0266   METH

                                                       B31
COLUMBIA UNIVERSITY,A BIBLIOGRAPHY OF THE FACULTY   BIBLIOG
OF POLITICAL SCIENCE OF COLUMBIA UNIVERSITY,   ACADEM
1880-1930. USA-45 LAW NAT/G LEGIS DIPLOM LEAD WAR   PHIL/SCI
GOV/REL ATTIT...TIME/SEQ 19/20. PAGE 24 E0478

                                                       B32
FLEMMING D.,THE UNITED STATES AND THE LEAGUE OF   INT/ORG
NATIONS, 1918-1920. FUT USA-45 NAT/G LEGIS TOP/EX   EDU/PROP
DEBATE CHOOSE PEACE ATTIT SOVEREIGN...TIME/SEQ
CON/ANAL CONGRESS LEAGUE/NAT 20 TREATY. PAGE 39
E0764

                                                       B32
GREAT BRIT COMM MINISTERS PWR,REPORT. UK LAW CONSTN   EX/STRUC
CONSULT LEGIS PARL/PROC SANCTION SOVEREIGN   NAT/G
...DECISION JURID 20 PARLIAMENT. PAGE 45 E0902   PWR
                                                       CONTROL

                                                       B32
LUNT D.C.,THE ROAD TO THE LAW. UK USA-45 LEGIS   ADJUD
EDU/PROP OWN ORD/FREE...DECISION TIME/SEQ NAT/COMP   LAW
16/20 AUSTRAL ENGLSH/LAW COMMON/LAW. PAGE 67 E1333   JURID
                                                       CT/SYS

                                                       B33
DANGERFIELD R.,IN DEFENSE OF THE SENATE. USA-45   LEGIS
CONSTN NAT/G EX/STRUC TOP/EX ATTIT KNOWL   DELIB/GP
...METH/CNCPT STAT TIME/SEQ TREND CON/ANAL CHARTS   DIPLOM
CONGRESS 20 TREATY. PAGE 28 E0565

                                                       B35
BEMIS S.F.,GUIDE TO THE DIPLOMATIC HISTORY OF THE   BIBLIOG/A
UNITED STATES, 17751921. NAT/G LEGIS TOP/EX   DIPLOM
PROB/SOLV CAP/ISM INT/TRADE TARIFFS ADJUD   USA-45
...CON/ANAL 18/20. PAGE 10 E0184

                                                       B35
LUCE R.,LEGISLATIVE PROBLEMS. CONSTN CHIEF JUDGE   TREND
BUDGET CONFER ETIQUET CONTROL MORAL PWR NEW/LIB   ADMIN
CONGRESS. PAGE 67 E1331   LEGIS

                                                       B35
MCLAUGHLIN A.C.,A CONSTITUTIONAL HISTORY OF THE   CONSTN
UNITED STATES. USA+45 USA-45 LOC/G NAT/G PROVS   DECISION
LEGIS JUDGE ADJUD...T 18/20. PAGE 71 E1422

                                                       B35
NORDSKOG J.E.,SOCIAL REFORM IN NORWAY. NORWAY INDUS   LABOR
NAT/G POL/PAR LEGIS ADJUD...SOC BIBLIOG SOC/INTEG   ADJUST
20. PAGE 78 E1555

                                                       B35
RAM J.,THE SCIENCE OF LEGAL JUDGMENT: A TREATISE...   LAW
UK CONSTN NAT/G LEGIS CREATE PROB/SOLV AGREE CT/SYS   JURID
...INT/LAW CONCPT 19 ENGLSH/LAW CANON/LAW CIVIL/LAW   EX/STRUC
CTS/WESTM. PAGE 83 E1672   ADJUD

                                                       B35
ROBSON W.A.,CIVILISATION AND THE GROWTH OF LAW.   LAW
UNIV CONSTN SOCIETY LEGIS ADJUD ATTIT PERCEPT MORAL   IDEA/COMP
ALL/IDEOS...CONCPT WORSHIP 20. PAGE 85 E1708   SOC

                                                       B36
CHAMBERLAIN J.P.,LEGISLATIVE PROCESS: NATION AND   CON/ANAL
STATE. LAW DELIB/GP ROUTINE. PAGE 21 E0414   PROVS
                                                       LEGIS
                                                       NAT/G

                                                       B36
GRAVES W.B.,AMERICAN STATE GOVERNMENT. CONSTN FINAN   NAT/G
EX/STRUC FORCES LEGIS BUDGET TAX CT/SYS REPRESENT   PROVS
GOV/REL...BIBLIOG/A 19/20. PAGE 45 E0900   ADMIN
                                                       FEDERAL

                                                       B36
HANSON L.,GOVERNMENT AND THE PRESS 1695-1763. UK   LAW
LOC/G LEGIS LICENSE CONTROL SANCTION CRIME ATTIT   JURID
ORD/FREE 17/18 PARLIAMENT AMEND/I. PAGE 50 E0996   PRESS
                                                       POLICY

                                                       B36
SCHULZ F.,PRINCIPLES OF ROMAN LAW. CONSTN FAM NAT/G   LAW
DOMIN CONTROL CT/SYS CRIME ISOLAT ATTIT ORD/FREE   LEGIS
PWR...JURID ROME/ANC ROMAN/LAW. PAGE 89 E1783   ADJUD
                                                       CONCPT

                                                       B37
BADEN A.L.,IMMIGRATION AND ITS RESTRICTION IN THE   BIBLIOG
US (PAMPHLET). USA-45 NAT/G LEGIS...GEOG 20   STRANGE
CONGRESS. PAGE 7 E0130   CONTROL
                                                       LAW

                                                       B37
RUTHERFORD M.L.,THE INFLUENCE OF THE AMERICAN BAR   ATTIT
ASSOCIATION ON PUBLIC OPINION AND LEGISLATION.   ADJUD
USA+45 LAW CONSTN LABOR LEGIS DOMIN EDU/PROP LEGIT   PROF/ORG
CT/SYS ROUTINE...TIME/SEQ 19/20 ABA. PAGE 87 E1739   JURID

                                                       B38
CLARK J.P.,THE RISE OF A NEW FEDERALISM. LEGIS   FEDERAL
TARIFFS EFFICIENCY NAT/LISM UTIL...JURID SOC   PROVS
GEN/LAWS BIBLIOG 19/20. PAGE 23 E0451   NAT/G
                                                       GOV/REL

                                                       B38
HOLDSWORTH W.S.,A HISTORY OF ENGLISH LAW; THE   LAW
CENTURIES OF SETTLEMENT AND REFORM (VOL. X). INDIA   LOC/G
UK CONSTN NAT/G CHIEF LEGIS ADMIN COLONIAL CT/SYS   EX/STRUC
CHOOSE ORD/FREE PWR...JURID 18 PARLIAMENT   ADJUD
COMMONWLTH COMMON/LAW. PAGE 54 E1077

                                                       B38
HOLDSWORTH W.S.,A HISTORY OF ENGLISH LAW; THE   LAW
CENTURIES OF SETTLEMENT AND REFORM (VOL. XII). UK   PROF/ORG
CONSTN STRATA LEGIS JUDGE ADJUD CT/SYS ATTIT   WRITING
...JURID CONCPT BIOG GEN/LAWS 18 ENGLSH/LAW   IDEA/COMP
BLACKSTN/W COMMON/LAW. PAGE 54 E1078

                                                       B38
HOLDSWORTH W.S.,A HISTORY OF ENGLISH LAW; THE   LAW
CENTURIES OF SETTLEMENT AND REFORM (VOL. XI). UK   COLONIAL
CONSTN NAT/G EX/STRUC DIPLOM ADJUD CT/SYS LEAD   LEGIS
CRIME ATTIT...INT/LAW JURID 18 CMN/WLTH PARLIAMENT   PARL/PROC
ENGLSH/LAW. PAGE 54 E1079

B38
POUND R.,THE FORMATIVE ERA OF AMERICAN LAW. CULTURE CONSTN
NAT/G PROVS LEGIS ADJUD CT/SYS PERSON SOVEREIGN   LAW
...POLICY IDEA/COMP GEN/LAWS 18/19. PAGE 82 E1637   CREATE
JURID

B39
MCILWAIN C.H.,CONSTITUTIONALISM AND THE CHANGING   CONSTN
WORLD. UK USA-45 LEGIS PRIVIL AUTHORIT SOVEREIGN   POLICY
...GOV/COMP 15/20 MAGNA/CART HOUSE/CMNS. PAGE 71   JURID
E1417

B39
SIEYES E.J.,LES DISCOURS DE SIEYES DANS LES DEBATS   CONSTN
CONSTITUTIONNELS DE L'AN III (2 ET 18 THERMIDOR).   ADJUD
FRANCE LAW NAT/G PROB/SOLV BAL/PWR GOV/REL 18 JURY.   LEGIS
PAGE 91 E1824   EX/STRUC

B40
FULLER G.H.,A SELECTED LIST OF RECENT REFERENCES ON   BIBLIOG/A
THE CONSTITUTION OF THE UNITED STATES (PAMPHLET).   CONSTN
CULTURE NAT/G LEGIS CONFER ADJUD GOV/REL CONSEN   LAW
POPULISM...JURID CONCPT 18/20 CONGRESS. PAGE 41   USA-45
E0820

B40
HART J.,AN INTRODUCTION TO ADMINISTRATIVE LAW, WITH   LAW
SELECTED CASES. USA-45 CONSTN SOCIETY NAT/G   ADMIN
EX/STRUC ADJUD CT/SYS LEAD CRIME ORD/FREE   LEGIS
...DECISION JURID 20 CASEBOOK. PAGE 50 E1002   PWR

B41
BIRDSALL P.,VERSAILLES TWENTY YEARS AFTER. MOD/EUR   DIPLOM
POL/PAR CHIEF CONSULT FORCES LEGIS REPAR PEACE   NAT/LISM
ORD/FREE...BIBLIOG 20 PRESIDENT TREATY. PAGE 12   WAR
E0231

B42
CARR R.K.,THE SUPREME COURT AND JUDICIAL REVIEW.   CT/SYS
NAT/G CHIEF LEGIS OP/RES LEAD GOV/REL GP/REL ATTIT   CONSTN
...POLICY DECISION 18/20 SUPREME/CT PRESIDENT   JURID
CONGRESS. PAGE 20 E0394   PWR

B42
FORTESCU J.,IN PRAISE OF ENGLISH LAW (1464) (TRANS.   LAW
BY S.B. CHRIMES). UK ELITES CHIEF FORCES CT/SYS   CONSTN
COERCE CRIME GOV/REL ILLEGIT...JURID GOV/COMP   LEGIS
GEN/LAWS 15. PAGE 39 E0774   ORD/FREE

C43
BENTHAM J.,"ON THE LIBERTY OF THE PRESS, AND PUBLIC   ORD/FREE
DISCUSSION" IN J. BOWRING, ED., THE WORKS OF JEREMY   PRESS
BENTHAM." SPAIN UK LAW ELITES NAT/G LEGIS INSPECT   CONFER
LEGIT WRITING CONTROL PRIVIL TOTALISM AUTHORIT   CONSERVE
...TRADIT 19 FREE/SPEE. PAGE 10 E0193

B44
BEARD C.A.,AMERICAN GOVERNMENT AND POLITICS (REV.   LEAD
ED.). CONSTN MUNIC POL/PAR PROVS EX/STRUC LEGIS   USA-45
TOP/EX CT/SYS GOV/REL...BIBLIOG T 18/20. PAGE 9   NAT/G
E0165   LOC/G

B44
SUAREZ F.,A TREATISE ON LAWS AND GOD THE LAWGIVER   LAW
(1612) IN SELECTIONS FROM THREE WORKS, VOL. II.   JURID
FRANCE ITALY UK CULTURE NAT/G SECT CHIEF LEGIS   GEN/LAWS
DOMIN LEGIT CT/SYS ORD/FREE PWR WORSHIP 16/17.   CATH
PAGE 94 E1892

S44
WRIGHT Q.,"CONSTITUTIONAL PROCEDURES OF THE US FOR   TOP/EX
CARRYING OUT OBLIGATIONS FOR MILITARY SANCTIONS."   FORCES
EUR+WWI FUT USA-45 WOR-45 CONSTN INTELL NAT/G   INT/LAW
CONSULT EX/STRUC LEGIS ROUTINE DRIVE...POLICY JURID   WAR
CONCPT OBS TREND TOT/POP 20. PAGE 108 E2153

B45
CLAGETT H.L.,A GUIDE TO THE LAW AND LEGAL   BIBLIOG
LITERATURE OF THE MEXICAN STATES. CONSTN LEGIS   JURID
JUDGE ADJUD ADMIN...INT/LAW CON/ANAL 20 MEXIC/AMER.   L/A+17C
PAGE 22 E0440   LAW

S46
CANTWELL F.V.,"PUBLIC OPINION AND THE LEGISLATIVE   CHARTS
PROCESS" USA+45 USA-45 NAT/G CT/SYS EXEC LEAD   DEBATE
DECISION. PAGE 19 E0374   LEGIS
ATTIT

B47
BORGESE G.,COMMON CAUSE. LAW CONSTN SOCIETY STRATA   WOR+45
ECO/DEV INT/ORG POL/PAR FORCES LEGIS TOP/EX CAP/ISM   NAT/G
DIPLOM ADMIN EXEC ATTIT PWR 20. PAGE 14 E0269   SOVEREIGN
REGION

B47
CLAGETT H.L.,A GUIDE TO THE LAW AND LEGAL   BIBLIOG/A

LITERATURE OF BOLIVIA. L/A+17C CONSTN LABOR LEGIS   JURID
ADMIN...CRIMLGY INT/LAW PHIL/SCI 16/20 BOLIV.   LAW
PAGE 22 E0441   CT/SYS

B47
CLAGETT H.L.,A GUIDE TO THE LAW AND LEGAL   BIBLIOG
LITERATURE OF CHILE, 1917-1946. CHILE CONSTN LABOR   L/A+17C
JUDGE ADJUD ADMIN...CRIMLGY INT/LAW JURID CON/ANAL   LAW
20. PAGE 22 E0442   LEGIS

B47
CLAGETT H.L.,A GUIDE TO THE LAW AND LEGAL   BIBLIOG
LITERATURE OF ECUADOR. ECUADOR CONSTN LABOR LEGIS   JURID
JUDGE ADJUD ADMIN CIVMIL/REL...CRIMLGY INT/LAW   LAW
CON/ANAL 20. PAGE 22 E0443   L/A+17C

B47
CLAGETT H.L.,A GUIDE TO THE LAW AND LEGAL   BIBLIOG
LITERATURE OF VENEZUELA. VENEZUELA CONSTN LABOR   L/A+17C
LEGIS JUDGE ADJUD ADMIN CIVMIL/REL...CRIMLGY JURID   INT/LAW
CON/ANAL 20. PAGE 23 E0446   LAW

B47
DE NOIA J.,GUIDE TO OFFICIAL PUBLICATIONS OF OTHER   BIBLIOG/A
AMERICAN REPUBLICS: ECUADOR (VOL. IX). ECUADOR LAW   CONSTN
FINAN LEGIS BUDGET CT/SYS 19/20. PAGE 30 E0589   NAT/G
EDU/PROP

B47
DE NOIA J.,GUIDE TO OFFICIAL PUBLICATIONS OF THE   BIBLIOG/A
OTHER AMERICAN REPUBLICS: EL SALVADOR. EL/SALVADR   CONSTN
LAW LEGIS EDU/PROP CT/SYS 20. PAGE 30 E0590   NAT/G
ADMIN

B47
DE NOIA J.,GUIDE TO OFFICIAL PUBLICATIONS OF THE   BIBLIOG/A
OTHER AMERICAN REPUBLICS: NICARAGUA (VOL. XIV).   EDU/PROP
NICARAGUA LAW LEGIS ADMIN CT/SYS...JURID 19/20.   NAT/G
PAGE 30 E0591   CONSTN

B47
DE NOIA J.,GUIDE TO OFFICIAL PUBLICATIONS OF THE   BIBLIOG/A
OTHER AMERICAN REPUBLICS: PANAMA (VOL. XV). PANAMA   CONSTN
LAW LEGIS EDU/PROP CT/SYS 20. PAGE 30 E0592   ADMIN
NAT/G

B47
HILL M.,IMMUNITIES AND PRIVILEGES OF INTERNATIONAL   INT/ORG
OFFICIALS. CANADA EUR+WWI NETHERLAND SWITZERLND LAW   ADMIN
LEGIS DIPLOM LEGIT RESPECT...TIME/SEQ LEAGUE/NAT UN
VAL/FREE 20. PAGE 52 E1046

B47
LOCKE J.,TWO TREATISES OF GOVERNMENT (1690). UK LAW   CONCPT
SOCIETY LEGIS LEGIT AGREE REV OWN HEREDITY MORAL   ORD/FREE
CONSERVE...POLICY MAJORIT 17 WILLIAM/3 NATURL/LAW.   NAT/G
PAGE 66 E1316   CONSEN

B47
MCILWAIN C.H.,CONSTITUTIONALISM: ANCIENT AND   CONSTN
MODERN. USA+45 ROMAN/EMP LAW CHIEF LEGIS CT/SYS   NAT/G
GP/REL ORD/FREE SOVEREIGN...POLICY TIME/SEQ   PARL/PROC
ROMAN/REP EUROPE. PAGE 71 E1419   GOV/COMP

B47
NEUBURGER O.,GUIDE TO OFFICIAL PUBLICATIONS OF   BIBLIOG/A
OTHER AMERICAN REPUBLICS: HONDURAS (VOL. XIII).   NAT/G
HONDURAS LAW LEGIS ADMIN CT/SYS...JURID 19/20.   EDU/PROP
PAGE 76 E1533   CONSTN

B47
NEUBURGER O.,GUIDE TO OFFICIAL PUBLICATIONS OF THE   BIBLIOG/A
OTHER AMERICAN REPUBLICS: HAITI (VOL. XII). HAITI   CONSTN
LAW FINAN LEGIS PRESS...JURID 20. PAGE 76 E1534   NAT/G
EDU/PROP

B48
BISHOP H.M.,BASIC ISSUES OF AMERICAN DEMOCRACY.   NAT/G
USA+45 USA-45 POL/PAR EX/STRUC LEGIS ADJUD FEDERAL   PARL/PROC
...BIBLIOG 18/20. PAGE 12 E0232   CONSTN

B48
CLAGETT H.L.,A GUIDE TO THE LAW AND LEGAL   BIBLIOG
LITERATURE OF ARGENTINA, 1917-1946. CONSTN LABOR   L/A+17C
JUDGE ADJUD ADMIN...CRIMLGY INT/LAW JURID CON/ANAL   LAW
20 ARGEN. PAGE 23 E0447   LEGIS

B48
CORWIN E.S.,LIBERTY AGAINST GOVERNMENT: THE RISE,   CONCPT
FLOWERING AND DECLINE OF A FAMOUS JURIDICAL   ORD/FREE
CONCEPT. LEGIS ADJUD CT/SYS SANCTION GOV/REL   JURID
FEDERAL CONSERVE NEW/LIB...OLD/LIB 18/20 ROMAN/LAW   CONSTN
COMMON/LAW. PAGE 26 E0514

B48
DE NOIA J.,GUIDE TO OFFICIAL PUBLICATIONS OF OTHER   BIBLIOG/A

AMERICAN REPUBLICS: PERU (VOL. XVII). PERU LAW   CONSTN
LEGIS ADMIN CT/SYS...JURID 19/20. PAGE 30 E0593   NAT/G
   EDU/PROP

   B48
HOLCOMBE A.N.,HUMAN RIGHTS IN THE MODERN WORLD.   ORD/FREE
WOR+45 LEGIS DIPLOM ADJUD PERSON...INT/LAW 20 UN   INT/ORG
TREATY CIVIL/LIB BILL/RIGHT. PAGE 54 E1071   CONSTN
   LAW

   B48
JESSUP P.C.,A MODERN LAW OF NATIONS. FUT WOR+45   INT/ORG
WOR-45 SOCIETY NAT/G DELIB/GP LEGIS BAL/PWR   ADJUD
EDU/PROP LEGIT PWR...INT/LAW JURID TIME/SEQ
LEAGUE/NAT 20. PAGE 58 E1166

   B48
KEIR D.L.,CASES IN CONSTITUTIONAL LAW. UK CHIEF   CONSTN
LEGIS DIPLOM TAX PARL/PROC CRIME GOV/REL...INT/LAW   LAW
JURID 17/20. PAGE 60 E1195   ADJUD
   CT/SYS

   B48
MEIKLEJOHN A.,FREE SPEECH AND ITS RELATION TO SELF-   LEGIS
GOVERNMENT. USA+45 USA-45 LAW DOMIN PRESS ORD/FREE   NAT/G
20 AMEND/I. PAGE 72 E1434   CONSTN
   PRIVIL

   B48
NEUBURGER O.,GUIDE TO OFFICIAL PUBLICATIONS OF THE   BIBLIOG/A
OTHER AMERICAN REPUBLICS: VENEZUELA (VOL. XIX).   NAT/G
VENEZUELA FINAN LEGIS PLAN BUDGET DIPLOM CT/SYS   CONSTN
PARL/PROC 19/20. PAGE 77 E1535   LAW

   S48
MILLER B.S.,"A LAW IS PASSED: THE ATOMIC ENERGY ACT   TEC/DEV
OF 1946." POL/PAR CHIEF CONFER DEBATE CONTROL   LEGIS
PARL/PROC ATTIT KNOWL...POLICY CONGRESS. PAGE 73   DECISION
E1457   LAW

   C48
WALKER H.,"THE LEGISLATIVE PROCESS; LAWMAKING IN   PARL/PROC
THE UNITED STATES." NAT/G POL/PAR PROVS EX/STRUC   LEGIS
OP/RES PROB/SOLV CT/SYS LOBBY GOV/REL...CHARTS   LAW
BIBLIOG T 18/20 CONGRESS. PAGE 105 E2094   CONSTN

   B49
BOYD A.M.,UNITED STATES GOVERNMENT PUBLICATIONS   BIBLIOG/A
(3RD ED.). USA+45 EX/STRUC LEGIS ADMIN...JURID   PRESS
CHARTS 20. PAGE 14 E0281   NAT/G
   EDU/PROP

   B49
DE HUSZAR G.B.,EQUALITY IN AMERICA: THE ISSUE OF   DISCRIM
MINORITY RIGHTS. USA+45 USA-45 LAW NEIGH SCHOOL   RACE/REL
LEGIS ACT/RES CHOOSE ATTIT RESPECT...ANTHOL 20   ORD/FREE
NEGRO. PAGE 29 E0585   PROB/SOLV

   B49
DENNING A.,FREEDOM UNDER THE LAW. MOD/EUR UK LAW   ORD/FREE
SOCIETY CHIEF EX/STRUC LEGIS ADJUD CT/SYS PERS/REL   JURID
PERSON 17/20 ENGLSH/LAW. PAGE 31 E0606   NAT/G

   B49
WORMUTH F.D.,THE ORIGINS OF MODERN   NAT/G
CONSTITUTIONALISM. GREECE UK LEGIS CREATE TEC/DEV   CONSTN
BAL/PWR DOMIN ADJUD REV WAR PWR...JURID ROMAN/REP   LAW
CROMWELL/O. PAGE 107 E2146

   B50
BAILEY S.K.,CONGRESS MAKES A LAW. USA+45 GP/REL   DECISION
SOC. PAGE 7 E0136   LEGIS
   LAW
   ECO/TAC

   B50
GRAVES W.B.,PUBLIC ADMINISTRATION: A COMPREHENSIVE   BIBLIOG
BIBLIOGRAPHY ON PUBLIC ADMINISTRATION IN THE UNITED   FINAN
STATES (PAMPHLET). USA+45 USA-45 LOC/G NAT/G LEGIS   CONTROL
ADJUD INGP/REL...MGT 20. PAGE 45 E0901   ADMIN

   B50
HURST J.W.,THE GROWTH OF AMERICAN LAW; THE LAW   LAW
MAKERS. USA-45 LOC/G NAT/G DELIB/GP JUDGE ADJUD   LEGIS
ADMIN ATTIT PWR...POLICY JURID BIBLIOG 18/20   CONSTN
CONGRESS SUPREME/CT ABA PRESIDENT. PAGE 56 E1115   CT/SYS

   B50
JENKINS W.S.,A GUIDE TO THE MICROFILM COLLECTION OF   BIBLIOG
EARLY STATE RECORDS. USA+45 CONSTN MUNIC LEGIS   PROVS
PRESS ADMIN CT/SYS 18/20. PAGE 58 E1152   AUD/VIS

   B50
WADE E.C.S.,CONSTITUTIONAL LAW; AN OUTLINE OF THE   CONSTN
LAW AND PRACTICE OF THE CONSTITUTION. UK LEGIS   NAT/G
DOMIN ADMIN GP/REL 16/20 CMN/WLTH PARLIAMENT   PARL/PROC

ENGLSH/LAW. PAGE 104 E2087   LAW

   B51
ANDERSON W.,STATE AND LOCAL GOVERNMENT IN THE   LOC/G
UNITED STATES. USA+45 CONSTN POL/PAR EX/STRUC LEGIS   MUNIC
BUDGET TAX ADJUD CT/SYS CHOOSE...CHARTS T 20.   PROVS
PAGE 5 E0094   GOV/REL

   B51
BISSAINTHE M.,DICTIONNAIRE DE BIBLIOGRAPHIE   BIBLIOG
HAITIENNE. HAITI ELITES AGRI LEGIS DIPLOM INT/TRADE   L/A+17C
WRITING ORD/FREE CATHISM...ART/METH GEOG 19/20   SOCIETY
NEGRO TREATY. PAGE 12 E0234   NAT/G

   B51
COOKE C.A.,CORPORATION TRUST AND COMPANY: AN ESSAY   LG/CO
IN LEGAL HISTORY. UK STRUCT LEGIS CAP/ISM GP/REL   FINAN
PROFIT 13/20 COMPNY/ACT. PAGE 25 E0499   ECO/TAC
   JURID

   B51
FRIEDMANN W.,LAW AND SOCIAL CHANGE IN CONTEMPORARY   LAW
BRITAIN. UK LABOR LG/CO LEGIS JUDGE CT/SYS ORD/FREE   ADJUD
NEW/LIB...DECISION JURID TREND METH/COMP BIBLIOG 20   SOCIETY
PARLIAMENT ENGLSH/LAW COMMON/LAW. PAGE 40 E0802   CONSTN

   B51
ROSSITER C.,THE SUPREME COURT AND THE COMMANDER IN   CT/SYS
CHIEF. LAW CONSTN DELIB/GP EX/STRUC LEGIS TOP/EX   CHIEF
ADJUD CONTROL...DECISION SOC/EXP PRESIDENT. PAGE 86   WAR
E1724   PWR

   B51
WHEARE K.C.,MODERN CONSTITUTIONS (HOME UNIVERSITY   CONSTN
LIBRARY). UNIV LAW NAT/G LEGIS...CONCPT TREND   CLASSIF
BIBLIOG. PAGE 106 E2115   PWR
   CREATE

   L51
KELSEN H.,"RECENT TRENDS IN THE LAW OF THE UNITED   INT/ORG
NATIONS." KOREA WOR+45 CONSTN LEGIS DIPLOM LEGIT   LAW
DETER WAR RIGID/FLEX HEALTH ORD/FREE RESPECT   INT/LAW
...JURID CON/ANAL UN VAL/FREE 20 NATO. PAGE 60
E1199

   L51
MANGONE G.,"THE IDEA AND PRACTICE OF WORLD   INT/ORG
GOVERNMENT." FUT WOR+45 WOR-45 ECO/DEV LEGIS CREATE   SOCIETY
LEGIT ROUTINE ATTIT MORAL PWR WEALTH...CONCPT   INT/LAW
GEN/LAWS 20. PAGE 68 E1358

   B52
APPADORAI A.,THE SUBSTANCE OF POLITICS (6TH ED.).   PHIL/SCI
EX/STRUC LEGIS DIPLOM CT/SYS CHOOSE FASCISM MARXISM   NAT/G
SOCISM...BIBLIOG T. PAGE 5 E0100

   B52
BENTHAM A.,HANDBOOK OF POLITICAL FALLACIES. FUT   POL/PAR
MOD/EUR LAW INTELL LOC/G MUNIC NAT/G DELIB/GP LEGIS
CREATE EDU/PROP CT/SYS ATTIT RIGID/FLEX KNOWL PWR
...RELATIV PSY SOC CONCPT SELF/OBS TREND STERTYP
TOT/POP. PAGE 10 E0189

   B52
BRIGGS H.W.,THE LAW OF NATIONS (2ND ED.). WOR+45   INT/LAW
WOR-45 NAT/G LEGIS WAR...ANTHOL 20 TREATY. PAGE 15   DIPLOM
E0301   JURID

   B52
CAHILL F.V.,JUDICIAL LEGISLATION: A STUDY IN   JURID
AMERICAN LEGAL THEORY. USA+45 USA-45 LAW NAT/G   ADJUD
GP/REL...POLICY PHIL/SCI SOC 20 HOLMES/OW. PAGE 18   LEGIS
E0359   CONTROL

   B52
DE GRAZIA A.,POLITICAL ORGANIZATION. CONSTN LOC/G   FEDERAL
MUNIC NAT/G CHIEF LEGIS TOP/EX ADJUD CT/SYS   LAW
PERS/REL...INT/LAW MYTH UN. PAGE 29 E0581   ADMIN

   B52
FLECHTHEIM O.K.,FUNDAMENTALS OF POLITICAL SCIENCE.   NAT/G
WOR+45 WOR-45 LAW POL/PAR EX/STRUC LEGIS ADJUD   DIPLOM
ATTIT PWR...INT/LAW. PAGE 38 E0760   IDEA/COMP
   CONSTN

   B52
GELLHORN W.,THE STATES AND SUBVERSION. USA+45   PROVS
USA-45 LOC/G DELIB/GP LEGIS EDU/PROP LEGIT CT/SYS   JURID
REGION PEACE ATTIT ORD/FREE SOCISM...INT CON/ANAL
20 CALIFORNIA MARYLAND ILLINOIS MICHIGAN NEW/YORK.
PAGE 43 E0845

   B52
HOLDSWORTH W.S.,A HISTORY OF ENGLISH LAW; THE   LAW
CENTURIES OF SETTLEMENT AND REFORM, 1701-1875 (VOL.   CONSTN
XIII). UK POL/PAR PROF/ORG LEGIS JUDGE WRITING   IDEA/COMP

ATTIT...JURID CONCPT BIOG GEN/LAWS 18/19 PARLIAMENT CT/SYS REFORMERS ENGLSH/LAW COMMON/LAW. PAGE 54 E1080

B52
JENNINGS W.I.,CONSTITUTIONAL LAWS OF THE CONSTN COMMONWEALTH. UK LAW CHIEF LEGIS TAX CT/SYS JURID PARL/PROC GOV/REL...INT/LAW 18/20 COMMONWLTH ADJUD ENGLSH/LAW COMMON/LAW. PAGE 58 E1165 COLONIAL

B52
THOM J.M.,GUIDE TO RESEARCH MATERIAL IN POLITICAL BIBLIOG/A SCIENCE (PAMPHLET). ELITES LOC/G MUNIC NAT/G LEGIS KNOWL DIPLOM ADJUD CIVMIL/REL GOV/REL PWR MGT. PAGE 96 E1916

L52
ROSTOW E.V.,"THE DEMOCRATIC CHARACTER OF JUDICIAL CONSTN REVIEW" (BMR)" USA+45 LAW NAT/G LEGIS TASK...JURID PROB/SOLV 20 SUPREME/CT. PAGE 86 E1725 ADJUD CT/SYS

L52
WRIGHT Q.,"CONGRESS AND THE TREATY-MAKING POWER." ROUTINE USA+45 WOR+45 CONSTN INTELL NAT/G CHIEF CONSULT DIPLOM EX/STRUC LEGIS TOP/EX CREATE GOV/REL DISPL DRIVE INT/LAW RIGID/FLEX...TREND TOT/POP CONGRESS CONGRESS 20 DELIB/GP TREATY. PAGE 108 E2154

S52
DE GRAZIA A.,"GENERAL THEORY OF APPORTIONMENT" APPORT (BMR)" USA+45 USA-45 CONSTN ELITES DELIB/GP PARTIC LEGIS REV CHOOSE...JURID 20. PAGE 29 E0582 PROVS REPRESENT

C52
LANCASTER L.W.,"GOVERNMENT IN RURAL AMERICA." GOV/REL USA+45 ECO/DEV AGRI SCHOOL FORCES LEGIS JUDGE LOC/G BUDGET TAX CT/SYS...CHARTS BIBLIOG. PAGE 62 E1248 MUNIC ADMIN

B53
BUTLER D.E.,THE ELECTORAL SYSTEM IN BRITAIN. CHOOSE 1918-1951. UK LAW POL/PAR SUFF...STAT BIBLIOG 20 LEGIS PARLIAMENT. PAGE 18 E0348 REPRESENT PARTIC

B53
GROSS B.M.,THE LEGISLATIVE STRUGGLE: A STUDY IN LEGIS SOCIAL COMBAT. STRUCT LOC/G POL/PAR JUDGE EDU/PROP DECISION DEBATE ETIQUET ADMIN LOBBY CHOOSE GOV/REL INGP/REL PERSON HEREDITY ALL/VALS...SOC PRESIDENT. PAGE 48 E0948 LEAD

B53
PADOVER S.K.,THE LIVING US CONSTITUTION. USA+45 CONSTN USA-45 POL/PAR ADJUD...DECISION AUD/VIS IDEA/COMP LEGIS 18/20 SUPREME/CT. PAGE 79 E1590 DELIB/GP BIOG

B53
UNESCO,A REGISTER OF LEGAL DOCUMENTATION IN THE BIBLIOG WORLD. WOR+45 WOR-45 NAT/G PROVS DELIB/GP LEGIS CONSTN 13/20. PAGE 98 E1959 LAW JURID

B54
BENTLEY A.F.,INQUIRY INTO INQUIRIES: ESSAYS IN EPIST SOCIAL THEORY. UNIV LEGIS ADJUD ADMIN LOBBY SOC ...PHIL/SCI PSY NEW/IDEA LING METH 20. PAGE 10 CONCPT E0200

B54
BROGAN D.W.,POLITICS IN AMERICA. LAW POL/PAR CHIEF NAT/G LEGIS LOBBY CHOOSE REPRESENT GP/REL RACE/REL CONSTN FEDERAL MORAL...BIBLIOG 20 PRESIDENT CONGRESS. USA+45 PAGE 16 E0304

B54
MANGONE G.,A SHORT HISTORY OF INTERNATIONAL INT/ORG ORGANIZATION. MOD/EUR USA+45 USA-45 WOR+45 WOR-45 INT/LAW LAW LEGIS CREATE LEGIT ROUTINE RIGID/FLEX PWR ...JURID CONCPT OBS TIME/SEQ STERTYP GEN/LAWS UN TOT/POP VAL/FREE 18/20. PAGE 68 E1359

B54
SCHWARTZ B.,FRENCH ADMINISTRATIVE LAW AND THE JURID COMMON-LAW WORLD. FRANCE CULTURE LOC/G NAT/G PROVS LAW DELIB/GP EX/STRUC LEGIS PROB/SOLV CT/SYS EXEC METH/COMP GOV/REL...IDEA/COMP ENGLSH/LAW. PAGE 89 E1786 ADJUD

B54
SINCO,PHILIPPINE POLITICAL LAW: PRINCIPLES AND LAW CONCEPTS (10TH ED.). PHILIPPINE LOC/G EX/STRUC CONSTN BAL/PWR ECO/TAC TAX ADJUD ADMIN CONTROL CT/SYS SUFF LEGIS ORD/FREE...T 20. PAGE 91 E1831

B54
US SENATE COMM ON FOREIGN REL,REVIEW OF THE UNITED BIBLIOG NATIONS CHARTER: A COLLECTION OF DOCUMENTS. LEGIS CONSTN DIPLOM ADMIN ARMS/CONT WAR REPRESENT SOVEREIGN INT/ORG ...INT/LAW 20 UN. PAGE 101 E2029 DEBATE

B54
WRIGHT Q.,PROBLEMS OF STABILITY AND PROGRESS IN INT/ORG INTERNATIONAL RELATIONSHIPS. FUT WOR+45 WOR-45 CONCPT SOCIETY LEGIS CREATE TEC/DEV ECO/TAC EDU/PROP ADJUD DIPLOM WAR PEACE ORD/FREE PWR...KNO/TEST TREND GEN/LAWS 20. PAGE 108 E2155

C54
BOWIE R.R.,"STUDIES IN FEDERALISM." AGRI FINAN FEDERAL LABOR EX/STRUC FORCES LEGIS DIPLOM INT/TRADE ADJUD EUR+WWI ...BIBLIOG 20 EEC. PAGE 14 E0279 INT/ORG CONSTN

C54
CALDWELL L.K.,"THE GOVERNMENT AND ADMINISTRATION OF PROVS NEW YORK." LOC/G MUNIC POL/PAR SCHOOL CHIEF LEGIS ADMIN PLAN TAX CT/SYS...MGT SOC/WK BIBLIOG 20 NEWYORK/C. CONSTN PAGE 19 E0365 EX/STRUC

B55
BERNSTEIN M.H.,REGULATING BUSINESS BY INDEPENDENT DELIB/GP COMMISSION. USA+45 USA-45 LG/CO CHIEF LEGIS CONTROL PROB/SOLV ADJUD SANCTION GP/REL ATTIT...TIME/SEQ CONSULT 19/20 MONOPOLY PRESIDENT CONGRESS. PAGE 11 E0214

B55
CHOWDHURI R.N.,INTERNATIONAL MANDATES AND DELIB/GP TRUSTEESHIP SYSTEMS. WOR+45 STRUCT ECO/UNDEV PLAN INT/ORG LEGIS DOMIN EDU/PROP LEGIT ADJUD EXEC SOVEREIGN PWR...CONCPT TIME/SEQ UN 20. PAGE 22 E0434

B55
CRAIG J.,BIBLIOGRAPHY OF PUBLIC ADMINISTRATION IN BIBLIOG AUSTRALIA. CONSTN FINAN EX/STRUC LEGIS PLAN DIPLOM GOV/REL RECEIVE ADJUD ROUTINE...HEAL 19/20 AUSTRAL ADMIN PARLIAMENT. PAGE 27 E0540 NAT/G

B55
CUSHMAN R.E.,LEADING CONSTITUTIONAL DECISIONS. CONSTN USA+45 USA-45 NAT/G EX/STRUC LEGIS JUDGE TAX PROB/SOLV FEDERAL...DECISION 20 SUPREME/CT CASEBOOK. PAGE 28 JURID E0559 CT/SYS

B55
FLIESS P.J.,FREEDOM OF THE PRESS IN THE GERMAN EDU/PROP REPUBLIC, 1918-1933. GERMANY LAW CONSTN POL/PAR ORD/FREE LEGIS WRITING ADMIN COERCE MURDER MARXISM...POLICY JURID BIBLIOG 20 WEIMAR/REP. PAGE 39 E0765 PRESS

B55
MAYERS L.,THE AMERICAN LEGAL SYSTEM. USA+45 USA-45 JURID NAT/G EX/STRUC ADMIN CONTROL FEDERAL 20 SUPREME/CT. CT/SYS PAGE 70 E1394 LEGIS ADJUD

B55
PULLEN W.R.,A CHECK LIST OF LEGISLATIVE JOURNALS BIBLIOG ISSUED SINCE 1937 BY THE STATES OF THE UNITED PROVS STATES OF AMERICA (PAMPHLET). USA+45 USA-45 LAW EDU/PROP WRITING ADJUD ADMIN...JURID 20. PAGE 83 E1662 LEGIS

B55
SERRANO MOSCOSO E.,A STATEMENT OF THE LAWS OF FINAN ECUADOR IN MATTERS AFFECTING BUSINESS (2ND ED.). ECO/UNDEV ECUADOR INDUS LABOR LG/CO NAT/G LEGIS TAX CONTROL LAW MARRIAGE 20. PAGE 90 E1805 CONSTN

B55
SMITH G.,A CONSTITUTIONAL AND LEGAL HISTORY OF CONSTN ENGLAND. UK ELITES NAT/G LEGIS ADJUD OWN HABITAT PARTIC POPULISM...JURID 20 ENGLSH/LAW. PAGE 92 E1844 LAW CT/SYS

B55
WHEARE K.C.,GOVERNMENT BY COMMITTEE; AN ESSAY ON DELIB/GP THE BRITISH CONSTITUTION. UK NAT/G LEGIS INSPECT CONSTN CONFER ADJUD ADMIN CONTROL TASK EFFICIENCY ROLE LEAD POPULISM 20. PAGE 106 E2116 GP/COMP

S55
BETH L.P.,"THE CASE FOR JUDICIAL PROTECTION OF CT/SYS CIVIL LIBERTIES" (BMR)" USA+45 CONSTN ELITES LEGIS JUDGE CONTROL...POLICY DECISION JURID 20 SUPREME/CT ADJUD CIVIL/LIB. PAGE 11 E0220 ORD/FREE

B56
BROWNE D.G.,THE RISE OF SCOTLAND YARD: A HISTORY OF CRIMLGY THE METROPOLITAN POLICE. UK MUNIC CHIEF ADMIN CRIME LEGIS GP/REL 19/20. PAGE 16 E0316 CONTROL FORCES

B56
DOUGLAS W.O.,WE THE JUDGES. INDIA USA+45 USA-45 LAW ADJUD
NAT/G SECT LEGIS LEGIS PRESS CRIME FEDERAL ORD/FREE CT/SYS
...POLICY GOV/COMP 19/20 WARRN/EARL MARSHALL/J CONSTN
SUPREME/CT. PAGE 32 E0640 GOV/REL

B56
EMDEN C.S.,THE PEOPLE AND THE CONSTITUTION (2ND CONSTN
ED.). UK LEGIS POPULISM 17/20 PARLIAMENT. PAGE 35 PARL/PROC
E0687 NAT/G
LAW

B56
HOGAN J.D.,AMERICAN SOCIAL LEGISLATION. USA+45 FAM STRUCT
AGE/Y ATTIT...JURID CONCPT TREND. PAGE 53 E1065 RECEIVE
LEGIS
LABOR

B56
KALNOKI BEDO A.,LEGAL SOURCES AND BIBLIOGRAPHY OF BIBLIOG
HUNGARY. COM HUNGARY CONSTN LEGIS JUDGE CT/SYS ADJUD
SANCTION CRIME 16/20. PAGE 59 E1181 LAW
JURID

B56
PEASLEE A.J.,CONSTITUTIONS OF NATIONS. WOR+45 LAW CONSTN
NAT/G EX/STRUC LEGIT CT/SYS ROUTINE CON/ANAL
CHOOSE ORD/FREE PWR SOVEREIGN...CHARTS TOT/POP.
PAGE 80 E1605

B56
SIPKOV I.,LEGAL SOURCES AND BIBLIOGRAPHY OF BIBLIOG
BULGARIA. BULGARIA COM LEGIS WRITING ADJUD CT/SYS LAW
...INT/LAW TREATY 20. PAGE 91 E1834 TOTALISM
MARXISM

B56
US HOUSE WAYS MEANS COMMITTEE,TRAFFIC IN, AND BIO/SOC
CONTROL OF NARCOTICS, BARBITURATES, AND CONTROL
AMPHETAMINES. CHINA/COM USA+45 SOCIETY LEGIS PROB/SOLV
ACT/RES EDU/PROP CT/SYS SANCTION PROFIT HEALTH CRIME
...HEAL PSY STAT 20. PAGE 100 E2011

B56
ZINN C.J.,HOW OUR LAWS ARE MADE: BROCHURE HOUSE OF LEGIS
REPRESENTATIVES DOCUMENT 451. LAW CONSTN CHIEF DELIB/GP
EX/STRUC PROB/SOLV HOUSE/REP SENATE. PAGE 108 E2171 PARL/PROC
ROUTINE

B57
NJ LAW AND LEGISLATIVE BURE,NEW JERSEY APPORT
LEGISLAVTIVE REAPPORTIONMENT (PAMPHLET). USA+45 LEGIS
ACT/RES ADJUD...STAT CHARTS 20 NEW/JERSEY. PAGE 2 CENSUS
E0041 REPRESENT

B57
BAYITCH S.A.,A GUIDE TO INTERAMERICAN LEGAL BIBLIOG
STUDIES: A SELECTIVE BIBLIOGRAPHY OF WORKS IN L/A+17C
ENGLISH. NAT/G LEGIS ADJUD CT/SYS CONGRESS 20. LAW
PAGE 8 E0157 JURID

B57
COMM. STUDY ORGAN. PEACE,STRENGTHENING THE UNITED INT/ORG
NATIONS. FUT USA+45 WOR+45 CONSTN NAT/G DELIB/GP ORD/FREE
FORCES LEGIS ECO/TAC LEGIT COERCE PEACE...JURID
CONCPT UN COLD/WAR 20. PAGE 24 E0482

B57
COSSIO C.,LA POLITICA COMO CONCIENCIA; MEDITACION POL/PAR
SOBRE LA ARGENTINA DE 1955. WOR+45 LEGIS EDU/PROP REV
PARL/PROC PARTIC ATTIT PWR CATHISM 20 ARGEN TOTALISM
PERON/JUAN. PAGE 26 E0517 JURID

B57
DIVINE R.A.,AMERICAN IMMIGRATION POLICY, 1924-52. GEOG
USA+45 USA-45 VOL/ASSN DELIB/GP ADJUD WAR ADJUST HABITAT
DISCRIM...POLICY JURID 20 DEPRESSION MIGRATION. LEGIS
PAGE 32 E0630 CONTROL

B57
HISS A.,IN THE COURT OF PUBLIC OPINION. USA+45 CRIME
DELIB/GP LEGIS LEGIT CT/SYS ATTIT 20 DEPT/STATE MARXISM
NIXON/RM HUAC HISS/ALGER. PAGE 53 E1053 BIOG
ADJUD

B57
JENNINGS I.,PARLIAMENT. UK FINAN INDUS POL/PAR PARL/PROC
DELIB/GP EX/STRUC PLAN CONTROL...MAJORIT JURID TOP/EX
PARLIAMENT. PAGE 58 E1163 MGT
LEGIS

B57
LONG H.A.,USURPERS - FOES OF FREE MAN. LAW NAT/G CT/SYS
CHIEF LEGIS DOMIN ADJUD REPRESENT GOV/REL ORD/FREE CENTRAL
LAISSEZ POPULISM...POLICY 18/20 SUPREME/CT FEDERAL

ROOSEVLT/F CONGRESS CON/INTERP. PAGE 66 E1325 CONSTN

B57
MEYER P.,ADMINISTRATIVE ORGANIZATION: A COMPARATIVE ADMIN
STUDY OF THE ORGANIZATION OF PUBLIC ADMINISTRATION. METH/COMP
DENMARK FRANCE NORWAY SWEDEN UK USA+45 ELITES LOC/G NAT/G
CONSULT LEGIS ADJUD CONTROL LEAD PWR SKILL CENTRAL
DECISION. PAGE 72 E1449

B57
SCHLOCHAUER H.J.,OFFENTLICHES RECHT. GERMANY/W CONSTN
FINAN EX/STRUC LEGIS DIPLOM FEDERAL ORD/FREE JURID
...INT/LAW 20. PAGE 88 E1757 ADMIN
CT/SYS

B57
US COMMISSION GOVT SECURITY,RECOMMENDATIONS; AREA: LEGIS
LEGISLATION. USA+45 USA-45 DELIB/GP PLAN TEC/DEV SANCTION
CIVMIL/REL ORD/FREE...POLICY DECISION 20 PRIVACY. CRIME
PAGE 99 E1982 CONTROL

B57
US SENATE COMM ON JUDICIARY,CIVIL RIGHTS - 1957. INT
USA+45 LAW NAT/G CONFER GOV/REL RACE/REL ORD/FREE LEGIS
PWR...JURID 20 SENATE CIV/RIGHTS. PAGE 102 E2039 DISCRIM
PARL/PROC

B57
US SENATE COMM ON JUDICIARY,HEARING BEFORE LEGIS
SUBCOMMITTEE ON COMMITTEE OF JUDICIARY, UNITED CONSTN
STATES SENATE: S. J. RES. 3. USA+45 NAT/G CONSULT CONFER
DELIB/GP DIPLOM ADJUD LOBBY REPRESENT 20 CONGRESS AGREE
TREATY. PAGE 102 E2040

B58
ALLEN C.K.,LAW IN THE MAKING. LEGIS ATTIT ORD/FREE LAW
SOVEREIGN POPULISM...JURID IDEA/COMP NAT/COMP CREATE
GEN/LAWS 20 ENGLSH/LAW. PAGE 4 E0069 CONSTN
SOCIETY

B58
BLOCH J.,STATES' RIGHTS: THE LAW OF THE LAND. PROVS
USA+45 USA-45 LAW CONSTN LEGIS CONTROL CT/SYS NAT/G
FEDERAL ORD/FREE...PREDICT 17/20 CONGRESS BAL/PWR
SUPREME/CT. PAGE 13 E0246 CENTRAL

B58
BRIERLY J.L.,THE BASIS OF OBLIGATION IN INT/LAW
INTERNATIONAL LAW, AND OTHER PAPERS. WOR+45 WOR-45 DIPLOM
LEGIS...JURID CONCPT NAT/COMP ANTHOL 20. PAGE 15 ADJUD
E0299 SOVEREIGN

B58
BUGEDA LANZAS J.,A STATEMENT OF THE LAWS OF CUBA IN JURID
MATTERS AFFECTING BUSINESS (2ND ED. REV., NAT/G
ENLARGED). CUBA L/A+17C LAW FINAN FAM LEGIS ACT/RES INDUS
ADMIN GP/REL...BIBLIOG 20 OAS. PAGE 17 E0327 WORKER

B58
BUREAU OF NATIONAL AFFAIRS,THE MCCLELLAN COMMITTEE DELIB/GP
HEARINGS - 1957. USA+45 LEGIS CONTROL CRIME CONFER
...CHARTS 20 CONGRESS AFL/CIO MCCLELLN/J. PAGE 17 LABOR
E0336 MGT

B58
CUNNINGHAM W.B.,COMPULSORY CONCILIATION AND POLICY
COLLECTIVE BARGAINING. CANADA NAT/G LEGIS ADJUD BARGAIN
CT/SYS GP/REL...MGT 20 NEW/BRUNS STRIKE CASEBOOK. LABOR
PAGE 28 E0555 INDUS

B58
HAND L.,THE BILL OF RIGHTS. USA+45 USA-45 CHIEF CONSTN
LEGIS BAL/PWR ROLE PWR 18/20 SUPREME/CT CONGRESS JURID
AMEND/V PRESIDENT AMEND/XIV. PAGE 50 E0994 ORD/FREE
CT/SYS

B58
HUNT B.I.,BIPARTISANSHIP: A CASE STUDY OF THE FOR/AID
FOREIGN ASSISTANCE PROGRAM, 1947-56 (DOCTORAL POL/PAR
THESIS). USA+45 INT/ORG CONSULT LEGIS TEC/DEV GP/REL
...BIBLIOG PRESIDENT TREATY NATO TRUMAN/HS DIPLOM
EISNHWR/DD CONGRESS. PAGE 56 E1114

B58
MACKENZIE W.J.M.,FREE ELECTIONS: AN ELEMENTARY EX/STRUC
TEXTBOOK. WOR+45 NAT/G POL/PAR LEGIS TOP/EX CHOOSE
EDU/PROP LEGIT CT/SYS ATTIT PWR...OBS CHARTS
STERTYP T CONGRESS PARLIAMENT 20. PAGE 67 E1342

B58
MASON A.T.,THE SUPREME COURT FROM TAFT TO WARREN. CT/SYS
EX/STRUC LEGIS ROLE 20 SUPREME/CT TAFT/WH HUGHES/CE JURID
STONE/HF. PAGE 69 E1376 ADJUD

B58
SPITZ D.,DEMOCRACY AND THE CHALLANGE OF POWER. FUT NAT/G

USA+45 USA-45 LAW SOCIETY STRUCT LOC/G POL/PAR PWR
PROVS DELIB/GP EX/STRUC LEGIS TOP/EX ACT/RES CREATE
DOMIN EDU/PROP LEGIT ADJUD ADMIN ATTIT DRIVE MORAL
ORD/FREE TOT/POP. PAGE 93 E1862

B58
STRONG C.F.,MODERN POLITICAL CONSTITUTIONS. LAW CONSTN
CHIEF DELIB/GP EX/STRUC LEGIS ADJUD CHOOSE FEDERAL IDEA/COMP
POPULISM...CONCPT BIBLIOG 20 UN. PAGE 94 E1887 NAT/G

B58
US SENATE COMM POST OFFICE,TO PROVIDE AN EFFECTIVE INT
SYSTEM OF PERSONNEL ADMINISTRATION. USA+45 NAT/G LEGIS
EX/STRUC PARL/PROC GOV/REL...JURID 20 SENATE CONFER
CIVIL/SERV. PAGE 103 E2060 ADMIN

B58
WESTIN A.F.,THE ANATOMY OF A CONSTITUTIONAL LAW CT/SYS
CASE. USA+45 LAW LEGIS ADMIN EXEC...DECISION MGT INDUS
SOC RECORD 20 SUPREME/CT. PAGE 105 E2113 ADJUD
CONSTN

B58
WHITNEY S.N.,ANTITRUST POLICIES: AMERICAN INDUS
EXPERIENCE IN TWENTY INDUSTRIES. USA+45 USA-45 LAW CONTROL
DELIB/GP LEGIS ADJUD CT/SYS GOV/REL ATTIT...ANTHOL LG/CO
20 MONOPOLY CASEBOOK. PAGE 106 E2119 MARKET

L58
INT. SOC. SCI. BULL.,"TECHNIQUES OF MEDIATION AND VOL/ASSN
CONCILIATION." EUR+WWI USA+45 SOCIETY INDUS INT/ORG DELIB/GP
LABOR NAT/G LEGIS DIPLOM EDU/PROP CHOOSE ATTIT INT/LAW
RIGID/FLEX...JURID CONCPT GEN/LAWS 20. PAGE 57
E1129

S58
FISHER F.M.,"THE MATHEMATICAL ANALYSIS OF SUPREME PROB/SOLV
COURT DECISIONS: THE USE AND ABUSE OF QUANTITATIVE CT/SYS
METHODS." USA+45 LAW EX/STRUC LEGIS JUDGE ROUTINE JURID
ATTIT DECISION. PAGE 38 E0757 MATH

S58
RIKER W.H.,"THE PARADOX OF VOTING AND CONGRESSIONAL PARL/PROC
RULES FOR VOTING ON AMENDMENTS." LAW DELIB/GP DECISION
EX/STRUC PROB/SOLV CONFER DEBATE EFFICIENCY ATTIT LEGIS
HOUSE/REP CONGRESS SENATE. PAGE 85 E1700 RATIONAL

S58
STAAR R.F.,"ELECTIONS IN COMMUNIST POLAND." EUR+WWI COM
SOCIETY INT/ORG NAT/G POL/PAR LEGIS ACT/RES ECO/TAC CHOOSE
EDU/PROP ADJUD ADMIN ROUTINE COERCE TOTALISM ATTIT POLAND
ORD/FREE PWR 20. PAGE 93 E1864

C58
BRODEN T.F.,"CONGRESSIONAL COMMITTEE REPORTS: THEIR LAW
ROLE AND HISTORY" USA-45 PARL/PROC ROLE. PAGE 15 DELIB/GP
E0303 LEGIS
DEBATE

N58
US HOUSE COMM FOREIGN AFFAIRS,HEARINGS ON DRAFT LEGIS
LEGISLATION TO AMEND FURTHER THE MUTUAL SECURITY DELIB/GP
ACT OF 1954 (PAMPHLET). USA+45 CONSULT FORCES CONFER
BUDGET DIPLOM DETER COST ORD/FREE...JURID 20 WEAPON
DEPT/DEFEN UN DEPT/STATE. PAGE 100 E2002

B59
BECK C.,CONTEMPT OF CONGRESS: A STUDY OF THE LEGIS
PROSECUTIONS INITIATED BY THE COMMITTEE ON UN- DELIB/GP
AMERICAN ACTIVITIES. USA+45 CONSTN DEBATE EXEC. PWR
PAGE 9 E0170 ADJUD

B59
COUNCIL OF STATE GOVERNORS,AMERICAN LEGISLATURES: LEGIS
STRUCTURE AND PROCEDURES. SUMMARY AND TABULATIONS CHARTS
OF A 1959 SURVEY. PUERT/RICO USA+45 PAY ADJUD ADMIN PROVS
APPORT...IDEA/COMP 20 GUAM VIRGIN/ISL. PAGE 27 REPRESENT
E0525

B59
GINSBURG M.,LAW AND OPINION IN ENGLAND. UK CULTURE JURID
KIN LABOR LEGIS EDU/PROP ADMIN CT/SYS CRIME OWN POLICY
HEALTH...ANTHOL 20 ENGLSH/LAW. PAGE 44 E0868 ECO/TAC

B59
GINZBURG B.,REDEDICATION TO FREEDOM. DELIB/GP LEGIS JURID
ATTIT MARXISM 20 SUPREME/CT CON/INTERP HUAC AMEND/I ORD/FREE
FBI. PAGE 44 E0871 CONSTN
NAT/G

B59
KERREMANS-RAMIOULL,LE PROBLEME DE LA DELINQUENCE BIBLIOG
JUVENILE (2ND ED.). FAM PUB/INST SCHOOL FORCES CRIME
LEGIS MORAL...CRIMLGY SOC 20. PAGE 60 E1205 AGE/Y
SOC/WK

B59
MOOS M.,THE CAMPUS AND THE STATE. LAW FINAN EDU/PROP
DELIB/GP LEGIS EXEC LOBBY GP/REL PWR...POLICY ACADEM
BIBLIOG. PAGE 74 E1489 PROVS
CONTROL

B59
PAULSEN M.G.,LEGAL INSTITUTIONS TODAY AND TOMORROW. JURID
UK USA+45 NAT/G PROF/ORG PROVS ADMIN PARL/PROC ADJUD
ORD/FREE NAT/COMP. PAGE 80 E1604 JUDGE
LEGIS

B59
REIFF H.,THE UNITED STATES AND THE TREATY LAW OF ADJUD
THE SEA. USA+45 USA-45 SEA SOCIETY INT/ORG CONSULT INT/LAW
DELIB/GP LEGIS DIPLOM LEGIT ATTIT ORD/FREE PWR
WEALTH...GEOG JURID TOT/POP 20 TREATY. PAGE 84
E1681

B59
REOCK E.C.,PROCEDURES AND STANDARDS FOR THE PROVS
APPORTIONMENT OF STATE LEGISLATURES (DOCTORAL LOC/G
THESIS). USA+45 POL/PAR LEGIS TEC/DEV ADJUD APPORT
BIBLIOG. PAGE 84 E1686 REPRESENT

B59
SPIRO H.J.,GOVERNMENT BY CONSTITUTIONS: THE NAT/G
POLITICAL SYSTEMS OF DEMOCRACY. CANADA EUR+WWI FUT CONSTN
USA+45 WOR+45 WOR-45 LEGIS TOP/EX LEGIT ADMIN
CT/SYS ORD/FREE PWR...TREND TOT/POP VAL/FREE 20.
PAGE 93 E1861

B59
SURRENCY E.C.,A GUIDE TO LEGAL RESEARCH. USA+45 NAT/G
ACADEM LEGIS ACT/RES ADMIN...DECISION METH/COMP PROVS
BIBLIOG METH. PAGE 94 E1894 ADJUD
JURID

B59
US CONGRESS JT ATOM ENRGY COMM,SELECTED MATERIALS NAT/G
ON FEDERAL-STATE COOPERATION IN THE ATOMIC ENERGY NUC/PWR
FIELD. USA+45 LAW LOC/G PROVS CONSULT LEGIS ADJUD GOV/REL
...POLICY BIBLIOG 20 AEC. PAGE 99 E1991 DELIB/GP

L59
COX A.,"THE ROLE OF LAW IN PRESERVING UNION LABOR
DEMOCRACY." EX/STRUC LEGIS PARTIC ROUTINE CHOOSE REPRESENT
INGP/REL ORD/FREE. PAGE 27 E0532 LAW
MAJORIT

L59
OBERER W.E.,"VOLUNTARY IMPARTIAL REVIEW OF LABOR: LABOR
SOME REFLECTIONS." DELIB/GP LEGIS PROB/SOLV ADJUD LAW
CONTROL COERCE PWR PLURISM POLICY. PAGE 78 E1570 PARTIC
INGP/REL

S59
BEANEY W.B.,"CIVIL LIBERTIES AND STATUTORY CT/SYS
CONSTRUCTION"(BMR)" USA+45 LEGIS BAL/PWR 20 ORD/FREE
SUPREME/CT. PAGE 8 E0162 ADJUD
LAW

S59
CHAPMAN B.,"THE FRENCH CONSEIL D'ETAT." FRANCE ADMIN
NAT/G CONSULT OP/RES PROB/SOLV PWR...OBS 20. LAW
PAGE 21 E0421 CT/SYS
LEGIS

S59
DERGE D.R.,"THE LAWYER AS DECISION-MAKER IN THE LEGIS
AMERICAN STATE LEGISLATURE." INTELL LOC/G POL/PAR LAW
CHOOSE AGE HEREDITY PERSON CONSERVE...JURID STAT DECISION
CHARTS. PAGE 31 E0607 LEAD

S59
MENDELSON W.,"JUDICIAL REVIEW AND PARTY POLITICS" CT/SYS
(BMR)" UK USA+45 USA-45 NAT/G LEGIS PROB/SOLV POL/PAR
EDU/PROP ADJUD EFFICIENCY...POLICY NAT/COMP 19/20 BAL/PWR
AUSTRAL SUPREME/CT. PAGE 72 E1436 JURID

B60
JUNZ A.J.,PRESENT TRENDS IN AMERICAN NATIONAL POL/PAR
GOVERNMENT. LEGIS DIPLOM ADMIN CT/SYS ORD/FREE CHOOSE
...CONCPT ANTHOL 20 CONGRESS PRESIDENT SUPREME/CT. CONSTN
PAGE 2 E0040 NAT/G

B60
ADRIAN C.R.,STATE AND LOCAL GOVERNMENTS: A STUDY IN LOC/G
THE POLITICAL PROCESS. USA+45 LAW FINAN MUNIC PROVS
POL/PAR LEGIS ADJUD EXEC CHOOSE REPRESENT. PAGE 3 GOV/REL
E0051 ATTIT

B60
BAKER G.E.,STATE CONSTITUTIONS - REAPPORTIONMENT. APPORT
USA+45 USA-45 CONSTN CHOOSE ATTIT ORD/FREE...JURID REPRESENT
20. PAGE 7 E0138 PROVS

BAKER G.E.,THE POLITICS OF REAPPORTIONMENT IN WASHINGTON STATE. LAW POL/PAR CREATE EDU/PROP PARL/PROC CHOOSE INGP/REL...CHARTS METH/COMP 20 WASHINGT/G LEAGUE/WV. PAGE 7 E0139
B60
VOL/ASSN
APPORT
PROVS
LEGIS

BLANSHARD P.,GOD AND MAN IN WASHINGTON. USA+45 CHIEF LEGIS LEGIT CT/SYS PRIVIL ATTIT ORD/FREE ...POLICY CONCPT 20 SUPREME/CT CONGRESS PRESIDENT CHURCH/STA. PAGE 12 E0242
B60
NAT/G
SECT
GP/REL
POL/PAR

CARPER E.T.,THE DEFENSE APPROPRIATIONS RIDER (PAMPHLET). USA+45 CONSTN CHIEF DELIB/GP LEGIS BUDGET LOBBY CIVMIL/REL...POLICY 20 CONGRESS EISNHWR/DD DEPT/DEFEN PRESIDENT BOSTON. PAGE 20 E0390
B60
GOV/REL
ADJUD
LAW
CONTROL

DILEY A.V.,INTRODUCTION TO THE STUDY OF THE LAW OF THE CONSTITUTION. FRANCE UK USA+45 USA-45 CONSULT FORCES TAX ADMIN FEDERAL ORD/FREE SOVEREIGN ...IDEA/COMP 20 ENGLSH/LAW CON/INTERP PARLIAMENT. PAGE 32 E0627
B60
CONSTN
LAW
LEGIS
GEN/LAWS

GELLHORN W.,AMERICAN RIGHTS: THE CONSTITUTION IN ACTION. USA+45 USA-45 LEGIS ADJUD COERCE RACE/REL DISCRIM MARXISM 20 SUPREME/CT. PAGE 43 E0846
B60
ORD/FREE
JURID
CT/SYS
CONSTN

HANBURY H.G.,ENGLISH COURTS OF LAW. UK EX/STRUC LEGIS CRIME ROLE 12/20 COMMON/LAW ENGLSH/LAW. PAGE 50 E0993
B60
JURID
CT/SYS
CONSTN
GOV/REL

HARVARD LAW SCHOOL LIBRARY,CURRENT LEGAL BIBLIOGRAPHY. USA+45 CONSTN LEGIS ADJUD CT/SYS POLICY. PAGE 51 E1006
B60
BIBLIOG
JURID
LAW
INT/LAW

HEYSE T.,PROBLEMS FONCIERS ET REGIME DES TERRES (ASPECTS ECONOMIQUES, JURIDIQUES ET SOCIAUX). AFR CONGO/BRAZ INT/ORG DIPLOM SOVEREIGN...GEOG TREATY 20. PAGE 52 E1037
B60
BIBLIOG
AGRI
ECO/UNDEV
LEGIS

LASKIN B.,CANADIAN CONSTITUTIONAL LAW: TEXT AND NOTES ON DISTRIBUTION OF LEGISLATIVE POWER (2ND ED.). CANADA LOC/G ECO/TAC TAX CONTROL CT/SYS CRIME FEDERAL PWR...JURID 20 PARLIAMENT. PAGE 63 E1259
B60
CONSTN
NAT/G
LAW
LEGIS

NAT'L MUNICIPAL LEAGUE,COMPENDIUM ON LEGISLATIVE APPORTIONMENT. USA+45 LOC/G NAT/G POL/PAR CT/SYS CHOOSE 20 SUPREME/CT CONGRESS. PAGE 76 E1523
B60
APPORT
REPRESENT
LEGIS
STAT

POWELL T.,THE SCHOOL BUS LAW: A CASE STUDY IN EDUCATION, RELIGION, AND POLITICS. USA+45 LAW NEIGH SECT LEGIS EDU/PROP ADJUD CT/SYS LOBBY CATHISM WORSHIP 20 CONNECTICT CHURCH/STA. PAGE 82 E1641
B60
JURID
SCHOOL

PRASAD B.,THE ORIGINS OF PROVINCIAL AUTONOMY. INDIA UK FINAN LOC/G FORCES LEGIS CONTROL CT/SYS PWR ...JURID 19/20. PAGE 82 E1646
B60
CENTRAL
PROVS
COLONIAL
NAT/G

SCHUBERT G.A.,CONSTITUTIONAL POLITICS: THE POLITICAL BEHAVIOR OF SUPREME COURT JUSTICES AND THE CONSTITUTIONAL POLICIES THEY MAKE. LAW ELITES CHIEF DELIB/GP EX/STRUC LEGIS DISCRIM ORD/FREE PWR ...POLICY MAJORIT CHARTS SUPREME/CT CONGRESS. PAGE 89 E1781
B60
CONSTN
CT/SYS
JURID
DECISION

US HOUSE COMM ON JUDICIARY,ESTABLISHMENT OF CONGRESSIONAL DISTRICTS. USA+45 PROB/SOLV 20 CONGRESS HOUSE/REP. PAGE 100 E2003
B60
APPORT
REPRESENT
LEGIS
LAW

US LIBRARY OF CONGRESS,INDEX TO LATIN AMERICAN LEGISLATION: 1950-1960 (2 VOLS.). NAT/G DELIB/GP ADMIN PARL/PROC 20. PAGE 101 E2019
B60
BIBLIOG/A
LEGIS
L/A+17C
JURID

US SENATE COMM ON JUDICIARY,FEDERAL ADMINISTRATIVE PROCEDURE. USA+45 CONSTN NAT/G PROB/SOLV CONFER GOV/REL...JURID INT 20 SENATE. PAGE 102 E2043
B60
PARL/PROC
LEGIS
ADMIN
LAW

US SENATE COMM ON JUDICIARY,ADMINISTRATIVE PROCEDURE LEGISLATION. USA+45 CONSTN NAT/G PROB/SOLV CONFER ROUTINE GOV/REL...INT 20 SENATE. PAGE 102 E2044
B60
PARL/PROC
LEGIS
ADMIN
JURID

BLACK H.,"THE BILL OF RIGHTS" (BMR)" USA+45 USA-45 LAW LEGIS CT/SYS FEDERAL PWR 18/20 CONGRESS SUPREME/CT BILL/RIGHT CIV/RIGHTS. PAGE 12 E0237
S60
CONSTN
ORD/FREE
NAT/G
JURID

POTTER P.B.,"RELATIVE VALUES OF INTERNATIONAL RELATIONS, LAW, AND ORGANIZATIONS." WOR+45 NAT/G LEGIT ADJUD ORD/FREE...CONCPT TOT/POP COLD/WAR 20. PAGE 81 E1633
S60
INT/ORG
LEGIS
DIPLOM
INT/LAW

ROURKE F.E.,"ADMINISTRATIVE SECRECY: A CONGRESSIONAL DILEMMA." DELIB/GP CT/SYS ATTIT ...MAJORIT DECISION JURID. PAGE 86 E1727
S60
LEGIS
EXEC
ORD/FREE
POLICY

RHODESIA-NYASA NATL ARCHIVES,A SELECT BIBLIOGRAPHY OF RECENT PUBLICATIONS CONCERNING THE FEDERATION OF RHODESIA AND NYASALAND (PAMPHLET). MALAWI RHODESIA LAW CULTURE STRUCT ECO/UNDEV LEGIS...GEOG 20. PAGE 84 E1689
N60
BIBLIOG
ADMIN
ORD/FREE
NAT/G

AUERBACH C.A.,THE LEGAL PROCESS. USA+45 DELIB/GP JUDGE CONFER ADJUD CONTROL...DECISION 20 SUPREME/CT. PAGE 6 E0116
B61
JURID
ADMIN
LEGIS
CT/SYS

AVERY M.W.,GOVERNMENT OF WASHINGTON STATE. USA+45 MUNIC DELIB/GP EX/STRUC LEGIS GIVE CT/SYS PARTIC REGION EFFICIENCY 20 WASHINGT/G GOVERNOR. PAGE 6 E0121
B61
PROVS
LOC/G
ADMIN
GOV/REL

BARBASH J.,LABOR'S GRASS ROOTS. CONSTN NAT/G EX/STRUC LEGIS WORKER LEAD...MAJORIT BIBLIOG. PAGE 8 E0147
B61
LABOR
INGP/REL
GP/REL
LAW

BAYITCH S.A.,LATIN AMERICA: A BIBLIOGRAPHICAL GUIDE. LAW CONSTN LEGIS JUDGE ADJUD CT/SYS 20. PAGE 8 E0158
B61
BIBLIOG
L/A+17C
NAT/G
JURID

BEASLEY K.E.,STATE SUPERVISION OF MUNICIPAL DEBT IN KANSAS - A CASE STUDY. USA+45 USA-45 FINAN PROVS BUDGET TAX ADJUD ADMIN CONTROL SUPEGO. PAGE 9 E0167
B61
MUNIC
LOC/G
LEGIS
JURID

CARROTHERS A.W.R.,LABOR ARBITRATION IN CANADA. CANADA LAW NAT/G CONSULT LEGIS WORKER ADJUD ADMIN CT/SYS 20. PAGE 20 E0396
B61
LABOR
MGT
GP/REL
BARGAIN

CHILDS M.W.,THE EROSION OF INDIVIDUAL LIBERTIES. NAT/G LEGIS ATTIT...JURID SOC CONCPT IDEA/COMP 20 SUPREME/CT AMEND/I. PAGE 22 E0430
B61
ADJUD
CT/SYS
ORD/FREE
CONSTN

GUIZOT F.P.G.,HISTORY OF THE ORIGIN OF REPRESENTATIVE GOVERNMENT IN EUROPE. CHRIST-17C FRANCE MOD/EUR SPAIN UK LAW CHIEF FORCES POPULISM ...MAJORIT TIME/SEQ GOV/COMP NAT/COMP 4/19 PARLIAMENT. PAGE 48 E0961
B61
LEGIS
REPRESENT
CONSTN
NAT/G

LA PONCE J.A.,THE GOVERNMENT OF THE FIFTH REPUBLIC: FRENCH POLITICAL PARTIES AND THE CONSTITUTION. ALGERIA FRANCE LAW NAT/G DELIB/GP LEGIS ECO/TAC MARXISM SOCISM...CHARTS BIBLIOG/A 20 DEGAULLE/C. PAGE 62 E1243
B61
PWR
POL/PAR
CONSTN
CHIEF

LEONI B.,FREEDOM AND THE LAW. WOR+45 SOCIETY ADJUD INGP/REL EFFICIENCY ATTIT DRIVE. PAGE 64 E1286
B61
JURID
ORD/FREE

LEGIS
CONTROL

B61
NELSON H.L.,LIBEL IN NEWS OF CONGRESSIONAL
INVESTIGATING COMMITTEES. USA+45 LAW PARL/PROC
PRIVIL RESPECT HOUSE/REP. PAGE 76 E1532
DELIB/GP
LEGIS
LICENSE
PRESS

B61
NEW JERSEY LEGISLATURE-SENATE,PUBLIC HEARINGS
BEFORE COMMITTEE ON REVISION AND AMENDMENT OF LAWS
ON SENATE BILL NO. 8. USA+45 FINAN PROVS WORKER
ACT/RES PLAN BUDGET TAX CRIME...IDEA/COMP 20
NEW/JERSEY URBAN/RNWL. PAGE 77 E1537
LEGIS
MUNIC
INDUS
PROB/SOLV

B61
PRITCHETT C.H.,CONGRESS VERSUS THE SUPREME COURT,
1957-1960. PROB/SOLV DOMIN EXEC GP/REL DISCRIM PWR
CONGRESS SUPREME/CT SUPREME/CT. PAGE 82 E1652
LEGIS
JURID
LAW

B61
RUEDA B.,A STATEMENT OF THE LAWS OF COLOMBIA IN
MATTERS AFFECTING BUSINESS (3RD ED.). INDUS FAM
LABOR LG/CO NAT/G LEGIS TAX CONTROL MARRIAGE 20
COLOMB. PAGE 86 E1733
FINAN
ECO/UNDEV
LAW
CONSTN

B61
TOMPKINS D.C.,CONFLICT OF INTEREST IN THE FEDERAL
GOVERNMENT: A BIBLIOGRAPHY. USA+45 EX/STRUC LEGIS
ADJUD ADMIN CRIME CONGRESS PRESIDENT. PAGE 96 E1932
BIBLIOG
ROLE
NAT/G
LAW

B61
US HOUSE COMM ON JUDICIARY,LEGISLATION RELATING TO
ORGANIZED CRIME. USA+45 DIST/IND DELIB/GP GAMBLE
SANCTION HOUSE/REP. PAGE 100 E2004
LEGIS
CONTROL
CRIME
LAW

B61
WARD R.E.,JAPANESE POLITICAL SCIENCE: A GUIDE TO
JAPANESE REFERENCE AND RESEARCH MATERIALS (2ND
ED.). LAW CONSTN STRATA NAT/G POL/PAR DELIB/GP
LEGIS ADMIN CHOOSE GP/REL...INT/LAW 19/20 CHINJAP.
PAGE 105 E2099
BIBLIOG/A
PHIL/SCI

B61
WINTERS J.M.,STATE CONSTITUTIONAL LIMITATIONS ON
SOLUTIONS OF METROPOLITAN AREA PROBLEMS. CONSTN
LEGIS LEAD REPRESENT DECISION. PAGE 107 E2134
MUNIC
REGION
LOC/G
LAW

L61
FELLMAN D.,"ACADEMIC FREEDOM IN AMERICAN LAW." LAW
CONSTN NAT/G VOL/ASSN PLAN PERSON KNOWL NEW/LIB.
PAGE 37 E0732
ACADEM
ORD/FREE
LEGIS
CULTURE

L61
KAUPER P.G.,"CHURCH AND STATE: COOPERATIVE
SEPARATISM." NAT/G LEGIS OP/RES TAX EDU/PROP GP/REL
TREND. PAGE 59 E1187
SECT
CONSTN
LAW
POLICY

S61
HARVEY W.B.,"THE RULE OF LAW IN HISTORICAL
PERSPECTIVE." USA+45 WOR+45 INTELL SOCIETY ECO/DEV
ECO/UNDEV NAT/G EX/STRUC LEGIS TOP/EX LEGIT SKILL
...CONCPT HIST/WRIT TOT/POP. PAGE 51 E1010
ACT/RES
LAW

B62
AMERICAN LAW INSTITUTE,FOREIGN RELATIONS LAW OF THE
UNITED STATES: RESTATEMENT, SECOND. USA+45 NAT/G
LEGIS ADJUD EXEC ROUTINE GOV/REL...INT/LAW JURID
CONCPT 20 TREATY. PAGE 4 E0082
PROF/ORG
LAW
DIPLOM
ORD/FREE

B62
BARLOW R.B.,CITIZENSHIP AND CONSCIENCE: STUDIES IN
THEORY AND PRACTICE OF RELIGIOUS TOLERATION IN
ENGLAND DURING EIGHTEENTH CENTURY. UK LAW VOL/ASSN
EDU/PROP SANCTION REV GP/REL MAJORITY ATTIT
ORD/FREE...BIBLIOG WORSHIP 18. PAGE 8 E0150
SECT
LEGIS
DISCRIM

B62
BICKEL A.,THE LEAST DANGEROUS BRANCH. USA+45 USA-45
CONSTN SCHOOL LEGIS ADJUD RACE/REL DISCRIM ORD/FREE
...JURID 18/20 SUPREME/CT CONGRESS MARSHALL/J
HOLMES/OW FRANKFUR/F. PAGE 12 E0226
LAW
NAT/G
CT/SYS

B62
BOCK E.A.,CASE STUDIES IN AMERICAN GOVERNMENT.
USA+45 ECO/DEV CHIEF EDU/PROP CT/SYS RACE/REL
ORD/FREE...JURID MGT PHIL/SCI PRESIDENT CASEBOOK.
PAGE 13 E0256
POLICY
LEGIS
IDEA/COMP
NAT/G

B62
BUREAU OF NATIONAL AFFAIRS,FEDERAL-STATE REGULATION
OF WELFARE FUNDS (REV. ED.). USA+45 LAW LEGIS
DEBATE AGE/O 20 CONGRESS. PAGE 17 E0337
WELF/ST
WEALTH
PLAN
SOC/WK

B62
CARPER E.T.,ILLINOIS GOES TO CONGRESS FOR ARMY
LAND. USA+45 LAW EXTR/IND PROVS REGION CIVMIL/REL
GOV/REL FEDERAL ATTIT 20 ILLINOIS SENATE CONGRESS
DIRKSEN/E DOUGLAS/P. PAGE 20 E0391
ADMIN
LOBBY
GEOG
LEGIS

B62
FROMAN L.A. JR.,PEOPLE AND POLITICS: AN ANALYSIS OF
THE AMERICAN POLITICAL SYSTEM. USA+45 CHIEF
DELIB/GP EX/STRUC LEGIS TOP/EX CT/SYS LOBBY
PERS/REL PWR...POLICY DECISION. PAGE 41 E0813
POL/PAR
PROB/SOLV
GOV/REL

B62
GANJI M.,INTERNATIONAL PROTECTION OF HUMAN RIGHTS.
WOR+45 CONSTN INT/TRADE CT/SYS SANCTION CRIME WAR
RACE/REL...CHARTS IDEA/COMP NAT/COMP BIBLIOG 20
TREATY NEGRO LEAGUE/NAT UN CIVIL/LIB. PAGE 42 E0831
ORD/FREE
DISCRIM
LEGIS
DELIB/GP

B62
HOOK S.,THE PARADOXES OF FREEDOM. UNIV CONSTN
INTELL LEGIS CONTROL REV CHOOSE SUPEGO...POLICY
JURID IDEA/COMP 19/20 CIV/RIGHTS. PAGE 55 E1095
CONCPT
MAJORIT
ORD/FREE
ALL/VALS

B62
HSUEH S.-S.,GOVERNMENT AND ADMINISTRATION OF HONG
KONG. CHIEF DELIB/GP LEGIS CT/SYS REPRESENT GOV/REL
20 HONG/KONG CITY/MGT CIVIL/SERV GOVERNOR. PAGE 55
E1106
ADMIN
LOC/G
COLONIAL
EX/STRUC

B62
LAWSON R.,INTERNATIONAL REGIONAL ORGANIZATIONS.
WOR+45 NAT/G VOL/ASSN CONSULT LEGIS EDU/PROP LEGIT
ADMIN EXEC ROUTINE HEALTH PWR WEALTH...JURID EEC
COLD/WAR 20 UN. PAGE 63 E1270
INT/ORG
DELIB/GP
REGION

B62
LITTLEFIELD N.,METROPOLITAN AREA PROBLEMS AND
MUNICIPAL HOME RULE. USA+45 PROVS ADMIN CONTROL
GP/REL PWR. PAGE 65 E1308
LOC/G
SOVEREIGN
JURID
LEGIS

B62
MASON A.T.,THE SUPREME COURT: PALADIUM OF FREEDOM.
USA-45 NAT/G POL/PAR CHIEF LEGIS ADJUD PARL/PROC
FEDERAL PWR...POLICY BIOG 18/20 SUPREME/CT
ROOSEVLT/F JEFFERSN/T MARSHALL/J HUGHES/CE. PAGE 69
E1378
CONSTN
CT/SYS
JURID

B62
MCGRATH J.J.,CHURCH AND STATE IN AMERICAN LAW:
CASES AND MATERIALS. USA+45 USA-45 LEGIS EDU/PROP
ADJUD CT/SYS PWR...ANTHOL 18/20 CHURCH/STA. PAGE 71
E1415
LAW
GOV/REL
SECT

B62
MURPHY W.F.,CONGRESS AND THE COURT. USA+45 LAW
LOBBY GP/REL RACE/REL ATTIT PWR...JURID INT BIBLIOG
CONGRESS SUPREME/CT WARRN/EARL. PAGE 75 E1509
LEGIS
CT/SYS
GOV/REL
ADJUD

B62
NAT'L MUNICIPAL LEAGUE,COMPENDIUM ON LEGISLATIVE
APPORTIONMENT. USA+45 LOC/G NAT/G POL/PAR PROVS
CT/SYS CHOOSE 20 SUPREME/CT CONGRESS. PAGE 76 E1524
APPORT
REPRESENT
LEGIS
STAT

B62
NATIONAL MUNICIPAL LEAGUE,COURT DECISIONS ON
LEGISLATIVE APPORTIONMENT (VOL. III). USA+45 JUDGE
ADJUD CONTROL ATTIT...DECISION JURID COURT/DIST
CASEBOOK. PAGE 76 E1528
PROVS
CT/SYS
APPORT
LEGIS

B62
PHILLIPS O.H.,CONSTITUTIONAL AND ADMINISTRATIVE LAW
(3RD ED.). UK INT/ORG LOC/G CHIEF EX/STRUC LEGIS
BAL/PWR ADJUD COLONIAL CT/SYS PWR...CHARTS 20.
PAGE 80 E1613
JURID
ADMIN
CONSTN
NAT/G

B62
PRESS C.,STATE MANUALS, BLUE BOOKS AND ELECTION
RESULTS. LAW LOC/G MUNIC LEGIS WRITING FEDERAL
SOVEREIGN...DECISION STAT CHARTS 20. PAGE 82 E1648
BIBLIOG
PROVS
ADMIN
CHOOSE

B62
US COMMISSION ON CIVIL RIGHTS,EQUAL PROTECTION OF
THE LAWS IN NORTH CAROLINA. USA+45 LOC/G NAT/G
CONSULT LEGIS WORKER PROB/SOLV EDU/PROP ADJUD
CHOOSE DISCRIM HEALTH 20 NEGRO NORTH/CAR
ORD/FREE
RESPECT
LAW
PROVS

CIV/RIGHTS. PAGE 99 E1984

B62
US COMMISSION ON CIVIL RIGHTS,HEARINGS BEFORE
UNITED STATES COMMISSION ON CIVIL RIGHTS. USA+45
ECO/DEV NAT/G CONSULT WORKER EDU/PROP ADJUD DISCRIM
ISOLAT HABITAT HEALTH RESPECT 20 NEGRO CIV/RIGHTS.
PAGE 99 E1985
ORD/FREE
LAW
ADMIN
LEGIS

L62
MANGIN G.,"L'ORGANIZATION JUDICIAIRE DES ETATS
D'AFRIQUE ET DE MADAGASCAR." ISLAM WOR+45 STRATA
STRUCT ECO/UNDEV NAT/G LEGIT EXEC...JURID TIME/SEQ
TOT/POP 20 SUPREME/CT. PAGE 68 E1357
AFR
LEGIS
COLONIAL
MADAGASCAR

L62
MURACCIOLE L.,"LA LOI FONDAMENTALE DE LA REPUBLIQUE
DU CONGO." WOR+45 SOCIETY ECO/UNDEV INT/ORG NAT/G
LEGIS PLAN LEGIT ADJUD COLONIAL ROUTINE ATTIT
SOVEREIGN 20 CONGO. PAGE 75 E1504
AFR
CONSTN

L62
N,"UNION INVESTMENT IN BUSINESS: A SOURCE OF UNION
CONFLICT OF INTEREST." LAW NAT/G LEGIS CONTROL
GP/REL INGP/REL DECISION. PAGE 76 E1515
LABOR
POLICY
FINAN
LG/CO

S62
GRAVEN J.,"LE MOUVEAU DROIT PENAL INTERNATIONAL."
UNIV STRUCT LEGIS ACT/RES CRIME ATTIT PERCEPT
PERSON...JURID CONCPT 20. PAGE 45 E0899
CT/SYS
PUB/INST
INT/ORG
INT/LAW

S62
SCHUBERT G.,"THE 1960 TERM OF THE SUPREME COURT: A
PSYCHOLOGICAL ANALYSIS." USA+45 LAW CT/SYS...STAT
SUPREME/CT. PAGE 88 E1772
DECISION
LEGIS
JUDGE
EX/STRUC

S62
SILVA R.C.,"LEGISLATIVE REPESENTATION - WITH
SPECIAL REFERENCE TO NEW YORK." LAW CONSTN LOC/G
NAT/G PROVS. PAGE 91 E1826
MUNIC
LEGIS
REPRESENT
APPORT

S62
THOMPSON D.,"THE UNITED KINGDOM AND THE TREATY OF
ROME." EUR+WWI INT/ORG NAT/G DELIB/GP LEGIS
INT/TRADE RIGID/FLEX...CONCPT EEC PARLIAMENT
CMN/WLTH 20. PAGE 96 E1918
ADJUD
JURID

C62
BACON F.,"OF JUDICATURE" (1612) IN F. BACON,
ESSAYS." ADJUD ADMIN SANCTION CRIME PWR...JURID
GEN/LAWS. PAGE 7 E0128
CT/SYS
LEGIS
LAW

C62
MORGAN G.G.,"SOVIET ADMINISTRATIVE LEGALITY: THE
ROLE OF THE ATTORNEY GENERAL'S OFFICE." COM USSR
CONTROL ROUTINE...CONCPT BIBLIOG 18/20. PAGE 74
E1493
LAW
CONSTN
LEGIS
ADMIN

N62
TWENTIETH CENTURY FUND,ONE MAN - ONE VOTE
(PAMPHLET). USA+45 CONSTN CONFER CT/SYS REGION
CONSEN FEDERAL ROLE...CENSUS 20 CONGRESS. PAGE 97
E1947
APPORT
LEGIS
REPRESENT
PROVS

N62
US ADVISORY COMN INTERGOV REL,APPORTIONMENT OF
STATE LEGISLATURES (PAMPHLET). LAW CONSTN EX/STRUC
LEGIS LEAD MAJORITY. PAGE 99 E1977
MUNIC
PROVS
REPRESENT
APPORT

B63
ADRIAN C.R.,GOVERNING OVER FIFTY STATES AND THEIR
COMMUNITIES. USA+45 CONSTN FINAN MUNIC NAT/G
POL/PAR EX/STRUC LEGIS ADMIN CONTROL CT/SYS
...CHARTS 20. PAGE 3 E0052
PROVS
LOC/G
GOV/REL
GOV/COMP

B63
ATTIA G.E.D.,LES FORCES ARMEES DES NATIONS UNIES EN
COREE ET AU MOYENORIENT. KOREA CONSTN NAT/G
DELIB/GP LEGIS PWR...IDEA/COMP NAT/COMP BIBLIOG UN
SUEZ. PAGE 6 E0114
FORCES
INT/LAW

B63
BADI J.,THE GOVERNMENT OF THE STATE OF ISRAEL: A
CRITICAL ACCOUNT OF ITS PARLIAMENT, EXECUTIVE, AND
JUDICIARY. ISRAEL ECO/DEV CHIEF DELIB/GP LEGIS
DIPLOM CT/SYS INGP/REL PEACE ORD/FREE...BIBLIOG 20
PARLIAMENT ARABS MIGRATION. PAGE 7 E0131
NAT/G
CONSTN
EX/STRUC
POL/PAR

B63
BROWN R.M.,THE SOUTH CAROLINA REGULATORS. USA-45
LEGIS LEGIT ADJUD COLONIAL CONTROL WAR...BIBLIOG/A
ORD/FREE
JURID

18 CHARLESTON SOUTH/CAR. PAGE 16 E0315
PWR
PROVS

B63
BURRUS B.R.,ADMINSTRATIVE LAW AND LOCAL GOVERNMENT.
USA+45 PROVS LEGIS LICENSE ADJUD ORD/FREE 20.
PAGE 18 E0347
EX/STRUC
LOC/G
JURID
CONSTN

B63
CARTER G.M.,FIVE AFRICAN STATES: RESPONSES TO
DIVERSITY. CONSTN CULTURE STRATA LEGIS PLAN ECO/TAC
DOMIN EDU/PROP CT/SYS EXEC CHOOSE ATTIT HEALTH
ORD/FREE PWR...TIME/SEQ TOT/POP VAL/FREE. PAGE 20
E0398
AFR
SOCIETY

B63
CORLEY R.N.,THE LEGAL ENVIRONMENT OF BUSINESS.
CONSTN LEGIS TAX ADMIN CT/SYS DISCRIM ATTIT PWR
...TREND 18/20. PAGE 26 E0509
NAT/G
INDUS
JURID
DECISION

B63
DAY R.E.,CIVIL RIGHTS USA: PUBLIC SCHOOLS, SOUTHERN
STATES - NORTH CAROLINA, 1963. USA+45 LOC/G NEIGH
LEGIS CREATE CT/SYS COERCE DISCRIM ATTIT...QU
CHARTS 20 NORTH/CAR NEGRO KKK CIV/RIGHTS. PAGE 29
E0579
EDU/PROP
ORD/FREE
RACE/REL
SANCTION

B63
DE GRAZIA A.,APPORTIONMENT AND REPRESENTATIVE
GOVERNMENT. CONSTN POL/PAR LEGIS PLAN ADJUD DISCRIM
RATIONAL...CONCPT STAT PREDICT TREND IDEA/COMP.
PAGE 29 E0583
REPRESENT
APPORT
NAT/G
MUNIC

B63
DECOTTIGNIES R.,LES NATIONALITES AFRICAINES. AFR
NAT/G PROB/SOLV DIPLOM COLONIAL ORD/FREE...CHARTS
GOV/COMP 20. PAGE 30 E0602
NAT/LISM
JURID
LEGIS
LAW

B63
GARNER U.F.,ADMINISTRATIVE LAW. UK LAW LOC/G NAT/G
EX/STRUC LEGIS JUDGE BAL/PWR BUDGET ADJUD CONTROL
CT/SYS...BIBLIOG 20. PAGE 42 E0840
ADMIN
JURID
PWR
GOV/REL

B63
GRANT D.R.,STATE AND LOCAL GOVERNMENT IN AMERICA.
USA+45 FINAN LOC/G MUNIC EX/STRUC FORCES EDU/PROP
ADMIN CHOOSE FEDERAL ATTIT...JURID 20. PAGE 45
E0897
PROVS
POL/PAR
LEGIS
CONSTN

B63
GRIFFITH J.A.G.,PRINCIPLES OF ADMINISTRATIVE LAW
(3RD ED.). UK CONSTN EX/STRUC LEGIS ADJUD CONTROL
CT/SYS PWR...CHARTS 20. PAGE 47 E0940
JURID
ADMIN
NAT/G
BAL/PWR

B63
GSOUSKI V.,LEGAL SOURCES AND BIBLIOGRAPHY OF THE
BALTIC STATES (ESTONIA, LATVIA, LITHUANIA). COM
ESTONIA LATVIA LITHUANIA NAT/G LEGIS CT/SYS
SANCTION CRIME 20. PAGE 48 E0957
BIBLIOG
ADJUD
LAW
JURID

B63
HACKER A.,CONGRESSIONAL DISTRICTING: THE ISSUE OF
EQUAL REPRESENTATION. FUT CT/SYS GEOG. PAGE 49
E0970
LEGIS
REPRESENT
APPORT

B63
HALEY A.G.,SPACE LAW AND GOVERNMENT. FUT USA+45
WOR+45 LEGIS ACT/RES CREATE ATTIT RIGID/FLEX
ORD/FREE PWR SOVEREIGN...POLICY JURID CONCPT CHARTS
VAL/FREE 20. PAGE 49 E0980
INT/ORG
LAW
SPACE

B63
LEAGUE WOMEN VOTERS NEW YORK,APPORTIONMENT WORKSHOP
KIT. USA+45 VOL/ASSN DELIB/GP LEGIS ATTIT ORD/FREE
...METH/COMP 20 SUPREME/CT NEW/YORK. PAGE 64 E1275
APPORT
REPRESENT
PROVS
JURID

B63
LEGISLATIVE REFERENCE SERVICE,DIGEST OF PUBLIC
GENERAL BILLS AND RESOLUTIONS. LAW COM/IND EDU/PROP
GOV/REL INGP/REL KNOWL...JURID 20 CONGRESS. PAGE 64
E1280
BIBLIOG/A
LEGIS
DELIB/GP
NAT/G

B63
MURPHY T.J.,CENSORSHIP: GOVERNMENT AND OBSCENITY.
USA+45 CULTURE LEGIS JUDGE EDU/PROP CONTROL
INGP/REL RATIONAL POPULISM...CATH JURID 20. PAGE 75
E1507
ORD/FREE
MORAL
LAW
CONSEN

B63
NATIONAL CIVIC REVIEW,REAPPORTIONMENT: A YEAR IN
APPORT

REVIEW (PAMPHLET). USA+45 LAW CT/SYS CHOOSE   REPRESENT
ORD/FREE PWR...ANTHOL 20 CONGRESS. PAGE 76 E1527   LEGIS
                                                     CONSTN

                                                     B63
NEWMAN E.S.,THE FREEDOM READER. USA+45 LEGIS TOP/EX RACE/REL
PLAN ADJUD CONTROL CT/SYS DISCRIM...DECISION ANTHOL LAW
20 SUPREME/CT CIV/RIGHTS. PAGE 77 E1541   POLICY
                                                     ORD/FREE

                                                     B63
PRITCHETT C.H.,THE THIRD BRANCH OF GOVERNMENT.   JURID
USA+45 USA-45 CONSTN SOCIETY INDUS SECT LEGIS JUDGE NAT/G
PROB/SOLV GOV/REL 20 SUPREME/CT CHURCH/STA. PAGE 82 ADJUD
E1654   CT/SYS

                                                     B63
REOCK E.C. JR.,POPULATION INEQUALITY AMONG COUNTIES APPORT
IN THE NEW JERSEY LEGISLATURE 1791-1962. PROVS   REPRESENT
ORD/FREE...CENSUS CHARTS 18/20 NEW/JERSEY. PAGE 84   LEGIS
E1687   JURID

                                                     B63
ROYAL INSTITUTE PUBLIC ADMIN,BRITISH PUBLIC   BIBLIOG
ADMINISTRATION. UK LAW FINAN INDUS LOC/G POL/PAR   ADMIN
LEGIS LOBBY PARL/PROC CHOOSE JURID. PAGE 86 E1729   MGT
                                                     NAT/G

                                                     B63
SARTORI G.,IL PARLAMENTO ITALIANO: 1946-1963. LAW   LEGIS
CONSTN ELITES POL/PAR LOBBY PRIVIL ATTIT PERSON   PARL/PROC
MORAL PWR SOC. PAGE 87 E1746   REPRESENT

                                                     B63
SCHMIDHAUSER J.R.,CONSTITUTIONAL LAW IN THE   LAW
POLITICAL PROCESS. SOCIETY LEGIS ADJUD CT/SYS   CONSTN
FEDERAL...SOC TREND IDEA/COMP ANTHOL T SUPREME/CT   JURID
SENATE CONGRESS HOUSE/REP. PAGE 88 E1761

                                                     B63
US COMN CIVIL RIGHTS,REPORT ON MISSISSIPPI. LAW   RACE/REL
LOC/G NAT/G LEGIS PLAN PROB/SOLV DISCRIM SOC/INTEG   CONSTN
20 MISSISSIPP NEGRO. PAGE 99 E1987   ORD/FREE
                                                     COERCE

                                                     B63
US CONGRESS: SENATE,HEARINGS OF THE COMMITTEE ON   LEGIS
THE JUDICIARY. USA+45 CONSTN NAT/G ADMIN GOV/REL 20 LAW
CONGRESS. PAGE 99 E1992   ORD/FREE
                                                     DELIB/GP

                                                     B63
US SENATE,DOCUMENTS ON INTERNATIONAL AS"ECTS OF   SPACE
EXPLORATION AND USE OF OUTER SPACE, 1954-62: STAFF   UTIL
REPORT FOR COMM AERON SPACE SCI. USA+45 USSR LEGIS   GOV/REL
LEAD CIVMIL/REL PEACE...POLICY INT/LAW ANTHOL 20   DIPLOM
CONGRESS NASA KHRUSH/N. PAGE 101 E2026

                                                     B63
US SENATE COMM ON JUDICIARY,ADMINISTRATIVE   PARL/PROC
CONFERENCE OF THE UNITED STATES. USA+45 CONSTN   JURID
NAT/G PROB/SOLV CONFER GOV/REL...INT 20 SENATE.   ADMIN
PAGE 102 E2048   LEGIS

                                                     L63
ROSE R.,"COMPARATIVE STUDIES IN POLITICAL FINANCE: FINAN
A SYMPOSIUM." ASIA EUR+WWI S/ASIA LAW CULTURE   POL/PAR
DELIB/GP LEGIS ACT/RES ECO/TAC EDU/PROP CHOOSE
ATTIT RIGID/FLEX SUPEGO PWR SKILL WEALTH...STAT
ANTHOL VAL/FREE. PAGE 85 E1714

                                                     S63
BECHHOEFER B.G.,"UNITED NATIONS PROCEDURES IN CASE   INT/ORG
OF VIOLATIONS OF DISARMAMENT AGREEMENTS." COM   DELIB/GP
USA+45 USSR LAW CONSTN NAT/G EX/STRUC FORCES LEGIS
BAL/PWR EDU/PROP CT/SYS ARMS/CONT ORD/FREE PWR
...POLICY STERTYP UN VAL/FREE 20. PAGE 9 E0169

                                                     S63
HARNETTY P.,"CANADA, SOUTH AFRICA AND THE   AFR
COMMONWEALTH." CANADA SOUTH/AFR LAW INT/ORG   ATTIT
VOL/ASSN DELIB/GP LEGIS TOP/EX ECO/TAC LEGIT DRIVE
MORAL...CONCPT CMN/WLTH 20. PAGE 50 E1000

                                                     C63
ATTIA G.E.O.,"LES FORCES ARMEES DES NATIONS UNIES   FORCES
EN COREE ET AU MOYENORIENT." KOREA CONSTN DELIB/GP   NAT/G
LEGIS PWR...IDEA/COMP NAT/COMP BIBLIOG UN SUEZ.   INT/LAW
PAGE 6 E0115

                                                     B64
ANDERSON J.W.,EISENHOWER, BROWNELL, AND THE   LAW
CONGRESS - THE TANGLED ORIGINS OF THE CIVIL RIGHTS   CONSTN
BILL OF 1956-1957. USA+45 POL/PAR LEGIS CREATE   POLICY
PROB/SOLV LOBBY GOV/REL RIGID/FLEX...NEW/IDEA 20   NAT/G
EISNHWR/DD CONGRESS BROWNELL/H CIV/RIGHTS. PAGE 5

E0090

                                                     B64
BERWANGER E.H.,WESTERN ANTI-NEGRO SENTIMENT AND   RACE/REL
LAWS 1846-60: A FACTOR IN THE SLAVERY EXTENSION   REGION
CONTROVERSY (PAPER). USA-45 LAW CONSTN LEGIS ADJUD   DISCRIM
...BIBLIOG 19 NEGRO. PAGE 11 E0218   ORD/FREE

                                                     B64
BROOKS T.R.,TOIL AND TROUBLE, A HISTORY OF AMERICAN INDUS
LABOR. WORKER BARGAIN CAP/ISM ADJUD AUTOMAT EXEC   LABOR
GP/REL RACE/REL EFFICIENCY INCOME PROFIT MARXISM   LEGIS
17/20 KENNEDY/JF AFL/CIO NEGRO. PAGE 16 E0310

                                                     B64
BUREAU OF NAT'L AFFAIRS,THE CIVIL RIGHTS ACT OF   LEGIS
1964. USA+45 LOC/G NAT/G DELIB/GP CONFER DEBATE   RACE/REL
DISCRIM...JURID 20 CONGRESS SUPREME/CT CIV/RIGHTS.   LAW
PAGE 17 E0333   CONSTN

                                                     B64
CHAPIN B.,THE AMERICAN LAW OF TREASON. USA-45 LAW   LEGIS
NAT/G JUDGE CRIME REV...BIBLIOG 18. PAGE 21 E0419   JURID
                                                     CONSTN
                                                     POLICY

                                                     B64
COUNCIL OF STATE GOVERNMENTS,LEGISLATIVE   LOC/G
APPORTIONMENT: A SUMMARY OF STATE ACTION. USA+45   PROVS
LEGIS REPRESENT...POLICY SUPREME/CT. PAGE 26 E0523   APPORT
                                                     CT/SYS

                                                     B64
DANELSKI D.J.,A SUPREME COURT JUSTICE IS APPOINTED. CHOOSE
CHIEF LEGIS CONFER DEBATE EXEC PERSON PWR...BIOG 20 JUDGE
CONGRESS PRESIDENT. PAGE 28 E0564   DECISION

                                                     B64
DIAS R.W.M.,A BIBLIOGRAPHY OF JURISPRUDENCE (2ND   BIBLIOG/A
ED.). VOL/ASSN LEGIS ADJUD CT/SYS OWN...INT/LAW   JURID
18/20. PAGE 31 E0619   LAW
                                                     CONCPT

                                                     B64
DUMON F.,LE BRESIL; SES INSTITUTIONS POLITIQUES ET   CONSTN
JUDICIARIES. BRAZIL POL/PAR CHIEF LEGIS ORD/FREE   JURID
19/20. PAGE 33 E0658   CT/SYS
                                                     GOV/REL

                                                     B64
ENDACOTT G.B.,GOVERNMENT AND PEOPLE IN HONG KONG   CONSTN
1841-1962: A CONSTITUTIONAL HISTORY. UK LEGIS ADJUD COLONIAL
REPRESENT ATTIT 19/20 HONG/KONG. PAGE 35 E0688   CONTROL
                                                     ADMIN

                                                     B64
EULAU H.,LAWYERS IN POLITICS: A STUDY IN   PROF/ORG
PROFESSIONAL CONVERGENCE. USA+45 POL/PAR DELIB/GP   JURID
GP/REL...QU 20. PAGE 35 E0701   LEGIS
                                                     ATTIT

                                                     B64
FULBRIGHT J.W.,OLD MYTHS AND NEW REALITIES. USA+45   DIPLOM
USSR LEGIS INT/TRADE DETER ATTIT...POLICY 20   INT/ORG
COLD/WAR TREATY. PAGE 41 E0818   ORD/FREE

                                                     B64
GARDNER L.C.,ECONOMIC ASPECTS OF NEW DEAL   ECO/TAC
DIPLOMACY. USA-45 WOR-45 LAW ECO/DEV INT/ORG NAT/G   DIPLOM
VOL/ASSN LEGIS TOP/EX EDU/PROP ORD/FREE PWR WEALTH
...POLICY TIME/SEQ VAL/FREE 20 ROOSEVLT/F. PAGE 42
E0836

                                                     B64
GARDNER R.N.,IN PURSUIT OF WORLD ORDER* US FOREIGN   OBS
POLICY AND INTERNATIONAL ORGANIZATIONS. USA+45 USSR INT/ORG
ECO/UNDEV FORCES LEGIS DIPLOM FOR/AID INT/TRADE   ALL/VALS
PEACE...INT/LAW PREDICT UN. PAGE 42 E0839

                                                     B64
GJUPANOVIC H.,LEGAL SOURCES AND BIBLIOGRAPHY OF   BIBLIOG/A
YUGOSLAVIA. COM YUGOSLAVIA LAW LEGIS DIPLOM ADMIN   JURID
PARL/PROC REGION CRIME CENTRAL 20. PAGE 44 E0873   CONSTN
                                                     ADJUD

                                                     B64
HALLER W.,DER SCHWEDISCHE JUSTITIEOMBUDSMAN.   JURID
DENMARK FINLAND NORWAY SWEDEN LEGIS ADJUD CONTROL   PARL/PROC
PERSON ORD/FREE...NAT/COMP 20 OMBUDSMAN. PAGE 50   ADMIN
E0986   CHIEF

                                                     B64
HANSON R.,FAIR REPRESENTATION COMES TO MARYLAND   APPORT
(PAMPHLET). BAL/PWR CT/SYS CHOOSE GOV/REL 20   REPRESENT
MARYLAND SUPREME/CT. PAGE 50 E0997   PROVS
                                                     LEGIS

HEGEL G.W.,HEGEL'S POLITICAL WRITINGS (TRANS. BY T.M. KNOX). GERMANY UK FINAN FORCES PARL/PROC CHOOSE REPRESENT...BIOG 19. PAGE 51 E1022
B64
CONSTN
LEGIS
JURID

HOLDSWORTH W.S.,A HISTORY OF ENGLISH LAW; THE CENTURIES OF DEVELOPMENT AND REFORM (VOL. XIV). UK CONSTN LOC/G NAT/G POL/PAR CHIEF EX/STRUC ADJUD COLONIAL ATTIT...INT/LAW JURID 18/19 TORY/PARTY COMMONWLTH WHIG/PARTY COMMON/LAW. PAGE 54 E1081
B64
LAW
LEGIS
LEAD
CT/SYS

HOLT S.,THE DICTIONARY OF AMERICAN GOVERNMENT. USA+45 LOC/G MUNIC PROVS LEGIS ADMIN JURID. PAGE 55 E1091
B64
DICTIONARY
INDEX
LAW
NAT/G

HOPKINSON T.,SOUTH AFRICA. SOUTH/AFR UK NAT/G POL/PAR LEGIS ECO/TAC PARL/PROC WAR...JURID AUD/VIS 19/20. PAGE 55 E1097
B64
SOCIETY
RACE/REL
DISCRIM

IRION F.C.,APPORTIONMENT OF THE NEW MEXICO LEGISLATURE. NAT/G LEGIS PRESS CT/SYS ATTIT ...POLICY TIME/SEQ 19/20 SUPREME/CT. PAGE 57 E1137
B64
APPORT
REPRESENT
GOV/REL
PROVS

KEEFE W.J.,THE AMERICAN LEGISLATIVE PROCESS: CONGRESS AND THE STATES. USA+45 LAW POL/PAR DELIB/GP DEBATE ADMIN LOBBY REPRESENT CONGRESS PRESIDENT. PAGE 60 E1191
B64
LEGIS
DECISION
PWR
PROVS

LEDERMAN W.R.,THE COURTS AND THE CANDIAN CONSTITUTION. CANADA PARL/PROC...POLICY JURID GOV/COMP ANTHOL 19/20 SUPREME/CT PARLIAMENT. PAGE 64 E1276
B64
CONSTN
CT/SYS
LEGIS
LAW

LOCKHART W.B.,CASES AND MATERIALS ON CONSTITUTIONAL RIGHTS AND LIBERTIES. USA+45 FORCES LEGIS DIPLOM PRESS CONTROL CRIME WAR PWR...AUD/VIS T WORSHIP 20 NEGRO. PAGE 66 E1317
B64
ORD/FREE
CONSTN
NAT/G

MAKI J.M.,COURT AND CONSTITUTION IN JAPAN: SELECTED SUPREME COURT DECISIONS, 1948-60. LAW AGRI FAM LEGIS BAL/PWR ADMIN CHOOSE...SOC ANTHOL CABINET 20 CHINJAP CIVIL/LIB. PAGE 68 E1355
B64
CONSTN
JURID
CT/SYS
CRIME

MASON A.T.,AMERICAN CONSTITUTIONAL LAW: INTRODUCTORY ESSAYS AND SELECTED CASES (3RD ED.). LAW LEGIS TAX ADJUD GOV/REL FEDERAL ORD/FREE PWR ...TIME/SEQ BIBLIOG T 19/20 SUPREME/CT. PAGE 69 E1379
B64
CONSTN
CT/SYS
JURID

MINAR D.W.,IDEAS AND POLITICS: THE AMERICAN EXPERIENCE. SECT CHIEF LEGIS CREATE ADJUD EXEC REV PWR...PHIL/SCI CONCPT IDEA/COMP 18/20 HAMILTON/A JEFFERSN/T DECLAR/IND JACKSON/A PRESIDENT. PAGE 73 E1464
B64
CONSTN
NAT/G
FEDERAL

MITAU G.T.,PROXIMATE SOLUTIONS: CASE PROBLEMS IN STATE AND LOCAL GOVERNMENT. USA+45 CONSTN NAT/G CHIEF LEGIS CT/SYS EXEC GOV/REL GP/REL PWR 20 CASEBOOK. PAGE 73 E1470
B64
PROVS
LOC/G
ADJUD

MITCHELL B.,A BIOGRAPHY OF THE CONSTITUTION OF THE UNITED STATES. USA+45 USA-45 PROVS CHIEF LEGIS DEBATE ADJUD SUFF FEDERAL...SOC 18/20 SUPREME/CT CONGRESS SENATE HOUSE/REP PRESIDENT. PAGE 73 E1472
B64
CONSTN
LAW
JURID

NEWMAN E.S.,CIVIL LIBERTY AND CIVIL RIGHTS. USA+45 USA-45 CONSTN PROVS FORCES LEGIS CT/SYS RACE/REL ATTIT...MAJORIT JURID WORSHIP 20 SUPREME/CT NEGRO CIV/RIGHTS CHURCH/STA. PAGE 77 E1543
B64
ORD/FREE
LAW
CONTROL
NAT/G

A CHECK LIST OF THE SPECIAL AND STANDING COMMITTEES OF THE AMERICAN BAR ASSOCIATION (VOL. II). USA+45 LEGIS PRESS CONFER...JURID CON/ANAL. PAGE 80 E1607
B64
BIBLIOG
LAW
VOL/ASSN

PRESS C.,A BIBLIOGRAPHIC INTRODUCTION TO AMERICAN STATE GOVERNMENT AND POLITICS (PAMPHLET). USA+45 USA-45 EX/STRUC ADJUD INGP/REL FEDERAL ORD/FREE 20. PAGE 82 E1649
B64
BIBLIOG
LEGIS
LOC/G
POL/PAR

RUSSELL R.B.,UNITED NATIONS EXPERIENCE WITH MILITARY FORCES: POLITICAL AND LEGAL ASPECTS. AFR KOREA WOR+45 LEGIS PROB/SOLV ADMIN CONTROL EFFICIENCY PEACE...POLICY INT/LAW BIBLIOG UN. PAGE 87 E1738
B64
FORCES
DIPLOM
SANCTION
ORD/FREE

SHAPIRO M.,LAW AND POLITICS IN THE SUPREME COURT: NEW APPROACHES TO POLITICAL JURISPRUDENCE. JUDGE PROB/SOLV LEGIT EXEC ROUTINE ATTIT ALL/VALS ...DECISION SOC. PAGE 90 E1811
B64
LEGIS
CT/SYS
LAW
JURID

STOICOIU V.,LEGAL SOURCES AND BIBLIOGRAPHY OF ROMANIA. COM ROMANIA LAW FINAN POL/PAR LEGIS JUDGE ADJUD CT/SYS PARL/PROC MARXISM 20. PAGE 93 E1874
B64
BIBLIOG/A
JURID
CONSTN
ADMIN

STOKES A.P.,CHURCH AND STATE IN THE UNITED STATES (3 VOLS.). USA+45 USA-45 NAT/G PROVS LEGIS CT/SYS SANCTION PRIVIL ORD/FREE 17/20 CHURCH/STA. PAGE 94 E1875
B64
SECT
CONSTN
POLICY

STRONG C.F.,HISTORY OF MODERN POLITICAL CONSTITUTIONS. STRUCT INT/ORG NAT/G LEGIS TEC/DEV DIPLOM INT/TRADE CT/SYS EXEC...METH/COMP T 12/20 UN. PAGE 94 E1888
B64
CONSTN
CONCPT

TELLADO A.,A STATEMENT OF THE LAWS OF THE DOMINICAN REPUBLIC IN MATTERS AFFECTING BUSINESS (3RD ED.). DOMIN/REP AGRI DIST/IND EXTR/IND FINAN FAM WORKER ECO/TAC TAX CT/SYS MARRIAGE OWN...BIBLIOG 20 MIGRATION. PAGE 95 E1913
B64
CONSTN
LEGIS
NAT/G
INDUS

TENBROCK J.,EQUAL UNDER LAW. USA-45 CONSTN POL/PAR EDU/PROP PARL/PROC ORD/FREE...BIBLIOG 19 AMEND/XIV. PAGE 95 E1914
B64
LEGIS
LAW
DISCRIM
DOMIN

US HOUSE COMM ON JUDICIARY,CONGRESSIONAL REDISTRICTING. USA+45 PROVS DELIB/GP 20 CONGRESS. PAGE 100 E2005
B64
APPORT
REPRESENT
LEGIS
LAW

US SENATE COMM ON JUDICIARY,CIVIL RIGHTS - THE PRESIDENT'S PROGRAM. USA+45 LAW PROB/SOLV PRESS ADJUD GOV/REL RACE/REL ORD/FREE PWR...JURID 20 SUPREME/CT SENATE CIV/RIGHTS PRESIDENT. PAGE 102 E2053
B64
INT
LEGIS
DISCRIM
PARL/PROC

US SENATE COMM ON JUDICIARY,ADMINISTRATIVE PROCEDURE ACT. USA+45 CONSTN NAT/G PROB/SOLV CONFER GOV/REL PWR...INT 20 SENATE. PAGE 102 E2054
B64
PARL/PROC
LEGIS
JURID
ADMIN

WRIGHT G.,RURAL REVOLUTION IN FRANCE: THE PEASANTRY IN THE TWENTIETH CENTURY. EUR+WWI MOD/EUR LAW CULTURE AGRI POL/PAR DELIB/GP LEGIS ECO/TAC EDU/PROP COERCE CHOOSE ATTIT RIGID/FLEX HEALTH ...STAT CENSUS CHARTS VAL/FREE 20. PAGE 107 E2148
B64
PWR
STRATA
FRANCE
REV

BERKS R.N.,"THE US AND WEAPONS CONTROL." WOR+45 LAW INT/ORG NAT/G LEGIS EXEC COERCE PEACE ATTIT RIGID/FLEX ALL/VALS PWR...POLICY TOT/POP 20. PAGE 11 E0204
L64
USA+45
PLAN
ARMS/CONT

BALDWIN G.B.,"THE DEPENDENCE OF SCIENCE ON LAW AND GOVERNMENT--THE INTERNATIONAL GEOPHYSICAL YEAR--A CASE STUDY." WOR+45 LAW INT/ORG PROF/ORG LEGIS PLAN EDU/PROP...TIME/SEQ VAL/FREE 20. PAGE 8 E0144
S64
NAT/G
KNOWL

DERWINSKI E.J.,"THE COST OF THE INTERNATIONAL COFFEE AGREEMENT." L/A+17C USA+45 WOR+45 ECO/UNDEV NAT/G VOL/ASSN LEGIS DIPLOM ECO/TAC FOR/AID LEGIT ATTIT...TIME/SEQ CONGRESS 20 TREATY. PAGE 31 E0608
S64
MARKET
DELIB/GP
INT/TRADE

BECKER T.L.,"POLITICAL BEHAVIORALISM AND MODERN JURISPRUDENCE." LEGIS JUDGE OP/RES ADJUD CT/SYS ATTIT PWR...BIBLIOG 20. PAGE 9 E0173
C64
DECISION
PROB/SOLV
JURID
GEN/LAWS

AMERICAN UNIVERSITY IN CAIRO,GUIDE TO UAR
GOVERNMENT PUBLICATIONS AT THE AUC LIBRARY
(PAMPHLET). ISLAM UAR USA+45 ECO/UNDEV...SOC STAT
20. PAGE 4 E0084

B65
BIBLIOG
NAT/G
LEGIS
LAW

BAR ASSOCIATION OF ST LOUIS,CONSTITUTIONAL FREEDOM
AND THE LAW. USA+45 LAW LABOR LEGIS EDU/PROP
...JURID CONCPT SUPREME/CT CIVIL/LIB CIV/RIGHTS.
PAGE 8 E0146

B65
ORD/FREE
CONSTN
RACE/REL
NAT/G

BARKER L.J.,FREEDOM, COURTS, POLITICS: STUDIES IN
CIVIL LIBERTIES. USA+45 LEGIS CREATE DOMIN PRESS
ADJUD LOBBY CRIME GP/REL RACE/REL MARXISM 20
CIVIL/LIB. PAGE 8 E0148

B65
JURID
CT/SYS
ATTIT
ORD/FREE

BLITZ L.F.,THE POLITICS AND ADMINISTRATION OF
NIGERIAN GOVERNMENT. NIGER CULTURE LOC/G LEGIS
DIPLOM COLONIAL CT/SYS SOVEREIGN...GEOG SOC ANTHOL
20. PAGE 13 E0245

B65
NAT/G
GOV/REL
POL/PAR

BOCK E.,GOVERNMENT REGULATION OF BUSINESS. USA+45
LAW EX/STRUC LEGIS EXEC ORD/FREE PWR...ANTHOL
CONGRESS. PAGE 13 E0255

B65
MGT
ADMIN
NAT/G
CONTROL

BREITEL C.D.,THE LAWMAKERS. USA+45 EX/STRUC LEGIS
JUDGE ATTIT ORD/FREE JURID. PAGE 15 E0290

B65
CT/SYS
ADJUD
FEDERAL
NAT/G

BRIGGS H.W.,THE INTERNATIONAL LAW COMMISSION. LAW
CONSTN LEGIS CREATE ADJUD CT/SYS ROUTINE TASK
EFFICIENCY...CLASSIF OBS UN. PAGE 15 E0302

B65
INT/LAW
DELIB/GP

CALIFORNIA LEGISLATURE,COMMITTEE ON ELECTIONS AND
REAPPORTIONMENT, FINAL REPORT. USA+45 LAW COMPUTER
TEC/DEV CHOOSE JURID. PAGE 19 E0366

B65
DELIB/GP
APPORT
LEGIS
ADJUD

CHARNAY J.P.,LE SUFFRAGE POLITIQUE EN FRANCE;
ELECTIONS PARLEMENTAIRES, ELECTION PRESIDENTIELLE,
REFERENDUMS. FRANCE CONSTN CHIEF DELIB/GP ECO/TAC
EDU/PROP CRIME INGP/REL MORAL ORD/FREE PWR CATHISM
20 PARLIAMENT PRESIDENT. PAGE 22 E0425

B65
CHOOSE
SUFF
NAT/G
LEGIS

CHRIMES S.B.,ENGLISH CONSTITUTIONAL HISTORY (3RD
ED.). UK CHIEF CONSULT DELIB/GP LEGIS CT/SYS 15/20
COMMON/LAW PARLIAMENT. PAGE 22 E0435

B65
CONSTN
BAL/PWR
NAT/G

COHN H.J.,THE GOVERNMENT OF THE RHINE PALATINATE IN
THE FIFTEENTH CENTURY. GERMANY FINAN LOC/G DELIB/GP
LEGIS CT/SYS CHOOSE CATHISM 14/15 PALATINATE.
PAGE 24 E0468

B65
PROVS
JURID
GP/REL
ADMIN

COLGNE A.B.,STATUTE MAKING (2ND ED.). LOC/G PROVS
CHOOSE MAJORITY...CHARTS DICTIONARY 20. PAGE 24
E0474

B65
LEGIS
LAW
CONSTN
NAT/G

CONGRESSIONAL QUARTERLY SERV,REVOLUTION IN CIVIL
RIGHTS. USA+45 USA-45 LEGIS ADJUD CT/SYS CHOOSE
DISCRIM...DECISION CONGRESS SUPREME/CT. PAGE 25
E0488

B65
LAW
CONSTN
RACE/REL
LOBBY

CONGRESSIONAL QUARTERLY SERV,POLITICS IN AMERICA,
1945-1964: THE POLITICS AND ISSUES OF THE POSTWAR
YEARS. USA+45 LAW FINAN CHIEF DIPLOM APPORT SUFF
...POLICY STAT TREND CHARTS 20 CONGRESS PRESIDENT.
PAGE 25 E0489

B65
CHOOSE
REPRESENT
POL/PAR
LEGIS

COOPER F.E.,STATE ADMINISTRATIVE LAW (2 VOLS.). LAW
LEGIS PLAN TAX ADJUD CT/SYS FEDERAL PWR...CONCPT
20. PAGE 25 E0501

B65
JURID
CONSTN
ADMIN
PROVS

FEERICK J.D.,FROM FAILING HANDS: THE STUDY OF
PRESIDENTIAL SUCCESSION. CONSTN NAT/G PROB/SOLV
LEAD PARL/PROC MURDER CHOOSE...NEW/IDEA BIBLIOG 20
KENNEDY/JF JOHNSON/LB PRESIDENT PRE/US/AM
VICE/PRES. PAGE 36 E0724

B65
EX/STRUC
CHIEF
LAW
LEGIS

FISCHER F.C.,THE GOVERNMENT OF MICHIGAN. USA+45
NAT/G PUB/INST EX/STRUC LEGIS BUDGET GIVE EDU/PROP
CT/SYS CHOOSE GOV/REL...T MICHIGAN. PAGE 38 E0753

B65
PROVS
LOC/G
ADMIN
CONSTN

FRYE R.J.,HOUSING AND URBAN RENEWAL IN ALABAMA.
USA+45 NEIGH LEGIS BUDGET ADJUD ADMIN PARTIC...MGT
20 ALABAMA URBAN/RNWL. PAGE 41 E0815

B65
MUNIC
PROB/SOLV
PLAN
GOV/REL

HOLDSWORTH W.S.,A HISTORY OF ENGLISH LAW; THE
CENTURIES OF SETTLEMENT AND REFORM (VOL. XV). UK
CONSTN SECT LEGIS JUDGE WRITING ADJUD CT/SYS CRIME
OWN...JURID IDEA/COMP 18 PARLIAMENT ENGLSH/LAW
COMMON/LAW. PAGE 54 E1082

B65
LAW
INDUS
PROF/ORG
ATTIT

HOWARD C.G.,LAW: ITS NATURE, FUNCTIONS, AND LIMITS.
USA+45 CONSTN LEGIS CREATE SANCTION ORD/FREE
...BIBLIOG 20. PAGE 55 E1101

B65
LAW
JURID
CONTROL
SOCIETY

KEEFE W.J.,THE AMERICAN LEGISLATIVE PROCESS. USA+45
CONSTN POL/PAR CT/SYS REPRESENT FEDERAL ATTIT
PLURISM...MAJORIT 20 CONGRESS PRESIDENT. PAGE 60
E1192

B65
LEGIS
NAT/G
CHIEF
GOV/REL

KING D.B.,LEGAL ASPECTS OF THE CIVIL RIGHTS
MOVEMENT. SERV/IND VOL/ASSN LEGIS EDU/PROP ADJUD
PARTIC CHOOSE...JURID SEGREGAT WORK. PAGE 61 E1215

B65
LAW
DISCRIM
TREND

LUGO-MARENCO J.J.,A STATEMENT OF THE LAWS OF
NICARAGUA IN MATTERS AFFECTING BUSINESS. NICARAGUA
AGRI DIST/IND EXTR/IND FINAN INDUS FAM WORKER
INT/TRADE TAX MARRIAGE OWN BIO/SOC 20 TREATY
RESOURCE/N MIGRATION. PAGE 67 E1332

B65
CONSTN
NAT/G
LEGIS
JURID

MCKAY R.B.,REAPPORTIONMENT: THE LAW AND POLITICS OF
EQUAL REPRESENTATION. FUT USA+45 PROVS BAL/PWR
ADJUD CHOOSE REPRESENT GOV/REL FEDERAL...JURID
BIBLIOG 20 SUPREME/CT CONGRESS. PAGE 71 E1420

B65
APPORT
MAJORIT
LEGIS
PWR

MCWHINNEY E.,JUDICIAL REVIEW IN THE ENGLISH-
SPEAKING WORLD (3RD ED.). CANADA UK WOR+45 LEGIS
CONTROL EXEC PARTIC...JURID 20 AUSTRAL. PAGE 71
E1431

B65
GOV/COMP
CT/SYS
ADJUD
CONSTN

MISHKIN P.J.,ON LAW IN COURTS. USA+45 LEGIS CREATE
ROLE 20. PAGE 73 E1468

B65
LAW
CT/SYS
ADJUD
CONSTN

MOSTECKY V.,SOVIET LEGAL BIBLIOGRAPHY. USSR LEGIS
PRESS WRITING CONFER ADJUD CT/SYS REV MARXISM
...INT/LAW JURID DICTIONARY 20. PAGE 75 E1503

B65
BIBLIOG/A
LAW
COM
CONSTN

NEGLEY G.,POLITICAL AUTHORITY AND MORAL JUDGMENT.
INTELL SOCIETY LEGIS SANCTION UTOPIA SOVEREIGN
MARXISM...INT/LAW LOG 20. PAGE 76 E1530

B65
MORAL
PWR
CONTROL

NJ LEGIS REAPPORT PLAN COMM,PUBLIC HEARING ON
REDISTRICTING AND REAPPORTIONMENT. USA+45 CONSTN
VOL/ASSN LEGIS DEBATE...POLICY GEOG CENSUS 20
NEW/JERSEY. PAGE 77 E1552

B65
APPORT
REPRESENT
PROVS
JURID

NWOGUGU E.I.,THE LEGAL PROBLEMS OF FOREIGN
INVESTMENT IN DEVELOPING COUNTRIES. WOR+45 INT/ORG
DELIB/GP LEGIS PROB/SOLV INT/TRADE TAX ADJUD
SANCTION...BIBLIOG 20 TREATY. PAGE 78 E1561

B65
FOR/AID
FINAN
INT/LAW
ECO/UNDEV

PEASLEE A.J.,CONSTITUTIONS OF NATIONS* THIRD
REVISED EDITION (VOLUME I* AFRICA). LAW EX/STRUC
LEGIS TOP/EX LEGIT CT/SYS ROUTINE ORD/FREE PWR
SOVEREIGN...CON/ANAL CHARTS. PAGE 80 E1606

B65
AFR
CHOOSE
CONSTN
NAT/G

SCHUBERT G.,REAPPORTIONMENT. LAW MUNIC POL/PAR PWR
GOV/COMP. PAGE 88 E1775

B65
REPRESENT
LOC/G
APPORT
LEGIS

SHARMA S.A., PARLIAMENTARY GOVERNMENT IN INDIA. INDIA FINAN LOC/G PROVS DELIB/GP PLAN ADMIN CT/SYS FEDERAL...JURID 20. PAGE 90 E1814
B65
NAT/G
CONSTN
PARL/PROC
LEGIS

SMITH C., THE OMBUDSMAN: A BIBLIOGRAPHY (PAMPHLET). DENMARK SWEDEN USA+45 LAW LEGIS JUDGE GOV/REL GP/REL...JURID 20. PAGE 92 E1841
B65
BIBLIOG
ADMIN
CT/SYS
ADJUD

SNOW J.H., REAPPORTIONMENT. LAW CONSTN NAT/G GOV/REL ORD/FREE...JURID 20 SUPREME/CT CONNECTICT. PAGE 92 E1848
B65
APPORT
ADJUD
LEGIS
PROVS

STOREY R.G., OUR UNALIENABLE RIGHTS. LAW SECT CT/SYS SUFF DISCRIM 17/20 CIVIL/LIB ENGLSH/LAW. PAGE 94 E1882
B65
CONSTN
JURID
ORD/FREE
LEGIS

SWISHER C.B., THE SUPREME COURT IN MODERN ROLE. COM COM/IND NAT/G FORCES LEGIS LOBBY PARTIC RACE/REL 20 SUPREME/CT. PAGE 95 E1901
B65
DELIB/GP
ATTIT
CT/SYS
ADJUD

US SENATE COMM ON JUDICIARY, HEARINGS BEFORE SUBCOMMITTEE ON ADMINISTRATIVE PRACTICE AND PROCEDURE ABOUT ADMINISTRATIVE PROCEDURE ACT 1965. USA+45 LEGIS EDU/PROP ADJUD GOV/REL INGP/REL EFFICIENCY...POLICY INT 20 CONGRESS. PAGE 103 E2055
B65
ROUTINE
DELIB/GP
ADMIN
NAT/G

WEINSTEIN J.B., "THE EFFECT OF THE FEDERAL REAPPORTIONMENT DECISIONS ON COUNTIES AND OTHER FORMS OF GOVERNMENT." LAW CONSTN LEGIS CHOOSE GOV/COMP. PAGE 105 E2108
L65
MUNIC
LOC/G
APPORT
REPRESENT

LUSKY L., "FOUR PROBLEMS IN LAWMAKING FOR PEACE." FORCES LEGIS CREATE ADJUD COERCE WAR MAJORITY PEACE PWR. PAGE 67 E1334
S65
ORD/FREE
INT/LAW
UTOPIA
RECORD

ANDERSON S.V., CANADIAN OMBUDSMAN PROPOSALS. CANADA LEGIS DEBATE PARL/PROC...MAJORIT JURID TIME/SEQ IDEA/COMP 20 OMBUDSMAN PARLIAMENT. PAGE 5 E0092
B66
NAT/G
CREATE
ADMIN
POL/PAR

ARCHER P., FREEDOM AT STAKE. UK LAW NAT/G LEGIS JUDGE CRIME MORAL...CONCPT 20 CIVIL/LIB. PAGE 5 E0103
B66
ORD/FREE
NAT/COMP
POLICY

BAKER G.E., THE REAPPORTIONMENT REVOLUTION: REPRESENTATION, POLITICAL POWER, AND THE SUPREME COURT. USA+45 MUNIC NAT/G POL/PAR PROVS PROB/SOLV CHOOSE ORD/FREE POPULISM...CONCPT CHARTS 20 SUPREME/CT. PAGE 7 E0140
B66
LEGIS
APPORT
REPRESENT
ADJUD

BEISER E.N., THE TREATMENT OF LEGISLATIVE APPORTIONMENT BY THE STATE AND FEDERAL COURTS (DISSERTATION). USA+45 CONSTN NAT/G PROVS LEGIS CHOOSE REPRESENT ATTIT...POLICY BIBLIOG 20 CONGRESS SUPREME/CT. PAGE 9 E0181
B66
CT/SYS
APPORT
ADJUD
PWR

CALIFORNIA STATE LIBRARY, REAPPORTIONMENT, A SELECTIVE BIBLIOGRAPHY. USA+45 LEGIS CT/SYS REPRESENT GOV/REL. PAGE 19 E0367
B66
BIBLIOG
APPORT
NAT/G
PROVS

CAMPBELL E., PARLIAMENTARY PRIVILEGE IN AUSTRALIA. UK LAW CONSTN COLONIAL ROLE ORD/FREE SOVEREIGN 18/20 COMMONWLTH AUSTRAL FREE/SPEE PARLIAMENT. PAGE 19 E0370
B66
LEGIS
PARL/PROC
JURID
PRIVIL

CONG QUARTERLY SERVICE, REPRESENTATION AND APPORTIONMENT. USA+45 USA-45 POL/PAR CT/SYS SUFF ...POLICY 20 CONGRESS SUPREME/CT. PAGE 25 E0486
B66
APPORT
LEGIS
REPRESENT
CONSTN

FENN DH J.R., BUSINESS DECISION MAKING AND GOVERNMENT POLICY. SERV/IND LEGIS LICENSE ADMIN
B66
DECISION
PLAN

CONTROL GP/REL INGP/REL 20 CASEBOOK. PAGE 37 E0736
NAT/G
LG/CO

FINK M., A SELECTIVE BIBLIOGRAPHY ON STATE CONSTITUTIONAL REVISION (PAMPHLET). USA+45 FINAN EX/STRUC LEGIS EDU/PROP ADMIN CT/SYS APPORT CHOOSE GOV/REL 20. PAGE 38 E0751
B66
BIBLIOG
PROVS
LOC/G
CONSTN

FRIED R.C., COMPARATIVE POLITICAL INSTITUTIONS. USSR EX/STRUC FORCES LEGIS JUDGE CONTROL REPRESENT ALL/IDEOS 20 CONGRESS BUREAUCRCY. PAGE 40 E0798
B66
NAT/G
PWR
EFFICIENCY
GOV/COMP

GHOSH P.K., THE CONSTITUTION OF INDIA: HOW IT HAS BEEN FRAMED. INDIA LOC/G DELIB/GP EX/STRUC PROB/SOLV BUDGET INT/TRADE CT/SYS CHOOSE...LING 20. PAGE 43 E0854
B66
CONSTN
NAT/G
LEGIS
FEDERAL

GOLDWIN R.A., APPORTIONMENT AND REPRESENTATION. MUNIC CT/SYS GP/REL ORD/FREE...POLICY ANTHOL 20 SUPREME/CT. PAGE 44 E0880
B66
APPORT
REPRESENT
LEGIS
CONSTN

GREENE L.E., GOVERNMENT IN TENNESSEE (2ND ED.). USA+45 DIST/IND INDUS POL/PAR EX/STRUC LEGIS PLAN BUDGET GIVE CT/SYS...MGT T 20 TENNESSEE. PAGE 46 E0909
B66
PROVS
LOC/G
CONSTN
ADMIN

HAMILTON H.D., REAPPORTIONING LEGISLATURES. USA+45 CONSTN POL/PAR PROVS LEGIS COMPUTER ADJUD CHOOSE ATTIT...ANTHOL 20 SUPREME/CT CONGRESS. PAGE 50 E0989
B66
APPORT
REPRESENT
PHIL/SCI
PWR

HANSON R., THE POLITICAL THICKET. USA+45 MUNIC POL/PAR LEGIS EXEC LOBBY CHOOSE...MAJORIT DECISION. PAGE 50 E0998
B66
APPORT
LAW
CONSTN
REPRESENT

HIDAYATULLAH M., DEMOCRACY IN INDIA AND THE JUDICIAL PROCESS. INDIA EX/STRUC LEGIS LEAD GOV/REL ATTIT ORD/FREE...MAJORIT CONCPT 20 NEHRU/J. PAGE 52 E1040
B66
NAT/G
CT/SYS
CONSTN
JURID

HOLDSWORTH W.S., A HISTORY OF ENGLISH LAW; THE CENTURIES OF SETTLEMENT AND REFORM (VOL. XVI). UK LOC/G NAT/G EX/STRUC LEGIS CT/SYS LEAD ATTIT ...POLICY DECISION JURID IDEA/COMP 18 PARLIAMENT. PAGE 54 E1083
B66
BIOG
PERSON
PROF/ORG
LAW

INSTITUTE COMP STUDY POL SYS, DOMINICAN REPUBLIC ELECTION FACT BOOK. DOMIN/REP LAW LEGIS REPRESENT ...JURID CHARTS 20. PAGE 57 E1126
B66
SUFF
CHOOSE
POL/PAR
NAT/G

LEHMANN L., LEGAL UND OPPORTUN - POLITISCHE JUSTIZ IN DER BUNDESREPUBLIK. GERMANY/W EDU/PROP ADJUD CONTROL PARL/PROC COERCE TOTALISM ATTIT 20 COM/PARTY. PAGE 64 E1281
B66
ORD/FREE
POL/PAR
JURID
LEGIS

MEDER A.E. JR., LEGISLATIVE APPORTIONMENT. USA+45 BAL/PWR REPRESENT ORD/FREE PWR...JURID 20 SUPREME/CT. PAGE 72 E1433
B66
APPORT
LEGIS
MATH
POLICY

POWERS E., CRIME AND PUNISHMENT IN EARLY MASSACHUSETTS 1620-1692: A DOCUMENTARY HISTORY. USA-45 SECT LEGIS COLONIAL ATTIT ORD/FREE MYSTISM 17 PRE/US/AM MASSACHU. PAGE 82 E1643
B66
CRIME
ADJUD
CT/SYS
PROVS

SHAPIRO M., FREEDOM OF SPEECH: THE SUPREME COURT AND JUDICIAL REVIEW. USA+45 LEGIS...CHARTS 20 SUPREME/CT FREE/SPEE. PAGE 90 E1812
B66
CT/SYS
ORD/FREE
CONSTN
JURID

SZLADITS C., A BIBLIOGRAPHY ON FOREIGN AND COMPARATIVE LAW (SUPPLEMENT 1964). FINAN FAM LABOR LG/CO LEGIS JUDGE ADMIN CRIME...CRIMLGY 20. PAGE 95 E1905
B66
BIBLIOG/A
CT/SYS
INT/LAW

TRESOLINI R.J., CASES IN AMERICAN NATIONAL
B66
NAT/G

GOVERNMENT AND POLITICS. LAW DIPLOM ADJUD LOBBY   LEGIS
FEDERAL ORD/FREE WEALTH...DECISION ANTHOL 20   CT/SYS
PRESIDENT. PAGE 97 E1940   POL/PAR

                                                        B66
US HOUSE COMM ON JUDICIARY,CIVIL COMMITMENT AND   BIO/SOC
TREATMENT OF NARCOTIC ADDICTS. USA+45 SOCIETY FINAN   CRIME
LEGIS PROB/SOLV GIVE CT/SYS SANCTION HEALTH   IDEA/COMP
...POLICY HEAL 20. PAGE 100 E2008   CONTROL

                                                        B66
US PRES COMN CRIME IN DC,REPORT OF THE US   CRIME
PRESIDENT'S COMMISSION ON CRIME IN THE DISTRICT OF   FORCES
COLUMBIA. LEGIS WORKER EDU/PROP ADJUD CONTROL   AGE/Y
CT/SYS GP/REL BIO/SOC HEALTH...CRIMLGY NEW/IDEA   SANCTION
STAT 20. PAGE 101 E2022

                                                        B66
US SENATE COMM ON JUDICIARY,HEARINGS ON FREE PRESS   PRESS
AND FAIR TRIAL (2 VOLS.). USA+45 CONSTN ELITES   LAW
LEGIS EDU/PROP CT/SYS LEAD CONGRESS. PAGE 103 E2057   CRIME
                                                        ORD/FREE

                                                        B66
WASHINGTON S.H.,BIBLIOGRAPHY: LABOR-MANAGEMENT   BIBLIOG
RELATIONS ACT, 1947 AS AMENDED BY LABOR-MANAGEMENT   LAW
REPORTING AND DISCLOSURE ACT, 1959. USA+45 CONSTN   LABOR
INDUS DELIB/GP LEGIS WORKER BARGAIN ECO/TAC ADJUD   MGT
GP/REL NEW/LIB...JURID CONGRESS. PAGE 105 E2100

                                                        B66
WILSON G.,CASES AND MATERIALS ON CONSTITUTIONAL AND   JURID
ADMINISTRATIVE LAW. UK LAW NAT/G EX/STRUC LEGIS   ADMIN
BAL/PWR BUDGET DIPLOM ADJUD CONTROL CT/SYS GOV/REL   CONSTN
ORD/FREE 20 PARLIAMENT ENGLSH/LAW. PAGE 106 E2126   PWR

                                                        S66
BURDETTE F.L.,"SELECTED ARTICLES AND DOCUMENTS ON   BIBLIOG
AMERICAN GOVERNMENT AND POLITICS." LAW LOC/G MUNIC   USA+45
NAT/G POL/PAR PROVS LEGIS BAL/PWR ADMIN EXEC   JURID
REPRESENT MGT. PAGE 17 E0331   CONSTN

                                                        S66
DETTER I.,"THE PROBLEM OF UNEQUAL TREATIES." CONSTN   SOVEREIGN
NAT/G LEGIS COLONIAL COERCE PWR...GEOG UN TIME   DOMIN
TREATY. PAGE 31 E0610   INT/LAW
                                                        ECO/UNDEV

                                                        S66
LANDE G.R.,"THE EFFECT OF THE RESOLUTIONS OF THE   LEGIS
UNITED NATIONS GENERAL ASSEMBLY." WOR+45 LAW   EFFICIENCY
INT/ORG NAT/G CHOOSE ISOLAT ATTIT...CLASSIF   RESPECT
GEN/METH UN. PAGE 62 E1249

                                                        S66
MATTHEWS D.G.,"PRELUDE-COUP D'ETAT-MILITARY   BIBLIOG
GOVERNMENT: A BIBLIOGRAPHICAL AND RESEARCH GUIDE TO   NAT/G
NIGERIAN POL AND GOVT, JAN, 1965-66." AFR NIGER LAW   ADMIN
CONSTN POL/PAR LEGIS CIVMIL/REL GOV/REL...STAT 20.   CHOOSE
PAGE 69 E1385

                                                        S66
NYC BAR ASSOCIATION RECORD,"PAPERBACKS FOR THE   BIBLIOG
BAR." USA+45 LEGIS ADJUD CT/SYS. PAGE 78 E1562   JURID
                                                        LAW
                                                        WRITING

                                                        S66
POLSBY N.W.,"BOOKS IN THE FIELD: POLITICAL   BIBLIOG/A
SCIENCE." LAW CONSTN LOC/G NAT/G LEGIS ADJUD PWR 20   ATTIT
SUPREME/CT. PAGE 81 E1627   ADMIN
                                                        JURID

                                                        B67
BAKER L.,BACK TO BACK: THE DUEL BETWEEN FDR AND THE   CHIEF
SUPREME COURT. ELITES LEGIS CREATE DOMIN INGP/REL   CT/SYS
PERSON PWR NEW/LIB 20 ROOSEVLT/F SUPREME/CT SENATE.   PARL/PROC
PAGE 7 E0142   GOV/REL

                                                        B67
BIBBY J.,ON CAPITOL HILL. POL/PAR LOBBY PARL/PROC   CONFER
GOV/REL PERS/REL...JURID PHIL/SCI OBS INT BIBLIOG   LEGIS
20 CONGRESS PRESIDENT. PAGE 12 E0224   CREATE
                                                        LEAD

                                                        B67
BROWN L.N.,FRENCH ADMINISTRATIVE LAW. FRANCE UK   EX/STRUC
CONSTN NAT/G LEGIS DOMIN CONTROL EXEC PARL/PROC PWR   LAW
...JURID METH/COMP GEN/METH. PAGE 16 E0314   IDEA/COMP
                                                        CT/SYS

                                                        B67
COWLING M.,1867 DISRAELI, GLADSTONE, AND   PARL/PROC
REVOLUTION: THE PASSING OF THE SECOND REFORM BILL.   POL/PAR
UK LEGIS LEAD LOBBY GP/REL INGP/REL...DECISION   ATTIT
BIBLIOG 19 REFORMERS. PAGE 27 E0531   LAW

                                                        B67
FESLER J.W.,THE FIFTY STATES AND THEIR LOCAL   PROVS
GOVERNMENTS. FUT USA+45 POL/PAR LEGIS PROB/SOLV   LOC/G
ADMIN CT/SYS CHOOSE GOV/REL FEDERAL...POLICY CHARTS
20 SUPREME/CT. PAGE 37 E0743

                                                        B67
FINCHER F.,THE GOVERNMENT OF THE UNITED STATES.   NAT/G
USA+45 USA-45 POL/PAR CHIEF CT/SYS LOBBY GP/REL   EX/STRUC
INGP/REL...CONCPT CHARTS BIBLIOG T 18/20 PRESIDENT   LEGIS
CONGRESS SUPREME/CT. PAGE 38 E0749   OP/RES

                                                        B67
GELLHORN W.,OMBUDSMEN AND OTHERS: CITIZENS'   NAT/COMP
PROTECTORS IN NINE COUNTRIES. WOR+45 LAW CONSTN   REPRESENT
LEGIS INSPECT ADJUD ADMIN CONTROL CT/SYS CHOOSE   INGP/REL
PERS/REL...STAT CHARTS 20. PAGE 43 E0847   PROB/SOLV

                                                        B67
JONES C.O.,EVERY SECOND YEAR: CONGRESSIONAL   EFFICIENCY
BEHAVIOR AND THE TWO-YEAR TERM. LAW POL/PAR   LEGIS
PROB/SOLV DEBATE CHOOSE PERS/REL COST FEDERAL PWR   TIME/SEQ
...CHARTS 20 CONGRESS SENATE HOUSE/REP. PAGE 59   NAT/G
E1172

                                                        B67
LONG E.V.,THE INTRUDERS: THE INVASION OF PRIVACY BY   LAW
GOVERNMENT AND INDUSTRY. USA+45 COM/IND INDUS LEGIS   PARTIC
TASK PERS/REL...JURID 20 CONGRESS. PAGE 66 E1324   NAT/G

                                                        B67
MCBRIDE J.H.,THE TEST BAN TREATY: MILITARY,   ARMS/CONT
TECHNOLOGICAL, AND POLITICAL IMPLICATIONS. USA+45   DIPLOM
USSR DELIB/GP FORCES LEGIS TEC/DEV BAL/PWR TREATY.   NUC/PWR
PAGE 70 E1399

                                                        B67
MEYERS M.,SOURCES OF THE AMERICAN REPUBLIC: A   COLONIAL
DOCUMENTARY HISTORY OF POLITICS, SOCIETY, AND   REV
THOUGHT (VOL. I, REV. ED.). USA-45 CULTURE STRUCT   WAR
NAT/G LEGIS LEAD ATTIT...JURID SOC ANTHOL 17/19
PRESIDENT. PAGE 72 E1450

                                                        B67
UNIVERSAL REFERENCE SYSTEM,LAW, JURISPRUDENCE, AND   BIBLIOG/A
JUDICIAL PROCESS (VOLUME VII). WOR+45 WOR-45 CONSTN   LAW
NAT/G LEGIS JUDGE CT/SYS...INT/LAW COMPUT/IR   JURID
GEN/METH METH. PAGE 99 E1976   ADJUD

                                                        B67
US SENATE COMM ON FOREIGN REL,CONSULAR CONVENTION   LEGIS
WITH THE SOVIET UNION. USA+45 USSR DELIB/GP LEAD   LOBBY
REPRESENT ATTIT ORD/FREE CONGRESS TREATY. PAGE 101   DIPLOM
E2031

                                                        L67
"A PROPOS DES INCITATIONS FINANCIERES AUX   LOC/G
GROUPEMENTS DES COMMUNES: ESSAI D'INTERPRETATION."   ECO/TAC
FRANCE NAT/G LEGIS ADMIN GOV/REL CENTRAL 20. PAGE 2   APPORT
E0037   ADJUD

                                                        L67
SCHUBERT G.,"THE RHETORIC OF CONSTITUTIONAL   CONSTN
CHANGE." USA+45 LAW CULTURE CHIEF LEGIS ADJUD   METH/COMP
CT/SYS ARMS/CONT ADJUST...CHARTS SIMUL. PAGE 89   ORD/FREE
E1777

                                                        S67
ADOKO A.,"THE CONSTITUTION OF UGANDA." AFR UGANDA   NAT/G
LOC/G CHIEF FORCES LEGIS ADJUD EXEC CHOOSE NAT/LISM   CONSTN
...IDEA/COMP 20. PAGE 3 E0050   ORD/FREE
                                                        LAW

                                                        S67
BRADLEY A.W.,"CONSTITUTION-MAKING IN UGANDA."   NAT/G
UGANDA LAW CHIEF DELIB/GP LEGIS ADMIN EXEC   CREATE
PARL/PROC RACE/REL ORD/FREE...GOV/COMP 20. PAGE 15   CONSTN
E0284   FEDERAL

                                                        S67
CLOGGER T.J.,"THE BIG EAR." UK USA+45 USSR LAW   DIPLOM
LEGIS CRIME GP/REL INGP/REL ATTIT 20 FBI ESPIONAGE.   ORD/FREE
PAGE 23 E0458   COM/IND
                                                        INSPECT

                                                        S67
CUMMINS L.,"THE FORMULATION OF THE "PLATT"   DIPLOM
AMENDMENT." CUBA L/A+17C NAT/G DELIB/GP CONFER   INT/LAW
...POLICY 20. PAGE 28 E0554   LEGIS

                                                        S67
FABREGA J.,"ANTECEDENTES EXTRANJEROS EN LA   CONSTN
CONSTITUCION PANAMENA." CUBA L/A+17C PANAMA URUGUAY   JURID
EX/STRUC LEGIS DIPLOM ORD/FREE 19/20 COLOMB   NAT/G
MEXIC/AMER. PAGE 36 E0709   PARL/PROC

GOSSETT W.T.,"ELECTING THE PRESIDENT: NEW HOPE FOR AN OLD IDEAL." FUT USA+45 USA-45 PROVS LEGIS PROB/SOLV WRITING DEBATE ADJUD REPRESENT...MAJORIT DECISION 20 HOUSE/REP PRESIDENT. PAGE 45 E0892
S67
CONSTN
CHIEF
CHOOSE
NAT/G

HAMILTON H.D.,"LEGISLATIVE CONSTITUENCIES: SINGLE-MEMBER DISTRICTS, MULTI-MEMBER DISTRICTS, AND FLOTERAL DISTRICTS." USA+45 LAW POL/PAR ADJUD RACE/REL...CHARTS METH/COMP 20. PAGE 50 E0990
S67
LEGIS
REPRESENT
APPORT
PLAN

HUBERT C.J.,"PLANNED UNIT DEVELOPMENT" LAW VOL/ASSN LEGIS EDU/PROP CT/SYS GOV/REL...NEW/IDEA 20 PLAN/UNIT. PAGE 56 E1107
S67
PLAN
MUNIC
HABITAT
ADJUD

MAYANJA A.,"THE GOVERNMENT'S PROPOSALS ON THE NEW CONSTITUTION." AFR UGANDA LAW CHIEF LEGIS ADJUD REPRESENT FEDERAL PWR 20. PAGE 69 E1390
S67
CONSTN
CONFER
ORD/FREE
NAT/G

RICHARDSON J.J.,"THE MAKING OF THE RESTRICTIVE TRADE PRACTICES ACT 1956 A CASE STUDY OF THE POLICY PROCESS IN BRITAIN." UK FINAN MARKET LG/CO POL/PAR CONSULT PRESS ADJUD ADMIN AGREE LOBBY SANCTION ATTIT 20. PAGE 84 E1695
S67
LEGIS
ECO/TAC
POLICY
INDUS

VAUGHN W.P.,"SEPARATE AND UNEQUAL: THE CIVIL RIGHTS ACT OF 1875 AND DEFEAT OF THE SCHOOL INTEGRATION CLAUSE." USA-45 LEGIS RACE/REL 19 CONGRESS. PAGE 103 E2073
S67
LAW
DISCRIM
EDU/PROP
PARL/PROC

BLACKSTONE W.,COMMENTARIES ON THE LAWS OF ENGLAND (4 VOLS.) (4TH ED.). UK CHIEF DELIB/GP LEGIS WORKER CT/SYS SANCTION CRIME OWN...CRIMLGY 18 ENGLSH/LAW. PAGE 12 E0238
B70
LAW
JURID
ADJUD
CONSTN

MAINE H.S.,LECTURES ON THE EARLY HISTORY OF INSTITUTIONS. IRELAND UK CONSTN ELITES STRUCT FAM KIN CHIEF LEGIS CT/SYS OWN SOVEREIGN...CONCPT 16 BENTHAM/J BREHON ROMAN/LAW. PAGE 68 E1351
B75
CULTURE
LAW
INGP/REL

BENTHAM J.,THE THEORY OF LEGISLATION. UK CREATE CRIME ATTIT ORD/FREE...CONCPT 18 REFORMERS. PAGE 10 E0196
B76
LEGIS
LAW
CRIMLGY
UTIL

WHITRIDGE L.I.,"LEGISLATIVE INQUESTS" USA-45 ADJUD GOV/REL SOVEREIGN 19/20 CONGRESS. PAGE 106 E2120
L86
CT/SYS
LEGIS
JURID
CONSTN

ADAMS J.,A DEFENSE OF THE CONSTITUTIONS OF GOVERNMENT OF THE UNITED STATES OF AMERICA. USA-45 STRATA CHIEF EX/STRUC LEGIS CT/SYS CONSERVE POPULISM...CONCPT CON/ANAL GOV/COMP. PAGE 3 E0048
B87
CONSTN
BAL/PWR
PWR
NAT/G

BURGESS J.W.,POLITICAL SCIENCE AND COMPARATIVE CONSTITUTIONAL LAW. FRANCE GERMANY UK USA-45 LEGIS DIPLOM ADJUD REPRESENT...CONCPT 19. PAGE 17 E0340
B90
CONSTN
LAW
LOC/G
NAT/G

SIDGWICK H.,THE ELEMENTS OF POLITICS. LOC/G NAT/G LEGIS DIPLOM ADJUD CONTROL EXEC PARL/PROC REPRESENT GOV/REL SOVEREIGN ALL/IDEOS 19 MILL/JS BENTHAM/J. PAGE 91 E1822
B91
POLICY
LAW
CONCPT

LOWELL A.L.,ESSAYS ON GOVERNMENT. UK USA-45 LEGIS PARL/PROC...POLICY PREDICT 19. PAGE 66 E1328
B92
CONSTN
ADJUD
CT/SYS
NAT/G

ESMEIN A.,ELEMENTS DE DROIT CONSTITUTIONNEL. FRANCE UK CHIEF EX/STRUC LEGIS ADJUD CT/SYS PARL/PROC REV GOV/REL ORD/FREE...JURID METH/COMP 18/19. PAGE 35 E0697
B96
LAW
CONSTN
NAT/G
CONCPT

POLLOCK F.,THE HISTORY OF ENGLISH LAW BEFORE THE TIME OF EDWARD I (2 VOLS, 2ND ED.). UK CULTURE LOC/G LEGIS LICENSE AGREE CONTROL CT/SYS SANCTION
B98
LAW
ADJUD
JURID

CRIME...TIME/SEQ 13 COMMON/LAW CANON/LAW. PAGE 81 E1626

LILLY W.S.,FIRST PRINCIPLES IN POLITICS. UNIV LAW LEGIS DOMIN ADJUD INGP/REL ORD/FREE SOVEREIGN ...JURID CONCPT 19 NATURL/LAW. PAGE 65 E1299
B99
NAT/G
CONSTN
MORAL
POLICY

LEGISLATION....SEE CONGRESS, LEGIS, SENATE, HOUSE/REP

LEGISLATIVE REFERENCE SERVICE E1280

LEGISLATIVE APPORTIONMENT....SEE APPORT

LEGISLATURES....SEE LEGIS

LEGIT....LEGITIMACY

CANON LAW ABSTRACTS. LEGIT CONFER CT/SYS INGP/REL MARRIAGE ATTIT MORAL WORSHIP 20. PAGE 2 E0026
N
BIBLIOG/A
CATHISM
SECT
LAW

DARBY W.E.,INTERNATIONAL TRIBUNALS. WOR-45 NAT/G ECO/TAC DOMIN LEGIT CT/SYS COERCE ORD/FREE PWR SOVEREIGN JURID. PAGE 29 E0567
B00
INT/ORG
ADJUD
PEACE
INT/LAW

DE TOCQUEVILLE A.,DEMOCRACY IN AMERICA (VOLUME ONE). LAW SOCIETY STRUCT NAT/G POL/PAR PROVS FORCES LEGIS TOP/EX DIPLOM LEGIT WAR PEACE ATTIT SOVEREIGN ...SELF/OBS TIME/SEQ CONGRESS 19. PAGE 30 E0594
B00
USA-45
TREND

GROTIUS H.,DE JURE BELLI AC PACIS. CHRIST-17C UNIV LAW SOCIETY PROVS LEGIT PEACE PERCEPT MORAL PWR ...CONCPT CON/ANAL GEN/LAWS. PAGE 48 E0952
B00
JURID
INT/LAW
WAR

HOLLAND T.E.,STUDIES IN INTERNATIONAL LAW. TURKEY USSR WOR-45 CONSTN NAT/G DIPLOM DOMIN LEGIT COERCE WAR PEACE ORD/FREE PWR SOVEREIGN...JURID CHARTS 20 PARLIAMENT SUEZ TREATY. PAGE 54 E1084
B00
INT/ORG
LAW
INT/LAW

LORIMER J.,THE INSTITUTES OF THE LAW OF NATIONS. WOR-45 CULTURE SOCIETY NAT/G VOL/ASSN DIPLOM LEGIT WAR PEACE DRIVE ORD/FREE SOVEREIGN...CONCPT RECORD INT TREND HYPO/EXP GEN/METH TOT/POP VAL/FREE 20. PAGE 66 E1327
B00
INT/ORG
LAW
INT/LAW

MAINE H.S.,ANCIENT LAW. MEDIT-7 CULTURE SOCIETY KIN SECT LEGIS LEGIT ROUTINE...JURID HIST/WRIT CON/ANAL TOT/POP VAL/FREE. PAGE 68 E1350
B00
FAM
LAW

BERKELEY G.,"DISCOURSE ON PASSIVE OBEDIENCE" (1712) THE WORKS... (VOL. IV)" UNIV DOMIN LEGIT CONTROL CRIME ADJUST CENTRAL MORAL ORD/FREE...POLICY WORSHIP. PAGE 10 E0202
C01
INGP/REL
SANCTION
RESPECT
GEN/LAWS

CRANDALL S.B.,TREATIES: THEIR MAKING AND ENFORCEMENT. MOD/EUR USA-45 CONSTN INT/ORG NAT/G LEGIS EDU/PROP LEGIT EXEC PEACE KNOWL MORAL...JURID CONGRESS 19/20 TREATY. PAGE 27 E0541
B04
LAW

DICEY A.,LAW AND PUBLIC OPINION IN ENGLAND. LAW CULTURE INTELL SOCIETY NAT/G SECT JUDGE LEGIT CHOOSE RIGID/FLEX KNOWL...OLD/LIB CONCPT STERTYP GEN/LAWS 20. PAGE 31 E0620
B05
ATTIT
UK

HOLLAND T.E.,LETTERS UPON WAR AND NEUTRALITY. WOR-45 NAT/G FORCES JUDGE ECO/TAC LEGIT CT/SYS NEUTRAL ROUTINE COERCE...JURID TIME/SEQ 20. PAGE 55 E1085
B09
LAW
INT/LAW
INT/ORG
WAR

REINSCH P.,PUBLIC INTERNATIONAL UNION. WOR-45 LAW LABOR INT/TRADE LEGIT PERSON ALL/VALS...SOCIALIST CONCPT TIME/SEQ TREND GEN/LAWS 19/20. PAGE 84 E1683
B11
FUT
INT/ORG
DIPLOM

BUTLER N.M.,THE INTERNATIONAL MIND. WOR-45 INT/ORG LEGIT PWR...JURID CONCPT 20. PAGE 18 E0350
B13
ADJUD
ORD/FREE
INT/LAW

VECCHIO G.D.,THE FORMAL BASES OF LAW (TRANS. BY J.
B14
LAW

LISLE). DOMIN LEGIT CONTROL COERCE UTIL MORAL PWR JURID
...CONCPT TIME/SEQ 17/20 COMMON/LAW NATURL/LAW. GEN/LAWS
PAGE 103 E2074 IDEA/COMP

B16
SALMOND J.W.,JURISPRUDENCE. UK LOC/G NAT/G LEGIS LAW
PROB/SOLV LICENSE LEGIT CRIME PERS/REL OWN ORD/FREE CT/SYS
...T 20. PAGE 87 E1742 JURID
ADJUD

L16
WRIGHT Q.,"THE ENFORCEMENT OF INTERNATIONAL LAW INT/ORG
THROUGH MUNICIPAL LAW IN THE US." USA-45 LOC/G LAW
NAT/G PUB/INST FORCES LEGIT CT/SYS PERCEPT ALL/VALS INT/LAW
...JURID 20. PAGE 107 E2149 WAR

B19
VANDERPOL A.,LA DOCTRINE SCOLASTIQUE DU DROIT DE WAR
GUERRE. CHRIST-17C FORCES DIPLOM LEGIT SUPEGO MORAL SECT
...BIOG AQUINAS/T SUAREZ/F CHRISTIAN. PAGE 103 INT/LAW
E2072

B20
DICKINSON E.,THE EQUALITY OF STATES IN LAW
INTERNATIONAL LAW. EUR+WWI INT/ORG NAT/G DIPLOM CONCPT
EDU/PROP LEGIT PEACE ATTIT ALL/VALS...JURID SOVEREIGN
TIME/SEQ LEAGUE/NAT. PAGE 31 E0622

B20
LIPPMAN W.,LIBERTY AND THE NEWS. USA+45 USA-45 LAW ORD/FREE
LEGIS DOMIN LEGIT ATTIT...POLICY SOC IDEA/COMP PRESS
METH/COMP 19/20. PAGE 65 E1300 COM/IND
EDU/PROP

B21
BRYCE J.,MODERN DEMOCRACIES. FUT NEW/ZEALND USA-45 NAT/G
LAW CONSTN POL/PAR PROVS VOL/ASSN EX/STRUC LEGIS TREND
LEGIT CT/SYS EXEC KNOWL CONGRESS AUSTRAL 20.
PAGE 16 E0322

B21
OPPENHEIM L.,THE FUTURE OF INTERNATIONAL LAW. INT/ORG
EUR+WWI MOD/EUR LAW LEGIS JUDGE LEGIT ORD/FREE CT/SYS
...JURID TIME/SEQ GEN/LAWS 20. PAGE 79 E1578 INT/LAW

B21
STOWELL E.C.,INTERVENTION IN INTERNATIONAL LAW. BAL/PWR
UNIV LAW SOCIETY INT/ORG ACT/RES PLAN LEGIT ROUTINE SOVEREIGN
WAR...JURID OBS GEN/LAWS 20. PAGE 94 E1884

B22
WRIGHT Q.,THE CONTROL OF AMERICAN FOREIGN NAT/G
RELATIONS. USA-45 WOR-45 CONSTN INT/ORG CONSULT EXEC
LEGIS LEGIT ROUTINE ORD/FREE PWR...POLICY JURID DIPLOM
CONCPT METH/CNCPT RECORD LEAGUE/NAT 20. PAGE 107
E2150

B23
HOLMES O.W. JR.,THE COMMON LAW. FUT WOR-45 CULTURE ADJUD
SOCIETY CREATE LEGIT ROUTINE ATTIT ALL/VALS...JURID CON/ANAL
METH/CNCPT TIME/SEQ GEN/LAWS TOT/POP VAL/FREE.
PAGE 55 E1087

S23
DEWEY J.,"ETHICS AND INTERNATIONAL RELATIONS." FUT LAW
WOR-45 SOCIETY INT/ORG VOL/ASSN DIPLOM LEGIT MORAL
ORD/FREE...JURID CONCPT GEN/METH 20. PAGE 31 E0618

B24
GENTILI A.,DE LEGATIONIBUS. CHRIST-17C NAT/G SECT DIPLOM
CONSULT LEGIT...POLICY CATH JURID CONCPT MYTH. INT/LAW
PAGE 43 E0848 INT/ORG
LAW

L25
HUDSON M.,"THE PERMANENT COURT OF INTERNATIONAL INT/ORG
JUSTICE AND THE QUESTION OF AMERICAN ADJUD
PARTICIPATION." WOR-45 LEGIT CT/SYS ORD/FREE DIPLOM
...JURID CONCPT TIME/SEQ GEN/LAWS VAL/FREE 20 ICJ. INT/LAW
PAGE 56 E1108

B26
HOCKING W.E.,PRESENT STATUS OF THE PHILOSOPHY OF JURID
LAW AND OF RIGHTS. UNIV CULTURE INTELL SOCIETY PHIL/SCI
NAT/G CREATE LEGIT SANCTION ALL/VALS SOC/INTEG ORD/FREE
18/20. PAGE 53 E1060

B27
LAUTERPACHT H.,PRIVATE LAW SOURCES AND ANALOGIES OF INT/ORG
INTERNATIONAL LAW. WOR-45 NAT/G DELIB/GP LEGIT ADJUD
COERCE ATTIT ORD/FREE PWR SOVEREIGN...JURID CONCPT PEACE
HIST/WRIT TIME/SEQ GEN/METH LEAGUE/NAT 20. PAGE 63 INT/LAW
E1264

B28
CORBETT P.E.,CANADA AND WORLD POLITICS. LAW CULTURE NAT/G

SOCIETY STRUCT MARKET INT/ORG FORCES ACT/RES PLAN CANADA
ECO/TAC LEGIT ORD/FREE PWR RESPECT...SOC CONCPT
TIME/SEQ TREND CMN/WLTH 20 LEAGUE/NAT. PAGE 26
E0504

B28
MAIR L.P.,THE PROTECTION OF MINORITIES. EUR+WWI LAW
WOR-45 CONSTN INT/ORG NAT/G LEGIT CT/SYS GP/REL SOVEREIGN
RACE/REL DISCRIM ORD/FREE RESPECT...JURID CONCPT
TIME/SEQ 20. PAGE 68 E1352

B28
YANG KUNG-SUN,THE BOOK OF LORD SHANG. LAW ECO/UNDEV ASIA
LOC/G NAT/G NEIGH PLAN ECO/TAC LEGIT ATTIT SKILL JURID
...CONCPT CON/ANAL WORK TOT/POP. PAGE 108 E2164

B29
CONWELL-EVANS T.P.,THE LEAGUE COUNCIL IN ACTION. DELIB/GP
EUR+WWI TURKEY UK USSR WOR-45 INT/ORG FORCES JUDGE INT/LAW
ECO/TAC EDU/PROP LEGIT ROUTINE ARMS/CONT COERCE
ATTIT PWR...MAJORIT GEOG JURID CONCPT LEAGUE/NAT
TOT/POP VAL/FREE TUNIS 20. PAGE 25 E0498

B29
MOLEY R.,POLITICS AND CRIMINAL PROSECUTION. USA-45 PWR
POL/PAR EX/STRUC LEGIT CONTROL LEAD ROUTINE CHOOSE CT/SYS
INGP/REL...JURID CHARTS 20. PAGE 74 E1481 CRIME
ADJUD

B30
WRIGHT Q.,MANDATES UNDER THE LEAGUE OF NATIONS. INT/ORG
WOR-45 CONSTN ECO/DEV ECO/UNDEV NAT/G DELIB/GP LAW
TOP/EX LEGIT ALL/VALS...JURID CONCPT LEAGUE/NAT 20. INT/LAW
PAGE 107 E2151

B31
STOWELL E.C.,INTERNATIONAL LAW. FUT UNIV WOR-45 INT/ORG
SOCIETY CONSULT EX/STRUC FORCES ACT/RES PLAN DIPLOM ROUTINE
EDU/PROP LEGIT DISPL PWR SKILL...POLICY CONCPT OBS INT/LAW
TREND TOT/POP 20. PAGE 94 E1885

B32
EAGLETON C.,INTERNATIONAL GOVERNMENT. BRAZIL FRANCE INT/ORG
GERMANY ITALY UK USSR WOR-45 DELIB/GP TOP/EX PLAN JURID
ECO/TAC EDU/PROP LEGIT ADJUD REGION ARMS/CONT DIPLOM
COERCE ATTIT PWR...GEOG MGT VAL/FREE LEAGUE/NAT 20. INT/LAW
PAGE 34 E0670

B32
MASTERS R.D.,INTERNATIONAL LAW IN INTERNATIONAL INT/ORG
COURTS. BELGIUM EUR+WWI FRANCE GERMANY MOD/EUR LAW
SWITZERLND WOR-45 SOCIETY STRATA STRUCT LEGIT EXEC INT/LAW
ALL/VALS...JURID HIST/WRIT TIME/SEQ TREND GEN/LAWS
20. PAGE 69 E1383

B32
MORLEY F.,THE SOCIETY OF NATIONS. EUR+WWI UNIV INT/ORG
WOR-45 LAW CONSTN ACT/RES PLAN EDU/PROP LEGIT CONCPT
ROUTINE...POLICY TIME/SEQ LEAGUE/NAT TOT/POP 20.
PAGE 75 E1496

B33
LAUTERPACHT H.,THE FUNCTION OF LAW IN THE INT/ORG
INTERNATIONAL COMMUNITY. WOR-45 NAT/G FORCES CREATE LAW
DOMIN LEGIT COERCE WAR PEACE ATTIT ORD/FREE PWR INT/LAW
SOVEREIGN...JURID CONCPT METH/CNCPT TIME/SEQ
GEN/LAWS GEN/METH LEAGUE/NAT TOT/POP VAL/FREE 20.
PAGE 63 E1265

B34
GONZALEZ PALENCIA A,ESTUDIO HISTORICO SOBRE LA LEGIT
CENSURA GUBERNATIVA EN ESPANA 1800-1833. NAT/G EDU/PROP
COERCE INGP/REL ATTIT AUTHORIT KNOWL...POLICY JURID PRESS
19. PAGE 44 E0884 CONTROL

B34
WOLFF C.,JUS GENTIUM METHODO SCIENTIFICA NAT/G
PERTRACTATUM. MOD/EUR INT/ORG VOL/ASSN LEGIT PEACE LAW
ATTIT...JURID 20. PAGE 107 E2140 INT/LAW
WAR

S35
MCMAHON A.H.,"INTERNATIONAL BOUNDARIES." WOR-45 GEOG
INT/ORG NAT/G LEGIT SKILL...CHARTS GEN/LAWS 20. VOL/ASSN
PAGE 71 E1423 INT/LAW

B37
RUTHERFORD M.L.,THE INFLUENCE OF THE AMERICAN BAR ATTIT
ASSOCIATION ON PUBLIC OPINION AND LEGISLATION. ADJUD
USA+45 USA-45 LAW CONSTN LABOR LEGIS DOMIN EDU/PROP LEGIT PROF/ORG
CT/SYS ROUTINE...TIME/SEQ 19/20 ABA. PAGE 87 E1739 JURID

B38
LEAGUE OF NATIONS-SECRETARIAT.,THE AIMS, METHODS ADJUD
AND ACTIVITY OF THE LEAGUE OF NATIONS. WOR+45 STRUCT
DIPLOM EDU/PROP LEGIT RIGID/FLEX ALL/VALS

...TIME/SEQ LEAGUE/NAT VAL/FREE 19/20. PAGE 64
E1273

B38
MCNAIR A.D.,THE LAW OF TREATIES: BRITISH PRACTICE
AND OPINIONS. UK CREATE DIPLOM LEGIT WRITING ADJUD
WAR...INT/LAW JURID TREATY. PAGE 71 E1424
AGREE
LAW
CT/SYS
NAT/G

B39
LAVES W.H.C.,INTERNATIONAL SECURITY. EUR+WWI
GERMANY UK USA-45 LAW NAT/G DELIB/GP TOP/EX COERCE
PWR...POLICY FASCIST CONCPT HIST/WRIT GEN/LAWS
LEAGUE/NAT NAZI 20. PAGE 63 E1267
ORD/FREE
LEGIT
ARMS/CONT
BAL/PWR

B39
WILSON G.G.,HANDBOOK OF INTERNATIONAL LAW. FUT UNIV
USA-45 WOR-45 SOCIETY LEGIT ATTIT DISPL DRIVE
ALL/VALS...INT/LAW TIME/SEQ TREND. PAGE 106 E2128
INT/ORG
LAW
CONCPT
WAR

B39
ZIMMERN A.,THE LEAGUE OF NATIONS AND THE RULE OF
LAW. WOR-45 STRUCT NAT/G DELIB/GP EX/STRUC ACT/RES
DOMIN LEGIT COERCE ORD/FREE PWR...POLICY RECORD
LEAGUE/NAT TOT/POP VAL/FREE 20 LEAGUE/NAT. PAGE 108
E2170
INT/ORG
LAW
DIPLOM

B40
CARR E.H.,THE TWENTY YEARS' CRISIS 1919-1939. FUT
WOR-45 BAL/PWR ECO/TAC LEGIT TOTALISM ATTIT
ALL/VALS...POLICY JURID CONCPT TIME/SEQ TREND
GEN/LAWS TOT/POP 20. PAGE 20 E0393
INT/ORG
DIPLOM
PEACE

B41
NIEMEYER G.,LAW WITHOUT FORCE: THE FUNCTION OF
POLITICS IN INTERNATIONAL LAW. PLAN INSPECT DIPLOM
REPAR LEGIT ADJUD WAR ORD/FREE...IDEA/COMP
METH/COMP GEN/LAWS 20. PAGE 77 E1549
COERCE
LAW
PWR
INT/LAW

S41
WRIGHT Q.,"FUNDAMENTAL PROBLEMS OF INTERNATIONAL
ORGANIZATION." UNIV WOR-45 STRUCT FORCES ACT/RES
CREATE DOMIN EDU/PROP LEGIT REGION NAT/LISM
ORD/FREE PWR RESPECT SOVEREIGN...JURID SOC CONCPT
METH/CNCPT TIME/SEQ 20. PAGE 107 E2152
INT/ORG
ATTIT
PEACE

B42
KELSEN H.,LAW AND PEACE IN INTERNATIONAL RELATIONS.
FUT WOR-45 NAT/G DELIB/GP DIPLOM LEGIT RIGID/FLEX
ORD/FREE SOVEREIGN...JURID CONCPT TREND STERTYP
GEN/LAWS LEAGUE/NAT 20. PAGE 60 E1197
INT/ORG
ADJUD
PEACE
INT/LAW

B43
CONOVER H.F.,THE BALKANS: A SELECTED LIST OF
REFERENCES. ALBANIA BULGARIA ROMANIA YUGOSLAVIA
INT/ORG PROB/SOLV DIPLOM LEGIT CONFER ADJUD WAR
NAT/LISM PEACE PWR 20 LEAGUE/NAT. PAGE 25 E0493
BIBLIOG
EUR+WWI

C43
BENTHAM J.,"ON THE LIBERTY OF THE PRESS, AND PUBLIC
DISCUSSION" IN J. BOWRING, ED., THE WORKS OF JEREMY
BENTHAM." SPAIN UK LAW ELITES NAT/G LEGIS INSPECT
LEGIT WRITING CONTROL PRIVIL TOTALISM AUTHORIT
...TRADIT 19 FREE/SPEE. PAGE 10 E0193
ORD/FREE
PRESS
CONFER
CONSERVE

B44
BRIERLY J.L.,THE OUTLOOK FOR INTERNATIONAL LAW. FUT
WOR-45 CONSTN NAT/G VOL/ASSN FORCES ECO/TAC DOMIN
LEGIT ADJUD ROUTINE PEACE ORD/FREE...INT/LAW JURID
METH LEAGUE/NAT 20. PAGE 15 E0298
INT/ORG
LAW

B44
CHENEY F.,CARTELS, COMBINES, AND TRUSTS: A SELECTED
LIST OF REFERENCES. GERMANY UK USA-45 WOR-45
DELIB/GP OP/RES BARGAIN CAP/ISM ECO/TAC INT/TRADE
LICENSE LEGIT CONFER PRICE 20. PAGE 22 E0428
BIBLIOG/A
LG/CO
ECO/DEV
INDUS

B44
FULLER G.H.,RENEGOTIATION OF WAR CONTRACTS: A
SELECTED LIST OF REFERENCES (PAMPHLET). USA-45
ECO/DEV LG/CO NAT/G OP/RES PLAN BAL/PWR LEGIT
CONTROL...MGT 20. PAGE 42 E0823
BIBLIOG
WAR
LAW
FINAN

B44
SUAREZ F.,A TREATISE ON LAWS AND GOD THE LAWGIVER
(1612) IN SELECTIONS FROM THREE WORKS, VOL. II.
FRANCE ITALY UK CULTURE NAT/G SECT CHIEF LEGIS
DOMIN LEGIT CT/SYS ORD/FREE PWR WORSHIP 16/17.
PAGE 94 E1892
LAW
JURID
GEN/LAWS
CATH

B45
BEVERIDGE W.,THE PRICE OF PEACE. GERMANY UK WOR+45
WOR-45 NAT/G FORCES CREATE LEGIT REGION WAR ATTIT
KNOWL ORD/FREE PWR...POLICY NEW/IDEA GEN/LAWS
LEAGUE/NAT 20 TREATY. PAGE 12 E0223
INT/ORG
TREND
PEACE

B45
HILL N.,CLAIMS TO TERRITORY IN INTERNATIONAL LAW
AND RELATIONS. WOR-45 NAT/G DOMIN EDU/PROP LEGIT
REGION ROUTINE ORD/FREE PWR WEALTH...GEOG INT/LAW
JURID 20. PAGE 52 E1047
INT/ORG
ADJUD
SOVEREIGN

B45
TINGSTERN H.,PEACE AND SECURITY AFTER WW II. WOR-45
DELIB/GP TOP/EX LEGIT CT/SYS COERCE PEACE ATTIT
PERCEPT...CONCPT LEAGUE/NAT 20. PAGE 96 E1927
INT/ORG
ORD/FREE
WAR
INT/LAW

B46
KEETON G.W.,MAKING INTERNATIONAL LAW WORK. FUT
WOR-45 NAT/G DELIB/GP FORCES LEGIT COERCE PEACE
ATTIT RIGID/FLEX ORD/FREE PWR...JURID CONCPT
HIST/WRIT GEN/METH LEAGUE/NAT 20. PAGE 60 E1193
INT/ORG
ADJUD
INT/LAW

B46
PATON G.W.,A TEXT-BOOK OF JURISPRUDENCE. CREATE
INSPECT LEGIT CT/SYS ROUTINE CRIME INGP/REL PRIVIL
...CONCPT BIBLIOG 20. PAGE 80 E1601
LAW
ADJUD
JURID
T

B47
HILL M.,IMMUNITIES AND PRIVILEGES OF INTERNATIONAL
OFFICIALS. CANADA EUR+WWI NETHERLAND SWITZERLND LAW
LEGIS DIPLOM LEGIT RESPECT...TIME/SEQ LEAGUE/NAT UN
VAL/FREE 20. PAGE 52 E1046
INT/ORG
ADMIN

B47
LOCKE J.,TWO TREATISES OF GOVERNMENT (1690). UK LAW
SOCIETY LEGIS LEGIT AGREE REV OWN HEREDITY MORAL
CONSERVE...POLICY MAJORIT 17 WILLIAM/3 NATURL/LAW.
PAGE 66 E1316
CONCPT
ORD/FREE
NAT/G
CONSEN

B48
FENWICK C.G.,INTERNATIONAL LAW. WOR+45 WOR-45
CONSTN NAT/G LEGIT CT/SYS REGION...CONCPT
LEAGUE/NAT UN 20. PAGE 37 E0737
INT/ORG
JURID
INT/LAW

B48
JESSUP P.C.,A MODERN LAW OF NATIONS. FUT WOR+45
WOR-45 SOCIETY NAT/G DELIB/GP LEGIS BAL/PWR
EDU/PROP LEGIT PWR...INT/LAW JURID TIME/SEQ
LEAGUE/NAT 20. PAGE 58 E1166
INT/ORG
ADJUD

L49
COMM. STUDY ORGAN. PEACE,"A TEN YEAR RECORD,
1939-1949." FUT WOR+45 LAW R+D CONSULT DELIB/GP
CREATE LEGIT ROUTINE ORD/FREE...TIME/SEQ UN 20.
PAGE 24 E0480
INT/ORG
CONSTN
PEACE

B50
JIMENEZ E.,VOTING AND HANDLING OF DISPUTES IN THE
SECURITY COUNCIL. WOR+45 CONSTN INT/ORG DIPLOM
LEGIT DETER CHOOSE MORAL ORD/FREE PWR...JURID
TIME/SEQ COLD/WAR UN 20. PAGE 59 E1168
DELIB/GP
ROUTINE

B50
STONE J.,THE PROVINCE AND FUNCTION OF LAW. UNIV
WOR+45 WOR-45 CULTURE INTELL SOCIETY ECO/DEV
ECO/UNDEV NAT/G LEGIT ROUTINE ATTIT PERCEPT PERSON
...JURID CONCPT GEN/LAWS GEN/METH 20. PAGE 94 E1877
INT/ORG
LAW

B51
PUSEY M.J.,CHARLES EVANS HUGHES (2 VOLS.). LAW
CONSTN NAT/G POL/PAR DIPLOM LEGIT WAR CHOOSE
PERS/REL DRIVE HEREDITY 19/20 DEPT/STATE LEAGUE/NAT
SUPREME/CT HUGHES/CE WWI. PAGE 83 E1663
BIOG
TOP/EX
ADJUD
PERSON

L51
KELSEN H.,"RECENT TRENDS IN THE LAW OF THE UNITED
NATIONS." KOREA WOR+45 CONSTN LEGIS DIPLOM LEGIT
DETER WAR RIGID/FLEX HEALTH ORD/FREE RESPECT
...JURID CON/ANAL UN VAL/FREE 20 NATO. PAGE 60
E1199
INT/ORG
LAW
INT/LAW

L51
LISSITZYN O.J.,"THE INTERNATIONAL COURT OF
JUSTICE." WOR+45 INT/ORG LEGIT ORD/FREE...CONCPT
TIME/SEQ TREND GEN/LAWS VAL/FREE 20 ICJ. PAGE 65
E1304
ADJUD
JURID
INT/LAW

L51
MANGONE G.,"THE IDEA AND PRACTICE OF WORLD
GOVERNMENT." FUT WOR+45 WOR-45 ECO/DEV LEGIS CREATE
LEGIT ROUTINE ATTIT MORAL PWR WEALTH...CONCPT
GEN/LAWS 20. PAGE 68 E1358
INT/ORG
SOCIETY
INT/LAW

B52
BUCKLAND W.W.,ROMAN LAW AND COMMON LAW: A
COMPARISON IN OUTLINE (2ND REV. ED.). UK FAM LEGIT
AGREE CT/SYS OWN...JURID ROMAN/REP ROMAN/LAW
COMMON/LAW. PAGE 17 E0325
IDEA/COMP
LAW
ADJUD
CONCPT

B52
GELLHORN W.,THE STATES AND SUBVERSION. USA+45   PROVS
USA-45 LOC/G DELIB/GP LEGIS EDU/PROP LEGIT CT/SYS   JURID
REGION PEACE ATTIT ORD/FREE SOCISM...INT CON/ANAL
20 CALIFORNIA MARYLAND ILLINOIS MICHIGAN NEW/YORK.
PAGE 43 E0845

B52
JACKSON E.,MEETING OF THE MINDS: A WAY TO PEACE   LABOR
THROUGH MEDIATION. WOR+45 INDUS INT/ORG NAT/G   JUDGE
DELIB/GP DIPLOM EDU/PROP LEGIT ORD/FREE...NEW/IDEA
SELF/OBS TIME/SEQ CHARTS GEN/LAWS TOT/POP 20 UN
TREATY. PAGE 57 E1139

B54
LANDHEER B.,RECOGNITION IN INTERNATIONAL LAW   BIBLIOG/A
(SELECTIVE BIBLIOGRAPHIES OF THE LIBRARY OF THE   INT/LAW
PEACE PALACE, VOL. II: PAMPHLET). NAT/G LEGIT   INT/ORG
SANCTION 20. PAGE 63 E1251   DIPLOM

B54
MANGONE G.,A SHORT HISTORY OF INTERNATIONAL   INT/ORG
ORGANIZATION. MOD/EUR USA+45 USA-45 WOR+45 WOR-45   INT/LAW
LAW LEGIS CREATE LEGIT ROUTINE RIGID/FLEX PWR
...JURID CONCPT OBS TIME/SEQ STERTYP GEN/LAWS UN
TOT/POP VAL/FREE 18/20. PAGE 68 E1359

B54
O'NEILL J.M.,CATHOLICS IN CONTROVERSY. USA+45 NAT/G   CATHISM
PROVS SCHOOL SECT EDU/PROP LEGIT CT/SYS SANCTION   CONSTN
GP/REL 20 SUPREME/CT CHURCH/STA. PAGE 78 E1569   POLICY
  LAW

L54
NICOLSON H.,"THE EVOLUTION OF DIPLOMATIC METHOD."   RIGID/FLEX
CHRIST-17C EUR+WWI FRANCE FUT ITALY MEDIT-7 MOD/EUR   METH/CNCPT
USA+45 USA-45 LAW NAT/G CREATE EDU/PROP LEGIT PEACE   DIPLOM
ATTIT ORD/FREE RESPECT SOVEREIGN. PAGE 77 E1548

B55
CHOWDHURI R.N.,INTERNATIONAL MANDATES AND   DELIB/GP
TRUSTEESHIP SYSTEMS. WOR+45 STRUCT ECO/UNDEV   PLAN
INT/ORG LEGIS DOMIN EDU/PROP LEGIT ADJUD EXEC PWR   SOVEREIGN
...CONCPT TIME/SEQ UN 20. PAGE 22 E0434

B56
ABELS J.,THE TRUMAN SCANDALS. USA+45 USA-45 POL/PAR   CRIME
TAX LEGIT CT/SYS CHOOSE PRIVIL MORAL WEALTH 20   ADMIN
TRUMAN/HS PRESIDENT CONGRESS. PAGE 2 E0043   CHIEF
  TRIBUTE

B56
ALEXANDER F.,THE CRIMINAL, THE JUDGE, AND THE   CRIME
PUBLIC. LAW CULTURE CONSULT LEGIT ADJUD SANCTION   CRIMLGY
ORD/FREE 20. PAGE 3 E0060   PSY
  ATTIT

B56
CORBETT P.E.,MORALS LAW, AND POWER IN INTERNATIONAL   SUPEGO
RELATIONS. WOR+45 WOR-45 INT/ORG VOL/ASSN DELIB/GP   CONCPT
CREATE BAL/PWR DIPLOM LEGIT ARMS/CONT MORAL...JURID   POLICY
GEN/LAWS TOT/POP LEAGUE/NAT 20. PAGE 26 E0506   INT/LAW

B56
PEASLEE A.J.,CONSTITUTIONS OF NATIONS. WOR+45 LAW   CONSTN
NAT/G EX/STRUC LEGIS TOP/EX LEGIT CT/SYS ROUTINE   CON/ANAL
CHOOSE ORD/FREE PWR SOVEREIGN...CHARTS TOT/POP.
PAGE 80 E1605

B56
SOHN L.B.,BASIC DOCUMENTS OF THE UNITED NATIONS.   DELIB/GP
WOR+45 LAW INT/ORG LEGIT EXEC ROUTINE CHOOSE PWR   CONSTN
...JURID CONCPT GEN/LAWS ANTHOL UN TOT/POP OAS FAO
ILO 20. PAGE 92 E1853

B56
WEIS P.,NATIONALITY AND STATELESSNESS IN   INT/ORG
INTERNATIONAL LAW. UK WOR+45 WOR-45 LAW CONSTN   SOVEREIGN
NAT/G DIPLOM EDU/PROP LEGIT ROUTINE RIGID/FLEX   INT/LAW
...JURID RECORD CMN/WLTH 20. PAGE 105 E2109

B57
BERLE A.A. JR.,ECONOMIC POWER AND FREE SOCIETY   LG/CO
(PAMPHLET). CLIENT CONSTN EX/STRUC ECO/TAC CONTROL   CAP/ISM
PARTIC PWR WEALTH MAJORIT. PAGE 11 E0205   INGP/REL
  LEGIT

B57
COMM. STUDY ORGAN. PEACE,STRENGTHENING THE UNITED   INT/ORG
NATIONS. FUT USA+45 WOR+45 CONSTN NAT/G DELIB/GP   ORD/FREE
FORCES LEGIS ECO/TAC LEGIT COERCE PEACE...JURID
CONCPT UN COLD/WAR 20. PAGE 24 E0482

B57
HISS A.,IN THE COURT OF PUBLIC OPINION. USA+45   CRIME

DELIB/GP LEGIS LEGIT CT/SYS ATTIT 20 DEPT/STATE   MARXISM
NIXON/RM HUAC HISS/ALGER. PAGE 53 E1053   BIOG
  ADJUD

B57
ROSENNE S.,THE INTERNATIONAL COURT OF JUSTICE.   INT/ORG
WOR+45 LAW DOMIN LEGIT PEACE PWR SOVEREIGN...JURID   CT/SYS
CONCPT RECORD TIME/SEQ CON/ANAL CHARTS UN TOT/POP   INT/LAW
VAL/FREE LEAGUE/NAT 20 ICJ. PAGE 86 E1716

B57
SCHUBERT G.A.,THE PRESIDENCY IN THE COURTS. CONSTN   PWR
FORCES DIPLOM TARIFFS ADJUD CONTROL WAR...DECISION   CT/SYS
MGT CHARTS 18/20 PRESIDENT CONGRESS SUPREME/CT.   LEGIT
PAGE 89 E1778   CHIEF

B57
WASSENBERGH H.A.,POST-WAR INTERNATIONAL CIVIL   COM/IND
AVIATION POLICY AND THE LAW OF THE AIR. WOR+45 AIR   NAT/G
INT/ORG DOMIN LEGIT PEACE ORD/FREE...POLICY JURID   INT/LAW
NEW/IDEA OBS TIME/SEQ TREND CHARTS 20 TREATY.
PAGE 105 E2101

B58
BOWETT D.W.,SELF-DEFENSE IN INTERNATIONAL LAW.   ADJUD
EUR+WWI MOD/EUR WOR+45 WOR-45 SOCIETY INT/ORG   CONCPT
CONSULT DIPLOM LEGIT COERCE ATTIT ORD/FREE...JURID   WAR
20 UN. PAGE 14 E0276   INT/LAW

B58
HENKIN L.,ARMS CONTROL AND INSPECTION IN AMERICAN   USA+45
LAW. LAW CONSTN INT/ORG LOC/G MUNIC NAT/G PROVS   JURID
EDU/PROP LEGIT EXEC NUC/PWR KNOWL ORD/FREE...OBS   ARMS/CONT
TOT/POP CONGRESS 20. PAGE 52 E1032

B58
MACKENZIE W.J.M.,FREE ELECTIONS: AN ELEMENTARY   EX/STRUC
TEXTBOOK. WOR+45 NAT/G POL/PAR LEGIS TOP/EX   CHOOSE
EDU/PROP LEGIT CT/SYS ATTIT PWR...OBS CHARTS
STERTYP T CONGRESS PARLIAMENT 20. PAGE 67 E1342

B58
RUSSELL R.B.,A HISTORY OF THE UNITED NATIONS   USA-45
CHARTER: THE ROLE OF THE UNITED STATES. SOCIETY   INT/ORG
NAT/G CONSULT DOMIN LEGIT ATTIT ORD/FREE PWR   CONSTN
...POLICY JURID CONCPT UN LEAGUE/NAT. PAGE 87 E1737

B58
SPITZ D.,DEMOCRACY AND THE CHALLANGE OF POWER. FUT   NAT/G
USA+45 USA-45 LAW SOCIETY STRUCT LOC/G POL/PAR   PWR
PROVS DELIB/GP EX/STRUC LEGIS TOP/EX ACT/RES CREATE
DOMIN EDU/PROP LEGIT ADJUD ADMIN ATTIT DRIVE MORAL
ORD/FREE TOT/POP. PAGE 93 E1862

L58
UNESCO,"TECHNIQUES OF MEDIATION AND CONCILIATION."   INT/ORG
EUR+WWI USA+45 WOR+45 INDUS FACE/GP EX/STRUC   CONSULT
EDU/PROP LEGIT PEACE ORD/FREE...INT/LAW TIME/SEQ   DIPLOM
LEAGUE/NAT 20. PAGE 98 E1961

B59
ANDERSON J.N.D.,ISLAMIC LAW IN THE MODERN WORLD.   ISLAM
FAM KIN SECT LEGIT ADJUD ATTIT DRIVE...TIME/SEQ   JURID
TREND GEN/LAWS 20 MUSLIM. PAGE 5 E0089

B59
CORBETT P.E.,LAW IN DIPLOMACY. UK USA+45 USSR   NAT/G
CONSTN SOCIETY INT/ORG JUDGE LEGIT ATTIT ORD/FREE   ADJUD
TOT/POP LEAGUE/NAT 20. PAGE 26 E0507   JURID
  DIPLOM

B59
FRIEDMANN W.G.,LAW IN A CHANGING SOCIETY. FUT   SOC
WOR+45 WOR-45 LAW SOCIETY STRUCT INT/TRADE LEGIT   JURID
ATTIT BIO/SOC HEALTH ORD/FREE SOVEREIGN...CONCPT
GEN/LAWS ILO 20. PAGE 41 E0803

B59
GOMEZ ROBLES J.,A STATEMENT OF THE LAWS OF   JURID
GUATEMALA IN MATTERS AFFECTING BUSINESS (2ND ED.   NAT/G
REV., ENLARGED). GUATEMALA L/A+17C LAW FINAN FAM   INDUS
WORKER ACT/RES DIPLOM ADJUD ADMIN GP/REL 20 OAS.   LEGIT
PAGE 44 E0881

B59
REIFF H.,THE UNITED STATES AND THE TREATY LAW OF   ADJUD
THE SEA. USA+45 USA-45 SEA SOCIETY INT/ORG CONSULT   INT/LAW
DELIB/GP LEGIS DIPLOM LEGIT ATTIT ORD/FREE PWR
WEALTH...GEOG JURID TOT/POP 20 TREATY. PAGE 84
E1681

B59
SCHNEIDER J.,TREATY-MAKING POWER OF INTERNATIONAL   INT/ORG
ORGANIZATIONS. FUT WOR+45 WOR-45 LAW NAT/G JUDGE   ROUTINE
DIPLOM LEGIT CT/SYS ORD/FREE PWR...INT/LAW JURID
GEN/LAWS TOT/POP UNESCO 20 TREATY. PAGE 88 E1762

SCHORN H.,DER RICHTER IM DRITTEN REICH; GESCHICHTE
UND DOKUMENTE. GERMANY NAT/G LEGIT CT/SYS INGP/REL
MORAL ORD/FREE RESPECT...JURID GP/COMP 20. PAGE 88
E1765
ADJUD
JUDGE
FASCISM
B59

SPIRO H.J.,GOVERNMENT BY CONSTITUTIONS: THE
POLITICAL SYSTEMS OF DEMOCRACY. CANADA EUR+WWI FUT
USA+45 WOR+45 WOR-45 LEGIS TOP/EX LEGIT ADMIN
CT/SYS ORD/FREE PWR...TREND TOT/POP VAL/FREE 20.
PAGE 93 E1861
NAT/G
CONSTN
B59

CARLSTON K.S.,"NATIONALIZATION: AN ANALYTIC
APPROACH." WOR+45 INT/ORG ECO/TAC DOMIN LEGIT ADJUD
COERCE ORD/FREE PWR WEALTH SOCISM...JURID CONCPT
TREND STERTYP TOT/POP VAL/FREE 20. PAGE 19 E0380
INDUS
NAT/G
NAT/LISM
SOVEREIGN
S59

CLOWARD R.A.,"ILLEGITIMATE MEANS, ANOMIE, AND
DEVIANT BEHAVIOR" STRUCT CRIME DRIVE PERSON...SOC
CONCPT NEW/IDEA 20 DURKHEIM/E MERTON/R. PAGE 23
E0459
ANOMIE
CRIMLGY
LEGIT
ADJUST
S59

DOMKE M.,"THE SETTLEMENT OF DISPUTES IN
INTERNATIONAL TRADE." USA+45 LAW STRATA STRUCT
JUDGE EDU/PROP PWR...METH/CNCPT 20. PAGE 32 E0634
CONSULT
LEGIT
INT/TRADE
S59

JENKS C.W.,"THE CHALLENGE OF UNIVERSALITY." FUT
UNIV CONSTN CULTURE CONSULT CREATE PLAN LEGIT ATTIT
MORAL ORD/FREE RESPECT...MAJORIT JURID 20. PAGE 58
E1155
INT/ORG
LAW
PEACE
INT/LAW
S59

SOHN L.B.,"THE DEFINITION OF AGGRESSION." FUT LAW
FORCES LEGIT ADJUD ROUTINE COERCE ORD/FREE PWR
...MAJORIT JURID QUANT COLD/WAR 20. PAGE 92 E1855
INT/ORG
CT/SYS
DETER
SOVEREIGN
S59

STONE J.,"CONFLICT MANAGEMENT THROUGH CONTEMPORARY
INTERNATIONAL LAW AND ORGANIZATION." WOR+45 LAW
NAT/G CREATE BAL/PWR DOMIN LEGIT ROUTINE COERCE
ATTIT ORD/FREE PWR SOVEREIGN...JURID 20. PAGE 94
E1880
INT/ORG
INT/LAW
S59

SUTTON F.X.,"REPRESENTATION AND THE NATURE OF
POLITICAL SYSTEMS." UNIV WOR-45 CULTURE SOCIETY
STRATA INT/ORG FORCES JUDGE DOMIN LEGIT EXEC REGION
REPRESENT ATTIT ORD/FREE RESPECT...SOC HIST/WRIT
TIME/SEQ. PAGE 95 E1896
NAT/G
CONCPT
S59

BERTHOLD O.,KAISER, VOLK UND AVIGNON. GERMANY CHIEF
LEGIT LEAD NAT/LISM CONSERVE 14 POPE CHRUCH/STA
LUDWIG/BAV JOHN/XXII. PAGE 11 E0217
DIPLOM
CATHISM
JURID
B60

BLANSHARD P.,GOD AND MAN IN WASHINGTON. USA+45
CHIEF LEGIS LEGIT CT/SYS PRIVIL ATTIT ORD/FREE
...POLICY CONCPT 20 SUPREME/CT CONGRESS PRESIDENT
CHURCH/STA. PAGE 12 E0242
NAT/G
SECT
GP/REL
POL/PAR
B60

ENGEL J.,THE SECURITY OF THE FREE WORLD. USSR
WOR+45 STRATA STRUCT ECO/DEV ECO/UNDEV INT/ORG
DELIB/GP FORCES DOMIN LEGIT ADJUD EXEC ARMS/CONT
COERCE...POLICY CONCPT NEW/IDEA TIME/SEQ GEN/LAWS
COLD/WAR WORK UN 20 NATO. PAGE 35 E0689
COM
TREND
DIPLOM
B60

GOLDSEN J.M.,INTERNATIONAL POLITICAL IMPLICATIONS
OF ACTIVITIES IN OUTER SPACE. FUT USA+45 WOR+45 AIR
LAW ACT/RES LEGIT ATTIT KNOWL ORD/FREE PWR...CONCPT
20. PAGE 44 E0879
R+D
SPACE
B60

JENNINGS R.,PROGRESS OF INTERNATIONAL LAW. FUT
WOR+45 WOR-45 SOCIETY NAT/G VOL/ASSN DELIB/GP
DIPLOM EDU/PROP LEGIT COERCE ATTIT DRIVE MORAL
ORD/FREE...JURID CONCPT OBS TIME/SEQ TREND
GEN/LAWS. PAGE 58 E1164
INT/ORG
LAW
INT/LAW
B60

LENCZOWSKI G.,OIL AND STATE IN THE MIDDLE EAST. FUT
IRAN LAW ECO/UNDEV EXTR/IND NAT/G TOP/EX PLAN
TEC/DEV ECO/TAC LEGIT ADMIN COERCE ATTIT ALL/VALS
PWR...CHARTS 20. PAGE 64 E1283
ISLAM
INDUS
NAT/LISM
B60

PRICE D.,THE SECRETARY OF STATE. USA+45 CONSTN
CONSULT
B60

ELITES INTELL CHIEF EX/STRUC TOP/EX LEGIT ATTIT PWR
SKILL...DECISION 20 CONGRESS. PAGE 82 E1650
DIPLOM
INT/LAW

KUNZ J.,"SANCTIONS IN INTERNATIONAL LAW." WOR+45
WOR-45 LEGIT ARMS/CONT COERCE PEACE ATTIT
...METH/CNCPT TIME/SEQ TREND 20. PAGE 62 E1234
INT/ORG
ADJUD
INT/LAW
L60

LAUTERPACHT E.,"THE SUEZ CANAL SETTLEMENT." FRANCE
ISLAM ISRAEL UAR UK BAL/PWR DIPLOM LEGIT...JURID
GEN/LAWS ANTHOL SUEZ VAL/FREE 20. PAGE 63 E1263
INT/ORG
LAW
L60

GRACIA-MORA M.R.,"INTERNATIONAL RESPONSIBILITY FOR
SUBVERSIVE ACTIVITIES AND HOSTILE PROPAGANDA BY
PRIVATE PERSONS AGAINST." COM EUR+WWI L/A+17C UK
USA+45 USSR WOR-45 CONSTN NAT/G LEGIT ADJUD REV
PEACE TOTALISM ORD/FREE...INT/LAW 20. PAGE 45 E0895
INT/ORG
JURID
SOVEREIGN
S60

POTTER P.B.,"RELATIVE VALUES OF INTERNATIONAL
RELATIONS, LAW, AND ORGANIZATIONS." WOR+45 NAT/G
LEGIT ADJUD ORD/FREE...CONCPT TOT/POP COLD/WAR 20.
PAGE 81 E1633
INT/ORG
LEGIS
DIPLOM
INT/LAW
S60

RHYNE C.S.,"LAW AS AN INSTRUMENT FOR PEACE." FUT
WOR+45 PLAN LEGIT ROUTINE ARMS/CONT NUC/PWR ATTIT
ORD/FREE...JURID METH/CNCPT TREND CON/ANAL HYPO/EXP
COLD/WAR 20. PAGE 84 E1690
ADJUD
EDU/PROP
INT/LAW
PEACE
S60

SCHACHTER O.,"THE ENFORCEMENT OF INTERNATIONAL
JUDICIAL AND ARBITRAL DECISIONS." WOR+45 NAT/G
ECO/TAC DOMIN LEGIT ROUTINE COERCE ATTIT DRIVE
ALL/VALS PWR...METH/CNCPT TREND TOT/POP 20 UN.
PAGE 87 E1750
INT/ORG
ADJUD
INT/LAW
S60

ANAND R.P.,COMPULSORY JURISDICTION OF INTERNATIONAL
COURT OF JUSTICE. FUT WOR+45 SOCIETY PLAN LEGIT
ADJUD ATTIT DRIVE PERSON ORD/FREE...JURID CONCPT
TREND 20 ICJ. PAGE 5 E0086
INT/ORG
COERCE
INT/LAW
B61

COWEN D.V.,THE FOUNDATIONS OF FREEDOM. AFR
SOUTH/AFR DOMIN LEGIT ADJUST DISCRIM TOTALISM ATTIT
ORD/FREE...MAJORIT JURID SOC/INTEG WORSHIP 20
NEGRO. PAGE 27 E0529
CONSTN
ELITES
RACE/REL
B61

MCDOUGAL M.S.,LAW AND MINIMUM WORLD PUBLIC ORDER.
WOR+45 SOCIETY NAT/G DELIB/GP EDU/PROP LEGIT ADJUD
COERCE ATTIT PERSON...JURID CONCPT RECORD TREND
TOT/POP 20. PAGE 70 E1406
INT/ORG
ORD/FREE
INT/LAW
B61

WECHSLER H.,PRINCIPLES, POLITICS AND FUNDAMENTAL
LAW: SELECTED ESSAYS. USA+45 USA-45 LAW SOCIETY
NAT/G PROVS DELIB/GP EX/STRUC ACT/RES LEGIT PERSON
KNOWL PWR...JURID 20 NUREMBERG. PAGE 105 E2106
CT/SYS
CONSTN
INT/LAW
B61

WRIGHT Q.,THE ROLE OF INTERNATIONAL LAW IN THE
ELIMINATION OF WAR. FUT WOR+45 WOR-45 NAT/G BAL/PWR
DIPLOM DOMIN LEGIT PWR...POLICY INT/LAW JURID
CONCPT TIME/SEQ TREND GEN/LAWS COLD/WAR 20.
PAGE 108 E2158
INT/ORG
ADJUD
ARMS/CONT
B61

SAND P.T.,"AN HISTORICAL SURVEY OF INTERNATIONAL
AIR LAW SINCE 1944." USA+45 USA-45 WOR+45 WOR-45
SOCIETY ECO/DEV NAT/G CONSULT EX/STRUC ACT/RES PLAN
LEGIT ROUTINE...JURID CONCPT METH/CNCPT TREND 20.
PAGE 87 E1744
INT/ORG
LAW
INT/LAW
SPACE
L61

TAUBENFELD H.J.,"A REGIME FOR OUTER SPACE." FUT
UNIV R+D ACT/RES PLAN BAL/PWR LEGIT ARMS/CONT
ORD/FREE...POLICY JURID TREND UN TOT/POP 20
COLD/WAR. PAGE 95 E1910
INT/ORG
ADJUD
SPACE
L61

CASTANEDA J.,"THE UNDERDEVELOPED NATIONS AND THE
DEVELOPMENT OF INTERNATIONAL LAW." FUT UNIV LAW
ACT/RES FOR/AID LEGIT PERCEPT SKILL...JURID
METH/CNCPT TIME/SEQ TOT/POP 20 UN. PAGE 21 E0405
INT/ORG
ECO/UNDEV
PEACE
INT/LAW
S61

HARVEY W.B.,"THE RULE OF LAW IN HISTORICAL
PERSPECTIVE." USA+45 WOR+45 INTELL SOCIETY ECO/DEV
ECO/UNDEV NAT/G EX/STRUC LEGIS TOP/EX LEGIT SKILL
...CONCPT HIST/WRIT TOT/POP. PAGE 51 E1010
ACT/RES
LAW
S61

LIPSON L.,"AN ARGUMENT ON THE LEGALITY OF
RECONNAISSANCE STATELLITES." COM USA+45 USSR WOR+45 LAW
AIR INTELL NAT/G CONSULT PLAN DIPLOM LEGIT ROUTINE SPACE
ATTIT...INT/LAW JURID CONCPT METH/CNCPT TREND
COLD/WAR 20. PAGE 65 E1302
S61
INT/ORG

MILLER E.,"LEGAL ASPECTS OF UN ACTION IN THE
CONGO." AFR CULTURE ADMIN PEACE DRIVE RIGID/FLEX
ORD/FREE...WELF/ST JURID OBS UN CONGO 20. PAGE 73
E1458
S61
INT/ORG
LEGIT

LEAGUE WOMEN VOTERS MASSACHU,THE MERIT SYSTEM IN
MASSACHUSETTS (PAMPHLET). USA+45 PROVS LEGIT PARTIC LAW
CHOOSE REPRESENT GOV/REL EFFICIENCY...POLICY SENIOR
GOV/COMP BIBLIOG 20 MASSACHU. PAGE 64 E1274 PROF/ORG
N61
LOC/G

BEBR G.,JUDICIAL CONTROL OF THE EUROPEAN
COMMUNITIES. EUR+WWI INT/ORG NAT/G DOMIN LEGIT PWR VOL/ASSN
...JURID CONCPT GEN/LAWS GEN/METH EEC 20. PAGE 9 INT/LAW
E0168
B62
ADJUD

CARLSTON K.S.,LAW AND ORGANIZATION IN WORLD
SOCIETY. WOR+45 FINAN ECO/TAC DOMIN LEGIT CT/SYS LAW
ROUTINE COERCE ORD/FREE PWR WEALTH...PLURIST
DECISION JURID MGT METH/CNCPT GEN/LAWS 20. PAGE 19
E0381
B62
INT/ORG

EVAN W.M.,LAW AND SOCIOLOGY: EXPLORATORY ESSAYS.
CONSULT ACT/RES OP/RES PROB/SOLV EDU/PROP LEGIT SOC
ADJUD CT/SYS GP/REL...PHIL/SCI ANTHOL SOC/INTEG 20. PROF/ORG
PAGE 35 E0703
B62
JURID

HADWEN J.G.,HOW UNITED NATIONS DECISIONS ARE MADE.
WOR+45 LAW EDU/PROP LEGIT ADMIN PWR...DECISION ROUTINE
SELF/OBS GEN/LAWS UN 20. PAGE 49 E0972
B62
INT/ORG

JENKS C.W.,THE PROPER LAW OF INTERNATIONAL
ORGANISATIONS. DIPLOM LEGIT AGREE CT/SYS SANCTION INT/ORG
REPRESENT SOVEREIGN...GEN/LAWS 20 UN UNESCO ILO ADJUD
NATO OAS. PAGE 58 E1158
B62
LAW
INT/LAW

LAWSON R.,INTERNATIONAL REGIONAL ORGANIZATIONS.
WOR+45 NAT/G VOL/ASSN CONSULT LEGIS EDU/PROP LEGIT DELIB/GP
ADMIN EXEC ROUTINE HEALTH PWR WEALTH...JURID EEC REGION
COLD/WAR 20 UN. PAGE 63 E1270
B62
INT/ORG

LILLICH R.B.,INTERNATIONAL CLAIMS: THEIR
ADJUDICATION BY NATIONAL COMMISSIONS. WOR+45 WOR-45 JURID
INT/ORG LEGIT CT/SYS TOT/POP 20. PAGE 65 E1297 INT/LAW
B62
ADJUD

MCDOUGAL M.S.,THE PUBLIC ORDER OF THE OCEANS.
WOR+45 WOR-45 SEA INT/ORG NAT/G CONSULT DELIB/GP ORD/FREE
DIPLOM LEGIT PEACE RIGID/FLEX...GEOG INT/LAW JURID
RECORD TOT/POP 20 TREATY. PAGE 70 E1407
B62
ADJUD

ROSENNE S.,THE WORLD COURT: WHAT IT IS AND HOW IT INT/ORG
WORKS. WOR+45 WOR-45 LAW CONSTN JUDGE EDU/PROP ADJUD
LEGIT ROUTINE CHOOSE PEACE ORD/FREE...JURID OBS INT/LAW
TIME/SEQ CHARTS UN TOT/POP VAL/FREE 20. PAGE 86
E1717
B62
INT/ORG

SCHWARZENBERGER G.,THE FRONTIERS OF INTERNATIONAL INT/ORG
LAW. WOR+45 WOR-45 NAT/G LEGIT CT/SYS ROUTINE MORAL LAW
ORD/FREE PWR...JURID SOC GEN/METH 20 COLD/WAR. INT/LAW
PAGE 89 E1789
B62

TRISKA J.F.,THE THEORY, LAW, AND POLICY OF SOVIET COM
TREATIES. WOR+45 WOR-45 CONSTN INT/ORG NAT/G LAW
VOL/ASSN DOMIN LEGIT COERCE ATTIT PWR RESPECT INT/LAW
...POLICY JURID CONCPT OBS SAMP TIME/SEQ TREND USSR
GEN/LAWS 20. PAGE 97 E1941
B62

WOETZEL R.K.,THE NURENBERG TRIALS IN INTERNATIONAL INT/ORG
LAW. CHRIST-17C MOD/EUR WOR+45 SOCIETY NAT/G ADJUD
DELIB/GP DOMIN LEGIT ROUTINE ATTIT DRIVE PERSON WAR
SUPEGO MORAL ORD/FREE...POLICY MAJORIT JURID PSY
SOC SELF/OBS RECORD NAZI TOT/POP. PAGE 107 E2138
B62

MANGIN G.,"L'ORGANIZATION JUDICIAIRE DES ETATS AFR
D'AFRIQUE ET DE MADAGASCAR." ISLAM WOR+45 STRATA LEGIS
L62

STRUCT ECO/UNDEV NAT/G LEGIT EXEC...JURID TIME/SEQ COLONIAL
TOT/POP 20 SUPREME/CT. PAGE 68 E1357 MADAGASCAR

MURACCIOLE L.,"LA LOI FONDAMENTALE DE LA REPUBLIQUE AFR
DU CONGO." WOR+45 SOCIETY ECO/UNDEV INT/ORG NAT/G CONSTN
LEGIS PLAN LEGIT ADJUD COLONIAL ROUTINE ATTIT
SOVEREIGN 20 CONGO. PAGE 75 E1504
L62

PETKOFF D.K.,"RECOGNITION AND NON-RECOGNITION OF INT/ORG
STATES AND GOVERNMENTS IN INTERNATIONAL LAW." ASIA LAW
COM USA+45 WOR+45 NAT/G ACT/RES DIPLOM DOMIN LEGIT INT/LAW
COERCE ORD/FREE PWR...CONCPT GEN/LAWS 20. PAGE 80
E1611
L62

STEIN E.,"MR HAMMARSKJOLD, THE CHARTER LAW AND THE CONCPT
FUTURE ROLE OF THE UNITED NATIONS SECRETARY- BIOG
GENERAL." WOR+45 CONSTN INT/ORG DELIB/GP FORCES
TOP/EX BAL/PWR LEGIT ROUTINE RIGID/FLEX PWR
...POLICY JURID OBS STERTYP UN COLD/WAR 20
HAMMARSK/D. PAGE 93 E1869
L62

CRANE R.D.,"LAW AND STRATEGY IN SPACE." FUT USA+45 CONCPT
WOR+45 AIR LAW INT/ORG NAT/G FORCES ACT/RES PLAN SPACE
BAL/PWR LEGIT ARMS/CONT COERCE ORD/FREE...POLICY
INT/LAW JURID SOC/EXP 20 TREATY. PAGE 27 E0542
S62

FALK R.A.,"THE REALITY OF INTERNATIONAL LAW." INT/ORG
WOR+45 NAT/G LEGIT COERCE DETER WAR MORAL ORD/FREE ADJUD
PWR SOVEREIGN...JURID CONCPT VAL/FREE COLD/WAR 20. NUC/PWR
PAGE 36 E0714 INT/LAW
S62

FENWICK C.G.,"ISSUES AT PUNTA DEL ESTE: NON- INT/ORG
INTERVENTION VS COLLECTIVE SECURITY." L/A+17C CUBA
USA+45 VOL/ASSN DELIB/GP ECO/TAC LEGIT ADJUD REGION
ORD/FREE OAS COLD/WAR 20. PAGE 37 E0738
S62

FINKELSTEIN L.S.,"THE UNITED NATIONS AND INT/ORG
ORGANIZATIONS FOR CONTROL OF ARMAMENT." FUT WOR+45 PWR
VOL/ASSN DELIB/GP TOP/EX CREATE EDU/PROP LEGIT ARMS/CONT
ADJUD NUC/PWR ATTIT RIGID/FLEX ORD/FREE...POLICY
DECISION CONCPT OBS TREND GEN/LAWS TOT/POP
COLD/WAR. PAGE 38 E0752
S62

GREEN L.C.,"POLITICAL OFFENSES, WAR CRIMES AND LAW
EXTRADITION." WOR+45 YUGOSLAVIA INT/ORG LEGIT CONCPT
ROUTINE WAR ORD/FREE SOVEREIGN...JURID NAZI 20 INT/LAW
INTERPOL. PAGE 46 E0906
S62

JOHNSON O.H.,"THE ENGLISH TRADITION IN LAW
INTERNATIONAL LAW." CHRIST-17C MOD/EUR EDU/PROP INT/LAW
LEGIT CT/SYS ORD/FREE...JURID CONCPT TIME/SEQ. UK
PAGE 59 E1170
S62

LISSITZYN O.J.,"SOME LEGAL IMPLICATIONS OF THE U-2 LAW
AND RB-47 INCIDENTS." FUT USA+45 USSR WOR+45 AIR CONCPT
NAT/G DIPLOM LEGIT MORAL ORD/FREE SOVEREIGN...JURID SPACE
GEN/LAWS GEN/METH COLD/WAR 20 U-2. PAGE 65 E1305 INT/LAW
S62

MCWHINNEY E.,"CO-EXISTENCE, THE CUBA CRISIS, AND CONCPT
COLD WAR-INTERNATIONAL WAR." CUBA USA+45 USSR INT/LAW
WOR+45 NAT/G TOP/EX BAL/PWR DIPLOM LEGIT
PEACE RIGID/FLEX ORD/FREE...STERTYP COLD/WAR 20.
PAGE 71 E1427
S62

MURACCIOLE L.,"LES MODIFICATIONS DE LA CONSTITUTION NAT/G
MALGACHE." AFR WOR+45 ECO/UNDEV LEGIT EXEC ALL/VALS STRUCT
...JURID 20. PAGE 75 E1505 SOVEREIGN
MADAGASCAR
S62

SCHACHTER O.,"DAG HAMMARSKJOLD AND THE RELATION OF ACT/RES
LAW TO POLITICS." FUT WOR+45 INT/ORG CONSULT PLAN ADJUD
TEC/DEV BAL/PWR DIPLOM LEGIT ATTIT PERCEPT ORD/FREE
...POLICY JURID CONCPT OBS TESTS STERTYP GEN/LAWS
20 HAMMARSK/D. PAGE 87 E1751
S62

VIGNES D.,"L'AUTORITE DES TRAITES INTERNATIONAUX EN STRUCT
DROIT INTERNE." EUR+WWI UNIV LAW CONSTN INTELL LEGIT
NAT/G POL/PAR DIPLOM ATTIT PERCEPT ALL/VALS FRANCE
...POLICY INT/LAW JURID CONCPT TIME/SEQ 20 TREATY.
PAGE 104 E2075
S62

C62

BACON F.,"OF THE TRUE GREATNESS OF KINGDOMS AND   WAR
ESTATES" (1612) IN F. BACON, ESSAYS." ELITES FORCES   PWR
DOMIN EDU/PROP LEGIT...POLICY GEN/LAWS 16/17   DIPLOM
TREATY. PAGE 7 E0129   CONSTN

B63

BOWETT D.W.,THE LAW OF INTERNATIONAL INSTITUTIONS.   INT/ORG
WOR+45 WOR-45 CONSTN DELIB/GP EX/STRUC JUDGE   ADJUD
EDU/PROP LEGIT CT/SYS EXEC ROUTINE RIGID/FLEX   DIPLOM
ORD/FREE PWR...JURID CONCPT ORG/CHARTS GEN/METH
LEAGUE/NAT OAS OEEC 20 UN. PAGE 14 E0277

B63

BROWN R.M.,THE SOUTH CAROLINA REGULATORS. USA-45   ORD/FREE
LEGIS LEGIT ADJUD COLONIAL CONTROL WAR...BIBLIOG/A   JURID
18 CHARLESTON SOUTH/CAR. PAGE 16 E0315   PWR
                                                          PROVS

B63

FALK R.A.,LAW, MORALITY, AND WAR IN THE   ADJUD
CONTEMPORARY WORLD. WOR+45 LAW INT/ORG EX/STRUC   ARMS/CONT
FORCES EDU/PROP LEGIT DETER NUC/PWR MORAL ORD/FREE   PEACE
...JURID TOT/POP 20. PAGE 36 E0715   INT/LAW

B63

FRIEDRICH C.J.,JUSTICE: NOMOS VI. UNIV LAW SANCTION   LEGIT
CRIME...CONCPT ANTHOL MARX/KARL LOCKE/JOHN   ADJUD
AQUINAS/T. PAGE 41 E0809   ORD/FREE
                                                          JURID

B63

HOWARD W.S.,AMERICAN SLAVERS AND THE FEDERAL LAW: DIST/IND
1837-1862. USA-45 NAT/G LEGIT COERCE RACE/REL   CRIMLGY
WEALTH...POLICY BIBLIOG/A 19. PAGE 55 E1102   LAW
                                                          EXEC

B63

A BIBLIOGRAPHY OF DOCTORAL DISSERTATIONS UNDERTAKEN   BIBLIOG
IN AMERICAN AND CANADIAN UNIVERSITIES ON RELIGION   ACADEM
AND POLITICS. LAW CONSTN DOMIN LEGIT ADJUD GP/REL   SECT
...POLICY 20. PAGE 62 E1241   JURID

B63

MOLLARD P.T.,LE REGIME JURIDIQUE DE LA PRESSE AU   PRESS
MAROC. MOROCCO CONTROL CRIME GP/REL ORD/FREE 20.   LAW
PAGE 74 E1482   LEAD
                                                          LEGIT

B63

REITZEL A.M.,DAS MAINZER KRONUNGSRECHT UND DIE   CHIEF
POLITISCHE PROBLEMATIK. GERMANY MUNIC LEGIT CATHISM   JURID
12/13. PAGE 84 E1684   CHOOSE
                                                          SECT

B63

YOUNGER R.D.,THE PEOPLE'S PANEL: THE GRAND JURY IN   CT/SYS
THE UNITED STATES, 1634-1941. USA-45 LAW LEGIT   JURID
CONTROL TASK GP/REL ROLE...TREND 17/20 GRAND/JURY.   CONSTN
PAGE 108 E2166   LOC/G

L63

LISSITZYN O.J.,"INTERNATIONAL LAW IN A DIVIDED   INT/ORG
WORLD." FUT WOR+45 CONSTN CULTURE ECO/DEV ECO/UNDEV   LAW
DIST/IND NAT/G FORCES ECO/TAC LEGIT ADJUD ADMIN
COERCE ATTIT HEALTH MORAL ORD/FREE PWR RESPECT
WEALTH VAL/FREE. PAGE 65 E1306

L63

MCDOUGAL M.S.,"THE ENJOYMENT AND ACQUISITION OF   PLAN
RESOURCES IN OUTER SPACE." CHRIST-17C FUT WOR+45   TREND
WOR-45 LAW EXTR/IND INT/ORG ACT/RES CREATE TEC/DEV
ECO/TAC LEGIT COERCE HEALTH KNOWL ORD/FREE PWR
WEALTH...JURID HIST/WRIT VAL/FREE. PAGE 70 E1408

S63

CAHIER P.,"LE DROIT INTERNE DES ORGANISATIONS   INT/ORG
INTERNATIONALES." UNIV CONSTN SOCIETY ECO/DEV R+D   JURID
NAT/G TOP/EX LEGIT ATTIT PERCEPT...TIME/SEQ 19/20.   DIPLOM
PAGE 18 E0357   INT/LAW

S63

FRIEDMANN W.G.,"THE USES OF 'GENERAL PRINCIPLES' IN   LAW
THE DEVELOPMENT OF INTERNATIONAL LAW." WOR+45 NAT/G   INT/LAW
DIPLOM INT/TRADE LEGIT ROUTINE RIGID/FLEX ORD/FREE   INT/ORG
...JURID CONCPT STERTYP GEN/METH 20. PAGE 41 E0804

S63

HARNETTY P.,"CANADA, SOUTH AFRICA AND THE   AFR
COMMONWEALTH." CANADA SOUTH/AFR LAW INT/ORG   ATTIT
VOL/ASSN DELIB/GP LEGIS TOP/EX ECO/TAC LEGIT DRIVE
MORAL...CONCPT CMN/WLTH 20. PAGE 50 E1000

S63

LEPAWSKY A.,"INTERNATIONAL DEVELOPMENT OF RIVER   INT/ORG
RESOURCES." CANADA EUR+WWI S/ASIA USA+45 SEA LEGIT   DELIB/GP

ADJUD ORD/FREE PWR WEALTH...MGT TIME/SEQ VAL/FREE
MEXIC/AMER 20. PAGE 64 E1287

S63

MCDOUGAL M.S.,"THE SOVIET-CUBAN QUARANTINE AND   ORD/FREE
SELF-DEFENSE." CUBA USA+45 USSR WOR+45 INT/ORG   LEGIT
NAT/G BAL/PWR NUC/PWR ATTIT...JURID CONCPT. PAGE 70   SOVEREIGN
E1409

S63

MODELSKI G.,"STUDY OF ALLIANCES." WOR+45 WOR-45   VOL/ASSN
INT/ORG NAT/G FORCES LEGIT ADMIN CHOOSE ALL/VALS   CON/ANAL
PWR SKILL...INT/LAW CONCPT GEN/LAWS 20 TREATY.   DIPLOM
PAGE 74 E1477

S63

TALLON D.,"L'ETUDE DU DROIT COMPARE COMME MOYEN DE   INT/ORG
RECHERCHER LES MATIERES SUSCEPTIBLES D'UNIFICATION   JURID
INTERNATIONALE." WOR+45 LAW SOCIETY VOL/ASSN   INT/LAW
CONSULT LEGIT CT/SYS RIGID/FLEX KNOWL 20. PAGE 95
E1906

S63

WEISSBERG G.,"MAPS AS EVIDENCE IN INTERNATIONAL   LAW
BOUNDARY DISPUTES: A REAPPRAISAL." CHINA/COM   GEOG
EUR+WWI INDIA MOD/EUR S/ASIA INT/ORG NAT/G LEGIT   SOVEREIGN
PERCEPT...JURID CHARTS 20. PAGE 105 E2110

S63

WENGLER W.,"LES CONFLITS DE LOIS ET LE PRINCIPE   JURID
D'EGALITE." UNIV LAW SOCIETY ACT/RES LEGIT ATTIT   CONCPT
PERCEPT 20. PAGE 105 E2111   INT/LAW

B64

COHEN M.,LAW AND POLITICS IN SPACE: SPECIFIC AND   DELIB/GP
URGENT PROBLEMS IN THE LAW OF OUTER SPACE.   LAW
CHINA/COM COM USA+45 USSR WOR+45 COM/IND INT/ORG   INT/LAW
NAT/G LEGIT NUC/PWR ATTIT BIO/SOC...JURID CONCPT   SPACE
CONGRESS 20 STALIN/J. PAGE 24 E0464

B64

FALK R.A.,THE ROLE OF DOMESTIC COURTS IN THE   LAW
INTERNATIONAL LEGAL ORDER. FUT WOR+45 INT/ORG NAT/G   INT/LAW
JUDGE EDU/PROP LEGIT CT/SYS...POLICY RELATIV JURID
CONCPT GEN/LAWS 20. PAGE 36 E0716

B64

FRIEDMANN W.G.,THE CHANGING STRUCTURE OF   ADJUD
INTERNATIONAL LAW. WOR+45 INT/ORG NAT/G PROVS LEGIT   TREND
ORD/FREE PWR...JURID CONCPT GEN/LAWS TOT/POP UN 20.   INT/LAW
PAGE 41 E0805

B64

SARTORIUS R.E.,THE JUSTIFICATION OF THE JUDICIAL   LAW
DECISION (DISSERTATION). PROB/SOLV LEGIT...JURID   PHIL/SCI
GEN/LAWS BIBLIOG 20. PAGE 87 E1747   CT/SYS
                                                        ADJUD

B64

SHAPIRO M.,LAW AND POLITICS IN THE SUPREME COURT: LEGIS
NEW APPROACHES TO POLITICAL JURISPRUDENCE. JUDGE   CT/SYS
PROB/SOLV LEGIT EXEC ROUTINE ATTIT ALL/VALS   LAW
...DECISION SOC. PAGE 90 E1811   JURID

B64

STANGER R.J.,ESSAYS ON INTERVENTION. PLAN PROB/SOLV   SOVEREIGN
BAL/PWR ADJUD COERCE WAR ROLE PWR...INT/LAW CONCPT   DIPLOM
20 UN INTERVENT. PAGE 93 E1865   POLICY
                                                        LEGIT

B64

UN PUB. INFORM. ORGAN.,EVERY MAN'S UNITED NATIONS.   INT/ORG
UNIV WOR+45 CONSTN CULTURE SOCIETY ECO/DEV   ROUTINE
ECO/UNDEV NAT/G ACT/RES PLAN ECO/TAC INT/TRADE
EDU/PROP LEGIT PEACE ATTIT ALL/VALS...POLICY HUM
INT/LAW CONCPT CHARTS UN TOT/POP 20. PAGE 97 E1954

L64

POUNDS N.J.G.,"THE POLITICS OF PARTITION." AFR ASIA   NAT/G
COM EUR+WWI FUT ISLAM S/ASIA USA+45 LAW ECO/DEV   NAT/LISM
ECO/UNDEV AGRI INDUS INT/ORG POL/PAR PROVS SECT
FORCES TOP/EX EDU/PROP LEGIT ATTIT MORAL ORD/FREE
PWR RESPECT WEALTH. PAGE 82 E1640

L64

WORLD PEACE FOUNDATION,"INTERNATIONAL   INT/ORG
ORGANIZATIONS: SUMMARY OF ACTIVITIES." INDIA   ROUTINE
PAKISTAN TURKEY WOR+45 CONSTN CONSULT EX/STRUC
ECO/TAC EDU/PROP LEGIT ORD/FREE...JURID SOC UN 20
CYPRESS. PAGE 107 E2145

S64

COHEN M.,"BASIC PRINCIPLES OF INTERNATIONAL LAW."   INT/ORG
UNIV WOR+45 WOR-45 BAL/PWR LEGIT ADJUD WAR ATTIT   INT/LAW
MORAL ORD/FREE PWR...JURID CONCPT MYTH TOT/POP 20.
PAGE 23 E0463

S64

DERWINSKI E.J.,"THE COST OF THE INTERNATIONAL
COFFEE AGREEMENT." L/A+17C USA+45 WOR+45 ECO/UNDEV
NAT/G VOL/ASSN LEGIS DIPLOM ECO/TAC FOR/AID LEGIT
ATTIT...TIME/SEQ CONGRESS 20 TREATY. PAGE 31 E0608

MARKET
DELIB/GP
INT/TRADE

S64

GARDNER R.N.,"THE SOVIET UNION AND THE UNITED
NATIONS." WOR+45 FINAN POL/PAR VOL/ASSN FORCES
ECO/TAC DOMIN EDU/PROP LEGIT ADJUD ADMIN ARMS/CONT
COERCE ATTIT ALL/VALS...POLICY MAJORIT CONCPT OBS
TIME/SEQ TREND STERTYP UN. PAGE 42 E0838

COM
INT/ORG
USSR

S64

GINSBURGS G.,"WARS OF NATIONAL LIBERATION - THE
SOVIET THESIS." COM USSR WOR+45 WOR-45 LAW CULTURE
INT/ORG DIPLOM LEGIT COLONIAL GUERRILLA WAR
NAT/LISM ATTIT PERSON MORAL PWR...JURID OBS TREND
MARX/KARL 20. PAGE 44 E0869

COERCE
CONCPT
INT/LAW
REV

S64

HICKEY D.,"THE PHILOSOPHICAL ARGUMENT FOR WORLD
GOVERNMENT." WOR+45 SOCIETY ACT/RES PLAN LEGIT
ADJUD PEACE PERCEPT PERSON ORD/FREE...HUM JURID
PHIL/SCI METH/CNCPT CON/ANAL STERTYP GEN/LAWS
TOT/POP 20. PAGE 52 E1039

FUT
INT/ORG

S64

KUNZ J.,"THE CHANGING SCIENCE OF INTERNATIONAL
LAW." FUT WOR+45 WOR-45 INT/ORG LEGIT ORD/FREE
...JURID TIME/SEQ GEN/LAWS 20. PAGE 62 E1235

ADJUD
CONCPT
INT/LAW

S64

LIPSON L.,"PEACEFUL COEXISTENCE." COM USSR WOR+45
LAW INT/ORG DIPLOM LEGIT ADJUD ORD/FREE...CONCPT
OBS TREND GEN/LAWS VAL/FREE COLD/WAR 20. PAGE 65
E1303

ATTIT
JURID
INT/LAW
PEACE

S64

PARADIES F.,"SOBRE LA HISTORIA DE LA LOGICA Y DE LA
LOGICA JURIDICA." LEGIT KNOWL...JURID METH/CNCPT
HIST/WRIT 20. PAGE 80 E1597

ADJUD

S64

SINGH N.,"THE CONTEMPORARY PRACTICE OF INDIA IN THE
FIELD OF INTERNATIONAL LAW." INDIA S/ASIA INT/ORG
NAT/G DOMIN EDU/PROP LEGIT KNOWL...CONCPT TOT/POP
20. PAGE 91 E1833

LAW
ATTIT
DIPLOM
INT/LAW

S64

SKUBISZEWSKI K.,"FORMS OF PARTICIPATION OF
INTERNATIONAL ORGANIZATION IN THE LAW MAKING
PROCESS." FUT WOR+45 NAT/G DELIB/GP DOMIN LEGIT
KNOWL PWR...JURID TREND 20. PAGE 92 E1837

INT/ORG
LAW
INT/LAW

B65

BAADE H.,THE SOVIET IMPACT ON INTERNATIONAL LAW.
INT/ORG INT/TRADE LEGIT COLONIAL ARMS/CONT REV WAR
...CON/ANAL ANTHOL TREATY. PAGE 6 E0124

INT/LAW
USSR
CREATE
ORD/FREE

B65

BROMBERG W.,CRIME AND THE MIND. LAW LEGIT ADJUD
CRIME MURDER AGE/Y ANOMIE BIO/SOC DRIVE SEX PSY.
PAGE 16 E0305

CRIMLGY
SOC
HEALTH
COERCE

B65

FRIEDMAN L.,SOUTHERN JUSTICE. USA+45 PUB/INST LEGIT
ADMIN CT/SYS DISCRIM...DECISION ANTHOL 20 NEGRO
SOUTH/US CIV/RIGHTS. PAGE 40 E0800

ADJUD
LAW
CONSTN
RACE/REL

B65

GINSBERG M.,ON JUSTICE IN SOCIETY. LAW EDU/PROP
LEGIT CT/SYS INGP/REL PRIVIL RATIONAL ATTIT MORAL
ORD/FREE...JURID 20. PAGE 44 E0867

ADJUD
ROLE
CONCPT

B65

HIGHSAW R.B.,CONFLICT AND CHANGE IN LOCAL
GOVERNMENT. USA+45 BUDGET ECO/TAC LEGIT ADJUD
ALABAMA. PAGE 52 E1044

GOV/REL
PROB/SOLV
LOC/G
BAL/PWR

B65

HOWE M.D.W.,THE GARDEN AND THE WILDERNESS. USA+45
LAW GIVE EDU/PROP LEGIT NAT/LISM ORD/FREE...POLICY
JURID SUPREME/CT CHURCH/STA. PAGE 55 E1103

CONSTN
SECT
NAT/G
GP/REL

B65

KARIS T.,THE TREASON TRIAL IN SOUTH AFRICA: A GUIDE
TO THE MICROFILM RECORD OF THE TRIAL. SOUTH/AFR LAW
ELITES NAT/G LEGIT CT/SYS RACE/REL DISCRIM...SOC
20. PAGE 59 E1185

BIBLIOG/A
ADJUD
CRIME
AFR

B65

MOELLER R.,LUDWIG DER BAYER UND DIE KURIE IM KAMPF
UM DAS REICH. GERMANY LAW SECT LEGIT LEAD GP/REL
CATHISM CONSERVE 14 LUDWIG/BAV POPE CHURCH/STA.
PAGE 74 E1478

JURID
CHIEF
CHOOSE
NAT/LISM

B65

PEASLEE A.J.,CONSTITUTIONS OF NATIONS* THIRD
REVISED EDITION (VOLUME I* AFRICA). LAW EX/STRUC
LEGIS TOP/EX LEGIT CT/SYS ROUTINE ORD/FREE PWR
SOVEREIGN...CON/ANAL CHARTS. PAGE 80 E1606

AFR
CHOOSE
CONSTN
NAT/G

B65

VONGLAHN G.,LAW AMONG NATIONS: AN INTRODUCTION TO
PUBLIC INTERNATIONAL LAW. UNIV WOR+45 LAW INT/ORG
NAT/G LEGIT EXEC RIGID/FLEX...CONCPT TIME/SEQ
GEN/LAWS UN TOT/POP 20. PAGE 104 E2084

CONSTN
JURID
INT/LAW

L65

RUBIN A.P.,"UNITED STATES CONTEMPORARY PRACTICE
RELATING TO INTERNATIONAL LAW." USA+45 WOR+45
CONSTN INT/ORG NAT/G DELIB/GP EX/STRUC DIPLOM DOMIN
CT/SYS ROUTINE ORD/FREE...CONCPT COLD/WAR 20.
PAGE 86 E1730

LAW
LEGIT
INT/LAW

L65

SHARMA S.P.,"THE INDIA-CHINA BORDER DISPUTE: AN
INDIAN PERSPECTIVE." ASIA CHINA/COM S/ASIA NAT/G
LEGIT CT/SYS NAT/LISM DRIVE MORAL ORD/FREE PWR 20.
PAGE 91 E1815

LAW
ATTIT
SOVEREIGN
INDIA

S65

AMRAM P.W.,"REPORT ON THE TENTH SESSION OF THE
HAGUE CONFERENCE ON PRIVATE INTERNATIONAL LAW."
USA+45 WOR+45 INT/ORG CREATE LEGIT ADJUD ALL/VALS
...JURID CONCPT METH/CNCPT OBS GEN/METH 20. PAGE 4
E0085

VOL/ASSN
DELIB/GP
INT/LAW

S65

BEVANS C.I.,"GHANA AND UNITED STATES - UNITED
KINGDOM AGREEMENTS." UK USA+45 LAW DELIB/GP
EX/STRUC ORD/FREE...JURID METH/CNCPT GEN/LAWS 20.
PAGE 11 E0222

NAT/G
LEGIT
GHANA
DIPLOM

S65

FALK R.A.,"INTERNATIONAL LEGAL ORDER." USA+45
INTELL FACE/GP INT/ORG LEGIT KNOWL...CONCPT
METH/CNCPT STYLE RECORD GEN/METH 20. PAGE 36 E0717

ATTIT
GEN/LAWS
INT/LAW

S65

GROSS L.,"PROBLEMS OF INTERNATIONAL ADJUDICATION
AND COMPLIANCE WITH INTERNATIONAL LAW: SOME SIMPLE
SOLUTIONS." WOR+45 SOCIETY NAT/G DOMIN LEGIT ADJUD
CT/SYS RIGID/FLEX HEALTH PWR...JURID NEW/IDEA
COLD/WAR 20. PAGE 48 E0951

LAW
METH/CNCPT
INT/LAW

S65

MAC CHESNEY B.,"SOME COMMENTS ON THE 'QUARANTINE'
OF CUBA." USA+45 WOR+45 NAT/G BAL/PWR DIPLOM LEGIT
ROUTINE ATTIT ORD/FREE...JURID METH/CNCPT 20.
PAGE 67 E1337

INT/ORG
LAW
CUBA
USSR

S65

STEIN E.,"TOWARD SUPREMACY OF TREATY-CONSTITUTION
BY JUDICIAL FIAT: ON THE MARGIN OF THE COSTA CASE."
EUR+WWI ITALY WOR+45 INT/ORG NAT/G LEGIT REGION
NAT/LISM PWR...JURID CONCPT TREND TOT/POP VAL/FREE
20. PAGE 93 E1870

ADJUD
CONSTN
SOVEREIGN
INT/LAW

B66

HAUSNER G.,JUSTICE IN JERUSALEM. GERMANY ISRAEL
SOCIETY KIN DIPLOM LEGIT CT/SYS PARTIC MURDER
MAJORITY ATTIT FASCISM...INT/LAW JURID 20 JEWS
WAR/TRIAL. PAGE 51 E1013

ADJUD
CRIME
RACE/REL
COERCE

L66

GREIG D.W.,"THE ADVISORY JURISDICTION OF THE
INTERNATIONAL COURT AND THE SETTLEMENT OF DISPUTES
BETWEEN STATES." ISRAEL KOREA FORCES BUDGET DOMIN
LEGIT ADJUD COST...RECORD UN CONGO/LEOP TREATY.
PAGE 46 E0915

INT/LAW
CT/SYS

S66

GREEN L.C.,"RHODESIAN OIL: BOOTLEGGERS OR PIRATES?"
AFR RHODESIA UK WOR+45 INT/ORG NAT/G DIPLOM LEGIT
COLONIAL SOVEREIGN 20 UN OAU. PAGE 46 E0907

INT/TRADE
SANCTION
INT/LAW
POLICY

S67

KETCHAM O.W.,"GUIDELINES FROM GAULT: REVOLUTIONARY
REQUIREMENTS AND REAPPRAISAL." LAW CONSTN CREATE
LEGIT ROUTINE SANCTION CRIME DISCRIM PRIVIL ROLE
...JURID NEW/IDEA 20 SUPREME/CT. PAGE 60 E1208

ADJUD
AGE/Y
CT/SYS

MC REYNOLDS D.,"THE RESISTANCE." USA+45 LAW ADJUD | S67 ATTIT
SANCTION INGP/REL PEACE 20. PAGE 70 E1398 | WAR
| LEGIT
| FORCES

REILLY T.J.,"FREEZING AND CONFISCATION OF CUBAN | S67 STRANGE
PROPERTY." CUBA USA+45 LAW DIPLOM LEGIT ADJUD | OWN
CONTROL. PAGE 84 E1682 | ECO/TAC

DUPRE L.,"TILL DEATH DO US PART?" UNIV FAM INSPECT | S68 MARRIAGE
LEGIT ADJUD SANCTION PERS/REL ANOMIE RIGID/FLEX SEX | CATH
...JURID IDEA/COMP 20 CHURCH/STA BIBLE CANON/LAW | LAW
CIVIL/LAW. PAGE 34 E0666

SHAPIRO J.P.,"SOVIET HISTORIOGRAPHY AND THE MOSCOW | S68 HIST/WRIT
TRIALS: AFTER THIRTY YEARS." USSR NAT/G LEGIT PRESS | EDU/PROP
CONTROL LEAD ATTIT MARXISM...NEW/IDEA METH 20 | SANCTION
TROTSKY/L STALIN/J KHRUSH/N. PAGE 90 E1810 | ADJUD

AUSTIN J.,LECTURES ON JURISPRUDENCE OR THE | B73 LAW
PHILOSOPHY OF POSITIVE LAW (VOL. II) (4TH ED., | ADJUD
REV.). UK CONSTN STRUCT PROB/SOLV LEGIT CT/SYS | JURID
SANCTION CRIME INGP/REL OWN SUPEGO ORD/FREE...T 19. | METH/CNCPT
PAGE 6 E0120

BROOKS S.,BRITAIN AND THE BOERS. AFR SOUTH/AFR UK | B99 WAR
CULTURE INSPECT LEGIT...INT/LAW 19/20 BOER/WAR. | DIPLOM
PAGE 16 E0309 | NAT/G

LEHMANN L. E1281

LEIBNITZ/G....GOTTFRIED WILHELM VON LEIBNITZ

HERRMANN K.,DAS STAATSDENKEN BEI LEIBNIZ. GP/REL | B58 NAT/G
ATTIT ORD/FREE...CONCPT IDEA/COMP 17 LEIBNITZ/G | JURID
CHURCH/STA. PAGE 52 E1034 | SECT
| EDU/PROP

LEISURE....UNOBLIGATED TIME EXPENDITURES

US LIBRARY OF CONGRESS,SOCIAL AND CULTURAL PROBLEMS | B42 BIBLIOG/A
IN WARTIME: APRIL 1941-MARCH 1942. WOR-45 CLIENT | WAR
SECT EDU/PROP CRIME LEISURE RACE/REL STRANGE ATTIT | SOC
DRIVE HEALTH...GEOG 20. PAGE 100 E2012 | CULTURE

US LIBRARY OF CONGRESS,SOCIAL AND CULTURAL PROBLEMS | B43 BIBLIOG/A
IN WARTIME: APRIL-DECEMBER (SUPPLEMENT 1). WOR-45 | WAR
SECT EDU/PROP CRIME LEISURE CIVMIL/REL RACE/REL | SOC
ATTIT DRIVE HEALTH...GEOG 20. PAGE 100 E2013 | CULTURE

US LIBRARY OF CONGRESS,SOCIAL AND CULTURAL PROBLEMS | B43 BIBLIOG/A
IN WARTIME: JANUARY-MAY 1943 (SUPPLEMENT 2). WOR-45 | WAR
FAM SECT PLAN EDU/PROP CRIME LEISURE RACE/REL DRIVE | SOC
HEALTH...GEOG 20 JEWS. PAGE 100 E2014 | CULTURE

MONEYPENNY P.,"UNIVERSITY PURPOSE, DISCIPLINE, AND | S67 ACADEM
DUE PROCESS." USA+45 EDU/PROP ADJUD LEISURE | AGE/Y
ORD/FREE. PAGE 74 E1484 | CONTROL
| ADMIN

LEITZ F. E1282

LENCZOWSKI G. E1283

LEND/LEASE....LEND-LEASE PROGRAM(S)

LENG S.C. E1284

LENIN/VI....VLADIMIR ILYICH LENIN

CHIU H.,"COMMUNIST CHINA'S ATTITUDE TOWARD | S66 INT/LAW
INTERNATIONAL LAW" CHINA/COM USSR LAW CONSTN DIPLOM | MARXISM
GP/REL 20 LENIN/VI. PAGE 22 E0431 | CONCPT
| IDEA/COMP

LENT G.E. E1285

LEONI B. E1286

LEPAWSKY A. E1287

LERNER M. E1288

LESAGE/J....J. LESAGE

LEVELLERS....LEVELLERS PARTY

LEVONTIN A.V. E1289

LEVY H.V. E1290

LEVY L.W. E1291,E1292

LEWIN J. E1293

LEWIS P.R. E1294

LEWIS/A....ARTHUR LEWIS

LEWIS/JL....JOHN L. LEWIS

LFNA....LEAGUE OF FREE NATIONS ASSOCIATION

LG/CO....LARGE COMPANY

PERSONNEL. USA+45 LAW LABOR LG/CO WORKER CREATE | N BIBLIOG/A
GOV/REL PERS/REL ATTIT WEALTH. PAGE 2 E0029 | ADMIN
| MGT
| GP/REL

GRIFFIN A.P.C.,A LIST OF BOOKS RELATING TO TRUSTS | B02 BIBLIOG/A
(2ND REV. ED.) (PAMPHLET). FRANCE GERMANY UK USA-45 | JURID
WOR-45 LAW ECO/DEV INDUS LG/CO NAT/G CAP/ISM | ECO/TAC
CENTRAL DISCRIM PWR LAISSEZ 19/20. PAGE 46 E0919 | VOL/ASSN

GRIFFIN A.P.C.,LIST OF MORE RECENT WORKS ON FEDERAL | B07 BIBLIOG/A
CONTROL OF COMMERCE AND CORPORATIONS (PAMPHLET). | NAT/G
USA-45 LAW ECO/DEV FINAN LG/CO TARIFFS TAX LICENSE | JURID
CENTRAL ORD/FREE WEALTH LAISSEZ 19/20. PAGE 47 | ECO/TAC
E0931

GRIFFIN A.P.C.,LIST OF WORKS RELATING TO GOVERNMENT | B08 BIBLIOG/A
REGULATION OF INSURANCE UNITED STATES AND FOREIGN | FINAN
COUNTRIES (2ND. ED.) (PAMPHLET). FRANCE GERMANY UK | LAW
USA-45 WOR-45 LG/CO LOC/G NAT/G LEGIS LICENSE ADJUD | CONTROL
LOBBY CENTRAL ORD/FREE 19/20. PAGE 47 E0933

BREWER D.J.,THE MOVEMENT OF COERCION (PAMPHLET). | N18 GP/REL
CONSTN INDUS ADJUD COERCE OWN WEALTH...OLD/LIB | LABOR
JURID 19 SUPREME/CT. PAGE 15 E0296 | LG/CO
| LAW

BUREAU OF NAT'L AFFAIRS INC.,A CURRENT LOOK AT: | N19 DISCRIM
(1) THE NEGRO AND TITLE VII, (2) SEX AND TITLE VII | SEX
(PAMPHLET). LAW LG/CO SML/CO RACE/REL...POLICY SOC | WORKER
STAT DEEP/QU TREND CON/ANAL CHARTS 20 NEGRO | MGT
CIV/RIGHTS. PAGE 17 E0334

MCCONNELL G.,THE STEEL SEIZURE OF 1952 (PAMPHLET). | N19 DELIB/GP
USA+45 FINAN INDUS PROC/MFG LG/CO EX/STRUC ADJUD | LABOR
CONTROL GP/REL ORD/FREE PWR 20 TRUMAN/HS PRESIDENT | PROB/SOLV
CONGRESS. PAGE 70 E1402 | NAT/G

LEITZ F.,DIE PUBLIZITAT DER AKTIENGESELLSCHAFT. | B29 LG/CO
BELGIUM FRANCE GERMANY UK FINAN PRESS GP/REL PROFIT | JURID
KNOWL 20. PAGE 64 E1282 | ECO/TAC
| NAT/COMP

CHENEY F.,CARTELS, COMBINES, AND TRUSTS: A SELECTED | B44 BIBLIOG/A
LIST OF REFERENCES. GERMANY UK USA-45 WOR-45 | LG/CO
DELIB/GP OP/RES BARGAIN CAP/ISM ECO/TAC INT/TRADE | ECO/DEV
LICENSE LEGIT CONFER PRICE 20. PAGE 22 E0428 | INDUS

FULLER G.H.,RENEGOTIATION OF WAR CONTRACTS: A | B44 BIBLIOG
SELECTED LIST OF REFERENCES (PAMPHLET). USA-45 | WAR
ECO/DEV LG/CO NAT/G OP/RES PLAN BAL/PWR LEGIT | LAW
CONTROL...MGT 20. PAGE 42 E0823 | FINAN

COOKE C.A.,CORPORATION TRUST AND COMPANY: AN ESSAY | B51 LG/CO
IN LEGAL HISTORY. UK STRUCT LEGIS CAP/ISM GP/REL | FINAN
PROFIT 13/20 COMPNY/ACT. PAGE 25 E0499 | ECO/TAC
| JURID

FRIEDMANN W.,LAW AND SOCIAL CHANGE IN CONTEMPORARY | B51 LAW
BRITAIN. UK LABOR LG/CO LEGIS JUDGE CT/SYS ORD/FREE | ADJUD
NEW/LIB...DECISION JURID TREND METH/COMP BIBLIOG 20 | SOCIETY
PARLIAMENT ENGLSH/LAW COMMON/LAW. PAGE 40 E0802 | CONSTN

B52
ANDREWS F.E.,CORPORATION GIVING. LAW TAX EDU/PROP
ADMIN...POLICY STAT CHARTS. PAGE 5 E0096
LG/CO
GIVE
SML/CO
FINAN

B54
FRIEDMAN W.,THE PUBLIC CORPORATION: A COMPARATIVE
SYMPOSIUM (UNIVERSITY OF TORONTO SCHOOL OF LAW
COMPARATIVE LAW SERIES, VOL. I). SWEDEN USA+45
INDUS INT/ORG NAT/G REGION CENTRAL FEDERAL...POLICY
JURID IDEA/COMP NAT/COMP ANTHOL 20 COMMONWLTH
MONOPOLY EUROPE. PAGE 40 E0801
LAW
SOCISM
LG/CO
OWN

B55
BERNSTEIN M.H.,REGULATING BUSINESS BY INDEPENDENT
COMMISSION. USA+45 USA-45 LG/CO CHIEF LEGIS
PROB/SOLV ADJUD SANCTION GP/REL ATTIT...TIME/SEQ
19/20 MONOPOLY PRESIDENT CONGRESS. PAGE 11 E0214
DELIB/GP
CONTROL
CONSULT

B55
SERRANO MOSCOSO E.,A STATEMENT OF THE LAWS OF
ECUADOR IN MATTERS AFFECTING BUSINESS (2ND ED.).
ECUADOR INDUS LABOR LG/CO NAT/G LEGIS TAX CONTROL
MARRIAGE 20. PAGE 90 E1805
FINAN
ECO/UNDEV
LAW
CONSTN

B57
BERLE A.A. JR.,ECONOMIC POWER AND FREE SOCIETY
(PAMPHLET). CLIENT CONSTN EX/STRUC ECO/TAC CONTROL
PARTIC PWR WEALTH MAJORIT. PAGE 11 E0205
LG/CO
CAP/ISM
INGP/REL
LEGIT

B58
WHITNEY S.N.,ANTITRUST POLICIES: AMERICAN
EXPERIENCE IN TWENTY INDUSTRIES. USA+45 USA-45 LAW
DELIB/GP LEGIS ADJUD CT/SYS GOV/REL ATTIT...ANTHOL
20 MONOPOLY CASEBOOK. PAGE 106 E2119
INDUS
CONTROL
LG/CO
MARKET

B59
FERRY W.H.,THE CORPORATION AND THE ECONOMY. CLIENT
LAW CONSTN LABOR NAT/G PLAN INT/TRADE PARTIC CONSEN
ORD/FREE PWR POLICY. PAGE 37 E0742
LG/CO
CONTROL
REPRESENT

B60
MUTHESIUS V.,DAS GESPENST DER WIRTSCHAFTLICHEN
MACHT. GERMANY/W ECO/DEV FINAN MARKET TAX...JURID
20. PAGE 75 E1513
ECO/TAC
NAT/G
CONCPT
LG/CO

B61
RUEDA B.,A STATEMENT OF THE LAWS OF COLOMBIA IN
MATTERS AFFECTING BUSINESS (3RD ED.). INDUS FAM
LABOR LG/CO NAT/G LEGIS TAX CONTROL MARRIAGE 20
COLOMB. PAGE 86 E1733
FINAN
ECO/UNDEV
LAW
CONSTN

L62
N,"UNION INVESTMENT IN BUSINESS: A SOURCE OF UNION
CONFLICT OF INTEREST." LAW NAT/G LEGIS CONTROL
GP/REL INGP/REL DECISION. PAGE 76 E1515
LABOR
POLICY
FINAN
LG/CO

N62
US SENATE COMM ON JUDICIARY,LEGISLATION TO
STRENGTHEN PENALTIES UNDER THE ANTITRUST LAWS
(PAMPHLET). USA+45 LG/CO CONFER CONTROL SANCTION
ORD/FREE 20 SENATE MONOPOLY. PAGE 102 E2045
LEAD
ADJUD
INDUS
ECO/TAC

B63
PATRA A.C.,THE ADMINISTRATION OF JUSTICE UNDER THE
EAST INDIA COMPANY IN BENGAL, BIHAR AND ORISSA.
INDIA UK LG/CO CAP/ISM INT/TRADE ADJUD COLONIAL
CONTROL CT/SYS...POLICY 20. PAGE 80 E1602
ADMIN
JURID
CONCPT

B63
US SENATE COMM ON JUDICIARY,ADMINISTERED PRICES.
USA+45 RATION ADJUD CONTROL LOBBY...POLICY 20
SENATE MONOPOLY. PAGE 102 E2047
LG/CO
PRICE
ADMIN
DECISION

B64
US SENATE COMM ON JUDICIARY,HEARINGS BEFORE
SUBCOMMITTEE ON ANTITRUST AND MONOPOLY: ECONOMIC
CONCENTRATION VOLUMES 1-5 JULY 1964-SEPT 1966.
USA+45 LAW FINAN ECO/TAC ADJUD COST EFFICIENCY
PRODUC...STAT CHARTS 20 CONGRESS MONOPOLY. PAGE 102
E2052
ECO/DEV
CONTROL
MARKET
LG/CO

S64
N,"QUASI-LEGISLATIVE ARBITRATION AGREEMENTS." LAW
LG/CO ECO/TAC SANCTION ATTIT POLICY. PAGE 76 E1516
ADJUD
ADJUST
LABOR
GP/REL

B66
FENN DH J.R.,BUSINESS DECISION MAKING AND
GOVERNMENT POLICY. SERV/IND LEGIS LICENSE ADMIN
DECISION
PLAN

CONTROL GP/REL INGP/REL 20 CASEBOOK. PAGE 37 E0736
NAT/G
LG/CO

B66
GRUNEWALD D.,PUBLIC POLICY AND THE MODERN
COOPERATION: SELECTED READINGS. USA+45 LAW MARKET
VOL/ASSN CAP/ISM INT/TRADE CENTRAL OWN...SOC ANTHOL
20. PAGE 48 E0954
LG/CO
POLICY
NAT/G
CONTROL

B66
SZLADITS C.,A BIBLIOGRAPHY ON FOREIGN AND
COMPARATIVE LAW (SUPPLEMENT 1964). FINAN FAM LABOR
LG/CO LEGIS JUDGE ADMIN CRIME...CRIMLGY 20. PAGE 95
E1905
BIBLIOG/A
CT/SYS
INT/LAW

B67
BEAL E.F.,THE PRACTICE OF COLLECTIVE BARGAINING
(3RD ED.). USA+45 WOR+45 ECO/DEV INDUS LG/CO
PROF/ORG WORKER ECO/TAC GP/REL WEALTH...JURID
METH/CNCPT. PAGE 8 E0160
BARGAIN
MGT
LABOR
ADJUD

B67
GABRIEL P.P.,THE INTERNATIONAL TRANSFER OF
CORPORATE SKILLS: MANAGEMENT CONTRACTS IN LESS
DEVELOPED COUNTRIES. CLIENT INDUS LG/CO PLAN
PROB/SOLV CAP/ISM ECO/TAC FOR/AID INT/TRADE RENT
ADMIN SKILL 20. PAGE 42 E0825
ECO/UNDEV
AGREE
MGT
CONSULT

L67
LAMBERT J.D.,"CORPORATE POLITICAL SPENDING AND
CAMPAIGN FINANCE." LAW CONSTN FINAN LABOR LG/CO
LOC/G NAT/G VOL/ASSN TEC/DEV ADJUD ADMIN PARTIC.
PAGE 62 E1247
USA+45
POL/PAR
CHOOSE
COST

S67
RICHARDSON J.J.,"THE MAKING OF THE RESTRICTIVE
TRADE PRACTICES ACT 1956 A CASE STUDY OF THE POLICY
PROCESS IN BRITAIN." UK FINAN MARKET LG/CO POL/PAR
CONSULT PRESS ADJUD ADMIN AGREE LOBBY SANCTION
ATTIT 20. PAGE 84 E1695
LEGIS
ECO/TAC
POLICY
INDUS

S67
WRAITH R.E.,"ADMINISTRATIVE CHANGE IN THE NEW
AFRICA." AFR LG/CO ADJUD INGP/REL PWR...RECORD
GP/COMP 20. PAGE 107 E2147
ADMIN
NAT/G
LOC/G
ECO/UNDEV

LIB/INTRNT....LIBERAL INTERNATIONAL

LIB/PARTY....LIBERAL PARTY (ALL NATIONS)

LIBERALISM....SEE NEW/LIB, WELF/ST, OLD/LIB, LAISSEZ

LIBERIA....SEE ALSO AFR

LIBERTY....SEE ORD/FREE

LIBRARY INTERNATIONAL REL E1295

LIBYA....SEE ALSO ISLAM

LICENSE....LEGAL PERMIT

B03
GRIFFIN A.P.C.,SELECT LIST OF BOOKS ON LABOR
PARTICULARLY RELATING TO STRIKES. FRANCE GERMANY
MOD/EUR UK USA-45 LAW NAT/G DELIB/GP WORKER BARGAIN
LICENSE PAY ADJUD 19/20. PAGE 46 E0924
BIBLIOG/A
GP/REL
MGT
LABOR

B04
GRIFFIN A.P.C.,A LIST OF BOOKS RELATING TO
RAILROADS IN THEIR RELATION TO THE GOVERNMENT AND
THE PUBLIC (PAMPHLET). USA-45 LAW ECO/DEV NAT/G
TEC/DEV CAP/ISM LICENSE CENTRAL LAISSEZ...DECISION
19/20. PAGE 47 E0925
BIBLIOG/A
SERV/IND
ADJUD
ECO/TAC

B07
GRIFFIN A.P.C.,LIST OF MORE RECENT WORKS ON FEDERAL
CONTROL OF COMMERCE AND CORPORATIONS (PAMPHLET).
USA-45 LAW ECO/DEV FINAN LG/CO TARIFFS TAX LICENSE
CENTRAL ORD/FREE WEALTH LAISSEZ 19/20. PAGE 47
E0931
BIBLIOG/A
NAT/G
JURID
ECO/TAC

B08
GRIFFIN A.P.C.,LIST OF WORKS RELATING TO GOVERNMENT
REGULATION OF INSURANCE UNITED STATES AND FOREIGN
COUNTRIES (2ND. ED.) (PAMPHLET). FRANCE GERMANY UK
USA-45 WOR-45 LG/CO LOC/G NAT/G LEGIS LICENSE ADJUD
LOBBY CENTRAL ORD/FREE 19/20. PAGE 47 E0933
BIBLIOG/A
FINAN
LAW
CONTROL

B10
COLORADO CIVIL SERVICE COMN,SECOND BIENNIAL REPORT
TO THE GOVERNOR, 1909-1910. USA+45 DELIB/GP LEGIS
LICENSE PAY 20 COLORADO CIVIL/SERV. PAGE 24 E0477
PROVS
LOC/G
ADMIN

FOUAD M.,LE REGIME DE LA PRESSE EN EGYPTE: THESE POUR LE DOCTORAT. UAR LICENSE EDU/PROP ADMIN SANCTION CRIME SUPEGO PWR...ART/METH JURID 19/20. PAGE 39 E0778
WORKER
B12
ORD/FREE
LEGIS
CONTROL
PRESS

SALMOND J.W.,JURISPRUDENCE. UK LOC/G NAT/G LEGIS PROB/SOLV LICENSE LEGIT CRIME PERS/REL OWN ORD/FREE ...T 20. PAGE 87 E1742
B16
LAW
CT/SYS
JURID
ADJUD

CLYDE W.M.,THE STRUGGLE FOR THE FREEDOM OF THE PRESS FROM CAXTON TO CROMWELL. UK LAW LOC/G SECT FORCES LICENSE WRITING SANCTION REV ATTIT PWR ...POLICY 15/17 PARLIAMENT CROMWELL/O MILTON/J. PAGE 23 E0460
B34
PRESS
ORD/FREE
CONTROL

HANSON L.,GOVERNMENT AND THE PRESS 1695-1763. UK LOC/G LEGIS LICENSE CONTROL SANCTION CRIME ATTIT ORD/FREE 17/18 PARLIAMENT AMEND/I. PAGE 50 E0996
B36
LAW
JURID
PRESS
POLICY

GILMORE M.P.,ARGUMENT FROM ROMAN LAW IN POLITICAL THOUGHT, 1200-1600. INTELL LICENSE CONTROL CT/SYS GOV/REL PRIVIL PWR...IDEA/COMP BIBLIOG 13/16. PAGE 44 E0866
B41
JURID
LAW
CONCPT
NAT/G

CHENEY F.,CARTELS, COMBINES, AND TRUSTS: A SELECTED LIST OF REFERENCES. GERMANY UK USA-45 WOR-45 DELIB/GP OP/RES BARGAIN CAP/ISM ECO/TAC INT/TRADE LICENSE LEGIT CONFER PRICE 20. PAGE 22 E0428
B44
BIBLIOG/A
LG/CO
ECO/DEV
INDUS

US LIBRARY OF CONGRESS,FREEDOM OF INFORMATION: SELECTIVE REPORT ON RECENT WRITINGS. USA+45 LAW CONSTN ELITES EDU/PROP PRESS LOBBY WAR TOTALISM ATTIT 20 UN UNESCO COLD/WAR. PAGE 101 E2018
B49
BIBLIOG/A
ORD/FREE
LICENSE
COM/IND

GIBBS C.R.,CONSTITUTIONAL AND STATUTORY PROVISIONS OF THE STATES (VOL. IX). USA+45 LICENSE ADJUD LEAD 20. PAGE 43 E0857
B51
PROVS
CONSTN
JURID
LOBBY

COUNCIL STATE GOVERNMENTS,OCCUPATIONAL LICENSING IN THE STATES. USA+45 PROVS ADMIN EXEC LOBBY 20. PAGE 27 E0526
B52
PROF/ORG
LICENSE
REPRESENT
EX/STRUC

NELSON H.L.,LIBEL IN NEWS OF CONGRESSIONAL INVESTIGATING COMMITTEES. USA+45 LAW PARL/PROC PRIVIL RESPECT HOUSE/REP. PAGE 76 E1532
B61
DELIB/GP
LEGIS
LICENSE
PRESS

SWAYZE H.,POLITICAL CONTROL OF LITERATURE IN THE USSR, 1946-1959. USSR NAT/G CREATE LICENSE...JURID 20. PAGE 95 E1898
B62
MARXISM
WRITING
CONTROL
DOMIN

BURRUS B.R.,ADMINSTRATIVE LAW AND LOCAL GOVERNMENT. USA+45 PROVS LEGIS LICENSE ADJUD ORD/FREE 20. PAGE 18 E0347
B63
EX/STRUC
LOC/G
JURID
CONSTN

SZLADITS C.,BIBLIOGRAPHY ON FOREIGN AND COMPARATIVE LAW: BOOKS AND ARTICLES IN ENGLISH (SUPPLEMENT 1962). FINAN INDUS JUDGE LICENSE ADMIN CT/SYS PARL/PROC OWN...INT/LAW CLASSIF METH/COMP NAT/COMP 20. PAGE 95 E1904
B64
BIBLIOG/A
JURID
ADJUD
LAW

DIZARD W.P.,TELEVISION* A WORLD VIEW. WOR+45 ECO/UNDEV TEC/DEV LICENSE LITERACY...STAT OBS INT QU TREND AUD/VIS BIBLIOG. PAGE 32 E0632
B66
COM/IND
ACT/RES
EDU/PROP
CREATE

FENN DH J.R.,BUSINESS DECISION MAKING AND GOVERNMENT POLICY. SERV/IND LEGIS LICENSE ADMIN CONTROL GP/REL INGP/REL 20 CASEBOOK. PAGE 37 E0736
B66
DECISION
PLAN
NAT/G
LG/CO

MC CONNELL J.P.,LAW AND BUSINESS: PATTERNS AND
B66
ECO/DEV

ISSUES IN COMMERCIAL LAW. USA+45 USA-45 LOC/G WORKER LICENSE CRIME REPRESENT GP/REL 20. PAGE 70 E1397
JURID
ADJUD
MGT

ELDRIDGE W.B.,NARCOTICS AND THE LAW: A CRITIQUE OF THE AMERICAN EXPERIMENT IN NARCOTIC DRUG CONTROL. PUB/INST ACT/RES PLAN LICENSE GP/REL EFFICIENCY ATTIT HEALTH...CRIMLGY HEAL STAT 20 ABA DEPT/HEW NARCO/ACT. PAGE 34 E0679
B67
LAW
INSPECT
BIO/SOC
JURID

DEUTSCH E.P.,"A JUDICIAL PATH TO WORLD PEACE." FUT WOR+45 CONSTN PROB/SOLV DIPLOM LICENSE ADJUD SANCTION CHOOSE REPRESENT NAT/LISM SOVEREIGN 20 ICJ. PAGE 31 E0611
S67
INT/LAW
INT/ORG
JURID
PEACE

WILLIG S.H.,"THE CONTROL OVER INTERSTATE DISTRIBUTION AND USE OF INVESTIGATIONAL DRUGS (IN THE UNITED STATES)" USA+45 NAT/G INT/TRADE LICENSE. PAGE 106 E2124
S67
DIST/IND
HEALTH
CONTROL
DELIB/GP

WILSON G.D.,"CRIMINAL SANCTIONS AGAINST PASSPORT AREA-RESTRICTION VIOLATIONS." USA+45 ADJUD CRIME GOV/REL DEPT/STATE CONGRESS. PAGE 106 E2127
S67
LAW
SANCTION
LICENSE
POLICY

POLLOCK F.,THE HISTORY OF ENGLISH LAW BEFORE THE TIME OF EDWARD I (2 VOLS, 2ND ED.). UK CULTURE LOC/G LEGIS LICENSE AGREE CONTROL CT/SYS SANCTION CRIME...TIME/SEQ 13 COMMON/LAW CANON/LAW. PAGE 81 E1626
B98
LAW
ADJUD
JURID

LIEBESNY H.J. E1210

LIECHTENST....LIECHTENSTEIN; SEE ALSO APPROPRIATE TIME/SPACE/CULTURE INDEX

LIGGETT E. E1296

LIGHTFT/PM....PHIL M. LIGHTFOOT

TAPER B.,GOMILLION VERSUS LIGHTFOOT: THE TUSKEGEE GERRYMANDER CASE. USA+45 LAW CONSTN LOC/G MUNIC CT/SYS 20 NEGRO CIV/RIGHTS GOMILLN/CG LIGHTFT/PM TUSKEGEE. PAGE 95 E1908
B62
APPORT
REPRESENT
RACE/REL
ADJUD

LIKERT/R....RENSIS LIKERT

LILLICH R.B. E1297,E1298

LILLY W.S. E1299

LIN/PIAO....LIN PIAO

LINCOLN G.A. E1589

LINCOLN/A....PRESIDENT ABRAHAM LINCOLN

LINDAHL/E....ERIK LINDAHL

LINDESMITH A. E0461

LING....LINGUISTICS, LANGUAGE

AFRICAN BIBLIOGRAPHIC CENTER,A CURRENT BIBLIOGRAPHY ON AFRICAN AFFAIRS. LAW CULTURE ECO/UNDEV LABOR SECT DIPLOM FOR/AID COLONIAL NAT/LISM...LING 20. PAGE 3 E0053
N
BIBLIOG/A
AFR
NAT/G
REGION

US BUREAU OF THE CENSUS,BIBLIOGRAPHY OF SOCIAL SCIENCE PERIODICALS AND MONOGRAPH SERIES. WOR+45 LAW DIPLOM EDU/PROP HEALTH...PSY SOC LING STAT. PAGE 99 E1980
N
BIBLIOG/A
CULTURE
NAT/G
SOCIETY

FAGUET E.,LE LIBERALISME. FRANCE PRESS ADJUD ADMIN DISCRIM CONSERVE SOCISM...TRADIT SOC LING WORSHIP PARLIAMENT. PAGE 36 E0711
B03
ORD/FREE
EDU/PROP
NAT/G
LAW

PRATT I.A.,MODERN EGYPT: A LIST OF REFERENCES TO MATERIAL IN THE NEW YORK PUBLIC LIBRARY. UAR ECO/UNDEV...GEOG JURID SOC LING 20. PAGE 82 E1647
B29
BIBLIOG
ISLAM
DIPLOM
NAT/G

HAMILTON W.H.,THE POWER TO GOVERN. ECO/DEV FINAN INDUS ECO/TAC INT/TRADE TARIFFS TAX CONTROL CT/SYS
B37
LING
CONSTN

WAR COST PWR 18/20 SUPREME/CT. PAGE 50 E0991   NAT/G
                                                               POLICY

LAW

                                                    B44
US LIBRARY OF CONGRESS,RUSSIA: A CHECK LIST   BIBLIOG
PRELIMINARY TO A BASIC BIBLIOGRAPHY OF MATERIALS IN   LAW
THE RUSSIAN LANGUAGE. COM USSR CULTURE EDU/PROP   SECT
MARXISM...ART/METH HUM LING 19/20. PAGE 101 E2015

                                                                                                    B64
                                                    HOHFELD W.N.,FUNDAMENTAL LEGAL CONCEPTIONS.   JURID
                                                    PROB/SOLV OWN PWR...DECISION LING IDEA/COMP   ADJUD
                                                    GEN/METH. PAGE 54 E1069   LAW
                                                                                                       METH/CNCPT
                                                    B46
AMERICAN DOCUMENTATION INST,CATALOGUE OF AUXILIARY   BIBLIOG
PUBLICATIONS IN MICROFILMS AND PHOTOPRINTS. USA-45   EDU/PROP
LAW AGRI CREATE TEC/DEV ADMIN...GEOG LING MATH 20.   PSY
PAGE 4 E0077

                                                                                                    B64
                                                    RAGHAVAN M.D.,INDIA IN CEYLONESE HISTORY, SOCIETY DIPLOM
                                                    AND CULTURE. CEYLON INDIA S/ASIA LAW SOCIETY   CULTURE
                                                    INT/TRADE ATTIT...ART/METH JURID SOC LING 20.   SECT
                                                    PAGE 83 E1668   STRUCT
                                                    S47
FRANKFURTER F.,"SOME REFLECTIONS ON THE READING OF   JURID
STATUTES" USA+45 USA-45 PROB/SOLV CT/SYS TASK   LAW
EFFICIENCY...LING 20. PAGE 40 E0791   ADJUD
                                                      WRITING

                                                                                                    B65
                                                    HAENSCH G.,PAN-AFRICANISM IN ACTION: AN ACCOUNT OF DICTIONARY
                                                    THE UAM TIC AND ALPHABETICAL IN GERMAN, ENGLISH,   DIPLOM
                                                    FRENCH AND SPANISH. WOR+45 INT/ORG NAT/G ARMS/CONT LING
                                                    WAR...INT/LAW IDEA/COMP TREATY. PAGE 49 E0974
                                                    B49
GROB F.,THE RELATIVITY OF WAR AND PEACE: A STUDY IN   WAR
LAW, HISTORY, AND POLITICS. WOR+45 WOR-45 LAW   PEACE
DIPLOM DEBATE...CONCPT LING IDEA/COMP BIBLIOG   INT/LAW
18/20. PAGE 48 E0944   STYLE

                                                                                                    B65
                                                    HARTUNG F.E.,CRIME, LAW, AND SOCIETY. LAW PUB/INST PERCEPT
                                                    CRIME PERS/REL AGE/Y BIO/SOC PERSON ROLE SUPEGO   CRIMLGY
                                                    ...LING GP/COMP GEN/LAWS 20. PAGE 50 E1004   DRIVE
                                                                                                       CONTROL
                                                    B50
EMBREE J.F.,BIBLIOGRAPHY OF THE PEOPLES AND   BIBLIOG/A
CULTURES OF MAINLAND SOUTHEAST ASIA. CAMBODIA LAOS   CULTURE
THAILAND VIETNAM LAW...GEOG HUM SOC MYTH LING   S/ASIA
CHARTS WORSHIP 20. PAGE 35 E0686

                                                                                                    B66
                                                    BRAIBANTI R.,RESEARCH ON THE BUREAUCRACY OF   HABITAT
                                                    PAKISTAN. PAKISTAN LAW CULTURE INTELL ACADEM LOC/G NAT/G
                                                    SECT PRESS CT/SYS...LING CHARTS 20 BUREAUCRCY.   ADMIN
                                                    PAGE 15 E0286   CONSTN
                                                    B54
AUSTIN J.,THE PROVINCE OF JURISPRUDENCE DETERMINED   CONCPT
AND THE USES OF THE STUDY OF JURISPRUDENCE. MORAL   LAW
...CLASSIF LING STYLE 19. PAGE 6 E0119   JURID
                                                      GEN/LAWS

                                                                                                    B66
                                                    GHOSH P.K.,THE CONSTITUTION OF INDIA: HOW IT HAS   CONSTN
                                                    BEEN FRAMED. INDIA LOC/G DELIB/GP EX/STRUC   NAT/G
                                                    PROB/SOLV BUDGET INT/TRADE CT/SYS CHOOSE...LING 20. LEGIS
                                                    PAGE 43 E0854   FEDERAL
                                                    B54
BENTLEY A.F.,INQUIRY INTO INQUIRIES: ESSAYS IN   EPIST
SOCIAL THEORY. UNIV LEGIS ADJUD ADMIN LOBBY   SOC
...PHIL/SCI PSY NEW/IDEA LING METH 20. PAGE 10   CONCPT
E0200

                                                                                                    B66
                                                    US DEPARTMENT OF STATE,RESEARCH ON AFRICA (EXTERNAL BIBLIOG/A
                                                    RESEARCH LIST NO 5-25). LAW CULTURE ECO/UNDEV   ASIA
                                                    POL/PAR DIPLOM EDU/PROP LEAD REGION MARXISM...GEOG S/ASIA
                                                    LING WORSHIP 20. PAGE 100 E1996   NAT/G
                                                    B55
TROTIER A.H.,DOCTORAL DISSERTATIONS ACCEPTED BY   BIBLIOG
AMERICAN UNIVERSITIES 1954-55. SECT DIPLOM HEALTH   ACADEM
...ART/METH GEOG INT/LAW SOC LING CHARTS 20.   USA+45
PAGE 97 E1943   WRITING

                                                                                                    B66
                                                    US DEPARTMENT OF STATE,RESEARCH ON THE USSR AND   BIBLIOG/A
                                                    EASTERN EUROPE (EXTERNAL RESEARCH LIST NO 1-25).   EUR+WWI
                                                    USSR LAW CULTURE SOCIETY NAT/G TEC/DEV DIPLOM   COM
                                                    EDU/PROP REGION...GEOG LING. PAGE 100 E1997   MARXISM
                                                    B56
RECASENS SICHES S.,TRATADO GENERAL DE SOCIOLOGIA.   SOC
CULTURE FAM NEIGH LEAD RACE/REL DISCRIM HABITAT   STRATA
ORD/FREE...JURID LING T SOC/INTEG 20. PAGE 84 E1677   KIN
                                                      GP/REL

                                                                                                    B66
                                                    WALL E.H.,THE COURT OF JUSTICE IN THE EUROPEAN   CT/SYS
                                                    COMMUNITIES: JURISDICTION AND PROCEDURE. EUR+WWI   INT/ORG
                                                    DIPLOM ADJUD ADMIN ROUTINE TASK...CONCPT LING 20.   LAW
                                                    PAGE 105 E2096   OP/RES
                                                    B57
BYRNES R.F.,BIBLIOGRAPHY OF AMERICAN PUBLICATIONS   BIBLIOG/A
ON EAST CENTRAL EUROPE, 1945-1957 (VOL. XXII). SECT   COM
DIPLOM EDU/PROP RACE/REL...ART/METH GEOG JURID SOC   MARXISM
LING 20 JEWS. PAGE 18 E0354   NAT/G

                                                                                                    S66
                                                    MATTHEWS D.G.,"ETHIOPIAN OUTLINE: A BIBLIOGRAPHIC   BIBLIOG
                                                    RESEARCH GUIDE." ETHIOPIA LAW STRUCT ECO/UNDEV AGRI NAT/G
                                                    LABOR SECT CHIEF DELIB/GP EX/STRUC ADMIN...LING   DIPLOM
                                                    ORG/CHARTS 20. PAGE 69 E1384   POL/PAR
                                                    B58
ORTIZ R.P.,ANNUARIO BIBLIOGRAFICO COLOMBIANO,   BIBLIOG
1951-1956. LAW RECEIVE EDU/PROP ADMIN...LING STAT   SOC
20 COLOMB. PAGE 79 E1582

                                                                                                    S66
                                                    SHEEHY E.P.,"SELECTED REFERENCE BOOKS OF   BIBLIOG/A
                                                    1965-1966." AGRI PERF/ART PRESS...GEOG HUM JURID   INDEX
                                                    SOC LING WORSHIP. PAGE 91 E1817   CLASSIF
                                                    L60
MILLER A.S.,"THE MYTH OF NEUTRALITY IN   ADJUD
CONSTITUTIONAL ADJUDICATION." LAW...DECISION JURID   CONSTN
LING TREND IDEA/COMP. PAGE 73 E1456   MYTH
                                                      UTIL

                                                    LINGUISTICS....SEE LING

                                                    LINK/AS....ARTHUR S. LINK
                                                    N61
VINER J.,THE INTELLECTUAL HISTORY OF LAISSEZ FAIRE   ATTIT
(PAMPHLET). WOR+45 WOR-45 LAW INTELL...POLICY LING   EDU/PROP
LOG 19/20. PAGE 104 E2077   LAISSEZ
                                                      ECO/TAC

                                                                                                    S66
                                                    GASS O.,"THE LITERATURE OF AMERICAN GOVERNMENT."   NEW/LIB
                                                    CONSTN DRIVE ORD/FREE...JURID CONCPT METH/CNCPT   CT/SYS
                                                    IDEA/COMP 20 WILSON/W BEARD/CA LINK/AS. PAGE 42   NAT/G
                                                    E0841
                                                    B62
FRIEDRICH C.J.,NOMOS V: THE PUBLIC INTEREST. UNIV   METH/CNCPT
ECO/TAC ADJUD UTIL ATTIT...POLICY LING LOG GEN/LAWS   CONCPT
20. PAGE 41 E0808   LAW
                                                      IDEA/COMP

                                                    B63
CHOJNACKI S.,REGISTER ON CURRENT RESEARCH ON   BIBLIOG
ETHIOPIA AND THE HORN OF AFRICA. ETHIOPIA LAW   ACT/RES
CULTURE AGRI SECT EDU/PROP ADMIN...GEOG HEAL LING   INTELL
20. PAGE 22 E0433   ACADEM

                                                                                                    B63
                                                    CRAIG A.,SUPPRESSED BOOKS: A HISTORY OF THE   BIBLIOG/A
                                                    CONCEPTION OF LITERARY OBSCENITY. WOR+45 WOR-45   LAW
                                                    CREATE EDU/PROP LITERACY ATTIT...ART/METH PSY   SEX
                                                    CONCPT 20. PAGE 27 E0538   CONTROL
                                                    B63
FISCHER-GALATI S.A.,RUMANIA; A BIBLIOGRAPHIC GUIDE   BIBLIOG/A
(PAMPHLET). ROMANIA INTELL ECO/DEV LABOR SECT   NAT/G
WEALTH...GEOG SOC/WK LING 20. PAGE 38 E0756   COM

B66
DIZARD W.P.,TELEVISION* A WORLD VIEW. WOR+45   COM/IND
ECO/UNDEV TEC/DEV LICENSE LITERACY...STAT OBS INT   ACT/RES
QU TREND AUD/VIS BIBLIOG. PAGE 32 E0632   EDU/PROP
                                                    CREATE

LITERARY ANALYSIS....SEE HUM

LITHUANIA....SEE ALSO USSR

B63
GSOUSKI V.,LEGAL SOURCES AND BIBLIOGRAPHY OF THE   BIBLIOG
BALTIC STATES (ESTONIA, LATVIA, LITHUANIA). COM   ADJUD
ESTONIA LATVIA LITHUANIA NAT/G LEGIS CT/SYS   LAW
SANCTION CRIME 20. PAGE 48 E0957   JURID

B63
KLESMENT J.,LEGAL SOURCES AND BIBLIOGRAPHY OF THE   BIBLIOG/A
BALTIC STATES (ESTONIA, LATVIA, LITHUANIA). COM   JURID
ESTONIA LATVIA LITHUANIA LAW FINAN ADJUD CT/SYS   CONSTN
REGION CENTRAL MARXISM 19/20. PAGE 61 E1223   ADMIN

LITTLEFIELD N. E1308

LIU/SHAO....LIU SHAO-CHI

LIVELY E. E1309

LIVINGSTON W.S. E1310

LIVNEH E. E1311

LIVNGSTN/D....DAVID LIVINGSTON

LIVY....LIVY

LLEWELLYN K.N. E1312,E1313

LLOYD/HD....HENRY D. LLOYD

LLOYD-GEO/D....DAVID LLOYD GEORGE

LOANS....SEE RENT+GIVE+FOR/AID+FINAN

LOBBY....PRESSURE GROUP

B08
GRIFFIN A.P.C.,LIST OF WORKS RELATING TO GOVERNMENT BIBLIOG/A
REGULATION OF INSURANCE UNITED STATES AND FOREIGN   FINAN
COUNTRIES (2ND. ED.) (PAMPHLET). FRANCE GERMANY UK   LAW
USA-45 WOR-45 LG/CO LOC/G NAT/G LEGIS LICENSE ADJUD CONTROL
LOBBY CENTRAL ORD/FREE 19/20. PAGE 47 E0933

N19
THE REGIONAL DIRECTOR AND THE PRESS (PAMPHLET).   PRESS
USA-45 COM/IND LOBBY ROLE 20 NLRB CINCINNATI   LABOR
BILL/RIGHT. PAGE 2 E0031   ORD/FREE
                                                    EDU/PROP

N19
CARPER E.T.,LOBBYING AND THE NATURAL GAS BILL   LOBBY
(PAMPHLET). USA+45 SERV/IND BARGAIN PAY DRIVE ROLE   ADJUD
WEALTH 20 CONGRESS SENATE EISNHWR/DD. PAGE 20 E0389 TRIBUTE
                                                    NAT/G

N19
HOGARTY R.A.,NEW JERSEY FARMERS AND MIGRANT HOUSING AGRI
RULES (PAMPHLET). USA+45 LAW ELITES FACE/GP LABOR   PROVS
PROF/ORG LOBBY PERS/REL RIGID/FLEX ROLE 20   WORKER
NEW/JERSEY. PAGE 53 E1067   HEALTH

L34
LLEWELLYN K.N.,"THE CONSTITUTION AS AN INSTITUTION" CONSTN
(BMR)" USA-45 PROB/SOLV LOBBY REPRESENT...DECISION   LAW
JURID 18/20 SUPREME/CT. PAGE 66 E1313   CONCPT
                                                    CT/SYS

B41
GELLHORN W.,FEDERAL ADMINISTRATIVE PROCEEDINGS.   EX/STRUC
USA+45 CLIENT FACE/GP NAT/G LOBBY REPRESENT PWR 20. LAW
PAGE 43 E0844   ADJUD
                                                    POLICY

B46
CORRY J.A.,DEMOCRATIC GOVERNMENT AND POLITICS.   NAT/G
WOR-45 EX/STRUC LOBBY TOTALISM...MAJORIT CONCPT   CONSTN
METH/COMP NAT/COMP 20. PAGE 26 E0511   POL/PAR
                                                    JURID

B47
HOCKING W.E.,FREEDOM OF THE PRESS: A FRAMEWORK OF   ORD/FREE
PRINCIPLE. WOR-45 SOCIETY NAT/G PROB/SOLV DEBATE   CONSTN
LOBBY...JURID PSY 20 AMEND/I. PAGE 53 E1061   PRESS
                                                    LAW

C48
WALKER H.,"THE LEGISLATIVE PROCESS; LAWMAKING IN   PARL/PROC
THE UNITED STATES." NAT/G POL/PAR PROVS EX/STRUC   LEGIS
OP/RES PROB/SOLV CT/SYS LOBBY GOV/REL...CHARTS   LAW
BIBLIOG T 18/20 CONGRESS. PAGE 105 E2094   CONSTN

B49
APPLEBY P.H.,POLICY AND ADMINISTRATION. USA+45   REPRESENT
NAT/G LOBBY PWR 20. PAGE 5 E0101   EXEC
                                                    ADMIN
                                                    CLIENT

B49
US LIBRARY OF CONGRESS,FREEDOM OF INFORMATION: BIBLIOG/A
SELECTIVE REPORT ON RECENT WRITINGS. USA+45 LAW   ORD/FREE
CONSTN ELITES EDU/PROP PRESS LOBBY WAR TOTALISM   LICENSE
ATTIT 20 UN UNESCO COLD/WAR. PAGE 101 E2018   COM/IND

B50
BURDETTE F.L.,LOBBYISTS IN ACTION (PAMPHLET).   LOBBY
CONSULT TEC/DEV INSPECT BARGAIN PARL/PROC SANCTION   ATTIT
20 CONGRESS. PAGE 17 E0329   POLICY
                                                    LAW

B51
GIBBS C.R.,CONSTITUTIONAL AND STATUTORY PROVISIONS   PROVS
OF THE STATES (VOL. IX). USA+45 LICENSE ADJUD LEAD   CONSTN
20. PAGE 43 E0857   JURID
                                                    LOBBY

B51
KEFAUVER E.,CRIME IN AMERICA. USA+45 USA-45 MUNIC   ELITES
NEIGH DELIB/GP TRIBUTE GAMBLE LOBBY SANCTION   CRIME
...AUD/VIS 20 CAPONE/AL MAFIA MIAMI CHICAGO   PWR
DETROIT. PAGE 60 E1194   FORCES

B52
APPLEBY P.H.,MORALITY AND ADMINISTRATION IN   REPRESENT
DEMOCRATIC GOVERNMENT. USA+45 CLIENT NAT/G EXEC   LOBBY
EFFICIENCY 20. PAGE 5 E0102   ADMIN
                                                    EX/STRUC

B52
COUNCIL STATE GOVERNMENTS,OCCUPATIONAL LICENSING IN PROF/ORG
THE STATES. USA+45 PROVS ADMIN EXEC LOBBY 20.   LICENSE
PAGE 27 E0526   REPRESENT
                                                    EX/STRUC

B52
PASCUAL R.R.,PARTYLESS DEMOCRACY. PHILIPPINE   POL/PAR
BARGAIN LOBBY CHOOSE EFFICIENCY ATTIT 20. PAGE 80   ORD/FREE
E1600   JURID
                                                    ECO/UNDEV

B53
GROSS B.M.,THE LEGISLATIVE STRUGGLE: A STUDY IN   LEGIS
SOCIAL COMBAT. STRUCT LOC/G POL/PAR JUDGE EDU/PROP   DECISION
DEBATE ETIQUET ADMIN LOBBY CHOOSE GOV/REL INGP/REL   PERSON
HEREDITY ALL/VALS...SOC PRESIDENT. PAGE 48 E0948   LEAD

B53
SECKLER-HUDSON C.,BIBLIOGRAPHY ON PUBLIC   BIBLIOG/A
ADMINISTRATION (4TH ED.). USA+45 LAW POL/PAR   ADMIN
DELIB/GP BUDGET ADJUD LOBBY GOV/REL GP/REL ATTIT   NAT/G
...JURID 20. PAGE 90 E1800   MGT

B54
BENTLEY A.F.,INQUIRY INTO INQUIRIES: ESSAYS IN   EPIST
SOCIAL THEORY. UNIV LEGIS ADJUD ADMIN LOBBY   SOC
...PHIL/SCI PSY NEW/IDEA LING METH 20. PAGE 10   CONCPT
E0200

B54
BROGAN D.W.,POLITICS IN AMERICA. LAW POL/PAR CHIEF   NAT/G
LEGIS LOBBY CHOOSE REPRESENT GP/REL RACE/REL   CONSTN
FEDERAL MORAL...BIBLIOG 20 PRESIDENT CONGRESS.   USA+45
PAGE 16 E0304

B56
REDFORD E.S.,PUBLIC ADMINISTRATION AND POLICY   EX/STRUC
FORMATION: STUDIES IN OIL, GAS, BANKING, RIVER   PROB/SOLV
DEVELOPMENT AND CORPORATE INVESTIGATIONS. USA+45   CONTROL
CLIENT NAT/G ADMIN LOBBY REPRESENT GOV/REL INGP/REL EXEC
20. PAGE 84 E1678

B57
US SENATE COMM ON JUDICIARY,HEARING BEFORE   LEGIS
SUBCOMMITTEE ON COMMITTEE OF JUDICIARY, UNITED   CONSTN
STATES SENATE: S. J. RES. 3. USA+45 NAT/G CONSULT   CONFER
DELIB/GP DIPLOM ADJUD LOBBY REPRESENT 20 CONGRESS   AGREE
TREATY. PAGE 102 E2040

B57
US SENATE SPEC COMM POLIT ACT,REPORT OF SPECIAL   LOBBY
COMMITTEE TO INVESTIGATE POLITICAL ACTIVITIES,   LAW
LOBBYING, AND CAMPAIGN CONTRIBUTIONS. USA+45   ECO/TAC

BARGAIN CRIME ATTIT...DECISION 20 CONGRESS. PARL/PROC
PAGE 103 E2061

B58

GARDINER H.C.,CATHOLIC VIEWPOINT ON CENSORSHIP. WRITING
DEBATE COERCE GP/REL...JURID CONCPT 20. PAGE 42 LOBBY
E0835 CATHISM
EDU/PROP

S58

VOSE C.E.,"LITIGATION AS A FORM OF PRESSURE GROUP CONTROL
ACTIVITY" (BMR)" USA+45 ADJUD ORD/FREE NAACP. CT/SYS
PAGE 104 E2085 VOL/ASSN
LOBBY

B59

MOOS M.,THE CAMPUS AND THE STATE. LAW FINAN EDU/PROP
DELIB/GP LEGIS EXEC LOBBY GP/REL PWR...POLICY ACADEM
BIBLIOG. PAGE 74 E1489 PROVS
CONTROL

B59

VOSE C.E.,CAUCASIANS ONLY: THE SUPREME COURT, THE CT/SYS
NAACP, AND THE RESTRICTIVE COVENANT CASES. USA+45 RACE/REL
LAW CONSTN LOBBY...SOC 20 NAACP SUPREME/CT NEGRO. DISCRIM
PAGE 104 E2086

S59

SCHEEHAN D.,"PUBLIC AND PRIVATE GROUPS AS LAW
IDENTIFIED IN THE FIELD OF TRADE REGULATIONS." CONTROL
USA+45 ADMIN REPRESENT GOV/REL. PAGE 87 E1753 ADJUD
LOBBY

B60

CARPER E.T.,THE DEFENSE APPROPRIATIONS RIDER GOV/REL
(PAMPHLET). USA+45 CONSTN CHIEF DELIB/GP LEGIS ADJUD
BUDGET LOBBY CIVMIL/REL...POLICY 20 CONGRESS LAW
EISNHWR/DD DEPT/DEFEN PRESIDENT BOSTON. PAGE 20 CONTROL
E0390

B60

MOCTEZUMA A.P.,EL CONFLICTO RELIGIOSO DE 1926 (2ND SECT
ED.). L/A+17C LAW NAT/G LOBBY COERCE GP/REL ATTIT ORD/FREE
...POLICY 20 MEXIC/AMER CHURCH/STA. PAGE 74 E1476 DISCRIM
REV

B60

POWELL T.,THE SCHOOL BUS LAW: A CASE STUDY IN JURID
EDUCATION, RELIGION, AND POLITICS. USA+45 LAW NEIGH SCHOOL
SECT LEGIS EDU/PROP ADJUD CT/SYS LOBBY CATHISM
WORSHIP 20 CONNECTICT CHURCH/STA. PAGE 82 E1641

B61

MASSEL M.S.,THE REGULATORY PROCESS (JOURNAL ADJUD
REPRINT). NAT/G LOBBY REPRESENT GOV/REL 20. PAGE 69 EX/STRUC
E1382 EXEC

B61

MURPHY E.F.,WATER PURITY: A STUDY IN LEGAL CONTROL SEA
OF NATURAL RESOURCES. LOC/G ACT/RES PLAN TEC/DEV LAW
LOBBY GP/REL COST ATTIT HEALTH ORD/FREE...HEAL PROVS
JURID 20 WISCONSIN WATER. PAGE 75 E1506 CONTROL

B61

SCOTT A.M.,POLITICS, USA: CASES ON THE AMERICAN CT/SYS
DEMOCRATIC PROCESS. USA+45 CHIEF FORCES DIPLOM CONSTN
LOBBY CHOOSE RACE/REL FEDERAL ATTIT...JURID ANTHOL NAT/G
T 20 PRESIDENT CONGRESS CIVIL/LIB. PAGE 90 E1795 PLAN

B61

SMITH J.W.,RELIGIOUS PERSPECTIVES IN AMERICAN SECT
CULTURE, VOL. 2: RELIGION IN AMERICAN LIFE. USA+45 DOMIN
CULTURE NAT/G EDU/PROP ADJUD LOBBY ATTIT...ART/METH SOCIETY
ANTHOL 20 CHURCH/STA BIBLE. PAGE 92 E1845 GP/REL

S61

ABLARD C.D.,"EX PARTE CONTACTS WITH FEDERAL EXEC
ADMINISTRATIVE AGENCIES." USA+45 CLIENT NAT/G ADJUD
DELIB/GP ADMIN PWR 20. PAGE 2 E0044 LOBBY
REPRESENT

B62

BERMAN D.M.,A BILL BECOMES A LAW: THE CIVIL RIGHTS DISCRIM
ACT OF 1960. USA+45 LAW POL/PAR LOBBY RACE/REL PARL/PROC
KNOWL...CHARTS 20 CONGRESS NEGRO CIV/RIGHTS. JURID
PAGE 11 E0206 GOV/REL

B62

CARPER E.T.,ILLINOIS GOES TO CONGRESS FOR ARMY ADMIN
LAND. USA+45 LAW EXTR/IND PROVS REGION CIVMIL/REL LOBBY
GOV/REL FEDERAL ATTIT 20 ILLINOIS SENATE CONGRESS GEOG
DIRKSEN/E DOUGLAS/P. PAGE 20 E0391 LEGIS

B62

FROMAN L.A. JR.,PEOPLE AND POLITICS: AN ANALYSIS OF POL/PAR
THE AMERICAN POLITICAL SYSTEM. USA+45 CHIEF PROB/SOLV

DELIB/GP EX/STRUC LEGIS TOP/EX CT/SYS LOBBY GOV/REL
PERS/REL PWR...POLICY DECISION. PAGE 41 E0813

B62

MURPHY W.F.,CONGRESS AND THE COURT. USA+45 LAW LEGIS
LOBBY GP/REL RACE/REL ATTIT PWR...JURID INT BIBLIOG CT/SYS
CONGRESS SUPREME/CT WARRN/EARL. PAGE 75 E1509 GOV/REL
ADJUD

B62

RICE C.E.,FREEDOM OF ASSOCIATION. USA+45 USA-45 LAW
POL/PAR LOBBY GP/REL...JURID BIBLIOG 18/20 NAT/G
SUPREME/CT PRE/US/AM. PAGE 84 E1691 CONSTN

L62

CAVERS D.F.,"ADMINISTRATIVE DECISION-MAKING IN REPRESENT
NUCLEAR FACILITIES LICENSING." USA+45 CLIENT ADMIN LOBBY
EXEC 20 AEC. PAGE 21 E0410 PWR
CONTROL

L62

ERDMANN H.H.,"ADMINISTRATIVE LAW AND FARM AGRI
ECONOMICS." USA+45 LOC/G NAT/G PLAN PROB/SOLV LOBBY ADMIN
...DECISION ANTHOL 20. PAGE 35 E0695 ADJUD
POLICY

B63

ROYAL INSTITUTE PUBLIC ADMIN,BRITISH PUBLIC BIBLIOG
ADMINISTRATION. UK LAW FINAN INDUS LOC/G POL/PAR ADMIN
LEGIS LOBBY PARL/PROC CHOOSE JURID. PAGE 86 E1729 MGT
NAT/G

B63

SARTORI G.,IL PARLAMENTO ITALIANO: 1946-1963. LAW LEGIS
CONSTN ELITES POL/PAR LOBBY PRIVIL ATTIT PERSON PARL/PROC
MORAL PWR SOC. PAGE 87 E1746 REPRESENT

B63

US SENATE COMM ON JUDICIARY,ADMINISTERED PRICES. LG/CO
USA+45 RATION ADJUD CONTROL LOBBY...POLICY 20 PRICE
SENATE MONOPOLY. PAGE 102 E2047 ADMIN
DECISION

B64

ANDERSON J.W.,EISENHOWER, BROWNELL, AND THE LAW
CONGRESS - THE TANGLED ORIGINS OF THE CIVIL RIGHTS CONSTN
BILL OF 1956-1957. USA+45 POL/PAR LEGIS CREATE POLICY
PROB/SOLV LOBBY GOV/REL RIGID/FLEX...NEW/IDEA 20 NAT/G
EISNHWR/DD CONGRESS BROWNELL/H CIV/RIGHTS. PAGE 5
E0090

B64

BENNETT H.A.,THE COMMISSION AND THE COMMON LAW: A ADJUD
STUDY IN ADMINISTRATIVE ADJUDICATION. LAW ADMIN DELIB/GP
CT/SYS LOBBY SANCTION GOV/REL 20 COMMON/LAW. DIST/IND
PAGE 10 E0188 POLICY

B64

FISK W.M.,ADMINISTRATIVE PROCEDURE IN A REGULATORY SERV/IND
AGENCY: THE CAB AND THE NEW YORK-CHICAGO CASE ECO/DEV
(PAMPHLET). USA+45 DIST/IND ADMIN CONTROL LOBBY AIR
GP/REL ROLE ORD/FREE NEWYORK/C CHICAGO CAB. PAGE 38 JURID
E0758

B64

HAMILTON H.D.,LEGISLATIVE APPORTIONMENT: KEY TO APPORT
POWER. USA+45 LAW CONSTN PROVS LOBBY CHOOSE ATTIT CT/SYS
SUPREME/CT. PAGE 50 E0988 LEAD
REPRESENT

B64

HANNA W.J.,POLITICS IN BLACK AFRICA: A SELECTIVE BIBLIOG
BIBLIOGRAPHY OF RELEVANT PERIODICAL LITERATURE. AFR NAT/LISM
LAW LOC/G MUNIC NAT/G POL/PAR LOBBY CHOOSE RACE/REL COLONIAL
SOVEREIGN 20. PAGE 50 E0995

B64

KEEFE W.J.,THE AMERICAN LEGISLATIVE PROCESS: LEGIS
CONGRESS AND THE STATES. USA+45 LAW POL/PAR DECISION
DELIB/GP DEBATE ADMIN LOBBY REPRESENT CONGRESS PWR
PRESIDENT. PAGE 60 E1191 PROVS

B65

BARKER L.J.,FREEDOM, COURTS, POLITICS: STUDIES IN JURID
CIVIL LIBERTIES. USA+45 LEGIS CREATE DOMIN PRESS CT/SYS
ADJUD LOBBY CRIME GP/REL RACE/REL MARXISM 20 ATTIT
CIVIL/LIB. PAGE 8 E0148 ORD/FREE

B65

CARTER G.M.,POLITICS IN EUROPE. EUR+WWI FRANCE GOV/COMP
GERMANY/W UK USSR LAW CONSTN POL/PAR VOL/ASSN PRESS OP/RES
LOBBY PWR...ANTHOL SOC/INTEG EEC. PAGE 20 E0399 ECO/DEV

B65

CONGRESSIONAL QUARTERLY SERV,REVOLUTION IN CIVIL LAW
RIGHTS. USA+45 USA-45 LEGIS ADJUD CT/SYS CHOOSE CONSTN

DISCRIM...DECISION CONGRESS SUPREME/CT. PAGE 25   RACE/REL
E0488   LOBBY

                                                            B65
SWISHER C.B.,THE SUPREME COURT IN MODERN ROLE. COM   DELIB/GP
COM/IND NAT/G FORCES LEGIS LOBBY PARTIC RACE/REL 20   ATTIT
SUPREME/CT. PAGE 95 E1901   CT/SYS
                                                         ADJUD

                                                            S65
LONG T.G.,"THE ADMINISTRATIVE PROCESS: AGONIZING   ADJUD
REAPPRAISAL IN THE FTC." NAT/G REPRESENT 20 FTC.   LOBBY
PAGE 66 E1326   ADMIN
                                                         EX/STRUC

                                                            B66
FELSHER H.,JUSTICE USA? USA+45 COM/IND JUDGE CT/SYS   ADJUD
MORAL ORD/FREE...SAMP/SIZ HYPO/EXP. PAGE 37 E0735   EDU/PROP
                                                         LOBBY

                                                            B66
HANSON R.,THE POLITICAL THICKET. USA+45 MUNIC   APPORT
POL/PAR LEGIS EXEC LOBBY CHOOSE...MAJORIT DECISION.   LAW
PAGE 50 E0998   CONSTN
                                                         REPRESENT

                                                            B66
HOLTZMAN A.,INTEREST GROUPS AND LOBBYING. USA+45   LOBBY
CHIEF ACT/RES ADJUD LEAD PARTIC CHOOSE...POLICY 20   NAT/G
CONGRESS. PAGE 55 E1092   EDU/PROP
                                                         GP/REL

                                                            B66
KUNSTLER W.M.,"DEEP IN MY HEART" USA+45 LAW   CT/SYS
PROF/ORG SECT LOBBY PARTIC CROWD DISCRIM ROLE   RACE/REL
...BIOG 20 KING/MAR/L NEGRO CIV/RIGHTS SOUTH/US.   ADJUD
PAGE 62 E1233   CONSULT

                                                            B66
MAGRATH C.P.,YAZOO: LAW AND POLITICS IN THE NEW   CT/SYS
REPUBLIC: THE CASE OF FLETCHER V. PECK. USA-45 LAW   DECISION
...BIBLIOG 19 SUPREME/CT YAZOO. PAGE 67 E1348   CONSTN
                                                         LOBBY

                                                            B66
MOSKOW M.H.,TEACHERS AND UNIONS. SCHOOL WORKER   EDU/PROP
ADJUD LOBBY ATTIT ORD/FREE 20. PAGE 75 E1501   PROF/ORG
                                                         LABOR
                                                         BARGAIN

                                                            B66
TRESOLINI R.J.,CASES IN AMERICAN NATIONAL   NAT/G
GOVERNMENT AND POLITICS. LAW DIPLOM ADJUD LOBBY   LEGIS
FEDERAL ORD/FREE WEALTH...DECISION ANTHOL 20   CT/SYS
PRESIDENT. PAGE 97 E1940   POL/PAR

                                                            B67
BAKKE E.W.,UNIONS, MANAGEMENT AND THE PUBLIC*   LABOR
READINGS AND TEXT. WORKER LOBBY...POLICY JURID   INDUS
ANTHOL T. PAGE 7 E0143   ADJUD
                                                         GP/REL

                                                            B67
BIBBY J.,ON CAPITOL HILL. POL/PAR LOBBY PARL/PROC   CONFER
GOV/REL PERS/REL...JURID PHIL/SCI OBS INT BIBLIOG   LEGIS
20 CONGRESS PRESIDENT. PAGE 12 E0224   CREATE
                                                         LEAD

                                                            B67
COWLING M.,1867 DISRAELI, GLADSTONE, AND   PARL/PROC
REVOLUTION: THE PASSING OF THE SECOND REFORM BILL.   POL/PAR
UK LEGIS LEAD LOBBY GP/REL INGP/REL...DECISION   ATTIT
BIBLIOG 19 REFORMERS. PAGE 27 E0531   LAW

                                                            B67
FINCHER F.,THE GOVERNMENT OF THE UNITED STATES.   NAT/G
USA+45 USA-45 POL/PAR CHIEF CT/SYS LOBBY GP/REL   EX/STRUC
INGP/REL...CONCPT CHARTS BIBLIOG T 18/20 PRESIDENT   LEGIS
CONGRESS SUPREME/CT. PAGE 38 E0749   OP/RES

                                                            B67
US SENATE COMM ON FOREIGN REL,CONSULAR CONVENTION   LEGIS
WITH THE SOVIET UNION. USA+45 USSR DELIB/GP LEAD   LOBBY
REPRESENT ATTIT ORD/FREE CONGRESS TREATY. PAGE 101   DIPLOM
E2031

                                                            S67
ANDERSON W.,"THE PERILS OF 'SHARING'." USA+45   BUDGET
ECO/TAC RECEIVE LOBBY GOV/REL CENTRAL COST INCOME   TAX
...POLICY PLURIST CONGRESS. PAGE 5 E0095   FEDERAL
                                                         LAW

                                                            S67
RICHARDSON J.J.,"THE MAKING OF THE RESTRICTIVE   LEGIS
TRADE PRACTICES ACT 1956 A CASE STUDY OF THE POLICY   ECO/TAC
PROCESS IN BRITAIN." UK FINAN MARKET LG/CO POL/PAR   POLICY

CONSULT PRESS ADJUD ADMIN AGREE LOBBY SANCTION   INDUS
ATTIT 20. PAGE 84 E1695

LOBBYING....SEE LOBBY

LOBINGIER C.S. E1314

LOBLE L.H. E1315

LOC/G....LOCAL GOVERNMENT

                                                            N
JOURNAL OF POLITICS. USA+45 USA-45 CONSTN POL/PAR   BIBLIOG/A
EX/STRUC LEGIS PROB/SOLV DIPLOM CT/SYS CHOOSE   NAT/G
RACE/REL 20. PAGE 1 E0011   LAW
                                                         LOC/G

                                                            N
POLITICAL SCIENCE QUARTERLY. USA+45 USA-45 LAW   BIBLIOG/A
CONSTN ECO/DEV INT/ORG LOC/G POL/PAR LEGIS LEAD   NAT/G
NUC/PWR...CONCPT 20. PAGE 1 E0013   DIPLOM
                                                         POLICY

                                                            N
DEUTSCHE BUCHEREI,JAHRESVERZEICHNIS DES DEUTSCHEN   BIBLIOG
SCHRIFTUMS. AUSTRIA EUR+WWI GERMANY SWITZERLND LAW   WRITING
LOC/G DIPLOM ADMIN...MGT SOC 19/20. PAGE 31 E0614   NAT/G

                                                            N
PUBLISHERS' CIRCULAR LIMITED,THE ENGLISH CATALOGUE   BIBLIOG
OF BOOKS. UK WOR+45 WOR-45 LAW CULTURE LOC/G NAT/G   ALL/VALS
ADMIN LEAD...MGT 19/20. PAGE 83 E1658   ALL/IDEOS
                                                         SOCIETY

                                                            N
US SUPERINTENDENT OF DOCUMENTS,EDUCATION (PRICE   BIBLIOG/A
LIST 31). USA+45 LAW FINAN LOC/G NAT/G DEBATE ADMIN   EDU/PROP
LEAD RACE/REL FEDERAL HEALTH POLICY. PAGE 103 E2062   ACADEM
                                                         SCHOOL

                                                            B04
FREUND E.,THE POLICE POWER; PUBLIC POLICY AND   CONSTN
CONSTITUTIONAL RIGHTS. USA-45 SOCIETY LOC/G NAT/G   LAW
FORCES LEGIS ADJUD CT/SYS OWN PWR...JURID 18/19   ORD/FREE
SUPREME/CT. PAGE 40 E0795   CONTROL

                                                            B05
GOODNOW F.J.,THE PRINCIPLES OF THE ADMINISTRATIVE   ADMIN
LAW OF THE UNITED STATES. USA-45 LAW STRUCT   NAT/G
EX/STRUC LEGIS BAL/PWR CONTROL GOV/REL PWR...JURID   PROVS
19/20 CIVIL/SERV. PAGE 45 E0887   LOC/G

                                                            B05
GRIFFIN A.P.C.,LIST OF REFERENCES ON PRIMARY   BIBLIOG/A
ELECTIONS (PAMPHLET). USA-45 LAW LOC/G DELIB/GP   POL/PAR
LEGIS OP/RES TASK REPRESENT CONSEN...DECISION 19/20   CHOOSE
CONGRESS. PAGE 47 E0928   POPULISM

                                                            B08
GRIFFIN A.P.C.,LIST OF WORKS RELATING TO GOVERNMENT   BIBLIOG/A
REGULATION OF INSURANCE UNITED STATES AND FOREIGN   FINAN
COUNTRIES (2ND. ED.) (PAMPHLET). FRANCE GERMANY UK   LAW
USA-45 WOR-45 LG/CO LOC/G NAT/G LEGIS LICENSE ADJUD   CONTROL
LOBBY CENTRAL ORD/FREE 19/20. PAGE 47 E0933

                                                            B09
JUSTINIAN,THE DIGEST (DIGESTA CORPUS JURIS CIVILIS)   JURID
(2 VOLS.) (TRANS. BY C. H. MONRO). ROMAN/EMP LAW   CT/SYS
FAM LOC/G LEGIS EDU/PROP CONTROL MARRIAGE OWN ROLE   NAT/G
CIVIL/LAW. PAGE 59 E1177   STRATA

                                                            B09
LOBINGIER C.S.,THE PEOPLE'S LAW OR POPULAR   CONSTN
PARTICIPATION IN LAW-MAKING. FRANCE SWITZERLND UK   LAW
LOC/G NAT/G PROVS LEGIS SUFF MAJORITY PWR POPULISM   PARTIC
...GOV/COMP BIBLIOG 19. PAGE 66 E1314

                                                            B10
COLORADO CIVIL SERVICE COMN,SECOND BIENNIAL REPORT   PROVS
TO THE GOVERNOR, 1909-1910. USA+45 DELIB/GP LEGIS   LOC/G
LICENSE PAY 20 COLORADO CIVIL/SERV. PAGE 24 E0477   ADMIN
                                                         WORKER

                                                            B12
MEYER H.H.B.,SELECT LIST OF REFERENCES ON THE   BIBLIOG/A
INITIATIVE, REFERENDUM, AND RECALL. MOD/EUR USA-45   NAT/G
LAW LOC/G MUNIC REPRESENT POPULISM 20 CONGRESS.   LEGIS
PAGE 72 E1446   CHOOSE

                                                            B15
SAWYER R.A.,A LIST OF WORKS ON COUNTY GOVERNMENT.   BIBLIOG/A
LAW FINAN MUNIC TOP/EX ROUTINE CRIME...CLASSIF   LOC/G
RECORD 19/20. PAGE 87 E1748   GOV/REL
                                                         ADMIN

SALMOND J.W.,JURISPRUDENCE. UK LOC/G NAT/G LEGIS   LAW
PROB/SOLV LICENSE LEGIT CRIME PERS/REL OWN ORD/FREE   CT/SYS
...T 20. PAGE 87 E1742   JURID
                                                          ADJUD
                                                          B16

SCHROEDER T.,FREE SPEECH FOR RADICALS (REV. ED.).   ORD/FREE
USA-45 CONSTN INDUS LOC/G FORCES SANCTION WAR ATTIT   CONTROL
SEX...JURID REFORMERS 20 FREE/SPEE. PAGE 88 E1767   LAW
                                                          PRESS
                                                          B16

WRIGHT Q.,"THE ENFORCEMENT OF INTERNATIONAL LAW   INT/ORG
THROUGH MUNICIPAL LAW IN THE US." USA-45 LOC/G   LAW
NAT/G PUB/INST FORCES LEGIT CT/SYS PERCEPT ALL/VALS   INT/LAW
...JURID 20. PAGE 107 E2149   WAR
                                                          L16

EYBERS G.W.,SELECT CONSTITUTIONAL DOCUMENTS   CONSTN
ILLUSTRATING SOUTH AFRICAN HISTORY 1795-1910.   LAW
SOUTH/AFR LOC/G LEGIS CT/SYS...JURID ANTHOL 18/20   NAT/G
NATAL CAPE/HOPE ORANGE/STA. PAGE 36 E0707   COLONIAL
                                                          B18

PORTER K.H.,A HISTORY OF SUFFRAGE IN THE UNITED   SUFF
STATES. USA-45 LAW CONSTN LOC/G NAT/G POL/PAR WAR   REPRESENT
DISCRIM OWN ATTIT SEX 18/20 NEGRO FEMALE/SEX.   CHOOSE
PAGE 81 E1629   PARTIC
                                                          B18

BLACHLY F.F.,"THE GOVERNMENT AND ADMINISTRATION OF   NAT/G
GERMANY." GERMANY CONSTN LOC/G PROVS DELIB/GP   GOV/REL
EX/STRUC FORCES LEGIS TOP/EX CT/SYS...BIBLIOG/A   ADMIN
19/20. PAGE 12 E0235   PHIL/SCI
                                                          C20

YANG KUNG-SUN,THE BOOK OF LORD SHANG. LAW ECO/UNDEV   ASIA
LOC/G NAT/G NEIGH PLAN ECO/TAC LEGIT ATTIT SKILL   JURID
...CONCPT CON/ANAL WORK TOT/POP. PAGE 108 E2164
                                                          B28

CAM H.M.,BIBLIOGRAPHY OF ENGLISH CONSTITUTIONAL   BIBLIOG/A
HISTORY (PAMPHLET). UK LAW LOC/G NAT/G POL/PAR SECT   CONSTN
DELIB/GP ADJUD ORD/FREE 19/20 PARLIAMENT. PAGE 19   ADMIN
E0369   PARL/PROC
                                                          B29

BUCK A.E.,"PUBLIC BUDGETING." USA-45 FINAN LOC/G   BUDGET
NAT/G LEGIS BAL/PAY COST...JURID TREND BIBLIOG/A   ROUTINE
20. PAGE 17 E0324   ADMIN
                                                          C29

BENTHAM J.,THE RATIONALE OF PUNISHMENT. UK LAW   CRIME
LOC/G NAT/G LEGIS CONTROL...JURID GEN/LAWS   SANCTION
COURT/SYS 19. PAGE 10 E0192   COERCE
                                                          ORD/FREE
                                                          B30

BIRD F.L.,THE RECALL OF PUBLIC OFFICERS; A STUDY OF   REPRESENT
THE OPERATION OF RECALL IN CALIFORNIA. LOC/G MUNIC   SANCTION
POL/PAR PROVS PROB/SOLV ADJUD PARTIC...CHARTS   CHOOSE
METH/COMP 20 CALIFORNIA RECALL. PAGE 12 E0230   LAW
                                                          B30

FAIRLIE J.A.,COUNTY GOVERNMENT AND ADMINISTRATION.   ADMIN
UK USA-45 NAT/G SCHOOL FORCES BUDGET TAX CT/SYS   GOV/REL
CHOOSE...JURID BIBLIOG 11/20. PAGE 36 E0713   LOC/G
                                                          MUNIC
                                                          B30

CLYDE W.M.,THE STRUGGLE FOR THE FREEDOM OF THE   PRESS
PRESS FROM CAXTON TO CROMWELL. UK LAW LOC/G SECT   ORD/FREE
FORCES LICENSE WRITING SANCTION REV ATTIT PWR   CONTROL
...POLICY 15/17 PARLIAMENT CROMWELL/O MILTON/J.
PAGE 23 E0460   B34

DE TOCQUEVILLE A.,DEMOCRACY IN AMERICA (4 VOLS.)   POPULISM
(TRANS. BY HENRY REEVE). CONSTN STRUCT LOC/G NAT/G   MAJORIT
POL/PAR PROVS ETIQUET CT/SYS MAJORITY ATTIT 18/19.   ORD/FREE
PAGE 30 E0595   SOCIETY
                                                          B35

KENNEDY W.P.,THE LAW AND CUSTOM OF THE SOUTH   CT/SYS
AFRICAN CONSTITUTION. AFR SOUTH/AFR KIN LOC/G PROVS   CONSTN
DIPLOM ADJUD ADMIN EXEC 20. PAGE 60 E1203   JURID
                                                          PARL/PROC
                                                          B35

MCLAUGHLIN A.C.,A CONSTITUTIONAL HISTORY OF THE   CONSTN
UNITED STATES. USA+45 USA-45 LOC/G NAT/G PROVS   DECISION
LEGIS JUDGE ADJUD...T 18/20. PAGE 71 E1422
                                                          B35

HANSON L.,GOVERNMENT AND THE PRESS 1695-1763. UK   LAW
                                                          B36

LOC/G LEGIS LICENSE CONTROL SANCTION CRIME ATTIT   JURID
ORD/FREE 17/18 PARLIAMENT AMEND/I. PAGE 50 E0996   PRESS
                                                          POLICY
                                                          B38

HOLDSWORTH W.S.,A HISTORY OF ENGLISH LAW; THE   LAW
CENTURIES OF SETTLEMENT AND REFORM (VOL. X). INDIA   LOC/G
UK CONSTN NAT/G CHIEF LEGIS ADMIN COLONIAL CT/SYS   EX/STRUC
CHOOSE ORD/FREE PWR...JURID 18 PARLIAMENT   ADJUD
COMMONWLTH COMMON/LAW. PAGE 54 E1077   B40

ANDERSON W.,FUNDAMENTALS OF AMERICAN GOVERNMENT.   NAT/G
USA-45 LAW POL/PAR CHIEF EX/STRUC BUDGET ADMIN   LOC/G
CT/SYS PARL/PROC CHOOSE FEDERAL...BIBLIOG 20.   GOV/REL
PAGE 5 E0093   CONSTN
                                                          N40

COUNTY GOVERNMENT IN THE UNITED STATES: A LIST OF   BIBLIOG/A
RECENT REFERENCES (PAMPHLET). USA-45 LAW PUB/INST   LOC/G
PLAN BUDGET CT/SYS CENTRAL 20. PAGE 52 E1027   ADMIN
                                                          MUNIC
                                                          B42

BLANCHARD L.R.,MARTINIQUE: A SELECTED LIST OF   BIBLIOG/A
REFERENCES (PAMPHLET). WEST/IND AGRI LOC/G SCHOOL   SOCIETY
...ART/METH GEOG JURID CHARTS 20. PAGE 12 E0241   CULTURE
                                                          COLONIAL
                                                          B44

BEARD C.A.,AMERICAN GOVERNMENT AND POLITICS (REV.   LEAD
ED.). CONSTN MUNIC POL/PAR PROVS EX/STRUC LEGIS   USA-45
TOP/EX CT/SYS GOV/REL...BIBLIOG T 18/20. PAGE 9   NAT/G
E0165   LOC/G
                                                          C44

JEFFERSON T.,"DEMOCRACY" (1816) IN BASIC WRITINGS."   POPULISM
USA-45 LOC/G NAT/G TAX CT/SYS CHOOSE ORD/FREE   MAJORIT
...GEN/LAWS 18/19 JEFFERSN/T. PAGE 58 E1151   REPRESENT
                                                          CONSTN
                                                          B45

CONOVER H.F.,THE GOVERNMENTS OF THE MAJOR FOREIGN   BIBLIOG
POWERS: A BIBLIOGRAPHY. FRANCE GERMANY ITALY UK   NAT/G
USSR CONSTN LOC/G POL/PAR EX/STRUC FORCES ADMIN   DIPLOM
CT/SYS CIVMIL/REL TOTALISM...POLICY 19/20. PAGE 25
E0494   B47

HARGRETT L.,A BIBLIOGRAPHY OF THE CONSTITUTIONS AND   BIBLIOG/A
LAWS OF THE AMERICAN INDIANS. USA-45 LOC/G GOV/REL   CONSTN
GP/REL 19/20 INDIAN/AM. PAGE 50 E0999   LAW
                                                          NAT/G
                                                          B47

HIRSHBERG H.S.,SUBJECT GUIDE TO UNITED STATES   BIBLIOG
GOVERNMENT PUBLICATIONS. USA+45 USA-45 LAW ADMIN   NAT/G
...SOC 20. PAGE 53 E1052   DIPLOM
                                                          LOC/G
                                                          B48

STOKES W.S.,BIBLIOGRAPHY OF STANDARD AND CLASSICAL   BIBLIOG
WORKS IN THE FIELDS OF AMERICAN POLITICAL SCIENCE.   NAT/G
USA+45 USA-45 POL/PAR PROVS FORCES DIPLOM ADMIN   LOC/G
CT/SYS APPORT 20 CONGRESS PRESIDENT. PAGE 94 E1876   CONSTN
                                                          B49

BRUCKER H.,FREEDOM OF INFORMATION. USA-45 LAW LOC/G   PRESS
ECO/TAC DOMIN PWR...NEW/IDEA BIBLIOG 17/20. PAGE 16   COM/IND
E0320   ORD/FREE
                                                          NAT/G
                                                          B50

GRAVES W.B.,PUBLIC ADMINISTRATION: A COMPREHENSIVE   BIBLIOG
BIBLIOGRAPHY ON PUBLIC ADMINISTRATION IN THE UNITED   FINAN
STATES (PAMPHLET). USA+45 USA-45 LOC/G NAT/G LEGIS   CONTROL
ADJUD INGP/REL...MGT 20. PAGE 45 E0901   ADMIN
                                                          B50

HURST J.W.,THE GROWTH OF AMERICAN LAW; THE LAW   LAW
MAKERS. USA-45 LOC/G NAT/G DELIB/GP JUDGE ADJUD   LEGIS
ADMIN ATTIT PWR...POLICY JURID BIBLIOG 18/20   CONSTN
CONGRESS SUPREME/CT ABA PRESIDENT. PAGE 56 E1115   CT/SYS
                                                          B50

MERRIAM C.E.,THE AMERICAN PARTY SYSTEM; AN   POL/PAR
INTRODUCTION TO THE STUDY OF POLITICAL PARTIES IN   CHOOSE
THE UNITED STATES (4TH ED.). USA+45 USA-45 LAW   SUFF
FINAN LOC/G NAT/G PROVS LEAD PARTIC CRIME ATTIT   REPRESENT
18/20 NEGRO CONGRESS PRESIDENT. PAGE 72 E1442   B50

WARD R.E.,A GUIDE TO JAPANESE REFERENCE AND   BIBLIOG/A
RESEARCH MATERIALS IN THE FIELD OF POLITICAL   ASIA
SCIENCE. LAW CONSTN LOC/G PRESS ADMIN...SOC   NAT/G
CON/ANAL METH 19/20 CHINJAP. PAGE 105 E2098   B50

B51
ANDERSON W.,STATE AND LOCAL GOVERNMENT IN THE
UNITED STATES. USA+45 CONSTN POL/PAR EX/STRUC LEGIS
BUDGET TAX ADJUD CT/SYS CHOOSE...CHARTS T 20.
PAGE 5 E0094

LOC/G
MUNIC
PROVS
GOV/REL

B52
BENTHAM A.,HANDBOOK OF POLITICAL FALLACIES. FUT
MOD/EUR LAW INTELL LOC/G MUNIC NAT/G DELIB/GP LEGIS
CREATE EDU/PROP CT/SYS ATTIT RIGID/FLEX KNOWL PWR
...RELATIV PSY SOC CONCPT SELF/OBS TREND STERTYP
TOT/POP. PAGE 10 E0189

POL/PAR

B52
DE GRAZIA A.,POLITICAL ORGANIZATION. CONSTN LOC/G
MUNIC NAT/G CHIEF LEGIS TOP/EX ADJUD CT/SYS
PERS/REL...INT/LAW MYTH UN. PAGE 29 E0581

FEDERAL
LAW
ADMIN

B52
GELLHORN W.,THE STATES AND SUBVERSION. USA+45
USA-45 LOC/G DELIB/GP LEGIS EDU/PROP LEGIT CT/SYS
REGION PEACE ATTIT ORD/FREE SOCISM...INT CON/ANAL
20 CALIFORNIA MARYLAND ILLINOIS MICHIGAN NEW/YORK.
PAGE 43 E0845

PROVS
JURID

B52
THOM J.M.,GUIDE TO RESEARCH MATERIAL IN POLITICAL
SCIENCE (PAMPHLET). ELITES LOC/G MUNIC NAT/G LEGIS
DIPLOM ADJUD CIVMIL/REL GOV/REL PWR MGT. PAGE 96
E1916

BIBLIOG/A
KNOWL

C52
LANCASTER L.W.,"GOVERNMENT IN RURAL AMERICA."
USA+45 ECO/DEV AGRI SCHOOL FORCES LEGIS JUDGE
BUDGET TAX CT/SYS...CHARTS BIBLIOG. PAGE 62 E1248

GOV/REL
LOC/G
MUNIC
ADMIN

B53
GROSS B.M.,THE LEGISLATIVE STRUGGLE: A STUDY IN
SOCIAL COMBAT. STRUCT LOC/G POL/PAR JUDGE EDU/PROP
DEBATE ETIQUET ADMIN LOBBY CHOOSE GOV/REL INGP/REL
HEREDITY ALL/VALS...SOC PRESIDENT. PAGE 48 E0948

LEGIS
DECISION
PERSON
LEAD

B53
STOUT H.M.,BRITISH GOVERNMENT. UK FINAN LOC/G
POL/PAR DELIB/GP DIPLOM ADMIN COLONIAL CHOOSE
ORD/FREE...JURID BIBLIOG 20 COMMONWLTH. PAGE 94
E1883

NAT/G
PARL/PROC
CONSTN
NEW/LIB

B54
BATTEN T.R.,PROBLEMS OF AFRICAN DEVELOPMENT (2ND
ED.). AFR LAW SOCIETY SCHOOL ECO/TAC TAX...GEOG
HEAL SOC 20. PAGE 8 E0154

ECO/UNDEV
AGRI
LOC/G
PROB/SOLV

B54
SCHWARTZ B.,FRENCH ADMINISTRATIVE LAW AND THE
COMMON-LAW WORLD. FRANCE CULTURE LOC/G NAT/G PROVS
DELIB/GP EX/STRUC LEGIS PROB/SOLV CT/SYS EXEC
GOV/REL...IDEA/COMP ENGLSH/LAW. PAGE 89 E1786

JURID
LAW
METH/COMP
ADJUD

B54
SINCO,PHILIPPINE POLITICAL LAW: PRINCIPLES AND
CONCEPTS (10TH ED.). PHILIPPINE LOC/G EX/STRUC
BAL/PWR ECO/TAC TAX ADJUD ADMIN CONTROL CT/SYS SUFF
ORD/FREE...T 20. PAGE 91 E1831

LAW
CONSTN
LEGIS

C54
CALDWELL L.K.,"THE GOVERNMENT AND ADMINISTRATION OF
NEW YORK." LOC/G MUNIC POL/PAR SCHOOL CHIEF LEGIS
PLAN TAX CT/SYS...MGT SOC/WK BIBLIOG 20 NEWYORK/C.
PAGE 19 E0365

PROVS
ADMIN
CONSTN
EX/STRUC

B55
GUAITA A.,BIBLIOGRAFIA ESPANOLA DE DERECHO
ADMINISTRATIVO (PAMPHLET). SPAIN LOC/G MUNIC NAT/G
PROVS JUDGE BAL/PWR GOV/REL OWN...JURID 18/19.
PAGE 48 E0959

BIBLIOG
ADMIN
CONSTN
PWR

B55
SWEET AND MAXWELL,A LEGAL BIBLIOGRAPHY OF THE
BRITISH COMMONWEALTH OF NATIONS (2ND ED. 7 VOLS.).
UK LOC/G MUNIC JUDGE ADJUD CRIME OWN...JURID 14/20
CMN/WLTH. PAGE 95 E1900

BIBLIOG/A
LAW
CONSTN
CT/SYS

B57
CHICAGO U LAW SCHOOL,CONFERENCE ON JUDICIAL
ADMINISTRATION. LOC/G MUNIC NAT/G PROVS...ANTHOL
20. PAGE 22 E0429

CT/SYS
ADJUD
ADMIN
GOV/REL

B57
MEYER P.,ADMINISTRATIVE ORGANIZATION: A COMPARATIVE
STUDY OF THE ORGANIZATION OF PUBLIC ADMINISTRATION.
DENMARK FRANCE NORWAY SWEDEN UK USA+45 ELITES LOC/G

ADMIN
METH/COMP
NAT/G

CONSULT LEGIS ADJUD CONTROL LEAD PWR SKILL
DECISION. PAGE 72 E1449

CENTRAL

B58
CABLE G.W.,THE NEGRO QUESTION: A SELECTION OF
WRITINGS ON CIVIL RIGHTS IN THE SOUTH. USA+45
STRATA LOC/G POL/PAR GIVE EDU/PROP WRITING CT/SYS
SANCTION CRIME CHOOSE WORSHIP 20 NEGRO CIV/RIGHTS
CONV/LEASE SOUTH/US. PAGE 18 E0355

RACE/REL
CULTURE
DISCRIM
ORD/FREE

B58
DAVIS K.C.,ADMINISTRATIVE LAW: CASES, TEXT,
PROBLEMS. LAW LOC/G NAT/G TOP/EX PAY CONTROL
GOV/REL INGP/REL FEDERAL 20 SUPREME/CT. PAGE 29
E0576

ADJUD
JURID
CT/SYS
ADMIN

B58
HENKIN L.,ARMS CONTROL AND INSPECTION IN AMERICAN
LAW. LAW CONSTN INT/ORG LOC/G MUNIC NAT/G PROVS
EDU/PROP LEGIT EXEC NUC/PWR KNOWL ORD/FREE...OBS
TOT/POP CONGRESS 20. PAGE 52 E1032

USA+45
JURID
ARMS/CONT

B58
SPITZ D.,DEMOCRACY AND THE CHALLANGE OF POWER. FUT
USA+45 USA-45 LAW SOCIETY STRUCT LOC/G POL/PAR
PROVS DELIB/GP EX/STRUC LEGIS TOP/EX ACT/RES CREATE
DOMIN EDU/PROP LEGIT ADJUD ADMIN ATTIT DRIVE MORAL
ORD/FREE TOT/POP. PAGE 93 E1862

NAT/G
PWR

B59
COUNCIL OF STATE GOVERNMENTS,STATE GOVERNMENT: AN
ANNOTATED BIBLIOGRAPHY (PAMPHLET). USA+45 LAW AGRI
INDUS WORKER PLAN TAX ADJUST AGE/Y ORD/FREE...HEAL
MGT 20. PAGE 26 E0521

BIBLIOG/A
PROVS
LOC/G
ADMIN

B59
DESMITH S.A.,JUDICIAL REVIEW OF ADMINISTRATIVE
ACTION. UK LOC/G CONSULT DELIB/GP ADMIN PWR
...DECISION JURID 20 ENGLSH/LAW. PAGE 31 E0609

ADJUD
NAT/G
PROB/SOLV
CT/SYS

B59
REOCK E.C.,PROCEDURES AND STANDARDS FOR THE
APPORTIONMENT OF STATE LEGISLATURES (DOCTORAL
THESIS). USA+45 POL/PAR LEGIS TEC/DEV ADJUD
BIBLIOG. PAGE 84 E1686

PROVS
LOC/G
APPORT
REPRESENT

B59
US CONGRESS JT ATOM ENRGY COMM,SELECTED MATERIALS
ON FEDERAL-STATE COOPERATION IN THE ATOMIC ENERGY
FIELD. USA+45 LAW LOC/G PROVS CONSULT LEGIS ADJUD
...POLICY BIBLIOG 20 AEC. PAGE 99 E1991

NAT/G
NUC/PWR
GOV/REL
DELIB/GP

S59
DERGE D.R.,"THE LAWYER AS DECISION-MAKER IN THE
AMERICAN STATE LEGISLATURE." INTELL LOC/G POL/PAR
CHOOSE AGE HEREDITY PERSON CONSERVE...JURID STAT
CHARTS. PAGE 31 E0607

LEGIS
LAW
DECISION
LEAD

N59
NATIONAL ASSN HOME BUILDERS,COMMUNITY FACILITIES: A
LIST OF SELECTED REFERENCES (PAMPHLET). USA+45
DIST/IND FINAN SERV/IND SCHOOL CREATE CONTROL
FEDERAL...JURID 20. PAGE 76 E1525

BIBLIOG/A
PLAN
LOC/G
MUNIC

B60
ADRIAN C.R.,STATE AND LOCAL GOVERNMENTS: A STUDY IN
THE POLITICAL PROCESS. USA+45 LAW FINAN MUNIC
POL/PAR LEGIS ADJUD EXEC CHOOSE REPRESENT. PAGE 3
E0051

LOC/G
PROVS
GOV/REL
ATTIT

B60
ALBI F.,TRATADO DE LOS MODOS DE GESTION DE LAS
CORPORACIONES LOCALES. SPAIN FINAN NAT/G BUDGET
CONTROL EXEC ROUTINE GOV/REL ORD/FREE SOVEREIGN
...MGT 20. PAGE 3 E0057

LOC/G
LAW
ADMIN
MUNIC

B60
BEEM H.D.,AN INTRODUCTION TO LEGAL BIBLIOGRAPHY FOT
THE NON-PROFESSIONAL STUDENT. LOC/G NAT/G TAX 20.
PAGE 9 E0177

BIBLIOG/A
JURID
METH
ADJUD

B60
HEAP D.,AN OUTLINE OF PLANNING LAW (3RD ED.). UK
LAW PROB/SOLV ADMIN CONTROL 20. PAGE 51 E1020

MUNIC
PLAN
JURID
LOC/G

B60
LASKIN B.,CANADIAN CONSTITUTIONAL LAW: TEXT AND
NOTES ON DISTRIBUTION OF LEGISLATIVE POWER (2ND
ED.). CANADA LOC/G ECO/TAC TAX CONTROL CT/SYS CRIME
FEDERAL PWR...JURID 20 PARLIAMENT. PAGE 63 E1259

CONSTN
NAT/G
LAW
LEGIS

NAT'L MUNICIPAL LEAGUE,COMPENDIUM ON LEGISLATIVE APPORTIONMENT. USA+45 LOC/G NAT/G POL/PAR PROVS CT/SYS CHOOSE 20 SUPREME/CT CONGRESS. PAGE 76 E1523
B60
APPORT
REPRESENT
LEGIS
STAT

PRASAD B.,THE ORIGINS OF PROVINCIAL AUTONOMY. INDIA UK FINAN LOC/G FORCES LEGIS CONTROL CT/SYS PWR ...JURID 19/20. PAGE 82 E1646
B60
CENTRAL
PROVS
COLONIAL
NAT/G

MARSHALL G.,"POLICE RESPONSIBILITY." UK LOC/G ADJUD ADMIN EXEC 20. PAGE 69 E1370
S60
CONTROL
REPRESENT
LAW
FORCES

AVERY M.W.,GOVERNMENT OF WASHINGTON STATE. USA+45 MUNIC DELIB/GP EX/STRUC LEGIS GIVE CT/SYS PARTIC REGION EFFICIENCY 20 WASHINGT/G GOVERNOR. PAGE 6 E0121
B61
PROVS
LOC/G
ADMIN
GOV/REL

BEASLEY K.E.,STATE SUPERVISION OF MUNICIPAL DEBT IN KANSAS - A CASE STUDY. USA+45 USA-45 FINAN PROVS BUDGET TAX ADJUD ADMIN CONTROL SUPEGO. PAGE 9 E0167
B61
MUNIC
LOC/G
LEGIS
JURID

BURDETTE F.L.,POLITICAL SCIENCE: A SELECTED BIBLIOGRAPHY OF BOOKS IN PRINT, WITH ANNOTATIONS (PAMPHLET). LAW LOC/G NAT/G POL/PAR PROVS DIPLOM EDU/PROP ADMIN CHOOSE ATTIT 20. PAGE 17 E0330
B61
BIBLIOG/A
GOV/COMP
CONCPT
ROUTINE

MURPHY E.F.,WATER PURITY: A STUDY IN LEGAL CONTROL OF NATURAL RESOURCES. LOC/G ACT/RES PLAN TEC/DEV LOBBY GP/REL COST ATTIT HEALTH ORD/FREE...HEAL JURID 20 WISCONSIN WATER. PAGE 75 E1506
B61
SEA
LAW
PROVS
CONTROL

POOLEY B.J.,PLANNING AND ZONING IN THE UNITED STATES. USA+45 MUNIC DELIB/GP ACT/RES PROB/SOLV TEC/DEV ADJUD ADMIN REGION 20 ZONING. PAGE 81 E1628
B61
PLAN
LOC/G
PROVS
LAW

PUGET H.,ESSAI DE BIBLIOGRAPHIE DES PRINCIPAUX OUVRAGES DE DROIT PUBLIC... QUI ONT PARU HORS DE FRANCE DE 1945 A 1958. EUR+WWI USA+45 CONSTN LOC/G ...METH 20. PAGE 83 E1660
B61
BIBLIOG
MGT
ADMIN
LAW

US COMMISSION ON CIVIL RIGHTS,JUSTICE: BOOK 5, 1961 REPORT OF THE U.S. COMMISSION ON CIVIL RIGHTS. LOC/G NAT/G RACE/REL...JURID 20 NEGRO CIV/RIGHTS INDIAN/AM JURY INDIAN/AM. PAGE 99 E1983
B61
DISCRIM
LAW
FORCES

WINTERS J.M.,STATE CONSTITUTIONAL LIMITATIONS ON SOLUTIONS OF METROPOLITAN AREA PROBLEMS. CONSTN LEGIS LEAD REPRESENT DECISION. PAGE 107 E2134
B61
MUNIC
REGION
LOC/G
LAW

GERWIG R.,"PUBLIC AUTHORITIES IN THE UNITED STATES." LAW CONSTN PROVS TAX ADMIN FEDERAL. PAGE 43 E0852
L61
LOC/G
MUNIC
GOV/REL
PWR

LEAGUE WOMEN VOTERS MASSACHU,THE MERIT SYSTEM IN MASSACHUSETTS (PAMPHLET). USA+45 PROVS LEGIT PARTIC CHOOSE REPRESENT GOV/REL EFFICIENCY...POLICY GOV/COMP BIBLIOG 20 MASSACHU. PAGE 64 E1274
N61
LOC/G
LAW
SENIOR
PROF/ORG

COSTA RICA UNIVERSIDAD BIBL,LISTA DE TESIS DE GRADO DE LA UNIVERSIDAD DE COSTA RICA. COSTA/RICA LAW LOC/G ADMIN LEAD...SOC 20. PAGE 26 E0518
B62
BIBLIOG/A
NAT/G
DIPLOM
ECO/UNDEV

HSUEH S.-.S.,GOVERNMENT AND ADMINISTRATION OF HONG KONG. CHIEF DELIB/GP LEGIS CT/SYS REPRESENT GOV/REL 20 HONG/KONG CITY/MGT CIVIL/SERV GOVERNOR. PAGE 55 E1106
B62
ADMIN
LOC/G
COLONIAL
EX/STRUC

INSTITUTE JUDICIAL ADMIN,JUDGES: THEIR TEMPORARY APPOINTMENT, ASSIGNMENT AND TRANSFER: SURVEY OF FED AND STATE CONSTN'S STATUTES, ROLES OF CT. USA+45 CONSTN PROVS CT/SYS GOV/REL PWR JURID. PAGE 57 E1128
B62
NAT/G
LOC/G
JUDGE
ADMIN

LITTLEFIELD N.,METROPOLITAN AREA PROBLEMS AND MUNICIPAL HOME RULE. USA+45 PROVS ADMIN CONTROL GP/REL PWR. PAGE 65 E1308
B62
LOC/G
SOVEREIGN
JURID
LEGIS

NAT'L MUNICIPAL LEAGUE,COMPENDIUM ON LEGISLATIVE APPORTIONMENT. USA+45 LOC/G NAT/G POL/PAR PROVS CT/SYS CHOOSE 20 SUPREME/CT CONGRESS. PAGE 76 E1524
B62
APPORT
REPRESENT
LEGIS
STAT

NEW YORK STATE LEGISLATURE,REPORT AND DRAFT OF PROPOSED LEGISLATION ON COURT REORGANIZATION. LAW PROVS DELIB/GP CREATE ADJUD 20 NEW/YORK. PAGE 77 E1538
B62
CT/SYS
JURID
MUNIC
LOC/G

PHILLIPS O.H.,CONSTITUTIONAL AND ADMINISTRATIVE LAW (3RD ED.). UK INT/ORG LOC/G CHIEF EX/STRUC LEGIS BAL/PWR ADJUD COLONIAL CT/SYS PWR...CHARTS 20. PAGE 80 E1613
B62
JURID
ADMIN
CONSTN
NAT/G

PRESS C.,STATE MANUALS, BLUE BOOKS AND ELECTION RESULTS. LAW LOC/G MUNIC LEGIS WRITING FEDERAL SOVEREIGN...DECISION STAT CHARTS 20. PAGE 82 E1648
B62
BIBLIOG
PROVS
ADMIN
CHOOSE

TAPER B.,GOMILLION VERSUS LIGHTFOOT: THE TUSKEGEE GERRYMANDER CASE. USA+45 LAW CONSTN LOC/G MUNIC CT/SYS 20 NEGRO CIV/RIGHTS GOMILLN/CG LIGHTFT/PM TUSKEGEE. PAGE 95 E1908
B62
APPORT
REPRESENT
RACE/REL
ADJUD

US COMMISSION ON CIVIL RIGHTS,EQUAL PROTECTION OF THE LAWS IN NORTH CAROLINA. USA+45 LOC/G NAT/G CONSULT LEGIS WORKER PROB/SOLV EDU/PROP ADJUD CHOOSE DISCRIM HEALTH 20 NEGRO NORTH/CAR CIV/RIGHTS. PAGE 99 E1984
B62
ORD/FREE
RESPECT
LAW
PROVS

ERDMANN H.H.,"ADMINISTRATIVE LAW AND FARM ECONOMICS." USA+45 LOC/G NAT/G PLAN PROB/SOLV LOBBY ...DECISION ANTHOL 20. PAGE 35 E0695
L62
AGRI
ADMIN
ADJUD
POLICY

SILVA R.C.,"LEGISLATIVE REPESENTATION - WITH SPECIAL REFERENCE TO NEW YORK." LAW CONSTN LOC/G NAT/G PROVS. PAGE 91 E1826
S62
MUNIC
LEGIS
REPRESENT
APPORT

ADRIAN C.R.,GOVERNING OVER FIFTY STATES AND THEIR COMMUNITIES. USA+45 CONSTN FINAN MUNIC NAT/G POL/PAR EX/STRUC LEGIS ADMIN CONTROL CT/SYS ...CHARTS 20. PAGE 3 E0052
B63
PROVS
LOC/G
GOV/REL
GOV/COMP

BURRUS B.R.,ADMINSTRATIVE LAW AND LOCAL GOVERNMENT. USA+45 PROVS LEGIS LICENSE ADJUD ORD/FREE 20. PAGE 18 E0347
B63
EX/STRUC
LOC/G
JURID
CONSTN

DAY R.E.,CIVIL RIGHTS USA: PUBLIC SCHOOLS, SOUTHERN STATES - NORTH CAROLINA, 1963. USA+45 LOC/G NEIGH LEGIS CREATE CT/SYS COERCE DISCRIM ATTIT...QU CHARTS 20 NORTH/CAR NEGRO KKK CIV/RIGHTS. PAGE 29 E0579
B63
EDU/PROP
ORD/FREE
RACE/REL
SANCTION

DOUGLAS W.O.,THE ANATOMY OF LIBERTY: THE RIGHTS OF MAN WITHOUT FORCE. WOR+45 ECO/DEV ECO/UNDEV LOC/G FORCES GOV/REL...SOC/WK 20. PAGE 32 E0643
B63
PEACE
LAW
DIPLOM
ORD/FREE

FORTES A.B.,HISTORIA ADMINISTRATIVA, JUDICIARIA E ECLESIASTICA DO RIO GRANDE DO SUL. BRAZIL L/A+17C LOC/G SECT COLONIAL CT/SYS ORD/FREE CATHISM 16/20. PAGE 39 E0773
B63
PROVS
ADMIN
JURID

FRIEDRICH C.J.,MAN AND HIS GOVERNMENT: AN EMPIRICAL THEORY OF POLITICS. UNIV LOC/G NAT/G ADJUD REV INGP/REL DISCRIM PWR BIBLIOG. PAGE 41 E0810
B63
PERSON
ORD/FREE
PARTIC
CONTROL

GALLAGHER J.F.,SUPERVISORIAL DISTRICTING IN CALIFORNIA COUNTIES: 1960-1963 (PAMPHLET). USA+45
B63
APPORT
REGION

ADJUD ADMIN PARTIC CHOOSE GP/REL...CENSUS 20   REPRESENT
CALIFORNIA. PAGE 42 E0828   LOC/G

                                                     B63
GARNER U.F.,ADMINISTRATIVE LAW. UK LAW LOC/G NAT/G   ADMIN
EX/STRUC LEGIS JUDGE BAL/PWR BUDGET ADJUD CONTROL   JURID
CT/SYS...BIBLIOG 20. PAGE 42 E0840   PWR
                                                     GOV/REL

                                                     B63
GOURNAY B.,PUBLIC ADMINISTRATION. FRANCE LAW CONSTN   BIBLIOG/A
AGRI FINAN LABOR SCHOOL EX/STRUC CHOOSE...MGT   ADMIN
METH/COMP 20. PAGE 45 E0894   NAT/G
                                                     LOC/G

                                                     B63
GRANT D.R.,STATE AND LOCAL GOVERNMENT IN AMERICA.   PROVS
USA+45 FINAN LOC/G MUNIC EX/STRUC FORCES EDU/PROP   POL/PAR
ADMIN CHOOSE FEDERAL ATTIT...JURID 20. PAGE 45   LEGIS
E0897   CONSTN

                                                     B63
LANOUE G.R.,A BIBLIOGRAPHY OF DOCTORAL   BIBLIOG
DISSERTATIONS ON POLITICS AND RELIGION. USA+45   NAT/G
USA-45 CONSTN PROVS DIPLOM CT/SYS MORAL...POLICY   LOC/G
JURID CONCPT 20. PAGE 63 E1252   SECT

                                                     B63
LIVINGSTON W.S.,FEDERALISM IN THE COMMONWEALTH - A   BIBLIOG
BIBLIOGRAPHICAL COMMENTARY. CANADA INDIA PAKISTAN   JURID
UK STRUCT LOC/G NAT/G POL/PAR...NAT/COMP 20   FEDERAL
AUSTRAL. PAGE 66 E1310   CONSTN

                                                     B63
LIVNEH E.,ISRAEL LEGAL BIBLIOGRAPHY IN EUROPEAN   BIBLIOG
LANGUAGES. ISRAEL LOC/G JUDGE TAX...INT/LAW 20.   LAW
PAGE 66 E1311   NAT/G
                                                     CONSTN

                                                     B63
PALOTAI O.C.,PUBLICATIONS OF THE INSTITUTE OF   BIBLIOG/A
GOVERNMENT, 1930-1962. LAW PROVS SCHOOL WORKER   ADMIN
ACT/RES OP/RES CT/SYS GOV/REL...CRIMLGY SOC/WK.   LOC/G
PAGE 79 E1594   FINAN

                                                     B63
ROYAL INSTITUTE PUBLIC ADMIN,BRITISH PUBLIC   BIBLIOG
ADMINISTRATION. UK LAW FINAN INDUS LOC/G POL/PAR   ADMIN
LEGIS LOBBY PARL/PROC CHOOSE JURID. PAGE 86 E1729   MGT
                                                     NAT/G

                                                     B63
US COMN CIVIL RIGHTS,REPORT ON MISSISSIPPI. LAW   RACE/REL
LOC/G NAT/G LEGIS PLAN PROB/SOLV DISCRIM SOC/INTEG   CONSTN
20 MISSISSIPP NEGRO. PAGE 99 E1987   ORD/FREE
                                                     COERCE

                                                     B63
YOUNGER R.D.,THE PEOPLE'S PANEL: THE GRAND JURY IN   CT/SYS
THE UNITED STATES, 1634-1941. USA-45 LAW LEGIT   JURID
CONTROL TASK GP/REL ROLE...TREND 17/20 GRAND/JURY.   CONSTN
PAGE 108 E2166   LOC/G

                                                     B64
BOUVIER-AJAM M.,MANUEL TECHNIQUE ET PRATIQUE DU   MUNIC
MAIRE ET DES ELUS ET AGENTS COMMUNAUX. FRANCE LOC/G   ADMIN
BUDGET CHOOSE GP/REL SUPEGO...JURID BIBLIOG 20   CHIEF
MAYOR COMMUNES. PAGE 14 E0274   NEIGH

                                                     B64
BUREAU OF NAT'L AFFAIRS,THE CIVIL RIGHTS ACT OF   LEGIS
1964. USA+45 LOC/G NAT/G DELIB/GP CONFER DEBATE   RACE/REL
DISCRIM...JURID 20 CONGRESS SUPREME/CT CIV/RIGHTS.   LAW
PAGE 17 E0333   CONSTN

                                                     B64
COUNCIL OF STATE GOVERNMENTS,LEGISLATIVE   LOC/G
APPORTIONMENT: A SUMMARY OF STATE ACTION. USA+45   PROVS
LEGIS REPRESENT...POLICY SUPREME/CT. PAGE 26 E0523   APPORT
                                                     CT/SYS

                                                     B64
HANNA W.J.,POLITICS IN BLACK AFRICA: A SELECTIVE   BIBLIOG
BIBLIOGRAPHY OF RELEVANT PERIODICAL LITERATURE. AFR   NAT/LISM
LAW LOC/G MUNIC NAT/G POL/PAR LOBBY CHOOSE RACE/REL   COLONIAL
SOVEREIGN 20. PAGE 50 E0995

                                                     B64
HOLDSWORTH W.S.,A HISTORY OF ENGLISH LAW; THE   LAW
CENTURIES OF DEVELOPMENT AND REFORM (VOL. XIV). UK   LEGIS
CONSTN LOC/G NAT/G POL/PAR CHIEF EX/STRUC ADJUD   LEAD
COLONIAL ATTIT...INT/LAW JURID 18/19 TORY/PARTY   CT/SYS
COMMONWLTH WHIG/PARTY COMMON/LAW. PAGE 54 E1081

                                                     B64
HOLT S.,THE DICTIONARY OF AMERICAN GOVERNMENT.   DICTIONARY

USA+45 LOC/G MUNIC PROVS LEGIS ADMIN JURID. PAGE 55   INDEX
E1091   LAW
                                                     NAT/G

                                                     B64
LIGGETT E.,BRITISH POLITICAL ISSUES: VOLUME 1. UK   POL/PAR
LAW CONSTN LOC/G NAT/G ADJUD 20. PAGE 65 E1296   GOV/REL
                                                     CT/SYS
                                                     DIPLOM

                                                     B64
MITAU G.T.,PROXIMATE SOLUTIONS: CASE PROBLEMS IN   PROVS
STATE AND LOCAL GOVERNMENT. USA+45 CONSTN NAT/G   LOC/G
CHIEF LEGIS CT/SYS EXEC GOV/REL GP/REL PWR 20   ADJUD
CASEBOOK. PAGE 73 E1470

                                                     B64
MITAU G.T.,INSOLUBLE PROBLEMS: CASE PROBLEMS ON THE   ADJUD
FUNCTIONS OF STATE AND LOCAL GOVERNMENT. USA+45 AIR   LOC/G
FINAN LABOR POL/PAR PROB/SOLV TAX RECEIVE CONTROL   PROVS
GP/REL 20 CASEBOOK ZONING. PAGE 73 E1471

                                                     B64
NATIONAL BOOK LEAGUE,THE COMMONWEALTH IN BOOKS: AN   BIBLIOG/A
ANNOTATED LIST. CANADA UK LOC/G SECT ADMIN...SOC   JURID
BIOG 20 CMN/WLTH. PAGE 76 E1526   NAT/G

                                                     B64
PRESS C.,A BIBLIOGRAPHIC INTRODUCTION TO AMERICAN   BIBLIOG
STATE GOVERNMENT AND POLITICS (PAMPHLET). USA+45   LEGIS
USA-45 EX/STRUC ADJUD INGP/REL FEDERAL ORD/FREE 20.   LOC/G
PAGE 82 E1649   POL/PAR

                                                     B64
RICHARDSON I.L.,BIBLIOGRAFIA BRASILEIRA DE   BIBLIOG
ADMINISTRACAO PUBLICA E ASSUNTOS CORRELATOS. BRAZIL   ADMIN
CONSTN FINAN LOC/G NAT/G POL/PAR PLAN DIPLOM   LAW
RECEIVE ATTIT...METH 20. PAGE 84 E1694

                                                     B65
BLITZ L.F.,THE POLITICS AND ADMINISTRATION OF   NAT/G
NIGERIAN GOVERNMENT. NIGER CULTURE LOC/G LEGIS   GOV/REL
DIPLOM COLONIAL CT/SYS SOVEREIGN...GEOG SOC ANTHOL   POL/PAR
20. PAGE 13 E0245

                                                     B65
CAMPBELL E.H.,SURVEYS, SUBDIVISIONS AND PLATTING,   CONSTN
AND BOUNDARIES: WASHINGTON STATE LAW AND JUDICIAL   PLAN
DECISIONS. USA+45 LAW LOC/G...DECISION JURID   GEOG
CON/ANAL BIBLIOG WASHINGT/G PARTITION WATER.   PROVS
PAGE 19 E0372

                                                     B65
CHARLTON K.,EDUCATION IN RENAISSANCE ENGLAND. ITALY   EDU/PROP
UK USA-45 WOR-45 LAW LOC/G NAT/G...IDEA/COMP 14/17   SCHOOL
HUMANISM. PAGE 21 E0423   ACADEM

                                                     B65
COHN H.J.,THE GOVERNMENT OF THE RHINE PALATINATE IN   PROVS
THE FIFTEENTH CENTURY. GERMANY FINAN LOC/G DELIB/GP   JURID
LEGIS CT/SYS CHOOSE CATHISM 14/15 PALATINATE.   GP/REL
PAGE 24 E0468   ADMIN

                                                     B65
COLGNE A.B.,STATUTE MAKING (2ND ED.). LOC/G PROVS   LEGIS
CHOOSE MAJORITY...CHARTS DICTIONARY 20. PAGE 24   LAW
E0474   CONSTN
                                                     NAT/G

                                                     B65
FERRELL J.S.,CASES AND MATERIALS ON LOCAL   APPORT
APPORTIONMENT. CONSTN LEAD GP/REL...DECISION   LOC/G
GOV/COMP. PAGE 37 E0740   REPRESENT
                                                     LAW

                                                     B65
FISCHER F.C.,THE GOVERNMENT OF MICHIGAN. USA+45   PROVS
NAT/G PUB/INST EX/STRUC LEGIS BUDGET GIVE EDU/PROP   LOC/G
CT/SYS CHOOSE GOV/REL...T MICHIGAN. PAGE 38 E0753   ADMIN
                                                     CONSTN

                                                     B65
HIGHSAW R.B.,CONFLICT AND CHANGE IN LOCAL   GOV/REL
GOVERNMENT. USA+45 BUDGET ECO/TAC LEGIT ADJUD   PROB/SOLV
ALABAMA. PAGE 52 E1044   LOC/G
                                                     BAL/PWR

                                                     B65
SCHUBERT G.,REAPPORTIONMENT. LAW MUNIC POL/PAR PWR   REPRESENT
GOV/COMP. PAGE 88 E1775   LOC/G
                                                     APPORT
                                                     LEGIS

                                                     B65
SHARMA S.A.,PARLIAMENTARY GOVERNMENT IN INDIA.   NAT/G
INDIA FINAN LOC/G PROVS DELIB/GP PLAN ADMIN CT/SYS   CONSTN

FEDERAL...JURID 20. PAGE 90 E1814   PARL/PROC
                                                           LEGIS

                                                               B65
SMITH R.C.,THEY CLOSED THEIR SCHOOLS. USA+45 NEIGH   RACE/REL
ADJUD CROWD CONSEN WEALTH...DECISION OBS INT 20   DISCRIM
NEGRO VIRGINIA. PAGE 92 E1846   LOC/G
                                                           SCHOOL

                                                               B65
US LIBRARY OF CONGRESS,INTERNAL SECURITY AND   CONTROL
SUBVERSION. USA+45 ACADEM LOC/G NAT/G PROVS   ADJUD
...POLICY ANARCH DECISION 20 CIVIL/SERV SUBVERT   LAW
SEDITION. PAGE 101 E2020   PLAN

                                                               L65
WEINSTEIN J.B.,"THE EFFECT OF THE FEDERAL   MUNIC
REAPPORTIONMENT DECISIONS ON COUNTIES AND OTHER   LOC/G
FORMS OF GOVERNMENT." LAW CONSTN LEGIS CHOOSE   APPORT
GOV/COMP. PAGE 105 E2108   REPRESENT

                                                               B66
AMERICAN JEWISH COMMITTEE,THE TYRANNY OF POVERTY   BIBLIOG/A
(PAMPHLET). USA+45 LAW ECO/DEV LOC/G MUNIC NAT/G   WEALTH
PUB/INST WORKER EDU/PROP CRIME...SOC/WK 20. PAGE 4   WELF/ST
E0080   PROB/SOLV

                                                               B66
AMERICAN JOURNAL COMP LAW,THE AMERICAN JOURNAL OF   IDEA/COMP
COMPARATIVE LAW READER. EUR+WWI USA+45 USA-45 LAW   JURID
CONSTN LOC/G MUNIC NAT/G DIPLOM...ANTHOL 20   INT/LAW
SUPREME/CT EURCT/JUST. PAGE 4 E0081   CT/SYS

                                                               B66
BRAIBANTI R.,RESEARCH ON THE BUREAUCRACY OF   HABITAT
PAKISTAN. PAKISTAN LAW CULTURE INTELL ACADEM LOC/G   NAT/G
SECT PRESS CT/SYS...LING CHARTS 20 BUREAUCRCY.   ADMIN
PAGE 15 E0286   CONSTN

                                                               B66
CARMEN I.H.,MOVIES, CENSORSHIP, AND THE LAW. LOC/G   EDU/PROP
NAT/G ATTIT ORD/FREE...DECISION INT IDEA/COMP   LAW
BIBLIOG 20 SUPREME/CT FILM. PAGE 19 E0383   ART/METH
                                                         CONSTN

                                                               B66
EPSTEIN F.T.,THE AMERICAN BIBLIOGRAPHY OF RUSSIAN   BIBLIOG
AND EAST EUROPEAN STUDIES FOR 1964. USSR LOC/G   COM
NAT/G POL/PAR FORCES ADMIN ARMS/CONT...JURID CONCPT   MARXISM
20 UN. PAGE 35 E0694   DIPLOM

                                                               B66
FINK M.,A SELECTIVE BIBLIOGRAPHY ON STATE   BIBLIOG
CONSTITUTIONAL REVISION (PAMPHLET). USA+45 FINAN   PROVS
EX/STRUC LEGIS EDU/PROP ADMIN CT/SYS APPORT CHOOSE   LOC/G
GOV/REL 20. PAGE 38 E0751   CONSTN

                                                               B66
GHOSH P.K.,THE CONSTITUTION OF INDIA: HOW IT HAS   CONSTN
BEEN FRAMED. INDIA LOC/G DELIB/GP EX/STRUC   NAT/G
PROB/SOLV BUDGET INT/TRADE CT/SYS CHOOSE...LING 20.   LEGIS
PAGE 43 E0854   FEDERAL

                                                               B66
GREENE L.E.,GOVERNMENT IN TENNESSEE (2ND ED.).   PROVS
USA+45 DIST/IND INDUS POL/PAR EX/STRUC LEGIS PLAN   LOC/G
BUDGET GIVE CT/SYS...MGT T 20 TENNESSEE. PAGE 46   CONSTN
E0909   ADMIN

                                                               B66
HOLDSWORTH W.S.,A HISTORY OF ENGLISH LAW; THE   BIOG
CENTURIES OF SETTLEMENT AND REFORM (VOL. XVI). UK   PERSON
LOC/G NAT/G EX/STRUC LEGIS CT/SYS LEAD ATTIT   PROF/ORG
...POLICY DECISION JURID IDEA/COMP 18 PARLIAMENT.   LAW
PAGE 54 E1083

                                                               B66
MC CONNELL J.P.,LAW AND BUSINESS: PATTERNS AND   ECO/DEV
ISSUES IN COMMERCIAL LAW. USA+45 USA-45 LOC/G   JURID
WORKER LICENSE CRIME REPRESENT GP/REL 20. PAGE 70   ADJUD
E1397   MGT

                                                               B66
US SENATE COMM ON JUDICIARY,SCHOOL PRAYER. USA+45   SCHOOL
LAW LOC/G SECT ADJUD WORSHIP 20 SENATE DEITY.   JURID
PAGE 103 E2058   NAT/G

                                                               L66
SEYLER W.C.,"DOCTORAL DISSERTATIONS IN POLITICAL   BIBLIOG
SCIENCE IN UNIVERSITIES OF THE UNITED STATES AND   LAW
CANADA." INT/ORG LOC/G ADMIN...INT/LAW MGT   NAT/G
GOV/COMP. PAGE 90 E1808

                                                               S66
BURDETTE F.L.,"SELECTED ARTICLES AND DOCUMENTS ON   BIBLIOG
AMERICAN GOVERNMENT AND POLITICS." LAW LOC/G MUNIC   USA+45

NAT/G POL/PAR PROVS LEGIS BAL/PWR ADMIN EXEC   JURID
REPRESENT MGT. PAGE 17 E0331   CONSTN

                                                               S66
POLSBY N.W.,"BOOKS IN THE FIELD: POLITICAL   BIBLIOG/A
SCIENCE." LAW CONSTN LOC/G NAT/G LEGIS ADJUD PWR 20   ATTIT
SUPREME/CT. PAGE 81 E1627   ADMIN
                                                        JURID

                                                               N66
BACHELDER G.L.,THE LITERATURE OF FEDERALISM: A   BIBLIOG
SELECTED BIBLIOGRAPHY (REV ED) (A PAMPHLET). USA+45   FEDERAL
USA-45 WOR+45 WOR-45 LAW CONSTN PROVS ADMIN CT/SYS   NAT/G
GOV/REL ROLE...CONCPT 19/20. PAGE 7 E0126   LOC/G

                                                               B67
BUREAU GOVERNMENT RES AND SERV,COUNTY GOVERNMENT   BIBLIOG/A
REORGANIZATION - A SELECTED ANNOTATED BIBLIOGRAPHY   APPORT
(PAPER). USA+45 USA-45 LAW CONSTN MUNIC PROVS   LOC/G
EX/STRUC CREATE PLAN PROB/SOLV REPRESENT GOV/REL   ADMIN
20. PAGE 17 E0332

                                                               B67
CHAPIN F.S. JR.,SELECTED REFERENCES ON URBAN   BIBLIOG
PLANNING METHODS AND TECHNIQUES. USA+45 LAW ECO/DEV   NEIGH
LOC/G NAT/G SCHOOL CONSULT CREATE PROB/SOLV TEC/DEV   MUNIC
SOC/WK. PAGE 21 E0420   PLAN

                                                               B67
FESLER J.W.,THE FIFTY STATES AND THEIR LOCAL   PROVS
GOVERNMENTS. FUT USA+45 POL/PAR LEGIS PROB/SOLV   LOC/G
ADMIN CT/SYS CHOOSE GOV/REL FEDERAL...POLICY CHARTS
20 SUPREME/CT. PAGE 37 E0743

                                                               B67
LENG S.C.,JUSTICE IN COMMUNIST CHINA: A SURVEY OF   CT/SYS
THE JUDICIAL SYSTEM OF THE CHINESE PEOPLE'S   ADJUD
REPUBLIC. CHINA/COM LAW CONSTN LOC/G NAT/G PROF/ORG   JURID
CONSULT FORCES ADMIN CRIME ORD/FREE...BIBLIOG 20   MARXISM
MAO. PAGE 64 E1284

                                                               B67
POGANY A.H.,POLITICAL SCIENCE AND INTERNATIONAL   BIBLIOG
RELATIONS, BOOKS RECOMMENDED FOR AMERICAN CATHOLIC   DIPLOM
COLLEGE LIBRARIES. INT/ORG LOC/G NAT/G FORCES
BAL/PWR ECO/TAC NUC/PWR...CATH INT/LAW TREATY 20.
PAGE 81 E1622

                                                               B67
UNIVERSAL REFERENCE SYSTEM,CURRENT EVENTS AND   BIBLIOG/A
PROBLEMS OF MODERN SOCIETY (VOLUME V). WOR+45 LOC/G   SOCIETY
MUNIC NAT/G PLAN EDU/PROP CRIME RACE/REL WEALTH   PROB/SOLV
...COMPUT/IR GEN/METH. PAGE 98 E1974   ATTIT

                                                               L67
"A PROPOS DES INCITATIONS FINANCIERES AUX   LOC/G
GROUPEMENTS DES COMMUNES: ESSAI D'INTERPRETATION."   ECO/TAC
FRANCE NAT/G LEGIS ADMIN GOV/REL CENTRAL 20. PAGE 2   APPORT
E0037   ADJUD

                                                               L67
LAMBERT J.D.,"CORPORATE POLITICAL SPENDING AND   USA+45
CAMPAIGN FINANCE." LAW CONSTN FINAN LABOR LG/CO   POL/PAR
LOC/G NAT/G VOL/ASSN TEC/DEV ADJUD ADMIN PARTIC.   CHOOSE
PAGE 62 E1247   COST

                                                               S67
ADOKO A.,"THE CONSTITUTION OF UGANDA." AFR UGANDA   NAT/G
LOC/G CHIEF FORCES LEGIS ADJUD EXEC CHOOSE NAT/LISM   CONSTN
...IDEA/COMP 20. PAGE 3 E0050   ORD/FREE
                                                       LAW

                                                               S67
SEIDLER G.L.,"MARXIST LEGAL THOUGHT IN POLAND."   MARXISM
POLAND SOCIETY R+D LOC/G NAT/G ACT/RES ADJUD CT/SYS   LAW
SUPEGO PWR...SOC TREND 20 MARX/KARL. PAGE 90 E1802   CONCPT
                                                       EFFICIENCY

                                                               S67
WRAITH R.E.,"ADMINISTRATIVE CHANGE IN THE NEW   ADMIN
AFRICA." AFR LG/CO ADJUD INGP/REL PWR...RECORD   NAT/G
GP/COMP 20. PAGE 107 E2147   LOC/G
                                                       ECO/UNDEV

                                                               B90
BURGESS J.W.,POLITICAL SCIENCE AND COMPARATIVE   CONSTN
CONSTITUTIONAL LAW. FRANCE GERMANY UK USA-45 LEGIS   LAW
DIPLOM ADJUD REPRESENT...CONCPT 19. PAGE 17 E0340   LOC/G
                                                       NAT/G

                                                               B91
SIDGWICK H.,THE ELEMENTS OF POLITICS. LOC/G NAT/G   POLICY
LEGIS DIPLOM ADJUD CONTROL EXEC PARL/PROC REPRESENT   LAW
GOV/REL SOVEREIGN ALL/IDEOS 19 MILL/JS BENTHAM/J.   CONCPT
PAGE 91 E1822

POLLOCK F..THE HISTORY OF ENGLISH LAW BEFORE THE   LAW
TIME OF EDWARD I (2 VOLS, 2ND ED.). UK CULTURE   ADJUD
LOC/G LEGIS LICENSE AGREE CONTROL CT/SYS SANCTION   JURID
CRIME...TIME/SEQ 13 COMMON/LAW CANON/LAW. PAGE 81
E1626
                                                        B98

LOCAL GOVERNMENT....SEE LOC/G

LOCKE J. E1316

LOCKE/JOHN....JOHN LOCKE
                                                        B63
    FRIEDRICH C.J..JUSTICE: NOMOS VI. UNIV LAW SANCTION LEGIT
    CRIME...CONCPT ANTHOL MARX/KARL LOCKE/JOHN   ADJUD
    AQUINAS/T. PAGE 41 E0809   ORD/FREE
                                                        JURID

LOCKHART W.B. E1317

LODGE/HC....HENRY CABOT LODGE

LOEVINGER L. E1318

LOEWENSTEIN K. E1319

LOFTON J. E1320

LOG....LOGIC
                                                        N
    BIBLIOGRAPHIE DE LA PHILOSOPHIE. LAW CULTURE SECT   BIBLIOG/A
    EDU/PROP MORAL...HUM METH/CNCPT 20. PAGE 1 E0018   PHIL/SCI
                                                        CONCPT
                                                        LOG
                                                        S18
    POWELL T.R.."THE LOGIC AND RHETORIC OF   CONSTN
    CONSTITUTIONAL LAW" (BMR)" USA+45 USA-45 DELIB/GP   LAW
    PROB/SOLV ADJUD CT/SYS...DECISION 20 SUPREME/CT   JURID
    CON/INTERP. PAGE 82 E1642   LOG
                                                        B46
    ROSS A..TOWARDS A REALISTIC JURISPRUDENCE: A   LAW
    CRITICISM OF THE DUALISM IN LAW (TRANS. BY ANNIE I. CONCPT
    FAUSBOLL). PLAN ADJUD CT/SYS ATTIT RIGID/FLEX   IDEA/COMP
    POPULISM...JURID PHIL/SCI LOG METH/COMP GEN/LAWS 20
    SCANDINAV. PAGE 86 E1720
                                                        B61
    NEWMAN R.P..RECOGNITION OF COMMUNIST CHINA? A STUDY MARXISM
    IN ARGUMENT. CHINA/COM NAT/G PROB/SOLV RATIONAL   ATTIT
    ...INT/LAW LOG IDEA/COMP BIBLIOG 20. PAGE 77 E1544 DIPLOM
                                                        POLICY
                                                        N61
    VINER J..THE INTELLECTUAL HISTORY OF LAISSEZ FAIRE ATTIT
    (PAMPHLET). WOR+45 WOR-45 LAW INTELL...POLICY LING EDU/PROP
    LOG 19/20. PAGE 104 E2077   LAISSEZ
                                                        ECO/TAC
                                                        B62
    FRIEDRICH C.J..NOMOS V: THE PUBLIC INTEREST. UNIV   METH/CNCPT
    ECO/TAC ADJUD UTIL ATTIT...POLICY LING LOG GEN/LAWS CONCPT
    20. PAGE 41 E0808   LAW
                                                        IDEA/COMP
                                                        B65
    NEGLEY G..POLITICAL AUTHORITY AND MORAL JUDGMENT.   MORAL
    INTELL SOCIETY LEGIS SANCTION UTOPIA SOVEREIGN   PWR
    MARXISM...INT/LAW LOG 20. PAGE 76 E1530   CONTROL
                                                        S67
    HORVATH B.."COMPARATIVE CONFLICTS LAW AND THE   INT/LAW
    CONCEPT OF CHANGING LAW." UNIV RATIONAL...JURID   IDEA/COMP
    LOG. PAGE 55 E1099   DIPLOM
                                                        CONCPT

LOGAN R.W. E1321

LOGIC....SEE LOG

LOGIST/MGT....LOGISTICS MANAGEMENT INSTITUTE

LONDON....LONDON, ENGLAND

LONDON INSTITUTE WORLD AFFAIRS E1322

LONDON SCHOOL ECONOMICS-POL E1323

LONG E.V. E1324

LONG H.A. E1325

LONG T.G. E1326

LONG/FAMLY....THE LONG FAMILY OF LOUISIANA

LONGE/FD....F.D. LONGE

LORIMER J. E1327

LOS/ANG....LOS ANGELES

LOUISIANA....LOUISIANA
                                                        B66
    O'NEILL C.E..CHURCH AND STATE IN FRENCH COLONIAL   COLONIAL
    LOUISIANA: POLICY AND POLITICS TO 1732. PROVS   NAT/G
    VOL/ASSN DELIB/GP ADJUD ADMIN GP/REL ATTIT DRIVE   SECT
    ...POLICY BIBLIOG 17/18 LOUISIANA CHURCH/STA.   PWR
    PAGE 78 E1568

LOUISVILLE....LOUISVILLE, KENTUCKY

LOUVERT/T....L'OUVERTURE TOUSSANT

LOVE....AFFECTION, FRIENDSHIP, SEX RELATIONS
                                                        B03
    CHANNING W.E..DISCOURSES ON WAR (1820-1840). LAW   WAR
    SECT DIPLOM INT/TRADE ALL/VALS. PAGE 21 E0418   PLAN
                                                        LOVE
                                                        ORD/FREE
                                                        B57
    BLOOMFIELD L.M..EGYPT, ISRAEL AND THE GULF OF   ISLAM
    AQABA: IN INTERNATIONAL LAW. LAW NAT/G CONSULT   INT/LAW
    FORCES PLAN ECO/TAC ROUTINE COERCE ATTIT DRIVE   UAR
    PERCEPT PERSON RIGID/FLEX LOVE PWR WEALTH...GEOG
    CONCPT MYTH TREND. PAGE 13 E0250
                                                        B58
    ALLEN C.K..ASPECTS OF JUSTICE. UK FAM COERCE CRIME JURID
    MARRIAGE AGE/Y LOVE 20 ENGLSH/LAW. PAGE 4 E0068   MORAL
                                                        ORD/FREE
                                                        S60
    SCHWELB E.."INTERNATIONAL CONVENTIONS ON HUMAN   INT/ORG
    RIGHTS." FUT WOR+45 LAW CONSTN CULTURE SOCIETY   HUM
    STRUCT INT/ORG NAT/G VOL/ASSN DELIB/GP PLAN ADJUD SUPEGO LOVE
    MORAL...SOC CONCPT STAT RECORD HIST/WRIT TREND 20
    UN. PAGE 89 E1790
                                                        S61
    LASSWELL H.D.."THE INTERPLAY OF ECONOMIC, POLITICAL JURID
    AND SOCIAL CRITERIA IN LEGAL POLICY." LAW LOVE   POLICY
    MORAL PWR RESPECT WEALTH...SOC IDEA/COMP. PAGE 63
    E1262
                                                        B63
    BROOKES E.H..POWER, LAW, RIGHT, AND LOVE: A STUDY   PWR
    IN POLITICAL VALUES. SOUTH/AFR NAT/G PERSON   ORD/FREE
    ...CONCPT IDEA/COMP 20. PAGE 16 E0308   JURID
                                                        LOVE
                                                        B63
    ROBERTSON A.H..HUMAN RIGHTS IN EUROPE. CONSTN   EUR+WWI
    SOCIETY INT/ORG NAT/G VOL/ASSN DELIB/GP ACT/RES   PERSON
    PLAN ADJUD REGION ROUTINE ATTIT LOVE ORD/FREE
    RESPECT...JURID SOC CONCPT SOC/EXP UN 20. PAGE 85
    E1705

LOVESTN/J....JAY LOVESTONE

LOWELL A.L. E1328

LOWENTHAL M. E1329

LOWITH....KARL LOWITH
                                                        B63
    HABERMAS J..THEORIE UND PRAXIS. RATIONAL PERSON   JURID
    ...PHIL/SCI ANTHOL 19/20 HEGEL/GWF MARX/KARL BLOCH REV
    LOWITH. PAGE 49 E0969   GEN/LAWS
                                                        MARXISM

LOWRY C.W. E1330

LOYALTY....SEE SUPEGO

LUA....LUA, OR LAWA: VILLAGE PEOPLES OF NORTHERN THAILAND

LUANDA....LUANDA, ANGOLA

LUBBOCK/TX....LUBBOCK, TEXAS

LUCE R. E1331

LUDWIG/BAV....LUDWIG THE BAVARIAN

BERTHOLD O.,KAISER, VOLK UND AVIGNON. GERMANY CHIEF   DIPLOM
LEGIT LEAD NAT/LISM CONSERVE 14 POPE CHRUCH/STA   CATHISM
LUDWIG/BAV JOHN/XXII. PAGE 11 E0217   JURID
B60

MOELLER R.,LUDWIG DER BAYER UND DIE KURIE IM KAMPF   JURID
UM DAS REICH. GERMANY LAW SECT LEGIT LEAD GP/REL   CHIEF
CATHISM CONSERVE 14 LUDWIG/BAV POPE CHURCH/STA.   CHOOSE
PAGE 74 E1478   NAT/LISM
B65

LUGO-MARENCO J.J. E1332

LUMBERING....SEE EXTR/IND

LUNT D.C. E1333

LUSKY L. E1334

LUTHER/M....MARTIN LUTHER

LUVALE....LUVALE TRIBE, CENTRAL AFRICA

LUXEMBOURG....SEE ALSO APPROPRIATE TIME/SPACE/CULTURE INDEX

BARTLETT J.L.,"AMERICAN BOND ISSUES IN THE EUROPEAN LAW
ECONOMIC COMMUNITY." EUR+WWI LUXEMBOURG USA+45   ECO/TAC
DIPLOM CONTROL BAL/PAY EEC. PAGE 8 E0153   FINAN
                                                     TAX
S67

LUZON....LUZON, PHILIPPINES

LYON J.T. E1744

LYONS F.S.L. E1335

────────────────── **M** ──────────────────

MAC CHESNEY B. E1337

MACAO....MACAO

MACAPAGL/D....DIOSDADO MACAPAGAL

MACARTHR/D....DOUGLAS MACARTHUR

MACDONALD A.F. E1338

MACHIAVELL....NICCOLO MACHIAVELLI

MACHIAVELLISM....SEE REALPOL, MACHIAVELL

BORGESE G.A.,GOLIATH: THE MARCH OF FASCISM. GERMANY POLICY
ITALY LAW POL/PAR SECT DIPLOM SOCISM...JURID MYTH   NAT/LISM
20 DANTE MACHIAVELL MUSSOLIN/B. PAGE 14 E0270   FASCISM
                                                     NAT/G
B37

BOTERO G.,THE REASON OF STATE AND THE GREATNESS OF   PHIL/SCI
CITIES. SECT CHIEF FORCES PLAN LEAD WAR MORAL   NEW/IDEA
...POLICY 16 MACHIAVELL TREATY. PAGE 14 E0272   CONTROL
B56

MACHOWSKI K. E1339

MACIVER R.M. E1340,E1341

MACKENZIE W.J.M. E1342

MACKINNON F. E1343

MACLEISH/A....ARCHIBALD MACLEISH

MACLEOD R.M. E1344

MACMILLN/H....HAROLD MACMILLAN, PRIME MINISTER

MACMULLEN R. E1345

MACOBY S. E0349

MACWHINNEY E. E1346

MADAGASCAR....SEE ALSO AFR

DUMON F.,LA COMMUNAUTE FRANCO-AFRO-MALGACHE: SES   JURID
ORIGINES, SES INSTITUTIONS, SON EVOLUTION. FRANCE   INT/ORG
MADAGASCAR POL/PAR DIPLOM ADMIN ATTIT...TREND T 20.   AFR
PAGE 33 E0657   CONSTN
B60

MANGIN G.,"L'ORGANIZATION JUDICIAIRE DES ETATS   AFR
D'AFRIQUE ET DE MADAGASCAR." ISLAM WOR+45 STRATA   LEGIS
STRUCT ECO/UNDEV NAT/G LEGIT EXEC...JURID TIME/SEQ   COLONIAL
L62

TOT/POP 20 SUPREME/CT. PAGE 68 E1357   MADAGASCAR

MURACCIOLE L.,"LES MODIFICATIONS DE LA CONSTITUTION NAT/G
MALGACHE." AFR WOR+45 ECO/UNDEV LEGIT EXEC ALL/VALS   STRUCT
...JURID 20. PAGE 75 E1505   SOVEREIGN
                                                     MADAGASCAR
S62

MADERO/F....FRANCISCO MADERO

MADISON/J....PRESIDENT JAMES MADISON

CAHN E.,THE GREAT RIGHTS. USA+45 NAT/G PROVS   CONSTN
CIVMIL/REL...IDEA/COMP ANTHOL BIBLIOG 18/20   LAW
MADISON/J BILL/RIGHT CIV/RIGHTS WARRN/EARL   ORD/FREE
BLACK/HL. PAGE 18 E0361   INGP/REL
B63

MAFIA....MAFIA

KEFAUVER E.,CRIME IN AMERICA. USA+45 USA-45 MUNIC   ELITES
NEIGH DELIB/GP TRIBUTE GAMBLE LOBBY SANCTION   CRIME
...AUD/VIS 20 CAPONE/AL MAFIA MIAMI CHICAGO   PWR
DETROIT. PAGE 60 E1194   FORCES
B51

HOEVELER H.J.,INTERNATIONALE BEKAMPFUNG DES   CRIMLGY
VERBRECHENS. AUSTRIA SWITZERLND WOR+45 INT/ORG   CRIME
CONTROL BIO/SOC...METH/COMP NAT/COMP 20 MAFIA   DIPLOM
SCOT/YARD FBI. PAGE 53 E1064   INT/LAW
B66

MAGGS P.B. E1347

MAGHREB....SEE ALSO ISLAM

MAGNA/CART....MAGNA CARTA

MCILWAIN C.H.,CONSTITUTIONALISM AND THE CHANGING   CONSTN
WORLD. UK USA-45 LEGIS PRIVIL AUTHORIT SOVEREIGN   POLICY
...GOV/COMP 15/20 MAGNA/CART HOUSE/CMNS. PAGE 71   JURID
E1417
B39

MAGON/F....FLORES MAGON

MAGRATH C.P. E1348

MAIMONIDES....MAIMONIDES

MAINE H.S. E1349,E1350,E1351

MAINE....MAINE

MAIR L.P. E1352

MAITLAND F.W. E1626

MAITLAND/F....FREDERIC WILLIAM MAITLAND

MAJORIT....MAJORITARIAN

YUKIO O.,THE VOICE OF JAPANESE DEMOCRACY, AN ESSAY   CONSTN
ON CONSTITUTIONAL LOYALTY (TRANS BY J. E. BECKER).   MAJORIT
ASIA POL/PAR DELIB/GP EX/STRUC RIGID/FLEX ORD/FREE   CHOOSE
PWR...POLICY JURID METH/COMP 19/20 CHINJAP.   NAT/G
PAGE 108 E2167
B18

GOOCH G.P.,ENGLISH DEMOCRATIC IDEAS IN THE   IDEA/COMP
SEVENTEENTH CENTURY (2ND ED.). UK LAW SECT FORCES   MAJORIT
DIPLOM LEAD PARL/PROC REV ATTIT AUTHORIT...ANARCH   EX/STRUC
CONCPT 17 PARLIAMENT CMN/WLTH REFORMERS. PAGE 45   CONSERVE
E0885
B27

CONWELL-EVANS T.P.,THE LEAGUE COUNCIL IN ACTION.   DELIB/GP
EUR+WWI TURKEY UK USSR WOR-45 INT/ORG FORCES JUDGE   INT/LAW
ECO/TAC EDU/PROP LEGIT ROUTINE ARMS/CONT COERCE
ATTIT PWR...MAJORIT GEOG JURID CONCPT LEAGUE/NAT
TOT/POP VAL/FREE TUNIS 20. PAGE 25 E0498
B29

DE TOCQUEVILLE A.,DEMOCRACY IN AMERICA (4 VOLS.)   POPULISM
(TRANS. BY HENRY REEVE). CONSTN STRUCT LOC/G NAT/G   MAJORIT
POL/PAR PROVS ETIQUET CT/SYS MAJORITY ATTIT 18/19.   ORD/FREE
PAGE 30 E0595   SOCIETY
B35

JEFFERSON T.,"DEMOCRACY" (1816) IN BASIC WRITINGS." POPULISM
USA-45 LOC/G NAT/G TAX CT/SYS CHOOSE ORD/FREE   MAJORIT
...GEN/LAWS 18/19 JEFFERSN/T. PAGE 58 E1151   REPRESENT
                                                     CONSTN
C44

CORRY J.A., DEMOCRATIC GOVERNMENT AND POLITICS. WOR-45 EX/STRUC LOBBY TOTALISM...MAJORIT CONCPT METH/COMP NAT/COMP 20. PAGE 26 E0511
NAT/G CONSTN POL/PAR JURID
B46

KONVITZ M.R., THE CONSTITUTION AND CIVIL RIGHTS. USA-45 NAT/G ADJUD GP/REL RACE/REL POPULISM ...MAJORIT 19/20 SUPREME/CT CIV/RIGHTS. PAGE 61 E1227
CONSTN LAW GOV/REL ORD/FREE
B47

LOCKE J., TWO TREATISES OF GOVERNMENT (1690). UK LAW SOCIETY LEGIS LEGIT AGREE REV OWN HEREDITY MORAL CONSERVE...POLICY MAJORIT 17 WILLIAM/3 NATURL/LAW. PAGE 66 E1316
CONCPT ORD/FREE NAT/G CONSEN
B47

THOREAU H.D., CIVIL DISOBEDIENCE (1849). USA-45 LAW CONSTN TAX COERCE REPRESENT GP/REL SUPEGO...MAJORIT CONCPT 19. PAGE 96 E1923
GEN/LAWS ORD/FREE POLICY
B49

HOLCOMBE A., "OUR MORE PERFECT UNION." USA+45 USA-45 POL/PAR JUDGE CT/SYS EQUILIB FEDERAL PWR...MAJORIT TREND BIBLIOG 18/20 CONGRESS PRESIDENT. PAGE 54 E1070
CONSTN NAT/G ADMIN PLAN
C50

BERLE A.A. JR., ECONOMIC POWER AND FREE SOCIETY (PAMPHLET). CLIENT CONSTN EX/STRUC ECO/TAC CONTROL PARTIC PWR WEALTH MAJORIT. PAGE 11 E0205
LG/CO CAP/ISM INGP/REL LEGIT
B57

JENNINGS I., PARLIAMENT. UK FINAN INDUS POL/PAR DELIB/GP EX/STRUC PLAN CONTROL...MAJORIT JURID PARLIAMENT. PAGE 58 E1163
PARL/PROC TOP/EX MGT LEGIS
B57

COX A., "THE ROLE OF LAW IN PRESERVING UNION DEMOCRACY." EX/STRUC LEGIS PARTIC ROUTINE CHOOSE INGP/REL ORD/FREE. PAGE 27 E0532
LABOR REPRESENT LAW MAJORIT
L59

JENKS C.W., "THE CHALLENGE OF UNIVERSALITY." FUT UNIV CONSTN CULTURE CONSULT CREATE PLAN LEGIT ATTIT MORAL ORD/FREE RESPECT...MAJORIT JURID 20. PAGE 58 E1155
INT/ORG LAW PEACE INT/LAW
S59

SOHN L.B., "THE DEFINITION OF AGGRESSION." FUT LAW FORCES LEGIT ADJUD ROUTINE COERCE ORD/FREE PWR ...MAJORIT JURID QUANT COLD/WAR 20. PAGE 92 E1855
INT/ORG CT/SYS DETER SOVEREIGN
S59

SCHUBERT G.A., CONSTITUTIONAL POLITICS: THE POLITICAL BEHAVIOR OF SUPREME COURT JUSTICES AND THE CONSTITUTIONAL POLICIES THEY MAKE. LAW ELITES CHIEF DELIB/GP EX/STRUC LEGIS DISCRIM ORD/FREE PWR ...POLICY MAJORIT CHARTS SUPREME/CT CONGRESS. PAGE 89 E1781
CONSTN CT/SYS JURID DECISION
B60

ROURKE F.E., "ADMINISTRATIVE SECRECY: A CONGRESSIONAL DILEMMA." DELIB/GP CT/SYS ATTIT ...MAJORIT DECISION JURID. PAGE 86 E1727
LEGIS EXEC ORD/FREE POLICY
S60

BARBASH J., LABOR'S GRASS ROOTS. CONSTN NAT/G EX/STRUC LEGIS WORKER LEAD...MAJORIT BIBLIOG. PAGE 8 E0147
LABOR INGP/REL GP/REL LAW
B61

CASSINELLI C.W., THE POLITICS OF FREEDOM. FUT UNIV LAW POL/PAR CHOOSE ORD/FREE...POLICY CONCPT MYTH BIBLIOG. PAGE 21 E0404
MAJORIT NAT/G PARL/PROC PARTIC
B61

COWEN D.V., THE FOUNDATIONS OF FREEDOM. AFR SOUTH/AFR DOMIN LEGIT ADJUST DISCRIM TOTALISM ATTIT ORD/FREE...MAJORIT JURID SOC/INTEG WORSHIP 20 NEGRO. PAGE 27 E0529
CONSTN ELITES RACE/REL
B61

FROEBEL J., THEORIE DER POLITIK, ALS ERGEBNIS EINER ERNEUERTEN PRUEFUNG DEMOKRATISCHER LEHRMEINUNGEN. WOR-45 SOCIETY POL/PAR SECT REV REPRESENT PWR SOVEREIGN...MAJORIT 19. PAGE 41 E0812
JURID ORD/FREE NAT/G
B61

GUIZOT F.P.G., HISTORY OF THE ORIGIN OF REPRESENTATIVE GOVERNMENT IN EUROPE. CHRIST-17C FRANCE MOD/EUR SPAIN UK LAW CHIEF FORCES POPULISM ...MAJORIT TIME/SEQ GOV/COMP NAT/COMP 4/19 PARLIAMENT. PAGE 48 E0961
LEGIS REPRESENT CONSTN NAT/G
B61

HIRSCHFIELD R.S., THE CONSTITUTION AND THE COURT. SCHOOL WAR RACE/REL EQUILIB ORD/FREE...POLICY MAJORIT DECISION JURID 18/20 PRESIDENT COLD/WAR CIVIL/LIB SUPREME/CT CONGRESS. PAGE 53 E1051
ADJUD PWR CONSTN LAW
B62

HOOK S., THE PARADOXES OF FREEDOM. UNIV CONSTN INTELL LEGIS CONTROL REV CHOOSE SUPEGO...POLICY JURID IDEA/COMP 19/20 CIV/RIGHTS. PAGE 55 E1095
CONCPT MAJORIT ORD/FREE ALL/VALS
B62

WOETZEL R.K., THE NURENBERG TRIALS IN INTERNATIONAL LAW. CHRIST-17C MOD/EUR WOR+45 SOCIETY NAT/G DELIB/GP DOMIN LEGIT ROUTINE ATTIT DRIVE PERSON SUPEGO MORAL ORD/FREE...POLICY MAJORIT JURID PSY SOC SELF/OBS RECORD NAZI TOT/POP. PAGE 107 E2138
INT/ORG ADJUD WAR
B62

JOUGHIN L., "ACADEMIC DUE PROCESS." DELIB/GP ADJUD ROUTINE ORD/FREE...POLICY MAJORIT TREND. PAGE 59 E1175
ACADEM LAW PROF/ORG CLIENT
S63

NEWMAN E.S., CIVIL LIBERTY AND CIVIL RIGHTS. USA+45 USA-45 CONSTN PROVS FORCES LEGIS CT/SYS RACE/REL ATTIT...MAJORIT JURID WORSHIP 20 SUPREME/CT NEGRO CIV/RIGHTS CHURCH/STA. PAGE 77 E1543
ORD/FREE LAW CONTROL NAT/G
B64

GARDNER R.N., "THE SOVIET UNION AND THE UNITED NATIONS." WOR+45 FINAN POL/PAR VOL/ASSN FORCES ECO/TAC DOMIN EDU/PROP LEGIT ADJUD ADMIN ARMS/CONT COERCE ATTIT ALL/VALS...POLICY MAJORIT CONCPT OBS TIME/SEQ TREND STERTYP UN. PAGE 42 E0838
COM INT/ORG USSR
S64

PRITCHETT C.H., "EQUAL PROTECTION AND THE URBAN MAJORITY." POL/PAR LEAD CHOOSE GP/REL PWR...MAJORIT DECISION. PAGE 83 E1655
MUNIC LAW REPRESENT APPORT
S64

KEEFE W.J., THE AMERICAN LEGISLATIVE PROCESS. USA+45 CONSTN POL/PAR CT/SYS REPRESENT FEDERAL ATTIT PLURALISM...MAJORIT 20 CONGRESS PRESIDENT. PAGE 60 E1192
LEGIS NAT/G CHIEF GOV/REL
B65

LASLEY J., THE WAR SYSTEM AND YOU. LAW FORCES ARMS/CONT NUC/PWR NAT/LISM ATTIT...MAJORIT IDEA/COMP UN WORSHIP. PAGE 63 E1261
MORAL PERSON DIPLOM WAR
B65

MCKAY R.B., REAPPORTIONMENT: THE LAW AND POLITICS OF EQUAL REPRESENTATION. FUT USA+45 PROVS BAL/PWR ADJUD CHOOSE REPRESENT GOV/REL FEDERAL...JURID BIBLIOG 20 SUPREME/CT CONGRESS. PAGE 71 E1420
APPORT MAJORIT LEGIS PWR
B65

NORDEN A., WAR AND NAZI CRIMINALS IN WEST GERMANY: STATE, ECONOMY, ADMINISTRATION, ARMY, JUSTICE, SCIENCE. GERMANY GERMANY/W MOD/EUR ECO/DEV ACADEM EX/STRUC FORCES DOMIN ADMIN CT/SYS...POLICY MAJORIT PACIFIST 20. PAGE 77 E1554
FASCIST WAR NAT/G TOP/EX
B65

ANDERSON S.V., CANADIAN OMBUDSMAN PROPOSALS. CANADA LEGIS DEBATE PARL/PROC...MAJORIT JURID TIME/SEQ IDEA/COMP 20 OMBUDSMAN PARLIAMENT. PAGE 5 E0092
NAT/G CREATE ADMIN POL/PAR
B66

DE TOCQUEVILLE A., DEMOCRACY IN AMERICA (1834-1840) (2 VOLS. IN I; TRANS. BY G. LAWRENCE). FRANCE CULTURE STRATA POL/PAR CT/SYS REPRESENT FEDERAL ORD/FREE SOVEREIGN...MAJORIT TREND GEN/LAWS 18/19. PAGE 30 E0596
POPULISM USA-45 CONSTN NAT/COMP
B66

HANSON R., THE POLITICAL THICKET. USA+45 MUNIC POL/PAR LEGIS EXEC LOBBY CHOOSE...MAJORIT DECISION. PAGE 50 E0998
APPORT LAW CONSTN REPRESENT
B66

B66
HIDAYATULLAH M.,DEMOCRACY IN INDIA AND THE JUDICIAL NAT/G
PROCESS. INDIA EX/STRUC LEGIS LEAD GOV/REL ATTIT   CT/SYS
ORD/FREE...MAJORIT CONCPT 20 NEHRU/J. PAGE 52 E1040   CONSTN
JURID

S67
GOSSETT W.T.,"ELECTING THE PRESIDENT: NEW HOPE FOR   CONSTN
AN OLD IDEAL." FUT USA+45 USA-45 PROVS LEGIS   CHIEF
PROB/SOLV WRITING DEBATE ADJUD REPRESENT...MAJORIT   CHOOSE
DECISION 20 HOUSE/REP PRESIDENT. PAGE 45 E0892   NAT/G

MAJORITY....BEHAVIOR OF MAJOR PARTS OF A GROUP; SEE ALSO
    CONSEN, MAJORIT

B09
LOBINGIER C.S.,THE PEOPLE'S LAW OR POPULAR   CONSTN
PARTICIPATION IN LAW-MAKING. FRANCE SWITZERLND UK   LAW
LOC/G NAT/G PROVS LEGIS SUFF MAJORITY PWR POPULISM   PARTIC
...GOV/COMP BIBLIOG 19. PAGE 66 E1314

B30
JORDAN E.,THEORY OF LEGISLATION: AN ESSAY ON THE   LEGIS
DYNAMICS OF PUBLIC MIND. NAT/G CREATE REPRESENT   CONCPT
MAJORITY ATTIT GEN/LAWS. PAGE 59 E1173   JURID
CT/SYS

B35
DE TOCQUEVILLE A.,DEMOCRACY IN AMERICA (4 VOLS.)   POPULISM
(TRANS. BY HENRY REEVE). CONSTN STRUC LOC/G NAT/G   MAJORIT
POL/PAR PROVS ETIQUET CT/SYS MAJORITY ATTIT 18/19.   ORD/FREE
PAGE 30 E0595   SOCIETY

B59
MORRIS C.,THE GREAT LEGAL PHILOSOPHERS: SELECTED   JURID
READINGS IN JURISPRUDENCE. UNIV INTELL SOCIETY   ADJUD
EDU/PROP MAJORITY UTOPIA PERSON KNOWL...ANTHOL.   PHIL/SCI
PAGE 75 E1497   IDEA/COMP

B59
SCHUBERT G.A.,QUANTITATIVE ANALYSIS OF JUDICIAL   JUDGE
BEHAVIOR. ADJUD LEAD CHOOSE INGP/REL MAJORITY ATTIT   CT/SYS
...DECISION JURID CHARTS GAME SIMUL SUPREME/CT.   PERSON
PAGE 89 E1780   QUANT

S59
MASON A.T.,"THE SUPREME COURT: TEMPLE AND FORUM"   CT/SYS
(BMR)" USA+45 USA-45 CONSTN DELIB/GP RACE/REL   JURID
MAJORITY ORD/FREE...DECISION SOC/INTEG 19/20   PWR
SUPREME/CT WARRN/EARL CIV/RIGHTS. PAGE 69 E1377   ATTIT

B62
BARLOW R.B.,CITIZENSHIP AND CONSCIENCE: STUDIES IN   SECT
THEORY AND PRACTICE OF RELIGIOUS TOLERATION IN   LEGIS
ENGLAND DURING EIGHTEENTH CENTURY. UK LAW VOL/ASSN   DISCRIM
EDU/PROP SANCTION REV GP/REL MAJORITY ATTIT
ORD/FREE...BIBLIOG WORSHIP 18. PAGE 8 E0150

N62
US ADVISORY COMN INTERGOV REL,APPORTIONMENT OF   MUNIC
STATE LEGISLATURES (PAMPHLET). LAW CONSTN EX/STRUC   PROVS
LEGIS LEAD MAJORITY. PAGE 99 E1977   REPRESENT
APPORT

B65
COLGNE A.B.,STATUTE MAKING (2ND ED.). LOC/G PROVS   LEGIS
CHOOSE MAJORITY...CHARTS DICTIONARY 20. PAGE 24   LAW
E0474   CONSTN
NAT/G

B65
SCHUBERT G.,THE JUDICIAL MIND: THE ATTITUDES AND   CT/SYS
IDEOLOGIES OF SUPREME COURT JUSTICES 1946-1963.   JUDGE
USA+45 ELITES NAT/G CONTROL PERS/REL MAJORITY   ATTIT
CONSERVE...DECISION JURID MODAL STAT TREND GP/COMP   NEW/LIB
GAME. PAGE 88 E1774

S65
LUSKY L.,"FOUR PROBLEMS IN LAWMAKING FOR PEACE."   ORD/FREE
FORCES LEGIS CREATE ADJUD COERCE WAR MAJORITY PEACE   INT/LAW
PWR. PAGE 67 E1334   UTOPIA
RECORD

B66
HAUSNER G.,JUSTICE IN JERUSALEM. GERMANY ISRAEL   ADJUD
SOCIETY KIN DIPLOM LEGIT CT/SYS PARTIC MURDER   CRIME
MAJORITY ATTIT FASCISM...INT/LAW JURID 20 JEWS   RACE/REL
WAR/TRIAL. PAGE 51 E1013   COERCE

B67
RAE D.,THE POLITICAL CONSEQUENCES OF ELECTORAL   POL/PAR
LAWS. EUR+WWI ICELAND ISRAEL NEW/ZEALND UK USA+45   CHOOSE
ADJUD APPORT GP/REL MAJORITY...MATH STAT CENSUS   NAT/COMP
CHARTS BIBLIOG 20 AUSTRAL. PAGE 83 E1667   REPRESENT

B91
DOLE C.F.,THE AMERICAN CITIZEN. USA-45 LAW PARTIC   NAT/G
ATTIT...INT/LAW 19. PAGE 32 E0633   MORAL
NAT/LISM
MAJORITY

MAJUMDAR B.B. E1353

MAKI J.M. E1354,E1355

MALAWI....SEE ALSO AFR

N60
RHODESIA-NYASA NATL ARCHIVES,A SELECT BIBLIOGRAPHY   BIBLIOG
OF RECENT PUBLICATIONS CONCERNING THE FEDERATION OF   ADMIN
RHODESIA AND NYASALAND (PAMPHLET). MALAWI RHODESIA   ORD/FREE
LAW CULTURE STRUCT ECO/UNDEV LEGIS...GEOG 20.   NAT/G
PAGE 84 E1689

B64
FRANCK T.M.,EAST AFRICAN UNITY THROUGH LAW. MALAWI   AFR
TANZANIA UGANDA UK ZAMBIA CONSTN INT/ORG NAT/G   FEDERAL
ADMIN ROUTINE TASK NAT/LISM ATTIT SOVEREIGN   REGION
...RECORD IDEA/COMP NAT/COMP. PAGE 40 E0785   INT/LAW

MALAYA....MALAYA

MALAYSIA....SEE ALSO S/ASIA

B64
GROVES H.E.,THE CONSTITUTION OF MALAYSIA. MALAYSIA   CONSTN
POL/PAR CHIEF CONSULT DELIB/GP CT/SYS PARL/PROC   NAT/G
CHOOSE FEDERAL ORD/FREE 20. PAGE 48 E0953   LAW

S67
DOUTY H.M.," REFERENCE TO DEVELOPING COUNTRIES."   TAX
JAMAICA MALAYSIA UK WOR+45 LAW FINAN ACT/RES BUDGET   ECO/UNDEV
CAP/ISM ECO/TAC TARIFFS RISK EFFICIENCY PROFIT   NAT/G
...CHARTS 20. PAGE 33 E0646

MALCOLM/X....MALCOLM X

MALDIVE....MALDIVE ISLAND; SEE ALSO S/ASIA, COMMONWLTH

MALE/SEX....MALE SEX

MALI....SEE ALSO AFR

MALTA....SEE ALSO APPROPRIATE TIME/SPACE/CULTURE INDEX

MALTHUS....THOMAS ROBERT MALTHUS

MANAGEMENT....SEE MGT, EX/STRUC, ADMIN

MANCHESTER....MANCHESTER, ENGLAND

MANCHU/DYN....MANCHU DYNASTY

MANGIN G. E1356,E1357

MANGONE G. E1358,E1359

MANITOBA....MANITOBA, CANADA

MANN S.Z. E1360

MANNERS....SEE ETIQUET

MANNHEIM H. E1361

MANNHEIM/K....KARL MANNHEIM

MANNING B. E1362

MANPOWER....SEE LABOR

MANSERGH N. E1363

MANTON/M....MART MANTON

B62
BORKIN J.,THE CORRUPT JUDGE. USA+45 CT/SYS ATTIT   ADJUD
SUPEGO MORAL RESPECT...BIBLIOG + SUPREME/CT   TRIBUTE
MANTON/M DAVIS/W JOHNSN/ALB. PAGE 14 E0271   CRIME

MANUFACTURING INDUSTRY....SEE PROC/MFG

MANVELL R. E1364

MAO....MAO TSE-TUNG

B67
LENG S.C.,JUSTICE IN COMMUNIST CHINA: A SURVEY OF   CT/SYS
THE JUDICIAL SYSTEM OF THE CHINESE PEOPLE'S   ADJUD

REPUBLIC. CHINA/COM LAW CONSTN LOC/G NAT/G PROF/ORG JURID
CONSULT FORCES ADMIN CRIME ORD/FREE...BIBLIOG 20   MARXISM
MAO. PAGE 64 E1284

MAPS....MAPS AND ATLASES; SEE ALSO CHARTS

B44
FULLER G.H.,TURKEY: A SELECTED LIST OF REFERENCES. BIBLIOG/A
ISLAM TURKEY CULTURE ECO/UNDEV AGRI DIPLOM NAT/LISM ALL/VALS
CONSERVE...GEOG HUM INT/LAW SOC 7/20 MAPS. PAGE 42 CONSERVE
E0824

MARAJO....MARAJO, A BRAZILIAN ISLAND

MARANHAO....MARANHAO, BRAZIL

MARCANT/V....VITO MARCANTONIO

MARCUSE/H....HERBERT MARCUSE

MARITAIN J. E1365

MARITAIN/J....JACQUES MARITAIN

MARITIME....MARITIME PROVINCES

B33
REID H.D.,RECUEIL DES COURS; TOME 45: LES   ORD/FREE
SERVITUDES INTERNATIONALES III. FRANCE CONSTN   DIPLOM
DELIB/GP PRESS CONTROL REV WAR CHOOSE PEACE MORAL   LAW
MARITIME TREATY. PAGE 84 E1680

MARKE J.J. E1366

MARKET RESEARCH....SEE MARKET

MARKET....MARKETING SYSTEM

N19
ATOMIC INDUSTRIAL FORUM,COMMENTARY ON LEGISLATION   NUC/PWR
TO PERMIT PRIVATE OWNERSHIP OF SPECIAL NUCLEAR   MARKET
MATERIAL (PAMPHLET). USA+45 DELIB/GP LEGIS PLAN OWN INDUS
...POLICY 20 AEC CONGRESS. PAGE 6 E0111   LAW

B28
CORBETT P.E.,CANADA AND WORLD POLITICS. LAW CULTURE NAT/G
SOCIETY STRUCT MARKET INT/ORG FORCES ACT/RES PLAN   CANADA
ECO/TAC LEGIT ORD/FREE PWR RESPECT...SOC CONCPT
TIME/SEQ TREND CMN/WLTH 20 LEAGUE/NAT. PAGE 26
E0504

B42
CROWE S.E.,THE BERLIN WEST AFRICA CONFERENCE,   AFR
1884-85. GERMANY ELITES MARKET INT/ORG DELIB/GP   CONFER
FORCES PROB/SOLV BAL/PWR CAP/ISM DOMIN COLONIAL   INT/TRADE
...INT/LAW 19. PAGE 28 E0548   DIPLOM

B47
TOWLE L.W.,INTERNATIONAL TRADE AND COMMERCIAL   MARKET
POLICY. WOR+45 LAW ECO/DEV FINAN INDUS NAT/G   INT/ORG
ECO/TAC WEALTH...TIME/SEQ ILO 20. PAGE 97 E1937   INT/TRADE

C49
BLODGETT R.H.,"COMPARATIVE ECONOMIC SYSTEMS (REV.   METH/COMP
ED.)" WOR-45 AGRI FINAN MARKET LABOR NAT/G PLAN   CONCPT
INT/TRADE PRICE...POLICY DECISION BIBLIOG 20.   ROUTINE
PAGE 13 E0248

B54
CAPLOW T.,THE SOCIOLOGY OF WORK. USA+45 USA-45   LABOR
STRATA MARKET FAM GP/REL INGP/REL ALL/VALS   WORKER
...DECISION STAT BIBLIOG SOC/INTEG 20. PAGE 19   INDUS
E0375   ROLE

B58
ATOMIC INDUSTRIAL FORUM,MANAGEMENT AND ATOMIC   NUC/PWR
ENERGY. WOR+45 SEA LAW MARKET NAT/G TEC/DEV INSPECT INDUS
INT/TRADE CONFER PEACE HEALTH...ANTHOL 20. PAGE 6   MGT
E0112   ECO/TAC

B58
WHITNEY S.N.,ANTITRUST POLICIES: AMERICAN   INDUS
EXPERIENCE IN TWENTY INDUSTRIES. USA+45 USA-45 LAW CONTROL
DELIB/GP LEGIS ADJUD CT/SYS GOV/REL ATTIT...ANTHOL LG/CO
20 MONOPOLY CASEBOOK. PAGE 106 E2119   MARKET

L59
COWAN T.A.,"A SYMPOSIUM ON GROUP INTERESTS AND THE ADJUD
LAW" USA+45 LAW MARKET LABOR PLAN INT/TRADE TAX   PWR
RACE/REL RIGID/FLEX...JURID ANTHOL 20. PAGE 27   INGP/REL
E0528   CREATE

B60
CONANT M.,ANTITRUST IN THE MOTION PICTURE INDUSTRY: PRICE
ECONOMIC AND LEGAL ANALYSIS. USA+45 MARKET ADJUST   CONTROL
DEMAND BIBLIOG. PAGE 24 E0484   LAW

ART/METH

B60
MUTHESIUS V.,DAS GESPENST DER WIRTSCHAFTLICHEN   ECO/TAC
MACHT. GERMANY/W ECO/DEV FINAN MARKET TAX...JURID   NAT/G
20. PAGE 75 E1513   CONCPT
                                                    LG/CO

B60
STEIN E.,AMERICAN ENTERPRISE IN THE EUROPEAN COMMON MARKET
MARKET: A LEGAL PROFILE. EUR+WWI FUT USA+45 SOCIETY ADJUD
STRUCT ECO/DEV NAT/G VOL/ASSN CONSULT PLAN TEC/DEV INT/LAW
ECO/TAC INT/TRADE ADMIN ATTIT RIGID/FLEX PWR...MGT
NEW/IDEA STAT TREND COMPUT/IR SIMUL EEC 20. PAGE 93
E1867

L60
STEIN E.,"LEGAL REMEDIES OF ENTERPRISES IN THE   MARKET
EUROPEAN ECONOMIC COMMUNITY." EUR+WWI FUT ECO/DEV   ADJUD
INDUS PLAN ECO/TAC ADMIN PWR...MGT MATH STAT TREND
CON/ANAL EEC 20. PAGE 93 E1868

B62
SHAW C.,LEGAL PROBLEMS IN INTERNATIONAL TRADE AND   INT/LAW
INVESTMENT. WOR+45 ECO/DEV ECO/UNDEV MARKET DIPLOM INT/TRADE
TAX INCOME ROLE...ANTHOL BIBLIOG 20 TREATY UN IMF   FINAN
GATT. PAGE 91 E1816   ECO/TAC

S63
WALKER H.,"THE INTERNATIONAL LAW OF COMMODITY   MARKET
AGREEMENTS." FUT WOR+45 ECO/DEV ECO/UNDEV FINAN   VOL/ASSN
INT/ORG NAT/G CONSULT CREATE PLAN ECO/TAC ATTIT   INT/LAW
PERCEPT...CONCPT GEN/LAWS TOT/POP GATT 20. PAGE 105 INT/TRADE
E2095

B64
US SENATE COMM ON JUDICIARY,HEARINGS BEFORE   ECO/DEV
SUBCOMMITTEE ON ANTITRUST AND MONOPOLY: ECONOMIC   CONTROL
CONCENTRATION VOLUMES 1-5 JULY 1964-SEPT 1966.   MARKET
USA+45 LAW FINAN ECO/TAC ADJUD COST EFFICIENCY   LG/CO
PRODUC...STAT CHARTS 20 CONGRESS MONOPOLY. PAGE 102
E2052

S64
DERWINSKI E.J.,"THE COST OF THE INTERNATIONAL   MARKET
COFFEE AGREEMENT." L/A+17C USA+45 WOR+45 ECO/UNDEV DELIB/GP
NAT/G VOL/ASSN LEGIS DIPLOM ECO/TAC FOR/AID LEGIT   INT/TRADE
ATTIT...TIME/SEQ CONGRESS 20 TREATY. PAGE 31 E0608

B65
US SENATE COMM ON JUDICIARY,ANTITRUST EXEMPTIONS   BAL/PAY
FOR AGREEMENTS RELATING TO BALANCE OF PAYMENTS.   ADJUD
FINAN ECO/TAC CONTROL WEALTH...POLICY 20 CONGRESS. MARKET
PAGE 103 E2056   INT/TRADE

B66
GRUNEWALD D.,PUBLIC POLICY AND THE MODERN   LG/CO
COOPERATION: SELECTED READINGS. USA+45 LAW MARKET   POLICY
VOL/ASSN CAP/ISM INT/TRADE CENTRAL OWN...SOC ANTHOL NAT/G
20. PAGE 48 E0954   CONTROL

B67
CAVES R.,AMERICAN INDUSTRY: STRUCTURE, CONDUCT,   ECO/DEV
PERFORMANCE (2ND ED.). USA+45 MARKET NAT/G ADJUD   INDUS
CONTROL GP/REL DEMAND WEALTH 20. PAGE 21 E0412   POLICY
                                                    ECO/TAC

B67
ROBINSON R.D., INTERNATIONAL MANAGEMENT. USA+45   INT/TRADE
FINAN R+D PLAN PRODUC...DECISION T. PAGE 67 E1336   MGT
                                                    INT/LAW
                                                    MARKET

L67
BERNHARD R.C.,"COMPETITION IN LAW AND ECONOMICS."   MARKET
LAW PLAN PRICE CONTROL PRODUC PROFIT...METH/CNCPT   POLICY
IDEA/COMP GEN/LAWS 20. PAGE 11 E0210   NAT/G
                                                    CT/SYS

S67
RICHARDSON J.J.,"THE MAKING OF THE RESTRICTIVE   LEGIS
TRADE PRACTICES ACT 1956 A CASE STUDY OF THE POLICY ECO/TAC
PROCESS IN BRITAIN." UK FINAN MARKET LG/CO POL/PAR POLICY
CONSULT PRESS ADJUD ADMIN AGREE LOBBY SANCTION   INDUS
ATTIT 20. PAGE 84 E1695

B82
POLLOCK F.,ESSAYS IN JURISPRUDENCE AND ETHICS. UNIV JURID
LAW FINAN MARKET WORKER INGP/REL MORAL...POLICY   CONCPT
GEN/LAWS. PAGE 81 E1625

MARKETING SYSTEM....SEE MARKET

MARNELL W.H. E1367

MARRIAGE....WEDLOCK; SEE ALSO LOVE

N
CANON LAW ABSTRACTS. LEGIT CONFER CT/SYS INGP/REL
MARRIAGE ATTIT MORAL WORSHIP 20. PAGE 2 E0026
   BIBLIOG/A
   CATHISM
   SECT
   LAW

B09
JUSTINIAN,THE DIGEST (DIGESTA CORPUS JURIS CIVILIS)
(2 VOLS.) (TRANS. BY C. H. MONRO). ROMAN/EMP LAW
FAM LOC/G LEGIS EDU/PROP CONTROL MARRIAGE OWN ROLE
CIVIL/LAW. PAGE 59 E1177
   JURID
   CT/SYS
   NAT/G
   STRATA

B42
HEGEL G.W.F.,PHILOSOPHY OF RIGHT. UNIV FAM SECT
CHIEF AGREE WAR MARRIAGE OWN ORD/FREE...POLICY
CONCPT. PAGE 51 E1023
   NAT/G
   LAW
   RATIONAL

S45
DAVIS A.,"CASTE, ECONOMY, AND VIOLENCE" (BMR)"
USA-45 LAW SOCIETY STRUCT SECT SANCTION COERCE
MARRIAGE SEX...PSY SOC SOC/INTEG 18/20 NEGRO
MISCEGEN SOUTH/US. PAGE 29 E0570
   STRATA
   RACE/REL
   DISCRIM

B55
CHARMATZ J.P.,COMPARATIVE STUDIES IN COMMUNITY
PROPERTY LAW. FRANCE USA+45...JURID GOV/COMP ANTHOL
20. PAGE 22 E0424
   MARRIAGE
   LAW
   OWN
   MUNIC

B55
SERRANO MOSCOSO E.,A STATEMENT OF THE LAWS OF
ECUADOR IN MATTERS AFFECTING BUSINESS (2ND ED.).
ECUADOR INDUS LABOR LG/CO NAT/G LEGIS TAX CONTROL
MARRIAGE 20. PAGE 90 E1805
   FINAN
   ECO/UNDEV
   LAW
   CONSTN

B55
WRONG D.H.,AMERICAN AND CANADIAN VIEWPOINTS. CANADA
USA+45 CONSTN STRATA FAM SECT WORKER ECO/TAC
EDU/PROP ADJUD MARRIAGE...IDEA/COMP 20. PAGE 108
E2161
   DIPLOM
   ATTIT
   NAT/COMP
   CULTURE

B57
INSTITUT DE DROIT INTL,TABLEAU GENERAL DES
RESOLUTIONS (1873-1956). LAW NEUTRAL CRIME WAR
MARRIAGE PEACE...JURID 19/20. PAGE 56 E1124
   INT/LAW
   DIPLOM
   ORD/FREE
   ADJUD

B58
ALLEN C.K.,ASPECTS OF JUSTICE. UK FAM COERCE CRIME
MARRIAGE AGE/Y LOVE 20 ENGLSH/LAW. PAGE 4 E0068
   JURID
   MORAL
   ORD/FREE

B61
HAGEN A.,STAAT UND KATHOLISCHE KIRCHE IN
WURTTEMBERG IN DEN JAHREN 1848-1862 (2 VOLS.).
GERMANY DELIB/GP EDU/PROP MARRIAGE CATHISM 19
CHURCH/STA. PAGE 49 E0975
   SECT
   PROVS
   GP/REL
   JURID

B61
RUEDA B.,A STATEMENT OF THE LAWS OF COLOMBIA IN
MATTERS AFFECTING BUSINESS (3RD ED.). INDUS FAM
LABOR LG/CO NAT/G LEGIS TAX CONTROL MARRIAGE 20
COLOMB. PAGE 86 E1733
   FINAN
   ECO/UNDEV
   LAW
   CONSTN

B64
FREISEN J.,STAAT UND KATHOLISCHE KIRCHE IN DEN
DEUTSCHEN BUNDESSTAATEN (2 VOLS.). GERMANY LAW FAM
NAT/G EDU/PROP GP/REL MARRIAGE WEALTH 19/20
CHURCH/STA. PAGE 40 E0793
   SECT
   CATHISM
   JURID
   PROVS

B64
TELLADO A.,A STATEMENT OF THE LAWS OF THE DOMINICAN
REPUBLIC IN MATTERS AFFECTING BUSINESS (3RD ED.).
DOMIN/REP AGRI DIST/IND EXTR/IND FINAN FAM WORKER
ECO/TAC TAX CT/SYS MARRIAGE OWN...BIBLIOG 20
MIGRATION. PAGE 95 E1913
   CONSTN
   LEGIS
   NAT/G
   INDUS

B65
LUGO-MARENCO J.J.,A STATEMENT OF THE LAWS OF
NICARAGUA IN MATTERS AFFECTING BUSINESS. NICARAGUA
AGRI DIST/IND EXTR/IND FINAN INDUS FAM WORKER
INT/TRADE TAX MARRIAGE OWN BIO/SOC 20 TREATY
RESOURCE/N MIGRATION. PAGE 67 E1332
   CONSTN
   NAT/G
   LEGIS
   JURID

L67
CICOUREL A.V.,"KINSHIP, MARRIAGE, AND DIVORCE IN
COMPARATIVE FAMILY LAW." UNIV LAW FAM KIN GEN/METH.
PAGE 22 E0438
   SOC
   PHIL/SCI
   MARRIAGE
   IDEA/COMP

S67
BOHANNAN P.,"INSTITUTIONS OF DIVORCE, FAMILY, AND
THE LAW." WOR+45 LAW CONSULT...JURID SOC. PAGE 13
E0258
   FAM
   MARRIAGE
   ADJUD
   SOCIETY

S68
DUPRE L.,"TILL DEATH DO US PART?" UNIV FAM INSPECT
LEGIT ADJUD SANCTION PERS/REL ANOMIE RIGID/FLEX SEX
...JURID IDEA/COMP 20 CHURCH/STA BIBLE CANON/LAW
CIVIL/LAW. PAGE 34 E0666
   MARRIAGE
   CATH
   LAW

B89
FICHTE J.G.,THE SCIENCE OF RIGHTS (TRANS. BY A.E.
KROEGER). WOR-45 FAM MUNIC NAT/G PROVS ADJUD CRIME
CHOOSE MARRIAGE SEX POPULISM 19 FICHTE/JG
NATURL/LAW. PAGE 37 E0744
   ORD/FREE
   CONSTN
   LAW
   CONCPT

MARS D. E1368

MARSH N.S. E1918

MARSHALL B. E1369

MARSHALL G. E1370

MARSHALL/A....ALFRED MARSHALL

MARSHALL/J....JOHN MARSHALL

B56
DOUGLAS W.O.,WE THE JUDGES. INDIA USA+45 USA-45 LAW
NAT/G SECT LEGIS PRESS CRIME FEDERAL ORD/FREE
...POLICY GOV/COMP 19/20 WARRN/EARL MARSHALL/J
SUPREME/CT. PAGE 32 E0640
   ADJUD
   CT/SYS
   CONSTN
   GOV/REL

B60
MENDELSON W.,CAPITALISM, DEMOCRACY, AND THE SUPREME
COURT. USA+45 USA-45 CONSTN DIPLOM GOV/REL ATTIT
ORD/FREE LAISSEZ...POLICY CHARTS PERS/COMP 18/20
SUPREME/CT MARSHALL/J HOLMES/OW TANEY/RB FIELD/JJ.
PAGE 72 E1437
   JUDGE
   CT/SYS
   JURID
   NAT/G

B62
BICKEL A.,THE LEAST DANGEROUS BRANCH. USA+45 USA-45
CONSTN SCHOOL LEGIS ADJUD RACE/REL DISCRIM ORD/FREE
...JURID 18/20 SUPREME/CT CONGRESS MARSHALL/J
HOLMES/OW FRANKFUR/F. PAGE 12 E0226
   LAW
   NAT/G
   CT/SYS

B62
MASON A.T.,THE SUPREME COURT: PALADIUM OF FREEDOM.
USA-45 NAT/G POL/PAR CHIEF LEGIS ADJUD PARL/PROC
FEDERAL PWR...POLICY BIOG 18/20 SUPREME/CT
ROOSEVLT/F JEFFERSN/T MARSHALL/J HUGHES/CE. PAGE 69
E1378
   CONSTN
   CT/SYS
   JURID

MARSHL/PLN....MARSHALL PLAN

MARTENS E. E1371

MARTI/JOSE....JOSE MARTI

MARTIN A. E1372

MARTIN L.J. E1373

MARTIN L.W. E1374

MARX C.M. E1375

MARX/KARL....KARL MARX

B63
FRIEDRICH C.J.,JUSTICE: NOMOS VI. UNIV LAW SANCTION
CRIME...CONCPT ANTHOL MARX/KARL LOCKE/JOHN
AQUINAS/T. PAGE 41 E0809
   LEGIT
   ADJUD
   ORD/FREE
   JURID

B63
HABERMAS J.,THEORIE UND PRAXIS. RATIONAL PERSON
...PHIL/SCI ANTHOL 19/20 HEGEL/GWF MARX/KARL BLOCH
LOWITH. PAGE 49 E0969
   JURID
   REV
   GEN/LAWS
   MARXISM

S64
CRANE R.D.,"BASIC PRINCIPLES IN SOVIET SPACE LAW."
FUT WOR+45 AIR INT/ORG DIPLOM DOMIN ARMS/CONT
COERCE NUC/PWR PEACE ATTIT DRIVE PWR...INT/LAW
METH/CNCPT NEW/IDEA OBS TREND GEN/LAWS VAL/FREE
MARX/KARL 20. PAGE 27 E0544
   COM
   LAW
   USSR
   SPACE

S64
GINSBURGS G.,"WARS OF NATIONAL LIBERATION - THE
SOVIET THESIS." COM USSR WOR+45 WOR-45 LAW CULTURE
INT/ORG DIPLOM LEGIT COLONIAL GUERRILLA WAR
NAT/LISM ATTIT PERSON MORAL PWR...JURID OBS TREND
MARX/KARL 20. PAGE 44 E0869
   COERCE
   CONCPT
   INT/LAW
   REV

S64
KARPOV P.V.,"PEACEFUL COEXISTENCE AND INTERNATIONAL
LAW." WOR+45 LAW SOCIETY INT/ORG VOL/ASSN FORCES
CREATE CAP/ISM DIPLOM ADJUD NUC/PWR PEACE MORAL
   COM
   ATTIT
   INT/LAW

ORD/FREE PWR MARXISM...MARXIST JURID CONCPT OBS
TREND COLD/WAR MARX/KARL 20. PAGE 59 E1186
USSR

S67
SEIDLER G.L.,"MARXIST LEGAL THOUGHT IN POLAND."
POLAND SOCIETY R+D LOC/G NAT/G ACT/RES ADJUD CT/SYS
SUPEGO PWR...SOC TREND 20 MARX/KARL. PAGE 90 E1802
MARXISM
LAW
CONCPT
EFFICIENCY

MARXISM....MARXISM, COMMUNISM; SEE ALSO MARXIST

N19
IN THE SHADOW OF FEAR; AMERICAN CIVIL LIBERTIES,
1948-49 (PAMPHLET). COM LAW LEGIS BAL/PWR EDU/PROP
CT/SYS RACE/REL DISCRIM MARXISM SOCISM 20 COLD/WAR
CONGRESS ACLU CIV/RIGHTS ESPIONAGE. PAGE 2 E0030
ORD/FREE
CONSTN
POLICY

N19
AMERICAN CIVIL LIBERTIES UNION,"WE HOLD THESE
TRUTHS" FREEDOM, JUSTICE, EQUALITY: REPORT ON CIVIL
LIBERTIES (A PERIODICAL PAMPHLET COVERING 1951-53).
USA+45 ACADEM NAT/G FORCES LEGIS COERCE CIVMIL/REL
GOV/REL DISCRIM PRIVIL MARXISM...OLD/LIB 20 ACLU UN
CIVIL/LIB. PAGE 4 E0076
ORD/FREE
LAW
RACE/REL
CONSTN

C20
DUNNING W.A.,"A HISTORY OF POLITICAL THINKERS FROM
ROUSSEAU TO SPENCER." NAT/G REV NAT/LISM UTIL
CONSERVE MARXISM POPULISM...JURID BIBLIOG 18/19.
PAGE 33 E0664
IDEA/COMP
PHIL/SCI
CONCPT
GEN/LAWS

B22
SCHROEDER T.,FREE SPEECH BIBLIOGRAPHY. EUR+WWI
WOR-45 NAT/G SECT ECO/TAC WRITING ADJUD ATTIT
MARXISM SOCISM 16/20. PAGE 88 E1768
BIBLIOG/A
ORD/FREE
CONTROL
LAW

B24
NAVILLE A.,LIBERTE, EGALITE, SOLIDARITE: ESSAIS
D'ANALYSE. STRATA FAM VOL/ASSN INT/TRADE GP/REL
MORAL MARXISM SOCISM...PSY TREATY. PAGE 76 E1529
ORD/FREE
SOC
IDEA/COMP
DIPLOM

B38
HARPER S.N.,THE GOVERNMENT OF THE SOVIET UNION. COM
USSR LAW CONSTN ECO/DEV PLAN TEC/DEV DIPLOM
INT/TRADE ADMIN REV NAT/LISM...POLICY 20. PAGE 50
E1001
MARXISM
NAT/G
LEAD
POL/PAR

B43
MICAUD C.A.,THE FRENCH RIGHT AND NAZI GERMANY
1933-1939: A STUDY OF PUBLIC OPINION. GERMANY UK
USSR POL/PAR ARMS/CONT COERCE DETER PEACE
RIGID/FLEX PWR MARXISM...FASCIST TREND 20
LEAGUE/NAT TREATY. PAGE 73 E1454
DIPLOM
AGREE

B44
US LIBRARY OF CONGRESS,RUSSIA: A CHECK LIST
PRELIMINARY TO A BASIC BIBLIOGRAPHY OF MATERIALS IN
THE RUSSIAN LANGUAGE. COM USSR CULTURE EDU/PROP
MARXISM...ART/METH HUM LING 19/20. PAGE 101 E2015
BIBLIOG
LAW
SECT

B48
YAKOBSON S.,FIVE HUNDRED RUSSIAN WORKS FOR COLLEGE
LIBRARIES (PAMPHLET). MOD/EUR USSR MARXISM SOCISM
...ART/METH GEOG HUM JURID SOC 13/20. PAGE 108
E2162
BIBLIOG
NAT/G
CULTURE
COM

B49
US DEPARTMENT OF STATE,SOVIET BIBLIOGRAPHY
(PAMPHLET). CHINA/COM COM USSR LAW AGRI INT/ORG
ECO/TAC EDU/PROP...POLICY GEOG 20. PAGE 99 E1994
BIBLIOG/A
MARXISM
CULTURE
DIPLOM

B50
BERMAN H.J.,JUSTICE IN RUSSIA: AN INTERPRETATION OF
SOVIET LAW. USSR LAW STRUCT LABOR FORCES AGREE
GP/REL ORD/FREE SOCISM...TIME/SEQ 20. PAGE 11 E0207
JURID
ADJUD
MARXISM
COERCE

B52
APPADORAI A.,THE SUBSTANCE OF POLITICS (6TH ED.).
EX/STRUC LEGIS DIPLOM CT/SYS CHOOSE FASCISM MARXISM
SOCISM...BIBLIOG T. PAGE 5 E0100
PHIL/SCI
NAT/G

B52
US DEPARTMENT OF STATE,RESEARCH ON EASTERN EUROPE
(EXCLUDING USSR). EUR+WWI LAW ECO/DEV NAT/G
PROB/SOLV DIPLOM ADMIN LEAD MARXISM...TREND 19/20.
PAGE 100 E1995
BIBLIOG
R+D
ACT/RES
COM

B55
BIBLIOGRAPHY ON THE COMMUNIST PROBLEM IN THE UNITED
STATES. USA-45 PRESS ADJUD ATTIT...BIOG 20. PAGE 2
E0033
BIBLIOG/A
MARXISM
POL/PAR
USA+45

B55
FLIESS P.J.,FREEDOM OF THE PRESS IN THE GERMAN
REPUBLIC. 1918-1933. GERMANY LAW CONSTN POL/PAR
LEGIS WRITING ADMIN COERCE MURDER MARXISM...POLICY
BIBLIOG 20 WEIMAR/REP. PAGE 39 E0765
EDU/PROP
ORD/FREE
JURID
PRESS

B55
MID-EUROPEAN LAW PROJECT,CHURCH AND STATE BEHIND
THE IRON CURTAIN. COM CZECHOSLVK HUNGARY POLAND
USSR CULTURE SECT EDU/PROP GOV/REL CATHISM...CHARTS
ANTHOL BIBLIOG WORSHIP 20 CHURCH/STA. PAGE 73 E1455
LAW
MARXISM
POLICY

B56
SIPKOV I.,LEGAL SOURCES AND BIBLIOGRAPHY OF
BULGARIA. BULGARIA COM LEGIS WRITING ADJUD CT/SYS
...INT/LAW TREATY 20. PAGE 91 E1834
BIBLIOG
LAW
TOTALISM
MARXISM

C56
FALL B.B.,"THE VIET-MINH REGIME." VIETNAM LAW
ECO/UNDEV POL/PAR FORCES DOMIN WAR ATTIT MARXISM
...BIOG PREDICT BIBLIOG/A 20. PAGE 36 E0720
NAT/G
ADMIN
EX/STRUC
LEAD

B57
BYRNES R.F.,BIBLIOGRAPHY OF AMERICAN PUBLICATIONS
ON EAST CENTRAL EUROPE, 1945-1957 (VOL. XXII). SECT
DIPLOM EDU/PROP RACE/REL...ART/METH GEOG JURID SOC
LING 20 JEWS. PAGE 18 E0354
BIBLIOG/A
COM
MARXISM
NAT/G

B57
HISS A.,IN THE COURT OF PUBLIC OPINION. USA+45
DELIB/GP LEGIS LEGIT CT/SYS ATTIT 20 DEPT/STATE
NIXON/RM HUAC HISS/ALGER. PAGE 53 E1053
CRIME
MARXISM
BIOG
ADJUD

B59
BOHMER A.,LEGAL SOURCES AND BIBLIOGRAPHY OF
CZECHOSLOVAKIA. COM CZECHOSLVK PARL/PROC SANCTION
CRIME MARXISM 20. PAGE 13 E0261
BIBLIOG
ADJUD
LAW
JURID

B59
EPSTEIN F.T.,EAST GERMANY: A SELECTED BIBLIOGRAPHY
(PAMPHLET). COM GERMANY/E LAW AGRI FINAN INDUS
LABOR POL/PAR EDU/PROP ADMIN AGE/Y 20. PAGE 35
E0693
BIBLIOG/A
INTELL
MARXISM
NAT/G

B59
GINZBURG B.,REDEDICATION TO FREEDOM. DELIB/GP LEGIS
ATTIT MARXISM 20 SUPREME/CT CON/INTERP HUAC AMEND/I
FBI. PAGE 44 E0871
JURID
ORD/FREE
CONSTN
NAT/G

B59
GSOVSKI V.,GOVERNMENT, LAW, AND COURTS IN THE
SOVIET UNION AND EASTERN EUROPE (2 VOLS.). COM USSR
AGRI INDUS WORKER CT/SYS CRIME...BIBLIOG 20
EUROPE/E. PAGE 48 E0958
ADJUD
MARXISM
CONTROL
ORD/FREE

B59
HOOK S.,POLITICAL POWER AND PERSONAL FREEDOM:
CRITICAL STUDIES IN DEMOCRACY, COMMUNISM AND CIVIL
RIGHTS. UNIV LAW SOCIETY DIPLOM TOTALISM MARXISM
SOCISM...PHIL/SCI IDEA/COMP 20 CIV/RIGHTS. PAGE 55
E1094
ORD/FREE
PWR
WELF/ST
CHOOSE

B60
FISCHER L.,THE SOVIETS IN WORLD AFFAIRS. CHINA/COM
COM EUR+WWI USSR INT/ORG CONFER LEAD ARMS/CONT REV
PWR...CHARTS 20 TREATY VERSAILLES. PAGE 38 E0755
DIPLOM
NAT/G
POLICY
MARXISM

B60
GELLHORN W.,AMERICAN RIGHTS: THE CONSTITUTION IN
ACTION. USA+45 USA-45 LEGIS ADJUD COERCE RACE/REL
DISCRIM MARXISM 20 SUPREME/CT. PAGE 43 E0846
ORD/FREE
JURID
CT/SYS
CONSTN

B61
LA PONCE J.A.,THE GOVERNMENT OF THE FIFTH REPUBLIC:
FRENCH POLITICAL PARTIES AND THE CONSTITUTION.
ALGERIA FRANCE LAW NAT/G DELIB/GP LEGIS ECO/TAC
MARXISM SOCISM...CHARTS BIBLIOG/A 20 DEGAULLE/C.
PAGE 62 E1243
PWR
POL/PAR
CONSTN
CHIEF

B61
NEWMAN R.P.,RECOGNITION OF COMMUNIST CHINA? A STUDY
IN ARGUMENT. CHINA/COM NAT/G PROB/SOLV RATIONAL
...INT/LAW LOG IDEA/COMP BIBLIOG 20. PAGE 77 E1544
MARXISM
ATTIT
DIPLOM
POLICY

B62
BOCHENSKI J.M.,HANDBOOK ON COMMUNISM. USSR WOR+45
LAW SOCIETY NAT/G POL/PAR SECT CRIME PERSON MARXISM
COM
DIPLOM

...SOC ANTHOL 20. PAGE 13 E0254   POLICY
                                                    CONCPT

                                                         B62
DOUGLAS W.O.,DEMOCRACY'S MANIFESTO. COM USA+45   DIPLOM
ECO/UNDEV INT/ORG FORCES PLAN NEUTRAL TASK MARXISM POLICY
...JURID 20 NATO SEATO. PAGE 32 E0642   NAT/G
                                                    ORD/FREE

                                                         B62
LEVY H.V.,LIBERDADE E JUSTICA SOCIAL (2ND ED.).   ORD/FREE
BRAZIL COM L/A+17C USSR INT/ORG PARTIC GP/REL   MARXISM
WEALTH 20 UN COM/PARTY. PAGE 65 E1290   CAP/ISM
                                                    LAW

                                                         B62
MCWHINNEY E.,CONSTITUTIONALISM IN GERMANY AND THE   CONSTN
FEDERAL CONSTITUTINAL COURT. GERMANY/W POL/PAR TV   CT/SYS
ADJUD CHOOSE EFFICIENCY ATTIT ORD/FREE MARXISM   CONTROL
...NEW/IDEA BIBLIOG 20. PAGE 71 E1428   NAT/G

                                                         B62
SWAYZE H.,POLITICAL CONTROL OF LITERATURE IN THE   MARXISM
USSR, 1946-1959. USSR NAT/G CREATE LICENSE...JURID WRITING
20. PAGE 95 E1898   CONTROL
                                                    DOMIN

                                                         B63
HABERMAS J.,THEORIE UND PRAXIS. RATIONAL PERSON   JURID
...PHIL/SCI ANTHOL 19/20 HEGEL/GWF MARX/KARL BLOCH REV
LOWITH. PAGE 49 E0969   GEN/LAWS
                                                    MARXISM

                                                         B63
KLESMENT J.,LEGAL SOURCES AND BIBLIOGRAPHY OF THE   BIBLIOG/A
BALTIC STATES (ESTONIA, LATVIA, LITHUANIA). COM   JURID
ESTONIA LATVIA LITHUANIA LAW FINAN ADJUD CT/SYS   CONSTN
REGION CENTRAL MARXISM 19/20. PAGE 61 E1223   ADMIN

                                                         B63
LAVROFF D.-.G.,LES LIBERTES PUBLIQUES EN UNION   ORD/FREE
SOVIETIQUE (REV. ED.). USSR NAT/G WORKER SANCTION   LAW
CRIME MARXISM NEW/LIB...JURID BIBLIOG WORSHIP 20.   ATTIT
PAGE 63 E1268   COM

                                                         B63
LIVELY E.,THE INVASION OF MISSISSIPPI. USA+45 LAW   RACE/REL
CONSTN NAT/G PROVS CT/SYS GOV/REL FEDERAL CONSERVE CROWD
...TRADIT 20 MISSISSIPP NEGRO NAACP WARRN/EARL   COERCE
KENNEDY/JF. PAGE 66 E1309   MARXISM

                                                         B63
PACHTER H.M.,COLLISION COURSE; THE CUBAN MISSILE   WAR
CRISIS AND COEXISTENCE. CUBA USA+45 DIPLOM   BAL/PWR
ARMS/CONT PEACE MARXISM...DECISION INT/LAW 20   NUC/PWR
COLD/WAR KHRUSH/N KENNEDY/JF CASTRO/F. PAGE 79   DETER
E1587

                                                         B63
US SENATE COMM ON JUDICIARY,CASTRO'S NETWORK IN THE PRESS
UNITED STATES. CUBA LAW DELIB/GP 20 SENATE   MARXISM
CASTRO/F. PAGE 102 E2050   DIPLOM
                                                    INSPECT

                                                         B64
BROOKS T.R.,TOIL AND TROUBLE, A HISTORY OF AMERICAN INDUS
LABOR. WORKER BARGAIN CAP/ISM ADJUD AUTOMAT EXEC   LABOR
GP/REL RACE/REL EFFICIENCY INCOME PROFIT MARXISM   LEGIS
17/20 KENNEDY/JF AFL/CIO NEGRO. PAGE 16 E0310

                                                         B64
DOOLIN D.J.,COMMUNIST CHINA: THE POLITICS OF   MARXISM
STUDENT OPPOSITION. CHINA/COM ELITES STRATA ACADEM DEBATE
NAT/G WRITING CT/SYS LEAD PARTIC COERCE TOTALISM   AGE/Y
20. PAGE 32 E0637   PWR

                                                         B64
DUBOIS J.,DANGER OVER PANAMA. FUT PANAMA SCHOOL   DIPLOM
PROB/SOLV EDU/PROP MARXISM...POLICY 19/20 TREATY   COERCE
INTERVENT CANAL/ZONE. PAGE 33 E0652

                                                         B64
FEIFER G.,JUSTICE IN MOSCOW. USSR LAW CRIME   ADJUD
...RECORD 20. PAGE 37 E0725   JURID
                                                    CT/SYS
                                                    MARXISM

                                                         B64
FREUD A.,OF HUMAN SOVEREIGNTY. WOR+45 INDUS SECT   NAT/LISM
ECO/TAC CRIME CHOOSE ATTIT MORAL MARXISM...POLICY   DIPLOM
BIBLIOG 20. PAGE 40 E0794   WAR
                                                    PEACE

                                                         B64
GRZYBOWSKI K.,THE SOCIALIST COMMONWEALTH OF   INT/LAW
NATIONS: ORGANIZATIONS AND INSTITUTIONS. FORCES   COM

                                                         B64
DIPLOM INT/TRADE ADJUD ADMIN LEAD WAR MARXISM   REGION
SOCISM...BIBLIOG 20 COMECON WARSAW/P. PAGE 48 E0956 INT/ORG

                                                         B64
GUMPLOWICZ L.,RECHTSSTAAT UND SOZIALISMUS. STRATA   JURID
ORD/FREE SOVEREIGN MARXISM...IDEA/COMP 16/20 KANT/I NAT/G
HOBBES/T. PAGE 48 E0962   SOCISM
                                                    CONCPT

                                                         B64
GUTTMANN A.,COMMUNISM, THE COURTS, AND THE   MARXISM
CONSTITUTION. USA+45 CT/SYS ORD/FREE...ANTHOL 20   POL/PAR
COM/PARTY CIV/RIGHTS. PAGE 48 E0965   CONSTN
                                                    LAW

                                                         B64
KISER S.L.,AMERICANISM IN ACTION. USA+45 LAW PROVS OLD/LIB
CAP/ISM DIPLOM RECEIVE CONTROL CT/SYS WAR FEDERAL   FOR/AID
ATTIT WEALTH 20 SUPREME/CT. PAGE 61 E1221   MARXISM
                                                    CONSTN

                                                         B64
LAPENNA I.,STATE AND LAW: SOVIET AND YUGOSLAV   JURID
THEORY. USSR YUGOSLAVIA STRATA STRUCT NAT/G DOMIN   COM
COERCE MARXISM...GOV/COMP IDEA/COMP 20. PAGE 63   LAW
E1253   SOVEREIGN

                                                         B64
SIEKANOWICZ P.,LEGAL SOURCES AND BIBLIOGRAPHY OF   BIBLIOG
POLAND. COM POLAND CONSTN NAT/G PARL/PROC SANCTION ADJUD
CRIME MARXISM 16/20. PAGE 91 E1823   LAW
                                                    JURID

                                                         B64
STOICOIU V.,LEGAL SOURCES AND BIBLIOGRAPHY OF   BIBLIOG/A
ROMANIA. COM ROMANIA LAW FINAN POL/PAR LEGIS JUDGE JURID
ADJUD CT/SYS PARL/PROC MARXISM 20. PAGE 93 E1874   CONSTN
                                                    ADMIN

                                                         B64
WAY H.F. JR.,LIBERTY IN THE BALANCE - CURRENT   ORD/FREE
ISSUES IN CIVIL LIBERTIES. USA+45 USA-45 DELIB/GP   EDU/PROP
RACE/REL DISCRIM TOTALISM MARXISM SOCISM...CONCPT   NAT/G
20 CONGRESS SUPREME/CT CIVIL/LIB. PAGE 105 E2104   JURID

                                                         S64
KARPOV P.V.,"PEACEFUL COEXISTENCE AND INTERNATIONAL COM
LAW." WOR+45 LAW SOCIETY INT/ORG VOL/ASSN FORCES   ATTIT
CREATE CAP/ISM DIPLOM ADJUD NUC/PWR PEACE MORAL   INT/LAW
ORD/FREE PWR MARXISM...MARXIST JURID CONCPT OBS   USSR
TREND COLD/WAR MARX/KARL 20. PAGE 59 E1186

                                                         B65
BARKER L.J.,FREEDOM, COURTS, POLITICS: STUDIES IN   JURID
CIVIL LIBERTIES. USA+45 LEGIS CREATE DOMIN PRESS   CT/SYS
ADJUD LOBBY CRIME GP/REL RACE/REL MARXISM 20   ATTIT
CIVIL/LIB. PAGE 8 E0148   ORD/FREE

                                                         B65
LAFAVE W.R.,LAW AND SOVIET SOCIETY. EX/STRUC DIPLOM JURID
DOMIN EDU/PROP PRESS ADMIN CRIME OWN MARXISM 20   CT/SYS
KHRUSH/N. PAGE 62 E1244   ADJUD
                                                    GOV/REL

                                                         B65
MOSTECKY V.,SOVIET LEGAL BIBLIOGRAPHY. USSR LEGIS   BIBLIOG/A
PRESS WRITING CONFER ADJUD CT/SYS REV MARXISM   LAW
...INT/LAW JURID DICTIONARY 20. PAGE 75 E1503   COM
                                                    CONSTN

                                                         B65
NEGLEY G.,POLITICAL AUTHORITY AND MORAL JUDGMENT.   MORAL
INTELL SOCIETY LEGIS SANCTION UTOPIA SOVEREIGN   PWR
MARXISM...INT/LAW LOG 20. PAGE 76 E1530   CONTROL

                                                         B66
DALLIN A.,POLITICS IN THE SOVIET UNION: 7 CASES.   MARXISM
COM USSR LAW POL/PAR CHIEF FORCES WRITING DOMIN   DOMIN
PARL/PROC CIVMIL/REL TOTALISM...ANTHOL 20 KHRUSH/N ORD/FREE
STALIN/J CASEBOOK COM/PARTY. PAGE 28 E0563   GOV/REL

                                                         B66
EPSTEIN F.T.,THE AMERICAN BIBLIOGRAPHY OF RUSSIAN   BIBLIOG
AND EAST EUROPEAN STUDIES FOR 1964. USSR LOC/G   COM
NAT/G POL/PAR FORCES ADMIN ARMS/CONT...JURID CONCPT MARXISM
20 UN. PAGE 35 E0694   DIPLOM

                                                         B66
OBERMANN E.,VERTEIDIGUNG PER FREIHEIT. GERMANY/W   FORCES
WOR+45 INT/ORG COERCE NUC/PWR WEAPON MARXISM 20 UN ORD/FREE
NATO WARSAW/P TREATY. PAGE 78 E1571   WAR
                                                    PEACE

                                                         B66
STUMPF S.E.,MORALITY AND THE LAW. USA+45 LAW   JURID
CULTURE PROB/SOLV DOMIN ADJUD CONTROL ADJUST   MORAL

ALL/IDEOS MARXISM...INT/LAW 20 SUPREME/CT. PAGE 94 CT/SYS
E1890

B66
THOMPSON J.M.,RUSSIA, BOLSHEVISM, AND THE   DIPLOM
VERSAILLES PEACE. RUSSIA USSR INT/ORG NAT/G   PEACE
DELIB/GP AGREE REV WAR PWR 20 TREATY VERSAILLES   MARXISM
BOLSHEVISM. PAGE 96 E1919

B66
US DEPARTMENT OF STATE,RESEARCH ON AFRICA (EXTERNAL BIBLIOG/A
RESEARCH LIST NO 5-25). LAW CULTURE ECO/UNDEV   ASIA
POL/PAR DIPLOM EDU/PROP LEAD REGION MARXISM...GEOG   S/ASIA
LING WORSHIP 20. PAGE 100 E1996   NAT/G

B66
US DEPARTMENT OF STATE,RESEARCH ON THE USSR AND   BIBLIOG/A
EASTERN EUROPE (EXTERNAL RESEARCH LIST NO 1-25).   EUR+WWI
USSR LAW CULTURE SOCIETY NAT/G TEC/DEV DIPLOM   COM
EDU/PROP REGION...GEOG LING. PAGE 100 E1997   MARXISM

B66
US DEPARTMENT OF STATE,RESEARCH ON WESTERN EUROPE, BIBLIOG/A
GREAT BRITAIN, AND CANADA (EXTERNAL RESEARCH LIST   EUR+WWI
NO 3-25). CANADA GERMANY/W UK LAW CULTURE NAT/G   DIPLOM
POL/PAR FORCES EDU/PROP REGION MARXISM...GEOG SOC
WORSHIP 20 CMN/WLTH. PAGE 100 E1998

B66
US HOUSE UNAMER ACTIV COMM,HEARINGS ON BILLS TO   LAW
MAKE PUNISHABLE ASSISTANCE TO ENEMIES OF US IN TIME SANCTION
OF UNDECLARED WAR. USA+45 VIETNAM/N EDU/PROP   VOL/ASSN
CONTROL WAR MARXISM HOUSE/REP. PAGE 100 E2010   GIVE

B66
US SENATE COMM AERO SPACE SCI,SOVIET SPACE   CONSULT
PROGRAMS, 1962-65: GOALS AND PURPOSES,   SPACE
ACHIEVEMENTS, PLANS, AND INTERNATIONAL   FUT
IMPLICATIONS. USA+45 USSR R+D FORCES PLAN EDU/PROP DIPLOM
PRESS ADJUD ARMS/CONT ATTIT MARXISM. PAGE 101 E2028

S66
CHIU H.,"COMMUNIST CHINA'S ATTITUDE TOWARD   INT/LAW
INTERNATIONAL LAW" CHINA/COM USSR LAW CONSTN DIPLOM MARXISM
GP/REL 20 LENIN/VI. PAGE 22 E0431   CONCPT
                                                    IDEA/COMP

B67
BAILEY N.A.,LATIN AMERICA IN WORLD POLITICS. PWR   L/A+17C
CONSERVE MARXISM...INT/LAW TREND BIBLIOG/A T OAS   DIPLOM
COLD/WAR. PAGE 7 E0134   INT/ORG
                                                    ATTIT

B67
LENG S.C.,JUSTICE IN COMMUNIST CHINA: A SURVEY OF   CT/SYS
THE JUDICIAL SYSTEM OF THE CHINESE PEOPLE'S   ADJUD
REPUBLIC. CHINA/COM LAW CONSTN LOC/G NAT/G PROF/ORG JURID
CONSULT FORCES ADMIN CRIME ORD/FREE...BIBLIOG 20   MARXISM
MAO. PAGE 64 E1284

B67
RAMUNDO B.A.,PEACEFUL COEXISTENCE: INTERNATIONAL   INT/LAW
LAW IN THE BUILDING OF COMMUNISM. USSR INT/ORG   PEACE
DIPLOM COLONIAL ARMS/CONT ROLE SOVEREIGN...POLICY   MARXISM
METH/COMP NAT/COMP BIBLIOG. PAGE 83 E1673   METH/CNCPT

B67
SLATER J.,THE OAS AND UNITED STATES FOREIGN POLICY. INT/ORG
KOREA L/A+17C USA+45 VOL/ASSN RISK COERCE PEACE   DIPLOM
ORD/FREE MARXISM...TREND 20 OAS. PAGE 92 E1838   ALL/IDEOS
                                                    ADJUD

S67
FLECHTHEIM O.K.,"BLOC FORMATION VS. DIALOGUE."   FUT
CONSTN ECO/DEV BAL/PWR PEACE ATTIT PWR COLD/WAR.   CAP/ISM
PAGE 38 E0761   MARXISM
                                                    DEBATE

S67
MIRONENKO Y.,"A NEW EXTENSION OF CRIMINAL LIABILITY ADJUD
IN THE USSR." COM USSR DOMIN EDU/PROP 20. PAGE 73   SANCTION
E1467   CRIME
                                                    MARXISM

S67
SEIDLER G.L.,"MARXIST LEGAL THOUGHT IN POLAND."   MARXISM
POLAND SOCIETY R+D LOC/G NAT/G ACT/RES ADJUD CT/SYS LAW
SUPEGO PWR...SOC TREND 20 MARX/KARL. PAGE 90 E1802 CONCPT
                                                    EFFICIENCY

S67
SHELDON C.H.,"PUBLIC OPINION AND HIGH COURTS: ATTIT
COMMUNIST PARTY CASES IN FOUR CONSTITUTIONAL   CT/SYS
SYSTEMS." CANADA GERMANY/W WOR+45 POL/PAR MARXISM   CONSTN
...METH/COMP NAT/COMP 20 AUSTRAL. PAGE 91 E1818   DECISION

S68
SHAPIRO J.P.,"SOVIET HISTORIOGRAPHY AND THE MOSCOW HIST/WRIT
TRIALS: AFTER THIRTY YEARS." USSR NAT/G LEGIT PRESS EDU/PROP
CONTROL LEAD ATTIT MARXISM...NEW/IDEA METH 20   SANCTION
TROTSKY/L STALIN/J KHRUSH/N. PAGE 90 E1810   ADJUD

MARXIST....MARXIST

S64
KARPOV P.V.,"PEACEFUL COEXISTENCE AND INTERNATIONAL COM
LAW." WOR+45 LAW SOCIETY INT/ORG VOL/ASSN FORCES   ATTIT
CREATE CAP/ISM DIPLOM ADJUD NUC/PWR PEACE MORAL   INT/LAW
ORD/FREE PWR MARXISM...MARXIST JURID CONCPT OBS   USSR
TREND COLD/WAR MARX/KARL 20. PAGE 59 E1186

S67
COHN K.,"CRIMES AGAINST HUMANITY." GERMANY INT/ORG WAR
SANCTION ATTIT ORD/FREE...MARXIST CRIMLGY 20 UN.   INT/LAW
PAGE 24 E0469   CRIME
                                                    ADJUD

MARYLAND....MARYLAND

B30
GREEN F.M.,CONSTITUTIONAL DEVELOPMENT IN THE SOUTH CONSTN
ATLANTIC STATES, 1776-1860: A STUDY IN THE   PROVS
EVOLUTION OF DEMOCRACY. USA-45 ELITES SOCIETY   PLURISM
STRATA ECO/DEV AGRI POL/PAR EX/STRUC LEGIS CT/SYS   REPRESENT
REGION...BIBLIOG 18/19 MARYLAND VIRGINIA GEORGIA
NORTH/CAR SOUTH/CAR. PAGE 46 E0905

B52
GELLHORN W.,THE STATES AND SUBVERSION. USA+45   PROVS
USA-45 LOC/G DELIB/GP LEGIS EDU/PROP LEGIT CT/SYS   JURID
REGION PEACE ATTIT ORD/FREE SOCISM...INT CON/ANAL
20 CALIFORNIA MARYLAND ILLINOIS MICHIGAN NEW/YORK.
PAGE 43 E0845

B64
HANSON R.,FAIR REPRESENTATION COMES TO MARYLAND   APPORT
(PAMPHLET). BAL/PWR CT/SYS CHOOSE GOV/REL 20   REPRESENT
MARYLAND SUPREME/CT. PAGE 50 E0997   PROVS
                                                    LEGIS

MASON A.T. E1376,E1377,E1378,E1379

MASON H.L. E1380

MASON J.B. E1381

MASS MEDIA....SEE EDU/PROP, COM/IND

MASSACHU....MASSACHUSETTS

N61
LEAGUE WOMEN VOTERS MASSACHU,THE MERIT SYSTEM IN   LOC/G
MASSACHUSETTS (PAMPHLET). USA+45 PROVS LEGIT PARTIC LAW
CHOOSE REPRESENT GOV/REL EFFICIENCY...POLICY   SENIOR
GOV/COMP BIBLIOG 20 MASSACHU. PAGE 64 E1274   PROF/ORG

B66
POWERS E.,CRIME AND PUNISHMENT IN EARLY   CRIME
MASSACHUSETTS 1620-1692: A DOCUMENTARY HISTORY.   ADJUD
USA-45 SECT LEGIS COLONIAL ATTIT ORD/FREE MYSTISM   CT/SYS
17 PRE/US/AM MASSACHU. PAGE 82 E1643   PROVS

MASSEL M.S. E1382

MASTERS R.D. E1383

MATH....MATHEMATICS

N19
RALSTON A.,A FRESH LOOK AT LEGISLATIVE   APPORT
APPORTIONMENT IN NEW JERSEY (PAMPHLET). USA+45   REPRESENT
CONSTN LEGIS OBJECTIVE...MATH METH 20 NEW/JERSEY.   PROVS
PAGE 83 E1671   JURID

B25
GODET M.,INDEX BIBLIOGRAPHICUS: INTERNATIONAL   BIBLIOG/A
CATALOGUE OF SOURCES OF CURRENT BIBLIOGRAPHIC   DIPLOM
INFORMATION. EUR+WWI MOD/EUR SOCIETY SECT TAX   EDU/PROP
...JURID PHIL/SCI SOC MATH. PAGE 44 E0876   LAW

B46
AMERICAN DOCUMENTATION INST,CATALOGUE OF AUXILIARY BIBLIOG
PUBLICATIONS IN MICROFILMS AND PHOTOPRINTS. USA+45 EDU/PROP
LAW AGRI CREATE TEC/DEV ADMIN...GEOG LING MATH 20. PSY
PAGE 4 E0077

S58
FISHER F.M.,"THE MATHEMATICAL ANALYSIS OF SUPREME   PROB/SOLV
COURT DECISIONS: THE USE AND ABUSE OF QUANTITATIVE CT/SYS
METHODS." USA+45 LAW EX/STRUC LEGIS JUDGE ROUTINE   JURID
ATTIT DECISION. PAGE 38 E0757   MATH

ROCHE J.P.,"POLITICAL SCIENCE AND SCIENCE FICTION" (BMR)" WOR+45 INTELL OP/RES ADJUD...JURID SOC IDEA/COMP 20. PAGE 85 E1709
S58 QUANT RATIONAL MATH METH

HARVARD UNIVERSITY LAW SCHOOL,INTERNATIONAL PROBLEMS OF FINANCIAL PROTECTION AGAINST NUCLEAR RISK. WOR+45 NAT/G DELIB/GP PROB/SOLV DIPLOM CONTROL ATTIT...POLICY INT/LAW MATH 20. PAGE 51 E1009
B59 NUC/PWR ADJUD INDUS FINAN

PUGWASH CONFERENCE,"ON BIOLOGICAL AND CHEMICAL WARFARE." WOR+45 SOCIETY PROC/MFG INT/ORG FORCES EDU/PROP ADJUD RIGID/FLEX ORD/FREE PWR...DECISION PSY NEW/IDEA MATH VAL/FREE 20. PAGE 83 E1661
S59 ACT/RES BIO/SOC WAR WEAPON

STEIN E.,"LEGAL REMEDIES OF ENTERPRISES IN THE EUROPEAN ECONOMIC COMMUNITY." EUR+WWI FUT ECO/DEV INDUS PLAN ECO/TAC ADMIN PWR...MGT MATH STAT TREND CON/ANAL EEC 20. PAGE 93 E1868
L60 MARKET ADJUD

NAGEL S.S.,"USING SIMPLE CALCULATIONS TO PREDICT JUDICIAL DECISIONS." ATTIT PERSON MATH. PAGE 76 E1517
S60 JURID LAW DECISION COMPUTER

WRIGHT Q.,"THE ESCALATION OF INTERNATIONAL CONFLICTS." WOR+45 WOR-45 FORCES DIPLOM RISK COST ATTIT ALL/VALS...INT/LAW QUANT STAT NAT/COMP. PAGE 108 E2160
S65 WAR PERCEPT PREDICT MATH

MEDER A.E. JR.,LEGISLATIVE APPORTIONMENT. USA+45 BAL/PWR REPRESENT ORD/FREE PWR...JURID 20 SUPREME/CT. PAGE 72 E1433
B66 APPORT LEGIS MATH POLICY

RAE D.,THE POLITICAL CONSEQUENCES OF ELECTORAL LAWS. EUR+WWI ICELAND ISRAEL NEW/ZEALND UK USA+45 ADJUD APPORT GP/REL MAJORITY...MATH STAT CENSUS CHARTS BIBLIOG 20 AUSTRAL. PAGE 83 E1667
B67 POL/PAR CHOOSE NAT/COMP REPRESENT

MATHEMATICS....SEE MATH, ALSO LOGIC, MATHEMATICS, AND LANGUAGE INDEX, P. XIV

MATTEI/E....ENRICO MATTEI

MATTHEWS D.G. E1384,E1385

MATTHEWS M.A. E1386,E1387,E1388

MATTHEWS R.O. E1389

MAU/MAU....MAU MAU

MAUD....MILITARY APPLICATIONS OF URANIUM DETONATION (MAUD) (U.K. - WWII)

MAURITANIA....SEE ALSO AFR

MAURRAS/C....CHARLES MAURRAS

MAYANJA A. E1390

MAYDA J. E1391

MAYER A.J. E1392

MAYER M. E1393

MAYERS L. E1394

MAYO L.H. E1395

MAYO/ELTON....ELTON MAYO

MAYOR....MAYOR; SEE ALSO MUNIC, CHIEF

BOUVIER-AJAM M.,MANUEL TECHNIQUE ET PRATIQUE DU MAIRE ET DES ELUS ET AGENTS COMMUNAUX. FRANCE LOC/G BUDGET CHOOSE GP/REL SUPEGO...JURID BIBLIOG 20 MAYOR COMMUNES. PAGE 14 E0274
B64 MUNIC ADMIN CHIEF NEIGH

MAZZINI J. E1396

MBEMBE....MBEMBE TRIBE

MC CONNELL J.P. E1397

MC REYNOLDS D. E1398

MCBRIDE J.H. E1399

MCCARTHY/E....EUGENE MCCARTHY

MCCARTHY/J....JOSEPH MCCARTHY

CAUGHEY J.W.,IN CLEAR AND PRESENT DANGER. USA+45 ADJUD COERCE ATTIT AUTHORIT...POLICY 20 COLD/WAR MCCARTHY/J. PAGE 21 E0408
B58 NAT/G CONTROL DOMIN ORD/FREE

MCCLEERY R. E1400

MCCLELLN/J....JOHN MCCLELLAN

BUREAU OF NATIONAL AFFAIRS,THE MCCLELLAN COMMITTEE HEARINGS - 1957. USA+45 LEGIS CONTROL CRIME ...CHARTS 20 CONGRESS AFL/CIO MCCLELLN/J. PAGE 17 E0336
B58 DELIB/GP CONFER LABOR MGT

MCCLINTOCK C.G. E1024

MCCLURE W. E1401

MCCONNELL G. E1402

MCDOUGAL M.S. E1403,E1404,E1405,E1406,E1407,E1408,E1409,E1410 , E1411,E1412

MCGEORGE H. E0590

MCGHEE G.C. E1413

MCGRATH J.J. E1414,E1415

MCILWAIN C.H. E1416,E1417,E1418,E1419

MCKAY R.B. E1420

MCKINLEY/W....PRESIDENT WILLIAM MCKINLEY

MCLAUGHLIN A.C. E1421,E1422

MCLUHAN/M....MARSHALL MCLUHAN

MCMAHON A.H. E1423

MCMAHON....MCMAHON LINE

MCNAIR A.D. E0325,E1424,E1425

MCNAMARA/R....ROBERT MCNAMARA

MCNAMEE B.J. E1426

MCQUIGG R.B. E0179

MCWHINNEY E. E1427,E1428,E1429,E1430,E1431

MDTA....MANPOWER DEVELOPMENT AND TRAINING ACT (1962)

MEAD/GH....GEORGE HERBERT MEAD

MEAD/MARG....MARGARET MEAD

MEADVIL/PA....MEADVILLE, PA.

MEAGHER R.F. E0806

MECHAM J.L. E1432

MEDER A.E. E1433

MEDIATION....SEE CONFER, CONSULT

MEDICAL CARE....SEE HEALTH

MEDITERRANEAN AND NEAR EAST, TO ISLAMIC PERIOD....SEE MEDIT-7

MEDIT-7....MEDITERRANEAN AND NEAR EAST TO THE ISLAMIC PERIOD (7TH CENTURY); SEE ALSO APPROPRIATE NATIONS

MAINE H.S.,ANCIENT LAW. MEDIT-7 CULTURE SOCIETY KIN FAM SECT LEGIS LEGIT ROUTINE...JURID HIST/WRIT CON/ANAL LAW TOT/POP VAL/FREE. PAGE 68 E1350
B00

PHILLIPSON C.,THE INTERNATIONAL LAW AND CUSTOM OF
B11 INT/ORG

ANCIENT GREECE AND ROME. MEDIT-7 UNIV INTELL
SOCIETY STRUCT NAT/G LEGIS EXEC PERSON...CONCPT OBS
CON/ANAL ROM/EMP. PAGE 80 E1614

LAW
INT/LAW

B20
VINOGRADOFF P.,OUTLINES OF HISTORICAL JURISPRUDENCE
(2 VOLS.). GREECE MEDIT-7 LAW CONSTN FACE/GP FAM
KIN MUNIC CRIME OWN...INT/LAW IDEA/COMP BIBLIOG.
PAGE 104 E2080

JURID
METH

C24
SHERMAN C.P.,"ROMAN LAW IN THE MODERN WORLD (2ND
ED.) (3 VOLS.)" MEDIT-7...JURID BIBLIOG. PAGE 91
E1819

LAW
ADJUD
OWN
CONSTN

B52
ETTINGHAUSEN R.,SELECTED AND ANNOTATED BIBLIOGRAPHY
OF BOOKS AND PERIODICALS IN WESTERN LANGUAGES
DEALING WITH NEAR AND MIDDLE EAST. LAW CULTURE SECT
...ART/METH GEOG SOC. PAGE 35 E0700

BIBLIOG/A
ISLAM
MEDIT-7

B54
NUSSBAUM D.,A CONCISE HISTORY OF THE LAW OF
NATIONS. ASIA CHRIST-17C EUR+WWI ISLAM MEDIT-7
MOD/EUR S/ASIA UNIV WOR+45 WOR-45 SOCIETY STRUCT
EXEC ATTIT ALL/VALS...CONCPT HIST/WRIT TIME/SEQ.
PAGE 78 E1560

INT/ORG
LAW
PEACE
INT/LAW

L54
NICOLSON H.,"THE EVOLUTION OF DIPLOMATIC METHOD."
CHRIST-17C EUR+WWI FRANCE FUT ITALY MEDIT-7 MOD/EUR
USA+45 USA-45 LAW NAT/G CREATE EDU/PROP LEGIT PEACE
ATTIT ORD/FREE RESPECT SOVEREIGN. PAGE 77 E1548

RIGID/FLEX
METH/CNCPT
DIPLOM

S64
GREENBERG S.,"JUDAISM AND WORLD JUSTICE." MEDIT-7
WOR+45 LAW CULTURE SOCIETY INT/ORG NAT/G FORCES
EDU/PROP ATTIT DRIVE PERSON SUPEGO ALL/VALS
...POLICY PSY CONCPT GEN/LAWS JEWS. PAGE 46 E0908

SECT
JURID
PEACE

C93
PLAYFAIR R.L.,"A BIBLIOGRAPHY OF MOROCCO." MOROCCO
CULTURE AGRI FORCES DIPLOM WAR HEALTH...GEOG JURID
SOC CHARTS. PAGE 81 E1620

BIBLIOG
ISLAM
MEDIT-7

MEIJI....MEIJI: THE REIGN OF EMPEROR MUTSUHITO OF JAPAN
(1868-1912)

MEIKLEJOHN A. E1434

MEIKLEJOHN D. E1435

MELANESIA....MELANESIA

MELINAT C.H. E1052

MENDELSON W. E1436,E1437,E1438,E1439

MENDELSSOHN S. E1440

MENDLOVITZ P. E0719

MENON/KRSH....KRISHNA MENON

MENSHEVIK....MENSHEVIKS

MENTAL DISORDERS....SEE HEALTH

MENTAL HEALTH....SEE HEALTH, PSY

MENTAL INSTITUTION....SEE PUB/INST

MENZIES/RG....ROBERT G. MENZIES

MERCANTLST....MERCANTILIST ECONOMIC THEORY

MERCIER/E....ERNEST MERCIER

MEREDITH/J....JAMES MEREDITH

MERGERS....SEE INDUS, EX/STRUC, FINAN

MERILLAT H.C.L. E1441

MERRIAM C.E. E1442

MERRITT R.L. E1443

MERTHYR....MERTHYR, WALES

MERTON R.K. E1444

MERTON/R....ROBERT MERTON

S59
CLOWARD R.A.,"ILLEGITIMATE MEANS, ANOMIE, AND
DEVIANT BEHAVIOR" STRUCT CRIME DRIVE PERSON...SOC
CONCPT NEW/IDEA 20 DURKHEIM/E MERTON/R. PAGE 23
E0459

ANOMIE
CRIMLGY
LEGIT
ADJUST

B64
CLINARD M.B.,ANOMIE AND DEVIANT BEHAVIOR: A
DISCUSSION AND CRITIQUE. SOCIETY FACE/GP CRIME
STRANGE ATTIT BIO/SOC DISPL RIGID/FLEX HEALTH...PSY
CONCPT BIBLIOG 20 MERTON/R. PAGE 23 E0456

PERSON
ANOMIE
KIN
NEIGH

MESOPOTAM....MESOPOTAMIA

METH....HEAVILY EMPHASIZED METHODOLOGY OR TECHNIQUE OF STUDY

N
AMERICAN POLITICAL SCIENCE REVIEW. USA+45 USA-45
WOR+45 WOR-45 INT/ORG ADMIN...INT/LAW PHIL/SCI
CONCPT METH 20 UN. PAGE 1 E0002

BIBLIOG/A
DIPLOM
NAT/G
GOV/COMP

B14
MCLAUGHLIN A.C.,CYCLOPEDIA OF AMERICAN GOVERNMENT
(3 VOLS.). LAW CONSTN POL/PAR ADMIN ROUTINE
...INT/LAW CONCPT BIBLIOG METH 20. PAGE 71 E1421

USA+45
NAT/G
DICTIONARY

N19
RALSTON A.,A FRESH LOOK AT LEGISLATIVE
APPORTIONMENT IN NEW JERSEY (PAMPHLET). USA+45
CONSTN LEGIS OBJECTIVE...MATH METH 20 NEW/JERSEY.
PAGE 83 E1671

APPORT
REPRESENT
PROVS
JURID

B20
VINOGRADOFF P.,OUTLINES OF HISTORICAL JURISPRUDENCE
(2 VOLS.). GREECE MEDIT-7 LAW CONSTN FACE/GP FAM
KIN MUNIC CRIME OWN...INT/LAW IDEA/COMP BIBLIOG.
PAGE 104 E2080

JURID
METH

B28
MACDONALD A.F.,ELEMENTS OF POLITICAL SCIENCE
RESEARCH. USA-45 ACADEM JUDGE EDU/PROP DEBATE ADJUD
EXEC...BIBLIOG METH T 20 CONGRESS. PAGE 67 E1338

LAW
FEDERAL
DECISION
CT/SYS

B31
BORCHARD E.H.,GUIDE TO THE LAW AND LEGAL LITERATURE
OF FRANCE. FRANCE FINAN INDUS LABOR SECT LEGIS
ADMIN COLONIAL CRIME OWN...INT/LAW 20. PAGE 14
E0266

BIBLIOG/A
LAW
CONSTN
METH

B36
CULVER D.C.,METHODOLOGY OF SOCIAL SCIENCE RESEARCH:
A BIBLIOGRAPHY. LAW CULTURE...CRIMLGY GEOG STAT OBS
INT QU HIST/WRIT CHARTS 20. PAGE 28 E0550

BIBLIOG/A
METH
SOC

B37
BEARDSLEY A.R.,LEGAL BIBLIOGRAPHY AND THE USE OF
LAW BOOKS. CONSTN CREATE PROB/SOLV...DECISION JURID
LAB/EXP. PAGE 9 E0166

BIBLIOG
LAW
METH
OP/RES

B44
BRIERLY J.L.,THE OUTLOOK FOR INTERNATIONAL LAW. FUT
WOR-45 CONSTN NAT/G VOL/ASSN FORCES ECO/TAC DOMIN
LEGIT ADJUD ROUTINE PEACE ORD/FREE...INT/LAW JURID
METH LEAGUE/NAT 20. PAGE 15 E0298

INT/ORG
LAW

B50
DOROSH J.T.,GUIDE TO SOVIET BIBLIOGRAPHIES. USSR
LAW AGRI SCHOOL SECT FORCES TEC/DEV...ART/METH GEOG
HUM SOC 20. PAGE 32 E0639

BIBLIOG
METH
CON/ANAL

B50
WARD R.E.,A GUIDE TO JAPANESE REFERENCE AND
RESEARCH MATERIALS IN THE FIELD OF POLITICAL
SCIENCE. LAW CONSTN LOC/G PRESS ADMIN...SOC
CON/ANAL METH 19/20 CHINJAP. PAGE 105 E2098

BIBLIOG/A
ASIA
NAT/G

B54
BENTLEY A.F.,INQUIRY INTO INQUIRIES: ESSAYS IN
SOCIAL THEORY. UNIV LEGIS ADJUD ADMIN LOBBY
...PHIL/SCI PSY NEW/IDEA LING METH 20. PAGE 10
E0200

EPIST
SOC
CONCPT

B54
HOEBEL E.A.,THE LAW OF PRIMITIVE MAN: A STUDY IN
COMPARATIVE LEGAL DYNAMICS. WOR-45...JURID SOC
IDEA/COMP METH 20. PAGE 53 E1063

LAW
CULTURE
GP/COMP
SOCIETY

B55
MOHL R.V.,DIE GESCHICHTE UND LITERATUR DER
STAATSWISSENSCHAFTEN (3 VOLS.). LAW NAT/G...JURID
METH/COMP METH. PAGE 74 E1480

PHIL/SCI
MOD/EUR

B56
COHEN A.,THE SUTHERLAND PAPERS. USA+45 USA-45 LAW   CRIMLGY
CONTROL CRIME AGE/Y...TREND ANTHOL BIBLIOG 20.   PHIL/SCI
PAGE 23 E0461   ACT/RES
                                                            METH

B56
SCHROEDER T.,METHODS OF CONSTITUTIONAL   ORD/FREE
CONSTRUCTION. LAW...METH 20. PAGE 88 E1769   CONSTN
                                                            JURID
                                                            EDU/PROP

B58
DEVLIN P.,THE CRIMINAL PROSECUTION IN ENGLAND. UK   CRIME
NAT/G ADMIN ROUTINE EFFICIENCY...JURID SOC 20.   LAW
PAGE 31 E0617   METH
                                                            CT/SYS

S58
ROCHE J.P.,"POLITICAL SCIENCE AND SCIENCE FICTION"   QUANT
(BMR)" WOR+45 INTELL OP/RES ADJUD...JURID SOC   RATIONAL
IDEA/COMP 20. PAGE 85 E1709   MATH
                                                            METH

B59
SIMPSON J.L.,INTERNATIONAL ARBITRATION: LAW AND   INT/LAW
PRACTICE. WOR+45 WOR-45 INT/ORG DELIB/GP ADJUD   DIPLOM
PEACE MORAL ORD/FREE...METH 18/20. PAGE 91 E1829   CT/SYS
                                                            CONSULT

B59
SURRENCY E.C.,A GUIDE TO LEGAL RESEARCH. USA+45   NAT/G
ACADEM LEGIS ACT/RES ADMIN...DECISION METH/COMP   PROVS
BIBLIOG METH. PAGE 94 E1894   ADJUD
                                                            JURID

B60
BEEM H.D.,AN INTRODUCTION TO LEGAL BIBLIOGRAPHY FOT   BIBLIOG/A
THE NON-PROFESSIONAL STUDENT. LOC/G NAT/G TAX 20.   JURID
PAGE 9 E0177   METH
                                                            ADJUD

S60
ULMER S.S.,"THE ANALYSIS OF BEHAVIOR PATTERNS ON   ATTIT
THE UNITED STATES SUPREME COURT" USA+45 LAW CT/SYS   ADJUD
PERS/REL RACE/REL PERSON...DECISION PSY SOC TREND   PROF/ORG
METH/COMP METH 20 SUPREME/CT CIVIL/LIB. PAGE 97   INGP/REL
E1951

B61
PUGET H.,ESSAI DE BIBLIOGRAPHIE DES PRINCIPAUX   BIBLIOG
OUVRAGES DE DROIT PUBLIC... QUI ONT PARU HORS DE   MGT
FRANCE DE 1945 A 1958. EUR+WWI USA+45 CONSTN LOC/G   ADMIN
...METH 20. PAGE 83 E1660   LAW

B62
MARS D.,SUGGESTED LIBRARY IN PUBLIC ADMINISTRATION.   BIBLIOG
FINAN DELIB/GP EX/STRUC WORKER COMPUTER ADJUD   ADMIN
...DECISION PSY SOC METH/COMP 20. PAGE 68 E1368   METH
                                                            MGT

B62
STERN R.L.,SUPREME COURT PRACTICE. USA+45 USA-45   CT/SYS
OP/RES...STYLE METH 20 SUPREME/CT. PAGE 93 E1872   ADJUD
                                                            JURID
                                                            ROUTINE

B64
MCDOUGAL M.S.,STUDIES IN WORLD PUBLIC ORDER. SPACE   INT/LAW
SEA INT/ORG CREATE AGREE NUC/PWR...POLICY PHIL/SCI   SOC
IDEA/COMP ANTHOL METH 20 UN. PAGE 71 E1411   DIPLOM

B64
RICHARDSON I.L.,BIBLIOGRAFIA BRASILEIRA DE   BIBLIOG
ADMINISTRACAO PUBLICA E ASSUNTOS CORRELATOS. BRAZIL   MGT
CONSTN FINAN LOC/G NAT/G POL/PAR PLAN DIPLOM   ADMIN
RECEIVE ATTIT...METH 20. PAGE 84 E1694   LAW

B65
PARRY C.,THE SOURCES AND EVIDENCES OF INTERNATIONAL   INT/LAW
LAW. WOR+45 WOR-45 DIPLOM AGREE SOVEREIGN...METH 20   ADJUD
TREATY UN LEAGUE/NAT. PAGE 80 E1599   INT/ORG
                                                            CT/SYS

B65
VON RENESSE E.A.,UNVOLLENDETE DEMOKRATIEN. AFR   ECO/UNDEV
ISLAM S/ASIA SOCIETY ACT/RES COLONIAL...JURID   NAT/COMP
CHARTS BIBLIOG METH 13/20. PAGE 104 E2083   SOVEREIGN

B66
BEDI A.S.,FREEDOM OF EXPRESSION AND SECURITY;   METH
COMPARATIVE STUDY OF FUNCTIONS OF SUPREME COURTS IN   CT/SYS
UNITED STATES AND INDIA. INDIA USA+45 LAW CONSTN   ADJUD
PROB/SOLV...DECISION JURID BIBLIOG 20 SUPREME/CT   ORD/FREE
FREE/SPEE AMEND/I. PAGE 9 E0175

B66
MACIVER R.M.,THE PREVENTION AND CONTROL OF   AGE/Y
DELINQUENCY. USA+45 STRATA PUB/INST ANOMIE ATTIT   PLAN
HABITAT PERSON HEALTH...CRIMLGY PSY SOC METH.   ADJUST
PAGE 67 E1341   CRIME

B66
RUNCIMAN W.G.,RELATIVE DEPRIVATION AND SOCIAL   STRATA
JUSTICE: A STUDY OF ATTITUDES TO SOCIAL INEQUALITY   STRUCT
IN TWENTIETH-CENTURY ENGLAND. UK LAW POL/PAR PWR   DISCRIM
...CONCPT NEW/IDEA SAMP METH 19/20. PAGE 86 E1734   ATTIT

B67
CLINARD M.B.,CRIMINAL BEHAVIOR SYSTEMS: A TYPOLOGY.   BIBLIOG
WOR+45 LAW SOCIETY STRUCT R+D AGE/Y ATTIT WEALTH   CRIME
...CLASSIF CHARTS METH/COMP METH. PAGE 23 E0457   CRIMLGY
                                                            PERSON

B67
DIEGUES M.,SOCIAL SCIENCE IN LATIN AMERICA. L/A+17C   METH
...JURID SOC ANTHOL 20. PAGE 31 E0624   ACADEM
                                                            EDU/PROP
                                                            ACT/RES

B67
UNIVERSAL REFERENCE SYSTEM,LAW, JURISPRUDENCE, AND   BIBLIOG/A
JUDICIAL PROCESS (VOLUME VII). WOR+45 WOR-45 CONSTN   LAW
NAT/G LEGIS JUDGE CT/SYS...INT/LAW COMPUT/IR   JURID
GEN/METH METH. PAGE 99 E1976   ADJUD

S67
GLASER D.,"NATIONAL GOALS AND INDICATORS FOR THE   CRIME
REDUCTION OF CRIME AND DELINQUENCY." FUT USA+45   CRIMLGY
NAT/G...CON/ANAL METH 20. PAGE 44 E0874   LAW
                                                            STAT

S67
HIRSCH W.Z.,"SOME ECONOMIC IMPLICATIONS OF CITY   ECO/TAC
PLANNING." LAW PROB/SOLV RATION EFFICIENCY...METH   JURID
20. PAGE 53 E1050   MUNIC
                                                            PLAN

S67
KONVITZ M.R.,"CIVIL LIBERTIES." USA+45 R+D...METH   LAW
20. PAGE 61 E1228   MORAL
                                                            ORD/FREE
                                                            NAT/G

S67
RUCKER B.W.,"WHAT SOLUTIONS DO PEOPLE ENDORSE IN   CONCPT
FREE PRESS-FAIR TRIAL DILEMMA?" LAW NAT/G CT/SYS   PRESS
ATTIT...NET/THEORY SAMP CHARTS IDEA/COMP METH 20.   ADJUD
PAGE 86 E1731   ORD/FREE

S68
SHAPIRO J.P.,"SOVIET HISTORIOGRAPHY AND THE MOSCOW   HIST/WRIT
TRIALS: AFTER THIRTY YEARS." USSR NAT/G LEGIT PRESS   EDU/PROP
CONTROL LEAD ATTIT MARXISM...NEW/IDEA METH 20   SANCTION
TROTSKY/L STALIN/J KHRUSH/N. PAGE 90 E1810   ADJUD

METH/CNCPT....METHODOLOGICAL CONCEPTS

METH/COMP....COMPARISON OF METHODS

N
INTERNATIONAL COMN JURISTS,AFRICAN CONFERENCE ON   CT/SYS
THE RULE OF LAW. AFR INT/ORG LEGIS DIPLOM CONFER   JURID
COLONIAL ORD/FREE...CONCPT METH/COMP 20. PAGE 57   DELIB/GP
E1131

N
CATHERINE R.,LA REVUE ADMINISTRATIVE. FRANCE LAW   ADMIN
NAT/G LEGIS...JURID BIBLIOG/A 20. PAGE 21 E0407   MGT
                                                          FINAN
                                                          METH/COMP

L11
POUND R.,"THE SCOPE AND PURPOSE OF SOCIOLOGICAL   JURID
JURISPRUDENCE."...GEN/LAWS 20 KANT/I HEGEL/GWF.   IDEA/COMP
PAGE 81 E1634   METH/COMP
                                                          SOC

B18
YUKIO O.,THE VOICE OF JAPANESE DEMOCRACY, AN ESSAY   CONSTN
ON CONSTITUTIONAL LOYALTY (TRANS BY J. E. BECKER).   MAJORIT
ASIA POL/PAR DELIB/GP EX/STRUC RIGID/FLEX ORD/FREE   CHOOSE
PWR...POLICY JURID METH/COMP 19/20 CHINJAP.   NAT/G
PAGE 108 E2167

N19
ARNOW K.,SELF-INSURANCE IN THE TREASURY (PAMPHLET).   ADMIN
USA+45 LAW RIGID/FLEX...POLICY METH/COMP 20   PLAN
DEPT/TREAS. PAGE 5 E0104   EFFICIENCY
                                                          NAT/G

LIPPMAN W.,LIBERTY AND THE NEWS. USA+45 USA-45 LAW
LEGIS DOMIN LEGIT ATTIT...POLICY SOC IDEA/COMP
METH/COMP 19/20. PAGE 65 E1300

ORD/FREE
PRESS
COM/IND
EDU/PROP

B20

COX G.C.,THE PUBLIC CONSCIENCE: A CASEBOOK IN
ETHICS....PHIL/SCI SOC CONCPT METH/COMP 20. PAGE 27
E0534

MORAL
ADJUD

B22

BIRD F.L.,THE RECALL OF PUBLIC OFFICERS; A STUDY OF
THE OPERATION OF RECALL IN CALIFORNIA. LOC/G MUNIC
POL/PAR PROVS PROB/SOLV ADJUD PARTIC...CHARTS
METH/COMP 20 CALIFORNIA RECALL. PAGE 12 E0230

REPRESENT
SANCTION
CHOOSE
LAW

B30

ENSOR R.C.K.,COURTS AND JUDGES IN FRANCE, GERMANY,
AND ENGLAND. FRANCE GERMANY UK LAW PROB/SOLV ADMIN
ROUTINE CRIME ROLE...METH/COMP 20 CIVIL/LAW.
PAGE 35 E0692

CT/SYS
EX/STRUC
ADJUD
NAT/COMP

B33

CUMMING J.,A CONTRIBUTION TOWARD A BIBLIOGRAPHY
DEALING WITH CRIME AND COGNATE SUBJECTS (3RD ED.).
UK LAW CULTURE PUB/INST ADJUD AGE BIO/SOC...PSY SOC
SOC/WK STAT METH/COMP 20. PAGE 28 E0552

BIBLIOG
CRIMLGY
FORCES
CT/SYS

B35

HALL J.,THEFT, LAW, AND SOCIETY. SOCIETY PROB/SOLV
...CRIMLGY SOC CONCPT TREND METH/COMP 18/20
LARCENY. PAGE 49 E0982

CRIME
LAW
ADJUD
ADJUST

B35

NIEMEYER G.,LAW WITHOUT FORCE: THE FUNCTION OF
POLITICS IN INTERNATIONAL LAW. PLAN INSPECT DIPLOM
REPAR LEGIT ADJUD WAR ORD/FREE...IDEA/COMP
METH/COMP GEN/LAWS 20. PAGE 77 E1549

COERCE
LAW
PWR
INT/LAW

B41

GURVITCH G.,SOCIOLOGY OF LAW. CONSTN SOCIETY CREATE
MORAL SOVEREIGN...POLICY EPIST JURID PHIL/SCI
IDEA/COMP METH/COMP HOLMES/OW HOBBES/T. PAGE 48
E0964

SOC
LAW
ADJUD

B42

CORRY J.A.,DEMOCRATIC GOVERNMENT AND POLITICS.
WOR-45 EX/STRUC LOBBY TOTALISM...MAJORIT CONCPT
METH/COMP NAT/COMP 20. PAGE 26 E0511

NAT/G
CONSTN
POL/PAR
JURID

B46

ROSS A.,TOWARDS A REALISTIC JURISPRUDENCE: A
CRITICISM OF THE DUALISM IN LAW (TRANS. BY ANNIE I.
FAUSBOLL). PLAN ADJUD CT/SYS ATTIT RIGID/FLEX
POPULISM...JURID PHIL/SCI LOG METH/COMP GEN/LAWS 20
SCANDINAV. PAGE 86 E1720

LAW
CONCPT
IDEA/COMP

B46

SLESSER H.,THE ADMINISTRATION OF THE LAW. UK CONSTN
EX/STRUC OP/RES PROB/SOLV CRIME ROLE...DECISION
METH/COMP 20 CIVIL/LAW ENGLSH/LAW CIVIL/LAW.
PAGE 92 E1839

LAW
CT/SYS
ADJUD

B48

BLODGETT R.H.,"COMPARATIVE ECONOMIC SYSTEMS (REV.
ED.)" WOR-45 AGRI FINAN MARKET LABOR NAT/G PLAN
INT/TRADE PRICE...POLICY DECISION BIBLIOG 20.
PAGE 13 E0248

METH/COMP
CONCPT
ROUTINE

C49

FRIEDMANN W.,LAW AND SOCIAL CHANGE IN CONTEMPORARY
BRITAIN. UK LABOR LG/CO LEGIS JUDGE CT/SYS ORD/FREE
NEW/LIB...DECISION JURID TREND METH/COMP BIBLIOG 20
PARLIAMENT ENGLSH/LAW COMMON/LAW. PAGE 40 E0802

LAW
ADJUD
SOCIETY
CONSTN

B51

CLAGETT H.L.,"THE ADMINISTRATION OF JUSTICE IN
LATIN AMERICA." L/A+17C ADMIN FEDERAL...JURID
METH/COMP BIBLIOG 20. PAGE 23 E0448

CT/SYS
ADJUD
JUDGE
CONSTN

C52

CALDWELL L.K.,RESEARCH METHODS IN PUBLIC
ADMINISTRATION; AN OUTLINE OF TOPICS AND READINGS
(PAMPHLET). LAW ACT/RES COMPUTER KNOWL...SOC STAT
GEN/METH 20. PAGE 18 E0364

BIBLIOG/A
METH/COMP
ADMIN
OP/RES

B53

US PRES CONF ADMIN PROCEDURE,REPORT (PAMPHLET).
USA+45 CONFER ADJUD...METH/COMP 20 PRESIDENT.
PAGE 101 E2024

NAT/G
DELIB/GP
ADJUST
ADMIN

N53

SCHWARTZ B.,FRENCH ADMINISTRATIVE LAW AND THE
COMMON-LAW WORLD. FRANCE CULTURE LOC/G NAT/G PROVS
DELIB/GP EX/STRUC LEGIS PROB/SOLV CT/SYS EXEC
GOV/REL...IDEA/COMP ENGLSH/LAW. PAGE 89 E1786

JURID
LAW
METH/COMP
ADJUD

B54

CAVAN R.S.,CRIMINOLOGY (2ND ED.). USA+45 LAW FAM
PUB/INST FORCES PLAN WAR AGE/Y PERSON ROLE SUPEGO
...CHARTS 20 FBI. PAGE 21 E0409

DRIVE
CRIMLGY
CONTROL
METH/COMP

B55

HOGAN W.N.,INTERNATIONAL CONFLICT AND COLLECTIVE
SECURITY: THE PRINCIPLE OF CONCERN IN INTERNATIONAL
ORGANIZATION. CONSTN EX/STRUC BAL/PWR DIPLOM ADJUD
CONTROL CENTRAL CONSEN PEACE...INT/LAW CONCPT
METH/COMP 20 UN LEAGUE/NAT. PAGE 53 E1066

INT/ORG
WAR
ORD/FREE
FORCES

B55

MOHL R.V.,DIE GESCHICHTE UND LITERATUR DER
STAATSWISSENSCHAFTEN (3 VOLS.). LAW NAT/G...JURID
METH/COMP METH. PAGE 74 E1480

PHIL/SCI
MOD/EUR

B55

MEYER P.,ADMINISTRATIVE ORGANIZATION: A COMPARATIVE
STUDY OF THE ORGANIZATION OF PUBLIC ADMINISTRATION.
DENMARK FRANCE NORWAY SWEDEN UK USA+45 ELITES LOC/G
CONSULT LEGIS ADJUD CONTROL LEAD PWR SKILL
DECISION. PAGE 72 E1449

ADMIN
METH/COMP
NAT/G
CENTRAL

B57

UNESCO,A REGISTER OF LEGAL DOCUMENTATION IN THE
WORLD (2ND ED.). CT/SYS...JURID IDEA/COMP METH/COMP
NAT/COMP 20. PAGE 98 E1960

BIBLIOG
LAW
INT/LAW
CONSTN

B57

LAW COMMISSION OF INDIA,REFORM OF JUDICIAL
ADMINISTRATION. INDIA TOP/EX ADMIN DISCRIM
EFFICIENCY...METH/COMP 20. PAGE 63 E1269

CT/SYS
ADJUD
GOV/REL
CONTROL

B58

OGDEN F.D.,THE POLL TAX IN THE SOUTH. USA+45 USA-45
CONSTN ADJUD ADMIN PARTIC CRIME...TIME/SEQ GOV/COMP
METH/COMP 18/20 SOUTH/US. PAGE 78 E1572

TAX
CHOOSE
RACE/REL
DISCRIM

B58

KNIERIEM A.,THE NUREMBERG TRIALS. EUR+WWI GERMANY
VOL/ASSN LEAD COERCE WAR INGP/REL TOTALISM SUPEGO
ORD/FREE...CONCPT METH/COMP. PAGE 61 E1225

INT/LAW
CRIME
PARTIC
JURID

B59

SURRENCY E.C.,A GUIDE TO LEGAL RESEARCH. USA+45
ACADEM LEGIS ACT/RES ADMIN...DECISION METH/COMP
BIBLIOG METH. PAGE 94 E1894

NAT/G
PROVS
ADJUD
JURID

B59

WAGNER W.J.,THE FEDERAL STATES AND THEIR JUDICIARY.
BRAZIL CANADA SWITZERLND USA+45 CONFER CT/SYS TASK
EFFICIENCY FEDERAL PWR...JURID BIBLIOG 20 AUSTRAL
MEXIC/AMER. PAGE 104 E2091

ADJUD
METH/COMP
PROB/SOLV
NAT/G

B59

BAKER G.E.,THE POLITICS OF REAPPORTIONMENT IN
WASHINGTON STATE. LAW POL/PAR CREATE EDU/PROP
PARL/PROC CHOOSE INGP/REL...CHARTS METH/COMP 20
WASHINGT/G LEAGUE/WV. PAGE 7 E0139

VOL/ASSN
APPORT
PROVS
LEGIS

B60

ULMER S.S.,"THE ANALYSIS OF BEHAVIOR PATTERNS ON
THE UNITED STATES SUPREME COURT" USA+45 LAW CT/SYS
PERS/REL RACE/REL PERSON...DECISION PSY SOC TREND
METH/COMP METH 20 SUPREME/CT CIVIL/LIB. PAGE 97
E1951

ATTIT
ADJUD
PROF/ORG
INGP/REL

S60

BAINS J.S.,STUDIES IN POLITICAL SCIENCE. INDIA
WOR+45 WOR-45 CONSTN BAL/PWR ADJUD ADMIN PARL/PROC
SOVEREIGN...SOC METH/COMP ANTHOL 17/20 UN. PAGE 7
E0137

DIPLOM
INT/LAW
NAT/G

B61

ROCHE J.P.,COURTS AND RIGHTS: THE AMERICAN
JUDICIARY IN ACTION (2ND ED.). UK USA+45 USA-45
STRUCT TEC/DEV SANCTION PERS/REL RACE/REL ORD/FREE
...METH/CNCPT GOV/COMP METH/COMP T 13/20. PAGE 85
E1710

JURID
CT/SYS
NAT/G
PROVS

B61

DIESING P.,REASON IN SOCIETY; FIVE TYPES OF
DECISIONS AND THEIR SOCIAL CONDITIONS. SOCIETY

RATIONAL
METH/COMP

B62

STRUCT LABOR CREATE TEC/DEV BARGAIN ADJUD ROLE   DECISION
...JURID BIBLIOG 20. PAGE 31 E0625   CONCPT

B62
MARS D.,SUGGESTED LIBRARY IN PUBLIC ADMINISTRATION. BIBLIOG
FINAN DELIB/GP EX/STRUC WORKER COMPUTER ADJUD   ADMIN
...DECISION PSY SOC METH/COMP 20. PAGE 68 E1368   METH
                                                     MGT

B63
GOURNAY B.,PUBLIC ADMINISTRATION. FRANCE LAW CONSTN BIBLIOG/A
AGRI FINAN LABOR SCHOOL EX/STRUC CHOOSE...MGT   ADMIN
METH/COMP 20. PAGE 45 E0894   NAT/G
                                                     LOC/G

B63
LEAGUE WOMEN VOTERS NEW YORK,APPORTIONMENT WORKSHOP APPORT
KIT. USA+45 VOL/ASSN DELIB/GP LEGIS ATTIT ORD/FREE   REPRESENT
...METH/COMP 20 SUPREME/CT NEW/YORK. PAGE 64 E1275   PROVS
                                                     JURID

B63
SCHUMAN S.I.,LEGAL POSITIVISM: ITS SCOPE AND   GEN/METH
LIMITATIONS. CONSTN NAT/G DIPLOM PARTIC UTOPIA   LAW
...POLICY DECISION PHIL/SCI CONCPT 20. PAGE 89   METH/COMP
E1784

B63
WADE H.W.R.,TOWARDS ADMINISTRATIVE JUSTICE. UK   ADJUD
USA+45 CONSTN CONSULT PROB/SOLV CT/SYS PARL/PROC   IDEA/COMP
...POLICY JURID METH/COMP 20 ENGLSH/LAW. PAGE 104   ADMIN
E2088

B64
COHEN M.L.,SELECTED BIBLIOGRAPHY OF FOREIGN AND   BIBLIOG/A
INTERNATIONAL LAW....IDEA/COMP METH/COMP 20.   JURID
PAGE 24 E0466   LAW
                                                     INT/LAW

B64
JENKS C.W.,THE PROSPECTS OF INTERNATIONAL   INT/LAW
ADJUDICATION. WOR+45 WOR-45 NAT/G DIPLOM CONTROL   ADJUD
PWR...POLICY JURID CONCPT METH/COMP 19/20 ICJ   CT/SYS
LEAGUE/NAT UN TREATY. PAGE 58 E1160   INT/ORG

B64
STRONG C.F.,HISTORY OF MODERN POLITICAL   CONSTN
CONSTITUTIONS. STRUCT INT/ORG NAT/G LEGIS TEC/DEV   CONCPT
DIPLOM INT/TRADE CT/SYS EXEC...METH/COMP T 12/20
UN. PAGE 94 E1888

B64
SZLADITS C.,BIBLIOGRAPHY ON FOREIGN AND COMPARATIVE BIBLIOG/A
LAW: BOOKS AND ARTICLES IN ENGLISH (SUPPLEMENT   JURID
1962). FINAN INDUS JUDGE LICENSE ADMIN CT/SYS   ADJUD
PARL/PROC OWN...INT/LAW CLASSIF METH/COMP NAT/COMP   LAW
20. PAGE 95 E1904

B65
CAVERS D.F.,THE CHOICE-OF-LAW PROCESS. PROB/SOLV   JURID
ADJUD CT/SYS CHOOSE RATIONAL...IDEA/COMP 16/20   DECISION
TREATY. PAGE 21 E0411   METH/COMP
                                                     ADMIN

B65
GAJENDRAGADKAR P.B.,LAW, LIBERTY AND SOCIAL   ORD/FREE
JUSTICE. INDIA CONSTN NAT/G SECT PLAN ECO/TAC PRESS LAW
POPULISM...SOC METH/COMP 20 HINDU. PAGE 42 E0826   ADJUD
                                                     JURID

B66
BEER U.,FRUCHTBARKEITSREGELUNG ALS KONSEQUENZ   CONTROL
VERANTWORTLICHER ELTERNSCHAFT. ASIA GERMANY/W INDIA GEOG
LAW ECO/DEV ECO/UNDEV TEC/DEV ECO/TAC BIO/SOC SEX   FAM
CATHISM...METH/COMP 20 CHINJAP BIRTH/CON. PAGE 9   SECT
E0178

B66
HOEVELER H.J.,INTERNATIONALE BEKAMPFUNG DES   CRIMLGY
VERBRECHENS. AUSTRIA SWITZERLND WOR+45 INT/ORG   CRIME
CONTROL BIO/SOC...METH/COMP NAT/COMP 20 MAFIA   DIPLOM
SCOT/YARD FBI. PAGE 53 E1064   INT/LAW

B66
WAINHOUSE D.W.,INTERNATIONAL PEACE OBSERVATION: A   PEACE
HISTORY AND FORECAST. INT/ORG PROB/SOLV BAL/PWR   DIPLOM
AGREE ARMS/CONT COERCE NUC/PWR...PREDICT METH/COMP
20 UN LEAGUE/NAT OAS TREATY. PAGE 104 E2092

B67
BOHANNAN P.,LAW AND WARFARE. CULTURE CT/SYS COERCE   METH/COMP
REV PEACE...JURID SOC CONCPT ANTHOL 20. PAGE 13   ADJUD
E0259   WAR
                                                     LAW

B67
BROWN L.N.,FRENCH ADMINISTRATIVE LAW. FRANCE UK   EX/STRUC
CONSTN NAT/G LEGIS DOMIN CONTROL EXEC PARL/PROC PWR LAW
...JURID METH/COMP GEN/METH. PAGE 16 E0314   IDEA/COMP
                                                     CT/SYS

B67
CLINARD M.B.,CRIMINAL BEHAVIOR SYSTEMS: A TYPOLOGY. BIBLIOG
WOR+45 LAW SOCIETY STRUCT R+D AGE/Y ATTIT WEALTH   CRIME
...CLASSIF CHARTS METH/COMP METH. PAGE 23 E0457   CRIMLGY
                                                     PERSON

B67
LOBLE L.H.,DELINQUENCY CAN BE STOPPED. FAM PUB/INST AGE/Y
CT/SYS ADJUST ATTIT...NEW/IDEA METH/COMP 20.   PROB/SOLV
PAGE 66 E1315   ADJUD
                                                     CRIME

B67
RAMUNDO B.A.,PEACEFUL COEXISTENCE: INTERNATIONAL   INT/LAW
LAW IN THE BUILDING OF COMMUNISM. USSR INT/ORG   PEACE
DIPLOM COLONIAL ARMS/CONT ROLE SOVEREIGN...POLICY   MARXISM
METH/COMP NAT/COMP BIBLIOG. PAGE 83 E1673   METH/CNCPT

L67
LENT G.E.,"TAX INCENTIVES FOR INVESTMENT IN   ECO/UNDEV
DEVELOPING COUNTRIES" WOR+45 LAW INDUS PLAN BUDGET   TAX
TARIFFS ADMIN...METH/COMP 20. PAGE 64 E1285   FINAN
                                                     ECO/TAC

L67
SCHUBERT G.,"THE RHETORIC OF CONSTITUTIONAL   CONSTN
CHANGE." USA+45 LAW CULTURE CHIEF LEGIS ADJUD   METH/COMP
CT/SYS ARMS/CONT ADJUST...CHARTS SIMUL. PAGE 89   ORD/FREE
E1777

S67
HAMILTON H.D.,"LEGISLATIVE CONSTITUENCIES: SINGLE-   LEGIS
MEMBER DISTRICTS, MULTI-MEMBER DISTRICTS, AND   REPRESENT
FLOTERAL DISTRICTS." USA+45 LAW POL/PAR ADJUD   APPORT
RACE/REL...CHARTS METH/COMP 20. PAGE 50 E0990   PLAN

S67
SHELDON C.H.,"PUBLIC OPINION AND HIGH COURTS: ATTIT
COMMUNIST PARTY CASES IN FOUR CONSTITUTIONAL   CT/SYS
SYSTEMS." CANADA GERMANY/W WOR+45 POL/PAR MARXISM   CONSTN
...METH/COMP NAT/COMP 20 AUSTRAL. PAGE 91 E1818   DECISION

B96
ESMEIN A.,ELEMENTS DE DROIT CONSTITUTIONNEL. FRANCE LAW
UK CHIEF EX/STRUC LEGIS ADJUD CT/SYS PARL/PROC REV   CONSTN
GOV/REL ORD/FREE...JURID METH/COMP 18/19. PAGE 35   NAT/G
E0697   CONCPT

METHOD, COMPARATIVE....SEE IDEA/COMP, METH/COMP

METHODOLOGY....SEE METH, PHIL/SCI, METHODOLOGICAL INDEXES,
    PP. XIII-XIV

METRO/COUN....METROPOLITAN COUNCIL

METROPOLITAN....SEE MUNIC

METTRNCH/K....PRINCE K. VON METTERNICH

MEXIC/AMER....MEXICAN-AMERICANS:

B08
GRIFFIN A.P.C.,LIST OF REFERENCES ON INTERNATIONAL   BIBLIOG/A
ARBITRATION. FRANCE L/A+17C USA-45 WOR-45 DIPLOM   INT/ORG
CONFER COLONIAL ARMS/CONT BAL/PAY EQUILIB SOVEREIGN INT/LAW
...DECISION 19/20 MEXIC/AMER. PAGE 47 E0932   DELIB/GP

B43
BEMIS S.F.,THE LATIN AMERICAN POLICY OF THE UNITED   DIPLOM
STATES: AN HISTORICAL INTERPRETATION. INT/ORG AGREE SOVEREIGN
COLONIAL WAR PEACE ATTIT ORD/FREE...POLICY INT/LAW   USA-45
CHARTS 18/20 MEXIC/AMER WILSON/W MONROE/DOC.   L/A+17C
PAGE 10 E0185

B45
CLAGETT H.L.,A GUIDE TO THE LAW AND LEGAL   BIBLIOG
LITERATURE OF THE MEXICAN STATES. CONSTN LEGIS   JURID
JUDGE ADJUD ADMIN...INT/LAW CON/ANAL 20 MEXIC/AMER. L/A+17C
PAGE 22 E0440   LAW

B45
VANCE H.L.,GUIDE TO THE LAW AND LEGAL LITERATURE OF BIBLIOG/A
MEXICO. LAW CONSTN FINAN LABOR FORCES ADJUD ADMIN   INT/LAW
...CRIMLGY PHIL/SCI CON/ANAL 20 MEXIC/AMER.   JURID
PAGE 103 E2070   CT/SYS

B59
WAGNER W.J.,THE FEDERAL STATES AND THEIR JUDICIARY. ADJUD

BRAZIL CANADA SWITZERLND USA+45 CONFER CT/SYS TASK   METH/COMP
EFFICIENCY FEDERAL PWR...JURID BIBLIOG 20 AUSTRAL   PROB/SOLV
MEXIC/AMER. PAGE 104 E2091   NAT/G

                                                        B60
GONZALEZ NAVARRO M.,LA COLONIZACION EN MEXICO,   ECO/UNDEV
1877-1910. AGRI NAT/G PLAN PROB/SOLV INCOME   GEOG
...POLICY JURID CENSUS 19/20 MEXIC/AMER MIGRATION.   HABITAT
PAGE 44 E0883   COLONIAL

                                                        B60
MOCTEZUMA A.P.,EL CONFLICTO RELIGIOSO DE 1926 (2ND   SECT
ED.). L/A+17C LAW NAT/G LOBBY COERCE GP/REL ATTIT   ORD/FREE
...POLICY 20 MEXIC/AMER CHURCH/STA. PAGE 74 E1476   DISCRIM
                                                        REV

                                                        S63
LEPAWSKY A.,"INTERNATIONAL DEVELOPMENT OF RIVER   INT/ORG
RESOURCES." CANADA EUR+WWI S/ASIA USA+45 SEA LEGIT   DELIB/GP
ADJUD ORD/FREE PWR WEALTH...MGT TIME/SEQ VAL/FREE
MEXIC/AMER 20. PAGE 64 E1287

                                                        S67
FABREGA J.,"ANTECEDENTES EXTRANJEROS EN LA   CONSTN
CONSTITUCION PANAMENA." CUBA L/A+17C PANAMA URUGUAY   JURID
EX/STRUC LEGIS DIPLOM ORD/FREE 19/20 COLOMB   NAT/G
MEXIC/AMER. PAGE 36 E0709   PARL/PROC

MEXICO....SEE ALSO L/A+17C

MEYER C.S. E1445

MEYER H.H.B. E0935,E1446,E1447,E1448

MEYER H.J. E0268

MEYER P. E1449

MEYERS M. E1450

MEYROWITZ H. E1451

MEZERIK A.G. E1452,E1453

MGT....MANAGEMENT

                                                        N
ADVANCED MANAGEMENT. INDUS EX/STRUC WORKER OP/RES   MGT
...DECISION BIBLIOG/A 20. PAGE 1 E0015   ADMIN
                                                        LABOR
                                                        GP/REL

                                                        N
ARBITRATION JOURNAL. WOR+45 LAW INDUS JUDGE DIPLOM   BIBLIOG
CT/SYS INGP/REL 20. PAGE 1 E0016   MGT
                                                        LABOR
                                                        ADJUD

                                                        N
AUSTRALIAN PUBLIC AFFAIRS INFORMATION SERVICE. LAW   BIBLIOG
...HEAL HUM MGT SOC CON/ANAL 20 AUSTRAL. PAGE 1   NAT/G
E0017   CULTURE
                                                        DIPLOM

                                                        N
LATIN AMERICA IN PERIODICAL LITERATURE. LAW TEC/DEV   BIBLIOG/A
DIPLOM RECEIVE EDU/PROP...GEOG HUM MGT 20. PAGE 2   L/A+17C
E0024   SOCIETY
                                                        ECO/UNDEV

                                                        N
PERSONNEL. USA+45 LAW LABOR LG/CO WORKER CREATE   BIBLIOG/A
GOV/REL PERS/REL ATTIT WEALTH. PAGE 2 E0029   ADMIN
                                                        MGT
                                                        GP/REL

                                                        N
CATHERINE R.,LA REVUE ADMINISTRATIVE. FRANCE LAW   ADMIN
NAT/G LEGIS...JURID BIBLIOG/A 20. PAGE 21 E0407   MGT
                                                        FINAN
                                                        METH/COMP

                                                        N
DEUTSCHE BUCHEREI,JAHRESVERZEICHNIS DER DEUTSCHEN   BIBLIOG
HOCHSCHULSCHRIFTEN. EUR+WWI GERMANY LAW ADMIN   WRITING
PERSON...MGT SOC 19/20. PAGE 31 E0613   ACADEM
                                                        INTELL

                                                        N
DEUTSCHE BUCHEREI,JAHRESVERZEICHNIS DES DEUTSCHEN   BIBLIOG
SCHRIFTUMS. AUSTRIA EUR+WWI GERMANY SWITZERLND LAW   WRITING
LOC/G DIPLOM ADMIN...MGT SOC 19/20. PAGE 31 E0614   NAT/G

                                                        N
PUBLISHERS' CIRCULAR LIMITED,THE ENGLISH CATALOGUE   BIBLIOG
OF BOOKS. UK WOR+45 WOR-45 LAW CULTURE LOC/G NAT/G   ALL/VALS
ADMIN LEAD...MGT 19/20. PAGE 83 E1658   ALL/IDEOS
                                                        SOCIETY

                                                        N
SOUTH AFRICA STATE LIBRARY,SOUTH AFRICAN NATIONAL   BIBLIOG
BIBLIOGRAPHY, SANB. SOUTH/AFR LAW NAT/G EDU/PROP   PRESS
...MGT PSY SOC 20. PAGE 93 E1858   WRITING

                                                        B03
GRIFFIN A.P.C.,LIST OF REFERENCES ON INDUSTRIAL   BIBLIOG/A
ARBITRATION (PAMPHLET). USA-45 STRATA VOL/ASSN   INDUS
DELIB/GP WORKER ADJUD GP/REL...MGT 19/20. PAGE 46   LABOR
E0921   BARGAIN

                                                        B03
GRIFFIN A.P.C.,SELECT LIST OF BOOKS ON LABOR   BIBLIOG/A
PARTICULARLY RELATING TO STRIKES. FRANCE GERMANY   GP/REL
MOD/EUR UK USA-45 LAW NAT/G DELIB/GP WORKER BARGAIN   MGT
LICENSE PAY ADJUD 19/20. PAGE 46 E0924   LABOR

                                                        B06
GRIFFIN A.P.C.,LIST OF BOOKS RELATING TO CHILD   BIBLIOG/A
LABOR (PAMPHLET). BELGIUM FRANCE GERMANY MOD/EUR UK   LAW
USA-45 ECO/DEV INDUS WORKER CAP/ISM PAY ROUTINE   LABOR
ALL/IDEOS...MGT SOC 19/20. PAGE 47 E0929   AGE/C

                                                        N19
BUREAU OF NAT'L AFFAIRS INC.,A CURRENT LOOK AT: DISCRIM
(1) THE NEGRO AND TITLE VII, (2) SEX AND TITLE VII   SEX
(PAMPHLET). LAW LG/CO SML/CO RACE/REL...POLICY SOC   WORKER
STAT DEEP/QU TREND CON/ANAL CHARTS 20 NEGRO   MGT
CIV/RIGHTS. PAGE 17 E0334

                                                        B32
EAGLETON C.,INTERNATIONAL GOVERNMENT. BRAZIL FRANCE   INT/ORG
GERMANY ITALY UK USSR WOR-45 DELIB/GP TOP/EX PLAN   JURID
ECO/TAC EDU/PROP LEGIT ADJUD REGION ARMS/CONT   DIPLOM
COERCE ATTIT PWR...GEOG MGT VAL/FREE LEAGUE/NAT 20.   INT/LAW
PAGE 34 E0670

                                                        B38
FIELD G.L.,THE SYNDICAL AND CORPORATIVE   FASCISM
INSTITUTIONS OF ITALIAN FASCISM. ITALY CONSTN   INDUS
STRATA LABOR EX/STRUC TOP/EX ADJUD ADMIN LEAD   NAT/G
TOTALISM AUTHORIT...MGT 20 MUSSOLIN/B. PAGE 38   WORKER
E0746

                                                        B44
FULLER G.H.,RENEGOTIATION OF WAR CONTRACTS: A   BIBLIOG
SELECTED LIST OF REFERENCES (PAMPHLET). USA-45   WAR
ECO/DEV LG/CO NAT/G OP/RES PLAN BAL/PWR LEGIT   LAW
CONTROL...MGT 20. PAGE 42 E0823   FINAN

                                                        B50
GRAVES W.B.,PUBLIC ADMINISTRATION: A COMPREHENSIVE   BIBLIOG
BIBLIOGRAPHY ON PUBLIC ADMINISTRATION IN THE UNITED   FINAN
STATES (PAMPHLET). USA+45 USA-45 LOC/G NAT/G LEGIS   CONTROL
ADJUD INGP/REL...MGT 20. PAGE 45 E0901   ADMIN

                                                        B52
THOM J.M.,GUIDE TO RESEARCH MATERIAL IN POLITICAL   BIBLIOG/A
SCIENCE (PAMPHLET). ELITES LOC/G MUNIC NAT/G LEGIS   KNOWL
DIPLOM ADJUD CIVMIL/REL GOV/REL PWR MGT. PAGE 96
E1916

                                                        B52
UNESCO,THESES DE SCIENCES SOCIALES: CATALOGUE   BIBLIOG
ANALYTIQUE INTERNATIONAL DE THESES INEDITES DE   ACADEM
DOCTORAT, 1940-1950. INT/ORG DIPLOM EDU/PROP...GEOG   WRITING
INT/LAW MGT PSY SOC 20. PAGE 98 E1958

                                                        B53
SECKLER-HUDSON C.,BIBLIOGRAPHY ON PUBLIC   BIBLIOG/A
ADMINISTRATION (4TH ED.). USA+45 LAW POL/PAR   ADMIN
DELIB/GP BUDGET ADJUD LOBBY GOV/REL GP/REL ATTIT   NAT/G
...JURID 20. PAGE 90 E1800   MGT

                                                        C54
CALDWELL L.K.,"THE GOVERNMENT AND ADMINISTRATION OF   PROVS
NEW YORK." LOC/G MUNIC POL/PAR SCHOOL CHIEF LEGIS   ADMIN
PLAN TAX CT/SYS...MGT SOC/WK BIBLIOG 20 NEWYORK/C.   CONSTN
PAGE 19 E0365   EX/STRUC

                                                        B57
JENNINGS I.,PARLIAMENT. UK FINAN INDUS POL/PAR   PARL/PROC
DELIB/GP EX/STRUC PLAN CONTROL...MAJORIT JURID   TOP/EX
PARLIAMENT. PAGE 58 E1163   MGT
                                                        LEGIS

                                                        B57
SCHUBERT G.A.,THE PRESIDENCY IN THE COURTS. CONSTN   PWR
FORCES DIPLOM TARIFFS ADJUD CONTROL WAR...DECISION   CT/SYS
MGT CHARTS 18/20 PRESIDENT CONGRESS SUPREME/CT.   LEGIT

PAGE 89 E1778   CHIEF

B58

AMERICAN SOCIETY PUBLIC ADMIN,STRENGTHENING   ADMIN
MANAGEMENT FOR DEMOCRATIC GOVERNMENT. USA+45 ACADEM NAT/G
EX/STRUC WORKER PLAN BUDGET CONFER CT/SYS   EXEC
EFFICIENCY ANTHOL. PAGE 4 E0083   MGT

B58

ATOMIC INDUSTRIAL FORUM,MANAGEMENT AND ATOMIC   NUC/PWR
ENERGY. WOR+45 SEA LAW MARKET NAT/G TEC/DEV INSPECT INDUS
INT/TRADE CONFER PEACE HEALTH...ANTHOL 20. PAGE 6   MGT
E0112   ECO/TAC

B58

BUREAU OF NATIONAL AFFAIRS,THE MCCLELLAN COMMITTEE   DELIB/GP
HEARINGS - 1957. USA+45 LEGIS CONTROL CRIME   CONFER
...CHARTS 20 CONGRESS AFL/CIO MCCLELLN/J. PAGE 17   LABOR
E0336   MGT

B58

CUNNINGHAM W.B.,COMPULSORY CONCILIATION AND   POLICY
COLLECTIVE BARGAINING. CANADA NAT/G LEGIS ADJUD   BARGAIN
CT/SYS GP/REL...MGT 20 NEW/BRUNS STRIKE CASEBOOK.   LABOR
PAGE 28 E0555   INDUS

B58

MOSER J.J.,JOHANN JACOB MOSER'S GESAMMELTE UND ZU   BIBLIOG
GEMEINNUTZIGEM GEBRAUCH EINGERICHTETE BIBLIOTHEK.   EXTR/IND
GERMANY PROC/MFG INT/TRADE...POLICY JURID MGT 18.   INDUS
PAGE 75 E1500

B58

SHARMA M.P.,PUBLIC ADMINISTRATION IN THEORY AND   MGT
PRACTICE. INDIA UK USA+45 USA-45 EX/STRUC ADJUD   ADMIN
...POLICY CONCPT NAT/COMP 20. PAGE 90 E1813   DELIB/GP
                                                    JURID

B58

WESTIN A.F.,THE ANATOMY OF A CONSTITUTIONAL LAW   CT/SYS
CASE. USA+45 LAW LEGIS ADMIN EXEC...DECISION MGT   INDUS
SOC RECORD 20 SUPREME/CT. PAGE 105 E2113   ADJUD
                                                    CONSTN

B59

COUNCIL OF STATE GOVERNMENTS,STATE GOVERNMENT: AN   BIBLIOG/A
ANNOTATED BIBLIOGRAPHY (PAMPHLET). USA+45 LAW AGRI   PROVS
INDUS WORKER PLAN TAX ADJUST AGE/Y ORD/FREE...HEAL   LOC/G
MGT 20. PAGE 26 E0521   ADMIN

B59

US SENATE COMM ON POST OFFICE,TO PROVIDE FOR AN   ADMIN
EFFECTIVE SYSTEM OF PERSONNEL ADMINISTRATION.   NAT/G
EFFICIENCY...MGT 20 CONGRESS CIVIL/SERV POSTAL/SYS   EX/STRUC
YARBROGH/R. PAGE 103 E2059   LAW

B60

ALBI F.,TRATADO DE LOS MODOS DE GESTION DE LAS   LOC/G
CORPORACIONES LOCALES. SPAIN FINAN NAT/G BUDGET   LAW
CONTROL EXEC ROUTINE GOV/REL ORD/FREE SOVEREIGN   ADMIN
...MGT 20. PAGE 3 E0057   MUNIC

B60

LEWIS P.R.,LITERATURE OF THE SOCIAL SCIENCES: AN   BIBLIOG/A
INTRODUCTORY SURVEY AND GUIDE. UK LAW INDUS DIPLOM   SOC
INT/TRADE ADMIN...MGT 19/20. PAGE 65 E1294

B60

STEIN E.,AMERICAN ENTERPRISE IN THE EUROPEAN COMMON MARKET
MARKET: A LEGAL PROFILE. EUR+WWI FUT USA+45 SOCIETY ADJUD
STRUCT ECO/DEV NAT/G VOL/ASSN CONSULT PLAN TEC/DEV   INT/LAW
ECO/TAC INT/TRADE ADMIN ATTIT RIGID/FLEX PWR...MGT
NEW/IDEA STAT TREND COMPUT/IR SIMUL EEC 20. PAGE 93
E1867

B60

WEBSTER J.A.,A GENERAL STUDY OF THE DEPARTMENT OF   ORD/FREE
DEFENSE INTERNAL SECURITY PROGRAM. USA+45 WORKER   PLAN
TEC/DEV ADJUD CONTROL CT/SYS EXEC GOV/REL COST   ADMIN
...POLICY DECISION MGT 20 DEPT/DEFEN SUPREME/CT.   NAT/G
PAGE 105 E2105

B60

WOETZEL R.K.,THE INTERNATIONAL CONTROL OF AIRSPACE   INT/ORG
AND OUTERSPACE. FUT WOR+45 AIR CONSTN STRUCT   JURID
CONSULT PLAN TEC/DEV ADJUD RIGID/FLEX KNOWL   SPACE
ORD/FREE PWR...TECHNIC GEOG MGT NEW/IDEA TREND   INT/LAW
COMPUT/IR VAL/FREE 20 TREATY. PAGE 107 E2137

L60

STEIN E.,"LEGAL REMEDIES OF ENTERPRISES IN THE   MARKET
EUROPEAN ECONOMIC COMMUNITY." EUR+WWI FUT ECO/DEV   ADJUD
INDUS PLAN ECO/TAC ADMIN PWR...MGT MATH STAT TREND
CON/ANAL EEC 20. PAGE 93 E1868

S60

MACKINNON F.,"THE UNIVERSITY: COMMUNITY OR   ACADEM
UTILITY?" CLIENT CONSTN INTELL FINAN NAT/G NEIGH   MGT
EDU/PROP PARTIC REPRESENT ROLE. PAGE 67 E1343   CONTROL
                                                    SERV/IND

B61

CARROTHERS A.W.R.,LABOR ARBITRATION IN CANADA.   LABOR
CANADA LAW NAT/G CONSULT LEGIS WORKER ADJUD ADMIN   MGT
CT/SYS 20. PAGE 20 E0396   GP/REL
                                                    BARGAIN

B61

PUGET H.,ESSAI DE BIBLIOGRAPHIE DES PRINCIPAUX   BIBLIOG
OUVRAGES DE DROIT PUBLIC... QUI ONT PARU HORS DE   MGT
FRANCE DE 1945 A 1958. EUR+WWI USA+45 CONSTN LOC/G   ADMIN
...METH 20. PAGE 83 E1660   LAW

B62

BOCK E.A.,CASE STUDIES IN AMERICAN GOVERNMENT.   POLICY
USA+45 ECO/DEV CHIEF EDU/PROP CT/SYS RACE/REL   LEGIS
ORD/FREE...JURID MGT PHIL/SCI PRESIDENT CASEBOOK.   IDEA/COMP
PAGE 13 E0256   NAT/G

B62

CARLSTON K.S.,LAW AND ORGANIZATION IN WORLD   INT/ORG
SOCIETY. WOR+45 FINAN ECO/TAC DOMIN LEGIT CT/SYS   LAW
ROUTINE COERCE ORD/FREE PWR WEALTH...PLURIST
DECISION JURID MGT METH/CNCPT GEN/LAWS 20. PAGE 19
E0381

B62

MARS D.,SUGGESTED LIBRARY IN PUBLIC ADMINISTRATION. BIBLIOG
FINAN DELIB/GP EX/STRUC WORKER COMPUTER ADJUD   ADMIN
...DECISION PSY SOC METH/COMP 20. PAGE 68 E1368   METH
                                                    MGT

S62

GANDOLFI A.,"REFLEXIONS SUR L'IMPOT DE CAPITATION   AFR
EN AFRIQUE NOIRE." GHANA SENEGAL LAW FINAN ACT/RES   CHOOSE
TEC/DEV ECO/TAC WEALTH...MGT TREND 20. PAGE 42
E0830

S62

MANGIN G.,"LES ACCORDS DE COOPERATION EN MATIERE DE INT/ORG
JUSTICE ENTRE LA FRANCE ET LES ETATS AFRICAINS ET   LAW
MALGACHE." AFR ISLAM WOR+45 STRUCT ECO/UNDEV NAT/G   FRANCE
DELIB/GP PERCEPT ALL/VALS...JURID MGT TIME/SEQ 20.
PAGE 68 E1356

B63

GINZBERG E.,DEMOCRATIC VALUES AND THE RIGHTS OF   LABOR
MANAGEMENT. LAW CONSTN REPRESENT GP/REL ROLE PWR   MGT
RESPECT POLICY. PAGE 44 E0870   DELIB/GP
                                                    ADJUD

B63

GOURNAY B.,PUBLIC ADMINISTRATION. FRANCE LAW CONSTN BIBLIOG/A
AGRI FINAN LABOR SCHOOL EX/STRUC CHOOSE...MGT   ADMIN
METH/COMP 20. PAGE 45 E0894   NAT/G
                                                    LOC/G

B63

HAUSMAN W.H.,MANAGING ECONOMIC DEVELOPMENT IN   ECO/UNDEV
AFRICA. AFR USA+45 LAW FINAN WORKER TEC/DEV WEALTH   PLAN
...ANTHOL 20. PAGE 51 E1012   FOR/AID
                                                    MGT

B63

ROYAL INSTITUTE PUBLIC ADMIN,BRITISH PUBLIC   BIBLIOG
ADMINISTRATION. UK LAW FINAN INDUS LOC/G POL/PAR   ADMIN
LEGIS LOBBY PARL/PROC CHOOSE JURID. PAGE 86 E1729   MGT
                                                    NAT/G

S63

LEPAWSKY A.,"INTERNATIONAL DEVELOPMENT OF RIVER   INT/ORG
RESOURCES." CANADA EUR+WWI S/ASIA USA+45 SEA LEGIT   DELIB/GP
ADJUD ORD/FREE PWR WEALTH...MGT TIME/SEQ VAL/FREE
MEXIC/AMER 20. PAGE 64 E1287

B64

JACKSON R.M.,THE MACHINERY OF JUSTICE IN ENGLAND.   CT/SYS
UK EDU/PROP CONTROL COST ORD/FREE...MGT 20   ADJUD
ENGLSH/LAW. PAGE 57 E1142   JUDGE
                                                    JURID

B64

RICHARDSON I.L.,BIBLIOGRAFIA BRASILEIRA DE   BIBLIOG
ADMINISTRACAO PUBLICA E ASSUNTOS CORRELATOS. BRAZIL MGT
CONSTN FINAN LOC/G NAT/G POL/PAR PLAN DIPLOM   ADMIN
RECEIVE ATTIT...METH 20. PAGE 84 E1694   LAW

B64

ROBINSON R.D.,INTERNATIONAL BUSINESS POLICY. AFR   ECO/TAC
INDIA L/A+17C USA+45 ELITES AGRI FOR/AID COERCE   DIST/IND
BAL/PAY...DECISION INT/LAW MGT 20. PAGE 85 E1706   COLONIAL

FINAN

B65

BOCK E.,GOVERNMENT REGULATION OF BUSINESS. USA+45 | MGT
LAW EX/STRUC LEGIS EXEC ORD/FREE PWR...ANTHOL | ADMIN
CONGRESS. PAGE 13 E0255 | NAT/G
| CONTROL

B65

FRYE R.J.,HOUSING AND URBAN RENEWAL IN ALABAMA. | MUNIC
USA+45 NEIGH LEGIS BUDGET ADJUD ADMIN PARTIC...MGT | PROB/SOLV
20 ALABAMA URBAN/RNWL. PAGE 41 E0815 | PLAN
| GOV/REL

B65

ROSS P.,THE GOVERNMENT AS A SOURCE OF UNION POWER. | LABOR
USA+45 LAW ECO/DEV PROB/SOLV ECO/TAC LEAD GP/REL | BARGAIN
...MGT 20. PAGE 86 E1723 | POLICY
| NAT/G

B65

UNIVERSAL REFERENCE SYSTEM,INTERNATIONAL AFFAIRS: | BIBLIOG/A
VOLUME I IN THE POLITICAL SCIENCE, GOVERNMENT, AND | GEN/METH
PUBLIC POLICY SERIES....DECISION ECOMETRIC GEOG | COMPUT/IR
INT/LAW JURID MGT PHIL/SCI PSY SOC. PAGE 98 E1972 | DIPLOM

B65

WEIL G.L.,A HANDBOOK ON THE EUROPEAN ECONOMIC | INT/TRADE
COMMUNITY. BELGIUM EUR+WWI FRANCE GERMANY/W ITALY | INT/ORG
CONSTN ECO/DEV CREATE PARTIC GP/REL...DECISION MGT | TEC/DEV
CHARTS 20 EEC. PAGE 105 E2107 | INT/LAW

B66

GREENE L.E.,GOVERNMENT IN TENNESSEE (2ND ED.). | PROVS
USA+45 DIST/IND INDUS POL/PAR EX/STRUC LEGIS PLAN | LOC/G
BUDGET GIVE CT/SYS...MGT T 20 TENNESSEE. PAGE 46 | CONSTN
E0909 | ADMIN

B66

MC CONNELL J.P.,LAW AND BUSINESS: PATTERNS AND | ECO/DEV
ISSUES IN COMMERCIAL LAW. USA+45 USA-45 LOC/G | JURID
WORKER LICENSE CRIME REPRESENT GP/REL 20. PAGE 70 | ADJUD
E1397 | MGT

B66

WASHINGTON S.H.,BIBLIOGRAPHY: LABOR-MANAGEMENT | BIBLIOG
RELATIONS ACT, 1947 AS AMENDED BY LABOR-MANAGEMENT | LAW
REPORTING AND DISCLOSURE ACT, 1959. USA+45 CONSTN | LABOR
INDUS DELIB/GP LEGIS WORKER BARGAIN ECO/TAC ADJUD | MGT
GP/REL NEW/LIB...JURID CONGRESS. PAGE 105 E2100

B66

YOUNG W.,EXISTING MECHANISMS OF ARMS CONTROL. | ARMS/CONT
PROC/MFG OP/RES DIPLOM TASK CENTRAL...MGT TREATY. | ADMIN
PAGE 108 E2165 | NUC/PWR
| ROUTINE

L66

SEYLER W.C.,"DOCTORAL DISSERTATIONS IN POLITICAL | BIBLIOG
SCIENCE IN UNIVERSITIES OF THE UNITED STATES AND | LAW
CANADA." INT/ORG LOC/G ADMIN...INT/LAW MGT | NAT/G
GOV/COMP. PAGE 90 E1808

S66

BURDETTE F.L.,"SELECTED ARTICLES AND DOCUMENTS ON | BIBLIOG
AMERICAN GOVERNMENT AND POLITICS." LAW LOC/G MUNIC | USA+45
NAT/G POL/PAR PROVS LEGIS BAL/PWR ADMIN EXEC | JURID
REPRESENT MGT. PAGE 17 E0331 | CONSTN

B67

BEAL E.F.,THE PRACTICE OF COLLECTIVE BARGAINING | BARGAIN
(3RD ED.). USA+45 WOR+45 ECO/DEV INDUS LG/CO | MGT
PROF/ORG WORKER ECO/TAC GP/REL WEALTH...JURID | LABOR
METH/CNCPT. PAGE 8 E0160 | ADJUD

B67

GABRIEL P.P.,THE INTERNATIONAL TRANSFER OF | ECO/UNDEV
CORPORATE SKILLS: MANAGEMENT CONTRACTS IN LESS | AGREE
DEVELOPED COUNTRIES. CLIENT INDUS LG/CO PLAN | MGT
PROB/SOLV CAP/ISM ECO/TAC FOR/AID INT/TRADE RENT | CONSULT
ADMIN SKILL 20. PAGE 42 E0825

B67

ROBINSON R.D., INTERNATIONAL MANAGEMENT. USA+45 | INT/TRADE
FINAN R+D PLAN PRODUC...DECISION T. PAGE 67 E1336 | MGT
| INT/LAW
| MARKET

B67

UNITED NATIONS,UNITED NATIONS PUBLICATIONS: | BIBLIOG/A
1945-1966. WOR+45 COM/IND DIST/IND FINAN TEC/DEV | INT/ORG
ADMIN...POLICY INT/LAW MGT CHARTS 20 UN UNESCO. | DIPLOM
PAGE 98 E1970 | WRITING

B67

UNIVERSAL REFERENCE SYSTEM,PUBLIC POLICY AND THE | BIBLIOG/A

POLICY

MANAGEMENT OF SCIENCE (VOLUME IX). FUT SPACE WOR+45 | MGT
LAW NAT/G TEC/DEV CONTROL NUC/PWR GOV/REL | PHIL/SCI
...COMPUT/IR GEN/METH. PAGE 99 E1975

S67

BERRODIN E.F.,"AT THE BARGAINING TABLE." LABOR | PROVS
DIPLOM ECO/TAC ADMIN...MGT 20 MICHIGAN. PAGE 11 | WORKER
E0216 | LAW
| BARGAIN

S67

CHAMBERLAIN N.W.,"STRIKES IN CONTEMPORARY CONTEXT." | LABOR
LAW INDUS NAT/G CHIEF CONFER COST ATTIT ORD/FREE | BARGAIN
...POLICY MGT 20. PAGE 21 E0415 | EFFICIENCY
| PROB/SOLV

S67

TYDINGS J.D.,"MODERNIZING THE ADMINISTRATION OF | CT/SYS
JUSTICE." PLAN ADMIN ROUTINE EFFICIENCY...JURID | MGT
SIMUL. PAGE 97 E1948 | COMPUTER
| CONSULT

MGT/OBJECT....MANAGEMENT BY OBJECTIVES

MIAMI....MIAMI, FLORIDA

B51

KEFAUVER E.,CRIME IN AMERICA. USA+45 USA-45 MUNIC | ELITES
NEIGH DELIB/GP TRIBUTE GAMBLE LOBBY SANCTION | CRIME
...AUD/VIS 20 CAPONE/AL MAFIA MIAMI CHICAGO | PWR
DETROIT. PAGE 60 E1194 | FORCES

MICAUD C.A. E1454

MICH/STA/U....MICHIGAN STATE UNIVERSITY

MICH/U....UNIVERSITY OF MICHIGAN

MICHIGAN STATE UNIVERSITY....SEE MICH/STA/U

MICHIGAN....MICHIGAN

B52

GELLHORN W.,THE STATES AND SUBVERSION. USA+45 | PROVS
USA-45 LOC/G DELIB/GP LEGIS EDU/PROP LEGIT CT/SYS | JURID
REGION PEACE ATTIT ORD/FREE SOCISM...INT CON/ANAL
20 CALIFORNIA MARYLAND ILLINOIS MICHIGAN NEW/YORK.
PAGE 43 E0845

B65

FISCHER F.C.,THE GOVERNMENT OF MICHIGAN. USA+45 | PROVS
NAT/G PUB/INST EX/STRUC LEGIS BUDGET GIVE EDU/PROP | LOC/G
CT/SYS CHOOSE GOV/REL...T MICHIGAN. PAGE 38 E0753 | ADMIN
| CONSTN

S67

BERRODIN E.F.,"AT THE BARGAINING TABLE." LABOR | PROVS
DIPLOM ECO/TAC ADMIN...MGT 20 MICHIGAN. PAGE 11 | WORKER
E0216 | LAW
| BARGAIN

MICRONESIA....MICRONESIA

MID/EAST....MIDDLE EAST

B55

KHADDURI M.,LAW IN THE MIDDLE EAST. LAW CONSTN | ADJUD
ACADEM FAM EDU/PROP CT/SYS SANCTION CRIME...INT/LAW | JURID
GOV/COMP ANTHOL 6/20 MID/EAST. PAGE 61 E1210 | ISLAM

B64

THANT U.,TOWARD WORLD PEACE. DELIB/GP TEC/DEV | DIPLOM
EDU/PROP WAR SOVEREIGN...INT/LAW 20 UN MID/EAST. | BIOG
PAGE 96 E1915 | PEACE
| COERCE

MIDDLETOWN....MIDDLETOWN: LOCATION OF LYND STUDY

MID-EUROPEAN LAW PROJECT E1455

MIDWEST/US....MIDWESTERN UNITED STATES

MIGRATION....MIGRATION; IMMIGRATION AND EMIGRATION; SEE
ALSO HABITAT, GEOG

B57

DIVINE R.A.,AMERICAN IMMIGRATION POLICY, 1924-52. | GEOG
USA+45 USA-45 VOL/ASSN DELIB/GP ADJUD WAR ADJUST | HABITAT
DISCRIM...POLICY JURID 20 DEPRESSION MIGRATION. | LEGIS
PAGE 32 E0630 | CONTROL

B57

US COMMISSION GOVT SECURITY,RECOMMENDATIONS; AREA: | POLICY
IMMIGRANT PROGRAM. USA+45 LAW WORKER DIPLOM | CONTROL
EDU/PROP WRITING ADMIN PEACE ATTIT...CONCPT ANTHOL | PLAN
20 MIGRATION SUBVERT. PAGE 99 E1981 | NAT/G

B60
GONZALEZ NAVARRO M.,LA COLONIZACION EN MEXICO,   ECO/UNDEV
1877-1910. AGRI NAT/G PLAN PROB/SOLV INCOME   GEOG
...POLICY JURID CENSUS 19/20 MEXIC/AMER MIGRATION.   HABITAT
PAGE 44 E0883   COLONIAL

B62
PAIKERT G.C.,THE GERMAN EXODUS. EUR+WWI GERMANY/W   INGP/REL
LAW CULTURE SOCIETY STRUCT INDUS NAT/LISM RESPECT   STRANGE
SOVEREIGN...CHARTS BIBLIOG SOC/INTEG 20 MIGRATION.   GEOG
PAGE 79 E1591   GP/REL

B63
BADI J.,THE GOVERNMENT OF THE STATE OF ISRAEL: A   NAT/G
CRITICAL ACCOUNT OF ITS PARLIAMENT, EXECUTIVE, AND   CONSTN
JUDICIARY. ISRAEL ECO/DEV CHIEF DELIB/GP LEGIS   EX/STRUC
DIPLOM CT/SYS INGP/REL PEACE ORD/FREE...BIBLIOG 20   POL/PAR
PARLIAMENT ARABS MIGRATION. PAGE 7 E0131

B64
TELLADO A.,A STATEMENT OF THE LAWS OF THE DOMINICAN CONSTN
REPUBLIC IN MATTERS AFFECTING BUSINESS (3RD ED.).   LEGIS
DOMIN/REP AGRI DIST/IND EXTR/IND FINAN FAM WORKER   NAT/G
ECO/TAC TAX CT/SYS MARRIAGE OWN...BIBLIOG 20   INDUS
MIGRATION. PAGE 95 E1913

B64
US HOUSE COMM ON JUDICIARY,IMMIGRATION HEARINGS.   NAT/G
DELIB/GP STRANGE HABITAT...GEOG JURID 20 CONGRESS   POLICY
MIGRATION. PAGE 100 E2006   DIPLOM
                                                     NAT/LISM

B65
LUGO-MARENCO J.J.,A STATEMENT OF THE LAWS OF   CONSTN
NICARAGUA IN MATTERS AFFECTING BUSINESS. NICARAGUA   NAT/G
AGRI DIST/IND EXTR/IND FINAN FAM WORKER   LEGIS
INT/TRADE TAX MARRIAGE OWN BIO/SOC 20 TREATY   JURID
RESOURCE/N MIGRATION. PAGE 67 E1332

MIL/ACAD....MILITARY ACADEMY

MILITARY....SEE FORCES

MILITARY APPLICATIONS OF URANIUM DETONATION....SEE MAUD

MILL/JAMES....JAMES MILL

MILL/JS....JOHN STUART MILL

B91
SIDGWICK H.,THE ELEMENTS OF POLITICS. LOC/G NAT/G   POLICY
LEGIS DIPLOM ADJUD CONTROL EXEC PARL/PROC REPRESENT LAW
GOV/REL SOVEREIGN ALL/IDEOS 19 MILL/JS BENTHAM/J.   CONCPT
PAGE 91 E1822

MILLER A.S. E1456

MILLER B.S. E1457

MILLER E. E1458

MILLER E.W. E1459

MILLER H.H. E1460

MILLER J.C. E1412

MILLER P. E1461

MILLER R.T. E2142

MILLIS W. E1462,E1463

MILLS/CW....C. WRIGHT MILLS

MILNER/A....ALFRED MILNER

MILTON/J....MILTON, JOHN

B34
CLYDE W.M.,THE STRUGGLE FOR THE FREEDOM OF THE   PRESS
PRESS FROM CAXTON TO CROMWELL. UK LAW LOC/G SECT   ORD/FREE
FORCES LICENSE WRITING SANCTION REV ATTIT PWR   CONTROL
...POLICY 15/17 PARLIAMENT CROMWELL/O MILTON/J.
PAGE 23 E0460

MINAR D.W. E1464

MINING....SEE EXTR/IND

MINISTERE DE L'EDUC NATIONALE E1465

MINISTRY OF OVERSEAS DEVELOPME E1466

MINNESOTA....MINNESOTA

MINORITY....SEE RACE/REL

MIRONENKO Y. E1467

MISCEGEN....MISCEGENATION

S45
DAVIS A.,"CASTE, ECONOMY, AND VIOLENCE" (BMR)"   STRATA
USA-45 LAW SOCIETY STRUCT SECT SANCTION COERCE   RACE/REL
MARRIAGE SEX...PSY SOC SOC/INTEG 18/20 NEGRO   DISCRIM
MISCEGEN SOUTH/US. PAGE 29 E0570

MISHKIN P.J. E1468

MISSION....MISSIONARIES

MISSISSIPPI ADVISORY COMMITTEE E1469

MISSISSIPP....MISSISSIPPI

N19
MISSISSIPPI ADVISORY COMMITTEE,REPORT ON   RACE/REL
MISSISSIPPI (PAMPHLET). USA+45 LAW PROVS FORCES   DISCRIM
ADJUD PWR...SOC/WK INT 20 MISSISSIPP NEGRO   COERCE
CIV/RIGHTS. PAGE 73 E1469   ORD/FREE

B63
LIVELY E.,THE INVASION OF MISSISSIPPI. USA+45 LAW   RACE/REL
CONSTN NAT/G PROVS CT/SYS GOV/REL FEDERAL CONSERVE   CROWD
...TRADIT 20 MISSISSIPP NEGRO NAACP WARRN/EARL   COERCE
KENNEDY/JF. PAGE 66 E1309   MARXISM

B63
US COMN CIVIL RIGHTS,REPORT ON MISSISSIPPI. LAW   RACE/REL
LOC/G NAT/G LEGIS PLAN PROB/SOLV DISCRIM SOC/INTEG   CONSTN
20 MISSISSIPP NEGRO. PAGE 99 E1987   ORD/FREE
                                                     COERCE

B64
DORMAN M.,WE SHALL OVERCOME. USA+45 ELITES ACADEM   RACE/REL
FORCES TOP/EX MURDER...JURID 20 CIV/RIGHTS   LAW
MISSISSIPP EVERS/MED CLEMSON. PAGE 32 E0638   DISCRIM

B64
FACTS ON FILE, INC.,CIVIL RIGHTS 1960-63: THE NEGRO DISCRIM
CAMPAIGN TO WIN EQUAL RIGHTS AND OPPORTUNITIES IN   PRESS
THE UNITED STATES. LAW CONSTN PARTIC SUFF 20 NEGRO   RACE/REL
CIV/RIGHTS MISSISSIPP. PAGE 36 E0710

MISSOURI....MISSOURI

S59
DWYER R.J.,"THE ADMINISTRATIVE ROLE IN   ADMIN
DESEGREGATION." USA+45 LAW PROB/SOLV LEAD RACE/REL   SCHOOL
ISOLAT STRANGE ROLE...POLICY SOC/INTEG MISSOURI   DISCRIM
NEGRO CIV/RIGHTS. PAGE 34 E0668   ATTIT

MITAU G.T. E1470,E1471

MITCHELL B. E1472

MITCHELL G.E. E1473

MITCHELL J.D.B. E1474

MITCHELL L.P. E1472

MNR....MOVIMIENTO NACIONALISTA REVOLUCIONARIO (BOLIVIA)

MO/BASIN....MISSOURI RIVER BASIN PLAN

MOB....SEE CROWD

MOBUTU/J....JOSEPH MOBUTU

MOCHE....MOCHE, PERU

MOCKFORD J. E1475

MOCTEZUMA A.P. E1476

MOD/EUR....MODERN EUROPE (1700-1918); SEE ALSO APPROPRIATE
  NATIONS

N
PUBLISHERS' CIRCULAR, THE OFFICIAL ORGAN OF THE   BIBLIOG
PUBLISHERS' ASSOCIATION OF GREAT BRITAIN AND   NAT/G
IRELAND. EUR+WWI MOD/EUR UK LAW PROB/SOLV DIPLOM   WRITING
COLONIAL ATTIT...HUM 19/20 CMN/WLTH. PAGE 2 E0025   LEAD

N
DE MARTENS G.F.,RECUEIL GENERALE DE TRAITES ET   BIBLIOG

AUTRES ACTES RELATIFS AUX RAPPORTS DE DROIT INTERNATIONAL (41 VOLS.). EUR+WWI MOD/EUR USA-45 ...INDEX TREATY 18/20. PAGE 30 E0587
INT/LAW DIPLOM

B00

MAINE H.S.,INTERNATIONAL LAW. MOD/EUR UNIV SOCIETY STRUCT ACT/RES EXEC WAR ATTIT PERSON ALL/VALS ...POLICY JURID CONCPT OBS TIME/SEQ TOT/POP. PAGE 68 E1349
INT/ORG LAW PEACE INT/LAW

B03

GRIFFIN A.P.C.,SELECT LIST OF BOOKS ON LABOR PARTICULARLY RELATING TO STRIKES. FRANCE GERMANY MOD/EUR UK USA-45 LAW NAT/G DELIB/GP WORKER BARGAIN LICENSE PAY ADJUD 19/20. PAGE 46 E0924
BIBLIOG/A GP/REL MGT LABOR

B04

CRANDALL S.B.,TREATIES: THEIR MAKING AND ENFORCEMENT. MOD/EUR USA-45 CONSTN INT/ORG NAT/G LEGIS EDU/PROP LEGIT EXEC PEACE KNOWL MORAL...JURID CONGRESS 19/20 TREATY. PAGE 27 E0541
LAW

B05

GRIFFIN A.P.C.,LIST OF BOOKS ON RAILROADS IN FOREIGN COUNTRIES. MOD/EUR ECO/DEV NAT/G CONTROL SOCISM...JURID 19/20 RAILROAD. PAGE 47 E0927
BIBLIOG/A SERV/IND ADMIN DIST/IND

B06

FOSTER J.W.,THE PRACTICE OF DIPLOMACY AS ILLUSTRATED IN THE FOREIGN RELATIONS OF THE UNITED STATES. MOD/EUR USA-45 NAT/G EX/STRUC ADMIN ...POLICY INT/LAW BIBLIOG 19/20. PAGE 39 E0777
DIPLOM ROUTINE PHIL/SCI

B06

GRIFFIN A.P.C.,LIST OF BOOKS RELATING TO CHILD LABOR (PAMPHLET). BELGIUM FRANCE GERMANY MOD/EUR UK USA-45 ECO/DEV INDUS WORKER CAP/ISM PAY ROUTINE ALL/IDEOS...MGT SOC 19/20. PAGE 47 E0929
BIBLIOG/A LAW LABOR AGE/C

B12

MEYER H.H.B.,SELECT LIST OF REFERENCES ON THE INITIATIVE, REFERENDUM, AND RECALL. MOD/EUR USA-45 LAW LOC/G MUNIC REPRESENT POPULISM 20 CONGRESS. PAGE 72 E1446
BIBLIOG/A NAT/G LEGIS CHOOSE

B13

BORCHARD E.M.,BIBLIOGRAPHY OF INTERNATIONAL LAW AND CONTINENTAL LAW. EUR+WWI MOD/EUR UK LAW INT/TRADE WAR PEACE...GOV/COMP NAT/COMP 19/20. PAGE 14 E0267
BIBLIOG INT/LAW JURID DIPLOM

B15

HOBSON J.A.,TOWARDS INTERNATIONAL GOVERNMENT. MOD/EUR STRUCT ECO/TAC EDU/PROP ADJUD ALL/VALS ...SOCIALIST CONCPT GEN/LAWS TOT/POP 20. PAGE 53 E1059
FUT INT/ORG CENTRAL

B16

ROOT E.,ADDRESSES ON INTERNATIONAL SUBJECTS. MOD/EUR UNIV USA-45 LAW SOCIETY EXEC ATTIT ALL/VALS ...POLICY JURID CONCPT 20 CHINJAP. PAGE 85 E1711
INT/ORG ACT/RES PEACE INT/LAW

N19

POUND R.,ORGANIZATION OF THE COURTS (PAMPHLET). MOD/EUR UK USA-45 ADJUD PWR...GOV/COMP 10/20 EUROPE. PAGE 82 E1635
CT/SYS JURID STRUCT ADMIN

B21

OPPENHEIM L.,THE FUTURE OF INTERNATIONAL LAW. EUR+WWI MOD/EUR LAW LEGIS JUDGE LEGIT ORD/FREE ...JURID TIME/SEQ GEN/LAWS 20. PAGE 79 E1578
INT/ORG CT/SYS INT/LAW

B22

BRYCE J.,INTERNATIONAL RELATIONS. CHRIST-17C EUR+WWI MOD/EUR CULTURE INTELL NAT/G DELIB/GP CREATE BAL/PWR DIPLOM ATTIT DRIVE RIGID/FLEX ALL/VALS...PLURIST JURID CONCPT TIME/SEQ GEN/LAWS TOT/POP. PAGE 16 E0323
INT/ORG POLICY

B22

MYERS D.P.,MANUAL OF COLLECTIONS OF TREATIES AND OF COLLECTIONS RELATING TO TREATIES. MOD/EUR INT/ORG LEGIS WRITING ADMIN SOVEREIGN...INT/LAW 19/20. PAGE 75 E1514
BIBLIOG/A DIPLOM CONFER

B25

GODET M.,INDEX BIBLIOGRAPHICUS: INTERNATIONAL CATALOGUE OF SOURCES OF CURRENT BIBLIOGRAPHIC INFORMATION. EUR+WWI MOD/EUR SOCIETY SECT TAX ...JURID PHIL/SCI SOC MATH. PAGE 44 E0876
BIBLIOG/A DIPLOM EDU/PROP LAW

B26

BEALE J.H.,A BIBLIOGRAPHY OF EARLY ENGLISH LAW
BIBLIOG/A

BOOKS. MOD/EUR UK PRESS ADJUD CT/SYS ATTIT...CHARTS 10/16. PAGE 8 E0161
JURID LAW

B26

INSTITUT INTERMEDIAIRE INTL,REPERTOIRE GENERAL DES TRAITES ET AUTRES ACTES DIPLOMATIQUES CONCLUS DEPUIS 1895 JUSQU'EN 1920. MOD/EUR WOR-45 INT/ORG VOL/ASSN DELIB/GP INT/TRADE WAR TREATY 19/20. PAGE 56 E1125
BIBLIOG DIPLOM

B30

BYNKERSHOEK C.,QUAESTIONUM JURIS PUBLICI LIBRI DUO. CHRIST-17C MOD/EUR CONSTN ELITES SOCIETY NAT/G PROVS EX/STRUC FORCES TOP/EX BAL/PWR DIPLOM ATTIT MORAL...TRADIT CONCPT. PAGE 18 E0352
INT/ORG LAW NAT/LISM INT/LAW

B32

MASTERS R.D.,INTERNATIONAL LAW IN INTERNATIONAL COURTS. BELGIUM EUR+WWI FRANCE GERMANY MOD/EUR SWITZERLND WOR-45 SOCIETY STRATA STRUCT LEGIT EXEC ALL/VALS...JURID HIST/WRIT TIME/SEQ TREND GEN/LAWS 20. PAGE 69 E1383
INT/ORG LAW INT/LAW

B34

CUMMINGS H.,LIBERTY UNDER LAW AND ADMINISTRATION. MOD/EUR USA-45 ADMIN ATTIT...JURID PHIL/SCI. PAGE 28 E0553
ORD/FREE LAW NAT/G SOCIETY

B34

WOLFF C.,JUS GENTIUM METHODO SCIENTIFICA PERTRACTATUM. MOD/EUR INT/ORG VOL/ASSN LEGIT PEACE ATTIT...JURID 20. PAGE 107 E2140
NAT/G LAW INT/LAW WAR

B36

MATTHEWS M.A.,DIPLOMACY: SELECT LIST ON DIPLOMACY, DIPLOMATIC AND CONSULAR PRACTICE, AND FOREIGN OFFICE ORGANIZATION (PAMPHLET). EUR+WWI MOD/EUR USA-45 WOR-45...INT/LAW 20. PAGE 69 E1387
BIBLIOG/A DIPLOM NAT/G

B36

MATTHEWS M.A.,INTERNATIONAL LAW: SELECT LIST OF WORKS IN ENGLISH ON PUBLIC INTERNATIONAL LAW: WITH COLLECTIONS OF CASES AND OPINIONS. CHRIST-17C EUR+WWI MOD/EUR WOR-45 CONSTN ADJUD JURID. PAGE 69 E1388
BIBLIOG/A INT/LAW ATTIT DIPLOM

B36

RUSSEL F.M.,THEORIES OF INTERNATIONAL RELATIONS. EUR+WWI FUT MOD/EUR USA-45 INT/ORG DIPLOM...JURID CONCPT. PAGE 86 E1735
PWR POLICY BAL/PWR SOVEREIGN

B37

THOMPSON J.W.,SECRET DIPLOMACY: A RECORD OF ESPIONAGE AND DOUBLE-DEALING: 1500-1815. CHRIST-17C MOD/EUR NAT/G WRITING RISK MORAL...ANTHOL BIBLIOG 16/19 ESPIONAGE. PAGE 96 E1920
DIPLOM CRIME

B40

MCILWAIN C.H.,CONSTITUTIONALISM, ANCIENT AND MODERN. CHRIST-17C MOD/EUR NAT/G CHIEF PROB/SOLV INSPECT AUTHORIT ORD/FREE PWR...TIME/SEQ ROMAN/REP. PAGE 71 E1418
CONSTN GEN/LAWS LAW

B41

BIRDSALL P.,VERSAILLES TWENTY YEARS AFTER. MOD/EUR POL/PAR CHIEF CONSULT FORCES LEGIS REPAR PEACE ORD/FREE...BIBLIOG 20 PRESIDENT TREATY. PAGE 12 E0231
DIPLOM NAT/LISM WAR

B42

FEILCHENFELD E.H.,THE INTERNATIONAL ECONOMIC LAW OF BELLIGERENT OCCUPATION. EUR+WWI MOD/EUR USA-45 INT/ORG DIPLOM ADJUD ARMS/CONT LEAGUE/NAT 20. PAGE 37 E0726
ECO/TAC INT/LAW WAR

B43

ANDERSON R.B.,SUPPLEMENT TO BEALE'S BIBLIOGRAPHY OF EARLY ENGLISH LAW BOOKS. MOD/EUR UK CONSTN PRESS ADJUD...CHARTS 10/15. PAGE 5 E0091
BIBLIOG/A JURID CT/SYS LAW

B43

SERENI A.P.,THE ITALIAN CONCEPTION OF INTERNATIONAL LAW. EUR+WWI MOD/EUR INT/ORG NAT/G DOMIN COERCE ORD/FREE FASCISM...OBS/ENVIR TREND 20. PAGE 90 E1804
LAW TIME/SEQ INT/LAW ITALY

B44

RUDIN H.R.,ARMISTICE 1918. FRANCE GERMANY MOD/EUR UK USA-45 NAT/G CHIEF DELIB/GP FORCES BAL/PWR REPAR ARMS/CONT 20 WILSON/W TREATY. PAGE 86 E1732
AGREE WAR PEACE DIPLOM

S44

GRIFFITH E.S.,"THE CHANGING PATTERN OF PUBLIC   LAW
POLICY FORMATION." MOD/EUR WOR+45 FINAN CHIEF   POLICY
CONFER ADMIN LEAD CONSERVE SOCISM TECHRACY...SOC   TEC/DEV
CHARTS CONGRESS. PAGE 47 E0938

B46

GRIFFIN G.G.,A GUIDE TO MANUSCRIPTS RELATING TO   BIBLIOG/A
AMERICAN HISTORY IN BRITISH DEPOSITORIES. CANADA   ALL/VALS
IRELAND MOD/EUR UK USA-45 LAW DIPLOM ADMIN COLONIAL NAT/G
WAR NAT/LISM SOVEREIGN...GEOG INT/LAW 15/19
CMN/WLTH. PAGE 47 E0936

B46

SCANLON H.L.,INTERNATIONAL LAW: A SELECTIVE LIST OF BIBLIOG/A
WORKS IN ENGLISH ON PUBLIC INTERNATIONAL LAW (A   INT/LAW
PAMPHLET). CHRIST-17C EUR+WWI MOD/EUR WOR-45 CT/SYS ADJUD
...JURID 20. PAGE 87 E1749   DIPLOM

B48

YAKOBSON S.,FIVE HUNDRED RUSSIAN WORKS FOR COLLEGE BIBLIOG
LIBRARIES (PAMPHLET). MOD/EUR USSR MARXISM SOCISM   NAT/G
...ART/METH GEOG HUM JURID SOC 13/20. PAGE 108   CULTURE
E2162   COM

B49

DENNING A.,FREEDOM UNDER THE LAW. MOD/EUR UK LAW   ORD/FREE
SOCIETY CHIEF EX/STRUC LEGIS ADJUD CT/SYS PERS/REL JURID
PERSON 17/20 ENGLSH/LAW. PAGE 31 E0606   NAT/G

B52

BENTHAM A.,HANDBOOK OF POLITICAL FALLACIES. FUT   POL/PAR
MOD/EUR LAW INTELL LOC/G MUNIC NAT/G DELIB/GP LEGIS
CREATE EDU/PROP CT/SYS ATTIT RIGID/FLEX KNOWL PWR
...RELATIV PSY SOC CONCPT SELF/OBS TREND STERTYP
TOT/POP. PAGE 10 E0189

C52

STUART G.H.,"AMERICAN DIPLOMATIC AND CONSULAR   DIPLOM
PRACTICE (2ND ED.)" EUR+WWI MOD/EUR USA-45 DELIB/GP ADMIN
INT/TRADE ADJUD...BIBLIOG 20. PAGE 94 E1889   INT/ORG

B54

HAMSON C.J.,EXECUTIVE DISCRETION AND JUDICIAL   ELITES
CONTROL; AN ASPECT OF THE FRENCH CONSEIL D'ETAT.   ADJUD
EUR+WWI FRANCE MOD/EUR UK NAT/G EX/STRUC PARTIC   NAT/COMP
CONSERVE...JURID BIBLIOG/A 18/20 SUPREME/CT.
PAGE 50 E0992

B54

MANGONE G.,A SHORT HISTORY OF INTERNATIONAL   INT/ORG
ORGANIZATION. MOD/EUR USA+45 USA-45 WOR+45 WOR-45   INT/LAW
LAW LEGIS CREATE LEGIT ROUTINE RIGID/FLEX PWR
...JURID CONCPT OBS TIME/SEQ STERTYP GEN/LAWS UN
TOT/POP VAL/FREE 18/20. PAGE 68 E1359

B54

NUSSBAUM D.,A CONCISE HISTORY OF THE LAW OF   INT/ORG
NATIONS. ASIA CHRIST-17C EUR+WWI ISLAM MEDIT-7   LAW
MOD/EUR S/ASIA UNIV WOR+45 WOR-45 SOCIETY STRUCT   PEACE
EXEC ATTIT ALL/VALS...CONCPT HIST/WRIT TIME/SEQ.   INT/LAW
PAGE 78 E1560

L54

NICOLSON H.,"THE EVOLUTION OF DIPLOMATIC METHOD."   RIGID/FLEX
CHRIST-17C EUR+WWI FRANCE FUT ITALY MEDIT-7 MOD/EUR METH/CNCPT
USA+45 USA-45 LAW NAT/G CREATE EDU/PROP LEGIT PEACE DIPLOM
ATTIT ORD/FREE RESPECT SOVEREIGN. PAGE 77 E1548

B55

MAZZINI J.,THE DUTIES OF MAN. MOD/EUR LAW SOCIETY   SUPEGO
FAM NAT/G POL/PAR SECT VOL/ASSN EX/STRUC ACT/RES   CONCPT
CREATE REV PEACE ATTIT ALL/VALS...GEN/LAWS WORK 19. NAT/LISM
PAGE 70 E1396

B55

MOHL R.V.,DIE GESCHICHTE UND LITERATUR DER   PHIL/SCI
STAATSWISSENSCHAFTEN (3 VOLS.). LAW NAT/G...JURID   MOD/EUR
METH/COMP METH. PAGE 74 E1480

B57

SINEY M.C.,THE ALLIED BLOCKADE OF GERMANY: DETER
1914-1916. EUR+WWI GERMANY MOD/EUR USA-45 DIPLOM   INT/TRADE
CONTROL NEUTRAL PWR 20. PAGE 91 E1832   INT/LAW
                                                   WAR

B58

BOWETT D.W.,SELF-DEFENSE IN INTERNATIONAL LAW.   ADJUD
EUR+WWI MOD/EUR WOR+45 WOR-45 SOCIETY INT/ORG   CONCPT
CONSULT DIPLOM LEGIT COERCE ATTIT ORD/FREE...JURID WAR
20 UN. PAGE 14 E0276   INT/LAW

B58

JENKS C.W.,THE COMMON LAW OF MANKIND. EUR+WWI   JURID
MOD/EUR SPACE WOR+45 INT/ORG BAL/PWR ARMS/CONT   SOVEREIGN
COERCE SUPEGO MORAL...TREND 20. PAGE 58 E1154

B59

MAYER A.J.,POLITICAL ORIGINS OF THE NEW DIPLOMACY, TREND
1917-1918. EUR+WWI MOD/EUR USA-45 WAR PWR...POLICY DIPLOM
INT/LAW BIBLIOG. PAGE 70 E1392

B61

GUIZOT F.P.G.,HISTORY OF THE ORIGIN OF   LEGIS
REPRESENTATIVE GOVERNMENT IN EUROPE. CHRIST-17C   REPRESENT
FRANCE MOD/EUR SPAIN UK LAW CHIEF FORCES POPULISM   CONSTN
...MAJORIT TIME/SEQ GOV/COMP NAT/COMP 4/19   NAT/G
PARLIAMENT. PAGE 48 E0961

B61

ROBERTSON A.H.,THE LAW OF INTERNATIONAL   RIGID/FLEX
INSTITUTIONS IN EUROPE. EUR+WWI MOD/EUR INT/ORG   ORD/FREE
NAT/G VOL/ASSN DELIB/GP...JURID TIME/SEQ TOT/POP 20
TREATY. PAGE 85 E1704

B62

HENDERSON W.O.,THE GENESIS OF THE COMMON MARKET.   ECO/DEV
EUR+WWI FRANCE MOD/EUR UK SEA COM/IND EXTR/IND   INT/TRADE
COLONIAL DISCRIM...TIME/SEQ CHARTS BIBLIOG 18/20   DIPLOM
EEC TREATY. PAGE 52 E1030

B62

WOETZEL R.K.,THE NURENBERG TRIALS IN INTERNATIONAL INT/ORG
LAW. CHRIST-17C MOD/EUR WOR+45 SOCIETY NAT/G   ADJUD
DELIB/GP DOMIN LEGIT ROUTINE ATTIT DRIVE PERSON   WAR
SUPEGO MORAL ORD/FREE...POLICY MAJORIT JURID PSY
SOC SELF/OBS RECORD NAZI TOT/POP. PAGE 107 E2138

S62

JOHNSON O.H.,"THE ENGLISH TRADITION IN   LAW
INTERNATIONAL LAW." CHRIST-17C MOD/EUR EDU/PROP   INT/LAW
LEGIT CT/SYS ORD/FREE...JURID CONCPT TIME/SEQ.   UK
PAGE 59 E1170

B63

LYONS F.S.L.,INTERNATIONALISM IN EUROPE 1815-1914. DIPLOM
LAW AGRI COM/IND DIST/IND LABOR SECT INT/TRADE   MOD/EUR
TARIFFS...BIBLIOG 19/20. PAGE 67 E1335   INT/ORG

S63

WEISSBERG G.,"MAPS AS EVIDENCE IN INTERNATIONAL   LAW
BOUNDARY DISPUTES: A REAPPRAISAL." CHINA/COM   GEOG
EUR+WWI INDIA MOD/EUR S/ASIA INT/ORG NAT/G LEGIT   SOVEREIGN
PERCEPT...JURID CHARTS 20. PAGE 105 E2110

B64

WRIGHT G.,RURAL REVOLUTION IN FRANCE: THE PEASANTRY PWR
IN THE TWENTIETH CENTURY. EUR+WWI MOD/EUR LAW   STRATA
CULTURE AGRI POL/PAR DELIB/GP LEGIS ECO/TAC   FRANCE
EDU/PROP COERCE CHOOSE ATTIT RIGID/FLEX HEALTH   REV
...STAT CENSUS CHARTS VAL/FREE 20. PAGE 107 E2148

B65

NORDEN A.,WAR AND NAZI CRIMINALS IN WEST GERMANY: FASCIST
STATE, ECONOMY, ADMINISTRATION, ARMY, JUSTICE,   WAR
SCIENCE. GERMANY GERMANY/W MOD/EUR ECO/DEV ACADEM   NAT/G
EX/STRUC FORCES DOMIN ADMIN CT/SYS...POLICY MAJORIT TOP/EX
PACIFIST 20. PAGE 77 E1554

B66

FEINE H.E.,REICH UND KIRCHE. CHRIST-17C MOD/EUR   JURID
ROMAN/EMP LAW CHOOSE ATTIT 10/19 CHURCH/STA   SECT
ROMAN/LAW. PAGE 37 E0728   NAT/G
                                                    GP/REL

B66

FUCHS W.P.,STAAT UND KIRCHE IM WANDEL DER   SECT
JAHRHUNDERTE. EUR+WWI MOD/EUR UK REV...JURID CONCPT NAT/G
4/20 EUROPE CHRISTIAN CHURCH/STA. PAGE 41 E0817   ORD/FREE
                                                    GP/REL

B67

BONGER W.A.,CRIMINALITY AND ECONOMIC CONDITIONS.   PERSON
MOD/EUR STRUCT INDUS WORKER EDU/PROP CRIME HABITAT CRIMLGY
ALL/VALS...JURID SOC 20 REFORMERS. PAGE 14 E0265   IDEA/COMP
                                                    ANOMIE

S67

WINES R.,"THE IMPERIAL CIRCLES, PRINCELY DIPLOMACY, NAT/G
AND IMPERIAL REFORM* 1681-1714." MOD/EUR DELIB/GP   NAT/LISM
BAL/PWR CONFER ADJUD PARL/PROC PARTIC ATTIT PWR   CENTRAL
17/18. PAGE 106 E2132   REGION

MODAL....MODAL TYPES, FASHIONS

S63

NAGEL S.S.,"A CONCEPTUAL SCHEME OF THE JUDICIAL   POLICY
PROCESS." ADJUD...DECISION NEW/IDEA AVERAGE MODAL   LAW
CHARTS. PAGE 76 E1518   JURID
                                                    DISCRIM

SCHUBERT G.,THE JUDICIAL MIND: THE ATTITUDES AND   CT/SYS
IDEOLOGIES OF SUPREME COURT JUSTICES 1946-1963.   JUDGE
USA+45 ELITES NAT/G CONTROL PERS/REL MAJORITY   ATTIT
CONSERVE...DECISION JURID MODAL STAT TREND GP/COMP   NEW/LIB
GAME. PAGE 88 E1774   B65

MODELS....SEE SIMUL, MATH, ALSO MODELS INDEX, P. XIV

MODELSKI G. E1477

MODERNIZATION....SEE MODERNIZE

MODERNIZE....MODERNIZATION

MOELLER R. E1478

MOEN N.W. E1479

MOHL R.V. E1480

MOLEY R. E1481

MOLLARD P.T. E1482

MONACO....SEE ALSO APPROPRIATE TIME/SPACE/CULTURE INDEX

MONARCH....SEE CHIEF, KING

MONARCHY....SEE CONSERVE, CHIEF, KING

MONCONDUIT F. E1483

MONETARY POLICY....SEE FINAN, PLAN

MONEY....SEE FINAN, ECO

MONEYPENNY P. E1484

MONGOLIA....SEE ALSO USSR

MONNIER J.P. E1485

MONOPOLY....MONOPOLIES, OLIGOPOLIES, AND ANTI-TRUST ACTIONS

BURRUS B.R.,INVESTIGATION AND DISCOVERY IN STATE   NAT/G
ANTITRUST (PAMPHLET). USA+45 USA-45 LEGIS ECO/TAC   PROVS
ADMIN CONTROL CT/SYS CRIME GOV/REL PWR...JURID   LAW
CHARTS 19/20 FTC MONOPOLY. PAGE 18 E0346   INSPECT
   N19

FRIEDMAN W.,THE PUBLIC CORPORATION: A COMPARATIVE   LAW
SYMPOSIUM (UNIVERSITY OF TORONTO SCHOOL OF LAW   SOCISM
COMPARATIVE LAW SERIES, VOL. I). SWEDEN USA+45   LG/CO
INDUS INT/ORG NAT/G REGION CENTRAL FEDERAL...POLICY   OWN
JURID IDEA/COMP NAT/COMP ANTHOL 20 COMMONWLTH
MONOPOLY EUROPE. PAGE 40 E0801   B54

BERNSTEIN M.H.,REGULATING BUSINESS BY INDEPENDENT   DELIB/GP
COMMISSION. USA+45 USA-45 LG/CO CHIEF LEGIS   CONTROL
PROB/SOLV ADJUD SANCTION GP/REL ATTIT...TIME/SEQ   CONSULT
19/20 MONOPOLY PRESIDENT CONGRESS. PAGE 11 E0214   B55

WHITNEY S.N.,ANTITRUST POLICIES: AMERICAN   INDUS
EXPERIENCE IN TWENTY INDUSTRIES. USA+45 USA-45 LAW   CONTROL
DELIB/GP LEGIS ADJUD CT/SYS GOV/REL ATTIT...ANTHOL   LG/CO
20 MONOPOLY CASEBOOK. PAGE 106 E2119   MARKET
   B58

US SENATE COMM ON JUDICIARY,LEGISLATION TO   LEAD
STRENGTHEN PENALTIES UNDER THE ANTITRUST LAWS   ADJUD
(PAMPHLET). USA+45 LG/CO CONFER CONTROL SANCTION   INDUS
ORD/FREE 20 SENATE MONOPOLY. PAGE 102 E2045   ECO/TAC
   N62

BOWIE R.R.,GOVERNMENT REGULATION OF BUSINESS: CASES   LAW
FROM THE NATIONAL REPORTER SYSTEM. USA+45 USA-45   CONTROL
NAT/G ECO/TAC ADJUD...ANTHOL 19/20 SUPREME/CT FTC   INDUS
FAIR/LABOR MONOPOLY. PAGE 14 E0280   CT/SYS
   B63

US SENATE COMM ON JUDICIARY,ADMINISTERED PRICES.   LG/CO
USA+45 RATION ADJUD CONTROL LOBBY...POLICY 20   PRICE
SENATE MONOPOLY. PAGE 102 E2047   ADMIN
   DECISION
   B63

US SENATE COMM ON JUDICIARY,HEARINGS BEFORE   ECO/DEV
SUBCOMMITTEE ON ANTITRUST AND MONOPOLY: ECONOMIC   CONTROL
CONCENTRATION VOLUMES 1-5 JULY 1964-SEPT 1966.   MARKET
USA+45 LAW FINAN ECO/TAC ADJUD COST EFFICIENCY   LG/CO
PRODUC...STAT CHARTS 20 CONGRESS MONOPOLY. PAGE 102
E2052   B64

HABERLER G.,A SURVEY OF INTERNATIONAL TRADE THEORY.   INT/TRADE
CANADA FRANCE GERMANY ECO/TAC TARIFFS AGREE COST   BAL/PAY
DEMAND WEALTH...ECOMETRIC 19/20 MONOPOLY TREATY.   DIPLOM
PAGE 49 E0968   POLICY
   B65

MONPIED E. E1486,E1487

MONROE/DOC....MONROE DOCTRINE

BEMIS S.F.,THE LATIN AMERICAN POLICY OF THE UNITED   DIPLOM
STATES: AN HISTORICAL INTERPRETATION. INT/ORG AGREE   SOVEREIGN
COLONIAL WAR PEACE ATTIT ORD/FREE...POLICY INT/LAW   USA-45
CHARTS 18/20 MEXIC/AMER WILSON/W MONROE/DOC.   L/A+17C
PAGE 10 E0185   B43

MONROE/J....PRESIDENT JAMES MONROE

MONTAGUE F.C. E0198

MONTANA....MONTANA

MONTECARLO....MONTE CARLO - OPERATIONAL RESEARCH
DECISION-MAKING MODEL

MONTESQ....MONTESQUIEU, CHARLES LOUIS DE SECONDAT

VILE M.J.C.,CONSTITUTIONALISM AND THE SEPARATION OF   CONSTN
POWERS. FRANCE UK USA+45 USA-45 NAT/G ADJUD CONTROL   BAL/PWR
GOV/REL...POLICY DECISION JURID GEN/LAWS 15/20   CONCPT
MONTESQ. PAGE 104 E2076   LAW
   B67

MONTGOMERY....MONTGOMERY, ALABAMA

MOODY M. E1488

MOOS M. E1489

MORAL....RECTITUDE, MORALITY, GOODNESS (ALSO IMMORALITY)

BIBLIOGRAPHIE DE LA PHILOSOPHIE. LAW CULTURE SECT   BIBLIOG/A
EDU/PROP MORAL...HUM METH/CNCPT 20. PAGE 1 E0018   PHIL/SCI
   CONCPT
   LOG
   N

CANON LAW ABSTRACTS. LEGIT CONFER CT/SYS INGP/REL   BIBLIOG/A
MARRIAGE ATTIT MORAL WORSHIP 20. PAGE 2 E0026   CATHISM
   SECT
   LAW
   N

BERNARD M.,FOUR LECTURES ON SUBJECTS CONNECTED WITH   LAW
DIPLOMACY. WOR-45 NAT/G VOL/ASSN RIGID/FLEX MORAL   ATTIT
PWR...JURID OBS GEN/LAWS GEN/METH 20 TREATY.   DIPLOM
PAGE 11 E0209   B00

GROTIUS H.,DE JURE BELLI AC PACIS. CHRIST-17C UNIV   JURID
LAW SOCIETY PROVS LEGIT PEACE PERCEPT MORAL PWR   INT/LAW
...CONCPT CON/ANAL GEN/LAWS. PAGE 48 E0952   WAR
   B00

BERKELEY G.,"DISCOURSE ON PASSIVE OBEDIENCE" (1712)   INGP/REL
THE WORKS... (VOL. IV)" UNIV DOMIN LEGIT CONTROL   SANCTION
CRIME ADJUST CENTRAL MORAL ORD/FREE...POLICY   RESPECT
WORSHIP. PAGE 10 E0202   GEN/LAWS
   C01

MOREL E.D.,THE BRITISH CASE IN FRENCH CONGO.   DIPLOM
CONGO/BRAZ FRANCE UK COERCE MORAL WEALTH...POLICY   INT/TRADE
INT/LAW 20 CONGO/LEOP. PAGE 74 E1490   COLONIAL
   AFR
   B03

CRANDALL S.B.,TREATIES: THEIR MAKING AND   LAW
ENFORCEMENT. MOD/EUR USA-45 CONSTN INT/ORG NAT/G
LEGIS EDU/PROP LEGIT EXEC PEACE KNOWL MORAL...JURID
CONGRESS 19/20 TREATY. PAGE 27 E0541   B04

CRAIG J.,ELEMENTS OF POLITICAL SCIENCE (3 VOLS.).   PHIL/SCI
CONSTN AGRI INDUS SCHOOL FORCES TAX CT/SYS SUFF   NAT/G
MORAL WEALTH...CONCPT 19 CIVIL/LIB. PAGE 27 E0539   ORD/FREE
   B14

VECCHIO G.D.,THE FORMAL BASES OF LAW (TRANS. BY J.   LAW
LISLE). DOMIN LEGIT CONTROL COERCE UTIL MORAL PWR   JURID
...CONCPT TIME/SEQ 17/20 COMMON/LAW NATURL/LAW.   GEN/LAWS
PAGE 103 E2074   IDEA/COMP
   B14

PUFENDORF S.,LAW OF NATURE AND OF NATIONS
(ABRIDGED). UNIV LAW NAT/G DIPLOM AGREE WAR PERSON
ALL/VALS PWR...POLICY 18 DEITY NATURL/LAW. PAGE 83
E1659
B16
CONCPT
INT/LAW
SECT
MORAL

DE VICTORIA F.,DE INDIS ET DE JURE BELLI (1557) IN
F. DE VICTORIA, DE INDIS ET DE JURE BELLI
REFLECTIONES. UNIV NAT/G SECT CHIEF PARTIC COERCE
PEACE MORAL...POLICY 16 INDIAN/AM CHRISTIAN
CONSCN/OBJ. PAGE 30 E0598
B17
WAR
INT/LAW
OWN

DUGUIT L.,LAW IN THE MODERN STATE (TRANS. BY FRIDA
AND HAROLD LASKI). CONSTN SOCIETY STRUCT MORAL
ORD/FREE SOVEREIGN 20. PAGE 33 E0655
B19
GEN/LAWS
CONCPT
NAT/G
LAW

VANDERPOL A.,LA DOCTRINE SCOLASTIQUE DU DROIT DE
GUERRE. CHRIST-17C FORCES DIPLOM LEGIT SUPEGO MORAL
...BIOG AQUINAS/T SUAREZ/F CHRISTIAN. PAGE 103
E2072
B19
WAR
SECT
INT/LAW

GIBB A.D.,JUDICIAL CORRUPTION IN THE UNITED KINGDOM
(PAMPHLET). UK DELIB/GP CT/SYS CRIME PERSON SUPEGO
17/20 SCOTLAND. PAGE 43 E0856
N19
MORAL
ATTIT
ADJUD

COX G.C.,THE PUBLIC CONSCIENCE: A CASEBOOK IN
ETHICS....PHIL/SCI SOC CONCPT METH/COMP 20. PAGE 27
E0534
B22
MORAL
ADJUD

DEWEY J.,"ETHICS AND INTERNATIONAL RELATIONS." FUT
WOR-45 SOCIETY INT/ORG VOL/ASSN DIPLOM LEGIT
ORD/FREE...JURID CONCPT GEN/METH 20. PAGE 31 E0618
S23
LAW
MORAL

NAVILLE A.,LIBERTE, EGALITE, SOLIDARITE: ESSAIS
D'ANALYSE. STRATA FAM VOL/ASSN INT/TRADE GP/REL
MORAL MARXISM SOCISM...PSY TREATY. PAGE 76 E1529
B24
ORD/FREE
SOC
IDEA/COMP
DIPLOM

JOHN OF SALISBURY,THE STATESMAN'S BOOK (1159)
(TRANS. BY J. DICKINSON). DOMIN GP/REL MORAL
ORD/FREE PWR CONSERVE...CATH CONCPT 12. PAGE 59
E1169
B27
NAT/G
SECT
CHIEF
LAW

HOBBES T.,THE ELEMENTS OF LAW, NATURAL AND POLITIC
(1650). STRATA NAT/G SECT CHIEF AGREE ATTIT
ALL/VALS MORAL ORD/FREE POPULISM...POLICY CONCPT.
PAGE 53 E1056
B28
PERSON
LAW
SOVEREIGN
CONSERVE

BUELL R.,INTERNATIONAL RELATIONS. WOR+45 WOR-45
CONSTN STRATA FORCES TOP/EX ADMIN ATTIT DRIVE
SUPEGO MORAL ORD/FREE PWR SOVEREIGN...JURID SOC
CONCPT 20. PAGE 17 E0326
B29
INT/ORG
BAL/PWR
DIPLOM

BURNS C.D.,POLITICAL IDEALS. WOR-45 LAW CULTURE
SOCIETY INT/ORG HEALTH MORAL...POLICY TOT/POP 20.
PAGE 18 E0344
B29
CONCPT
GEN/LAWS

BYNKERSHOEK C.,QUAESTIONUM JURIS PUBLICI LIBRI DUO.
CHRIST-17C MOD/EUR CONSTN ELITES SOCIETY NAT/G
PROVS EX/STRUC FORCES TOP/EX BAL/PWR DIPLOM ATTIT
MORAL...TRADIT CONCPT. PAGE 18 E0352
B30
INT/ORG
LAW
NAT/LISM
INT/LAW

GENTILI A.,DE JURE BELLI, LIBRI TRES (1612) (VOL.
2). FORCES DIPLOM AGREE PEACE SOVEREIGN. PAGE 43
E0849
B33
WAR
INT/LAW
MORAL
SUPEGO

REID H.D.,RECUEIL DES COURS; TOME 45: LES
SERVITUDES INTERNATIONALES III. FRANCE CONSTN
DELIB/GP PRESS CONTROL REV WAR CHOOSE PEACE MORAL
MARITIME TREATY. PAGE 84 E1680
B33
ORD/FREE
DIPLOM
LAW

LUCE R.,LEGISLATIVE PROBLEMS. CONSTN CHIEF JUDGE
BUDGET CONFER ETIQUET CONTROL MORAL PWR NEW/LIB
CONGRESS. PAGE 67 E1331
B35
TREND
ADMIN
LEGIS

ROBSON W.A.,CIVILISATION AND THE GROWTH OF LAW.
UNIV CONSTN SOCIETY LEGIS ADJUD ATTIT PERCEPT MORAL
ALL/IDEOS...CONCPT WORSHIP 20. PAGE 85 E1708
B35
LAW
IDEA/COMP
SOC

THOMPSON J.W.,SECRET DIPLOMACY: A RECORD OF
ESPIONAGE AND DOUBLE-DEALING: 1500-1815. CHRIST-17C
MOD/EUR NAT/G WRITING RISK MORAL...ANTHOL BIBLIOG
16/19 ESPIONAGE. PAGE 96 E1920
B37
DIPLOM
CRIME

HADDOW A.,"POLITICAL SCIENCE IN AMERICAN COLLEGES
AND UNIVERSITIES 1636-1900." CONSTN MORAL...POLICY
INT/LAW CON/ANAL BIBLIOG T 17/20. PAGE 49 E0971
C39
USA-45
LAW
ACADEM
KNOWL

GURVITCH G.,"MAJOR PROBLEMS OF THE SOCIOLOGY OF
LAW." CULTURE SANCTION KNOWL MORAL...POLICY EPIST
JURID WORSHIP. PAGE 48 E0963
S40
SOC
LAW
PHIL/SCI

CRAIG A.,ABOVE ALL LIBERTIES. FRANCE UK USA-45 LAW
CONSTN CULTURE INTELL NAT/G SECT JUDGE...IDEA/COMP
BIBLIOG 18/20. PAGE 27 E0536
B42
ORD/FREE
MORAL
WRITING
EDU/PROP

GURVITCH G.,SOCIOLOGY OF LAW. CONSTN SOCIETY CREATE
MORAL SOVEREIGN...POLICY EPIST JURID PHIL/SCI
IDEA/COMP METH/COMP HOLMES/OW HOBBES/T. PAGE 48
E0964
B42
SOC
LAW
ADJUD

CRAIG A.,"ABOVE ALL LIBERTIES." FRANCE UK LAW
CULTURE INTELL SECT ORD/FREE 18/20. PAGE 27 E0537
C42
BIBLIOG/A
EDU/PROP
WRITING
MORAL

BENTHAM J.,"PRINCIPLES OF INTERNATIONAL LAW" IN J.
BOWRING, ED., THE WORKS OF JEREMY BENTHAM." UNIV
NAT/G PLAN PROB/SOLV DIPLOM CONTROL SANCTION MORAL
ORD/FREE PWR SOVEREIGN 19. PAGE 10 E0194
C43
INT/LAW
JURID
WAR
PEACE

LOCKE J.,TWO TREATISES OF GOVERNMENT (1690). UK LAW
SOCIETY LEGIS LEGIT AGREE REV OWN HEREDITY MORAL
CONSERVE...POLICY MAJORIT 17 WILLIAM/3 NATURL/LAW.
PAGE 66 E1316
B47
CONCPT
ORD/FREE
NAT/G
CONSEN

MORGENTHAL H.J.,POLITICS AMONG NATIONS: THE
STRUGGLE FOR POWER AND PEACE. FUT WOR+45 INT/ORG
OP/RES PROB/SOLV BAL/PWR CONTROL ATTIT MORAL
...INT/LAW BIBLIOG 20 COLD/WAR. PAGE 75 E1494
B48
DIPLOM
PEACE
PWR
POLICY

ALEXANDER L.,"WAR CRIMES, THEIR SOCIAL-
PSYCHOLOGICAL ASPECTS." EUR+WWI GERMANY LAW CULTURE
ELITES KIN POL/PAR PUB/INST FORCES DOMIN EDU/PROP
COERCE CRIME ATTIT SUPEGO HEALTH MORAL PWR FASCISM
...PSY OBS TREND GEN/LAWS NAZI 20. PAGE 3 E0061
S48
DRIVE
WAR

MORGENTHAU H.J.,"THE TWILIGHT OF INTERNATIONAL
MORALITY" (BMR)" WOR+45 WOR-45 BAL/PWR WAR NAT/LISM
PEACE...POLICY INT/LAW IDEA/COMP 15/20 TREATY
INTERVENT. PAGE 75 E1495
S48
MORAL
DIPLOM
NAT/G

JIMENEZ E.,VOTING AND HANDLING OF DISPUTES IN THE
SECURITY COUNCIL. WOR+45 CONSTN INT/ORG DIPLOM
LEGIT DETER CHOOSE MORAL ORD/FREE PWR...JURID
TIME/SEQ COLD/WAR UN 20. PAGE 59 E1168
B50
DELIB/GP
ROUTINE

MANGONE G.,"THE IDEA AND PRACTICE OF WORLD
GOVERNMENT." FUT WOR+45 WOR-45 ECO/DEV LEGIS CREATE
LEGIT ROUTINE ATTIT MORAL PWR WEALTH...CONCPT
GEN/LAWS 20. PAGE 68 E1358
L51
INT/ORG
SOCIETY
INT/LAW

FORSTER A.,THE TROUBLE MAKERS. USA+45 LAW CULTURE
SOCIETY STRUCT VOL/ASSN CROWD GP/REL MORAL...PSY
SOC CONCPT 20 NEGRO JEWS. PAGE 39 E0771
B52
DISCRIM
SECT
RACE/REL
ATTIT

LIPPMANN W.,ISOLATION AND ALLIANCES: AN AMERICAN
SPEAKS TO THE BRITISH. USA+45 USA-45 INT/ORG AGREE
COERCE DETER WAR PEACE MORAL 20 TREATY INTERVENT.
PAGE 65 E1301
B52
DIPLOM
SOVEREIGN
COLONIAL
ATTIT

AUSTIN J.,THE PROVINCE OF JURISPRUDENCE DETERMINED
AND THE USES OF THE STUDY OF JURISPRUDENCE. MORAL
...CLASSIF LING STYLE 19. PAGE 6 E0119
B54
CONCPT
LAW
JURID
GEN/LAWS

B54

BROGAN D.W.,POLITICS IN AMERICA. LAW POL/PAR CHIEF   NAT/G
LEGIS LOBBY CHOOSE REPRESENT GP/REL RACE/REL   CONSTN
FEDERAL MORAL...BIBLIOG 20 PRESIDENT CONGRESS.   USA+45
PAGE 16 E0304

B55

BEISEL A.R.,CONTROL OVER ILLEGAL ENFORCEMENT OF THE   ORD/FREE
CRIMINAL LAW: ROLE OF THE SUPREME COURT. CONSTN   LAW
ROUTINE MORAL PWR...SOC 20 SUPREME/CT. PAGE 9 E0180   CRIME

B56

ABELS J.,THE TRUMAN SCANDALS. USA+45 USA-45 POL/PAR   CRIME
TAX LEGIT CT/SYS CHOOSE PRIVIL MORAL WEALTH 20   ADMIN
TRUMAN/HS PRESIDENT CONGRESS. PAGE 2 E0043   CHIEF
                                                     TRIBUTE

B56

BOTERO G.,THE REASON OF STATE AND THE GREATNESS OF   PHIL/SCI
CITIES. SECT CHIEF FORCES PLAN LEAD WAR MORAL   NEW/IDEA
...POLICY 16 MACHIAVELL TREATY. PAGE 14 E0272   CONTROL

B56

CALLISON I.P.,COURTS OF INJUSTICE. USA+45 PROF/ORG   CT/SYS
ADJUD CRIME PERSON MORAL PWR RESPECT SKILL 20.   JUDGE
PAGE 19 E0368   JURID

B56

CORBETT P.E.,MORALS LAW, AND POWER IN INTERNATIONAL   SUPEGO
RELATIONS. WOR+45 WOR-45 INT/ORG VOL/ASSN DELIB/GP   CONCPT
CREATE BAL/PWR DIPLOM LEGIT ARMS/CONT MORAL...JURID   POLICY
GEN/LAWS TOT/POP LEAGUE/NAT 20. PAGE 26 E0506   INT/LAW

B56

FIELD G.C.,POLITICAL THEORY. POL/PAR REPRESENT   CONCPT
MORAL SOVEREIGN...JURID IDEA/COMP. PAGE 38 E0745   NAT/G
                                                     ORD/FREE
                                                     DIPLOM

B56

PERKINS D.,CHARLES EVANS HUGHES AND THE AMERICAN   PERSON
DEMOCRATIC STATESMANSHIP. USA+45 USA-45 NAT/G   BIOG
POL/PAR DELIB/GP JUDGE PLAN MORAL PWR...HIST/WRIT   DIPLOM
LEAGUE/NAT 20. PAGE 80 E1609

B57

BERNS W.,FREEDOM, VIRTUE AND THE FIRST AMENDMENT.   JURID
USA+45 USA-45 CONSTN INTELL JUDGE ADJUD RIGID/FLEX   ORD/FREE
MORAL...CONCPT 20 AMEND/I. PAGE 11 E0211   CT/SYS
                                                     LAW

B57

DE VISSCHER C.,THEORY AND REALITY IN PUBLIC   INT/ORG
INTERNATIONAL LAW. WOR+45 WOR-45 SOCIETY NAT/G   LAW
CT/SYS ATTIT MORAL ORD/FREE PWR...JURID CONCPT   INT/LAW
METH/CNCPT TIME/SEQ GEN/LAWS LEAGUE/NAT TOT/POP
VAL/FREE COLD/WAR. PAGE 30 E0599

S57

FRANKFURTER F.,"THE SUPREME COURT IN THE MIRROR OF   EDU/PROP
JUSTICES" (BMR)" USA+45 USA-45 INTELL INSPECT   ADJUD
EFFICIENCY ROLE KNOWL MORAL 18/20 SUPREME/CT.   CT/SYS
PAGE 40 E0792   PERSON

B58

ALLEN C.K.,ASPECTS OF JUSTICE. UK FAM COERCE CRIME   JURID
MARRIAGE AGE/Y LOVE 20 ENGLSH/LAW. PAGE 4 E0068   MORAL
                                                     ORD/FREE

B58

JENKS C.W.,THE COMMON LAW OF MANKIND. EUR+WWI   JURID
MOD/EUR SPACE WOR+45 INT/ORG BAL/PWR ARMS/CONT   SOVEREIGN
COERCE SUPEGO MORAL...TREND 20. PAGE 58 E1154

B58

SPITZ D.,DEMOCRACY AND THE CHALLANGE OF POWER. FUT   NAT/G
USA+45 USA-45 LAW SOCIETY STRUCT LOC/G POL/PAR   PWR
PROVS DELIB/GP EX/STRUC LEGIS TOP/EX ACT/RES CREATE
DOMIN EDU/PROP LEGIT ADJUD ADMIN ATTIT DRIVE MORAL
ORD/FREE TOT/POP. PAGE 93 E1862

B59

KERREMANS-RAMIOULL,LE PROBLEME DE LA DELINQUENCE   BIBLIOG
JUVENILE (2ND ED.). FAM PUB/INST SCHOOL FORCES   CRIME
LEGIS MORAL...CRIMLGY SOC 20. PAGE 60 E1205   AGE/Y
                                                     SOC/WK

B59

NICHOLS R.F.,RELIGION AND AMERICAN DEMOCRACY.   NAT/G
USA+45 USA-45 LAW CHOOSE SUFF MORAL ORD/FREE   SECT
POPULISM...POLICY BIBLIOG 16/20 PRE/US/AM   CONSTN
CHRISTIAN. PAGE 77 E1547   CONCPT

B59

SCHORN H.,DER RICHTER IM DRITTEN REICH; GESCHICHTE   ADJUD

UND DOKUMENTE. GERMANY NAT/G LEGIT CT/SYS INGP/REL   JUDGE
MORAL ORD/FREE RESPECT...JURID GP/COMP 20. PAGE 88   FASCISM
E1765

B59

SIMPSON J.L.,INTERNATIONAL ARBITRATION: LAW AND   INT/LAW
PRACTICE. WOR+45 WOR-45 INT/ORG DELIB/GP ADJUD   DIPLOM
PEACE MORAL ORD/FREE...METH 18/20. PAGE 91 E1829   CT/SYS
                                                     CONSULT

S59

JENKS C.W.,"THE CHALLENGE OF UNIVERSALITY." FUT   INT/ORG
UNIV CONSTN CULTURE CONSULT CREATE PLAN LEGIT ATTIT   LAW
MORAL ORD/FREE RESPECT...MAJORIT JURID 20. PAGE 58   PEACE
E1155   INT/LAW

B60

GIBNEY F.,THE OPERATORS. USA+45 LAW STRATA BIO/SOC   CRIME
MORAL ORD/FREE SOC. PAGE 43 E0858   CULTURE
                                                     ANOMIE
                                                     CRIMLGY

B60

JENKS C.W.,HUMAN RIGHTS AND INTERNATIONAL LABOR   CONCPT
STANDARDS. WOR+45 CONSTN LABOR VOL/ASSN DELIB/GP
ACT/RES EDU/PROP MORAL RESPECT...JURID SOC TREND
GEN/LAWS WORK ILO 20. PAGE 58 E1156

B60

JENNINGS R.,PROGRESS OF INTERNATIONAL LAW. FUT   INT/ORG
WOR+45 WOR-45 SOCIETY NAT/G VOL/ASSN DELIB/GP   LAW
DIPLOM EDU/PROP LEGIT COERCE ATTIT DRIVE MORAL   INT/LAW
ORD/FREE...JURID CONCPT OBS TIME/SEQ TREND
GEN/LAWS. PAGE 58 E1164

S60

SCHWELB E.,"INTERNATIONAL CONVENTIONS ON HUMAN   INT/ORG
RIGHTS." FUT WOR+45 LAW CONSTN CULTURE SOCIETY   HUM
STRUCT VOL/ASSN DELIB/GP PLAN ADJUD SUPEGO LOVE
MORAL...SOC CONCPT STAT RECORD HIST/WRIT TREND 20
UN. PAGE 89 E1790

S60

THOMPSON K.W.,"MORAL PURPOSE IN FOREIGN POLICY: MORAL
REALITIES AND ILLUSIONS." WOR+45 WOR-45 LAW CULTURE   JURID
SOCIETY INT/ORG PLAN ADJUD ADMIN COERCE RIGID/FLEX   DIPLOM
SUPEGO KNOWL ORD/FREE PWR...SOC TREND SOC/EXP
TOT/POP 20. PAGE 96 E1921

S60

WRIGHT Q.,"LEGAL ASPECTS OF THE U-2 INCIDENT." COM   PWR
USA+45 USSR STRUCT NAT/G FORCES PLAN TEC/DEV ADJUD   POLICY
RIGID/FLEX MORAL ORD/FREE...DECISION INT/LAW JURID   SPACE
PSY TREND GEN/LAWS COLD/WAR VAL/FREE 20 U-2.
PAGE 108 E2157

B61

BEDFORD S.,THE FACES OF JUSTICE: A TRAVELLER'S   CT/SYS
REPORT. AUSTRIA FRANCE GERMANY/W SWITZERLND UK UNIV   ORD/FREE
WOR+45 WOR-45 CULTURE PARTIC GOV/REL MORAL...JURID   PERSON
OBS GOV/COMP 20. PAGE 9 E0174   LAW

L61

SILVING H.,"IN RE EICHMANN: A DILEMMA OF LAW AND   CT/SYS
MORALITY" WOR+45 INSPECT ADJUST MORAL...JURID 20   INT/LAW
WAR/TRIAL EICHMANN/A NATURL/LAW. PAGE 91 E1828   CONCPT

S61

LASSWELL H.D.,"THE INTERPLAY OF ECONOMIC, POLITICAL   JURID
AND SOCIAL CRITERIA IN LEGAL POLICY." LAW LOVE   POLICY
MORAL PWR RESPECT WEALTH...SOC IDEA/COMP. PAGE 63
E1262

S61

RICHSTEIN A.R.,"LEGAL RULES IN NUCLEAR WEAPONS   NUC/PWR
EMPLOYMENTS." FUT WOR+45 LAW SOCIETY FORCES PLAN   TEC/DEV
WEAPON RIGID/FLEX...HEAL CONCPT TREND VAL/FREE 20.   MORAL
PAGE 85 E1696   ARMS/CONT

B62

BORKIN J.,THE CORRUPT JUDGE. USA+45 CT/SYS ATTIT   ADJUD
SUPEGO MORAL RESPECT...BIBLIOG + SUPREME/CT   TRIBUTE
MANTON/M DAVIS/W JOHNSN/ALB. PAGE 14 E0271   CRIME

B62

CRANSTON M.,WHAT ARE HUMAN RIGHTS? UNIV WOR+45   LAW
INT/ORG ADMIN...POLICY CONCPT METH/CNCPT GEN/LAWS   ORD/FREE
20. PAGE 28 E0545   JURID
                                                     IDEA/COMP

B62

ROSTOW E.V.,THE SOVEREIGN PREROGATIVE: THE SUPREME   JURID
COURT AND THE QUEST FOR LAW. CONSTN CT/SYS FEDERAL   PROF/ORG
MORAL SOVEREIGN 20 SUPREME/CT. PAGE 86 E1726   ATTIT
                                                     ORD/FREE

SCHWARZENBERGER G.,THE FRONTIERS OF INTERNATIONAL
LAW. WOR+45 WOR-45 NAT/G LEGIT CT/SYS ROUTINE MORAL
ORD/FREE PWR...JURID SOC GEN/METH 20 COLD/WAR.
PAGE 89 E1789
INT/ORG
LAW
INT/LAW
B62

WOETZEL R.K.,THE NURENBERG TRIALS IN INTERNATIONAL
LAW. CHRIST-17C MOD/EUR WOR+45 SOCIETY NAT/G
DELIB/GP DOMIN LEGIT ROUTINE ATTIT DRIVE PERSON
SUPEGO MORAL ORD/FREE...POLICY MAJORIT JURID PSY
SOC SELF/OBS RECORD NAZI TOT/POP. PAGE 107 E2138
INT/ORG
ADJUD
WAR
B62

FALK R.A.,"THE REALITY OF INTERNATIONAL LAW."
WOR+45 NAT/G LEGIT COERCE DETER WAR MORAL ORD/FREE
PWR SOVEREIGN...JURID CONCPT VAL/FREE COLD/WAR 20.
PAGE 36 E0714
INT/ORG
ADJUD
NUC/PWR
INT/LAW
S62

LISSITZYN O.J.,"SOME LEGAL IMPLICATIONS OF THE U-2
AND RB-47 INCIDENTS." FUT USA+45 USSR WOR+45 AIR
NAT/G DIPLOM LEGIT MORAL ORD/FREE SOVEREIGN...JURID
GEN/LAWS GEN/METH COLD/WAR 20 U-2. PAGE 65 E1305
LAW
CONCPT
SPACE
INT/LAW
S62

BLACK C.L. JR.,THE OCCASIONS OF JUSTICE: ESSAYS
MOSTLY ON LAW. USA+45 JUDGE RACE/REL DISCRIM ATTIT
MORAL ORD/FREE 20 SUPREME/CT BLACK. PAGE 12 E0236
JURID
CONSTN
CT/SYS
LAW
B63

DILLIARD I.,ONE MAN'S STAND FOR FREEDOM: MR.
JUSTICE BLACK AND THE BILL OF RIGHTS. USA+45
POL/PAR SECT DELIB/GP FORCES ADJUD CONTROL WAR
DISCRIM MORAL...BIBLIOG 20 NEGRO SUPREME/CT
BILL/RIGHT BLACK/HL. PAGE 32 E0628
CONSTN
JURID
JUDGE
ORD/FREE
B63

FALK R.A.,LAW, MORALITY, AND WAR IN THE
CONTEMPORARY WORLD. WOR+45 LAW INT/ORG EX/STRUC
FORCES EDU/PROP LEGIT DETER NUC/PWR MORAL ORD/FREE
...JURID TOT/POP 20. PAGE 36 E0715
ADJUD
ARMS/CONT
PEACE
INT/LAW
B63

LANOUE G.R.,A BIBLIOGRAPHY OF DOCTORAL
DISSERTATIONS ON POLITICS AND RELIGION. USA+45
USA-45 CONSTN PROVS DIPLOM CT/SYS MORAL...POLICY
JURID CONCPT 20. PAGE 63 E1252
BIBLIOG
NAT/G
LOC/G
SECT
B63

MURPHY T.J.,CENSORSHIP: GOVERNMENT AND OBSCENITY.
USA+45 CULTURE LEGIS JUDGE EDU/PROP CONTROL
INGP/REL RATIONAL POPULISM...CATH JURID 20. PAGE 75
E1507
ORD/FREE
MORAL
LAW
CONSEN
B63

SARTORI G.,IL PARLAMENTO ITALIANO: 1946-1963. LAW
CONSTN ELITES POL/PAR LOBBY PRIVIL ATTIT PERSON
MORAL PWR SOC. PAGE 87 E1746
LEGIS
PARL/PROC
REPRESENT
B63

SMITH E.A.,CHURCH AND STATE IN YOUR COMMUNITY.
USA+45 PROVS SCHOOL ACT/RES CT/SYS PARTIC ATTIT
MORAL ORD/FREE CATHISM 20 PROTESTANT CHURCH/STA.
PAGE 92 E1842
GP/REL
SECT
NAT/G
NEIGH
B63

LISSITZYN O.J.,"INTERNATIONAL LAW IN A DIVIDED
WORLD." FUT WOR+45 CONSTN CULTURE ECO/DEV ECO/UNDEV
DIST/IND NAT/G FORCES ECO/TAC LEGIT ADJUD ADMIN
COERCE ATTIT HEALTH MORAL ORD/FREE PWR RESPECT
WEALTH VAL/FREE. PAGE 65 E1306
INT/ORG
LAW
L63

HARNETTY P.,"CANADA, SOUTH AFRICA AND THE
COMMONWEALTH." CANADA SOUTH/AFR LAW INT/ORG
VOL/ASSN DELIB/GP LEGIS TOP/EX ECO/TAC LEGIT DRIVE
MORAL...CONCPT CMN/WLTH 20. PAGE 50 E1000
AFR
ATTIT
S63

FREUD A.,OF HUMAN SOVEREIGNTY. WOR+45 INDUS SECT
ECO/TAC CRIME CHOOSE ATTIT MORAL MARXISM...POLICY
BIBLIOG 20. PAGE 40 E0794
NAT/LISM
DIPLOM
WAR
PEACE
B64

NICE R.W.,TREASURY OF LAW. WOR+45 WOR-45 SECT ADJUD
MORAL ORD/FREE...INT/LAW JURID PHIL/SCI ANTHOL.
PAGE 77 E1545
LAW
WRITING
PERS/REL
DIPLOM
B64

SHKLAR J.N.,LEGALISM. CREATE PROB/SOLV CT/SYS
...POLICY CRIMLGY DECISION JURID METH/CNCPT.
PAGE 91 E1821
MORAL
LAW
NEW/IDEA
B64

US AIR FORCE ACADEMY ASSEMBLY.OUTER SPACE: FINAL
REPORT APRIL 1-4, 1964. FUT USA+45 WOR+45 LAW
DELIB/GP CONFER ARMS/CONT WAR PEACE ATTIT MORAL
...ANTHOL 20 NASA. PAGE 99 E1979
SPACE
CIVMIL/REL
NUC/PWR
DIPLOM
B64

POUNDS N.J.G.,"THE POLITICS OF PARTITION." AFR ASIA
COM EUR+WWI FUT ISLAM S/ASIA USA-45 LAW ECO/DEV
ECO/UNDEV AGRI INDUS INT/ORG POL/PAR PROVS SECT
FORCES TOP/EX EDU/PROP LEGIT ATTIT MORAL ORD/FREE
PWR RESPECT WEALTH. PAGE 82 E1640
NAT/G
NAT/LISM
L64

CARNEGIE ENDOWMENT INT. PEACE."HUMAN RIGHTS (ISSUES
BEFORE THE NINETEENTH GENERAL ASSEMBLY)." AFR
WOR+45 LAW CONSTN NAT/G EDU/PROP GP/REL DISCRIM
PEACE ATTIT MORAL ORD/FREE...INT/LAW PSY CONCPT
RECORD UN 20. PAGE 20 E0385
INT/ORG
PERSON
RACE/REL
S64

CARNEGIE ENDOWMENT INT. PEACE."LEGAL QUESTIONS
(ISSUES BEFORE THE NINETEENTH GENERAL ASSEMBLY)."
WOR+45 CONSTN NAT/G DELIB/GP ADJUD PEACE MORAL
ORD/FREE...RECORD UN 20 TREATY. PAGE 20 E0386
INT/ORG
LAW
INT/LAW
S64

COHEN M.,"BASIC PRINCIPLES OF INTERNATIONAL LAW."
UNIV WOR+45 WOR-45 BAL/PWR LEGIT ADJUD WAR ATTIT
MORAL ORD/FREE PWR...JURID CONCPT MYTH TOT/POP 20.
PAGE 23 E0463
INT/ORG
INT/LAW
S64

GINSBURGS G.,"WARS OF NATIONAL LIBERATION - THE
SOVIET THESIS." COM USSR WOR+45 WOR-45 LAW CULTURE
INT/ORG DIPLOM LEGIT COLONIAL GUERRILLA WAR
NAT/LISM ATTIT PERSON MORAL PWR...JURID OBS TREND
MARX/KARL 20. PAGE 44 E0869
COERCE
CONCPT
INT/LAW
REV
S64

KARPOV P.V.,"PEACEFUL COEXISTENCE AND INTERNATIONAL
LAW." WOR+45 LAW SOCIETY INT/ORG VOL/ASSN FORCES
CREATE CAP/ISM DIPLOM ADJUD NUC/PWR PEACE MORAL
ORD/FREE PWR MARXISM...MARXIST JURID CONCPT OBS
TREND COLD/WAR MARX/KARL 20. PAGE 59 E1186
COM
ATTIT
INT/LAW
USSR
S64

SCHWELB E.,"OPERATION OF THE EUROPEAN CONVENTION ON
HUMAN RIGHTS." EUR+WWI LAW SOCIETY CREATE EDU/PROP
ADJUD ADMIN PEACE ATTIT ORD/FREE PWR...POLICY
INT/LAW CONCPT OBS GEN/LAWS UN VAL/FREE ILO 20
ECHR. PAGE 89 E1791
INT/ORG
MORAL
S64

MISSISSIPPI BLACK PAPER: (FIFTY-SEVEN NEGRO AND
WHITE CITIZENS' TESTIMONY OF POLICE BRUTALITY...).
USA+45 LAW SOCIETY CT/SYS SANCTION CRIME MORAL
ORD/FREE RESPECT 20 NEGRO. PAGE 2 E0035
COERCE
RACE/REL
DISCRIM
FORCES
B65

ANDRUS H.L.,LIBERALISM, CONSERVATISM, MORMONISM.
USA+45 PLAN ADJUD CONTROL HAPPINESS ORD/FREE
CONSERVE NEW/LIB WORSHIP 20. PAGE 5 E0097
SECT
UTOPIA
MORAL
B65

CHARNAY J.P.,LE SUFFRAGE POLITIQUE EN FRANCE;
ELECTIONS PARLEMENTAIRES, ELECTION PRESIDENTIELLE,
REFERENDUMS. FRANCE CONSTN CHIEF DELIB/GP ECO/TAC
EDU/PROP CRIME INGP/REL MORAL ORD/FREE PWR CATHISM
20 PARLIAMENT PRESIDENT. PAGE 22 E0425
CHOOSE
SUFF
NAT/G
LEGIS
B65

GINSBERG M.,ON JUSTICE IN SOCIETY. LAW EDU/PROP
LEGIT CT/SYS INGP/REL PRIVIL RATIONAL ATTIT MORAL
ORD/FREE...JURID 20. PAGE 44 E0867
ADJUD
ROLE
CONCPT
B65

ISORNI J.,LES CAS DE CONSCIENCE DE L'AVOCAT.
FRANCE LAW ACT/RES CT/SYS PARTIC ROLE MORAL 20.
PAGE 57 E1138
SUPEGO
JURID
CRIME
B65

KAMISAR Y.,CRIMINAL JUSTICE IN OUR TIME. USA+45
FORCES JUDGE PROB/SOLV COERCE MORAL 20 CIVIL/LIB
CIV/RIGHTS. PAGE 59 E1182
ORD/FREE
CRIME
CT/SYS
LAW
B65

LASLEY J.,THE WAR SYSTEM AND YOU. LAW FORCES
ARMS/CONT NUC/PWR NAT/LISM ATTIT...MAJORIT
IDEA/COMP UN WORSHIP. PAGE 63 E1261
MORAL
PERSON
DIPLOM
WAR
B65

MURPHY W.F.,WIRETAPPING ON TRIAL: A CASE STUDY IN
JURID
B65

THE JUDICIAL PROCESS. CONSTN ELITES CT/SYS CRIME LAW
MORAL ORD/FREE...DECISION SUPREME/CT. PAGE 75 E1511 POLICY

  B65
NEGLEY G.,POLITICAL AUTHORITY AND MORAL JUDGMENT. MORAL
INTELL SOCIETY LEGIS SANCTION UTOPIA SOVEREIGN PWR
MARXISM...INT/LAW LOG 20. PAGE 76 E1530 CONTROL

  L65
SHARMA S.P.,"THE INDIA-CHINA BORDER DISPUTE: AN LAW
INDIAN PERSPECTIVE." ASIA CHINA/COM S/ASIA NAT/G ATTIT
LEGIT CT/SYS NAT/LISM DRIVE MORAL ORD/FREE PWR 20. SOVEREIGN
PAGE 91 E1815 INDIA

  B66
ARCHER P.,FREEDOM AT STAKE. UK LAW NAT/G LEGIS ORD/FREE
JUDGE CRIME MORAL...CONCPT 20 CIVIL/LIB. PAGE 5 NAT/COMP
E0103 POLICY

  B66
BEELEY A.L.,THE BAIL SYSTEM IN CHICAGO. LAW MUNIC JURID
PUB/INST EFFICIENCY MORAL...CRIMLGY METH/CNCPT STAT CT/SYS
20 CHICAGO. PAGE 9 E0176 CRIME
 ADJUD

  B66
FELSHER H.,JUSTICE USA? USA+45 COM/IND JUDGE CT/SYS ADJUD
MORAL ORD/FREE...SAMP/SIZ HYPO/EXP. PAGE 37 E0735 EDU/PROP
 LOBBY

  B66
GARCON M.,LETTRE OUVERTE A LA JUSTICE. FRANCE NAT/G ORD/FREE
PROB/SOLV PAY EFFICIENCY MORAL 20. PAGE 42 E0834 ADJUD
 CT/SYS

  B66
LOFTON J.,JUSTICE AND THE PRESS. EDU/PROP GOV/REL PRESS
MORAL 20. PAGE 66 E1320 JURID
 CT/SYS
 ORD/FREE

  B66
MACMULLEN R.,ENEMIES OF THE ROMAN EMPIRE: TREASON, CRIME
UNREST, AND ALIENATION IN THE EMPIRE. ROMAN/EMP ADJUD
MUNIC CONTROL LEAD ATTIT PERSON MYSTISM...PHIL/SCI MORAL
BIBLIOG. PAGE 67 E1345 SOCIETY

  B66
NANTWI E.K.,THE ENFORCEMENT OF INTERNATIONAL INT/LAW
JUDICIAL DECISIONS AND ARBITAL AWARDS IN PUBLIC ADJUD
INTERNATIONAL LAW. WOR+45 WOR-45 JUDGE PROB/SOLV SOVEREIGN
DIPLOM CT/SYS SUPEGO MORAL PWR RESPECT...METH/CNCPT INT/ORG
18/20 CASEBOOK. PAGE 76 E1520

  B66
STUMPF S.E.,MORALITY AND THE LAW. USA+45 LAW JURID
CULTURE PROB/SOLV DOMIN ADJUD CONTROL ADJUST MORAL
ALL/IDEOS MARXISM...INT/LAW 20 SUPREME/CT. PAGE 94 CT/SYS
E1890

  S67
KONVITZ M.R.,"CIVIL LIBERTIES." USA+45 R+D...METH LAW
20. PAGE 61 E1228 MORAL
 ORD/FREE
 NAT/G

  S67
MACLEOD R.M.,"LAW, MEDICINE AND PUBLIC OPINION: THE LAW
RESISTANCE TO COMPULSORY HEALTH LEGISLATION HEALTH
1870-1907." UK CONSTN SECT DELIB/GP DEBATE ATTIT
PARL/PROC GP/REL MORAL 19. PAGE 67 E1344

  B82
POLLOCK F.,ESSAYS IN JURISPRUDENCE AND ETHICS. UNIV JURID
LAW FINAN MARKET WORKER INGP/REL MORAL...POLICY CONCPT
GEN/LAWS. PAGE 81 E1625

  L84
ELLMAKER E.G.,"REVELATION OF RIGHTS." JUDGE DISCRIM ORD/FREE
SUPEGO...JURID PHIL/SCI CONCPT 17/18. PAGE 35 E0685 ADMIN
 MORAL
 NAT/G

  B90
GODWIN W.,POLITICAL JUSTICE. UK ELITES OWN KNOWL ORD/FREE
MORAL WEALTH...JURID 18/19. PAGE 44 E0877 SOVEREIGN
 STRUCT
 CONCPT

  B91
BENTHAM J.,A FRAGMENT ON GOVERNMENT (1776). CONSTN SOVEREIGN
MUNIC NAT/G SECT AGREE HAPPINESS UTIL MORAL LAW
ORD/FREE...JURID CONCPT. PAGE 10 E0198 DOMIN

  B91
DOLE C.F.,THE AMERICAN CITIZEN. USA-45 LAW PARTIC NAT/G

ATTIT...INT/LAW 19. PAGE 32 E0633 MORAL
 NAT/LISM
 MAJORITY

  B96
DE VATTEL E.,THE LAW OF NATIONS. AGRI FINAN CHIEF LAW
DIPLOM INT/TRADE AGREE OWN ALL/VALS MORAL ORD/FREE CONCPT
SOVEREIGN...GEN/LAWS 18 NATURL/LAW WOLFF/C. PAGE 30 NAT/G
E0597 INT/LAW

  B99
LILLY W.S.,FIRST PRINCIPLES IN POLITICS. UNIV LAW NAT/G
LEGIS DOMIN ADJUD INGP/REL ORD/FREE SOVEREIGN CONSTN
...JURID CONCPT 19 NATURL/LAW. PAGE 65 E1299 MORAL
 POLICY

MORALITY....SEE MORAL, CULTURE, ALL/VALS, LAW/ETHIC

MORE/THOM....SIR THOMAS MORE

MOREL E.D. E1490

MORELAND C.C. E1491

MORENO F.J. E1492

MORGAN G.G. E1493

MORGENTH/H.... HANS MORGENTHAU

MORGENTHAU H.J. E1495,E1494

MORL/MINTO....MORLEY-MINTO - ERA OF BRITISH RULE IN INDIA
 (1905-1910)

MORLEY F. E1496

MORLEY/J....JOHN MORLEY

MORMON....MORMON PEOPLE AND MORMON FAITH

MOROCCO....SEE ALSO ISLAM

  B57
CONOVER H.F.,NORTH AND NORTHEAST AFRICA; A SELECTED BIBLIOG/A
ANNOTATED LIST OF WRITINGS. ALGERIA MOROCCO SUDAN DIPLOM
UAR CULTURE INT/ORG PROB/SOLV ADJUD NAT/LISM PWR AFR
WEALTH...SOC 20 UN. PAGE 25 E0496 ECO/UNDEV

  B63
MOLLARD P.T.,LE REGIME JURIDIQUE DE LA PRESSE AU PRESS
MAROC. MOROCCO CONTROL CRIME GP/REL ORD/FREE 20. LAW
PAGE 74 E1482 LEAD
 LEGIT

  B63
ROBERT J.,LA MONARCHIE MAROCAINE. MOROCCO LABOR CHIEF
MUNIC POL/PAR EX/STRUC ORD/FREE PWR...JURID TREND T CONSERVE
20. PAGE 85 E1702 ADMIN
 CONSTN

  C93
PLAYFAIR R.L.,"A BIBLIOGRAPHY OF MOROCCO." MOROCCO BIBLIOG
CULTURE AGRI FORCES DIPLOM WAR HEALTH...GEOG JURID ISLAM
SOC CHARTS. PAGE 81 E1620 MEDIT-7

MORRIS C. E1468,E1497

MORRIS R.B. E1498,E1499

MORRIS/CW....C.W. MORRIS

MORRIS/G....G. MORRIS

MORROW/DW....DWIGHT W. MORROW

MOSCA/G....GAETANO MOSCA

MOSCOW....MOSCOW, U.S.S.R.

MOSER J.J. E1500

MOSKOW M.H. E1501

MOSKOWITZ M. E1502

MOSSI....MOSSI TRIBE

MOSTECKY V. E1503

MOTIVATION....SEE DRIVE

MOYNI/RPRT....MOYNIHAN REPORT

MOYNIHAN REPORT....SEE MOYNI/RPRT

MOZAMBIQUE....MOZAMBIQUE

MUCKRAKER....MUCKRAKERS

MUGWUMP....MUGWUMP

MULATTO....MULATTO

MULTIVAR....MULTIVARIATE ANALYSIS

MUNIC....CITIES, TOWNS, VILLAGES

```
                                                        B12
MEYER H.H.B.,SELECT LIST OF REFERENCES ON THE       BIBLIOG/A
INITIATIVE, REFERENDUM, AND RECALL. MOD/EUR USA-45  NAT/G
LAW LOC/G MUNIC REPRESENT POPULISM 20 CONGRESS.     LEGIS
PAGE 72 E1446                                       CHOOSE


                                                        B15
SAWYER R.A.,A LIST OF WORKS ON COUNTY GOVERNMENT.   BIBLIOG/A
LAW FINAN MUNIC TOP/EX ROUTINE CRIME...CLASSIF      LOC/G
RECORD 19/20. PAGE 87 E1748                         GOV/REL
                                                    ADMIN

                                                        B19
LONDON SCHOOL ECONOMICS-POL,ANNUAL DIGEST OF PUBLIC BIBLIOG/A
INTERNATIONAL LAW CASES. INT/ORG MUNIC NAT/G PROVS  INT/LAW
ADMIN NEUTRAL WAR GOV/REL PRIVIL 20. PAGE 66 E1323  ADJUD
                                                    DIPLOM

                                                        N19
JANOWITZ M.,SOCIAL CONTROL OF ESCALATED RIOTS       CROWD
(PAMPHLET). USA+45 USA-45 LAW SOCIETY MUNIC FORCES  ORD/FREE
PROB/SOLV EDU/PROP TV CRIME ATTIT...BIBLIOG 20      CONTROL
NEGRO CIV/RIGHTS. PAGE 58 E1148                     RACE/REL

                                                        B20
VINOGRADOFF P.,OUTLINES OF HISTORICAL JURISPRUDENCE JURID
(2 VOLS.). GREECE MEDIT-7 LAW CONSTN FACE/GP FAM    METH
KIN MUNIC CRIME OWN...INT/LAW IDEA/COMP BIBLIOG.
PAGE 104 E2080

                                                        B28
BENTHAM J.,A COMMENT OF THE COMMENTARIES (1765-69). LAW
MUNIC SECT ADJUD AGREE CT/SYS CONSEN HAPPINESS      CONCPT
ORD/FREE 18. PAGE 10 E0191                          IDEA/COMP

                                                        B30
BIRD F.L.,THE RECALL OF PUBLIC OFFICERS; A STUDY OF REPRESENT
THE OPERATION OF RECALL IN CALIFORNIA. LOC/G MUNIC  SANCTION
POL/PAR PROVS PROB/SOLV ADJUD PARTIC...CHARTS       CHOOSE
METH/COMP 20 CALIFORNIA RECALL. PAGE 12 E0230       LAW

                                                        B30
FAIRLIE J.A.,COUNTY GOVERNMENT AND ADMINISTRATION.  ADMIN
UK USA-45 NAT/G SCHOOL FORCES BUDGET TAX CT/SYS     GOV/REL
CHOOSE...JURID BIBLIOG 11/20. PAGE 36 E0713         LOC/G
                                                    MUNIC

                                                        N40
COUNTY GOVERNMENT IN THE UNITED STATES: A LIST OF   BIBLIOG/A
RECENT REFERENCES (PAMPHLET). USA-45 LAW PUB/INST   LOC/G
PLAN BUDGET CT/SYS CENTRAL 20. PAGE 52 E1027        ADMIN
                                                    MUNIC

                                                        B43
CLAGETT H.L.,A GUIDE TO THE LAW AND LEGAL           BIBLIOG
LITERATURE OF PARAGUAY. PARAGUAY CONSTN COM/IND     JURID
LABOR MUNIC JUDGE ADMIN CT/SYS...CRIMLGY INT/LAW    LAW
CON/ANAL 20. PAGE 22 E0439                          L/A+17C

                                                        B44
BEARD C.A.,AMERICAN GOVERNMENT AND POLITICS (REV.   LEAD
ED.). CONSTN MUNIC POL/PAR PROVS EX/STRUC LEGIS     USA-45
TOP/EX CT/SYS GOV/REL...BIBLIOG T 18/20. PAGE 9     NAT/G
E0165                                               LOC/G

                                                        B47
CLAGETT H.L.,A GUIDE TO THE LAW AND LEGAL           BIBLIOG
LITERATURE OF PERU. PERU CONSTN COM/IND LABOR MUNIC L/A+17C
JUDGE ADMIN CT/SYS...CRIMLGY INT/LAW JURID 20.      PHIL/SCI
PAGE 23 E0444                                       LAW

                                                        B47
CLAGETT H.L.,A GUIDE TO THE LAW AND LEGAL           BIBLIOG
```

```
LITERATURE OF URUGUAY. URUGUAY CONSTN COM/IND FINAN LAW
LABOR MUNIC JUDGE PRESS ADMIN CT/SYS...INT/LAW      JURID
PHIL/SCI 20. PAGE 23 E0445                          L/A+17C

                                                        S47
ANGELL R.C.,"THE SOCIAL INTEGRATION OF AMERICAN     MUNIC
CITIES OF MORE THAN 1000,000 POPULATION" (BMR)      CENSUS
USA+45 SOCIETY CRIME ADJUST WEALTH...GEOG SOC       GP/REL
CONCPT INDICATOR SAMP CHARTS SOC/INTEG 20. PAGE 5
E0098

                                                        B50
BROWN E.S.,MANUAL OF GOVERNMENT PUBLICATIONS.       BIBLIOG/A
WOR+45 WOR-45 CONSTN INT/ORG MUNIC PROVS DIPLOM     NAT/G
ADMIN 20. PAGE 16 E0313                             LAW

                                                        B50
JENKINS W.S.,A GUIDE TO THE MICROFILM COLLECTION OF BIBLIOG
EARLY STATE RECORDS. USA+45 CONSTN MUNIC LEGIS      PROVS
PRESS ADMIN CT/SYS 18/20. PAGE 58 E1152             AUD/VIS

                                                        B51
ANDERSON W.,STATE AND LOCAL GOVERNMENT IN THE       LOC/G
UNITED STATES. USA+45 CONSTN POL/PAR EX/STRUC LEGIS MUNIC
BUDGET TAX ADJUD CT/SYS CHOOSE...CHARTS T 20.       PROVS
PAGE 5 E0094                                        GOV/REL

                                                        B51
KEFAUVER E.,CRIME IN AMERICA. USA+45 USA-45 MUNIC   ELITES
NEIGH DELIB/GP TRIBUTE GAMBLE LOBBY SANCTION        CRIME
...AUD/VIS 20 CAPONE/AL MAFIA MIAMI CHICAGO         PWR
DETROIT. PAGE 60 E1194                              FORCES

                                                        B52
BENTHAM A.,HANDBOOK OF POLITICAL FALLACIES. FUT     POL/PAR
MOD/EUR LAW INTELL LOC/G MUNIC NAT/G DELIB/GP LEGIS
CREATE EDU/PROP CT/SYS ATTIT RIGID/FLEX KNOWL PWR
...RELATIV PSY SOC CONCPT SELF/OBS TREND STERTYP
TOT/POP. PAGE 10 E0189

                                                        B52
DE GRAZIA A.,POLITICAL ORGANIZATION. CONSTN LOC/G   FEDERAL
MUNIC NAT/G CHIEF LEGIS TOP/EX ADJUD CT/SYS         LAW
PERS/REL...INT/LAW MYTH UN. PAGE 29 E0581           ADMIN

                                                        B52
THOM J.M.,GUIDE TO RESEARCH MATERIAL IN POLITICAL   BIBLIOG/A
SCIENCE (PAMPHLET). ELITES LOC/G MUNIC NAT/G LEGIS  KNOWL
DIPLOM ADJUD CIVMIL/REL GOV/REL PWR MGT. PAGE 96
E1916

                                                        C52
LANCASTER L.W.,"GOVERNMENT IN RURAL AMERICA."       GOV/REL
USA+45 ECO/DEV AGRI SCHOOL FORCES LEGIS JUDGE       LOC/G
BUDGET TAX CT/SYS...CHARTS BIBLIOG. PAGE 62 E1248   MUNIC
                                                    ADMIN

                                                        B53
MAJUMDAR B.B.,PROBLEMS OF PUBLIC ADMINISTRATION IN  ECO/UNDEV
INDIA. INDIA INDUS PLAN BUDGET ADJUD CENTRAL DEMAND GOV/REL
WEALTH...WELF/ST ANTHOL 20 CIVIL/SERV. PAGE 68      ADMIN
E1353                                               MUNIC

                                                        C54
CALDWELL L.K.,"THE GOVERNMENT AND ADMINISTRATION OF PROVS
NEW YORK." LOC/G MUNIC POL/PAR SCHOOL CHIEF LEGIS   ADMIN
PLAN TAX CT/SYS...MGT SOC/WK BIBLIOG 20 NEWYORK/C.  CONSTN
PAGE 19 E0365                                       EX/STRUC

                                                        B55
CHARMATZ J.P.,COMPARATIVE STUDIES IN COMMUNITY      MARRIAGE
PROPERTY LAW. FRANCE USA+45...JURID GOV/COMP ANTHOL LAW
20. PAGE 22 E0424                                   OWN
                                                    MUNIC

                                                        B55
GUAITA A.,BIBLIOGRAFIA ESPANOLA DE DERECHO          BIBLIOG
ADMINISTRATIVO (PAMPHLET). SPAIN LOC/G MUNIC NAT/G  ADMIN
PROVS JUDGE BAL/PWR GOV/REL OWN...JURID 18/19.      CONSTN
PAGE 48 E0959                                       PWR

                                                        B55
SWEET AND MAXWELL,A LEGAL BIBLIOGRAPHY OF THE       BIBLIOG/A
BRITISH COMMONWEALTH OF NATIONS (2ND ED.  7 VOLS.). LAW
UK LOC/G MUNIC JUDGE ADJUD CRIME OWN...JURID 14/20  CONSTN
CMN/WLTH. PAGE 95 E1900                             CT/SYS

                                                        B56
BROWNE D.G.,THE RISE OF SCOTLAND YARD: A HISTORY OF CRIMLGY
THE METROPOLITAN POLICE. UK MUNIC CHIEF ADMIN CRIME LEGIS
GP/REL 19/20. PAGE 16 E0316                         CONTROL
                                                    FORCES

                                                        S56
ROSENBERG M.,"POWER AND DESEGREGATION." USA+45      PWR
STRATA MUNIC GP/REL. PAGE 85 E1715                  DISCRIM
```

DECISION
LAW

B57
CHICAGO U LAW SCHOOL,CONFERENCE ON JUDICIAL
ADMINISTRATION. LOC/G MUNIC NAT/G PROVS...ANTHOL
20. PAGE 22 E0429

CT/SYS
ADJUD
ADMIN
GOV/REL

S57
KNEIER C.M.,"MISLEADING THE VOTERS." CONSTN LEAD
CHOOSE PERS/REL. PAGE 61 E1224

MUNIC
REPRESENT
LAW
ATTIT

B58
HENKIN L.,ARMS CONTROL AND INSPECTION IN AMERICAN
LAW. LAW CONSTN INT/ORG LOC/G MUNIC NAT/G PROVS
EDU/PROP LEGIT EXEC NUC/PWR KNOWL ORD/FREE...OBS
TOT/POP CONGRESS 20. PAGE 52 E1032

USA+45
JURID
ARMS/CONT

N59
NATIONAL ASSN HOME BUILDERS,COMMUNITY FACILITIES: A
LIST OF SELECTED REFERENCES (PAMPHLET). USA+45
DIST/IND FINAN SERV/IND SCHOOL CREATE CONTROL
FEDERAL...JURID 20. PAGE 76 E1525

BIBLIOG/A
PLAN
LOC/G
MUNIC

B60
ADRIAN C.R.,STATE AND LOCAL GOVERNMENTS: A STUDY IN
THE POLITICAL PROCESS. USA+45 LAW FINAN MUNIC
POL/PAR LEGIS ADJUD EXEC CHOOSE REPRESENT. PAGE 3
E0051

LOC/G
PROVS
GOV/REL
ATTIT

B60
ALBI F.,TRATADO DE LOS MODOS DE GESTION DE LAS
CORPORACIONES LOCALES. SPAIN FINAN NAT/G BUDGET
CONTROL EXEC ROUTINE GOV/REL ORD/FREE SOVEREIGN
...MGT 20. PAGE 3 E0057

LOC/G
LAW
ADMIN
MUNIC

B60
AMERICAN ASSOCIATION LAW LIB,INDEX TO FOREIGN LEGAL
PERIODICALS. WOR+45 MUNIC...IDEA/COMP 20. PAGE 4
E0075

INDEX
LAW
JURID
DIPLOM

B60
HEAP D.,AN OUTLINE OF PLANNING LAW (3RD ED.). UK
LAW PROB/SOLV ADMIN CONTROL 20. PAGE 51 E1020

MUNIC
PLAN
JURID
LOC/G

B61
AVERY M.W.,GOVERNMENT OF WASHINGTON STATE. USA+45
MUNIC DELIB/GP EX/STRUC LEGIS GIVE CT/SYS PARTIC
REGION EFFICIENCY 20 WASHINGT/G GOVERNOR. PAGE 6
E0121

PROVS
LOC/G
ADMIN
GOV/REL

B61
BEASLEY K.E.,STATE SUPERVISION OF MUNICIPAL DEBT IN
KANSAS - A CASE STUDY. USA+45 USA-45 FINAN PROVS
BUDGET TAX ADJUD ADMIN CONTROL SUPEGO. PAGE 9 E0167

MUNIC
LOC/G
LEGIS
JURID

B61
MERTON R.K.,CONTEMPORARY SOCIAL PROBLEMS: AN
INTRODUCTION TO THE SOCIOLOGY OF DEVIANT BEHAVIOR
AND SOCIAL DISORGANIZATION. FAM MUNIC FORCES WORKER
PROB/SOLV INGP/REL RACE/REL ISOLAT...CRIMLGY GEOG
PSY T 20 NEGRO. PAGE 72 E1444

CRIME
ANOMIE
STRANGE
SOC

B61
NEW JERSEY LEGISLATURE-SENATE,PUBLIC HEARINGS
BEFORE COMMITTEE ON REVISION AND AMENDMENT OF LAWS
ON SENATE BILL NO. 8. USA+45 FINAN PROVS WORKER
ACT/RES PLAN BUDGET TAX CRIME...IDEA/COMP 20
NEW/JERSEY URBAN/RNWL. PAGE 77 E1537

LEGIS
MUNIC
INDUS
PROB/SOLV

B61
POOLEY B.J.,PLANNING AND ZONING IN THE UNITED
STATES. USA+45 MUNIC DELIB/GP ACT/RES PROB/SOLV
TEC/DEV ADJUD ADMIN REGION 20 ZONING. PAGE 81 E1628

PLAN
LOC/G
PROVS
LAW

B61
WINTERS J.M.,STATE CONSTITUTIONAL LIMITATIONS ON
SOLUTIONS OF METROPOLITAN AREA PROBLEMS. CONSTN
LEGIS LEAD REPRESENT DECISION. PAGE 107 E2134

MUNIC
REGION
LOC/G
LAW

L61
GERWIG R.,"PUBLIC AUTHORITIES IN THE UNITED
STATES." LAW CONSTN PROVS TAX ADMIN FEDERAL.
PAGE 43 E0852

LOC/G
MUNIC
GOV/REL
PWR

B62
BOYD W.J.,PATTERNS OF APPORTIONMENT (PAMPHLET). LAW
CONSTN CHOOSE GOV/COMP. PAGE 14 E0282

MUNIC
PROVS
REPRESENT
APPORT

B62
CURRY J.E.,RACE TENSIONS AND THE POLICE. LAW MUNIC
NEIGH TEC/DEV RUMOR CONTROL COERCE GP/REL ATTIT
...SOC 20 NEGRO. PAGE 28 E0558

FORCES
RACE/REL
CROWD
ORD/FREE

B62
NEW YORK STATE LEGISLATURE,REPORT AND DRAFT OF
PROPOSED LEGISLATION ON COURT REORGANIZATION. LAW
PROVS DELIB/GP CREATE ADJUD 20 NEW/YORK. PAGE 77
E1538

CT/SYS
JURID
MUNIC
LOC/G

B62
PRESS C.,STATE MANUALS, BLUE BOOKS AND ELECTION
RESULTS. LAW LOC/G MUNIC LEGIS WRITING FEDERAL
SOVEREIGN...DECISION STAT CHARTS 20. PAGE 82 E1648

BIBLIOG
PROVS
ADMIN
CHOOSE

B62
TAPER B.,GOMILLION VERSUS LIGHTFOOT: THE TUSKEGEE
GERRYMANDER CASE. USA+45 LAW CONSTN LOC/G MUNIC
CT/SYS 20 NEGRO CIV/RIGHTS GOMILLN/CG LIGHTFT/PM
TUSKEGEE. PAGE 95 E1908

APPORT
REPRESENT
RACE/REL
ADJUD

B62
WINTERS J.M.,INTERSTATE METROPOLITAN AREAS. CONSTN
LEAD CHOOSE PWR DECISION. PAGE 107 E2135

MUNIC
LAW
REGION
GOV/REL

S62
SILVA R.C.,"LEGISLATIVE REPESENTATION - WITH
SPECIAL REFERENCE TO NEW YORK." LAW CONSTN LOC/G
NAT/G PROVS. PAGE 91 E1826

MUNIC
LEGIS
REPRESENT
APPORT

N62
US ADVISORY COMN INTERGOV REL,APPORTIONMENT OF
STATE LEGISLATURES (PAMPHLET). LAW CONSTN EX/STRUC
LEGIS LEAD MAJORITY. PAGE 99 E1977

MUNIC
PROVS
REPRESENT
APPORT

B63
ADRIAN C.R.,GOVERNING OVER FIFTY STATES AND THEIR
COMMUNITIES. USA+45 CONSTN FINAN MUNIC NAT/G
POL/PAR EX/STRUC LEGIS ADMIN CONTROL CT/SYS
...CHARTS 20. PAGE 3 E0052

PROVS
LOC/G
GOV/REL
GOV/COMP

B63
DE GRAZIA A.,APPORTIONMENT AND REPRESENTATIVE
GOVERNMENT. CONSTN POL/PAR LEGIS PLAN ADJUD DISCRIM
RATIONAL...CONCPT STAT PREDICT TREND IDEA/COMP.
PAGE 29 E0583

REPRESENT
APPORT
NAT/G
MUNIC

B63
GRANT D.R.,STATE AND LOCAL GOVERNMENT IN AMERICA.
USA+45 FINAN LOC/G MUNIC EX/STRUC FORCES EDU/PROP
ADMIN CHOOSE FEDERAL ATTIT...JURID 20. PAGE 45
E0897

PROVS
POL/PAR
LEGIS
CONSTN

B63
REITZEL A.M.,DAS MAINZER KRONUNGSRECHT UND DIE
POLITISCHE PROBLEMATIK. GERMANY MUNIC LEGIT CATHISM
12/13. PAGE 84 E1684

CHIEF
JURID
CHOOSE
SECT

B63
ROBERT J.,LA MONARCHIE MAROCAINE. MOROCCO LABOR
MUNIC POL/PAR EX/STRUC ORD/FREE PWR...JURID TREND T
20. PAGE 85 E1702

CHIEF
CONSERVE
ADMIN
CONSTN

S63
BRAUSCH G.E.,"AFRICAN ETHNOCRACIES: SOME
SOCIOLOGICAL IMPLICATIONS OF CONSTITUTIONAL CHANGE
IN EMERGENT TERRITORIES OF AFRICA." AFR CONSTN
FACE/GP MUNIC NAT/G DOMIN ATTIT ALL/VALS
...HIST/WRIT GEN/LAWS VAL/FREE 20. PAGE 15 E0289

LAW
SOC
ELITES

B64
BOUVIER-AJAM M.,MANUEL TECHNIQUE ET PRATIQUE DU
MAIRE ET DES ELUS ET AGENTS COMMUNAUX. FRANCE LOC/G
BUDGET CHOOSE GP/REL SUPEGO...JURID BIBLIOG 20
MAYOR COMMUNES. PAGE 14 E0274

MUNIC
ADMIN
CHIEF
NEIGH

B64
HAAR C.M.,LAW AND LAND: ANGLO-AMERICAN PLANNING
PRACTICE. UK USA+45 NAT/G TEC/DEV BUDGET CT/SYS
INGP/REL EFFICIENCY OWN...JURID 20. PAGE 49 E0967

LAW
PLAN
MUNIC
NAT/COMP

B64
HANNA W.J.,POLITICS IN BLACK AFRICA: A SELECTIVE   BIBLIOG
BIBLIOGRAPHY OF RELEVANT PERIODICAL LITERATURE. AFR   NAT/LISM
LAW LOC/G MUNIC NAT/G POL/PAR LOBBY CHOOSE RACE/REL   COLONIAL
SOVEREIGN 20. PAGE 50 E0995

B64
HOLT S.,THE DICTIONARY OF AMERICAN GOVERNMENT.   DICTIONARY
USA+45 LOC/G MUNIC PROVS LEGIS ADMIN JURID. PAGE 55   INDEX
E1091   LAW
                                                       NAT/G

S64
PRITCHETT C.H.,"EQUAL PROTECTION AND THE URBAN   MUNIC
MAJORITY." POL/PAR LEAD CHOOSE GP/REL PWR...MAJORIT   LAW
DECISION. PAGE 83 E1655   REPRESENT
                                                       APPORT

B65
FRYE R.J.,HOUSING AND URBAN RENEWAL IN ALABAMA.   MUNIC
USA+45 NEIGH LEGIS BUDGET ADJUD ADMIN PARTIC...MGT   PROB/SOLV
20 ALABAMA URBAN/RNWL. PAGE 41 E0815   PLAN
                                                       GOV/REL

B65
HOWE R.,THE STORY OF SCOTLAND YARD: A HISTORY OF   CRIMLGY
THE CID FROM THE EARLIEST TIMES TO THE PRESENT DAY.   CRIME
UK MUNIC EDU/PROP 6/20 SCOT/YARD. PAGE 55 E1104   FORCES
                                                       ADMIN

B65
SCHUBERT G.,REAPPORTIONMENT. LAW MUNIC POL/PAR PWR   REPRESENT
GOV/COMP. PAGE 88 E1775   LOC/G
                                                       APPORT
                                                       LEGIS

B65
US OFFICE ECONOMIC OPPORTUNITY,CATALOG OF FEDERAL   BIBLIOG
PROGRAMS FOR INDIVIDUAL AND COMMUNITY IMPROVEMENT.   CLIENT
USA+45 GIVE RECEIVE ADMIN HEALTH KNOWL SKILL WEALTH   ECO/TAC
CHARTS. PAGE 101 E2021   MUNIC

L65
WEINSTEIN J.B.,"THE EFFECT OF THE FEDERAL   MUNIC
REAPPORTIONMENT DECISIONS ON COUNTIES AND OTHER   LOC/G
FORMS OF GOVERNMENT." LAW CONSTN LEGIS CHOOSE   APPORT
GOV/COMP. PAGE 105 E2108   REPRESENT

S65
DIXON R.G.,"NEW CONSTITUTIONAL FORMS FOR   MUNIC
METROPOLIS: REAPPORTIONED COUNTY BOARDS; LOCAL   REGION
COUNCILS OF GOVERNMENT." LAW CONSTN LEAD APPORT   GOV/COMP
REPRESENT DECISION. PAGE 32 E0631   PLAN

B66
AMERICAN JEWISH COMMITTEE,THE TYRANNY OF POVERTY   BIBLIOG/A
(PAMPHLET). USA+45 LAW ECO/DEV LOC/G MUNIC NAT/G   WEALTH
PUB/INST WORKER EDU/PROP CRIME...SOC/WK 20. PAGE 4   WELF/ST
E0080   PROB/SOLV

B66
AMERICAN JOURNAL COMP LAW,THE AMERICAN JOURNAL OF   IDEA/COMP
COMPARATIVE LAW READER. EUR+WWI USA+45 USA-45 LAW   JURID
CONSTN LOC/G MUNIC NAT/G DIPLOM...ANTHOL 20   INT/LAW
SUPREME/CT EURCT/JUST. PAGE 4 E0081   CT/SYS

B66
BAKER G.E.,THE REAPPORTIONMENT REVOLUTION;   LEGIS
REPRESENTATION, POLITICAL POWER, AND THE SUPREME   APPORT
COURT. USA+45 MUNIC NAT/G POL/PAR PROVS PROB/SOLV   REPRESENT
CHOOSE ORD/FREE POPULISM...CONCPT CHARTS 20   ADJUD
SUPREME/CT. PAGE 7 E0140

B66
BEELEY A.L.,THE BAIL SYSTEM IN CHICAGO. LAW MUNIC   JURID
PUB/INST EFFICIENCY MORAL...CRIMLGY METH/CNCPT STAT   CT/SYS
20 CHICAGO. PAGE 9 E0176   CRIME
                                                       ADJUD

B66
GOLDWIN R.A.,APPORTIONMENT AND REPRESENTATION.   APPORT
MUNIC CT/SYS GP/REL ORD/FREE...POLICY ANTHOL 20   REPRESENT
SUPREME/CT. PAGE 44 E0880   LEGIS
                                                       CONSTN

B66
HANSON R.,THE POLITICAL THICKET. USA+45 MUNIC   APPORT
POL/PAR LEGIS EXEC LOBBY CHOOSE...MAJORIT DECISION.   LAW
PAGE 50 E0998   CONSTN
                                                       REPRESENT

B66
MACMULLEN R.,ENEMIES OF THE ROMAN EMPIRE: TREASON,   CRIME
UNREST, AND ALIENATION IN THE EMPIRE. ROMAN/EMP   ADJUD
MUNIC CONTROL LEAD ATTIT PERSON MYSTISM...PHIL/SCI   MORAL

BIBLIOG. PAGE 67 E1345   SOCIETY

B66
OSTERMANN R.,A REPORT IN DEPTH ON CRIME IN AMERICA.   CRIME
FUT USA+45 MUNIC PUB/INST TEC/DEV MURDER EFFICIENCY   FORCES
ATTIT BIO/SOC...PSY 20. PAGE 79 E1584   CONTROL
                                                       LAW

B66
SMITH E.A.,CHURCH-STATE RELATIONS IN ECUMENICAL   NAT/G
PERSPECTIVE. WOR+45 LAW MUNIC INGP/REL DISCRIM   SECT
ATTIT SUPEGO ORD/FREE CATHISM...PHIL/SCI IDEA/COMP   GP/REL
20 PROTESTANT ECUMENIC CHURCH/STA CHRISTIAN.   ADJUD
PAGE 92 E1843

S66
BURDETTE F.L.,"SELECTED ARTICLES AND DOCUMENTS ON   BIBLIOG
AMERICAN GOVERNMENT AND POLITICS." LAW LOC/G MUNIC   USA+45
NAT/G POL/PAR PROVS LEGIS BAL/PWR ADMIN EXEC   JURID
REPRESENT MGT. PAGE 17 E0331   CONSTN

N66
CONGRESSIONAL QUARTERLY SERV,HOUSING A NATION   HABITAT
(PAMPHLET). USA+45 LAW STRUCT DIST/IND DELIB/GP   NAT/G
...GEOG CHARTS 20 DEPT/HUD. PAGE 25 E0490   PLAN
                                                       MUNIC

B67
BERNSTEIN S.,ALTERNATIVES TO VIOLENCE: ALIENATED   AGE/Y
YOUTH AND RIOTS, RACE AND POVERTY. MUNIC PUB/INST   SOC/WK
SCHOOL INGP/REL RACE/REL UTOPIA DRIVE HABITAT ROLE   NEIGH
WEALTH...INT 20. PAGE 11 E0215   CRIME

B67
BUREAU GOVERNMENT RES AND SERV,COUNTY GOVERNMENT   BIBLIOG/A
REORGANIZATION - A SELECTED ANNOTATED BIBLIOGRAPHY   APPORT
(PAPER). USA+45 USA-45 LAW CONSTN MUNIC PROVS   LOC/G
EX/STRUC CREATE PLAN PROB/SOLV REPRESENT GOV/REL   ADMIN
20. PAGE 17 E0332

B67
CHAPIN F.S. JR.,SELECTED REFERENCES ON URBAN   BIBLIOG
PLANNING METHODS AND TECHNIQUES. USA+45 LAW ECO/DEV   NEIGH
LOC/G NAT/G SCHOOL CONSULT CREATE PROB/SOLV TEC/DEV   MUNIC
SOC/WK. PAGE 21 E0420   PLAN

B67
GRAHAM H.D.,CRISIS IN PRINT: DESEGREGATION AND THE   PRESS
PRESS IN TENNESSEE. LAW SOCIETY MUNIC POL/PAR   PROVS
EDU/PROP LEAD REPRESENT DISCRIM ATTIT...IDEA/COMP   POLICY
BIBLIOG/A SOC/INTEG 20 TENNESSEE SUPREME/CT   RACE/REL
SOUTH/US. PAGE 45 E0896

B67
GREENE L.S.,AMERICAN GOVERNMENT POLICIES AND   POLICY
FUNCTIONS. USA+45 LAW AGRI DIST/IND LABOR MUNIC   NAT/G
BUDGET DIPLOM EDU/PROP ORD/FREE...BIBLIOG T 20.   ADMIN
PAGE 46 E0910   DECISION

B67
HODGKINSON R.G.,THE ORIGINS OF THE NATIONAL HEALTH   HEAL
SERVICE: THE MEDICAL SERVICES OF THE NEW POOR LAW,   NAT/G
1834-1871. UK INDUS MUNIC WORKER PROB/SOLV   POLICY
EFFICIENCY ATTIT HEALTH WEALTH SOCISM...JURID   LAW
SOC/WK 19/20. PAGE 53 E1062

B67
UNIVERSAL REFERENCE SYSTEM,CURRENT EVENTS AND   BIBLIOG/A
PROBLEMS OF MODERN SOCIETY (VOLUME V). WOR+45 LOC/G   SOCIETY
MUNIC NAT/G PLAN EDU/PROP CRIME RACE/REL WEALTH   PROB/SOLV
...COMPUT/IR GEN/METH. PAGE 98 E1974   ATTIT

L67
CARMICHAEL D.M.,"FORTY YEARS OF WATER POLLUTION   HEALTH
CONTROL IN WISCONSIN: A CASE STUDY." LAW EXTR/IND   CONTROL
INDUS MUNIC DELIB/GP PLAN PROB/SOLV SANCTION   ADMIN
...CENSUS CHARTS 20 WISCONSIN. PAGE 20 E0384   ADJUD

S67
HIRSCH W.Z.,"SOME ECONOMIC IMPLICATIONS OF CITY   ECO/TAC
PLANNING." LAW PROB/SOLV RATION EFFICIENCY...METH   JURID
20. PAGE 53 E1050   MUNIC
                                                       PLAN

S67
HUBERT C.J.,"PLANNED UNIT DEVELOPMENT" LAW VOL/ASSN   PLAN
LEGIS EDU/PROP CT/SYS GOV/REL...NEW/IDEA 20   MUNIC
PLAN/UNIT. PAGE 56 E1107   HABITAT
                                                       ADJUD

B89
FICHTE J.G.,THE SCIENCE OF RIGHTS (TRANS. BY A.E.   ORD/FREE
KROEGER). WOR-45 FAM MUNIC NAT/G PROVS ADJUD CRIME   CONSTN
CHOOSE MARRIAGE SEX POPULISM 19 FICHTE/JG   LAW
NATURL/LAW. PAGE 37 E0744   CONCPT

BENTHAM J.,A FRAGMENT ON GOVERNMENT (1776). CONSTN
MUNIC NAT/G SECT AGREE HAPPINESS UTIL MORAL
ORD/FREE...JURID CONCPT. PAGE 10 E0198
CONSTN
SOVEREIGN
LAW
DOMIN
B91

MUNICH....MUNICH, GERMANY

MUNICIPALITIES....SEE MUNIC

MURACCIOLE L. E1504,E1505

MURDER....MURDER, ASSASSINATION; SEE ALSO CRIME

FLIESS P.J.,FREEDOM OF THE PRESS IN THE GERMAN
REPUBLIC, 1918-1933. GERMANY LAW CONSTN POL/PAR
LEGIS WRITING ADMIN COERCE MURDER MARXISM...POLICY
BIBLIOG 20 WEIMAR/REP. PAGE 39 E0765
EDU/PROP
ORD/FREE
JURID
PRESS
B55

CLINARD M.B.,SOCIOLOGY OF DEVIANT BEHAVIOR. FAM
CONTROL MURDER DISCRIM PERSON...PSY SOC T SOC/INTEG
20. PAGE 23 E0455
BIO/SOC
CRIME
SEX
ANOMIE
B57

BELL D.,"THE RACKET RIDDEN LONGSHOREMEN" (BMR)"
USA+45 SEA WORKER MURDER ROLE...SOC 20 NEWYORK/C.
PAGE 9 E0182
CRIME
LABOR
DIST/IND
ELITES
S59

DORMAN M.,WE SHALL OVERCOME. USA+45 ELITES ACADEM
FORCES TOP/EX MURDER...JURID 20 CIV/RIGHTS
MISSISSIPP EVERS/MED CLEMSON. PAGE 32 E0638
RACE/REL
LAW
DISCRIM
B64

BELL J.,THE JOHNSON TREATMENT: HOW LYNDON JOHNSON
TOOK OVER THE PRESIDENCY AND MADE IT HIS OWN.
USA+45 DELIB/GP DIPLOM ADJUD MURDER CHOOSE PERSON
PWR...POLICY OBS INT TIME 20 JOHNSON/LB KENNEDY/JF
PRESIDENT CONGRESS. PAGE 10 E0183
INGP/REL
TOP/EX
CONTROL
NAT/G
B65

BROMBERG W.,CRIME AND THE MIND. LAW LEGIT ADJUD
CRIME MURDER AGE/Y ANOMIE BIO/SOC DRIVE SEX PSY.
PAGE 16 E0305
CRIMLGY
SOC
HEALTH
COERCE
B65

FEERICK J.D.,FROM FAILING HANDS: THE STUDY OF
PRESIDENTIAL SUCCESSION. CONSTN NAT/G PROB/SOLV
LEAD PARL/PROC MURDER CHOOSE...NEW/IDEA BIBLIOG 20
KENNEDY/JF JOHNSON/LB PRESIDENT PRE/US/AM
VICE/PRES. PAGE 36 E0724
EX/STRUC
CHIEF
LAW
LEGIS
B65

HAUSNER G.,JUSTICE IN JERUSALEM. GERMANY ISRAEL
SOCIETY KIN DIPLOM LEGIT CT/SYS PARTIC MURDER
MAJORITY ATTIT FASCISM...INT/LAW JURID 20 JEWS
WAR/TRIAL. PAGE 51 E1013
ADJUD
CRIME
RACE/REL
COERCE
B66

OSTERMANN R.,A REPORT IN DEPTH ON CRIME IN AMERICA.
FUT USA+45 MUNIC PUB/INST TEC/DEV MURDER EFFICIENCY
ATTIT BIO/SOC...PSY 20. PAGE 79 E1584
CRIME
FORCES
CONTROL
LAW
B66

MANVELL R.,THE INCOMPARABLE CRIME. GERMANY ACT/RES
DEATH...BIBLIOG 20 JEWS. PAGE 68 E1364
MURDER
CRIME
WAR
HIST/WRIT
B67

MURNGIN....MURNGIN, AN AUSTRALIAN TRIBE

MURPHY E.F. E1506

MURPHY T.J. E1507

MURPHY W.F. E1508,E1509,E1510,E1511

MURRAY/JC....JOHN COURTNEY MURRAY

MUSCAT....MUSCAT AND OMAN; SEE ALSO ISLAM

MUSIC....MUSIC AND SONGS

STEVENS R.E.,REFERENCE BOOKS IN THE SOCIAL SCIENCES
AND HUMANITIES. CULTURE PERF/ART SECT EDU/PROP
...JURID PSY SOC/WK STAT 20 MUSIC. PAGE 93 E1873
BIBLIOG/A
SOC
HUM
ART/METH
B66

MUSIKER R. E1512

MUSLIM....MUSLIM PEOPLE AND RELIGION

ANDERSON J.N.D.,ISLAMIC LAW IN THE MODERN WORLD.
FAM KIN SECT LEGIT ADJUD ATTIT DRIVE...TIME/SEQ
TREND GEN/LAWS 20 MUSLIM. PAGE 5 E0089
ISLAM
JURID
B59

MUSLIM/LG....MUSLIM LEAGUE

MUSSOLIN/B....BENITO MUSSOLINI

BORGESE G.A.,GOLIATH: THE MARCH OF FASCISM. GERMANY
ITALY LAW POL/PAR SECT DIPLOM SOCISM...JURID MYTH
20 DANTE MACHIAVELL MUSSOLIN/B. PAGE 14 E0270
POLICY
NAT/LISM
FASCISM
NAT/G
B37

FIELD G.L.,THE SYNDICAL AND CORPORATIVE
INSTITUTIONS OF ITALIAN FASCISM. ITALY CONSTN
STRATA LABOR EX/STRUC TOP/EX ADJUD ADMIN LEAD
TOTALISM AUTHORIT...MGT 20 MUSSOLIN/B. PAGE 38
E0746
FASCISM
INDUS
NAT/G
WORKER
B38

MUTHER J.E. E1737

MUTHESIUS V. E1513

MYERS D.P. E1514

MYRDAL/G....GUNNAR MYRDAL

MYSTIC....MYSTICAL

MYSTICISM....SEE MYSTISM

MYSTISM....MYSTICISM

MACMULLEN R.,ENEMIES OF THE ROMAN EMPIRE: TREASON,
UNREST, AND ALIENATION IN THE EMPIRE. ROMAN/EMP
MUNIC CONTROL LEAD ATTIT PERSON MYSTISM...PHIL/SCI
BIBLIOG. PAGE 67 E1345
CRIME
ADJUD
MORAL
SOCIETY
B66

POWERS E.,CRIME AND PUNISHMENT IN EARLY
MASSACHUSETTS 1620-1692: A DOCUMENTARY HISTORY.
USA-45 SECT LEGIS COLONIAL ATTIT ORD/FREE MYSTISM
17 PRE/US/AM MASSACHU. PAGE 82 E1643
CRIME
ADJUD
CT/SYS
PROVS
B66

MYTH....FICTION

GENTILI A.,DE LEGATIONIBUS. CHRIST-17C NAT/G SECT
CONSULT LEGIT...POLICY CATH JURID CONCPT MYTH.
PAGE 43 E0848
DIPLOM
INT/LAW
INT/ORG
LAW
B24

BORGESE G.A.,GOLIATH: THE MARCH OF FASCISM. GERMANY
ITALY LAW POL/PAR SECT DIPLOM SOCISM...JURID MYTH
20 DANTE MACHIAVELL MUSSOLIN/B. PAGE 14 E0270
POLICY
NAT/LISM
FASCISM
NAT/G
B37

LERNER M.,"CONSTITUTION AND COURT AS SYMBOLS"
(BMR)" USA+45 USA-45 DOMIN PWR SOVEREIGN...PSY MYTH
18/20 SUPREME/CT. PAGE 64 E1288
CONSTN
CT/SYS
ATTIT
EDU/PROP
L37

DE HUSZAR G.B.,NEW PERSPECTIVES ON PEACE. UNIV
CULTURE SOCIETY ECO/DEV ECO/UNDEV NAT/G FORCES
CREATE ECO/TAC DOMIN ADJUD COERCE DRIVE ORD/FREE
...GEOG JURID PSY SOC CONCPT TOT/POP. PAGE 29 E0584
ATTIT
MYTH
PEACE
WAR
B44

FRANK J.,LAW AND THE MODERN MIND. UNIV LAW CT/SYS
RATIONAL ATTIT...CONCPT 20 HOLMES/OW JURY. PAGE 40
E0787
JURID
ADJUD
IDEA/COMP
MYTH
B49

EMBREE J.F.,BIBLIOGRAPHY OF THE PEOPLES AND
CULTURES OF MAINLAND SOUTHEAST ASIA. CAMBODIA LAOS
THAILAND VIETNAM LAW...GEOG HUM SOC MYTH LING
CHARTS WORSHIP 20. PAGE 35 E0686
BIBLIOG/A
CULTURE
S/ASIA
B50

FRANK J.,COURTS ON TRIAL: MYTH AND REALITY IN
AMERICAN JUSTICE. LAW CONSULT PROB/SOLV EDU/PROP
ADJUD ROUTINE ORD/FREE...GEN/LAWS T 20.
PAGE 40 E0788
JURID
CT/SYS
MYTH
CONSTN
B50

DE GRAZIA A.,POLITICAL ORGANIZATION. CONSTN LOC/G
FEDERAL
B52

MUNIC NAT/G CHIEF LEGIS TOP/EX ADJUD CT/SYS
PERS/REL...INT/LAW MYTH UN. PAGE 29 E0581
LAW
ADMIN

S55
CAHN E.,"A DANGEROUS MYTH IN THE SCHOOL SEGREGATION
CASES" (BMR)" USA+45 CONSTN PROVS ADJUD DISCRIM
...POLICY MYTH SOC/INTEG 20 SUPREME/CT AMEND/XIV.
PAGE 18 E0360
JURID
SCHOOL
RACE/REL

B57
BLOOMFIELD L.M.,EGYPT, ISRAEL AND THE GULF OF
AQABA: IN INTERNATIONAL LAW. LAW NAT/G CONSULT
FORCES PLAN ECO/TAC ROUTINE COERCE ATTIT DRIVE
PERCEPT PERSON RIGID/FLEX LOVE PWR WEALTH...GEOG
CONCPT MYTH TREND. PAGE 13 E0250
ISLAM
INT/LAW
UAR

B57
LEVONTIN A.V.,THE MYTH OF INTERNATIONAL SECURITY: A
JURIDICAL AND CRITICAL ANALYSIS. FUT WOR+45 WOR-45
LAW NAT/G VOL/ASSN ACT/RES BAL/PWR ATTIT ORD/FREE
...JURID METH/CNCPT TIME/SEQ TREND STERTYP 20.
PAGE 64 E1289
INT/ORG
INT/LAW
SOVEREIGN
MYTH

L60
MILLER A.S.,"THE MYTH OF NEUTRALITY IN
CONSTITUTIONAL ADJUDICATION." LAW...DECISION JURID
LING TREND IDEA/COMP. PAGE 73 E1456
ADJUD
CONSTN
MYTH
UTIL

B61
CASSINELLI C.W.,THE POLITICS OF FREEDOM. FUT UNIV
LAW POL/PAR CHOOSE ORD/FREE...POLICY CONCPT MYTH
BIBLIOG. PAGE 21 E0404
MAJORIT
NAT/G
PARL/PROC
PARTIC

S64
COHEN M.,"BASIC PRINCIPLES OF INTERNATIONAL LAW."
UNIV WOR+45 WOR-45 LAW NAT/G ADJUD WAR ATTIT
MORAL ORD/FREE PWR...JURID CONCPT MYTH TOT/POP 20.
PAGE 23 E0463
INT/ORG
INT/LAW

S64
KHAN M.Z.,"ISLAM AND INTERNATIONAL RELATIONS." FUT
WOR+45 LAW CULTURE SOCIETY NAT/G SECT DELIB/GP
FORCES EDU/PROP ATTIT PERSON SUPEGO ALL/VALS
...POLICY PSY CONCPT MYTH HIST/WRIT GEN/LAWS.
PAGE 61 E1211
ISLAM
INT/ORG
DIPLOM

B65
STONE J.,HUMAN LAW AND HUMAN JUSTICE. JUDGE...SOC
MYTH IDEA/COMP. PAGE 94 E1881
CONCPT
SANCTION
JURID

S65
KHOURI F.J.,"THE JORDON RIVER CONTROVERSY." LAW
SOCIETY ECO/UNDEV AGRI FINAN INDUS SECT FORCES
ACT/RES PLAN TEC/DEV ECO/TAC EDU/PROP COERCE ATTIT
DRIVE PERCEPT RIGID/FLEX ALL/VALS...GEOG SOC MYTH
WORK. PAGE 61 E1212
ISLAM
INT/ORG
ISRAEL
JORDAN

————————— N —————————

NAACP....NATIONAL ASSOCIATION FOR THE ADVANCEMENT OF
COLORED PEOPLE

S58
VOSE C.E.,"LITIGATION AS A FORM OF PRESSURE GROUP
ACTIVITY" (BMR)" USA+45 ADJUD ORD/FREE NAACP.
PAGE 104 E2085
CONTROL
CT/SYS
VOL/ASSN
LOBBY

B59
VOSE C.E.,CAUCASIANS ONLY: THE SUPREME COURT, THE
NAACP, AND THE RESTRICTIVE COVENANT CASES. USA+45
LAW CONSTN LOBBY...SOC 20 NAACP SUPREME/CT NEGRO.
PAGE 104 E2086
CT/SYS
RACE/REL
DISCRIM

B63
LIVELY E.,THE INVASION OF MISSISSIPPI. USA+45 LAW
CONSTN NAT/G PROVS CT/SYS GOV/REL FEDERAL CONSERVE
...TRADIT 20 MISSISSIPP NEGRO NAACP WARRN/EARL
KENNEDY/JF. PAGE 66 E1309
RACE/REL
CROWD
COERCE
MARXISM

NABALOI....NABALOI TRIBE, PHILIPPINES

NAFTA....NORTH ATLANTIC FREE TRADE AREA

NAGEL S.S. E1517,E1518,E1519

NAM....NATIONAL ASSOCIATION OF MANUFACTURERS

NAM/TIEN....NAM TIEN

NANTWI E.K. E1520

NAPOLEON/B....NAPOLEON BONAPARTE

NARAIN I. E1521

NARAYAN/J....JAYPRAKASH NARAYAN

NARCO/ACT....UNIFORM NARCOTIC DRUG ACT

B67
ELDRIDGE W.B.,NARCOTICS AND THE LAW: A CRITIQUE OF
THE AMERICAN EXPERIMENT IN NARCOTIC DRUG CONTROL.
PUB/INST ACT/RES PLAN LICENSE GP/REL EFFICIENCY
ATTIT HEALTH...CRIMLGY HEAL STAT 20 ABA DEPT/HEW
NARCO/ACT. PAGE 34 E0679
LAW
INSPECT
BIO/SOC
JURID

NASA E1522

NASA....NATIONAL AERONAUTIC AND SPACE ADMINISTRATION

B62
US CONGRESS,COMMUNICATIONS SATELLITE LEGISLATION:
HEARINGS BEFORE COMM ON AERON AND SPACE SCIENCES ON
BILLS S2550 AND 2814. WOR+45 LAW VOL/ASSN PLAN
DIPLOM CONTROL OWN PEACE...NEW/IDEA CONGRESS NASA.
PAGE 99 E1990
SPACE
COM/IND
ADJUD
GOV/REL

B63
US SENATE,DOCUMENTS ON INTERNATIONAL AS"ECTS OF
EXPLORATION AND USE OF OUTER SPACE, 1954-62: STAFF
REPORT FOR COMM AERON SPACE SCI. USA+45 USSR LEGIS
LEAD CIVMIL/REL PEACE...POLICY INT/LAW ANTHOL 20
CONGRESS NASA KHRUSH/N. PAGE 101 E2026
SPACE
UTIL
GOV/REL
DIPLOM

B64
NASA,PROCEEDINGS OF CONFERENCE ON THE LAW OF SPACE
AND OF SATELLITE COMMUNICATIONS: CHICAGO 1963. FUT
WOR+45 DELIB/GP PROB/SOLV TEC/DEV CONFER ADJUD
NUC/PWR...POLICY IDEA/COMP 20 NASA. PAGE 76 E1522
SPACE
COM/IND
LAW
DIPLOM

B64
US AIR FORCE ACADEMY ASSEMBLY,OUTER SPACE: FINAL
REPORT APRIL 1-4, 1964. FUT USA+45 WOR+45 LAW
DELIB/GP CONFER ARMS/CONT WAR PEACE ATTIT MORAL
...ANTHOL 20 NASA. PAGE 99 E1979
SPACE
CIVMIL/REL
NUC/PWR
DIPLOM

B65
US SENATE,US INTERNATIONAL SPACE PROGRAMS, 1959-65:
STAFF REPORT FOR COMM ON AERONAUTICAL AND SPACE
SCIENCES. WOR+45 VOL/ASSN CIVMIL/REL 20 CONGRESS
NASA TREATY. PAGE 101 E2027
SPACE
DIPLOM
PLAN
GOV/REL

NASHVILLE....NASHVILLE, TENNESSEE

NASSER/G....GAMAL ABDUL NASSER

NAT/COMP....COMPARISON OF NATIONS

N
AMERICAN JOURNAL OF INTERNATIONAL LAW. WOR+45
WOR-45 CONSTN INT/ORG NAT/G CT/SYS ARMS/CONT WAR
...DECISION JURID NAT/COMP 20. PAGE 1 E0001
BIBLIOG/A
INT/LAW
DIPLOM
ADJUD

N
NEUE POLITISCHE LITERATUR; BERICHTE UBER DAS
INTERNATIONALE SCHRIFTTUM ZUR POLITIK. WOR+45 LAW
CONSTN POL/PAR ADMIN LEAD GOV/REL...POLICY
IDEA/COMP. PAGE 2 E0028
BIBLIOG/A
DIPLOM
NAT/G
NAT/COMP

B01
BRYCE J.,STUDIES IN HISTORY AND JURISPRUDENCE (2
VOLS.). ICELAND SOUTH/AFR UK LAW PROB/SOLV
SOVEREIGN...PHIL/SCI NAT/COMP ROME/ANC ROMAN/LAW.
PAGE 16 E0321
IDEA/COMP
CONSTN
JURID

B13
BORCHARD E.M.,BIBLIOGRAPHY OF INTERNATIONAL LAW AND
CONTINENTAL LAW. EUR+WWI MOD/EUR UK LAW INT/TRADE
WAR PEACE...GOV/COMP NAT/COMP 19/20. PAGE 14 E0267
BIBLIOG
INT/LAW
JURID
DIPLOM

B18
WILSON W.,THE STATE: ELEMENTS OF HISTORICAL AND
PRACTICAL POLITICS. FRANCE GERMANY ITALY UK USSR
CONSTN EX/STRUC LEGIS CT/SYS WAR PWR...POLICY
GOV/COMP 20. PAGE 106 E2131
NAT/G
JURID
CONCPT
NAT/COMP

B24
HOLDSWORTH W.S.,A HISTORY OF ENGLISH LAW: THE
COMMON LAW AND ITS RIVALS (VOL. IV). UK SEA AGRI
CHIEF ADJUD CONTROL CRIME GOV/REL...INT/LAW JURID
NAT/COMP 16/17 PARLIAMENT COMMON/LAW CANON/LAW
ENGLSH/LAW. PAGE 54 E1075
LAW
LEGIS
CT/SYS
CONSTN

B28
HOLDSWORTH W.S.,THE HISTORIANS OF ANGLO-AMERICAN
LAW. UK USA-45 INTELL LEGIS RESPECT...BIOG NAT/COMP
17/20 COMMON/LAW. PAGE 54 E1076
HIST/WRIT
LAW
JURID

LEITZ F.,DIE PUBLIZITAT DER AKTIENGESELLSCHAFT. LG/CO
BELGIUM FRANCE GERMANY UK FINAN PRESS GP/REL PROFIT JURID
KNOWL 20. PAGE 64 E1282 ECO/TAC
NAT/COMP
B29

LUNT D.C.,THE ROAD TO THE LAW. UK USA+45 LEGIS ADJUD
EDU/PROP OWN ORD/FREE...DECISION TIME/SEQ NAT/COMP LAW
16/20 AUSTRAL ENGLSH/LAW COMMON/LAW. PAGE 67 E1333 JURID
CT/SYS
B32

ENSOR R.C.K.,COURTS AND JUDGES IN FRANCE, GERMANY, CT/SYS
AND ENGLAND. FRANCE GERMANY UK LAW PROB/SOLV ADMIN EX/STRUC
ROUTINE CRIME ROLE...METH/COMP 20 CIVIL/LAW. ADJUD
PAGE 35 E0692 NAT/COMP
B33

CORRY J.A.,DEMOCRATIC GOVERNMENT AND POLITICS. NAT/G
WOR-45 EX/STRUC LOBBY TOTALISM...MAJORIT CONCPT CONSTN
METH/COMP NAT/COMP 20. PAGE 26 E0511 POL/PAR
JURID
B46

ENKE S.,INTERNATIONAL ECONOMICS. UK USA+45 USSR INT/TRADE
INT/ORG BAL/PWR BARGAIN CAP/ISM BAL/PAY...NAT/COMP FINAN
20 TREATY. PAGE 35 E0691 TARIFFS
ECO/TAC
B47

FRIEDMAN W.,THE PUBLIC CORPORATION: A COMPARATIVE LAW
SYMPOSIUM (UNIVERSITY OF TORONTO SCHOOL OF LAW SOCISM
COMPARATIVE LAW SERIES, VOL. I). SWEDEN USA+45 LG/CO
INDUS INT/ORG NAT/G REGION CENTRAL FEDERAL...POLICY OWN
JURID IDEA/COMP NAT/COMP ANTHOL 20 COMMONWLTH
MONOPOLY EUROPE. PAGE 40 E0801
B54

HAMSON C.J.,EXECUTIVE DISCRETION AND JUDICIAL ELITES
CONTROL; AN ASPECT OF THE FRENCH CONSEIL D'ETAT. ADJUD
EUR+WWI FRANCE MOD/EUR UK NAT/G EX/STRUC PARTIC NAT/COMP
CONSERVE...JURID BIBLIOG/A 18/20 SUPREME/CT.
PAGE 50 E0992
B54

WRONG D.H.,AMERICAN AND CANADIAN VIEWPOINTS. CANADA DIPLOM
USA+45 CONSTN STRATA FAM SECT WORKER ECO/TAC ATTIT
EDU/PROP ADJUD MARRIAGE...IDEA/COMP 20. PAGE 108 NAT/COMP
E2161 CULTURE
B55

DONALDSON A.G.,SOME COMPARATIVE ASPECTS OF IRISH CONSTN
LAW. IRELAND NAT/G DIPLOM ADMIN CT/SYS LEAD ATTIT LAW
SOVEREIGN...JURID BIBLIOG/A 12/20 CMN/WLTH. PAGE 32 NAT/COMP
E0635 INT/LAW
B57

PALMER N.D.,INTERNATIONAL RELATIONS. WOR+45 INT/ORG DIPLOM
NAT/G ECO/TAC EDU/PROP COLONIAL WAR PWR SOVEREIGN BAL/PWR
...POLICY T 20 TREATY. PAGE 79 E1593 NAT/COMP
B57

UNESCO,A REGISTER OF LEGAL DOCUMENTATION IN THE BIBLIOG
WORLD (2ND ED.). CT/SYS...JURID IDEA/COMP METH/COMP LAW
NAT/COMP 20. PAGE 98 E1960 INT/LAW
CONSTN
B57

ALLEN C.K.,LAW IN THE MAKING. LEGIS ATTIT ORD/FREE LAW
SOVEREIGN POPULISM...JURID IDEA/COMP NAT/COMP CREATE
GEN/LAWS 20 ENGLSH/LAW. PAGE 4 E0069 CONSTN
SOCIETY
B58

BRIERLY J.L.,THE BASIS OF OBLIGATION IN INT/LAW
INTERNATIONAL LAW. AND OTHER PAPERS. WOR+45 WOR-45 DIPLOM
LEGIS...JURID CONCPT NAT/COMP ANTHOL 20. PAGE 15 ADJUD
E0299 SOVEREIGN
B58

SHARMA M.P.,PUBLIC ADMINISTRATION IN THEORY AND MGT
PRACTICE. INDIA UK USA+45 USA-45 EX/STRUC ADJUD ADMIN
...POLICY CONCPT NAT/COMP 20. PAGE 90 E1813 DELIB/GP
JURID
B58

KIRCHHEIMER O.,GEGENWARTSPROBLEME DER DIPLOM
ASYLGEWAHRUNG. DOMIN GP/REL ATTIT...NAT/COMP 20. INT/LAW
PAGE 61 E1217 JURID
ORD/FREE
B59

PAULSEN M.G.,LEGAL INSTITUTIONS TODAY AND TOMORROW. JURID
UK USA+45 NAT/G PROF/ORG PROVS ADMIN PARL/PROC ADJUD
B59

ORD/FREE NAT/COMP. PAGE 80 E1604 JUDGE
LEGIS

WILDNER H.,DIE TECHNIK DER DIPLOMATIE. TOP/EX ROLE DIPLOM
ORD/FREE...INT/LAW JURID IDEA/COMP NAT/COMP 20. POLICY
PAGE 106 E2122 DELIB/GP
NAT/G
B59

MENDELSON W.,"JUDICIAL REVIEW AND PARTY POLITICS" CT/SYS
(BMR)" UK USA+45 USA-45 NAT/G LEGIS PROB/SOLV POL/PAR
EDU/PROP ADJUD EFFICIENCY...POLICY NAT/COMP 19/20 BAL/PWR
AUSTRAL SUPREME/CT. PAGE 72 E1436 JURID
S59

CASTBERG F.,FREEDOM OF SPEECH IN THE WEST. FRANCE ORD/FREE
GERMANY USA+45 USA-45 LAW CONSTN CHIEF PRESS SANCTION
DISCRIM...CONCPT 18/20. PAGE 21 E0406 ADJUD
NAT/COMP
B60

PINTO F.B.M.,ENRIQUECIMENTO ILICITO NO EXERCICIO DE ADMIN
CARGOS PUBLICOS. BRAZIL L/A+17C USA+45 ELITES NAT/G
TRIBUTE CONTROL INGP/REL ORD/FREE PWR...NAT/COMP CRIME
20. PAGE 81 E1617 LAW
B60

GUIZOT F.P.G.,HISTORY OF THE ORIGIN OF LEGIS
REPRESENTATIVE GOVERNMENT IN EUROPE. CHRIST-17C REPRESENT
FRANCE MOD/EUR SPAIN UK LAW CHIEF FORCES POPULISM CONSTN
...MAJORIT TIME/SEQ GOV/COMP NAT/COMP 4/19 NAT/G
PARLIAMENT. PAGE 48 E0961
B61

FATOUROS A.A.,GOVERNMENT GUARANTEES TO FOREIGN NAT/G
INVESTORS. WOR+45 ECO/UNDEV INDUS WORKER ADJUD FINAN
...NAT/COMP BIBLIOG TREATY. PAGE 36 E0722 INT/TRADE
ECO/DEV
B62

GANJI M.,INTERNATIONAL PROTECTION OF HUMAN RIGHTS. ORD/FREE
WOR+45 CONSTN INT/TRADE CT/SYS SANCTION CRIME WAR DISCRIM
RACE/REL...CHARTS IDEA/COMP NAT/COMP BIBLIOG 20 LEGIS
TREATY NEGRO LEAGUE/NAT UN CIVIL/LIB. PAGE 42 E0831 DELIB/GP
B62

GRZYBOWSKI K.,SOVIET LEGAL INSTITUTIONS. USA+45 ADJUD
USSR ECO/DEV NAT/G EDU/PROP CONTROL CT/SYS CRIME LAW
OWN ATTIT PWR SOCISM...NAT/COMP 20. PAGE 48 E0955 JURID
B62

ATTIA G.E.D.,LES FORCES ARMEES DES NATIONS UNIES EN FORCES
COREE ET AU MOYENORIENT. KOREA CONSTN NAT/G INT/LAW
DELIB/GP LEGIS PWR...IDEA/COMP NAT/COMP BIBLIOG UN
SUEZ. PAGE 6 E0114
B63

GEERTZ C.,OLD SOCIETIES AND NEW STATES: THE QUEST ECO/UNDEV
FOR MODERNITY IN ASIA AND AFRICA. AFR ASIA LAW TEC/DEV
CULTURE SECT EDU/PROP REV...GOV/COMP NAT/COMP 20. NAT/LISM
PAGE 42 E0842 SOVEREIGN
B63

LIVINGSTON W.S.,FEDERALISM IN THE COMMONWEALTH - A BIBLIOG
BIBLIOGRAPHICAL COMMENTARY. CANADA INDIA PAKISTAN JURID
UK STRUCT LOC/G NAT/G POL/PAR...NAT/COMP 20 FEDERAL
AUSTRAL. PAGE 66 E1310 CONSTN
B63

BOLGAR V.,"THE PUBLIC INTEREST: A JURISPRUDENTIAL CONCPT
AND COMPARATIVE OVERVIEW OF SYMPOSIUM ON ORD/FREE
FUNDAMENTAL CONCEPTS OF PUBLIC LAW" COM FRANCE CONTROL
GERMANY SWITZERLND LAW ADJUD ADMIN AGREE LAISSEZ NAT/COMP
...JURID GEN/LAWS 20 EUROPE/E. PAGE 14 E0264
L63

ATTIA G.E.O.,"LES FORCES ARMEES DES NATIONS UNIES FORCES
EN COREE ET AU MOYENORIENT." KOREA CONSTN DELIB/GP NAT/G
LEGIS PWR...IDEA/COMP NAT/COMP BIBLIOG UN SUEZ. INT/LAW
PAGE 6 E0115
C63

CURRIE D.P.,FEDERALISM AND THE NEW NATIONS OF FEDERAL
AFRICA. CANADA USA+45 INT/TRADE TAX GP/REL AFR
...NAT/COMP SOC/INTEG 20. PAGE 28 E0556 ECO/UNDEV
INT/LAW
B64

FRANCK T.M.,EAST AFRICAN UNITY THROUGH LAW. MALAWI AFR
TANZANIA UGANDA UK ZAMBIA CONSTN INT/ORG NAT/G FEDERAL
ADMIN ROUTINE TASK NAT/LISM ATTIT SOVEREIGN REGION
...RECORD IDEA/COMP NAT/COMP. PAGE 40 E0785 INT/LAW
B64

GESELLSCHAFT RECHTSVERGLEICH,BIBLIOGRAPHIE DES BIBLIOG/A
B64

DEUTSCHEN RECHTS (BIBLIOGRAPHY OF GERMAN LAW, TRANS. BY COURTLAND PETERSON). GERMANY FINAN INDUS LABOR SECT FORCES CT/SYS PARL/PROC CRIME...INT/LAW SOC NAT/COMP 20. PAGE 43 E0853
JURID CONSTN ADMIN

B64
HAAR C.M.,LAW AND LAND: ANGLO-AMERICAN PLANNING PRACTICE. UK USA+45 NAT/G TEC/DEV BUDGET CT/SYS INGP/REL EFFICIENCY OWN...JURID 20. PAGE 49 E0967
LAW PLAN MUNIC NAT/COMP

B64
HALLER W.,DER SCHWEDISCHE JUSTITIEOMBUDSMAN. DENMARK FINLAND NORWAY SWEDEN LEGIS ADJUD CONTROL PERSON ORD/FREE...NAT/COMP 20 OMBUDSMAN. PAGE 50 E0986
JURID PARL/PROC ADMIN CHIEF

B64
SZLADITS C.,BIBLIOGRAPHY ON FOREIGN AND COMPARATIVE LAW: BOOKS AND ARTICLES IN ENGLISH (SUPPLEMENT 1962). FINAN INDUS JUDGE LICENSE ADMIN CT/SYS PARL/PROC OWN...INT/LAW CLASSIF METH/COMP NAT/COMP 20. PAGE 95 E1904
BIBLIOG/A JURID ADJUD LAW

B65
O'CONNELL D.P.,INTERNATIONAL LAW (2 VOLS.). WOR+45 WOR-45 ECO/DEV ECO/UNDEV INT/ORG NAT/G AGREE ...POLICY JURID CONCPT NAT/COMP 20 TREATY. PAGE 78 E1566
INT/LAW DIPLOM CT/SYS

B65
VON RENESSE E.A.,UNVOLLENDETE DEMOKRATIEN. AFR ISLAM S/ASIA SOCIETY ACT/RES COLONIAL...JURID CHARTS BIBLIOG METH 13/20. PAGE 104 E2083
ECO/UNDEV NAT/COMP SOVEREIGN

B65
WHITEMAN M.M.,DIGEST OF INTERNATIONAL LAW* VOLUME 5. DEPARTMENT OF STATE PUBLICATION 7873. USA+45 WOR+45 OP/RES...CONCPT CLASSIF RECORD IDEA/COMP. PAGE 106 E2118
INT/LAW NAT/G NAT/COMP

S65
MARTIN A.,"PROLIFERATION." FUT WOR+45 PROB/SOLV REGION ADJUST...PREDICT NAT/COMP UN TREATY. PAGE 69 E1372
RECORD NUC/PWR ARMS/CONT VOL/ASSN

S65
WRIGHT Q.,"THE ESCALATION OF INTERNATIONAL CONFLICTS." WOR+45 WOR-45 FORCES DIPLOM RISK COST ATTIT ALL/VALS...INT/LAW QUANT STAT NAT/COMP. PAGE 108 E2160
WAR PERCEPT PREDICT MATH

B66
ARCHER P.,FREEDOM AT STAKE. UK LAW NAT/G LEGIS JUDGE CRIME MORAL...CONCPT 20 CIVIL/LIB. PAGE 5 E0103
ORD/FREE NAT/COMP POLICY

B66
DE TOCQUEVILLE A,DEMOCRACY IN AMERICA (1834-1840) (2 VOLS. IN I; TRANS. BY G. LAWRENCE). FRANCE CULTURE STRATA POL/PAR CT/SYS REPRESENT FEDERAL ORD/FREE SOVEREIGN...MAJORIT TREND GEN/LAWS 18/19. PAGE 30 E0596
POPULISM USA-45 CONSTN NAT/COMP

B66
DOUMA J.,BIBLIOGRAPHY ON THE INTERNATIONAL COURT INCLUDING THE PERMANENT COURT, 1918-1964. WOR+45 WOR-45 DELIB/GP WAR PRIVIL...JURID NAT/COMP 20 UN LEAGUE/NAT. PAGE 33 E0645
BIBLIOG/A INT/ORG CT/SYS DIPLOM

B66
HAY P.,FEDERALISM AND SUPRANATIONAL ORGANIZATIONS: PATTERNS FOR NEW LEGAL STRUCTURES. EUR+WWI LAW NAT/G VOL/ASSN DIPLOM PWR...NAT/COMP TREATY EEC. PAGE 51 E1014
SOVEREIGN FEDERAL INT/ORG INT/LAW

B66
HOEVELER H.J.,INTERNATIONALE BEKAMPFUNG DES VERBRECHENS. AUSTRIA SWITZERLND WOR+45 INT/ORG CONTROL BIO/SOC...METH/COMP NAT/COMP 20 MAFIA SCOT/YARD FBI. PAGE 53 E1064
CRIMLGY CRIME DIPLOM INT/LAW

B66
HOYT E.C.,NATIONAL POLICY AND INTERNATIONAL LAW* CASE STUDIES FROM AMERICAN CANAL POLICY* MONOGRAPH NO. 1 -- 1966-1967. PANAMA UK ELITES BAL/PWR EFFICIENCY...CLASSIF NAT/COMP SOC/EXP COLOMB TREATY. PAGE 55 E1105
INT/LAW USA-45 DIPLOM PWR

B67
GELLHORN W.,OMBUDSMEN AND OTHERS: CITIZENS' PROTECTORS IN NINE COUNTRIES. WOR+45 LAW CONSTN LEGIS INSPECT ADJUD ADMIN CONTROL CT/SYS CHOOSE PERS/REL...STAT CHARTS 20. PAGE 43 E0847
NAT/COMP REPRESENT INGP/REL PROB/SOLV

B67
RAE D.,THE POLITICAL CONSEQUENCES OF ELECTORAL LAWS. EUR+WWI ICELAND ISRAEL NEW/ZEALND UK USA+45 ADJUD APPORT GP/REL MAJORITY...MATH STAT CENSUS CHARTS BIBLIOG 20 AUSTRAL. PAGE 83 E1667
POL/PAR CHOOSE NAT/COMP REPRESENT

B67
RAMUNDO B.A.,PEACEFUL COEXISTENCE: INTERNATIONAL LAW IN THE BUILDING OF COMMUNISM. USSR INT/ORG DIPLOM COLONIAL ARMS/CONT ROLE SOVEREIGN...POLICY METH/COMP NAT/COMP BIBLIOG. PAGE 83 E1673
INT/LAW PEACE MARXISM METH/CNCPT

S67
SHELDON C.H.,"PUBLIC OPINION AND HIGH COURTS: COMMUNIST PARTY CASES IN FOUR CONSTITUTIONAL SYSTEMS." CANADA GERMANY/W WOR+45 POL/PAR MARXISM ...METH/COMP NAT/COMP 20 AUSTRAL. PAGE 91 E1818
ATTIT CT/SYS CONSTN DECISION

S68
DUGARD J.,"THE REVOCATION OF THE MANDATE FOR SOUTH WEST AFRICA." SOUTH/AFR WOR+45 STRATA NAT/G DELIB/GP DIPLOM ADJUD SANCTION CHOOSE RACE/REL ...POLICY NAT/COMP 20 AFRICA/SW UN TRUST/TERR LEAGUE/NAT. PAGE 33 E0654
AFR INT/ORG DISCRIM COLONIAL

NAT/FARMER....NATIONAL FARMERS' ASSOCIATION

NAT/G....NATIONAL GOVERNMENT

NAT/LISM....NATIONALISM

N
BACKGROUND; JOURNAL OF INTERNATIONAL STUDIES ASSOCIATION. INT/ORG FORCES ACT/RES EDU/PROP COERCE NAT/LISM PEACE ATTIT...INT/LAW CONCPT 20. PAGE 1 E0004
BIBLIOG DIPLOM POLICY

N
AFRICAN BIBLIOGRAPHIC CENTER.A CURRENT BIBLIOGRAPHY ON AFRICAN AFFAIRS. LAW CULTURE ECO/UNDEV LABOR SECT DIPLOM FOR/AID COLONIAL NAT/LISM...LING 20. PAGE 3 E0053
BIBLIOG/A AFR NAT/G REGION

N
ASIA FOUNDATION.LIBRARY NOTES. LAW CONSTN CULTURE SOCIETY ECO/UNDEV INT/ORG NAT/G COLONIAL LEAD REGION NAT/LISM ATTIT 20 UN. PAGE 6 E0107
BIBLIOG/A ASIA S/ASIA DIPLOM

B00
GRIFFIN A.P.C.,LIST OF BOOKS RELATING TO THE THEORY OF COLONIZATION, GOVERNMENT OF DEPENDENCIES, PROTECTORATES, AND RELATED TOPICS. FRANCE GERMANY ITALY SPAIN UK USA-45 WOR+45 ECO/TAC ADMIN CONTROL REGION NAT/LISM ALL/VALS PWR...INT/LAW SOC 16/19. PAGE 46 E0917
BIBLIOG/A COLONIAL GOV/REL DOMIN

B04
GRIFFIN A.P.C.,REFERENCES ON CHINESE IMMIGRATIONS (PAMPHLET). USA-45 KIN NAT/LISM ATTIT...SOC 19/20. PAGE 47 E0926
BIBLIOG/A STRANGE JURID RACE/REL

C20
DUNNING W.A.,"A HISTORY OF POLITICAL THINKERS FROM ROUSSEAU TO SPENCER." NAT/G REV NAT/LISM UTIL CONSERVE MARXISM POPULISM...JURID BIBLIOG 18/19. PAGE 33 E0664
IDEA/COMP PHIL/SCI CONCPT GEN/LAWS

B30
BYNKERSHOEK C.,QUAESTIONUM JURIS PUBLICI LIBRI DUO. CHRIST-17C MOD/EUR CONSTN ELITES SOCIETY NAT/G PROVS EX/STRUC FORCES TOP/EX BAL/PWR DIPLOM ATTIT MORAL...TRADIT CONCPT. PAGE 18 E0352
INT/ORG LAW NAT/LISM INT/LAW

B35
FOREIGN AFFAIRS BIBLIOGRAPHY: A SELECTED AND ANNOTATED LIST OF BOOKS ON INTERNATIONAL RELATIONS 1919-1962 (4 VOLS.). CONSTN FORCES COLONIAL ARMS/CONT WAR NAT/LISM PEACE ATTIT DRIVE...POLICY INT/LAW 20. PAGE 2 E0032
BIBLIOG/A DIPLOM INT/ORG

B36
BRIERLY J.L.,THE LAW OF NATIONS (2ND ED.). WOR+45 WOR-45 INT/ORG AGREE CONTROL COERCE WAR NAT/LISM PEACE PWR 16/20 TREATY LEAGUE/NAT. PAGE 15 E0297
DIPLOM INT/LAW NAT/G

B37
BORGESE G.A.,GOLIATH: THE MARCH OF FASCISM. GERMANY ITALY LAW POL/PAR SECT DIPLOM SOCISM...JURID MYTH 20 DANTE MACHIAVELL MUSSOLIN/B. PAGE 14 E0270
POLICY NAT/LISM FASCISM NAT/G

B38
CLARK J.P.,THE RISE OF A NEW FEDERALISM. LEGIS TARIFFS EFFICIENCY NAT/LISM UTIL...JURID SOC
FEDERAL PROVS

GEN/LAWS BIBLIOG 19/20. PAGE 23 E0451   NAT/G
GOV/REL

B38
GRISWOLD A.W.,THE FAR EASTERN POLICY OF THE UNITED DIPLOM
STATES. ASIA S/ASIA USA-45 INT/ORG INT/TRADE WAR POLICY
NAT/LISM...BIBLIOG 19/20 LEAGUE/NAT ROOSEVLT/T CHIEF
ROOSEVLT/F WILSON/W TREATY. PAGE 47 E0943

B38
HARPER S.N.,THE GOVERNMENT OF THE SOVIET UNION. COM MARXISM
USSR LAW CONSTN ECO/DEV PLAN TEC/DEV DIPLOM NAT/G
INT/TRADE ADMIN REV NAT/LISM...POLICY 20. PAGE 50 LEAD
E1001 POL/PAR

B41
BIRDSALL P.,VERSAILLES TWENTY YEARS AFTER. MOD/EUR DIPLOM
POL/PAR CHIEF CONSULT FORCES LEGIS REPAR PEACE NAT/LISM
ORD/FREE...BIBLIOG 20 PRESIDENT TREATY. PAGE 12 WAR
E0231

S41
WRIGHT Q.,"FUNDAMENTAL PROBLEMS OF INTERNATIONAL INT/ORG
ORGANIZATION." UNIV WOR-45 STRUCT FORCES ACT/RES ATTIT
CREATE DOMIN EDU/PROP LEGIT REGION NAT/LISM PEACE
ORD/FREE PWR RESPECT SOVEREIGN...JURID SOC CONCPT
METH/CNCPT TIME/SEQ 20. PAGE 107 E2152

B43
CONOVER H.F.,THE BALKANS: A SELECTED LIST OF BIBLIOG
REFERENCES. ALBANIA BULGARIA ROMANIA YUGOSLAVIA EUR+WWI
INT/ORG PROB/SOLV DIPLOM LEGIT CONFER ADJUD WAR
NAT/LISM PEACE PWR 20 LEAGUE/NAT. PAGE 25 E0493

B44
FULLER G.H.,TURKEY: A SELECTED LIST OF REFERENCES. BIBLIOG/A
ISLAM TURKEY CULTURE ECO/UNDEV AGRI DIPLOM NAT/LISM ALL/VALS
CONSERVE...GEOG HUM INT/LAW SOC 7/20 MAPS. PAGE 42
E0824

B45
REVES E.,THE ANATOMY OF PEACE. WOR-45 LAW CULTURE ACT/RES
NAT/G PLAN TEC/DEV EDU/PROP WAR NAT/LISM ATTIT CONCPT
ALL/VALS SOVEREIGN...POLICY HUM TIME/SEQ 20. NUC/PWR
PAGE 84 E1688 PEACE

B45
WOOLBERT R.G.,FOREIGN AFFAIRS BIBLIOGRAPHY, BIBLIOG/A
1932-1942. INT/ORG SECT INT/TRADE COLONIAL RACE/REL DIPLOM
NAT/LISM...GEOG INT/LAW GOV/COMP IDEA/COMP 20. WAR
PAGE 107 E2144

B46
GRIFFIN G.G.,A GUIDE TO MANUSCRIPTS RELATING TO BIBLIOG/A
AMERICAN HISTORY IN BRITISH DEPOSITORIES. CANADA ALL/VALS
IRELAND MOD/EUR UK USA-45 LAW DIPLOM ADMIN COLONIAL NAT/G
WAR NAT/LISM SOVEREIGN...GEOG INT/LAW 15/19
CMN/WLTH. PAGE 47 E0936

B47
HYDE C.C.,INTERNATIONAL LAW, CHIEFLY AS INTERPRETED INT/LAW
AND APPLIED BY THE UNITED STATES (3 VOLS., 2ND REV. DIPLOM
ED.). USA-45 WOR+45 WOR-45 INT/ORG CT/SYS WAR NAT/G
NAT/LISM PEACE ORD/FREE...JURID 19/20 TREATY. POLICY
PAGE 56 E1119

S48
MORGENTHAU H.J.,"THE TWILIGHT OF INTERNATIONAL MORAL
MORALITY" (BMR)" WOR+45 WOR-45 BAL/PWR WAR NAT/LISM DIPLOM
PEACE...POLICY INT/LAW IDEA/COMP 15/20 TREATY NAT/G
INTERVENT. PAGE 75 E1495

B51
BIDDLE F.,THE FEAR OF FREEDOM. USA+45 LAW NAT/G ANOMIE
PUB/INST PROB/SOLV DOMIN CONTROL SANCTION REV INGP/REL
NAT/LISM 20. PAGE 12 E0227 VOL/ASSN
ORD/FREE

S52
MCDOUGAL M.S.,"THE COMPARATIVE STUDY OF LAW FOR PLAN
POLICY PURPOSES." FUT NAT/G POL/PAR CONSULT ADJUD JURID
PWR SOVEREIGN...METH/CNCPT IDEA/COMP SIMUL 20. NAT/LISM
PAGE 70 E1403

B55
BURR R.N.,DOCUMENTS ON INTER-AMERICAN COOPERATION: BIBLIOG
VOL. I, 1810-1881; VOL. II, 1881-1948. DELIB/GP DIPLOM
BAL/PWR INT/TRADE REPRESENT NAT/LISM PEACE HABITAT INT/ORG
ORD/FREE PWR SOVEREIGN...INT/LAW 20 OAS. PAGE 18 L/A+17C
E0345

B55
MAZZINI J.,THE DUTIES OF MAN. MOD/EUR LAW SOCIETY SUPEGO
FAM NAT/G POL/PAR SECT VOL/ASSN EX/STRUC ACT/RES CONCPT
CREATE REV PEACE ATTIT ALL/VALS...GEN/LAWS WORK 19. NAT/LISM
PAGE 70 E1396

C56
TYLER P.,"IMMIGRATION AND THE UNITED STATES." CULTURE
USA+45 USA-45 LAW SECT INGP/REL RACE/REL NAT/LISM GP/REL
ATTIT...BIBLIOG SOC/INTEG 19/20. PAGE 97 E1949 DISCRIM

B57
CONOVER H.F.,NORTH AND NORTHEAST AFRICA: A SELECTED BIBLIOG/A
ANNOTATED LIST OF WRITINGS. ALGERIA MOROCCO SUDAN DIPLOM
UAR CULTURE INT/ORG PROB/SOLV ADJUD NAT/LISM PWR AFR
WEALTH...SOC 20 UN. PAGE 25 E0496 ECO/UNDEV

B58
DUCLOUX L.,FROM BLACKMAIL TO TREASON. FRANCE PLAN COERCE
DIPLOM EDU/PROP PRESS RUMOR NAT/LISM...CRIMLGY 20. CRIME
PAGE 33 E0653 NAT/G
PWR

B58
MASON H.L.,TOYNBEE'S APPROACH TO WORLD POLITICS. DIPLOM
AFR USA+45 USSR LAW WAR NAT/LISM ALL/IDEOS...HUM CONCPT
BIBLIOG. PAGE 69 E1380 PHIL/SCI
SECT

B58
MOSKOWITZ M.,HUMAN RIGHTS AND WORLD ORDER. INT/ORG DIPLOM
PLAN GP/REL NAT/LISM SOVEREIGN...CONCPT 20 UN INT/LAW
TREATY CIV/RIGHTS. PAGE 75 E1502 ORD/FREE

B59
BROOKES E.H.,THE COMMONWEALTH TODAY. UK ROMAN/EMP FEDERAL
INT/ORG RACE/REL NAT/LISM SOVEREIGN...TREND DIPLOM
SOC/INTEG 20. PAGE 16 E0307 JURID
IDEA/COMP

B59
PANHUYS H.F.,THE ROLE OF NATIONALITY IN INT/LAW
INTERNATIONAL LAW. ADJUD CRIME WAR STRANGE...JURID NAT/LISM
TREND. PAGE 80 E1596 INGP/REL

B59
SCOTT F.R.,CIVIL LIBERTIES AND CANADIAN FEDERALISM. ORD/FREE
CANADA LAW ADJUD CT/SYS GOV/REL 20 CIV/RIGHTS. FEDERAL
PAGE 90 E1797 NAT/LISM
CONSTN

B59
VITTACHI T.,EMERGENCY '58. CEYLON UK STRUCT NAT/G RACE/REL
FORCES ADJUD CRIME REV NAT/LISM 20. PAGE 104 E2081 DISCRIM
DIPLOM
SOVEREIGN

S59
CARLSTON K.S.,"NATIONALIZATION: AN ANALYTIC INDUS
APPROACH." WOR+45 INT/ORG ECO/TAC DOMIN LEGIT ADJUD NAT/G
COERCE ORD/FREE PWR WEALTH SOCISM...JURID CONCPT NAT/LISM
TREND STERTYP TOT/POP VAL/FREE 20. PAGE 19 E0380 SOVEREIGN

B60
BERTHOLD O.,KAISER, VOLK UND AVIGNON. GERMANY CHIEF DIPLOM
LEGIT LEAD NAT/LISM CONSERVE 14 POPE CHRUCH/STA CATHISM
LUDWIG/BAV JOHN/XXII. PAGE 11 E0217 JURID

B60
LENCZOWSKI G.,OIL AND STATE IN THE MIDDLE EAST. FUT ISLAM
IRAN LAW ECO/UNDEV EXTR/IND NAT/G TOP/EX PLAN INDUS
TEC/DEV ECO/TAC LEGIT ADMIN COERCE ATTIT ALL/VALS NAT/LISM
PWR...CHARTS 20. PAGE 64 E1283

S60
NICHOLS J.P.,"HAZARDS OF AMERICAN PRIVATE FINAN
INVESTMENT IN UNDERDEVELOPED COUNTRIES." FUT ECO/UNDEV
L/A+17C USA+45 USA-45 EXTR/IND CONSULT BAL/PWR CAP/ISM
ECO/TAC DOMIN ADJUD ATTIT SOVEREIGN WEALTH NAT/LISM
...HIST/WRIT TIME/SEQ TREND VAL/FREE 20. PAGE 77
E1546

B62
PAIKERT G.C.,THE GERMAN EXODUS. EUR+WWI GERMANY/W INGP/REL
LAW CULTURE SOCIETY STRUCT INDUS NAT/LISM RESPECT STRANGE
SOVEREIGN...CHARTS BIBLIOG SOC/INTEG 20 MIGRATION. GEOG
PAGE 79 E1591 GP/REL

B62
PERKINS D.,AMERICA'S QUEST FOR PEACE. USA+45 WOR+45 INT/LAW
DIPLOM CONFER NAT/LISM ATTIT 20 UN TREATY. PAGE 80 INT/ORG
E1610 ARMS/CONT
PEACE

B62
ROSENZWEIG F.,HEGEL UND DER STAAT. GERMANY SOCIETY JURID
FAM POL/PAR NAT/LISM...BIOG 19. PAGE 86 E1718 NAT/G
CONCPT
PHIL/SCI

B63
DECOTTIGNIES R.,LES NATIONALITES AFRICAINES. AFR NAT/LISM
NAT/G PROB/SOLV DIPLOM COLONIAL ORD/FREE...CHARTS JURID
GOV/COMP 20. PAGE 30 E0602 LEGIS
LAW

B63
ELIAS T.O.,GOVERNMENT AND POLITICS IN AFRICA. AFR
CONSTN CULTURE SOCIETY NAT/G POL/PAR DIPLOM NAT/LISM
REPRESENT PERSON...SOC TREND BIBLIOG 4/20. PAGE 34 COLONIAL
E0681 LAW

B63
ELIAS T.O.,THE NIGERIAN LEGAL SYSTEM. NIGERIA LAW CT/SYS
FAM KIN SECT ADMIN NAT/LISM...JURID 18/20 ADJUD
ENGLSH/LAW COMMON/LAW. PAGE 34 E0682 COLONIAL
PROF/ORG

B63
GEERTZ C.,OLD SOCIETIES AND NEW STATES: THE QUEST ECO/UNDEV
FOR MODERNITY IN ASIA AND AFRICA. AFR ASIA LAW TEC/DEV
CULTURE SECT EDU/PROP REV...GOV/COMP NAT/COMP 20. NAT/LISM
PAGE 42 E0842 SOVEREIGN

B63
LEWIN J.,POLITICS AND LAW IN SOUTH AFRICA. NAT/LISM
SOUTH/AFR UK POL/PAR BAL/PWR ECO/TAC COLONIAL POLICY
CONTROL GP/REL DISCRIM PWR 20 NEGRO. PAGE 65 E1293 LAW
RACE/REL

B63
RAVENS J.P.,STAAT UND KATHOLISCHE KIRCHE IN GP/REL
PREUSSENS POLNISCHEN TEILUNGSGEBIETEN. GERMANY CATHISM
POLAND PRUSSIA PROVS DIPLOM EDU/PROP DEBATE SECT
NAT/LISM...JURID 18 CHURCH/STA. PAGE 83 E1674 NAT/G

B64
FRANCK T.M.,EAST AFRICAN UNITY THROUGH LAW. MALAWI AFR
TANZANIA UGANDA UK ZAMBIA CONSTN INT/ORG NAT/G FEDERAL
ADMIN ROUTINE TASK NAT/LISM ATTIT SOVEREIGN REGION
...RECORD IDEA/COMP NAT/COMP. PAGE 40 E0785 INT/LAW

B64
FREUD A.,OF HUMAN SOVEREIGNTY. WOR+45 INDUS SECT NAT/LISM
ECO/TAC CRIME CHOOSE ATTIT MORAL MARXISM...POLICY DIPLOM
BIBLIOG 20. PAGE 40 E0794 WAR
PEACE

B64
HANNA W.J.,POLITICS IN BLACK AFRICA: A SELECTIVE BIBLIOG
BIBLIOGRAPHY OF RELEVANT PERIODICAL LITERATURE. AFR NAT/LISM
LAW LOC/G MUNIC NAT/G POL/PAR LOBBY CHOOSE RACE/REL COLONIAL
SOVEREIGN 20. PAGE 50 E0995

B64
ROBERTS HL,FOREIGN AFFAIRS BIBLIOGRAPHY, 1952-1962. BIBLIOG/A
ECO/DEV SECT PLAN FOR/AID INT/TRADE ARMS/CONT DIPLOM
NAT/LISM ATTIT...INT/LAW GOV/COMP IDEA/COMP 20. INT/ORG
PAGE 85 E1703 WAR

B64
SCHMEISER D.A.,CIVIL LIBERTIES IN CANADA. CANADA ORD/FREE
LAW SECT PRESS RACE/REL NAT/LISM PRIVIL 20 CONSTN
COMMONWLTH PARLIAMENT CIVIL/LIB CHURCH/STA. PAGE 88 ADJUD
E1758 EDU/PROP

B64
US HOUSE COMM ON JUDICIARY,IMMIGRATION HEARINGS. NAT/G
DELIB/GP STRANGE HABITAT...GEOG JURID 20 CONGRESS POLICY
MIGRATION. PAGE 100 E2006 DIPLOM
NAT/LISM

B64
WRIGHT Q.,A STUDY OF WAR. LAW NAT/G PROB/SOLV WAR
BAL/PWR NAT/LISM PEACE ATTIT SOVEREIGN...CENSUS CONCPT
SOC/INTEG. PAGE 108 E2159 DIPLOM
CONTROL

L64
POUNDS N.J.G.,"THE POLITICS OF PARTITION." AFR ASIA NAT/G
COM EUR+WWI FUT ISLAM S/ASIA USA-45 LAW ECO/DEV NAT/LISM
ECO/UNDEV AGRI INDUS INT/ORG POL/PAR PROVS SECT
FORCES TOP/EX EDU/PROP LEGIT ATTIT MORAL ORD/FREE
PWR RESPECT WEALTH. PAGE 82 E1640

S64
GINSBURGS G.,"WARS OF NATIONAL LIBERATION - THE COERCE
SOVIET THESIS." COM USSR WOR+45 WOR-45 LAW CULTURE CONCPT
INT/ORG DIPLOM LEGIT COLONIAL GUERRILLA WAR INT/LAW
NAT/LISM ATTIT PERSON MORAL PWR...JURID OBS TREND REV
MARX/KARL 20. PAGE 44 E0869

B65
COWEN Z.,THE BRITISH COMMONWEALTH OF NATIONS IN A JURID
CHANGING WORLD. UK ECO/UNDEV INT/ORG ECO/TAC DIPLOM
INT/TRADE COLONIAL WAR GP/REL RACE/REL SOVEREIGN PARL/PROC

SOC/INTEG 20 TREATY EEC COMMONWLTH. PAGE 27 E0530 NAT/LISM

B65
HOWE M.D.W.,THE GARDEN AND THE WILDERNESS. USA+45 CONSTN
LAW GIVE EDU/PROP LEGIT NAT/LISM ORD/FREE...POLICY SECT
JURID SUPREME/CT CHURCH/STA. PAGE 55 E1103 NAT/G
GP/REL

B65
INST INTL DES CIVILISATION DIF,THE CONSTITUTIONS CONSTN
AND ADMINISTRATIVE INSTITUTIONS OF THE NEW STATES. ADMIN
AFR ISLAM S/ASIA NAT/G POL/PAR DELIB/GP EX/STRUC ADJUD
CONFER EFFICIENCY NAT/LISM...JURID SOC 20. PAGE 56 ECO/UNDEV
E1123

B65
KUPER H.,AFRICAN LAW. LAW FAM KIN SECT JUDGE ADJUST AFR
NAT/LISM 17/20. PAGE 62 E1236 CT/SYS
ADJUD
COLONIAL

B65
LASLEY J.,THE WAR SYSTEM AND YOU. LAW FORCES MORAL
ARMS/CONT NUC/PWR NAT/LISM ATTIT...MAJORIT PERSON
IDEA/COMP UN WORSHIP. PAGE 63 E1261 DIPLOM
WAR

B65
MOELLER R.,LUDWIG DER BAYER UND DIE KURIE IM KAMPF JURID
UM DAS REICH. GERMANY LAW SECT LEGIT LEAD GP/REL CHIEF
CATHISM CONSERVE 14 LUDWIG/BAV POPE CHURCH/STA. CHOOSE
PAGE 74 E1478 NAT/LISM

B65
O'BRIEN W.V.,THE NEW NATIONS IN INTERNATIONAL LAW INT/LAW
AND DIPLOMACY* THE YEAR BOOK OF WORLD POLITY* CULTURE
VOLUME III. USA+45 ECO/UNDEV INT/ORG FORCES DIPLOM SOVEREIGN
COLONIAL NEUTRAL REV NAT/LISM ATTIT RESPECT. ANTHOL
PAGE 78 E1565

B65
US HOUSE COMM ON JUDICIARY,IMMIGRATION AND GP/REL
NATIONALITY. LAW...POLICY 20. PAGE 100 E2007 NAT/LISM
NAT/G
JURID

L65
SHARMA S.P.,"THE INDIA-CHINA BORDER DISPUTE: AN LAW
INDIAN PERSPECTIVE." ASIA CHINA/COM S/ASIA NAT/G ATTIT
LEGIT CT/SYS NAT/LISM DRIVE MORAL ORD/FREE PWR 20. SOVEREIGN
PAGE 91 E1815 INDIA

S65
STEIN E.,"TOWARD SUPREMACY OF TREATY-CONSTITUTION ADJUD
BY JUDICIAL FIAT: ON THE MARGIN OF THE COSTA CASE." CONSTN
EUR+WWI ITALY WOR+45 INT/ORG NAT/G LEGIT REGION SOVEREIGN
NAT/LISM PWR...JURID CONCPT TREND TOT/POP VAL/FREE INT/LAW
20. PAGE 93 E1870

B66
HOPKINS J.F.K.,ARABIC PERIODICAL LITERATURE, 1961. BIBLIOG/A
ISLAM LAW CULTURE SECT...GEOG HEAL PHIL/SCI PSY SOC NAT/LISM
20. PAGE 55 E1096 TEC/DEV
INDUS

B67
NIVEN R.,NIGERIA. NIGERIA CONSTN INDUS EX/STRUC NAT/G
COLONIAL REV NAT/LISM...CHARTS 19/20. PAGE 77 E1550 REGION
CHOOSE
GP/REL

B67
PADELFORD N.J.,THE DYNAMICS OF INTERNATIONAL DIPLOM
POLITICS (2ND ED.). WOR+45 LAW INT/ORG FORCES NAT/G
TEC/DEV REGION NAT/LISM PEACE ATTIT PWR ALL/IDEOS POLICY
UN COLD/WAR NATO TREATY. PAGE 79 E1589 DECISION

S67
ADOKO A.,"THE CONSTITUTION OF UGANDA." AFR UGANDA NAT/G
LOC/G CHIEF FORCES LEGIS ADJUD EXEC CHOOSE NAT/LISM CONSTN
...IDEA/COMP 20. PAGE 3 E0050 ORD/FREE
LAW

S67
DEUTSCH E.P.,"A JUDICIAL PATH TO WORLD PEACE." FUT INT/LAW
WOR+45 CONSTN PROB/SOLV DIPLOM LICENSE ADJUD INT/ORG
SANCTION CHOOSE REPRESENT NAT/LISM SOVEREIGN 20 JURID
ICJ. PAGE 31 E0611 PEACE

S67
DOYLE S.E.,"COMMUNICATION SATELLITES* INTERNAL TEC/DEV
ORGANIZATION FOR DEVELOPMENT AND CONTROL." USA+45 SPACE
R+D ACT/RES DIPLOM NAT/LISM...POLICY INT/LAW COM/IND
PREDICT UN. PAGE 33 E0647 INT/ORG

MATTHEWS R.O.,"THE SUEZ CANAL DISPUTE* A CASE STUDY
IN PEACEFUL SETTLEMENT." FRANCE ISRAEL UAR UK NAT/G
CONTROL LEAD COERCE WAR NAT/LISM ROLE ORD/FREE PWR
...INT/LAW UN 20. PAGE 69 E1389
      S67
PEACE
DIPLOM
ADJUD

WINES R.,"THE IMPERIAL CIRCLES, PRINCELY DIPLOMACY,
AND IMPERIAL REFORM* 1681-1714." MOD/EUR DELIB/GP
BAL/PWR CONFER ADJUD PARL/PROC PARTIC ATTIT PWR
17/18. PAGE 106 E2132
      S67
NAT/G
NAT/LISM
CENTRAL
REGION

DOLE C.F.,THE AMERICAN CITIZEN. USA-45 LAW PARTIC
ATTIT...INT/LAW 19. PAGE 32 E0633
      B91
NAT/G
MORAL
NAT/LISM
MAJORITY

NAT/SAFETY....NATIONAL SAFETY COUNCIL

NAT/SERV....COMPULSORY NATIONAL SERVICE

NAT/UNITY....NATIONAL UNITY COMMITTEE (TURKEY)

NAT'L MUNICIPAL LEAGUE E1523,E1524

NATAL....SEE ALSO SOUTH AFRICA

EYBERS G.W.,SELECT CONSTITUTIONAL DOCUMENTS
ILLUSTRATING SOUTH AFRICAN HISTORY 1795-1910.
SOUTH/AFR LOC/G LEGIS CT/SYS...JURID ANTHOL 18/20
NATAL CAPE/HOPE ORANGE/STA. PAGE 36 E0707
      B18
CONSTN
LAW
NAT/G
COLONIAL

NATIONAL AERONAUTIC AND SPACE ADMINISTRATION....SEE NASA

NATIONAL ASSOCIATION FOR THE ADVANCEMENT OF COLORED
    PEOPLE....SEE NAACP

NATIONAL ASSOCIATION OF MANUFACTURERS....SEE NAM

NATIONAL BELLAS HESS....SEE BELLAS/HES

NATIONAL COUNCIL OF CHURCHES....SEE NCC

NATIONAL DEBT....SEE DEBT

NATIONAL DIRECTORY (IRELAND)....SEE DIRECT/NAT

NATIONAL EDUCATION ASSOCIATION....SEE NEA

NATIONAL FARMERS' ASSOCIATION....SEE NAT/FARMER

NATIONAL GUARD....SEE NATL/GUARD

NATIONAL INSTITUTE OF HEALTH....SEE NIH

NATIONAL INSTITUTE OF PUBLIC ADMINISTRATION....SEE NIPA

NATIONAL LABOR RELATIONS BOARD....SEE NLRB

NATIONAL LIBERATION COUNCIL IN GHANA....SEE NLC

NATIONAL LIBERATION FRONT (OF SOUTH VIETNAM)....SEE NLF

NATIONAL RECOVERY ADMINISTRATION....SEE NRA

NATIONAL SAFETY COUNCIL....SEE NAT/SAFETY

NATIONAL SCIENCE FOUNDATION....SEE NSF

NATIONAL SECURITY COUNCIL....SEE NSC

NATIONAL SECURITY....SEE ORD/FREE

NATIONAL SOCIAL SCIENCE FOUNDATION....SEE NSSF

NATIONAL UNITY COMMITTEE....SEE NUC

NATIONAL WEALTH....SEE NAT/G+WEALTH

NATIONAL ASSN HOME BUILDERS E1525

NATIONAL BOOK LEAGUE E1526

NATIONAL CIVIC REVIEW E1527

NATIONAL MUNICIPAL LEAGUE E1528

NATIONALISM....SEE NAT/LISM

NATIONALIST CHINA....SEE TAIWAN

NATIONALIZATION....SEE SOCISM

NATL/GUARD....NATIONAL GUARD

NATO....NORTH ATLANTIC TREATY ORGANIZATION; SEE ALSO
    VOL/ASSN, INT/ORG, FORCES, DETER

KAFKA G.,FREIHEIT UND ANARCHIE. SECT COERCE DETER
WAR ATTIT...IDEA/COMP 20 NATO. PAGE 59 E1179
      B49
CONCPT
ORD/FREE
JURID
INT/ORG

KELSEN H.,"RECENT TRENDS IN THE LAW OF THE UNITED
NATIONS." KOREA WOR+45 CONSTN LEGIS DIPLOM LEGIT
DETER WAR RIGID/FLEX HEALTH ORD/FREE RESPECT
...JURID CON/ANAL UN VAL/FREE 20 NATO. PAGE 60
E1199
      L51
INT/ORG
LAW
INT/LAW

HUNT B.I.,BIPARTISANSHIP: A CASE STUDY OF THE
FOREIGN ASSISTANCE PROGRAM, 1947-56 (DOCTORAL
THESIS). USA+45 INT/ORG CONSULT LEGIS TEC/DEV
...BIBLIOG PRESIDENT TREATY NATO TRUMAN/HS
EISNHWR/DD CONGRESS. PAGE 56 E1114
      B58
FOR/AID
POL/PAR
GP/REL
DIPLOM

ENGEL J.,THE SECURITY OF THE FREE WORLD. USSR
WOR+45 STRATA STRUCT ECO/DEV ECO/UNDEV INT/ORG
DELIB/GP FORCES DOMIN LEGIT ADJUD EXEC ARMS/CONT
COERCE...POLICY CONCPT NEW/IDEA TIME/SEQ GEN/LAWS
COLD/WAR WORK UN 20 NATO. PAGE 35 E0689
      B60
COM
TREND
DIPLOM

CONFERENCE ATLANTIC COMMUNITY,AN INTRODUCTORY
BIBLIOGRAPHY. COM WOR+45 FORCES DIPLOM ECO/TAC WAR
...INT/LAW HIST/WRIT COLD/WAR NATO. PAGE 25 E0485
      B61
BIBLIOG/A
CON/ANAL
INT/ORG

DOUGLAS W.O.,DEMOCRACY'S MANIFESTO. COM USA+45
ECO/UNDEV INT/ORG FORCES PLAN NEUTRAL TASK MARXISM
...JURID 20 NATO SEATO. PAGE 32 E0642
      B62
DIPLOM
POLICY
NAT/G
ORD/FREE

JENKS C.W.,THE PROPER LAW OF INTERNATIONAL
ORGANISATIONS. DIPLOM LEGIT AGREE CT/SYS SANCTION
REPRESENT SOVEREIGN...GEN/LAWS 20 UN UNESCO ILO
NATO OAS. PAGE 58 E1158
      B62
LAW
INT/ORG
ADJUD
INT/LAW

ELLERT R.B.,NATO 'FAIR TRIAL' SAFEGUARDS: PRECURSOR
TO AN INTERNATIONAL BILL OF PROCEDURAL RIGHTS.
WOR+45 FORCES CRIME CIVMIL/REL ATTIT ORD/FREE 20
NATO. PAGE 34 E0683
      B63
JURID
INT/LAW
INT/ORG
CT/SYS

ECONOMIDES C.P.,LE POUVOIR DE DECISION DES
ORGANISATIONS INTERNATIONALES EUROPEENNES. DIPLOM
DOMIN INGP/REL EFFICIENCY...INT/LAW JURID 20 NATO
OEEC EEC COUNCL/EUR EURATOM. PAGE 34 E0673
      B64
INT/ORG
PWR
DECISION
GP/COMP

FOX A.B.,"NATO AND CONGRESS." CONSTN DELIB/GP
EX/STRUC FORCES TOP/EX BUDGET NUC/PWR GOV/REL
...GP/COMP CONGRESS NATO TREATY. PAGE 39 E0779
      S65
CONTROL
DIPLOM

OBERMANN E.,VERTEIDIGUNG PER FREIHEIT. GERMANY/W
WOR+45 INT/ORG COERCE NUC/PWR WEAPON MARXISM 20 UN
NATO WARSAW/P TREATY. PAGE 78 E1571
      B66
FORCES
ORD/FREE
WAR
PEACE

BLAISDELL D.C.,"INTERNATIONAL ORGANIZATION." FUT
WOR+45 ECO/DEV DELIB/GP FORCES EFFICIENCY PEACE
ORD/FREE...INT/LAW 20 UN LEAGUE/NAT NATO. PAGE 12
E0239
      C66
BIBLIOG
INT/ORG
DIPLOM
ARMS/CONT

PADELFORD N.J.,THE DYNAMICS OF INTERNATIONAL
POLITICS (2ND ED.). WOR+45 LAW INT/ORG FORCES
TEC/DEV REGION NAT/LISM PEACE ATTIT PWR ALL/IDEOS
UN COLD/WAR NATO TREATY. PAGE 79 E1589
      B67
DIPLOM
NAT/G
POLICY
DECISION

NATURL/LAW....NATURAL LAW

VECCHIO G.D.,THE FORMAL BASES OF LAW (TRANS. BY J.
LISLE). DOMIN LEGIT CONTROL COERCE UTIL MORAL PWR
...CONCPT TIME/SEQ 17/20 COMMON/LAW NATURL/LAW.
PAGE 103 E2074
      B14
LAW
JURID
GEN/LAWS
IDEA/COMP

PUFENDORF S.,LAW OF NATURE AND OF NATIONS
(ABRIDGED). UNIV LAW NAT/G DIPLOM AGREE WAR PERSON
ALL/VALS PWR...POLICY 18 DEITY NATURL/LAW. PAGE 83
E1659
      B16
CONCPT
INT/LAW
SECT
MORAL

B30
BURLAMAQUI J.J.,PRINCIPLES OF NATURAL AND POLITIC   LAW
LAW (2 VOLS.) (1747-51). EX/STRUC LEGIS AGREE   NAT/G
CT/SYS CHOOSE ROLE SOVEREIGN 18 NATURL/LAW. PAGE 17 ORD/FREE
E0342   CONCPT

B47
LOCKE J.,TWO TREATISES OF GOVERNMENT (1690). UK LAW CONCPT
SOCIETY LEGIS LEGIT AGREE REV OWN HEREDITY MORAL   ORD/FREE
CONSERVE...POLICY MAJORIT 17 WILLIAM/3 NATURL/LAW.   NAT/G
PAGE 66 E1316   CONSEN

B56
LASLETT P.,PHILOSOPHY, POLITICS AND SOCIETY. UNIV   CONSTN
CRIME SOVEREIGN...JURID PHIL/SCI ANTHOL PLATO   ATTIT
NATURL/LAW. PAGE 63 E1260   CONCPT
                                                     GEN/LAWS

B59
ROSS A.,ON LAW AND JUSTICE. USA+45 RATIONAL   JURID
...IDEA/COMP GEN/LAWS 20 SCANDINAV NATURL/LAW.   PHIL/SCI
PAGE 86 E1722   LAW
                                                     CONCPT

L61
SILVING H.,"IN RE EICHMANN: A DILEMMA OF LAW AND   CT/SYS
MORALITY" WOR+45 INSPECT ADJUST MORAL...JURID 20   INT/LAW
WAR/TRIAL EICHMANN/A NATURL/LAW. PAGE 91 E1828   CONCPT

B64
GIANNELLA D.A.,RELIGION AND THE PUBLIC ORDER: AN   SECT
ANNUAL REVIEW OF CHURCH AND STATE, AND OF RELIGION, NAT/G
LAW, AND SOCIETY. USA+45 LAW SOCIETY FAM POL/PAR   CONSTN
SCHOOL GIVE EDU/PROP GP/REL...JURID GEN/LAWS   ORD/FREE
BIBLIOG/A 20 CHURCH/STA BIRTH/CON CONSCN/OBJ
NATURL/LAW. PAGE 43 E0855

B89
FICHTE J.G.,THE SCIENCE OF RIGHTS (TRANS. BY A.E.   ORD/FREE
KROEGER). WOR-45 FAM MUNIC NAT/G PROVS ADJUD CRIME   CONSTN
CHOOSE MARRIAGE SEX POPULISM 19 FICHTE/JG   LAW
NATURL/LAW. PAGE 37 E0744   CONCPT

B96
DE VATTEL E.,THE LAW OF NATIONS. AGRI FINAN CHIEF   LAW
DIPLOM INT/TRADE AGREE OWN ALL/VALS MORAL ORD/FREE   CONCPT
SOVEREIGN...GEN/LAWS 18 NATURL/LAW WOLFF/C. PAGE 30 NAT/G
E0597   INT/LAW

B99
LILLY W.S.,FIRST PRINCIPLES IN POLITICS. UNIV LAW   NAT/G
LEGIS DOMIN ADJUD INGP/REL ORD/FREE SOVEREIGN   CONSTN
...JURID CONCPT 19 NATURL/LAW. PAGE 65 E1299   MORAL
                                                     POLICY

NAVAHO....NAVAHO INDIANS

NAVAL/RES....OFFICE OF NAVAL RESEARCH

NAVILLE A. E1529

NAVY....NAVY (ALL NATIONS)

NAWAS M.K. E1833

NAZI....NAZI MOVEMENT (ALL NATIONS); SEE ALSO GERMANY,
   NAT/LISM, FASCIST

B39
LAVES W.H.C.,INTERNATIONAL SECURITY. EUR+WWI   ORD/FREE
GERMANY UK USA LAW NAT/G DELIB/GP TOP/EX COERCE   LEGIT
PWR...POLICY FASCIST CONCPT HIST/WRIT GEN/LAWS   ARMS/CONT
LEAGUE/NAT NAZI 20. PAGE 63 E1267   BAL/PWR

B47
GORDON D.L.,THE HIDDEN WEAPON: THE STORY OF   INT/ORG
ECONOMIC WARFARE. EUR+WWI USA-45 LAW FINAN INDUS   ECO/TAC
NAT/G CONSULT FORCES PLAN DOMIN PWR WEALTH   INT/TRADE
...INT/LAW CONCPT OBS TOT/POP NAZI 20. PAGE 45   WAR
E0891

S48
ALEXANDER L.,"WAR CRIMES, THEIR SOCIAL-   DRIVE
PSYCHOLOGICAL ASPECTS." EUR+WWI GERMANY LAW CULTURE WAR
ELITES KIN POL/PAR PUB/INST FORCES DOMIN EDU/PROP
COERCE CRIME ATTIT SUPEGO HEALTH MORAL PWR FASCISM
...PSY OBS TREND GEN/LAWS NAZI 20. PAGE 3 E0061

B62
HEYDECKER J.J.,THE NUREMBERG TRIAL: HISTORY OF NAZI LAW
GERMANY AS REVEALED THROUGH THE TESTIMONY AT   CRIME
NUREMBERG. EUR+WWI GERMANY VOL/ASSN LEAD COERCE   PARTIC
CROWD INGP/REL RACE/REL SUPEGO ORD/FREE...CONCPT 20 TOTALISM
NAZI ANTI/SEMIT NUREMBERG JEWS. PAGE 52 E1036

B62
WOETZEL R.K.,THE NURENBERG TRIALS IN INTERNATIONAL   INT/ORG
LAW. CHRIST-17C MOD/EUR WOR+45 SOCIETY NAT/G   ADJUD
DELIB/GP DOMIN LEGIT ROUTINE ATTIT DRIVE PERSON   WAR
SUPEGO MORAL ORD/FREE...POLICY MAJORIT JURID PSY
SOC SELF/OBS RECORD NAZI TOT/POP. PAGE 107 E2138

S62
GREEN L.C.,"POLITICAL OFFENSES, WAR CRIMES AND   LAW
EXTRADITION." WOR+45 YUGOSLAVIA INT/ORG LEGIT   CONCPT
ROUTINE WAR ORD/FREE SOVEREIGN...JURID NAZI 20   INT/LAW
INTERPOL. PAGE 46 E0906

B66
FISCHER H.,EINER IM VORDERGRUND: TARAS   FASCISM
BORODAJKEWYCZ. AUSTRIA POL/PAR PROF/ORG EDU/PROP   LAW
CT/SYS ORD/FREE 20 NAZI. PAGE 38 E0754   ATTIT
                                                     PRESS

NCC....NATIONAL COUNCIL OF CHURCHES

NE/WIN....NE WIN

NEA....NATIONAL EDUCATION ASSOCIATION

NEAR EAST....SEE MEDIT-7, ISLAM

NEBRASKA....NEBRASKA

B55
ZABEL O.H.,GOD AND CAESAR IN NEBRASKA: A STUDY OF   SECT
LEGAL RELATIONSHIP OF CHURCH AND STATE, 1854-1954.   PROVS
TAX GIVE ADMIN CONTROL GP/REL ROLE...GP/COMP 19/20   LAW
NEBRASKA. PAGE 108 E2168   EDU/PROP

NEG/INCOME....NEGATIVE INCOME TAX

NEGATIVE INCOME TAX....SEE NEG/INCOME

NEGLEY G. E1530

NEGRITO....NEGRITO TRIBE, PHILIPPINES

NEGRO....NEGRO;

B06
GRIFFIN A.P.C.,SELECT LIST OF REFERENCES ON THE   BIBLIOG/A
NEGRO QUESTION (REV. ED.). USA-45 CONSTN SCHOOL   RACE/REL
SUFF ADJUST...JURID SOC/INTEG 19/20 NEGRO. PAGE 47   DISCRIM
E0930   ATTIT

B12
GRIFFIN A.P.C.,SELECT LIST OF REFERENCES ON   BIBLIOG/A
IMPEACHMENT (REV. ED.) (PAMPHLET). USA-45 LAW PROVS CONSTN
ADJUD ATTIT...JURID 19/20 NEGRO. PAGE 47 E0935   NAT/G
                                                     LEGIS

B18
PORTER K.H.,A HISTORY OF SUFFRAGE IN THE UNITED   SUFF
STATES. USA-45 LAW CONSTN LOC/G NAT/G POL/PAR WAR   REPRESENT
DISCRIM OWN ATTIT SEX 18/20 NEGRO FEMALE/SEX.   CHOOSE
PAGE 81 E1629   PARTIC

N19
BUREAU OF NAT'L AFFAIRS INC.,A CURRENT LOOK AT: DISCRIM
(1) THE NEGRO AND TITLE VII, (2) SEX AND TITLE VII   SEX
(PAMPHLET). LAW LG/CO SML/CO RACE/REL...POLICY SOC   WORKER
STAT DEEP/QU TREND CON/ANAL CHARTS 20 NEGRO   MGT
CIV/RIGHTS. PAGE 17 E0334

N19
JANOWITZ M.,SOCIAL CONTROL OF ESCALATED RIOTS   CROWD
(PAMPHLET). USA+45 USA-45 LAW SOCIETY MUNIC FORCES   ORD/FREE
PROB/SOLV EDU/PROP TV CRIME ATTIT...BIBLIOG 20   CONTROL
NEGRO CIV/RIGHTS. PAGE 58 E1148   RACE/REL

N19
MISSISSIPPI ADVISORY COMMITTEE,REPORT ON   RACE/REL
MISSISSIPPI (PAMPHLET). USA+45 LAW PROVS FORCES   DISCRIM
ADJUD PWR...SOC/WK INT 20 MISSISSIPP NEGRO   COERCE
CIV/RIGHTS. PAGE 73 E1469   ORD/FREE

S45
DAVIS A.,"CASTE, ECONOMY, AND VIOLENCE" (BMR)"   STRATA
USA-45 LAW SOCIETY SECT SANCTION COERCE   RACE/REL
MARRIAGE SEX...PSY SOC SOC/INTEG 18/20 NEGRO   DISCRIM
MISCEGEN SOUTH/US. PAGE 29 E0570

B49
DE HUSZAR G.B.,EQUALITY IN AMERICA: THE ISSUE OF   DISCRIM
MINORITY RIGHTS. USA+45 USA-45 LAW NEIGH SCHOOL   RACE/REL
LEGIS ACT/RES CHOOSE ATTIT RESPECT...ANTHOL 20   ORD/FREE
NEGRO. PAGE 29 E0585   PROB/SOLV

B50
FRAGA IRIBARNE M.,RAZAS Y RACISMO IN NORTEAMERICA.   RACE/REL

USA+45 CONSTN STRATA NAT/G PROVS ATTIT...SOC CONCPT JURID
19/20 NEGRO. PAGE 39 E0783
LAW
DISCRIM

B50
MERRIAM C.E.,THE AMERICAN PARTY SYSTEM: AN POL/PAR
INTRODUCTION TO THE STUDY OF POLITICAL PARTIES IN CHOOSE
THE UNITED STATES (4TH ED.). USA+45 USA-45 LAW SUFF
FINAN LOC/G NAT/G PROVS LEAD PARTIC CRIME ATTIT REPRESENT
18/20 NEGRO CONGRESS PRESIDENT. PAGE 72 E1442

B51
BISSAINTHE M.,DICTIONNAIRE DE BIBLIOGRAPHIE BIBLIOG
HAITIENNE. HAITI ELITES AGRI LEGIS DIPLOM INT/TRADE L/A+17C
WRITING ORD/FREE CATHISM...ART/METH GEOG 19/20 SOCIETY
NEGRO TREATY. PAGE 12 E0234 NAT/G

B52
DU BOIS W.E.B.,IN BATTLE FOR PEACE. AFR USA+45 PEACE
COLONIAL CT/SYS PERS/REL PERSON ORD/FREE...JURID 20 RACE/REL
NEGRO CIVIL/LIB. PAGE 33 E0650 DISCRIM
BIOG

B52
FORSTER A.,THE TROUBLE MAKERS. USA+45 LAW CULTURE DISCRIM
SOCIETY STRUCT VOL/ASSN CROWD GP/REL MORAL...PSY SECT
SOC CONCPT 20 NEGRO JEWS. PAGE 39 E0771 RACE/REL
ATTIT

B57
ROWAN C.T.,GO SOUTH TO SORROW. USA+45 STRUCT NAT/G RACE/REL
EDU/PROP LEAD COERCE ISOLAT DRIVE SUPEGO RESPECT DISCRIM
...PREDICT 20 NEGRO SUPREME/CT SOUTH/US CIV/RIGHTS. ANOMIE
PAGE 86 E1728 LAW

B58
CABLE G.W.,THE NEGRO QUESTION: A SELECTION OF RACE/REL
WRITINGS ON CIVIL RIGHTS IN THE SOUTH. USA+45 CULTURE
STRATA LOC/G POL/PAR GIVE EDU/PROP WRITING CT/SYS DISCRIM
SANCTION CRIME CHOOSE WORSHIP 20 NEGRO CIV/RIGHTS ORD/FREE
CONV/LEASE SOUTH/US. PAGE 18 E0355

B59
HAYS B.,A SOUTHERN MODERATE SPEAKS. LAW PROVS SECT
SCHOOL KNOWL...JURID SOC SELF/OBS BIOG 20 NEGRO DISCRIM
SUPREME/CT. PAGE 51 E1015 CT/SYS
RACE/REL

B59
TOMPKINS D.C.,SUPREME COURT OF THE UNITED STATES: A BIBLIOG/A
BIBLIOGRAPHY. LAW JUDGE ADJUD GOV/REL DISCRIM CT/SYS
...JURID 18/20 SUPREME/CT NEGRO. PAGE 96 E1931 CONSTN
NAT/G

B59
VOSE C.E.,CAUCASIANS ONLY: THE SUPREME COURT, THE CT/SYS
NAACP, AND THE RESTRICTIVE COVENANT CASES. USA+45 RACE/REL
LAW CONSTN LOBBY...SOC 20 NAACP SUPREME/CT NEGRO. DISCRIM
PAGE 104 E2086

S59
DWYER R.J.,"THE ADMINISTRATIVE ROLE IN ADMIN
DESEGREGATION." USA+45 LAW PROB/SOLV LEAD RACE/REL SCHOOL
ISOLAT STRANGE ROLE...POLICY SOC/INTEG MISSOURI DISCRIM
NEGRO CIV/RIGHTS. PAGE 34 E0668 ATTIT

S59
MURPHY W.F.,"LOWER COURT CHECKS ON SUPREME COURT CT/SYS
POWER" (BMR)" USA+45 NAT/G PROVS SCHOOL GOV/REL BAL/PWR
RACE/REL DISCRIM ATTIT...DECISION JURID 20 CONTROL
SUPREME/CT NEGRO. PAGE 75 E1508 ADJUD

B60
FELLMAN D.,THE SUPREME COURT AND EDUCATION. ACADEM CT/SYS
NAT/G PROVS DELIB/GP ADJUD ORD/FREE...POLICY JURID SECT
WORSHIP 20 SUPREME/CT NEGRO CHURCH/STA. PAGE 37 RACE/REL
E0731 SCHOOL

B61
COWEN D.V.,THE FOUNDATIONS OF FREEDOM. AFR CONSTN
SOUTH/AFR DOMIN LEGIT ADJUST DISCRIM TOTALISM ATTIT ELITES
ORD/FREE...MAJORIT JURID SOC/INTEG WORSHIP 20 RACE/REL
NEGRO. PAGE 27 E0529

B61
MERTON R.K.,CONTEMPORARY SOCIAL PROBLEMS: AN CRIME
INTRODUCTION TO THE SOCIOLOGY OF DEVIANT BEHAVIOR ANOMIE
AND SOCIAL DISORGANIZATION. FAM MUNIC FORCES WORKER STRANGE
PROB/SOLV INGP/REL RACE/REL ISOLAT...CRIMLGY GEOG SOC
PSY T 20 NEGRO. PAGE 72 E1444

B61
US COMMISSION ON CIVIL RIGHTS,JUSTICE: BOOK 5, 1961 DISCRIM
REPORT OF THE U.S. COMMISSION ON CIVIL RIGHTS. LAW
LOC/G NAT/G RACE/REL...JURID 20 NEGRO CIV/RIGHTS FORCES
INDIAN/AM JURY INDIAN/AM. PAGE 99 E1983

B62
BERMAN D.M.,A BILL BECOMES A LAW: THE CIVIL RIGHTS DISCRIM
ACT OF 1960. USA+45 LAW POL/PAR LOBBY RACE/REL PARL/PROC
KNOWL...CHARTS 20 CONGRESS NEGRO CIV/RIGHTS. JURID
PAGE 11 E0206 GOV/REL

B62
CURRY J.E.,RACE TENSIONS AND THE POLICE. LAW MUNIC FORCES
NEIGH TEC/DEV RUMOR CONTROL COERCE GP/REL ATTIT RACE/REL
...SOC 20 NEGRO. PAGE 28 E0558 CROWD
ORD/FREE

B62
GANJI M.,INTERNATIONAL PROTECTION OF HUMAN RIGHTS. ORD/FREE
WOR+45 CONSTN INT/TRADE CT/SYS SANCTION CRIME WAR DISCRIM
RACE/REL...CHARTS IDEA/COMP NAT/COMP BIBLIOG 20 LEGIS
TREATY NEGRO LEAGUE/NAT UN CIVIL/LIB. PAGE 42 E0831 DELIB/GP

B62
MITCHELL G.E.,THE ANGRY BLACK SOUTH. USA+45 LAW RACE/REL
CONSTN SCHOOL DELIB/GP EDU/PROP CONTROL SUFF ANOMIE DISCRIM
DRIVE...ANTHOL 20 NEGRO CIV/RIGHTS SOUTH/US. ADJUST
PAGE 74 E1473 ORD/FREE

B62
TAPER B.,GOMILLION VERSUS LIGHTFOOT: THE TUSKEGEE APPORT
GERRYMANDER CASE. USA+45 LAW CONSTN LOC/G MUNIC REPRESENT
CT/SYS 20 NEGRO CIV/RIGHTS GOMILLN/CG LIGHTFT/PM RACE/REL
TUSKEGEE. PAGE 95 E1908 ADJUD

B62
US COMMISSION ON CIVIL RIGHTS,EQUAL PROTECTION OF ORD/FREE
THE LAWS IN NORTH CAROLINA. USA+45 LOC/G NAT/G RESPECT
CONSULT LEGIS WORKER PROB/SOLV EDU/PROP ADJUD LAW
CHOOSE DISCRIM HEALTH 20 NEGRO NORTH/CAR PROVS
CIV/RIGHTS. PAGE 99 E1984

B62
US COMMISSION ON CIVIL RIGHTS,HEARINGS BEFORE ORD/FREE
UNITED STATES COMMISSION ON CIVIL RIGHTS. USA+45 LAW
ECO/DEV NAT/G CONSULT WORKER EDU/PROP ADJUD DISCRIM ADMIN
ISOLAT HABITAT HEALTH RESPECT 20 NEGRO CIV/RIGHTS. LEGIS
PAGE 99 E1985

B63
DAY R.E.,CIVIL RIGHTS USA: PUBLIC SCHOOLS, SOUTHERN EDU/PROP
STATES - NORTH CAROLINA, 1963. USA+45 LOC/G NEIGH ORD/FREE
LEGIS CREATE CT/SYS COERCE DISCRIM ATTIT...QU RACE/REL
CHARTS 20 NORTH/CAR NEGRO KKK CIV/RIGHTS. PAGE 29 SANCTION
E0579

B63
DILLIARD I.,ONE MAN'S STAND FOR FREEDOM: MR. CONSTN
JUSTICE BLACK AND THE BILL OF RIGHTS. USA+45 JURID
POL/PAR SECT DELIB/GP FORCES ADJUD CONTROL WAR JUDGE
DISCRIM MORAL...BIBLIOG 20 NEGRO SUPREME/CT ORD/FREE
BILL/RIGHT BLACK/HL. PAGE 32 E0628

B63
JACOBS P.,STATE OF UNIONS. USA+45 STRATA TOP/EX LABOR
GP/REL RACE/REL DEMAND DISCRIM ATTIT PWR 20 ECO/TAC
CONGRESS NEGRO HOFFA/J. PAGE 57 E1145 BARGAIN
DECISION

B63
LEWIN J.,POLITICS AND LAW IN SOUTH AFRICA. NAT/LISM
SOUTH/AFR UK POL/PAR BAL/PWR ECO/TAC COLONIAL POLICY
CONTROL GP/REL DISCRIM PWR 20 NEGRO. PAGE 65 E1293 LAW
RACE/REL

B63
LIVELY E.,THE INVASION OF MISSISSIPPI. USA+45 LAW RACE/REL
CONSTN NAT/G PROVS CT/SYS GOV/REL FEDERAL CONSERVE CROWD
...TRADIT 20 MISSISSIPP NEGRO NAACP WARRN/EARL COERCE
KENNEDY/JF. PAGE 66 E1309 MARXISM

B63
US COMMISSION ON CIVIL RIGHTS,FREEDOM TO THE FREE. RACE/REL
USA+45 USA-45 LAW VOL/ASSN CT/SYS ATTIT PWR...JURID DISCRIM
BIBLIOG 17/20 SUPREME/CT NEGRO CIV/RIGHTS. PAGE 99 NAT/G
E1986 POLICY

B63
US COMN CIVIL RIGHTS,REPORT ON MISSISSIPPI. LAW RACE/REL
LOC/G NAT/G LEGIS PLAN PROB/SOLV DISCRIM SOC/INTEG CONSTN
20 MISSISSIPP NEGRO. PAGE 99 E1987 ORD/FREE
COERCE

B64
BERWANGER E.H.,WESTERN ANTI-NEGRO SENTIMENT AND RACE/REL
LAWS 1846-60: A FACTOR IN THE SLAVERY EXTENSION REGION
CONTROVERSY (PAPER). USA-45 LAW CONSTN LEGIS ADJUD DISCRIM
...BIBLIOG 19 NEGRO. PAGE 11 E0218 ORD/FREE

B64

BROOKS T.R.,TOIL AND TROUBLE. A HISTORY OF AMERICAN   INDUS
LABOR. WORKER BARGAIN CAP/ISM ADJUD AUTOMAT EXEC   LABOR
GP/REL RACE/REL EFFICIENCY INCOME PROFIT MARXISM   LEGIS
17/20 KENNEDY/JF AFL/CIO NEGRO. PAGE 16 E0310

B64

FACTS ON FILE, INC.,CIVIL RIGHTS 1960-63: THE NEGRO DISCRIM
CAMPAIGN TO WIN EQUAL RIGHTS AND OPPORTUNITIES IN   PRESS
THE UNITED STATES. LAW CONSTN PARTIC SUFF 20 NEGRO   RACE/REL
CIV/RIGHTS MISSISSIPP. PAGE 36 E0710

B64

LOCKHART W.B.,CASES AND MATERIALS ON CONSTITUTIONAL   ORD/FREE
RIGHTS AND LIBERTIES. USA+45 FORCES LEGIS DIPLOM   CONSTN
PRESS CONTROL CRIME WAR PWR...AUD/VIS T WORSHIP 20   NAT/G
NEGRO. PAGE 66 E1317

B64

MARSHALL B.,FEDERALISM AND CIVIL RIGHTS. USA+45   FEDERAL
PROVS BAL/PWR CONTROL CT/SYS PARTIC SOVEREIGN   ORD/FREE
...JURID 20 NEGRO CIV/RIGHTS. PAGE 68 E1369   CONSTN
                                                     FORCES

B64

NEWMAN E.S.,CIVIL LIBERTY AND CIVIL RIGHTS. USA+45   ORD/FREE
USA-45 CONSTN PROVS FORCES LEGIS CT/SYS RACE/REL   LAW
ATTIT...MAJORIT JURID WORSHIP 20 SUPREME/CT NEGRO   CONTROL
CIV/RIGHTS CHURCH/STA. PAGE 77 E1543   NAT/G

B65

MISSISSIPPI BLACK PAPER: (FIFTY-SEVEN NEGRO AND   COERCE
WHITE CITIZENS' TESTIMONY OF POLICE BRUTALITY...).   RACE/REL
USA+45 LAW SOCIETY CT/SYS SANCTION CRIME MORAL   DISCRIM
ORD/FREE RESPECT 20 NEGRO. PAGE 2 E0035   FORCES

B65

CARTER R.L.,EQUALITY. LAW LABOR NEIGH SCHOOL   POLICY
RACE/REL 20 NEGRO. PAGE 20 E0402   DISCRIM
                                                     PLAN
                                                     CREATE

B65

EHLE J.,THE FREE MEN. USA+45 NAT/G PROVS FORCES   RACE/REL
JUDGE ADJUD ATTIT...POLICY SOC SOC/INTEG 20 NEGRO.   ORD/FREE
PAGE 34 E0677   DISCRIM

B65

FRIEDMAN L.,SOUTHERN JUSTICE. USA+45 PUB/INST LEGIT   ADJUD
ADMIN CT/SYS DISCRIM...DECISION ANTHOL 20 NEGRO   LAW
SOUTH/US CIV/RIGHTS. PAGE 40 E0800   CONSTN
                                                     RACE/REL

B65

IANNIELLO L.,MILESTONES ALONG THE MARCH: TWELVE   RACE/REL
HISTORIC CIVIL RIGHTS DOCUMENTS--FROM WORLD WAR II   DISCRIM
TO SELMA. USA+45 LAW FORCES TOP/EX PARTIC SUFF...T   CONSTN
20 NEGRO CIV/RIGHTS TRUMAN/HS SUPREME/CT   NAT/G
KENNEDY/JF. PAGE 56 E1121

B65

ROSE A.M.,MINORITY PROBLEMS: A TEXTBOOK OF READINGS   RACE/REL
IN INTERGROUP RELATIONS. UNIV USA+45 LAW SCHOOL   DISCRIM
WORKER PROB/SOLV GP/REL PERSON...PSY ANTHOL WORSHIP   ISOLAT
20 NEGRO INDIAN/AM JEWS EUROPE. PAGE 85 E1713   ACT/RES

B65

SCHROEDER O.,DEFACTO SEGREGATION AND CIVIL RIGHTS.   ANTHOL
LAW PROVS SCHOOL WORKER ATTIT HABITAT HEALTH WEALTH   DISCRIM
...JURID CHARTS 19/20 NEGRO SUPREME/CT KKK. PAGE 88   RACE/REL
E1766   ORD/FREE

B65

SMITH R.C.,THEY CLOSED THEIR SCHOOLS. USA+45 NEIGH   RACE/REL
ADJUD CROWD CONSEN WEALTH...DECISION OBS INT 20   DISCRIM
NEGRO VIRGINIA. PAGE 92 E1846   LOC/G
                                                     SCHOOL

B66

KUNSTLER W.M.,"DEEP IN MY HEART" USA+45 LAW   CT/SYS
PROF/ORG SECT LOBBY PARTIC CROWD DISCRIM ROLE   RACE/REL
...BIOG 20 KING/MAR/L NEGRO CIV/RIGHTS SOUTH/US.   ADJUD
PAGE 62 E1233   CONSULT

B66

MILLER E.W.,THE NEGRO IN AMERICA: A BIBLIOGRAPHY.   BIBLIOG
USA+45 LAW EDU/PROP REV GOV/REL GP/REL INGP/REL   DISCRIM
ADJUST HABITAT PERSON HEALTH ORD/FREE SOC/INTEG 20   RACE/REL
NEGRO. PAGE 73 E1459

B66

SKOLNICK J.H.,JUSTICE WITHOUT TRIAL: LAW   FORCES
ENFORCEMENT IN DEMOCRATIC SOCIETY. USA+45 LAW   CRIMLGY
TRIBUTE RACE/REL BIO/SOC PERSON...PSY SOC 20 NEGRO   CRIME
BUREAUCRCY PROSTITUTN. PAGE 92 E1836

L67

HOWARD A.E.D.,"MR. JUSTICE BLACK: THE NEGRO PROTEST   ADJUD
MOVEMENT AND THE RULE OF LAW." USA+45 CONSTN CT/SYS   JUDGE
CHOOSE GP/REL...DECISION JURID NEGRO SUPREME/CT.   LAW
PAGE 55 E1100   REPRESENT

S67

"THE FEDERAL AGRICULTURAL STABILIZATION PROGRAM AND   AGRI
THE NEGRO." LAW CONSTN PLAN REPRESENT DISCRIM   CONTROL
ORD/FREE 20 NEGRO CONGRESS. PAGE 2 E0039   NAT/G
                                                     RACE/REL

S67

EDGEWORTH A.B. JR.,"CIVIL RIGHTS PLUS THREE YEARS: WORKER
BANKS AND THE ANTI-DISCRIMINATION LAW" USA+45   DISCRIM
SOCIETY DELIB/GP RACE/REL EFFICIENCY 20 NEGRO   FINAN
CIV/RIGHTS. PAGE 34 E0675   LAW

NEHRU/J....JAWAHARLAL NEHRU

B66

HIDAYATULLAH M.,DEMOCRACY IN INDIA AND THE JUDICIAL   NAT/G
PROCESS. INDIA EX/STRUC LEGIS LEAD GOV/REL ATTIT   CT/SYS
ORD/FREE...MAJORIT CONCPT 20 NEHRU/J. PAGE 52 E1040   CONSTN
                                                     JURID

NEHRU/PM....PANDIT MOTILAL NEHRU

NEIGH....NEIGHBORHOOD

B28

YANG KUNG-SUN,THE BOOK OF LORD SHANG. LAW ECO/UNDEV   ASIA
LOC/G NAT/G NEIGH PLAN ECO/TAC LEGIT ATTIT SKILL   JURID
...CONCPT CON/ANAL WORK TOT/POP. PAGE 108 E2164

S38

CLEMMER D.,"LEADERSHIP PHENOMENA IN A PRISON   PUB/INST
COMMUNITY." NEIGH PLAN CHOOSE PERSON ROLE...OBS   CRIMLGY
INT. PAGE 23 E0452   LEAD
                                                     CLIENT

B49

DE HUSZAR G.B.,EQUALITY IN AMERICA: THE ISSUE OF   DISCRIM
MINORITY RIGHTS. USA+45 USA-45 LAW NEIGH SCHOOL   RACE/REL
LEGIS ACT/RES CHOOSE ATTIT RESPECT...ANTHOL 20   ORD/FREE
NEGRO. PAGE 29 E0585   PROB/SOLV

B51

KEFAUVER E.,CRIME IN AMERICA. USA+45 USA-45 MUNIC   ELITES
NEIGH DELIB/GP TRIBUTE GAMBLE LOBBY SANCTION   CRIME
...AUD/VIS 20 CAPONE/AL MAFIA MIAMI CHICAGO   PWR
DETROIT. PAGE 60 E1194   FORCES

B56

RECASENS SICHES S.,TRATADO GENERAL DE SOCIOLOGIA.   SOC
CULTURE FAM NEIGH LEAD RACE/REL DISCRIM HABITAT   STRATA
ORD/FREE...JURID LING T SOC/INTEG 20. PAGE 84 E1677   KIN
                                                     GP/REL

S57

GOODE W.J.,"COMMUNITY WITHIN A COMMUNITY: THE   PROF/ORG
PROFESSIONS." STRATA STRUCT SANCTION INGP/REL...SOC   NEIGH
GP/COMP. PAGE 45 E0886   CLIENT
                                                     CONTROL

S58

CRESSEY D.R.,"ACHIEVEMENT OF AN UNSTATED   PUB/INST
ORGANIZATIONAL GOAL: AN OBSERVATION ON PRISONS."   CLIENT
OP/RES PROB/SOLV PERS/REL ANOMIE ATTIT ROLE RESPECT   NEIGH
CRIMLGY. PAGE 28 E0546   INGP/REL

B60

CARTER R.F.,COMMUNITIES AND THEIR SCHOOLS. USA+45   SCHOOL
LAW FINAN PROVS BUDGET TAX LEAD PARTIC CHOOSE...SOC   ACT/RES
INT QU 20. PAGE 20 E0401   NEIGH
                                                     INGP/REL

B60

POWELL T.,THE SCHOOL BUS LAW: A CASE STUDY IN   JURID
EDUCATION, RELIGION, AND POLITICS. USA+45 LAW NEIGH   SCHOOL
SECT LEGIS EDU/PROP ADJUD CT/SYS LOBBY CATHISM
WORSHIP 20 CONNECTICT CHURCH/STA. PAGE 82 E1641

S60

MACKINNON F.,"THE UNIVERSITY: COMMUNITY OR   ACADEM
UTILITY?" CLIENT CONSTN INTELL FINAN NAT/G NEIGH   MGT
EDU/PROP PARTIC REPRESENT ROLE. PAGE 67 E1343   CONTROL
                                                     SERV/IND

B62

CURRY J.E.,RACE TENSIONS AND THE POLICE. LAW MUNIC   FORCES
NEIGH TEC/DEV RUMOR CONTROL COERCE GP/REL ATTIT   RACE/REL
...SOC 20 NEGRO. PAGE 28 E0558   CROWD
                                                     ORD/FREE

B63
DAY R.E.,CIVIL RIGHTS USA: PUBLIC SCHOOLS, SOUTHERN   EDU/PROP
STATES - NORTH CAROLINA, 1963. USA+45 LOC/G NEIGH   ORD/FREE
LEGIS CREATE CT/SYS COERCE DISCRIM ATTIT...QU   RACE/REL
CHARTS 20 NORTH/CAR NEGRO KKK CIV/RIGHTS. PAGE 29   SANCTION
E0579

B63
SMITH E.A.,CHURCH AND STATE IN YOUR COMMUNITY.   GP/REL
USA+45 PROVS SCHOOL ACT/RES CT/SYS PARTIC ATTIT   SECT
MORAL ORD/FREE CATHISM 20 PROTESTANT CHURCH/STA.   NAT/G
PAGE 92 E1842   NEIGH

B64
BOUVIER-AJAM M.,MANUEL TECHNIQUE ET PRATIQUE DU   MUNIC
MAIRE ET DES ELUS ET AGENTS COMMUNAUX. FRANCE LOC/G   ADMIN
BUDGET CHOOSE GP/REL SUPEGO...JURID BIBLIOG 20   CHIEF
MAYOR COMMUNES. PAGE 14 E0274   NEIGH

B64
CHEIN I.,THE ROAD TO H; NARCOTICS, DELINQUENCY, AND   BIO/SOC
SOCIAL POLICY. USA+45 NEIGH CRIME INGP/REL ATTIT   AGE/Y
PERSON...SOC/WK 20 NEWYORK/C. PAGE 22 E0426   POLICY
                                                      ANOMIE

B64
CLINARD M.B.,ANOMIE AND DEVIANT BEHAVIOR: A   PERSON
DISCUSSION AND CRITIQUE. SOCIETY FACE/GP CRIME   ANOMIE
STRANGE ATTIT BIO/SOC DISPL RIGID/FLEX HEALTH...PSY   KIN
CONCPT BIBLIOG 20 MERTON/R. PAGE 23 E0456   NEIGH

B65
CARTER R.L.,EQUALITY. LAW LABOR NEIGH SCHOOL   POLICY
RACE/REL 20 NEGRO. PAGE 20 E0402   DISCRIM
                                                      PLAN
                                                      CREATE

B65
FRYE R.J.,HOUSING AND URBAN RENEWAL IN ALABAMA.   MUNIC
USA+45 NEIGH LEGIS BUDGET ADJUD ADMIN PARTIC...MGT   PROB/SOLV
20 ALABAMA URBAN/RNWL. PAGE 41 E0815   PLAN
                                                      GOV/REL

B65
SMITH R.C.,THEY CLOSED THEIR SCHOOLS. USA+45 NEIGH   RACE/REL
ADJUD CROWD CONSEN WEALTH...DECISION OBS INT 20   DISCRIM
NEGRO VIRGINIA. PAGE 92 E1846   LOC/G
                                                      SCHOOL

B67
BERNSTEIN S.,ALTERNATIVES TO VIOLENCE: ALIENATED   AGE/Y
YOUTH AND RIOTS, RACE AND POVERTY. MUNIC PUB/INST   SOC/WK
SCHOOL INGP/REL RACE/REL UTOPIA DRIVE HABITAT ROLE   NEIGH
WEALTH...INT 20. PAGE 11 E0215   CRIME

B67
BRAGER G.A.,COMMUNITY ACTION AGAINST POVERTY.   NEIGH
USA+45 LAW STRATA INGP/REL INCOME NEW/LIB...POLICY   WEALTH
WELF/ST ANTHOL. PAGE 15 E0285   SOC/WK
                                                      CREATE

B67
CHAPIN F.S. JR.,SELECTED REFERENCES ON URBAN   BIBLIOG
PLANNING METHODS AND TECHNIQUES. USA+45 LAW ECO/DEV   NEIGH
LOC/G NAT/G SCHOOL CONSULT CREATE PROB/SOLV TEC/DEV   MUNIC
SOC/WK. PAGE 21 E0420   PLAN

NELSON D.H. E1531

NELSON H.L. E1532

NEOLITHIC....NEOLITHIC PERIOD

NEPAL....SEE ALSO S/ASIA

NET/THEORY....NETWORK THEORY

B63
FAWCETT J.E.S.,THE BRITISH COMMONWEALTH IN   INT/LAW
INTERNATIONAL LAW. LAW INT/ORG NAT/G VOL/ASSN   STRUCT
OP/RES DIPLOM ADJUD CENTRAL CONSEN...NET/THEORY   COLONIAL
CMN/WLTH TREATY. PAGE 36 E0723

B66
FALK R.A.,THE STRATEGY OF WORLD ORDER* 4 VOLUMES.   ORD/FREE
WOR+45 ECO/UNDEV ACADEM INT/ORG ACT/RES DIPLOM   GEN/LAWS
ARMS/CONT WAR...NET/THEORY SIMUL BIBLIOG UN.   ANTHOL
PAGE 36 E0719   INT/LAW

S67
RUCKER B.W.,"WHAT SOLUTIONS DO PEOPLE ENDORSE IN   CONCPT
FREE PRESS-FAIR TRIAL DILEMMA?" LAW NAT/G CT/SYS   PRESS
ATTIT...NET/THEORY SAMP CHARTS IDEA/COMP METH 20.   ADJUD
PAGE 86 E1731   ORD/FREE

NETH/IND....NETHERLAND EAST INDIES (PRE-INDONESIA)

B45
US LIBRARY OF CONGRESS,NETHERLANDS EAST INDIES.   BIBLIOG/A
INDONESIA LAW CULTURE AGRI INDUS SCHOOL COLONIAL   S/ASIA
HEALTH...GEOG JURID SOC 19/20 NETH/IND. PAGE 101   NAT/G
E2017

NETHERLAND....NETHERLANDS; SEE ALSO APPROPRIATE TIME/SPACE/
    CULTURE INDEX

L00
HISTORICUS,"LETTERS AND SOME QUESTIONS OF   WEALTH
INTERNATIONAL LAW." FRANCE NETHERLAND UK USA-45   JURID
WOR-45 LAW NAT/G COERCE...SOC CONCPT GEN/LAWS   WAR
TOT/POP 19 CIVIL/WAR. PAGE 53 E1054   INT/LAW

B47
HILL M.,IMMUNITIES AND PRIVILEGES OF INTERNATIONAL   INT/ORG
OFFICIALS. CANADA EUR+WWI NETHERLAND SWITZERLND LAW   ADMIN
LEGIS DIPLOM LEGIT RESPECT...TIME/SEQ LEAGUE/NAT UN
VAL/FREE 20. PAGE 52 E1046

S63
RIGAUX F.,"LA SIGNIFICATION DES ACTES JUDICIARES A   CONSULT
L'ETRANGER." EUR+WWI ITALY NETHERLAND LAW ACT/RES   CT/SYS
DRIVE...JURID GEN/LAWS TOT/POP 20. PAGE 85 E1699   GERMANY

B65
CONRING E.,KIRCHE UND STAAT NACH DER LEHRE DER   SECT
NIEDERLANDISCHEN CALVINISTEN IN DER ERSTEN HALFTE   JURID
DES 17. JAHRHUNDERTS. NETHERLAND GP/REL...CONCPT 17   NAT/G
CHURCH/STA. PAGE 25 E0497   ORD/FREE

NETWORK THEORY....SEE NET/THEORY

NEUBURGER O. E1533,E1534,E1535

NEUMANN F. E1536

NEUTRAL....POLITICAL NONALIGNMENT, LEGAL NEUTRALITY

B'
LALL A.S.,NEGOTIATING DISARMAMENT* THE EIGHTEEN   OBS
NATION DISARMAMENT CONFERENCE* THE FIRST TWO YEARS,   ARMS/CONT
1962-1964. ASIA FRANCE INDIA USA+45 USSR PROB/SOLV   DIPLOM
ADJUD NEUTRAL ATTIT...IDEA/COMP COLD/WAR. PAGE 62   OP/RES
E1246

B09
HOLLAND T.E.,LETTERS UPON WAR AND NEUTRALITY.   LAW
WOR-45 NAT/G FORCES JUDGE ECO/TAC LEGIT CT/SYS   INT/LAW
NEUTRAL ROUTINE COERCE...JURID TIME/SEQ 20. PAGE 55   INT/ORG
E1085   WAR

B15
INTERNATIONAL LAW ASSOCIATION,A FORTY YEARS'   BIBLIOG
CATALOGUE OF THE BOOKS, PAMPHLETS AND PAPERS IN THE   LAW
LIBRARY OF THE INTERNATIONAL LAW ASSOCIATION.   INT/LAW
INT/ORG DIPLOM ADJUD NEUTRAL...IDEA/COMP 19/20.
PAGE 57 E1134

B19
LONDON SCHOOL ECONOMICS-POL,ANNUAL DIGEST OF PUBLIC   BIBLIOG/A
INTERNATIONAL LAW CASES. INT/ORG MUNIC NAT/G PROVS   INT/LAW
ADMIN NEUTRAL WAR GOV/REL PRIVIL 20. PAGE 66 E1323   ADJUD
                                                      DIPLOM

B37
KETCHAM E.H.,PRELIMINARY SELECT BIBLIOGRAPHY OF   BIBLIOG
INTERNATIONAL LAW (PAMPHLET). WOR-45 LAW INT/ORG   DIPLOM
NAT/G PROB/SOLV CT/SYS NEUTRAL WAR 19/20. PAGE 60   ADJUD
E1207   INT/LAW

B40
CONOVER H.F.,FOREIGN RELATIONS OF THE UNITED   BIBLIOG/A
STATES: A LIST OF RECENT BOOKS (PAMPHLET). ASIA   USA-45
CANADA L/A+17C UK INT/ORG INT/TRADE TARIFFS NEUTRAL   DIPLOM
WAR PEACE...INT/LAW CON/ANAL 20 CHINJAP. PAGE 25
E0492

N47
FOX W.T.R.,UNITED STATES POLICY IN A TWO POWER   DIPLOM
WORLD. COM USA+45 USSR FORCES DOMIN AGREE NEUTRAL   FOR/AID
NUC/PWR ORD/FREE SOVEREIGN 20 COLD/WAR TREATY   POLICY
EUROPE/W INTERVENT. PAGE 39 E0780

L49
MARX C.M.,"ADMINISTRATIVE ETHICS AND THE RULE OF   ADMIN
LAW." USA+45 ELITES ACT/RES DOMIN NEUTRAL ROUTINE   LAW
INGP/REL ORD/FREE...JURID IDEA/COMP. PAGE 69 E1375

B53
OPPENHEIM L.,INTERNATIONAL LAW: A TREATISE (7TH   INT/LAW
ED., 2 VOLS.). LAW CONSTN PROB/SOLV INT/TRADE ADJUD   INT/ORG
AGREE NEUTRAL WAR ORD/FREE SOVEREIGN...BIBLIOG 20   DIPLOM
LEAGUE/NAT UN ILO. PAGE 79 E1579

POTTER P.B.,"NEUTRALITY, 1955." WOR+45 WOR-45   **S56**
INT/ORG NAT/G WAR ATTIT...POLICY IDEA/COMP 17/20   NEUTRAL
LEAGUE/NAT UN COLD/WAR. PAGE 81 E1631   INT/LAW
   DIPLOM
   CONCPT

INSTITUT DE DROIT INTL,TABLEAU GENERAL DES   **B57**
RESOLUTIONS (1873-1956). LAW NEUTRAL CRIME WAR   INT/LAW
MARRIAGE PEACE...JURID 19/20. PAGE 56 E1124   DIPLOM
   ORD/FREE
   ADJUD

SINEY M.C.,THE ALLIED BLOCKADE OF GERMANY: **B57**
1914-1916. EUR+WWI GERMANY MOD/EUR USA-45 DIPLOM   DETER
CONTROL NEUTRAL PWR 20. PAGE 91 E1832   INT/TRADE
   INT/LAW
   WAR

RIENOW R.,CONTEMPORARY INTERNATIONAL POLITICS.   **B61**
WOR+45 INT/ORG BAL/PWR EDU/PROP COLONIAL NEUTRAL   DIPLOM
REGION WAR PEACE...INT/LAW 20 COLD/WAR UN. PAGE 85   PWR
E1698   POLICY
   NAT/G

SYATAUW J.J.G.,SOME NEWLY ESTABLISHED ASIAN STATES   **B61**
AND THE DEVELOPMENT OF INTERNATIONAL LAW. BURMA   INT/LAW
CEYLON INDIA INDONESIA ECO/UNDEV COLONIAL NEUTRAL   ADJUST
WAR PEACE SOVEREIGN...CHARTS 19/20. PAGE 95 E1902   SOCIETY
   S/ASIA

DOUGLAS W.O.,DEMOCRACY'S MANIFESTO. COM USA+45   **B62**
ECO/UNDEV INT/ORG FORCES PLAN NEUTRAL TASK MARXISM   DIPLOM
...JURID 20 NATO SEATO. PAGE 32 E0642   POLICY
   NAT/G
   ORD/FREE

GYORGY A.,PROBLEMS IN INTERNATIONAL RELATIONS. COM   **B62**
CT/SYS NUC/PWR ALL/IDEOS 20 UN EEC ECSC. PAGE 49   DIPLOM
E0966   NEUTRAL
   BAL/PWR
   REV

JACOBINI H.B.,INTERNATIONAL LAW: A TEXT. DIPLOM   **B62**
ADJUD NEUTRAL WAR PEACE T. PAGE 57 E1143   INT/LAW
   CT/SYS
   CONCPT

OSSENBECK F.J.,OPEN SPACE AND PEACE. CHINA/COM FUT   **B64**
USA+45 USSR LAW PROB/SOLV TEC/DEV EDU/PROP NEUTRAL   SPACE
PEACE...AUD/VIS ANTHOL 20. PAGE 79 E1583   ORD/FREE
   DIPLOM
   CREATE

MORRIS R.B.,THE PEACEMAKERS; THE GREAT POWERS AND   **B65**
AMERICAN INDEPENDENCE. BAL/PWR CONFER COLONIAL   SOVEREIGN
NEUTRAL PEACE ORD/FREE TREATY 18 PRE/US/AM. PAGE 75   REV
E1499   DIPLOM

O'BRIEN W.V.,THE NEW NATIONS IN INTERNATIONAL LAW   **B65**
AND DIPLOMACY* THE YEAR BOOK OF WORLD POLITY*   INT/LAW
VOLUME III. USA+45 ECO/UNDEV INT/ORG FORCES DIPLOM   CULTURE
COLONIAL NEUTRAL REV NAT/LISM ATTIT RESPECT.   SOVEREIGN
PAGE 78 E1565   ANTHOL

BROWNLIE I.,"SOME LEGAL ASPECTS OF THE USE OF   **S65**
NUCLEAR WEAPONS." UK NEUTRAL DETER UN TREATY.   LAW
PAGE 16 E0317   NUC/PWR
   WAR
   INT/LAW

CANFIELD L.H.,THE PRESIDENCY OF WOODROW WILSON: **B66**
PRELUDE TO A WORLD IN CRISIS. USA-45 ADJUD NEUTRAL   PERSON
WAR CHOOSE INGP/REL PEACE ORD/FREE 20 WILSON/W   POLICY
PRESIDENT TREATY LEAGUE/NAT. PAGE 19 E0373   DIPLOM
   GOV/REL

DYCK H.V.,WEIMAR GERMANY AND SOVIET RUSSIA   **B66**
1926-1933. EUR+WWI GERMANY UK USSR ECO/TAC   DIPLOM
INT/TRADE NEUTRAL WAR ATTIT 20 WEIMAR/REP TREATY.   GOV/REL
PAGE 34 E0669   POLICY

LEVY L.W.,JUDICIAL REVIEW AND THE SUPREME COURT.   **B67**
USA+45 USA-45 NEUTRAL ATTIT ORD/FREE...POLICY   ADJUD
DECISION BIBLIOG 18/20 BILL/RIGHT SUPREME/CT.   CONSTN
PAGE 65 E1292   LAW
   CT/SYS

LEGAULT A.,"ORGANISATION ET CONDUITE DES OPERATIONS   **L67**
DE MAINTIEN DE LA PAIX." FORCES ACT/RES ADJUD AGREE   INT/ORG
CONTROL NEUTRAL TASK PRIVIL ORD/FREE 20 UN. PAGE 64   PEACE
E1279   WAR
   INT/LAW

NEVADA....NEVADA

NEW LIBERALISM....SEE NEW/LIB

NEW STATES....SEE ECO/UNDEV+GEOGRAPHIC AREA+COLONIAL+
     NAT/LISM

NEW JERSEY LEGISLATURE-SENATE E1537

NEW YORK STATE LEGISLATURE E1538

NEW YORK STATE LIBRARY E1539

NEW/BRUNS....NEW BRUNSWICK, CANADA

CUNNINGHAM W.B.,COMPULSORY CONCILIATION AND   **B58**
COLLECTIVE BARGAINING. CANADA NAT/G LEGIS ADJUD   POLICY
CT/SYS GP/REL...MGT 20 NEW/BRUNS STRIKE CASEBOOK.   BARGAIN
PAGE 28 E0555   LABOR
   INDUS

NEW/DEAL....NEW DEAL OF F.D.R.'S ADMINISTRATION

AUERBACH J.S.,LABOR AND LIBERTY; THE LA FOLLETTE   **B66**
COMMITTEE AND THE NEW DEAL. USA-45 LAW LEAD RESPECT   DELIB/GP
SOCISM...BIBLIOG 20 CONGRESS BILL/RIGHT LAFOLLET/R   LABOR
NEW/DEAL. PAGE 6 E0117   CONSTN
   ORD/FREE

COHEN M.R.,LAW AND THE SOCIAL ORDER: ESSAYS IN   **B67**
LEGAL PHILOSOPHY. USA-45 CONSULT WORKER ECO/TAC   JURID
ATTIT WEALTH...POLICY WELF/ST SOC 20 NEW/DEAL   LABOR
DEPRESSION. PAGE 24 E0467   IDEA/COMP

NEW/DELHI....NEW DELHI (UNCTAD MEETING OF DEVELOPED AND
     UNDERDEVELOPED NATIONS IN 1968)

NEW/ECO/MN....NEW ECONOMIC MECHANISM OF HUNGARY

NEW/ECONOM....NEW ECONOMICS

NEW/ENGLND....NEW ENGLAND

NEW/FRONTR....NEW FRONTIER OF J.F.KENNEDY

NEW/GUINEA....NEW GUINEA

NEW/HAMPSH....NEW HAMPSHIRE

NEW/HEBRID....NEW HEBRIDES

NEW/IDEA....NEW CONCEPT

NEW/JERSEY....NEW JERSEY

HOGARTY R.A.,NEW JERSEY FARMERS AND MIGRANT HOUSING AGRI   **N19**
RULES (PAMPHLET). USA+45 LAW ELITES FACE/GP LABOR   PROVS
PROF/ORG LOBBY PERS/REL RIGID/FLEX ROLE 20   WORKER
NEW/JERSEY. PAGE 53 E1067   HEALTH

RALSTON A.,A FRESH LOOK AT LEGISLATIVE   **N19**
APPORTIONMENT IN NEW JERSEY (PAMPHLET). USA+45   APPORT
CONSTN LEGIS OBJECTIVE...MATH METH 20 NEW/JERSEY.   REPRESENT
PAGE 83 E1671   PROVS
   JURID

NJ LAW AND LEGISLATIVE BURE,NEW JERSEY   **B57**
LEGISLAVTIVE REAPPORTIONMENT (PAMPHLET). USA+45   APPORT
ACT/RES ADJUD...STAT CHARTS 20 NEW/JERSEY. PAGE 2   LEGIS
E0041   CENSUS
   REPRESENT

NEW JERSEY LEGISLATURE-SENATE,PUBLIC HEARINGS   **B61**
BEFORE COMMITTEE ON REVISION AND AMENDMENT OF LAWS   LEGIS
ON SENATE BILL NO. 8. USA+45 FINAN PROVS WORKER   MUNIC
ACT/RES PLAN BUDGET TAX CRIME...IDEA/COMP 20   INDUS
NEW/JERSEY URBAN/RNWL. PAGE 77 E1537   PROB/SOLV

REOCK E.C. JR.,POPULATION INEQUALITY AMONG COUNTIES   **B63**
IN THE NEW JERSEY LEGISLATURE 1791-1962. PROVS   APPORT
ORD/FREE...CENSUS CHARTS 18/20 NEW/JERSEY. PAGE 84   REPRESENT
E1687   LEGIS
   JURID

NJ LEGIS REAPPORT PLAN COMM,PUBLIC HEARING ON   **B65**
REDISTRICTING AND REAPPORTIONMENT. USA+45 CONSTN   APPORT
VOL/ASSN LEGIS DEBATE...POLICY GEOG CENSUS 20   REPRESENT
NEW/JERSEY. PAGE 77 E1552   PROVS
   JURID

NEW/LEFT....THE NEW LEFT

NEW/LIB....NEW LIBERALISM

LUCE R.,LEGISLATIVE PROBLEMS. CONSTN CHIEF JUDGE
BUDGET CONFER ETIQUET CONTROL MORAL PWR NEW/LIB
CONGRESS. PAGE 67 E1331
B35
TREND
ADMIN
LEGIS

CORWIN E.S.,LIBERTY AGAINST GOVERNMENT: THE RISE,
FLOWERING AND DECLINE OF A FAMOUS JURIDICAL
CONCEPT. LEGIS ADJUD CT/SYS SANCTION GOV/REL
FEDERAL CONSERVE NEW/LIB...OLD/LIB 18/20 ROMAN/LAW
COMMON/LAW. PAGE 26 E0514
B48
CONCPT
ORD/FREE
JURID
CONSTN

FRIEDMANN W.,LAW AND SOCIAL CHANGE IN CONTEMPORARY
BRITAIN. UK LABOR LG/CO LEGIS JUDGE CT/SYS ORD/FREE
NEW/LIB...DECISION JURID TREND METH/COMP BIBLIOG 20
PARLIAMENT ENGLSH/LAW COMMON/LAW. PAGE 40 E0802
B51
LAW
ADJUD
SOCIETY
CONSTN

STOUT H.M.,BRITISH GOVERNMENT. UK FINAN LOC/G
POL/PAR DELIB/GP DIPLOM ADMIN COLONIAL CHOOSE
ORD/FREE...JURID BIBLIOG 20 COMMONWLTH. PAGE 94
E1883
B53
NAT/G
PARL/PROC
CONSTN
NEW/LIB

DUNNILL F.,THE CIVIL SERVICE. UK LAW PLAN ADMIN
EFFICIENCY DRIVE NEW/LIB...STAT CHARTS 20
PARLIAMENT CIVIL/SERV. PAGE 33 E0662
B56
PERSON
WORKER
STRATA
SOC/WK

BERNS W.,FREEDOM, VIRTUE, AND THE FIRST AMENDMENT.
USA+45 LAW CONSTN PROB/SOLV NEW/LIB...JURID 20
SUPREME/CT AMEND/I. PAGE 11 E0212
B57
ADJUD
CT/SYS
ORD/FREE

FELLMAN D.,"ACADEMIC FREEDOM IN AMERICAN LAW." LAW
CONSTN NAT/G VOL/ASSN PLAN PERSON KNOWL NEW/LIB.
PAGE 37 E0732
L61
ACADEM
ORD/FREE
LEGIS
CULTURE

LAVROFF D.-.G.,LES LIBERTES PUBLIQUES EN UNION
SOVIETIQUE (REV. ED.). USSR NAT/G WORKER SANCTION
CRIME MARXISM NEW/LIB...JURID BIBLIOG WORSHIP 20.
PAGE 63 E1268
B63
ORD/FREE
LAW
ATTIT
COM

ANDRUS H.L.,LIBERALISM, CONSERVATISM, MORMONISM.
USA+45 PLAN ADJUD CONTROL HAPPINESS ORD/FREE
CONSERVE NEW/LIB WORSHIP 20. PAGE 5 E0097
B65
SECT
UTOPIA
MORAL

SCHUBERT G.,THE JUDICIAL MIND: THE ATTITUDES AND
IDEOLOGIES OF SUPREME COURT JUSTICES 1946-1963.
USA+45 ELITES NAT/G CONTROL PERS/REL MAJORITY
CONSERVE...DECISION JURID MODAL STAT TREND GP/COMP
GAME. PAGE 88 E1774
B65
CT/SYS
JUDGE
ATTIT
NEW/LIB

WASHINGTON S.H.,BIBLIOGRAPHY: LABOR-MANAGEMENT
RELATIONS ACT, 1947 AS AMENDED BY LABOR-MANAGEMENT
REPORTING AND DISCLOSURE ACT, 1959. USA+45 CONSTN
INDUS DELIB/GP LEGIS WORKER BARGAIN ECO/TAC ADJUD
GP/REL NEW/LIB...JURID CONGRESS. PAGE 105 E2100
B66
BIBLIOG
LAW
LABOR
MGT

GASS O.,"THE LITERATURE OF AMERICAN GOVERNMENT."
CONSTN DRIVE ORD/FREE...JURID CONCPT METH/CNCPT
IDEA/COMP 20 WILSON/W BEARD/CA LINK/AS. PAGE 42
E0841
S66
NEW/LIB
CT/SYS
NAT/G

BAKER L.,BACK TO BACK: THE DUEL BETWEEN FDR AND THE
SUPREME COURT. ELITES LEGIS CREATE DOMIN INGP/REL
PERSON PWR NEW/LIB 20 ROOSEVLT/F SUPREME/CT SENATE.
PAGE 7 E0142
B67
CHIEF
CT/SYS
PARL/PROC
GOV/REL

BRAGER G.A.,COMMUNITY ACTION AGAINST POVERTY.
USA+45 LAW STRATA INGP/REL INCOME NEW/LIB...POLICY
WELF/ST ANTHOL. PAGE 15 E0285
B67
NEIGH
WEALTH
SOC/WK
CREATE

NEW/MEXICO....NEW MEXICO

NEW/YORK....NEW YORK STATE

GELLHORN W.,THE STATES AND SUBVERSION. USA+45
USA-45 LOC/G DELIB/GP LEGIS EDU/PROP LEGIT CT/SYS
REGION PEACE ATTIT ORD/FREE SOCISM...INT CON/ANAL
B52
PROVS
JURID

20 CALIFORNIA MARYLAND ILLINOIS MICHIGAN NEW/YORK.
PAGE 43 E0845

NEW YORK STATE LEGISLATURE,REPORT AND DRAFT OF
PROPOSED LEGISLATION ON COURT REORGANIZATION. LAW
PROVS DELIB/GP CREATE ADJUD 20 NEW/YORK. PAGE 77
E1538
B62
CT/SYS
JURID
MUNIC
LOC/G

LEAGUE WOMEN VOTERS NEW YORK,APPORTIONMENT WORKSHOP
KIT. USA+45 VOL/ASSN DELIB/GP LEGIS ATTIT ORD/FREE
...METH/COMP 20 SUPREME/CT NEW/YORK. PAGE 64 E1275
B63
APPORT
REPRESENT
PROVS
JURID

HEWITT W.H.,ADMINISTRATION OF CRIMINAL JUSTICE IN
NEW YORK. LAW PROB/SOLV ADJUD ADMIN...CRIMLGY
CHARTS T 20 NEW/YORK. PAGE 52 E1035
B67
CRIME
ROLE
CT/SYS
FORCES

NEW/YORK/C....NEW YORK CITY

NEW/ZEALND....NEW ZEALAND; SEE ALSO S/ASIA, COMMONWLTH

INDEX TO LEGAL PERIODICALS. CANADA NEW/ZEALND UK
USA+45 USA-45 CONSTN LEGIS JUDGE ADJUD ADMIN
CONTROL CT/SYS FEDERAL...CRIMLGY INT/LAW 20
CMN/WLTH AUSTRAL. PAGE 1 E0006
N
BIBLIOG
INDEX
LAW
JURID

BRYCE J.,MODERN DEMOCRACIES. FUT NEW/ZEALND USA-45
LAW CONSTN POL/PAR PROVS VOL/ASSN EX/STRUC LEGIS
LEGIT CT/SYS EXEC KNOWL CONGRESS AUSTRAL 20.
PAGE 16 E0322
B21
NAT/G
TREND

EDWARDS C.D.,TRADE REGULATIONS OVERSEAS. IRELAND
NEW/ZEALND SOUTH/AFR NAT/G CAP/ISM TARIFFS CONTROL
...POLICY JURID 20 EEC CHINJAP. PAGE 34 E0676
B66
INT/TRADE
DIPLOM
INT/LAW
ECO/TAC

RAE D.,THE POLITICAL CONSEQUENCES OF ELECTORAL
LAWS. EUR+WWI ICELAND ISRAEL NEW/ZEALND UK USA+45
ADJUD APPORT GP/REL MAJORITY...MATH STAT CENSUS
CHARTS BIBLIOG 20 AUSTRAL. PAGE 83 E1667
B67
POL/PAR
CHOOSE
NAT/COMP
REPRESENT

NEWARK/NJ....NEWARK, N.J.

NEWBURY C.W. E1540

NEWFNDLND....NEWFOUNDLAND, CANADA

NEWMAN E.S. E1541,E1542,E1543

NEWMAN R.P. E1544

NEWY/TIMES....NEW YORK TIMES

NEWYORK/C....NEW YORK CITY

CALDWELL L.K.,"THE GOVERNMENT AND ADMINISTRATION OF
NEW YORK." LOC/G MUNIC POL/PAR SCHOOL CHIEF LEGIS
PLAN TAX CT/SYS...MGT SOC/WK BIBLIOG 20 NEWYORK/C.
PAGE 19 E0365
C54
PROVS
ADMIN
CONSTN
EX/STRUC

LARROWE C.P.,SHAPE-UP AND HIRING HALL. TRIBUTE
ADJUD CONTROL SANCTION COERCE CRIME GP/REL PWR
...CHARTS 20 AFL/CIO NEWYORK/C SEATTLE. PAGE 63
E1256
B55
LABOR
INDUS
WORKER
NAT/G

BELL D.,"THE RACKET RIDDEN LONGSHOREMEN" (BMR)"
USA+45 SEA WORKER MURDER ROLE...SOC 20 NEWYORK/C.
PAGE 9 E0182
S59
CRIME
LABOR
DIST/IND
ELITES

CHEIN I.,THE ROAD TO H: NARCOTICS, DELINQUENCY, AND
SOCIAL POLICY. USA+45 NEIGH CRIME INGP/REL ATTIT
PERSON...SOC/WK 20 NEWYORK/C. PAGE 22 E0426
B64
BIO/SOC
AGE/Y
POLICY
ANOMIE

FISK W.M.,ADMINISTRATIVE PROCEDURE IN A REGULATORY
AGENCY: THE CAB AND THE NEW YORK-CHICAGO CASE
(PAMPHLET). USA+45 DIST/IND ADMIN CONTROL LOBBY
GP/REL ROLE ORD/FREE NEWYORK/C CHICAGO CAB. PAGE 38
E0758
B64
SERV/IND
ECO/DEV
AIR
JURID

NICARAGUA....NICARAGUA; SEE ALSO L/A+17C

B47
DE NOIA J..GUIDE TO OFFICIAL PUBLICATIONS OF THE   BIBLIOG/A
OTHER AMERICAN REPUBLICS: NICARAGUA (VOL. XIV).   EDU/PROP
NICARAGUA LAW LEGIS ADMIN CT/SYS...JURID 19/20.   NAT/G
PAGE 30 E0591   CONSTN

B65
LUGO-MARENCO J.J..A STATEMENT OF THE LAWS OF   CONSTN
NICARAGUA IN MATTERS AFFECTING BUSINESS. NICARAGUA   NAT/G
AGRI DIST/IND EXTR/IND FINAN INDUS FAM WORKER   LEGIS
INT/TRADE TAX MARRIAGE OWN BIO/SOC 20 TREATY   JURID
RESOURCE/N MIGRATION. PAGE 67 E1332

B67
OPERATIONS AND POLICY RESEARCH,NICARAGUA: ELECTION   POL/PAR
FACTBOOK: FEBRUARY 5, 1967 (PAMPHLET). NICARAGUA   CHOOSE
LAW NAT/G LEAD REPRESENT...STAT BIOG CHARTS 20.   PLAN
PAGE 79 E1577   ATTIT

NICE R.W. E1545

NICHOLAS/I....CZAR NICHOLAS I

NICHOLS J.P. E1546

NICHOLS R.F. E1547

NICHOLSON T.L. E1867

NICOLSON H. E1548

NICOLSON/A....SIR ARTHUR NICOLSON

NIEBUHR/R....REINHOLD NIEBUHR

NIEBURG/HL....H.L. NIEBURG

NIEMEYER G. E0254,E1549

NIETZSCH/F....FRIEDRICH NIETZSCHE

NIGERIA....SEE ALSO AFR

B65
BLITZ L.F..THE POLITICS AND ADMINISTRATION OF   NAT/G
NIGERIAN GOVERNMENT. NIGER CULTURE LOC/G LEGIS   GOV/REL
DIPLOM COLONIAL CT/SYS SOVEREIGN...GEOG SOC ANTHOL   POL/PAR
20. PAGE 13 E0245

S66
MATTHEWS D.G.,"PRELUDE-COUP D'ETAT-MILITARY   BIBLIOG
GOVERNMENT: A BIBLIOGRAPHICAL AND RESEARCH GUIDE TO   NAT/G
NIGERIAN POL AND GOVT, JAN, 1965-66." AFR NIGER LAW   ADMIN
CONSTN POL/PAR LEGIS CIVMIL/REL GOV/REL...STAT 20.   CHOOSE
PAGE 69 E1385

B63
ELIAS T.O..THE NIGERIAN LEGAL SYSTEM. NIGERIA LAW   CT/SYS
FAM KIN SECT ADMIN NAT/LISM...JURID 18/20   ADJUD
ENGLSH/LAW COMMON/LAW. PAGE 34 E0682   COLONIAL
                                                        PROF/ORG

B65
PROEHL P.O..FOREIGN ENTERPRISE IN NIGERIA. NIGERIA   ECO/UNDEV
FINAN LABOR NAT/G TAX 20. PAGE 83 E1656   ECO/TAC
                                                        JURID
                                                        CAP/ISM

B66
KEAY E.A..THE NATIVE AND CUSTOMARY COURTS OF   AFR
NIGERIA. NIGERIA CONSTN ELITES NAT/G TOP/EX PARTIC   ADJUD
REGION...DECISION JURID 19/20. PAGE 60 E1190   LAW

B67
NIVEN R..NIGERIA. NIGERIA CONSTN INDUS EX/STRUC   NAT/G
COLONIAL REV NAT/LISM...CHARTS 19/20. PAGE 77 E1550   REGION
                                                        CHOOSE
                                                        GP/REL

NIH....NATIONAL INSTITUTE OF HEALTH

NIPA....NATIONAL INSTITUTE OF PUBLIC ADMINISTRATION

NISBET R.A. E1444

NISEI....NISEI: JAPANESE AMERICANS

NIVEN R. E1550

NIXON H.C. E0897

NIXON/RM....PRESIDENT RICHARD M. NIXON

B57
HISS A..IN THE COURT OF PUBLIC OPINION. USA+45   CRIME
DELIB/GP LEGIS LEGIT CT/SYS ATTIT 20 DEPT/STATE   MARXISM
NIXON/RM HUAC HISS/ALGER. PAGE 53 E1053   BIOG
                                                        ADJUD

NIZARD L. E1551

NJ LEGIS REAPPORT PLAN COMM E1552

NKRUMAH/K....KWAME NKRUMAH

NLC....NATIONAL LIBERATION COUNCIL IN GHANA

NLF....NATIONAL LIBERATION FRONT OF SOUTH VIETNAM

NLRB....NATIONAL LABOR RELATIONS BOARD

N19
THE REGIONAL DIRECTOR AND THE PRESS (PAMPHLET).   PRESS
USA-45 COM/IND LOBBY ROLE 20 NLRB CINCINNATI   LABOR
BILL/RIGHT. PAGE 2 E0031   ORD/FREE
                                                        EDU/PROP

B37
BUREAU OF NATIONAL AFFAIRS,LABOR RELATIONS   LABOR
REFERENCE MANUAL VOL 1, 1935-1937. BARGAIN DEBATE   ADMIN
ROUTINE INGP/REL 20 NLRB. PAGE 17 E0335   ADJUD
                                                       NAT/G

B55
BLOOM G.F..ECONOMICS OF LABOR RELATIONS. USA+45 LAW   ECO/DEV
CONSULT WORKER CAP/ISM PAY ADJUD CONTROL EFFICIENCY   ECO/TAC
ORD/FREE...CHARTS 19/20 AFL/CIO NLRB DEPT/LABOR.   LABOR
PAGE 13 E0249   GOV/REL

S60
MANN S.Z.,"POLICY FORMULATION IN THE EXECUTIVE   EXEC
BRANCH: THE TAFT-HARTLEY EXPERIENCE." USA+45 LABOR   GOV/REL
CHIEF INGP/REL 20 NLRB. PAGE 68 E1360   EX/STRUC
                                                       PROB/SOLV

NOBILITY....SEE ELITES

NOBLEMAN E.E. E1553

NOMAD/MAX....MAX NOMAD

NOMADISM....SEE GEOG

NONALIGNED NATIONS....SEE THIRD/WRLD

NON-WHITE....SEE RACE/REL

NONVIOLENT....NONVIOLENCE (CONCEPT)

NORDEN A. E1554

NORDSKOG J.E. E1555

NORGAARD C.A. E1556

NORMS....SEE AVERAGE, ALSO APPROPRIATE VALUES AND DIMENSIONS
         OF GROUPS, STAT, LOG, ETC.

NORTH AFRICA....SEE AFRICA/N, ISLAM

NORTH ATLANTIC FREE TRADE AREA....SEE NAFTA

NORTH ATLANTIC TREATY ORGANIZATION....SEE NATO

NORTH KOREA....SEE KOREA/N

NORTH VIETNAM....SEE VIETNAM/N

NORTH/AMER....NORTH AMERICA, EXCLUSIVE OF CENTRAL AMERICA

NORTH/CAR....NORTH CAROLINA

B30
GREEN F.M..CONSTITUTIONAL DEVELOPMENT IN THE SOUTH   CONSTN
ATLANTIC STATES, 1776-1860: A STUDY IN THE   PROVS
EVOLUTION OF DEMOCRACY. USA-45 ELITES SOCIETY   PLURISM
STRATA ECO/DEV AGRI POL/PAR EX/STRUC LEGIS CT/SYS   REPRESENT
REGION...BIBLIOG 18/19 MARYLAND VIRGINIA GEORGIA
NORTH/CAR SOUTH/CAR. PAGE 46 E0905

B62
US COMMISSION ON CIVIL RIGHTS,EQUAL PROTECTION OF   ORD/FREE
THE LAWS IN NORTH CAROLINA. USA+45 LOC/G NAT/G   RESPECT
CONSULT LEGIS WORKER PROB/SOLV EDU/PROP ADJUD   LAW
CHOOSE DISCRIM HEALTH 20 NEGRO NORTH/CAR   PROVS
CIV/RIGHTS. PAGE 99 E1984

B63
DAY R.E..CIVIL RIGHTS USA: PUBLIC SCHOOLS, SOUTHERN   EDU/PROP

STATES - NORTH CAROLINA, 1963. USA+45 LOC/G NEIGH   ORD/FREE
LEGIS CREATE CT/SYS COERCE DISCRIM ATTIT...QU   RACE/REL
CHARTS 20 NORTH/CAR NEGRO KKK CIV/RIGHTS. PAGE 29   SANCTION
E0579

NORTH/DAK....NORTH DAKOTA

NORTH/US....NORTHERN UNITED STATES

NORTHERN RHODESIA....SEE ZAMBIA

NORTHRUP H.R. E0249

NORTHW/TER....NORTHWEST TERRITORIES, CANADA

NORTHWST/U....NORTHWESTERN UNIVERSITY

NORTON T.J. E1557

NORWAY....SEE ALSO APPROPRIATE TIME/SPACE/CULTURE INDEX

                                                              B35
NORDSKOG J.E.,SOCIAL REFORM IN NORWAY. NORWAY INDUS LABOR
NAT/G POL/PAR LEGIS ADJUD...SOC BIBLIOG SOC/INTEG   ADJUST
20. PAGE 78 E1555

                                                              B53
ORFIELD L.B.,THE GROWTH OF SCANDINAVIAN LAW.   JURID
DENMARK ICELAND NORWAY SWEDEN LAW DIPLOM...BIBLIOG   CT/SYS
9/20. PAGE 79 E1581   NAT/G

                                                              B57
MEYER P.,ADMINISTRATIVE ORGANIZATION: A COMPARATIVE ADMIN
STUDY OF THE ORGANIZATION OF PUBLIC ADMINISTRATION. METH/COMP
DENMARK FRANCE NORWAY SWEDEN UK USA+45 ELITES LOC/G NAT/G
CONSULT LEGIS ADJUD CONTROL LEAD PWR SKILL   CENTRAL
DECISION. PAGE 72 E1449

                                                              B62
SOWLE C.R.,POLICE POWER AND INDIVIDUAL FREEDOM: THE FORCES
QUEST FOR BALANCE. CANADA EUR+WWI ISRAEL NORWAY   ORD/FREE
USA+45 LAW CONSTN SOCIETY CONTROL ROUTINE SANCTION   IDEA/COMP
GP/REL 20 CHINJAP. PAGE 93 E1859

                                                              B64
FRYDENSBERG P.,PEACE-KEEPING: EXPERIENCE AND   INT/ORG
EVALUATION: THE OSLO PAPERS. NORWAY FORCES PLAN   DIPLOM
CONTROL...INT/LAW 20 UN. PAGE 41 E0814   PEACE
                                                     COERCE

                                                              B64
HALLER W.,DER SCHWEDISCHE JUSTITIEOMBUDSMAN.   JURID
DENMARK FINLAND NORWAY SWEDEN LEGIS ADJUD CONTROL   PARL/PROC
PERSON ORD/FREE...NAT/COMP 20 OMBUDSMAN. PAGE 50   ADMIN
E0986   CHIEF

NOTZ R.L. E1558

NOVA/SCOT....NOVA SCOTIA, CANADA

NOVOGROD J.C. E1113

NOVOTNY/A....A. NOVOTNY

NRA....NATIONAL RECOVERY ADMINISTRATION

NSC....NATIONAL SECURITY COUNCIL

NSF....NATIONAL SCIENCE FOUNDATION

NSSF....NATIONAL SOCIAL SCIENCE FOUNDATION

NUC....NATIONAL UNITY COMMITTEE (TURKEY)

NUC/PWR....NUCLEAR POWER, INCLUDING NUCLEAR WEAPONS

                                                              N
POLITICAL SCIENCE QUARTERLY. USA+45 USA-45 LAW   BIBLIOG/A
CONSTN ECO/DEV INT/ORG LOC/G POL/PAR LEGIS LEAD   NAT/G
NUC/PWR...CONCPT 20. PAGE 1 E0013   DIPLOM
                                                     POLICY

                                                              N
FOREIGN AFFAIRS. SPACE WOR+45 WOR-45 CULTURE   BIBLIOG
ECO/UNDEV FINAN NAT/G TEC/DEV INT/TRADE ARMS/CONT   DIPLOM
NUC/PWR...POLICY 20 UN EURATOM ECSC EEC. PAGE 1   INT/ORG
E0021   INT/LAW

                                                              N
AIR UNIVERSITY LIBRARY,INDEX TO MILITARY   BIBLIOG/A
PERIODICALS. FUT SPACE WOR+45 REGION ARMS/CONT   FORCES
NUC/PWR WAR PEACE INT/LAW. PAGE 3 E0056   NAT/G
                                                     DIPLOM

                                                              N19
ATOMIC INDUSTRIAL FORUM,COMMENTARY ON LEGISLATION   NUC/PWR
TO PERMIT PRIVATE OWNERSHIP OF SPECIAL NUCLEAR   MARKET
MATERIAL (PAMPHLET). USA+45 DELIB/GP LEGIS PLAN OWN INDUS
...POLICY 20 AEC CONGRESS. PAGE 6 E0111   LAW

                                                              N19
MEZERIK A.G.,ATOM TESTS AND RADIATION HAZARDS   NUC/PWR
(PAMPHLET). WOR+45 INT/ORG DIPLOM DETER 20 UN   ARMS/CONT
TREATY. PAGE 73 E1452   CONFER
                                                     HEALTH

                                                              N19
MEZERIK AG,OUTER SPACE: UN, US, USSR (PAMPHLET).   SPACE
USSR DELIB/GP FORCES DETER NUC/PWR SOVEREIGN   CONTROL
...POLICY 20 UN TREATY. PAGE 73 E1453   DIPLOM
                                                     INT/ORG

                                                              B45
GALLOWAY E.,ABSTRACTS OF POSTWAR LITERATURE (VOL.   BIBLIOG/A
IV) JAN.-JULY, 1945 NOS. 901-1074. POLAND USA+45   NUC/PWR
USSR WOR+45 INDUS LABOR PLAN ECO/TAC INT/TRADE TAX   NAT/G
EDU/PROP ADMIN COLONIAL INT/LAW. PAGE 42 E0829   DIPLOM

                                                              B45
REVES E.,THE ANATOMY OF PEACE. WOR-45 LAW CULTURE   ACT/RES
NAT/G PLAN TEC/DEV EDU/PROP WAR NAT/LISM ATTIT   CONCPT
ALL/VALS SOVEREIGN...POLICY HUM TIME/SEQ 20.   NUC/PWR
PAGE 84 E1688   PEACE

                                                              N47
FOX W.T.R.,UNITED STATES POLICY IN A TWO POWER   DIPLOM
WORLD. COM USA+45 USSR FORCES DOMIN AGREE NEUTRAL   FOR/AID
NUC/PWR ORD/FREE SOVEREIGN 20 COLD/WAR TREATY   POLICY
EUROPE/W INTERVENT. PAGE 39 E0780

                                                              B55
COMM. STUDY ORGAN. PEACE,REPORTS. WOR-45 ECO/DEV   WOR+45
ECO/UNDEV VOL/ASSN CONSULT FORCES PLAN TEC/DEV   INT/ORG
DOMIN EDU/PROP NUC/PWR ATTIT PWR WEALTH...JURID   ARMS/CONT
STERTYP FAO ILO 20 UN. PAGE 24 E0481

                                                              B58
ATOMIC INDUSTRIAL FORUM,MANAGEMENT AND ATOMIC   NUC/PWR
ENERGY. WOR+45 SEA LAW MARKET NAT/G TEC/DEV INSPECT INDUS
INT/TRADE CONFER PEACE HEALTH...ANTHOL 20. PAGE 6   MGT
E0112   ECO/TAC

                                                              B58
HENKIN L.,ARMS CONTROL AND INSPECTION IN AMERICAN   USA+45
LAW. LAW CONSTN INT/ORG LOC/G MUNIC NAT/G PROVS   JURID
EDU/PROP LEGIT EXEC NUC/PWR KNOWL ORD/FREE...OBS   ARMS/CONT
TOT/POP CONGRESS 20. PAGE 52 E1032

                                                              B58
SOC OF COMP LEGIS AND INT LAW,THE LAW OF THE SEA... INT/LAW
(PAMPHLET). WOR+45 NAT/G INT/TRADE ADJUD CONTROL   INT/ORG
NUC/PWR WAR PEACE ATTIT ORD/FREE...JURID CHARTS 20   DIPLOM
UN TREATY RESOURCE/N. PAGE 92 E1850   SEA

                                                              B59
COMM. STUDY ORGAN. PEACE,ORGANIZING PEACE IN THE   INT/ORG
NUCLEAR AGE. FUT CONSULT DELIB/GP DOMIN ADJUD   ACT/RES
ROUTINE COERCE ORD/FREE...TECHNIC INT/LAW JURID   NUC/PWR
NEW/IDEA UN COLD/WAR 20. PAGE 24 E0483

                                                              B59
HARVARD UNIVERSITY LAW SCHOOL,INTERNATIONAL   NUC/PWR
PROBLEMS OF FINANCIAL PROTECTION AGAINST NUCLEAR   ADJUD
RISK. WOR+45 NAT/G DELIB/GP PROB/SOLV DIPLOM   INDUS
CONTROL ATTIT...POLICY INT/LAW MATH 20. PAGE 51   FINAN
E1009

                                                              B59
MAYDA J.,ATOMIC ENERGY AND LAW. ECO/UNDEV FINAN   NUC/PWR
TEC/DEV FOR/AID EFFICIENCY PRODUC WEALTH...POLICY   L/A+17C
TECHNIC 20. PAGE 70 E1391   LAW
                                                     ADMIN

                                                              B59
U OF MICHIGAN LAW SCHOOL,ATOMS AND THE LAW. USA+45   NUC/PWR
PROVS WORKER PROB/SOLV DIPLOM ADMIN GOV/REL ANTHOL. NAT/G
PAGE 97 E1950   CONTROL
                                                     LAW

                                                              B59
US CONGRESS JT ATOM ENRGY COMM,SELECTED MATERIALS   NAT/G
ON FEDERAL-STATE COOPERATION IN THE ATOMIC ENERGY   NUC/PWR
FIELD. USA+45 LAW LOC/G PROVS CONSULT LEGIS ADJUD   GOV/REL
...POLICY BIBLIOG 20 AEC. PAGE 99 E1991   DELIB/GP

                                                              S59
CORY R.H. JR.,"INTERNATIONAL INSPECTION FROM   STRUCT
PROPOSALS TO REALIZATION." WOR+45 TEC/DEV ECO/TAC   PSY
ADJUD ORD/FREE PWR WEALTH...RECORD VAL/FREE 20.   ARMS/CONT
PAGE 26 E0516   NUC/PWR

E1587

ATOMIC INDUSTRIAL FORUM,ATOMS FOR INDUSTRY: WORLD
FORUM. WOR+45 FINAN COST UTIL...JURID ANTHOL 20.
PAGE 6 E0113
B60 NUC/PWR INDUS PLAN PROB/SOLV

UNITED WORLD FEDERALISTS,UNITED WORLD FEDERALISTS;
PANORAMA OF RECENT BOOKS, FILMS, AND JOURNALS ON
WORLD FEDERATION, THE UN, AND WORLD PEACE. CULTURE
ECO/UNDEV PROB/SOLV FOR/AID ARMS/CONT NUC/PWR
...INT/LAW PHIL/SCI 20 UN. PAGE 98 E1971
B60 BIBLIOG/A DIPLOM INT/ORG PEACE

O'BRIEN W.,"THE ROLE OF FORCE IN THE INTERNATIONAL
JURIDICAL ORDER." WOR+45 NAT/G FORCES DOMIN ADJUD
ARMS/CONT DETER NUC/PWR WAR ATTIT PWR...CATH
INT/LAW JURID CONCPT TREND STERTYP GEN/LAWS 20.
PAGE 78 E1564
S60 INT/ORG COERCE

RHYNE C.S.,"LAW AS AN INSTRUMENT FOR PEACE." FUT
WOR+45 PLAN LEGIT ROUTINE ARMS/CONT NUC/PWR ATTIT
ORD/FREE...JURID METH/CNCPT TREND CON/ANAL HYPO/EXP
COLD/WAR 20. PAGE 84 E1690
S60 ADJUD EDU/PROP INT/LAW PEACE

SANDERS R.,"NUCLEAR DYNAMITE: A NEW DIMENSION IN
FOREIGN POLICY." FUT WOR+45 ECO/DEV CONSULT TEC/DEV
PERCEPT...CONT/OBS TIME/SEQ TREND GEN/LAWS TOT/POP
20 TREATY. PAGE 87 E1745
S60 INDUS PWR DIPLOM NUC/PWR

MACHOWSKI K.,"SELECTED PROBLEMS OF NATIONAL
SOVEREIGNTY WITH REFERENCE TO THE LAW OF OUTER
SPACE." FUT WOR+45 AIR LAW INTELL SOCIETY ECO/DEV
PLAN EDU/PROP DETER DRIVE PERCEPT SOVEREIGN
...POLICY INT/LAW OBS TREND TOT/POP 20. PAGE 67
E1339
S61 UNIV ACT/RES NUC/PWR SPACE

RICHSTEIN A.R.,"LEGAL RULES IN NUCLEAR WEAPONS
EMPLOYMENTS." FUT WOR+45 LAW SOCIETY FORCES PLAN
WEAPON RIGID/FLEX...HEAL CONCPT TREND VAL/FREE 20.
PAGE 85 E1696
S61 NUC/PWR TEC/DEV MORAL ARMS/CONT

DUPRE J.S.,SCIENCE AND THE NATION: POLICY AND
POLITICS. USA+45 LAW ACADEM FORCES ADMIN CIVMIL/REL
GOV/REL EFFICIENCY PEACE...TREND 20 SCI/ADVSRY.
PAGE 34 E0665
B62 R+D INDUS TEC/DEV NUC/PWR

GYORGY A.,PROBLEMS IN INTERNATIONAL RELATIONS. COM
CT/SYS NUC/PWR ALL/IDEOS 20 UN EEC ECSC. PAGE 49
E0966
B62 DIPLOM NEUTRAL BAL/PWR REV

WADSWORTH J.J.,THE PRICE OF PEACE. WOR+45 TEC/DEV
CONTROL NUC/PWR PEACE ATTIT TREATY 20. PAGE 104
E2089
B62 DIPLOM INT/ORG ARMS/CONT POLICY

FALK R.A.,"THE REALITY OF INTERNATIONAL LAW."
WOR+45 NAT/G LEGIT COERCE DETER WAR MORAL ORD/FREE
PWR SOVEREIGN...JURID CONCPT VAL/FREE COLD/WAR 20.
PAGE 36 E0714
S62 INT/ORG ADJUD NUC/PWR INT/LAW

FINKELSTEIN L.S.,"THE UNITED NATIONS AND
ORGANIZATIONS FOR CONTROL OF ARMAMENT." FUT WOR+45
VOL/ASSN DELIB/GP TOP/EX CREATE EDU/PROP LEGIT
ADJUD NUC/PWR ATTIT RIGID/FLEX ORD/FREE...POLICY
DECISION CONCPT OBS TREND GEN/LAWS TOT/POP
COLD/WAR. PAGE 38 E0752
S62 INT/ORG PWR ARMS/CONT

DEENER D.R.,CANADA - UNITED STATES TREATY
RELATIONS. CANADA USA+45 USA-45 NAT/G FORCES PLAN
PROB/SOLV AGREE NUC/PWR...TREND 18/20 TREATY.
PAGE 30 E0603
B63 DIPLOM INT/LAW POLICY

FALK R.A.,LAW, MORALITY, AND WAR IN THE
CONTEMPORARY WORLD. WOR+45 LAW INT/ORG EX/STRUC
FORCES EDU/PROP LEGIT DETER NUC/PWR MORAL ORD/FREE
...JURID TOT/POP 20. PAGE 36 E0715
B63 ADJUD ARMS/CONT PEACE INT/LAW

PACHTER H.M.,COLLISION COURSE; THE CUBAN MISSILE
CRISIS AND COEXISTENCE. CUBA USA+45 DIPLOM
ARMS/CONT PEACE MARXISM...DECISION INT/LAW 20
COLD/WAR KHRUSH/N KENNEDY/JF CASTRO/F. PAGE 79
B63 WAR BAL/PWR NUC/PWR DETER

BOHN L.,"WHOSE NUCLEAR TEST: NON-PHYSICAL
INSPECTION AND TEST BAN." WOR+45 R+D INT/ORG
VOL/ASSN ORD/FREE...GEN/LAWS GEN/METH COLD/WAR 20.
PAGE 13 E0262
S63 ADJUD ARMS/CONT TEC/DEV NUC/PWR

CLEVELAND H.,"CRISIS DIPLOMACY." USA+45 WOR+45 LAW
FORCES TASK NUC/PWR PWR 20. PAGE 23 E0454
S63 DECISION DIPLOM PROB/SOLV POLICY

MCDOUGAL M.S.,"THE SOVIET-CUBAN QUARANTINE AND
SELF-DEFENSE." CUBA USA+45 USSR WOR+45 INT/ORG
NAT/G BAL/PWR NUC/PWR ATTIT...JURID CONCPT. PAGE 70
E1409
S63 ORD/FREE LEGIT SOVEREIGN

MEYROWITZ H.,"LES JURISTES DEVANT L'ARME NUCLEAIRE."
FUT WOR+45 INTELL SOCIETY BAL/PWR DETER WAR...JURID
CONCPT 20. PAGE 72 E1451
S63 ACT/RES ADJUD INT/LAW NUC/PWR

BLOUSTEIN E.J.,NUCLEAR ENERGY, PUBLIC POLICY, AND
THE LAW. USA+45 NAT/G ADJUD ADMIN GP/REL OWN PEACE
ATTIT HEALTH...ANTHOL 20. PAGE 13 E0251
B64 TEC/DEV LAW POLICY NUC/PWR

COHEN M.,LAW AND POLITICS IN SPACE: SPECIFIC AND
URGENT PROBLEMS IN THE LAW OF OUTER SPACE.
CHINA/COM COM USA+45 WOR+45 COM/IND INT/ORG
NAT/G LEGIT NUC/PWR ATTIT BIO/SOC...JURID CONCPT
CONGRESS 20 STALIN/J. PAGE 24 E0464
B64 DELIB/GP LAW INT/LAW SPACE

MCDOUGAL M.S.,STUDIES IN WORLD PUBLIC ORDER. SPACE
SEA INT/ORG CREATE AGREE NUC/PWR...POLICY PHIL/SCI
IDEA/COMP ANTHOL METH 20 UN. PAGE 71 E1411
B64 INT/LAW SOC DIPLOM

NASA,PROCEEDINGS OF CONFERENCE ON THE LAW OF SPACE
AND OF SATELLITE COMMUNICATIONS: CHICAGO 1963. FUT
WOR+45 DELIB/GP PROB/SOLV TEC/DEV CONFER ADJUD
NUC/PWR...POLICY IDEA/COMP 20 NASA. PAGE 76 E1522
B64 SPACE COM/IND LAW DIPLOM

REGALA R.,WORLD PEACE THROUGH DIPLOMACY AND LAW.
S/ASIA WOR+45 ECO/UNDEV INT/ORG FORCES PLAN
PROB/SOLV FOR/AID NUC/PWR WAR...POLICY INT/LAW 20.
PAGE 84 E1679
B64 DIPLOM PEACE ADJUD

SCHWARTZ M.D.,CONFERENCE ON SPACE SCIENCE AND SPACE
LAW. FUT COM/IND NAT/G FORCES ACT/RES PLAN BUDGET
DIPLOM NUC/PWR WEAPON...POLICY ANTHOL 20. PAGE 89
E1788
B64 SPACE LAW PEACE TEC/DEV

US AIR FORCE ACADEMY ASSEMBLY,OUTER SPACE: FINAL
REPORT APRIL 1-4, 1964. FUT USA+45 WOR+45 LAW
DELIB/GP CONFER ARMS/CONT WAR PEACE ATTIT MORAL
...ANTHOL 20 NASA. PAGE 99 E1979
B64 SPACE CIVMIL/REL NUC/PWR DIPLOM

WILLIAMS S.P.,TOWARD A GENUINE WORLD SECURITY
SYSTEM (PAMPHLET). WOR+45 INT/ORG FORCES PLAN
NUC/PWR ORD/FREE...INT/LAW CONCPT UN PRESIDENT.
PAGE 106 E2123
B64 BIBLIOG/A ARMS/CONT DIPLOM PEACE

CRANE R.D.,"BASIC PRINCIPLES IN SOVIET SPACE LAW."
FUT WOR+45 AIR INT/ORG DIPLOM DOMIN ARMS/CONT
COERCE NUC/PWR PEACE ATTIT DRIVE PWR...INT/LAW
METH/CNCPT NEW/IDEA OBS TREND GEN/LAWS VAL/FREE
MARX/KARL 20. PAGE 27 E0544
S64 COM LAW USSR SPACE

KARPOV P.V.,"PEACEFUL COEXISTENCE AND INTERNATIONAL
LAW." WOR+45 LAW SOCIETY INT/ORG VOL/ASSN FORCES
CREATE CAP/ISM DIPLOM ADJUD NUC/PWR PEACE MORAL
ORD/FREE PWR MARXISM...MARXIST JURID CONCPT OBS
TREND COLD/WAR MARX/KARL 20. PAGE 59 E1186
S64 COM ATTIT INT/LAW USSR

MAGGS P.B.,"SOVIET VIEWPOINT ON NUCLEAR WEAPONS IN
INTERNATIONAL LAW." USSR WOR+45 INT/ORG FORCES
DIPLOM ARMS/CONT ATTIT ORD/FREE PWR...POLICY JURID
CONCPT OBS TREND CON/ANAL GEN/LAWS VAL/FREE 20.
PAGE 67 E1347
S64 COM LAW INT/LAW NUC/PWR

B65

GOTLIEB A.,DISARMAMENT AND INTERNATIONAL LAW* A   INT/LAW
STUDY OF THE ROLE OF LAW IN THE DISARMAMENT   INT/ORG
PROCESS. USA+45 USSR PROB/SOLV CONFER ADMIN ROUTINE   ARMS/CONT
NUC/PWR ORD/FREE SOVEREIGN UN TREATY. PAGE 45 E0893   IDEA/COMP

B65

LASLEY J.,THE WAR SYSTEM AND YOU. LAW FORCES   MORAL
ARMS/CONT NUC/PWR NAT/LISM ATTIT...MAJORIT   PERSON
IDEA/COMP UN WORSHIP. PAGE 63 E1261   DIPLOM
                                                        WAR

S65

BROWNLIE I.,"SOME LEGAL ASPECTS OF THE USE OF   LAW
NUCLEAR WEAPONS." UK NEUTRAL DETER UN TREATY.   NUC/PWR
PAGE 16 E0317   WAR
                                                        INT/LAW

S65

FOX A.B.,"NATO AND CONGRESS." CONSTN DELIB/GP   CONTROL
EX/STRUC FORCES TOP/EX BUDGET NUC/PWR GOV/REL   DIPLOM
...GP/COMP CONGRESS NATO TREATY. PAGE 39 E0779

S65

HIBBS A.R.,"SPACE TECHNOLOGY* THE THREAT AND THE   SPACE
PROMISE." FUT VOL/ASSN TEC/DEV NUC/PWR COST   ARMS/CONT
EFFICIENCY UTIL UN TREATY. PAGE 52 E1038   PREDICT

S65

MARTIN A.,"PROLIFERATION." FUT WOR+45 PROB/SOLV   RECORD
REGION ADJUST...PREDICT NAT/COMP UN TREATY. PAGE 69   NUC/PWR
E1372   ARMS/CONT
                                                        VOL/ASSN

C65

SEARA M.V.,"COSMIC INTERNATIONAL LAW." LAW ACADEM   SPACE
ACT/RES DIPLOM COLONIAL CONTROL NUC/PWR SOVEREIGN   INT/LAW
...GEN/LAWS BIBLIOG UN. PAGE 90 E1799   IDEA/COMP
                                                        INT/ORG

B66

INTL ATOMIC ENERGY AGENCY,INTERNATIONAL CONVENTIONS   DIPLOM
ON CIVIL LIABILITY FOR NUCLEAR DAMAGE. FUT WOR+45   INT/ORG
ADJUD WAR COST PEACE SOVEREIGN...JURID 20. PAGE 57   DELIB/GP
E1135   NUC/PWR

B66

JACOBSON H.K.,DIPLOMATS, SCIENTISTS, AND   DIPLOM
POLITICIANS* THE UNITED STATES AND THE NUCLEAR TEST   ARMS/CONT
BAN NEGOTIATIONS. USA+45 USSR ACT/RES PLAN CONFER   TECHRACY
DETER NUC/PWR CONSEN ORD/FREE...INT TREATY. PAGE 57   INT/ORG
E1146

B66

OBERMANN E.,VERTEIDIGUNG PER FREIHEIT. GERMANY/W   FORCES
WOR+45 INT/ORG COERCE NUC/PWR WEAPON MARXISM 20 UN   ORD/FREE
NATO WARSAW/P TREATY. PAGE 78 E1571   WAR
                                                        PEACE

B66

SALTER L.M.,RESOLUTION OF INTERNATIONAL CONFLICT.   PROB/SOLV
USA+45 INT/ORG SECT DIPLOM ECO/TAC FOR/AID DETER   PEACE
NUC/PWR WAR 20. PAGE 87 E1743   INT/LAW
                                                        POLICY

B66

UNITED NATIONS,INTERNATIONAL SPACE BIBLIOGRAPHY.   BIBLIOG
FUT INT/ORG TEC/DEV DIPLOM ARMS/CONT NUC/PWR   SPACE
...JURID SOC UN. PAGE 98 E1969   PEACE
                                                        R+D

B66

WAINHOUSE D.W.,INTERNATIONAL PEACE OBSERVATION: A   PEACE
HISTORY AND FORECAST. INT/ORG PROB/SOLV BAL/PWR   DIPLOM
AGREE ARMS/CONT COERCE NUC/PWR...PREDICT METH/COMP
20 UN LEAGUE/NAT OAS TREATY. PAGE 104 E2092

B66

YOUNG W.,EXISTING MECHANISMS OF ARMS CONTROL.   ARMS/CONT
PROC/MFG OP/RES DIPLOM TASK CENTRAL...MGT TREATY.   ADMIN
PAGE 108 E2165   NUC/PWR
                                                        ROUTINE

S66

BROWNLIE I.,"NUCLEAR PROLIFERATION* SOME PROBLEMS   NUC/PWR
OF CONTROL." USA+45 USSR ECO/UNDEV INT/ORG FORCES   ARMS/CONT
TEC/DEV REGION CONSEN...RECORD TREATY. PAGE 16   VOL/ASSN
E0318   ORD/FREE

B67

GARCIA ROBLES A.,THE DENUCLEARIZATION OF LATIN   NUC/PWR
AMERICA (TRANS. BY MARJORIE URQUIDI). LAW PLAN   ARMS/CONT
DIPLOM...ANTHOL 20 TREATY UN. PAGE 42 E0833   L/A+17C
                                                        INT/ORG

B67

MARTIN L.W.,THE SEA IN MODERN STRATEGY. LAW ECO/TAC   ROLE
WAR. PAGE 69 E1374   PWR
                                                        NUC/PWR
                                                        DIPLOM

B67

MCBRIDE J.H.,THE TEST BAN TREATY: MILITARY,   ARMS/CONT
TECHNOLOGICAL, AND POLITICAL IMPLICATIONS. USA+45   DIPLOM
USSR DELIB/GP FORCES LEGIS TEC/DEV BAL/PWR TREATY.   NUC/PWR
PAGE 70 E1399

B67

POGANY A.H.,POLITICAL SCIENCE AND INTERNATIONAL   BIBLIOG
RELATIONS, BOOKS RECOMMENDED FOR AMERICAN CATHOLIC   DIPLOM
COLLEGE LIBRARIES. INT/ORG LOC/G NAT/G FORCES
BAL/PWR ECO/TAC NUC/PWR...CATH INT/LAW TREATY 20.
PAGE 81 E1622

B67

UNIVERSAL REFERENCE SYSTEM,PUBLIC POLICY AND THE   BIBLIOG/A
MANAGEMENT OF SCIENCE (VOLUME IX). FUT SPACE WOR+45   POLICY
LAW NAT/G TEC/DEV CONTROL NUC/PWR GOV/REL   MGT
...COMPUT/IR GEN/METH. PAGE 99 E1975   PHIL/SCI

B67

US SENATE COMM ON FOREIGN REL,TREATY ON OUTER   SPACE
SPACE. WOR+45 AIR FORCES PROB/SOLV NUC/PWR SENATE   DIPLOM
TREATY UN. PAGE 101 E2032   ARMS/CONT
                                                      LAW

B67

US SENATE COMM ON FOREIGN REL,UNITED STATES   ARMS/CONT
ARMAMENT AND DISARMAMENT PROBLEMS. USA+45 AIR   WEAPON
BAL/PWR DIPLOM FOR/AID NUC/PWR ORD/FREE SENATE   FORCES
TREATY. PAGE 102 E2035   PROB/SOLV

S67

EYRAUD M.,"LA FRANCE FACE A UN EVENTUEL TRAITE DE   NUC/PWR
NON DISSEMINATION DES ARMES NUCLEAIRES." FRANCE   ARMS/CONT
USA+45 EXTR/IND INDUS R+D INT/ORG ACT/RES TEC/DEV   POLICY
AGREE PRODUC ATTIT 20 TREATY AEC EURATOM. PAGE 36
E0708

NUCLEAR POWER....SEE NUC/PWR

NUCLEAR WAR....SEE NUC/PWR+COERCE, WAR

NUMELIN R. E1559

NUMERICAL INDICES....SEE INDEX

NUREMBERG....NUREMBERG WAR TRIALS; SEE ALSO WAR/TRIAL

B55

BENTON W.E.,NUREMBERG: GERMAN VIEWS OF THE WAR   CRIME
TRIALS. EUR+WWI GERMANY VOL/ASSN LEAD PARTIC COERCE   WAR
INGP/REL RACE/REL TOTALISM SUPEGO ORD/FREE...ANTHOL   LAW
NUREMBERG. PAGE 10 E0201   JURID

B61

WECHSLER H.,PRINCIPLES, POLITICS AND FUNDAMENTAL   CT/SYS
LAW: SELECTED ESSAYS. USA+45 USA-45 LAW SOCIETY   CONSTN
NAT/G PROVS DELIB/GP EX/STRUC ACT/RES LEGIT PERSON   INT/LAW
KNOWL PWR...JURID 20 NUREMBERG. PAGE 105 E2106

B62

HEYDECKER J.J.,THE NUREMBERG TRIAL: HISTORY OF NAZI   LAW
GERMANY AS REVEALED THROUGH THE TESTIMONY AT   CRIME
NUREMBERG. EUR+WWI GERMANY VOL/ASSN LEAD COERCE   PARTIC
CROWD INGP/REL RACE/REL SUPEGO ORD/FREE...CONCPT 20   TOTALISM
NAZI ANTI/SEMIT NUREMBERG JEWS. PAGE 52 E1036

NUSSBAUM D. E1560

NWOGUGU E.I. E1561

NYASALAND....SEE MALAWI

NYATURU....NYATURU, A TRIBE OF TANGANYIKA

NYC....NEW YORK CITY

NYC BAR ASSOCIATION RECORD E1562

O'BRIEN F.W. E1563

O'BRIEN W. E1564

O'BRIEN W.V. E1565

O'CONNELL D.P. E1566

O'HIGGINS P. E1567

O'NEIL R.M. E1598

O'NEILL C.E. E1568

O'NEILL J.M. E1569

OAS....ORGANIZATION OF AMERICAN STATES; SEE ALSO INT/ORG,
VOL/ASSN

N19
PAN AMERICAN UNION,INFORME DE LA MISION DE   CHOOSE
ASISTENCIA TECNICA DE LA OEA A LA REPUBLICA DE   SUFF
HONDURAS EN MATERIA ELECTORAL (PAMPHLET). HONDURAS   POL/PAR
CONSTN ORD/FREE...JURID OBS 20 OAS. PAGE 80 E1595   NAT/G

B55
BURR R.N.,DOCUMENTS ON INTER-AMERICAN COOPERATION: BIBLIOG
VOL. I, 1810-1881; VOL. II, 1881-1948. DELIB/GP   DIPLOM
BAL/PWR INT/TRADE REPRESENT NAT/LISM PEACE HABITAT   INT/ORG
ORD/FREE PWR SOVEREIGN...INT/LAW 20 OAS. PAGE 18   L/A+17C
E0345

B56
SOHN L.B.,BASIC DOCUMENTS OF THE UNITED NATIONS.   DELIB/GP
WOR+45 LAW INT/ORG LEGIT EXEC ROUTINE CHOOSE PWR   CONSTN
...JURID CONCPT GEN/LAWS ANTHOL UN TOT/POP OAS FAO
ILO 20. PAGE 92 E1853

B57
JENKS C.W.,THE INTERNATIONAL PROTECTION OF TRADE   LABOR
UNION FREEDOM. FUT WOR+45 WOR-45 VOL/ASSN DELIB/GP   INT/ORG
CT/SYS REGION ROUTINE...JURID METH/CNCPT RECORD
TIME/SEQ CHARTS ILO WORK OAS 20. PAGE 58 E1153

B58
BUGEDA LANZAS J.,A STATEMENT OF THE LAWS OF CUBA IN   JURID
MATTERS AFFECTING BUSINESS (2ND ED. REV.,   NAT/G
ENLARGED). CUBA L/A+17C LAW FINAN FAM LEGIS ACT/RES   INDUS
ADMIN GP/REL...BIBLIOG 20 OAS. PAGE 17 E0327   WORKER

B59
GOMEZ ROBLES J.,A STATEMENT OF THE LAWS OF   JURID
GUATEMALA IN MATTERS AFFECTING BUSINESS (2ND ED.   NAT/G
REV., ENLARGED). GUATEMALA L/A+17C LAW FINAN FAM   INDUS
WORKER ACT/RES DIPLOM ADJUD ADMIN GP/REL 20 OAS.   LEGIT
PAGE 44 E0881

B61
MECHAM J.L.,THE UNITED STATES AND INTER-AMERICAN   DIPLOM
SECURITY, 1889-1960. L/A+17C USA+45 USA-45 CONSTN   WAR
FORCES INT/TRADE PEACE TOTALISM ATTIT...JURID 19/20   ORD/FREE
UN OAS. PAGE 72 E1432   INT/ORG

B62
ALEXANDROWICZ C.H.,WORLD ECONOMIC AGENCIES: LAW AND   INT/LAW
PRACTICE. WOR+45 DIST/IND FINAN LABOR CONSULT   INT/ORG
INT/TRADE TARIFFS REPRESENT HEALTH...JURID 20 UN   DIPLOM
GATT EEC OAS ECSC. PAGE 3 E0063   ADJUD

B62
JENKS C.W.,THE PROPER LAW OF INTERNATIONAL   LAW
ORGANISATIONS. DIPLOM LEGIT AGREE CT/SYS SANCTION   INT/ORG
REPRESENT SOVEREIGN...GEN/LAWS 20 UN UNESCO ILO   ADJUD
NATO OAS. PAGE 58 E1158   INT/LAW

S62
FENWICK C.G.,"ISSUES AT PUNTA DEL ESTE: NON-   INT/ORG
INTERVENTION VS COLLECTIVE SECURITY." L/A+17C   CUBA
USA+45 VOL/ASSN DELIB/GP ECO/TAC LEGIT ADJUD REGION
ORD/FREE OAS COLD/WAR 20. PAGE 37 E0738

B63
BOWETT D.W.,THE LAW OF INTERNATIONAL INSTITUTIONS.   INT/ORG
WOR+45 WOR-45 CONSTN DELIB/GP EX/STRUC JUDGE   ADJUD
EDU/PROP LEGIT CT/SYS EXEC ROUTINE RIGID/FLEX   DIPLOM
ORD/FREE PWR...JURID CONCPT ORG/CHARTS GEN/METH
LEAGUE/NAT OAS OEEC 20 UN. PAGE 14 E0277

B66
WAINHOUSE D.W.,INTERNATIONAL PEACE OBSERVATION: A   PEACE
HISTORY AND FORECAST. INT/ORG PROB/SOLV BAL/PWR   DIPLOM
AGREE ARMS/CONT COERCE NUC/PWR...PREDICT METH/COMP
20 UN LEAGUE/NAT OAS TREATY. PAGE 104 E2092

B67
BAILEY N.A.,LATIN AMERICA IN WORLD POLITICS. PWR   L/A+17C
CONSERVE MARXISM...INT/LAW TREND BIBLIOG/A T OAS   DIPLOM
COLD/WAR. PAGE 7 E0134   INT/ORG
                                                          ATTIT

B67
SLATER J.,THE OAS AND UNITED STATES FOREIGN POLICY.   INT/ORG
KOREA L/A+17C USA+45 VOL/ASSN RISK COERCE PEACE   DIPLOM
ORD/FREE MARXISM...TREND 20 OAS. PAGE 92 E1838   ALL/IDEOS
                                                          ADJUD

S67
TOMASEK R.D.,"THE CHILEAN-BOLIVIAN LAUCA RIVER   INT/ORG

DISPUTE AND THE OAS." CHILE L/A+17C PROB/SOLV ADJUD DIPLOM
CONTROL PEACE 20 BOLIV OAS. PAGE 96 E1930   GEOG
                                                          WAR

B68
GREGG R.W.,INTERNATIONAL ORGANIZATION IN THE   INT/ORG
WESTERN HEMISPHERE. L/A+17C USA+45 CULTURE PLAN   DIPLOM
DOMIN AGREE CONTROL DETER PWR...GEOG 20 OAS TREATY.   ECO/UNDEV
PAGE 46 E0913

OATMAN M.E. E0235

OAU....ORGANIZATION FOR AFRICAN UNITY

S66
GREEN L.C.,"RHODESIAN OIL: BOOTLEGGERS OR PIRATES?"   INT/TRADE
AFR RHODESIA UK WOR+45 INT/ORG NAT/G DIPLOM LEGIT   SANCTION
COLONIAL SOVEREIGN 20 UN OAU. PAGE 46 E0907   INT/LAW
                                                          POLICY

OBERER W.E. E1570

OBERLIN....OBERLIN, OHIO

OBERMANN E. E1571

OBESITY....SEE HEALTH, EATING

OBJECTIVE....OBJECTIVE, OBJECTIVITY

N19
RALSTON A.,A FRESH LOOK AT LEGISLATIVE   APPORT
APPORTIONMENT IN NEW JERSEY (PAMPHLET). USA+45   REPRESENT
CONSTN LEGIS OBJECTIVE...MATH METH 20 NEW/JERSEY.   PROVS
PAGE 83 E1671   JURID

S36
CORWIN E.S.,"THE CONSTITUTION AS INSTRUMENT AND AS   CONSTN
SYMBOL." USA+45 ECO/DEV INDUS CAP/ISM SANCTION   LAW
RIGID/FLEX ORD/FREE LAISSEZ OBJECTIVE 20 CONGRESS   ADJUD
SUPREME/CT. PAGE 26 E0512   PWR

S48
BRADEN G.D.,"THE SEARCH FOR OBJECTIVITY IN   CONSTN
CONSTITUTIONAL LAW" (BMR)" USA+45 USA-45 LAW NAT/G   CT/SYS
CONTROL ORD/FREE PWR OBJECTIVE...JURID 20   IDEA/COMP
SUPREME/CT. PAGE 15 E0283   POLICY

B57
KELSEN H.,WHAT IS JUSTICE. WOR+45 WOR-45...CONCPT   JURID
BIBLE. PAGE 60 E1201   ORD/FREE
                                                          OBJECTIVE
                                                          PHIL/SCI

B61
WASSERSTROM R.A.,THE JUDICIAL DECISION: TOWARD A   JUDGE
THEORY OF LEGAL JUSTIFICATION. ACT/RES RATIONAL   LAW
PERCEPT KNOWL OBJECTIVE...DECISION JURID. PAGE 105   ADJUD
E2102

B64
ENGEL S.,LAW, STATE, AND INTERNATIONAL LEGAL ORDER.   JURID
WOR+45 NAT/G ORD/FREE RELATISM...INT/LAW IDEA/COMP   OBJECTIVE
ANTHOL 20 KELSEN/H. PAGE 35 E0690   CONCPT
                                                          DEBATE

OBLIGATION....SEE SUPEGO

OBS....OBSERVATION; SEE ALSO DIRECT OBSERVATION METHOD
INDEX, P. XIV

B'
LALL A.S.,NEGOTIATING DISARMAMENT* THE EIGHTEEN   OBS
NATION DISARMAMENT CONFERENCE* THE FIRST TWO YEARS,   ARMS/CONT
1962-1964. ASIA FRANCE INDIA USA+45 USSR PROB/SOLV   DIPLOM
ADJUD NEUTRAL ATTIT...IDEA/COMP COLD/WAR. PAGE 62   OP/RES
E1246

B00
BERNARD M.,FOUR LECTURES ON SUBJECTS CONNECTED WITH   LAW
DIPLOMACY. WOR-45 NAT/G VOL/ASSN RIGID/FLEX MORAL   ATTIT
PWR...JURID OBS GEN/LAWS GEN/METH 20 TREATY.   DIPLOM
PAGE 11 E0209

B00
MAINE H.S.,INTERNATIONAL LAW. MOD/EUR UNIV SOCIETY   INT/ORG
STRUCT ACT/RES EXEC WAR ATTIT PERSON ALL/VALS   LAW
...POLICY JURID CONCPT OBS TIME/SEQ TOT/POP.   PEACE
PAGE 68 E1349   INT/LAW

B11
PHILLIPSON C.,THE INTERNATIONAL LAW AND CUSTOM OF   INT/ORG
ANCIENT GREECE AND ROME. MEDIT-7 UNIV INTELL   LAW
SOCIETY STRUCT NAT/G LEGIS EXEC PERSON...CONCPT OBS   INT/LAW
CON/ANAL ROM/EMP. PAGE 80 E1614

ROOT E., "THE EFFECT OF DEMOCRACY ON INTERNATIONAL LAW." USA-45 WOR-45 INTELL SOCIETY INT/ORG NAT/G CONSULT ACT/RES CREATE PLAN EDU/PROP PEACE SKILL ...CONCPT METH/CNCPT OBS 20. PAGE 85 E1712
S17
LEGIS
JURID
INT/LAW

PAN AMERICAN UNION, INFORME DE LA MISION DE ASISTENCIA TECNICA DE LA OEA A LA REPUBLICA DE HONDURAS EN MATERIA ELECTORAL (PAMPHLET). HONDURAS CONSTN ORD/FREE...JURID OBS 20 OAS. PAGE 80 E1595
N19
CHOOSE
SUFF
POL/PAR
NAT/G

STOWELL E.C., INTERVENTION IN INTERNATIONAL LAW. UNIV LAW SOCIETY INT/ORG ACT/RES PLAN LEGIT ROUTINE WAR...JURID OBS GEN/LAWS 20. PAGE 94 E1884
B21
BAL/PWR
SOVEREIGN

FEIS H., "RESEARCH ACTIVITIES OF THE LEAGUE OF NATIONS." EUR+WWI WOR-45 R+D INT/ORG CT/SYS ARMS/CONT WEALTH...OBS RECORD LEAGUE/NAT ILO 20. PAGE 37 E0729
L29
CONSULT
KNOWL
PEACE

STOWELL E.C., INTERNATIONAL LAW. FUT UNIV WOR-45 SOCIETY CONSULT EX/STRUC FORCES ACT/RES PLAN DIPLOM EDU/PROP LEGIT DISPL PWR SKILL...POLICY CONCPT OBS TREND TOT/POP 20. PAGE 94 E1885
B31
INT/ORG
ROUTINE
INT/LAW

CULVER D.C., METHODOLOGY OF SOCIAL SCIENCE RESEARCH: A BIBLIOGRAPHY. LAW CULTURE...CRIMLGY GEOG STAT OBS INT QU HIST/WRIT CHARTS 20. PAGE 28 E0550
B36
BIBLIOG/A
METH
SOC

CLEMMER D., "LEADERSHIP PHENOMENA IN A PRISON COMMUNITY." NEIGH PLAN CHOOSE PERSON ROLE...OBS INT. PAGE 23 E0452
S38
PUB/INST
CRIMLGY
LEAD
CLIENT

PUTTKAMMER E.W., WAR AND THE LAW. UNIV USA-45 CONSTN CULTURE SOCIETY NAT/G POL/PAR ROUTINE ALL/VALS ...JURID CONCPT OBS WORK VAL/FREE 20. PAGE 83 E1664
B44
INT/ORG
LAW
WAR
INT/LAW

WRIGHT Q., "CONSTITUTIONAL PROCEDURES OF THE US FOR CARRYING OUT OBLIGATIONS FOR MILITARY SANCTIONS." EUR+WWI FUT USA-45 WOR-45 CONSTN INTELL NAT/G CONSULT EX/STRUC LEGIS ROUTINE DRIVE...POLICY JURID CONCPT OBS TREND TOT/POP 20. PAGE 108 E2153
S44
TOP/EX
FORCES
INT/LAW
WAR

GORDON D.L., THE HIDDEN WEAPON: THE STORY OF ECONOMIC WARFARE. EUR+WWI USA-45 LAW FINAN INDUS NAT/G CONSULT FORCES PLAN DOMIN PWR WEALTH ...INT/LAW CONCPT OBS TOT/POP NAZI 20. PAGE 45 E0891
B47
INT/ORG
ECO/TAC
INT/TRADE
WAR

ALEXANDER L., "WAR CRIMES, THEIR SOCIAL-PSYCHOLOGICAL ASPECTS." EUR+WWI GERMANY LAW CULTURE ELITES KIN POL/PAR PUB/INST FORCES DOMIN EDU/PROP COERCE CRIME ATTIT SUPEGO HEALTH MORAL PWR FASCISM ...PSY OBS TREND GEN/LAWS NAZI 20. PAGE 3 E0061
S48
DRIVE
WAR

KIRK G., "MATERIALS FOR THE STUDY OF INTERNATIONAL RELATIONS." FUT UNIV WOR+45 INTELL EDU/PROP ROUTINE PEACE ATTIT...INT/LAW JURID CONCPT OBS. PAGE 61 E1219
S49
INT/ORG
ACT/RES
DIPLOM

MACIVER R.M., GREAT EXPRESSIONS OF HUMAN RIGHTS. LAW CONSTN CULTURE INTELL SOCIETY R+D INT/ORG ATTIT DRIVE...JURID OBS HIST/WRIT GEN/LAWS. PAGE 67 E1340
B50
UNIV
CONCPT

COHEN M.B., "PERSONALITY AS A FACTOR IN ADMINISTRATIVE DECISIONS." ADJUD PERS/REL ANOMIE SUPEGO...OBS SELF/OBS INT. PAGE 24 E0465
S51
PERSON
ADMIN
PROB/SOLV
PSY

MANGONE G., A SHORT HISTORY OF INTERNATIONAL ORGANIZATION. MOD/EUR USA+45 USA-45 WOR+45 WOR-45 LAW LEGIS CREATE LEGIT ROUTINE RIGID/FLEX PWR ...JURID CONCPT OBS TIME/SEQ STERTYP GEN/LAWS UN TOT/POP VAL/FREE 18/20. PAGE 68 E1359
B54
INT/ORG
INT/LAW

WASSENBERGH H.A., POST-WAR INTERNATIONAL CIVIL AVIATION POLICY AND THE LAW OF THE AIR. WOR+45 AIR INT/ORG DOMIN LEGIT PEACE ORD/FREE...POLICY JURID NEW/IDEA OBS TIME/SEQ TREND CHARTS 20 TREATY.
B57
COM/IND
NAT/G
INT/LAW

PAGE 105 E2101

HENKIN L., ARMS CONTROL AND INSPECTION IN AMERICAN LAW. LAW CONSTN INT/ORG LOC/G MUNIC NAT/G PROVS EDU/PROP LEGIT EXEC NUC/PWR KNOWL ORD/FREE...OBS TOT/POP CONGRESS 20. PAGE 52 E1032
B58
USA+45
JURID
ARMS/CONT

MACKENZIE W.J.M., FREE ELECTIONS: AN ELEMENTARY TEXTBOOK. WOR+45 NAT/G POL/PAR LEGIS TOP/EX EDU/PROP LEGIT CT/SYS ATTIT PWR...OBS CHARTS STERTYP T CONGRESS PARLIAMENT 20. PAGE 67 E1342
B58
EX/STRUC
CHOOSE

CHAPMAN B., "THE FRENCH CONSEIL D'ETAT." FRANCE NAT/G CONSULT OP/RES PROB/SOLV PWR...OBS 20. PAGE 21 E0421
S59
ADMIN
LAW
CT/SYS
LEGIS

JENNINGS R., PROGRESS OF INTERNATIONAL LAW. FUT WOR+45 WOR-45 SOCIETY NAT/G VOL/ASSN DELIB/GP DIPLOM EDU/PROP LEGIT COERCE DRIVE MORAL ORD/FREE...JURID CONCPT OBS TIME/SEQ TREND GEN/LAWS. PAGE 58 E1164
B60
INT/ORG
LAW
INT/LAW

BEDFORD S., THE FACES OF JUSTICE: A TRAVELLER'S REPORT. AUSTRIA FRANCE GERMANY/W SWITZERLND UK UNIV WOR+45 WOR-45 CULTURE PARTIC GOV/REL MORAL...JURID OBS GOV/COMP 20. PAGE 9 E0174
B61
CT/SYS
ORD/FREE
PERSON
LAW

MACHOWSKI K., "SELECTED PROBLEMS OF NATIONAL SOVEREIGNTY WITH REFERENCE TO THE LAW OF OUTER SPACE." FUT WOR+45 AIR LAW INTELL SOCIETY ECO/DEV PLAN EDU/PROP DETER DRIVE PERCEPT SOVEREIGN ...POLICY INT/LAW OBS TREND TOT/POP 20. PAGE 67 E1339
S61
UNIV
ACT/RES
NUC/PWR
SPACE

MILLER E., "LEGAL ASPECTS OF UN ACTION IN THE CONGO." AFR CULTURE ADMIN PEACE DRIVE RIGID/FLEX ORD/FREE...WELF/ST JURID OBS UN CONGO 20. PAGE 73 E1458
S61
INT/ORG
LEGIT

ASSOCIATION BAR OF NYC, REPORT ON ADMISSION PROCEDURES TO NEW YORK STATE MENTAL HOSPITALS. LAW CONSTN INGP/REL RESPECT...PSY OBS RECORD. PAGE 6 E0108
B62
PUB/INST
HEALTH
CLIENT
ROUTINE

ROSENNE S., THE WORLD COURT: WHAT IT IS AND HOW IT WORKS. WOR+45 WOR-45 LAW CONSTN JUDGE EDU/PROP LEGIT ROUTINE CHOOSE PEACE ORD/FREE...JURID OBS TIME/SEQ CHARTS UN TOT/POP VAL/FREE 20. PAGE 86 E1717
B62
INT/ORG
ADJUD
INT/LAW

TRISKA J.F., THE THEORY, LAW, AND POLICY OF SOVIET TREATIES. WOR+45 WOR-45 CONSTN INT/ORG NAT/G VOL/ASSN DELIB/GP LEGIS LEGIT COERCE ATTIT PWR RESPECT ...POLICY JURID CONCPT OBS SAMP TIME/SEQ TREND GEN/LAWS 20. PAGE 97 E1941
B62
COM
LAW
INT/LAW
USSR

NIZARD L., "CUBAN QUESTION AND SECURITY COUNCIL." L/A+17C USA+45 ECO/UNDEV NAT/G POL/PAR DELIB/GP ECO/TAC PWR...RELATIV OBS TIME/SEQ TREND GEN/LAWS UN 20 UN. PAGE 77 E1551
L62
INT/ORG
JURID
DIPLOM
CUBA

STEIN E., "MR HAMMARSKJOLD, THE CHARTER LAW AND THE FUTURE ROLE OF THE UNITED NATIONS SECRETARY-GENERAL." WOR+45 WOR-45 CONSTN INT/ORG DELIB/GP FORCES TOP/EX BAL/PWR LEGIT ROUTINE RIGID/FLEX PWR ...POLICY JURID OBS STERTYP UN COLD/WAR 20 HAMMARSK/D. PAGE 93 E1869
L62
CONCPT
BIOG

FINKELSTEIN L.S., "THE UNITED NATIONS AND ORGANIZATIONS FOR CONTROL OF ARMAMENT." FUT WOR+45 VOL/ASSN DELIB/GP TOP/EX CREATE EDU/PROP LEGIT ADJUD NUC/PWR ATTIT RIGID/FLEX ORD/FREE...POLICY DECISION CONCPT OBS TREND GEN/LAWS TOT/POP COLD/WAR. PAGE 38 E0752
S62
INT/ORG
PWR
ARMS/CONT

SCHACHTER O., "DAG HAMMARSKJOLD AND THE RELATION OF LAW TO POLITICS." FUT WOR+45 INT/ORG CONSULT PLAN TEC/DEV BAL/PWR DIPLOM LEGIT ATTIT PERCEPT ORD/FREE ...POLICY JURID CONCPT OBS TESTS STERTYP GEN/LAWS 20 HAMMARSK/D. PAGE 87 E1751
S62
ACT/RES
ADJUD

S63

GERHARD H.,"COMMODITY TRADE STABILIZATION THROUGH   PLAN
INTERNATIONAL AGREEMENTS." WOR+45 ECO/DEV ECO/UNDEV   ECO/TAC
NAT/G ROUTINE ORD/FREE...INT/LAW OBS TREND GEN/METH   INT/TRADE
TOT/POP 20. PAGE 43 E0850

B64

GARDNER R.N.,IN PURSUIT OF WORLD ORDER* US FOREIGN   OBS
POLICY AND INTERNATIONAL ORGANIZATIONS. USA+45 USSR   INT/ORG
ECO/UNDEV FORCES LEGIS DIPLOM FOR/AID INT/TRADE   ALL/VALS
PEACE...INT/LAW PREDICT UN. PAGE 42 E0839

B64

IKLE F.C.,HOW NATIONS NEGOTIATE. COM EUR+WWI USA+45   NAT/G
INTELL INT/ORG VOL/ASSN DELIB/GP ACT/RES CREATE   PWR
DOMIN EDU/PROP ADJUD ROUTINE ATTIT PERSON ORD/FREE   POLICY
RESPECT SKILL...PSY SOC OBS VAL/FREE. PAGE 56 E1122

S64

CRANE R.D.,"BASIC PRINCIPLES IN SOVIET SPACE LAW."   COM
FUT WOR+45 AIR INT/ORG DIPLOM DOMIN ARMS/CONT   LAW
COERCE NUC/PWR PEACE ATTIT DRIVE PWR...INT/LAW   USSR
METH/CNCPT NEW/IDEA OBS TREND GEN/LAWS VAL/FREE   SPACE
MARX/KARL 20. PAGE 27 E0544

S64

GARDNER R.N.,"THE SOVIET UNION AND THE UNITED   COM
NATIONS." WOR+45 FINAN POL/PAR VOL/ASSN FORCES   INT/ORG
ECO/TAC DOMIN EDU/PROP LEGIT ADJUD ADMIN ARMS/CONT   USSR
COERCE ATTIT ALL/VALS...POLICY MAJORIT CONCPT OBS
TIME/SEQ TREND STERTYP UN. PAGE 42 E0838

S64

GINSBURGS G.,"WARS OF NATIONAL LIBERATION - THE   COERCE
SOVIET THESIS." COM USSR WOR+45 LAW CULTURE   CONCPT
INT/ORG DIPLOM LEGIT COLONIAL GUERRILLA WAR   INT/LAW
NAT/LISM ATTIT PERSON MORAL PWR...JURID OBS TREND   REV
MARX/KARL 20. PAGE 44 E0869

S64

KARPOV P.V.,"PEACEFUL COEXISTENCE AND INTERNATIONAL   COM
LAW." WOR+45 LAW SOCIETY INT/ORG VOL/ASSN FORCES   ATTIT
CREATE CAP/ISM DIPLOM ADJUD NUC/PWR PEACE MORAL   INT/LAW
ORD/FREE PWR MARXISM...MARXIST JURID CONCPT OBS   USSR
TREND COLD/WAR MARX/KARL 20. PAGE 59 E1186

S64

LIPSON L.,"PEACEFUL COEXISTENCE." COM USSR WOR+45   ATTIT
LAW INT/ORG DIPLOM LEGIT ADJUD ORD/FREE...CONCPT   JURID
OBS TREND GEN/LAWS VAL/FREE COLD/WAR 20. PAGE 65   INT/LAW
E1303   PEACE

S64

MAGGS P.B.,"SOVIET VIEWPOINT ON NUCLEAR WEAPONS IN   COM
INTERNATIONAL LAW." USSR WOR+45 INT/ORG FORCES   LAW
DIPLOM ARMS/CONT ATTIT ORD/FREE PWR...POLICY JURID   INT/LAW
CONCPT OBS TREND CON/ANAL GEN/LAWS VAL/FREE 20.   NUC/PWR
PAGE 67 E1347

S64

SCHWELB E.,"OPERATION OF THE EUROPEAN CONVENTION ON   INT/ORG
HUMAN RIGHTS." EUR+WWI LAW SOCIETY CREATE EDU/PROP   MORAL
ADJUD ADMIN PEACE ATTIT ORD/FREE PWR...POLICY
INT/LAW CONCPT OBS GEN/LAWS UN VAL/FREE ILO 20
ECHR. PAGE 89 E1791

B65

BELL J.,THE JOHNSON TREATMENT: HOW LYNDON JOHNSON   INGP/REL
TOOK OVER THE PRESIDENCY AND MADE IT HIS OWN.   TOP/EX
USA+45 DELIB/GP DIPLOM ADJUD MURDER CHOOSE PERSON   CONTROL
PWR...POLICY OBS INT TIME 20 JOHNSON/LB KENNEDY/JF   NAT/G
PRESIDENT CONGRESS. PAGE 10 E0183

B65

BRIGGS H.W.,THE INTERNATIONAL LAW COMMISSION. LAW   INT/LAW
CONSTN LEGIS CREATE ADJUD CT/SYS ROUTINE TASK   DELIB/GP
EFFICIENCY...CLASSIF OBS UN. PAGE 15 E0302

B65

SMITH R.C.,THEY CLOSED THEIR SCHOOLS. USA+45 NEIGH   RACE/REL
ADJUD CROWD CONSEN WEALTH...DECISION OBS INT 20   DISCRIM
NEGRO VIRGINIA. PAGE 92 E1846   LOC/G
                                                       SCHOOL

B65

WHITE G.M.,THE USE OF EXPERTS BY INTERNATIONAL   INT/LAW
TRIBUNALS. WOR+45 WOR-45 INT/ORG NAT/G PAY ADJUD   ROUTINE
COST...OBS BIBLIOG 20. PAGE 106 E2117   CONSULT
                                                       CT/SYS

S65

AMRAM P.W.,"REPORT ON THE TENTH SESSION OF THE   VOL/ASSN
HAGUE CONFERENCE ON PRIVATE INTERNATIONAL LAW."   DELIB/GP
USA+45 WOR+45 INT/ORG CREATE LEGIT ADJUD ALL/VALS   INT/LAW
...JURID CONCPT METH/CNCPT OBS GEN/METH 20. PAGE 4
E0085

B66

CARLIN J.E.,LAWYER'S ETHICS. CLIENT STRUCT CONSULT   ATTIT
PERS/REL PWR...JURID OBS CHARTS 20. PAGE 19 E0378   PROF/ORG
                                                       INT

B66

DIZARD W.P.,TELEVISION* A WORLD VIEW. WOR+45   COM/IND
ECO/UNDEV TEC/DEV LICENSE LITERACY...STAT OBS INT   ACT/RES
QU TREND AUD/VIS BIBLIOG. PAGE 32 E0632   EDU/PROP
                                                       CREATE

B66

MERILLAT H.C.L.,LEGAL ADVISERS AND INTERNATIONAL   INT/ORG
ORGANIZATIONS. LAW NAT/G CONSULT OP/RES ADJUD   INT/LAW
SANCTION TASK CONSEN ORG/CHARTS. PAGE 72 E1441   CREATE
                                                       OBS

B67

BIBBY J.,ON CAPITOL HILL. POL/PAR LOBBY PARL/PROC   CONFER
GOV/REL PERS/REL...JURID PHIL/SCI OBS INT BIBLIOG   LEGIS
20 CONGRESS PRESIDENT. PAGE 12 E0224   CREATE
                                                       LEAD

OBS/ENVIR....SOCIAL MILIEU OF AND RESISTANCES TO OBSERVATIONS

B43

SERENI A.P.,THE ITALIAN CONCEPTION OF INTERNATIONAL   LAW
LAW. EUR+WWI MOD/EUR INT/ORG NAT/G DOMIN COERCE   TIME/SEQ
ORD/FREE FASCISM...OBS/ENVIR TREND 20. PAGE 90   INT/LAW
E1804   ITALY

B62

STERN A.C.,AIR POLLUTION (2 VOLS.). LAW INDUS   AIR
PROB/SOLV TEC/DEV INSPECT RISK BIO/SOC HABITAT   OP/RES
...OBS/ENVIR TESTS SAMP 20 POLLUTION. PAGE 93 E1871   CONTROL
                                                       HEALTH

OBSCENITY....OBSCENITY

OBSERVATION....SEE DIRECT-OBSERVATION METHOD INDEX, P. XIV

OBSOLESCNC....OBSOLESCENCE, PLANNED

OCCUPATION....SEE WORKER

OCEANIA....OCEANIA: AUSTRALIA, NEW ZEALAND, MALAYSIA,
    MELANESIA, MICRONESIA, AND POLYNESIA

ODEGARD/P....PETER ODEGARD

B63

US SENATE COMM ON JUDICIARY,PACIFICA FOUNDATION.   DELIB/GP
USA+45 LAW COM/IND 20 ODEGARD/P BINNS/JJ SCHINDLR/P   EDU/PROP
HEALEY/D THOMAS/TK. PAGE 102 E2051   ORD/FREE
                                                       ATTIT

ODINGA/O....OGINGA ODINGA

OECD....ORGANIZATION FOR ECONOMIC COOPERATION AND
    DEVELOPMENT

OEEC....ORGANIZATION FOR EUROPEAN ECONOMIC COOPERATION;
    SEE ALSO VOL/ASSN, INT/ORG

B63

BOWETT D.W.,THE LAW OF INTERNATIONAL INSTITUTIONS.   INT/ORG
WOR+45 WOR-45 CONSTN DELIB/GP EX/STRUC JUDGE   ADJUD
EDU/PROP LEGIT CT/SYS EXEC ROUTINE RIGID/FLEX   DIPLOM
ORD/FREE PWR...JURID CONCPT ORG/CHARTS GEN/METH
LEAGUE/NAT OAS OEEC 20 UN. PAGE 14 E0277

B64

ECONOMIDES C.P.,LE POUVOIR DE DECISION DES   INT/ORG
ORGANISATIONS INTERNATIONALES EUROPEENNES. DIPLOM   PWR
DOMIN INGP/REL EFFICIENCY...INT/LAW JURID 20 NATO   DECISION
OEEC EEC COUNCL/EUR EURATOM. PAGE 34 E0673   GP/COMP

B65

SOPER T.,EVOLVING COMMONWEALTH. AFR CANADA INDIA   INT/ORG
IRELAND UK LAW CONSTN POL/PAR DOMIN CONTROL WAR PWR   COLONIAL
...AUD/VIS 18/20 COMMONWLTH OEEC. PAGE 93 E1857   VOL/ASSN

OEO....OFFICE OF ECONOMIC OPPORTUNITY

OEP....OFFICE OF EMERGENCY PLANNING

OFFICE OF ECONOMIC OPPORTUNITY....SEE OEO

OFFICE OF EMERGENCY PLANNING....SEE OEP

OFFICE OF PRICE ADMINISTRATION....SEE OPA

OGDAL M.S. E1192

OGDEN F.D. E1572

OGUL M.S. E1191

OHIO....OHIO

OHLIN/HECK....OHLIN-HECKSCHER THEORY OF COMMODITY TRADE

OKELLO/J....JOHN OKELLO

OKINAWA....OKINAWA

OKINSHEVICH L.A. E1573

OKLAHOMA....OKLAHOMA

OLAS....ORGANIZATION FOR LATIN AMERICAN SOLIDARITY

OLD LIBERAL....SEE OLD/LIB

OLD/LIB....OLD LIBERAL

DICEY A.,LAW AND PUBLIC OPINION IN ENGLAND. LAW **B05** ATTIT
CULTURE INTELL SOCIETY NAT/G SECT JUDGE LEGIT UK
CHOOSE RIGID/FLEX KNOWL...OLD/LIB CONCPT STERTYP
GEN/LAWS 20. PAGE 31 E0620

BREWER D.J.,THE MOVEMENT OF COERCION (PAMPHLET). **N18** GP/REL
CONSTN INDUS ADJUD COERCE OWN WEALTH...OLD/LIB LABOR
JURID 19 SUPREME/CT. PAGE 15 E0296 LG/CO
LAW

AMERICAN CIVIL LIBERTIES UNION,"WE HOLD THESE **N19** ORD/FREE
TRUTHS" FREEDOM, JUSTICE, EQUALITY: REPORT ON CIVIL LAW
LIBERTIES (A PERIODICAL PAMPHLET COVERING 1951-53). RACE/REL
USA+45 ACADEM NAT/G FORCES LEGIS COERCE CIVMIL/REL CONSTN
GOV/REL DISCRIM PRIVIL MARXISM...OLD/LIB 20 ACLU UN
CIVIL/LIB. PAGE 4 E0076

CORWIN E.S.,LIBERTY AGAINST GOVERNMENT: THE RISE, **B48** CONCPT
FLOWERING AND DECLINE OF A FAMOUS JURIDICAL ORD/FREE
CONCEPT. LEGIS ADJUD CT/SYS SANCTION GOV/REL JURID
FEDERAL CONSERVE NEW/LIB...OLD/LIB 18/20 ROMAN/LAW CONSTN
COMMON/LAW. PAGE 26 E0514

JENKS C.W.,INTERNATIONAL IMMUNITIES. PLAN EDU/PROP **B61** INT/ORG
ADMIN PERCEPT...OLD/LIB JURID CONCPT TREND TOT/POP. DIPLOM
PAGE 58 E1157

KISER S.L.,AMERICANISM IN ACTION. USA+45 LAW PROVS **B64** OLD/LIB
CAP/ISM DIPLOM RECEIVE CONTROL CT/SYS WAR FEDERAL FOR/AID
ATTIT WEALTH 20 SUPREME/CT. PAGE 61 E1221 MARXISM
CONSTN

COHN M.M.,AN INTRODUCTION TO THE STUDY OF THE **B92** CONSTN
CONSTITUTION. USA-45 USA+45 SOCIETY NAT/G EX/STRUC JURID
HABITAT...PSY CONCPT 18/20. PAGE 24 E0470 OLD/LIB

SMITH A.,LECTURES ON JUSTICE, POLICE, REVENUE AND **B96** DIPLOM
ARMS (1763). UK LAW FAM FORCES TARIFFS AGREE COERCE JURID
INCOME OWN WEALTH LAISSEZ...GEN/LAWS 17/18. PAGE 92 OLD/LIB
E1840 TAX

OLIGARCHY....SEE ELITES

OLIGOPOLY....SEE MONOPOLY

OLIN/MTHSN....OLIN MATHIESON

OLIVARES....OLIVARES, HEAD OF SPAIN DURING CATALAN REV.,
1640

OLIVER C.T. E1574

OLSON W.C. E1575

OMBUDSMAN....OMBUDSMAN; DOMESTIC GRIEVANCE ORGAN

JUSTICE,THE CITIZEN AND THE ADMINISTRATION: THE **B61** INGP/REL
REDRESS OF GRIEVANCES (PAMPHLET). EUR+WWI UK LAW CONSULT
CONSTN STRATA NAT/G CT/SYS PARTIC COERCE...NEW/IDEA ADJUD

IDEA/COMP 20 OMBUDSMAN. PAGE 59 E1176 REPRESENT

UTLEY T.E.,OCCASION FOR OMBUDSMAN. UK CREATE **B61** PROB/SOLV
CONTROL 20 OMBUDSMAN. PAGE 103 E2065 INGP/REL
REPRESENT
ADJUD

HALLER W.,DER SCHWEDISCHE JUSTITIEOMBUDSMAN. **B64** JURID
DENMARK FINLAND NORWAY SWEDEN LEGIS ADJUD CONTROL PARL/PROC
PERSON ORD/FREE...NAT/COMP 20 OMBUDSMAN. PAGE 50 ADMIN
E0986 CHIEF

AARON T.J.,THE CONTROL OF POLICE DISCRETION: THE **B66** CONTROL
DANISH EXPERIENCE. DENMARK LAW CREATE ADMIN FORCES
INGP/REL SUPEGO PWR 20 OMBUDSMAN. PAGE 2 E0042 REPRESENT
PROB/SOLV

ANDERSON S.V.,CANADIAN OMBUDSMAN PROPOSALS. CANADA **B66** NAT/G
LEGIS DEBATE PARL/PROC...MAJORIT JURID TIME/SEQ CREATE
IDEA/COMP 20 OMBUDSMAN PARLIAMENT. PAGE 5 E0092 ADMIN
POL/PAR

ONTARIO....ONTARIO, CANADA

HILL D.G.,"HUMAN RIGHTS LEGISLATION IN ONTARIO." **S67** DELIB/GP
CANADA R+D VOL/ASSN CONSULT INSPECT EDU/PROP ADJUD ORD/FREE
AGREE TASK GP/REL INGP/REL DISCRIM 20 CIV/RIGHTS LAW
ONTARIO CIVIL/LIB. PAGE 52 E1045 POLICY

OP/RES....OPERATIONS RESEARCH; SEE ALSO CREATE

ADVANCED MANAGEMENT. INDUS EX/STRUC WORKER OP/RES **N** MGT
...DECISION BIBLIOG/A 20. PAGE 1 E0015 ADMIN
LABOR
GP/REL

LALL A.S.,NEGOTIATING DISARMAMENT* THE EIGHTEEN **B'** OBS
NATION DISARMAMENT CONFERENCE* THE FIRST TWO YEARS, ARMS/CONT
1962-1964. ASIA FRANCE INDIA USA+45 USSR PROB/SOLV DIPLOM
ADJUD NEUTRAL ATTIT...IDEA/COMP COLD/WAR. PAGE 62 OP/RES
E1246

GRIFFIN A.P.C.,LIST OF REFERENCES ON PRIMARY **B05** BIBLIOG/A
ELECTIONS (PAMPHLET). USA-45 LAW LOC/G DELIB/GP POL/PAR
LEGIS OP/RES TASK REPRESENT CONSEN...DECISION 19/20 CHOOSE
CONGRESS. PAGE 47 E0928 POPULISM

BEARDSLEY A.R.,LEGAL BIBLIOGRAPHY AND THE USE OF **B37** BIBLIOG
LAW BOOKS. CONSTN CREATE PROB/SOLV...DECISION JURID LAW
LAB/EXP. PAGE 9 E0166 METH
OP/RES

GILL N.N.,"PERMANENT ADVISORY COMMISSIONS IN THE **S40** DELIB/GP
FEDERAL GOVERNMENT." CLIENT FINAN OP/RES EDU/PROP NAT/G
PARTIC ROUTINE INGP/REL KNOWL SKILL...CLASSIF DECISION
TREND. PAGE 43 E0860

CARR R.K.,THE SUPREME COURT AND JUDICIAL REVIEW. **B42** CT/SYS
NAT/G CHIEF LEGIS OP/RES LEAD GOV/REL GP/REL ATTIT CONSTN
...POLICY DECISION 18/20 SUPREME/CT PRESIDENT JURID
CONGRESS. PAGE 20 E0394 PWR

CHENEY F.,CARTELS, COMBINES, AND TRUSTS: A SELECTED **B44** BIBLIOG/A
LIST OF REFERENCES. GERMANY UK USA+45 WOR-45 LG/CO
DELIB/GP OP/RES BARGAIN CAP/ISM ECO/TAC INT/TRADE ECO/DEV
LICENSE LEGIT CONFER PRICE 20. PAGE 22 E0428 INDUS

FULLER G.H.,RENEGOTIATION OF WAR CONTRACTS: A **B44** BIBLIOG
SELECTED LIST OF REFERENCES (PAMPHLET). USA-45 WAR
ECO/DEV LG/CO NAT/G OP/RES PLAN BAL/PWR LEGIT LAW
CONTROL...MGT 20. PAGE 42 E0823 FINAN

MORGENTHAL H.J.,POLITICS AMONG NATIONS: THE **B48** DIPLOM
STRUGGLE FOR POWER AND PEACE. FUT WOR+45 INT/ORG PEACE
OP/RES PROB/SOLV BAL/PWR CONTROL ATTIT MORAL PWR
...INT/LAW BIBLIOG 20 COLD/WAR. PAGE 75 E1494 POLICY

SLESSER H.,THE ADMINISTRATION OF THE LAW. UK CONSTN **B48** LAW
EX/STRUC OP/RES PROB/SOLV CRIME ROLE...DECISION CT/SYS
METH/COMP 20 CIVIL/LAW ENGLSH/LAW CIVIL/LAW. ADJUD
PAGE 92 E1839

WALKER H.,"THE LEGISLATIVE PROCESS: LAWMAKING IN THE UNITED STATES." NAT/G POL/PAR PROVS EX/STRUC OP/RES PROB/SOLV CT/SYS LOBBY GOV/REL...CHARTS BIBLIOG T 18/20 CONGRESS. PAGE 105 E2094
C48
PARL/PROC
LEGIS
LAW
CONSTN

CALDWELL L.K.,RESEARCH METHODS IN PUBLIC ADMINISTRATION: AN OUTLINE OF TOPICS AND READINGS (PAMPHLET). LAW ACT/RES COMPUTER KNOWL...SOC STAT GEN/METH 20. PAGE 18 E0364
B53
BIBLIOG/A
METH/COMP
ADMIN
OP/RES

LANDHEER B.,FUNDAMENTALS OF PUBLIC INTERNATIONAL LAW (SELECTIVE BIBLIOGRAPHIES OF THE LIBRARY OF THE PEACE PALACE, VOL. I; PAMPH). INT/ORG OP/RES PEACE ...IDEA/COMP 20. PAGE 62 E1250
B53
BIBLIOG/A
INT/LAW
DIPLOM
PHIL/SCI

CRESSEY D.R.,"ACHIEVEMENT OF AN UNSTATED ORGANIZATIONAL GOAL: AN OBSERVATION ON PRISONS." OP/RES PROB/SOLV PERS/REL ANOMIE ATTIT ROLE RESPECT CRIMLGY. PAGE 28 E0546
S58
PUB/INST
CLIENT
NEIGH
INGP/REL

ROCHE J.P.,"POLITICAL SCIENCE AND SCIENCE FICTION" (BMR)" WOR+45 INTELL OP/RES ADJUD...JURID SOC IDEA/COMP 20. PAGE 85 E1709
S58
QUANT
RATIONAL
MATH
METH

CHAPMAN B.,"THE FRENCH CONSEIL D'ETAT." FRANCE NAT/G CONSULT OP/RES PROB/SOLV PWR...OBS 20. PAGE 21 E0421
S59
ADMIN
LAW
CT/SYS
LEGIS

KAUPER P.G.,"CHURCH AND STATE: COOPERATIVE SEPARATISM." NAT/G LEGIS OP/RES TAX EDU/PROP GP/REL TREND. PAGE 59 E1187
L61
SECT
CONSTN
LAW
POLICY

EVAN W.M.,LAW AND SOCIOLOGY: EXPLORATORY ESSAYS. CONSULT ACT/RES OP/RES PROB/SOLV EDU/PROP LEGIT ADJUD CT/SYS GP/REL...PHIL/SCI ANTHOL SOC/INTEG 20. PAGE 35 E0703
B62
JURID
SOC
PROF/ORG

STERN A.C.,AIR POLLUTION (2 VOLS.). LAW INDUS PROB/SOLV TEC/DEV INSPECT RISK BIO/SOC HABITAT ...OBS/ENVIR TESTS SAMP 20 POLLUTION. PAGE 93 E1871
B62
AIR
OP/RES
CONTROL
HEALTH

STERN R.L.,SUPREME COURT PRACTICE. USA+45 USA-45 OP/RES...STYLE METH 20 SUPREME/CT. PAGE 93 E1872
B62
CT/SYS
ADJUD
JURID
ROUTINE

ECOLE NATIONALE D'ADMIN,BIBLIOGRAPHIE SELECTIVE D'OUVRAGES DE LANGUE FRANCAISE TRAITANT DES PROBLEMES GOUVERNEMENTAUX ET ADMINISTRATIFS. NAT/G FORCES ACT/RES OP/RES PLAN PROB/SOLV BUDGET ADJUD COLONIAL LEAD 20. PAGE 34 E0672
B63
BIBLIOG
AFR
ADMIN
EX/STRUC

FAWCETT J.E.S.,THE BRITISH COMMONWEALTH IN INTERNATIONAL LAW. LAW INT/ORG NAT/G VOL/ASSN OP/RES DIPLOM ADJUD CENTRAL CONSEN...NET/THEORY CMN/WLTH TREATY. PAGE 36 E0723
B63
INT/LAW
STRUCT
COLONIAL

PALOTAI O.C.,PUBLICATIONS OF THE INSTITUTE OF GOVERNMENT, 1930-1962. LAW PROVS SCHOOL WORKER ACT/RES OP/RES CT/SYS GOV/REL...CRIMLGY SOC/WK. PAGE 79 E1594
B63
BIBLIOG/A
ADMIN
LOC/G
FINAN

BOWETT D.W.,UNITED NATIONS FORCES* A LEGAL STUDY. CYPRUS ISRAEL KOREA LAW CONSTN ACT/RES CREATE BUDGET CONTROL TASK PWR...INT/LAW IDEA/COMP UN CONGO/LEOP SUEZ. PAGE 14 E0278
B64
OP/RES
FORCES
ARMS/CONT

KAHNG T.J.,LAW, POLITICS, AND THE SECURITY COUNCIL* AN INQUIRY INTO THE HANDLING OF LEGAL QUESTIONS. LAW CONSTN NAT/G ACT/RES OP/RES CT/SYS TASK PWR ...INT/LAW BIBLIOG UN. PAGE 59 E1180
B64
DELIB/GP
ADJUD
ROUTINE

BECKER T.L.,"POLITICAL BEHAVIORALISM AND MODERN JURISPRUDENCE." LEGIS JUDGE OP/RES ADJUD CT/SYS ATTIT PWR...BIBLIOG 20. PAGE 9 E0173
C64
DECISION
PROB/SOLV
JURID

CARTER G.M.,POLITICS IN EUROPE. EUR+WWI FRANCE GERMANY/W UK USSR LAW CONSTN POL/PAR VOL/ASSN PRESS LOBBY PWR...ANTHOL SOC/INTEG EEC. PAGE 20 E0399
B65
GOV/COMP
OP/RES
ECO/DEV

WHITEMAN M.M.,DIGEST OF INTERNATIONAL LAW* VOLUME 5, DEPARTMENT OF STATE PUBLICATION 7873. USA+45 WOR+45 OP/RES...CONCPT CLASSIF RECORD IDEA/COMP. PAGE 106 E2118
B65
INT/LAW
NAT/G
NAT/COMP

DAVIS K.,BUSINESS AND ITS ENVIRONMENT. LAW ECO/DEV INDUS OP/RES ADMIN CONTROL ROUTINE GP/REL PROFIT POLICY. PAGE 29 E0573
B66
EX/STRUC
PROB/SOLV
CAP/ISM
EXEC

MERILLAT H.C.L.,LEGAL ADVISERS AND INTERNATIONAL ORGANIZATIONS. LAW NAT/G CONSULT OP/RES ADJUD SANCTION TASK CONSEN ORG/CHARTS. PAGE 72 E1441
B66
INT/ORG
INT/LAW
CREATE
OBS

WALL E.H.,THE COURT OF JUSTICE IN THE EUROPEAN COMMUNITIES: JURISDICTION AND PROCEDURE. EUR+WWI DIPLOM ADJUD ADMIN ROUTINE TASK...CONCPT LING 20. PAGE 105 E2096
B66
CT/SYS
INT/ORG
LAW
OP/RES

YOUNG W.,EXISTING MECHANISMS OF ARMS CONTROL. PROC/MFG OP/RES DIPLOM TASK CENTRAL...MGT TREATY. PAGE 108 E2165
B66
ARMS/CONT
ADMIN
NUC/PWR
ROUTINE

ZAWODNY J.K.,"GUIDE TO THE STUDY OF INTERNATIONAL RELATIONS." OP/RES PRESS...STAT INT 20. PAGE 108 E2169
C66
BIBLIOG/A
DIPLOM
INT/LAW
INT/ORG

ASCH S.H.,POLICE AUTHORITY AND THE RIGHTS OF THE INDIVIDUAL. CONSTN DOMIN ADJUD CT/SYS...JURID 20. PAGE 6 E0106
B67
FORCES
OP/RES
ORD/FREE

FINCHER F.,THE GOVERNMENT OF THE UNITED STATES. USA+45 USA-45 POL/PAR CHIEF CT/SYS LOBBY GP/REL INGP/REL...CONCPT CHARTS BIBLIOG T 18/20 PRESIDENT CONGRESS SUPREME/CT. PAGE 38 E0749
B67
NAT/G
EX/STRUC
LEGIS
OP/RES

MORENO F.J.,"THE SPANISH COLONIAL SYSTEM: A FUNCTIONAL APPROACH." SPAIN WOR-45 LAW CHIEF DIPLOM ADJUD CIVMIL/REL AUTHORIT ROLE PWR...CONCPT 17/20. PAGE 74 E1492
S67
COLONIAL
CONTROL
NAT/G
OP/RES

HALL A.B.,"DETERMINATION OF METHODS FOR ASCERTAINING THE FACTORS THAT INFLUENCE JUDICIAL DECISIONS IN CASES INVOLVING DUE PROCESS" LAW JUDGE DEBATE EFFICIENCY OPTIMAL UTIL...SOC CONCPT PROBABIL STAT SAMP. PAGE 49 E0981
S26
ADJUD
DECISION
CONSTN
JURID

B18

EYBERS G.W.,SELECT CONSTITUTIONAL DOCUMENTS CONSTN
ILLUSTRATING SOUTH AFRICAN HISTORY 1795-1910. LAW
SOUTH/AFR LOC/G LEGIS CT/SYS...JURID ANTHOL 18/20 NAT/G
NATAL CAPE/HOPE ORANGE/STA. PAGE 36 E0707 COLONIAL

ORD/FREE....SECURITY, ORDER, RESTRAINT, LIBERTY, FREEDOM

N

INTERNATIONAL COMN JURISTS,AFRICAN CONFERENCE ON CT/SYS
THE RULE OF LAW. AFR INT/ORG LEGIS DIPLOM CONFER JURID
COLONIAL ORD/FREE...CONCPT METH/COMP 20. PAGE 57 DELIB/GP
E1131

B00

DARBY W.E.,INTERNATIONAL TRIBUNALS. WOR-45 NAT/G INT/ORG
ECO/TAC DOMIN LEGIT CT/SYS COERCE ORD/FREE PWR ADJUD
SOVEREIGN JURID. PAGE 29 E0567 PEACE
INT/LAW

B00

HOLLAND T.E.,STUDIES IN INTERNATIONAL LAW. TURKEY INT/ORG
USSR WOR-45 CONSTN NAT/G DIPLOM DOMIN LEGIT COERCE LAW
WAR PEACE ORD/FREE PWR SOVEREIGN...JURID CHARTS 20 INT/LAW
PARLIAMENT SUEZ TREATY. PAGE 54 E1084

B00

LORIMER J.,THE INSTITUTES OF THE LAW OF NATIONS. INT/ORG
WOR-45 CULTURE SOCIETY NAT/G VOL/ASSN DIPLOM LEGIT LAW
WAR PEACE DRIVE ORD/FREE SOVEREIGN...CONCPT RECORD INT/LAW
INT TREND HYPO/EXP GEN/METH TOT/POP VAL/FREE 20.
PAGE 66 E1327

B01

GRIFFIN A.P.C.,LIST OF BOOKS ON SAMOA (PAMPHLET). BIBLIOG/A
GERMANY S/ASIA UK USA-45 WOR-45 ECO/UNDEV REGION COLONIAL
ALL/VALS ORD/FREE ALL/IDEOS...GEOG INT/LAW 19 SAMOA DIPLOM
GUAM. PAGE 46 E0918

C01

BERKELEY G.,"DISCOURSE ON PASSIVE OBEDIENCE" (1712) INGP/REL
THE WORKS... (VOL. IV)" UNIV DOMIN LEGIT CONTROL SANCTION
CRIME ADJUST CENTRAL MORAL ORD/FREE...POLICY RESPECT
WORSHIP. PAGE 10 E0202 GEN/LAWS

B03

CHANNING W.E.,DISCOURSES ON WAR (1820-1840). LAW WAR
SECT DIPLOM INT/TRADE ALL/VALS. PAGE 21 E0418 PLAN
LOVE
ORD/FREE

B03

FAGUET E.,LE LIBERALISME. FRANCE PRESS ADJUD ADMIN ORD/FREE
DISCRIM CONSERVE SOCISM...TRADIT SOC LING WORSHIP EDU/PROP
PARLIAMENT. PAGE 36 E0711 NAT/G
LAW

B04

BURKE E.,A LETTER TO THE SHERIFFS OF BRISTOL LEGIS
(1777). USA-45 LAW ECO/TAC COLONIAL CT/SYS REV ADJUD
GP/REL ORD/FREE...POLICY 18 PARLIAMENT BURKE/EDM. CRIME
PAGE 17 E0341

B04

FREUND E.,THE POLICE POWER; PUBLIC POLICY AND CONSTN
CONSTITUTIONAL RIGHTS. USA-45 SOCIETY LOC/G NAT/G LAW
FORCES LEGIS ADJUD CT/SYS OWN PWR...JURID 18/19 ORD/FREE
SUPREME/CT. PAGE 40 E0795 CONTROL

C05

DUNNING W.A.,"HISTORY OF POLITICAL THEORIES FROM PHIL/SCI
LUTHER TO MONTESQUIEU." LAW NAT/G SECT DIPLOM REV CONCPT
WAR ORD/FREE SOVEREIGN CONSERVE...TRADIT BIBLIOG GEN/LAWS
16/18. PAGE 33 E0663

B07

GRIFFIN A.P.C.,LIST OF MORE RECENT WORKS ON FEDERAL BIBLIOG/A
CONTROL OF COMMERCE AND CORPORATIONS (PAMPHLET). NAT/G
USA-45 LAW ECO/DEV FINAN LG/CO TARIFFS TAX LICENSE JURID
CENTRAL ORD/FREE WEALTH LAISSEZ 19/20. PAGE 47 ECO/TAC
E0931

B08

GRIFFIN A.P.C.,LIST OF WORKS RELATING TO GOVERNMENT BIBLIOG/A
REGULATION OF INSURANCE UNITED STATES AND FOREIGN FINAN
COUNTRIES (2ND. ED.) (PAMPHLET). FRANCE GERMANY UK LAW
USA-45 WOR-45 LG/CO LOC/G NAT/G LEGIS LICENSE ADJUD CONTROL
LOBBY CENTRAL ORD/FREE 19/20. PAGE 47 E0933

B12

FOUAD M.,LE REGIME DE LA PRESSE EN EGYPTE: THESE ORD/FREE
POUR LE DOCTORAT. UAR LICENSE EDU/PROP ADMIN LEGIS
SANCTION CRIME SUPEGO PWR...ART/METH JURID 19/20. CONTROL
PAGE 39 E0778 PRESS

B13

BUTLER N.M.,THE INTERNATIONAL MIND. WOR-45 INT/ORG ADJUD
LEGIT PWR...JURID CONCPT 20. PAGE 18 E0350 ORD/FREE
INT/LAW

B14

CRAIG J.,ELEMENTS OF POLITICAL SCIENCE (3 VOLS.). PHIL/SCI
CONSTN AGRI INDUS SCHOOL FORCES TAX CT/SYS SUFF NAT/G
MORAL WEALTH...CONCPT 19 CIVIL/LIB. PAGE 27 E0539 ORD/FREE

B14

FIGGIS J.N.,CHURCHES IN THE MODERN STATE (2ND ED.). SECT
LAW CHIEF BAL/PWR PWR...CONCPT CHURCH/STA POPE. NAT/G
PAGE 38 E0748 SOCIETY
ORD/FREE

B16

SALMOND J.W.,JURISPRUDENCE. UK LOC/G NAT/G LEGIS LAW
PROB/SOLV LICENSE LEGIT CRIME PERS/REL OWN ORD/FREE CT/SYS
...T 20. PAGE 87 E1742 JURID
ADJUD

B16

SCHROEDER T.,FREE SPEECH FOR RADICALS (REV. ED.). ORD/FREE
USA-45 CONSTN INDUS LOC/G FORCES SANCTION WAR ATTIT CONTROL
SEX...JURID REFORMERS 20 FREE/SPEE. PAGE 88 E1767 LAW
PRESS

B18

YUKIO O.,THE VOICE OF JAPANESE DEMOCRACY, AN ESSAY CONSTN
ON CONSTITUTIONAL LOYALTY (TRANS BY J. E. BECKER). MAJORIT
ASIA POL/PAR DELIB/GP EX/STRUC RIGID/FLEX ORD/FREE CHOOSE
PWR...POLICY JURID METH/COMP 19/20 CHINJAP. NAT/G
PAGE 108 E2167

B19

DUGUIT L.,LAW IN THE MODERN STATE (TRANS. BY FRIDA GEN/LAWS
AND HAROLD LASKI). CONSTN SOCIETY STRUCT MORAL CONCPT
ORD/FREE SOVEREIGN 20. PAGE 33 E0655 NAT/G
LAW

N19

IN THE SHADOW OF FEAR; AMERICAN CIVIL LIBERTIES, ORD/FREE
1948-49 (PAMPHLET). COM LAW LEGIS BAL/PWR EDU/PROP CONSTN
CT/SYS RACE/REL DISCRIM MARXISM SOCISM 20 COLD/WAR POLICY
CONGRESS ACLU CIV/RIGHTS ESPIONAGE. PAGE 2 E0030

N19

THE REGIONAL DIRECTOR AND THE PRESS (PAMPHLET). PRESS
USA-45 COM/IND LOBBY ROLE 20 NLRB CINCINNATI LABOR
BILL/RIGHT. PAGE 2 E0031 ORD/FREE
EDU/PROP

N19

AMERICAN CIVIL LIBERTIES UNION,"WE HOLD THESE ORD/FREE
TRUTHS" FREEDOM, JUSTICE, EQUALITY: REPORT ON CIVIL LAW
LIBERTIES (A PERIODICAL PAMPHLET COVERING 1951-53) RACE/REL
USA+45 ACADEM NAT/G FORCES LEGIS COERCE CIVMIL/REL CONSTN
GOV/REL DISCRIM PRIVIL MARXISM...OLD/LIB 20 ACLU UN
CIVIL/LIB. PAGE 4 E0076

N19

BRENNAN W.J. JR.,THE BILL OF RIGHTS AND THE STATES CONSTN
(PAMPHLET). USA+45 USA-45 LEGIS BAL/PWR ADJUD PROVS
CT/SYS FEDERAL PWR SOVEREIGN 18/20 SUPREME/CT GOV/REL
BILL/RIGHT. PAGE 15 E0293 ORD/FREE

N19

COUTROT A.,THE FIGHT OVER THE 1959 PRIVATE SCHOOL
EDUCATION LAW IN FRANCE (PAMPHLET). FRANCE NAT/G PARL/PROC
SECT GIVE EDU/PROP GP/REL ATTIT RIGID/FLEX ORD/FREE CATHISM
20 CHURCH/STA. PAGE 27 E0527 LAW

N19

JANOWITZ M.,SOCIAL CONTROL OF ESCALATED RIOTS CROWD
(PAMPHLET). USA+45 USA-45 LAW SOCIETY MUNIC FORCES ORD/FREE
PROB/SOLV EDU/PROP TV CRIME ATTIT...BIBLIOG 20 CONTROL
NEGRO CIV/RIGHTS. PAGE 58 E1148 RACE/REL

N19

MCCONNELL G.,THE STEEL SEIZURE OF 1952 (PAMPHLET). DELIB/GP
USA+45 FINAN INDUS PROC/MFG LG/CO EX/STRUC ADJUD LABOR
CONTROL GP/REL ORD/FREE PWR 20 TRUMAN/HS PRESIDENT PROB/SOLV
CONGRESS. PAGE 70 E1402 NAT/G

N19

MISSISSIPPI ADVISORY COMMITTEE,REPORT ON RACE/REL
MISSISSIPPI (PAMPHLET). USA+45 LAW PROVS FORCES DISCRIM
ADJUD PWR...SOC/WK INT 20 MISSISSIPP NEGRO COERCE
CIV/RIGHTS. PAGE 73 E1469 ORD/FREE

N19

PAN AMERICAN UNION,INFORME DE LA MISION DE CHOOSE
ASISTENCIA TECNICA DE LA OEA A LA REPUBLICA DE SUFF
HONDURAS EN MATERIA ELECTORAL (PAMPHLET). HONDURAS POL/PAR
CONSTN ORD/FREE...JURID OBS 20 OAS. PAGE 80 E1595 NAT/G

TAYLOR H.,WHY THE PENDING TREATY WITH COLOMBIA SHOULD BE RATIFIED (PAMPHLET). PANAMA USA-45 DELIB/GP INT/TRADE REV ORD/FREE...JURID TREATY 18/19 ROOSEVLT/T TAFT/WH COLOMB. PAGE 95 E1912
N19 INT/LAW DIPLOM

COX H.,ECONOMIC LIBERTY. UNIV LAW INT/TRADE RATION TARIFFS RACE/REL SOCISM POLICY. PAGE 27 E0535
B20 NAT/G ORD/FREE ECO/TAC PERSON

LIPPMAN W.,LIBERTY AND THE NEWS. USA+45 USA-45 LAW LEGIS DOMIN LEGIT ATTIT...POLICY SOC IDEA/COMP METH/COMP 19/20. PAGE 65 E1300
B20 ORD/FREE PRESS COM/IND EDU/PROP

CARDOZO B.N.,THE NATURE OF THE JUDICIAL PROCESS. ROUTINE ORD/FREE...POLICY 20. PAGE 19 E0377
B21 JURID CT/SYS LEAD DECISION

OPPENHEIM L.,THE FUTURE OF INTERNATIONAL LAW. EUR+WWI MOD/EUR LAW LEGIS JUDGE LEGIT ORD/FREE ...JURID TIME/SEQ GEN/LAWS 20. PAGE 79 E1578
B21 INT/ORG CT/SYS INT/LAW

SCHROEDER T.,FREE SPEECH BIBLIOGRAPHY. EUR+WWI WOR-45 NAT/G SECT ECO/TAC WRITING ADJUD ATTIT MARXISM SOCISM 16/20. PAGE 88 E1768
B22 BIBLIOG/A ORD/FREE CONTROL LAW

WRIGHT Q.,THE CONTROL OF AMERICAN FOREIGN RELATIONS. USA-45 WOR-45 CONSTN INT/ORG CONSULT LEGIS LEGIT ROUTINE ORD/FREE PWR...POLICY JURID CONCPT METH/CNCPT RECORD LEAGUE/NAT 20. PAGE 107 E2150
B22 NAT/G EXEC DIPLOM

DE MONTESQUIEU C.,THE SPIRIT OF LAWS (2 VOLS.) (TRANS. BY THOMAS NUGENT). FRANCE FINAN SECT INT/TRADE TAX COERCE REV DISCRIM HABITAT ORD/FREE 19 ALEMBERT/J CIVIL/LAW. PAGE 30 E0588
B23 JURID LAW CONCPT GEN/LAWS

DEWEY J.,"ETHICS AND INTERNATIONAL RELATIONS." FUT WOR-45 SOCIETY INT/ORG VOL/ASSN DIPLOM LEGIT ORD/FREE...JURID CONCPT GEN/METH 20. PAGE 31 E0618
S23 LAW MORAL

HALL W.E.,A TREATISE ON INTERNATIONAL LAW. WOR-45 CONSTN INT/ORG NAT/G DIPLOM ORD/FREE LEAGUE/NAT 20 TREATY. PAGE 49 E0985
B24 PWR JURID WAR INT/LAW

NAVILLE A.,LIBERTE, EGALITE, SOLIDARITE: ESSAIS D'ANALYSE. STRATA FAM VOL/ASSN INT/TRADE GP/REL MORAL MARXISM SOCISM...PSY TREATY. PAGE 76 E1529
B24 ORD/FREE SOC IDEA/COMP DIPLOM

BARNES H.E.,"SOCIOLOGY AND POLITICAL THEORY: A CONSIDERATION OF THE SOCIOLOGICAL BASIS OF POLITICS." LAW CONSTN NAT/G DIPLOM DOMIN ROUTINE REV ORD/FREE SOVEREIGN...PHIL/SCI CLASSIF BIBLIOG 18/20. PAGE 8 E0151
C24 CONCPT STRUCT SOC

HUDSON M.,"THE PERMANENT COURT OF INTERNATIONAL JUSTICE AND THE QUESTION OF AMERICAN PARTICIPATION." WOR-45 LEGIT CT/SYS ORD/FREE ...JURID CONCPT TIME/SEQ GEN/LAWS VAL/FREE 20 ICJ. PAGE 56 E1108
L25 INT/ORG ADJUD DIPLOM INT/LAW

FORTESCUE J.,THE GOVERNANCE OF ENGLAND (1471-76). UK LAW FINAN SECT LEGIS PROB/SOLV TAX DOMIN ADMIN GP/REL COST ORD/FREE PWR 14/15. PAGE 39 E0776
B26 CONSERVE CONSTN CHIEF NAT/G

HOCKING W.E.,PRESENT STATUS OF THE PHILOSOPHY OF LAW AND OF RIGHTS. UNIV CULTURE INTELL SOCIETY NAT/G CREATE LEGIT SANCTION ALL/VALS SOC/INTEG 18/20. PAGE 53 E1060
B26 JURID PHIL/SCI ORD/FREE

DICKINSON J.,ADMINISTRATIVE JUSTICE AND THE SUPREMACY OF LAW IN THE UNITED STATES. USA-45 LAW INDUS DOMIN EDU/PROP CONTROL EXEC GP/REL ORD/FREE
B27 CT/SYS ADJUD ADMIN

...POLICY JURID 19/20. PAGE 31 E0623
NAT/G

JOHN OF SALISBURY,THE STATESMAN'S BOOK (1159) (TRANS. BY J. DICKINSON). DOMIN GP/REL MORAL ORD/FREE PWR CONSERVE...CATH CONCPT 12. PAGE 59 E1169
B27 NAT/G SECT CHIEF LAW

LAUTERPACHT H.,PRIVATE LAW SOURCES AND ANALOGIES OF INTERNATIONAL LAW. WOR-45 NAT/G DELIB/GP LEGIT COERCE ATTIT ORD/FREE PWR SOVEREIGN...JURID CONCPT HIST/WRIT TIME/SEQ GEN/METH LEAGUE/NAT 20. PAGE 63 E1264
B27 INT/ORG ADJUD PEACE INT/LAW

RYAN J.A.,DECLINING LIVERTY AND OTHER ESSAYS. USA-45 SECT DELIB/GP ATTIT PWR SOCISM 20 SUPREME/CT. PAGE 87 E1740
B27 ORD/FREE LEGIS JURID NAT/G

BENTHAM J.,A COMMENT OF THE COMMENTARIES (1765-69). MUNIC SECT ADJUD AGREE CT/SYS CONSEN HAPPINESS ORD/FREE 18. PAGE 10 E0191
B28 LAW CONCPT IDEA/COMP

BUTLER G.,THE DEVELOPMENT OF INTERNATIONAL LAW. WOR-45 SOCIETY NAT/G KNOWL ORD/FREE PWR...JURID CONCPT HIST/WRIT GEN/LAWS. PAGE 18 E0349
B28 LAW INT/LAW DIPLOM INT/ORG

CORBETT P.E.,CANADA AND WORLD POLITICS. LAW CULTURE SOCIETY STRUCT MARKET INT/ORG FORCES ACT/RES PLAN ECO/TAC LEGIT ORD/FREE PWR RESPECT...SOC CONCPT TIME/SEQ TREND CMN/WLTH 20 LEAGUE/NAT. PAGE 26 E0504
B28 NAT/G CANADA

HOBBES T.,THE ELEMENTS OF LAW, NATURAL AND POLITIC (1650). STRATA NAT/G SECT CHIEF AGREE ATTIT ALL/VALS MORAL ORD/FREE POPULISM...POLICY CONCPT. PAGE 53 E1056
B28 PERSON LAW SOVEREIGN CONSERVE

MAIR L.P.,THE PROTECTION OF MINORITIES. EUR+WWI WOR-45 CONSTN INT/ORG NAT/G LEGIT CT/SYS GP/REL RACE/REL DISCRIM ORD/FREE RESPECT...JURID CONCPT TIME/SEQ 20. PAGE 68 E1352
B28 LAW SOVEREIGN

NORTON T.J.,LOSING LIBERTY JUDICIALLY. PROVS LEGIS BAL/PWR CT/SYS...JURID 18/20 SUPREME/CT CIV/RIGHTS CONGRESS. PAGE 78 E1557
B28 NAT/G ORD/FREE CONSTN JUDGE

BUELL R.,INTERNATIONAL RELATIONS. WOR+45 WOR-45 CONSTN STRATA FORCES TOP/EX ADMIN ATTIT DRIVE SUPEGO MORAL ORD/FREE PWR SOVEREIGN...JURID SOC CONCPT 20. PAGE 17 E0326
B29 INT/ORG BAL/PWR DIPLOM

CAM H.M.,BIBLIOGRAPHY OF ENGLISH CONSTITUTIONAL HISTORY (PAMPHLET). UK LAW LOC/G NAT/G POL/PAR SECT DELIB/GP ADJUD ORD/FREE 19/20 PARLIAMENT. PAGE 19 E0369
B29 BIBLIOG/A CONSTN ADMIN PARL/PROC

STURZO L.,THE INTERNATIONAL COMMUNITY AND THE RIGHT OF WAR (TRANS. BY BARBARA BARCLAY CARTER). CULTURE CREATE PROB/SOLV DIPLOM ADJUD CONTROL PEACE PERSON ORD/FREE...INT/LAW IDEA/COMP PACIFIST 20 LEAGUE/NAT. PAGE 94 E1891
B29 INT/ORG PLAN WAR CONCPT

BENTHAM J.,THE RATIONALE OF PUNISHMENT. UK LAW LOC/G NAT/G LEGIS CONTROL...JURID GEN/LAWS COURT/SYS 19. PAGE 10 E0192
B30 CRIME SANCTION COERCE ORD/FREE

BURLAMAQUI J.J.,PRINCIPLES OF NATURAL AND POLITIC LAW (2 VOLS.) (1747-51). EX/STRUC LEGIS AGREE CT/SYS CHOOSE ROLE SOVEREIGN 18 NATURL/LAW. PAGE 17 E0342
B30 LAW NAT/G ORD/FREE CONCPT

LUNT D.C.,THE ROAD TO THE LAW. UK USA-45 LEGIS EDU/PROP OWN ORD/FREE...DECISION TIME/SEQ NAT/COMP 16/20 AUSTRAL ENGLSH/LAW COMMON/LAW. PAGE 67 E1333
B32 ADJUD LAW JURID CT/SYS

LAUTERPACHT H.,THE FUNCTION OF LAW IN THE
B33 INT/ORG

INTERNATIONAL COMMUNITY. WOR-45 NAT/G FORCES CREATE LAW DOMIN LEGIT COERCE WAR PEACE ATTIT ORD/FREE PWR SOVEREIGN...JURID CONCPT METH/CNCPT TIME/SEQ GEN/LAWS GEN/METH LEAGUE/NAT TOT/POP VAL/FREE 20. PAGE 63 E1265   INT/LAW

B33
REID H.D.,RECUEIL DES COURS; TOME 45: LES SERVITUDES INTERNATIONALES III. FRANCE CONSTN DELIB/GP PRESS CONTROL REV WAR CHOOSE PEACE MORAL MARITIME TREATY. PAGE 84 E1680   ORD/FREE DIPLOM LAW

B34
CLYDE W.M.,THE STRUGGLE FOR THE FREEDOM OF THE PRESS FROM CAXTON TO CROMWELL. UK LAW LOC/G SECT FORCES LICENSE WRITING SANCTION REV ATTIT PWR ...POLICY 15/17 PARLIAMENT CROMWELL/O MILTON/J. PAGE 23 E0460   PRESS ORD/FREE CONTROL

B34
CUMMINGS H.,LIBERTY UNDER LAW AND ADMINISTRATION. MOD/EUR USA-45 ADMIN ATTIT...JURID PHIL/SCI. PAGE 28 E0553   ORD/FREE LAW NAT/G SOCIETY

B35
DE TOCQUEVILLE A.,DEMOCRACY IN AMERICA (4 VOLS.) (TRANS. BY HENRY REEVE). CONSTN STRUCT LOC/G NAT/G POL/PAR PROVS ETIQUET CT/SYS MAJORITY ATTIT 18/19. PAGE 30 E0595   POPULISM MAJORIT ORD/FREE SOCIETY

B35
HUDSON M.,BY PACIFIC MEANS. WOR-45 EDU/PROP ORD/FREE...CONCPT TIME/SEQ GEN/LAWS LEAGUE/NAT TOT/POP 20 TREATY. PAGE 56 E1110   INT/ORG CT/SYS PEACE

B36
HANSON L.,GOVERNMENT AND THE PRESS 1695-1763. UK LOC/G LEGIS LICENSE CONTROL SANCTION CRIME ATTIT ORD/FREE 17/18 PARLIAMENT AMEND/I. PAGE 50 E0996   LAW JURID PRESS POLICY

B36
KONRAD F.,DIE PERSONLICHE FREIHEIT IM NATIONALSOZIALISTISCHEN DEUTSCHEN REICHE. GERMANY JUDGE ADJUD GP/REL FASCISM 20 CIVIL/LIB. PAGE 61 E1226   ORD/FREE JURID CONSTN CONCPT

B36
SCHULZ F.,PRINCIPLES OF ROMAN LAW. CONSTN FAM NAT/G DOMIN CONTROL CT/SYS CRIME ISOLAT ATTIT ORD/FREE PWR...JURID ROME/ANC ROMAN/LAW. PAGE 89 E1783   LAW LEGIS ADJUD CONCPT

S36
CORWIN E.S.,"THE CONSTITUTION AS INSTRUMENT AND AS SYMBOL." USA-45 ECO/DEV INDUS CAP/ISM SANCTION RIGID/FLEX ORD/FREE LAISSEZ OBJECTIVE 20 CONGRESS SUPREME/CT. PAGE 26 E0512   CONSTN LAW ADJUD PWR

B38
FRANKFURTER F.,MR. JUSTICE HOLMES AND THE SUPREME COURT. USA-45 CONSTN SOCIETY FEDERAL OWN ATTIT ORD/FREE PWR...POLICY JURID 20 SUPREME/CT HOLMES/OW BILL/RIGHT. PAGE 40 E0790   CREATE CT/SYS DECISION LAW

B38
HOLDSWORTH W.S.,A HISTORY OF ENGLISH LAW; THE CENTURIES OF SETTLEMENT AND REFORM (VOL. X). INDIA UK CONSTN NAT/G CHIEF LEGIS ADMIN COLONIAL CT/SYS CHOOSE ORD/FREE PWR...JURID 18 PARLIAMENT COMMONWLTH COMMON/LAW. PAGE 54 E1077   LAW LOC/G EX/STRUC ADJUD

B39
BENES E.,INTERNATIONAL SECURITY. GERMANY UK NAT/G DELIB/GP PLAN BAL/PWR ATTIT ORD/FREE PWR LEAGUE/NAT 20 TREATY. PAGE 10 E0186   EUR+WWI INT/ORG WAR

B39
LAVES W.H.C.,INTERNATIONAL SECURITY. EUR+WWI GERMANY UK USA-45 LAW NAT/G DELIB/GP TOP/EX COERCE PWR...POLICY FASCIST CONCPT HIST/WRIT GEN/LAWS LEAGUE/NAT NAZI 20. PAGE 63 E1267   ORD/FREE LEGIT ARMS/CONT BAL/PWR

B39
TIMASHEFF N.S.,AN INTRODUCTION TO THE SOCIOLOGY OF LAW. CRIME ANOMIE ATTIT DRIVE ORD/FREE...JURID PSY CONCPT. PAGE 96 E1926   SOC BIBLIOG PWR

B39
ZIMMERN A.,THE LEAGUE OF NATIONS AND THE RULE OF LAW. WOR-45 STRUCT NAT/G DELIB/GP EX/STRUC BAL/PWR DOMIN LEGIT COERCE ORD/FREE PWR...POLICY RECORD LEAGUE/NAT TOT/POP VAL/FREE 20 LEAGUE/NAT. PAGE 108 E2170   INT/ORG LAW DIPLOM

B40
HART J.,AN INTRODUCTION TO ADMINISTRATIVE LAW, WITH SELECTED CASES. USA-45 CONSTN SOCIETY NAT/G EX/STRUC ADJUD CT/SYS LEAD CRIME ORD/FREE ...DECISION JURID 20 CASEBOOK. PAGE 50 E1002   LAW ADMIN LEGIS PWR

B40
HOBBES T.,A DIALOGUE BETWEEN A PHILOSOPHER AND A STUDENT OF THE COMMON LAWS OF ENGLAND (1667?). UK SECT DOMIN ADJUD CRIME INCOME OWN UTIL ORD/FREE PWR SOVEREIGN...JURID GEN/LAWS 17. PAGE 53 E1057   CT/SYS CHIEF SANCTION

B40
MCILWAIN C.H.,CONSTITUTIONALISM, ANCIENT AND MODERN. CHRIST-17C MOD/EUR NAT/G CHIEF PROB/SOLV INSPECT AUTHORIT ORD/FREE PWR...TIME/SEQ ROMAN/REP. PAGE 71 E1418   CONSTN GEN/LAWS LAW

B41
BIRDSALL P.,VERSAILLES TWENTY YEARS AFTER. MOD/EUR POL/PAR CHIEF CONSULT FORCES LEGIS REPAR PEACE ORD/FREE...BIBLIOG 20 PRESIDENT TREATY. PAGE 12 E0231   DIPLOM NAT/LISM WAR

B41
CHAFEE Z. JR.,FREE SPEECH IN THE UNITED STATES. USA-45 ADJUD CONTROL CRIME WAR...BIBLIOG 20 FREE/SPEE AMEND/I SUPREME/CT. PAGE 21 E0413   ORD/FREE CONSTN ATTIT JURID

B41
MCCLURE W.,INTERNATIONAL EXECUTIVE AGREEMENTS. USA-45 WOR-45 INT/ORG NAT/G DELIB/GP ADJUD ROUTINE ORD/FREE PWR...TIME/SEQ TREND CON/ANAL. PAGE 70 E1401   TOP/EX DIPLOM

B41
NIEMEYER G.,LAW WITHOUT FORCE: THE FUNCTION OF POLITICS IN INTERNATIONAL LAW. PLAN INSPECT DIPLOM REPAR LEGIT ADJUD WAR ORD/FREE...IDEA/COMP METH/COMP GEN/LAWS 20. PAGE 77 E1549   COERCE LAW PWR INT/LAW

L41
COMM. STUDY ORGAN. PEACE,"ORGANIZATION OF PEACE." USA-45 WOR-45 STRATA NAT/G ACT/RES DIPLOM ECO/TAC EDU/PROP ADJUD ATTIT ORD/FREE PWR...SOC CONCPT ANTHOL LEAGUE/NAT 20. PAGE 24 E0479   INT/ORG PLAN PEACE

S41
WRIGHT Q.,"FUNDAMENTAL PROBLEMS OF INTERNATIONAL ORGANIZATION." UNIV WOR-45 STRUCT FORCES ACT/RES CREATE DOMIN EDU/PROP LEGIT REGION NAT/LISM ORD/FREE PWR RESPECT SOVEREIGN...JURID SOC CONCPT METH/CNCPT TIME/SEQ 20. PAGE 107 E2152   INT/ORG ATTIT PEACE

B42
CRAIG A.,ABOVE ALL LIBERTIES. FRANCE UK USA-45 LAW CONSTN CULTURE INTELL NAT/G SECT JUDGE...IDEA/COMP BIBLIOG 18/20. PAGE 27 E0536   ORD/FREE MORAL WRITING EDU/PROP

B42
FORTESCU J.,IN PRAISE OF ENGLISH LAW (1464) (TRANS. BY S.B. CHRIMES). UK ELITES CHIEF FORCES CT/SYS COERCE CRIME GOV/REL ILLEGIT...JURID GOV/COMP GEN/LAWS 15. PAGE 39 E0774   LAW CONSTN LEGIS ORD/FREE

B42
HEGEL G.W.F.,PHILOSOPHY OF RIGHT. UNIV FAM SECT CHIEF AGREE WAR MARRIAGE OWN ORD/FREE...POLICY CONCPT. PAGE 51 E1023   NAT/G LAW RATIONAL

B42
KELSEN H.,LAW AND PEACE IN INTERNATIONAL RELATIONS. FUT WOR-45 NAT/G DELIB/GP DIPLOM LEGIT RIGID/FLEX ORD/FREE SOVEREIGN...JURID CONCPT TREND STERTYP GEN/LAWS LEAGUE/NAT 20. PAGE 60 E1197   INT/ORG ADJUD PEACE INT/LAW

C42
CRAIG A.,"ABOVE ALL LIBERTIES." FRANCE UK LAW CULTURE INTELL SECT ORD/FREE 18/20. PAGE 27 E0537   BIBLIOG/A EDU/PROP WRITING MORAL

B43
BEMIS S.F.,THE LATIN AMERICAN POLICY OF THE UNITED STATES: AN HISTORICAL INTERPRETATION. INT/ORG AGREE COLONIAL WAR PEACE ATTIT ORD/FREE...POLICY INT/LAW CHARTS 18/20 MEXIC/AMER WILSON/W MONROE/DOC. PAGE 10 E0185   DIPLOM SOVEREIGN USA-45 L/A+17C

B43
SERENI A.P.,THE ITALIAN CONCEPTION OF INTERNATIONAL LAW. EUR+WWI MOD/EUR INT/ORG NAT/G DOMIN COERCE ORD/FREE FASCISM...OBS/ENVIR TREND 20. PAGE 90 E1804   LAW TIME/SEQ INT/LAW ITALY

ORD/FREE
COM/IND

BENTHAM J.,"ON THE LIBERTY OF THE PRESS, AND PUBLIC
DISCUSSION" IN J. BOWRING, ED., THE WORKS OF JEREMY
BENTHAM." SPAIN UK LAW ELITES NAT/G LEGIS INSPECT
LEGIT WRITING CONTROL PRIVIL TOTALISM AUTHORIT
...TRADIT 19 FREE/SPEE. PAGE 10 E0193
— C43 ORD/FREE PRESS CONFER CONSERVE

BENTHAM J.,"PRINCIPLES OF INTERNATIONAL LAW" IN J.
BOWRING, ED., THE WORKS OF JEREMY BENTHAM." UNIV
NAT/G PLAN PROB/SOLV DIPLOM CONTROL SANCTION MORAL
ORD/FREE PWR SOVEREIGN 19. PAGE 10 E0194
— C43 INT/LAW JURID WAR PEACE

ADLER M.J.,HOW TO THINK ABOUT WAR AND PEACE. WOR-45
LAW SOCIETY EX/STRUC DIPLOM KNOWL ORD/FREE...POLICY
TREND GEN/LAWS 20. PAGE 3 E0049
— B44 INT/ORG CREATE ARMS/CONT PEACE

BRIERLY J.L.,THE OUTLOOK FOR INTERNATIONAL LAW. FUT
WOR-45 CONSTN NAT/G VOL/ASSN FORCES ECO/TAC DOMIN
LEGIT ADJUD ROUTINE PEACE ORD/FREE...INT/LAW JURID
METH LEAGUE/NAT 20. PAGE 15 E0298
— B44 INT/ORG LAW

DE HUSZAR G.B.,NEW PERSPECTIVES ON PEACE. UNIV
CULTURE SOCIETY ECO/DEV ECO/UNDEV NAT/G FORCES
CREATE ECO/TAC DOMIN ADJUD COERCE DRIVE ORD/FREE
...GEOG JURID PSY SOC CONCPT TOT/POP. PAGE 29 E0584
— B44 ATTIT MYTH PEACE WAR

FULLER G.H.,MILITARY GOVERNMENT: A LIST OF
REFERENCES (A PAMPHLET). ITALY UK USA-45 WOR-45 LAW
FORCES DOMIN ADMIN ARMS/CONT ORD/FREE PWR
...DECISION 20 CHINJAP. PAGE 41 E0822
— B44 BIBLIOG DIPLOM CIVMIL/REL SOVEREIGN

HUDSON M.,INTERNATIONAL TRIBUNALS PAST AND FUTURE.
FUT WOR-45 LAW EDU/PROP ADJUD ORD/FREE...CONCPT
TIME/SEQ TREND GEN/LAWS TOT/POP VAL/FREE 18/20.
PAGE 56 E1111
— B44 INT/ORG STRUCT INT/LAW

SUAREZ F.,A TREATISE ON LAWS AND GOD THE LAWGIVER
(1612) IN SELECTIONS FROM THREE WORKS, VOL. II.
FRANCE ITALY UK CULTURE NAT/G SECT CHIEF LEGIS
DOMIN LEGIT CT/SYS ORD/FREE PWR WORSHIP 16/17.
PAGE 94 E1892
— B44 LAW JURID GEN/LAWS CATH

JEFFERSON T.,"DEMOCRACY" (1816) IN BASIC WRITINGS."
USA-45 LOC/G NAT/G TAX CT/SYS CHOOSE ORD/FREE
...GEN/LAWS 18/19 JEFFERSN/T. PAGE 58 E1151
— C44 POPULISM MAJORIT REPRESENT CONSTN

BEVERIDGE W.,THE PRICE OF PEACE. GERMANY UK WOR+45
WOR-45 NAT/G FORCES CREATE LEGIT REGION WAR ATTIT
KNOWL ORD/FREE PWR...POLICY NEW/IDEA GEN/LAWS
LEAGUE/NAT 20 TREATY. PAGE 12 E0223
— B45 INT/ORG TREND PEACE

HILL N.,CLAIMS TO TERRITORY IN INTERNATIONAL LAW
AND RELATIONS. WOR-45 NAT/G DOMIN EDU/PROP LEGIT
REGION ROUTINE ORD/FREE PWR WEALTH...GEOG INT/LAW
JURID 20. PAGE 52 E1047
— B45 INT/ORG ADJUD SOVEREIGN

TINGSTERN H.,PEACE AND SECURITY AFTER WW II. WOR-45
DELIB/GP TOP/EX LEGIT CT/SYS COERCE PEACE ATTIT
PERCEPT...CONCPT LEAGUE/NAT 20. PAGE 96 E1927
— B45 INT/ORG ORD/FREE WAR INT/LAW

WEST R.,CONSCIENCE AND SOCIETY: A STUDY OF THE
PSYCHOLOGICAL PREREQUISITES OF LAW AND ORDER. FUT
UNIV LAW SOCIETY STRUCT DIPLOM WAR PERS/REL SUPEGO
...SOC 20. PAGE 105 E2112
— B45 COERCE INT/LAW ORD/FREE PERSON

GILLIN J.L.,SOCIAL PATHOLOGY. SOCIETY SECT CRIME
ANOMIE DISPL ORD/FREE WEALTH...CRIMLGY PSY WORSHIP.
PAGE 44 E0864
— B46 SOC ADJUST CULTURE INGP/REL

KEETON G.W.,MAKING INTERNATIONAL LAW WORK. FUT
WOR-45 NAT/G DELIB/GP FORCES LEGIT COERCE PEACE
ATTIT RIGID/FLEX ORD/FREE PWR...JURID CONCPT
HIST/WRIT GEN/METH LEAGUE/NAT 20. PAGE 60 E1193
— B46 INT/ORG ADJUD INT/LAW

ERNST M.L.,"THE FIRST FREEDOM." USA-45 LAW R+D
PRESS 20. PAGE 35 E0696
— L46 BIBLIOG EDU/PROP

HOCKING W.E.,FREEDOM OF THE PRESS: A FRAMEWORK OF
PRINCIPLE. WOR-45 SOCIETY NAT/G PROB/SOLV DEBATE
LOBBY...JURID PSY 20 AMEND/I. PAGE 53 E1061
— B47 ORD/FREE CONSTN PRESS LAW

HYDE C.C.,INTERNATIONAL LAW, CHIEFLY AS INTERPRETED
AND APPLIED BY THE UNITED STATES (3 VOLS., 2ND REV.
ED.). USA+45 WOR+45 INT/ORG CT/SYS WAR
NAT/LISM PEACE ORD/FREE...JURID 19/20 TREATY.
PAGE 56 E1119
— B47 INT/LAW DIPLOM NAT/G POLICY

KONVITZ M.R.,THE CONSTITUTION AND CIVIL RIGHTS.
USA-45 NAT/G ADJUD GP/REL RACE/REL POPULISM
...MAJORIT 19/20 SUPREME/CT CIV/RIGHTS. PAGE 61
E1227
— B47 CONSTN LAW GOV/REL ORD/FREE

LOCKE J.,TWO TREATISES OF GOVERNMENT (1690). UK LAW
SOCIETY LEGIS LEGIT AGREE REV OWN HEREDITY MORAL
CONSERVE...POLICY MAJORIT 17 WILLIAM/3 NATURL/LAW.
PAGE 66 E1316
— B47 CONCPT ORD/FREE NAT/G CONSEN

MCILWAIN C.H.,CONSTITUTIONALISM: ANCIENT AND
MODERN. USA+45 ROMAN/EMP LAW CHIEF LEGIS CT/SYS
GP/REL ORD/FREE SOVEREIGN...POLICY TIME/SEQ
ROMAN/REP EUROPE. PAGE 71 E1419
— B47 CONSTN NAT/G PARL/PROC GOV/COMP

FOX W.T.R.,UNITED STATES POLICY IN A TWO POWER
WORLD. COM USA+45 USSR FORCES DOMIN AGREE NEUTRAL
NUC/PWR ORD/FREE SOVEREIGN 20 COLD/WAR TREATY
EUROPE/W INTERVENT. PAGE 39 E0780
— N47 DIPLOM FOR/AID POLICY

CORWIN E.S.,LIBERTY AGAINST GOVERNMENT. UK USA-45
ROMAN/EMP LAW CONSTN PERS/REL OWN ATTIT 1/20
ROMAN/LAW ENGLSH/LAW AMEND/XIV. PAGE 26 E0513
— B48 JURID ORD/FREE CONCPT

CORWIN E.S.,LIBERTY AGAINST GOVERNMENT: THE RISE,
FLOWERING AND DECLINE OF A FAMOUS JURIDICAL
CONCEPT. LEGIS ADJUD CT/SYS SANCTION GOV/REL
FEDERAL CONSERVE NEW/LIB...OLD/LIB 18/20 ROMAN/LAW
COMMON/LAW. PAGE 26 E0514
— B48 CONCPT ORD/FREE JURID CONSTN

HOLCOMBE A.N.,HUMAN RIGHTS IN THE MODERN WORLD.
WOR+45 LEGIS DIPLOM ADJUD PERSON...INT/LAW 20 UN
TREATY CIVIL/LIB BILL/RIGHT. PAGE 54 E1071
— B48 ORD/FREE INT/ORG CONSTN LAW

MEIKLEJOHN A.,FREE SPEECH AND ITS RELATION TO SELF-
GOVERNMENT. USA+45 USA-45 LAW DOMIN PRESS ORD/FREE
20 AMEND/I. PAGE 72 E1434
— B48 LEGIS NAT/G CONSTN PRIVIL

BRADEN G.D.,"THE SEARCH FOR OBJECTIVITY IN
CONSTITUTIONAL LAW" (BMR)" USA+45 USA-45 LAW NAT/G
CONTROL ORD/FREE PWR OBJECTIVE...JURID 20
SUPREME/CT. PAGE 15 E0283
— S48 CONSTN CT/SYS IDEA/COMP POLICY

BRUCKER H.,FREEDOM OF INFORMATION. USA-45 LAW LOC/G
ECO/TAC DOMIN PWR...NEW/IDEA BIBLIOG 17/20. PAGE 16
E0320
— B49 PRESS COM/IND ORD/FREE NAT/G

DE HUSZAR G.B.,EQUALITY IN AMERICA: THE ISSUE OF
MINORITY RIGHTS. USA+45 USA-45 LAW NEIGH SCHOOL
LEGIS ACT/RES CHOOSE ATTIT RESPECT...ANTHOL 20
NEGRO. PAGE 29 E0585
— B49 DISCRIM RACE/REL ORD/FREE PROB/SOLV

DENNING A.,FREEDOM UNDER THE LAW. MOD/EUR UK LAW
SOCIETY CHIEF EX/STRUC LEGIS ADJUD CT/SYS PERS/REL
PERSON 17/20 ENGLSH/LAW. PAGE 31 E0606
— B49 ORD/FREE JURID NAT/G

KAFKA G.,FREIHEIT UND ANARCHIE. SECT COERCE DETER
WAR ATTIT...IDEA/COMP 20 NATO. PAGE 59 E1179
— B49 CONCPT ORD/FREE JURID INT/ORG

SCHONS D.,BOOK CENSORSHIP IN NEW SPAIN (NEW WORLD
STUDIES, BOOK II). SPAIN LAW CULTURE INSPECT ADJUD
— B49 CHRIST-17C EDU/PROP

CT/SYS SANCTION GP/REL ORD/FREE 14/17. PAGE 88   CONTROL
E1764   PRESS

                                                  B49
SUMMERS R.E..FEDERAL INFORMATION CONTROLS IN   ADJUD
PEACETIME. USA+45 COM/IND DOMIN INGP/REL ATTIT   CONTROL
ORD/FREE 20. PAGE 94 E1893   EDU/PROP
                                                  PRESS

                                                  B49
THOREAU H.D..CIVIL DISOBEDIENCE (1849). USA-45 LAW GEN/LAWS
CONSTN TAX COERCE REPRESENT GP/REL SUPEGO...MAJORIT ORD/FREE
CONCPT 19. PAGE 96 E1923   POLICY

                                                  B49
US LIBRARY OF CONGRESS.FREEDOM OF INFORMATION: BIBLIOG/A
SELECTIVE REPORT ON RECENT WRITINGS. USA+45 LAW   ORD/FREE
CONSTN ELITES EDU/PROP PRESS LOBBY WAR TOTALISM   LICENSE
ATTIT 20 UN UNESCO COLD/WAR. PAGE 101 E2018   COM/IND

                                                  B49
WALINE M..LE CONTROLE JURIDICTIONNEL DE   JURID
L'ADMINISTRATION. BELGIUM FRANCE UAR JUDGE BAL/PWR ADMIN
ADJUD CONTROL CT/SYS...GP/COMP 20. PAGE 104 E2093 PWR
                                                  ORD/FREE

                                                  L49
COMM. STUDY ORGAN. PEACE."A TEN YEAR RECORD,   INT/ORG
1939-1949." FUT WOR+45 LAW R+D CONSULT DELIB/GP   CONSTN
CREATE LEGIT ROUTINE ORD/FREE...TIME/SEQ UN 20.   PEACE
PAGE 24 E0480

                                                  L49
MARX C.M.."ADMINISTRATIVE ETHICS AND THE RULE OF   ADMIN
LAW." USA+45 ELITES ACT/RES DOMIN NEUTRAL ROUTINE LAW
INGP/REL ORD/FREE...JURID IDEA/COMP. PAGE 69 E1375

                                                  B50
BERMAN H.J..JUSTICE IN RUSSIA; AN INTERPRETATION OF JURID
SOVIET LAW. USSR LAW STRUCT LABOR FORCES AGREE   ADJUD
GP/REL ORD/FREE SOCISM...TIME/SEQ 20. PAGE 11 E0207 MARXISM
                                                  COERCE

                                                  B50
FRANK J..COURTS ON TRIAL: MYTH AND REALITY IN   JURID
AMERICAN JUSTICE. LAW CONSULT PROB/SOLV EDU/PROP   CT/SYS
ADJUD ROUTINE ROLE ORD/FREE...GEN/LAWS T 20.   MYTH
PAGE 40 E0788   CONSTN

                                                  B50
JIMENEZ E..VOTING AND HANDLING OF DISPUTES IN THE DELIB/GP
SECURITY COUNCIL. WOR+45 CONSTN INT/ORG DIPLOM   ROUTINE
LEGIT DETER CHOOSE MORAL ORD/FREE PWR...JURID
TIME/SEQ COLD/WAR UN 20. PAGE 59 E1168

                                                  B50
ROSS A..CONSTITUTION OF THE UNITED NATIONS. CONSTN PEACE
CONSULT DELIB/GP ECO/TAC...INT/LAW JURID 20 UN   DIPLOM
LEAGUE/NAT. PAGE 86 E1721   ORD/FREE
                                                  INT/ORG

                                                  B51
BIDDLE F..THE FEAR OF FREEDOM. USA+45 LAW NAT/G   ANOMIE
PUB/INST PROB/SOLV DOMIN CONTROL SANCTION REV   INGP/REL
NAT/LISM 20. PAGE 12 E0227   VOL/ASSN
                                                  ORD/FREE

                                                  B51
BISSAINTHE M..DICTIONNAIRE DE BIBLIOGRAPHIE   BIBLIOG
HAITIENNE. HAITI ELITES AGRI LEGIS DIPLOM INT/TRADE L/A+17C
WRITING ORD/FREE CATHISM...ART/METH GEOG 19/20   SOCIETY
NEGRO TREATY. PAGE 12 E0234   NAT/G

                                                  B51
DAVIS K.C..ADMINISTRATIVE LAW. USA+45 USA-45 NAT/G ADMIN
PROB/SOLV BAL/PWR CONTROL ORD/FREE...POLICY 20   JURID
SUPREME/CT. PAGE 29 E0574   EX/STRUC
                                                  ADJUD

                                                  B51
FITCH R.E..THE LIMITS OF LIBERTY. COERCE...JURID   ORD/FREE
GEN/LAWS. PAGE 38 E0759   CONCPT
                                                  PWR

                                                  B51
FRIEDMANN W..LAW AND SOCIAL CHANGE IN CONTEMPORARY LAW
BRITAIN. UK LABOR LG/CO LEGIS JUDGE CT/SYS ORD/FREE ADJUD
NEW/LIB...DECISION JURID TREND METH/COMP BIBLIOG 20 SOCIETY
PARLIAMENT ENGLSH/LAW COMMON/LAW. PAGE 40 E0802   CONSTN

                                                  B51
HUXLEY J..FREEDOM AND CULTURE. UNIV LAW SOCIETY R+D CULTURE
ACADEM SCHOOL CREATE SANCTION ATTIT KNOWL...HUM   ORD/FREE
ANTHOL 20. PAGE 56 E1118   PHIL/SCI
                                                  IDEA/COMP

                                                  B51
KELSEN H..THE LAW OF THE UNITED NATIONS. WOR+45   INT/ORG
STRUCT RIGID/FLEX ORD/FREE...INT/LAW JURID CONCPT ADJUD
CON/ANAL GEN/METH UN TOT/POP VAL/FREE 20. PAGE 60
E1198

                                                  L51
KELSEN H.."RECENT TRENDS IN THE LAW OF THE UNITED INT/ORG
NATIONS." KOREA WOR+45 CONSTN LEGIS DIPLOM LEGIT   LAW
DETER WAR RIGID/FLEX HEALTH ORD/FREE RESPECT   INT/LAW
...JURID CON/ANAL UN VAL/FREE 20 NATO. PAGE 60
E1199

                                                  L51
LISSITZYN O.J.."THE INTERNATIONAL COURT OF   ADJUD
JUSTICE." WOR+45 INT/ORG LEGIT ORD/FREE...CONCPT   JURID
TIME/SEQ TREND GEN/LAWS VAL/FREE 20 ICJ. PAGE 65   INT/LAW
E1304

                                                  B52
COLEMAN J.W. JR..DEATH AT THE COURT-HOUSE. CONTROL CROWD
COERCE 20 KENTUCKY. PAGE 24 E0472   ORD/FREE
                                                  CRIME
                                                  CT/SYS

                                                  B52
DU BOIS W.E.B..IN BATTLE FOR PEACE. AFR USA+45   PEACE
COLONIAL CT/SYS PERS/REL PERSON ORD/FREE...JURID 20 RACE/REL
NEGRO CIVIL/LIB. PAGE 33 E0650   DISCRIM
                                                  BIOG

                                                  B52
GELLHORN W..THE STATES AND SUBVERSION. USA+45   PROVS
USA-45 LOC/G DELIB/GP LEGIS EDU/PROP LEGIT CT/SYS JURID
REGION PEACE ATTIT ORD/FREE SOCISM...INT CON/ANAL
20 CALIFORNIA MARYLAND ILLINOIS MICHIGAN NEW/YORK.
PAGE 43 E0845

                                                  B52
JACKSON E..MEETING OF THE MINDS: A WAY TO PEACE   LABOR
THROUGH MEDIATION. WOR+45 INDUS INT/ORG NAT/G   JUDGE
DELIB/GP DIPLOM EDU/PROP LEGIT ORD/FREE...NEW/IDEA
SELF/OBS TIME/SEQ CHARTS GEN/LAWS TOT/POP 20 UN
TREATY. PAGE 57 E1139

                                                  B52
KELSEN H..PRINCIPLES OF INTERNATIONAL LAW. WOR+45 ADJUD
WOR-45 INT/ORG ORD/FREE...JURID GEN/LAWS TOT/POP   CONSTN
20. PAGE 60 E1200   INT/LAW

                                                  B52
MORRIS R.B..FAIR TRIAL. USA-45 JUDGE ORD/FREE   ADJUD
...JURID 20. PAGE 75 E1498   CT/SYS
                                                  CRIME
                                                  LAW

                                                  B52
PASCUAL R.R..PARTYLESS DEMOCRACY. PHILIPPINE   POL/PAR
BARGAIN LOBBY CHOOSE EFFICIENCY ATTIT 20. PAGE 80 ORD/FREE
E1600   JURID
                                                  ECO/UNDEV

                                                  B53
COKE E..INSTITUTES OF THE LAWS OF ENGLAND   JURID
(1628-1658). UK LAW ADJUD PERS/REL ORD/FREE   OWN
...CRIMLGY 11/17. PAGE 24 E0471   CT/SYS
                                                  CONSTN

                                                  B53
KIRK R..THE CONSERVATIVE MIND. POL/PAR ORD/FREE   CONSERVE
...JURID CONCPT 18/20. PAGE 61 E1220   PERSON
                                                  PHIL/SCI
                                                  IDEA/COMP

                                                  B53
OPPENHEIM L..INTERNATIONAL LAW: A TREATISE (7TH   INT/LAW
ED., 2 VOLS.). LAW CONSTN PROB/SOLV INT/TRADE ADJUD INT/ORG
AGREE NEUTRAL WAR ORD/FREE SOVEREIGN...BIBLIOG 20 DIPLOM
LEAGUE/NAT UN ILO. PAGE 79 E1579

                                                  B53
STOUT H.M..BRITISH GOVERNMENT. UK FINAN LOC/G   NAT/G
POL/PAR DELIB/GP DIPLOM ADMIN COLONIAL CHOOSE   PARL/PROC
ORD/FREE...JURID BIBLIOG 20 COMMONWLTH. PAGE 94   CONSTN
E1883   NEW/LIB

                                                  B54
ELIAS T.O..GROUNDWORK OF NIGERIAN LAW. AFR LEAD   JURID
CRIME INGP/REL ORD/FREE 17/20. PAGE 34 E0680   CT/SYS
                                                  CONSTN
                                                  CONSULT

                                                  B54
JAMES L.F..THE SUPREME COURT IN AMERICAN LIFE.   ADJUD
USA+45 USA-45 CONSTN CRIME GP/REL INGP/REL RACE/REL CT/SYS
CONSEN FEDERAL PERSON ORD/FREE 18/20 SUPREME/CT   JURID

DEPRESSION CIV/RIGHTS CHURCH/STA FREE/SPEE. PAGE 58 DECISION
E1147

B54
SINCO,PHILIPPINE POLITICAL LAW: PRINCIPLES AND | LAW
CONCEPTS (10TH ED.). PHILIPPINE LOC/G EX/STRUC | CONSTN
BAL/PWR ECO/TAC TAX ADJUD ADMIN CONTROL CT/SYS SUFF | LEGIS
ORD/FREE...T 20. PAGE 91 E1831

B54
WRIGHT Q.,PROBLEMS OF STABILITY AND PROGRESS IN | INT/ORG
INTERNATIONAL RELATIONSHIPS. FUT WOR+45 WOR-45 | CONCPT
SOCIETY LEGIS CREATE TEC/DEV ECO/TAC EDU/PROP ADJUD | DIPLOM
WAR PEACE ORD/FREE PWR...KNO/TEST TREND GEN/LAWS
20. PAGE 108 E2155

L54
NICOLSON H.,"THE EVOLUTION OF DIPLOMATIC METHOD." | RIGID/FLEX
CHRIST-17C EUR+WWI FRANCE FUT ITALY MEDIT-7 MOD/EUR | METH/CNCPT
USA+45 USA-45 LAW NAT/G CREATE EDU/PROP LEGIT PEACE | DIPLOM
ATTIT ORD/FREE RESPECT SOVEREIGN. PAGE 77 E1548

B55
BEISEL A.R.,CONTROL OVER ILLEGAL ENFORCEMENT OF THE | ORD/FREE
CRIMINAL LAW: ROLE OF THE SUPREME COURT. CONSTN | LAW
ROUTINE MORAL PWR...SOC 20 SUPREME/CT. PAGE 9 E0180 | CRIME

B55
BENTON W.E.,NUREMBERG: GERMAN VIEWS OF THE WAR | CRIME
TRIALS. EUR+WWI GERMANY VOL/ASSN LEAD PARTIC COERCE | WAR
INGP/REL RACE/REL TOTALISM SUPEGO ORD/FREE...ANTHOL | LAW
NUREMBERG. PAGE 10 E0201 | JURID

B55
BLOOM G.F.,ECONOMICS OF LABOR RELATIONS. USA+45 LAW | ECO/DEV
CONSULT WORKER CAP/ISM PAY ADJUD CONTROL EFFICIENCY | ECO/TAC
ORD/FREE...CHARTS 19/20 AFL/CIO NLRB DEPT/LABOR. | LABOR
PAGE 13 E0249 | GOV/REL

B55
BURR R.N.,DOCUMENTS ON INTER-AMERICAN COOPERATION: | BIBLIOG
VOL. I, 1810-1881; VOL. II, 1881-1948. DELIB/GP | DIPLOM
BAL/PWR INT/TRADE REPRESENT NAT/LISM PEACE HABITAT | INT/ORG
ORD/FREE PWR SOVEREIGN...INT/LAW 20 OAS. PAGE 18 | L/A+17C
E0345

B55
CHENERY W.L.,FREEDOM OF THE PRESS. USA+45 USA-45 | ORD/FREE
LAW NAT/G DOMIN EDU/PROP 17/20. PAGE 22 E0427 | COM/IND
| PRESS
| CONSTN

B55
DE ARAGAO J.G.,LA JURIDICTION ADMINISTRATIVE AU | EX/STRUC
BRESIL. BRAZIL ADJUD COLONIAL CT/SYS REV FEDERAL | ADMIN
ORD/FREE...BIBLIOG 19/20. PAGE 29 E0580 | NAT/G

B55
FLIESS P.J.,FREEDOM OF THE PRESS IN THE GERMAN | EDU/PROP
REPUBLIC, 1918-1933. GERMANY LAW CONSTN POL/PAR | ORD/FREE
LEGIS WRITING ADMIN COERCE MURDER MARXISM...POLICY | JURID
BIBLIOG 20 WEIMAR/REP. PAGE 39 E0765 | PRESS

B55
GRINDEL C.W.,CONCEPT OF FREEDOM. WOR+45 WOR-45 LAW | ORD/FREE
LABOR NAT/G SECT EDU/PROP 20. PAGE 47 E0942 | DIPLOM
| CONCPT
| GP/REL

B55
HOGAN W.N.,INTERNATIONAL CONFLICT AND COLLECTIVE | INT/ORG
SECURITY: THE PRINCIPLE OF CONCERN IN INTERNATIONAL | WAR
ORGANIZATION. CONSTN EX/STRUC BAL/PWR DIPLOM ADJUD | ORD/FREE
CONTROL CENTRAL CONSEN PEACE...INT/LAW CONCPT | FORCES
METH/COMP 20 UN LEAGUE/NAT. PAGE 53 E1066

B55
SVARLIEN O.,AN INTRODUCTION TO THE LAW OF NATIONS. | INT/LAW
SEA AIR INT/ORG NAT/G CHIEF ADMIN AGREE WAR PRIVIL | DIPLOM
ORD/FREE SOVEREIGN...BIBLIOG 16/20. PAGE 95 E1897

B55
UN HEADQUARTERS LIBRARY,BIBLIOGRAPHIE DE LA CHARTE | BIBLIOG/A
DES NATIONS UNIES. CHINA/COM KOREA WOR+45 VOL/ASSN | INT/ORG
CONFER ADMIN COERCE PEACE ATTIT ORD/FREE SOVEREIGN | DIPLOM
...INT/LAW 20 UNESCO UN. PAGE 97 E1953

S55
BETH L.P.,"THE CASE FOR JUDICIAL PROTECTION OF | CT/SYS
CIVIL LIBERTIES" (BMR)" USA+45 CONSTN ELITES LEGIS | JUDGE
CONTROL...POLICY DECISION JURID 20 SUPREME/CT | ADJUD
CIVIL/LIB. PAGE 11 E0220 | ORD/FREE

B56
ALEXANDER F.,THE CRIMINAL, THE JUDGE, AND THE | CRIME
PUBLIC. LAW CULTURE CONSULT LEGIT ADJUD SANCTION | CRIMLGY

ORD/FREE 20. PAGE 3 E0060 | PSY
| ATTIT

B56
DOUGLAS W.O.,WE THE JUDGES. INDIA USA+45 USA-45 LAW | ADJUD
NAT/G SECT LEGIS PRESS CRIME FEDERAL ORD/FREE | CT/SYS
...POLICY GOV/COMP 19/20 WARRN/EARL MARSHALL/J | CONSTN
SUPREME/CT. PAGE 32 E0640 | GOV/REL

B56
FIELD G.C.,POLITICAL THEORY. POL/PAR REPRESENT | CONCPT
MORAL SOVEREIGN...JURID IDEA/COMP. PAGE 38 E0745 | NAT/G
| ORD/FREE
| DIPLOM

B56
HURST J.W.,LAW AND THE CONDITIONS OF FREEDOM IN THE | LAW
NINETEENTH CENTURY UNITED STATES. USA-45 CONSTN | ORD/FREE
STRUCT ADMIN GP/REL FEDERAL HABITAT...JURID 19. | POLICY
PAGE 56 E1116 | NAT/G

B56
JESSUP P.C.,TRANSNATIONAL LAW. FUT WOR+45 JUDGE | LAW
CREATE ADJUD ORD/FREE...CONCPT VAL/FREE 20. PAGE 59 | JURID
E1167 | INT/LAW

B56
KUPER L.,PASSIVE RESISTANCE IN SOUTH AFRICA. | ORD/FREE
SOUTH/AFR LAW NAT/G POL/PAR VOL/ASSN DISCRIM | RACE/REL
...POLICY SOC AUD/VIS 20. PAGE 62 E1237 | ATTIT

B56
PEASLEE A.J.,CONSTITUTIONS OF NATIONS. WOR+45 LAW | CONSTN
NAT/G EX/STRUC LEGIS TOP/EX LEGIT CT/SYS ROUTINE | CON/ANAL
CHOOSE ORD/FREE PWR SOVEREIGN...CHARTS TOT/POP.
PAGE 80 E1605

B56
RECASENS SICHES S.,TRATADO GENERAL DE SOCIOLOGIA. | SOC
CULTURE FAM NEIGH LEAD RACE/REL DISCRIM HABITAT | STRATA
ORD/FREE...JURID LING T SOC/INTEG 20. PAGE 84 E1677 | KIN
| GP/REL

B56
SCHROEDER T.,METHODS OF CONSTITUTIONAL | ORD/FREE
CONSTRUCTION. LAW...METH 20. PAGE 88 E1769 | CONSTN
| JURID
| EDU/PROP

B56
SOHN L.B.,CASES ON UNITED NATIONS LAW. STRUCT | INT/ORG
DELIB/GP WAR PEACE ORD/FREE...DECISION ANTHOL 20 | INT/LAW
UN. PAGE 92 E1854 | ADMIN
| ADJUD

B56
SUTHERLAND A.E.,THE LAW AND ONE MAN AMONG MANY. | JURID
USA+45 INTELL ADJUD CT/SYS 20. PAGE 95 E1895 | INGP/REL
| ORD/FREE
| CONCPT

B56
WIGGINS J.R.,FREEDOM OR SECRECY. USA+45 USA-45 | ORD/FREE
DELIB/GP EX/STRUC FORCES ADJUD SANCTION KNOWL PWR | PRESS
...AUD/VIS CONGRESS 20. PAGE 106 E2121 | NAT/G
| CONTROL

B57
BERNS W.,FREEDOM, VIRTUE AND THE FIRST AMENDMENT. | JURID
USA+45 USA-45 CONSTN INTELL JUDGE ADJUD RIGID/FLEX | ORD/FREE
MORAL...CONCPT 20 AMEND/I. PAGE 11 E0211 | CT/SYS
| LAW

B57
BERNS W.,FREEDOM, VIRTUE, AND THE FIRST AMENDMENT. | ADJUD
USA-45 LAW CONSTN PROB/SOLV NEW/LIB...JURID 20 | CT/SYS
SUPREME/CT AMEND/I. PAGE 11 E0212 | ORD/FREE

B57
COMM. STUDY ORGAN. PEACE,STRENGTHENING THE UNITED | INT/ORG
NATIONS. FUT USA+45 WOR+45 CONSTN NAT/G DELIB/GP | ORD/FREE
FORCES LEGIS ECO/TAC LEGIT COERCE PEACE...JURID
CONCPT UN COLD/WAR 20. PAGE 24 E0482

B57
DE VISSCHER C.,THEORY AND REALITY IN PUBLIC | INT/ORG
INTERNATIONAL LAW. WOR+45 WOR-45 SOCIETY NAT/G | LAW
CT/SYS ATTIT MORAL ORD/FREE PWR...JURID CONCPT | INT/LAW
METH/CNCPT TIME/SEQ GEN/LAWS LEAGUE/NAT TOT/POP
VAL/FREE COLD/WAR. PAGE 30 E0599

B57
DUMBAULD E.,THE BILL OF RIGHTS AND WHAT IT MEANS | CONSTN
TODAY. USA+45 USA-45 CT/SYS...JURID STYLE TIME/SEQ | LAW
BIBLIOG 18/20 BILL/RIGHT. PAGE 33 E0656 | ADJUD
| ORD/FREE

FAIRCHILD H.P.,THE ANATOMY OF FREEDOM. USA+45
ACADEM SCHOOL SECT CAP/ISM PRESS CHOOSE SOCISM.
PAGE 36 E0712
ORD/FREE
CONCPT
NAT/G
JURID
B57

INSTITUT DE DROIT INTL,TABLEAU GENERAL DES
RESOLUTIONS (1873-1956). LAW NEUTRAL CRIME WAR
MARRIAGE PEACE...JURID 19/20. PAGE 56 E1124
INT/LAW
DIPLOM
ORD/FREE
ADJUD
B57

KELSEN H.,WHAT IS JUSTICE. WOR+45 WOR-45...CONCPT
BIBLE. PAGE 60 E1201
JURID
ORD/FREE
OBJECTIVE
PHIL/SCI
B57

LEVONTIN A.V.,THE MYTH OF INTERNATIONAL SECURITY: A
JURIDICAL AND CRITICAL ANALYSIS. FUT WOR+45 WOR-45
LAW NAT/G VOL/ASSN ACT/RES BAL/PWR ATTIT ORD/FREE
...JURID METH/CNCPT TIME/SEQ TREND STERTYP 20.
PAGE 64 E1289
INT/ORG
INT/LAW
SOVEREIGN
MYTH
B57

LONG H.A.,USURPERS - FOES OF FREE MAN. LAW NAT/G
CHIEF LEGIS DOMIN ADJUD REPRESENT GOV/REL ORD/FREE
LAISSEZ POPULISM...POLICY 18/20 SUPREME/CT
ROOSEVLT/F CONGRESS CON/INTERP. PAGE 66 E1325
CT/SYS
CENTRAL
FEDERAL
CONSTN
B57

MILLS W.,INDIVIDUAL FREEDOM AND COMMON DEFENSE
(PAMPHLET). USA+45 USSR NAT/G EDU/PROP CRIME CHOOSE
20 COLD/WAR. PAGE 73 E1463
ORD/FREE
CONSTN
INGP/REL
FORCES
B57

MORELAND C.C.,EQUAL JUSTICE UNDER LAW. USA+45
USA-45 PROF/ORG PROVS JUDGE...POLICY JURID. PAGE 74
E1491
CONSTN
ADJUD
CT/SYS
ORD/FREE
B57

NEUMANN F.,THE DEMOCRATIC AND THE AUTHORITARIAN
STATE: ESSAYS IN POLITICAL AND LEGAL THEORY. USA+45
USA-45 CONTROL REV GOV/REL PEACE ALL/IDEOS
...INT/LAW CONCPT GEN/LAWS BIBLIOG 20. PAGE 77
E1536
DOMIN
NAT/G
ORD/FREE
POLICY
B57

POUND R.,THE DEVELOPMENT OF CONSTITUTIONAL
GUARANTEES OF LIBERTY. UK USA-45 CHIEF COLONIAL REV
...JURID CONCPT 15/20. PAGE 82 E1638
LAW
CONSTN
ORD/FREE
ATTIT
B57

SCHLOCHAUER H.J.,OFFENTLICHES RECHT. GERMANY/W
FINAN EX/STRUC LEGIS DIPLOM FEDERAL ORD/FREE
...INT/LAW 20. PAGE 88 E1757
CONSTN
JURID
ADMIN
CT/SYS
B57

SINCLAIR T.C.,THE POLITICS OF JUDICIAL REVIEW
1937-1957. USA+45 USA-45 NAT/G 20 SUPREME/CT
CIVIL/LIB. PAGE 91 E1830
JURID
ATTIT
ORD/FREE
RACE/REL
B57

US COMMISSION GOVT SECURITY,RECOMMENDATIONS; AREA:
LEGISLATION. USA+45 USA-45 DELIB/GP PLAN TEC/DEV
CIVMIL/REL ORD/FREE...POLICY DECISION 20 PRIVACY.
PAGE 99 E1982
LEGIS
SANCTION
CRIME
CONTROL
B57

US SENATE COMM ON JUDICIARY,CIVIL RIGHTS - 1957.
USA+45 LAW NAT/G CONFER GOV/REL RACE/REL ORD/FREE
PWR...JURID 20 SENATE CIV/RIGHTS. PAGE 102 E2039
INT
LEGIS
DISCRIM
PARL/PROC
B57

WASSENBERGH H.A.,POST-WAR INTERNATIONAL CIVIL
AVIATION POLICY AND THE LAW OF THE AIR. WOR+45 AIR
INT/ORG DOMIN LEGIT PEACE ORD/FREE...POLICY JURID
NEW/IDEA OBS TIME/SEQ TREND CHARTS 20 TREATY.
PAGE 105 E2101
COM/IND
NAT/G
INT/LAW
B57

ALLEN C.K.,ASPECTS OF JUSTICE. UK FAM COERCE CRIME
MARRIAGE AGE/Y LOVE 20 ENGLSH/LAW. PAGE 4 E0068
JURID
MORAL
ORD/FREE
B58

ALLEN C.K.,LAW IN THE MAKING. LEGIS ATTIT ORD/FREE
SOVEREIGN POPULISM...JURID IDEA/COMP NAT/COMP
LAW
CREATE
B58

GEN/LAWS 20 ENGLSH/LAW. PAGE 4 E0069
CONSTN
SOCIETY

BLOCH J.,STATES' RIGHTS: THE LAW OF THE LAND.
USA+45 USA-45 LAW CONSTN LEGIS CONTROL CT/SYS
FEDERAL ORD/FREE...PREDICT 17/20 CONGRESS
SUPREME/CT. PAGE 13 E0246
PROVS
NAT/G
BAL/PWR
CENTRAL
B58

BOWETT D.W.,SELF-DEFENSE IN INTERNATIONAL LAW.
EUR+WWI MOD/EUR WOR+45 WOR-45 SOCIETY INT/ORG
CONSULT DIPLOM LEGIT COERCE ATTIT ORD/FREE...JURID
20 UN. PAGE 14 E0276
ADJUD
CONCPT
WAR
INT/LAW
B58

CABLE G.W.,THE NEGRO QUESTION: A SELECTION OF
WRITINGS ON CIVIL RIGHTS IN THE SOUTH. USA+45
STRATA LOC/G POL/PAR GIVE EDU/PROP WRITING CT/SYS
SANCTION CRIME CHOOSE WORSHIP 20 NEGRO CIV/RIGHTS
CONV/LEASE SOUTH/US. PAGE 18 E0355
RACE/REL
CULTURE
DISCRIM
ORD/FREE
B58

CAUGHEY J.W.,IN CLEAR AND PRESENT DANGER. USA+45
ADJUD COERCE ATTIT AUTHORIT...POLICY 20 COLD/WAR
MCCARTHY/J. PAGE 21 E0408
NAT/G
CONTROL
DOMIN
ORD/FREE
B58

DOUGLAS W.O.,THE RIGHT OF THE PEOPLE. USA+45
EDU/PROP CONTROL REPRESENT PRIVIL...IDEA/COMP 20.
PAGE 32 E0641
ORD/FREE
CONSTN
CT/SYS
CIVMIL/REL
B58

FELLMAN D.,THE DEFENDANT'S RIGHTS. USA+45 NAT/G
CONSULT CT/SYS SUPEGO ORD/FREE...BIBLIOG SUPREME/CT
CIVIL/SERV. PAGE 37 E0730
CONSTN
LAW
CRIME
ADJUD
B58

HAND L.,THE BILL OF RIGHTS. USA+45 USA-45 CHIEF
LEGIS BAL/PWR ROLE PWR 18/20 SUPREME/CT CONGRESS
AMEND/V PRESIDENT AMEND/XIV. PAGE 50 E0994
CONSTN
JURID
ORD/FREE
CT/SYS
B58

HENKIN L.,ARMS CONTROL AND INSPECTION IN AMERICAN
LAW. LAW CONSTN INT/ORG LOC/G MUNIC NAT/G PROVS
EDU/PROP LEGIT EXEC NUC/PWR KNOWL ORD/FREE...OBS
TOT/POP CONGRESS 20. PAGE 52 E1032
USA+45
JURID
ARMS/CONT
B58

HERRMANN K.,DAS STAATSDENKEN BEI LEIBNIZ. GP/REL
ATTIT ORD/FREE...CONCPT IDEA/COMP 17 LEIBNITZ/G
CHURCH/STA. PAGE 52 E1034
NAT/G
JURID
SECT
EDU/PROP
B58

MOSKOWITZ M.,HUMAN RIGHTS AND WORLD ORDER. INT/ORG
PLAN GP/REL NAT/LISM SOVEREIGN...CONCPT 20 UN
TREATY CIV/RIGHTS. PAGE 75 E1502
DIPLOM
INT/LAW
ORD/FREE
B58

PALMER E.E.,CIVIL LIBERTIES. USA+45 ADJUD CT/SYS
PARTIC OWN LAISSEZ POPULISM...JURID CONCPT ANTHOL
20 SUPREME/CT CIVIL/LIB. PAGE 79 E1592
ORD/FREE
CONSTN
RACE/REL
LAW
B58

RUSSELL R.B.,A HISTORY OF THE UNITED NATIONS
CHARTER: THE ROLE OF THE UNITED STATES. SOCIETY
NAT/G CONSULT DOMIN LEGIT ATTIT ORD/FREE PWR
...POLICY JURID CONCPT UN LEAGUE/NAT. PAGE 87 E1737
USA-45
INT/ORG
CONSTN
B58

SOC OF COMP LEGIS AND INT LAW,THE LAW OF THE SEA...
(PAMPHLET). WOR+45 NAT/G INT/TRADE ADJUD CONTROL
NUC/PWR WAR PEACE ATTIT ORD/FREE...JURID CHARTS 20
UN TREATY RESOURCE/N. PAGE 92 E1850
INT/LAW
INT/ORG
DIPLOM
SEA
B58

SPITZ D.,DEMOCRACY AND THE CHALLANGE OF POWER. FUT
USA+45 USA-45 LAW SOCIETY STRUCT LOC/G POL/PAR
PROVS DELIB/GP EX/STRUC LEGIS TOP/EX ACT/RES CREATE
DOMIN EDU/PROP LEGIT ADJUD ADMIN ATTIT DRIVE MORAL
ORD/FREE TOT/POP. PAGE 93 E1862
NAT/G
PWR
B58

STONE J.,AGGRESSION AND WORLD ORDER: A CRITIQUE OF
UNITED NATIONS THEORIES OF AGGRESSION. LAW CONSTN
DELIB/GP PROB/SOLV BAL/PWR DIPLOM DEBATE ADJUD
CRIME PWR...POLICY IDEA/COMP 20 UN SUEZ LEAGUE/NAT.
PAGE 94 E1879
ORD/FREE
INT/ORG
WAR
CONCPT
B58

UNESCO,"TECHNIQUES OF MEDIATION AND CONCILIATION." INT/ORG EUR+WWI USA+45 WOR+45 INDUS FACE/GP EX/STRUC CONSULT EDU/PROP LEGIT PEACE ORD/FREE...INT/LAW TIME/SEQ DIPLOM LEAGUE/NAT 20. PAGE 98 E1961   L58

MCDOUGAL M.S.,"PERSPECTIVES FOR A LAW OF OUTER INT/ORG SPACE." FUT WOR+45 AIR CONSULT DELIB/GP TEC/DEV SPACE CT/SYS ORD/FREE...POLICY JURID 20 UN. PAGE 70 E1404 INT/LAW   S58

STAAR R.F.,"ELECTIONS IN COMMUNIST POLAND." EUR+WWI COM SOCIETY INT/ORG NAT/G POL/PAR LEGIS ACT/RES ECO/TAC CHOOSE EDU/PROP ADJUD ADMIN ROUTINE COERCE TOTALISM ATTIT POLAND ORD/FREE PWR 20. PAGE 93 E1864   S58

VOSE C.E.,"LITIGATION AS A FORM OF PRESSURE GROUP CONTROL ACTIVITY" (BMR)" USA+45 ADJUD ORD/FREE NAACP. CT/SYS PAGE 104 E2085   VOL/ASSN   LOBBY   S58

US HOUSE COMM FOREIGN AFFAIRS,HEARINGS ON DRAFT LEGIS LEGISLATION TO AMEND FURTHER THE MUTUAL SECURITY DELIB/GP ACT OF 1954 (PAMPHLET). USA+45 CONSULT FORCES CONFER BUDGET DIPLOM DETER COST ORD/FREE...JURID 20 WEAPON DEPT/DEFEN UN DEPT/STATE. PAGE 100 E2002   N58

ABRAHAM H.J.,COURTS AND JUDGES: AN INTRODUCTION TO CT/SYS THE JUDICIAL PROCESS. USA+45 CONSTN ELITES NAT/G PERSON ORD/FREE PWR 19/20 SUPREME/CT. PAGE 2 E0045 JURID   ADJUD   B59

COMM. STUDY ORGAN. PEACE,ORGANIZING PEACE IN THE INT/ORG NUCLEAR AGE. FUT CONSULT DELIB/GP DOMIN ADJUD ACT/RES ROUTINE COERCE ORD/FREE...TECHNIC INT/LAW JURID NUC/PWR NEW/IDEA UN COLD/WAR 20. PAGE 24 E0483   B59

CORBETT P.E.,LAW IN DIPLOMACY. UK USA+45 USSR NAT/G CONSTN SOCIETY INT/ORG JUDGE LEGIT ATTIT ORD/FREE ADJUD TOT/POP LEAGUE/NAT 20. PAGE 26 E0507 JURID   DIPLOM   B59

COUNCIL OF STATE GOVERNMENTS,STATE GOVERNMENT: AN BIBLIOG/A ANNOTATED BIBLIOGRAPHY (PAMPHLET). USA+45 LAW AGRI PROVS INDUS WORKER PLAN TAX ADJUST AGE/Y ORD/FREE...HEAL LOC/G MGT 20. PAGE 26 E0521 ADMIN   B59

DASH S.,THE EAVESDROPPERS. USA+45 DELIB/GP TEC/DEV CRIME ORD/FREE...POLICY CRIMLGY JURID 20 PRIVACY. PAGE 29 CONTROL E0569   ACT/RES   LAW   B59

DAVIS K.C.,ADMINISTRATIVE LAW TEXT. USA+45 NAT/G ADJUD DELIB/GP EX/STRUC CONTROL ORD/FREE...T 20 ADMIN SUPREME/CT. PAGE 29 E0577 JURID   CT/SYS   B59

ELLIOTT S.D.,IMPROVING OUR COURTS. LAW EX/STRUC CT/SYS PLAN PROB/SOLV ADJUD ADMIN TASK CRIME EFFICIENCY JURID ORD/FREE 20. PAGE 34 E0684 GOV/REL   NAT/G   B59

FELLMANN D.,THE LIMITS OF FREEDOM. USA+45 USA-45 CONCPT NAT/G SECT ROLE ORD/FREE WORSHIP 18/20 FREE/SPEE. JURID PAGE 37 E0734 CONSTN   B59

FERRY W.H.,THE CORPORATION AND THE ECONOMY. CLIENT LG/CO LAW CONSTN LABOR NAT/G PLAN INT/TRADE PARTIC CONSEN CONTROL ORD/FREE PWR POLICY. PAGE 37 E0742 REPRESENT   B59

FRIEDMANN W.G.,LAW IN A CHANGING SOCIETY. FUT SOC WOR+45 WOR-45 LAW SOCIETY STRUCT INT/TRADE LEGIT JURID ATTIT BIO/SOC HEALTH ORD/FREE SOVEREIGN...CONCPT GEN/LAWS ILO 20. PAGE 41 E0803   B59

GINZBURG B.,REDEDICATION TO FREEDOM. DELIB/GP LEGIS JURID ATTIT MARXISM 20 SUPREME/CT CON/INTERP HUAC AMEND/I ORD/FREE FBI. PAGE 44 E0871 CONSTN   NAT/G   B59

GSOVSKI V.,GOVERNMENT, LAW, AND COURTS IN THE ADJUD

SOVIET UNION AND EASTERN EUROPE (2 VOLS.). COM USSR MARXISM AGRI INDUS WORKER CT/SYS CRIME...BIBLIOG 20 CONTROL EUROPE/E. PAGE 48 E0958 ORD/FREE   B59

HOOK S.,POLITICAL POWER AND PERSONAL FREEDOM: ORD/FREE CRITICAL STUDIES IN DEMOCRACY, COMMUNISM AND CIVIL PWR RIGHTS. UNIV LAW SOCIETY DIPLOM TOTALISM MARXISM WELF/ST SOCISM...PHIL/SCI IDEA/COMP 20 CIV/RIGHTS. PAGE 55 CHOOSE E1094   B59

KIRCHHEIMER O.,GEGENWARTSPROBLEME DER DIPLOM ASYLGEWAHRUNG. DOMIN GP/REL ATTIT...NAT/COMP 20. INT/LAW PAGE 61 E1217 JURID   ORD/FREE   B59

KNIERIEM A.,THE NUREMBERG TRIALS. EUR+WWI GERMANY INT/LAW VOL/ASSN LEAD COERCE WAR INGP/REL TOTALISM SUPEGO CRIME ORD/FREE...CONCPT METH/COMP. PAGE 61 E1225 PARTIC   JURID   B59

LAPIERE R.,THE FREUDIAN ETHIC. USA+45 FAM EDU/PROP PSY CONTROL CRIME ADJUST AGE DRIVE PERCEPT PERSON SEX ORD/FREE ...SOC 20 FREUD/S. PAGE 63 E1254 SOCIETY   B59

LOEWENSTEIN K.,VERFASSUNGSRECHT UND CONSTN VERFASSUNGSPRAXIS DER VEREINIGTEN STAATEN. USA+45 POL/PAR USA-45 COLONIAL CT/SYS GP/REL RACE/REL ORD/FREE EX/STRUC ...JURID 18/20 SUPREME/CT CONGRESS PRESIDENT NAT/G BILL/RIGHT CIVIL/LIB. PAGE 66 E1319   B59

NICHOLS R.F.,RELIGION AND AMERICAN DEMOCRACY. NAT/G USA+45 USA-45 LAW CHOOSE SUFF MORAL ORD/FREE SECT POPULISM...POLICY BIBLIOG 16/20 PRE/US/AM CONSTN CHRISTIAN. PAGE 77 E1547 CONCPT   B59

PAULSEN M.G.,LEGAL INSTITUTIONS TODAY AND TOMORROW. JURID UK USA+45 NAT/G PROF/ORG PROVS ADMIN PARL/PROC ADJUD ORD/FREE NAT/COMP. PAGE 80 E1604 JUDGE   LEGIS   B59

REIFF H.,THE UNITED STATES AND THE TREATY LAW OF ADJUD THE SEA. USA+45 USA-45 SEA SOCIETY INT/ORG CONSULT INT/LAW DELIB/GP LEGIS DIPLOM LEGIT ATTIT ORD/FREE PWR WEALTH...GEOG JURID TOT/POP 20 TREATY. PAGE 84 E1681   B59

SCHNEIDER J.,TREATY-MAKING POWER OF INTERNATIONAL INT/ORG ORGANIZATIONS. FUT WOR+45 WOR-45 LAW NAT/G JUDGE ROUTINE DIPLOM LEGIT CT/SYS ORD/FREE PWR...INT/LAW JURID GEN/LAWS TOT/POP UNESCO 20 TREATY. PAGE 88 E1762   B59

SCHORN H.,DER RICHTER IM DRITTEN REICH; GESCHICHTE ADJUD UND DOKUMENTE. GERMANY NAT/G LEGIT CT/SYS INGP/REL JUDGE MORAL ORD/FREE RESPECT...JURID GP/COMP 20. PAGE 88 FASCISM E1765   B59

SCOTT F.R.,CIVIL LIBERTIES AND CANADIAN FEDERALISM. ORD/FREE CANADA LAW ADJUD CT/SYS GOV/REL 20 CIV/RIGHTS. FEDERAL PAGE 90 E1797 NAT/LISM   CONSTN   B59

SIMPSON J.L.,INTERNATIONAL ARBITRATION: LAW AND INT/LAW PRACTICE. WOR+45 WOR-45 INT/ORG DELIB/GP ADJUD DIPLOM PEACE MORAL ORD/FREE...METH 18/20. PAGE 91 E1829 CT/SYS   CONSULT   B59

SISSON C.H.,THE SPIRIT OF BRITISH ADMINISTRATION GOV/COMP AND SOME EUROPEAN COMPARISONS. FRANCE GERMANY/W ADMIN SWEDEN UK LAW EX/STRUC INGP/REL EFFICIENCY ORD/FREE ELITES ...DECISION 20. PAGE 91 E1835 ATTIT   B59

SPIRO H.J.,GOVERNMENT BY CONSTITUTIONS: THE NAT/G POLITICAL SYSTEMS OF DEMOCRACY. CANADA EUR+WWI FUT CONSTN USA+45 WOR+45 WOR-45 LEGIS TOP/EX LEGIT ADMIN CT/SYS ORD/FREE PWR...TREND TOT/POP VAL/FREE 20. PAGE 93 E1861   B59

WILDNER H.,DIE TECHNIK DER DIPLOMATIE. TOP/EX ROLE DIPLOM ORD/FREE...INT/LAW JURID IDEA/COMP NAT/COMP 20. POLICY PAGE 106 E2122 DELIB/GP   NAT/G   B59

COX A.,"THE ROLE OF LAW IN PRESERVING UNION
DEMOCRACY." EX/STRUC LEGIS PARTIC ROUTINE CHOOSE
INGP/REL ORD/FREE. PAGE 27 E0532
L59
LABOR
REPRESENT
LAW
MAJORIT

BEANEY W.B.,"CIVIL LIBERTIES AND STATUTORY
CONSTRUCTION"(BMR)" USA+45 LEGIS BAL/PWR 20
SUPREME/CT. PAGE 8 E0162
S59
CT/SYS
ORD/FREE
ADJUD
LAW

CARLSTON K.S.,"NATIONALIZATION: AN ANALYTIC
APPROACH." WOR+45 INT/ORG ECO/TAC DOMIN LEGIT ADJUD
COERCE ORD/FREE PWR WEALTH SOCISM...JURID CONCPT
TREND STERTYP TOT/POP VAL/FREE 20. PAGE 19 E0380
S59
INDUS
NAT/G
NAT/LISM
SOVEREIGN

CORY R.H. JR.,"INTERNATIONAL INSPECTION FROM
PROPOSALS TO REALIZATION." WOR+45 TEC/DEV ECO/TAC
ADJUD ORD/FREE PWR WEALTH...RECORD VAL/FREE 20.
PAGE 26 E0516
S59
STRUCT
PSY
ARMS/CONT
NUC/PWR

JENKS C.W.,"THE CHALLENGE OF UNIVERSALITY." FUT
UNIV CONSTN CULTURE CONSULT CREATE PLAN LEGIT ATTIT
MORAL ORD/FREE RESPECT...MAJORIT JURID 20. PAGE 58
E1155
S59
INT/ORG
LAW
PEACE
INT/LAW

MASON A.T.,"THE SUPREME COURT: TEMPLE AND FORUM"
(BMR)" USA+45 USA-45 CONSTN DELIB/GP RACE/REL
MAJORITY ORD/FREE...DECISION SOC/INTEG 19/20
SUPREME/CT WARRN/EARL CIV/RIGHTS. PAGE 69 E1377
S59
CT/SYS
JURID
PWR
ATTIT

PUGWASH CONFERENCE,"ON BIOLOGICAL AND CHEMICAL
WARFARE." WOR+45 SOCIETY PROC/MFG INT/ORG FORCES
EDU/PROP ADJUD RIGID/FLEX ORD/FREE PWR...DECISION
PSY NEW/IDEA MATH VAL/FREE 20. PAGE 83 E1661
S59
ACT/RES
BIO/SOC
WAR
WEAPON

SOHN L.B.,"THE DEFINITION OF AGGRESSION." FUT LAW
FORCES LEGIT ADJUD ROUTINE COERCE ORD/FREE PWR
...MAJORIT JURID QUANT COLD/WAR 20. PAGE 92 E1855
S59
INT/ORG
CT/SYS
DETER
SOVEREIGN

STONE J.,"CONFLICT MANAGEMENT THROUGH CONTEMPORARY
INTERNATIONAL LAW AND ORGANIZATION." WOR+45 LAW
NAT/G CREATE BAL/PWR DOMIN LEGIT ROUTINE COERCE
ATTIT ORD/FREE PWR SOVEREIGN...JURID 20. PAGE 94
E1880
S59
INT/ORG
INT/LAW

SUTTON F.X.,"REPRESENTATION AND THE NATURE OF
POLITICAL SYSTEMS." UNIV WOR-45 CULTURE SOCIETY
STRATA INT/ORG FORCES JUDGE DOMIN LEGIT EXEC REGION
REPRESENT ATTIT ORD/FREE RESPECT...SOC HIST/WRIT
TIME/SEQ. PAGE 95 E1896
S59
NAT/G
CONCPT

TIPTON J.B.,"PARTICIPATION OF THE UNITED STATES IN
THE INTERNATIONAL LABOR ORGANIZATION." USA+45 LAW
STRUCT ECO/DEV ECO/UNDEV INDUS TEC/DEV ECO/TAC
ADMIN PERCEPT ORD/FREE SKILL...STAT HIST/WRIT
GEN/METH ILO WORK 20. PAGE 96 E1928
S59
LABOR
INT/ORG

COLLINS I.,"THE GOVERNMENT AND THE NEWSPAPER PRESS
IN FRANCE, 1814-1881. FRANCE LAW ADMIN CT/SYS
...CON/ANAL BIBLIOG 19. PAGE 24 E0475
C59
PRESS
ORD/FREE
NAT/G
EDU/PROP

JUNZ A.J.,PRESENT TRENDS IN AMERICAN NATIONAL
GOVERNMENT. LEGIS DIPLOM ADMIN CT/SYS ORD/FREE
...CONCPT ANTHOL 20 CONGRESS PRESIDENT SUPREME/CT.
PAGE 2 E0040
B60
POL/PAR
CHOOSE
CONSTN
NAT/G

ALBI F.,TRATADO DE LOS MODOS DE GESTION DE LAS
CORPORACIONES LOCALES. SPAIN FINAN NAT/G BUDGET
CONTROL EXEC ROUTINE GOV/REL ORD/FREE SOVEREIGN
...MGT 20. PAGE 3 E0057
B60
LOC/G
LAW
ADMIN
MUNIC

BAKER G.E.,STATE CONSTITUTIONS - REAPPORTIONMENT.
USA+45 USA-45 CONSTN CHOOSE ATTIT ORD/FREE...JURID
20. PAGE 7 E0138
B60
APPORT
REPRESENT
PROVS
LEGIS

BLANSHARD P.,GOD AND MAN IN WASHINGTON. USA+45
B60
NAT/G

CHIEF LEGIS LEGIT CT/SYS PRIVIL ATTIT ORD/FREE
...POLICY CONCPT 20 SUPREME/CT CONGRESS PRESIDENT
CHURCH/STA. PAGE 12 E0242
SECT
GP/REL
POL/PAR

CASTBERG F.,FREEDOM OF SPEECH IN THE WEST. FRANCE
GERMANY USA+45 USA-45 LAW CONSTN CHIEF PRESS
DISCRIM...CONCPT 18/20. PAGE 21 E0406
B60
ORD/FREE
SANCTION
ADJUD
NAT/COMP

DILEY A.V.,INTRODUCTION TO THE STUDY OF THE LAW OF
THE CONSTITUTION. FRANCE UK USA+45 USA-45 CONSULT
FORCES TAX ADMIN FEDERAL ORD/FREE SOVEREIGN
...IDEA/COMP 20 ENGLSH/LAW CON/INTERP PARLIAMENT.
PAGE 32 E0627
B60
CONSTN
LAW
LEGIS
GEN/LAWS

FELLMAN D.,THE SUPREME COURT AND EDUCATION. ACADEM
NAT/G PROVS DELIB/GP ADJUD ORD/FREE...POLICY JURID
WORSHIP 20 SUPREME/CT NEGRO CHURCH/STA. PAGE 37
E0731
B60
CT/SYS
SECT
RACE/REL
SCHOOL

GELLHORN W.,AMERICAN RIGHTS: THE CONSTITUTION IN
ACTION. USA+45 USA-45 LEGIS ADJUD COERCE RACE/REL
DISCRIM MARXISM 20 SUPREME/CT. PAGE 43 E0846
B60
ORD/FREE
JURID
CT/SYS
CONSTN

GIBNEY F.,THE OPERATORS. USA+45 LAW STRATA BIO/SOC
MORAL ORD/FREE SOC. PAGE 43 E0858
B60
CRIME
CULTURE
ANOMIE
CRIMLGY

GOLDSEN J.M.,INTERNATIONAL POLITICAL IMPLICATIONS
OF ACTIVITIES IN OUTER SPACE. FUT USA+45 WOR+45 AIR
LAW ACT/RES LEGIT ATTIT KNOWL ORD/FREE PWR...CONCPT
20. PAGE 44 E0879
B60
R+D
SPACE

JENNINGS R.,PROGRESS OF INTERNATIONAL LAW. FUT
WOR+45 WOR-45 SOCIETY NAT/G VOL/ASSN DELIB/GP
DIPLOM EDU/PROP LEGIT COERCE ATTIT DRIVE MORAL
ORD/FREE...JURID CONCPT OBS TIME/SEQ TREND
GEN/LAWS. PAGE 58 E1164
B60
INT/ORG
LAW
INT/LAW

MENDELSON W.,CAPITALISM, DEMOCRACY, AND THE SUPREME
COURT. USA+45 USA-45 CONSTN DIPLOM GOV/REL ATTIT
ORD/FREE LAISSEZ...POLICY CHARTS PERS/COMP 18/20
SUPREME/CT MARSHALL/J HOLMES/OW TANEY/RB FIELD/JJ.
PAGE 72 E1437
B60
JUDGE
CT/SYS
JURID
NAT/G

MOCTEZUMA A.P.,EL CONFLICTO RELIGIOSO DE 1926 (2ND
ED.). L/A+17C LAW NAT/G LOBBY COERCE GP/REL ATTIT
...POLICY 20 MEXIC/AMER CHURCH/STA. PAGE 74 E1476
B60
SECT
ORD/FREE
DISCRIM
REV

PAUL A.M.,CONSERVATIVE CRISIS AND THE RULE OF LAW.
USA-45 LABOR WORKER ATTIT ORD/FREE CONSERVE LAISSEZ
...DECISION JURID 19 SUPREME/CT. PAGE 80 E1603
B60
CONSTN
ADJUD
STRUCT
PROF/ORG

PINTO F.B.M.,ENRIQUECIMENTO ILICITO NO EXERCICIO DE
CARGOS PUBLICOS. BRAZIL L/A+17C USA+45 ELITES
TRIBUTE CONTROL INGP/REL ORD/FREE PWR...NAT/COMP
20. PAGE 81 E1617
B60
ADMIN
NAT/G
CRIME
LAW

SCHEIBER H.N.,THE WILSON ADMINISTRATION AND CIVIL
LIBERTIES 1917-1921. LAW GOV/REL ATTIT 20 WILSON/W
CIVIL/LIB. PAGE 87 E1754
B60
ORD/FREE
WAR
NAT/G
CONTROL

SCHUBERT G.A.,CONSTITUTIONAL POLITICS: THE
POLITICAL BEHAVIOR OF SUPREME COURT JUSTICES AND
THE CONSTITUTIONAL POLICIES THEY MAKE. LAW ELITES
CHIEF DELIB/GP EX/STRUC LEGIS DISCRIM ORD/FREE PWR
...POLICY MAJORIT CHARTS SUPREME/CT CONGRESS.
PAGE 89 E1781
B60
CONSTN
CT/SYS
JURID
DECISION

WEBSTER J.A.,A GENERAL STUDY OF THE DEPARTMENT OF
DEFENSE INTERNAL SECURITY PROGRAM. USA+45 WORKER
TEC/DEV ADJUD CONTROL CT/SYS EXEC GOV/REL COST
...POLICY DECISION MGT 20 DEPT/DEFEN SUPREME/CT.
PAGE 105 E2105
B60
ORD/FREE
PLAN
ADMIN
NAT/G

WOETZEL R.K.,THE INTERNATIONAL CONTROL OF AIRSPACE
B60
INT/ORG

AND OUTERSPACE. FUT WOR+45 AIR CONSTN STRUCT
CONSULT PLAN TEC/DEV ADJUD RIGID/FLEX KNOWL
ORD/FREE PWR...TECHNIC GEOG MGT NEW/IDEA TREND
COMPUT/IR VAL/FREE 20 TREATY. PAGE 107 E2137
 JURID
 SPACE
 INT/LAW

L60

DEAN A.W.."SECOND GENEVA CONFERENCE OF THE LAW OF
THE SEA: THE FIGHT FOR FREEDOM OF THE SEAS." FUT
USA+45 USSR WOR+45 WOR-45 SEA CONSTN STRUCT PLAN
INT/TRADE ADJUD ADMIN ORD/FREE...DECISION RECORD
TREND GEN/LAWS 20 TREATY. PAGE 30 E0600
 INT/ORG
 JURID
 INT/LAW

S60

BLACK H.."THE BILL OF RIGHTS" (BMR)" USA+45 USA-45
LAW LEGIS CT/SYS FEDERAL PWR 18/20 CONGRESS
SUPREME/CT BILL/RIGHT CIV/RIGHTS. PAGE 12 E0237
 CONSTN
 ORD/FREE
 NAT/G
 JURID

S60

GRACIA-MORA M.R.."INTERNATIONAL RESPONSIBILITY FOR
SUBVERSIVE ACTIVITIES AND HOSTILE PROPAGANDA BY
PRIVATE PERSONS AGAINST." COM EUR+WWI L/A+17C UK
USA+45 USSR WOR-45 CONSTN NAT/G LEGIT ADJUD REV
PEACE TOTALISM ORD/FREE...INT/LAW 20. PAGE 45 E0895
 INT/ORG
 JURID
 SOVEREIGN

S60

POTTER P.B.."RELATIVE VALUES OF INTERNATIONAL
RELATIONS, LAW, AND ORGANIZATIONS." WOR+45 NAT/G
LEGIT ADJUD ORD/FREE...CONCPT TOT/POP COLD/WAR 20.
PAGE 81 E1633
 INT/ORG
 LEGIS
 DIPLOM
 INT/LAW

S60

RHYNE C.S.."LAW AS AN INSTRUMENT FOR PEACE." FUT
WOR+45 PLAN LEGIT ROUTINE ARMS/CONT NUC/PWR ATTIT
ORD/FREE...JURID METH/CNCPT TREND CON/ANAL HYPO/EXP
COLD/WAR 20. PAGE 84 E1690
 ADJUD
 EDU/PROP
 INT/LAW
 PEACE

S60

ROURKE F.E.."ADMINISTRATIVE SECRECY: A
CONGRESSIONAL DILEMMA." DELIB/GP CT/SYS ATTIT
...MAJORIT DECISION JURID. PAGE 86 E1727
 LEGIS
 EXEC
 ORD/FREE
 POLICY

S60

THOMPSON K.W.."MORAL PURPOSE IN FOREIGN POLICY:
REALITIES AND ILLUSIONS." WOR+45 WOR-45 LAW CULTURE
SOCIETY INT/ORG PLAN ADJUD ADMIN COERCE RIGID/FLEX
SUPEGO KNOWL ORD/FREE PWR...SOC TREND SOC/EXP
TOT/POP 20. PAGE 96 E1921
 MORAL
 JURID
 DIPLOM

S60

WRIGHT Q.."LEGAL ASPECTS OF THE U-2 INCIDENT." COM
USA+45 USSR STRUCT NAT/G FORCES PLAN TEC/DEV ADJUD
RIGID/FLEX MORAL ORD/FREE...DECISION INT/LAW JURID
PSY TREND GEN/LAWS COLD/WAR VAL/FREE 20 U-2.
PAGE 108 E2157
 PWR
 POLICY
 SPACE

N60

RHODESIA-NYASA NATL ARCHIVES.A SELECT BIBLIOGRAPHY
OF RECENT PUBLICATIONS CONCERNING THE FEDERATION OF
RHODESIA AND NYASALAND (PAMPHLET). MALAWI RHODESIA
LAW CULTURE STRUCT ECO/UNDEV LEGIS...GEOG 20.
PAGE 84 E1689
 BIBLIOG
 ADMIN
 ORD/FREE
 NAT/G

B61

ANAND R.P.."COMPULSORY JURISDICTION OF INTERNATIONAL
COURT OF JUSTICE. FUT WOR+45 SOCIETY PLAN LEGIT
ADJUD ATTIT DRIVE PERSON ORD/FREE...JURID CONCPT
TREND 20 ICJ. PAGE 5 E0086
 INT/ORG
 COERCE
 INT/LAW

B61

BEDFORD S.,THE FACES OF JUSTICE: A TRAVELLER'S
REPORT. AUSTRIA FRANCE GERMANY/W SWITZERLND UK UNIV
WOR+45 WOR-45 CULTURE PARTIC GOV/REL MORAL...JURID
OBS GOV/COMP 20. PAGE 9 E0174
 CT/SYS
 ORD/FREE
 PERSON
 LAW

B61

BRENNAN D.G.,ARMS CONTROL, DISARMAMENT, AND
NATIONAL SECURITY. WOR+45 NAT/G FORCES CREATE
PROB/SOLV PARTIC WAR PEACE...DECISION INT/LAW
ANTHOL BIBLIOG 20. PAGE 15 E0291
 ARMS/CONT
 ORD/FREE
 DIPLOM
 POLICY

B61

CASSINELLI C.W.,THE POLITICS OF FREEDOM. FUT UNIV
LAW POL/PAR CHOOSE ORD/FREE...POLICY CONCPT MYTH
BIBLIOG. PAGE 21 E0404
 MAJORIT
 NAT/G
 PARL/PROC
 PARTIC

B61

CHILDS M.W.,THE EROSION OF INDIVIDUAL LIBERTIES.
NAT/G LEGIS ATTIT...JURID SOC CONCPT IDEA/COMP 20
SUPREME/CT AMEND/I. PAGE 22 E0430
 ADJUD
 CT/SYS
 ORD/FREE
 CONSTN

B61

COWEN D.V.,THE FOUNDATIONS OF FREEDOM. AFR
 CONSTN

SOUTH/AFR DOMIN LEGIT ADJUST DISCRIM TOTALSM ATTIT ELITES
ORD/FREE...MAJORIT JURID SOC/INTEG WORSHIP 20
NEGRO. PAGE 27 E0529
 RACE/REL

B61

FREUND P.A.,THE SUPREME COURT OF THE UNITED STATES:
ITS BUSINESS, PURPOSES, AND PERFORMANCE. CONSTN
CRIME CONSEN ORD/FREE...DECISION 20 SUPREME/CT
CIVIL/LIB. PAGE 40 E0797
 CT/SYS
 JURID
 ADJUD
 FEDERAL

B61

FROEBEL J.,THEORIE DER POLITIK, ALS ERGEBNIS EINER
ERNEUERTEN PRUEFUNG DEMOKRATISCHER LEHRMEINUNGEN.
WOR-45 SOCIETY POL/PAR SECT REV REPRESENT PWR
SOVEREIGN...MAJORIT 19. PAGE 41 E0812
 JURID
 ORD/FREE
 NAT/G

B61

JACOBS C.E.,JUSTICE FRANKFURTER AND CIVIL
LIBERTIES. USA+45 USA-45 LAW NAT/G PROB/SOLV PRESS
PERS/REL...JURID WORSHIP 20 SUPREME/CT FRANKFUR/F
CIVIL/LIB. PAGE 57 E1144
 BIOG
 CONSTN
 ADJUD
 ORD/FREE

B61

LEONI B.,FREEDOM AND THE LAW. WOR+45 SOCIETY ADJUD
INGP/REL EFFICIENCY ATTIT DRIVE. PAGE 64 E1286
 JURID
 ORD/FREE
 LEGIS
 CONTROL

B61

MCDOUGAL M.S.,LAW AND MINIMUM WORLD PUBLIC ORDER.
WOR+45 SOCIETY NAT/G DELIB/GP EDU/PROP LEGIT ADJUD
COERCE ATTIT PERSON...JURID CONCPT RECORD TREND
TOT/POP 20. PAGE 70 E1406
 INT/ORG
 ORD/FREE
 INT/LAW

B61

MECHAM J.L.,THE UNITED STATES AND INTER-AMERICAN
SECURITY, 1889-1960. L/A+17C USA+45 USA-45 CONSTN
FORCES INT/TRADE PEACE TOTALSM ATTIT...JURID 19/20
UN OAS. PAGE 72 E1432
 DIPLOM
 WAR
 ORD/FREE
 INT/ORG

B61

MURPHY E.F.,WATER PURITY: A STUDY IN LEGAL CONTROL
OF NATURAL RESOURCES. LOC/G ACT/RES PLAN TEC/DEV
LOBBY GP/REL COST ATTIT HEALTH ORD/FREE...HEAL
JURID 20 WISCONSIN WATER. PAGE 75 E1506
 SEA
 LAW
 PROVS
 CONTROL

B61

ROBERTSON A.H.,THE LAW OF INTERNATIONAL
INSTITUTIONS IN EUROPE. EUR+WWI MOD/EUR INT/ORG
NAT/G VOL/ASSN DELIB/GP...JURID TIME/SEQ TOT/POP 20
TREATY. PAGE 85 E1704
 RIGID/FLEX
 ORD/FREE

B61

ROCHE J.P.,COURTS AND RIGHTS: THE AMERICAN
JUDICIARY IN ACTION (2ND ED.). UK USA+45 USA-45
STRUCT TEC/DEV SANCTION PERS/REL RACE/REL ORD/FREE
...METH/CNCPT GOV/COMP METH/COMP T 13/20. PAGE 85
E1710
 JURID
 CT/SYS
 NAT/G
 PROVS

B61

US CONGRESS,CONSTITUTIONAL RIGHTS OF THE MENTALLY
ILL. USA+45 LAW PUB/INST DELIB/GP ADJUD ORD/FREE
...PSY QU 20 CONGRESS. PAGE 99 E1989
 HEALTH
 CONSTN
 JURID
 CONFER

L61

FELLMAN D.."ACADEMIC FREEDOM IN AMERICAN LAW." LAW
CONSTN NAT/G VOL/ASSN PLAN PERSON KNOWL NEW/LIB.
PAGE 37 E0732
 ACADEM
 ORD/FREE
 LEGIS
 CULTURE

L61

TAUBENFELD H.J.."A REGIME FOR OUTER SPACE." FUT
UNIV R+D ACT/RES PLAN BAL/PWR LEGIT ARMS/CONT
ORD/FREE...POLICY JURID TREND UN TOT/POP 20
COLD/WAR. PAGE 95 E1910
 INT/ORG
 ADJUD
 SPACE

S61

AGNEW P.C.."INTRODUCING CHANGE IN A MENTAL
HOSPITAL." CLIENT WORKER PROB/SOLV INGP/REL
PERS/REL ADJUST. PAGE 3 E0054
 ORD/FREE
 PUB/INST
 PSY
 ADMIN

S61

MILLER E.."LEGAL ASPECTS OF UN ACTION IN THE
CONGO." AFR CULTURE ADMIN PEACE DRIVE RIGID/FLEX
ORD/FREE...WELF/ST JURID OBS UN CONGO 20. PAGE 73
E1458
 INT/ORG
 LEGIT

N61

DELEGACION NACIONAL DE PRENSA,FALANGE ESPANOL
TRADICIONALISTA Y DE LAS JUNTAS OFENSIVAS
NACIONALES SINDICALISTAS. IX CONSEJO NACIONAL
(PAMPHLET). LAW VOL/ASSN TOTALSM AUTHORIT ORD/FREE
FASCISM...ANTHOL 20 FRANCO/F FALANGIST. PAGE 31
E0605
 EDU/PROP
 FASCIST
 CONFER
 POL/PAR

B62
AMERICAN LAW INSTITUTE,FOREIGN RELATIONS LAW OF THE PROF/ORG
UNITED STATES: RESTATEMENT, SECOND. USA+45 NAT/G LAW
LEGIS ADJUD EXEC ROUTINE GOV/REL...INT/LAW JURID DIPLOM
CONCPT 20 TREATY. PAGE 4 E0082 ORD/FREE

B62
BARLOW R.B.,CITIZENSHIP AND CONSCIENCE: STUDIES IN SECT
THEORY AND PRACTICE OF RELIGIOUS TOLERATION IN LEGIS
ENGLAND DURING EIGHTEENTH CENTURY. UK LAW VOL/ASSN DISCRIM
EDU/PROP SANCTION REV GP/REL MAJORITY ATTIT
ORD/FREE...BIBLIOG WORSHIP 18. PAGE 8 E0150

B62
BICKEL A.,THE LEAST DANGEROUS BRANCH. USA+45 USA-45 LAW
CONSTN SCHOOL LEGIS ADJUD RACE/REL DISCRIM ORD/FREE NAT/G
...JURID 18/20 SUPREME/CT CONGRESS MARSHALL/J CT/SYS
HOLMES/OW FRANKFUR/F. PAGE 12 E0226

B62
BOCK E.A.,CASE STUDIES IN AMERICAN GOVERNMENT. POLICY
USA+45 ECO/DEV CHIEF EDU/PROP CT/SYS RACE/REL LEGIS
ORD/FREE...JURID MGT PHIL/SCI PRESIDENT CASEBOOK. IDEA/COMP
PAGE 13 E0256 NAT/G

B62
BRANDT R.B.,SOCIAL JUSTICE. UNIV LAW GP/REL PWR ORD/FREE
ALL/IDEOS...POLICY SOC ANTHOL 20. PAGE 15 E0287 CONSTN
CONCPT

B62
CARLSTON K.S.,LAW AND ORGANIZATION IN WORLD INT/ORG
SOCIETY. WOR+45 FINAN ECO/TAC DOMIN LEGIT CT/SYS LAW
ROUTINE COERCE ORD/FREE PWR WEALTH...PLURIST
DECISION JURID MGT METH/CNCPT GEN/LAWS 20. PAGE 19
E0381

B62
CRANSTON M.,WHAT ARE HUMAN RIGHTS? UNIV WOR+45 LAW
INT/ORG MORAL...POLICY CONCPT METH/CNCPT GEN/LAWS ORD/FREE
20. PAGE 28 E0545 JURID
IDEA/COMP

B62
CURRY J.E.,RACE TENSIONS AND THE POLICE. LAW MUNIC FORCES
NEIGH TEC/DEV RUMOR CONTROL COERCE GP/REL ATTIT RACE/REL
...SOC 20 NEGRO. PAGE 28 E0558 CROWD
ORD/FREE

B62
DAVIS F.J.,SOCIETY AND THE LAW. USA+45 CONSTN LAW
ACADEM FAM CONSULT ACT/RES GP/REL ORD/FREE SOC
ENGLSH/LAW 20. PAGE 29 E0572 CULTURE
STRUCT

B62
DE LAVALLE H.,A STATEMENT OF THE LAWS OF PERU IN CONSTN
MATTERS AFFECTING BUSINESS (3RD ED.). PERU WORKER JURID
INT/TRADE INCOME ORD/FREE...INT/LAW 20. PAGE 30 FINAN
E0586 TAX

B62
DOUGLAS W.O.,DEMOCRACY'S MANIFESTO. COM USA+45 DIPLOM
ECO/UNDEV INT/ORG FORCES PLAN NEUTRAL TASK MARXISM POLICY
...JURID 20 NATO SEATO. PAGE 32 E0642 NAT/G
ORD/FREE

B62
DUROSELLE J.B.,HISTOIRE DIPLOMATIQUE DE 1919 A NOS DIPLOM
JOURS (3RD ED.). FRANCE INT/ORG CHIEF FORCES CONFER WOR+45
ARMS/CONT WAR PEACE ORD/FREE...T TREATY 20 WOR-45
COLD/WAR. PAGE 34 E0667

B62
GANJI M.,INTERNATIONAL PROTECTION OF HUMAN RIGHTS. ORD/FREE
WOR+45 CONSTN INT/TRADE CT/SYS SANCTION CRIME WAR DISCRIM
RACE/REL...CHARTS IDEA/COMP NAT/COMP BIBLIOG 20 LEGIS
TREATY NEGRO LEAGUE/NAT UN CIVIL/LIB. PAGE 42 E0831 DELIB/GP

B62
HEYDECKER J.J.,THE NUREMBERG TRIAL: HISTORY OF NAZI LAW
GERMANY AS REVEALED THROUGH THE TESTIMONY AT CRIME
NUREMBERG. EUR+WWI GERMANY VOL/ASSN LEAD COERCE PARTIC
CROWD INGP/REL RACE/REL SUPEGO ORD/FREE...CONCPT 20 TOTALISM
NAZI ANTI/SEMIT NUREMBERG JEWS. PAGE 52 E1036

B62
HIRSCHFIELD R.S.,THE CONSTITUTION AND THE COURT. ADJUD
SCHOOL WAR RACE/REL EQUILIB ORD/FREE...POLICY PWR
MAJORIT DECISION JURID 18/20 PRESIDENT COLD/WAR CONSTN
CIVIL/LIB SUPREME/CT CONGRESS. PAGE 53 E1051 LAW

B62
HOOK S.,THE PARADOXES OF FREEDOM. UNIV CONSTN CONCPT
INTELL LEGIS CONTROL REV CHOOSE SUPEGO...POLICY MAJORIT

JURID IDEA/COMP 19/20 CIV/RIGHTS. PAGE 55 E1095 ORD/FREE
ALL/VALS

B62
INTERNAT CONGRESS OF JURISTS,EXECUTIVE ACTION AND JURID
THE RULE OF RULE: REPORTION PROCEEDINGS OF INT'T EXEC
CONGRESS OF JURISTS,--RIO DE JANEIRO, BRAZIL. WOR+45 ORD/FREE
ACADEM CONSULT JUDGE EDU/PROP ADJUD CT/SYS INGP/REL CONTROL
PERSON DEPT/DEFEN. PAGE 57 E1130

B62
KAUPER P.G.,CIVIL LIBERTIES AND THE CONSTITUTION. LAW
USA+45 SECT EDU/PROP WRITING ADJUD SEX ORD/FREE 20 CONSTN
SUPREME/CT CIVIL/LIB CHURCH/STA. PAGE 60 E1188 CT/SYS
DECISION

B62
LEVY H.V.,LIBERDADE E JUSTICA SOCIAL (2ND ED.). ORD/FREE
BRAZIL COM L/A+17C USSR INT/ORG PARTIC GP/REL MARXISM
WEALTH 20 UN COM/PARTY. PAGE 65 E1290 CAP/ISM
LAW

B62
MCDOUGAL M.S.,THE PUBLIC ORDER OF THE OCEANS. ADJUD
WOR+45 WOR-45 SEA INT/ORG NAT/G CONSULT DELIB/GP ORD/FREE
DIPLOM LEGIT PEACE RIGID/FLEX...GEOG INT/LAW JURID
RECORD TOT/POP 20 TREATY. PAGE 70 E1407

B62
MCWHINNEY E.,CONSTITUTIONALISM IN GERMANY AND THE CONSTN
FEDERAL CONSTITUTINAL COURT. GERMANY/W POL/PAR TV CT/SYS
ADJUD CHOOSE EFFICIENCY ATTIT ORD/FREE MARXISM CONTROL
...NEW/IDEA BIBLIOG 20. PAGE 71 E1428 NAT/G

B62
MITCHELL G.E.,THE ANGRY BLACK SOUTH. USA+45 LAW RACE/REL
CONSTN SCHOOL DELIB/GP EDU/PROP CONTROL SUFF ANOMIE DISCRIM
DRIVE...ANTHOL 20 NEGRO CIV/RIGHTS SOUTH/US. ADJUST
PAGE 74 E1473 ORD/FREE

B62
NORGAARD C.A.,THE POSITION OF THE INDIVIDUAL IN INT/LAW
INTERNATIONAL LAW. INT/ORG SUPEGO ORD/FREE DIPLOM
SOVEREIGN...CONCPT 20 UN. PAGE 78 E1556 CRIME
JURID

B62
OTTENBERG M.,THE FEDERAL INVESTIGATORS. USA+45 LAW FORCES
COM/IND DIST/IND WORKER DIPLOM INT/TRADE CONTROL INSPECT
FEDERAL HEALTH ORD/FREE FBI CIA FTC SEC FDA. NAT/G
PAGE 79 E1585 CRIME

B62
ROSENNE S.,THE WORLD COURT: WHAT IT IS AND HOW IT INT/ORG
WORKS. WOR+45 WOR-45 LAW CONSTN JUDGE EDU/PROP ADJUD
LEGIT ROUTINE CHOOSE PEACE ORD/FREE...JURID OBS INT/LAW
TIME/SEQ CHARTS UN TOT/POP VAL/FREE 20. PAGE 86
E1717

B62
ROSTOW E.V.,THE SOVEREIGN PREROGATIVE: THE SUPREME JURID
COURT AND THE QUEST FOR LAW. CONSTN CT/SYS FEDERAL PROF/ORG
MORAL SOVEREIGN 20 SUPREME/CT. PAGE 86 E1726 ATTIT
ORD/FREE

B62
SCHWARZENBERGER G.,THE FRONTIERS OF INTERNATIONAL INT/ORG
LAW. WOR+45 WOR-45 NAT/G LEGIT CT/SYS ROUTINE MORAL LAW
ORD/FREE PWR...JURID SOC GEN/METH 20 COLD/WAR. INT/LAW
PAGE 89 E1789

B62
SOWLE C.R.,POLICE POWER AND INDIVIDUAL FREEDOM: THE FORCES
QUEST FOR BALANCE. CANADA EUR+WWI ISRAEL NORWAY ORD/FREE
USA+45 LAW CONSTN SOCIETY CONTROL ROUTINE SANCTION IDEA/COMP
GP/REL 20 CHINJAP. PAGE 93 E1859

B62
THOMPSON K.W.,AMERICAN DIPLOMACY AND EMERGENT NAT/G
PATTERNS. USA+45 USA-45 WOR+45 WOR-45 LAW DELIB/GP BAL/PWR
FORCES TOP/EX DIPLOM ATTIT DRIVE RIGID/FLEX
ORD/FREE PWR SOVEREIGN...POLICY 20. PAGE 96 E1922

B62
US AIR FORCE,THE MILITARY JUSTICE SYSTEM (REV. JURID
ED.). USA+45 DELIB/GP...IDEA/COMP 20. PAGE 99 E1978 FORCES
ADJUD
ORD/FREE

B62
US COMMISSION ON CIVIL RIGHTS,EQUAL PROTECTION OF ORD/FREE
THE LAWS IN NORTH CAROLINA. USA+45 LOC/G NAT/G RESPECT
CONSULT LEGIS WORKER PROB/SOLV EDU/PROP ADJUD LAW
CHOOSE DISCRIM HEALTH 20 NEGRO NORTH/CAR PROVS
CIV/RIGHTS. PAGE 99 E1984

US COMMISSION ON CIVIL RIGHTS.HEARINGS BEFORE
UNITED STATES COMMISSION ON CIVIL RIGHTS. USA+45
ECO/DEV NAT/G CONSULT WORKER EDU/PROP ADJUD DISCRIM
ISOLAT HABITAT HEALTH RESPECT 20 NEGRO CIV/RIGHTS.
PAGE 99 E1985
   B62
   ORD/FREE
   LAW
   ADMIN
   LEGIS

US SENATE COMM ON JUDICIARY.CONSTITUTIONAL RIGHTS
OF MILITARY PERSONNEL. USA+45 USA-45 FORCES DIPLOM
WAR CONGRESS. PAGE 102 E2046
   B62
   CONSTN
   ORD/FREE
   JURID
   CT/SYS

WOETZEL R.K..THE NURENBERG TRIALS IN INTERNATIONAL
LAW. CHRIST-17C MOD/EUR WOR+45 SOCIETY NAT/G
DELIB/GP DOMIN LEGIT ROUTINE ATTIT DRIVE PERSON
SUPEGO MORAL ORD/FREE...POLICY MAJORIT JURID PSY
SOC SELF/OBS RECORD NAZI TOT/POP. PAGE 107 E2138
   B62
   INT/ORG
   ADJUD
   WAR

PETKOFF D.K.."RECOGNITION AND NON-RECOGNITION OF
STATES AND GOVERNMENTS IN INTERNATIONAL LAW." ASIA
COM USA+45 WOR+45 NAT/G ACT/RES DIPLOM DOMIN LEGIT
COERCE ORD/FREE PWR...CONCPT GEN/LAWS 20. PAGE 80
E1611
   L62
   INT/ORG
   LAW
   INT/LAW

SPAETH H.J.."JUDICIAL POWER AS A VARIABLE
MOTIVATING SUPREME COURT BEHAVIOR." DELIB/GP ADJUD
RATIONAL ATTIT PERSON ORD/FREE...CLASSIF STAT
GEN/METH. PAGE 93 E1860
   L62
   JUDGE
   DECISION
   PERS/COMP
   PSY

CRANE R.D.."LAW AND STRATEGY IN SPACE." FUT USA+45
WOR+45 AIR LAW INT/ORG NAT/G FORCES ACT/RES PLAN
BAL/PWR LEGIT ARMS/CONT COERCE ORD/FREE...POLICY
INT/LAW JURID SOC/EXP 20 TREATY. PAGE 27 E0542
   S62
   CONCPT
   SPACE

FALK R.A.."THE REALITY OF INTERNATIONAL LAW."
WOR+45 NAT/G LEGIT COERCE DETER WAR MORAL ORD/FREE
PWR SOVEREIGN...JURID CONCPT VAL/FREE COLD/WAR 20.
PAGE 36 E0714
   S62
   INT/ORG
   ADJUD
   NUC/PWR
   INT/LAW

FENWICK C.G.."ISSUES AT PUNTA DEL ESTE: NON-
INTERVENTION VS COLLECTIVE SECURITY." L/A-17C
USA+45 VOL/ASSN DELIB/GP ECO/TAC LEGIT ADJUD REGION
ORD/FREE OAS COLD/WAR 20. PAGE 37 E0738
   S62
   INT/ORG
   CUBA

FINKELSTEIN L.S.."THE UNITED NATIONS AND
ORGANIZATIONS FOR CONTROL OF ARMAMENT." FUT WOR+45
VOL/ASSN DELIB/GP TOP/EX CREATE EDU/PROP LEGIT
ADJUD NUC/PWR ATTIT RIGID/FLEX ORD/FREE...POLICY
DECISION CONCPT OBS TREND GEN/LAWS TOT/POP
COLD/WAR. PAGE 38 E0752
   S62
   INT/ORG
   PWR
   ARMS/CONT

GREEN L.C.."POLITICAL OFFENSES, WAR CRIMES AND
EXTRADITION." WOR+45 YUGOSLAVIA INT/ORG LEGIT
ROUTINE WAR ORD/FREE SOVEREIGN...JURID NAZI 20
INTERPOL. PAGE 46 E0906
   S62
   LAW
   CONCPT
   INT/LAW

GREENSPAN M.."INTERNATIONAL LAW AND ITS PROTECTION
FOR PARTICIPANTS IN UNCONVENTIONAL WARFARE." WOR+45
LAW INT/ORG NAT/G POL/PAR COERCE REV ORD/FREE
...INT/LAW TOT/POP 20. PAGE 46 E0912
   S62
   FORCES
   JURID
   GUERRILLA
   WAR

JOHNSON O.H.."THE ENGLISH TRADITION IN
INTERNATIONAL LAW." CHRIST-17C MOD/EUR EDU/PROP
LEGIT CT/SYS ORD/FREE...JURID CONCPT TIME/SEQ.
PAGE 59 E1170
   S62
   LAW
   INT/LAW
   UK

LISSITZYN O.J.."SOME LEGAL IMPLICATIONS OF THE U-2
AND RB-47 INCIDENTS." FUT USA+45 USSR WOR+45 AIR
NAT/G DIPLOM LEGIT MORAL ORD/FREE SOVEREIGN...JURID
GEN/LAWS GEN/METH COLD/WAR 20 U-2. PAGE 65 E1305
   S62
   LAW
   CONCPT
   SPACE
   INT/LAW

MCWHINNEY E.."CO-EXISTENCE, THE CUBA CRISIS, AND
COLD WAR-INTERNATIONAL WAR." CUBA USA+45 USSR
WOR+45 NAT/G TOP/EX BAL/PWR DIPLOM DOMIN LEGIT
PEACE RIGID/FLEX ORD/FREE...STERTYP COLD/WAR 20.
PAGE 71 E1427
   S62
   CONCPT
   INT/LAW

SCHACHTER O.."DAG HAMMARSKJOLD AND THE RELATION OF
LAW TO POLITICS." FUT WOR+45 INT/ORG CONSULT PLAN
TEC/DEV BAL/PWR DIPLOM LEGIT ATTIT PERCEPT ORD/FREE
...POLICY JURID CONCPT OBS TESTS STERTYP GEN/LAWS
20 HAMMARSK/D. PAGE 87 E1751
   S62
   ACT/RES
   ADJUD

US SENATE COMM ON JUDICIARY.LEGISLATION TO
STRENGTHEN PENALTIES UNDER THE ANTITRUST LAWS
(PAMPHLET). USA+45 LG/CO CONFER CONTROL SANCTION
ORD/FREE 20 SENATE MONOPOLY. PAGE 102 E2045
   N62
   LEAD
   ADJUD
   INDUS
   ECO/TAC

BADI J..THE GOVERNMENT OF THE STATE OF ISRAEL: A
CRITICAL ACCOUNT OF ITS PARLIAMENT, EXECUTIVE, AND
JUDICIARY. ISRAEL ECO/DEV CHIEF DELIB/GP LEGIS
DIPLOM CT/SYS INGP/REL PEACE ORD/FREE...BIBLIOG 20
PARLIAMENT ARABS MIGRATION. PAGE 7 E0131
   B63
   NAT/G
   CONSTN
   EX/STRUC
   POL/PAR

BLACK C.L. JR..THE OCCASIONS OF JUSTICE: ESSAYS
MOSTLY ON LAW. USA+45 JUDGE RACE/REL DISCRIM ATTIT
MORAL ORD/FREE 20 SUPREME/CT BLACK. PAGE 12 E0236
   B63
   JURID
   CONSTN
   CT/SYS
   LAW

BOWETT D.W..THE LAW OF INTERNATIONAL INSTITUTIONS.
WOR+45 WOR-45 CONSTN DELIB/GP EX/STRUC JUDGE
EDU/PROP LEGIT CT/SYS EXEC ROUTINE RIGID/FLEX
ORD/FREE PWR...JURID CONCPT ORG/CHARTS GEN/METH
LEAGUE/NAT OAS OEEC 20 UN. PAGE 14 E0277
   B63
   INT/ORG
   ADJUD
   DIPLOM

BROOKES E.H..POWER, LAW, RIGHT, AND LOVE: A STUDY
IN POLITICAL VALUES. SOUTH/AFR NAT/G PERSON
...CONCPT IDEA/COMP 20. PAGE 16 E0308
   B63
   PWR
   ORD/FREE
   JURID
   LOVE

BROWN R.M..THE SOUTH CAROLINA REGULATORS. USA-45
LEGIS LEGIT ADJUD COLONIAL CONTROL WAR...BIBLIOG/A
18 CHARLESTON SOUTH/CAR. PAGE 16 E0315
   B63
   ORD/FREE
   JURID
   PWR
   PROVS

BURRUS B.R..ADMINSTRATIVE LAW AND LOCAL GOVERNMENT.
USA+45 PROVS LEGIS LICENSE ADJUD ORD/FREE 20.
PAGE 18 E0347
   B63
   EX/STRUC
   LOC/G
   JURID
   CONSTN

CAHN E..THE GREAT RIGHTS. USA+45 NAT/G PROVS
CIVMIL/REL...IDEA/COMP ANTHOL BIBLIOG 18/20
MADISON/J BILL/RIGHT CIV/RIGHTS WARRN/EARL
BLACK/HL. PAGE 18 E0361
   B63
   CONSTN
   LAW
   ORD/FREE
   INGP/REL

CARTER G.M..FIVE AFRICAN STATES: RESPONSES TO
DIVERSITY. CONSTN CULTURE STRATA LEGIS PLAN ECO/TAC
DOMIN EDU/PROP CT/SYS EXEC CHOOSE ATTIT HEALTH
ORD/FREE PWR...TIME/SEQ TOT/POP VAL/FREE. PAGE 20
E0398
   B63
   AFR
   SOCIETY

COUNCIL OF STATE GOVERNMENTS.INCREASED RIGHTS FOR
DEFENDANTS IN STATE CRIMINAL PROSECUTIONS. USA+45
GOV/REL INGP/REL FEDERAL ORD/FREE...JURID 20
SUPREME/CT. PAGE 26 E0522
   B63
   CT/SYS
   ADJUD
   PROVS
   CRIME

DAY R.E..CIVIL RIGHTS USA: PUBLIC SCHOOLS, SOUTHERN
STATES - NORTH CAROLINA, 1963. USA+45 LOC/G NEIGH
LEGIS CREATE CT/SYS COERCE DISCRIM ATTIT...QU
CHARTS 20 NORTH/CAR NEGRO KKK CIV/RIGHTS. PAGE 29
E0579
   B63
   EDU/PROP
   ORD/FREE
   RACE/REL
   SANCTION

DECOTTIGNIES R..LES NATIONALITES AFRICAINES. AFR
NAT/G PROB/SOLV DIPLOM COLONIAL ORD/FREE...CHARTS
GOV/COMP 20. PAGE 30 E0602
   B63
   NAT/LISM
   JURID
   LEGIS
   LAW

DILLIARD I..ONE MAN'S STAND FOR FREEDOM: MR.
JUSTICE BLACK AND THE BILL OF RIGHTS. USA+45
POL/PAR SECT DELIB/GP FORCES ADJUD CONTROL WAR
DISCRIM MORAL...BIBLIOG 20 NEGRO SUPREME/CT
BILL/RIGHT BLACK/HL. PAGE 32 E0628
   B63
   CONSTN
   JURID
   JUDGE
   ORD/FREE

DOUGLAS W.O..THE ANATOMY OF LIBERTY: THE RIGHTS OF
MAN WITHOUT FORCE. WOR+45 ECO/DEV ECO/UNDEV LOC/G
FORCES GOV/REL...SOC/WK 20. PAGE 32 E0643
   B63
   PEACE
   LAW
   DIPLOM
   ORD/FREE

ELLERT R.B..NATO 'FAIR TRIAL' SAFEGUARDS: PRECURSOR
TO AN INTERNATIONAL BILL OF PROCEDURAL RIGHTS.
WOR+45 FORCES CRIME CIVMIL/REL ATTIT ORD/FREE 20
NATO. PAGE 34 E0683
   B63
   JURID
   INT/LAW
   INT/ORG
   CT/SYS

FALK R.A.,LAW, MORALITY, AND WAR IN THE   B63   ADJUD
CONTEMPORARY WORLD. WOR+45 LAW INT/ORG EX/STRUC   ARMS/CONT
FORCES EDU/PROP LEGIT DETER NUC/PWR MORAL ORD/FREE   PEACE
...JURID TOT/POP 20. PAGE 36 E0715   INT/LAW

FORTES A.B.,HISTORIA ADMINISTRATIVA, JUDICIARIA E   B63   PROVS
ECLESIASTICA DO RIO GRANDE DO SUL. BRAZIL L/A+17C   ADMIN
LOC/G SECT COLONIAL CT/SYS ORD/FREE CATHISM 16/20.   JURID
PAGE 39 E0773

FRAENKEL O.K.,THE SUPREME COURT AND CIVIL   B63   ORD/FREE
LIBERTIES: HOW THE COURT HAS PROTECTED THE BILL OF   CONSTN
RIGHTS. NAT/G CT/SYS CHOOSE PERS/REL RACE/REL   ADJUD
DISCRIM PERSON...DECISION 20 SUPREME/CT CIVIL/LIB   JURID
BILL/RIGHT. PAGE 39 E0782

FRIEDRICH C.J.,JUSTICE: NOMOS VI. UNIV LAW SANCTION   B63   LEGIT
CRIME...CONCPT ANTHOL MARX/KARL LOCKE/JOHN   ADJUD
AQUINAS/T. PAGE 41 E0809   ORD/FREE
    JURID

FRIEDRICH C.J.,MAN AND HIS GOVERNMENT: AN EMPIRICAL   B63   PERSON
THEORY OF POLITICS. UNIV LOC/G NAT/G ADJUD REV   ORD/FREE
INGP/REL DISCRIM PWR BIBLIOG. PAGE 41 E0810   PARTIC
    CONTROL

HALEY A.G.,SPACE LAW AND GOVERNMENT. FUT USA+45   B63   INT/ORG
WOR+45 LEGIS ACT/RES CREATE ATTIT RIGID/FLEX   LAW
ORD/FREE PWR SOVEREIGN...POLICY JURID CONCPT CHARTS   SPACE
VAL/FREE 20. PAGE 49 E0980

HALL J.,COMPARATIVE LAW AND SOCIAL THEORY. WOR+45   B63   LAW
CONSTN CULTURE DOMIN CT/SYS ORD/FREE...PLURIST   SOC
JURID CONCPT NEW/IDEA GEN/LAWS VAL/FREE. PAGE 49
E0984

JENKS C.W.,LAW, FREEDOM, AND WELFARE. WOR+45 GIVE   B63   INT/LAW
ADJUD WAR PEACE HABITAT ORD/FREE. PAGE 58 E1159   DIPLOM
    SOVEREIGN
    PROB/SOLV

LAVROFF D.-.G.,LES LIBERTES PUBLIQUES EN UNION   B63   ORD/FREE
SOVIETIQUE (REV. ED.). USSR NAT/G WORKER SANCTION   LAW
CRIME MARXISM NEW/LIB...JURID BIBLIOG WORSHIP 20.   ATTIT
PAGE 63 E1268   COM

LEAGUE WOMEN VOTERS NEW YORK,APPORTIONMENT WORKSHOP   B63   APPORT
KIT. USA+45 VOL/ASSN DELIB/GP LEGIS ATTIT ORD/FREE   REPRESENT
...METH/COMP 20 SUPREME/CT NEW/YORK. PAGE 64 E1275   PROVS
    JURID

LEVY L.W.,JEFFERSON AND CIVIL LIBERTIES: THE DARKER   B63   BIOG
SIDE. USA-45 LAW INTELL ACADEM FORCES PRESS REV   ORD/FREE
INGP/REL PERSON 18/19 JEFFERSN/T CIVIL/LIB. PAGE 65   CONSTN
E1291   ATTIT

LOWRY C.W.,TO PRAY OR NOT TO PRAY. ADJUD SANCTION   B63   SECT
GP/REL ORD/FREE PWR CATHISM WORSHIP 20 SUPREME/CT   CT/SYS
CHRISTIAN CHRUCH/STA. PAGE 67 E1330   CONSTN
    PRIVIL

MCDOUGAL M.S.,LAW AND PUBLIC ORDER IN SPACE. FUT   B63   SPACE
USA+45 ACT/RES TEC/DEV ADJUD...POLICY INT/LAW JURID   ORD/FREE
20. PAGE 70 E1410   DIPLOM
    DECISION

MOLLARD P.T.,LE REGIME JURIDIQUE DE LA PRESSE AU   B63   PRESS
MAROC. MOROCCO CONTROL CRIME GP/REL ORD/FREE 20.   LAW
PAGE 74 E1482   LEAD
    LEGIT

MURPHY T.J.,CENSORSHIP: GOVERNMENT AND OBSCENITY.   B63   ORD/FREE
USA+45 CULTURE LEGIS JUDGE EDU/PROP CONTROL   MORAL
INGP/REL RATIONAL POPULISM...CATH JURID 20. PAGE 75   LAW
E1507   CONSEN

NATIONAL CIVIC REVIEW,REAPPORTIONMENT: A YEAR IN   B63   APPORT
REVIEW (PAMPHLET). USA+45 LAW CT/SYS CHOOSE   REPRESENT
ORD/FREE PWR...ANTHOL 20 CONGRESS. PAGE 76 E1527   LEGIS
    CONSTN

NEWMAN E.S.,THE FREEDOM READER. USA+45 LEGIS TOP/EX   B63   RACE/REL
PLAN ADJUD CONTROL CT/SYS DISCRIM...DECISION ANTHOL   LAW
20 SUPREME/CT CIV/RIGHTS. PAGE 77 E1541   POLICY
    ORD/FREE

REALE M.,PLURALISMO E LIBERDADE. STRUCT ADJUST   B63   CONCPT
ATTIT 20 CIVIL/LIB. PAGE 84 E1676   ORD/FREE
    JURID
    INGP/REL

REOCK E.C. JR.,POPULATION INEQUALITY AMONG COUNTIES   B63   APPORT
IN THE NEW JERSEY LEGISLATURE 1791-1962. PROVS   REPRESENT
ORD/FREE...CENSUS CHARTS 18/20 NEW/JERSEY. PAGE 84   LEGIS
E1687   JURID

ROBERT J.,LA MONARCHIE MAROCAINE. MOROCCO LABOR   B63   CHIEF
MUNIC POL/PAR EX/STRUC ORD/FREE PWR...JURID TREND T   CONSERVE
20. PAGE 85 E1702   ADMIN
    CONSTN

ROBERTSON A.H.,HUMAN RIGHTS IN EUROPE. CONSTN   B63   EUR+WWI
SOCIETY INT/ORG NAT/G VOL/ASSN DELIB/GP ACT/RES   PERSON
PLAN ADJUD REGION ROUTINE ATTIT LOVE ORD/FREE
RESPECT...JURID SOC CONCPT SOC/EXP UN 20. PAGE 85
E1705

ROSNER G.,THE UNITED NATIONS EMERGENCY FORCE.   B63   INT/ORG
FRANCE ISRAEL UAR UK WOR+45 CREATE WAR PEACE   FORCES
ORD/FREE PWR...INT/LAW JURID HIST/WRIT TIME/SEQ UN.
PAGE 86 E1719

SMITH E.A.,CHURCH AND STATE IN YOUR COMMUNITY.   B63   GP/REL
USA+45 PROVS SCHOOL ACT/RES CT/SYS PARTIC ATTIT   SECT
MORAL ORD/FREE CATHISM 20 PROTESTANT CHURCH/STA.   NAT/G
PAGE 92 E1842   NEIGH

STREET H.,FREEDOM: THE INDIVIDUAL AND THE LAW. UK   B63   ORD/FREE
COM/IND EDU/PROP PRESS RUMOR TV PWR 20 CIVIL/LIB   NAT/G
FILM. PAGE 94 E1886   JURID
    PARL/PROC

TUSSMAN J.,THE SUPREME COURT ON RACIAL   B63   CT/SYS
DISCRIMINATION. USA+45 USA-45 NAT/G PROB/SOLV ADJUD   DISCRIM
RACE/REL ORD/FREE...JURID 20 SUPREME/CT CIV/RIGHTS.   ATTIT
PAGE 97 E1946   LAW

US COMN CIVIL RIGHTS,REPORT ON MISSISSIPPI. LAW   B63   RACE/REL
LOC/G NAT/G LEGIS PLAN PROB/SOLV DISCRIM SOC/INTEG   CONSTN
20 MISSISSIPP NEGRO. PAGE 99 E1987   ORD/FREE
    COERCE

US CONGRESS: SENATE,HEARINGS OF THE COMMITTEE ON   B63   LEGIS
THE JUDICIARY. USA+45 CONSTN NAT/G ADMIN GOV/REL 20   LAW
CONGRESS. PAGE 99 E1992   ORD/FREE
    DELIB/GP

US SENATE COMM ON JUDICIARY,US PERSONNEL SECURITY   B63   PLAN
PRACTICES. USA+45 DELIB/GP ADJUD ADMIN ORD/FREE   NAT/G
...CHARTS 20 CONGRESS CIVIL/SERV. PAGE 102 E2049   CONTROL
    WORKER

US SENATE COMM ON JUDICIARY,PACIFICA FOUNDATION.   B63   DELIB/GP
USA+45 LAW COM/IND 20 ODEGARD/P BINNS/JJ SCHINDLR/P   EDU/PROP
HEALEY/D THOMAS/TK. PAGE 102 E2051   ORD/FREE
    ATTIT

VAN SLYCK P.,PEACE: THE CONTROL OF NATIONAL POWER.   B63   ARMS/CONT
CUBA WOR+45 FINAN NAT/G FORCES PROB/SOLV TEC/DEV   PEACE
BAL/PWR ADMIN CONTROL ORD/FREE...POLICY INT/LAW UN   INT/ORG
COLD/WAR TREATY. PAGE 103 E2069   DIPLOM

BOLGAR V.,"THE PUBLIC INTEREST: A JURISPRUDENTIAL   L63   CONCPT
AND COMPARATIVE OVERVIEW OF SYMPOSIUM ON   ORD/FREE
FUNDAMENTAL CONCEPTS OF PUBLIC LAW" COM FRANCE   CONTROL
GERMANY SWITZERLND LAW ADJUD ADMIN AGREE LAISSEZ   NAT/COMP
...JURID GEN/LAWS 20 EUROPE/E. PAGE 14 E0264

LISSITZYN O.J.,"INTERNATIONAL LAW IN A DIVIDED   L63   INT/ORG
WORLD." FUT WOR+45 CONSTN CULTURE ECO/DEV ECO/UNDEV   LAW

DIST/IND NAT/G FORCES ECO/TAC LEGIT ADJUD ADMIN
COERCE ATTIT HEALTH MORAL ORD/FREE PWR RESPECT
WEALTH VAL/FREE. PAGE 65 E1306

L63

MCDOUGAL M.S.,"THE ENJOYMENT AND ACQUISITION OF   PLAN
RESOURCES IN OUTER SPACE." CHRIST-17C FUT WOR+45   TREND
WOR-45 LAW EXTR/IND INT/ORG ACT/RES CREATE
TEC/DEV ECO/TAC LEGIT COERCE HEALTH KNOWL ORD/FREE PWR
WEALTH...JURID HIST/WRIT VAL/FREE. PAGE 70 E1408

S63

ALGER C.F.,"HYPOTHESES ON RELATIONSHIPS BETWEEN THE   INT/ORG
ORGANIZATION OF INTERNATIONAL SOCIETY AND   LAW
INTERNATIONAL ORDER." WOR+45 WOR-45 ORD/FREE PWR
...JURID GEN/LAWS VAL/FREE 20. PAGE 3 E0066

S63

BECHHOEFER B.G.,"UNITED NATIONS PROCEDURES IN CASE   INT/ORG
OF VIOLATIONS OF DISARMAMENT AGREEMENTS." COM   DELIB/GP
USA+45 USSR LAW CONSTN NAT/G EX/STRUC FORCES LEGIS
BAL/PWR EDU/PROP CT/SYS ARMS/CONT ORD/FREE PWR
...POLICY STERTYP UN VAL/FREE 20. PAGE 9 E0169

S63

BERMAN H.J.,"THE DILEMMA OF SOVIET LAW REFORM."   COM
NAT/G POL/PAR CT/SYS ALL/VALS ORD/FREE PWR...POLICY   LAW
JURID VAL/FREE 20. PAGE 11 E0208   USSR

S63

BOHN L.,"WHOSE NUCLEAR TEST: NON-PHYSICAL   ADJUD
INSPECTION AND TEST BAN." WOR+45 R+D INT/ORG   ARMS/CONT
VOL/ASSN ORD/FREE...GEN/LAWS GEN/METH COLD/WAR 20.   TEC/DEV
PAGE 13 E0262   NUC/PWR

S63

FRIEDMANN W.G.,"THE USES OF 'GENERAL PRINCIPLES' IN   LAW
THE DEVELOPMENT OF INTERNATIONAL LAW." WOR+45 NAT/G   INT/LAW
DIPLOM INT/TRADE LEGIT ROUTINE RIGID/FLEX ORD/FREE   INT/ORG
...JURID CONCPT STERTYP GEN/METH 20. PAGE 41 E0804

S63

GERHARD H.,"COMMODITY TRADE STABILIZATION THROUGH   PLAN
INTERNATIONAL AGREEMENTS." WOR+45 ECO/DEV ECO/UNDEV   ECO/TAC
NAT/G ROUTINE ORD/FREE...INT/LAW OBS TREND GEN/METH   INT/TRADE
TOT/POP 20. PAGE 43 E0850

S63

JOUGHIN L.,"ACADEMIC DUE PROCESS." DELIB/GP ADJUD   ACADEM
ROUTINE ORD/FREE...POLICY MAJORIT TREND. PAGE 59   LAW
E1175   PROF/ORG
                                                        CLIENT

S63

LEPAWSKY A.,"INTERNATIONAL DEVELOPMENT OF RIVER   INT/ORG
RESOURCES." CANADA EUR+WWI S/ASIA USA+45 SEA LEGIT   DELIB/GP
ADJUD ORD/FREE PWR WEALTH...MGT TIME/SEQ VAL/FREE
MEXIC/AMER 20. PAGE 64 E1287

S63

MCDOUGAL M.S.,"THE SOVIET-CUBAN QUARANTINE AND   ORD/FREE
SELF-DEFENSE." CUBA USA+45 USSR WOR+45 INT/ORG   LEGIT
NAT/G BAL/PWR NUC/PWR ATTIT...JURID CONCPT. PAGE 70   SOVEREIGN
E1409

B64

ANASTAPLO G.,NOTES ON THE FIRST AMENDMENT TO THE   ORD/FREE
CONSTITUTION OF THE UNITED STATES (PART TWO).   CONSTN
USA+45 USA-45 NAT/G JUDGE DEBATE SUPEGO PWR   CT/SYS
SOVEREIGN 18/20 SUPREME/CT CONGRESS AMEND/I. PAGE 5   ATTIT
E0088

B64

BERWANGER E.H.,WESTERN ANTI-NEGRO SENTIMENT AND   RACE/REL
LAWS 1846-60: A FACTOR IN THE SLAVERY EXTENSION   REGION
CONTROVERSY (PAPER). USA-45 LAW CONSTN LEGIS ADJUD   DISCRIM
...BIBLIOG 19 NEGRO. PAGE 11 E0218   ORD/FREE

B64

BUREAU OF NATIONAL AFFAIRS,STATE FAIR EMPLOYMENT   PROVS
LAWS AND THEIR ADMINISTRATION. INDUS ADJUD PERS/REL   DISCRIM
RACE/REL ATTIT ORD/FREE WEALTH 20. PAGE 17 E0338   WORKER
                                                        JURID

B64

DUMON F.,LE BRESIL; SES INSTITUTIONS POLITIQUES ET   CONSTN
JUDICIARIES. BRAZIL POL/PAR CHIEF LEGIS ORD/FREE   JURID
19/20. PAGE 33 E0658   CT/SYS
                                                        GOV/REL

B64

ENGEL S.,LAW, STATE, AND INTERNATIONAL LEGAL ORDER.   JURID
WOR+45 NAT/G ORD/FREE RELATISM...INT/LAW IDEA/COMP   OBJECTIVE
ANTHOL 20 KELSEN/H. PAGE 35 E0690   CONCPT
                                                        DEBATE

B64

FISK W.M.,ADMINISTRATIVE PROCEDURE IN A REGULATORY   SERV/IND
AGENCY: THE CAB AND THE NEW YORK-CHICAGO CASE   ECO/DEV
(PAMPHLET). USA+45 DIST/IND ADMIN CONTROL LOBBY   AIR
GP/REL ROLE ORD/FREE NEWYORK/C CHICAGO CAB. PAGE 38   JURID
E0758

B64

FRIEDMANN W.G.,THE CHANGING STRUCTURE OF   ADJUD
INTERNATIONAL LAW. WOR+45 INT/ORG NAT/G PROVS LEGIT   TREND
ORD/FREE PWR...JURID CONCPT GEN/LAWS TOT/POP UN 20.   INT/LAW
PAGE 41 E0805

B64

FULBRIGHT J.W.,OLD MYTHS AND NEW REALITIES. USA+45   DIPLOM
USSR LEGIS INT/TRADE DETER ATTIT...POLICY 20   INT/ORG
COLD/WAR TREATY. PAGE 41 E0818   ORD/FREE

B64

GARDNER L.C.,ECONOMIC ASPECTS OF NEW DEAL   ECO/TAC
DIPLOMACY. USA+45 WOR-45 LAW ECO/DEV INT/ORG NAT/G   DIPLOM
VOL/ASSN LEGIS TOP/EX EDU/PROP ORD/FREE PWR WEALTH
...POLICY TIME/SEQ VAL/FREE 20 ROOSEVLT/F. PAGE 42
E0836

B64

GIANNELLA D.A.,RELIGION AND THE PUBLIC ORDER: AN   SECT
ANNUAL REVIEW OF CHURCH AND STATE, AND OF RELIGION,   NAT/G
LAW, AND SOCIETY. USA+45 LAW SOCIETY FAM POL/PAR   CONSTN
SCHOOL GIVE EDU/PROP GP/REL...JURID GEN/LAWS   ORD/FREE
BIBLIOG/A 20 CHURCH/STA BIRTH/CON CONSCN/OBJ
NATURL/LAW. PAGE 43 E0855

B64

GROVES H.E.,THE CONSTITUTION OF MALAYSIA. MALAYSIA   CONSTN
POL/PAR CHIEF CONSULT DELIB/GP CT/SYS PARL/PROC   NAT/G
CHOOSE FEDERAL ORD/FREE 20. PAGE 48 E0953   LAW

B64

GUMPLOWICZ L.,RECHTSSTAAT UND SOZIALISMUS. STRATA   JURID
ORD/FREE SOVEREIGN MARXISM...IDEA/COMP 16/20 KANT/I   NAT/G
HOBBES/T. PAGE 48 E0962   SOCISM
                                                        CONCPT

B64

GUTTMANN A.,COMMUNISM, THE COURTS, AND THE   MARXISM
CONSTITUTION. USA+45 CT/SYS ORD/FREE...ANTHOL 20   POL/PAR
COM/PARTY CIV/RIGHTS. PAGE 48 E0965   CONSTN
                                                        LAW

B64

HALLER W.,DER SCHWEDISCHE JUSTITIEOMBUDSMAN.   JURID
DENMARK FINLAND NORWAY SWEDEN LEGIS ADJUD CONTROL   PARL/PROC
PERSON ORD/FREE...NAT/COMP 20 OMBUDSMAN. PAGE 50   ADMIN
E0986   CHIEF

B64

IKLE F.C.,HOW NATIONS NEGOTIATE. COM EUR+WWI USA+45   NAT/G
INTELL INT/ORG VOL/ASSN DELIB/GP ACT/RES CREATE   PWR
DOMIN EDU/PROP ADJUD ROUTINE ATTIT PERSON ORD/FREE   POLICY
RESPECT SKILL...PSY SOC OBS VAL/FREE. PAGE 56 E1122

B64

JACKSON R.M.,THE MACHINERY OF JUSTICE IN ENGLAND.   CT/SYS
UK EDU/PROP CONTROL COST ORD/FREE...MGT 20   ADJUD
ENGLSH/LAW. PAGE 57 E1142   JUDGE
                                                        JURID

B64

KAUPER P.G.,RELIGION AND THE CONSTITUTION. USA+45   CONSTN
USA-45 LAW NAT/G SCHOOL SECT GP/REL ATTIT...BIBLIOG   JURID
WORSHIP 18/20 SUPREME/CT FREE/SPEE CHURCH/STA.   ORD/FREE
PAGE 60 E1189

B64

KOREA (REPUBLIC) SUPREME COURT,KOREAN LEGAL SYSTEM.   JURID
KOREA/S WOR+45 LAW LEAD ROUTINE GOV/REL ORD/FREE 20   CT/SYS
SUPREME/CT. PAGE 61 E1229   CONSTN
                                                        CRIME

B64

LOCKHART W.B.,CASES AND MATERIALS ON CONSTITUTIONAL   ORD/FREE
RIGHTS AND LIBERTIES. USA+45 FORCES LEGIS DIPLOM   CONSTN
PRESS CONTROL CRIME WAR PWR...AUD/VIS T WORSHIP 20   NAT/G
NEGRO. PAGE 66 E1317

B64

MAKI J.M.,COURT AND CONSTITUTION IN JAPAN; SELECTED   CT/SYS
SUPREME COURT DECISIONS, 1948-60. FAM LABOR GOV/REL   CONSTN
HABITAT ORD/FREE...DECISION JURID 20 CHINJAP   PROB/SOLV
SUPREME/CT CIV/RIGHTS. PAGE 68 E1354   LAW

B64

MARNELL W.H.,THE FIRST AMENDMENT: THE HISTORY OF   CONSTN
RELIGIOUS FREEDOM IN AMERICA. WOR+45 WOR-45 PROVS   SECT
CREATE CT/SYS...POLICY BIBLIOG/A WORSHIP 16/20.   ORD/FREE

PAGE 68 E1367   GOV/REL

B64

MARSHALL B.,FEDERALISM AND CIVIL RIGHTS. USA+45   FEDERAL
PROVS BAL/PWR CONTROL CT/SYS PARTIC SOVEREIGN   ORD/FREE
...JURID 20 NEGRO CIV/RIGHTS. PAGE 68 E1369   CONSTN
   FORCES

B64

MASON A.T.,AMERICAN CONSTITUTIONAL LAW: CONSTN
INTRODUCTORY ESSAYS AND SELECTED CASES (3RD ED.).   CT/SYS
LAW LEGIS TAX ADJUD GOV/REL FEDERAL ORD/FREE PWR   JURID
...TIME/SEQ BIBLIOG T 19/20 SUPREME/CT. PAGE 69
E1379

B64

NEWMAN E.S.,POLICE, THE LAW, AND PERSONAL FREEDOM.   JURID
USA+45 CONSTN JUDGE CT/SYS CRIME PERS/REL RESPECT   FORCES
...CRIMLGY 20. PAGE 77 E1542   ORD/FREE
   ADJUD

B64

NEWMAN E.S.,CIVIL LIBERTY AND CIVIL RIGHTS. USA+45   ORD/FREE
USA-45 CONSTN PROVS FORCES LEGIS CT/SYS RACE/REL   LAW
ATTIT...MAJORIT JURID WORSHIP 20 SUPREME/CT NEGRO   CONTROL
CIV/RIGHTS CHURCH/STA. PAGE 77 E1543   NAT/G

B64

NICE R.W.,TREASURY OF LAW. WOR+45 WOR-45 SECT ADJUD   LAW
MORAL ORD/FREE...INT/LAW JURID PHIL/SCI ANTHOL.   WRITING
PAGE 77 E1545   PERS/REL
   DIPLOM

B64

OSSENBECK F.J.,OPEN SPACE AND PEACE. CHINA/COM FUT   SPACE
USA+45 USSR LAW PROB/SOLV TEC/DEV EDU/PROP NEUTRAL   ORD/FREE
PEACE...AUD/VIS ANTHOL 20. PAGE 79 E1583   DIPLOM
   CREATE

B64

PRESS C.,A BIBLIOGRAPHIC INTRODUCTION TO AMERICAN   BIBLIOG
STATE GOVERNMENT AND POLITICS (PAMPHLET). USA+45   LEGIS
USA-45 EX/STRUC ADJUD INGP/REL FEDERAL ORD/FREE 20.   LOC/G
PAGE 82 E1649   POL/PAR

B64

RUSSELL R.B.,UNITED NATIONS EXPERIENCE WITH   FORCES
MILITARY FORCES: POLITICAL AND LEGAL ASPECTS. AFR   DIPLOM
KOREA WOR+45 LEGIS PROB/SOLV ADMIN CONTROL   SANCTION
EFFICIENCY PEACE...POLICY INT/LAW BIBLIOG UN.   ORD/FREE
PAGE 87 E1738

B64

SCHMEISER D.A.,CIVIL LIBERTIES IN CANADA. CANADA   ORD/FREE
LAW SECT PRESS RACE/REL NAT/LISM PRIVIL 20   CONSTN
COMMONWLTH PARLIAMENT CIVIL/LIB CHURCH/STA. PAGE 88   ADJUD
E1758   EDU/PROP

B64

SCHWELB E.,HUMAN RIGHTS AND THE INTERNATIONAL   INT/ORG
COMMUNITY. WOR+45 WOR-45 NAT/G SECT DELIB/GP DIPLOM   ORD/FREE
PEACE RESPECT TREATY 20 UN. PAGE 89 E1792   INT/LAW

B64

STOKES A.P.,CHURCH AND STATE IN THE UNITED STATES   SECT
(3 VOLS.). USA+45 USA-45 NAT/G PROVS LEGIS CT/SYS   CONSTN
SANCTION PRIVIL ORD/FREE 17/20 CHURCH/STA. PAGE 94   POLICY
E1875

B64

TENBROCK J.,EQUAL UNDER LAW. USA-45 CONSTN POL/PAR   LEGIS
EDU/PROP PARL/PROC ORD/FREE...BIBLIOG 19 AMEND/XIV.   LAW
PAGE 95 E1914   DISCRIM
   DOMIN

B64

US SENATE COMM ON JUDICIARY,CIVIL RIGHTS - THE   INT
PRESIDENT'S PROGRAM. USA+45 LAW PROB/SOLV PRESS   LEGIS
ADJUD GOV/REL RACE/REL ORD/FREE PWR...JURID 20   DISCRIM
SUPREME/CT SENATE CIV/RIGHTS PRESIDENT. PAGE 102   PARL/PROC
E2053

B64

WAY H.F. JR.,LIBERTY IN THE BALANCE - CURRENT   ORD/FREE
ISSUES IN CIVIL LIBERTIES. USA+45 USA-45 DELIB/GP   EDU/PROP
RACE/REL DISCRIM TOTALISM MARXISM SOCISM...CONCPT   NAT/G
20 CONGRESS SUPREME/CT CIVIL/LIB. PAGE 105 E2104   JURID

B64

WILLIAMS S.P.,TOWARD A GENUINE WORLD SECURITY   BIBLIOG/A
SYSTEM (PAMPHLET). WOR+45 INT/ORG FORCES PLAN   ARMS/CONT
NUC/PWR ORD/FREE...INT/LAW CONCPT UN PRESIDENT.   DIPLOM
PAGE 106 E2123   PEACE

L64

POUNDS N.J.G.,"THE POLITICS OF PARTITION." AFR ASIA   NAT/G

COM EUR+WWI FUT ISLAM S/ASIA USA-45 LAW ECO/DEV   NAT/LISM
ECO/UNDEV AGRI INDUS INT/ORG POL/PAR PROVS SECT
FORCES TOP/EX EDU/PROP LEGIT ATTIT MORAL ORD/FREE
PWR RESPECT WEALTH. PAGE 82 E1640

L64

WORLD PEACE FOUNDATION,"INTERNATIONAL   INT/ORG
ORGANIZATIONS: SUMMARY OF ACTIVITIES." INDIA   ROUTINE
PAKISTAN TURKEY WOR+45 CONSTN CONSULT EX/STRUC
ECO/TAC EDU/PROP LEGIT ORD/FREE...JURID SOC UN 20
CYPRESS. PAGE 107 E2145

S64

CARNEGIE ENDOWMENT INT. PEACE,"HUMAN RIGHTS (ISSUES   INT/ORG
BEFORE THE NINETEENTH GENERAL ASSEMBLY)." AFR   PERSON
WOR+45 LAW CONSTN NAT/G EDU/PROP GP/REL DISCRIM   RACE/REL
PEACE ATTIT MORAL ORD/FREE...INT/LAW PSY CONCPT
RECORD UN 20. PAGE 20 E0385

S64

CARNEGIE ENDOWMENT INT. PEACE,"LEGAL QUESTIONS   INT/ORG
(ISSUES BEFORE THE NINETEENTH GENERAL ASSEMBLY)."   LAW
WOR+45 CONSTN NAT/G DELIB/GP ADJUD PEACE MORAL   INT/LAW
ORD/FREE...RECORD UN 20 TREATY. PAGE 20 E0386

S64

COHEN M.,"BASIC PRINCIPLES OF INTERNATIONAL LAW."   INT/ORG
UNIV WOR+45 WOR-45 BAL/PWR LEGIT ADJUD WAR ATTIT   INT/LAW
MORAL ORD/FREE PWR...JURID CONCPT MYTH TOT/POP 20.
PAGE 23 E0463

S64

HICKEY D.,"THE PHILOSOPHICAL ARGUMENT FOR WORLD   FUT
GOVERNMENT." WOR+45 SOCIETY ACT/RES PLAN LEGIT   INT/ORG
ADJUD PEACE PERCEPT PERSON ORD/FREE...HUM JURID
PHIL/SCI METH/CNCPT CON/ANAL STERTYP GEN/LAWS
TOT/POP 20. PAGE 52 E1039

S64

KARPOV P.V.,"PEACEFUL COEXISTENCE AND INTERNATIONAL   COM
LAW." WOR+45 LAW SOCIETY INT/ORG VOL/ASSN FORCES   ATTIT
CREATE CAP/ISM DIPLOM ADJUD NUC/PWR PEACE MORAL   INT/LAW
ORD/FREE PWR MARXISM...MARXIST JURID CONCPT OBS   USSR
TREND COLD/WAR MARX/KARL 20. PAGE 59 E1186

S64

KUNZ J.,"THE CHANGING SCIENCE OF INTERNATIONAL   ADJUD
LAW." FUT WOR+45 WOR-45 INT/ORG LEGIT ORD/FREE   CONCPT
...JURID TIME/SEQ GEN/LAWS 20. PAGE 62 E1235   INT/LAW

S64

LIPSON L.,"PEACEFUL COEXISTENCE." COM USSR WOR+45   ATTIT
LAW INT/ORG DIPLOM LEGIT ADJUD ORD/FREE...CONCPT   JURID
OBS TREND GEN/LAWS VAL/FREE COLD/WAR 20. PAGE 65   INT/LAW
E1303   PEACE

S64

MAGGS P.B.,"SOVIET VIEWPOINT ON NUCLEAR WEAPONS IN   COM
INTERNATIONAL LAW." USSR WOR+45 INT/ORG FORCES   LAW
DIPLOM ARMS/CONT ATTIT ORD/FREE PWR...POLICY JURID   INT/LAW
CONCPT OBS TREND CON/ANAL GEN/LAWS VAL/FREE 20.   NUC/PWR
PAGE 67 E1347

S64

SCHWELB E.,"OPERATION OF THE EUROPEAN CONVENTION ON   INT/ORG
HUMAN RIGHTS." EUR+WWI LAW SOCIETY CREATE EDU/PROP   MORAL
ADJUD ADMIN PEACE ATTIT ORD/FREE PWR...POLICY
INT/LAW CONCPT OBS GEN/LAWS UN VAL/FREE ILO 20
ECHR. PAGE 89 E1791

B65

MISSISSIPPI BLACK PAPER: (FIFTY-SEVEN NEGRO AND   COERCE
WHITE CITIZENS' TESTIMONY OF POLICE BRUTALITY...).   RACE/REL
USA+45 LAW SOCIETY CT/SYS SANCTION CRIME MORAL   DISCRIM
ORD/FREE RESPECT 20 NEGRO. PAGE 2 E0035   FORCES

B65

AMERICAN ASSEMBLY COLUMBIA U,THE COURTS, THE   CT/SYS
PUBLIC, AND THE LAW EXPLOSION. USA+45 ELITES PROVS   ADJUD
EDU/PROP CRIME CHOOSE PERSON ORD/FREE PWR 20.   NAT/G
PAGE 4 E0074

B65

ANDRUS H.L.,LIBERALISM, CONSERVATISM, MORMONISM.   SECT
USA+45 PLAN ADJUD CONTROL HAPPINESS ORD/FREE   UTOPIA
CONSERVE NEW/LIB WORSHIP 20. PAGE 5 E0097   MORAL

B65

ANTIEU C.J.,RELIGION UNDER THE STATE CONSTITUTIONS.   SECT
USA+45 LAW SCHOOL TAX SANCTION PRIVIL ORD/FREE   CONSTN
...JURID 20 SUPREME/CT CHURCH/STA. PAGE 5 E0099   PROVS
   GP/REL

B65

ASSOCIATION BAR OF NYC,RADIO, TELEVISION, AND THE   AUD/VIS
ADMINISTRATION OF JUSTICE: A DOCUMENTED SURVEY OF   ATTIT

MATERIALS. USA+45 DELIB/GP FORCES PRESS ADJUD CONTROL CT/SYS CRIME...INT IDEA/COMP BIBLIOG. PAGE 6 E0109 — ORD/FREE

B65
BAADE H.,THE SOVIET IMPACT ON INTERNATIONAL LAW. INT/ORG INT/TRADE LEGIT COLONIAL ARMS/CONT REV WAR ...CON/ANAL ANTHOL TREATY. PAGE 6 E0124 — INT/LAW USSR CREATE ORD/FREE

B65
BAR ASSOCIATION OF ST LOUIS,CONSTITUTIONAL FREEDOM AND THE LAW. USA+45 LAW LABOR LEGIS EDU/PROP ...JURID CONCPT SUPREME/CT CIVIL/LIB CIV/RIGHTS. PAGE 8 E0146 — ORD/FREE CONSTN RACE/REL NAT/G

B65
BARKER L.J.,FREEDOM, COURTS, POLITICS: STUDIES IN CIVIL LIBERTIES. USA+45 LEGIS CREATE DOMIN PRESS ADJUD LOBBY CRIME GP/REL RACE/REL MARXISM 20 CIVIL/LIB. PAGE 8 E0148 — JURID CT/SYS ATTIT ORD/FREE

B65
BERKOWITZ M.,AMERICAN NATIONAL SECURITY: A READER IN THEORY AND POLICY. USA+45 INT/ORG FORCES BAL/PWR DIPLOM ECO/TAC DETER PWR...INT/LAW ANTHOL BIBLIOG 20 UN. PAGE 11 E0203 — ORD/FREE WAR ARMS/CONT POLICY

B65
BOCK E.,GOVERNMENT REGULATION OF BUSINESS. USA+45 LAW EX/STRUC LEGIS EXEC ORD/FREE PWR...ANTHOL CONGRESS. PAGE 13 E0255 — MGT ADMIN NAT/G CONTROL

B65
BREITEL C.D.,THE LAWMAKERS. USA+45 EX/STRUC LEGIS JUDGE ATTIT ORD/FREE JURID. PAGE 15 E0290 — CT/SYS ADJUD FEDERAL NAT/G

B65
CHARNAY J.P.,LE SUFFRAGE POLITIQUE EN FRANCE; ELECTIONS PARLEMENTAIRES, ELECTION PRESIDENTIELLE, REFERENDUMS. FRANCE CONSTN CHIEF DELIB/GP ECO/TAC EDU/PROP CRIME INGP/REL MORAL ORD/FREE PWR CATHISM 20 PARLIAMENT PRESIDENT. PAGE 22 E0425 — CHOOSE SUFF NAT/G LEGIS

B65
CONRING E.,KIRCHE UND STAAT NACH DER LEHRE DER NIEDERLANDISCHEN CALVINISTEN IN DER ERSTEN HALFTE DES 17. JAHRHUNDERTS. NETHERLAND GP/REL...CONCPT 17 CHURCH/STA. PAGE 25 E0497 — SECT JURID NAT/G ORD/FREE

B65
EHLE J.,THE FREE MEN. USA+45 NAT/G PROVS FORCES JUDGE ADJUD ATTIT...POLICY SOC SOC/INTEG 20 NEGRO. PAGE 34 E0677 — RACE/REL ORD/FREE DISCRIM

B65
FELLMAN D.,RELIGION IN AMERICAN PUBLIC LAW. USA+45 USA-45 NAT/G PROVS ADJUD SANCTION GP/REL PRIVIL ORD/FREE...JURID TIME/SEQ 18/20 SUPREME/CT CHURCH/STA. PAGE 37 E0733 — SECT CONSTN LAW POLICY

B65
GAJENDRAGADKAR P.B.,LAW, LIBERTY AND SOCIAL JUSTICE. INDIA CONSTN NAT/G SECT PLAN ECO/TAC PRESS POPULISM...SOC METH/COMP 20 HINDU. PAGE 42 E0826 — ORD/FREE LAW ADJUD JURID

B65
GINSBERG M.,ON JUSTICE IN SOCIETY. LAW EDU/PROP LEGIT CT/SYS INGP/REL PRIVIL RATIONAL ATTIT MORAL ORD/FREE...JURID 20. PAGE 44 E0867 — ADJUD ROLE CONCPT

B65
GLUECK S.,ROSCOE POUND AND CRIMINAL JUSTICE. SOCIETY FAM GOV/REL AGE/Y ATTIT ORD/FREE...CRIMLGY BIOG ANTHOL SOC/INTEG 19/20. PAGE 44 E0875 — CT/SYS CRIME LAW ADJUD

B65
GOTLIEB A.,DISARMAMENT AND INTERNATIONAL LAW* A STUDY OF THE ROLE OF LAW IN THE DISARMAMENT PROCESS. USA+45 USSR PROB/SOLV CONFER ADMIN ROUTINE NUC/PWR ORD/FREE SOVEREIGN UN TREATY. PAGE 45 E0893 — INT/LAW INT/ORG ARMS/CONT IDEA/COMP

B65
HOWARD C.G.,LAW: ITS NATURE, FUNCTIONS, AND LIMITS. USA+45 CONSTN LEGIS CREATE SANCTION ORD/FREE ...BIBLIOG 20. PAGE 55 E1101 — LAW JURID CONTROL SOCIETY

B65
HOWE M.D.W.,THE GARDEN AND THE WILDERNESS. USA+45 LAW GIVE EDU/PROP LEGIT NAT/LISM ORD/FREE...POLICY — CONSTN SECT

JURID SUPREME/CT CHURCH/STA. PAGE 55 E1103 — NAT/G GP/REL

B65
JENKS C.W.,SPACE LAW. DIPLOM DEBATE CONTROL ORD/FREE TREATY 20 UN. PAGE 58 E1161 — SPACE INT/LAW JURID INT/ORG

B65
KAMISAR Y.,CRIMINAL JUSTICE IN OUR TIME. USA+45 FORCES JUDGE PROB/SOLV COERCE MORAL 20 CIVIL/LIB CIV/RIGHTS. PAGE 59 E1182 — ORD/FREE CRIME CT/SYS LAW

B65
MEIKLEJOHN D.,FREEDOM AND THE PUBLIC: PUBLIC AND PRIVATE MORALITY IN AMERICA. USA+45 USA-45...POLICY JURID IDEA/COMP. PAGE 72 E1435 — NAT/G CONCPT ORD/FREE

B65
MILLIS W.,AN END TO ARMS. LAW INT/ORG FORCES ACT/RES CREATE DIPLOM WAR...POLICY HUM NEW/IDEA HYPO/EXP. PAGE 73 E1462 — FUT PWR ARMS/CONT ORD/FREE

B65
MONCONDUIT F.,LA COMMISSION EUROPEENNE DES DROITS DE L'HOMME. DIPLOM AGREE GP/REL ORD/FREE PWR ...BIBLIOG 20 TREATY. PAGE 74 E1483 — INT/LAW INT/ORG ADJUD JURID

B65
MORRIS R.B.,THE PEACEMAKERS: THE GREAT POWERS AND AMERICAN INDEPENDENCE. BAL/PWR CONFER COLONIAL NEUTRAL PEACE ORD/FREE TREATY 18 PRE/US/AM. PAGE 75 E1499 — SOVEREIGN REV DIPLOM

B65
MURPHY W.F.,WIRETAPPING ON TRIAL: A CASE STUDY IN THE JUDICIAL PROCESS. CONSTN ELITES CT/SYS CRIME MORAL ORD/FREE...DECISION SUPREME/CT. PAGE 75 E1511 — JURID LAW POLICY

B65
NEWBURY C.W.,BRITISH POLICY TOWARDS WEST AFRICA: SELECT DOCUMENTS 1786-1874. AFR UK INT/TRADE DOMIN ADMIN COLONIAL CT/SYS COERCE ORD/FREE...BIBLIOG/A 18/19. PAGE 77 E1540 — DIPLOM POLICY NAT/G WRITING

B65
PADELFORD N.,THE UNITED NATIONS IN THE BALANCE* ACCOMPLISHMENTS AND PROSPECTS. NAT/G VOL/ASSN DIPLOM ADMIN COLONIAL CT/SYS REGION WAR ORD/FREE ...ANTHOL UN. PAGE 79 E1588 — INT/ORG CONTROL

B65
PARKER D.,CIVIL LIBERTIES CASE STUDIES AND THE LAW. SECT ADJUD...CONCPT WORSHIP 20 SUPREME/CT CIV/RIGHTS FREE/SPEE. PAGE 80 E1598 — ORD/FREE JURID CONSTN JUDGE

B65
PEASLEE A.J.,CONSTITUTIONS OF NATIONS* THIRD REVISED EDITION (VOLUME I* AFRICA). LAW EX/STRUC LEGIS TOP/EX LEGIT CT/SYS ROUTINE ORD/FREE PWR SOVEREIGN...CON/ANAL CHARTS. PAGE 80 E1606 — AFR CHOOSE CONSTN NAT/G

B65
SCHROEDER O.,DEFACTO SEGREGATION AND CIVIL RIGHTS. LAW PROVS SCHOOL WORKER ATTIT HABITAT HEALTH WEALTH ...JURID CHARTS 19/20 NEGRO SUPREME/CT KKK. PAGE 88 E1766 — ANTHOL DISCRIM RACE/REL ORD/FREE

B65
SCHUBERT G.,THE POLITICAL ROLE OF THE COURTS IN JUDICIAL POLICY MAKING. USA+45 CONSTN JUDGE FEEDBACK CHOOSE RACE/REL ORD/FREE...TRADIT PSY BIBLIOG/A 20 KENNEDY/JF SUPREME/CT. PAGE 89 E1776 — CT/SYS POLICY DECISION

B65
SNOW J.H.,REAPPORTIONMENT. LAW CONSTN NAT/G GOV/REL ORD/FREE...JURID 20 SUPREME/CT CONNECTICT. PAGE 92 E1848 — APPORT ADJUD LEGIS PROVS

B65
STOREY R.G.,OUR UNALIENABLE RIGHTS. LAW SECT CT/SYS SUFF DISCRIM 17/20 CIVIL/LIB ENGLSH/LAW. PAGE 94 E1882 — CONSTN JURID ORD/FREE LEGIS

B65
TRESOLINI R.J.,AMERICAN CONSTITUTIONAL LAW. USA+45 USA-45 NAT/G ADJUD ORD/FREE PWR...POLICY BIOG 20 SUPREME/CT CASEBOOK. PAGE 97 E1939 — CONSTN CT/SYS JURID LAW

WILSON J.F.,CHURCH AND STATE IN AMERICAN HISTORY. USA+45 USA-45 ADJUD CT/SYS ORD/FREE SOVEREIGN ...ANTHOL BIBLIOG/A 17/20 CHURCH/STA. PAGE 106 E2129
SECT NAT/G GP/REL CONTROL
B65

RUBIN A.P.,"UNITED STATES CONTEMPORARY PRACTICE RELATING TO INTERNATIONAL LAW." USA+45 WOR+45 CONSTN INT/ORG NAT/G DELIB/GP EX/STRUC DIPLOM DOMIN CT/SYS ROUTINE ORD/FREE...CONCPT COLD/WAR 20. PAGE 86 E1730
LAW LEGIT INT/LAW
L65

SHARMA S.P.,"THE INDIA-CHINA BORDER DISPUTE: AN INDIAN PERSPECTIVE." ASIA CHINA/COM S/ASIA NAT/G LEGIT CT/SYS NAT/LISM DRIVE MORAL ORD/FREE PWR 20. PAGE 91 E1815
LAW ATTIT SOVEREIGN INDIA
L65

BEVANS C.I.,"GHANA AND UNITED STATES - UNITED KINGDOM AGREEMENTS." UK USA+45 LAW DELIB/GP EX/STRUC ORD/FREE...JURID METH/CNCPT GEN/LAWS 20. PAGE 11 E0222
NAT/G LEGIT GHANA DIPLOM
S65

LUSKY L.,"FOUR PROBLEMS IN LAWMAKING FOR PEACE." FORCES LEGIS CREATE ADJUD COERCE WAR MAJORITY PEACE PWR. PAGE 67 E1334
ORD/FREE INT/LAW UTOPIA RECORD
S65

MAC CHESNEY B.,"SOME COMMENTS ON THE 'QUARANTINE' OF CUBA." USA+45 WOR+45 NAT/G BAL/PWR DIPLOM LEGIT ROUTINE ATTIT ORD/FREE...JURID METH/CNCPT 20. PAGE 67 E1337
INT/ORG LAW CUBA USSR
S65

MCWHINNEY E.,"CHANGING INTERNATIONAL LAW METHOD AND OBJECTIVES IN THE ERA OF THE SOVIET-WESTERN DETENTE." COM USA+45 NAT/G BAL/PWR CT/SYS ATTIT ORD/FREE...HUM JURID NEW/IDEA COLD/WAR VAL/FREE 20. PAGE 71 E1430
LAW TREND
S65

ARCHER P.,FREEDOM AT STAKE. UK LAW NAT/G LEGIS JUDGE CRIME MORAL...CONCPT 20 CIVIL/LIB. PAGE 5 E0103
ORD/FREE NAT/COMP POLICY
B66

AUERBACH J.S.,LABOR AND LIBERTY; THE LA FOLLETTE COMMITTEE AND THE NEW DEAL. USA-45 LAW LEAD RESPECT SOCISM...BIBLIOG 20 CONGRESS BILL/RIGHT LAFOLLET/R NEW/DEAL. PAGE 6 E0117
DELIB/GP LABOR CONSTN ORD/FREE
B66

BAKER G.E.,THE REAPPORTIONMENT REVOLUTION; REPRESENTATION, POLITICAL POWER, AND THE SUPREME COURT. USA+45 MUNIC NAT/G POL/PAR PROVS PROB/SOLV CHOOSE ORD/FREE POPULISM...CONCPT CHARTS 20 SUPREME/CT. PAGE 7 E0140
LEGIS APPORT REPRESENT ADJUD
B66

BEDI A.S.,FREEDOM OF EXPRESSION AND SECURITY; COMPARATIVE STUDY OF FUNCTIONS OF SUPREME COURTS IN UNITED STATES AND INDIA. INDIA USA+45 LAW CONSTN PROB/SOLV...DECISION JURID BIBLIOG 20 SUPREME/CT FREE/SPEE AMEND/I. PAGE 9 E0175
METH CT/SYS ADJUD ORD/FREE
B66

CAHN E.,CONFRONTING INJUSTICE. USA+45 PROB/SOLV TAX EDU/PROP PRESS CT/SYS GP/REL DISCRIM BIO/SOC ...IDEA/COMP BIBLIOG WORSHIP 20 BILL/RIGHT. PAGE 18 E0362
ORD/FREE CONSTN ADJUD
B66

CAMPBELL E.,PARLIAMENTARY PRIVILEGE IN AUSTRALIA. UK LAW CONSTN COLONIAL ROLE ORD/FREE SOVEREIGN 18/20 COMMONWLTH AUSTRAL FREE/SPEE PARLIAMENT. PAGE 19 E0370
LEGIS PARL/PROC JURID PRIVIL
B66

CANFIELD L.H.,THE PRESIDENCY OF WOODROW WILSON: PRELUDE TO A WORLD IN CRISIS. USA-45 ADJUD NEUTRAL WAR CHOOSE INGP/REL PEACE ORD/FREE 20 WILSON/W PRESIDENT TREATY LEAGUE/NAT. PAGE 19 E0373
PERSON POLICY DIPLOM GOV/REL
B66

CARMEN I.H.,MOVIES, CENSORSHIP, AND THE LAW. LOC/G NAT/G ATTIT ORD/FREE...DECISION INT IDEA/COMP BIBLIOG 20 SUPREME/CT FILM. PAGE 19 E0383
EDU/PROP LAW ART/METH CONSTN
B66

COUNCIL OF EUROPE,EUROPEAN CONVENTION ON HUMAN
ORD/FREE
B66

RIGHTS - COLLECTED TEXTS (5TH ED.). EUR+WWI DIPLOM ADJUD CT/SYS...INT/LAW 20 ECHR. PAGE 26 E0520
DELIB/GP INT/ORG JURID

DALLIN A.,POLITICS IN THE SOVIET UNION: 7 CASES. COM USSR LAW POL/PAR CHIEF FORCES WRITING CONTROL PARL/PROC CIVMIL/REL TOTALISM...ANTHOL 20 KHRUSH/N STALIN/J CASEBOOK COM/PARTY. PAGE 28 E0563
MARXISM DOMIN ORD/FREE GOV/REL
B66

DE TOCQUEVILLE A,DEMOCRACY IN AMERICA (1834-1840) (2 VOLS. IN I; TRANS. BY G. LAWRENCE). FRANCE CULTURE STRATA POL/PAR CT/SYS REPRESENT FEDERAL ORD/FREE SOVEREIGN...MAJORIT TREND GEN/LAWS 18/19. PAGE 30 E0596
POPULISM USA-45 CONSTN NAT/COMP
B66

FALK R.A.,THE STRATEGY OF WORLD ORDER* 4 VOLUMES. WOR+45 ECO/UNDEV ACADEM INT/ORG ACT/RES DIPLOM ARMS/CONT WAR...NET/THEORY SIMUL BIBLIOG UN. PAGE 36 E0719
ORD/FREE GEN/LAWS ANTHOL INT/LAW
B66

FELSHER H.,JUSTICE USA? USA+45 COM/IND JUDGE CT/SYS MORAL ORD/FREE...SAMP/SIZ HYPO/EXP. PAGE 37 E0735
ADJUD EDU/PROP LOBBY
B66

FISCHER H.,EINER IM VORDERGRUND: TARAS BORODAJKEWYCZ. AUSTRIA POL/PAR PROF/ORG EDU/PROP CT/SYS ORD/FREE 20 NAZI. PAGE 38 E0754
FASCISM LAW ATTIT PRESS
B66

FUCHS W.P.,STAAT UND KIRCHE IM WANDEL DER JAHRHUNDERTE. EUR+WWI MOD/EUR UK REV...JURID CONCPT 4/20 EUROPE CHRISTIAN CHURCH/STA. PAGE 41 E0817
SECT NAT/G ORD/FREE GP/REL
B66

GARCON M.,LETTRE OUVERTE A LA JUSTICE. FRANCE NAT/G PROB/SOLV PAY EFFICIENCY MORAL 20. PAGE 42 E0834
ORD/FREE ADJUD CT/SYS
B66

GILLMOR D.M.,FREE PRESS AND FAIR TRIAL. UK USA+45 CONSTN PROB/SOLV PRESS CONTROL CRIME DISCRIM RESPECT...AUD/VIS 20 CIVIL/LIB. PAGE 44 E0865
ORD/FREE ADJUD ATTIT EDU/PROP
B66

GOLDWIN R.A.,APPORTIONMENT AND REPRESENTATION. MUNIC CT/SYS GP/REL ORD/FREE...POLICY ANTHOL 20 SUPREME/CT. PAGE 44 E0880
APPORT REPRESENT LEGIS CONSTN
B66

HARVEY W.B.,LAW AND SOCIAL CHANGE IN GHANA. AFR GHANA CONSULT CONTROL CT/SYS INGP/REL 20. PAGE 51 E1011
JURID CONSTN LEAD ORD/FREE
B66

HIDAYATULLAH M.,DEMOCRACY IN INDIA AND THE JUDICIAL PROCESS. INDIA EX/STRUC LEGIS LEAD GOV/REL ATTIT ORD/FREE...MAJORIT CONCPT 20 NEHRU/J. PAGE 52 E1040
NAT/G CT/SYS CONSTN JURID
B66

JACOBSON H.K.,DIPLOMATS, SCIENTISTS, AND POLITICIANS* THE UNITED STATES AND THE NUCLEAR TEST BAN NEGOTIATIONS. USA+45 USSR ACT/RES PLAN CONFER DETER NUC/PWR CONSEN ORD/FREE...INT TREATY. PAGE 57 E1146
DIPLOM ARMS/CONT TECHRACY INT/ORG
B66

LEHMANN L.,LEGAL UND OPPORTUN - POLITISCHE JUSTIZ IN DER BUNDESREPUBLIK. GERMANY/W EDU/PROP ADJUD CONTROL PARL/PROC COERCE TOTALISM ATTIT 20 COM/PARTY. PAGE 64 E1281
ORD/FREE POL/PAR JURID LEGIS
B66

LOFTON J.,JUSTICE AND THE PRESS. EDU/PROP GOV/REL MORAL 20. PAGE 66 E1320
PRESS JURID CT/SYS ORD/FREE
B66

MCNAIR A.D.,THE LEGAL EFFECTS OF WAR. UK FINAN DIPLOM ORD/FREE 20 ENGLSH/LAW. PAGE 71 E1425
JURID WAR INT/TRADE LABOR
B66

MEDER A.E. JR.,LEGISLATIVE APPORTIONMENT. USA+45
APPORT
B66

BAL/PWR REPRESENT ORD/FREE PWR...JURID 20
SUPREME/CT. PAGE 72 E1433
LEGIS
MATH
POLICY

B66

MENDELSON W.,JUSTICES BLACK AND FRANKFURTER:
CONFLICT IN THE COURT (2ND ED.). NAT/G PROVS
PROB/SOLV BAL/PWR CONTROL FEDERAL ISOLAT ANOMIE
ORD/FREE...DECISION 20 SUPREME/CT BLACK/HL
FRANKFUR/F. PAGE 72 E1439
JURID
ADJUD
IDEA/COMP
ROLE

B66

MILLER E.W.,THE NEGRO IN AMERICA: A BIBLIOGRAPHY.
USA+45 LAW EDU/PROP REV GOV/REL GP/REL INGP/REL
ADJUST HABITAT PERSON HEALTH ORD/FREE SOC/INTEG 20
NEGRO. PAGE 73 E1459
BIBLIOG
DISCRIM
RACE/REL

B66

MOSKOW M.H.,TEACHERS AND UNIONS. SCHOOL WORKER
ADJUD LOBBY ATTIT ORD/FREE 20. PAGE 75 E1501
EDU/PROP
PROF/ORG
LABOR
BARGAIN

B66

OBERMANN E.,VERTEIDIGUNG PER FREIHEIT. GERMANY/W
WOR+45 INT/ORG COERCE NUC/PWR WEAPON MARXISM 20 UN
NATO WARSAW/P TREATY. PAGE 78 E1571
FORCES
ORD/FREE
WAR
PEACE

B66

POLLACK R.S.,THE INDIVIDUAL'S RIGHTS AND
INTERNATIONAL ORGANIZATION. LAW INT/ORG DELIB/GP
SUPEGO...JURID SOC/INTEG 20 TREATY UN. PAGE 81
E1623
INT/LAW
ORD/FREE
DIPLOM
PERSON

B66

POWERS E.,CRIME AND PUNISHMENT IN EARLY
MASSACHUSETTS 1620-1692: A DOCUMENTARY HISTORY.
USA-45 LAW LEGIS COLONIAL ATTIT ORD/FREE MYSTISM
17 PRE/US/AM MASSACHU. PAGE 82 E1643
CRIME
ADJUD
CT/SYS
PROVS

B66

SHAPIRO M.,FREEDOM OF SPEECH: THE SUPREME COURT AND
JUDICIAL REVIEW. USA+45 LEGIS...CHARTS 20
SUPREME/CT FREE/SPEE. PAGE 90 E1812
CT/SYS
ORD/FREE
CONSTN
JURID

B66

SMITH E.A.,CHURCH-STATE RELATIONS IN ECUMENICAL
PERSPECTIVE. WOR+45 LAW MUNIC INGP/REL DISCRIM
ATTIT SUPEGO ORD/FREE CATHISM...PHIL/SCI IDEA/COMP
20 PROTESTANT ECUMENIC CHURCH/STA CHRISTIAN.
PAGE 92 E1843
NAT/G
SECT
GP/REL
ADJUD

B66

SOBEL N.R.,THE NEW CONFESSION STANDARDS, MIRANDA V.
ARIZONA. USA+45 USA-45 LAW PROF/ORG EDU/PROP 20
SUPREME/CT. PAGE 92 E1849
JURID
CT/SYS
ORD/FREE
ADJUD

B66

SWEET E.C.,CIVIL LIBERTIES IN AMERICA. LAW CONSTN
NAT/G PRESS CT/SYS DISCRIM ATTIT WORSHIP 20
CIVIL/LIB. PAGE 95 E1899
ADJUD
ORD/FREE
SUFF
COERCE

B66

TRESOLINI R.J.,CASES IN AMERICAN NATIONAL
GOVERNMENT AND POLITICS. LAW DIPLOM ADJUD LOBBY
FEDERAL ORD/FREE WEALTH...DECISION ANTHOL 20
PRESIDENT. PAGE 97 E1940
NAT/G
LEGIS
CT/SYS
POL/PAR

B66

US SENATE COMM ON JUDICIARY,HEARINGS ON FREE PRESS
AND FAIR TRIAL (2 VOLS.). USA+45 CONSTN ELITES
LEGIS EDU/PROP CT/SYS LEAD CONGRESS. PAGE 103 E2057
PRESS
LAW
CRIME
ORD/FREE

B66

WILSON G.,CASES AND MATERIALS ON CONSTITUTIONAL AND
ADMINISTRATIVE LAW. UK LAW NAT/G EX/STRUC LEGIS
BAL/PWR BUDGET DIPLOM ADJUD CONTROL CT/SYS GOV/REL
ORD/FREE 20 PARLIAMENT ENGLSH/LAW. PAGE 106 E2126
JURID
ADMIN
CONSTN
PWR

S66

BROWNLIE I.,"NUCLEAR PROLIFERATION* SOME PROBLEMS
OF CONTROL." USA+45 USSR ECO/UNDEV INT/ORG FORCES
TEC/DEV REGION CONSEN...RECORD TREATY. PAGE 16
E0318
NUC/PWR
ARMS/CONT
VOL/ASSN
ORD/FREE

S66

GASS O.,"THE LITERATURE OF AMERICAN GOVERNMENT."
CONSTN DRIVE ORD/FREE...JURID CONCPT METH/CNCPT
IDEA/COMP 20 WILSON/W BEARD/CA LINK/AS. PAGE 42
E0841
NEW/LIB
CT/SYS
NAT/G

C66

BLAISDELL D.C.,"INTERNATIONAL ORGANIZATION." FUT
WOR+45 ECO/DEV DELIB/GP FORCES EFFICIENCY PEACE
ORD/FREE...INT/LAW 20 UN LEAGUE/NAT NATO. PAGE 12
E0239
BIBLIOG
INT/ORG
DIPLOM
ARMS/CONT

B67

ASCH S.H.,POLICE AUTHORITY AND THE RIGHTS OF THE
INDIVIDUAL. CONSTN DOMIN ADJUD CT/SYS...JURID 20.
PAGE 6 E0106
FORCES
OP/RES
ORD/FREE

B67

GREENE L.S.,AMERICAN GOVERNMENT POLICIES AND
FUNCTIONS. USA+45 LAW AGRI DIST/IND LABOR MUNIC
BUDGET DIPLOM EDU/PROP ORD/FREE...BIBLIOG T 20.
PAGE 46 E0910
POLICY
NAT/G
ADMIN
DECISION

B67

INTERNATIONAL CONCILIATION,ISSUES BEFORE THE 22ND
GENERAL ASSEMBLY. WOR+45 ECO/UNDEV FINAN BAL/PWR
BUDGET INT/TRADE STRANGE ORD/FREE...INT/LAW 20 UN
COLD/WAR. PAGE 57 E1132
PROB/SOLV
INT/ORG
DIPLOM
PEACE

B67

LAWYERS COMM AMER POLICY VIET,VIETNAM AND
INTERNATIONAL LAW: AN ANALYSIS OF THE LEGALITY OF
THE US MILITARY INVOLVEMENT. VIETNAM LAW INT/ORG
COERCE WEAPON PEACE ORD/FREE 20 UN SEATO TREATY.
PAGE 64 E1271
INT/LAW
DIPLOM
ADJUD
WAR

B67

LENG S.C.,JUSTICE IN COMMUNIST CHINA: A SURVEY OF
THE JUDICIAL SYSTEM OF THE CHINESE PEOPLE'S
REPUBLIC. CHINA/COM LAW CONSTN LOC/G NAT/G PROF/ORG
CONSULT FORCES ADMIN CRIME ORD/FREE...BIBLIOG 20
MAO. PAGE 64 E1284
CT/SYS
ADJUD
JURID
MARXISM

B67

LEVY L.W.,JUDICIAL REVIEW AND THE SUPREME COURT.
USA+45 USA-45 NEUTRAL ATTIT ORD/FREE...POLICY
DECISION BIBLIOG 18/20 BILL/RIGHT SUPREME/CT.
PAGE 65 E1292
ADJUD
CONSTN
LAW
CT/SYS

B67

PLANO J.C.,FORGING WORLD ORDER: THE POLITICS OF
INTERNATIONAL ORGANIZATION. PROB/SOLV DIPLOM
CONTROL CENTRAL RATIONAL ORD/FREE...INT/LAW CHARTS
BIBLIOG 20 UN LEAGUE/NAT. PAGE 81 E1618
INT/ORG
ADMIN
JURID

B67

SLATER J.,THE OAS AND UNITED STATES FOREIGN POLICY.
KOREA L/A-17C USA+45 VOL/ASSN RISK COERCE PEACE
ORD/FREE MARXISM...TREND 20 OAS. PAGE 92 E1838
INT/ORG
DIPLOM
ALL/IDEOS
ADJUD

B67

US SENATE COMM ON FOREIGN REL,CONSULAR CONVENTION
WITH THE SOVIET UNION. USA+45 USSR DELIB/GP LEAD
REPRESENT ATTIT ORD/FREE CONGRESS TREATY. PAGE 101
E2031
LEGIS
LOBBY
DIPLOM

B67

US SENATE COMM ON FOREIGN REL,UNITED STATES
ARMAMENT AND DISARMAMENT PROBLEMS. USA+45 AIR
BAL/PWR DIPLOM FOR/AID NUC/PWR ORD/FREE SENATE
TREATY. PAGE 102 E2035
ARMS/CONT
WEAPON
FORCES
PROB/SOLV

L67

BAADE H.W.,"THE ACQUIRED RIGHTS OF INTERNATIONAL
PUBLIC SERVANTS: A CASE STUDY IN RECEPTION OF
PUBLIC LAW." WOR+45 DELIB/GP DIPLOM ORD/FREE
...INT/LAW JURID UN. PAGE 7 E0125
INT/ORG
WORKER
ADJUD
LAW

L67

BARRON J.A.,"ACCESS TO THE PRESS." USA+45 TEC/DEV
PRESS TV ADJUD AUD/VIS. PAGE 8 E0152
ORD/FREE
COM/IND
EDU/PROP
LAW

L67

HITCHMAN J.M.,"THE PLATT AMENDMENT REVISITED: A
BIBLIOGRAPHICAL SURVEY." CUBA ACADEM DELIB/GP
ORD/FREE...HIST/WRIT 20. PAGE 53 E1055
ATTIT
DIPLOM
SOVEREIGN
INT/LAW

L67

LEGAULT A.,"ORGANISATION ET CONDUITE DES OPERATIONS
DE MAINTIEN DE LA PAIX." FORCES ACT/RES ADJUD AGREE
CONTROL NEUTRAL TASK PRIVIL ORD/FREE 20 UN. PAGE 64
E1279
INT/ORG
PEACE
WAR
INT/LAW

L67

SCHUBERT G.,"THE RHETORIC OF CONSTITUTIONAL
CHANGE." USA+45 LAW CULTURE CHIEF LEGIS ADJUD
CT/SYS ARMS/CONT ADJUST...CHARTS SIMUL. PAGE 89
E1777
CONSTN
METH/COMP
ORD/FREE

"THE STATE OF ZONING ADMINISTRATION IN ILLINOIS:
PROCEDURAL REQUIREMENTS OF JUDICIAL INTERVENTION."
USA+45 LAW CONSTN DELIB/GP ADJUD CT/SYS ORD/FREE
ILLINOIS. PAGE 2 E0038
ADMIN
CONTROL
HABITAT
PLAN
S67

"THE FEDERAL AGRICULTURAL STABILIZATION PROGRAM AND
THE NEGRO." LAW CONSTN PLAN REPRESENT DISCRIM
ORD/FREE 20 NEGRO CONGRESS. PAGE 2 E0039
AGRI
CONTROL
NAT/G
RACE/REL
S67

ADOKO A.,"THE CONSTITUTION OF UGANDA." AFR UGANDA
LOC/G CHIEF FORCES LEGIS ADJUD EXEC CHOOSE NAT/LISM
...IDEA/COMP 20. PAGE 3 E0050
NAT/G
CONSTN
ORD/FREE
LAW
S67

ALEXANDER B.,"GIBRALTAR" SPAIN UK CONSTN WORKER
PROB/SOLV FOR/AID RECEIVE CONTROL 20. PAGE 3 E0059
DIPLOM
INT/ORG
ORD/FREE
ECO/TAC
S67

BRADLEY A.W.,"CONSTITUTION-MAKING IN UGANDA."
UGANDA LAW CHIEF DELIB/GP LEGIS ADMIN EXEC
PARL/PROC RACE/REL ORD/FREE...GOV/COMP 20. PAGE 15
E0284
NAT/G
CREATE
CONSTN
FEDERAL
S67

CHAMBERLAIN N.W.,"STRIKES IN CONTEMPORARY CONTEXT."
LAW INDUS NAT/G CHIEF CONFER COST ATTIT ORD/FREE
...POLICY MGT 20. PAGE 21 E0415
LABOR
BARGAIN
EFFICIENCY
PROB/SOLV
S67

CLOGGER T.J.,"THE BIG EAR." UK USA+45 USSR LAW
LEGIS CRIME GP/REL INGP/REL ATTIT 20 FBI ESPIONAGE.
PAGE 23 E0458
DIPLOM
ORD/FREE
COM/IND
INSPECT
S67

COHN K.,"CRIMES AGAINST HUMANITY." GERMANY INT/ORG
SANCTION ATTIT ORD/FREE...MARXIST CRIMLGY 20 UN.
PAGE 24 E0469
WAR
INT/LAW
CRIME
ADJUD
S67

DANIEL C.,"FREEDOM, EQUITY, AND THE WAR ON
POVERTY." USA+45 WORKER ECO/TAC JURID. PAGE 29
E0566
WEALTH
INCOME
SOCIETY
ORD/FREE
S67

FABREGA J.,"ANTECEDENTES EXTRANJEROS EN LA
CONSTITUCION PANAMENA." CUBA L/A+17C PANAMA URUGUAY
EX/STRUC LEGIS DIPLOM ORD/FREE 19/20 COLOMB
MEXIC/AMER. PAGE 36 E0709
CONSTN
JURID
NAT/G
PARL/PROC
S67

HILL D.G.,"HUMAN RIGHTS LEGISLATION IN ONTARIO."
CANADA R+D VOL/ASSN CONSULT INSPECT EDU/PROP ADJUD
AGREE TASK GP/REL INGP/REL DISCRIM 20 CIV/RIGHTS
ONTARIO CIVIL/LIB. PAGE 52 E1045
DELIB/GP
ORD/FREE
LAW
POLICY
S67

KIM R.C.C.,"THE SUPREME COURT: ORALLE WITHOUT
TRUTH." USA+45 EDU/PROP RACE/REL ADJUST ALL/VALS
ORD/FREE...DECISION WORSHIP SUPREME/CT. PAGE 61
E1214
CT/SYS
PROB/SOLV
ADJUD
REPRESENT
S67

KONVITZ M.R.,"CIVIL LIBERTIES." USA+45 R+D...METH
20. PAGE 61 E1228
LAW
MORAL
ORD/FREE
NAT/G
S67

MATTHEWS R.O.,"THE SUEZ CANAL DISPUTE* A CASE STUDY
IN PEACEFUL SETTLEMENT." FRANCE ISRAEL UAR UK NAT/G
CONTROL LEAD COERCE WAR NAT/LISM ROLE ORD/FREE PWR
...INT/LAW UN 20. PAGE 69 E1389
PEACE
DIPLOM
ADJUD
S67

MAYANJA A.,"THE GOVERNMENT'S PROPOSALS ON THE NEW
CONSTITUTION." AFR UGANDA LAW CHIEF LEGIS ADJUD
REPRESENT FEDERAL PWR 20. PAGE 69 E1390
CONSTN
CONFER
ORD/FREE
NAT/G
S67

MAYER M.,"THE IDEA OF JUSTICE AND THE POOR." USA+45
CLIENT CONSULT RENT ADJUD DISCRIM KNOWL 20. PAGE 70
E1393
INCOME
WEALTH
LAW
ORD/FREE
S67

MONEYPENNY P.,"UNIVERSITY PURPOSE, DISCIPLINE, AND
DUE PROCESS." USA+45 EDU/PROP ADJUD LEISURE
ORD/FREE. PAGE 74 E1484
ACADEM
AGE/Y
CONTROL
ADMIN
S67

PEMBERTON J., JR.,"CONSTITUTIONAL PROBLEMS IN
RESTRAINT ON THE MEDIA." CONSTN PROB/SOLV EDU/PROP
CONFER CONTROL JURID. PAGE 80 E1608
LAW
PRESS
ORD/FREE
S67

RUCKER B.W.,"WHAT SOLUTIONS DO PEOPLE ENDORSE IN
FREE PRESS-FAIR TRIAL DILEMMA?" LAW NAT/G CT/SYS
ATTIT...NET/THEORY SAMP CHARTS IDEA/COMP METH 20.
PAGE 86 E1731
CONCPT
PRESS
ADJUD
ORD/FREE
S67

SHAFFER T.L.,"DIRECT RESTRAINT ON THE PRESS."
USA+45 EDU/PROP CONTROL...JURID NEW/IDEA ABA.
PAGE 90 E1809
LAW
PRESS
ORD/FREE
ADJUD
S67

AUSTIN J.,LECTURES ON JURISPRUDENCE OR THE
PHILOSOPHY OF POSITIVE LAW (VOL. II) (4TH ED.,
REV.). UK CONSTN STRUCT PROB/SOLV LEGIT CT/SYS
SANCTION CRIME INGP/REL OWN SUPEGO ORD/FREE...T 19.
PAGE 6 E0120
LAW
ADJUD
JURID
METH/CNCPT
B73

BENTHAM J.,THE THEORY OF LEGISLATION. UK CREATE
CRIME ATTIT ORD/FREE...CONCPT 18 REFORMERS. PAGE 10
E0196
LEGIS
LAW
CRIMLGY
UTIL
B76

ELLMAKER E.G.,"REVELATION OF RIGHTS." JUDGE DISCRIM
SUPEGO...JURID PHIL/SCI CONCPT 17/18. PAGE 35 E0685
ORD/FREE
ADMIN
MORAL
NAT/G
L84

GOODNOW F.J.,"AN EXECUTIVE AND THE COURTS: JUDICIAL
REMEDIES AGAINST ADMINISTRATIVE ACTION" FRANCE UK
USA-45 WOR-45 LAW CONSTN SANCTION ORD/FREE 19.
PAGE 45 E0888
CT/SYS
GOV/REL
ADMIN
ADJUD
L86

FICHTE J.G.,THE SCIENCE OF RIGHTS (TRANS. BY A.E.
KROEGER). WOR-45 FAM MUNIC NAT/G PROVS ADJUD CRIME
CHOOSE MARRIAGE SEX POPULISM 19 FICHTE/JG
NATURL/LAW. PAGE 37 E0744
ORD/FREE
CONSTN
LAW
CONCPT
B89

GODWIN W.,POLITICAL JUSTICE. UK ELITES OWN KNOWL
MORAL WEALTH...JURID 18/19. PAGE 44 E0877
ORD/FREE
SOVEREIGN
STRUCT
CONCPT
B90

BENTHAM J.,A FRAGMENT ON GOVERNMENT (1776). CONSTN
MUNIC NAT/G SECT AGREE HAPPINESS UTIL MORAL
ORD/FREE...JURID CONCPT. PAGE 10 E0198
SOVEREIGN
LAW
DOMIN
B91

DE VATTEL E.,THE LAW OF NATIONS. AGRI FINAN CHIEF
DIPLOM INT/TRADE AGREE OWN ALL/VALS MORAL ORD/FREE
SOVEREIGN...GEN/LAWS 18 NATURL/LAW WOLFF/C. PAGE 30
E0597
LAW
CONCPT
NAT/G
INT/LAW
B96

ESMEIN A.,ELEMENTS DE DROIT CONSTITUTIONNEL. FRANCE
UK CHIEF EX/STRUC LEGIS ADJUD CT/SYS PARL/PROC REV
GOV/REL ORD/FREE...JURID METH/COMP 18/19. PAGE 35
E0697
LAW
CONSTN
NAT/G
CONCPT
B96

LILLY W.S.,FIRST PRINCIPLES IN POLITICS. UNIV LAW
LEGIS DOMIN ADJUD INGP/REL ORD/FREE SOVEREIGN
...JURID CONCPT 19 NATURL/LAW. PAGE 65 E1299
NAT/G
CONSTN
MORAL
POLICY
B99

ORDER....SEE ORD/FREE

OREGON....OREGON

ORFIELD L.B. E1581

ORG/CHARTS....ORGANIZATIONAL CHARTS, BLUEPRINTS

ORGANIZATION FOR AFRICAN UNITY....SEE OAU

ORGANIZATION FOR ECONOMIC COOPERATION AND DEVELOPMENT....
    SEE OECD

ORGANIZATION FOR EUROPEAN ECONOMIC COOPERATION....SEE OEEC

ORGANIZATION FOR LATIN AMERICAN SOLIDARITY....SEE OLAS

ORGANIZATION OF AMERICAN STATES....SEE OAS

ORGANIZATION, INTERNATIONAL....SEE INT/ORG

ORGANIZATION, LABOR....SEE LABOR

ORGANIZATION, POLITICAL....SEE POL/PAR

ORGANIZATION, PROFESSIONAL....SEE PROF/ORG

ORGANIZATION, VOLUNTARY....SEE VOL/ASSN

ORGANIZATIONAL BEHAVIOR, NONEXECUTIVE....SEE ADMIN

ORGANIZATIONAL CHARTS....SEE ORG/CHARTS

ORTHO/GK....GREEK ORTHODOX CHURCH

ORTHO/RUSS....RUSSIAN ORTHODOX CATHOLIC

ORTIZ R.P. E1582

ORWELL/G....GEORGE ORWELL

OSHOGBO....OSHOGBO, WEST AFRICA

OSSENBECK F.J. E1583

OSTERMANN R. E1584

OTTENBERG M. E1585

OTTOMAN....OTTOMAN EMPIRE

OTTOSON H.W. E1586

OUTER SPACE....SEE SPACE

OUTER/MONG....OUTER MONGOLIA

OVERSEAS DEVELOPMENT INSTITUTE....SEE OVRSEA/DEV

OVIMBUNDU....OVIMBUNDU PEOPLES OF ANGOLA

OVRSEA/DEV....OVERSEAS DEVELOPMENT INSTITUTE

OWEN/RBT....ROBERT OWEN

OWI....OFFICE OF WAR INFORMATION

OWN....OWNERSHIP, OWNER

B04
FREUND E.,THE POLICE POWER; PUBLIC POLICY AND CONSTN
CONSTITUTIONAL RIGHTS. USA-45 SOCIETY LOC/G NAT/G LAW
FORCES LEGIS ADJUD CT/SYS OWN PWR...JURID 18/19 ORD/FREE
SUPREME/CT. PAGE 40 E0795 CONTROL

B09
JUSTINIAN,THE DIGEST (DIGESTA CORPUS JURIS CIVILIS) JURID
(2 VOLS.) (TRANS. BY C. H. MONRO). ROMAN/EMP LAW CT/SYS
FAM LOC/G LEGIS EDU/PROP CONTROL MARRIAGE OWN ROLE NAT/G
CIVIL/LAW. PAGE 59 E1177 STRATA

B16
SALMOND J.W.,JURISPRUDENCE. UK LOC/G NAT/G LEGIS LAW
PROB/SOLV LICENSE LEGIT CRIME PERS/REL OWN ORD/FREE CT/SYS
...T 20. PAGE 87 E1742 JURID
ADJUD

B17
DE VICTORIA F.,DE INDIS ET DE JURE BELLI (1557) IN WAR
F. DE VICTORIA, DE INDIS ET DE JURE BELLI INT/LAW
REFLECTIONES. UNIV NAT/G SECT CHIEF PARTIC COERCE OWN
PEACE MORAL...POLICY 16 INDIAN/AM CHRISTIAN
CONSCN/OBJ. PAGE 30 E0598

B18
PORTER K.H.,A HISTORY OF SUFFRAGE IN THE UNITED SUFF
STATES. USA-45 LAW CONSTN LOC/G NAT/G POL/PAR WAR REPRESENT
DISCRIM OWN ATTIT SEX 18/20 NEGRO FEMALE/SEX. CHOOSE
PAGE 81 E1629 PARTIC

N18
BREWER D.J.,THE MOVEMENT OF COERCION (PAMPHLET). GP/REL
CONSTN INDUS ADJUD COERCE OWN WEALTH...OLD/LIB LABOR
JURID 19 SUPREME/CT. PAGE 15 E0296 LG/CO
LAW

N19
ATOMIC INDUSTRIAL FORUM,COMMENTARY ON LEGISLATION NUC/PWR
TO PERMIT PRIVATE OWNERSHIP OF SPECIAL NUCLEAR MARKET
MATERIAL (PAMPHLET). USA+45 DELIB/GP LEGIS PLAN OWN INDUS
...POLICY 20 AEC CONGRESS. PAGE 6 E0111 LAW

B20
VINOGRADOFF P.,OUTLINES OF HISTORICAL JURISPRUDENCE JURID
(2 VOLS.). GREECE MEDIT-7 LAW CONSTN FACE/GP FAM METH
KIN MUNIC CRIME OWN...INT/LAW IDEA/COMP BIBLIOG.
PAGE 104 E2080

C24
SHERMAN C.P.,"ROMAN LAW IN THE MODERN WORLD (2ND LAW
ED.) (3 VOLS.)" MEDIT-7...JURID BIBLIOG. PAGE 91 ADJUD
E1819 OWN
CONSTN

B31
BORCHARD E.H.,GUIDE TO THE LAW AND LEGAL LITERATURE BIBLIOG/A
OF FRANCE. FRANCE FINAN INDUS LABOR SECT LEGIS LAW
ADMIN COLONIAL CRIME OWN...INT/LAW 20. PAGE 14 CONSTN
E0266 METH

B32
LUNT D.C.,THE ROAD TO THE LAW. UK USA-45 LEGIS ADJUD
EDU/PROP OWN ORD/FREE...DECISION TIME/SEQ NAT/COMP LAW
16/20 AUSTRAL ENGLSH/LAW COMMON/LAW. PAGE 67 E1333 JURID
CT/SYS

B38
FRANKFURTER F.,MR. JUSTICE HOLMES AND THE SUPREME CREATE
COURT. USA-45 CONSTN SOCIETY FEDERAL OWN ATTIT CT/SYS
ORD/FREE PWR...POLICY JURID 20 SUPREME/CT HOLMES/OW DECISION
BILL/RIGHT. PAGE 40 E0790 LAW

B40
HOBBES T.,A DIALOGUE BETWEEN A PHILOSOPHER AND A CT/SYS
STUDENT OF THE COMMON LAWS OF ENGLAND (1667?). UK CHIEF
SECT DOMIN ADJUD CRIME INCOME OWN UTIL ORD/FREE PWR SANCTION
SOVEREIGN...JURID GEN/LAWS 17. PAGE 53 E1057

B42
HEGEL G.W.F.,PHILOSOPHY OF RIGHT. UNIV FAM SECT NAT/G
CHIEF AGREE WAR MARRIAGE OWN ORD/FREE...POLICY LAW
CONCPT. PAGE 51 E1023 RATIONAL

B47
LOCKE J.,TWO TREATISES OF GOVERNMENT (1690). UK LAW CONCPT
SOCIETY LEGIS LEGIT AGREE REV OWN HEREDITY MORAL ORD/FREE
CONSERVE...POLICY MAJORIT 17 WILLIAM/3 NATURL/LAW. NAT/G
PAGE 66 E1316 CONSEN

B48
CORWIN E.S.,LIBERTY AGAINST GOVERNMENT. UK USA-45 JURID
ROMAN/EMP LAW CONSTN PERS/REL OWN ATTIT 1/20 ORD/FREE
ROMAN/LAW ENGLSH/LAW AMEND/XIV. PAGE 26 E0513 CONCPT

B52
BUCKLAND W.W.,ROMAN LAW AND COMMON LAW; A IDEA/COMP
COMPARISON IN OUTLINE (2ND REV. ED.). UK FAM LEGIT LAW
AGREE CT/SYS OWN...JURID ROMAN/REP ROMAN/LAW ADJUD
COMMON/LAW. PAGE 17 E0325 CONCPT

B53
COKE E.,INSTITUTES OF THE LAWS OF ENGLAND JURID
(1628-1658). UK LAW ADJUD PERS/REL ORD/FREE OWN
...CRIMLGY 11/17. PAGE 24 E0471 CT/SYS
CONSTN

B54
FRIEDMAN W.,THE PUBLIC CORPORATION: A COMPARATIVE LAW
SYMPOSIUM (UNIVERSITY OF TORONTO SCHOOL OF LAW SOCISM
COMPARATIVE LAW SERIES, VOL. I). SWEDEN USA+45 LG/CO
INDUS INT/ORG NAT/G REGION CENTRAL FEDERAL...POLICY OWN
JURID IDEA/COMP NAT/COMP ANTHOL 20 COMMONWLTH
MONOPOLY EUROPE. PAGE 40 E0801

B55
CHARMATZ J.P.,COMPARATIVE STUDIES IN COMMUNITY MARRIAGE
PROPERTY LAW. FRANCE USA+45...JURID GOV/COMP ANTHOL LAW
20. PAGE 22 E0424 OWN
MUNIC

B55
GUAITA A.,BIBLIOGRAFIA ESPANOLA DE DERECHO BIBLIOG
ADMINISTRATIVO (PAMPHLET). SPAIN LOC/G MUNIC NAT/G ADMIN
PROVS JUDGE BAL/PWR GOV/REL OWN...JURID 18/19. CONSTN
PAGE 48 E0959 PWR

B55
SMITH G.,A CONSTITUTIONAL AND LEGAL HISTORY OF CONSTN
ENGLAND. UK ELITES NAT/G LEGIS ADJUD OWN HABITAT PARTIC
POPULISM...JURID 20 ENGLSH/LAW. PAGE 92 E1844 LAW
CT/SYS

B55

SWEET AND MAXWELL, A LEGAL BIBLIOGRAPHY OF THE BRITISH COMMONWEALTH OF NATIONS (2ND ED. 7 VOLS.). UK LOC/G MUNIC JUDGE ADJUD CRIME OWN...JURID 14/20 CMN/WLTH. PAGE 95 E1900

BIBLIOG/A
LAW
CONSTN
CT/SYS

B58

PALMER E.E., CIVIL LIBERTIES. USA+45 ADJUD CT/SYS PARTIC OWN LAISSEZ POPULISM...JURID CONCPT ANTHOL 20 SUPREME/CT CIVIL/LIB. PAGE 79 E1592

ORD/FREE
CONSTN
RACE/REL
LAW

B59

GINSBURG M., LAW AND OPINION IN ENGLAND. UK CULTURE KIN LABOR LEGIS EDU/PROP ADMIN CT/SYS CRIME OWN HEALTH...ANTHOL 20 ENGLSH/LAW. PAGE 44 E0868

JURID
POLICY
ECO/TAC

B61

ALFRED H., PUBLIC OWNERSHIP IN THE USA: GOALS AND PRIORITIES. LAW INDUS INT/TRADE ADJUD GOV/REL EFFICIENCY PEACE SOCISM...POLICY ANTHOL 20 TVA. PAGE 3 E0064

CONTROL
OWN
ECO/DEV
ECO/TAC

B61

LARSON A., WHEN NATIONS DISAGREE. USA+45 WOR+45 INT/ORG ADJUD COERCE CRIME OWN SOVEREIGN...POLICY JURID 20. PAGE 63 E1258

INT/LAW
DIPLOM
WAR

B62

GRZYBOWSKI K., SOVIET LEGAL INSTITUTIONS. USA+45 USSR ECO/DEV NAT/G EDU/PROP CONTROL CT/SYS CRIME OWN ATTIT PWR SOCISM...NAT/COMP 20. PAGE 48 E0955

ADJUD
LAW
JURID

B62

US CONGRESS, COMMUNICATIONS SATELLITE LEGISLATION: HEARINGS BEFORE COMM ON AERON AND SPACE SCIENCES ON BILLS S2550 AND 2814. WOR+45 LAW VOL/ASSN PLAN DIPLOM CONTROL OWN PEACE...NEW/IDEA CONGRESS NASA. PAGE 99 E1990

SPACE
COM/IND
ADJUD
GOV/REL

B64

BLOUSTEIN E.J., NUCLEAR ENERGY, PUBLIC POLICY, AND THE LAW. USA+45 NAT/G ADJUD ADMIN GP/REL OWN PEACE ATTIT HEALTH...ANTHOL 20. PAGE 13 E0251

TEC/DEV
LAW
POLICY
NUC/PWR

B64

DIAS R.W.M., A BIBLIOGRAPHY OF JURISPRUDENCE (2ND ED.). VOL/ASSN LEGIS ADJUD CT/SYS OWN...INT/LAW 18/20. PAGE 31 E0619

BIBLIOG/A
JURID
LAW
CONCPT

B64

HAAR C.M., LAW AND LAND: ANGLO-AMERICAN PLANNING PRACTICE. UK USA+45 NAT/G TEC/DEV BUDGET CT/SYS INGP/REL EFFICIENCY OWN...JURID 20. PAGE 49 E0967

LAW
PLAN
MUNIC
NAT/COMP

B64

HOHFELD W.N., FUNDAMENTAL LEGAL CONCEPTIONS. PROB/SOLV OWN PWR...DECISION LING IDEA/COMP GEN/METH. PAGE 54 E1069

JURID
ADJUD
LAW
METH/CNCPT

B64

SZLADITS C., BIBLIOGRAPHY ON FOREIGN AND COMPARATIVE LAW: BOOKS AND ARTICLES IN ENGLISH (SUPPLEMENT 1962). FINAN INDUS JUDGE LICENSE ADMIN CT/SYS PARL/PROC OWN...INT/LAW CLASSIF METH/COMP NAT/COMP 20. PAGE 95 E1904

BIBLIOG/A
JURID
ADJUD
LAW

B64

TELLADO A., A STATEMENT OF THE LAWS OF THE DOMINICAN REPUBLIC IN MATTERS AFFECTING BUSINESS (3RD ED.). DOMIN/REP AGRI DIST/IND EXTR/IND FINAN FAM WORKER ECO/TAC TAX CT/SYS MARRIAGE OWN...BIBLIOG 20 MIGRATION. PAGE 95 E1913

CONSTN
LEGIS
NAT/G
INDUS

B65

FALK R.A., THE AFTERMATH OF SABBATINO: BACKGROUND PAPERS AND PROCEEDINGS OF SEVENTH HAMMARSKJOLD FORUM. USA+45 LAW ACT/RES ADJUD ROLE...BIBLIOG 20 EXPROPRIAT SABBATINO HARLAN/JM. PAGE 36 E0718

SOVEREIGN
CT/SYS
INT/LAW
OWN

B65

HOLDSWORTH W.S., A HISTORY OF ENGLISH LAW; THE CENTURIES OF SETTLEMENT AND REFORM (VOL. XV). UK CONSTN SECT LEGIS JUDGE WRITING ADJUD CT/SYS CRIME OWN...JURID IDEA/COMP 18 PARLIAMENT ENGLSH/LAW COMMON/LAW. PAGE 54 E1082

LAW
INDUS
PROF/ORG
ATTIT

B65

LAFAVE W.R., LAW AND SOVIET SOCIETY. EX/STRUC DIPLOM DOMIN EDU/PROP PRESS ADMIN CRIME OWN MARXISM 20 KHRUSH/N. PAGE 62 E1244

JURID
CT/SYS
ADJUD

B65

LUGO-MARENCO J.J., A STATEMENT OF THE LAWS OF NICARAGUA IN MATTERS AFFECTING BUSINESS. NICARAGUA AGRI DIST/IND EXTR/IND FINAN INDUS FAM WORKER INT/TRADE TAX MARRIAGE OWN BIO/SOC 20 TREATY RESOURCE/N MIGRATION. PAGE 67 E1332

CONSTN
NAT/G
LEGIS
JURID

B66

COPLIN W.D., THE FUNCTIONS OF INTERNATIONAL LAW. WOR+45 ECO/DEV ECO/UNDEV ADJUD COLONIAL WAR OWN SOVEREIGN...POLICY GEN/LAWS 20. PAGE 25 E0503

INT/LAW
DIPLOM
INT/ORG

B66

GRUNEWALD D., PUBLIC POLICY AND THE MODERN COOPERATION: SELECTED READINGS. USA+45 LAW MARKET VOL/ASSN CAP/ISM INT/TRADE CENTRAL OWN...SOC ANTHOL 20. PAGE 48 E0954

LG/CO
POLICY
NAT/G
CONTROL

S67

REILLY T.J., "FREEZING AND CONFISCATION OF CUBAN PROPERTY." CUBA USA+45 LAW DIPLOM LEGIT ADJUD CONTROL. PAGE 84 E1682

STRANGE
OWN
ECO/TAC

B70

BLACKSTONE W., COMMENTARIES ON THE LAWS OF ENGLAND (4 VOLS.) (4TH ED.). UK CHIEF DELIB/GP LEGIS WORKER CT/SYS SANCTION CRIME OWN...CRIMLGY 18 ENGLSH/LAW. PAGE 12 E0238

LAW
JURID
ADJUD
CONSTN

B73

AUSTIN J., LECTURES ON JURISPRUDENCE OR THE PHILOSOPHY OF POSITIVE LAW (VOL. II) (4TH ED., REV.). UK CONSTN STRUCT PROB/SOLV LEGIT CT/SYS SANCTION CRIME INGP/REL OWN SUPEGO ORD/FREE...T 19. PAGE 6 E0120

LAW
ADJUD
JURID
METH/CNCPT

B75

MAINE H.S., LECTURES ON THE EARLY HISTORY OF INSTITUTIONS. IRELAND UK CONSTN ELITES STRUCT FAM KIN CHIEF LEGIS JUDGE CT/SYS OWN SOVEREIGN...CONCPT 16 BENTHAM/J BREHON ROMAN/LAW. PAGE 68 E1351

CULTURE
LAW
INGP/REL

B90

GODWIN W., POLITICAL JUSTICE. UK ELITES OWN KNOWL MORAL WEALTH...JURID 18/19. PAGE 44 E0877

ORD/FREE
SOVEREIGN
STRUCT
CONCPT

B96

DE VATTEL E., THE LAW OF NATIONS. AGRI FINAN CHIEF DIPLOM INT/TRADE AGREE OWN ALL/VALS MORAL ORD/FREE SOVEREIGN...GEN/LAWS 18 NATURL/LAW WOLFF/C. PAGE 30 E0597

LAW
CONCPT
NAT/G
INT/LAW

B96

SMITH A., LECTURES ON JUSTICE, POLICE, REVENUE AND ARMS (1763). UK LAW FAM FORCES TARIFFS AGREE COERCE INCOME OWN WEALTH LAISSEZ...GEN/LAWS 17/18. PAGE 92 E1840

DIPLOM
JURID
OLD/LIB
TAX

OXFORD/GRP....OXFORD GROUP

P

PACHTER H.M. E1587

PACIFIC/IS....PACIFIC ISLANDS: US TRUST TERRITORY OF THE PACIFIC ISLANDS - CAROLINE ISLANDS, MARSHALL ISLANDS, AND MARIANA ISLANDS

PACIFISM....SEE ALSO ARMS/CONT, PEACE

B50

MONPIED E., BIBLIOGRAPHIE FEDERALISTE: OUVRAGES CHOISIS (VOL. I, MIMEOGRAPHED PAPER). EUR+WWI DIPLOM ADMIN REGION ATTIT PACIFISM SOCISM...INT/LAW 19/20. PAGE 74 E1486

BIBLIOG/A
FEDERAL
CENTRAL
INT/ORG

PACIFIST....PACIFIST; SEE ALSO PEACE

B29

STURZO L., THE INTERNATIONAL COMMUNITY AND THE RIGHT OF WAR (TRANS. BY BARBARA BARCLAY CARTER). CULTURE CREATE PROB/SOLV DIPLOM ADJUD CONTROL PEACE PERSON ORD/FREE...INT/LAW IDEA/COMP PACIFIST 20 LEAGUE/NAT. PAGE 94 E1891

INT/ORG
PLAN
WAR
CONCPT

B65

NORDEN A., WAR AND NAZI CRIMINALS IN WEST GERMANY: STATE, ECONOMY, ADMINISTRATION, ARMY, JUSTICE. SCIENCE. GERMANY GERMANY/W MOD/EUR ECO/DEV ACADEM EX/STRUC FORCES DOMIN ADMIN CT/SYS...POLICY MAJORIT PACIFIST 20. PAGE 77 E1554

FASCIST
WAR
NAT/G
TOP/EX

PADELFORD N. E1588

PADELFORD N.J. E1589

PADOVER S.K. E1590,E1920

PAIKERT G.C. E1591

PAIN....SEE HEALTH

PAKISTAN....SEE ALSO S/ASIA

B63
LIVINGSTON W.S.,FEDERALISM IN THE COMMONWEALTH - A BIBLIOG
BIBLIOGRAPHICAL COMMENTARY. CANADA INDIA PAKISTAN JURID
UK STRUCT LOC/G NAT/G POL/PAR...NAT/COMP 20 FEDERAL
AUSTRAL. PAGE 66 E1310 CONSTN

B64
GOODNOW H.F.,THE CIVIL SERVICE OF PAKISTAN: ADMIN
BUREAUCRACY IN A NEW NATION. INDIA PAKISTAN S/ASIA GOV/REL
ECO/UNDEV PROVS CHIEF PARTIC CHOOSE EFFICIENCY PWR LAW
...BIBLIOG 20. PAGE 45 E0889 NAT/G

L64
WORLD PEACE FOUNDATION,"INTERNATIONAL INT/ORG
ORGANIZATIONS: SUMMARY OF ACTIVITIES." INDIA ROUTINE
PAKISTAN TURKEY WOR+45 CONSTN CONSULT EX/STRUC
ECO/TAC EDU/PROP LEGIT ORD/FREE...JURID SOC UN 20
CYPRESS. PAGE 107 E2145

B66
BRAIBANTI R.,RESEARCH ON THE BUREAUCRACY OF HABITAT
PAKISTAN. PAKISTAN LAW CULTURE INTELL ACADEM LOC/G NAT/G
SECT PRESS CT/SYS...LING CHARTS 20 BUREAUCRCY. ADMIN
PAGE 15 E0286 CONSTN

PAKISTAN/E....EAST PAKISTAN

PALATINATE.... SEE ALSO GERMANY

B65
COHN H.J.,THE GOVERNMENT OF THE RHINE PALATINATE IN PROVS
THE FIFTEENTH CENTURY. GERMANY FINAN LOC/G DELIB/GP JURID
LEGIS CT/SYS CHOOSE CATHISM 14/15 PALATINATE. GP/REL
PAGE 24 E0468 ADMIN

PALESTINE....PALESTINE (PRE-1948 ISRAEL); SEE ALSO ISRAEL

PALMER E.E. E1592

PALMER N.D. E1593

PALOTAI O.C. E1594

PAN AMERICAN UNION E1595

PANAF/FREE....PAN AFRICAN FREEDOM MOVEMENT

PANAFR/ISM....PAN-AFRICANISM

PANAMA CANAL ZONE....SEE CANAL/ZONE

PANAMA....PANAMA

N19
TAYLOR H.,WHY THE PENDING TREATY WITH COLOMBIA INT/LAW
SHOULD BE RATIFIED (PAMPHLET). PANAMA USA-45 DIPLOM
DELIB/GP INT/TRADE REV ORD/FREE...JURID TREATY
18/19 ROOSEVLT/T TAFT/WH COLOMB. PAGE 95 E1912

B47
DE NOIA J.,GUIDE TO OFFICIAL PUBLICATIONS OF THE BIBLIOG/A
OTHER AMERICAN REPUBLICS: PANAMA (VOL. XV). PANAMA CONSTN
LAW LEGIS EDU/PROP CT/SYS 20. PAGE 30 E0592 ADMIN
NAT/G

B64
DUBOIS J.,DANGER OVER PANAMA. FUT PANAMA SCHOOL DIPLOM
PROB/SOLV EDU/PROP MARXISM...POLICY 19/20 TREATY COERCE
INTERVENT CANAL/ZONE. PAGE 33 E0652

B66
HOYT E.C.,NATIONAL POLICY AND INTERNATIONAL LAW* INT/LAW
CASE STUDIES FROM AMERICAN CANAL POLICY* MONOGRAPH USA-45
NO. 1 -- 1966-1967. PANAMA UK ELITES BAL/PWR DIPLOM
EFFICIENCY...CLASSIF NAT/COMP SOC/EXP COLOMB PWR
TREATY. PAGE 55 E1105

S67
FABREGA J.,"ANTECEDENTES EXTRANJEROS EN LA CONSTN
CONSTITUCION PANAMENA." CUBA L/A+17C PANAMA URUGUAY JURID
EX/STRUC LEGIS DIPLOM ORD/FREE 19/20 COLOMB NAT/G
MEXIC/AMER. PAGE 36 E0709 PARL/PROC

PANHUYS H.F. E1596

PANJAB, PANJABI PEOPLE....SEE PUNJAB

PANKHURST R. E0433

PAPUA....PAPUA

PARADIES F. E1597

PARAGUAY....SEE ALSO L/A+17C

B43
CLAGETT H.L.,A GUIDE TO THE LAW AND LEGAL BIBLIOG
LITERATURE OF PARAGUAY. PARAGUAY CONSTN COM/IND JURID
LABOR MUNIC JUDGE ADMIN CT/SYS...CRIMLGY INT/LAW LAW
CON/ANAL 20. PAGE 22 E0439 L/A+17C

PARETO/V....VILFREDO PARETO

PARIS....PARIS, FRANCE

PARITY....SEE ECO

PARK/R....ROBERT PARK

PARKER D. E1598

PARKER/H....HENRY PARKER

PARKFOREST....PARK FOREST, ILLINOIS

PARL/PROC....PARLIAMENTARY PROCESSES; SEE ALSO LEGIS

NRE
MEYER C.S.,ELIZABETH I AND THE RELIGIOUS SETTLEMENT GP/REL
OF 1559. UK ELITES CHIEF LEGIS DISCRIM CATHISM 16 SECT
CHURCH/STA ELIZABTH/I. PAGE 72 E1445 LAW
PARL/PROC

B08
WILSON W.,CONSTITUTIONAL GOVERNMENT IN THE UNITED NAT/G
STATES. USA-45 LAW POL/PAR PROVS CHIEF LEGIS GOV/REL
BAL/PWR ADJUD EXEC FEDERAL PWR 18/20 SUPREME/CT CONSTN
HOUSE/REP SENATE. PAGE 106 E2130 PARL/PROC

B10
MCILWAIN C.H.,THE HIGH COURT OF PARLIAMENT AND ITS LAW
SUPREMACY B1910 1878 408. UK EX/STRUC PARL/PROC LEGIS
GOV/REL INGP/REL PRIVIL 12/20 PARLIAMENT CONSTN
ENGLSH/LAW. PAGE 71 E1416 NAT/G

N19
BAILEY S.D.,VETO IN THE SECURITY COUNCIL DELIB/GP
(PAMPHLET). COM USSR WOR+45 BAL/PWR PARL/PROC INT/ORG
ARMS/CONT PRIVIL PWR...INT/LAW TREND CHARTS 20 UN DIPLOM
SUEZ. PAGE 7 E0135

N19
COUTROT A.,THE FIGHT OVER THE 1959 PRIVATE SCHOOL
EDUCATION LAW IN FRANCE (PAMPHLET). FRANCE NAT/G PARL/PROC
SECT GIVE EDU/PROP GP/REL ATTIT RIGID/FLEX ORD/FREE CATHISM
20 CHURCH/STA. PAGE 27 E0527 LAW

B23
ROBERT H.M.,PARLIAMENTARY LAW. POL/PAR LEGIS PARTIC PARL/PROC
CHOOSE REPRESENT GP/REL. PAGE 85 E1701 DELIB/GP
NAT/G
JURID

B27
GOOCH G.P.,ENGLISH DEMOCRATIC IDEAS IN THE IDEA/COMP
SEVENTEENTH CENTURY (2ND ED.). UK LAW SECT FORCES MAJORIT
DIPLOM LEAD PARL/PROC REV ATTIT AUTHORIT...ANARCH EX/STRUC
CONCPT 17 PARLIAMENT CMN/WLTH REFORMERS. PAGE 45 CONSERVE
E0885

B29
CAM H.M.,BIBLIOGRAPHY OF ENGLISH CONSTITUTIONAL BIBLIOG/A
HISTORY (PAMPHLET). UK LAW LOC/G NAT/G POL/PAR SECT CONSTN
DELIB/GP ADJUD ORD/FREE 19/20 PARLIAMENT. PAGE 19 ADMIN
E0369 PARL/PROC

B32
GREAT BRIT COMM MINISTERS PWR,REPORT. UK LAW CONSTN EX/STRUC
CONSULT LEGIS PARL/PROC SANCTION SOVEREIGN NAT/G
...DECISION JURID 20 PARLIAMENT. PAGE 45 E0902 PWR
CONTROL

B35
KENNEDY W.P.,THE LAW AND CUSTOM OF THE SOUTH CT/SYS
AFRICAN CONSTITUTION. AFR SOUTH/AFR KIN LOC/G PROVS CONSTN
DIPLOM ADJUD ADMIN EXEC 20. PAGE 60 E1203 JURID
PARL/PROC

HUDSON M.O.,INTERNATIONAL LEGISLATION: 1929-1931.   B36
WOR-45 SEA AIR AGRI FINAN LABOR DIPLOM ECO/TAC   INT/LAW
REPAR CT/SYS ARMS/CONT WAR WEAPON...JURID 20 TREATY PARL/PROC
LEAGUE/NAT. PAGE 56 E1112   ADJUD
                                                    LAW

HOLDSWORTH W.S.,A HISTORY OF ENGLISH LAW; THE   B38
CENTURIES OF SETTLEMENT AND REFORM (VOL. XI). UK   LAW
CONSTN NAT/G EX/STRUC DIPLOM ADJUD CT/SYS LEAD   COLONIAL
CRIME ATTIT...INT/LAW JURID 18 CMN/WLTH PARLIAMENT LEGIS
ENGLSH/LAW. PAGE 54 E1079   PARL/PROC

ANDERSON W.,FUNDAMENTALS OF AMERICAN GOVERNMENT.   B40
USA-45 LAW POL/PAR CHIEF EX/STRUC BUDGET ADMIN   NAT/G
CT/SYS PARL/PROC CHOOSE FEDERAL...BIBLIOG 20.   LOC/G
PAGE 5 E0093   GOV/REL
                                                    CONSTN

MCILWAIN C.H.,CONSTITUTIONALISM: ANCIENT AND   B47
MODERN. USA+45 ROMAN/EMP LAW CHIEF LEGIS CT/SYS   CONSTN
GP/REL ORD/FREE SOVEREIGN...POLICY TIME/SEQ   NAT/G
ROMAN/REP EUROPE. PAGE 71 E1419   PARL/PROC
                                                    GOV/COMP

BISHOP H.M.,BASIC ISSUES OF AMERICAN DEMOCRACY.   B48
USA+45 USA-45 POL/PAR EX/STRUC LEGIS ADJUD FEDERAL NAT/G
...BIBLIOG 18/20. PAGE 12 E0232   PARL/PROC
                                                    CONSTN

KEIR D.L.,CASES IN CONSTITUTIONAL LAW. UK CHIEF   B48
LEGIS DIPLOM TAX PARL/PROC CRIME GOV/REL...INT/LAW CONSTN
JURID 17/20. PAGE 60 E1195   LAW
                                                    ADJUD
                                                    CT/SYS

NEUBURGER O.,GUIDE TO OFFICIAL PUBLICATIONS OF THE   B48
OTHER AMERICAN REPUBLICS: VENEZUELA (VOL. XIX).   BIBLIOG/A
VENEZUELA FINAN LEGIS PLAN BUDGET DIPLOM CT/SYS   NAT/G
PARL/PROC 19/20. PAGE 77 E1535   CONSTN
                                                    LAW

MILLER B.S.,"A LAW IS PASSED: THE ATOMIC ENERGY ACT   S48
OF 1946." POL/PAR CHIEF CONFER DEBATE CONTROL   TEC/DEV
PARL/PROC ATTIT KNOWL...POLICY CONGRESS. PAGE 73   LEGIS
E1457   DECISION
                                                    LAW

WALKER H.,"THE LEGISLATIVE PROCESS; LAWMAKING IN   C48
THE UNITED STATES." NAT/G POL/PAR PROVS EX/STRUC   PARL/PROC
OP/RES PROB/SOLV CT/SYS LOBBY GOV/REL...CHARTS   LEGIS
BIBLIOG T 18/20 CONGRESS. PAGE 105 E2094   LAW
                                                    CONSTN

BURDETTE F.L.,LOBBYISTS IN ACTION (PAMPHLET).   B50
CONSULT TEC/DEV INSPECT BARGAIN PARL/PROC SANCTION LOBBY
20 CONGRESS. PAGE 17 E0329   ATTIT
                                                    POLICY
                                                    LAW

WADE E.C.S.,CONSTITUTIONAL LAW; AN OUTLINE OF THE   B50
LAW AND PRACTICE OF THE CONSTITUTION. UK LEGIS   CONSTN
DOMIN ADMIN GP/REL 16/20 CMN/WLTH PARLIAMENT   NAT/G
ENGLSH/LAW. PAGE 104 E2087   PARL/PROC
                                                    LAW

JENNINGS W.I.,CONSTITUTIONAL LAWS OF THE   B52
COMMONWEALTH. UK LAW CHIEF LEGIS TAX CT/SYS   CONSTN
PARL/PROC GOV/REL...INT/LAW 18/20 COMMONWLTH   JURID
ENGLSH/LAW COMMON/LAW. PAGE 58 E1165   ADJUD
                                                    COLONIAL

STOUT H.M.,BRITISH GOVERNMENT. UK FINAN LOC/G   B53
POL/PAR DELIB/GP DIPLOM ADMIN COLONIAL CHOOSE   NAT/G
ORD/FREE...JURID BIBLIOG 20 COMMONWLTH. PAGE 94   PARL/PROC
E1883   CONSTN
                                                    NEW/LIB

EMDEN C.S.,THE PEOPLE AND THE CONSTITUTION (2ND   B56
ED.). UK LEGIS POPULISM 17/20 PARLIAMENT. PAGE 35   CONSTN
E0687   PARL/PROC
                                                    NAT/G
                                                    LAW

ZINN C.J.,HOW OUR LAWS ARE MADE: BROCHURE HOUSE OF   B56
REPRESENTATIVES DOCUMENT 451. LAW CONSTN CHIEF   LEGIS
EX/STRUC PROB/SOLV HOUSE/REP SENATE. PAGE 108 E2171 DELIB/GP
                                                    PARL/PROC
                                                    ROUTINE

COSSIO C.,LA POLITICA COMO CONCIENCIA; MEDITACION   B57
SOBRE LA ARGENTINA DE 1955. WOR+45 LEGIS EDU/PROP   POL/PAR
PARL/PROC PARTIC ATTIT PWR CATHISM 20 ARGEN   REV
PERON/JUAN. PAGE 26 E0517   TOTALISM
                                                    JURID

JENNINGS I.,PARLIAMENT. UK FINAN INDUS POL/PAR   B57
DELIB/GP EX/STRUC PLAN CONTROL...MAJORIT JURID   PARL/PROC
PARLIAMENT. PAGE 58 E1163   TOP/EX
                                                    MGT
                                                    LEGIS

US SENATE COMM ON JUDICIARY,CIVIL RIGHTS - 1957.   B57
USA+45 LAW NAT/G CONFER GOV/REL RACE/REL ORD/FREE   INT
PWR...JURID 20 SENATE CIV/RIGHTS. PAGE 102 E2039   LEGIS
                                                    DISCRIM
                                                    PARL/PROC

US SENATE SPEC COMM POLIT ACT,REPORT OF SPECIAL   B57
COMMITTEE TO INVESTIGATE POLITICAL ACTIVITIES,   LOBBY
LOBBYING, AND CAMPAIGN CONTRIBUTIONS. USA+45   LAW
BARGAIN CRIME ATTIT...DECISION 20 CONGRESS.   ECO/TAC
PAGE 103 E2061   PARL/PROC

EUSDEN J.D.,PURITANS, LAWYERS, AND POLITICS IN   B58
EARLY SEVENTEENTH-CENTURY ENGLAND. UK CT/SYS   GP/REL
PARL/PROC RATIONAL PWR SOVEREIGN...IDEA/COMP   SECT
BIBLIOG 17 PURITAN COMMON/LAW. PAGE 35 E0702   NAT/G
                                                    LAW

JAPAN MINISTRY OF JUSTICE,CRIMINAL JUSTICE IN   B58
JAPAN. LAW PROF/ORG PUB/INST FORCES CONTROL CT/SYS CONSTN
PARL/PROC 20 CHINJAP. PAGE 58 E1149   CRIME
                                                    JURID
                                                    ADMIN

MOEN N.W.,THE GOVERNMENT OF SCOTLAND 1603 - 1625.   B58
UK JUDGE ADMIN GP/REL PWR 17 SCOTLAND COMMON/LAW.   CHIEF
PAGE 74 E1479   JURID
                                                    CONTROL
                                                    PARL/PROC

US SENATE COMM POST OFFICE,TO PROVIDE AN EFFECTIVE   B58
SYSTEM OF PERSONNEL ADMINISTRATION. USA+45 NAT/G   INT
EX/STRUC PARL/PROC GOV/REL...JURID 20 SENATE   LEGIS
CIVIL/SERV. PAGE 103 E2060   CONFER
                                                    ADMIN

RIKER W.H.,"THE PARADOX OF VOTING AND CONGRESSIONAL   S58
RULES FOR VOTING ON AMENDMENTS." LAW DELIB/GP   PARL/PROC
EX/STRUC PROB/SOLV CONFER DEBATE EFFICIENCY ATTIT   DECISION
HOUSE/REP CONGRESS SENATE. PAGE 85 E1700   LEGIS
                                                    RATIONAL

BRODEN T.F.,"CONGRESSIONAL COMMITTEE REPORTS: THEIR   C58
ROLE AND HISTORY" USA-45 PARL/PROC ROLE. PAGE 15   LAW
E0303   DELIB/GP
                                                    LEGIS
                                                    DEBATE

RAJAN M.S.,"UNITED NATIONS AND DOMESTIC   C58
JURISDICTION." WOR+45 WOR-45 PARL/PROC...IDEA/COMP INT/LAW
BIBLIOG 20 UN. PAGE 83 E1670   DIPLOM
                                                    CONSTN
                                                    INT/ORG

BOHMER A.,LEGAL SOURCES AND BIBLIOGRAPHY OF   B59
CZECHOSLOVAKIA. COM CZECHOSLVK PARL/PROC SANCTION   BIBLIOG
CRIME MARXISM 20. PAGE 13 E0261   ADJUD
                                                    LAW
                                                    JURID

PAULSEN M.G.,LEGAL INSTITUTIONS TODAY AND TOMORROW.   B59
UK USA+45 NAT/G PROF/ORG PROVS ADMIN PARL/PROC   JURID
ORD/FREE NAT/COMP. PAGE 80 E1604   ADJUD
                                                    JUDGE
                                                    LEGIS

SQUIBB G.D.,THE HIGH COURT OF CHIVALRY. UK NAT/G   B59
FORCES ADJUD WAR 14/20 PARLIAMENT ENGLSH/LAW.   CT/SYS
PAGE 93 E1863   PARL/PROC
                                                    JURID

BAKER G.E.,THE POLITICS OF REAPPORTIONMENT IN   B60
WASHINGTON STATE. LAW POL/PAR CREATE EDU/PROP   VOL/ASSN
PARL/PROC CHOOSE INGP/REL...CHARTS METH/COMP 20   APPORT
WASHINGT/G LEAGUE/WV. PAGE 7 E0139   PROVS
                                                    LEGIS

RIENOW R.,INTRODUCTION TO GOVERNMENT (2ND ED.). UK   B60
USA+45 USSR POL/PAR ADMIN REV CHOOSE SUFF FEDERAL   CONSTN
PWR...JURID GOV/COMP T 20. PAGE 85 E1697   PARL/PROC
                                                    REPRESENT
                                                    AUTHORIT

US LIBRARY OF CONGRESS,INDEX TO LATIN AMERICAN   B60
LEGISLATION: 1950-1960 (2 VOLS.). NAT/G DELIB/GP   BIBLIOG/A
ADMIN PARL/PROC 20. PAGE 101 E2019   LEGIS
                                                    L/A+17C
                                                    JURID

US SENATE COMM ON JUDICIARY,FEDERAL ADMINISTRATIVE PARL/PROC
PROCEDURE. USA+45 CONSTN NAT/G PROB/SOLV CONFER LEGIS
GOV/REL...JURID INT 20 SENATE. PAGE 102 E2043 ADMIN
                                                                                          B60
                                                                          LAW

US SENATE COMM ON JUDICIARY,ADMINISTRATIVE PARL/PROC
PROCEDURE LEGISLATION. USA+45 CONSTN NAT/G LEGIS
PROB/SOLV CONFER ROUTINE GOV/REL...INT 20 SENATE. ADMIN
                                                                                          B60
PAGE 102 E2044   JURID

BAINS J.S.,STUDIES IN POLITICAL SCIENCE. INDIA DIPLOM
WOR+45 WOR-45 CONSTN BAL/PWR ADJUD ADMIN PARL/PROC INT/LAW
SOVEREIGN...SOC METH/COMP ANTHOL 17/20 UN. PAGE 7 NAT/G
                                                                                          B61
E0137

CASSINELLI C.W.,THE POLITICS OF FREEDOM. FUT UNIV MAJORIT
LAW POL/PAR CHOOSE ORD/FREE...POLICY CONCPT MYTH NAT/G
BIBLIOG. PAGE 21 E0404 PARL/PROC
                                                                                          B61
                                                                          PARTIC

NELSON H.L.,LIBEL IN NEWS OF CONGRESSIONAL DELIB/GP
INVESTIGATING COMMITTEES. USA+45 LAW PARL/PROC LEGIS
PRIVIL RESPECT HOUSE/REP. PAGE 76 E1532 LICENSE
                                                                                          B61
                                                                          PRESS

BERMAN D.M.,A BILL BECOMES A LAW: THE CIVIL RIGHTS DISCRIM
ACT OF 1960. USA+45 LAW POL/PAR LOBBY RACE/REL PARL/PROC
KNOWL...CHARTS 20 CONGRESS NEGRO CIV/RIGHTS. JURID
                                                                                          B62
PAGE 11 E0206   GOV/REL

MASON A.T.,THE SUPREME COURT: PALADIUM OF FREEDOM. CONSTN
USA-45 NAT/G POL/PAR CHIEF LEGIS ADJUD PARL/PROC CT/SYS
FEDERAL PWR...POLICY BIOG 18/20 SUPREME/CT JURID
                                                                                          B62
ROOSEVLT/F JEFFERSN/T MARSHALL/J HUGHES/CE. PAGE 69
E1378

ROYAL INSTITUTE PUBLIC ADMIN,BRITISH PUBLIC BIBLIOG
ADMINISTRATION. UK LAW FINAN INDUS LOC/G POL/PAR ADMIN
LEGIS LOBBY PARL/PROC CHOOSE JURID. PAGE 86 E1729 MGT
                                                                                          B63
                                                                          NAT/G

SARTORI G.,IL PARLAMENTO ITALIANO: 1946-1963. LAW LEGIS
CONSTN ELITES POL/PAR LOBBY PRIVIL ATTIT PERSON PARL/PROC
MORAL PWR SOC. PAGE 87 E1746 REPRESENT
                                                                                          B63

STREET H.,FREEDOM: THE INDIVIDUAL AND THE LAW. UK ORD/FREE
COM/IND EDU/PROP PRESS RUMOR TV PWR 20 CIVIL/LIB NAT/G
FILM. PAGE 94 E1886 JURID
                                                                                          B63
                                                                          PARL/PROC

US SENATE COMM ON JUDICIARY,ADMINISTRATIVE PARL/PROC
CONFERENCE OF THE UNITED STATES. USA+45 CONSTN JURID
NAT/G PROB/SOLV CONFER GOV/REL...INT 20 SENATE. ADMIN
                                                                                          B63
PAGE 102 E2048   LEGIS

WADE H.W.R.,TOWARDS ADMINISTRATIVE JUSTICE. UK ADJUD
USA+45 CONSTN CONSULT PROB/SOLV CT/SYS PARL/PROC IDEA/COMP
...POLICY JURID METH/COMP 20 ENGLSH/LAW. PAGE 104 ADMIN
                                                                                          B63
E2088

FORBES A.H.,CURRENT RESEARCH IN BRITISH STUDIES. UK BIBLIOG
CONSTN CULTURE POL/PAR SECT DIPLOM ADMIN...JURID PERSON
BIOG WORSHIP 20. PAGE 39 E0769 NAT/G
                                                                                          B64
                                                                          PARL/PROC

GESELLSCHAFT RECHTSVERGLEICH,BIBLIOGRAPHIE DES BIBLIOG/A
DEUTSCHEN RECHTS (BIBLIOGRAPHY OF GERMAN LAW, JURID
TRANS. BY COURTLAND PETERSON). GERMANY FINAN INDUS CONSTN
LABOR SECT FORCES CT/SYS PARL/PROC CRIME...INT/LAW ADMIN
                                                                                          B64
SOC NAT/COMP 20. PAGE 43 E0853

GJUPANOVIC H.,LEGAL SOURCES AND BIBLIOGRAPHY OF BIBLIOG/A
YUGOSLAVIA. COM YUGOSLAVIA LAW LEGIS DIPLOM ADMIN JURID
PARL/PROC REGION CRIME CENTRAL 20. PAGE 44 E0873 CONSTN
                                                                                          B64
                                                                          ADJUD

GROVES H.E.,THE CONSTITUTION OF MALAYSIA. MALAYSIA CONSTN
POL/PAR CHIEF CONSULT DELIB/GP CT/SYS PARL/PROC NAT/G
CHOOSE FEDERAL ORD/FREE 20. PAGE 48 E0953 LAW
                                                                                          B64

HALLER W.,DER SCHWEDISCHE JUSTITIEOMBUDSMAN. JURID
DENMARK FINLAND NORWAY SWEDEN LEGIS ADJUD CONTROL PARL/PROC
PERSON ORD/FREE...NAT/COMP 20 OMBUDSMAN. PAGE 50 ADMIN
                                                                                          B64
E0986   CHIEF

HEGEL G.W.,HEGEL'S POLITICAL WRITINGS (TRANS. BY CONSTN
T.M. KNOX). GERMANY UK FINAN FORCES PARL/PROC LEGIS
CHOOSE REPRESENT...BIOG 19. PAGE 51 E1022 JURID
                                                                                          B64

HOPKINSON T.,SOUTH AFRICA. SOUTH/AFR UK NAT/G SOCIETY
POL/PAR LEGIS ECO/TAC PARL/PROC WAR...JURID AUD/VIS RACE/REL
19/20. PAGE 55 E1097 DISCRIM
                                                                                          B64

LEDERMAN W.R.,THE COURTS AND THE CANDIAN CONSTN
CONSTITUTION. CANADA PARL/PROC...POLICY JURID CT/SYS
GOV/COMP ANTHOL 19/20 SUPREME/CT PARLIAMENT. LEGIS
PAGE 64 E1276   LAW
                                                                                          B64

SIEKANOWICZ P.,LEGAL SOURCES AND BIBLIOGRAPHY OF BIBLIOG
POLAND. COM POLAND CONSTN NAT/G PARL/PROC SANCTION ADJUD
CRIME MARXISM 16/20. PAGE 91 E1823 LAW
                                                                                          B64
                                                                          JURID

STOICOIU V.,LEGAL SOURCES AND BIBLIOGRAPHY OF BIBLIOG/A
ROMANIA. COM ROMANIA LAW FINAN POL/PAR LEGIS JUDGE JURID
ADJUD CT/SYS PARL/PROC MARXISM 20. PAGE 93 E1874 CONSTN
                                                                                          B64
                                                                          ADMIN

SZLADITS C.,BIBLIOGRAPHY ON FOREIGN AND COMPARATIVE BIBLIOG/A
LAW: BOOKS AND ARTICLES IN ENGLISH (SUPPLEMENT JURID
1962). FINAN INDUS JUDGE LICENSE ADMIN CT/SYS ADJUD
PARL/PROC OWN...INT/LAW CLASSIF METH/COMP NAT/COMP LAW
                                                                                          B64
20. PAGE 95 E1904

TENBROCK J.,EQUAL UNDER LAW. USA-45 CONSTN POL/PAR LEGIS
EDU/PROP PARL/PROC ORD/FREE...BIBLIOG 19 AMEND/XIV. LAW
PAGE 95 E1914   DISCRIM
                                                                                          B64
                                                                          DOMIN

US SENATE COMM ON JUDICIARY,CIVIL RIGHTS - THE INT
PRESIDENT'S PROGRAM. USA+45 LAW PROB/SOLV PRESS LEGIS
ADJUD GOV/REL RACE/REL ORD/FREE PWR...JURID 20 DISCRIM
SUPREME/CT SENATE CIV/RIGHTS PRESIDENT. PAGE 102 PARL/PROC
                                                                                          B64
E2053

US SENATE COMM ON JUDICIARY,ADMINISTRATIVE PARL/PROC
PROCEDURE ACT. USA+45 CONSTN NAT/G PROB/SOLV CONFER LEGIS
GOV/REL PWR...INT 20 SENATE. PAGE 102 E2054 JURID
                                                                                          B64
                                                                          ADMIN

COWEN Z.,THE BRITISH COMMONWEALTH OF NATIONS IN A JURID
CHANGING WORLD. UK ECO/UNDEV INT/ORG ECO/TAC DIPLOM
INT/TRADE COLONIAL WAR GP/REL RACE/REL SOVEREIGN PARL/PROC
SOC/INTEG 20 TREATY EEC COMMONWLTH. PAGE 27 E0530 NAT/LISM
                                                                                          B65

FEERICK J.D.,FROM FAILING HANDS: THE STUDY OF EX/STRUC
PRESIDENTIAL SUCCESSION. CONSTN NAT/G PROB/SOLV CHIEF
LEAD PARL/PROC MURDER CHOOSE...NEW/IDEA BIBLIOG 20 LAW
KENNEDY/JF JOHNSON/LB PRESIDENT PRE/US/AM LEGIS
                                                                                          B65
VICE/PRES. PAGE 36 E0724

PYLEE M.V.,CONSTITUTIONAL GOVERNMENT IN INDIA (2ND CONSTN
REV. ED.). INDIA POL/PAR EX/STRUC DIPLOM COLONIAL NAT/G
CT/SYS PARL/PROC PRIVIL...JURID 16/20. PAGE 83 PROVS
E1665   FEDERAL
                                                                                          B65

SHARMA S.A.,PARLIAMENTARY GOVERNMENT IN INDIA. NAT/G
INDIA FINAN LOC/G PROVS DELIB/GP PLAN ADMIN CT/SYS CONSTN
FEDERAL...JURID 20. PAGE 90 E1814 PARL/PROC
                                                                                          B65
                                                                          LEGIS

ANDERSON S.V.,CANADIAN OMBUDSMAN PROPOSALS. CANADA NAT/G
LEGIS DEBATE PARL/PROC...MAJORIT JURID TIME/SEQ CREATE
IDEA/COMP 20 OMBUDSMAN PARLIAMENT. PAGE 5 E0092 ADMIN
                                                                                          B66
                                                                          POL/PAR

BURNS A.C.,PARLIAMENT AS AN EXPORT. WOR+45 CONSTN PARL/PROC
BARGAIN DEBATE ROUTINE GOV/REL EFFICIENCY...ANTHOL POL/PAR
COMMONWLTH PARLIAMENT. PAGE 17 E0343 CT/SYS
                                                                                          B66
                                                                          CHIEF

CAMPBELL E.,PARLIAMENTARY PRIVILEGE IN AUSTRALIA. LEGIS
UK LAW CONSTN COLONIAL ROLE ORD/FREE SOVEREIGN PARL/PROC
18/20 COMMONWLTH AUSTRAL FREE/SPEE PARLIAMENT. JURID
PAGE 19 E0370   PRIVIL
B66

DALLIN A.,POLITICS IN THE SOVIET UNION: 7 CASES. MARXISM
COM USSR LAW POL/PAR CHIEF FORCES WRITING CONTROL DOMIN
PARL/PROC CIVMIL/REL TOTALISM...ANTHOL 20 KHRUSH/N ORD/FREE
STALIN/J CASEBOOK COM/PARTY. PAGE 28 E0563   GOV/REL
B66

LEHMANN L.,LEGAL UND OPPORTUN - POLITISCHE JUSTIZ ORD/FREE
IN DER BUNDESREPUBLIK. GERMANY/W EDU/PROP ADJUD POL/PAR
CONTROL PARL/PROC COERCE TOTALISM ATTIT 20   JURID
COM/PARTY. PAGE 64 E1281   LEGIS
B66

BAKER L.,BACK TO BACK: THE DUEL BETWEEN FDR AND THE CHIEF
SUPREME COURT. ELITES LEGIS CREATE DOMIN INGP/REL CT/SYS
PERSON PWR NEW/LIB 20 ROOSEVLT/F SUPREME/CT SENATE. PARL/PROC
PAGE 7 E0142   GOV/REL
B67

BIBBY J.,ON CAPITOL HILL. POL/PAR LOBBY PARL/PROC CONFER
GOV/REL PERS/REL...JURID PHIL/SCI OBS INT BIBLIOG LEGIS
20 CONGRESS PRESIDENT. PAGE 12 E0224   CREATE
                                                 LEAD
B67

BROWN L.N.,FRENCH ADMINISTRATIVE LAW. FRANCE UK EX/STRUC
CONSTN NAT/G LEGIS DOMIN CONTROL EXEC PARL/PROC PWR LAW
...JURID METH/COMP GEN/METH. PAGE 16 E0314   IDEA/COMP
                                                 CT/SYS
B67

COWLING M.,1867 DISRAELI, GLADSTONE, AND   PARL/PROC
REVOLUTION: THE PASSING OF THE SECOND REFORM BILL. POL/PAR
UK LEGIS LEAD LOBBY GP/REL INGP/REL...DECISION   ATTIT
BIBLIOG 19 REFORMERS. PAGE 27 E0531   LAW
B67

BRADLEY A.W.,"CONSTITUTION-MAKING IN UGANDA."   NAT/G
UGANDA LAW CHIEF DELIB/GP LEGIS ADMIN EXEC   CREATE
PARL/PROC RACE/REL ORD/FREE...GOV/COMP 20. PAGE 15 CONSTN
E0284   FEDERAL
S67

FABREGA J.,"ANTECEDENTES EXTRANJEROS EN LA   CONSTN
CONSTITUCION PANAMENA." CUBA L/A+17C PANAMA URUGUAY JURID
EX/STRUC LEGIS DIPLOM ORD/FREE 19/20 COLOMB   NAT/G
MEXIC/AMER. PAGE 36 E0709   PARL/PROC
S67

MACLEOD R.M.,"LAW, MEDICINE AND PUBLIC OPINION: THE LAW
RESISTANCE TO COMPULSORY HEALTH LEGISLATION   HEALTH
1870-1907." UK CONSTN SECT DELIB/GP DEBATE   ATTIT
PARL/PROC GP/REL MORAL 19. PAGE 67 E1344
S67

VAUGHN W.P.,"SEPARATE AND UNEQUAL: THE CIVIL RIGHTS LAW
ACT OF 1875 AND DEFEAT OF THE SCHOOL INTEGRATION DISCRIM
CLAUSE." USA-45 LEGIS RACE/REL 19 CONGRESS.   EDU/PROP
PAGE 103 E2073   PARL/PROC
S67

WINES R.,"THE IMPERIAL CIRCLES, PRINCELY DIPLOMACY, NAT/G
AND IMPERIAL REFORM* 1681-1714." MOD/EUR DELIB/GP NAT/LISM
BAL/PWR CONFER ADJUD PARL/PROC PARTIC ATTIT PWR CENTRAL
17/18. PAGE 106 E2132   REGION
B91

SIDGWICK H.,THE ELEMENTS OF POLITICS. LOC/G NAT/G POLICY
LEGIS DIPLOM ADJUD CONTROL EXEC PARL/PROC REPRESENT LAW
GOV/REL SOVEREIGN ALL/IDEOS 19 MILL/JS BENTHAM/J. CONCPT
PAGE 91 E1822
B92

LOWELL A.L.,ESSAYS ON GOVERNMENT. UK USA-45 LEGIS CONSTN
PARL/PROC...POLICY PREDICT 19. PAGE 66 E1328   ADJUD
                                                 CT/SYS
                                                 NAT/G
B96

ESMEIN A.,ELEMENTS DE DROIT CONSTITUTIONNEL. FRANCE LAW
UK LAW CHIEF EX/STRUC LEGIS ADJUD CT/SYS PARL/PROC REV CONSTN
GOV/REL ORD/FREE...JURID METH/COMP 18/19. PAGE 35 NAT/G
E0697   CONCPT

PARLIAMENTARY PROCESSES....SEE PARL/PROC

PARLIAMENT....PARLIAMENT (ALL NATIONS); SEE ALSO LEGIS

CANADIAN GOVERNMENT PUBLICATIONS (1955-). CANADA BIBLIOG/A
AGRI FINAN LABOR FORCES INT/TRADE HEALTH...JURID 20 NAT/G
PARLIAMENT. PAGE 1 E0005   DIPLOM
                                                  INT/ORG
N

HOLLAND T.E.,STUDIES IN INTERNATIONAL LAW. TURKEY INT/ORG
USSR WOR-45 CONSTN NAT/G DIPLOM LEGIT COERCE   LAW
WAR PEACE ORD/FREE PWR SOVEREIGN...JURID CHARTS 20 INT/LAW
PARLIAMENT SUEZ TREATY. PAGE 54 E1084
B00

FAGUET E.,LE LIBERALISME. FRANCE PRESS ADJUD ADMIN ORD/FREE
DISCRIM CONSERVE SOCISM...TRADIT SOC LING WORSHIP EDU/PROP
PARLIAMENT. PAGE 36 E0711   NAT/G
                                                   LAW
B03

GRIFFIN A.P.C.,LISTS PUBLISHED 1902-03: LABOR   BIBLIOG/A
PARTICULARLY RELATING TO STRIKES (PAMPHLET). UK LABOR
USA-45 FINAN WORKER PLAN BARGAIN CRIME GOV/REL   GP/REL
...POLICY 19/20 PARLIAMENT. PAGE 46 E0923   ECO/TAC
B03

BURKE E.,A LETTER TO THE SHERIFFS OF BRISTOL   LEGIS
(1777). USA-45 LAW ECO/TAC COLONIAL CT/SYS REV   ADJUD
GP/REL ORD/FREE...POLICY 18 PARLIAMENT BURKE/EDM. CRIME
PAGE 17 E0541
B04

MCILWAIN C.H.,THE HIGH COURT OF PARLIAMENT AND ITS LAW
SUPREMACY B1910 1878 408. UK EX/STRUC PARL/PROC LEGIS
GOV/REL INGP/REL PRIVIL 12/20 PARLIAMENT   CONSTN
ENGLSH/LAW. PAGE 71 E1416   NAT/G
B10

HOLDSWORTH W.S.,A HISTORY OF ENGLISH LAW; THE   LAW
COMMON LAW AND ITS RIVALS (VOL. V). UK SEA EX/STRUC LEGIS
WRITING ADMIN...INT/LAW JURID CONCPT IDEA/COMP   ADJUD
WORSHIP 16/17 PARLIAMENT ENGLSH/LAW COMMON/LAW. CT/SYS
PAGE 54 E1073
B24

HOLDSWORTH W.S.,A HISTORY OF ENGLISH LAW; THE   LAW
COMMON LAW AND ITS RIVALS (VOL. VI). UK STRATA   CONSTN
EX/STRUC ADJUD ADMIN CONTROL CT/SYS...JURID CONCPT LEGIS
GEN/LAWS 17 COMMONWLTH PARLIAMENT ENGLSH/LAW   CHIEF
COMMON/LAW. PAGE 54 E1074
B24

HOLDSWORTH W.S.,A HISTORY OF ENGLISH LAW; THE   LAW
COMMON LAW AND ITS RIVALS (VOL. IV). UK SEA AGRI LEGIS
CHIEF ADJUD CONTROL CRIME GOV/REL...INT/LAW JURID CT/SYS
NAT/COMP 16/17 PARLIAMENT COMMON/LAW CANON/LAW   CONSTN
ENGLSH/LAW. PAGE 54 E1075
B24

GOOCH G.P.,ENGLISH DEMOCRATIC IDEAS IN THE   IDEA/COMP
SEVENTEENTH CENTURY (2ND ED.). UK LAW SECT FORCES MAJORIT
DIPLOM LEAD PARL/PROC REV ATTIT AUTHORIT...ANARCH EX/STRUC
CONCPT 17 PARLIAMENT CMN/WLTH REFORMERS. PAGE 45 CONSERVE
E0885
B27

CAM H.M.,BIBLIOGRAPHY OF ENGLISH CONSTITUTIONAL BIBLIOG/A
HISTORY (PAMPHLET). UK LAW LOC/G NAT/G POL/PAR SECT CONSTN
DELIB/GP ADJUD ORD/FREE 19/20 PARLIAMENT. PAGE 19 ADMIN
E0369   PARL/PROC
B29

GREAT BRIT COMM MINISTERS PWR,REPORT. UK LAW CONSTN EX/STRUC
CONSULT LEGIS PARL/PROC SANCTION SOVEREIGN   NAT/G
...DECISION JURID 20 PARLIAMENT. PAGE 45 E0902   PWR
                                                 CONTROL
B32

CLYDE W.M.,THE STRUGGLE FOR THE FREEDOM OF THE   PRESS
PRESS FROM CAXTON TO CROMWELL. UK LAW LOC/G SECT ORD/FREE
FORCES LICENSE WRITING SANCTION REV ATTIT PWR   CONTROL
...POLICY 15/17 PARLIAMENT CROMWELL/O MILTON/J.
PAGE 23 E0460
B34

HANSON L.,GOVERNMENT AND THE PRESS 1695-1763. UK LAW
LOC/G LEGIS LICENSE CONTROL SANCTION CRIME ATTIT JURID
ORD/FREE 17/18 PARLIAMENT AMEND/I. PAGE 50 E0996 PRESS
                                                 POLICY
B36

HOLDSWORTH W.S.,A HISTORY OF ENGLISH LAW; THE   LAW
CENTURIES OF SETTLEMENT AND REFORM (VOL. X). INDIA LOC/G
UK CONSTN NAT/G CHIEF LEGIS ADMIN COLONIAL CT/SYS EX/STRUC
CHOOSE ORD/FREE PWR...JURID 18 PARLIAMENT   ADJUD
COMMONWLTH COMMON/LAW. PAGE 54 E1077
B38

B38
HOLDSWORTH W.S.,A HISTORY OF ENGLISH LAW: THE
CENTURIES OF SETTLEMENT AND REFORM (VOL. XI). UK
CONSTN NAT/G EX/STRUC DIPLOM ADJUD CT/SYS LEAD
CRIME ATTIT...INT/LAW JURID 18 CMN/WLTH PARLIAMENT
ENGLSH/LAW. PAGE 54 E1079
LAW
COLONIAL
LEGIS
PARL/PROC

B50
WADE E.C.S.,CONSTITUTIONAL LAW: AN OUTLINE OF THE
LAW AND PRACTICE OF THE CONSTITUTION. UK LEGIS
DOMIN ADMIN GP/REL 16/20 CMN/WLTH PARLIAMENT
ENGLSH/LAW. PAGE 104 E2087
CONSTN
NAT/G
PARL/PROC
LAW

B51
FRIEDMANN W.,LAW AND SOCIAL CHANGE IN CONTEMPORARY
BRITAIN. UK LABOR LG/CO LEGIS JUDGE CT/SYS ORD/FREE
NEW/LIB...DECISION JURID TREND METH/COMP BIBLIOG 20
PARLIAMENT ENGLSH/LAW COMMON/LAW. PAGE 40 E0802
LAW
ADJUD
SOCIETY
CONSTN

B52
HOLDSWORTH W.S.,A HISTORY OF ENGLISH LAW: THE
CENTURIES OF SETTLEMENT AND REFORM. 1701-1875 (VOL.
XIII). UK POL/PAR PROF/ORG LEGIS JUDGE WRITING
ATTIT...JURID CONCPT BIOG GEN/LAWS 18/19 PARLIAMENT
REFORMERS ENGLSH/LAW COMMON/LAW. PAGE 54 E1080
LAW
CONSTN
IDEA/COMP
CT/SYS

B53
BUTLER D.E.,THE ELECTORAL SYSTEM IN BRITAIN,
1918-1951. UK LAW POL/PAR SUFF...STAT BIBLIOG 20
PARLIAMENT. PAGE 18 E0348
CHOOSE
LEGIS
REPRESENT
PARTIC

B55
CRAIG J.,BIBLIOGRAPHY OF PUBLIC ADMINISTRATION IN
AUSTRALIA. CONSTN FINAN EX/STRUC LEGIS PLAN DIPLOM
RECEIVE ADJUD ROUTINE...HEAL 19/20 AUSTRAL
PARLIAMENT. PAGE 27 E0540
BIBLIOG
GOV/REL
ADMIN
NAT/G

S55
CARR C.,"LEGISLATIVE CONTROL OF ADMINISTRATIVE
RULES AND REGULATIONS: PARLIAMENTARY SUPERVISION IN
BRITAIN." DELIB/GP CONTROL ROLE PWR PARLIAMENT.
PAGE 20 E0392
EXEC
REPRESENT
JURID

B56
DUNNILL F.,THE CIVIL SERVICE. UK LAW PLAN ADMIN
EFFICIENCY DRIVE NEW/LIB...STAT CHARTS 20
PARLIAMENT CIVIL/SERV. PAGE 33 E0662
PERSON
WORKER
STRATA
SOC/WK

B56
EMDEN C.S.,THE PEOPLE AND THE CONSTITUTION (2ND
ED.). UK LEGIS POPULISM 17/20 PARLIAMENT. PAGE 35
E0687
CONSTN
PARL/PROC
NAT/G
LAW

B57
JENNINGS I.,PARLIAMENT. UK FINAN INDUS POL/PAR
DELIB/GP EX/STRUC PLAN CONTROL...MAJORIT JURID
PARLIAMENT. PAGE 58 E1163
PARL/PROC
TOP/EX
MGT
LEGIS

B58
MACKENZIE W.J.M.,FREE ELECTIONS: AN ELEMENTARY
TEXTBOOK. WOR+45 NAT/G POL/PAR LEGIS TOP/EX
EDU/PROP LEGIT CT/SYS ATTIT PWR...OBS CHARTS
STERTYP T CONGRESS PARLIAMENT 20. PAGE 67 E1342
EX/STRUC
CHOOSE

B59
SQUIBB G.D.,THE HIGH COURT OF CHIVALRY. UK NAT/G
FORCES ADJUD WAR 14/20 PARLIAMENT ENGLSH/LAW.
PAGE 93 E1863
CT/SYS
PARL/PROC
JURID

B60
DILEY A.V.,INTRODUCTION TO THE STUDY OF THE LAW OF
THE CONSTITUTION. FRANCE UK USA+45 USA-45 CONSULT
FORCES TAX ADMIN FEDERAL ORD/FREE SOVEREIGN
...IDEA/COMP 20 ENGLSH/LAW CON/INTERP PARLIAMENT.
PAGE 32 E0627
CONSTN
LAW
LEGIS
GEN/LAWS

B60
LASKIN B.,CANADIAN CONSTITUTIONAL LAW: TEXT AND
NOTES ON DISTRIBUTION OF LEGISLATIVE POWER (2ND
ED.). CANADA LOC/G ECO/TAC TAX CONTROL CT/SYS CRIME
FEDERAL PWR...JURID 20 PARLIAMENT. PAGE 63 E1259
CONSTN
NAT/G
LAW
LEGIS

B61
GUIZOT F.P.G.,HISTORY OF THE ORIGIN OF
REPRESENTATIVE GOVERNMENT IN EUROPE. CHRIST-17C
FRANCE MOD/EUR SPAIN UK LAW CHIEF FORCES POPULISM
...MAJORIT TIME/SEQ GOV/COMP NAT/COMP 4/19
PARLIAMENT. PAGE 48 E0961
LEGIS
REPRESENT
CONSTN
NAT/G

S62
THOMPSON D.,"THE UNITED KINGDOM AND THE TREATY OF
ROME." EUR+WWI INT/ORG NAT/G DELIB/GP LEGIS
ADJUD
JURID

INT/TRADE RIGID/FLEX...CONCPT EEC PARLIAMENT
CMN/WLTH 20. PAGE 96 E1918

B63
BADI J.,THE GOVERNMENT OF THE STATE OF ISRAEL: A
CRITICAL ACCOUNT OF ITS PARLIAMENT, EXECUTIVE, AND
JUDICIARY. ISRAEL ECO/DEV CHIEF DELIB/GP LEGIS
DIPLOM CT/SYS INGP/REL PEACE ORD/FREE...BIBLIOG 20
PARLIAMENT ARABS MIGRATION. PAGE 7 E0131
NAT/G
CONSTN
EX/STRUC
POL/PAR

B64
LEDERMAN W.R.,THE COURTS AND THE CANDIAN
CONSTITUTION. CANADA PARL/PROC...POLICY JURID
GOV/COMP ANTHOL 19/20 SUPREME/CT PARLIAMENT.
PAGE 64 E1276
CONSTN
CT/SYS
LEGIS
LAW

B64
SCHMEISER D.A.,CIVIL LIBERTIES IN CANADA. CANADA
LAW SECT PRESS RACE/REL NAT/LISM PRIVIL 20
COMMONWLTH PARLIAMENT CIVIL/LIB CHURCH/STA. PAGE 88
E1758
ORD/FREE
CONSTN
ADJUD
EDU/PROP

B65
CHARNAY J.P.,LE SUFFRAGE POLITIQUE EN FRANCE:
ELECTIONS PARLEMENTAIRES, ELECTION PRESIDENTIELLE,
REFERENDUMS. FRANCE CONSTN CHIEF DELIB/GP ECO/TAC
EDU/PROP CRIME INGP/REL MORAL ORD/FREE PWR CATHISM
20 PARLIAMENT PRESIDENT. PAGE 22 E0425
CHOOSE
SUFF
NAT/G
LEGIS

B65
CHRIMES S.B.,ENGLISH CONSTITUTIONAL HISTORY (3RD
ED.). UK CHIEF CONSULT DELIB/GP LEGIS CT/SYS 15/20
COMMON/LAW PARLIAMENT. PAGE 22 E0435
CONSTN
BAL/PWR
NAT/G

B65
HOLDSWORTH W.S.,A HISTORY OF ENGLISH LAW: THE
CENTURIES OF SETTLEMENT AND REFORM (VOL. XV). UK
CONSTN SECT LEGIS JUDGE WRITING ADJUD CT/SYS CRIME
OWN...JURID IDEA/COMP 18 PARLIAMENT ENGLSH/LAW
COMMON/LAW. PAGE 54 E1082
LAW
INDUS
PROF/ORG
ATTIT

B66
ANDERSON S.V.,CANADIAN OMBUDSMAN PROPOSALS. CANADA
LEGIS DEBATE PARL/PROC...MAJORIT JURID TIME/SEQ
IDEA/COMP 20 OMBUDSMAN PARLIAMENT. PAGE 5 E0092
NAT/G
CREATE
ADMIN
POL/PAR

B66
BURNS A.C.,PARLIAMENT AS AN EXPORT. WOR+45 CONSTN
BARGAIN DEBATE ROUTINE GOV/REL EFFICIENCY...ANTHOL
COMMONWLTH PARLIAMENT. PAGE 17 E0343
PARL/PROC
POL/PAR
CT/SYS
CHIEF

B66
CAMPBELL E.,PARLIAMENTARY PRIVILEGE IN AUSTRALIA.
UK LAW CONSTN COLONIAL ROLE ORD/FREE SOVEREIGN
18/20 COMMONWLTH AUSTRAL FREE/SPEE PARLIAMENT.
PAGE 19 E0370
LEGIS
PARL/PROC
JURID
PRIVIL

B66
HOLDSWORTH W.S.,A HISTORY OF ENGLISH LAW: THE
CENTURIES OF SETTLEMENT AND REFORM (VOL. XVI). UK
LOC/G NAT/G EX/STRUC LEGIS CT/SYS LEAD ATTIT
...POLICY DECISION JURID IDEA/COMP 18 PARLIAMENT.
PAGE 54 E1083
BIOG
PERSON
PROF/ORG
LAW

B66
WILSON G.,CASES AND MATERIALS ON CONSTITUTIONAL AND
ADMINISTRATIVE LAW. UK LAW NAT/G EX/STRUC LEGIS
BAL/PWR BUDGET DIPLOM ADJUD CONTROL CT/SYS GOV/REL
ORD/FREE 20 PARLIAMENT ENGLSH/LAW. PAGE 106 E2126
JURID
ADMIN
CONSTN
PWR

PARNELL/CS....CHARLES STEWART PARNELL

PAROLE....SEE PUB/INST, ROUTINE, CRIME

PARRY C. E1599

PARSONS/T....TALCOTT PARSONS

PARTH/SASS....PARTHO-SASSANIAN EMPIRE

PARTHEMOS G.S. E0910

PARTIC....PARTICIPATION: CIVIC ACTIVITY AND NONACTIVITY

S05
PHILLIPS J.B.,"MODIFICATIONS OF THE JURY SYSTEM."
PARTIC EFFICIENCY ATTIT PERCEPT...TREND 19
SUPREME/CT JURY. PAGE 80 E1612
JURID
DELIB/GP
PERS/REL
POLICY

B09
LOBINGIER C.S.,THE PEOPLE'S LAW OR POPULAR
PARTICIPATION IN LAW-MAKING. FRANCE SWITZERLND UK
LOC/G NAT/G PROVS LEGIS SUFF MAJORITY PWR POPULISM
CONSTN
LAW
PARTIC

...GOV/COMP BIBLIOG 19. PAGE 66 E1314

B17
DE VICTORIA F.,DE INDIS ET DE JURE BELLI (1557) IN WAR
F. DE VICTORIA, DE INDIS ET DE JURE BELLI INT/LAW
REFLECTIONES. UNIV NAT/G SECT CHIEF PARTIC COERCE OWN
PEACE MORAL...POLICY 16 INDIAN/AM CHRISTIAN
CONSCN/OBJ. PAGE 30 E0598

B18
PORTER K.H.,A HISTORY OF SUFFRAGE IN THE UNITED SUFF
STATES. USA-45 LAW CONSTN LOC/G NAT/G POL/PAR WAR REPRESENT
DISCRIM OWN ATTIT SEX 18/20 NEGRO FEMALE/SEX. CHOOSE
PAGE 81 E1629 PARTIC

B23
ROBERT H.M.,PARLIAMENTARY LAW. POL/PAR LEGIS PARTIC PARL/PROC
CHOOSE REPRESENT GP/REL. PAGE 85 E1701 DELIB/GP
NAT/G
JURID

B30
BIRD F.L.,THE RECALL OF PUBLIC OFFICERS; A STUDY OF REPRESENT
THE OPERATION OF RECALL IN CALIFORNIA. LOC/G MUNIC SANCTION
POL/PAR PROVS PROB/SOLV ADJUD PARTIC...CHARTS CHOOSE
METH/COMP 20 CALIFORNIA RECALL. PAGE 12 E0230 LAW

B34
EVANS I.L.,NATIVE POLICY IN SOUTHERN AFRICA. AFR
RHODESIA SOUTH/AFR UK STRUCT PARTIC RACE/REL ATTIT COLONIAL
WEALTH SOC/INTEG AFRICA/SW. PAGE 35 E0705 DOMIN
LAW

B36
HERRING E.P.,PUBLIC ADMINISTRATION AND THE PUBLIC GP/REL
INTEREST. LABOR NAT/G PARTIC EFFICIENCY 20. PAGE 52 DECISION
E1033 PROB/SOLV
ADMIN

S40
GILL N.N.,"PERMANENT ADVISORY COMMISSIONS IN THE DELIB/GP
FEDERAL GOVERNMENT." CLIENT FINAN OP/RES EDU/PROP NAT/G
PARTIC ROUTINE INGP/REL KNOWL SKILL...CLASSIF DECISION
TREND. PAGE 43 E0860

B50
MERRIAM C.E.,THE AMERICAN PARTY SYSTEM; AN POL/PAR
INTRODUCTION TO THE STUDY OF POLITICAL PARTIES IN CHOOSE
THE UNITED STATES (4TH ED.). USA+45 USA-45 LAW SUFF
FINAN LOC/G NAT/G PROVS LEAD PARTIC CRIME ATTIT REPRESENT
18/20 NEGRO CONGRESS PRESIDENT. PAGE 72 E1442

S52
DE GRAZIA A.,"GENERAL THEORY OF APPORTIONMENT" APPORT
(BMR)" USA+45 USA-45 CONSTN ELITES DELIB/GP PARTIC LEGIS
REV CHOOSE...JURID 20. PAGE 29 E0582 PROVS
REPRESENT

B53
BUTLER D.E.,THE ELECTORAL SYSTEM IN BRITAIN, CHOOSE
1918-1951. UK LAW POL/PAR SUFF...STAT BIBLIOG 20 LEGIS
PARLIAMENT. PAGE 18 E0348 REPRESENT
PARTIC

B54
HAMSON C.J.,EXECUTIVE DISCRETION AND JUDICIAL ELITES
CONTROL; AN ASPECT OF THE FRENCH CONSEIL D'ETAT. ADJUD
EUR+WWI FRANCE MOD/EUR UK NAT/G EX/STRUC PARTIC NAT/COMP
CONSERVE...JURID BIBLIOG/A 18/20 SUPREME/CT.
PAGE 50 E0992

B55
BENTON W.E.,NUREMBERG: GERMAN VIEWS OF THE WAR CRIME
TRIALS. EUR+WWI GERMANY VOL/ASSN LEAD PARTIC COERCE WAR
INGP/REL RACE/REL TOTALISM SUPEGO ORD/FREE...ANTHOL LAW
NUREMBERG. PAGE 10 E0201 JURID

B55
SMITH G.,A CONSTITUTIONAL AND LEGAL HISTORY OF CONSTN
ENGLAND. UK ELITES NAT/G LEGIS ADJUD OWN HABITAT PARTIC
POPULISM...JURID 20 ENGLSH/LAW. PAGE 92 E1844 LAW
CT/SYS

B57
BERLE A.A. JR.,ECONOMIC POWER AND FREE SOCIETY LG/CO
(PAMPHLET). CLIENT CONSTN EX/STRUC ECO/TAC CONTROL CAP/ISM
PARTIC PWR WEALTH MAJORIT. PAGE 11 E0205 INGP/REL
LEGIT

B57
COSSIO C.,LA POLITICA COMO CONCIENCIA; MEDITACION POL/PAR
SOBRE LA ARGENTINA DE 1955. WOR+45 LEGIS EDU/PROP REV
PARL/PROC PARTIC ATTIT PWR CATHISM 20 ARGEN TOTALISM
PERON/JUAN. PAGE 26 E0517 JURID

B58
OGDEN F.D.,THE POLL TAX IN THE SOUTH. USA+45 USA-45 TAX
CONSTN ADJUD ADMIN PARTIC CRIME...TIME/SEQ GOV/COMP CHOOSE
METH/COMP 18/20 SOUTH/US. PAGE 78 E1572 RACE/REL
DISCRIM

B58
PALMER E.E.,CIVIL LIBERTIES. USA+45 ADJUD CT/SYS ORD/FREE
PARTIC OWN LAISSEZ POPULISM...JURID CONCPT ANTHOL CONSTN
20 SUPREME/CT CIVIL/LIB. PAGE 79 E1592 RACE/REL
LAW

B59
FERRY W.H.,THE CORPORATION AND THE ECONOMY. CLIENT LG/CO
LAW CONSTN LABOR NAT/G PLAN INT/TRADE PARTIC CONSEN CONTROL
ORD/FREE PWR POLICY. PAGE 37 E0742 REPRESENT

B59
KNIERIEM A.,THE NUREMBERG TRIALS. EUR+WWI GERMANY INT/LAW
VOL/ASSN LEAD COERCE WAR INGP/REL TOTALISM SUPEGO CRIME
ORD/FREE...CONCPT METH/COMP. PAGE 61 E1225 PARTIC
JURID

L59
COX A.,"THE ROLE OF LAW IN PRESERVING UNION LABOR
DEMOCRACY." EX/STRUC LEGIS PARTIC ROUTINE CHOOSE REPRESENT
INGP/REL ORD/FREE. PAGE 27 E0532 LAW
MAJORIT

L59
OBERER W.E.,"VOLUNTARY IMPARTIAL REVIEW OF LABOR: LABOR
SOME REFLECTIONS." DELIB/GP LEGIS PROB/SOLV ADJUD LAW
CONTROL COERCE PWR PLURISM POLICY. PAGE 78 E1570 PARTIC
INGP/REL

B60
CARTER R.F.,COMMUNITIES AND THEIR SCHOOLS. USA+45 SCHOOL
LAW FINAN PROVS BUDGET TAX LEAD PARTIC CHOOSE...SOC ACT/RES
INT QU 20. PAGE 20 E0401 NEIGH
INGP/REL

S60
MACKINNON F.,"THE UNIVERSITY: COMMUNITY OR ACADEM
UTILITY?" CLIENT CONSTN INTELL FINAN NAT/G NEIGH MGT
EDU/PROP PARTIC REPRESENT ROLE. PAGE 67 E1343 CONTROL
SERV/IND

B61
AVERY M.W.,GOVERNMENT OF WASHINGTON STATE. USA+45 PROVS
MUNIC DELIB/GP EX/STRUC LEGIS GIVE CT/SYS PARTIC LOC/G
REGION EFFICIENCY 20 WASHINGT/G GOVERNOR. PAGE 6 ADMIN
E0121 GOV/REL

B61
BEDFORD S.,THE FACES OF JUSTICE: A TRAVELLER'S CT/SYS
REPORT. AUSTRIA FRANCE GERMANY/W SWITZERLND UK UNIV ORD/FREE
WOR+45 WOR-45 CULTURE PARTIC GOV/REL MORAL...JURID PERSON
OBS GOV/COMP 20. PAGE 9 E0174 LAW

B61
BRENNAN D.G.,ARMS CONTROL, DISARMAMENT, AND ARMS/CONT
NATIONAL SECURITY. WOR+45 NAT/G FORCES CREATE ORD/FREE
PROB/SOLV PARTIC WAR PEACE...DECISION INT/LAW DIPLOM
ANTHOL BIBLIOG 20. PAGE 15 E0291 POLICY

B61
CASSINELLI C.W.,THE POLITICS OF FREEDOM. FUT UNIV MAJORIT
LAW POL/PAR CHOOSE ORD/FREE...POLICY CONCPT MYTH NAT/G
BIBLIOG. PAGE 21 E0404 PARL/PROC
PARTIC

B61
JUSTICE,THE CITIZEN AND THE ADMINISTRATION: THE INGP/REL
REDRESS OF GRIEVANCES (PAMPHLET). EUR+WWI UK LAW CONSULT
CONSTN STRATA NAT/G CT/SYS PARTIC COERCE...NEW/IDEA ADJUD
IDEA/COMP 20 OMBUDSMAN. PAGE 59 E1176 REPRESENT

N61
LEAGUE WOMEN VOTERS MASSACHU,THE MERIT SYSTEM IN LOC/G
MASSACHUSETTS (PAMPHLET). USA+45 PROVS LEGIT PARTIC LAW
CHOOSE REPRESENT GOV/REL EFFICIENCY...POLICY SENIOR
GOV/COMP BIBLIOG 20 MASSACHU. PAGE 64 E1274 PROF/ORG

B62
GALENSON W.,TRADE UNIONS MONOGRAPH SERIES (A SERIES LABOR
OF NINE TEXTS). DELIB/GP LEAD PARTIC...DECISION INGP/REL
ORG/CHARTS. PAGE 42 E0827 CONSTN
REPRESENT

B62
HEYDECKER J.J.,THE NUREMBERG TRIAL: HISTORY OF NAZI LAW
GERMANY AS REVEALED THROUGH THE TESTIMONY AT CRIME
NUREMBERG. EUR+WWI GERMANY VOL/ASSN LEAD COERCE PARTIC
CROWD INGP/REL RACE/REL SUPEGO ORD/FREE...CONCPT 20 TOTALISM
NAZI ANTI/SEMIT NUREMBERG JEWS. PAGE 52 E1036

LEVY H.V.,LIBERDADE E JUSTICA SOCIAL (2ND ED.). ORD/FREE   B62
BRAZIL COM L/A+17C USSR INT/ORG PARTIC GP/REL MARXISM
WEALTH 20 UN COM/PARTY. PAGE 65 E1290 CAP/ISM
  LAW

FRIEDRICH C.J.,MAN AND HIS GOVERNMENT: AN EMPIRICAL PERSON   B63
THEORY OF POLITICS. UNIV LOC/G NAT/G ADJUD REV ORD/FREE
INGP/REL DISCRIM PWR BIBLIOG. PAGE 41 E0810 PARTIC
  CONTROL

GALLAGHER J.F.,SUPERVISORIAL DISTRICTING IN APPORT   B63
CALIFORNIA COUNTIES: 1960-1963 (PAMPHLET). USA+45 REGION
ADJUD ADMIN PARTIC CHOOSE GP/REL...CENSUS 20 REPRESENT
CALIFORNIA. PAGE 42 E0828 LOC/G

HORRELL M.,LEGISLATION AND RACE RELATIONS LAW   B63
(PAMPHLET). SOUTH/AFR SCHOOL TAX DOMIN CONTROL 20. RACE/REL
PAGE 55 E1098 DISCRIM
  PARTIC

SCHUMAN S.I.,LEGAL POSITIVISM: ITS SCOPE AND GEN/METH   B63
LIMITATIONS. CONSTN NAT/G DIPLOM PARTIC UTOPIA LAW
...POLICY DECISION PHIL/SCI CONCPT 20. PAGE 89 METH/COMP
E1784

SMITH E.A.,CHURCH AND STATE IN YOUR COMMUNITY. GP/REL   B63
USA+45 PROVS SCHOOL ACT/RES CT/SYS PARTIC ATTIT SECT
MORAL ORD/FREE CATHISM 20 PROTESTANT CHURCH/STA. NAT/G
PAGE 92 E1842 NEIGH

US PRES COMN REGIS AND VOTING,REPORT ON CHOOSE   N63
REGISTRATION AND VOTING (PAMPHLET). USA+45 POL/PAR LAW
CHIEF EDU/PROP PARTIC REPRESENT ATTIT...PSY CHARTS SUFF
20. PAGE 101 E2023 INSPECT

DOOLIN D.J.,COMMUNIST CHINA: THE POLITICS OF MARXISM   B64
STUDENT OPPOSITION. CHINA/COM ELITES STRATA ACADEM DEBATE
NAT/G WRITING CT/SYS LEAD PARTIC COERCE TOTALISM AGE/Y
20. PAGE 32 E0637 PWR

FACTS ON FILE, INC.,CIVIL RIGHTS 1960-63: THE NEGRO DISCRIM   B64
CAMPAIGN TO WIN EQUAL RIGHTS AND OPPORTUNITIES IN PRESS
THE UNITED STATES. LAW CONSTN PARTIC SUFF 20 NEGRO RACE/REL
CIV/RIGHTS MISSISSIPP. PAGE 36 E0710

GOODNOW H.F.,THE CIVIL SERVICE OF PAKISTAN: ADMIN   B64
BUREAUCRACY IN A NEW NATION. INDIA PAKISTAN S/ASIA GOV/REL
ECO/UNDEV PROVS CHIEF PARTIC CHOOSE EFFICIENCY PWR LAW
...BIBLIOG 20. PAGE 45 E0889 NAT/G

MARSHALL B.,FEDERALISM AND CIVIL RIGHTS. USA+45 FEDERAL   B64
PROVS BAL/PWR CONTROL CT/SYS PARTIC SOVEREIGN ORD/FREE
...JURID 20 NEGRO CIV/RIGHTS. PAGE 68 E1369 CONSTN
  FORCES

BAKER H.R.,"INMATE SELF-GOVERNMENT." ACT/RES CREATE PUB/INST   S64
CONTROL PARTIC ATTIT RIGID/FLEX QU. PAGE 7 E0141 CRIME
  INGP/REL
  REPRESENT

FRYE R.J.,HOUSING AND URBAN RENEWAL IN ALABAMA. MUNIC   B65
USA+45 NEIGH LEGIS BUDGET ADJUD ADMIN PARTIC...MGT PROB/SOLV
20 ALABAMA URBAN/RNWL. PAGE 41 E0815 PLAN
  GOV/REL

IANNIELLO L.,MILESTONES ALONG THE MARCH: TWELVE RACE/REL   B65
HISTORIC CIVIL RIGHTS DOCUMENTS--FROM WORLD WAR II DISCRIM
TO SELMA. USA+45 LAW FORCES TOP/EX PARTIC SUFF...T CONSTN
20 NEGRO CIV/RIGHTS TRUMAN/HS SUPREME/CT NAT/G
KENNEDY/JF. PAGE 56 E1121

ISORNI J.,LES CAS DE CONSCIENCE DE L'AVOCAT. SUPEGO   B65
FRANCE LAW ACT/RES CT/SYS PARTIC ROLE MORAL 20. JURID
PAGE 57 E1138 CRIME

KING D.B.,LEGAL ASPECTS OF THE CIVIL RIGHTS LAW   B65
MOVEMENT. SERV/IND VOL/ASSN LEGIS EDU/PROP ADJUD DISCRIM
PARTIC CHOOSE...JURID SEGREGAT WORK. PAGE 61 E1215 TREND

MCWHINNEY E.,JUDICIAL REVIEW IN THE ENGLISH- GOV/COMP   B65
SPEAKING WORLD (3RD ED.). CANADA UK WOR+45 LEGIS CT/SYS
CONTROL EXEC PARTIC...JURID 20 AUSTRAL. PAGE 71 ADJUD
E1431 CONSTN

SWISHER C.B.,THE SUPREME COURT IN MODERN ROLE. COM DELIB/GP   B65
COM/IND NAT/G FORCES LEGIS LOBBY PARTIC RACE/REL 20 ATTIT
SUPREME/CT. PAGE 95 E1901 CT/SYS
  ADJUD

WEIL G.L.,A HANDBOOK ON THE EUROPEAN ECONOMIC INT/TRADE   B65
COMMUNITY. BELGIUM EUR+WWI FRANCE GERMANY/W ITALY INT/ORG
CONSTN ECO/DEV CREATE PARTIC GP/REL...DECISION MGT TEC/DEV
CHARTS 20 EEC. PAGE 105 E2107 INT/LAW

HAUSNER G.,JUSTICE IN JERUSALEM. GERMANY ISRAEL ADJUD   B66
SOCIETY KIN DIPLOM LEGIT CT/SYS PARTIC MURDER CRIME
MAJORITY ATTIT FASCISM...INT/LAW JURID 20 JEWS RACE/REL
WAR/TRIAL. PAGE 51 E1013 COERCE

HOLTZMAN A.,INTEREST GROUPS AND LOBBYING. USA+45 LOBBY   B66
CHIEF ACT/RES ADJUD LEAD PARTIC CHOOSE...POLICY 20 NAT/G
CONGRESS. PAGE 55 E1092 EDU/PROP
  GP/REL

KEAY E.A.,THE NATIVE AND CUSTOMARY COURTS OF AFR   B66
NIGERIA. NIGERIA CONSTN ELITES NAT/G TOP/EX PARTIC ADJUD
REGION...DECISION JURID 19/20. PAGE 60 E1190 LAW

KUNSTLER W.M.,"DEEP IN MY HEART" USA+45 LAW CT/SYS   B66
PROF/ORG SECT LOBBY PARTIC CROWD DISCRIM ROLE RACE/REL
...BIOG 20 KING/MAR/L NEGRO CIV/RIGHTS SOUTH/US. ADJUD
PAGE 62 E1233 CONSULT

LONG E.V.,THE INTRUDERS: THE INVASION OF PRIVACY BY LAW   B67
GOVERNMENT AND INDUSTRY. USA+45 COM/IND INDUS LEGIS PARTIC
TASK PERS/REL...JURID 20 CONGRESS. PAGE 66 E1324 NAT/G

LAMBERT J.D.,"CORPORATE POLITICAL SPENDING AND USA+45   L67
CAMPAIGN FINANCE." LAW CONSTN FINAN LABOR LG/CO POL/PAR
LOC/G NAT/G VOL/ASSN TEC/DEV ADJUD ADMIN PARTIC. CHOOSE
PAGE 62 E1247 COST

WINES R.,"THE IMPERIAL CIRCLES, PRINCELY DIPLOMACY, NAT/G   S67
AND IMPERIAL REFORM* 1681-1714." MOD/EUR DELIB/GP NAT/LISM
BAL/PWR CONFER ADJUD PARL/PROC PARTIC ATTIT PWR CENTRAL
17/18. PAGE 106 E2132 REGION

CHIU H.,"COMMUNIST CHINA'S ATTITUDE TOWARD THE INT/LAW   L68
UNITED NATIONS: A LEGAL ANALYSIS." CHINA/COM WOR+45 SOVEREIGN
LAW NAT/G DIPLOM CONFER ADJUD PARTIC ATTIT...POLICY INT/ORG
TREND 20 UN. PAGE 22 E0432 REPRESENT

DOLE C.F.,THE AMERICAN CITIZEN. USA-45 LAW PARTIC NAT/G   B91
ATTIT...INT/LAW 19. PAGE 32 E0633 MORAL
  NAT/LISM
  MAJORITY

PARTIES, POLITICAL....SEE POL/PAR

PARTITION....PARTITIONS AND PARTITIONING - DIVISION OF AN
   EXISTING POLITICAL-GEOGRAPHICAL ENTITY INTO TWO OR
   MORE AUTONOMOUS ZONES

CAMPBELL E.H.,SURVEYS, SUBDIVISIONS AND PLATTING, CONSTN   B65
AND BOUNDARIES: WASHINGTON STATE LAW AND JUDICIAL PLAN
DECISIONS. USA+45 LAW LOC/G...DECISION JURID GEOG
CON/ANAL BIBLIOG WASHINGT/G PARTITION WATER. PROVS
PAGE 19 E0372

PASCUAL R.R. E1600

PASSPORT....SEE LICENSE

PATENT....PATENT

PATENT/OFF....U.S. PATENT OFFICE

PATHAN....PATHAN PEOPLE (PAKISTAN, AFGHANISTAN)

PATHET/LAO....PATHET LAO

PATON G.W. E1601

PATRA A.C. E1602

PATRIOTISM....SEE NAT/LISM

PAUL A.M. E1603

PAULING/L....LINUS PAULING

PAULSEN M.G. E1604

PAY....EARNINGS; SEE ALSO INCOME

B03
GRIFFIN A.P.C.,SELECT LIST OF BOOKS ON LABOR | BIBLIOG/A
PARTICULARLY RELATING TO STRIKES. FRANCE GERMANY | GP/REL
MOD/EUR UK USA-45 LAW NAT/G DELIB/GP WORKER BARGAIN | MGT
LICENSE PAY ADJUD 19/20. PAGE 46 E0924 | LABOR

B06
GRIFFIN A.P.C.,LIST OF BOOKS RELATING TO CHILD | BIBLIOG/A
LABOR (PAMPHLET). BELGIUM FRANCE GERMANY MOD/EUR UK | LAW
USA-45 ECO/DEV INDUS WORKER CAP/ISM PAY ROUTINE | LABOR
ALL/IDEOS...MGT SOC 19/20. PAGE 47 E0929 | AGE/C

B10
COLORADO CIVIL SERVICE COMN,SECOND BIENNIAL REPORT | PROVS
TO THE GOVERNOR, 1909-1910. USA-45 DELIB/GP LEGIS | LOC/G
LICENSE PAY 20 COLORADO CIVIL/SERV. PAGE 24 E0477 | ADMIN
| WORKER

N19
CARPER E.T.,LOBBYING AND THE NATURAL GAS BILL | LOBBY
(PAMPHLET). USA+45 SERV/IND BARGAIN PAY DRIVE ROLE | ADJUD
WEALTH 20 CONGRESS SENATE EISNHWR/DD. PAGE 20 E0389 | TRIBUTE
| NAT/G

C43
BENTHAM J.,"THE RATIONALE OF REWARD" IN J. BOWRING, | SANCTION
ED., THE WORKS OF JEREMY BENTHAM (VOL. 2)" LAW | ECO/TAC
WORKER CREATE INSPECT PAY ROUTINE HAPPINESS PRODUC | INCOME
SUPEGO WEALTH METH/CNCPT. PAGE 10 E0195 | PWR

B55
BLOOM G.F.,ECONOMICS OF LABOR RELATIONS. USA+45 LAW | ECO/DEV
CONSULT WORKER CAP/ISM PAY ADJUD CONTROL EFFICIENCY | ECO/TAC
ORD/FREE...CHARTS 19/20 AFL/CIO NLRB DEPT/LABOR. | LABOR
PAGE 13 E0249 | GOV/REL

B58
DAVIS K.C.,ADMINISTRATIVE LAW; CASES, TEXT, | ADJUD
PROBLEMS. LAW LOC/G NAT/G TOP/EX PAY CONTROL | JURID
GOV/REL INGP/REL FEDERAL 20 SUPREME/CT. PAGE 29 | CT/SYS
E0576 | ADMIN

B59
COUNCIL OF STATE GOVERNORS,AMERICAN LEGISLATURES: | LEGIS
STRUCTURE AND PROCEDURES. SUMMARY AND TABULATIONS | CHARTS
OF A 1959 SURVEY. PUERT/RICO USA+45 PAY ADJUD ADMIN | PROVS
APPORT...IDEA/COMP 20 GUAM VIRGIN/ISL. PAGE 27 | REPRESENT
E0525

B61
AYLMER G.,THE KING'S SERVANTS. UK ELITES CHIEF PAY | ADMIN
CT/SYS WEALTH 17 CROMWELL/O CHARLES/I. PAGE 6 E0122 | ROUTINE
| EX/STRUC
| NAT/G

B65
WHITE G.M.,THE USE OF EXPERTS BY INTERNATIONAL | INT/LAW
TRIBUNALS. WOR+45 WOR-45 INT/ORG NAT/G PAY ADJUD | ROUTINE
COST...OBS BIBLIOG 20. PAGE 106 E2117 | CONSULT
| CT/SYS

B66
GARCON M.,LETTRE OUVERTE A LA JUSTICE. FRANCE NAT/G | ORD/FREE
PROB/SOLV PAY EFFICIENCY MORAL 20. PAGE 42 E0834 | ADJUD
| CT/SYS

B66
PLATE H.,PARTEIFINANZIERUNG UND GRUNDESETZ. GERMANY | POL/PAR
NAT/G PLAN GIVE PAY INCOME WEALTH...JURID 20. | CONSTN
PAGE 81 E1619 | FINAN

S67
CREYKE G. JR.,"THE PAYMENT GAP IN FEDERAL | CONSTRUC
CONSTRUCTION CONTRACTS." USA+45 LAW FINAN ECO/TAC | PAY
CONTROL CT/SYS SUPREME/CT. PAGE 28 E0547 | COST
| NAT/G

PAYNE E.M. E1426

PEACE W.H. E1473

PEACE OF WESTPHALIA....SEE WESTPHALIA

PEACE....SEE ALSO ORD/FREE

PEACE CORPS....SEE PEACE/CORP

N
BACKGROUND; JOURNAL OF INTERNATIONAL STUDIES | BIBLIOG
ASSOCIATION. INT/ORG FORCES ACT/RES EDU/PROP COERCE | DIPLOM
NAT/LISM PEACE ATTIT...INT/LAW CONCPT 20. PAGE 1 | POLICY
E0004

N
JOURNAL OF INTERNATIONAL AFFAIRS. WOR+45 ECO/UNDEV | BIBLIOG
POL/PAR ECO/TAC WAR PEACE PERSON ALL/IDEOS | DIPLOM
...INT/LAW TREND. PAGE 1 E0010 | INT/ORG
| NAT/G

N
BIBLIOGRAPHIE DER SOZIALWISSENSCHAFTEN. WOR-45 | BIBLIOG
CONSTN SOCIETY ECO/DEV ECO/UNDEV DIPLOM LEAD WAR | LAW
PEACE...PHIL/SCI SOC 19/20. PAGE 1 E0019 | CONCPT
| NAT/G

N
AIR UNIVERSITY LIBRARY,INDEX TO MILITARY | BIBLIOG/A
PERIODICALS. FUT SPACE WOR+45 REGION ARMS/CONT | FORCES
NUC/PWR WAR PEACE INT/LAW. PAGE 3 E0056 | NAT/G
| DIPLOM

N
TURNER R.K.,BIBLIOGRAPHY ON WORLD ORGANIZATION. | BIBLIOG/A
INT/TRADE CT/SYS ARMS/CONT WEALTH...INT/LAW 20. | INT/ORG
PAGE 97 E1944 | PEACE
| WAR

N
UNITED NATIONS,UNITED NATIONS PUBLICATIONS. WOR+45 | BIBLIOG
ECO/UNDEV AGRI FINAN FORCES ADMIN LEAD WAR PEACE | INT/ORG
...POLICY INT/LAW 20 UN. PAGE 98 E1965 | DIPLOM

B00
DARBY W.E.,INTERNATIONAL TRIBUNALS. WOR-45 NAT/G | INT/ORG
ECO/TAC DOMIN LEGIT CT/SYS COERCE ORD/FREE PWR | ADJUD
SOVEREIGN JURID. PAGE 29 E0567 | PEACE
| INT/LAW

B00
DE TOCQUEVILLE A.,DEMOCRACY IN AMERICA (VOLUME | USA-45
ONE). LAW SOCIETY STRUCT NAT/G POL/PAR PROVS FORCES | TREND
LEGIS TOP/EX DIPLOM LEGIT WAR PEACE ATTIT SOVEREIGN
...SELF/OBS TIME/SEQ CONGRESS 19. PAGE 30 E0594

B00
GROTIUS H.,DE JURE BELLI AC PACIS. CHRIST-17C UNIV | JURID
LAW SOCIETY PROVS LEGIT PEACE PERCEPT MORAL PWR | INT/LAW
...CONCPT CON/ANAL GEN/LAWS. PAGE 48 E0952 | WAR

B00
HOLLAND T.E.,STUDIES IN INTERNATIONAL LAW. TURKEY | INT/ORG
USSR WOR-45 CONSTN NAT/G DIPLOM DOMIN LEGIT COERCE | LAW
WAR PEACE ORD/FREE PWR SOVEREIGN...JURID CHARTS 20 | INT/LAW
PARLIAMENT SUEZ TREATY. PAGE 54 E1084

B00
LORIMER J.,THE INSTITUTES OF THE LAW OF NATIONS. | INT/ORG
WOR+45 CULTURE SOCIETY NAT/G VOL/ASSN DIPLOM LEGIT | LAW
WAR PEACE DRIVE ORD/FREE SOVEREIGN...CONCPT RECORD | INT/LAW
INT TREND HYPO/EXP GEN/METH TOT/POP VAL/FREE 20.
PAGE 66 E1327

B00
MAINE H.S.,INTERNATIONAL LAW. MOD/EUR UNIV SOCIETY | INT/ORG
STRUCT ACT/RES EXEC WAR ATTIT PERSON ALL/VALS | LAW
...POLICY JURID CONCPT OBS TIME/SEQ TOT/POP. | PEACE
PAGE 68 E1349 | INT/LAW

B04
CRANDALL S.B.,TREATIES: THEIR MAKING AND | LAW
ENFORCEMENT. MOD/EUR USA-45 CONSTN INT/ORG NAT/G
LEGIS EDU/PROP LEGIT EXEC PEACE KNOWL MORAL...JURID
CONGRESS 19/20 TREATY. PAGE 27 E0541

B13
ADAMS B.,THE THEORY OF SOCIAL REVOLUTIONS. FUT | CAP/ISM
USA-45 GP/REL PEACE...NEW/IDEA 20. PAGE 3 E0047 | REV
| SOCIETY
| CT/SYS

B13
BORCHARD E.M.,BIBLIOGRAPHY OF INTERNATIONAL LAW AND | BIBLIOG
CONTINENTAL LAW. EUR+WWI MOD/EUR UK LAW INT/TRADE | INT/LAW
WAR PEACE...GOV/COMP NAT/COMP 19/20. PAGE 14 E0267 | JURID
| DIPLOM

B16
ROOT E.,ADDRESSES ON INTERNATIONAL SUBJECTS. | INT/ORG
MOD/EUR UNIV USA-45 LAW SOCIETY EXEC ATTIT ALL/VALS | ACT/RES
...POLICY JURID CONCPT 20 CHINJAP. PAGE 85 E1711 | PEACE
| INT/LAW

B17

DE VICTORIA F.,DE INDIS ET DE JURE BELLI (1557) IN   WAR
F. DE VICTORIA, DE INDIS ET DE JURE BELLI   INT/LAW
REFLECTIONES. UNIV NAT/G SECT CHIEF PARTIC COERCE   OWN
PEACE MORAL...POLICY 16 INDIAN/AM CHRISTIAN
CONSCN/OBJ. PAGE 30 E0598

S17

ROOT E.,"THE EFFECT OF DEMOCRACY ON INTERNATIONAL   LEGIS
LAW." USA-45 WOR-45 INTELL SOCIETY INT/ORG NAT/G   JURID
CONSULT ACT/RES CREATE PLAN EDU/PROP PEACE SKILL   INT/LAW
...CONCPT METH/CNCPT OBS 20. PAGE 85 E1712

B20

DICKINSON E.,THE EQUALITY OF STATES IN   LAW
INTERNATIONAL LAW. WOR-45 INT/ORG NAT/G DIPLOM   CONCPT
EDU/PROP LEGIT PEACE ATTIT ALL/VALS...JURID   SOVEREIGN
TIME/SEQ LEAGUE/NAT. PAGE 31 E0622

B27

LAUTERPACHT H.,PRIVATE LAW SOURCES AND ANALOGIES OF   INT/ORG
INTERNATIONAL LAW. WOR-45 NAT/G DELIB/GP LEGIT   ADJUD
COERCE ATTIT ORD/FREE PWR SOVEREIGN...JURID CONCPT   PEACE
HIST/WRIT TIME/SEQ GEN/METH LEAGUE/NAT 20. PAGE 63   INT/LAW
E1264

B29

STURZO L.,THE INTERNATIONAL COMMUNITY AND THE RIGHT   INT/ORG
OF WAR (TRANS. BY BARBARA BARCLAY CARTER). CULTURE   PLAN
CREATE PROB/SOLV DIPLOM ADJUD CONTROL PEACE PERSON   WAR
ORD/FREE...INT/LAW IDEA/COMP PACIFIST 20   CONCPT
LEAGUE/NAT. PAGE 94 E1891

L29

FEIS H.,"RESEARCH ACTIVITIES OF THE LEAGUE OF   CONSULT
NATIONS." EUR+WWI WOR-45 R+D INT/ORG CT/SYS   KNOWL
ARMS/CONT WEALTH...OBS RECORD LEAGUE/NAT ILO 20.   PEACE
PAGE 37 E0729

B32

FLEMMING D.,THE UNITED STATES AND THE LEAGUE OF   INT/ORG
NATIONS, 1918-1920. FUT USA-45 NAT/G LEGIS TOP/EX   EDU/PROP
DEBATE CHOOSE PEACE ATTIT SOVEREIGN...TIME/SEQ
CON/ANAL CONGRESS LEAGUE/NAT 20 TREATY. PAGE 39
E0764

B33

GENTILI A.,DE JURE BELLI, LIBRI TRES (1612) (VOL.   WAR
2). FORCES DIPLOM AGREE PEACE SOVEREIGN. PAGE 43   INT/LAW
E0849   MORAL
                                                          SUPEGO

B33

LAUTERPACHT H.,THE FUNCTION OF LAW IN THE   INT/ORG
INTERNATIONAL COMMUNITY. WOR-45 NAT/G FORCES CREATE   LAW
DOMIN LEGIT COERCE WAR PEACE ATTIT ORD/FREE PWR   INT/LAW
SOVEREIGN...JURID CONCPT METH/CNCPT TIME/SEQ
GEN/LAWS GEN/METH LEAGUE/NAT TOT/POP VAL/FREE 20.
PAGE 63 E1265

B33

REID H.D.,RECUEIL DES COURS; TOME 45: LES   ORD/FREE
SERVITUDES INTERNATIONALES III. FRANCE CONSTN   DIPLOM
DELIB/GP PRESS CONTROL REV WAR CHOOSE PEACE MORAL   LAW
MARITIME TREATY. PAGE 84 E1680

B34

WOLFF C.,JUS GENTIUM METHODO SCIENTIFICA   NAT/G
PERTRACTATUM. MOD/EUR INT/ORG VOL/ASSN LEGIT PEACE   LAW
ATTIT...JURID 20. PAGE 107 E2140   INT/LAW
                                                          WAR

B35

FOREIGN AFFAIRS BIBLIOGRAPHY: A SELECTED AND   BIBLIOG/A
ANNOTATED LIST OF BOOKS ON INTERNATIONAL RELATIONS   DIPLOM
1919-1962 (4 VOLS.). CONSTN FORCES COLONIAL   INT/ORG
ARMS/CONT WAR NAT/LISM PEACE ATTIT DRIVE...POLICY
INT/LAW 20. PAGE 2 E0032

B35

HUDSON M.,BY PACIFIC MEANS. WOR-45 EDU/PROP   INT/ORG
ORD/FREE...CONCPT TIME/SEQ GEN/LAWS LEAGUE/NAT   CT/SYS
TOT/POP 20 TREATY. PAGE 56 E1110   PEACE

B36

BRIERLY J.L.,THE LAW OF NATIONS (2ND ED.). WOR+45   DIPLOM
WOR-45 INT/ORG AGREE CONTROL COERCE WAR NAT/LISM   INT/LAW
PEACE PWR 16/20 TREATY LEAGUE/NAT. PAGE 15 E0297   NAT/G

B38

HAGUE PERMANENT CT INTL JUSTIC.WORLD COURT REPORTS: INT/ORG
COLLECTION OF THE JUDGEMENTS ORDERS AND OPINIONS   CT/SYS
VOLUME 3 1932-35. WOR-45 LAW DELIB/GP CONFER WAR   DIPLOM
PEACE ATTIT...DECISION ANTHOL 20 WORLD/CT CASEBOOK.   ADJUD
PAGE 49 E0976

B38

SAINT-PIERRE C.I.,SCHEME FOR LASTING PEACE (TRANS.   INT/ORG
BY H. BELLOT). INDUS NAT/G CHIEF FORCES INT/TRADE   PEACE
CT/SYS WAR PWR SOVEREIGN WEALTH...POLICY 18.   AGREE
PAGE 87 E1741   INT/LAW

B40

CARR E.H.,THE TWENTY YEARS' CRISIS 1919-1939. FUT   INT/ORG
WOR-45 BAL/PWR ECO/TAC LEGIT TOTALISM ATTIT   DIPLOM
ALL/VALS...POLICY JURID CONCPT TIME/SEQ TREND   PEACE
GEN/LAWS TOT/POP 20. PAGE 20 E0393

B40

CONOVER H.F.,FOREIGN RELATIONS OF THE UNITED   BIBLIOG/A
STATES: A LIST OF RECENT BOOKS (PAMPHLET). ASIA   USA-45
CANADA L/A+17C UK INT/ORG INT/TRADE TARIFFS NEUTRAL   DIPLOM
WAR PEACE...INT/LAW CON/ANAL 20 CHINJAP. PAGE 25
E0492

B41

BIRDSALL P.,VERSAILLES TWENTY YEARS AFTER. MOD/EUR   DIPLOM
POL/PAR CHIEF CONSULT FORCES LEGIS REPAR PEACE   NAT/LISM
ORD/FREE...BIBLIOG 20 PRESIDENT TREATY. PAGE 12   WAR
E0231

L41

COMM. STUDY ORGAN. PEACE,"ORGANIZATION OF PEACE."   INT/ORG
USA-45 WOR-45 STRATA NAT/G ACT/RES DIPLOM ECO/TAC   PLAN
EDU/PROP ADJUD ATTIT ORD/FREE PWR...SOC CONCPT   PEACE
ANTHOL LEAGUE/NAT 20. PAGE 24 E0479

S41

WRIGHT Q.,"FUNDAMENTAL PROBLEMS OF INTERNATIONAL   INT/ORG
ORGANIZATION." UNIV WOR-45 STRUCT FORCES ACT/RES   ATTIT
CREATE DOMIN EDU/PROP LEGIT REGION NAT/LISM   PEACE
ORD/FREE PWR RESPECT SOVEREIGN...JURID SOC CONCPT
METH/CNCPT TIME/SEQ 20. PAGE 107 E2152

B42

FULLER G.H.,DEFENSE FINANCING: A SUPPLEMENTARY LIST   BIBLIOG/A
OF REFERENCES (PAMPHLET). CANADA UK USA-45 ECO/DEV   FINAN
NAT/G DELIB/GP BUDGET ADJUD ARMS/CONT WEAPON COST   FORCES
PEACE PWR 20 AUSTRAL CHINJAP CONGRESS. PAGE 41   DIPLOM
E0821

B42

HAMBRO C.J.,HOW TO WIN THE PEACE. ECO/TAC EDU/PROP   FUT
ADJUD PERSON ALL/VALS...SOCIALIST TREND GEN/LAWS   INT/ORG
20. PAGE 50 E0987   PEACE

B42

KELSEN H.,LAW AND PEACE IN INTERNATIONAL RELATIONS.   INT/ORG
FUT WOR-45 NAT/G DELIB/GP DIPLOM LEGIT RIGID/FLEX   ADJUD
ORD/FREE SOVEREIGN...JURID CONCPT TREND STERTYP   PEACE
GEN/LAWS LEAGUE/NAT 20. PAGE 60 E1197   INT/LAW

B43

BEMIS S.F.,THE LATIN AMERICAN POLICY OF THE UNITED   DIPLOM
STATES: AN HISTORICAL INTERPRETATION. INT/ORG AGREE   SOVEREIGN
COLONIAL WAR PEACE ATTIT ORD/FREE...POLICY INT/LAW   USA-45
CHARTS 18/20 MEXIC/AMER WILSON/W MONROE/DOC.   L/A+17C
PAGE 10 E0185

B43

CONOVER H.F.,THE BALKANS: A SELECTED LIST OF   BIBLIOG
REFERENCES. ALBANIA BULGARIA ROMANIA YUGOSLAVIA   EUR+WWI
INT/ORG PROB/SOLV DIPLOM LEGIT CONFER ADJUD WAR
NAT/LISM PEACE PWR 20 LEAGUE/NAT. PAGE 25 E0493

B43

HAGUE PERMANENT CT INTL JUSTIC.WORLD COURT REPORTS: INT/ORG
COLLECTION OF THE JUDGEMENTS ORDERS AND OPINIONS   CT/SYS
VOLUME 4 1936-42. WOR-45 CONFER PEACE ATTIT   DIPLOM
...DECISION JURID ANTHOL 20 WORLD/CT CASEBOOK.   ADJUD
PAGE 49 E0977

B43

MICAUD C.A.,THE FRENCH RIGHT AND NAZI GERMANY   DIPLOM
1933-1939: A STUDY OF PUBLIC OPINION. GERMANY UK   AGREE
USSR POL/PAR ARMS/CONT COERCE DETER PEACE
RIGID/FLEX PWR MARXISM...FASCIST TREND 20
LEAGUE/NAT TREATY. PAGE 73 E1454

C43

BENTHAM J.,"PRINCIPLES OF INTERNATIONAL LAW" IN J.   INT/LAW
BOWRING, ED., THE WORKS OF JEREMY BENTHAM." UNIV   JURID
NAT/G PLAN PROB/SOLV DIPLOM CONTROL SANCTION MORAL   WAR
ORD/FREE PWR SOVEREIGN 19. PAGE 10 E0194   PEACE

B44

ADLER M.J.,HOW TO THINK ABOUT WAR AND PEACE. WOR-45   INT/ORG
LAW SOCIETY EX/STRUC DIPLOM KNOWL ORD/FREE...POLICY   CREATE
TREND GEN/LAWS 20. PAGE 3 E0049   ARMS/CONT
                                                     PEACE

BRIERLY J.L.,THE OUTLOOK FOR INTERNATIONAL LAW. FUT INT/ORG
WOR-45 CONSTN NAT/G VOL/ASSN FORCES ECO/TAC DOMIN LAW
LEGIT ADJUD ROUTINE PEACE ORD/FREE...INT/LAW JURID
METH LEAGUE/NAT 20. PAGE 15 E0298
B44

DE HUSZAR G.B.,NEW PERSPECTIVES ON PEACE. UNIV ATTIT
CULTURE SOCIETY ECO/DEV ECO/UNDEV NAT/G FORCES MYTH
CREATE ECO/TAC DOMIN ADJUD COERCE DRIVE ORD/FREE PEACE
...GEOG JURID PSY SOC CONCPT TOT/POP. PAGE 29 E0584 WAR
B44

RUDIN H.R.,ARMISTICE 1918. FRANCE GERMANY MOD/EUR AGREE
UK USA+45 NAT/G CHIEF DELIB/GP FORCES BAL/PWR REPAR WAR
ARMS/CONT 20 WILSON/W TREATY. PAGE 86 E1732 PEACE
DIPLOM
B44

BEVERIDGE W.,THE PRICE OF PEACE. GERMANY UK WOR+45 INT/ORG
WOR-45 NAT/G FORCES CREATE LEGIT REGION WAR ATTIT TREND
KNOWL ORD/FREE PWR...POLICY NEW/IDEA GEN/LAWS PEACE
LEAGUE/NAT 20 TREATY. PAGE 12 E0223
B45

REVES E.,THE ANATOMY OF PEACE. WOR-45 LAW CULTURE ACT/RES
NAT/G PLAN TEC/DEV EDU/PROP WAR NAT/LISM ATTIT CONCPT
ALL/VALS SOVEREIGN...POLICY HUM TIME/SEQ 20. NUC/PWR
PAGE 84 E1688 PEACE
B45

TINGSTERN H.,PEACE AND SECURITY AFTER WW II. WOR-45 INT/ORG
DELIB/GP TOP/EX LEGIT CT/SYS COERCE PEACE ATTIT ORD/FREE
PERCEPT...CONCPT LEAGUE/NAT 20. PAGE 96 E1927 WAR
INT/LAW
B45

KEETON G.W.,MAKING INTERNATIONAL LAW WORK. FUT INT/ORG
WOR-45 NAT/G DELIB/GP FORCES LEGIT COERCE PEACE ADJUD
ATTIT RIGID/FLEX ORD/FREE PWR...JURID CONCPT INT/LAW
HIST/WRIT GEN/METH LEAGUE/NAT 20. PAGE 60 E1193
B46

HYDE C.C.,INTERNATIONAL LAW, CHIEFLY AS INTERPRETED INT/LAW
AND APPLIED BY THE UNITED STATES (3 VOLS., 2ND REV. DIPLOM
ED.). USA-45 WOR+45 WOR-45 INT/ORG CT/SYS WAR NAT/G
NAT/LISM PEACE ORD/FREE...JURID 19/20 TREATY. POLICY
PAGE 56 E1119
B47

MORGENTHAL H.J.,POLITICS AMONG NATIONS: THE DIPLOM
STRUGGLE FOR POWER AND PEACE. FUT WOR+45 INT/ORG PEACE
OP/RES PROB/SOLV BAL/PWR CONTROL ATTIT MORAL PWR
...INT/LAW BIBLIOG 20 COLD/WAR. PAGE 75 E1494 POLICY
B48

MORGENTHAU H.J.,"THE TWILIGHT OF INTERNATIONAL MORAL
MORALITY" (BMR)" WOR+45 WOR-45 BAL/PWR WAR NAT/LISM DIPLOM
PEACE...POLICY INT/LAW IDEA/COMP 15/20 TREATY NAT/G
INTERVENT. PAGE 75 E1495
S48

GROB F.,THE RELATIVITY OF WAR AND PEACE: A STUDY IN WAR
LAW, HISTORY, AND POLITICS. WOR+45 WOR-45 LAW PEACE
DIPLOM DEBATE...CONCPT LING IDEA/COMP BIBLIOG INT/LAW
18/20. PAGE 48 E0944 STYLE
B49

COMM. STUDY ORGAN. PEACE,"A TEN YEAR RECORD, INT/ORG
1939-1949." FUT WOR+45 LAW R+D CONSULT DELIB/GP CONSTN
CREATE LEGIT ROUTINE ORD/FREE...TIME/SEQ UN 20. PEACE
PAGE 24 E0480
L49

KIRK G.,"MATERIALS FOR THE STUDY OF INTERNATIONAL INT/ORG
RELATIONS." FUT UNIV WOR+45 INTELL EDU/PROP ROUTINE ACT/RES
PEACE ATTIT...INT/LAW JURID CONCPT OBS. PAGE 61 DIPLOM
E1219
S49

LAUTERPACHT H.,INTERNATIONAL LAW AND HUMAN RIGHTS. DELIB/GP
USA+45 CONSTN STRUCT INT/ORG ACT/RES EDU/PROP PEACE LAW
PERSON ALL/VALS...CONCPT CON/ANAL GEN/LAWS UN 20. INT/LAW
PAGE 63 E1266
B50

ROSS A.,CONSTITUTION OF THE UNITED NATIONS. CONSTN PEACE
CONSULT DELIB/GP ECO/TAC...INT/LAW JURID 20 UN DIPLOM
LEAGUE/NAT. PAGE 86 E1721 ORD/FREE
INT/ORG
B50

NUMELIN R.,"THE BEGINNINGS OF DIPLOMACY." INT/TRADE DIPLOM
WAR GP/REL PEACE STRANGE ATTIT...INT/LAW CONCPT KIN
BIBLIOG. PAGE 78 E1559 CULTURE
LAW
C50

CORBETT P.E.,LAW AND SOCIETY IN THE RELATIONS OF INT/LAW
STATES. FUT WOR+45 WOR-45 CONTROL WAR PEACE PWR DIPLOM
...POLICY JURID 16/20 TREATY. PAGE 26 E0505 INT/ORG
B51

DU BOIS W.E.B.,IN BATTLE FOR PEACE. AFR USA+45 PEACE
COLONIAL CT/SYS PERS/REL PERSON ORD/FREE...JURID 20 RACE/REL
NEGRO CIVIL/LIB. PAGE 33 E0650 DISCRIM
BIOG
B52

FERRELL R.H.,PEACE IN THEIR TIME. FRANCE UK USA-45 PEACE
INT/ORG NAT/G FORCES CREATE AGREE ARMS/CONT COERCE DIPLOM
WAR TREATY 20 WILSON/W LEAGUE/NAT BRIAND/A. PAGE 37
E0741
B52

GELLHORN W.,THE STATES AND SUBVERSION. USA+45 PROVS
USA-45 LOC/G DELIB/GP LEGIS EDU/PROP LEGIT CT/SYS JURID
REGION PEACE ATTIT ORD/FREE SOCISM...INT CON/ANAL
20 CALIFORNIA MARYLAND ILLINOIS MICHIGAN NEW/YORK.
PAGE 43 E0845
B52

LIPPMANN W.,ISOLATION AND ALLIANCES: AN AMERICAN DIPLOM
SPEAKS TO THE BRITISH. USA+45 USA-45 INT/ORG AGREE SOVEREIGN
COERCE DETER WAR PEACE MORAL 20 TREATY INTERVENT. COLONIAL
PAGE 65 E1301 ATTIT
B52

VANDENBOSCH A.,THE UN: BACKGROUND, ORGANIZATION, DELIB/GP
FUNCTIONS, ACTIVITIES. WOR+45 LAW CONSTN STRUCT TIME/SEQ
INT/ORG CONSULT BAL/PWR EDU/PROP EXEC ALL/VALS PEACE
...POLICY CONCPT UN 20. PAGE 103 E2071
B52

LANDHEER B.,FUNDAMENTALS OF PUBLIC INTERNATIONAL BIBLIOG/A
LAW (SELECTIVE BIBLIOGRAPHIES OF THE LIBRARY OF THE INT/LAW
PEACE PALACE, VOL. I; PAMPH). INT/ORG OP/RES PEACE DIPLOM
...IDEA/COMP 20. PAGE 62 E1250 PHIL/SCI
B53

NUSSBAUM D.,A CONCISE HISTORY OF THE LAW OF INT/ORG
NATIONS. ASIA CHRIST-17C EUR+WWI ISLAM MEDIT-7 LAW
MOD/EUR S/ASIA UNIV WOR+45 WOR-45 SOCIETY STRUCT PEACE
EXEC ATTIT ALL/VALS...CONCPT HIST/WRIT TIME/SEQ. INT/LAW
PAGE 78 E1560
B54

WRIGHT Q.,PROBLEMS OF STABILITY AND PROGRESS IN INT/ORG
INTERNATIONAL RELATIONSHIPS. FUT WOR+45 WOR-45 CONCPT
SOCIETY LEGIS CREATE TEC/DEV ECO/TAC EDU/PROP ADJUD DIPLOM
WAR PEACE ORD/FREE PWR...KNO/TEST TREND GEN/LAWS
20. PAGE 108 E2155
B54

NICOLSON H.,"THE EVOLUTION OF DIPLOMATIC METHOD." RIGID/FLEX
CHRIST-17C EUR+WWI FRANCE FUT ITALY MEDIT-7 MOD/EUR METH/CNCPT
USA+45 USA-45 LAW NAT/G CREATE EDU/PROP LEGIT PEACE DIPLOM
ATTIT ORD/FREE RESPECT SOVEREIGN. PAGE 77 E1548
L54

BURR R.N.,DOCUMENTS ON INTER-AMERICAN COOPERATION: BIBLIOG
VOL. I, 1810-1881; VOL. II, 1881-1948. DELIB/GP DIPLOM
BAL/PWR INT/TRADE REPRESENT NAT/LISM PEACE HABITAT INT/ORG
ORD/FREE PWR SOVEREIGN...INT/LAW 20 OAS. PAGE 18 L/A+17C
E0345
B55

HOGAN W.N.,INTERNATIONAL CONFLICT AND COLLECTIVE INT/ORG
SECURITY: THE PRINCIPLE OF CONCERN IN INTERNATIONAL WAR
ORGANIZATION. CONSTN EX/STRUC BAL/PWR DIPLOM ADJUD ORD/FREE
CONTROL CENTRAL CONSEN PEACE...INT/LAW CONCPT FORCES
METH/COMP 20 UN LEAGUE/NAT. PAGE 53 E1066
B55

KHADDURI M.,WAR AND PEACE IN THE LAW OF ISLAM. ISLAM
CONSTN CULTURE SOCIETY STRATA NAT/G PROVS SECT JURID
FORCES TOP/EX CREATE DOMIN EDU/PROP ADJUD COERCE PEACE
ATTIT RIGID/FLEX ALL/VALS...CONCPT TIME/SEQ TOT/POP WAR
VAL/FREE. PAGE 61 E1209
B55

MAZZINI J.,THE DUTIES OF MAN. MOD/EUR LAW SOCIETY SUPEGO
FAM NAT/G POL/PAR SECT VOL/ASSN EX/STRUC ACT/RES CONCPT
CREATE REV PEACE ATTIT ALL/VALS...GEN/LAWS WORK 19. NAT/LISM
PAGE 70 E1396
B55

UN HEADQUARTERS LIBRARY,BIBLIOGRAPHIE DE LA CHARTE BIBLIOG/A
DES NATIONS UNIES. CHINA/COM KOREA WOR+45 VOL/ASSN INT/ORG
CONFER ADMIN COERCE PEACE ATTIT ORD/FREE SOVEREIGN DIPLOM
...INT/LAW 20 UNESCO UN. PAGE 97 E1953
B55

                                                              S55
WRIGHT Q.,"THE PEACEFUL ADJUSTMENT OF INTERNATIONAL   R+D
RELATIONS: PROBLEMS AND RESEARCH APPROACHES." UNIV   METH/CNCPT
INTELL EDU/PROP ADJUD ROUTINE KNOWL SKILL...INT/LAW   PEACE
JURID PHIL/SCI CLASSIF 20. PAGE 108 E2156

                                                              B56
SOHN L.B.,CASES ON UNITED NATIONS LAW. STRUCT   INT/ORG
DELIB/GP WAR PEACE ORD/FREE...DECISION ANTHOL 20   INT/LAW
UN. PAGE 92 E1854   ADMIN
                                                        ADJUD

                                                              B57
ALIGHIERI D.,ON WORLD GOVERNMENT. ROMAN/EMP LAW   POLICY
SOCIETY INT/ORG NAT/G POL/PAR ADJUD WAR GP/REL   CONCPT
PEACE WORSHIP 15 WORLDUNITY DANTE. PAGE 4 E0067   DIPLOM
                                                        SECT

                                                              B57
COMM. STUDY ORGAN. PEACE,STRENGTHENING THE UNITED   INT/ORG
NATIONS. FUT USA+45 WOR+45 CONSTN NAT/G DELIB/GP   ORD/FREE
FORCES LEGIS ECO/TAC LEGIT COERCE PEACE...JURID
CONCPT UN COLD/WAR 20. PAGE 24 E0482

                                                              B57
INSTITUT DE DROIT INTL,TABLEAU GENERAL DES   INT/LAW
RESOLUTIONS (1873-1956). LAW NEUTRAL CRIME WAR   DIPLOM
MARRIAGE PEACE...JURID 19/20. PAGE 56 E1124   ORD/FREE
                                                        ADJUD

                                                              B57
NEUMANN F.,THE DEMOCRATIC AND THE AUTHORITARIAN   DOMIN
STATE: ESSAYS IN POLITICAL AND LEGAL THEORY. USA+45   NAT/G
USA-45 CONTROL REV GOV/REL PEACE ALL/IDEOS   ORD/FREE
...INT/LAW CONCPT GEN/LAWS BIBLIOG 20. PAGE 77   POLICY
E1536

                                                              B57
ROSENNE S.,THE INTERNATIONAL COURT OF JUSTICE.   INT/ORG
WOR+45 LAW DOMIN LEGIT PEACE PWR SOVEREIGN...JURID   CT/SYS
CONCPT RECORD TIME/SEQ CON/ANAL CHARTS UN TOT/POP   INT/LAW
VAL/FREE LEAGUE/NAT 20 ICJ. PAGE 86 E1716

                                                              B57
US COMMISSION GOVT SECURITY,RECOMMENDATIONS; AREA: POLICY
IMMIGRANT PROGRAM. USA+45 LAW WORKER DIPLOM   CONTROL
EDU/PROP WRITING ADMIN PEACE ATTIT...CONCPT ANTHOL   PLAN
20 MIGRATION SUBVERT. PAGE 99 E1981   NAT/G

                                                              B57
WASSENBERGH H.A.,POST-WAR INTERNATIONAL CIVIL   COM/IND
AVIATION POLICY AND THE LAW OF THE AIR. WOR+45 AIR   NAT/G
INT/ORG DOMIN LEGIT PEACE ORD/FREE...POLICY JURID   INT/LAW
NEW/IDEA OBS TIME/SEQ TREND CHARTS 20 TREATY.
PAGE 105 E2101

                                                              B58
ATOMIC INDUSTRIAL FORUM,MANAGEMENT AND ATOMIC   NUC/PWR
ENERGY. WOR+45 SEA LAW MARKET NAT/G TEC/DEV INSPECT   INDUS
INT/TRADE CONFER PEACE HEALTH...ANTHOL 20. PAGE 6   MGT
E0112   ECO/TAC

                                                              B58
SCHOEDER P.W.,THE AXIS ALLIANCE AND JAPANESE-   AGREE
AMERICAN RELATIONS 1941. ASIA GERMANY UK USA-45   DIPLOM
PEACE ATTIT...POLICY BIBLIOG 20 CHINJAP TREATY.   WAR
PAGE 88 E1763

                                                              B58
SOC OF COMP LEGIS AND INT LAW,THE LAW OF THE SEA...   INT/LAW
(PAMPHLET). WOR+45 NAT/G INT/TRADE ADJUD CONTROL   INT/ORG
NUC/PWR WAR PEACE ATTIT ORD/FREE...JURID CHARTS 20   DIPLOM
UN TREATY RESOURCE/N. PAGE 92 E1850   SEA

                                                              L58
UNESCO,"TECHNIQUES OF MEDIATION AND CONCILIATION."   INT/ORG
EUR+WWI USA+45 WOR+45 INDUS FACE/GP EX/STRUC   CONSULT
EDU/PROP LEGIT PEACE ORD/FREE...INT/LAW TIME/SEQ   DIPLOM
LEAGUE/NAT 20. PAGE 98 E1961

                                                              B59
SIMPSON J.L.,INTERNATIONAL ARBITRATION: LAW AND   INT/LAW
PRACTICE. WOR+45 WOR-45 INT/ORG DELIB/GP ADJUD   DIPLOM
PEACE MORAL ORD/FREE...METH 18/20. PAGE 91 E1829   CT/SYS
                                                        CONSULT

                                                              S59
JENKS C.W.,"THE CHALLENGE OF UNIVERSALITY." FUT   INT/ORG
UNIV CONSTN CULTURE CONSULT CREATE PLAN LEGIT ATTIT   LAW
MORAL ORD/FREE RESPECT...MAJORIT JURID 20. PAGE 58   PEACE
E1155   INT/LAW

                                                              B60
CLARK G.,WORLD PEACE THROUGH WORLD LAW. FUT WOR+45   INT/ORG
CONSULT FORCES ACT/RES CREATE PLAN ADMIN ROUTINE   LAW
ARMS/CONT DETER ATTIT PWR...JURID VAL/FREE UNESCO   PEACE

20 UN. PAGE 23 E0449   INT/LAW

                                                              B60
UNITED WORLD FEDERALISTS,UNITED WORLD FEDERALISTS;   BIBLIOG/A
PANORAMA OF RECENT BOOKS, FILMS, AND JOURNALS ON   DIPLOM
WORLD FEDERATION. THE UN, AND WORLD PEACE. CULTURE   INT/ORG
ECO/UNDEV PROB/SOLV FOR/AID ARMS/CONT NUC/PWR   PEACE
...INT/LAW PHIL/SCI 20 UN. PAGE 98 E1971

                                                              L60
KUNZ J.,"SANCTIONS IN INTERNATIONAL LAW." WOR+45   INT/ORG
WOR-45 LEGIT ARMS/CONT COERCE PEACE ATTIT   ADJUD
...METH/CNCPT TIME/SEQ TREND 20. PAGE 62 E1234   INT/LAW

                                                              S60
GRACIA-MORA M.R.,"INTERNATIONAL RESPONSIBILITY FOR   INT/ORG
SUBVERSIVE ACTIVITIES AND HOSTILE PROPAGANDA BY   JURID
PRIVATE PERSONS AGAINST." COM EUR+WWI L/A+17C UK   SOVEREIGN
USA+45 USSR WOR-45 CONSTN NAT/G LEGIT ADJUD REV
PEACE TOTALISM ORD/FREE...INT/LAW 20. PAGE 45 E0895

                                                              S60
RHYNE C.S.,"LAW AS AN INSTRUMENT FOR PEACE." FUT   ADJUD
WOR+45 PLAN LEGIT ROUTINE ARMS/CONT NUC/PWR ATTIT   EDU/PROP
ORD/FREE...JURID METH/CNCPT TREND CON/ANAL HYPO/EXP   INT/LAW
COLD/WAR 20. PAGE 84 E1690   PEACE

                                                              B61
ALFRED H.,PUBLIC OWNERSHIP IN THE USA: GOALS AND   CONTROL
PRIORITIES. LAW INDUS INT/TRADE ADJUD GOV/REL   OWN
EFFICIENCY PEACE SOCISM...POLICY ANTHOL 20 TVA.   ECO/DEV
PAGE 3 E0064   ECO/TAC

                                                              B61
BRENNAN D.G.,ARMS CONTROL, DISARMAMENT, AND   ARMS/CONT
NATIONAL SECURITY. WOR+45 NAT/G FORCES CREATE   ORD/FREE
PROB/SOLV PARTIC WAR PEACE...DECISION INT/LAW   DIPLOM
ANTHOL BIBLIOG 20. PAGE 15 E0291   POLICY

                                                              B61
MECHAM J.L.,THE UNITED STATES AND INTER-AMERICAN   DIPLOM
SECURITY: 1889-1960. L/A+17C USA+45 USA-45 CONSTN   WAR
FORCES INT/TRADE PEACE TOTALISM ATTIT...JURID 19/20   ORD/FREE
UN OAS. PAGE 72 E1432   INT/ORG

                                                              B61
RIENOW R.,CONTEMPORARY INTERNATIONAL POLITICS.   DIPLOM
WOR+45 INT/ORG BAL/PWR EDU/PROP COLONIAL NEUTRAL   PWR
REGION WAR PEACE...INT/LAW 20 COLD/WAR UN. PAGE 85   POLICY
E1698   NAT/G

                                                              B61
SYATAUW J.J.G.,SOME NEWLY ESTABLISHED ASIAN STATES   INT/LAW
AND THE DEVELOPMENT OF INTERNATIONAL LAW. BURMA   ADJUST
CEYLON INDIA INDONESIA ECO/UNDEV COLONIAL NEUTRAL   SOCIETY
WAR PEACE SOVEREIGN...CHARTS 19/20. PAGE 95 E1902   S/ASIA

                                                              S61
CASTANEDA J.,"THE UNDERDEVELOPED NATIONS AND THE   INT/ORG
DEVELOPMENT OF INTERNATIONAL LAW." FUT UNIV LAW   ECO/UNDEV
ACT/RES FOR/AID LEGIT PERCEPT SKILL...JURID   PEACE
METH/CNCPT TIME/SEQ TOT/POP 20 UN. PAGE 21 E0405   INT/LAW

                                                              S61
JACKSON E.,"THE FUTURE DEVELOPMENT OF THE UNITED   INT/ORG
NATIONS: SOME SUGGESTIONS FOR RESEARCH." FUT LAW   PWR
CONSTN ECO/DEV FINAN PEACE WEALTH...WELF/ST CONCPT
UN 20. PAGE 57 E1140

                                                              S61
MILLER E.,"LEGAL ASPECTS OF UN ACTION IN THE   INT/ORG
CONGO." AFR CULTURE ADMIN PEACE DRIVE RIGID/FLEX   LEGIT
ORD/FREE...WELF/ST JURID OBS UN CONGO 20. PAGE 73
E1458

                                                              B62
BIBLIOTHEQUE PALAIS DE LA PAIX,CATALOGUE OF THE   BIBLIOG
PEACE PALACE LIBRARY, SUPPLEMENT 1937-1952 (7   INT/LAW
VOLS.). WOR+45 WOR-45 INT/ORG NAT/G ADJUD WAR PEACE   DIPLOM
...JURID 20. PAGE 12 E0225

                                                              B62
DUPRE J.S.,SCIENCE AND THE NATION: POLICY AND   R+D
POLITICS. USA+45 LAW ACADEM FORCES ADMIN CIVMIL/REL   INDUS
GOV/REL EFFICIENCY PEACE...TREND 20 SCI/ADVSRY.   TEC/DEV
PAGE 34 E0665   NUC/PWR

                                                              B62
DUROSELLE J.B.,HISTOIRE DIPLOMATIQUE DE 1919 A NOS   DIPLOM
JOURS (3RD ED.). FRANCE INT/ORG CHIEF FORCES CONFER   WOR+45
ARMS/CONT WAR PEACE ORD/FREE...T TREATY 20   WOR-45
COLD/WAR. PAGE 34 E0667

                                                              B62
JACOBINI H.B.,INTERNATIONAL LAW: A TEXT. DIPLOM   INT/LAW
ADJUD NEUTRAL WAR PEACE T. PAGE 57 E1143   CT/SYS

CONCPT

MCDOUGAL M.S.,THE PUBLIC ORDER OF THE OCEANS. B62
WOR+45 WOR-45 SEA INT/ORG NAT/G CONSULT DELIB/GP ADJUD
DIPLOM LEGIT PEACE RIGID/FLEX...GEOG INT/LAW JURID ORD/FREE
RECORD TOT/POP 20 TREATY. PAGE 70 E1407

B62
PERKINS D.,AMERICA'S QUEST FOR PEACE. USA+45 WOR+45 INT/LAW
DIPLOM CONFER NAT/LISM ATTIT 20 UN TREATY. PAGE 80 INT/ORG
E1610 ARMS/CONT
PEACE

B62
ROSENNE S.,THE WORLD COURT: WHAT IT IS AND HOW IT INT/ORG
WORKS. WOR+45 WOR-45 LAW CONSTN JUDGE EDU/PROP ADJUD
LEGIT ROUTINE CHOOSE PEACE ORD/FREE...JURID OBS INT/LAW
TIME/SEQ CHARTS UN TOT/POP VAL/FREE 20. PAGE 86
E1717

B62
US CONGRESS,COMMUNICATIONS SATELLITE LEGISLATION: SPACE
HEARINGS BEFORE COMM ON AERON AND SPACE SCIENCES ON COM/IND
BILLS S2550 AND 2814. WOR+45 LAW VOL/ASSN PLAN ADJUD
DIPLOM CONTROL OWN PEACE...NEW/IDEA CONGRESS NASA. GOV/REL
PAGE 99 E1990

B62
WADSWORTH J.J.,THE PRICE OF PEACE. WOR+45 TEC/DEV DIPLOM
CONTROL NUC/PWR PEACE ATTIT TREATY 20. PAGE 104 INT/ORG
E2089 ARMS/CONT
POLICY

S62
MCWHINNEY E.,"CO-EXISTENCE, THE CUBA CRISIS, AND CONCPT
COLD WAR-INTERNATIONAL WAR." CUBA USA+45 USSR INT/LAW
WOR+45 NAT/G TOP/EX BAL/PWR DIPLOM DOMIN LEGIT
PEACE RIGID/FLEX ORD/FREE...STERTYP COLD/WAR 20.
PAGE 71 E1427

B63
BADI J.,THE GOVERNMENT OF THE STATE OF ISRAEL: A NAT/G
CRITICAL ACCOUNT OF ITS PARLIAMENT, EXECUTIVE, AND CONSTN
JUDICIARY. ISRAEL ECO/DEV CHIEF DELIB/GP LEGIS EX/STRUC
DIPLOM CT/SYS INGP/REL PEACE ORD/FREE...BIBLIOG 20 POL/PAR
PARLIAMENT ARABS MIGRATION. PAGE 7 E0131

B63
DOUGLAS W.O.,THE ANATOMY OF LIBERTY: THE RIGHTS OF PEACE
MAN WITHOUT FORCE. WOR+45 ECO/DEV ECO/UNDEV LOC/G LAW
FORCES GOV/REL...SOC/WK 20. PAGE 32 E0643 DIPLOM
ORD/FREE

B63
DUNN F.S.,PEACE-MAKING AND THE SETTLEMENT WITH POLICY
JAPAN. ASIA USA+45 USA-45 FORCES BAL/PWR ECO/TAC PEACE
CONFER WAR PWR SOVEREIGN 20 CHINJAP COLD/WAR PLAN
TREATY. PAGE 33 E0661 DIPLOM

B63
FALK R.A.,LAW, MORALITY, AND WAR IN THE ADJUD
CONTEMPORARY WORLD. WOR+45 LAW INT/ORG EX/STRUC ARMS/CONT
FORCES EDU/PROP LEGIT DETER NUC/PWR MORAL ORD/FREE PEACE
...JURID TOT/POP 20. PAGE 36 E0715 INT/LAW

B63
JENKS C.W.,LAW, FREEDOM, AND WELFARE. WOR+45 GIVE INT/LAW
ADJUD WAR PEACE HABITAT ORD/FREE. PAGE 58 E1159 DIPLOM
SOVEREIGN
PROB/SOLV

B63
PACHTER H.M.,COLLISION COURSE; THE CUBAN MISSILE WAR
CRISIS AND COEXISTENCE. CUBA USA+45 DIPLOM BAL/PWR
ARMS/CONT PEACE MARXISM...DECISION INT/LAW 20 NUC/PWR
COLD/WAR KHRUSH/N KENNEDY/JF CASTRO/F. PAGE 79 DETER
E1587

B63
ROSNER G.,THE UNITED NATIONS EMERGENCY FORCE. INT/ORG
FRANCE ISRAEL UAR UK WOR+45 CREATE WAR PEACE FORCES
ORD/FREE PWR...INT/LAW JURID HIST/WRIT TIME/SEQ UN.
PAGE 86 E1719

B63
US SENATE,DOCUMENTS ON INTERNATIONAL ASPECTS OF SPACE
EXPLORATION AND USE OF OUTER SPACE, 1954-62: STAFF UTIL
REPORT FOR COMM AERON SPACE SCI. USA+45 USSR LEGIS GOV/REL
LEAD CIVMIL/REL PEACE...POLICY INT/LAW ANTHOL 20 DIPLOM
CONGRESS NASA KHRUSH/N. PAGE 101 E2026

B63
VAN SLYCK P.,PEACE: THE CONTROL OF NATIONAL POWER. ARMS/CONT
CUBA WOR+45 FINAN NAT/G FORCES PROB/SOLV TEC/DEV PEACE
BAL/PWR ADMIN CONTROL ORD/FREE...POLICY INT/LAW UN INT/ORG

COLD/WAR TREATY. PAGE 103 E2069 DIPLOM

S63
GARDNER R.N.,"COOPERATION IN OUTER SPACE." FUT USSR INT/ORG
WOR+45 AIR LAW COM/IND CONSULT DELIB/GP CREATE ACT/RES
KNOWL 20 TREATY. PAGE 42 E0837 PEACE
SPACE

B64
BLOUSTEIN E.J.,NUCLEAR ENERGY, PUBLIC POLICY, AND TEC/DEV
THE LAW. USA+45 NAT/G ADJUD ADMIN GP/REL OWN PEACE LAW
ATTIT HEALTH...ANTHOL 20. PAGE 13 E0251 POLICY
NUC/PWR

B64
FREUD A.,OF HUMAN SOVEREIGNTY. WOR+45 INDUS SECT NAT/LISM
ECO/TAC CRIME CHOOSE ATTIT MORAL MARXISM...POLICY DIPLOM
BIBLIOG 20. PAGE 40 E0794 WAR
PEACE

B64
FRYDENSBERG P.,PEACE-KEEPING: EXPERIENCE AND INT/ORG
EVALUATION: THE OSLO PAPERS. NORWAY FORCES PLAN DIPLOM
CONTROL...INT/LAW 20 UN. PAGE 41 E0814 PEACE
COERCE

B64
GARDNER R.N.,IN PURSUIT OF WORLD ORDER* US FOREIGN OBS
POLICY AND INTERNATIONAL ORGANIZATIONS. USA+45 USSR INT/ORG
ECO/UNDEV FORCES LEGIS DIPLOM FOR/AID INT/TRADE ALL/VALS
PEACE...INT/LAW PREDICT UN. PAGE 42 E0839

B64
MCWHINNEY E.,"PEACEFUL COEXISTENCE" AND SOVIET- PEACE
WESTERN INTERNATIONAL LAW. USSR DIPLOM LEAD...JURID IDEA/COMP
20 COLD/WAR. PAGE 71 E1429 INT/LAW
ATTIT

B64
OSSENBECK F.J.,OPEN SPACE AND PEACE. CHINA/COM FUT SPACE
USA+45 USSR LAW PROB/SOLV TEC/DEV EDU/PROP NEUTRAL ORD/FREE
PEACE...AUD/VIS ANTHOL 20. PAGE 79 E1583 DIPLOM
CREATE

B64
REGALA R.,WORLD PEACE THROUGH DIPLOMACY AND LAW. DIPLOM
S/ASIA WOR+45 ECO/UNDEV INT/ORG FORCES PLAN PEACE
PROB/SOLV FOR/AID NUC/PWR WAR...POLICY INT/LAW 20. ADJUD
PAGE 84 E1679

B64
RUSSELL R.B.,UNITED NATIONS EXPERIENCE WITH FORCES
MILITARY FORCES: POLITICAL AND LEGAL ASPECTS. AFR DIPLOM
KOREA WOR+45 LEGIS PROB/SOLV ADMIN CONTROL SANCTION
EFFICIENCY PEACE...POLICY INT/LAW BIBLIOG UN. ORD/FREE
PAGE 87 E1738

B64
SCHWARTZ M.D.,CONFERENCE ON SPACE SCIENCE AND SPACE SPACE
LAW. FUT COM/IND NAT/G FORCES ACT/RES PLAN BUDGET LAW
DIPLOM NUC/PWR WEAPON...POLICY ANTHOL 20. PAGE 89 PEACE
E1788 TEC/DEV

B64
SCHWELB E.,HUMAN RIGHTS AND THE INTERNATIONAL INT/ORG
COMMUNITY. WOR+45 WOR-45 NAT/G SECT DELIB/GP DIPLOM ORD/FREE
PEACE RESPECT TREATY 20 UN. PAGE 89 E1792 INT/LAW

B64
SEGAL R.,SANCTIONS AGAINST SOUTH AFRICA. AFR SANCTION
SOUTH/AFR NAT/G INT/TRADE RACE/REL PEACE PWR DISCRIM
...INT/LAW ANTHOL 20 UN. PAGE 90 E1801 ECO/TAC
POLICY

B64
TAUBENFELD H.J.,SPACE AND SOCIETY. USA+45 LAW SPACE
FORCES CREATE TEC/DEV ADJUD CONTROL COST PEACE SOCIETY
...PREDICT ANTHOL 20. PAGE 95 E1911 ADJUST
DIPLOM

B64
THANT U.,TOWARD WORLD PEACE. DELIB/GP TEC/DEV DIPLOM
EDU/PROP WAR SOVEREIGN...INT/LAW 20 UN MID/EAST. BIOG
PAGE 96 E1915 PEACE
COERCE

B64
UN PUB. INFORM. ORGAN.,EVERY MAN'S UNITED NATIONS. INT/ORG
UNIV WOR+45 CONSTN CULTURE SOCIETY ECO/DEV ROUTINE
ECO/UNDEV NAT/G ACT/RES PLAN ECO/TAC INT/TRADE
EDU/PROP LEGIT PEACE ATTIT ALL/VALS...POLICY HUM
INT/LAW CONCPT CHARTS UN TOT/POP 20. PAGE 97 E1954

B64
US AIR FORCE ACADEMY ASSEMBLY,OUTER SPACE: FINAL SPACE
REPORT APRIL 1-4, 1964. FUT USA+45 WOR+45 LAW CIVMIL/REL

DELIB/GP CONFER ARMS/CONT WAR PEACE ATTIT MORAL
...ANTHOL 20 NASA. PAGE 99 E1979
    NUC/PWR
    DIPLOM

B64
WILLIAMS S.P.,TOWARD A GENUINE WORLD SECURITY
SYSTEM (PAMPHLET). WOR+45 INT/ORG FORCES PLAN
NUC/PWR ORD/FREE...INT/LAW CONCPT UN PRESIDENT.
PAGE 106 E2123
    BIBLIOG/A
    ARMS/CONT
    DIPLOM
    PEACE

B64
WRIGHT Q.,A STUDY OF WAR. LAW NAT/G PROB/SOLV
BAL/PWR NAT/LISM PEACE ATTIT SOVEREIGN...CENSUS
SOC/INTEG. PAGE 108 E2159
    WAR
    CONCPT
    DIPLOM
    CONTROL

L64
BERKS R.N.,"THE US AND WEAPONS CONTROL." WOR+45 LAW
INT/ORG LEGIS EXEC COERCE PEACE ATTIT
RIGID/FLEX ALL/VALS PWR...POLICY TOT/POP 20.
PAGE 11 E0204
    USA+45
    PLAN
    ARMS/CONT

S64
CARNEGIE ENDOWMENT INT. PEACE,"HUMAN RIGHTS (ISSUES
BEFORE THE NINETEENTH GENERAL ASSEMBLY)." AFR
WOR+45 LAW CONSTN NAT/G EDU/PROP GP/REL DISCRIM
PEACE ATTIT MORAL ORD/FREE...INT/LAW PSY CONCPT
RECORD UN 20. PAGE 20 E0385
    INT/ORG
    PERSON
    RACE/REL

S64
CARNEGIE ENDOWMENT INT. PEACE,"LEGAL QUESTIONS
(ISSUES BEFORE THE NINETEENTH GENERAL ASSEMBLY)."
WOR+45 CONSTN NAT/G DELIB/GP ADJUD PEACE MORAL
ORD/FREE...RECORD UN 20 TREATY. PAGE 20 E0386
    INT/ORG
    LAW
    INT/LAW

S64
CRANE R.D.,"BASIC PRINCIPLES IN SOVIET SPACE LAW."
FUT WOR+45 AIR INT/ORG DIPLOM DOMIN ARMS/CONT
COERCE NUC/PWR PEACE ATTIT DRIVE PWR...INT/LAW
METH/CNCPT NEW/IDEA OBS TREND GEN/LAWS VAL/FREE
MARX/KARL 20. PAGE 27 E0544
    COM
    LAW
    USSR
    SPACE

S64
GREENBERG S.,"JUDAISM AND WORLD JUSTICE." MEDIT-7
WOR+45 LAW CULTURE SOCIETY INT/ORG NAT/G FORCES
EDU/PROP ATTIT DRIVE PERSON SUPEGO ALL/VALS
...POLICY PSY CONCPT GEN/LAWS JEWS. PAGE 46 E0908
    SECT
    JURID
    PEACE

S64
HICKEY D.,"THE PHILOSOPHICAL ARGUMENT FOR WORLD
GOVERNMENT." WOR+45 SOCIETY ACT/RES PLAN LEGIT
ADJUD PEACE PERCEPT PERSON ORD/FREE...HUM JURID
PHIL/SCI METH/CNCPT CON/ANAL STERTYP GEN/LAWS
TOT/POP 20. PAGE 52 E1039
    FUT
    INT/ORG

S64
KARPOV P.V.,"PEACEFUL COEXISTENCE AND INTERNATIONAL
LAW." WOR+45 LAW SOCIETY INT/ORG VOL/ASSN FORCES
CREATE CAP/ISM DIPLOM ADJUD NUC/PWR PEACE MORAL
ORD/FREE PWR MARXISM...MARXIST JURID CONCPT OBS
TREND COLD/WAR MARX/KARL 20. PAGE 59 E1186
    COM
    ATTIT
    INT/LAW
    USSR

S64
LIPSON L.,"PEACEFUL COEXISTENCE." COM USSR WOR+45
LAW INT/ORG DIPLOM LEGIT ADJUD ORD/FREE...CONCPT
OBS TREND GEN/LAWS VAL/FREE COLD/WAR 20. PAGE 65
E1303
    ATTIT
    JURID
    INT/LAW
    PEACE

S64
MCGHEE G.C.,"EAST-WEST RELATIONS TODAY." WOR+45
PROB/SOLV BAL/PWR PEACE 20 COLD/WAR. PAGE 71 E1413
    IDEA/COMP
    DIPLOM
    ADJUD

S64
SCHWELB E.,"OPERATION OF THE EUROPEAN CONVENTION ON
HUMAN RIGHTS." EUR+WWI LAW SOCIETY CREATE EDU/PROP
ADJUD ADMIN PEACE ATTIT ORD/FREE PWR...POLICY
INT/LAW CONCPT OBS GEN/LAWS UN VAL/FREE ILO 20
ECHR. PAGE 89 E1791
    INT/ORG
    MORAL

B65
FORGAC A.A.,NEW DIPLOMACY AND THE UNITED NATIONS.
FRANCE GERMANY UK USSR INT/ORG DELIB/GP EX/STRUC
PEACE...INT/LAW CONCPT UN. PAGE 39 E0770
    DIPLOM
    ETIQUET
    NAT/G

B65
MORRIS R.B.,THE PEACEMAKERS; THE GREAT POWERS AND
AMERICAN INDEPENDENCE. BAL/PWR CONFER COLONIAL
NEUTRAL PEACE ORD/FREE TREATY 18 PRE/US/AM. PAGE 75
E1499
    SOVEREIGN
    REV
    DIPLOM

S65
FRIEDHEIM R.,"THE 'SATISFIED' AND 'DISSATISFIED'
STATES NEGOTIATE INTERNATIONAL LAW* A CASE STUDY."
DIPLOM CONFER ADJUD CONSEN PEACE ATTIT UN. PAGE 40
E0799
    INT/LAW
    RECORD

S65
HAZARD J.N.,"CO-EXISTENCE LAW BOWS OUT." WOR+45 R+D
INT/ORG VOL/ASSN CONSULT DELIB/GP ACT/RES CREATE
PEACE KNOWL...JURID CONCPT COLD/WAR VAL/FREE 20.
PAGE 51 E1018
    PROF/ORG
    ADJUD

S65
LUSKY L.,"FOUR PROBLEMS IN LAWMAKING FOR PEACE."
FORCES LEGIS CREATE ADJUD COERCE WAR MAJORITY PEACE
PWR. PAGE 67 E1334
    ORD/FREE
    INT/LAW
    UTOPIA
    RECORD

B66
CANFIELD L.H.,THE PRESIDENCY OF WOODROW WILSON:
PRELUDE TO A WORLD IN CRISIS. USA-45 ADJUD NEUTRAL
WAR CHOOSE INGP/REL PEACE ORD/FREE 20 WILSON/W
PRESIDENT TREATY LEAGUE/NAT. PAGE 19 E0373
    PERSON
    POLICY
    DIPLOM
    GOV/REL

B66
CLARK G.,WORLD PEACE THROUGH WORLD LAW; TWO
ALTERNATIVE PLANS. WOR+45 DELIB/GP FORCES TAX
CONFER ADJUD SANCTION ARMS/CONT WAR CHOOSE PRIVIL
20 UN COLD/WAR. PAGE 23 E0450
    INT/LAW
    PEACE
    PLAN
    INT/ORG

B66
INTL ATOMIC ENERGY AGENCY,INTERNATIONAL CONVENTIONS
ON CIVIL LIABILITY FOR NUCLEAR DAMAGE. FUT WOR+45
ADJUD WAR COST PEACE SOVEREIGN...JURID 20. PAGE 57
E1135
    DIPLOM
    INT/ORG
    DELIB/GP
    NUC/PWR

B66
OBERMANN E.,VERTEIDIGUNG PER FREIHEIT. GERMANY/W
WOR+45 INT/ORG COERCE NUC/PWR WEAPON MARXISM 20 UN
NATO WARSAW/P TREATY. PAGE 78 E1571
    FORCES
    ORD/FREE
    WAR
    PEACE

B66
SALTER L.M.,RESOLUTION OF INTERNATIONAL CONFLICT.
USA+45 INT/ORG SECT DIPLOM ECO/TAC FOR/AID DETER
NUC/PWR WAR 20. PAGE 87 E1743
    PROB/SOLV
    PEACE
    INT/LAW
    POLICY

B66
THOMPSON J.M.,RUSSIA, BOLSHEVISM, AND THE
VERSAILLES PEACE. RUSSIA USSR INT/ORG NAT/G
DELIB/GP AGREE REV WAR PWR 20 TREATY VERSAILLES
BOLSHEVISM. PAGE 96 E1919
    DIPLOM
    PEACE
    MARXISM

B66
UNITED NATIONS,INTERNATIONAL SPACE BIBLIOGRAPHY.
FUT INT/ORG TEC/DEV DIPLOM ARMS/CONT NUC/PWR
...JURID SOC UN. PAGE 98 E1969
    BIBLIOG
    SPACE
    PEACE
    R+D

B66
WAINHOUSE D.W.,INTERNATIONAL PEACE OBSERVATION: A
HISTORY AND FORECAST. INT/ORG PROB/SOLV BAL/PWR
AGREE ARMS/CONT COERCE NUC/PWR...PREDICT METH/COMP
20 UN LEAGUE/NAT OAS TREATY. PAGE 104 E2092
    PEACE
    DIPLOM

C66
BLAISDELL D.C.,"INTERNATIONAL ORGANIZATION." FUT
WOR+45 ECO/DEV DELIB/GP FORCES EFFICIENCY PEACE
ORD/FREE...INT/LAW 20 UN LEAGUE/NAT NATO. PAGE 12
E0239
    BIBLIOG
    INT/ORG
    DIPLOM
    ARMS/CONT

B67
BOHANNAN P.,LAW AND WARFARE. CULTURE CT/SYS COERCE
REV PEACE...JURID SOC CONCPT ANTHOL 20. PAGE 13
E0259
    METH/COMP
    ADJUD
    WAR
    LAW

B67
HOLCOMBE A.N.,A STRATEGY OF PEACE IN A CHANGING
WORLD. USA+45 WOR+45 LAW NAT/G CREATE DIPLOM
ARMS/CONT WAR...CHARTS 20 UN COLD/WAR. PAGE 54
E1072
    PEACE
    PLAN
    INT/ORG
    INT/LAW

B67
INTERNATIONAL CONCILIATION,ISSUES BEFORE THE 22ND
GENERAL ASSEMBLY. WOR+45 ECO/UNDEV FINAN BAL/PWR
BUDGET INT/TRADE STRANGE ORD/FREE...INT/LAW 20 UN
COLD/WAR. PAGE 57 E1132
    PROB/SOLV
    INT/ORG
    DIPLOM
    PEACE

B67
LAWYERS COMM AMER POLICY VIET,VIETNAM AND
INTERNATIONAL LAW: AN ANALYSIS OF THE LEGALITY OF
THE US MILITARY INVOLVEMENT. VIETNAM LAW INT/ORG
COERCE WEAPON PEACE ORD/FREE 20 UN SEATO TREATY.
PAGE 64 E1271
    INT/LAW
    DIPLOM
    ADJUD
    WAR

B67
PADELFORD N.J.,THE DYNAMICS OF INTERNATIONAL
POLITICS (2ND ED.). WOR+45 LAW INT/ORG FORCES
TEC/DEV REGION NAT/LISM PEACE ATTIT PWR ALL/IDEOS
UN COLD/WAR NATO TREATY. PAGE 79 E1589
    DIPLOM
    NAT/G
    POLICY
    DECISION

RAMUNDO B.A.,PEACEFUL COEXISTENCE: INTERNATIONAL LAW IN THE BUILDING OF COMMUNISM. USSR INT/ORG DIPLOM COLONIAL ARMS/CONT ROLE SOVEREIGN...POLICY METH/COMP NAT/COMP BIBLIOG. PAGE 83 E1673
INT/LAW
PEACE
MARXISM
METH/CNCPT
B67

SLATER J.,THE OAS AND UNITED STATES FOREIGN POLICY. KOREA L/A+17C USA+45 VOL/ASSN RISK COERCE PEACE ORD/FREE MARXISM...TREND 20 OAS. PAGE 92 E1838
INT/ORG
DIPLOM
ALL/IDEOS
ADJUD
B67

US DEPARTMENT OF STATE,TREATIES IN FORCE. USA+45 WOR+45 AGREE WAR PEACE 20 TREATY. PAGE 100 E1999
BIBLIOG
DIPLOM
INT/ORG
DETER
B67

US SENATE COMM ON FOREIGN REL,A SELECT CHRONOLOGY AND BACKGROUND DOCUMENTS RELATING TO THE MIDDLE EAST. ISRAEL UAR LAW INT/ORG FORCES PROB/SOLV CONFER CONSEN PEACE ATTIT...POLICY 20 UN SENATE TRUMAN/HS. PAGE 101 E2033
ISLAM
TIME/SEQ
DIPLOM
B67

"FOCUS ON WORLD LAW." WOR+45 NAT/G CT/SYS PEACE ...BIBLIOG 20 UN. PAGE 2 E0036
INT/LAW
INT/ORG
PROB/SOLV
CONCPT
L67

LEGAULT A.,"ORGANISATION ET CONDUITE DES OPERATIONS DE MAINTIEN DE LA PAIX." FORCES ACT/RES ADJUD AGREE CONTROL NEUTRAL TASK PRIVIL ORD/FREE 20 UN. PAGE 64 E1279
INT/ORG
PEACE
WAR
INT/LAW
L67

DEUTSCH E.P.,"A JUDICIAL PATH TO WORLD PEACE." FUT WOR+45 CONSTN PROB/SOLV DIPLOM LICENSE ADJUD SANCTION CHOOSE REPRESENT NAT/LISM SOVEREIGN 20 ICJ. PAGE 31 E0611
INT/LAW
INT/ORG
JURID
PEACE
S67

FLECHTHEIM O.K.,"BLOC FORMATION VS. DIALOGUE." CONSTN ECO/DEV BAL/PWR PEACE ATTIT PWR COLD/WAR. PAGE 38 E0761
FUT
CAP/ISM
MARXISM
DEBATE
S67

MATTHEWS R.O.,"THE SUEZ CANAL DISPUTE* A CASE STUDY IN PEACEFUL SETTLEMENT." FRANCE ISRAEL UAR UK NAT/G CONTROL LEAD COERCE WAR NAT/LISM ROLE ORD/FREE PWR ...INT/LAW UN 20. PAGE 69 E1389
PEACE
DIPLOM
ADJUD
S67

MC REYNOLDS D.,"THE RESISTANCE." USA+45 LAW ADJUD SANCTION INGP/REL PEACE 20. PAGE 70 E1398
ATTIT
WAR
LEGIT
FORCES
S67

STEEL R.,"WHAT CAN THE UN DO?" RHODESIA ECO/UNDEV DIPLOM ECO/TAC SANCTION...INT/LAW UN. PAGE 93 E1866
INT/ORG
BAL/PWR
PEACE
FOR/AID
S67

TOMASEK R.D.,"THE CHILEAN-BOLIVIAN LAUCA RIVER DISPUTE AND THE OAS." CHILE L/A+17C PROB/SOLV ADJUD CONTROL PEACE 20 BOLIV OAS. PAGE 96 E1930
INT/ORG
DIPLOM
GEOG
WAR
S67

HULL R.H.,LAW AND VIETNAM. COM VIETNAM CONSTN INT/ORG FORCES DIPLOM AGREE COERCE DETER WEAPON PEACE ATTIT 20 UN TREATY. PAGE 56 E1113
POLICY
LAW
WAR
INT/LAW
B68

PEACE/CORP....PEACE CORPS

PEACEFUL COEXISTENCE....SEE PEACE+COLD/WAR

PEARSON/L....LESTER PEARSON

PEASLEE A.J. E1605,E1606

PEASNT/WAR....PEASANT WAR (1525)

PEMBERTON J., E1608

PENN/WM....WILLIAM PENN

PENNSYLVAN....PENNSYLVANIA

BALDWIN L.D.,WHISKEY REBELS; THE STORY OF A FRONTIER UPRISING. USA-45 LAW ADJUD LEAD COERCE PWR ...BIBLIOG/A 18 PENNSYLVAN FEDERALIST. PAGE 8 E0145
REV
POL/PAR
TAX
TIME/SEQ
B39

PENOLOGY....SEE CRIME

PENTAGON....PENTAGON

PEOPLE'S REPUBLIC OF CHINA....SEE CHINA/COM
PEPPER H.W.T. E0646
PERCEPT....PERCEPTION AND COGNITION

GROTIUS H.,DE JURE BELLI AC PACIS. CHRIST-17C UNIV LAW SOCIETY PROVS LEGIT PEACE PERCEPT MORAL PWR ...CONCPT CON/ANAL GEN/LAWS. PAGE 48 E0952
JURID
INT/LAW
WAR
B00

PHILLIPS J.B.,"MODIFICATIONS OF THE JURY SYSTEM." PARTIC EFFICIENCY ATTIT PERCEPT...TREND 19 SUPREME/CT JURY. PAGE 80 E1612
JURID
DELIB/GP
PERS/REL
POLICY
S05

WRIGHT Q.,"THE ENFORCEMENT OF INTERNATIONAL LAW THROUGH MUNICIPAL LAW IN THE US." USA-45 LOC/G NAT/G PUB/INST FORCES LEGIT CT/SYS PERCEPT ALL/VALS ...JURID 20. PAGE 107 E2149
INT/ORG
LAW
INT/LAW
WAR
L16

HUDSON M.,"THE TEACHING OF INTERNATIONAL LAW IN AMERICA." USA-45 LAW CONSULT ACT/RES CREATE EDU/PROP ATTIT RIGID/FLEX...JURID CONCPT RECORD HIST/WRIT TREND GEN/LAWS 18/20. PAGE 56 E1109
PERCEPT
KNOWL
INT/LAW
L28

ROBSON W.A.,CIVILISATION AND THE GROWTH OF LAW. UNIV CONSTN SOCIETY LEGIS ADJUD ATTIT PERCEPT MORAL ALL/IDEOS...CONCPT WORSHIP 20. PAGE 85 E1708
LAW
IDEA/COMP
SOC
B35

TINGSTERN H.,PEACE AND SECURITY AFTER WW II. WOR-45 DELIB/GP TOP/EX LEGIT CT/SYS COERCE PEACE ATTIT PERCEPT...CONCPT LEAGUE/NAT 20. PAGE 96 E1927
INT/ORG
ORD/FREE
WAR
INT/LAW
B45

MARITAIN J.,HUMAN RIGHTS: COMMENTS AND INTERPRETATIONS. COM UNIV WOR+45 LAW CONSTN CULTURE SOCIETY ECO/DEV ECO/UNDEV SCHOOL DELIB/GP EDU/PROP ATTIT PERCEPT ALL/VALS...HUM SOC TREND UNESCO 20. PAGE 68 E1365
INT/ORG
CONCPT
B49

STONE J.,THE PROVINCE AND FUNCTION OF LAW. UNIV WOR+45 WOR-45 CULTURE INTELL SOCIETY ECO/DEV ECO/UNDEV NAT/G LEGIT ROUTINE ATTIT PERCEPT PERSON ...JURID CONCPT GEN/LAWS GEN/METH 20. PAGE 94 E1877
INT/ORG
LAW
B50

BEANEY W.M.,THE RIGHT TO COUNSEL IN AMERICAN COURTS. UK USA-45 USA+45 LAW NAT/G PROVS COLONIAL PERCEPT 18/20 SUPREME/CT AMEND/VI AMEND/XIV ENGLSH/LAW. PAGE 8 E0163
ADJUD
CONSTN
CT/SYS
B55

BLOOMFIELD L.M.,EGYPT, ISRAEL AND THE GULF OF AQABA: IN INTERNATIONAL LAW. LAW NAT/G CONSULT FORCES PLAN ECO/TAC ROUTINE COERCE ATTIT DRIVE PERCEPT PERSON RIGID/FLEX LOVE PWR WEALTH...GEOG CONCPT MYTH TREND. PAGE 13 E0250
ISLAM
INT/LAW
UAR
B57

LAPIERE R.,THE FREUDIAN ETHIC. USA+45 FAM EDU/PROP CONTROL CRIME ADJUST AGE DRIVE PERCEPT PERSON SEX ...SOC 20 FREUD/S. PAGE 63 E1254
PSY
ORD/FREE
SOCIETY
B59

TIPTON J.B.,"PARTICIPATION OF THE UNITED STATES IN THE INTERNATIONAL LABOR ORGANIZATION." USA+45 LAW STRUCT ECO/DEV ECO/UNDEV INDUS TEC/DEV ECO/TAC ADMIN PERCEPT ORD/FREE SKILL...STAT HIST/WRIT GEN/METH ILO WORK 20. PAGE 96 E1928
LABOR
INT/ORG
S59

SANDERS R.,"NUCLEAR DYNAMITE: A NEW DIMENSION IN FOREIGN POLICY." FUT WOR+45 ECO/DEV CONSULT TEC/DEV PERCEPT...CONT/OBS TIME/SEQ TREND GEN/LAWS TOT/POP 20 TREATY. PAGE 87 E1745
INDUS
PWR
DIPLOM
NUC/PWR
S60

JENKS C.W.,INTERNATIONAL IMMUNITIES. PLAN EDU/PROP ADMIN PERCEPT...OLD/LIB JURID CONCPT TREND TOT/POP. PAGE 58 E1157
INT/ORG
DIPLOM
B61

KAPLAN M.A.,THE POLITICAL FOUNDATIONS OF
INTERNATIONAL LAW. WOR+45 WOR-45 CULTURE SOCIETY
ECO/DEV DIPLOM PERCEPT...TECHNIC METH/CNCPT.
PAGE 59 E1184
INT/ORG
LAW
B61

WASSERSTROM R.A.,THE JUDICIAL DECISION: TOWARD A
THEORY OF LEGAL JUSTIFICATION. ACT/RES RATIONAL
PERCEPT KNOWL OBJECTIVE...DECISION JURID. PAGE 105
E2102
JUDGE
LAW
ADJUD
B61

CASTANEDA J.,"THE UNDERDEVELOPED NATIONS AND THE
DEVELOPMENT OF INTERNATIONAL LAW." FUT UNIV LAW
ACT/RES FOR/AID LEGIT PERCEPT SKILL...JURID
METH/CNCPT TIME/SEQ TOT/POP 20 UN. PAGE 21 E0405
INT/ORG
ECO/UNDEV
PEACE
INT/LAW
S61

MACHOWSKI K.,"SELECTED PROBLEMS OF NATIONAL
SOVEREIGNTY WITH REFERENCE TO THE LAW OF OUTER
SPACE." FUT WOR+45 AIR LAW INTELL SOCIETY ECO/DEV
PLAN EDU/PROP DETER DRIVE PERCEPT SOVEREIGN
...POLICY INT/LAW OBS TREND TOT/POP 20. PAGE 67
E1339
UNIV
ACT/RES
NUC/PWR
SPACE
S61

GRAVEN J.,"LE MOUVEAU DROIT PENAL INTERNATIONAL."
UNIV STRUCT LEGIS ACT/RES CRIME ATTIT PERCEPT
PERSON...JURID CONCPT 20. PAGE 45 E0899
CT/SYS
PUB/INST
INT/ORG
INT/LAW
S62

MANGIN G.,"LES ACCORDS DE COOPERATION EN MATIERE DE
JUSTICE ENTRE LA FRANCE ET LES ETATS AFRICAINS ET
MALGACHE." AFR ISLAM WOR+45 STRUCT ECO/UNDEV NAT/G
DELIB/GP PERCEPT ALL/VALS...JURID MGT TIME/SEQ 20.
PAGE 68 E1356
INT/ORG
LAW
FRANCE
S62

MONNIER J.P.,"LA SUCCESSION D'ETATS EN MATIERE DE
RESPONSABILITE INTERNATIONALE." UNIV CONSTN INTELL
SOCIETY ADJUD ROUTINE PERCEPT SUPEGO...GEN/LAWS
TOT/POP 20. PAGE 74 E1485
NAT/G
JURID
INT/LAW
S62

SCHACHTER O.,"DAG HAMMARSKJOLD AND THE RELATION OF
LAW TO POLITICS." FUT WOR+45 INT/ORG CONSULT PLAN
TEC/DEV BAL/PWR DIPLOM LEGIT ATTIT PERCEPT ORD/FREE
...POLICY JURID CONCPT OBS TESTS STERTYP GEN/LAWS
20 HAMMARSK/D. PAGE 87 E1751
ACT/RES
ADJUD
S62

VIGNES D.,"L'AUTORITE DES TRAITES INTERNATIONAUX EN
DROIT INTERNE." EUR+WWI UNIV LAW CONSTN INTELL
NAT/G POL/PAR DIPLOM ATTIT PERCEPT ALL/VALS
...POLICY INT/LAW JURID CONCPT TIME/SEQ 20 TREATY.
PAGE 104 E2075
STRUCT
LEGIT
FRANCE
S62

CAHIER P.,"LE DROIT INTERNE DES ORGANISATIONS
INTERNATIONALES." UNIV CONSTN SOCIETY ECO/DEV R+D
NAT/G TOP/EX LEGIT ATTIT PERCEPT...TIME/SEQ 19/20.
PAGE 18 E0357
INT/ORG
JURID
DIPLOM
INT/LAW
S63

WALKER H.,"THE INTERNATIONAL LAW OF COMMODITY
AGREEMENTS." FUT WOR+45 ECO/DEV ECO/UNDEV FINAN
INT/ORG NAT/G CONSULT CREATE PLAN ECO/TAC ATTIT
PERCEPT...CONCPT GEN/LAWS TOT/POP GATT 20. PAGE 105
E2095
MARKET
VOL/ASSN
INT/LAW
INT/TRADE
S63

WEISSBERG G.,"MAPS AS EVIDENCE IN INTERNATIONAL
BOUNDARY DISPUTES: A REAPPRAISAL." CHINA/COM
EUR+WWI INDIA MOD/EUR S/ASIA INT/ORG NAT/G LEGIT
PERCEPT...JURID CHARTS 20. PAGE 105 E2110
LAW
GEOG
SOVEREIGN
S63

WENGLER W.,"LES CONFLITS DE LOIS ET LE PRINCIPE
D'EGALITE." UNIV LAW SOCIETY ACT/RES LEGIT ATTIT
PERCEPT 20. PAGE 105 E2111
JURID
CONCPT
INT/LAW
S63

HICKEY D.,"THE PHILOSOPHICAL ARGUMENT FOR WORLD
GOVERNMENT." WOR+45 SOCIETY ACT/RES PLAN LEGIT
ADJUD PEACE PERCEPT PERSON ORD/FREE...HUM JURID
PHIL/SCI METH/CNCPT CON/ANAL STERTYP GEN/LAWS
TOT/POP 20. PAGE 52 E1039
FUT
INT/ORG
S64

HARTUNG F.E.,CRIME, LAW, AND SOCIETY. LAW PUB/INST
CRIME PERS/REL AGE/Y BIO/SOC PERSON ROLE SUPEGO
...LING GP/COMP GEN/LAWS 20. PAGE 50 E1004
PERCEPT
CRIMLGY
DRIVE
CONTROL
B65

KHOURI F.J.,"THE JORDON RIVER CONTROVERSY." LAW
SOCIETY ECO/UNDEV AGRI FINAN INDUS SECT FORCES
ACT/RES PLAN TEC/DEV ECO/TAC EDU/PROP COERCE ATTIT
DRIVE PERCEPT RIGID/FLEX ALL/VALS...GEOG SOC MYTH
WORK. PAGE 61 E1212
ISLAM
INT/ORG
ISRAEL
JORDAN
S65

WRIGHT Q.,"THE ESCALATION OF INTERNATIONAL
CONFLICTS." WOR+45 WOR-45 FORCES DIPLOM RISK COST
ATTIT ALL/VALS...INT/LAW QUANT STAT NAT/COMP.
PAGE 108 E2160
WAR
PERCEPT
PREDICT
MATH
S65

PERCEPTION....SEE PERCEPT

PERCY/CHAS....CHARLES PERCY

PERF/ART....PERFORMING ARTS

COUNCIL BRITISH NATIONAL BIB,BRITISH NATIONAL
BIBLIOGRAPHY. UK AGRI CONSTRUC PERF/ART POL/PAR
SECT CREATE INT/TRADE LEAD...HUM JURID PHIL/SCI 20.
PAGE 26 E0519
BIBLIOG/A
NAT/G
TEC/DEV
DIPLOM
B50

STEVENS R.E.,REFERENCE BOOKS IN THE SOCIAL SCIENCES
AND HUMANITIES. CULTURE PERF/ART SECT EDU/PROP
...JURID PSY SOC/WK STAT 20 MUSIC. PAGE 93 E1873
BIBLIOG/A
SOC
HUM
ART/METH
B66

SHEEHY E.P.,"SELECTED REFERENCE BOOKS OF
1965-1966." AGRI PERF/ART PRESS...GEOG HUM JURID
SOC LING WORSHIP. PAGE 91 E1817
BIBLIOG/A
INDEX
CLASSIF
S66

PERFORMING ARTS....SEE PERF/ART; ALSO ART/METH

PERKINS D. E1609,E1610

PERKINS H.C. E1593

PERON/JUAN....JUAN PERON

COSSIO C.,LA POLITICA COMO CONCIENCIA; MEDITACION
SOBRE LA ARGENTINA DE 1955. WOR+45 LEGIS EDU/PROP
PARL/PROC PARTIC ATTIT PWR CATHISM 20 ARGEN
PERON/JUAN. PAGE 26 E0517
POL/PAR
REV
TOTALISM
JURID
B57

PERS/COMP....COMPARISON OF PERSONS

SCHMIDHAUSER J.R.,JUDICIAL BEHAVIOR AND THE
SECTIONAL CRISIS OF 1837-1860. USA-45 ADJUD CT/SYS
INGP/REL ATTIT HABITAT...DECISION PSY STAT CHARTS
SIMUL. PAGE 88 E1759
JUDGE
POL/PAR
PERS/COMP
PERSON
N13

BORGATTA E.F.,SOCIAL WORKERS' PERCEPTIONS OF
CLIENTS. SERV/IND ROUTINE PERS/REL DRIVE PERSON
RESPECT...SOC PERS/COMP 20. PAGE 14 E0268
SOC/WK
ATTIT
CLIENT
PROB/SOLV
B60

MENDELSON W.,CAPITALISM, DEMOCRACY, AND THE SUPREME
COURT. USA+45 USA-45 CONSTN DIPLOM GOV/REL ATTIT
ORD/FREE LAISSEZ...POLICY CHARTS PERS/COMP 18/20
SUPREME/CT MARSHALL/J HOLMES/OW TANEY/RB FIELD/JJ.
PAGE 72 E1437
JUDGE
CT/SYS
JURID
NAT/G
B60

SPAETH H.J.,"JUDICIAL POWER AS A VARIABLE
MOTIVATING SUPREME COURT BEHAVIOR." DELIB/GP ADJUD
RATIONAL ATTIT PERSON ORD/FREE...CLASSIF STAT
GEN/METH. PAGE 93 E1860
JUDGE
DECISION
PERS/COMP
PSY
L62

GREY D.L.,"INTERVIEWING AT THE COURT." USA+45
ELITES COM/IND ACT/RES PRESS CT/SYS PERSON...SOC
INT 20 SUPREME/CT. PAGE 46 E0916
JUDGE
ATTIT
PERS/COMP
GP/COMP
S67

PERS/REL....RELATIONS BETWEEN PERSONS AND INTERPERSONAL
    COMMUNICATION

PERSONNEL. USA+45 LAW LABOR LG/CO WORKER CREATE
GOV/REL PERS/REL ATTIT WEALTH. PAGE 2 E0029
BIBLIOG/A
ADMIN
MGT
GP/REL
N

PHILLIPS J.B.,"MODIFICATIONS OF THE JURY SYSTEM."
PARTIC EFFICIENCY ATTIT PERCEPT...TREND 19
JURID
DELIB/GP
S05

SUPREME/CT JURY. PAGE 80 E1612
PERS/REL
POLICY

B16
SALMOND J.W.,JURISPRUDENCE. UK LOC/G NAT/G LEGIS
PROB/SOLV LICENSE LEGIT CRIME PERS/REL OWN ORD/FREE
...T 20. PAGE 87 E1742
LAW
CT/SYS
JURID
ADJUD

N19
HOGARTY R.A.,NEW JERSEY FARMERS AND MIGRANT HOUSING
RULES (PAMPHLET). USA+45 LAW ELITES FACE/GP LABOR
PROF/ORG LOBBY PERS/REL RIGID/FLEX ROLE 20
NEW/JERSEY. PAGE 53 E1067
AGRI
PROVS
WORKER
HEALTH

L30
LLEWELLYN K.N.,"A REALISTIC JURISPRUDENCE - THE
NEXT STEP." PROB/SOLV ADJUD GP/REL PERS/REL
IDEA/COMP. PAGE 66 E1312
LAW
CONCPT
JURID
GEN/LAWS

B45
WEST R.,CONSCIENCE AND SOCIETY: A STUDY OF THE
PSYCHOLOGICAL PREREQUISITES OF LAW AND ORDER. FUT
UNIV LAW SOCIETY STRUCT DIPLOM WAR PERS/REL SUPEGO
...SOC 20. PAGE 105 E2112
COERCE
INT/LAW
ORD/FREE
PERSON

B48
CORWIN E.S.,LIBERTY AGAINST GOVERNMENT. UK USA-45
ROMAN/EMP LAW CONSTN PERS/REL OWN ATTIT 1/20
ROMAN/LAW ENGLSH/LAW AMEND/XIV. PAGE 26 E0513
JURID
ORD/FREE
CONCPT

B49
DENNING A.,FREEDOM UNDER THE LAW. MOD/EUR UK LAW
SOCIETY CHIEF EX/STRUC LEGIS ADJUD CT/SYS PERS/REL
PERSON 17/20 ENGLSH/LAW. PAGE 31 E0606
ORD/FREE
JURID
NAT/G

B51
PUSEY M.J.,CHARLES EVANS HUGHES (2 VOLS.). LAW
CONSTN NAT/G POL/PAR DIPLOM LEGIT WAR CHOOSE
PERS/REL DRIVE HEREDITY 19/20 DEPT/STATE LEAGUE/NAT
SUPREME/CT HUGHES/CE WWI. PAGE 83 E1663
BIOG
TOP/EX
ADJUD
PERSON

S51
COHEN M.B.,"PERSONALITY AS A FACTOR IN
ADMINISTRATIVE DECISIONS." ADJUD PERS/REL ANOMIE
SUPEGO...OBS SELF/OBS INT. PAGE 24 E0465
PERSON
ADMIN
PROB/SOLV
PSY

B52
DE GRAZIA A.,POLITICAL ORGANIZATION. CONSTN LOC/G
MUNIC NAT/G CHIEF LEGIS TOP/EX ADJUD CT/SYS
PERS/REL...INT/LAW MYTH UN. PAGE 29 E0581
FEDERAL
LAW
ADMIN

B52
DU BOIS W.E.B.,IN BATTLE FOR PEACE. AFR USA+45
COLONIAL CT/SYS PERS/REL PERSON ORD/FREE...JURID 20
NEGRO CIVIL/LIB. PAGE 33 E0650
PEACE
RACE/REL
DISCRIM
BIOG

B53
COKE E.,INSTITUTES OF THE LAWS OF ENGLAND
(1628-1658). UK LAW ADJUD PERS/REL ORD/FREE
...CRIMLGY 11/17. PAGE 24 E0471
JURID
OWN
CT/SYS
CONSTN

S57
KNEIER C.M.,"MISLEADING THE VOTERS." CONSTN LEAD
CHOOSE PERS/REL. PAGE 61 E1224
MUNIC
REPRESENT
LAW
ATTIT

B58
CLEMMER D.,THE PRISON COMMUNITY. CULTURE CONTROL
LEAD ROUTINE PERS/REL PERSON...SOC METH/CNCPT.
PAGE 23 E0453
PUB/INST
CRIMLGY
CLIENT
INGP/REL

L58
BEVAN W.,"JURY BEHAVIOR AS A FUNCTION OF THE
PRESTIGE OF THE FOREMAN AND THE NATURE OF HIS
LEADERSHIP" (BMR)" DELIB/GP DOMIN ADJUD LEAD
PERS/REL ATTIT...PSY STAT INT QU CHARTS SOC/EXP 20
JURY. PAGE 11 E0221
PERSON
EDU/PROP
DECISION
CT/SYS

S58
CRESSEY D.R.,"ACHIEVEMENT OF AN UNSTATED
ORGANIZATIONAL GOAL: AN OBSERVATION ON PRISONS."
OP/RES PROB/SOLV PERS/REL ANOMIE ATTIT ROLE RESPECT
CRIMLGY. PAGE 28 E0546
PUB/INST
CLIENT
NEIGH
INGP/REL

C58
FRIEDRICH C.J.,"AUTHORITY, REASON AND DISCRETION"
IN C. FRIEDRICH'S AUTHORITY (BMR)" UNIV EX/STRUC
ADJUD ADMIN CONTROL INGP/REL ATTIT PERSON PWR.
PAGE 41 E0807
AUTHORIT
CHOOSE
RATIONAL
PERS/REL

B60
BORGATTA E.F.,SOCIAL WORKERS' PERCEPTIONS OF
CLIENTS. SERV/IND ROUTINE PERS/REL DRIVE PERSON
RESPECT...SOC PERS/COMP 20. PAGE 14 E0268
SOC/WK
ATTIT
CLIENT
PROB/SOLV

S60
ULMER S.S.,"THE ANALYSIS OF BEHAVIOR PATTERNS ON
THE UNITED STATES SUPREME COURT" USA+45 LAW CT/SYS
PERS/REL RACE/REL PERSON...DECISION PSY SOC TREND
METH/COMP METH 20 SUPREME/CT CIVIL/LIB. PAGE 97
E1951
ATTIT
ADJUD
PROF/ORG
INGP/REL

C60
MCCLEERY R.,"COMMUNICATION PATTERNS AS BASES OF
SYSTEMS OF AUTHORITY AND POWER" IN THEORETICAL
STUDIES IN SOCIAL ORGAN. OF PRISON-BMR. USA+45
SOCIETY STRUCT EDU/PROP ADMIN CONTROL COERCE CRIME
GP/REL AUTHORIT...SOC 20. PAGE 70 E1400
PERS/REL
PUB/INST
PWR
DOMIN

B61
JACOBS C.E.,JUSTICE FRANKFURTER AND CIVIL
LIBERTIES. USA+45 USA-45 LAW NAT/G PROB/SOLV PRESS
PERS/REL...JURID WORSHIP 20 SUPREME/CT FRANKFUR/F
CIVIL/LIB. PAGE 57 E1144
BIOG
CONSTN
ADJUD
ORD/FREE

B61
ROCHE J.P.,COURTS AND RIGHTS: THE AMERICAN
JUDICIARY IN ACTION (2ND ED.). UK USA+45 USA-45
STRUCT TEC/DEV SANCTION PERS/REL RACE/REL ORD/FREE
...METH/CNCPT GOV/COMP METH/COMP T 13/20. PAGE 85
E1710
JURID
CT/SYS
NAT/G
PROVS

S61
AGNEW P.C.,"INTRODUCING CHANGE IN A MENTAL
HOSPITAL." CLIENT WORKER PROB/SOLV INGP/REL
PERS/REL ADJUST. PAGE 3 E0054
ORD/FREE
PUB/INST
PSY
ADMIN

B62
FROMAN L.A. JR.,PEOPLE AND POLITICS: AN ANALYSIS OF
THE AMERICAN POLITICAL SYSTEM. USA+45 CHIEF
DELIB/GP EX/STRUC LEGIS TOP/EX CT/SYS LOBBY
PERS/REL PWR...POLICY DECISION. PAGE 41 E0813
POL/PAR
PROB/SOLV
GOV/REL

B63
FRAENKEL O.K.,THE SUPREME COURT AND CIVIL
LIBERTIES: HOW THE COURT HAS PROTECTED THE BILL OF
RIGHTS. NAT/G CT/SYS CHOOSE PERS/REL RACE/REL
DISCRIM PERSON...DECISION 20 SUPREME/CT CIVIL/LIB
BILL/RIGHT. PAGE 39 E0782
ORD/FREE
CONSTN
ADJUD
JURID

S63
HILLS R.J.,"THE REPRESENTATIVE FUNCTION: NEGLECTED
DIMENSION OF LEADERSHIP BEHAVIOR" USA+45 CLIENT
STRUCT SCHOOL PERS/REL...STAT QU SAMP LAB/EXP 20.
PAGE 53 E1048
LEAD
ADMIN
EXEC
ACT/RES

B64
BUREAU OF NATIONAL AFFAIRS,STATE FAIR EMPLOYMENT
LAWS AND THEIR ADMINISTRATION. INDUS ADJUD PERS/REL
RACE/REL ATTIT ORD/FREE WEALTH 20. PAGE 17 E0338
PROVS
DISCRIM
WORKER
JURID

B64
MURPHY W.F.,ELEMENTS OF JUDICIAL STRATEGY. CONSTN
JUDGE PERS/REL PERSON 19/20 SUPREME/CT. PAGE 75
E1510
CT/SYS
ADJUD
JURID

B64
NEWMAN E.S.,POLICE, THE LAW, AND PERSONAL FREEDOM.
USA+45 CONSTN JUDGE CT/SYS CRIME PERS/REL RESPECT
...CRIMLGY 20. PAGE 77 E1542
JURID
FORCES
ORD/FREE
ADJUD

B64
NICE R.W.,TREASURY OF LAW. WOR+45 WOR-45 SECT ADJUD
MORAL ORD/FREE...INT/LAW JURID PHIL/SCI ANTHOL.
PAGE 77 E1545
LAW
WRITING
PERS/REL
DIPLOM

B64
TODD A.,JUSTICE ON TRIAL: THE CASE OF LOUIS D.
BRANDEIS. TOP/EX DISCRIM...JURID 20 WILSON/W
CONGRESS SUPREME/CT BRANDEIS/L SENATE. PAGE 96
E1929
PERSON
RACE/REL
PERS/REL
NAT/G

B65
HARTUNG F.E.,CRIME, LAW, AND SOCIETY. LAW PUB/INST
CRIME PERS/REL AGE/Y BIO/SOC PERSON ROLE SUPEGO
...LING GP/COMP GEN/LAWS 20. PAGE 50 E1004
PERCEPT
CRIMLGY
DRIVE
CONTROL

B65
SCHUBERT G.,THE JUDICIAL MIND: THE ATTITUDES AND
CT/SYS

IDEOLOGIES OF SUPREME COURT JUSTICES 1946-1963.   JUDGE
USA+45 ELITES NAT/G CONTROL PERS/REL MAJORITY   ATTIT
CONSERVE...DECISION JURID MODAL STAT TREND GP/COMP   NEW/LIB
GAME. PAGE 88 E1774

                                                       B66
BAHRO H.,DAS KINDSCHAFTSRECHT IN DER UNION DER   JURID
SOZIALISTITSCHEN SOWJETREPUBLIKEN. USSR SECT   AGE/C
EDU/PROP CONTROL PWR...SOC/WK 20. PAGE 7 E0133   PERS/REL
                                                       SUPEGO

                                                       B66
CARLIN J.E.,LAWYER'S ETHICS. CLIENT STRUCT CONSULT   ATTIT
PERS/REL PWR...JURID OBS CHARTS 20. PAGE 19 E0378   PROF/ORG
                                                       INT

                                                       B67
BIBBY J.,ON CAPITOL HILL. POL/PAR LOBBY PARL/PROC   CONFER
GOV/REL PERS/REL...JURID PHIL/SCI OBS INT BIBLIOG   LEGIS
20 CONGRESS PRESIDENT. PAGE 12 E0224   CREATE
                                                       LEAD

                                                       B67
GELLHORN W.,OMBUDSMEN AND OTHERS: CITIZENS'   NAT/COMP
PROTECTORS IN NINE COUNTRIES. WOR+45 LAW CONSTN   REPRESENT
LEGIS INSPECT ADJUD ADMIN CONTROL CT/SYS CHOOSE   INGP/REL
PERS/REL...STAT CHARTS 20. PAGE 43 E0847   PROB/SOLV

                                                       B67
JONES C.O.,EVERY SECOND YEAR: CONGRESSIONAL   EFFICIENCY
BEHAVIOR AND THE TWO-YEAR TERM. LAW POL/PAR   LEGIS
PROB/SOLV DEBATE CHOOSE PERS/REL COST FEDERAL PWR   TIME/SEQ
...CHARTS 20 CONGRESS SENATE HOUSE/REP. PAGE 59   NAT/G
E1172

                                                       B67
KING W.L.,MELVILLE WESTON FULLER: CHIEF JUSTICE OF   BIOG
THE UNITED STATES, 1888-1910. USA-45 CONSTN FINAN   CT/SYS
LABOR TAX GOV/REL PERS/REL ATTIT PERSON PWR...JURID   LAW
BIBLIOG 19/20 SUPREME/CT FULLER/MW HOLMES/OW.   ADJUD
PAGE 61 E1216

                                                       B67
LONG E.V.,THE INTRUDERS: THE INVASION OF PRIVACY BY   LAW
GOVERNMENT AND INDUSTRY. USA+45 COM/IND INDUS LEGIS   PARTIC
TASK PERS/REL...JURID 20 CONGRESS. PAGE 66 E1324   NAT/G

                                                       S67
BLAKEY G.R.,"ORGANIZED CRIME IN THE UNITED STATES."   CRIME
USA+45 USA-45 STRUCT LABOR NAT/G VOL/ASSN ADMIN   ELITES
PERS/REL PWR...CRIMLGY INT 17/20. PAGE 12 E0240   CONTROL

                                                       S67
CARTER R.M.,"SOME FACTORS IN SENTENCING POLICY."   ADJUD
LAW PUB/INST CRIME PERS/REL...POLICY JURID SOC   CT/SYS
TREND CON/ANAL CHARTS SOC/EXP 20. PAGE 20 E0403   ADMIN

                                                       S68
DUPRE L.,"TILL DEATH DO US PART?" UNIV FAM INSPECT   MARRIAGE
LEGIT ADJUD SANCTION PERS/REL ANOMIE RIGID/FLEX SEX   CATH
...JURID IDEA/COMP 20 CHURCH/STA BIBLE CANON/LAW   LAW
CIVIL/LAW. PAGE 34 E0666

PERS/TEST....PERSONALITY TESTS

PERSIA....PERSIA: ANCIENT IRAN

PERSON....PERSONALITY AND HUMAN NATURE

                                                       N
JOURNAL OF INTERNATIONAL AFFAIRS. WOR+45 ECO/UNDEV   BIBLIOG
POL/PAR ECO/TAC WAR PEACE PERSON ALL/IDEOS   DIPLOM
...INT/LAW TREND. PAGE 1 E0010   INT/ORG
                                                      NAT/G

                                                       N
DEUTSCHE BIBLIOGRAPHIE, HALBJAHRESVERZEICHNIS.   BIBLIOG
WOR+45 LAW ADMIN PERSON. PAGE 1 E0020   NAT/G
                                                      DIPLOM

                                                       N
DEUTSCHE BUCHEREI,JAHRESVERZEICHNIS DER DEUTSCHEN   BIBLIOG
HOCHSCHULSCHRIFTEN. EUR+WWI GERMANY LAW ADMIN   WRITING
PERSON...MGT SOC 19/20. PAGE 31 E0613   ACADEM
                                                      INTELL

                                                       N
DEUTSCHE BUCHEREI,DEUTSCHES BUCHERVERZEICHNIS.   BIBLIOG
GERMANY LAW CULTURE POL/PAR ADMIN LEAD ATTIT PERSON   NAT/G
...SOC 20. PAGE 31 E0615   DIPLOM
                                                      ECO/DEV

                                                       B00
MAINE H.S.,INTERNATIONAL LAW. MOD/EUR UNIV SOCIETY   INT/ORG
STRUCT ACT/RES EXEC WAR ATTIT PERSON ALL/VALS   LAW
...POLICY JURID CONCPT OBS TIME/SEQ TOT/POP.   PEACE

PAGE 68 E1349   INT/LAW

                                                       B11
PHILLIPSON C.,THE INTERNATIONAL LAW AND CUSTOM OF   INT/ORG
ANCIENT GREECE AND ROME. MEDIT-7 UNIV INTELL   LAW
SOCIETY STRUCT NAT/G LEGIS EXEC PERSON...CONCPT OBS   INT/LAW
CON/ANAL ROM/EMP. PAGE 80 E1614

                                                       B11
REINSCH P.,PUBLIC INTERNATIONAL UNION. WOR-45 LAW   FUT
LABOR INT/TRADE LEGIT PERSON ALL/VALS...SOCIALIST   INT/ORG
CONCPT TIME/SEQ TREND GEN/LAWS 19/20. PAGE 84 E1683   DIPLOM

                                                       N13
SCHMIDHAUSER J.R.,JUDICIAL BEHAVIOR AND THE   JUDGE
SECTIONAL CRISIS OF 1837-1860. USA-45 ADJUD CT/SYS   POL/PAR
INGP/REL ATTIT HABITAT...DECISION PSY STAT CHARTS   PERS/COMP
SIMUL. PAGE 88 E1759   PERSON

                                                       B16
PUFENDORF S.,LAW OF NATURE AND OF NATIONS   CONCPT
(ABRIDGED). UNIV LAW NAT/G DIPLOM AGREE WAR PERSON   INT/LAW
ALL/VALS PWR...POLICY 18 DEITY NATURL/LAW. PAGE 83   SECT
E1659   MORAL

                                                       N19
GIBB A.D.,JUDICIAL CORRUPTION IN THE UNITED KINGDOM   MORAL
(PAMPHLET). UK DELIB/GP CT/SYS CRIME PERSON SUPEGO   ATTIT
17/20 SCOTLAND. PAGE 43 E0856   ADJUD

                                                       B20
COX H.,ECONOMIC LIBERTY. UNIV LAW INT/TRADE RATION   NAT/G
TARIFFS RACE/REL SOCISM POLICY. PAGE 27 E0535   ORD/FREE
                                                      ECO/TAC
                                                      PERSON

                                                       B22
FARRAND M.,THE FRAMING OF THE CONSTITUTION OF THE   CONSTN
UNITED STATES (1913). USA-45 EX/STRUC PROB/SOLV   DELIB/GP
PERSON. PAGE 36 E0721   LEGIS
                                                      CT/SYS

                                                       B28
HOBBES T.,THE ELEMENTS OF LAW, NATURAL AND POLITIC   PERSON
(1650). STRATA NAT/G SECT CHIEF AGREE ATTIT   LAW
ALL/VALS MORAL ORD/FREE POPULISM...POLICY CONCPT.   SOVEREIGN
PAGE 53 E1056   CONSERVE

                                                       B29
STURZO L.,THE INTERNATIONAL COMMUNITY AND THE RIGHT   INT/ORG
OF WAR (TRANS. BY BARBARA BARCLAY CARTER). CULTURE   PLAN
CREATE PROB/SOLV DIPLOM ADJUD CONTROL PEACE PERSON   WAR
ORD/FREE...INT/LAW IDEA/COMP PACIFIST 20   CONCPT
LEAGUE/NAT. PAGE 94 E1891

                                                       B38
POUND R.,THE FORMATIVE ERA OF AMERICAN LAW. CULTURE   CONSTN
NAT/G PROVS LEGIS ADJUD CT/SYS PERSON SOVEREIGN   LAW
...POLICY IDEA/COMP GEN/LAWS 18/19. PAGE 82 E1637   CREATE
                                                      JURID

                                                       S38
CLEMMER D.,"LEADERSHIP PHENOMENA IN A PRISON   PUB/INST
COMMUNITY." NEIGH PLAN CHOOSE PERSON ROLE...OBS   CRIMLGY
INT. PAGE 23 E0452   LEAD
                                                      CLIENT

                                                       B41
EVANS C.,AMERICAN BIBLIOGRAPHY... (12 VOLUMES).   BIBLIOG
USA-45 LAW DIPLOM ADMIN PERSON...HUM SOC 17/18.   NAT/G
PAGE 35 E0704   ALL/VALS
                                                      ALL/IDEOS

                                                       B42
HAMBRO C.J.,HOW TO WIN THE PEACE. ECO/TAC EDU/PROP   FUT
ADJUD PERSON ALL/VALS...SOCIALIST TREND GEN/LAWS   INT/ORG
20. PAGE 50 E0987   PEACE

                                                       B45
WEST R.,CONSCIENCE AND SOCIETY: A STUDY OF THE   COERCE
PSYCHOLOGICAL PREREQUISITES OF LAW AND ORDER. FUT   INT/LAW
UNIV LAW SOCIETY STRUCT DIPLOM WAR PERS/REL SUPEGO   ORD/FREE
...SOC 20. PAGE 105 E2112   PERSON

                                                       B48
HOLCOMBE A.N.,HUMAN RIGHTS IN THE MODERN WORLD.   ORD/FREE
WOR+45 LEGIS DIPLOM ADJUD PERSON...INT/LAW 20 UN   INT/ORG
TREATY CIVIL/LIB BILL/RIGHT. PAGE 54 E1071   CONSTN
                                                      LAW

                                                       B49
DENNING A.,FREEDOM UNDER THE LAW. MOD/EUR UK LAW   ORD/FREE
SOCIETY CHIEF EX/STRUC LEGIS ADJUD CT/SYS PERS/REL   JURID
PERSON 17/20 ENGLSH/LAW. PAGE 31 E0606   NAT/G

B50
LAUTERPACHT H.,INTERNATIONAL LAW AND HUMAN RIGHTS. DELIB/GP
USA+45 CONSTN STRUCT INT/ORG ACT/RES EDU/PROP PEACE LAW
PERSON ALL/VALS...CONCPT CON/ANAL GEN/LAWS UN 20. INT/LAW
PAGE 63 E1266

B50
STONE J.,THE PROVINCE AND FUNCTION OF LAW. UNIV   INT/ORG
WOR+45 WOR-45 CULTURE INTELL SOCIETY ECO/DEV   LAW
ECO/UNDEV NAT/G LEGIT ROUTINE ATTIT PERCEPT PERSON
...JURID CONCPT GEN/LAWS GEN/METH 20. PAGE 94 E1877

B51
PUSEY M.J.,CHARLES EVANS HUGHES (2 VOLS.). LAW   BIOG
CONSTN NAT/G POL/PAR DIPLOM LEGIT WAR CHOOSE   TOP/EX
PERS/REL DRIVE HEREDITY 19/20 DEPT/STATE LEAGUE/NAT ADJUD
SUPREME/CT HUGHES/CE WWI. PAGE 83 E1663   PERSON

S51
COHEN M.B.,"PERSONALITY AS A FACTOR IN   PERSON
ADMINISTRATIVE DECISIONS." ADJUD PERS/REL ANOMIE   ADMIN
SUPEGO...OBS SELF/OBS INT. PAGE 24 E0465   PROB/SOLV
                                                   PSY

B52
DU BOIS W.E.B.,IN BATTLE FOR PEACE. AFR USA+45   PEACE
COLONIAL CT/SYS PERS/REL PERSON ORD/FREE...JURID 20 RACE/REL
NEGRO CIVIL/LIB. PAGE 33 E0650   DISCRIM
                                                   BIOG

B53
GROSS B.M.,THE LEGISLATIVE STRUGGLE: A STUDY IN   LEGIS
SOCIAL COMBAT. STRUCT LOC/G POL/PAR JUDGE EDU/PROP DECISION
DEBATE ETIQUET ADMIN LOBBY CHOOSE GOV/REL INGP/REL PERSON
HEREDITY ALL/VALS...SOC PRESIDENT. PAGE 48 E0948   LEAD

B53
KIRK R.,THE CONSERVATIVE MIND. POL/PAR ORD/FREE   CONSERVE
...JURID CONCPT 18/20. PAGE 61 E1220   PERSON
                                                   PHIL/SCI
                                                   IDEA/COMP

B54
JAMES L.F.,THE SUPREME COURT IN AMERICAN LIFE.   ADJUD
USA+45 USA-45 CONSTN CRIME GP/REL INGP/REL RACE/REL CT/SYS
CONSEN FEDERAL PERSON ORD/FREE 18/20 SUPREME/CT   JURID
DEPRESSION CIV/RIGHTS CHURCH/STA FREE/SPEE. PAGE 58 DECISION
E1147

B55
CAVAN R.S.,CRIMINOLOGY (2ND ED.). USA+45 LAW FAM   DRIVE
PUB/INST FORCES PLAN WAR AGE/Y PERSON ROLE SUPEGO   CRIMLGY
...CHARTS 20 FBI. PAGE 21 E0409   CONTROL
                                                   METH/COMP

B56
CALLISON I.P.,COURTS OF INJUSTICE. USA+45 PROF/ORG CT/SYS
ADJUD CRIME PERSON MORAL PWR RESPECT SKILL 20.   JUDGE
PAGE 19 E0368   JURID

B56
DUNNILL F.,THE CIVIL SERVICE. UK LAW PLAN ADMIN   PERSON
EFFICIENCY DRIVE NEW/LIB...STAT CHARTS 20   WORKER
PARLIAMENT CIVIL/SERV. PAGE 33 E0662   STRATA
                                                   SOC/WK

B56
PERKINS D.,CHARLES EVANS HUGHES AND THE AMERICAN   PERSON
DEMOCRATIC STATESMANSHIP. USA+45 USA-45 NAT/G   BIOG
POL/PAR DELIB/GP JUDGE PLAN MORAL PWR...HIST/WRIT   DIPLOM
LEAGUE/NAT 20. PAGE 80 E1609

B57
BLOOMFIELD L.M.,EGYPT, ISRAEL AND THE GULF OF   ISLAM
AQABA: IN INTERNATIONAL LAW. LAW NAT/G CONSULT   INT/LAW
FORCES PLAN ECO/TAC ROUTINE COERCE ATTIT DRIVE   UAR
PERCEPT PERSON RIGID/FLEX LOVE PWR WEALTH...GEOG
CONCPT MYTH TREND. PAGE 13 E0250

B57
CLINARD M.B.,SOCIOLOGY OF DEVIANT BEHAVIOR. FAM   BIO/SOC
CONTROL MURDER DISCRIM PERSON...PSY SOC T SOC/INTEG CRIME
20. PAGE 23 E0455   SEX
                                                   ANOMIE

B57
COOPER F.E.,THE LAWYER AND ADMINISTRATIVE AGENCIES. CONSULT
USA+45 CLIENT LAW PROB/SOLV CT/SYS PERSON ROLE.   ADMIN
PAGE 25 E0500   ADJUD
                                                   DELIB/GP

S57
FRANKFURTER F.,"THE SUPREME COURT IN THE MIRROR OF EDU/PROP
JUSTICES" (BMR)" USA+45 USA-45 INTELL INSPECT   ADJUD
EFFICIENCY ROLE KNOWL MORAL 18/20 SUPREME/CT.   CT/SYS
PAGE 40 E0792   PERSON

B58
CLEMMER D.,THE PRISON COMMUNITY. CULTURE CONTROL   PUB/INST
LEAD ROUTINE PERS/REL PERSON...SOC METH/CNCPT.   CRIMLGY
PAGE 23 E0453   CLIENT
                                                   INGP/REL

L58
BEVAN W.,"JURY BEHAVIOR AS A FUNCTION OF THE   PERSON
PRESTIGE OF THE FOREMAN AND THE NATURE OF HIS   EDU/PROP
LEADERSHIP" (BMR)" DELIB/GP DOMIN ADJUD LEAD   DECISION
PERS/REL ATTIT...PSY STAT INT QU CHARTS SOC/EXP 20 CT/SYS
JURY. PAGE 11 E0221

S58
SCHUBERT G.A.,"THE STUDY OF JUDICIAL DECISION-   JUDGE
MAKING AS AN ASPECT OF POLITICAL BEHAVIOR." PLAN   DECISION
ADJUD CT/SYS INGP/REL PERSON...PHIL/SCI SOC QUANT   CON/ANAL
STAT CHARTS IDEA/COMP SOC/EXP. PAGE 89 E1779   GAME

C58
FRIEDRICH C.J.,"AUTHORITY, REASON AND DISCRETION"   AUTHORIT
IN C. FRIEDRICH'S AUTHORITY (BMR)" UNIV EX/STRUC   CHOOSE
ADJUD ADMIN CONTROL INGP/REL ATTIT PERSON PWR.   RATIONAL
PAGE 41 E0807   PERS/REL

B59
ABRAHAM H.J.,COURTS AND JUDGES: AN INTRODUCTION TO CT/SYS
THE JUDICIAL PROCESS. USA+45 CONSTN ELITES NAT/G   PERSON
ORD/FREE PWR 19/20 SUPREME/CT. PAGE 2 E0045   JURID
                                                   ADJUD

B59
CHRISTMAN H.M.,THE PUBLIC PAPERS OF CHIEF JUSTICE   LAW
EARL WARREN. CONSTN POL/PAR EDU/PROP SANCTION   CT/SYS
HEALTH...TREND 20 SUPREME/CT WARRN/EARL. PAGE 22   PERSON
E0436   ADJUD

B59
LAPIERE R.,THE FREUDIAN ETHIC. USA+45 FAM EDU/PROP PSY
CONTROL CRIME ADJUST AGE DRIVE PERCEPT PERSON SEX   ORD/FREE
...SOC 20 FREUD/S. PAGE 63 E1254   SOCIETY

B59
MORRIS C.,THE GREAT LEGAL PHILOSOPHERS: SELECTED   JURID
READINGS IN JURISPRUDENCE. UNIV INTELL SOCIETY   ADJUD
EDU/PROP MAJORITY UTOPIA PERSON KNOWL...ANTHOL.   PHIL/SCI
PAGE 75 E1497   IDEA/COMP

B59
SCHUBERT G.A.,QUANTITATIVE ANALYSIS OF JUDICIAL   JUDGE
BEHAVIOR. ADJUD LEAD CHOOSE INGP/REL MAJORITY ATTIT CT/SYS
...DECISION JURID CHARTS GAME SIMUL SUPREME/CT.   PERSON
PAGE 89 E1780   QUANT

S59
CLOWARD R.A.,"ILLEGITIMATE MEANS, ANOMIE, AND   ANOMIE
DEVIANT BEHAVIOR" STRUCT CRIME DRIVE PERSON...SOC   CRIMLGY
CONCPT NEW/IDEA 20 DURKHEIM/E MERTON/R. PAGE 23   LEGIT
E0459   ADJUST

S59
DERGE D.R.,"THE LAWYER AS DECISION-MAKER IN THE   LEGIS
AMERICAN STATE LEGISLATURE." INTELL LOC/G POL/PAR   LAW
CHOOSE AGE HEREDITY PERSON CONSERVE...JURID STAT   DECISION
CHARTS. PAGE 31 E0607   LEAD

B60
BORGATTA E.F.,SOCIAL WORKERS' PERCEPTIONS OF   SOC/WK
CLIENTS. SERV/IND ROUTINE PERS/REL DRIVE PERSON   ATTIT
RESPECT...SOC PERS/COMP 20. PAGE 14 E0268   CLIENT
                                                   PROB/SOLV

S60
NAGEL S.S.,"USING SIMPLE CALCULATIONS TO PREDICT   JURID
JUDICIAL DECISIONS." ATTIT PERSON MATH. PAGE 76   LAW
E1517   DECISION
                                                   COMPUTER

S60
ULMER S.S.,"THE ANALYSIS OF BEHAVIOR PATTERNS ON   ATTIT
THE UNITED STATES SUPREME COURT" USA+45 LAW CT/SYS ADJUD
PERS/REL RACE/REL PERSON...DECISION PSY SOC TREND   PROF/ORG
METH/COMP METH 20 SUPREME/CT CIVIL/LIB. PAGE 97   INGP/REL
E1951

B61
ANAND R.P.,COMPULSORY JURISDICTION OF INTERNATIONAL INT/ORG
COURT OF JUSTICE. FUT WOR+45 SOCIETY PLAN LEGIT   COERCE
ADJUD ATTIT DRIVE PERSON ORD/FREE...JURID CONCPT   INT/LAW
TREND 20 ICJ. PAGE 5 E0086

B61
BEDFORD S.,THE FACES OF JUSTICE: A TRAVELLER'S   CT/SYS
REPORT. AUSTRIA FRANCE GERMANY/W SWITZERLND UK UNIV ORD/FREE
WOR+45 WOR-45 CULTURE PARTIC GOV/REL MORAL...JURID PERSON

OBS GOV/COMP 20. PAGE 9 E0174   LAW

B61

MCDOUGAL M.S.,LAW AND MINIMUM WORLD PUBLIC ORDER.   INT/ORG
WOR+45 SOCIETY NAT/G DELIB/GP EDU/PROP LEGIT ADJUD   ORD/FREE
COERCE ATTIT PERSON...JURID CONCPT RECORD TREND   INT/LAW
TOT/POP 20. PAGE 70 E1406

B61

WECHSLER H.,PRINCIPLES, POLITICS AND FUNDAMENTAL   CT/SYS
LAW: SELECTED ESSAYS. USA+45 USA-45 LAW SOCIETY   CONSTN
NAT/G PROVS DELIB/GP EX/STRUC ACT/RES LEGIT PERSON   INT/LAW
KNOWL PWR...JURID 20 NUREMBERG. PAGE 105 E2106

L61

FELLMAN D.,"ACADEMIC FREEDOM IN AMERICAN LAW." LAW   ACADEM
CONSTN NAT/G VOL/ASSN PLAN PERSON KNOWL NEW/LIB.   ORD/FREE
PAGE 37 E0732   LEGIS
                                                     CULTURE

S61

SCHUBERT G.,"A PSYCHOMETRIC MODEL OF THE SUPREME   JUDGE
COURT." DELIB/GP ADJUD CHOOSE ATTIT...DECISION   CT/SYS
JURID PSY QUANT STAT HYPO/EXP GEN/METH SUPREME/CT.   PERSON
PAGE 88 E1771   SIMUL

B62

BOCHENSKI J.M.,HANDBOOK ON COMMUNISM. USSR WOR+45   COM
LAW SOCIETY NAT/G POL/PAR SECT CRIME PERSON MARXISM   DIPLOM
...SOC ANTHOL 20. PAGE 13 E0254   POLICY
                                                     CONCPT

B62

INTERNAT CONGRESS OF JURISTS,EXECUTIVE ACTION AND   JURID
THE RULE OF RULE: REPORTION PROCEEDINGS OF INT'T   EXEC
CONGRESS OF JURISTS-RIO DE JANEIRO, BRAZIL. WOR+45   ORD/FREE
ACADEM CONSULT JUDGE EDU/PROP ADJUD CT/SYS INGP/REL   CONTROL
PERSON DEPT/DEFEN. PAGE 57 E1130

B62

WOETZEL R.K.,THE NURENBERG TRIALS IN INTERNATIONAL   INT/ORG
LAW. CHRIST-17C MOD/EUR WOR+45 SOCIETY NAT/G   ADJUD
DELIB/GP DOMIN LEGIT ROUTINE ATTIT DRIVE PERSON   WAR
SUPEGO MORAL ORD/FREE...POLICY MAJORIT JURID PSY
SOC SELF/OBS RECORD NAZI TOT/POP. PAGE 107 E2138

L62

SPAETH H.J.,"JUDICIAL POWER AS A VARIABLE   JUDGE
MOTIVATING SUPREME COURT BEHAVIOR." DELIB/GP ADJUD   DECISION
RATIONAL ATTIT PERSON ORD/FREE...CLASSIF STAT   PERS/COMP
GEN/METH. PAGE 93 E1860   PSY

S62

GRAVEN J.,"LE MOUVEAU DROIT PENAL INTERNATIONAL."   CT/SYS
UNIV STRUCT LEGIS ACT/RES CRIME ATTIT PERCEPT   PUB/INST
PERSON...JURID CONCPT 20. PAGE 45 E0899   INT/ORG
                                                     INT/LAW

B63

BROOKES E.H.,POWER, LAW, RIGHT, AND LOVE: A STUDY   PWR
IN POLITICAL VALUES. SOUTH/AFR NAT/G PERSON   ORD/FREE
...CONCPT IDEA/COMP 20. PAGE 16 E0308   JURID
                                                     LOVE

B63

DUNHAM A.,MR. JUSTICE. ADJUD PWR...JURID ANTHOL   BIOG
18/20 SUPREME/CT. PAGE 33 E0659   PERSON
                                                     LAW
                                                     CT/SYS

B63

ELIAS T.O.,GOVERNMENT AND POLITICS IN AFRICA.   AFR
CONSTN CULTURE SOCIETY NAT/G POL/PAR DIPLOM   NAT/LISM
REPRESENT PERSON...SOC TREND BIBLIOG 4/20. PAGE 34   COLONIAL
E0681   LAW

B63

FRAENKEL O.K.,THE SUPREME COURT AND CIVIL   ORD/FREE
LIBERTIES: HOW THE COURT HAS PROTECTED THE BILL OF   CONSTN
RIGHTS. NAT/G CT/SYS CHOOSE PERS/REL RACE/REL   ADJUD
DISCRIM PERSON...DECISION 20 SUPREME/CT CIVIL/LIB   JURID
BILL/RIGHT. PAGE 39 E0782

B63

FRIEDRICH C.J.,MAN AND HIS GOVERNMENT: AN EMPIRICAL   PERSON
THEORY OF POLITICS. UNIV LOC/G NAT/G ADJUD REV   ORD/FREE
INGP/REL DISCRIM PWR BIBLIOG. PAGE 41 E0810   PARTIC
                                                     CONTROL

B63

HABERMAS J.,THEORIE UND PRAXIS. RATIONAL PERSON   JURID
...PHIL/SCI ANTHOL 19/20 HEGEL/GWF MARX/KARL BLOCH   REV
LOWITH. PAGE 49 E0969   GEN/LAWS
                                                     MARXISM

B63

LEVY L.W.,JEFFERSON AND CIVIL LIBERTIES: THE DARKER   BIOG
SIDE. USA-45 LAW INTELL ACADEM FORCES PRESS REV   ORD/FREE
INGP/REL PERSON 18/19 JEFFERSN/T CIVIL/LIB. PAGE 65   CONSTN
E1291   ATTIT

B63

ROBERTSON A.H.,HUMAN RIGHTS IN EUROPE. CONSTN   EUR+WWI
SOCIETY INT/ORG NAT/G VOL/ASSN DELIB/GP ACT/RES   PERSON
PLAN ADJUD REGION ROUTINE ATTIT LOVE ORD/FREE
RESPECT...JURID SOC CONCPT SOC/EXP UN 20. PAGE 85
E1705

B63

SARTORI G.,IL PARLAMENTO ITALIANO: 1946-1963. LAW   LEGIS
CONSTN ELITES POL/PAR LOBBY PRIVIL ATTIT PERSON   PARL/PROC
MORAL PWR SOC. PAGE 87 E1746   REPRESENT

S63

MENDELSON W.,"THE NEO-BEHAVIORAL APPROACH TO THE   DECISION
JUDICIAL PROCESS: A CRITIQUE" ADJUD PERSON...SOC   JURID
RECORD IDEA/COMP. PAGE 72 E1438   JUDGE

B64

CHEIN I.,THE ROAD TO H: NARCOTICS, DELINQUENCY, AND   BIO/SOC
SOCIAL POLICY. USA+45 NEIGH CRIME INGP/REL ATTIT   AGE/Y
PERSON...SOC/WK 20 NEWYORK/C. PAGE 22 E0426   POLICY
                                                     ANOMIE

B64

CLINARD M.B.,ANOMIE AND DEVIANT BEHAVIOR: A   PERSON
DISCUSSION AND CRITIQUE. SOCIETY FACE/GP CRIME   ANOMIE
STRANGE ATTIT BIO/SOC DISPL RIGID/FLEX HEALTH...PSY   KIN
CONCPT BIBLIOG 20 MERTON/R. PAGE 23 E0456   NEIGH

B64

DANELSKI D.J.,A SUPREME COURT JUSTICE IS APPOINTED.   CHOOSE
CHIEF LEGIS CONFER DEBATE EXEC PERSON PWR...BIOG 20   JUDGE
CONGRESS PRESIDENT. PAGE 28 E0564   DECISION

B64

FORBES A.H.,CURRENT RESEARCH IN BRITISH STUDIES. UK   BIBLIOG
CONSTN CULTURE POL/PAR SECT DIPLOM ADMIN...JURID   PERSON
BIOG WORSHIP 20. PAGE 39 E0769   NAT/G
                                                     PARL/PROC

B64

GRASMUCK E.L.,COERCITIO STAAT UND KIRCHE IM   GP/REL
DONATISTENSTREIT. CHRIST-17C ROMAN/EMP LAW PROVS   NAT/G
DEBATE PERSON SOVEREIGN...JURID CONCPT 4/5   SECT
AUGUSTINE CHURCH/STA ROMAN/LAW. PAGE 45 E0898   COERCE

B64

GRIFFITH W.E.,THE SINO-SOVIET RIFT. ASIA CHINA/COM   ATTIT
COM CUBA USSR YUGOSLAVIA NAT/G POL/PAR VOL/ASSN   TIME/SEQ
DELIB/GP FORCES TOP/EX DIPLOM EDU/PROP DRIVE PERSON   BAL/PWR
PWR...TREND 20 TREATY. PAGE 47 E0941   SOCISM

B64

HALLER W.,DER SCHWEDISCHE JUSTITIEOMBUDSMAN.   JURID
DENMARK FINLAND NORWAY SWEDEN LEGIS ADJUD CONTROL   PARL/PROC
PERSON ORD/FREE...NAT/COMP 20 OMBUDSMAN. PAGE 50   ADMIN
E0986   CHIEF

B64

IKLE F.C.,HOW NATIONS NEGOTIATE. COM EUR+WWI USA+45   NAT/G
INTELL INT/ORG VOL/ASSN DELIB/GP ACT/RES CREATE   PWR
DOMIN EDU/PROP ADJUD ROUTINE ATTIT PERSON ORD/FREE   POLICY
RESPECT SKILL...PSY SOC OBS VAL/FREE. PAGE 56 E1122

B64

MURPHY W.F.,ELEMENTS OF JUDICIAL STRATEGY. CONSTN   CT/SYS
JUDGE PERS/REL PERSON 19/20 SUPREME/CT. PAGE 75   ADJUD
E1510   JURID

B64

SCHUBERT G.A.,JUDICIAL BEHAVIOR: A READER IN THEORY   ATTIT
AND RESEARCH. POL/PAR CT/SYS ROLE SUPEGO PWR   PERSON
...DECISION JURID REGRESS CHARTS SIMUL ANTHOL 20.   ADJUD
PAGE 89 E1782   ACT/RES

B64

TODD A.,JUSTICE ON TRIAL: THE CASE OF LOUIS D.   PERSON
BRANDEIS. TOP/EX DISCRIM...JURID 20 WILSON/W   RACE/REL
CONGRESS SUPREME/CT BRANDEIS/L SENATE. PAGE 96   PERS/REL
E1929   NAT/G

S64

CARNEGIE ENDOWMENT INT. PEACE,"HUMAN RIGHTS (ISSUES   INT/ORG
BEFORE THE NINETEENTH GENERAL ASSEMBLY)." AFR   PERSON
WOR+45 LAW CONSTN NAT/G EDU/PROP GP/REL DISCRIM   RACE/REL
PEACE ATTIT MORAL ORD/FREE...INT/LAW PSY CONCPT
RECORD UN 20. PAGE 20 E0385

S64

GINSBURGS G.,"WARS OF NATIONAL LIBERATION - THE   COERCE

SOVIET THESIS." COM USSR WOR+45 WOR-45 LAW CULTURE | CONCPT
INT/ORG DIPLOM LEGIT COLONIAL GUERRILLA WAR | INT/LAW
NAT/LISM ATTIT PERSON MORAL PWR...JURID OBS TREND | REV
MARX/KARL 20. PAGE 44 E0869

S64
GREENBERG S.,"JUDAISM AND WORLD JUSTICE." MEDIT-7 | SECT
WOR+45 LAW CULTURE SOCIETY INT/ORG NAT/G FORCES | JURID
EDU/PROP ATTIT DRIVE PERSON SUPEGO ALL/VALS | PEACE
...POLICY PSY CONCPT GEN/LAWS JEWS. PAGE 46 E0908

S64
HICKEY D.,"THE PHILOSOPHICAL ARGUMENT FOR WORLD | FUT
GOVERNMENT." WOR+45 SOCIETY ACT/RES PLAN LEGIT | INT/ORG
ADJUD PEACE PERCEPT PERSON ORD/FREE...HUM JURID
PHIL/SCI METH/CNCPT CON/ANAL STERTYP GEN/LAWS
TOT/POP 20. PAGE 52 E1039

S64
KHAN M.Z.,"ISLAM AND INTERNATIONAL RELATIONS." FUT | ISLAM
WOR+45 LAW CULTURE SOCIETY NAT/G SECT DELIB/GP | INT/ORG
FORCES EDU/PROP ATTIT PERSON SUPEGO ALL/VALS | DIPLOM
...POLICY PSY CONCPT MYTH HIST/WRIT GEN/LAWS.
PAGE 61 E1211

B65
AMERICAN ASSEMBLY COLUMBIA U.,THE COURTS, THE | CT/SYS
PUBLIC, AND THE LAW EXPLOSION. USA+45 ELITES PROVS | ADJUD
EDU/PROP CRIME CHOOSE PERSON ORD/FREE PWR 20. | NAT/G
PAGE 4 E0074

B65
BELL J.,THE JOHNSON TREATMENT: HOW LYNDON JOHNSON | INGP/REL
TOOK OVER THE PRESIDENCY AND MADE IT HIS OWN. | TOP/EX
USA+45 DELIB/GP DIPLOM ADJUD MURDER CHOOSE PERSON | CONTROL
PWR...POLICY OBS INT TIME 20 JOHNSON/LB KENNEDY/JF | NAT/G
PRESIDENT CONGRESS. PAGE 10 E0183

B65
HARTUNG F.E.,CRIME, LAW, AND SOCIETY. LAW PUB/INST | PERCEPT
CRIME PERS/REL AGE/Y BIO/SOC PERSON ROLE SUPEGO | CRIMLGY
...LING GP/COMP GEN/LAWS 20. PAGE 50 E1004 | DRIVE
| CONTROL

B65
LASLEY J.,THE WAR SYSTEM AND YOU. LAW FORCES | MORAL
ARMS/CONT NUC/PWR NAT/LISM ATTIT...MAJORIT | PERSON
IDEA/COMP UN WORSHIP. PAGE 63 E1261 | DIPLOM
| WAR

B65
ROSE A.M.,MINORITY PROBLEMS: A TEXTBOOK OF READINGS | RACE/REL
IN INTERGROUP RELATIONS. UNIV USA+45 LAW SCHOOL | DISCRIM
WORKER PROB/SOLV GP/REL PERSON...PSY ANTHOL WORSHIP | ISOLAT
20 NEGRO INDIAN/AM JEWS EUROPE. PAGE 85 E1713 | ACT/RES

B66
BAXTER M.G.,DANIEL WEBSTER & THE SUPREME COURT. LAW | CONSTN
NAT/G PROF/ORG DEBATE ADJUD LEAD FEDERAL PERSON. | CT/SYS
PAGE 8 E0156 | JURID

B66
CANFIELD L.H.,THE PRESIDENCY OF WOODROW WILSON: | PERSON
PRELUDE TO A WORLD IN CRISIS. USA-45 ADJUD NEUTRAL | POLICY
WAR CHOOSE INGP/REL PEACE ORD/FREE 20 WILSON/W | DIPLOM
PRESIDENT TREATY LEAGUE/NAT. PAGE 19 E0373 | GOV/REL

B66
HOLDSWORTH W.S.,A HISTORY OF ENGLISH LAW: THE | BIOG
CENTURIES OF SETTLEMENT AND REFORM (VOL. XVI). UK | PERSON
LOC/G NAT/G EX/STRUC LEGIS CT/SYS LEAD ATTIT | PROF/ORG
...POLICY DECISION JURID IDEA/COMP 18 PARLIAMENT. | LAW
PAGE 54 E1083

B66
HOLMES O.W.,JUSTICE HOLMES, EX CATHEDRA. USA+45 | BIOG
USA-45 LAW INTELL ADMIN ATTIT...BIBLIOG 20 | PERSON
SUPREME/CT HOLMES/OW. PAGE 55 E1088 | CT/SYS
| ADJUD

B66
MACIVER R.M.,THE PREVENTION AND CONTROL OF | AGE/Y
DELINQUENCY. USA+45 STRATA PUB/INST ANOMIE ATTIT | PLAN
HABITAT PERSON HEALTH...CRIMLGY PSY SOC METH. | ADJUST
PAGE 67 E1341 | CRIME

B66
MACMULLEN R.,ENEMIES OF THE ROMAN EMPIRE: TREASON, | CRIME
UNREST, AND ALIENATION IN THE EMPIRE. ROMAN/EMP | ADJUD
MUNIC CONTROL LEAD ATTIT PERSON MYSTISM...PHIL/SCI | MORAL
BIBLIOG. PAGE 67 E1345 | SOCIETY

B66
MILLER E.W.,THE NEGRO IN AMERICA: A BIBLIOGRAPHY. | BIBLIOG
USA+45 LAW EDU/PROP REV GOV/REL GP/REL INGP/REL | DISCRIM
ADJUST HABITAT PERSON HEALTH ORD/FREE SOC/INTEG 20 | RACE/REL

NEGRO. PAGE 73 E1459

B66
POLLACK R.S.,THE INDIVIDUAL'S RIGHTS AND | INT/LAW
INTERNATIONAL ORGANIZATION. LAW INT/ORG DELIB/GP | ORD/FREE
SUPEGO...JURID SOC/INTEG 20 TREATY UN. PAGE 81 | DIPLOM
E1623 | PERSON

B66
SKOLNICK J.H.,JUSTICE WITHOUT TRIAL: LAW | FORCES
ENFORCEMENT IN DEMOCRATIC SOCIETY. USA+45 LAW | CRIMLGY
TRIBUTE RACE/REL BIO/SOC PERSON...PSY SOC 20 NEGRO | CRIME
BUREAUCRCY PROSTITUTN. PAGE 92 E1836

B67
BAKER L.,BACK TO BACK: THE DUEL BETWEEN FDR AND THE | CHIEF
SUPREME COURT. ELITES LEGIS CREATE DOMIN INGP/REL | CT/SYS
PERSON PWR NEW/LIB 20 ROOSEVLT/F SUPREME/CT SENATE. | PARL/PROC
PAGE 7 E0142 | GOV/REL

B67
BONGER W.A.,CRIMINALITY AND ECONOMIC CONDITIONS. | PERSON
MOD/EUR STRUCT INDUS WORKER EDU/PROP CRIME HABITAT | CRIMLGY
ALL/VALS...JURID SOC 20 REFORMERS. PAGE 14 E0265 | IDEA/COMP
| ANOMIE

B67
CLINARD M.B.,CRIMINAL BEHAVIOR SYSTEMS: A TYPOLOGY. | BIBLIOG
WOR+45 LAW SOCIETY STRUCT R+D AGE/Y ATTIT WEALTH | CRIME
...CLASSIF CHARTS METH/COMP METH. PAGE 23 E0457 | CRIMLGY
| PERSON

B67
DEBOLD R.C.,LSD, MAN AND SOCIETY. USA+45 LAW | HEALTH
SOCIETY SECT CONTROL SANCTION STRANGE ATTIT...HEAL | DRIVE
CHARTS ANTHOL BIBLIOG. PAGE 30 E0601 | PERSON
| BIO/SOC

B67
KING W.L.,MELVILLE WESTON FULLER: CHIEF JUSTICE OF | BIOG
THE UNITED STATES, 1888-1910. USA-45 CONSTN FINAN | CT/SYS
LABOR TAX GOV/REL PERS/REL ATTIT PERSON PWR...JURID | LAW
BIBLIOG 19/20 SUPREME/CT FULLER/MW HOLMES/OW. | ADJUD
PAGE 61 E1216

L67
FRANCK T.M.,"SOME PSYCHOLOGICAL FACTORS IN | DIPLOM
INTERNATIONAL THIRD-PARTY DECISION-MAKING." UNIV | ADJUD
SOCIETY PROB/SOLV DISCRIM ATTIT HABITAT...DECISION | PERSON
PSY. PAGE 40 E0786 | CONSULT

S67
GREY D.L.,"INTERVIEWING AT THE COURT." USA+45 | JUDGE
ELITES COM/IND ACT/RES PRESS CT/SYS PERSON...SOC | ATTIT
INT 20 SUPREME/CT. PAGE 46 E0916 | PERS/COMP
| GP/COMP

PERSONAL RELATIONS....SEE PERS/REL

PERSONALITY....SEE PERSON, ALSO PERSONALITY INDEX, P. XIII

PERSUASION....SEE LOBBY, EDU/PROP

PERU....SEE ALSO L/A+17C

B47
CLAGETT H.L.,A GUIDE TO THE LAW AND LEGAL | BIBLIOG
LITERATURE OF PERU. PERU CONSTN COM/IND LABOR MUNIC | L/A+17C
JUDGE ADMIN CT/SYS...CRIMLGY INT/LAW JURID 20. | PHIL/SCI
PAGE 23 E0444 | LAW

B48
DE NOIA J.,GUIDE TO OFFICIAL PUBLICATIONS OF OTHER | BIBLIOG/A
AMERICAN REPUBLICS: PERU (VOL. XVII). PERU LAW | CONSTN
LEGIS ADMIN CT/SYS...JURID 19/20. PAGE 30 E0593 | NAT/G
| EDU/PROP

B62
DE LAVALLE H.,A STATEMENT OF THE LAWS OF PERU IN | CONSTN
MATTERS AFFECTING BUSINESS (3RD ED.). PERU WORKER | JURID
INT/TRADE INCOME ORD/FREE...INT/LAW 20. PAGE 30 | FINAN
E0586 | TAX

PETAIN/HP....H.P. PETAIN

PETERS....PETERS V. NEW YORK

PETKOFF D.K. E1611

PHIL/SCI....SCIENTIFIC METHOD AND PHILOSOPHY OF SCIENCE

B
DEUTSCHE BIBLIOTH FRANKF A M.DEUTSCHE | BIBLIOG
BIBLIOGRAPHIE. EUR+WWI GERMANY ECO/DEV FORCES | LAW

DIPLOM LEAD...POLICY PHIL/SCI SOC 20. PAGE 31 E0612 ADMIN
NAT/G

N
AMERICAN POLITICAL SCIENCE REVIEW. USA+45 USA-45   BIBLIOG/A
WOR+45 WOR-45 INT/ORG ADMIN...INT/LAW PHIL/SCI   DIPLOM
CONCPT METH 20 UN. PAGE 1 E0002   NAT/G
                                                   GOV/COMP

N
BIBLIOGRAPHIE DE LA PHILOSOPHIE. LAW CULTURE SECT BIBLIOG/A
EDU/PROP MORAL...HUM METH/CNCPT 20. PAGE 1 E0018   PHIL/SCI
                                                   CONCPT
                                                   LOG

N
BIBLIOGRAPHIE DER SOZIALWISSENSCHAFTEN. WOR-45   BIBLIOG
CONSTN SOCIETY ECO/DEV ECO/UNDEV DIPLOM LEAD WAR   LAW
PEACE...PHIL/SCI SOC 19/20. PAGE 1 E0019   CONCPT
                                                   NAT/G

N
THE JAPAN SCIENCE REVIEW: LAW AND POLITICS: LIST OF BIBLIOG
BOOKS AND ARTICLES ON LAW AND POLITICS. CONSTN AGRI LAW
INDUS LABOR DIPLOM TAX ADMIN CRIME...INT/LAW SOC 20 S/ASIA
CHINJAP. PAGE 2 E0027   PHIL/SCI

N
AMER COUNCIL OF LEARNED SOCIET.THE ACLS CONSTITUENT BIBLIOG/A
SOCIETY JOURNAL PROJECT. FUT USA+45 LAW NAT/G PLAN HUM
DIPLOM PHIL/SCI. PAGE 4 E0072   COMPUT/IR
                                                    COMPUTER

B01
BRYCE J.,STUDIES IN HISTORY AND JURISPRUDENCE (2   IDEA/COMP
VOLS.). ICELAND SOUTH/AFR UK LAW PROB/SOLV   CONSTN
SOVEREIGN...PHIL/SCI NAT/COMP ROME/ANC ROMAN/LAW.   JURID
PAGE 16 E0321

C05
DUNNING W.A.,"HISTORY OF POLITICAL THEORIES FROM   PHIL/SCI
LUTHER TO MONTESQUIEU." LAW NAT/G SECT DIPLOM REV   CONCPT
WAR ORD/FREE SOVEREIGN CONSERVE...TRADIT BIBLIOG   GEN/LAWS
16/18. PAGE 33 E0663

B06
FOSTER J.W.,THE PRACTICE OF DIPLOMACY AS   DIPLOM
ILLUSTRATED IN THE FOREIGN RELATIONS OF THE UNITED ROUTINE
STATES. MOD/EUR USA-45 NAT/G EX/STRUC ADMIN   PHIL/SCI
...POLICY INT/LAW BIBLIOG 19/20. PAGE 39 E0777

B14
CRAIG J.,ELEMENTS OF POLITICAL SCIENCE (3 VOLS.). PHIL/SCI
CONSTN AGRI INDUS SCHOOL FORCES TAX CT/SYS SUFF   NAT/G
MORAL WEALTH...CONCPT 19 CIVIL/LIB. PAGE 27 E0539 ORD/FREE

B16
CARLYLE A.J.,BIBLIOGRAPHY OF POLITICAL THEORY   BIBLIOG/A
(PAMPHLET). FRANCE GERMANY UK USA-45...JURID 9/19. CONCPT
PAGE 19 E0382   PHIL/SCI

C20
BLACHLY F.F.,"THE GOVERNMENT AND ADMINISTRATION OF NAT/G
GERMANY." GERMANY CONSTN LOC/G PROVS DELIB/GP   GOV/REL
EX/STRUC FORCES LEGIS TOP/EX CT/SYS...BIBLIOG/A   ADMIN
19/20. PAGE 12 E0235   PHIL/SCI

C20
DUNNING W.A.,"A HISTORY OF POLITICAL THINKERS FROM IDEA/COMP
ROUSSEAU TO SPENCER." NAT/G REV NAT/LISM UTIL   PHIL/SCI
CONSERVE MARXISM POPULISM...JURID BIBLIOG 18/19.   CONCPT
PAGE 33 E0664   GEN/LAWS

L21
HALDEMAN E.,"SERIALS OF AN INTERNATIONAL   BIBLIOG
CHARACTER." WOR-45 DIPLOM...ART/METH GEOG HEAL HUM PHIL/SCI
INT/LAW JURID PSY SOC. PAGE 49 E0978

B22
COX G.C.,THE PUBLIC CONSCIENCE: A CASEBOOK IN   MORAL
ETHICS....PHIL/SCI SOC CONCPT METH/COMP 20. PAGE 27 ADJUD
E0534

B23
POUND R.,INTERPRETATIONS OF LEGAL HISTORY. CULTURE LAW
...PHIL/SCI NEW/IDEA CLASSIF SIMUL GEN/LAWS 19/20. IDEA/COMP
PAGE 82 E1636   JURID

C24
BARNES H.E.,"SOCIOLOGY AND POLITICAL THEORY: A   CONCPT
CONSIDERATION OF THE SOCIOLOGICAL BASIS OF   STRUCT
POLITICS." LAW CONSTN NAT/G DIPLOM DOMIN ROUTINE   SOC
REV ORD/FREE SOVEREIGN...PHIL/SCI CLASSIF BIBLIOG
18/20. PAGE 8 E0151

B25
GODET M.,INDEX BIBLIOGRAPHICUS: INTERNATIONAL   BIBLIOG/A
CATALOGUE OF SOURCES OF CURRENT BIBLIOGRAPHIC   DIPLOM
INFORMATION. EUR+WWI MOD/EUR SOCIETY SECT TAX   EDU/PROP
...JURID PHIL/SCI SOC MATH. PAGE 44 E0876   LAW

B26
HOCKING W.E.,PRESENT STATUS OF THE PHILOSOPHY OF   JURID
LAW AND OF RIGHTS. UNIV CULTURE INTELL SOCIETY   PHIL/SCI
NAT/G CREATE LEGIT SANCTION ALL/VALS SOC/INTEG   ORD/FREE
18/20. PAGE 53 E1060

B31
COLUMBIA UNIVERSITY,A BIBLIOGRAPHY OF THE FACULTY BIBLIOG
OF POLITICAL SCIENCE OF COLUMBIA UNIVERSITY,   ACADEM
1880-1930. USA-45 LAW NAT/G LEGIS DIPLOM LEAD WAR PHIL/SCI
GOV/REL ATTIT...TIME/SEQ 19/20. PAGE 24 E0478

B34
CUMMINGS H.,LIBERTY UNDER LAW AND ADMINISTRATION. ORD/FREE
MOD/EUR USA-45 ADMIN ATTIT...JURID PHIL/SCI.   LAW
PAGE 28 E0553   NAT/G
                                                    SOCIETY

S37
TIMASHEFF N.S.,"WHAT IS SOCIOLOGY OF LAW?" (BMR)" LAW
UNIV INTELL PWR...EPIST JURID PHIL/SCI IDEA/COMP. SOC
PAGE 96 E1925   SOCIETY

C39
SCOTT J.B.,"LAW, THESTATE, AND THE INTERNATIONAL   LAW
COMMUNITY (2 VOLS.)" INTELL INT/ORG NAT/G SECT   PHIL/SCI
INT/TRADE WAR...INT/LAW GEN/LAWS BIBLIOG. PAGE 90 DIPLOM
E1798   CONCPT

S40
GURVITCH G.,"MAJOR PROBLEMS OF THE SOCIOLOGY OF   SOC
LAW." CULTURE SANCTION KNOWL MORAL...POLICY EPIST LAW
JURID WORSHIP. PAGE 48 E0963   PHIL/SCI

B42
GURVITCH G.,SOCIOLOGY OF LAW. CONSTN SOCIETY CREATE SOC
MORAL SOVEREIGN...POLICY EPIST JURID PHIL/SCI   LAW
IDEA/COMP METH/COMP HOLMES/OW HOBBES/T. PAGE 48   ADJUD
E0964

B45
VANCE H.L.,GUIDE TO THE LAW AND LEGAL LITERATURE OF BIBLIOG/A
MEXICO. LAW CONSTN FINAN LABOR FORCES ADJUD ADMIN INT/LAW
...CRIMLGY PHIL/SCI CON/ANAL 20 MEXIC/AMER.   JURID
PAGE 103 E2070   CT/SYS

B46
ROSS A.,TOWARDS A REALISTIC JURISPRUDENCE: A   LAW
CRITICISM OF THE DUALISM IN LAW (TRANS. BY ANNIE I. CONCPT
FAUSBOLL). PLAN ADJUD CT/SYS ATTIT RIGID/FLEX   IDEA/COMP
POPULISM...JURID PHIL/SCI LOG METH/COMP GEN/LAWS 20
SCANDINAV. PAGE 86 E1720

B47
CLAGETT H.L.,A GUIDE TO THE LAW AND LEGAL   BIBLIOG/A
LITERATURE OF BOLIVIA. L/A+17C CONSTN LABOR LEGIS JURID
ADMIN...CRIMLGY INT/LAW PHIL/SCI 16/20 BOLIV.   LAW
PAGE 22 E0441   CT/SYS

B47
CLAGETT H.L.,A GUIDE TO THE LAW AND LEGAL   BIBLIOG
LITERATURE OF PERU. PERU CONSTN COM/IND LABOR MUNIC L/A+17C
JUDGE ADMIN CT/SYS...CRIMLGY INT/LAW JURID 20.   PHIL/SCI
PAGE 23 E0444   LAW

B47
CLAGETT H.L.,A GUIDE TO THE LAW AND LEGAL   BIBLIOG
LITERATURE OF URUGUAY. URUGUAY CONSTN COM/IND FINAN L/A+17C
LABOR MUNIC JUDGE PRESS ADMIN CT/SYS...INT/LAW   JURID
PHIL/SCI 20. PAGE 23 E0445   L/A+17C

B48
GRIFFITH E.S.,RESEARCH IN POLITICAL SCIENCE: THE   BIBLIOG
WORK OF PANELS OF RESEARCH COMMITTEE, APSA. WOR+45 PHIL/SCI
WOR-45 COM/IND R+D FORCES ACT/RES WAR...GOV/COMP   DIPLOM
ANTHOL 20. PAGE 47 E0939   JURID

B50
COUNCIL BRITISH NATIONAL BIB,BRITISH NATIONAL   BIBLIOG/A
BIBLIOGRAPHY. UK AGRI CONSTRUC PERF/ART POL/PAR   NAT/G
SECT CREATE INT/TRADE LEAD...HUM JURID PHIL/SCI 20. TEC/DEV
PAGE 26 E0519   DIPLOM

B51
HUXLEY J.,FREEDOM AND CULTURE. UNIV LAW SOCIETY R+D CULTURE
ACADEM SCHOOL CREATE SANCTION ATTIT KNOWL...HUM   ORD/FREE
ANTHOL 20. PAGE 56 E1118   PHIL/SCI
                                                   IDEA/COMP

B52
APPADORAI A.,THE SUBSTANCE OF POLITICS (6TH ED.). PHIL/SCI
EX/STRUC LEGIS DIPLOM CT/SYS CHOOSE FASCISM MARXISM NAT/G
SOCISM...BIBLIOG T. PAGE 5 E0100

B52
CAHILL F.V.,JUDICIAL LEGISLATION: A STUDY IN JURID
AMERICAN LEGAL THEORY. USA+45 USA-45 LAW NAT/G ADJUD
GP/REL...POLICY PHIL/SCI SOC 20 HOLMES/OW. PAGE 18 LEGIS
E0359 CONTROL

B53
KIRK R.,THE CONSERVATIVE MIND. POL/PAR ORD/FREE CONSERVE
...JURID CONCPT 18/20. PAGE 61 E1220 PERSON
PHIL/SCI
IDEA/COMP

B53
LANDHEER B.,FUNDAMENTALS OF PUBLIC INTERNATIONAL BIBLIOG/A
LAW (SELECTIVE BIBLIOGRAPHIES OF THE LIBRARY OF THE INT/LAW
PEACE PALACE, VOL. I: PAMPH). INT/ORG OP/RES PEACE DIPLOM
...IDEA/COMP 20. PAGE 62 E1250 PHIL/SCI

B53
MARKE J.J.,A CATALOGUE OF THE LAW COLLECTION AT NEW BIBLIOG/A
YORK UNIVERSITY, WITH SELECTED ANNOTATIONS. ACADEM LAW
ADJUD CT/SYS...CONCPT BIOG 20. PAGE 68 E1366 PHIL/SCI
IDEA/COMP

B54
BENTLEY A.F.,INQUIRY INTO INQUIRIES: ESSAYS IN EPIST
SOCIAL THEORY. UNIV LEGIS ADJUD ADMIN LOBBY SOC
...PHIL/SCI PSY NEW/IDEA LING METH 20. PAGE 10 CONCPT
E0200

B55
JAPAN MOMBUSHO DAIGAKU GAKIYUT,BIBLIOGRAPHY OF THE BIBLIOG
STUDIES ON LAW AND POLITICS (PAMPHLET). CONSTN LAW
INDUS LABOR DIPLOM TAX ADMIN...CRIMLGY INT/LAW 20 PHIL/SCI
CHINJAP. PAGE 58 E1150

B55
MOHL R.V.,DIE GESCHICHTE UND LITERATUR DER PHIL/SCI
STAATSWISSENSCHAFTEN (3 VOLS.). LAW NAT/G...JURID MOD/EUR
METH/COMP METH. PAGE 74 E1480

S55
WRIGHT Q.,"THE PEACEFUL ADJUSTMENT OF INTERNATIONAL R+D
RELATIONS: PROBLEMS AND RESEARCH APPROACHES." UNIV METH/CNCPT
INTELL EDU/PROP ADJUD ROUTINE KNOWL SKILL...INT/LAW PEACE
JURID PHIL/SCI CLASSIF 20. PAGE 108 E2156

B56
BOTERO G.,THE REASON OF STATE AND THE GREATNESS OF PHIL/SCI
CITIES. SECT CHIEF FORCES PLAN LEAD WAR MORAL NEW/IDEA
...POLICY 16 MACHIAVELL TREATY. PAGE 14 E0272 CONTROL

B56
COHEN A.,THE SUTHERLAND PAPERS. USA+45 USA-45 LAW CRIMLGY
CONTROL CRIME AGE/Y...TREND ANTHOL BIBLIOG 20. PHIL/SCI
PAGE 23 E0461 ACT/RES
METH

B56
LASLETT P.,PHILOSOPHY, POLITICS AND SOCIETY. UNIV CONSTN
CRIME SOVEREIGN...JURID PHIL/SCI ANTHOL PLATO ATTIT
NATURL/LAW. PAGE 63 E1260 CONCPT
GEN/LAWS

B57
KELSEN H.,WHAT IS JUSTICE. WOR+45 WOR-45...CONCPT JURID
BIBLE. PAGE 60 E1201 ORD/FREE
OBJECTIVE
PHIL/SCI

B58
MASON H.L.,TOYNBEE'S APPROACH TO WORLD POLITICS. DIPLOM
AFR USA+45 USSR LAW WAR NAT/LISM ALL/IDEOS...HUM CONCPT
BIBLIOG. PAGE 69 E1380 PHIL/SCI
SECT

S58
SCHUBERT G.A.,"THE STUDY OF JUDICIAL DECISION- JUDGE
MAKING AS AN ASPECT OF POLITICAL BEHAVIOR." PLAN DECISION
ADJUD CT/SYS INGP/REL PERSON...PHIL/SCI SOC QUANT CON/ANAL
STAT CHARTS IDEA/COMP SOC/EXP. PAGE 89 E1779 GAME

B59
HOOK S.,POLITICAL POWER AND PERSONAL FREEDOM: ORD/FREE
CRITICAL STUDIES IN DEMOCRACY, COMMUNISM AND CIVIL PWR
RIGHTS. UNIV LAW SOCIETY DIPLOM TOTALISM MARXISM WELF/ST
SOCISM...PHIL/SCI IDEA/COMP 20 CIV/RIGHTS. PAGE 55 CHOOSE
E1094

B59
MORRIS C.,THE GREAT LEGAL PHILOSOPHERS: SELECTED JURID

B59
READINGS IN JURISPRUDENCE. UNIV INTELL SOCIETY ADJUD
EDU/PROP MAJORITY UTOPIA PERSON KNOWL...ANTHOL. PHIL/SCI
PAGE 75 E1497 IDEA/COMP

B59
ROSS A.,ON LAW AND JUSTICE. USA+45 RATIONAL JURID
...IDEA/COMP GEN/LAWS 20 SCANDINAV NATURL/LAW. PHIL/SCI
PAGE 86 E1722 LAW
CONCPT

B60
UNITED WORLD FEDERALISTS,UNITED WORLD FEDERALISTS: BIBLIOG/A
PANORAMA OF RECENT BOOKS, FILMS, AND JOURNALS ON DIPLOM
WORLD FEDERATION, THE UN, AND WORLD PEACE. CULTURE INT/ORG
ECO/UNDEV PROB/SOLV FOR/AID ARMS/CONT NUC/PWR PEACE
...INT/LAW PHIL/SCI 20 UN. PAGE 98 E1971

B61
WARD R.E.,JAPANESE POLITICAL SCIENCE: A GUIDE TO BIBLIOG/A
JAPANESE REFERENCE AND RESEARCH MATERIALS (2ND PHIL/SCI
ED.). LAW CONSTN STRATA NAT/G POL/PAR DELIB/GP
LEGIS ADMIN CHOOSE GP/REL...INT/LAW 19/20 CHINJAP.
PAGE 105 E2099

B62
BOCK E.A.,CASE STUDIES IN AMERICAN GOVERNMENT. POLICY
USA+45 ECO/DEV CHIEF EDU/PROP CT/SYS RACE/REL LEGIS
ORD/FREE...JURID MGT PHIL/SCI PRESIDENT CASEBOOK. IDEA/COMP
PAGE 13 E0256 NAT/G

B62
EVAN W.M.,LAW AND SOCIOLOGY: EXPLORATORY ESSAYS. JURID
CONSULT ACT/RES OP/RES PROB/SOLV EDU/PROP LEGIT SOC
ADJUD CT/SYS GP/REL...PHIL/SCI ANTHOL SOC/INTEG 20. PROF/ORG
PAGE 35 E0703

B62
ROSENZWEIG F.,HEGEL UND DER STAAT. GERMANY SOCIETY JURID
FAM POL/PAR NAT/LISM...BIOG 19. PAGE 86 E1718 NAT/G
CONCPT
PHIL/SCI

B62
SCHWARTZ L.E.,INTERNATIONAL ORGANIZATIONS AND SPACE INT/ORG
COOPERATION. VOL/ASSN CONSULT CREATE TEC/DEV DIPLOM
SANCTION...POLICY INT/LAW PHIL/SCI 20 UN. PAGE 89 R+D
E1787 SPACE

B63
HABERMAS J.,THEORIE UND PRAXIS. RATIONAL PERSON JURID
...PHIL/SCI ANTHOL 19/20 HEGEL/GWF MARX/KARL BLOCH REV
LOWITH. PAGE 49 E0969 GEN/LAWS
MARXISM

B63
SCHUMAN S.I.,LEGAL POSITIVISM: ITS SCOPE AND GEN/METH
LIMITATIONS. CONSTN NAT/G DIPLOM PARTIC UTOPIA LAW
...POLICY DECISION PHIL/SCI CONCPT 20. PAGE 89 METH/COMP
E1784

L63
LOEVINGER L.,"JURIMETRICS* THE METHODOLOGY OF LEGAL COMPUT/IR
INQUIRY." COMPUTER CREATE PLAN TEC/DEV AUTOMAT JURID
CT/SYS EFFICIENCY...DECISION PHIL/SCI NEW/IDEA GEN/METH
QUANT PREDICT. PAGE 66 E1318 ADJUD

B64
HURST W.H.,JUSTICE HOLMES ON LEGAL HISTORY. USA-45 ADJUD
LAW SOCIETY NAT/G WRITING...POLICY PHIL/SCI SOC JURID
CONCPT 20 HOLMES/OW SUPREME/CT ENGLSH/LAW. PAGE 56 BIOG
E1117

B64
MCDOUGAL M.S.,STUDIES IN WORLD PUBLIC ORDER. SPACE INT/LAW
SEA INT/ORG CREATE AGREE NUC/PWR...POLICY PHIL/SCI SOC
IDEA/COMP ANTHOL METH 20 UN. PAGE 71 E1411 DIPLOM

B64
MINAR D.W.,IDEAS AND POLITICS: THE AMERICAN CONSTN
EXPERIENCE. SECT CHIEF LEGIS CREATE ADJUD EXEC REV NAT/G
PWR...PHIL/SCI CONCPT IDEA/COMP 18/20 HAMILTON/A FEDERAL
JEFFERSN/T DECLAR/IND JACKSON/A PRESIDENT. PAGE 73
E1464

B64
NICE R.W.,TREASURY OF LAW. WOR+45 WOR-45 SECT ADJUD LAW
MORAL ORD/FREE...INT/LAW JURID PHIL/SCI ANTHOL. WRITING
PAGE 77 E1545 PERS/REL
DIPLOM

B64
SARTORIUS R.E.,THE JUSTIFICATION OF THE JUDICIAL LAW
DECISION (DISSERTATION). PROB/SOLV LEGIT...JURID PHIL/SCI
GEN/LAWS BIBLIOG 20. PAGE 87 E1747 CT/SYS
ADJUD

S64

HICKEY D.,"THE PHILOSOPHICAL ARGUMENT FOR WORLD   FUT
GOVERNMENT." WOR+45 SOCIETY ACT/RES PLAN LEGIT   INT/ORG
ADJUD PEACE PERCEPT PERSON ORD/FREE...HUM JURID
PHIL/SCI METH/CNCPT CON/ANAL STERTYP GEN/LAWS
TOT/POP 20. PAGE 52 E1039

B65

UNIVERSAL REFERENCE SYSTEM,INTERNATIONAL AFFAIRS: BIBLIOG/A
VOLUME I IN THE POLITICAL SCIENCE, GOVERNMENT, AND   GEN/METH
PUBLIC POLICY SERIES....DECISION ECOMETRIC GEOG   COMPUT/IR
INT/LAW JURID MGT PHIL/SCI PSY SOC. PAGE 98 E1972   DIPLOM

B66

HAMILTON H.D.,REAPPORTIONING LEGISLATURES. USA+45   APPORT
CONSTN POL/PAR PROVS LEGIS COMPUTER ADJUD CHOOSE   REPRESENT
ATTIT...ANTHOL 20 SUPREME/CT CONGRESS. PAGE 50   PHIL/SCI
E0989   PWR

B66

HOPKINS J.F.K.,ARABIC PERIODICAL LITERATURE, 1961.   BIBLIOG/A
ISLAM LAW CULTURE SECT...GEOG HEAL PHIL/SCI PSY SOC   NAT/LISM
20. PAGE 55 E1096   TEC/DEV
                                                        INDUS

B66

KUNST H.,EVANGELISCHES STAATSLEXIKON. LAW CONSTN   JURID
POL/PAR...PHIL/SCI CONCPT DICTIONARY. PAGE 62 E1232   SECT
                                                        SOC
                                                        NAT/G

B66

MACMULLEN R.,ENEMIES OF THE ROMAN EMPIRE: TREASON,   CRIME
UNREST, AND ALIENATION IN THE EMPIRE. ROMAN/EMP   ADJUD
MUNIC CONTROL LEAD ATTIT PERSON MYSTISM...PHIL/SCI   MORAL
BIBLIOG. PAGE 67 E1345   SOCIETY

B66

OLSON W.C.,THE THEORY AND PRACTICE OF INTERNATIONAL   DIPLOM
RELATIONS (2ND ED.). WOR+45 LEAD SUPEGO...INT/LAW   NAT/G
PHIL/SCI. PAGE 79 E1575   INT/ORG
                                                        POLICY

B66

SMITH E.A.,CHURCH-STATE RELATIONS IN ECUMENICAL   NAT/G
PERSPECTIVE. WOR+45 LAW MUNIC INGP/REL DISCRIM   SECT
ATTIT SUPEGO ORD/FREE CATHISM...PHIL/SCI IDEA/COMP   GP/REL
20 PROTESTANT ECUMENIC CHURCH/STA CHRISTIAN.   ADJUD
PAGE 92 E1843

S66

SHKLAR J.,"SELECTED ARTICLES AND DOCUMENTS ON   BIBLIOG
POLITICAL THEORY." ADJUD REV...JURID PHIL/SCI   ELITES
IDEA/COMP. PAGE 91 E1820   PWR

B67

BIBBY J.,ON CAPITOL HILL. POL/PAR LOBBY PARL/PROC   CONFER
GOV/REL PERS/REL...JURID PHIL/SCI OBS INT BIBLIOG   LEGIS
20 CONGRESS PRESIDENT. PAGE 12 E0224   CREATE
                                                        LEAD

B67

UNIVERSAL REFERENCE SYSTEM,PUBLIC POLICY AND THE   BIBLIOG/A
MANAGEMENT OF SCIENCE (VOLUME IX). FUT SPACE WOR+45   POLICY
LAW NAT/G TEC/DEV CONTROL NUC/PWR GOV/REL   MGT
...COMPUT/IR GEN/METH. PAGE 99 E1975   PHIL/SCI

L67

CICOUREL A.V.,"KINSHIP, MARRIAGE, AND DIVORCE IN   SOC
COMPARATIVE FAMILY LAW." UNIV LAW FAM KIN GEN/METH.   PHIL/SCI
PAGE 22 E0438   MARRIAGE
                                                        IDEA/COMP

L84

ELLMAKER E.G.,"REVELATION OF RIGHTS." JUDGE DISCRIM   ORD/FREE
SUPEGO...JURID PHIL/SCI CONCPT 17/18. PAGE 35 E0685   ADMIN
                                                        MORAL
                                                        NAT/G

PHILADELPH....PHILADELPHIA, PENNSYLVANIA

PHILANTHROPY....SEE GIVE+WEALTH

PHILIP/J....JOHN PHILIP

PHILIPPINE....PHILIPPINES; SEE ALSO S/ASIA

PHILIPPINES....SEE PHILIPPINE; S/ASIA

B52

PASCUAL R.R.,PARTYLESS DEMOCRACY. PHILIPPINE   POL/PAR
BARGAIN LOBBY CHOOSE EFFICIENCY ATTIT 20. PAGE 80   ORD/FREE
E1600   JURID
                                                        ECO/UNDEV

B54

SINCO,PHILIPPINE POLITICAL LAW: PRINCIPLES AND   LAW
CONCEPTS (10TH ED.). PHILIPPINE LOC/G EX/STRUC   CONSTN
BAL/PWR ECO/TAC TAX ADJUD ADMIN CONTROL CT/SYS SUFF   LEGIS
ORD/FREE...T 20. PAGE 91 E1831

PHILLIP/IV....PHILLIP IV OF SPAIN

PHILLIPS G.G. E2087

PHILLIPS J.B. E1612

PHILLIPS O.H. E1613

PHILLIPS/F....F. PHILLIPS - POLICE CHIEF, N.Y.C.

PHILLIPSON C. E1614

PHILOSOPHR....PHILOSOPHER

PHILOSOPHY....SEE GEN/LAWS. PHILOSOPHY OF SCIENCE....SEE
    PHIL/SCI

PHILOSOPHY OF SCIENCE....SEE PHIL/SCI

PHOTOGRAPHS....SEE AUD/VIS

PHS....PUBLIC HEALTH SERVICE

PICKLES D. E1615

PIERCE R.A. E1616

PIERCE/F....PRESIDENT FRANKLIN PIERCE

PIGOU/AC....ARTHUR CECIL PIGOU

PINCUS/J....JOHN PINCUS

PINTO F.B.M. E1617

PITTSBURGH....PITTSBURGH, PENNSYLVANIA

PLAN....PLANNING

N

AMER COUNCIL OF LEARNED SOCIET,THE ACLS CONSTITUENT   BIBLIOG/A
SOCIETY JOURNAL PROJECT. FUT USA+45 LAW NAT/G PLAN   HUM
DIPLOM PHIL/SCI. PAGE 4 E0072   COMPUT/IR
                                                        COMPUTER

B03

CHANNING W.E.,DISCOURSES ON WAR (1820-1840). LAW   WAR
SECT DIPLOM INT/TRADE ALL/VALS. PAGE 21 E0418   PLAN
                                                        LOVE
                                                        ORD/FREE

B03

GRIFFIN A.P.C.,LISTS PUBLISHED 1902-03: LABOR   BIBLIOG/A
PARTICULARLY RELATING TO STRIKES (PAMPHLET). UK   LABOR
USA-45 FINAN WORKER PLAN BARGAIN CRIME GOV/REL   GP/REL
...POLICY 19/20 PARLIAMENT. PAGE 46 E0923   ECO/TAC

S17

ROOT E.,"THE EFFECT OF DEMOCRACY ON INTERNATIONAL   LEGIS
LAW." USA-45 WOR-45 INTELL SOCIETY INT/ORG NAT/G   JURID
CONSULT ACT/RES CREATE PLAN EDU/PROP PEACE SKILL   INT/LAW
...CONCPT METH/CNCPT OBS 20. PAGE 85 E1712

N19

ARNOW K.,SELF-INSURANCE IN THE TREASURY (PAMPHLET).   ADMIN
USA+45 LAW RIGID/FLEX...POLICY METH/COMP 20   PLAN
DEPT/TREAS. PAGE 5 E0104   EFFICIENCY
                                                        NAT/G

N19

ATOMIC INDUSTRIAL FORUM,COMMENTARY ON LEGISLATION   NUC/PWR
TO PERMIT PRIVATE OWNERSHIP OF SPECIAL NUCLEAR   MARKET
MATERIAL (PAMPHLET). USA+45 DELIB/GP LEGIS PLAN OWN   INDUS
...POLICY 20 AEC CONGRESS. PAGE 6 E0111   LAW

N19

OPERATIONS AND POLICY RESEARCH,URUGUAY: ELECTION   POL/PAR
FACTBOOK: NOVEMBER 27, 1966 (PAMPHLET). URUGUAY LAW   CHOOSE
NAT/G LEAD REPRESENT...STAT BIOG CHARTS 20. PAGE 79   PLAN
E1576   ATTIT

B21

STOWELL E.C.,INTERVENTION IN INTERNATIONAL LAW.   BAL/PWR
UNIV LAW SOCIETY INT/ORG ACT/RES PLAN LEGIT ROUTINE   SOVEREIGN
WAR...JURID OBS GEN/LAWS 20. PAGE 94 E1884   WAR

B28

CORBETT P.E.,CANADA AND WORLD POLITICS. LAW CULTURE   NAT/G
SOCIETY STRUCT MARKET INT/ORG FORCES ACT/RES PLAN   CANADA
ECO/TAC LEGIT ORD/FREE PWR RESPECT...SOC CONCPT

TIME/SEQ TREND CMN/WLTH 20 LEAGUE/NAT. PAGE 26
E0504

B28
YANG KUNG-SUN,THE BOOK OF LORD SHANG. LAW ECO/UNDEV ASIA
LOC/G NAT/G NEIGH PLAN ECO/TAC LEGIT ATTIT SKILL JURID
...CONCPT CON/ANAL WORK TOT/POP. PAGE 108 E2164

B29
STURZO L.,THE INTERNATIONAL COMMUNITY AND THE RIGHT INT/ORG
OF WAR (TRANS. BY BARBARA BARCLAY CARTER). CULTURE PLAN
CREATE PROB/SOLV DIPLOM ADJUD CONTROL PEACE PERSON WAR
ORD/FREE...INT/LAW IDEA/COMP PACIFIST 20 CONCPT
LEAGUE/NAT. PAGE 94 E1891

L29
DARWIN L.,"WHAT IS EUGENICS." USA-45 LAW SOCIETY PLAN
FACE/GP FAM ACT/RES ECO/TAC HEALTH...HEAL TREND BIO/SOC
STERTYP 20. PAGE 29 E0568

B31
STOWELL E.C.,INTERNATIONAL LAW. FUT UNIV WOR-45 INT/ORG
SOCIETY CONSULT EX/STRUC FORCES ACT/RES PLAN DIPLOM ROUTINE
EDU/PROP LEGIT DISPL PWR SKILL...POLICY CONCPT OBS INT/LAW
TREND TOT/POP 20. PAGE 94 E1885

B32
EAGLETON C.,INTERNATIONAL GOVERNMENT. BRAZIL FRANCE INT/ORG
GERMANY ITALY UK USSR WOR-45 DELIB/GP TOP/EX PLAN JURID
ECO/TAC EDU/PROP LEGIT ADJUD REGION ARMS/CONT DIPLOM
COERCE ATTIT PWR...GEOG MGT VAL/FREE LEAGUE/NAT 20. INT/LAW
PAGE 34 E0670

B32
MORLEY F.,THE SOCIETY OF NATIONS. EUR+WWI UNIV INT/ORG
WOR-45 LAW CONSTN ACT/RES PLAN EDU/PROP LEGIT CONCPT
ROUTINE...POLICY TIME/SEQ LEAGUE/NAT TOT/POP 20.
PAGE 75 E1496

B38
HARPER S.N.,THE GOVERNMENT OF THE SOVIET UNION. COM MARXISM
USSR LAW CONSTN EX/STRUC PLAN TEC/DEV DIPLOM NAT/G
INT/TRADE ADMIN REV NAT/LISM...POLICY 20. PAGE 50 LEAD
E1001 POL/PAR

S38
CLEMMER D.,"LEADERSHIP PHENOMENA IN A PRISON PUB/INST
COMMUNITY." NEIGH PLAN CHOOSE PERSON ROLE...OBS CRIMLGY
INT. PAGE 23 E0452 LEAD
CLIENT

B39
BENES E.,INTERNATIONAL SECURITY. GERMANY UK NAT/G EUR+WWI
DELIB/GP PLAN BAL/PWR ATTIT ORD/FREE PWR LEAGUE/NAT INT/ORG
20 TREATY. PAGE 10 E0186 WAR

B40
WOLFERS A.,BRITAIN AND FRANCE BETWEEN TWO WORLD DIPLOM
WARS. FRANCE UK INT/ORG NAT/G PLAN BARGAIN ECO/TAC WAR
AGREE ISOLAT ALL/IDEOS...DECISION GEOG 20 TREATY POLICY
VERSAILLES INTERVENT. PAGE 107 E2139

N40
COUNTY GOVERNMENT IN THE UNITED STATES: A LIST OF BIBLIOG/A
RECENT REFERENCES (PAMPHLET). USA-45 LAW PUB/INST LOC/G
PLAN BUDGET CT/SYS CENTRAL 20. PAGE 52 E1027 ADMIN
MUNIC

B41
NIEMEYER G.,LAW WITHOUT FORCE: THE FUNCTION OF COERCE
POLITICS IN INTERNATIONAL LAW. PLAN INSPECT DIPLOM LAW
REPAR LEGIT ADJUD WAR ORD/FREE...IDEA/COMP PWR
METH/COMP GEN/LAWS 20. PAGE 77 E1549 INT/LAW

L41
COMM. STUDY ORGAN. PEACE,"ORGANIZATION OF PEACE." INT/ORG
USA-45 WOR-45 STRATA NAT/G ACT/RES ECO/TAC PLAN
EDU/PROP ADJUD ATTIT ORD/FREE PWR...SOC CONCPT PEACE
ANTHOL LEAGUE/NAT 20. PAGE 24 E0479

B43
US LIBRARY OF CONGRESS,SOCIAL AND CULTURAL PROBLEMS BIBLIOG/A
IN WARTIME: JANUARY-MAY 1943 (SUPPLEMENT 2). WOR-45 WAR
FAM SECT PLAN EDU/PROP CRIME LEISURE RACE/REL DRIVE SOC
HEALTH...GEOG 20 JEWS. PAGE 100 E2014 CULTURE

C43
BENTHAM J.,"PRINCIPLES OF INTERNATIONAL LAW" IN J. INT/LAW
BOWRING, ED., THE WORKS OF JEREMY BENTHAM." UNIV JURID
NAT/G PLAN PROB/SOLV DIPLOM CONTROL SANCTION MORAL WAR
ORD/FREE PWR SOVEREIGN 19. PAGE 10 E0194 PEACE

B44
FULLER G.H.,RENEGOTIATION OF WAR CONTRACTS: A BIBLIOG
SELECTED LIST OF REFERENCES (PAMPHLET). USA-45 WAR
ECO/DEV LG/CO NAT/G OP/RES PLAN BAL/PWR LEGIT LAW

CONTROL...MGT 20. PAGE 42 E0823 FINAN

B45
GALLOWAY E.,ABSTRACTS OF POSTWAR LITERATURE (VOL. BIBLIOG/A
IV) JAN.-JULY, 1945 NOS. 901-1074. POLAND USA+45 NUC/PWR
USSR WOR+45 INDUS LABOR PLAN ECO/TAC INT/TRADE TAX NAT/G
EDU/PROP ADMIN COLONIAL INT/LAW. PAGE 42 E0829 DIPLOM

B45
REVES E.,THE ANATOMY OF PEACE. WOR-45 LAW CULTURE ACT/RES
NAT/G PLAN TEC/DEV EDU/PROP WAR NAT/LISM ATTIT CONCPT
ALL/VALS SOVEREIGN...POLICY HUM TIME/SEQ 20. NUC/PWR
PAGE 84 E1688 PEACE

B46
ROSS A.,TOWARDS A REALISTIC JURISPRUDENCE: A LAW
CRITICISM OF THE DUALISM IN LAW (TRANS. BY ANNIE I. CONCPT
FAUSBOLL). PLAN ADJUD CT/SYS ATTIT RIGID/FLEX IDEA/COMP
POPULISM...JURID PHIL/SCI LOG METH/COMP GEN/LAWS 20
SCANDINAV. PAGE 86 E1720

B47
GORDON D.L.,THE HIDDEN WEAPON: THE STORY OF INT/ORG
ECONOMIC WARFARE. EUR+WWI USA-45 LAW FINAN INDUS ECO/TAC
NAT/G CONSULT FORCES PLAN DOMIN PWR WEALTH INT/TRADE
...INT/LAW CONCPT OBS TOT/POP NAZI 20. PAGE 45 WAR
E0891

B48
NEUBURGER O.,GUIDE TO OFFICIAL PUBLICATIONS OF THE BIBLIOG/A
OTHER AMERICAN REPUBLICS: VENEZUELA (VOL. XIX). NAT/G
VENEZUELA FINAN LEGIS PLAN BUDGET DIPLOM CT/SYS CONSTN
PARL/PROC 19/20. PAGE 77 E1535 LAW

C49
BLODGETT R.H.,"COMPARATIVE ECONOMIC SYSTEMS (REV. METH/COMP
ED.)" WOR-45 AGRI FINAN MARKET LABOR NAT/G PLAN CONCPT
INT/TRADE PRICE...POLICY DECISION BIBLIOG 20. ROUTINE
PAGE 13 E0248

C50
HOLCOMBE A.,"OUR MORE PERFECT UNION." USA+45 USA-45 CONSTN
POL/PAR JUDGE CT/SYS EQUILIB FEDERAL PWR...MAJORIT NAT/G
TREND BIBLIOG 18/20 CONGRESS PRESIDENT. PAGE 54 ADMIN
E1070 PLAN

S52
MCDOUGAL M.S.,"THE COMPARATIVE STUDY OF LAW FOR PLAN
POLICY PURPOSES." FUT NAT/G POL/PAR CONSULT ADJUD JURID
PWR SOVEREIGN...METH/CNCPT IDEA/COMP SIMUL 20. NAT/LISM
PAGE 70 E1403

B53
MAJUMDAR B.B.,PROBLEMS OF PUBLIC ADMINISTRATION IN ECO/UNDEV
INDIA. INDIA INDUS PLAN BUDGET ADJUD CENTRAL DEMAND GOV/REL
WEALTH...WELF/ST ANTHOL 20 CIVIL/SERV. PAGE 68 ADMIN
E1353 MUNIC

B54
BINANI G.D.,INDIA AT A GLANCE (REV. ED.). INDIA INDEX
COM/IND FINAN INDUS LABOR PROVS SCHOOL PLAN DIPLOM CON/ANAL
INT/TRADE ADMIN...JURID 20. PAGE 12 E0229 NAT/G
ECO/UNDEV

C54
CALDWELL L.K.,"THE GOVERNMENT AND ADMINISTRATION OF PROVS
NEW YORK." LOC/G MUNIC POL/PAR SCHOOL CHIEF LEGIS ADMIN
PLAN TAX CT/SYS...MGT SOC/WK BIBLIOG 20 NEWYORK/C. CONSTN
PAGE 19 E0365 EX/STRUC

C54
GUINS G.C.,"SOVIET LAW AND SOVIET SOCIETY." COM LAW
USSR STRATA FAM NAT/G WORKER DOMIN RACE/REL STRUCT
...BIBLIOG 20. PAGE 48 E0960 PLAN

B55
CAVAN R.S.,CRIMINOLOGY (2ND ED.). USA+45 LAW FAM DRIVE
PUB/INST FORCES PLAN WAR AGE/Y PERSON ROLE SUPEGO CRIMLGY
...CHARTS 20 FBI. PAGE 21 E0409 CONTROL
METH/COMP

B55
CHOWDHURI R.N.,INTERNATIONAL MANDATES AND DELIB/GP
TRUSTEESHIP SYSTEMS. WOR+45 STRUCT ECO/UNDEV PLAN
INT/ORG LEGIS DOMIN EDU/PROP LEGIT ADJUD EXEC PWR SOVEREIGN
...CONCPT TIME/SEQ UN 20. PAGE 22 E0434

B55
COMM. STUDY ORGAN. PEACE,REPORTS. WOR-45 ECO/DEV WOR+45
ECO/UNDEV VOL/ASSN CONSULT FORCES PLAN TEC/DEV INT/ORG
DOMIN EDU/PROP NUC/PWR ATTIT PWR WEALTH...JURID ARMS/CONT
STERTYP FAO ILO 20 UN. PAGE 24 E0481

B55
CRAIG J.,BIBLIOGRAPHY OF PUBLIC ADMINISTRATION IN BIBLIOG
AUSTRALIA. CONSTN FINAN EX/STRUC LEGIS PLAN DIPLOM GOV/REL

RECEIVE ADJUD ROUTINE...HEAL 19/20 AUSTRAL   ADMIN
PARLIAMENT. PAGE 27 E0540   NAT/G

                                                   B56
BOTERO G.,THE REASON OF STATE AND THE GREATNESS OF PHIL/SCI
CITIES. SECT CHIEF FORCES PLAN LEAD WAR MORAL   NEW/IDEA
...POLICY 16 MACHIAVELL TREATY. PAGE 14 E0272   CONTROL

                                                   B56
DUNNILL F.,THE CIVIL SERVICE. UK LAW PLAN ADMIN   PERSON
EFFICIENCY DRIVE NEW/LIB...STAT CHARTS 20   WORKER
PARLIAMENT CIVIL/SERV. PAGE 33 E0662   STRATA
                                                   SOC/WK

                                                   B56
ESTEP R.,AN AIR POWER BIBLIOGRAPHY. USA+45 TEC/DEV BIBLIOG/A
BUDGET DIPLOM EDU/PROP DETER CIVMIL/REL...DECISION FORCES
INT/LAW 20. PAGE 35 E0698   WEAPON
                                                   PLAN

                                                   B56
NOTZ R.L.,FEDERAL GRANTS-IN-AID TO STATES: ANALYSIS GIVE
OF LAWS IN FORCE ON SEPTEMBER 10, 1956. USA+45 LAW NAT/G
SCHOOL PLAN ECO/TAC TAX RECEIVE...HEAL JURID 20.   PROVS
PAGE 78 E1558   GOV/REL

                                                   B56
PERKINS D.,CHARLES EVANS HUGHES AND THE AMERICAN   PERSON
DEMOCRATIC STATESMANSHIP. USA+45 USA-45 NAT/G   BIOG
POL/PAR DELIB/GP JUDGE PLAN MORAL PWR...HIST/WRIT DIPLOM
LEAGUE/NAT 20. PAGE 80 E1609

                                                   B57
BLOOMFIELD L.M.,EGYPT, ISRAEL AND THE GULF OF   ISLAM
AQABA: IN INTERNATIONAL LAW. LAW NAT/G CONSULT   INT/LAW
FORCES PLAN ECO/TAC ROUTINE COERCE ATTIT DRIVE   UAR
PERCEPT PERSON RIGID/FLEX LOVE PWR WEALTH...GEOG
CONCPT MYTH TREND. PAGE 13 E0250

                                                   B57
FREUND G.,UNHOLY ALLIANCE. EUR+WWI GERMANY USSR   DIPLOM
FORCES ECO/TAC CONTROL WAR PWR...TREND TREATY.   PLAN
PAGE 40 E0796   POLICY

                                                   B57
JENNINGS I.,PARLIAMENT. UK FINAN INDUS POL/PAR   PARL/PROC
DELIB/GP EX/STRUC PLAN CONTROL...MAJORIT JURID   TOP/EX
PARLIAMENT. PAGE 58 E1163   MGT
                                                   LEGIS

                                                   B57
US COMMISSION GOVT SECURITY,RECOMMENDATIONS; AREA: POLICY
IMMIGRANT PROGRAM. USA+45 LAW WORKER DIPLOM   CONTROL
EDU/PROP WRITING ADMIN PEACE ATTIT...CONCPT ANTHOL PLAN
20 MIGRATION SUBVERT. PAGE 99 E1981   NAT/G

                                                   B57
US COMMISSION GOVT SECURITY,RECOMMENDATIONS; AREA: LEGIS
LEGISLATION. USA+45 USA-45 DELIB/GP PLAN TEC/DEV   SANCTION
CIVMIL/REL ORD/FREE...POLICY DECISION 20 PRIVACY. CRIME
PAGE 99 E1982   CONTROL

                                                   B57
US SENATE COMM ON JUDICIARY,LIMITATION OF APPELLATE CT/SYS
JURISDICTION OF THE SUPREME COURT. USA+45 LAW NAT/G ADJUD
DELIB/GP PLAN ADMIN CONTROL PWR...DECISION 20   POLICY
CONGRESS SUPREME/CT. PAGE 102 E2041   GOV/REL

                                                   B58
AMERICAN SOCIETY PUBLIC ADMIN,STRENGTHENING   ADMIN
MANAGEMENT FOR DEMOCRATIC GOVERNMENT. USA+45 ACADEM NAT/G
EX/STRUC WORKER PLAN BUDGET CONFER CT/SYS   EXEC
EFFICIENCY ANTHOL. PAGE 4 E0083   MGT

                                                   B58
CHAMBERLIN E.H.,LABOR UNIONS AND PUBLIC POLICY.   LABOR
PLAN BARGAIN SANCTION INGP/REL JURID. PAGE 21 E0416 WEALTH
                                                   PWR
                                                   NAT/G

                                                   B58
DUCLOUX L.,FROM BLACKMAIL TO TREASON. FRANCE PLAN COERCE
DIPLOM EDU/PROP PRESS RUMOR NAT/LISM...CRIMLGY 20. CRIME
PAGE 33 E0653   NAT/G
                                                   PWR

                                                   B58
MOSKOWITZ M.,HUMAN RIGHTS AND WORLD ORDER. INT/ORG DIPLOM
PLAN GP/REL NAT/LISM SOVEREIGN...CONCPT 20 UN   INT/LAW
TREATY CIV/RIGHTS. PAGE 75 E1502   ORD/FREE

                                                   S58
SCHUBERT G.A.,"THE STUDY OF JUDICIAL DECISION-   JUDGE
MAKING AS AN ASPECT OF POLITICAL BEHAVIOR." PLAN   DECISION
ADJUD CT/SYS INGP/REL PERSON...PHIL/SCI SOC QUANT CON/ANAL
STAT CHARTS IDEA/COMP SOC/EXP. PAGE 89 E1779   GAME

                                                   B59
COUNCIL OF STATE GOVERNMENTS,STATE GOVERNMENT: AN BIBLIOG/A
ANNOTATED BIBLIOGRAPHY (PAMPHLET). USA+45 LAW AGRI PROVS
INDUS WORKER PLAN TAX ADJUST AGE/Y ORD/FREE...HEAL LOC/G
MGT 20. PAGE 26 E0521   ADMIN

                                                   B59
ELLIOTT S.D.,IMPROVING OUR COURTS. LAW EX/STRUC   CT/SYS
PLAN PROB/SOLV ADJUD ADMIN TASK CRIME EFFICIENCY   JURID
ORD/FREE 20. PAGE 34 E0684   GOV/REL
                                                   NAT/G

                                                   B59
FERRY W.H.,THE CORPORATION AND THE ECONOMY. CLIENT LG/CO
LAW CONSTN LABOR NAT/G PLAN INT/TRADE PARTIC CONSEN CONTROL
ORD/FREE PWR POLICY. PAGE 37 E0742   REPRESENT

                                                   B59
HALEY A.G.,FIRST COLLOQUIUM ON THE LAW OF OUTER   SPACE
SPACE. WOR+45 INT/ORG ACT/RES PLAN BAL/PWR CONFER LAW
ATTIT PWR...POLICY JURID CHARTS ANTHOL 20. PAGE 49 SOVEREIGN
E0979   CONTROL

                                                   B59
COLUMBIA U. BUREAU OF APPL SOC RES, ATTITUDES OF   ATTIT
PROMINENT AMERICANS TOWARD "WORLD PEACE THROUGH   ACT/RES
WORLD LAW" (SUPRA-NATL ORGANIZATION FOR WAR   INT/LAW
PREVENTION). USA+45 USSR ELITES FORCES PLAN   STAT
PROB/SOLV CONTROL WAR PWR...POLICY SOC QU IDEA/COMP
20 UN. PAGE 82 E1644

                                                   L59
COWAN T.A.,"A SYMPOSIUM ON GROUP INTERESTS AND THE ADJUD
LAW" USA+45 LAW MARKET LABOR PLAN INT/TRADE TAX   PWR
RACE/REL RIGID/FLEX...JURID ANTHOL 20. PAGE 27   INGP/REL
E0528   CREATE

                                                   S59
JENKS C.W.,"THE CHALLENGE OF UNIVERSALITY." FUT   INT/ORG
UNIV CONSTN CULTURE CONSULT CREATE PLAN LEGIT ATTIT LAW
MORAL ORD/FREE RESPECT...MAJORIT JURID 20. PAGE 58 PEACE
E1155   INT/LAW

                                                   N59
NATIONAL ASSN HOME BUILDERS,COMMUNITY FACILITIES: A BIBLIOG/A
LIST OF SELECTED REFERENCES (PAMPHLET). USA+45   PLAN
DIST/IND FINAN SERV/IND SCHOOL CREATE CONTROL   LOC/G
FEDERAL...JURID 20. PAGE 76 E1525   MUNIC

                                                   B60
ATOMIC INDUSTRIAL FORUM,ATOMS FOR INDUSTRY: WORLD NUC/PWR
FORUM. WOR+45 FINAN COST UTIL...JURID ANTHOL 20.   INDUS
PAGE 6 E0113   PLAN
                                                   PROB/SOLV

                                                   B60
CLARK G.,WORLD PEACE THROUGH WORLD LAW. FUT WOR+45 INT/ORG
CONSULT FORCES ACT/RES CREATE PLAN ADMIN ROUTINE   LAW
ARMS/CONT DETER ATTIT PWR...JURID VAL/FREE UNESCO PEACE
20 UN. PAGE 23 E0449   INT/LAW

                                                   B60
GONZALEZ NAVARRO M.,LA COLONIZACION EN MEXICO,   ECO/UNDEV
1877-1910. AGRI NAT/G PLAN PROB/SOLV INCOME   GEOG
...POLICY JURID CENSUS 19/20 MEXIC/AMER MIGRATION. HABITAT
PAGE 44 E0883   COLONIAL

                                                   B60
HEAP D.,AN OUTLINE OF PLANNING LAW (3RD ED.). UK   MUNIC
LAW PROB/SOLV ADMIN CONTROL 20. PAGE 51 E1020   PLAN
                                                   JURID
                                                   LOC/G

                                                   B60
LENCZOWSKI G.,OIL AND STATE IN THE MIDDLE EAST. FUT ISLAM
IRAN LAW ECO/UNDEV EXTR/IND NAT/G TOP/EX PLAN   INDUS
TEC/DEV ECO/TAC LEGIT ADMIN COERCE ATTIT ALL/VALS NAT/LISM
PWR...CHARTS 20. PAGE 64 E1283

                                                   B60
SCHUBERT G.,THE PUBLIC INTEREST. USA+45 CONSULT   POLICY
PLAN PROB/SOLV ADJUD ADMIN GP/REL PWR ALL/IDEOS 20. DELIB/GP
PAGE 88 E1770   REPRESENT
                                                   POL/PAR

                                                   B60
STEIN E.,AMERICAN ENTERPRISE IN THE EUROPEAN COMMON MARKET
MARKET: A LEGAL PROFILE. EUR+WWI FUT USA+45 SOCIETY ADJUD
STRUCT ECO/DEV NAT/G VOL/ASSN CONSULT PLAN TEC/DEV INT/LAW
ECO/TAC INT/TRADE ADMIN ATTIT RIGID/FLEX PWR...MGT
NEW/IDEA STAT TREND COMPUT/IR SIMUL EEC 20. PAGE 93
E1867

                                                   B60
WEBSTER J.A.,A GENERAL STUDY OF THE DEPARTMENT OF ORD/FREE

DEFENSE INTERNAL SECURITY PROGRAM. USA+45 WORKER   PLAN
TEC/DEV ADJUD CONTROL CT/SYS EXEC GOV/REL COST   ADMIN
...POLICY DECISION MGT 20 DEPT/DEFEN SUPREME/CT.   NAT/G
PAGE 105 E2105

                                B60
WOETZEL R.K.,THE INTERNATIONAL CONTROL OF AIRSPACE   INT/ORG
AND OUTERSPACE. FUT WOR+45 AIR CONSTN STRUCT   JURID
CONSULT PLAN TEC/DEV ADJUD RIGID/FLEX KNOWL   SPACE
ORD/FREE PWR...TECHNIC GEOG MGT NEW/IDEA TREND   INT/LAW
COMPUT/IR VAL/FREE 20 TREATY. PAGE 107 E2137

                                L60
DEAN A.W.,"SECOND GENEVA CONFERENCE OF THE LAW OF   INT/ORG
THE SEA: THE FIGHT FOR FREEDOM OF THE SEAS." FUT   JURID
USA+45 USSR WOR+45 WOR-45 SEA CONSTN STRUCT PLAN   INT/LAW
INT/TRADE ADJUD ADMIN ORD/FREE...DECISION RECORD
TREND GEN/LAWS 20 TREATY. PAGE 30 E0600

                                L60
STEIN E.,"LEGAL REMEDIES OF ENTERPRISES IN THE   MARKET
EUROPEAN ECONOMIC COMMUNITY." EUR+WWI FUT ECO/DEV ADJUD
INDUS PLAN ECO/TAC ADMIN PWR...MGT MATH STAT TREND
CON/ANAL EEC 20. PAGE 93 E1868

                                S60
RHYNE C.S.,"LAW AS AN INSTRUMENT FOR PEACE." FUT   ADJUD
WOR+45 PLAN LEGIT ROUTINE ARMS/CONT NUC/PWR ATTIT EDU/PROP
ORD/FREE...JURID METH/CNCPT. TREND CON/ANAL HYPO/EXP INT/LAW
COLD/WAR 20. PAGE 84 E1690   PEACE

                                S60
SCHWELB E.,"INTERNATIONAL CONVENTIONS ON HUMAN   INT/ORG
RIGHTS." FUT WOR+45 LAW ADJUD INTELL SOCIETY   HUM
STRUCT VOL/ASSN DELIB/GP PLAN ADJUD SUPEGO LOVE
MORAL...SOC CONCPT STAT RECORD HIST/WRIT TREND 20
UN. PAGE 89 E1790

                                S60
THOMPSON K.W.,"MORAL PURPOSE IN FOREIGN POLICY: MORAL
REALITIES AND ILLUSIONS." WOR+45 WOR-45 LAW CULTURE JURID
SOCIETY INT/ORG PLAN ADJUD ADMIN COERCE RIGID/FLEX DIPLOM
SUPEGO KNOWL ORD/FREE PWR...SOC TREND SOC/EXP
TOT/POP 20. PAGE 96 E1921

                                S60
WRIGHT Q.,"LEGAL ASPECTS OF THE U-2 INCIDENT." COM PWR
USA+45 USSR STRUCT NAT/G FORCES PLAN TEC/DEV ADJUD POLICY
RIGID/FLEX MORAL ORD/FREE...DECISION INT/LAW JURID SPACE
PSY TREND GEN/LAWS COLD/WAR VAL/FREE 20 U-2.
PAGE 108 E2157

                                B61
ANAND R.P.,COMPULSORY JURISDICTION OF INTERNATIONAL INT/ORG
COURT OF JUSTICE. FUT WOR+45 SOCIETY PLAN LEGIT   COERCE
ADJUD ATTIT DRIVE PERSON ORD/FREE...JURID CONCPT   INT/LAW
TREND 20 ICJ. PAGE 5 E0086

                                B61
JENKS C.W.,INTERNATIONAL IMMUNITIES. PLAN EDU/PROP INT/ORG
ADMIN PERCEPT...OLD/LIB JURID CONCPT TREND TOT/POP. DIPLOM
PAGE 58 E1157

                                B61
MURPHY E.F.,WATER PURITY: A STUDY IN LEGAL CONTROL SEA
OF NATURAL RESOURCES. LOC/G ACT/RES PLAN TEC/DEV   LAW
LOBBY GP/REL COST ATTIT HEALTH ORD/FREE...HEAL   PROVS
JURID 20 WISCONSIN WATER. PAGE 75 E1506   CONTROL

                                B61
NEW JERSEY LEGISLATURE-SENATE,PUBLIC HEARINGS   LEGIS
BEFORE COMMITTEE ON REVISION AND AMENDMENT OF LAWS MUNIC
ON SENATE BILL NO. 8. USA+45 FINAN PROVS WORKER   INDUS
ACT/RES PLAN BUDGET TAX CRIME...IDEA/COMP 20   PROB/SOLV
NEW/JERSEY URBAN/RNWL. PAGE 77 E1537

                                B61
POOLEY B.J.,PLANNING AND ZONING IN THE UNITED   PLAN
STATES. USA+45 MUNIC DELIB/GP ACT/RES PROB/SOLV   LOC/G
TEC/DEV ADJUD ADMIN REGION 20 ZONING. PAGE 81 E1628 PROVS
                                LAW

                                B61
SCOTT A.M.,POLITICS, USA; CASES ON THE AMERICAN   CT/SYS
DEMOCRATIC PROCESS. USA+45 CHIEF FORCES DIPLOM   CONSTN
LOBBY CHOOSE RACE/REL FEDERAL ATTIT...JURID ANTHOL NAT/G
T 20 PRESIDENT CONGRESS CIVIL/LIB. PAGE 90 E1795   PLAN

                                L61
FELLMAN D.,"ACADEMIC FREEDOM IN AMERICAN LAW." LAW ACADEM
CONSTN NAT/G VOL/ASSN PLAN PERSON KNOWL NEW/LIB.   ORD/FREE
PAGE 37 E0732   LEGIS
                                CULTURE

                                L61
SAND P.T.,"AN HISTORICAL SURVEY OF INTERNATIONAL   INT/ORG

AIR LAW SINCE 1944." USA+45 USA-45 WOR+45 WOR-45   LAW
SOCIETY ECO/DEV NAT/G CONSULT EX/STRUC ACT/RES PLAN INT/LAW
LEGIT ROUTINE...JURID CONCPT METH/CNCPT TREND 20.   SPACE
PAGE 87 E1744

                                L61
TAUBENFELD H.J.,"A REGIME FOR OUTER SPACE." FUT   INT/ORG
UNIV R+D ACT/RES PLAN BAL/PWR LEGIT ARMS/CONT   ADJUD
ORD/FREE...POLICY JURID TREND UN TOT/POP 20   SPACE
COLD/WAR. PAGE 95 E1910

                                S61
ALGER C.F.,"NON-RESOLUTION CONSEQUENCES OF THE   INT/ORG
UNITED NATIONS AND THEIR EFFECT ON INTERNATIONAL   DRIVE
CONFLICT." WOR+45 CONSTN ECO/DEV NAT/G CONSULT   BAL/PWR
DELIB/GP TOP/EX ACT/RES PLAN DIPLOM EDU/PROP
ROUTINE ATTIT ALL/VALS...INT/LAW TOT/POP UN 20.
PAGE 3 E0065

                                S61
LIPSON L.,"AN ARGUMENT ON THE LEGALITY OF   INT/ORG
RECONNAISSANCE STATELLITES." COM USA+45 USSR WOR+45 LAW
AIR INTELL NAT/G CONSULT PLAN DIPLOM LEGIT ROUTINE SPACE
ATTIT...INT/LAW JURID CONCPT METH/CNCPT TREND
COLD/WAR 20. PAGE 65 E1302

                                S61
MACHOWSKI K.,"SELECTED PROBLEMS OF NATIONAL   UNIV
SOVEREIGNTY WITH REFERENCE TO THE LAW OF OUTER   ACT/RES
SPACE." FUT WOR+45 AIR LAW INTELL SOCIETY ECO/DEV   NUC/PWR
PLAN EDU/PROP DETER DRIVE PERCEPT SOVEREIGN   SPACE
...POLICY INT/LAW OBS TREND TOT/POP 20. PAGE 67
E1339

                                S61
RICHSTEIN A.R.,"LEGAL RULES IN NUCLEAR WEAPONS   NUC/PWR
EMPLOYMENTS." FUT WOR+45 LAW SOCIETY FORCES PLAN   TEC/DEV
WEAPON RIGID/FLEX...HEAL CONCPT TREND VAL/FREE 20. MORAL
PAGE 85 E1696   ARMS/CONT

                                B62
BUREAU OF NATIONAL AFFAIRS,FEDERAL-STATE REGULATION WELF/ST
OF WELFARE FUNDS (REV. ED.). USA+45 LAW LEGIS   WEALTH
DEBATE AGE/O 20 CONGRESS. PAGE 17 E0337   PLAN
                                SOC/WK

                                B62
DOUGLAS W.O.,DEMOCRACY'S MANIFESTO. COM USA+45   DIPLOM
ECO/UNDEV INT/ORG FORCES PLAN NEUTRAL TASK MARXISM POLICY
...JURID 20 NATO SEATO. PAGE 32 E0642   NAT/G
                                ORD/FREE

                                B62
UNECA LIBRARY,NEW ACQUISITIONS IN THE UNECA   BIBLIOG
LIBRARY. LAW NAT/G PLAN PROB/SOLV TEC/DEV ADMIN   AFR
REGION...GEOG SOC 20 UN. PAGE 98 E1956   ECO/UNDEV
                                INT/ORG

                                B62
US CONGRESS,COMMUNICATIONS SATELLITE LEGISLATION: SPACE
HEARINGS BEFORE COMM ON AERON AND SPACE SCIENCES ON COM/IND
BILLS S2550 AND 2814. WOR+45 LAW VOL/ASSN PLAN   ADJUD
DIPLOM CONTROL OWN PEACE...NEW/IDEA CONGRESS NASA. GOV/REL
PAGE 99 E1990

                                L62
ERDMANN H.H.,"ADMINISTRATIVE LAW AND FARM   AGRI
ECONOMICS." USA+45 LOC/G NAT/G PLAN PROB/SOLV LOBBY ADMIN
...DECISION ANTHOL 20. PAGE 35 E0695   ADJUD
                                POLICY

                                L62
MURACCIOLE L.,"LA LOI FONDAMENTALE DE LA REPUBLIQUE AFR
DU CONGO." WOR+45 SOCIETY ECO/UNDEV INT/ORG NAT/G   CONSTN
LEGIS PLAN LEGIT ADJUD COLONIAL ROUTINE ATTIT
SOVEREIGN 20 CONGO. PAGE 75 E1504

                                S62
CRANE R.D.,"LAW AND STRATEGY IN SPACE." FUT USA+45 CONCPT
WOR+45 AIR LAW INT/ORG NAT/G FORCES ACT/RES PLAN   SPACE
BAL/PWR LEGIT ARMS/CONT COERCE ORD/FREE...POLICY
INT/LAW JURID SOC/EXP 20 TREATY. PAGE 27 E0542

                                S62
SCHACHTER O.,"DAG HAMMARSKJOLD AND THE RELATION OF ACT/RES
LAW TO POLITICS." FUT WOR+45 INT/ORG CONSULT PLAN   ADJUD
TEC/DEV BAL/PWR DIPLOM LEGIT ATTIT PERCEPT ORD/FREE
...POLICY JURID CONCPT OBS TESTS STERTYP GEN/LAWS
20 HAMMARSK/D. PAGE 87 E1751

                                B63
CARTER G.M.,FIVE AFRICAN STATES: RESPONSES TO   AFR
DIVERSITY. CONSTN CULTURE STRATA LEGIS PLAN ECO/TAC SOCIETY
DOMIN EDU/PROP CT/SYS EXEC CHOOSE ATTIT HEALTH
ORD/FREE PWR...TIME/SEQ TOT/POP VAL/FREE. PAGE 20
E0398

DE GRAZIA A.,APPORTIONMENT AND REPRESENTATIVE
GOVERNMENT. CONSTN POL/PAR LEGIS PLAN ADJUD DISCRIM
RATIONAL...CONCPT STAT PREDICT TREND IDEA/COMP.
PAGE 29 E0583

B63
REPRESENT
APPORT
NAT/G
MUNIC

DEENER D.R.,CANADA - UNITED STATES TREATY
RELATIONS. CANADA USA+45 USA-45 NAT/G FORCES PLAN
PROB/SOLV AGREE NUC/PWR...TREND 18/20 TREATY.
PAGE 30 E0603

B63
DIPLOM
INT/LAW
POLICY

DUNN F.S.,PEACE-MAKING AND THE SETTLEMENT WITH
JAPAN. ASIA USA+45 USA-45 FORCES BAL/PWR ECO/TAC
CONFER WAR PWR SOVEREIGN 20 CHINJAP COLD/WAR
TREATY. PAGE 33 E0661

B63
POLICY
PEACE
PLAN
DIPLOM

ECOLE NATIONALE D'ADMIN.BIBLIOGRAPHIE SELECTIVE
D'OUVRAGES DE LANGUE FRANCAISE TRAITANT DES
PROBLEMES GOUVERNEMENTAUX ET ADMINISTRATIFS. NAT/G
FORCES ACT/RES OP/RES PLAN PROB/SOLV BUDGET ADJUD
COLONIAL LEAD 20. PAGE 34 E0672

B63
BIBLIOG
AFR
ADMIN
EX/STRUC

HAUSMAN W.H.,MANAGING ECONOMIC DEVELOPMENT IN
AFRICA. AFR USA+45 LAW FINAN WORKER TEC/DEV WEALTH
...ANTHOL 20. PAGE 51 E1012

B63
ECO/UNDEV
PLAN
FOR/AID
MGT

NEWMAN E.S.,THE FREEDOM READER. USA+45 LEGIS TOP/EX
PLAN ADJUD CONTROL CT/SYS DISCRIM...DECISION ANTHOL
20 SUPREME/CT CIV/RIGHTS. PAGE 77 E1541

B63
RACE/REL
LAW
POLICY
ORD/FREE

PRYOR F.L.,THE COMMUNIST FOREIGN TRADE SYSTEM. COM
CZECHOSLVK GERMANY YUGOSLAVIA LAW ECO/DEV DIST/IND
POL/PAR PLAN DOMIN TOTALSM DRIVE RIGID/FLEX WEALTH
...STAT STAND/INT CHARTS 20. PAGE 83 E1657

B63
ATTIT
ECO/TAC

ROBERTSON A.H.,HUMAN RIGHTS IN EUROPE. CONSTN
SOCIETY INT/ORG NAT/G VOL/ASSN DELIB/GP ACT/RES
PLAN ADJUD REGION ROUTINE ATTIT LOVE ORD/FREE
RESPECT...JURID SOC CONCPT SOC/EXP UN 20. PAGE 85
E1705

B63
EUR+WWI
PERSON

US COMN CIVIL RIGHTS,REPORT ON MISSISSIPPI. LAW
LOC/G NAT/G LEGIS PLAN PROB/SOLV DISCRIM SOC/INTEG
20 MISSISSIPP NEGRO. PAGE 99 E1987

B63
RACE/REL
CONSTN
ORD/FREE
COERCE

US SENATE COMM ON JUDICIARY.US PERSONNEL SECURITY
PRACTICES. USA+45 DELIB/GP ADMIN ORD/FREE
...CHARTS 20 CONGRESS CIVIL/SERV. PAGE 102 E2049

B63
PLAN
NAT/G
CONTROL
WORKER

LOEVINGER L.,"JURIMETRICS* THE METHODOLOGY OF LEGAL
INQUIRY." COMPUTER CREATE PLAN TEC/DEV AUTOMAT
CT/SYS EFFICIENCY...DECISION PHIL/SCI NEW/IDEA
QUANT PREDICT. PAGE 66 E1318

L63
COMPUT/IR
JURID
GEN/METH
ADJUD

MCDOUGAL M.S.,"THE ENJOYMENT AND ACQUISITION OF
RESOURCES IN OUTER SPACE." CHRIST-17C FUT WOR+45
WOR-45 LAW EXTR/IND INT/ORG ACT/RES CREATE TEC/DEV
ECO/TAC LEGIT COERCE HEALTH KNOWL ORD/FREE PWR
WEALTH...JURID HIST/WRIT VAL/FREE. PAGE 70 E1408

L63
PLAN
TREND

GERHARD H.,"COMMODITY TRADE STABILIZATION THROUGH
INTERNATIONAL AGREEMENTS." WOR+45 ECO/DEV ECO/UNDEV
NAT/G ROUTINE ORD/FREE...INT/LAW OBS TREND GEN/METH
TOT/POP 20. PAGE 43 E0850

S63
PLAN
ECO/TAC
INT/TRADE

WALKER H.,"THE INTERNATIONAL LAW OF COMMODITY
AGREEMENTS." FUT WOR+45 ECO/DEV ECO/UNDEV FINAN
INT/ORG NAT/G CONSULT CREATE PLAN ECO/TAC ATTIT
PERCEPT...CONCPT GEN/LAWS TOT/POP GATT 20. PAGE 105
E2095

S63
MARKET
VOL/ASSN
INT/LAW
INT/TRADE

BOGEN J.I.,FINANCIAL HANDBOOK (4TH ED.). UNIV LAW
PLAN TAX RISK 20. PAGE 13 E0257

B64
FINAN
DICTIONARY

FRYDENSBERG P.,PEACE-KEEPING: EXPERIENCE AND
EVALUATION: THE OSLO PAPERS. NORWAY FORCES PLAN

B64
INT/ORG
DIPLOM

CONTROL...INT/LAW 20 UN. PAGE 41 E0814

PEACE
COERCE

HAAR C.M.,LAW AND LAND: ANGLO-AMERICAN PLANNING
PRACTICE. UK USA+45 NAT/G TEC/DEV BUDGET CT/SYS
INGP/REL EFFICIENCY OWN...JURID 20. PAGE 49 E0967

B64
LAW
PLAN
MUNIC
NAT/COMP

OPPENHEIMER M.,A MANUAL FOR DIRECT ACTION. USA+45
SCHOOL FORCES ADJUD CT/SYS SUFF RACE/REL DISCRIM
...POLICY CHARTS 20. PAGE 79 E1580

B64
PLAN
VOL/ASSN
JURID
LEAD

REGALA R.,WORLD PEACE THROUGH DIPLOMACY AND LAW.
S/ASIA WOR+45 ECO/UNDEV INT/ORG FORCES PLAN
PROB/SOLV FOR/AID NUC/PWR WAR...POLICY INT/LAW 20.
PAGE 84 E1679

B64
DIPLOM
PEACE
ADJUD

RICHARDSON I.L.,BIBLIOGRAFIA BRASILEIRA DE
ADMINISTRACAO PUBLICA E ASSUNTOS CORRELATOS. BRAZIL
CONSTN FINAN LOC/G NAT/G POL/PAR PLAN DIPLOM
RECEIVE ATTIT...METH 20. PAGE 84 E1694

B64
BIBLIOG
MGT
ADMIN
LAW

ROBERTS HL,FOREIGN AFFAIRS BIBLIOGRAPHY, 1952-1962.
ECO/DEV SECT PLAN FOR/AID INT/TRADE ARMS/CONT
NAT/LISM ATTIT...INT/LAW GOV/COMP IDEA/COMP 20.
PAGE 85 E1703

B64
BIBLIOG/A
DIPLOM
INT/ORG
WAR

SCHWARTZ M.D.,CONFERENCE ON SPACE SCIENCE AND SPACE
LAW. FUT COM/IND NAT/G FORCES ACT/RES PLAN BUDGET
DIPLOM NUC/PWR WEAPON...POLICY ANTHOL 20. PAGE 89
E1788

B64
SPACE
LAW
PEACE
TEC/DEV

STANGER R.J.,ESSAYS ON INTERVENTION. PLAN PROB/SOLV
BAL/PWR ADJUD COERCE WAR ROLE PWR...INT/LAW CONCPT
20 UN INTERVENT. PAGE 93 E1865

B64
SOVEREIGN
DIPLOM
POLICY
LEGIT

UN PUB. INFORM. ORGAN.,EVERY MAN'S UNITED NATIONS.
UNIV WOR+45 CONSTN CULTURE SOCIETY ECO/DEV
ECO/UNDEV NAT/G ACT/RES PLAN ECO/TAC INT/TRADE
EDU/PROP LEGIT PEACE ATTIT ALL/VALS...POLICY HUM
INT/LAW CONCPT CHARTS UN TOT/POP 20. PAGE 97 E1954

B64
INT/ORG
ROUTINE

WILLIAMS S.P.,TOWARD A GENUINE WORLD SECURITY
SYSTEM (PAMPHLET). WOR+45 INT/ORG FORCES PLAN
NUC/PWR ORD/FREE...INT/LAW CONCPT UN PRESIDENT.
PAGE 106 E2123

B64
BIBLIOG/A
ARMS/CONT
DIPLOM
PEACE

BERKS R.N.,"THE US AND WEAPONS CONTROL." WOR+45 LAW
INT/ORG NAT/G LEGIS EXEC COERCE PEACE ATTIT
RIGID/FLEX ALL/VALS PWR...POLICY TOT/POP 20.
PAGE 11 E0204

L64
USA+45
PLAN
ARMS/CONT

BALDWIN G.B.,"THE DEPENDENCE OF SCIENCE ON LAW AND
GOVERNMENT--THE INTERNATIONAL GEOPHYSICAL YEAR--A
CASE STUDY." WOR+45 LAW INT/ORG PROF/ORG LEGIS PLAN
EDU/PROP...TIME/SEQ VAL/FREE 20. PAGE 8 E0144

S64
NAT/G
KNOWL

HICKEY D.,"THE PHILOSOPHICAL ARGUMENT FOR WORLD
GOVERNMENT." WOR+45 SOCIETY ACT/RES PLAN LEGIT
ADJUD PEACE PERCEPT PERSON ORD/FREE...HUM JURID
PHIL/SCI METH/CNCPT CON/ANAL STERTYP GEN/LAWS
TOT/POP 20. PAGE 52 E1039

S64
FUT
INT/ORG

ANDRUS H.L.,LIBERALISM, CONSERVATISM, MORMONISM.
USA+45 PLAN ADJUD CONTROL HAPPINESS ORD/FREE
CONSERVE NEW/LIB WORSHIP 20. PAGE 5 E0097

B65
SECT
UTOPIA
MORAL

CAMPBELL E.H.,SURVEYS, SUBDIVISIONS AND PLATTING,
AND BOUNDARIES: WASHINGTON STATE LAW AND JUDICIAL
DECISIONS. USA+45 LAW LOC/G...DECISION JURID
CON/ANAL BIBLIOG WASHINGT/G PARTITION WATER.
PAGE 19 E0372

B65
CONSTN
PLAN
GEOG
PROVS

CARTER R.L.,EQUALITY. LAW LABOR NEIGH SCHOOL
RACE/REL 20 NEGRO. PAGE 20 E0402

B65
POLICY
DISCRIM
PLAN
CREATE

CONGRESSIONAL QUARTERLY SERV,FEDERAL ROLE IN EDUCATION (PAMPHLET). LAW SCHOOL PLAN TAX ADJUD ...CHARTS SOC/INTEG 20 PRESIDENT. PAGE 25 E0487
B65
ACADEM
DISCRIM
RECEIVE
FEDERAL

COOPER F.E.,STATE ADMINISTRATIVE LAW (2 VOLS.). LAW LEGIS PLAN TAX ADJUD CT/SYS FEDERAL PWR...CONCPT 20. PAGE 25 E0501
B65
JURID
CONSTN
ADMIN
PROVS

FRYE R.J.,HOUSING AND URBAN RENEWAL IN ALABAMA. USA+45 NEIGH LEGIS BUDGET ADJUD ADMIN PARTIC...MGT 20 ALABAMA URBAN/RNWL. PAGE 41 E0815
B65
MUNIC
PROB/SOLV
PLAN
GOV/REL

GAJENDRAGADKAR P.B.,LAW, LIBERTY AND SOCIAL JUSTICE. INDIA CONSTN NAT/G SECT PLAN ECO/TAC PRESS POPULISM...SOC METH/COMP 20 HINDU. PAGE 42 E0826
B65
ORD/FREE
LAW
ADJUD
JURID

JOHNSTON D.M.,THE INTERNATIONAL LAW OF FISHERIES: A FRAMEWORK FOR POLICYORIENTED INQUIRIES. WOR+45 ACT/RES PLAN PROB/SOLV CONTROL SOVEREIGN. PAGE 59 E1171
B65
CONCPT
EXTR/IND
JURID
DIPLOM

SHARMA S.A.,PARLIAMENTARY GOVERNMENT IN INDIA. INDIA FINAN LOC/G PROVS DELIB/GP PLAN ADMIN CT/SYS FEDERAL...JURID 20. PAGE 90 E1814
B65
NAT/G
CONSTN
PARL/PROC
LEGIS

US LIBRARY OF CONGRESS,INTERNAL SECURITY AND SUBVERSION. USA+45 ACADEM LOC/G NAT/G PROVS ...POLICY ANARCH DECISION 20 CIVIL/SERV SUBVERT SEDITION. PAGE 101 E2020
B65
CONTROL
ADJUD
LAW
PLAN

US SENATE,US INTERNATIONAL SPACE PROGRAMS, 1959-65: STAFF REPORT FOR COMM ON AERONAUTICAL AND SPACE SCIENCES. WOR+45 VOL/ASSN CIVMIL/REL 20 CONGRESS NASA TREATY. PAGE 101 E2027
B65
SPACE
DIPLOM
PLAN
GOV/REL

DIXON R.G.,"NEW CONSTITUTIONAL FORMS FOR METROPOLIS: REAPPORTIONED COUNTY BOARDS; LOCAL COUNCILS OF GOVERNMENT." LAW CONSTN LEAD APPORT REPRESENT DECISION. PAGE 32 E0631
S65
MUNIC
REGION
GOV/COMP
PLAN

KHOURI F.J.,"THE JORDON RIVER CONTROVERSY." LAW SOCIETY ECO/UNDEV AGRI FINAN INDUS SECT FORCES ACT/RES PLAN TEC/DEV ECO/TAC EDU/PROP COERCE ATTIT DRIVE PERCEPT RIGID/FLEX ALL/VALS...GEOG SOC MYTH WORK. PAGE 61 E1212
S65
ISLAM
INT/ORG
ISRAEL
JORDAN

PRABHAKAR P.,"SURVEY OF RESEARCH AND SOURCE MATERIALS; THE SINO-INDIAN BORDER DISPUTE." CHINA/COM INDIA LAW NAT/G PLAN BAL/PWR WAR...POLICY 20 COLD/WAR. PAGE 82 E1645
S65
BIBLIOG
ASIA
S/ASIA
DIPLOM

CLARK G.,WORLD PEACE THROUGH WORLD LAW; TWO ALTERNATIVE PLANS. WOR+45 DELIB/GP FORCES TAX CONFER ADJUD SANCTION ARMS/CONT WAR CHOOSE PRIVIL 20 UN COLD/WAR. PAGE 23 E0450
B66
INT/LAW
PEACE
PLAN
INT/ORG

FENN DH J.R.,BUSINESS DECISION MAKING AND GOVERNMENT POLICY. SERV/IND LEGIS LICENSE ADMIN CONTROL GP/REL INGP/REL 20 CASEBOOK. PAGE 37 E0736
B66
DECISION
PLAN
NAT/G
LG/CO

FRIEDMANN W.G.,INTERNATIONAL FINANCIAL AID. USA+45 ECO/DEV ECO/UNDEV NAT/G VOL/ASSN EX/STRUC PLAN RENT GIVE BAL/PAY PWR...GEOG INT/LAW STAT TREND UN EEC COMECON. PAGE 41 E0806
B66
INT/ORG
FOR/AID
TEC/DEV
ECO/TAC

GREENE L.E.,GOVERNMENT IN TENNESSEE (2ND ED.). USA+45 DIST/IND INDUS POL/PAR EX/STRUC LEGIS PLAN BUDGET GIVE CT/SYS...MGT T 20 TENNESSEE. PAGE 46 E0909
B66
PROVS
LOC/G
CONSTN
ADMIN

JACOBSON H.K.,DIPLOMATS, SCIENTISTS, AND POLITICIANS* THE UNITED STATES AND THE NUCLEAR TEST BAN NEGOTIATIONS. USA+45 USSR ACT/RES PLAN CONFER DETER NUC/PWR CONSEN ORD/FREE...INT TREATY. PAGE 57
B66
DIPLOM
ARMS/CONT
TECHRACY
INT/ORG

E1146

MACIVER R.M.,THE PREVENTION AND CONTROL OF DELINQUENCY. USA+45 STRATA PUB/INST ANOMIE ATTIT HABITAT PERSON HEALTH...CRIMLGY PSY SOC METH. PAGE 67 E1341
B66
AGE/Y
PLAN
ADJUST
CRIME

PLATE H.,PARTEIFINANZIERUNG UND GRUNDESETZ. GERMANY NAT/G PLAN GIVE PAY INCOME WEALTH...JURID 20. PAGE 81 E1619
B66
POL/PAR
CONSTN
FINAN

US SENATE COMM AERO SPACE SCI,SOVIET SPACE PROGRAMS, 1962-65; GOALS AND PURPOSES, ACHIEVEMENTS, PLANS, AND INTERNATIONAL IMPLICATIONS. USA+45 USSR R+D FORCES PLAN EDU/PROP PRESS ADJUD ARMS/CONT ATTIT MARXISM. PAGE 101 E2028
B66
CONSULT
SPACE
FUT
DIPLOM

CONGRESSIONAL QUARTERLY SERV,HOUSING A NATION (PAMPHLET). USA+45 LAW STRUCT DIST/IND DELIB/GP ...GEOG CHARTS 20 DEPT/HUD. PAGE 25 E0490
N66
HABITAT
NAT/G
PLAN
MUNIC

BUREAU GOVERNMENT RES AND SERV,COUNTY GOVERNMENT REORGANIZATION - A SELECTED ANNOTATED BIBLIOGRAPHY (PAPER). USA+45 USA-45 LAW CONSTN MUNIC PROVS EX/STRUC CREATE PLAN PROB/SOLV REPRESENT GOV/REL 20. PAGE 17 E0332
B67
BIBLIOG/A
APPORT
LOC/G
ADMIN

CHAPIN F.S. JR.,SELECTED REFERENCES ON URBAN PLANNING METHODS AND TECHNIQUES. USA+45 LAW ECO/DEV LOC/G NAT/G SCHOOL CONSULT CREATE PROB/SOLV TEC/DEV SOC/WK. PAGE 21 E0420
B67
BIBLIOG
NEIGH
MUNIC
PLAN

ELDRIDGE W.B.,NARCOTICS AND THE LAW: A CRITIQUE OF THE AMERICAN EXPERIMENT IN NARCOTIC DRUG CONTROL. PUB/INST ACT/RES PLAN LICENSE GP/REL EFFICIENCY ATTIT HEALTH...CRIMLGY HEAL STAT 20 ABA DEPT/HEW NARCO/ACT. PAGE 34 E0679
B67
LAW
INSPECT
BIO/SOC
JURID

GABRIEL P.P.,THE INTERNATIONAL TRANSFER OF CORPORATE SKILLS: MANAGEMENT CONTRACTS IN LESS DEVELOPED COUNTRIES. CLIENT INDUS LG/CO PLAN PROB/SOLV CAP/ISM ECO/TAC FOR/AID INT/TRADE RENT ADMIN SKILL 20. PAGE 42 E0825
B67
ECO/UNDEV
AGREE
MGT
CONSULT

GARCIA ROBLES A.,THE DENUCLEARIZATION OF LATIN AMERICA (TRANS. BY MARJORIE URQUIDI). LAW PLAN DIPLOM...ANTHOL 20 TREATY UN. PAGE 42 E0833
B67
NUC/PWR
ARMS/CONT
L/A+17C
INT/ORG

HOLCOMBE A.N.,A STRATEGY OF PEACE IN A CHANGING WORLD. USA+45 WOR+45 LAW NAT/G CREATE DIPLOM ARMS/CONT WAR...CHARTS 20 UN COLD/WAR. PAGE 54 E1072
B67
PEACE
PLAN
INT/ORG
INT/LAW

ROBINSON R.D., INTERNATIONAL MANAGEMENT. USA+45 FINAN R+D PLAN PRODUC...DECISION T. PAGE 67 E1336
B67
INT/TRADE
MGT
INT/LAW
MARKET

OPERATIONS AND POLICY RESEARCH,NICARAGUA: ELECTION FACTBOOK: FEBRUARY 5, 1967 (PAMPHLET). NICARAGUA LAW NAT/G LEAD REPRESENT...STAT BIOG CHARTS 20. PAGE 79 E1577
B67
POL/PAR
CHOOSE
PLAN
ATTIT

UNIVERSAL REFERENCE SYSTEM,CURRENT EVENTS AND PROBLEMS OF MODERN SOCIETY (VOLUME V). WOR+45 LOC/G MUNIC NAT/G PLAN EDU/PROP CRIME RACE/REL WEALTH ...COMPUT/IR GEN/METH. PAGE 98 E1974
B67
BIBLIOG/A
SOCIETY
PROB/SOLV
ATTIT

BERNHARD R.C.,"COMPETITION IN LAW AND ECONOMICS." LAW PLAN PRICE CONTROL PRODUC PROFIT...METH/CNCPT IDEA/COMP GEN/LAWS 20. PAGE 11 E0210
L67
MARKET
POLICY
NAT/G
CT/SYS

CARMICHAEL D.M.,"FORTY YEARS OF WATER POLLUTION CONTROL IN WISCONSIN: A CASE STUDY." LAW EXTR/IND INDUS MUNIC DELIB/GP PLAN PROB/SOLV SANCTION ...CENSUS CHARTS 20 WISCONSIN. PAGE 20 E0384
L67
HEALTH
CONTROL
ADMIN
ADJUD

LENT G.E.,"TAX INCENTIVES FOR INVESTMENT IN DEVELOPING COUNTRIES" WOR+45 LAW INDUS PLAN BUDGET TARIFFS ADMIN...METH/COMP 20. PAGE 64 E1285
L67
ECO/UNDEV
TAX
FINAN
ECO/TAC

"THE STATE OF ZONING ADMINISTRATION IN ILLINOIS: PROCEDURAL REQUIREMENTS OF JUDICIAL INTERVENTION." USA+45 LAW CONSTN DELIB/GP ADJUD CT/SYS ORD/FREE ILLINOIS. PAGE 2 E0038
S67
ADMIN
CONTROL
HABITAT
PLAN

"THE FEDERAL AGRICULTURAL STABILIZATION PROGRAM AND THE NEGRO." LAW CONSTN PLAN REPRESENT DISCRIM ORD/FREE 20 NEGRO CONGRESS. PAGE 2 E0039
S67
AGRI
CONTROL
NAT/G
RACE/REL

HAMILTON H.D.,"LEGISLATIVE CONSTITUENCIES: SINGLE-MEMBER DISTRICTS, MULTI-MEMBER DISTRICTS, AND FLOTERAL DISTRICTS." USA+45 LAW POL/PAR ADJUD RACE/REL...CHARTS METH/COMP 20. PAGE 50 E0990
S67
LEGIS
REPRESENT
APPORT
PLAN

HIRSCH W.Z.,"SOME ECONOMIC IMPLICATIONS OF CITY PLANNING." LAW PROB/SOLV RATION EFFICIENCY...METH 20. PAGE 53 E1050
S67
ECO/TAC
JURID
MUNIC
PLAN

HUBERT C.J.,"PLANNED UNIT DEVELOPMENT" LAW VOL/ASSN LEGIS EDU/PROP CT/SYS GOV/REL...NEW/IDEA 20 PLAN/UNIT. PAGE 56 E1107
S67
PLAN
MUNIC
HABITAT
ADJUD

KENNEDY R.F.,"TOWARD A NATION WHERE THE LAW IS KING." PLAN CT/SYS CRIME INGP/REL...JURID SOC. PAGE 60 E1202
S67
CRIMLGY
ADJUST
LAW
PUB/INST

TRAYNOR R.J.,"WHO CAN BEST JUDGE THE JUDGES?" USA+45 PLAN PROB/SOLV ATTIT...DECISION JURID 20. PAGE 97 E1938
S67
CHOOSE
ADJUD
REPRESENT
CT/SYS

TYDINGS J.D.,"MODERNIZING THE ADMINISTRATION OF JUSTICE." PLAN ADMIN ROUTINE EFFICIENCY...JURID SIMUL. PAGE 97 E1948
S67
CT/SYS
MGT
COMPUTER
CONSULT

GREGG R.W.,INTERNATIONAL ORGANIZATION IN THE WESTERN HEMISPHERE. L/A+17C USA+45 CULTURE PLAN DOMIN AGREE CONTROL DETER PWR...GEOG 20 OAS TREATY. PAGE 46 E0913
B68
INT/ORG
DIPLOM
ECO/UNDEV

PLAN/UNIT....PLANNED UNIT DEVELOPMENT

HUBERT C.J.,"PLANNED UNIT DEVELOPMENT" LAW VOL/ASSN LEGIS EDU/PROP CT/SYS GOV/REL...NEW/IDEA 20 PLAN/UNIT. PAGE 56 E1107
S67
PLAN
MUNIC
HABITAT
ADJUD

PLANO J.C. E1618

PLATE H. E1619

PLATO....PLATO

LASLETT P.,PHILOSOPHY, POLITICS AND SOCIETY. UNIV CRIME SOVEREIGN...JURID PHIL/SCI ANTHOL PLATO NATURL/LAW. PAGE 63 E1260
B56
CONSTN
ATTIT
CONCPT
GEN/LAWS

HALL J.,STUDIES IN JURISPRUDENCE AND CRIMINAL THEORY. USA-45 LAW CULTURE CREATE SUPEGO...CRIMLGY PSY /20 PLATO. PAGE 49 E0983
B58
JURID
CRIME
CONCPT
CT/SYS

PLAYFAIR R.L. E1620

PLEKHNV/GV....G.V. PLEKHANOV

PLISCHKE E. E1621

PLUMMER C. E0776

PLUNKITT/G....G.W. PLUNKITT, TAMMANY BOSS

PLURALISM....SEE PLURISM, PLURIST

PLURISM....PLURALISM, SOCIO-POLITICAL ORDER OF AUTONOMOUS GROUPS

GREEN F.M.,CONSTITUTIONAL DEVELOPMENT IN THE SOUTH ATLANTIC STATES, 1776-1860; A STUDY IN THE EVOLUTION OF DEMOCRACY. USA-45 ELITES SOCIETY STRATA ECO/DEV AGRI POL/PAR EX/STRUC LEGIS CT/SYS REGION...BIBLIOG 18/19 MARYLAND VIRGINIA GEORGIA NORTH/CAR SOUTH/CAR. PAGE 46 E0905
B30
CONSTN
PROVS
PLURISM
REPRESENT

OBERER W.E.,"VOLUNTARY IMPARTIAL REVIEW OF LABOR: SOME REFLECTIONS." DELIB/GP LEGIS PROB/SOLV ADJUD CONTROL COERCE PWR PLURISM POLICY. PAGE 78 E1570
L59
LABOR
LAW
PARTIC
INGP/REL

KEEFE W.J.,THE AMERICAN LEGISLATIVE PROCESS. USA+45 CONSTN POL/PAR CT/SYS REPRESENT FEDERAL ATTIT PLURISM...MAJORIT 20 CONGRESS PRESIDENT. PAGE 60 E1192
B65
LEGIS
NAT/G
CHIEF
GOV/REL

PLURIST....PLURALIST

BRYCE J.,INTERNATIONAL RELATIONS. CHRIST-17C EUR+WWI MOD/EUR CULTURE INTELL NAT/G DELIB/GP CREATE BAL/PWR DIPLOM ATTIT DRIVE RIGID/FLEX ALL/VALS...PLURIST JURID CONCPT TIME/SEQ GEN/LAWS TOT/POP. PAGE 16 E0323
B22
INT/ORG
POLICY

CARLSTON K.S.,LAW AND ORGANIZATION IN WORLD SOCIETY. WOR+45 FINAN ECO/TAC DOMIN LEGIT CT/SYS ROUTINE COERCE ORD/FREE PWR WEALTH...PLURIST DECISION JURID MGT METH/CNCPT GEN/LAWS 20. PAGE 19 E0381
B62
INT/ORG
LAW

HALL J.,COMPARATIVE LAW AND SOCIAL THEORY. WOR+45 CONSTN CULTURE DOMIN CT/SYS ORD/FREE...PLURIST JURID CONCPT NEW/IDEA GEN/LAWS VAL/FREE. PAGE 49 E0984
B63
LAW
SOC

ANDERSON W.,"THE PERILS OF 'SHARING'." USA+45 ECO/TAC RECEIVE LOBBY GOV/REL CENTRAL COST INCOME ...POLICY PLURIST CONGRESS. PAGE 5 E0095
S67
BUDGET
TAX
FEDERAL
LAW

POGANY A.H. E1622

POGANY H.L. E1622

POL....POLITICAL AND POWER PROCESS

POL/PAR....POLITICAL PARTIES

ANNALS OF THE AMERICAN ACADEMY OF POLITICAL AND SOCIAL SCIENCE. AFR ASIA S/ASIA WOR+45 POL/PAR DIPLOM CRIME REV...SOC BIOG 20. PAGE 1 E0003
N
BIBLIOG/A
NAT/G
CULTURE
ATTIT

JOURNAL OF INTERNATIONAL AFFAIRS. WOR+45 ECO/UNDEV POL/PAR ECO/TAC WAR PEACE PERSON ALL/IDEOS ...INT/LAW TREND. PAGE 1 E0010
N
BIBLIOG
DIPLOM
INT/ORG
NAT/G

JOURNAL OF POLITICS. USA+45 USA-45 CONSTN POL/PAR EX/STRUC LEGIS PROB/SOLV DIPLOM CT/SYS CHOOSE RACE/REL 20. PAGE 1 E0011
N
BIBLIOG/A
NAT/G
LAW
LOC/G

MIDWEST JOURNAL OF POLITICAL SCIENCE. USA+45 CONSTN ECO/DEV LEGIS PROB/SOLV CT/SYS LEAD GOV/REL ATTIT POLICY. PAGE 1 E0012
N
BIBLIOG/A
NAT/G
DIPLOM
POL/PAR

POLITICAL SCIENCE QUARTERLY. USA+45 USA-45 LAW CONSTN ECO/DEV INT/ORG LOC/G POL/PAR LEGIS LEAD NUC/PWR...CONCPT 20. PAGE 1 E0013
N
BIBLIOG/A
NAT/G
DIPLOM
POLICY

HANDBOOK OF LATIN AMERICAN STUDIES. LAW CULTURE ECO/UNDEV POL/PAR ADMIN LEAD...SOC 20. PAGE 1 E0022
N
BIBLIOG/A
L/A+17C
NAT/G
DIPLOM

NEUE POLITISCHE LITERATUR; BERICHTE UBER DAS INTERNATIONALE SCHRIFTTUM ZUR POLITIK. WOR+45 LAW CONSTN POL/PAR ADMIN LEAD GOV/REL...POLICY IDEA/COMP. PAGE 2 E0028
BIBLIOG/A DIPLOM NAT/G NAT/COMP
N

CORNELL UNIVERSITY LIBRARY,SOUTHEAST ASIA ACCESSIONS LIST. LAW SOCIETY STRUCT ECO/UNDEV POL/PAR TEC/DEV DIPLOM LEAD REGION. PAGE 26 E0510
BIBLIOG S/ASIA NAT/G CULTURE
N

DEUTSCHE BUCHEREI,DEUTSCHES BUCHERVERZEICHNIS. GERMANY LAW CULTURE POL/PAR ADMIN LEAD ATTIT PERSON ...SOC 20. PAGE 31 E0615
BIBLIOG NAT/G DIPLOM ECO/DEV
N

DE TOCQUEVILLE A.,DEMOCRACY IN AMERICA (VOLUME ONE). LAW SOCIETY STRUCT NAT/G POL/PAR PROVS FORCES LEGIS TOP/EX DIPLOM LEGIT WAR PEACE ATTIT SOVEREIGN ...SELF/OBS TIME/SEQ CONGRESS 19. PAGE 30 E0594
USA-45 TREND
B00

GRIFFIN A.P.C.,LIST OF REFERENCES ON PRIMARY ELECTIONS (PAMPHLET). USA-45 LAW LOC/G DELIB/GP LEGIS OP/RES TASK REPRESENT CONSEN...DECISION 19/20 CONGRESS. PAGE 47 E0928
BIBLIOG/A POL/PAR CHOOSE POPULISM
B05

WILSON W.,CONSTITUTIONAL GOVERNMENT IN THE UNITED STATES. USA-45 LAW POL/PAR PROVS CHIEF LEGIS BAL/PWR ADJUD EXEC FEDERAL PWR 18/20 SUPREME/CT HOUSE/REP SENATE. PAGE 106 E2130
NAT/G GOV/REL CONSTN PARL/PROC
B08

SCHMIDHAUSER J.R.,JUDICIAL BEHAVIOR AND THE SECTIONAL CRISIS OF 1837-1860. USA-45 ADJUD CT/SYS INGP/REL ATTIT HABITAT...DECISION PSY STAT CHARTS SIMUL. PAGE 88 E1759
JUDGE POL/PAR PERS/COMP PERSON
N13

MCLAUGHLIN A.C.,CYCLOPEDIA OF AMERICAN GOVERNMENT (3 VOLS.). LAW CONSTN POL/PAR ADMIN ROUTINE ...INT/LAW CONCPT BIBLIOG METH 20. PAGE 71 E1421
USA+45 NAT/G DICTIONARY
B14

PORTER K.H.,A HISTORY OF SUFFRAGE IN THE UNITED STATES. USA-45 LAW CONSTN LOC/G NAT/G POL/PAR WAR DISCRIM OWN ATTIT SEX 18/20 NEGRO FEMALE/SEX. PAGE 81 E1629
SUFF REPRESENT CHOOSE PARTIC
B18

YUKIO O.,THE VOICE OF JAPANESE DEMOCRACY, AN ESSAY ON CONSTITUTIONAL LOYALTY (TRANS BY J. E. BECKER). ASIA POL/PAR DELIB/GP EX/STRUC RIGID/FLEX ORD/FREE PWR...POLICY JURID METH/COMP 19/20 CHINJAP. PAGE 108 E2167
CONSTN MAJORIT CHOOSE NAT/G
B18

OPERATIONS AND POLICY RESEARCH,URUGUAY: ELECTION FACTBOOK: NOVEMBER 27, 1966 (PAMPHLET). URUGUAY LAW NAT/G LEAD REPRESENT...STAT BIOG CHARTS 20. PAGE 79 E1576
POL/PAR CHOOSE PLAN ATTIT
N19

PAN AMERICAN UNION,INFORME DE LA MISION DE ASISTENCIA TECNICA DE LA OEA A LA REPUBLICA DE HONDURAS EN MATERIA ELECTORAL (PAMPHLET). HONDURAS CONSTN ORD/FREE...JURID OBS 20 OAS. PAGE 80 E1595
CHOOSE SUFF POL/PAR NAT/G
N19

BRYCE J.,MODERN DEMOCRACIES. FUT NEW/ZEALND USA-45 LAW CONSTN POL/PAR PROVS VOL/ASSN EX/STRUC LEGIS LEGIT CT/SYS EXEC KNOWL CONGRESS AUSTRAL 20. PAGE 16 E0322
NAT/G TREND
B21

ROBERT H.M.,PARLIAMENTARY LAW. POL/PAR LEGIS PARTIC CHOOSE REPRESENT GP/REL. PAGE 85 E1701
PARL/PROC DELIB/GP NAT/G JURID
B23

CAM H.M.,BIBLIOGRAPHY OF ENGLISH CONSTITUTIONAL HISTORY (PAMPHLET). UK LAW LOC/G NAT/G POL/PAR SECT DELIB/GP ADJUD ORD/FREE 19/20 PARLIAMENT. PAGE 19 E0369
BIBLIOG/A CONSTN ADMIN PARL/PROC
B29

MOLEY R.,POLITICS AND CRIMINAL PROSECUTION. USA-45 POL/PAR EX/STRUC LEGIT CONTROL LEAD ROUTINE CHOOSE INGP/REL...JURID CHARTS 20. PAGE 74 E1481
PWR CT/SYS CRIME ADJUD
B29

BIRD F.L.,THE RECALL OF PUBLIC OFFICERS; A STUDY OF THE OPERATION OF RECALL IN CALIFORNIA. LOC/G MUNIC POL/PAR PROVS PROB/SOLV ADJUD PARTIC...CHARTS METH/COMP 20 CALIFORNIA RECALL. PAGE 12 E0230
REPRESENT SANCTION CHOOSE LAW
B30

GREEN F.M.,CONSTITUTIONAL DEVELOPMENT IN THE SOUTH ATLANTIC STATES, 1776-1860; A STUDY IN THE EVOLUTION OF DEMOCRACY. USA-45 ELITES SOCIETY STRATA ECO/DEV AGRI POL/PAR EX/STRUC LEGIS CT/SYS REGION...BIBLIOG 18/19 MARYLAND VIRGINIA GEORGIA NORTH/CAR SOUTH/CAR. PAGE 46 E0905
CONSTN PROVS PLURISM REPRESENT
B30

BURCHFIELD L.,STUDENT'S GUIDE TO MATERIALS IN POLITICAL SCIENCE. FINAN INT/ORG NAT/G POL/PAR DIPLOM PRESS ADMIN...BIOG 18/19. PAGE 17 E0328
BIBLIOG INDEX LAW
B35

DE TOCQUEVILLE A.,DEMOCRACY IN AMERICA (4 VOLS.) (TRANS. BY HENRY REEVE). CONSTN STRUCT LOC/G NAT/G POL/PAR PROVS ETIQUET CT/SYS MAJORITY ATTIT 18/19. PAGE 30 E0595
POPULISM MAJORIT ORD/FREE SOCIETY
B35

NORDSKOG J.E.,SOCIAL REFORM IN NORWAY. NORWAY INDUS NAT/G POL/PAR LEGIS ADJUD...SOC BIBLIOG SOC/INTEG 20. PAGE 78 E1555
LABOR ADJUST
B35

BORGESE G.A.,GOLIATH: THE MARCH OF FASCISM. GERMANY ITALY LAW POL/PAR SECT DIPLOM SOCISM...JURID MYTH 20 DANTE MACHIAVELL MUSSOLIN/B. PAGE 14 E0270
POLICY NAT/LISM FASCISM NAT/G
B37

HARPER S.N.,THE GOVERNMENT OF THE SOVIET UNION. COM USSR LAW CONSTN ECO/DEV PLAN TEC/DEV DIPLOM INT/TRADE ADMIN REV NAT/LISM...POLICY 20. PAGE 50 E1001
MARXISM NAT/G LEAD POL/PAR
B38

BALDWIN L.D.,WHISKEY REBELS; THE STORY OF A FRONTIER UPRISING. USA-45 LAW ADJUD LEAD COERCE PWR ...BIBLIOG/A 18 PENNSYLVAN FEDERALIST. PAGE 8 E0145
REV POL/PAR TAX TIME/SEQ
B39

ANDERSON W.,FUNDAMENTALS OF AMERICAN GOVERNMENT. USA-45 LAW POL/PAR CHIEF EX/STRUC BUDGET ADMIN CT/SYS PARL/PROC CHOOSE FEDERAL...BIBLIOG 20. PAGE 5 E0093
NAT/G LOC/G GOV/REL CONSTN
B40

GERTH H.,"THE NAZI PARTY: ITS LEADERSHIP AND COMPOSITION" (BMR)" GERMANY ELITES STRATA STRUCT EX/STRUC FORCES ECO/TAC CT/SYS CHOOSE TOTALISM AGE/Y AUTHORIT PWR 20. PAGE 43 E0851
POL/PAR DOMIN LEAD ADMIN
S40

BIRDSALL P.,VERSAILLES TWENTY YEARS AFTER. MOD/EUR POL/PAR CHIEF CONSULT FORCES LEGIS REPAR PEACE ORD/FREE...BIBLIOG 20 PRESIDENT TREATY. PAGE 12 E0231
DIPLOM NAT/LISM WAR
B41

MICAUD C.A.,THE FRENCH RIGHT AND NAZI GERMANY 1933-1939: A STUDY OF PUBLIC OPINION. GERMANY UK USSR POL/PAR ARMS/CONT COERCE DETER PEACE RIGID/FLEX PWR MARXISM...FASCIST TREND 20 LEAGUE/NAT TREATY. PAGE 73 E1454
DIPLOM AGREE
B43

BEARD C.A.,AMERICAN GOVERNMENT AND POLITICS (REV. ED.). CONSTN MUNIC POL/PAR PROVS EX/STRUC LEGIS TOP/EX CT/SYS GOV/REL...BIBLIOG T 18/20. PAGE 9 E0165
LEAD USA-45 NAT/G LOC/G
B44

PUTTKAMMER E.W.,WAR AND THE LAW. UNIV USA-45 CONSTN CULTURE SOCIETY NAT/G POL/PAR ROUTINE ALL/VALS ...JURID CONCPT OBS WORK VAL/FREE 20. PAGE 83 E1664
INT/ORG LAW WAR INT/LAW
B44

MASON J.B.,"THE JUDICIAL SYSTEM OF THE NAZI PARTY." GERMANY ELITES POL/PAR DOMIN CONTROL SANCTION TOTALISM...JURID 20 HITLER/A. PAGE 69 E1381
FASCISM CT/SYS ADJUD LAW
S44

CONOVER H.F.,THE GOVERNMENTS OF THE MAJOR FOREIGN POWERS: A BIBLIOGRAPHY. FRANCE GERMANY ITALY UK USSR CONSTN LOC/G POL/PAR EX/STRUC FORCES ADMIN
BIBLIOG NAT/G DIPLOM
B45

CT/SYS CIVMIL/REL TOTALISM...POLICY 19/20. PAGE 25
E0494

B46
CORRY J.A.,DEMOCRATIC GOVERNMENT AND POLITICS.   NAT/G
WOR-45 EX/STRUC LOBBY TOTALISM...MAJORIT CONCPT   CONSTN
METH/COMP NAT/COMP 20. PAGE 26 E0511   POL/PAR
  JURID

B47
BORGESE G.,COMMON CAUSE. LAW CONSTN SOCIETY STRATA   WOR+45
ECO/DEV INT/ORG POL/PAR FORCES LEGIS TOP/EX CAP/ISM   NAT/G
DIPLOM ADMIN EXEC ATTIT PWR 20. PAGE 14 E0269   SOVEREIGN
  REGION

B48
BISHOP H.M.,BASIC ISSUES OF AMERICAN DEMOCRACY.   NAT/G
USA+45 USA-45 POL/PAR EX/STRUC LEGIS ADJUD FEDERAL   PARL/PROC
...BIBLIOG 18/20. PAGE 12 E0232   CONSTN

B48
STOKES W.S.,BIBLIOGRAPHY OF STANDARD AND CLASSICAL   BIBLIOG
WORKS IN THE FIELDS OF AMERICAN POLITICAL SCIENCE.   NAT/G
USA+45 USA-45 POL/PAR PROVS FORCES DIPLOM ADMIN   LOC/G
CT/SYS APPORT 20 CONGRESS PRESIDENT. PAGE 94 E1876   CONSTN

S48
ALEXANDER L.,"WAR CRIMES, THEIR SOCIAL-   DRIVE
PSYCHOLOGICAL ASPECTS." EUR+WWI GERMANY LAW CULTURE   WAR
ELITES KIN POL/PAR PUB/INST FORCES DOMIN EDU/PROP
COERCE CRIME ATTIT SUPEGO HEALTH MORAL PWR FASCISM
...PSY OBS TREND GEN/LAWS NAZI 20. PAGE 3 E0061

S48
MILLER B.S.,"A LAW IS PASSED: THE ATOMIC ENERGY ACT   TEC/DEV
OF 1946." POL/PAR CHIEF CONFER DEBATE CONTROL   LEGIS
PARL/PROC ATTIT KNOWL...POLICY CONGRESS. PAGE 73   DECISION
E1457   LAW

C48
WALKER H.,"THE LEGISLATIVE PROCESS; LAWMAKING IN   PARL/PROC
THE UNITED STATES." NAT/G POL/PAR PROVS EX/STRUC   LEGIS
OP/RES PROB/SOLV CT/SYS LOBBY GOV/REL...CHARTS   LAW
BIBLIOG T 18/20 CONGRESS. PAGE 105 E2094   CONSTN

B50
COUNCIL BRITISH NATIONAL BIB,BRITISH NATIONAL   BIBLIOG/A
BIBLIOGRAPHY. UK AGRI CONSTRUC PERF/ART POL/PAR   NAT/G
SECT CREATE INT/TRADE LEAD...HUM JURID PHIL/SCI 20.   TEC/DEV
PAGE 26 E0519   DIPLOM

B50
MERRIAM C.E.,THE AMERICAN PARTY SYSTEM; AN   POL/PAR
INTRODUCTION TO THE STUDY OF POLITICAL PARTIES IN   CHOOSE
THE UNITED STATES (4TH ED.). USA+45 USA-45 LAW   SUFF
FINAN LOC/G NAT/G PROVS LEAD PARTIC CRIME ATTIT   REPRESENT
18/20 NEGRO CONGRESS PRESIDENT. PAGE 72 E1442

C50
HOLCOMBE A.,"OUR MORE PERFECT UNION." USA+45 USA-45   CONSTN
POL/PAR JUDGE CT/SYS EQUILIB FEDERAL PWR...MAJORIT   NAT/G
TREND BIBLIOG 18/20 CONGRESS PRESIDENT. PAGE 54   ADMIN
E1070   PLAN

B51
ANDERSON W.,STATE AND LOCAL GOVERNMENT IN THE   LOC/G
UNITED STATES. USA+45 CONSTN POL/PAR EX/STRUC LEGIS   MUNIC
BUDGET TAX ADJUD CT/SYS CHOOSE...CHARTS T 20.   PROVS
PAGE 5 E0094   GOV/REL

B51
PUSEY M.J.,CHARLES EVANS HUGHES (2 VOLS.). LAW   BIOG
CONSTN NAT/G POL/PAR DIPLOM LEGIT WAR CHOOSE   TOP/EX
PERS/REL DRIVE HEREDITY 19/20 DEPT/STATE LEAGUE/NAT   ADJUD
SUPREME/CT HUGHES/CE WWI. PAGE 83 E1663   PERSON

B52
BENTHAM A.,HANDBOOK OF POLITICAL FALLACIES. FUT   POL/PAR
MOD/EUR LAW INTELL LOC/G MUNIC NAT/G DELIB/GP LEGIS
CREATE EDU/PROP CT/SYS ATTIT RIGID/FLEX KNOWL PWR
...RELATIV PSY SOC CONCPT SELF/OBS TREND STERTYP
TOT/POP. PAGE 10 E0189

B52
FLECHTHEIM O.K.,FUNDAMENTALS OF POLITICAL SCIENCE.   NAT/G
WOR+45 WOR-45 LAW POL/PAR EX/STRUC LEGIS ADJUD   DIPLOM
ATTIT PWR...INT/LAW. PAGE 38 E0760   IDEA/COMP
  CONSTN

B52
HOLDSWORTH W.S.,A HISTORY OF ENGLISH LAW; THE   LAW
CENTURIES OF SETTLEMENT AND REFORM, 1701-1875 (VOL.   CONSTN
XIII). UK POL/PAR PROF/ORG LEGIS JUDGE WRITING   IDEA/COMP
ATTIT...JURID CONCPT BIOG GEN/LAWS 18/19 PARLIAMENT   CT/SYS
REFORMERS ENGLSH/LAW COMMON/LAW. PAGE 54 E1080

B52
PASCUAL R.R.,PARTYLESS DEMOCRACY. PHILIPPINE   POL/PAR
BARGAIN LOBBY CHOOSE EFFICIENCY ATTIT 20. PAGE 80   ORD/FREE
E1600   JURID
  ECO/UNDEV

S52
MCDOUGAL M.S.,"THE COMPARATIVE STUDY OF LAW FOR   PLAN
POLICY PURPOSES." FUT NAT/G POL/PAR CONSULT ADJUD   JURID
PWR SOVEREIGN...METH/CNCPT IDEA/COMP SIMUL 20.   NAT/LISM
PAGE 70 E1403

B53
BUTLER D.E.,THE ELECTORAL SYSTEM IN BRITAIN,   CHOOSE
1918-1951. UK LAW POL/PAR SUFF...STAT BIBLIOG 20   LEGIS
PARLIAMENT. PAGE 18 E0348   REPRESENT
  PARTIC

B53
GROSS B.M.,THE LEGISLATIVE STRUGGLE: A STUDY IN   LEGIS
SOCIAL COMBAT. STRUCT LOC/G POL/PAR JUDGE EDU/PROP   DECISION
DEBATE ETIQUET ADMIN LOBBY CHOOSE GOV/REL INGP/REL   PERSON
HEREDITY ALL/VALS...SOC PRESIDENT. PAGE 48 E0948   LEAD

B53
KIRK R.,THE CONSERVATIVE MIND. POL/PAR ORD/FREE   CONSERVE
...JURID CONCPT 18/20. PAGE 61 E1220   PERSON
  PHIL/SCI
  IDEA/COMP

B53
PADOVER S.K.,THE LIVING US CONSTITUTION. USA+45   CONSTN
USA-45 POL/PAR ADJUD...DECISION AUD/VIS IDEA/COMP   LEGIS
18/20 SUPREME/CT. PAGE 79 E1590   DELIB/GP
  BIOG

B53
SECKLER-HUDSON C.,BIBLIOGRAPHY ON PUBLIC   BIBLIOG/A
ADMINISTRATION (4TH ED.). USA+45 LAW POL/PAR   ADMIN
DELIB/GP BUDGET ADJUD LOBBY GOV/REL GP/REL ATTIT   NAT/G
...JURID 20. PAGE 90 E1800   MGT

B53
STOUT H.M.,BRITISH GOVERNMENT. UK FINAN LOC/G   NAT/G
POL/PAR DELIB/GP DIPLOM ADMIN COLONIAL CHOOSE   PARL/PROC
ORD/FREE...JURID BIBLIOG 20 COMMONWLTH. PAGE 94   CONSTN
E1883   NEW/LIB

B54
BROGAN D.W.,POLITICS IN AMERICA. LAW POL/PAR CHIEF   NAT/G
LEGIS LOBBY CHOOSE REPRESENT GP/REL RACE/REL   CONSTN
FEDERAL MORAL...BIBLIOG 20 PRESIDENT CONGRESS.   USA+45
PAGE 16 E0304

C54
CALDWELL L.K.,"THE GOVERNMENT AND ADMINISTRATION OF   PROVS
NEW YORK." LOC/G MUNIC POL/PAR SCHOOL CHIEF LEGIS   ADMIN
PLAN TAX CT/SYS...MGT SOC/WK BIBLIOG 20 NEWYORK/C.   CONSTN
PAGE 19 E0365   EX/STRUC

B55
BIBLIOGRAPHY ON THE COMMUNIST PROBLEM IN THE UNITED   BIBLIOG/A
STATES. USA-45 PRESS ADJUD ATTIT...BIOG 20. PAGE 2   MARXISM
E0033   POL/PAR
  USA+45

B55
FLIESS P.J.,FREEDOM OF THE PRESS IN THE GERMAN   EDU/PROP
REPUBLIC, 1918-1933. GERMANY LAW CONSTN POL/PAR   ORD/FREE
LEGIS WRITING ADMIN COERCE MURDER MARXISM...POLICY   JURID
BIBLIOG 20 WEIMAR/REP. PAGE 39 E0765   PRESS

B55
MAZZINI J.,THE DUTIES OF MAN. MOD/EUR LAW SOCIETY   SUPEGO
FAM NAT/G POL/PAR SECT VOL/ASSN EX/STRUC ACT/RES   CONCPT
CREATE REV PEACE ATTIT ALL/VALS...GEN/LAWS WORK 19.   NAT/LISM
PAGE 70 E1396

B56
ABELS J.,THE TRUMAN SCANDALS. USA+45 USA-45 POL/PAR   CRIME
TAX LEGIT CT/SYS CHOOSE PRIVIL MORAL WEALTH 20   ADMIN
TRUMAN/HS PRESIDENT CONGRESS. PAGE 2 E0043   CHIEF
  TRIBUTE

B56
FIELD G.C.,POLITICAL THEORY. POL/PAR REPRESENT   CONCPT
MORAL SOVEREIGN...JURID IDEA/COMP. PAGE 38 E0745   NAT/G
  ORD/FREE
  DIPLOM

B56
KUPER L.,PASSIVE RESISTANCE IN SOUTH AFRICA.   ORD/FREE
SOUTH/AFR LAW NAT/G POL/PAR VOL/ASSN DISCRIM   RACE/REL
...POLICY SOC AUD/VIS 20. PAGE 62 E1237   ATTIT

PERKINS D.,CHARLES EVANS HUGHES AND THE AMERICAN DEMOCRATIC STATESMANSHIP. USA+45 USA-45 NAT/G POL/PAR DELIB/GP JUDGE PLAN MORAL PWR...HIST/WRIT LEAGUE/NAT 20. PAGE 80 E1609
B56
PERSON
BIOG
DIPLOM

FALL B.B.,"THE VIET-MINH REGIME." VIETNAM LAW ECO/UNDEV POL/PAR FORCES DOMIN WAR ATTIT MARXISM ...BIOG PREDICT BIBLIOG/A 20. PAGE 36 E0720
C56
NAT/G
ADMIN
EX/STRUC
LEAD

ALIGHIERI D.,ON WORLD GOVERNMENT. ROMAN/EMP LAW SOCIETY INT/ORG NAT/G POL/PAR ADJUD WAR GP/REL PEACE WORSHIP 15 WORLDUNITY DANTE. PAGE 4 E0067
B57
POLICY
CONCPT
DIPLOM
SECT

COSSIO C.,LA POLITICA COMO CONCIENCIA; MEDITACION SOBRE LA ARGENTINA DE 1955. WOR+45 LEGIS EDU/PROP PARL/PROC PARTIC ATTIT PWR CATHISM 20 ARGEN PERON/JUAN. PAGE 26 E0517
B57
POL/PAR
REV
TOTALISM
JURID

JENNINGS I.,PARLIAMENT. UK FINAN INDUS POL/PAR DELIB/GP EX/STRUC PLAN CONTROL...MAJORIT JURID PARLIAMENT. PAGE 58 E1163
B57
PARL/PROC
TOP/EX
MGT
LEGIS

CABLE G.W.,THE NEGRO QUESTION: A SELECTION OF WRITINGS ON CIVIL RIGHTS IN THE SOUTH. USA+45 STRATA LOC/G POL/PAR GIVE EDU/PROP WRITING CT/SYS SANCTION CRIME CHOOSE WORSHIP 20 NEGRO CIV/RIGHTS CONV/LEASE SOUTH/US. PAGE 18 E0355
B58
RACE/REL
CULTURE
DISCRIM
ORD/FREE

HUNT B.I.,BIPARTISANSHIP: A CASE STUDY OF THE FOREIGN ASSISTANCE PROGRAM, 1947-56 (DOCTORAL THESIS). USA+45 INT/ORG CONSULT LEGIS TEC/DEV ...BIBLIOG PRESIDENT TREATY NATO TRUMAN/HS EISNHWR/DD CONGRESS. PAGE 56 E1114
B58
FOR/AID
POL/PAR
GP/REL
DIPLOM

KAPLAN H.E.,THE LAW OF CIVIL SERVICE. USA+45 LAW POL/PAR CT/SYS CRIME GOV/REL...POLICY JURID 20. PAGE 59 E1183
B58
ADJUD
NAT/G
ADMIN
CONSTN

MACKENZIE W.J.M.,FREE ELECTIONS: AN ELEMENTARY TEXTBOOK. WOR+45 NAT/G POL/PAR LEGIS TOP/EX EDU/PROP LEGIT CT/SYS ATTIT PWR...OBS CHARTS STERTYP T CONGRESS PARLIAMENT 20. PAGE 67 E1342
B58
EX/STRUC
CHOOSE

SPITZ D.,DEMOCRACY AND THE CHALLANGE OF POWER. FUT USA+45 USA-45 LAW SOCIETY STRUCT LOC/G POL/PAR PROVS DELIB/GP EX/STRUC LEGIS TOP/EX ACT/RES CREATE DOMIN EDU/PROP LEGIT ADJUD ADMIN ATTIT DRIVE MORAL ORD/FREE TOT/POP. PAGE 93 E1862
B58
NAT/G
PWR

DAHL R.A.,"DECISION-MAKING IN A DEMOCRACY: THE SUPREME COURT AS A NATIONAL POLICY-MAKER" (BMR)" USA+45 USA-45 POL/PAR ADJUD GOV/REL PWR...POLICY JURID 19/20 SUPREME/CT. PAGE 28 E0561
S58
CT/SYS
CONSTN
DECISION
NAT/G

STAAR R.F.,"ELECTIONS IN COMMUNIST POLAND." EUR+WWI SOCIETY INT/ORG NAT/G POL/PAR LEGIS ACT/RES ECO/TAC EDU/PROP ADJUD ADMIN ROUTINE COERCE TOTALISM ATTIT ORD/FREE PWR 20. PAGE 93 E1864
S58
COM
CHOOSE
POLAND

CHRISTMAN H.M.,THE PUBLIC PAPERS OF CHIEF JUSTICE EARL WARREN. CONSTN POL/PAR EDU/PROP SANCTION HEALTH...TREND 20 SUPREME/CT WARRN/EARL. PAGE 22 E0436
B59
LAW
CT/SYS
PERSON
ADJUD

EPSTEIN F.T.,EAST GERMANY: A SELECTED BIBLIOGRAPHY (PAMPHLET). COM GERMANY/E LAW AGRI FINAN INDUS LABOR POL/PAR EDU/PROP ADMIN AGE/Y 20. PAGE 35 E0693
B59
BIBLIOG/A
INTELL
MARXISM
NAT/G

LOEWENSTEIN K.,VERFASSUNGSRECHT UND VERFASSUNGSPRAXIS DER VEREINIGTEN STAATEN. USA+45 USA-45 COLONIAL CT/SYS GP/REL RACE/REL ORD/FREE ...JURID 18/20 SUPREME/CT CONGRESS PRESIDENT BILL/RIGHT CIVIL/LIB. PAGE 66 E1319
B59
CONSTN
POL/PAR
EX/STRUC
NAT/G

REOCK E.C.,PROCEDURES AND STANDARDS FOR THE
B59
PROVS

APPORTIONMENT OF STATE LEGISLATURES (DOCTORAL THESIS). USA+45 POL/PAR LEGIS TEC/DEV ADJUD BIBLIOG. PAGE 84 E1686
LOC/G
APPORT
REPRESENT

DERGE D.R.,"THE LAWYER AS DECISION-MAKER IN THE AMERICAN STATE LEGISLATURE." INTELL LOC/G POL/PAR CHOOSE AGE HEREDITY PERSON CONSERVE...JURID STAT CHARTS. PAGE 31 E0607
S59
LEGIS
LAW
DECISION
LEAD

MENDELSON W.,"JUDICIAL REVIEW AND PARTY POLITICS" (BMR)" UK USA+45 USA-45 NAT/G LEGIS PROB/SOLV EDU/PROP ADJUD EFFICIENCY...POLICY NAT/COMP 19/20 AUSTRAL SUPREME/CT. PAGE 72 E1436
S59
CT/SYS
POL/PAR
BAL/PWR
JURID

JUNZ A.J.,PRESENT TRENDS IN AMERICAN NATIONAL GOVERNMENT. LEGIS DIPLOM ADMIN CT/SYS ORD/FREE ...CONCPT ANTHOL 20 CONGRESS PRESIDENT SUPREME/CT. PAGE 2 E0040
B60
POL/PAR
CHOOSE
CONSTN
NAT/G

ADRIAN C.R.,STATE AND LOCAL GOVERNMENTS: A STUDY IN THE POLITICAL PROCESS. USA+45 LAW FINAN MUNIC POL/PAR LEGIS ADJUD EXEC CHOOSE REPRESENT. PAGE 3 E0051
B60
LOC/G
PROVS
GOV/REL
ATTIT

BAKER G.E.,THE POLITICS OF REAPPORTIONMENT IN WASHINGTON STATE. LAW POL/PAR CREATE EDU/PROP PARL/PROC CHOOSE INGP/REL...CHARTS METH/COMP 20 WASHINGT/G LEAGUE/WV. PAGE 7 E0139
B60
VOL/ASSN
APPORT
PROVS
LEGIS

BAYLEY D.H.,VIOLENT AGITATION AND THE DEMOCRATIC PROCESS IN INDIA. INDIA LAW POL/PAR 20. PAGE 8 E0159
B60
COERCE
CROWD
CONSTN
PROB/SOLV

BLANSHARD P.,GOD AND MAN IN WASHINGTON. USA+45 CHIEF LEGIS LEGIT CT/SYS PRIVIL ORD/FREE ...POLICY CONCPT 20 SUPREME/CT CONGRESS PRESIDENT CHURCH/STA. PAGE 12 E0242
B60
NAT/G
SECT
GP/REL
POL/PAR

DUMON F.,LA COMMUNAUTE FRANCO-AFRO-MALGACHE: SES ORIGINES, SES INSTITUTIONS, SON EVOLUTION. FRANCE MADAGASCAR POL/PAR DIPLOM ADMIN ATTIT...TREND T 20. PAGE 33 E0657
B60
JURID
INT/ORG
AFR
CONSTN

LA PONCE J.A.,THE PROTECTION OF MINORITIES. WOR+45 WOR-45 NAT/G POL/PAR SUFF...INT/LAW CLASSIF GP/COMP GOV/COMP BIBLIOG 17/20 CIVIL/LIB CIV/RIGHTS. PAGE 62 E1242
B60
INGP/REL
DOMIN
SOCIETY
RACE/REL

NAT'L MUNICIPAL LEAGUE,COMPENDIUM ON LEGISLATIVE APPORTIONMENT. USA+45 LOC/G NAT/G POL/PAR PROVS CT/SYS CHOOSE 20 SUPREME/CT CONGRESS. PAGE 76 E1523
B60
APPORT
REPRESENT
LEGIS
STAT

RIENOW R.,INTRODUCTION TO GOVERNMENT (2ND ED.). UK USA+45 USSR POL/PAR ADMIN REV CHOOSE SUFF FEDERAL PWR...JURID GOV/COMP T 20. PAGE 85 E1697
B60
CONSTN
PARL/PROC
REPRESENT
AUTHORIT

SCHUBERT G.,THE PUBLIC INTEREST. USA+45 CONSULT PLAN PROB/SOLV ADJUD ADMIN GP/REL PWR ALL/IDEOS 20. PAGE 88 E1770
B60
POLICY
DELIB/GP
REPRESENT
POL/PAR

BENNETT G.,THE KENYATTA ELECTION: KENYA 1960-1961. AFR INGP/REL RACE/REL CONSEN ATTIT 20 KENYATTA. PAGE 10 E0187
B61
CHOOSE
POL/PAR
LAW
SUFF

BURDETTE F.L.,POLITICAL SCIENCE: A SELECTED BIBLIOGRAPHY OF BOOKS IN PRINT, WITH ANNOTATIONS (PAMPHLET). LAW LOC/G NAT/G POL/PAR DIPLOM EDU/PROP ADMIN CHOOSE ATTIT 20. PAGE 17 E0330
B61
BIBLIOG/A
GOV/COMP
CONCPT
ROUTINE

CARNELL F.,THE POLITICS OF THE NEW STATES: A SELECT ANNOTATED BIBLIOGRAPHY WITH SPECIAL REFERENCE TO THE COMMONWEALTH. CONSTN ELITES LABOR NAT/G POL/PAR EX/STRUC DIPLOM ADJUD ADMIN...GOV/COMP 20 COMMONWLTH. PAGE 20 E0387
B61
BIBLIOG/A
AFR
ASIA
COLONIAL

B61
CASSINELLI C.W.,THE POLITICS OF FREEDOM. FUT UNIV   MAJORIT
LAW POL/PAR CHOOSE ORD/FREE...POLICY CONCPT MYTH   NAT/G
BIBLIOG. PAGE 21 E0404   PARL/PROC
  PARTIC

B61
FROEBEL J.,THEORIE DER POLITIK. ALS ERGEBNIS EINER   JURID
ERNEUERTEN PRUEFUNG DEMOKRATISCHER LEHRMEINUNGEN.   ORD/FREE
WOR-45 SOCIETY POL/PAR SECT REV REPRESENT PWR   NAT/G
SOVEREIGN...MAJORIT 19. PAGE 41 E0812

B61
LA PONCE J.A.,THE GOVERNMENT OF THE FIFTH REPUBLIC: PWR
FRENCH POLITICAL PARTIES AND THE CONSTITUTION.   POL/PAR
ALGERIA FRANCE LAW NAT/G DELIB/GP LEGIS ECO/TAC   CONSTN
MARXISM SOCISM...CHARTS BIBLIOG/A 20 DEGAULLE/C.   CHIEF
PAGE 62 E1243

B61
WARD R.E.,JAPANESE POLITICAL SCIENCE: A GUIDE TO   BIBLIOG/A
JAPANESE REFERENCE AND RESEARCH MATERIALS (2ND   PHIL/SCI
ED.). LAW CONSTN STRATA NAT/G POL/PAR DELIB/GP
LEGIS ADMIN CHOOSE GP/REL...INT/LAW 19/20 CHINJAP.
PAGE 105 E2099

N61
DELEGACION NACIONAL DE PRENSA,FALANGE ESPANOL   EDU/PROP
TRADICIONALISTA Y DE LAS JUNTAS OFENSIVAS   FASCIST
NACIONALES SINDICALISTAS. IX CONSEJO NACIONAL   CONFER
(PAMPHLET). LAW VOL/ASSN TOTALISM AUTHORIT ORD/FREE   POL/PAR
FASCISM...ANTHOL 20 FRANCO/F FALANGIST. PAGE 31
E0605

B62
BERMAN D.M.,A BILL BECOMES A LAW: THE CIVIL RIGHTS   DISCRIM
ACT OF 1960. USA+45 LAW POL/PAR LOBBY RACE/REL   PARL/PROC
KNOWL...CHARTS 20 CONGRESS NEGRO CIV/RIGHTS.   JURID
PAGE 11 E0206   GOV/REL

B62
BOCHENSKI J.M.,HANDBOOK ON COMMUNISM. USSR WOR+45   COM
LAW SOCIETY NAT/G POL/PAR SECT CRIME PERSON MARXISM   DIPLOM
...SOC ANTHOL 20. PAGE 13 E0254   POLICY
  CONCPT

B62
FROMAN L.A. JR.,PEOPLE AND POLITICS: AN ANALYSIS OF   POL/PAR
THE AMERICAN POLITICAL SYSTEM. USA+45 CHIEF   PROB/SOLV
DELIB/GP EX/STRUC LEGIS TOP/EX CT/SYS LOBBY   GOV/REL
PERS/REL PWR...POLICY DECISION. PAGE 41 E0813

B62
MASON A.T.,THE SUPREME COURT: PALADIUM OF FREEDOM.   CONSTN
USA-45 NAT/G POL/PAR CHIEF LEGIS ADJUD PARL/PROC   CT/SYS
FEDERAL PWR...POLICY BIOG 18/20 SUPREME/CT   JURID
ROOSEVLT/F JEFFERSN/T MARSHALL/J HUGHES/CE. PAGE 69
E1378

B62
MCWHINNEY E.,CONSTITUTIONALISM IN GERMANY AND THE   CONSTN
FEDERAL CONSTITUTINAL COURT. GERMANY/W POL/PAR TV   CT/SYS
ADJUD CHOOSE EFFICIENCY ATTIT ORD/FREE MARXISM   CONTROL
...NEW/IDEA BIBLIOG 20. PAGE 71 E1428   NAT/G

B62
NAT'L MUNICIPAL LEAGUE,COMPENDIUM ON LEGISLATIVE   APPORT
APPORTIONMENT. USA+45 LOC/G NAT/G POL/PAR PROVS   REPRESENT
CT/SYS CHOOSE 20 SUPREME/CT CONGRESS. PAGE 76 E1524   LEGIS
  STAT

B62
RICE C.E.,FREEDOM OF ASSOCIATION. USA+45 USA-45   LAW
POL/PAR LOBBY GP/REL...JURID BIBLIOG 18/20   NAT/G
SUPREME/CT PRE/US/AM. PAGE 84 E1691   CONSTN

B62
ROSENZWEIG F.,HEGEL UND DER STAAT. GERMANY SOCIETY   JURID
FAM POL/PAR NAT/LISM...BIOG 19. PAGE 86 E1718   NAT/G
  CONCPT
  PHIL/SCI

B62
SILVA R.C.,RUM, RELIGION, AND VOTES: 1928 RE-   POL/PAR
EXAMINED. USA-45 LAW SECT DISCRIM CATHISM...CORREL   CHOOSE
STAT 20 PRESIDENT SMITH/ALF DEMOCRAT. PAGE 91 E1827   GP/COMP
  ATTIT

L62
NIZARD L.,"CUBAN QUESTION AND SECURITY COUNCIL."   INT/ORG
L/A+17C USA+45 ECO/UNDEV NAT/G POL/PAR DELIB/GP   JURID
ECO/TAC PWR...RELATIV OBS TIME/SEQ TREND GEN/LAWS   DIPLOM
UN 20 UN. PAGE 77 E1551   CUBA

S62
GREENSPAN M.,"INTERNATIONAL LAW AND ITS PROTECTION   FORCES

FOR PARTICIPANTS IN UNCONVENTIONAL WARFARE." WOR+45   JURID
LAW INT/ORG NAT/G POL/PAR COERCE REV ORD/FREE   GUERRILLA
...INT/LAW TOT/POP 20. PAGE 46 E0912   WAR

S62
VIGNES D.,"L'AUTORITE DES TRAITES INTERNATIONAUX EN   STRUCT
DROIT INTERNE." EUR+WWI UNIV LAW CONSTN INTELL   LEGIT
NAT/G POL/PAR DIPLOM ATTIT PERCEPT ALL/VALS   FRANCE
...POLICY INT/LAW JURID CONCPT TIME/SEQ 20 TREATY.
PAGE 104 E2075

B63
ADRIAN C.R.,GOVERNING OVER FIFTY STATES AND THEIR   PROVS
COMMUNITIES. USA+45 CONSTN FINAN MUNIC NAT/G   LOC/G
POL/PAR EX/STRUC LEGIS ADMIN CONTROL CT/SYS   GOV/REL
...CHARTS 20. PAGE 3 E0052   GOV/COMP

B63
BADI J.,THE GOVERNMENT OF THE STATE OF ISRAEL: A   NAT/G
CRITICAL ACCOUNT OF ITS PARLIAMENT, EXECUTIVE, AND   CONSTN
JUDICIARY. ISRAEL ECO/DEV CHIEF DELIB/GP LEGIS   EX/STRUC
DIPLOM CT/SYS INGP/REL PEACE ORD/FREE...BIBLIOG 20   POL/PAR
PARLIAMENT ARABS MIGRATION. PAGE 7 E0131

B63
DE GRAZIA A.,APPORTIONMENT AND REPRESENTATIVE   REPRESENT
GOVERNMENT. CONSTN POL/PAR LEGIS PLAN ADJUD DISCRIM   APPORT
RATIONAL...CONCPT STAT PREDICT TREND IDEA/COMP.   NAT/G
PAGE 29 E0583   MUNIC

B63
DILLIARD I.,ONE MAN'S STAND FOR FREEDOM: MR.   CONSTN
JUSTICE BLACK AND THE BILL OF RIGHTS. USA+45   JURID
POL/PAR SECT DELIB/GP FORCES ADJUD CONTROL WAR   JUDGE
DISCRIM MORAL...BIBLIOG 20 NEGRO SUPREME/CT   ORD/FREE
BILL/RIGHT BLACK/HL. PAGE 32 E0628

B63
ELIAS T.O.,GOVERNMENT AND POLITICS IN AFRICA.   AFR
CONSTN CULTURE SOCIETY NAT/G POL/PAR DIPLOM   NAT/LISM
REPRESENT PERSON...SOC TREND BIBLIOG 4/20. PAGE 34   COLONIAL
E0681   LAW

B63
GRANT D.R.,STATE AND LOCAL GOVERNMENT IN AMERICA.   PROVS
USA+45 FINAN LOC/G MUNIC EX/STRUC FORCES EDU/PROP   POL/PAR
ADMIN CHOOSE FEDERAL ATTIT...JURID 20. PAGE 45   LEGIS
E0897   CONSTN

B63
LEWIN J.,POLITICS AND LAW IN SOUTH AFRICA.   NAT/LISM
SOUTH/AFR UK POL/PAR BAL/PWR ECO/TAC COLONIAL   POLICY
CONTROL GP/REL DISCRIM PWR 20 NEGRO. PAGE 65 E1293   LAW
  RACE/REL

B63
LIVINGSTON W.S.,FEDERALISM IN THE COMMONWEALTH - A   BIBLIOG
BIBLIOGRAPHICAL COMMENTARY. CANADA INDIA PAKISTAN   JURID
UK STRUCT LOC/G NAT/G POL/PAR...NAT/COMP 20   FEDERAL
AUSTRAL. PAGE 66 E1310   CONSTN

B63
PRYOR F.L.,THE COMMUNIST FOREIGN TRADE SYSTEM. COM   ATTIT
CZECHOSLVK GERMANY YUGOSLAVIA LAW ECO/DEV DIST/IND   ECO/TAC
POL/PAR PLAN DOMIN TOTALISM DRIVE RIGID/FLEX WEALTH
...STAT STAND/INT CHARTS 20. PAGE 83 E1657

B63
RICHARDS P.G.,PATRONAGE IN BRITISH GOVERNMENT.   EX/STRUC
ELITES DELIB/GP TOP/EX PROB/SOLV CONTROL CT/SYS   REPRESENT
EXEC PWR. PAGE 84 E1693   POL/PAR
  ADMIN

B63
ROBERT J.,LA MONARCHIE MAROCAINE. MOROCCO LABOR   CHIEF
MUNIC POL/PAR EX/STRUC ORD/FREE PWR...JURID TREND T   CONSERVE
20. PAGE 85 E1702   ADMIN
  CONSTN

B63
ROYAL INSTITUTE PUBLIC ADMIN,BRITISH PUBLIC   BIBLIOG
ADMINISTRATION. UK LAW FINAN INDUS LOC/G POL/PAR   ADMIN
LEGIS LOBBY PARL/PROC CHOOSE JURID. PAGE 86 E1729   MGT
  NAT/G

B63
SARTORI G.,IL PARLAMENTO ITALIANO: 1946-1963. LAW   LEGIS
CONSTN ELITES POL/PAR LOBBY PRIVIL ATTIT PERSON   PARL/PROC
MORAL PWR SOC. PAGE 87 E1746   REPRESENT

B63
VINES K.N.,STUDIES IN JUDICIAL POLITICS: TULANE   CT/SYS
STUDIES IN POLITICAL SCIENCE (VOL. 8). POL/PAR   GOV/REL
JUDGE ADJUD SANCTION CRIME CHOOSE PWR...JURID STAT   PROVS
TIME/SEQ CHARTS. PAGE 104 E2079

L63
ROSE R., "COMPARATIVE STUDIES IN POLITICAL FINANCE: FINAN
A SYMPOSIUM." ASIA EUR+WWI S/ASIA LAW CULTURE   POL/PAR
DELIB/GP LEGIS ACT/RES ECO/TAC EDU/PROP CHOOSE
ATTIT RIGID/FLEX SUPEGO PWR SKILL WEALTH...STAT
ANTHOL VAL/FREE. PAGE 85 E1714

S63
BERMAN H.J., "THE DILEMMA OF SOVIET LAW REFORM."   COM
NAT/G POL/PAR CT/SYS ALL/VALS ORD/FREE PWR...POLICY   LAW
JURID VAL/FREE 20. PAGE 11 E0208   USSR

S63
MACWHINNEY E., "LES CONCEPT SOVIETIQUE DE   NAT/G
'COEXISTENCE PACIFIQUE' ET LES RAPPORTS JURIDIQUES   CONCPT
ENTRE L'URSS ET LES ETATS OCIDENTAUX." COM FUT   DIPLOM
WOR+45 LAW CULTURE INTELL POL/PAR ACT/RES BAL/PWR   USSR
...INT/LAW 20. PAGE 67 E1346

N63
US PRES COMN REGIS AND VOTING, REPORT ON   CHOOSE
REGISTRATION AND VOTING (PAMPHLET). USA+45 POL/PAR   LAW
CHIEF EDU/PROP PARTIC REPRESENT ATTIT...PSY CHARTS   SUFF
20. PAGE 101 E2023   INSPECT

B64
ANDERSON J.W., EISENHOWER, BROWNELL, AND THE   LAW
CONGRESS - THE TANGLED ORIGINS OF THE CIVIL RIGHTS   CONSTN
BILL OF 1956-1957. USA+45 POL/PAR LEGIS CREATE   POLICY
PROB/SOLV LOBBY GOV/REL RIGID/FLEX...NEW/IDEA 20   NAT/G
EISNHWR/DD CONGRESS BROWNELL/H CIV/RIGHTS. PAGE 5
E0090

B64
DUMON F., LE BRESIL; SES INSTITUTIONS POLITIQUES ET   CONSTN
JUDICIARIES. BRAZIL POL/PAR CHIEF LEGIS ORD/FREE   JURID
19/20. PAGE 33 E0658   CT/SYS
                                                      GOV/REL

B64
EULAU H., LAWYERS IN POLITICS: A STUDY IN   PROF/ORG
PROFESSIONAL CONVERGENCE. USA+45 POL/PAR DELIB/GP   JURID
GP/REL...QU 20. PAGE 35 E0701   LEGIS
                                                      ATTIT

B64
FORBES A.H., CURRENT RESEARCH IN BRITISH STUDIES. UK BIBLIOG
CONSTN CULTURE POL/PAR SECT DIPLOM ADMIN...JURID   PERSON
BIOG WORSHIP 20. PAGE 39 E0769   NAT/G
                                                      PARL/PROC

B64
GIANNELLA D.A., RELIGION AND THE PUBLIC ORDER: AN   SECT
ANNUAL REVIEW OF CHURCH AND STATE, AND OF RELIGION,   NAT/G
LAW, AND SOCIETY. USA+45 LAW SOCIETY FAM POL/PAR   CONSTN
SCHOOL GIVE EDU/PROP GP/REL...JURID GEN/LAWS   ORD/FREE
BIBLIOG/A 20 CHURCH/STA BIRTH/CON CONSCN/OBJ
NATURL/LAW. PAGE 43 E0855

B64
GRIFFITH W.E., THE SINO-SOVIET RIFT. ASIA CHINA/COM   ATTIT
COM CUBA USSR YUGOSLAVIA NAT/G POL/PAR VOL/ASSN   TIME/SEQ
DELIB/GP FORCES TOP/EX DIPLOM EDU/PROP DRIVE PERSON   BAL/PWR
PWR...TREND 20 TREATY. PAGE 47 E0941   SOCISM

B64
GROVES H.E., THE CONSTITUTION OF MALAYSIA. MALAYSIA   CONSTN
POL/PAR CHIEF CONSULT DELIB/GP CT/SYS PARL/PROC   NAT/G
CHOOSE FEDERAL ORD/FREE 20. PAGE 48 E0953   LAW

B64
GUTTMANN A., COMMUNISM, THE COURTS, AND THE   MARXISM
CONSTITUTION. USA+45 CT/SYS ORD/FREE...ANTHOL 20   POL/PAR
COM/PARTY CIV/RIGHTS. PAGE 48 E0965   CONSTN
                                                      LAW

B64
HANNA W.J., POLITICS IN BLACK AFRICA: A SELECTIVE   BIBLIOG
BIBLIOGRAPHY OF RELEVANT PERIODICAL LITERATURE. AFR   NAT/LISM
LAW LOC/G MUNIC NAT/G POL/PAR LOBBY CHOOSE RACE/REL   COLONIAL
SOVEREIGN 20. PAGE 50 E0995

B64
HENKE W., DAS RECHT DER POLITISCHEN PARTEIEN.   POL/PAR
GERMANY/W LAW CT/SYS GP/REL SUPEGO 20. PAGE 52   JURID
E1031   CONSTN
                                                      NAT/G

B64
HOLDSWORTH W.S., A HISTORY OF ENGLISH LAW; THE   LAW
CENTURIES OF DEVELOPMENT AND REFORM (VOL. XIV). UK   LEGIS
CONSTN LOC/G NAT/G POL/PAR CHIEF EX/STRUC ADJUD   LEAD
COLONIAL ATTIT...INT/LAW JURID 18/19 TORY/PARTY   CT/SYS
COMMONWLTH WHIG/PARTY COMMON/LAW. PAGE 54 E1081

B64
HOPKINSON T., SOUTH AFRICA. SOUTH/AFR UK NAT/G   SOCIETY
POL/PAR LEGIS ECO/TAC PARL/PROC WAR...JURID AUD/VIS   RACE/REL
19/20. PAGE 55 E1097   DISCRIM

B64
KEEFE W.J., THE AMERICAN LEGISLATIVE PROCESS: LEGIS
CONGRESS AND THE STATES. USA+45 LAW POL/PAR   DECISION
DELIB/GP DEBATE ADMIN LOBBY REPRESENT CONGRESS   PWR
PRESIDENT. PAGE 60 E1191   PROVS

B64
LIGGETT E., BRITISH POLITICAL ISSUES: VOLUME 1. UK   POL/PAR
LAW CONSTN LOC/G NAT/G ADJUD 20. PAGE 65 E1296   GOV/REL
                                                      CT/SYS
                                                      DIPLOM

B64
MITAU G.T., INSOLUBLE PROBLEMS: CASE PROBLEMS ON THE ADJUD
FUNCTIONS OF STATE AND LOCAL GOVERNMENT. USA+45 AIR   LOC/G
FINAN LABOR POL/PAR PROB/SOLV TAX RECEIVE CONTROL   PROVS
GP/REL 20 CASEBOOK ZONING. PAGE 73 E1471

B64
PRESS C., A BIBLIOGRAPHIC INTRODUCTION TO AMERICAN   BIBLIOG
STATE GOVERNMENT AND POLITICS (PAMPHLET). USA+45   LEGIS
USA-45 EX/STRUC ADJUD INGP/REL FEDERAL ORD/FREE 20.   LOC/G
PAGE 82 E1649   POL/PAR

B64
RICHARDSON I.L., BIBLIOGRAFIA BRASILEIRA DE   BIBLIOG
ADMINISTRACAO PUBLICA E ASSUNTOS CORRELATOS. BRAZIL   MGT
CONSTN FINAN LOC/G NAT/G POL/PAR PLAN DIPLOM   ADMIN
RECEIVE ATTIT...METH 20. PAGE 84 E1694   LAW

B64
SCHUBERT G.A., JUDICIAL BEHAVIOR: A READER IN THEORY ATTIT
AND RESEARCH. POL/PAR CT/SYS ROLE SUPEGO PWR   PERSON
...DECISION JURID REGRESS CHARTS SIMUL ANTHOL 20.   ADJUD
PAGE 89 E1782   ACT/RES

B64
STOICOIU V., LEGAL SOURCES AND BIBLIOGRAPHY OF   BIBLIOG/A
ROMANIA. COM ROMANIA LAW FINAN POL/PAR LEGIS JUDGE   JURID
ADJUD CT/SYS PARL/PROC MARXISM 20. PAGE 93 E1874   CONSTN
                                                      ADMIN

B64
TENBROCK J., EQUAL UNDER LAW. USA-45 CONSTN POL/PAR   LEGIS
EDU/PROP PARL/PROC ORD/FREE...BIBLIOG 19 AMEND/XIV.   LAW
PAGE 95 E1914   DISCRIM
                                                      DOMIN

B64
WRIGHT G., RURAL REVOLUTION IN FRANCE: THE PEASANTRY PWR
IN THE TWENTIETH CENTURY. EUR+WWI MOD/EUR LAW   STRATA
CULTURE AGRI POL/PAR DELIB/GP LEGIS ECO/TAC   FRANCE
EDU/PROP COERCE CHOOSE ATTIT RIGID/FLEX HEALTH   REV
...STAT CENSUS CHARTS VAL/FREE 20. PAGE 107 E2148

L64
POUNDS N.J.G., "THE POLITICS OF PARTITION." AFR ASIA NAT/G
COM EUR+WWI FUT ISLAM S/ASIA USA-45 LAW ECO/DEV   NAT/LISM
ECO/UNDEV AGRI INDUS INT/ORG POL/PAR PROVS SECT
FORCES TOP/EX EDU/PROP LEGIT ATTIT MORAL ORD/FREE
PWR RESPECT WEALTH. PAGE 82 E1640

S64
GARDNER R.N., "THE SOVIET UNION AND THE UNITED   COM
NATIONS." WOR+45 FINAN POL/PAR VOL/ASSN FORCES   INT/ORG
ECO/TAC DOMIN EDU/PROP LEGIT ADJUD ADMIN ARMS/CONT   USSR
COERCE ATTIT ALL/VALS...POLICY MAJORIT CONCPT OBS
TIME/SEQ TREND STERTYP UN. PAGE 42 E0838

S64
PRITCHETT C.H., "EQUAL PROTECTION AND THE URBAN   MUNIC
MAJORITY." POL/PAR LEAD CHOOSE GP/REL PWR...MAJORIT   LAW
DECISION. PAGE 83 E1655   REPRESENT
                                                      APPORT

B65
BLITZ L.F., THE POLITICS AND ADMINISTRATION OF   NAT/G
NIGERIAN GOVERNMENT. NIGER CULTURE LOC/G LEGIS   GOV/REL
DIPLOM COLONIAL CT/SYS SOVEREIGN...GEOG SOC ANTHOL   POL/PAR
20. PAGE 13 E0245

B65
CARTER G.M., POLITICS IN EUROPE. EUR+WWI FRANCE   GOV/COMP
GERMANY/W UK USSR LAW CONSTN POL/PAR VOL/ASSN PRESS   OP/RES
LOBBY PWR...ANTHOL SOC/INTEG EEC. PAGE 20 E0399   ECO/DEV

B65
CHROUST A.H., THE RISE OF THE LEGAL PROFESSION IN   JURID
AMERICA (3 VOLS.). STRATA STRUCT POL/PAR PROF/ORG   USA-45
COLONIAL LEAD REV SKILL...SOC 17/20. PAGE 22 E0437   CT/SYS
                                                      LAW

B65
CONGRESSIONAL QUARTERLY SERV.POLITICS IN AMERICA. CHOOSE
1945-1964: THE POLITICS AND ISSUES OF THE POSTWAR REPRESENT
YEARS. USA+45 LAW FINAN CHIEF DIPLOM APPORT SUFF POL/PAR
...POLICY STAT TREND CHARTS 20 CONGRESS PRESIDENT. LEGIS
PAGE 25 E0489

B65
INST INTL DES CIVILISATION DIF.THE CONSTITUTIONS CONSTN
AND ADMINISTRATIVE INSTITUTIONS OF THE NEW STATES. ADMIN
AFR ISLAM S/ASIA NAT/G POL/PAR DELIB/GP EX/STRUC ADJUD
CONFER EFFICIENCY NAT/LISM...JURID SOC 20. PAGE 56 ECO/UNDEV
E1123

B65
KEEFE W.J.,THE AMERICAN LEGISLATIVE PROCESS. USA+45 LEGIS
CONSTN POL/PAR CT/SYS REPRESENT FEDERAL ATTIT NAT/G
PLURISM...MAJORIT 20 CONGRESS PRESIDENT. PAGE 60 CHIEF
E1192 GOV/REL

B65
PYLEE M.V.,CONSTITUTIONAL GOVERNMENT IN INDIA (2ND CONSTN
REV. ED.). INDIA POL/PAR EX/STRUC DIPLOM COLONIAL NAT/G
CT/SYS PARL/PROC PRIVIL...JURID 16/20. PAGE 83 PROVS
E1665 FEDERAL

B65
SCHUBERT G.,REAPPORTIONMENT. LAW MUNIC POL/PAR PWR REPRESENT
GOV/COMP. PAGE 88 E1775 LOC/G
APPORT
LEGIS

B65
SOPER T.,EVOLVING COMMONWEALTH. AFR CANADA INDIA INT/ORG
IRELAND UK LAW CONSTN POL/PAR DOMIN CONTROL WAR PWR COLONIAL
...AUD/VIS 18/20 COMMONWLTH OEEC. PAGE 93 E1857 VOL/ASSN

B66
ANDERSON S.V.,CANADIAN OMBUDSMAN PROPOSALS. CANADA NAT/G
LEGIS DEBATE PARL/PROC...MAJORIT JURID TIME/SEQ CREATE
IDEA/COMP 20 OMBUDSMAN PARLIAMENT. PAGE 5 E0092 ADMIN
POL/PAR

B66
BAKER G.E.,THE REAPPORTIONMENT REVOLUTION: LEGIS
REPRESENTATION, POLITICAL POWER, AND THE SUPREME APPORT
COURT. USA+45 MUNIC NAT/G POL/PAR PROVS PROB/SOLV REPRESENT
CHOOSE ORD/FREE POPULISM...CONCPT CHARTS 20 ADJUD
SUPREME/CT. PAGE 7 E0140

B66
BURNS A.C.,PARLIAMENT AS AN EXPORT. WOR+45 CONSTN PARL/PROC
BARGAIN DEBATE ROUTINE GOV/REL EFFICIENCY...ANTHOL POL/PAR
COMMONWLTH PARLIAMENT. PAGE 17 E0343 CT/SYS
CHIEF

B66
CONG QUARTERLY SERVICE.REPRESENTATION AND APPORT
APPORTIONMENT. USA+45 USA-45 POL/PAR CT/SYS SUFF LEGIS
...POLICY 20 CONGRESS SUPREME/CT. PAGE 25 E0486 REPRESENT
CONSTN

B66
DALLIN A.,POLITICS IN THE SOVIET UNION: 7 CASES. MARXISM
COM USSR LAW POL/PAR CHIEF FORCES WRITING CONTROL DOMIN
PARL/PROC CIVMIL/REL TOTALISM...ANTHOL 20 KHRUSH/N ORD/FREE
STALIN/J CASEBOOK COM/PARTY. PAGE 28 E0563 GOV/REL

B66
DE TOCQUEVILLE A.DEMOCRACY IN AMERICA (1834-1840) POPULISM
(2 VOLS. IN I; TRANS. BY G. LAWRENCE). FRANCE USA-45
CULTURE STRATA POL/PAR CT/SYS REPRESENT FEDERAL CONSTN
ORD/FREE SOVEREIGN...MAJORIT TREND GEN/LAWS 18/19. NAT/COMP
PAGE 30 E0596

B66
EPSTEIN F.T.,THE AMERICAN BIBLIOGRAPHY OF RUSSIAN BIBLIOG
AND EAST EUROPEAN STUDIES FOR 1964. USSR LOC/G COM
NAT/G POL/PAR FORCES ADMIN ARMS/CONT...JURID CONCPT MARXISM
20 UN. PAGE 35 E0694 DIPLOM

B66
FISCHER H.,EINER IM VORDERGRUND: TARAS FASCISM
BORODAJKEWYCZ. AUSTRIA POL/PAR PROF/ORG EDU/PROP LAW
CT/SYS ORD/FREE 20 NAZI. PAGE 38 E0754 ATTIT
PRESS

B66
GREENE L.E.,GOVERNMENT IN TENNESSEE (2ND ED.). PROVS
USA+45 DIST/IND INDUS POL/PAR EX/STRUC LEGIS PLAN LOC/G
BUDGET GIVE CT/SYS...MGT T 20 TENNESSEE. PAGE 46 CONSTN
E0909 ADMIN

B66
HAMILTON H.D.,REAPPORTIONING LEGISLATURES. USA+45 APPORT

B66
CONSTN POL/PAR PROVS LEGIS COMPUTER ADJUD CHOOSE REPRESENT
ATTIT...ANTHOL 20 SUPREME/CT CONGRESS. PAGE 50 PHIL/SCI
E0989 PWR

B66
HANSON R.,THE POLITICAL THICKET. USA+45 MUNIC APPORT
POL/PAR LEGIS EXEC LOBBY CHOOSE...MAJORIT DECISION. LAW
PAGE 50 E0998 CONSTN
REPRESENT

B66
INSTITUTE COMP STUDY POL SYS.DOMINICAN REPUBLIC SUFF
ELECTION FACT BOOK. DOMIN/REP LAW LEGIS REPRESENT CHOOSE
...JURID CHARTS 20. PAGE 57 E1126 POL/PAR
NAT/G

B66
KUNST H.,EVANGELISCHES STAATSLEXIKON. LAW CONSTN JURID
POL/PAR...PHIL/SCI CONCPT DICTIONARY. PAGE 62 E1232 SECT
SOC
NAT/G

B66
LEHMANN L.,LEGAL UND OPPORTUN - POLITISCHE JUSTIZ ORD/FREE
IN DER BUNDESREPUBLIK. GERMANY/W EDU/PROP ADJUD POL/PAR
CONTROL PARL/PROC COERCE TOTALISM ATTIT 20 JURID
COM/PARTY. PAGE 64 E1281 LEGIS

B66
PLATE H.,PARTEIFINANZIERUNG UND GRUNDESETZ. GERMANY POL/PAR
NAT/G PLAN GIVE PAY INCOME WEALTH...JURID 20. CONSTN
PAGE 81 E1619 FINAN

B66
RUNCIMAN W.G.,RELATIVE DEPRIVATION AND SOCIAL STRATA
JUSTICE: A STUDY OF ATTITUDES TO SOCIAL INEQUALITY STRUCT
IN TWENTIETH-CENTURY ENGLAND. UK LAW POL/PAR PWR DISCRIM
...CONCPT NEW/IDEA SAMP METH 19/20. PAGE 86 E1734 ATTIT

B66
TRESOLINI R.J.,CASES IN AMERICAN NATIONAL NAT/G
GOVERNMENT AND POLITICS. LAW DIPLOM ADJUD LOBBY LEGIS
FEDERAL ORD/FREE WEALTH...DECISION ANTHOL 20 CT/SYS
PRESIDENT. PAGE 97 E1940 POL/PAR

B66
US DEPARTMENT OF STATE.RESEARCH ON AFRICA (EXTERNAL BIBLIOG/A
RESEARCH LIST NO 5-25). LAW CULTURE ECO/UNDEV ASIA
POL/PAR DIPLOM EDU/PROP LEAD REGION MARXISM...GEOG S/ASIA
LING WORSHIP 20. PAGE 100 E1996 NAT/G

B66
US DEPARTMENT OF STATE.RESEARCH ON WESTERN EUROPE, BIBLIOG/A
GREAT BRITAIN, AND CANADA (EXTERNAL RESEARCH LIST EUR+WWI
NO 3-25). CANADA GERMANY/W UK LAW CULTURE NAT/G DIPLOM
POL/PAR FORCES EDU/PROP REGION MARXISM...GEOG SOC
WORSHIP 20 CMN/WLTH. PAGE 100 E1998

S66
BURDETTE F.L.,"SELECTED ARTICLES AND DOCUMENTS ON BIBLIOG
AMERICAN GOVERNMENT AND POLITICS." LAW LOC/G MUNIC USA+45
NAT/G POL/PAR PROVS LEGIS BAL/PWR ADMIN EXEC JURID
REPRESENT MGT. PAGE 17 E0331 CONSTN

S66
MATTHEWS D.G.,"ETHIOPIAN OUTLINE: A BIBLIOGRAPHIC BIBLIOG
RESEARCH GUIDE." ETHIOPIA LAW STRUCT ECO/UNDEV AGRI NAT/G
LABOR SECT CHIEF DELIB/GP EX/STRUC ADMIN...LING DIPLOM
ORG/CHARTS 20. PAGE 69 E1384 POL/PAR

S66
MATTHEWS D.G.,"PRELUDE-COUP D'ETAT-MILITARY BIBLIOG
GOVERNMENT: A BIBLIOGRAPHICAL AND RESEARCH GUIDE TO NAT/G
NIGERIAN POL AND GOVT, JAN, 1965-66." AFR NIGER LAW ADMIN
CONSTN POL/PAR LEGIS CIVMIL/REL GOV/REL...STAT 20. CHOOSE
PAGE 69 E1385

B67
BIBBY J.,ON CAPITOL HILL. POL/PAR LOBBY PARL/PROC CONFER
GOV/REL PERS/REL...JURID PHIL/SCI OBS INT BIBLIOG LEGIS
20 CONGRESS PRESIDENT. PAGE 12 E0224 CREATE
LEAD

B67
BOULTON D.,OBJECTION OVERRULED. UK LAW POL/PAR FORCES
DIPLOM ADJUD SANCTION DEATH WAR CIVMIL/REL 20. SOCISM
PAGE 14 E0273 SECT

B67
COWLING M.,1867 DISRAELI, GLADSTONE, AND PARL/PROC
REVOLUTION: THE PASSING OF THE SECOND REFORM BILL. POL/PAR
UK LEGIS LEAD LOBBY GP/REL INGP/REL...DECISION ATTIT
BIBLIOG 19 REFORMERS. PAGE 27 E0531 LAW

B67
FESLER J.W.,THE FIFTY STATES AND THEIR LOCAL PROVS

GOVERNMENTS. FUT USA+45 POL/PAR LEGIS PROB/SOLV
ADMIN CT/SYS CHOOSE GOV/REL FEDERAL...POLICY CHARTS
20 SUPREME/CT. PAGE 37 E0743
    LOC/G

    B67
FINCHER F.,THE GOVERNMENT OF THE UNITED STATES.
USA+45 USA-45 POL/PAR CHIEF CT/SYS LOBBY GP/REL
INGP/REL...CONCPT CHARTS BIBLIOG T 18/20 PRESIDENT
CONGRESS SUPREME/CT. PAGE 38 E0749
    NAT/G
    EX/STRUC
    LEGIS
    OP/RES

    B67
GRAHAM H.D.,CRISIS IN PRINT: DESEGREGATION AND THE
PRESS IN TENNESSEE. LAW SOCIETY MUNIC POL/PAR
EDU/PROP LEAD REPRESENT DISCRIM ATTIT...IDEA/COMP
BIBLIOG/A SOC/INTEG 20 TENNESSEE SUPREME/CT
SOUTH/US. PAGE 45 E0896
    PRESS
    PROVS
    POLICY
    RACE/REL

    B67
JONES C.O.,EVERY SECOND YEAR: CONGRESSIONAL
BEHAVIOR AND THE TWO-YEAR TERM. LAW POL/PAR
PROB/SOLV DEBATE CHOOSE PERS/REL COST FEDERAL PWR
...CHARTS 20 CONGRESS SENATE HOUSE/REP. PAGE 59
E1172
    EFFICIENCY
    LEGIS
    TIME/SEQ
    NAT/G

    B67
OPERATIONS AND POLICY RESEARCH,NICARAGUA: ELECTION
FACTBOOK: FEBRUARY 5, 1967 (PAMPHLET). NICARAGUA
LAW NAT/G LEAD REPRESENT...STAT BIOG CHARTS 20.
PAGE 79 E1577
    POL/PAR
    CHOOSE
    PLAN
    ATTIT

    B67
RAE D.,THE POLITICAL CONSEQUENCES OF ELECTORAL
LAWS. EUR+WWI ICELAND ISRAEL NEW/ZEALND UK USA+45
ADJUD APPORT GP/REL MAJORITY...MATH STAT CENSUS
CHARTS BIBLIOG 20 AUSTRAL. PAGE 83 E1667
    POL/PAR
    CHOOSE
    NAT/COMP
    REPRESENT

    L67
LAMBERT J.D.,"CORPORATE POLITICAL SPENDING AND
CAMPAIGN FINANCE." LAW CONSTN FINAN LABOR LG/CO
LOC/G NAT/G VOL/ASSN TEC/DEV ADJUD ADMIN PARTIC.
PAGE 62 E1247
    USA+45
    POL/PAR
    CHOOSE
    COST

    S67
HAMILTON H.D.,"LEGISLATIVE CONSTITUENCIES: SINGLE-
MEMBER DISTRICTS, MULTI-MEMBER DISTRICTS, AND
FLOTERAL DISTRICTS." USA+45 LAW POL/PAR ADJUD
RACE/REL...CHARTS METH/COMP 20. PAGE 50 E0990
    LEGIS
    REPRESENT
    APPORT
    PLAN

    S67
RICHARDSON J.J.,"THE MAKING OF THE RESTRICTIVE
TRADE PRACTICES ACT 1956 A CASE STUDY OF THE POLICY
PROCESS IN BRITAIN." UK FINAN MARKET LG/CO POL/PAR
CONSULT PRESS ADJUD ADMIN AGREE LOBBY SANCTION
ATTIT 20. PAGE 84 E1695
    LEGIS
    ECO/TAC
    POLICY
    INDUS

    S67
SHELDON C.H.,"PUBLIC OPINION AND HIGH COURTS:
COMMUNIST PARTY CASES IN FOUR CONSTITUTIONAL
SYSTEMS." CANADA GERMANY/W WOR+45 POL/PAR MARXISM
...METH/COMP NAT/COMP 20 AUSTRAL. PAGE 91 E1818
    ATTIT
    CT/SYS
    CONSTN
    DECISION

POLAND....SEE ALSO COM

    B45
GALLOWAY E.,ABSTRACTS OF POSTWAR LITERATURE (VOL.
IV) JAN.-JULY, 1945 NOS. 901-1074. POLAND USA+45
USSR WOR+45 INDUS LABOR PLAN ECO/TAC INT/TRADE TAX
EDU/PROP ADMIN COLONIAL INT/LAW. PAGE 42 E0829
    BIBLIOG/A
    NUC/PWR
    NAT/G
    DIPLOM

    B55
MID-EUROPEAN LAW PROJECT,CHURCH AND STATE BEHIND
THE IRON CURTAIN. COM CZECHOSLVK HUNGARY POLAND
USSR CULTURE SECT EDU/PROP GOV/REL CATHISM...CHARTS
ANTHOL BIBLIOG WORSHIP 20 CHURCH/STA. PAGE 73 E1455
    LAW
    MARXISM
    POLICY

    S58
STAAR R.F.,"ELECTIONS IN COMMUNIST POLAND." EUR+WWI
SOCIETY INT/ORG NAT/G POL/PAR LEGIS ACT/RES ECO/TAC
EDU/PROP ADJUD ADMIN ROUTINE COERCE TOTALISM ATTIT
ORD/FREE PWR 20. PAGE 93 E1864
    COM
    CHOOSE
    POLAND

    B63
RAVENS J.P.,STAAT UND KATHOLISCHE KIRCHE IN
PREUSSENS POLNISCHEN TEILUNGSGEBIETEN. GERMANY
POLAND PRUSSIA PROVS DIPLOM EDU/PROP DEBATE
NAT/LISM...JURID 18 CHURCH/STA. PAGE 83 E1674
    GP/REL
    CATHISM
    SECT
    NAT/G

    B64
SIEKANOWICZ P.,LEGAL SOURCES AND BIBLIOGRAPHY OF
POLAND. COM POLAND CONSTN NAT/G PARL/PROC SANCTION
CRIME MARXISM 16/20. PAGE 91 E1823
    BIBLIOG
    ADJUD
    LAW
    JURID

    S67
SEIDLER G.L.,"MARXIST LEGAL THOUGHT IN POLAND."
POLAND SOCIETY R+D LOC/G NAT/G ACT/RES ADJUD CT/SYS
    MARXISM
    LAW

SUPEGO PWR...SOC TREND 20 MARX/KARL. PAGE 90 E1802
    CONCPT
    EFFICIENCY

POLICE....SEE FORCES

POLICY....ETHICS OF PUBLIC POLICIES

POLIT/ACTN....POLITICAL ACTION COMMITTEE

POLITBURO....POLITBURO (U.S.S.R.)

POLITICAL FINANCING....SEE FINAN

POLITICAL MACHINE....SEE ADMIN

POLITICAL MOVEMENT....SEE IDEOLOGICAL TOPIC INDEX

POLITICAL ORGANIZATION....SEE POL/PAR

POLITICAL PROCESS....SEE LEGIS

POLITICAL SYSTEMS....SEE IDEOLOGICAL TOPIC INDEX

POLITICAL SYSTEMS THEORY....SEE NET THEORY

POLITICAL THEORY....SEE IDEOLOGICAL TOPIC INDEX

POLK/JAMES....PRESIDENT JAMES POLK

POLLACK R.S. E1623

POLLACK/N....NORMAN POLLACK

POLLOCK E.M. E1045

POLLOCK F. E1624,E1625,E1626

POLLUTION....AIR OR WATER POLLUTION

    B62
STERN A.C.,AIR POLLUTION (2 VOLS.). LAW INDUS
PROB/SOLV TEC/DEV INSPECT RISK BIO/SOC HABITAT
...OBS/ENVIR TESTS SAMP 20 POLLUTION. PAGE 93 E1871
    AIR
    OP/RES
    CONTROL
    HEALTH

POLSBY N.W. E1627

POLYNESIA....POLYNESIA

POOLE R.E. E1272

POOLEY B.J. E1628

POONA....POONA, INDIA

POPE....POPE

    B14
FIGGIS J.N.,CHURCHES IN THE MODERN STATE (2ND ED.).
LAW CHIEF BAL/PWR PWR...CONCPT CHURCH/STA POPE.
PAGE 38 E0748
    SECT
    NAT/G
    SOCIETY
    ORD/FREE

    B60
BERTHOLD O.,KAISER, VOLK UND AVIGNON. GERMANY CHIEF
LEGIT LEAD NAT/LISM CONSERVE 14 POPE CHRUCH/STA
LUDWIG/BAV JOHN/XXII. PAGE 11 E0217
    DIPLOM
    CATHISM
    JURID

    B65
MOELLER R.,LUDWIG DER BAYER UND DIE KURIE IM KAMPF
UM DAS REICH. GERMANY LAW SECT LEGIT LEAD GP/REL
CATHISM CONSERVE 14 LUDWIG/BAV POPE CHURCH/STA.
PAGE 74 E1478
    JURID
    CHIEF
    CHOOSE
    NAT/LISM

POPPER/K....KARL POPPER

POPULATION....SEE GEOG, CENSUS

POPULISM....MAJORITARIANISM

    B05
GRIFFIN A.P.C.,LIST OF REFERENCES ON PRIMARY
ELECTIONS (PAMPHLET). USA-45 LAW LOC/G DELIB/GP
LEGIS OP/RES TASK REPRESENT CONSEN...DECISION 19/20
CONGRESS. PAGE 47 E0928
    BIBLIOG/A
    POL/PAR
    CHOOSE
    POPULISM

    B09
LOBINGIER C.S.,THE PEOPLE'S LAW OR POPULAR
PARTICIPATION IN LAW-MAKING. FRANCE SWITZERLND UK
LOC/G NAT/G PROVS LEGIS SUFF MAJORITY PWR POPULISM
    CONSTN
    LAW
    PARTIC

...GOV/COMP BIBLIOG 19. PAGE 66 E1314

B12
BEARD C.A.,THE SUPREME COURT AND THE CONSTITUTION.   CONSTN
LAW NAT/G PROVS LEGIS GOV/REL ATTIT POPULISM   CT/SYS
SUPREME/CT. PAGE 9 E0164   ADJUD
                                                            CONTROL

B12
MEYER H.H.B.,SELECT LIST OF REFERENCES ON THE   BIBLIOG/A
INITIATIVE, REFERENDUM, AND RECALL. MOD/EUR USA-45   NAT/G
LAW LOC/G MUNIC REPRESENT POPULISM 20 CONGRESS.   LEGIS
PAGE 72 E1446   CHOOSE

C20
DUNNING W.A.,"A HISTORY OF POLITICAL THINKERS FROM   IDEA/COMP
ROUSSEAU TO SPENCER." NAT/G REV NAT/LISM UTIL   PHIL/SCI
CONSERVE MARXISM POPULISM...JURID BIBLIOG 18/19.   CONCPT
PAGE 33 E0664   GEN/LAWS

B28
HOBBES T.,THE ELEMENTS OF LAW, NATURAL AND POLITIC   PERSON
(1650). STRATA NAT/G SECT CHIEF AGREE ATTIT   LAW
ALL/VALS MORAL ORD/FREE POPULISM...POLICY CONCPT.   SOVEREIGN
PAGE 53 E1056   CONSERVE

B35
DE TOCQUEVILLE A.,DEMOCRACY IN AMERICA (4 VOLS.)   POPULISM
(TRANS. BY HENRY REEVE). CONSTN STRUCT LOC/G MAJORIT   MAJORIT
POL/PAR PROVS ETIQUET CT/SYS MAJORITY ATTIT 18/19.   ORD/FREE
PAGE 30 E0595   SOCIETY

B40
FULLER G.H.,A SELECTED LIST OF RECENT REFERENCES ON   BIBLIOG/A
THE CONSTITUTION OF THE UNITED STATES (PAMPHLET).   CONSTN
CULTURE NAT/G LEGIS CONFER ADJUD GOV/REL CONSEN   LAW
POPULISM...JURID CONCPT 18/20 CONGRESS. PAGE 41   USA-45
E0820

C44
JEFFERSON T.,"DEMOCRACY" (1816) IN BASIC WRITINGS."   POPULISM
USA-45 LOC/G NAT/G TAX CT/SYS CHOOSE ORD/FREE   MAJORIT
...GEN/LAWS 18/19 JEFFERSN/T. PAGE 58 E1151   REPRESENT
                                                       CONSTN

B46
ROSS A.,TOWARDS A REALISTIC JURISPRUDENCE: A   LAW
CRITICISM OF THE DUALISM IN LAW (TRANS. BY ANNIE I.   CONCPT
FAUSBOLL). PLAN ADJUD CT/SYS ATTIT RIGID/FLEX   IDEA/COMP
POPULISM...JURID PHIL/SCI LOG METH/COMP GEN/LAWS 20
SCANDINAV. PAGE 86 E1720

B47
KONVITZ M.R.,THE CONSTITUTION AND CIVIL RIGHTS.   CONSTN
USA-45 NAT/G ADJUD GP/REL RACE/REL POPULISM   LAW
...MAJORIT 19/20 SUPREME/CT CIV/RIGHTS. PAGE 61   GOV/REL
E1227   ORD/FREE

B55
SMITH G.,A CONSTITUTIONAL AND LEGAL HISTORY OF   CONSTN
ENGLAND. UK ELITES NAT/G LEGIS ADJUD OWN HABITAT   PARTIC
POPULISM...JURID 20 ENGLSH/LAW. PAGE 92 E1844   LAW
                                                       CT/SYS

B55
WHEARE K.C.,GOVERNMENT BY COMMITTEE; AN ESSAY ON   DELIB/GP
THE BRITISH CONSTITUTION. UK NAT/G LEGIS INSPECT   CONSTN
CONFER ADJUD ADMIN CONTROL TASK EFFICIENCY ROLE   LEAD
POPULISM 20. PAGE 106 E2116   GP/COMP

B56
EMDEN C.S.,THE PEOPLE AND THE CONSTITUTION (2ND   CONSTN
ED.). UK LEGIS POPULISM 17/20 PARLIAMENT. PAGE 35   PARL/PROC
E0687   NAT/G
                                                       LAW

B57
LONG H.A.,USURPERS - FOES OF FREE MAN. LAW NAT/G   CT/SYS
CHIEF LEGIS DOMIN ADJUD REPRESENT GOV/REL ORD/FREE   CENTRAL
LAISSEZ POPULISM...POLICY 18/20 SUPREME/CT   FEDERAL
ROOSEVLT/F CONGRESS CON/INTERP. PAGE 66 E1325   CONSTN

B58
ALLEN C.K.,LAW IN THE MAKING. LEGIS ATTIT ORD/FREE   LAW
SOVEREIGN POPULISM...JURID IDEA/COMP NAT/COMP   CREATE
GEN/LAWS 20 ENGLSH/LAW. PAGE 4 E0069   CONSTN
                                                       SOCIETY

B58
PALMER E.E.,CIVIL LIBERTIES. USA+45 ADJUD CT/SYS   ORD/FREE
PARTIC OWN LAISSEZ POPULISM...JURID CONCPT ANTHOL   CONSTN
20 SUPREME/CT CIVIL/LIB. PAGE 79 E1592   RACE/REL
                                                       LAW

B58
STRONG C.F.,MODERN POLITICAL CONSTITUTIONS. LAW   CONSTN

CHIEF DELIB/GP EX/STRUC LEGIS ADJUD CHOOSE FEDERAL   IDEA/COMP
POPULISM...CONCPT BIBLIOG 20 UN. PAGE 94 E1887   NAT/G

B59
NICHOLS R.F.,RELIGION AND AMERICAN DEMOCRACY.   NAT/G
USA+45 USA-45 LAW CHOOSE SUFF MORAL ORD/FREE   SECT
POPULISM...POLICY BIBLIOG 16/20 PRE/US/AM   CONSTN
CHRISTIAN. PAGE 77 E1547   CONCPT

B61
GUIZOT F.P.G.,HISTORY OF THE ORIGIN OF   LEGIS
REPRESENTATIVE GOVERNMENT IN EUROPE. CHRIST-17C   REPRESENT
FRANCE MOD/EUR SPAIN UK LAW CHIEF FORCES POPULISM   CONSTN
...MAJORIT TIME/SEQ GOV/COMP NAT/COMP 4/19   NAT/G
PARLIAMENT. PAGE 48 E0961

B63
MURPHY T.J.,CENSORSHIP: GOVERNMENT AND OBSCENITY.   ORD/FREE
USA+45 CULTURE LEGIS JUDGE EDU/PROP CONTROL   MORAL
INGP/REL RATIONAL POPULISM...CATH JURID 20. PAGE 75   LAW
E1507   CONSEN

B65
GAJENDRAGADKAR P.B.,LAW, LIBERTY AND SOCIAL   ORD/FREE
JUSTICE. INDIA CONSTN NAT/G SECT PLAN ECO/TAC PRESS   LAW
POPULISM...SOC METH/COMP 20 HINDU. PAGE 42 E0826   ADJUD
                                                       JURID

B66
BAKER G.E.,THE REAPPORTIONMENT REVOLUTION;   LEGIS
REPRESENTATION, POLITICAL POWER, AND THE SUPREME   APPORT
COURT. USA+45 MUNIC NAT/G POL/PAR PROVS PROB/SOLV   REPRESENT
CHOOSE ORD/FREE POPULISM...CONCPT CHARTS 20   ADJUD
SUPREME/CT. PAGE 7 E0140

B66
DE TOCQUEVILLE A.DEMOCRACY IN AMERICA (1834-1840)   POPULISM
(2 VOLS. IN 1; TRANS. BY G. LAWRENCE). FRANCE   USA+45
CULTURE STRATA POL/PAR CT/SYS REPRESENT FEDERAL   CONSTN
ORD/FREE SOVEREIGN...MAJORIT TREND GEN/LAWS 18/19.   NAT/COMP
PAGE 30 E0596

B87
ADAMS J.,A DEFENSE OF THE CONSTITUTIONS OF   CONSTN
GOVERNMENT OF THE UNITED STATES OF AMERICA. USA-45   BAL/PWR
STRATA CHIEF EX/STRUC LEGIS CT/SYS CONSERVE   PWR
POPULISM...CONCPT CON/ANAL GOV/COMP. PAGE 3 E0048   NAT/G

B89
FICHTE J.G.,THE SCIENCE OF RIGHTS (TRANS. BY A.E.   ORD/FREE
KROEGER). WOR-45 FAM MUNIC NAT/G PROVS ADJUD CRIME   CONSTN
CHOOSE MARRIAGE SEX POPULISM 19 FICHTE/JG   LAW
NATURL/LAW. PAGE 37 E0744   CONCPT

PORTER K.H. E1629

PORTUGAL....SEE ALSO APPROPRIATE TIME/SPACE/CULTURE INDEX

POSPISIL L. E1630

POSTAL/SYS....POSTAL SYSTEMS

B59
US SENATE COMM ON POST OFFICE,TO PROVIDE FOR AN   ADMIN
EFFECTIVE SYSTEM OF PERSONNEL ADMINISTRATION.   NAT/G
EFFICIENCY...MGT 20 CONGRESS CIVIL/SERV POSTAL/SYS   EX/STRUC
YARBROGH/R. PAGE 103 E2059   LAW

POSTOFFICE....POST OFFICE DEPARTMENT

POTSDAM....POTSDAM

POTTER P.B. E1631,E1632,E1633

POUND R. E1634,E1635,E1636,E1637,E1638,E1639

POUND/ROS....ROSCOE POUND

POUNDS N.J.G. E1640

POVERTY....SEE WEALTH, INCOME

POVRTY/WAR....WAR ON POVERTY; SEE ALSC JOHNSN/LB

POWELL T. E1641

POWELL T.R. E1642

POWELL/AC....ADAM CLAYTON POWELL

POWER....SEE PWR

POWERS E. E1643

PPBS....PLANNING-PROGRAMMING-BUDGETING SYSTEM

PRABHAKAR P. E1645

PRAGMATICS....SEE LOG

PRASAD B. E1646

PRATT G.N. E1744

PRATT I.A. E1647

PRE/AMER....PRE-EUROPEAN AMERICAS

PRE/US/AM....PRE-1776 UNITED STATES (THE COLONIES)

B59
NICHOLS R.F.,RELIGION AND AMERICAN DEMOCRACY. NAT/G
USA+45 USA-45 LAW CHOOSE SUFF MORAL ORD/FREE SECT
POPULISM...POLICY BIBLIOG 16/20 PRE/US/AM CONSTN
CHRISTIAN. PAGE 77 E1547 CONCPT

B62
RICE C.E.,FREEDOM OF ASSOCIATION. USA+45 USA-45 LAW
POL/PAR LOBBY GP/REL...JURID BIBLIOG 18/20 NAT/G
SUPREME/CT PRE/US/AM. PAGE 84 E1691 CONSTN

B65
FEERICK J.D.,FROM FAILING HANDS: THE STUDY OF EX/STRUC
PRESIDENTIAL SUCCESSION. CONSTN NAT/G PROB/SOLV CHIEF
LEAD PARL/PROC MURDER CHOOSE...NEW/IDEA BIBLIOG 20 LAW
KENNEDY/JF JOHNSON/LB PRESIDENT PRE/US/AM LEGIS
VICE/PRES. PAGE 36 E0724

B65
MILLER H.H.,THE CASE FOR LIBERTY. USA-45 LAW JUDGE COLONIAL
CT/SYS...AUD/VIS 18 PRE/US/AM CASEBOOK. PAGE 73 JURID
E1460 PROB/SOLV

B65
MORRIS R.B.,THE PEACEMAKERS: THE GREAT POWERS AND SOVEREIGN
AMERICAN INDEPENDENCE. BAL/PWR CONFER COLONIAL REV
NEUTRAL PEACE ORD/FREE TREATY 18 PRE/US/AM. PAGE 75 DIPLOM
E1499

B66
POWERS E.,CRIME AND PUNISHMENT IN EARLY CRIME
MASSACHUSETTS 1620-1692: A DOCUMENTARY HISTORY. ADJUD
USA-45 SECT LEGIS COLONIAL ATTIT ORD/FREE MYSTISM CT/SYS
17 PRE/US/AM MASSACHU. PAGE 82 E1643 PROVS

PREDICT....PREDICTION OF FUTURE EVENTS, SEE ALSO FUT

C56
FALL B.B.,"THE VIET-MINH REGIME." VIETNAM LAW NAT/G
ECO/UNDEV POL/PAR FORCES DOMIN WAR ATTIT MARXISM ADMIN
...BIOG PREDICT BIBLIOG/A 20. PAGE 36 E0720 EX/STRUC
LEAD

B57
ROWAN C.T.,GO SOUTH TO SORROW. USA+45 STRUCT NAT/G RACE/REL
EDU/PROP LEAD COERCE ISOLAT DRIVE SUPEGO RESPECT DISCRIM
...PREDICT 20 NEGRO SUPREME/CT SOUTH/US CIV/RIGHTS. ANOMIE
PAGE 86 E1728 LAW

B58
BLOCH J.,STATES' RIGHTS: THE LAW OF THE LAND. PROVS
USA+45 USA-45 LAW CONSTN LEGIS CONTROL CT/SYS NAT/G
FEDERAL ORD/FREE...PREDICT 17/20 CONGRESS BAL/PWR
SUPREME/CT. PAGE 13 E0246 CENTRAL

B63
DE GRAZIA A.,APPORTIONMENT AND REPRESENTATIVE REPRESENT
GOVERNMENT. CONSTN POL/PAR LEGIS PLAN ADJUD DISCRIM APPORT
RATIONAL...CONCPT STAT PREDICT TREND IDEA/COMP. NAT/G
PAGE 29 E0583 MUNIC

L63
LOEVINGER L.,"JURIMETRICS* THE METHODOLOGY OF LEGAL COMPUT/IR
INQUIRY." COMPUTER CREATE PLAN TEC/DEV AUTOMAT JURID
CT/SYS EFFICIENCY...DECISION PHIL/SCI NEW/IDEA GEN/METH
QUANT PREDICT. PAGE 66 E1318 ADJUD

B64
GARDNER R.N.,IN PURSUIT OF WORLD ORDER* US FOREIGN OBS
POLICY AND INTERNATIONAL ORGANIZATIONS. USA+45 USSR INT/ORG
ECO/UNDEV FORCES LEGIS DIPLOM FOR/AID INT/TRADE ALL/VALS
PEACE...INT/LAW PREDICT UN. PAGE 42 E0839

B64
TAUBENFELD H.J.,SPACE AND SOCIETY. USA+45 LAW SPACE
FORCES CREATE TEC/DEV ADJUD CONTROL COST PEACE SOCIETY
...PREDICT ANTHOL 20. PAGE 95 E1911 ADJUST
DIPLOM

B65
FLEMING R.W.,THE LABOR ARBITRATION PROCESS. USA+45 GP/REL
LAW BARGAIN ADJUD ROUTINE SANCTION COST...PREDICT LABOR
CHARTS TIME 20. PAGE 38 E0763 CONSULT
DELIB/GP

S65
HIBBS A.R.,"SPACE TECHNOLOGY* THE THREAT AND THE SPACE
PROMISE." FUT VOL/ASSN TEC/DEV NUC/PWR COST ARMS/CONT
EFFICIENCY UTIL UN TREATY. PAGE 52 E1038 PREDICT

S65
MARTIN A.,"PROLIFERATION." FUT WOR+45 PROB/SOLV RECORD
REGION ADJUST...PREDICT NAT/COMP UN TREATY. PAGE 69 NUC/PWR
E1372 ARMS/CONT
VOL/ASSN

S65
WRIGHT Q.,"THE ESCALATION OF INTERNATIONAL WAR
CONFLICTS." WOR+45 WOR-45 FORCES DIPLOM RISK COST PERCEPT
ATTIT ALL/VALS...INT/LAW QUANT STAT NAT/COMP. PREDICT
PAGE 108 E2160 MATH

B66
HAYS P.R.,LABOR ARBITRATION: A DISSENTING VIEW. GP/REL
USA+45 LAW DELIB/GP BARGAIN ADJUD...PREDICT 20. LABOR
PAGE 51 E1016 CONSULT
CT/SYS

B66
WAINHOUSE D.W.,INTERNATIONAL PEACE OBSERVATION: A PEACE
HISTORY AND FORECAST. INT/ORG PROB/SOLV BAL/PWR DIPLOM
AGREE ARMS/CONT COERCE NUC/PWR...PREDICT METH/COMP
20 UN LEAGUE/NAT OAS TREATY. PAGE 104 E2092

B67
AMDS W.E.,DELINQUENCY PREVENTION: THEORY AND AGE/Y
PRACTICE. USA+45 SOCIETY FAM SCHOOL SECT FORCES CRIME
PROB/SOLV...HEAL JURID PREDICT ANTHOL. PAGE 4 E0071 PUB/INST
LAW

S67
DOYLE S.E.,"COMMUNICATION SATELLITES* INTERNAL TEC/DEV
ORGANIZATION FOR DEVELOPMENT AND CONTROL." USA+45 SPACE
R+D ACT/RES DIPLOM NAT/LISM...POLICY INT/LAW COM/IND
PREDICT UN. PAGE 33 E0647 INT/ORG

B92
LOWELL A.L.,ESSAYS ON GOVERNMENT. UK USA-45 LEGIS CONSTN
PARL/PROC...POLICY PREDICT 19. PAGE 66 E1328 ADJUD
CT/SYS
NAT/G

PREDICTION....SEE PREDICT, FUT

PREFECT....PREFECTS AND PREFECTORALISM

PREHIST....PREHISTORIC SOCIETY, PRIOR TO 3000 B.C.

PREJUDICE....SEE DISCRIM

PRESIDENT....PRESIDENCY (ALL NATIONS); SEE ALSO CHIEF

N
US SUPERINTENDENT OF DOCUMENTS,POLITICAL SCIENCE: BIBLIOG/A
GOVERNMENT, CRIME, DISTRICT OF COLUMBIA (PRICE LIST NAT/G
54). USA+45 LAW CONSTN EX/STRUC WORKER ADJUD ADMIN CRIME
CT/SYS CHOOSE INGP/REL RACE/REL CONGRESS PRESIDENT.
PAGE 103 E2063

B03
GRIFFIN A.P.C.,LIST OF BOOKS ON THE CONSTITUTION OF BIBLIOG/A
THE UNITED STATES (PAMPHLET). USA-45 NAT/G EX/STRUC CONSTN
JUDGE TOP/EX CT/SYS 18/20 CONGRESS PRESIDENT LAW
SUPREME/CT. PAGE 46 E0920 JURID

N19
MCCONNELL G.,THE STEEL SEIZURE OF 1952 (PAMPHLET). DELIB/GP
USA+45 FINAN INDUS PROC/MFG LG/CO EX/STRUC ADJUD LABOR
CONTROL GP/REL ORD/FREE PWR 20 TRUMAN/HS PRESIDENT PROB/SOLV
CONGRESS. PAGE 70 E1402 NAT/G

B33
HELLMAN F.S.,SELECTED LIST OF REFERENCES ON THE BIBLIOG/A
CONSTITUTIONAL POWERS OF THE PRESIDENT INCLUDING JURID
POWERS RECENTLY DELEGATED. USA-45 NAT/G EX/STRUC LAW
TOP/EX CENTRAL FEDERAL PWR 20 PRESIDENT. PAGE 51 CONSTN
E1025

B38
HELLMAN F.S.,THE SUPREME COURT ISSUE: SELECTED LIST BIBLIOG/A
OF REFERENCES. USA-45 NAT/G CHIEF EX/STRUC JUDGE CONSTN
ATTIT...JURID 20 PRESIDENT ROOSEVLT/F SUPREME/CT. CT/SYS

PRESIDENT

PAGE 51 E1026   LAW

B41
BIRDSALL P.,VERSAILLES TWENTY YEARS AFTER. MOD/EUR DIPLOM
POL/PAR CHIEF CONSULT FORCES LEGIS REPAR PEACE NAT/LISM
ORD/FREE...BIBLIOG 20 PRESIDENT TREATY. PAGE 12 WAR
E0231

B42
CARR R.K.,THE SUPREME COURT AND JUDICIAL REVIEW. CT/SYS
NAT/G CHIEF LEGIS OP/RES LEAD GOV/REL GP/REL ATTIT CONSTN
...POLICY DECISION 18/20 SUPREME/CT PRESIDENT JURID
CONGRESS. PAGE 20 E0394 PWR

B48
STOKES W.S.,BIBLIOGRAPHY OF STANDARD AND CLASSICAL BIBLIOG
WORKS IN THE FIELDS OF AMERICAN POLITICAL SCIENCE. NAT/G
USA+45 USA-45 POL/PAR PROVS FORCES DIPLOM LOC/G
CT/SYS APPORT 20 CONGRESS PRESIDENT. PAGE 94 E1876 CONSTN

B50
HURST J.W.,THE GROWTH OF AMERICAN LAW; THE LAW LAW
MAKERS. USA-45 LOC/G NAT/G DELIB/GP JUDGE ADJUD LEGIS
ADMIN ATTIT PWR...POLICY JURID BIBLIOG 18/20 CONSTN
CONGRESS SUPREME/CT ABA PRESIDENT. PAGE 56 E1115 CT/SYS

B50
MERRIAM C.E.,THE AMERICAN PARTY SYSTEM; AN POL/PAR
INTRODUCTION TO THE STUDY OF POLITICAL PARTIES IN CHOOSE
THE UNITED STATES (4TH ED.). USA+45 USA-45 LAW SUFF
FINAN LOC/G NAT/G PROVS LEAD PARTIC CRIME ATTIT REPRESENT
18/20 NEGRO CONGRESS PRESIDENT. PAGE 72 E1442

C50
HOLCOMBE A.,"OUR MORE PERFECT UNION." USA+45 USA-45 CONSTN
POL/PAR JUDGE CT/SYS EQUILIB FEDERAL PWR...MAJORIT NAT/G
TREND BIBLIOG 18/20 CONGRESS PRESIDENT. PAGE 54 ADMIN
E1070 PLAN

B51
ROSSITER C.,THE SUPREME COURT AND THE COMMANDER IN CT/SYS
CHIEF. LAW CONSTN DELIB/GP EX/STRUC LEGIS TOP/EX CHIEF
ADJUD CONTROL...DECISION SOC/EXP PRESIDENT. PAGE 86 WAR
E1724 PWR

B53
GROSS B.M.,THE LEGISLATIVE STRUGGLE: A STUDY IN LEGIS
SOCIAL COMBAT. STRUCT LOC/G POL/PAR JUDGE EDU/PROP DECISION
DEBATE ETIQUET ADMIN LOBBY CHOOSE GOV/REL INGP/REL PERSON
HEREDITY ALL/VALS...SOC PRESIDENT. PAGE 48 E0948 LEAD

N53
US PRES CONF ADMIN PROCEDURE,REPORT (PAMPHLET). NAT/G
USA+45 CONFER ADJUD...METH/COMP 20 PRESIDENT. DELIB/GP
PAGE 101 E2024 ADJUST
ADMIN

B54
BROGAN D.W.,POLITICS IN AMERICA. LAW POL/PAR CHIEF NAT/G
LEGIS LOBBY CHOOSE REPRESENT GP/REL RACE/REL CONSTN
FEDERAL MORAL...BIBLIOG 20 PRESIDENT CONGRESS. USA+45
PAGE 16 E0304

B55
BERNSTEIN M.H.,REGULATING BUSINESS BY INDEPENDENT DELIB/GP
COMMISSION. USA+45 USA-45 LG/CO CHIEF LEGIS CONTROL
PROB/SOLV ADJUD SANCTION GP/REL ATTIT...TIME/SEQ CONSULT
19/20 MONOPOLY PRESIDENT CONGRESS. PAGE 11 E0214

B56
ABELS J.,THE TRUMAN SCANDALS. USA+45 USA-45 POL/PAR CRIME
TAX LEGIT CT/SYS CHOOSE PRIVIL MORAL WEALTH 20 ADMIN
TRUMAN/HS PRESIDENT CONGRESS. PAGE 2 E0043 CHIEF
TRIBUTE

S56
TANENHAUS J.,"THE SUPREME COURT AND PRESIDENTIAL CT/SYS
POWER." USA+45 USA-45 NAT/G ADJUD GOV/REL FEDERAL PWR
20 PRESIDENT. PAGE 95 E1907 CONTROL
CHIEF

B57
SCHUBERT G.A.,THE PRESIDENCY IN THE COURTS. CONSTN PWR
FORCES DIPLOM TARIFFS ADJUD CONTROL WAR...DECISION CT/SYS
MGT CHARTS 18/20 PRESIDENT CONGRESS SUPREME/CT. LEGIT
PAGE 89 E1778 CHIEF

B58
HAND L.,THE BILL OF RIGHTS. USA+45 USA-45 CHIEF CONSTN
LEGIS BAL/PWR ROLE PWR 18/20 SUPREME/CT CONGRESS JURID
AMEND/V PRESIDENT AMEND/XIV. PAGE 50 E0994 ORD/FREE
CT/SYS

B58
HUNT B.I.,BIPARTISANSHIP: A CASE STUDY OF THE FOR/AID
FOREIGN ASSISTANCE PROGRAM, 1947-56 (DOCTORAL POL/PAR

THESIS). USA+45 INT/ORG CONSULT LEGIS TEC/DEV GP/REL
...BIBLIOG PRESIDENT TREATY NATO TRUMAN/HS DIPLOM
EISNHWR/DD CONGRESS. PAGE 56 E1114

B58
US CONGRESS,FREEDOM OF INFORMATION AND SECRECY IN CHIEF
GOVERNMENT (2 VOLS.). USA+45 DELIB/GP EX/STRUC PRIVIL
EDU/PROP PWR 20 CONGRESS PRESIDENT. PAGE 99 E1988 CONSTN
LAW

B59
LOEWENSTEIN K.,VERFASSUNGSRECHT UND CONSTN
VERFASSUNGSPRAXIS DER VEREINIGTEN STAATEN. USA+45 POL/PAR
USA-45 COLONIAL CT/SYS GP/REL RACE/REL ORD/FREE EX/STRUC
...JURID 18/20 SUPREME/CT CONGRESS PRESIDENT NAT/G
BILL/RIGHT CIVIL/LIB. PAGE 66 E1319

B59
US SENATE COMM ON JUDICIARY,EXECUTIVE PRIVILEGE. CHIEF
USA+45 DELIB/GP CONTROL KNOWL PWR 20 CONGRESS PRIVIL
PRESIDENT. PAGE 102 E2042 CONSTN
LAW

B60
JUNZ A.J.,PRESENT TRENDS IN AMERICAN NATIONAL POL/PAR
GOVERNMENT. LEGIS DIPLOM ADMIN CT/SYS ORD/FREE CHOOSE
...CONCPT ANTHOL 20 CONGRESS PRESIDENT SUPREME/CT. CONSTN
PAGE 2 E0040 NAT/G

B60
BLANSHARD P.,GOD AND MAN IN WASHINGTON. USA+45 NAT/G
CHIEF LEGIS LEGIT CT/SYS PRIVIL ATTIT ORD/FREE SECT
...POLICY CONCPT 20 SUPREME/CT CONGRESS PRESIDENT GP/REL
CHURCH/STA. PAGE 12 E0242 POL/PAR

B60
CARPER E.T.,THE DEFENSE APPROPRIATIONS RIDER GOV/REL
(PAMPHLET). USA+45 CONSTN CHIEF DELIB/GP LEGIS ADJUD
BUDGET LOBBY CIVMIL/REL...POLICY 20 CONGRESS LAW
EISNHWR/DD DEPT/DEFEN PRESIDENT BOSTON. PAGE 20 CONTROL
E0390

B61
KURLAND P.B.,RELIGION AND THE LAW. USA+45 USA-45 SECT
CONSTN PROVS CHIEF ADJUD SANCTION PRIVIL CATHISM NAT/G
...POLICY 17/20 SUPREME/CT PRESIDENT CHURCH/STA. CT/SYS
PAGE 62 E1239 GP/REL

B61
SCOTT A.M.,POLITICS, USA; CASES ON THE AMERICAN CT/SYS
DEMOCRATIC PROCESS. USA+45 CHIEF FORCES DIPLOM CONSTN
LOBBY CHOOSE RACE/REL FEDERAL ATTIT...JURID ANTHOL NAT/G
T 20 PRESIDENT CONGRESS CIVIL/LIB. PAGE 90 E1795 PLAN

B61
TOMPKINS D.C.,CONFLICT OF INTEREST IN THE FEDERAL BIBLIOG
GOVERNMENT: A BIBLIOGRAPHY. USA+45 EX/STRUC LEGIS ROLE
ADJUD ADMIN CRIME CONGRESS PRESIDENT. PAGE 96 E1932 NAT/G
LAW

B62
BOCK E.A.,CASE STUDIES IN AMERICAN GOVERNMENT. POLICY
USA+45 ECO/DEV CHIEF EDU/PROP CT/SYS RACE/REL LEGIS
ORD/FREE...JURID MGT PHIL/SCI PRESIDENT CASEBOOK. IDEA/COMP
PAGE 13 E0256 NAT/G

B62
HIRSCHFIELD R.S.,THE CONSTITUTION AND THE COURT. ADJUD
SCHOOL WAR RACE/REL EQUILIB ORD/FREE...POLICY PWR
MAJORIT DECISION JURID 18/20 PRESIDENT COLD/WAR CONSTN
CIVIL/LIB SUPREME/CT CONGRESS. PAGE 53 E1051 LAW

B62
SILVA R.C.,RUM, RELIGION, AND VOTES: 1928 RE- POL/PAR
EXAMINED. USA-45 LAW SECT DISCRIM CATHISM...CORREL CHOOSE
STAT 20 PRESIDENT SMITH/ALF DEMOCRAT. PAGE 91 E1827 GP/COMP
ATTIT

B64
DANELSKI D.J.,A SUPREME COURT JUSTICE IS APPOINTED. CHOOSE
CHIEF LEGIS CONFER DEBATE EXEC PERSON PWR...BIOG 20 JUDGE
CONGRESS PRESIDENT. PAGE 28 E0564 DECISION

B64
KEEFE W.J.,THE AMERICAN LEGISLATIVE PROCESS: LEGIS
CONGRESS AND THE STATES. USA+45 LAW POL/PAR DECISION
DELIB/GP DEBATE ADMIN LOBBY REPRESENT CONGRESS PWR
PRESIDENT. PAGE 60 E1191 PROVS

B64
MINAR D.W.,IDEAS AND POLITICS: THE AMERICAN CONSTN
EXPERIENCE. SECT CHIEF LEGIS CREATE ADJUD EXEC REV NAT/G
PWR...PHIL/SCI CONCPT IDEA/COMP 18/20 HAMILTON/A FEDERAL
JEFFERSN/T DECLAR/IND JACKSON/A PRESIDENT. PAGE 73
E1464

MITCHELL B.,A BIOGRAPHY OF THE CONSTITUTION OF THE UNITED STATES. USA+45 USA-45 PROVS CHIEF LEGIS DEBATE ADJUD SUFF FEDERAL...SOC 18/20 SUPREME/CT CONGRESS SENATE HOUSE/REP PRESIDENT. PAGE 73 E1472
B64 CONSTN LAW JURID

TOMPKINS D.C.,PRESIDENTIAL SUCCESSION. USA+45 CHIEF ADJUD 20 PRESIDENT CONGRESS. PAGE 96 E1933
B64 BIBLIOG/A EX/STRUC CONSTN TOP/EX

US SENATE COMM ON JUDICIARY,CIVIL RIGHTS - THE PRESIDENT'S PROGRAM. USA+45 LAW PROB/SOLV PRESS ADJUD GOV/REL RACE/REL ORD/FREE PWR...JURID 20 SUPREME/CT SENATE CIV/RIGHTS PRESIDENT. PAGE 102 E2053
B64 INT LEGIS DISCRIM PARL/PROC

WILLIAMS S.P.,TOWARD A GENUINE WORLD SECURITY SYSTEM (PAMPHLET). WOR+45 INT/ORG FORCES PLAN NUC/PWR ORD/FREE...INT/LAW CONCPT UN PRESIDENT. PAGE 106 E2123
B64 BIBLIOG/A ARMS/CONT DIPLOM PEACE

BELL J.,THE JOHNSON TREATMENT: HOW LYNDON JOHNSON TOOK OVER THE PRESIDENCY AND MADE IT HIS OWN. USA+45 DELIB/GP DIPLOM ADJUD MURDER CHOOSE PERSON PWR...POLICY OBS INT TIME 20 JOHNSON/LB KENNEDY/JF PRESIDENT CONGRESS. PAGE 10 E0183
B65 INGP/REL TOP/EX CONTROL NAT/G

CHARNAY J.P.,LE SUFFRAGE POLITIQUE EN FRANCE; ELECTIONS PARLEMENTAIRES, ELECTION PRESIDENTIELLE, REFERENDUMS. FRANCE CONSTN CHIEF DELIB/GP ECO/TAC EDU/PROP CRIME INGP/REL MORAL ORD/FREE PWR CATHISM 20 PARLIAMENT PRESIDENT. PAGE 22 E0425
B65 CHOOSE SUFF NAT/G LEGIS

CONGRESSIONAL QUARTERLY SERV,FEDERAL ROLE IN EDUCATION (PAMPHLET). LAW SCHOOL PLAN TAX ADJUD ...CHARTS SOC/INTEG 20 PRESIDENT. PAGE 25 E0487
B65 ACADEM DISCRIM RECEIVE FEDERAL

CONGRESSIONAL QUARTERLY SERV,POLITICS IN AMERICA, 1945-1964: THE POLITICS AND ISSUES OF THE POSTWAR YEARS. USA+45 LAW FINAN CHIEF DIPLOM APPORT SUFF ...POLICY STAT TREND CHARTS 20 CONGRESS PRESIDENT. PAGE 25 E0489
B65 CHOOSE REPRESENT POL/PAR LEGIS

FEERICK J.D.,FROM FAILING HANDS: THE STUDY OF PRESIDENTIAL SUCCESSION. CONSTN NAT/G PROB/SOLV LEAD PARL/PROC MURDER CHOOSE...NEW/IDEA BIBLIOG 20 KENNEDY/JF JOHNSON/LB PRESIDENT PRE/US/AM VICE/PRES. PAGE 36 E0724
B65 EX/STRUC CHIEF LAW LEGIS

KEEFE W.J.,THE AMERICAN LEGISLATIVE PROCESS. USA+45 CONSTN POL/PAR CT/SYS REPRESENT FEDERAL ATTIT PLURISM...MAJORIT 20 CONGRESS PRESIDENT. PAGE 60 E1192
B65 LEGIS NAT/G CHIEF GOV/REL

CANFIELD L.H.,THE PRESIDENCY OF WOODROW WILSON: PRELUDE TO A WORLD IN CRISIS. USA-45 ADJUD NEUTRAL WAR CHOOSE INGP/REL PEACE ORD/FREE 20 WILSON/W PRESIDENT TREATY LEAGUE/NAT. PAGE 19 E0373
B66 PERSON POLICY DIPLOM GOV/REL

TRESOLINI R.J.,CASES IN AMERICAN NATIONAL GOVERNMENT AND POLITICS. LAW DIPLOM ADJUD LOBBY FEDERAL ORD/FREE WEALTH...DECISION ANTHOL 20 PRESIDENT. PAGE 97 E1940
B66 NAT/G LEGIS CT/SYS POL/PAR

BIBBY J.,ON CAPITOL HILL. POL/PAR LOBBY PARL/PROC GOV/REL PERS/REL...JURID PHIL/SCI OBS INT BIBLIOG 20 CONGRESS PRESIDENT. PAGE 12 E0224
B67 CONFER LEGIS CREATE LEAD

FINCHER F.,THE GOVERNMENT OF THE UNITED STATES. USA+45 USA-45 POL/PAR CHIEF CT/SYS LOBBY GP/REL INGP/REL...CONCPT CHARTS BIBLIOG T 18/20 PRESIDENT CONGRESS SUPREME/CT. PAGE 38 E0749
B67 NAT/G EX/STRUC LEGIS OP/RES

MEYERS M.,SOURCES OF THE AMERICAN REPUBLIC; A DOCUMENTARY HISTORY OF POLITICS, SOCIETY, AND THOUGHT (VOL. I, REV. ED.). USA-45 CULTURE STRUCT NAT/G LEGIS LEAD ATTIT...JURID SOC ANTHOL 17/19 PRESIDENT. PAGE 72 E1450
B67 COLONIAL REV WAR

GOSSETT W.T.,"ELECTING THE PRESIDENT: NEW HOPE FOR AN OLD IDEAL." FUT USA+45 USA-45 PROVS LEGIS PROB/SOLV WRITING DEBATE ADJUD REPRESENT...MAJORIT DECISION 20 HOUSE/REP PRESIDENT. PAGE 45 E0892
S67 CONSTN CHIEF CHOOSE NAT/G

PRESS C. E1648,E1649

PRESS....PRESS, OPERATIONS OF ALL PRINTED MEDIA, EXCEPT FILM AND TV (Q.V.), JOURNALISM; SEE ALSO COM/IND

SOUTH AFRICA STATE LIBRARY,SOUTH AFRICAN NATIONAL BIBLIOGRAPHY, SANB. SOUTH/AFR LAW NAT/G EDU/PROP ...MGT PSY SOC 20. PAGE 93 E1858
N BIBLIOG PRESS WRITING

FAGUET E.,LE LIBERALISME. FRANCE PRESS ADJUD ADMIN DISCRIM CONSERVE SOCISM...TRADIT SOC LING WORSHIP PARLIAMENT. PAGE 36 E0711
B03 ORD/FREE EDU/PROP NAT/G LAW

FOUAD M.,LE REGIME DE LA PRESSE EN EGYPTE: THESE POUR LE DOCTORAT. UAR LICENSE EDU/PROP ADMIN SANCTION CRIME SUPEGO PWR...ART/METH JURID 19/20. PAGE 39 E0778
B12 ORD/FREE LEGIS CONTROL PRESS

SCHROEDER T.,FREE SPEECH FOR RADICALS (REV. ED.). USA-45 CONSTN INDUS LOC/G FORCES SANCTION WAR ATTIT SEX...JURID REFORMERS 20 FREE/SPEE. PAGE 88 E1767
B16 ORD/FREE CONTROL LAW PRESS

THE REGIONAL DIRECTOR AND THE PRESS (PAMPHLET). USA-45 COM/IND LOBBY ROLE 20 NLRB CINCINNATI BILL/RIGHT. PAGE 2 E0031
N19 PRESS LABOR ORD/FREE EDU/PROP

LIPPMAN W.,LIBERTY AND THE NEWS. USA+45 USA-45 LAW LEGIS DOMIN LEGIT ATTIT...POLICY SOC IDEA/COMP METH/COMP 19/20. PAGE 65 E1300
B20 ORD/FREE PRESS COM/IND EDU/PROP

BEALE J.H.,A BIBLIOGRAPHY OF EARLY ENGLISH LAW BOOKS. MOD/EUR UK PRESS ADJUD CT/SYS ATTIT...CHARTS 10/16. PAGE 8 E0161
B26 BIBLIOG/A JURID LAW

LEITZ F.,DIE PUBLIZITAT DER AKTIENGESELLSCHAFT. BELGIUM FRANCE GERMANY UK FINAN PRESS GP/REL PROFIT KNOWL 20. PAGE 64 E1282
B29 LG/CO JURID ECO/TAC NAT/COMP

REID H.D.,RECUEIL DES COURS; TOME 45: LES SERVITUDES INTERNATIONALES III. FRANCE CONSTN DELIB/GP PRESS CONTROL REV WAR CHOOSE PEACE MORAL MARITIME TREATY. PAGE 84 E1680
B33 ORD/FREE DIPLOM LAW

CLYDE W.M.,THE STRUGGLE FOR THE FREEDOM OF THE PRESS FROM CAXTON TO CROMWELL. UK LAW LOC/G SECT FORCES LICENSE WRITING SANCTION REV ATTIT PWR ...POLICY 15/17 PARLIAMENT CROMWELL/O MILTON/J. PAGE 23 E0460
B34 PRESS ORD/FREE CONTROL

GONZALEZ PALENCIA A,ESTUDIO HISTORICO SOBRE LA CENSURA GUBERNATIVA EN ESPANA 1800-1833. NAT/G COERCE INGP/REL ATTIT AUTHORIT KNOWL...POLICY JURID 19. PAGE 44 E0884
B34 LEGIT EDU/PROP PRESS CONTROL

BURCHFIELD L.,STUDENT'S GUIDE TO MATERIALS IN POLITICAL SCIENCE. FINAN INT/ORG NAT/G POL/PAR DIPLOM PRESS ADMIN...BIOG 18/19. PAGE 17 E0328
B35 BIBLIOG INDEX LAW

HANSON L.,GOVERNMENT AND THE PRESS 1695-1763. UK LOC/G LEGIS LICENSE CONTROL SANCTION CRIME ATTIT ORD/FREE 17/18 PARLIAMENT AMEND/I. PAGE 50 E0996
B36 LAW JURID PRESS POLICY

ANDERSON R.B.,SUPPLEMENT TO BEALE'S BIBLIOGRAPHY OF EARLY ENGLISH LAW BOOKS. MOD/EUR UK CONSTN PRESS ADJUD...CHARTS 10/15. PAGE 5 E0091
B43 BIBLIOG/A JURID CT/SYS LAW

BENTHAM J.,"ON THE LIBERTY OF THE PRESS, AND PUBLIC DISCUSSION" IN J. BOWRING, ED., THE WORKS OF JEREMY
C43 ORD/FREE PRESS

B64
FACTS ON FILE, INC.,CIVIL RIGHTS 1960-63: THE NEGRO DISCRIM
CAMPAIGN TO WIN EQUAL RIGHTS AND OPPORTUNITIES IN PRESS
THE UNITED STATES. LAW CONSTN PARTIC SUFF 20 NEGRO RACE/REL
CIV/RIGHTS MISSISSIPP. PAGE 36 E0710

B64
IRION F.C.,APPORTIONMENT OF THE NEW MEXICO APPORT
LEGISLATURE. NAT/G LEGIS PRESS CT/SYS ATTIT REPRESENT
...POLICY TIME/SEQ 19/20 SUPREME/CT. PAGE 57 E1137 GOV/REL
PROVS

B64
LOCKHART W.B.,CASES AND MATERIALS ON CONSTITUTIONAL ORD/FREE
RIGHTS AND LIBERTIES. USA+45 FORCES LEGIS DIPLOM CONSTN
PRESS CONTROL CRIME WAR PWR...AUD/VIS T WORSHIP 20 NAT/G
NEGRO. PAGE 66 E1317

B64
A CHECK LIST OF THE SPECIAL AND STANDING COMMITTEES BIBLIOG
OF THE AMERICAN BAR ASSOCIATION (VOL. II). USA+45 LAW
LEGIS PRESS CONFER...JURID CON/ANAL. PAGE 80 E1607 VOL/ASSN

B64
SCHMEISER D.A.,CIVIL LIBERTIES IN CANADA. CANADA ORD/FREE
LAW SECT PRESS RACE/REL NAT/LISM PRIVIL 20 CONSTN
COMMONWLTH PARLIAMENT CIVIL/LIB CHURCH/STA. PAGE 88 ADJUD
E1758 EDU/PROP

B64
US SENATE COMM ON JUDICIARY,CIVIL RIGHTS - THE INT
PRESIDENT'S PROGRAM. USA+45 LAW PROB/SOLV PRESS LEGIS
ADJUD GOV/REL RACE/REL ORD/FREE PWR...JURID 20 DISCRIM
SUPREME/CT SENATE CIV/RIGHTS PRESIDENT. PAGE 102 PARL/PROC
E2053

B65
ASSOCIATION BAR OF NYC,RADIO, TELEVISION, AND THE AUD/VIS
ADMINISTRATION OF JUSTICE: A DOCUMENTED SURVEY OF ATTIT
MATERIALS. USA+45 DELIB/GP FORCES PRESS ADJUD ORD/FREE
CONTROL CT/SYS CRIME...INT IDEA/COMP BIBLIOG.
PAGE 6 E0109

B65
BARKER L.J.,FREEDOM, COURTS, POLITICS: STUDIES IN JURID
CIVIL LIBERTIES. USA+45 LEGIS CREATE DOMIN PRESS CT/SYS
ADJUD LOBBY CRIME GP/REL RACE/REL MARXISM 20 ATTIT
CIVIL/LIB. PAGE 8 E0148 ORD/FREE

B65
CARTER G.M.,POLITICS IN EUROPE. EUR+WWI FRANCE GOV/COMP
GERMANY/W UK USSR LAW CONSTN POL/PAR VOL/ASSN PRESS OP/RES
LOBBY PWR...ANTHOL SOC/INTEG EEC. PAGE 20 E0399 ECO/DEV

B65
GAJENDRAGADKAR P.B.,LAW, LIBERTY AND SOCIAL ORD/FREE
JUSTICE. INDIA CONSTN NAT/G SECT PLAN ECO/TAC PRESS LAW
POPULISM...SOC METH/COMP 20 HINDU. PAGE 42 E0826 ADJUD
JURID

B65
LAFAVE W.R.,LAW AND SOVIET SOCIETY. EX/STRUC DIPLOM JURID
DOMIN EDU/PROP PRESS ADMIN CRIME OWN MARXISM 20 CT/SYS
KHRUSH/N. PAGE 62 E1244 ADJUD
GOV/REL

B65
MOSTECKY V.,SOVIET LEGAL BIBLIOGRAPHY. USSR LEGIS BIBLIOG/A
PRESS WRITING CONFER ADJUD CT/SYS REV MARXISM LAW
...INT/LAW JURID DICTIONARY 20. PAGE 75 E1503 COM
CONSTN

B65
UNESCO,HANDBOOK OF INTERNATIONAL EXCHANGES. COM/IND INDEX
R+D ACADEM PROF/ORG VOL/ASSN CREATE TEC/DEV INT/ORG
EDU/PROP AGREE 20 TREATY. PAGE 98 E1963 DIPLOM
PRESS

B66
BRAIBANTI R.,RESEARCH ON THE BUREAUCRACY OF HABITAT
PAKISTAN. PAKISTAN LAW CULTURE INTELL ACADEM LOC/G NAT/G
SECT PRESS CT/SYS...LING CHARTS 20 BUREAUCRCY. ADMIN
PAGE 15 E0286 CONSTN

B66
CAHN E.,CONFRONTING INJUSTICE. USA+45 PROB/SOLV TAX ORD/FREE
EDU/PROP PRESS CT/SYS GP/REL DISCRIM BIO/SOC CONSTN
...IDEA/COMP BIBLIOG WORSHIP 20 BILL/RIGHT. PAGE 18 ADJUD
E0362

B66
FISCHER H.,EINER IM VORDERGRUND: TARAS FASCISM
BORODAJKEWYCZ. AUSTRIA POL/PAR PROF/ORG EDU/PROP LAW
CT/SYS ORD/FREE 20 NAZI. PAGE 38 E0754 ATTIT

B66
GILLMOR D.M.,FREE PRESS AND FAIR TRIAL. UK USA+45 ORD/FREE
CONSTN PROB/SOLV PRESS CONTROL CRIME DISCRIM ADJUD
RESPECT...AUD/VIS 20 CIVIL/LIB. PAGE 44 E0865 ATTIT
EDU/PROP

B66
LOFTON J.,JUSTICE AND THE PRESS. EDU/PROP GOV/REL PRESS
MORAL 20. PAGE 66 E1320 JURID
CT/SYS
ORD/FREE

B66
SWEET E.C.,CIVIL LIBERTIES IN AMERICA. LAW CONSTN ADJUD
NAT/G PRESS CT/SYS DISCRIM ATTIT WORSHIP 20 ORD/FREE
CIVIL/LIB. PAGE 95 E1899 SUFF
COERCE

B66
US SENATE COMM AERO SPACE SCI,SOVIET SPACE CONSULT
PROGRAMS, 1962-65: GOALS AND PURPOSES, SPACE
ACHIEVEMENTS, PLANS, AND INTERNATIONAL FUT
IMPLICATIONS. USA+45 USSR R+D FORCES PLAN EDU/PROP DIPLOM
PRESS ADJUD ARMS/CONT ATTIT MARXISM. PAGE 101 E2028

B66
US SENATE COMM ON JUDICIARY,HEARINGS ON FREE PRESS PRESS
AND FAIR TRIAL (2 VOLS.). USA+45 CONSTN ELITES LAW
LEGIS EDU/PROP CT/SYS LEAD CONGRESS. PAGE 103 E2057 CRIME
ORD/FREE

S66
SHEEHY E.P.,"SELECTED REFERENCE BOOKS OF BIBLIOG/A
1965-1966." AGRI PERF/ART PRESS...GEOG HUM JURID INDEX
SOC LING WORSHIP. PAGE 91 E1817 CLASSIF

C66
ZAWODNY J.K.,"GUIDE TO THE STUDY OF INTERNATIONAL BIBLIOG/A
RELATIONS." OP/RES PRESS...STAT INT 20. PAGE 108 DIPLOM
E2169 INT/LAW
INT/ORG

B67
BOLES D.E.,THE TWO SWORDS. USA+45 USA-45 LAW CONSTN SCHOOL
SOCIETY FINAN PRESS CT/SYS...HEAL JURID BIBLIOG EDU/PROP
WORSHIP 20 SUPREME/CT CHURCH/STA. PAGE 13 E0263 ADJUD

B67
COX A.,CIVIL RIGHTS, THE CONSTITUTION, AND THE LAW
COURTS. CONSTN EDU/PROP CRIME DISCRIM ATTIT...JURID FEDERAL
20. PAGE 27 E0533 RACE/REL
PRESS

B67
FRIENDLY A.,CRIME AND PUBLICITY. TV CT/SYS SUPEGO PRESS
20. PAGE 41 E0811 CRIME
ROLE
LAW

B67
GRAHAM H.D.,CRISIS IN PRINT: DESEGREGATION AND THE PRESS
PRESS IN TENNESSEE. LAW SOCIETY MUNIC POL/PAR PROVS
EDU/PROP LEAD REPRESENT DISCRIM ATTIT...IDEA/COMP POLICY
BIBLIOG/A SOC/INTEG 20 TENNESSEE SUPREME/CT RACE/REL
SOUTH/US. PAGE 45 E0896

L67
BARRON J.A.,"ACCESS TO THE PRESS." USA+45 TEC/DEV ORD/FREE
PRESS TV ADJUD AUD/VIS. PAGE 8 E0152 COM/IND
EDU/PROP
LAW

S67
GREY D.L.,"INTERVIEWING AT THE COURT." USA+45 JUDGE
ELITES COM/IND ACT/RES PRESS CT/SYS PERSON...SOC ATTIT
INT 20 SUPREME/CT. PAGE 46 E0916 PERS/COMP
GP/COMP

S67
GRIFFIN H.C.,"PREJUDICIAL PUBLICITY: SEARCH FOR A LAW
CIVIL REMEDY." EDU/PROP CONTROL DISCRIM...JURID 20. SANCTION
PAGE 47 E0937 PRESS
ADJUD

S67
PEMBERTON J., JR.,"CONSTITUTIONAL PROBLEMS IN LAW
RESTRAINT ON THE MEDIA." CONSTN PROB/SOLV EDU/PROP PRESS
CONFER CONTROL JURID. PAGE 80 E1608 ORD/FREE

S67
READ J.S.,"CENSORED." UGANDA CONSTN INTELL SOCIETY EDU/PROP
NAT/G DIPLOM PRESS WRITING ADJUD ADMIN COLONIAL AFR
RISK...IDEA/COMP 20. PAGE 84 E1675 CREATE

RICHARDSON J.J.,"THE MAKING OF THE RESTRICTIVE TRADE PRACTICES ACT 1956 A CASE STUDY OF THE POLICY PROCESS IN BRITAIN." UK FINAN MARKET LG/CO POL/PAR CONSULT PRESS ADJUD ADMIN AGREE LOBBY SANCTION ATTIT 20. PAGE 84 E1695
S67
LEGIS
ECO/TAC
POLICY
INDUS

RUCKER B.W.,"WHAT SOLUTIONS DO PEOPLE ENDORSE IN FREE PRESS-FAIR TRIAL DILEMMA?" LAW NAT/G CT/SYS ATTIT...NET/THEORY SAMP CHARTS IDEA/COMP METH 20. PAGE 86 E1731
S67
CONCPT
PRESS
ADJUD
ORD/FREE

SHAFFER T.L.,"DIRECT RESTRAINT ON THE PRESS." USA+45 EDU/PROP CONTROL...JURID NEW/IDEA ABA. PAGE 90 E1809
S67
LAW
PRESS
ORD/FREE
ADJUD

SHAPIRO J.P.,"SOVIET HISTORIOGRAPHY AND THE MOSCOW TRIALS: AFTER THIRTY YEARS." USSR NAT/G LEGIT PRESS CONTROL LEAD ATTIT MARXISM...NEW/IDEA METH 20 TROTSKY/L STALIN/J KHRUSH/N. PAGE 90 E1810
S68
HIST/WRIT
EDU/PROP
SANCTION
ADJUD

PRESSURE GROUPS....SEE LOBBY

PRICE D. E1650

PRICE CONTROL....SEE PRICE, COST, PLAN, RATION

PRICE....SEE ALSO COST

CHENEY F.,CARTELS, COMBINES, AND TRUSTS: A SELECTED LIST OF REFERENCES. GERMANY UK USA-45 WOR-45 DELIB/GP OP/RES BARGAIN CAP/ISM ECO/TAC INT/TRADE LICENSE LEGIT CONFER PRICE 20. PAGE 22 E0428
B44
BIBLIOG/A
LG/CO
ECO/DEV
INDUS

BLODGETT R.H.,"COMPARATIVE ECONOMIC SYSTEMS (REV. ED.)" WOR-45 AGRI FINAN MARKET LABOR NAT/G PLAN INT/TRADE PRICE...POLICY DECISION BIBLIOG 20. PAGE 13 E0248
C49
METH/COMP
CONCPT
ROUTINE

INSTITUTE DES RELATIONS INTL,LES ASPECTS ECONOMIQUES DU REARMEMENT (ETUDE DE L'INSTITUT DES RELATIONS INTERNATIONALES A BRUXELLES). BELGIUM UK USA+45 EXTR/IND FINAN FORCES WORKER PROB/SOLV DIPLOM PRICE...POLICY 20 TREATY. PAGE 57 E1127
B51
WEAPON
DEMAND
ECO/TAC
INT/TRADE

CONANT M.,ANTITRUST IN THE MOTION PICTURE INDUSTRY: ECONOMIC AND LEGAL ANALYSIS. USA+45 MARKET ADJUST DEMAND BIBLIOG. PAGE 24 E0484
B60
PRICE
CONTROL
LAW
ART/METH

US SENATE COMM ON JUDICIARY,ADMINISTERED PRICES. USA+45 RATION ADJUD CONTROL LOBBY...POLICY 20 SENATE MONOPOLY. PAGE 102 E2047
B63
LG/CO
PRICE
ADMIN
DECISION

HAEFELE E.T.,GOVERNMENT CONTROLS ON TRANSPORT. AFR RHODESIA TANZANIA DIPLOM ECO/TAC TARIFFS PRICE ADJUD CONTROL REGION EFFICIENCY...POLICY 20 CONGO. PAGE 49 E0973
B65
ECO/UNDEV
DIST/IND
FINAN
NAT/G

BERNHARD R.C.,"COMPETITION IN LAW AND ECONOMICS." LAW PLAN PRICE CONTROL PRODUC PROFIT...METH/CNCPT IDEA/COMP GEN/LAWS 20. PAGE 11 E0210
L67
MARKET
POLICY
NAT/G
CT/SYS

PRICING....SEE PRICE

PRIMARIES....ELECTORAL PRIMARIES

PRIME/MIN....PRIME MINISTER

PRINCETN/U....PRINCETON UNIVERSITY

PRISON....PRISONS; SEE ALSO PUB/INST

PRITCHETT C.H. E1651,E1652,E1653,E1654,E1655

PRIVACY....PRIVACY AND ITS INVASION

US COMMISSION GOVT SECURITY,RECOMMENDATIONS; AREA: LEGISLATION. USA+45 USA-45 DELIB/GP PLAN TEC/DEV CIVMIL/REL ORD/FREE...POLICY DECISION 20 PRIVACY. PAGE 99 E1982
B57
LEGIS
SANCTION
CRIME
CONTROL

DASH S.,THE EAVESDROPPERS. USA+45 DELIB/GP TEC/DEV ORD/FREE...POLICY CRIMLGY JURID 20 PRIVACY. PAGE 29 E0569
B59
CRIME
CONTROL
ACT/RES
LAW

PRIVIL....PRIVILEGED, AS CONDITION

MCILWAIN C.H.,THE HIGH COURT OF PARLIAMENT AND ITS SUPREMACY B1910 1878 408. UK EX/STRUC PARL/PROC GOV/REL INGP/REL PRIVIL 12/20 PARLIAMENT ENGLSH/LAW. PAGE 71 E1416
B10
LAW
LEGIS
CONSTN
NAT/G

LONDON SCHOOL ECONOMICS-POL,ANNUAL DIGEST OF PUBLIC INTERNATIONAL LAW CASES. INT/ORG MUNIC NAT/G PROVS ADMIN NEUTRAL WAR GOV/REL PRIVIL 20. PAGE 66 E1323
B19
BIBLIOG/A
INT/LAW
ADJUD
DIPLOM

AMERICAN CIVIL LIBERTIES UNION,"WE HOLD THESE TRUTHS" FREEDOM, JUSTICE, EQUALITY: REPORT ON CIVIL LIBERTIES (A PERIODICAL PAMPHLET COVERING 1951-53). USA+45 ACADEM NAT/G FORCES LEGIS COERCE CIVMIL/REL GOV/REL DISCRIM PRIVIL MARXISM...OLD/LIB 20 ACLU UN CIVIL/LIB. PAGE 4 E0076
N19
ORD/FREE
LAW
RACE/REL
CONSTN

BAILEY S.D.,VETO IN THE SECURITY COUNCIL (PAMPHLET). COM USSR WOR+45 BAL/PWR PARL/PROC ARMS/CONT PRIVIL PWR...INT/LAW TREND CHARTS 20 UN SUEZ. PAGE 7 E0135
N19
DELIB/GP
INT/ORG
DIPLOM

MCILWAIN C.H.,CONSTITUTIONALISM AND THE CHANGING WORLD. UK USA-45 LEGIS PRIVIL AUTHORIT SOVEREIGN ...GOV/COMP 15/20 MAGNA/CART HOUSE/CMNS. PAGE 71 E1417
B39
CONSTN
POLICY
JURID

GILMORE M.P.,ARGUMENT FROM ROMAN LAW IN POLITICAL THOUGHT, 1200-1600. INTELL LICENSE CONTROL CT/SYS GOV/REL PRIVIL PWR...IDEA/COMP BIBLIOG 13/16. PAGE 44 E0866
B41
JURID
LAW
CONCPT
NAT/G

BENTHAM J.,"ON THE LIBERTY OF THE PRESS, AND PUBLIC DISCUSSION" IN J. BOWRING, ED., THE WORKS OF JEREMY BENTHAM." SPAIN UK LAW ELITES NAT/G LEGIS INSPECT LEGIT WRITING CONTROL PRIVIL TOTALISM AUTHORIT ...TRADIT 19 FREE/SPEE. PAGE 10 E0193
C43
ORD/FREE
PRESS
CONFER
CONSERVE

PATON G.W.,A TEXT-BOOK OF JURISPRUDENCE. CREATE INSPECT LEGIT CT/SYS ROUTINE CRIME INGP/REL PRIVIL ...CONCPT BIBLIOG 20. PAGE 80 E1601
B46
LAW
ADJUD
JURID
T

MEIKLEJOHN A.,FREE SPEECH AND ITS RELATION TO SELF-GOVERNMENT. USA+45 USA-45 LAW DOMIN PRESS ORD/FREE 20 AMEND/I. PAGE 72 E1434
B48
LEGIS
NAT/G
CONSTN
PRIVIL

SVARLIEN O.,AN INTRODUCTION TO THE LAW OF NATIONS. SEA AIR INT/ORG NAT/G CHIEF ADMIN AGREE WAR PRIVIL ORD/FREE SOVEREIGN...BIBLIOG 16/20. PAGE 95 E1897
B55
INT/LAW
DIPLOM

ABELS J.,THE TRUMAN SCANDALS. USA+45 USA-45 POL/PAR TAX LEGIT CT/SYS CHOOSE PRIVIL MORAL WEALTH 20 TRUMAN/HS PRESIDENT CONGRESS. PAGE 2 E0043
B56
CRIME
ADMIN
CHIEF
TRIBUTE

DOUGLAS W.O.,THE RIGHT OF THE PEOPLE. USA+45 EDU/PROP CONTROL REPRESENT PRIVIL...IDEA/COMP 20. PAGE 32 E0641
B58
ORD/FREE
CONSTN
CT/SYS
CIVMIL/REL

US CONGRESS,FREEDOM OF INFORMATION AND SECRECY IN GOVERNMENT (2 VOLS.). USA+45 DELIB/GP EX/STRUC EDU/PROP PWR 20 CONGRESS PRESIDENT. PAGE 99 E1988
B58
CHIEF
PRIVIL
CONSTN
LAW

US SENATE COMM ON JUDICIARY,EXECUTIVE PRIVILEGE. USA+45 DELIB/GP CONTROL KNOWL PWR 20 CONGRESS PRESIDENT. PAGE 102 E2042
B59
CHIEF
PRIVIL
CONSTN
LAW

BLANSHARD P.,GOD AND MAN IN WASHINGTON. USA+45
B60
NAT/G

CHIEF LEGIS LEGIT CT/SYS PRIVIL ATTIT ORD/FREE ...POLICY CONCPT 20 SUPREME/CT CONGRESS PRESIDENT CHURCH/STA. PAGE 12 E0242
SECT
GP/REL
POL/PAR

B61
KURLAND P.B.,RELIGION AND THE LAW. USA+45 USA-45 CONSTN PROVS CHIEF ADJUD SANCTION PRIVIL CATHISM ...POLICY 17/20 SUPREME/CT PRESIDENT CHURCH/STA. PAGE 62 E1239
SECT
NAT/G
CT/SYS
GP/REL

B61
NELSON H.L.,LIBEL IN NEWS OF CONGRESSIONAL INVESTIGATING COMMITTEES. USA+45 LAW PARL/PROC PRIVIL RESPECT HOUSE/REP. PAGE 76 E1532
DELIB/GP
LEGIS
LICENSE
PRESS

B62
TUSSMAN J.,THE SUPREME COURT ON CHURCH AND STATE. USA+45 USA-45 SANCTION PRIVIL...POLICY JURID 19/20 SUPREME/CT CHURCH/STA. PAGE 97 E1945
CT/SYS
SECT
ADJUD

B63
DRINAN R.F.,RELIGION, THE COURTS, AND PUBLIC POLICY. USA+45 CONSTN BUDGET TAX GIVE ADJUD SANCTION GP/REL PRIVIL 20 CHURCH/STA. PAGE 33 E0649
SECT
CT/SYS
POLICY
SCHOOL

B63
LOWRY C.W.,TO PRAY OR NOT TO PRAY. ADJUD SANCTION GP/REL ORD/FREE PWR CATHISM WORSHIP 20 SUPREME/CT CHRISTIAN CHRUCH/STA. PAGE 67 E1330
SECT
CT/SYS
CONSTN
PRIVIL

B63
SARTORI G.,IL PARLAMENTO ITALIANO: 1946-1963. LAW CONSTN ELITES POL/PAR LOBBY PRIVIL ATTIT PERSON MORAL PWR SOC. PAGE 87 E1746
LEGIS
PARL/PROC
REPRESENT

B64
AHLUWALIA K.,THE LEGAL STATUS, PRIVILEGES AND IMMUNITIES OF SPECIALIZED AGENCIES OF UN AND CERTAIN OTHER INTERNATIONAL ORGANIZATIONS. WOR+45 LAW CONSULT DELIB/GP FORCES. PAGE 3 E0055
PRIVIL
DIPLOM
INT/ORG
INT/LAW

B64
SCHMEISER D.A.,CIVIL LIBERTIES IN CANADA. CANADA LAW SECT PRESS RACE/REL NAT/LISM PRIVIL 20 COMMONWLTH PARLIAMENT CIVIL/LIB CHURCH/STA. PAGE 88 E1758
ORD/FREE
CONSTN
ADJUD
EDU/PROP

B64
STOKES A.P.,CHURCH AND STATE IN THE UNITED STATES (3 VOLS.). USA+45 USA-45 NAT/G PROVS LEGIS CT/SYS SANCTION PRIVIL ORD/FREE 17/20 CHURCH/STA. PAGE 94 E1875
SECT
CONSTN
POLICY

B65
ANTIEU C.J.,RELIGION UNDER THE STATE CONSTITUTIONS. USA+45 LAW SCHOOL TAX SANCTION PRIVIL ORD/FREE ...JURID 20 SUPREME/CT CHURCH/STA. PAGE 5 E0099
SECT
CONSTN
PROVS
GP/REL

B65
FELLMAN D.,RELIGION IN AMERICAN PUBLIC LAW. USA+45 USA-45 NAT/G PROVS ADJUD SANCTION GP/REL PRIVIL ORD/FREE...JURID TIME/SEQ 18/20 SUPREME/CT CHURCH/STA. PAGE 37 E0733
SECT
CONSTN
LAW
POLICY

B65
GINSBERG M.,ON JUSTICE IN SOCIETY. LAW EDU/PROP LEGIT CT/SYS INGP/REL PRIVIL RATIONAL ATTIT MORAL ORD/FREE...JURID 20. PAGE 44 E0867
ADJUD
ROLE
CONCPT

B65
PYLEE M.V.,CONSTITUTIONAL GOVERNMENT IN INDIA (2ND REV. ED.). INDIA POL/PAR EX/STRUC DIPLOM COLONIAL CT/SYS PARL/PROC PRIVIL...JURID 16/20. PAGE 83 E1665
CONSTN
NAT/G
PROVS
FEDERAL

B66
CAMPBELL E.,PARLIAMENTARY PRIVILEGE IN AUSTRALIA. UK LAW CONSTN COLONIAL ROLE ORD/FREE SOVEREIGN 18/20 COMMONWLTH AUSTRAL FREE/SPEE PARLIAMENT. PAGE 19 E0370
LEGIS
PARL/PROC
JURID
PRIVIL

B66
CLARK G.,WORLD PEACE THROUGH WORLD LAW: TWO ALTERNATIVE PLANS. WOR+45 DELIB/GP FORCES TAX CONFER ADJUD SANCTION ARMS/CONT WAR CHOOSE PRIVIL 20 UN COLD/WAR. PAGE 23 E0450
INT/LAW
PEACE
PLAN
INT/ORG

B66
DOUMA J.,BIBLIOGRAPHY ON THE INTERNATIONAL COURT INCLUDING THE PERMANENT COURT, 1918-1964. WOR+45 WOR-45 DELIB/GP WAR PRIVIL...JURID NAT/COMP 20 UN LEAGUE/NAT. PAGE 33 E0645
BIBLIOG/A
INT/ORG
CT/SYS
DIPLOM

B66
LEE L.T.,VIENNA CONVENTION ON CONSULAR RELATIONS. WOR+45 LAW INT/ORG CONFER GP/REL PRIVIL...INT/LAW 20 TREATY VIENNA/CNV. PAGE 64 E1277
AGREE
DIPLOM
ADMIN

B67
US SENATE COMM ON FOREIGN REL,USIA FOREIGN SERVICE PERSONNEL SYSTEM. USA+45 LAW CONSULT ADMIN 20 USIA. PAGE 102 E2038
DIPLOM
EDU/PROP
PRIVIL
PROF/ORG

L67
LEGAULT A.,"ORGANISATION ET CONDUITE DES OPERATIONS INT/ORG DE MAINTIEN DE LA PAIX." FORCES ACT/RES ADJUD AGREE PEACE CONTROL NEUTRAL TASK PRIVIL ORD/FREE 20 UN. PAGE 64 WAR E1279
INT/LAW

S67
KETCHAM O.W.,"GUIDELINES FROM GAULT: REVOLUTIONARY REQUIREMENTS AND REAPPRAISAL." LAW CONSTN CREATE LEGIT ROUTINE SANCTION CRIME DISCRIM PRIVIL ROLE ...JURID NEW/IDEA 20 SUPREME/CT. PAGE 60 E1208
ADJUD
AGE/Y
CT/SYS

PRIVILEGE....SEE PRIVIL

PROB/SOLV....PROBLEM SOLVING

N
INTERNATIONAL AFFAIRS. WOR+45 WOR-45 ECO/UNDEV INT/ORG NAT/G PROB/SOLV FOR/AID WAR...POLICY 20. PAGE 1 E0007
BIBLIOG/A
DIPLOM
INT/LAW
INT/TRADE

N
JOURNAL OF POLITICS. USA+45 USA-45 CONSTN POL/PAR EX/STRUC LEGIS PROB/SOLV DIPLOM CT/SYS CHOOSE RACE/REL 20. PAGE 1 E0011
BIBLIOG/A
NAT/G
LAW
LOC/G

N
MIDWEST JOURNAL OF POLITICAL SCIENCE. USA+45 CONSTN ECO/DEV LEGIS PROB/SOLV CT/SYS LEAD GOV/REL ATTIT POLICY. PAGE 1 E0012
BIBLIOG/A
NAT/G
DIPLOM
POL/PAR

N
INTERNATIONAL BIBLIOGRAPHY ON CRIME AND DELINQUENCY. USA+45 LAW FORCES PROB/SOLV AGE/Y 20. PAGE 1 E0023
BIBLIOG/A
CRIME
ANOMIE
CRIMLGY

N
PUBLISHERS' CIRCULAR, THE OFFICIAL ORGAN OF THE PUBLISHERS' ASSOCIATION OF GREAT BRITAIN AND IRELAND. EUR+WWI MOD/EUR UK LAW PROB/SOLV DIPLOM COLONIAL ATTIT...HUM 19/20 CMN/WLTH. PAGE 2 E0025
BIBLIOG
NAT/G
WRITING
LEAD

N
NEW YORK STATE LIBRARY,CHECKLIST OF OFFICIAL PUBLICATIONS OF THE STATE OF NEW YORK. USA+45 USA-45 LAW PROB/SOLV LEAD ATTIT 19/20. PAGE 77 E1539
BIBLIOG
PROVS
WRITING
GOV/REL

N
UNESCO,INTERNATIONAL BIBLIOGRAPHY OF POLITICAL SCIENCE (VOLUMES 1-8). WOR+45 LAW NAT/G EX/STRUC LEGIS PROB/SOLV DIPLOM ADMIN GOV/REL 20 UNESCO. PAGE 98 E1957
BIBLIOG
CONCPT
IDEA/COMP

B'
LALL A.S.,NEGOTIATING DISARMAMENT* THE EIGHTEEN NATION DISARMAMENT CONFERENCE* THE FIRST TWO YEARS, 1962-1964. ASIA FRANCE INDIA USA+45 USSR PROB/SOLV ADJUD NEUTRAL ATTIT...IDEA/COMP COLD/WAR. PAGE 62 E1246
OBS
ARMS/CONT
DIPLOM
OP/RES

B01
BRYCE J.,STUDIES IN HISTORY AND JURISPRUDENCE (2 VOLS.). ICELAND SOUTH/AFR UK LAW PROB/SOLV SOVEREIGN...PHIL/SCI NAT/COMP ROME/ANC ROMAN/LAW. PAGE 16 E0321
IDEA/COMP
CONSTN
JURID

B16
SALMOND J.W.,JURISPRUDENCE. UK LOC/G NAT/G LEGIS PROB/SOLV LICENSE LEGIT CRIME PERS/REL OWN ORD/FREE ...T 20. PAGE 87 E1742
LAW
CT/SYS
JURID
ADJUD

S18
POWELL T.R.,"THE LOGIC AND RHETORIC OF CONSTITUTIONAL LAW" (BMR)" USA+45 USA-45 DELIB/GP PROB/SOLV ADJUD CT/SYS...DECISION 20 SUPREME/CT CON/INTERP. PAGE 82 E1642
CONSTN
LAW
JURID
LOG

JANOWITZ M.,SOCIAL CONTROL OF ESCALATED RIOTS   N19
(PAMPHLET). USA+45 USA-45 LAW SOCIETY MUNIC FORCES   CROWD
PROB/SOLV EDU/PROP TV CRIME ATTIT...BIBLIOG 20   ORD/FREE
NEGRO CIV/RIGHTS. PAGE 58 E1148   CONTROL
                                                     RACE/REL

MCCONNELL G.,THE STEEL SEIZURE OF 1952 (PAMPHLET).   N19
USA+45 FINAN INDUS PROC/MFG LG/CO EX/STRUC ADJUD   DELIB/GP
CONTROL GP/REL ORD/FREE PWR 20 TRUMAN/HS PRESIDENT   LABOR
CONGRESS. PAGE 70 E1402   PROB/SOLV
                                                     NAT/G

FARRAND M.,THE FRAMING OF THE CONSTITUTION OF THE   B22
UNITED STATES (1913). USA-45 EX/STRUC PROB/SOLV   CONSTN
PERSON. PAGE 36 E0721   DELIB/GP
                                                     LEGIS
                                                     CT/SYS

FORTESCUE J.,THE GOVERNANCE OF ENGLAND (1471-76).   B26
UK LAW FINAN SECT LEGIS PROB/SOLV TAX DOMIN ADMIN   CONSERVE
GP/REL COST ORD/FREE PWR 14/15. PAGE 39 E0776   CONSTN
                                                     CHIEF
                                                     NAT/G

FRANKFURTER F.,THE BUSINESS OF THE SUPREME COURT; A B28
STUDY IN THE FEDERAL JUDICIAL SYSTEM. USA+45 CONSTN CT/SYS
EX/STRUC PROB/SOLV GP/REL ATTIT PWR...POLICY JURID   ADJUD
18/20 SUPREME/CT CONGRESS. PAGE 40 E0789   LAW
                                                     FEDERAL

STURZO L.,THE INTERNATIONAL COMMUNITY AND THE RIGHT B29
OF WAR (TRANS. BY BARBARA BARCLAY CARTER). CULTURE   INT/ORG
CREATE PROB/SOLV DIPLOM ADJUD CONTROL PEACE PERSON   PLAN
ORD/FREE...INT/LAW IDEA/COMP PACIFIST 20   WAR
LEAGUE/NAT. PAGE 94 E1891   CONCPT

BIRD F.L.,THE RECALL OF PUBLIC OFFICERS; A STUDY OF B30
THE OPERATION OF RECALL IN CALIFORNIA. LOC/G MUNIC   REPRESENT
POL/PAR PROVS PROB/SOLV ADJUD PARTIC...CHARTS   SANCTION
METH/COMP 20 CALIFORNIA RECALL. PAGE 12 E0230   CHOOSE
                                                     LAW

LLEWELLYN K.N.,"A REALISTIC JURISPRUDENCE - THE   L30
NEXT STEP." PROB/SOLV ADJUD GP/REL PERS/REL   LAW
IDEA/COMP. PAGE 66 E1312   CONCPT
                                                     JURID
                                                     GEN/LAWS

ENSOR R.C.K.,COURTS AND JUDGES IN FRANCE, GERMANY,   B33
AND ENGLAND. FRANCE GERMANY UK LAW PROB/SOLV ADMIN   CT/SYS
ROUTINE CRIME ROLE...METH/COMP 20 CIVIL/LAW.   EX/STRUC
PAGE 35 E0692   ADJUD
                                                     NAT/COMP

CULVER D.C.,BIBLIOGRAPHY OF CRIME AND CRIMINAL   B34
JUSTICE, 1927-1931. LAW CULTURE PUB/INST PROB/SOLV   BIBLIOG/A
CT/SYS...PSY SOC STAT 20. PAGE 28 E0549   CRIMLGY
                                                     ADJUD
                                                     FORCES

LLEWELLYN K.N.,"THE CONSTITUTION AS AN INSTITUTION" L34
(BMR)" USA-45 PROB/SOLV LOBBY REPRESENT...DECISION   CONSTN
JURID 18/20 SUPREME/CT. PAGE 66 E1313   LAW
                                                     CONCPT
                                                     CT/SYS

BEMIS S.F.,GUIDE TO THE DIPLOMATIC HISTORY OF THE   B35
UNITED STATES, 17751921. NAT/G LEGIS TOP/EX   BIBLIOG/A
PROB/SOLV CAP/ISM INT/TRADE TARIFFS ADJUD   DIPLOM
...CON/ANAL 18/20. PAGE 10 E0184   USA-45

HALL J.,THEFT, LAW, AND SOCIETY. SOCIETY PROB/SOLV   B35
...CRIMLGY SOC CONCPT TREND METH/COMP 18/20   CRIME
LARCENCY. PAGE 49 E0982   LAW
                                                     ADJUD
                                                     ADJUST

RAM J.,THE SCIENCE OF LEGAL JUDGMENT: A TREATISE... B35
UK CONSTN NAT/G LEGIS CREATE PROB/SOLV AGREE CT/SYS LAW
...INT/LAW CONCPT 19 ENGLSH/LAW CANON/LAW CIVIL/LAW JURID
CTS/WESTM. PAGE 83 E1672   EX/STRUC
                                                     ADJUD

HERRING E.P.,PUBLIC ADMINISTRATION AND THE PUBLIC   B36
INTEREST. LABOR NAT/G PARTIC EFFICIENCY 20. PAGE 52 GP/REL
E1033   DECISION
                                                     PROB/SOLV
                                                     ADMIN

BEARDSLEY A.R.,LEGAL BIBLIOGRAPHY AND THE USE OF   B37
LAW BOOKS. CONSTN CREATE PROB/SOLV...DECISION JURID BIBLIOG
LAB/EXP. PAGE 9 E0166   METH
                                                     OP/RES

KETCHAM E.H.,PRELIMINARY SELECT BIBLIOGRAPHY OF   B37
INTERNATIONAL LAW (PAMPHLET). WOR-45 LAW INT/ORG   BIBLIOG
NAT/G PROB/SOLV CT/SYS NEUTRAL WAR 19/20. PAGE 60   DIPLOM
E1207   ADJUD
                                                     INT/LAW

CULVER D.C.,BIBLIOGRAPHY OF CRIME AND CRIMINAL   B39
JUSTICE, 1932-1937. USA-45 LAW CULTURE PUB/INST   BIBLIOG/A
PROB/SOLV CT/SYS...PSY SOC STAT 20. PAGE 28 E0551   CRIMLGY
                                                     ADJUD
                                                     FORCES

SIEYES E.J.,LES DISCOURS DE SIEYES DANS LES DEBATS   B39
CONSTITUTIONNELS DE L'AN III (2 ET 18 THERMIDOR).   CONSTN
FRANCE LAW NAT/G PROB/SOLV BAL/PWR GOV/REL 18 JURY. ADJUD
PAGE 91 E1824   LEGIS
                                                     EX/STRUC

MCILWAIN C.H.,CONSTITUTIONALISM, ANCIENT AND   B40
MODERN. CHRIST-17C MOD/EUR NAT/G CHIEF PROB/SOLV   CONSTN
INSPECT AUTHORIT ORD/FREE PWR...TIME/SEQ ROMAN/REP. GEN/LAWS
PAGE 71 E1418   LAW

CROWE S.E.,THE BERLIN WEST AFRICA CONFERENCE,   B42
1884-85. GERMANY ELITES MARKET INT/ORG DELIB/GP   AFR
FORCES PROB/SOLV BAL/PWR CAP/ISM DOMIN COLONIAL   CONFER
...INT/LAW 19. PAGE 28 E0548   INT/TRADE
                                                     DIPLOM

CONOVER H.F.,THE BALKANS: A SELECTED LIST OF   B43
REFERENCES. ALBANIA BULGARIA ROMANIA YUGOSLAVIA   BIBLIOG
INT/ORG PROB/SOLV DIPLOM LEGIT CONFER ADJUD WAR   EUR+WWI
NAT/LISM PEACE PWR 20 LEAGUE/NAT. PAGE 25 E0493

BENTHAM J.,"PRINCIPLES OF INTERNATIONAL LAW" IN J.   C43
BOWRING, ED., THE WORKS OF JEREMY BENTHAM." UNIV   INT/LAW
NAT/G PLAN PROB/SOLV DIPLOM CONTROL SANCTION MORAL   JURID
ORD/FREE PWR SOVEREIGN 19. PAGE 10 E0194   WAR
                                                     PEACE

HOCKING W.E.,FREEDOM OF THE PRESS: A FRAMEWORK OF   B47
PRINCIPLE. WOR-45 SOCIETY NAT/G PROB/SOLV DEBATE   ORD/FREE
LOBBY...JURID PSY 20 AMEND/I. PAGE 53 E1061   CONSTN
                                                     PRESS
                                                     LAW

FRANKFURTER F.,"SOME REFLECTIONS ON THE READING OF   S47
STATUTES" USA+45 USA-45 PROB/SOLV CT/SYS TASK   JURID
EFFICIENCY...LING 20. PAGE 40 E0791   LAW
                                                     ADJUD
                                                     WRITING

MORGENTHAL H.J.,POLITICS AMONG NATIONS: THE   B48
STRUGGLE FOR POWER AND PEACE. FUT WOR+45 INT/ORG   DIPLOM
OP/RES PROB/SOLV BAL/PWR CONTROL ATTIT MORAL   PEACE
...INT/LAW BIBLIOG 20 COLD/WAR. PAGE 75 E1494   PWR
                                                     POLICY

SLESSER H.,THE ADMINISTRATION OF THE LAW. UK CONSTN B48
EX/STRUC OP/RES PROB/SOLV CRIME ROLE...DECISION   LAW
METH/COMP 20 CIVIL/LAW ENGLSH/LAW CIVIL/LAW.   CT/SYS
PAGE 92 E1839   ADJUD

WALKER H.,"THE LEGISLATIVE PROCESS; LAWMAKING IN   C48
THE UNITED STATES." NAT/G POL/PAR PROVS EX/STRUC   PARL/PROC
OP/RES PROB/SOLV CT/SYS LOBBY GOV/REL...CHARTS   LEGIS
BIBLIOG T 18/20 CONGRESS. PAGE 105 E2094   LAW
                                                     CONSTN

DE HUSZAR G.B.,EQUALITY IN AMERICA: THE ISSUE OF   B49
MINORITY RIGHTS. USA+45 USA-45 LAW NEIGH SCHOOL   DISCRIM
LEGIS ACT/RES CHOOSE ATTIT RESPECT...ANTHOL 20   RACE/REL
NEGRO. PAGE 29 E0585   ORD/FREE
                                                     PROB/SOLV

FRANK J.,COURTS ON TRIAL: MYTH AND REALITY IN   B50
AMERICAN JUSTICE. LAW CONSULT PROB/SOLV EDU/PROP   JURID
ADJUD ROUTINE ROLE ORD/FREE...GEN/LAWS T 20.   CT/SYS
PAGE 40 E0788   MYTH
                                                     CONSTN

US FEDERAL BUREAU INVESTIGAT,BIBLIOGRAPHY OF CRIME   B50
AND KINDRED SUBJECTS (PAPER). USA+45 PROB/SOLV   BIBLIOG/A
TREND. PAGE 100 E2001   CRIME
                                                     LAW
                                                     CRIMLGY

BIDDLE F.,THE FEAR OF FREEDOM. USA+45 LAW NAT/G   B51
PUB/INST PROB/SOLV DOMIN CONTROL SANCTION REV   ANOMIE
NAT/LISM 20. PAGE 12 E0227   INGP/REL
                                                     VOL/ASSN
                                                     ORD/FREE

DAVIS K.C.,ADMINISTRATIVE LAW. USA+45 USA-45 NAT/G
PROB/SOLV BAL/PWR CONTROL ORD/FREE...POLICY 20
SUPREME/CT. PAGE 29 E0574
B51 ADMIN JURID EX/STRUC ADJUD

INSTITUTE DES RELATIONS INTL,LES ASPECTS
ECONOMIQUES DU REARMEMENT (ETUDE DE L'INSTITUT DES
RELATIONS INTERNATIONALES A BRUXELLES). BELGIUM UK
USA+45 EXTR/IND FINAN FORCES WORKER PROB/SOLV
DIPLOM PRICE...POLICY 20 TREATY. PAGE 57 E1127
B51 WEAPON DEMAND ECO/TAC INT/TRADE

COHEN M.B.,"PERSONALITY AS A FACTOR IN
ADMINISTRATIVE DECISIONS." ADJUD PERS/REL ANOMIE
SUPEGO...OBS SELF/OBS INT. PAGE 24 E0465
S51 PERSON ADMIN PROB/SOLV PSY

US DEPARTMENT OF STATE,RESEARCH ON EASTERN EUROPE
(EXCLUDING USSR). EUR+WWI LAW ECO/DEV NAT/G
PROB/SOLV DIPLOM ADMIN LEAD MARXISM...TREND 19/20.
PAGE 100 E1995
B52 BIBLIOG R+D ACT/RES COM

ROSTOW E.V.,"THE DEMOCRATIC CHARACTER OF JUDICIAL
REVIEW" (BMR)" USA+45 LAW NAT/G LEGIS TASK...JURID
20 SUPREME/CT. PAGE 86 E1725
L52 CONSTN PROB/SOLV ADJUD CT/SYS

OPPENHEIM L.,INTERNATIONAL LAW: A TREATISE (7TH
ED., 2 VOLS.). LAW CONSTN PROB/SOLV INT/TRADE ADJUD
AGREE NEUTRAL WAR ORD/FREE SOVEREIGN...BIBLIOG 20
LEAGUE/NAT UN ILO. PAGE 79 E1579
B53 INT/LAW INT/ORG DIPLOM

BATTEN T.R.,PROBLEMS OF AFRICAN DEVELOPMENT (2ND
ED.). AFR LAW SOCIETY SCHOOL ECO/TAC TAX...GEOG
HEAL SOC 20. PAGE 8 E0154
B54 ECO/UNDEV AGRI LOC/G PROB/SOLV

SCHWARTZ B.,FRENCH ADMINISTRATIVE LAW AND THE
COMMON-LAW WORLD. FRANCE CULTURE LOC/G NAT/G PROVS
DELIB/GP EX/STRUC LEGIS PROB/SOLV CT/SYS EXEC
GOV/REL...IDEA/COMP ENGLSH/LAW. PAGE 89 E1786
B54 JURID LAW METH/COMP ADJUD

BERNSTEIN M.H.,REGULATING BUSINESS BY INDEPENDENT
COMMISSION. USA+45 USA-45 LG/CO CHIEF LEGIS
PROB/SOLV ADJUD SANCTION GP/REL ATTIT...TIME/SEQ
19/20 MONOPOLY PRESIDENT CONGRESS. PAGE 11 E0214
B55 DELIB/GP CONTROL CONSULT

CUSHMAN R.E.,LEADING CONSTITUTIONAL DECISIONS.
USA+45 USA-45 NAT/G EX/STRUC LEGIS JUDGE TAX
FEDERAL...DECISION 20 SUPREME/CT CASEBOOK. PAGE 28
E0559
B55 CONSTN PROB/SOLV JURID CT/SYS

REDFORD E.S.,PUBLIC ADMINISTRATION AND POLICY
FORMATION: STUDIES IN OIL, GAS, BANKING, RIVER
DEVELOPMENT AND CORPORATE INVESTIGATIONS. USA+45
CLIENT NAT/G ADMIN LOBBY REPRESENT GOV/REL INGP/REL EXEC
20. PAGE 84 E1678
B56 EX/STRUC PROB/SOLV CONTROL

US HOUSE WAYS MEANS COMMITTEE,TRAFFIC IN, AND
CONTROL OF NARCOTICS, BARBITURATES, AND
AMPHETAMINES. CHINA/COM USA+45 SOCIETY LEGIS
ACT/RES EDU/PROP CT/SYS SANCTION PROFIT HEALTH
...HEAL PSY STAT 20. PAGE 100 E2011
B56 BIO/SOC CONTROL PROB/SOLV CRIME

ZINN C.J.,HOW OUR LAWS ARE MADE: BROCHURE HOUSE OF
REPRESENTATIVES DOCUMENT 451. LAW CONSTN CHIEF
EX/STRUC PROB/SOLV HOUSE/REP SENATE. PAGE 108 E2171
B56 LEGIS DELIB/GP PARL/PROC ROUTINE

AUMANN F.R.,"THE ISTRUMENTALITIES OF JUSTICE: THEIR
FORMS, FUNCTIONS, AND LIMITATIONS." WOR+45 WOR-45
JUDGE PROB/SOLV ROUTINE ATTIT...BIBLIOG 20. PAGE 6
E0118
C56 JURID ADMIN CT/SYS ADJUD

BERNS W.,FREEDOM, VIRTUE, AND THE FIRST AMENDMENT.
USA+45 LAW CONSTN PROB/SOLV NEW/LIB...JURID 20
SUPREME/CT AMEND/I. PAGE 11 E0212
B57 ADJUD CT/SYS ORD/FREE

CONOVER H.F.,NORTH AND NORTHEAST AFRICA; A SELECTED
ANNOTATED LIST OF WRITINGS. ALGERIA MOROCCO SUDAN
B57 BIBLIOG/A DIPLOM

UAR CULTURE INT/ORG PROB/SOLV ADJUD NAT/LISM PWR
WEALTH...SOC 20 UN. PAGE 25 E0496
AFR ECO/UNDEV

COOPER F.E.,THE LAWYER AND ADMINISTRATIVE AGENCIES.
USA+45 CLIENT LAW PROB/SOLV CT/SYS PERSON ROLE.
PAGE 25 E0500
B57 CONSULT ADMIN ADJUD DELIB/GP

HINDERLING A.,DIE REFORMATORISCHE
VERWALTUNGSGERICHTSBARKEIT. GERMANY/W PROB/SOLV
ADJUD SUPEGO PWR...CONCPT 20. PAGE 53 E1049
B57 ADMIN CT/SYS JURID CONTROL

CARPENTER W.S.,FOUNDATIONS OF MODERN JURISPRUDENCE. LAW
UNIV PROB/SOLV ADJUD CT/SYS CRIME ATTIT...CONCPT
18/20. PAGE 20 E0388
B58 LAW JURID

DAVIS K.C.,ADMINISTRATIVE LAW TREATISE (VOLS. I AND
IV). NAT/G JUDGE PROB/SOLV ADJUD GP/REL 20
SUPREME/CT. PAGE 29 E0575
B58 ADMIN JURID CT/SYS EX/STRUC

STONE J.,AGGRESSION AND WORLD ORDER: A CRITIQUE OF
UNITED NATIONS THEORIES OF AGGRESSION. LAW CONSTN
DELIB/GP PROB/SOLV BAL/PWR DIPLOM DEBATE ADJUD
CRIME PWR...POLICY IDEA/COMP 20 UN SUEZ LEAGUE/NAT.
PAGE 94 E1879
B58 ORD/FREE INT/ORG WAR CONCPT

CRESSEY D.R.,"ACHIEVEMENT OF AN UNSTATED
ORGANIZATIONAL GOAL: AN OBSERVATION ON PRISONS."
OP/RES PROB/SOLV PERS/REL ANOMIE ATTIT ROLE RESPECT
CRIMLGY. PAGE 28 E0546
S58 PUB/INST CLIENT NEIGH INGP/REL

FISHER F.M.,"THE MATHEMATICAL ANALYSIS OF SUPREME
COURT DECISIONS: THE USE AND ABUSE OF QUANTITATIVE
METHODS." USA+45 LAW EX/STRUC LEGIS JUDGE ROUTINE
ATTIT DECISION. PAGE 38 E0757
S58 PROB/SOLV CT/SYS JURID MATH

RIKER W.H.,"THE PARADOX OF VOTING AND CONGRESSIONAL
RULES FOR VOTING ON AMENDMENTS." LAW DELIB/GP
EX/STRUC PROB/SOLV CONFER DEBATE EFFICIENCY ATTIT
HOUSE/REP CONGRESS SENATE. PAGE 85 E1700
S58 PARL/PROC DECISION LEGIS RATIONAL

DESMITH S.A.,JUDICIAL REVIEW OF ADMINISTRATIVE
ACTION. UK LOC/G CONSULT DELIB/GP ADMIN PWR
...DECISION JURID 20 ENGLSH/LAW. PAGE 31 E0609
B59 ADJUD NAT/G PROB/SOLV CT/SYS

ELLIOTT S.D.,IMPROVING OUR COURTS. LAW EX/STRUC
PLAN PROB/SOLV ADJUD ADMIN TASK CRIME EFFICIENCY
ORD/FREE 20. PAGE 34 E0684
B59 CT/SYS JURID GOV/REL NAT/G

HARVARD UNIVERSITY LAW SCHOOL,INTERNATIONAL
PROBLEMS OF FINANCIAL PROTECTION AGAINST NUCLEAR
RISK. WOR+45 NAT/G DELIB/GP PROB/SOLV DIPLOM
CONTROL ATTIT...POLICY INT/LAW MATH 20. PAGE 51
E1009
B59 NUC/PWR ADJUD INDUS FINAN

COLUMBIA U. BUREAU OF APPL SOC RES, ATTITUDES OF
PROMINENT AMERICANS TOWARD "WORLD PEACE THROUGH
WORLD LAW" (SUPRA-NATL ORGANIZATION FOR WAR
PREVENTION). USA+45 USSR ELITES FORCES PLAN
PROB/SOLV CONTROL WAR PWR...POLICY SOC QU IDEA/COMP
20 UN. PAGE 82 E1644
B59 ATTIT ACT/RES INT/LAW STAT

U OF MICHIGAN LAW SCHOOL,ATOMS AND THE LAW. USA+45
PROVS WORKER PROB/SOLV DIPLOM ADMIN GOV/REL ANTHOL.
PAGE 97 E1950
B59 NUC/PWR NAT/G CONTROL LAW

WAGNER W.J.,THE FEDERAL STATES AND THEIR JUDICIARY.
BRAZIL CANADA SWITZERLND USA+45 CONFER CT/SYS TASK
EFFICIENCY FEDERAL PWR...JURID BIBLIOG 20 AUSTRAL
MEXIC/AMER. PAGE 104 E2091
B59 ADJUD METH/COMP PROB/SOLV NAT/G

OBERER W.E.,"VOLUNTARY IMPARTIAL REVIEW OF LABOR:
SOME REFLECTIONS." DELIB/GP LEGIS PROB/SOLV ADJUD
CONTROL COERCE PWR PLURISM POLICY. PAGE 78 E1570
L59 LABOR LAW PARTIC INGP/REL

                                                    S59
CHAPMAN B.,"THE FRENCH CONSEIL D'ETAT." FRANCE   ADMIN
NAT/G CONSULT OP/RES PROB/SOLV PWR...OBS 20.   LAW
PAGE 21 E0421   CT/SYS
                                                    LEGIS

                                                    S59
DWYER R.J.,"THE ADMINISTRATIVE ROLE IN   ADMIN
DESEGREGATION." USA+45 LAW PROB/SOLV LEAD RACE/REL SCHOOL
ISOLAT STRANGE ROLE...POLICY SOC/INTEG MISSOURI   DISCRIM
NEGRO CIV/RIGHTS. PAGE 34 E0668   ATTIT

                                                    S59
MENDELSON W.,"JUDICIAL REVIEW AND PARTY POLITICS"   CT/SYS
(BMR)" UK USA+45 USA-45 NAT/G LEGIS PROB/SOLV   POL/PAR
EDU/PROP ADJUD EFFICIENCY...POLICY NAT/COMP 19/20   BAL/PWR
AUSTRAL SUPREME/CT. PAGE 72 E1436   JURID

                                                    B60
ATOMIC INDUSTRIAL FORUM,ATOMS FOR INDUSTRY: WORLD   NUC/PWR
FORUM. WOR+45 FINAN COST UTIL...JURID ANTHOL 20.   INDUS
PAGE 6 E0113   PLAN
                                                    PROB/SOLV

                                                    B60
BAYLEY D.H.,VIOLENT AGITATION AND THE DEMOCRATIC   COERCE
PROCESS IN INDIA. INDIA LAW POL/PAR 20. PAGE 8   CROWD
E0159   CONSTN
                                                    PROB/SOLV

                                                    B60
BORGATTA E.F.,SOCIAL WORKERS' PERCEPTIONS OF   SOC/WK
CLIENTS. SERV/IND ROUTINE PERS/REL DRIVE PERSON   ATTIT
RESPECT...SOC PERS/COMP 20. PAGE 14 E0268   CLIENT
                                                    PROB/SOLV

                                                    B60
DAVIS K.C.,ADMINISTRATIVE LAW AND GOVERNMENT.   ADMIN
USA+45 EX/STRUC PROB/SOLV ADJUD GP/REL PWR...POLICY JURID
20 SUPREME/CT. PAGE 29 E0578   CT/SYS
                                                    NAT/G

                                                    B60
GONZALEZ NAVARRO M.,LA COLONIZACION EN MEXICO,   ECO/UNDEV
1877-1910. AGRI NAT/G PLAN PROB/SOLV INCOME   GEOG
...POLICY JURID CENSUS 19/20 MEXIC/AMER MIGRATION. HABITAT
PAGE 44 E0883   COLONIAL

                                                    B60
HEAP D.,AN OUTLINE OF PLANNING LAW (3RD ED.). UK   MUNIC
LAW PROB/SOLV ADMIN CONTROL 20. PAGE 51 E1020   PLAN
                                                    JURID
                                                    LOC/G

                                                    B60
SCHUBERT G.,THE PUBLIC INTEREST. USA+45 CONSULT   POLICY
PLAN PROB/SOLV ADJUD ADMIN GP/REL PWR ALL/IDEOS 20. DELIB/GP
PAGE 88 E1770   REPRESENT
                                                    POL/PAR

                                                    B60
UNITED WORLD FEDERALISTS,UNITED WORLD FEDERALISTS; BIBLIOG/A
PANORAMA OF RECENT BOOKS, FILMS, AND JOURNALS ON   DIPLOM
WORLD FEDERATION, THE UN, AND WORLD PEACE. CULTURE INT/ORG
ECO/UNDEV PROB/SOLV FOR/AID ARMS/CONT NUC/PWR   PEACE
...INT/LAW PHIL/SCI 20 UN. PAGE 98 E1971

                                                    B60
US HOUSE COMM ON JUDICIARY,ESTABLISHMENT OF   APPORT
CONGRESSIONAL DISTRICTS. USA+45 PROB/SOLV 20   REPRESENT
CONGRESS HOUSE/REP. PAGE 100 E2003   LEGIS
                                                    LAW

                                                    B60
US SENATE COMM ON JUDICIARY,FEDERAL ADMINISTRATIVE PARL/PROC
PROCEDURE. USA+45 CONSTN NAT/G PROB/SOLV CONFER   LEGIS
GOV/REL...JURID INT 20 SENATE. PAGE 102 E2043   ADMIN
                                                    LAW

                                                    B60
US SENATE COMM ON JUDICIARY,ADMINISTRATIVE   PARL/PROC
PROCEDURE LEGISLATION. USA+45 CONSTN NAT/G   LEGIS
PROB/SOLV CONFER ROUTINE GOV/REL...INT 20 SENATE.   ADMIN
PAGE 102 E2044   JURID

                                                    S60
MANN S.Z.,"POLICY FORMULATION IN THE EXECUTIVE   EXEC
BRANCH: THE TAFT-HARTLEY EXPERIENCE." USA+45 LABOR GOV/REL
CHIEF INGP/REL 20 NLRB. PAGE 68 E1360   EX/STRUC
                                                    PROB/SOLV

                                                    C60
HAZARD J.N.,"SETTLING DISPUTES IN SOVIET SOCIETY: ADJUD
THE FORMATIVE YEARS OF LEGAL INSTITUTIONS." USSR   LAW
NAT/G PROF/ORG PROB/SOLV CONTROL CT/SYS ROUTINE REV COM
CENTRAL...JURID BIBLIOG 20. PAGE 51 E1017   POLICY

                                                    B61
BRENNAN D.G.,ARMS CONTROL, DISARMAMENT, AND   ARMS/CONT
NATIONAL SECURITY. WOR+45 NAT/G FORCES CREATE   ORD/FREE
PROB/SOLV PARTIC WAR PEACE...DECISION INT/LAW   DIPLOM
ANTHOL BIBLIOG 20. PAGE 15 E0291   POLICY

                                                    B61
JACOBS C.E.,JUSTICE FRANKFURTER AND CIVIL   BIOG
LIBERTIES. USA+45 USA-45 LAW NAT/G PROB/SOLV PRESS CONSTN
PERS/REL...JURID WORSHIP 20 SUPREME/CT FRANKFUR/F   ADJUD
CIVIL/LIB. PAGE 57 E1144   ORD/FREE

                                                    B61
MERTON R.K.,CONTEMPORARY SOCIAL PROBLEMS: AN   CRIME
INTRODUCTION TO THE SOCIOLOGY OF DEVIANT BEHAVIOR   ANOMIE
AND SOCIAL DISORGANIZATION. FAM MUNIC FORCES WORKER STRANGE
PROB/SOLV INGP/REL RACE/REL ISOLAT...CRIMLGY GEOG   SOC
PSY T 20 NEGRO. PAGE 72 E1444

                                                    B61
NEW JERSEY LEGISLATURE-SENATE,PUBLIC HEARINGS   LEGIS
BEFORE COMMITTEE ON REVISION AND AMENDMENT OF LAWS MUNIC
ON SENATE BILL NO. 8. USA+45 FINAN PROVS WORKER   INDUS
ACT/RES PLAN BUDGET TAX CRIME...IDEA/COMP 20   PROB/SOLV
NEW/JERSEY URBAN/RNWL. PAGE 77 E1537

                                                    B61
NEWMAN R.P.,RECOGNITION OF COMMUNIST CHINA? A STUDY MARXISM
IN ARGUMENT. CHINA/COM NAT/G PROB/SOLV RATIONAL   ATTIT
...INT/LAW LOG IDEA/COMP BIBLIOG 20. PAGE 77 E1544 DIPLOM
                                                    POLICY

                                                    B61
POOLEY B.J.,PLANNING AND ZONING IN THE UNITED   PLAN
STATES. USA+45 MUNIC DELIB/GP ACT/RES PROB/SOLV   LOC/G
TEC/DEV ADJUD ADMIN REGION 20 ZONING. PAGE 81 E1628 PROVS
                                                    LAW

                                                    B61
PRITCHETT C.H.,CONGRESS VERSUS THE SUPREME COURT,   LEGIS
1957-1960. PROB/SOLV DOMIN EXEC GP/REL DISCRIM PWR JURID
CONGRESS SUPREME/CT SUPREME/CT. PAGE 82 E1652   LAW

                                                    B61
UTLEY T.E.,OCCASION FOR OMBUDSMAN. UK CREATE   PROB/SOLV
CONTROL 20 OMBUDSMAN. PAGE 103 E2065   INGP/REL
                                                    REPRESENT
                                                    ADJUD

                                                    S61
AGNEW P.C.,"INTRODUCING CHANGE IN A MENTAL   ORD/FREE
HOSPITAL." CLIENT WORKER PROB/SOLV INGP/REL   PUB/INST
PERS/REL ADJUST. PAGE 3 E0054   PSY
                                                    ADMIN

                                                    B62
BISHOP W.W. JR.,INTERNATIONAL LAW: CASES AND   INT/LAW
MATERIALS. WOR+45 INT/ORG FORCES PROB/SOLV AGREE   DIPLOM
WAR...JURID IDEA/COMP T 20 TREATY. PAGE 12 E0233   CONCPT
                                                    CT/SYS

                                                    B62
DONNELLY R.C.,CRIMINAL LAW: PROBLEMS FOR DECISION   CRIME
IN THE PROMULGATION, INVOCATION AND ADMINISTRATION LAW
OF A LAW OF CRIMES. USA+45 SANCTION BIO/SOC   ADJUD
...DECISION JURID BIBLIOG 20. PAGE 32 E0636   PROB/SOLV

                                                    B62
EVAN W.M.,LAW AND SOCIOLOGY: EXPLORATORY ESSAYS.   JURID
CONSULT ACT/RES OP/RES PROB/SOLV EDU/PROP LEGIT   SOC
ADJUD CT/SYS GP/REL...PHIL/SCI ANTHOL SOC/INTEG 20. PROF/ORG
PAGE 35 E0703

                                                    B62
FROMAN L.A. JR.,PEOPLE AND POLITICS: AN ANALYSIS OF POL/PAR
THE AMERICAN POLITICAL SYSTEM. USA+45 CHIEF   PROB/SOLV
DELIB/GP EX/STRUC LEGIS TOP/EX CT/SYS LOBBY   GOV/REL
PERS/REL PWR...POLICY DECISION. PAGE 41 E0813

                                                    B62
SIGLIANO R E.,THE COURTS. USA+45 USA-45 LAW CONSTN ADJUD
NAT/G ROUTINE CHOOSE 18/20 SUPREME/CT. PAGE 91   PROB/SOLV
E1825   CT/SYS
                                                    JUDGE

                                                    B62
STERN A.C.,AIR POLLUTION (2 VOLS.). LAW INDUS   AIR
PROB/SOLV TEC/DEV INSPECT RISK BIO/SOC HABITAT   OP/RES
...OBS/ENVIR TESTS SAMP 20 POLLUTION. PAGE 93 E1871 CONTROL
                                                    HEALTH

                                                    B62
UNECA LIBRARY,NEW ACQUISITIONS IN THE UNECA   BIBLIOG
LIBRARY. LAW NAT/G PLAN PROB/SOLV TEC/DEV ADMIN   AFR
REGION...GEOG SOC 20 UN. PAGE 98 E1956   ECO/UNDEV

INT/ORG

B62

US COMMISSION ON CIVIL RIGHTS,EQUAL PROTECTION OF THE LAWS IN NORTH CAROLINA. USA+45 LOC/G NAT/G CONSULT LEGIS WORKER PROB/SOLV EDU/PROP ADJUD CHOOSE DISCRIM HEALTH 20 NEGRO NORTH/CAR CIV/RIGHTS. PAGE 99 E1984
ORD/FREE
RESPECT
LAW
PROVS

L62

ERDMANN H.H.,"ADMINISTRATIVE LAW AND FARM ECONOMICS." USA+45 LOC/G NAT/G PLAN PROB/SOLV LOBBY ...DECISION ANTHOL 20. PAGE 35 E0695
AGRI
ADMIN
ADJUD
POLICY

C62

LILLICH R.B.,"INTERNATIONAL CLAIMS: THEIR ADJUDICATION BY NATIONAL COMMISSIONS." WOR+45 WOR-45 NAT/G ADJUD...JURID BIBLIOG 18/20. PAGE 65 E1298
INT/LAW
DIPLOM
PROB/SOLV

B63

DECOTTIGNIES R.,LES NATIONALITES AFRICAINES. AFR NAT/G PROB/SOLV DIPLOM COLONIAL ORD/FREE...CHARTS GOV/COMP 20. PAGE 30 E0602
NAT/LISM
JURID
LEGIS
LAW

B63

DEENER D.R.,CANADA - UNITED STATES TREATY RELATIONS. CANADA USA+45 USA-45 NAT/G FORCES PLAN PROB/SOLV AGREE NUC/PWR...TREND 18/20 TREATY. PAGE 30 E0603
DIPLOM
INT/LAW
POLICY

B63

ECOLE NATIONALE D'ADMIN,BIBLIOGRAPHIE SELECTIVE D'OUVRAGES DE LANGUE FRANCAISE TRAITANT DES PROBLEMES GOUVERNEMENTAUX ET ADMINISTRATIFS. NAT/G FORCES ACT/RES OP/RES PLAN PROB/SOLV BUDGET ADJUD COLONIAL LEAD 20. PAGE 34 E0672
BIBLIOG
AFR
ADMIN
EX/STRUC

B63

JENKS C.W.,LAW, FREEDOM, AND WELFARE. WOR+45 GIVE ADJUD WAR PEACE HABITAT ORD/FREE. PAGE 58 E1159
INT/LAW
DIPLOM
SOVEREIGN
PROB/SOLV

B63

OTTOSON H.W.,LAND USE POLICY AND PROBLEMS IN THE UNITED STATES. USA+45 USA-45 LAW AGRI INDUS NAT/G GP/REL...CHARTS ANTHOL 19/20 HOMEST/ACT. PAGE 79 E1586
PROB/SOLV
UTIL
HABITAT
POLICY

B63

PRITCHETT C.H.,THE ROOSEVELT COURT. USA-45 LAW INGP/REL...CHARTS 20 SUPREME/CT. PAGE 82 E1653
DECISION
PROB/SOLV
CT/SYS
JURID

B63

PRITCHETT C.H.,THE THIRD BRANCH OF GOVERNMENT. USA+45 USA-45 CONSTN SOCIETY INDUS SECT LEGIS JUDGE PROB/SOLV GOV/REL 20 SUPREME/CT CHURCH/STA. PAGE 82 E1654
JURID
NAT/G
ADJUD
CT/SYS

B63

RICHARDS P.G.,PATRONAGE IN BRITISH GOVERNMENT. ELITES DELIB/GP TOP/EX PROB/SOLV CONTROL CT/SYS EXEC PWR. PAGE 84 E1693
EX/STRUC
REPRESENT
POL/PAR
ADMIN

B63

TUSSMAN J.,THE SUPREME COURT ON RACIAL DISCRIMINATION. USA+45 USA-45 NAT/G PROB/SOLV ADJUD RACE/REL ORD/FREE...JURID 20 SUPREME/CT CIV/RIGHTS. PAGE 97 E1946
CT/SYS
DISCRIM
ATTIT
LAW

B63

US COMN CIVIL RIGHTS,REPORT ON MISSISSIPPI. LAW LOC/G NAT/G LEGIS PLAN PROB/SOLV DISCRIM SOC/INTEG 20 MISSISSIPP NEGRO. PAGE 99 E1987
RACE/REL
CONSTN
ORD/FREE
COERCE

B63

US SENATE COMM ON JUDICIARY,ADMINISTRATIVE CONFERENCE OF THE UNITED STATES. USA+45 CONSTN NAT/G PROB/SOLV CONFER GOV/REL...INT 20 SENATE. PAGE 102 E2048
PARL/PROC
JURID
ADMIN
LEGIS

B63

VAN SLYCK P.,PEACE: THE CONTROL OF NATIONAL POWER. CUBA WOR+45 FINAN NAT/G FORCES PROB/SOLV TEC/DEV BAL/PWR ADMIN CONTROL ORD/FREE...POLICY INT/LAW UN COLD/WAR TREATY. PAGE 103 E2069
ARMS/CONT
PEACE
INT/ORG
DIPLOM

B63

WADE H.W.R.,TOWARDS ADMINISTRATIVE JUSTICE. UK
ADJUD

USA+45 CONSTN CONSULT PROB/SOLV CT/SYS PARL/PROC ...POLICY JURID METH/COMP 20 ENGLSH/LAW. PAGE 104 E2088
IDEA/COMP
ADMIN

S63

CLEVELAND H.,"CRISIS DIPLOMACY." USA+45 WOR+45 LAW FORCES TASK NUC/PWR PWR 20. PAGE 23 E0454
DECISION
DIPLOM
PROB/SOLV
POLICY

B64

ANDERSON J.W.,EISENHOWER, BROWNELL, AND THE CONGRESS - THE TANGLED ORIGINS OF THE CIVIL RIGHTS BILL OF 1956-1957. USA+45 POL/PAR LEGIS CREATE PROB/SOLV LOBBY GOV/REL RIGID/FLEX...NEW/IDEA 20 EISNHWR/DD CONGRESS BROWNELL/H CIV/RIGHTS. PAGE 5 E0090
LAW
CONSTN
POLICY
NAT/G

B64

DRESSLER D.,READINGS IN CRIMINOLOGY AND PENOLOGY. UNIV CULTURE PUB/INST FORCES ACT/RES PROB/SOLV ANOMIE BIO/SOC SUPEGO...GEOG PSY ANTHOL 20. PAGE 33 E0648
CRIMLGY
CRIME
ADJUD
ADJUST

B64

DUBOIS J.,DANGER OVER PANAMA. FUT PANAMA SCHOOL PROB/SOLV EDU/PROP MARXISM...POLICY 19/20 TREATY INTERVENT CANAL/ZONE. PAGE 33 E0652
DIPLOM
COERCE

B64

HOHFELD W.N.,FUNDAMENTAL LEGAL CONCEPTIONS. PROB/SOLV OWN PWR...DECISION LING IDEA/COMP GEN/METH. PAGE 54 E1069
JURID
ADJUD
LAW
METH/CNCPT

B64

MAKI J.M.,COURT AND CONSTITUTION IN JAPAN; SELECTED SUPREME COURT DECISIONS, 1948-60. FAM LABOR GOV/REL HABITAT ORD/FREE...DECISION JURID 20 CHINJAP SUPREME/CT CIV/RIGHTS. PAGE 68 E1354
CT/SYS
CONSTN
PROB/SOLV
LAW

B64

MITAU G.T.,INSOLUBLE PROBLEMS: CASE PROBLEMS ON THE FUNCTIONS OF STATE AND LOCAL GOVERNMENT. USA+45 AIR FINAN LABOR POL/PAR PROB/SOLV TAX RECEIVE CONTROL GP/REL 20 CASEBOOK ZONING. PAGE 73 E1471
ADJUD
LOC/G
PROVS

B64

NASA,PROCEEDINGS OF CONFERENCE ON THE LAW OF SPACE AND OF SATELLITE COMMUNICATIONS: CHICAGO 1963. FUT WOR+45 DELIB/GP PROB/SOLV TEC/DEV CONFER ADJUD NUC/PWR...POLICY IDEA/COMP 20 NASA. PAGE 76 E1522
SPACE
COM/IND
LAW
DIPLOM

B64

OSSENBECK F.J.,OPEN SPACE AND PEACE. CHINA/COM FUT USA+45 USSR LAW PROB/SOLV TEC/DEV EDU/PROP NEUTRAL PEACE...AUD/VIS ANTHOL 20. PAGE 79 E1583
SPACE
ORD/FREE
DIPLOM
CREATE

B64

REGALA R.,WORLD PEACE THROUGH DIPLOMACY AND LAW. S/ASIA WOR+45 ECO/UNDEV INT/ORG FORCES PLAN PROB/SOLV FOR/AID NUC/PWR WAR...POLICY INT/LAW 20. PAGE 84 E1679
DIPLOM
PEACE
ADJUD

B64

RICE C.E.,THE SUPREME COURT AND PUBLIC PRAYER. CONSTN SCHOOL SECT PROB/SOLV TAX ATTIT WORSHIP 18/20 SUPREME/CT CHURCH/STA. PAGE 84 E1692
JURID
POLICY
NAT/G

B64

RUSSELL R.B.,UNITED NATIONS EXPERIENCE WITH MILITARY FORCES: POLITICAL AND LEGAL ASPECTS. AFR KOREA WOR+45 LEGIS PROB/SOLV ADMIN CONTROL EFFICIENCY PEACE...POLICY INT/LAW BIBLIOG UN. PAGE 87 E1738
FORCES
DIPLOM
SANCTION
ORD/FREE

B64

SARTORIUS R.E.,THE JUSTIFICATION OF THE JUDICIAL DECISION (DISSERTATION). PROB/SOLV LEGIT...JURID GEN/LAWS BIBLIOG 20. PAGE 87 E1747
LAW
PHIL/SCI
CT/SYS
ADJUD

B64

SHAPIRO M.,LAW AND POLITICS IN THE SUPREME COURT: NEW APPROACHES TO POLITICAL JURISPRUDENCE. JUDGE PROB/SOLV LEGIT EXEC ROUTINE ATTIT ALL/VALS ...DECISION SOC. PAGE 90 E1811
LEGIS
CT/SYS
LAW
JURID

B64

SHKLAR J.N.,LEGALISM. CREATE PROB/SOLV CT/SYS ...POLICY CRIMLGY DECISION JURID METH/CNCPT. PAGE 91 E1821
MORAL
LAW
NEW/IDEA

B64

STANGER R.J.,ESSAYS ON INTERVENTION. PLAN PROB/SOLV
SOVEREIGN

BAL/PWR ADJUD COERCE WAR ROLE PWR...INT/LAW CONCPT 20 UN INTERVENT. PAGE 93 E1865   DIPLOM POLICY LEGIT

US SENATE COMM ON JUDICIARY,CIVIL RIGHTS - THE PRESIDENT'S PROGRAM. USA+45 LAW PROB/SOLV PRESS ADJUD GOV/REL RACE/REL ORD/FREE PWR...JURID 20 SUPREME/CT SENATE CIV/RIGHTS PRESIDENT. PAGE 102 E2053   B64 INT LEGIS DISCRIM PARL/PROC

US SENATE COMM ON JUDICIARY,ADMINISTRATIVE PROCEDURE ACT. USA+45 CONSTN NAT/G PROB/SOLV CONFER GOV/REL PWR...INT 20 SENATE. PAGE 102 E2054   B64 PARL/PROC LEGIS JURID ADMIN

WRIGHT Q.,A STUDY OF WAR. LAW NAT/G PROB/SOLV BAL/PWR NAT/LISM PEACE ATTIT SOVEREIGN...CENSUS SOC/INTEG. PAGE 108 E2159   B64 WAR CONCPT DIPLOM CONTROL

MAYO L.H.,"LEGAL-POLICY DECISION PROCESS: ALTERNATIVE THINKING AND THE PREDICTIVE FUNCTION." PROB/SOLV EFFICIENCY RATIONAL. PAGE 70 E1395   L64 DECISION SIMUL JURID TEC/DEV

MCGHEE G.C.,"EAST-WEST RELATIONS TODAY." WOR+45 PROB/SOLV BAL/PWR PEACE 20 COLD/WAR. PAGE 71 E1413   S64 IDEA/COMP DIPLOM ADJUD

BECKER T.L.,"POLITICAL BEHAVIORALISM AND MODERN JURISPRUDENCE." LEGIS JUDGE OP/RES ADJUD CT/SYS ATTIT PWR...BIBLIOG 20. PAGE 9 E0173   C64 DECISION PROB/SOLV JURID GEN/LAWS

CORWIN E.S.,"AMERICAN CONSTITUTIONAL HISTORY." LAW NAT/G PROB/SOLV EQUILIB FEDERAL ATTIT PWR...JURID BIBLIOG 20. PAGE 26 E0515   C64 ANTHOL JUDGE ADJUD CT/SYS

CAVERS D.F.,THE CHOICE-OF-LAW PROCESS. PROB/SOLV ADJUD CT/SYS CHOOSE RATIONAL...IDEA/COMP 16/20 TREATY. PAGE 21 E0411   B65 JURID DECISION METH/COMP ADMIN

FEERICK J.D.,FROM FAILING HANDS: THE STUDY OF PRESIDENTIAL SUCCESSION. CONSTN NAT/G PROB/SOLV LEAD PARL/PROC MURDER CHOOSE...NEW/IDEA BIBLIOG 20 KENNEDY/JF JOHNSON/LB PRESIDENT PRE/US/AM VICE/PRES. PAGE 36 E0724   B65 EX/STRUC CHIEF LAW LEGIS

FRYE R.J.,HOUSING AND URBAN RENEWAL IN ALABAMA. USA+45 NEIGH LEGIS BUDGET ADJUD ADMIN PARTIC...MGT 20 ALABAMA URBAN/RNWL. PAGE 41 E0815   B65 MUNIC PROB/SOLV PLAN GOV/REL

GOTLIEB A.,DISARMAMENT AND INTERNATIONAL LAW* A STUDY OF THE ROLE OF LAW IN THE DISARMAMENT PROCESS. USA+45 USSR PROB/SOLV CONFER ADMIN ROUTINE NUC/PWR ORD/FREE SOVEREIGN UN TREATY. PAGE 45 E0893   B65 INT/LAW INT/ORG ARMS/CONT IDEA/COMP

HIGHSAW R.B.,CONFLICT AND CHANGE IN LOCAL GOVERNMENT. USA+45 BUDGET ECO/TAC LEGIT ADJUD ALABAMA. PAGE 52 E1044   B65 GOV/REL PROB/SOLV LOC/G BAL/PWR

JOHNSTON D.M.,THE INTERNATIONAL LAW OF FISHERIES: A FRAMEWORK FOR POLICYORIENTED INQUIRIES. WOR+45 ACT/RES PLAN PROB/SOLV CONTROL SOVEREIGN. PAGE 59 E1171   B65 CONCPT EXTR/IND JURID DIPLOM

KAMISAR Y.,CRIMINAL JUSTICE IN OUR TIME. USA+45 FORCES JUDGE PROB/SOLV COERCE MORAL 20 CIVIL/LIB CIV/RIGHTS. PAGE 59 E1182   B65 ORD/FREE CRIME CT/SYS LAW

MILLER H.H.,THE CASE FOR LIBERTY. USA-45 LAW JUDGE CT/SYS...AUD/VIS 18 PRE/US/AM CASEBOOK. PAGE 73 E1460   B65 COLONIAL JURID PROB/SOLV

NWOGUGU E.I.,THE LEGAL PROBLEMS OF FOREIGN   B65 FOR/AID

INVESTMENT IN DEVELOPING COUNTRIES. WOR+45 INT/ORG DELIB/GP LEGIS PROB/SOLV INT/TRADE TAX ADJUD SANCTION...BIBLIOG 20 TREATY. PAGE 78 E1561   FINAN INT/LAW ECO/UNDEV

RADZINOWICZ L.,THE NEED FOR CRIMINOLOGY AND A PROPOSAL FOR AN INSTITUTE OF CRIMINOLOGY. FUT UK USA+45 SOCIETY ACT/RES PROB/SOLV CRIME...PSY SOC BIBLIOG 20. PAGE 83 E1666   B65 CRIMLGY PROF/ORG ACADEM CONTROL

ROSE A.M.,MINORITY PROBLEMS: A TEXTBOOK OF READINGS IN INTERGROUP RELATIONS. UNIV USA+45 LAW SCHOOL WORKER PROB/SOLV GP/REL PERSON...PSY ANTHOL WORSHIP 20 NEGRO INDIAN/AM JEWS EUROPE. PAGE 85 E1713   B65 RACE/REL DISCRIM ISOLAT ACT/RES

ROSS P.,THE GOVERNMENT AS A SOURCE OF UNION POWER. USA+45 LAW ECO/DEV PROB/SOLV ECO/TAC LEAD GP/REL ...MGT 20. PAGE 86 E1723   B65 LABOR BARGAIN POLICY NAT/G

MARTIN A.,"PROLIFERATION." FUT WOR+45 PROB/SOLV REGION ADJUST...PREDICT NAT/COMP UN TREATY. PAGE 69 E1372   S65 RECORD NUC/PWR ARMS/CONT VOL/ASSN

AARON T.J.,THE CONTROL OF POLICE DISCRETION: THE DANISH EXPERIENCE. DENMARK LAW CREATE ADMIN INGP/REL SUPEGO PWR 20 OMBUDSMAN. PAGE 2 E0042   B66 CONTROL FORCES REPRESENT PROB/SOLV

AMERICAN JEWISH COMMITTEE,GROUP RELATIONS IN THE UNITED STATES: PROBLEMS AND PERSPECTIVES: A SELECTED, ANNOTATED BIBLIOGRAPHY (PAMPHLET). LAW CONSTN STRATA SCHOOL SECT PROB/SOLV ATTIT...POLICY WELF/ST SOC/WK 20. PAGE 4 E0079   B66 BIBLIOG/A USA+45 STRUCT GP/REL

AMERICAN JEWISH COMMITTEE,THE TYRANNY OF POVERTY (PAMPHLET). USA+45 LAW ECO/DEV LOC/G MUNIC NAT/G PUB/INST WORKER EDU/PROP CRIME...SOC/WK 20. PAGE 4 E0080   B66 BIBLIOG/A WEALTH WELF/ST PROB/SOLV

BAKER G.E.,THE REAPPORTIONMENT REVOLUTION; REPRESENTATION, POLITICAL POWER, AND THE SUPREME COURT. USA+45 MUNIC NAT/G POL/PAR PROVS PROB/SOLV CHOOSE ORD/FREE POPULISM...CONCPT CHARTS 20 SUPREME/CT. PAGE 7 E0140   B66 LEGIS APPORT REPRESENT ADJUD

BEDI A.S.,FREEDOM OF EXPRESSION AND SECURITY; COMPARATIVE STUDY OF FUNCTIONS OF SUPREME COURTS IN UNITED STATES AND INDIA. INDIA USA+45 LAW CONSTN PROB/SOLV...DECISION JURID BIBLIOG 20 SUPREME/CT FREE/SPEE AMEND/I. PAGE 9 E0175   B66 METH CT/SYS ADJUD ORD/FREE

CAHN E.,CONFRONTING INJUSTICE. USA+45 PROB/SOLV TAX EDU/PROP PRESS CT/SYS GP/REL DISCRIM BIO/SOC ...IDEA/COMP BIBLIOG WORSHIP 20 BILL/RIGHT. PAGE 18 E0362   B66 ORD/FREE CONSTN ADJUD

DAVIS K.,BUSINESS AND ITS ENVIRONMENT. LAW ECO/DEV INDUS OP/RES ADMIN CONTROL ROUTINE GP/REL PROFIT POLICY. PAGE 29 E0573   B66 EX/STRUC PROB/SOLV CAP/ISM EXEC

GARCON M.,LETTRE OUVERTE A LA JUSTICE. FRANCE NAT/G PROB/SOLV PAY EFFICIENCY MORAL 20. PAGE 42 E0834   B66 ORD/FREE ADJUD CT/SYS

GHOSH P.K.,THE CONSTITUTION OF INDIA: HOW IT HAS BEEN FRAMED. INDIA LOC/G DELIB/GP EX/STRUC PROB/SOLV BUDGET INT/TRADE CT/SYS CHOOSE...LING 20. PAGE 43 E0854   B66 CONSTN NAT/G LEGIS FEDERAL

GILLMOR D.M.,FREE PRESS AND FAIR TRIAL. UK USA+45 CONSTN PROB/SOLV PRESS CONTROL CRIME DISCRIM RESPECT...AUD/VIS 20 CIVIL/LIB. PAGE 44 E0865   B66 ORD/FREE ADJUD ATTIT EDU/PROP

KURLAND P.B.,THE SUPREME COURT REVIEW. USA+45 USA-45 LAW LABOR SUFF...ANTHOL 20 SUPREME/CT. PAGE 62 E1240   B66 JURID PROB/SOLV ADJUD NAT/G

MENDELSON W.,JUSTICES BLACK AND FRANKFURTER: CONFLICT IN THE COURT (2ND ED.). NAT/G PROVS PROB/SOLV BAL/PWR CONTROL FEDERAL ISOLAT ANOMIE ORD/FREE...DECISION 20 SUPREME/CT BLACK/HL FRANKFUR/F. PAGE 72 E1439
B66 JURID ADJUD IDEA/COMP ROLE

NANTWI E.K.,THE ENFORCEMENT OF INTERNATIONAL JUDICIAL DECISIONS AND ARBITAL AWARDS IN PUBLIC INTERNATIONAL LAW. WOR+45 WOR-45 JUDGE PROB/SOLV DIPLOM CT/SYS SUPEGO MORAL PWR RESPECT...METH/CNCPT 18/20 CASEBOOK. PAGE 76 E1520
B66 INT/LAW ADJUD SOVEREIGN INT/ORG

SALTER L.M.,RESOLUTION OF INTERNATIONAL CONFLICT. USA+45 INT/ORG SECT DIPLOM ECO/TAC FOR/AID DETER NUC/PWR WAR 20. PAGE 87 E1743
B66 PROB/SOLV PEACE INT/LAW POLICY

STUMPF S.E.,MORALITY AND THE LAW. USA+45 LAW CULTURE PROB/SOLV DOMIN ADJUD CONTROL ADJUST ALL/IDEOS MARXISM...INT/LAW 20 SUPREME/CT. PAGE 94 E1890
B66 JURID MORAL CT/SYS

US HOUSE COMM ON JUDICIARY,CIVIL COMMITMENT AND TREATMENT OF NARCOTIC ADDICTS. USA+45 SOCIETY FINAN LEGIS PROB/SOLV GIVE CT/SYS SANCTION HEALTH ...POLICY HEAL 20. PAGE 100 E2008
B66 BIO/SOC CRIME IDEA/COMP CONTROL

WAINHOUSE D.W.,INTERNATIONAL PEACE OBSERVATION: A HISTORY AND FORECAST. INT/ORG PROB/SOLV BAL/PWR AGREE ARMS/CONT COERCE NUC/PWR...PREDICT METH/COMP 20 UN LEAGUE/NAT OAS TREATY. PAGE 104 E2092
B66 PEACE DIPLOM

HOLSTI K.J.,"RESOLVING INTERNATIONAL CONFLICTS* A TAXONOMY OF BEHAVIOR AND SOME FIGURES ON PROCEDURES." WOR+45 WOR-45 INT/ORG ADJUD EFFICIENCY ...STAT IDEA/COMP. PAGE 55 E1089
L66 DIPLOM PROB/SOLV WAR CLASSIF

AMDS W.E.,DELINQUENCY PREVENTION: THEORY AND PRACTICE. USA+45 SOCIETY FAM SCHOOL SECT FORCES PROB/SOLV...HEAL JURID PREDICT ANTHOL. PAGE 4 E0071
B67 AGE/Y CRIME PUB/INST LAW

BUREAU GOVERNMENT RES AND SERV,COUNTY GOVERNMENT REORGANIZATION - A SELECTED ANNOTATED BIBLIOGRAPHY (PAPER). USA+45 USA-45 LAW CONSTN MUNIC PROVS EX/STRUC CREATE PLAN PROB/SOLV REPRESENT GOV/REL 20. PAGE 17 E0332
B67 BIBLIOG/A APPORT LOC/G ADMIN

CHAPIN F.S. JR.,SELECTED REFERENCES ON URBAN PLANNING METHODS AND TECHNIQUES. USA+45 LAW ECO/DEV LOC/G NAT/G SCHOOL CONSULT CREATE PROB/SOLV TEC/DEV SOC/WK. PAGE 21 E0420
B67 BIBLIOG NEIGH MUNIC PLAN

FESLER J.W.,THE FIFTY STATES AND THEIR LOCAL GOVERNMENTS. FUT USA+45 POL/PAR LEGIS PROB/SOLV ADMIN CT/SYS CHOOSE GOV/REL FEDERAL...POLICY CHARTS 20 SUPREME/CT. PAGE 37 E0743
B67 PROVS LOC/G

GABRIEL P.P.,THE INTERNATIONAL TRANSFER OF CORPORATE SKILLS: MANAGEMENT CONTRACTS IN LESS DEVELOPED COUNTRIES. CLIENT INDUS LG/CO PLAN PROB/SOLV CAP/ISM ECO/TAC FOR/AID INT/TRADE RENT ADMIN SKILL 20. PAGE 42 E0825
B67 ECO/UNDEV AGREE MGT CONSULT

GELLHORN W.,OMBUDSMEN AND OTHERS: CITIZENS' PROTECTORS IN NINE COUNTRIES. WOR+45 LAW CONSTN LEGIS INSPECT ADJUD ADMIN CONTROL CT/SYS CHOOSE PERS/REL...STAT CHARTS 20. PAGE 43 E0847
B67 NAT/COMP REPRESENT INGP/REL PROB/SOLV

HEWITT W.H.,ADMINISTRATION OF CRIMINAL JUSTICE IN NEW YORK. LAW PROB/SOLV ADJUD ADMIN...CRIMLGY CHARTS T 20 NEW/YORK. PAGE 52 E1035
B67 CRIME ROLE CT/SYS FORCES

HODGKINSON R.G.,THE ORIGINS OF THE NATIONAL HEALTH SERVICE: THE MEDICAL SERVICES OF THE NEW POOR LAW, 1834-1871. UK INDUS MUNIC WORKER PROB/SOLV EFFICIENCY ATTIT HEALTH WEALTH SOCISM...JURID SOC/WK 19/20. PAGE 53 E1062
B67 HEAL NAT/G POLICY LAW

INTERNATIONAL CONCILIATION,ISSUES BEFORE THE 22ND GENERAL ASSEMBLY. WOR+45 ECO/UNDEV FINAN BAL/PWR BUDGET INT/TRADE STRANGE ORD/FREE...INT/LAW 20 UN COLD/WAR. PAGE 57 E1132
B67 PROB/SOLV INT/ORG DIPLOM PEACE

JONES C.O.,EVERY SECOND YEAR: CONGRESSIONAL BEHAVIOR AND THE TWO-YEAR TERM. LAW POL/PAR PROB/SOLV DEBATE CHOOSE PERS/REL COST FEDERAL PWR ...CHARTS 20 CONGRESS SENATE HOUSE/REP. PAGE 59 E1172
B67 EFFICIENCY LEGIS TIME/SEQ NAT/G

LAFAVE W.R.,INTERNATIONAL TRADE, INVESTMENT, AND ORGANIZATION. INDUS PROB/SOLV TARIFFS CONTROL ...TREND ANTHOL BIBLIOG 20 EEC. PAGE 62 E1245
B67 INT/TRADE INT/LAW INT/ORG

LOBLE L.H.,DELINQUENCY CAN BE STOPPED. FAM PUB/INST CT/SYS ADJUST ATTIT...NEW/IDEA METH/COMP 20. PAGE 66 E1315
B67 AGE/Y PROB/SOLV ADJUD CRIME

MCDOUGAL M.S.,THE INTERPRETATION OF AGREEMENTS AND WORLD PUBLIC ORDER: PRINCIPLES OF CONTENT AND PROCEDURE. WOR+45 CONSTN PROB/SOLV TEC/DEV ...CON/ANAL TREATY. PAGE 71 E1412
B67 INT/LAW STRUCT ECO/UNDEV DIPLOM

PLANO J.C.,FORGING WORLD ORDER: THE POLITICS OF INTERNATIONAL ORGANIZATION. PROB/SOLV DIPLOM CONTROL CENTRAL RATIONAL ORD/FREE...INT/LAW CHARTS BIBLIOG 20 UN LEAGUE/NAT. PAGE 81 E1618
B67 INT/ORG ADMIN JURID

UNIVERSAL REFERENCE SYSTEM,CURRENT EVENTS AND PROBLEMS OF MODERN SOCIETY (VOLUME V). WOR+45 LOC/G MUNIC NAT/G PLAN EDU/PROP CRIME RACE/REL WEALTH ...COMPUT/IR GEN/METH. PAGE 98 E1974
B67 BIBLIOG/A SOCIETY PROB/SOLV ATTIT

US SENATE COMM ON FOREIGN REL,TREATY ON OUTER SPACE. WOR+45 AIR FORCES PROB/SOLV NUC/PWR SENATE TREATY UN. PAGE 101 E2032
B67 SPACE DIPLOM ARMS/CONT LAW

US SENATE COMM ON FOREIGN REL,A SELECT CHRONOLOGY AND BACKGROUND DOCUMENTS RELATING TO THE MIDDLE EAST. ISRAEL UAR LAW INT/ORG FORCES PROB/SOLV CONFER CONSEN PEACE ATTIT...POLICY 20 UN SENATE TRUMAN/HS. PAGE 101 E2033
B67 ISLAM TIME/SEQ DIPLOM

US SENATE COMM ON FOREIGN REL,UNITED STATES ARMAMENT AND DISARMAMENT PROBLEMS. USA+45 AIR BAL/PWR DIPLOM FOR/AID NUC/PWR ORD/FREE SENATE TREATY. PAGE 102 E2035
B67 ARMS/CONT WEAPON FORCES PROB/SOLV

"FOCUS ON WORLD LAW." WOR+45 NAT/G CT/SYS PEACE ...BIBLIOG 20 UN. PAGE 2 E0036
L67 INT/LAW INT/ORG PROB/SOLV CONCPT

CARMICHAEL D.M.,"FORTY YEARS OF WATER POLLUTION CONTROL IN WISCONSIN: A CASE STUDY." LAW EXTR/IND INDUS MUNIC DELIB/GP PLAN PROB/SOLV SANCTION ...CENSUS CHARTS 20 WISCONSIN. PAGE 20 E0384
L67 HEALTH CONTROL ADMIN ADJUD

FRANCK T.M.,"SOME PSYCHOLOGICAL FACTORS IN INTERNATIONAL THIRD-PARTY DECISION-MAKING." UNIV SOCIETY PROB/SOLV DISCRIM ATTIT HABITAT...DECISION PSY. PAGE 40 E0786
L67 DIPLOM ADJUD PERSON CONSULT

WAELBROECK M.,"THE APPLICATION OF EEC LAW BY NATIONAL COURTS." EUR+WWI INT/ORG CT/SYS...JURID EEC TREATY. PAGE 104 E2090
L67 INT/LAW NAT/G LAW PROB/SOLV

ALEXANDER B.,"GIBRALTAR" SPAIN UK CONSTN WORKER PROB/SOLV FOR/AID RECEIVE CONTROL 20. PAGE 3 E0059
S67 DIPLOM INT/ORG ORD/FREE ECO/TAC

CHAMBERLAIN N.W.,"STRIKES IN CONTEMPORARY CONTEXT." LAW INDUS NAT/G CHIEF CONFER COST ATTIT ORD/FREE ...POLICY MGT 20. PAGE 21 E0415
S67 LABOR BARGAIN EFFICIENCY PROB/SOLV

CHAMBLISS W.J.,"TYPES OF DEVIANCE AND THE   S67   CRIME
EFFECTIVENESS OF LEGAL SANCTIONS" SOCIETY PROB/SOLV   SANCTION
ADJUD CONTROL DETER. PAGE 21 E0417   EFFICIENCY
                                                                   LAW

DEUTSCH E.P.,"A JUDICIAL PATH TO WORLD PEACE." FUT   S67   INT/LAW
WOR+45 CONSTN PROB/SOLV DIPLOM LICENSE ADJUD   INT/ORG
SANCTION CHOOSE REPRESENT NAT/LISM SOVEREIGN 20   JURID
ICJ. PAGE 31 E0611   PEACE

GOSSETT W.T.,"ELECTING THE PRESIDENT: NEW HOPE FOR   S67   CONSTN
AN OLD IDEAL." FUT USA+45 USA-45 PROVS LEGIS   CHIEF
PROB/SOLV WRITING DEBATE ADJUD REPRESENT...MAJORIT   CHOOSE
DECISION 20 HOUSE/REP PRESIDENT. PAGE 45 E0892   NAT/G

HIRSCH W.Z.,"SOME ECONOMIC IMPLICATIONS OF CITY   S67   ECO/TAC
PLANNING." LAW PROB/SOLV RATION EFFICIENCY...METH   JURID
20. PAGE 53 E1050   MUNIC
                                                                   PLAN

KIM R.C.C.,"THE SUPREME COURT: ORALLE WITHOUT   S67   CT/SYS
TRUTH." USA+45 EDU/PROP RACE/REL ADJUST ALL/VALS   PROB/SOLV
ORD/FREE...DECISION WORSHIP SUPREME/CT. PAGE 61   ADJUD
E1214   REPRESENT

LARSEN P.B.,"THE UNITED STATES-ITALY AIR TRANSPORT   S67   INT/LAW
ARBITRATION: PROBLEMS OF TREATY INTERPRETATION AND   ADJUD
ENFORCEMENT." ITALY USA+45 AIR PROB/SOLV DIPLOM   INT/TRADE
DEBATE CONTROL CT/SYS...DECISION TREATY. PAGE 63   DIST/IND
E1257

LAY S.H.,"EXCLUSIVE GOVERNMENTAL LIABILITY FOR   S67   NAT/G
SPACE ACCIDENTS." USA+45 LAW FINAN SERV/IND TEC/DEV   SUPEGO
ADJUD. PAGE 64 E1272   SPACE
                                                                   PROB/SOLV

PEMBERTON J., JR.,"CONSTITUTIONAL PROBLEMS IN   S67   LAW
RESTRAINT ON THE MEDIA." CONSTN PROB/SOLV EDU/PROP   PRESS
CONFER CONTROL JURID. PAGE 80 E1608   ORD/FREE

SCHELLING T.C.,"ECONOMICS AND CRIMINAL ENTERPRISE."   S67   CRIME
LAW FORCES BARGAIN ECO/TAC CONTROL GAMBLE ROUTINE   PROB/SOLV
ADJUST DEMAND INCOME PROFIT CRIMLGY. PAGE 87 E1756   CONCPT

TOMASEK R.D.,"THE CHILEAN-BOLIVIAN LAUCA RIVER   S67   INT/ORG
DISPUTE AND THE OAS." CHILE L/A+17C PROB/SOLV ADJUD   DIPLOM
CONTROL PEACE 20 BOLIV OAS. PAGE 96 E1930   GEOG
                                                                   WAR

TRAYNOR R.J.,"WHO CAN BEST JUDGE THE JUDGES?"   S67   CHOOSE
USA+45 PLAN PROB/SOLV ATTIT...DECISION JURID 20.   ADJUD
PAGE 97 E1938   REPRESENT
                                                                   CT/SYS

AUSTIN J.,LECTURES ON JURISPRUDENCE OR THE   B73   LAW
PHILOSOPHY OF POSITIVE LAW (VOL. II) (4TH ED.,   ADJUD
REV.). UK CONSTN STRUCT PROB/SOLV LEGIT CT/SYS   JURID
SANCTION CRIME INGP/REL OWN SUPEGO ORD/FREE...T 19.   METH/CNCPT
PAGE 6 E0120

CADWALDER J.L.,DIGEST OF THE PUBLISHED OPINIONS OF   B77   BIBLIOG
THE ATTORNEYS-GENERAL, AND OF THE LEADING DECISIONS   CT/SYS
OF THE FEDERAL COURTS (REV ED). USA-45 NAT/G JUDGE   DECISION
PROB/SOLV DIPLOM ATTIT...POLICY INT/LAW ANTHOL 19.   ADJUD
PAGE 18 E0356

PROBABIL....PROBABILITY; SEE ALSO GAMBLE

HALL A.B.,"DETERMINATION OF METHODS FOR   S26   ADJUD
ASCERTAINING THE FACTORS THAT INFLUENCE JUDICIAL   DECISION
DECISIONS IN CASES INVOLVING DUE PROCESS" LAW JUDGE   CONSTN
DEBATE EFFICIENCY OPTIMAL UTIL...SOC CONCPT   JURID
PROBABIL STAT SAMP. PAGE 49 E0981

PROBABILITY....SEE PROBABIL

PROBLEM SOLVING....SEE PROB/SOLV

PROC/MFG....PROCESSING OR MANUFACTURING INDUSTRIES

MCCONNELL G.,THE STEEL SEIZURE OF 1952 (PAMPHLET).   N19   DELIB/GP
USA+45 FINAN INDUS PROC/MFG LG/CO EX/STRUC ADJUD   LABOR
CONTROL GP/REL ORD/FREE PWR 20 TRUMAN/HS PRESIDENT   PROB/SOLV
CONGRESS. PAGE 70 E1402   NAT/G

MOSER J.J.,JOHANN JACOB MOSER'S GESAMMELTE UND ZU   B58   BIBLIOG
GEMEINNUTZIGEM GEBRAUCH EINGERICHTETE BIBLIOTHEK.   EXTR/IND
GERMANY PROC/MFG INT/TRADE...POLICY JURID MGT 18.   INDUS
PAGE 75 E1500

PUGWASH CONFERENCE."ON BIOLOGICAL AND CHEMICAL   S59   ACT/RES
WARFARE." WOR+45 SOCIETY PROC/MFG INT/ORG FORCES   BIO/SOC
EDU/PROP ADJUD RIGID/FLEX ORD/FREE PWR...DECISION   WAR
PSY NEW/IDEA MATH VAL/FREE 20. PAGE 83 E1661   WEAPON

YOUNG W.,EXISTING MECHANISMS OF ARMS CONTROL.   B66   ARMS/CONT
PROC/MFG OP/RES DIPLOM TASK CENTRAL...MGT TREATY.   ADMIN
PAGE 108 E2165   NUC/PWR
                                                                   ROUTINE

PROCEDURAL SYSTEMS....SEE ROUTINE, ALSO PROCESSES AND
    PRACTICES INDEX

PROCESSING OR MANUFACTURING INDUSTRY....SEE PROC/MFG

PRODUC....PRODUCTIVITY; SEE ALSO PLAN

BENTHAM J.,"THE RATIONALE OF REWARD" IN J. BOWRING,   C43   SANCTION
ED., THE WORKS OF JEREMY BENTHAM (VOL. 2)" LAW   ECO/TAC
WORKER CREATE INSPECT PAY ROUTINE HAPPINESS PRODUC   INCOME
SUPEGO WEALTH METH/CNCPT. PAGE 10 E0195   PWR

MAYDA J.,ATOMIC ENERGY AND LAW. ECO/UNDEV FINAN   B59   NUC/PWR
TEC/DEV FOR/AID EFFICIENCY PRODUC WEALTH...POLICY   L/A+17C
TECHNIC 20. PAGE 70 E1391   LAW
                                                                   ADMIN

INTNTL COTTON ADVISORY COMMITT,GOVERNMENT   B62   ECO/TAC
REGULATIONS ON COTTON, 1962 (PAMPHLET). WOR+45   LAW
RATION PRODUC...CHARTS 20. PAGE 57 E1136   CONTROL
                                                                   AGRI

US SENATE COMM ON JUDICIARY,HEARINGS BEFORE   B64   ECO/DEV
SUBCOMMITTEE ON ANTITRUST AND MONOPOLY: ECONOMIC   CONTROL
CONCENTRATION VOLUMES 1-5 JULY 1964-SEPT 1966.   MARKET
USA+45 LAW FINAN ECO/TAC ADJUD COST EFFICIENCY   LG/CO
PRODUC...STAT CHARTS 20 CONGRESS MONOPOLY. PAGE 102
E2052

ROBINSON R.D., INTERNATIONAL MANAGEMENT. USA+45   B67   INT/TRADE
FINAN R+D PLAN PRODUC...DECISION T. PAGE 67 E1336   MGT
                                                                   INT/LAW
                                                                   MARKET

BERNHARD R.C.,"COMPETITION IN LAW AND ECONOMICS."   L67   MARKET
LAW PLAN PRICE CONTROL PRODUC PROFIT...METH/CNCPT   POLICY
IDEA/COMP GEN/LAWS 20. PAGE 11 E0210   NAT/G
                                                                   CT/SYS

EYRAUD M.,"LA FRANCE FACE A UN EVENTUEL TRAITE DE   S67   NUC/PWR
NON DISSEMINATION DES ARMES NUCLEAIRES." FRANCE   ARMS/CONT
USA+45 EXTR/IND INDUS R+D INT/ORG ACT/RES TEC/DEV   POLICY
AGREE PRODUC ATTIT 20 TREATY AEC EURATOM. PAGE 36
E0708

PRODUCTIVITY....SEE PRODUC

PROEHL P.O. E1656

PROF/ORG....PROFESSIONAL ORGANIZATIONS

HOGARTY R.A.,NEW JERSEY FARMERS AND MIGRANT HOUSING   N19   AGRI
RULES (PAMPHLET). USA+45 LAW ELITES FACE/GP LABOR   PROVS
PROF/ORG LOBBY PERS/REL RIGID/FLEX ROLE 20   WORKER
NEW/JERSEY. PAGE 53 E1067   HEALTH

RUTHERFORD M.L.,THE INFLUENCE OF THE AMERICAN BAR   B37   ATTIT
ASSOCIATION ON PUBLIC OPINION AND LEGISLATION.   ADJUD
USA+45 LAW CONSTN LABOR LEGIS DOMIN EDU/PROP LEGIT   PROF/ORG
CT/SYS ROUTINE...TIME/SEQ 19/20 ABA. PAGE 87 E1739   JURID

HOLDSWORTH W.S.,A HISTORY OF ENGLISH LAW; THE   B38   LAW

CENTURIES OF SETTLEMENT AND REFORM (VOL. XII). UK CONSTN STRATA LEGIS JUDGE ADJUD CT/SYS ATTIT ...JURID CONCPT BIOG GEN/LAWS 18 ENGLSH/LAW BLACKSTN/W COMMON/LAW. PAGE 54 E1078
PROF/ORG
WRITING
IDEA/COMP

B52

COUNCIL STATE GOVERNMENTS,OCCUPATIONAL LICENSING IN THE STATES. USA+45 PROVS ADMIN EXEC LOBBY 20. PAGE 27 E0526
PROF/ORG
LICENSE
REPRESENT
EX/STRUC

B52

HOLDSWORTH W.S.,A HISTORY OF ENGLISH LAW; THE CENTURIES OF SETTLEMENT AND REFORM, 1701-1875 (VOL. XIII). UK POL/PAR PROF/ORG LEGIS JUDGE WRITING ATTIT...JURID CONCPT BIOG GEN/LAWS 18/19 PARLIAMENT REFORMERS ENGLSH/LAW COMMON/LAW. PAGE 54 E1080
LAW
CONSTN
IDEA/COMP
CT/SYS

B56

CALLISON I.P.,COURTS OF INJUSTICE. USA+45 PROF/ORG ADJUD CRIME PERSON MORAL PWR RESPECT SKILL 20. PAGE 19 E0368
CT/SYS
JUDGE
JURID

B57

MORELAND C.C.,EQUAL JUSTICE UNDER LAW. USA+45 USA-45 PROF/ORG PROVS JUDGE...POLICY JURID. PAGE 74 E1491
CONSTN
ADJUD
CT/SYS
ORD/FREE

S57

GOODE W.J.,"COMMUNITY WITHIN A COMMUNITY: THE PROFESSIONS." STRATA STRUCT SANCTION INGP/REL...SOC GP/COMP. PAGE 45 E0886
PROF/ORG
NEIGH
CLIENT
CONTROL

B58

JAPAN MINISTRY OF JUSTICE,CRIMINAL JUSTICE IN JAPAN. LAW PROF/ORG PUB/INST FORCES CONTROL CT/SYS PARL/PROC 20 CHINJAP. PAGE 58 E1149
CONSTN
CRIME
JURID
ADMIN

B59

PAULSEN M.G.,LEGAL INSTITUTIONS TODAY AND TOMORROW. UK USA+45 NAT/G PROF/ORG PROVS ADMIN PARL/PROC ORD/FREE NAT/COMP. PAGE 80 E1604
JURID
ADJUD
JUDGE
LEGIS

B60

PAUL A.M.,CONSERVATIVE CRISIS AND THE RULE OF LAW. USA-45 LABOR WORKER ATTIT ORD/FREE CONSERVE LAISSEZ ...DECISION JURID 19 SUPREME/CT. PAGE 80 E1603
CONSTN
ADJUD
STRUCT
PROF/ORG

S60

ULMER S.S.,"THE ANALYSIS OF BEHAVIOR PATTERNS ON THE UNITED STATES SUPREME COURT" USA+45 LAW CT/SYS PERS/REL RACE/REL PERSON...DECISION PSY SOC TREND METH/COMP METH 20 SUPREME/CT CIVIL/LIB. PAGE 97 E1951
ATTIT
ADJUD
PROF/ORG
INGP/REL

C60

HAZARD J.N.,"SETTLING DISPUTES IN SOVIET SOCIETY: THE FORMATIVE YEARS OF LEGAL INSTITUTIONS." USSR NAT/G PROF/ORG PROB/SOLV CONTROL CT/SYS ROUTINE REV CENTRAL...JURID BIBLIOG 20. PAGE 51 E1017
ADJUD
LAW
COM
POLICY

B61

WESTIN A.F.,THE SUPREME COURT: VIEWS FROM INSIDE. USA+45 NAT/G PROF/ORG PROVS DELIB/GP INGP/REL DISCRIM ATTIT...POLICY DECISION JURID ANTHOL 20 SUPREME/CT CONGRESS CIVIL/LIB. PAGE 106 E2114
CT/SYS
LAW
ADJUD
GOV/REL

N61

LEAGUE WOMEN VOTERS MASSACHU,THE MERIT SYSTEM IN MASSACHUSETTS (PAMPHLET). USA+45 PROVS LEGIT PARTIC CHOOSE REPRESENT GOV/REL EFFICIENCY...POLICY GOV/COMP BIBLIOG 20 MASSACHU. PAGE 64 E1274
LOC/G
LAW
SENIOR
PROF/ORG

B62

AMERICAN LAW INSTITUTE,FOREIGN RELATIONS LAW OF THE UNITED STATES: RESTATEMENT, SECOND. USA+45 NAT/G LEGIS ADJUD EXEC ROUTINE GOV/REL...INT/LAW JURID CONCPT 20 TREATY. PAGE 4 E0082
PROF/ORG
LAW
DIPLOM
ORD/FREE

B62

EVAN W.M.,LAW AND SOCIOLOGY: EXPLORATORY ESSAYS. CONSULT ACT/RES OP/RES PROB/SOLV EDU/PROP LEGIT ADJUD CT/SYS GP/REL...PHIL/SCI ANTHOL SOC/INTEG 20. PAGE 35 E0703
JURID
SOC
PROF/ORG

B62

MILLER P.,THE LEGAL MIND IN AMERICA. PROF/ORG JUDGE ADJUD CT/SYS 18/19 SUPREME/CT. PAGE 73 E1461
JURID
CONSTN
NAT/G
CONCPT

B62

ROSTOW E.V.,THE SOVEREIGN PREROGATIVE: THE SUPREME COURT AND THE QUEST FOR LAW. CONSTN CT/SYS FEDERAL MORAL SOVEREIGN 20 SUPREME/CT. PAGE 86 E1726
JURID
PROF/ORG
ATTIT
ORD/FREE

B63

ELIAS T.O.,THE NIGERIAN LEGAL SYSTEM. NIGERIA LAW FAM KIN SECT ADMIN NAT/LISM...JURID 18/20 ENGLSH/LAW COMMON/LAW. PAGE 34 E0682
CT/SYS
ADJUD
COLONIAL
PROF/ORG

S63

JOUGHIN L.,"ACADEMIC DUE PROCESS." DELIB/GP ADJUD ROUTINE ORD/FREE...POLICY MAJORIT TREND. PAGE 59 E1175
ACADEM
LAW
PROF/ORG
CLIENT

B64

EULAU H.,LAWYERS IN POLITICS: A STUDY IN PROFESSIONAL CONVERGENCE. USA+45 POL/PAR DELIB/GP GP/REL...QU 20. PAGE 35 E0701
PROF/ORG
JURID
LEGIS
ATTIT

S64

BALDWIN G.B.,"THE DEPENDENCE OF SCIENCE ON LAW AND GOVERNMENT--THE INTERNATIONAL GEOPHYSICAL YEAR--A CASE STUDY." WOR+45 LAW INT/ORG PROF/ORG LEGIS PLAN EDU/PROP...TIME/SEQ VAL/FREE 20. PAGE 8 E0144
NAT/G
KNOWL

B65

CHROUST A.H.,THE RISE OF THE LEGAL PROFESSION IN AMERICA (3 VOLS.). STRATA STRUCT POL/PAR PROF/ORG COLONIAL LEAD REV SKILL...SOC 17/20. PAGE 22 E0437
JURID
USA-45
CT/SYS
LAW

B65

HOLDSWORTH W.S.,A HISTORY OF ENGLISH LAW; THE CENTURIES OF SETTLEMENT AND REFORM (VOL. XV). UK CONSTN SECT LEGIS JUDGE WRITING ADJUD CT/SYS CRIME OWN...JURID IDEA/COMP 18 PARLIAMENT ENGLSH/LAW COMMON/LAW. PAGE 54 E1082
LAW
INDUS
PROF/ORG
ATTIT

B65

MARTENS E.,DIE HANNOVERSCHE KIRCHENKOMMISSION. GERMANY LAW INT/ORG PROVS SECT CONFER GP/REL CATHISM 16/20. PAGE 69 E1371
JURID
DELIB/GP
CONSTN
PROF/ORG

B65

RADZINOWICZ L.,THE NEED FOR CRIMINOLOGY AND A PROPOSAL FOR AN INSTITUTE OF CRIMINOLOGY. FUT UK USA+45 SOCIETY ACT/RES PROB/SOLV CRIME...PSY SOC BIBLIOG 20. PAGE 83 E1666
CRIMLGY
PROF/ORG
ACADEM
CONTROL

B65

RENNER K.,MENSCH UND GESELLSCHAFT - GRUNDRISS EINER SOZIOLOGIE (2ND ED.). STRATA FAM LABOR PROF/ORG WAR ...JURID CLASSIF 20. PAGE 84 E1685
SOC
STRUCT
NAT/G
SOCIETY

B65

UNESCO,INTERNATIONAL ORGANIZATIONS IN THE SOCIAL SCIENCES(REV. ED.). LAW ADMIN ATTIT...CRIMLGY GEOG INT/LAW PSY SOC STAT 20 UNESCO. PAGE 98 E1962
INT/ORG
R+D
PROF/ORG
ACT/RES

B65

UNESCO,HANDBOOK OF INTERNATIONAL EXCHANGES. COM/IND R+D ACADEM PROF/ORG VOL/ASSN CREATE TEC/DEV EDU/PROP AGREE 20 TREATY. PAGE 98 E1963
INDEX
INT/ORG
DIPLOM
PRESS

S65

HAZARD J.N.,"CO-EXISTENCE LAW BOWS OUT." WOR+45 R+D INT/ORG VOL/ASSN CONSULT DELIB/GP ACT/RES CREATE PEACE KNOWL...JURID CONCPT COLD/WAR VAL/FREE 20. PAGE 51 E1018
PROF/ORG
ADJUD

B66

BAXTER M.G.,DANIEL WEBSTER & THE SUPREME COURT. LAW NAT/G PROF/ORG DEBATE ADJUD LEAD FEDERAL PERSON. PAGE 8 E0156
CONSTN
CT/SYS
JURID

B66

BRENNAN J.T.,THE COST OF THE AMERICAN JUDICIAL SYSTEM. USA+45 PROF/ORG TV ADMIN EFFICIENCY. PAGE 15 E0292
COST
CT/SYS
ADJUD
JURID

B66

CARLIN J.E.,LAWYER'S ETHICS. CLIENT STRUCT CONSULT PERS/REL PWR...JURID OBS CHARTS 20. PAGE 19 E0378
ATTIT
PROF/ORG
INT

FISCHER H.,EINER IM VORDERGRUND: TARAS FASCISM
BORODAJKEWYCZ. AUSTRIA POL/PAR PROF/ORG EDU/PROP LAW
CT/SYS ORD/FREE 20 NAZI. PAGE 38 E0754 ATTIT
PRESS
B66

HOLDSWORTH W.S.,A HISTORY OF ENGLISH LAW; THE BIOG
CENTURIES OF SETTLEMENT AND REFORM (VOL. XVI). UK PERSON
LOC/G NAT/G EX/STRUC LEGIS CT/SYS LEAD ATTIT PROF/ORG
...POLICY DECISION JURID IDEA/COMP 18 PARLIAMENT. LAW
PAGE 54 E1083
B66

KUNSTLER W.M.,"DEEP IN MY HEART" USA+45 LAW CT/SYS
PROF/ORG SECT LOBBY PARTIC CROWD DISCRIM ROLE RACE/REL
...BIOG 20 KING/MAR/L NEGRO CIV/RIGHTS SOUTH/US. ADJUD
PAGE 62 E1233 CONSULT
B66

MOSKOW M.H.,TEACHERS AND UNIONS. SCHOOL WORKER EDU/PROP
ADJUD LOBBY ATTIT ORD/FREE 20. PAGE 75 E1501 PROF/ORG
LABOR
BARGAIN
B66

SOBEL N.R.,THE NEW CONFESSION STANDARDS, MIRANDA V. JURID
ARIZONA. USA+45 USA-45 LAW PROF/ORG EDU/PROP 20 CT/SYS
SUPREME/CT. PAGE 92 E1849 ORD/FREE
ADJUD
B66

BEAL E.F.,THE PRACTICE OF COLLECTIVE BARGAINING BARGAIN
(3RD ED.). USA+45 WOR+45 ECO/DEV INDUS LG/CO MGT
PROF/ORG WORKER ECO/TAC GP/REL WEALTH...JURID LABOR
METH/CNCPT. PAGE 8 E0160 ADJUD
B67

LENG S.C.,JUSTICE IN COMMUNIST CHINA: A SURVEY OF CT/SYS
THE JUDICIAL SYSTEM OF THE CHINESE PEOPLE'S ADJUD
REPUBLIC. CHINA/COM LAW CONSTN LOC/G NAT/G PROF/ORG JURID
CONSULT FORCES ADMIN CRIME ORD/FREE...BIBLIOG 20 MARXISM
MAO. PAGE 64 E1284
B67

US SENATE COMM ON FOREIGN REL,USIA FOREIGN SERVICE DIPLOM
PERSONNEL SYSTEM. USA+45 LAW CONSULT ADMIN 20 USIA. EDU/PROP
PAGE 102 E2038 PRIVIL
PROF/ORG

PROFESSIONAL ORGANIZATION....SEE PROF/ORG

PROFIT....SEE ALSO ECO

LEITZ F.,DIE PUBLIZITAT DER AKTIENGESELLSCHAFT. LG/CO
BELGIUM FRANCE GERMANY UK FINAN PRESS GP/REL PROFIT JURID
KNOWL 20. PAGE 64 E1282 ECO/TAC
NAT/COMP
B29

COOKE C.A.,CORPORATION TRUST AND COMPANY: AN ESSAY LG/CO
IN LEGAL HISTORY. UK STRUCT LEGIS CAP/ISM GP/REL FINAN
PROFIT 13/20 COMPNY/ACT. PAGE 25 E0499 ECO/TAC
JURID
B51

US HOUSE WAYS MEANS COMMITTEE,TRAFFIC IN, AND BIO/SOC
CONTROL OF NARCOTICS, BARBITURATES, AND CONTROL
AMPHETAMINES. CHINA/COM USA+45 SOCIETY LEGIS PROB/SOLV
ACT/RES EDU/PROP CT/SYS SANCTION PROFIT HEALTH CRIME
...HEAL PSY STAT 20. PAGE 100 E2011
B56

BROOKS T.R.,TOIL AND TROUBLE, A HISTORY OF AMERICAN INDUS
LABOR. WORKER BARGAIN CAP/ISM ADJUD AUTOMAT EXEC LABOR
GP/REL RACE/REL EFFICIENCY INCOME PROFIT MARXISM LEGIS
17/20 KENNEDY/JF AFL/CIO NEGRO. PAGE 16 E0310
B64

DAVIS K.,BUSINESS AND ITS ENVIRONMENT. LAW ECO/DEV EX/STRUC
INDUS OP/RES ADMIN CONTROL ROUTINE GP/REL PROFIT PROB/SOLV
POLICY. PAGE 29 E0573 CAP/ISM
EXEC
B66

BERNHARD R.C.,"COMPETITION IN LAW AND ECONOMICS." MARKET
LAW PLAN PRICE CONTROL PRODUC PROFIT...METH/CNCPT POLICY
IDEA/COMP GEN/LAWS 20. PAGE 11 E0210 NAT/G
CT/SYS
L67

DOUTY H.M.," REFERENCE TO DEVELOPING COUNTRIES." TAX
JAMAICA MALAYSIA UK WOR+45 LAW FINAN ACT/RES BUDGET ECO/UNDEV
CAP/ISM ECO/TAC TARIFFS RISK EFFICIENCY PROFIT NAT/G
...CHARTS 20. PAGE 33 E0646
S67

SCHELLING T.C.,"ECONOMICS AND CRIMINAL ENTERPRISE." CRIME
LAW FORCES BARGAIN ECO/TAC CONTROL GAMBLE ROUTINE PROB/SOLV
ADJUST DEMAND INCOME PROFIT CRIMLGY. PAGE 87 E1756 CONCPT
S67

PROFUMO/J....JOHN PROFUMO, THE PROFUMO AFFAIR

PROG/TEAC....PROGRAMMED INSTRUCTION

EWALD R.F.,"ONE OF MANY POSSIBLE GAMES." ACADEM SIMUL
INT/ORG ARMS/CONT...INT/LAW GAME. PAGE 36 E0706 HYPO/EXP
PROG/TEAC
RECORD
S66

PROGRAMMED INSTRUCTION....SEE PROG/TEAC

PROGRAMMING....SEE COMPUTER

PROGRSV/M....PROGRESSIVE MOVEMENT (ALL NATIONS)

PROJ/TEST....PROJECTIVE TESTS

PROJECTION....SEE DISPL

PROPAGANDA....SEE EDU/PROP

PROPERTY TAX....SEE PROPERTY/TX

PROPERTY/TX....PROPERTY TAX

PROSTITUTN....SEE ALSO SEX + CRIME

SKOLNICK J.H.,JUSTICE WITHOUT TRIAL: LAW FORCES
ENFORCEMENT IN DEMOCRATIC SOCIETY. USA+45 LAW CRIMLGY
TRIBUTE RACE/REL BIO/SOC PERSON...PSY SOC 20 NEGRO CRIME
BUREAUCRCY PROSTITUTN. PAGE 92 E1836
B66

PROTECTNSM....PROTECTIONISM

PROTEST....SEE COERCE

PROTESTANT....PROTESTANTS, PROTESTANTISM

GONNER R.,DAS KIRCHENPATRONATRECHT IM JURID
GROSSHERZOGTUM BADEN. GERMANY LAW PROVS DEBATE SECT
ATTIT CATHISM 14/19 PROTESTANT CHRISTIAN CHURCH/STA NAT/G
BADEN. PAGE 44 E0882 GP/REL
B62

SMITH E.A.,CHURCH AND STATE IN YOUR COMMUNITY. GP/REL
USA+45 PROVS SCHOOL ACT/RES CT/SYS PARTIC ATTIT SECT
MORAL ORD/FREE CATHISM 20 PROTESTANT CHURCH/STA. NAT/G
PAGE 92 E1842 NEIGH
B63

SMITH E.A.,CHURCH-STATE RELATIONS IN ECUMENICAL NAT/G
PERSPECTIVE. WOR+45 LAW MUNIC INGP/REL DISCRIM SECT
ATTIT SUPEGO ORD/FREE CATHISM...PHIL/SCI IDEA/COMP GP/REL
20 PROTESTANT ECUMENIC CHURCH/STA CHRISTIAN. ADJUD
PAGE 92 E1843
B66

PROUDHON/P....PIERRE JOSEPH PROUDHON

PROVS....STATE AND PROVINCES

KEITT L.,AN ANNOTATED BIBLIOGRAPHY OF BIBLIOG/A
BIBLIOGRAPHIES OF STATUTORY MATERIALS OF THE UNITED LAW
STATES. CHRIST-17C USA-45 LEGIS ADJUD COLONIAL CONSTN
CT/SYS...JURID 16/20. PAGE 60 E1196 PROVS
N

NEW YORK STATE LIBRARY,CHECKLIST OF OFFICIAL BIBLIOG
PUBLICATIONS OF THE STATE OF NEW YORK. USA+45 PROVS
USA-45 LAW PROB/SOLV LEAD ATTIT 19/20. PAGE 77 WRITING
E1539 GOV/REL
N

DE TOCQUEVILLE A.,DEMOCRACY IN AMERICA (VOLUME USA-45
ONE). LAW SOCIETY STRUCT NAT/G POL/PAR PROVS FORCES TREND
LEGIS TOP/EX DIPLOM LEGIT WAR PEACE ATTIT SOVEREIGN
...SELF/OBS TIME/SEQ CONGRESS 19. PAGE 30 E0594
B00

GROTIUS H.,DE JURE BELLI AC PACIS. CHRIST-17C UNIV JURID
LAW SOCIETY PROVS LEGIT PEACE PERCEPT MORAL PWR INT/LAW
...CONCPT CON/ANAL GEN/LAWS. PAGE 48 E0952 WAR
B00

GOODNOW F.J.,THE PRINCIPLES OF THE ADMINISTRATIVE ADMIN
B05

LAW OF THE UNITED STATES. USA-45 LAW STRUCT
EX/STRUC LEGIS BAL/PWR CONTROL GOV/REL PWR...JURID
19/20 CIVIL/SERV. PAGE 45 E0887
NAT/G
PROVS
LOC/G

B08

WILSON W.,CONSTITUTIONAL GOVERNMENT IN THE UNITED
STATES. USA-45 LAW POL/PAR PROVS CHIEF LEGIS
BAL/PWR ADJUD EXEC FEDERAL PWR 18/20 SUPREME/CT
HOUSE/REP SENATE. PAGE 106 E2130
NAT/G
GOV/REL
CONSTN
PARL/PROC

B09

LOBINGIER C.S.,THE PEOPLE'S LAW OR POPULAR
PARTICIPATION IN LAW-MAKING. FRANCE SWITZERLND UK
LOC/G NAT/G PROVS LEGIS SUFF MAJORITY PWR POPULISM
...GOV/COMP BIBLIOG 19. PAGE 66 E1314
CONSTN
LAW
PARTIC

B10

COLORADO CIVIL SERVICE COMN,SECOND BIENNIAL REPORT
TO THE GOVERNOR, 1909-1910. USA-45 DELIB/GP LEGIS
LICENSE PAY 20 COLORADO CIVIL/SERV. PAGE 24 E0477
PROVS
LOC/G
ADMIN
WORKER

B12

BEARD C.A.,THE SUPREME COURT AND THE CONSTITUTION.
LAW NAT/G PROVS LEGIS GOV/REL ATTIT POPULISM
SUPREME/CT. PAGE 9 E0164
CONSTN
CT/SYS
ADJUD
CONTROL

B12

GRIFFIN A.P.C.,SELECT LIST OF REFERENCES ON
IMPEACHMENT (REV. ED.) (PAMPHLET). USA-45 LAW PROVS
ADJUD ATTIT...JURID 19/20 NEGRO. PAGE 47 E0935
BIBLIOG/A
CONSTN
NAT/G
LEGIS

B19

LONDON SCHOOL ECONOMICS-POL,ANNUAL DIGEST OF PUBLIC
INTERNATIONAL LAW CASES. INT/ORG MUNIC NAT/G PROVS
ADMIN NEUTRAL WAR GOV/REL PRIVIL 20. PAGE 66 E1323
BIBLIOG/A
INT/LAW
ADJUD
DIPLOM

N19

BRENNAN W.J. JR.,THE BILL OF RIGHTS AND THE STATES
(PAMPHLET). USA-45 USA-45 LEGIS BAL/PWR ADJUD
CT/SYS FEDERAL PWR SOVEREIGN 18/20 SUPREME/CT
BILL/RIGHT. PAGE 15 E0293
CONSTN
PROVS
GOV/REL
ORD/FREE

N19

BURRUS B.R.,INVESTIGATION AND DISCOVERY IN STATE
ANTITRUST (PAMPHLET). USA+45 USA-45 LEGIS ECO/TAC
ADMIN CONTROL CT/SYS CRIME GOV/REL PWR...JURID
CHARTS 19/20 FTC MONOPOLY. PAGE 18 E0346
NAT/G
PROVS
LAW
INSPECT

N19

HOGARTY R.A.,NEW JERSEY FARMERS AND MIGRANT HOUSING
RULES (PAMPHLET). USA+45 LAW ELITES FACE/GP LABOR
PROF/ORG LOBBY PERS/REL RIGID/FLEX ROLE 20
NEW/JERSEY. PAGE 53 E1067
AGRI
PROVS
WORKER
HEALTH

N19

MISSISSIPPI ADVISORY COMMITTEE,REPORT ON
MISSISSIPPI (PAMPHLET). USA+45 LAW PROVS FORCES
ADJUD PWR...SOC/WK INT 20 MISSISSIPP NEGRO
CIV/RIGHTS. PAGE 73 E1469
RACE/REL
DISCRIM
COERCE
ORD/FREE

N19

RALSTON A.,A FRESH LOOK AT LEGISLATIVE
APPORTIONMENT IN NEW JERSEY (PAMPHLET). USA+45
CONSTN LEGIS OBJECTIVE...MATH METH 20 NEW/JERSEY.
PAGE 83 E1671
APPORT
REPRESENT
PROVS
JURID

C20

BLACHLY F.F.,"THE GOVERNMENT AND ADMINISTRATION OF
GERMANY." GERMANY CONSTN LOC/G PROVS DELIB/GP
EX/STRUC FORCES LEGIS TOP/EX CT/SYS...BIBLIOG/A
19/20. PAGE 12 E0235
NAT/G
GOV/REL
ADMIN
PHIL/SCI

B21

BRYCE J.,MODERN DEMOCRACIES. FUT NEW/ZEALND USA-45
LAW CONSTN POL/PAR PROVS VOL/ASSN EX/STRUC LEGIS
LEGIT CT/SYS EXEC KNOWL CONGRESS AUSTRAL 20.
PAGE 16 E0322
NAT/G
TREND

B28

NORTON T.J.,LOSING LIBERTY JUDICIALLY. PROVS LEGIS
BAL/PWR CT/SYS...JURID 18/20 SUPREME/CT CIV/RIGHTS
CONGRESS. PAGE 78 E1557
NAT/G
ORD/FREE
CONSTN
JUDGE

B30

BIRD F.L.,THE RECALL OF PUBLIC OFFICERS; A STUDY OF
THE OPERATION OF RECALL IN CALIFORNIA. LOC/G MUNIC
POL/PAR PROVS PROB/SOLV ADJUD PARTIC...CHARTS
METH/COMP 20 CALIFORNIA RECALL. PAGE 12 E0230
REPRESENT
SANCTION
CHOOSE
LAW

B30

BYNKERSHOEK C.,QUAESTIONUM JURIS PUBLICI LIBRI DUO.
INT/ORG

CHRIST-17C MOD/EUR CONSTN ELITES SOCIETY NAT/G
PROVS EX/STRUC FORCES TOP/EX BAL/PWR DIPLOM ATTIT
MORAL...TRADIT CONCPT. PAGE 18 E0352
LAW
NAT/LISM
INT/LAW

B30

GREEN F.M.,CONSTITUTIONAL DEVELOPMENT IN THE SOUTH
ATLANTIC STATES, 1776-1860; A STUDY IN THE
EVOLUTION OF DEMOCRACY. USA-45 ELITES SOCIETY
STRATA ECO/DEV AGRI POL/PAR EX/STRUC LEGIS CT/SYS
REGION...BIBLIOG 18/19 MARYLAND VIRGINIA GEORGIA
NORTH/CAR SOUTH/CAR. PAGE 46 E0905
CONSTN
PROVS
PLURISM
REPRESENT

B35

DE TOCQUEVILLE A.,DEMOCRACY IN AMERICA (4 VOLS.)
(TRANS. BY HENRY REEVE). CONSTN STRUCT LOC/G NAT/G
POL/PAR PROVS ETIQUET CT/SYS MAJORITY ATTIT 18/19.
PAGE 30 E0595
POPULISM
MAJORIT
ORD/FREE
SOCIETY

B35

KENNEDY W.P.,THE LAW AND CUSTOM OF THE SOUTH
AFRICAN CONSTITUTION. AFR SOUTH/AFR KIN LOC/G PROVS
DIPLOM ADJUD ADMIN EXEC 20. PAGE 60 E1203
CT/SYS
CONSTN
JURID
PARL/PROC

B35

MCLAUGHLIN A.C.,A CONSTITUTIONAL HISTORY OF THE
UNITED STATES. USA+45 USA-45 LOC/G NAT/G PROVS
LEGIS JUDGE ADJUD...T 18/20. PAGE 71 E1422
CONSTN
DECISION

B36

CHAMBERLAIN J.P.,LEGISLATIVE PROCESS: NATION AND
STATE. LAW DELIB/GP ROUTINE. PAGE 21 E0414
CON/ANAL
PROVS
LEGIS
NAT/G

B36

GRAVES W.B.,AMERICAN STATE GOVERNMENT. CONSTN FINAN
EX/STRUC FORCES LEGIS BUDGET TAX CT/SYS REPRESENT
GOV/REL...BIBLIOG/A 19/20. PAGE 45 E0900
NAT/G
PROVS
ADMIN
FEDERAL

B38

CLARK J.P.,THE RISE OF A NEW FEDERALISM. LEGIS
TARIFFS EFFICIENCY NAT/LISM UTIL...JURID SOC
GEN/LAWS BIBLIOG 19/20. PAGE 23 E0451
FEDERAL
PROVS
NAT/G
GOV/REL

B38

POUND R.,THE FORMATIVE ERA OF AMERICAN LAW. CULTURE
NAT/G PROVS LEGIS ADJUD CT/SYS PERSON SOVEREIGN
...POLICY IDEA/COMP GEN/LAWS 18/19. PAGE 82 E1637
CONSTN
LAW
CREATE
JURID

B44

BEARD C.A.,AMERICAN GOVERNMENT AND POLITICS (REV.
ED.). CONSTN MUNIC POL/PAR PROVS EX/STRUC LEGIS
TOP/EX CT/SYS GOV/REL...BIBLIOG T 18/20. PAGE 9
E0165
LEAD
USA-45
NAT/G
LOC/G

B45

US LIBRARY OF CONGRESS,CONSTITUTIONAL AND STATUTORY
PROVISIONS OF THE STATES (VOL. I). USA-45 CREATE
TAX CT/SYS CHOOSE SUFF INCOME PWR 20. PAGE 101
E2016
CONSTN
FEDERAL
PROVS
JURID

B48

STOKES W.S.,BIBLIOGRAPHY OF STANDARD AND CLASSICAL
WORKS IN THE FIELDS OF AMERICAN POLITICAL SCIENCE.
USA+45 USA-45 POL/PAR PROVS FORCES DIPLOM ADMIN
CT/SYS APPORT 20 CONGRESS PRESIDENT. PAGE 94 E1876
BIBLIOG
NAT/G
LOC/G
CONSTN

C48

WALKER H.,"THE LEGISLATIVE PROCESS; LAWMAKING IN
THE UNITED STATES." NAT/G POL/PAR PROVS EX/STRUC
OP/RES PROB/SOLV CT/SYS LOBBY GOV/REL...CHARTS
BIBLIOG T 18/20 CONGRESS. PAGE 105 E2094
PARL/PROC
LEGIS
LAW
CONSTN

B50

BROWN E.S.,MANUAL OF GOVERNMENT PUBLICATIONS.
WOR+45 WOR-45 CONSTN INT/ORG MUNIC PROVS DIPLOM
ADMIN 20. PAGE 16 E0313
BIBLIOG/A
NAT/G
LAW

B50

FRAGA IRIBARNE M.,RAZAS Y RACISMO IN NORTEAMERICA.
USA+45 CONSTN STRATA NAT/G PROVS ATTIT...SOC CONCPT
19/20 NEGRO. PAGE 39 E0783
RACE/REL
JURID
LAW
DISCRIM

B50

JENKINS W.S.,A GUIDE TO THE MICROFILM COLLECTION OF
EARLY STATE RECORDS. USA+45 CONSTN MUNIC LEGIS
PRESS ADMIN CT/SYS 18/20. PAGE 58 E1152
BIBLIOG
PROVS
AUD/VIS

B50

MERRIAM C.E.,THE AMERICAN PARTY SYSTEM; AN
INTRODUCTION TO THE STUDY OF POLITICAL PARTIES IN
POL/PAR
CHOOSE

THE UNITED STATES (4TH ED.). USA+45 USA-45 LAW FINAN LOC/G NAT/G PROVS LEAD PARTIC CRIME ATTIT 18/20 NEGRO CONGRESS PRESIDENT. PAGE 72 E1442
SUFF REPRESENT

B51
ANDERSON W.,STATE AND LOCAL GOVERNMENT IN THE UNITED STATES. USA+45 CONSTN POL/PAR EX/STRUC LEGIS BUDGET TAX ADJUD CT/SYS CHOOSE...CHARTS T 20. PAGE 5 E0094
LOC/G MUNIC PROVS GOV/REL

B51
CAMPBELL E.H.,UNITED STATES CITIZENSHIP AND QUALIFICATIONS FOR VOTING IN WASHINGTON. USA+45 NAT/G PROVS...CHARTS BIBLIOG 20 WASHINGT/G. PAGE 19 E0371
LAW CONSTN SUFF CHOOSE

B51
GIBBS C.R.,CONSTITUTIONAL AND STATUTORY PROVISIONS OF THE STATES (VOL. IX). USA+45 LICENSE ADJUD LEAD 20. PAGE 43 E0857
PROVS CONSTN JURID LOBBY

B52
COUNCIL STATE GOVERNMENTS,OCCUPATIONAL LICENSING IN THE STATES. USA+45 PROVS ADMIN EXEC LOBBY 20. PAGE 27 E0526
PROF/ORG LICENSE REPRESENT EX/STRUC

B52
GELLHORN W.,THE STATES AND SUBVERSION. USA+45 USA-45 LOC/G DELIB/GP LEGIS EDU/PROP LEGIT CT/SYS REGION PEACE ATTIT ORD/FREE SOCISM...INT CON/ANAL 20 CALIFORNIA MARYLAND ILLINOIS MICHIGAN NEW/YORK. PAGE 43 E0845
PROVS JURID

S52
DE GRAZIA A.,"GENERAL THEORY OF APPORTIONMENT" (BMR)" USA+45 USA-45 CONSTN ELITES DELIB/GP PARTIC REV CHOOSE...JURID 20. PAGE 29 E0582
APPORT LEGIS PROVS REPRESENT

B53
UNESCO,A REGISTER OF LEGAL DOCUMENTATION IN THE WORLD. WOR+45 WOR-45 NAT/G PROVS DELIB/GP LEGIS 13/20. PAGE 98 E1959
BIBLIOG CONSTN LAW JURID

B54
BINANI G.D.,INDIA AT A GLANCE (REV. ED.). INDIA COM/IND FINAN INDUS LABOR PROVS SCHOOL PLAN DIPLOM INT/TRADE ADMIN...JURID 20. PAGE 12 E0229
INDEX CON/ANAL NAT/G ECO/UNDEV

B54
O'NEILL J.M.,CATHOLICS IN CONTROVERSY. USA+45 NAT/G PROVS SCHOOL SECT EDU/PROP LEGIT CT/SYS SANCTION GP/REL 20 SUPREME/CT CHURCH/STA. PAGE 78 E1569
CATHISM CONSTN POLICY LAW

B54
SCHWARTZ B.,FRENCH ADMINISTRATIVE LAW AND THE COMMON-LAW WORLD. FRANCE CULTURE LOC/G NAT/G PROVS DELIB/GP EX/STRUC LEGIS PROB/SOLV CT/SYS EXEC GOV/REL...IDEA/COMP ENGLSH/LAW. PAGE 89 E1786
JURID LAW METH/COMP ADJUD

C54
CALDWELL L.K.,"THE GOVERNMENT AND ADMINISTRATION OF NEW YORK." LOC/G MUNIC POL/PAR SCHOOL CHIEF LEGIS PLAN TAX CT/SYS...MGT SOC/WK BIBLIOG 20 NEWYORK/C. PAGE 19 E0365
PROVS ADMIN CONSTN EX/STRUC

B55
BEANEY W.M.,THE RIGHT TO COUNSEL IN AMERICAN COURTS. UK USA+45 USA-45 LAW NAT/G PROVS COLONIAL PERCEPT 18/20 SUPREME/CT AMEND/VI AMEND/XIV ENGLSH/LAW. PAGE 8 E0163
ADJUD CONSTN CT/SYS

B55
GUAITA A.,BIBLIOGRAFIA ESPANOLA DE DERECHO ADMINISTRATIVO (PAMPHLET). SPAIN LOC/G MUNIC NAT/G PROVS JUDGE BAL/PWR GOV/REL OWN...JURID 18/19. PAGE 48 E0959
BIBLIOG ADMIN CONSTN PWR

B55
KHADDURI M.,WAR AND PEACE IN THE LAW OF ISLAM. CONSTN CULTURE SOCIETY STRATA NAT/G PROVS SECT FORCES TOP/EX CREATE DOMIN EDU/PROP ADJUD COERCE ATTIT RIGID/FLEX ALL/VALS...CONCPT TIME/SEQ TOT/POP VAL/FREE. PAGE 61 E1209
ISLAM JURID PEACE WAR

B55
PULLEN W.R.,A CHECK LIST OF LEGISLATIVE JOURNALS ISSUED SINCE 1937 BY THE STATES OF THE UNITED STATES OF AMERICA (PAMPHLET). USA+45 USA-45 LAW WRITING ADJUD ADMIN...JURID 20. PAGE 83 E1662
BIBLIOG PROVS EDU/PROP LEGIS

B55
ZABEL O.H.,GOD AND CAESAR IN NEBRASKA: A STUDY OF LEGAL RELATIONSHIP OF CHURCH AND STATE, 1854-1954. TAX GIVE ADMIN CONTROL GP/REL ROLE...GP/COMP 19/20 NEBRASKA. PAGE 108 E2168
SECT PROVS LAW EDU/PROP

S55
CAHN E.,"A DANGEROUS MYTH IN THE SCHOOL SEGREGATION CASES" (BMR)" USA+45 CONSTN PROVS ADJUD DISCRIM ...POLICY MYTH SOC/INTEG 20 SUPREME/CT AMEND/XIV. PAGE 18 E0360
JURID SCHOOL RACE/REL

B56
NOTZ R.L.,FEDERAL GRANTS-IN-AID TO STATES: ANALYSIS OF LAWS IN FORCE ON SEPTEMBER 10, 1956. USA+45 LAW SCHOOL PLAN ECO/TAC TAX RECEIVE...HEAL JURID 20. PAGE 78 E1558
GIVE NAT/G PROVS GOV/REL

B57
CHICAGO U LAW SCHOOL,CONFERENCE ON JUDICIAL ADMINISTRATION. LOC/G MUNIC NAT/G PROVS...ANTHOL 20. PAGE 22 E0429
CT/SYS ADJUD ADMIN GOV/REL

B57
MORELAND C.C.,EQUAL JUSTICE UNDER LAW. USA+45 USA-45 PROF/ORG PROVS JUDGE...POLICY JURID. PAGE 74 E1491
CONSTN ADJUD CT/SYS ORD/FREE

B58
BLOCH J.,STATES' RIGHTS: THE LAW OF THE LAND. USA+45 USA-45 LAW CONSTN LEGIS CONTROL CT/SYS FEDERAL ORD/FREE...PREDICT 17/20 CONGRESS SUPREME/CT. PAGE 13 E0246
PROVS NAT/G BAL/PWR CENTRAL

B58
HENKIN L.,ARMS CONTROL AND INSPECTION IN AMERICAN LAW. LAW CONSTN INT/ORG LOC/G MUNIC NAT/G PROVS EDU/PROP LEGIT EXEC NUC/PWR KNOWL ORD/FREE...OBS TOT/POP CONGRESS 20. PAGE 52 E1032
USA+45 JURID ARMS/CONT

B58
O'BRIEN F.W.,JUSTICE REED AND THE FIRST AMENDMENT, THE RELIGION CLAUSES. USA+45 USA-45 NAT/G PROVS CONTROL FEDERAL...POLICY JURID TIME/SEQ 20 SUPREME/CT CHRUCH/STA AMEND/I REED/STAN. PAGE 78 E1563
ADJUD SECT CT/SYS

B58
SPITZ D.,DEMOCRACY AND THE CHALLANGE OF POWER. FUT USA+45 USA-45 LAW SOCIETY STRUCT LOC/G POL/PAR PROVS DELIB/GP EX/STRUC LEGIS TOP/EX ACT/RES CREATE DOMIN EDU/PROP LEGIT ADJUD ADMIN ATTIT DRIVE MORAL ORD/FREE TOT/POP. PAGE 93 E1862
NAT/G PWR

B58
WOOD J.E.,CHURCH AND STATE IN SCRIPTURE HISTORY AND CONSTITUTIONAL LAW. LAW CONSTN SOCIETY PROVS VOL/ASSN BAL/PWR COLONIAL CT/SYS ATTIT...BIBLIOG 20 SUPREME/CT CHURCH/STA BIBLE. PAGE 107 E2142
GP/REL SECT NAT/G ADJUD

B59
COUNCIL OF STATE GOVERNMENTS,STATE GOVERNMENT: AN ANNOTATED BIBLIOGRAPHY (PAMPHLET). USA+45 LAW AGRI INDUS WORKER PLAN TAX ADJUST AGE/Y ORD/FREE...HEAL MGT 20. PAGE 26 E0521
BIBLIOG/A PROVS LOC/G ADMIN

B59
COUNCIL OF STATE GOVERNORS,AMERICAN LEGISLATURES: STRUCTURE AND PROCEDURES. SUMMARY AND TABULATIONS OF A 1959 SURVEY. PUERT/RICO USA+45 PAY ADJUD ADMIN APPORT...IDEA/COMP 20 GUAM VIRGIN/ISL. PAGE 27 E0525
LEGIS CHARTS PROVS REPRESENT

B59
HAYS B.,A SOUTHERN MODERATE SPEAKS. LAW PROVS SCHOOL KNOWL...JURID SOC SELF/OBS BIOG 20 NEGRO SUPREME/CT. PAGE 51 E1015
SECT DISCRIM CT/SYS RACE/REL

B59
MOOS M.,THE CAMPUS AND THE STATE. LAW FINAN DELIB/GP LEGIS EXEC LOBBY GP/REL PWR...POLICY BIBLIOG. PAGE 74 E1489
EDU/PROP ACADEM PROVS CONTROL

B59
PAULSEN M.G.,LEGAL INSTITUTIONS TODAY AND TOMORROW. UK USA+45 NAT/G PROF/ORG PROVS ADMIN PARL/PROC ORD/FREE NAT/COMP. PAGE 80 E1604
JURID ADJUD JUDGE LEGIS

B59
REOCK E.C.,PROCEDURES AND STANDARDS FOR THE APPORTIONMENT OF STATE LEGISLATURES (DOCTORAL
PROVS LOC/G

THESIS). USA+45 POL/PAR LEGIS TEC/DEV ADJUD | APPORT
BIBLIOG. PAGE 84 E1686 | REPRESENT

B59

SURRENCY E.C., A GUIDE TO LEGAL RESEARCH. USA+45 | NAT/G
ACADEM LEGIS ACT/RES ADMIN...DECISION METH/COMP | PROVS
BIBLIOG METH. PAGE 94 E1894 | ADJUD
| JURID

B59

U OF MICHIGAN LAW SCHOOL, ATOMS AND THE LAW. USA+45 | NUC/PWR
PROVS WORKER PROB/SOLV DIPLOM ADMIN GOV/REL ANTHOL. | NAT/G
PAGE 97 E1950 | CONTROL
| LAW

B59

US CONGRESS JT ATOM ENRGY COMM, SELECTED MATERIALS | NAT/G
ON FEDERAL-STATE COOPERATION IN THE ATOMIC ENERGY | NUC/PWR
FIELD. USA+45 LAW LOC/G PROVS CONSULT LEGIS ADJUD | GOV/REL
...POLICY BIBLIOG 20 AEC. PAGE 99 E1991 | DELIB/GP

S59

MURPHY W.F., "LOWER COURT CHECKS ON SUPREME COURT | CT/SYS
POWER" (BMR)" USA+45 NAT/G PROVS SCHOOL GOV/REL | BAL/PWR
RACE/REL DISCRIM ATTIT...DECISION JURID 20 | CONTROL
SUPREME/CT NEGRO. PAGE 75 E1508 | ADJUD

B60

ADRIAN C.R., STATE AND LOCAL GOVERNMENTS: A STUDY IN | LOC/G
THE POLITICAL PROCESS. USA+45 LAW FINAN MUNIC | PROVS
POL/PAR LEGIS ADJUD EXEC CHOOSE REPRESENT. PAGE 3 | GOV/REL
E0051 | ATTIT

B60

BAKER G.E., STATE CONSTITUTIONS - REAPPORTIONMENT. | APPORT
USA+45 USA-45 CONSTN CHOOSE ATTIT ORD/FREE...JURID | REPRESENT
20. PAGE 7 E0138 | PROVS
| LEGIS

B60

BAKER G.E., THE POLITICS OF REAPPORTIONMENT IN | VOL/ASSN
WASHINGTON STATE. LAW POL/PAR CREATE EDU/PROP | APPORT
PARL/PROC CHOOSE INGP/REL...CHARTS METH/COMP 20 | PROVS
WASHINGT/G LEAGUE/WV. PAGE 7 E0139 | LEGIS

B60

CARTER R.F., COMMUNITIES AND THEIR SCHOOLS. USA+45 | SCHOOL
LAW FINAN PROVS BUDGET TAX LEAD PARTIC CHOOSE...SOC | ACT/RES
INT QU 20. PAGE 20 E0401 | NEIGH
| INGP/REL

B60

FELLMAN D., THE SUPREME COURT AND EDUCATION. ACADEM | CT/SYS
NAT/G PROVS DELIB/GP ADJUD ORD/FREE...POLICY JURID | SECT
WORSHIP 20 SUPREME/CT NEGRO CHURCH/STA. PAGE 37 | RACE/REL
E0731 | SCHOOL

B60

NAT'L MUNICIPAL LEAGUE, COMPENDIUM ON LEGISLATIVE | APPORT
APPORTIONMENT. USA+45 LOC/G NAT/G POL/PAR PROVS | REPRESENT
CT/SYS CHOOSE 20 SUPREME/CT CONGRESS. PAGE 76 E1523 | LEGIS
| STAT

B60

PRASAD B., THE ORIGINS OF PROVINCIAL AUTONOMY. INDIA | CENTRAL
UK FINAN LOC/G FORCES LEGIS CONTROL CT/SYS PWR | PROVS
...JURID 19/20. PAGE 82 E1646 | COLONIAL
| NAT/G

B61

AVERY M.W., GOVERNMENT OF WASHINGTON STATE. USA+45 | PROVS
MUNIC DELIB/GP EX/STRUC LEGIS GIVE CT/SYS PARTIC | LOC/G
REGION EFFICIENCY 20 WASHINGT/G GOVERNOR. PAGE 6 | ADMIN
E0121 | GOV/REL

B61

BEASLEY K.E., STATE SUPERVISION OF MUNICIPAL DEBT IN | MUNIC
KANSAS - A CASE STUDY. USA+45 USA-45 FINAN PROVS | LOC/G
BUDGET TAX ADJUD ADMIN CONTROL SUPEGO. PAGE 9 E0167 | LEGIS
| JURID

B61

BURDETTE F.L., POLITICAL SCIENCE: A SELECTED | BIBLIOG/A
BIBLIOGRAPHY OF BOOKS IN PRINT, WITH ANNOTATIONS | GOV/COMP
(PAMPHLET). LAW LOC/G NAT/G POL/PAR PROVS DIPLOM | CONCPT
EDU/PROP ADMIN CHOOSE ATTIT 20. PAGE 17 E0330 | ROUTINE

B61

HAGEN A., STAAT UND KATHOLISCHE KIRCHE IN | SECT
WURTTEMBERG IN DEN JAHREN 1848-1862 (2 VOLS.). | PROVS
GERMANY DELIB/GP EDU/PROP MARRIAGE CATHISM 19 | GP/REL
CHURCH/STA. PAGE 49 E0975 | JURID

B61

KURLAND P.B., RELIGION AND THE LAW. USA+45 USA-45 | SECT
CONSTN PROVS CHIEF ADJUD SANCTION PRIVIL CATHISM | NAT/G

...POLICY 17/20 SUPREME/CT PRESIDENT CHURCH/STA. | CT/SYS
PAGE 62 E1239 | GP/REL

B61

MURPHY E.F., WATER PURITY: A STUDY IN LEGAL CONTROL | SEA
OF NATURAL RESOURCES. LOC/G ACT/RES PLAN TEC/DEV | LAW
LOBBY GP/REL COST ATTIT HEALTH ORD/FREE...HEAL | PROVS
JURID 20 WISCONSIN WATER. PAGE 75 E1506 | CONTROL

B61

NEW JERSEY LEGISLATURE-SENATE, PUBLIC HEARINGS | LEGIS
BEFORE COMMITTEE ON REVISION AND AMENDMENT OF LAWS | MUNIC
ON SENATE BILL NO. 8. USA+45 FINAN PROVS WORKER | INDUS
ACT/RES PLAN BUDGET TAX CRIME...IDEA/COMP 20 | PROB/SOLV
NEW/JERSEY URBAN/RNWL. PAGE 77 E1537

B61

POOLEY B.J., PLANNING AND ZONING IN THE UNITED | PLAN
STATES. USA+45 MUNIC DELIB/GP ACT/RES PROB/SOLV | LOC/G
TEC/DEV ADJUD ADMIN REGION 20 ZONING. PAGE 81 E1628 | PROVS
| LAW

B61

ROCHE J.P., COURTS AND RIGHTS: THE AMERICAN | JURID
JUDICIARY IN ACTION (2ND ED.). UK USA+45 USA-45 | CT/SYS
STRUCT TEC/DEV SANCTION PERS/REL RACE/REL ORD/FREE | NAT/G
...METH/CNCPT GOV/COMP METH/COMP T 13/20. PAGE 85 | PROVS
E1710

B61

WECHSLER H., PRINCIPLES, POLITICS AND FUNDAMENTAL | CT/SYS
LAW: SELECTED ESSAYS. USA+45 USA-45 LAW SOCIETY | CONSTN
NAT/G PROVS DELIB/GP EX/STRUC ACT/RES LEGIT PERSON | INT/LAW
KNOWL PWR...JURID 20 NUREMBERG. PAGE 105 E2106

B61

WESTIN A.F., THE SUPREME COURT: VIEWS FROM INSIDE. | CT/SYS
USA+45 NAT/G PROF/ORG PROVS DELIB/GP INGP/REL | LAW
DISCRIM ATTIT...POLICY DECISION JURID ANTHOL 20 | ADJUD
SUPREME/CT CONGRESS CIVIL/LIB. PAGE 106 E2114 | GOV/REL

L61

GERWIG R., "PUBLIC AUTHORITIES IN THE UNITED | LOC/G
STATES." LAW CONSTN PROVS TAX ADMIN FEDERAL. | MUNIC
PAGE 43 E0852 | GOV/REL
| PWR

L61

MCNAMEE B.J., "CONFLICT OF INTEREST: STATE | LAW
GOVERNMENT EMPLOYEES." USA+45 PROVS 20. PAGE 71 | REPRESENT
E1426 | ADMIN
| CONTROL

N61

LEAGUE WOMEN VOTERS MASSACHU, THE MERIT SYSTEM IN | LOC/G
MASSACHUSETTS (PAMPHLET). USA+45 PROVS LEGIT PARTIC | LAW
CHOOSE REPRESENT GOV/REL EFFICIENCY...POLICY | SENIOR
GOV/COMP BIBLIOG 20 MASSACHU. PAGE 64 E1274 | PROF/ORG

B62

BOYD W.J., PATTERNS OF APPORTIONMENT (PAMPHLET). LAW | MUNIC
CONSTN CHOOSE GOV/COMP. PAGE 14 E0282 | PROVS
| REPRESENT
| APPORT

B62

CARPER E.T., ILLINOIS GOES TO CONGRESS FOR ARMY | ADMIN
LAND. USA+45 LAW EXTR/IND PROVS REGION CIVMIL/REL | LOBBY
GOV/REL FEDERAL ATTIT 20 ILLINOIS SENATE CONGRESS | GEOG
DIRKSEN/E DOUGLAS/P. PAGE 20 E0391 | LEGIS

B62

GONNER R., DAS KIRCHENPATRONATRECHT IM | JURID
GROSSHERZOGTUM BADEN. GERMANY LAW PROVS DEBATE | SECT
ATTIT CATHISM 14/19 PROTESTANT CHRISTIAN CHURCH/STA | NAT/G
BADEN. PAGE 44 E0882 | GP/REL

B62

INSTITUTE JUDICIAL ADMIN, JUDGES: THEIR TEMPORARY | NAT/G
APPOINTMENT, ASSIGNMENT AND TRANSFER: SURVEY OF FED | LOC/G
AND STATE CONSTN'S STATUTES, ROLES OF CT. USA+45 | JUDGE
CONSTN PROVS CT/SYS GOV/REL PWR JURID. PAGE 57 | ADMIN
E1128

B62

LITTLEFIELD N., METROPOLITAN AREA PROBLEMS AND | LOC/G
MUNICIPAL HOME RULE. USA+45 PROVS ADMIN CONTROL | SOVEREIGN
GP/REL PWR. PAGE 65 E1308 | JURID
| LEGIS

B62

MCGRATH J.J., CHURCH AND STATE IN AMERICAN LAW. LAW | SECT
PROVS SCHOOL TAX GIVE CT/SYS GP/REL...POLICY ANTHOL | ADJUD
18/20 SUPREME/CT CHURCH/STA CASEBOOK. PAGE 71 E1414 | CONSTN
| NAT/G

NAT'L MUNICIPAL LEAGUE,COMPENDIUM ON LEGISLATIVE APPORTIONMENT. USA+45 LOC/G NAT/G POL/PAR PROVS CT/SYS CHOOSE 20 SUPREME/CT CONGRESS. PAGE 76 E1524
B62
APPORT
REPRESENT
LEGIS
STAT

NATIONAL MUNICIPAL LEAGUE,COURT DECISIONS ON LEGISLATIVE APPORTIONMENT (VOL. III). USA+45 JUDGE ADJUD CONTROL ATTIT...DECISION JURID COURT/DIST CASEBOOK. PAGE 76 E1528
B62
PROVS
CT/SYS
APPORT
LEGIS

NEW YORK STATE LEGISLATURE,REPORT AND DRAFT OF PROPOSED LEGISLATION ON COURT REORGANIZATION. LAW PROVS DELIB/GP CREATE ADJUD 20 NEW/YORK. PAGE 77 E1538
B62
CT/SYS
JURID
MUNIC
LOC/G

PRESS C.,STATE MANUALS, BLUE BOOKS AND ELECTION RESULTS. LAW LOC/G MUNIC LEGIS WRITING FEDERAL SOVEREIGN...DECISION STAT CHARTS 20. PAGE 82 E1648
B62
BIBLIOG
PROVS
ADMIN
CHOOSE

US COMMISSION ON CIVIL RIGHTS,EQUAL PROTECTION OF THE LAWS IN NORTH CAROLINA. USA+45 LOC/G NAT/G CONSULT LEGIS WORKER PROB/SOLV EDU/PROP ADJUD CHOOSE DISCRIM HEALTH 20 NEGRO NORTH/CAR CIV/RIGHTS. PAGE 99 E1984
B62
ORD/FREE
RESPECT
LAW
PROVS

SILVA R.C.,"LEGISLATIVE REPESENTATION - WITH SPECIAL REFERENCE TO NEW YORK." LAW CONSTN LOC/G NAT/G PROVS. PAGE 91 E1826
S62
MUNIC
LEGIS
REPRESENT
APPORT

TWENTIETH CENTURY FUND,ONE MAN - ONE VOTE (PAMPHLET). USA+45 CONSTN CONFER CT/SYS REGION CONSEN FEDERAL ROLE...CENSUS 20 CONGRESS. PAGE 97 E1947
N62
APPORT
LEGIS
REPRESENT
PROVS

US ADVISORY COMN INTERGOV REL,APPORTIONMENT OF STATE LEGISLATURES (PAMPHLET). LAW CONSTN EX/STRUC LEGIS LEAD MAJORITY. PAGE 99 E1977
N62
MUNIC
PROVS
REPRESENT
APPORT

ADRIAN C.R.,GOVERNING OVER FIFTY STATES AND THEIR COMMUNITIES. USA+45 CONSTN FINAN MUNIC NAT/G POL/PAR EX/STRUC LEGIS ADMIN CONTROL CT/SYS ...CHARTS 20. PAGE 3 E0052
B63
PROVS
LOC/G
GOV/REL
GOV/COMP

BROWN R.M.,THE SOUTH CAROLINA REGULATORS. USA-45 LEGIS LEGIT ADJUD COLONIAL CONTROL WAR...BIBLIOG/A 18 CHARLESTON SOUTH/CAR. PAGE 16 E0315
B63
ORD/FREE
JURID
PWR
PROVS

BURRUS B.R.,ADMINSTRATIVE LAW AND LOCAL GOVERNMENT. USA+45 PROVS LEGIS LICENSE ADJUD ORD/FREE 20. PAGE 18 E0347
B63
EX/STRUC
LOC/G
JURID
CONSTN

CAHN E.,THE GREAT RIGHTS. USA+45 NAT/G PROVS CIVMIL/REL...IDEA/COMP ANTHOL BIBLIOG 18/20 MADISON/J BILL/RIGHT CIV/RIGHTS WARRN/EARL BLACK/HL. PAGE 18 E0361
B63
CONSTN
LAW
ORD/FREE
INGP/REL

COUNCIL OF STATE GOVERNMENTS,INCREASED RIGHTS FOR DEFENDANTS IN STATE CRIMINAL PROSECUTIONS. USA+45 GOV/REL INGP/REL FEDERAL ORD/FREE...JURID 20 SUPREME/CT. PAGE 26 E0522
B63
CT/SYS
ADJUD
PROVS
CRIME

FORTES A.B.,HISTORIA ADMINISTRATIVA, JUDICIARIA E ECLESIASTICA DO RIO GRANDE DO SUL. BRAZIL L/A+17C LOC/G SECT COLONIAL CT/SYS ORD/FREE CATHISM 16/20. PAGE 39 E0773
B63
PROVS
ADMIN
JURID

GRANT D.R.,STATE AND LOCAL GOVERNMENT IN AMERICA. USA+45 FINAN LOC/G MUNIC EX/STRUC FORCES EDU/PROP ADMIN CHOOSE FEDERAL ATTIT...JURID 20. PAGE 45 E0897
B63
PROVS
POL/PAR
LEGIS
CONSTN

LANOUE G.R.,A BIBLIOGRAPHY OF DOCTORAL DISSERTATIONS ON POLITICS AND RELIGION. USA+45 USA-45 CONSTN PROVS DIPLOM CT/SYS MORAL...POLICY JURID CONCPT 20. PAGE 63 E1252
B63
BIBLIOG
NAT/G
LOC/G
SECT

LEAGUE WOMEN VOTERS NEW YORK,APPORTIONMENT WORKSHOP KIT. USA+45 VOL/ASSN DELIB/GP LEGIS ATTIT ORD/FREE ...METH/COMP 20 SUPREME/CT NEW/YORK. PAGE 64 E1275
B63
APPORT
REPRESENT
PROVS
JURID

LIVELY E.,THE INVASION OF MISSISSIPPI. USA+45 LAW CONSTN NAT/G PROVS CT/SYS GOV/REL FEDERAL CONSERVE ...TRADIT 20 MISSISSIPP NEGRO NAACP WARRN/EARL KENNEDY/JF. PAGE 66 E1309
B63
RACE/REL
CROWD
COERCE
MARXISM

PALOTAI O.C.,PUBLICATIONS OF THE INSTITUTE OF GOVERNMENT, 1930-1962. LAW PROVS SCHOOL WORKER ACT/RES OP/RES CT/SYS GOV/REL...CRIMLGY SOC/WK. PAGE 79 E1594
B63
BIBLIOG/A
ADMIN
LOC/G
FINAN

RAVENS J.P.,STAAT UND KATHOLISCHE KIRCHE IN PREUSSENS POLNISCHEN TEILUNGSGEBIETEN. GERMANY POLAND PRUSSIA PROVS DIPLOM EDU/PROP DEBATE NAT/LISM...JURID 18 CHURCH/STA. PAGE 83 E1674
B63
GP/REL
CATHISM
SECT
NAT/G

REOCK E.C. JR.,POPULATION INEQUALITY AMONG COUNTIES IN THE NEW JERSEY LEGISLATURE 1791-1962. PROVS ORD/FREE...CENSUS CHARTS 18/20 NEW/JERSEY. PAGE 84 E1687
B63
APPORT
REPRESENT
LEGIS
JURID

SMITH E.A.,CHURCH AND STATE IN YOUR COMMUNITY. USA+45 PROVS SCHOOL ACT/RES CT/SYS PARTIC ATTIT MORAL ORD/FREE CATHISM 20 PROTESTANT CHURCH/STA. PAGE 92 E1842
B63
GP/REL
SECT
NAT/G
NEIGH

VINES K.N.,STUDIES IN JUDICIAL POLITICS: TULANE STUDIES IN POLITICAL SCIENCE (VOL. 8). POL/PAR JUDGE ADJUD SANCTION CRIME CHOOSE PWR...JURID STAT TIME/SEQ CHARTS. PAGE 104 E2079
B63
CT/SYS
GOV/REL
PROVS

BUREAU OF NATIONAL AFFAIRS,STATE FAIR EMPLOYMENT LAWS AND THEIR ADMINISTRATION. INDUS ADJUD PERS/REL RACE/REL ATTIT ORD/FREE WEALTH 20. PAGE 17 E0338
B64
PROVS
DISCRIM
WORKER
JURID

COUNCIL OF STATE GOVERNMENTS,LEGISLATIVE APPORTIONMENT: A SUMMARY OF STATE ACTION. USA+45 LEGIS REPRESENT...POLICY SUPREME/CT. PAGE 26 E0523
B64
LOC/G
PROVS
APPORT
CT/SYS

FEINE H.E.,DIE BESETZUNG DER REICHSBISTUMER VOM WESTFALISCHEN FRIEDEN BIS ZUR SAKULARISATION. GERMANY EDU/PROP GP/REL AGE 17/19. PAGE 37 E0727
B64
CHOOSE
SECT
JURID
PROVS

FREISEN J.,STAAT UND KATHOLISCHE KIRCHE IN DEN DEUTSCHEN BUNDESSTAATEN (2 VOLS.). GERMANY LAW FAM NAT/G EDU/PROP GP/REL MARRIAGE WEALTH 19/20 CHURCH/STA. PAGE 40 E0793
B64
SECT
CATHISM
JURID
PROVS

FRIEDMANN W.G.,THE CHANGING STRUCTURE OF INTERNATIONAL LAW. WOR+45 INT/ORG NAT/G PROVS LEGIT ORD/FREE PWR...JURID CONCPT GEN/LAWS TOT/POP UN 20. PAGE 41 E0805
B64
ADJUD
TREND
INT/LAW

GOODNOW H.F.,THE CIVIL SERVICE OF PAKISTAN: BUREAUCRACY IN A NEW NATION. INDIA PAKISTAN S/ASIA ECO/UNDEV PROVS CHIEF PARTIC CHOOSE EFFICIENCY PWR ...BIBLIOG 20. PAGE 45 E0889
B64
ADMIN
GOV/REL
LAW
NAT/G

GRASMUCK E.L.,COERCITIO STAAT UND KIRCHE IM DONATISTENSTREIT. CHRIST-17C ROMAN/EMP LAW PROVS DEBATE PERSON SOVEREIGN...JURID CONCPT 4/5 AUGUSTINE CHURCH/STA ROMAN/LAW. PAGE 45 E0898
B64
GP/REL
NAT/G
SECT
COERCE

HAMILTON H.D.,LEGISLATIVE APPORTIONMENT; KEY TO POWER. USA+45 LAW CONSTN PROVS LOBBY CHOOSE ATTIT SUPREME/CT. PAGE 50 E0988
B64
APPORT
CT/SYS
LEAD
REPRESENT

HANSON R.,FAIR REPRESENTATION COMES TO MARYLAND (PAMPHLET). BAL/PWR CT/SYS CHOOSE GOV/REL 20 MARYLAND SUPREME/CT. PAGE 50 E0997
B64
APPORT
REPRESENT
PROVS
LEGIS

CHURCH/STA. PAGE 9 E0179 NAT/G

HOLT S.,THE DICTIONARY OF AMERICAN GOVERNMENT.
USA+45 LOC/G MUNIC PROVS LEGIS ADMIN JURID. PAGE 55
E1091
B64
DICTIONARY
INDEX
LAW
NAT/G

IRION F.C.,APPORTIONMENT OF THE NEW MEXICO
LEGISLATURE. NAT/G LEGIS PRESS CT/SYS ATTIT
...POLICY TIME/SEQ 19/20 SUPREME/CT. PAGE 57 E1137
B64
APPORT
REPRESENT
GOV/REL
PROVS

KEEFE W.J.,THE AMERICAN LEGISLATIVE PROCESS:
CONGRESS AND THE STATES. USA+45 LAW POL/PAR
DELIB/GP DEBATE ADMIN LOBBY REPRESENT CONGRESS
PRESIDENT. PAGE 60 E1191
B64
LEGIS
DECISION
PWR
PROVS

KISER S.L.,AMERICANISM IN ACTION. USA+45 LAW PROVS
CAP/ISM DIPLOM RECEIVE CONTROL CT/SYS WAR FEDERAL
ATTIT WEALTH 20 SUPREME/CT. PAGE 61 E1221
B64
OLD/LIB
FOR/AID
MARXISM
CONSTN

MARNELL W.H.,THE FIRST AMENDMENT: THE HISTORY OF
RELIGIOUS FREEDOM IN AMERICA. WOR+45 WOR-45 PROVS
CREATE CT/SYS...POLICY BIBLIOG/A WORSHIP 16/20.
PAGE 68 E1367
B64
CONSTN
SECT
ORD/FREE
GOV/REL

MARSHALL B.,FEDERALISM AND CIVIL RIGHTS. USA+45
PROVS BAL/PWR CONTROL CT/SYS PARTIC SOVEREIGN
...JURID 20 NEGRO CIV/RIGHTS. PAGE 68 E1369
B64
FEDERAL
ORD/FREE
CONSTN
FORCES

MITAU G.T.,PROXIMATE SOLUTIONS: CASE PROBLEMS IN
STATE AND LOCAL GOVERNMENT. USA+45 CONSTN NAT/G
CHIEF LEGIS CT/SYS EXEC GOV/REL GP/REL PWR 20
CASEBOOK. PAGE 73 E1470
B64
PROVS
LOC/G
ADJUD

MITAU G.T.,INSOLUBLE PROBLEMS: CASE PROBLEMS ON THE
FUNCTIONS OF STATE AND LOCAL GOVERNMENT. USA+45 AIR
FINAN LABOR POL/PAR PROB/SOLV TAX RECEIVE CONTROL
GP/REL 20 CASEBOOK ZONING. PAGE 73 E1471
B64
ADJUD
LOC/G
PROVS

MITCHELL B.,A BIOGRAPHY OF THE CONSTITUTION OF THE
UNITED STATES. USA+45 USA-45 PROVS CHIEF LEGIS
DEBATE ADJUD SUFF FEDERAL...SOC 18/20 SUPREME/CT
CONGRESS SENATE HOUSE/REP PRESIDENT. PAGE 73 E1472
B64
CONSTN
LAW
JURID

NEWMAN E.S.,CIVIL LIBERTY AND CIVIL RIGHTS. USA+45
USA-45 CONSTN PROVS FORCES LEGIS CT/SYS RACE/REL
ATTIT...MAJORIT JURID WORSHIP 20 SUPREME/CT NEGRO
CIV/RIGHTS CHURCH/STA. PAGE 77 E1543
B64
ORD/FREE
LAW
CONTROL
NAT/G

STOKES A.P.,CHURCH AND STATE IN THE UNITED STATES
(3 VOLS.). USA+45 USA-45 NAT/G PROVS LEGIS CT/SYS
SANCTION PRIVIL ORD/FREE 17/20 CHURCH/STA. PAGE 94
E1875
B64
SECT
CONSTN
POLICY

US HOUSE COMM ON JUDICIARY,CONGRESSIONAL
REDISTRICTING. USA+45 PROVS DELIB/GP 20 CONGRESS.
PAGE 100 E2005
B64
APPORT
REPRESENT
LEGIS
LAW

POUNDS N.J.G.,"THE POLITICS OF PARTITION." AFR ASIA
COM EUR+WWI FUT ISLAM S/ASIA USA-45 LAW ECO/DEV
ECO/UNDEV AGRI INDUS INT/ORG POL/PAR PROVS SECT
FORCES TOP/EX EDU/PROP LEGIT ATTIT MORAL ORD/FREE
PWR RESPECT WEALTH. PAGE 82 E1640
L64
NAT/G
NAT/LISM

AMERICAN ASSEMBLY COLUMBIA U,THE COURTS, THE
PUBLIC, AND THE LAW EXPLOSION. USA+45 ELITES PROVS
EDU/PROP CRIME CHOOSE PERSON ORD/FREE PWR 20.
PAGE 4 E0074
B65
CT/SYS
ADJUD
NAT/G

ANTIEU C.J.,RELIGION UNDER THE STATE CONSTITUTIONS.
USA+45 LAW SCHOOL TAX SANCTION PRIVIL ORD/FREE
...JURID 20 SUPREME/CT CHURCH/STA. PAGE 5 E0099
B65
SECT
CONSTN
PROVS
GP/REL

BEGGS D.W.,AMERICA'S SCHOOLS AND CHURCHES: PARTNERS
IN CONFLICT. USA+45 PROVS EDU/PROP ADJUD DISCRIM
ATTIT...IDEA/COMP ANTHOL BIBLIOG WORSHIP 20
B65
SECT
GP/REL
SCHOOL

CAMPBELL E.H.,SURVEYS, SUBDIVISIONS AND PLATTING,
AND BOUNDARIES: WASHINGTON STATE LAW AND JUDICIAL
DECISIONS. USA+45 LAW LOC/G...DECISION JURID
CON/ANAL BIBLIOG WASHINGT/G PARTITION WATER.
PAGE 19 E0372
B65
CONSTN
PLAN
GEOG
PROVS

COHN H.J.,THE GOVERNMENT OF THE RHINE PALATINATE IN
THE FIFTEENTH CENTURY. GERMANY FINAN LOC/G DELIB/GP
LEGIS CT/SYS CHOOSE CATHISM 14/15 PALATINATE.
PAGE 24 E0468
B65
PROVS
JURID
GP/REL
ADMIN

COLGNE A.B.,STATUTE MAKING (2ND ED.). LOC/G PROVS
CHOOSE MAJORITY...CHARTS DICTIONARY 20. PAGE 24
E0474
B65
LEGIS
LAW
CONSTN
NAT/G

COOPER F.E.,STATE ADMINISTRATIVE LAW (2 VOLS.). LAW
LEGIS PLAN TAX ADJUD CT/SYS FEDERAL PWR...CONCPT
20. PAGE 25 E0501
B65
JURID
CONSTN
ADMIN
PROVS

EHLE J.,THE FREE MEN. USA+45 NAT/G PROVS FORCES
JUDGE ADJUD ATTIT...POLICY SOC SOC/INTEG 20 NEGRO.
PAGE 34 E0677
B65
RACE/REL
ORD/FREE
DISCRIM

FELLMAN D.,RELIGION IN AMERICAN PUBLIC LAW. USA+45
USA-45 NAT/G PROVS ADJUD SANCTION GP/REL PRIVIL
ORD/FREE...JURID TIME/SEQ 18/20 SUPREME/CT
CHURCH/STA. PAGE 37 E0733
B65
SECT
CONSTN
LAW
POLICY

FISCHER F.C.,THE GOVERNMENT OF MICHIGAN. USA+45
NAT/G PUB/INST EX/STRUC LEGIS BUDGET GIVE EDU/PROP
CT/SYS CHOOSE GOV/REL...T MICHIGAN. PAGE 38 E0753
B65
PROVS
LOC/G
ADMIN
CONSTN

KAAS L.,DIE GEISTLICHE GERICHTSBARKEIT DER
KATHOLISCHEN KIRCHE IN PREUSSEN (2 VOLS.). PRUSSIA
CONSTN NAT/G PROVS SECT ADJUD ADMIN ATTIT 16/20.
PAGE 59 E1178
B65
JURID
CATHISM
GP/REL
CT/SYS

MARTENS E.,DIE HANNOVERSCHE KIRCHENKOMMISSION.
GERMANY LAW INT/ORG PROVS SECT CONFER GP/REL
CATHISM 16/20. PAGE 69 E1371
B65
JURID
DELIB/GP
CONSTN
PROF/ORG

MCKAY R.B.,REAPPORTIONMENT: THE LAW AND POLITICS OF
EQUAL REPRESENTATION. FUT USA+45 PROVS BAL/PWR
ADJUD CHOOSE REPRESENT GOV/REL FEDERAL...JURID
BIBLIOG 20 SUPREME/CT CONGRESS. PAGE 71 E1420
B65
APPORT
MAJORIT
LEGIS
PWR

NJ LEGIS REAPPORT PLAN COMM,PUBLIC HEARING ON
REDISTRICTING AND REAPPORTIONMENT. USA+45 CONSTN
VOL/ASSN LEGIS DEBATE...POLICY GEOG CENSUS 20
NEW/JERSEY. PAGE 77 E1552
B65
APPORT
REPRESENT
PROVS
JURID

PYLEE M.V.,CONSTITUTIONAL GOVERNMENT IN INDIA (2ND
REV. ED.). INDIA POL/PAR EX/STRUC DIPLOM COLONIAL
CT/SYS PARL/PROC PRIVIL...JURID 16/20. PAGE 83
E1665
B65
CONSTN
NAT/G
PROVS
FEDERAL

SCHROEDER O.,DEFACTO SEGREGATION AND CIVIL RIGHTS.
LAW PROVS SCHOOL WORKER ATTIT HABITAT HEALTH WEALTH
...JURID CHARTS 19/20 NEGRO SUPREME/CT KKK. PAGE 88
E1766
B65
ANTHOL
DISCRIM
RACE/REL
ORD/FREE

SHARMA S.A.,PARLIAMENTARY GOVERNMENT IN INDIA.
INDIA FINAN LOC/G PROVS DELIB/GP PLAN ADMIN CT/SYS
FEDERAL...JURID 20. PAGE 90 E1814
B65
NAT/G
CONSTN
PARL/PROC
LEGIS

SNOW J.H.,REAPPORTIONMENT. LAW CONSTN NAT/G GOV/REL
ORD/FREE...JURID 20 SUPREME/CT CONNECTICT. PAGE 92
E1848
B65
APPORT
ADJUD
LEGIS
PROVS

US LIBRARY OF CONGRESS,INTERNAL SECURITY AND
SUBVERSION. USA+45 ACADEM LOC/G NAT/G PROVS
...POLICY ANARCH DECISION 20 CIVIL/SERV SUBVERT
B65
CONTROL
ADJUD
LAW

SEDITION. PAGE 101 E2020   PLAN

ACT/RES

B66
BAKER G.E.,THE REAPPORTIONMENT REVOLUTION; LEGIS
REPRESENTATION, POLITICAL POWER, AND THE SUPREME APPORT
COURT. USA+45 MUNIC NAT/G POL/PAR PROVS PROB/SOLV REPRESENT
CHOOSE ORD/FREE POPULISM...CONCPT CHARTS 20 ADJUD
SUPREME/CT. PAGE 7 E0140

B66
BEISER E.N.,THE TREATMENT OF LEGISLATIVE CT/SYS
APPORTIONMENT BY THE STATE AND FEDERAL COURTS APPORT
(DISSERTATION). USA+45 CONSTN NAT/G PROVS LEGIS ADJUD
CHOOSE REPRESENT ATTIT...POLICY BIBLIOG 20 CONGRESS PWR
SUPREME/CT. PAGE 9 E0181

B66
CALIFORNIA STATE LIBRARY,REAPPORTIONMENT, A BIBLIOG
SELECTIVE BIBLIOGRAPHY. USA+45 LEGIS CT/SYS APPORT
REPRESENT GOV/REL. PAGE 19 E0367 NAT/G
PROVS

B66
FINK M.,A SELECTIVE BIBLIOGRAPHY ON STATE BIBLIOG
CONSTITUTIONAL REVISION (PAMPHLET). USA+45 FINAN PROVS
EX/STRUC LEGIS EDU/PROP ADMIN CT/SYS APPORT CHOOSE LOC/G
GOV/REL 20. PAGE 38 E0751 CONSTN

B66
GREENE L.E.,GOVERNMENT IN TENNESSEE (2ND ED.). PROVS
USA+45 DIST/IND INDUS POL/PAR EX/STRUC LEGIS PLAN LOC/G
BUDGET GIVE CT/SYS...MGT T 20 TENNESSEE. PAGE 46 CONSTN
E0909 ADMIN

B66
HAMILTON H.D.,REAPPORTIONING LEGISLATURES. USA+45 APPORT
CONSTN POL/PAR PROVS LEGIS COMPUTER ADJUD CHOOSE REPRESENT
ATTIT...ANTHOL 20 SUPREME/CT CONGRESS. PAGE 50 PHIL/SCI
E0989 PWR

B66
MENDELSON W.,JUSTICES BLACK AND FRANKFURTER: JURID
CONFLICT IN THE COURT (2ND ED.). NAT/G PROVS ADJUD
PROB/SOLV BAL/PWR CONTROL FEDERAL ISOLAT ANOMIE IDEA/COMP
ORD/FREE...DECISION 20 SUPREME/CT BLACK/HL ROLE
FRANKFUR/F. PAGE 72 E1439

B66
O'NEILL C.E.,CHURCH AND STATE IN FRENCH COLONIAL COLONIAL
LOUISIANA: POLICY AND POLITICS TO 1732. PROVS NAT/G
VOL/ASSN DELIB/GP ADJUD ADMIN GP/REL ATTIT DRIVE SECT
...POLICY BIBLIOG 17/18 LOUISIANA CHURCH/STA. PWR
PAGE 78 E1568

B66
POWERS E.,CRIME AND PUNISHMENT IN EARLY CRIME
MASSACHUSETTS 1620-1692: A DOCUMENTARY HISTORY. ADJUD
USA-45 SECT LEGIS COLONIAL ATTIT ORD/FREE MYSTISM CT/SYS
17 PRE/US/AM MASSACHU. PAGE 82 E1643 PROVS

S66
BURDETTE F.L.,"SELECTED ARTICLES AND DOCUMENTS ON BIBLIOG
AMERICAN GOVERNMENT AND POLITICS." LAW LOC/G MUNIC USA+45
NAT/G POL/PAR PROVS LEGIS BAL/PWR ADMIN EXEC JURID
REPRESENT MGT. PAGE 17 E0331 CONSTN

N66
BACHELDER G.L.,THE LITERATURE OF FEDERALISM: A BIBLIOG
SELECTED BIBLIOGRAPHY (REV ED) (A PAMPHLET). USA+45 FEDERAL
USA-45 WOR+45 WOR-45 LAW CONSTN PROVS ADMIN CT/SYS NAT/G
GOV/REL ROLE...CONCPT 19/20. PAGE 7 E0126 LOC/G

B67
BUREAU GOVERNMENT RES AND SERV,COUNTY GOVERNMENT BIBLIOG/A
REORGANIZATION - A SELECTED ANNOTATED BIBLIOGRAPHY APPORT
(PAPER). USA+45 USA-45 LAW CONSTN MUNIC PROVS LOC/G
EX/STRUC CREATE PLAN PROB/SOLV REPRESENT GOV/REL ADMIN
20. PAGE 17 E0332

B67
FESLER J.W.,THE FIFTY STATES AND THEIR LOCAL PROVS
GOVERNMENTS. FUT USA+45 POL/PAR LEGIS PROB/SOLV LOC/G
ADMIN CT/SYS CHOOSE GOV/REL FEDERAL...POLICY CHARTS
20 SUPREME/CT. PAGE 37 E0743

B67
GRAHAM H.D.,CRISIS IN PRINT: DESEGREGATION AND THE PRESS
PRESS IN TENNESSEE. LAW SOCIETY MUNIC POL/PAR PROVS
EDU/PROP LEAD REPRESENT DISCRIM ATTIT...IDEA/COMP POLICY
BIBLIOG/A SOC/INTEG 20 TENNESSEE SUPREME/CT RACE/REL
SOUTH/US. PAGE 45 E0896

L67
NAGEL S.S.,"DISPARITIES IN CRIMINAL PROCEDURE." ADJUD
STRATA NAT/G PROVS EDU/PROP RACE/REL AGE HABITAT DISCRIM
SEX...JURID CHARTS 20. PAGE 76 E1519 STRUCT

S67
BERRODIN E.F.,"AT THE BARGAINING TABLE." LABOR PROVS
DIPLOM ECO/TAC ADMIN...MGT 20 MICHIGAN. PAGE 11 WORKER
E0216 LAW
BARGAIN

S67
GOSSETT W.T.,"ELECTING THE PRESIDENT: NEW HOPE FOR CONSTN
AN OLD IDEAL." FUT USA+45 USA-45 PROVS LEGIS CHIEF
PROB/SOLV WRITING DEBATE ADJUD REPRESENT...MAJORIT CHOOSE
DECISION 20 HOUSE/REP PRESIDENT. PAGE 45 E0892 NAT/G

S67
RAI H.,"DISTRICT MAGISTRATE AND POLICE STRUCT
SUPERINTENDENT IN INDIA: THE CONTROVERSY OF DUAL CONTROL
CONTROL" INDIA LAW PROVS ADMIN PWR 19/20. PAGE 83 ROLE
E1669 FORCES

B89
FICHTE J.G.,THE SCIENCE OF RIGHTS (TRANS. BY A.E. ORD/FREE
KROEGER). WOR-45 FAM MUNIC NAT/G PROVS ADJUD CRIME CONSTN
CHOOSE MARRIAGE SEX POPULISM 19 FICHTE/JG LAW
NATURL/LAW. PAGE 37 E0744 CONCPT

PRUITT/DG....DEAN G. PRUITT

PRUSSIA....PRUSSIA

B63
RAVENS J.P.,STAAT UND KATHOLISCHE KIRCHE IN GP/REL
PREUSSENS POLNISCHEN TEILUNGSGEBIETEN. GERMANY CATHISM
POLAND PRUSSIA PROVS DIPLOM EDU/PROP DEBATE SECT
NAT/LISM...JURID 18 CHURCH/STA. PAGE 83 E1674 NAT/G

B65
KAAS L.,DIE GEISTLICHE GERICHTSBARKEIT DER JURID
KATHOLISCHEN KIRCHE IN PREUSSEN (2 VOLS.). PRUSSIA CATHISM
CONSTN NAT/G PROVS SECT ADJUD ADMIN ATTIT 16/20. GP/REL
PAGE 59 E1178 CT/SYS

PRYOR F.L. E1657

PSY....PSYCHOLOGY

N
SOUTH AFRICA STATE LIBRARY,SOUTH AFRICAN NATIONAL BIBLIOG
BIBLIOGRAPHY, SANB. SOUTH/AFR LAW NAT/G EDU/PROP PRESS
...MGT PSY SOC 20. PAGE 93 E1858 WRITING

N
US BUREAU OF THE CENSUS,BIBLIOGRAPHY OF SOCIAL BIBLIOG/A
SCIENCE PERIODICALS AND MONOGRAPH SERIES. WOR+45 CULTURE
LAW DIPLOM EDU/PROP HEALTH...PSY SOC LING STAT. NAT/G
PAGE 99 E1980 SOCIETY

N13
SCHMIDHAUSER J.R.,JUDICIAL BEHAVIOR AND THE JUDGE
SECTIONAL CRISIS OF 1837-1860. USA-45 ADJUD CT/SYS POL/PAR
INGP/REL ATTIT HABITAT...DECISION PSY STAT CHARTS PERS/COMP
SIMUL. PAGE 88 E1759 PERSON

L21
HALDEMAN E.,"SERIALS OF AN INTERNATIONAL BIBLIOG
CHARACTER." WOR-45 DIPLOM...ART/METH GEOG HEAL HUM PHIL/SCI
INT/LAW JURID PSY SOC. PAGE 49 E0978

B24
NAVILLE A.,LIBERTE, EGALITE, SOLIDARITE: ESSAIS ORD/FREE
D'ANALYSE. STRATA FAM VOL/ASSN INT/TRADE GP/REL SOC
MORAL MARXISM SOCISM...PSY TREATY. PAGE 76 E1529 IDEA/COMP
DIPLOM

B34
CULVER D.C.,BIBLIOGRAPHY OF CRIME AND CRIMINAL BIBLIOG/A
JUSTICE, 1927-1931. LAW CULTURE PUB/INST PROB/SOLV CRIMLGY
CT/SYS...PSY SOC STAT 20. PAGE 28 E0549 ADJUD
FORCES

B35
CUMMING J.,A CONTRIBUTION TOWARD A BIBLIOGRAPHY BIBLIOG
DEALING WITH CRIME AND COGNATE SUBJECTS (3RD ED.). CRIMLGY
UK LAW CULTURE PUB/INST ADJUD AGE BIO/SOC...PSY SOC FORCES
SOC/WK STAT METH/COMP 20. PAGE 28 E0552 CT/SYS

L37
LERNER M.,"CONSTITUTION AND COURT AS SYMBOLS" CONSTN
(BMR)" USA+45 USA-45 DOMIN PWR SOVEREIGN...PSY MYTH CT/SYS
18/20 SUPREME/CT. PAGE 64 E1288 ATTIT
EDU/PROP

B39
CULVER D.C.,BIBLIOGRAPHY OF CRIME AND CRIMINAL BIBLIOG/A
JUSTICE, 1932-1937. USA-45 LAW CULTURE PUB/INST CRIMLGY
PROB/SOLV CT/SYS...PSY SOC STAT 20. PAGE 28 E0551 ADJUD

FORCES

B39

TIMASHEFF N.S.,AN INTRODUCTION TO THE SOCIOLOGY OF
LAW. CRIME ANOMIE ATTIT DRIVE ORD/FREE...JURID PSY
CONCPT. PAGE 96 E1926

SOC
BIBLIOG
PWR

B44

DE HUSZAR G.B.,NEW PERSPECTIVES ON PEACE. UNIV
CULTURE SOCIETY ECO/DEV ECO/UNDEV NAT/G FORCES
CREATE ECO/TAC DOMIN ADJUD COERCE DRIVE ORD/FREE
...GEOG JURID PSY SOC CONCPT TOT/POP. PAGE 29 E0584

ATTIT
MYTH
PEACE
WAR

S45

DAVIS A.,"CASTE, ECONOMY, AND VIOLENCE" (BMR)"
USA-45 LAW SOCIETY STRUCT SECT SANCTION COERCE
MARRIAGE SEX...PSY SOC SOC/INTEG 18/20 NEGRO
MISCEGEN SOUTH/US. PAGE 29 E0570

STRATA
RACE/REL
DISCRIM

B46

AMERICAN DOCUMENTATION INST,CATALOGUE OF AUXILIARY
PUBLICATIONS IN MICROFILMS AND PHOTOPRINTS. USA-45
LAW AGRI CREATE TEC/DEV ADMIN...GEOG LING MATH 20.
PAGE 4 E0077

BIBLIOG
EDU/PROP
PSY

B46

GILLIN J.L.,SOCIAL PATHOLOGY. SOCIETY SECT CRIME
ANOMIE DISPL ORD/FREE WEALTH...CRIMLGY PSY WORSHIP.
PAGE 44 E0864

SOC
ADJUST
CULTURE
INGP/REL

B47

HOCKING W.E.,FREEDOM OF THE PRESS: A FRAMEWORK OF
PRINCIPLE. WOR-45 SOCIETY NAT/G PROB/SOLV DEBATE
LOBBY...JURID PSY 20 AMEND/I. PAGE 53 E1061

ORD/FREE
CONSTN
PRESS
LAW

S48

ALEXANDER L.,"WAR CRIMES, THEIR SOCIAL-
PSYCHOLOGICAL ASPECTS." EUR+WWI GERMANY LAW CULTURE
ELITES KIN POL/PAR PUB/INST FORCES DOMIN EDU/PROP
COERCE CRIME ATTIT SUPEGO HEALTH MORAL PWR FASCISM
...PSY OBS TREND GEN/LAWS NAZI 20. PAGE 3 E0061

DRIVE
WAR

S51

COHEN M.B.,"PERSONALITY AS A FACTOR IN
ADMINISTRATIVE DECISIONS." ADJUD PERS/REL ANOMIE
SUPEGO...OBS SELF/OBS INT. PAGE 24 E0465

PERSON
ADMIN
PROB/SOLV
PSY

B52

BENTHAM A.,HANDBOOK OF POLITICAL FALLACIES. FUT
MOD/EUR LAW INTELL LOC/G MUNIC NAT/G LEGIS
CREATE EDU/PROP CT/SYS ATTIT RIGID/FLEX KNOWL PWR
...RELATIV PSY SOC CONCPT SELF/OBS TREND STERTYP
TOT/POP. PAGE 10 E0189

POL/PAR

B52

FORSTER A.,THE TROUBLE MAKERS. USA+45 LAW CULTURE
SOCIETY STRUCT VOL/ASSN CROWD GP/REL MORAL...PSY
SOC CONCPT 20 NEGRO JEWS. PAGE 39 E0771

DISCRIM
SECT
RACE/REL
ATTIT

B52

UNESCO,THESES DE SCIENCES SOCIALES: CATALOGUE
ANALYTIQUE INTERNATIONAL DE THESES INEDITES DE
DOCTORAT, 1940-1950. INT/ORG DIPLOM EDU/PROP...GEOG
INT/LAW MGT PSY SOC 20. PAGE 98 E1958

BIBLIOG
ACADEM
WRITING

B54

BENTLEY A.F.,INQUIRY INTO INQUIRIES: ESSAYS IN
SOCIAL THEORY. UNIV LEGIS ADJUD ADMIN LOBBY
...PHIL/SCI PSY NEW/IDEA LING METH 20. PAGE 10
E0200

EPIST
SOC
CONCPT

B56

ALEXANDER F.,THE CRIMINAL, THE JUDGE, AND THE
PUBLIC. LAW CULTURE CONSULT LEGIT ADJUD SANCTION
ORD/FREE 20. PAGE 3 E0060

CRIME
CRIMLGY
PSY
ATTIT

B56

US HOUSE WAYS MEANS COMMITTEE,TRAFFIC IN, AND
CONTROL OF NARCOTICS, BARBITURATES, AND
AMPHETAMINES. CHINA/COM USA+45 SOCIETY LEGIS
ACT/RES EDU/PROP CT/SYS SANCTION PROFIT HEALTH
...HEAL PSY STAT 20. PAGE 100 E2011

BIO/SOC
CONTROL
PROB/SOLV
CRIME

B57

CLINARD M.B.,SOCIOLOGY OF DEVIANT BEHAVIOR. FAM
CONTROL MURDER DISCRIM PERSON...PSY SOC T SOC/INTEG
20. PAGE 23 E0455

BIO/SOC
CRIME
SEX
ANOMIE

B58

HALL J.,STUDIES IN JURISPRUDENCE AND CRIMINAL

JURID

THEORY. USA-45 LAW CULTURE CREATE SUPEGO...CRIMLGY
PSY /20 PLATO. PAGE 49 E0983

CRIME
CONCPT
CT/SYS

L58

BEVAN W.,"JURY BEHAVIOR AS A FUNCTION OF THE
PRESTIGE OF THE FOREMAN AND THE NATURE OF HIS
LEADERSHIP" (BMR)" DELIB/GP DOMIN ADJUD LEAD
PERS/REL ATTIT...PSY STAT INT QU CHARTS SOC/EXP 20
JURY. PAGE 11 E0221

PERSON
EDU/PROP
DECISION
CT/SYS

B59

HOBSBAWM E.J.,PRIMITIVE REBELS: STUDIES IN ARCHAIC
FORMS OF SOCIAL MOVEMENT IN THE 19TH AND 20TH
CENTURIES. ITALY SPAIN CULTURE VOL/ASSN RISK CROWD
GP/REL INGP/REL ISOLAT TOTALISM...PSY SOC 18/20.
PAGE 53 E1058

SOCIETY
CRIME
REV
GUERRILLA

B59

LAPIERE R.,THE FREUDIAN ETHIC. USA+45 FAM EDU/PROP
CONTROL CRIME ADJUST AGE DRIVE PERCEPT PERSON SEX
...SOC 20 FREUD/S. PAGE 63 E1254

PSY
ORD/FREE
SOCIETY

S59

CORY R.H. JR.,"INTERNATIONAL INSPECTION FROM
PROPOSALS TO REALIZATION." WOR+45 TEC/DEV ECO/TAC
ADJUD ORD/FREE PWR WEALTH...RECORD VAL/FREE 20.
PAGE 26 E0516

STRUCT
PSY
ARMS/CONT
NUC/PWR

S59

PUGWASH CONFERENCE,"ON BIOLOGICAL AND CHEMICAL
WARFARE." WOR+45 SOCIETY PROC/MFG INT/ORG FORCES
EDU/PROP ADJUD RIGID/FLEX ORD/FREE PWR...DECISION
PSY NEW/IDEA MATH VAL/FREE 20. PAGE 83 E1661

ACT/RES
BIO/SOC
WAR
WEAPON

C59

EASTON D.,"POLITICAL ANTHROPOLOGY" IN BIENNIAL
REVIEW OF ANTHROPOLOGY" UNIV LAW CULTURE ELITES
SOCIETY CREATE...PSY CONCPT GP/COMP GEN/METH 20.
PAGE 34 E0671

SOC
BIBLIOG/A
NEW/IDEA

S60

ULMER S.S.,"THE ANALYSIS OF BEHAVIOR PATTERNS ON
THE UNITED STATES SUPREME COURT" USA+45 LAW CT/SYS
PERS/REL RACE/REL PERSON...DECISION PSY SOC TREND
METH/COMP METH 20 SUPREME/CT CIVIL/LIB. PAGE 97
E1951

ATTIT
ADJUD
PROF/ORG
INGP/REL

S60

WRIGHT Q.,"LEGAL ASPECTS OF THE U-2 INCIDENT." COM
USA+45 USSR STRUCT NAT/G FORCES PLAN TEC/DEV ADJUD
RIGID/FLEX MORAL ORD/FREE...DECISION INT/LAW JURID
PSY TREND GEN/LAWS COLD/WAR VAL/FREE 20 U-2.
PAGE 108 E2157

PWR
POLICY
SPACE

B61

MERTON R.K.,CONTEMPORARY SOCIAL PROBLEMS: AN
INTRODUCTION TO THE SOCIOLOGY OF DEVIANT BEHAVIOR
AND SOCIAL DISORGANIZATION. FAM MUNIC FORCES WORKER
PROB/SOLV INGP/REL RACE/REL ISOLAT...CRIMLGY GEOG
PSY T 20 NEGRO. PAGE 72 E1444

CRIME
ANOMIE
STRANGE
SOC

B61

US CONGRESS,CONSTITUTIONAL RIGHTS OF THE MENTALLY
ILL. USA+45 LAW PUB/INST DELIB/GP ADJUD ORD/FREE
...PSY QU 20 CONGRESS. PAGE 99 E1989

HEALTH
CONSTN
JURID
CONFER

S61

AGNEW P.C.,"INTRODUCING CHANGE IN A MENTAL
HOSPITAL." CLIENT WORKER PROB/SOLV INGP/REL
PERS/REL ADJUST. PAGE 3 E0054

ORD/FREE
PUB/INST
PSY
ADMIN

S61

SCHUBERT G.,"A PSYCHOMETRIC MODEL OF THE SUPREME
COURT." DELIB/GP ADJUD CHOOSE ATTIT...DECISION
JURID PSY QUANT STAT HYPO/EXP GEN/METH SUPREME/CT.
PAGE 88 E1771

JUDGE
CT/SYS
PERSON
SIMUL

B62

ASSOCIATION BAR OF NYC,REPORT ON ADMISSION
PROCEDURES TO NEW YORK STATE MENTAL HOSPITALS. LAW
CONSTN INGP/REL RESPECT...PSY OBS RECORD. PAGE 6
E0108

PUB/INST
HEALTH
CLIENT
ROUTINE

B62

MARS D.,SUGGESTED LIBRARY IN PUBLIC ADMINISTRATION.
FINAN DELIB/GP EX/STRUC WORKER COMPUTER ADJUD
...DECISION PSY SOC METH/COMP 20. PAGE 68 E1368

BIBLIOG
ADMIN
METH
MGT

B62

WOETZEL R.K.,THE NURENBERG TRIALS IN INTERNATIONAL
LAW. CHRIST-17C MOD/EUR WOR+45 SOCIETY NAT/G
DELIB/GP DOMIN LEGIT ROUTINE ATTIT DRIVE PERSON

INT/ORG
ADJUD
WAR

SUPEGO MORAL ORD/FREE...POLICY MAJORIT JURID PSY
SOC SELF/OBS RECORD NAZI TOT/POP. PAGE 107 E2138

L62

SPAETH H.J.,"JUDICIAL POWER AS A VARIABLE   JUDGE
MOTIVATING SUPREME COURT BEHAVIOR." DELIB/GP ADJUD   DECISION
RATIONAL ATTIT PERSON ORD/FREE...CLASSIF STAT   PERS/COMP
GEN/METH. PAGE 93 E1860   PSY

B63

CRAIG A.,SUPPRESSED BOOKS: A HISTORY OF THE   BIBLIOG/A
CONCEPTION OF LITERARY OBSCENITY. WOR+45 WOR-45   LAW
CREATE EDU/PROP LITERACY ATTIT...ART/METH PSY   SEX
CONCPT 20. PAGE 27 E0538   CONTROL

C63

SCHUBERT G.,"JUDICIAL DECISION-MAKING." FORCES LEAD   ADJUD
ATTIT DRIVE...POLICY PSY STAT CHARTS ANTHOL BIBLIOG   DECISION
20. PAGE 88 E1773   JUDGE
                                                           CT/SYS

N63

US PRES COMN REGIS AND VOTING,REPORT ON   CHOOSE
REGISTRATION AND VOTING (PAMPHLET). USA+45 POL/PAR   LAW
CHIEF EDU/PROP PARTIC REPRESENT ATTIT...PSY CHARTS   SUFF
20. PAGE 101 E2023   INSPECT

B64

CLINARD M.B.,ANOMIE AND DEVIANT BEHAVIOR: A   PERSON
DISCUSSION AND CRITIQUE. SOCIETY FACE/GP CRIME   ANOMIE
STRANGE ATTIT BIO/SOC DISPL RIGID/FLEX HEALTH...PSY   KIN
CONCPT BIBLIOG 20 MERTON/R. PAGE 23 E0456   NEIGH

B64

DRESSLER D.,READINGS IN CRIMINOLOGY AND PENOLOGY.   CRIMLGY
UNIV CULTURE PUB/INST FORCES ACT/RES PROB/SOLV   CRIME
ANOMIE BIO/SOC SUPEGO...GEOG PSY ANTHOL 20. PAGE 33   ADJUD
E0648   ADJUST

B64

IKLE F.C.,HOW NATIONS NEGOTIATE. COM EUR+WWI USA+45   NAT/G
INTELL INT/ORG VOL/ASSN DELIB/GP ACT/RES CREATE   PWR
DOMIN EDU/PROP ADJUD ROUTINE ATTIT PERSON ORD/FREE   POLICY
RESPECT SKILL...PSY SOC OBS VAL/FREE. PAGE 56 E1122

S64

CARNEGIE ENDOWMENT INT. PEACE,"HUMAN RIGHTS (ISSUES   INT/ORG
BEFORE THE NINETEENTH GENERAL ASSEMBLY)." AFR   PERSON
WOR+45 LAW CONSTN NAT/G EDU/PROP GP/REL DISCRIM   RACE/REL
PEACE ATTIT MORAL ORD/FREE...INT/LAW PSY CONCPT
RECORD UN 20. PAGE 20 E0385

S64

GREENBERG S.,"JUDAISM AND WORLD JUSTICE." MEDIT-7   SECT
WOR+45 LAW CULTURE SOCIETY INT/ORG NAT/G FORCES   JURID
EDU/PROP ATTIT DRIVE PERSON SUPEGO ALL/VALS   PEACE
...POLICY PSY CONCPT GEN/LAWS JEWS. PAGE 46 E0908

S64

KHAN M.Z.,"ISLAM AND INTERNATIONAL RELATIONS." FUT   ISLAM
WOR+45 LAW CULTURE SOCIETY NAT/G SECT DELIB/GP   INT/ORG
FORCES EDU/PROP ATTIT PERSON SUPEGO ALL/VALS   DIPLOM
...POLICY PSY CONCPT MYTH HIST/WRIT GEN/LAWS.
PAGE 61 E1211

B65

BROMBERG W.,CRIME AND THE MIND. LAW LEGIT ADJUD   CRIMLGY
CRIME MURDER AGE/Y ANOMIE BIO/SOC DRIVE SEX PSY.   SOC
PAGE 16 E0305   HEALTH
                                                          COERCE

B65

RADZINOWICZ L.,THE NEED FOR CRIMINOLOGY AND A   CRIMLGY
PROPOSAL FOR AN INSTITUTE OF CRIMINOLOGY. FUT UK   PROF/ORG
USA+45 SOCIETY ACT/RES PROB/SOLV CRIME...PSY SOC   ACADEM
BIBLIOG 20. PAGE 83 E1666   CONTROL

B65

ROSE A.M.,MINORITY PROBLEMS: A TEXTBOOK OF READINGS   RACE/REL
IN INTERGROUP RELATIONS. UNIV USA+45 LAW SCHOOL   DISCRIM
WORKER PROB/SOLV GP/REL PERSON...PSY ANTHOL WORSHIP   ISOLAT
20 NEGRO INDIAN/AM JEWS EUROPE. PAGE 85 E1713   ACT/RES

B65

SCHUBERT G.,THE POLITICAL ROLE OF THE COURTS IN   CT/SYS
JUDICIAL POLICY MAKING. USA+45 CONSTN JUDGE   POLICY
FEEDBACK CHOOSE RACE/REL ORD/FREE...TRADIT PSY   DECISION
BIBLIOG/A 20 KENNEDY/JF SUPREME/CT. PAGE 89 E1776

B65

UNESCO,INTERNATIONAL ORGANIZATIONS IN THE SOCIAL   INT/ORG
SCIENCES(REV. ED.). LAW ADMIN ATTIT...CRIMLGY GEOG   R+D
INT/LAW PSY SOC STAT 20 UNESCO. PAGE 98 E1962   PROF/ORG
                                                          ACT/RES

B65

UNIVERSAL REFERENCE SYSTEM,INTERNATIONAL AFFAIRS: BIBLIOG/A
VOLUME I IN THE POLITICAL SCIENCE, GOVERNMENT, AND   GEN/METH
PUBLIC POLICY SERIES...DECISION ECOMETRIC GEOG   COMPUT/IR
INT/LAW JURID MGT PHIL/SCI PSY SOC. PAGE 98 E1972   DIPLOM

B66

HOPKINS J.F.K.,ARABIC PERIODICAL LITERATURE, 1961.   BIBLIOG/A
ISLAM LAW CULTURE SECT...GEOG HEAL PHIL/SCI PSY SOC   NAT/LISM
20. PAGE 55 E1096   TEC/DEV
                                                          INDUS

B66

MACIVER R.M.,THE PREVENTION AND CONTROL OF   AGE/Y
DELINQUENCY. USA+45 STRATA PUB/INST ANOMIE ATTIT   PLAN
HABITAT PERSON HEALTH...CRIMLGY PSY SOC METH.   ADJUST
PAGE 67 E1341   CRIME

B66

OSTERMANN R.,A REPORT IN DEPTH ON CRIME IN AMERICA.   CRIME
FUT USA+45 MUNIC PUB/INST TEC/DEV MURDER EFFICIENCY   FORCES
ATTIT BIO/SOC...PSY 20. PAGE 79 E1584   CONTROL
                                                        LAW

B66

SKOLNICK J.H.,JUSTICE WITHOUT TRIAL: LAW   FORCES
ENFORCEMENT IN DEMOCRATIC SOCIETY. USA+45 LAW   CRIMLGY
TRIBUTE RACE/REL BIO/SOC PERSON...PSY SOC 20 NEGRO   CRIME
BUREAUCRCY PROSTITUTN. PAGE 92 E1836

B66

STEVENS R.E.,REFERENCE BOOKS IN THE SOCIAL SCIENCES   BIBLIOG/A
AND HUMANITIES. CULTURE PERF/ART SECT EDU/PROP   SOC
...JURID PSY SOC/WK STAT 20 MUSIC. PAGE 93 E1873   HUM
                                                        ART/METH

L67

FRANCK T.M.,"SOME PSYCHOLOGICAL FACTORS IN   DIPLOM
INTERNATIONAL THIRD-PARTY DECISION-MAKING." UNIV   ADJUD
SOCIETY PROB/SOLV DISCRIM ATTIT HABITAT...DECISION   PERSON
PSY. PAGE 40 E0786   CONSULT

S67

GIBSON G.H.,"LABOR PIRACY ON THE BRANDYWINE."   ECO/TAC
USA-45 INDUS R+D VOL/ASSN CAP/ISM ADJUD DRIVE...PSY   CREATE
19. PAGE 43 E0859   TEC/DEV
                                                        WORKER

B92

COHN M.M.,AN INTRODUCTION TO THE STUDY OF THE   CONSTN
CONSTITUTION. USA+45 USA-45 SOCIETY NAT/G EX/STRUC   JURID
HABITAT...PSY CONCPT 18/20. PAGE 24 E0470   OLD/LIB

PSY/WAR....PSYCHOLOGICAL WARFARE; SEE ALSO PSY + EDU/PROP +
    WAR

PSYCHIATRY....SEE PSY

PSYCHOANALYSIS....SEE BIOG, PSY

PSYCHO-DRAMA....SEE SELF/OBS

PSYCHOLOGICAL WARFARE....SEE PSY+EDU/PROP+WAR

PSYCHOLOGY....SEE PSY

PUB/INST....MENTAL, CORRECTIONAL, AND OTHER HABITATIONAL
    INSTITUTIONS

L16

WRIGHT Q.,"THE ENFORCEMENT OF INTERNATIONAL LAW   INT/ORG
THROUGH MUNICIPAL LAW IN THE US." USA-45 LOC/G   LAW
NAT/G PUB/INST FORCES LEGIT CT/SYS PERCEPT ALL/VALS   INT/LAW
...JURID 20. PAGE 107 E2149   WAR

B34

CULVER D.C.,BIBLIOGRAPHY OF CRIME AND CRIMINAL   BIBLIOG/A
JUSTICE, 1927-1931. LAW CULTURE PUB/INST PROB/SOLV   CRIMLGY
CT/SYS...PSY SOC STAT 20. PAGE 28 E0549   ADJUD
                                                        FORCES

B35

CUMMING J.,A CONTRIBUTION TOWARD A BIBLIOGRAPHY   BIBLIOG
DEALING WITH CRIME AND COGNATE SUBJECTS (3RD ED.).   CRIMLGY
UK LAW CULTURE PUB/INST ADJUD AGE BIO/SOC...PSY SOC   FORCES
SOC/WK STAT METH/COMP 20. PAGE 28 E0552   CT/SYS

S38

CLEMMER D.,"LEADERSHIP PHENOMENA IN A PRISON   PUB/INST
COMMUNITY." NEIGH PLAN CHOOSE PERSON ROLE...OBS   CRIMLGY
INT. PAGE 23 E0452   LEAD
                                                        CLIENT

B39

CULVER D.C.,BIBLIOGRAPHY OF CRIME AND CRIMINAL   BIBLIOG/A
JUSTICE, 1932-1937. USA-45 LAW CULTURE PUB/INST   CRIMLGY

PROB/SOLV CT/SYS...PSY SOC STAT 20. PAGE 28 E0551 — ADJUD FORCES

N40
COUNTY GOVERNMENT IN THE UNITED STATES: A LIST OF RECENT REFERENCES (PAMPHLET). USA-45 LAW PUB/INST PLAN BUDGET CT/SYS CENTRAL 20. PAGE 52 E1027 — BIBLIOG/A LOC/G ADMIN MUNIC

S48
ALEXANDER L.,"WAR CRIMES, THEIR SOCIAL-PSYCHOLOGICAL ASPECTS." EUR+WWI GERMANY LAW CULTURE ELITES KIN POL/PAR PUB/INST FORCES DOMIN EDU/PROP COERCE CRIME ATTIT SUPEGO HEALTH MORAL PWR FASCISM ...PSY OBS TREND GEN/LAWS NAZI 20. PAGE 3 E0061 — DRIVE WAR

B51
BIDDLE F.,THE FEAR OF FREEDOM. USA+45 LAW NAT/G PUB/INST PROB/SOLV DOMIN CONTROL SANCTION REV NAT/LISM 20. PAGE 12 E0227 — ANOMIE INGP/REL VOL/ASSN ORD/FREE

B55
CAVAN R.S.,CRIMINOLOGY (2ND ED.). USA+45 LAW FAM PUB/INST FORCES PLAN WAR AGE/Y PERSON ROLE SUPEGO ...CHARTS 20 FBI. PAGE 21 E0409 — DRIVE CRIMLGY CONTROL METH/COMP

B58
CLEMMER D.,THE PRISON COMMUNITY. CULTURE CONTROL LEAD ROUTINE PERS/REL PERSON...SOC METH/CNCPT. PAGE 23 E0453 — PUB/INST CRIMLGY CLIENT INGP/REL

B58
JAPAN MINISTRY OF JUSTICE,CRIMINAL JUSTICE IN JAPAN. LAW PROF/ORG PUB/INST FORCES CONTROL CT/SYS PARL/PROC 20 CHINJAP. PAGE 58 E1149 — CONSTN CRIME JURID ADMIN

S58
CRESSEY D.R.,"ACHIEVEMENT OF AN UNSTATED ORGANIZATIONAL GOAL: AN OBSERVATION ON PRISONS." OP/RES PROB/SOLV PERS/REL ANOMIE ATTIT ROLE RESPECT CRIMLGY. PAGE 28 E0546 — PUB/INST CLIENT NEIGH INGP/REL

B59
KERREMANS-RAMIOULL,LE PROBLEME DE LA DELINQUENCE JUVENILE (2ND ED.). FAM PUB/INST SCHOOL FORCES LEGIS MORAL...CRIMLGY SOC 20. PAGE 60 E1205 — BIBLIOG CRIME AGE/Y SOC/WK

C60
MCCLEERY R.,"COMMUNICATION PATTERNS AS BASES OF SYSTEMS OF AUTHORITY AND POWER" IN THEORETICAL STUDIES IN SOCIAL ORGAN. OF PRISON-BMR. USA+45 SOCIETY STRUCT EDU/PROP ADMIN CONTROL COERCE CRIME GP/REL AUTHORIT...SOC 20. PAGE 70 E1400 — PERS/REL PUB/INST PWR DOMIN

B61
DAVIS B.F.,THE DESPERATE AND THE DAMNED. USA+45 LAW DEATH ANOMIE...CRIMLGY 20 SAN/QUENTN. PAGE 29 E0571 — PUB/INST SANCTION CRIME

B61
US CONGRESS,CONSTITUTIONAL RIGHTS OF THE MENTALLY ILL. USA+45 LAW PUB/INST DELIB/GP ADJUD ORD/FREE ...PSY QU 20 CONGRESS. PAGE 99 E1989 — HEALTH CONSTN JURID CONFER

S61
AGNEW P.C.,"INTRODUCING CHANGE IN A MENTAL HOSPITAL." CLIENT WORKER PROB/SOLV INGP/REL PERS/REL ADJUST. PAGE 3 E0054 — ORD/FREE PUB/INST PSY ADMIN

B62
ASSOCIATION BAR OF NYC,REPORT ON ADMISSION PROCEDURES TO NEW YORK STATE MENTAL HOSPITALS. LAW CONSTN INGP/REL RESPECT...PSY OBS RECORD. PAGE 6 E0108 — PUB/INST HEALTH CLIENT ROUTINE

S62
GRAVEN J.,"LE MOUVEAU DROIT PENAL INTERNATIONAL." UNIV STRUCT LEGIS ACT/RES CRIME ATTIT PERCEPT PERSON...JURID CONCPT 20. PAGE 45 E0899 — CT/SYS PUB/INST INT/ORG INT/LAW

B64
DRESSLER D.,READINGS IN CRIMINOLOGY AND PENOLOGY. UNIV CULTURE PUB/INST FORCES ACT/RES PROB/SOLV ANOMIE BIO/SOC SUPEGO...GEOG PSY ANTHOL 20. PAGE 33 E0648 — CRIMLGY CRIME ADJUD ADJUST

S64
BAKER H.R.,"INMATE SELF-GOVERNMENT." ACT/RES CREATE — PUB/INST

CONTROL PARTIC ATTIT RIGID/FLEX QU. PAGE 7 E0141 — CRIME INGP/REL REPRESENT

B65
FISCHER F.C.,THE GOVERNMENT OF MICHIGAN. USA+45 NAT/G PUB/INST EX/STRUC LEGIS BUDGET GIVE EDU/PROP CT/SYS CHOOSE GOV/REL...T MICHIGAN. PAGE 38 E0753 — PROVS LOC/G ADMIN CONSTN

B65
FRIEDMAN L.,SOUTHERN JUSTICE. USA+45 PUB/INST LEGIT ADMIN CT/SYS DISCRIM...DECISION ANTHOL 20 NEGRO SOUTH/US CIV/RIGHTS. PAGE 40 E0800 — ADJUD LAW CONSTN RACE/REL

B65
HARTUNG F.E.,CRIME, LAW, AND SOCIETY. LAW PUB/INST CRIME PERS/REL AGE/Y BIO/SOC PERSON ROLE SUPEGO ...LING GP/COMP GEN/LAWS 20. PAGE 50 E1004 — PERCEPT CRIMLGY DRIVE CONTROL

B66
AMERICAN JEWISH COMMITTEE,THE TYRANNY OF POVERTY (PAMPHLET). USA+45 LAW ECO/DEV LOC/G MUNIC NAT/G PUB/INST WORKER EDU/PROP CRIME...SOC/WK 20. PAGE 4 E0080 — BIBLIOG/A WEALTH WELF/ST PROB/SOLV

B66
BEELEY A.L.,THE BAIL SYSTEM IN CHICAGO. LAW MUNIC PUB/INST EFFICIENCY MORAL...CRIMLGY METH/CNCPT STAT 20 CHICAGO. PAGE 9 E0176 — JURID CT/SYS CRIME ADJUD

B66
COUNCIL OF STATE GOVERNMENTS,THE HANDBOOK ON INTERSTATE CRIME CONTROL. USA+45 PUB/INST DELIB/GP AGREE AGE/Y 20 INTST/CRIM. PAGE 27 E0524 — CRIME GOV/REL CONTROL JURID

B66
MACIVER R.M.,THE PREVENTION AND CONTROL OF DELINQUENCY. USA+45 STRATA PUB/INST ANOMIE ATTIT HABITAT PERSON HEALTH...CRIMLGY PSY SOC METH. PAGE 67 E1341 — AGE/Y PLAN ADJUST CRIME

B66
OSTERMANN R.,A REPORT IN DEPTH ON CRIME IN AMERICA. FUT USA+45 MUNIC PUB/INST TEC/DEV MURDER EFFICIENCY ATTIT BIO/SOC...PSY 20. PAGE 79 E1584 — CRIME FORCES CONTROL LAW

B67
AMDS W.E.,DELINQUENCY PREVENTION: THEORY AND PRACTICE. USA+45 SOCIETY FAM SCHOOL SECT FORCES PROB/SOLV...HEAL JURID PREDICT ANTHOL. PAGE 4 E0071 — AGE/Y CRIME PUB/INST LAW

B67
BERNSTEIN S.,ALTERNATIVES TO VIOLENCE: ALIENATED YOUTH AND RIOTS, RACE AND POVERTY. MUNIC PUB/INST SCHOOL INGP/REL RACE/REL UTOPIA DRIVE HABITAT ROLE WEALTH...INT 20. PAGE 11 E0215 — AGE/Y SOC/WK NEIGH CRIME

B67
ELDRIDGE W.B.,NARCOTICS AND THE LAW: A CRITIQUE OF THE AMERICAN EXPERIMENT IN NARCOTIC DRUG CONTROL. PUB/INST ACT/RES PLAN LICENSE GP/REL EFFICIENCY ATTIT HEALTH...CRIMLGY HEAL STAT 20 ABA DEPT/HEW NARCO/ACT. PAGE 34 E0679 — LAW INSPECT BIO/SOC JURID

B67
LOBLE L.H.,DELINQUENCY CAN BE STOPPED. FAM PUB/INST CT/SYS ADJUST ATTIT...NEW/IDEA METH/COMP 20. PAGE 66 E1315 — AGE/Y PROB/SOLV ADJUD CRIME

S67
CARTER R.M.,"SOME FACTORS IN SENTENCING POLICY." LAW PUB/INST CRIME PERS/REL...POLICY JURID SOC TREND CON/ANAL CHARTS SOC/EXP 20. PAGE 20 E0403 — ADJUD CT/SYS ADMIN

S67
KENNEDY R.F.,"TOWARD A NATION WHERE THE LAW IS KING." PLAN CT/SYS CRIME INGP/REL...JURID SOC. PAGE 60 E1202 — CRIMLGY ADJUST LAW PUB/INST

PUB/TRANS....PUBLIC TRANSPORTATION

PUBL/WORKS....PUBLIC WORKS

PUBLIC ADMINISTRATION....SEE ADMIN

PUBLIC OPINION....SEE ATTIT

PUBLIC POLICY....SEE PLAN

PUBLIC RELATIONS....SEE NAT/G+RELATIONS INDEX

PUBLIC WORKS....SEE PUBL/WORKS

PUBLIC/EDU....PUBLIC EDUCATION ASSOCIATION

PUBLIC/REL....PUBLIC RELATIONS; SEE ALSO RELATIONS
    INDEX

PUBLIC/USE....PUBLIC USE

PUBLISHERS' CIRCULAR LIMITED E1658

PUEBLO....PUEBLO INCIDENT; SEE ALSO KOREA/N

PUERT/RICN....PUERTO RICAN

PUERT/RICO....PUERTO RICO; SEE ALSO L/A+17C

B59
COUNCIL OF STATE GOVERNORS,AMERICAN LEGISLATURES: LEGIS
STRUCTURE AND PROCEDURES. SUMMARY AND TABULATIONS   CHARTS
OF A 1959 SURVEY. PUERT/RICO USA+45 PAY ADJUD ADMIN PROVS
APPORT...IDEA/COMP 20 GUAM VIRGIN/ISL. PAGE 27   REPRESENT
E0525

PUFENDORF S. E1659

PUGET H. E1660

PUGWASH CONFERENCE E1661

PULLEN W.R. E1662

PULLMAN....PULLMAN, ILLINOIS

PUNISHMENT....SEE ADJUD, LAW, LEGIT, SANCTION

PUNJAB....THE PUNJAB AND ITS PEOPLES

PUNTA DEL ESTE....SEE PUNTA/ESTE

PUNTA/ESTE....PUNTA DEL ESTE

PURCELL F.P. E0285

PURGE....PURGES

PURHAM/M....MARGERY PURHAM

PURITAN....PURITANS

B58
EUSDEN J.D.,PURITANS, LAWYERS, AND POLITICS IN   GP/REL
EARLY SEVENTEENTH-CENTURY ENGLAND. UK CT/SYS   SECT
PARL/PROC RATIONAL PWR SOVEREIGN...IDEA/COMP   NAT/G
BIBLIOG 17 PURITAN COMMON/LAW. PAGE 35 E0702   LAW

PUSEY M.J. E1663

PUTTKAMMER E.W. E1664

PWR....POWER, PARTICIPATION IN DECISION-MAKING

B00
BERNARD M.,FOUR LECTURES ON SUBJECTS CONNECTED WITH LAW
DIPLOMACY. WOR-45 NAT/G VOL/ASSN RIGID/FLEX MORAL   ATTIT
PWR...JURID OBS GEN/LAWS GEN/METH 20 TREATY.   DIPLOM
PAGE 11 E0209

B00
DARBY W.E.,INTERNATIONAL TRIBUNALS. WOR-45 NAT/G   INT/ORG
ECO/TAC DOMIN LEGIT CT/SYS COERCE ORD/FREE PWR   ADJUD
SOVEREIGN JURID. PAGE 29 E0567   PEACE
                                                     INT/LAW

B00
GRIFFIN A.P.C.,LIST OF BOOKS RELATING TO THE THEORY BIBLIOG/A
OF COLONIZATION, GOVERNMENT OF DEPENDENCIES,   COLONIAL
PROTECTORATES, AND RELATED TOPICS. FRANCE GERMANY   GOV/REL
ITALY SPAIN UK USA-45 WOR-45 ECO/TAC ADMIN CONTROL   DOMIN
REGION NAT/LISM ALL/VALS PWR...INT/LAW SOC 16/19.
PAGE 46 E0917

B00
GROTIUS H.,DE JURE BELLI AC PACIS. CHRIST-17C UNIV   JURID
LAW SOCIETY PROVS LEGIT PEACE PERCEPT MORAL PWR   INT/LAW
...CONCPT CON/ANAL GEN/LAWS. PAGE 48 E0952   WAR

B00
HOLLAND T.E.,STUDIES IN INTERNATIONAL LAW. TURKEY   INT/ORG
USSR WOR-45 CONSTN NAT/G DIPLOM DOMIN LEGIT COERCE   LAW
WAR PEACE ORD/FREE PWR SOVEREIGN...JURID CHARTS 20   INT/LAW
PARLIAMENT SUEZ TREATY. PAGE 54 E1084

B02
GRIFFIN A.P.C.,A LIST OF BOOKS RELATING TO TRUSTS   BIBLIOG/A
(2ND REV. ED.) (PAMPHLET). FRANCE GERMANY UK USA-45 JURID
WOR-45 LAW ECO/DEV INDUS LG/CO NAT/G CAP/ISM   ECO/TAC
CENTRAL DISCRIM PWR LAISSEZ 19/20. PAGE 46 E0919   VOL/ASSN

B04
FREUND E.,THE POLICE POWER; PUBLIC POLICY AND   CONSTN
CONSTITUTIONAL RIGHTS. USA-45 SOCIETY LOC/G NAT/G   LAW
FORCES LEGIS ADJUD CT/SYS OWN PWR...JURID 18/19   ORD/FREE
SUPREME/CT. PAGE 40 E0795   CONTROL

B05
GOODNOW F.J.,THE PRINCIPLES OF THE ADMINISTRATIVE   ADMIN
LAW OF THE UNITED STATES. USA-45 LAW STRUCT   NAT/G
EX/STRUC LEGIS BAL/PWR CONTROL GOV/REL PWR...JURID   PROVS
19/20 CIVIL/SERV. PAGE 45 E0887   LOC/G

B08
WILSON W.,CONSTITUTIONAL GOVERNMENT IN THE UNITED   NAT/G
STATES. USA-45 LAW POL/PAR PROVS CHIEF LEGIS   GOV/REL
BAL/PWR ADJUD EXEC FEDERAL PWR 18/20 SUPREME/CT   CONSTN
HOUSE/REP SENATE. PAGE 106 E2130   PARL/PROC

B09
LOBINGIER C.S.,THE PEOPLE'S LAW OR POPULAR   CONSTN
PARTICIPATION IN LAW-MAKING. FRANCE SWITZERLND UK   LAW
LOC/G NAT/G PROVS LEGIS SUFF MAJORITY PWR POPULISM   PARTIC
...GOV/COMP BIBLIOG 19. PAGE 66 E1314

B12
FOUAD M.,LE REGIME DE LA PRESSE EN EGYPTE: THESE   ORD/FREE
POUR LE DOCTORAT. UAR LICENSE EDU/PROP ADMIN   LEGIS
SANCTION CRIME SUPEGO PWR...ART/METH JURID 19/20.   CONTROL
PAGE 39 E0778   PRESS

B13
BUTLER N.M.,THE INTERNATIONAL MIND. WOR-45 INT/ORG   ADJUD
LEGIT PWR...JURID CONCPT 20. PAGE 18 E0350   ORD/FREE
                                                     INT/LAW

B14
FIGGIS J.N.,CHURCHES IN THE MODERN STATE (2ND ED.). SECT
LAW CHIEF BAL/PWR PWR...CONCPT CHURCH/STA POPE.   NAT/G
PAGE 38 E0748   SOCIETY
                                                     ORD/FREE

B14
VECCHIO G.D.,THE FORMAL BASES OF LAW (TRANS. BY J.   LAW
LISLE). DOMIN LEGIT CONTROL COERCE UTIL MORAL PWR   JURID
...CONCPT TIME/SEQ 17/20 COMMON/LAW NATURL/LAW.   GEN/LAWS
PAGE 103 E2074   IDEA/COMP

B16
PUFENDORF S.,LAW OF NATURE AND OF NATIONS   CONCPT
(ABRIDGED). UNIV LAW NAT/G DIPLOM AGREE WAR PERSON   INT/LAW
ALL/VALS PWR...POLICY 18 DEITY NATURL/LAW. PAGE 83   SECT
E1659   MORAL

B18
WILSON W.,THE STATE: ELEMENTS OF HISTORICAL AND   NAT/G
PRACTICAL POLITICS. FRANCE GERMANY ITALY UK USSR   JURID
CONSTN EX/STRUC LEGIS CT/SYS WAR PWR...POLICY   CONCPT
GOV/COMP 20. PAGE 106 E2131   NAT/COMP

B18
YUKIO O.,THE VOICE OF JAPANESE DEMOCRACY. AN ESSAY   CONSTN
ON CONSTITUTIONAL LOYALTY (TRANS BY J. E. BECKER).   MAJORIT
ASIA POL/PAR DELIB/GP EX/STRUC RIGID/FLEX ORD/FREE   CHOOSE
PWR...POLICY JURID METH/COMP 19/20 CHINJAP.   NAT/G
PAGE 108 E2167

N19
BAILEY S.D.,VETO IN THE SECURITY COUNCIL   DELIB/GP
(PAMPHLET). COM USSR WOR+45 BAL/PWR PARL/PROC   INT/ORG
ARMS/CONT PRIVIL PWR...INT/LAW TREND CHARTS 20 UN   DIPLOM
SUEZ. PAGE 7 E0135

N19
BRENNAN W.J. JR.,THE BILL OF RIGHTS AND THE STATES   CONSTN
(PAMPHLET). USA+45 USA-45 LEGIS BAL/PWR ADJUD   PROVS
CT/SYS FEDERAL PWR SOVEREIGN 18/20 SUPREME/CT   GOV/REL
BILL/RIGHT. PAGE 15 E0293   ORD/FREE

N19
BURRUS B.R.,INVESTIGATION AND DISCOVERY IN STATE   NAT/G
ANTITRUST (PAMPHLET). USA+45 USA-45 LEGIS ECO/TAC   PROVS
ADMIN CONTROL CT/SYS CRIME GOV/REL PWR...JURID   LAW
CHARTS 19/20 FTC MONOPOLY. PAGE 18 E0346   INSPECT

N19

MCCONNELL G.,THE STEEL SEIZURE OF 1952 (PAMPHLET). DELIB/GP
USA+45 FINAN INDUS PROC/MFG LG/CO EX/STRUC ADJUD LABOR
CONTROL GP/REL ORD/FREE PWR 20 TRUMAN/HS PRESIDENT PROB/SOLV
CONGRESS. PAGE 70 E1402 NAT/G

N19

MISSISSIPPI ADVISORY COMMITTEE,REPORT ON RACE/REL
MISSISSIPPI (PAMPHLET). USA+45 LAW PROVS FORCES DISCRIM
ADJUD PWR...SOC/WK INT 20 MISSISSIPP NEGRO COERCE
CIV/RIGHTS. PAGE 73 E1469 ORD/FREE

N19

POUND R.,ORGANIZATION OF THE COURTS (PAMPHLET). CT/SYS
MOD/EUR UK USA-45 ADJUD PWR...GOV/COMP 10/20 JURID
EUROPE. PAGE 82 E1635 STRUCT
ADMIN

B20

MEYER H.H.B.,LIST OF REFERENCES ON THE TREATY- BIBLIOG
MAKING POWER. USA-45 CONTROL PWR...INT/LAW TIME/SEQ DIPLOM
18/20 TREATY. PAGE 72 E1448 CONSTN

B22

WRIGHT Q.,THE CONTROL OF AMERICAN FOREIGN NAT/G
RELATIONS. USA-45 WOR-45 CONSTN INT/ORG CONSULT EXEC
LEGIS LEGIT ROUTINE ORD/FREE PWR...POLICY JURID DIPLOM
CONCPT METH/CNCPT RECORD LEAGUE/NAT 20. PAGE 107
E2150

B24

HALL W.E.,A TREATISE ON INTERNATIONAL LAW. WOR-45 PWR
CONSTN INT/ORG NAT/G DIPLOM ORD/FREE LEAGUE/NAT 20 JURID
TREATY. PAGE 49 E0985 WAR
INT/LAW

B26

FORTESCUE J.,THE GOVERNANCE OF ENGLAND (1471-76). CONSERVE
UK LAW FINAN SECT LEGIS PROB/SOLV TAX DOMIN ADMIN CONSTN
GP/REL COST ORD/FREE PWR 14/15. PAGE 39 E0776 CHIEF
NAT/G

B27

JOHN OF SALISBURY,THE STATESMAN'S BOOK (1159) NAT/G
(TRANS. BY J. DICKINSON). DOMIN GP/REL MORAL SECT
ORD/FREE PWR CONSERVE...CATH CONCPT 12. PAGE 59 CHIEF
E1169 LAW

B27

LAUTERPACHT H.,PRIVATE LAW SOURCES AND ANALOGIES OF INT/ORG
INTERNATIONAL LAW. WOR-45 NAT/G ADJUD LEGIT ADJUD
COERCE ATTIT ORD/FREE PWR SOVEREIGN...JURID CONCPT PEACE
HIST/WRIT TIME/SEQ GEN/METH LEAGUE/NAT 20. PAGE 63 INT/LAW
E1264

B27

RYAN J.A.,DECLINING LIVERTY AND OTHER ESSAYS. ORD/FREE
USA-45 SECT DELIB/GP ATTIT PWR SOCISM 20 LEGIS
SUPREME/CT. PAGE 87 E1740 JURID
NAT/G

B28

BUTLER G.,THE DEVELOPMENT OF INTERNATIONAL LAW. LAW
WOR-45 SOCIETY NAT/G KNOWL ORD/FREE PWR...JURID INT/LAW
CONCPT HIST/WRIT GEN/LAWS. PAGE 18 E0349 DIPLOM
INT/ORG

B28

CORBETT P.E.,CANADA AND WORLD POLITICS. LAW CULTURE NAT/G
SOCIETY STRUCT MARKET INT/ORG FORCES ACT/RES PLAN CANADA
ECO/TAC LEGIT ORD/FREE PWR RESPECT...SOC CONCPT
TIME/SEQ TREND CMN/WLTH 20 LEAGUE/NAT. PAGE 26
E0504

B28

FRANKFURTER F.,THE BUSINESS OF THE SUPREME COURT; A CT/SYS
STUDY IN THE FEDERAL JUDICIAL SYSTEM. USA-45 CONSTN ADJUD
EX/STRUC PROB/SOLV GP/REL ATTIT PWR...POLICY JURID LAW
18/20 SUPREME/CT CONGRESS. PAGE 40 E0789 FEDERAL

B29

BUELL R.,INTERNATIONAL RELATIONS. WOR+45 WOR-45 INT/ORG
CONSTN STRATA FORCES TOP/EX ADMIN ATTIT DRIVE BAL/PWR
SUPEGO MORAL ORD/FREE PWR SOVEREIGN...JURID SOC DIPLOM
CONCPT 20. PAGE 17 E0326

B29

CONWELL-EVANS T.P.,THE LEAGUE COUNCIL IN ACTION. DELIB/GP
EUR+WWI TURKEY UK USSR WOR-45 INT/ORG FORCES JUDGE INT/LAW
ECO/TAC EDU/PROP LEGIT ROUTINE ARMS/CONT COERCE
ATTIT PWR...MAJORIT GEOG JURID CONCPT LEAGUE/NAT
TOT/POP VAL/FREE TUNIS 20. PAGE 25 E0498

B29

MOLEY R.,POLITICS AND CRIMINAL PROSECUTION. USA-45 PWR
POL/PAR EX/STRUC LEGIT CONTROL LEAD ROUTINE CHOOSE CT/SYS

INGP/REL...JURID CHARTS 20. PAGE 74 E1481 CRIME
ADJUD

B31

STOWELL E.C.,INTERNATIONAL LAW. FUT UNIV WOR-45 INT/ORG
SOCIETY CONSULT EX/STRUC FORCES ACT/RES PLAN DIPLOM ROUTINE
EDU/PROP LEGIT DISPL PWR SKILL...POLICY CONCPT OBS INT/LAW
TREND TOT/POP 20. PAGE 94 E1885

B32

EAGLETON C.,INTERNATIONAL GOVERNMENT. BRAZIL FRANCE INT/ORG
GERMANY ITALY UK USSR WOR-45 DELIB/GP TOP/EX PLAN JURID
ECO/TAC EDU/PROP LEGIT ADJUD REGION ARMS/CONT DIPLOM
COERCE ATTIT PWR...GEOG MGT VAL/FREE LEAGUE/NAT 20. INT/LAW
PAGE 34 E0670

B32

GREAT BRIT COMM MINISTERS PWR,REPORT. UK LAW CONSTN EX/STRUC
CONSULT LEGIS PARL/PROC SANCTION SOVEREIGN NAT/G
...DECISION JURID 20 PARLIAMENT. PAGE 45 E0902 PWR
CONTROL

B33

HELLMAN F.S.,SELECTED LIST OF REFERENCES ON THE BIBLIOG/A
CONSTITUTIONAL POWERS OF THE PRESIDENT INCLUDING JURID
POWERS RECENTLY DELEGATED. USA-45 NAT/G EX/STRUC LAW
TOP/EX CENTRAL FEDERAL PWR 20 PRESIDENT. PAGE 51 CONSTN
E1025

B33

LAUTERPACHT H.,THE FUNCTION OF LAW IN THE INT/ORG
INTERNATIONAL COMMUNITY. WOR-45 NAT/G FORCES CREATE LAW
DOMIN LEGIT COERCE WAR PEACE ATTIT ORD/FREE PWR INT/LAW
SOVEREIGN...JURID CONCPT METH/CNCPT TIME/SEQ
GEN/LAWS GEN/METH LEAGUE/NAT TOT/POP VAL/FREE 20.
PAGE 63 E1265

B34

CLYDE W.M.,THE STRUGGLE FOR THE FREEDOM OF THE PRESS
PRESS FROM CAXTON TO CROMWELL. UK LAW LOC/G SECT ORD/FREE
FORCES LICENSE WRITING SANCTION REV ATTIT PWR CONTROL
...POLICY 15/17 PARLIAMENT CROMWELL/O MILTON/J.
PAGE 23 E0460

B35

LUCE R.,LEGISLATIVE PROBLEMS. CONSTN CHIEF JUDGE TREND
BUDGET CONFER ETIQUET CONTROL MORAL PWR NEW/LIB ADMIN
CONGRESS. PAGE 67 E1331 LEGIS

B36

BRIERLY J.L.,THE LAW OF NATIONS (2ND ED.). WOR+45 DIPLOM
WOR-45 INT/ORG AGREE CONTROL COERCE WAR NAT/LISM INT/LAW
PEACE PWR 16/20 TREATY LEAGUE/NAT. PAGE 15 E0297 NAT/G

B36

RUSSEL F.M.,THEORIES OF INTERNATIONAL RELATIONS. PWR
EUR+WWI FUT MOD/EUR USA-45 INT/ORG DIPLOM...JURID POLICY
CONCPT. PAGE 86 E1735 BAL/PWR
SOVEREIGN

B36

SCHULZ F.,PRINCIPLES OF ROMAN LAW. CONSTN FAM NAT/G LAW
DOMIN CONTROL CT/SYS CRIME ISOLAT ATTIT ORD/FREE LEGIS
PWR...JURID ROME/ANC ROMAN/LAW. PAGE 89 E1783 ADJUD
CONCPT

S36

CORWIN E.S.,"THE CONSTITUTION AS INSTRUMENT AND AS CONSTN
SYMBOL." USA-45 ECO/DEV INDUS CAP/ISM SANCTION LAW
RIGID/FLEX ORD/FREE LAISSEZ OBJECTIVE 20 CONGRESS ADJUD
SUPREME/CT. PAGE 26 E0512 PWR

B37

HAMILTON W.H.,THE POWER TO GOVERN. ECO/DEV FINAN LING
INDUS ECO/TAC INT/TRADE TARIFFS TAX CONTROL CT/SYS CONSTN
WAR COST PWR 18/20 SUPREME/CT. PAGE 50 E0991 NAT/G
POLICY

L37

LERNER M.,"CONSTITUTION AND COURT AS SYMBOLS" CONSTN
(BMR)" USA+45 USA-45 DOMIN PWR SOVEREIGN...PSY MYTH CT/SYS
18/20 SUPREME/CT. PAGE 64 E1288 ATTIT
EDU/PROP

S37

TIMASHEFF N.S.,"WHAT IS SOCIOLOGY OF LAW?" (BMR)" LAW
UNIV INTELL PWR...EPIST JURID PHIL/SCI IDEA/COMP. SOC
PAGE 96 E1925 SOCIETY

B38

FRANKFURTER F.,MR. JUSTICE HOLMES AND THE SUPREME CREATE
COURT. USA-45 CONSTN SOCIETY FEDERAL OWN ATTIT CT/SYS
ORD/FREE PWR...POLICY JURID 20 SUPREME/CT HOLMES/OW DECISION
BILL/RIGHT. PAGE 40 E0790 LAW

B38

HOLDSWORTH W.S.,A HISTORY OF ENGLISH LAW; THE CENTURIES OF SETTLEMENT AND REFORM (VOL. X). INDIA UK CONSTN NAT/G CHIEF LEGIS ADMIN COLONIAL CT/SYS CHOOSE ORD/FREE PWR...JURID 18 PARLIAMENT COMMONWLTH COMMON/LAW. PAGE 54 E1077
LAW
LOC/G
EX/STRUC
ADJUD

B38

SAINT-PIERRE C.I.,SCHEME FOR LASTING PEACE (TRANS. BY H. BELLOT). INDUS NAT/G CHIEF FORCES INT/TRADE CT/SYS WAR PWR SOVEREIGN WEALTH...POLICY 18. PAGE 87 E1741
INT/ORG
PEACE
AGREE
INT/LAW

B39

BALDWIN L.D.,WHISKEY REBELS; THE STORY OF A FRONTIER UPRISING. USA+45 LAW ADJUD LEAD COERCE PWR ...BIBLIOG/A 18 PENNSYLVAN FEDERALIST. PAGE 8 E0145
REV
POL/PAR
TAX
TIME/SEQ

B39

BENES E.,INTERNATIONAL SECURITY. GERMANY UK NAT/G DELIB/GP PLAN BAL/PWR ATTIT ORD/FREE PWR LEAGUE/NAT 20 TREATY. PAGE 10 E0186
EUR+WWI
INT/ORG
WAR

B39

LAVES W.H.C.,INTERNATIONAL SECURITY. EUR+WWI GERMANY UK USA+45 LAW NAT/G DELIB/GP TOP/EX COERCE PWR...POLICY FASCIST CONCPT HIST/WRIT GEN/LAWS LEAGUE/NAT NAZI 20. PAGE 63 E1267
ORD/FREE
LEGIT
ARMS/CONT
BAL/PWR

B39

TIMASHEFF N.S.,AN INTRODUCTION TO THE SOCIOLOGY OF LAW. CRIME ANOMIE ATTIT DRIVE ORD/FREE...JURID PSY CONCPT. PAGE 96 E1926
SOC
BIBLIOG
PWR

B39

ZIMMERN A.,THE LEAGUE OF NATIONS AND THE RULE OF LAW. WOR-45 STRUCT NAT/G DELIB/GP EX/STRUC BAL/PWR DOMIN LEGIT COERCE ORD/FREE PWR...POLICY RECORD LEAGUE/NAT TOT/POP VAL/FREE 20 LEAGUE/NAT. PAGE 108 E2170
INT/ORG
LAW
DIPLOM

B40

HART J.,AN INTRODUCTION TO ADMINISTRATIVE LAW, WITH SELECTED CASES. USA+45 CONSTN SOCIETY NAT/G EX/STRUC ADJUD CT/SYS LEAD CRIME ORD/FREE ...DECISION JURID 20 CASEBOOK. PAGE 50 E1002
LAW
ADMIN
LEGIS
PWR

B40

HOBBES T.,A DIALOGUE BETWEEN A PHILOSOPHER AND A STUDENT OF THE COMMON LAWS OF ENGLAND (1667?). UK SECT DOMIN ADJUD CRIME INCOME OWN UTIL ORD/FREE PWR SOVEREIGN...JURID GEN/LAWS 17. PAGE 53 E1057
CT/SYS
CHIEF
SANCTION

B40

MCILWAIN C.H.,CONSTITUTIONALISM, ANCIENT AND MODERN. CHRIST-17C MOD/EUR NAT/G CHIEF PROB/SOLV INSPECT AUTHORIT ORD/FREE PWR...TIME/SEQ ROMAN/REP. PAGE 71 E1418
CONSTN
GEN/LAWS
LAW

S40

GERTH H.,"THE NAZI PARTY: ITS LEADERSHIP AND COMPOSITION" (BMR)" GERMANY ELITES STRATA STRUCT EX/STRUC FORCES ECO/TAC CT/SYS CHOOSE TOTALISM AGE/Y AUTHORIT PWR 20. PAGE 43 E0851
POL/PAR
DOMIN
LEAD
ADMIN

B41

GELLHORN W.,FEDERAL ADMINISTRATIVE PROCEEDINGS. USA+45 CLIENT FACE/GP NAT/G LOBBY REPRESENT PWR 20. PAGE 43 E0844
EX/STRUC
LAW
ADJUD
POLICY

B41

GILMORE M.P.,ARGUMENT FROM ROMAN LAW IN POLITICAL THOUGHT, 1200-1600. INTELL LICENSE CONTROL CT/SYS GOV/REL PRIVIL PWR...IDEA/COMP BIBLIOG 13/16. PAGE 44 E0866
JURID
LAW
CONCPT
NAT/G

B41

MCCLURE W.,INTERNATIONAL EXECUTIVE AGREEMENTS. USA+45 WOR-45 INT/ORG NAT/G DELIB/GP ADJUD ROUTINE ORD/FREE PWR...TIME/SEQ TREND CON/ANAL. PAGE 70 E1401
TOP/EX
DIPLOM

B41

NIEMEYER G.,LAW WITHOUT FORCE: THE FUNCTION OF POLITICS IN INTERNATIONAL LAW. PLAN INSPECT DIPLOM REPAR LEGIT ADJUD WAR ORD/FREE...IDEA/COMP METH/COMP GEN/LAWS 20. PAGE 77 E1549
COERCE
LAW
PWR
INT/LAW

L41

COMM. STUDY ORGAN. PEACE,"ORGANIZATION OF PEACE." USA-45 WOR-45 STRATA NAT/G ACT/RES DIPLOM ECO/TAC EDU/PROP ADJUD ATTIT ORD/FREE PWR...SOC CONCPT ANTHOL LEAGUE/NAT 20. PAGE 24 E0479
INT/ORG
PLAN
PEACE

S41

WRIGHT Q.,"FUNDAMENTAL PROBLEMS OF INTERNATIONAL ORGANIZATION." UNIV WOR-45 STRUCT FORCES ACT/RES CREATE DOMIN EDU/PROP LEGIT REGION NAT/LISM ORD/FREE PWR RESPECT SOVEREIGN...JURID SOC CONCPT METH/CNCPT TIME/SEQ 20. PAGE 107 E2152
INT/ORG
ATTIT
PEACE

B42

CARR R.K.,THE SUPREME COURT AND JUDICIAL REVIEW. NAT/G CHIEF LEGIS OP/RES LEAD GOV/REL GP/REL ATTIT ...POLICY DECISION 18/20 SUPREME/CT PRESIDENT CONGRESS. PAGE 20 E0394
CT/SYS
CONSTN
JURID
PWR

B42

FULLER G.H.,DEFENSE FINANCING: A SUPPLEMENTARY LIST OF REFERENCES (PAMPHLET). CANADA UK USA-45 ECO/DEV NAT/G DELIB/GP BUDGET ADJUD ARMS/CONT WEAPON COST PEACE PWR 20 AUSTRAL CHINJAP CONGRESS. PAGE 41 E0821
BIBLIOG/A
FINAN
FORCES
DIPLOM

B43

CONOVER H.F.,THE BALKANS: A SELECTED LIST OF REFERENCES. ALBANIA BULGARIA ROMANIA YUGOSLAVIA INT/ORG PROB/SOLV DIPLOM LEGIT CONFER ADJUD WAR NAT/LISM PEACE PWR 20 LEAGUE/NAT. PAGE 25 E0493
BIBLIOG
EUR+WWI

B43

MICAUD C.A.,THE FRENCH RIGHT AND NAZI GERMANY 1933-1939: A STUDY OF PUBLIC OPINION. GERMANY UK USSR POL/PAR ARMS/CONT COERCE DETER PEACE RIGID/FLEX PWR MARXISM...FASCIST TREND 20 LEAGUE/NAT TREATY. PAGE 73 E1454
DIPLOM
AGREE

C43

BENTHAM J.,"PRINCIPLES OF INTERNATIONAL LAW" IN J. BOWRING, ED., THE WORKS OF JEREMY BENTHAM." UNIV NAT/G PLAN PROB/SOLV DIPLOM CONTROL SANCTION MORAL ORD/FREE PWR SOVEREIGN 19. PAGE 10 E0194
INT/LAW
JURID
WAR
PEACE

C43

BENTHAM J.,"THE RATIONALE OF REWARD" IN J. BOWRING, ED., THE WORKS OF JEREMY BENTHAM (VOL. 2)" LAW WORKER CREATE INSPECT PAY ROUTINE HAPPINESS PRODUC SUPEGO WEALTH METH/CNCPT. PAGE 10 E0195
SANCTION
ECO/TAC
INCOME
PWR

B44

FULLER G.H.,MILITARY GOVERNMENT: A LIST OF REFERENCES (A PAMPHLET). ITALY UK USA-45 WOR-45 LAW FORCES DOMIN ADMIN ARMS/CONT ORD/FREE PWR ...DECISION 20 CHINJAP. PAGE 41 E0822
BIBLIOG
DIPLOM
CIVMIL/REL
SOVEREIGN

B44

SUAREZ F.,A TREATISE ON LAWS AND GOD THE LAWGIVER (1612) IN SELECTIONS FROM THREE WORKS, VOL. II. FRANCE ITALY UK CULTURE NAT/G SECT CHIEF LEGIS DOMIN LEGIT CT/SYS ORD/FREE PWR WORSHIP 16/17. PAGE 94 E1892
LAW
JURID
GEN/LAWS
CATH

B45

BEVERIDGE W.,THE PRICE OF PEACE. GERMANY UK WOR+45 WOR-45 NAT/G FORCES CREATE LEGIT REGION WAR ATTIT KNOWL ORD/FREE PWR...POLICY NEW/IDEA GEN/LAWS LEAGUE/NAT 20 TREATY. PAGE 12 E0223
INT/ORG
TREND
PEACE

B45

HILL N.,CLAIMS TO TERRITORY IN INTERNATIONAL LAW AND RELATIONS. WOR-45 NAT/G DOMIN EDU/PROP LEGIT REGION ROUTINE ORD/FREE PWR WEALTH...GEOG INT/LAW JURID 20. PAGE 52 E1047
INT/ORG
ADJUD
SOVEREIGN

B45

US LIBRARY OF CONGRESS,CONSTITUTIONAL AND STATUTORY PROVISIONS OF THE STATES (VOL. I). USA-45 CREATE TAX CT/SYS CHOOSE SUFF INCOME PWR 20. PAGE 101 E2016
CONSTN
FEDERAL
PROVS
JURID

B46

KEETON G.W.,MAKING INTERNATIONAL LAW WORK. FUT WOR-45 NAT/G DELIB/GP FORCES LEGIT COERCE PEACE ATTIT RIGID/FLEX ORD/FREE PWR...JURID CONCPT HIST/WRIT GEN/METH LEAGUE/NAT 20. PAGE 60 E1193
INT/ORG
ADJUD
INT/LAW

B47

BORGESE G.,COMMON CAUSE. LAW CONSTN SOCIETY STRATA ECO/DEV INT/ORG POL/PAR FORCES LEGIS TOP/EX CAP/ISM DIPLOM ADMIN EXEC ATTIT PWR 20. PAGE 14 E0269
WOR+45
NAT/G
SOVEREIGN
REGION

B47

GORDON D.L.,THE HIDDEN WEAPON: THE STORY OF ECONOMIC WARFARE. EUR+WWI USA-45 LAW FINAN INDUS NAT/G CONSULT FORCES PLAN DOMIN PWR WEALTH ...INT/LAW CONCPT OBS TOT/POP NAZI 20. PAGE 45 E0891
INT/ORG
ECO/TAC
INT/TRADE
WAR

JESSUP P.C.,A MODERN LAW OF NATIONS. FUT WOR+45 WOR-45 SOCIETY NAT/G DELIB/GP LEGIS BAL/PWR EDU/PROP LEGIT PWR...INT/LAW JURID TIME/SEQ LEAGUE/NAT 20. PAGE 58 E1166
INT/ORG
ADJUD
B48

MORGENTHAL H.J.,POLITICS AMONG NATIONS: THE STRUGGLE FOR POWER AND PEACE. FUT WOR+45 INT/ORG OP/RES PROB/SOLV BAL/PWR CONTROL ATTIT MORAL ...INT/LAW BIBLIOG 20 COLD/WAR. PAGE 75 E1494
DIPLOM
PEACE
PWR
POLICY
B48

ALEXANDER L.,"WAR CRIMES, THEIR SOCIAL-PSYCHOLOGICAL ASPECTS." EUR+WWI GERMANY LAW CULTURE ELITES KIN POL/PAR PUB/INST FORCES DOMIN EDU/PROP COERCE CRIME ATTIT SUPEGO HEALTH MORAL PWR FASCISM ...PSY OBS TREND GEN/LAWS NAZI 20. PAGE 3 E0061
DRIVE
WAR
S48

BRADEN G.D.,"THE SEARCH FOR OBJECTIVITY IN CONSTITUTIONAL LAW" (BMR)" USA+45 USA-45 LAW NAT/G CONTROL ORD/FREE PWR OBJECTIVE...JURID 20 SUPREME/CT. PAGE 15 E0283
CONSTN
CT/SYS
IDEA/COMP
POLICY
S48

APPLEBY P.H.,POLICY AND ADMINISTRATION. USA+45 NAT/G LOBBY PWR 20. PAGE 5 E0101
REPRESENT
EXEC
ADMIN
CLIENT
B49

BRUCKER H.,FREEDOM OF INFORMATION. USA-45 LAW LOC/G ECO/TAC DOMIN PWR...NEW/IDEA BIBLIOG 17/20. PAGE 16 E0320
PRESS
COM/IND
ORD/FREE
NAT/G
B49

WALINE M.,LE CONTROLE JURIDICTIONNEL DE L'ADMINISTRATION. BELGIUM FRANCE UAR JUDGE BAL/PWR ADJUD CONTROL CT/SYS...GP/COMP 20. PAGE 104 E2093
JURID
ADMIN
PWR
ORD/FREE
B49

WORMUTH F.D.,THE ORIGINS OF MODERN CONSTITUTIONALISM. GREECE UK LEGIS CREATE TEC/DEV BAL/PWR DOMIN ADJUD REV WAR PWR...JURID ROMAN/REP CROMWELL/O. PAGE 107 E2146
NAT/G
CONSTN
LAW
B49

HURST J.W.,THE GROWTH OF AMERICAN LAW; THE LAW MAKERS. USA-45 LOC/G NAT/G DELIB/GP JUDGE ADJUD ADMIN ATTIT PWR...POLICY JURID BIBLIOG 18/20 CONGRESS SUPREME/CT ABA PRESIDENT. PAGE 56 E1115
LAW
LEGIS
CONSTN
CT/SYS
B50

JIMENEZ E.,VOTING AND HANDLING OF DISPUTES IN THE SECURITY COUNCIL. WOR+45 CONSTN INT/ORG DIPLOM LEGIT DETER CHOOSE MORAL ORD/FREE PWR...JURID TIME/SEQ COLD/WAR UN 20. PAGE 59 E1168
DELIB/GP
ROUTINE
B50

HOLCOMBE A.,"OUR MORE PERFECT UNION." USA+45 USA-45 CONSTN POL/PAR JUDGE CT/SYS EQUILIB FEDERAL PWR...MAJORIT TREND BIBLIOG 18/20 CONGRESS PRESIDENT. PAGE 54 E1070
CONSTN
NAT/G
ADMIN
PLAN
C50

CORBETT P.E.,LAW AND SOCIETY IN THE RELATIONS OF STATES. FUT WOR+45 WOR-45 CONTROL WAR PEACE PWR ...POLICY JURID 16/20 TREATY. PAGE 26 E0505
INT/LAW
DIPLOM
INT/ORG
B51

FITCH R.E.,THE LIMITS OF LIBERTY. COERCE...JURID GEN/LAWS. PAGE 38 E0759
ORD/FREE
CONCPT
PWR
B51

KEFAUVER E.,CRIME IN AMERICA. USA+45 USA-45 MUNIC NEIGH DELIB/GP TRIBUTE GAMBLE LOBBY SANCTION ...AUD/VIS 20 CAPONE/AL MAFIA MIAMI CHICAGO DETROIT. PAGE 60 E1194
ELITES
CRIME
PWR
FORCES
B51

ROSSITER C.,THE SUPREME COURT AND THE COMMANDER IN CHIEF. LAW CONSTN DELIB/GP EX/STRUC LEGIS TOP/EX ADJUD CONTROL...DECISION SOC/EXP PRESIDENT. PAGE 86 E1724
CT/SYS
CHIEF
WAR
PWR
B51

WHEARE K.C.,MODERN CONSTITUTIONS (HOME UNIVERSITY LIBRARY). UNIV LAW NAT/G LEGIS...CONCPT TREND BIBLIOG. PAGE 106 E2115
CONSTN
CLASSIF
PWR
CREATE
B51

MANGONE G.,"THE IDEA AND PRACTICE OF WORLD GOVERNMENT." FUT WOR+45 WOR-45 ECO/DEV LEGIS CREATE LEGIT ROUTINE ATTIT MORAL PWR WEALTH...CONCPT GEN/LAWS 20. PAGE 68 E1358
INT/ORG
SOCIETY
INT/LAW
L51

BENTHAM A.,HANDBOOK OF POLITICAL FALLACIES. FUT MOD/EUR LAW INTELL LOC/G MUNIC NAT/G DELIB/GP LEGIS CREATE EDU/PROP CT/SYS ATTIT RIGID/FLEX KNOWL PWR ...RELATIV PSY SOC CONCPT SELF/OBS TREND STERTYP TOT/POP. PAGE 10 E0189
POL/PAR
B52

FLECHTHEIM O.K.,FUNDAMENTALS OF POLITICAL SCIENCE. WOR+45 WOR-45 LAW POL/PAR EX/STRUC LEGIS ADJUD ATTIT PWR...INT/LAW. PAGE 38 E0760
NAT/G
DIPLOM
IDEA/COMP
CONSTN
B52

THOM J.M.,GUIDE TO RESEARCH MATERIAL IN POLITICAL SCIENCE (PAMPHLET). ELITES LOC/G MUNIC NAT/G LEGIS DIPLOM ADJUD CIVMIL/REL GOV/REL PWR MGT. PAGE 96 E1916
BIBLIOG/A
KNOWL
B52

MCDOUGAL M.S.,"THE COMPARATIVE STUDY OF LAW FOR POLICY PURPOSES." FUT NAT/G POL/PAR CONSULT ADJUD PWR SOVEREIGN...METH/CNCPT IDEA/COMP SIMUL 20. PAGE 70 E1403
PLAN
JURID
NAT/LISM
S52

MANGONE G.,A SHORT HISTORY OF INTERNATIONAL ORGANIZATION. MOD/EUR USA+45 USA-45 WOR+45 WOR-45 LAW LEGIS CREATE LEGIT ROUTINE RIGID/FLEX PWR ...JURID CONCPT OBS TIME/SEQ STERTYP GEN/LAWS UN TOT/POP VAL/FREE 18/20. PAGE 68 E1359
INT/ORG
INT/LAW
B54

WRIGHT Q.,PROBLEMS OF STABILITY AND PROGRESS IN INTERNATIONAL RELATIONSHIPS. FUT WOR+45 WOR-45 SOCIETY LEGIS CREATE TEC/DEV ECO/TAC EDU/PROP ADJUD WAR PEACE ORD/FREE PWR...KNO/TEST TREND GEN/LAWS 20. PAGE 108 E2155
INT/ORG
CONCPT
DIPLOM
B54

COOPER L.,"ADMINISTRATIVE JUSTICE." UK ADMIN REPRESENT PWR...POLICY 20. PAGE 25 E0502
LAW
ADJUD
CONTROL
EX/STRUC
S54

BEISEL A.R.,CONTROL OVER ILLEGAL ENFORCEMENT OF THE CRIMINAL LAW: ROLE OF THE SUPREME COURT. CONSTN ROUTINE MORAL PWR...SOC 20 SUPREME/CT. PAGE 9 E0180
ORD/FREE
LAW
CRIME
B55

BURR R.N.,DOCUMENTS ON INTER-AMERICAN COOPERATION: VOL. I, 1810-1881; VOL. II, 1881-1948. DELIB/GP BAL/PWR INT/TRADE REPRESENT NAT/LISM PEACE HABITAT ORD/FREE PWR SOVEREIGN...INT/LAW 20 OAS. PAGE 18 E0345
BIBLIOG
DIPLOM
INT/ORG
L/A+17C
B55

CHOWDHURI R.N.,INTERNATIONAL MANDATES AND TRUSTEESHIP SYSTEMS. WOR+45 STRUCT ECO/UNDEV INT/ORG LEGIS DOMIN EDU/PROP LEGIT ADJUD EXEC PWR ...CONCPT TIME/SEQ UN 20. PAGE 22 E0434
DELIB/GP
PLAN
SOVEREIGN
B55

COMM. STUDY ORGAN. PEACE,REPORTS. WOR-45 ECO/DEV ECO/UNDEV VOL/ASSN CONSULT FORCES PLAN TEC/DEV DOMIN EDU/PROP NUC/PWR ATTIT PWR WEALTH...JURID STERTYP FAO ILO 20 UN. PAGE 24 E0481
WOR+45
INT/ORG
ARMS/CONT
B55

GUAITA A.,BIBLIOGRAFIA ESPANOLA DE DERECHO ADMINISTRATIVO (PAMPHLET). SPAIN LOC/G MUNIC NAT/G PROVS JUDGE BAL/PWR GOV/REL OWN...JURID 18/19. PAGE 48 E0959
BIBLIOG
ADMIN
CONSTN
PWR
B55

LARROWE C.P.,SHAPE-UP AND HIRING HALL. TRIBUTE ADJUD CONTROL SANCTION COERCE CRIME GP/REL PWR ...CHARTS 20 AFL/CIO NEWYORK/C SEATTLE. PAGE 63 E1256
LABOR
INDUS
WORKER
NAT/G
B55

CARR C.,"LEGISLATIVE CONTROL OF ADMINISTRATIVE RULES AND REGULATIONS: PARLIAMENTARY SUPERVISION IN BRITAIN." DELIB/GP CONTROL ROLE PWR PARLIAMENT. PAGE 20 E0392
EXEC
REPRESENT
JURID
S55

CALLISON I.P.,COURTS OF INJUSTICE. USA+45 PROF/ORG ADJUD CRIME PERSON MORAL PWR RESPECT SKILL 20.
CT/SYS
JUDGE
B56

PAGE 19 E0368   JURID

STUDY OF THE ORGANIZATION OF PUBLIC ADMINISTRATION. METH/COMP
DENMARK FRANCE NORWAY SWEDEN UK USA+45 ELITES LOC/G NAT/G
CONSULT LEGIS ADJUD CONTROL LEAD PWR SKILL   CENTRAL
DECISION. PAGE 72 E1449

B56
PEASLEE A.J.,CONSTITUTIONS OF NATIONS. WOR+45 LAW   CONSTN
NAT/G EX/STRUC LEGIS TOP/EX LEGIT CT/SYS ROUTINE   CON/ANAL
CHOOSE ORD/FREE PWR SOVEREIGN...CHARTS TOT/POP.
PAGE 80 E1605

B57
PALMER N.D.,INTERNATIONAL RELATIONS. WOR+45 INT/ORG DIPLOM
NAT/G ECO/TAC EDU/PROP COLONIAL WAR PWR SOVEREIGN BAL/PWR
...POLICY T 20 TREATY. PAGE 79 E1593   NAT/COMP

B56
PERKINS D.,CHARLES EVANS HUGHES AND THE AMERICAN PERSON
DEMOCRATIC STATESMANSHIP. USA+45 USA-45 NAT/G   BIOG
POL/PAR DELIB/GP JUDGE PLAN MORAL PWR...HIST/WRIT DIPLOM
LEAGUE/NAT 20. PAGE 80 E1609

B57
ROSENNE S.,THE INTERNATIONAL COURT OF JUSTICE.   INT/ORG
WOR+45 LAW DOMIN LEGIT PEACE PWR SOVEREIGN...JURID CT/SYS
CONCPT RECORD TIME/SEQ CON/ANAL CHARTS UN TOT/POP INT/LAW
VAL/FREE LEAGUE/NAT 20 ICJ. PAGE 86 E1716

B56
SOHN L.B.,BASIC DOCUMENTS OF THE UNITED NATIONS. DELIB/GP
WOR+45 LAW INT/ORG LEGIT EXEC ROUTINE CHOOSE PWR CONSTN
...JURID CONCPT GEN/LAWS ANTHOL UN TOT/POP OAS FAO
ILO 20. PAGE 92 E1853

B57
SCHUBERT G.A.,THE PRESIDENCY IN THE COURTS. CONSTN PWR
FORCES DIPLOM TARIFFS ADJUD CONTROL WAR...DECISION CT/SYS
MGT CHARTS 18/20 PRESIDENT CONGRESS SUPREME/CT.   LEGIT
PAGE 89 E1778   CHIEF

B56
US HOUSE RULES COMM,HEARINGS BEFORE A SPECIAL   ADMIN
SUBCOMMITTEE: ESTABLISHMENT OF A STANDING COMMITTEE DOMIN
ON ADMINISTRATIVE PROCEDURE, PRACTICE. USA+45 LAW DELIB/GP
EX/STRUC ADJUD CONTROL EXEC GOV/REL EFFICIENCY PWR NAT/G
...POLICY INT 20 CONGRESS. PAGE 100 E2009

B57
SINEY M.C.,THE ALLIED BLOCKADE OF GERMANY: DETER
1914-1916. EUR+WWI GERMANY MOD/EUR USA-45 DIPLOM INT/TRADE
CONTROL NEUTRAL PWR 20. PAGE 91 E1832   INT/LAW
                                 WAR

B56
WIGGINS J.R.,FREEDOM OR SECRECY. USA+45 USA-45   ORD/FREE
DELIB/GP EX/STRUC FORCES ADJUD SANCTION KNOWL PWR PRESS
...AUD/VIS CONGRESS 20. PAGE 106 E2121   NAT/G
                                 CONTROL

B57
US SENATE COMM ON JUDICIARY,CIVIL RIGHTS - 1957. INT
USA+45 LAW NAT/G CONFER GOV/REL RACE/REL ORD/FREE LEGIS
PWR...JURID 20 SENATE CIV/RIGHTS. PAGE 102 E2039 DISCRIM
                                 PARL/PROC

L56
CARRINGTON P.D.,"POLITICAL QUESTIONS: THE JUDICIAL ADJUD
CHECK ON THE EXECUTIVE." USA+45 LAW CHIEF 20.   EXEC
PAGE 20 E0395   PWR
                                 REPRESENT

B57
US SENATE COMM ON JUDICIARY,LIMITATION OF APPELLATE CT/SYS
JURISDICTION OF THE SUPREME COURT. USA+45 LAW NAT/G ADJUD
DELIB/GP PLAN ADMIN CONTROL PWR...DECISION 20   POLICY
CONGRESS SUPREME/CT. PAGE 102 E2041   GOV/REL

S56
ROSENBERG M.,"POWER AND DESEGREGATION." USA+45   PWR
STRATA MUNIC GP/REL. PAGE 85 E1715   DISCRIM
                                 DECISION
                                 LAW

B58
CHAMBERLIN E.H.,LABOR UNIONS AND PUBLIC POLICY.   LABOR
PLAN BARGAIN SANCTION INGP/REL JURID. PAGE 21 E0416 WEALTH
                                 PWR
                                 NAT/G

S56
TANENHAUS J.,"THE SUPREME COURT AND PRESIDENTIAL CT/SYS
POWER." USA+45 USA-45 NAT/G ADJUD GOV/REL FEDERAL PWR
20 PRESIDENT. PAGE 95 E1907   CONTROL
                                 CHIEF

B58
DUCLOUX L.,FROM BLACKMAIL TO TREASON. FRANCE PLAN COERCE
DIPLOM EDU/PROP PRESS RUMOR NAT/LISM...CRIMLGY 20. CRIME
PAGE 33 E0653   NAT/G
                                 PWR

B57
BERLE A.A. JR.,ECONOMIC POWER AND FREE SOCIETY   LG/CO
(PAMPHLET). CLIENT CONSTN EX/STRUC ECO/TAC CONTROL CAP/ISM
PARTIC PWR WEALTH MAJORIT. PAGE 11 E0205   INGP/REL
                                 LEGIT

B58
EUSDEN J.D.,PURITANS, LAWYERS, AND POLITICS IN   GP/REL
EARLY SEVENTEENTH-CENTURY ENGLAND. UK CT/SYS   SECT
PARL/PROC RATIONAL PWR SOVEREIGN...IDEA/COMP   NAT/G
BIBLIOG 17 PURITAN COMMON/LAW. PAGE 35 E0702   LAW

B57
BLOOMFIELD L.M.,EGYPT, ISRAEL AND THE GULF OF   ISLAM
AQABA: IN INTERNATIONAL LAW. LAW NAT/G CONSULT   INT/LAW
FORCES PLAN ECO/TAC ROUTINE COERCE ATTIT DRIVE   UAR
PERCEPT PERSON RIGID/FLEX LOVE PWR WEALTH...GEOG
CONCPT MYTH TREND. PAGE 13 E0250

B58
HAND L.,THE BILL OF RIGHTS. USA+45 USA-45 CHIEF   CONSTN
LEGIS BAL/PWR ROLE PWR 18/20 SUPREME/CT CONGRESS JURID
AMEND/V PRESIDENT AMEND/XIV. PAGE 50 E0994   ORD/FREE
                                 CT/SYS

B57
CONOVER H.F.,NORTH AND NORTHEAST AFRICA: A SELECTED BIBLIOG/A
ANNOTATED LIST OF WRITINGS. ALGERIA MOROCCO SUDAN DIPLOM
UAR CULTURE INT/ORG PROB/SOLV ADJUD NAT/LISM PWR AFR
WEALTH...SOC 20 UN. PAGE 25 E0496   ECO/UNDEV

B58
MACKENZIE W.J.M.,FREE ELECTIONS: AN ELEMENTARY   EX/STRUC
TEXTBOOK. WOR+45 NAT/G POL/PAR LEGIS TOP/EX   CHOOSE
EDU/PROP LEGIT CT/SYS ATTIT PWR...OBS CHARTS
STERTYP T CONGRESS PARLIAMENT 20. PAGE 67 E1342

B57
COSSIO C.,LA POLITICA COMO CONCIENCIA: MEDITACION POL/PAR
SOBRE LA ARGENTINA DE 1955. WOR+45 LEGIS EDU/PROP REV
PARL/PROC PARTIC ATTIT PWR CATHISM 20 ARGEN   TOTALISM
PERON/JUAN. PAGE 26 E0517   JURID

B58
MOEN N.W.,THE GOVERNMENT OF SCOTLAND 1603 - 1625. CHIEF
UK JUDGE ADMIN GP/REL PWR 17 SCOTLAND COMMON/LAW. JURID
PAGE 74 E1479   CONTROL
                                 PARL/PROC

B57
DE VISSCHER C.,THEORY AND REALITY IN PUBLIC   INT/ORG
INTERNATIONAL LAW. WOR+45 WOR-45 SOCIETY NAT/G   LAW
CT/SYS ATTIT MORAL ORD/FREE PWR...JURID CONCPT   INT/LAW
METH/CNCPT TIME/SEQ GEN/LAWS LEAGUE/NAT TOT/POP
VAL/FREE COLD/WAR. PAGE 30 E0599

B58
RUSSELL R.B.,A HISTORY OF THE UNITED NATIONS   USA-45
CHARTER: THE ROLE OF THE UNITED STATES. SOCIETY   INT/ORG
NAT/G CONSULT DOMIN LEGIT ATTIT ORD/FREE PWR   CONSTN
...POLICY JURID CONCPT UN LEAGUE/NAT. PAGE 87 E1737

B57
FREUND G.,UNHOLY ALLIANCE. EUR+WWI GERMANY USSR   DIPLOM
FORCES ECO/TAC CONTROL WAR PWR...TREND TREATY.   PLAN
PAGE 40 E0796   POLICY

B58
SPITZ D.,DEMOCRACY AND THE CHALLANGE OF POWER. FUT NAT/G
USA+45 USA-45 LAW SOCIETY STRUCT LOC/G POL/PAR   PWR
PROVS DELIB/GP EX/STRUC LEGIS TOP/EX ACT/RES CREATE
DOMIN EDU/PROP LEGIT ADJUD ADMIN ATTIT DRIVE MORAL
ORD/FREE TOT/POP. PAGE 93 E1862

B57
HINDERLING A.,DIE REFORMATORISCHE   ADMIN
VERWALTUNGSGERICHTSBARKEIT. GERMANY/W PROB/SOLV   CT/SYS
ADJUD SUPEGO PWR...CONCPT 20. PAGE 53 E1049   JURID
                                 CONTROL

B58
STONE J.,AGGRESSION AND WORLD ORDER: A CRITIQUE OF ORD/FREE
UNITED NATIONS THEORIES OF AGGRESSION. LAW CONSTN INT/ORG
DELIB/GP PROB/SOLV BAL/PWR DIPLOM DEBATE ADJUD   WAR
CRIME PWR...POLICY IDEA/COMP 20 UN SUEZ LEAGUE/NAT. CONCPT
PAGE 94 E1879

B57
MEYER P.,ADMINISTRATIVE ORGANIZATION: A COMPARATIVE ADMIN

US CONGRESS,FREEDOM OF INFORMATION AND SECRECY IN
GOVERNMENT (2 VOLS.). USA+45 DELIB/GP EX/STRUC
EDU/PROP PWR 20 CONGRESS PRESIDENT. PAGE 99 E1988
CHIEF B58
PRIVIL
CONSTN
LAW

DAHL R.A.,"DECISION-MAKING IN A DEMOCRACY: THE
SUPREME COURT AS A NATIONAL POLICY-MAKER" (BMR)"
USA+45 USA-45 POL/PAR ADJUD GOV/REL PWR...POLICY
JURID 19/20 SUPREME/CT. PAGE 28 E0561
CT/SYS S58
CONSTN
DECISION
NAT/G

STAAR R.F.,"ELECTIONS IN COMMUNIST POLAND." EUR+WWI
SOCIETY INT/ORG NAT/G POL/PAR ACT/RES ECO/TAC
EDU/PROP ADJUD ADMIN ROUTINE COERCE TOTALISM ATTIT
ORD/FREE PWR 20. PAGE 93 E1864
COM S58
CHOOSE
POLAND

FRIEDRICH C.J.,"AUTHORITY, REASON AND DISCRETION"
IN C. FRIEDRICH'S AUTHORITY (BMR)" UNIV EX/STRUC
ADJUD ADMIN CONTROL INGP/REL ATTIT PERSON PWR.
PAGE 41 E0807
AUTHORIT C58
CHOOSE
RATIONAL
PERS/REL

ABRAHAM H.J.,COURTS AND JUDGES: AN INTRODUCTION TO
THE JUDICIAL PROCESS. USA+45 CONSTN ELITES NAT/G
ORD/FREE PWR 19/20 SUPREME/CT. PAGE 2 E0045
CT/SYS B59
PERSON
JURID
ADJUD

BECK C.,CONTEMPT OF CONGRESS: A STUDY OF THE
PROSECUTIONS INITIATED BY THE COMMITTEE ON UN-
AMERICAN ACTIVITIES. USA+45 CONSTN DEBATE EXEC.
PAGE 9 E0170
LEGIS B59
DELIB/GP
PWR
ADJUD

BROMWICH L.,UNION CONSTITUTIONS. CONSTN EX/STRUC
PRESS ADJUD CONTROL CHOOSE REPRESENT PWR SAMP.
PAGE 16 E0306
LABOR B59
ROUTINE
INGP/REL
RACE/REL

DESMITH S.A.,JUDICIAL REVIEW OF ADMINISTRATIVE
ACTION. UK LOC/G CONSULT DELIB/GP ADMIN PWR
...DECISION JURID 20 ENGLSH/LAW. PAGE 31 E0609
ADJUD B59
NAT/G
PROB/SOLV
CT/SYS

FERRY W.H.,THE CORPORATION AND THE ECONOMY. CLIENT
LAW CONSTN LABOR NAT/G PLAN INT/TRADE PARTIC CONSEN
ORD/FREE PWR POLICY. PAGE 37 E0742
LG/CO B59
CONTROL
REPRESENT

GREENSPAN M.,THE MODERN LAW OF LAND WARFARE. WOR+45
INT/ORG NAT/G DELIB/GP FORCES ATTIT...POLICY
HYPO/EXP STERTYP 20. PAGE 46 E0911
ADJUD B59
PWR
WAR

HALEY A.G.,FIRST COLLOQUIUM ON THE LAW OF OUTER
SPACE. WOR+45 INT/ORG ACT/RES PLAN BAL/PWR CONFER
ATTIT PWR...POLICY JURID CHARTS ANTHOL 20. PAGE 49
E0979
SPACE B59
LAW
SOVEREIGN
CONTROL

HOOK S.,POLITICAL POWER AND PERSONAL FREEDOM:
CRITICAL STUDIES IN DEMOCRACY, COMMUNISM AND CIVIL
RIGHTS. UNIV LAW SOCIETY DIPLOM TOTALISM MARXISM
SOCISM...PHIL/SCI IDEA/COMP 20 CIV/RIGHTS. PAGE 55
E1094
ORD/FREE B59
PWR
WELF/ST
CHOOSE

MAYER A.J.,POLITICAL ORIGINS OF THE NEW DIPLOMACY,
1917-1918. EUR+WWI MOD/EUR USA-45 WAR PWR...POLICY
INT/LAW BIBLIOG. PAGE 70 E1392
TREND B59
DIPLOM

MOOS M.,THE CAMPUS AND THE STATE. LAW FINAN
DELIB/GP LEGIS EXEC LOBBY GP/REL PWR...POLICY
BIBLIOG. PAGE 74 E1489
EDU/PROP B59
ACADEM
PROVS
CONTROL

COLUMBIA U. BUREAU OF APPL SOC RES, ATTITUDES OF
PROMINENT AMERICANS TOWARD "WORLD PEACE THROUGH
WORLD LAW" (SUPRA-NATL ORGANIZATION FOR WAR
PREVENTION). USA+45 USSR ELITES FORCES PLAN
PROB/SOLV CONTROL WAR PWR...POLICY SOC QU IDEA/COMP
20 UN. PAGE 82 E1644
ATTIT B59
ACT/RES
INT/LAW
STAT

REIFF H.,THE UNITED STATES AND THE TREATY LAW OF
THE SEA. USA+45 USA-45 SEA SOCIETY INT/ORG CONSULT
DELIB/GP LEGIS DIPLOM LEGIT ATTIT ORD/FREE PWR
WEALTH...GEOG JURID TOT/POP 20 TREATY. PAGE 84
E1681
ADJUD B59
INT/LAW

SCHNEIDER J.,TREATY-MAKING POWER OF INTERNATIONAL
ORGANIZATIONS. FUT WOR+45 WOR-45 LAW NAT/G JUDGE
DIPLOM LEGIT CT/SYS ORD/FREE PWR...INT/LAW JURID
GEN/LAWS TOT/POP UNESCO 20 TREATY. PAGE 88 E1762
INT/ORG B59
ROUTINE

SPIRO H.J.,GOVERNMENT BY CONSTITUTIONS: THE
POLITICAL SYSTEMS OF DEMOCRACY. CANADA EUR+WWI FUT
USA+45 WOR+45 WOR-45 LEGIS TOP/EX LEGIT ADMIN
CT/SYS ORD/FREE PWR...TREND TOT/POP VAL/FREE 20.
PAGE 93 E1861
NAT/G B59
CONSTN

US SENATE COMM ON JUDICIARY,EXECUTIVE PRIVILEGE.
USA+45 DELIB/GP CONTROL KNOWL PWR 20 CONGRESS
PRESIDENT. PAGE 102 E2042
CHIEF B59
PRIVIL
CONSTN
LAW

WAGNER W.J.,THE FEDERAL STATES AND THEIR JUDICIARY.
BRAZIL CANADA SWITZERLND USA+45 CONFER CT/SYS TASK
EFFICIENCY FEDERAL PWR...JURID BIBLIOG 20 AUSTRAL
MEXIC/AMER. PAGE 104 E2091
ADJUD B59
METH/COMP
PROB/SOLV
NAT/G

COWAN T.A.,"A SYMPOSIUM ON GROUP INTERESTS AND THE
LAW" USA+45 LAW MARKET LABOR PLAN INT/TRADE TAX
RACE/REL RIGID/FLEX...JURID ANTHOL 20. PAGE 27
E0528
ADJUD L59
PWR
INGP/REL
CREATE

OBERER W.E.,"VOLUNTARY IMPARTIAL REVIEW OF LABOR:
SOME REFLECTIONS." DELIB/GP LEGIS PROB/SOLV ADJUD
CONTROL COERCE PWR PLURISM POLICY. PAGE 78 E1570
LABOR L59
LAW
PARTIC
INGP/REL

CARLSTON K.S.,"NATIONALIZATION: AN ANALYTIC
APPROACH." WOR+45 INT/ORG ECO/TAC DOMIN LEGIT ADJUD
COERCE ORD/FREE PWR WEALTH SOCISM...JURID CONCPT
TREND STERTYP TOT/POP VAL/FREE 20. PAGE 19 E0380
INDUS S59
NAT/G
NAT/LISM
SOVEREIGN

CHAPMAN B.,"THE FRENCH CONSEIL D'ETAT." FRANCE
NAT/G CONSULT OP/RES PROB/SOLV PWR...OBS 20.
PAGE 21 E0421
ADMIN S59
LAW
CT/SYS
LEGIS

CORY R.H. JR.,"INTERNATIONAL INSPECTION FROM
PROPOSALS TO REALIZATION." WOR+45 TEC/DEV ECO/TAC
ADJUD ORD/FREE PWR WEALTH...RECORD VAL/FREE 20.
PAGE 26 E0516
STRUCT S59
PSY
ARMS/CONT
NUC/PWR

DOMKE M.,"THE SETTLEMENT OF DISPUTES IN
INTERNATIONAL TRADE." USA+45 LAW STRATA STRUCT
JUDGE EDU/PROP PWR...METH/CNCPT 20. PAGE 32 E0634
CONSULT S59
LEGIT
INT/TRADE

MASON A.T.,"THE SUPREME COURT: TEMPLE AND FORUM"
(BMR)" USA+45 USA-45 CONSTN DELIB/GP RACE/REL
MAJORITY ORD/FREE...DECISION SOC/INTEG 19/20
SUPREME/CT WARRN/EARL CIV/RIGHTS. PAGE 69 E1377
CT/SYS S59
JURID
PWR
ATTIT

PUGWASH CONFERENCE,"ON BIOLOGICAL AND CHEMICAL
WARFARE." WOR+45 SOCIETY PROC/MFG INT/ORG FORCES
EDU/PROP ADJUD RIGID/FLEX ORD/FREE PWR...DECISION
PSY NEW/IDEA MATH VAL/FREE 20. PAGE 83 E1661
ACT/RES S59
BIO/SOC
WAR
WEAPON

SOHN L.B.,"THE DEFINITION OF AGGRESSION." FUT LAW
FORCES LEGIT ADJUD ROUTINE COERCE ORD/FREE PWR
...MAJORIT JURID QUANT COLD/WAR 20. PAGE 92 E1855
INT/ORG S59
CT/SYS
DETER
SOVEREIGN

STONE J.,"CONFLICT MANAGEMENT THROUGH CONTEMPORARY
INTERNATIONAL LAW AND ORGANIZATION." WOR+45 LAW
NAT/G CREATE BAL/PWR DOMIN LEGIT ROUTINE COERCE
ATTIT ORD/FREE PWR SOVEREIGN...JURID 20. PAGE 94
E1880
INT/ORG S59
INT/LAW

CLARK G.,WORLD PEACE THROUGH WORLD LAW. FUT WOR+45
CONSULT FORCES ACT/RES CREATE PLAN ADMIN ROUTINE
ARMS/CONT DETER ATTIT PWR...JURID VAL/FREE UNESCO
20 UN. PAGE 23 E0449
INT/ORG B60
LAW
PEACE
INT/LAW

DAVIS K.C.,ADMINISTRATIVE LAW AND GOVERNMENT.
USA+45 EX/STRUC PROB/SOLV ADJUD GP/REL PWR...POLICY
20 SUPREME/CT. PAGE 29 E0578
ADMIN B60
JURID
CT/SYS

NAT/G

B60

FISCHER L.,THE SOVIETS IN WORLD AFFAIRS. CHINA/COM DIPLOM
COM EUR+WWI USSR INT/ORG CONFER LEAD ARMS/CONT REV NAT/G
PWR...CHARTS 20 TREATY VERSAILLES. PAGE 38 E0755 POLICY
MARXISM

B60

GOLDSEN J.M.,INTERNATIONAL POLITICAL IMPLICATIONS R+D
OF ACTIVITIES IN OUTER SPACE. FUT USA+45 WOR+45 AIR SPACE
LAW ACT/RES LEGIT ATTIT KNOWL ORD/FREE PWR...CONCPT
20. PAGE 44 E0879

B60

LASKIN B.,CANADIAN CONSTITUTIONAL LAW: TEXT AND CONSTN
NOTES ON DISTRIBUTION OF LEGISLATIVE POWER (2ND LAW
ED.). CANADA LOC/G ECO/TAC TAX CONTROL CT/SYS CRIME LEGIS
FEDERAL PWR...JURID 20 PARLIAMENT. PAGE 63 E1259

B60

LENCZOWSKI G.,OIL AND STATE IN THE MIDDLE EAST. FUT ISLAM
IRAN LAW ECO/UNDEV EXTR/IND NAT/G TOP/EX PLAN INDUS
TEC/DEV ECO/TAC LEGIT ADMIN COERCE ATTIT ALL/VALS NAT/LISM
PWR...CHARTS 20. PAGE 64 E1283

B60

PINTO F.B.M.,ENRIQUECIMENTO ILICITO NO EXERCICIO DE ADMIN
CARGOS PUBLICOS. BRAZIL L/A+17C USA+45 ELITES NAT/G
TRIBUTE CONTROL INGP/REL ORD/FREE PWR...NAT/COMP CRIME
20. PAGE 81 E1617 LAW

B60

PRASAD B.,THE ORIGINS OF PROVINCIAL AUTONOMY. INDIA CENTRAL
UK FINAN LOC/G FORCES LEGIS CONTROL CT/SYS PWR PROVS
...JURID 19/20. PAGE 82 E1646 COLONIAL
NAT/G

B60

PRICE D.,THE SECRETARY OF STATE. USA+45 CONSTN CONSULT
ELITES INTELL CHIEF EX/STRUC TOP/EX LEGIT ATTIT PWR DIPLOM
SKILL...DECISION 20 CONGRESS. PAGE 82 E1650 INT/LAW

B60

RIENOW R.,INTRODUCTION TO GOVERNMENT (2ND ED.). UK CONSTN
USA+45 USSR POL/PAR ADMIN REV CHOOSE SUFF FEDERAL PARL/PROC
PWR...JURID GOV/COMP T 20. PAGE 85 E1697 REPRESENT
AUTHORIT

B60

SCHMIDHAUSER J.R.,THE SUPREME COURT: ITS POLITICS, JUDGE
PERSONALITIES, AND PROCEDURES. LAW DELIB/GP JURID
EX/STRUC TOP/EX ADJUD CT/SYS CHOOSE RATIONAL PWR DECISION
SUPREME/CT. PAGE 88 E1760

B60

SCHUBERT G.,THE PUBLIC INTEREST. USA+45 CONSULT POLICY
PLAN PROB/SOLV ADJUD ADMIN GP/REL PWR ALL/IDEOS 20. DELIB/GP
PAGE 88 E1770 REPRESENT
POL/PAR

B60

SCHUBERT G.A.,CONSTITUTIONAL POLITICS: THE CONSTN
POLITICAL BEHAVIOR OF SUPREME COURT JUSTICES AND CT/SYS
THE CONSTITUTIONAL POLICIES THEY MAKE. LAW ELITES JURID
CHIEF DELIB/GP EX/STRUC LEGIS DISCRIM ORD/FREE PWR DECISION
...POLICY MAJORIT CHARTS SUPREME/CT CONGRESS.
PAGE 89 E1781

B60

STEIN E.,AMERICAN ENTERPRISE IN THE EUROPEAN COMMON MARKET
MARKET: A LEGAL PROFILE. EUR+WWI FUT USA+45 SOCIETY ADJUD
STRUCT ECO/DEV NAT/G VOL/ASSN CONSULT PLAN TEC/DEV INT/LAW
ECO/TAC INT/TRADE ADMIN ATTIT RIGID/FLEX PWR...MGT
NEW/IDEA STAT TREND COMPUT/IR SIMUL EEC 20. PAGE 93
E1867

B60

WOETZEL R.K.,THE INTERNATIONAL CONTROL OF AIRSPACE INT/ORG
AND OUTERSPACE. FUT WOR+45 AIR CONSTN STRUCT JURID
CONSULT PLAN TEC/DEV ADJUD RIGID/FLEX KNOWL SPACE
ORD/FREE PWR...TECHNIC GEOG MGT NEW/IDEA TREND INT/LAW
COMPUT/IR VAL/FREE 20 TREATY. PAGE 107 E2137

L60

STEIN E.,"LEGAL REMEDIES OF ENTERPRISES IN THE MARKET
EUROPEAN ECONOMIC COMMUNITY." EUR+WWI FUT ECO/DEV ADJUD
INDUS PLAN ECO/TAC ADMIN PWR...MGT MATH STAT TREND
CON/ANAL EEC 20. PAGE 93 E1868

S60

BLACK H.,"THE BILL OF RIGHTS" (BMR)" USA+45 USA-45 CONSTN
LAW LEGIS CT/SYS FEDERAL PWR 18/20 CONGRESS ORD/FREE
SUPREME/CT BILL/RIGHT CIV/RIGHTS. PAGE 12 E0237 NAT/G
JURID

S60

O'BRIEN W.,"THE ROLE OF FORCE IN THE INTERNATIONAL INT/ORG
JURIDICAL ORDER." WOR+45 NAT/G FORCES DOMIN ADJUD COERCE
ARMS/CONT DETER NUC/PWR WAR ATTIT PWR...CATH
INT/LAW JURID CONCPT TREND STERTYP GEN/LAWS 20.
PAGE 78 E1564

S60

SANDERS R.,"NUCLEAR DYNAMITE: A NEW DIMENSION IN INDUS
FOREIGN POLICY." FUT WOR+45 ECO/DEV CONSULT TEC/DEV PWR
PERCEPT...CONT/OBS TIME/SEQ TREND GEN/LAWS TOT/POP DIPLOM
20 TREATY. PAGE 87 E1745 NUC/PWR

S60

SCHACHTER O.,"THE ENFORCEMENT OF INTERNATIONAL INT/ORG
JUDICIAL AND ARBITRAL DECISIONS." WOR+45 NAT/G ADJUD
ECO/TAC DOMIN LEGIT ROUTINE COERCE ATTIT DRIVE INT/LAW
ALL/VALS PWR...METH/CNCPT TREND TOT/POP 20 UN.
PAGE 87 E1750

S60

THOMPSON K.W.,"MORAL PURPOSE IN FOREIGN POLICY: MORAL
REALITIES AND ILLUSIONS." WOR+45 WOR-45 LAW CULTURE JURID
SOCIETY INT/ORG PLAN ADJUD ADMIN COERCE RIGID/FLEX DIPLOM
SUPEGO KNOWL ORD/FREE PWR...SOC TREND SOC/EXP
TOT/POP 20. PAGE 96 E1921

S60

WRIGHT Q.,"LEGAL ASPECTS OF THE U-2 INCIDENT." COM PWR
USA+45 USSR STRUCT NAT/G FORCES PLAN TEC/DEV ADJUD POLICY
RIGID/FLEX MORAL ORD/FREE...DECISION INT/LAW JURID SPACE
PSY TREND GEN/LAWS COLD/WAR VAL/FREE 20 U-2.
PAGE 108 E2157

C60

MCCLEERY R.,"COMMUNICATION PATTERNS AS BASES OF PERS/REL
SYSTEMS OF AUTHORITY AND POWER" IN THEORETICAL PUB/INST
STUDIES IN SOCIAL ORGAN. OF PRISON-BMR. USA+45 PWR
SOCIETY STRUCT EDU/PROP ADMIN CONTROL COERCE CRIME DOMIN
GP/REL AUTHORIT...SOC 20. PAGE 70 E1400

B61

FROEBEL J.,THEORIE DER POLITIK, ALS ERGEBNIS EINER JURID
ERNEUERTEN PRUEFUNG DEMOKRATISCHER LEHRMEINUNGEN. ORD/FREE
WOR-45 SOCIETY POL/PAR SECT REV REPRESENT PWR NAT/G
SOVEREIGN...MAJORIT 19. PAGE 41 E0812

B61

LA PONCE J.A.,THE GOVERNMENT OF THE FIFTH REPUBLIC: PWR
FRENCH POLITICAL PARTIES AND THE CONSTITUTION. POL/PAR
ALGERIA FRANCE LAW NAT/G DELIB/GP LEGIS ECO/TAC CONSTN
MARXISM SOCISM...CHARTS BIBLIOG/A 20 DEGAULLE/C. CHIEF
PAGE 62 E1243

B61

PRITCHETT C.H.,CONGRESS VERSUS THE SUPREME COURT. LEGIS
1957-1960. PROB/SOLV DOMIN EXEC GP/REL DISCRIM PWR JURID
CONGRESS SUPREME/CT SUPREME/CT. PAGE 82 E1652 LAW

B61

RIENOW R.,CONTEMPORARY INTERNATIONAL POLITICS. DIPLOM
WOR+45 INT/ORG BAL/PWR EDU/PROP COLONIAL NEUTRAL PWR
REGION WAR PEACE...INT/LAW 20 COLD/WAR UN. PAGE 85 POLICY
E1698 NAT/G

B61

WECHSLER H.,PRINCIPLES, POLITICS AND FUNDAMENTAL CT/SYS
LAW: SELECTED ESSAYS. USA+45 USA-45 LAW SOCIETY CONSTN
NAT/G PROVS DELIB/GP EX/STRUC ACT/RES LEGIT PERSON INT/LAW
KNOWL PWR...JURID 20 NUREMBERG. PAGE 105 E2106

B61

WRIGHT Q.,THE ROLE OF INTERNATIONAL LAW IN THE INT/ORG
ELIMINATION OF WAR. FUT WOR+45 WOR-45 NAT/G BAL/PWR ADJUD
DIPLOM DOMIN LEGIT PWR...POLICY INT/LAW JURID ARMS/CONT
CONCPT TIME/SEQ TREND GEN/LAWS COLD/WAR 20.
PAGE 108 E2158

L61

GERWIG R.,"PUBLIC AUTHORITIES IN THE UNITED LOC/G
STATES." LAW CONSTN PROVS TAX ADMIN FEDERAL. MUNIC
PAGE 43 E0852 GOV/REL
PWR

S61

ABLARD C.D.,"EX PARTE CONTACTS WITH FEDERAL EXEC
ADMINISTRATIVE AGENCIES." USA+45 CLIENT NAT/G ADJUD
DELIB/GP ADMIN PWR 20. PAGE 2 E0044 LOBBY
REPRESENT

S61

JACKSON E.,"THE FUTURE DEVELOPMENT OF THE UNITED INT/ORG
NATIONS: SOME SUGGESTIONS FOR RESEARCH." FUT LAW PWR
CONSTN ECO/DEV FINAN PEACE WEALTH...WELF/ST CONCPT
UN 20. PAGE 57 E1140

S61

LASSWELL H.D.,"THE INTERPLAY OF ECONOMIC, POLITICAL JURID
AND SOCIAL CRITERIA IN LEGAL POLICY." LAW LOVE POLICY
MORAL PWR RESPECT WEALTH...SOC IDEA/COMP. PAGE 63
E1262

B62

AMER SOCIETY POL & LEGAL PHIL,THE PUBLIC INTEREST: CONCPT
NOMOS V. LAW EDU/PROP...SOC METH/CNCPT ANTHOL. ATTIT
PAGE 4 E0073 PWR
GEN/LAWS

B62

BEBR G.,JUDICIAL CONTROL OF THE EUROPEAN ADJUD
COMMUNITIES. EUR+WWI INT/ORG NAT/G DOMIN LEGIT PWR VOL/ASSN
...JURID CONCPT GEN/LAWS GEN/METH EEC 20. PAGE 9 INT/LAW
E0168

B62

BRANDT R.B.,SOCIAL JUSTICE. UNIV LAW GP/REL PWR ORD/FREE
ALL/IDEOS...POLICY SOC ANTHOL 20. PAGE 15 E0287 CONSTN
CONCPT

B62

CARLSTON K.S.,LAW AND ORGANIZATION IN WORLD INT/ORG
SOCIETY. WOR+45 FINAN ECO/TAC DOMIN LEGIT CT/SYS LAW
ROUTINE COERCE ORD/FREE PWR WEALTH...PLURIST
DECISION JURID MGT METH/CNCPT GEN/LAWS 20. PAGE 19
E0381

B62

FROMAN L.A. JR.,PEOPLE AND POLITICS: AN ANALYSIS OF POL/PAR
THE AMERICAN POLITICAL SYSTEM. USA+45 CHIEF PROB/SOLV
DELIB/GP EX/STRUC LEGIS TOP/EX CT/SYS LOBBY GOV/REL
PERS/REL PWR...POLICY DECISION. PAGE 41 E0813

B62

GRZYBOWSKI K.,SOVIET LEGAL INSTITUTIONS. USA+45 ADJUD
USSR ECO/DEV NAT/G EDU/PROP CONTROL CT/SYS CRIME LAW
OWN ATTIT PWR SOCISM...NAT/COMP 20. PAGE 48 E0955 JURID

B62

HADWEN J.G.,HOW UNITED NATIONS DECISIONS ARE MADE. INT/ORG
WOR+45 LAW EDU/PROP LEGIT ADMIN PWR...DECISION ROUTINE
SELF/OBS GEN/LAWS UN 20. PAGE 49 E0972

B62

HIRSCHFIELD R.S.,THE CONSTITUTION AND THE COURT. ADJUD
SCHOOL WAR RACE/REL EQUILIB ORD/FREE...POLICY PWR
MAJORIT DECISION JURID 18/20 PRESIDENT COLD/WAR CONSTN
CIVIL/LIB SUPREME/CT CONGRESS. PAGE 53 E1051 LAW

B62

INSTITUTE JUDICIAL ADMIN,JUDGES: THEIR TEMPORARY NAT/G
APPOINTMENT, ASSIGNMENT AND TRANSFER: SURVEY OF FED LOC/G
AND STATE CONSTN'S STATUTES. ROLES OF CT. USA+45 JUDGE
CONSTN PROVS CT/SYS GOV/REL PWR JURID. PAGE 57 ADMIN
E1128

B62

LAWSON R.,INTERNATIONAL REGIONAL ORGANIZATIONS. INT/ORG
WOR+45 NAT/G VOL/ASSN CONSULT LEGIS EDU/PROP LEGIT DELIB/GP
ADMIN EXEC ROUTINE HEALTH PWR WEALTH...JURID EEC REGION
COLD/WAR 20 UN. PAGE 63 E1270

B62

LITTLEFIELD N.,METROPOLITAN AREA PROBLEMS AND LOC/G
MUNICIPAL HOME RULE. USA+45 PROVS ADMIN CONTROL SOVEREIGN
GP/REL PWR. PAGE 65 E1308 JURID
LEGIS

B62

MASON A.T.,THE SUPREME COURT: PALADIUM OF FREEDOM. CONSTN
USA+45 NAT/G POL/PAR CHIEF LEGIS ADJUD PARL/PROC CT/SYS
FEDERAL PWR...POLICY BIOG 18/20 SUPREME/CT JURID
ROOSEVLT/F JEFFERSN/T MARSHALL/J HUGHES/CE. PAGE 69
E1378

B62

MCGRATH J.J.,CHURCH AND STATE IN AMERICAN LAW: LAW
CASES AND MATERIALS. USA+45 USA-45 LEGIS EDU/PROP GOV/REL
ADJUD CT/SYS PWR...ANTHOL 18/20 CHURCH/STA. PAGE 71 SECT
E1415

B62

MURPHY W.F.,CONGRESS AND THE COURT. USA+45 LAW LEGIS
LOBBY GP/REL RACE/REL ATTIT PWR...JURID INT BIBLIOG CT/SYS
CONGRESS SUPREME/CT WARRN/EARL. PAGE 75 E1509 GOV/REL
ADJUD

B62

PHILLIPS O.H.,CONSTITUTIONAL AND ADMINISTRATIVE LAW JURID
(3RD ED.). UK INT/ORG LOC/G CHIEF EX/STRUC LEGIS ADMIN
BAL/PWR ADJUD COLONIAL CT/SYS PWR...CHARTS 20. CONSTN
PAGE 80 E1613 NAT/G

B62

SCHWARZENBERGER G.,THE FRONTIERS OF INTERNATIONAL INT/ORG
LAW. WOR+45 WOR-45 NAT/G LEGIT CT/SYS ROUTINE MORAL LAW
ORD/FREE PWR...JURID SOC GEN/METH 20 COLD/WAR. INT/LAW
PAGE 89 E1789

B62

SOMMER T.,DEUTSCHLAND UND JAPAN ZWISCHEN DEN DIPLOM
MACHTEN. GERMANY DELIB/GP BAL/PWR AGREE COERCE WAR
TOTALISM PWR 20 CHINJAP TREATY. PAGE 93 E1856 ATTIT

B62

THOMPSON K.W.,AMERICAN DIPLOMACY AND EMERGENT NAT/G
PATTERNS. USA+45 USA-45 WOR+45 WOR-45 LAW DELIB/GP BAL/PWR
FORCES TOP/EX DIPLOM ATTIT DRIVE RIGID/FLEX
ORD/FREE PWR SOVEREIGN...POLICY 20. PAGE 96 E1922

B62

TRISKA J.F.,THE THEORY, LAW, AND POLICY OF SOVIET COM
TREATIES. WOR+45 WOR-45 CONSTN INT/ORG NAT/G LAW
VOL/ASSN DOMIN LEGIT COERCE ATTIT PWR RESPECT INT/LAW
...POLICY JURID CONCPT OBS SAMP TIME/SEQ TREND USSR
GEN/LAWS 20. PAGE 97 E1941

B62

WINTERS J.M.,INTERSTATE METROPOLITAN AREAS. CONSTN MUNIC
LEAD CHOOSE PWR DECISION. PAGE 107 E2135 LAW
REGION
GOV/REL

L62

CAVERS D.F.,"ADMINISTRATIVE DECISION-MAKING IN REPRESENT
NUCLEAR FACILITIES LICENSING." USA+45 CLIENT ADMIN LOBBY
EXEC 20 AEC. PAGE 21 E0410 PWR
CONTROL

L62

NIZARD L.,"CUBAN QUESTION AND SECURITY COUNCIL." INT/ORG
L/A+17C USA+45 ECO/UNDEV NAT/G POL/PAR DELIB/GP JURID
ECO/TAC PWR...RELATIV OBS TIME/SEQ TREND GEN/LAWS DIPLOM
UN 20 UN. PAGE 77 E1551 CUBA

L62

PETKOFF D.K.,"RECOGNITION AND NON-RECOGNITION OF INT/ORG
STATES AND GOVERNMENTS IN INTERNATIONAL LAW." ASIA LAW
COM USA+45 WOR+45 NAT/G ACT/RES DIPLOM DOMIN LEGIT INT/LAW
COERCE ORD/FREE PWR...CONCPT GEN/LAWS 20. PAGE 80
E1611

L62

STEIN E.,"MR HAMMARSKJOLD, THE CHARTER LAW AND THE CONCPT
FUTURE ROLE OF THE UNITED NATIONS SECRETARY- BIOG
GENERAL." WOR+45 CONSTN INT/ORG DELIB/GP FORCES
TOP/EX BAL/PWR LEGIT ROUTINE RIGID/FLEX PWR
...POLICY JURID OBS STERTYP UN COLD/WAR 20
HAMMARSK/D. PAGE 93 E1869

L62

UNITED NATIONS,"CAPITAL PUNISHMENT." WOR+45 CULTURE LAW
NAT/G ROUTINE COERCE HEALTH PWR...POLICY SOC QU STAT
CHARTS VAL/FREE 20. PAGE 98 E1967

S62

CRANE R.D.,"SOVIET ATTITUDE TOWARD INTERNATIONAL LAW
SPACE LAW." COM FUT USA+45 USSR AIR CONSTN DELIB/GP ATTIT
DOMIN PWR...JURID TREND TOT/POP 20. PAGE 27 E0543 INT/LAW
SPACE

S62

FALK R.A.,"THE REALITY OF INTERNATIONAL LAW." INT/ORG
WOR+45 NAT/G LEGIT COERCE DETER WAR MORAL ORD/FREE ADJUD
PWR SOVEREIGN...JURID CONCPT VAL/FREE COLD/WAR 20. NUC/PWR
PAGE 36 E0714 INT/LAW

S62

FINKELSTEIN L.S.,"THE UNITED NATIONS AND INT/ORG
ORGANIZATIONS FOR CONTROL OF ARMAMENT." FUT WOR+45 PWR
VOL/ASSN DELIB/GP TOP/EX CREATE EDU/PROP LEGIT ARMS/CONT
ADJUD NUC/PWR ATTIT RIGID/FLEX ORD/FREE...POLICY
DECISION CONCPT OBS TREND GEN/LAWS TOT/POP
COLD/WAR. PAGE 38 E0752

C62

BACON F.,"OF JUDICATURE" (1612) IN F. BACON, CT/SYS
ESSAYS." ADJUD ADMIN SANCTION CRIME PWR...JURID LEGIS
GEN/LAWS. PAGE 7 E0128 LAW

C62

BACON F.,"OF THE TRUE GREATNESS OF KINGDOMS AND WAR
ESTATES" (1612) IN F. BACON, ESSAYS." ELITES FORCES PWR
DOMIN EDU/PROP LEGIT...POLICY GEN/LAWS 16/17 DIPLOM
TREATY. PAGE 7 E0129 CONSTN

B63

ATTIA G.E.D.,LES FORCES ARMEES DES NATIONS UNIES EN FORCES
COREE ET AU MOYENORIENT. KOREA CONSTN NAT/G INT/LAW

DELIB/GP LEGIS PWR...IDEA/COMP NAT/COMP BIBLIOG UN
SUEZ. PAGE 6 E0114

B63
BOWETT D.W.,THE LAW OF INTERNATIONAL INSTITUTIONS. INT/ORG
WOR+45 WOR-45 CONSTN DELIB/GP EX/STRUC JUDGE ADJUD
EDU/PROP LEGIT CT/SYS EXEC ROUTINE RIGID/FLEX DIPLOM
ORD/FREE PWR...JURID CONCPT ORG/CHARTS GEN/METH
LEAGUE/NAT OAS OEEC 20 UN. PAGE 14 E0277

B63
BROOKES E.H.,POWER, LAW, RIGHT, AND LOVE: A STUDY PWR
IN POLITICAL VALUES. SOUTH/AFR NAT/G PERSON ORD/FREE
...CONCPT IDEA/COMP 20. PAGE 16 E0308 JURID
LOVE

B63
BROWN R.M.,THE SOUTH CAROLINA REGULATORS. USA-45 ORD/FREE
LEGIS LEGIT ADJUD COLONIAL CONTROL WAR...BIBLIOG/A JURID
18 CHARLESTON SOUTH/CAR. PAGE 16 E0315 PWR
PROVS

B63
CARTER G.M.,FIVE AFRICAN STATES: RESPONSES TO AFR
DIVERSITY. CONSTN CULTURE STRATA LEGIS PLAN ECO/TAC SOCIETY
DOMIN EDU/PROP CT/SYS EXEC CHOOSE ATTIT HEALTH
ORD/FREE PWR...TIME/SEQ TOT/POP VAL/FREE. PAGE 20
E0398

B63
CORLEY R.N.,THE LEGAL ENVIRONMENT OF BUSINESS. NAT/G
CONSTN LEGIS TAX ADMIN CT/SYS DISCRIM ATTIT PWR INDUS
...TREND 18/20. PAGE 26 E0509 JURID
DECISION

B63
DUNHAM A.,MR. JUSTICE. ADJUD PWR...JURID ANTHOL BIOG
18/20 SUPREME/CT. PAGE 33 E0659 PERSON
LAW
CT/SYS

B63
DUNN F.S.,PEACE-MAKING AND THE SETTLEMENT WITH POLICY
JAPAN. ASIA USA-45 USA-45 FORCES BAL/PWR ECO/TAC PEACE
CONFER WAR PWR SOVEREIGN 20 CHINJAP COLD/WAR PLAN
TREATY. PAGE 33 E0661 DIPLOM

B63
FRIEDRICH C.J.,MAN AND HIS GOVERNMENT: AN EMPIRICAL PERSON
THEORY OF POLITICS. UNIV LOC/G NAT/G ADJUD REV ORD/FREE
INGP/REL DISCRIM PWR BIBLIOG. PAGE 41 E0810 PARTIC
CONTROL

B63
GARNER U.F.,ADMINISTRATIVE LAW. UK LAW LOC/G NAT/G ADMIN
EX/STRUC LEGIS JUDGE BAL/PWR BUDGET ADJUD CONTROL JURID
CT/SYS...BIBLIOG 20. PAGE 42 E0840 PWR
GOV/REL

B63
GINZBERG E.,DEMOCRATIC VALUES AND THE RIGHTS OF LABOR
MANAGEMENT. LAW CONSTN REPRESENT GP/REL ROLE PWR MGT
RESPECT POLICY. PAGE 44 E0870 DELIB/GP
ADJUD

B63
GRIFFITH J.A.G.,PRINCIPLES OF ADMINISTRATIVE LAW JURID
(3RD ED.) UK CONSTN EX/STRUC LEGIS ADJUD CONTROL ADMIN
CT/SYS PWR...CHARTS 20. PAGE 47 E0940 NAT/G
BAL/PWR

B63
HALEY A.G.,SPACE LAW AND GOVERNMENT. FUT USA+45 INT/ORG
WOR+45 LEGIS ACT/RES CREATE ATTIT RIGID/FLEX LAW
ORD/FREE PWR SOVEREIGN...POLICY JURID CONCPT CHARTS SPACE
VAL/FREE 20. PAGE 49 E0980

B63
JACOBS P.,STATE OF UNIONS. USA+45 STRATA TOP/EX LABOR
GP/REL RACE/REL DEMAND DISCRIM ATTIT PWR 20 ECO/TAC
CONGRESS NEGRO HOFFA/J. PAGE 57 E1145 BARGAIN
DECISION

B63
LEWIN J.,POLITICS AND LAW IN SOUTH AFRICA. NAT/LISM
SOUTH/AFR UK POL/PAR BAL/PWR ECO/TAC COLONIAL POLICY
CONTROL GP/REL DISCRIM PWR 20 NEGRO. PAGE 65 E1293 LAW
RACE/REL

B63
LOWRY C.W.,TO PRAY OR NOT TO PRAY. ADJUD SANCTION SECT
GP/REL ORD/FREE PWR CATHISM WORSHIP 20 SUPREME/CT CT/SYS
CHRISTIAN CHRUCH/STA. PAGE 67 E1330 CONSTN
PRIVIL

B63
NATIONAL CIVIC REVIEW,REAPPORTIONMENT: A YEAR IN APPORT
REVIEW (PAMPHLET). USA+45 LAW CT/SYS CHOOSE REPRESENT
ORD/FREE PWR...ANTHOL 20 CONGRESS. PAGE 76 E1527 LEGIS
CONSTN

B63
RICHARDS P.G.,PATRONAGE IN BRITISH GOVERNMENT. EX/STRUC
ELITES DELIB/GP TOP/EX PROB/SOLV CONTROL CT/SYS REPRESENT
EXEC PWR. PAGE 84 E1693 POL/PAR
ADMIN

B63
ROBERT J.,LA MONARCHIE MAROCAINE. MOROCCO LABOR CHIEF
MUNIC POL/PAR EX/STRUC ORD/FREE PWR...JURID TREND T CONSERVE
20. PAGE 85 E1702 ADMIN
CONSTN

B63
ROSNER G.,THE UNITED NATIONS EMERGENCY FORCE. INT/ORG
FRANCE ISRAEL UAR UK WOR+45 CREATE WAR PEACE FORCES
ORD/FREE PWR...INT/LAW JURID HIST/WRIT TIME/SEQ UN.
PAGE 86 E1719

B63
SARTORI G.,IL PARLAMENTO ITALIANO: 1946-1963. LAW LEGIS
CONSTN ELITES POL/PAR LOBBY PRIVIL ATTIT PERSON PARL/PROC
MORAL PWR SOC. PAGE 87 E1746 REPRESENT

B63
SCOTT A.M.,THE SUPREME COURT V. THE CONSTITUTION. PWR
USA+45 CONTROL ATTIT ROLE...POLICY CONCPT 20 CT/SYS
SUPREME/CT. PAGE 90 E1796 NAT/G
CONSTN

B63
STREET H.,FREEDOM: THE INDIVIDUAL AND THE LAW. UK ORD/FREE
COM/IND EDU/PROP PRESS RUMOR TV PWR 20 CIVIL/LIB NAT/G
FILM. PAGE 94 E1886 JURID
PARL/PROC

B63
US COMMISSION ON CIVIL RIGHTS,FREEDOM TO THE FREE. RACE/REL
USA+45 USA-45 LAW VOL/ASSN CT/SYS ATTIT PWR...JURID DISCRIM
BIBLIOG 17/20 SUPREME/CT NEGRO CIV/RIGHTS. PAGE 99 NAT/G
E1986 POLICY

B63
VINES K.N.,STUDIES IN JUDICIAL POLITICS: TULANE CT/SYS
STUDIES IN POLITICAL SCIENCE (VOL. 8). POL/PAR GOV/REL
JUDGE ADJUD SANCTION CRIME CHOOSE PWR...JURID STAT PROVS
TIME/SEQ CHARTS. PAGE 104 E2079

L63
LISSITZYN O.J.,"INTERNATIONAL LAW IN A DIVIDED INT/ORG
WORLD." FUT WOR+45 CONSTN CULTURE ECO/DEV ECO/UNDEV LAW
DIST/IND NAT/G FORCES ECO/TAC LEGIT ADJUD ADMIN
COERCE ATTIT HEALTH MORAL ORD/FREE PWR RESPECT
WEALTH VAL/FREE. PAGE 65 E1306

L63
MCDOUGAL M.S.,"THE ENJOYMENT AND ACQUISITION OF PLAN
RESOURCES IN OUTER SPACE." CHRIST-17C FUT WOR+45 TREND
WOR-45 LAW EXTR/IND INT/ORG ACT/RES CREATE TEC/DEV
ECO/TAC LEGIT COERCE HEALTH KNOWL ORD/FREE PWR
WEALTH...JURID HIST/WRIT VAL/FREE. PAGE 70 E1408

L63
ROSE R.,"COMPARATIVE STUDIES IN POLITICAL FINANCE: FINAN
A SYMPOSIUM." ASIA EUR+WWI S/ASIA LAW CULTURE POL/PAR
DELIB/GP LEGIS ACT/RES ECO/TAC EDU/PROP CHOOSE
ATTIT RIGID/FLEX SUPEGO PWR SKILL WEALTH...STAT
ANTHOL VAL/FREE. PAGE 85 E1714

S63
ALGER C.F.,"HYPOTHESES ON RELATIONSHIPS BETWEEN THE INT/ORG
ORGANIZATION OF INTERNATIONAL SOCIETY AND LAW
INTERNATIONAL ORDER." WOR+45 WOR-45 ORD/FREE PWR
...JURID GEN/LAWS VAL/FREE 20. PAGE 3 E0066

S63
BECHHOEFER B.G.,"UNITED NATIONS PROCEDURES IN CASE INT/ORG
OF VIOLATIONS OF DISARMAMENT AGREEMENTS." COM DELIB/GP
USA+45 USSR LAW CONSTN NAT/G EX/STRUC FORCES LEGIS
BAL/PWR EDU/PROP CT/SYS ARMS/CONT ORD/FREE PWR
...POLICY STERTYP UN VAL/FREE 20. PAGE 9 E0169

S63
BERMAN H.J.,"THE DILEMMA OF SOVIET LAW REFORM." COM
NAT/G POL/PAR CT/SYS ALL/VALS ORD/FREE PWR...POLICY LAW
JURID VAL/FREE 20. PAGE 11 E0208 USSR

S63
CLEVELAND H.,"CRISIS DIPLOMACY." USA+45 WOR+45 LAW DECISION
FORCES TASK NUC/PWR PWR 20. PAGE 23 E0454 DIPLOM
PROB/SOLV

POLICY

S63

GIRAUD E.,"L'INTERDICTION DU RECOURS A LA FORCE, LA INT/ORG
THEORIE ET LA PRATIQUE DES NATIONS UNIES." ALGERIA FORCES
COM CUBA HUNGARY WOR+45 ADJUD TOTALISM ATTIT DIPLOM
RIGID/FLEX PWR...POLICY JURID CONCPT UN 20 CONGO.
PAGE 44 E0872

S63

LEPAWSKY A.,"INTERNATIONAL DEVELOPMENT OF RIVER INT/ORG
RESOURCES." CANADA EUR+WWI S/ASIA USA+45 SEA LEGIT DELIB/GP
ADJUD ORD/FREE PWR WEALTH...MGT TIME/SEQ VAL/FREE
MEXIC/AMER 20. PAGE 64 E1287

S63

MODELSKI G.,"STUDY OF ALLIANCES." WOR+45 WOR-45 VOL/ASSN
INT/ORG NAT/G FORCES LEGIT ADMIN CHOOSE ALL/VALS CON/ANAL
PWR SKILL...INT/LAW CONCPT GEN/LAWS 20 TREATY. DIPLOM
PAGE 74 E1477

C63

ATTIA G.E.O.,"LES FORCES ARMEES DES NATIONS UNIES FORCES
EN COREE ET AU MOYENORIENT." KOREA CONSTN DELIB/GP NAT/G
LEGIS PWR...IDEA/COMP NAT/COMP BIBLIOG UN SUEZ. INT/LAW
PAGE 6 E0115

B64

ANASTAPLO G.,NOTES ON THE FIRST AMENDMENT TO THE ORD/FREE
CONSTITUTION OF THE UNITED STATES (PART TWO). CONSTN
USA+45 USA-45 NAT/G JUDGE DEBATE SUPEGO PWR CT/SYS
SOVEREIGN 18/20 SUPREME/CT CONGRESS AMEND/I. PAGE 5 ATTIT
E0088

B64

BOWETT D.W.,UNITED NATIONS FORCES* A LEGAL STUDY. OP/RES
CYPRUS ISRAEL KOREA LAW CONSTN ACT/RES CREATE FORCES
BUDGET CONTROL TASK PWR...INT/LAW IDEA/COMP UN ARMS/CONT
CONGO/LEOP SUEZ. PAGE 14 E0278

B64

DANELSKI D.J.,A SUPREME COURT JUSTICE IS APPOINTED. CHOOSE
CHIEF LEGIS CONFER DEBATE EXEC PERSON PWR...BIOG 20 JUDGE
CONGRESS PRESIDENT. PAGE 28 E0564 DECISION

B64

DOOLIN D.J.,COMMUNIST CHINA: THE POLITICS OF MARXISM
STUDENT OPPOSITION. CHINA/COM ELITES STRATA ACADEM DEBATE
NAT/G WRITING CT/SYS LEAD PARTIC COERCE TOTALISM AGE/Y
20. PAGE 32 E0637 PWR

B64

ECONOMIDES C.P.,LE POUVOIR DE DECISION DES INT/ORG
ORGANISATIONS INTERNATIONALES EUROPEENNES. DIPLOM PWR
DOMIN INGP/REL EFFICIENCY...INT/LAW JURID 20 NATO DECISION
OEEC EEC COUNCL/EUR EURATOM. PAGE 34 E0673 GP/COMP

B64

FRIEDMANN W.G.,THE CHANGING STRUCTURE OF ADJUD
INTERNATIONAL LAW. WOR+45 INT/ORG NAT/G PROVS LEGIT TREND
ORD/FREE PWR...JURID CONCPT GEN/LAWS TOT/POP UN 20. INT/LAW
PAGE 41 E0805

B64

GARDNER L.C.,ECONOMIC ASPECTS OF NEW DEAL ECO/TAC
DIPLOMACY. USA-45 WOR-45 LAW ECO/DEV INT/ORG NAT/G DIPLOM
VOL/ASSN LEGIS TOP/EX EDU/PROP ORD/FREE PWR WEALTH
...POLICY TIME/SEQ VAL/FREE 20 ROOSEVLT/F. PAGE 42
E0836

B64

GOODNOW H.F.,THE CIVIL SERVICE OF PAKISTAN: ADMIN
BUREAUCRACY IN A NEW NATION. INDIA PAKISTAN S/ASIA GOV/REL
ECO/UNDEV PROVS CHIEF PARTIC CHOOSE EFFICIENCY PWR LAW
...BIBLIOG 20. PAGE 45 E0889 NAT/G

B64

GRIFFITH W.E.,THE SINO-SOVIET RIFT. ASIA CHINA/COM ATTIT
COM CUBA USSR YUGOSLAVIA NAT/G POL/PAR VOL/ASSN TIME/SEQ
DELIB/GP FORCES TOP/EX DIPLOM EDU/PROP DRIVE PERSON BAL/PWR
PWR...TREND 20 TREATY. PAGE 47 E0941 SOCISM

B64

HEKHUIS D.J.,INTERNATIONAL STABILITY: MILITARY, TEC/DEV
ECONOMIC AND POLITICAL DIMENSIONS. FUT WOR+45 LAW DETER
ECO/UNDEV INT/ORG NAT/G VOL/ASSN FORCES ACT/RES REGION
BAL/PWR PWR WEALTH...STAT UN 20. PAGE 51 E1024

B64

HOHFELD W.N.,FUNDAMENTAL LEGAL CONCEPTIONS. JURID
PROB/SOLV OWN PWR...DECISION LING IDEA/COMP ADJUD
GEN/METH. PAGE 54 E1069 LAW
METH/CNCPT

B64

IKLE F.C.,HOW NATIONS NEGOTIATE. COM EUR+WWI USA+45 NAT/G

INTELL INT/ORG VOL/ASSN DELIB/GP ACT/RES CREATE PWR
DOMIN EDU/PROP ADJUD ROUTINE ATTIT PERSON ORD/FREE POLICY
RESPECT SKILL...PSY SOC OBS VAL/FREE. PAGE 56 E1122

B64

JENKS C.W.,THE PROSPECTS OF INTERNATIONAL INT/LAW
ADJUDICATION. WOR+45 WOR-45 NAT/G DIPLOM CONTROL ADJUD
PWR...POLICY JURID CONCPT METH/COMP 19/20 ICJ CT/SYS
LEAGUE/NAT UN TREATY. PAGE 58 E1160 INT/ORG

B64

KAHNG T.J.,LAW, POLITICS, AND THE SECURITY COUNCIL* DELIB/GP
AN INQUIRY INTO THE HANDLING OF LEGAL QUESTIONS. ADJUD
LAW CONSTN NAT/G ACT/RES OP/RES CT/SYS TASK PWR ROUTINE
...INT/LAW BIBLIOG UN. PAGE 59 E1180

B64

KEEFE W.J.,THE AMERICAN LEGISLATIVE PROCESS: LEGIS
CONGRESS AND THE STATES. USA+45 LAW POL/PAR DECISION
DELIB/GP DEBATE ADMIN LOBBY REPRESENT CONGRESS PWR
PRESIDENT. PAGE 60 E1191 PROVS

B64

LOCKHART W.B.,CASES AND MATERIALS ON CONSTITUTIONAL ORD/FREE
RIGHTS AND LIBERTIES. USA+45 FORCES LEGIS DIPLOM CONSTN
PRESS CONTROL CRIME WAR PWR...AUD/VIS T WORSHIP 20 NAT/G
NEGRO. PAGE 66 E1317

B64

MANNING B.,FEDERAL CONFLICT OF INTEREST LAW. USA+45 LAW
NAT/G PWR 20. PAGE 68 E1362 CONTROL
ADMIN
JURID

B64

MASON A.T.,AMERICAN CONSTITUTIONAL LAW: CONSTN
INTRODUCTORY ESSAYS AND SELECTED CASES (3RD ED.). CT/SYS
LAW LEGIS TAX ADJUD GOV/REL FEDERAL ORD/FREE PWR JURID
...TIME/SEQ BIBLIOG T 19/20 SUPREME/CT. PAGE 69
E1379

B64

MINAR D.W.,IDEAS AND POLITICS: THE AMERICAN CONSTN
EXPERIENCE. SECT CHIEF LEGIS CREATE ADJUD EXEC REV NAT/G
PWR...PHIL/SCI CONCPT IDEA/COMP 18/20 HAMILTON/A FEDERAL
JEFFERSN/T DECLAR/IND JACKSON/A PRESIDENT. PAGE 73
E1464

B64

MITAU G.T.,PROXIMATE SOLUTIONS: CASE PROBLEMS IN PROVS
STATE AND LOCAL GOVERNMENT. USA+45 CONSTN NAT/G LOC/G
CHIEF LEGIS CT/SYS EXEC GOV/REL GP/REL PWR 20 ADJUD
CASEBOOK. PAGE 73 E1470

B64

SCHUBERT G.A.,JUDICIAL BEHAVIOR: A READER IN THEORY ATTIT
AND RESEARCH. POL/PAR CT/SYS ROLE SUPEGO PWR PERSON
...DECISION JURID REGRESS CHARTS SIMUL ANTHOL 20. ADJUD
PAGE 89 E1782 ACT/RES

B64

SEGAL R.,SANCTIONS AGAINST SOUTH AFRICA. AFR SANCTION
SOUTH/AFR NAT/G INT/TRADE RACE/REL PEACE PWR DISCRIM
...INT/LAW ANTHOL 20 UN. PAGE 90 E1801 ECO/TAC
POLICY

B64

STANGER R.J.,ESSAYS ON INTERVENTION. PLAN PROB/SOLV SOVEREIGN
BAL/PWR ADJUD COERCE WAR ROLE PWR...INT/LAW CONCPT DIPLOM
20 UN INTERVENT. PAGE 93 E1865 POLICY
LEGIT

B64

US SENATE COMM ON JUDICIARY,CIVIL RIGHTS - THE INT
PRESIDENT'S PROGRAM. USA+45 LAW PROB/SOLV PRESS LEGIS
ADJUD GOV/REL RACE/REL ORD/FREE PWR...JURID 20 DISCRIM
SUPREME/CT SENATE CIV/RIGHTS PRESIDENT. PAGE 102 PARL/PROC
E2053

B64

US SENATE COMM ON JUDICIARY,ADMINISTRATIVE PARL/PROC
PROCEDURE ACT. USA+45 CONSTN NAT/G PROB/SOLV CONFER LEGIS
GOV/REL PWR...INT 20 SENATE. PAGE 102 E2054 JURID
ADMIN

B64

WRIGHT G.,RURAL REVOLUTION IN FRANCE: THE PEASANTRY PWR
IN THE TWENTIETH CENTURY. EUR+WWI MOD/EUR LAW STRATA
CULTURE AGRI POL/PAR DELIB/GP LEGIS ECO/TAC FRANCE
EDU/PROP COERCE CHOOSE ATTIT RIGID/FLEX HEALTH REV
...STAT CENSUS CHARTS VAL/FREE 20. PAGE 107 E2148

L64

BERKS R.N.,"THE US AND WEAPONS CONTROL." WOR+45 LAW USA+45
INT/ORG NAT/G LEGIS EXEC COERCE PEACE ATTIT PLAN
RIGID/FLEX ALL/VALS PWR...POLICY TOT/POP 20. ARMS/CONT

PAGE 11 E0204

L64

POUNDS N.J.G.,"THE POLITICS OF PARTITION." AFR ASIA NAT/G
COM EUR+WWI FUT ISLAM S/ASIA USA-45 LAW ECO/DEV NAT/LISM
ECO/UNDEV AGRI INDUS INT/ORG POL/PAR PROVS SECT
FORCES TOP/EX EDU/PROP LEGIT ATTIT MORAL ORD/FREE
PWR RESPECT WEALTH. PAGE 82 E1640

S64

COHEN M.,"BASIC PRINCIPLES OF INTERNATIONAL LAW." INT/ORG
UNIV WOR+45 WOR-45 BAL/PWR LEGIT ADJUD WAR ATTIT INT/LAW
MORAL ORD/FREE PWR...JURID CONCPT MYTH TOT/POP 20.
PAGE 23 E0463

S64

CRANE R.D.,"BASIC PRINCIPLES IN SOVIET SPACE LAW." COM
FUT WOR+45 INT/ORG DIPLOM DOMIN ARMS/CONT LAW
COERCE NUC/PWR PEACE ATTIT DRIVE PWR...INT/LAW USSR
METH/CNCPT NEW/IDEA OBS TREND GEN/LAWS VAL/FREE SPACE
MARX/KARL 20. PAGE 27 E0544

S64

GINSBURGS G.,"WARS OF NATIONAL LIBERATION - THE COERCE
SOVIET THESIS." COM USSR WOR+45 WOR-45 LAW CULTURE CONCPT
INT/ORG DIPLOM LEGIT COLONIAL GUERRILLA WAR INT/LAW
NAT/LISM ATTIT PERSON MORAL PWR...JURID OBS TREND REV
MARX/KARL 20. PAGE 44 E0869

S64

KARPOV P.V.,"PEACEFUL COEXISTENCE AND INTERNATIONAL COM
LAW." WOR+45 LAW SOCIETY INT/ORG VOL/ASSN FORCES ATTIT
CREATE CAP/ISM DIPLOM ADJUD NUC/PWR PEACE MORAL INT/LAW
ORD/FREE PWR MARXISM...MARXIST JURID CONCPT OBS USSR
TREND COLD/WAR MARX/KARL 20. PAGE 59 E1186

S64

MAGGS P.B.,"SOVIET VIEWPOINT ON NUCLEAR WEAPONS IN COM
INTERNATIONAL LAW." USSR WOR+45 INT/ORG FORCES LAW
DIPLOM ARMS/CONT ATTIT ORD/FREE PWR...POLICY JURID INT/LAW
CONCPT OBS TREND CON/ANAL GEN/LAWS VAL/FREE 20. NUC/PWR
PAGE 67 E1347

S64

PRITCHETT C.H.,"EQUAL PROTECTION AND THE URBAN MUNIC
MAJORITY." POL/PAR LEAD CHOOSE GP/REL PWR...MAJORIT LAW
DECISION. PAGE 83 E1655 REPRESENT
APPORT

S64

SCHWELB E.,"OPERATION OF THE EUROPEAN CONVENTION ON INT/ORG
HUMAN RIGHTS." EUR+WWI LAW SOCIETY CREATE EDU/PROP MORAL
ADJUD ADMIN PEACE ATTIT ORD/FREE PWR...POLICY
INT/LAW CONCPT OBS GEN/LAWS UN VAL/FREE ILO 20
ECHR. PAGE 89 E1791

S64

SKUBISZEWSKI K.,"FORMS OF PARTICIPATION OF INT/ORG
INTERNATIONAL ORGANIZATION IN THE LAW MAKING LAW
PROCESS." FUT WOR+45 NAT/G DELIB/GP DOMIN LEGIT INT/LAW
KNOWL PWR...JURID TREND 20. PAGE 92 E1837

S64

TRISKA J.F.,"SOVIET TREATY LAW: A QUANTITATIVE COM
ANALYSIS." WOR+45 LAW ECO/UNDEV AGRI COM/IND INDUS ECO/TAC
CREATE TEC/DEV DIPLOM ATTIT PWR WEALTH...JURID SAMP INT/LAW
TIME/SEQ TREND CHARTS VAL/FREE 20 TREATY. PAGE 97 USSR
E1942

C64

BECKER T.L.,"POLITICAL BEHAVIORALISM AND MODERN DECISION
JURISPRUDENCE." LEGIS JUDGE OP/RES ADJUD CT/SYS PROB/SOLV
ATTIT PWR...BIBLIOG 20. PAGE 9 E0173 JURID
GEN/LAWS

C64

CORWIN E.S.,"AMERICAN CONSTITUTIONAL HISTORY." LAW ANTHOL
NAT/G PROB/SOLV EQUILIB FEDERAL ATTIT PWR...JURID JUDGE
BIBLIOG 20. PAGE 26 E0515 ADJUD
CT/SYS

B65

AMERICAN ASSEMBLY COLUMBIA U.THE COURTS, THE CT/SYS
PUBLIC, AND THE LAW EXPLOSION. USA+45 ELITES PROVS ADJUD
EDU/PROP CRIME CHOOSE PERSON ORD/FREE PWR 20. NAT/G
PAGE 4 E0074

B65

BELL J.,THE JOHNSON TREATMENT: HOW LYNDON JOHNSON INGP/REL
TOOK OVER THE PRESIDENCY AND MADE IT HIS OWN. TOP/EX
USA+45 DELIB/GP DIPLOM ADJUD MURDER CHOOSE PERSON CONTROL
PWR...POLICY OBS INT TIME 20 JOHNSON/LB KENNEDY/JF NAT/G
PRESIDENT CONGRESS. PAGE 10 E0183

B65

BERKOWITZ M.,AMERICAN NATIONAL SECURITY: A READER ORD/FREE

IN THEORY AND POLICY. USA+45 INT/ORG FORCES BAL/PWR WAR
DIPLOM ECO/TAC DETER PWR...INT/LAW ANTHOL BIBLIOG ARMS/CONT
20 UN. PAGE 11 E0203 POLICY

B65

BOCK E.,GOVERNMENT REGULATION OF BUSINESS. USA+45 MGT
LAW EX/STRUC LEGIS EXEC ORD/FREE PWR...ANTHOL ADMIN
CONGRESS. PAGE 13 E0255 NAT/G
CONTROL

B65

CARTER G.M.,POLITICS IN EUROPE. EUR+WWI FRANCE GOV/COMP
GERMANY/W UK USSR LAW CONSTN POL/PAR VOL/ASSN PRESS OP/RES
LOBBY PWR...ANTHOL SOC/INTEG EEC. PAGE 20 E0399 ECO/DEV

B65

CHARNAY J.P.,LE SUFFRAGE POLITIQUE EN FRANCE; CHOOSE
ELECTIONS PARLEMENTAIRES, ELECTION PRESIDENTIELLE, SUFF
REFERENDUMS. FRANCE CONSTN CHIEF DELIB/GP ECO/TAC NAT/G
EDU/PROP CRIME INGP/REL MORAL ORD/FREE PWR CATHISM LEGIS
20 PARLIAMENT PRESIDENT. PAGE 22 E0425

B65

COOPER F.E.,STATE ADMINISTRATIVE LAW (2 VOLS.). LAW JURID
LEGIS PLAN TAX ADJUD CT/SYS FEDERAL PWR...CONCPT CONSTN
20. PAGE 25 E0501 ADMIN
PROVS

B65

MCKAY R.B.,REAPPORTIONMENT: THE LAW AND POLITICS OF APPORT
EQUAL REPRESENTATION. FUT USA+45 PROVS BAL/PWR MAJORIT
ADJUD CHOOSE REPRESENT GOV/REL FEDERAL...JURID LEGIS
BIBLIOG 20 SUPREME/CT CONGRESS. PAGE 71 E1420 PWR

B65

MILLIS W.,AN END TO ARMS. LAW INT/ORG FORCES FUT
ACT/RES CREATE DIPLOM WAR...POLICY HUM NEW/IDEA PWR
HYPO/EXP. PAGE 73 E1462 ARMS/CONT
ORD/FREE

B65

MONCONDUIT F.,LA COMMISSION EUROPEENNE DES DROITS INT/LAW
DE L'HOMME. DIPLOM AGREE GP/REL ORD/FREE PWR INT/ORG
...BIBLIOG 20 TREATY. PAGE 74 E1483 ADJUD
JURID

B65

NEGLEY G.,POLITICAL AUTHORITY AND MORAL JUDGMENT. MORAL
INTELL SOCIETY LEGIS SANCTION UTOPIA SOVEREIGN PWR
MARXISM...INT/LAW LOG 20. PAGE 76 E1530 CONTROL

B65

PEASLEE A.J.,CONSTITUTIONS OF NATIONS* THIRD AFR
REVISED EDITION (VOLUME I* AFRICA). LAW EX/STRUC CHOOSE
LEGIS TOP/EX LEGIT CT/SYS ROUTINE ORD/FREE PWR CONSTN
SOVEREIGN...CON/ANAL CHARTS. PAGE 80 E1606 NAT/G

B65

SCHUBERT G.,REAPPORTIONMENT. LAW MUNIC POL/PAR PWR REPRESENT
GOV/COMP. PAGE 88 E1775 LOC/G
APPORT
LEGIS

B65

SOPER T.,EVOLVING COMMONWEALTH. AFR CANADA INDIA INT/ORG
IRELAND UK LAW CONSTN POL/PAR DOMIN CONTROL WAR PWR COLONIAL
...AUD/VIS 18/20 COMMONWLTH OEEC. PAGE 93 E1857 VOL/ASSN

B65

THOMAS A.V.,NONINTERVENTION: THE LAW AND ITS IMPORT INT/LAW
IN THE AMERICAS. L/A+17C USA+45 USA-45 WOR+45 PWR
DIPLOM ADJUD...JURID IDEA/COMP 20 UN INTERVENT. COERCE
PAGE 96 E1917

B65

TRESOLINI R.J.,AMERICAN CONSTITUTIONAL LAW. USA+45 CONSTN
USA-45 NAT/G ADJUD ORD/FREE PWR...POLICY BIOG 20 CT/SYS
SUPREME/CT CASEBOOK. PAGE 97 E1939 JURID
LAW

L65

SHARMA S.P.,"THE INDIA-CHINA BORDER DISPUTE: AN LAW
INDIAN PERSPECTIVE." ASIA CHINA/COM S/ASIA NAT/G ATTIT
LEGIT CT/SYS NAT/LISM DRIVE MORAL ORD/FREE PWR 20. SOVEREIGN
PAGE 91 E1815 INDIA

S65

GROSS L.,"PROBLEMS OF INTERNATIONAL ADJUDICATION LAW
AND COMPLIANCE WITH INTERNATIONAL LAW: SOME SIMPLE METH/CNCPT
SOLUTIONS." WOR+45 SOCIETY NAT/G DOMIN LEGIT ADJUD INT/LAW
CT/SYS RIGID/FLEX HEALTH PWR...JURID NEW/IDEA
COLD/WAR 20. PAGE 48 E0951

S65

LUSKY L.,"FOUR PROBLEMS IN LAWMAKING FOR PEACE." ORD/FREE
FORCES LEGIS CREATE ADJUD COERCE WAR MAJORITY PEACE INT/LAW

UTOPIA
RECORD

S65

STEIN E.,"TOWARD SUPREMACY OF TREATY-CONSTITUTION
BY JUDICIAL FIAT: ON THE MARGIN OF THE COSTA CASE."
EUR+WWI ITALY WOR+45 INT/ORG NAT/G LEGIT REGION
NAT/LISM PWR...JURID CONCPT TREND TOT/POP VAL/FREE
20. PAGE 93 E1870

ADJUD
CONSTN
SOVEREIGN
INT/LAW

S65

ULMER S.S.,"TOWARD A THEORY OF SUBGROUP FORMATION
IN THE UNITED STATES SUPREME COURT." USA+45 ROUTINE
CHOOSE PWR...JURID STAT CON/ANAL SIMUL SUPREME/CT.
PAGE 97 E1952

CT/SYS
ADJUD
ELITES
INGP/REL

C65

SCHEINGOLD S.A.,"THE RULE OF LAW IN EUROPEAN
INTEGRATION: THE PATH OF THE SCHUMAN PLAN." EUR+WWI
JUDGE ADJUD FEDERAL ATTIT PWR...RECORD INT BIBLIOG
EEC ECSC. PAGE 87 E1755

INT/LAW
CT/SYS
REGION
CENTRAL

B66

AARON T.J.,THE CONTROL OF POLICE DISCRETION: THE
DANISH EXPERIENCE. DENMARK LAW CREATE ADMIN
INGP/REL SUPEGO PWR 20 OMBUDSMAN. PAGE 2 E0042

CONTROL
FORCES
REPRESENT
PROB/SOLV

B66

BAHRO H.,DAS KINDSCHAFTSRECHT IN DER UNION DER
SOZIALISTITSCHEN SOWJETREPUBLIKEN. USSR SECT
EDU/PROP CONTROL PWR...SOC/WK 20. PAGE 7 E0133

JURID
AGE/C
PERS/REL
SUPEGO

B66

BEISER E.N.,THE TREATMENT OF LEGISLATIVE
APPORTIONMENT BY THE STATE AND FEDERAL COURTS
(DISSERTATION). USA+45 CONSTN NAT/G PROVS LEGIS
CHOOSE REPRESENT ATTIT...POLICY BIBLIOG 20 CONGRESS
SUPREME/CT. PAGE 9 E0181

CT/SYS
APPORT
ADJUD
PWR

B66

CARLIN J.E.,LAWYER'S ETHICS. CLIENT STRUCT CONSULT
PERS/REL PWR...JURID OBS CHARTS 20. PAGE 19 E0378

ATTIT
PROF/ORG
INT

B66

FRIED R.C.,COMPARATIVE POLITICAL INSTITUTIONS. USSR
EX/STRUC FORCES LEGIS JUDGE CONTROL REPRESENT
ALL/IDEOS 20 CONGRESS BUREAUCRCY. PAGE 40 E0798

NAT/G
PWR
EFFICIENCY
GOV/COMP

B66

FRIEDMANN W.G.,INTERNATIONAL FINANCIAL AID. USA+45
ECO/DEV ECO/UNDEV NAT/G VOL/ASSN EX/STRUC PLAN RENT
GIVE BAL/PAY PWR...GEOG INT/LAW STAT TREND UN EEC
COMECON. PAGE 41 E0806

INT/ORG
FOR/AID
TEC/DEV
ECO/TAC

B66

HAMILTON H.D.,REAPPORTIONING LEGISLATURES. USA+45
CONSTN POL/PAR PROVS LEGIS COMPUTER ADJUD CHOOSE
ATTIT...ANTHOL 20 SUPREME/CT CONGRESS. PAGE 50
E0989

APPORT
REPRESENT
PHIL/SCI
PWR

B66

HAY P.,FEDERALISM AND SUPRANATIONAL ORGANIZATIONS:
PATTERNS FOR NEW LEGAL STRUCTURES. EUR+WWI LAW
NAT/G VOL/ASSN DIPLOM PWR...NAT/COMP TREATY EEC.
PAGE 51 E1014

SOVEREIGN
FEDERAL
INT/ORG
INT/LAW

B66

HOYT E.C.,NATIONAL POLICY AND INTERNATIONAL LAW*
CASE STUDIES FROM AMERICAN CANAL POLICY* MONOGRAPH
NO. 1 -- 1966-1967. PANAMA UK ELITES BAL/PWR
EFFICIENCY...CLASSIF NAT/COMP SOC/EXP COLOMB
TREATY. PAGE 55 E1105

INT/LAW
USA-45
DIPLOM
PWR

B66

MEDER A.E. JR.,LEGISLATIVE APPORTIONMENT. USA+45
BAL/PWR REPRESENT ORD/FREE PWR...JURID 20
SUPREME/CT. PAGE 72 E1433

APPORT
LEGIS
MATH
POLICY

B66

NANTWI E.K.,THE ENFORCEMENT OF INTERNATIONAL
JUDICIAL DECISIONS AND ARBITAL AWARDS IN PUBLIC
INTERNATIONAL LAW. WOR+45 WOR-45 JUDGE PROB/SOLV
DIPLOM CT/SYS SUPEGO MORAL PWR RESPECT...METH/CNCPT
18/20 CASEBOOK. PAGE 76 E1520

INT/LAW
ADJUD
SOVEREIGN
INT/ORG

B66

O'NEILL C.E.,CHURCH AND STATE IN FRENCH COLONIAL
LOUISIANA: POLICY AND POLITICS TO 1732. PROVS
VOL/ASSN DELIB/GP ADJUD ADMIN GP/REL ATTIT DRIVE
...POLICY BIBLIOG 17/18 LOUISIANA CHURCH/STA.
PAGE 78 E1568

COLONIAL
NAT/G
SECT
PWR

B66

RUNCIMAN W.G.,RELATIVE DEPRIVATION AND SOCIAL
JUSTICE: A STUDY OF ATTITUDES TO SOCIAL INEQUALITY
IN TWENTIETH-CENTURY ENGLAND. UK LAW POL/PAR PWR
...CONCPT NEW/IDEA SAMP METH 19/20. PAGE 86 E1734

STRATA
STRUCT
DISCRIM
ATTIT

B66

THOMPSON J.M.,RUSSIA, BOLSHEVISM, AND THE
VERSAILLES PEACE. RUSSIA USSR INT/ORG NAT/G
DELIB/GP AGREE REV WAR PWR 20 TREATY VERSAILLES
BOLSHEVISM. PAGE 96 E1919

DIPLOM
PEACE
MARXISM

B66

WILSON G.,CASES AND MATERIALS ON CONSTITUTIONAL AND
ADMINISTRATIVE LAW. UK LAW NAT/G EX/STRUC LEGIS
BAL/PWR BUDGET DIPLOM ADJUD CONTROL CT/SYS GOV/REL
ORD/FREE 20 PARLIAMENT ENGLSH/LAW. PAGE 106 E2126

JURID
ADMIN
CONSTN
PWR

L66

HIGGINS R.,"THE INTERNATIONAL COURT AND SOUTH WEST
AFRICA* SOME IMPLICATIONS OF THE JUDGMENT." AFR LAW
ECO/UNDEV JUDGE RACE/REL COST PWR...INT/LAW TREND
UN TREATY. PAGE 52 E1043

SOUTH/AFR
COLONIAL
CT/SYS
ADJUD

S66

DETTER I.,"THE PROBLEM OF UNEQUAL TREATIES." CONSTN
NAT/G LEGIS COLONIAL COERCE PWR...GEOG UN TIME
TREATY. PAGE 31 E0610

SOVEREIGN
DOMIN
INT/LAW
ECO/UNDEV

S66

POLSBY N.W.,"BOOKS IN THE FIELD: POLITICAL
SCIENCE." LAW CONSTN LOC/G NAT/G LEGIS ADJUD PWR 20
SUPREME/CT. PAGE 81 E1627

BIBLIOG/A
ATTIT
ADMIN
JURID

S66

SHKLAR J.,"SELECTED ARTICLES AND DOCUMENTS ON
POLITICAL THEORY." ADJUD REV...JURID PHIL/SCI
IDEA/COMP. PAGE 91 E1820

BIBLIOG
ELITES
PWR

B67

BAILEY N.A.,LATIN AMERICA IN WORLD POLITICS. PWR
CONSERVE MARXISM...INT/LAW TREND BIBLIOG/A T OAS
COLD/WAR. PAGE 7 E0134

L/A+17C
DIPLOM
INT/ORG
ATTIT

B67

BAKER L.,BACK TO BACK: THE DUEL BETWEEN FDR AND THE
SUPREME COURT. ELITES LEGIS CREATE DOMIN INGP/REL
PERSON PWR NEW/LIB 20 ROOSEVLT/F SUPREME/CT SENATE.
PAGE 7 E0142

CHIEF
CT/SYS
PARL/PROC
GOV/REL

B67

BROWN L.N.,FRENCH ADMINISTRATIVE LAW. FRANCE UK
CONSTN NAT/G LEGIS DOMIN CONTROL EXEC PARL/PROC PWR
...JURID METH/COMP GEN/METH. PAGE 16 E0314

EX/STRUC
LAW
IDEA/COMP
CT/SYS

B67

HOLSTI K.J.,INTERNATIONAL POLITICS* A FRAMEWORK FOR
ANALYSIS. WOR+45 WOR-45 NAT/G EDU/PROP DETER WAR
WEAPON PWR BIBLIOG. PAGE 55 E1090

DIPLOM
BARGAIN
POLICY
INT/LAW

B67

JONES C.O.,EVERY SECOND YEAR: CONGRESSIONAL
BEHAVIOR AND THE TWO-YEAR TERM. LAW POL/PAR
PROB/SOLV DEBATE CHOOSE PERS/REL COST FEDERAL PWR
...CHARTS 20 CONGRESS SENATE HOUSE/REP. PAGE 59
E1172

EFFICIENCY
LEGIS
TIME/SEQ
NAT/G

B67

KING W.L.,MELVILLE WESTON FULLER: CHIEF JUSTICE OF
THE UNITED STATES, 1888-1910. USA-45 CONSTN FINAN
LABOR TAX GOV/REL PERS/REL ATTIT PERSON PWR...JURID
BIBLIOG 19/20 SUPREME/CT FULLER/MW HOLMES/OW.
PAGE 61 E1216

BIOG
CT/SYS
LAW
ADJUD

B67

MARTIN L.W.,THE SEA IN MODERN STRATEGY. LAW ECO/TAC
WAR. PAGE 69 E1374

ROLE
PWR
NUC/PWR
DIPLOM

B67

PADELFORD N.J.,THE DYNAMICS OF INTERNATIONAL
POLITICS (2ND ED.). WOR+45 LAW INT/ORG FORCES
TEC/DEV REGION NAT/LISM PEACE ATTIT PWR ALL/IDEOS
UN COLD/WAR NATO TREATY. PAGE 79 E1589

DIPLOM
NAT/G
POLICY
DECISION

S67

BLAKEY G.R.,"ORGANIZED CRIME IN THE UNITED STATES."
USA+45 USA-45 STRUCT LABOR NAT/G VOL/ASSN ADMIN
PERS/REL PWR...CRIMLGY INT 17/20. PAGE 12 E0240

CRIME
ELITES
CONTROL

S67

FLECHTHEIM O.K.,"BLOC FORMATION VS. DIALOGUE." FUT
CONSTN ECO/DEV BAL/PWR PEACE ATTIT PWR COLD/WAR. CAP/ISM
PAGE 38 E0761   MARXISM
                                                                    DEBATE

S67

MATTHEWS R.O.,"THE SUEZ CANAL DISPUTE* A CASE STUDY PEACE
IN PEACEFUL SETTLEMENT." FRANCE ISRAEL UAR UK NAT/G DIPLOM
CONTROL LEAD COERCE WAR NAT/LISM ROLE ORD/FREE PWR ADJUD
...INT/LAW UN 20. PAGE 69 E1389

S67

MAYANJA A.,"THE GOVERNMENT'S PROPOSALS ON THE NEW CONSTN
CONSTITUTION." AFR UGANDA LAW CHIEF LEGIS ADJUD CONFER
REPRESENT FEDERAL PWR 20. PAGE 69 E1390 ORD/FREE
                                                                    NAT/G

S67

MORENO F.J.,"THE SPANISH COLONIAL SYSTEM: A COLONIAL
FUNCTIONAL APPROACH." SPAIN WOR-45 LAW CHIEF DIPLOM CONTROL
ADJUD CIVMIL/REL AUTHORIT ROLE PWR...CONCPT 17/20. NAT/G
PAGE 74 E1492 OP/RES

S67

POSPISIL L.,"LEGAL LEVELS AND MULTIPLICITY OF LEGAL LAW
SYSTEMS IN HUMAN SOCIETIES." WOR+45 CENTRAL PWR STRATA
...SOC CHARTS GP/COMP GEN/LAWS. PAGE 81 E1630 JURID
                                                                    STRUCT

S67

RAI H.,"DISTRICT MAGISTRATE AND POLICE STRUCT
SUPERINTENDENT IN INDIA: THE CONTROVERSY OF DUAL CONTROL
CONTROL" INDIA LAW PROVS ADMIN PWR 19/20. PAGE 83 ROLE
E1669 FORCES

S67

SEIDLER G.L.,"MARXIST LEGAL THOUGHT IN POLAND." MARXISM
POLAND SOCIETY R+D LOC/G NAT/G ACT/RES ADJUD CT/SYS LAW
SUPEGO PWR...SOC TREND 20 MARX/KARL. PAGE 90 E1802 CONCPT
                                                                    EFFICIENCY

S67

WINES R.,"THE IMPERIAL CIRCLES, PRINCELY DIPLOMACY, NAT/G
AND IMPERIAL REFORM* 1681-1714." MOD/EUR DELIB/GP NAT/LISM
BAL/PWR CONFER ADJUD PARL/PROC PARTIC ATTIT PWR CENTRAL
17/18. PAGE 106 E2132 REGION

S67

WRAITH R.E.,"ADMINISTRATIVE CHANGE IN THE NEW ADMIN
AFRICA." AFR LG/CO ADJUD INGP/REL PWR...RECORD NAT/G
GP/COMP 20. PAGE 107 E2147 LOC/G
                                                                    ECO/UNDEV

B68

GREGG R.W.,INTERNATIONAL ORGANIZATION IN THE INT/ORG
WESTERN HEMISPHERE. L/A+17C USA+45 CULTURE PLAN DIPLOM
DOMIN AGREE CONTROL DETER PWR...GEOG 20 OAS TREATY. ECO/UNDEV
PAGE 46 E0913

B87

ADAMS J.,A DEFENSE OF THE CONSTITUTIONS OF CONSTN
GOVERNMENT OF THE UNITED STATES OF AMERICA. USA-45 BAL/PWR
STRATA CHIEF EX/STRUC LEGIS CT/SYS CONSERVE PWR
POPULISM...CONCPT CON/ANAL GOV/COMP. PAGE 3 E0048 NAT/G

PYLEE M.V. E1665

Q

QU....QUESTIONNAIRES; SEE ALSO QUESTIONNAIRES INDEX, P. XIV

B36

CULVER D.C.,METHODOLOGY OF SOCIAL SCIENCE RESEARCH: BIBLIOG/A
A BIBLIOGRAPHY. LAW CULTURE...CRIMLGY GEOG STAT OBS METH
INT QU HIST/WRIT CHARTS 20. PAGE 28 E0550 SOC

B56

FRANCIS R.G.,SERVICE AND PROCEDURE IN BUREAUCRACY. CLIENT
EXEC LEAD ROUTINE...QU 20. PAGE 39 E0784 ADMIN
                                                                    INGP/REL
                                                                    REPRESENT

L58

BEVAN W.,"JURY BEHAVIOR AS A FUNCTION OF THE PERSON
PRESTIGE OF THE FOREMAN AND THE NATURE OF HIS EDU/PROP
LEADERSHIP" (BMR)" DELIB/GP DOMIN ADJUD LEAD DECISION
PERS/REL ATTIT...PSY STAT INT QU CHARTS SOC/EXP 20 CT/SYS
JURY. PAGE 11 E0221

B59

COLUMBIA U. BUREAU OF APPL SOC RES, ATTITUDES OF ATTIT
PROMINENT AMERICANS TOWARD "WORLD PEACE THROUGH ACT/RES
WORLD LAW" (SUPRA-NATL ORGANIZATION FOR WAR INT/LAW
PREVENTION). USA+45 USSR ELITES FORCES PLAN STAT
PROB/SOLV CONTROL WAR PWR...POLICY SOC QU IDEA/COMP
20 UN. PAGE 82 E1644

B60

CARTER R.F.,COMMUNITIES AND THEIR SCHOOLS. USA+45 SCHOOL
LAW FINAN PROVS BUDGET TAX LEAD PARTIC CHOOSE...SOC ACT/RES
INT QU 20. PAGE 20 E0401 NEIGH
                                                                    INGP/REL

B61

US CONGRESS,CONSTITUTIONAL RIGHTS OF THE MENTALLY HEALTH
ILL. USA+45 LAW PUB/INST DELIB/GP ADJUD ORD/FREE CONSTN
...PSY QU 20 CONGRESS. PAGE 99 E1989 JURID
                                                                    CONFER

L62

UNITED NATIONS,"CAPITAL PUNISHMENT." WOR+45 CULTURE LAW
NAT/G ROUTINE COERCE HEALTH PWR...POLICY SOC QU STAT
CHARTS VAL/FREE 20. PAGE 98 E1967

B63

DAY R.E.,CIVIL RIGHTS USA: PUBLIC SCHOOLS, SOUTHERN EDU/PROP
STATES - NORTH CAROLINA, 1963. USA+45 LOC/G NEIGH ORD/FREE
LEGIS CREATE CT/SYS COERCE DISCRIM ATTIT...QU RACE/REL
CHARTS 20 NORTH/CAR NEGRO KKK CIV/RIGHTS. PAGE 29 SANCTION
E0579

S63

HILLS R.J.,"THE REPRESENTATIVE FUNCTION: NEGLECTED LEAD
DIMENSION OF LEADERSHIP BEHAVIOR" USA+45 CLIENT ADMIN
STRUCT SCHOOL PERS/REL...STAT QU SAMP LAB/EXP 20. EXEC
PAGE 53 E1048 ACT/RES

B64

EULAU H.,LAWYERS IN POLITICS: A STUDY IN PROF/ORG
PROFESSIONAL CONVERGENCE. USA+45 POL/PAR DELIB/GP JURID
GP/REL...QU 20. PAGE 35 E0701 LEGIS
                                                                    ATTIT

S64

BAKER H.R.,"INMATE SELF-GOVERNMENT." ACT/RES CREATE PUB/INST
CONTROL PARTIC ATTIT RIGID/FLEX QU. PAGE 7 E0141 CRIME
                                                                    INGP/REL
                                                                    REPRESENT

B66

DIZARD W.P.,TELEVISION* A WORLD VIEW. WOR+45 COM/IND
ECO/UNDEV TEC/DEV LICENSE LITERACY...STAT OBS INT ACT/RES
QU TREND AUD/VIS BIBLIOG. PAGE 32 E0632 EDU/PROP
                                                                    CREATE

QU/SEMANT....SEMANTIC AND SOCIAL PROBLEMS OF QUESTIONNAIRES

QUAKER....QUAKER

QUANT....QUANTIFICATION

S58

ROCHE J.P.,"POLITICAL SCIENCE AND SCIENCE FICTION" QUANT
(BMR)" WOR+45 INTELL OP/RES ADJUD...JURID SOC RATIONAL
IDEA/COMP 20. PAGE 85 E1709 MATH
                                                                    METH

S58

SCHUBERT G.A.,"THE STUDY OF JUDICIAL DECISION- JUDGE
MAKING AS AN ASPECT OF POLITICAL BEHAVIOR." PLAN DECISION
ADJUD CT/SYS INGP/REL PERSON...PHIL/SCI SOC QUANT CON/ANAL
STAT CHARTS IDEA/COMP SOC/EXP. PAGE 89 E1779 GAME

B59

SCHUBERT G.A.,QUANTITATIVE ANALYSIS OF JUDICIAL JUDGE
BEHAVIOR. ADJUD LEAD CHOOSE INGP/REL MAJORITY ATTIT CT/SYS
...DECISION JURID CHARTS GAME SIMUL SUPREME/CT. PERSON
PAGE 89 E1780 QUANT

S59

SOHN L.B.,"THE DEFINITION OF AGGRESSION." FUT LAW INT/ORG
FORCES LEGIT ADJUD ROUTINE COERCE ORD/FREE PWR CT/SYS
...MAJORIT JURID QUANT COLD/WAR 20. PAGE 92 E1855 DETER
                                                                    SOVEREIGN

S61

SCHUBERT G.,"A PSYCHOMETRIC MODEL OF THE SUPREME JUDGE
COURT." DELIB/GP ADJUD CHOOSE ATTIT...DECISION CT/SYS
JURID PSY QUANT STAT HYPO/EXP GEN/METH SUPREME/CT. PERSON
PAGE 88 E1771 SIMUL

L63

LOEVINGER L.,"JURIMETRICS* THE METHODOLOGY OF LEGAL COMPUT/IR
INQUIRY." COMPUTER CREATE PLAN TEC/DEV AUTOMAT JURID
CT/SYS EFFICIENCY...DECISION PHIL/SCI NEW/IDEA GEN/METH
QUANT PREDICT. PAGE 66 E1318 ADJUD

S65

WRIGHT Q.,"THE ESCALATION OF INTERNATIONAL WAR
CONFLICTS." WOR+45 WOR-45 FORCES DIPLOM RISK COST PERCEPT
ATTIT ALL/VALS...INT/LAW QUANT STAT NAT/COMP. PREDICT
PAGE 108 E2160 MATH

QUANTIFICATION....SEE QUANT

QUANTITATIVE CONTENT ANALYSIS....SEE CON/ANAL

QUEBEC....QUEBEC, CANADA

QUESTIONNAIRES....SEE QU

QUICK C.W. E1215

QUINNEY R. E0457

R

R+D....RESEARCH AND DEVELOPMENT GROUP

L29
FEIS H.,"RESEARCH ACTIVITIES OF THE LEAGUE OF
NATIONS." EUR+WWI WOR-45 R+D INT/ORG CT/SYS
ARMS/CONT WEALTH...OBS RECORD LEAGUE/NAT ILO 20.
PAGE 37 E0729
CONSULT
KNOWL
PEACE

S40
FLORIN J.,"BOLSHEVIST AND NATIONAL SOCIALIST
DOCTRINES OF INTERNATIONAL LAW." EUR+WWI GERMANY
USSR R+D INT/ORG NAT/G DIPLOM DOMIN EDU/PROP SOCISM
...CONCPT TIME/SEQ 20. PAGE 39 E0768
LAW
ATTIT
TOTALISM
INT/LAW

L46
ERNST M.L.,"THE FIRST FREEDOM." USA-45 LAW R+D
PRESS 20. PAGE 35 E0696
BIBLIOG
EDU/PROP
ORD/FREE
COM/IND

B48
GRIFFITH E.S.,RESEARCH IN POLITICAL SCIENCE: THE
WORK OF PANELS OF RESEARCH COMMITTEE, APSA. WOR+45
WOR-45 COM/IND R+D FORCES ACT/RES WAR...GOV/COMP
ANTHOL 20. PAGE 47 E0939
BIBLIOG
PHIL/SCI
DIPLOM
JURID

L49
COMM. STUDY ORGAN. PEACE,"A TEN YEAR RECORD,
1939-1949." FUT WOR+45 LAW R+D CONSULT DELIB/GP
CREATE LEGIT ROUTINE ORD/FREE...TIME/SEQ UN 20.
PAGE 24 E0480
INT/ORG
CONSTN
PEACE

B50
MACIVER R.M.,GREAT EXPRESSIONS OF HUMAN RIGHTS. LAW
CONSTN CULTURE INTELL SOCIETY R+D INT/ORG ATTIT
DRIVE...JURID OBS HIST/WRIT GEN/LAWS. PAGE 67 E1340
UNIV
CONCPT

B51
HUXLEY J.,FREEDOM AND CULTURE. UNIV LAW SOCIETY R+D
ACADEM SCHOOL CREATE SANCTION ATTIT KNOWL...HUM
ANTHOL 20. PAGE 56 E1118
CULTURE
ORD/FREE
PHIL/SCI
IDEA/COMP

B52
US DEPARTMENT OF STATE,RESEARCH ON EASTERN EUROPE
(EXCLUDING USSR). EUR+WWI LAW ECO/DEV NAT/G
PROB/SOLV DIPLOM ADMIN LEAD MARXISM...TREND 19/20.
PAGE 100 E1995
BIBLIOG
R+D
ACT/RES
COM

S55
WRIGHT Q.,"THE PEACEFUL ADJUSTMENT OF INTERNATIONAL
RELATIONS: PROBLEMS AND RESEARCH APPROACHES." UNIV
INTELL EDU/PROP ADJUD ROUTINE KNOWL SKILL...INT/LAW
JURID PHIL/SCI CLASSIF 20. PAGE 108 E2156
R+D
METH/CNCPT
PEACE

B60
GOLDSEN J.M.,INTERNATIONAL POLITICAL IMPLICATIONS
OF ACTIVITIES IN OUTER SPACE. FUT USA+45 WOR+45 AIR
LAW ACT/RES LEGIT ATTIT KNOWL ORD/FREE PWR...CONCPT
20. PAGE 44 E0879
R+D
SPACE

L61
TAUBENFELD H.J.,"A TREATY FOR ANTARCTICA." FUT
USA+45 INTELL INT/ORG LABOR 20 TREATY ANTARCTICA.
PAGE 95 E1909
R+D
ACT/RES
DIPLOM

L61
TAUBENFELD H.J.,"A REGIME FOR OUTER SPACE." FUT
UNIV R+D ACT/RES PLAN BAL/PWR LEGIT ARMS/CONT
ORD/FREE...POLICY JURID TREND UN TOT/POP 20
COLD/WAR. PAGE 95 E1910
INT/ORG
ADJUD
SPACE

B62
DUPRE J.S.,SCIENCE AND THE NATION: POLICY AND
POLITICS. USA+45 LAW ACADEM FORCES ADMIN CIVMIL/REL
GOV/REL EFFICIENCY PEACE...TREND 20 SCI/ADVSRY.
PAGE 34 E0665
R+D
INDUS
TEC/DEV
NUC/PWR

B62
SCHWARTZ L.E.,INTERNATIONAL ORGANIZATIONS AND SPACE
COOPERATION. VOL/ASSN CONSULT CREATE TEC/DEV
SANCTION...POLICY INT/LAW PHIL/SCI 20 UN. PAGE 89
E1787
INT/ORG
DIPLOM
R+D
SPACE

L62
"AMERICAN BEHAVIORAL SCIENTIST." USSR LAW NAT/G
...SOC 20 UN. PAGE 2 E0034
BIBLIOG
AFR
R+D

S63
BOHN L.,"WHOSE NUCLEAR TEST: NON-PHYSICAL
INSPECTION AND TEST BAN." WOR+45 R+D INT/ORG
VOL/ASSN ORD/FREE...GEN/LAWS GEN/METH COLD/WAR 20.
PAGE 13 E0262
ADJUD
ARMS/CONT
TEC/DEV
NUC/PWR

S63
CAHIER P.,"LE DROIT INTERNE DES ORGANISATIONS
INTERNATIONALES." UNIV CONSTN SOCIETY ECO/DEV R+D
NAT/G TOP/EX LEGIT ATTIT PERCEPT...TIME/SEQ 19/20.
PAGE 18 E0357
INT/ORG
JURID
DIPLOM
INT/LAW

B65
UNESCO,INTERNATIONAL ORGANIZATIONS IN THE SOCIAL
SCIENCES(REV. ED.). LAW ADMIN ATTIT...CRIMLGY GEOG
INT/LAW PSY SOC STAT 20 UNESCO. PAGE 98 E1962
INT/ORG
R+D
PROF/ORG
ACT/RES

B65
UNESCO,HANDBOOK OF INTERNATIONAL EXCHANGES. COM/IND
R+D ACADEM PROF/ORG VOL/ASSN CREATE TEC/DEV
EDU/PROP AGREE 20 TREATY. PAGE 98 E1963
INDEX
INT/ORG
DIPLOM
PRESS

S65
HAZARD J.N.,"CO-EXISTENCE LAW BOWS OUT." WOR+45 R+D
INT/ORG VOL/ASSN CONSULT DELIB/GP ACT/RES CREATE
PEACE KNOWL...JURID CONCPT COLD/WAR VAL/FREE 20.
PAGE 51 E1018
PROF/ORG
ADJUD

B66
UNITED NATIONS,INTERNATIONAL SPACE BIBLIOGRAPHY.
FUT INT/ORG TEC/DEV DIPLOM ARMS/CONT NUC/PWR
...JURID SOC UN. PAGE 98 E1969
BIBLIOG
SPACE
PEACE
R+D

B66
US SENATE COMM AERO SPACE SCI,SOVIET SPACE
PROGRAMS, 1962-65; GOALS AND PURPOSES,
ACHIEVEMENTS, PLANS, AND INTERNATIONAL
IMPLICATIONS. USA+45 USSR R+D FORCES PLAN EDU/PROP
PRESS ADJUD ARMS/CONT ATTIT MARXISM. PAGE 101 E2028
CONSULT
SPACE
FUT
DIPLOM

B67
CLINARD M.B.,CRIMINAL BEHAVIOR SYSTEMS: A TYPOLOGY.
WOR+45 LAW SOCIETY STRUCT R+D AGE/Y ATTIT WEALTH
...CLASSIF CHARTS METH/COMP METH. PAGE 23 E0457
BIBLIOG
CRIME
CRIMLGY
PERSON

B67
ROBINSON R.D., INTERNATIONAL MANAGEMENT. USA+45
FINAN R+D PLAN PRODUC...DECISION T. PAGE 67 E1336
INT/TRADE
MGT
INT/LAW
MARKET

S67
DOYLE S.E.,"COMMUNICATION SATELLITES* INTERNAL
ORGANIZATION FOR DEVELOPMENT AND CONTROL." USA+45
R+D ACT/RES DIPLOM NAT/LISM...POLICY INT/LAW
PREDICT UN. PAGE 33 E0647
TEC/DEV
SPACE
COM/IND
INT/ORG

S67
EYRAUD M.,"LA FRANCE FACE A UN EVENTUEL TRAITE DE
NON DISSEMINATION DES ARMES NUCLEAIRES." FRANCE
USA+45 EXTR/IND INDUS R+D INT/ORG ACT/RES TEC/DEV
AGREE PRODUC ATTIT 20 TREATY AEC EURATOM. PAGE 36
E0708
NUC/PWR
ARMS/CONT
POLICY

S67
GIBSON G.H.,"LABOR PIRACY ON THE BRANDYWINE."
USA-45 INDUS R+D VOL/ASSN CAP/ISM ADJUD DRIVE...PSY
19. PAGE 43 E0859
ECO/TAC
CREATE
TEC/DEV
WORKER

S67
HILL D.G.,"HUMAN RIGHTS LEGISLATION IN ONTARIO."
CANADA R+D VOL/ASSN CONSULT INSPECT EDU/PROP ADJUD
AGREE TASK GP/REL INGP/REL DISCRIM 20 CIV/RIGHTS
ONTARIO CIVIL/LIB. PAGE 52 E1045
DELIB/GP
ORD/FREE
LAW
POLICY

S67
KONVITZ M.R.,"CIVIL LIBERTIES." USA+45 R+D...METH
20. PAGE 61 E1228
LAW
MORAL
ORD/FREE
NAT/G

S67
SEIDLER G.L.,"MARXIST LEGAL THOUGHT IN POLAND."
POLAND SOCIETY R+D LOC/G NAT/G ACT/RES ADJUD CT/SYS
SUPEGO PWR...SOC TREND 20 MARX/KARL. PAGE 90 E1802
MARXISM
LAW
CONCPT
EFFICIENCY

RACE....SEE RACE/REL, KIN

RACE/REL....RACE RELATIONS; SEE ALSO DISCRIM, ISOLAT, KIN

N
JOURNAL OF POLITICS. USA+45 USA-45 CONSTN POL/PAR   BIBLIOG/A
EX/STRUC LEGIS PROB/SOLV DIPLOM CT/SYS CHOOSE   NAT/G
RACE/REL 20. PAGE 1 E0011   LAW
                                                       LOC/G

N
US SUPERINTENDENT OF DOCUMENTS,EDUCATION (PRICE   BIBLIOG/A
LIST 31). USA+45 LAW FINAN LOC/G NAT/G DEBATE ADMIN   EDU/PROP
LEAD RACE/REL FEDERAL HEALTH POLICY. PAGE 103 E2062   ACADEM
                                                       SCHOOL

N
US SUPERINTENDENT OF DOCUMENTS,POLITICAL SCIENCE: BIBLIOG/A
GOVERNMENT, CRIME, DISTRICT OF COLUMBIA (PRICE LIST   NAT/G
54). USA+45 LAW CONSTN EX/STRUC WORKER ADJUD ADMIN   CRIME
CT/SYS CHOOSE INGP/REL RACE/REL CONGRESS PRESIDENT.
PAGE 103 E2063

B04
GRIFFIN A.P.C.,REFERENCES ON CHINESE IMMIGRATIONS   BIBLIOG/A
(PAMPHLET). USA-45 KIN NAT/LISM ATTIT...SOC 19/20.   STRANGE
PAGE 47 E0926   JURID
                                                       RACE/REL

B06
GRIFFIN A.P.C.,SELECT LIST OF REFERENCES ON THE   BIBLIOG/A
NEGRO QUESTION (REV. ED.). USA-45 CONSTN SCHOOL   RACE/REL
SUFF ADJUST...JURID SOC/INTEG 19/20 NEGRO. PAGE 47   DISCRIM
E0930   ATTIT

B10
MENDELSSOHN S.,MENDELSSOHN'S SOUTH AFRICA   BIBLIOG/A
BIBLIOGRAPHY (VOL. I). SOUTH/AFR RACE/REL...GEOG   CULTURE
JURID 19/20. PAGE 72 E1440

N19
IN THE SHADOW OF FEAR; AMERICAN CIVIL LIBERTIES,   ORD/FREE
1948-49 (PAMPHLET). COM LAW LEGIS BAL/PWR EDU/PROP   CONSTN
CT/SYS RACE/REL DISCRIM MARXISM SOCISM 20 COLD/WAR   POLICY
CONGRESS ACLU CIV/RIGHTS ESPIONAGE. PAGE 2 E0030

N19
AMERICAN CIVIL LIBERTIES UNION,"WE HOLD THESE   ORD/FREE
TRUTHS" FREEDOM, JUSTICE, EQUALITY: REPORT ON CIVIL   LAW
LIBERTIES (A PERIODICAL PAMPHLET COVERING 1951-53).   RACE/REL
USA+45 ACADEM NAT/G FORCES LEGIS COERCE CIVMIL/REL   CONSTN
GOV/REL DISCRIM PRIVIL MARXISM...OLD/LIB 20 ACLU UN
CIVIL/LIB. PAGE 4 E0076

N19
BUREAU OF NAT'L AFFAIRS INC.,A CURRENT LOOK AT: DISCRIM
(1) THE NEGRO AND TITLE VII, (2) SEX AND TITLE VII   SEX
(PAMPHLET). LAW LG/CO SML/CO RACE/REL...POLICY SOC   WORKER
STAT DEEP/QU TREND CON/ANAL CHARTS 20 NEGRO   MGT
CIV/RIGHTS. PAGE 17 E0334

N19
JANOWITZ M.,SOCIAL CONTROL OF ESCALATED RIOTS   CROWD
(PAMPHLET). USA+45 USA-45 LAW SOCIETY MUNIC FORCES   ORD/FREE
PROB/SOLV EDU/PROP TV CRIME ATTIT...BIBLIOG 20   CONTROL
NEGRO CIV/RIGHTS. PAGE 58 E1148   RACE/REL

N19
MISSISSIPPI ADVISORY COMMITTEE,REPORT ON   RACE/REL
MISSISSIPPI (PAMPHLET). USA+45 LAW PROVS FORCES   DISCRIM
ADJUD PWR...SOC/WK INT 20 MISSISSIPP NEGRO   COERCE
CIV/RIGHTS. PAGE 73 E1469   ORD/FREE

B20
COX H.,ECONOMIC LIBERTY. UNIV LAW INT/TRADE RATION   NAT/G
TARIFFS RACE/REL SOCISM POLICY. PAGE 27 E0535   ORD/FREE
                                                       ECO/TAC
                                                       PERSON

B28
MAIR L.P.,THE PROTECTION OF MINORITIES. EUR+WWI   LAW
WOR-45 CONSTN INT/ORG NAT/G LEGIT CT/SYS GP/REL   SOVEREIGN
RACE/REL DISCRIM ORD/FREE RESPECT...JURID CONCPT
TIME/SEQ 20. PAGE 68 E1352

B33
GILLETTE J.M.,CURRENT SOCIAL PROBLEMS. CONTROL   GEOG
CRIME AGE/Y BIO/SOC...SOC 20. PAGE 43 E0861   HEALTH
                                                       RACE/REL
                                                       FAM

B34
EVANS I.L.,NATIVE POLICY IN SOUTHERN AFRICA.   AFR
RHODESIA SOUTH/AFR UK STRUCT PARTIC RACE/REL ATTIT   COLONIAL
WEALTH SOC/INTEG AFRICA/SW. PAGE 35 E0705   DOMIN
                                                       LAW

B42
GILLETTE J.M.,PROBLEMS OF A CHANGING SOCIAL ORDER.   BIO/SOC
USA+45 STRATA FAM CONTROL CRIME RACE/REL HEALTH   ADJUST
WEALTH...GEOG GP/COMP. PAGE 43 E0862   ATTIT
                                                       SOC/WK

B42
US LIBRARY OF CONGRESS,SOCIAL AND CULTURAL PROBLEMS   BIBLIOG/A
IN WARTIME: APRIL 1941-MARCH 1942. WOR-45 CLIENT   WAR
SECT EDU/PROP CRIME LEISURE RACE/REL STRANGE ATTIT   SOC
DRIVE HEALTH...GEOG 20. PAGE 100 E2012   CULTURE

B43
US LIBRARY OF CONGRESS,SOCIAL AND CULTURAL PROBLEMS   BIBLIOG/A
IN WARTIME: APRIL-DECEMBER (SUPPLEMENT 1). WOR-45   WAR
SECT EDU/PROP CRIME LEISURE CIVMIL/REL RACE/REL   SOC
ATTIT DRIVE HEALTH...GEOG 20. PAGE 100 E2013   CULTURE

B43
US LIBRARY OF CONGRESS,SOCIAL AND CULTURAL PROBLEMS   BIBLIOG/A
IN WARTIME: JANUARY-MAY 1943 (SUPPLEMENT 2). WOR-45   WAR
FAM SECT PLAN EDU/PROP CRIME LEISURE RACE/REL DRIVE   SOC
HEALTH...GEOG 20 JEWS. PAGE 100 E2014   CULTURE

B45
WOOLBERT R.G.,FOREIGN AFFAIRS BIBLIOGRAPHY,   BIBLIOG/A
1932-1942. INT/ORG SECT INT/TRADE COLONIAL RACE/REL   DIPLOM
NAT/LISM...GEOG INT/LAW GOV/COMP IDEA/COMP 20.   WAR
PAGE 107 E2144

S45
DAVIS A.,"CASTE, ECONOMY, AND VIOLENCE" (BMR)"   STRATA
USA-45 LAW SOCIETY STRUCT SECT SANCTION COERCE   RACE/REL
MARRIAGE SEX...PSY SOC SOC/INTEG 18/20 NEGRO   DISCRIM
MISCEGEN SOUTH/US. PAGE 29 E0570

B47
KONVITZ M.R.,THE CONSTITUTION AND CIVIL RIGHTS.   CONSTN
USA-45 NAT/G ADJUD GP/REL RACE/REL POPULISM   LAW
...MAJORIT 19/20 SUPREME/CT CIV/RIGHTS. PAGE 61   GOV/REL
E1227   ORD/FREE

B49
DE HUSZAR G.B.,EQUALITY IN AMERICA: THE ISSUE OF   DISCRIM
MINORITY RIGHTS. USA+45 USA-45 LAW NEIGH SCHOOL   RACE/REL
LEGIS ACT/RES CHOOSE ATTIT RESPECT...ANTHOL 20   ORD/FREE
NEGRO. PAGE 29 E0585   PROB/SOLV

B50
FRAGA IRIBARNE M.,RAZAS Y RACISMO IN NORTEAMERICA.   RACE/REL
USA+45 CONSTN STRATA NAT/G PROVS ATTIT...SOC CONCPT   JURID
19/20 NEGRO. PAGE 39 E0783   LAW
                                                       DISCRIM

B52
DU BOIS W.E.B.,IN BATTLE FOR PEACE. AFR USA+45   PEACE
COLONIAL CT/SYS PERS/REL PERSON ORD/FREE...JURID 20   RACE/REL
NEGRO CIVIL/LIB. PAGE 33 E0650   DISCRIM
                                                       BIOG

B52
FORSTER A.,THE TROUBLE MAKERS. USA+45 LAW CULTURE   DISCRIM
SOCIETY STRUCT VOL/ASSN CROWD GP/REL MORAL...PSY   SECT
SOC CONCPT 20 NEGRO JEWS. PAGE 39 E0771   RACE/REL
                                                       ATTIT

B52
WALTER P.A.F.,RACE AND CULTURE RELATIONS. FAM   RACE/REL
HEALTH WEALTH...POLICY CRIMLGY GEOG BIBLIOG T 20.   DISCRIM
PAGE 105 E2097   GP/REL
                                                       CONCPT

B54
BROGAN D.W.,POLITICS IN AMERICA. LAW POL/PAR CHIEF   NAT/G
LEGIS LOBBY CHOOSE REPRESENT GP/REL RACE/REL   CONSTN
FEDERAL MORAL...BIBLIOG 20 PRESIDENT CONGRESS.   USA+45
PAGE 16 E0304

B54
JAMES L.F.,THE SUPREME COURT IN AMERICAN LIFE.   ADJUD
USA+45 USA-45 CONSTN CRIME GP/REL INGP/REL RACE/REL   CT/SYS
CONSEN FEDERAL PERSON ORD/FREE 18/20 SUPREME/CT   JURID
DEPRESSION CIV/RIGHTS CHURCH/STA FREE/SPEE. PAGE 58   DECISION
E1147

C54
GUINS G.C.,"SOVIET LAW AND SOVIET SOCIETY." COM   LAW
USSR STRATA FAM NAT/G WORKER DOMIN RACE/REL   STRUCT
...BIBLIOG 20. PAGE 48 E0960   PLAN

B55
BENTON W.E.,NUREMBERG: GERMAN VIEWS OF THE WAR   CRIME
TRIALS. EUR+WWI GERMANY VOL/ASSN LEAD PARTIC COERCE   WAR
INGP/REL RACE/REL TOTALISM SUPEGO ORD/FREE...ANTHOL   LAW
NUREMBERG. PAGE 10 E0201   JURID

CAHN E.,"A DANGEROUS MYTH IN THE SCHOOL SEGREGATION CASES" (BMR)" USA+45 CONSTN PROVS ADJUD DISCRIM ...POLICY MYTH SOC/INTEG 20 SUPREME/CT AMEND/XIV. PAGE 18 E0360
S55
JURID
SCHOOL
RACE/REL

KUPER L.,PASSIVE RESISTANCE IN SOUTH AFRICA. SOUTH/AFR LAW NAT/G POL/PAR VOL/ASSN DISCRIM ...POLICY SOC AUD/VIS 20. PAGE 62 E1237
B56
ORD/FREE
RACE/REL
ATTIT

RECASENS SICHES S.,TRATADO GENERAL DE SOCIOLOGIA. CULTURE FAM NEIGH LEAD RACE/REL DISCRIM HABITAT ORD/FREE...JURID LING T SOC/INTEG 20. PAGE 84 E1677
B56
SOC
STRATA
KIN
GP/REL

TYLER P.,"IMMIGRATION AND THE UNITED STATES." USA+45 USA-45 LAW SECT INGP/REL RACE/REL NAT/LISM ATTIT...BIBLIOG SOC/INTEG 19/20. PAGE 97 E1949
C56
CULTURE
GP/REL
DISCRIM

BYRNES R.F.,BIBLIOGRAPHY OF AMERICAN PUBLICATIONS ON EAST CENTRAL EUROPE, 1945-1957 (VOL. XXII). SECT DIPLOM EDU/PROP RACE/REL...ART/METH GEOG JURID SOC LING 20 JEWS. PAGE 18 E0354
B57
BIBLIOG/A
COM
MARXISM
NAT/G

ROWAN C.T.,GO SOUTH TO SORROW. USA+45 STRUCT NAT/G EDU/PROP LEAD COERCE ISOLAT DRIVE SUPEGO RESPECT ...PREDICT 20 NEGRO SUPREME/CT SOUTH/US CIV/RIGHTS. PAGE 86 E1728
B57
RACE/REL
DISCRIM
ANOMIE
LAW

SINCLAIR T.C.,THE POLITICS OF JUDICIAL REVIEW 1937-1957. USA+45 USA-45 NAT/G 20 SUPREME/CT CIVIL/LIB. PAGE 91 E1830
B57
JURID
ATTIT
ORD/FREE
RACE/REL

US SENATE COMM ON JUDICIARY,CIVIL RIGHTS - 1957. USA+45 LAW NAT/G CONFER GOV/REL RACE/REL ORD/FREE PWR...JURID 20 SENATE CIV/RIGHTS. PAGE 102 E2039
B57
INT
LEGIS
DISCRIM
PARL/PROC

CABLE G.W.,THE NEGRO QUESTION: A SELECTION OF WRITINGS ON CIVIL RIGHTS IN THE SOUTH. USA+45 STRATA LOC/G POL/PAR GIVE EDU/PROP WRITING CT/SYS SANCTION CRIME CHOOSE WORSHIP 20 NEGRO CIV/RIGHTS CONV/LEASE SOUTH/US. PAGE 18 E0355
B58
RACE/REL
CULTURE
DISCRIM
ORD/FREE

MUSIKER R.,GUIDE TO SOUTH AFRICAN REFERENCE BOOKS. SOUTH/AFR SOCIETY SECT EDU/PROP PRESS RACE/REL ...JURID SOC/WK 20. PAGE 75 E1512
B58
BIBLIOG/A
SOC
GEOG

OGDEN F.D.,THE POLL TAX IN THE SOUTH. USA+45 USA-45 CONSTN ADJUD ADMIN PARTIC CRIME...TIME/SEQ GOV/COMP METH/COMP 18/20 SOUTH/US. PAGE 78 E1572
B58
TAX
CHOOSE
RACE/REL
DISCRIM

PALMER E.E.,CIVIL LIBERTIES. USA+45 ADJUD CT/SYS PARTIC OWN LAISSEZ POPULISM...JURID CONCPT ANTHOL 20 SUPREME/CT CIVIL/LIB. PAGE 79 E1592
B58
ORD/FREE
CONSTN
RACE/REL
LAW

BROMWICH L.,UNION CONSTITUTIONS. CONSTN EX/STRUC PRESS ADJUD CONTROL CHOOSE REPRESENT PWR SAMP. PAGE 16 E0306
B59
LABOR
ROUTINE
INGP/REL
RACE/REL

BROOKES E.H.,THE COMMONWEALTH TODAY. UK ROMAN/EMP INT/ORG RACE/REL NAT/LISM SOVEREIGN...TREND SOC/INTEG 20. PAGE 16 E0307
B59
FEDERAL
DIPLOM
JURID
IDEA/COMP

HAYS B.,A SOUTHERN MODERATE SPEAKS. LAW PROVS SCHOOL KNOWL...JURID SOC SELF/OBS BIOG 20 NEGRO SUPREME/CT. PAGE 51 E1015
B59
SECT
DISCRIM
CT/SYS
RACE/REL

LOEWENSTEIN K.,VERFASSUNGSRECHT UND VERFASSUNGSPRAXIS DER VEREINIGTEN STAATEN. USA+45 USA-45 COLONIAL CT/SYS GP/REL RACE/REL ORD/FREE ...JURID 18/20 SUPREME/CT CONGRESS PRESIDENT BILL/RIGHT CIVIL/LIB. PAGE 66 E1319
B59
CONSTN
POL/PAR
EX/STRUC
NAT/G

VITTACHIT,EMERGENCY '58. CEYLON UK STRUCT NAT/G FORCES ADJUD CRIME REV NAT/LISM 20. PAGE 104 E2081
B59
RACE/REL
DISCRIM
DIPLOM
SOVEREIGN

VOSE C.E.,CAUCASIANS ONLY: THE SUPREME COURT, THE NAACP, AND THE RESTRICTIVE COVENANT CASES. USA+45 LAW CONSTN LOBBY...SOC 20 NAACP SUPREME/CT NEGRO. PAGE 104 E2086
B59
CT/SYS
RACE/REL
DISCRIM

COWAN T.A.,"A SYMPOSIUM ON GROUP INTERESTS AND THE LAW" USA+45 LAW MARKET LABOR PLAN INT/TRADE TAX RACE/REL RIGID/FLEX...JURID ANTHOL 20. PAGE 27 E0528
L59
ADJUD
PWR
INGP/REL
CREATE

DWYER R.J.,"THE ADMINISTRATIVE ROLE IN DESEGREGATION." USA+45 LAW PROB/SOLV LEAD RACE/REL ISOLAT STRANGE ROLE...POLICY SOC/INTEG MISSOURI NEGRO CIV/RIGHTS. PAGE 34 E0668
S59
ADMIN
SCHOOL
DISCRIM
ATTIT

MASON A.T.,"THE SUPREME COURT: TEMPLE AND FORUM" (BMR)" USA+45 USA-45 CONSTN DELIB/GP RACE/REL MAJORITY ORD/FREE...DECISION SOC/INTEG 19/20 SUPREME/CT WARRN/EARL CIV/RIGHTS. PAGE 69 E1377
S59
CT/SYS
JURID
PWR
ATTIT

MURPHY W.F.,"LOWER COURT CHECKS ON SUPREME COURT POWER" (BMR)" USA+45 NAT/G PROVS SCHOOL GOV/REL RACE/REL DISCRIM ATTIT...DECISION JURID 20 SUPREME/CT NEGRO. PAGE 75 E1508
S59
CT/SYS
BAL/PWR
CONTROL
ADJUD

FELLMAN D.,THE SUPREME COURT AND EDUCATION. ACADEM NAT/G PROVS DELIB/GP ADJUD ORD/FREE...POLICY JURID WORSHIP 20 SUPREME/CT NEGRO CHURCH/STA. PAGE 37 E0731
B60
CT/SYS
SECT
RACE/REL
SCHOOL

GELLHORN W.,AMERICAN RIGHTS: THE CONSTITUTION IN ACTION. USA+45 USA-45 LEGIS ADJUD COERCE RACE/REL DISCRIM MARXISM 20 SUPREME/CT. PAGE 43 E0846
B60
ORD/FREE
JURID
CT/SYS
CONSTN

LA PONCE J.A.,THE PROTECTION OF MINORITIES. WOR+45 WOR-45 NAT/G POL/PAR SUFF...INT/LAW CLASSIF GP/COMP GOV/COMP BIBLIOG 17/20 CIVIL/LIB CIV/RIGHTS. PAGE 62 E1242
B60
INGP/REL
DOMIN
SOCIETY
RACE/REL

ULMER S.S.,"THE ANALYSIS OF BEHAVIOR PATTERNS ON THE UNITED STATES SUPREME COURT" USA+45 LAW CT/SYS PERS/REL RACE/REL PERSON...DECISION PSY SOC TREND METH/COMP METH 20 SUPREME/CT CIVIL/LIB. PAGE 97 E1951
S60
ATTIT
ADJUD
PROF/ORG
INGP/REL

BENNETT G.,THE KENYATTA ELECTION: KENYA 1960-1961. AFR INGP/REL RACE/REL CONSEN ATTIT 20 KENYATTA. PAGE 10 E0187
B61
CHOOSE
POL/PAR
LAW
SUFF

COWEN D.V.,THE FOUNDATIONS OF FREEDOM. AFR SOUTH/AFR DOMIN LEGIT ADJUST DISCRIM TOTALSM ATTIT ORD/FREE...MAJORIT JURID SOC/INTEG WORSHIP 20 NEGRO. PAGE 27 E0529
B61
CONSTN
ELITES
RACE/REL

MERTON R.K.,CONTEMPORARY SOCIAL PROBLEMS: AN INTRODUCTION TO THE SOCIOLOGY OF DEVIANT BEHAVIOR AND SOCIAL DISORGANIZATION. FAM MUNIC FORCES WORKER PROB/SOLV INGP/REL RACE/REL ISOLAT...CRIMLGY GEOG PSY T 20 NEGRO. PAGE 72 E1444
B61
CRIME
ANOMIE
STRANGE
SOC

ROCHE J.P.,COURTS AND RIGHTS: THE AMERICAN JUDICIARY IN ACTION (2ND ED.). UK USA+45 USA-45 STRUCT TEC/DEV SANCTION PERS/REL RACE/REL ORD/FREE ...METH/CNCPT GOV/COMP METH/COMP T 13/20. PAGE 85 E1710
B61
JURID
CT/SYS
NAT/G
PROVS

SCOTT A.M.,POLITICS, USA; CASES ON THE AMERICAN DEMOCRATIC PROCESS. USA+45 CHIEF FORCES DIPLOM LOBBY CHOOSE RACE/REL FEDERAL ATTIT...JURID ANTHOL T 20 PRESIDENT CONGRESS CIVIL/LIB. PAGE 90 E1795
B61
CT/SYS
CONSTN
NAT/G
PLAN

US COMMISSION ON CIVIL RIGHTS,JUSTICE: BOOK 5, 1961 REPORT OF THE U.S. COMMISSION ON CIVIL RIGHTS.
B61
DISCRIM
LAW

LOC/G NAT/G RACE/REL...JURID 20 NEGRO CIV/RIGHTS FORCES
INDIAN/AM JURY INDIAN/AM. PAGE 99 E1983

B62
BERMAN D.M.,A BILL BECOMES A LAW: THE CIVIL RIGHTS DISCRIM
ACT OF 1960. USA+45 LAW POL/PAR LOBBY RACE/REL PARL/PROC
KNOWL...CHARTS 20 CONGRESS NEGRO CIV/RIGHTS. JURID
PAGE 11 E0206 GOV/REL

B62
BICKEL A.,THE LEAST DANGEROUS BRANCH. USA+45 USA-45 LAW
CONSTN SCHOOL LEGIS ADJUD RACE/REL DISCRIM ORD/FREE NAT/G
...JURID 18/20 SUPREME/CT CONGRESS MARSHALL/J CT/SYS
HOLMES/OW FRANKFUR/F. PAGE 12 E0226

B62
BOCK E.A.,CASE STUDIES IN AMERICAN GOVERNMENT. POLICY
USA+45 ECO/DEV CHIEF EDU/PROP CT/SYS RACE/REL LEGIS
ORD/FREE...JURID MGT PHIL/SCI PRESIDENT CASEBOOK. IDEA/COMP
PAGE 13 E0256 NAT/G

B62
CURRY J.E.,RACE TENSIONS AND THE POLICE. LAW MUNIC FORCES
NEIGH TEC/DEV RUMOR CONTROL COERCE GP/REL ATTIT RACE/REL
...SOC 20 NEGRO. PAGE 28 E0558 CROWD
ORD/FREE

B62
GANJI M.,INTERNATIONAL PROTECTION OF HUMAN RIGHTS. ORD/FREE
WOR+45 CONSTN INT/TRADE CT/SYS SANCTION CRIME WAR DISCRIM
RACE/REL...CHARTS IDEA/COMP NAT/COMP BIBLIOG 20 LEGIS
TREATY NEGRO LEAGUE/NAT UN CIVIL/LIB. PAGE 42 E0831 DELIB/GP

B62
HEYDECKER J.J.,THE NUREMBERG TRIAL: HISTORY OF NAZI LAW
GERMANY AS REVEALED THROUGH THE TESTIMONY AT CRIME
NUREMBERG. EUR+WWI GERMANY VOL/ASSN LEAD COERCE PARTIC
CROWD INGP/REL RACE/REL SUPEGO ORD/FREE...CONCPT 20 TOTALISM
NAZI ANTI/SEMIT NUREMBERG JEWS. PAGE 52 E1036

B62
HIRSCHFIELD R.S.,THE CONSTITUTION AND THE COURT. ADJUD
SCHOOL WAR RACE/REL EQUILIB ORD/FREE...POLICY PWR
MAJORIT DECISION JURID 18/20 PRESIDENT COLD/WAR CONSTN
CIVIL/LIB SUPREME/CT CONGRESS. PAGE 53 E1051 LAW

B62
MITCHELL G.E.,THE ANGRY BLACK SOUTH. USA+45 LAW RACE/REL
CONSTN SCHOOL DELIB/GP EDU/PROP CONTROL SUFF ANOMIE DISCRIM
DRIVE...ANTHOL 20 NEGRO CIV/RIGHTS SOUTH/US. ADJUST
PAGE 74 E1473 ORD/FREE

B62
MURPHY W.F.,CONGRESS AND THE COURT. USA+45 LAW LEGIS
LOBBY GP/REL RACE/REL ATTIT PWR...JURID INT BIBLIOG CT/SYS
CONGRESS SUPREME/CT WARRN/EARL. PAGE 75 E1509 GOV/REL
ADJUD

B62
TAPER B.,GOMILLION VERSUS LIGHTFOOT: THE TUSKEGEE APPORT
GERRYMANDER CASE. USA+45 LAW CONSTN LOC/G MUNIC REPRESENT
CT/SYS 20 NEGRO CIV/RIGHTS GOMILLN/CG LIGHTFT/PM RACE/REL
TUSKEGEE. PAGE 95 E1908 ADJUD

C62
ABRAHAM H.J.,"THE JUDICIAL PROCESS." USA+45 USA-45 BIBLIOG
LAW NAT/G ADMIN CT/SYS INGP/REL RACE/REL DISCRIM CONSTN
...JURID IDEA/COMP 19/20. PAGE 2 E0046 JUDGE
ADJUD

B63
BLACK C.L. JR.,THE OCCASIONS OF JUSTICE: ESSAYS JURID
MOSTLY ON LAW. USA+45 JUDGE RACE/REL DISCRIM ATTIT CONSTN
MORAL ORD/FREE 20 SUPREME/CT BLACK. PAGE 12 E0236 CT/SYS
LAW

B63
DAY R.E.,CIVIL RIGHTS USA: PUBLIC SCHOOLS, SOUTHERN EDU/PROP
STATES - NORTH CAROLINA, 1963. USA+45 LOC/G NEIGH ORD/FREE
LEGIS CREATE CT/SYS COERCE DISCRIM ATTIT...QU RACE/REL
CHARTS 20 NORTH/CAR NEGRO KKK CIV/RIGHTS. PAGE 29 SANCTION
E0579

B63
FRAENKEL O.K.,THE SUPREME COURT AND CIVIL ORD/FREE
LIBERTIES: HOW THE COURT HAS PROTECTED THE BILL OF CONSTN
RIGHTS. NAT/G CT/SYS CHOOSE PERS/REL RACE/REL ADJUD
DISCRIM PERSON...DECISION 20 SUPREME/CT CIVIL/LIB JURID
BILL/RIGHT. PAGE 39 E0782

B63
HORRELL M.,LEGISLATION AND RACE RELATIONS LAW
(PAMPHLET). SOUTH/AFR SCHOOL TAX DOMIN CONTROL 20. RACE/REL
PAGE 55 E1098 DISCRIM
PARTIC

B63
HOWARD W.S.,AMERICAN SLAVERS AND THE FEDERAL LAW: DIST/IND
1837-1862. USA-45 NAT/G LEGIT COERCE RACE/REL CRIMLGY
WEALTH...POLICY BIBLIOG/A 19. PAGE 55 E1102 LAW
EXEC

B63
JACOBS P.,STATE OF UNIONS. USA+45 STRATA TOP/EX LABOR
GP/REL RACE/REL DEMAND DISCRIM ATTIT PWR 20 ECO/TAC
CONGRESS NEGRO HOFFA/J. PAGE 57 E1145 BARGAIN
DECISION

B63
LEWIN J.,POLITICS AND LAW IN SOUTH AFRICA. NAT/LISM
SOUTH/AFR UK POL/PAR BAL/PWR ECO/TAC COLONIAL POLICY
CONTROL GP/REL DISCRIM PWR 20 NEGRO. PAGE 65 E1293 LAW
RACE/REL

B63
LIVELY E.,THE INVASION OF MISSISSIPPI. USA+45 LAW RACE/REL
CONSTN NAT/G PROVS CT/SYS GOV/REL FEDERAL CONSERVE CROWD
...TRADIT 20 MISSISSIPP NEGRO NAACP WARRN/EARL COERCE
KENNEDY/JF. PAGE 66 E1309 MARXISM

B63
NEWMAN E.S.,THE FREEDOM READER. USA+45 LEGIS TOP/EX RACE/REL
PLAN ADJUD CONTROL CT/SYS DISCRIM...DECISION ANTHOL LAW
20 SUPREME/CT CIV/RIGHTS. PAGE 77 E1541 POLICY
ORD/FREE

B63
TUSSMAN J.,THE SUPREME COURT ON RACIAL CT/SYS
DISCRIMINATION. USA+45 USA-45 NAT/G PROB/SOLV ADJUD DISCRIM
RACE/REL ORD/FREE...JURID 20 SUPREME/CT CIV/RIGHTS. ATTIT
PAGE 97 E1946 LAW

B63
US COMMISSION ON CIVIL RIGHTS,FREEDOM TO THE FREE. RACE/REL
USA+45 USA-45 LAW VOL/ASSN CT/SYS ATTIT PWR...JURID DISCRIM
BIBLIOG 17/20 SUPREME/CT NEGRO CIV/RIGHTS. PAGE 99 NAT/G
E1986 POLICY

B63
US COMN CIVIL RIGHTS,REPORT ON MISSISSIPPI. LAW RACE/REL
LOC/G NAT/G LEGIS PLAN PROB/SOLV DISCRIM SOC/INTEG CONSTN
20 MISSISSIPP NEGRO. PAGE 99 E1987 ORD/FREE
COERCE

S63
VINES K.N.,"THE ROLE OF THE CIRCUIT COURT OF REGION
APPEALS IN THE FEDERAL JUDICIAL PROCESS: A CASE ADJUD
STUDY." USA+45 STRATA JUDGE RESPECT...DECISION CT/SYS
JURID CHARTS GP/COMP. PAGE 104 E2078 RACE/REL

B64
BERWANGER E.H.,WESTERN ANTI-NEGRO SENTIMENT AND RACE/REL
LAWS 1846-60: A FACTOR IN THE SLAVERY EXTENSION REGION
CONTROVERSY (PAPER). USA-45 LAW CONSTN LEGIS ADJUD DISCRIM
...BIBLIOG 19 NEGRO. PAGE 11 E0218 ORD/FREE

B64
BROOKS T.R.,TOIL AND TROUBLE, A HISTORY OF AMERICAN INDUS
LABOR. WORKER BARGAIN CAP/ISM ADJUD AUTOMAT EXEC LABOR
GP/REL RACE/REL EFFICIENCY INCOME PROFIT MARXISM LEGIS
17/20 KENNEDY/JF AFL/CIO NEGRO. PAGE 16 E0310

B64
BUREAU OF NAT'L AFFAIRS,THE CIVIL RIGHTS ACT OF LEGIS
1964. USA+45 LOC/G NAT/G DELIB/GP CONFER DEBATE RACE/REL
DISCRIM...JURID 20 CONGRESS SUPREME/CT CIV/RIGHTS. LAW
PAGE 17 E0333 CONSTN

B64
BUREAU OF NATIONAL AFFAIRS,STATE FAIR EMPLOYMENT PROVS
LAWS AND THEIR ADMINISTRATION. INDUS ADJUD PERS/REL DISCRIM
RACE/REL ATTIT ORD/FREE WEALTH 20. PAGE 17 E0338 WORKER
JURID

B64
DORMAN M.,WE SHALL OVERCOME. USA+45 ELITES ACADEM RACE/REL
FORCES TOP/EX MURDER...JURID 20 CIV/RIGHTS LAW
MISSISSIPP EVERS/MED CLEMSON. PAGE 32 E0638 DISCRIM

B64
FACTS ON FILE, INC.,CIVIL RIGHTS 1960-63: THE NEGRO DISCRIM
CAMPAIGN TO WIN EQUAL RIGHTS AND OPPORTUNITIES IN PRESS
THE UNITED STATES. LAW CONSTN PARTIC SUFF 20 NEGRO RACE/REL
CIV/RIGHTS MISSISSIPP. PAGE 36 E0710

B64
HANNA W.J.,POLITICS IN BLACK AFRICA: A SELECTIVE BIBLIOG
BIBLIOGRAPHY OF RELEVANT PERIODICAL LITERATURE. AFR NAT/LISM
LAW LOC/G MUNIC NAT/G POL/PAR LOBBY CHOOSE RACE/REL COLONIAL
SOVEREIGN 20. PAGE 50 E0995

HOPKINSON T.,SOUTH AFRICA. SOUTH/AFR UK NAT/G
POL/PAR LEGIS ECO/TAC PARL/PROC WAR...JURID AUD/VIS
19/20. PAGE 55 E1097

B64
SOCIETY
RACE/REL
DISCRIM

NEWMAN E.S.,CIVIL LIBERTY AND CIVIL RIGHTS. USA+45
USA-45 CONSTN PROVS FORCES LEGIS CT/SYS RACE/REL
ATTIT...MAJORIT JURID WORSHIP 20 SUPREME/CT NEGRO
CIV/RIGHTS CHURCH/STA. PAGE 77 E1543

B64
ORD/FREE
LAW
CONTROL
NAT/G

OPPENHEIMER M.,A MANUAL FOR DIRECT ACTION. USA+45
SCHOOL FORCES ADJUD CT/SYS SUFF RACE/REL DISCRIM
...POLICY CHARTS 20. PAGE 79 E1580

B64
PLAN
VOL/ASSN
JURID
LEAD

SCHMEISER D.A.,CIVIL LIBERTIES IN CANADA. CANADA
LAW SECT PRESS RACE/REL NAT/LISM PRIVIL 20
COMMONWLTH PARLIAMENT CIVIL/LIB CHURCH/STA. PAGE 88
E1758

B64
ORD/FREE
CONSTN
EDU/PROP

SEGAL R.,SANCTIONS AGAINST SOUTH AFRICA. AFR
SOUTH/AFR NAT/G INT/TRADE RACE/REL PEACE PWR
...INT/LAW ANTHOL 20 UN. PAGE 90 E1801

B64
SANCTION
DISCRIM
ECO/TAC
POLICY

TODD A.,JUSTICE ON TRIAL: THE CASE OF LOUIS D.
BRANDEIS. TOP/EX DISCRIM...JURID 20 WILSON/W
CONGRESS SUPREME/CT BRANDEIS/L SENATE. PAGE 96
E1929

B64
PERSON
RACE/REL
PERS/REL
NAT/G

US SENATE COMM ON JUDICIARY,CIVIL RIGHTS - THE
PRESIDENT'S PROGRAM. USA+45 LAW PROB/SOLV PRESS
ADJUD GOV/REL RACE/REL ORD/FREE PWR...JURID 20
SUPREME/CT SENATE CIV/RIGHTS PRESIDENT. PAGE 102
E2053

B64
INT
LEGIS
DISCRIM
PARL/PROC

WAY H.F. JR.,LIBERTY IN THE BALANCE - CURRENT
ISSUES IN CIVIL LIBERTIES. USA+45 USA-45 DELIB/GP
RACE/REL DISCRIM TOTALISM MARXISM SOCISM...CONCPT
20 CONGRESS SUPREME/CT CIVIL/LIB. PAGE 105 E2104

B64
ORD/FREE
EDU/PROP
NAT/G
JURID

CARNEGIE ENDOWMENT INT. PEACE,"HUMAN RIGHTS (ISSUES
BEFORE THE NINETEENTH GENERAL ASSEMBLY)." AFR
WOR+45 LAW CONSTN NAT/G EDU/PROP GP/REL DISCRIM
PEACE ATTIT MORAL ORD/FREE...INT/LAW PSY CONCPT
RECORD UN 20. PAGE 20 E0385

S64
INT/ORG
PERSON
RACE/REL

MISSISSIPPI BLACK PAPER: (FIFTY-SEVEN NEGRO AND
WHITE CITIZENS' TESTIMONY OF POLICE BRUTALITY...).
USA+45 LAW SOCIETY CT/SYS SANCTION CRIME MORAL
ORD/FREE RESPECT 20 NEGRO. PAGE 2 E0035

B65
COERCE
RACE/REL
DISCRIM
FORCES

BAR ASSOCIATION OF ST LOUIS,CONSTITUTIONAL FREEDOM
AND THE LAW. USA+45 LAW LABOR LEGIS EDU/PROP
...JURID CONCPT SUPREME/CT CIVIL/LIB CIV/RIGHTS.
PAGE 8 E0146

B65
ORD/FREE
CONSTN
RACE/REL
NAT/G

BARKER L.J.,FREEDOM, COURTS, POLITICS: STUDIES IN
CIVIL LIBERTIES. USA+45 LEGIS CREATE DOMIN PRESS
ADJUD LOBBY CRIME GP/REL RACE/REL MARXISM 20
CIVIL/LIB. PAGE 8 E0148

B65
JURID
CT/SYS
ATTIT
ORD/FREE

CARTER R.L.,EQUALITY. LAW LABOR NEIGH SCHOOL
RACE/REL 20 NEGRO. PAGE 20 E0402

B65
POLICY
DISCRIM
PLAN
CREATE

CONGRESSIONAL QUARTERLY SERV,REVOLUTION IN CIVIL
RIGHTS. USA+45 USA-45 LEGIS ADJUD CT/SYS CHOOSE
DISCRIM...DECISION CONGRESS SUPREME/CT. PAGE 25
E0488

B65
LAW
CONSTN
RACE/REL
LOBBY

COWEN Z.,THE BRITISH COMMONWEALTH OF NATIONS IN A
CHANGING WORLD. UK ECO/UNDEV INT/ORG ECO/TAC
INT/TRADE COLONIAL WAR GP/REL RACE/REL SOVEREIGN
SOC/INTEG 20 TREATY EEC COMMONWLTH. PAGE 27 E0530

B65
JURID
DIPLOM
PARL/PROC
NAT/LISM

EHLE J.,THE FREE MEN. USA+45 NAT/G PROVS FORCES
JUDGE ADJUD ATTIT...POLICY SOC SOC/INTEG 20 NEGRO.
PAGE 34 E0677

B65
RACE/REL
ORD/FREE
DISCRIM

FRIEDMAN L.,SOUTHERN JUSTICE. USA+45 PUB/INST LEGIT
ADMIN CT/SYS DISCRIM...DECISION ANTHOL 20 NEGRO
SOUTH/US CIV/RIGHTS. PAGE 40 E0800

B65
ADJUD
LAW
CONSTN
RACE/REL

GILLETTE W.,THE RIGHT TO VOTE: POLITICS AND THE
PASSAGE OF THE FIFTEENTH AMENDMENT. USA-45 LAW LEAD
DISCRIM SEGREGAT CONGRESS. PAGE 44 E0863

B65
RACE/REL
CONSTN

IANNIELLO L.,MILESTONES ALONG THE MARCH: TWELVE
HISTORIC CIVIL RIGHTS DOCUMENTS--FROM WORLD WAR II
TO SELMA. USA+45 LAW FORCES TOP/EX PARTIC SUFF...T
20 NEGRO CIV/RIGHTS TRUMAN/HS SUPREME/CT
KENNEDY/JF. PAGE 56 E1121

B65
RACE/REL
DISCRIM
CONSTN
NAT/G

KARIS T.,THE TREASON TRIAL IN SOUTH AFRICA: A GUIDE
TO THE MICROFILM RECORD OF THE TRIAL. SOUTH/AFR LAW
ELITES NAT/G LEGIT CT/SYS RACE/REL DISCRIM...SOC
20. PAGE 59 E1185

B65
BIBLIOG/A
ADJUD
CRIME
AFR

ROSE A.M.,MINORITY PROBLEMS: A TEXTBOOK OF READINGS
IN INTERGROUP RELATIONS. UNIV USA+45 LAW SCHOOL
WORKER PROB/SOLV GP/REL PERSON...PSY ANTHOL WORSHIP
20 NEGRO INDIAN/AM JEWS EUROPE. PAGE 85 E1713

B65
RACE/REL
DISCRIM
ISOLAT
ACT/RES

SCHROEDER O.,DEFACTO SEGREGATION AND CIVIL RIGHTS.
LAW PROVS SCHOOL WORKER ATTIT HABITAT HEALTH WEALTH
...JURID CHARTS 19/20 NEGRO SUPREME/CT KKK. PAGE 88
E1766

B65
ANTHOL
DISCRIM
RACE/REL
ORD/FREE

SCHUBERT G.,THE POLITICAL ROLE OF THE COURTS IN
JUDICIAL POLICY MAKING. USA+45 CONSTN JUDGE
FEEDBACK CHOOSE RACE/REL ORD/FREE...TRADIT PSY
BIBLIOG/A 20 KENNEDY/JF SUPREME/CT. PAGE 89 E1776

B65
CT/SYS
POLICY
DECISION

SMITH R.C.,THEY CLOSED THEIR SCHOOLS. USA+45 NEIGH
ADJUD CROWD CONSEN WEALTH...DECISION OBS INT 20
NEGRO VIRGINIA. PAGE 92 E1846

B65
RACE/REL
DISCRIM
LOC/G
SCHOOL

SWISHER C.B.,THE SUPREME COURT IN MODERN ROLE. COM
COM/IND NAT/G FORCES LEGIS LOBBY PARTIC RACE/REL 20
SUPREME/CT. PAGE 95 E1901

B65
DELIB/GP
ATTIT
CT/SYS
ADJUD

HAUSNER G.,JUSTICE IN JERUSALEM. GERMANY ISRAEL
SOCIETY KIN DIPLOM LEGIT CT/SYS PARTIC MURDER
MAJORITY ATTIT FASCISM...INT/LAW JURID 20 JEWS
WAR/TRIAL. PAGE 51 E1013

B66
ADJUD
CRIME
RACE/REL
COERCE

KUNSTLER W.M.,"DEEP IN MY HEART" USA+45 LAW
PROF/ORG SECT LOBBY PARTIC CROWD DISCRIM ROLE
...BIOG 20 KING/MAR/L NEGRO CIV/RIGHTS SOUTH/US.
PAGE 62 E1233

B66
CT/SYS
RACE/REL
ADJUD
CONSULT

MILLER E.W.,THE NEGRO IN AMERICA: A BIBLIOGRAPHY.
USA+45 LAW EDU/PROP REV GOV/REL GP/REL INGP/REL
ADJUST HABITAT PERSON HEALTH ORD/FREE SOC/INTEG 20
NEGRO. PAGE 73 E1459

B66
BIBLIOG
DISCRIM
RACE/REL

SKOLNICK J.H.,JUSTICE WITHOUT TRIAL: LAW
ENFORCEMENT IN DEMOCRATIC SOCIETY. USA+45 LAW
TRIBUTE RACE/REL BIO/SOC PERSON...PSY SOC 20 NEGRO
BUREAUCRCY PROSTITUTN. PAGE 92 E1836

B66
FORCES
CRIMLGY
CRIME

HIGGINS R.,"THE INTERNATIONAL COURT AND SOUTH WEST
AFRICA* SOME IMPLICATIONS OF THE JUDGMENT." AFR LAW
ECO/UNDEV JUDGE RACE/REL COST PWR...INT/LAW TREND
UN TREATY. PAGE 52 E1043

L66
SOUTH/AFR
COLONIAL
CT/SYS
ADJUD

BERNSTEIN S.,ALTERNATIVES TO VIOLENCE: ALIENATED
YOUTH AND RIOTS, RACE AND POVERTY. MUNIC PUB/INST
SCHOOL INGP/REL RACE/REL UTOPIA DRIVE HABITAT ROLE
WEALTH...INT 20. PAGE 11 E0215

B67
AGE/Y
SOC/WK
NEIGH
CRIME

COX A.,CIVIL RIGHTS, THE CONSTITUTION, AND THE
COURTS. CONSTN EDU/PROP CRIME DISCRIM ATTIT...JURID
20. PAGE 27 E0533

B67
LAW
FEDERAL
RACE/REL
PRESS

GRAHAM H.D.,CRISIS IN PRINT: DESEGREGATION AND THE PRESS IN TENNESSEE. LAW SOCIETY MUNIC POL/PAR EDU/PROP LEAD REPRESENT DISCRIM ATTIT...IDEA/COMP BIBLIOG/A SOC/INTEG 20 TENNESSEE SUPREME/CT SOUTH/US. PAGE 45 E0896
B67 PRESS PROVS POLICY RACE/REL

NARAIN I.,THE POLITICS OF RACIALISM. INDIA SOUTH/AFR LAW NAT/G RACE/REL ATTIT 20. PAGE 76 E1521
B67 DISCRIM COLONIAL HIST/WRIT

RUSSELL B.,WAR CRIMES IN VIETNAM. USA+45 VIETNAM FORCES DIPLOM WEAPON RACE/REL DISCRIM ISOLAT BIO/SOC 20 COLD/WAR RUSSELL/B. PAGE 87 E1736
B67 WAR CRIME ATTIT POLICY

UNIVERSAL REFERENCE SYSTEM,CURRENT EVENTS AND PROBLEMS OF MODERN SOCIETY (VOLUME V). WOR+45 LOC/G MUNIC NAT/G PLAN EDU/PROP CRIME RACE/REL WEALTH ...COMPUT/IR GEN/METH. PAGE 98 E1974
B67 BIBLIOG/A SOCIETY PROB/SOLV ATTIT

NAGEL S.S.,"DISPARITIES IN CRIMINAL PROCEDURE." STRATA NAT/G PROVS EDU/PROP RACE/REL AGE HABITAT SEX...JURID CHARTS 20. PAGE 76 E1519
L67 ADJUD DISCRIM STRUCT ACT/RES

"THE FEDERAL AGRICULTURAL STABILIZATION PROGRAM AND THE NEGRO." LAW CONSTN PLAN REPRESENT DISCRIM ORD/FREE 20 NEGRO CONGRESS. PAGE 2 E0039
S67 AGRI CONTROL NAT/G RACE/REL

BRADLEY A.W.,"CONSTITUTION-MAKING IN UGANDA." UGANDA LAW CHIEF DELIB/GP LEGIS ADMIN EXEC PARL/PROC RACE/REL ORD/FREE...GOV/COMP 20. PAGE 15 E0284
S67 NAT/G CREATE CONSTN FEDERAL

EDGEWORTH A.B. JR.,"CIVIL RIGHTS PLUS THREE YEARS: BANKS AND THE ANTI-DISCRIMINATION LAW" USA+45 SOCIETY DELIB/GP RACE/REL EFFICIENCY 20 NEGRO CIV/RIGHTS. PAGE 34 E0675
S67 WORKER DISCRIM FINAN LAW

HAMILTON H.D.,"LEGISLATIVE CONSTITUENCIES: SINGLE-MEMBER DISTRICTS, MULTI-MEMBER DISTRICTS, AND FLOTERAL DISTRICTS." USA+45 LAW POL/PAR ADJUD RACE/REL...CHARTS METH/COMP 20. PAGE 50 E0990
S67 LEGIS REPRESENT APPORT PLAN

KIM R.C.C.,"THE SUPREME COURT: ORALLE WITHOUT TRUTH." USA+45 EDU/PROP RACE/REL ADJUST ALL/VALS ORD/FREE...DECISION WORSHIP SUPREME/CT. PAGE 61 E1214
S67 CT/SYS PROB/SOLV ADJUD REPRESENT

SCOTT A.,"TWENTY-FIVE YEARS OF OPINION ON INTEGRATION IN TEXAS." USA+45 USA-45 DISCRIM ...KNO/TEST TREND CHARTS 20 TEXAS. PAGE 89 E1794
S67 ATTIT ADJUST RACE/REL LAW

VAUGHN W.P.,"SEPARATE AND UNEQUAL: THE CIVIL RIGHTS ACT OF 1875 AND DEFEAT OF THE SCHOOL INTEGRATION CLAUSE." USA-45 LEGIS RACE/REL 19 CONGRESS. PAGE 103 E2073
S67 LAW DISCRIM EDU/PROP PARL/PROC

DUGARD J.,"THE REVOCATION OF THE MANDATE FOR SOUTH WEST AFRICA." SOUTH/AFR WOR+45 STRATA NAT/G DELIB/GP DIPLOM ADJUD SANCTION CHOOSE RACE/REL ...POLICY NAT/COMP 20 AFRICA/SW UN TRUST/TERR LEAGUE/NAT. PAGE 33 E0654
S68 AFR INT/ORG DISCRIM COLONIAL

RADZINOWICZ L. E1666

RAE D. E1667

RAF....ROYAL AIR FORCE

RAGHAVAN M.D. E1668

RAHMAN/TA....TUNKU ABDUL RAHMAN

RAI H. E1669

RAILROAD....RAILROADS AND RAILWAY SYSTEMS

GRIFFIN A.P.C.,LIST OF BOOKS ON RAILROADS IN FOREIGN COUNTRIES. MOD/EUR ECO/DEV NAT/G CONTROL
B05 BIBLIOG/A SERV/IND

SOCISM...JURID 19/20 RAILROAD. PAGE 47 E0927
ADMIN DIST/IND

RAJAN M.S. E1670

RAJARATAM/S....S. RAJARATAM

RAJASTHAN....RAJASTHAN

RALSTON A. E1671

RAM J. E1672

RAMA RAO T.V. E0229

RAMUNDO B.A. E1673

RANDOMNESS....SEE PROB/SOLV

RANKE/L....LEOPOLD VON RANKE

RANKING SYSTEMS....SEE SENIOR

RANKOVIC/A....ALEXANDER RANKOVIC, YUGOSLAVIAOS FORMER VICE PRESIDENT

RATION....RATIONING

FULLER G.A.,DEMOBILIZATION: A SELECTED LIST OF REFERENCES. USA+45 LAW AGRI LABOR WORKER ECO/TAC RATION RECEIVE EDU/PROP ROUTINE ARMS/CONT ALL/VALS 20. PAGE 41 E0819
N BIBLIOG/A INDUS FORCES NAT/G

GRIFFIN A.P.C.,LISTS PUBLISHED 1902-03: GOVERNMENT OWNERSHIP OF RAILROADS (PAMPHLET). USA-45 LAW NAT/G RATION GOV/REL CENTRAL SOCISM...POLICY 19/20. PAGE 46 E0922
B03 BIBLIOG DIST/IND CONTROL ADJUD

COX H.,ECONOMIC LIBERTY. UNIV LAW INT/TRADE RATION TARIFFS RACE/REL SOCISM POLICY. PAGE 27 E0535
B20 NAT/G ORD/FREE ECO/TAC PERSON

INTNTL COTTON ADVISORY COMMITT,GOVERNMENT REGULATIONS ON COTTON, 1962 (PAMPHLET). WOR+45 RATION PRODUC...CHARTS 20. PAGE 57 E1136
B62 ECO/TAC LAW CONTROL AGRI

US SENATE COMM ON JUDICIARY,ADMINISTERED PRICES. USA+45 RATION ADJUD CONTROL LOBBY...POLICY 20 SENATE MONOPOLY. PAGE 102 E2047
B63 LG/CO PRICE ADMIN DECISION

HIRSCH W.Z.,"SOME ECONOMIC IMPLICATIONS OF CITY PLANNING." LAW PROB/SOLV RATION EFFICIENCY...METH 20. PAGE 53 E1050
S67 ECO/TAC JURID MUNIC PLAN

RATIONAL....RATIONALITY

HEGEL G.W.F.,PHILOSOPHY OF RIGHT. UNIV FAM SECT CHIEF AGREE WAR MARRIAGE OWN ORD/FREE...POLICY CONCPT. PAGE 51 E1023
B42 NAT/G LAW RATIONAL

FRANK J.,LAW AND THE MODERN MIND. UNIV LAW CT/SYS RATIONAL ATTIT...CONCPT 20 HOLMES/OW JURY. PAGE 40 E0787
B49 JURID ADJUD IDEA/COMP MYTH

FIELD G.L.,"LAW AS AN OBJECTIVE POLITICAL CONCEPT" (BMR)" UNIV SOCIETY RATIONAL JURID. PAGE 38 E0747
S49 LAW CONCPT METH/CNCPT SANCTION

EUSDEN J.D.,PURITANS, LAWYERS, AND POLITICS IN EARLY SEVENTEENTH-CENTURY ENGLAND. UK CT/SYS PARL/PROC RATIONAL PWR SOVEREIGN...IDEA/COMP BIBLIOG 17 PURITAN COMMON/LAW. PAGE 35 E0702
B58 GP/REL SECT NAT/G LAW

RIKER W.H.,"THE PARADOX OF VOTING AND CONGRESSIONAL RULES FOR VOTING ON AMENDMENTS." LAW DELIB/GP EX/STRUC PROB/SOLV CONFER DEBATE EFFICIENCY ATTIT HOUSE/REP CONGRESS SENATE. PAGE 85 E1700
S58 PARL/PROC DECISION LEGIS RATIONAL

ROCHE J.P.,"POLITICAL SCIENCE AND SCIENCE FICTION" QUANT
(BMR)" WOR+45 INTELL OP/RES ADJUD...JURID SOC   RATIONAL
IDEA/COMP 20. PAGE 85 E1709   MATH
                                         S58   METH

FRIEDRICH C.J.,"AUTHORITY, REASON AND DISCRETION"   AUTHORIT
IN C. FRIEDRICH'S AUTHORITY (BMR)" UNIV EX/STRUC   CHOOSE
ADJUD ADMIN CONTROL INGP/REL ATTIT PERSON PWR.   RATIONAL
PAGE 41 E0807   PERS/REL
                                         C58

ROSS A.,ON LAW AND JUSTICE. USA+45 RATIONAL   JURID
...IDEA/COMP GEN/LAWS 20 SCANDINAV NATURL/LAW.   PHIL/SCI
PAGE 86 E1722   LAW
                                         B59   CONCPT

SCHMIDHAUSER J.R.,THE SUPREME COURT: ITS POLITICS, JUDGE
PERSONALITIES, AND PROCEDURES. LAW DELIB/GP   JURID
EX/STRUC TOP/EX ADJUD CT/SYS CHOOSE RATIONAL PWR   DECISION
SUPREME/CT. PAGE 88 E1760
                                         B60

NEWMAN R.P.,RECOGNITION OF COMMUNIST CHINA? A STUDY MARXISM
IN ARGUMENT. CHINA/COM NAT/G PROB/SOLV RATIONAL   ATTIT
...INT/LAW LOG IDEA/COMP BIBLIOG 20. PAGE 77 E1544 DIPLOM
                                         B61   POLICY

WASSERSTROM R.A.,THE JUDICIAL DECISION: TOWARD A   JUDGE
THEORY OF LEGAL JUSTIFICATION. ACT/RES RATIONAL   LAW
PERCEPT KNOWL OBJECTIVE...DECISION JURID. PAGE 105 ADJUD
E2102
                                         B61

DIESING P.,REASON IN SOCIETY; FIVE TYPES OF   RATIONAL
DECISIONS AND THEIR SOCIAL CONDITIONS. SOCIETY   METH/COMP
STRUCT LABOR CREATE TEC/DEV BARGAIN ADJUD ROLE   DECISION
...JURID BIBLIOG 20. PAGE 31 E0625   CONCPT
                                         B62

SPAETH H.J.,"JUDICIAL POWER AS A VARIABLE   JUDGE
MOTIVATING SUPREME COURT BEHAVIOR." DELIB/GP ADJUD DECISION
RATIONAL ATTIT PERSON ORD/FREE...CLASSIF STAT   PERS/COMP
GEN/METH. PAGE 93 E1860   PSY
                                         L62

DE GRAZIA A.,APPORTIONMENT AND REPRESENTATIVE   REPRESENT
GOVERNMENT. CONSTN POL/PAR LEGIS PLAN ADJUD DISCRIM APPORT
RATIONAL...CONCPT STAT PREDICT TREND IDEA/COMP.   NAT/G
PAGE 29 E0583   MUNIC
                                         B63

HABERMAS J.,THEORIE UND PRAXIS. RATIONAL PERSON   JURID
...PHIL/SCI ANTHOL 19/20 HEGEL/GWF MARX/KARL BLOCH REV
LOWITH. PAGE 49 E0969   GEN/LAWS
                                         B63   MARXISM

MURPHY T.J.,CENSORSHIP: GOVERNMENT AND OBSCENITY.   ORD/FREE
USA+45 CULTURE LEGIS JUDGE EDU/PROP CONTROL   MORAL
INGP/REL RATIONAL POPULISM...CATH JURID 20. PAGE 75 LAW
E1507   CONSEN
                                         B63

MAYO L.H.,"LEGAL-POLICY DECISION PROCESS: DECISION
ALTERNATIVE THINKING AND THE PREDICTIVE FUNCTION." SIMUL
PROB/SOLV EFFICIENCY RATIONAL. PAGE 70 E1395   JURID
                                         L64   TEC/DEV

CAVERS D.F.,THE CHOICE-OF-LAW PROCESS. PROB/SOLV   JURID
ADJUD CT/SYS CHOOSE RATIONAL...IDEA/COMP 16/20   DECISION
TREATY. PAGE 21 E0411   METH/COMP
                                         B65   ADMIN

GINSBERG M.,ON JUSTICE IN SOCIETY. LAW EDU/PROP   ADJUD
LEGIT CT/SYS INGP/REL PRIVIL RATIONAL ATTIT MORAL   ROLE
ORD/FREE...JURID 20. PAGE 44 E0867   CONCPT
                                         B65

PLANO J.C.,FORGING WORLD ORDER: THE POLITICS OF   INT/ORG
INTERNATIONAL ORGANIZATION. PROB/SOLV DIPLOM   ADMIN
CONTROL CENTRAL RATIONAL ORD/FREE...INT/LAW CHARTS JURID
BIBLIOG 20 UN LEAGUE/NAT. PAGE 81 E1618
                                         B67

HORVATH B.,"COMPARATIVE CONFLICTS LAW AND THE   INT/LAW
CONCEPT OF CHANGING LAW." UNIV RATIONAL...JURID   IDEA/COMP
LOG. PAGE 55 E1099   DIPLOM
                                         S67   CONCPT

RAVENS J.P. E1674

READ J.S. E1675

REAGAN/RON....RONALD REAGAN

REALE M. E1676

REALPOL....REALPOLITIK, PRACTICAL POLITICS

REC/INT....RECORDING OF INTERVIEWS

RECALL....RECALL PROCEDURE

                                         B30
BIRD F.L.,THE RECALL OF PUBLIC OFFICERS; A STUDY OF REPRESENT
THE OPERATION OF RECALL IN CALIFORNIA. LOC/G MUNIC SANCTION
POL/PAR PROVS PROB/SOLV ADJUD PARTIC...CHARTS   CHOOSE
METH/COMP 20 CALIFORNIA RECALL. PAGE 12 E0230   LAW

RECASENS SICHES S. E1677

RECEIVE....RECEIVING (IN WELFARE SENSE)

                                         N
FULLER G.A.,DEMOBILIZATION: A SELECTED LIST OF   BIBLIOG/A
REFERENCES. USA+45 LAW AGRI LABOR WORKER ECO/TAC   INDUS
RATION RECEIVE EDU/PROP ROUTINE ARMS/CONT ALL/VALS FORCES
20. PAGE 41 E0819   NAT/G

                                         N
LATIN AMERICA IN PERIODICAL LITERATURE. LAW TEC/DEV BIBLIOG/A
DIPLOM RECEIVE EDU/PROP...GEOG HUM MGT 20. PAGE 2   L/A+17C
E0024   SOCIETY
                                                    ECO/UNDEV

                                         B19
SMITH R.H.,JUSTICE AND THE POOR. LAW RECEIVE ADJUD CT/SYS
CRIME GOV/REL COST...JURID SOC/WK CONCPT STAT   DISCRIM
CHARTS GP/COMP 20. PAGE 92 E1847   WEALTH

                                         B55
CRAIG J.,BIBLIOGRAPHY OF PUBLIC ADMINISTRATION IN   BIBLIOG
AUSTRALIA. CONSTN FINAN EX/STRUC LEGIS PLAN DIPLOM GOV/REL
RECEIVE ADJUD ROUTINE...HEAL 19/20 AUSTRAL   ADMIN
PARLIAMENT. PAGE 27 E0540   NAT/G

                                         B56
HOGAN J.D.,AMERICAN SOCIAL LEGISLATION. USA+45 FAM STRUCT
AGE/Y ATTIT...JURID CONCPT TREND. PAGE 53 E1065   RECEIVE
                                                    LEGIS
                                                    LABOR

                                         B56
NOTZ R.L.,FEDERAL GRANTS-IN-AID TO STATES: ANALYSIS GIVE
OF LAWS IN FORCE ON SEPTEMBER 10, 1956. USA+45 LAW NAT/G
SCHOOL PLAN ECO/TAC TAX RECEIVE...HEAL JURID 20.   PROVS
PAGE 78 E1558   GOV/REL

                                         B58
ORTIZ R.P.,ANNUARIO BIBLIOGRAFICO COLOMBIANO,   BIBLIOG
1951-1956. LAW RECEIVE EDU/PROP ADMIN...LING STAT   SOC
20 COLOMB. PAGE 79 E1582

                                         B64
KISER S.L.,AMERICANISM IN ACTION. USA+45 LAW PROVS OLD/LIB
CAP/ISM DIPLOM RECEIVE CONTROL CT/SYS WAR FEDERAL   FOR/AID
ATTIT WEALTH 20 SUPREME/CT. PAGE 61 E1221   MARXISM
                                                    CONSTN

                                         B64
MITAU G.T.,INSOLUBLE PROBLEMS: CASE PROBLEMS ON THE ADJUD
FUNCTIONS OF STATE AND LOCAL GOVERNMENT. USA+45 AIR LOC/G
FINAN LABOR POL/PAR PROB/SOLV TAX RECEIVE CONTROL   PROVS
GP/REL 20 CASEBOOK ZONING. PAGE 73 E1471

                                         B64
RICHARDSON I.L.,BIBLIOGRAFIA BRASILEIRA DE   BIBLIOG
ADMINISTRACAO PUBLICA E ASSUNTOS CORRELATOS. BRAZIL MGT
CONSTN FINAN LOC/G NAT/G POL/PAR PLAN DIPLOM   ADMIN
RECEIVE ATTIT...METH 20. PAGE 84 E1694   LAW

                                         B65
CONGRESSIONAL QUARTERLY SERV,FEDERAL ROLE IN   ACADEM
EDUCATION (PAMPHLET). LAW SCHOOL PLAN TAX ADJUD   DISCRIM
...CHARTS SOC/INTEG 20 PRESIDENT. PAGE 25 E0487   RECEIVE
                                                    FEDERAL

                                         B65
US OFFICE ECONOMIC OPPORTUNITY,CATALOG OF FEDERAL   BIBLIOG
PROGRAMS FOR INDIVIDUAL AND COMMUNITY IMPROVEMENT. CLIENT
USA+45 GIVE RECEIVE ADMIN HEALTH KNOWL SKILL WEALTH ECO/TAC
CHARTS. PAGE 101 E2021   MUNIC

                                         S67
ALEXANDER B.,"GIBRALTAR" SPAIN UK CONSTN WORKER   DIPLOM

PROB/SOLV FOR/AID RECEIVE CONTROL 20. PAGE 3 E0059   INT/ORG ORD/FREE ECO/TAC

S67

ANDERSON W.,"THE PERILS OF 'SHARING'." USA+45 ECO/TAC RECEIVE LOBBY GOV/REL CENTRAL COST INCOME ...POLICY PLURIST CONGRESS. PAGE 5 E0095   BUDGET TAX FEDERAL LAW

RECIFE....RECIFE, BRAZIL

RECIPROCITY....SEE SANCTION

RECONSTRUCTION PERIOD....SEE CIVIL/WAR

RECORD....RECORDING OF DIRECT OBSERVATIONS

B00

LORIMER J.,THE INSTITUTES OF THE LAW OF NATIONS. WOR-45 CULTURE SOCIETY NAT/G VOL/ASSN DIPLOM LEGIT WAR PEACE DRIVE ORD/FREE SOVEREIGN...CONCPT RECORD INT TREND HYPO/EXP GEN/METH TOT/POP VAL/FREE 20. PAGE 66 E1327   INT/ORG LAW INT/LAW

B15

SAWYER R.A.,A LIST OF WORKS ON COUNTY GOVERNMENT. LAW FINAN MUNIC TOP/EX ROUTINE CRIME...CLASSIF RECORD 19/20. PAGE 87 E1748   BIBLIOG/A LOC/G GOV/REL ADMIN

B22

WRIGHT Q.,THE CONTROL OF AMERICAN FOREIGN RELATIONS. USA-45 WOR-45 CONSTN INT/ORG CONSULT LEGIS LEGIT ROUTINE ORD/FREE PWR...POLICY JURID CONCPT METH/CNCPT RECORD LEAGUE/NAT 20. PAGE 107 E2150   NAT/G EXEC DIPLOM

L28

HUDSON M.,"THE TEACHING OF INTERNATIONAL LAW IN AMERICA." USA-45 LAW CONSULT ACT/RES CREATE EDU/PROP ATTIT RIGID/FLEX...JURID CONCPT RECORD HIST/WRIT TREND GEN/LAWS 18/20. PAGE 56 E1109   PERCEPT KNOWL INT/LAW

L29

FEIS H.,"RESEARCH ACTIVITIES OF THE LEAGUE OF NATIONS." EUR+WWI WOR-45 R+D INT/ORG CT/SYS ARMS/CONT WEALTH...OBS RECORD LEAGUE/NAT ILO 20. PAGE 37 E0729   CONSULT KNOWL PEACE

B39

ZIMMERN A.,THE LEAGUE OF NATIONS AND THE RULE OF LAW. WOR-45 STRUCT NAT/G DELIB/GP EX/STRUC BAL/PWR DOMIN LEGIT COERCE ORD/FREE PWR...POLICY RECORD LEAGUE/NAT TOT/POP VAL/FREE 20 LEAGUE/NAT. PAGE 108 E2170   INT/ORG LAW DIPLOM

B56

WEIS P.,NATIONALITY AND STATELESSNESS IN INTERNATIONAL LAW. UK WOR+45 WOR-45 LAW CONSTN NAT/G DIPLOM EDU/PROP LEGIT ROUTINE RIGID/FLEX ...JURID RECORD CMN/WLTH 20. PAGE 105 E2109   INT/ORG SOVEREIGN INT/LAW

B57

JENKS C.W.,THE INTERNATIONAL PROTECTION OF TRADE UNION FREEDOM. FUT WOR+45 WOR-45 VOL/ASSN DELIB/GP CT/SYS REGION ROUTINE...JURID METH/CNCPT RECORD TIME/SEQ CHARTS ILO WORK OAS 20. PAGE 58 E1153   LABOR INT/ORG

B57

ROSENNE S.,THE INTERNATIONAL COURT OF JUSTICE. WOR+45 LAW DOMIN LEGIT PEACE PWR SOVEREIGN...JURID CONCPT RECORD TIME/SEQ CON/ANAL CHARTS UN TOT/POP VAL/FREE LEAGUE/NAT 20 ICJ. PAGE 86 E1716   INT/ORG CT/SYS INT/LAW

B58

WESTIN A.F.,THE ANATOMY OF A CONSTITUTIONAL LAW CASE. USA+45 LAW LEGIS ADMIN EXEC...DECISION MGT SOC RECORD 20 SUPREME/CT. PAGE 105 E2113   CT/SYS INDUS ADJUD CONSTN

S59

CORY R.H. JR.,"INTERNATIONAL INSPECTION FROM PROPOSALS TO REALIZATION." WOR+45 TEC/DEV ECO/TAC ADJUD ORD/FREE PWR WEALTH...RECORD VAL/FREE 20. PAGE 26 E0516   STRUCT PSY ARMS/CONT NUC/PWR

L60

DEAN A.W.,"SECOND GENEVA CONFERENCE OF THE LAW OF THE SEA: THE FIGHT FOR FREEDOM OF THE SEAS." FUT USA+45 USSR WOR+45 WOR-45 SEA CONSTN STRUCT PLAN INT/TRADE ADJUD ADMIN ORD/FREE...DECISION RECORD TREND GEN/LAWS 20 TREATY. PAGE 30 E0600   INT/ORG JURID INT/LAW

S60

SCHWELB E.,"INTERNATIONAL CONVENTIONS ON HUMAN   INT/ORG

RIGHTS." FUT WOR+45 LAW CONSTN CULTURE SOCIETY STRUCT VOL/ASSN DELIB/GP PLAN ADJUD SUPEGO LOVE MORAL...SOC CONCPT STAT RECORD HIST/WRIT TREND 20 UN. PAGE 89 E1790   HUM

B61

MCDOUGAL M.S.,LAW AND MINIMUM WORLD PUBLIC ORDER. WOR+45 SOCIETY NAT/G DELIB/GP EDU/PROP LEGIT ADJUD COERCE ATTIT PERSON...JURID CONCPT RECORD TREND TOT/POP 20. PAGE 70 E1406   INT/ORG ORD/FREE INT/LAW

B62

ASSOCIATION BAR OF NYC,REPORT ON ADMISSION PROCEDURES TO NEW YORK STATE MENTAL HOSPITALS. LAW CONSTN INGP/REL RESPECT...PSY OBS RECORD. PAGE 6 E0108   PUB/INST HEALTH CLIENT ROUTINE

B62

MCDOUGAL M.S.,THE PUBLIC ORDER OF THE OCEANS. WOR+45 WOR-45 SEA INT/ORG NAT/G CONSULT DELIB/GP DIPLOM LEGIT PEACE RIGID/FLEX...GEOG INT/LAW JURID RECORD TOT/POP 20 TREATY. PAGE 70 E1407   ADJUD ORD/FREE

B62

WOETZEL R.K.,THE NURENBERG TRIALS IN INTERNATIONAL LAW. CHRIST-17C MOD/EUR WOR+45 SOCIETY NAT/G DELIB/GP DOMIN LEGIT ROUTINE ATTIT DRIVE PERSON SUPEGO MORAL ORD/FREE...POLICY MAJORIT JURID PSY SOC SELF/OBS RECORD NAZI TOT/POP. PAGE 107 E2138   INT/ORG ADJUD WAR

S63

MENDELSON W.,"THE NEO-BEHAVIORAL APPROACH TO THE JUDICIAL PROCESS: A CRITIQUE" ADJUD PERSON...SOC RECORD IDEA/COMP. PAGE 72 E1438   DECISION JURID JUDGE

B64

DUBISSON M.,LA COUR INTERNATIONALE DE JUSTICE. FRANCE LAW CONSTN JUDGE DOMIN ADJUD...INT/LAW CLASSIF RECORD ORG/CHARTS UN. PAGE 33 E0651   CT/SYS INT/ORG

B64

FEIFER G.,JUSTICE IN MOSCOW. USSR LAW CRIME ...RECORD 20. PAGE 37 E0725   ADJUD JURID CT/SYS MARXISM

B64

FRANCK T.M.,EAST AFRICAN UNITY THROUGH LAW. MALAWI TANZANIA UGANDA UK ZAMBIA CONSTN INT/ORG NAT/G ADMIN ROUTINE TASK NAT/LISM ATTIT SOVEREIGN ...RECORD IDEA/COMP NAT/COMP. PAGE 40 E0785   AFR FEDERAL REGION INT/LAW

S64

CARNEGIE ENDOWMENT INT. PEACE,"HUMAN RIGHTS (ISSUES BEFORE THE NINETEENTH GENERAL ASSEMBLY)." AFR WOR+45 LAW CONSTN NAT/G EDU/PROP GP/REL DISCRIM PEACE ATTIT MORAL ORD/FREE...INT/LAW PSY CONCPT RECORD UN 20. PAGE 20 E0385   INT/ORG PERSON RACE/REL

S64

CARNEGIE ENDOWMENT INT. PEACE,"LEGAL QUESTIONS (ISSUES BEFORE THE NINETEENTH GENERAL ASSEMBLY)." WOR+45 CONSTN NAT/G DELIB/GP ADJUD PEACE MORAL ORD/FREE...RECORD UN 20 TREATY. PAGE 20 E0386   INT/ORG LAW INT/LAW

B65

WHITEMAN M.M.,DIGEST OF INTERNATIONAL LAW* VOLUME 5. DEPARTMENT OF STATE PUBLICATION 7873. USA+45 WOR+45 OP/RES...CONCPT CLASSIF RECORD IDEA/COMP. PAGE 106 E2118   INT/LAW NAT/G NAT/COMP

S65

FALK R.A.,"INTERNATIONAL LEGAL ORDER." USA+45 INTELL FACE/GP INT/ORG LEGIT KNOWL...CONCPT METH/CNCPT STYLE RECORD GEN/METH 20. PAGE 36 E0717   ATTIT GEN/LAWS INT/LAW

S65

FRIEDHEIM R.,"THE 'SATISFIED' AND 'DISSATISFIED' STATES NEGOTIATE INTERNATIONAL LAW* A CASE STUDY." DIPLOM CONFER ADJUD CONSEN PEACE ATTIT UN. PAGE 40 E0799   INT/LAW RECORD

S65

LUSKY L.,"FOUR PROBLEMS IN LAWMAKING FOR PEACE." FORCES LEGIS CREATE ADJUD COERCE WAR MAJORITY PEACE PWR. PAGE 67 E1334   ORD/FREE INT/LAW UTOPIA RECORD

S65

MARTIN A.,"PROLIFERATION." FUT WOR+45 PROB/SOLV REGION ADJUST...PREDICT NAT/COMP UN TREATY. PAGE 69 E1372   RECORD NUC/PWR ARMS/CONT VOL/ASSN

C65

SCHEINGOLD S.A.,"THE RULE OF LAW IN EUROPEAN   INT/LAW

INTEGRATION: THE PATH OF THE SCHUMAN PLAN." EUR+WWI CT/SYS
JUDGE ADJUD FEDERAL ATTIT PWR...RECORD INT BIBLIOG REGION
EEC ECSC. PAGE 87 E1755   CENTRAL

                                                             L66
GREIG D.W.,"THE ADVISORY JURISDICTION OF THE   INT/LAW
INTERNATIONAL COURT AND THE SETTLEMENT OF DISPUTES   CT/SYS
BETWEEN STATES." ISRAEL KOREA FORCES BUDGET DOMIN
LEGIT ADJUD COST...RECORD UN CONGO/LEOP TREATY.
PAGE 46 E0915

                                                             L66
KRENZ F.E.,"THE REFUGEE AS A SUBJECT OF   INT/LAW
INTERNATIONAL LAW." FUT LAW NAT/G CREATE ADJUD   DISCRIM
ISOLAT STRANGE...RECORD UN. PAGE 62 E1230   NEW/IDEA

                                                             L66
YALEM R.J.,"THE STUDY OF INTERNATIONAL   VOL/ASSN
ORGANIZATION, 1920-1965* A SURVEY OF THE   INT/ORG
LITERATURE." WOR+45 WOR-45 REGION...INT/LAW CLASSIF   BIBLIOG/A
RECORD HIST/WRIT CON/ANAL IDEA/COMP UN. PAGE 108
E2163

                                                             S66
ANAND R.P.,"ATTITUDE OF THE ASIAN-AFRICAN STATES   INT/LAW
TOWARD CERTAIN PROBLEMS OF INTERNATIONAL LAW."   ATTIT
L/A+17C S/ASIA ECO/UNDEV CREATE CONFER ADJUD   ASIA
COLONIAL...RECORD GP/COMP UN. PAGE 5 E0087   AFR

                                                             S66
BROWNLIE I.,"NUCLEAR PROLIFERATION* SOME PROBLEMS   NUC/PWR
OF CONTROL." USA+45 USSR ECO/UNDEV INT/ORG FORCES   ARMS/CONT
TEC/DEV REGION CONSEN...RECORD TREATY. PAGE 16   VOL/ASSN
E0318   ORD/FREE

                                                             S66
EWALD R.F.,"ONE OF MANY POSSIBLE GAMES." ACADEM   SIMUL
INT/ORG ARMS/CONT...INT/LAW GAME. PAGE 36 E0706   HYPO/EXP
                                                         PROG/TEAC
                                                         RECORD

                                                             S66
FINE R.I.,"PEACE-KEEPING COSTS AND ARTICLE 19 OF   FORCES
THE UN CHARTER* AN INVITATION TO RESPONSIBILITY."   COST
INT/ORG NAT/G ADJUD CT/SYS CHOOSE CONSEN...RECORD   CONSTN
IDEA/COMP UN. PAGE 38 E0750

                                                             S67
WRAITH R.E.,"ADMINISTRATIVE CHANGE IN THE NEW   ADMIN
AFRICA." AFR LG/CO ADJUD INGP/REL PWR...RECORD   NAT/G
GP/COMP 20. PAGE 107 E2147   LOC/G
                                                         ECO/UNDEV

RECTITUDE....SEE MORAL

RED/GUARD....RED GUARD

REDFIELD/R....ROBERT REDFIELD

REDFORD E.S. E1678

REED/STAN....JUSTICE STANLEY REED

                                                             B58
O'BRIEN F.W.,JUSTICE REED AND THE FIRST AMENDMENT,   ADJUD
THE RELIGION CLAUSES. USA+45 USA-45 NAT/G PROVS   SECT
CONTROL FEDERAL...POLICY JURID TIME/SEQ 20   CT/SYS
SUPREME/CT CHRUCH/STA AMEND/I REED/STAN. PAGE 78
E1563

REFERENDUM....REFERENDUM; SEE ALSO PARTIC

REFORMERS....REFORMERS

                                                             B16
SCHROEDER T.,FREE SPEECH FOR RADICALS (REV. ED.).   ORD/FREE
USA-45 CONSTN INDUS LOC/G FORCES SANCTION WAR ATTIT   CONTROL
SEX...JURID REFORMERS 20 FREE/SPEE. PAGE 88 E1767   LAW
                                                         PRESS

                                                             B27
GOOCH G.P.,ENGLISH DEMOCRATIC IDEAS IN THE   IDEA/COMP
SEVENTEENTH CENTURY (2ND ED.). UK LAW SECT FORCES   MAJORIT
DIPLOM LEAD PARL/PROC REV ATTIT AUTHORIT...ANARCH   EX/STRUC
CONCPT 17 PARLIAMENT CMN/WLTH REFORMERS. PAGE 45   CONSERVE
E0885

                                                             B52
HOLDSWORTH W.S.,A HISTORY OF ENGLISH LAW; THE   LAW
CENTURIES OF SETTLEMENT AND REFORM, 1701-1875 (VOL.   CONSTN
XIII). UK POL/PAR PROF/ORG LEGIS JUDGE WRITING   IDEA/COMP
ATTIT...JURID CONCPT BIOG GEN/LAWS 18/19 PARLIAMENT   CT/SYS

REFORMERS ENGLSH/LAW COMMON/LAW. PAGE 54 E1080

                                                             B67
BONGER W.A.,CRIMINALITY AND ECONOMIC CONDITIONS.   PERSON
MOD/EUR STRUCT INDUS WORKER EDU/PROP CRIME HABITAT   CRIMLGY
ALL/VALS...JURID SOC 20 REFORMERS. PAGE 14 E0265   IDEA/COMP
                                                         ANOMIE

                                                             B67
COWLING M.,1867 DISRAELI, GLADSTONE, AND   PARL/PROC
REVOLUTION; THE PASSING OF THE SECOND REFORM BILL.   POL/PAR
UK LEGIS LEAD LOBBY GP/REL INGP/REL...DECISION   ATTIT
BIBLIOG 19 REFORMERS. PAGE 27 E0531   LAW

                                                             B76
BENTHAM J.,THE THEORY OF LEGISLATION. UK CREATE   LEGIS
CRIME ATTIT ORD/FREE...CONCPT 18 REFORMERS. PAGE 10   LAW
E0196   CRIMLGY
                                                         UTIL

REGALA R. E1679

REGION....REGIONALISM

                                                             N
AFRICAN BIBLIOGRAPHIC CENTER,A CURRENT BIBLIOGRAPHY   BIBLIOG/A
ON AFRICAN AFFAIRS. LAW CULTURE ECO/UNDEV LABOR   AFR
SECT DIPLOM FOR/AID COLONIAL NAT/LISM...LING 20.   NAT/G
PAGE 3 E0053   REGION

                                                             N
AIR UNIVERSITY LIBRARY,INDEX TO MILITARY   BIBLIOG/A
PERIODICALS. FUT SPACE WOR+45 REGION ARMS/CONT   FORCES
NUC/PWR WAR PEACE INT/LAW. PAGE 3 E0056   NAT/G
                                                         DIPLOM

                                                             N
ASIA FOUNDATION,LIBRARY NOTES. LAW CONSTN CULTURE   BIBLIOG/A
SOCIETY ECO/UNDEV INT/ORG NAT/G COLONIAL LEAD   ASIA
REGION NAT/LISM ATTIT 20 UN. PAGE 6 E0107   S/ASIA
                                                         DIPLOM

                                                             N
CORNELL UNIVERSITY LIBRARY,SOUTHEAST ASIA   BIBLIOG
ACCESSIONS LIST. LAW SOCIETY STRUCT ECO/UNDEV   S/ASIA
POL/PAR TEC/DEV DIPLOM LEAD REGION. PAGE 26 E0510   NAT/G
                                                         CULTURE

                                                             B00
GRIFFIN A.P.C.,LIST OF BOOKS RELATING TO THE THEORY   BIBLIOG/A
OF COLONIZATION, GOVERNMENT OF DEPENDENCIES,   COLONIAL
PROTECTORATES, AND RELATED TOPICS. FRANCE GERMANY   GOV/REL
ITALY SPAIN UK USA-45 WOR-45 ECO/TAC ADMIN CONTROL   DOMIN
REGION NAT/LISM ALL/VALS PWR...INT/LAW SOC 16/19.
PAGE 46 E0917

                                                             B01
GRIFFIN A.P.C.,LIST OF BOOKS ON SAMOA (PAMPHLET).   BIBLIOG/A
GERMANY S/ASIA UK USA-45 WOR-45 ECO/UNDEV REGION   COLONIAL
ALL/VALS ORD/FREE ALL/IDEOS...GEOG INT/LAW 19 SAMOA   DIPLOM
GUAM. PAGE 46 E0918

                                                             B30
GREEN F.M.,CONSTITUTIONAL DEVELOPMENT IN THE SOUTH   CONSTN
ATLANTIC STATES, 1776-1860; A STUDY IN THE   PROVS
EVOLUTION OF DEMOCRACY. USA-45 ELITES SOCIETY   PLURISM
STRATA ECO/DEV AGRI POL/PAR EX/STRUC LEGIS CT/SYS   REPRESENT
REGION...BIBLIOG 18/19 MARYLAND VIRGINIA GEORGIA
NORTH/CAR SOUTH/CAR. PAGE 46 E0905

                                                             B32
EAGLETON C.,INTERNATIONAL GOVERNMENT. BRAZIL FRANCE   INT/ORG
GERMANY ITALY UK USSR WOR-45 DELIB/GP TOP/EX PLAN   JURID
ECO/TAC EDU/PROP LEGIT ADJUD REGION ARMS/CONT   DIPLOM
COERCE ATTIT PWR...GEOG MGT VAL/FREE LEAGUE/NAT 20.   INT/LAW
PAGE 34 E0670

                                                             B37
SCHUSTER E.,GUIDE TO LAW AND LEGAL LITERATURE OF   BIBLIOG/A
CENTRAL AMERICAN REPUBLICS. L/A+17C INT/ORG ADJUD   REGION
SANCTION CRIME...JURID 19/20. PAGE 89 E1785   CT/SYS
                                                         LAW

                                                             S41
WRIGHT Q.,"FUNDAMENTAL PROBLEMS OF INTERNATIONAL   INT/ORG
ORGANIZATION." UNIV WOR-45 STRUCT FORCES ACT/RES   ATTIT
CREATE DOMIN EDU/PROP LEGIT REGION NAT/LISM   PEACE
ORD/FREE PWR RESPECT SOVEREIGN...JURID SOC CONCPT
METH/CNCPT TIME/SEQ 20. PAGE 107 E2152

                                                             B45
BEVERIDGE W.,THE PRICE OF PEACE. GERMANY UK WOR+45   INT/ORG
WOR-45 NAT/G FORCES CREATE LEGIT REGION WAR ATTIT   TREND
KNOWL ORD/FREE PWR...POLICY NEW/IDEA GEN/LAWS   PEACE
LEAGUE/NAT 20 TREATY. PAGE 12 E0223

B45

HILL N.,CLAIMS TO TERRITORY IN INTERNATIONAL LAW AND RELATIONS. WOR-45 NAT/G DOMIN EDU/PROP LEGIT REGION ROUTINE ORD/FREE PWR WEALTH...GEOG INT/LAW JURID 20. PAGE 52 E1047
INT/ORG
ADJUD
SOVEREIGN

B47

BORGESE G.,COMMON CAUSE. LAW CONSTN SOCIETY STRATA ECO/DEV INT/ORG POL/PAR FORCES LEGIS TOP/EX CAP/ISM DIPLOM ADMIN EXEC ATTIT PWR 20. PAGE 14 E0269
WOR+45
NAT/G
SOVEREIGN
REGION

B48

FENWICK C.G.,INTERNATIONAL LAW. WOR+45 WOR-45 CONSTN NAT/G LEGIT CT/SYS REGION...CONCPT LEAGUE/NAT UN 20. PAGE 37 E0737
INT/ORG
JURID
INT/LAW

B50

MONPIED E.,BIBLIOGRAPHIE FEDERALISTE: OUVRAGES CHOISIS (VOL. I. MIMEOGRAPHED PAPER). EUR+WWI DIPLOM ADMIN REGION ATTIT PACIFISM SOCISM...INT/LAW 19/20. PAGE 74 E1486
BIBLIOG/A
FEDERAL
CENTRAL
INT/ORG

N51

MONPIED E.,FEDERALIST BIBLIOGRAPHY: ARTICLES AND DOCUMENTS PUBLISHED IN BRITISH PERIODICALS 1945-1951 (MIMEOGRAPHED). EUR+WWI UK WOR-45 DIPLOM REGION ATTIT SOCISM...INT/LAW 20. PAGE 74 E1487
BIBLIOG/A
INT/ORG
FEDERAL
CENTRAL

B52

GELLHORN W.,THE STATES AND SUBVERSION. USA+45 USA-45 LOC/G DELIB/GP LEGIS EDU/PROP LEGIT CT/SYS REGION PEACE ATTIT ORD/FREE SOCISM...INT CON/ANAL 20 CALIFORNIA MARYLAND ILLINOIS MICHIGAN NEW/YORK. PAGE 43 E0845
PROVS
JURID

B54

FRIEDMAN W.,THE PUBLIC CORPORATION: A COMPARATIVE SYMPOSIUM (UNIVERSITY OF TORONTO SCHOOL OF LAW COMPARATIVE LAW SERIES, VOL. I). SWEDEN USA+45 INDUS INT/ORG NAT/G REGION CENTRAL FEDERAL...POLICY JURID IDEA/COMP NAT/COMP ANTHOL 20 COMMONWLTH MONOPOLY EUROPE. PAGE 40 E0801
LAW
SOCISM
LG/CO
OWN

B57

JENKS C.W.,THE INTERNATIONAL PROTECTION OF TRADE UNION FREEDOM. FUT WOR+45 WOR-45 VOL/ASSN DELIB/GP CT/SYS REGION ROUTINE...JURID METH/CNCPT RECORD TIME/SEQ CHARTS ILO WORK OAS 20. PAGE 58 E1153
LABOR
INT/ORG

S59

SUTTON F.X.,"REPRESENTATION AND THE NATURE OF POLITICAL SYSTEMS." UNIV WOR-45 CULTURE SOCIETY STRATA INT/ORG FORCES JUDGE DOMIN LEGIT EXEC REGION REPRESENT ATTIT ORD/FREE RESPECT...SOC HIST/WRIT TIME/SEQ. PAGE 95 E1896
NAT/G
CONCPT

B61

AVERY M.W.,GOVERNMENT OF WASHINGTON STATE. USA+45 MUNIC DELIB/GP EX/STRUC LEGIS GIVE CT/SYS PARTIC REGION EFFICIENCY 20 WASHINGT/G GOVERNOR. PAGE 6 E0121
PROVS
LOC/G
ADMIN
GOV/REL

B61

POOLEY B.J.,PLANNING AND ZONING IN THE UNITED STATES. USA+45 MUNIC DELIB/GP ACT/RES PROB/SOLV TEC/DEV ADJUD ADMIN REGION 20 ZONING. PAGE 81 E1628
PLAN
LOC/G
PROVS
LAW

B61

RIENOW R.,CONTEMPORARY INTERNATIONAL POLITICS. WOR+45 INT/ORG BAL/PWR EDU/PROP COLONIAL NEUTRAL REGION WAR PEACE...INT/LAW 20 COLD/WAR UN. PAGE 85 E1698
DIPLOM
PWR
POLICY
NAT/G

B61

WINTERS J.M.,STATE CONSTITUTIONAL LIMITATIONS ON SOLUTIONS OF METROPOLITAN AREA PROBLEMS. CONSTN LEGIS LEAD REPRESENT DECISION. PAGE 107 E2134
MUNIC
REGION
LOC/G
LAW

B62

CARPER E.T.,ILLINOIS GOES TO CONGRESS FOR ARMY LAND. USA+45 LAW EXTR/IND PROVS REGION CIVMIL/REL GOV/REL FEDERAL ATTIT 20 ILLINOIS SENATE CONGRESS DIRKSEN/E DOUGLAS/P. PAGE 20 E0391
ADMIN
LOBBY
GEOG
LEGIS

B62

LAWSON R.,INTERNATIONAL REGIONAL ORGANIZATIONS. WOR+45 NAT/G VOL/ASSN CONSULT LEGIS EDU/PROP LEGIT ADMIN EXEC ROUTINE HEALTH PWR WEALTH...JURID EEC COLD/WAR 20 UN. PAGE 63 E1270
INT/ORG
DELIB/GP
REGION

B62

UNECA LIBRARY,NEW ACQUISITIONS IN THE UNECA LIBRARY. LAW NAT/G PLAN PROB/SOLV TEC/DEV ADMIN
BIBLIOG
AFR

REGION...GEOG SOC 20 UN. PAGE 98 E1956
ECO/UNDEV
INT/ORG

B62

WINTERS J.M.,INTERSTATE METROPOLITAN AREAS. CONSTN LEAD CHOOSE PWR DECISION. PAGE 107 E2135
MUNIC
LAW
REGION
GOV/REL

S62

FENWICK C.G.,"ISSUES AT PUNTA DEL ESTE: NON-INTERVENTION VS COLLECTIVE SECURITY." L/A+17C USA+45 VOL/ASSN DELIB/GP ECO/TAC LEGIT ADJUD REGION ORD/FREE OAS COLD/WAR 20. PAGE 37 E0738
INT/ORG
CUBA

N62

TWENTIETH CENTURY FUND,ONE MAN - ONE VOTE (PAMPHLET). USA+45 CONSTN CONFER CT/SYS REGION CONSEN FEDERAL ROLE...CENSUS 20 CONGRESS. PAGE 97 E1947
APPORT
LEGIS
REPRESENT
PROVS

B63

GALLAGHER J.F.,SUPERVISORIAL DISTRICTING IN CALIFORNIA COUNTIES: 1960-1963 (PAMPHLET). USA+45 ADJUD ADMIN PARTIC CHOOSE GP/REL...CENSUS 20 CALIFORNIA. PAGE 42 E0828
APPORT
REGION
REPRESENT
LOC/G

B63

KLESMENT J.,LEGAL SOURCES AND BIBLIOGRAPHY OF THE BALTIC STATES (ESTONIA, LATVIA, LITHUANIA). COM ESTONIA LATVIA LITHUANIA LAW FINAN ADJUD CT/SYS REGION CENTRAL MARXISM 19/20. PAGE 61 E1223
BIBLIOG/A
JURID
CONSTN
ADMIN

B63

ROBERTSON A.H.,HUMAN RIGHTS IN EUROPE. CONSTN SOCIETY INT/ORG NAT/G VOL/ASSN DELIB/GP ACT/RES PLAN ADJUD REGION ROUTINE ATTIT LOVE ORD/FREE RESPECT...JURID SOC CONCPT SOC/EXP UN 20. PAGE 85 E1705
EUR+WWI
PERSON

S63

VINES K.N.,"THE ROLE OF THE CIRCUIT COURT OF APPEALS IN THE FEDERAL JUDICIAL PROCESS: A CASE STUDY." USA+45 STRATA JUDGE RESPECT...DECISION JURID CHARTS GP/COMP. PAGE 104 E2078
REGION
ADJUD
CT/SYS
RACE/REL

B64

BERWANGER E.H.,WESTERN ANTI-NEGRO SENTIMENT AND LAWS 1846-60: A FACTOR IN THE SLAVERY EXTENSION CONTROVERSY (PAPER). USA-45 LAW CONSTN LEGIS ADJUD ...BIBLIOG 19 NEGRO. PAGE 11 E0218
RACE/REL
REGION
DISCRIM
ORD/FREE

B64

FRANCK T.M.,EAST AFRICAN UNITY THROUGH LAW. MALAWI TANZANIA UGANDA UK ZAMBIA CONSTN INT/ORG NAT/G ADMIN ROUTINE TASK NAT/LISM ATTIT SOVEREIGN ...RECORD IDEA/COMP NAT/COMP. PAGE 40 E0785
AFR
FEDERAL
REGION
INT/LAW

B64

GJUPANOVIC H.,LEGAL SOURCES AND BIBLIOGRAPHY OF YUGOSLAVIA. COM YUGOSLAVIA LAW LEGIS DIPLOM ADMIN PARL/PROC REGION CRIME CENTRAL 20. PAGE 44 E0873
BIBLIOG/A
JURID
CONSTN
ADJUD

B64

GRZYBOWSKI K.,THE SOCIALIST COMMONWEALTH OF NATIONS: ORGANIZATIONS AND INSTITUTIONS. FORCES DIPLOM INT/TRADE ADJUD ADMIN LEAD WAR MARXISM SOCISM...BIBLIOG 20 COMECON WARSAW/P. PAGE 48 E0956
INT/LAW
COM
REGION
INT/ORG

B64

HEKHUIS D.J.,INTERNATIONAL STABILITY: MILITARY, ECONOMIC AND POLITICAL DIMENSIONS. FUT WOR+45 LAW ECO/UNDEV INT/ORG NAT/G VOL/ASSN FORCES ACT/RES BAL/PWR PWR WEALTH...STAT UN 20. PAGE 51 E1024
TEC/DEV
DETER
REGION

B65

HAEFELE E.T.,GOVERNMENT CONTROLS ON TRANSPORT. AFR RHODESIA TANZANIA DIPLOM ECO/TAC TARIFFS PRICE ADJUD CONTROL REGION EFFICIENCY...POLICY 20 CONGO. PAGE 49 E0973
ECO/UNDEV
DIST/IND
FINAN
NAT/G

B65

PADELFORD N.,THE UNITED NATIONS IN THE BALANCE* ACCOMPLISHMENTS AND PROSPECTS. NAT/G VOL/ASSN DIPLOM ADMIN COLONIAL CT/SYS REGION WAR ORD/FREE ...ANTHOL UN. PAGE 79 E1588
INT/ORG
CONTROL

S65

DIXON R.G.,"NEW CONSTITUTIONAL FORMS FOR METROPOLIS: REAPPORTIONED COUNTY BOARDS; LOCAL COUNCILS OF GOVERNMENT." LAW CONSTN LEAD APPORT REPRESENT DECISION. PAGE 32 E0631
MUNIC
REGION
GOV/COMP
PLAN

S65

MARTIN A.,"PROLIFERATION." FUT WOR+45 PROB/SOLV
RECORD

REGION ADJUST...PREDICT NAT/COMP UN TREATY. PAGE 69   NUC/PWR
E1372   ARMS/CONT
                                                       VOL/ASSN

                                                       S65
STEIN E.,"TOWARD SUPREMACY OF TREATY-CONSTITUTION   ADJUD
BY JUDICIAL FIAT: ON THE MARGIN OF THE COSTA CASE."   CONSTN
EUR+WWI ITALY WOR+45 INT/ORG NAT/G LEGIT REGION   SOVEREIGN
NAT/LISM PWR...JURID CONCPT TREND TOT/POP VAL/FREE   INT/LAW
20. PAGE 93 E1870

                                                       C65
SCHEINGOLD S.A.,"THE RULE OF LAW IN EUROPEAN   INT/LAW
INTEGRATION: THE PATH OF THE SCHUMAN PLAN." EUR+WWI   CT/SYS
JUDGE ADJUD FEDERAL ATTIT PWR...RECORD INT BIBLIOG   REGION
EEC ECSC. PAGE 87 E1755   CENTRAL

                                                       B66
KEAY E.A.,THE NATIVE AND CUSTOMARY COURTS OF   AFR
NIGERIA. NIGERIA CONSTN ELITES NAT/G TOP/EX PARTIC   ADJUD
REGION...DECISION JURID 19/20. PAGE 60 E1190   LAW

                                                       B66
US DEPARTMENT OF STATE,RESEARCH ON AFRICA (EXTERNAL   BIBLIOG/A
RESEARCH LIST NO 5-25). LAW CULTURE ECO/UNDEV   ASIA
POL/PAR DIPLOM EDU/PROP LEAD REGION MARXISM...GEOG   S/ASIA
LING WORSHIP 20. PAGE 100 E1996   NAT/G

                                                       B66
US DEPARTMENT OF STATE,RESEARCH ON THE USSR AND   BIBLIOG/A
EASTERN EUROPE (EXTERNAL RESEARCH LIST NO 1-25).   EUR+WWI
USSR LAW CULTURE SOCIETY NAT/G TEC/DEV DIPLOM   COM
EDU/PROP REGION...GEOG LING. PAGE 100 E1997   MARXISM

                                                       B66
US DEPARTMENT OF STATE,RESEARCH ON WESTERN EUROPE,   BIBLIOG/A
GREAT BRITAIN, AND CANADA (EXTERNAL RESEARCH LIST   EUR+WWI
NO 3-25). CANADA GERMANY/W UK LAW CULTURE NAT/G   DIPLOM
POL/PAR FORCES EDU/PROP REGION MARXISM...GEOG SOC
WORSHIP 20 CMN/WLTH. PAGE 100 E1998

                                                       L66
YALEM R.J.,"THE STUDY OF INTERNATIONAL   VOL/ASSN
ORGANIZATION, 1920-1965* A SURVEY OF THE   INT/ORG
LITERATURE." WOR+45 WOR-45 REGION...INT/LAW CLASSIF   BIBLIOG/A
RECORD HIST/WRIT CON/ANAL IDEA/COMP UN. PAGE 108
E2163

                                                       S66
BROWNLIE I.,"NUCLEAR PROLIFERATION* SOME PROBLEMS   NUC/PWR
OF CONTROL." USA+45 USSR ECO/UNDEV INT/ORG FORCES   ARMS/CONT
TEC/DEV REGION CONSEN...RECORD TREATY. PAGE 16   VOL/ASSN
E0318   ORD/FREE

                                                       B67
NIVEN R.,NIGERIA. NIGERIA CONSTN INDUS EX/STRUC   NAT/G
COLONIAL REV NAT/LISM...CHARTS 19/20. PAGE 77 E1550   REGION
                                                       CHOOSE
                                                       GP/REL

                                                       B67
PADELFORD N.J.,THE DYNAMICS OF INTERNATIONAL   DIPLOM
POLITICS (2ND ED.). WOR+45 LAW INT/ORG FORCES   NAT/G
TEC/DEV REGION NAT/LISM PEACE ATTIT PWR ALL/IDEOS   POLICY
UN COLD/WAR NATO TREATY. PAGE 79 E1589   DECISION

                                                       S67
WINES R.,"THE IMPERIAL CIRCLES, PRINCELY DIPLOMACY,   NAT/G
AND IMPERIAL REFORM* 1681-1714." MOD/EUR DELIB/GP   NAT/LISM
BAL/PWR CONFER ADJUD PARL/PROC PARTIC ATTIT PWR   CENTRAL
17/18. PAGE 106 E2132   REGION

                                                       N67
US SENATE COMM ON FOREIGN REL,SURVEY OF THE   INT/TRADE
ALLIANCE FOR PROGRESS: FOREIGN TRADE POLICIES   REGION
(PAMPHLET). L/A+17C LAW ECO/UNDEV ECO/TAC TARIFFS   AGREE
20 GATT LAFTA UN. PAGE 102 E2037   INT/ORG

REGRESS....REGRESSION ANALYSIS; SEE ALSO CON/ANAL

                                                       B64
SCHUBERT G.A.,JUDICIAL BEHAVIOR: A READER IN THEORY   ATTIT
AND RESEARCH. POL/PAR CT/SYS ROLE SUPEGO PWR   PERSON
...DECISION JURID REGRESS CHARTS SIMUL ANTHOL 20.   ADJUD
PAGE 89 E1782   ACT/RES

REGRESSION ANALYSIS....SEE REGRESS

REHABILITN....REHABILITATION

REID H.D. E1680

REIFF H. E1681

REILLY T.J. E1682

REINHARDT J.M. E0861,E0862

REINSCH P. E1683

REITZEL A.M. E1684

RELATIONS AMONG GROUPS....SEE GP/REL

RELATISM....RELATIVISM

                                                       B64
ENGEL S.,LAW, STATE, AND INTERNATIONAL LEGAL ORDER.   JURID
WOR+45 NAT/G ORD/FREE RELATISM...INT/LAW IDEA/COMP   OBJECTIVE
ANTHOL 20 KELSEN/H. PAGE 35 E0690   CONCPT
                                                       DEBATE

RELATIV....RELATIVITY

                                                       B52
BENTHAM A.,HANDBOOK OF POLITICAL FALLACIES. FUT   POL/PAR
MOD/EUR LAW INTELL LOC/G MUNIC NAT/G DELIB/GP LEGIS
CREATE EDU/PROP CT/SYS ATTIT RIGID/FLEX KNOWL PWR
...RELATIV PSY SOC CONCPT SELF/OBS TREND STERTYP
TOT/POP. PAGE 10 E0189

                                                       L62
NIZARD L.,"CUBAN QUESTION AND SECURITY COUNCIL."   INT/ORG
L/A+17C USA+45 ECO/UNDEV NAT/G POL/PAR DELIB/GP   JURID
ECO/TAC PWR...RELATIV OBS TIME/SEQ TREND GEN/LAWS   DIPLOM
UN 20 UN. PAGE 77 E1551   CUBA

                                                       B64
FALK R.A.,THE ROLE OF DOMESTIC COURTS IN THE   LAW
INTERNATIONAL LEGAL ORDER. FUT WOR+45 INT/ORG NAT/G   INT/LAW
JUDGE ADJUD FEDERAL ATTIT PWR...POLICY RELATIV JURID
CONCPT GEN/LAWS 20. PAGE 36 E0716

RELATIVISM....SEE RELATISM, RELATIV

RELATIVITY....SEE RELATIV

RELIGION....SEE SECT, WORSHIP

RELIGIOUS GROUP....SEE SECT

RENAISSAN....RENAISSANCE

RENNER K. E1685

RENT....RENTING

                                                       B66
FRIEDMANN W.G.,INTERNATIONAL FINANCIAL AID. USA+45   INT/ORG
ECO/DEV ECO/UNDEV NAT/G VOL/ASSN EX/STRUC PLAN RENT   FOR/AID
GIVE BAL/PAY PWR...GEOG INT/LAW STAT TREND UN EEC   TEC/DEV
COMECON. PAGE 41 E0806   ECO/TAC

                                                       B67
GABRIEL P.P.,THE INTERNATIONAL TRANSFER OF   ECO/UNDEV
CORPORATE SKILLS: MANAGEMENT CONTRACTS IN LESS   AGREE
DEVELOPED COUNTRIES. CLIENT INDUS LG/CO PLAN   MGT
PROB/SOLV CAP/ISM ECO/TAC FOR/AID INT/TRADE RENT   CONSULT
ADMIN SKILL 20. PAGE 42 E0825

                                                       S67
MAYER M.,"THE IDEA OF JUSTICE AND THE POOR." USA+45   INCOME
CLIENT CONSULT RENT ADJUD DISCRIM KNOWL 20. PAGE 70   WEALTH
E1393   LAW
                                                       ORD/FREE

REOCK E.C. E1686,E1687

REP/CONVEN....REPUBLICAN (PARTY - U.S.) NATIONAL CONVENTION

REPAR....REPARATIONS; SEE ALSO INT/REL, SANCTION

                                                       B36
HUDSON M.O.,INTERNATIONAL LEGISLATION: 1929-1931.   INT/LAW
WOR-45 SEA AIR AGRI FINAN LABOR DIPLOM ECO/TAC   PARL/PROC
REPAR CT/SYS ARMS/CONT WAR WEAPON...JURID 20 TREATY   ADJUD
LEAGUE/NAT. PAGE 56 E1112   LAW

                                                       B41
BIRDSALL P.,VERSAILLES TWENTY YEARS AFTER. MOD/EUR   DIPLOM
POL/PAR CHIEF CONSULT FORCES LEGIS REPAR PEACE   NAT/LISM
ORD/FREE...BIBLIOG 20 PRESIDENT TREATY. PAGE 12   WAR
E0231

                                                       B41
NIEMEYER G.,LAW WITHOUT FORCE: THE FUNCTION OF   COERCE
POLITICS IN INTERNATIONAL LAW. PLAN INSPECT DIPLOM   LAW
REPAR LEGIT ADJUD WAR ORD/FREE...IDEA/COMP   PWR

METH/COMP GEN/LAWS 20. PAGE 77 E1549   INT/LAW

B44
RUDIN H.R.,ARMISTICE 1918. FRANCE GERMANY MOD/EUR AGREE
UK USA-45 NAT/G CHIEF DELIB/GP FORCES BAL/PWR REPAR WAR
ARMS/CONT 20 WILSON/W TREATY. PAGE 86 E1732   PEACE
                                              DIPLOM

B49
JACKSON R.H.,INTERNATIONAL CONFERENCE ON MILITARY DIPLOM
TRIALS. FRANCE GERMANY UK USA+45 USSR VOL/ASSN   INT/ORG
DELIB/GP REPAR ADJUD CT/SYS CRIME WAR 20 WAR/TRIAL. INT/LAW
PAGE 57 E1141   CIVMIL/REL

B66
BROWNLIE I.,PRINCIPLES OF PUBLIC INTERNATIONAL LAW. INT/LAW
WOR+45 WOR-45 LAW JUDGE REPAR ADJUD SOVEREIGN   DIPLOM
...JURID T. PAGE 16 E0319   INT/ORG

REPARATIONS....SEE REPAR

REPRESENT....REPRESENTATION; SEE ALSO LEGIS

B00
GREELY A.W.,PUBLIC DOCUMENTS OF THE FIRST FOURTEEN BIBLIOG/A
CONGRESSES, 1789-1817. USA-45 LEAD REPRESENT ATTIT NAT/G
18/19 CONGRESS. PAGE 45 E0904   LAW
                                              LEGIS

B05
GRIFFIN A.P.C.,LIST OF REFERENCES ON PRIMARY   BIBLIOG/A
ELECTIONS (PAMPHLET). USA-45 LAW LOC/G DELIB/GP   POL/PAR
LEGIS OP/RES TASK REPRESENT CONSEN...DECISION 19/20 CHOOSE
CONGRESS. PAGE 47 E0928   POPULISM

B08
GRIFFIN A.P.C.,REFERENCES ON CORRUPT PRACTICES IN   BIBLIOG/A
ELECTIONS (PAMPHLET). USA-45 LAW CONSTN TRIBUTE   CHOOSE
CRIME REPRESENT...JURID 19/20. PAGE 47 E0934   SUFF
                                              APPORT

B12
MEYER H.H.B.,SELECT LIST OF REFERENCES ON THE   BIBLIOG/A
INITIATIVE, REFERENDUM, AND RECALL. MOD/EUR USA-45 NAT/G
LAW LOC/G MUNIC REPRESENT POPULISM 20 CONGRESS.   LEGIS
PAGE 72 E1446   CHOOSE

B18
PORTER K.H.,A HISTORY OF SUFFRAGE IN THE UNITED   SUFF
STATES. USA-45 LAW CONSTN LOC/G NAT/G POL/PAR WAR   REPRESENT
DISCRIM OWN ATTIT SEX 18/20 NEGRO FEMALE/SEX.   CHOOSE
PAGE 81 E1629   PARTIC

N19
OPERATIONS AND POLICY RESEARCH,URUGUAY: ELECTION   POL/PAR
FACTBOOK: NOVEMBER 27, 1966 (PAMPHLET). URUGUAY LAW CHOOSE
NAT/G LEAD REPRESENT...STAT BIOG CHARTS 20. PAGE 79 PLAN
E1576   ATTIT

N19
RALSTON A.,A FRESH LOOK AT LEGISLATIVE   APPORT
APPORTIONMENT IN NEW JERSEY (PAMPHLET). USA+45   REPRESENT
CONSTN LEGIS OBJECTIVE...MATH METH 20 NEW/JERSEY.   PROVS
PAGE 83 E1671   JURID

B23
ROBERT H.M.,PARLIAMENTARY LAW. POL/PAR LEGIS PARTIC PARL/PROC
CHOOSE REPRESENT GP/REL. PAGE 85 E1701   DELIB/GP
                                              NAT/G
                                              JURID

B30
BIRD F.L.,THE RECALL OF PUBLIC OFFICERS; A STUDY OF REPRESENT
THE OPERATION OF RECALL IN CALIFORNIA. LOC/G MUNIC SANCTION
POL/PAR PROVS PROB/SOLV ADJUD PARTIC...CHARTS   CHOOSE
METH/COMP 20 CALIFORNIA RECALL. PAGE 12 E0230   LAW

B30
GREEN F.M.,CONSTITUTIONAL DEVELOPMENT IN THE SOUTH CONSTN
ATLANTIC STATES, 1776-1860; A STUDY IN THE   PROVS
EVOLUTION OF DEMOCRACY. USA-45 ELITES SOCIETY   PLURISM
STRATA ECO/DEV AGRI POL/PAR EX/STRUC LEGIS CT/SYS   REPRESENT
REGION...BIBLIOG 18/19 MARYLAND VIRGINIA GEORGIA
NORTH/CAR SOUTH/CAR. PAGE 46 E0905

B30
JORDAN E.,THEORY OF LEGISLATION: AN ESSAY ON THE   LEGIS
DYNAMICS OF PUBLIC MIND. NAT/G CREATE REPRESENT   CONCPT
MAJORITY ATTIT GEN/LAWS. PAGE 59 E1173   JURID
                                              CT/SYS

L34
LLEWELLYN K.N.,"THE CONSTITUTION AS AN INSTITUTION" CONSTN
(BMR)" USA-45 PROB/SOLV LOBBY REPRESENT...DECISION   LAW
JURID 18/20 SUPREME/CT. PAGE 66 E1313   CONCPT
                                              CT/SYS

B36
GRAVES W.B.,AMERICAN STATE GOVERNMENT. CONSTN FINAN NAT/G
EX/STRUC FORCES LEGIS BUDGET TAX CT/SYS REPRESENT   PROVS
GOV/REL...BIBLIOG/A 19/20. PAGE 45 E0900   ADMIN
                                              FEDERAL

B41
GELLHORN W.,FEDERAL ADMINISTRATIVE PROCEEDINGS.   EX/STRUC
USA+45 CLIENT FACE/GP NAT/G LOBBY REPRESENT PWR 20. LAW
PAGE 43 E0844   ADJUD
                                              POLICY

C44
JEFFERSON T.,"DEMOCRACY" (1816) IN BASIC WRITINGS." POPULISM
USA-45 LOC/G NAT/G TAX CT/SYS CHOOSE ORD/FREE   MAJORIT
...GEN/LAWS 18/19 JEFFERSN/T. PAGE 58 E1151   REPRESENT
                                              CONSTN

B49
APPLEBY P.H.,POLICY AND ADMINISTRATION. USA+45   REPRESENT
NAT/G LOBBY PWR 20. PAGE 5 E0101   EXEC
                                              ADMIN
                                              CLIENT

B49
THOREAU H.D.,CIVIL DISOBEDIENCE (1849). USA-45 LAW GEN/LAWS
CONSTN TAX COERCE REPRESENT GP/REL SUPEGO...MAJORIT ORD/FREE
CONCPT 19. PAGE 96 E1923   POLICY

S49
PRITCHETT C.H.,"THE PRESIDENT AND THE SUPREME   GOV/REL
COURT." NAT/G CONTROL REPRESENT FEDERAL 20. PAGE 82 CT/SYS
E1651   CHIEF

B50
MERRIAM C.E.,THE AMERICAN PARTY SYSTEM; AN   POL/PAR
INTRODUCTION TO THE STUDY OF POLITICAL PARTIES IN   CHOOSE
THE UNITED STATES (4TH ED.). USA+45 USA-45 LAW   SUFF
FINAN LOC/G NAT/G PROVS LEAD PARTIC CRIME ATTIT   REPRESENT
18/20 NEGRO CONGRESS PRESIDENT. PAGE 72 E1442

S50
ROBINSON W.S.,"BIAS, PROBABILITY AND TRIAL BY JURY" REPRESENT
(BMR)" USA+45 USA-45 SOCIETY...SOC CONCPT. PAGE 85 JURID
E1707   CT/SYS
                                              DECISION

B52
APPLEBY P.H.,MORALITY AND ADMINISTRATION IN   REPRESENT
DEMOCRATIC GOVERNMENT. USA+45 CLIENT NAT/G EXEC   LOBBY
EFFICIENCY 20. PAGE 5 E0102   ADMIN
                                              EX/STRUC

B52
COUNCIL STATE GOVERNMENTS,OCCUPATIONAL LICENSING IN PROF/ORG
THE STATES. USA+45 PROVS ADMIN EXEC LOBBY 20.   LICENSE
PAGE 27 E0526   REPRESENT
                                              EX/STRUC

S52
DE GRAZIA A.,"GENERAL THEORY OF APPORTIONMENT"   APPORT
(BMR)" USA+45 USA-45 CONSTN ELITES DELIB/GP PARTIC LEGIS
REV CHOOSE...JURID 20. PAGE 29 E0582   PROVS
                                              REPRESENT

B53
BUTLER D.E.,THE ELECTORAL SYSTEM IN BRITAIN,   CHOOSE
1918-1951. UK LAW POL/PAR SUFF...STAT BIBLIOG 20   LEGIS
PARLIAMENT. PAGE 18 E0348   REPRESENT
                                              PARTIC

B54
BROGAN D.W.,POLITICS IN AMERICA. LAW POL/PAR CHIEF NAT/G
LEGIS LOBBY CHOOSE REPRESENT GP/REL RACE/REL   CONSTN
FEDERAL MORAL...BIBLIOG 20 PRESIDENT CONGRESS.   USA+45
PAGE 16 E0304

B54
US SENATE COMM ON FOREIGN REL,REVIEW OF THE UNITED BIBLIOG
NATIONS CHARTER: A COLLECTION OF DOCUMENTS. LEGIS   CONSTN
DIPLOM ADMIN ARMS/CONT WAR REPRESENT SOVEREIGN   INT/ORG
...INT/LAW 20 UN. PAGE 101 E2029   DEBATE

S54
COOPER L.,"ADMINISTRATIVE JUSTICE." UK ADMIN   LAW
REPRESENT PWR...POLICY 20. PAGE 25 E0502   ADJUD
                                            CONTROL
                                            EX/STRUC

S54
HART J.,"ADMINISTRATION AND THE COURTS." USA+45   ADMIN
NAT/G REPRESENT 20. PAGE 50 E1003   GOV/REL
                                            CT/SYS
                                            FEDERAL

BURR R.N.,DOCUMENTS ON INTER-AMERICAN COOPERATION: VOL. I, 1810-1881; VOL. II, 1881-1948. DELIB/GP BAL/PWR INT/TRADE REPRESENT NAT/LISM PEACE HABITAT ORD/FREE PWR SOVEREIGN...INT/LAW 20 OAS. PAGE 18 E0345
BIBLIOG DIPLOM INT/ORG L/A+17C
B55

CARR C.,"LEGISLATIVE CONTROL OF ADMINISTRATIVE RULES AND REGULATIONS: PARLIAMENTARY SUPERVISION IN BRITAIN." DELIB/GP CONTROL ROLE PWR PARLIAMENT. PAGE 20 E0392
EXEC REPRESENT JURID
S55

FIELD G.C.,POLITICAL THEORY. POL/PAR REPRESENT MORAL SOVEREIGN...JURID IDEA/COMP. PAGE 38 E0745
CONCPT NAT/G ORD/FREE DIPLOM
B56

FRANCIS R.G.,SERVICE AND PROCEDURE IN BUREAUCRACY. EXEC LEAD ROUTINE...QU 20. PAGE 39 E0784
CLIENT ADMIN INGP/REL REPRESENT
B56

REDFORD E.S.,PUBLIC ADMINISTRATION AND POLICY FORMATION: STUDIES IN OIL, GAS, BANKING, RIVER DEVELOPMENT AND CORPORATE INVESTIGATIONS. USA+45 CLIENT NAT/G ADMIN LOBBY REPRESENT GOV/REL INGP/REL 20. PAGE 84 E1678
EX/STRUC PROB/SOLV CONTROL EXEC
B56

CARRINGTON P.D.,"POLITICAL QUESTIONS: THE JUDICIAL CHECK ON THE EXECUTIVE." USA+45 LAW CHIEF 20. PAGE 20 E0395
ADJUD EXEC PWR REPRESENT
L56

NOBLEMAN E.E.,"THE DELEGATION OF PRESIDENTIAL FUNCTIONS: CONSTITUTIONAL AND LEGAL ASPECTS." USA+45 CONSTN NAT/G CONTROL 20. PAGE 77 E1553
CHIEF REPRESENT EX/STRUC LAW
S56

NJ LAW AND LEGISLATIVE BURE,NEW JERSEY LEGISLAVTIVE REAPPORTIONMENT (PAMPHLET). USA+45 ACT/RES ADJUD...STAT CHARTS 20 NEW/JERSEY. PAGE 2 E0041
APPORT LEGIS CENSUS REPRESENT
B57

LONG H.A.,USURPERS - FOES OF FREE MAN. LAW NAT/G CHIEF LEGIS DOMIN ADJUD REPRESENT GOV/REL ORD/FREE LAISSEZ POPULISM...POLICY 18/20 SUPREME/CT ROOSEVLT/F CONGRESS CON/INTERP. PAGE 66 E1325
CT/SYS CENTRAL FEDERAL CONSTN
B57

US SENATE COMM ON JUDICIARY,HEARING BEFORE SUBCOMMITTEE ON COMMITTEE OF JUDICIARY, UNITED STATES SENATE: S. J. RES. 3. USA+45 NAT/G CONSULT DELIB/GP DIPLOM ADJUD LOBBY REPRESENT 20 CONGRESS TREATY. PAGE 102 E2040
LEGIS CONSTN CONFER AGREE
B57

KNEIER C.M.,"MISLEADING THE VOTERS." CONSTN LEAD CHOOSE PERS/REL. PAGE 61 E1224
MUNIC REPRESENT LAW ATTIT
S57

DOUGLAS W.O.,THE RIGHT OF THE PEOPLE. USA+45 EDU/PROP CONTROL REPRESENT PRIVIL...IDEA/COMP 20. PAGE 32 E0641
ORD/FREE CONSTN CT/SYS CIVMIL/REL
B58

BROMWICH L.,UNION CONSTITUTIONS. CONSTN EX/STRUC PRESS ADJUD CONTROL CHOOSE REPRESENT PWR SAMP. PAGE 16 E0306
LABOR ROUTINE INGP/REL RACE/REL
B59

COUNCIL OF STATE GOVERNORS,AMERICAN LEGISLATURES: STRUCTURE AND PROCEDURES. SUMMARY AND TABULATIONS OF A 1959 SURVEY. PUERT/RICO USA+45 PAY ADJUD ADMIN APPORT...IDEA/COMP 20 GUAM VIRGIN/ISL. PAGE 27 E0525
LEGIS CHARTS PROVS REPRESENT
B59

FERRY W.H.,THE CORPORATION AND THE ECONOMY. CLIENT LAW CONSTN LABOR NAT/G PLAN INT/TRADE PARTIC CONSEN ORD/FREE PWR POLICY. PAGE 37 E0742
LG/CO CONTROL REPRESENT
B59

REOCK E.C.,PROCEDURES AND STANDARDS FOR THE APPORTIONMENT OF STATE LEGISLATURES (DOCTORAL
PROVS LOC/G
B59

THESIS). USA+45 POL/PAR LEGIS TEC/DEV ADJUD BIBLIOG. PAGE 84 E1686
APPORT REPRESENT

COX A.,"THE ROLE OF LAW IN PRESERVING UNION DEMOCRACY." EX/STRUC LEGIS PARTIC ROUTINE CHOOSE INGP/REL ORD/FREE. PAGE 27 E0532
LABOR REPRESENT LAW MAJORIT
L59

HECTOR L.J.,"GOVERNMENT BY ANONYMITY: WHO WRITES OUR REGULATORY OPINIONS?" USA+45 NAT/G TOP/EX CONTROL EXEC. PAGE 51 E1021
ADJUD REPRESENT EX/STRUC ADMIN
L59

SCHEEHAN D.,"PUBLIC AND PRIVATE GROUPS AS IDENTIFIED IN THE FIELD OF TRADE REGULATIONS." USA+45 ADMIN REPRESENT GOV/REL. PAGE 87 E1753
LAW CONTROL ADJUD LOBBY
S59

SUTTON F.X.,"REPRESENTATION AND THE NATURE OF POLITICAL SYSTEMS." UNIV WOR-45 CULTURE SOCIETY STRATA INT/ORG FORCES JUDGE DOMIN LEGIT EXEC REGION REPRESENT ATTIT ORD/FREE RESPECT...SOC HIST/WRIT TIME/SEQ. PAGE 95 E1896
NAT/G CONCPT
S59

ADRIAN C.R.,STATE AND LOCAL GOVERNMENTS: A STUDY IN THE POLITICAL PROCESS. USA+45 LAW FINAN MUNIC POL/PAR LEGIS ADJUD EXEC CHOOSE REPRESENT. PAGE 3 E0051
LOC/G PROVS GOV/REL ATTIT
B60

BAKER G.E.,STATE CONSTITUTIONS - REAPPORTIONMENT. USA+45 USA-45 CONSTN CHOOSE ATTIT ORD/FREE...JURID 20. PAGE 7 E0138
APPORT REPRESENT PROVS LEGIS
B60

NAT'L MUNICIPAL LEAGUE,COMPENDIUM ON LEGISLATIVE APPORTIONMENT. USA+45 LOC/G NAT/G POL/PAR PROVS CT/SYS CHOOSE 20 SUPREME/CT CONGRESS. PAGE 76 E1523
APPORT REPRESENT LEGIS STAT
B60

RIENOW R.,INTRODUCTION TO GOVERNMENT (2ND ED.). UK USA+45 USSR POL/PAR ADMIN REV CHOOSE SUFF FEDERAL PWR...JURID GOV/COMP T 20. PAGE 85 E1697
CONSTN PARL/PROC REPRESENT AUTHORIT
B60

SCHUBERT G.,THE PUBLIC INTEREST. USA+45 CONSULT PLAN PROB/SOLV ADJUD ADMIN GP/REL PWR ALL/IDEOS 20. PAGE 88 E1770
POLICY DELIB/GP REPRESENT POL/PAR
B60

US HOUSE COMM ON JUDICIARY,ESTABLISHMENT OF CONGRESSIONAL DISTRICTS. USA+45 PROB/SOLV 20 CONGRESS HOUSE/REP. PAGE 100 E2003
APPORT REPRESENT LEGIS LAW
B60

FUCHS R.F.,"FAIRNESS AND EFFECTIVENESS IN ADMINISTRATIVE AGENCY ORGANIZATION AND PROCEDURES." USA+45 ADJUD ADMIN REPRESENT. PAGE 41 E0816
EFFICIENCY EX/STRUC EXEC POLICY
L60

MACKINNON F.,"THE UNIVERSITY: COMMUNITY OR UTILITY?" CLIENT CONSTN INTELL FINAN NAT/G NEIGH EDU/PROP PARTIC REPRESENT ROLE. PAGE 67 E1343
ACADEM MGT CONTROL SERV/IND
S60

MARSHALL G.,"POLICE RESPONSIBILITY." UK LOC/G ADJUD ADMIN EXEC 20. PAGE 69 E1370
CONTROL REPRESENT LAW FORCES
S60

FROEBEL J.,THEORIE DER POLITIK, ALS ERGEBNIS EINER ERNEUERTEN PRUEFUNG DEMOKRATISCHER LEHRMEINUNGEN. WOR-45 SOCIETY POL/PAR SECT REV REPRESENT PWR SOVEREIGN...MAJORIT 19. PAGE 41 E0812
JURID ORD/FREE NAT/G
B61

GUIZOT F.P.G.,HISTORY OF THE ORIGIN OF REPRESENTATIVE GOVERNMENT IN EUROPE. CHRIST-17C FRANCE MOD/EUR SPAIN UK LAW CHIEF FORCES POPULISM ...MAJORIT TIME/SEQ GOV/COMP NAT/COMP 4/19 PARLIAMENT. PAGE 48 E0961
LEGIS REPRESENT CONSTN NAT/G
B61

JUSTICE,THE CITIZEN AND THE ADMINISTRATION: THE
REDRESS OF GRIEVANCES (PAMPHLET). EUR+WWI UK LAW
CONSTN STRATA NAT/G CT/SYS PARTIC COERCE...NEW/IDEA
IDEA/COMP 20 OMBUDSMAN. PAGE 59 E1176

B61 INGP/REL CONSULT ADJUD REPRESENT

MASSEL M.S.,THE REGULATORY PROCESS (JOURNAL
REPRINT). NAT/G LOBBY REPRESENT GOV/REL 20. PAGE 69
E1382

B61 ADJUD EX/STRUC EXEC

UTLEY T.E.,OCCASION FOR OMBUDSMAN. UK CREATE
CONTROL 20 OMBUDSMAN. PAGE 103 E2065

B61 PROB/SOLV INGP/REL REPRESENT ADJUD

WINTERS J.M.,STATE CONSTITUTIONAL LIMITATIONS ON
SOLUTIONS OF METROPOLITAN AREA PROBLEMS. CONSTN
LEGIS LEAD REPRESENT DECISION. PAGE 107 E2134

B61 MUNIC REGION LOC/G LAW

MCNAMEE B.J.,"CONFLICT OF INTEREST: STATE
GOVERNMENT EMPLOYEES." USA+45 PROVS 20. PAGE 71
E1426

L61 LAW REPRESENT ADMIN CONTROL

ABLARD C.D.,"EX PARTE CONTACTS WITH FEDERAL
ADMINISTRATIVE AGENCIES." USA+45 CLIENT NAT/G
DELIB/GP ADMIN PWR 20. PAGE 2 E0044

S61 EXEC ADJUD LOBBY REPRESENT

BAER E.,"THE GENERAL ACCOUNTING OFFICE: THE FEDERAL
GOVERNMENT'S AUDITOR." USA+45 NAT/G REPRESENT 20
GENACCOUNT. PAGE 7 E0132

S61 ADJUD EX/STRUC EXEC LAW

LEAGUE WOMEN VOTERS MASSACHU,THE MERIT SYSTEM IN
MASSACHUSETTS (PAMPHLET). USA+45 PROVS LEGIT PARTIC
CHOOSE REPRESENT GOV/REL EFFICIENCY...POLICY
GOV/COMP BIBLIOG 20 MASSACHU. PAGE 64 E1274

N61 LOC/G LAW SENIOR PROF/ORG

ALEXANDROWICZ C.H.,WORLD ECONOMIC AGENCIES: LAW AND
PRACTICE. WOR+45 DIST/IND FINAN LABOR CONSULT
INT/TRADE TARIFFS REPRESENT HEALTH...JURID 20 UN
GATT EEC OAS ECSC. PAGE 3 E0063

B62 INT/LAW INT/ORG DIPLOM ADJUD

BOYD W.J.,PATTERNS OF APPORTIONMENT (PAMPHLET). LAW
CONSTN CHOOSE GOV/COMP. PAGE 14 E0282

B62 MUNIC PROVS REPRESENT APPORT

GALENSON W.,TRADE UNIONS MONOGRAPH SERIES (A SERIES
OF NINE TEXTS). DELIB/GP LEAD PARTIC...DECISION
ORG/CHARTS. PAGE 42 E0827

B62 LABOR INGP/REL CONSTN REPRESENT

HSUEH S.-S.,GOVERNMENT AND ADMINISTRATION OF HONG
KONG. CHIEF DELIB/GP LEGIS CT/SYS REPRESENT GOV/REL
20 HONG/KONG CITY/MGT CIVIL/SERV GOVERNOR. PAGE 55
E1106

B62 ADMIN LOC/G COLONIAL EX/STRUC

JENKS C.W.,THE PROPER LAW OF INTERNATIONAL
ORGANISATIONS. DIPLOM LEGIT AGREE CT/SYS SANCTION
REPRESENT SOVEREIGN...GEN/LAWS 20 UN UNESCO ILO
NATO OAS. PAGE 58 E1158

B62 LAW INT/ORG ADJUD INT/LAW

NAT'L MUNICIPAL LEAGUE,COMPENDIUM ON LEGISLATIVE
APPORTIONMENT. USA+45 LOC/G NAT/G POL/PAR PROVS
CT/SYS CHOOSE 20 SUPREME/CT CONGRESS. PAGE 76 E1524

B62 APPORT REPRESENT LEGIS STAT

TAPER B.,GOMILLION VERSUS LIGHTFOOT: THE TUSKEGEE
GERRYMANDER CASE. USA+45 LAW CONSTN LOC/G MUNIC
CT/SYS 20 NEGRO CIV/RIGHTS GOMILLN/CG LIGHTFT/PM
TUSKEGEE. PAGE 95 E1908

B62 APPORT REPRESENT RACE/REL ADJUD

CAVERS D.F.,"ADMINISTRATIVE DECISION-MAKING IN
NUCLEAR FACILITIES LICENSING." USA+45 CLIENT ADMIN
EXEC 20 AEC. PAGE 21 E0410

L62 REPRESENT LOBBY PWR CONTROL

SILVA R.C.,"LEGISLATIVE REPESENTATION - WITH
SPECIAL REFERENCE TO NEW YORK." LAW CONSTN LOC/G
NAT/G PROVS. PAGE 91 E1826

S62 MUNIC LEGIS REPRESENT APPORT

TWENTIETH CENTURY FUND,ONE MAN - ONE VOTE
(PAMPHLET). USA+45 CONSTN CONFER CT/SYS REGION
CONSEN FEDERAL ROLE...CENSUS 20 CONGRESS. PAGE 97
E1947

N62 APPORT LEGIS REPRESENT PROVS

US ADVISORY COMN INTERGOV REL,APPORTIONMENT OF
STATE LEGISLATURES (PAMPHLET). LAW CONSTN EX/STRUC
LEGIS LEAD MAJORITY. PAGE 99 E1977

N62 MUNIC PROVS REPRESENT APPORT

DE GRAZIA A.,APPORTIONMENT AND REPRESENTATIVE
GOVERNMENT. CONSTN POL/PAR LEGIS PLAN ADJUD DISCRIM
RATIONAL...CONCPT STAT PREDICT TREND IDEA/COMP.
PAGE 29 E0583

B63 REPRESENT APPORT NAT/G MUNIC

ELIAS T.O.,GOVERNMENT AND POLITICS IN AFRICA.
CONSTN CULTURE SOCIETY NAT/G POL/PAR DIPLOM
REPRESENT PERSON...SOC TREND BIBLIOG 4/20. PAGE 34
E0681

B63 AFR NAT/LISM COLONIAL LAW

GALLAGHER J.F.,SUPERVISORIAL DISTRICTING IN
CALIFORNIA COUNTIES: 1960-1963 (PAMPHLET). USA+45
ADJUD ADMIN PARTIC CHOOSE GP/REL...CENSUS 20
CALIFORNIA. PAGE 42 E0828

B63 APPORT REGION REPRESENT LOC/G

GINZBERG E.,DEMOCRATIC VALUES AND THE RIGHTS OF
MANAGEMENT. LAW CONSTN REPRESENT GP/REL ROLE PWR
RESPECT POLICY. PAGE 44 E0870

B63 LABOR MGT DELIB/GP ADJUD

HACKER A.,CONGRESSIONAL DISTRICTING: THE ISSUE OF
EQUAL REPRESENTATION. FUT CT/SYS GEOG. PAGE 49
E0970

B63 LEGIS REPRESENT APPORT

LEAGUE WOMEN VOTERS NEW YORK,APPORTIONMENT WORKSHOP
KIT. USA+45 VOL/ASSN DELIB/GP LEGIS ATTIT ORD/FREE
...METH/COMP 20 SUPREME/CT NEW/YORK. PAGE 64 E1275

B63 APPORT REPRESENT PROVS JURID

NATIONAL CIVIC REVIEW,REAPPORTIONMENT: A YEAR IN
REVIEW (PAMPHLET). USA+45 LAW CT/SYS CHOOSE
ORD/FREE PWR...ANTHOL 20 CONGRESS. PAGE 76 E1527

B63 APPORT REPRESENT LEGIS CONSTN

REOCK E.C. JR.,POPULATION INEQUALITY AMONG COUNTIES
IN THE NEW JERSEY LEGISLATURE 1791-1962. PROVS
ORD/FREE...CENSUS CHARTS 18/20 NEW/JERSEY. PAGE 84
E1687

B63 APPORT REPRESENT LEGIS JURID

RICHARDS P.G.,PATRONAGE IN BRITISH GOVERNMENT.
ELITES DELIB/GP TOP/EX PROB/SOLV CONTROL CT/SYS
EXEC PWR. PAGE 84 E1693

B63 EX/STRUC REPRESENT POL/PAR ADMIN

SARTORI G.,IL PARLAMENTO ITALIANO: 1946-1963. LAW
CONSTN ELITES POL/PAR LOBBY PRIVIL ATTIT PERSON
MORAL PWR SOC. PAGE 87 E1746

B63 LEGIS PARL/PROC REPRESENT

WOLL P.,ADMINISTRATIVE LAW: THE INFORMAL PROCESS.
USA+45 NAT/G CONTROL EFFICIENCY 20. PAGE 107 E2141

B63 ADMIN ADJUD REPRESENT EX/STRUC

US PRES COMN REGIS AND VOTING,REPORT ON
REGISTRATION AND VOTING (PAMPHLET). USA+45 POL/PAR
CHIEF EDU/PROP PARTIC REPRESENT ATTIT...PSY CHARTS
20. PAGE 101 E2023

N63 CHOOSE LAW SUFF INSPECT

COUNCIL OF STATE GOVERNMENTS,LEGISLATIVE
APPORTIONMENT: A SUMMARY OF STATE ACTION. USA+45
LEGIS REPRESENT...POLICY SUPREME/CT. PAGE 26 E0523

B64 LOC/G PROVS APPORT CT/SYS

ENDACOTT G.B.,GOVERNMENT AND PEOPLE IN HONG KONG

B64 CONSTN

1841-1962: A CONSTITUTIONAL HISTORY. UK LEGIS ADJUD REPRESENT ATTIT 19/20 HONG/KONG. PAGE 35 E0688

COLONIAL CONTROL ADMIN

B64

HAMILTON H.D., LEGISLATIVE APPORTIONMENT: KEY TO POWER. USA+45 LAW CONSTN PROVS LOBBY CHOOSE ATTIT SUPREME/CT. PAGE 50 E0988

APPORT CT/SYS LEAD REPRESENT

B64

HANSON R., FAIR REPRESENTATION COMES TO MARYLAND (PAMPHLET). BAL/PWR CT/SYS CHOOSE GOV/REL 20 MARYLAND SUPREME/CT. PAGE 50 E0997

APPORT REPRESENT PROVS LEGIS

B64

HEGEL G.W., HEGEL'S POLITICAL WRITINGS (TRANS. BY T.M. KNOX). GERMANY UK FINAN FORCES PARL/PROC CHOOSE REPRESENT...BIOG 19. PAGE 51 E1022

CONSTN LEGIS JURID

B64

IRION F.C., APPORTIONMENT OF THE NEW MEXICO LEGISLATURE. NAT/G LEGIS PRESS CT/SYS ATTIT ...POLICY TIME/SEQ 19/20 SUPREME/CT. PAGE 57 E1137

APPORT REPRESENT GOV/REL PROVS

B64

KEEFE W.J., THE AMERICAN LEGISLATIVE PROCESS: CONGRESS AND THE STATES. USA+45 LAW POL/PAR DELIB/GP DEBATE ADMIN LOBBY REPRESENT CONGRESS PRESIDENT. PAGE 60 E1191

LEGIS DECISION PWR PROVS

B64

NELSON D.H., ADMINISTRATIVE AGENCIES OF THE USA: THEIR DECISIONS AND AUTHORITY. USA+45 NAT/G CONTROL CT/SYS REPRESENT...DECISION 20. PAGE 76 E1531

ADMIN EX/STRUC ADJUD LAW

B64

US HOUSE COMM ON JUDICIARY, CONGRESSIONAL REDISTRICTING. USA+45 PROVS DELIB/GP 20 CONGRESS. PAGE 100 E2005

APPORT REPRESENT LEGIS LAW

S64

BAKER H.R., "INMATE SELF-GOVERNMENT." ACT/RES CREATE CONTROL PARTIC ATTIT RIGID/FLEX QU. PAGE 7 E0141

PUB/INST CRIME INGP/REL REPRESENT

S64

PRITCHETT C.H., "EQUAL PROTECTION AND THE URBAN MAJORITY." POL/PAR LEAD CHOOSE GP/REL PWR...MAJORIT DECISION. PAGE 83 E1655

MUNIC LAW REPRESENT APPORT

B65

CONGRESSIONAL QUARTERLY SERV, POLITICS IN AMERICA, 1945-1964: THE POLITICS AND ISSUES OF THE POSTWAR YEARS. USA+45 LAW FINAN CHIEF DIPLOM APPORT SUFF ...POLICY STAT TREND CHARTS 20 CONGRESS PRESIDENT. PAGE 25 E0489

CHOOSE REPRESENT POL/PAR LEGIS

B65

FERRELL J.S., CASES AND MATERIALS ON LOCAL APPORTIONMENT. CONSTN LEAD GP/REL...DECISION GOV/COMP. PAGE 37 E0740

APPORT LOC/G REPRESENT LAW

B65

KEEFE W.J., THE AMERICAN LEGISLATIVE PROCESS. USA+45 CONSTN POL/PAR CT/SYS REPRESENT FEDERAL ATTIT PLURISM...MAJORIT 20 CONGRESS PRESIDENT. PAGE 60 E1192

LEGIS NAT/G CHIEF GOV/REL

B65

MCKAY R.B., REAPPORTIONMENT: THE LAW AND POLITICS OF EQUAL REPRESENTATION. FUT USA+45 PROVS BAL/PWR ADJUD CHOOSE REPRESENT GOV/REL FEDERAL...JURID BIBLIOG 20 SUPREME/CT CONGRESS. PAGE 71 E1420

APPORT MAJORIT LEGIS PWR

B65

NJ LEGIS REAPPORT PLAN COMM, PUBLIC HEARING ON REDISTRICTING AND REAPPORTIONMENT. USA+45 CONSTN VOL/ASSN LEGIS DEBATE...POLICY GEOG CENSUS 20 NEW/JERSEY. PAGE 77 E1552

APPORT REPRESENT PROVS JURID

B65

SCHUBERT G., REAPPORTIONMENT. LAW MUNIC POL/PAR PWR GOV/COMP. PAGE 88 E1775

REPRESENT LOC/G APPORT LEGIS

L65

WEINSTEIN J.B., "THE EFFECT OF THE FEDERAL

MUNIC

REAPPORTIONMENT DECISIONS ON COUNTIES AND OTHER FORMS OF GOVERNMENT." LAW CONSTN LEGIS CHOOSE GOV/COMP. PAGE 105 E2108

LOC/G APPORT REPRESENT

S65

DIXON R.G., "NEW CONSTITUTIONAL FORMS FOR METROPOLIS: REAPPORTIONED COUNTY BOARDS; LOCAL COUNCILS OF GOVERNMENT." LAW CONSTN LEAD APPORT REPRESENT DECISION. PAGE 32 E0631

MUNIC REGION GOV/COMP PLAN

S65

LONG T.G., "THE ADMINISTRATIVE PROCESS: AGONIZING REAPPRAISAL IN THE FTC." NAT/G REPRESENT 20 FTC. PAGE 66 E1326

ADJUD LOBBY ADMIN EX/STRUC

B66

AARON T.J., THE CONTROL OF POLICE DISCRETION: THE DANISH EXPERIENCE. DENMARK LAW CREATE ADMIN INGP/REL SUPEGO PWR 20 OMBUDSMAN. PAGE 2 E0042

CONTROL FORCES REPRESENT PROB/SOLV

B66

BAKER G.E., THE REAPPORTIONMENT REVOLUTION: REPRESENTATION, POLITICAL POWER, AND THE SUPREME COURT. USA+45 MUNIC NAT/G POL/PAR PROVS PROB/SOLV CHOOSE ORD/FREE POPULISM...CONCPT CHARTS 20 SUPREME/CT. PAGE 7 E0140

LEGIS APPORT REPRESENT ADJUD

B66

BEISER E.N., THE TREATMENT OF LEGISLATIVE APPORTIONMENT BY THE STATE AND FEDERAL COURTS (DISSERTATION). USA+45 CONSTN NAT/G PROVS LEGIS CHOOSE REPRESENT ATTIT...POLICY BIBLIOG 20 CONGRESS SUPREME/CT. PAGE 9 E0181

CT/SYS APPORT ADJUD PWR

B66

CALIFORNIA STATE LIBRARY, REAPPORTIONMENT, A SELECTIVE BIBLIOGRAPHY. USA+45 LEGIS CT/SYS REPRESENT GOV/REL. PAGE 19 E0367

BIBLIOG APPORT NAT/G PROVS

B66

CONG QUARTERLY SERVICE, REPRESENTATION AND APPORTIONMENT. USA+45 POL/PAR CT/SYS SUFF ...POLICY 20 CONGRESS SUPREME/CT. PAGE 25 E0486

APPORT LEGIS REPRESENT CONSTN

B66

DE TOCQUEVILLE A, DEMOCRACY IN AMERICA (1834-1840) (2 VOLS. IN I; TRANS. BY G. LAWRENCE). FRANCE CULTURE STRATA POL/PAR CT/SYS REPRESENT FEDERAL ORD/FREE SOVEREIGN...MAJORIT TREND GEN/LAWS 18/19. PAGE 30 E0596

POPULISM USA-45 CONSTN NAT/COMP

B66

FRIED R.C., COMPARATIVE POLITICAL INSTITUTIONS. USSR EX/STRUC FORCES LEGIS JUDGE CONTROL REPRESENT ALL/IDEOS 20 CONGRESS BUREAUCRCY. PAGE 40 E0798

NAT/G PWR EFFICIENCY GOV/COMP

B66

GOLDWIN R.A., APPORTIONMENT AND REPRESENTATION. MUNIC CT/SYS GP/REL ORD/FREE...POLICY ANTHOL 20 SUPREME/CT. PAGE 44 E0880

APPORT REPRESENT LEGIS CONSTN

B66

HAMILTON H.D., REAPPORTIONING LEGISLATURES. USA+45 CONSTN POL/PAR PROVS LEGIS COMPUTER ADJUD CHOOSE ATTIT...ANTHOL 20 SUPREME/CT CONGRESS. PAGE 50 E0989

APPORT REPRESENT PHIL/SCI PWR

B66

HANSON R., THE POLITICAL THICKET. USA+45 MUNIC POL/PAR LEGIS EXEC LOBBY CHOOSE...MAJORIT DECISION. PAGE 50 E0998

APPORT LAW CONSTN REPRESENT

B66

INSTITUTE COMP STUDY POL SYS, DOMINICAN REPUBLIC ELECTION FACT BOOK. DOMIN/REP LAW LEGIS REPRESENT ...JURID CHARTS 20. PAGE 57 E1126

SUFF CHOOSE POL/PAR NAT/G

B66

MC CONNELL J.P., LAW AND BUSINESS: PATTERNS AND ISSUES IN COMMERCIAL LAW. USA+45 USA-45 LOC/G WORKER LICENSE CRIME REPRESENT GP/REL 20. PAGE 70 E1397

ECO/DEV JURID ADJUD MGT

B66

MEDER A.E. JR., LEGISLATIVE APPORTIONMENT. USA+45 BAL/PWR REPRESENT ORD/FREE PWR...JURID 20 SUPREME/CT. PAGE 72 E1433

APPORT LEGIS MATH POLICY

BURDETTE F.L.,"SELECTED ARTICLES AND DOCUMENTS ON AMERICAN GOVERNMENT AND POLITICS." LAW LOC/G MUNIC NAT/G POL/PAR PROVS LEGIS BAL/PWR ADMIN EXEC REPRESENT MGT. PAGE 17 E0331
BIBLIOG USA+45 JURID CONSTN
S66

BUREAU GOVERNMENT RES AND SERV,COUNTY GOVERNMENT REORGANIZATION - A SELECTED ANNOTATED BIBLIOGRAPHY (PAPER). USA+45 USA-45 LAW CONSTN MUNIC PROVS EX/STRUC CREATE PLAN PROB/SOLV REPRESENT GOV/REL 20. PAGE 17 E0332
BIBLIOG/A APPORT LOC/G ADMIN
B67

GELLHORN W.,OMBUDSMEN AND OTHERS: CITIZENS' PROTECTORS IN NINE COUNTRIES. WOR+45 LAW CONSTN LEGIS INSPECT ADJUD ADMIN CONTROL CT/SYS CHOOSE PERS/REL...STAT CHARTS 20. PAGE 43 E0847
NAT/COMP REPRESENT INGP/REL PROB/SOLV
B67

GRAHAM H.D.,CRISIS IN PRINT: DESEGREGATION AND THE PRESS IN TENNESSEE. LAW SOCIETY MUNIC POL/PAR EDU/PROP LEAD REPRESENT DISCRIM ATTIT...IDEA/COMP BIBLIOG/A SOC/INTEG 20 TENNESSEE SUPREME/CT SOUTH/US. PAGE 45 E0896
PRESS PROVS POLICY RACE/REL
B67

OPERATIONS AND POLICY RESEARCH,NICARAGUA: ELECTION FACTBOOK: FEBRUARY 5, 1967 (PAMPHLET). NICARAGUA LAW NAT/G LEAD REPRESENT...STAT BIOG CHARTS 20. PAGE 79 E1577
POL/PAR CHOOSE PLAN ATTIT
B67

RAE D.,THE POLITICAL CONSEQUENCES OF ELECTORAL LAWS. EUR+WWI ICELAND ISRAEL NEW/ZEALND UK USA+45 ADJUD APPORT GP/REL MAJORITY...MATH STAT CENSUS CHARTS BIBLIOG 20 AUSTRAL. PAGE 83 E1667
POL/PAR CHOOSE NAT/COMP REPRESENT
B67

US SENATE COMM ON FOREIGN REL,CONSULAR CONVENTION WITH THE SOVIET UNION. USA+45 USSR DELIB/GP LEAD REPRESENT ATTIT ORD/FREE CONGRESS TREATY. PAGE 101 E2031
LEGIS LOBBY DIPLOM
B67

HOWARD A.E.D.,"MR. JUSTICE BLACK: THE NEGRO PROTEST MOVEMENT AND THE RULE OF LAW." USA+45 CONSTN CT/SYS CHOOSE GP/REL...DECISION JURID NEGRO SUPREME/CT. PAGE 55 E1100
ADJUD JUDGE LAW REPRESENT
L67

"THE FEDERAL AGRICULTURAL STABILIZATION PROGRAM AND THE NEGRO." LAW CONSTN PLAN REPRESENT DISCRIM ORD/FREE 20 NEGRO CONGRESS. PAGE 2 E0039
AGRI CONTROL NAT/G RACE/REL
S67

DEUTSCH E.P.,"A JUDICIAL PATH TO WORLD PEACE." FUT WOR+45 CONSTN PROB/SOLV DIPLOM LICENSE ADJUD SANCTION CHOOSE REPRESENT NAT/LISM SOVEREIGN 20 ICJ. PAGE 31 E0611
INT/LAW INT/ORG JURID PEACE
S67

GOSSETT W.T.,"ELECTING THE PRESIDENT: NEW HOPE FOR AN OLD IDEAL." FUT USA+45 USA-45 PROVS LEGIS PROB/SOLV WRITING DEBATE ADJUD REPRESENT...MAJORIT DECISION 20 HOUSE/REP PRESIDENT. PAGE 45 E0892
CONSTN CHIEF CHOOSE NAT/G
S67

HAMILTON H.D.,"LEGISLATIVE CONSTITUENCIES: SINGLE-MEMBER DISTRICTS, MULTI-MEMBER DISTRICTS, AND FLOTERAL DISTRICTS." USA+45 LAW POL/PAR ADJUD RACE/REL...CHARTS METH/COMP 20. PAGE 50 E0990
LEGIS REPRESENT APPORT PLAN
S67

KIM R.C.C.,"THE SUPREME COURT: ORALLE WITHOUT TRUTH." USA+45 EDU/PROP RACE/REL ADJUST ALL/VALS ORD/FREE...DECISION WORSHIP SUPREME/CT. PAGE 61 E1214
CT/SYS PROB/SOLV ADJUD REPRESENT
S67

MAYANJA A.,"THE GOVERNMENT'S PROPOSALS ON THE NEW CONSTITUTION." AFR UGANDA LAW CHIEF LEGIS ADJUD REPRESENT FEDERAL PWR 20. PAGE 69 E1390
CONSTN CONFER ORD/FREE NAT/G
S67

TRAYNOR R.J.,"WHO CAN BEST JUDGE THE JUDGES?" USA+45 PLAN PROB/SOLV ATTIT...DECISION JURID 20. PAGE 97 E1938
CHOOSE ADJUD REPRESENT CT/SYS
S67

CHIU H.,"COMMUNIST CHINA'S ATTITUDE TOWARD THE UNITED NATIONS: A LEGAL ANALYSIS." CHINA/COM WOR+45
INT/LAW SOVEREIGN
L68

LAW NAT/G DIPLOM CONFER ADJUD PARTIC ATTIT...POLICY TREND 20 UN. PAGE 22 E0432
INT/ORG REPRESENT
B90

BURGESS J.W.,POLITICAL SCIENCE AND COMPARATIVE CONSTITUTIONAL LAW. FRANCE GERMANY UK USA-45 LEGIS DIPLOM ADJUD REPRESENT...CONCPT 19. PAGE 17 E0340
CONSTN LAW LOC/G NAT/G
B90

SIDGWICK H.,THE ELEMENTS OF POLITICS. LOC/G NAT/G LEGIS DIPLOM ADJUD CONTROL EXEC PARL/PROC REPRESENT GOV/REL SOVEREIGN ALL/IDEOS 19 MILL/JS BENTHAM/J. PAGE 91 E1822
POLICY LAW CONCPT
B91

REPUBLIC OF CHINA....SEE TAIWAN

REPUBLICAN....REPUBLICAN PARTY (ALL NATIONS)

RESEARCH....SEE ACT/RES, OP/RES R+D, CREATE

RESEARCH AND DEVELOPMENT GROUP....SEE R+D

RESIST/INT....SOCIAL RESISTANCE TO INTERVIEWS

RESOURCE/N....NATURAL RESOURCES

SOC OF COMP LEGIS AND INT LAW,THE LAW OF THE SEA... (PAMPHLET). WOR+45 NAT/G INT/TRADE ADJUD CONTROL NUC/PWR WAR PEACE ATTIT ORD/FREE...JURID CHARTS 20 UN TREATY RESOURCE/N. PAGE 92 E1850
INT/LAW INT/ORG DIPLOM SEA
B58

LUGO-MARENCO J.J.,A STATEMENT OF THE LAWS OF NICARAGUA IN MATTERS AFFECTING BUSINESS. NICARAGUA AGRI DIST/IND EXTR/IND FINAN INDUS FAM WORKER INT/TRADE TAX MARRIAGE OWN BIO/SOC 20 TREATY RESOURCE/N MIGRATION. PAGE 67 E1332
CONSTN NAT/G LEGIS JURID
B65

RESPECT....RESPECT, SOCIAL CLASS, STRATIFICATION (CONTEMPT)

BERKELEY G.,"DISCOURSE ON PASSIVE OBEDIENCE" (1712) THE WORKS... (VOL. IV)" UNIV DOMIN LEGIT CONTROL CRIME ADJUST CENTRAL MORAL ORD/FREE...POLICY WORSHIP. PAGE 10 E0202
INGP/REL SANCTION RESPECT GEN/LAWS
C01

CORBETT P.E.,CANADA AND WORLD POLITICS. LAW CULTURE SOCIETY STRUCT MARKET INT/ORG FORCES ACT/RES PLAN ECO/TAC LEGIT ORD/FREE PWR RESPECT...SOC CONCPT TIME/SEQ TREND CMN/WLTH 20 LEAGUE/NAT. PAGE 26 E0504
NAT/G CANADA
B28

HOLDSWORTH W.S.,THE HISTORIANS OF ANGLO-AMERICAN LAW. UK USA-45 INTELL LEGIS RESPECT...BIOG NAT/COMP 17/20 COMMON/LAW. PAGE 54 E1076
HIST/WRIT LAW JURID
B28

MAIR L.P.,THE PROTECTION OF MINORITIES. EUR+WWI WOR-45 CONSTN INT/ORG NAT/G LEGIT CT/SYS GP/REL RACE/REL DISCRIM ORD/FREE RESPECT...JURID CONCPT TIME/SEQ 20. PAGE 68 E1352
LAW SOVEREIGN
B28

WRIGHT Q.,"FUNDAMENTAL PROBLEMS OF INTERNATIONAL ORGANIZATION." UNIV WOR-45 STRUCT FORCES ACT/RES CREATE DOMIN EDU/PROP LEGIT REGION NAT/LISM ORD/FREE PWR RESPECT SOVEREIGN...JURID SOC CONCPT METH/CNCPT TIME/SEQ 20. PAGE 107 E2152
INT/ORG ATTIT PEACE
S41

HILL M.,IMMUNITIES AND PRIVILEGES OF INTERNATIONAL OFFICIALS. CANADA EUR+WWI NETHERLAND SWITZERLND LAW LEGIS DIPLOM LEGIT RESPECT...TIME/SEQ LEAGUE/NAT UN VAL/FREE 20. PAGE 52 E1046
INT/ORG ADMIN
B47

DE HUSZAR G.B.,EQUALITY IN AMERICA: THE ISSUE OF MINORITY RIGHTS. USA+45 USA-45 LAW NEIGH SCHOOL LEGIS ACT/RES CHOOSE ATTIT RESPECT...ANTHOL 20 NEGRO. PAGE 29 E0585
DISCRIM RACE/REL ORD/FREE PROB/SOLV
B49

KELSEN H.,"RECENT TRENDS IN THE LAW OF THE UNITED NATIONS." KOREA WOR+45 CONSTN LEGIS DIPLOM LEGIT DETER WAR RIGID/FLEX HEALTH ORD/FREE RESPECT ...JURID CON/ANAL UN VAL/FREE 20 NATO. PAGE 60 E1199
INT/ORG LAW INT/LAW
L51

NICOLSON H.,"THE EVOLUTION OF DIPLOMATIC METHOD."
RIGID/FLEX
L54

CHRIST-17C EUR+WWI FRANCE FUT ITALY MEDIT-7 MOD/EUR METH/CNCPT
USA+45 USA-45 LAW NAT/G CREATE EDU/PROP LEGIT PEACE DIPLOM
ATTIT ORD/FREE RESPECT SOVEREIGN. PAGE 77 E1548

B56
CALLISON I.P.,COURTS OF INJUSTICE. USA+45 PROF/ORG CT/SYS
ADJUD CRIME PERSON MORAL PWR RESPECT SKILL 20. JUDGE
PAGE 19 E0368 JURID

B57
ROWAN C.T.,GO SOUTH TO SORROW. USA+45 STRUCT NAT/G RACE/REL
EDU/PROP LEAD COERCE ISOLAT DRIVE SUPEGO RESPECT DISCRIM
...PREDICT 20 NEGRO SUPREME/CT SOUTH/US CIV/RIGHTS. ANOMIE
PAGE 86 E1728 LAW

S58
CRESSEY D.R.,"ACHIEVEMENT OF AN UNSTATED PUB/INST
ORGANIZATIONAL GOAL: AN OBSERVATION ON PRISONS." CLIENT
OP/RES PROB/SOLV PERS/REL ANOMIE ATTIT ROLE RESPECT NEIGH
CRIMLGY. PAGE 28 E0546 INGP/REL

B59
SCHORN H.,DER RICHTER IM DRITTEN REICH; GESCHICHTE ADJUD
UND DOKUMENTE. GERMANY NAT/G LEGIT CT/SYS INGP/REL JUDGE
MORAL ORD/FREE RESPECT...JURID GP/COMP 20. PAGE 88 FASCISM
E1765

S59
JENKS C.W.,"THE CHALLENGE OF UNIVERSALITY." FUT INT/ORG
UNIV CONSTN CULTURE CONSULT CREATE PLAN LEGIT ATTIT LAW
MORAL ORD/FREE RESPECT...MAJORIT JURID 20. PAGE 58 PEACE
E1155 INT/LAW

S59
SUTTON F.X.,"REPRESENTATION AND THE NATURE OF NAT/G
POLITICAL SYSTEMS." UNIV WOR-45 CULTURE SOCIETY CONCPT
STRATA INT/ORG FORCES JUDGE DOMIN LEGIT EXEC REGION
REPRESENT ATTIT ORD/FREE RESPECT...SOC HIST/WRIT
TIME/SEQ. PAGE 95 E1896

B60
BORGATTA E.F.,SOCIAL WORKERS' PERCEPTIONS OF SOC/WK
CLIENTS. SERV/IND ROUTINE PERS/REL DRIVE PERSON ATTIT
RESPECT...SOC PERS/COMP 20. PAGE 14 E0268 CLIENT
PROB/SOLV

B60
JENKS C.W.,HUMAN RIGHTS AND INTERNATIONAL LABOR CONCPT
STANDARDS. WOR+45 CONSTN LABOR VOL/ASSN DELIB/GP
ACT/RES EDU/PROP MORAL RESPECT...JURID SOC TREND
GEN/LAWS WORK ILO 20. PAGE 58 E1156

B61
NELSON H.L.,LIBEL IN NEWS OF CONGRESSIONAL DELIB/GP
INVESTIGATING COMMITTEES. USA+45 LAW PARL/PROC LEGIS
PRIVIL RESPECT HOUSE/REP. PAGE 76 E1532 LICENSE
PRESS

S61
LASSWELL H.D.,"THE INTERPLAY OF ECONOMIC, POLITICAL JURID
AND SOCIAL CRITERIA IN LEGAL POLICY." LAW LOVE POLICY
MORAL PWR RESPECT WEALTH...SOC IDEA/COMP. PAGE 63
E1262

B62
ASSOCIATION BAR OF NYC,REPORT ON ADMISSION PUB/INST
PROCEDURES TO NEW YORK STATE MENTAL HOSPITALS. LAW HEALTH
CONSTN INGP/REL RESPECT...PSY OBS RECORD. PAGE 6 CLIENT
E0108 ROUTINE

B62
BORKIN J.,THE CORRUPT JUDGE. USA+45 CT/SYS ATTIT ADJUD
SUPEGO MORAL RESPECT...BIBLIOG + SUPREME/CT TRIBUTE
MANTON/M DAVIS/W JOHNSN/ALB. PAGE 14 E0271 CRIME

B62
PAIKERT G.C.,THE GERMAN EXODUS. EUR+WWI GERMANY/W INGP/REL
LAW CULTURE SOCIETY STRUCT INDUS NAT/LISM RESPECT STRANGE
SOVEREIGN...CHARTS BIBLIOG SOC/INTEG 20 MIGRATION. GEOG
PAGE 79 E1591 GP/REL

B62
TRISKA J.F.,THE THEORY, LAW, AND POLICY OF SOVIET COM
TREATIES. WOR+45 WOR-45 CONSTN INT/ORG NAT/G LAW
VOL/ASSN DOMIN LEGIT COERCE ATTIT PWR RESPECT INT/LAW
...POLICY JURID CONCPT OBS SAMP TIME/SEQ TREND USSR
GEN/LAWS 20. PAGE 97 E1941

B62
US COMMISSION ON CIVIL RIGHTS,EQUAL PROTECTION OF ORD/FREE
THE LAWS IN NORTH CAROLINA. USA+45 LOC/G NAT/G RESPECT
CONSULT LEGIS WORKER PROB/SOLV EDU/PROP ADJUD LAW
CHOOSE DISCRIM HEALTH 20 NEGRO NORTH/CAR CIV/RIGHTS. PROVS
CIV/RIGHTS. PAGE 99 E1984

B62
US COMMISSION ON CIVIL RIGHTS,HEARINGS BEFORE ORD/FREE
UNITED STATES COMMISSION ON CIVIL RIGHTS. USA+45 LAW
ECO/DEV NAT/G CONSULT WORKER EDU/PROP ADJUD DISCRIM ADMIN
ISOLAT HABITAT HEALTH RESPECT 20 NEGRO CIV/RIGHTS. LEGIS
PAGE 99 E1985

L62
GROSS L.,"IMMUNITIES AND PRIVILEGES OF DELIGATIONS INT/ORG
TO THE UNITED NATIONS." USA+45 WOR+45 STRATA NAT/G LAW
VOL/ASSN CONSULT DIPLOM EDU/PROP ROUTINE RESPECT ELITES
...POLICY INT/LAW CONCPT UN 20. PAGE 48 E0950

B63
GINZBERG E.,DEMOCRATIC VALUES AND THE RIGHTS OF LABOR
MANAGEMENT. LAW CONSTN REPRESENT GP/REL ROLE PWR MGT
RESPECT POLICY. PAGE 44 E0870 DELIB/GP
ADJUD

B63
ROBERTSON A.H.,HUMAN RIGHTS IN EUROPE. CONSTN EUR+WWI
SOCIETY INT/ORG NAT/G VOL/ASSN DELIB/GP ACT/RES PERSON
PLAN ADJUD REGION ROUTINE ATTIT LOVE ORD/FREE
RESPECT...JURID SOC CONCPT SOC/EXP UN 20. PAGE 85
E1705

L63
LISSITZYN O.J.,"INTERNATIONAL LAW IN A DIVIDED INT/ORG
WORLD." FUT WOR+45 CONSTN CULTURE ECO/DEV ECO/UNDEV LAW
DIST/IND NAT/G FORCES ECO/TAC LEGIT ADJUD ADMIN
COERCE ATTIT HEALTH MORAL ORD/FREE PWR RESPECT
WEALTH VAL/FREE. PAGE 65 E1306

S63
VINES K.N.,"THE ROLE OF THE CIRCUIT COURT OF REGION
APPEALS IN THE FEDERAL JUDICIAL PROCESS: A CASE ADJUD
STUDY." USA+45 STRATA JUDGE RESPECT...DECISION CT/SYS
JURID CHARTS GP/COMP. PAGE 104 E2078 RACE/REL

B64
IKLE F.C.,HOW NATIONS NEGOTIATE. COM EUR+WWI USA+45 NAT/G
INTELL INT/ORG VOL/ASSN DELIB/GP ACT/RES CREATE PWR
DOMIN EDU/PROP ADJUD ROUTINE ATTIT PERSON ORD/FREE POLICY
RESPECT SKILL...PSY SOC OBS VAL/FREE. PAGE 56 E1122

B64
NEWMAN E.S.,POLICE, THE LAW, AND PERSONAL FREEDOM. JURID
USA+45 CONSTN JUDGE CT/SYS CRIME PERS/REL RESPECT FORCES
...CRIMLGY 20. PAGE 77 E1542 ORD/FREE
ADJUD

B64
SCHWELB E.,HUMAN RIGHTS AND THE INTERNATIONAL INT/ORG
COMMUNITY. WOR+45 WOR-45 NAT/G SECT DELIB/GP DIPLOM ORD/FREE
PEACE RESPECT TREATY 20 UN. PAGE 89 E1792 INT/LAW

L64
POUNDS N.J.G.,"THE POLITICS OF PARTITION." AFR ASIA NAT/G
COM EUR+WWI FUT ISLAM S/ASIA USA-45 LAW ECO/DEV NAT/LISM
ECO/UNDEV AGRI INDUS INT/ORG POL/PAR PROVS SECT
FORCES TOP/EX EDU/PROP LEGIT ATTIT MORAL ORD/FREE
PWR RESPECT WEALTH. PAGE 82 E1640

B65
MISSISSIPPI BLACK PAPER: (FIFTY-SEVEN NEGRO AND COERCE
WHITE CITIZENS' TESTIMONY OF POLICE BRUTALITY...). RACE/REL
USA+45 LAW SOCIETY CT/SYS SANCTION CRIME MORAL DISCRIM
ORD/FREE RESPECT 20 NEGRO. PAGE 2 E0035 FORCES

B65
O'BRIEN W.V.,THE NEW NATIONS IN INTERNATIONAL LAW INT/LAW
AND DIPLOMACY* THE YEAR BOOK OF WORLD POLITY* CULTURE
VOLUME III. USA+45 ECO/UNDEV INT/ORG FORCES DIPLOM SOVEREIGN
COLONIAL NEUTRAL REV NAT/LISM ATTIT RESPECT. ANTHOL
PAGE 78 E1565

B66
AUERBACH J.S.,LABOR AND LIBERTY; THE LA FOLLETTE DELIB/GP
COMMITTEE AND THE NEW DEAL. USA-45 LAW LEAD RESPECT LABOR
SOCISM...BIBLIOG 20 CONGRESS BILL/RIGHT LAFOLLET/R CONSTN
NEW/DEAL. PAGE 6 E0117 ORD/FREE

B66
GILLMOR D.M.,FREE PRESS AND FAIR TRIAL. UK USA+45 ORD/FREE
CONSTN PROB/SOLV PRESS CONTROL CRIME DISCRIM ADJUD
RESPECT...AUD/VIS 20 CIVIL/LIB. PAGE 44 E0865 ATTIT
EDU/PROP

B66
NANTWI E.K.,THE ENFORCEMENT OF INTERNATIONAL INT/LAW
JUDICIAL DECISIONS AND ARBITAL AWARDS IN PUBLIC ADJUD
INTERNATIONAL LAW. WOR+45 WOR-45 JUDGE PROB/SOLV SOVEREIGN
DIPLOM CT/SYS SUPEGO MORAL PWR RESPECT...METH/CNCPT INT/ORG
18/20 CASEBOOK. PAGE 76 E1520

LANDE G.R.,"THE EFFECT OF THE RESOLUTIONS OF THE UNITED NATIONS GENERAL ASSEMBLY." WOR+45 LAW INT/ORG NAT/G CHOOSE ISOLAT ATTIT...CLASSIF GEN/METH UN. PAGE 62 E1249
S66 LEGIS EFFICIENCY RESPECT

RESPONSIBILITY....SEE SUPEGO, RESPECT

RESPONSIVENESS....SEE RIGID/FLEX

RESTRAINT....SEE ORD/FREE

RETIREMENT....SEE SENIOR, ADMIN

REUTHER/W....WALTER REUTHER

REV....REVOLUTION; SEE ALSO WAR

ANNALS OF THE AMERICAN ACADEMY OF POLITICAL AND SOCIAL SCIENCE. AFR ASIA S/ASIA WOR+45 POL/PAR DIPLOM CRIME REV...SOC BIOG 20. PAGE 1 E0003
N BIBLIOG/A NAT/G CULTURE ATTIT

BURKE E.,A LETTER TO THE SHERIFFS OF BRISTOL (1777). USA-45 LAW ECO/TAC COLONIAL CT/SYS REV GP/REL ORD/FREE...POLICY 18 PARLIAMENT BURKE/EDM. PAGE 17 E0341
B04 LEGIS ADJUD CRIME

DUNNING W.A.,"HISTORY OF POLITICAL THEORIES FROM LUTHER TO MONTESQUIEU." LAW NAT/G SECT DIPLOM REV WAR ORD/FREE SOVEREIGN CONSERVE...TRADIT BIBLIOG 16/18. PAGE 33 E0663
C05 PHIL/SCI CONCPT GEN/LAWS

ADAMS B.,THE THEORY OF SOCIAL REVOLUTIONS. FUT USA-45 GP/REL PEACE...NEW/IDEA 20. PAGE 3 E0047
B13 CAP/ISM REV SOCIETY CT/SYS

TAYLOR H.,WHY THE PENDING TREATY WITH COLOMBIA SHOULD BE RATIFIED (PAMPHLET). PANAMA USA-45 DELIB/GP INT/TRADE REV ORD/FREE...JURID TREATY 18/19 ROOSEVLT/T TAFT/WH COLOMB. PAGE 95 E1912
N19 INT/LAW DIPLOM

DUNNING W.A.,"A HISTORY OF POLITICAL THINKERS FROM ROUSSEAU TO SPENCER." NAT/G REV NAT/LISM UTIL CONSERVE MARXISM POPULISM...JURID BIBLIOG 18/19. PAGE 33 E0664
C20 IDEA/COMP PHIL/SCI CONCPT GEN/LAWS

DE MONTESQUIEU C.,THE SPIRIT OF LAWS (2 VOLS.) (TRANS. BY THOMAS NUGENT). FRANCE FINAN SECT INT/TRADE TAX COERCE REV DISCRIM HABITAT ORD/FREE 19 ALEMBERT/J CIVIL/LAW. PAGE 30 E0588
B23 JURID LAW CONCPT GEN/LAWS

BARNES H.E.,"SOCIOLOGY AND POLITICAL THEORY: A CONSIDERATION OF THE SOCIOLOGICAL BASIS OF POLITICS." LAW CONSTN NAT/G DIPLOM DOMIN ROUTINE REV ORD/FREE SOVEREIGN...PHIL/SCI CLASSIF BIBLIOG 18/20. PAGE 8 E0151
C24 CONCPT STRUCT SOC

GOOCH G.P.,ENGLISH DEMOCRATIC IDEAS IN THE SEVENTEENTH CENTURY (2ND ED.). UK LAW SECT FORCES DIPLOM LEAD PARL/PROC REV ATTIT AUTHORIT...ANARCH CONCPT 17 PARLIAMENT CMN/WLTH REFORMERS. PAGE 45 E0885
B27 IDEA/COMP MAJORIT EX/STRUC CONSERVE

REID H.D.,RECUEIL DES COURS; TOME 45: LES SERVITUDES INTERNATIONALES III. FRANCE CONSTN DELIB/GP PRESS CONTROL REV WAR CHOOSE PEACE MORAL MARITIME TREATY. PAGE 84 E1680
B33 ORD/FREE DIPLOM LAW

CLYDE W.M.,THE STRUGGLE FOR THE FREEDOM OF THE PRESS FROM CAXTON TO CROMWELL. UK LAW LOC/G SECT FORCES LICENSE WRITING SANCTION REV ATTIT PWR ...POLICY 15/17 PARLIAMENT CROMWELL/O MILTON/J. PAGE 23 E0460
B34 PRESS ORD/FREE CONTROL

HARPER S.N.,THE GOVERNMENT OF THE SOVIET UNION. COM USSR LAW CONSTN ECO/DEV PLAN TEC/DEV DIPLOM INT/TRADE ADMIN REV NAT/LISM...POLICY 20. PAGE 50 E1001
B38 MARXISM NAT/G LEAD POL/PAR

BALDWIN L.D.,WHISKEY REBELS; THE STORY OF A FRONTIER UPRISING. USA-45 LAW ADJUD LEAD COERCE PWR ...BIBLIOG/A 18 PENNSYLVAN FEDERALIST. PAGE 8 E0145
B39 REV POL/PAR TAX TIME/SEQ

LOCKE J.,TWO TREATISES OF GOVERNMENT (1690). UK LAW SOCIETY LEGIS LEGIT AGREE REV OWN HEREDITY MORAL CONSERVE...POLICY MAJORIT 17 WILLIAM/3 NATURL/LAW. PAGE 66 E1316
B47 CONCPT ORD/FREE NAT/G CONSEN

WORMUTH F.D.,THE ORIGINS OF MODERN CONSTITUTIONALISM. GREECE UK LEGIS CREATE TEC/DEV BAL/PWR DOMIN ADJUD REV WAR PWR...JURID ROMAN/REP CROMWELL/O. PAGE 107 E2146
B49 NAT/G CONSTN LAW

BIDDLE F.,THE FEAR OF FREEDOM. USA+45 LAW NAT/G PUB/INST PROB/SOLV DOMIN CONTROL SANCTION REV NAT/LISM 20. PAGE 12 E0227
B51 ANOMIE INGP/REL VOL/ASSN ORD/FREE

LEEK J.H.,"TREASON AND THE CONSTITUTION" (BMR)" USA+45 USA-45 EDU/PROP COLONIAL CT/SYS REV WAR ATTIT...TREND 18/20 SUPREME/CT CON/INTERP SMITH/ACT COMMON/LAW. PAGE 64 E1278
S51 CONSTN JURID CRIME NAT/G

DE GRAZIA A.,"GENERAL THEORY OF APPORTIONMENT" (BMR)" USA+45 USA-45 CONSTN ELITES DELIB/GP PARTIC REV CHOOSE...JURID 20. PAGE 29 E0582
S52 APPORT LEGIS PROVS REPRESENT

DE ARAGAO J.G.,LA JURIDICTION ADMINISTRATIVE AU BRESIL. BRAZIL ADJUD COLONIAL CT/SYS REV FEDERAL ORD/FREE...BIBLIOG 19/20. PAGE 29 E0580
B55 EX/STRUC ADMIN NAT/G

MAZZINI J.,THE DUTIES OF MAN. MOD/EUR LAW SOCIETY FAM NAT/G POL/PAR SECT VOL/ASSN EX/STRUC ACT/RES CREATE REV PEACE ATTIT ALL/VALS...GEN/LAWS WORK 19. PAGE 70 E1396
B55 SUPEGO CONCPT NAT/LISM

COSSIO C.,LA POLITICA COMO CONCIENCIA; MEDITACION SOBRE LA ARGENTINA DE 1955. WOR+45 LEGIS EDU/PROP PARL/PROC PARTIC ATTIT PWR CATHISM 20 ARGEN PERON/JUAN. PAGE 26 E0517
B57 POL/PAR REV TOTALISM JURID

NEUMANN F.,THE DEMOCRATIC AND THE AUTHORITARIAN STATE: ESSAYS IN POLITICAL AND LEGAL THEORY. USA+45 USA-45 CONTROL REV GOV/REL PEACE ALL/IDEOS ...INT/LAW CONCPT GEN/LAWS BIBLIOG 20. PAGE 77 E1536
B57 DOMIN NAT/G ORD/FREE POLICY

POUND R.,THE DEVELOPMENT OF CONSTITUTIONAL GUARANTEES OF LIBERTY. UK USA-45 CHIEF COLONIAL REV ...JURID CONCPT 15/20. PAGE 82 E1638
B57 LAW CONSTN ORD/FREE ATTIT

HOBSBAWM E.J.,PRIMITIVE REBELS; STUDIES IN ARCHAIC FORMS OF SOCIAL MOVEMENT IN THE 19TH AND 20TH CENTURIES. ITALY SPAIN CULTURE VOL/ASSN RISK CROWD GP/REL INGP/REL ISOLAT TOTALISM...PSY SOC 18/20. PAGE 53 E1058
B59 SOCIETY CRIME REV GUERRILLA

OKINSHEVICH L.A.,LATIN AMERICA IN SOVIET WRITINGS, 1945-1958: A BIBLIOGRAPHY. USSR LAW ECO/UNDEV LABOR DIPLOM EDU/PROP REV...GEOG SOC 20. PAGE 78 E1573
B59 BIBLIOG WRITING COM L/A+17C

VITTACHIT,EMERGENCY '58. CEYLON UK STRUCT NAT/G FORCES ADJUD CRIME REV NAT/LISM 20. PAGE 104 E2081
B59 RACE/REL DISCRIM DIPLOM SOVEREIGN

FISCHER L.,THE SOVIETS IN WORLD AFFAIRS. CHINA/COM COM EUR+WWI USSR INT/ORG CONFER LEAD ARMS/CONT REV PWR...CHARTS 20 TREATY VERSAILLES. PAGE 38 E0755
B60 DIPLOM NAT/G POLICY MARXISM

MOCTEZUMA A.P.,EL CONFLICTO RELIGIOSO DE 1926 (2ND ED.). L/A+17C LAW NAT/G LOBBY COERCE GP/REL ATTIT ...POLICY 20 MEXIC/AMER CHURCH/STA. PAGE 74 E1476
B60 SECT ORD/FREE DISCRIM REV

B60
RIENOW R.,INTRODUCTION TO GOVERNMENT (2ND ED.). UK
USA+45 USSR POL/PAR ADMIN REV CHOOSE SUFF FEDERAL
PWR...JURID GOV/COMP T 20. PAGE 85 E1697

CONSTN
PARL/PROC
REPRESENT
AUTHORIT

S60
GRACIA-MORA M.R.,"INTERNATIONAL RESPONSIBILITY FOR
SUBVERSIVE ACTIVITIES AND HOSTILE PROPAGANDA BY
PRIVATE PERSONS AGAINST." COM EUR+WWI L/A+17C UK
USA+45 USSR WOR-45 CONSTN NAT/G LEGIT ADJUD REV
PEACE TOTALISM ORD/FREE...INT/LAW 20. PAGE 45 E0895

INT/ORG
JURID
SOVEREIGN

C60
HAZARD J.N.,"SETTLING DISPUTES IN SOVIET SOCIETY:
THE FORMATIVE YEARS OF LEGAL INSTITUTIONS." USSR
NAT/G PROF/ORG PROB/SOLV CONTROL CT/SYS ROUTINE REV
CENTRAL...JURID BIBLIOG 20. PAGE 51 E1017

ADJUD
LAW
COM
POLICY

B61
FROEBEL J.,THEORIE DER POLITIK, ALS ERGEBNIS EINER
ERNEUERTEN PRUEFUNG DEMOKRATISCHER LEHRMEINUNGEN.
WOR-45 SOCIETY POL/PAR SECT REV REPRESENT PWR
SOVEREIGN...MAJORIT 19. PAGE 41 E0812

JURID
ORD/FREE
NAT/G

B62
BARLOW R.B.,CITIZENSHIP AND CONSCIENCE: STUDIES IN
THEORY AND PRACTICE OF RELIGIOUS TOLERATION IN
ENGLAND DURING EIGHTEENTH CENTURY. UK LAW VOL/ASSN
EDU/PROP SANCTION REV GP/REL MAJORITY ATTIT
ORD/FREE...BIBLIOG WORSHIP 18. PAGE 8 E0150

SECT
LEGIS
DISCRIM

B62
GYORGY A.,PROBLEMS IN INTERNATIONAL RELATIONS. COM
CT/SYS NUC/PWR ALL/IDEOS 20 UN EEC ECSC. PAGE 49
E0966

DIPLOM
NEUTRAL
BAL/PWR
REV

B62
HOOK S.,THE PARADOXES OF FREEDOM. UNIV CONSTN
INTELL LEGIS CONTROL REV CHOOSE SUPEGO...POLICY
JURID IDEA/COMP 19/20 CIV/RIGHTS. PAGE 55 E1095

CONCPT
MAJORIT
ORD/FREE
ALL/VALS

S62
GREENSPAN M.,"INTERNATIONAL LAW AND ITS PROTECTION
FOR PARTICIPANTS IN UNCONVENTIONAL WARFARE." WOR+45
LAW INT/ORG NAT/G POL/PAR COERCE REV ORD/FREE
...INT/LAW TOT/POP 20. PAGE 46 E0912

FORCES
JURID
GUERRILLA
WAR

B63
FRIEDRICH C.J.,MAN AND HIS GOVERNMENT: AN EMPIRICAL
THEORY OF POLITICS. UNIV LOC/G NAT/G ADJUD REV
INGP/REL DISCRIM PWR BIBLIOG. PAGE 41 E0810

PERSON
ORD/FREE
PARTIC
CONTROL

B63
GEERTZ C.,OLD SOCIETIES AND NEW STATES: THE QUEST
FOR MODERNITY IN ASIA AND AFRICA. AFR ASIA LAW
CULTURE SECT EDU/PROP REV...GOV/COMP NAT/COMP 20.
PAGE 42 E0842

ECO/UNDEV
TEC/DEV
NAT/LISM
SOVEREIGN

B63
HABERMAS J.,THEORIE UND PRAXIS. RATIONAL PERSON
...PHIL/SCI ANTHOL 19/20 HEGEL/GWF MARX/KARL BLOCH
LOWITH. PAGE 49 E0969

JURID
REV
GEN/LAWS
MARXISM

B63
LEVY L.W.,JEFFERSON AND CIVIL LIBERTIES: THE DARKER
SIDE. USA-45 LAW INTELL ACADEM FORCES PRESS REV
INGP/REL PERSON 18/19 JEFFERSN/T CIVIL/LIB. PAGE 65
E1291

BIOG
ORD/FREE
CONSTN
ATTIT

B64
CHAPIN B.,THE AMERICAN LAW OF TREASON. USA-45 LAW
NAT/G JUDGE CRIME REV...BIBLIOG 18. PAGE 21 E0419

LEGIS
JURID
CONSTN
POLICY

B64
MINAR D.W.,IDEAS AND POLITICS: THE AMERICAN
EXPERIENCE. SECT CHIEF LEGIS CREATE ADJUD EXEC REV
PWR...PHIL/SCI CONCPT IDEA/COMP 18/20 HAMILTON/A
JEFFERSN/T DECLAR/IND JACKSON/A PRESIDENT. PAGE 73
E1464

CONSTN
NAT/G
FEDERAL

B64
WRIGHT G.,RURAL REVOLUTION IN FRANCE: THE PEASANTRY
IN THE TWENTIETH CENTURY. EUR+WWI MOD/EUR LAW
CULTURE AGRI POL/PAR DELIB/GP LEGIS ECO/TAC
EDU/PROP COERCE CHOOSE ATTIT RIGID/FLEX HEALTH
...STAT CENSUS CHARTS VAL/FREE 20. PAGE 107 E2148

PWR
STRATA
FRANCE
REV

S64
GINSBURGS G.,"WARS OF NATIONAL LIBERATION - THE
SOVIET THESIS." COM USSR WOR+45 WOR-45 LAW CULTURE
INT/ORG DIPLOM LEGIT COLONIAL GUERRILLA WAR
NAT/LISM ATTIT PERSON MORAL PWR...JURID OBS TREND
MARX/KARL 20. PAGE 44 E0869

COERCE
CONCPT
INT/LAW
REV

B65
BAADE H.,THE SOVIET IMPACT ON INTERNATIONAL LAW.
INT/ORG INT/TRADE LEGIT COLONIAL ARMS/CONT REV WAR
...CON/ANAL ANTHOL TREATY. PAGE 6 E0124

INT/LAW
USSR
CREATE
ORD/FREE

B65
CHROUST A.H.,THE RISE OF THE LEGAL PROFESSION IN
AMERICA (3 VOLS.). STRATA STRUCT POL/PAR PROF/ORG
COLONIAL LEAD REV SKILL...SOC 17/20. PAGE 22 E0437

JURID
USA-45
CT/SYS
LAW

B65
MORRIS R.B.,THE PEACEMAKERS; THE GREAT POWERS AND
AMERICAN INDEPENDENCE. BAL/PWR CONFER COLONIAL
NEUTRAL PEACE ORD/FREE TREATY 18 PRE/US/AM. PAGE 75
E1499

SOVEREIGN
REV
DIPLOM

B65
MOSTECKY V.,SOVIET LEGAL BIBLIOGRAPHY. USSR LEGIS
PRESS WRITING CONFER ADJUD CT/SYS REV MARXISM
...INT/LAW JURID DICTIONARY 20. PAGE 75 E1503

BIBLIOG/A
LAW
COM
CONSTN

B65
O'BRIEN W.V.,THE NEW NATIONS IN INTERNATIONAL LAW
AND DIPLOMACY* THE YEAR BOOK OF WORLD POLITY*
VOLUME III. USA+45 ECO/UNDEV INT/ORG FORCES DIPLOM
COLONIAL NEUTRAL REV NAT/LISM ATTIT RESPECT.
PAGE 78 E1565

INT/LAW
CULTURE
SOVEREIGN
ANTHOL

B66
FUCHS W.P.,STAAT UND KIRCHE IM WANDEL DER
JAHRHUNDERTE. EUR+WWI MOD/EUR UK REV...JURID CONCPT
4/20 EUROPE CHRISTIAN CHURCH/STA. PAGE 41 E0817

SECT
NAT/G
ORD/FREE
GP/REL

B66
MILLER E.W.,THE NEGRO IN AMERICA: A BIBLIOGRAPHY.
USA+45 LAW EDU/PROP REV GOV/REL GP/REL INGP/REL
ADJUST HABITAT PERSON HEALTH ORD/FREE SOC/INTEG 20
NEGRO. PAGE 73 E1459

BIBLIOG
DISCRIM
RACE/REL

B66
THOMPSON J.M.,RUSSIA, BOLSHEVISM, AND THE
VERSAILLES PEACE. RUSSIA USSR INT/ORG NAT/G
DELIB/GP AGREE REV WAR PWR 20 TREATY VERSAILLES
BOLSHEVISM. PAGE 96 E1919

DIPLOM
PEACE
MARXISM

S66
SHKLAR J.,"SELECTED ARTICLES AND DOCUMENTS ON
POLITICAL THEORY." ADJUD REV...JURID PHIL/SCI
IDEA/COMP. PAGE 91 E1820

BIBLIOG
ELITES
PWR

B67
BOHANNAN P.,LAW AND WARFARE. CULTURE CT/SYS COERCE
REV PEACE...JURID SOC CONCPT ANTHOL 20. PAGE 13
E0259

METH/COMP
ADJUD
WAR
LAW

B67
MEYERS M.,SOURCES OF THE AMERICAN REPUBLIC; A
DOCUMENTARY HISTORY OF POLITICS, SOCIETY, AND
THOUGHT (VOL. I, REV. ED.). USA-45 CULTURE STRUCT
NAT/G LEGIS LEAD ATTIT...JURID SOC ANTHOL 17/19
PRESIDENT. PAGE 72 E1450

COLONIAL
REV
WAR

B67
NIVEN R.,NIGERIA. NIGERIA CONSTN INDUS EX/STRUC
COLONIAL REV NAT/LISM...CHARTS 19/20. PAGE 77 E1550

NAT/G
REGION
CHOOSE
GP/REL

B89
FERNEUIL T.,LES PRINCIPES DE 1789 ET LA SCIENCE
SOCIALE. FRANCE NAT/G REV ATTIT...CONCPT TREND
IDEA/COMP 18/19. PAGE 37 E0739

CONSTN
POLICY
LAW

B96
ESMEIN A.,ELEMENTS DE DROIT CONSTITUTIONNEL. FRANCE
UK CHIEF EX/STRUC LEGIS ADJUD CT/SYS PARL/PROC REV
GOV/REL ORD/FREE...JURID METH/COMP 18/19. PAGE 35
E0697

LAW
CONSTN
NAT/G
CONCPT

REVES E. E1688

REVOLUTION....SEE REV

REWARD....SEE SANCTION

RHODE/ISL....RHODE ISLAND

RHODES/C....CECIL RHODES

RHODESIA....SEE ALSO AFR

B34
EVANS I.L.,NATIVE POLICY IN SOUTHERN AFRICA. AFR
RHODESIA SOUTH/AFR UK STRUCT PARTIC RACE/REL ATTIT COLONIAL
WEALTH SOC/INTEG AFRICA/SW. PAGE 35 E0705 DOMIN
LAW

N60
RHODESIA-NYASA NATL ARCHIVES.A SELECT BIBLIOGRAPHY BIBLIOG
OF RECENT PUBLICATIONS CONCERNING THE FEDERATION OF ADMIN
RHODESIA AND NYASALAND (PAMPHLET). MALAWI RHODESIA ORD/FREE
LAW CULTURE STRUCT ECO/UNDEV LEGIS...GEOG 20. NAT/G
PAGE 84 E1689

B65
HAEFELE E.T.,GOVERNMENT CONTROLS ON TRANSPORT. AFR ECO/UNDEV
RHODESIA TANZANIA DIPLOM ECO/TAC TARIFFS PRICE DIST/IND
ADJUD CONTROL REGION EFFICIENCY...POLICY 20 CONGO. FINAN
PAGE 49 E0973 NAT/G

S66
GREEN L.C.,"RHODESIAN OIL: BOOTLEGGERS OR PIRATES?" INT/TRADE
AFR RHODESIA UK WOR+45 INT/ORG NAT/G DIPLOM LEGIT SANCTION
COLONIAL SOVEREIGN 20 UN OAU. PAGE 46 E0907 INT/LAW
POLICY

S67
STEEL R.,"WHAT CAN THE UN DO?" RHODESIA ECO/UNDEV INT/ORG
DIPLOM ECO/TAC SANCTION...INT/LAW UN. PAGE 93 E1866 BAL/PWR
PEACE
FOR/AID

RHODESIA-NYASA NATL ARCHIVES E1689

RHYNE C.S. E1690

RICARDO/D....DAVID RICARDO

RICE C.E. E1691,E1692

RICHARD/H....HENRY RICHARD (WELSH POLITICIAN - 19TH CENTURY)

RICHARDS P.G. E1693

RICHARDSON I.L. E1694

RICHARDSON J.J. E1695

RICHARDSON S.S. E1190

RICHSTEIN A.R. E1696

RIENOW R. E1697,E1698

RIESMAN/D....DAVID RIESMAN

RIGAUX F. E1699

RIGGS R.E. E1618

RIGGS/FRED....FRED W. RIGGS

RIGHTS/MAN....RIGHTS OF MAN

RIGID/FLEX....DEGREE OF RESPONSIVENESS TO NEW IDEAS, METHODS,
AND PEOPLE

B00
BERNARD M.,FOUR LECTURES ON SUBJECTS CONNECTED WITH LAW
DIPLOMACY. WOR-45 NAT/G VOL/ASSN RIGID/FLEX MORAL ATTIT
PWR...JURID OBS GEN/LAWS GEN/METH 20 TREATY. DIPLOM
PAGE 11 E0209

B05
DICEY A.,LAW AND PUBLIC OPINION IN ENGLAND. LAW ATTIT
CULTURE INTELL SOCIETY NAT/G SECT JUDGE LEGIT UK
CHOOSE RIGID/FLEX KNOWL...OLD/LIB CONCPT STERTYP
GEN/LAWS 20. PAGE 31 E0620

B18
YUKIO O.,THE VOICE OF JAPANESE DEMOCRACY, AN ESSAY CONSTN
ON CONSTITUTIONAL LOYALTY (TRANS BY J. E. BECKER). MAJORIT
ASIA POL/PAR DELIB/GP EX/STRUC RIGID/FLEX ORD/FREE CHOOSE
PWR...POLICY JURID METH/COMP 19/20 CHINJAP. NAT/G
PAGE 108 E2167

N19
ARNOW K.,SELF-INSURANCE IN THE TREASURY (PAMPHLET). ADMIN
USA+45 LAW RIGID/FLEX...POLICY METH/COMP 20 PLAN
DEPT/TREAS. PAGE 5 E0104 EFFICIENCY
NAT/G

N19
COUTROT A.,THE FIGHT OVER THE 1959 PRIVATE SCHOOL
EDUCATION LAW IN FRANCE (PAMPHLET). FRANCE NAT/G PARL/PROC
SECT GIVE EDU/PROP GP/REL ATTIT RIGID/FLEX ORD/FREE CATHISM
20 CHURCH/STA. PAGE 27 E0527 LAW

N19
HOGARTY R.A.,NEW JERSEY FARMERS AND MIGRANT HOUSING AGRI
RULES (PAMPHLET). USA+45 LAW ELITES FACE/GP LABOR PROVS
PROF/ORG LOBBY PERS/REL RIGID/FLEX ROLE 20 WORKER
NEW/JERSEY. PAGE 53 E1067 HEALTH

B22
BRYCE J.,INTERNATIONAL RELATIONS. CHRIST-17C INT/ORG
EUR+WWI MOD/EUR CULTURE INTELL NAT/G DELIB/GP POLICY
CREATE BAL/PWR DIPLOM ATTIT DRIVE RIGID/FLEX
ALL/VALS...PLURIST JURID CONCPT TIME/SEQ GEN/LAWS
TOT/POP. PAGE 16 E0323

L28
HUDSON M.,"THE TEACHING OF INTERNATIONAL LAW IN PERCEPT
AMERICA." USA-45 LAW CONSULT ACT/RES CREATE KNOWL
EDU/PROP ATTIT RIGID/FLEX...JURID CONCPT RECORD INT/LAW
HIST/WRIT TREND GEN/LAWS 18/20. PAGE 56 E1109

S36
CORWIN E.S.,"THE CONSTITUTION AS INSTRUMENT AND AS CONSTN
SYMBOL." USA-45 ECO/DEV INDUS CAP/ISM SANCTION LAW
RIGID/FLEX ORD/FREE LAISSEZ OBJECTIVE 20 CONGRESS ADJUD
SUPREME/CT. PAGE 26 E0512 PWR

B38
LEAGUE OF NATIONS-SECRETARIAT.,THE AIMS, METHODS ADJUD
AND ACTIVITY OF THE LEAGUE OF NATIONS. WOR+45 STRUCT
DIPLOM EDU/PROP LEGIT RIGID/FLEX ALL/VALS
...TIME/SEQ LEAGUE/NAT VAL/FREE 19/20. PAGE 64
E1273

B42
KELSEN H.,LAW AND PEACE IN INTERNATIONAL RELATIONS. INT/ORG
FUT WOR-45 NAT/G DELIB/GP DIPLOM LEGIT RIGID/FLEX ADJUD
ORD/FREE SOVEREIGN...JURID CONCPT TREND STERTYP PEACE
GEN/LAWS LEAGUE/NAT 20. PAGE 60 E1197 INT/LAW

B43
MICAUD C.A.,THE FRENCH RIGHT AND NAZI GERMANY DIPLOM
1933-1939: A STUDY OF PUBLIC OPINION. GERMANY UK AGREE
USSR POL/PAR ARMS/CONT COERCE DETER PEACE
RIGID/FLEX PWR MARXISM...FASCIST TREND 20
LEAGUE/NAT TREATY. PAGE 73 E1454

B46
KEETON G.W.,MAKING INTERNATIONAL LAW WORK. FUT INT/ORG
WOR-45 NAT/G DELIB/GP FORCES LEGIT COERCE PEACE ADJUD
ATTIT RIGID/FLEX ORD/FREE PWR...JURID CONCPT INT/LAW
HIST/WRIT GEN/METH LEAGUE/NAT 20. PAGE 60 E1193

B46
ROSS A.,TOWARDS A REALISTIC JURISPRUDENCE: A LAW
CRITICISM OF THE DUALISM IN LAW (TRANS. BY ANNIE I. CONCPT
FAUSBOLL). PLAN ADJUD CT/SYS ATTIT RIGID/FLEX IDEA/COMP
POPULISM...JURID PHIL/SCI LOG METH/COMP GEN/LAWS 20
SCANDINAV. PAGE 86 E1720

B51
KELSEN H.,THE LAW OF THE UNITED NATIONS. WOR+45 INT/ORG
STRUCT RIGID/FLEX ORD/FREE...INT/LAW JURID CONCPT ADJUD
CON/ANAL GEN/METH UN TOT/POP VAL/FREE 20. PAGE 60
E1198

L51
KELSEN H.,"RECENT TRENDS IN THE LAW OF THE UNITED INT/ORG
NATIONS." KOREA WOR+45 CONSTN LEGIS DIPLOM LEGIT LAW
DETER WAR RIGID/FLEX HEALTH ORD/FREE RESPECT INT/LAW
...JURID CON/ANAL UN VAL/FREE 20 NATO. PAGE 60
E1199

B52
BENTHAM A.,HANDBOOK OF POLITICAL FALLACIES. FUT POL/PAR
MOD/EUR LAW INTELL LOC/G MUNIC NAT/G DELIB/GP LEGIS
CREATE EDU/PROP CT/SYS ATTIT RIGID/FLEX KNOWL PWR
...RELATIV PSY SOC CONCPT SELF/OBS TREND STERTYP
TOT/POP. PAGE 10 E0189

L52
WRIGHT Q.,"CONGRESS AND THE TREATY-MAKING POWER." ROUTINE
USA+45 WOR+45 CONSTN INTELL NAT/G CHIEF CONSULT DIPLOM
EX/STRUC LEGIS TOP/EX CREATE GOV/REL DISPL DRIVE INT/LAW
RIGID/FLEX...TREND TOT/POP CONGRESS CONGRESS 20 DELIB/GP
TREATY. PAGE 108 E2154

B54
MANGONE G.,A SHORT HISTORY OF INTERNATIONAL INT/ORG
ORGANIZATION. MOD/EUR USA+45 USA-45 WOR+45 WOR-45 INT/LAW
LAW LEGIS CREATE LEGIT ROUTINE RIGID/FLEX PWR

...JURID CONCPT OBS TIME/SEQ STERTYP GEN/LAWS UN
TOT/POP VAL/FREE 18/20. PAGE 68 E1359

L54
NICOLSON H.,"THE EVOLUTION OF DIPLOMATIC METHOD." RIGID/FLEX
CHRIST-17C EUR+WWI FRANCE FUT ITALY MEDIT-7 MOD/EUR METH/CNCPT
USA+45 USA-45 LAW NAT/G CREATE EDU/PROP LEGIT PEACE DIPLOM
ATTIT ORD/FREE RESPECT SOVEREIGN. PAGE 77 E1548

B55
KHADDURI M.,WAR AND PEACE IN THE LAW OF ISLAM. ISLAM
CONSTN CULTURE SOCIETY STRATA NAT/G PROVS SECT JURID
FORCES TOP/EX CREATE DOMIN EDU/PROP ADJUD COERCE PEACE
ATTIT RIGID/FLEX ALL/VALS...CONCPT TIME/SEQ TOT/POP WAR
VAL/FREE. PAGE 61 E1209

B56
WEIS P.,NATIONALITY AND STATELESSNESS IN INT/ORG
INTERNATIONAL LAW. UK WOR+45 WOR-45 LAW CONSTN SOVEREIGN
NAT/G DIPLOM EDU/PROP LEGIT ROUTINE RIGID/FLEX INT/LAW
...JURID RECORD CMN/WLTH 20. PAGE 105 E2109

B57
BERNS W.,FREEDOM, VIRTUE AND THE FIRST AMENDMENT. JURID
USA+45 USA-45 CONSTN INTELL JUDGE ADJUD RIGID/FLEX ORD/FREE
MORAL...CONCPT 20 AMEND/I. PAGE 11 E0211 CT/SYS
LAW

B57
BLOOMFIELD L.M.,EGYPT, ISRAEL AND THE GULF OF ISLAM
AQABA: IN INTERNATIONAL LAW. LAW NAT/G CONSULT INT/LAW
FORCES PLAN ECO/TAC ROUTINE COERCE ATTIT DRIVE UAR
PERCEPT PERSON RIGID/FLEX LOVE PWR WEALTH...GEOG
CONCPT MYTH TREND. PAGE 13 E0250

L58
INT. SOC. SCI. BULL.,"TECHNIQUES OF MEDIATION AND VOL/ASSN
CONCILIATION." EUR+WWI USA+45 SOCIETY INDUS INT/ORG DELIB/GP
LABOR NAT/G LEGIS DIPLOM EDU/PROP CHOOSE ATTIT INT/LAW
RIGID/FLEX...JURID CONCPT GEN/LAWS 20. PAGE 57
E1129

L59
COWAN T.A.,"A SYMPOSIUM ON GROUP INTERESTS AND THE ADJUD
LAW" USA+45 LAW MARKET LABOR PLAN INT/TRADE TAX PWR
RACE/REL RIGID/FLEX...JURID ANTHOL 20. PAGE 27 INGP/REL
E0528 CREATE

S59
PUGWASH CONFERENCE.,"ON BIOLOGICAL AND CHEMICAL ACT/RES
WARFARE." WOR+45 SOCIETY PROC/MFG INT/ORG FORCES BIO/SOC
EDU/PROP ADJUD RIGID/FLEX ORD/FREE PWR...DECISION WAR
PSY NEW/IDEA MATH VAL/FREE 20. PAGE 83 E1661 WEAPON

B60
STEIN E.,AMERICAN ENTERPRISE IN THE EUROPEAN COMMON MARKET
MARKET: A LEGAL PROFILE. EUR+WWI FUT USA+45 SOCIETY ADJUD
STRUCT ECO/DEV NAT/G VOL/ASSN CONSULT PLAN TEC/DEV INT/LAW
ECO/TAC INT/TRADE ADMIN ATTIT RIGID/FLEX PWR...MGT
NEW/IDEA STAT TREND COMPUT/IR SIMUL EEC 20. PAGE 93
E1867

B60
WOETZEL R.K.,THE INTERNATIONAL CONTROL OF AIRSPACE INT/ORG
AND OUTERSPACE. FUT WOR+45 AIR CONSTN STRUCT JURID
CONSULT PLAN TEC/DEV ADJUD RIGID/FLEX KNOWL SPACE
ORD/FREE PWR...TECHNIC GEOG MGT NEW/IDEA TREND INT/LAW
COMPUT/IR VAL/FREE 20 TREATY. PAGE 107 E2137

S60
THOMPSON K.W.,"MORAL PURPOSE IN FOREIGN POLICY: MORAL
REALITIES AND ILLUSIONS." WOR+45 WOR-45 LAW CULTURE JURID
SOCIETY INT/ORG PLAN ADJUD ADMIN COERCE RIGID/FLEX DIPLOM
SUPEGO KNOWL ORD/FREE PWR...SOC TREND SOC/EXP
TOT/POP 20. PAGE 96 E1921

S60
WRIGHT Q.,"LEGAL ASPECTS OF THE U-2 INCIDENT." COM PWR
USA+45 USSR STRUCT NAT/G FORCES PLAN TEC/DEV ADJUD POLICY
RIGID/FLEX MORAL ORD/FREE...DECISION INT/LAW JURID SPACE
PSY TREND GEN/LAWS COLD/WAR VAL/FREE 20 U-2.
PAGE 108 E2157

B61
ROBERTSON A.H.,THE LAW OF INTERNATIONAL RIGID/FLEX
INSTITUTIONS IN EUROPE. EUR+WWI MOD/EUR INT/ORG ORD/FREE
NAT/G VOL/ASSN DELIB/GP...JURID TIME/SEQ TOT/POP 20
TREATY. PAGE 85 E1704

S61
MILLER E.,"LEGAL ASPECTS OF UN ACTION IN THE INT/ORG
CONGO." AFR CULTURE ADMIN PEACE DRIVE RIGID/FLEX LEGIT
ORD/FREE...WELF/ST JURID OBS UN CONGO 20. PAGE 73
E1458

S61
RICHSTEIN A.R.,"LEGAL RULES IN NUCLEAR WEAPONS NUC/PWR
EMPLOYMENTS." FUT WOR+45 LAW SOCIETY FORCES PLAN TEC/DEV
WEAPON RIGID/FLEX...HEAL CONCPT TREND VAL/FREE 20. MORAL
PAGE 85 E1696 ARMS/CONT

B62
MCDOUGAL M.S.,THE PUBLIC ORDER OF THE OCEANS. ADJUD
WOR+45 WOR-45 SEA INT/ORG NAT/G CONSULT DELIB/GP ORD/FREE
DIPLOM LEGIT PEACE RIGID/FLEX...GEOG INT/LAW JURID
RECORD TOT/POP 20 TREATY. PAGE 70 E1407

B62
THOMPSON K.W.,AMERICAN DIPLOMACY AND EMERGENT NAT/G
PATTERNS. USA+45 USA-45 WOR+45 WOR-45 LAW DELIB/GP BAL/PWR
FORCES TOP/EX DIPLOM ATTIT DRIVE RIGID/FLEX
ORD/FREE PWR SOVEREIGN...POLICY 20. PAGE 96 E1922

L62
STEIN E.,"MR HAMMARSKJOLD, THE CHARTER LAW AND THE CONCPT
FUTURE ROLE OF THE UNITED NATIONS SECRETARY- BIOG
GENERAL." WOR+45 CONSTN INT/ORG DELIB/GP FORCES
TOP/EX BAL/PWR LEGIT ROUTINE RIGID/FLEX PWR
...POLICY JURID OBS STERTYP UN COLD/WAR 20
HAMMARSK/D. PAGE 93 E1869

S62
BIERZANECK R.,"LA NON-RECONAISSANCE ET LE DROIT EDU/PROP
INTERNATIONAL CONTEMPORAIN." EUR+WWI FUT WOR+45 LAW JURID
ECO/DEV ATTIT RIGID/FLEX...CONCPT TIME/SEQ TOT/POP DIPLOM
20. PAGE 12 E0228 INT/LAW

S62
FINKELSTEIN L.S.,"THE UNITED NATIONS AND INT/ORG
ORGANIZATIONS FOR CONTROL OF ARMAMENT." FUT WOR+45 PWR
VOL/ASSN DELIB/GP TOP/EX CREATE EDU/PROP LEGIT ARMS/CONT
ADJUD NUC/PWR ATTIT RIGID/FLEX ORD/FREE...POLICY
DECISION CONCPT OBS TREND GEN/LAWS TOT/POP
COLD/WAR. PAGE 38 E0752

S62
MCWHINNEY E.,"CO-EXISTENCE, THE CUBA CRISIS, AND CONCPT
COLD WAR-INTERNATIONAL WAR." CUBA USA+45 USSR INT/LAW
WOR+45 NAT/G TOP/EX BAL/PWR DIPLOM DOMIN LEGIT
PEACE RIGID/FLEX ORD/FREE...STERTYP COLD/WAR 20.
PAGE 71 E1427

S62
THOMPSON D.,"THE UNITED KINGDOM AND THE TREATY OF ADJUD
ROME." EUR+WWI INT/ORG NAT/G DELIB/GP LEGIS JURID
INT/TRADE RIGID/FLEX...CONCPT EEC PARLIAMENT
CMN/WLTH 20. PAGE 96 E1918

B63
BOWETT D.W.,THE LAW OF INTERNATIONAL INSTITUTIONS. INT/ORG
WOR+45 WOR-45 CONSTN DELIB/GP EX/STRUC JUDGE ADJUD
EDU/PROP LEGIT CT/SYS EXEC ROUTINE RIGID/FLEX DIPLOM
ORD/FREE PWR...JURID CONCPT ORG/CHARTS GEN/METH
LEAGUE/NAT OAS OEEC 20 UN. PAGE 14 E0277

B63
HALEY A.G.,SPACE LAW AND GOVERNMENT. FUT USA+45 INT/ORG
WOR+45 SOCIETY ACT/RES CREATE RIGID/FLEX LAW
ORD/FREE PWR SOVEREIGN...POLICY JURID CONCPT CHARTS SPACE
VAL/FREE 20. PAGE 49 E0980

B63
PRYOR F.L.,THE COMMUNIST FOREIGN TRADE SYSTEM. COM ATTIT
CZECHOSLVK GERMANY YUGOSLAVIA LAW ECO/DEV DIST/IND ECO/TAC
POL/PAR PLAN DOMIN TOTALISM DRIVE RIGID/FLEX WEALTH
...STAT STAND/INT CHARTS 20. PAGE 83 E1657

L63
ROSE R.,"COMPARATIVE STUDIES IN POLITICAL FINANCE: FINAN
A SYMPOSIUM." ASIA EUR+WWI S/ASIA LAW CULTURE POL/PAR
DELIB/GP LEGIS ACT/RES ECO/TAC EDU/PROP CHOOSE
ATTIT RIGID/FLEX SUPEGO PWR SKILL WEALTH...STAT
ANTHOL VAL/FREE. PAGE 85 E1714

S63
FRIEDMANN W.G.,"THE USES OF 'GENERAL PRINCIPLES' IN LAW
THE DEVELOPMENT OF INTERNATIONAL LAW." WOR+45 NAT/G INT/LAW
DIPLOM INT/TRADE LEGIT ROUTINE RIGID/FLEX ORD/FREE INT/ORG
...JURID CONCPT STERTYP GEN/METH 20. PAGE 41 E0804

S63
GIRAUD E.,"L'INTERDICTION DU RECOURS A LA FORCE, LA INT/ORG
THEORIE ET LA PRATIQUE DES NATIONS UNIES." ALGERIA FORCES
COM CUBA HUNGARY WOR+45 ADJUD TOTALISM ATTIT DIPLOM
RIGID/FLEX PWR...POLICY JURID CONCPT UN 20 CONGO.
PAGE 44 E0872

S63
TALLON D.,"L'ETUDE DU DROIT COMPARE COMME MOYEN DE INT/ORG
RECHERCHER LES MATIERES SUSCEPTIBLES D'UNIFICATION JURID
INTERNATIONALE." WOR+45 LAW SOCIETY VOL/ASSN INT/LAW

CONSULT LEGIT CT/SYS RIGID/FLEX KNOWL 20. PAGE 95
E1906

B64

ANDERSON J.W.,EISENHOWER, BROWNELL, AND THE
CONGRESS - THE TANGLED ORIGINS OF THE CIVIL RIGHTS
BILL OF 1956-1957. USA+45 POL/PAR LEGIS CREATE
PROB/SOLV LOBBY GOV/REL RIGID/FLEX...NEW/IDEA 20
EISNHWR/DD CONGRESS BROWNELL/H CIV/RIGHTS. PAGE 5
E0090
          LAW
          CONSTN
          POLICY
          NAT/G

B64

CLINARD M.B.,ANOMIE AND DEVIANT BEHAVIOR: A
DISCUSSION AND CRITIQUE. SOCIETY FACE/GP CRIME
STRANGE ATTIT BIO/SOC DISPL RIGID/FLEX HEALTH...PSY
CONCPT BIBLIOG 20 MERTON/R. PAGE 23 E0456
          PERSON
          ANOMIE
          KIN
          NEIGH

B64

WRIGHT G.,RURAL REVOLUTION IN FRANCE: THE PEASANTRY
IN THE TWENTIETH CENTURY. EUR+WWI MOD/EUR LAW
CULTURE AGRI POL/PAR DELIB/GP LEGIS ECO/TAC
EDU/PROP COERCE CHOOSE ATTIT RIGID/FLEX HEALTH
...STAT CENSUS CHARTS VAL/FREE 20. PAGE 107 E2148
          PWR
          STRATA
          FRANCE
          REV

L64

BERKS R.N.,"THE US AND WEAPONS CONTROL." WOR+45 LAW
INT/ORG NAT/G LEGIS EXEC COERCE PEACE ATTIT
RIGID/FLEX ALL/VALS PWR...POLICY TOT/POP 20.
PAGE 11 E0204
          USA+45
          PLAN
          ARMS/CONT

S64

BAKER H.R.,"INMATE SELF-GOVERNMENT." ACT/RES CREATE
CONTROL PARTIC ATTIT RIGID/FLEX QU. PAGE 7 E0141
          PUB/INST
          CRIME
          INGP/REL
          REPRESENT

B65

VONGLAHN G.,LAW AMONG NATIONS: AN INTRODUCTION TO
PUBLIC INTERNATIONAL LAW. UNIV WOR+45 LAW INT/ORG
NAT/G LEGIT EXEC RIGID/FLEX...CONCPT TIME/SEQ
GEN/LAWS UN TOT/POP 20. PAGE 104 E2084
          CONSTN
          JURID
          INT/LAW

S65

GROSS L.,"PROBLEMS OF INTERNATIONAL ADJUDICATION
AND COMPLIANCE WITH INTERNATIONAL LAW: SOME SIMPLE
SOLUTIONS." WOR+45 SOCIETY NAT/G DOMIN LEGIT ADJUD
CT/SYS RIGID/FLEX HEALTH PWR...JURID NEW/IDEA
COLD/WAR 20. PAGE 48 E0951
          LAW
          METH/CNCPT
          INT/LAW

S65

KHOURI F.J.,"THE JORDON RIVER CONTROVERSY." LAW
SOCIETY ECO/UNDEV AGRI FINAN INDUS SECT FORCES
ACT/RES PLAN TEC/DEV ECO/TAC EDU/PROP COERCE ATTIT
DRIVE PERCEPT RIGID/FLEX ALL/VALS...GEOG SOC MYTH
WORK. PAGE 61 E1212
          ISLAM
          INT/ORG
          ISRAEL
          JORDAN

S68

DUPRE L.,"TILL DEATH DO US PART?" UNIV FAM INSPECT
LEGIT ADJUD SANCTION PERS/REL ANOMIE RIGID/FLEX SEX
...JURID IDEA/COMP 20 CHURCH/STA BIBLE CANON/LAW
CIVIL/LAW. PAGE 34 E0666
          MARRIAGE
          CATH
          LAW

RIKER W.H. E1700

RIO/PACT....RIO PACT

RIOT....RIOTS; SEE ALSO CROWD

RIPS R.E. E0281

RISK....SEE ALSO GAMBLE

B37

THOMPSON J.W.,SECRET DIPLOMACY: A RECORD OF
ESPIONAGE AND DOUBLE-DEALING: 1500-1815. CHRIST-17C
MOD/EUR NAT/G WRITING RISK MORAL...ANTHOL BIBLIOG
16/19 ESPIONAGE. PAGE 96 E1920
          DIPLOM
          CRIME

B59

HOBSBAWM E.J.,PRIMITIVE REBELS; STUDIES IN ARCHAIC
FORMS OF SOCIAL MOVEMENT IN THE 19TH AND 20TH
CENTURIES. ITALY SPAIN CULTURE VOL/ASSN RISK CROWD
GP/REL INGP/REL ISOLAT TOTALISM...PSY SOC 18/20.
PAGE 53 E1058
          SOCIETY
          CRIME
          REV
          GUERRILLA

B62

STERN A.C.,AIR POLLUTION (2 VOLS.). LAW INDUS
PROB/SOLV TEC/DEV INSPECT RISK BIO/SOC HABITAT
...OBS/ENVIR TESTS SAMP 20 POLLUTION. PAGE 93 E1871
          AIR
          OP/RES
          CONTROL
          HEALTH

B64

BOGEN J.I.,FINANCIAL HANDBOOK (4TH ED.). UNIV LAW
PLAN TAX RISK 20. PAGE 13 E0257
          FINAN
          DICTIONARY

S65

WRIGHT Q.,"THE ESCALATION OF INTERNATIONAL
CONFLICTS." WOR+45 WOR-45 FORCES DIPLOM RISK COST
ATTIT ALL/VALS...INT/LAW QUANT STAT NAT/COMP.
PAGE 108 E2160
          WAR
          PERCEPT
          PREDICT
          MATH

B67

SLATER J.,THE OAS AND UNITED STATES FOREIGN POLICY.
KOREA L/A+17C USA+45 VOL/ASSN RISK COERCE PEACE
ORD/FREE MARXISM...TREND 20 OAS. PAGE 92 E1838
          INT/ORG
          DIPLOM
          ALL/IDEOS
          ADJUD

S67

DOUTY H.M.," REFERENCE TO DEVELOPING COUNTRIES."
JAMAICA MALAYSIA UK WOR+45 LAW FINAN ACT/RES BUDGET
CAP/ISM ECO/TAC TARIFFS RISK EFFICIENCY PROFIT
...CHARTS 20. PAGE 33 E0646
          TAX
          ECO/UNDEV
          NAT/G

S67

READ J.S.,"CENSORED." UGANDA CONSTN INTELL SOCIETY
NAT/G DIPLOM PRESS WRITING ADJUD ADMIN COLONIAL
RISK...IDEA/COMP 20. PAGE 84 E1675
          EDU/PROP
          AFR
          CREATE

RITCHIE/JM....JESS M. RITCHIE

RITSCHL/H....HANS RITSCHL

RITUAL....RITUALS AND SYMBOLIC CEREMONIES; SEE ALSO WORSHIP,
SECT

RKFDV....REICHSKOMMISSARIAT FUR DIE FESTIGUNG DEUTSCHEN
VOLKSTUMS

RKO....R.K.O.

ROBERT H.M. E1701

ROBERT J. E1702

ROBERTS H.L. E1703

ROBERTSON A.H. E1704,E1705

ROBESPR/M....MAXIMILIAN FRANCOIS ROBESPIERRE

ROBINSN/JH....JAMES HARVEY ROBINSON

ROBINSON R.D. E1336,E1706

ROBINSON W.S. E1707

ROBINSON/H....HENRY ROBINSON

ROBSON W.A. E1708

ROCHE J.P. E1709,E1710

RODBRTUS/C....CARL RODBERTUS

ROLE....ROLE, REFERENCE GROUP, CROSS-PRESSURES

B09

JUSTINIAN,THE DIGEST (DIGESTA CORPUS JURIS CIVILIS)
(2 VOLS.) (TRANS. BY C. H. MONRO). ROMAN/EMP LAW
FAM LOC/G LEGIS EDU/PROP CONTROL MARRIAGE OWN ROLE
CIVIL/LAW. PAGE 59 E1177
          JURID
          CT/SYS
          NAT/G
          STRATA

N19

THE REGIONAL DIRECTOR AND THE PRESS (PAMPHLET).
USA+45 COM/IND LOBBY ROLE 20 NLRB CINCINNATI
BILL/RIGHT. PAGE 2 E0031
          PRESS
          LABOR
          ORD/FREE
          EDU/PROP

N19

CARPER E.T.,LOBBYING AND THE NATURAL GAS BILL
(PAMPHLET). USA+45 SERV/IND BARGAIN PAY DRIVE ROLE
WEALTH 20 CONGRESS SENATE EISNHWR/DD. PAGE 20 E0389
          LOBBY
          ADJUD
          TRIBUTE
          NAT/G

N19

HOGARTY R.A.,NEW JERSEY FARMERS AND MIGRANT HOUSING
RULES (PAMPHLET). USA+45 LAW ELITES FACE/GP LABOR
PROF/ORG LOBBY PERS/REL RIGID/FLEX ROLE 20
NEW/JERSEY. PAGE 53 E1067
          AGRI
          PROVS
          WORKER
          HEALTH

B30

BURLAMAQUI J.J.,PRINCIPLES OF NATURAL AND POLITIC
LAW (2 VOLS.) (1747-51). EX/STRUC LEGIS AGREE
CT/SYS CHOOSE ROLE SOVEREIGN 18 NATURL/LAW. PAGE 17
E0342
          LAW
          NAT/G
          ORD/FREE
          CONCPT

B33

ENSOR R.C.K.,COURTS AND JUDGES IN FRANCE, GERMANY,
AND ENGLAND. FRANCE GERMANY UK LAW PROB/SOLV ADMIN
ROUTINE CRIME ROLE...METH/COMP 20 CIVIL/LAW.
PAGE 35 E0692
          CT/SYS
          EX/STRUC
          ADJUD
          NAT/COMP

S38

CLEMMER D.,"LEADERSHIP PHENOMENA IN A PRISON COMMUNITY." NEIGH PLAN CHOOSE PERSON ROLE...OBS INT. PAGE 23 E0452
PUB/INST
CRIMLGY
LEAD
CLIENT

B48

SLESSER H.,THE ADMINISTRATION OF THE LAW. UK CONSTN LAW EX/STRUC OP/RES PROB/SOLV CRIME ROLE...DECISION METH/COMP 20 CIVIL/LAW ENGLSH/LAW CIVIL/LAW. PAGE 92 E1839
LAW
CT/SYS
ADJUD

B50

FRANK J.,COURTS ON TRIAL: MYTH AND REALITY IN AMERICAN JUSTICE. LAW CONSULT PROB/SOLV EDU/PROP ADJUD ROUTINE ROLE ORD/FREE...GEN/LAWS T 20. PAGE 40 E0788
JURID
CT/SYS
MYTH
CONSTN

B54

CAPLOW T.,THE SOCIOLOGY OF WORK. USA+45 USA-45 STRATA MARKET FAM GP/REL INGP/REL ALL/VALS ...DECISION STAT BIBLIOG SOC/INTEG 20. PAGE 19 E0375
LABOR
WORKER
INDUS
ROLE

B55

CAVAN R.S.,CRIMINOLOGY (2ND ED.). USA+45 LAW FAM PUB/INST FORCES PLAN WAR AGE/Y PERSON ROLE SUPEGO ...CHARTS 20 FBI. PAGE 21 E0409
DRIVE
CRIMLGY
CONTROL
METH/COMP

B55

WHEARE K.C.,GOVERNMENT BY COMMITTEE; AN ESSAY ON THE BRITISH CONSTITUTION. UK NAT/G LEGIS INSPECT CONFER ADJUD ADMIN CONTROL TASK EFFICIENCY ROLE POPULISM 20. PAGE 106 E2116
DELIB/GP
CONSTN
LEAD
GP/COMP

B55

ZABEL O.H.,GOD AND CAESAR IN NEBRASKA: A STUDY OF LEGAL RELATIONSHIP OF CHURCH AND STATE, 1854-1954. TAX GIVE ADMIN CONTROL GP/REL ROLE...GP/COMP 19/20 NEBRASKA. PAGE 108 E2168
SECT
PROVS
LAW
EDU/PROP

S55

CARR C.,"LEGISLATIVE CONTROL OF ADMINISTRATIVE RULES AND REGULATIONS: PARLIAMENTARY SUPERVISION IN BRITAIN." DELIB/GP CONTROL ROLE PWR PARLIAMENT. PAGE 20 E0392
EXEC
REPRESENT
JURID

B57

COOPER F.E.,THE LAWYER AND ADMINISTRATIVE AGENCIES. USA+45 CLIENT LAW PROB/SOLV CT/SYS PERSON ROLE. PAGE 25 E0500
CONSULT
ADMIN
ADJUD
DELIB/GP

S57

FRANKFURTER F.,"THE SUPREME COURT IN THE MIRROR OF JUSTICES" (BMR)" USA+45 USA-45 INTELL INSPECT EFFICIENCY ROLE KNOWL MORAL 18/20 SUPREME/CT. PAGE 40 E0792
EDU/PROP
ADJUD
CT/SYS
PERSON

B58

HAND L.,THE BILL OF RIGHTS. USA+45 USA-45 CHIEF LEGIS BAL/PWR ROLE PWR 18/20 SUPREME/CT CONGRESS AMEND/V PRESIDENT AMEND/XIV. PAGE 50 E0994
CONSTN
JURID
ORD/FREE
CT/SYS

B58

MASON A.T.,THE SUPREME COURT FROM TAFT TO WARREN. EX/STRUC LEGIS ROLE 20 SUPREME/CT TAFT/WH HUGHES/CE STONE/HF. PAGE 69 E1376
CT/SYS
JURID
ADJUD

S58

CRESSEY D.R.,"ACHIEVEMENT OF AN UNSTATED ORGANIZATIONAL GOAL: AN OBSERVATION ON PRISONS." OP/RES PROB/SOLV PERS/REL ANOMIE ATTIT ROLE RESPECT CRIMLGY. PAGE 28 E0546
PUB/INST
CLIENT
NEIGH
INGP/REL

C58

BRODEN T.F.,"CONGRESSIONAL COMMITTEE REPORTS: THEIR ROLE AND HISTORY" USA-45 PARL/PROC ROLE. PAGE 15 E0303
LAW
DELIB/GP
LEGIS
DEBATE

B59

FELLMANN D.,THE LIMITS OF FREEDOM. USA+45 USA-45 NAT/G SECT ROLE ORD/FREE WORSHIP 18/20 FREE/SPEE. PAGE 37 E0734
CONCPT
JURID
CONSTN

B59

WILDNER H.,DIE TECHNIK DER DIPLOMATIE. TOP/EX ROLE ORD/FREE...INT/LAW JURID IDEA/COMP NAT/COMP 20. PAGE 106 E2122
DIPLOM
POLICY
DELIB/GP
NAT/G

S59

BELL D.,"THE RACKET RIDDEN LONGSHOREMEN" (BMR)" USA+45 SEA WORKER MURDER ROLE...SOC 20 NEWYORK/C. PAGE 9 E0182
CRIME
LABOR
DIST/IND
ELITES

S59

DWYER R.J.,"THE ADMINISTRATIVE ROLE IN DESEGREGATION." USA+45 LAW PROB/SOLV LEAD RACE/REL ISOLAT STRANGE ROLE...POLICY SOC/INTEG MISSOURI NEGRO CIV/RIGHTS. PAGE 34 E0668
ADMIN
SCHOOL
DISCRIM
ATTIT

B60

HANBURY H.G.,ENGLISH COURTS OF LAW. UK EX/STRUC LEGIS CRIME ROLE 12/20 COMMON/LAW ENGLSH/LAW. PAGE 50 E0993
JURID
CT/SYS
CONSTN
GOV/REL

S60

MACKINNON F.,"THE UNIVERSITY: COMMUNITY OR UTILITY?" CLIENT CONSTN INTELL FINAN NAT/G NEIGH EDU/PROP PARTIC REPRESENT ROLE. PAGE 67 E1343
ACADEM
MGT
CONTROL
SERV/IND

B61

TOMPKINS D.C.,CONFLICT OF INTEREST IN THE FEDERAL GOVERNMENT: A BIBLIOGRAPHY. USA+45 EX/STRUC LEGIS ADJUD ADMIN CRIME CONGRESS PRESIDENT. PAGE 96 E1932
BIBLIOG
ROLE
NAT/G
LAW

B62

DIESING P.,REASON IN SOCIETY; FIVE TYPES OF DECISIONS AND THEIR SOCIAL CONDITIONS. SOCIETY STRUCT LABOR CREATE TEC/DEV BARGAIN ADJUD ROLE ...JURID BIBLIOG 20. PAGE 31 E0625
RATIONAL
METH/COMP
DECISION
CONCPT

B62

SHAW C.,LEGAL PROBLEMS IN INTERNATIONAL TRADE AND INVESTMENT. WOR+45 ECO/DEV ECO/UNDEV MARKET DIPLOM TAX INCOME ROLE...ANTHOL BIBLIOG 20 TREATY UN IMF GATT. PAGE 91 E1816
INT/LAW
INT/TRADE
FINAN
ECO/TAC

N62

TWENTIETH CENTURY FUND,ONE MAN - ONE VOTE (PAMPHLET). USA+45 CONSTN CONFER CT/SYS REGION CONSEN FEDERAL ROLE...CENSUS 20 CONGRESS. PAGE 97 E1947
APPORT
LEGIS
REPRESENT
PROVS

B63

GINZBERG E.,DEMOCRATIC VALUES AND THE RIGHTS OF MANAGEMENT. LAW CONSTN REPRESENT GP/REL ROLE PWR RESPECT POLICY. PAGE 44 E0870
LABOR
MGT
DELIB/GP
ADJUD

B63

SCOTT A.M.,THE SUPREME COURT V. THE CONSTITUTION. USA+45 CONTROL ATTIT ROLE...POLICY CONCPT 20 SUPREME/CT. PAGE 90 E1796
PWR
CT/SYS
NAT/G
CONSTN

B63

YOUNGER R.D.,THE PEOPLE'S PANEL: THE GRAND JURY IN THE UNITED STATES, 1634-1941. USA+45 LAW LEGIT CONTROL TASK GP/REL ROLE...TREND 17/20 GRAND/JURY. PAGE 108 E2166
CT/SYS
JURID
CONSTN
LOC/G

B64

FISK W.M.,ADMINISTRATIVE PROCEDURE IN A REGULATORY AGENCY: THE CAB AND THE NEW YORK-CHICAGO CASE (PAMPHLET). USA+45 DIST/IND ADMIN CONTROL LOBBY GP/REL ROLE ORD/FREE NEWYORK/C CHICAGO CAB. PAGE 38 E0758
SERV/IND
ECO/DEV
AIR
JURID

B64

SCHUBERT G.A.,JUDICIAL BEHAVIOR: A READER IN THEORY AND RESEARCH. POL/PAR CT/SYS ROLE SUPEGO PWR ...DECISION JURID REGRESS CHARTS SIMUL ANTHOL 20. PAGE 89 E1782
ATTIT
PERSON
ADJUD
ACT/RES

B64

STANGER R.J.,ESSAYS ON INTERVENTION. PLAN PROB/SOLV BAL/PWR ADJUD COERCE WAR ROLE PWR...INT/LAW CONCPT 20 UN INTERVENT. PAGE 93 E1865
SOVEREIGN
DIPLOM
POLICY
LEGIT

B65

FALK R.A.,THE AFTERMATH OF SABBATINO: BACKGROUND PAPERS AND PROCEEDINGS OF SEVENTH HAMMARSKJOLD FORUM. USA+45 LAW ACT/RES ADJUD ROLE...BIBLIOG 20 EXPROPRIAT SABBATINO HARLAN/JM. PAGE 36 E0718
SOVEREIGN
CT/SYS
INT/LAW
OWN

B65

GINSBERG M.,ON JUSTICE IN SOCIETY. LAW EDU/PROP LEGIT CT/SYS INGP/REL PRIVIL RATIONAL ATTIT MORAL ORD/FREE...JURID 20. PAGE 44 E0867
ADJUD
ROLE
CONCPT

HARTUNG F.E..CRIME, LAW, AND SOCIETY. LAW PUB/INST
CRIME PERS/REL AGE/Y BIO/SOC PERSON ROLE SUPEGO
...LING GP/COMP GEN/LAWS 20. PAGE 50 E1004

B65
PERCEPT
CRIMLGY
DRIVE
CONTROL

ISORNI J..LES CAS DE CONSCIENCE DE L'AVOCAT.
FRANCE LAW ACT/RES CT/SYS PARTIC ROLE MORAL 20.
PAGE 57 E1138

B65
SUPEGO
JURID
CRIME

KRISLOV S..THE SUPREME COURT IN THE POLITICAL
PROCESS. USA+45 LAW SOCIETY STRUCT WORKER ADMIN
ROLE...JURID SOC 20 SUPREME/CT. PAGE 62 E1231

B65
ADJUD
DECISION
CT/SYS
CONSTN

MISHKIN P.J..ON LAW IN COURTS. USA+45 LEGIS CREATE
ROLE 20. PAGE 73 E1468

B65
LAW
CT/SYS
ADJUD
CONSTN

CAMPBELL E..PARLIAMENTARY PRIVILEGE IN AUSTRALIA.
UK LAW CONSTN COLONIAL ROLE ORD/FREE SOVEREIGN
18/20 COMMONWLTH AUSTRAL FREE/SPEE PARLIAMENT.
PAGE 19 E0370

B66
LEGIS
PARL/PROC
JURID
PRIVIL

KUNSTLER W.M.."DEEP IN MY HEART" USA+45 LAW
PROF/ORG SECT LOBBY PARTIC CROWD DISCRIM ROLE
...BIOG 20 KING/MAR/L NEGRO CIV/RIGHTS SOUTH/US.
PAGE 62 E1233

B66
CT/SYS
RACE/REL
ADJUD
CONSULT

MENDELSON W..JUSTICES BLACK AND FRANKFURTER:
CONFLICT IN THE COURT (2ND ED.). NAT/G PROVS
PROB/SOLV BAL/PWR CONTROL FEDERAL ISOLAT ANOMIE
ORD/FREE...DECISION 20 SUPREME/CT BLACK/HL
FRANKFUR/F. PAGE 72 E1439

B66
JURID
ADJUD
IDEA/COMP
ROLE

BACHELDER G.L..THE LITERATURE OF FEDERALISM: A
SELECTED BIBLIOGRAPHY (REV ED) (A PAMPHLET). USA+45
USA-45 WOR+45 WOR-45 LAW CONSTN PROVS ADMIN CT/SYS
GOV/REL ROLE...CONCPT 19/20. PAGE 7 E0126

N66
BIBLIOG
FEDERAL
NAT/G
LOC/G

BERNSTEIN S..ALTERNATIVES TO VIOLENCE: ALIENATED
YOUTH AND RIOTS, RACE AND POVERTY. MUNIC PUB/INST
SCHOOL INGP/REL RACE/REL UTOPIA DRIVE HABITAT ROLE
WEALTH...INT 20. PAGE 11 E0215

B67
AGE/Y
SOC/WK
NEIGH
CRIME

FRIENDLY A..CRIME AND PUBLICITY. TV CT/SYS SUPEGO
20. PAGE 41 E0811

B67
PRESS
CRIME
ROLE
LAW

HEWITT W.H..ADMINISTRATION OF CRIMINAL JUSTICE IN
NEW YORK. LAW PROB/SOLV ADJUD ADMIN...CRIMLGY
CHARTS T 20 NEW/YORK. PAGE 52 E1035

B67
CRIME
ROLE
CT/SYS
FORCES

MARTIN L.W..THE SEA IN MODERN STRATEGY. LAW ECO/TAC
WAR. PAGE 69 E1374

B67
ROLE
PWR
NUC/PWR
DIPLOM

RAMUNDO B.A..PEACEFUL COEXISTENCE: INTERNATIONAL
LAW IN THE BUILDING OF COMMUNISM. USSR INT/ORG
DIPLOM COLONIAL ARMS/CONT ROLE SOVEREIGN...POLICY
METH/COMP NAT/COMP BIBLIOG. PAGE 83 E1673

B67
INT/LAW
PEACE
MARXISM
METH/CNCPT

BLUMBERG A.S.."THE PRACTICE OF LAW AS CONFIDENCE
GAME; ORGANIZATIONAL COOPTATION OF A PROFESSION."
USA+45 CLIENT SOCIETY CONSULT ROLE JURID. PAGE 13
E0252

L67
CT/SYS
ADJUD
GP/REL
ADMIN

KETCHAM O.W.."GUIDELINES FROM GAULT: REVOLUTIONARY
REQUIREMENTS AND REAPPRAISAL." LAW CONSTN CREATE
LEGIT ROUTINE SANCTION CRIME DISCRIM PRIVIL ROLE
...JURID NEW/IDEA 20 SUPREME/CT. PAGE 60 E1208

S67
ADJUD
AGE/Y
CT/SYS

MATTHEWS R.O.."THE SUEZ CANAL DISPUTE* A CASE STUDY
IN PEACEFUL SETTLEMENT." FRANCE ISRAEL UAR UK NAT/G
CONTROL LEAD COERCE WAR NAT/LISM ROLE ORD/FREE PWR
...INT/LAW UN 20. PAGE 69 E1389

S67
PEACE
DIPLOM
ADJUD

MITCHELL J.D.B.."THE CONSTITUTIONAL IMPLICATIONS OF
JUDICIAL CONTROL OF THE ADMINISTRATION IN THE
UNITED KINGDOM." UK LAW ADJUD ADMIN GOV/REL ROLE
...GP/COMP 20. PAGE 74 E1474

S67
CONSTN
CT/SYS
CONTROL
EX/STRUC

MORENO F.J.."THE SPANISH COLONIAL SYSTEM: A
FUNCTIONAL APPROACH." SPAIN WOR-45 LAW CHIEF DIPLOM
ADJUD CIVMIL/REL AUTHORIT ROLE PWR...CONCPT 17/20.
PAGE 74 E1492

S67
COLONIAL
CONTROL
NAT/G
OP/RES

RAI H.."DISTRICT MAGISTRATE AND POLICE
SUPERINTENDENT IN INDIA: THE CONTROVERSY OF DUAL
CONTROL" INDIA LAW PROVS ADMIN PWR 19/20. PAGE 83
E1669

S67
STRUCT
CONTROL
ROLE
FORCES

ROMAN CATHOLIC....SEE CATH, CATHISM

ROMAN/EMP....ROMAN EMPIRE

JUSTINIAN,THE DIGEST (DIGESTA CORPUS JURIS CIVILIS)
(2 VOLS.) (TRANS. BY C. H. MONRO). ROMAN/EMP LAW
FAM LOC/G LEGIS EDU/PROP CONTROL MARRIAGE OWN ROLE
CIVIL/LAW. PAGE 59 E1177

B09
JURID
CT/SYS
NAT/G
STRATA

PHILLIPSON C..THE INTERNATIONAL LAW AND CUSTOM OF
ANCIENT GREECE AND ROME. MEDIT-7 UNIV INTELL
SOCIETY STRUCT NAT/G LEGIS EXEC PERSON...CONCPT OBS
CON/ANAL ROM/EMP. PAGE 80 E1614

B11
INT/ORG
LAW
INT/LAW

MCILWAIN C.H..CONSTITUTIONALISM: ANCIENT AND
MODERN. USA+45 ROMAN/EMP LAW CHIEF LEGIS CT/SYS
GP/REL ORD/FREE SOVEREIGN...POLICY TIME/SEQ
ROMAN/REP EUROPE. PAGE 71 E1419

B47
CONSTN
NAT/G
PARL/PROC
GOV/COMP

CORWIN E.S..LIBERTY AGAINST GOVERNMENT. UK USA-45
ROMAN/EMP LAW CONSTN PERS/REL OWN ATTIT 1/20
ROMAN/LAW ENGLSH/LAW AMEND/XIV. PAGE 26 E0513

B48
JURID
ORD/FREE
CONCPT

ALIGHIERI D..ON WORLD GOVERNMENT. ROMAN/EMP LAW
SOCIETY INT/ORG NAT/G POL/PAR ADJUD WAR GP/REL
PEACE WORSHIP 15 WORLDUNITY DANTE. PAGE 4 E0067

B57
POLICY
CONCPT
DIPLOM
SECT

BROOKES E.H..THE COMMONWEALTH TODAY. UK ROMAN/EMP
INT/ORG RACE/REL NAT/LISM SOVEREIGN...TREND
SOC/INTEG 20. PAGE 16 E0307

B59
FEDERAL
DIPLOM
JURID
IDEA/COMP

GRASMUCK E.L..COERCITIO STAAT UND KIRCHE IM
DONATISTENSTREIT. CHRIST-17C ROMAN/EMP LAW PROVS
DEBATE PERSON SOVEREIGN...JURID CONCPT 4/5
AUGUSTINE CHURCH/STA ROMAN/LAW. PAGE 45 E0898

B64
GP/REL
NAT/G
SECT
COERCE

COLEMAN-NORTON P.R..ROMAN STATE AND CHRISTIAN
CHURCH: A COLLECTION OF LEGAL DOCUMENTS TO A.D. 535
(3 VOLS.). CHRIST-17C ROMAN/EMP...ANTHOL DICTIONARY
6 CHRISTIAN CHURCH/STA. PAGE 24 E0473

B66
GP/REL
NAT/G
SECT
LAW

FEINE H.E..REICH UND KIRCHE. CHRIST-17C MOD/EUR
ROMAN/EMP LAW CHOOSE ATTIT 10/19 CHURCH/STA
ROMAN/LAW. PAGE 37 E0728

B66
JURID
SECT
NAT/G
GP/REL

MACMULLEN R..ENEMIES OF THE ROMAN EMPIRE: TREASON,
UNREST, AND ALIENATION IN THE EMPIRE. ROMAN/EMP
MUNIC CONTROL LEAD ATTIT PERSON MYSTISM...PHIL/SCI
BIBLIOG. PAGE 67 E1345

B66
CRIME
ADJUD
MORAL
SOCIETY

ROMAN/LAW....ROMAN LAW

BRYCE J..STUDIES IN HISTORY AND JURISPRUDENCE (2
VOLS.). ICELAND SOUTH/AFR UK LAW PROB/SOLV
SOVEREIGN...PHIL/SCI NAT/COMP ROME/ANC ROMAN/LAW.
PAGE 16 E0321

B01
IDEA/COMP
CONSTN
JURID

SCHULZ F..PRINCIPLES OF ROMAN LAW. CONSTN FAM NAT/G
DOMIN CONTROL CT/SYS CRIME ISOLAT ATTIT ORD/FREE
PWR...JURID ROME/ANC ROMAN/LAW. PAGE 89 E1783

B36
LAW
LEGIS
ADJUD
CONCPT

CORWIN E.S.,LIBERTY AGAINST GOVERNMENT. UK USA-45 **JURID**
ROMAN/EMP LAW CONSTN PERS/REL OWN ATTIT 1/20 **ORD/FREE**
ROMAN/LAW ENGLSH/LAW AMEND/XIV. PAGE 26 E0513 **CONCPT**
B48

CORWIN E.S.,LIBERTY AGAINST GOVERNMENT: THE RISE, **CONCPT**
FLOWERING AND DECLINE OF A FAMOUS JURIDICAL **ORD/FREE**
CONCEPT. LEGIS ADJUD CT/SYS SANCTION GOV/REL **JURID**
FEDERAL CONSERVE NEW/LIB...OLD/LIB 18/20 ROMAN/LAW **CONSTN**
COMMON/LAW. PAGE 26 E0514
B48

BUCKLAND W.W.,ROMAN LAW AND COMMON LAW; A **IDEA/COMP**
COMPARISON IN OUTLINE (2ND REV. ED.). UK FAM LEGIT **LAW**
AGREE CT/SYS OWN...JURID ROMAN/REP ROMAN/LAW **ADJUD**
COMMON/LAW. PAGE 17 E0325 **CONCPT**
B52

GRASMUCK E.L.,COERCITIO STAAT UND KIRCHE IM **GP/REL**
DONATISTENSTREIT. CHRIST-17C ROMAN/EMP LAW PROVS **NAT/G**
DEBATE PERSON SOVEREIGN...JURID CONCPT 4/5 **SECT**
AUGUSTINE CHURCH/STA ROMAN/LAW. PAGE 45 E0898 **COERCE**
B64

FEINE H.E.,REICH UND KIRCHE. CHRIST-17C MOD/EUR **JURID**
ROMAN/EMP LAW CHOOSE ATTIT 10/19 CHURCH/STA **SECT**
ROMAN/LAW. PAGE 37 E0728 **NAT/G**
GP/REL
B66

MAINE H.S.,LECTURES ON THE EARLY HISTORY OF **CULTURE**
INSTITUTIONS. IRELAND UK CONSTN ELITES STRUCT FAM **LAW**
KIN CHIEF LEGIS CT/SYS OWN SOVEREIGN...CONCPT 16 **INGP/REL**
BENTHAM/J BREHON ROMAN/LAW. PAGE 68 E1351
B75

ROMAN/REP....ROMAN REPUBLIC

MCILWAIN C.H.,CONSTITUTIONALISM, ANCIENT AND **CONSTN**
MODERN. CHRIST-17C MOD/EUR NAT/G CHIEF PROB/SOLV **GEN/LAWS**
INSPECT AUTHORIT ORD/FREE PWR...TIME/SEQ ROMAN/REP. **LAW**
PAGE 71 E1418
B40

MCILWAIN C.H.,CONSTITUTIONALISM: ANCIENT AND **CONSTN**
MODERN. USA+45 ROMAN/EMP LAW CHIEF LEGIS CT/SYS **NAT/G**
GP/REL ORD/FREE SOVEREIGN...POLICY TIME/SEQ **PARL/PROC**
ROMAN/REP EUROPE. PAGE 71 E1419 **GOV/COMP**
B47

WORMUTH F.D.,THE ORIGINS OF MODERN **NAT/G**
CONSTITUTIONALISM. GREECE UK LEGIS CREATE TEC/DEV **CONSTN**
BAL/PWR DOMIN ADJUD REV WAR PWR...JURID ROMAN/REP **LAW**
CROMWELL/O. PAGE 107 E2146
B49

BUCKLAND W.W.,ROMAN LAW AND COMMON LAW; A **IDEA/COMP**
COMPARISON IN OUTLINE (2ND REV. ED.). UK FAM LEGIT **LAW**
AGREE CT/SYS OWN...JURID ROMAN/REP ROMAN/LAW **ADJUD**
COMMON/LAW. PAGE 17 E0325 **CONCPT**
B52

ROMANIA....SEE ALSO COM

CONOVER H.F.,THE BALKANS: A SELECTED LIST OF **BIBLIOG**
REFERENCES. ALBANIA BULGARIA ROMANIA YUGOSLAVIA **EUR+WWI**
INT/ORG PROB/SOLV DIPLOM LEGIT CONFER ADJUD WAR
NAT/LISM PEACE PWR 20 LEAGUE/NAT. PAGE 25 E0493
B43

FISCHER-GALATI S.A.,RUMANIA; A BIBLIOGRAPHIC GUIDE **BIBLIOG/A**
(PAMPHLET). ROMANIA INTELL ECO/DEV LABOR SECT **NAT/G**
WEALTH...GEOG SOC/WK LING 20. PAGE 38 E0756 **COM**
LAW
B63

STOICOIU V.,LEGAL SOURCES AND BIBLIOGRAPHY OF **BIBLIOG/A**
ROMANIA. COM ROMANIA LAW FINAN POL/PAR LEGIS JUDGE **JURID**
ADJUD CT/SYS PARL/PROC MARXISM 20. PAGE 93 E1874 **CONSTN**
ADMIN
B64

ROME....ROME

ROME/ANC....ANCIENT ROME; SEE ALSO ROMAN/EMP,ROMAN/REP

BRYCE J.,STUDIES IN HISTORY AND JURISPRUDENCE (2 **IDEA/COMP**
VOLS.). ICELAND SOUTH/AFR UK LAW PROB/SOLV **CONSTN**
SOVEREIGN...PHIL/SCI NAT/COMP ROME/ANC ROMAN/LAW. **JURID**
PAGE 16 E0321
B01

SCHULZ F.,PRINCIPLES OF ROMAN LAW. CONSTN FAM NAT/G **LAW**
DOMIN CONTROL CT/SYS CRIME ISOLAT ATTIT ORD/FREE **LEGIS**
B36

PWR...JURID ROME/ANC ROMAN/LAW. PAGE 89 E1783 **ADJUD**
CONCPT

ROMNEY/GEO....GEORGE ROMNEY

ROOSEVLT/F....PRESIDENT FRANKLIN D. ROOSEVELT

GRISWOLD A.W.,THE FAR EASTERN POLICY OF THE UNITED **DIPLOM**
STATES. ASIA S/ASIA USA-45 INT/ORG INT/TRADE WAR **POLICY**
NAT/LISM...BIBLIOG 19/20 LEAGUE/NAT ROOSEVLT/T **CHIEF**
ROOSEVLT/F WILSON/W TREATY. PAGE 47 E0943
B38

HELLMAN F.S.,THE SUPREME COURT ISSUE: SELECTED LIST **BIBLIOG/A**
OF REFERENCES. USA-45 NAT/G CHIEF EX/STRUC JUDGE **CONSTN**
ATTIT...JURID 20 PRESIDENT ROOSEVLT/F SUPREME/CT. **CT/SYS**
PAGE 51 E1026 **LAW**
B38

LONG H.A.,USURPERS - FOES OF FREE MAN. LAW NAT/G **CT/SYS**
CHIEF LEGIS DOMIN ADJUD REPRESENT GOV/REL ORD/FREE **CENTRAL**
LAISSEZ POPULISM...POLICY 18/20 SUPREME/CT **FEDERAL**
ROOSEVLT/F CONGRESS CON/INTERP. PAGE 66 E1325 **CONSTN**
B57

MASON A.T.,THE SUPREME COURT: PALADIUM OF FREEDOM. **CONSTN**
USA-45 NAT/G POL/PAR CHIEF LEGIS ADJUD PARL/PROC **CT/SYS**
FEDERAL PWR...POLICY BIOG 18/20 SUPREME/CT **JURID**
ROOSEVLT/F JEFFERSN/T MARSHALL/J HUGHES/CE. PAGE 69
E1378
B62

GARDNER L.C.,ECONOMIC ASPECTS OF NEW DEAL **ECO/TAC**
DIPLOMACY. USA-45 WOR-45 LAW ECO/DEV INT/ORG NAT/G **DIPLOM**
VOL/ASSN LEGIS TOP/EX EDU/PROP ORD/FREE PWR WEALTH
...POLICY TIME/SEQ VAL/FREE 20 ROOSEVLT/F. PAGE 42
E0836
B64

BAKER L.,BACK TO BACK: THE DUEL BETWEEN FDR AND THE **CHIEF**
SUPREME COURT. ELITES LEGIS CREATE DOMIN INGP/REL **CT/SYS**
PERSON PWR NEW/LIB 20 ROOSEVLT/F SUPREME/CT SENATE. **PARL/PROC**
PAGE 7 E0142 **GOV/REL**
B67

ROOSEVLT/T....PRESIDENT THEODORE ROOSEVELT

TAYLOR H.,WHY THE PENDING TREATY WITH COLOMBIA **INT/LAW**
SHOULD BE RATIFIED (PAMPHLET). PANAMA USA-45 **DIPLOM**
DELIB/GP INT/TRADE REV ORD/FREE...JURID TREATY
18/19 ROOSEVLT/T TAFT/WH COLOMB. PAGE 95 E1912
N19

GRISWOLD A.W.,THE FAR EASTERN POLICY OF THE UNITED **DIPLOM**
STATES. ASIA S/ASIA USA-45 INT/ORG INT/TRADE WAR **POLICY**
NAT/LISM...BIBLIOG 19/20 LEAGUE/NAT ROOSEVLT/T **CHIEF**
ROOSEVLT/F WILSON/W TREATY. PAGE 47 E0943
B38

ROOT E. E1711,E1712

ROSBERG C.G. E0187

ROSE A.M. E1713

ROSE C.B. E1713

ROSE R. E1714

ROSEN M. E0735

ROSENBERG M. E1715

ROSENNE S. E1716,E1717

ROSENZWEIG F. E1718

ROSNER G. E1719

ROSS A. E1720,E1721,E1722

ROSS P. E1723

ROSS/EH....EDWARD H. ROSS

ROSSITER C. E1724

ROSSMOOR....ROSSMOOR LEISURE WORLD, SEAL BEACH, CAL.

ROSTOW E.V. E0280,E1725,E1726

ROURKE F.E. E1489,E1727

ROUSSEAU/J....JEAN JACQUES ROUSSEAU

ROUSSOS G. E1487

N

FULLER G.A.,DEMOBILIZATION: A SELECTED LIST OF BIBLIOG/A
REFERENCES. USA+45 LAW AGRI LABOR WORKER ECO/TAC INDUS
RATION RECEIVE EDU/PROP ROUTINE ARMS/CONT ALL/VALS FORCES
20. PAGE 41 E0819 NAT/G

B00

MAINE H.S.,ANCIENT LAW. MEDIT-7 CULTURE SOCIETY KIN FAM
SECT LEGIS LEGIT ROUTINE...JURID HIST/WRIT CON/ANAL LAW
TOT/POP VAL/FREE. PAGE 68 E1350

B06

FOSTER J.W.,THE PRACTICE OF DIPLOMACY AS DIPLOM
ILLUSTRATED IN THE FOREIGN RELATIO..S OF THE UNITED ROUTINE
STATES. MOD/EUR USA+45 NAT/G EX/STRUC ADMIN PHIL/SCI
...POLICY INT/LAW BIBLIOG 19/20. PAGE 39 E0777

B06

GRIFFIN A.P.C.,LIST OF BOOKS RELATING TO CHILD BIBLIOG/A
LABOR (PAMPHLET). BELGIUM FRANCE GERMANY MOD/EUR UK LAW
USA+45 ECO/DEV INDUS WORKER CAP/ISM PAY ROUTINE LABOR
ALL/IDEOS...MGT SOC 19/20. PAGE 47 E0929 AGE/C

B09

HOLLAND T.E.,LETTERS UPON WAR AND NEUTRALITY. LAW
WOR-45 NAT/G FORCES JUDGE ECO/TAC LEGIT CT/SYS INT/LAW
NEUTRAL ROUTINE COERCE...JURID TIME/SEQ 20. PAGE 55 INT/ORG
E1085 WAR

B14

MCLAUGHLIN A.C.,CYCLOPEDIA OF AMERICAN GOVERNMENT USA+45
(3 VOLS.). LAW CONSTN POL/PAR ADMIN ROUTINE NAT/G
...INT/LAW CONCPT BIBLIOG METH 20. PAGE 71 E1421 DICTIONARY

B15

SAWYER R.A.,A LIST OF WORKS ON COUNTY GOVERNMENT. BIBLIOG/A
LAW FINAN MUNIC TOP/EX ROUTINE CRIME...CLASSIF LOC/G
RECORD 19/20. PAGE 87 E1748 GOV/REL
ADMIN

B21

CARDOZO B.N.,THE NATURE OF THE JUDICIAL PROCESS. JURID
ROUTINE ORD/FREE...POLICY 20. PAGE 19 E0377 CT/SYS
LEAD
DECISION

B21

STOWELL E.C.,INTERVENTION IN INTERNATIONAL LAW. BAL/PWR
UNIV LAW SOCIETY INT/ORG ACT/RES PLAN LEGIT ROUTINE SOVEREIGN
WAR...JURID OBS GEN/LAWS 20. PAGE 94 E1884

B22

WRIGHT Q.,THE CONTROL OF AMERICAN FOREIGN NAT/G
RELATIONS. USA+45 WOR-45 CONSTN INT/ORG CONSULT EXEC
LEGIS LEGIT ROUTINE ORD/FREE PWR...POLICY JURID DIPLOM
CONCPT METH/CNCPT RECORD LEAGUE/NAT 20. PAGE 107
E2150

B23

HOLMES O.W. JR.,THE COMMON LAW. FUT WOR-45 CULTURE ADJUD
SOCIETY CREATE LEGIT ROUTINE ATTIT ALL/VALS...JURID CON/ANAL
METH/CNCPT TIME/SEQ GEN/LAWS TOT/POP VAL/FREE.
PAGE 55 E1087

C24

BARNES H.E.,"SOCIOLOGY AND POLITICAL THEORY: A CONCPT
CONSIDERATION OF THE SOCIOLOGICAL BASIS OF STRUCT
POLITICS." LAW CONSTN NAT/G DIPLOM DOMIN ROUTINE SOC
REV ORD/FREE SOVEREIGN...PHIL/SCI CLASSIF BIBLIOG
18/20. PAGE 8 E0151

B29

CONWELL-EVANS T.P.,THE LEAGUE COUNCIL IN ACTION. DELIB/GP
EUR+WWI TURKEY UK USSR WOR-45 INT/ORG FORCES JUDGE INT/LAW
ECO/TAC EDU/PROP LEGIT ROUTINE ARMS/CONT COERCE
ATTIT PWR...MAJORIT GEOG JURID CONCPT LEAGUE/NAT
TOT/POP VAL/FREE TUNIS 20. PAGE 25 E0498

B29

MOLEY R.,POLITICS AND CRIMINAL PROSECUTION. USA-45 PWR
POL/PAR EX/STRUC LEGIT CONTROL LEAD ROUTINE CHOOSE CT/SYS
INGP/REL...JURID CHARTS 20. PAGE 74 E1481 CRIME
ADJUD

C29

BUCK A.E.,"PUBLIC BUDGETING." USA-45 FINAN LOC/G BUDGET
NAT/G LEGIS BAL/PAY COST...JURID TREND BIBLIOG/A ROUTINE
20. PAGE 17 E0324 ADMIN

B31

STOWELL E.C.,INTERNATIONAL LAW. FUT UNIV WOR-45 INT/ORG
SOCIETY CONSULT EX/STRUC FORCES ACT/RES PLAN DIPLOM ROUTINE
EDU/PROP LEGIT DISPL PWR SKILL...POLICY CONCPT OBS INT/LAW
TREND TOT/POP 20. PAGE 94 E1885

B32

MORLEY F.,THE SOCIETY OF NATIONS. EUR+WWI UNIV INT/ORG
WOR-45 LAW CONSTN ACT/RES PLAN EDU/PROP LEGIT CONCPT
ROUTINE...POLICY TIME/SEQ LEAGUE/NAT TOT/POP 20.
PAGE 75 E1496

B33

ENSOR R.C.K.,COURTS AND JUDGES IN FRANCE, GERMANY, CT/SYS
AND ENGLAND. FRANCE GERMANY UK LAW PROB/SOLV ADMIN EX/STRUC
ROUTINE CRIME ROLE...METH/COMP 20 CIVIL/LAW. ADJUD
PAGE 35 E0692 NAT/COMP

B36

CHAMBERLAIN J.P.,LEGISLATIVE PROCESS: NATION AND CON/ANAL
STATE. LAW DELIB/GP ROUTINE. PAGE 21 E0414 PROVS
LEGIS
NAT/G

B37

BUREAU OF NATIONAL AFFAIRS,LABOR RELATIONS LABOR
REFERENCE MANUAL VOL 1, 1935-1937. BARGAIN DEBATE ADMIN
ROUTINE INGP/REL 20 NLRB. PAGE 17 E0335 ADJUD
NAT/G

B37

RUTHERFORD M.L.,THE INFLUENCE OF THE AMERICAN BAR ATTIT
ASSOCIATION ON PUBLIC OPINION AND LEGISLATION. ADJUD
USA+45 LAW CONSTN LABOR LEGIS DOMIN EDU/PROP LEGIT PROF/ORG
CT/SYS ROUTINE...TIME/SEQ 19/20 ABA. PAGE 87 E1739 JURID

S40

GILL N.N.,"PERMANENT ADVISORY COMMISSIONS IN THE DELIB/GP
FEDERAL GOVERNMENT." CLIENT FINAN OP/RES EDU/PROP NAT/G
PARTIC ROUTINE INGP/REL KNOWL SKILL...CLASSIF DECISION
TREND. PAGE 43 E0860

B41

MCCLURE W.,INTERNATIONAL EXECUTIVE AGREEMENTS. TOP/EX
USA-45 WOR-45 INT/ORG NAT/G DELIB/GP ADJUD ROUTINE DIPLOM
ORD/FREE PWR...TIME/SEQ TREND CON/ANAL. PAGE 70
E1401

C43

BENTHAM J.,"THE RATIONALE OF REWARD" IN J. BOWRING, SANCTION
ED., THE WORKS OF JEREMY BENTHAM (VOL. 2)" LAW ECO/TAC
WORKER CREATE INSPECT PAY ROUTINE HAPPINESS PRODUC INCOME
SUPEGO WEALTH METH/CNCPT. PAGE 10 E0195 PWR

B44

BRIERLY J.L.,THE OUTLOOK FOR INTERNATIONAL LAW. FUT INT/ORG
WOR-45 CONSTN NAT/G VOL/ASSN FORCES ECO/TAC DOMIN LAW
LEGIT ADJUD ROUTINE PEACE ORD/FREE...INT/LAW JURID
METH LEAGUE/NAT 20. PAGE 15 E0298

B44

PUTTKAMMER E.W.,WAR AND THE LAW. UNIV USA+45 CONSTN INT/ORG
CULTURE SOCIETY NAT/G POL/PAR ROUTINE ALL/VALS LAW
...JURID CONCPT OBS WORK VAL/FREE 20. PAGE 83 E1664 WAR
INT/LAW

S44

WRIGHT Q.,"CONSTITUTIONAL PROCEDURES OF THE US FOR TOP/EX
CARRYING OUT OBLIGATIONS FOR MILITARY SANCTIONS." FORCES
EUR+WWI FUT USA-45 WOR-45 CONSTN INTELL NAT/G INT/LAW
CONSULT EX/STRUC LEGIS ROUTINE DRIVE...POLICY JURID WAR
CONCPT OBS TREND TOT/POP 20. PAGE 108 E2153

B45

HILL N.,CLAIMS TO TERRITORY IN INTERNATIONAL LAW INT/ORG
AND RELATIONS. WOR-45 NAT/G DOMIN EDU/PROP LEGIT ADJUD
REGION ROUTINE ORD/FREE PWR WEALTH...GEOG INT/LAW SOVEREIGN
JURID 20. PAGE 52 E1047

B46

PATON G.W.,A TEXT-BOOK OF JURISPRUDENCE. CREATE LAW
INSPECT LEGIT CT/SYS ROUTINE CRIME INGP/REL PRIVIL ADJUD
...CONCPT BIBLIOG 20. PAGE 80 E1601 JURID
T

L49

COMM. STUDY ORGAN. PEACE,"A TEN YEAR RECORD, INT/ORG
1939-1949." FUT WOR+45 LAW R+D CONSULT DELIB/GP CONSTN
CREATE LEGIT ROUTINE ORD/FREE...TIME/SEQ UN 20. PEACE
PAGE 24 E0480

L49

MARX C.M.,"ADMINISTRATIVE ETHICS AND THE RULE OF ADMIN
LAW." USA+45 ELITES ACT/RES DOMIN NEUTRAL ROUTINE LAW
INGP/REL ORD/FREE...JURID IDEA/COMP. PAGE 69 E1375

S49

KIRK G.,"MATERIALS FOR THE STUDY OF INTERNATIONAL INT/ORG
RELATIONS." FUT UNIV WOR+45 INTELL EDU/PROP ROUTINE ACT/RES
PEACE ATTIT...INT/LAW JURID CONCPT OBS. PAGE 61 DIPLOM
E1219

BLODGETT R.H.,"COMPARATIVE ECONOMIC SYSTEMS (REV. ED.)" WOR-45 AGRI FINAN MARKET LABOR NAT/G PLAN INT/TRADE PRICE...POLICY DECISION BIBLIOG 20. PAGE 13 E0248
C49
METH/COMP
CONCPT
ROUTINE

FRANK J.,COURTS ON TRIAL: MYTH AND REALITY IN AMERICAN JUSTICE. LAW CONSULT PROB/SOLV EDU/PROP ADJUD ROUTINE ROLE ORD/FREE...GEN/LAWS T 20. PAGE 40 E0788
B50
JURID
CT/SYS
MYTH
CONSTN

JIMENEZ E.,VOTING AND HANDLING OF DISPUTES IN THE SECURITY COUNCIL. WOR+45 CONSTN INT/ORG DIPLOM LEGIT DETER CHOOSE MORAL ORD/FREE PWR...JURID TIME/SEQ COLD/WAR UN 20. PAGE 59 E1168
B50
DELIB/GP
ROUTINE

STONE J.,THE PROVINCE AND FUNCTION OF LAW. UNIV WOR+45 WOR-45 CULTURE INTELL SOCIETY ECO/DEV ECO/UNDEV NAT/G LEGIT ROUTINE ATTIT PERCEPT PERSON ...JURID CONCPT GEN/LAWS GEN/METH 20. PAGE 94 E1877
B50
INT/ORG
LAW

MANGONE G.,"THE IDEA AND PRACTICE OF WORLD GOVERNMENT." FUT WOR+45 WOR-45 ECO/DEV LEGIS CREATE LEGIT ROUTINE ATTIT MORAL PWR WEALTH...CONCPT GEN/LAWS 20. PAGE 68 E1358
L51
INT/ORG
SOCIETY
INT/LAW

WRIGHT Q.,"CONGRESS AND THE TREATY-MAKING POWER." USA+45 WOR+45 CONSTN INTELL NAT/G CHIEF CONSULT EX/STRUC LEGIS TOP/EX CREATE GOV/REL DISPL DRIVE RIGID/FLEX...TREND TOT/POP CONGRESS CONGRESS 20 TREATY. PAGE 108 E2154
L52
ROUTINE
DIPLOM
INT/LAW
DELIB/GP

MANGONE G.,A SHORT HISTORY OF INTERNATIONAL ORGANIZATION. MOD/EUR USA+45 USA-45 WOR+45 WOR-45 LAW LEGIS CREATE LEGIT ROUTINE RIGID/FLEX PWR ...JURID CONCPT OBS TIME/SEQ STERTYP GEN/LAWS UN TOT/POP VAL/FREE 18/20. PAGE 68 E1359
B54
INT/ORG
INT/LAW

BEISEL A.R.,CONTROL OVER ILLEGAL ENFORCEMENT OF THE CRIMINAL LAW: ROLE OF THE SUPREME COURT. CONSTN ROUTINE MORAL PWR...SOC 20 SUPREME/CT. PAGE 9 E0180
B55
ORD/FREE
LAW
CRIME

BRAUN K.,LABOR DISPUTES AND THEIR SETTLEMENT. ECO/TAC ROUTINE TASK GP/REL...DECISION GEN/LAWS. PAGE 15 E0288
B55
INDUS
LABOR
BARGAIN
ADJUD

CRAIG J.,BIBLIOGRAPHY OF PUBLIC ADMINISTRATION IN AUSTRALIA. CONSTN FINAN EX/STRUC LEGIS PLAN DIPLOM RECEIVE ADJUD ROUTINE...HEAL 19/20 AUSTRAL PARLIAMENT. PAGE 27 E0540
B55
BIBLIOG
GOV/REL
ADMIN
NAT/G

WRIGHT Q.,"THE PEACEFUL ADJUSTMENT OF INTERNATIONAL RELATIONS: PROBLEMS AND RESEARCH APPROACHES." UNIV INTELL EDU/PROP ADJUD ROUTINE KNOWL SKILL...INT/LAW JURID PHIL/SCI CLASSIF 20. PAGE 108 E2156
S55
R+D
METH/CNCPT
PEACE

FRANCIS R.G.,SERVICE AND PROCEDURE IN BUREAUCRACY. EXEC LEAD ROUTINE...QU 20. PAGE 39 E0784
B56
CLIENT
ADMIN
INGP/REL
REPRESENT

PEASLEE A.J.,CONSTITUTIONS OF NATIONS. WOR+45 LAW NAT/G EX/STRUC LEGIS TOP/EX LEGIT CT/SYS ROUTINE CHOOSE ORD/FREE PWR SOVEREIGN...CHARTS TOT/POP. PAGE 80 E1605
B56
CONSTN
CON/ANAL

SOHN L.B.,BASIC DOCUMENTS OF THE UNITED NATIONS. WOR+45 LAW INT/ORG LEGIT EXEC ROUTINE CHOOSE PWR ...JURID CONCPT GEN/LAWS ANTHOL UN TOT/POP OAS FAO ILO 20. PAGE 92 E1853
B56
DELIB/GP
CONSTN

SYKES G.M.,CRIME AND SOCIETY. LAW STRATA STRUCT ACT/RES ROUTINE ANOMIE WEALTH...POLICY SOC/INTEG 20. PAGE 95 E1903
B56
CRIMLGY
CRIME
CULTURE
INGP/REL

WEIS P.,NATIONALITY AND STATELESSNESS IN INTERNATIONAL LAW. UK WOR+45 WOR-45 LAW CONSTN NAT/G DIPLOM EDU/PROP LEGIT ROUTINE RIGID/FLEX
B56
INT/ORG
SOVEREIGN
INT/LAW

...JURID RECORD CMN/WLTH 20. PAGE 105 E2109

ZINN C.J.,HOW OUR LAWS ARE MADE: BROCHURE HOUSE OF REPRESENTATIVES DOCUMENT 451. LAW CONSTN CHIEF EX/STRUC PROB/SOLV HOUSE/REP SENATE. PAGE 108 E2171
B56
LEGIS
DELIB/GP
PARL/PROC
ROUTINE

AUMANN F.R.,"THE ISTRUMENTALITIES OF JUSTICE: THEIR FORMS, FUNCTIONS, AND LIMITATIONS." WOR+45 WOR-45 JUDGE PROB/SOLV ROUTINE ATTIT...BIBLIOG 20. PAGE 6 E0118
C56
JURID
ADMIN
CT/SYS
ADJUD

BLOOMFIELD L.M.,EGYPT, ISRAEL AND THE GULF OF AQABA: IN INTERNATIONAL LAW. LAW NAT/G CONSULT FORCES PLAN ECO/TAC ROUTINE COERCE ATTIT DRIVE PERCEPT PERSON RIGID/FLEX LOVE PWR WEALTH...GEOG CONCPT MYTH TREND. PAGE 13 E0250
B57
ISLAM
INT/LAW
UAR

JENKS C.W.,THE INTERNATIONAL PROTECTION OF TRADE UNION FREEDOM. FUT WOR+45 WOR-45 VOL/ASSN DELIB/GP CT/SYS REGION ROUTINE...JURID METH/CNCPT RECORD TIME/SEQ CHARTS ILO WORK OAS 20. PAGE 58 E1153
B57
LABOR
INT/ORG

CLEMMER D.,THE PRISON COMMUNITY. CULTURE CONTROL LEAD ROUTINE PERS/REL PERSON...SOC METH/CNCPT. PAGE 23 E0453
B58
PUB/INST
CRIMLGY
CLIENT
INGP/REL

DEVLIN P.,THE CRIMINAL PROSECUTION IN ENGLAND. UK NAT/G ADMIN ROUTINE EFFICIENCY...JURID SOC 20. PAGE 31 E0617
B58
CRIME
LAW
METH
CT/SYS

FISHER F.M.,"THE MATHEMATICAL ANALYSIS OF SUPREME COURT DECISIONS: THE USE AND ABUSE OF QUANTITATIVE METHODS." USA+45 LAW EX/STRUC LEGIS JUDGE ROUTINE ATTIT DECISION. PAGE 38 E0757
S58
PROB/SOLV
CT/SYS
JURID
MATH

STAAR R.F.,"ELECTIONS IN COMMUNIST POLAND." EUR+WWI SOCIETY INT/ORG NAT/G POL/PAR LEGIS ACT/RES ECO/TAC EDU/PROP ADJUD ADMIN ROUTINE COERCE TOTALISM ATTIT ORD/FREE PWR 20. PAGE 93 E1864
S58
COM
CHOOSE
POLAND

BROMWICH L.,UNION CONSTITUTIONS. CONSTN EX/STRUC PRESS ADJUD CONTROL CHOOSE REPRESENT PWR SAMP. PAGE 16 E0306
B59
LABOR
ROUTINE
INGP/REL
RACE/REL

COMM. STUDY ORGAN. PEACE,ORGANIZING PEACE IN THE NUCLEAR AGE. FUT CONSULT DELIB/GP DOMIN ADJUD ROUTINE COERCE ORD/FREE...TECHNIC INT/LAW JURID NEW/IDEA UN COLD/WAR 20. PAGE 24 E0483
B59
INT/ORG
ACT/RES
NUC/PWR

SCHNEIDER J.,TREATY-MAKING POWER OF INTERNATIONAL ORGANIZATIONS. FUT WOR+45 WOR-45 LAW NAT/G JUDGE DIPLOM LEGIT CT/SYS ORD/FREE PWR...INT/LAW JURID GEN/LAWS TOT/POP UNESCO 20 TREATY. PAGE 88 E1762
B59
INT/ORG
ROUTINE

COX A.,"THE ROLE OF LAW IN PRESERVING UNION DEMOCRACY." EX/STRUC LEGIS PARTIC ROUTINE CHOOSE INGP/REL ORD/FREE. PAGE 27 E0532
L59
LABOR
REPRESENT
LAW
MAJORIT

POTTER P.B.,"OBSTACLES AND ALTERNATIVES TO INTERNATIONAL LAW." WOR+45 NAT/G VOL/ASSN DELIB/GP BAL/PWR DOMIN ROUTINE...JURID VAL/FREE 20. PAGE 81 E1632
S59
INT/ORG
LAW
DIPLOM
INT/LAW

SOHN L.B.,"THE DEFINITION OF AGGRESSION." FUT LAW FORCES LEGIT ADJUD ROUTINE COERCE ORD/FREE PWR ...MAJORIT JURID QUANT COLD/WAR 20. PAGE 92 E1855
S59
INT/ORG
CT/SYS
DETER
SOVEREIGN

STONE J.,"CONFLICT MANAGEMENT THROUGH CONTEMPORARY INTERNATIONAL LAW AND ORGANIZATION." WOR+45 LAW NAT/G CREATE BAL/PWR DOMIN LEGIT ROUTINE COERCE ATTIT ORD/FREE PWR SOVEREIGN...JURID 20. PAGE 94 E1880
S59
INT/ORG
INT/LAW

ALBI F.,TRATADO DE LOS MODOS DE GESTION DE LAS
B60
LOC/G

CORPORACIONES LOCALES. SPAIN FINAN NAT/G BUDGET CONTROL EXEC ROUTINE GOV/REL ORD/FREE SOVEREIGN ...MGT 20. PAGE 3 E0057
LAW
ADMIN
MUNIC

B60
BORGATTA E.F.,SOCIAL WORKERS' PERCEPTIONS OF CLIENTS. SERV/IND ROUTINE PERS/REL DRIVE PERSON RESPECT...SOC PERS/COMP 20. PAGE 14 E0268
SOC/WK
ATTIT
CLIENT
PROB/SOLV

B60
CLARK G.,WORLD PEACE THROUGH WORLD LAW. FUT WOR+45 CONSULT FORCES ACT/RES CREATE PLAN ADMIN ROUTINE ARMS/CONT DETER ATTIT PWR...JURID VAL/FREE UNESCO 20 UN. PAGE 23 E0449
INT/ORG
LAW
PEACE
INT/LAW

B60
US SENATE COMM ON JUDICIARY,ADMINISTRATIVE PROCEDURE LEGISLATION. USA+45 CONSTN NAT/G PROB/SOLV CONFER ROUTINE GOV/REL...INT 20 SENATE. PAGE 102 E2044
PARL/PROC
LEGIS
ADMIN
JURID

S60
RHYNE C.S.,"LAW AS AN INSTRUMENT FOR PEACE." FUT WOR+45 PLAN LEGIT ROUTINE ARMS/CONT NUC/PWR ATTIT ORD/FREE...JURID METH/CNCPT TREND CON/ANAL HYPO/EXP COLD/WAR 20. PAGE 84 E1690
ADJUD
EDU/PROP
INT/LAW
PEACE

S60
SCHACHTER O.,"THE ENFORCEMENT OF INTERNATIONAL JUDICIAL AND ARBITRAL DECISIONS." WOR+45 NAT/G ECO/TAC DOMIN LEGIT ROUTINE COERCE ATTIT DRIVE ALL/VALS PWR...METH/CNCPT TREND TOT/POP 20 UN. PAGE 87 E1750
INT/ORG
ADJUD
INT/LAW

C60
HAZARD J.N.,"SETTLING DISPUTES IN SOVIET SOCIETY: THE FORMATIVE YEARS OF LEGAL INSTITUTIONS." USSR NAT/G PROF/ORG PROB/SOLV CONTROL CT/SYS ROUTINE REV CENTRAL...JURID BIBLIOG 20. PAGE 51 E1017
ADJUD
LAW
COM
POLICY

B61
AYLMER G.,THE KING'S SERVANTS. UK ELITES CHIEF PAY CT/SYS WEALTH 17 CROMWELL/O CHARLES/I. PAGE 6 E0122
ADMIN
ROUTINE
EX/STRUC
NAT/G

B61
BURDETTE F.L.,POLITICAL SCIENCE: A SELECTED BIBLIOGRAPHY OF BOOKS IN PRINT, WITH ANNOTATIONS (PAMPHLET). LAW LOC/G NAT/G POL/PAR PROVS DIPLOM EDU/PROP ADMIN CHOOSE ATTIT 20. PAGE 17 E0330
BIBLIOG/A
GOV/COMP
CONCPT
ROUTINE

L61
SAND P.T.,"AN HISTORICAL SURVEY OF INTERNATIONAL AIR LAW SINCE 1944." USA+45 USA-45 WOR+45 WOR-45 SOCIETY ECO/DEV NAT/G CONSULT EX/STRUC ACT/RES PLAN LEGIT ROUTINE...JURID CONCPT METH/CNCPT TREND 20. PAGE 87 E1744
INT/ORG
LAW
INT/LAW
SPACE

S61
ALGER C.F.,"NON-RESOLUTION CONSEQUENCES OF THE UNITED NATIONS AND THEIR EFFECT ON INTERNATIONAL CONFLICT." WOR+45 CONSTN ECO/DEV NAT/G CONSULT DELIB/GP TOP/EX ACT/RES PLAN DIPLOM EDU/PROP ROUTINE ATTIT ALL/VALS...INT/LAW TOT/POP UN 20. PAGE 3 E0065
INT/ORG
DRIVE
BAL/PWR

S61
LIPSON L.,"AN ARGUMENT ON THE LEGALITY OF RECONNAISSANCE STATELLITES." COM USA+45 USSR WOR+45 AIR INTELL NAT/G CONSULT PLAN DIPLOM LEGIT ROUTINE ATTIT...INT/LAW JURID CONCPT METH/CNCPT TREND COLD/WAR 20. PAGE 65 E1302
INT/ORG
LAW
SPACE

B62
AMERICAN LAW INSTITUTE,FOREIGN RELATIONS LAW OF THE UNITED STATES: RESTATEMENT, SECOND. USA+45 NAT/G LEGIS ADJUD EXEC ROUTINE GOV/REL...INT/LAW JURID CONCPT 20 TREATY. PAGE 4 E0082
PROF/ORG
LAW
DIPLOM
ORD/FREE

B62
ASSOCIATION BAR OF NYC,REPORT ON ADMISSION PROCEDURES TO NEW YORK STATE MENTAL HOSPITALS. LAW CONSTN INGP/REL RESPECT...PSY OBS RECORD. PAGE 6 E0108
PUB/INST
HEALTH
CLIENT
ROUTINE

B62
CARLSTON K.S.,LAW AND ORGANIZATION IN WORLD SOCIETY. WOR+45 FINAN ECO/TAC DOMIN LEGIT CT/SYS ROUTINE COERCE ORD/FREE PWR WEALTH...PLURIST DECISION JURID MGT METH/CNCPT GEN/LAWS 20. PAGE 19 E0381
INT/ORG
LAW

B62
HADWEN J.G.,HOW UNITED NATIONS DECISIONS ARE MADE.
INT/ORG

WOR+45 LAW EDU/PROP LEGIT ADMIN PWR...DECISION SELF/OBS GEN/LAWS UN 20. PAGE 49 E0972
ROUTINE

B62
LAWSON R.,INTERNATIONAL REGIONAL ORGANIZATIONS. WOR+45 NAT/G VOL/ASSN CONSULT LEGIS EDU/PROP LEGIT ADMIN EXEC ROUTINE HEALTH PWR WEALTH...JURID EEC COLD/WAR 20 UN. PAGE 63 E1270
INT/ORG
DELIB/GP
REGION

B62
ROSENNE S.,THE WORLD COURT: WHAT IT IS AND HOW IT WORKS. WOR+45 WOR-45 LAW CONSTN JUDGE EDU/PROP LEGIT ROUTINE CHOOSE PEACE ORD/FREE...JURID OBS TIME/SEQ CHARTS UN TOT/POP VAL/FREE 20. PAGE 86 E1717
INT/ORG
ADJUD
INT/LAW

B62
SCHWARZENBERGER G.,THE FRONTIERS OF INTERNATIONAL LAW. WOR+45 WOR-45 NAT/G LEGIT CT/SYS ROUTINE MORAL ORD/FREE PWR...JURID SOC GEN/METH 20 COLD/WAR. PAGE 89 E1789
INT/ORG
LAW
INT/LAW

B62
SIGLIANO R E.,THE COURTS. USA+45 USA-45 LAW CONSTN NAT/G ROUTINE CHOOSE 18/20 SUPREME/CT. PAGE 91 E1825
ADJUD
PROB/SOLV
CT/SYS
JUDGE

B62
SOWLE C.R.,POLICE POWER AND INDIVIDUAL FREEDOM: THE QUEST FOR BALANCE. CANADA EUR+WWI ISRAEL NORWAY USA+45 LAW CONSTN SOCIETY CONTROL ROUTINE SANCTION GP/REL 20 CHINJAP. PAGE 93 E1859
FORCES
ORD/FREE
IDEA/COMP

B62
STERN R.L.,SUPREME COURT PRACTICE. USA+45 USA-45 OP/RES...STYLE METH 20 SUPREME/CT. PAGE 93 E1872
CT/SYS
ADJUD
JURID
ROUTINE

B62
WOETZEL R.K.,THE NURENBERG TRIALS IN INTERNATIONAL LAW. CHRIST-17C MOD/EUR WOR+45 SOCIETY NAT/G DELIB/GP DOMIN LEGIT ROUTINE ATTIT DRIVE PERSON SUPEGO MORAL ORD/FREE...POLICY MAJORIT JURID PSY SOC SELF/OBS RECORD NAZI TOT/POP. PAGE 107 E2138
INT/ORG
ADJUD
WAR

L62
GROSS L.,"IMMUNITIES AND PRIVILEGES OF DELIGATIONS TO THE UNITED NATIONS." USA+45 WOR+45 STRATA NAT/G VOL/ASSN CONSULT DIPLOM EDU/PROP ROUTINE RESPECT ...POLICY INT/LAW CONCPT UN 20. PAGE 48 E0950
INT/ORG
LAW
ELITES

L62
MURACCIOLE L.,"LA LOI FONDAMENTALE DE LA REPUBLIQUE DU CONGO." WOR+45 SOCIETY ECO/UNDEV INT/ORG NAT/G LEGIS PLAN LEGIT ADJUD COLONIAL ROUTINE ATTIT SOVEREIGN 20 CONGO. PAGE 75 E1504
AFR
CONSTN

L62
STEIN E.,"MR HAMMARSKJOLD, THE CHARTER LAW AND THE FUTURE ROLE OF THE UNITED NATIONS SECRETARY-GENERAL." WOR+45 CONSTN INT/ORG DELIB/GP FORCES TOP/EX BAL/PWR LEGIT ROUTINE RIGID/FLEX PWR ...POLICY JURID OBS STERTYP UN COLD/WAR 20 HAMMARSK/D. PAGE 93 E1869
CONCPT
BIOG

L62
UNITED NATIONS,"CAPITAL PUNISHMENT." WOR+45 CULTURE NAT/G ROUTINE COERCE HEALTH PWR...POLICY SOC QU CHARTS VAL/FREE 20. PAGE 98 E1967
LAW
STAT

S62
GREEN L.C.,"POLITICAL OFFENSES, WAR CRIMES AND EXTRADITION." WOR+45 YUGOSLAVIA INT/ORG LEGIT ROUTINE WAR ORD/FREE SOVEREIGN...JURID NAZI 20 INTERPOL. PAGE 46 E0906
LAW
CONCPT
INT/LAW

S62
MONNIER J.P.,"LA SUCCESSION D'ETATS EN MATIERE DE RESPONSABILITE INTERNATIONALE." UNIV CONSTN INTELL SOCIETY ADJUD ROUTINE PERCEPT SUPEGO...GEN/LAWS TOT/POP 20. PAGE 74 E1485
NAT/G
JURID
INT/LAW

C62
MORGAN G.G.,"SOVIET ADMINISTRATIVE LEGALITY: THE ROLE OF THE ATTORNEY GENERAL'S OFFICE." COM USSR CONTROL ROUTINE...CONCPT BIBLIOG 18/20. PAGE 74 E1493
LAW
CONSTN
LEGIS
ADMIN

C62
VAN DER SPRENKEL S.,"LEGAL INSTITUTIONS IN MANCHU CHINA." ASIA STRUCT CT/SYS ROUTINE GOV/REL GP/REL ...CONCPT BIBLIOG 17/20. PAGE 103 E2068
LAW
JURID
ADMIN
ADJUD

BOWETT D.W.,THE LAW OF INTERNATIONAL INSTITUTIONS. INT/ORG
WOR+45 WOR-45 CONSTN DELIB/GP EX/STRUC JUDGE   ADJUD
EDU/PROP LEGIT CT/SYS EXEC ROUTINE RIGID/FLEX   DIPLOM
ORD/FREE PWR...JURID CONCPT ORG/CHARTS GEN/METH
LEAGUE/NAT OAS OEEC 20 UN. PAGE 14 E0277
                                              B63

ROBERTSON A.H.,HUMAN RIGHTS IN EUROPE. CONSTN   EUR+WWI
SOCIETY INT/ORG NAT/G VOL/ASSN DELIB/GP ACT/RES   PERSON
PLAN ADJUD REGION ROUTINE ATTIT LOVE ORD/FREE
RESPECT...JURID SOC CONCPT SOC/EXP UN 20. PAGE 85
E1705
                                              S63

FRIEDMANN W.G.,"THE USES OF 'GENERAL PRINCIPLES' IN   LAW
THE DEVELOPMENT OF INTERNATIONAL LAW." WOR+45 NAT/G   INT/LAW
DIPLOM INT/TRADE LEGIT ROUTINE RIGID/FLEX ORD/FREE   INT/ORG
...JURID CONCPT STERTYP GEN/METH 20. PAGE 41 E0804
                                              S63

GERHARD H.,"COMMODITY TRADE STABILIZATION THROUGH   PLAN
INTERNATIONAL AGREEMENTS." WOR+45 ECO/DEV ECO/UNDEV   ECO/TAC
NAT/G ROUTINE ORD/FREE...INT/LAW OBS TREND GEN/METH   INT/TRADE
TOT/POP 20. PAGE 43 E0850
                                              S63

JOUGHIN L.,"ACADEMIC DUE PROCESS." DELIB/GP ADJUD   ACADEM
ROUTINE ORD/FREE...POLICY MAJORIT TREND. PAGE 59   LAW
E1175   PROF/ORG
                                                      CLIENT
                                              B64

FRANCK T.M.,EAST AFRICAN UNITY THROUGH LAW. MALAWI   AFR
TANZANIA UGANDA UK ZAMBIA CONSTN INT/ORG NAT/G   FEDERAL
ADMIN ROUTINE TASK NAT/LISM ATTIT SOVEREIGN   REGION
...RECORD IDEA/COMP NAT/COMP. PAGE 40 E0785   INT/LAW
                                              B64

IKLE F.C.,HOW NATIONS NEGOTIATE. COM EUR+WWI USA+45   NAT/G
INTELL INT/ORG VOL/ASSN DELIB/GP ACT/RES CREATE   PWR
DOMIN EDU/PROP ADJUD ROUTINE ATTIT PERSON ORD/FREE   POLICY
RESPECT SKILL...PSY SOC OBS VAL/FREE. PAGE 56 E1122
                                              B64

KAHNG T.J.,LAW, POLITICS, AND THE SECURITY COUNCIL*   DELIB/GP
AN INQUIRY INTO THE HANDLING OF LEGAL QUESTIONS.   ADJUD
LAW CONSTN NAT/G ACT/RES OP/RES CT/SYS TASK PWR   ROUTINE
...INT/LAW BIBLIOG UN. PAGE 59 E1180
                                              B64

KOREA (REPUBLIC) SUPREME COURT,KOREAN LEGAL SYSTEM.   JURID
KOREA/S WOR+45 LAW LEAD ROUTINE GOV/REL ORD/FREE 20   CT/SYS
SUPREME/CT. PAGE 61 E1229   CONSTN
                                                      CRIME
                                              B64

SHAPIRO M.,LAW AND POLITICS IN THE SUPREME COURT: LEGIS
NEW APPROACHES TO POLITICAL JURISPRUDENCE. JUDGE   CT/SYS
PROB/SOLV LEGIT EXEC ROUTINE ATTIT ALL/VALS   LAW
...DECISION SOC. PAGE 90 E1811   JURID
                                              B64

UN PUB. INFORM. ORGAN.,EVERY MAN'S UNITED NATIONS.   INT/ORG
UNIV WOR+45 CONSTN CULTURE SOCIETY ECO/DEV   ROUTINE
ECO/UNDEV NAT/G ACT/RES PLAN ECO/TAC INT/TRADE
EDU/PROP LEGIT PEACE ATTIT ALL/VALS...POLICY HUM
INT/LAW CONCPT CHARTS UN TOT/POP 20. PAGE 97 E1954
                                              L64

WORLD PEACE FOUNDATION.,"INTERNATIONAL   INT/ORG
ORGANIZATIONS: SUMMARY OF ACTIVITIES." INDIA   ROUTINE
PAKISTAN TURKEY WOR+45 CONSTN CONSULT EX/STRUC
ECO/TAC EDU/PROP LEGIT ORD/FREE...JURID SOC UN 20
CYPRESS. PAGE 107 E2145
                                              B65

BRIGGS H.W.,THE INTERNATIONAL LAW COMMISSION. LAW   INT/LAW
CONSTN LEGIS CREATE ADJUD CT/SYS ROUTINE TASK   DELIB/GP
EFFICIENCY...CLASSIF OBS UN. PAGE 15 E0302
                                              B65

FLEMING R.W.,THE LABOR ARBITRATION PROCESS. USA+45   GP/REL
LAW BARGAIN ADJUD ROUTINE SANCTION COST...PREDICT   LABOR
CHARTS TIME 20. PAGE 38 E0763   CONSULT
                                                      DELIB/GP
                                              B65

GOTLIEB A.,DISARMAMENT AND INTERNATIONAL LAW* A   INT/LAW
STUDY OF THE ROLE OF LAW IN THE DISARMAMENT   INT/ORG
PROCESS. USA+45 USSR PROB/SOLV CONFER ADMIN ROUTINE   ARMS/CONT
NUC/PWR ORD/FREE SOVEREIGN UN TREATY. PAGE 45 E0893   IDEA/COMP
                                              B65

PEASLEE A.J.,CONSTITUTIONS OF NATIONS* THIRD   AFR
REVISED EDITION (VOLUME I* AFRICA). LAW EX/STRUC   CHOOSE

LEGIS TOP/EX LEGIT CT/SYS ROUTINE ORD/FREE PWR   CONSTN
SOVEREIGN...CON/ANAL CHARTS. PAGE 80 E1606   NAT/G
                                              B65

US SENATE COMM ON JUDICIARY,HEARINGS BEFORE   ROUTINE
SUBCOMMITTEE ON ADMINISTRATIVE PRACTICE AND   DELIB/GP
PROCEDURE ABOUT ADMINISTRATIVE PROCEDURE ACT 1965.   ADMIN
USA+45 LEGIS EDU/PROP ADJUD GOV/REL INGP/REL   NAT/G
EFFICIENCY...POLICY INT 20 CONGRESS. PAGE 103 E2055
                                              B65

WHITE G.M.,THE USE OF EXPERTS BY INTERNATIONAL   INT/LAW
TRIBUNALS. WOR+45 WOR-45 INT/ORG NAT/G PAY ADJUD   ROUTINE
COST...OBS BIBLIOG 20. PAGE 106 E2117   CONSULT
                                                      CT/SYS
                                              L65

FORTE W.E.,"THE FOOD AND DRUG ADMINISTRATION, THE   CONTROL
FEDERAL TRADE COMMISSION AND THE DECEPTIVE   HEALTH
PACKAGING." ROUTINE...JURID 20 FTC. PAGE 39 E0772   ADJUD
                                                      INDUS
                                              L65

RUBIN A.P.,"UNITED STATES CONTEMPORARY PRACTICE   LAW
RELATING TO INTERNATIONAL LAW." USA+45 WOR+45   LEGIT
CONSTN INT/ORG NAT/G DELIB/GP EX/STRUC DIPLOM DOMIN   INT/LAW
CT/SYS ROUTINE ORD/FREE...CONCPT COLD/WAR 20.
PAGE 86 E1730
                                              S65

MAC CHESNEY B.,"SOME COMMENTS ON THE 'QUARANTINE'   INT/ORG
OF CUBA." USA+45 WOR+45 NAT/G BAL/PWR DIPLOM LEGIT   LAW
ROUTINE ATTIT ORD/FREE...JURID METH/CNCPT 20.   CUBA
PAGE 67 E1337   USSR
                                              S65

ULMER S.S.,"TOWARD A THEORY OF SUBGROUP FORMATION   CT/SYS
IN THE UNITED STATES SUPREME COURT." USA+45 ROUTINE   ADJUD
CHOOSE PWR...JURID STAT CON/ANAL SIMUL SUPREME/CT.   ELITES
PAGE 97 E1952   INGP/REL
                                              B66

BURNS A.C.,PARLIAMENT AS AN EXPORT. WOR+45 CONSTN   PARL/PROC
BARGAIN DEBATE ROUTINE GOV/REL EFFICIENCY...ANTHOL   POL/PAR
COMMONWLTH PARLIAMENT. PAGE 17 E0343   CT/SYS
                                                      CHIEF
                                              B66

DAVIS K.,BUSINESS AND ITS ENVIRONMENT. LAW ECO/DEV   EX/STRUC
INDUS OP/RES ADMIN CONTROL ROUTINE GP/REL PROFIT   PROB/SOLV
POLICY. PAGE 29 E0573   CAP/ISM
                                                      EXEC
                                              B66

WALL E.H.,THE COURT OF JUSTICE IN THE EUROPEAN   CT/SYS
COMMUNITIES: JURISDICTION AND PROCEDURE. EUR+WWI   INT/ORG
DIPLOM ADJUD ADMIN ROUTINE TASK...CONCPT LING 20.   LAW
PAGE 105 E2096   OP/RES
                                              B66

YOUNG W.,EXISTING MECHANISMS OF ARMS CONTROL.   ARMS/CONT
PROC/MFG OP/RES DIPLOM TASK CENTRAL...MGT TREATY.   ADMIN
PAGE 108 E2165   NUC/PWR
                                                      ROUTINE
                                              B67

US PRES TASK FORCE ADMIN JUS,TASK FORCE REPORT: THE   CT/SYS
COURTS. USA+45 CONSULT CONFER...JURID CHARTS.   ADJUD
PAGE 101 E2025   ROUTINE
                                                      ADMIN
                                              S67

KETCHAM O.W.,"GUIDELINES FROM GAULT: REVOLUTIONARY   ADJUD
REQUIREMENTS AND REAPPRAISAL." LAW CONSTN CREATE   AGE/Y
LEGIT ROUTINE SANCTION CRIME DISCRIM PRIVIL ROLE   CT/SYS
...JURID NEW/IDEA 20 SUPREME/CT. PAGE 60 E1208
                                              S67

SCHELLING T.C.,"ECONOMICS AND CRIMINAL ENTERPRISE."   CRIME
LAW FORCES BARGAIN ECO/TAC CONTROL GAMBLE ROUTINE   PROB/SOLV
ADJUST DEMAND INCOME PROFIT CRIMLGY. PAGE 87 E1756   CONCPT
                                              S67

TYDINGS J.D.,"MODERNIZING THE ADMINISTRATION OF   CT/SYS
JUSTICE." PLAN ADMIN ROUTINE EFFICIENCY...JURID   MGT
SIMUL. PAGE 97 E1948   COMPUTER
                                                      CONSULT

RUBIN A.P. E1730

RUCKER B.W. E1731

RUDIN H.R. E1732

RUEDA B. E1733

RUEF/ABE....ABRAHAM RUEF

RULES/COMM....RULES COMMITTEES OF CONGRESS

RUMOR....SEE ALSO PERS/REL

B58
DUCLOUX L.,FROM BLACKMAIL TO TREASON. FRANCE PLAN   COERCE
DIPLOM EDU/PROP PRESS RUMOR NAT/LISM...CRIMLGY 20.   CRIME
PAGE 33 E0653   NAT/G
                                                          PWR

B62
CURRY J.E.,RACE TENSIONS AND THE POLICE. LAW MUNIC   FORCES
NEIGH TEC/DEV RUMOR CONTROL COERCE GP/REL ATTIT   RACE/REL
...SOC 20 NEGRO. PAGE 28 E0558   CROWD
                                                          ORD/FREE

B63
STREET H.,FREEDOM: THE INDIVIDUAL AND THE LAW. UK   ORD/FREE
COM/IND EDU/PROP PRESS RUMOR TV PWR 20 CIVIL/LIB   NAT/G
FILM. PAGE 94 E1886   JURID
                                                          PARL/PROC

RUNCIMAN W.G. E1734

RURAL....RURAL AREAS, PEOPLE, ETC.

RUSK/DEAN....DEAN RUSK

RUSKIN/J....JOHN RUSKIN

RUSSEL F.M. E1735

RUSSELL B. E1736

RUSSELL R.B. E1737,E1738

RUSSELL/B....BERTRAND RUSSELL

B67
RUSSELL B.,WAR CRIMES IN VIETNAM. USA+45 VIETNAM   WAR
FORCES DIPLOM WEAPON RACE/REL DISCRIM ISOLAT   CRIME
BIO/SOC 20 COLD/WAR RUSSELL/B. PAGE 87 E1736   ATTIT
                                                          POLICY

RUSSIA....PRE-REVOLUTIONARY RUSSIA; SEE ALSO APPROPRIATE
          TIME/SPACE/CULTURE INDEX

B66
THOMPSON J.M.,RUSSIA, BOLSHEVISM, AND THE   DIPLOM
VERSAILLES PEACE. RUSSIA USSR INT/ORG NAT/G   PEACE
DELIB/GP AGREE REV WAR PWR 20 TREATY VERSAILLES   MARXISM
BOLSHEVISM. PAGE 96 E1919

RUTHERFORD M.L. E1739

RWANDA....SEE ALSO AFR

RYAN F.M. E0230

RYAN J.A. E1740

RYUKYUS....RYUKYU ISLANDS

S

S/AFR....SOUTH AFRICA, SEE ALSO AFR

S/ASIA....SOUTHEAST ASIA; SEE ALSO APPROPRIATE NATIONS

N
ANNALS OF THE AMERICAN ACADEMY OF POLITICAL AND   BIBLIOG/A
SOCIAL SCIENCE. AFR ASIA S/ASIA WOR+45 POL/PAR   NAT/G
DIPLOM CRIME REV...SOC BIOG 20. PAGE 1 E0003   CULTURE
                                                         ATTIT

N
INTERNATIONAL STUDIES. ASIA S/ASIA WOR+45 ECO/UNDEV   BIBLIOG/A
INT/ORG NAT/G LEAD ATTIT WEALTH...SOC 20. PAGE 1   DIPLOM
E0009   INT/LAW
                                                        INT/TRADE

N
THE JAPAN SCIENCE REVIEW: LAW AND POLITICS: LIST OF   BIBLIOG
BOOKS AND ARTICLES ON LAW AND POLITICS. CONSTN AGRI   LAW
INDUS LABOR DIPLOM TAX ADMIN CRIME...INT/LAW SOC 20   S/ASIA
CHINJAP. PAGE 2 E0027   PHIL/SCI

N
ASIA FOUNDATION,LIBRARY NOTES. LAW CONSTN CULTURE   BIBLIOG/A
SOCIETY ECO/UNDEV INT/ORG NAT/G COLONIAL LEAD   ASIA
REGION NAT/LISM ATTIT 20 UN. PAGE 6 E0107   S/ASIA
                                                        DIPLOM

N
CORNELL UNIVERSITY LIBRARY,SOUTHEAST ASIA   BIBLIOG
ACCESSIONS LIST. LAW SOCIETY STRUCT ECO/UNDEV   S/ASIA
POL/PAR TEC/DEV DIPLOM LEAD REGION. PAGE 26 E0510   NAT/G
                                                        CULTURE

B01
GRIFFIN A.P.C.,LIST OF BOOKS ON SAMOA (PAMPHLET).   BIBLIOG/A
GERMANY S/ASIA UK USA-45 WOR-45 ECO/UNDEV REGION   COLONIAL
ALL/VALS ORD/FREE ALL/IDEOS...GEOG INT/LAW 19 SAMOA   DIPLOM
GUAM. PAGE 46 E0918

B01
GRONING J.,BIBLIOTHECA JURIS GENTIUM COMMUNIS, QUA   BIBLIOG
PRAECIPUORUM, ASIAE, AFRICAE, ET AMERICAE,   JURID
POPULORUM DE JURIS NATURAE... AFR ASIA S/ASIA   LAW
USA-45 16/17. PAGE 48 E0946   NAT/G

B03
GRONING J.,BIBLIOTHECA JURIS GENTIUM EXOTICA. AFR   BIBLIOG
ASIA S/ASIA USA-45 16/17. PAGE 48 E0947   JURID
                                                        NAT/G
                                                        LAW

B38
GRISWOLD A.W.,THE FAR EASTERN POLICY OF THE UNITED   DIPLOM
STATES. ASIA S/ASIA USA-45 INT/ORG INT/TRADE WAR   POLICY
NAT/LISM...BIBLIOG 19/20 LEAGUE/NAT ROOSEVLT/T   CHIEF
ROOSEVLT/F WILSON/W TREATY. PAGE 47 E0943

B45
US LIBRARY OF CONGRESS,NETHERLANDS EAST INDIES.   BIBLIOG/A
INDONESIA LAW CULTURE AGRI INDUS SCHOOL COLONIAL   S/ASIA
HEALTH...GEOG JURID SOC 19/20 NETH/IND. PAGE 101   NAT/G
E2017

B50
EMBREE J.F.,BIBLIOGRAPHY OF THE PEOPLES AND   BIBLIOG/A
CULTURES OF MAINLAND SOUTHEAST ASIA. CAMBODIA LAOS   CULTURE
THAILAND VIETNAM LAW...GEOG HUM SOC MYTH LING   S/ASIA
CHARTS WORSHIP 20. PAGE 35 E0686

B54
NUSSBAUM D.,A CONCISE HISTORY OF THE LAW OF   INT/ORG
NATIONS. ASIA CHRIST-17C EUR+WWI ISLAM MEDIT-7   LAW
MOD/EUR S/ASIA UNIV WOR+45 WOR-45 SOCIETY STRUCT   PEACE
EXEC ATTIT ALL/VALS...CONCPT HIST/WRIT TIME/SEQ.   INT/LAW
PAGE 78 E1560

B58
ALEXANDROWICZ,A BIBLIOGRAPHY OF INDIAN LAW. INDIA   BIBLIOG
S/ASIA CONSTN CT/SYS...INT/LAW 19/20. PAGE 3 E0062   LAW
                                                       ADJUD
                                                       JURID

B61
SYATAUW J.J.G.,SOME NEWLY ESTABLISHED ASIAN STATES   INT/LAW
AND THE DEVELOPMENT OF INTERNATIONAL LAW. BURMA   ADJUST
CEYLON INDIA INDONESIA ECO/UNDEV COLONIAL NEUTRAL   SOCIETY
WAR PEACE SOVEREIGN...CHARTS 19/20. PAGE 95 E1902   S/ASIA

L62
CORET A.,"L'INDEPENDANCE DU SAMOA OCCIDENTAL."   NAT/G
S/ASIA LAW INT/ORG EXEC ALL/VALS SAMOA UN 20.   STRUCT
PAGE 26 E0508   SOVEREIGN

L63
ROSE R.,"COMPARATIVE STUDIES IN POLITICAL FINANCE: FINAN
A SYMPOSIUM." ASIA EUR+WWI S/ASIA LAW CULTURE   POL/PAR
DELIB/GP LEGIS ACT/RES ECO/TAC EDU/PROP CHOOSE
ATTIT RIGID/FLEX SUPEGO PWR SKILL WEALTH...STAT
ANTHOL VAL/FREE. PAGE 85 E1714

S63
LEPAWSKY A.,"INTERNATIONAL DEVELOPMENT OF RIVER   INT/ORG
RESOURCES." CANADA EUR+WWI S/ASIA USA+45 SEA LEGIT   DELIB/GP
ADJUD ORD/FREE PWR WEALTH...MGT TIME/SEQ VAL/FREE
MEXIC/AMER 20. PAGE 64 E1287

S63
WEISSBERG G.,"MAPS AS EVIDENCE IN INTERNATIONAL   LAW
BOUNDARY DISPUTES: A REAPPRAISAL." CHINA/COM   GEOG
EUR+WWI INDIA MOD/EUR S/ASIA INT/ORG NAT/G LEGIT   SOVEREIGN
PERCEPT...JURID CHARTS 20. PAGE 105 E2110

B64
GOODNOW H.F.,THE CIVIL SERVICE OF PAKISTAN: ADMIN
BUREAUCRACY IN A NEW NATION. INDIA PAKISTAN S/ASIA   GOV/REL
ECO/UNDEV PROVS CHIEF PARTIC CHOOSE EFFICIENCY PWR   LAW
...BIBLIOG 20. PAGE 45 E0889   NAT/G

RAGHAVAN M.D.,INDIA IN CEYLONESE HISTORY, SOCIETY AND CULTURE. CEYLON INDIA S/ASIA LAW SOCIETY INT/TRADE ATTIT...ART/METH JURID SOC LING 20. PAGE 83 E1668
DIPLOM CULTURE SECT STRUCT
B64

REGALA R.,WORLD PEACE THROUGH DIPLOMACY AND LAW. S/ASIA WOR+45 ECO/UNDEV INT/ORG FORCES PLAN PROB/SOLV FOR/AID NUC/PWR WAR...POLICY INT/LAW 20. PAGE 84 E1679
DIPLOM PEACE ADJUD
B64

POUNDS N.J.G.,"THE POLITICS OF PARTITION." AFR ASIA COM EUR+WWI FUT ISLAM S/ASIA USA-45 LAW ECO/DEV ECO/UNDEV AGRI INDUS INT/ORG POL/PAR PROVS SECT FORCES TOP/EX EDU/PROP LEGIT ATTIT MORAL ORD/FREE PWR RESPECT WEALTH. PAGE 82 E1640
NAT/G NAT/LISM
L64

SINGH N.,"THE CONTEMPORARY PRACTICE OF INDIA IN THE FIELD OF INTERNATIONAL LAW." INDIA S/ASIA INT/ORG NAT/G DOMIN EDU/PROP LEGIT KNOWL...CONCPT TOT/POP 20. PAGE 91 E1833
LAW ATTIT DIPLOM INT/LAW
S64

INST INTL DES CIVILISATION DIF,THE CONSTITUTIONS AND ADMINISTRATIVE INSTITUTIONS OF THE NEW STATES. AFR ISLAM S/ASIA NAT/G POL/PAR DELIB/GP EX/STRUC CONFER EFFICIENCY NAT/LISM...JURID SOC 20. PAGE 56 E1123
CONSTN ADMIN ADJUD ECO/UNDEV
B65

VON RENESSE E.A.,UNVOLLENDETE DEMOKRATIEN. AFR ISLAM S/ASIA SOCIETY ACT/RES COLONIAL...JURID CHARTS BIBLIOG METH 13/20. PAGE 104 E2083
ECO/UNDEV NAT/COMP SOVEREIGN
B65

SHARMA S.P.,"THE INDIA-CHINA BORDER DISPUTE: AN INDIAN PERSPECTIVE." ASIA CHINA/COM S/ASIA NAT/G LEGIT CT/SYS NAT/LISM DRIVE MORAL ORD/FREE PWR 20. PAGE 91 E1815
LAW ATTIT SOVEREIGN INDIA
L65

PRABHAKAR P.,"SURVEY OF RESEARCH AND SOURCE MATERIALS; THE SINO-INDIAN BORDER DISPUTE." CHINA/COM INDIA LAW NAT/G PLAN BAL/PWR WAR...POLICY 20 COLD/WAR. PAGE 82 E1645
BIBLIOG ASIA S/ASIA DIPLOM
S65

US DEPARTMENT OF STATE,RESEARCH ON AFRICA (EXTERNAL RESEARCH LIST NO 5-25). LAW CULTURE ECO/UNDEV POL/PAR DIPLOM EDU/PROP LEAD REGION MARXISM...GEOG LING WORSHIP 20. PAGE 100 E1996
BIBLIOG/A ASIA S/ASIA NAT/G
B66

US SENATE COMM ON FOREIGN REL,ASIAN DEVELOPMENT BANK ACT. USA+45 LAW DIPLOM...CHARTS 20 BLACK/EUG S/EASTASIA. PAGE 101 E2030
FOR/AID FINAN ECO/UNDEV S/ASIA
B66

ANAND R.P.,"ATTITUDE OF THE ASIAN-AFRICAN STATES TOWARD CERTAIN PROBLEMS OF INTERNATIONAL LAW." L/A+17C S/ASIA ECO/UNDEV CREATE CONFER ADJUD COLONIAL...RECORD GP/COMP UN. PAGE 5 E0087
INT/LAW ATTIT ASIA AFR
S66

WATT A.,THE EVOLUTION OF AUSTRALIAN FOREIGN POLICY 1938-65. ASIA S/ASIA USA+45 USA-45 INT/ORG NAT/G FORCES FOR/AID TREATY 20 AUSTRAL. PAGE 105 E2103
DIPLOM WAR
B67

S/EASTASIA....SOUTHEAST ASIA: CAMBODIA, LAOS, NORTH AND SOUTH VIETNAM, AND THAILAND

US SENATE COMM ON FOREIGN REL,ASIAN DEVELOPMENT BANK ACT. USA+45 LAW DIPLOM...CHARTS 20 BLACK/EUG S/EASTASIA. PAGE 101 E2030
FOR/AID FINAN ECO/UNDEV S/ASIA
B66

SABAH....SABAH, MALAYSIA

SABBATINO....SABBATINO CASE

FALK R.A.,THE AFTERMATH OF SABBATINO: BACKGROUND PAPERS AND PROCEEDINGS OF SEVENTH HAMMARSKJOLD FORUM. USA+45 LAW ACT/RES ADJUD ROLE...BIBLIOG 20 EXPROPRIAT SABBATINO HARLAN/JM. PAGE 36 E0718
SOVEREIGN CT/SYS INT/LAW OWN
B65

SAINT AUGUSTINE....SEE AUGUSTINE

SAINT/PIER....JACQUES SAINT-PIERRE

SAINT-PIERRE C.I. E1741

SAINTSIMON....COMTE DE SAINT-SIMON

SALARY....SEE WORKER, WEALTH, ROUTINE

SALAZAR/A....ANTONIO DE OLIVERA SALAZAR

SALERA V. E0691

SALIENCE....SALIENCE

SALINGER/P....PIERRE SALINGER

SALMOND J.W. E1742

SALO....SALO REPUBLIC

SALTER L.M. E1743

SAMBURU....SAMBURU TRIBE OF EAST AFRICA

GRIFFIN A.P.C.,LIST OF BOOKS ON SAMOA (PAMPHLET). GERMANY S/ASIA UK USA-45 WOR-45 ECO/UNDEV REGION ALL/VALS ORD/FREE ALL/IDEOS...GEOG INT/LAW 19 SAMOA GUAM. PAGE 46 E0918
BIBLIOG/A COLONIAL DIPLOM
B01

CORET A.,"L'INDEPENDANCE DU SAMOA OCCIDENTAL." S/ASIA LAW INT/ORG EXEC ALL/VALS SAMOA UN 20. PAGE 26 E0508
NAT/G STRUCT SOVEREIGN
L62

SAMP....SAMPLE SURVEY

HALL A.B.,"DETERMINATION OF METHODS FOR ASCERTAINING THE FACTORS THAT INFLUENCE JUDICIAL DECISIONS IN CASES INVOLVING DUE PROCESS" LAW JUDGE DEBATE EFFICIENCY OPTIMAL UTIL...SOC CONCPT PROBABIL STAT SAMP. PAGE 49 E0981
ADJUD DECISION CONSTN JURID
S26

ANGELL R.C.,"THE SOCIAL INTEGRATION OF AMERICAN CITIES OF MORE THAN 1000,000 POPULATION" (BMR)" USA+45 SOCIETY CRIME ADJUST WEALTH...GEOG SOC CONCPT INDICATOR SAMP CHARTS SOC/INTEG 20. PAGE 5 E0098
MUNIC CENSUS GP/REL
S47

BROMWICH L.,UNION CONSTITUTIONS. CONSTN EX/STRUC PRESS ADJUD CONTROL CHOOSE REPRESENT PWR SAMP. PAGE 16 E0306
LABOR ROUTINE INGP/REL RACE/REL
B59

STERN A.C.,AIR POLLUTION (2 VOLS.). LAW INDUS PROB/SOLV TEC/DEV INSPECT RISK BIO/SOC HABITAT ...OBS/ENVIR TESTS SAMP 20 POLLUTION. PAGE 93 E1871
AIR OP/RES CONTROL HEALTH
B62

TRISKA J.F.,THE THEORY, LAW, AND POLICY OF SOVIET TREATIES. WOR+45 WOR-45 CONSTN INT/ORG NAT/G VOL/ASSN DOMIN LEGIT COERCE ATTIT PWR RESPECT ...POLICY JURID CONCPT OBS SAMP TIME/SEQ TREND GEN/LAWS 20. PAGE 97 E1941
COM LAW INT/LAW USSR
B62

HILLS R.J.,"THE REPRESENTATIVE FUNCTION: NEGLECTED DIMENSION OF LEADERSHIP BEHAVIOR" USA+45 CLIENT STRUCT SCHOOL PERS/REL...STAT QU SAMP LAB/EXP 20. PAGE 53 E1048
LEAD ADMIN EXEC ACT/RES
S63

TRISKA J.F.,"SOVIET TREATY LAW: A QUANTITATIVE ANALYSIS." WOR+45 LAW ECO/UNDEV AGRI COM/IND INDUS CREATE TEC/DEV DIPLOM ATTIT PWR WEALTH...JURID SAMP TIME/SEQ TREND CHARTS VAL/FREE 20 TREATY. PAGE 97 E1942
COM ECO/TAC INT/LAW USSR
S64

RUNCIMAN W.G.,RELATIVE DEPRIVATION AND SOCIAL JUSTICE: A STUDY OF ATTITUDES TO SOCIAL INEQUALITY IN TWENTIETH-CENTURY ENGLAND. UK LAW POL/PAR PWR ...CONCPT NEW/IDEA SAMP METH 19/20. PAGE 86 E1734
STRATA STRUCT DISCRIM ATTIT
B66

RUCKER B.W.,"WHAT SOLUTIONS DO PEOPLE ENDORSE IN FREE PRESS-FAIR TRIAL DILEMMA?" LAW NAT/G CT/SYS ATTIT...NET/THEORY SAMP CHARTS IDEA/COMP METH 20. PAGE 86 E1731
CONCPT PRESS ADJUD ORD/FREE
S67

SAMP/SIZ....SIZES AND TECHNIQUES OF SAMPLING

B66
FELSHER H..JUSTICE USA? USA+45 COM/IND JUDGE CT/SYS ADJUD
MORAL ORD/FREE...SAMP/SIZ HYPO/EXP. PAGE 37 E0735   EDU/PROP
                                                      LOBBY

SAMPLE....SEE SAMP

SAMPLE AND SAMPLING....SEE UNIVERSES AND SAMPLING INDEX,
   P. XIV

SAMUELSN/P....PAUL SAMUELSON

SAN/FRAN....SAN FRANCISCO

SAN/MARINO....SAN MARINO

SAN/MARTIN....JOSE DE SAN MARTIN

SAN/QUENTN....SAN QUENTIN PRISON

                                                      B61
DAVIS B.F..THE DESPERATE AND THE DAMNED. USA+45 LAW PUB/INST
DEATH ANOMIE...CRIMLGY 20 SAN/QUENTN. PAGE 29 E0571   SANCTION
                                                      CRIME

SANCTION....SANCTION OF LAW AND SEMI-LEGAL PRIVATE
   ASSOCIATIONS AND SOCIAL GROUPS

                                                      C01
BERKELEY G.."DISCOURSE ON PASSIVE OBEDIENCE" (1712) INGP/REL
THE WORKS... (VOL. IV)" UNIV DOMIN LEGIT CONTROL   SANCTION
CRIME ADJUST CENTRAL MORAL ORD/FREE...POLICY   RESPECT
WORSHIP. PAGE 10 E0202   GEN/LAWS

                                                      B12
FOUAD M..LE REGIME DE LA PRESSE EN EGYPTE: THESE   ORD/FREE
POUR LE DOCTORAT. UAR LICENSE EDU/PROP ADMIN   LEGIS
SANCTION CRIME SUPEGO PWR...ART/METH JURID 19/20.   CONTROL
PAGE 39 E0778   PRESS

                                                      B16
SCHROEDER T..FREE SPEECH FOR RADICALS (REV. ED.).   ORD/FREE
USA-45 CONSTN INDUS LOC/G FORCES SANCTION WAR ATTIT   CONTROL
SEX...JURID REFORMERS 20 FREE/SPEE. PAGE 88 E1767   LAW
                                                      PRESS

                                                      B26
HOCKING W.E..PRESENT STATUS OF THE PHILOSOPHY OF   JURID
LAW AND OF RIGHTS. UNIV CULTURE INTELL SOCIETY   PHIL/SCI
NAT/G CREATE LEGIT SANCTION ALL/VALS SOC/INTEG   ORD/FREE
18/20. PAGE 53 E1060

                                                      B30
BENTHAM J..THE RATIONALE OF PUNISHMENT. UK LAW   CRIME
LOC/G NAT/G LEGIS CONTROL...JURID GEN/LAWS   SANCTION
COURT/SYS 19. PAGE 10 E0192   COERCE
                                                      ORD/FREE

                                                      B30
BIRD F.L..THE RECALL OF PUBLIC OFFICERS; A STUDY OF REPRESENT
THE OPERATION OF RECALL IN CALIFORNIA. LOC/G MUNIC   SANCTION
POL/PAR PROVS PROB/SOLV ADJUD PARTIC...CHARTS   CHOOSE
METH/COMP 20 CALIFORNIA RECALL. PAGE 12 E0230   LAW

                                                      B32
GREAT BRIT COMM MINISTERS PWR.REPORT. UK LAW CONSTN EX/STRUC
CONSULT LEGIS PARL/PROC SANCTION SOVEREIGN   NAT/G
...DECISION JURID 20 PARLIAMENT. PAGE 45 E0902   PWR
                                                      CONTROL

                                                      B34
CLYDE W.M..THE STRUGGLE FOR THE FREEDOM OF THE   PRESS
PRESS FROM CAXTON TO CROMWELL. UK LAW LOC/G SECT   ORD/FREE
FORCES LICENSE WRITING SANCTION REV ATTIT PWR   CONTROL
...POLICY 15/17 PARLIAMENT CROMWELL/O MILTON/J.
PAGE 23 E0460

                                                      B36
HANSON L..GOVERNMENT AND THE PRESS 1695-1763. UK   LAW
LOC/G LEGIS LICENSE CONTROL SANCTION CRIME ATTIT   JURID
ORD/FREE 17/18 PARLIAMENT AMEND/I. PAGE 50 E0996   PRESS
                                                      POLICY

                                                      S36
CORWIN E.S.."THE CONSTITUTION AS INSTRUMENT AND AS   CONSTN
SYMBOL." USA-45 ECO/DEV INDUS CAP/ISM SANCTION   LAW
RIGID/FLEX ORD/FREE LAISSEZ OBJECTIVE 20 CONGRESS   ADJUD
SUPREME/CT. PAGE 26 E0512   PWR

                                                      B37
SCHUSTER E..GUIDE TO LAW AND LEGAL LITERATURE OF   BIBLIOG/A
CENTRAL AMERICAN REPUBLICS. L/A+17C INT/ORG ADJUD   REGION

SANCTION CRIME...JURID 19/20. PAGE 89 E1785   CT/SYS
                                                      LAW

                                                      B40
HOBBES T..A DIALOGUE BETWEEN A PHILOSOPHER AND A   CT/SYS
STUDENT OF THE COMMON LAWS OF ENGLAND (1667?). UK   CHIEF
SECT DOMIN ADJUD CRIME INCOME OWN UTIL ORD/FREE PWR   SANCTION
SOVEREIGN...JURID GEN/LAWS 17. PAGE 53 E1057

                                                      S40
GURVITCH G.."MAJOR PROBLEMS OF THE SOCIOLOGY OF   SOC
LAW." CULTURE SANCTION KNOWL MORAL...POLICY EPIST   LAW
JURID WORSHIP. PAGE 48 E0963   PHIL/SCI

                                                      C43
BENTHAM J.."PRINCIPLES OF INTERNATIONAL LAW" IN J.   INT/LAW
BOWRING, ED., THE WORKS OF JEREMY BENTHAM." UNIV   JURID
NAT/G PLAN PROB/SOLV DIPLOM CONTROL SANCTION MORAL   WAR
ORD/FREE PWR SOVEREIGN 19. PAGE 10 E0194   PEACE

                                                      C43
BENTHAM J.."THE RATIONALE OF REWARD" IN J. BOWRING, SANCTION
ED., THE WORKS OF JEREMY BENTHAM (VOL. 2)" LAW   ECO/TAC
WORKER CREATE INSPECT PAY ROUTINE HAPPINESS PRODUC   INCOME
SUPEGO WEALTH METH/CNCPT. PAGE 10 E0195   PWR

                                                      S44
MASON J.B.."THE JUDICIAL SYSTEM OF THE NAZI PARTY." FASCISM
GERMANY ELITES POL/PAR DOMIN CONTROL SANCTION   CT/SYS
TOTALISM...JURID 20 HITLER/A. PAGE 69 E1381   ADJUD
                                                      LAW

                                                      S45
DAVIS A.."CASTE, ECONOMY, AND VIOLENCE" (BMR)"   STRATA
USA-45 LAW SOCIETY STRUCT SECT SANCTION COERCE   RACE/REL
MARRIAGE SEX...PSY SOC SOC/INTEG 18/20 NEGRO   DISCRIM
MISCEGEN SOUTH/US. PAGE 29 E0570

                                                      B48
CORWIN E.S..LIBERTY AGAINST GOVERNMENT: THE RISE,   CONCPT
FLOWERING AND DECLINE OF A FAMOUS JURIDICAL   ORD/FREE
CONCEPT. LEGIS ADJUD CT/SYS SANCTION GOV/REL   JURID
FEDERAL CONSERVE NEW/LIB...OLD/LIB 18/20 ROMAN/LAW   CONSTN
COMMON/LAW. PAGE 26 E0514

                                                      B49
SCHONS D..BOOK CENSORSHIP IN NEW SPAIN (NEW WORLD   CHRIST-17C
STUDIES, BOOK II). SPAIN LAW CULTURE INSPECT ADJUD   EDU/PROP
CT/SYS SANCTION GP/REL ORD/FREE 14/17. PAGE 88   CONTROL
E1764   PRESS

                                                      S49
FIELD G.L.."LAW AS AN OBJECTIVE POLITICAL CONCEPT"   LAW
(BMR)" UNIV SOCIETY RATIONAL JURID. PAGE 38 E0747   CONCPT
                                                      METH/CNCPT
                                                      SANCTION

                                                      B50
BURDETTE F.L..LOBBYISTS IN ACTION (PAMPHLET).   LOBBY
CONSULT TEC/DEV INSPECT BARGAIN PARL/PROC SANCTION   ATTIT
20 CONGRESS. PAGE 17 E0329   POLICY
                                                      LAW

                                                      B51
BIDDLE F..THE FEAR OF FREEDOM. USA+45 LAW NAT/G   ANOMIE
PUB/INST PROB/SOLV DOMIN CONTROL SANCTION REV   INGP/REL
NAT/LISM 20. PAGE 12 E0227   VOL/ASSN
                                                      ORD/FREE

                                                      B51
HUXLEY J..FREEDOM AND CULTURE. UNIV LAW SOCIETY R+D CULTURE
ACADEM SCHOOL CREATE SANCTION ATTIT KNOWL...HUM   ORD/FREE
ANTHOL 20. PAGE 56 E1118   PHIL/SCI
                                                      IDEA/COMP

                                                      B51
KEFAUVER E..CRIME IN AMERICA. USA+45 USA-45 MUNIC   ELITES
NEIGH DELIB/GP TRIBUTE GAMBLE LOBBY SANCTION   CRIME
...AUD/VIS 20 CAPONE/AL MAFIA MIAMI CHICAGO   PWR
DETROIT. PAGE 60 E1194   FORCES

                                                      B54
LANDHEER B..RECOGNITION IN INTERNATIONAL LAW   BIBLIOG/A
(SELECTIVE BIBLIOGRAPHIES OF THE LIBRARY OF THE   INT/LAW
PEACE PALACE, VOL. II; PAMPHLET). NAT/G LEGIT   INT/ORG
SANCTION 20. PAGE 63 E1251   DIPLOM

                                                      B54
O'NEILL J.M..CATHOLICS IN CONTROVERSY. USA+45 NAT/G CATHISM
PROVS SCHOOL SECT EDU/PROP LEGIT CT/SYS SANCTION   CONSTN
GP/REL 20 SUPREME/CT CHURCH/STA. PAGE 78 E1569   POLICY
                                                      LAW

                                                      B55
BERNSTEIN M.H..REGULATING BUSINESS BY INDEPENDENT   DELIB/GP
COMMISSION. USA+45 USA-45 LG/CO CHIEF LEGIS   CONTROL

PROB/SOLV ADJUD SANCTION GP/REL ATTIT...TIME/SEQ
19/20 MONOPOLY PRESIDENT CONGRESS. PAGE 11 E0214
CONSULT

B55

KHADDURI M.,LAW IN THE MIDDLE EAST. LAW CONSTN
ACADEM FAM EDU/PROP CT/SYS SANCTION CRIME...INT/LAW
GOV/COMP ANTHOL 6/20 MID/EAST. PAGE 61 E1210
ADJUD
JURID
ISLAM

B55

LARROWE C.P.,SHAPE-UP AND HIRING HALL. TRIBUTE
ADJUD CONTROL SANCTION COERCE CRIME GP/REL PWR
...CHARTS 20 AFL/CIO NEWYORK/C SEATTLE. PAGE 63
E1256
LABOR
INDUS
WORKER
NAT/G

B56

ALEXANDER F.,THE CRIMINAL, THE JUDGE, AND THE
PUBLIC. LAW CULTURE CONSULT LEGIT ADJUD SANCTION
ORD/FREE 20. PAGE 3 E0060
CRIME
CRIMLGY
PSY
ATTIT

B56

KALNOKI BEDO A.,LEGAL SOURCES AND BIBLIOGRAPHY OF
HUNGARY. COM HUNGARY CONSTN LEGIS JUDGE CT/SYS
SANCTION CRIME 16/20. PAGE 59 E1181
BIBLIOG
ADJUD
LAW
JURID

B56

US HOUSE WAYS MEANS COMMITTEE,TRAFFIC IN, AND
CONTROL OF NARCOTICS, BARBITURATES, AND
AMPHETAMINES. CHINA/COM USA+45 SOCIETY LEGIS
ACT/RES EDU/PROP CT/SYS SANCTION PROFIT HEALTH
...HEAL PSY STAT 20. PAGE 100 E2011
BIO/SOC
CONTROL
PROB/SOLV
CRIME

B56

WIGGINS J.R.,FREEDOM OR SECRECY. USA+45 USA-45
DELIB/GP EX/STRUC FORCES ADJUD SANCTION KNOWL PWR
...AUD/VIS CONGRESS 20. PAGE 106 E2121
ORD/FREE
PRESS
NAT/G
CONTROL

B57

US COMMISSION GOVT SECURITY,RECOMMENDATIONS; AREA:
LEGISLATION. USA+45 USA-45 DELIB/GP PLAN TEC/DEV
CIVMIL/REL ORD/FREE...POLICY DECISION 20 PRIVACY.
PAGE 99 E1982
LEGIS
SANCTION
CRIME
CONTROL

S57

GOODE W.J.,"COMMUNITY WITHIN A COMMUNITY: THE
PROFESSIONS." STRATA STRUCT SANCTION INGP/REL...SOC
GP/COMP. PAGE 45 E0886
PROF/ORG
NEIGH
CLIENT
CONTROL

B58

CABLE G.W.,THE NEGRO QUESTION: A SELECTION OF
WRITINGS ON CIVIL RIGHTS IN THE SOUTH. USA+45
STRATA LOC/G POL/PAR GIVE EDU/PROP WRITING CT/SYS
SANCTION CRIME CHOOSE WORSHIP 20 NEGRO CIV/RIGHTS
CONV/LEASE SOUTH/US. PAGE 18 E0355
RACE/REL
CULTURE
DISCRIM
ORD/FREE

B58

CHAMBERLIN E.H.,LABOR UNIONS AND PUBLIC POLICY.
PLAN BARGAIN SANCTION INGP/REL JURID. PAGE 21 E0416
LABOR
WEALTH
PWR
NAT/G

B59

BOHMER A.,LEGAL SOURCES AND BIBLIOGRAPHY OF
CZECHOSLOVAKIA. COM CZECHOSLVK PARL/PROC SANCTION
CRIME MARXISM 20. PAGE 13 E0261
BIBLIOG
ADJUD
LAW
JURID

B59

CHRISTMAN H.M.,THE PUBLIC PAPERS OF CHIEF JUSTICE
EARL WARREN. CONSTN POL/PAR EDU/PROP SANCTION
HEALTH...TREND 20 SUPREME/CT WARRN/EARL. PAGE 22
E0436
LAW
CT/SYS
PERSON
ADJUD

B60

CASTBERG F.,FREEDOM OF SPEECH IN THE WEST. FRANCE
GERMANY USA+45 USA-45 LAW CONSTN CHIEF PRESS
DISCRIM...CONCPT 18/20. PAGE 21 E0406
ORD/FREE
SANCTION
ADJUD
NAT/COMP

B61

DAVIS B.F.,THE DESPERATE AND THE DAMNED. USA+45 LAW
DEATH ANOMIE...CRIMLGY 20 SAN/QUENTN. PAGE 29 E0571
PUB/INST
SANCTION
CRIME

B61

KURLAND P.B.,RELIGION AND THE LAW. USA+45 USA-45
CONSTN PROVS CHIEF ADJUD SANCTION PRIVIL CATHISM
...POLICY 17/20 SUPREME/CT PRESIDENT CHURCH/STA.
PAGE 62 E1239
SECT
NAT/G
CT/SYS
GP/REL

B61

ROCHE J.P.,COURTS AND RIGHTS: THE AMERICAN
JUDICIARY IN ACTION (2ND ED.). UK USA+45 USA-45
JURID
CT/SYS

STRUCT TEC/DEV SANCTION PERS/REL RACE/REL ORD/FREE
...METH/CNCPT GOV/COMP METH/COMP T 13/20. PAGE 85
E1710
NAT/G
PROVS

B61

US HOUSE COMM ON JUDICIARY,LEGISLATION RELATING TO
ORGANIZED CRIME. USA+45 DIST/IND DELIB/GP GAMBLE
SANCTION HOUSE/REP. PAGE 100 E2004
LEGIS
CONTROL
CRIME
LAW

B62

BARLOW R.B.,CITIZENSHIP AND CONSCIENCE: STUDIES IN
THEORY AND PRACTICE OF RELIGIOUS TOLERATION IN
ENGLAND DURING EIGHTEENTH CENTURY. UK LAW VOL/ASSN
EDU/PROP SANCTION REV GP/REL MAJORITY ATTIT
ORD/FREE...BIBLIOG WORSHIP 18. PAGE 8 E0150
SECT
LEGIS
DISCRIM

B62

DONNELLY R.C.,CRIMINAL LAW: PROBLEMS FOR DECISION
IN THE PROMULGATION, INVOCATION AND ADMINISTRATION
OF A LAW OF CRIMES. USA+45 SANCTION BIO/SOC
...DECISION JURID BIBLIOG 20. PAGE 32 E0636
CRIME
LAW
ADJUD
PROB/SOLV

B62

GANJI M.,INTERNATIONAL PROTECTION OF HUMAN RIGHTS.
WOR+45 CONSTN INT/TRADE CT/SYS SANCTION CRIME WAR
RACE/REL...CHARTS IDEA/COMP NAT/COMP BIBLIOG 20
TREATY NEGRO LEAGUE/NAT UN CIVIL/LIB. PAGE 42 E0831
ORD/FREE
DISCRIM
LEGIS
DELIB/GP

B62

JENKS C.W.,THE PROPER LAW OF INTERNATIONAL
ORGANISATIONS. DIPLOM LEGIT AGREE CT/SYS SANCTION
REPRESENT SOVEREIGN...GEN/LAWS 20 UN UNESCO ILO
NATO OAS. PAGE 58 E1158
LAW
INT/ORG
ADJUD
INT/LAW

B62

SCHWARTZ L.E.,INTERNATIONAL ORGANIZATIONS AND SPACE
COOPERATION. VOL/ASSN CONSULT CREATE TEC/DEV
SANCTION...POLICY INT/LAW PHIL/SCI 20 UN. PAGE 89
E1787
INT/ORG
DIPLOM
R+D
SPACE

B62

SOWLE C.R.,POLICE POWER AND INDIVIDUAL FREEDOM: THE
QUEST FOR BALANCE. CANADA EUR+WWI ISRAEL NORWAY
USA+45 LAW CONSTN SOCIETY CONTROL ROUTINE SANCTION
GP/REL 20 CHINJAP. PAGE 93 E1859
FORCES
ORD/FREE
IDEA/COMP

B62

TUSSMAN J.,THE SUPREME COURT ON CHURCH AND STATE.
USA+45 USA-45 SANCTION PRIVIL...POLICY JURID 19/20
SUPREME/CT CHURCH/STA. PAGE 97 E1945
CT/SYS
SECT
ADJUD

C62

BACON F.,"OF JUDICATURE" (1612) IN F. BACON,
ESSAYS." ADJUD ADMIN SANCTION CRIME PWR...JURID
GEN/LAWS. PAGE 7 E0128
CT/SYS
LEGIS
LAW

N62

US SENATE COMM ON JUDICIARY,LEGISLATION TO
STRENGTHEN PENALTIES UNDER THE ANTITRUST LAWS
(PAMPHLET). USA+45 LG/CO CONFER CONTROL SANCTION
ORD/FREE 20 SENATE MONOPOLY. PAGE 102 E2045
LEAD
ADJUD
INDUS
ECO/TAC

B63

DAY R.E.,CIVIL RIGHTS USA: PUBLIC SCHOOLS, SOUTHERN
STATES - NORTH CAROLINA, 1963. USA+45 LOC/G NEIGH
LEGIS CREATE CT/SYS COERCE DISCRIM ATTIT...QU
CHARTS 20 NORTH/CAR NEGRO KKK CIV/RIGHTS. PAGE 29
E0579
EDU/PROP
ORD/FREE
RACE/REL
SANCTION

B63

DRINAN R.F.,RELIGION, THE COURTS, AND PUBLIC
POLICY. USA+45 CONSTN BUDGET TAX GIVE ADJUD
SANCTION GP/REL PRIVIL 20 CHURCH/STA. PAGE 33 E0649
SECT
CT/SYS
POLICY
SCHOOL

B63

FRIEDRICH C.J.,JUSTICE: NOMOS VI. UNIV LAW SANCTION
CRIME...CONCPT ANTHOL MARX/KARL LOCKE/JOHN
AQUINAS/T. PAGE 41 E0809
LEGIT
ADJUD
ORD/FREE
JURID

B63

GSOUSKI V.,LEGAL SOURCES AND BIBLIOGRAPHY OF THE
BALTIC STATES (ESTONIA, LATVIA, LITHUANIA). COM
ESTONIA LATVIA LITHUANIA NAT/G LEGIS CT/SYS
SANCTION CRIME 20. PAGE 48 E0957
BIBLIOG
ADJUD
LAW
JURID

B63

LAVROFF D.--G.,LES LIBERTES PUBLIQUES EN UNION
SOVIETIQUE (REV. ED.). USSR NAT/G WORKER SANCTION
CRIME MARXISM NEW/LIB...JURID BIBLIOG WORSHIP 20.
PAGE 63 E1268
ORD/FREE
LAW
ATTIT
COM

B63

LOWRY C.W.,TO PRAY OR NOT TO PRAY. ADJUD SANCTION
SECT

GP/REL ORD/FREE PWR CATHISM WORSHIP 20 SUPREME/CT CHRISTIAN CHRUCH/STA. PAGE 67 E1330
CT/SYS CONSTN PRIVIL

B63
VINES K.N.,STUDIES IN JUDICIAL POLITICS: TULANE STUDIES IN POLITICAL SCIENCE (VOL. 8). POL/PAR JUDGE ADJUD SANCTION CRIME CHOOSE PWR...JURID STAT TIME/SEQ CHARTS. PAGE 104 E2079
CT/SYS GOV/REL PROVS

B64
BENNETT H.A.,THE COMMISSION AND THE COMMON LAW: A STUDY IN ADMINISTRATIVE ADJUDICATION. LAW ADMIN CT/SYS LOBBY SANCTION GOV/REL 20 COMMON/LAW. PAGE 10 E0188
ADJUD DELIB/GP DIST/IND POLICY

B64
RUSSELL R.B.,UNITED NATIONS EXPERIENCE WITH MILITARY FORCES: POLITICAL AND LEGAL ASPECTS. AFR KOREA WOR+45 LEGIS PROB/SOLV ADMIN CONTROL EFFICIENCY PEACE...POLICY INT/LAW BIBLIOG UN. PAGE 87 E1738
FORCES DIPLOM SANCTION ORD/FREE

B64
SEGAL R.,SANCTIONS AGAINST SOUTH AFRICA. AFR SOUTH/AFR NAT/G INT/TRADE RACE/REL PEACE PWR ...INT/LAW ANTHOL 20 UN. PAGE 90 E1801
SANCTION DISCRIM ECO/TAC POLICY

B64
SIEKANOWICZ P.,LEGAL SOURCES AND BIBLIOGRAPHY OF POLAND. COM POLAND CONSTN NAT/G PARL/PROC SANCTION CRIME MARXISM 16/20. PAGE 91 E1823
BIBLIOG ADJUD LAW JURID

B64
STOKES A.P.,CHURCH AND STATE IN THE UNITED STATES (3 VOL5.). USA+45 USA-45 NAT/G PROVS LEGIS CT/SYS SANCTION PRIVIL ORD/FREE 17/20 CHURCH/STA. PAGE 94 E1875
SECT CONSTN POLICY

S64
N.,"QUASI-LEGISLATIVE ARBITRATION AGREEMENTS." LAW LG/CO ECO/TAC SANCTION ATTIT POLICY. PAGE 76 E1516
ADJUD ADJUST LABOR GP/REL

B65
MISSISSIPPI BLACK PAPER: (FIFTY-SEVEN NEGRO AND WHITE CITIZENS' TESTIMONY OF POLICE BRUTALITY...). USA+45 LAW SOCIETY CT/SYS SANCTION CRIME MORAL ORD/FREE RESPECT 20 NEGRO. PAGE 2 E0035
COERCE RACE/REL DISCRIM FORCES

B65
ANTIEU C.J.,RELIGION UNDER THE STATE CONSTITUTIONS. USA+45 LAW SCHOOL TAX SANCTION PRIVIL ORD/FREE ...JURID 20 SUPREME/CT CHURCH/STA. PAGE 5 E0099
SECT CONSTN PROVS GP/REL

B65
FELLMAN D.,RELIGION IN AMERICAN PUBLIC LAW. USA+45 USA-45 NAT/G PROVS ADJUD SANCTION GP/REL PRIVIL ORD/FREE...JURID TIME/SEQ 18/20 SUPREME/CT CHURCH/STA. PAGE 37 E0733
SECT CONSTN LAW POLICY

B65
FLEMING R.W.,THE LABOR ARBITRATION PROCESS. USA+45 LAW BARGAIN ADJUD ROUTINE SANCTION COST...PREDICT CHARTS TIME 20. PAGE 38 E0763
GP/REL LABOR CONSULT DELIB/GP

B65
HOWARD C.G.,LAW: ITS NATURE, FUNCTIONS, AND LIMITS. USA+45 CONSTN LEGIS CREATE SANCTION ORD/FREE ...BIBLIOG 20. PAGE 55 E1101
LAW JURID CONTROL SOCIETY

B65
NEGLEY G.,POLITICAL AUTHORITY AND MORAL JUDGMENT. INTELL SOCIETY LEGIS SANCTION UTOPIA SOVEREIGN MARXISM...INT/LAW LOG 20. PAGE 76 E1530
MORAL PWR CONTROL

B65
NWOGUGU E.I.,THE LEGAL PROBLEMS OF FOREIGN INVESTMENT IN DEVELOPING COUNTRIES. WOR+45 INT/ORG DELIB/GP LEGIS PROB/SOLV INT/TRADE TAX ADJUD SANCTION...BIBLIOG 20 TREATY. PAGE 78 E1561
FOR/AID FINAN INT/LAW ECO/UNDEV

B65
STONE J.,HUMAN LAW AND HUMAN JUSTICE. JUDGE...SOC MYTH IDEA/COMP. PAGE 94 E1881
CONCPT SANCTION JURID

B66
CLARK G.,WORLD PEACE THROUGH WORLD LAW; TWO ALTERNATIVE PLANS. WOR+45 DELIB/GP FORCES TAX
INT/LAW PEACE

CONFER ADJUD SANCTION ARMS/CONT WAR CHOOSE PRIVIL 20 UN COLD/WAR. PAGE 23 E0450
PLAN INT/ORG

B66
HOGUE A.R.,ORIGINS OF THE COMMON LAW. UK STRUCT AGRI CT/SYS SANCTION CONSERVE 12/14 ENGLSH/LAW COMMON/LAW. PAGE 54 E1068
LAW SOCIETY CONSTN

B66
MERILLAT H.C.L.,LEGAL ADVISERS AND INTERNATIONAL ORGANIZATIONS. LAW NAT/G CONSULT OP/RES ADJUD SANCTION TASK CONSEN ORG/CHARTS. PAGE 72 E1441
INT/ORG INT/LAW CREATE OBS

B66
US HOUSE COMM ON JUDICIARY,CIVIL COMMITMENT AND TREATMENT OF NARCOTIC ADDICTS. USA+45 SOCIETY FINAN LEGIS PROB/SOLV GIVE CT/SYS SANCTION HEALTH ...POLICY HEAL 20. PAGE 100 E2008
BIO/SOC CRIME IDEA/COMP CONTROL

B66
US HOUSE UNAMER ACTIV COMM,HEARINGS ON BILLS TO MAKE PUNISHABLE ASSISTANCE TO ENEMIES OF US IN TIME OF UNDECLARED WAR. USA+45 VIETNAM/N EDU/PROP CONTROL WAR MARXISM HOUSE/REP. PAGE 100 E2010
LAW SANCTION VOL/ASSN GIVE

B66
US PRES COMN CRIME IN DC,REPORT OF THE US PRESIDENT'S COMMISSION ON CRIME IN THE DISTRICT OF COLUMBIA. LEGIS WORKER EDU/PROP ADJUD CONTROL CT/SYS GP/REL BIO/SOC HEALTH...CRIMLGY NEW/IDEA STAT 20. PAGE 101 E2022
CRIME FORCES AGE/Y SANCTION

S66
GREEN L.C.,"RHODESIAN OIL: BOOTLEGGERS OR PIRATES?" AFR RHODESIA UK WOR+45 INT/ORG NAT/G DIPLOM LEGIT COLONIAL SOVEREIGN 20 UN OAU. PAGE 46 E0907
INT/TRADE SANCTION INT/LAW POLICY

B67
BOULTON D.,OBJECTION OVERRULED. UK LAW POL/PAR DIPLOM ADJUD SANCTION DEATH WAR CIVMIL/REL 20. PAGE 14 E0273
FORCES SOCISM SECT

B67
DEBOLD R.C.,LSD, MAN AND SOCIETY. USA+45 LAW SOCIETY SECT CONTROL SANCTION STRANGE ATTIT...HEAL CHARTS ANTHOL BIBLIOG. PAGE 30 E0601
HEALTH DRIVE PERSON BIO/SOC

L67
CARMICHAEL D.M.,"FORTY YEARS OF WATER POLLUTION CONTROL IN WISCONSIN: A CASE STUDY." LAW EXTR/IND INDUS MUNIC DELIB/GP PLAN PROB/SOLV SANCTION ...CENSUS CHARTS 20 WISCONSIN. PAGE 20 E0384
HEALTH CONTROL ADMIN ADJUD

S67
CHAMBLISS W.J.,"TYPES OF DEVIANCE AND THE EFFECTIVENESS OF LEGAL SANCTIONS" SOCIETY PROB/SOLV ADJUD CONTROL DETER. PAGE 21 E0417
CRIME SANCTION EFFICIENCY LAW

S67
COHN K.,"CRIMES AGAINST HUMANITY." GERMANY INT/ORG SANCTION ATTIT ORD/FREE...MARXIST CRIMLGY 20 UN. PAGE 24 E0469
WAR INT/LAW CRIME ADJUD

S67
DEUTSCH E.P.,"A JUDICIAL PATH TO WORLD PEACE." FUT WOR+45 CONSTN PROB/SOLV DIPLOM LICENSE ADJUD SANCTION CHOOSE REPRESENT NAT/LISM SOVEREIGN 20 ICJ. PAGE 31 E0611
INT/LAW INT/ORG JURID PEACE

S67
GRIFFIN H.C.,"PREJUDICIAL PUBLICITY: SEARCH FOR A CIVIL REMEDY." EDU/PROP CONTROL DISCRIM...JURID 20. PAGE 47 E0937
LAW SANCTION PRESS ADJUD

S67
KETCHAM O.W.,"GUIDELINES FROM GAULT: REVOLUTIONARY REQUIREMENTS AND REAPPRAISAL." LAW CONSTN CREATE LEGIT ROUTINE SANCTION CRIME DISCRIM PRIVIL ROLE ...JURID NEW/IDEA 20 SUPREME/CT. PAGE 60 E1208
ADJUD AGE/Y CT/SYS

S67
MC REYNOLDS D.,"THE RESISTANCE." USA+45 LAW ADJUD SANCTION INGP/REL PEACE 20. PAGE 70 E1398
ATTIT WAR LEGIT FORCES

S67
MIRONENKO Y.,"A NEW EXTENSION OF CRIMINAL LIABILITY IN THE USSR." COM USSR DOMIN EDU/PROP 20. PAGE 73 E1467
ADJUD SANCTION CRIME

MARXISM

S67

RICHARDSON J.J.,"THE MAKING OF THE RESTRICTIVE
TRADE PRACTICES ACT 1956 A CASE STUDY OF THE POLICY
PROCESS IN BRITAIN." UK FINAN MARKET LG/CO POL/PAR
CONSULT PRESS ADJUD ADMIN AGREE LOBBY SANCTION
ATTIT 20. PAGE 84 E1695

LEGIS
ECO/TAC
POLICY
INDUS

S67

STEEL R.,"WHAT CAN THE UN DO?" RHODESIA ECO/UNDEV
DIPLOM ECO/TAC SANCTION...INT/LAW UN. PAGE 93 E1866

INT/ORG
BAL/PWR
PEACE
FOR/AID

S67

WILSON G.D.,"CRIMINAL SANCTIONS AGAINST PASSPORT
AREA-RESTRICTION VIOLATIONS." USA+45 ADJUD CRIME
GOV/REL DEPT/STATE CONGRESS. PAGE 106 E2127

LAW
SANCTION
LICENSE
POLICY

S68

DUGARD J.,"THE REVOCATION OF THE MANDATE FOR SOUTH
WEST AFRICA." SOUTH/AFR WOR+45 STRATA NAT/G
DELIB/GP DIPLOM ADJUD SANCTION CHOOSE RACE/REL
...POLICY NAT/COMP 20 AFRICA/SW UN TRUST/TERR
LEAGUE/NAT. PAGE 33 E0654

AFR
INT/ORG
DISCRIM
COLONIAL

S68

DUPRE L.,"TILL DEATH DO US PART?" UNIV FAM INSPECT
LEGIT ADJUD SANCTION PERS/REL ANOMIE RIGID/FLEX SEX
...JURID IDEA/COMP 20 CHURCH/STA BIBLE CANON/LAW
CIVIL/LAW. PAGE 34 E0666

MARRIAGE
CATH
LAW

S68

SHAPIRO J.P.,"SOVIET HISTORIOGRAPHY AND THE MOSCOW
TRIALS: AFTER THIRTY YEARS." USSR NAT/G LEGIT PRESS
CONTROL LEAD ATTIT MARXISM...NEW/IDEA METH 20
TROTSKY/L STALIN/J KHRUSH/N. PAGE 90 E1810

HIST/WRIT
EDU/PROP
SANCTION
ADJUD

B70

BLACKSTONE W.,COMMENTARIES ON THE LAWS OF ENGLAND
(4 VOLS.) (4TH ED.). UK CHIEF DELIB/GP LEGIS WORKER
CT/SYS SANCTION CRIME OWN...CRIMLGY 18 ENGLSH/LAW.
PAGE 12 E0238

LAW
JURID
ADJUD
CONSTN

B73

AUSTIN J.,LECTURES ON JURISPRUDENCE OR THE
PHILOSOPHY OF POSITIVE LAW (VOL. II) (4TH ED.,
REV.). UK CONSTN STRUCT PROB/SOLV LEGIT CT/SYS
SANCTION CRIME INGP/REL OWN SUPEGO ORD/FREE...T 19.
PAGE 6 E0120

LAW
ADJUD
JURID
METH/CNCPT

L86

GOODNOW F.J.,"AN EXECUTIVE AND THE COURTS: JUDICIAL
REMEDIES AGAINST ADMINISTRATIVE ACTION" FRANCE UK
USA-45 WOR-45 LAW CONSTN SANCTION ORD/FREE 19.
PAGE 45 E0888

CT/SYS
GOV/REL
ADMIN
ADJUD

B98

POLLOCK F.,THE HISTORY OF ENGLISH LAW BEFORE THE
TIME OF EDWARD I (2 VOLS, 2ND ED.). UK CULTURE
LOC/G LEGIS LICENSE AGREE CONTROL CT/SYS SANCTION
CRIME...TIME/SEQ 13 COMMON/LAW CANON/LAW. PAGE 81
E1626

LAW
ADJUD
JURID

SAND P.T. E1744

SANDERS R. E1745

SANFORD S.A. E0665

SANTAYAN/G....GEORGE SANTAYANA

SAO/PAULO....SAO PAULO, BRAZIL

SAPIR/EDW....EDWARD SAPIR

SARAWAK....SARAWAK, MALAYSIA

SARTORI G. E1746

SARTORIUS R.E. E1747

SARTRE/J....JEAN-PAUL SARTRE

SARVODAYA....SARVODAYA - GANDHIAN SOCIALIST POLITICAL IDEAL
OF UNIVERSAL MATERIAL AND SPIRITUAL WELFARE; SEE ALSO
GANDHI/M

SASKATCH....SASKATCHEWAN, CANADA

SATELLITE....SPACE SATELLITES

SATISFACTION....SEE HAPPINESS

SAUDI/ARAB....SAUDI ARABIA; SEE ALSO ISLAM

SAWYER R.A. E1748

SAX/JOSEPH....JOSEPH SAX

SAY/EMIL....EMIL SAY

SBA....SMALL BUSINESS ADMINISTRATION

SCALES....SEE TESTS AND SCALES INDEX, P. XIV

SCANDINAV....SCANDINAVIAN COUNTRIES

B46

ROSS A.,TOWARDS A REALISTIC JURISPRUDENCE: A
CRITICISM OF THE DUALISM IN LAW (TRANS. BY ANNIE I.
FAUSBOLL). PLAN ADJUD CT/SYS ATTIT RIGID/FLEX
POPULISM...JURID PHIL/SCI LOG METH/COMP GEN/LAWS 20
SCANDINAV. PAGE 86 E1720

LAW
CONCPT
IDEA/COMP

B59

ROSS A.,ON LAW AND JUSTICE. USA+45 RATIONAL
...IDEA/COMP GEN/LAWS 20 SCANDINAV NATURL/LAW.
PAGE 86 E1722

JURID
PHIL/SCI
LAW
CONCPT

SCANLON H.L. E1749

SCANLON/H....HUGH SCANLON

SCHACHTER O. E1750,E1751

SCHECHTER A.H. E1752

SCHEIBER H.N. E1754

SCHEINGOLD S.A. E1755

SCHELLING T.C. E1756

SCHEURER/K....AUGUSTE SCHEURER-KESTNER

SCHINDLR/P....PAULINE SCHINDLER

B63

US SENATE COMM ON JUDICIARY,PACIFICA FOUNDATION.
USA+45 LAW COM/IND 20 ODEGARD/P BINNS/JJ SCHINDLR/P
HEALEY/D THOMAS/TK. PAGE 102 E2051

DELIB/GP
EDU/PROP
ORD/FREE
ATTIT

SCHIZO....SCHIZOPHRENIA

SCHLOCHAUER H.J. E1757

SCHMEISER D.A. E1758

SCHMIDHAUSER J.R. E1759,E1760,E1761

SCHNEIDER J. E1762

SCHOEDER P.W. E1763

SCHOLASTIC....SCHOLASTICISM (MEDIEVAL)

SCHONS D. E1764

SCHOOL....SCHOOLS, EXCEPT UNIVERSITIES

N

TEXTBOOKS IN PRINT. WOR+45 WOR-45 LAW DIPLOM
ALL/VALS ALL/IDEOS...SOC T 19/20. PAGE 1 E0014

BIBLIOG
SCHOOL
KNOWL

N

US SUPERINTENDENT OF DOCUMENTS,EDUCATION (PRICE
LIST 31). USA+45 LAW FINAN LOC/G NAT/G DEBATE ADMIN
LEAD RACE/REL FEDERAL HEALTH POLICY. PAGE 103 E2062

BIBLIOG/A
EDU/PROP
ACADEM
SCHOOL

B06

GRIFFIN A.P.C.,SELECT LIST OF REFERENCES ON THE
NEGRO QUESTION (REV. ED.). USA-45 CONSTN SCHOOL
SUFF ADJUST...JURID SOC/INTEG 19/20 NEGRO. PAGE 47
E0930

BIBLIOG/A
RACE/REL
DISCRIM
ATTIT

B14

CRAIG J.,ELEMENTS OF POLITICAL SCIENCE (3 VOLS.).
CONSTN AGRI INDUS SCHOOL FORCES TAX CT/SYS SUFF
MORAL WEALTH...CONCPT 19 CIVIL/LIB. PAGE 27 E0539

PHIL/SCI
NAT/G
ORD/FREE

N19
COUTROT A.,THE FIGHT OVER THE 1959 PRIVATE
EDUCATION LAW IN FRANCE (PAMPHLET). FRANCE NAT/G
SECT GIVE EDU/PROP GP/REL ATTIT RIGID/FLEX ORD/FREE
20 CHURCH/STA. PAGE 27 E0527
SCHOOL
PARL/PROC
CATHISM
LAW

B30
FAIRLIE J.A.,COUNTY GOVERNMENT AND ADMINISTRATION.
UK USA-45 NAT/G SCHOOL FORCES BUDGET TAX CT/SYS
CHOOSE...JURID BIBLIOG 11/20. PAGE 36 E0713
ADMIN
GOV/REL
LOC/G
MUNIC

B42
BLANCHARD L.R.,MARTINIQUE: A SELECTED LIST OF
REFERENCES (PAMPHLET). WEST/IND AGRI LOC/G SCHOOL
...ART/METH GEOG JURID CHARTS 20. PAGE 12 E0241
BIBLIOG/A
SOCIETY
CULTURE
COLONIAL

B45
US LIBRARY OF CONGRESS,NETHERLANDS EAST INDIES.
INDONESIA LAW CULTURE AGRI INDUS SCHOOL COLONIAL
HEALTH...GEOG JURID SOC 19/20 NETH/IND. PAGE 101
E2017
BIBLIOG/A
S/ASIA
NAT/G

B49
DE HUSZAR G.B.,EQUALITY IN AMERICA: THE ISSUE OF
MINORITY RIGHTS. USA+45 USA-45 LAW NEIGH SCHOOL
LEGIS ACT/RES CHOOSE ATTIT RESPECT...ANTHOL 20
NEGRO. PAGE 29 E0585
DISCRIM
RACE/REL
ORD/FREE
PROB/SOLV

B49
MARITAIN J.,HUMAN RIGHTS: COMMENTS AND
INTERPRETATIONS. COM UNIV WOR+45 LAW CONSTN CULTURE
SOCIETY ECO/DEV ECO/UNDEV SCHOOL DELIB/GP EDU/PROP
ATTIT PERCEPT ALL/VALS...HUM SOC TREND UNESCO 20.
PAGE 68 E1365
INT/ORG
CONCPT

B50
DOROSH J.T.,GUIDE TO SOVIET BIBLIOGRAPHIES. USSR
LAW AGRI SCHOOL SECT FORCES TEC/DEV...ART/METH GEOG
HUM SOC 20. PAGE 32 E0639
BIBLIOG
METH
CON/ANAL

B51
HUXLEY J.,FREEDOM AND CULTURE. UNIV LAW SOCIETY R+D
ACADEM SCHOOL CREATE SANCTION ATTIT KNOWL...HUM
ANTHOL 20. PAGE 56 E1118
CULTURE
ORD/FREE
PHIL/SCI
IDEA/COMP

C52
LANCASTER L.W.,"GOVERNMENT IN RURAL AMERICA."
USA+45 ECO/DEV AGRI SCHOOL FORCES LEGIS JUDGE
BUDGET TAX CT/SYS...CHARTS BIBLIOG. PAGE 62 E1248
GOV/REL
LOC/G
MUNIC
ADMIN

B54
BATTEN T.R.,PROBLEMS OF AFRICAN DEVELOPMENT (2ND
ED.). AFR LAW SOCIETY SCHOOL ECO/TAC TAX...GEOG
HEAL SOC 20. PAGE 8 E0154
ECO/UNDEV
AGRI
LOC/G
PROB/SOLV

B54
BINANI G.D.,INDIA AT A GLANCE (REV. ED.). INDIA
COM/IND FINAN INDUS LABOR PROVS SCHOOL PLAN DIPLOM
INT/TRADE ADMIN...JURID 20. PAGE 12 E0229
INDEX
CON/ANAL
NAT/G
ECO/UNDEV

B54
O'NEILL J.M.,CATHOLICS IN CONTROVERSY. USA+45 NAT/G
PROVS SCHOOL SECT EDU/PROP LEGIT CT/SYS SANCTION
GP/REL 20 SUPREME/CT CHURCH/STA. PAGE 78 E1569
CATHISM
CONSTN
POLICY
LAW

C54
CALDWELL L.K.,"THE GOVERNMENT AND ADMINISTRATION OF
NEW YORK." LOC/G MUNIC POL/PAR SCHOOL CHIEF LEGIS
PLAN TAX CT/SYS...MGT SOC/WK BIBLIOG 20 NEWYORK/C.
PAGE 19 E0365
PROVS
ADMIN
CONSTN
EX/STRUC

S55
CAHN E.,"A DANGEROUS MYTH IN THE SCHOOL SEGREGATION
CASES" (BMR)" USA+45 CONSTN PROVS ADJUD DISCRIM
...POLICY MYTH SOC/INTEG 20 SUPREME/CT AMEND/XIV.
PAGE 18 E0360
JURID
SCHOOL
RACE/REL

B56
NOTZ R.L.,FEDERAL GRANTS-IN-AID TO STATES: ANALYSIS
OF LAWS IN FORCE ON SEPTEMBER 10, 1956. USA+45 LAW
SCHOOL PLAN ECO/TAC TAX RECEIVE...HEAL JURID 20.
PAGE 78 E1558
GIVE
NAT/G
PROVS
GOV/REL

B57
FAIRCHILD H.P.,THE ANATOMY OF FREEDOM. USA+45
ACADEM SCHOOL SECT CAP/ISM PRESS CHOOSE SOCISM.
PAGE 36 E0712
ORD/FREE
CONCPT
NAT/G
JURID

B59
HAYS B.,A SOUTHERN MODERATE SPEAKS. LAW PROVS
SCHOOL KNOWL...JURID SOC SELF/OBS BIOG 20 NEGRO
SUPREME/CT. PAGE 51 E1015
SECT
DISCRIM
CT/SYS
RACE/REL

B59
KERREMANS-RAMIOULL,LE PROBLEME DE LA DELINQUENCE
JUVENILE (2ND ED.). FAM PUB/INST SCHOOL FORCES
LEGIS MORAL...CRIMLGY SOC 20. PAGE 60 E1205
BIBLIOG
CRIME
AGE/Y
SOC/WK

S59
DWYER R.J.,"THE ADMINISTRATIVE ROLE IN
DESEGREGATION." USA+45 LAW PROB/SOLV LEAD RACE/REL
ISOLAT STRANGE ROLE...POLICY SOC/INTEG MISSOURI
NEGRO CIV/RIGHTS. PAGE 34 E0668
ADMIN
SCHOOL
DISCRIM
ATTIT

S59
MURPHY W.F.,"LOWER COURT CHECKS ON SUPREME COURT
POWER" (BMR)" USA+45 NAT/G PROVS SCHOOL GOV/REL
RACE/REL DISCRIM ATTIT...DECISION JURID 20
SUPREME/CT NEGRO. PAGE 75 E1508
CT/SYS
BAL/PWR
CONTROL
ADJUD

N59
NATIONAL ASSN HOME BUILDERS,COMMUNITY FACILITIES: A
LIST OF SELECTED REFERENCES (PAMPHLET). USA+45
DIST/IND FINAN SERV/IND SCHOOL CREATE CONTROL
FEDERAL...JURID 20. PAGE 76 E1525
BIBLIOG/A
PLAN
LOC/G
MUNIC

B60
CARTER R.F.,COMMUNITIES AND THEIR SCHOOLS. USA+45
LAW FINAN PROVS BUDGET TAX LEAD PARTIC CHOOSE...SOC
INT QU 20. PAGE 20 E0401
SCHOOL
ACT/RES
NEIGH
INGP/REL

B60
FELLMAN D.,THE SUPREME COURT AND EDUCATION. ACADEM
NAT/G PROVS DELIB/GP ADJUD ORD/FREE...POLICY JURID
WORSHIP 20 SUPREME/CT NEGRO CHURCH/STA. PAGE 37
E0731
CT/SYS
SECT
RACE/REL
SCHOOL

B60
POWELL T.,THE SCHOOL BUS LAW: A CASE STUDY IN
EDUCATION, RELIGION, AND POLITICS. USA+45 LAW NEIGH
SECT LEGIS EDU/PROP ADJUD CT/SYS LOBBY CATHISM
WORSHIP 20 CONNECTICT CHURCH/STA. PAGE 82 E1641
JURID
SCHOOL

B62
BICKEL A.,THE LEAST DANGEROUS BRANCH. USA+45 USA-45
CONSTN SCHOOL LEGIS ADJUD RACE/REL DISCRIM ORD/FREE
...JURID 18/20 SUPREME/CT CONGRESS MARSHALL/J
HOLMES/OW FRANKFUR/F. PAGE 12 E0226
LAW
NAT/G
CT/SYS

B62
HIRSCHFIELD R.S.,THE CONSTITUTION AND THE COURT.
SCHOOL WAR RACE/REL EQUILIB ORD/FREE...POLICY
MAJORIT DECISION JURID 18/20 PRESIDENT COLD/WAR
CIVIL/LIB SUPREME/CT CONGRESS. PAGE 53 E1051
ADJUD
PWR
CONSTN
LAW

B62
MCGRATH J.J.,CHURCH AND STATE IN AMERICAN LAW. LAW
PROVS SCHOOL TAX GIVE CT/SYS GP/REL...POLICY ANTHOL
18/20 SUPREME/CT CHURCH/STA CASEBOOK. PAGE 71 E1414
SECT
ADJUD
CONSTN
NAT/G

B62
MITCHELL G.E.,THE ANGRY BLACK SOUTH. USA+45 LAW
CONSTN SCHOOL DELIB/GP EDU/PROP CONTROL SUFF ANOMIE
DRIVE...ANTHOL 20 NEGRO CIV/RIGHTS SOUTH/US.
PAGE 74 E1473
RACE/REL
DISCRIM
ADJUST
ORD/FREE

B63
DRINAN R.F.,RELIGION, THE COURTS, AND PUBLIC
POLICY. USA+45 CONSTN BUDGET TAX GIVE ADJUD
SANCTION GP/REL PRIVIL 20 CHURCH/STA. PAGE 33 E0649
SECT
CT/SYS
POLICY
SCHOOL

B63
GOURNAY B.,PUBLIC ADMINISTRATION. FRANCE LAW CONSTN
AGRI FINAN LABOR SCHOOL EX/STRUC CHOOSE...MGT
METH/COMP 20. PAGE 45 E0894
BIBLIOG/A
ADMIN
NAT/G
LOC/G

B63
HORRELL M.,LEGISLATION AND RACE RELATIONS
(PAMPHLET). SOUTH/AFR SCHOOL TAX DOMIN CONTROL 20.
PAGE 55 E1098
LAW
RACE/REL
DISCRIM
PARTIC

B63
PALOTAI O.C.,PUBLICATIONS OF THE INSTITUTE OF
GOVERNMENT, 1930-1962. LAW PROVS SCHOOL WORKER
ACT/RES OP/RES CT/SYS GOV/REL...CRIMLGY SOC/WK.
PAGE 79 E1594
BIBLIOG/A
ADMIN
LOC/G
FINAN

SMITH E.A.,CHURCH AND STATE IN YOUR COMMUNITY. GP/REL
USA+45 PROVS SCHOOL ACT/RES CT/SYS PARTIC ATTIT SECT
MORAL ORD/FREE CATHISM 20 PROTESTANT CHURCH/STA. NAT/G
PAGE 92 E1842 NEIGH
B63

HILLS R.J.,"THE REPRESENTATIVE FUNCTION: NEGLECTED LEAD
DIMENSION OF LEADERSHIP BEHAVIOR" USA+45 CLIENT ADMIN
STRUCT SCHOOL PERS/REL...STAT QU SAMP LAB/EXP 20. EXEC
PAGE 53 E1048 ACT/RES
S63

DUBOIS J.,DANGER OVER PANAMA. FUT PANAMA SCHOOL DIPLOM
PROB/SOLV EDU/PROP MARXISM...POLICY 19/20 TREATY COERCE
INTERVENT CANAL/ZONE. PAGE 33 E0652
B64

GIANNELLA D.A.,RELIGION AND THE PUBLIC ORDER: AN SECT
ANNUAL REVIEW OF CHURCH AND STATE, AND OF RELIGION, NAT/G
LAW, AND SOCIETY. USA+45 LAW SOCIETY FAM POL/PAR CONSTN
SCHOOL GIVE EDU/PROP GP/REL...JURID GEN/LAWS ORD/FREE
BIBLIOG/A 20 CHURCH/STA BIRTH/CON CONSCN/OBJ
NATURL/LAW. PAGE 43 E0855
B64

KAUPER P.G.,RELIGION AND THE CONSTITUTION. USA+45 CONSTN
USA-45 LAW NAT/G SCHOOL SECT GP/REL ATTIT...BIBLIOG JURID
WORSHIP 18/20 SUPREME/CT FREE/SPEE CHURCH/STA. ORD/FREE
PAGE 60 E1189
B64

OPPENHEIMER M.,A MANUAL FOR DIRECT ACTION. USA+45 PLAN
SCHOOL FORCES ADJUD CT/SYS SUFF RACE/REL DISCRIM VOL/ASSN
...POLICY CHARTS 20. PAGE 79 E1580 JURID
LEAD
B64

RICE C.E.,THE SUPREME COURT AND PUBLIC PRAYER. JURID
CONSTN SCHOOL SECT PROB/SOLV TAX ATTIT WORSHIP POLICY
18/20 SUPREME/CT CHURCH/STA. PAGE 84 E1692 NAT/G
B64

ANTIEU C.J.,RELIGION UNDER THE STATE CONSTITUTIONS. SECT
USA+45 LAW SCHOOL TAX SANCTION PRIVIL ORD/FREE CONSTN
...JURID 20 SUPREME/CT CHURCH/STA. PAGE 5 E0099 PROVS
GP/REL
B65

BEGGS D.W.,AMERICA'S SCHOOLS AND CHURCHES: PARTNERS SECT
IN CONFLICT. USA+45 PROVS EDU/PROP ADJUD DISCRIM GP/REL
ATTIT...IDEA/COMP ANTHOL BIBLIOG WORSHIP 20 SCHOOL
CHURCH/STA. PAGE 9 E0179 NAT/G
B65

CARTER R.L.,EQUALITY. LAW LABOR NEIGH SCHOOL POLICY
RACE/REL 20 NEGRO. PAGE 20 E0402 DISCRIM
PLAN
CREATE
B65

CHARLTON K.,EDUCATION IN RENAISSANCE ENGLAND. ITALY EDU/PROP
UK USA+45 WOR-45 LAW LOC/G NAT/G...IDEA/COMP 14/17 SCHOOL
HUMANISM. PAGE 21 E0423 ACADEM
B65

CONGRESSIONAL QUARTERLY SERV,FEDERAL ROLE IN ACADEM
EDUCATION (PAMPHLET). LAW SCHOOL PLAN TAX ADJUD DISCRIM
...CHARTS SOC/INTEG 20 PRESIDENT. PAGE 25 E0487 RECEIVE
FEDERAL
B65

ROSE A.M.,MINORITY PROBLEMS: A TEXTBOOK OF READINGS RACE/REL
IN INTERGROUP RELATIONS. UNIV USA+45 LAW SCHOOL DISCRIM
WORKER PROB/SOLV GP/REL PERSON...PSY ANTHOL WORSHIP ISOLAT
20 NEGRO INDIAN/AM JEWS EUROPE. PAGE 85 E1713 ACT/RES
B65

SCHROEDER O.,DEFACTO SEGREGATION AND CIVIL RIGHTS. ANTHOL
LAW PROVS SCHOOL WORKER ATTIT HABITAT HEALTH WEALTH DISCRIM
...JURID CHARTS 19/20 NEGRO SUPREME/CT KKK. PAGE 88 RACE/REL
E1766 ORD/FREE
B65

SMITH R.C.,THEY CLOSED THEIR SCHOOLS. USA+45 NEIGH RACE/REL
ADJUD CROWD CONSEN WEALTH...DECISION OBS INT 20 DISCRIM
NEGRO VIRGINIA. PAGE 92 E1846 LOC/G
SCHOOL
B65

AMERICAN JEWISH COMMITTEE,GROUP RELATIONS IN THE BIBLIOG/A
UNITED STATES: PROBLEMS AND PERSPECTIVES: A USA+45
SELECTED, ANNOTATED BIBLIOGRAPHY (PAMPHLET). LAW STRUCT
CONSTN STRATA SCHOOL SECT PROB/SOLV ATTIT...POLICY GP/REL
WELF/ST SOC/WK 20. PAGE 4 E0079
B66

DOUGLAS W.O.,THE BIBLE AND THE SCHOOLS. USA+45 SECT
CULTURE ADJUD INGP/REL AGE/C AGE/Y ATTIT KNOWL NAT/G
WORSHIP 20 SUPREME/CT CHURCH/STA BIBLE CHRISTIAN. SCHOOL
PAGE 32 E0644 GP/REL
B66

MOSKOW M.H.,TEACHERS AND UNIONS. SCHOOL WORKER EDU/PROP
ADJUD LOBBY ATTIT ORD/FREE 20. PAGE 75 E1501 PROF/ORG
LABOR
BARGAIN
B66

TIEDT S.W.,THE ROLE OF THE FEDERAL GOVERNMENT IN NAT/G
EDUCATION. FUT USA+45 USA-45 CONSTN SECT BUDGET EDU/PROP
CT/SYS GOV/REL 18/20 SUPREME/CT. PAGE 96 E1924 GIVE
SCHOOL
B66

US SENATE COMM ON JUDICIARY,SCHOOL PRAYER. USA+45 SCHOOL
LAW LOC/G SECT ADJUD WORSHIP 20 SENATE DEITY. JURID
PAGE 103 E2058 NAT/G
B66

AMDS W.E.,DELINQUENCY PREVENTION: THEORY AND AGE/Y
PRACTICE. USA+45 SOCIETY FAM SCHOOL SECT FORCES CRIME
PROB/SOLV...HEAL JURID PREDICT ANTHOL. PAGE 4 E0071 PUB/INST
LAW
B67

BERNSTEIN S.,ALTERNATIVES TO VIOLENCE: ALIENATED AGE/Y
YOUTH AND RIOTS, RACE AND POVERTY. MUNIC PUB/INST SOC/WK
SCHOOL INGP/REL RACE/REL UTOPIA DRIVE HABITAT ROLE NEIGH
WEALTH...INT 20. PAGE 11 E0215 CRIME
B67

BOLES D.E.,THE TWO SWORDS. USA+45 USA-45 LAW CONSTN SCHOOL
SOCIETY FINAN PRESS CT/SYS...HEAL JURID BIBLIOG EDU/PROP
WORSHIP 20 SUPREME/CT CHURCH/STA. PAGE 13 E0263 ADJUD
B67

CHAPIN F.S. JR.,SELECTED REFERENCES ON URBAN BIBLIOG
PLANNING METHODS AND TECHNIQUES. USA+45 LAW ECO/DEV NEIGH
LOC/G NAT/G SCHOOL CONSULT CREATE PROB/SOLV TEC/DEV MUNIC
SOC/WK. PAGE 21 E0420 PLAN
B67

SCHORN H. E1765

SCHROEDER O. E1766

SCHROEDER T. E1767,E1768,E1769

SCHUBERT G. E1770,E1771,E1772,E1773,E1774,E1775,E1776,E1777

SCHUBERT G.A. E1778,E1779,E1780,E1781,E1782

SCHUESSLER K. E0461

SCHULZ F. E1783

SCHUMAN S.I. E1784

SCHUMCHR/K....KURT SCHUMACHER

SCHUMPTR/J....JOSEPH SCHUMPETER

SCHUSTER E. E1785

SCHWARTZ B. E1786

SCHWARTZ L.E. E1787

SCHWARTZ M.D. E1788

SCHWARTZ R.D. E0636

SCHWARTZ R.F. E0569

SCHWARZENBERGER G. E1193,E1789

SCHWELB E. E1790,E1791,E1792

SCHWERIN K. E1793

SCHWINN....ARNOLD, SCHWINN + COMPANY

SCI/ADVSRY....SCIENCE ADVISORY COMMISSION

DUPRE J.S.,SCIENCE AND THE NATION: POLICY AND R+D
POLITICS. USA+45 LAW ACADEM FORCES ADMIN CIVMIL/REL INDUS
GOV/REL EFFICIENCY PEACE...TREND 20 SCI/ADVSRY. TEC/DEV
PAGE 34 E0665 NUC/PWR
B62

SCIENCE....SEE PHIL/SCI, CREATE

SCIENCE ADVISORY COMMISSION....SEE SCI/ADVSRY

SCIENTIFIC METHOD....SEE PHIL/SCI

SCOT/YARD....SCOTLAND YARD - LONDON POLICE HEADQUARTERS AND
    DETECTIVE BUREAU

B65
HOWE R.,THE STORY OF SCOTLAND YARD: A HISTORY OF   CRIMLGY
THE CID FROM THE EARLIEST TIMES TO THE PRESENT DAY.   CRIME
UK MUNIC EDU/PROP 6/20 SCOT/YARD. PAGE 55 E1104   FORCES
                                                        ADMIN

B66
HOEVELER H.J.,INTERNATIONALE BEKAMPFUNG DES   CRIMLGY
VERBRECHENS. AUSTRIA SWITZERLND WOR+45 INT/ORG   CRIME
CONTROL BIO/SOC...METH/COMP NAT/COMP 20 MAFIA   DIPLOM
SCOT/YARD FBI. PAGE 53 E1064   INT/LAW

SCOTLAND....SCOTLAND

N19
GIBB A.D.,JUDICIAL CORRUPTION IN THE UNITED KINGDOM   MORAL
(PAMPHLET). UK DELIB/GP CT/SYS CRIME PERSON SUPEGO   ATTIT
17/20 SCOTLAND. PAGE 43 E0856   ADJUD

B58
MOEN N.W.,THE GOVERNMENT OF SCOTLAND 1603 - 1625.   CHIEF
UK JUDGE ADMIN GP/REL PWR 17 SCOTLAND COMMON/LAW.   JURID
PAGE 74 E1479   CONTROL
                                                        PARL/PROC

SCOTT A. E1794

SCOTT A.M. E1795,E1796

SCOTT F.R. E1797

SCOTT G.B. E0598

SCOTT J.B. E0849,E1798

SCREENING AND SELECTION....SEE CHOOSE, SAMP

SDR....SPECIAL DRAWING RIGHTS

SDS....STUDENTS FOR A DEMOCRATIC SOCIETY

SEA....LOCALE OF SUBJECT ACTIVITY IS AQUATIC

B24
HOLDSWORTH W.S.,A HISTORY OF ENGLISH LAW; THE   LAW
COMMON LAW AND ITS RIVALS (VOL. V). UK SEA EX/STRUC   LEGIS
WRITING ADMIN...INT/LAW JURID CONCPT IDEA/COMP   ADJUD
WORSHIP 16/17 PARLIAMENT ENGLSH/LAW COMMON/LAW.   CT/SYS
PAGE 54 E1073

B24
HOLDSWORTH W.S.,A HISTORY OF ENGLISH LAW; THE   LAW
COMMON LAW AND ITS RIVALS (VOL. IV). UK SEA AGRI   LEGIS
CHIEF ADJUD CONTROL CRIME GOV/REL...INT/LAW JURID   CT/SYS
NAT/COMP 16/17 PARLIAMENT COMMON/LAW CANON/LAW.   CONSTN
ENGLSH/LAW. PAGE 54 E1075

B36
HUDSON M.O.,INTERNATIONAL LEGISLATION: 1929-1931.   INT/LAW
WOR-45 SEA AIR AGRI FINAN LABOR DIPLOM ECO/TAC   PARL/PROC
REPAR CT/SYS ARMS/CONT WAR WEAPON...JURID 20 TREATY   ADJUD
LEAGUE/NAT. PAGE 56 E1112   LAW

B55
SVARLIEN O.,AN INTRODUCTION TO THE LAW OF NATIONS.   INT/LAW
SEA AIR INT/ORG NAT/G CHIEF ADMIN AGREE WAR PRIVIL   DIPLOM
ORD/FREE SOVEREIGN...BIBLIOG 16/20. PAGE 95 E1897

B58
ATOMIC INDUSTRIAL FORUM,MANAGEMENT AND ATOMIC   NUC/PWR
ENERGY. WOR+45 SEA LAW MARKET NAT/G TEC/DEV INSPECT   INDUS
INT/TRADE CONFER PEACE HEALTH...ANTHOL 20. PAGE 6   MGT
E0112   ECO/TAC

B58
SOC OF COMP LEGIS AND INT LAW,THE LAW OF THE SEA...   INT/LAW
(PAMPHLET). WOR+45 NAT/G INT/TRADE ADJUD CONTROL   INT/ORG
NUC/PWR WAR PEACE ATTIT ORD/FREE...JURID CHARTS 20   DIPLOM
UN TREATY RESOURCE/N. PAGE 92 E1850   SEA

B59
REIFF H.,THE UNITED STATES AND THE TREATY LAW OF   ADJUD
THE SEA. USA+45 USA-45 SEA SOCIETY INT/ORG CONSULT   INT/LAW
DELIB/GP LEGIS DIPLOM LEGIT ATTIT ORD/FREE PWR
WEALTH...GEOG JURID TOT/POP 20 TREATY. PAGE 84
E1681

S59
BELL D.,"THE RACKET RIDDEN LONGSHOREMEN" (BMR)"   CRIME

USA+45 SEA WORKER MURDER ROLE...SOC 20 NEWYORK/C.   LABOR
PAGE 9 E0182   DIST/IND
                                                        ELITES

L60
DEAN A.W.,"SECOND GENEVA CONFERENCE OF THE LAW OF   INT/ORG
THE SEA: THE FIGHT FOR FREEDOM OF THE SEAS." FUT   JURID
USA+45 USSR WOR+45 WOR-45 SEA CONSTN STRUCT PLAN   INT/LAW
INT/TRADE ADJUD ADMIN ORD/FREE...DECISION RECORD
TREND GEN/LAWS 20 TREATY. PAGE 30 E0600

B61
MURPHY E.F.,WATER PURITY: A STUDY IN LEGAL CONTROL   SEA
OF NATURAL RESOURCES. LOC/G ACT/RES PLAN TEC/DEV   LAW
LOBBY GP/REL COST ATTIT HEALTH ORD/FREE...HEAL   PROVS
JURID 20 WISCONSIN WATER. PAGE 75 E1506   CONTROL

B62
COLOMBOS C.J.,THE INTERNATIONAL LAW OF THE SEA.   INT/LAW
WOR+45 EXTR/IND DIPLOM INT/TRADE TARIFFS AGREE WAR   SEA
...TIME/SEQ 20 TREATY. PAGE 24 E0476   JURID
                                                        ADJUD

B62
HENDERSON W.O.,THE GENESIS OF THE COMMON MARKET.   ECO/DEV
EUR+WWI FRANCE MOD/EUR UK SEA COM/IND EXTR/IND   INT/TRADE
COLONIAL DISCRIM...TIME/SEQ CHARTS BIBLIOG 18/20   DIPLOM
EEC TREATY. PAGE 52 E1030

B62
MCDOUGAL M.S.,THE PUBLIC ORDER OF THE OCEANS.   ADJUD
WOR+45 WOR-45 SEA INT/ORG NAT/G CONSULT DELIB/GP   ORD/FREE
DIPLOM LEGIT PEACE RIGID/FLEX...GEOG INT/LAW JURID
RECORD TOT/POP 20 TREATY. PAGE 70 E1407

S63
LEPAWSKY A.,"INTERNATIONAL DEVELOPMENT OF RIVER   INT/ORG
RESOURCES." CANADA EUR+WWI S/ASIA USA+45 SEA LEGIT   DELIB/GP
ADJUD ORD/FREE PWR WEALTH...MGT TIME/SEQ VAL/FREE
MEXIC/AMER 20. PAGE 64 E1287

B64
MCDOUGAL M.S.,STUDIES IN WORLD PUBLIC ORDER. SPACE   INT/LAW
SEA INT/ORG CREATE AGREE NUC/PWR...POLICY PHIL/SCI   SOC
IDEA/COMP ANTHOL METH 20 UN. PAGE 71 E1411   DIPLOM

SEARA M.V. E1799

SEATO....SOUTH EAST ASIA TREATY ORGANIZATION; SEE ALSO
    INT/ORG, VOL/ASSN, FORCES, DETER

B62
DOUGLAS W.O.,DEMOCRACY'S MANIFESTO. COM USA+45   DIPLOM
ECO/UNDEV INT/ORG FORCES PLAN NEUTRAL TASK MARXISM   POLICY
...JURID 20 NATO SEATO. PAGE 32 E0642   NAT/G
                                                        ORD/FREE

B67
LAWYERS COMM AMER POLICY VIET,VIETNAM AND   INT/LAW
INTERNATIONAL LAW: AN ANALYSIS OF THE LEGALITY OF   DIPLOM
THE US MILITARY INVOLVEMENT. VIETNAM LAW INT/ORG   ADJUD
COERCE WEAPON PEACE ORD/FREE 20 UN SEATO TREATY.   WAR
PAGE 64 E1271

SEATTLE....SEATTLE, WASHINGTON

B55
LARROWE C.P.,SHAPE-UP AND HIRING HALL. TRIBUTE   LABOR
ADJUD CONTROL SANCTION COERCE CRIME GP/REL PWR   INDUS
...CHARTS 20 AFL/CIO NEWYORK/C SEATTLE. PAGE 63   WORKER
E1256   NAT/G

SEC/EXCHNG....SECURITY EXCHANGE COMMISSION

B62
OTTENBERG M.,THE FEDERAL INVESTIGATORS. USA+45 LAW   FORCES
COM/IND DIST/IND WORKER DIPLOM INT/TRADE CONTROL   INSPECT
FEDERAL HEALTH ORD/FREE FBI CIA FTC SEC FDA.   NAT/G
PAGE 79 E1585   CRIME

SEC/EXCHNG....SECURITY EXCHANGE COMMISSION

SEC/REFORM....SECOND REFORM ACT OF 1867 (U.K.)

SEC/STATE....U.S. SECRETARY OF STATE

SECKLER-HUDSON C. E1800

SECT....CHURCH, SECT, RELIGIOUS GROUP

CONOVER H.F.,OFFICIAL PUBLICATIONS OF BRITISH EAST AFRICA (PAMPHLET). UK LAW ECO/UNDEV AGRI EXTR/IND SECT LEGIS BUDGET TAX...HEAL STAT 20. PAGE 25 E0491
N BIBLIOG/A AFR ADMIN COLONIAL

BIBLIOGRAPHIE DE LA PHILOSOPHIE. LAW CULTURE SECT EDU/PROP MORAL...HUM METH/CNCPT 20. PAGE 1 E0018
N BIBLIOG/A PHIL/SCI CONCPT LOG

CANON LAW ABSTRACTS. LEGIT CONFER CT/SYS INGP/REL MARRIAGE ATTIT MORAL WORSHIP 20. PAGE 2 E0026
N BIBLIOG/A CATHISM SECT LAW

AFRICAN BIBLIOGRAPHIC CENTER,A CURRENT BIBLIOGRAPHY ON AFRICAN AFFAIRS. LAW CULTURE ECO/UNDEV LABOR SECT DIPLOM FOR/AID COLONIAL NAT/LISM...LING 20. PAGE 3 E0053
N BIBLIOG/A AFR NAT/G REGION

MEYER C.S.,ELIZABETH I AND THE RELIGIOUS SETTLEMENT OF 1559. UK ELITES CHIEF LEGIS DISCRIM CATHISM 16 CHURCH/STA ELIZABTH/I. PAGE 72 E1445
NRE GP/REL SECT LAW PARL/PROC

MAINE H.S.,ANCIENT LAW. MEDIT-7 CULTURE SOCIETY KIN SECT LEGIS LEGIT ROUTINE...JURID HIST/WRIT CON/ANAL TOT/POP VAL/FREE. PAGE 68 E1350
B00 FAM LAW

CHANNING W.E.,DISCOURSES ON WAR (1820-1840). LAW SECT DIPLOM INT/TRADE ALL/VALS. PAGE 21 E0418
B03 WAR PLAN LOVE ORD/FREE

DICEY A.,LAW AND PUBLIC OPINION IN ENGLAND. LAW CULTURE INTELL SOCIETY NAT/G SECT JUDGE LEGIT CHOOSE RIGID/FLEX KNOWL...OLD/LIB CONCPT STERTYP GEN/LAWS 20. PAGE 31 E0620
B05 ATTIT UK

DUNNING W.A.,"HISTORY OF POLITICAL THEORIES FROM LUTHER TO MONTESQUIEU." LAW NAT/G SECT DIPLOM REV WAR ORD/FREE SOVEREIGN CONSERVE...TRADIT BIBLIOG 16/18. PAGE 33 E0663
C05 PHIL/SCI CONCPT GEN/LAWS

FIGGIS J.N.,CHURCHES IN THE MODERN STATE (2ND ED.). SECT LAW CHIEF BAL/PWR PWR...CONCPT CHURCH/STA POPE. PAGE 38 E0748
B14 SECT NAT/G SOCIETY ORD/FREE

PUFENDORF S.,LAW OF NATURE AND OF NATIONS (ABRIDGED). UNIV LAW NAT/G DIPLOM AGREE WAR PERSON ALL/VALS PWR...POLICY 18 DEITY NATURL/LAW. PAGE 83 E1659
B16 CONCPT INT/LAW SECT MORAL

DE VICTORIA F.,DE INDIS ET DE JURE BELLI (1557) IN F. DE VICTORIA, DE INDIS ET DE JURE BELLI REFLECTIONES. UNIV NAT/G SECT CHIEF PARTIC COERCE PEACE MORAL...POLICY 16 INDIAN/AM CHRISTIAN CONSCN/OBJ. PAGE 30 E0598
B17 WAR INT/LAW OWN

VANDERPOL A.,LA DOCTRINE SCOLASTIQUE DU DROIT DE GUERRE. CHRIST-17C FORCES DIPLOM LEGIT SUPEGO MORAL ...BIOG AQUINAS/T SUAREZ/F CHRISTIAN. PAGE 103 E2072
B19 WAR SECT INT/LAW

COUTROT A.,THE FIGHT OVER THE 1959 PRIVATE EDUCATION LAW IN FRANCE (PAMPHLET). FRANCE NAT/G SECT GIVE EDU/PROP GP/REL ATTIT RIGID/FLEX ORD/FREE 20 CHURCH/STA. PAGE 27 E0527
N19 SCHOOL PARL/PROC CATHISM LAW

SCHROEDER T.,FREE SPEECH BIBLIOGRAPHY. EUR+WWI WOR-45 NAT/G SECT ECO/TAC WRITING ADJUD ATTIT MARXISM SOCISM 16/20. PAGE 88 E1768
B22 BIBLIOG/A ORD/FREE CONTROL LAW

DE MONTESQUIEU C.,THE SPIRIT OF LAWS (2 VOLS.) (TRANS. BY THOMAS NUGENT). FRANCE FINAN SECT INT/TRADE TAX COERCE REV DISCRIM HABITAT ORD/FREE 19 ALEMBERT/J CIVIL/LAW. PAGE 30 E0588
B23 JURID LAW CONCPT GEN/LAWS

GENTILI A.,DE LEGATIONIBUS. CHRIST-17C NAT/G SECT CONSULT LEGIT...POLICY CATH JURID CONCPT MYTH. PAGE 43 E0848
B24 DIPLOM INT/LAW INT/ORG LAW

GODET M.,INDEX BIBLIOGRAPHICUS: INTERNATIONAL CATALOGUE OF SOURCES OF CURRENT BIBLIOGRAPHIC INFORMATION. EUR+WWI MOD/EUR SOCIETY SECT TAX ...JURID PHIL/SCI SOC MATH. PAGE 44 E0876
B25 BIBLIOG/A DIPLOM EDU/PROP LAW

FORTESCUE J.,THE GOVERNANCE OF ENGLAND (1471-76). UK LAW FINAN SECT LEGIS PROB/SOLV TAX DOMIN ADMIN GP/REL COST ORD/FREE PWR 14/15. PAGE 39 E0776
B26 CONSERVE CONSTN CHIEF NAT/G

GOOCH G.P.,ENGLISH DEMOCRATIC IDEAS IN THE SEVENTEENTH CENTURY (2ND ED.). UK LAW SECT FORCES DIPLOM LEAD PARL/PROC REV ATTIT AUTHORIT...ANARCH CONCPT 17 PARLIAMENT CMN/WLTH REFORMERS. PAGE 45 E0885
B27 IDEA/COMP MAJORIT EX/STRUC CONSERVE

JOHN OF SALISBURY,THE STATESMAN'S BOOK (1159) (TRANS. BY J. DICKINSON). DOMIN GP/REL MORAL ORD/FREE PWR CONSERVE...CATH CONCPT 12. PAGE 59 E1169
B27 NAT/G SECT CHIEF LAW

RYAN J.A.,DECLINING LIVERTY AND OTHER ESSAYS. USA-45 SECT DELIB/GP ATTIT PWR SOCISM 20 SUPREME/CT. PAGE 87 E1740
B27 ORD/FREE LEGIS JURID NAT/G

BENTHAM J.,A COMMENT OF THE COMMENTARIES (1765-69). LAW MUNIC SECT ADJUD AGREE CT/SYS CONSEN HAPPINESS ORD/FREE 18. PAGE 10 E0191
B28 CONCPT IDEA/COMP

HOBBES T.,THE ELEMENTS OF LAW, NATURAL AND POLITIC (1650). STRATA NAT/G SECT CHIEF AGREE ATTIT ALL/VALS MORAL ORD/FREE POPULISM...POLICY CONCPT. PAGE 53 E1056
B28 PERSON LAW SOVEREIGN CONSERVE

CAM H.M.,BIBLIOGRAPHY OF ENGLISH CONSTITUTIONAL HISTORY (PAMPHLET). UK LAW LOC/G NAT/G POL/PAR SECT DELIB/GP ADJUD ORD/FREE 19/20 PARLIAMENT. PAGE 19 E0369
B29 BIBLIOG/A CONSTN ADMIN PARL/PROC

BORCHARD E.H.,GUIDE TO THE LAW AND LEGAL LITERATURE OF FRANCE. FRANCE FINAN INDUS LABOR SECT LEGIS ADMIN COLONIAL CRIME OWN...INT/LAW 20. PAGE 14 E0266
B31 BIBLIOG/A LAW CONSTN METH

AMERICAN FOREIGN LAW ASSN,BIOGRAPHICAL NOTES ON THE LAWS AND LEGAL LITERATURE OF URUGUAY AND CURACAO. URUGUAY CONSTN FINAN SECT FORCES JUDGE DIPLOM INT/TRADE ADJUD CT/SYS CRIME 20. PAGE 4 E0078
B33 BIBLIOG/A LAW JURID ADMIN

CLYDE W.M.,THE STRUGGLE FOR THE FREEDOM OF THE PRESS FROM CAXTON TO CROMWELL. UK LAW LOC/G SECT FORCES LICENSE WRITING SANCTION REV ATTIT PWR ...POLICY 15/17 PARLIAMENT CROMWELL/O MILTON/J. PAGE 23 E0460
B34 PRESS ORD/FREE CONTROL

BORGESE G.A.,GOLIATH: THE MARCH OF FASCISM. GERMANY ITALY LAW POL/PAR SECT DIPLOM SOCISM...JURID MYTH 20 DANTE MACHIAVELL MUSSOLIN/B. PAGE 14 E0270
B37 POLICY NAT/LISM FASCISM NAT/G

SCOTT J.B.,"LAW, THESTATE, AND THE INTERNATIONAL COMMUNITY (2 VOLS.)" INTELL INT/ORG NAT/G SECT INT/TRADE WAR...INT/LAW GEN/LAWS BIBLIOG. PAGE 90 E1798
C39 LAW PHIL/SCI DIPLOM CONCPT

HOBBES T.,A DIALOGUE BETWEEN A PHILOSOPHER AND A STUDENT OF THE COMMON LAWS OF ENGLAND (1667?). UK SECT DOMIN ADJUD CRIME INCOME OWN UTIL ORD/FREE PWR SOVEREIGN...JURID GEN/LAWS 17. PAGE 53 E1057
B40 CT/SYS CHIEF SANCTION

CRAIG A.,ABOVE ALL LIBERTIES. FRANCE UK USA-45 LAW CONSTN CULTURE INTELL NAT/G SECT JUDGE...IDEA/COMP BIBLIOG 18/20. PAGE 27 E0536
B42 ORD/FREE MORAL WRITING EDU/PROP

B42
HEGEL G.W.F.,PHILOSOPHY OF RIGHT. UNIV FAM SECT NAT/G
CHIEF AGREE WAR MARRIAGE OWN ORD/FREE...POLICY LAW
CONCPT. PAGE 51 E1023 RATIONAL

B42
US LIBRARY OF CONGRESS,SOCIAL AND CULTURAL PROBLEMS BIBLIOG/A
IN WARTIME: APRIL 1941-MARCH 1942. WOR-45 CLIENT WAR
SECT EDU/PROP CRIME LEISURE RACE/REL STRANGE ATTIT SOC
DRIVE HEALTH...GEOG 20. PAGE 100 E2012 CULTURE

C42
CRAIG A.,"ABOVE ALL LIBERTIES." FRANCE UK LAW BIBLIOG/A
CULTURE INTELL SECT ORD/FREE 18/20. PAGE 27 E0537 EDU/PROP
WRITING
MORAL

B43
US LIBRARY OF CONGRESS,SOCIAL AND CULTURAL PROBLEMS BIBLIOG/A
IN WARTIME: APRIL-DECEMBER (SUPPLEMENT 1). WOR-45 WAR
SECT EDU/PROP CRIME LEISURE CIVMIL/REL RACE/REL SOC
ATTIT DRIVE HEALTH...GEOG 20. PAGE 100 E2013 CULTURE

B43
US LIBRARY OF CONGRESS,SOCIAL AND CULTURAL PROBLEMS BIBLIOG/A
IN WARTIME: JANUARY-MAY 1943 (SUPPLEMENT 2). WOR-45 WAR
FAM SECT PLAN EDU/PROP CRIME LEISURE RACE/REL DRIVE SOC
HEALTH...GEOG 20 JEWS. PAGE 100 E2014 CULTURE

B44
SUAREZ F.,A TREATISE ON LAWS AND GOD THE LAWGIVER LAW
(1612) IN SELECTIONS FROM THREE WORKS, VOL. II. JURID
FRANCE ITALY UK CULTURE NAT/G SECT CHIEF LEGIS GEN/LAWS
DOMIN LEGIT CT/SYS ORD/FREE PWR WORSHIP 16/17. CATH
PAGE 94 E1892

B44
US LIBRARY OF CONGRESS,RUSSIA: A CHECK LIST BIBLIOG
PRELIMINARY TO A BASIC BIBLIOGRAPHY OF MATERIALS IN LAW
THE RUSSIAN LANGUAGE. COM USSR CULTURE EDU/PROP SECT
MARXISM...ART/METH HUM LING 19/20. PAGE 101 E2015

B45
CONOVER H.F.,THE NAZI STATE: WAR CRIMES AND WAR BIBLIOG
CRIMINALS. GERMANY CULTURE NAT/G SECT FORCES DIPLOM WAR
INT/TRADE EDU/PROP...INT/LAW BIOG HIST/WRIT CRIME
TIME/SEQ 20. PAGE 25 E0495

B45
WOOLBERT R.G.,FOREIGN AFFAIRS BIBLIOGRAPHY, BIBLIOG/A
1932-1942. INT/ORG SECT INT/TRADE COLONIAL RACE/REL DIPLOM
NAT/LISM...GEOG INT/LAW GOV/COMP IDEA/COMP 20. WAR
PAGE 107 E2144

S45
DAVIS A.,"CASTE, ECONOMY, AND VIOLENCE" (BMR)" STRATA
USA+45 USA-45 LAW STRUCT SECT SANCTION COERCE RACE/REL
MARRIAGE SEX...PSY SOC SOC/INTEG 18/20 NEGRO DISCRIM
MISCEGEN SOUTH/US. PAGE 29 E0570

B46
GILLIN J.L.,SOCIAL PATHOLOGY. SOCIETY SECT CRIME SOC
ANOMIE DISPL ORD/FREE WEALTH...CRIMLGY PSY WORSHIP. ADJUST
PAGE 44 E0864 CULTURE
INGP/REL

B49
HOLLERAN M.P.,CHURCH AND STATE IN GUATEMALA. SECT
GUATEMALA LAW STRUCT CATHISM...SOC SOC/INTEG 17/20 NAT/G
CHURCH/STA. PAGE 55 E1086 GP/REL
CULTURE

B49
KAFKA G.,FREIHEIT UND ANARCHIE. SECT COERCE DETER CONCPT
WAR ATTIT...IDEA/COMP 20 NATO. PAGE 59 E1179 ORD/FREE
JURID
INT/ORG

B50
COUNCIL BRITISH NATIONAL BIB,BRITISH NATIONAL BIBLIOG/A
BIBLIOGRAPHY. UK AGRI CONSTRUC PERF/ART POL/PAR NAT/G
SECT CREATE INT/TRADE LEAD...HUM JURID PHIL/SCI 20. TEC/DEV
PAGE 26 E0519 DIPLOM

B50
DOROSH J.T.,GUIDE TO SOVIET BIBLIOGRAPHIES. USSR BIBLIOG
LAW AGRI SCHOOL SECT FORCES TEC/DEV...ART/METH GEOG METH
HUM SOC 20. PAGE 32 E0639 CON/ANAL

B52
ETTINGHAUSEN R.,SELECTED AND ANNOTATED BIBLIOGRAPHY BIBLIOG/A
OF BOOKS AND PERIODICALS IN WESTERN LANGUAGES ISLAM
DEALING WITH NEAR AND MIDDLE EAST. LAW CULTURE SECT MEDIT-7
...ART/METH GEOG SOC. PAGE 35 E0700

B52
FORSTER A.,THE TROUBLE MAKERS. USA+45 LAW CULTURE DISCRIM
SOCIETY STRUCT VOL/ASSN CROWD GP/REL MORAL...PSY SECT
SOC CONCPT 20 NEGRO JEWS. PAGE 39 E0771 RACE/REL
ATTIT

B53
AYMARD A.,HISTOIRE GENERALE DES CIVILISATIONS (7 BIBLIOG/A
VOLS.). WOR+45 WOR-45 LAW SECT CREATE ATTIT SOC
...ART/METH WORSHIP. PAGE 6 E0123

B54
O'NEILL J.M.,CATHOLICS IN CONTROVERSY. USA+45 NAT/G CATHISM
PROVS SCHOOL SECT EDU/PROP LEGIT CT/SYS SANCTION CONSTN
GP/REL 20 SUPREME/CT CHURCH/STA. PAGE 78 E1569 POLICY
LAW

B55
GRINDEL C.W.,CONCEPT OF FREEDOM. WOR+45 WOR-45 LAW ORD/FREE
LABOR NAT/G SECT EDU/PROP 20. PAGE 47 E0942 DIPLOM
CONCPT
GP/REL

B55
KHADDURI M.,WAR AND PEACE IN THE LAW OF ISLAM. ISLAM
CONSTN CULTURE SOCIETY STRATA NAT/G PROVS SECT JURID
FORCES TOP/EX CREATE DOMIN EDU/PROP ADJUD COERCE PEACE
ATTIT RIGID/FLEX ALL/VALS...CONCPT TIME/SEQ TOT/POP WAR
VAL/FREE. PAGE 61 E1209

B55
MAZZINI J.,THE DUTIES OF MAN. MOD/EUR LAW SOCIETY SUPEGO
FAM NAT/G POL/PAR SECT VOL/ASSN EX/STRUC ACT/RES CONCPT
CREATE REV PEACE ATTIT ALL/VALS...GEN/LAWS WORK 19. NAT/LISM
PAGE 70 E1396

B55
MID-EUROPEAN LAW PROJECT,CHURCH AND STATE BEHIND LAW
THE IRON CURTAIN. COM CZECHOSLVK HUNGARY POLAND MARXISM
USSR CULTURE SECT EDU/PROP GOV/REL CATHISM...CHARTS POLICY
ANTHOL BIBLIOG WORSHIP 20 CHURCH/STA. PAGE 73 E1455

B55
TROTIER A.H.,DOCTORAL DISSERTATIONS ACCEPTED BY BIBLIOG
AMERICAN UNIVERSITIES 1954-55. SECT DIPLOM HEALTH ACADEM
...ART/METH GEOG INT/LAW SOC LING CHARTS 20. USA+45
PAGE 97 E1943 WRITING

B55
WRONG D.H.,AMERICAN AND CANADIAN VIEWPOINTS. CANADA DIPLOM
USA+45 CONSTN STRATA FAM SECT WORKER ECO/TAC ATTIT
EDU/PROP ADJUD MARRIAGE...IDEA/COMP 20. PAGE 108 NAT/COMP
E2161 CULTURE

B55
ZABEL O.H.,GOD AND CAESAR IN NEBRASKA: A STUDY OF SECT
LEGAL RELATIONSHIP OF CHURCH AND STATE, 1854-1954. PROVS
TAX GIVE ADMIN CONTROL GP/REL ROLE...GP/COMP 19/20 LAW
NEBRASKA. PAGE 108 E2168 EDU/PROP

B56
BOTERO G.,THE REASON OF STATE AND THE GREATNESS OF PHIL/SCI
CITIES. SECT CHIEF FORCES PLAN LEAD WAR MORAL NEW/IDEA
...POLICY 16 MACHIAVELL TREATY. PAGE 14 E0272 CONTROL

B56
DOUGLAS W.O.,WE THE JUDGES. INDIA USA+45 USA-45 LAW ADJUD
NAT/G SECT LEGIS CRIME FEDERAL ORD/FREE CT/SYS
...POLICY GOV/COMP 19/20 WARRN/EARL MARSHALL/J CONSTN
SUPREME/CT. PAGE 32 E0640 GOV/REL

C56
TYLER P.,"IMMIGRATION AND THE UNITED STATES." CULTURE
USA+45 USA-45 LAW SECT INGP/REL RACE/REL NAT/LISM GP/REL
ATTIT...BIBLIOG SOC/INTEG 19/20. PAGE 97 E1949 DISCRIM

B57
ALIGHIERI D.,ON WORLD GOVERNMENT. ROMAN/EMP LAW POLICY
SOCIETY INT/ORG NAT/G POL/PAR ADJUD WAR GP/REL CONCPT
PEACE WORSHIP 15 WORLDUNITY DANTE. PAGE 4 E0067 DIPLOM
SECT

B57
BYRNES R.F.,BIBLIOGRAPHY OF AMERICAN PUBLICATIONS BIBLIOG/A
ON EAST CENTRAL EUROPE, 1945-1957 (VOL. XXII). SECT COM
DIPLOM EDU/PROP RACE/REL...ART/METH GEOG JURID SOC MARXISM
LING 20 JEWS. PAGE 18 E0354 NAT/G

B57
FAIRCHILD H.P.,THE ANATOMY OF FREEDOM. USA+45 ORD/FREE
ACADEM SCHOOL SECT CAP/ISM PRESS CHOOSE SOCISM. CONCPT
PAGE 36 E0712 NAT/G
JURID

B58
EUSDEN J.D.,PURITANS, LAWYERS, AND POLITICS IN GP/REL

EARLY SEVENTEENTH-CENTURY ENGLAND. UK CT/SYS — SECT / NAT/G / LAW
PARL/PROC RATIONAL PWR SOVEREIGN...IDEA/COMP
BIBLIOG 17 PURITAN COMMON/LAW. PAGE 35 E0702

B58
HERRMANN K.,DAS STAATSDENKEN BEI LEIBNIZ. GP/REL — NAT/G / JURID / SECT / EDU/PROP
ATTIT ORD/FREE...CONCPT IDEA/COMP 17 LEIBNITZ/G
CHURCH/STA. PAGE 52 E1034

B58
KURL S.,ESTONIA: A SELECTED BIBLIOGRAPHY. USSR — BIBLIOG / CULTURE / NAT/G
ESTONIA LAW INTELL SECT...ART/METH GEOG HUM SOC 20.
PAGE 62 E1238

B58
MASON H.L.,TOYNBEE'S APPROACH TO WORLD POLITICS. — DIPLOM / CONCPT / PHIL/SCI / SECT
AFR USA+45 USSR LAW WAR NAT/LISM ALL/IDEOS...HUM
BIBLIOG. PAGE 69 E1380

B58
MUSIKER R.,GUIDE TO SOUTH AFRICAN REFERENCE BOOKS. — BIBLIOG/A / SOC / GEOG
SOUTH/AFR SOCIETY SECT EDU/PROP PRESS RACE/REL
...JURID SOC/WK 20. PAGE 75 E1512

B58
O'BRIEN F.W.,JUSTICE REED AND THE FIRST AMENDMENT, — ADJUD / SECT / CT/SYS
THE RELIGION CLAUSES. USA+45 USA-45 NAT/G PROVS
CONTROL FEDERAL...POLICY JURID TIME/SEQ 20
SUPREME/CT CHRUCH/STA AMEND/I REED/STAN. PAGE 78
E1563

B58
WOOD J.E.,CHURCH AND STATE IN SCRIPTURE HISTORY AND — GP/REL / SECT / NAT/G / ADJUD
CONSTITUTIONAL LAW. LAW CONSTN SOCIETY PROVS
VOL/ASSN BAL/PWR COLONIAL CT/SYS ATTIT...BIBLIOG 20
SUPREME/CT CHURCH/STA BIBLE. PAGE 107 E2142

B59
ANDERSON J.N.D.,ISLAMIC LAW IN THE MODERN WORLD. — ISLAM / JURID
FAM KIN SECT LEGIT ADJUD ATTIT DRIVE...TIME/SEQ
TREND GEN/LAWS 20 MUSLIM. PAGE 5 E0089

B59
FELLMANN D.,THE LIMITS OF FREEDOM. USA+45 USA-45 — CONCPT / JURID / CONSTN
NAT/G SECT ROLE ORD/FREE WORSHIP 18/20 FREE/SPEE.
PAGE 37 E0734

B59
HAYS B.,A SOUTHERN MODERATE SPEAKS. LAW PROVS — SECT / DISCRIM / CT/SYS / RACE/REL
SCHOOL KNOWL...JURID SOC SELF/OBS BIOG 20 NEGRO
SUPREME/CT. PAGE 51 E1015

B59
NICHOLS R.F.,RELIGION AND AMERICAN DEMOCRACY. — NAT/G / SECT / CONSTN / CONCPT
USA+45 USA-45 LAW CHOOSE SUFF MORAL ORD/FREE
POPULISM...POLICY BIBLIOG 16/20 PRE/US/AM
CHRISTIAN. PAGE 77 E1547

B60
BLANSHARD P.,GOD AND MAN IN WASHINGTON. USA+45 — NAT/G / SECT / GP/REL / POL/PAR
CHIEF LEGIS LEGIT CT/SYS PRIVIL ATTIT ORD/FREE
...POLICY CONCPT 20 SUPREME/CT CONGRESS PRESIDENT
CHURCH/STA. PAGE 12 E0242

B60
FELLMAN D.,THE SUPREME COURT AND EDUCATION. ACADEM — CT/SYS / SECT / RACE/REL / SCHOOL
NAT/G PROVS DELIB/GP ADJUD ORD/FREE...POLICY JURID
WORSHIP 20 SUPREME/CT NEGRO CHURCH/STA. PAGE 37
E0731

B60
MOCTEZUMA A.P.,EL CONFLICTO RELIGIOSO DE 1926 (2ND — SECT / ORD/FREE / DISCRIM / REV
ED.). L/A+17C LAW NAT/G LOBBY COERCE GP/REL ATTIT
...POLICY 20 MEXIC/AMER CHURCH/STA. PAGE 74 E1476

B60
POWELL T.,THE SCHOOL BUS LAW: A CASE STUDY IN — JURID / SCHOOL
EDUCATION, RELIGION, AND POLITICS. USA+45 LAW NEIGH
SECT LEGIS EDU/PROP ADJUD CT/SYS LOBBY CATHISM
WORSHIP 20 CONNECTICT CHURCH/STA. PAGE 82 E1641

B61
FROEBEL J.,THEORIE DER POLITIK, ALS ERGEBNIS EINER — JURID / ORD/FREE / NAT/G
ERNEUERTEN PRUEFUNG DEMOKRATISCHER LEHRMEINUNGEN.
WOR-45 SOCIETY POL/PAR SECT REV REPRESENT PWR
SOVEREIGN...MAJORIT 19. PAGE 41 E0812

B61
HAGEN A.,STAAT UND KATHOLISCHE KIRCHE IN — SECT / PROVS / GP/REL / JURID
WURTTEMBERG IN DEN JAHREN 1848-1862 (2 VOLS.).
GERMANY DELIB/GP EDU/PROP MARRIAGE CATHISM 19
CHURCH/STA. PAGE 49 E0975

B61
KURLAND P.B.,RELIGION AND THE LAW. USA+45 USA-45 — SECT / NAT/G / CT/SYS / GP/REL
CONSTN PROVS CHIEF ADJUD SANCTION PRIVIL CATHISM
...POLICY 17/20 SUPREME/CT PRESIDENT CHURCH/STA.
PAGE 62 E1239

B61
SMITH J.W.,RELIGIOUS PERSPECTIVES IN AMERICAN — SECT / DOMIN / SOCIETY / GP/REL
CULTURE, VOL. 2, RELIGION IN AMERICAN LIFE. USA+45
CULTURE NAT/G EDU/PROP ADJUD LOBBY ATTIT...ART/METH
ANTHOL 20 CHURCH/STA BIBLE. PAGE 92 E1845

L61
KAUPER P.G.,"CHURCH AND STATE: COOPERATIVE — SECT / CONSTN / LAW / POLICY
SEPARATISM." NAT/G LEGIS OP/RES TAX EDU/PROP GP/REL
TREND. PAGE 59 E1187

B62
BARLOW R.B.,CITIZENSHIP AND CONSCIENCE: STUDIES IN — SECT / LEGIS / DISCRIM
THEORY AND PRACTICE OF RELIGIOUS TOLERATION IN
ENGLAND DURING EIGHTEENTH CENTURY. UK LAW VOL/ASSN
EDU/PROP SANCTION REV GP/REL MAJORITY ATTIT
ORD/FREE...BIBLIOG WORSHIP 18. PAGE 8 E0150

B62
BOCHENSKI J.M.,HANDBOOK ON COMMUNISM. USSR WOR+45 — COM / DIPLOM / POLICY / CONCPT
LAW SOCIETY NAT/G POL/PAR SECT CRIME PERSON MARXISM
...SOC ANTHOL 20. PAGE 13 E0254

B62
GONNER R.,DAS KIRCHENPATRONATRECHT IM — JURID / SECT / NAT/G / GP/REL
GROSSHERZOGTUM BADEN. GERMANY LAW PROVS DEBATE
ATTIT CATHISM 14/19 PROTESTANT CHRISTIAN CHURCH/STA
BADEN. PAGE 44 E0882

B62
KAUPER P.G.,CIVIL LIBERTIES AND THE CONSTITUTION. — LAW / CONSTN / CT/SYS / DECISION
USA+45 SECT EDU/PROP WRITING ADJUD SEX ORD/FREE 20
SUPREME/CT CIVIL/LIB CHURCH/STA. PAGE 60 E1188

B62
KIDDER F.E.,THESES ON PAN AMERICAN TOPICS. LAW — BIBLIOG / CHRIST-17C / L/A+17C / SOCIETY
CULTURE NAT/G SECT DIPLOM HEALTH...ART/METH GEOG
SOC 13/20. PAGE 61 E1213

B62
MCGRATH J.J.,CHURCH AND STATE IN AMERICAN LAW. LAW — SECT / ADJUD / CONSTN / NAT/G
PROVS SCHOOL TAX GIVE CT/SYS GP/REL...POLICY ANTHOL
18/20 SUPREME/CT CHURCH/STA CASEBOOK. PAGE 71 E1414

B62
MCGRATH J.J.,CHURCH AND STATE IN AMERICAN LAW: — LAW / GOV/REL / SECT
CASES AND MATERIALS. USA+45 USA-45 LEGIS EDU/PROP
ADJUD CT/SYS PWR...ANTHOL 18/20 CHURCH/STA. PAGE 71
E1415

B62
SILVA R.C.,RUM, RELIGION, AND VOTES: 1928 RE- — POL/PAR / CHOOSE / GP/COMP / ATTIT
EXAMINED. USA-45 LAW SECT DISCRIM CATHISM...CORREL
STAT 20 PRESIDENT SMITH/ALF DEMOCRAT. PAGE 91 E1827

B62
TUSSMAN J.,THE SUPREME COURT ON CHURCH AND STATE. — CT/SYS / SECT / ADJUD
USA+45 USA-45 SANCTION PRIVIL...POLICY JURID 19/20
SUPREME/CT CHURCH/STA. PAGE 97 E1945

B63
CHOJNACKI S.,REGISTER ON CURRENT RESEARCH ON — BIBLIOG / ACT/RES / INTELL / ACADEM
ETHIOPIA AND THE HORN OF AFRICA. ETHIOPIA LAW
CULTURE AGRI SECT EDU/PROP ADMIN...GEOG HEAL LING
20. PAGE 22 E0433

B63
DILLIARD I.,ONE MAN'S STAND FOR FREEDOM: MR. — CONSTN / JURID / JUDGE / ORD/FREE
JUSTICE BLACK AND THE BILL OF RIGHTS. USA+45
POL/PAR SECT DELIB/GP FORCES ADJUD CONTROL WAR
DISCRIM MORAL...BIBLIOG 20 NEGRO SUPREME/CT
BILL/RIGHT BLACK/HL. PAGE 32 E0628

B63
DRINAN R.F.,RELIGION, THE COURTS, AND PUBLIC — SECT / CT/SYS / POLICY / SCHOOL
POLICY. USA+45 CONSTN BUDGET TAX GIVE ADJUD
SANCTION GP/REL PRIVIL 20 CHURCH/STA. PAGE 33 E0649

B63
ELIAS T.O.,THE NIGERIAN LEGAL SYSTEM. NIGERIA LAW — CT/SYS / ADJUD / COLONIAL
FAM KIN SECT ADMIN NAT/LISM...JURID 18/20
ENGLSH/LAW COMMON/LAW. PAGE 34 E0682

PROF/ORG

SOC NAT/COMP 20. PAGE 43 E0853

B63
FISCHER-GALATI S.A.,RUMANIA; A BIBLIOGRAPHIC GUIDE BIBLIOG/A
(PAMPHLET). ROMANIA INTELL ECO/DEV LABOR SECT NAT/G
WEALTH...GEOG SOC/WK LING 20. PAGE 38 E0756 COM
LAW

B64
GIANNELLA D.A.,RELIGION AND THE PUBLIC ORDER: AN SECT
ANNUAL REVIEW OF CHURCH AND STATE, AND OF RELIGION, NAT/G
LAW, AND SOCIETY. USA+45 LAW SOCIETY FAM POL/PAR CONSTN
SCHOOL GIVE EDU/PROP GP/REL...JURID GEN/LAWS ORD/FREE
BIBLIOG/A 20 CHURCH/STA BIRTH/CON CONSCN/OBJ
NATURL/LAW. PAGE 43 E0855

B63
FORTES A.B.,HISTORIA ADMINISTRATIVA, JUDICIARIA E PROVS
ECLESIASTICA DO RIO GRANDE DO SUL. BRAZIL L/A+17C ADMIN
LOC/G SECT COLONIAL CT/SYS ORD/FREE CATHISM 16/20. JURID
PAGE 39 E0773

B64
GRASMUCK E.L.,COERCITIO STAAT UND KIRCHE IM GP/REL
DONATISTENSTREIT. CHRIST-17C ROMAN/EMP LAW PROVS NAT/G
DEBATE PERSON SOVEREIGN...JURID CONCPT 4/5 SECT
AUGUSTINE CHURCH/STA ROMAN/LAW. PAGE 45 E0898 COERCE

B63
GEERTZ C.,OLD SOCIETIES AND NEW STATES: THE QUEST ECO/UNDEV
FOR MODERNITY IN ASIA AND AFRICA. AFR ASIA LAW TEC/DEV
CULTURE SECT EDU/PROP REV...GOV/COMP NAT/COMP 20. NAT/LISM
PAGE 42 E0842 SOVEREIGN

B64
KAUPER P.G.,RELIGION AND THE CONSTITUTION. USA+45 CONSTN
USA-45 LAW NAT/G SCHOOL SECT GP/REL ATTIT...BIBLIOG JURID
WORSHIP 18/20 SUPREME/CT FREE/SPEE CHURCH/STA. ORD/FREE
PAGE 60 E1189

B63
A BIBLIOGRAPHY OF DOCTORAL DISSERTATIONS UNDERTAKEN BIBLIOG
IN AMERICAN AND CANADIAN UNIVERSITIES ON RELIGION ACADEM
AND POLITICS. LAW CONSTN DOMIN LEGIT ADJUD GP/REL SECT
...POLICY 20. PAGE 62 E1241 JURID

B64
MARNELL W.H.,THE FIRST AMENDMENT: THE HISTORY OF CONSTN
RELIGIOUS FREEDOM IN AMERICA. WOR+45 WOR-45 PROVS SECT
CREATE CT/SYS...POLICY BIBLIOG/A WORSHIP 16/20. ORD/FREE
PAGE 68 E1367 GOV/REL

B63
LANOUE G.R.,A BIBLIOGRAPHY OF DOCTORAL BIBLIOG
DISSERTATIONS ON POLITICS AND RELIGION. USA+45 NAT/G
USA-45 CONSTN PROVS DIPLOM CT/SYS MORAL...POLICY LOC/G
JURID CONCPT 20. PAGE 63 E1252 SECT

B64
MINAR D.W.,IDEAS AND POLITICS: THE AMERICAN CONSTN
EXPERIENCE. SECT CHIEF LEGIS CREATE ADJUD EXEC REV NAT/G
PWR...PHIL/SCI CONCPT IDEA/COMP 18/20 HAMILTON/A FEDERAL
JEFFERSN/T DECLAR/IND JACKSON/A PRESIDENT. PAGE 73
E1464

B63
LOWRY C.W.,TO PRAY OR NOT TO PRAY. ADJUD SANCTION SECT
GP/REL ORD/FREE PWR CATHISM WORSHIP 20 SUPREME/CT CT/SYS
CHRISTIAN CHRUCH/STA. PAGE 67 E1330 CONSTN
PRIVIL

B64
NATIONAL BOOK LEAGUE,THE COMMONWEALTH IN BOOKS: AN BIBLIOG/A
ANNOTATED LIST. CANADA UK LOC/G SECT ADMIN...SOC JURID
BIOG 20 CMN/WLTH. PAGE 76 E1526 NAT/G

B63
LYONS F.S.L.,INTERNATIONALISM IN EUROPE 1815-1914. DIPLOM
LAW AGRI COM/IND DIST/IND LABOR SECT INT/TRADE MOD/EUR
TARIFFS...BIBLIOG 19/20. PAGE 67 E1335 INT/ORG

B64
NICE R.W.,TREASURY OF LAW. WOR+45 WOR-45 SECT ADJUD LAW
MORAL ORD/FREE...INT/LAW JURID PHIL/SCI ANTHOL. WRITING
PAGE 77 E1545 PERS/REL
DIPLOM

B63
PRITCHETT C.H.,THE THIRD BRANCH OF GOVERNMENT. JURID
USA+45 USA-45 CONSTN SOCIETY INDUS SECT LEGIS JUDGE NAT/G
PROB/SOLV GOV/REL 20 SUPREME/CT CHURCH/STA. PAGE 82 ADJUD
E1654 CT/SYS

B64
RAGHAVAN M.D.,INDIA IN CEYLONESE HISTORY, SOCIETY DIPLOM
AND CULTURE. CEYLON INDIA S/ASIA LAW SOCIETY CULTURE
INT/TRADE ATTIT...ART/METH JURID SOC LING 20. SECT
PAGE 83 E1668 STRUCT

B63
RAVENS J.P.,STAAT UND KATHOLISCHE KIRCHE IN GP/REL
PREUSSENS POLNISCHEN TEILUNGSGEBIETEN. GERMANY CATHISM
POLAND PRUSSIA PROVS DIPLOM EDU/PROP DEBATE SECT
NAT/LISM...JURID 18 CHURCH/STA. PAGE 83 E1674 NAT/G

B64
RICE C.E.,THE SUPREME COURT AND PUBLIC PRAYER. JURID
CONSTN SCHOOL SECT PROB/SOLV TAX ATTIT WORSHIP POLICY
18/20 SUPREME/CT CHURCH/STA. PAGE 84 E1692 NAT/G

B63
REITZEL A.M.,DAS MAINZER KRONUNGSRECHT UND DIE CHIEF
POLITISCHE PROBLEMATIK. GERMANY MUNIC LEGIT CATHISM JURID
12/13. PAGE 84 E1684 CHOOSE
SECT

B64
ROBERTS HL,FOREIGN AFFAIRS BIBLIOGRAPHY, 1952-1962. BIBLIOG/A
ECO/DEV SECT PLAN FOR/AID INT/TRADE ARMS/CONT DIPLOM
NAT/LISM ATTIT...INT/LAW GOV/COMP IDEA/COMP 20. INT/ORG
PAGE 85 E1703 WAR

B63
SMITH E.A.,CHURCH AND STATE IN YOUR COMMUNITY. GP/REL
USA+45 PROVS SCHOOL ACT/RES CT/SYS PARTIC ATTIT SECT
MORAL ORD/FREE CATHISM 20 PROTESTANT CHURCH/STA. NAT/G
PAGE 92 E1842 NEIGH

B64
SCHMEISER D.A.,CIVIL LIBERTIES IN CANADA. CANADA ORD/FREE
LAW SECT PRESS RACE/REL NAT/LISM PRIVIL 20 CONSTN
COMMONWLTH PARLIAMENT CIVIL/LIB CHURCH/STA. PAGE 88 ADJUD
E1758 EDU/PROP

B64
FEINE H.E.,DIE BESETZUNG DER REICHSBISTUMER VOM CHOOSE
WESTFALISCHEN FRIEDEN BIS ZUR SAKULARISATION. SECT
GERMANY EDU/PROP GP/REL AGE 17/19. PAGE 37 E0727 JURID
PROVS

B64
SCHWELB E.,HUMAN RIGHTS AND THE INTERNATIONAL INT/ORG
COMMUNITY. WOR+45 WOR-45 NAT/G SECT DELIB/GP DIPLOM ORD/FREE
PEACE RESPECT TREATY 20 UN. PAGE 89 E1792 INT/LAW

B64
FORBES A.H.,CURRENT RESEARCH IN BRITISH STUDIES. UK BIBLIOG
CONSTN CULTURE POL/PAR SECT DIPLOM ADMIN...JURID PERSON
BIOG WORSHIP 20. PAGE 39 E0769 NAT/G
PARL/PROC

B64
STOKES A.P.,CHURCH AND STATE IN THE UNITED STATES SECT
(3 VOLS.). USA+45 USA-45 NAT/G PROVS LEGIS CT/SYS CONSTN
SANCTION PRIVIL ORD/FREE 17/20 CHURCH/STA. PAGE 94 POLICY
E1875

B64
FREISEN J.,STAAT UND KATHOLISCHE KIRCHE IN DEN SECT
DEUTSCHEN BUNDESSTAATEN (2 VOLS.). GERMANY LAW FAM CATHISM
NAT/G EDU/PROP GP/REL MARRIAGE WEALTH 19/20 JURID
CHURCH/STA. PAGE 40 E0793 PROVS

L64
POUNDS N.J.G.,"THE POLITICS OF PARTITION." AFR ASIA NAT/G
COM EUR+WWI FUT ISLAM S/ASIA USA-45 LAW ECO/DEV NAT/LISM
ECO/UNDEV AGRI INDUS INT/ORG POL/PAR PROVS SECT
FORCES TOP/EX EDU/PROP LEGIT ATTIT MORAL ORD/FREE
PWR RESPECT WEALTH. PAGE 82 E1640

B64
FREUD A.,OF HUMAN SOVEREIGNTY. WOR+45 INDUS SECT NAT/LISM
ECO/TAC CRIME CHOOSE ATTIT MORAL MARXISM...POLICY DIPLOM
BIBLIOG 20. PAGE 40 E0794 WAR
PEACE

S64
GREENBERG S.,"JUDAISM AND WORLD JUSTICE." MEDIT-7 SECT
WOR+45 LAW CULTURE SOCIETY INT/ORG NAT/G FORCES JURID
EDU/PROP ATTIT DRIVE PERSON SUPEGO ALL/VALS PEACE
...POLICY PSY CONCPT GEN/LAWS JEWS. PAGE 46 E0908

B64
GESELLSCHAFT RECHTSVERGLEICH,BIBLIOGRAPHIE DES BIBLIOG/A
DEUTSCHEN RECHTS (BIBLIOGRAPHY OF GERMAN LAW, JURID
TRANS. BY COURTLAND PETERSON). GERMANY FINAN INDUS CONSTN
LABOR SECT FORCES CT/SYS PARL/PROC CRIME...INT/LAW ADMIN

S64
KHAN M.Z.,"ISLAM AND INTERNATIONAL RELATIONS." FUT ISLAM
WOR+45 LAW CULTURE SOCIETY NAT/G SECT DELIB/GP INT/ORG

FORCES EDU/PROP ATTIT PERSON SUPEGO ALL/VALS   DIPLOM
...POLICY PSY CONCPT MYTH HIST/WRIT GEN/LAWS.
PAGE 61 E1211

B65
ANDRUS H.L.,LIBERALISM, CONSERVATISM, MORMONISM.   SECT
USA+45 PLAN ADJUD CONTROL HAPPINESS ORD/FREE   UTOPIA
CONSERVE NEW/LIB WORSHIP 20. PAGE 5 E0097   MORAL

B65
ANTIEU C.J.,RELIGION UNDER THE STATE CONSTITUTIONS. SECT
USA+45 LAW SCHOOL TAX SANCTION PRIVIL ORD/FREE   CONSTN
...JURID 20 SUPREME/CT CHURCH/STA. PAGE 5 E0099   PROVS
                                          GP/REL

B65
BEGGS D.W.,AMERICA'S SCHOOLS AND CHURCHES: PARTNERS SECT
IN CONFLICT. USA+45 PROVS EDU/PROP ADJUD DISCRIM GP/REL
ATTIT...IDEA/COMP ANTHOL BIBLIOG WORSHIP 20   SCHOOL
CHURCH/STA. PAGE 9 E0179   NAT/G

B65
BOVY L.,LE MOUVEMENT SYNDICAL OUEST AFRICAIN   BIBLIOG
D'EXPRESSION FRANCAISE. AFR SECT...JURID SOC 20. SOCISM
PAGE 14 E0275   ECO/UNDEV
                                          IDEA/COMP

B65
CONRING E.,KIRCHE UND STAAT NACH DER LEHRE DER   SECT
NIEDERLANDISCHEN CALVINISTEN IN DER ERSTEN HALFTE JURID
DES 17. JAHRHUNDERTS. NETHERLAND GP/REL...CONCPT 17 NAT/G
CHURCH/STA. PAGE 25 E0497   ORD/FREE

B65
FELLMAN D.,RELIGION IN AMERICAN PUBLIC LAW. USA+45 SECT
USA-45 NAT/G PROVS ADJUD SANCTION GP/REL PRIVIL   CONSTN
ORD/FREE...JURID TIME/SEQ 18/20 SUPREME/CT   LAW
CHURCH/STA. PAGE 37 E0733   POLICY

B65
GAJENDRAGADKAR P.B.,LAW, LIBERTY AND SOCIAL   ORD/FREE
JUSTICE. INDIA CONSTN NAT/G SECT PLAN ECO/TAC PRESS LAW
POPULISM...SOC METH/COMP 20 HINDU. PAGE 42 E0826   ADJUD
                                          JURID

B65
HIGGINS R.,CONFLICT OF INTERESTS* INTERNATIONAL LAW INT/LAW
IN A DIVIDED WORLD. ASIA USSR ECO/DEV ECO/UNDEV   IDEA/COMP
SECT INT/TRADE COLD/WAR WORSHIP. PAGE 52 E1042   ADJUST

B65
HOLDSWORTH W.S.,A HISTORY OF ENGLISH LAW; THE   LAW
CENTURIES OF SETTLEMENT AND REFORM (VOL. XV). UK INDUS
CONSTN SECT LEGIS JUDGE WRITING ADJUD CT/SYS CRIME PROF/ORG
OWN...JURID IDEA/COMP 18 PARLIAMENT ENGLSH/LAW   ATTIT
COMMON/LAW. PAGE 54 E1082

B65
HOWE M.D.W.,THE GARDEN AND THE WILDERNESS. USA+45 CONSTN
LAW GIVE EDU/PROP LEGIT NAT/LISM ORD/FREE...POLICY SECT
JURID SUPREME/CT CHURCH/STA. PAGE 55 E1103   NAT/G
                                          GP/REL

B65
KAAS L.,DIE GEISTLICHE GERICHTSBARKEIT DER   JURID
KATHOLISCHEN KIRCHE IN PREUSSEN (2 VOLS.). PRUSSIA CATHISM
CONSTN NAT/G PROVS SECT ADJUD ADMIN ATTIT 16/20. GP/REL
PAGE 59 E1178   CT/SYS

B65
KUPER H.,AFRICAN LAW. LAW FAM KIN SECT JUDGE ADJUST AFR
NAT/LISM 17/20. PAGE 62 E1236   CT/SYS
                                          ADJUD
                                          COLONIAL

B65
MARTENS E.,DIE HANNOVERSCHE KIRCHENKOMMISSION.   JURID
GERMANY LAW INT/ORG PROVS SECT CONFER GP/REL   DELIB/GP
CATHISM 16/20. PAGE 69 E1371   CONSTN
                                            PROF/ORG

B65
MOELLER R.,LUDWIG DER BAYER UND DIE KURIE IM KAMPF JURID
UM DAS REICH. GERMANY LAW SECT LEGIT LEAD GP/REL CHIEF
CATHISM CONSERVE 14 LUDWIG/BAV POPE CHURCH/STA.   CHOOSE
PAGE 74 E1478   NAT/LISM

B65
PARKER D.,CIVIL LIBERTIES CASE STUDIES AND THE LAW. ORD/FREE
SECT ADJUD...CONCPT WORSHIP 20 SUPREME/CT   JURID
CIV/RIGHTS FREE/SPEE. PAGE 80 E1598   CONSTN
                                          JUDGE

B65
STOREY R.G.,OUR UNALIENABLE RIGHTS. LAW SECT CT/SYS CONSTN
SUFF DISCRIM 17/20 CIVIL/LIB ENGLSH/LAW. PAGE 94 JURID

E1882   ORD/FREE
                                   LEGIS

B65
WILSON J.F.,CHURCH AND STATE IN AMERICAN HISTORY. SECT
USA+45 USA-45 ADJUD CT/SYS ORD/FREE SOVEREIGN   NAT/G
...ANTHOL BIBLIOG/A 17/20 CHURCH/STA. PAGE 106   GP/REL
E2129   CONTROL

S65
KHOURI F.J.,"THE JORDON RIVER CONTROVERSY." LAW   ISLAM
SOCIETY ECO/UNDEV AGRI FINAN INDUS SECT FORCES   INT/ORG
ACT/RES PLAN TEC/DEV ECO/TAC EDU/PROP COERCE ATTIT ISRAEL
DRIVE PERCEPT RIGID/FLEX ALL/VALS...GEOG SOC MYTH JORDAN
WORK. PAGE 61 E1212

B66
AMERICAN JEWISH COMMITTEE,GROUP RELATIONS IN THE BIBLIOG/A
UNITED STATES: PROBLEMS AND PERSPECTIVES: A   USA+45
SELECTED, ANNOTATED BIBLIOGRAPHY (PAMPHLET). LAW STRUCT
CONSTN STRATA SCHOOL SECT PROB/SOLV ATTIT...POLICY GP/REL
WELF/ST SOC/WK 20. PAGE 4 E0079

B66
BAHRO H.,DAS KINDSCHAFTSRECHT IN DER UNION DER   JURID
SOZIALISTITSCHEN SOWJETREPUBLIKEN. USSR SECT   AGE/C
EDU/PROP CONTROL PWR...SOC/WK 20. PAGE 7 E0133   PERS/REL
                                          SUPEGO

B66
BEER U.,FRUCHTBARKEITSREGELUNG ALS KONSEQUENZ   CONTROL
VERANTWORTLICHER ELTERNSCHAFT. ASIA GERMANY/W INDIA GEOG
LAW ECO/DEV ECO/UNDEV TEC/DEV ECO/TAC BIO/SOC SEX FAM
CATHISM...METH/COMP 20 CHINJAP BIRTH/CON. PAGE 9 SECT
E0178

B66
BRAIBANTI R.,RESEARCH ON THE BUREAUCRACY OF   HABITAT
PAKISTAN. PAKISTAN LAW CULTURE INTELL ACADEM LOC/G NAT/G
SECT PRESS CT/SYS...LING CHARTS 20 BUREAUCRCY.   ADMIN
PAGE 15 E0286   CONSTN

B66
COLEMAN-NORTON P.R.,ROMAN STATE AND CHRISTIAN   GP/REL
CHURCH: A COLLECTION OF LEGAL DOCUMENTS TO A.D. 535 NAT/G
(3 VOLS.). CHRIST-17C ROMAN/EMP...ANTHOL DICTIONARY SECT
6 CHRISTIAN CHURCH/STA. PAGE 24 E0473   LAW

B66
DOUGLAS W.O.,THE BIBLE AND THE SCHOOLS. USA+45   SECT
CULTURE ADJUD INGP/REL AGE/C AGE/Y ATTIT KNOWL   NAT/G
WORSHIP 20 SUPREME/CT CHURCH/STA BIBLE CHRISTIAN. SCHOOL
PAGE 32 E0644   GP/REL

B66
FEINE H.E.,REICH UND KIRCHE. CHRIST-17C MOD/EUR   JURID
ROMAN/EMP LAW CHOOSE ATTIT 10/19 CHURCH/STA   SECT
ROMAN/LAW. PAGE 37 E0728   NAT/G
                                          GP/REL

B66
FUCHS W.P.,STAAT UND KIRCHE IM WANDEL DER   SECT
JAHRHUNDERTE. EUR+WWI MOD/EUR UK REV...JURID CONCPT NAT/G
4/20 EUROPE CHRISTIAN CHURCH/STA. PAGE 41 E0817   ORD/FREE
                                          GP/REL

B66
HOPKINS J.F.K.,ARABIC PERIODICAL LITERATURE, 1961. BIBLIOG/A
ISLAM LAW CULTURE SECT...GEOG HEAL PHIL/SCI PSY SOC NAT/LISM
20. PAGE 55 E1096   TEC/DEV
                                          INDUS

B66
KERR M.H.,ISLAMIC REFORM: THE POLITICAL AND LEGAL LAW
THEORIES OF MUHAMMAD 'ABDUH AND RASHID RIDA. NAT/G CONCPT
SECT LEAD SOVEREIGN CONSERVE...JURID BIBLIOG   ISLAM
WORSHIP 20. PAGE 60 E1204

B66
KUNST H.,EVANGELISCHES STAATSLEXIKON. LAW CONSTN JURID
POL/PAR...PHIL/SCI CONCPT DICTIONARY. PAGE 62 E1232 SECT
                                          SOC
                                          NAT/G

B66
KUNSTLER W.M.,"DEEP IN MY HEART" USA+45 LAW   CT/SYS
PROF/ORG SECT LOBBY PARTIC CROWD DISCRIM ROLE   RACE/REL
...BIOG 20 KING/MAR/L NEGRO CIV/RIGHTS SOUTH/US.   ADJUD
PAGE 62 E1233   CONSULT

B66
O'NEILL C.E.,CHURCH AND STATE IN FRENCH COLONIAL COLONIAL
LOUISIANA: POLICY AND POLITICS TO 1732. PROVS   NAT/G
VOL/ASSN DELIB/GP ADJUD ADMIN GP/REL ATTIT DRIVE SECT
...POLICY BIBLIOG 17/18 LOUISIANA CHURCH/STA.   PWR
PAGE 78 E1568

B66

POWERS E.,CRIME AND PUNISHMENT IN EARLY   CRIME
MASSACHUSETTS 1620-1692: A DOCUMENTARY HISTORY.   ADJUD
USA-45 SECT LEGIS COLONIAL ATTIT ORD/FREE MYSTISM   CT/SYS
17 PRE/US/AM MASSACHU. PAGE 82 E1643   PROVS

B66

SALTER L.M.,RESOLUTION OF INTERNATIONAL CONFLICT.   PROB/SOLV
USA+45 INT/ORG SECT DIPLOM ECO/TAC FOR/AID DETER   PEACE
NUC/PWR WAR 20. PAGE 87 E1743   INT/LAW
                                                          POLICY

B66

SMITH E.A.,CHURCH-STATE RELATIONS IN ECUMENICAL   NAT/G
PERSPECTIVE. WOR+45 LAW MUNIC INGP/REL DISCRIM   SECT
ATTIT SUPEGO ORD/FREE CATHISM...PHIL/SCI IDEA/COMP   GP/REL
20 PROTESTANT ECUMENIC CHURCH/STA CHRISTIAN.   ADJUD
PAGE 92 E1843

B66

STEVENS R.E.,REFERENCE BOOKS IN THE SOCIAL SCIENCES   BIBLIOG/A
AND HUMANITIES. CULTURE PERF/ART SECT EDU/PROP   SOC
...JURID PSY SOC/WK STAT 20 MUSIC. PAGE 93 E1873   HUM
                                                          ART/METH

B66

TIEDT S.W.,THE ROLE OF THE FEDERAL GOVERNMENT IN   NAT/G
EDUCATION. FUT USA+45 USA-45 CONSTN SECT BUDGET   EDU/PROP
CT/SYS GOV/REL 18/20 SUPREME/CT. PAGE 96 E1924   GIVE
                                                          SCHOOL

B66

US SENATE COMM ON JUDICIARY,SCHOOL PRAYER. USA+45   SCHOOL
LAW LOC/G SECT ADJUD WORSHIP 20 SENATE DEITY.   JURID
PAGE 103 E2058   NAT/G

S66

MATTHEWS D.G.,"ETHIOPIAN OUTLINE: A BIBLIOGRAPHIC   BIBLIOG
RESEARCH GUIDE." ETHIOPIA LAW STRUCT ECO/UNDEV AGRI   NAT/G
LABOR SECT CHIEF DELIB/GP EX/STRUC ADMIN...LING   DIPLOM
ORG/CHARTS 20. PAGE 69 E1384   POL/PAR

B67

AMDS W.E.,DELINQUENCY PREVENTION: THEORY AND   AGE/Y
PRACTICE. USA+45 SOCIETY FAM SCHOOL SECT FORCES   CRIME
PROB/SOLV...HEAL JURID PREDICT ANTHOL. PAGE 4 E0071   PUB/INST
                                                          LAW

B67

BOULTON D.,OBJECTION OVERRULED. UK LAW POL/PAR   FORCES
DIPLOM ADJUD SANCTION DEATH WAR CIVMIL/REL 20.   SOCISM
PAGE 14 E0273   SECT

B67

DEBOLD R.C.,LSD, MAN AND SOCIETY. USA+45 LAW   HEALTH
SOCIETY SECT CONTROL SANCTION STRANGE ATTIT...HEAL   DRIVE
CHARTS ANTHOL BIBLIOG. PAGE 30 E0601   PERSON
                                                          BIO/SOC

S67

MACLEOD R.M.,"LAW, MEDICINE AND PUBLIC OPINION: THE   LAW
RESISTANCE TO COMPULSORY HEALTH LEGISLATION   HEALTH
1870-1907." UK CONSTN SECT DELIB/GP DEBATE   ATTIT
PARL/PROC GP/REL MORAL 19. PAGE 67 E1344

B91

BENTHAM J.,A FRAGMENT ON GOVERNMENT (1776). CONSTN   SOVEREIGN
MUNIC NAT/G SECT AGREE HAPPINESS UTIL MORAL   LAW
ORD/FREE...JURID CONCPT. PAGE 10 E0198   DOMIN

B97

JENKS E.J.,LAW AND POLITICS IN THE MIDDLE AGES.   LAW
CHRIST-17C CULTURE STRUCT KIN NAT/G SECT CT/SYS   SOCIETY
GP/REL...CLASSIF CHARTS IDEA/COMP BIBLIOG 8/16.   ADJUST
PAGE 58 E1162

SECUR/COUN....UNITED NATIONS SECURITY COUNCIL

SECUR/PROG....SECURITY PROGRAM

SECURITIES....SEE FINAN

SECURITY....SEE ORD/FREE

SECURITY COUNCIL....SEE UN+DELIB/GP+PWR

SEDITION....SEDITION

B65

US LIBRARY OF CONGRESS,INTERNAL SECURITY AND   CONTROL
SUBVERSION. USA+45 ACADEM LOC/G NAT/G PROVS   ADJUD

...POLICY ANARCH DECISION 20 CIVIL/SERV SUBVERT   LAW
SEDITION. PAGE 101 E2020   PLAN

SEEK....SEARCH FOR EDUCATION, ELEVATION, AND KNOWLEDGE

SEGAL R. E1801

SEGREGAT....SEGREGATION

B65

GILLETTE W.,THE RIGHT TO VOTE: POLITICS AND THE   RACE/REL
PASSAGE OF THE FIFTEENTH AMENDMENT. USA-45 LAW LEAD   CONSTN
DISCRIM SEGREGAT CONGRESS. PAGE 44 E0863

B65

KING D.B.,LEGAL ASPECTS OF THE CIVIL RIGHTS   LAW
MOVEMENT. SERV/IND VOL/ASSN LEGIS EDU/PROP ADJUD   DISCRIM
PARTIC CHOOSE...JURID SEGREGAT WORK. PAGE 61 E1215   TREND

SEGREGATION....SEE NEGRO, SOUTH/US, RACE/REL, SOC/INTEG,
    CIV/RIGHTS, DISCRIM, MISCEGEN, ISOLAT, SCHOOL,
    STRANGE, ANOMIE, SEGREGAT

SEIDLER G.L. E1802

SELASSIE/H....HAILE SELASSIE

SELBORNE/W....WILLIAM SELBORNE

SELEC/SERV....SELECTIVE SERVICE

SELF/OBS....SELF/OBSERVATION

B00

DE TOCQUEVILLE A.,DEMOCRACY IN AMERICA (VOLUME   USA-45
ONE). LAW SOCIETY STRUCT NAT/G POL/PAR PROVS FORCES   TREND
LEGIS TOP/EX DIPLOM LEGIT WAR PEACE ATTIT SOVEREIGN
...SELF/OBS TIME/SEQ CONGRESS 19. PAGE 30 E0594

S51

COHEN M.B.,"PERSONALITY AS A FACTOR IN   PERSON
ADMINISTRATIVE DECISIONS." ADJUD PERS/REL ANOMIE   ADMIN
SUPEGO...OBS SELF/OBS INT. PAGE 24 E0465   PROB/SOLV
                                                        PSY

B52

BENTHAM A.,HANDBOOK OF POLITICAL FALLACIES. FUT   POL/PAR
MOD/EUR LAW INTELL LOC/G MUNIC NAT/G DELIB/GP LEGIS
CREATE EDU/PROP CT/SYS ATTIT RIGID/FLEX KNOWL PWR
...RELATIV PSY SOC CONCPT SELF/OBS TREND STERTYP
TOT/POP. PAGE 10 E0189

B52

JACKSON E.,MEETING OF THE MINDS: A WAY TO PEACE   LABOR
THROUGH MEDIATION. WOR+45 INDUS INT/ORG NAT/G   JUDGE
DELIB/GP DIPLOM EDU/PROP LEGIT ORD/FREE...NEW/IDEA
SELF/OBS TIME/SEQ CHARTS GEN/LAWS TOT/POP 20 UN
TREATY. PAGE 57 E1139

B59

HAYS B.,A SOUTHERN MODERATE SPEAKS. LAW PROVS   SECT
SCHOOL KNOWL...JURID SOC SELF/OBS BIOG 20 NEGRO   DISCRIM
SUPREME/CT. PAGE 51 E1015   CT/SYS
                                                        RACE/REL

B62

HADWEN J.G.,HOW UNITED NATIONS DECISIONS ARE MADE.   INT/ORG
WOR+45 LAW EDU/PROP LEGIT ADMIN PWR...DECISION   ROUTINE
SELF/OBS GEN/LAWS UN 20. PAGE 49 E0972

B62

WOETZEL R.K.,THE NURENBERG TRIALS IN INTERNATIONAL   INT/ORG
LAW. CHRIST-17C MOD/EUR WOR+45 SOCIETY NAT/G   ADJUD
DELIB/GP DOMIN LEGIT ROUTINE ATTIT DRIVE PERSON   WAR
SUPEGO MORAL ORD/FREE...POLICY MAJORIT JURID PSY
SOC SELF/OBS RECORD NAZI TOT/POP. PAGE 107 E2138

SEMANTICS...SEE LOG

SEN B. E1803

SEN/SPACE....UNITED STATES SENATE SPECIAL COMMITTEE ON
    SPACE ASTRONAUTICS

SENATE SPECIAL COMMITTEE ON SPACE ASTRONAUTICS....SEE
    SEN/SPACE

SENATE....SENATE (ALL NATIONS); SEE ALSO CONGRESS, LEGIS

B08

WILSON W.,CONSTITUTIONAL GOVERNMENT IN THE UNITED   NAT/G
STATES. USA-45 LAW POL/PAR PROVS CHIEF LEGIS   GOV/REL
BAL/PWR ADJUD EXEC FEDERAL PWR 18/20 SUPREME/CT   CONSTN
HOUSE/REP SENATE. PAGE 106 E2130   PARL/PROC

CARPER E.T.,LOBBYING AND THE NATURAL GAS BILL (PAMPHLET). USA+45 SERV/IND BARGAIN PAY DRIVE ROLE WEALTH 20 CONGRESS SENATE EISNHWR/DD. PAGE 20 E0389
N19
LOBBY
ADJUD
TRIBUTE
NAT/G

ZINN C.J.,HOW OUR LAWS ARE MADE: BROCHURE HOUSE OF REPRESENTATIVES DOCUMENT 451. LAW CONSTN CHIEF EX/STRUC PROB/SOLV HOUSE/REP SENATE. PAGE 108 E2171
B56
LEGIS
DELIB/GP
PARL/PROC
ROUTINE

US SENATE COMM ON JUDICIARY,CIVIL RIGHTS - 1957. USA+45 LAW NAT/G CONFER GOV/REL RACE/REL ORD/FREE PWR...JURID 20 SENATE CIV/RIGHTS. PAGE 102 E2039
B57
INT
LEGIS
DISCRIM
PARL/PROC

US SENATE COMM POST OFFICE,TO PROVIDE AN EFFECTIVE SYSTEM OF PERSONNEL ADMINISTRATION. USA+45 NAT/G EX/STRUC PARL/PROC GOV/REL...JURID 20 SENATE CIVIL/SERV. PAGE 103 E2060
B58
INT
LEGIS
CONFER
ADMIN

RIKER W.H.,"THE PARADOX OF VOTING AND CONGRESSIONAL RULES FOR VOTING ON AMENDMENTS." LAW DELIB/GP EX/STRUC PROB/SOLV CONFER DEBATE EFFICIENCY ATTIT HOUSE/REP CONGRESS SENATE. PAGE 85 E1700
S58
PARL/PROC
DECISION
LEGIS
RATIONAL

BYRD E.M. JR.,TREATIES AND EXECUTIVE AGREEMENTS IN THE UNITED STATES: THEIR SEPARATE ROLES AND LIMITATIONS. USA+45 USA-45 EX/STRUC TARIFFS CT/SYS GOV/REL FEDERAL...IDEA/COMP BIBLIOG SUPREME/CT SENATE CONGRESS. PAGE 18 E0353
B60
CHIEF
INT/LAW
DIPLOM

US SENATE COMM ON JUDICIARY,FEDERAL ADMINISTRATIVE PROCEDURE. USA+45 CONSTN NAT/G PROB/SOLV CONFER GOV/REL...JURID INT 20 SENATE. PAGE 102 E2043
B60
PARL/PROC
LEGIS
ADMIN
LAW

US SENATE COMM ON JUDICIARY,ADMINISTRATIVE PROCEDURE LEGISLATION. USA+45 CONSTN NAT/G PROB/SOLV CONFER ROUTINE GOV/REL...INT 20 SENATE. PAGE 102 E2044
B60
PARL/PROC
LEGIS
ADMIN
JURID

CARPER E.T.,ILLINOIS GOES TO CONGRESS FOR ARMY LAND. USA+45 LAW EXTR/IND PROVS REGION CIVMIL/REL GOV/REL FEDERAL ATTIT 20 ILLINOIS SENATE CONGRESS DIRKSEN/E DOUGLAS/P. PAGE 20 E0391
B62
ADMIN
LOBBY
GEOG
LEGIS

US SENATE COMM ON JUDICIARY,LEGISLATION TO STRENGTHEN PENALTIES UNDER THE ANTITRUST LAWS (PAMPHLET). USA+45 LG/CO CONFER CONTROL SANCTION ORD/FREE 20 SENATE MONOPOLY. PAGE 102 E2045
N62
LEAD
ADJUD
INDUS
ECO/TAC

SCHMIDHAUSER J.R.,CONSTITUTIONAL LAW IN THE POLITICAL PROCESS. SOCIETY LEGIS ADJUD CT/SYS FEDERAL...SOC TREND IDEA/COMP ANTHOL T SUPREME/CT SENATE CONGRESS HOUSE/REP. PAGE 88 E1761
B63
LAW
CONSTN
JURID

US SENATE COMM ON JUDICIARY,ADMINISTERED PRICES. USA+45 RATION ADJUD CONTROL LOBBY...POLICY 20 SENATE MONOPOLY. PAGE 102 E2047
B63
LG/CO
PRICE
ADMIN
DECISION

US SENATE COMM ON JUDICIARY,ADMINISTRATIVE CONFERENCE OF THE UNITED STATES. USA+45 CONSTN NAT/G PROB/SOLV CONFER GOV/REL...INT 20 SENATE. PAGE 102 E2048
B63
PARL/PROC
JURID
ADMIN
LEGIS

US SENATE COMM ON JUDICIARY,CASTRO'S NETWORK IN THE UNITED STATES. CUBA LAW DELIB/GP 20 SENATE CASTRO/F. PAGE 102 E2050
B63
PRESS
MARXISM
DIPLOM
INSPECT

MITCHELL B.,A BIOGRAPHY OF THE CONSTITUTION OF THE UNITED STATES. USA+45 USA-45 PROVS CHIEF LEGIS DEBATE ADJUD SUFF FEDERAL...SOC 18/20 SUPREME/CT CONGRESS SENATE HOUSE/REP PRESIDENT. PAGE 73 E1472
B64
CONSTN
LAW
JURID

TODD A.,JUSTICE ON TRIAL: THE CASE OF LOUIS D. BRANDEIS. TOP/EX DISCRIM...JURID 20 WILSON/W CONGRESS SUPREME/CT BRANDEIS/L SENATE. PAGE 96 E1929
B64
PERSON
RACE/REL
PERS/REL
NAT/G

US SENATE COMM ON JUDICIARY,CIVIL RIGHTS - THE PRESIDENT'S PROGRAM. USA+45 LAW PROB/SOLV PRESS ADJUD GOV/REL RACE/REL ORD/FREE PWR...JURID 20 SUPREME/CT SENATE CIV/RIGHTS PRESIDENT. PAGE 102 E2053
B64
INT
LEGIS
DISCRIM
PARL/PROC

US SENATE COMM ON JUDICIARY,ADMINISTRATIVE PROCEDURE ACT. USA+45 CONSTN NAT/G PROB/SOLV CONFER GOV/REL PWR...INT 20 SENATE. PAGE 102 E2054
B64
PARL/PROC
LEGIS
JURID
ADMIN

US SENATE COMM ON JUDICIARY,SCHOOL PRAYER. USA+45 LAW LOC/G SECT ADJUD WORSHIP 20 SENATE DEITY. PAGE 103 E2058
B66
SCHOOL
JURID
NAT/G

BAKER L.,BACK TO BACK: THE DUEL BETWEEN FDR AND THE SUPREME COURT. ELITES LEGIS CREATE DOMIN INGP/REL PERSON PWR NEW/LIB 20 ROOSEVLT/F SUPREME/CT SENATE. PAGE 7 E0142
B67
CHIEF
CT/SYS
PARL/PROC
GOV/REL

JONES C.O.,EVERY SECOND YEAR: CONGRESSIONAL BEHAVIOR AND THE TWO-YEAR TERM. LAW POL/PAR PROB/SOLV DEBATE CHOOSE PERS/REL COST FEDERAL PWR ...CHARTS 20 CONGRESS SENATE HOUSE/REP. PAGE 59 E1172
B67
EFFICIENCY
LEGIS
TIME/SEQ
NAT/G

US SENATE COMM ON FOREIGN REL,TREATY ON OUTER SPACE. WOR+45 AIR FORCES PROB/SOLV NUC/PWR SENATE TREATY UN. PAGE 101 E2032
B67
SPACE
DIPLOM
ARMS/CONT
LAW

US SENATE COMM ON FOREIGN REL,A SELECT CHRONOLOGY AND BACKGROUND DOCUMENTS RELATING TO THE MIDDLE EAST. ISRAEL UAR LAW INT/ORG FORCES PROB/SOLV CONFER CONSEN PEACE ATTIT...POLICY 20 UN SENATE TRUMAN/HS. PAGE 101 E2033
B67
ISLAM
TIME/SEQ
DIPLOM

US SENATE COMM ON FOREIGN REL,INTER-AMERICAN DEVELOPMENT BANK ACT AMENDMENT. L/A+17C USA+45 DELIB/GP DIPLOM FOR/AID BAL/PAY...CHARTS SENATE. PAGE 102 E2034
B67
LAW
FINAN
INT/ORG
ECO/UNDEV

US SENATE COMM ON FOREIGN REL,UNITED STATES ARMAMENT AND DISARMAMENT PROBLEMS. USA+45 AIR BAL/PWR DIPLOM FOR/AID NUC/PWR ORD/FREE SENATE TREATY. PAGE 102 E2035
B67
ARMS/CONT
WEAPON
FORCES
PROB/SOLV

US SENATE COMM ON FOREIGN REL,FOREIGN ASSISTANCE ACT OF 1967. VIETNAM WOR+45 DELIB/GP CONFER CONTROL WAR WEAPON BAL/PAY...CENSUS CHARTS SENATE. PAGE 102 E2036
B67
FOR/AID
LAW
DIPLOM
POLICY

SENEGAL....SEE ALSO AFR

GANDOLFI A.,"REFLEXIONS SUR L'IMPOT DE CAPITATION EN AFRIQUE NOIRE." GHANA SENEGAL LAW FINAN ACT/RES TEC/DEV ECO/TAC WEALTH...MGT TREND 20. PAGE 42 E0830
S62
AFR
CHOOSE

SENIOR....SENIORITY; SEE ALSO ADMIN, ROUTINE

LEAGUE WOMEN VOTERS MASSACHU,THE MERIT SYSTEM IN MASSACHUSETTS (PAMPHLET). USA+45 PROVS LEGIT PARTIC CHOOSE REPRESENT GOV/REL EFFICIENCY...POLICY GOV/COMP BIBLIOG 20 MASSACHU. PAGE 64 E1274
N61
LOC/G
LAW
SENIOR
PROF/ORG

SEPARATION....SEE ISOLAT, DISCRIM, RACE/REL

SERBIA....SERBIA

SERENI A.P. E1804

SERRANO MOSCOSO E. E1805

SERV/IND....SERVICE INDUSTRY

GRIFFIN A.P.C.,A LIST OF BOOKS RELATING TO RAILROADS IN THEIR RELATION TO THE GOVERNMENT AND THE PUBLIC (PAMPHLET). USA-45 LAW ECO/DEV NAT/G TEC/DEV CAP/ISM LICENSE CENTRAL LAISSEZ...DECISION 19/20. PAGE 47 E0925
B04
BIBLIOG/A
SERV/IND
ADJUD
ECO/TAC

GRIFFIN A.P.C.,LIST OF BOOKS ON RAILROADS IN FOREIGN COUNTRIES. MOD/EUR ECO/DEV NAT/G CONTROL SOCISM...JURID 19/20 RAILROAD. PAGE 47 E0927
B05
BIBLIOG/A
SERV/IND
ADMIN
DIST/IND

CARPER E.T.,LOBBYING AND THE NATURAL GAS BILL (PAMPHLET). USA+45 SERV/IND BARGAIN PAY DRIVE ROLE WEALTH 20 CONGRESS SENATE EISNHWR/DD. PAGE 20 E0389
N19
LOBBY
ADJUD
TRIBUTE
NAT/G

NATIONAL ASSN HOME BUILDERS,COMMUNITY FACILITIES: A LIST OF SELECTED REFERENCES (PAMPHLET). USA+45 DIST/IND FINAN SERV/IND SCHOOL CREATE CONTROL FEDERAL...JURID 20. PAGE 76 E1525
N59
BIBLIOG/A
PLAN
LOC/G
MUNIC

BORGATTA E.F.,SOCIAL WORKERS' PERCEPTIONS OF CLIENTS. SERV/IND ROUTINE PERS/REL DRIVE PERSON RESPECT...SOC PERS/COMP 20. PAGE 14 E0268
B60
SOC/WK
ATTIT
CLIENT
PROB/SOLV

MACKINNON F.,"THE UNIVERSITY: COMMUNITY OR UTILITY?" CLIENT CONSTN INTELL FINAN NAT/G NEIGH EDU/PROP PARTIC REPRESENT ROLE. PAGE 67 E1343
S60
ACADEM
MGT
CONTROL
SERV/IND

FISK W.M.,ADMINISTRATIVE PROCEDURE IN A REGULATORY AGENCY: THE CAB AND THE NEW YORK-CHICAGO CASE (PAMPHLET). USA+45 DIST/IND ADMIN CONTROL LOBBY GP/REL ROLE ORD/FREE NEWYORK/C CHICAGO CAB. PAGE 38 E0758
B64
SERV/IND
ECO/DEV
AIR
JURID

KING D.B.,LEGAL ASPECTS OF THE CIVIL RIGHTS MOVEMENT. SERV/IND VOL/ASSN LEGIS EDU/PROP ADJUD PARTIC CHOOSE...JURID SEGREGAT WORK. PAGE 61 E1215
B65
LAW
DISCRIM
TREND

FENN DH J.R.,BUSINESS DECISION MAKING AND GOVERNMENT POLICY. SERV/IND LEGIS LICENSE ADMIN CONTROL GP/REL INGP/REL 20 CASEBOOK. PAGE 37 E0736
B66
DECISION
PLAN
NAT/G
LG/CO

LAY S.H.,"EXCLUSIVE GOVERNMENTAL LIABILITY FOR SPACE ACCIDENTS." USA+45 LAW FINAN SERV/IND TEC/DEV ADJUD. PAGE 64 E1272
S67
NAT/G
SUPEGO
SPACE
PROB/SOLV

SERVAN/JJ....JEAN JACQUES SERVAN-SCHREIBER

SERVICE INDUSTRY....SEE SERV/IND

SESTER J. E0882

SET THEORY....SEE CLASSIF

SETARO F.C. E1806

SEVENTHDAY....SEVENTH DAY ADVENTISTS

SEX DIFFERENCES....SEE SEX

SEX....SEE ALSO BIO/SOC

SCHROEDER T.,FREE SPEECH FOR RADICALS (REV. ED.). USA-45 CONSTN INDUS LOC/G FORCES SANCTION WAR ATTIT SEX...JURID REFORMERS 20 FREE/SPEE. PAGE 88 E1767
B16
ORD/FREE
CONTROL
LAW
PRESS

PORTER K.H.,A HISTORY OF SUFFRAGE IN THE UNITED STATES. USA-45 LAW CONSTN LOC/G NAT/G POL/PAR WAR DISCRIM OWN ATTIT SEX 18/20 NEGRO FEMALE/SEX. PAGE 81 E1629
B18
SUFF
REPRESENT
CHOOSE
PARTIC

BUREAU OF NAT'L AFFAIRS INC.,A CURRENT LOOK AT: (1) THE NEGRO AND TITLE VII, (2) SEX AND TITLE VII (PAMPHLET). LAW LG/CO SML/CO RACE/REL...POLICY SOC STAT DEEP/QU TREND CON/ANAL CHARTS 20 NEGRO CIV/RIGHTS. PAGE 17 E0334
N19
DISCRIM
SEX
WORKER
MGT

DAVIS A.,"CASTE, ECONOMY, AND VIOLENCE" (BMR)" USA-45 LAW SOCIETY STRUCT SECT SANCTION COERCE MARRIAGE SEX...PSY SOC SOC/INTEG 18/20 NEGRO MISCEGEN SOUTH/US. PAGE 29 E0570
S45
STRATA
RACE/REL
DISCRIM

CLINARD M.B.,SOCIOLOGY OF DEVIANT BEHAVIOR. FAM CONTROL MURDER DISCRIM PERSON...PSY SOC T SOC/INTEG 20. PAGE 23 E0455
B57
BIO/SOC
CRIME
SEX
ANOMIE

LAPIERE R.,THE FREUDIAN ETHIC. USA+45 FAM EDU/PROP CONTROL CRIME ADJUST AGE DRIVE PERCEPT PERSON SEX ...SOC 20 FREUD/S. PAGE 63 E1254
B59
PSY
ORD/FREE
SOCIETY

KAUPER P.G.,CIVIL LIBERTIES AND THE CONSTITUTION. USA+45 SECT EDU/PROP WRITING ADJUD SEX ORD/FREE 20 SUPREME/CT CIVIL/LIB CHURCH/STA. PAGE 60 E1188
B62
LAW
CONSTN
CT/SYS
DECISION

CRAIG A.,SUPPRESSED BOOKS: A HISTORY OF THE CONCEPTION OF LITERARY OBSCENITY. WOR+45 WOR-45 CREATE EDU/PROP LITERACY ATTIT...ART/METH PSY CONCPT 20. PAGE 27 E0538
B63
BIBLIOG/A
LAW
SEX
CONTROL

BROMBERG W.,CRIME AND THE MIND. LAW LEGIT ADJUD CRIME MURDER AGE/Y ANOMIE BIO/SOC DRIVE SEX PSY. PAGE 16 E0305
B65
CRIMLGY
SOC
HEALTH
COERCE

BEER U.,FRUCHTBARKEITSREGELUNG ALS KONSEQUENZ VERANTWORTLICHER ELTERNSCHAFT. ASIA GERMANY/W INDIA LAW ECO/DEV ECO/UNDEV TEC/DEV ECO/TAC BIO/SOC SEX CATHISM...METH/COMP 20 CHINJAP BIRTH/CON. PAGE 9 E0178
B66
CONTROL
GEOG
FAM
SECT

NAGEL S.S.,"DISPARITIES IN CRIMINAL PROCEDURE." STRATA NAT/G PROVS EDU/PROP RACE/REL AGE HABITAT SEX...JURID CHARTS 20. PAGE 76 E1519
L67
ADJUD
DISCRIM
STRUCT
ACT/RES

DUPRE L.,"TILL DEATH DO US PART?" UNIV FAM INSPECT LEGIT ADJUD SANCTION PERS/REL ANOMIE RIGID/FLEX SEX ...JURID IDEA/COMP 20 CHURCH/STA BIBLE CANON/LAW CIVIL/LAW. PAGE 34 E0666
S68
MARRIAGE
CATH
LAW

FICHTE J.G.,THE SCIENCE OF RIGHTS (TRANS. BY A.E. KROEGER). WOR-45 FAM MUNIC NAT/G PROVS ADJUD CRIME CHOOSE MARRIAGE SEX POPULISM 19 FICHTE/JG NATURL/LAW. PAGE 37 E0744
B89
ORD/FREE
CONSTN
LAW
CONCPT

SEXUAL BEHAVIOR....SEE SEX, PERSON

SEYID MUHAMMAD V.A. E1807

SEYLER W.C. E1808

SHACK W.A. E0433

SHAFFER T.L. E1809

SHANGHAI....SHANGHAI

SHAPIRO D.L. E1050

SHAPIRO J.P. E1810

SHAPIRO M. E1811,E1812

SHARMA M.P. E1813

SHARMA S.A. E1814

SHARMA S.P. E1815

SHASTRI/LB....LAL BAHADUR SHASTRI

SHAW C. E1816

SHAW P.C. E0126
SHEEHAN D. F1753
SHEEHY E.P. E1817

SHELDON C.H. E1818

SHEPPARD/S....SAMUEL SHEPPARD

SHERMAN C.P. E1819

SHERMN/ACT....SHERMAN ANTI-TRUST ACT; SEE ALSO MONOPOLY

SHIPMAN S.S. E0257

SHKLAR J. E1820,E1821

SHOUP/C....C. SHOUP

SHRIVER/S....SARGENT SHRIVER

SIBERIA....SIBERIA

SIBRON....SIBRON V. NEW YORK

SICILY....SICILY

SICKNESS....SEE HEALTH

SIDGWICK H. E1822

SIDGWICK/H....HENRY SIDGWICK

SIEKANOWICZ P. E1823

SIER/LEONE....SIERRA LEONE; SEE ALSO AFR

SIEYES E.J. E1824

SIGLIANO R E. E1825

SIHANOUK....NORODOM SIHANOUK

SIKKIM....SEE ALSO S/ASIA

SILVA R.C. E1826,E1827

SILVER....SILVER STANDARD AND POLICIES RELATING TO SILVER

SILVING H. E1828

SIMMEL/G....GEORG SIMMEL

SIMPSON J.L. E1829

SIMPSON....SIMPSON V. UNION OIL COMPANY

SIMUL....SCIENTIFIC MODELS

		N13
SCHMIDHAUSER J.R.,JUDICIAL BEHAVIOR AND THE SECTIONAL CRISIS OF 1837-1860. USA-45 ADJUD CT/SYS INGP/REL ATTIT HABITAT...DECISION PSY STAT CHARTS SIMUL. PAGE 88 E1759	JUDGE POL/PAR PERS/COMP PERSON	

		B23
POUND R.,INTERPRETATIONS OF LEGAL HISTORY. CULTURE ...PHIL/SCI NEW/IDEA CLASSIF SIMUL GEN/LAWS 19/20. PAGE 82 E1636	LAW IDEA/COMP JURID	

		S52
MCDOUGAL M.S.,"THE COMPARATIVE STUDY OF LAW FOR POLICY PURPOSES." FUT NAT/G POL/PAR CONSULT ADJUD PWR SOVEREIGN...METH/CNCPT IDEA/COMP SIMUL 20. PAGE 70 E1403	PLAN JURID NAT/LISM	

		B59
SCHUBERT G.A.,QUANTITATIVE ANALYSIS OF JUDICIAL BEHAVIOR. ADJUD LEAD CHOOSE INGP/REL MAJORITY ATTIT ...DECISION JURID CHARTS GAME SIMUL SUPREME/CT. PAGE 89 E1780	JUDGE CT/SYS PERSON QUANT	

		B60
STEIN E.,AMERICAN ENTERPRISE IN THE EUROPEAN COMMON MARKET: A LEGAL PROFILE. EUR+WWI FUT USA+45 SOCIETY STRUCT ECO/DEV NAT/G VOL/ASSN CONSULT PLAN TEC/DEV ECO/TAC INT/TRADE ADMIN ATTIT RIGID/FLEX PWR...MGT NEW/IDEA STAT TREND COMPUT/IR SIMUL EEC 20. PAGE 93 E1867	MARKET ADJUD INT/LAW	

		S61
SCHUBERT G.,"A PSYCHOMETRIC MODEL OF THE SUPREME COURT." DELIB/GP ADJUD CHOOSE ATTIT...DECISION JURID PSY QUANT STAT HYPO/EXP GEN/METH SUPREME/CT. PAGE 88 E1771	JUDGE CT/SYS PERSON SIMUL	

		B64
SCHUBERT G.A.,JUDICIAL BEHAVIOR: A READER IN THEORY AND RESEARCH. POL/PAR CT/SYS ROLE SUPEGO PWR ...DECISION JURID REGRESS CHARTS SIMUL ANTHOL 20. PAGE 89 E1782	ATTIT PERSON ADJUD ACT/RES	

		L64
MAYO L.H.,"LEGAL-POLICY DECISION PROCESS: ALTERNATIVE THINKING AND THE PREDICTIVE FUNCTION." PROB/SOLV EFFICIENCY RATIONAL. PAGE 70 E1395	DECISION SIMUL JURID TEC/DEV	

		S65
ULMER S.S.,"TOWARD A THEORY OF SUBGROUP FORMATION IN THE UNITED STATES SUPREME COURT." USA+45 ROUTINE CHOOSE PWR...JURID STAT CON/ANAL SIMUL SUPREME/CT. PAGE 97 E1952	CT/SYS ADJUD ELITES INGP/REL	

		B66
FALK R.A.,THE STRATEGY OF WORLD ORDER* 4 VOLUMES. WOR+45 ECO/UNDEV ACADEM INT/ORG ACT/RES DIPLOM ARMS/CONT WAR...NET/THEORY SIMUL BIBLIOG UN. PAGE 36 E0719	ORD/FREE GEN/LAWS ANTHOL INT/LAW	

		S66
EWALD R.F.,"ONE OF MANY POSSIBLE GAMES." ACADEM INT/ORG ARMS/CONT...INT/LAW GAME. PAGE 36 E0706	SIMUL HYPO/EXP PROG/TEAC RECORD	

		L67
SCHUBERT G.,"THE RHETORIC OF CONSTITUTIONAL CHANGE." USA+45 LAW CULTURE CHIEF LEGIS ADJUD CT/SYS ARMS/CONT ADJUST...CHARTS SIMUL. PAGE 89 E1777	CONSTN METH/COMP ORD/FREE	

		S67
TYDINGS J.D.,"MODERNIZING THE ADMINISTRATION OF JUSTICE." PLAN ADMIN ROUTINE EFFICIENCY...JURID SIMUL. PAGE 97 E1948	CT/SYS MGT COMPUTER CONSULT	

SIMULATION....SEE SIMUL, MODELS INDEX

SINAI....SINAI

SINCLAIR T.C. E1830

SINCO V.G. E1831

SIND....SIND - REGION OF PAKISTAN

SINEY M.C. E1832

SINGAPORE....SINGAPORE; SEE ALSO MALAYSIA

SINGH N. E1833

SINO/SOV....SINO-SOVIET RELATIONSHIPS

SINYAVSK/A....ANDREY SINYAVSKY

SIPKOV I. E1834

SIRS....SALARY INFORMATION RETRIEVAL SYSTEM

SISSON C.H. E1835

SKILL....DEXTERITY

		S17
ROOT E.,"THE EFFECT OF DEMOCRACY ON INTERNATIONAL LAW." USA+45 WOR+45 INTELL SOCIETY INT/ORG NAT/G CONSULT ACT/RES CREATE PLAN EDU/PROP PEACE SKILL ...CONCPT METH/CNCPT OBS 20. PAGE 85 E1712	LEGIS JURID INT/LAW	

		B28
YANG KUNG-SUN,THE BOOK OF LORD SHANG. LAW ECO/UNDEV LOC/G NAT/G NEIGH PLAN ECO/TAC LEGIT ATTIT SKILL ...CONCPT CON/ANAL WORK TOT/POP. PAGE 108 E2164	ASIA JURID	

		B31
STOWELL E.C.,INTERNATIONAL LAW. FUT UNIV WOR-45 SOCIETY CONSULT EX/STRUC FORCES ACT/RES PLAN DIPLOM EDU/PROP LEGIT DISPL PWR SKILL...POLICY CONCPT OBS TREND TOT/POP 20. PAGE 94 E1885	INT/ORG ROUTINE INT/LAW	

		S35
MCMAHON A.H.,"INTERNATIONAL BOUNDARIES." WOR-45 INT/ORG NAT/G LEGIT SKILL...CHARTS GEN/LAWS 20. PAGE 71 E1423	GEOG VOL/ASSN INT/LAW	

		S40
GILL N.N.,"PERMANENT ADVISORY COMMISSIONS IN THE FEDERAL GOVERNMENT." CLIENT FINAN OP/RES EDU/PROP PARTIC ROUTINE INGP/REL KNOWL SKILL...CLASSIF TREND. PAGE 43 E0860	DELIB/GP NAT/G DECISION	

		S55
WRIGHT Q.,"THE PEACEFUL ADJUSTMENT OF INTERNATIONAL RELATIONS: PROBLEMS AND RESEARCH APPROACHES." UNIV INTELL EDU/PROP ADJUD ROUTINE KNOWL SKILL...INT/LAW JURID PHIL/SCI CLASSIF 20. PAGE 108 E2156	R+D METH/CNCPT PEACE	

B56
CALLISON I.P.,COURTS OF INJUSTICE. USA+45 PROF/ORG CT/SYS
ADJUD CRIME PERSON MORAL PWR RESPECT SKILL 20. JUDGE
PAGE 19 E0368 JURID

B57
MEYER P.,ADMINISTRATIVE ORGANIZATION: A COMPARATIVE ADMIN
STUDY OF THE ORGANIZATION OF PUBLIC ADMINISTRATION. METH/COMP
DENMARK FRANCE NORWAY SWEDEN UK USA+45 ELITES LOC/G NAT/G
CONSULT LEGIS ADJUD CONTROL LEAD PWR SKILL CENTRAL
DECISION. PAGE 72 E1449

S59
TIPTON J.B.,"PARTICIPATION OF THE UNITED STATES IN LABOR
THE INTERNATIONAL LABOR ORGANIZATION." USA+45 LAW INT/ORG
STRUCT ECO/DEV ECO/UNDEV INDUS TEC/DEV ECO/TAC
ADMIN PERCEPT ORD/FREE SKILL...STAT HIST/WRIT
GEN/METH ILO WORK 20. PAGE 96 E1928

B60
PRICE D.,THE SECRETARY OF STATE. USA+45 CONSTN CONSULT
ELITES INTELL CHIEF EX/STRUC TOP/EX LEGIT ATTIT PWR DIPLOM
SKILL...DECISION 20 CONGRESS. PAGE 82 E1650 INT/LAW

S61
CASTANEDA J.,"THE UNDERDEVELOPED NATIONS AND THE INT/ORG
DEVELOPMENT OF INTERNATIONAL LAW." FUT UNIV LAW ECO/UNDEV
ACT/RES FOR/AID LEGIT PERCEPT SKILL...JURID PEACE
METH/CNCPT TIME/SEQ TOT/POP 20 UN. PAGE 21 E0405 INT/LAW

S61
HARVEY W.B.,"THE RULE OF LAW IN HISTORICAL ACT/RES
PERSPECTIVE." USA+45 WOR+45 INTELL SOCIETY ECO/DEV LAW
ECO/UNDEV NAT/G EX/STRUC LEGIS TOP/EX LEGIT SKILL
...CONCPT HIST/WRIT TOT/POP. PAGE 51 E1010

L63
ROSE R.,"COMPARATIVE STUDIES IN POLITICAL FINANCE: FINAN
A SYMPOSIUM." ASIA EUR+WWI S/ASIA LAW CULTURE POL/PAR
DELIB/GP LEGIS ACT/RES ECO/TAC EDU/PROP CHOOSE
ATTIT RIGID/FLEX SUPEGO PWR SKILL WEALTH...STAT
ANTHOL VAL/FREE. PAGE 85 E1714

S63
MODELSKI G.,"STUDY OF ALLIANCES." WOR+45 WOR-45 VOL/ASSN
INT/ORG NAT/G FORCES LEGIT ADMIN CHOOSE ALL/VALS CON/ANAL
PWR SKILL...INT/LAW CONCPT GEN/LAWS 20 TREATY. DIPLOM
PAGE 74 E1477

B64
IKLE F.C.,HOW NATIONS NEGOTIATE. COM EUR+WWI USA+45 NAT/G
INTELL INT/ORG VOL/ASSN DELIB/GP ACT/RES CREATE PWR
DOMIN EDU/PROP ADJUD ROUTINE ATTIT PERSON ORD/FREE POLICY
RESPECT SKILL...PSY SOC OBS VAL/FREE. PAGE 56 E1122

B65
CHROUST A.H.,THE RISE OF THE LEGAL PROFESSION IN JURID
AMERICA (3 VOLS.). STRATA STRUCT POL/PAR PROF/ORG USA-45
COLONIAL LEAD REV SKILL...SOC 17/20. PAGE 22 E0437 CT/SYS
LAW

B65
US OFFICE ECONOMIC OPPORTUNITY,CATALOG OF FEDERAL BIBLIOG
PROGRAMS FOR INDIVIDUAL AND COMMUNITY IMPROVEMENT. CLIENT
USA+45 GIVE RECEIVE ADMIN HEALTH KNOWL SKILL WEALTH ECO/TAC
CHARTS. PAGE 101 E2021 MUNIC

B67
GABRIEL P.P.,THE INTERNATIONAL TRANSFER OF ECO/UNDEV
CORPORATE SKILLS: MANAGEMENT CONTRACTS IN LESS AGREE
DEVELOPED COUNTRIES. CLIENT INDUS LG/CO PLAN MGT
PROB/SOLV CAP/ISM ECO/TAC FOR/AID INT/TRADE RENT CONSULT
ADMIN SKILL 20. PAGE 42 E0825

SKOLNICK J.H. E1836

SKUBISZEWSKI K. E1837

SLATER J. E1838

SLAV/MACED....SLAVO-MACEDONIANS

SLAVERY....SEE ORD/FREE, DOMIN

SLAVS....SLAVS - PERTAINING TO THE SLAVIC PEOPLE AND
SLAVOPHILISM

SLEEP....SLEEPING AND FATIGUE

SLESSER H. E1839

SLUMS....SLUMS

SLUSSER R.M. E1941

SMITH A. E1840

SMITH A.A. E0504

SMITH C. E1841
SMITH D.T. E1766
SMITH E.A. E1842,E1843

SMITH G. E1844

SMITH G.D. E0371

SMITH J.W. E1845

SMITH R.C. E1846

SMITH R.H. E1847

SMITH/ACT....SMITH ACT

S51
LEEK J.H.,"TREASON AND THE CONSTITUTION" (BMR)" CONSTN
USA+45 USA-45 EDU/PROP COLONIAL CT/SYS REV WAR JURID
ATTIT...TREND 18/20 SUPREME/CT CON/INTERP SMITH/ACT CRIME
COMMON/LAW. PAGE 64 E1278 NAT/G

SMITH/ADAM....ADAM SMITH

B88
BENTHAM J.,DEFENCE OF USURY (1787). UK LAW NAT/G TAX
TEC/DEV ECO/TAC CONTROL ATTIT...CONCPT IDEA/COMP 18 FINAN
SMITH/ADAM. PAGE 10 E0197 ECO/DEV
POLICY

SMITH/ALF....ALFRED E. SMITH

B62
SILVA R.C.,RUM, RELIGION, AND VOTES: 1928 RE- POL/PAR
EXAMINED. USA-45 LAW SECT DISCRIM CATHISM...CORREL CHOOSE
STAT 20 PRESIDENT SMITH/ALF DEMOCRAT. PAGE 91 E1827 GP/COMP
ATTIT

SMITH/IAN....IAN SMITH

SMITH/JOS....JOSEPH SMITH

SMITH/LEVR....SMITH-LEVER ACT

SML/CO....SMALL COMPANY

N19
BUREAU OF NAT'L AFFAIRS INC.,A CURRENT LOOK AT: DISCRIM
(1) THE NEGRO AND TITLE VII, (2) SEX AND TITLE VII SEX
(PAMPHLET). LAW LG/CO SML/CO RACE/REL...POLICY SOC WORKER
STAT DEEP/QU TREND CON/ANAL CHARTS 20 NEGRO MGT
CIV/RIGHTS. PAGE 17 E0334

B52
ANDREWS F.E.,CORPORATION GIVING. LAW TAX EDU/PROP LG/CO
ADMIN...POLICY STAT CHARTS. PAGE 5 E0096 GIVE
SML/CO
FINAN

SMUTS/JAN....JAN CHRISTIAN SMUTS

SNCC....STUDENT NONVIOLENT COORDINATING COMMITTEE; SEE ALSO
STUDNT/PWR

SNOW J.H. E1848

SOBEL N.R. E1849

SOC....SOCIOLOGY

N
LIBRARY INTERNATIONAL REL,INTERNATIONAL INFORMATION BIBLIOG/A
SERVICE. WOR+45 CULTURE INT/ORG FORCES...GEOG HUM DIPLOM
SOC. PAGE 65 E1295 INT/TRADE
INT/LAW

B
DEUTSCHE BIBLIOTH FRANKF A M,DEUTSCHE BIBLIOG
BIBLIOGRAPHIE. EUR+WWI GERMANY ECO/DEV FORCES LAW
DIPLOM LEAD...POLICY PHIL/SCI SOC 20. PAGE 31 E0612 ADMIN
NAT/G

N
ANNALS OF THE AMERICAN ACADEMY OF POLITICAL AND BIBLIOG/A
SOCIAL SCIENCE. AFR ASIA S/ASIA WOR+45 POL/PAR NAT/G
DIPLOM CRIME REV...SOC BIOG 20. PAGE 1 E0003 CULTURE
ATTIT

N
INTERNATIONAL STUDIES. ASIA S/ASIA WOR+45 ECO/UNDEV BIBLIOG/A
INT/ORG NAT/G LEAD ATTIT WEALTH...SOC 20. PAGE 1 DIPLOM
E0009 INT/LAW

INT/TRADE

TEXTBOOKS IN PRINT. WOR+45 WOR-45 LAW DIPLOM
ALL/VALS ALL/IDEOS...SOC T 19/20. PAGE 1 E0014
N
BIBLIOG
SCHOOL
KNOWL

AUSTRALIAN PUBLIC AFFAIRS INFORMATION SERVICE. LAW
...HEAL HUM MGT SOC CON/ANAL 20 AUSTRAL. PAGE 1
E0017
N
BIBLIOG
NAT/G
CULTURE
DIPLOM

BIBLIOGRAPHIE DER SOZIALWISSENSCHAFTEN. WOR-45
CONSTN SOCIETY ECO/DEV ECO/UNDEV DIPLOM LEAD WAR
PEACE...PHIL/SCI SOC 19/20. PAGE 1 E0019
N
BIBLIOG
LAW
CONCPT
NAT/G

HANDBOOK OF LATIN AMERICAN STUDIES. LAW CULTURE
ECO/UNDEV POL/PAR ADMIN LEAD...SOC 20. PAGE 1 E0022
N
BIBLIOG/A
L/A+17C
NAT/G
DIPLOM

THE JAPAN SCIENCE REVIEW: LAW AND POLITICS: LIST OF
BOOKS AND ARTICLES ON LAW AND POLITICS. CONSTN AGRI
INDUS LABOR DIPLOM TAX ADMIN CRIME...INT/LAW SOC 20
CHINJAP. PAGE 2 E0027
N
BIBLIOG
LAW
S/ASIA
PHIL/SCI

ATLANTIC INSTITUTE,ATLANTIC STUDIES. COM EUR+WWI
USA+45 CULTURE STRUCT ECO/DEV FORCES LEAD ARMS/CONT
...INT/LAW JURID SOC. PAGE 6 E0110
N
BIBLIOG/A
DIPLOM
POLICY
GOV/REL

DEUTSCHE BUCHEREI,JAHRESVERZEICHNIS DER DEUTSCHEN
HOCHSCHULSCHRIFTEN. EUR+WWI GERMANY LAW ADMIN
PERSON...MGT SOC 19/20. PAGE 31 E0613
N
BIBLIOG
WRITING
ACADEM
INTELL

DEUTSCHE BUCHEREI,JAHRESVERZEICHNIS DES DEUTSCHEN
SCHRIFTUMS. AUSTRIA EUR+WWI GERMANY SWITZERLND LAW
LOC/G DIPLOM ADMIN...MGT SOC 19/20. PAGE 31 E0614
N
BIBLIOG
WRITING
NAT/G

DEUTSCHE BUCHEREI,DEUTSCHES BUCHERVERZEICHNIS.
GERMANY LAW CULTURE POL/PAR ADMIN LEAD ATTIT PERSON
...SOC 20. PAGE 31 E0615
N
BIBLIOG
NAT/G
DIPLOM
ECO/DEV

MINISTERE DE L'EDUC NATIONALE,CATALOGUE DES THESES
DE DOCTORAT SOUTENUES DEVANT LES UNIVERSITAIRES
FRANCAISES. FRANCE LAW DIPLOM ADMIN...HUM SOC 20.
PAGE 73 E1465
N
BIBLIOG
ACADEM
KNOWL
NAT/G

SOUTH AFRICA STATE LIBRARY,SOUTH AFRICAN NATIONAL
BIBLIOGRAPHY. SANB. SOUTH/AFR LAW NAT/G EDU/PROP
...MGT PSY SOC 20. PAGE 93 E1858
N
BIBLIOG
PRESS
WRITING

US BUREAU OF THE CENSUS,BIBLIOGRAPHY OF SOCIAL
SCIENCE PERIODICALS AND MONOGRAPH SERIES. WOR+45
LAW DIPLOM EDU/PROP HEALTH...PSY SOC LING STAT.
PAGE 99 E1980
N
BIBLIOG/A
CULTURE
NAT/G
SOCIETY

GRIFFIN A.P.C.,LIST OF BOOKS RELATING TO THE THEORY
OF COLONIZATION, GOVERNMENT OF DEPENDENCIES,
PROTECTORATES, AND RELATED TOPICS. FRANCE GERMANY
ITALY SPAIN UK USA-45 WOR-45 ECO/TAC ADMIN CONTROL
REGION NAT/LISM ALL/VALS PWR...INT/LAW SOC 16/19.
PAGE 46 E0917
B00
BIBLIOG/A
COLONIAL
GOV/REL
DOMIN

HISTORICUS,"LETTERS AND SOME QUESTIONS OF
INTERNATIONAL LAW." FRANCE NETHERLAND UK USA-45
WOR-45 LAW NAT/G COERCE...SOC CONCPT GEN/LAWS
TOT/POP 19 CIVIL/WAR. PAGE 53 E1054
L00
WEALTH
JURID
WAR
INT/LAW

FAGUET E.,LE LIBERALISME. FRANCE PRESS ADJUD ADMIN
DISCRIM CONSERVE SOCISM...TRADIT SOC LING WORSHIP
PARLIAMENT. PAGE 36 E0711
B03
ORD/FREE
EDU/PROP
NAT/G
LAW

GRIFFIN A.P.C.,REFERENCES ON CHINESE IMMIGRATIONS
(PAMPHLET). USA-45 KIN NAT/LISM ATTIT...SOC 19/20.
PAGE 47 E0926
B04
BIBLIOG/A
STRANGE
JURID
RACE/REL

GRIFFIN A.P.C.,LIST OF BOOKS RELATING TO CHILD
LABOR (PAMPHLET). BELGIUM FRANCE GERMANY MOD/EUR UK
USA-45 ECO/DEV INDUS WORKER CAP/ISM PAY ROUTINE
ALL/IDEOS...MGT SOC 19/20. PAGE 47 E0929
B06
BIBLIOG/A
LAW
LABOR
AGE/C

POUND R.,"THE SCOPE AND PURPOSE OF SOCIOLOGICAL
JURISPRUDENCE."...GEN/LAWS 20 KANT/I HEGEL/GWF.
PAGE 81 E1634
L11
JURID
IDEA/COMP
METH/COMP
SOC

BUREAU OF NAT'L AFFAIRS INC.,A CURRENT LOOK AT:
(1) THE NEGRO AND TITLE VII, (2) SEX AND TITLE VII
(PAMPHLET). LAW LG/CO SML/CO RACE/REL...POLICY SOC
STAT DEEP/QU TREND CON/ANAL CHARTS 20 NEGRO
CIV/RIGHTS. PAGE 17 E0334
N19
DISCRIM
SEX
WORKER
MGT

LIPPMAN W.,LIBERTY AND THE NEWS. USA+45 USA-45 LAW
LEGIS DOMIN LEGIT ATTIT...POLICY SOC IDEA/COMP
METH/COMP 19/20. PAGE 65 E1300
B20
ORD/FREE
PRESS
COM/IND
EDU/PROP

HALDEMAN E.,"SERIALS OF AN INTERNATIONAL
CHARACTER." WOR-45 DIPLOM...ART/METH GEOG HEAL HUM
INT/LAW JURID PSY SOC. PAGE 49 E0978
L21
BIBLIOG
PHIL/SCI

COX G.C.,THE PUBLIC CONSCIENCE: A CASEBOOK IN
ETHICS....PHIL/SCI SOC CONCPT METH/COMP 20. PAGE 27
E0534
B22
MORAL
ADJUD   /

NAVILLE A.,LIBERTE, EGALITE, SOLIDARITE: ESSAIS
D'ANALYSE. STRATA FAM VOL/ASSN INT/TRADE GP/REL
MORAL MARXISM SOCISM...PSY TREATY. PAGE 76 E1529
B24
ORD/FREE
SOC
IDEA/COMP
DIPLOM

BARNES H.E.,"SOCIOLOGY AND POLITICAL THEORY: A
CONSIDERATION OF THE SOCIOLOGICAL BASIS OF
POLITICS." LAW CONSTN NAT/G DIPLOM DOMIN ROUTINE
REV ORD/FREE SOVEREIGN...PHIL/SCI CLASSIF BIBLIOG
18/20. PAGE 8 E0151
C24
CONCPT
STRUCT
SOC

GODET M.,INDEX BIBLIOGRAPHICUS: INTERNATIONAL
CATALOGUE OF SOURCES OF CURRENT BIBLIOGRAPHIC
INFORMATION. EUR+WWI MOD/EUR SOCIETY SECT TAX
...JURID PHIL/SCI SOC MATH. PAGE 44 E0876
B25
BIBLIOG/A
DIPLOM
EDU/PROP
LAW

HALL A.B.,"DETERMINATION OF METHODS FOR
ASCERTAINING THE FACTORS THAT INFLUENCE JUDICIAL
DECISIONS IN CASES INVOLVING DUE PROCESS" LAW JUDGE
DEBATE EFFICIENCY OPTIMAL UTIL...SOC CONCPT
PROBABIL STAT SAMP. PAGE 49 E0981
S26
ADJUD
DECISION
CONSTN
JURID

CORBETT P.E.,CANADA AND WORLD POLITICS. LAW CULTURE
SOCIETY STRUCT MARKET INT/ORG FORCES ACT/RES PLAN
ECO/TAC LEGIT ORD/FREE PWR RESPECT...SOC CONCPT
TIME/SEQ TREND CMN/WLTH 20 LEAGUE/NAT. PAGE 26
E0504
B28
NAT/G
CANADA

BUELL R.,INTERNATIONAL RELATIONS. WOR+45 WOR-45
CONSTN STRATA FORCES TOP/EX ADMIN ATTIT DRIVE
SUPEGO MORAL ORD/FREE PWR SOVEREIGN...JURID SOC
CONCPT 20. PAGE 17 E0326
B29
INT/ORG
BAL/PWR
DIPLOM

PRATT I.A.,MODERN EGYPT: A LIST OF REFERENCES TO
MATERIAL IN THE NEW YORK PUBLIC LIBRARY. UAR
ECO/UNDEV...GEOG JURID SOC LING 20. PAGE 82 E1647
B29
BIBLIOG
ISLAM
DIPLOM
NAT/G

GILLETTE J.M.,CURRENT SOCIAL PROBLEMS. CONTROL
CRIME AGE/Y BIO/SOC...SOC 20. PAGE 43 E0861
B33
GEOG
HEALTH
RACE/REL
FAM

CULVER D.C.,BIBLIOGRAPHY OF CRIME AND CRIMINAL
JUSTICE, 1927-1931. LAW CULTURE PUB/INST PROB/SOLV
CT/SYS...PSY SOC STAT 20. PAGE 28 E0549
B34
BIBLIOG/A
CRIMLGY
ADJUD
FORCES

CUMMING J.,A CONTRIBUTION TOWARD A BIBLIOGRAPHY
DEALING WITH CRIME AND COGNATE SUBJECTS (3RD ED.).
B35
BIBLIOG
CRIMLGY

UK LAW CULTURE PUB/INST ADJUD AGE BIO/SOC...PSY SOC FORCES SOC/WK STAT METH/COMP 20. PAGE 28 E0552   CT/SYS

B35

HALL J.,THEFT, LAW, AND SOCIETY. SOCIETY PROB/SOLV CRIME ...CRIMLGY SOC CONCPT TREND METH/COMP 18/20 LAW LARCENCY. PAGE 49 E0982   ADJUD   ADJUST

B35

NORDSKOG J.E.,SOCIAL REFORM IN NORWAY. NORWAY INDUS LABOR NAT/G POL/PAR LEGIS ADJUD...SOC BIBLIOG SOC/INTEG ADJUST 20. PAGE 78 E1555

B35

ROBSON W.A.,CIVILISATION AND THE GROWTH OF LAW. LAW UNIV CONSTN SOCIETY LEGIS ADJUD ATTIT PERCEPT MORAL IDEA/COMP ALL/IDEOS...CONCPT WORSHIP 20. PAGE 85 E1708   SOC

B36

CULVER D.C.,METHODOLOGY OF SOCIAL SCIENCE RESEARCH: BIBLIOG/A A BIBLIOGRAPHY. LAW CULTURE...CRIMLGY GEOG STAT OBS METH INT QU HIST/WRIT CHARTS 20. PAGE 28 E0550   SOC

B36

EHRLICH E.,FUNDAMENTAL PRINCIPLES OF THE SOCIOLOGY LAW OF LAW (TRANS. BY WALTER L. MOLL). UNIV SOCIETY JURID ADJUD CT/SYS...POLICY GP/COMP GEN/LAWS GEN/METH. SOC PAGE 34 E0678   CONCPT

S37

TIMASHEFF N.S.,"WHAT IS SOCIOLOGY OF LAW?" (BMR)" LAW UNIV INTELL PWR...EPIST JURID PHIL/SCI IDEA/COMP. SOC PAGE 96 E1925   SOCIETY

B38

CLARK J.P.,THE RISE OF A NEW FEDERALISM. LEGIS FEDERAL TARIFFS EFFICIENCY NAT/LISM UTIL...JURID SOC PROVS GEN/LAWS BIBLIOG 19/20. PAGE 23 E0451   NAT/G   GOV/REL

B39

CULVER D.C.,BIBLIOGRAPHY OF CRIME AND CRIMINAL BIBLIOG/A JUSTICE. 1932-1937. USA-45 LAW CULTURE PUB/INST CRIMLGY PROB/SOLV CT/SYS...PSY SOC STAT 20. PAGE 28 E0551 ADJUD   FORCES

B39

TIMASHEFF N.S.,AN INTRODUCTION TO THE SOCIOLOGY OF SOC LAW. CRIME ANOMIE ATTIT DRIVE ORD/FREE...JURID PSY BIBLIOG CONCPT. PAGE 96 E1926   PWR

S40

GURVITCH G.,"MAJOR PROBLEMS OF THE SOCIOLOGY OF SOC LAW." CULTURE SANCTION KNOWL MORAL...POLICY EPIST LAW JURID WORSHIP. PAGE 48 E0963   PHIL/SCI

B41

EVANS C.,AMERICAN BIBLIOGRAPHY... (12 VOLUMES). BIBLIOG USA-45 LAW DIPLOM ADMIN PERSON...HUM SOC 17/18. NAT/G PAGE 35 E0704   ALL/VALS   ALL/IDEOS

L41

COMM. STUDY ORGAN. PEACE,"ORGANIZATION OF PEACE." INT/ORG USA-45 WOR-45 STRATA NAT/G ACT/RES DIPLOM ECO/TAC PLAN EDU/PROP ADJUD ATTIT ORD/FREE PWR...SOC CONCPT PEACE ANTHOL LEAGUE/NAT 20. PAGE 24 E0479

S41

WRIGHT Q.,"FUNDAMENTAL PROBLEMS OF INTERNATIONAL INT/ORG ORGANIZATION." UNIV WOR-45 STRUCT FORCES ACT/RES ATTIT CREATE DOMIN EDU/PROP LEGIT REGION NAT/LISM PEACE ORD/FREE PWR RESPECT SOVEREIGN...JURID SOC CONCPT METH/CNCPT TIME/SEQ 20. PAGE 107 E2152

B42

GURVITCH G.,SOCIOLOGY OF LAW. CONSTN SOCIETY CREATE SOC MORAL SOVEREIGN...POLICY EPIST JURID PHIL/SCI LAW IDEA/COMP METH/COMP HOLMES/OW HOBBES/T. PAGE 48 ADJUD E0964

B42

US LIBRARY OF CONGRESS,SOCIAL AND CULTURAL PROBLEMS BIBLIOG/A IN WARTIME: APRIL 1941-MARCH 1942. WOR-45 CLIENT WAR SECT EDU/PROP CRIME LEISURE RACE/REL STRANGE ATTIT SOC DRIVE HEALTH...GEOG 20. PAGE 100 E2012   CULTURE

B43

US LIBRARY OF CONGRESS,SOCIAL AND CULTURAL PROBLEMS BIBLIOG/A IN WARTIME: APRIL-DECEMBER (SUPPLEMENT 1). WOR-45 WAR SECT EDU/PROP CRIME LEISURE CIVMIL/REL RACE/REL SOC ATTIT DRIVE HEALTH...GEOG 20. PAGE 100 E2013   CULTURE

B43

US LIBRARY OF CONGRESS,SOCIAL AND CULTURAL PROBLEMS BIBLIOG/A

IN WARTIME: JANUARY-MAY 1943 (SUPPLEMENT 2). WOR-45 WAR FAM SECT PLAN EDU/PROP CRIME LEISURE RACE/REL DRIVE SOC HEALTH...GEOG 20 JEWS. PAGE 100 E2014   CULTURE

B44

DE HUSZAR G.B.,NEW PERSPECTIVES ON PEACE. UNIV ATTIT CULTURE SOCIETY ECO/DEV ECO/UNDEV NAT/G FORCES MYTH CREATE ECO/TAC DOMIN ADJUD COERCE DRIVE ORD/FREE PEACE ...GEOG JURID PSY SOC CONCPT TOT/POP. PAGE 29 E0584 WAR

B44

FULLER G.H.,TURKEY: A SELECTED LIST OF REFERENCES. BIBLIOG/A ISLAM TURKEY CULTURE ECO/UNDEV AGRI DIPLOM NAT/LISM ALL/VALS CONSERVE...GEOG HUM INT/LAW SOC 7/20 MAPS. PAGE 42 E0824

S44

GRIFFITH E.S.,"THE CHANGING PATTERN OF PUBLIC LAW POLICY FORMATION." MOD/EUR WOR+45 FINAN CHIEF POLICY CONFER ADMIN LEAD CONSERVE SOCISM TECHRACY...SOC TEC/DEV CHARTS CONGRESS. PAGE 47 E0938

B45

US LIBRARY OF CONGRESS,NETHERLANDS EAST INDIES. BIBLIOG/A INDONESIA LAW CULTURE AGRI INDUS SCHOOL COLONIAL S/ASIA HEALTH...GEOG JURID SOC 19/20 NETH/IND. PAGE 101 NAT/G E2017

B45

WEST R.,CONSCIENCE AND SOCIETY: A STUDY OF THE COERCE PSYCHOLOGICAL PREREQUISITES OF LAW AND ORDER. FUT INT/LAW UNIV LAW SOCIETY STRUCT DIPLOM WAR PERS/REL SUPEGO ORD/FREE ...SOC 20. PAGE 105 E2112   PERSON

S45

DAVIS A.,"CASTE, ECONOMY, AND VIOLENCE" (BMR)" STRATA USA-45 LAW SOCIETY STRUCT SECT SANCTION COERCE RACE/REL MARRIAGE SEX...PSY SOC SOC/INTEG 18/20 NEGRO DISCRIM MISCEGEN SOUTH/US. PAGE 29 E0570

B46

GILLIN J.L.,SOCIAL PATHOLOGY. SOCIETY SECT CRIME SOC ANOMIE DISPL ORD/FREE WEALTH...CRIMLGY PSY WORSHIP. ADJUST PAGE 44 E0864   CULTURE   INGP/REL

B47

HIRSHBERG H.S.,SUBJECT GUIDE TO UNITED STATES BIBLIOG GOVERNMENT PUBLICATIONS. USA+45 USA-45 LAW ADMIN NAT/G ...SOC 20. PAGE 53 E1052   DIPLOM   LOC/G

S47

ANGELL R.C.,"THE SOCIAL INTEGRATION OF AMERICAN MUNIC CITIES OF MORE THAN 1000,000 POPULATION" (BMR)" CENSUS USA+45 SOCIETY CRIME ADJUST WEALTH...GEOG SOC GP/REL CONCPT INDICATOR SAMP CHARTS SOC/INTEG 20. PAGE 5 E0098

B48

YAKOBSON S.,FIVE HUNDRED RUSSIAN WORKS FOR COLLEGE BIBLIOG LIBRARIES (PAMPHLET). MOD/EUR USSR MARXISM SOCISM NAT/G ...ART/METH GEOG HUM JURID SOC 13/20. PAGE 108 CULTURE E2162   COM

B49

HOLLERAN M.P.,CHURCH AND STATE IN GUATEMALA. SECT GUATEMALA LAW STRUCT CATHISM...SOC SOC/INTEG 17/20 NAT/G CHURCH/STA. PAGE 55 E1086   GP/REL   CULTURE

B49

MARITAIN J.,HUMAN RIGHTS: COMMENTS AND INT/ORG INTERPRETATIONS. COM UNIV WOR+45 LAW CONSTN CULTURE CONCPT SOCIETY ECO/DEV ECO/UNDEV SCHOOL DELIB/GP EDU/PROP ATTIT PERCEPT ALL/VALS...HUM SOC TREND UNESCO 20. PAGE 68 E1365

B50

BAILEY S.K.,CONGRESS MAKES A LAW. USA+45 GP/REL DECISION SOC. PAGE 7 E0136   LEGIS   LAW   ECO/TAC

B50

DOROSH J.T.,GUIDE TO SOVIET BIBLIOGRAPHIES. USSR BIBLIOG LAW AGRI SCHOOL SECT FORCES TEC/DEV...ART/METH GEOG METH HUM SOC 20. PAGE 32 E0639   CON/ANAL

B50

EMBREE J.F.,BIBLIOGRAPHY OF THE PEOPLES AND BIBLIOG/A CULTURES OF MAINLAND SOUTHEAST ASIA. CAMBODIA LAOS CULTURE THAILAND VIETNAM LAW...GEOG HUM SOC MYTH LING S/ASIA CHARTS WORSHIP 20. PAGE 35 E0686

B50
FRAGA IRIBARNE M.,RAZAS Y RACISMO IN NORTEAMERICA.   RACE/REL
USA+45 CONSTN STRATA NAT/G PROVS ATTIT...SOC CONCPT   JURID
19/20 NEGRO. PAGE 39 E0783   LAW
                                                            DISCRIM

B50
WARD R.E.,A GUIDE TO JAPANESE REFERENCE AND   BIBLIOG/A
RESEARCH MATERIALS IN THE FIELD OF POLITICAL   ASIA
SCIENCE. LAW CONSTN LOC/G PRESS ADMIN...SOC   NAT/G
CON/ANAL METH 19/20 CHINJAP. PAGE 105 E2098

S50
ROBINSON W.S.,"BIAS, PROBABILITY AND TRIAL BY JURY"   REPRESENT
(BMR)" USA+45 USA-45 SOCIETY...SOC CONCPT. PAGE 85   JURID
E1707   CT/SYS
                                                            DECISION

B52
BENTHAM A.,HANDBOOK OF POLITICAL FALLACIES. FUT   POL/PAR
MOD/EUR LAW INTELL LOC/G MUNIC NAT/G DELIB/GP LEGIS
CREATE EDU/PROP CT/SYS ATTIT RIGID/FLEX KNOWL PWR
...RELATIV PSY SOC CONCPT SELF/OBS TREND STERTYP
TOT/POP. PAGE 10 E0189

B52
CAHILL F.V.,JUDICIAL LEGISLATION: A STUDY IN   JURID
AMERICAN LEGAL THEORY. USA+45 USA-45 LAW NAT/G   ADJUD
GP/REL...POLICY PHIL/SCI SOC 20 HOLMES/OW. PAGE 18   LEGIS
E0359   CONTROL

B52
DILLON D.R.,LATIN AMERICA, 1935-1949; A SELECTED   BIBLIOG
BIBLIOGRAPHY. LAW EDU/PROP...SOC 20. PAGE 32 E0629   L/A+17C
                                                            NAT/G
                                                            DIPLOM

B52
ETTINGHAUSEN R.,SELECTED AND ANNOTATED BIBLIOGRAPHY BIBLIOG/A
OF BOOKS AND PERIODICALS IN WESTERN LANGUAGES   ISLAM
DEALING WITH NEAR AND MIDDLE EAST. LAW CULTURE SECT   MEDIT-7
...ART/METH GEOG SOC. PAGE 35 E0700

B52
FORSTER A.,THE TROUBLE MAKERS. USA+45 LAW CULTURE   DISCRIM
SOCIETY STRUCT VOL/ASSN CROWD GP/REL MORAL...PSY   SECT
SOC CONCPT 20 NEGRO JEWS. PAGE 39 E0771   RACE/REL
                                                            ATTIT

B52
UNESCO,THESES DE SCIENCES SOCIALES: CATALOGUE   BIBLIOG
ANALYTIQUE INTERNATIONAL DE THESES INEDITES DE   ACADEM
DOCTORAT, 1940-1950. INT/ORG DIPLOM EDU/PROP...GEOG WRITING
INT/LAW MGT PSY SOC 20. PAGE 98 E1958

B53
AYMARD A.,HISTOIRE GENERALE DES CIVILISATIONS (7   BIBLIOG/A
VOLS.). WOR+45 WOR-45 LAW SECT CREATE ATTIT   SOC
...ART/METH WORSHIP. PAGE 6 E0123

B53
CALDWELL L.K.,RESEARCH METHODS IN PUBLIC   BIBLIOG/A
ADMINISTRATION; AN OUTLINE OF TOPICS AND READINGS   METH/COMP
(PAMPHLET). LAW ACT/RES COMPUTER KNOWL...SOC STAT   ADMIN
GEN/METH 20. PAGE 18 E0364   OP/RES

B53
GROSS B.M.,THE LEGISLATIVE STRUGGLE: A STUDY IN   LEGIS
SOCIAL COMBAT. STRUCT LOC/G POL/PAR JUDGE EDU/PROP   DECISION
DEBATE ETIQUET ADMIN LOBBY CHOOSE GOV/REL INGP/REL   PERSON
HEREDITY ALL/VALS...SOC PRESIDENT. PAGE 48 E0948   LEAD

B53
PIERCE R.A.,RUSSIAN CENTRAL ASIA, 1867-1917: A   BIBLIOG
SELECTED BIBLIOGRAPHY (PAMPHLET). USSR LAW CULTURE   COLONIAL
NAT/G EDU/PROP WAR...GEOG SOC 19/20. PAGE 81 E1616   ADMIN
                                                            COM

B54
BATTEN T.R.,PROBLEMS OF AFRICAN DEVELOPMENT (2ND   ECO/UNDEV
ED.). AFR LAW SOCIETY SCHOOL ECO/TAC TAX...GEOG   AGRI
HEAL SOC 20. PAGE 8 E0154   LOC/G
                                                            PROB/SOLV

B54
BENTLEY A.F.,INQUIRY INTO INQUIRIES: ESSAYS IN   EPIST
SOCIAL THEORY. UNIV LEGIS ADJUD ADMIN LOBBY   SOC
...PHIL/SCI PSY NEW/IDEA LING METH 20. PAGE 10   CONCPT
E0200

B54
CARTER P.G.,STATISTICAL BULLETINS: AN ANNOTATED   BIBLIOG/A
BIBLIOGRAPHY OF THE GENERAL STATISTICAL BULLETINS   WOR+45
AND MAJOR POL SUBDIV OF WORLD. CULTURE AGRI FINAN   NAT/G
INDUS LABOR TEC/DEV INT/TRADE CT/SYS WEALTH   STAT
...CRIMLGY SOC 20. PAGE 20 E0400

B54
HOEBEL E.A.,THE LAW OF PRIMITIVE MAN: A STUDY IN   LAW
COMPARATIVE LEGAL DYNAMICS. WOR-45...JURID SOC   CULTURE
IDEA/COMP METH 20. PAGE 53 E1063   GP/COMP
                                                            SOCIETY

B54
TOTOK W.,HANDBUCH DER BIBLIOGRAPHISCHEN   BIBLIOG/A
NACHSCHLAGEWERKE. GERMANY LAW CULTURE ADMIN...SOC   NAT/G
20. PAGE 97 E1936   DIPLOM
                                                            POLICY

B55
BEISEL A.R.,CONTROL OVER ILLEGAL ENFORCEMENT OF THE ORD/FREE
CRIMINAL LAW: ROLE OF THE SUPREME COURT. CONSTN   LAW
ROUTINE MORAL PWR...SOC 20 SUPREME/CT. PAGE 9 E0180   CRIME

B55
TROTIER A.H.,DOCTORAL DISSERTATIONS ACCEPTED BY   BIBLIOG
AMERICAN UNIVERSITIES 1954-55. SECT DIPLOM HEALTH   ACADEM
...ART/METH GEOG INT/LAW SOC LING CHARTS 20.   USA+45
PAGE 97 E1943   WRITING

B56
KUPER L.,PASSIVE RESISTANCE IN SOUTH AFRICA.   ORD/FREE
SOUTH/AFR LAW NAT/G POL/PAR VOL/ASSN DISCRIM   RACE/REL
...POLICY SOC AUD/VIS 20. PAGE 62 E1237   ATTIT

B56
RECASENS SICHES S.,TRATADO GENERAL DE SOCIOLOGIA.   SOC
CULTURE FAM NEIGH LEAD RACE/REL DISCRIM HABITAT   STRATA
ORD/FREE...JURID LING T SOC/INTEG 20. PAGE 84 E1677   KIN
                                                            GP/REL

B57
BYRNES R.F.,BIBLIOGRAPHY OF AMERICAN PUBLICATIONS   BIBLIOG/A
ON EAST CENTRAL EUROPE, 1945-1957 (VOL. XXII). SECT   COM
DIPLOM EDU/PROP RACE/REL...ART/METH GEOG JURID SOC   MARXISM
LING 20 JEWS. PAGE 18 E0354   NAT/G

B57
CLINARD M.B.,SOCIOLOGY OF DEVIANT BEHAVIOR. FAM   BIO/SOC
CONTROL MURDER DISCRIM PERSON...PSY SOC T SOC/INTEG   CRIME
20. PAGE 23 E0455   SEX
                                                            ANOMIE

B57
CONOVER H.F.,NORTH AND NORTHEAST AFRICA; A SELECTED BIBLIOG/A
ANNOTATED LIST OF WRITINGS. ALGERIA MOROCCO SUDAN   DIPLOM
UAR CULTURE INT/ORG PROB/SOLV ADJUD NAT/LISM PWR   AFR
WEALTH...SOC 20 UN. PAGE 25 E0496   ECO/UNDEV

S57
GOODE W.J.,"COMMUNITY WITHIN A COMMUNITY: THE   PROF/ORG
PROFESSIONS." STRATA STRUCT SANCTION INGP/REL...SOC   NEIGH
GP/COMP. PAGE 45 E0886   CLIENT
                                                           CONTROL

B58
CLEMMER D.,THE PRISON COMMUNITY. CULTURE CONTROL   PUB/INST
LEAD ROUTINE PERS/REL PERSON...SOC METH/CNCPT.   CRIMLGY
PAGE 23 E0453   CLIENT
                                                           INGP/REL

B58
DEVLIN P.,THE CRIMINAL PROSECUTION IN ENGLAND. UK   CRIME
NAT/G ADMIN ROUTINE EFFICIENCY...JURID SOC 20.   LAW
PAGE 31 E0617   METH
                                                          CT/SYS

B58
KURL S.,ESTONIA: A SELECTED BIBLIOGRAPHY. USSR   BIBLIOG
ESTONIA LAW INTELL SECT...ART/METH GEOG HUM SOC 20.   CULTURE
PAGE 62 E1238   NAT/G

B58
MUSIKER R.,GUIDE TO SOUTH AFRICAN REFERENCE BOOKS.   BIBLIOG/A
SOUTH/AFR SOCIETY SECT EDU/PROP PRESS RACE/REL   SOC
...JURID SOC/WK 20. PAGE 75 E1512   GEOG

B58
ORTIZ R.P.,ANNUARIO BIBLIOGRAFICO COLOMBIANO,   BIBLIOG
1951-1956. LAW RECEIVE EDU/PROP ADMIN...LING STAT   SOC
20 COLOMB. PAGE 79 E1582

B58
WESTIN A.F.,THE ANATOMY OF A CONSTITUTIONAL LAW   CT/SYS
CASE. USA+45 LAW LEGIS ADMIN EXEC...DECISION MGT   INDUS
SOC RECORD 20 SUPREME/CT. PAGE 105 E2113   ADJUD
                                                          CONSTN

S58
ROCHE J.P.,"POLITICAL SCIENCE AND SCIENCE FICTION"   QUANT
(BMR)" WOR+45 INTELL OP/RES ADJUD...JURID SOC   RATIONAL
IDEA/COMP 20. PAGE 85 E1709   MATH

METH

S58

SCHUBERT G.A.,"THE STUDY OF JUDICIAL DECISION-
MAKING AS AN ASPECT OF POLITICAL BEHAVIOR." PLAN
ADJUD CT/SYS INGP/REL PERSON...PHIL/SCI SOC QUANT
STAT CHARTS IDEA/COMP SOC/EXP. PAGE 89 E1779

JUDGE
DECISION
CON/ANAL
GAME

B59

FRIEDMANN W.G.,LAW IN A CHANGING SOCIETY. FUT
WOR+45 WOR-45 LAW SOCIETY STRUCT INT/TRADE LEGIT
ATTIT BIO/SOC HEALTH ORD/FREE SOVEREIGN...CONCPT
GEN/LAWS ILO 20. PAGE 41 E0803

SOC
JURID

B59

HAYS B.,A SOUTHERN MODERATE SPEAKS. LAW PROVS
SCHOOL KNOWL...JURID SOC SELF/OBS BIOG 20 NEGRO
SUPREME/CT. PAGE 51 E1015

SECT
DISCRIM
CT/SYS
RACE/REL

B59

HOBSBAWM E.J.,PRIMITIVE REBELS; STUDIES IN ARCHAIC
FORMS OF SOCIAL MOVEMENT IN THE 19TH AND 20TH
CENTURIES. ITALY SPAIN CULTURE VOL/ASSN RISK CROWD
GP/REL INGP/REL ISOLAT TOTALISM...PSY SOC 18/20.
PAGE 53 E1058

SOCIETY
CRIME
REV
GUERRILLA

B59

KERREMANS-RAMIOULL,LE PROBLEME DE LA DELINQUENCE
JUVENILE (2ND ED.). FAM PUB/INST SCHOOL FORCES
LEGIS MORAL...CRIMLGY SOC 20. PAGE 60 E1205

BIBLIOG
CRIME
AGE/Y
SOC/WK

B59

LAPIERE R.,THE FREUDIAN ETHIC. USA+45 FAM EDU/PROP
CONTROL CRIME ADJUST AGE DRIVE PERCEPT PERSON SEX
...SOC 20 FREUD/S. PAGE 63 E1254

PSY
ORD/FREE
SOCIETY

B59

OKINSHEVICH L.A.,LATIN AMERICA IN SOVIET WRITINGS,
1945-1958: A BIBLIOGRAPHY. USSR LAW ECO/UNDEV LABOR
DIPLOM EDU/PROP REV...GEOG SOC 20. PAGE 78 E1573

BIBLIOG
WRITING
COM
L/A+17C

B59

COLUMBIA U. BUREAU OF APPL SOC RES, ATTITUDES OF
PROMINENT AMERICANS TOWARD "WORLD PEACE THROUGH
WORLD LAW" (SUPRA-NATL ORGANIZATION FOR WAR
PREVENTION). USA+45 USSR ELITES FORCES PLAN
PROB/SOLV CONTROL WAR PWR...POLICY SOC QU IDEA/COMP
20 UN. PAGE 82 E1644

ATTIT
ACT/RES
INT/LAW
STAT

B59

VOSE C.E.,CAUCASIANS ONLY: THE SUPREME COURT, THE
NAACP, AND THE RESTRICTIVE COVENANT CASES. USA+45
LAW CONSTN LOBBY...SOC 20 NAACP SUPREME/CT NEGRO.
PAGE 104 E2086

CT/SYS
RACE/REL
DISCRIM

S59

BELL D.,"THE RACKET RIDDEN LONGSHOREMEN" (BMR)"
USA+45 SEA WORKER MURDER ROLE...SOC 20 NEWYORK/C.
PAGE 9 E0182

CRIME
LABOR
DIST/IND
ELITES

S59

CLOWARD R.A.,"ILLEGITIMATE MEANS, ANOMIE, AND
DEVIANT BEHAVIOR" STRUCT CRIME DRIVE PERSON...SOC
CONCPT NEW/IDEA 20 DURKHEIM/E MERTON/R. PAGE 23
E0459

ANOMIE
CRIMLGY
LEGIT
ADJUST

S59

SUTTON F.X.,"REPRESENTATION AND THE NATURE OF
POLITICAL SYSTEMS." UNIV WOR-45 CULTURE SOCIETY
STRATA INT/ORG FORCES JUDGE DOMIN LEGIT EXEC REGION
REPRESENT ATTIT ORD/FREE RESPECT...SOC HIST/WRIT
TIME/SEQ. PAGE 95 E1896

NAT/G
CONCPT

C59

EASTON D.,"POLITICAL ANTHROPOLOGY" IN BIENNIAL
REVIEW OF ANTHROPOLOGY" UNIV LAW CULTURE ELITES
SOCIETY CREATE...PSY CONCPT GP/COMP GEN/METH 20.
PAGE 34 E0671

SOC
BIBLIOG/A
NEW/IDEA

B60

BORGATTA E.F.,SOCIAL WORKERS' PERCEPTIONS OF
CLIENTS. SERV/IND ROUTINE PERS/REL DRIVE PERSON
RESPECT...SOC PERS/COMP 20. PAGE 14 E0268

SOC/WK
ATTIT
CLIENT
PROB/SOLV

B60

CARTER R.F.,COMMUNITIES AND THEIR SCHOOLS. USA+45
LAW FINAN PROVS BUDGET TAX LEAD PARTIC CHOOSE...SOC
INT QU 20. PAGE 20 E0401

SCHOOL
ACT/RES
NEIGH
INGP/REL

B60

FLORES R.H.,CATALOGO DE TESIS DOCTORALES DE LAS
FACULTADES DE LA UNIVERSIDAD DE EL SALVADOR.
EL/SALVADR LAW DIPLOM ADMIN LEAD GOV/REL...SOC
19/20. PAGE 39 E0767

BIBLIOG
ACADEM
L/A+17C
NAT/G

B60

GIBNEY F.,THE OPERATORS. USA+45 LAW STRATA BIO/SOC
MORAL ORD/FREE SOC. PAGE 43 E0858

CRIME
CULTURE
ANOMIE
CRIMLGY

B60

JENKS C.W.,HUMAN RIGHTS AND INTERNATIONAL LABOR
STANDARDS. WOR+45 CONSTN LABOR VOL/ASSN DELIB/GP
ACT/RES EDU/PROP MORAL RESPECT...JURID SOC TREND
GEN/LAWS WORK ILO 20. PAGE 58 E1156

CONCPT

B60

LEWIS P.R.,LITERATURE OF THE SOCIAL SCIENCES: AN
INTRODUCTORY SURVEY AND GUIDE. UK LAW INDUS DIPLOM
INT/TRADE ADMIN...MGT 19/20. PAGE 65 E1294

BIBLIOG/A
SOC

S60

SCHWELB E.,"INTERNATIONAL CONVENTIONS ON HUMAN
RIGHTS." FUT WOR+45 LAW CONSTN CULTURE SOCIETY
STRUCT VOL/ASSN DELIB/GP PLAN ADJUD SUPEGO LOVE
MORAL...SOC CONCPT STAT RECORD HIST/WRIT TREND 20
UN. PAGE 89 E1790

INT/ORG
HUM

S60

THOMPSON K.W.,"MORAL PURPOSE IN FOREIGN POLICY:
REALITIES AND ILLUSIONS." WOR+45 WOR-45 LAW CULTURE
SOCIETY INT/ORG PLAN ADJUD ADMIN COERCE RIGID/FLEX
SUPEGO KNOWL ORD/FREE PWR...SOC TREND SOC/EXP
TOT/POP 20. PAGE 96 E1921

MORAL
JURID
DIPLOM

S60

ULMER S.S.,"THE ANALYSIS OF BEHAVIOR PATTERNS ON
THE UNITED STATES SUPREME COURT" USA+45 CT/SYS
PERS/REL RACE/REL PERSON...DECISION PSY SOC TREND
METH/COMP METH 20 SUPREME/CT CIVIL/LIB. PAGE 97
E1951

ATTIT
ADJUD
PROF/ORG
INGP/REL

C60

MCCLEERY R.,"COMMUNICATION PATTERNS AS BASES OF
SYSTEMS OF AUTHORITY AND POWER" IN THEORETICAL
STUDIES IN SOCIAL ORGAN. OF PRISON-BMR. USA+45
SOCIETY STRUCT EDU/PROP ADMIN CONTROL COERCE CRIME
GP/REL AUTHORIT...SOC 20. PAGE 70 E1400

PERS/REL
PUB/INST
PWR
DOMIN

B61

BAINS J.S.,STUDIES IN POLITICAL SCIENCE. INDIA
WOR+45 WOR-45 CONSTN BAL/PWR ADJUD ADMIN PARL/PROC
SOVEREIGN...SOC METH/COMP ANTHOL 17/20 UN. PAGE 7
E0137

DIPLOM
INT/LAW
NAT/G

B61

CHILDS M.W.,THE EROSION OF INDIVIDUAL LIBERTIES.
NAT/G LEGIS ATTIT...JURID SOC CONCPT IDEA/COMP 20
SUPREME/CT AMEND/I. PAGE 22 E0430

ADJUD
CT/SYS
ORD/FREE
CONSTN

B61

FLINN M.W.,AN ECONOMIC AND SOCIAL HISTORY OF
BRITAIN, 1066-1939. UK LAW STRATA STRUCT AGRI
DIST/IND INDUS WORKER INT/TRADE WAR...CENSUS 11/20.
PAGE 39 E0766

SOCIETY
SOC

B61

MERTON R.K.,CONTEMPORARY SOCIAL PROBLEMS: AN
INTRODUCTION TO THE SOCIOLOGY OF DEVIANT BEHAVIOR
AND SOCIAL DISORGANIZATION. FAM MUNIC FORCES WORKER
PROB/SOLV INGP/REL RACE/REL ISOLAT...CRIMLGY GEOG
PSY T 20 NEGRO. PAGE 72 E1444

CRIME
ANOMIE
STRANGE
SOC

S61

LASSWELL H.D.,"THE INTERPLAY OF ECONOMIC, POLITICAL
AND SOCIAL CRITERIA IN LEGAL POLICY." LAW LOVE
MORAL PWR RESPECT WEALTH...SOC IDEA/COMP. PAGE 63
E1262

JURID
POLICY

B62

AMER SOCIETY POL & LEGAL PHIL,THE PUBLIC INTEREST:
NOMOS V. LAW EDU/PROP...SOC METH/CNCPT ANTHOL.
PAGE 4 E0073

CONCPT
ATTIT
PWR
GEN/LAWS

B62

BOCHENSKI J.M.,HANDBOOK ON COMMUNISM. USSR WOR+45
LAW SOCIETY NAT/G POL/PAR SECT CRIME PERSON MARXISM
...SOC ANTHOL 20. PAGE 13 E0254

COM
DIPLOM
POLICY
CONCPT

B62

BRANDT R.B.,SOCIAL JUSTICE. UNIV LAW GP/REL PWR

ORD/FREE

ALL/IDEOS...POLICY SOC ANTHOL 20. PAGE 15 E0287   CONSTN
CONCPT

B62

COSTA RICA UNIVERSIDAD BIBL,LISTA DE TESIS DE GRADO BIBLIOG/A
DE LA UNIVERSIDAD DE COSTA RICA. COSTA/RICA LAW   NAT/G
LOC/G ADMIN LEAD...SOC 20. PAGE 26 E0518   DIPLOM
ECO/UNDEV

B62

CURRY J.E.,RACE TENSIONS AND THE POLICE. LAW MUNIC   FORCES
NEIGH TEC/DEV RUMOR CONTROL COERCE GP/REL ATTIT   RACE/REL
...SOC 20 NEGRO. PAGE 28 E0558   CROWD
ORD/FREE

B62

DAVIS F.J.,SOCIETY AND THE LAW. USA+45 CONSTN   LAW
ACADEM FAM CONSULT ACT/RES GP/REL ORD/FREE   SOC
ENGLSH/LAW 20. PAGE 29 E0572   CULTURE
STRUCT

B62

EVAN W.M.,LAW AND SOCIOLOGY: EXPLORATORY ESSAYS.   JURID
CONSULT ACT/RES OP/RES PROB/SOLV TEC/DEV PROP LEGIT   SOC
ADJUD CT/SYS GP/REL...PHIL/SCI ANTHOL SOC/INTEG 20.   PROF/ORG
PAGE 35 E0703

B62

KIDDER F.E.,THESES ON PAN AMERICAN TOPICS. LAW   BIBLIOG
CULTURE NAT/G SECT DIPLOM HEALTH...ART/METH GEOG   CHRIST-17C
SOC 13/20. PAGE 61 E1213   L/A+17C
SOCIETY

B62

MARS D.,SUGGESTED LIBRARY IN PUBLIC ADMINISTRATION.   BIBLIOG
FINAN DELIB/GP EX/STRUC WORKER COMPUTER ADJUD   ADMIN
...DECISION PSY SOC METH/COMP 20. PAGE 68 E1368   METH
MGT

B62

SCHWARZENBERGER G.,THE FRONTIERS OF INTERNATIONAL   INT/ORG
LAW. WOR+45 WOR-45 NAT/G LEGIT CT/SYS ROUTINE MORAL   LAW
ORD/FREE PWR...JURID SOC GEN/METH 20 COLD/WAR.   INT/LAW
PAGE 89 E1789

B62

UNECA LIBRARY,NEW ACQUISITIONS IN THE UNECA   BIBLIOG
LIBRARY. LAW NAT/G PLAN PROB/SOLV TEC/DEV ADMIN   AFR
REGION...GEOG SOC 20 UN. PAGE 98 E1956   ECO/UNDEV
INT/ORG

B62

WOETZEL R.K.,THE NURENBERG TRIALS IN INTERNATIONAL   INT/ORG
LAW. CHRIST-17C MOD/EUR WOR+45 SOCIETY NAT/G   ADJUD
DELIB/GP DOMIN LEGIT ROUTINE ATTIT DRIVE PERSON   WAR
SUPEGO MORAL ORD/FREE...POLICY MAJORIT JURID PSY
SOC SELF/OBS RECORD NAZI TOT/POP. PAGE 107 E2138

L62

"AMERICAN BEHAVIORAL SCIENTIST." USSR LAW NAT/G   BIBLIOG
...SOC 20 UN. PAGE 2 E0034   AFR
R+D

L62

UNITED NATIONS,"CAPITAL PUNISHMENT." WOR+45 CULTURE   LAW
NAT/G ROUTINE COERCE HEALTH PWR...POLICY SOC QU   STAT
CHARTS VAL/FREE 20. PAGE 98 E1967

B63

ELIAS T.O.,GOVERNMENT AND POLITICS IN AFRICA.   AFR
CONSTN CULTURE SOCIETY NAT/G POL/PAR DIPLOM   NAT/LISM
REPRESENT PERSON...SOC TREND BIBLIOG 4/20. PAGE 34   COLONIAL
E0681   LAW

B63

HALL J.,COMPARATIVE LAW AND SOCIAL THEORY. WOR+45   LAW
CONSTN CULTURE DOMIN CT/SYS ORD/FREE...PLURIST   SOC
JURID CONCPT NEW/IDEA GEN/LAWS VAL/FREE. PAGE 49
E0984

B63

ROBERTSON A.H.,HUMAN RIGHTS IN EUROPE. CONSTN   EUR+WWI
SOCIETY INT/ORG NAT/G VOL/ASSN DELIB/GP ACT/RES   PERSON
PLAN ADJUD REGION ROUTINE ATTIT LOVE ORD/FREE
RESPECT...JURID SOC CONCPT SOC/EXP UN 20. PAGE 85
E1705

B63

SARTORI G.,IL PARLAMENTO ITALIANO: 1946-1963. LAW   LEGIS
CONSTN ELITES POL/PAR LOBBY PRIVIL ATTIT PERSON   PARL/PROC
MORAL PWR SOC. PAGE 87 E1746   REPRESENT

B63

SCHMIDHAUSER J.R.,CONSTITUTIONAL LAW IN THE   LAW
POLITICAL PROCESS. SOCIETY LEGIS ADJUD CT/SYS   CONSTN
FEDERAL...SOC TREND IDEA/COMP ANTHOL T SUPREME/CT   JURID

SENATE CONGRESS HOUSE/REP. PAGE 88 E1761

S63

BRAUSCH G.E.,"AFRICAN ETHNOCRACIES: SOME   LAW
SOCIOLOGICAL IMPLICATIONS OF CONSTITUTIONAL CHANGE   SOC
IN EMERGENT TERRITORIES OF AFRICA." AFR CONSTN   ELITES
FACE/GP MUNIC NAT/G DOMIN ATTIT ALL/VALS
...HIST/WRIT GEN/LAWS VAL/FREE 20. PAGE 15 E0289

S63

MENDELSON W.,"THE NEO-BEHAVIORAL APPROACH TO THE   DECISION
JUDICIAL PROCESS: A CRITIQUE" ADJUD PERSON...SOC   JURID
RECORD IDEA/COMP. PAGE 72 E1438   JUDGE

B64

BERNSTEIN H.,A BOOKSHELF ON BRAZIL. BRAZIL ADMIN   BIBLIOG/A
COLONIAL...HUM JURID SOC 20. PAGE 11 E0213   NAT/G
L/A+17C
ECO/UNDEV

B64

GESELLSCHAFT RECHTSVERGLEICH,BIBLIOGRAPHIE DES   BIBLIOG/A
DEUTSCHEN RECHTS (BIBLIOGRAPHY OF GERMAN LAW,   JURID
TRANS. BY COURTLAND PETERSON). GERMANY FINAN INDUS   CONSTN
LABOR SECT FORCES CT/SYS PARL/PROC CRIME...INT/LAW   ADMIN
SOC NAT/COMP 20. PAGE 43 E0853

B64

HURST W.H.,JUSTICE HOLMES ON LEGAL HISTORY. USA-45   ADJUD
LAW SOCIETY NAT/G WRITING...POLICY PHIL/SCI SOC   JURID
CONCPT 20 HOLMES/OW SUPREME/CT ENGLSH/LAW. PAGE 56   BIOG
E1117

B64

IKLE F.C.,HOW NATIONS NEGOTIATE. COM EUR+WWI USA+45   NAT/G
INTELL INT/ORG VOL/ASSN DELIB/GP ACT/RES CREATE   PWR
DOMIN EDU/PROP ADJUD ROUTINE ATTIT PERSON ORD/FREE   POLICY
RESPECT SKILL...PSY SOC OBS VAL/FREE. PAGE 56 E1122

B64

MAKI J.M.,COURT AND CONSTITUTION IN JAPAN: SELECTED   CONSTN
SUPREME COURT DECISIONS, 1948-60. LAW AGRI FAM   JURID
LEGIS BAL/PWR ADMIN CHOOSE...SOC ANTHOL CABINET 20   CT/SYS
CHINJAP CIVIL/LIB. PAGE 68 E1355   CRIME

B64

MCDOUGAL M.S.,STUDIES IN WORLD PUBLIC ORDER. SPACE   INT/LAW
SEA INT/ORG CREATE AGREE NUC/PWR...POLICY PHIL/SCI   SOC
IDEA/COMP ANTHOL METH 20 UN. PAGE 71 E1411   DIPLOM

B64

MITCHELL B.,A BIOGRAPHY OF THE CONSTITUTION OF THE   CONSTN
UNITED STATES. USA+45 USA-45 PROVS CHIEF LEGIS   LAW
DEBATE ADJUD SUFF FEDERAL...SOC 16/20 SUPREME/CT   JURID
CONGRESS SENATE HOUSE/REP PRESIDENT. PAGE 73 E1472

B64

NATIONAL BOOK LEAGUE,THE COMMONWEALTH IN BOOKS: AN   BIBLIOG/A
ANNOTATED LIST. CANADA UK LOC/G SECT ADMIN...SOC   JURID
BIOG 20 CMN/WLTH. PAGE 76 E1526   NAT/G

B64

RAGHAVAN M.D.,INDIA IN CEYLONESE HISTORY, SOCIETY   DIPLOM
AND CULTURE. CEYLON INDIA S/ASIA LAW SOCIETY   CULTURE
INT/TRADE ATTIT...ART/METH JURID SOC LING 20.   SECT
PAGE 83 E1668   STRUCT

B64

SHAPIRO M.,LAW AND POLITICS IN THE SUPREME COURT: LEGIS
NEW APPROACHES TO POLITICAL JURISPRUDENCE. JUDGE   CT/SYS
PROB/SOLV LEGIT EXEC ROUTINE ATTIT ALL/VALS   LAW
...DECISION SOC. PAGE 90 E1811   JURID

L64

WORLD PEACE FOUNDATION,"INTERNATIONAL   INT/ORG
ORGANIZATIONS: SUMMARY OF ACTIVITIES." INDIA   ROUTINE
PAKISTAN TURKEY WOR+45 CONSTN CONSULT EX/STRUC
ECO/TAC EDU/PROP LEGIT ORD/FREE...JURID SOC UN 20
CYPRESS. PAGE 107 E2145

B65

AMERICAN UNIVERSITY IN CAIRO,GUIDE TO UAR   BIBLIOG
GOVERNMENT PUBLICATIONS AT THE AUC LIBRARY   NAT/G
(PAMPHLET). ISLAM UAR USA+45 ECO/UNDEV...SOC STAT   LEGIS
20. PAGE 4 E0084   LAW

B65

BLITZ L.F.,THE POLITICS AND ADMINISTRATION OF   NAT/G
NIGERIAN GOVERNMENT. NIGER CULTURE LOC/G LEGIS   GOV/REL
DIPLOM COLONIAL CT/SYS SOVEREIGN...GEOG SOC ANTHOL   POL/PAR
20. PAGE 13 E0245

B65

BOVY L.,LE MOUVEMENT SYNDICAL OUEST AFRICAIN   BIBLIOG
D'EXPRESSION FRANCAISE. AFR SECT...JURID SOC 20.   SOCISM
PAGE 14 E0275   ECO/UNDEV

IDEA/COMP

NAT/G

B65
BROMBERG W.,CRIME AND THE MIND. LAW LEGIT ADJUD | CRIMLGY
CRIME MURDER AGE/Y ANOMIE BIO/SOC DRIVE SEX PSY. | SOC
PAGE 16 E0305 | HEALTH
| COERCE

B65
CHROUST A.H.,THE RISE OF THE LEGAL PROFESSION IN | JURID
AMERICA (3 VOLS.). STRATA STRUCT POL/PAR PROF/ORG | USA-45
COLONIAL LEAD REV SKILL...SOC 17/20. PAGE 22 E0437 | CT/SYS
| LAW

B65
EHLE J.,THE FREE MEN. USA+45 NAT/G PROVS FORCES | RACE/REL
JUDGE ADJUD ATTIT...POLICY SOC SOC/INTEG 20 NEGRO. | ORD/FREE
PAGE 34 E0677 | DISCRIM

B65
GAJENDRAGADKAR P.B.,LAW, LIBERTY AND SOCIAL | ORD/FREE
JUSTICE. INDIA CONSTN NAT/G SECT PLAN ECO/TAC PRESS | LAW
POPULISM...SOC METH/COMP 20 HINDU. PAGE 42 E0826 | ADJUD
| JURID

B65
INST INTL DES CIVILISATION DIF,THE CONSTITUTIONS | CONSTN
AND ADMINISTRATIVE INSTITUTIONS OF THE NEW STATES. | ADMIN
AFR ISLAM S/ASIA NAT/G POL/PAR DELIB/GP EX/STRUC | ADJUD
CONFER EFFICIENCY NAT/LISM...JURID SOC 20. PAGE 56 | ECO/UNDEV
E1123

B65
KARIS T.,THE TREASON TRIAL IN SOUTH AFRICA: A GUIDE | BIBLIOG/A
TO THE MICROFILM RECORD OF THE TRIAL. SOUTH/AFR LAW | ADJUD
ELITES NAT/G LEGIT CT/SYS RACE/REL DISCRIM...SOC | CRIME
20. PAGE 59 E1185 | AFR

B65
KRISLOV S.,THE SUPREME COURT IN THE POLITICAL | ADJUD
PROCESS. USA+45 LAW SOCIETY STRUCT WORKER ADMIN | DECISION
ROLE...JURID SOC 20 SUPREME/CT. PAGE 62 E1231 | CT/SYS
| CONSTN

B65
RADZINOWICZ L.,THE NEED FOR CRIMINOLOGY AND A | CRIMLGY
PROPOSAL FOR AN INSTITUTE OF CRIMINOLOGY. FUT UK | PROF/ORG
USA+45 SOCIETY ACT/RES PROB/SOLV CRIME...PSY SOC | ACADEM
BIBLIOG 20. PAGE 83 E1666 | CONTROL

B65
RENNER K.,MENSCH UND GESELLSCHAFT - GRUNDRISS EINER | SOC
SOZIOLOGIE (2ND ED.). STRATA FAM LABOR PROF/ORG WAR | STRUCT
...JURID CLASSIF 20. PAGE 84 E1685 | NAT/G
| SOCIETY

B65
STONE J.,HUMAN LAW AND HUMAN JUSTICE. JUDGE...SOC | CONCPT
MYTH IDEA/COMP. PAGE 94 E1881 | SANCTION
| JURID

B65
UNESCO,INTERNATIONAL ORGANIZATIONS IN THE SOCIAL | INT/ORG
SCIENCES(REV. ED.). LAW ADMIN ATTIT...CRIMLGY GEOG | R+D
INT/LAW PSY SOC STAT 20 UNESCO. PAGE 98 E1962 | PROF/ORG
| ACT/RES

B65
UNIVERSAL REFERENCE SYSTEM,INTERNATIONAL AFFAIRS: | BIBLIOG/A
VOLUME I IN THE POLITICAL SCIENCE, GOVERNMENT, AND | GEN/METH
PUBLIC POLICY SERIES....DECISION ECOMETRIC GEOG | COMPUT/IR
INT/LAW JURID MGT PHIL/SCI PSY SOC. PAGE 98 E1972 | DIPLOM

S65
KHOURI F.J.,"THE JORDON RIVER CONTROVERSY." LAW | ISLAM
SOCIETY ECO/UNDEV AGRI FINAN INDUS SECT FORCES | INT/ORG
ACT/RES PLAN TEC/DEV ECO/TAC EDU/PROP COERCE ATTIT | ISRAEL
DRIVE PERCEPT RIGID/FLEX ALL/VALS...GEOG SOC MYTH | JORDAN
WORK. PAGE 61 E1212

B66
GRUNEWALD D.,,PUBLIC POLICY AND THE MODERN | LG/CO
COOPERATION: SELECTED READINGS. USA+45 LAW MARKET | POLICY
VOL/ASSN CAP/ISM INT/TRADE CENTRAL OWN...SOC ANTHOL | NAT/G
20. PAGE 48 E0954 | CONTROL

B66
HOPKINS J.F.K.,ARABIC PERIODICAL LITERATURE, 1961. | BIBLIOG/A
ISLAM LAW CULTURE SECT...GEOG HEAL PHIL/SCI PSY SOC | NAT/LISM
20. PAGE 55 E1096 | TEC/DEV
| INDUS

B66
KUNST H.,EVANGELISCHES STAATSLEXIKON. LAW CONSTN | JURID
POL/PAR...PHIL/SCI CONCPT DICTIONARY. PAGE 62 E1232 | SECT
| SOC

B66
MACIVER R.M.,THE PREVENTION AND CONTROL OF | AGE/Y
DELINQUENCY. USA+45 STRATA PUB/INST ANOMIE ATTIT | PLAN
HABITAT PERSON HEALTH...CRIMLGY PSY SOC METH. | ADJUST
PAGE 67 E1341 | CRIME

B66
SKOLNICK J.H.,JUSTICE WITHOUT TRIAL: LAW | FORCES
ENFORCEMENT IN DEMOCRATIC SOCIETY. USA+45 LAW | CRIMLGY
TRIBUTE RACE/REL BIO/SOC PERSON...PSY SOC 20 NEGRO | CRIME
BUREAUCRCY PROSTITUTN. PAGE 92 E1836

B66
STEVENS R.E.,REFERENCE BOOKS IN THE SOCIAL SCIENCES | BIBLIOG/A
AND HUMANITIES. CULTURE PERF/ART SECT EDU/PROP | SOC
...JURID PSY SOC/WK STAT 20 MUSIC. PAGE 93 E1873 | HUM
| ART/METH

B66
UNITED NATIONS,INTERNATIONAL SPACE BIBLIOGRAPHY. | BIBLIOG
FUT INT/ORG TEC/DEV DIPLOM ARMS/CONT NUC/PWR | SPACE
...JURID SOC UN. PAGE 98 E1969 | PEACE
| R+D

B66
US DEPARTMENT OF STATE,RESEARCH ON WESTERN EUROPE, | BIBLIOG/A
GREAT BRITAIN, AND CANADA (EXTERNAL RESEARCH LIST | EUR+WWI
NO 3-25). CANADA GERMANY/W UK LAW CULTURE NAT/G | DIPLOM
POL/PAR FORCES EDU/PROP REGION MARXISM...GEOG SOC
WORSHIP 20 CMN/WLTH. PAGE 100 E1998

S66
SHEEHY E.P.,"SELECTED REFERENCE BOOKS OF | BIBLIOG/A
1965-1966." AGRI PERF/ART PRESS...GEOG HUM JURID | INDEX
SOC LING WORSHIP. PAGE 91 E1817 | CLASSIF

B67
BOHANNAN P.,LAW AND WARFARE. CULTURE CT/SYS COERCE | METH/COMP
REV PEACE...JURID SOC CONCPT ANTHOL 20. PAGE 13 | ADJUD
E0259 | WAR
| LAW

B67
BONGER W.A.,CRIMINALITY AND ECONOMIC CONDITIONS. | PERSON
MOD/EUR STRUCT INDUS WORKER EDU/PROP CRIME HABITAT | CRIMLGY
ALL/VALS...JURID SOC 20 REFORMERS. PAGE 14 E0265 | IDEA/COMP
| ANOMIE

B67
COHEN M.R.,LAW AND THE SOCIAL ORDER: ESSAYS IN | JURID
LEGAL PHILOSOPHY. USA-45 CONSULT WORKER ECO/TAC | LABOR
ATTIT WEALTH...POLICY WELF/ST SOC 20 NEW/DEAL | IDEA/COMP
DEPRESSION. PAGE 24 E0467

B67
DIEGUES M.,SOCIAL SCIENCE IN LATIN AMERICA. L/A+17C | METH
...JURID SOC ANTHOL 20. PAGE 31 E0624 | ACADEM
| EDU/PROP
| ACT/RES

B67
MEYERS M.,SOURCES OF THE AMERICAN REPUBLIC: A | COLONIAL
DOCUMENTARY HISTORY OF POLITICS, SOCIETY, AND | REV
THOUGHT (VOL. I, REV. ED.). USA-45 CULTURE STRUCT | WAR
NAT/G LEGIS LEAD ATTIT...JURID SOC ANTHOL 17/19
PRESIDENT. PAGE 72 E1450

B67
UNIVERSAL REFERENCE SYSTEM,BIBLIOGRAPHY OF | BIBLIOG/A
BIBLIOGRAPHIES IN POLITICAL SCIENCE, GOVERNMENT, | NAT/G
AND PUBLIC POLICY (VOLUME III). WOR+45 WOR-45 LAW | DIPLOM
ADMIN...SOC CON/ANAL COMPUT/IR GEN/METH. PAGE 98 | POLICY
E1973

L67
CICOUREL A.V.,"KINSHIP, MARRIAGE, AND DIVORCE IN | SOC
COMPARATIVE FAMILY LAW." UNIV LAW FAM KIN GEN/METH. | PHIL/SCI
PAGE 22 E0438 | MARRIAGE
| IDEA/COMP

S67
BOHANNAN P.,"INSTITUTIONS OF DIVORCE, FAMILY, AND | FAM
THE LAW." WOR+45 LAW CONSULT...JURID SOC. PAGE 13 | MARRIAGE
E0258 | ADJUD
| SOCIETY

S67
CARTER R.M.,"SOME FACTORS IN SENTENCING POLICY." | ADJUD
LAW PUB/INST CRIME PERS/REL...POLICY JURID SOC | CT/SYS
TREND CON/ANAL CHARTS SOC/EXP 20. PAGE 20 E0403 | ADMIN

S67
GREY D.L.,"INTERVIEWING AT THE COURT." USA+45 | JUDGE
ELITES COM/IND ACT/RES PRESS CT/SYS PERSON...SOC | ATTIT

INT 20 SUPREME/CT. PAGE 46 E0916

PERS/COMP
GP/COMP

S67

KENNEDY R.F.,"TOWARD A NATION WHERE THE LAW IS KING." PLAN CT/SYS CRIME INGP/REL...JURID SOC. PAGE 60 E1202

CRIMLGY
ADJUST
LAW
PUB/INST

S67

POSPISIL L.,"LEGAL LEVELS AND MULTIPLICITY OF LEGAL SYSTEMS IN HUMAN SOCIETIES." WOR+45 CENTRAL PWR ...SOC CHARTS GP/COMP GEN/LAWS. PAGE 81 E1630

LAW
STRATA
JURID
STRUCT

S67

SEIDLER G.L.,"MARXIST LEGAL THOUGHT IN POLAND." POLAND SOCIETY R+D LOC/G NAT/G ACT/RES ADJUD CT/SYS SUPEGO PWR...SOC TREND 20 MARX/KARL. PAGE 90 E1802

MARXISM
LAW
CONCPT
EFFICIENCY

C93

PLAYFAIR R.L.,"A BIBLIOGRAPHY OF MOROCCO." MOROCCO CULTURE AGRI FORCES DIPLOM WAR HEALTH...GEOG JURID SOC CHARTS. PAGE 81 E1620

BIBLIOG
ISLAM
MEDIT-7

SOC OF COMP LEGIS AND INT LAW E1850

SOC/DEMPAR....SOCIAL DEMOCRATIC PARTY (USE WITH SPECIFIC NATION)

SOC/EXP....."SOCIAL" EXPERIMENTATION UNDER UNCONTROLLED CONDITIONS

B51

ROSSITER C.,THE SUPREME COURT AND THE COMMANDER IN CHIEF. LAW CONSTN DELIB/GP EX/STRUC LEGIS TOP/EX ADJUD CONTROL...DECISION SOC/EXP PRESIDENT. PAGE 86 E1724

CT/SYS
CHIEF
WAR
PWR

L58

BEVAN W.,"JURY BEHAVIOR AS A FUNCTION OF THE PRESTIGE OF THE FOREMAN AND THE NATURE OF HIS LEADERSHIP" (BMR)" DELIB/GP DOMIN ADJUD LEAD PERS/REL ATTIT...PSY STAT INT QU CHARTS SOC/EXP 20 JURY. PAGE 11 E0221

PERSON
EDU/PROP
DECISION
CT/SYS

S58

SCHUBERT G.A.,"THE STUDY OF JUDICIAL DECISION-MAKING AS AN ASPECT OF POLITICAL BEHAVIOR." PLAN ADJUD CT/SYS INGP/REL PERSON...PHIL/SCI SOC QUANT STAT CHARTS IDEA/COMP SOC/EXP. PAGE 89 E1779

JUDGE
DECISION
CON/ANAL
GAME

S60

THOMPSON K.W.,"MORAL PURPOSE IN FOREIGN POLICY: REALITIES AND ILLUSIONS." WOR+45 WOR-45 LAW CULTURE SOCIETY INT/ORG PLAN ADJUD ADMIN COERCE RIGID/FLEX SUPEGO KNOWL ORD/FREE PWR...SOC TREND SOC/EXP TOT/POP 20. PAGE 96 E1921

MORAL
JURID
DIPLOM

S62

CRANE R.D.,"LAW AND STRATEGY IN SPACE." FUT USA+45 WOR+45 AIR LAW INT/ORG NAT/G FORCES ACT/RES PLAN BAL/PWR LEGIT ARMS/CONT COERCE ORD/FREE...POLICY INT/LAW JURID SOC/EXP 20 TREATY. PAGE 27 E0542

CONCPT
SPACE

B63

ROBERTSON A.H.,HUMAN RIGHTS IN EUROPE. CONSTN SOCIETY INT/ORG NAT/G VOL/ASSN DELIB/GP ACT/RES PLAN ADJUD REGION ROUTINE ATTIT LOVE ORD/FREE RESPECT...JURID SOC CONCPT SOC/EXP UN 20. PAGE 85 E1705

EUR+WWI
PERSON

B66

HOYT E.C.,NATIONAL POLICY AND INTERNATIONAL LAW* CASE STUDIES FROM AMERICAN CANAL POLICY* MONOGRAPH NO. 1 -- 1966-1967. PANAMA UK ELITES BAL/PWR EFFICIENCY...CLASSIF NAT/COMP SOC/EXP COLOMB TREATY. PAGE 55 E1105

INT/LAW
USA-45
DIPLOM
PWR

S67

CARTER R.M.,"SOME FACTORS IN SENTENCING POLICY." LAW PUB/INST CRIME PERS/REL...POLICY JURID SOC TREND CON/ANAL CHARTS SOC/EXP 20. PAGE 20 E0403

ADJUD
CT/SYS
ADMIN

SOC/INTEG....SOCIAL INTEGRATION; SEE ALSO CONSEN, RACE/REL

B06

GRIFFIN A.P.C.,SELECT LIST OF REFERENCES ON THE NEGRO QUESTION (REV. ED.). USA-45 CONSTN SCHOOL SUFF ADJUST...JURID SOC/INTEG 19/20 NEGRO. PAGE 47 E0930

BIBLIOG/A
RACE/REL
DISCRIM
ATTIT

B26

HOCKING W.E.,PRESENT STATUS OF THE PHILOSOPHY OF LAW AND OF RIGHTS. UNIV CULTURE INTELL SOCIETY

JURID
PHIL/SCI

NAT/G CREATE LEGIT SANCTION ALL/VALS SOC/INTEG 18/20. PAGE 53 E1060

ORD/FREE

B34

EVANS I.L.,NATIVE POLICY IN SOUTHERN AFRICA. RHODESIA SOUTH/AFR UK STRUCT PARTIC RACE/REL ATTIT WEALTH SOC/INTEG AFRICA/SW. PAGE 35 E0705

AFR
COLONIAL
DOMIN
LAW

B35

NORDSKOG J.E.,SOCIAL REFORM IN NORWAY. NORWAY INDUS NAT/G POL/PAR LEGIS ADJUD...SOC BIBLIOG SOC/INTEG 20. PAGE 78 E1555

LABOR
ADJUST

S45

DAVIS A.,"CASTE, ECONOMY, AND VIOLENCE" (BMR)" USA+45 LAW SOCIETY STRUCT SECT SANCTION COERCE MARRIAGE SEX...PSY SOC SOC/INTEG 18/20 NEGRO MISCEGEN SOUTH/US. PAGE 29 E0570

STRATA
RACE/REL
DISCRIM

S47

ANGELL R.C.,"THE SOCIAL INTEGRATION OF AMERICAN CITIES OF MORE THAN 1000,000 POPULATION" (BMR)" USA+45 SOCIETY CRIME ADJUST WEALTH...GEOG SOC CONCPT INDICATOR SAMP CHARTS SOC/INTEG 20. PAGE 5 E0098

MUNIC
CENSUS
GP/REL

B49

HOLLERAN M.P.,CHURCH AND STATE IN GUATEMALA. GUATEMALA LAW STRUCT CATHISM...SOC SOC/INTEG 17/20 CHURCH/STA. PAGE 55 E1086

SECT
NAT/G
GP/REL
CULTURE

B54

CAPLOW T.,THE SOCIOLOGY OF WORK. USA+45 USA-45 STRATA MARKET FAM GP/REL INGP/REL ALL/VALS ...DECISION STAT BIBLIOG SOC/INTEG 20. PAGE 19 E0375

LABOR
WORKER
INDUS
ROLE

S55

CAHN E.,"A DANGEROUS MYTH IN THE SCHOOL SEGREGATION CASES" (BMR)" USA+45 CONSTN PROVS ADJUD DISCRIM ...POLICY MYTH SOC/INTEG 20 SUPREME/CT AMEND/XIV. PAGE 18 E0360

JURID
SCHOOL
RACE/REL

B56

RECASENS SICHES S.,TRATADO GENERAL DE SOCIOLOGIA. CULTURE FAM NEIGH LEAD RACE/REL DISCRIM HABITAT ORD/FREE...JURID LING T SOC/INTEG 20. PAGE 84 E1677

SOC
STRATA
KIN
GP/REL

B56

SYKES G.M.,CRIME AND SOCIETY. LAW STRATA STRUCT ACT/RES ROUTINE ANOMIE WEALTH...POLICY SOC/INTEG 20. PAGE 95 E1903

CRIMLGY
CRIME
CULTURE
INGP/REL

C56

TYLER P.,"IMMIGRATION AND THE UNITED STATES." USA+45 USA-45 LAW SECT INGP/REL RACE/REL NAT/LISM ATTIT...BIBLIOG SOC/INTEG 19/20. PAGE 97 E1949

CULTURE
GP/REL
DISCRIM

B57

CLINARD M.B.,SOCIOLOGY OF DEVIANT BEHAVIOR. FAM CONTROL MURDER DISCRIM PERSON...PSY SOC T SOC/INTEG 20. PAGE 23 E0455

BIO/SOC
CRIME
SEX
ANOMIE

B59

BROOKES E.H.,THE COMMONWEALTH TODAY. UK ROMAN/EMP INT/ORG RACE/REL NAT/LISM SOVEREIGN...TREND SOC/INTEG 20. PAGE 16 E0307

FEDERAL
DIPLOM
JURID
IDEA/COMP

S59

DWYER R.J.,"THE ADMINISTRATIVE ROLE IN DESEGREGATION." USA+45 LAW PROB/SOLV LEAD RACE/REL ISOLAT STRANGE ROLE...POLICY SOC/INTEG MISSOURI NEGRO CIV/RIGHTS. PAGE 34 E0668

ADMIN
SCHOOL
DISCRIM
ATTIT

S59

MASON A.T.,"THE SUPREME COURT: TEMPLE AND FORUM" (BMR)" USA+45 USA-45 CONSTN DELIB/GP RACE/REL MAJORITY ORD/FREE...DECISION SOC/INTEG 19/20 SUPREME/CT WARRN/EARL CIV/RIGHTS. PAGE 69 E1377

CT/SYS
JURID
PWR
ATTIT

B61

COWEN D.V.,THE FOUNDATIONS OF FREEDOM. AFR SOUTH/AFR DOMIN LEGIT ADJUST DISCRIM TOTALISM ATTIT ORD/FREE...MAJORIT JURID SOC/INTEG WORSHIP 20 NEGRO. PAGE 27 E0529

CONSTN
ELITES
RACE/REL

B62

EVAN W.M.,LAW AND SOCIOLOGY: EXPLORATORY ESSAYS. CONSULT ACT/RES OP/RES PROB/SOLV EDU/PROP LEGIT ADJUD CT/SYS GP/REL...PHIL/SCI ANTHOL SOC/INTEG 20. PROF/ORG

JURID
SOC
PROF/ORG

PAGE 35 E0703

B62
PAIKERT G.C.,THE GERMAN EXODUS. EUR+WWI GERMANY/W   INGP/REL
LAW CULTURE SOCIETY STRUCT INDUS NAT/LISM RESPECT   STRANGE
SOVEREIGN...CHARTS BIBLIOG SOC/INTEG 20 MIGRATION.   GEOG
PAGE 79 E1591   GP/REL

B63
US COMN CIVIL RIGHTS,REPORT ON MISSISSIPPI. LAW   RACE/REL
LOC/G NAT/G LEGIS PLAN PROB/SOLV DISCRIM SOC/INTEG CONSTN
20 MISSISSIPP NEGRO. PAGE 99 E1987   ORD/FREE
                                                    COERCE

B64
CURRIE D.P.,FEDERALISM AND THE NEW NATIONS OF   FEDERAL
AFRICA. CANADA USA+45 INT/TRADE TAX GP/REL   AFR
...NAT/COMP SOC/INTEG 20. PAGE 28 E0556   ECO/UNDEV
                                                    INT/LAW

B64
WRIGHT Q.,A STUDY OF WAR. LAW NAT/G PROB/SOLV   WAR
BAL/PWR NAT/LISM PEACE ATTIT SOVEREIGN...CENSUS   CONCPT
SOC/INTEG. PAGE 108 E2159   DIPLOM
                                                    CONTROL

B65
CARTER G.M.,POLITICS IN EUROPE. EUR+WWI FRANCE   GOV/COMP
GERMANY/W UK USSR LAW CONSTN POL/PAR VOL/ASSN PRESS OP/RES
LOBBY PWR...ANTHOL SOC/INTEG EEC. PAGE 20 E0399   ECO/DEV

B65
CONGRESSIONAL QUARTERLY SERV,FEDERAL ROLE IN   ACADEM
EDUCATION (PAMPHLET). LAW SCHOOL PLAN TAX ADJUD   DISCRIM
...CHARTS SOC/INTEG 20 PRESIDENT. PAGE 25 E0487   RECEIVE
                                                    FEDERAL

B65
COWEN Z.,THE BRITISH COMMONWEALTH OF NATIONS IN A   JURID
CHANGING WORLD. UK ECO/UNDEV INT/ORG ECO/TAC   DIPLOM
INT/TRADE COLONIAL WAR GP/REL RACE/REL SOVEREIGN   PARL/PROC
SOC/INTEG 20 TREATY EEC COMMONWLTH. PAGE 27 E0530   NAT/LISM

B65
EHLE J.,THE FREE MEN. USA+45 NAT/G PROVS FORCES   RACE/REL
JUDGE ADJUD ATTIT...POLICY SOC SOC/INTEG 20 NEGRO. ORD/FREE
PAGE 34 E0677   DISCRIM

B65
GLUECK S.,ROSCOE POUND AND CRIMINAL JUSTICE.   CT/SYS
SOCIETY FAM GOV/REL AGE/Y ATTIT ORD/FREE...CRIMLGY CRIME
BIOG ANTHOL SOC/INTEG 19/20. PAGE 44 E0875   LAW
                                                    ADJUD

B66
MILLER E.W.,THE NEGRO IN AMERICA: A BIBLIOGRAPHY.   BIBLIOG
USA+45 LAW EDU/PROP REV GOV/REL GP/REL INGP/REL   DISCRIM
ADJUST HABITAT PERSON HEALTH ORD/FREE SOC/INTEG 20 RACE/REL
NEGRO. PAGE 73 E1459

B66
POLLACK R.S.,THE INDIVIDUAL'S RIGHTS AND   INT/LAW
INTERNATIONAL ORGANIZATION. LAW INT/ORG DELIB/GP   ORD/FREE
SUPEGO...JURID SOC/INTEG 20 TREATY UN. PAGE 81   DIPLOM
E1623   PERSON

B67
GRAHAM H.D.,CRISIS IN PRINT: DESEGREGATION AND THE PRESS
PRESS IN TENNESSEE. LAW SOCIETY MUNIC POL/PAR   PROVS
EDU/PROP LEAD REPRESENT DISCRIM ATTIT...IDEA/COMP   POLICY
BIBLIOG/A SOC/INTEG 20 TENNESSEE SUPREME/CT   RACE/REL
SOUTH/US. PAGE 45 E0896

SOC/PAR....SOCIALIST PARTY (USE WITH SPECIFIC NATION)

SOC/REVPAR....SOCIALIST REVOLUTIONARY PARTY (USE WITH
     SPECIFIC NATION)

SOC/SECUR....SOCIAL SECURITY

SOC/WK....SOCIAL WORK, SOCIAL SERVICE ORGANIZATION

N
INTERNATIONAL BOOK NEWS, 1928-1934. ECO/UNDEV FINAN BIBLIOG/A
INDUS LABOR INT/TRADE CONFER ADJUD COLONIAL...HEAL DIPLOM
SOC/WK CHARTS 20 LEAGUE/NAT. PAGE 1 E0008   INT/LAW
                                                    INT/ORG

B19
SMITH R.H.,JUSTICE AND THE POOR. LAW RECEIVE ADJUD CT/SYS
CRIME GOV/REL COST...JURID SOC/WK CONCPT STAT   DISCRIM
CHARTS GP/COMP 20. PAGE 92 E1847   WEALTH

N19
MISSISSIPPI ADVISORY COMMITTEE,REPORT ON   RACE/REL
MISSISSIPPI (PAMPHLET). USA+45 LAW PROVS FORCES   DISCRIM

ADJUD PWR...SOC/WK INT 20 MISSISSIPP NEGRO   COERCE
CIV/RIGHTS. PAGE 73 E1469   ORD/FREE

B35
CUMMING J.,A CONTRIBUTION TOWARD A BIBLIOGRAPHY   BIBLIOG
DEALING WITH CRIME AND COGNATE SUBJECTS (3RD ED.). CRIMLGY
UK LAW CULTURE PUB/INST ADJUD AGE BIO/SOC...PSY SOC FORCES
SOC/WK STAT METH/COMP 20. PAGE 28 E0552   CT/SYS

B42
GILLETTE J.M.,PROBLEMS OF A CHANGING SOCIAL ORDER. BIO/SOC
USA+45 STRATA FAM CONTROL CRIME RACE/REL HEALTH   ADJUST
WEALTH...GEOG GP/COMP. PAGE 43 E0862   ATTIT
                                                    SOC/WK

B45
UNCIO CONFERENCE LIBRARY,SHORT TITLE CLASSIFIED   BIBLIOG
CATALOG. WOR-45 DOMIN COLONIAL WAR...SOC/WK 20   DIPLOM
LEAGUE/NAT UN. PAGE 98 E1955   INT/ORG
                                                    INT/LAW

C54
CALDWELL L.K.,"THE GOVERNMENT AND ADMINISTRATION OF PROVS
NEW YORK." LOC/G MUNIC POL/PAR SCHOOL CHIEF LEGIS   ADMIN
PLAN TAX CT/SYS...MGT SOC/WK BIBLIOG 20 NEWYORK/C. CONSTN
PAGE 19 E0365   EX/STRUC

B56
DUNNILL F.,THE CIVIL SERVICE. UK LAW PLAN ADMIN   PERSON
EFFICIENCY DRIVE NEW/LIB...STAT CHARTS 20   WORKER
PARLIAMENT CIVIL/SERV. PAGE 33 E0662   STRATA
                                                    SOC/WK

B58
MUSIKER R.,GUIDE TO SOUTH AFRICAN REFERENCE BOOKS. BIBLIOG/A
SOUTH/AFR SOCIETY SECT EDU/PROP PRESS RACE/REL   SOC
...JURID SOC/WK 20. PAGE 75 E1512   GEOG

B59
KERREMANS-RAMIOULL,LE PROBLEME DE LA DELINQUENCE   BIBLIOG
JUVENILE (2ND ED.). FAM PUB/INST SCHOOL FORCES   CRIME
LEGIS MORAL...CRIMLGY SOC 20. PAGE 60 E1205   AGE/Y
                                                    SOC/WK

B60
BORGATTA E.F.,SOCIAL WORKERS' PERCEPTIONS OF   SOC/WK
CLIENTS. SERV/IND ROUTINE PERS/REL DRIVE PERSON   ATTIT
RESPECT...SOC PERS/COMP 20. PAGE 14 E0268   CLIENT
                                                    PROB/SOLV

B62
BUREAU OF NATIONAL AFFAIRS,FEDERAL-STATE REGULATION WELF/ST
OF WELFARE FUNDS (REV. ED.). USA+45 LAW LEGIS   WEALTH
DEBATE AGE/O 20 CONGRESS. PAGE 17 E0337   PLAN
                                                    SOC/WK

B63
DOUGLAS W.O.,THE ANATOMY OF LIBERTY: THE RIGHTS OF PEACE
MAN WITHOUT FORCE. WOR+45 ECO/DEV ECO/UNDEV LOC/G   LAW
FORCES GOV/REL...SOC/WK 20. PAGE 32 E0643   DIPLOM
                                                    ORD/FREE

B63
FISCHER-GALATI S.A.,RUMANIA; A BIBLIOGRAPHIC GUIDE BIBLIOG/A
(PAMPHLET). ROMANIA INTELL ECO/DEV LABOR SECT   NAT/G
WEALTH...GEOG SOC/WK LING 20. PAGE 38 E0756   COM
                                                    LAW

B63
PALOTAI O.C.,PUBLICATIONS OF THE INSTITUTE OF   BIBLIOG/A
GOVERNMENT, 1930-1962. LAW PROVS SCHOOL WORKER   ADMIN
ACT/RES OP/RES CT/SYS GOV/REL...CRIMLGY SOC/WK.   LOC/G
PAGE 79 E1594   FINAN

B64
CHEIN I.,THE ROAD TO H; NARCOTICS, DELINQUENCY, AND BIO/SOC
SOCIAL POLICY. USA+45 NEIGH CRIME INGP/REL ATTIT   AGE/Y
PERSON...SOC/WK 20 NEWYORK/C. PAGE 22 E0426   POLICY
                                                    ANOMIE

B66
AMERICAN JEWISH COMMITTEE,GROUP RELATIONS IN THE   BIBLIOG/A
UNITED STATES: PROBLEMS AND PERSPECTIVES: A   USA+45
SELECTED, ANNOTATED BIBLIOGRAPHY (PAMPHLET). LAW   STRUCT
CONSTN STRATA SCHOOL SECT PROB/SOLV ATTIT...POLICY GP/REL
WELF/ST SOC/WK 20. PAGE 4 E0079

B66
AMERICAN JEWISH COMMITTEE,THE TYRANNY OF POVERTY   BIBLIOG/A
(PAMPHLET). USA+45 LAW ECO/DEV LOC/G MUNIC NAT/G   WEALTH
PUB/INST WORKER EDU/PROP CRIME...SOC/WK 20. PAGE 4 WELF/ST
E0080   PROB/SOLV

B66
BAHRO H.,DAS KINDSCHAFTSRECHT IN DER UNION DER   JURID
SOZIALISTITSCHEN SOWJETREPUBLIKEN. USSR SECT   AGE/C

EDU/PROP CONTROL PWR...SOC/WK 20. PAGE 7 E0133   PERS/REL
SUPEGO

B66
STEVENS R.E.,REFERENCE BOOKS IN THE SOCIAL SCIENCES   BIBLIOG/A
AND HUMANITIES. CULTURE PERF/ART SECT EDU/PROP   SOC
...JURID PSY SOC/WK STAT 20 MUSIC. PAGE 93 E1873   HUM
ART/METH

B67
BERNSTEIN S.,ALTERNATIVES TO VIOLENCE: ALIENATED   AGE/Y
YOUTH AND RIOTS, RACE AND POVERTY. MUNIC PUB/INST   SOC/WK
SCHOOL INGP/REL RACE/REL UTOPIA DRIVE HABITAT ROLE   NEIGH
WEALTH...INT 20. PAGE 11 E0215   CRIME

B67
BRAGER G.A.,COMMUNITY ACTION AGAINST POVERTY.   NEIGH
USA+45 LAW STRATA INGP/REL INCOME NEW/LIB...POLICY   WEALTH
WELF/ST ANTHOL. PAGE 15 E0285   SOC/WK
CREATE

B67
CHAPIN F.S. JR.,SELECTED REFERENCES ON URBAN   BIBLIOG
PLANNING METHODS AND TECHNIQUES. USA+45 LAW ECO/DEV   NEIGH
LOC/G NAT/G SCHOOL CONSULT CREATE PROB/SOLV TEC/DEV   MUNIC
SOC/WK. PAGE 21 E0420   PLAN

B67
HODGKINSON R.G.,THE ORIGINS OF THE NATIONAL HEALTH   HEAL
SERVICE: THE MEDICAL SERVICES OF THE NEW POOR LAW,   NAT/G
1834-1871. UK INDUS MUNIC WORKER PROB/SOLV   POLICY
EFFICIENCY ATTIT HEALTH WEALTH SOCISM...JURID   LAW
SOC/WK 19/20. PAGE 53 E1062

SOCIAL ANALYSIS....SEE SOC

SOCIAL CLASS....SEE STRATA

SOCIAL INSTITUTIONS....SEE INSTITUTIONAL INDEX

SOCIAL MOBILITY....SEE STRATA

SOCIAL PSYCHOLOGY (GROUPS)....SEE SOC

SOCIAL PSYCHOLOGY (INDIVIDUALS)....SEE PSY

SOCIAL STRUCTURE....SEE STRUCT

SOCIAL WORK....SEE SOC/WK

SOCIAL STRUCTURE....SEE STRUCT, STRATA

SOCIALISM....SEE SOCISM, SOCIALIST

SOCIALIST....NON-COMMUNIST SOCIALIST; SEE ALSO SOCISM

B11
REINSCH P.,PUBLIC INTERNATIONAL UNION. WOR-45 LAW   FUT
LABOR INT/TRADE LEGIT PERSON ALL/VALS...SOCIALIST   INT/ORG
CONCPT TIME/SEQ TREND GEN/LAWS 19/20. PAGE 84 E1683   DIPLOM

B15
HOBSON J.A.,TOWARDS INTERNATIONAL GOVERNMENT.   FUT
MOD/EUR STRUCT ECO/TAC EDU/PROP ADJUD ALL/VALS   INT/ORG
...SOCIALIST CONCPT GEN/LAWS TOT/POP 20. PAGE 53   CENTRAL
E1059

B42
HAMBRO C.J.,HOW TO WIN THE PEACE. ECO/TAC EDU/PROP   FUT
ADJUD PERSON ALL/VALS...SOCIALIST TREND GEN/LAWS   INT/ORG
20. PAGE 50 E0987   PEACE

SOCIALIZATION....SEE ADJUST

SOCIETE DES NATIONS E1851

SOCIETY....SOCIETY AS A WHOLE

SOCIOLOGY....SEE SOC

SOCIOLOGY OF KNOWLEDGE....SEE EPIST

SOCISM....SOCIALISM; SEE ALSO SOCIALIST

B03
FAGUET E.,LE LIBERALISME. FRANCE PRESS ADJUD ADMIN   ORD/FREE
DISCRIM CONSERVE SOCISM...TRADIT SOC LING WORSHIP   EDU/PROP
PARLIAMENT. PAGE 36 E0711   NAT/G
LAW

B03
GRIFFIN A.P.C.,LISTS PUBLISHED 1902-03: GOVERNMENT   BIBLIOG
OWNERSHIP OF RAILROADS (PAMPHLET). USA-45 LAW NAT/G   DIST/IND
RATION GOV/REL CENTRAL SOCISM...POLICY 19/20.   CONTROL
PAGE 46 E0922   ADJUD

B05
GRIFFIN A.P.C.,LIST OF BOOKS ON RAILROADS IN   BIBLIOG/A
FOREIGN COUNTRIES. MOD/EUR ECO/DEV NAT/G CONTROL   SERV/IND
SOCISM...JURID 19/20 RAILROAD. PAGE 47 E0927   ADMIN
DIST/IND

B12
POLLOCK F.,THE GENIUS OF THE COMMON LAW. CHRIST-17C   LAW
UK FINAN CHIEF ACT/RES ADMIN GP/REL ATTIT SOCISM   CULTURE
...ANARCH JURID. PAGE 81 E1624   CREATE

N19
IN THE SHADOW OF FEAR; AMERICAN CIVIL LIBERTIES,   ORD/FREE
1948-49 (PAMPHLET). COM LAW LEGIS BAL/PWR EDU/PROP   CONSTN
CT/SYS RACE/REL DISCRIM MARXISM SOCISM 20 COLD/WAR   POLICY
CONGRESS ACLU CIV/RIGHTS ESPIONAGE. PAGE 2 E0030

B20
COX H.,ECONOMIC LIBERTY. UNIV LAW INT/TRADE RATION   NAT/G
TARIFFS RACE/REL SOCISM POLICY. PAGE 27 E0535   ORD/FREE
ECO/TAC
PERSON

B22
SCHROEDER T.,FREE SPEECH BIBLIOGRAPHY. EUR+WWI   BIBLIOG/A
WOR-45 NAT/G SECT ECO/TAC WRITING ADJUD ATTIT   ORD/FREE
MARXISM SOCISM 16/20. PAGE 88 E1768   CONTROL
LAW

B24
NAVILLE A.,LIBERTE, EGALITE, SOLIDARITE: ESSAIS   ORD/FREE
D'ANALYSE. STRATA FAM VOL/ASSN INT/TRADE GP/REL   SOC
MORAL MARXISM SOCISM...PSY TREATY. PAGE 76 E1529   IDEA/COMP
DIPLOM

B27
RYAN J.A.,DECLINING LIVERTY AND OTHER ESSAYS.   ORD/FREE
USA-45 SECT DELIB/GP ATTIT PWR SOCISM 20   LEGIS
SUPREME/CT. PAGE 87 E1740   JURID
NAT/G

B37
BORGESE G.A.,GOLIATH: THE MARCH OF FASCISM. GERMANY   POLICY
ITALY LAW POL/PAR SECT DIPLOM SOCISM...JURID MYTH   NAT/LISM
20 DANTE MACHIAVELL MUSSOLIN/B. PAGE 14 E0270   FASCISM
NAT/G

S40
FLORIN J.,"BOLSHEVIST AND NATIONAL SOCIALIST   LAW
DOCTRINES OF INTERNATIONAL LAW." EUR+WWI GERMANY   ATTIT
USSR R+D INT/ORG NAT/G DIPLOM DOMIN EDU/PROP SOCISM   TOTALISM
...CONCPT TIME/SEQ 20. PAGE 39 E0768   INT/LAW

S44
GRIFFITH E.S.,"THE CHANGING PATTERN OF PUBLIC   LAW
POLICY FORMATION." MOD/EUR WOR+45 FINAN CHIEF   POLICY
CONFER ADMIN LEAD CONSERVE SOCISM TECHRACY...SOC   TEC/DEV
CHARTS CONGRESS. PAGE 47 E0938

B48
YAKOBSON S.,FIVE HUNDRED RUSSIAN WORKS FOR COLLEGE   BIBLIOG
LIBRARIES (PAMPHLET). MOD/EUR USSR MARXISM SOCISM   NAT/G
...ART/METH GEOG HUM JURID SOC 13/20. PAGE 108   CULTURE
E2162   COM

B50
BERMAN H.J.,JUSTICE IN RUSSIA; AN INTERPRETATION OF   JURID
SOVIET LAW. USSR LAW STRUCT LABOR FORCES AGREE   ADJUD
GP/REL ORD/FREE SOCISM...TIME/SEQ 20. PAGE 11 E0207   MARXISM
COERCE

B50
MONPIED E.,BIBLIOGRAPHIE FEDERALISTE: OUVRAGES   BIBLIOG/A
CHOISIS (VOL. I, MIMEOGRAPHED PAPER). EUR+WWI   FEDERAL
DIPLOM ADMIN REGION ATTIT PACIFISM SOCISM...INT/LAW   CENTRAL
19/20. PAGE 74 E1486   INT/ORG

N51
MONPIED E.,FEDERALIST BIBLIOGRAPHY: ARTICLES AND   BIBLIOG/A
DOCUMENTS PUBLISHED IN BRITISH PERIODICALS   INT/ORG
1945-1951 (MIMEOGRAPHED). EUR+WWI UK WOR+45 DIPLOM   FEDERAL
REGION ATTIT SOCISM...INT/LAW 20. PAGE 74 E1487   CENTRAL

B52
APPADORAI A.,THE SUBSTANCE OF POLITICS (6TH ED.).   PHIL/SCI
EX/STRUC LEGIS DIPLOM CT/SYS CHOOSE FASCISM MARXISM   NAT/G
SOCISM...BIBLIOG T. PAGE 5 E0100

B52
GELLHORN W.,THE STATES AND SUBVERSION. USA+45   PROVS

USA-45 LOC/G DELIB/GP LEGIS EDU/PROP LEGIT CT/SYS   JURID
REGION PEACE ATTIT ORD/FREE SOCISM...INT CON/ANAL
20 CALIFORNIA MARYLAND ILLINOIS MICHIGAN NEW/YORK.
PAGE 43 E0845

                                                     B54
FRIEDMAN W.,THE PUBLIC CORPORATION: A COMPARATIVE   LAW
SYMPOSIUM (UNIVERSITY OF TORONTO SCHOOL OF LAW   SOCISM
COMPARATIVE LAW SERIES. VOL. I). SWEDEN USA+45   LG/CO
INDUS INT/ORG NAT/G REGION CENTRAL FEDERAL...POLICY OWN
JURID IDEA/COMP NAT/COMP ANTHOL 20 COMMONWLTH
MONOPOLY EUROPE. PAGE 40 E0801

                                                     B57
FAIRCHILD H.P.,THE ANATOMY OF FREEDOM. USA+45   ORD/FREE
ACADEM SCHOOL SECT CAP/ISM PRESS CHOOSE SOCISM.   CONCPT
PAGE 36 E0712   NAT/G
                                                     JURID

                                                     B59
HOOK S.,POLITICAL POWER AND PERSONAL FREEDOM: ORD/FREE
CRITICAL STUDIES IN DEMOCRACY, COMMUNISM AND CIVIL   PWR
RIGHTS. UNIV LAW SOCIETY DIPLOM TOTALISM MARXISM   WELF/ST
SOCISM...PHIL/SCI IDEA/COMP 20 CIV/RIGHTS. PAGE 55   CHOOSE
E1094

                                                     S59
CARLSTON K.S.,"NATIONALIZATION: AN ANALYTIC   INDUS
APPROACH." WOR+45 INT/ORG ECO/TAC DOMIN LEGIT ADJUD NAT/G
COERCE ORD/FREE PWR WEALTH SOCISM...JURID CONCPT   NAT/LISM
TREND STERTYP TOT/POP VAL/FREE 20. PAGE 19 E0380   SOVEREIGN

                                                     B61
ALFRED H.,PUBLIC OWNERSHIP IN THE USA: GOALS AND   CONTROL
PRIORITIES. LAW INDUS INT/TRADE ADJUD GOV/REL   OWN
EFFICIENCY PEACE SOCISM...POLICY ANTHOL 20 TVA.   ECO/DEV
PAGE 3 E0064   ECO/TAC

                                                     B61
LA PONCE J.A.,THE GOVERNMENT OF THE FIFTH REPUBLIC: PWR
FRENCH POLITICAL PARTIES AND THE CONSTITUTION.   POL/PAR
ALGERIA FRANCE LAW NAT/G DELIB/GP LEGIS ECO/TAC   CONSTN
MARXISM SOCISM...CHARTS BIBLIOG/A 20 DEGAULLE/C.   CHIEF
PAGE 62 E1243

                                                     B62
GRZYBOWSKI K.,SOVIET LEGAL INSTITUTIONS. USA+45   ADJUD
USSR ECO/DEV NAT/G EDU/PROP CONTROL CT/SYS CRIME   LAW
OWN ATTIT PWR SOCISM...NAT/COMP 20. PAGE 48 E0955   JURID

                                                     B64
GRIFFITH W.E.,THE SINO-SOVIET RIFT. ASIA CHINA/COM   ATTIT
COM CUBA USSR YUGOSLAVIA NAT/G POL/PAR VOL/ASSN   TIME/SEQ
DELIB/GP FORCES TOP/EX DIPLOM EDU/PROP DRIVE PERSON BAL/PWR
PWR...TREND 20 TREATY. PAGE 47 E0941   SOCISM

                                                     B64
GRZYBOWSKI K.,THE SOCIALIST COMMONWEALTH OF   INT/LAW
NATIONS: ORGANIZATIONS AND INSTITUTIONS. FORCES   COM
DIPLOM INT/TRADE ADJUD ADMIN LEAD WAR MARXISM   REGION
SOCISM...BIBLIOG 20 COMECON WARSAW/P. PAGE 48 E0956 INT/ORG

                                                     B64
GUMPLOWICZ L.,RECHTSSTAAT UND SOZIALISMUS. STRATA   JURID
ORD/FREE SOVEREIGN MARXISM...IDEA/COMP 16/20 KANT/I NAT/G
HOBBES/T. PAGE 48 E0962   SOCISM
                                                     CONCPT

                                                     B64
WAY H.F. JR.,LIBERTY IN THE BALANCE - CURRENT   ORD/FREE
ISSUES IN CIVIL LIBERTIES. USA+45 USA-45 DELIB/GP   EDU/PROP
RACE/REL DISCRIM TOTALISM MARXISM SOCISM...CONCPT   NAT/G
20 CONGRESS SUPREME/CT CIVIL/LIB. PAGE 105 E2104   JURID

                                                     B65
BOVY L.,LE MOUVEMENT SYNDICAL OUEST AFRICAIN   BIBLIOG
D'EXPRESSION FRANCAISE. AFR SECT...JURID SOC 20.   SOCISM
PAGE 14 E0275   ECO/UNDEV
                                                     IDEA/COMP

                                                     B66
AUERBACH J.S.,LABOR AND LIBERTY; THE LA FOLLETTE   DELIB/GP
COMMITTEE AND THE NEW DEAL. USA-45 LAW LEAD RESPECT LABOR
SOCISM...BIBLIOG 20 CONGRESS BILL/RIGHT LAFOLLET/R   CONSTN
NEW/DEAL. PAGE 6 E0117   ORD/FREE

                                                     B67
BOULTON D.,OBJECTION OVERRULED. UK LAW POL/PAR   FORCES
DIPLOM ADJUD SANCTION DEATH WAR CIVMIL/REL 20.   SOCISM
PAGE 14 E0273   SECT

                                                     B67
HODGKINSON R.G.,THE ORIGINS OF THE NATIONAL HEALTH   HEAL
SERVICE: THE MEDICAL SERVICES OF THE NEW POOR LAW,   NAT/G
1834-1871. UK INDUS MUNIC WORKER PROB/SOLV   POLICY
EFFICIENCY ATTIT HEALTH WEALTH SOCISM...JURID   LAW

SOC/WK 19/20. PAGE 53 E1062

SOCRATES....SOCRATES

SOHN L.B. E0449,E0450,E1852,E1853,E1854,E1855

SOLOMONS....THE SOLOMON ISLANDS

SOMALIA....SOMALIA; SEE ALSO AFR

SOMMER T. E1856

SONDERMANN F.A. E1575

SONGAI....SONGAI EMPIRES (AFRICA)

SOPER T. E1857

SOREL/G....GEORGES SOREL

SOUPHANGOU....PRINCE SOUPHANGOU-VONG (LEADER OF PATHET LAO)

SOUTH KOREA....SEE KOREA/S

SOUTH VIETNAM....SEE VIETNAM

SOUTH WEST AFRICA....SEE AFRICA/SW

SOUTH AFRICA STATE LIBRARY E1858

SOUTH/AFR....UNION OF SOUTH AFRICA

                                                     N
SOUTH AFRICA STATE LIBRARY,SOUTH AFRICAN NATIONAL   BIBLIOG
BIBLIOGRAPHY, SANB. SOUTH/AFR LAW NAT/G EDU/PROP   PRESS
...MGT PSY SOC 20. PAGE 93 E1858   WRITING

                                                     B00
BATY T.,INTERNATIONAL LAW IN SOUTH AFRICA. AFR   JURID
SOUTH/AFR LAW CONFER 19/20. PAGE 8 E0155   WAR
                                                     SOVEREIGN
                                                     COLONIAL

                                                     B01
BRYCE J.,STUDIES IN HISTORY AND JURISPRUDENCE (2   IDEA/COMP
VOLS.). ICELAND SOUTH/AFR UK LAW PROB/SOLV   CONSTN
SOVEREIGN...PHIL/SCI NAT/COMP ROME/ANC ROMAN/LAW.   JURID
PAGE 16 E0321

                                                     B10
MENDELSSOHN S.,MENDELSSOHN'S SOUTH AFRICA   BIBLIOG/A
BIBLIOGRAPHY (VOL. I). SOUTH/AFR RACE/REL...GEOG   CULTURE
JURID 19/20. PAGE 72 E1440

                                                     B18
EYBERS G.W.,SELECT CONSTITUTIONAL DOCUMENTS   CONSTN
ILLUSTRATING SOUTH AFRICAN HISTORY 1795-1910.   LAW
SOUTH/AFR LOC/G LEGIS CT/SYS...JURID ANTHOL 18/20   NAT/G
NATAL CAPE/HOPE ORANGE/STA. PAGE 36 E0707   COLONIAL

                                                     B34
EVANS I.L.,NATIVE POLICY IN SOUTHERN AFRICA.   AFR
RHODESIA SOUTH/AFR UK STRUCT PARTIC RACE/REL ATTIT   COLONIAL
WEALTH SOC/INTEG AFRICA/SW. PAGE 35 E0705   DOMIN
                                                     LAW

                                                     B35
KENNEDY W.P.,THE LAW AND CUSTOM OF THE SOUTH   CT/SYS
AFRICAN CONSTITUTION. AFR SOUTH/AFR KIN LOC/G PROVS CONSTN
DIPLOM ADJUD ADMIN EXEC 20. PAGE 60 E1203   JURID
                                                     PARL/PROC

                                                     B50
MOCKFORD J.,SOUTH-WEST AFRICA AND THE INTERNATIONAL COLONIAL
COURT (PAMPHLET). AFR GERMANY SOUTH/AFR UK   SOVEREIGN
ECO/UNDEV DIPLOM CONTROL DISCRIM...DECISION JURID   INT/LAW
20 AFRICA/SW. PAGE 74 E1475   DOMIN

                                                     B56
KUPER L.,PASSIVE RESISTANCE IN SOUTH AFRICA.   ORD/FREE
SOUTH/AFR LAW NAT/G POL/PAR VOL/ASSN DISCRIM   RACE/REL
...POLICY SOC AUD/VIS 20. PAGE 62 E1237   ATTIT

                                                     B58
MUSIKER R.,GUIDE TO SOUTH AFRICAN REFERENCE BOOKS.   BIBLIOG/A
SOUTH/AFR SOCIETY SECT EDU/PROP PRESS RACE/REL   SOC
...JURID SOC/WK 20. PAGE 75 E1512   GEOG

                                                     B61
COWEN D.V.,THE FOUNDATIONS OF FREEDOM. AFR   CONSTN
SOUTH/AFR DOMIN LEGIT ADJUST DISCRIM TOTALISM ATTIT ELITES
ORD/FREE...MAJORIT JURID SOC/INTEG WORSHIP 20   RACE/REL

NEGRO. PAGE 27 E0529

SOUTH/DAK....SOUTH DAKOTA

SOUTH/US....SOUTH (UNITED STATES)

B63
BROOKES E.H.,POWER, LAW, RIGHT, AND LOVE: A STUDY   PWR
IN POLITICAL VALUES. SOUTH/AFR NAT/G PERSON   ORD/FREE
...CONCPT IDEA/COMP 20. PAGE 16 E0308   JURID
  LOVE

B63
HORRELL M.,LEGISLATION AND RACE RELATIONS   LAW
(PAMPHLET). SOUTH/AFR SCHOOL TAX DOMIN CONTROL 20.   RACE/REL
PAGE 55 E1098   DISCRIM
  PARTIC

B63
JOSEPH H.,IF THIS BE TREASON. SOUTH/AFR 20. PAGE 59   AFR
E1174   LAW
  CT/SYS
  CRIME

B63
LEWIN J.,POLITICS AND LAW IN SOUTH AFRICA.   NAT/LISM
SOUTH/AFR UK POL/PAR BAL/PWR ECO/TAC COLONIAL   POLICY
CONTROL GP/REL DISCRIM PWR 20 NEGRO. PAGE 65 E1293   LAW
  RACE/REL

S63
HARNETTY P.,"CANADA, SOUTH AFRICA AND THE   AFR
COMMONWEALTH." CANADA SOUTH/AFR LAW INT/ORG   ATTIT
VOL/ASSN DELIB/GP LEGIS TOP/EX ECO/TAC LEGIT DRIVE
MORAL...CONCPT CMN/WLTH 20. PAGE 50 E1000

B64
HOPKINSON T.,SOUTH AFRICA. SOUTH/AFR UK NAT/G   SOCIETY
POL/PAR LEGIS ECO/TAC PARL/PROC WAR...JURID AUD/VIS   RACE/REL
19/20. PAGE 55 E1097   DISCRIM

B64
SEGAL R.,SANCTIONS AGAINST SOUTH AFRICA. AFR   SANCTION
SOUTH/AFR NAT/G INT/TRADE RACE/REL PEACE PWR   DISCRIM
...INT/LAW ANTHOL 20 UN. PAGE 90 E1801   ECO/TAC
  POLICY

B65
KARIS T.,THE TREASON TRIAL IN SOUTH AFRICA: A GUIDE   BIBLIOG/A
TO THE MICROFILM RECORD OF THE TRIAL. SOUTH/AFR LAW   ADJUD
ELITES NAT/G LEGIT CT/SYS RACE/REL DISCRIM...SOC   CRIME
20. PAGE 59 E1185   AFR

B66
EDWARDS C.D.,TRADE REGULATIONS OVERSEAS. IRELAND   INT/TRADE
NEW/ZEALND SOUTH/AFR NAT/G CAP/ISM TARIFFS CONTROL   DIPLOM
...POLICY JURID 20 EEC CHINJAP. PAGE 34 E0676   INT/LAW
  ECO/TAC

L66
HIGGINS R.,"THE INTERNATIONAL COURT AND SOUTH WEST   SOUTH/AFR
AFRICA: SOME IMPLICATIONS OF THE JUDGMENT." AFR LAW   COLONIAL
ECO/UNDEV JUDGE RACE/REL COST PWR...INT/LAW TREND   CT/SYS
UN TREATY. PAGE 52 E1043   ADJUD

B67
NARAIN I.,THE POLITICS OF RACIALISM. INDIA   DISCRIM
SOUTH/AFR LAW NAT/G RACE/REL ATTIT 20. PAGE 76   COLONIAL
E1521   HIST/WRIT

S68
DUGARD J.,"THE REVOCATION OF THE MANDATE FOR SOUTH   AFR
WEST AFRICA." SOUTH/AFR WOR+45 STRATA NAT/G   INT/ORG
DELIB/GP DIPLOM ADJUD SANCTION CHOOSE RACE/REL   DISCRIM
...POLICY NAT/COMP 20 AFRICA/SW UN TRUST/TERR   COLONIAL
LEAGUE/NAT. PAGE 33 E0654

B99
BROOKS S.,BRITAIN AND THE BOERS. AFR SOUTH/AFR UK   WAR
CULTURE INSPECT LEGIT...INT/LAW 19/20 BOER/WAR.   DIPLOM
PAGE 16 E0309   NAT/G

SOUTH/AMER....SOUTH AMERICA

SOUTH/CAR....SOUTH CAROLINA

B30
GREEN F.M.,CONSTITUTIONAL DEVELOPMENT IN THE SOUTH   CONSTN
ATLANTIC STATES, 1776-1860; A STUDY IN THE   PROVS
EVOLUTION OF DEMOCRACY. USA-45 ELITES SOCIETY   PLURISM
STRATA ECO/DEV AGRI POL/PAR EX/STRUC LEGIS CT/SYS   REPRESENT
REGION...BIBLIOG 18/19 MARYLAND VIRGINIA GEORGIA
NORTH/CAR SOUTH/CAR. PAGE 46 E0905

B63
BROWN R.M.,THE SOUTH CAROLINA REGULATORS. USA-45   ORD/FREE
LEGIS LEGIT ADJUD COLONIAL CONTROL WAR...BIBLIOG/A   JURID
18 CHARLESTON SOUTH/CAR. PAGE 16 E0315   PWR
  PROVS

S45
DAVIS A.,"CASTE, ECONOMY, AND VIOLENCE" (BMR)"   STRATA
USA-45 LAW SOCIETY STRUCT SECT SANCTION COERCE   RACE/REL
MARRIAGE SEX...PSY SOC SOC/INTEG 18/20 NEGRO   DISCRIM
MISCEGEN SOUTH/US. PAGE 29 E0570

B57
ROWAN C.T.,GO SOUTH TO SORROW. USA+45 STRUCT NAT/G   RACE/REL
EDU/PROP LEAD COERCE ISOLAT DRIVE SUPEGO RESPECT   DISCRIM
...PREDICT 20 NEGRO SUPREME/CT SOUTH/US CIV/RIGHTS.   ANOMIE
PAGE 86 E1728   LAW

B58
CABLE G.W.,THE NEGRO QUESTION: A SELECTION OF   RACE/REL
WRITINGS ON CIVIL RIGHTS IN THE SOUTH. USA+45   CULTURE
STRATA LOC/G POL/PAR GIVE EDU/PROP WRITING CT/SYS   DISCRIM
SANCTION CRIME CHOOSE WORSHIP 20 NEGRO CIV/RIGHTS   ORD/FREE
CONV/LEASE SOUTH/US. PAGE 18 E0355

B58
OGDEN F.D.,THE POLL TAX IN THE SOUTH. USA+45 USA-45   TAX
CONSTN ADJUD ADMIN PARTIC CRIME...TIME/SEQ GOV/COMP   CHOOSE
METH/COMP 18/20 SOUTH/US. PAGE 78 E1572   RACE/REL
  DISCRIM

B62
MITCHELL G.E.,THE ANGRY BLACK SOUTH. USA+45 LAW   RACE/REL
CONSTN SCHOOL DELIB/GP EDU/PROP CONTROL SUFF ANOMIE   DISCRIM
DRIVE...ANTHOL 20 NEGRO CIV/RIGHTS SOUTH/US.   ADJUST
PAGE 74 E1473   ORD/FREE

B65
FRIEDMAN L.,SOUTHERN JUSTICE. USA+45 PUB/INST LEGIT   ADJUD
ADMIN CT/SYS DISCRIM...DECISION ANTHOL 20 NEGRO   LAW
SOUTH/US CIV/RIGHTS. PAGE 40 E0800   CONSTN
  RACE/REL

B66
KUNSTLER W.M.,"DEEP IN MY HEART" USA+45 LAW   CT/SYS
PROF/ORG SECT LOBBY PARTIC CROWD DISCRIM ROLE   RACE/REL
...BIOG 20 KING/MAR/L NEGRO CIV/RIGHTS SOUTH/US.   ADJUD
PAGE 62 E1233   CONSULT

B67
GRAHAM H.D.,CRISIS IN PRINT: DESEGREGATION AND THE   PRESS
PRESS IN TENNESSEE. LAW SOCIETY MUNIC POL/PAR   PROVS
EDU/PROP LEAD REPRESENT DISCRIM ATTIT...IDEA/COMP   POLICY
BIBLIOG/A SOC/INTEG 20 TENNESSEE SUPREME/CT   RACE/REL
SOUTH/US. PAGE 45 E0896

SOUTHEAST ASIA....SEE S/EASTASIA, S/ASIA

SOUTHEAST ASIA TREATY ORGANIZATION....SEE SEATO

SOUTHERN RHODESIA....SEE RHODESIA, COMMONWLTH

SOVEREIGN....SOVEREIGNTY

B00
BATY T.,INTERNATIONAL LAW IN SOUTH AFRICA. AFR   JURID
SOUTH/AFR LAW CONFER 19/20. PAGE 8 E0155   WAR
  SOVEREIGN
  COLONIAL

B00
DARBY W.E.,INTERNATIONAL TRIBUNALS. WOR-45 NAT/G   INT/ORG
ECO/TAC DOMIN LEGIT CT/SYS COERCE ORD/FREE PWR   ADJUD
SOVEREIGN JURID. PAGE 29 E0567   PEACE
  INT/LAW

B00
DE TOCQUEVILLE A.,DEMOCRACY IN AMERICA (VOLUME   USA-45
ONE). LAW SOCIETY STRUCT NAT/G POL/PAR PROVS FORCES   TREND
LEGIS TOP/EX DIPLOM LEGIT WAR PEACE ATTIT SOVEREIGN
...SELF/OBS TIME/SEQ CONGRESS 19. PAGE 30 E0594

B00
HOLLAND T.E.,STUDIES IN INTERNATIONAL LAW. TURKEY   INT/ORG
USSR WOR-45 CONSTN NAT/G DIPLOM DOMIN LEGIT COERCE   LAW
WAR PEACE ORD/FREE PWR SOVEREIGN...JURID CHARTS 20   INT/LAW
PARLIAMENT SUEZ TREATY. PAGE 54 E1084

B00
LORIMER J.,THE INSTITUTES OF THE LAW OF NATIONS.   INT/ORG
WOR-45 CULTURE SOCIETY NAT/G VOL/ASSN DIPLOM LEGIT   LAW
WAR PEACE DRIVE ORD/FREE SOVEREIGN...CONCPT RECORD   INT/LAW
INT TREND HYPO/EXP GEN/METH TOT/POP VAL/FREE 20.
PAGE 66 E1327

B01
BRYCE J.,STUDIES IN HISTORY AND JURISPRUDENCE (2   IDEA/COMP
VOLS.). ICELAND SOUTH/AFR UK LAW PROB/SOLV   CONSTN

SOVEREIGN...PHIL/SCI NAT/COMP ROME/ANC ROMAN/LAW. JURID
PAGE 16 E0321

C05
DUNNING W.A.."HISTORY OF POLITICAL THEORIES FROM PHIL/SCI
LUTHER TO MONTESQUIEU." LAW NAT/G SECT DIPLOM REV CONCPT
WAR ORD/FREE SOVEREIGN CONSERVE...TRADIT BIBLIOG GEN/LAWS
16/18. PAGE 33 E0663

B08
GRIFFIN A.P.C..LIST OF REFERENCES ON INTERNATIONAL BIBLIOG/A
ARBITRATION. FRANCE L/A+17C USA-45 WOR-45 DIPLOM INT/ORG
CONFER COLONIAL ARMS/CONT BAL/PAY EQUILIB SOVEREIGN INT/LAW
...DECISION 19/20 MEXIC/AMER. PAGE 47 E0932 DELIB/GP

B19
DUGUIT L..LAW IN THE MODERN STATE (TRANS. BY FRIDA GEN/LAWS
AND HAROLD LASKI). CONSTN SOCIETY STRUCT MORAL CONCPT
ORD/FREE SOVEREIGN 20. PAGE 33 E0655 NAT/G
LAW

N19
BRENNAN W.J. JR..THE BILL OF RIGHTS AND THE STATES CONSTN
(PAMPHLET). USA+45 USA-45 LEGIS BAL/PWR ADJUD PROVS
CT/SYS FEDERAL PWR SOVEREIGN 18/20 SUPREME/CT GOV/REL
BILL/RIGHT. PAGE 15 E0293 ORD/FREE

N19
MEZERIK AG,OUTER SPACE: UN, US, USSR (PAMPHLET). SPACE
USSR DELIB/GP FORCES DETER NUC/PWR SOVEREIGN CONTROL
...POLICY 20 UN TREATY. PAGE 73 E1453 DIPLOM
INT/ORG

B20
DICKINSON E..THE EQUALITY OF STATES IN LAW
INTERNATIONAL LAW. WOR-45 INT/ORG NAT/G DIPLOM CONCPT
EDU/PROP LEGIT PEACE ATTIT ALL/VALS...JURID SOVEREIGN
TIME/SEQ LEAGUE/NAT. PAGE 31 E0622

B21
STOWELL E.C..INTERVENTION IN INTERNATIONAL LAW. BAL/PWR
UNIV LAW SOCIETY INT/ORG ACT/RES PLAN LEGIT ROUTINE SOVEREIGN
WAR...JURID OBS GEN/LAWS 20. PAGE 94 E1884

B22
MYERS D.P..MANUAL OF COLLECTIONS OF TREATIES AND OF BIBLIOG/A
COLLECTIONS RELATING TO TREATIES. MOD/EUR INT/ORG DIPLOM
LEGIS WRITING ADMIN SOVEREIGN...INT/LAW 19/20. CONFER
PAGE 75 E1514

C24
BARNES H.E.."SOCIOLOGY AND POLITICAL THEORY: A CONCPT
CONSIDERATION OF THE SOCIOLOGICAL BASIS OF STRUCT
POLITICS." LAW CONSTN NAT/G DIPLOM DOMIN ROUTINE SOC
REV ORD/FREE SOVEREIGN...PHIL/SCI CLASSIF BIBLIOG
18/20. PAGE 8 E0151

B27
LAUTERPACHT H..PRIVATE LAW SOURCES AND ANALOGIES OF INT/ORG
INTERNATIONAL LAW. WOR-45 NAT/G DELIB/GP LEGIT ADJUD
COERCE ATTIT ORD/FREE PWR SOVEREIGN...JURID CONCPT PEACE
HIST/WRIT TIME/SEQ GEN/METH LEAGUE/NAT. PAGE 63 INT/LAW
E1264

B28
HOBBES T..THE ELEMENTS OF LAW, NATURAL AND POLITIC PERSON
(1650). STRATA NAT/G SECT CHIEF AGREE ATTIT LAW
ALL/VALS MORAL ORD/FREE POPULISM...POLICY CONCPT. SOVEREIGN
PAGE 53 E1056 CONSERVE

B28
MAIR L.P..THE PROTECTION OF MINORITIES. EUR+WWI LAW
WOR-45 CONSTN INT/ORG NAT/G LEGIT CT/SYS GP/REL SOVEREIGN
RACE/REL DISCRIM ORD/FREE RESPECT...JURID CONCPT
TIME/SEQ 20. PAGE 68 E1352

B29
BUELL R..INTERNATIONAL RELATIONS. WOR+45 WOR-45 INT/ORG
CONSTN STRATA FORCES TOP/EX ADMIN ATTIT DRIVE BAL/PWR
SUPEGO MORAL ORD/FREE PWR SOVEREIGN...JURID SOC DIPLOM
CONCPT 20. PAGE 17 E0326

B30
BURLAMAQUI J.J..PRINCIPLES OF NATURAL AND POLITIC LAW
LAW (2 VOLS.) (1747-51). EX/STRUC LEGIS AGREE NAT/G
CT/SYS CHOOSE ROLE SOVEREIGN 18 NATURL/LAW. PAGE 17 ORD/FREE
E0342 CONCPT

B30
WILLOUGHBY W.W..PRINCIPLES OF THE CONSTITUTIONAL CONSTN
LAW OF THE UNITED STATES. USA-45 ADJUD FEDERAL NAT/G
SOVEREIGN 18/20 COMMON/LAW. PAGE 106 E2125 CONCPT
JURID

B32
FLEMMING D..THE UNITED STATES AND THE LEAGUE OF INT/ORG

NATIONS, 1918-1920. FUT USA-45 NAT/G LEGIS TOP/EX EDU/PROP
DEBATE CHOOSE PEACE ATTIT SOVEREIGN...TIME/SEQ
CON/ANAL CONGRESS LEAGUE/NAT 20 TREATY. PAGE 39
E0764

B32
GREAT BRIT COMM MINISTERS PWR,REPORT. UK LAW CONSTN EX/STRUC
CONSULT LEGIS PARL/PROC SANCTION SOVEREIGN NAT/G
...DECISION JURID 20 PARLIAMENT. PAGE 45 E0902 PWR
CONTROL

B33
GENTILI A..DE JURE BELLI, LIBRI TRES (1612) (VOL. WAR
2). FORCES DIPLOM AGREE PEACE SOVEREIGN. PAGE 43 INT/LAW
E0849 MORAL
SUPEGO

B33
LAUTERPACHT H..THE FUNCTION OF LAW IN THE INT/ORG
INTERNATIONAL COMMUNITY. WOR-45 NAT/G FORCES CREATE LAW
DOMIN LEGIT COERCE WAR PEACE ATTIT ORD/FREE PWR INT/LAW
SOVEREIGN...JURID CONCPT METH/CNCPT TIME/SEQ
GEN/LAWS GEN/METH LEAGUE/NAT TOT/POP VAL/FREE 20.
PAGE 63 E1265

B36
RUSSEL F.M..THEORIES OF INTERNATIONAL RELATIONS. PWR
EUR+WWI FUT MOD/EUR USA-45 INT/ORG DIPLOM...JURID POLICY
CONCPT. PAGE 86 E1735 BAL/PWR
SOVEREIGN

L37
LERNER M.."CONSTITUTION AND COURT AS SYMBOLS" CONSTN
(BMR)" USA+45 USA-45 DOMIN PWR SOVEREIGN...PSY MYTH CT/SYS
18/20 SUPREME/CT. PAGE 64 E1288 ATTIT
EDU/PROP

B38
POUND R..THE FORMATIVE ERA OF AMERICAN LAW. CULTURE CONSTN
NAT/G PROVS LEGIS ADJUD CT/SYS PERSON SOVEREIGN LAW
...POLICY IDEA/COMP GEN/LAWS 18/19. PAGE 82 E1637 CREATE
JURID

B38
SAINT-PIERRE C.I..SCHEME FOR LASTING PEACE (TRANS. INT/ORG
BY H. BELLOT). INDUS NAT/G CHIEF FORCES INT/TRADE PEACE
CT/SYS WAR PWR SOVEREIGN WEALTH...POLICY 18. AGREE
PAGE 87 E1741 INT/LAW

B39
MCILWAIN C.H..CONSTITUTIONALISM AND THE CHANGING CONSTN
WORLD. UK USA-45 LEGIS PRIVIL AUTHORIT SOVEREIGN POLICY
...GOV/COMP 15/20 MAGNA/CART HOUSE/CMNS. PAGE 71 JURID
E1417

B40
HOBBES T..A DIALOGUE BETWEEN A PHILOSOPHER AND A CT/SYS
STUDENT OF THE COMMON LAWS OF ENGLAND (1667?). UK CHIEF
SECT DOMIN ADJUD CRIME INCOME OWN UTIL ORD/FREE PWR SANCTION
SOVEREIGN...JURID GEN/LAWS 17. PAGE 53 E1057

S41
WRIGHT Q.."FUNDAMENTAL PROBLEMS OF INTERNATIONAL INT/ORG
ORGANIZATION." UNIV WOR-45 STRUCT FORCES ACT/RES ATTIT
CREATE DOMIN EDU/PROP LEGIT REGION NAT/LISM PEACE
ORD/FREE PWR RESPECT SOVEREIGN...JURID SOC CONCPT
METH/CNCPT TIME/SEQ 20. PAGE 107 E2152

B42
GURVITCH G..SOCIOLOGY OF LAW. CONSTN SOCIETY CREATE SOC
MORAL SOVEREIGN...POLICY EPIST JURID PHIL/SCI LAW
IDEA/COMP METH/COMP HOLMES/OW HOBBES/T. PAGE 48 ADJUD
E0964

B42
KELSEN H..LAW AND PEACE IN INTERNATIONAL RELATIONS. INT/ORG
FUT WOR-45 NAT/G DELIB/GP DIPLOM LEGIT RIGID/FLEX ADJUD
ORD/FREE SOVEREIGN...JURID CONCPT TREND STERTYP PEACE
GEN/LAWS LEAGUE/NAT 20. PAGE 60 E1197 INT/LAW

B43
BEMIS S.F..THE LATIN AMERICAN POLICY OF THE UNITED DIPLOM
STATES: AN HISTORICAL INTERPRETATION. INT/ORG AGREE SOVEREIGN
COLONIAL WAR PEACE ATTIT ORD/FREE...POLICY INT/LAW USA-45
CHARTS 18/20 MEXIC/AMER WILSON/W MONROE/DOC. L/A+17C
PAGE 10 E0185

C43
BENTHAM J.."PRINCIPLES OF INTERNATIONAL LAW" IN J. INT/LAW
BOWRING, ED., THE WORKS OF JEREMY BENTHAM." UNIV JURID
NAT/G PLAN PROB/SOLV DIPLOM CONTROL SANCTION MORAL WAR
ORD/FREE PWR SOVEREIGN 19. PAGE 10 E0194 PEACE

B44
FULLER G.H..MILITARY GOVERNMENT: A LIST OF BIBLIOG
REFERENCES (A PAMPHLET). ITALY UK USA-45 WOR-45 LAW DIPLOM

FORCES DOMIN ADMIN ARMS/CONT ORD/FREE PWR
...DECISION 20 CHINJAP. PAGE 41 E0822

CIVMIL/REL
SOVEREIGN

B45

HILL N.,CLAIMS TO TERRITORY IN INTERNATIONAL LAW
AND RELATIONS. WOR-45 NAT/G DOMIN EDU/PROP LEGIT
REGION ROUTINE ORD/FREE PWR WEALTH...GEOG INT/LAW
JURID 20. PAGE 52 E1047

INT/ORG
ADJUD
SOVEREIGN

B45

REVES E.,THE ANATOMY OF PEACE. WOR-45 LAW CULTURE
NAT/G PLAN TEC/DEV EDU/PROP WAR NAT/LISM ATTIT
ALL/VALS SOVEREIGN...POLICY HUM TIME/SEQ 20.
PAGE 84 E1688

ACT/RES
CONCPT
NUC/PWR
PEACE

B46

GRIFFIN G.G.,A GUIDE TO MANUSCRIPTS RELATING TO
AMERICAN HISTORY IN BRITISH DEPOSITORIES. CANADA
IRELAND MOD/EUR UK USA-45 LAW DIPLOM ADMIN COLONIAL
WAR NAT/LISM SOVEREIGN...GEOG INT/LAW 15/19
CMN/WLTH. PAGE 47 E0936

BIBLIOG/A
ALL/VALS
NAT/G

B47

BORGESE G.,COMMON CAUSE. LAW CONSTN SOCIETY STRATA
ECO/DEV INT/ORG POL/PAR FORCES LEGIS TOP/EX CAP/ISM
DIPLOM ADMIN EXEC ATTIT PWR 20. PAGE 14 E0269

WOR+45
NAT/G
SOVEREIGN
REGION

B47

MCILWAIN C.H.,CONSTITUTIONALISM: ANCIENT AND
MODERN. USA+45 ROMAN/EMP LAW CHIEF LEGIS CT/SYS
GP/REL ORD/FREE SOVEREIGN...POLICY TIME/SEQ
ROMAN/REP EUROPE. PAGE 71 E1419

CONSTN
NAT/G
PARL/PROC
GOV/COMP

N47

FOX W.T.R.,UNITED STATES POLICY IN A TWO POWER
WORLD. COM USA+45 USSR FORCES DOMIN AGREE NEUTRAL
NUC/PWR ORD/FREE SOVEREIGN 20 COLD/WAR TREATY
EUROPE/W INTERVENT. PAGE 39 E0780

DIPLOM
FOR/AID
POLICY

B50

MOCKFORD J.,SOUTH-WEST AFRICA AND THE INTERNATIONAL
COURT (PAMPHLET). AFR GERMANY SOUTH/AFR UK
ECO/UNDEV DIPLOM CONTROL DISCRIM...DECISION JURID
20 AFRICA/SW. PAGE 74 E1475

COLONIAL
SOVEREIGN
INT/LAW
DOMIN

B52

LIPPMANN W.,ISOLATION AND ALLIANCES: AN AMERICAN
SPEAKS TO THE BRITISH. USA+45 USA-45 INT/ORG AGREE
COERCE DETER WAR PEACE MORAL 20 TREATY INTERVENT.
PAGE 65 E1301

DIPLOM
SOVEREIGN
COLONIAL
ATTIT

S52

MCDOUGAL M.S.,"THE COMPARATIVE STUDY OF LAW FOR
POLICY PURPOSES." FUT NAT/G POL/PAR CONSULT ADJUD
PWR SOVEREIGN...METH/CNCPT IDEA/COMP SIMUL 20.
PAGE 70 E1403

PLAN
JURID
NAT/LISM

B53

OPPENHEIM L.,INTERNATIONAL LAW: A TREATISE (7TH
ED., 2 VOLS.). LAW CONSTN PROB/SOLV INT/TRADE ADJUD
AGREE NEUTRAL WAR ORD/FREE SOVEREIGN...BIBLIOG 20
LEAGUE/NAT UN ILO. PAGE 79 E1579

INT/LAW
INT/ORG
DIPLOM

B54

STONE J.,LEGAL CONTROLS OF INTERNATIONAL CONFLICT:
A TREATISE ON THE DYNAMICS OF DISPUTES AND WAR LAW.
WOR+45 WOR-45 NAT/G DIPLOM CT/SYS SOVEREIGN...JURID
CONCPT METH/CNCPT GEN/LAWS TOT/POP VAL/FREE
COLD/WAR LEAGUE/NAT 20. PAGE 94 E1878

INT/ORG
LAW
WAR
INT/LAW

B54

US SENATE COMM ON FOREIGN REL,REVIEW OF THE UNITED
NATIONS CHARTER: A COLLECTION OF DOCUMENTS. LEGIS
DIPLOM ADMIN ARMS/CONT WAR REPRESENT SOVEREIGN
...INT/LAW 20 UN. PAGE 101 E2029

BIBLIOG
CONSTN
INT/ORG
DEBATE

L54

NICOLSON H.,"THE EVOLUTION OF DIPLOMATIC METHOD."
CHRIST-17C EUR+WWI FRANCE FUT ITALY MEDIT-7 MOD/EUR
USA+45 USA-45 LAW NAT/G CREATE EDU/PROP LEGIT PEACE
ATTIT ORD/FREE RESPECT SOVEREIGN. PAGE 77 E1548

RIGID/FLEX
METH/CNCPT
DIPLOM

B55

BURR R.N.,DOCUMENTS ON INTER-AMERICAN COOPERATION:
VOL. I, 1810-1881; VOL. II, 1881-1948. DELIB/GP
BAL/PWR INT/TRADE REPRESENT NAT/LISM PEACE HABITAT
ORD/FREE PWR SOVEREIGN...INT/LAW 20 OAS. PAGE 18
E0345

BIBLIOG
DIPLOM
INT/ORG
L/A+17C

B55

CHOWDHURI R.N.,INTERNATIONAL MANDATES AND
TRUSTEESHIP SYSTEMS. WOR+45 STRUCT ECO/UNDEV
INT/ORG LEGIS DOMIN EDU/PROP LEGIT ADJUD EXEC PWR
...CONCPT TIME/SEQ UN 20. PAGE 22 E0434

DELIB/GP
PLAN
SOVEREIGN

B55

SVARLIEN O.,AN INTRODUCTION TO THE LAW OF NATIONS.
SEA AIR INT/ORG NAT/G CHIEF ADMIN AGREE WAR PRIVIL
ORD/FREE SOVEREIGN...BIBLIOG 16/20. PAGE 95 E1897

INT/LAW
DIPLOM

B55

UN HEADQUARTERS LIBRARY,BIBLIOGRAPHIE DE LA CHARTE
DES NATIONS UNIES. CHINA/COM KOREA WOR+45 VOL/ASSN
CONFER ADMIN COERCE PEACE ATTIT ORD/FREE SOVEREIGN
...INT/LAW 20 UNESCO UN. PAGE 97 E1953

BIBLIOG/A
INT/ORG
DIPLOM

B56

FIELD G.C.,POLITICAL THEORY. POL/PAR REPRESENT
MORAL SOVEREIGN...JURID IDEA/COMP. PAGE 38 E0745

CONCPT
NAT/G
ORD/FREE
DIPLOM

B56

LASLETT P.,PHILOSOPHY, POLITICS AND SOCIETY. UNIV
CRIME SOVEREIGN...JURID PHIL/SCI ANTHOL PLATO
NATURL/LAW. PAGE 63 E1260

CONSTN
ATTIT
CONCPT
GEN/LAWS

B56

PEASLEE A.J.,CONSTITUTIONS OF NATIONS. WOR+45 LAW
NAT/G EX/STRUC LEGIS TOP/EX LEGIT CT/SYS ROUTINE
CHOOSE ORD/FREE PWR SOVEREIGN...CHARTS TOT/POP.
PAGE 80 E1605

CONSTN
CON/ANAL

B56

WEIS P.,NATIONALITY AND STATELESSNESS IN
INTERNATIONAL LAW. UK WOR+45 WOR-45 LAW CONSTN
NAT/G DIPLOM EDU/PROP LEGIT ROUTINE RIGID/FLEX
...JURID RECORD CMN/WLTH 20. PAGE 105 E2109

INT/ORG
SOVEREIGN
INT/LAW

B57

DONALDSON A.G.,SOME COMPARATIVE ASPECTS OF IRISH
LAW. IRELAND NAT/G DIPLOM ADMIN CT/SYS LEAD ATTIT
SOVEREIGN...JURID BIBLIOG/A 12/20 CMN/WLTH. PAGE 32
E0635

CONSTN
LAW
NAT/COMP
INT/LAW

B57

LEVONTIN A.V.,THE MYTH OF INTERNATIONAL SECURITY: A
JURIDICAL AND CRITICAL ANALYSIS. FUT WOR+45 WOR-45
LAW NAT/G VOL/ASSN ACT/RES BAL/PWR ATTIT ORD/FREE
...JURID METH/CNCPT TIME/SEQ TREND STERTYP 20.
PAGE 64 E1289

INT/ORG
INT/LAW
SOVEREIGN
MYTH

B57

PALMER N.D.,INTERNATIONAL RELATIONS. WOR+45 INT/ORG
NAT/G ECO/TAC EDU/PROP COLONIAL WAR PWR SOVEREIGN
...POLICY T 20 TREATY. PAGE 79 E1593

DIPLOM
BAL/PWR
NAT/COMP

B57

ROSENNE S.,THE INTERNATIONAL COURT OF JUSTICE.
WOR+45 LAW DOMIN LEGIT PEACE PWR SOVEREIGN...JURID
CONCPT RECORD TIME/SEQ CON/ANAL CHARTS UN TOT/POP
VAL/FREE LEAGUE/NAT 20 ICJ. PAGE 86 E1716

INT/ORG
CT/SYS
INT/LAW

B58

ALLEN C.K.,LAW IN THE MAKING. LEGIS ATTIT ORD/FREE
SOVEREIGN POPULISM...JURID IDEA/COMP NAT/COMP
GEN/LAWS 20 ENGLSH/LAW. PAGE 4 E0069

LAW
CREATE
CONSTN
SOCIETY

B58

BRIERLY J.L.,THE BASIS OF OBLIGATION IN
INTERNATIONAL LAW, AND OTHER PAPERS. WOR+45 WOR-45
LEGIS...JURID CONCPT NAT/COMP ANTHOL 20. PAGE 15
E0299

INT/LAW
DIPLOM
ADJUD
SOVEREIGN

B58

EUSDEN J.D.,PURITANS, LAWYERS, AND POLITICS IN
EARLY SEVENTEENTH-CENTURY ENGLAND. UK CT/SYS
PARL/PROC RATIONAL PWR SOVEREIGN...IDEA/COMP
BIBLIOG 17 PURITAN COMMON/LAW. PAGE 35 E0702

GP/REL
SECT
NAT/G
LAW

B58

JENKS C.W.,THE COMMON LAW OF MANKIND. EUR+WWI
MOD/EUR SPACE WOR+45 INT/ORG BAL/PWR ARMS/CONT
COERCE SUPEGO MORAL...TREND 20. PAGE 58 E1154

JURID
SOVEREIGN

B58

MANSERGH N.,COMMONWEALTH PERSPECTIVES. GHANA UK LAW
VOL/ASSN CONFER HEALTH SOVEREIGN...GEOG CHARTS
ANTHOL 20 CMN/WLTH AUSTRAL. PAGE 68 E1363

DIPLOM
COLONIAL
INT/ORG
INGP/REL

B58

MOSKOWITZ M.,HUMAN RIGHTS AND WORLD ORDER. INT/ORG
PLAN GP/REL NAT/LISM SOVEREIGN...CONCPT 20 UN
TREATY CIV/RIGHTS. PAGE 75 E1502

DIPLOM
INT/LAW
ORD/FREE

B59

BROOKES E.H.,THE COMMONWEALTH TODAY. UK ROMAN/EMP
INT/ORG RACE/REL NAT/LISM SOVEREIGN...TREND

FEDERAL
DIPLOM

SOC/INTEG 20. PAGE 16 E0307   JURID
                                                     IDEA/COMP

                                                        B59
FRIEDMANN W.G.,LAW IN A CHANGING SOCIETY. FUT   SOC
WOR+45 WOR-45 LAW SOCIETY STRUCT INT/TRADE LEGIT   JURID
ATTIT BIO/SOC HEALTH ORD/FREE SOVEREIGN...CONCPT
GEN/LAWS ILO 20. PAGE 41 E0803

                                                        B59
HALEY A.G.,FIRST COLLOQUIUM ON THE LAW OF OUTER   SPACE
SPACE. WOR+45 INT/ORG ACT/RES PLAN BAL/PWR CONFER   LAW
ATTIT PWR...POLICY JURID CHARTS ANTHOL 20. PAGE 49   SOVEREIGN
E0979   CONTROL

                                                        B59
VITTACHIT,EMERGENCY '58. CEYLON UK STRUCT NAT/G   RACE/REL
FORCES ADJUD CRIME REV NAT/LISM 20. PAGE 104 E2081   DISCRIM
                                                     DIPLOM
                                                     SOVEREIGN

                                                        B59
WOETZEL R.K.,DIE INTERNATIONALE KONTROLLE DER   SPACE
HOHEREN LUFTSCHICHTEN UND DES WELTRAUMS. INT/ORG   INT/LAW
NAT/G CONTROL SUPEGO...JURID CONCPT 20. PAGE 107   DIPLOM
E2136   SOVEREIGN

                                                        S59
CARLSTON K.S.,"NATIONALIZATION: AN ANALYTIC   INDUS
APPROACH." WOR+45 INT/ORG ECO/TAC DOMIN LEGIT ADJUD   NAT/G
COERCE ORD/FREE PWR WEALTH SOCISM...JURID CONCPT   NAT/LISM
TREND STERTYP TOT/POP VAL/FREE 20. PAGE 19 E0380   SOVEREIGN

                                                        S59
SOHN L.B.,"THE DEFINITION OF AGGRESSION." FUT LAW   INT/ORG
FORCES LEGIT ADJUD ROUTINE COERCE ORD/FREE PWR   CT/SYS
...MAJORIT JURID QUANT COLD/WAR 20. PAGE 92 E1855   DETER
                                                     SOVEREIGN

                                                        S59
STONE J.,"CONFLICT MANAGEMENT THROUGH CONTEMPORARY   INT/ORG
INTERNATIONAL LAW AND ORGANIZATION." WOR+45 LAW   INT/LAW
NAT/G CREATE BAL/PWR DOMIN LEGIT ROUTINE COERCE
ATTIT ORD/FREE PWR SOVEREIGN...JURID 20. PAGE 94
E1880

                                                        B60
ALBI F.,TRATADO DE LOS MODOS DE GESTION DE LAS   LOC/G
CORPORACIONES LOCALES. SPAIN FINAN NAT/G BUDGET   LAW
CONTROL EXEC ROUTINE GOV/REL ORD/FREE SOVEREIGN   ADMIN
...MGT 20. PAGE 3 E0057   MUNIC

                                                        B60
DILEY A.V.,INTRODUCTION TO THE STUDY OF THE LAW OF   CONSTN
THE CONSTITUTION. FRANCE UK USA+45 USA-45 CONSULT   LAW
FORCES TAX ADMIN FEDERAL ORD/FREE SOVEREIGN   LEGIS
...IDEA/COMP 20 ENGLSH/LAW CON/INTERP PARLIAMENT.   GEN/LAWS
PAGE 32 E0627

                                                        B60
HEYSE T.,PROBLEMS FONCIERS ET REGIME DES TERRES   BIBLIOG
(ASPECTS ECONOMIQUES, JURIDIQUES ET SOCIAUX). AFR   AGRI
CONGO/BRAZ INT/ORG DIPLOM SOVEREIGN...GEOG TREATY   ECO/UNDEV
20. PAGE 52 E1037   LEGIS

                                                        S60
GRACIA-MORA M.R.,"INTERNATIONAL RESPONSIBILITY FOR   INT/ORG
SUBVERSIVE ACTIVITIES AND HOSTILE PROPAGANDA BY   JURID
PRIVATE PERSONS AGAINST." COM EUR+WWI L/A+17C UK   SOVEREIGN
USA+45 USSR WOR-45 CONSTN NAT/G LEGIT ADJUD REV
PEACE TOTALISM ORD/FREE...INT/LAW 20. PAGE 45 E0895

                                                        S60
NICHOLS J.P.,"HAZARDS OF AMERICAN PRIVATE   FINAN
INVESTMENT IN UNDERDEVELOPED COUNTRIES." FUT   ECO/UNDEV
L/A+17C USA+45 USA-45 EXTR/IND CONSULT BAL/PWR   CAP/ISM
ECO/TAC DOMIN ADJUD ATTIT SOVEREIGN WEALTH   NAT/LISM
...HIST/WRIT TIME/SEQ TREND VAL/FREE 20. PAGE 77
E1546

                                                        B61
BAINS J.S.,STUDIES IN POLITICAL SCIENCE. INDIA   DIPLOM
WOR+45 WOR-45 CONSTN BAL/PWR ADJUD ADMIN PARL/PROC   INT/LAW
SOVEREIGN...SOC METH/COMP ANTHOL 17/20 UN. PAGE 7   NAT/G
E0137

                                                        B61
FROEBEL J.,THEORIE DER POLITIK, ALS ERGEBNIS EINER   JURID
ERNEUERTEN PRUEFUNG DEMOKRATISCHER LEHRMEINUNGEN.   ORD/FREE
WOR-45 SOCIETY POL/PAR SECT REV REPRESENT PWR   NAT/G
SOVEREIGN...MAJORIT 19. PAGE 41 E0812

                                                        B61
LARSON A.,WHEN NATIONS DISAGREE. USA+45 WOR+45   INT/LAW
INT/ORG ADJUD COERCE CRIME OWN SOVEREIGN...POLICY   DIPLOM
JURID 20. PAGE 63 E1258   WAR

                                                        B61
SYATAUW J.J.G.,SOME NEWLY ESTABLISHED ASIAN STATES   INT/LAW
AND THE DEVELOPMENT OF INTERNATIONAL LAW. BURMA   ADJUST
CEYLON INDIA INDONESIA ECO/UNDEV COLONIAL NEUTRAL   SOCIETY
WAR PEACE SOVEREIGN...CHARTS 19/20. PAGE 95 E1902   S/ASIA

                                                        S61
MACHOWSKI K.,"SELECTED PROBLEMS OF NATIONAL   UNIV
SOVEREIGNTY WITH REFERENCE TO THE LAW OF OUTER   ACT/RES
SPACE." FUT WOR+45 AIR LAW INTELL SOCIETY ECO/DEV   NUC/PWR
PLAN EDU/PROP DETER DRIVE PERCEPT SOVEREIGN   SPACE
...POLICY INT/LAW OBS TREND TOT/POP 20. PAGE 67
E1339

                                                        B62
JENKS C.W.,THE PROPER LAW OF INTERNATIONAL   LAW
ORGANISATIONS. DIPLOM LEGIT AGREE CT/SYS SANCTION   INT/ORG
REPRESENT SOVEREIGN...GEN/LAWS 20 UN UNESCO ILO   ADJUST
NATO OAS. PAGE 58 E1158   INT/LAW

                                                        B62
LITTLEFIELD N.,METROPOLITAN AREA PROBLEMS AND   LOC/G
MUNICIPAL HOME RULE. USA+45 PROVS ADMIN CONTROL   SOVEREIGN
GP/REL PWR. PAGE 65 E1308   JURID
                                                     LEGIS

                                                        B62
NORGAARD C.A.,THE POSITION OF THE INDIVIDUAL IN   INT/LAW
INTERNATIONAL LAW. INT/ORG SUPEGO ORD/FREE   DIPLOM
SOVEREIGN...CONCPT 20 UN. PAGE 78 E1556   CRIME
                                                     JURID

                                                        B62
PAIKERT G.C.,THE GERMAN EXODUS. EUR+WWI GERMANY/W   INGP/REL
LAW CULTURE SOCIETY STRUCT INDUS NAT/LISM RESPECT   STRANGE
SOVEREIGN...CHARTS BIBLIOG SOC/INTEG 20 MIGRATION.   GEOG
PAGE 79 E1591   GP/REL

                                                        B62
PRESS C.,STATE MANUALS, BLUE BOOKS AND ELECTION   BIBLIOG
RESULTS. LAW LOC/G MUNIC LEGIS WRITING FEDERAL   PROVS
SOVEREIGN...DECISION STAT CHARTS 20. PAGE 82 E1648   ADMIN
                                                     CHOOSE

                                                        B62
ROSTOW E.V.,THE SOVEREIGN PREROGATIVE: THE SUPREME   JURID
COURT AND THE QUEST FOR LAW. CONSTN CT/SYS FEDERAL   PROF/ORG
MORAL SOVEREIGN 20 SUPREME/CT. PAGE 86 E1726   ATTIT
                                                     ORD/FREE

                                                        B62
THOMPSON K.W.,AMERICAN DIPLOMACY AND EMERGENT   NAT/G
PATTERNS. USA+45 USA-45 WOR+45 WOR-45 LAW DELIB/GP   BAL/PWR
FORCES TOP/EX DIPLOM ATTIT DRIVE RIGID/FLEX
ORD/FREE PWR SOVEREIGN...POLICY 20. PAGE 96 E1922

                                                        L62
CORET A.,"L'INDEPENDANCE DU SAMOA OCCIDENTAL."   NAT/G
S/ASIA LAW INT/ORG EXEC ALL/VALS SAMOA UN 20.   STRUCT
PAGE 26 E0508   SOVEREIGN

                                                        L62
MURACCIOLE L.,"LA LOI FONDAMENTALE DE LA REPUBLIQUE   AFR
DU CONGO." WOR+45 SOCIETY ECO/UNDEV INT/ORG NAT/G   CONSTN
LEGIS PLAN LEGIT ADJUD COLONIAL ROUTINE ATTIT
SOVEREIGN 20 CONGO. PAGE 75 E1504

                                                        S62
FALK R.A.,"THE REALITY OF INTERNATIONAL LAW."   INT/ORG
WOR+45 NAT/G LEGIT COERCE DETER WAR MORAL ORD/FREE   ADJUD
PWR SOVEREIGN...JURID CONCPT VAL/FREE COLD/WAR 20.   NUC/PWR
PAGE 36 E0714   INT/LAW

                                                        S62
GREEN L.C.,"POLITICAL OFFENSES, WAR CRIMES AND   LAW
EXTRADITION." WOR+45 YUGOSLAVIA INT/ORG LEGIT   CONCPT
ROUTINE WAR ORD/FREE SOVEREIGN...JURID NAZI 20   INT/LAW
INTERPOL. PAGE 46 E0906

                                                        S62
LISSITZYN O.J.,"SOME LEGAL IMPLICATIONS OF THE U-2   LAW
AND RB-47 INCIDENTS." FUT USA+45 USSR WOR+45 AIR   CONCPT
NAT/G DIPLOM LEGIT MORAL ORD/FREE SOVEREIGN...JURID   SPACE
GEN/LAWS GEN/METH COLD/WAR 20 U-2. PAGE 65 E1305   INT/LAW

                                                        S62
MURACCIOLE L.,"LES MODIFICATIONS DE LA CONSTITUTION   NAT/G
MALGACHE." AFR WOR+45 ECO/UNDEV LEGIT EXEC ALL/VALS   STRUCT
...JURID 20. PAGE 75 E1505   SOVEREIGN
                                                     MADAGASCAR

                                                        B63
DUNN F.S.,PEACE-MAKING AND THE SETTLEMENT WITH   POLICY
JAPAN. ASIA USA+45 USA-45 FORCES BAL/PWR ECO/TAC   PEACE
CONFER WAR PWR SOVEREIGN 20 CHINJAP COLD/WAR   PLAN

TREATY. PAGE 33 E0661   DIPLOM   PAGE 96 E1915   PEACE
                                                                                                              COERCE

                                               B63
GEERTZ C.,OLD SOCIETIES AND NEW STATES: THE QUEST   ECO/UNDEV   B64
FOR MODERNITY IN ASIA AND AFRICA. AFR ASIA LAW   TEC/DEV   WRIGHT Q.,A STUDY OF WAR. LAW NAT/G PROB/SOLV   WAR
CULTURE SECT EDU/PROP REV...GOV/COMP NAT/COMP 20.   NAT/LISM   BAL/PWR NAT/LISM PEACE ATTIT SOVEREIGN...CENSUS CONCPT
PAGE 42 E0842   SOVEREIGN SOC/INTEG. PAGE 108 E2159   DIPLOM
                                                                                                              CONTROL
                                               B63
HALEY A.G.,SPACE LAW AND GOVERNMENT. FUT USA+45   INT/ORG   B65
WOR+45 LEGIS ACT/RES CREATE ATTIT RIGID/FLEX   LAW   BLITZ L.F.,THE POLITICS AND ADMINISTRATION OF NAT/G
ORD/FREE PWR SOVEREIGN...POLICY JURID CONCPT CHARTS SPACE   NIGERIAN GOVERNMENT. NIGER CULTURE LOC/G LEGIS GOV/REL
VAL/FREE 20. PAGE 49 E0980   DIPLOM COLONIAL CT/SYS SOVEREIGN...GEOG SOC ANTHOL POL/PAR
                                                               20. PAGE 13 E0245
                                               B63
HIGGINS R.,THE DEVELOPMENT OF INTERNATIONAL LAW   INT/ORG   B65
THROUGH THE POLITICAL ORGANS OF THE UNITED NATIONS. INT/LAW   COWEN Z.,THE BRITISH COMMONWEALTH OF NATIONS IN A JURID
WOR+45 FORCES DIPLOM AGREE COERCE ATTIT SOVEREIGN   TEC/DEV   CHANGING WORLD. UK ECO/UNDEV INT/ORG ECO/TAC   DIPLOM
...BIBLIOG 20 UN TREATY. PAGE 52 E1041   JURID   INT/TRADE COLONIAL WAR GP/REL RACE/REL SOVEREIGN PARL/PROC
                                                               SOC/INTEG 20 TREATY EEC COMMONWLTH. PAGE 27 E0530 NAT/LISM
                                               B63
JENKS C.W.,LAW, FREEDOM, AND WELFARE. WOR+45 GIVE   INT/LAW   B65
ADJUD WAR PEACE HABITAT ORD/FREE. PAGE 58 E1159   DIPLOM   FALK R.A.,THE AFTERMATH OF SABBATINO: BACKGROUND SOVEREIGN
                                                    SOVEREIGN PAPERS AND PROCEEDINGS OF SEVENTH HAMMARSKJOLD   CT/SYS
                                                    PROB/SOLV FORUM. USA+45 LAW ACT/RES ADJUD ROLE...BIBLIOG 20 INT/LAW
                                                               EXPROPRIAT SABBATINO HARLAN/JM. PAGE 36 E0718   OWN
                                               S63
MCDOUGAL M.S.,"THE SOVIET-CUBAN QUARANTINE AND   ORD/FREE   B65
SELF-DEFENSE." CUBA USA+45 USSR WOR+45 INT/ORG   LEGIT   GOTLIEB A.,DISARMAMENT AND INTERNATIONAL LAW* A INT/LAW
NAT/G BAL/PWR NUC/PWR ATTIT...JURID CONCPT. PAGE 70 SOVEREIGN STUDY OF THE ROLE OF LAW IN THE DISARMAMENT   INT/ORG
E1409   PROCESS. USA+45 USSR PROB/SOLV CONFER ADMIN ROUTINE ARMS/CONT
                                                               NUC/PWR ORD/FREE SOVEREIGN UN TREATY. PAGE 45 E0893 IDEA/COMP
                                               S63
WEISSBERG G.,"MAPS AS EVIDENCE IN INTERNATIONAL   LAW   B65
BOUNDARY DISPUTES: A REAPPRAISAL." CHINA/COM   GEOG   JOHNSTON D.M.,THE INTERNATIONAL LAW OF FISHERIES: A CONCPT
EUR+WWI INDIA MOD/EUR S/ASIA INT/ORG NAT/G LEGIT   SOVEREIGN FRAMEWORK FOR POLICYORIENTED INQUIRIES. WOR+45 EXTR/IND
PERCEPT...JURID CHARTS 20. PAGE 105 E2110   ACT/RES PLAN PROB/SOLV CONTROL SOVEREIGN. PAGE 59 JURID
                                                               E1171   DIPLOM
                                               B64
ANASTAPLO G.,NOTES ON THE FIRST AMENDMENT TO THE   ORD/FREE   B65
CONSTITUTION OF THE UNITED STATES (PART TWO).   CONSTN   MORRIS R.B.,THE PEACEMAKERS: THE GREAT POWERS AND SOVEREIGN
USA+45 USA-45 NAT/G JUDGE DEBATE SUPEGO PWR   CT/SYS   AMERICAN INDEPENDENCE. BAL/PWR CONFER COLONIAL REV
SOVEREIGN 18/20 SUPREME/CT CONGRESS AMEND/I. PAGE 5 ATTIT   NEUTRAL PEACE ORD/FREE TREATY 18 PRE/US/AM. PAGE 75 DIPLOM
E0088   E1499

                                               B64   B65
FRANCK T.M.,EAST AFRICAN UNITY THROUGH LAW. MALAWI   AFR   NEGLEY G.,POLITICAL AUTHORITY AND MORAL JUDGMENT. MORAL
TANZANIA UGANDA UK ZAMBIA CONSTN INT/ORG NAT/G   FEDERAL   INTELL SOCIETY LEGIS SANCTION UTOPIA SOVEREIGN PWR
ADMIN ROUTINE TASK NAT/LISM ATTIT SOVEREIGN   REGION   MARXISM...INT/LAW LOG 20. PAGE 76 E1530   CONTROL
...RECORD IDEA/COMP NAT/COMP. PAGE 40 E0785   INT/LAW
                                                                                                              B65
                                               B64   O'BRIEN W.V.,THE NEW NATIONS IN INTERNATIONAL LAW INT/LAW
GRASMUCK E.L.,COERCITIO STAAT UND KIRCHE IM   GP/REL   AND DIPLOMACY* THE YEAR BOOK OF WORLD POLITY*   CULTURE
DONATISTENSTREIT. CHRIST-17C ROMAN/EMP LAW PROVS   NAT/G   VOLUME III. USA+45 ECO/UNDEV INT/ORG FORCES DIPLOM SOVEREIGN
DEBATE PERSON SOVEREIGN...JURID CONCPT 4/5   SECT   COLONIAL NEUTRAL REV NAT/LISM ATTIT RESPECT.   ANTHOL
AUGUSTINE CHURCH/STA ROMAN/LAW. PAGE 45 E0898   COERCE   PAGE 78 E1565

                                               B64   B65
GUMPLOWICZ L.,RECHTSSTAAT UND SOZIALISMUS. STRATA   JURID   PARRY C.,THE SOURCES AND EVIDENCES OF INTERNATIONAL INT/LAW
ORD/FREE SOVEREIGN MARXISM...IDEA/COMP 16/20 KANT/I NAT/G   LAW. WOR+45 WOR-45 DIPLOM AGREE SOVEREIGN...METH 20 ADJUD
HOBBES/T. PAGE 48 E0962   SOCISM   TREATY UN LEAGUE/NAT. PAGE 80 E1599   INT/ORG
                                                    CONCPT   CT/SYS
                                               B64   B65
HANNA W.J.,POLITICS IN BLACK AFRICA: A SELECTIVE   BIBLIOG   PEASLEE A.J.,CONSTITUTIONS OF NATIONS* THIRD   AFR
BIBLIOGRAPHY OF RELEVANT PERIODICAL LITERATURE. AFR NAT/LISM   REVISED EDITION (VOLUME I* AFRICA). LAW EX/STRUC CHOOSE
LAW LOC/G MUNIC NAT/G POL/PAR LOBBY CHOOSE RACE/REL COLONIAL   LEGIS TOP/EX LEGIT CT/SYS ROUTINE ORD/FREE PWR   CONSTN
SOVEREIGN 20. PAGE 50 E0995   SOVEREIGN...CON/ANAL CHARTS. PAGE 80 E1606   NAT/G

                                               B64   B65
LAPENNA I.,STATE AND LAW: SOVIET AND YUGOSLAV   JURID   VON RENESSE E.A.,UNVOLLENDETE DEMOKRATIEN. AFR ECO/UNDEV
THEORY. USSR YUGOSLAVIA STRATA STRUCT NAT/G DOMIN   COM   ISLAM S/ASIA SOCIETY ACT/RES COLONIAL...JURID   NAT/COMP
COERCE MARXISM...GOV/COMP IDEA/COMP 20. PAGE 63   LAW   CHARTS BIBLIOG METH 13/20. PAGE 104 E2083   SOVEREIGN
E1253   SOVEREIGN
                                                                                                              B65
                                               B64   WILSON J.F.,CHURCH AND STATE IN AMERICAN HISTORY. SECT
MARSHALL B.,FEDERALISM AND CIVIL RIGHTS. USA+45   FEDERAL   USA+45 USA-45 ADJUD CT/SYS ORD/FREE SOVEREIGN   NAT/G
PROVS BAL/PWR CONTROL CT/SYS PARTIC SOVEREIGN   ORD/FREE   ...ANTHOL BIBLIOG/A 17/20 CHURCH/STA. PAGE 106   GP/REL
...JURID 20 NEGRO CIV/RIGHTS. PAGE 68 E1369   CONSTN   E2129   CONTROL
                                                    FORCES
                                                                                                              L65
                                               B64   SHARMA S.P.,"THE INDIA-CHINA BORDER DISPUTE: AN LAW
SCHECHTER A.H.,INTERPRETATION OF AMBIGUOUS   INT/LAW   INDIAN PERSPECTIVE." ASIA CHINA/COM S/ASIA NAT/G ATTIT
DOCUMENTS BY INTERNATIONAL ADMINISTRATIVE   DIPLOM   LEGIT CT/SYS NAT/LISM DRIVE MORAL ORD/FREE PWR 20. SOVEREIGN
TRIBUNALS. WOR+45 EX/STRUC INT/TRADE CT/SYS   INT/ORG   PAGE 91 E1815   INDIA
SOVEREIGN 20 UN ILO EURCT/JUST. PAGE 87 E1752   ADJUD
                                                                                                              S65
                                               B64   STEIN E.,"TOWARD SUPREMACY OF TREATY-CONSTITUTION ADJUD
STANGER R.J.,ESSAYS ON INTERVENTION. PLAN PROB/SOLV SOVEREIGN BY JUDICIAL FIAT: ON THE MARGIN OF THE COSTA CASE." CONSTN
BAL/PWR ADJUD COERCE WAR ROLE PWR...INT/LAW CONCPT   DIPLOM   EUR+WWI ITALY WOR+45 INT/ORG NAT/G LEGIT REGION SOVEREIGN
20 UN INTERVENT. PAGE 93 E1865   POLICY   NAT/LISM PWR...JURID CONCPT TREND TOT/POP VAL/FREE INT/LAW
                                                    LEGIT   20. PAGE 93 E1870

                                               B64   C65
THANT U.,TOWARD WORLD PEACE. DELIB/GP TEC/DEV   DIPLOM   SEARA M.V.,"COSMIC INTERNATIONAL LAW." LAW ACADEM SPACE
EDU/PROP WAR SOVEREIGN...INT/LAW 20 UN MID/EAST.   BIOG   ACT/RES DIPLOM COLONIAL CONTROL NUC/PWR SOVEREIGN INT/LAW

...GEN/LAWS BIBLIOG UN. PAGE 90 E1799   IDEA/COMP
                                                          INT/ORG

                                                          JURID
                                                          CONSTN

                                               B66
BROWNLIE I.,PRINCIPLES OF PUBLIC INTERNATIONAL LAW. INT/LAW
WOR+45 WOR-45 LAW JUDGE REPAR ADJUD SOVEREIGN   DIPLOM
...JURID T. PAGE 16 E0319   INT/ORG

                                                          B90
GODWIN W.,POLITICAL JUSTICE. UK ELITES OWN KNOWL   ORD/FREE
MORAL WEALTH...JURID 18/19. PAGE 44 E0877   SOVEREIGN
                                                    STRUCT
                                                    CONCPT

                                               B66
CAMPBELL E.,PARLIAMENTARY PRIVILEGE IN AUSTRALIA. LEGIS
UK LAW CONSTN COLONIAL ROLE ORD/FREE SOVEREIGN   PARL/PROC
18/20 COMMONWLTH AUSTRAL FREE/SPEE PARLIAMENT.   JURID
PAGE 19 E0370   PRIVIL

                                                          B91
BENTHAM J.,A FRAGMENT ON GOVERNMENT (1776). CONSTN SOVEREIGN
MUNIC NAT/G SECT AGREE HAPPINESS UTIL MORAL   LAW
ORD/FREE...JURID CONCPT. PAGE 10 E0198   DOMIN

                                               B66
COPLIN W.D.,THE FUNCTIONS OF INTERNATIONAL LAW.   INT/LAW
WOR+45 ECO/DEV ECO/UNDEV ADJUD COLONIAL WAR OWN   DIPLOM
SOVEREIGN...POLICY GEN/LAWS 20. PAGE 25 E0503   INT/ORG

                                                          B91
SIDGWICK H.,THE ELEMENTS OF POLITICS. LOC/G NAT/G   POLICY
LEGIS DIPLOM ADJUD CONTROL EXEC PARL/PROC REPRESENT LAW
GOV/REL SOVEREIGN ALL/IDEOS 19 MILL/JS BENTHAM/J.   CONCPT
PAGE 91 E1822

                                               B66
DE TOCQUEVILLE A.,DEMOCRACY IN AMERICA (1834-1840) POPULISM
(2 VOLS. IN I; TRANS. BY G. LAWRENCE). FRANCE   USA-45
CULTURE STRATA POL/PAR CT/SYS REPRESENT FEDERAL   CONSTN
ORD/FREE SOVEREIGN...MAJORIT TREND GEN/LAWS 18/19. NAT/COMP
PAGE 30 E0596

                                                          B96
DE VATTEL E.,THE LAW OF NATIONS. AGRI FINAN CHIEF   LAW
DIPLOM INT/TRADE AGREE OWN ALL/VALS MORAL ORD/FREE CONCPT
SOVEREIGN...GEN/LAWS 18 NATURL/LAW WOLFF/C. PAGE 30 NAT/G
E0597   INT/LAW

                                               B66
HAY P.,FEDERALISM AND SUPRANATIONAL ORGANIZATIONS: SOVEREIGN
PATTERNS FOR NEW LEGAL STRUCTURES. EUR+WWI LAW   FEDERAL
NAT/G VOL/ASSN DIPLOM PWR...NAT/COMP TREATY EEC.   INT/ORG
PAGE 51 E1014   INT/LAW

                                                          B99
LILLY W.S.,FIRST PRINCIPLES IN POLITICS. UNIV LAW   NAT/G
LEGIS DOMIN ADJUD INGP/REL ORD/FREE SOVEREIGN   CONSTN
...JURID CONCPT 19 NATURL/LAW. PAGE 65 E1299   MORAL
                                                    POLICY

                                               B66
INTL ATOMIC ENERGY AGENCY,INTERNATIONAL CONVENTIONS DIPLOM
ON CIVIL LIABILITY FOR NUCLEAR DAMAGE. FUT WOR+45   INT/ORG
ADJUD WAR COST PEACE SOVEREIGN...JURID 20. PAGE 57 DELIB/GP
E1135   NUC/PWR

SOVEREIGNTY.....SEE SOVEREIGN

SOVIET UNION.....SEE USSR

SOWLE C.R. E1859

SPACE....OUTER SPACE, SPACE LAW

                                               B66
KERR M.H.,ISLAMIC REFORM: THE POLITICAL AND LEGAL   LAW
THEORIES OF MUHAMMAD 'ABDUH AND RASHID RIDA. NAT/G CONCPT
SECT LEAD SOVEREIGN CONSERVE...JURID BIBLIOG   ISLAM
WORSHIP 20. PAGE 60 E1204

                                                          N
FOREIGN AFFAIRS. SPACE WOR+45 WOR-45 CULTURE   BIBLIOG
ECO/UNDEV FINAN NAT/G TEC/DEV INT/TRADE ARMS/CONT   DIPLOM
NUC/PWR...POLICY 20 UN EURATOM ECSC EEC. PAGE 1   INT/ORG
E0021   INT/LAW

                                               B66
NANTWI E.K.,THE ENFORCEMENT OF INTERNATIONAL   INT/LAW
JUDICIAL DECISIONS AND ARBITAL AWARDS IN PUBLIC   ADJUD
INTERNATIONAL LAW. WOR+45 WOR-45 JUDGE PROB/SOLV   SOVEREIGN
DIPLOM CT/SYS SUPEGO MORAL PWR RESPECT...METH/CNCPT INT/ORG
18/20 CASEBOOK. PAGE 76 E1520

                                                          N
AIR UNIVERSITY LIBRARY,INDEX TO MILITARY   BIBLIOG/A
PERIODICALS. FUT SPACE WOR+45 REGION ARMS/CONT   FORCES
NUC/PWR WAR PEACE INT/LAW. PAGE 3 E0056   NAT/G
                                                    DIPLOM

                                               S66
DETTER I.,"THE PROBLEM OF UNEQUAL TREATIES." CONSTN SOVEREIGN
NAT/G LEGIS COLONIAL COERCE PWR...GEOG UN TIME   DOMIN
TREATY. PAGE 31 E0610   INT/LAW
                                                    ECO/UNDEV

                                                          N19
MEZERIK AG,OUTER SPACE: UN, US, USSR (PAMPHLET).   SPACE
USSR DELIB/GP FORCES DETER NUC/PWR SOVEREIGN   CONTROL
...POLICY 20 UN TREATY. PAGE 73 E1453   DIPLOM
                                                    INT/ORG

                                               S66
GREEN L.C.,"RHODESIAN OIL: BOOTLEGGERS OR PIRATES?" INT/TRADE
AFR RHODESIA UK WOR+45 INT/ORG NAT/G DIPLOM LEGIT   SANCTION
COLONIAL SOVEREIGN 20 UN OAU. PAGE 46 E0907   INT/LAW
                                                    POLICY

                                                          B58
JENKS C.W.,THE COMMON LAW OF MANKIND. EUR+WWI   JURID
MOD/EUR SPACE WOR+45 INT/ORG BAL/PWR ARMS/CONT   SOVEREIGN
COERCE SUPEGO MORAL...TREND 20. PAGE 58 E1154

                                               B67
RAMUNDO B.A.,PEACEFUL COEXISTENCE: INTERNATIONAL   INT/LAW
LAW IN THE BUILDING OF COMMUNISM. USSR INT/ORG   PEACE
DIPLOM COLONIAL ARMS/CONT ROLE SOVEREIGN...POLICY   MARXISM
METH/COMP NAT/COMP BIBLIOG. PAGE 83 E1673   METH/CNCPT

                                                          S58
MCDOUGAL M.S.,"PERSPECTIVES FOR A LAW OF OUTER   INT/ORG
SPACE." FUT WOR+45 AIR CONSULT DELIB/GP TEC/DEV   SPACE
CT/SYS ORD/FREE...POLICY JURID 20 UN. PAGE 70 E1404 INT/LAW

                                               L67
HITCHMAN J.M.,"THE PLATT AMENDMENT REVISITED: A   ATTIT
BIBLIOGRAPHICAL SURVEY." CUBA ACADEM DELIB/GP   DIPLOM
ORD/FREE...HIST/WRIT 20. PAGE 53 E1055   SOVEREIGN
                                                    INT/LAW

                                                          B59
HALEY A.G.,FIRST COLLOQUIUM ON THE LAW OF OUTER   SPACE
SPACE. WOR+45 INT/ORG ACT/RES PLAN BAL/PWR CONFER   LAW
ATTIT PWR...POLICY JURID CHARTS ANTHOL 20. PAGE 49 SOVEREIGN
E0979   CONTROL

                                               S67
DEUTSCH E.P.,"A JUDICIAL PATH TO WORLD PEACE." FUT INT/LAW
WOR+45 CONSTN PROB/SOLV DIPLOM LICENSE ADJUD   INT/ORG
SANCTION CHOOSE REPRESENT NAT/LISM SOVEREIGN 20   JURID
ICJ. PAGE 31 E0611   PEACE

                                                          B59
WOETZEL R.K.,DIE INTERNATIONALE KONTROLLE DER   SPACE
HOHEREN LUFTSCHICHTEN UND DES WELTRAUMS. INT/ORG   INT/LAW
NAT/G CONTROL SUPEGO...JURID CONCPT 20. PAGE 107   DIPLOM
E2136   SOVEREIGN

                                               L68
CHIU H.,"COMMUNIST CHINA'S ATTITUDE TOWARD THE   INT/LAW
UNITED NATIONS: A LEGAL ANALYSIS." CHINA/COM WOR+45 SOVEREIGN
LAW NAT/G DIPLOM CONFER ADJUD PARTIC ATTIT...POLICY INT/ORG
TREND 20 UN. PAGE 22 E0432   REPRESENT

                                                          B60
GOLDSEN J.M.,INTERNATIONAL POLITICAL IMPLICATIONS   R+D
OF ACTIVITIES IN OUTER SPACE. FUT USA+45 WOR+45 AIR SPACE
LAW ACT/RES LEGIT ATTIT KNOWL ORD/FREE PWR...CONCPT
20. PAGE 44 E0879

                                               B75
MAINE H.S.,LECTURES ON THE EARLY HISTORY OF   CULTURE
INSTITUTIONS. IRELAND UK CONSTN ELITES STRUCT FAM   LAW
KIN CHIEF LEGIS CT/SYS OWN SOVEREIGN...CONCPT 16   INGP/REL
BENTHAM/J BREHON ROMAN/LAW. PAGE 68 E1351

                                                          B60
WOETZEL R.K.,THE INTERNATIONAL CONTROL OF AIRSPACE INT/ORG
AND OUTERSPACE. FUT WOR+45 AIR CONSTN STRUCT   JURID
CONSULT PLAN TEC/DEV ADJUD RIGID/FLEX KNOWL   SPACE
ORD/FREE PWR...TECHNIC GEOG MGT NEW/IDEA TREND   INT/LAW
COMPUT/IR VAL/FREE 20 TREATY. PAGE 107 E2137

                                               L86
WHITRIDGE L.I.,"LEGISLATIVE INQUESTS" USA+45 ADJUD CT/SYS
GOV/REL SOVEREIGN 19/20 CONGRESS. PAGE 106 E2120   LEGIS

                                                          S60
WRIGHT Q.,"LEGAL ASPECTS OF THE U-2 INCIDENT." COM PWR
USA+45 USSR STRUCT NAT/G FORCES PLAN TEC/DEV ADJUD POLICY

RIGID/FLEX MORAL ORD/FREE...DECISION INT/LAW JURID SPACE
PSY TREND GEN/LAWS COLD/WAR VAL/FREE 20 U-2.
PAGE 108 E2157

L61
SAND P.T.,"AN HISTORICAL SURVEY OF INTERNATIONAL   INT/ORG
AIR LAW SINCE 1944." USA+45 USA-45 WOR+45 WOR-45   LAW
SOCIETY ECO/DEV NAT/G CONSULT EX/STRUC ACT/RES PLAN INT/LAW
LEGIT ROUTINE...JURID CONCPT METH/CNCPT TREND 20.   SPACE
PAGE 87 E1744

L61
TAUBENFELD H.J.,"A REGIME FOR OUTER SPACE." FUT   INT/ORG
UNIV R+D ACT/RES PLAN BAL/PWR LEGIT ARMS/CONT   ADJUD
ORD/FREE...POLICY JURID TREND UN TOT/POP 20   SPACE
COLD/WAR. PAGE 95 E1910

S61
LIPSON L.,"AN ARGUMENT ON THE LEGALITY OF   INT/ORG
RECONNAISSANCE SATELLITES." COM USA+45 USSR WOR+45 LAW
AIR INTELL NAT/G CONSULT PLAN DIPLOM LEGIT ROUTINE   SPACE
ATTIT...INT/LAW JURID CONCPT METH/CNCPT TREND
COLD/WAR 20. PAGE 65 E1302

S61
MACHOWSKI K.,"SELECTED PROBLEMS OF NATIONAL   UNIV
SOVEREIGNTY WITH REFERENCE TO THE LAW OF OUTER   ACT/RES
SPACE." FUT WOR+45 AIR LAW INTELL SOCIETY ECO/DEV   NUC/PWR
PLAN EDU/PROP DETER DRIVE PERCEPT SOVEREIGN   SPACE
...POLICY INT/LAW OBS TREND TOT/POP 20. PAGE 67
E1339

B62
SCHWARTZ L.E.,INTERNATIONAL ORGANIZATIONS AND SPACE INT/ORG
COOPERATION. VOL/ASSN CONSULT CREATE TEC/DEV   DIPLOM
SANCTION...POLICY INT/LAW PHIL/SCI 20 UN. PAGE 89   R+D
E1787   SPACE

B62
US CONGRESS,COMMUNICATIONS SATELLITE LEGISLATION: SPACE
HEARINGS BEFORE COMM ON AERON AND SPACE SCIENCES ON COM/IND
BILLS S2550 AND 2814. WOR+45 LAW VOL/ASSN PLAN   ADJUD
DIPLOM CONTROL OWN PEACE...NEW/IDEA CONGRESS NASA.   GOV/REL
PAGE 99 E1990

S62
CRANE R.D.,"LAW AND STRATEGY IN SPACE." FUT USA+45 CONCPT
WOR+45 AIR LAW INT/ORG NAT/G FORCES ACT/RES PLAN   SPACE
BAL/PWR LEGIT ARMS/CONT COERCE ORD/FREE...POLICY
INT/LAW JURID SOC/EXP 20 TREATY. PAGE 27 E0542

S62
CRANE R.D.,"SOVIET ATTITUDE TOWARD INTERNATIONAL   LAW
SPACE LAW." COM FUT USA+45 USSR AIR CONSTN DELIB/GP ATTIT
DOMIN PWR...JURID TREND TOT/POP 20. PAGE 27 E0543   INT/LAW
                                                    SPACE

S62
LISSITZYN O.J.,"SOME LEGAL IMPLICATIONS OF THE U-2 LAW
AND RB-47 INCIDENTS." FUT USA+45 USSR WOR+45 AIR   CONCPT
NAT/G LEGIT MORAL ORD/FREE SOVEREIGN...JURID   SPACE
GEN/LAWS GEN/METH COLD/WAR 20 U-2. PAGE 65 E1305   INT/LAW

B63
HALEY A.G.,SPACE LAW AND GOVERNMENT. FUT USA+45   INT/ORG
WOR+45 LEGIS ACT/RES CREATE ATTIT RIGID/FLEX   LAW
ORD/FREE PWR SOVEREIGN...POLICY JURID CONCPT CHARTS SPACE
VAL/FREE 20. PAGE 49 E0980

B63
MCDOUGAL M.S.,LAW AND PUBLIC ORDER IN SPACE. FUT   SPACE
USA+45 ACT/RES TEC/DEV ADJUD...POLICY INT/LAW JURID ORD/FREE
20. PAGE 70 E1410   DIPLOM
                                                    DECISION

B63
US SENATE,DOCUMENTS ON INTERNATIONAL AS"ECTS OF   SPACE
EXPLORATION AND USE OF OUTER SPACE, 1954-62: STAFF UTIL
REPORT FOR COMM AERON SPACE SCI. USA+45 USSR LEGIS GOV/REL
LEAD CIVMIL/REL PEACE...POLICY INT/LAW ANTHOL 20   DIPLOM
CONGRESS NASA KHRUSH/N. PAGE 101 E2026

S63
GARDNER R.N.,"COOPERATION IN OUTER SPACE." FUT USSR INT/ORG
WOR+45 AIR LAW COM/IND CONSULT DELIB/GP CREATE   ACT/RES
KNOWL 20 TREATY. PAGE 42 E0837   PEACE
                                                    SPACE

B64
COHEN M.,LAW AND POLITICS IN SPACE: SPECIFIC AND   DELIB/GP
URGENT PROBLEMS IN THE LAW OF OUTER SPACE.   LAW
CHINA/COM COM USA+45 USSR WOR+45 COM/IND INT/ORG   INT/LAW
NAT/G LEGIT NUC/PWR ATTIT BIO/SOC...JURID CONCPT   SPACE
CONGRESS 20 STALIN/J. PAGE 24 E0464

B64
MCDOUGAL M.S.,STUDIES IN WORLD PUBLIC ORDER. SPACE INT/LAW
SEA INT/ORG CREATE AGREE NUC/PWR...POLICY PHIL/SCI SOC
IDEA/COMP ANTHOL METH 20 UN. PAGE 71 E1411   DIPLOM

B64
NASA,PROCEEDINGS OF CONFERENCE ON THE LAW OF SPACE SPACE
AND OF SATELLITE COMMUNICATIONS: CHICAGO 1963. FUT COM/IND
WOR+45 DELIB/GP PROB/SOLV TEC/DEV CONFER ADJUD   LAW
NUC/PWR...POLICY IDEA/COMP 20 NASA. PAGE 76 E1522   DIPLOM

B64
OSSENBECK F.J.,OPEN SPACE AND PEACE. CHINA/COM FUT SPACE
USA+45 USSR LAW PROB/SOLV TEC/DEV EDU/PROP NEUTRAL ORD/FREE
PEACE...AUD/VIS ANTHOL 20. PAGE 79 E1583   DIPLOM
                                                    CREATE

B64
SCHWARTZ M.D.,CONFERENCE ON SPACE SCIENCE AND SPACE SPACE
LAW. FUT COM/IND NAT/G FORCES ACT/RES PLAN BUDGET   LAW
DIPLOM NUC/PWR WEAPON...POLICY ANTHOL 20. PAGE 89   PEACE
E1788   TEC/DEV

B64
TAUBENFELD H.J.,SPACE AND SOCIETY. USA+45 LAW   SPACE
FORCES CREATE TEC/DEV ADJUD CONTROL COST PEACE   SOCIETY
...PREDICT ANTHOL 20. PAGE 95 E1911   ADJUST
                                                    DIPLOM

B64
US AIR FORCE ACADEMY ASSEMBLY,OUTER SPACE: FINAL   SPACE
REPORT APRIL 1-4, 1964. FUT USA+45 WOR+45 LAW   CIVMIL/REL
DELIB/GP CONFER ARMS/CONT WAR PEACE ATTIT MORAL   NUC/PWR
...ANTHOL 20 NASA. PAGE 99 E1979   DIPLOM

S64
CRANE R.D.,"BASIC PRINCIPLES IN SOVIET SPACE LAW." COM
FUT WOR+45 AIR INT/ORG DIPLOM DOMIN ARMS/CONT   LAW
COERCE NUC/PWR PEACE ATTIT DRIVE PWR...INT/LAW   USSR
METH/CNCPT NEW/IDEA OBS TREND GEN/LAWS VAL/FREE   SPACE
MARX/KARL 20. PAGE 27 E0544

B65
JENKS C.W.,SPACE LAW. DIPLOM DEBATE CONTROL   SPACE
ORD/FREE TREATY 20 UN. PAGE 58 E1161   INT/LAW
                                                    JURID
                                                    INT/ORG

B65
US SENATE,US INTERNATIONAL SPACE PROGRAMS, 1959-65: SPACE
STAFF REPORT FOR COMM ON AERONAUTICAL AND SPACE   DIPLOM
SCIENCES. WOR+45 VOL/ASSN CIVMIL/REL 20 CONGRESS   PLAN
NASA TREATY. PAGE 101 E2027   GOV/REL

S65
HIBBS A.R.,"SPACE TECHNOLOGY* THE THREAT AND THE   SPACE
PROMISE." FUT VOL/ASSN TEC/DEV NUC/PWR COST   ARMS/CONT
EFFICIENCY UTIL UN TREATY. PAGE 52 E1038   PREDICT

C65
SEARA M.V.,"COSMIC INTERNATIONAL LAW." LAW ACADEM   SPACE
ACT/RES DIPLOM COLONIAL CONTROL NUC/PWR SOVEREIGN   INT/LAW
...GEN/LAWS BIBLIOG UN. PAGE 90 E1799   IDEA/COMP
                                                    INT/ORG

B66
UNITED NATIONS,INTERNATIONAL SPACE BIBLIOGRAPHY.   BIBLIOG
FUT INT/ORG TEC/DEV DIPLOM ARMS/CONT NUC/PWR   SPACE
...JURID SOC UN. PAGE 98 E1969   PEACE
                                                    R+D

B66
US SENATE COMM AERO SPACE SCI,SOVIET SPACE   CONSULT
PROGRAMS, 1962-65: GOALS AND PURPOSES,   SPACE
ACHIEVEMENTS, PLANS, AND INTERNATIONAL   FUT
IMPLICATIONS. USA+45 USSR R+D FORCES PLAN EDU/PROP DIPLOM
PRESS ADJUD ARMS/CONT ATTIT MARXISM. PAGE 101 E2028

B67
UNIVERSAL REFERENCE SYSTEM,PUBLIC POLICY AND THE   BIBLIOG/A
MANAGEMENT OF SCIENCE (VOLUME IX). FUT SPACE WOR+45 POLICY
LAW NAT/G TEC/DEV CONTROL NUC/PWR GOV/REL   MGT
...COMPUT/IR GEN/METH. PAGE 99 E1975   PHIL/SCI

B67
US SENATE COMM ON FOREIGN REL,TREATY ON OUTER   SPACE
SPACE. WOR+45 AIR FORCES PROB/SOLV NUC/PWR SENATE   DIPLOM
TREATY UN. PAGE 101 E2032   ARMS/CONT
                                                    LAW

S67
DOYLE S.E.,"COMMUNICATION SATELLITES* INTERNAL   TEC/DEV
ORGANIZATION FOR DEVELOPMENT AND CONTROL." USA+45   SPACE
R+D ACT/RES DIPLOM NAT/LISM...POLICY INT/LAW   COM/IND
PREDICT UN. PAGE 33 E0647   INT/ORG

LAY S.H.,"EXCLUSIVE GOVERNMENTAL LIABILITY FOR
SPACE ACCIDENTS." USA+45 LAW FINAN SERV/IND TEC/DEV
ADJUD. PAGE 64 E1272

S67
NAT/G
SUPEGO
SPACE
PROB/SOLV

SPAETH H.J. E1860

SPAIN....SPAIN

GRIFFIN A.P.C.,LIST OF BOOKS RELATING TO THE THEORY
OF COLONIZATION, GOVERNMENT OF DEPENDENCIES,
PROTECTORATES, AND RELATED TOPICS. FRANCE GERMANY
ITALY SPAIN UK USA-45 WOR-45 ECO/TAC ADMIN CONTROL
REGION NAT/LISM ALL/VALS PWR...INT/LAW SOC 16/19.
PAGE 46 E0917

B00
BIBLIOG/A
COLONIAL
GOV/REL
DOMIN

BENTHAM J.,"ON THE LIBERTY OF THE PRESS, AND PUBLIC
DISCUSSION" IN J. BOWRING, ED., THE WORKS OF JEREMY
BENTHAM." SPAIN UK LAW ELITES NAT/G LEGIS INSPECT
LEGIT WRITING CONTROL PRIVIL TOTALISM AUTHORIT
...TRADIT 19 FREE/SPEE. PAGE 10 E0193

C43
ORD/FREE
PRESS
CONFER
CONSERVE

SCHONS D.,BOOK CENSORSHIP IN NEW SPAIN (NEW WORLD
STUDIES, BOOK II). SPAIN LAW CULTURE INSPECT ADJUD
CT/SYS SANCTION GP/REL ORD/FREE 14/17. PAGE 88
E1764

B49
CHRIST-17C
EDU/PROP
CONTROL
PRESS

GUAITA A.,BIBLIOGRAFIA ESPANOLA DE DERECHO
ADMINISTRATIVO (PAMPHLET). SPAIN LOC/G MUNIC NAT/G
PROVS JUDGE BAL/PWR GOV/REL OWN...JURID 18/19.
PAGE 48 E0959

B55
BIBLIOG
ADMIN
CONSTN
PWR

HOBSBAWM E.J.,PRIMITIVE REBELS; STUDIES IN ARCHAIC
FORMS OF SOCIAL MOVEMENT IN THE 19TH AND 20TH
CENTURIES. ITALY SPAIN CULTURE VOL/ASSN RISK CROWD
GP/REL INGP/REL ISOLAT TOTALISM...PSY SOC 18/20.
PAGE 53 E1058

B59
SOCIETY
CRIME
REV
GUERRILLA

ALBI F.,TRATADO DE LOS MODOS DE GESTION DE LAS
CORPORACIONES LOCALES. SPAIN FINAN NAT/G BUDGET
CONTROL EXEC ROUTINE GOV/REL ORD/FREE SOVEREIGN
...MGT 20. PAGE 3 E0057

B60
LOC/G
LAW
ADMIN
MUNIC

GUIZOT F.P.G.,HISTORY OF THE ORIGIN OF
REPRESENTATIVE GOVERNMENT IN EUROPE. CHRIST-17C
FRANCE MOD/EUR SPAIN UK LAW CHIEF FORCES POPULISM
...MAJORIT TIME/SEQ GOV/COMP NAT/COMP 4/19
PARLIAMENT. PAGE 48 E0961

B61
LEGIS
REPRESENT
CONSTN
NAT/G

ALEXANDER B.,"GIBRALTAR" SPAIN UK CONSTN WORKER
PROB/SOLV FOR/AID RECEIVE CONTROL 20. PAGE 3 E0059

S67
DIPLOM
INT/ORG
ORD/FREE
ECO/TAC

MORENO F.J.,"THE SPANISH COLONIAL SYSTEM: A
FUNCTIONAL APPROACH." SPAIN WOR-45 LAW CHIEF DIPLOM
ADJUD CIVMIL/REL AUTHORIT ROLE PWR...CONCPT 17/20.
PAGE 74 E1492

S67
COLONIAL
CONTROL
NAT/G
OP/RES

SPAN/AMER....SPANISH-AMERICAN CULTURE

SPEAKER OF THE HOUSE....SEE CONGRESS, HOUSE/REP, LEGIS,
PARLIAMENT

SPEAR/BRWN....SPEARMAN BROWN PREDICTION FORMULA

SPECIALIZATION....SEE TASK, SKILL

SPECULATION....SEE GAMBLE, RISK

SPENCER/H....HERBERT SPENCER

SPENGLER/O....OSWALD SPENGLER

SPINOZA/B....BARUCH (OR BENEDICT) SPINOZA

SPIRO H.J. E1861

SPITZ D. E1862

SPOCK/B....BENJAMIN SPOCK

SPORTS....SPORTS AND ATHLETIC COMPETITIONS

SPRAGUE J.D. E0701

SQUIBB G.D. E1863

SRAFFA/P....PIERO SRAFFA

SST....SUPERSONIC TRANSPORT

ST/LOUIS....ST. LOUIS, MISSOURI

ST/PAUL....SAINT PAUL, MINNESOTA

STAAR R.F. E1864

STAGES....SEE TIME/SEQ

STALIN/J....JOSEPH STALIN

COHEN M.,LAW AND POLITICS IN SPACE: SPECIFIC AND
URGENT PROBLEMS IN THE LAW OF OUTER SPACE.
CHINA/COM COM USA+45 USSR WOR+45 COM/IND INT/ORG
NAT/G LEGIT NUC/PWR ATTIT BIO/SOC...JURID CONCPT
CONGRESS 20 STALIN/J. PAGE 24 E0464

B64
DELIB/GP
LAW
INT/LAW
SPACE

DALLIN A.,POLITICS IN THE SOVIET UNION: 7 CASES.
COM USSR LAW POL/PAR CHIEF FORCES WRITING CONTROL
PARL/PROC CIVMIL/REL TOTALISM...ANTHOL 20 KHRUSH/N
STALIN/J CASEBOOK COM/PARTY. PAGE 28 E0563

B66
MARXISM
DOMIN
ORD/FREE
GOV/REL

SHAPIRO J.P.,"SOVIET HISTORIOGRAPHY AND THE MOSCOW
TRIALS: AFTER THIRTY YEARS." USSR NAT/G LEGIT PRESS
CONTROL LEAD ATTIT MARXISM...NEW/IDEA METH 20
TROTSKY/L STALIN/J KHRUSH/N. PAGE 90 E1810

S68
HIST/WRIT
EDU/PROP
SANCTION
ADJUD

STAMMLER/R....RUDOLF STAMMLER

STAND/INT....STANDARDIZED INTERVIEWS

PRYOR F.L.,THE COMMUNIST FOREIGN TRADE SYSTEM. COM
CZECHOSLVK GERMANY YUGOSLAVIA LAW ECO/DEV DIST/IND
POL/PAR PLAN DOMIN TOTALISM DRIVE RIGID/FLEX WEALTH
...STAT STAND/INT CHARTS 20. PAGE 83 E1657

B63
ATTIT
ECO/TAC

STANDARDIZED INTERVIEWS....SEE STAND/INT

STANFORD/U....STANFORD UNIVERSITY

STANGER R.J. E1865

STANKIEW/W....W.J. STANKIEWICZ

STAR/CARR....STAR-CARR, A PREHISTORIC SOCIETY

STAT....STATISTICS

CONOVER H.F.,OFFICIAL PUBLICATIONS OF BRITISH EAST
AFRICA (PAMPHLET). UK LAW ECO/UNDEV AGRI EXTR/IND
SECT LEGIS BUDGET TAX...HEAL STAT 20. PAGE 25 E0491

N
BIBLIOG/A
AFR
ADMIN
COLONIAL

MINISTRY OF OVERSEAS DEVELOPME,TECHNICAL CO-
OPERATION -- A BIBLIOGRAPHY. UK LAW SOCIETY DIPLOM
ECO/TAC FOR/AID...STAT 20 CMN/WLTH. PAGE 73 E1466

N
BIBLIOG
TEC/DEV
ECO/DEV
NAT/G

US BUREAU OF THE CENSUS,BIBLIOGRAPHY OF SOCIAL
SCIENCE PERIODICALS AND MONOGRAPH SERIES. WOR+45
LAW DIPLOM EDU/PROP HEALTH...PSY SOC LING STAT.
PAGE 99 E1980

N
BIBLIOG/A
CULTURE
NAT/G
SOCIETY

SCHMIDHAUSER J.R.,JUDICIAL BEHAVIOR AND THE
SECTIONAL CRISIS OF 1837-1860. USA-45 ADJUD CT/SYS
INGP/REL ATTIT HABITAT...DECISION PSY STAT CHARTS
SIMUL. PAGE 88 E1759

N13
JUDGE
POL/PAR
PERS/COMP
PERSON

SMITH R.H.,JUSTICE AND THE POOR. LAW RECEIVE ADJUD
CRIME GOV/REL COST...JURID SOC/WK CONCPT STAT
CHARTS GP/COMP 20. PAGE 92 E1847

B19
CT/SYS
DISCRIM
WEALTH

BUREAU OF NAT'L AFFAIRS INC.,A CURRENT LOOK AT:
(1) THE NEGRO AND TITLE VII, (2) SEX AND TITLE VII
(PAMPHLET). LAW LG/CO SML/CO RACE/REL...POLICY SOC

N19
DISCRIM
SEX
WORKER

STAT DEEP/QU TREND CON/ANAL CHARTS 20 NEGRO   MGT
CIV/RIGHTS. PAGE 17 E0334

N19
OPERATIONS AND POLICY RESEARCH,URUGUAY: ELECTION   POL/PAR
FACTBOOK: NOVEMBER 27, 1966 (PAMPHLET). URUGUAY LAW   CHOOSE
NAT/G LEAD REPRESENT...STAT BIOG CHARTS 20. PAGE 79   PLAN
E1576   ATTIT

S26
HALL A.B.,"DETERMINATION OF METHODS FOR   ADJUD
ASCERTAINING THE FACTORS THAT INFLUENCE JUDICIAL   DECISION
DECISIONS IN CASES INVOLVING DUE PROCESS" LAW JUDGE   CONSTN
DEBATE EFFICIENCY OPTIMAL UTIL...SOC CONCPT   JURID
PROBABIL STAT SAMP. PAGE 49 E0981

B33
DANGERFIELD R.,IN DEFENSE OF THE SENATE. USA-45   LEGIS
CONSTN NAT/G EX/STRUC TOP/EX ATTIT KNOWL   DELIB/GP
...METH/CNCPT STAT TIME/SEQ TREND CON/ANAL CHARTS   DIPLOM
CONGRESS 20 TREATY. PAGE 28 E0565

B34
CULVER D.C.,BIBLIOGRAPHY OF CRIME AND CRIMINAL   BIBLIOG/A
JUSTICE, 1927-1931. LAW CULTURE PUB/INST PROB/SOLV   CRIMLGY
CT/SYS...PSY SOC STAT 20. PAGE 28 E0549   ADJUD
  FORCES

B35
CUMMING J.,A CONTRIBUTION TOWARD A BIBLIOGRAPHY   BIBLIOG
DEALING WITH CRIME AND COGNATE SUBJECTS (3RD ED.).   CRIMLGY
UK LAW CULTURE PUB/INST ADJUD AGE BIO/SOC...PSY SOC   FORCES
SOC/WK STAT METH/COMP 20. PAGE 28 E0552   CT/SYS

B36
CULVER D.C.,METHODOLOGY OF SOCIAL SCIENCE RESEARCH: BIBLIOG/A
A BIBLIOGRAPHY. LAW CULTURE...CRIMLGY GEOG STAT OBS   METH
INT QU HIST/WRIT CHARTS 20. PAGE 28 E0550   SOC

B39
CULVER D.C.,BIBLIOGRAPHY OF CRIME AND CRIMINAL   BIBLIOG/A
JUSTICE, 1932-1937. USA-45 LAW CULTURE PUB/INST   CRIMLGY
PROB/SOLV CT/SYS...PSY SOC STAT 20. PAGE 28 E0551   ADJUD
  FORCES

B52
ANDREWS F.E.,CORPORATION GIVING. LAW TAX EDU/PROP   LG/CO
ADMIN...POLICY STAT CHARTS. PAGE 5 E0096   GIVE
  SML/CO
  FINAN

B53
BUTLER D.E.,THE ELECTORAL SYSTEM IN BRITAIN,   CHOOSE
1918-1951. UK LAW POL/PAR SUFF...STAT BIBLIOG 20   LEGIS
PARLIAMENT. PAGE 18 E0348   REPRESENT
  PARTIC

B53
CALDWELL L.K.,RESEARCH METHODS IN PUBLIC   BIBLIOG/A
ADMINISTRATION: AN OUTLINE OF TOPICS AND READINGS   METH/COMP
(PAMPHLET). LAW ACT/RES COMPUTER KNOWL...SOC STAT   ADMIN
GEN/METH 20. PAGE 18 E0364   OP/RES

B54
CAPLOW T.,THE SOCIOLOGY OF WORK. USA+45 USA-45   LABOR
STRATA MARKET FAM GP/REL INGP/REL ALL/VALS   WORKER
...DECISION STAT BIBLIOG SOC/INTEG 20. PAGE 19   INDUS
E0375   ROLE

B54
CARTER P.G.,STATISTICAL BULLETINS: AN ANNOTATED   BIBLIOG/A
BIBLIOGRAPHY OF THE GENERAL STATISTICAL BULLETINS   WOR+45
AND MAJOR POL SUBDIV OF WORLD. CULTURE AGRI FINAN   NAT/G
INDUS LABOR TEC/DEV INT/TRADE CT/SYS WEALTH   STAT
...CRIMLGY SOC 20. PAGE 20 E0400

B56
DUNNILL F.,THE CIVIL SERVICE. UK LAW PLAN ADMIN   PERSON
EFFICIENCY DRIVE NEW/LIB...STAT CHARTS 20   WORKER
PARLIAMENT CIVIL/SERV. PAGE 33 E0662   STRATA
  SOC/WK

B56
US HOUSE WAYS MEANS COMMITTEE,TRAFFIC IN, AND   BIO/SOC
CONTROL OF NARCOTICS, BARBITURATES, AND   CONTROL
AMPHETAMINES. CHINA/COM USA+45 SOCIETY LEGIS   PROB/SOLV
ACT/RES EDU/PROP CT/SYS SANCTION PROFIT HEALTH   CRIME
...HEAL PSY STAT 20. PAGE 100 E2011

B57
NJ LAW AND LEGISLATIVE BURE,NEW JERSEY   APPORT
LEGISLAVTIVE REAPPORTIONMENT (PAMPHLET). USA+45   LEGIS
ACT/RES ADJUD...STAT CHARTS 20 NEW/JERSEY. PAGE 2   CENSUS
E0041   REPRESENT

B58
ORTIZ R.P.,ANNUARIO BIBLIOGRAFICO COLOMBIANO,   BIBLIOG
1951-1956. LAW RECEIVE EDU/PROP ADMIN...LING STAT   SOC
20 COLOMB. PAGE 79 E1582

L58
BEVAN W.,"JURY BEHAVIOR AS A FUNCTION OF THE   PERSON
PRESTIGE OF THE FOREMAN AND THE NATURE OF HIS   EDU/PROP
LEADERSHIP" (BMR)" DELIB/GP DOMIN ADJUD LEAD   DECISION
PERS/REL ATTIT...PSY STAT INT QU CHARTS SOC/EXP 20   CT/SYS
JURY. PAGE 11 E0221

S58
SCHUBERT G.A.,"THE STUDY OF JUDICIAL DECISION-   JUDGE
MAKING AS AN ASPECT OF POLITICAL BEHAVIOR." PLAN   DECISION
ADJUD CT/SYS INGP/REL PERSON...PHIL/SCI SOC QUANT   CON/ANAL
STAT CHARTS IDEA/COMP SOC/EXP. PAGE 89 E1779   GAME

B59
PO414COLUMBIA BUR OF APP SOC R,ATTITUDES OF   ATTIT
PROMINENT AMERICANS TOWARD "WORLD PEACE THROUGH   ACT/RES
WORLD LAW" (SUPRA-NATL ORGANIZATION FOR WAR   INT/LAW
PREVENTION). USA+45 USSR ELITES FORCES PLAN   STAT
PROB/SOLV CONTROL WAR PWR...POLICY SOC QU IDEA/COMP
20 UN. PAGE 82 E1644

S59
DERGE D.R.,"THE LAWYER AS DECISION-MAKER IN THE   LEGIS
AMERICAN STATE LEGISLATURE." INTELL LOC/G POL/PAR   LAW
CHOOSE AGE HEREDITY PERSON CONSERVE...JURID STAT   DECISION
CHARTS. PAGE 31 E0607   LEAD

S59
TIPTON J.B.,"PARTICIPATION OF THE UNITED STATES IN   LABOR
THE INTERNATIONAL LABOR ORGANIZATION." USA+45 LAW   INT/ORG
STRUCT ECO/DEV ECO/UNDEV INDUS TEC/DEV ECO/TAC
ADMIN PERCEPT ORD/FREE SKILL...STAT HIST/WRIT
GEN/METH ILO WORK 20. PAGE 96 E1928

B60
NAT'L MUNICIPAL LEAGUE,COMPENDIUM ON LEGISLATIVE   APPORT
APPORTIONMENT. USA+45 LOC/G NAT/G POL/PAR PROVS   REPRESENT
CT/SYS CHOOSE 20 SUPREME/CT CONGRESS. PAGE 76 E1523   LEGIS
  STAT

B60
STEIN E.,AMERICAN ENTERPRISE IN THE EUROPEAN COMMON   MARKET
MARKET: A LEGAL PROFILE. EUR+WWI FUT USA+45 SOCIETY   ADJUD
STRUCT ECO/DEV NAT/G VOL/ASSN CONSULT PLAN TEC/DEV   INT/LAW
ECO/TAC INT/TRADE ADMIN ATTIT RIGID/FLEX PWR...MGT
NEW/IDEA STAT TREND COMPUT/IR SIMUL EEC 20. PAGE 93
E1867

L60
STEIN E.,"LEGAL REMEDIES OF ENTERPRISES IN THE   MARKET
EUROPEAN ECONOMIC COMMUNITY." EUR+WWI FUT ECO/DEV   ADJUD
INDUS PLAN ECO/TAC ADMIN PWR...MGT MATH STAT TREND
CON/ANAL EEC 20. PAGE 93 E1868

S60
SCHWELB E.,"INTERNATIONAL CONVENTIONS ON HUMAN   INT/ORG
RIGHTS." FUT WOR+45 LAW CONSTN CULTURE SOCIETY   HUM
STRUCT VOL/ASSN DELIB/GP PLAN ADJUD SUPEGO LOVE
MORAL...SOC CONCPT STAT RECORD HIST/WRIT TREND 20
UN. PAGE 89 E1790

S61
SCHUBERT G.,"A PSYCHOMETRIC MODEL OF THE SUPREME   JUDGE
COURT." DELIB/GP ADJUD CHOOSE ATTIT...DECISION   CT/SYS
JURID PSY QUANT STAT HYPO/EXP GEN/METH SUPREME/CT.   PERSON
PAGE 88 E1771   SIMUL

B62
NAT'L MUNICIPAL LEAGUE,COMPENDIUM ON LEGISLATIVE   APPORT
APPORTIONMENT. USA+45 LOC/G NAT/G POL/PAR PROVS   REPRESENT
CT/SYS CHOOSE 20 SUPREME/CT CONGRESS. PAGE 76 E1524   LEGIS
  STAT

B62
PRESS C.,STATE MANUALS, BLUE BOOKS AND ELECTION   BIBLIOG
RESULTS. LAW LOC/G MUNIC LEGIS WRITING FEDERAL   PROVS
SOVEREIGN...DECISION STAT CHARTS 20. PAGE 82 E1648   ADMIN
  CHOOSE

B62
SILVA R.C.,RUM, RELIGION, AND VOTES: 1928 RE-   POL/PAR
EXAMINED. USA-45 LAW SECT DISCRIM CATHISM...CORREL   CHOOSE
STAT 20 PRESIDENT SMITH/ALF DEMOCRAT. PAGE 91 E1827   GP/COMP
  ATTIT

L62
SCHWERIN K.,"LAW LIBRARIES AND FOREIGN LAW   BIBLIOG
COLLECTION IN THE USA." USA+45 USA-45...INT/LAW   LAW
STAT 20. PAGE 89 E1793   ACADEM
  ADMIN

SPAETH H.J.,"JUDICIAL POWER AS A VARIABLE
MOTIVATING SUPREME COURT BEHAVIOR." DELIB/GP ADJUD
RATIONAL ATTIT PERSON ORD/FREE...CLASSIF STAT
GEN/METH. PAGE 93 E1860
`L62 JUDGE DECISION PERS/COMP PSY`

UNITED NATIONS,"CAPITAL PUNISHMENT." WOR+45 CULTURE
NAT/G ROUTINE COERCE HEALTH PWR...POLICY SOC QU
CHARTS VAL/FREE 20. PAGE 98 E1967
`L62 LAW STAT`

SCHUBERT G.,"THE 1960 TERM OF THE SUPREME COURT: A
PSYCHOLOGICAL ANALYSIS." USA+45 LAW CT/SYS...STAT
SUPREME/CT. PAGE 88 E1772
`S62 DECISION LEGIS JUDGE EX/STRUC`

DE GRAZIA A.,APPORTIONMENT AND REPRESENTATIVE
GOVERNMENT. CONSTN POL/PAR LEGIS PLAN ADJUD DISCRIM
RATIONAL...CONCPT STAT PREDICT TREND IDEA/COMP.
PAGE 29 E0583
`B63 REPRESENT APPORT NAT/G MUNIC`

PRYOR F.L.,THE COMMUNIST FOREIGN TRADE SYSTEM. COM
CZECHOSLVK GERMANY YUGOSLAVIA LAW ECO/DEV DIST/IND
POL/PAR PLAN DOMIN TOTALISM DRIVE RIGID/FLEX WEALTH
...STAT STAND/INT CHARTS 20. PAGE 83 E1657
`B63 ATTIT ECO/TAC`

VINES K.N.,STUDIES IN JUDICIAL POLITICS: TULANE
STUDIES IN POLITICAL SCIENCE (VOL. 8). POL/PAR
JUDGE ADJUD SANCTION CRIME CHOOSE PWR...JURID STAT
TIME/SEQ CHARTS. PAGE 104 E2079
`B63 CT/SYS GOV/REL PROVS`

ROSE R.,"COMPARATIVE STUDIES IN POLITICAL FINANCE:
A SYMPOSIUM." ASIA EUR+WWI S/ASIA LAW CULTURE
DELIB/GP LEGIS ACT/RES ECO/TAC EDU/PROP CHOOSE
ATTIT RIGID/FLEX SUPEGO PWR SKILL WEALTH...STAT
ANTHOL VAL/FREE. PAGE 85 E1714
`L63 FINAN POL/PAR`

HILLS R.J.,"THE REPRESENTATIVE FUNCTION: NEGLECTED
DIMENSION OF LEADERSHIP BEHAVIOR" USA+45 CLIENT
STRUCT SCHOOL PERS/REL...STAT QU SAMP LAB/EXP 20.
PAGE 53 E1048
`S63 LEAD ADMIN EXEC ACT/RES`

SCHUBERT G.,"JUDICIAL DECISION-MAKING." FORCES LEAD
ATTIT DRIVE...POLICY PSY STAT CHARTS ANTHOL BIBLIOG
20. PAGE 88 E1773
`C63 ADJUD DECISION JUDGE CT/SYS`

BECKER T.L.,POLITICAL BEHAVIORALISM AND MODERN
JURISPRUDENCE* A WORKING THEORY AND STUDY IN
JUDICIAL DECISION-MAKING. CONSTN...JURID STAT
GEN/METH INDEX. PAGE 9 E0172
`B64 JUDGE LAW DECISION CT/SYS`

HEKHUIS D.J.,INTERNATIONAL STABILITY: MILITARY,
ECONOMIC AND POLITICAL DIMENSIONS. FUT WOR+45
ECO/UNDEV INT/ORG NAT/G VOL/ASSN FORCES ACT/RES
BAL/PWR PWR WEALTH...STAT UN 20. PAGE 51 E1024
`B64 TEC/DEV DETER REGION`

US SENATE COMM ON JUDICIARY,HEARINGS BEFORE
SUBCOMMITTEE ON ANTITRUST AND MONOPOLY: ECONOMIC
CONCENTRATION VOLUMES 1-5 JULY 1964-SEPT 1966.
USA+45 LAW FINAN ECO/TAC ADJUD COST EFFICIENCY
PRODUC...STAT CHARTS 20 CONGRESS MONOPOLY. PAGE 102
E2052
`B64 ECO/DEV CONTROL MARKET LG/CO`

WRIGHT G.,RURAL REVOLUTION IN FRANCE: THE PEASANTRY
IN THE TWENTIETH CENTURY. EUR+WWI MOD/EUR LAW
CULTURE AGRI POL/PAR DELIB/GP LEGIS ECO/TAC
EDU/PROP COERCE CHOOSE ATTIT RIGID/FLEX HEALTH
...STAT CENSUS CHARTS VAL/FREE 20. PAGE 107 E2148
`B64 PWR STRATA FRANCE REV`

AMERICAN UNIVERSITY IN CAIRO,GUIDE TO UAR
GOVERNMENT PUBLICATIONS AT THE AUC LIBRARY
(PAMPHLET). ISLAM UAR USA+45 ECO/UNDEV...SOC STAT
20. PAGE 4 E0084
`B65 BIBLIOG NAT/G LEGIS LAW`

CONGRESSIONAL QUARTERLY SERV,POLITICS IN AMERICA,
1945-1964: THE POLITICS AND ISSUES OF THE POSTWAR
YEARS. USA+45 LAW FINAN CHIEF DIPLOM APPORT SUFF
...POLICY STAT TREND CHARTS 20 CONGRESS PRESIDENT.
PAGE 25 E0489
`B65 CHOOSE REPRESENT POL/PAR LEGIS`

SCHUBERT G.,THE JUDICIAL MIND: THE ATTITUDES AND
`B65 CT/SYS`

IDEOLOGIES OF SUPREME COURT JUSTICES 1946-1963.
USA+45 ELITES NAT/G CONTROL PERS/REL MAJORITY
CONSERVE...DECISION JURID MODAL STAT TREND GP/COMP
GAME. PAGE 88 E1774
`JUDGE ATTIT NEW/LIB`

UNESCO,INTERNATIONAL ORGANIZATIONS IN THE SOCIAL
SCIENCES(REV. ED.). LAW ADMIN ATTIT...CRIMLGY GEOG
INT/LAW PSY SOC STAT 20 UNESCO. PAGE 98 E1962
`B65 INT/ORG R+D PROF/ORG ACT/RES`

ULMER S.S.,"TOWARD A THEORY OF SUBGROUP FORMATION
IN THE UNITED STATES SUPREME COURT." USA+45 ROUTINE
CHOOSE PWR...JURID STAT CON/ANAL SIMUL SUPREME/CT.
PAGE 97 E1952
`S65 CT/SYS ADJUD ELITES INGP/REL`

WRIGHT Q.,"THE ESCALATION OF INTERNATIONAL
CONFLICTS." WOR+45 WOR-45 FORCES DIPLOM RISK COST
ATTIT ALL/VALS...INT/LAW QUANT STAT NAT/COMP.
PAGE 108 E2160
`S65 WAR PERCEPT PREDICT MATH`

BEELEY A.L.,THE BAIL SYSTEM IN CHICAGO. LAW MUNIC
PUB/INST EFFICIENCY MORAL...CRIMLGY METH/CNCPT STAT
20 CHICAGO. PAGE 9 E0176
`B66 JURID CT/SYS CRIME ADJUD`

DIZARD W.P.,TELEVISION* A WORLD VIEW. WOR+45
ECO/UNDEV TEC/DEV LICENSE LITERACY...STAT OBS INT
QU TREND AUD/VIS BIBLIOG. PAGE 32 E0632
`B66 COM/IND ACT/RES EDU/PROP CREATE`

FLEISCHER B.M.,THE ECONOMICS OF DELINQUENCY. UNIV
WORKER STRANGE ANOMIE...STAT CHARTS 20. PAGE 38
E0762
`B66 STRATA INCOME AGE/Y CRIME`

FRIEDMANN W.G.,INTERNATIONAL FINANCIAL AID. USA+45
ECO/DEV ECO/UNDEV NAT/G VOL/ASSN EX/STRUC PLAN RENT
GIVE BAL/PAY PWR...GEOG INT/LAW STAT TREND UN EEC
COMECON. PAGE 41 E0806
`B66 INT/ORG FOR/AID TEC/DEV ECO/TAC`

STEVENS R.E.,REFERENCE BOOKS IN THE SOCIAL SCIENCES
AND HUMANITIES. CULTURE PERF/ART SECT EDU/PROP
...JURID PSY SOC/WK STAT 20 MUSIC. PAGE 93 E1873
`B66 BIBLIOG/A SOC HUM ART/METH`

US PRES COMN CRIME IN DC,REPORT OF THE US
PRESIDENT'S COMMISSION ON CRIME IN THE DISTRICT OF
COLUMBIA. LEGIS WORKER EDU/PROP ADJUD CONTROL
CT/SYS GP/REL BIO/SOC HEALTH...CRIMLGY NEW/IDEA
STAT 20. PAGE 101 E2022
`B66 CRIME FORCES AGE/Y SANCTION`

HOLSTI K.J.,"RESOLVING INTERNATIONAL CONFLICTS* A
TAXONOMY OF BEHAVIOR AND SOME FIGURES ON
PROCEDURES." WOR+45 WOR-45 INT/ORG ADJUD EFFICIENCY
...STAT IDEA/COMP. PAGE 55 E1089
`L66 DIPLOM PROB/SOLV WAR CLASSIF`

MATTHEWS D.G.,"PRELUDE-COUP D'ETAT-MILITARY
GOVERNMENT: A BIBLIOGRAPHICAL AND RESEARCH GUIDE TO
NIGERIAN POL AND GOVT, JAN, 1965-66." AFR NIGER LAW
CONSTN POL/PAR LEGIS CIVMIL/REL GOV/REL...STAT 20.
PAGE 69 E1385
`S66 BIBLIOG NAT/G ADMIN CHOOSE`

ZAWODNY J.K.,"GUIDE TO THE STUDY OF INTERNATIONAL
RELATIONS." OP/RES PRESS...STAT INT 20. PAGE 108
E2169
`C66 BIBLIOG/A DIPLOM INT/LAW INT/ORG`

ELDRIDGE W.B.,NARCOTICS AND THE LAW: A CRITIQUE OF
THE AMERICAN EXPERIMENT IN NARCOTIC DRUG CONTROL.
PUB/INST ACT/RES PLAN LICENSE GP/REL EFFICIENCY
ATTIT HEALTH...CRIMLGY HEAL STAT 20 ABA DEPT/HEW
NARCO/ACT. PAGE 34 E0679
`B67 LAW INSPECT BIO/SOC JURID`

GELLHORN W.,OMBUDSMEN AND OTHERS: CITIZENS'
PROTECTORS IN NINE COUNTRIES. WOR+45 LAW CONSTN
LEGIS INSPECT ADJUD ADMIN CONTROL CT/SYS CHOOSE
PERS/REL...STAT CHARTS 20. PAGE 43 E0847
`B67 NAT/COMP REPRESENT INGP/REL PROB/SOLV`

OPERATIONS AND POLICY RESEARCH,NICARAGUA: ELECTION
FACTBOOK: FEBRUARY 5, 1967 (PAMPHLET). NICARAGUA
LAW NAT/G LEAD REPRESENT...STAT BIOG CHARTS 20.
`B67 POL/PAR CHOOSE PLAN`

ATTIT

                                                            B67
RAE D.,THE POLITICAL CONSEQUENCES OF ELECTORAL   POL/PAR
LAWS. EUR+WWI ICELAND ISRAEL NEW/ZEALND UK USA+45   CHOOSE
ADJUD APPORT GP/REL MAJORITY...MATH STAT CENSUS   NAT/COMP
CHARTS BIBLIOG 20 AUSTRAL. PAGE 83 E1667   REPRESENT

                                                            S67
GLASER D.,"NATIONAL GOALS AND INDICATORS FOR THE   CRIME
REDUCTION OF CRIME AND DELINQUENCY." FUT USA+45   CRIMLGY
NAT/G...CON/ANAL METH 20. PAGE 44 E0874   LAW
                                                      STAT

STATE GOVERNMENT....SEE PROVS

STATE DEPARTMENT....SEE DEPT/STATE

STATISTICS....SEE STAT, ALSO LOGIC, MATHEMATICS, AND
      LANGUAGE INDEX, P. XIV

STAUB H. E0060

STEEL R. E1866

STEIN E. E1146,E1867,E1868,E1869,E1870

STEINBERG E.B. E0973

STEREOTYPE....SEE STERTYP

STERN A.C. E1871

STERN R.L. E1872

STERN/GANG....STERN GANG (PALESTINE)

STERTYP....STEREOTYPE

                                                            B05
DICEY A.,LAW AND PUBLIC OPINION IN ENGLAND. LAW   ATTIT
CULTURE INTELL SOCIETY NAT/G SECT JUDGE LEGIT   UK
CHOOSE RIGID/FLEX KNOWL...OLD/LIB CONCPT STERTYP
GEN/LAWS 20. PAGE 31 E0620

                                                            L29
DARWIN L.,"WHAT IS EUGENICS." USA-45 LAW SOCIETY   PLAN
FACE/GP FAM ACT/RES ECO/TAC HEALTH...HEAL TREND   BIO/SOC
STERTYP 20. PAGE 29 E0568

                                                            B42
KELSEN H.,LAW AND PEACE IN INTERNATIONAL RELATIONS.   INT/ORG
FUT WOR-45 NAT/G DELIB/GP DIPLOM LEGIT RIGID/FLEX   ADJUD
ORD/FREE SOVEREIGN...JURID CONCPT TREND STERTYP   PEACE
GEN/LAWS LEAGUE/NAT 20. PAGE 60 E1197   INT/LAW

                                                            B52
BENTHAM A.,HANDBOOK OF POLITICAL FALLACIES. FUT   POL/PAR
MOD/EUR LAW INTELL LOC/G MUNIC NAT/G DELIB/GP LEGIS
CREATE EDU/PROP CT/SYS ATTIT RIGID/FLEX KNOWL PWR
...RELATIV PSY SOC CONCPT SELF/OBS TREND STERTYP
TOT/POP. PAGE 10 E0189

                                                            B54
MANGONE G.,A SHORT HISTORY OF INTERNATIONAL   INT/ORG
ORGANIZATION. MOD/EUR USA+45 USA-45 WOR+45 WOR-45   INT/LAW
LAW LEGIS CREATE LEGIT ROUTINE RIGID/FLEX PWR
...JURID CONCPT OBS TIME/SEQ STERTYP GEN/LAWS UN
TOT/POP VAL/FREE 18/20. PAGE 68 E1359

                                                            B55
COMM. STUDY ORGAN. PEACE,REPORTS. WOR-45 ECO/DEV   WOR+45
ECO/UNDEV VOL/ASSN CONSULT FORCES PLAN TEC/DEV   INT/ORG
DOMIN EDU/PROP NUC/PWR ATTIT PWR WEALTH...JURID   ARMS/CONT
STERTYP FAO ILO 20 UN. PAGE 24 E0481

                                                            B57
LEVONTIN A.V.,THE MYTH OF INTERNATIONAL SECURITY: A   INT/ORG
JURIDICAL AND CRITICAL ANALYSIS. FUT WOR+45 WOR-45   INT/LAW
LAW NAT/G VOL/ASSN ACT/RES BAL/PWR ATTIT ORD/FREE   SOVEREIGN
...JURID METH/CNCPT TIME/SEQ TREND STERTYP 20.   MYTH
PAGE 64 E1289

                                                            B58
MACKENZIE W.J.M.,FREE ELECTIONS: AN ELEMENTARY   EX/STRUC
TEXTBOOK. WOR+45 NAT/G POL/PAR LEGIS TOP/EX   CHOOSE
EDU/PROP LEGIT CT/SYS ATTIT PWR...OBS CHARTS
STERTYP T CONGRESS PARLIAMENT 20. PAGE 67 E1342

                                                            B59
GREENSPAN M.,THE MODERN LAW OF LAND WARFARE. WOR+45   ADJUD
INT/ORG NAT/G DELIB/GP FORCES ATTIT...POLICY   PWR
HYPO/EXP STERTYP 20. PAGE 46 E0911   WAR

                                                            S59
CARLSTON K.S.,"NATIONALIZATION: AN ANALYTIC   INDUS
APPROACH." WOR+45 INT/ORG ECO/TAC DOMIN LEGIT ADJUD   NAT/G
COERCE ORD/FREE PWR WEALTH SOCISM...JURID CONCPT   NAT/LISM
TREND STERTYP TOT/POP VAL/FREE 20. PAGE 19 E0380   SOVEREIGN

                                                            S60
O'BRIEN W.,"THE ROLE OF FORCE IN THE INTERNATIONAL   INT/ORG
JURIDICAL ORDER." WOR+45 NAT/G FORCES DOMIN ADJUD   COERCE
ARMS/CONT DETER NUC/PWR WAR ATTIT PWR...CATH
INT/LAW JURID CONCPT TREND STERTYP GEN/LAWS 20.
PAGE 78 E1564

                                                            L62
STEIN E.,"MR HAMMARSKJOLD, THE CHARTER LAW AND THE   CONCPT
FUTURE ROLE OF THE UNITED NATIONS SECRETARY-   BIOG
GENERAL." WOR+45 CONSTN INT/ORG DELIB/GP FORCES
TOP/EX BAL/PWR LEGIT ROUTINE RIGID/FLEX PWR
...POLICY JURID OBS STERTYP UN COLD/WAR 20
HAMMARSK/D. PAGE 93 E1869

                                                            S62
MCWHINNEY E.,"CO-EXISTENCE, THE CUBA CRISIS, AND   CONCPT
COLD WAR-INTERNATIONAL WAR." CUBA USA+45 USSR   INT/LAW
WOR+45 NAT/G TOP/EX BAL/PWR DIPLOM DOMIN LEGIT
PEACE RIGID/FLEX ORD/FREE...STERTYP COLD/WAR 20.
PAGE 71 E1427

                                                            S62
SCHACHTER O.,"DAG HAMMARSKJOLD AND THE RELATION OF   ACT/RES
LAW TO POLITICS." FUT WOR+45 INT/ORG CONSULT PLAN   ADJUD
TEC/DEV BAL/PWR DIPLOM LEGIT ATTIT PERCEPT ORD/FREE
...POLICY JURID CONCPT OBS TESTS STERTYP GEN/LAWS
20 HAMMARSK/D. PAGE 87 E1751

                                                            S63
BECHHOEFER B.G.,"UNITED NATIONS PROCEDURES IN CASE   INT/ORG
OF VIOLATIONS OF DISARMAMENT AGREEMENTS." WOR+45   DELIB/GP
USA+45 USSR LAW CONSTN NAT/G EX/STRUC FORCES LEGIS
BAL/PWR EDU/PROP CT/SYS ARMS/CONT ORD/FREE PWR
...POLICY STERTYP UN VAL/FREE 20. PAGE 9 E0169

                                                            S63
FRIEDMANN W.G.,"THE USES OF 'GENERAL PRINCIPLES' IN   LAW
THE DEVELOPMENT OF INTERNATIONAL LAW." WOR+45 NAT/G   INT/LAW
DIPLOM INT/TRADE LEGIT ROUTINE RIGID/FLEX ORD/FREE   INT/ORG
...JURID CONCPT STERTYP GEN/METH 20. PAGE 41 E0804

                                                            S64
GARDNER R.N.,"THE SOVIET UNION AND THE UNITED   COM
NATIONS." WOR+45 FINAN POL/PAR VOL/ASSN FORCES   INT/ORG
ECO/TAC DOMIN EDU/PROP LEGIT ADJUD ADMIN ARMS/CONT   USSR
COERCE ATTIT ALL/VALS...POLICY MAJORIT CONCPT OBS
TIME/SEQ TREND STERTYP UN. PAGE 42 E0838

                                                            S64
HICKEY D.,"THE PHILOSOPHICAL ARGUMENT FOR WORLD   FUT
GOVERNMENT." WOR+45 SOCIETY ACT/RES PLAN LEGIT   INT/ORG
ADJUD PEACE PERCEPT PERSON ORD/FREE...HUM JURID
PHIL/SCI METH/CNCPT CON/ANAL STERTYP GEN/LAWS
TOT/POP 20. PAGE 52 E1039

STEVENS R.E. E1873

STEVENSN/A....ADLAI STEVENSON

STEWARD/JH....JULIAN H. STEWARD

STIMSON/HL....HENRY L. STIMSON

STOCHASTIC PROCESSES....SEE PROB/SOLV, MODELS INDEX

STOCKHOLM....STOCKHOLM

STOICOIU V. E1874

STOKES A.P. E1875

STOKES W.S. E1876

STOKES/CB....CARL B. STOKES

STOL....SHORT TAKE-OFF AND LANDING AIRCRAFT

STONE J. E1877,E1878,E1879,E1880,E1881

STONE R.C. E0784

STONE/HF....HARLAN FISKE STONE

                                                            B58
MASON A.T.,THE SUPREME COURT FROM TAFT TO WARREN.   CT/SYS
EX/STRUC LEGIS ROLE 20 SUPREME/CT TAFT/WH HUGHES/CE   JURID
STONE/HF. PAGE 69 E1376   ADJUD

STONE/IF....I.F. STONE

STOREY–STRATA

STOREY R.G. E1882

STORING/HJ....H.J. STORING

STOUT H.M. E1883

STOWELL E.C. E1884,E1885

STRANGE....ESTRANGEMENT, ALIENATION, IMPERSONALITY

B04
GRIFFIN A.P.C.,REFERENCES ON CHINESE IMMIGRATIONS
(PAMPHLET). USA-45 KIN NAT/LISM ATTIT...SOC 19/20.
PAGE 47 E0926
BIBLIOG/A
STRANGE
JURID
RACE/REL

B37
BADEN A.L.,IMMIGRATION AND ITS RESTRICTION IN THE
US (PAMPHLET). USA-45 NAT/G LEGIS...GEOG 20
CONGRESS. PAGE 7 E0130
BIBLIOG
STRANGE
CONTROL
LAW

B42
US LIBRARY OF CONGRESS,SOCIAL AND CULTURAL PROBLEMS
IN WARTIME: APRIL 1941-MARCH 1942. WOR-45 CLIENT
SECT EDU/PROP CRIME LEISURE RACE/REL STRANGE ATTIT
DRIVE HEALTH...GEOG 20. PAGE 100 E2012
BIBLIOG/A
WAR
SOC
CULTURE

C50
NUMELIN R.,"THE BEGINNINGS OF DIPLOMACY." INT/TRADE
WAR GP/REL PEACE STRANGE ATTIT...INT/LAW CONCPT
BIBLIOG. PAGE 78 E1559
DIPLOM
KIN
CULTURE
LAW

B59
PANHUYS H.F.,THE ROLE OF NATIONALITY IN
INTERNATIONAL LAW. ADJUD CRIME WAR STRANGE...JURID
TREND. PAGE 80 E1596
INT/LAW
NAT/LISM
INGP/REL

S59
DWYER R.J.,"THE ADMINISTRATIVE ROLE IN
DESEGREGATION." USA+45 LAW PROB/SOLV LEAD RACE/REL
ISOLAT STRANGE ROLE...POLICY SOC/INTEG MISSOURI
NEGRO CIV/RIGHTS. PAGE 34 E0668
ADMIN
SCHOOL
DISCRIM
ATTIT

B61
MERTON R.K.,CONTEMPORARY SOCIAL PROBLEMS: AN
INTRODUCTION TO THE SOCIOLOGY OF DEVIANT BEHAVIOR
AND SOCIAL DISORGANIZATION. FAM MUNIC FORCES WORKER
PROB/SOLV INGP/REL RACE/REL ISOLAT...CRIMLGY GEOG
PSY T 20 NEGRO. PAGE 72 E1444
CRIME
ANOMIE
STRANGE
SOC

B62
PAIKERT G.C.,THE GERMAN EXODUS. EUR+WWI GERMANY/W
LAW CULTURE SOCIETY STRUCT INDUS NAT/LISM RESPECT
SOVEREIGN...CHARTS BIBLIOG SOC/INTEG 20 MIGRATION.
PAGE 79 E1591
INGP/REL
STRANGE
GEOG
GP/REL

B64
CLINARD M.B.,ANOMIE AND DEVIANT BEHAVIOR: A
DISCUSSION AND CRITIQUE. SOCIETY FACE/GP CRIME
STRANGE ATTIT BIO/SOC DISPL RIGID/FLEX HEALTH...PSY
CONCPT BIBLIOG 20 MERTON/R. PAGE 23 E0456
PERSON
ANOMIE
KIN
NEIGH

B64
US HOUSE COMM ON JUDICIARY,IMMIGRATION HEARINGS.
DELIB/GP STRANGE HABITAT...GEOG JURID 20 CONGRESS
MIGRATION. PAGE 100 E2006
NAT/G
POLICY
DIPLOM
NAT/LISM

B66
FLEISCHER B.M.,THE ECONOMICS OF DELINQUENCY. UNIV
WORKER STRANGE ANOMIE...STAT CHARTS 20. PAGE 38
E0762
STRATA
INCOME
AGE/Y
CRIME

L66
KRENZ F.E.,"THE REFUGEE AS A SUBJECT OF
INTERNATIONAL LAW." FUT LAW NAT/G CREATE ADJUD
ISOLAT STRANGE...RECORD UN. PAGE 62 E1230
INT/LAW
DISCRIM
NEW/IDEA

B67
DEBOLD R.C.,LSD, MAN AND SOCIETY. USA+45 LAW
SOCIETY SECT CONTROL SANCTION STRANGE ATTIT...HEAL
CHARTS ANTHOL BIBLIOG. PAGE 30 E0601
HEALTH
DRIVE
PERSON
BIO/SOC

B67
INTERNATIONAL CONCILIATION,ISSUES BEFORE THE 22ND
GENERAL ASSEMBLY. WOR+45 ECO/UNDEV FINAN BAL/PWR
BUDGET INT/TRADE STRANGE ORD/FREE...INT/LAW 20 UN
COLD/WAR. PAGE 57 E1132
PROB/SOLV
INT/ORG
DIPLOM
PEACE

S67
REILLY T.J.,"FREEZING AND CONFISCATION OF CUBAN
PROPERTY." CUBA USA+45 LAW DIPLOM LEGIT ADJUD
STRANGE
OWN

CONTROL. PAGE 84 E1682
ECO/TAC

STRASBOURG....STRASBOURG PLAN

STRATA....SOCIAL STRATA, CLASS DIVISION

B03
GRIFFIN A.P.C.,LIST OF REFERENCES ON INDUSTRIAL
ARBITRATION (PAMPHLET). USA-45 STRATA VOL/ASSN
DELIB/GP WORKER ADJUD GP/REL...MGT 19/20. PAGE 46
E0921
BIBLIOG/A
INDUS
LABOR
BARGAIN

B09
JUSTINIAN,THE DIGEST (DIGESTA CORPUS JURIS CIVILIS)
(2 VOLS.) (TRANS. BY C. H. MONRO). ROMAN/EMP LAW
FAM LOC/G LEGIS EDU/PROP CONTROL MARRIAGE OWN ROLE
CIVIL/LAW. PAGE 59 E1177
JURID
CT/SYS
NAT/G
STRATA

B24
HOLDSWORTH W.S.,A HISTORY OF ENGLISH LAW: THE
COMMON LAW AND ITS RIVALS (VOL. VI). UK STRATA
EX/STRUC ADJUD ADMIN CONTROL CT/SYS...JURID CONCPT
GEN/LAWS 17 COMMONWLTH PARLIAMENT ENGLSH/LAW
COMMON/LAW. PAGE 54 E1074
LAW
CONSTN
LEGIS
CHIEF

B24
NAVILLE A.,LIBERTE, EGALITE, SOLIDARITE: ESSAIS
D'ANALYSE. STRATA FAM VOL/ASSN INT/TRADE GP/REL
MORAL MARXISM SOCISM...PSY TREATY. PAGE 76 E1529
ORD/FREE
SOC
IDEA/COMP
DIPLOM

B28
HOBBES T.,THE ELEMENTS OF LAW, NATURAL AND POLITIC
(1650). STRATA NAT/G SECT CHIEF AGREE ATTIT
ALL/VALS MORAL ORD/FREE POPULISM...POLICY CONCPT.
PAGE 53 E1056
PERSON
LAW
SOVEREIGN
CONSERVE

B29
BUELL R.,INTERNATIONAL RELATIONS. WOR+45 WOR-45
CONSTN STRATA FORCES TOP/EX ADMIN ATTIT DRIVE
SUPEGO MORAL ORD/FREE PWR SOVEREIGN...JURID SOC
CONCPT 20. PAGE 17 E0326
INT/ORG
BAL/PWR
DIPLOM

B30
GREEN F.M.,CONSTITUTIONAL DEVELOPMENT IN THE SOUTH
ATLANTIC STATES, 1776-1860: A STUDY IN THE
EVOLUTION OF DEMOCRACY. USA-45 ELITES SOCIETY
STRATA ECO/DEV AGRI POL/PAR EX/STRUC LEGIS CT/SYS
REGION...BIBLIOG 18/19 MARYLAND VIRGINIA GEORGIA
NORTH/CAR SOUTH/CAR. PAGE 46 E0905
CONSTN
PROVS
PLURISM
REPRESENT

B32
MASTERS R.D.,INTERNATIONAL LAW IN INTERNATIONAL
COURTS. BELGIUM EUR+WWI FRANCE GERMANY MOD/EUR
SWITZERLND WOR-45 SOCIETY STRATA STRUCT LEGIT EXEC
ALL/VALS...JURID HIST/WRIT TIME/SEQ TREND GEN/LAWS
20. PAGE 69 E1383
INT/ORG
LAW
INT/LAW

B38
FIELD G.L.,THE SYNDICAL AND CORPORATIVE
INSTITUTIONS OF ITALIAN FASCISM. ITALY CONSTN
STRATA LABOR EX/STRUC TOP/EX ADJUD ADMIN LEAD
TOTALISM AUTHORIT...MGT 20 MUSSOLIN/B. PAGE 38
E0746
FASCISM
INDUS
NAT/G
WORKER

B38
HOLDSWORTH W.S.,A HISTORY OF ENGLISH LAW: THE
CENTURIES OF SETTLEMENT AND REFORM (VOL. XII). UK
CONSTN STRATA LEGIS JUDGE ADJUD CT/SYS ATTIT
...JURID CONCPT BIOG GEN/LAWS 18 ENGLSH/LAW
BLACKSTN/W COMMON/LAW. PAGE 54 E1078
LAW
PROF/ORG
WRITING
IDEA/COMP

S40
GERTH H.,"THE NAZI PARTY: ITS LEADERSHIP AND
COMPOSITION" (BMR)" GERMANY ELITES STRATA STRUCT
EX/STRUC FORCES ECO/TAC CT/SYS CHOOSE TOTALISM
AGE/Y AUTHORIT PWR 20. PAGE 43 E0851
POL/PAR
DOMIN
LEAD
ADMIN

L41
COMM. STUDY ORGAN. PEACE,"ORGANIZATION OF PEACE."
USA-45 WOR-45 STRATA NAT/G ACT/RES DIPLOM ECO/TAC
EDU/PROP ADJUD ATTIT ORD/FREE PWR...SOC CONCPT
ANTHOL LEAGUE/NAT 20. PAGE 24 E0479
INT/ORG
PLAN
PEACE

B42
GILLETTE J.M.,PROBLEMS OF A CHANGING SOCIAL ORDER.
USA+45 STRATA FAM CONTROL CRIME RACE/REL HEALTH
WEALTH...GEOG GP/COMP. PAGE 43 E0862
BIO/SOC
ADJUST
ATTIT
SOC/WK

S45
DAVIS A.,"CASTE, ECONOMY, AND VIOLENCE" (BMR)"
USA-45 LAW SOCIETY STRUCT SECT SANCTION COERCE
MARRIAGE SEX...PSY SOC SOC/INTEG 18/20 NEGRO
MISCEGEN SOUTH/US. PAGE 29 E0570
STRATA
RACE/REL
DISCRIM

BORGESE G.,COMMON CAUSE. LAW CONSTN SOCIETY STRATA ECO/DEV INT/ORG POL/PAR FORCES LEGIS TOP/EX CAP/ISM DIPLOM ADMIN EXEC ATTIT PWR 20. PAGE 14 E0269
B47
WOR+45 NAT/G SOVEREIGN REGION

FRAGA IRIBARNE M.,RAZAS Y RACISMO IN NORTEAMERICA. USA+45 CONSTN STRATA NAT/G PROVS ATTIT...SOC CONCPT 19/20 NEGRO. PAGE 39 E0783
B50
RACE/REL JURID LAW DISCRIM

CAPLOW T.,THE SOCIOLOGY OF WORK. USA+45 USA-45 STRATA MARKET FAM GP/REL INGP/REL ALL/VALS ...DECISION STAT BIBLIOG SOC/INTEG 20. PAGE 19 E0375
B54
LABOR WORKER INDUS ROLE

GUINS G.C.,"SOVIET LAW AND SOVIET SOCIETY." COM USSR STRATA FAM NAT/G WORKER DOMIN RACE/REL ...BIBLIOG 20. PAGE 48 E0960
C54
LAW STRUCT PLAN

KHADDURI M.,WAR AND PEACE IN THE LAW OF ISLAM. CONSTN CULTURE SOCIETY STRATA NAT/G PROVS SECT FORCES TOP/EX CREATE DOMIN EDU/PROP ADJUD COERCE ATTIT RIGID/FLEX ALL/VALS...CONCPT TIME/SEQ TOT/POP VAL/FREE. PAGE 61 E1209
B55
ISLAM JURID PEACE WAR

WRONG D.H.,AMERICAN AND CANADIAN VIEWPOINTS. CANADA USA+45 CONSTN STRATA FAM SECT WORKER ECO/TAC EDU/PROP ADJUD MARRIAGE...IDEA/COMP 20. PAGE 108 E2161
B55
DIPLOM ATTIT NAT/COMP CULTURE

DUNNILL F.,THE CIVIL SERVICE. UK LAW PLAN ADMIN EFFICIENCY DRIVE NEW/LIB...STAT CHARTS 20 PARLIAMENT CIVIL/SERV. PAGE 33 E0662
B56
PERSON WORKER STRATA SOC/WK

RECASENS SICHES S.,TRATADO GENERAL DE SOCIOLOGIA. CULTURE FAM NEIGH LEAD RACE/REL DISCRIM HABITAT ORD/FREE...JURID LING T SOC/INTEG 20. PAGE 84 E1677
B56
SOC STRATA KIN GP/REL

SYKES G.M.,CRIME AND SOCIETY. LAW STRATA STRUCT ACT/RES ROUTINE ANOMIE WEALTH...POLICY SOC/INTEG 20. PAGE 95 E1903
B56
CRIMLGY CRIME CULTURE INGP/REL

ROSENBERG M.,"POWER AND DESEGREGATION." USA+45 STRATA MUNIC GP/REL. PAGE 85 E1715
S56
PWR DISCRIM DECISION LAW

GOODE W.J.,"COMMUNITY WITHIN A COMMUNITY: THE PROFESSIONS." STRATA STRUCT SANCTION INGP/REL...SOC GP/COMP. PAGE 45 E0886
S57
PROF/ORG NEIGH CLIENT CONTROL

CABLE G.W.,THE NEGRO QUESTION: A SELECTION OF WRITINGS ON CIVIL RIGHTS IN THE SOUTH. USA+45 STRATA LOC/G POL/PAR GIVE EDU/PROP WRITING CT/SYS SANCTION CRIME CHOOSE WORSHIP 20 NEGRO CIV/RIGHTS CONV/LEASE SOUTH/US. PAGE 18 E0355
B58
RACE/REL CULTURE DISCRIM ORD/FREE

BRIGGS A.,CHARTIST STUDIES. UK LAW NAT/G WORKER EDU/PROP COERCE SUFF GP/REL ATTIT...ANTHOL 19. PAGE 15 E0300
B59
INDUS STRATA LABOR POLICY

DOMKE M.,"THE SETTLEMENT OF DISPUTES IN INTERNATIONAL TRADE." USA+45 LAW STRATA STRUCT JUDGE EDU/PROP PWR...METH/CNCPT 20. PAGE 32 E0634
S59
CONSULT LEGIT INT/TRADE

SUTTON F.X.,"REPRESENTATION AND THE NATURE OF POLITICAL SYSTEMS." UNIV WOR-45 CULTURE SOCIETY STRATA INT/ORG FORCES JUDGE DOMIN LEGIT EXEC REGION REPRESENT ATTIT ORD/FREE RESPECT...SOC HIST/WRIT TIME/SEQ. PAGE 95 E1896
S59
NAT/G CONCPT

ENGEL J.,THE SECURITY OF THE FREE WORLD. USSR WOR+45 STRATA STRUCT ECO/DEV ECO/UNDEV INT/ORG DELIB/GP FORCES DOMIN LEGIT ADJUD EXEC ARMS/CONT COERCE...POLICY CONCPT NEW/IDEA TIME/SEQ GEN/LAWS
B60
COM TREND DIPLOM

COLD/WAR WORK UN 20 NATO. PAGE 35 E0689

GIBNEY F.,THE OPERATORS. USA+45 LAW STRATA BIO/SOC MORAL ORD/FREE SOC. PAGE 43 E0858
B60
CRIME CULTURE ANOMIE CRIMLGY

FLINN M.W.,AN ECONOMIC AND SOCIAL HISTORY OF BRITAIN, 1066-1939. UK LAW STRATA STRUCT AGRI DIST/IND INDUS WORKER INT/TRADE WAR...CENSUS 11/20. PAGE 39 E0766
B61
SOCIETY SOC

JUSTICE,THE CITIZEN AND THE ADMINISTRATION: THE REDRESS OF GRIEVANCES (PAMPHLET). EUR+WWI UK LAW CONSTN STRATA NAT/G CT/SYS PARTIC COERCE...NEW/IDEA IDEA/COMP 20 OMBUDSMAN. PAGE 59 E1176
B61
INGP/REL CONSULT ADJUD REPRESENT

WARD R.E.,JAPANESE POLITICAL SCIENCE: A GUIDE TO JAPANESE REFERENCE AND RESEARCH MATERIALS (2ND ED.). LAW CONSTN STRATA NAT/G POL/PAR DELIB/GP LEGIS ADMIN CHOOSE GP/REL...INT/LAW 19/20 CHINJAP. PAGE 105 E2099
B61
BIBLIOG/A PHIL/SCI

GROSS L.,"IMMUNITIES AND PRIVILEGES OF DELIGATIONS TO THE UNITED NATIONS." USA+45 WOR+45 STRATA NAT/G VOL/ASSN CONSULT DIPLOM EDU/PROP ROUTINE RESPECT ...POLICY INT/LAW CONCPT UN 20. PAGE 48 E0950
L62
INT/ORG LAW ELITES

MANGIN G.,"L'ORGANIZATION JUDICIAIRE DES ETATS D'AFRIQUE ET DE MADAGASCAR." ISLAM WOR+45 STRATA STRUCT ECO/UNDEV NAT/G LEGIT EXEC...JURID TIME/SEQ TOT/POP 20 SUPREME/CT. PAGE 68 E1357
L62
AFR LEGIS COLONIAL MADAGASCAR

CARTER G.M.,FIVE AFRICAN STATES: RESPONSES TO DIVERSITY. CONSTN CULTURE STRATA LEGIS PLAN ECO/TAC DOMIN EDU/PROP CT/SYS EXEC CHOOSE ATTIT HEALTH ORD/FREE PWR...TIME/SEQ TOT/POP VAL/FREE. PAGE 20 E0398
B63
AFR SOCIETY

JACOBS P.,STATE OF UNIONS. USA+45 STRATA TOP/EX GP/REL RACE/REL DEMAND DISCRIM ATTIT PWR 20 CONGRESS NEGRO HOFFA/J. PAGE 57 E1145
B63
LABOR ECO/TAC BARGAIN DECISION

VINES K.N.,"THE ROLE OF THE CIRCUIT COURT OF APPEALS IN THE FEDERAL JUDICIAL PROCESS: A CASE STUDY." USA+45 STRATA JUDGE RESPECT...DECISION JURID CHARTS GP/COMP. PAGE 104 E2078
S63
REGION ADJUD CT/SYS RACE/REL

DOOLIN D.J.,COMMUNIST CHINA: THE POLITICS OF STUDENT OPPOSITION. CHINA/COM ELITES STRATA ACADEM NAT/G WRITING CT/SYS LEAD PARTIC COERCE TOTALISM 20. PAGE 32 E0637
B64
MARXISM DEBATE AGE/Y PWR

GUMPLOWICZ L.,RECHTSSTAAT UND SOZIALISMUS. STRATA ORD/FREE SOVEREIGN MARXISM...IDEA/COMP 16/20 KANT/I HOBBES/T. PAGE 48 E0962
B64
JURID NAT/G SOCISM CONCPT

LAPENNA I.,STATE AND LAW: SOVIET AND YUGOSLAV THEORY. USSR YUGOSLAVIA STRATA STRUCT NAT/G DOMIN COERCE MARXISM...GOV/COMP IDEA/COMP 20. PAGE 63 E1253
B64
JURID COM LAW SOVEREIGN

WRIGHT G.,RURAL REVOLUTION IN FRANCE: THE PEASANTRY IN THE TWENTIETH CENTURY. EUR+WWI MOD/EUR LAW CULTURE AGRI POL/PAR DELIB/GP LEGIS ECO/TAC EDU/PROP COERCE CHOOSE ATTIT RIGID/FLEX HEALTH ...STAT CENSUS CHARTS VAL/FREE 20. PAGE 107 E2148
B64
PWR STRATA FRANCE REV

CHROUST A.H.,THE RISE OF THE LEGAL PROFESSION IN AMERICA (3 VOLS.). STRATA STRUCT POL/PAR PROF/ORG COLONIAL LEAD REV SKILL...SOC 17/20. PAGE 22 E0437
B65
JURID USA-45 CT/SYS LAW

RENNER K.,MENSCH UND GESELLSCHAFT - GRUNDRISS EINER SOZIOLOGIE (2ND ED.). STRATA FAM LABOR PROF/ORG WAR ...JURID CLASSIF 20. PAGE 84 E1685
B65
SOC STRUCT NAT/G SOCIETY

AMERICAN JEWISH COMMITTEE.GROUP RELATIONS IN THE
UNITED STATES: PROBLEMS AND PERSPECTIVES: A
SELECTED, ANNOTATED BIBLIOGRAPHY (PAMPHLET). LAW
CONSTN STRATA SCHOOL SECT PROB/SOLV ATTIT...POLICY
WELF/ST SOC/WK 20. PAGE 4 E0079
   B66 BIBLIOG/A USA+45 STRUCT GP/REL

DE TOCQUEVILLE A.DEMOCRACY IN AMERICA (1834-1840)
(2 VOLS. IN I; TRANS. BY G. LAWRENCE). FRANCE
CULTURE STRATA POL/PAR CT/SYS REPRESENT FEDERAL
ORD/FREE SOVEREIGN...MAJORIT TREND GEN/LAWS 18/19.
PAGE 30 E0596
   B66 POPULISM USA-45 CONSTN NAT/COMP

FLEISCHER B.M.,THE ECONOMICS OF DELINQUENCY. UNIV
WORKER STRANGE ANOMIE...STAT CHARTS 20. PAGE 38
E0762
   B66 STRATA INCOME AGE/Y CRIME

MACIVER R.M.,THE PREVENTION AND CONTROL OF
DELINQUENCY. USA+45 STRATA PUB/INST ANOMIE ATTIT
HABITAT PERSON HEALTH...CRIMLGY PSY SOC METH.
PAGE 67 E1341
   B66 AGE/Y PLAN ADJUST CRIME

RUNCIMAN W.G.,RELATIVE DEPRIVATION AND SOCIAL
JUSTICE: A STUDY OF ATTITUDES TO SOCIAL INEQUALITY
IN TWENTIETH-CENTURY ENGLAND. UK LAW POL/PAR PWR
...CONCPT NEW/IDEA SAMP METH 19/20. PAGE 86 E1734
   B66 STRATA STRUCT DISCRIM ATTIT

BRAGER G.A.,COMMUNITY ACTION AGAINST POVERTY.
USA+45 LAW STRATA INGP/REL INCOME NEW/LIB...POLICY
WELF/ST ANTHOL. PAGE 15 E0285
   B67 NEIGH WEALTH SOC/WK CREATE

NAGEL S.S.,"DISPARITIES IN CRIMINAL PROCEDURE."
STRATA NAT/G PROVS EDU/PROP RACE/REL AGE HABITAT
SEX...JURID CHARTS 20. PAGE 76 E1519
   L67 ADJUD DISCRIM STRUCT ACT/RES

POSPISIL L.,"LEGAL LEVELS AND MULTIPLICITY OF LEGAL
SYSTEMS IN HUMAN SOCIETIES." WOR+45 CENTRAL PWR
...SOC CHARTS GP/COMP GEN/LAWS. PAGE 81 E1630
   S67 LAW STRATA JURID STRUCT

DUGARD J.,"THE REVOCATION OF THE MANDATE FOR SOUTH
WEST AFRICA." SOUTH/AFR WOR+45 STRATA NAT/G
DELIB/GP DIPLOM ADJUD SANCTION CHOOSE RACE/REL
...POLICY NAT/COMP 20 AFRICA/SW UN TRUST/TERR
LEAGUE/NAT. PAGE 33 E0654
   S68 AFR INT/ORG DISCRIM COLONIAL

ADAMS J.,A DEFENSE OF THE CONSTITUTIONS OF
GOVERNMENT OF THE UNITED STATES OF AMERICA. USA+45
STRATA CHIEF EX/STRUC LEGIS CT/SYS CONSERVE
POPULISM...CONCPT CON/ANAL GOV/COMP. PAGE 3 E0048
   B87 CONSTN BAL/PWR PWR NAT/G

STRATEGY....SEE PLAN, DECISION

STRATIFICATION....SEE STRATA

STREET H. E0940,E1886

STRESEMANN, GUSTAV....SEE STRESEMN/G

STRESEMN/G....GUSTAV STRESEMANN

BRETTON H.L.,STRESEMANN AND THE REVISION OF
VERSAILLES: A FIGHT FOR REASON. EUR+WWI GERMANY
FORCES BUDGET ARMS/CONT WAR SUPEGO...BIBLIOG 20
TREATY VERSAILLES STRESEMN/G. PAGE 15 E0294
   B53 POLICY DIPLOM BIOG

STRESS....SEE PERSON, DRIVE

STRIKE....STRIKE OF WORKERS

CUNNINGHAM W.B.,COMPULSORY CONCILIATION AND
COLLECTIVE BARGAINING. CANADA NAT/G LEGIS ADJUD
CT/SYS GP/REL...MGT 20 NEW/BRUNS STRIKE CASEBOOK.
PAGE 28 E0555
   B58 POLICY BARGAIN LABOR INDUS

STRIKES....SEE LABOR, GP/REL, FINAN, STRIKE

STRONG C.F. E1887,E1888

STRUC/FUNC....STRUCTURAL-FUNCTIONAL THEORY

STRUCT...SOCIAL STRUCTURE

ATLANTIC INSTITUTE.ATLANTIC STUDIES. COM EUR+WWI
USA+45 CULTURE STRUCT ECO/DEV FORCES LEAD ARMS/CONT
...INT/LAW JURID SOC. PAGE 6 E0110
   N BIBLIOG/A DIPLOM POLICY GOV/REL

CORNELL UNIVERSITY LIBRARY.SOUTHEAST ASIA
ACCESSIONS LIST. LAW SOCIETY STRUCT ECO/UNDEV
POL/PAR TEC/DEV DIPLOM LEAD REGION. PAGE 26 E0510
   N BIBLIOG S/ASIA NAT/G CULTURE

DE TOCQUEVILLE A.,DEMOCRACY IN AMERICA (VOLUME
ONE). LAW SOCIETY STRUCT NAT/G POL/PAR PROVS FORCES
LEGIS TOP/EX DIPLOM LEGIT WAR PEACE ATTIT SOVEREIGN
...SELF/OBS TIME/SEQ CONGRESS 19. PAGE 30 E0594
   B00 USA-45 TREND

MAINE H.S.,INTERNATIONAL LAW. MOD/EUR UNIV SOCIETY
STRUCT ACT/RES EXEC WAR ATTIT PERSON ALL/VALS
...POLICY JURID CONCPT OBS TIME/SEQ TOT/POP.
PAGE 68 E1349
   B00 INT/ORG LAW PEACE INT/LAW

GOODNOW F.J.,THE PRINCIPLES OF THE ADMINISTRATIVE
LAW OF THE UNITED STATES. USA-45 LAW STRUCT
EX/STRUC LEGIS BAL/PWR CONTROL GOV/REL PWR...JURID
19/20 CIVIL/SERV. PAGE 45 E0887
   B05 ADMIN NAT/G PROVS LOC/G

PHILLIPSON C.,THE INTERNATIONAL LAW AND CUSTOM OF
ANCIENT GREECE AND ROME. MEDIT-7 UNIV INTELL
SOCIETY STRUCT NAT/G LEGIS EXEC PERSON...CONCPT OBS
CON/ANAL ROM/EMP. PAGE 80 E1614
   B11 INT/ORG LAW INT/LAW

HOBSON J.A.,TOWARDS INTERNATIONAL GOVERNMENT.
MOD/EUR STRUCT ECO/TAC EDU/PROP ADJUD ALL/VALS
...SOCIALIST CONCPT GEN/LAWS TOT/POP 20. PAGE 53
E1059
   B15 FUT INT/ORG CENTRAL

DUGUIT L.,LAW IN THE MODERN STATE (TRANS. BY FRIDA
AND HAROLD LASKI). CONSTN SOCIETY STRUCT MORAL
ORD/FREE SOVEREIGN 20. PAGE 33 E0655
   B19 GEN/LAWS CONCPT NAT/G LAW

POUND R.,ORGANIZATION OF THE COURTS (PAMPHLET).
MOD/EUR UK USA-45 ADJUD PWR...GOV/COMP 10/20
EUROPE. PAGE 82 E1635
   N19 CT/SYS JURID STRUCT ADMIN

BARNES H.E.,"SOCIOLOGY AND POLITICAL THEORY: A
CONSIDERATION OF THE SOCIOLOGICAL BASIS OF
POLITICS." LAW CONSTN NAT/G DIPLOM DOMIN ROUTINE
REV ORD/FREE SOVEREIGN...PHIL/SCI CLASSIF BIBLIOG
18/20. PAGE 8 E0151
   C24 CONCPT STRUCT SOC

CORBETT P.E.,CANADA AND WORLD POLITICS. LAW CULTURE
SOCIETY STRUCT MARKET INT/ORG FORCES ACT/RES PLAN
ECO/TAC LEGIT ORD/FREE PWR RESPECT...SOC CONCPT
TIME/SEQ TREND CMN/WLTH 20 LEAGUE/NAT. PAGE 26
E0504
   B28 NAT/G CANADA

MASTERS R.D.,INTERNATIONAL LAW IN INTERNATIONAL
COURTS. BELGIUM EUR+WWI FRANCE GERMANY MOD/EUR
SWITZERLND WOR-45 SOCIETY STRATA STRUCT LEGIT EXEC
ALL/VALS...JURID HIST/WRIT TIME/SEQ TREND GEN/LAWS
20. PAGE 69 E1383
   B32 INT/ORG LAW INT/LAW

EVANS I.L.,NATIVE POLICY IN SOUTHERN AFRICA.
RHODESIA SOUTH/AFR UK STRUCT PARTIC RACE/REL ATTIT
WEALTH SOC/INTEG AFRICA/SW. PAGE 35 E0705
   B34 AFR COLONIAL DOMIN LAW

DE TOCQUEVILLE A.,DEMOCRACY IN AMERICA (4 VOLS.)
(TRANS. BY HENRY REEVE). CONSTN STRUCT LOC/G NAT/G
POL/PAR PROVS ETIQUET CT/SYS MAJORITY ATTIT 18/19.
PAGE 30 E0595
   B35 POPULISM MAJORIT ORD/FREE SOCIETY

LEAGUE OF NATIONS-SECRETARIAT.,THE AIMS, METHODS
AND ACTIVITY OF THE LEAGUE OF NATIONS. WOR+45
DIPLOM EDU/PROP LEGIT RIGID/FLEX ALL/VALS
...TIME/SEQ LEAGUE/NAT VAL/FREE 19/20. PAGE 64
E1273
   B38 ADJUD STRUCT

ZIMMERN A.,THE LEAGUE OF NATIONS AND THE RULE OF
   B39 INT/ORG

LAW. WOR-45 STRUCT NAT/G DELIB/GP EX/STRUC BAL/PWR LAW
DOMIN LEGIT COERCE ORD/FREE PWR...POLICY RECORD DIPLOM
LEAGUE/NAT TOT/POP VAL/FREE 20 LEAGUE/NAT. PAGE 108
E2170

S40
GERTH H.,"THE NAZI PARTY: ITS LEADERSHIP AND POL/PAR
COMPOSITION" (BMR)" GERMANY ELITES STRATA STRUCT DOMIN
EX/STRUC FORCES ECO/TAC CT/SYS CHOOSE TOTALISM LEAD
AGE/Y AUTHORIT PWR 20. PAGE 43 E0851 ADMIN

S41
WRIGHT Q.,"FUNDAMENTAL PROBLEMS OF INTERNATIONAL INT/ORG
ORGANIZATION." UNIV WOR-45 STRUCT FORCES ACT/RES ATTIT
CREATE DOMIN EDU/PROP LEGIT REGION NAT/LISM PEACE
ORD/FREE PWR RESPECT SOVEREIGN...JURID SOC CONCPT
METH/CNCPT TIME/SEQ 20. PAGE 107 E2152

B44
HUDSON M.,INTERNATIONAL TRIBUNALS PAST AND FUTURE. INT/ORG
FUT WOR-45 LAW EDU/PROP ADJUD ORD/FREE...CONCPT STRUCT
TIME/SEQ TREND GEN/LAWS TOT/POP VAL/FREE 18/20. INT/LAW
PAGE 56 E1111

B45
WEST R.,CONSCIENCE AND SOCIETY: A STUDY OF THE COERCE
PSYCHOLOGICAL PREREQUISITES OF LAW AND ORDER. FUT INT/LAW
UNIV LAW SOCIETY STRUCT DIPLOM WAR PERS/REL SUPEGO ORD/FREE
...SOC 20. PAGE 105 E2112 PERSON

S45
DAVIS A.,"CASTE, ECONOMY, AND VIOLENCE" (BMR)" STRATA
USA-45 LAW SOCIETY STRUCT SECT SANCTION COERCE RACE/REL
MARRIAGE SEX...PSY SOC SOC/INTEG 18/20 NEGRO DISCRIM
MISCEGEN SOUTH/US. PAGE 29 E0570

B46
MANNHEIM H.,CRIMINAL JUSTICE AND SOCIAL ADJUD
RECONSTRUCTION. USA+45 EDU/PROP CRIME ANOMIE LAW
...JURID BIBLIOG 20. PAGE 68 E1361 STRUCT
ADJUST

B49
HOLLERAN M.P.,CHURCH AND STATE IN GUATEMALA. SECT
GUATEMALA LAW STRUCT CATHISM...SOC SOC/INTEG 17/20 NAT/G
CHURCH/STA. PAGE 55 E1086 GP/REL
CULTURE

B50
BERMAN H.J.,JUSTICE IN RUSSIA; AN INTERPRETATION OF JURID
SOVIET LAW. USSR LAW STRUCT LABOR FORCES AGREE ADJUD
GP/REL ORD/FREE SOCISM...TIME/SEQ 20. PAGE 11 E0207 MARXISM
COERCE

B50
LAUTERPACHT H.,INTERNATIONAL LAW AND HUMAN RIGHTS. DELIB/GP
USA+45 CONSTN STRUCT INT/ORG ACT/RES EDU/PROP PEACE LAW
PERSON ALL/VALS...CONCPT CON/ANAL GEN/LAWS UN 20. INT/LAW
PAGE 63 E1266

B51
COOKE C.A.,CORPORATION TRUST AND COMPANY: AN ESSAY LG/CO
IN LEGAL HISTORY. UK STRUCT LEGIS CAP/ISM GP/REL FINAN
PROFIT 13/20 COMPANY/ACT. PAGE 25 E0499 ECO/TAC
JURID

B51
KELSEN H.,THE LAW OF THE UNITED NATIONS. WOR+45 INT/ORG
STRUCT RIGID/FLEX ORD/FREE...INT/LAW JURID CONCPT ADJUD
CON/ANAL GEN/METH UN TOT/POP VAL/FREE 20. PAGE 60
E1198

B52
FORSTER A.,THE TROUBLE MAKERS. USA+45 LAW CULTURE DISCRIM
SOCIETY STRUCT VOL/ASSN CROWD GP/REL MORAL...PSY SECT
SOC CONCPT 20 NEGRO JEWS. PAGE 39 E0771 RACE/REL
ATTIT

B52
VANDENBOSCH A.,THE UN: BACKGROUND, ORGANIZATION, DELIB/GP
FUNCTIONS, ACTIVITIES. WOR+45 LAW CONSTN STRUCT TIME/SEQ
INT/ORG CONSULT BAL/PWR EDU/PROP EXEC ALL/VALS PEACE
...POLICY CONCPT UN 20. PAGE 103 E2071

B53
GROSS B.M.,THE LEGISLATIVE STRUGGLE: A STUDY IN LEGIS
SOCIAL COMBAT. STRUCT LOC/G POL/PAR JUDGE EDU/PROP DECISION
DEBATE ETIQUET ADMIN LOBBY CHOOSE GOV/REL INGP/REL PERSON
HEREDITY ALL/VALS...SOC PRESIDENT. PAGE 48 E0948 LEAD

B54
NUSSBAUM D.,A CONCISE HISTORY OF THE LAW OF INT/ORG
NATIONS. ASIA CHRIST-17C EUR+WWI ISLAM MEDIT-7 LAW
MOD/EUR S/ASIA UNIV WOR+45 WOR-45 SOCIETY STRUCT PEACE
EXEC ATTIT ALL/VALS...CONCPT HIST/WRIT TIME/SEQ. INT/LAW
PAGE 78 E1560

C54
GUINS G.C.,"SOVIET LAW AND SOVIET SOCIETY." COM LAW
USSR STRATA FAM NAT/G WORKER DOMIN RACE/REL STRUCT
...BIBLIOG 20. PAGE 48 E0960 PLAN

B55
CHOWDHURI R.N.,INTERNATIONAL MANDATES AND DELIB/GP
TRUSTEESHIP SYSTEMS. WOR+45 STRUCT ECO/UNDEV PLAN
INT/ORG LEGIS DOMIN EDU/PROP LEGIT ADJUD EXEC PWR SOVEREIGN
...CONCPT TIME/SEQ UN 20. PAGE 22 E0434

B56
CARLSTON K.S.,LAW AND STRUCTURES OF SOCIAL ACTION. JURID
LAW SOCIETY ECO/DEV DIPLOM CONTROL ATTIT...DECISION INT/LAW
CONCPT 20. PAGE 19 E0379 INGP/REL
STRUCT

B56
HOGAN J.D.,AMERICAN SOCIAL LEGISLATION. USA+45 FAM STRUCT
AGE/Y ATTIT...JURID CONCPT TREND. PAGE 53 E1065 RECEIVE
LEGIS
LABOR

B56
HURST J.W.,LAW AND THE CONDITIONS OF FREEDOM IN THE LAW
NINETEENTH CENTURY UNITED STATES. USA-45 CONSTN ORD/FREE
STRUCT ADMIN GP/REL FEDERAL HABITAT...JURID 19. POLICY
PAGE 56 E1116 NAT/G

B56
SOHN L.B.,CASES ON UNITED NATIONS LAW. STRUCT INT/ORG
DELIB/GP WAR PEACE ORD/FREE...DECISION ANTHOL 20 INT/LAW
UN. PAGE 92 E1854 ADMIN
ADJUD

B56
SYKES G.M.,CRIME AND SOCIETY. LAW STRATA STRUCT CRIMLGY
ACT/RES ROUTINE ANOMIE WEALTH...POLICY SOC/INTEG CRIME
20. PAGE 95 E1903 CULTURE
INGP/REL

B57
ROWAN C.T.,GO SOUTH TO SORROW. USA+45 STRUCT NAT/G RACE/REL
EDU/PROP LEAD COERCE ISOLAT DRIVE SUPEGO RESPECT DISCRIM
...PREDICT 20 NEGRO SUPREME/CT SOUTH/US CIV/RIGHTS. ANOMIE
PAGE 86 E1728 LAW

S57
GOODE W.J.,"COMMUNITY WITHIN A COMMUNITY: THE PROF/ORG
PROFESSIONS." STRATA STRUCT SANCTION INGP/REL...SOC NEIGH
GP/COMP. PAGE 45 E0886 CLIENT
CONTROL

B58
SPITZ D.,DEMOCRACY AND THE CHALLANGE OF POWER. FUT NAT/G
USA+45 USA-45 LAW SOCIETY STRUCT LOC/G POL/PAR PWR
PROVS DELIB/GP EX/STRUC LEGIS TOP/EX ACT/RES CREATE
DOMIN EDU/PROP LEGIT ADJUD ADMIN ATTIT DRIVE MORAL
ORD/FREE TOT/POP. PAGE 93 E1862

B59
FRIEDMANN W.G.,LAW IN A CHANGING SOCIETY. FUT SOC
WOR+45 WOR-45 LAW SOCIETY STRUCT INT/TRADE LEGIT JURID
ATTIT BIO/SOC HEALTH ORD/FREE SOVEREIGN...CONCPT
GEN/LAWS ILO 20. PAGE 41 E0803

B59
VITTACHI,EMERGENCY '58. CEYLON UK STRUCT NAT/G RACE/REL
FORCES ADJUD CRIME REV NAT/LISM 20. PAGE 104 E2081 DISCRIM
DIPLOM
SOVEREIGN

S59
CLOWARD R.A.,"ILLEGITIMATE MEANS, ANOMIE, AND ANOMIE
DEVIANT BEHAVIOR" STRUCT CRIME DRIVE PERSON...SOC CRIMLGY
CONCPT NEW/IDEA 20 DURKHEIM/E MERTON/R. PAGE 23 LEGIT
E0459 ADJUST

S59
CORY R.H. JR.,"INTERNATIONAL INSPECTION FROM STRUCT
PROPOSALS TO REALIZATION." WOR+45 TEC/DEV ECO/TAC PSY
ADJUD ORD/FREE PWR WEALTH...RECORD VAL/FREE 20. ARMS/CONT
PAGE 26 E0516 NUC/PWR

S59
DOMKE M.,"THE SETTLEMENT OF DISPUTES IN CONSULT
INTERNATIONAL TRADE." USA+45 LAW STRATA STRUCT LEGIT
JUDGE EDU/PROP PWR...METH/CNCPT 20. PAGE 32 E0634 INT/TRADE

S59
TIPTON J.B.,"PARTICIPATION OF THE UNITED STATES IN LABOR
THE INTERNATIONAL LABOR ORGANIZATION." USA+45 LAW INT/ORG
STRUCT ECO/DEV ECO/UNDEV INDUS TEC/DEV ECO/TAC
ADMIN PERCEPT ORD/FREE SKILL...STAT HIST/WRIT
GEN/METH ILO WORK 20. PAGE 96 E1928

ENGEL J.,THE SECURITY OF THE FREE WORLD. USSR
WOR+45 STRATA STRUCT ECO/DEV ECO/UNDEV INT/ORG
DELIB/GP FORCES DOMIN LEGIT ADJUD EXEC ARMS/CONT
COERCE...POLICY CONCPT NEW/IDEA TIME/SEQ GEN/LAWS
COLD/WAR WORK UN 20 NATO. PAGE 35 E0689
 B60
 COM
 TREND
 DIPLOM

PAUL A.M.,CONSERVATIVE CRISIS AND THE RULE OF LAW.
USA-45 LABOR WORKER ATTIT ORD/FREE CONSERVE LAISSEZ
...DECISION JURID 19 SUPREME/CT. PAGE 80 E1603
 B60
 CONSTN
 ADJUD
 STRUCT
 PROF/ORG

STEIN E.,AMERICAN ENTERPRISE IN THE EUROPEAN COMMON
MARKET: A LEGAL PROFILE. EUR+WWI FUT USA+45 SOCIETY
STRUCT ECO/DEV NAT/G VOL/ASSN CONSULT PLAN TEC/DEV
ECO/TAC INT/TRADE ADMIN ATTIT RIGID/FLEX PWR...MGT
NEW/IDEA STAT TREND COMPUT/IR SIMUL EEC 20. PAGE 93
E1867
 B60
 MARKET
 INT/LAW

WOETZEL R.K.,THE INTERNATIONAL CONTROL OF AIRSPACE
AND OUTERSPACE. FUT WOR+45 AIR CONSTN STRUCT
CONSULT PLAN TEC/DEV ADJUD RIGID/FLEX KNOWL
ORD/FREE PWR...TECHNIC GEOG MGT NEW/IDEA TREND
COMPUT/IR VAL/FREE 20 TREATY. PAGE 107 E2137
 B60
 INT/ORG
 JURID
 SPACE
 INT/LAW

DEAN A.W.,"SECOND GENEVA CONFERENCE OF THE LAW OF
THE SEA: THE FIGHT FOR FREEDOM OF THE SEAS." FUT
USA+45 USSR WOR+45 WOR-45 SEA CONSTN STRUCT PLAN
INT/TRADE ADJUD ADMIN ORD/FREE...DECISION RECORD
TREND GEN/LAWS 20 TREATY. PAGE 30 E0600
 L60
 INT/ORG
 JURID
 INT/LAW

SCHWELB E.,"INTERNATIONAL CONVENTIONS ON HUMAN
RIGHTS." FUT WOR+45 LAW CONSTN CULTURE SOCIETY
STRUCT VOL/ASSN DELIB/GP PLAN ADJUD SUPEGO LOVE
MORAL...SOC CONCPT STAT RECORD HIST/WRIT TREND 20
UN. PAGE 89 E1790
 S60
 INT/ORG
 HUM

WRIGHT Q.,"LEGAL ASPECTS OF THE U-2 INCIDENT." COM
USA+45 USSR STRUCT NAT/G FORCES PLAN TEC/DEV ADJUD
RIGID/FLEX MORAL ORD/FREE...DECISION INT/LAW JURID
PSY TREND GEN/LAWS COLD/WAR VAL/FREE 20 U-2.
PAGE 108 E2157
 S60
 PWR
 POLICY
 SPACE

MCCLEERY R.,"COMMUNICATION PATTERNS AS BASES OF
SYSTEMS OF AUTHORITY AND POWER" IN THEORETICAL
STUDIES IN SOCIAL ORGAN. OF PRISON-BMR. USA+45
SOCIETY STRUCT EDU/PROP ADMIN CONTROL COERCE CRIME
GP/REL AUTHORIT...SOC 20. PAGE 70 E1400
 C60
 PERS/REL
 PUB/INST
 PWR
 DOMIN

RHODESIA-NYASA NATL ARCHIVES,A SELECT BIBLIOGRAPHY
OF RECENT PUBLICATIONS CONCERNING THE FEDERATION OF
RHODESIA AND NYASALAND (PAMPHLET). MALAWI RHODESIA
LAW CULTURE STRUCT ECO/UNDEV LEGIS...GEOG 20.
PAGE 84 E1689
 N60
 BIBLIOG
 ADMIN
 ORD/FREE
 NAT/G

FLINN M.W.,AN ECONOMIC AND SOCIAL HISTORY OF
BRITAIN, 1066-1939. UK LAW STRATA STRUCT AGRI
DIST/IND INDUS WORKER INT/TRADE WAR...CENSUS 11/20.
PAGE 39 E0766
 B61
 SOCIETY
 SOC

ROCHE J.P.,COURTS AND RIGHTS: THE AMERICAN
JUDICIARY IN ACTION (2ND ED.). UK USA+45 USA-45
STRUCT TEC/DEV SANCTION PERS/REL RACE/REL ORD/FREE
...METH/CNCPT GOV/COMP METH/COMP T 13/20. PAGE 85
E1710
 B61
 JURID
 CT/SYS
 NAT/G
 PROVS

DAVIS F.J.,SOCIETY AND THE LAW. USA+45 CONSTN
ACADEM FAM CONSULT ACT/RES GP/REL ORD/FREE
ENGLSH/LAW 20. PAGE 29 E0572
 B62
 LAW
 SOC
 CULTURE
 STRUCT

DIESING P.,REASON IN SOCIETY: FIVE TYPES OF
DECISIONS AND THEIR SOCIAL CONDITIONS. SOCIETY
STRUCT LABOR CREATE TEC/DEV BARGAIN ADJUD ROLE
...JURID BIBLIOG 20. PAGE 31 E0625
 B62
 RATIONAL
 METH/COMP
 DECISION
 CONCPT

PAIKERT G.C.,THE GERMAN EXODUS. EUR+WWI GERMANY/W
LAW CULTURE SOCIETY STRUCT INDUS NAT/LISM RESPECT
SOVEREIGN...CHARTS BIBLIOG SOC/INTEG 20 MIGRATION.
PAGE 79 E1591
 B62
 INGP/REL
 STRANGE
 GEOG
 GP/REL

CORET A.,"L'INDEPENDANCE DU SAMOA OCCIDENTAL."
S/ASIA LAW INT/ORG EXEC ALL/VALS SAMOA UN 20.
PAGE 26 E0508
 L62
 NAT/G
 STRUCT
 SOVEREIGN

MANGIN G.,"L'ORGANIZATION JUDICIAIRE DES ETATS
D'AFRIQUE ET DE MADAGASCAR." ISLAM WOR+45 STRATA
STRUCT ECO/UNDEV NAT/G LEGIT EXEC...JURID TIME/SEQ
TOT/POP 20 SUPREME/CT. PAGE 68 E1357
 L62
 AFR
 LEGIS
 COLONIAL
 MADAGASCAR

GRAVEN J.,"LE MOUVEAU DROIT PENAL INTERNATIONAL."
UNIV STRUCT LEGIS ACT/RES CRIME ATTIT PERCEPT
PERSON...JURID CONCPT 20. PAGE 45 E0899
 S62
 CT/SYS
 PUB/INST
 INT/ORG
 INT/LAW

MANGIN G.,"LES ACCORDS DE COOPERATION EN MATIERE DE
JUSTICE ENTRE LA FRANCE ET LES ETATS AFRICAINS ET
MALGACHE." AFR ISLAM WOR+45 STRUCT ECO/UNDEV NAT/G
DELIB/GP PERCEPT ALL/VALS...JURID MGT TIME/SEQ 20.
PAGE 68 E1356
 S62
 INT/ORG
 LAW
 FRANCE

MURACCIOLE L.,"LES MODIFICATIONS DE LA CONSTITUTION
MALGACHE." AFR WOR+45 ECO/UNDEV LEGIT EXEC ALL/VALS
...JURID 20. PAGE 75 E1505
 S62
 NAT/G
 STRUCT
 SOVEREIGN
 MADAGASCAR

VIGNES D.,"L'AUTORITE DES TRAITES INTERNATIONAUX EN
DROIT INTERNE." EUR+WWI UNIV LAW CONSTN INTELL
NAT/G POL/PAR DIPLOM ATTIT PERCEPT ALL/VALS
...POLICY INT/LAW JURID CONCPT TIME/SEQ 20 TREATY.
PAGE 104 E2075
 S62
 STRUCT
 LEGIT
 FRANCE

VAN DER SPRENKEL S.,"LEGAL INSTITUTIONS IN MANCHU
CHINA." ASIA STRUCT CT/SYS ROUTINE GOV/REL GP/REL
...CONCPT BIBLIOG 17/20. PAGE 103 E2068
 C62
 LAW
 JURID
 ADMIN
 ADJUD

FAWCETT J.E.S.,THE BRITISH COMMONWEALTH IN
INTERNATIONAL LAW. LAW INT/ORG NAT/G VOL/ASSN
OP/RES DIPLOM ADJUD CENTRAL CONSEN...NET/THEORY
CMN/WLTH TREATY. PAGE 36 E0723
 B63
 INT/LAW
 STRUCT
 COLONIAL

LIVINGSTON W.S.,FEDERALISM IN THE COMMONWEALTH - A
BIBLIOGRAPHICAL COMMENTARY. CANADA INDIA PAKISTAN
UK STRUCT LOC/G NAT/G POL/PAR...NAT/COMP 20
AUSTRAL. PAGE 66 E1310
 B63
 BIBLIOG
 JURID
 FEDERAL
 CONSTN

REALE M.,PLURALISMO E LIBERDADE. STRUCT ADJUST
ATTIT 20 CIVIL/LIB. PAGE 84 E1676
 B63
 CONCPT
 ORD/FREE
 JURID
 INGP/REL

HILLS R.J.,"THE REPRESENTATIVE FUNCTION: NEGLECTED
DIMENSION OF LEADERSHIP BEHAVIOR" USA+45 CLIENT
STRUCT SCHOOL PERS/REL...STAT QU SAMP LAB/EXP 20.
PAGE 53 E1048
 S63
 LEAD
 ADMIN
 EXEC
 ACT/RES

LAPENNA I.,STATE AND LAW: SOVIET AND YUGOSLAV
THEORY. USSR YUGOSLAVIA STRATA STRUCT NAT/G DOMIN
COERCE MARXISM...GOV/COMP IDEA/COMP 20. PAGE 63
E1253
 B64
 JURID
 COM
 LAW
 SOVEREIGN

RAGHAVAN M.D.,INDIA IN CEYLONESE HISTORY, SOCIETY
AND CULTURE. CEYLON INDIA S/ASIA LAW SOCIETY
INT/TRADE ATTIT...ART/METH JURID SOC LING 20.
PAGE 83 E1668
 B64
 DIPLOM
 CULTURE
 SECT
 STRUCT

STRONG C.F.,HISTORY OF MODERN POLITICAL
CONSTITUTIONS. STRUCT INT/ORG NAT/G LEGIS TEC/DEV
DIPLOM INT/TRADE CT/SYS EXEC...METH/COMP T 12/20
UN. PAGE 94 E1888
 B64
 CONSTN
 CONCPT

CHROUST A.H.,THE RISE OF THE LEGAL PROFESSION IN
AMERICA (3 VOLS.). STRATA STRUCT POL/PAR PROF/ORG
COLONIAL LEAD REV SKILL...SOC 17/20. PAGE 22 E0437
 B65
 JURID
 USA-45
 CT/SYS
 LAW

KRISLOV S.,THE SUPREME COURT IN THE POLITICAL
PROCESS. USA+45 LAW SOCIETY STRUCT WORKER ADMIN
ROLE...JURID SOC 20 SUPREME/CT. PAGE 62 E1231
 B65
 ADJUD
 DECISION
 CT/SYS
 CONSTN

B65
RENNER K.,MENSCH UND GESELLSCHAFT - GRUNDRISS EINER SOC SOZIOLOGIE (2ND ED.). STRATA FAM LABOR PROF/ORG WAR ...JURID CLASSIF 20. PAGE 84 E1685
SOC
STRUCT
NAT/G
SOCIETY

B66
AMERICAN JEWISH COMMITTEE,GROUP RELATIONS IN THE UNITED STATES: PROBLEMS AND PERSPECTIVES: A SELECTED, ANNOTATED BIBLIOGRAPHY (PAMPHLET). LAW CONSTN STRATA SCHOOL SECT PROB/SOLV ATTIT...POLICY WELF/ST SOC/WK 20. PAGE 4 E0079
BIBLIOG/A
USA/+45
STRUCT
GP/REL

B66
CARLIN J.E.,LAWYER'S ETHICS. CLIENT STRUCT CONSULT PERS/REL PWR...JURID OBS CHARTS 20. PAGE 19 E0378
ATTIT
PROF/ORG
INT

B66
HOGUE A.R.,ORIGINS OF THE COMMON LAW. UK STRUCT AGRI CT/SYS SANCTION CONSERVE 12/14 ENGLSH/LAW COMMON/LAW. PAGE 54 E1068
LAW
SOCIETY
CONSTN

B66
RUNCIMAN W.G.,RELATIVE DEPRIVATION AND SOCIAL JUSTICE: A STUDY OF ATTITUDES TO SOCIAL INEQUALITY IN TWENTIETH-CENTURY ENGLAND. UK LAW POL/PAR PWR ...CONCPT NEW/IDEA SAMP METH 19/20. PAGE 86 E1734
STRATA
STRUCT
DISCRIM
ATTIT

S66
MATTHEWS D.G.,"ETHIOPIAN OUTLINE: A BIBLIOGRAPHIC RESEARCH GUIDE." ETHIOPIA LAW STRUCT ECO/UNDEV AGRI LABOR SECT CHIEF DELIB/GP EX/STRUC ADMIN...LING ORG/CHARTS 20. PAGE 69 E1384
BIBLIOG
NAT/G
DIPLOM
POL/PAR

N66
CONGRESSIONAL QUARTERLY SERV,HOUSING A NATION (PAMPHLET). USA+45 LAW STRUCT DIST/IND DELIB/GP ...GEOG CHARTS 20 DEPT/HUD. PAGE 25 E0490
HABITAT
NAT/G
PLAN
MUNIC

B67
BONGER W.A.,CRIMINALITY AND ECONOMIC CONDITIONS. MOD/EUR STRUCT INDUS WORKER EDU/PROP CRIME HABITAT ALL/VALS...JURID SOC 20 REFORMERS. PAGE 14 E0265
PERSON
CRIMLGY
IDEA/COMP
ANOMIE

B67
CLINARD M.B.,CRIMINAL BEHAVIOR SYSTEMS: A TYPOLOGY. WOR+45 LAW SOCIETY STRUCT R+D AGE/Y ATTIT WEALTH ...CLASSIF CHARTS METH/COMP METH. PAGE 23 E0457
BIBLIOG
CRIME
CRIMLGY
PERSON

B67
MCDOUGAL M.S.,THE INTERPRETATION OF AGREEMENTS AND WORLD PUBLIC ORDER: PRINCIPLES OF CONTENT AND PROCEDURE. WOR+45 CONSTN PROB/SOLV TEC/DEV ...CON/ANAL TREATY. PAGE 71 E1412
INT/LAW
STRUCT
ECO/UNDEV
DIPLOM

B67
MEYERS M.,SOURCES OF THE AMERICAN REPUBLIC; A DOCUMENTARY HISTORY OF POLITICS, SOCIETY, AND THOUGHT (VOL. I, REV. ED.). USA-45 CULTURE STRUCT NAT/G LEGIS LEAD ATTIT...JURID SOC ANTHOL 17/19 PRESIDENT. PAGE 72 E1450
COLONIAL
REV
WAR

L67
NAGEL S.S.,"DISPARITIES IN CRIMINAL PROCEDURE." STRATA NAT/G PROVS EDU/PROP RACE/REL AGE HABITAT SEX...JURID CHARTS 20. PAGE 76 E1519
ADJUD
DISCRIM
STRUCT
ACT/RES

S67
BLAKEY G.R.,"ORGANIZED CRIME IN THE UNITED STATES." USA+45 USA-45 STRUCT LABOR NAT/G VOL/ASSN ADMIN PERS/REL PWR...CRIMLGY INT 17/20. PAGE 12 E0240
CRIME
ELITES
CONTROL

S67
POSPISIL L.,"LEGAL LEVELS AND MULTIPLICITY OF LEGAL SYSTEMS IN HUMAN SOCIETIES." WOR+45 CENTRAL PWR ...SOC CHARTS GP/COMP GEN/LAWS. PAGE 81 E1630
LAW
STRATA
JURID
STRUCT

S67
RAI H.,"DISTRICT MAGISTRATE AND POLICE SUPERINTENDENT IN INDIA: THE CONTROVERSY OF DUAL CONTROL" INDIA LAW PROVS ADMIN PWR 19/20. PAGE 83 E1669
STRUCT
CONTROL
ROLE
FORCES

B73
AUSTIN J.,LECTURES ON JURISPRUDENCE OR THE PHILOSOPHY OF POSITIVE LAW (VOL. II) (4TH ED., REV.). UK CONSTN STRUCT PROB/SOLV LEGIT CT/SYS SANCTION CRIME INGP/REL OWN SUPEGO ORD/FREE...T 19. PAGE 6 E0120
LAW
ADJUD
JURID
METH/CNCPT

B75
MAINE H.S.,LECTURES ON THE EARLY HISTORY OF INSTITUTIONS. IRELAND UK CONSTN ELITES STRUCT FAM KIN CHIEF LEGIS CT/SYS OWN SOVEREIGN...CONCPT 16 BENTHAM/J BREHON ROMAN/LAW. PAGE 68 E1351
CULTURE
LAW
INGP/REL

B90
GODWIN W.,POLITICAL JUSTICE. UK ELITES OWN KNOWL MORAL WEALTH...JURID 18/19. PAGE 44 E0877
ORD/FREE
SOVEREIGN
STRUCT
CONCPT

B97
JENKS E.J.,LAW AND POLITICS IN THE MIDDLE AGES. CHRIST-17C CULTURE STRUCT KIN NAT/G SECT CT/SYS GP/REL...CLASSIF CHARTS IDEA/COMP BIBLIOG 8/16. PAGE 58 E1162
LAW
SOCIETY
ADJUST

STRUVE/P....PETER STRUVE

STUART G.H. E1889

STUART/DYN....THE STUART DYNASTY

STUDENT NONVIOLENT COORDINATING COMMITTEE....SEE SNCC, STUDNT/PWR

STUDENTS FOR A DEMOCRATIC SOCIETY....SEE SDS

STUDNT/PWR....STUDENT POWER: STUDENT PROTESTS AND PROTEST MOVEMENTS

STUMBERG G.W. E0266

STUMPF S.E. E1890

STURZO L. E1891

STYLE....STYLES OF SCIENTIFIC COMMUNICATION

B49
GROB F.,THE RELATIVITY OF WAR AND PEACE: A STUDY IN LAW, HISTORY, AND POLITICS. WOR+45 WOR-45 LAW DIPLOM DEBATE...CONCPT LING IDEA/COMP BIBLIOG 18/20. PAGE 48 E0944
WAR
PEACE
INT/LAW
STYLE

B54
AUSTIN J.,THE PROVINCE OF JURISPRUDENCE DETERMINED AND THE USES OF THE STUDY OF JURISPRUDENCE. MORAL ...CLASSIF LING STYLE 19. PAGE 6 E0119
CONCPT
LAW
JURID
GEN/LAWS

B57
DUMBAULD E.,THE BILL OF RIGHTS AND WHAT IT MEANS TODAY. USA+45 USA-45 CT/SYS...JURID STYLE TIME/SEQ BIBLIOG 18/20 BILL/RIGHT. PAGE 33 E0656
CONSTN
LAW
ADJUD
ORD/FREE

B62
STERN R.L.,SUPREME COURT PRACTICE. USA+45 USA-45 OP/RES...STYLE METH 20 SUPREME/CT. PAGE 93 E1872
CT/SYS
ADJUD
JURID
ROUTINE

S65
FALK R.A.,"INTERNATIONAL LEGAL ORDER." USA+45 INTELL FACE/GP INT/ORG LEGIT KNOWL...CONCPT METH/CNCPT STYLE RECORD GEN/METH 20. PAGE 36 E0717
ATTIT
GEN/LAWS
INT/LAW

SUAREZ F. E1892

SUAREZ/F....FRANCISCO SUAREZ

B19
VANDERPOL A.,LA DOCTRINE SCOLASTIQUE DU DROIT DE GUERRE. CHRIST-17C FORCES DIPLOM LEGIT SUPEGO MORAL ...BIOG AQUINAS/T SUAREZ/F CHRISTIAN. PAGE 103 E2072
WAR
SECT
INT/LAW

SUBMARINE....SUBMARINES AND SUBMARINE WARFARE

SUBSIDIES....SEE FINAN

SUBURBS....SUBURBS

SUBVERT....SUBVERSION

B57
US COMMISSION GOVT SECURITY,RECOMMENDATIONS; AREA: IMMIGRANT PROGRAM. USA+45 LAW WORKER DIPLOM EDU/PROP WRITING ADMIN PEACE ATTIT...CONCPT ANTHOL
POLICY
CONTROL
PLAN

20 MIGRATION SUBVERT. PAGE 99 E1981 — NAT/G

B65
US LIBRARY OF CONGRESS,INTERNAL SECURITY AND
SUBVERSION. USA+45 ACADEM LOC/G NAT/G PROVS
...POLICY ANARCH DECISION 20 CIVIL/SERV SUBVERT
SEDITION. PAGE 101 E2020 — CONTROL ADJUD LAW PLAN

SUCCESSION....SUCCESSION (POLITICAL)

SUDAN....SEE ALSO AFR

B57
CONOVER H.F.,NORTH AND NORTHEAST AFRICA; A SELECTED
ANNOTATED LIST OF WRITINGS. ALGERIA MOROCCO SUDAN
UAR CULTURE INT/ORG PROB/SOLV ADJUD NAT/LISM PWR
WEALTH...SOC 20 UN. PAGE 25 E0496 — BIBLIOG/A DIPLOM AFR ECO/UNDEV

SUDETENLND....SUDETENLAND

SUEZ CRISIS....SEE NAT/LISM+COERCE, ALSO INDIVIDUAL
NATIONS, SUEZ

SUEZ....SUEZ CANAL

B00
HOLLAND T.E.,STUDIES IN INTERNATIONAL LAW. TURKEY
USSR WOR-45 CONSTN NAT/G DIPLOM DOMIN LEGIT COERCE
WAR PEACE ORD/FREE PWR SOVEREIGN...JURID CHARTS 20
PARLIAMENT SUEZ TREATY. PAGE 54 E1084 — INT/ORG LAW INT/LAW

N19
BAILEY S.D.,VETO IN THE SECURITY COUNCIL
(PAMPHLET). COM USSR WOR+45 CONSTN NAT/G PARL/PROC
ARMS/CONT PRIVIL PWR...INT/LAW TREND CHARTS 20 UN
SUEZ. PAGE 7 E0135 — DELIB/GP INT/ORG DIPLOM

B58
STONE J.,AGGRESSION AND WORLD ORDER: A CRITIQUE OF
UNITED NATIONS THEORIES OF AGGRESSION. LAW CONSTN
DELIB/GP PROB/SOLV BAL/PWR DIPLOM DEBATE ADJUD
CRIME PWR...POLICY IDEA/COMP 20 UN SUEZ LEAGUE/NAT.
PAGE 94 E1879 — ORD/FREE INT/ORG WAR CONCPT

L60
LAUTERPACHT E.,"THE SUEZ CANAL SETTLEMENT." FRANCE
ISLAM ISRAEL UAR UK BAL/PWR DIPLOM LEGIT...JURID
GEN/LAWS ANTHOL SUEZ VAL/FREE 20. PAGE 63 E1263 — INT/ORG LAW

B63
ATTIA G.E.D.,LES FORCES ARMEES DES NATIONS UNIES EN
COREE ET AU MOYENORIENT. KOREA CONSTN NAT/G
DELIB/GP LEGIS PWR...IDEA/COMP NAT/COMP BIBLIOG UN
SUEZ. PAGE 6 E0114 — FORCES INT/LAW

C63
ATTIA G.E.O.,"LES FORCES ARMEES DES NATIONS UNIES
EN COREE ET AU MOYENORIENT." KOREA CONSTN DELIB/GP
LEGIS PWR...IDEA/COMP NAT/COMP BIBLIOG UN SUEZ.
PAGE 6 E0115 — FORCES NAT/G INT/LAW

B64
BOWETT D.W.,UNITED NATIONS FORCES* A LEGAL STUDY.
CYPRUS ISRAEL KOREA LAW CONSTN ACT/RES CREATE
BUDGET CONTROL TASK PWR...INT/LAW IDEA/COMP UN
CONGO/LEOP SUEZ. PAGE 14 E0278 — OP/RES FORCES ARMS/CONT

SUFF....SUFFRAGE; SEE ALSO CHOOSE

B06
GRIFFIN A.P.C.,SELECT LIST OF REFERENCES ON THE
NEGRO QUESTION (REV. ED.). USA-45 CONSTN SCHOOL
SUFF ADJUST...JURID SOC/INTEG 19/20 NEGRO. PAGE 47
E0930 — BIBLIOG/A RACE/REL DISCRIM ATTIT

B08
GRIFFIN A.P.C.,REFERENCES ON CORRUPT PRACTICES IN
ELECTIONS (PAMPHLET). USA-45 LAW CONSTN TRIBUTE
CRIME REPRESENT...JURID 19/20. PAGE 47 E0934 — BIBLIOG/A CHOOSE SUFF APPORT

B09
LOBINGIER C.S.,THE PEOPLE'S LAW OR POPULAR
PARTICIPATION IN LAW-MAKING. FRANCE SWITZERLND UK
LOC/G NAT/G PROVS LEGIS SUFF MAJORITY PWR POPULISM
...GOV/COMP BIBLIOG 19. PAGE 66 E1314 — CONSTN LAW PARTIC

B14
CRAIG J.,ELEMENTS OF POLITICAL SCIENCE (3 VOLS.).
CONSTN AGRI INDUS SCHOOL FORCES TAX CT/SYS SUFF
MORAL WEALTH...CONCPT 19 CIVIL/LIB. PAGE 27 E0539 — PHIL/SCI NAT/G ORD/FREE

B18
PORTER K.H.,A HISTORY OF SUFFRAGE IN THE UNITED
STATES. USA-45 LAW CONSTN LOC/G NAT/G POL/PAR WAR
DISCRIM OWN ATTIT SEX 18/20 NEGRO FEMALE/SEX. — SUFF REPRESENT CHOOSE

PAGE 81 E1629 — PARTIC

N19
PAN AMERICAN UNION,INFORME DE LA MISION DE
ASISTENCIA TECNICA DE LA OEA A LA REPUBLICA DE
HONDURAS EN MATERIA ELECTORAL (PAMPHLET). HONDURAS
CONSTN ORD/FREE...JURID OBS 20 OAS. PAGE 80 E1595 — CHOOSE SUFF POL/PAR NAT/G

B45
US LIBRARY OF CONGRESS,CONSTITUTIONAL AND STATUTORY
PROVISIONS OF THE STATES (VOL. I). USA-45 CREATE
TAX CT/SYS CHOOSE SUFF INCOME PWR 20. PAGE 101
E2016 — CONSTN FEDERAL PROVS JURID

B50
MERRIAM C.E.,THE AMERICAN PARTY SYSTEM; AN
INTRODUCTION TO THE STUDY OF POLITICAL PARTIES IN
THE UNITED STATES (4TH ED.). USA+45 USA-45 LAW
FINAN LOC/G NAT/G PROVS LEAD PARTIC CRIME ATTIT
18/20 NEGRO CONGRESS PRESIDENT. PAGE 72 E1442 — POL/PAR CHOOSE SUFF REPRESENT

B51
CAMPBELL E.H.,UNITED STATES CITIZENSHIP AND
QUALIFICATIONS FOR VOTING IN WASHINGTON. USA+45
NAT/G PROVS...CHARTS BIBLIOG 20 WASHINGT/G. PAGE 19
E0371 — LAW CONSTN SUFF CHOOSE

B53
BUTLER D.E.,THE ELECTORAL SYSTEM IN BRITAIN,
1918-1951. UK LAW POL/PAR SUFF...STAT BIBLIOG 20
PARLIAMENT. PAGE 18 E0348 — CHOOSE LEGIS REPRESENT PARTIC

B54
SINCO,PHILIPPINE POLITICAL LAW: PRINCIPLES AND
CONCEPTS (10TH ED.). PHILIPPINE LOC/G EX/STRUC
BAL/PWR ECO/TAC TAX ADJUD ADMIN CONTROL CT/SYS SUFF
ORD/FREE...T 20. PAGE 91 E1831 — LAW CONSTN LEGIS

B59
BRIGGS A.,CHARTIST STUDIES. UK LAW NAT/G WORKER
EDU/PROP COERCE SUFF GP/REL ATTIT...ANTHOL 19.
PAGE 15 E0300 — INDUS STRATA LABOR POLICY

B59
NICHOLS R.F.,RELIGION AND AMERICAN DEMOCRACY.
USA+45 USA-45 LAW CHOOSE SUFF MORAL ORD/FREE
POPULISM...POLICY BIBLIOG 16/20 PRE/US/AM
CHRISTIAN. PAGE 77 E1547 — NAT/G SECT CONSTN CONCPT

B60
LA PONCE J.A.,THE PROTECTION OF MINORITIES. WOR+45
WOR-45 NAT/G POL/PAR SUFF...INT/LAW CLASSIF GP/COMP
GOV/COMP BIBLIOG 17/20 CIVIL/LIB CIV/RIGHTS.
PAGE 62 E1242 — INGP/REL DOMIN SOCIETY RACE/REL

B60
RIENOW R.,INTRODUCTION TO GOVERNMENT (2ND ED.). UK
USA+45 USSR POL/PAR ADMIN REV CHOOSE SUFF FEDERAL
PWR...JURID GOV/COMP T 20. PAGE 85 E1697 — CONSTN PARL/PROC REPRESENT AUTHORIT

B61
BENNETT G.,THE KENYATTA ELECTION: KENYA 1960-1961.
AFR INGP/REL RACE/REL CONSEN ATTIT 20 KENYATTA.
PAGE 10 E0187 — CHOOSE POL/PAR LAW SUFF

B62
MITCHELL G.E.,THE ANGRY BLACK SOUTH. USA+45 LAW
CONSTN SCHOOL DELIB/GP EDU/PROP CONTROL SUFF ANOMIE
DRIVE...ANTHOL 20 NEGRO CIV/RIGHTS SOUTH/US.
PAGE 74 E1473 — RACE/REL DISCRIM ADJUST ORD/FREE

N63
US PRES COMN REGIS AND VOTING,REPORT ON
REGISTRATION AND VOTING (PAMPHLET). USA+45 POL/PAR
CHIEF EDU/PROP PARTIC REPRESENT ATTIT...PSY CHARTS
20. PAGE 101 E2023 — CHOOSE LAW SUFF INSPECT

B64
FACTS ON FILE, INC.,CIVIL RIGHTS 1960-63: THE NEGRO
CAMPAIGN TO WIN EQUAL RIGHTS AND OPPORTUNITIES IN
THE UNITED STATES. LAW CONSTN PARTIC SUFF 20 NEGRO
CIV/RIGHTS MISSISSIPP. PAGE 36 E0710 — DISCRIM PRESS RACE/REL

B64
MITCHELL B.,A BIOGRAPHY OF THE CONSTITUTION OF THE
UNITED STATES. USA+45 USA-45 PROVS CHIEF LEGIS
DEBATE ADJUD SUFF FEDERAL...SOC 18/20 SUPREME/CT
CONGRESS SENATE HOUSE/REP PRESIDENT. PAGE 73 E1472 — CONSTN LAW JURID

B64
OPPENHEIMER M.,A MANUAL FOR DIRECT ACTION. USA+45
SCHOOL FORCES ADJUD CT/SYS SUFF RACE/REL DISCRIM — PLAN VOL/ASSN

...POLICY CHARTS 20. PAGE 79 E1580 — JURID LEAD

B65
CHARNAY J.P.,LE SUFFRAGE POLITIQUE EN FRANCE; ELECTIONS PARLEMENTAIRES, ELECTION PRESIDENTIELLE, REFERENDUMS. FRANCE CONSTN CHIEF DELIB/GP ECO/TAC EDU/PROP CRIME INGP/REL MORAL ORD/FREE PWR CATHISM 20 PARLIAMENT PRESIDENT. PAGE 22 E0425 — CHOOSE SUFF NAT/G LEGIS

B65
CONGRESSIONAL QUARTERLY SERV,POLITICS IN AMERICA, 1945-1964: THE POLITICS AND ISSUES OF THE POSTWAR YEARS. USA+45 LAW FINAN CHIEF DIPLOM APPORT SUFF ...POLICY STAT TREND CHARTS 20 CONGRESS PRESIDENT. PAGE 25 E0489 — CHOOSE REPRESENT POL/PAR LEGIS

B65
IANNIELLO L.,MILESTONES ALONG THE MARCH: TWELVE HISTORIC CIVIL RIGHTS DOCUMENTS--FROM WORLD WAR II TO SELMA. USA+45 LAW FORCES TOP/EX PARTIC SUFF...T 20 NEGRO CIV/RIGHTS TRUMAN/HS SUPREME/CT KENNEDY/JF. PAGE 56 E1121 — RACE/REL DISCRIM CONSTN NAT/G

B65
STOREY R.G.,OUR UNALIENABLE RIGHTS. LAW SECT CT/SYS SUFF DISCRIM 17/20 CIVIL/LIB ENGLSH/LAW. PAGE 94 E1882 — CONSTN JURID ORD/FREE LEGIS

B66
CONG QUARTERLY SERVICE,REPRESENTATION AND APPORTIONMENT. USA+45 USA-45 POL/PAR CT/SYS SUFF ...POLICY 20 CONGRESS SUPREME/CT. PAGE 25 E0486 — APPORT LEGIS REPRESENT CONSTN

B66
INSTITUTE COMP STUDY POL SYS,DOMINICAN REPUBLIC ELECTION FACT BOOK. DOMIN/REP LAW LEGIS REPRESENT ...JURID CHARTS 20. PAGE 57 E1126 — SUFF CHOOSE POL/PAR NAT/G

B66
KURLAND P.B.,THE SUPREME COURT REVIEW. USA+45 USA-45 LAW LABOR SUFF...ANTHOL 20 SUPREME/CT. PAGE 62 E1240 — JURID PROB/SOLV ADJUD NAT/G

B66
SWEET E.C.,CIVIL LIBERTIES IN AMERICA. LAW CONSTN NAT/G PRESS CT/SYS DISCRIM ATTIT WORSHIP 20 CIVIL/LIB. PAGE 95 E1899 — ADJUD ORD/FREE SUFF COERCE

SUFFRAGE....SEE SUFF

SUICIDE....SUICIDE AND RELATED SELF-DESTRUCTIVENESS

SUKARNO/A....ACHMED SUKARNO

SUMATRA....SUMATRA

SUMER....SUMER, A PRE- OR EARLY HISTORIC SOCIETY

SUMMERS R.E. E1893

SUMMERS R.S. E1101

SUN/YAT....SUN YAT-SEN

SUPEGO....CONSCIENCE, SUPEREGO, RESPONSIBILITY

B12
FOUAD M.,LE REGIME DE LA PRESSE EN EGYPTE: THESE POUR LE DOCTORAT. UAR LICENSE EDU/PROP ADMIN SANCTION CRIME SUPEGO PWR...ART/METH JURID 19/20. PAGE 39 E0778 — ORD/FREE LEGIS CONTROL PRESS

B19
VANDERPOL A.,LA DOCTRINE SCOLASTIQUE DU DROIT DE GUERRE. CHRIST-17C FORCES DIPLOM LEGIT SUPEGO MORAL ...BIOG AQUINAS/T SUAREZ/F CHRISTIAN. PAGE 103 E2072 — WAR SECT INT/LAW

N19
GIBB A.D.,JUDICIAL CORRUPTION IN THE UNITED KINGDOM (PAMPHLET). UK DELIB/GP CT/SYS CRIME PERSON SUPEGO 17/20 SCOTLAND. PAGE 43 E0856 — MORAL ATTIT ADJUD

B29
BUELL R.,INTERNATIONAL RELATIONS. WOR+45 WOR-45 CONSTN STRATA FORCES TOP/EX ADMIN ATTIT DRIVE SUPEGO MORAL ORD/FREE PWR SOVEREIGN...JURID SOC CONCPT 20. PAGE 17 E0326 — INT/ORG BAL/PWR DIPLOM

B33
GENTILI A.,DE JURE BELLI, LIBRI TRES (1612) (VOL. 2). FORCES DIPLOM AGREE PEACE SOVEREIGN. PAGE 43 E0849 — WAR INT/LAW MORAL SUPEGO

C43
BENTHAM J.,"THE RATIONALE OF REWARD" IN J. BOWRING, ED., THE WORKS OF JEREMY BENTHAM (VOL. 2)." LAW WORKER CREATE INSPECT PAY ROUTINE HAPPINESS PRODUC SUPEGO WEALTH METH/CNCPT. PAGE 10 E0195 — SANCTION ECO/TAC INCOME PWR

B45
WEST R.,CONSCIENCE AND SOCIETY: A STUDY OF THE PSYCHOLOGICAL PREREQUISITES OF LAW AND ORDER. FUT UNIV LAW SOCIETY STRUCT DIPLOM WAR PERS/REL SUPEGO ...SOC 20. PAGE 105 E2112 — COERCE INT/LAW ORD/FREE PERSON

S48
ALEXANDER L.,"WAR CRIMES, THEIR SOCIAL-PSYCHOLOGICAL ASPECTS." EUR+WWI GERMANY LAW CULTURE ELITES KIN POL/PAR PUB/INST FORCES DOMIN EDU/PROP COERCE CRIME ATTIT SUPEGO HEALTH MORAL PWR FASCISM ...PSY OBS TREND GEN/LAWS NAZI 20. PAGE 3 E0061 — DRIVE WAR

B49
THOREAU H.D.,CIVIL DISOBEDIENCE (1849). USA-45 LAW CONSTN TAX COERCE REPRESENT GP/REL SUPEGO...MAJORIT CONCPT 19. PAGE 96 E1923 — GEN/LAWS ORD/FREE POLICY

S51
COHEN M.B.,"PERSONALITY AS A FACTOR IN ADMINISTRATIVE DECISIONS." ADJUD PERS/REL ANOMIE SUPEGO...OBS SELF/OBS INT. PAGE 24 E0465 — PERSON ADMIN PROB/SOLV PSY

B53
BRETTON H.L.,STRESEMANN AND THE REVISION OF VERSAILLES: A FIGHT FOR REASON. EUR+WWI GERMANY FORCES BUDGET ARMS/CONT WAR SUPEGO...BIBLIOG 20 TREATY VERSAILLES STRESEMN/G. PAGE 15 E0294 — POLICY DIPLOM BIOG

B55
BENTON W.E.,NUREMBERG: GERMAN VIEWS OF THE WAR TRIALS. EUR+WWI GERMANY VOL/ASSN LEAD PARTIC COERCE INGP/REL RACE/REL TOTALISM SUPEGO ORD/FREE...ANTHOL NUREMBERG. PAGE 10 E0201 — CRIME WAR LAW JURID

B55
CAVAN R.S.,CRIMINOLOGY (2ND ED.). USA+45 LAW FAM PUB/INST FORCES PLAN WAR AGE/Y PERSON ROLE SUPEGO ...CHARTS 20 FBI. PAGE 21 E0409 — DRIVE CRIMLGY CONTROL METH/COMP

B55
MAZZINI J.,THE DUTIES OF MAN. MOD/EUR LAW SOCIETY FAM NAT/G POL/PAR SECT VOL/ASSN EX/STRUC ACT/RES CREATE REV PEACE ATTIT ALL/VALS...GEN/LAWS WORK 19. PAGE 70 E1396 — SUPEGO CONCPT NAT/LISM

B56
CORBETT P.E.,MORALS LAW, AND POWER IN INTERNATIONAL RELATIONS. WOR+45 WOR-45 INT/ORG VOL/ASSN DELIB/GP CREATE BAL/PWR DIPLOM LEGIT ARMS/CONT MORAL...JURID GEN/LAWS TOT/POP LEAGUE/NAT 20. PAGE 26 E0506 — SUPEGO CONCPT POLICY INT/LAW

B57
HINDERLING A.,DIE REFORMATORISCHE VERWALTUNGSGERICHTSBARKEIT. GERMANY/W PROB/SOLV ADJUD SUPEGO PWR...CONCPT 20. PAGE 53 E1049 — ADMIN CT/SYS JURID CONTROL

B57
ROWAN C.T.,GO SOUTH TO SORROW. USA+45 STRUCT NAT/G EDU/PROP LEAD COERCE ISOLAT DRIVE SUPEGO RESPECT ...PREDICT 20 NEGRO SUPREME/CT SOUTH/US CIV/RIGHTS. PAGE 86 E1728 — RACE/REL DISCRIM ANOMIE LAW

B58
FELLMAN D.,THE DEFENDANT'S RIGHTS. USA+45 NAT/G CONSULT CT/SYS SUPEGO ORD/FREE...BIBLIOG SUPREME/CT CIVIL/SERV. PAGE 37 E0730 — CONSTN LAW CRIME ADJUD

B58
HALL J.,STUDIES IN JURISPRUDENCE AND CRIMINAL THEORY. USA-45 LAW CULTURE CREATE SUPEGO...CRIMLGY PSY /20 PLATO. PAGE 49 E0983 — JURID CRIME CONCPT CT/SYS

B58
JENKS C.W.,THE COMMON LAW OF MANKIND. EUR+WWI MOD/EUR SPACE WOR+45 INT/ORG BAL/PWR ARMS/CONT COERCE SUPEGO MORAL...TREND 20. PAGE 58 E1154 — JURID SOVEREIGN

KNIERIEM A.,THE NUREMBERG TRIALS. EUR+WWI GERMANY VOL/ASSN LEAD COERCE WAR INGP/REL TOTALISM SUPEGO ORD/FREE...CONCPT METH/COMP. PAGE 61 E1225
B59
INT/LAW
CRIME
PARTIC
JURID

WOETZEL R.K.,DIE INTERNATIONALE KONTROLLE DER HOHEREN LUFTSCHICHTEN UND DES WELTRAUMS. INT/ORG NAT/G CONTROL SUPEGO...JURID CONCPT 20. PAGE 107 E2136
B59
SPACE
INT/LAW
DIPLOM
SOVEREIGN

SCHWELB E.,"INTERNATIONAL CONVENTIONS ON HUMAN RIGHTS." FUT WOR+45 LAW CONSTN CULTURE SOCIETY STRUCT VOL/ASSN DELIB/GP PLAN ADJUD SUPEGO LOVE MORAL...SOC CONCPT STAT RECORD HIST/WRIT TREND 20 UN. PAGE 89 E1790
S60
INT/ORG
HUM

THOMPSON K.W.,"MORAL PURPOSE IN FOREIGN POLICY: REALITIES AND ILLUSIONS." WOR+45 WOR-45 LAW CULTURE SOCIETY INT/ORG PLAN ADJUD ADMIN COERCE RIGID/FLEX SUPEGO KNOWL ORD/FREE PWR...SOC TREND SOC/EXP TOT/POP 20. PAGE 96 E1921
S60
MORAL
JURID
DIPLOM

BEASLEY K.E.,STATE SUPERVISION OF MUNICIPAL DEBT IN KANSAS - A CASE STUDY. USA+45 USA-45 FINAN PROVS BUDGET TAX ADJUD ADMIN CONTROL SUPEGO. PAGE 9 E0167
B61
MUNIC
LOC/G
LEGIS
JURID

BORKIN J.,THE CORRUPT JUDGE. USA+45 CT/SYS ATTIT SUPEGO MORAL RESPECT...BIBLIOG + SUPREME/CT MANTON/M DAVIS/W JOHNSN/ALB. PAGE 14 E0271
B62
ADJUD
TRIBUTE
CRIME

HEYDECKER J.J.,THE NUREMBERG TRIAL: HISTORY OF NAZI GERMANY AS REVEALED THROUGH THE TESTIMONY AT NUREMBERG. EUR+WWI GERMANY VOL/ASSN LEAD COERCE CROWD INGP/REL RACE/REL SUPEGO ORD/FREE...CONCPT 20 NAZI ANTI/SEMIT NUREMBERG JEWS. PAGE 52 E1036
B62
LAW
CRIME
PARTIC
TOTALISM

HOOK S.,THE PARADOXES OF FREEDOM. UNIV CONSTN INTELL LEGIS CONTROL REV CHOOSE SUPEGO...POLICY JURID IDEA/COMP 19/20 CIV/RIGHTS. PAGE 55 E1095
B62
CONCPT
MAJORIT
ORD/FREE
ALL/VALS

NORGAARD C.A.,THE POSITION OF THE INDIVIDUAL IN INTERNATIONAL LAW. INT/ORG SUPEGO ORD/FREE SOVEREIGN...CONCPT 20 UN. PAGE 78 E1556
B62
INT/LAW
DIPLOM
CRIME
JURID

WOETZEL R.K.,THE NURENBERG TRIALS IN INTERNATIONAL LAW. CHRIST-17C MOD/EUR WOR+45 SOCIETY NAT/G DELIB/GP DOMIN LEGIT ROUTINE ATTIT DRIVE PERSON SUPEGO MORAL ORD/FREE...POLICY MAJORIT JURID PSY SOC SELF/OBS RECORD NAZI TOT/POP. PAGE 107 E2138
B62
INT/ORG
ADJUD
WAR

MONNIER J.P.,"LA SUCCESSION D'ETATS EN MATIERE DE RESPONSABILITE INTERNATIONALE." UNIV CONSTN INTELL SOCIETY ADJUD ROUTINE PERCEPT SUPEGO...GEN/LAWS TOT/POP 20. PAGE 74 E1485
S62
NAT/G
JURID
INT/LAW

ROSE R.,"COMPARATIVE STUDIES IN POLITICAL FINANCE: A SYMPOSIUM." ASIA EUR+WWI S/ASIA LAW CULTURE DELIB/GP LEGIS ACT/RES ECO/TAC EDU/PROP CHOOSE ATTIT RIGID/FLEX SUPEGO PWR SKILL WEALTH...STAT ANTHOL VAL/FREE. PAGE 85 E1714
L63
FINAN
POL/PAR

ANASTAPLO G.,NOTES ON THE FIRST AMENDMENT TO THE CONSTITUTION OF THE UNITED STATES (PART TWO). USA+45 USA-45 NAT/G JUDGE DEBATE SUPEGO PWR SOVEREIGN 18/20 SUPREME/CT CONGRESS AMEND/I. PAGE 5 E0088
B64
ORD/FREE
CONSTN
CT/SYS
ATTIT

BOUVIER-AJAM M.,MANUEL TECHNIQUE ET PRATIQUE DU MAIRE ET DES ELUS ET AGENTS COMMUNAUX. FRANCE LOC/G BUDGET CHOOSE GP/REL SUPEGO...JURID BIBLIOG 20 MAYOR COMMUNES. PAGE 14 E0274
B64
MUNIC
ADMIN
CHIEF
NEIGH

DRESSLER D.,READINGS IN CRIMINOLOGY AND PENOLOGY. UNIV CULTURE PUB/INST FORCES ACT/RES PROB/SOLV ANOMIE BIO/SOC SUPEGO...GEOG PSY ANTHOL 20. PAGE 33 E0648
B64
CRIMLGY
CRIME
ADJUD
ADJUST

HENKE W.,DAS RECHT DER POLITISCHEN PARTEIEN. GERMANY/W LAW CT/SYS GP/REL SUPEGO 20. PAGE 52 E1031
B64
POL/PAR
JURID
CONSTN
NAT/G

SCHUBERT G.A.,JUDICIAL BEHAVIOR: A READER IN THEORY AND RESEARCH. POL/PAR CT/SYS ROLE SUPEGO PWR ...DECISION JURID REGRESS CHARTS SIMUL ANTHOL 20. PAGE 89 E1782
B64
ATTIT
PERSON
ADJUD
ACT/RES

GREENBERG S.,"JUDAISM AND WORLD JUSTICE." MEDIT-7 WOR+45 LAW CULTURE SOCIETY INT/ORG NAT/G FORCES EDU/PROP ATTIT DRIVE PERSON SUPEGO ALL/VALS ...POLICY PSY CONCPT GEN/LAWS JEWS. PAGE 46 E0908
S64
SECT
JURID
PEACE

KHAN M.Z.,"ISLAM AND INTERNATIONAL RELATIONS." FUT WOR+45 LAW CULTURE SOCIETY NAT/G SECT DELIB/GP FORCES EDU/PROP ATTIT PERSON SUPEGO ALL/VALS ...POLICY PSY CONCPT MYTH HIST/WRIT GEN/LAWS. PAGE 61 E1211
S64
ISLAM
INT/ORG
DIPLOM

HARTUNG F.E.,CRIME, LAW, AND SOCIETY. LAW PUB/INST CRIME PERS/REL AGE/Y BIO/SOC PERSON ROLE SUPEGO ...LING GP/COMP GEN/LAWS 20. PAGE 50 E1004
B65
PERCEPT
CRIMLGY
DRIVE
CONTROL

ISORNI J.,LES CAS DE CONSCIENCE DE L'AVOCAT. FRANCE LAW ACT/RES CT/SYS PARTIC ROLE MORAL 20. PAGE 57 E1138
B65
SUPEGO
JURID
CRIME

AARON T.J.,THE CONTROL OF POLICE DISCRETION: THE DANISH EXPERIENCE. DENMARK LAW CREATE ADMIN INGP/REL SUPEGO PWR 20 OMBUDSMAN. PAGE 2 E0042
B66
CONTROL
FORCES
REPRESENT
PROB/SOLV

BAHRO H.,DAS KINDSCHAFTSRECHT IN DER UNION DER SOZIALISTITSCHEN SOWJETREPUBLIKEN. USSR SECT EDU/PROP CONTROL PWR...SOC/WK 20. PAGE 7 E0133
B66
JURID
AGE/C
PERS/REL
SUPEGO

NANTWI E.K.,THE ENFORCEMENT OF INTERNATIONAL JUDICIAL DECISIONS AND ARBITAL AWARDS IN PUBLIC INTERNATIONAL LAW. WOR+45 WOR-45 JUDGE PROB/SOLV DIPLOM CT/SYS SUPEGO MORAL PWR RESPECT...METH/CNCPT 18/20 CASEBOOK. PAGE 76 E1520
B66
INT/LAW
ADJUD
SOVEREIGN
INT/ORG

OLSON W.C.,THE THEORY AND PRACTICE OF INTERNATIONAL RELATIONS (2ND ED.). WOR+45 LEAD SUPEGO...INT/LAW PHIL/SCI. PAGE 79 E1575
B66
DIPLOM
NAT/G
INT/ORG
POLICY

POLLACK R.S.,THE INDIVIDUAL'S RIGHTS AND INTERNATIONAL ORGANIZATION. LAW INT/ORG DELIB/GP SUPEGO...JURID SOC/INTEG 20 TREATY UN. PAGE 81 E1623
B66
INT/LAW
ORD/FREE
DIPLOM
PERSON

SMITH E.A.,CHURCH-STATE RELATIONS IN ECUMENICAL PERSPECTIVE. WOR+45 LAW MUNIC INGP/REL DISCRIM ATTIT SUPEGO ORD/FREE CATHISM...PHIL/SCI IDEA/COMP 20 PROTESTANT ECUMENIC CHURCH/STA CHRISTIAN. PAGE 92 E1843
B66
NAT/G
SECT
GP/REL
ADJUD

FRIENDLY A.,CRIME AND PUBLICITY. TV CT/SYS SUPEGO 20. PAGE 41 E0811
B67
PRESS
CRIME
ROLE
LAW

LAY S.H.,"EXCLUSIVE GOVERNMENTAL LIABILITY FOR SPACE ACCIDENTS." USA+45 LAW FINAN SERV/IND TEC/DEV ADJUD. PAGE 64 E1272
S67
NAT/G
SUPEGO
SPACE
PROB/SOLV

SEIDLER G.L.,"MARXIST LEGAL THOUGHT IN POLAND." POLAND SOCIETY R+D LOC/G NAT/G ACT/RES ADJUD CT/SYS SUPEGO PWR...SOC TREND 20 MARX/KARL. PAGE 90 E1802
S67
MARXISM
LAW
CONCPT
EFFICIENCY

AUSTIN J.,LECTURES ON JURISPRUDENCE OR THE PHILOSOPHY OF POSITIVE LAW (VOL. II) (4TH ED., REV.). UK CONSTN STRUCT PROB/SOLV LEGIT CT/SYS
B73
LAW
ADJUD
JURID

SANCTION CRIME INGP/REL OWN SUPEGO ORD/FREE...T 19. METH/CNCPT
PAGE 6 E0120

L84
ELLMAKER E.G.,"REVELATION OF RIGHTS." JUDGE DISCRIM ORD/FREE
SUPEGO...JURID PHIL/SCI CONCPT 17/18. PAGE 35 E0685   ADMIN
                                                       MORAL
                                                       NAT/G

SUPERVISION....SEE EXEC, CONTROL, LEAD, TASK

SUPREME/CT....SUPREME COURT (ALL NATIONS)

B03
GRIFFIN A.P.C.,LIST OF BOOKS ON THE CONSTITUTION OF   BIBLIOG/A
THE UNITED STATES (PAMPHLET). USA-45 NAT/G EX/STRUC   CONSTN
JUDGE TOP/EX CT/SYS 18/20 CONGRESS PRESIDENT   LAW
SUPREME/CT. PAGE 46 E0920   JURID

B04
FREUND E.,THE POLICE POWER; PUBLIC POLICY AND   CONSTN
CONSTITUTIONAL RIGHTS. USA-45 SOCIETY LOC/G NAT/G   LAW
FORCES LEGIS ADJUD CT/SYS OWN PWR...JURID 18/19   ORD/FREE
SUPREME/CT. PAGE 40 E0795   CONTROL

S05
PHILLIPS J.B.,"MODIFICATIONS OF THE JURY SYSTEM."   JURID
PARTIC EFFICIENCY ATTIT PERCEPT...TREND 19   DELIB/GP
SUPREME/CT JURY. PAGE 80 E1612   PERS/REL
                                                       POLICY

B08
WILSON W.,CONSTITUTIONAL GOVERNMENT IN THE UNITED   NAT/G
STATES. USA-45 LAW POL/PAR PROVS BAL/PWR ADJUD   GOV/REL
EXEC FEDERAL PWR 18/20 SUPREME/CT   CONSTN
HOUSE/REP SENATE. PAGE 106 E2130   PARL/PROC

B12
BEARD C.A.,THE SUPREME COURT AND THE CONSTITUTION.   CONSTN
LAW NAT/G PROVS LEGIS GOV/REL ATTIT POPULISM   CT/SYS
SUPREME/CT. PAGE 9 E0164   ADJUD
                                                       CONTROL

S18
POWELL T.R.,"THE LOGIC AND RHETORIC OF   CONSTN
CONSTITUTIONAL LAW" (BMR)" USA+45 USA-45 DELIB/GP   LAW
PROB/SOLV ADJUD CT/SYS...DECISION 20 SUPREME/CT   JURID
CON/INTERP. PAGE 82 E1642   LOG

N18
BREWER D.J.,THE MOVEMENT OF COERCION (PAMPHLET).   GP/REL
CONSTN INDUS ADJUD COERCE OWN WEALTH...OLD/LIB   LABOR
JURID 19 SUPREME/CT. PAGE 15 E0296   LG/CO
                                                       LAW

N19
BRENNAN W.J. JR.,THE BILL OF RIGHTS AND THE STATES   CONSTN
(PAMPHLET). USA+45 USA-45 LEGIS ADJUD   PROVS
CT/SYS FEDERAL PWR SOVEREIGN 18/20 SUPREME/CT   GOV/REL
BILL/RIGHT. PAGE 15 E0293   ORD/FREE

B27
RYAN J.A.,DECLINING LIVERTY AND OTHER ESSAYS.   ORD/FREE
USA-45 SECT DELIB/GP ATTIT PWR SOCISM 20   LEGIS
SUPREME/CT. PAGE 87 E1740   JURID
                                                       NAT/G

B28
FRANKFURTER F.,THE BUSINESS OF THE SUPREME COURT; A   CT/SYS
STUDY IN THE FEDERAL JUDICIAL SYSTEM. USA-45 CONSTN   ADJUD
EX/STRUC PROB/SOLV GP/REL ATTIT PWR...POLICY JURID   LAW
18/20 SUPREME/CT CONGRESS. PAGE 40 E0789   FEDERAL

B28
NORTON T.J.,LOSING LIBERTY JUDICIALLY. PROVS LEGIS   NAT/G
BAL/PWR CT/SYS...JURID 18/20 SUPREME/CT CIV/RIGHTS   ORD/FREE
CONGRESS. PAGE 78 E1557   CONSTN
                                                       JUDGE

L34
LLEWELLYN K.N.,"THE CONSTITUTION AS AN INSTITUTION"   CONSTN
(BMR)" USA-45 PROB/SOLV LOBBY REPRESENT...DECISION   LAW
JURID 18/20 SUPREME/CT. PAGE 66 E1313   CONCPT
                                                       CT/SYS

S36
CORWIN E.S.,"THE CONSTITUTION AS INSTRUMENT AND AS   CONSTN
SYMBOL." USA-45 ECO/DEV INDUS CAP/ISM SANCTION   LAW
RIGID/FLEX ORD/FREE LAISSEZ OBJECTIVE 20 CONGRESS   ADJUD
SUPREME/CT. PAGE 26 E0512   PWR

B37
HAMILTON W.H.,THE POWER TO GOVERN. ECO/DEV FINAN   LING
INDUS ECO/TAC INT/TRADE TARIFFS TAX CONTROL CT/SYS   CONSTN

WAR COST PWR 18/20 SUPREME/CT. PAGE 50 E0991   NAT/G
                                                       POLICY

L37
LERNER M.,"CONSTITUTION AND COURT AS SYMBOLS"   CONSTN
(BMR)" USA+45 USA-45 DOMIN PWR SOVEREIGN...PSY MYTH   CT/SYS
18/20 SUPREME/CT. PAGE 64 E1288   ATTIT
                                                       EDU/PROP

B38
FRANKFURTER F.,MR. JUSTICE HOLMES AND THE SUPREME   CREATE
COURT. USA-45 CONSTN SOCIETY FEDERAL OWN ATTIT   CT/SYS
ORD/FREE PWR...POLICY JURID 20 SUPREME/CT HOLMES/OW   DECISION
BILL/RIGHT. PAGE 40 E0790   LAW

B38
HELLMAN F.S.,THE SUPREME COURT ISSUE: SELECTED LIST   BIBLIOG/A
OF REFERENCES. USA-45 NAT/G CHIEF EX/STRUC JUDGE   CONSTN
ATTIT...JURID 20 PRESIDENT ROOSEVLT/F SUPREME/CT.   CT/SYS
PAGE 51 E1026   LAW

B41
CHAFEE Z. JR.,FREE SPEECH IN THE UNITED STATES.   ORD/FREE
USA-45 ADJUD CONTROL CRIME WAR...BIBLIOG 20   CONSTN
FREE/SPEE AMEND/I SUPREME/CT. PAGE 21 E0413   ATTIT
                                                       JURID

B42
CARR R.K.,THE SUPREME COURT AND JUDICIAL REVIEW.   CT/SYS
NAT/G CHIEF LEGIS OP/RES LEAD GOV/REL GP/REL ATTIT   CONSTN
...POLICY DECISION 18/20 SUPREME/CT PRESIDENT   JURID
CONGRESS. PAGE 20 E0394   PWR

B47
KONVITZ M.R.,THE CONSTITUTION AND CIVIL RIGHTS.   CONSTN
USA-45 NAT/G ADJUD GP/REL RACE/REL POPULISM   LAW
...MAJORIT 19/20 SUPREME/CT CIV/RIGHTS. PAGE 61   GOV/REL
E1227   ORD/FREE

S48
BRADEN G.D.,"THE SEARCH FOR OBJECTIVITY IN   CONSTN
CONSTITUTIONAL LAW" (BMR)" USA+45 USA-45 LAW NAT/G   CT/SYS
CONTROL ORD/FREE PWR OBJECTIVE...JURID 20   IDEA/COMP
SUPREME/CT. PAGE 15 E0283   POLICY

B50
HURST J.W.,THE GROWTH OF AMERICAN LAW; THE LAW   LAW
MAKERS. USA-45 LOC/G NAT/G DELIB/GP JUDGE ADJUD   LEGIS
ADMIN ATTIT PWR...POLICY JURID BIBLIOG 18/20   CONSTN
CONGRESS SUPREME/CT ABA PRESIDENT. PAGE 56 E1115   CT/SYS

B51
DAVIS K.C.,ADMINISTRATIVE LAW. USA+45 USA-45 NAT/G   ADMIN
PROB/SOLV BAL/PWR CONTROL ORD/FREE...POLICY 20   JURID
SUPREME/CT. PAGE 29 E0574   EX/STRUC
                                                       ADJUD

B51
PUSEY M.J.,CHARLES EVANS HUGHES (2 VOLS.). LAW   BIOG
CONSTN NAT/G POL/PAR DIPLOM LEGIT WAR CHOOSE   TOP/EX
PERS/REL DRIVE HEREDITY 19/20 DEPT/STATE LEAGUE/NAT   ADJUD
SUPREME/CT HUGHES/CE WWI. PAGE 83 E1663   PERSON

B51
WOOD V.,DUE PROCESS OF LAW 1932-1949: SUPREME   CONSTN
COURT'S USE OF A CONSTITUTIONAL TOOL. USA+45 USA-45   TREND
SOCIETY TAX CRIME...POLICY CHARTS 20 SUPREME/CT.   ADJUD
PAGE 107 E2143   GOV/REL

S51
LEEK J.H.,"TREASON AND THE CONSTITUTION" (BMR)"   CONSTN
USA+45 USA-45 EDU/PROP COLONIAL CT/SYS REV WAR   JURID
ATTIT...TREND 18/20 SUPREME/CT CON/INTERP SMITH/ACT   CRIME
COMMON/LAW. PAGE 64 E1278   NAT/G

L52
ROSTOW E.V.,"THE DEMOCRATIC CHARACTER OF JUDICIAL   CONSTN
REVIEW" (BMR)" USA+45 LAW NAT/G LEGIS TASK...JURID   PROB/SOLV
20 SUPREME/CT. PAGE 86 E1725   ADJUD
                                                       CT/SYS

B53
PADOVER S.K.,THE LIVING US CONSTITUTION. USA+45   CONSTN
USA-45 POL/PAR ADJUD...DECISION AUD/VIS IDEA/COMP   LEGIS
18/20 SUPREME/CT. PAGE 79 E1590   DELIB/GP
                                                       BIOG

B54
HAMSON C.J.,EXECUTIVE DISCRETION AND JUDICIAL   ELITES
CONTROL; AN ASPECT OF THE FRENCH CONSEIL D'ETAT.   ADJUD
EUR+WWI FRANCE MOD/EUR UK NAT/G EX/STRUC PARTIC   NAT/COMP
CONSERVE...JURID BIBLIOG/A 18/20 SUPREME/CT.
PAGE 50 E0992

B54
JAMES L.F.,THE SUPREME COURT IN AMERICAN LIFE.   ADJUD

USA+45 USA-45 CONSTN CRIME GP/REL INGP/REL RACE/REL CT/SYS
CONSEN FEDERAL PERSON ORD/FREE 18/20 SUPREME/CT JURID
DEPRESSION CIV/RIGHTS CHURCH/STA FREE/SPEE. PAGE 58 DECISION
E1147

B54
O'NEILL J.M.,CATHOLICS IN CONTROVERSY. USA+45 NAT/G CATHISM
PROVS SCHOOL SECT EDU/PROP LEGIT CT/SYS SANCTION CONSTN
GP/REL 20 SUPREME/CT CHURCH/STA. PAGE 78 E1569 POLICY
LAW

B55
BEANEY W.M.,THE RIGHT TO COUNSEL IN AMERICAN ADJUD
COURTS. UK USA+45 USA-45 LAW NAT/G PROVS COLONIAL CONSTN
PERCEPT 18/20 SUPREME/CT AMEND/VI AMEND/XIV CT/SYS
ENGLSH/LAW. PAGE 8 E0163

B55
BEISEL A.R.,CONTROL OVER ILLEGAL ENFORCEMENT OF THE ORD/FREE
CRIMINAL LAW: ROLE OF THE SUPREME COURT. CONSTN LAW
ROUTINE MORAL PWR...SOC 20 SUPREME/CT. PAGE 9 E0180 CRIME

B55
CUSHMAN R.E.,LEADING CONSTITUTIONAL DECISIONS. CONSTN
USA+45 USA-45 NAT/G EX/STRUC LEGIS JUDGE TAX PROB/SOLV
FEDERAL...DECISION 20 SUPREME/CT CASEBOOK. PAGE 28 JURID
E0559 CT/SYS

B55
MAYERS L.,THE AMERICAN LEGAL SYSTEM. USA+45 USA-45 JURID
NAT/G EX/STRUC ADMIN CONTROL FEDERAL 20 SUPREME/CT. CT/SYS
PAGE 70 E1394 LEGIS
ADJUD

S55
BETH L.P.,"THE CASE FOR JUDICIAL PROTECTION OF CT/SYS
CIVIL LIBERTIES" (BMR)" USA+45 CONSTN ELITES LEGIS JUDGE
CONTROL...POLICY DECISION JURID 20 SUPREME/CT ADJUD
CIVIL/LIB. PAGE 11 E0220 ORD/FREE

S55
CAHN E.,"A DANGEROUS MYTH IN THE SCHOOL SEGREGATION JURID
CASES" (BMR)" USA+45 CONSTN PROVS ADJUD DISCRIM SCHOOL
...POLICY MYTH SOC/INTEG 20 SUPREME/CT AMEND/XIV. RACE/REL
PAGE 18 E0360

B56
DOUGLAS W.O.,WE THE JUDGES. INDIA USA+45 USA-45 LAW ADJUD
NAT/G SECT LEGIS PRESS CRIME FEDERAL ORD/FREE CT/SYS
...POLICY GOV/COMP 19/20 WARRN/EARL MARSHALL/J CONSTN
SUPREME/CT. PAGE 32 E0640 GOV/REL

B57
BERNS W.,FREEDOM, VIRTUE, AND THE FIRST AMENDMENT. ADJUD
USA-45 LAW CONSTN PROB/SOLV NEW/LIB...JURID 20 CT/SYS
SUPREME/CT AMEND/I. PAGE 11 E0212 ORD/FREE

B57
LONG H.A.,USURPERS - FOES OF FREE MAN. LAW NAT/G CT/SYS
CHIEF LEGIS DOMIN ADJUD REPRESENT GOV/REL ORD/FREE CENTRAL
LAISSEZ POPULISM...POLICY 18/20 SUPREME/CT FEDERAL
ROOSEVLT/F CONGRESS CON/INTERP. PAGE 66 E1325 CONSTN

B57
ROWAN C.T.,GO SOUTH TO SORROW. USA+45 STRUCT NAT/G RACE/REL
EDU/PROP LEAD COERCE ISOLAT DRIVE SUPEGO RESPECT DISCRIM
...PREDICT 20 NEGRO SUPREME/CT SOUTH/US CIV/RIGHTS. ANOMIE
PAGE 86 E1728 LAW

B57
SCHUBERT G.A.,THE PRESIDENCY IN THE COURTS. CONSTN PWR
FORCES DIPLOM TARIFFS ADJUD CONTROL WAR...DECISION CT/SYS
MGT CHARTS 18/20 PRESIDENT CONGRESS SUPREME/CT. LEGIT
PAGE 89 E1778 CHIEF

B57
SINCLAIR T.C.,THE POLITICS OF JUDICIAL REVIEW JURID
1937-1957. USA+45 USA-45 NAT/G 20 SUPREME/CT ATTIT
CIVIL/LIB. PAGE 91 E1830 ORD/FREE
RACE/REL

B57
US SENATE COMM ON JUDICIARY,LIMITATION OF APPELLATE CT/SYS
JURISDICTION OF THE SUPREME COURT. USA+45 LAW NAT/G ADJUD
DELIB/GP PLAN ADMIN CONTROL PWR...DECISION 20 POLICY
CONGRESS SUPREME/CT. PAGE 102 E2041 GOV/REL

S57
FRANKFURTER F.,"THE SUPREME COURT IN THE MIRROR OF EDU/PROP
JUSTICES" (BMR)" USA+45 USA-45 INTELL INSPECT ADJUD
EFFICIENCY ROLE KNOWL MORAL 18/20 SUPREME/CT. CT/SYS
PAGE 40 E0792 PERSON

B58
BLOCH J.,STATES' RIGHTS: THE LAW OF THE LAND. PROVS
USA+45 USA-45 LAW CONSTN LEGIS CONTROL CT/SYS NAT/G

FEDERAL ORD/FREE...PREDICT 17/20 CONGRESS BAL/PWR
SUPREME/CT. PAGE 13 E0246 CENTRAL

B58
DAVIS K.C.,ADMINISTRATIVE LAW TREATISE (VOLS. I AND ADMIN
IV). NAT/G JUDGE PROB/SOLV ADJUD GP/REL 20 JURID
SUPREME/CT. PAGE 29 E0575 CT/SYS
EX/STRUC

B58
DAVIS K.C.,ADMINISTRATIVE LAW: CASES, TEXT, ADJUD
PROBLEMS. LAW LOC/G NAT/G TOP/EX PAY CONTROL JURID
GOV/REL INGP/REL FEDERAL 20 SUPREME/CT. PAGE 29 CT/SYS
E0576 ADMIN

B58
FELLMAN D.,THE DEFENDANT'S RIGHTS. USA+45 NAT/G CONSTN
CONSULT CT/SYS SUPEGO ORD/FREE...BIBLIOG SUPREME/CT LAW
CIVIL/SERV. PAGE 37 E0730 CRIME
ADJUD

B58
HAND L.,THE BILL OF RIGHTS. USA+45 USA-45 CHIEF CONSTN
LEGIS BAL/PWR ROLE PWR 18/20 SUPREME/CT CONGRESS JURID
AMEND/V PRESIDENT AMEND/XIV. PAGE 50 E0994 ORD/FREE
CT/SYS

B58
MASON A.T.,THE SUPREME COURT FROM TAFT TO WARREN. CT/SYS
EX/STRUC LEGIS ROLE 20 SUPREME/CT TAFT/WH HUGHES/CE JURID
STONE/HF. PAGE 69 E1376 ADJUD

B58
O'BRIEN F.W.,JUSTICE REED AND THE FIRST AMENDMENT, ADJUD
THE RELIGION CLAUSES. USA+45 USA-45 NAT/G PROVS SECT
CONTROL FEDERAL...POLICY JURID TIME/SEQ 20 CT/SYS
SUPREME/CT CHRUCH/STA AMEND/I REED/STAN. PAGE 78
E1563

B58
PALMER E.E.,CIVIL LIBERTIES. USA+45 ADJUD CT/SYS ORD/FREE
PARTIC OWN LAISSEZ POPULISM...JURID CONCPT ANTHOL CONSTN
20 SUPREME/CT CIVIL/LIB. PAGE 79 E1592 RACE/REL
LAW

B58
WESTIN A.F.,THE ANATOMY OF A CONSTITUTIONAL LAW CT/SYS
CASE. USA+45 LAW LEGIS ADMIN EXEC...DECISION MGT INDUS
SOC RECORD 20 SUPREME/CT. PAGE 105 E2113 ADJUD
CONSTN

B58
WOOD J.E.,CHURCH AND STATE IN SCRIPTURE HISTORY AND GP/REL
CONSTITUTIONAL LAW. LAW CONSTN SOCIETY PROVS SECT
VOL/ASSN BAL/PWR COLONIAL CT/SYS ATTIT...BIBLIOG 20 NAT/G
SUPREME/CT CHURCH/STA BIBLE. PAGE 107 E2142 ADJUD

S58
DAHL R.A.,"DECISION-MAKING IN A DEMOCRACY: THE CT/SYS
SUPREME COURT AS A NATIONAL POLICY-MAKER" (BMR)" CONSTN
USA+45 USA-45 POL/PAR ADJUD GOV/REL PWR...POLICY DECISION
JURID 19/20 SUPREME/CT. PAGE 28 E0561 NAT/G

B59
ABRAHAM H.J.,COURTS AND JUDGES: AN INTRODUCTION TO CT/SYS
THE JUDICIAL PROCESS. USA+45 CONSTN ELITES NAT/G PERSON
ORD/FREE PWR 19/20 SUPREME/CT. PAGE 2 E0045 JURID
ADJUD

B59
CHRISTMAN H.M.,THE PUBLIC PAPERS OF CHIEF JUSTICE LAW
EARL WARREN. CONSTN POL/PAR EDU/PROP SANCTION CT/SYS
HEALTH...TREND 20 SUPREME/CT WARRN/EARL. PAGE 22 PERSON
E0436 ADJUD

B59
DAVIS K.C.,ADMINISTRATIVE LAW TEXT. USA+45 NAT/G ADJUD
DELIB/GP EX/STRUC CONTROL ORD/FREE...T 20 ADMIN
SUPREME/CT. PAGE 29 E0577 JURID
CT/SYS

B59
GINZBURG B.,REDEDICATION TO FREEDOM. DELIB/GP LEGIS JURID
ATTIT MARXISM 20 SUPREME/CT CON/INTERP HUAC AMEND/I ORD/FREE
FBI. PAGE 44 E0871 CONSTN
NAT/G

B59
HAYS B.,A SOUTHERN MODERATE SPEAKS. LAW PROVS SECT
SCHOOL KNOWL...JURID SOC SELF/OBS BIOG 20 NEGRO DISCRIM
SUPREME/CT. PAGE 51 E1015 CT/SYS
RACE/REL

B59
LOEWENSTEIN K.,VERFASSUNGSRECHT UND CONSTN
VERFASSUNGSPRAXIS DER VEREINIGTEN STAATEN. USA+45 POL/PAR

USA-45 COLONIAL CT/SYS GP/REL RACE/REL ORD/FREE   EX/STRUC
...JURID 18/20 SUPREME/CT CONGRESS PRESIDENT   NAT/G
BILL/RIGHT CIVIL/LIB. PAGE 66 E1319

B59

SCHUBERT G.A.,QUANTITATIVE ANALYSIS OF JUDICIAL   JUDGE
BEHAVIOR. ADJUD LEAD CHOOSE INGP/REL MAJORITY ATTIT   CT/SYS
...DECISION JURID CHARTS GAME SIMUL SUPREME/CT.   PERSON
PAGE 89 E1780   QUANT

B59

TOMPKINS D.C.,SUPREME COURT OF THE UNITED STATES: A   BIBLIOG/A
BIBLIOGRAPHY. LAW JUDGE ADJUD GOV/REL DISCRIM   CT/SYS
...JURID 18/20 SUPREME/CT NEGRO. PAGE 96 E1931   CONSTN
     NAT/G

B59

VOSE C.E.,CAUCASIANS ONLY: THE SUPREME COURT, THE   CT/SYS
NAACP, AND THE RESTRICTIVE COVENANT CASES. USA+45   RACE/REL
LAW CONSTN LOBBY...SOC 20 NAACP SUPREME/CT NEGRO.   DISCRIM
PAGE 104 E2086

S59

BEANEY W.B.,"CIVIL LIBERTIES AND STATUTORY   CT/SYS
CONSTRUCTION"(BMR)" USA+45 LEGIS BAL/PWR 20   ORD/FREE
SUPREME/CT. PAGE 8 E0162   ADJUD
     LAW

S59

MASON A.T.,"THE SUPREME COURT: TEMPLE AND FORUM"   CT/SYS
(BMR)" USA+45 USA-45 CONSTN DELIB/GP RACE/REL   JURID
MAJORITY ORD/FREE...DECISION SOC/INTEG 19/20   PWR
SUPREME/CT WARRN/EARL CIV/RIGHTS. PAGE 69 E1377   ATTIT

S59

MENDELSON W.,"JUDICIAL REVIEW AND PARTY POLITICS"   CT/SYS
(BMR)" UK USA+45 USA-45 NAT/G LEGIS PROB/SOLV   POL/PAR
EDU/PROP ADJUD EFFICIENCY...POLICY NAT/COMP 19/20   BAL/PWR
AUSTRAL SUPREME/CT. PAGE 72 E1436   JURID

S59

MURPHY W.F.,"LOWER COURT CHECKS ON SUPREME COURT   CT/SYS
POWER" (BMR)" USA+45 NAT/G PROVS SCHOOL GOV/REL   BAL/PWR
RACE/REL DISCRIM ATTIT...DECISION JURID 20   CONTROL
SUPREME/CT NEGRO. PAGE 75 E1508   ADJUD

B60

)B JUNZ A.J.,PRESENT TRENDS IN AMERICAN NATIONAL   POL/PAR
GOVERNMENT. LEGIS DIPLOM ADMIN CT/SYS ORD/FREE   CHOOSE
...CONCPT ANTHOL 20 CONGRESS PRESIDENT SUPREME/CT.   CONSTN
PAGE 2 E0040   NAT/G

B60

BLANSHARD P.,GOD AND MAN IN WASHINGTON. USA+45   NAT/G
CHIEF LEGIS LEGIT CT/SYS PRIVIL ATTIT ORD/FREE   SECT
...POLICY CONCPT 20 SUPREME/CT CONGRESS PRESIDENT   GP/REL
CHURCH/STA. PAGE 12 E0242   POL/PAR

B60

BYRD E.M. JR.,TREATIES AND EXECUTIVE AGREEMENTS IN   CHIEF
THE UNITED STATES: THEIR SEPARATE ROLES AND   INT/LAW
LIMITATIONS. USA+45 USA-45 EX/STRUC TARIFFS CT/SYS   DIPLOM
GOV/REL FEDERAL...IDEA/COMP BIBLIOG SUPREME/CT
SENATE CONGRESS. PAGE 18 E0353

B60

DAVIS K.C.,ADMINISTRATIVE LAW AND GOVERNMENT.   ADMIN
USA+45 EX/STRUC PROB/SOLV ADJUD GP/REL PWR...POLICY   JURID
20 SUPREME/CT. PAGE 29 E0578   CT/SYS
     NAT/G

B60

FELLMAN D.,THE SUPREME COURT AND EDUCATION. ACADEM   CT/SYS
NAT/G PROVS DELIB/GP ADJUD ORD/FREE...POLICY JURID   SECT
WORSHIP 20 SUPREME/CT NEGRO CHURCH/STA. PAGE 37   RACE/REL
E0731   SCHOOL

B60

GELLHORN W.,AMERICAN RIGHTS: THE CONSTITUTION IN   ORD/FREE
ACTION. USA+45 USA-45 LEGIS ADJUD COERCE RACE/REL   JURID
DISCRIM MARXISM 20 SUPREME/CT. PAGE 43 E0846   CT/SYS
     CONSTN

B60

MENDELSON W.,CAPITALISM, DEMOCRACY, AND THE SUPREME   JUDGE
COURT. USA+45 USA-45 CONSTN DIPLOM GOV/REL ATTIT   CT/SYS
ORD/FREE LAISSEZ...POLICY CHARTS PERS/COMP 18/20   JURID
SUPREME/CT MARSHALL/J HOLMES/OW TANEY/RB FIELD/JJ.   NAT/G
PAGE 72 E1437

B60

NAT'L MUNICIPAL LEAGUE.COMPENDIUM ON LEGISLATIVE   APPORT
APPORTIONMENT. USA+45 LOC/G NAT/G POL/PAR PROVS   REPRESENT
CT/SYS CHOOSE 20 SUPREME/CT CONGRESS. PAGE 76 E1523   LEGIS
     STAT

B60

PAUL A.M.,CONSERVATIVE CRISIS AND THE RULE OF LAW.   CONSTN
USA-45 LABOR WORKER ATTIT ORD/FREE CONSERVE LAISSEZ   ADJUD
...DECISION JURID 19 SUPREME/CT. PAGE 80 E1603   STRUCT
     PROF/ORG

B60

SCHMIDHAUSER J.R.,THE SUPREME COURT: ITS POLITICS,   JUDGE
PERSONALITIES, AND PROCEDURES. LAW DELIB/GP   JURID
EX/STRUC TOP/EX ADJUD CT/SYS CHOOSE RATIONAL PWR   DECISION
SUPREME/CT. PAGE 88 E1760

B60

SCHUBERT G.A.,CONSTITUTIONAL POLITICS: THE   CONSTN
POLITICAL BEHAVIOR OF SUPREME COURT JUSTICES AND   CT/SYS
THE CONSTITUTIONAL POLICIES THEY MAKE. LAW ELITES   JURID
CHIEF DELIB/GP EX/STRUC LEGIS DISCRIM ORD/FREE PWR   DECISION
...POLICY MAJORIT CHARTS SUPREME/CT CONGRESS.
PAGE 89 E1781

B60

WEBSTER J.A.,A GENERAL STUDY OF THE DEPARTMENT OF   ORD/FREE
DEFENSE INTERNAL SECURITY PROGRAM. USA+45 WORKER   PLAN
TEC/DEV ADJUD CONTROL CT/SYS EXEC GOV/REL COST   ADMIN
...POLICY DECISION MGT 20 DEPT/DEFEN SUPREME/CT.   NAT/G
PAGE 105 E2105

S60

BLACK H.,"THE BILL OF RIGHTS" (BMR)" USA+45 USA-45   CONSTN
LAW LEGIS CT/SYS FEDERAL PWR 18/20 CONGRESS   ORD/FREE
SUPREME/CT BILL/RIGHT CIV/RIGHTS. PAGE 12 E0237   NAT/G
     JURID

S60

ULMER S.S.,"THE ANALYSIS OF BEHAVIOR PATTERNS ON   ATTIT
THE UNITED STATES SUPREME COURT" USA+45 LAW ADJUD   ADJUD
PERS/REL RACE/REL PERSON...DECISION PSY SOC TREND   PROF/ORG
METH/COMP METH 20 SUPREME/CT CIVIL/LIB. PAGE 97   INGP/REL
E1951

B61

AUERBACH C.A.,THE LEGAL PROCESS. USA+45 DELIB/GP   JURID
JUDGE CONFER ADJUD CONTROL...DECISION 20   ADMIN
SUPREME/CT. PAGE 6 E0116   LEGIS
     CT/SYS

B61

CHILDS M.W.,THE EROSION OF INDIVIDUAL LIBERTIES.   ADJUD
NAT/G LEGIS ATTIT...JURID SOC CONCPT IDEA/COMP 20   CT/SYS
SUPREME/CT AMEND/I. PAGE 22 E0430   ORD/FREE
     CONSTN

B61

FREUND P.A.,THE SUPREME COURT OF THE UNITED STATES: CT/SYS
ITS BUSINESS, PURPOSES, AND PERFORMANCE. CONSTN   JURID
CRIME CONSEN ORD/FREE...DECISION 20 SUPREME/CT   ADJUD
CIVIL/LIB. PAGE 40 E0797   FEDERAL

B61

JACOBS C.E.,JUSTICE FRANKFURTER AND CIVIL   BIOG
LIBERTIES. USA+45 USA-45 LAW NAT/G PROB/SOLV PRESS   CONSTN
PERS/REL...JURID WORSHIP 20 SUPREME/CT FRANKFUR/F   ADJUD
CIVIL/LIB. PAGE 57 E1144   ORD/FREE

B61

KURLAND P.B.,RELIGION AND THE LAW. USA+45 USA-45   SECT
CONSTN PROVS CHIEF ADJUD SANCTION PRIVIL CATHISM   NAT/G
...POLICY 17/20 SUPREME/CT PRESIDENT CHURCH/STA.   CT/SYS
PAGE 62 E1239   GP/REL

B61

PRITCHETT C.H.,CONGRESS VERSUS THE SUPREME COURT,   LEGIS
1957-1960. PROB/SOLV DOMIN EXEC GP/REL DISCRIM PWR   JURID
CONGRESS SUPREME/CT SUPREME/CT. PAGE 82 E1652   LAW

B61

PRITCHETT C.H.,CONGRESS VERSUS THE SUPREME COURT,   LEGIS
1957-1960. PROB/SOLV DOMIN EXEC GP/REL DISCRIM PWR   JURID
CONGRESS SUPREME/CT SUPREME/CT. PAGE 82 E1652   LAW

B61

WESTIN A.F.,THE SUPREME COURT: VIEWS FROM INSIDE.   CT/SYS
USA+45 NAT/G PROF/ORG PROVS DELIB/GP INGP/REL   LAW
DISCRIM ATTIT...POLICY DECISION JURID ANTHOL 20   ADJUD
SUPREME/CT CONGRESS CIVIL/LIB. PAGE 106 E2114   GOV/REL

S61

SCHUBERT G.,"A PSYCHOMETRIC MODEL OF THE SUPREME   JUDGE
COURT." DELIB/GP ADJUD CHOOSE ATTIT...DECISION   CT/SYS
JURID PSY QUANT STAT HYPO/EXP GEN/METH SUPREME/CT.   PERSON
PAGE 88 E1771   SIMUL

B62

BICKEL A.,THE LEAST DANGEROUS BRANCH. USA+45 USA-45   LAW
CONSTN SCHOOL LEGIS ADJUD RACE/REL DISCRIM ORD/FREE   NAT/G
...JURID 18/20 SUPREME/CT CONGRESS MARSHALL/J   CT/SYS

HOLMES/OW FRANKFUR/F. PAGE 12 E0226

B62

BORKIN J.,THE CORRUPT JUDGE. USA+45 CT/SYS ATTIT ADJUD
SUPEGO MORAL RESPECT...BIBLIOG + SUPREME/CT TRIBUTE
MANTON/M DAVIS/W JOHNSN/ALB. PAGE 14 E0271 CRIME

B62

HIRSCHFIELD R.S.,THE CONSTITUTION AND THE COURT. ADJUD
SCHOOL WAR RACE/REL EQUILIB ORD/FREE...POLICY PWR
MAJORIT DECISION JURID 18/20 PRESIDENT COLD/WAR CONSTN
CIVIL/LIB SUPREME/CT CONGRESS. PAGE 53 E1051 LAW

B62

KAUPER P.G.,CIVIL LIBERTIES AND THE CONSTITUTION. LAW
USA+45 SECT EDU/PROP WRITING ADJUD SEX ORD/FREE 20 CONSTN
SUPREME/CT CIVIL/LIB CHURCH/STA. PAGE 60 E1188 CT/SYS
DECISION

B62

MASON A.T.,THE SUPREME COURT: PALADIUM OF FREEDOM. CONSTN
USA-45 NAT/G POL/PAR CHIEF LEGIS ADJUD PARL/PROC CT/SYS
FEDERAL PWR...POLICY BIOG 18/20 SUPREME/CT JURID
ROOSEVLT/F JEFFERSN/T MARSHALL/J HUGHES/CE. PAGE 69
E1378

B62

MCGRATH J.J.,CHURCH AND STATE IN AMERICAN LAW. LAW
PROVS SCHOOL TAX GIVE CT/SYS GP/REL...POLICY ANTHOL SECT
18/20 SUPREME/CT CHURCH/STA CASEBOOK. PAGE 71 E1414 ADJUD
CONSTN
NAT/G

B62

MILLER P.,THE LEGAL MIND IN AMERICA. PROF/ORG JUDGE JURID
ADJUD CT/SYS 18/19 SUPREME/CT. PAGE 73 E1461 CONSTN
NAT/G
CONCPT

B62

MURPHY W.F.,CONGRESS AND THE COURT. USA+45 LAW LEGIS
LOBBY GP/REL RACE/REL ATTIT PWR...JURID INT BIBLIOG CT/SYS
CONGRESS SUPREME/CT WARRN/EARL. PAGE 75 E1509 GOV/REL
ADJUD

B62

NAT'L MUNICIPAL LEAGUE,COMPENDIUM ON LEGISLATIVE APPORT
APPORTIONMENT. USA+45 LOC/G NAT/G POL/PAR PROVS REPRESENT
CT/SYS CHOOSE 20 SUPREME/CT CONGRESS. PAGE 76 E1524 LEGIS
STAT

B62

RICE C.E.,FREEDOM OF ASSOCIATION. USA+45 USA-45 LAW
POL/PAR LOBBY GP/REL...JURID BIBLIOG 18/20 NAT/G
SUPREME/CT PRE/US/AM. PAGE 84 E1691 CONSTN

B62

ROSTOW E.V.,THE SOVEREIGN PREROGATIVE: THE SUPREME JURID
COURT AND THE QUEST FOR LAW. CONSTN CT/SYS FEDERAL PROF/ORG
MORAL SOVEREIGN 20 SUPREME/CT. PAGE 86 E1726 ATTIT
ORD/FREE

B62

SIGLIANO R E.,THE COURTS. USA+45 USA-45 LAW CONSTN ADJUD
NAT/G ROUTINE CHOOSE 18/20 SUPREME/CT. PAGE 91 PROB/SOLV
E1825 CT/SYS
JUDGE

B62

STERN R.L.,SUPREME COURT PRACTICE. USA+45 USA-45 CT/SYS
OP/RES...STYLE METH 20 SUPREME/CT. PAGE 93 E1872 ADJUD
JURID
ROUTINE

B62

TUSSMAN J.,THE SUPREME COURT ON CHURCH AND STATE. CT/SYS
USA+45 USA-45 SANCTION PRIVIL...POLICY JURID 19/20 SECT
SUPREME/CT CHURCH/STA. PAGE 97 E1945 ADJUD

L62

MANGIN G.,"L'ORGANIZATION JUDICIAIRE DES ETATS AFR
D'AFRIQUE ET DE MADAGASCAR." ISLAM WOR+45 STRATA LEGIS
STRUCT ECO/UNDEV NAT/G LEGIT EXEC...JURID TIME/SEQ COLONIAL
TOT/POP 20 SUPREME/CT. PAGE 68 E1357 MADAGASCAR

S62

SCHUBERT G.,"THE 1960 TERM OF THE SUPREME COURT: A DECISION
PSYCHOLOGICAL ANALYSIS." USA+45 LAW CT/SYS...STAT LEGIS
SUPREME/CT. PAGE 88 E1772 JUDGE
EX/STRUC

B63

BLACK C.L. JR.,THE OCCASIONS OF JUSTICE: ESSAYS JURID
MOSTLY ON LAW. USA+45 JUDGE RACE/REL DISCRIM ATTIT CONSTN
MORAL ORD/FREE 20 SUPREME/CT BLACK. PAGE 12 E0236 CT/SYS
LAW

B63

BOWIE R.R.,GOVERNMENT REGULATION OF BUSINESS: CASES LAW
FROM THE NATIONAL REPORTER SYSTEM. USA+45 USA-45 CONTROL
NAT/G ECO/TAC ADJUD...ANTHOL 19/20 SUPREME/CT FTC INDUS
FAIR/LABOR MONOPOLY. PAGE 14 E0280 CT/SYS

B63

COUNCIL OF STATE GOVERNMENTS,INCREASED RIGHTS FOR CT/SYS
DEFENDANTS IN STATE CRIMINAL PROSECUTIONS. USA+45 ADJUD
GOV/REL INGP/REL FEDERAL ORD/FREE...JURID 20 PROVS
SUPREME/CT. PAGE 26 E0522 CRIME

B63

DILLIARD I.,ONE MAN'S STAND FOR FREEDOM: MR. CONSTN
JUSTICE BLACK AND THE BILL OF RIGHTS. USA+45 JURID
POL/PAR SECT DELIB/GP FORCES ADJUD CONTROL WAR JUDGE
DISCRIM MORAL...BIBLIOG 20 NEGRO SUPREME/CT ORD/FREE
BILL/RIGHT BLACK/HL. PAGE 32 E0628

B63

DUNHAM A.,MR. JUSTICE. ADJUD PWR...JURID ANTHOL BIOG
18/20 SUPREME/CT. PAGE 33 E0659 PERSON
LAW
CT/SYS

B63

FRAENKEL O.K.,THE SUPREME COURT AND CIVIL ORD/FREE
LIBERTIES: HOW THE COURT HAS PROTECTED THE BILL OF CONSTN
RIGHTS. NAT/G CT/SYS CHOOSE PERS/REL RACE/REL ADJUD
DISCRIM PERSON...DECISION 20 SUPREME/CT CIVIL/LIB JURID
BILL/RIGHT. PAGE 39 E0782

B63

HYNEMAN C.S.,THE SUPREME COURT ON TRIAL. ADJUD LEAD CT/SYS
GP/REL FEDERAL...IDEA/COMP 20 SUPREME/CT. PAGE 56 JURID
E1120 POLICY
NAT/G

B63

LEAGUE WOMEN VOTERS NEW YORK,APPORTIONMENT WORKSHOP APPORT
KIT. USA+45 VOL/ASSN DELIB/GP LEGIS ATTIT ORD/FREE REPRESENT
...METH/COMP 20 SUPREME/CT NEW/YORK. PAGE 64 E1275 PROVS
JURID

B63

LOWRY C.W.,TO PRAY OR NOT TO PRAY. ADJUD SANCTION SECT
GP/REL ORD/FREE PWR CATHISM WORSHIP 20 SUPREME/CT CT/SYS
CHRISTIAN CHRUCH/STA. PAGE 67 E1330 CONSTN
PRIVIL

B63

NEWMAN E.S.,THE FREEDOM READER. USA+45 LEGIS TOP/EX RACE/REL
PLAN ADJUD CONTROL CT/SYS DISCRIM...DECISION ANTHOL LAW
20 SUPREME/CT CIV/RIGHTS. PAGE 77 E1541 POLICY
ORD/FREE

B63

PRITCHETT C.H.,THE ROOSEVELT COURT. USA-45 LAW DECISION
INGP/REL...CHARTS 20 SUPREME/CT. PAGE 82 E1653 PROB/SOLV
CT/SYS
JURID

B63

PRITCHETT C.H.,THE THIRD BRANCH OF GOVERNMENT. JURID
USA+45 USA-45 CONSTN SOCIETY INDUS SECT LEGIS JUDGE NAT/G
PROB/SOLV GOV/REL 20 SUPREME/CT CHURCH/STA. PAGE 82 ADJUD
E1654 CT/SYS

B63

SCHMIDHAUSER J.R.,CONSTITUTIONAL LAW IN THE LAW
POLITICAL PROCESS. SOCIETY LEGIS ADJUD CT/SYS CONSTN
FEDERAL...SOC TREND IDEA/COMP ANTHOL T SUPREME/CT JURID
SENATE CONGRESS HOUSE/REP. PAGE 88 E1761

B63

SCOTT A.M.,THE SUPREME COURT V. THE CONSTITUTION. PWR
USA+45 CONTROL ATTIT ROLE...POLICY CONCPT 20 CT/SYS
SUPREME/CT. PAGE 90 E1796 NAT/G
CONSTN

B63

TUSSMAN J.,THE SUPREME COURT ON RACIAL CT/SYS
DISCRIMINATION. USA+45 USA-45 NAT/G PROB/SOLV ADJUD DISCRIM
RACE/REL ORD/FREE...JURID 20 SUPREME/CT CIV/RIGHTS. ATTIT
PAGE 97 E1946 LAW

B63

US COMMISSION ON CIVIL RIGHTS,FREEDOM TO THE FREE. RACE/REL
USA+45 USA-45 LAW VOL/ASSN CT/SYS ATTIT PWR...JURID DISCRIM
BIBLIOG 17/20 SUPREME/CT NEGRO CIV/RIGHTS. PAGE 99 NAT/G
E1986 POLICY

B64

ANASTAPLO G.,NOTES ON THE FIRST AMENDMENT TO THE ORD/FREE
CONSTITUTION OF THE UNITED STATES (PART TWO). CONSTN
USA+45 USA-45 NAT/G JUDGE DEBATE SUPEGO PWR CT/SYS

SOVEREIGN 18/20 SUPREME/CT CONGRESS AMEND/I. PAGE 5 ATTIT
E0088

ATTIT...MAJORIT JURID WORSHIP 20 SUPREME/CT NEGRO
CIV/RIGHTS CHURCH/STA. PAGE 77 E1543   CONTROL NAT/G

B64

BUREAU OF NAT'L AFFAIRS,THE CIVIL RIGHTS ACT OF
1964. USA+45 LOC/G NAT/G DELIB/GP CONFER DEBATE
DISCRIM...JURID 20 CONGRESS SUPREME/CT CIV/RIGHTS.
PAGE 17 E0333   LEGIS RACE/REL LAW CONSTN

B64

RICE C.E.,THE SUPREME COURT AND PUBLIC PRAYER.
CONSTN SCHOOL SECT PROB/SOLV TAX ATTIT WORSHIP
18/20 SUPREME/CT CHURCH/STA. PAGE 84 E1692   JURID POLICY NAT/G

B64

COUNCIL OF STATE GOVERNMENTS,LEGISLATIVE
APPORTIONMENT: A SUMMARY OF STATE ACTION. USA+45
LEGIS REPRESENT...POLICY SUPREME/CT. PAGE 26 E0523   LOC/G PROVS APPORT CT/SYS

B64

TODD A.,JUSTICE ON TRIAL: THE CASE OF LOUIS D.
BRANDEIS. TOP/EX DISCRIM...JURID 20 WILSON/W
CONGRESS SUPREME/CT BRANDEIS/L SENATE. PAGE 96
E1929   PERSON RACE/REL PERS/REL NAT/G

B64

DIETZE G.,ESSAYS ON THE AMERICAN CONSTITUTION: A
COMMEMORATIVE VOLUME IN HONOR OF ALPHEUS T. MASON.
USA+45 USA-45 LAW INTELL...POLICY BIOG IDEA/COMP
ANTHOL SUPREME/CT. PAGE 32 E0626   FEDERAL CONSTN DIPLOM CT/SYS

B64

US SENATE COMM ON JUDICIARY,CIVIL RIGHTS - THE
PRESIDENT'S PROGRAM. USA+45 USA-45 LAW PROB/SOLV PRESS
ADJUD GOV/REL RACE/REL ORD/FREE PWR...JURID 20
SUPREME/CT SENATE CIV/RIGHTS PRESIDENT. PAGE 102
E2053   INT LEGIS DISCRIM PARL/PROC

B64

HAMILTON H.D.,LEGISLATIVE APPORTIONMENT; KEY TO
POWER. USA+45 LAW CONSTN PROVS LOBBY CHOOSE ATTIT
SUPREME/CT. PAGE 50 E0988   APPORT CT/SYS LEAD REPRESENT

B64

WAY H.F. JR.,LIBERTY IN THE BALANCE - CURRENT
ISSUES IN CIVIL LIBERTIES. USA+45 USA-45 DELIB/GP
RACE/REL DISCRIM TOTALISM MARXISM SOCISM...CONCPT
20 CONGRESS SUPREME/CT CIVIL/LIB. PAGE 105 E2104   ORD/FREE EDU/PROP NAT/G JURID

B64

HANSON R.,FAIR REPRESENTATION COMES TO MARYLAND
(PAMPHLET). BAL/PWR CT/SYS CHOOSE GOV/REL 20
MARYLAND SUPREME/CT. PAGE 50 E0997   APPORT REPRESENT PROVS LEGIS

B65

ANTIEU C.J.,RELIGION UNDER THE STATE CONSTITUTIONS.
USA+45 LAW SCHOOL TAX SANCTION PRIVIL ORD/FREE
...JURID 20 SUPREME/CT CHURCH/STA. PAGE 5 E0099   SECT CONSTN PROVS GP/REL

B64

HURST W.H.,JUSTICE HOLMES ON LEGAL HISTORY. USA-45
LAW SOCIETY NAT/G WRITING...POLICY PHIL/SCI SOC
CONCPT 20 HOLMES/OW SUPREME/CT ENGLSH/LAW. PAGE 56
E1117   ADJUD JURID BIOG

B65

BAR ASSOCIATION OF ST LOUIS,CONSTITUTIONAL FREEDOM
AND THE LAW. USA+45 USA-45 LAW LABOR LEGIS EDU/PROP
...JURID CONCPT SUPREME/CT CIVIL/LIB CIV/RIGHTS.
PAGE 8 E0146   ORD/FREE CONSTN RACE/REL NAT/G

B64

IRION F.C.,APPORTIONMENT OF THE NEW MEXICO
LEGISLATURE. NAT/G LEGIS PRESS CT/SYS ATTIT
...POLICY TIME/SEQ 19/20 SUPREME/CT. PAGE 57 E1137   APPORT REPRESENT GOV/REL PROVS

B65

CONGRESSIONAL QUARTERLY SERV,REVOLUTION IN CIVIL
RIGHTS. USA+45 USA-45 LEGIS ADJUD CT/SYS CHOOSE
DISCRIM...DECISION CONGRESS SUPREME/CT. PAGE 25
E0488   LAW CONSTN RACE/REL LOBBY

B64

KAUPER P.G.,RELIGION AND THE CONSTITUTION. USA+45
USA-45 LAW NAT/G SCHOOL SECT GP/REL ATTIT...BIBLIOG
WORSHIP 18/20 SUPREME/CT FREE/SPEE CHURCH/STA.
PAGE 60 E1189   CONSTN JURID ORD/FREE

B65

FELLMAN D.,RELIGION IN AMERICAN PUBLIC LAW. USA+45
USA-45 NAT/G PROVS ADJUD SANCTION GP/REL PRIVIL
ORD/FREE...JURID TIME/SEQ 18/20 SUPREME/CT
CHURCH/STA. PAGE 37 E0733   SECT CONSTN LAW POLICY

B64

KISER S.L.,AMERICANISM IN ACTION. USA+45 LAW PROVS
CAP/ISM DIPLOM RECEIVE CONTROL CT/SYS WAR FEDERAL
ATTIT WEALTH 20 SUPREME/CT. PAGE 61 E1221   OLD/LIB FOR/AID MARXISM CONSTN

B65

HOWE M.D.W.,THE GARDEN AND THE WILDERNESS. USA+45
LAW GIVE EDU/PROP LEGIT NAT/LISM ORD/FREE...POLICY
JURID SUPREME/CT CHURCH/STA. PAGE 55 E1103   CONSTN SECT NAT/G GP/REL

B64

KOREA (REPUBLIC) SUPREME COURT,KOREAN LEGAL SYSTEM.
KOREA/S WOR+45 LAW LEAD ROUTINE GOV/REL ORD/FREE 20
SUPREME/CT. PAGE 61 E1229   JURID CT/SYS CONSTN CRIME

B65

IANNIELLO L.,MILESTONES ALONG THE MARCH: TWELVE
HISTORIC CIVIL RIGHTS DOCUMENTS--FROM WORLD WAR II
TO SELMA. USA+45 LAW FORCES TOP/EX PARTIC SUFF...T
20 NEGRO CIV/RIGHTS TRUMAN/HS SUPREME/CT
KENNEDY/JF. PAGE 56 E1121   RACE/REL DISCRIM CONSTN NAT/G

B64

LEDERMAN W.R.,THE COURTS AND THE CANDIAN
CONSTITUTION. CANADA PARL/PROC...POLICY JURID
GOV/COMP ANTHOL 19/20 SUPREME/CT PARLIAMENT.
PAGE 64 E1276   CONSTN CT/SYS LEGIS LAW

B65

KRISLOV S.,THE SUPREME COURT IN THE POLITICAL
PROCESS. USA+45 LAW SOCIETY STRUCT WORKER ADMIN
ROLE...JURID SOC 20 SUPREME/CT. PAGE 62 E1231   ADJUD DECISION CT/SYS CONSTN

B64

MAKI J.M.,COURT AND CONSTITUTION IN JAPAN; SELECTED
SUPREME COURT DECISIONS, 1948-60. FAM LABOR GOV/REL
HABITAT ORD/FREE...DECISION JURID 20 CHINJAP
SUPREME/CT CIV/RIGHTS. PAGE 68 E1354   CT/SYS CONSTN PROB/SOLV LAW

B65

MCKAY R.B.,REAPPORTIONMENT: THE LAW AND POLITICS OF
EQUAL REPRESENTATION. FUT USA+45 PROVS BAL/PWR
ADJUD CHOOSE REPRESENT GOV/REL FEDERAL...JURID
BIBLIOG 20 SUPREME/CT CONGRESS. PAGE 71 E1420   APPORT MAJORIT LEGIS PWR

B64

MASON A.T.,AMERICAN CONSTITUTIONAL LAW:
INTRODUCTORY ESSAYS AND SELECTED CASES (3RD ED.).
LAW LEGIS TAX ADJUD GOV/REL FEDERAL ORD/FREE PWR
...TIME/SEQ BIBLIOG T 19/20 SUPREME/CT. PAGE 69
E1379   CONSTN CT/SYS JURID

B65

MURPHY W.F.,WIRETAPPING ON TRIAL: A CASE STUDY IN
THE JUDICIAL PROCESS. CONSTN ELITES CT/SYS CRIME
MORAL ORD/FREE...DECISION SUPREME/CT. PAGE 75 E1511   JURID LAW POLICY

B64

MITCHELL B.,A BIOGRAPHY OF THE CONSTITUTION OF THE
UNITED STATES. USA+45 USA-45 PROVS CHIEF LEGIS
DEBATE ADJUD SUFF FEDERAL...SOC 18/20 SUPREME/CT
CONGRESS SENATE HOUSE/REP PRESIDENT. PAGE 73 E1472   CONSTN LAW JURID

B65

PARKER D.,CIVIL LIBERTIES CASE STUDIES AND THE LAW.
SECT ADJUD...CONCPT WORSHIP 20 SUPREME/CT
CIV/RIGHTS FREE/SPEE. PAGE 80 E1598   ORD/FREE JURID CONSTN JUDGE

B64

MURPHY W.F.,ELEMENTS OF JUDICIAL STRATEGY. CONSTN
JUDGE PERS/REL PERSON 19/20 SUPREME/CT. PAGE 75
E1510   CT/SYS ADJUD JURID

B65

SCHROEDER O.,DEFACTO SEGREGATION AND CIVIL RIGHTS.
LAW PROVS SCHOOL WORKER ATTIT HABITAT HEALTH WEALTH
...JURID CHARTS 19/20 NEGRO SUPREME/CT KKK. PAGE 88
E1766   ANTHOL DISCRIM RACE/REL ORD/FREE

B64

NEWMAN E.S.,CIVIL LIBERTY AND CIVIL RIGHTS. USA+45
USA-45 CONSTN PROVS FORCES LEGIS CT/SYS RACE/REL   ORD/FREE LAW

B65

SCHUBERT G.,THE POLITICAL ROLE OF THE COURTS IN
JUDICIAL POLICY MAKING. USA+45 CONSTN JUDGE   CT/SYS POLICY

FEEDBACK CHOOSE RACE/REL ORD/FREE...TRADIT PSY   DECISION
BIBLIOG/A 20 KENNEDY/JF SUPREME/CT. PAGE 89 E1776

                                                        B65
SNOW J.H.,REAPPORTIONMENT. LAW CONSTN NAT/G GOV/REL   APPORT
ORD/FREE...JURID 20 SUPREME/CT CONNECTICT. PAGE 92   ADJUD
E1848   LEGIS
                                                      PROVS

                                                        B65
SWISHER C.B.,THE SUPREME COURT IN MODERN ROLE. COM   DELIB/GP
COM/IND NAT/G FORCES LEGIS LOBBY PARTIC RACE/REL 20 ATTIT
SUPREME/CT. PAGE 95 E1901   CT/SYS
                                                      ADJUD

                                                        B65
TRESOLINI R.J.,AMERICAN CONSTITUTIONAL LAW. USA+45   CONSTN
USA-45 NAT/G ADJUD ORD/FREE PWR...POLICY BIOG 20   CT/SYS
SUPREME/CT CASEBOOK. PAGE 97 E1939   JURID
                                                      LAW

                                                        S65
ULMER S.S.,"TOWARD A THEORY OF SUBGROUP FORMATION   CT/SYS
IN THE UNITED STATES SUPREME COURT." USA+45 ROUTINE ADJUD
CHOOSE PWR...JURID STAT CON/ANAL SIMUL SUPREME/CT.   ELITES
PAGE 97 E1952   INGP/REL

                                                        B66
AMERICAN JOURNAL COMP LAW,THE AMERICAN JOURNAL OF   IDEA/COMP
COMPARATIVE LAW READER. EUR+WWI USA+45 USA-45 LAW   JURID
CONSTN LOC/G MUNIC NAT/G DIPLOM...ANTHOL 20   INT/LAW
SUPREME/CT EURCT/JUST. PAGE 4 E0081   CT/SYS

                                                        B66
BAKER G.E.,THE REAPPORTIONMENT REVOLUTION;   LEGIS
REPRESENTATION, POLITICAL POWER, AND THE SUPREME   APPORT
COURT. USA+45 MUNIC NAT/G POL/PAR PROVS PROB/SOLV   REPRESENT
CHOOSE ORD/FREE POPULISM...CONCPT CHARTS 20   ADJUD
SUPREME/CT. PAGE 7 E0140

                                                        B66
BEDI A.S.,FREEDOM OF EXPRESSION AND SECURITY;   METH
COMPARATIVE STUDY OF FUNCTIONS OF SUPREME COURTS IN CT/SYS
UNITED STATES AND INDIA. INDIA USA+45 LAW CONSTN   ADJUD
PROB/SOLV...DECISION JURID BIBLIOG 20 SUPREME/CT   ORD/FREE
FREE/SPEE AMEND/I. PAGE 9 E0175

                                                        B66
BEISER E.N.,THE TREATMENT OF LEGISLATIVE   CT/SYS
APPORTIONMENT BY THE STATE AND FEDERAL COURTS   APPORT
(DISSERTATION). USA+45 CONSTN NAT/G PROVS LEGIS   ADJUD
CHOOSE REPRESENT ATTIT...POLICY BIBLIOG 20 CONGRESS PWR
SUPREME/CT. PAGE 9 E0181

                                                        B66
CARMEN I.H.,MOVIES, CENSORSHIP, AND THE LAW. LOC/G   EDU/PROP
NAT/G ATTIT ORD/FREE...DECISION INT IDEA/COMP   LAW
BIBLIOG 20 SUPREME/CT FILM. PAGE 19 E0383   ART/METH
                                                     CONSTN

                                                        B66
CONG QUARTERLY SERVICE,REPRESENTATION AND   APPORT
APPORTIONMENT. USA+45 USA-45 POL/PAR CT/SYS SUFF   LEGIS
...POLICY 20 CONGRESS SUPREME/CT. PAGE 25 E0486   REPRESENT
                                                     CONSTN

                                                        B66
DOUGLAS W.O.,THE BIBLE AND THE SCHOOLS. USA+45   SECT
CULTURE ADJUD INGP/REL AGE/C AGE/Y ATTIT KNOWL   NAT/G
WORSHIP 20 SUPREME/CT CHURCH/STA BIBLE CHRISTIAN.   SCHOOL
PAGE 32 E0644   GP/REL

                                                        B66
GOLDWIN R.A.,APPORTIONMENT AND REPRESENTATION.   APPORT
MUNIC CT/SYS GP/REL ORD/FREE...POLICY ANTHOL 20   REPRESENT
SUPREME/CT. PAGE 44 E0880   LEGIS
                                                     CONSTN

                                                        B66
HAMILTON H.D.,REAPPORTIONING LEGISLATURES. USA+45   APPORT
CONSTN POL/PAR PROVS LEGIS COMPUTER ADJUD CHOOSE   REPRESENT
ATTIT...ANTHOL 20 SUPREME/CT CONGRESS. PAGE 50   PHIL/SCI
E0989   PWR

                                                        B66
HOLMES O.W.,JUSTICE HOLMES, EX CATHEDRA. USA+45   BIOG
USA-45 LAW INTELL ADMIN ATTIT...BIBLIOG 20   PERSON
SUPREME/CT HOLMES/OW. PAGE 55 E1088   CT/SYS
                                                     ADJUD

                                                        B66
KURLAND P.B.,THE SUPREME COURT REVIEW. USA+45   JURID
USA-45 LAW LABOR SUFF...ANTHOL 20 SUPREME/CT.   PROB/SOLV
PAGE 62 E1240   ADJUD
                                                     NAT/G

                                                        B66
MAGRATH C.P.,YAZOO; LAW AND POLITICS IN THE NEW   CT/SYS
REPUBLIC: THE CASE OF FLETCHER V. PECK. USA-45 LAW   DECISION
...BIBLIOG 19 SUPREME/CT YAZOO. PAGE 67 E1348   CONSTN
                                                     LOBBY

                                                        B66
MEDER A.E. JR.,LEGISLATIVE APPORTIONMENT. USA+45   APPORT
BAL/PWR REPRESENT ORD/FREE PWR...JURID 20   LEGIS
SUPREME/CT. PAGE 72 E1433   MATH
                                                     POLICY

                                                        B66
MENDELSON W.,JUSTICES BLACK AND FRANKFURTER: JURID
CONFLICT IN THE COURT (2ND ED.). NAT/G PROVS   ADJUD
PROB/SOLV BAL/PWR CONTROL FEDERAL ISOLAT ANOMIE   IDEA/COMP
ORD/FREE...DECISION 20 SUPREME/CT BLACK/HL   ROLE
FRANKFUR/F. PAGE 72 E1439

                                                        B66
SHAPIRO M.,FREEDOM OF SPEECH: THE SUPREME COURT AND CT/SYS
JUDICIAL REVIEW. USA+45 LEGIS...CHARTS 20   ORD/FREE
SUPREME/CT FREE/SPEE. PAGE 90 E1812   CONSTN
                                                     JURID

                                                        B66
SOBEL N.R.,THE NEW CONFESSION STANDARDS, MIRANDA V. JURID
ARIZONA. USA+45 USA-45 LAW PROF/ORG EDU/PROP 20   CT/SYS
SUPREME/CT. PAGE 92 E1849   ORD/FREE
                                                     ADJUD

                                                        B66
STUMPF S.E.,MORALITY AND THE LAW. USA+45 LAW   JURID
CULTURE PROB/SOLV DOMIN ADJUD CONTROL ADJUST   MORAL
ALL/IDEOS MARXISM...INT/LAW 20 SUPREME/CT. PAGE 94   CT/SYS
E1890

                                                        B66
TIEDT S.W.,THE ROLE OF THE FEDERAL GOVERNMENT IN   NAT/G
EDUCATION. FUT USA+45 USA-45 CONSTN SECT BUDGET   EDU/PROP
CT/SYS GOV/REL 18/20 SUPREME/CT. PAGE 96 E1924   GIVE
                                                     SCHOOL

                                                        S66
POLSBY N.W.,"BOOKS IN THE FIELD: POLITICAL   BIBLIOG/A
SCIENCE." LAW CONSTN LOC/G NAT/G LEGIS ADJUD PWR 20 ATTIT
SUPREME/CT. PAGE 81 E1627   ADMIN
                                                     JURID

                                                        B67
BAKER L.,BACK TO BACK: THE DUEL BETWEEN FDR AND THE CHIEF
SUPREME COURT. ELITES LEGIS CREATE DOMIN INGP/REL   CT/SYS
PERSON PWR NEW/LIB 20 ROOSEVLT/F SUPREME/CT SENATE. PARL/PROC
PAGE 7 E0142   GOV/REL

                                                        B67
BOLES D.E.,THE TWO SWORDS. USA+45 USA-45 LAW CONSTN SCHOOL
SOCIETY FINAN PRESS CT/SYS...HEAL JURID BIBLIOG   EDU/PROP
WORSHIP 20 SUPREME/CT CHURCH/STA. PAGE 13 E0263   ADJUD

                                                        B67
FESLER J.W.,THE FIFTY STATES AND THEIR LOCAL   PROVS
GOVERNMENTS. FUT USA+45 POL/PAR LEGIS PROB/SOLV   LOC/G
ADMIN CT/SYS CHOOSE GOV/REL FEDERAL...POLICY CHARTS
20 SUPREME/CT. PAGE 37 E0743

                                                        B67
FINCHER F.,THE GOVERNMENT OF THE UNITED STATES.   NAT/G
USA+45 USA-45 POL/PAR CHIEF CT/SYS LOBBY GP/REL   EX/STRUC
INGP/REL...CONCPT CHARTS BIBLIOG T 18/20 PRESIDENT   LEGIS
CONGRESS SUPREME/CT. PAGE 38 E0749   OP/RES

                                                        B67
GRAHAM H.D.,CRISIS IN PRINT: DESEGREGATION AND THE   PRESS
PRESS IN TENNESSEE. LAW SOCIETY MUNIC POL/PAR   PROVS
EDU/PROP LEAD REPRESENT DISCRIM ATTIT...IDEA/COMP   POLICY
BIBLIOG/A SOC/INTEG 20 TENNESSEE SUPREME/CT   RACE/REL
SOUTH/US. PAGE 45 E0896

                                                        B67
KING W.L.,MELVILLE WESTON FULLER: CHIEF JUSTICE OF   BIOG
THE UNITED STATES, 1888-1910. USA-45 CONSTN FINAN   CT/SYS
LABOR TAX GOV/REL PERS/REL ATTIT PERSON PWR...JURID LAW
BIBLIOG 19/20 SUPREME/CT FULLER/MW HOLMES/OW.   ADJUD
PAGE 61 E1216

                                                        B67
LEVY L.W.,JUDICIAL REVIEW AND THE SUPREME COURT.   ADJUD
USA+45 USA-45 NEUTRAL ATTIT ORD/FREE...POLICY   CONSTN
DECISION BIBLIOG 18/20 BILL/RIGHT SUPREME/CT.   LAW
PAGE 65 E1292   CT/SYS

                                                        L67
HOWARD A.E.D.,"MR. JUSTICE BLACK: THE NEGRO PROTEST ADJUD
MOVEMENT AND THE RULE OF LAW." USA+45 CONSTN CT/SYS JUDGE
CHOOSE GP/REL...DECISION JURID NEGRO SUPREME/CT.   LAW

PAGE 55 E1100   REPRESENT

S67
CREYKE G. JR.."THE PAYMENT GAP IN FEDERAL   CONSTRUC
CONSTRUCTION CONTRACTS." USA+45 LAW FINAN ECO/TAC   PAY
CONTROL CT/SYS SUPREME/CT. PAGE 28 E0547   COST
                                                     NAT/G

S67
GREY D.L.."INTERVIEWING AT THE COURT." USA+45   JUDGE
ELITES COM/IND ACT/RES PRESS CT/SYS PERSON...SOC   ATTIT
INT 20 SUPREME/CT. PAGE 46 E0916   PERS/COMP
                                                     GP/COMP

S67
KETCHAM O.W.."GUIDELINES FROM GAULT: REVOLUTIONARY   ADJUD
REQUIREMENTS AND REAPPRAISAL." LAW CONSTN CREATE   AGE/Y
LEGIT ROUTINE SANCTION CRIME DISCRIM PRIVIL ROLE   CT/SYS
...JURID NEW/IDEA 20 SUPREME/CT. PAGE 60 E1208

S67
KIM R.C.C.."THE SUPREME COURT: ORALLE WITHOUT   CT/SYS
TRUTH." USA+45 EDU/PROP RACE/REL ADJUST ALL/VALS   PROB/SOLV
ORD/FREE...DECISION WORSHIP SUPREME/CT. PAGE 61   ADJUD
E1214   REPRESENT

SURPLUS.....SEE DEMAND,PLAN

SURRENCY E.C. E1894

SURVEY ANALYSIS....SEE SAMP/SIZ

SUTHERLAND A.E. E1895

SUTTHOFF J. E0401

SUTTON F.X. E1896

SVARLIEN O. E1897

SWATANTRA....SWATANTRA - COALITION RIGHT-WING PARTY IN INDIA

SWAYZE H. E1898

SWEDEN....SEE ALSO APPROPRIATE TIME/SPACE/CULTURE INDEX

B53
ORFIELD L.B..THE GROWTH OF SCANDINAVIAN LAW.   JURID
DENMARK ICELAND NORWAY SWEDEN LAW DIPLOM...BIBLIOG   CT/SYS
9/20. PAGE 79 E1581   NAT/G

B54
FRIEDMAN W..THE PUBLIC CORPORATION: A COMPARATIVE   LAW
SYMPOSIUM (UNIVERSITY OF TORONTO SCHOOL OF LAW   SOCISM
COMPARATIVE LAW SERIES, VOL. I). SWEDEN USA+45   LG/CO
INDUS INT/ORG NAT/G REGION CENTRAL FEDERAL...POLICY OWN
JURID IDEA/COMP NAT/COMP ANTHOL 20 COMMONWLTH
MONOPOLY EUROPE. PAGE 40 E0801

B57
MEYER P..ADMINISTRATIVE ORGANIZATION: A COMPARATIVE ADMIN
STUDY OF THE ORGANIZATION OF PUBLIC ADMINISTRATION. METH/COMP
DENMARK FRANCE NORWAY SWEDEN UK USA+45 ELITES LOC/G NAT/G
CONSULT LEGIS ADJUD CONTROL LEAD PWR SKILL   CENTRAL
DECISION. PAGE 72 E1449

B59
SISSON C.H..THE SPIRIT OF BRITISH ADMINISTRATION   GOV/COMP
AND SOME EUROPEAN COMPARISONS. FRANCE GERMANY/W   ADMIN
SWEDEN UK LAW EX/STRUC INGP/REL EFFICIENCY ORD/FREE ELITES
...DECISION 20. PAGE 91 E1835   ATTIT

B64
HALLER W..DER SCHWEDISCHE JUSTITIEOMBUDSMAN.   JURID
DENMARK FINLAND NORWAY SWEDEN LEGIS ADJUD CONTROL   PARL/PROC
PERSON ORD/FREE...NAT/COMP 20 OMBUDSMAN. PAGE 50   ADMIN
E0986   CHIEF

B65
SMITH C..THE OMBUDSMAN: A BIBLIOGRAPHY (PAMPHLET).   BIBLIOG
DENMARK SWEDEN USA+45 LAW LEGIS JUDGE GOV/REL   ADMIN
GP/REL...JURID 20. PAGE 92 E1841   CT/SYS
                                                     ADJUD

SWEET E.C. E1899

SWEET AND MAXWELL E1900

SWISHER C.B. E1901

SWITZERLND....SWITZERLAND; SEE ALSO APPROPRIATE TIME/SPACE/
      CULTURE INDEX

N
DEUTSCHE BUCHEREI.JAHRESVERZEICHNIS DES DEUTSCHEN   BIBLIOG
SCHRIFTUMS. AUSTRIA EUR+WWI GERMANY SWITZERLND LAW   WRITING

LOC/G DIPLOM ADMIN...MGT SOC 19/20. PAGE 31 E0614   NAT/G

B09
LOBINGIER C.S..THE PEOPLE'S LAW OR POPULAR   CONSTN
PARTICIPATION IN LAW-MAKING. FRANCE SWITZERLND UK   LAW
LOC/G NAT/G PROVS LEGIS SUFF MAJORITY PWR POPULISM   PARTIC
...GOV/COMP BIBLIOG 19. PAGE 66 E1314

B32
MASTERS R.D..INTERNATIONAL LAW IN INTERNATIONAL   INT/ORG
COURTS. BELGIUM EUR+WWI FRANCE GERMANY MOD/EUR   LAW
SWITZERLND USA+45 SOCIETY STRATA STRUCT LEGIT EXEC   INT/LAW
ALL/VALS...JURID HIST/WRIT TIME/SEQ TREND GEN/LAWS
20. PAGE 69 E1383

B47
HILL M..IMMUNITIES AND PRIVILEGES OF INTERNATIONAL   INT/ORG
OFFICIALS. CANADA EUR+WWI NETHERLAND SWITZERLND LAW ADMIN
LEGIS DIPLOM LEGIT RESPECT...TIME/SEQ LEAGUE/NAT UN
VAL/FREE 20. PAGE 52 E1046

B47
INTERNATIONAL COURT OF JUSTICE,CHARTER OF THE   INT/LAW
UNITED NATIONS, STATUTE AND RULES OF COURT AND   INT/ORG
OTHER CONSTITUTIONAL DOCUMENTS. SWITZERLND LAW   CT/SYS
ADJUD INGP/REL...JURID 20 ICJ UN. PAGE 57 E1133   DIPLOM

B59
WAGNER W.J..THE FEDERAL STATES AND THEIR JUDICIARY. ADJUD
BRAZIL CANADA SWITZERLND USA+45 CONFER CT/SYS TASK   METH/COMP
EFFICIENCY FEDERAL PWR...JURID BIBLIOG 20 AUSTRAL   PROB/SOLV
MEXIC/AMER. PAGE 104 E2091   NAT/G

B61
BEDFORD S..THE FACES OF JUSTICE: A TRAVELLER'S   CT/SYS
REPORT. AUSTRIA FRANCE GERMANY/W SWITZERLND UK UNIV ORD/FREE
WOR+45 WOR-45 CULTURE PARTIC GOV/REL MORAL...JURID   PERSON
OBS GOV/COMP 20. PAGE 9 E0174   LAW

L63
BOLGAR V.."THE PUBLIC INTEREST: A JURISPRUDENTIAL   CONCPT
AND COMPARATIVE OVERVIEW OF SYMPOSIUM ON   ORD/FREE
FUNDAMENTAL CONCEPTS OF PUBLIC LAW" COM FRANCE   CONTROL
GERMANY SWITZERLND LAW ADJUD ADMIN AGREE LAISSEZ   NAT/COMP
...JURID GEN/LAWS 20 EUROPE/E. PAGE 14 E0264

B66
HOEVELER H.J..INTERNATIONALE BEKAMPFUNG DES   CRIMLGY
VERBRECHENS. AUSTRIA SWITZERLND WOR+45 INT/ORG   CRIME
CONTROL BIO/SOC...METH/COMP NAT/COMP 20 MAFIA   DIPLOM
SCOT/YARD FBI. PAGE 53 E1064   INT/LAW

SYATAUW J.J.G. E1902

SYKES G.M. E1903

SYNANON....SYNANON: COMMUNITY OF FORMER DRUG ADDICTS AND
      CRIMINALS

SYNTAX....SEE LOG

SYRIA....SEE ALSO UAR

SYS/QU....SYSTEMATIZING AND ANALYZING QUESTIONNAIRES

SYSTEMS....SEE ROUTINE, COMPUTER

SZASZ/T....THOMAS SZASZ

SZLADITS C. E1904,E1905

─────────────────────────── T ───────────────────────────

T....TEXTBOOK

N
TEXTBOOKS IN PRINT. WOR+45 WOR-45 LAW DIPLOM   BIBLIOG
ALL/VALS ALL/IDEOS...SOC T 19/20. PAGE 1 E0014   SCHOOL
                                                     KNOWL

B16
SALMOND J.W..JURISPRUDENCE. UK LOC/G NAT/G LEGIS   LAW
PROB/SOLV LICENSE LEGIT CRIME PERS/REL OWN ORD/FREE CT/SYS
...T 20. PAGE 87 E1742   JURID
                                                     ADJUD

B28
MACDONALD A.F..ELEMENTS OF POLITICAL SCIENCE   LAW
RESEARCH. USA-45 ACADEM JUDGE EDU/PROP DEBATE ADJUD FEDERAL
EXEC...BIBLIOG METH T 20 CONGRESS. PAGE 67 E1338   DECISION
                                                     CT/SYS

B35
MCLAUGHLIN A.C..A CONSTITUTIONAL HISTORY OF THE   CONSTN
UNITED STATES. USA+45 USA-45 LOC/G NAT/G PROVS   DECISION
LEGIS JUDGE ADJUD...T 18/20. PAGE 71 E1422

T

HADDOW A.,"POLITICAL SCIENCE IN AMERICAN COLLEGES AND UNIVERSITIES 1636-1900." CONSTN MORAL...POLICY INT/LAW CON/ANAL BIBLIOG T 17/20. PAGE 49 E0971
C39
USA-45
LAW
ACADEM
KNOWL

BEARD C.A.,AMERICAN GOVERNMENT AND POLITICS (REV. ED.). CONSTN MUNIC POL/PAR PROVS EX/STRUC LEGIS TOP/EX CT/SYS GOV/REL...BIBLIOG T 18/20. PAGE 9 E0165
B44
LEAD
USA-45
NAT/G
LOC/G

PATON G.W.,A TEXT-BOOK OF JURISPRUDENCE. CREATE INSPECT LEGIT CT/SYS ROUTINE CRIME INGP/REL PRIVIL ...CONCPT BIBLIOG 20. PAGE 80 E1601
B46
LAW
ADJUD
JURID
T

WALKER H.,"THE LEGISLATIVE PROCESS; LAWMAKING IN THE UNITED STATES." NAT/G POL/PAR PROVS EX/STRUC OP/RES PROB/SOLV CT/SYS LOBBY GOV/REL...CHARTS BIBLIOG T 18/20 CONGRESS. PAGE 105 E2094
C48
PARL/PROC
LEGIS
LAW
CONSTN

FRANK J.,COURTS ON TRIAL: MYTH AND REALITY IN AMERICAN JUSTICE. LAW CONSULT PROB/SOLV EDU/PROP ADJUD ROUTINE ROLE ORD/FREE...GEN/LAWS T 20. PAGE 40 E0788
B50
JURID
CT/SYS
MYTH
CONSTN

ANDERSON W.,STATE AND LOCAL GOVERNMENT IN THE UNITED STATES. USA+45 CONSTN POL/PAR EX/STRUC LEGIS BUDGET TAX ADJUD CT/SYS CHOOSE...CHARTS T 20. PAGE 5 E0094
B51
LOC/G
MUNIC
PROVS
GOV/REL

APPADORAI A.,THE SUBSTANCE OF POLITICS (6TH ED.). EX/STRUC LEGIS DIPLOM CT/SYS CHOOSE FASCISM MARXISM SOCISM...BIBLIOG T. PAGE 5 E0100
B52
PHIL/SCI
NAT/G

WALTER P.A.F.,RACE AND CULTURE RELATIONS. FAM HEALTH WEALTH...POLICY CRIMLGY GEOG BIBLIOG T 20. PAGE 105 E2097
B52
RACE/REL
DISCRIM
GP/REL
CONCPT

SINCO,PHILIPPINE POLITICAL LAW: PRINCIPLES AND CONCEPTS (10TH ED.). PHILIPPINE LOC/G EX/STRUC BAL/PWR ECO/TAC TAX ADJUD ADMIN CONTROL CT/SYS SUFF ORD/FREE...T 20. PAGE 91 E1831
B54
LAW
CONSTN
LEGIS

RECASENS SICHES S.,TRATADO GENERAL DE SOCIOLOGIA. CULTURE FAM NEIGH LEAD RACE/REL DISCRIM HABITAT ORD/FREE...JURID LING T SOC/INTEG 20. PAGE 84 E1677
B56
SOC
STRATA
KIN
GP/REL

CLINARD M.B.,SOCIOLOGY OF DEVIANT BEHAVIOR. FAM CONTROL MURDER DISCRIM PERSON...PSY SOC T SOC/INTEG 20. PAGE 23 E0455
B57
BIO/SOC
CRIME
SEX
ANOMIE

PALMER N.D.,INTERNATIONAL RELATIONS. WOR+45 INT/ORG NAT/G ECO/TAC EDU/PROP COLONIAL WAR PWR SOVEREIGN ...POLICY T 20 TREATY. PAGE 79 E1593
B57
DIPLOM
BAL/PWR
NAT/COMP

MACKENZIE W.J.M.,FREE ELECTIONS: AN ELEMENTARY TEXTBOOK. WOR+45 NAT/G POL/PAR LEGIS TOP/EX EDU/PROP LEGIT CT/SYS ATTIT PWR...OBS CHARTS STERTYP T CONGRESS PARLIAMENT 20. PAGE 67 E1342
B58
EX/STRUC
CHOOSE

DAVIS K.C.,ADMINISTRATIVE LAW TEXT. USA+45 NAT/G DELIB/GP EX/STRUC CONTROL ORD/FREE...T 20 SUPREME/CT. PAGE 29 E0577
B59
ADJUD
ADMIN
JURID
CT/SYS

DUMON F.,LA COMMUNAUTE FRANCO-AFRO-MALGACHE: SES ORIGINES, SES INSTITUTIONS, SON EVOLUTION. FRANCE MADAGASCAR POL/PAR DIPLOM ADMIN ATTIT...TREND T 20. PAGE 33 E0657
B60
JURID
INT/ORG
AFR
CONSTN

RIENOW R.,INTRODUCTION TO GOVERNMENT (2ND ED.). UK USA+45 USSR POL/PAR ADMIN REV CHOOSE SUFF FEDERAL PWR...JURID GOV/COMP T 20. PAGE 85 E1697
B60
CONSTN
PARL/PROC
REPRESENT
AUTHORIT

MERTON R.K.,CONTEMPORARY SOCIAL PROBLEMS: AN
B61
CRIME

INTRODUCTION TO THE SOCIOLOGY OF DEVIANT BEHAVIOR AND SOCIAL DISORGANIZATION. FAM MUNIC FORCES WORKER PROB/SOLV INGP/REL RACE/REL ISOLAT...CRIMLGY GEOG PSY T 20 NEGRO. PAGE 72 E1444
ANOMIE
STRANGE
SOC

ROCHE J.P.,COURTS AND RIGHTS: THE AMERICAN JUDICIARY IN ACTION (2ND ED.). UK USA+45 USA-45 STRUCT TEC/DEV SANCTION PERS/REL RACE/REL ORD/FREE ...METH/CNCPT GOV/COMP METH/COMP T 13/20. PAGE 85 E1710
B61
JURID
CT/SYS
NAT/G
PROVS

SCOTT A.M.,POLITICS, USA; CASES ON THE AMERICAN DEMOCRATIC PROCESS. USA+45 CHIEF FORCES DIPLOM LOBBY CHOOSE RACE/REL FEDERAL ATTIT...JURID ANTHOL T 20 PRESIDENT CONGRESS CIVIL/LIB. PAGE 90 E1795
B61
CT/SYS
CONSTN
NAT/G
PLAN

BISHOP W.W. JR.,INTERNATIONAL LAW: CASES AND MATERIALS. WOR+45 INT/ORG FORCES PROB/SOLV AGREE WAR...JURID IDEA/COMP T 20 TREATY. PAGE 12 E0233
B62
INT/LAW
DIPLOM
CONCPT
CT/SYS

DUROSELLE J.B.,HISTOIRE DIPLOMATIQUE DE 1919 A NOS JOURS (3RD ED.). FRANCE INT/ORG CHIEF FORCES CONFER ARMS/CONT WAR PEACE ORD/FREE...T TREATY 20 COLD/WAR. PAGE 34 E0667
B62
DIPLOM
WOR+45
WOR-45

JACOBINI H.B.,INTERNATIONAL LAW: A TEXT. DIPLOM ADJUD NEUTRAL WAR PEACE T. PAGE 57 E1143
B62
INT/LAW
CT/SYS
CONCPT

ROBERT J.,LA MONARCHIE MAROCAINE. MOROCCO LABOR MUNIC POL/PAR EX/STRUC ORD/FREE PWR...JURID TREND T 20. PAGE 85 E1702
B63
CHIEF
CONSERVE
ADMIN
CONSTN

SCHMIDHAUSER J.R.,CONSTITUTIONAL LAW IN THE POLITICAL PROCESS. SOCIETY LEGIS ADJUD CT/SYS FEDERAL...SOC TREND IDEA/COMP ANTHOL T SUPREME/CT SENATE CONGRESS HOUSE/REP. PAGE 88 E1761
B63
LAW
CONSTN
JURID

LOCKHART W.B.,CASES AND MATERIALS ON CONSTITUTIONAL RIGHTS AND LIBERTIES. USA+45 FORCES LEGIS DIPLOM PRESS CONTROL CRIME WAR PWR...AUD/VIS T WORSHIP 20 NEGRO. PAGE 66 E1317
B64
ORD/FREE
CONSTN
NAT/G

MASON A.T.,AMERICAN CONSTITUTIONAL LAW: INTRODUCTORY ESSAYS AND SELECTED CASES (3RD ED.). LAW LEGIS TAX ADJUD GOV/REL FEDERAL ORD/FREE PWR ...TIME/SEQ BIBLIOG T 19/20 SUPREME/CT. PAGE 69 E1379
B64
CONSTN
CT/SYS
JURID

STRONG C.F.,HISTORY OF MODERN POLITICAL CONSTITUTIONS. STRUCT INT/ORG NAT/G LEGIS TEC/DEV DIPLOM INT/TRADE CT/SYS EXEC...METH/COMP T 12/20 UN. PAGE 94 E1888
B64
CONSTN
CONCPT

FISCHER F.C.,THE GOVERNMENT OF MICHIGAN. USA+45 NAT/G PUB/INST EX/STRUC LEGIS BUDGET GIVE EDU/PROP CT/SYS CHOOSE GOV/REL...T MICHIGAN. PAGE 38 E0753
B65
PROVS
LOC/G
ADMIN
CONSTN

IANNIELLO L.,MILESTONES ALONG THE MARCH: TWELVE HISTORIC CIVIL RIGHTS DOCUMENTS--FROM WORLD WAR II TO SELMA. USA+45 LAW FORCES TOP/EX PARTIC SUFF...T 20 NEGRO CIV/RIGHTS TRUMAN/HS SUPREME/CT KENNEDY/JF. PAGE 56 E1121
B65
RACE/REL
DISCRIM
CONSTN
NAT/G

BROWNLIE I.,PRINCIPLES OF PUBLIC INTERNATIONAL LAW. WOR+45 WOR-45 LAW JUDGE REPAR ADJUD SOVEREIGN ...JURID T. PAGE 16 E0319
B66
INT/LAW
DIPLOM
INT/ORG

GREENE L.E.,GOVERNMENT IN TENNESSEE (2ND ED.). USA+45 DIST/IND INDUS POL/PAR EX/STRUC LEGIS PLAN BUDGET GIVE CT/SYS...MGT T 20 TENNESSEE. PAGE 46 E0909
B66
PROVS
LOC/G
CONSTN
ADMIN

BAILEY N.A.,LATIN AMERICA IN WORLD POLITICS. PWR CONSERVE MARXISM...INT/LAW TREND BIBLIOG/A T OAS COLD/WAR. PAGE 7 E0134
B67
L/A+17C
DIPLOM
INT/ORG
ATTIT

B67
BAKKE E.W.,UNIONS, MANAGEMENT AND THE PUBLIC*   LABOR
READINGS AND TEXT. WORKER LOBBY...POLICY JURID   INDUS
ANTHOL T. PAGE 7 E0143   ADJUD
                                                   GP/REL

B67
CAHIER P.,LE DROIT DIPLOMATIQUE CONTEMPORAIN.   INT/LAW
INT/ORG CHIEF ADMIN...T 20. PAGE 18 E0358   DIPLOM
                                                   JURID

B67
ESTEY M.,THE UNIONS: STRUCTURE, DEVELOPMENT, AND   LABOR
MANAGEMENT. FUT USA+45 ADJUD CONTROL INGP/REL DRIVE EX/STRUC
...DECISION T 20 AFL/CIO. PAGE 35 E0699   ADMIN
                                                   GOV/REL

B67
FINCHER F.,THE GOVERNMENT OF THE UNITED STATES.   NAT/G
USA+45 USA-45 POL/PAR CHIEF CT/SYS LOBBY GP/REL   EX/STRUC
INGP/REL...CONCPT CHARTS BIBLIOG T 18/20 PRESIDENT LEGIS
CONGRESS SUPREME/CT. PAGE 38 E0749   OP/RES

B67
GREENE L.S.,AMERICAN GOVERNMENT POLICIES AND   POLICY
FUNCTIONS. USA+45 LAW AGRI DIST/IND LABOR MUNIC   NAT/G
BUDGET DIPLOM EDU/PROP ORD/FREE...BIBLIOG T 20.   ADMIN
PAGE 46 E0910   DECISION

B67
HEWITT W.H.,ADMINISTRATION OF CRIMINAL JUSTICE IN CRIME
NEW YORK. LAW PROB/SOLV ADJUD ADMIN...CRIMLGY   ROLE
CHARTS T 20 NEW/YORK. PAGE 52 E1035   CT/SYS
                                                   FORCES

B67
ROBINSON R.D., INTERNATIONAL MANAGEMENT. USA+45   INT/TRADE
FINAN R+D PLAN PRODUC...DECISION T. PAGE 67 E1336   MGT
                                                   INT/LAW
                                                   MARKET

B73
AUSTIN J.,LECTURES ON JURISPRUDENCE OR THE   LAW
PHILOSOPHY OF POSITIVE LAW (VOL. II) (4TH ED.,   ADJUD
REV.). UK CONSTN STRUCT PROB/SOLV LEGIT CT/SYS   JURID
SANCTION CRIME INGP/REL OWN SUPEGO ORD/FREE...T 19. METH/CNCPT
PAGE 6 E0120

TABOOS....SEE CULTURE

TAFT/HART....TAFT-HARTLEY ACT

TAFT/RA....ROBERT A. TAFT

TAFT/WH....PRESIDENT WILLIAM HOWARD TAFT

N19
TAYLOR H.,WHY THE PENDING TREATY WITH COLOMBIA   INT/LAW
SHOULD BE RATIFIED (PAMPHLET). PANAMA USA-45   DIPLOM
DELIB/GP INT/TRADE REV ORD/FREE...JURID TREATY
18/19 ROOSEVLT/T TAFT/WH COLOMB. PAGE 95 E1912

B58
MASON A.T.,THE SUPREME COURT FROM TAFT TO WARREN. CT/SYS
EX/STRUC LEGIS ROLE 20 SUPREME/CT TAFT/WH HUGHES/CE JURID
STONE/HF. PAGE 69 E1376   ADJUD

TAHITI....TAHITI

TAIWAN....TAIWAN AND REPUBLIC OF CHINA

TALLON D. E1906

TAMMANY....TAMMANY HALL

TANENHAUS J. E1907

TANEY/RB....ROGER B. TANEY

B60
MENDELSON W.,CAPITALISM, DEMOCRACY, AND THE SUPREME JUDGE
COURT. USA+45 USA-45 CONSTN DIPLOM GOV/REL ATTIT   CT/SYS
ORD/FREE LAISSEZ...POLICY CHARTS PERS/COMP 18/20   JURID
SUPREME/CT MARSHALL/J HOLMES/OW TANEY/RB FIELD/JJ. NAT/G
PAGE 72 E1437

TANGANYIKA....SEE TANZANIA

TANZANIA....TANZANIA; SEE ALSO AFR

B64
FRANCK T.M.,EAST AFRICAN UNITY THROUGH LAW. MALAWI AFR
TANZANIA UGANDA UK ZAMBIA CONSTN INT/ORG NAT/G   FEDERAL
ADMIN ROUTINE TASK NAT/LISM ATTIT SOVEREIGN   REGION
...RECORD IDEA/COMP NAT/COMP. PAGE 40 E0785   INT/LAW

B65
HAEFELE E.T.,GOVERNMENT CONTROLS ON TRANSPORT. AFR ECO/UNDEV
RHODESIA TANZANIA DIPLOM ECO/TAC TARIFFS PRICE   DIST/IND
ADJUD CONTROL REGION EFFICIENCY...POLICY 20 CONGO. FINAN
PAGE 49 E0973   NAT/G

TAPER B. E1908

TARIFFS....SEE ALSO INT/TRADE,GATT

B07
GRIFFIN A.P.C.,LIST OF MORE RECENT WORKS ON FEDERAL BIBLIOG/A
CONTROL OF COMMERCE AND CORPORATIONS (PAMPHLET).   NAT/G
USA-45 LAW ECO/DEV FINAN LG/CO TARIFFS TAX LICENSE JURID
CENTRAL ORD/FREE WEALTH LAISSEZ 19/20. PAGE 47   ECO/TAC
E0931

B20
COX H.,ECONOMIC LIBERTY. UNIV LAW INT/TRADE RATION NAT/G
TARIFFS RACE/REL SOCISM POLICY. PAGE 27 E0535   ORD/FREE
                                                   ECO/TAC
                                                   PERSON

B34
US TARIFF COMMISSION,THE TARIFF: A BIBLIOGRAPHY: A BIBLIOG/A
SELECT LIST OF REFERENCES. USA-45 LAW DIPLOM TAX   TARIFFS
ADMIN...POLICY TREATY 20. PAGE 103 E2064   ECO/TAC

B35
BEMIS S.F.,GUIDE TO THE DIPLOMATIC HISTORY OF THE BIBLIOG/A
UNITED STATES, 17751921. NAT/G LEGIS TOP/EX   DIPLOM
PROB/SOLV CAP/ISM INT/TRADE TARIFFS ADJUD   USA-45
...CON/ANAL 18/20. PAGE 10 E0184

B37
HAMILTON W.H.,THE POWER TO GOVERN. ECO/DEV FINAN   LING
INDUS ECO/TAC INT/TRADE TARIFFS TAX CONTROL CT/SYS CONSTN
WAR COST PWR 18/20 SUPREME/CT. PAGE 50 E0991   NAT/G
                                                   POLICY

B38
CLARK J.P.,THE RISE OF A NEW FEDERALISM. LEGIS   FEDERAL
TARIFFS EFFICIENCY NAT/LISM UTIL...JURID SOC   PROVS
GEN/LAWS BIBLIOG 19/20. PAGE 23 E0451   NAT/G
                                                   GOV/REL

B40
CONOVER H.F.,FOREIGN RELATIONS OF THE UNITED   BIBLIOG/A
STATES: A LIST OF RECENT BOOKS (PAMPHLET). ASIA   USA-45
CANADA L/A+17C UK INT/ORG INT/TRADE TARIFFS NEUTRAL DIPLOM
WAR PEACE...INT/LAW CON/ANAL 20 CHINJAP. PAGE 25
E0492

B47
ENKE S.,INTERNATIONAL ECONOMICS. UK USA+45 USSR   INT/TRADE
INT/ORG BAL/PWR BARGAIN CAP/ISM BAL/PAY...NAT/COMP FINAN
20 TREATY. PAGE 35 E0691   TARIFFS
                                                   ECO/TAC

B57
SCHUBERT G.A.,THE PRESIDENCY IN THE COURTS. CONSTN PWR
FORCES DIPLOM TARIFFS ADJUD CONTROL WAR...DECISION CT/SYS
MGT CHARTS 18/20 PRESIDENT CONGRESS SUPREME/CT.   LEGIT
PAGE 89 E1778   CHIEF

B58
SEYID MUHAMMAD V.A.,THE LEGAL FRAMEWORK OF WORLD   INT/LAW
TRADE. WOR+45 INT/ORG DIPLOM CONTROL...BIBLIOG 20 VOL/ASSN
TREATY UN IMF GATT. PAGE 90 E1807   INT/TRADE
                                                   TARIFFS

B60
BYRD E.M. JR.,TREATIES AND EXECUTIVE AGREEMENTS IN CHIEF
THE UNITED STATES: THEIR SEPARATE ROLES AND   INT/LAW
LIMITATIONS. USA+45 USA-45 EX/STRUC TARIFFS CT/SYS DIPLOM
GOV/REL FEDERAL...IDEA/COMP BIBLIOG SUPREME/CT
SENATE CONGRESS. PAGE 18 E0353

B62
ALEXANDROWICZ C.H.,WORLD ECONOMIC AGENCIES: LAW AND INT/LAW
PRACTICE. WOR+45 DIST/IND FINAN LABOR CONSULT   INT/ORG
INT/TRADE TARIFFS REPRESENT HEALTH...JURID 20 UN   DIPLOM
GATT EEC OAS ECSC. PAGE 3 E0063   ADJUD

B62
COLOMBOS C.J.,THE INTERNATIONAL LAW OF THE SEA.   INT/LAW
WOR+45 EXTR/IND DIPLOM INT/TRADE TARIFFS AGREE WAR SEA
...TIME/SEQ 20 TREATY. PAGE 24 E0476   JURID
                                                   ADJUD

B63
LYONS F.S.L.,INTERNATIONALISM IN EUROPE 1815-1914. DIPLOM
LAW AGRI COM/IND DIST/IND LABOR SECT INT/TRADE   MOD/EUR
TARIFFS...BIBLIOG 19/20. PAGE 67 E1335   INT/ORG

HABERLER G.,A SURVEY OF INTERNATIONAL TRADE THEORY.   INT/TRADE   B65
CANADA FRANCE GERMANY ECO/TAC TARIFFS AGREE COST   BAL/PAY
DEMAND WEALTH...ECOMETRIC 19/20 MONOPOLY TREATY.   DIPLOM
PAGE 49 E0968   POLICY

HAEFELE E.T.,GOVERNMENT CONTROLS ON TRANSPORT. AFR   ECO/UNDEV   B65
RHODESIA TANZANIA DIPLOM ECO/TAC TARIFFS PRICE   DIST/IND
ADJUD CONTROL REGION EFFICIENCY...POLICY 20 CONGO.   FINAN
PAGE 49 E0973   NAT/G

EDWARDS C.D.,TRADE REGULATIONS OVERSEAS. IRELAND   INT/TRADE   B66
NEW/ZEALND SOUTH/AFR NAT/G CAP/ISM TARIFFS CONTROL   DIPLOM
...POLICY JURID 20 EEC CHINJAP. PAGE 34 E0676   INT/LAW
  ECO/TAC

LAFAVE W.R.,INTERNATIONAL TRADE, INVESTMENT, AND   INT/TRADE   B67
ORGANIZATION. INDUS PROB/SOLV TARIFFS CONTROL   INT/LAW
...TREND ANTHOL BIBLIOG 20 EEC. PAGE 62 E1245   INT/ORG

LENT G.E.,"TAX INCENTIVES FOR INVESTMENT IN   ECO/UNDEV   L67
DEVELOPING COUNTRIES" WOR+45 LAW INDUS PLAN BUDGET   TAX
TARIFFS ADMIN...METH/COMP 20. PAGE 64 E1285   FINAN
  ECO/TAC

DOUTY H.M.," REFERENCE TO DEVELOPING COUNTRIES."   TAX   S67
JAMAICA MALAYSIA UK WOR+45 LAW FINAN ACT/RES BUDGET   ECO/UNDEV
CAP/ISM ECO/TAC TARIFFS RISK EFFICIENCY PROFIT   NAT/G
...CHARTS 20. PAGE 33 E0646

US SENATE COMM ON FOREIGN REL,SURVEY OF THE   INT/TRADE   N67
ALLIANCE FOR PROGRESS: FOREIGN TRADE POLICIES   REGION
(PAMPHLET). L/A+17C LAW ECO/UNDEV ECO/TAC TARIFFS   AGREE
20 GATT LAFTA UN. PAGE 102 E2037   INT/ORG

SMITH A.,LECTURES ON JUSTICE, POLICE, REVENUE AND   DIPLOM   B96
ARMS (1763). UK LAW FAM FORCES TARIFFS AGREE COERCE   JURID
INCOME OWN WEALTH LAISSEZ...GEN/LAWS 17/18. PAGE 92   OLD/LIB
E1840   TAX

TARTARS....TARTARS

TASK....SPECIFIC SELF-ASSIGNED OR OTHER ASSIGNED OPERATIONS

GRIFFIN A.P.C.,LIST OF REFERENCES ON PRIMARY   BIBLIOG/A   B05
ELECTIONS (PAMPHLET). USA-45 LAW LOC/G DELIB/GP   POL/PAR
LEGIS OP/RES TASK REPRESENT CONSEN...DECISION 19/20   CHOOSE
CONGRESS. PAGE 47 E0928   POPULISM

FRANKFURTER F.,"SOME REFLECTIONS ON THE READING OF   JURID   S47
STATUTES" USA+45 USA-45 PROB/SOLV CT/SYS TASK   LAW
EFFICIENCY...LING 20. PAGE 40 E0791   ADJUD
  WRITING

LOWENTHAL M.,THE FEDERAL BUREAU OF INVESTIGATION.   FORCES   B50
USA+45 SOCIETY ADMIN TASK CRIME INGP/REL...CRIMLGY   NAT/G
20 FBI ESPIONAGE. PAGE 67 E1329   ATTIT
  LAW

ROSTOW E.V.,"THE DEMOCRATIC CHARACTER OF JUDICIAL   CONSTN   L52
REVIEW" (BMR)" USA+45 LAW NAT/G LEGIS TASK...JURID   PROB/SOLV
20 SUPREME/CT. PAGE 86 E1725   ADJUD
  CT/SYS

BRAUN K.,LABOR DISPUTES AND THEIR SETTLEMENT.   INDUS   B55
ECO/TAC ROUTINE TASK GP/REL...DECISION GEN/LAWS.   LABOR
PAGE 15 E0288   BARGAIN
  ADJUD

WHEARE K.C.,GOVERNMENT BY COMMITTEE; AN ESSAY ON   DELIB/GP   B55
THE BRITISH CONSTITUTION. UK NAT/G LEGIS INSPECT   CONSTN
CONFER ADJUD ADMIN CONTROL TASK EFFICIENCY ROLE   LEAD
POPULISM 20. PAGE 106 E2116   GP/COMP

ELLIOTT S.D.,IMPROVING OUR COURTS. LAW EX/STRUC   CT/SYS   B59
PLAN PROB/SOLV ADJUD ADMIN TASK CRIME EFFICIENCY   JURID
ORD/FREE 20. PAGE 34 E0684   GOV/REL
  NAT/G

WAGNER W.J.,THE FEDERAL STATES AND THEIR JUDICIARY.   ADJUD   B59

BRAZIL CANADA SWITZERLND USA+45 CONFER CT/SYS TASK   METH/COMP
EFFICIENCY FEDERAL PWR...JURID BIBLIOG 20 AUSTRAL   PROB/SOLV
MEXIC/AMER. PAGE 104 E2091   NAT/G

DOUGLAS W.O.,DEMOCRACY'S MANIFESTO. COM USA+45   DIPLOM   B62
ECO/UNDEV INT/ORG FORCES PLAN NEUTRAL TASK MARXISM   POLICY
...JURID 20 NATO SEATO. PAGE 32 E0642   NAT/G
  ORD/FREE

YOUNGER R.D.,THE PEOPLE'S PANEL: THE GRAND JURY IN   CT/SYS   B63
THE UNITED STATES, 1634-1941. USA-45 LAW LEGIT   JURID
CONTROL TASK GP/REL ROLE...TREND 17/20 GRAND/JURY.   CONSTN
PAGE 108 E2166   LOC/G

CLEVELAND H.,"CRISIS DIPLOMACY." USA+45 WOR+45 LAW   DECISION   S63
FORCES TASK NUC/PWR PWR 20. PAGE 23 E0454   DIPLOM
  PROB/SOLV
  POLICY

BOWETT D.W.,UNITED NATIONS FORCES* A LEGAL STUDY.   OP/RES   B64
CYPRUS ISRAEL KOREA LAW CONSTN ACT/RES CREATE   FORCES
BUDGET CONTROL TASK PWR...INT/LAW IDEA/COMP UN   ARMS/CONT
CONGO/LEOP SUEZ. PAGE 14 E0278

FRANCK T.M.,EAST AFRICAN UNITY THROUGH LAW. MALAWI   AFR   B64
TANZANIA UGANDA UK ZAMBIA CONSTN INT/ORG NAT/G   FEDERAL
ADMIN ROUTINE TASK NAT/LISM ATTIT SOVEREIGN   REGION
...RECORD IDEA/COMP NAT/COMP. PAGE 40 E0785   INT/LAW

KAHNG T.J.,LAW, POLITICS, AND THE SECURITY COUNCIL*   DELIB/GP   B64
AN INQUIRY INTO THE HANDLING OF LEGAL QUESTIONS.   ADJUD
LAW CONSTN NAT/G ACT/RES OP/RES CT/SYS TASK PWR   ROUTINE
...INT/LAW BIBLIOG UN. PAGE 59 E1180

BRIGGS H.W.,THE INTERNATIONAL LAW COMMISSION. LAW   INT/LAW   B65
CONSTN LEGIS CREATE ADJUD CT/SYS ROUTINE TASK   DELIB/GP
EFFICIENCY...CLASSIF OBS UN. PAGE 15 E0302

SEN B.,A DIPLOMAT'S HANDBOOK OF INTERNATIONAL LAW   DIPLOM   B65
AND PRACTICE. WOR+45 NAT/G ADJUST. PAGE 90 E1803   INT/LAW
  TASK
  LAW

MERILLAT H.C.L.,LEGAL ADVISERS AND INTERNATIONAL   INT/ORG   B66
ORGANIZATIONS. LAW NAT/G CONSULT OP/RES ADJUD   INT/LAW
SANCTION TASK CONSEN ORG/CHARTS. PAGE 72 E1441   CREATE
  OBS

WALL E.H.,THE COURT OF JUSTICE IN THE EUROPEAN   CT/SYS   B66
COMMUNITIES: JURISDICTION AND PROCEDURE. EUR+WWI   INT/ORG
DIPLOM ADJUD ADMIN ROUTINE TASK...CONCPT LING 20.   LAW
PAGE 105 E2096   OP/RES

YOUNG W.,EXISTING MECHANISMS OF ARMS CONTROL.   ARMS/CONT   B66
PROC/MFG OP/RES DIPLOM TASK CENTRAL...MGT TREATY.   ADMIN
PAGE 108 E2165   NUC/PWR
  ROUTINE

LONG E.V.,THE INTRUDERS: THE INVASION OF PRIVACY BY   LAW   B67
GOVERNMENT AND INDUSTRY. USA+45 COM/IND INDUS LEGIS   PARTIC
TASK PERS/REL...JURID 20 CONGRESS. PAGE 66 E1324   NAT/G

LEGAULT A.,"ORGANISATION ET CONDUITE DES OPERATIONS   INT/ORG   L67
DE MAINTIEN DE LA PAIX." FORCES ACT/RES ADJUD AGREE   PEACE
CONTROL NEUTRAL TASK PRIVIL ORD/FREE 20 UN. PAGE 64   WAR
E1279   INT/LAW

HILL D.G.,"HUMAN RIGHTS LEGISLATION IN ONTARIO."   DELIB/GP   S67
CANADA R+D VOL/ASSN CONSULT INSPECT EDU/PROP ADJUD   ORD/FREE
AGREE TASK GP/REL INGP/REL DISCRIM 20 CIV/RIGHTS   LAW
ONTARIO CIVIL/LIB. PAGE 52 E1045   POLICY

TAUBENFELD H.J. E1909,E1910,E1911

TAX....TAXING, TAXATION

CONOVER H.F.,OFFICIAL PUBLICATIONS OF BRITISH EAST   BIBLIOG/A   N
AFRICA (PAMPHLET). UK LAW ECO/UNDEV AGRI EXTR/IND   AFR
SECT LEGIS BUDGET TAX...HEAL STAT 20. PAGE 25 E0491   ADMIN
  COLONIAL

THE JAPAN SCIENCE REVIEW: LAW AND POLITICS: LIST OF
BOOKS AND ARTICLES ON LAW AND POLITICS. CONSTN AGRI
INDUS LABOR DIPLOM TAX ADMIN CRIME...INT/LAW SOC 20
CHINJAP. PAGE 2 E0027
N / BIBLIOG LAW S/ASIA PHIL/SCI

GRIFFIN A.P.C.,LIST OF MORE RECENT WORKS ON FEDERAL
CONTROL OF COMMERCE AND CORPORATIONS (PAMPHLET).
USA-45 LAW ECO/DEV FINAN LG/CO TARIFFS TAX LICENSE
CENTRAL ORD/FREE WEALTH LAISSEZ 19/20. PAGE 47
E0931
B07 / BIBLIOG/A NAT/G JURID ECO/TAC

CRAIG J.,ELEMENTS OF POLITICAL SCIENCE (3 VOLS.).
CONSTN AGRI INDUS SCHOOL FORCES TAX CT/SYS SUFF
MORAL WEALTH...CONCPT 19 CIVIL/LIB. PAGE 27 E0539
B14 / PHIL/SCI NAT/G ORD/FREE

DE MONTESQUIEU C.,THE SPIRIT OF LAWS (2 VOLS.)
(TRANS. BY THOMAS NUGENT). FRANCE FINAN SECT
INT/TRADE TAX COERCE REV DISCRIM HABITAT ORD/FREE
19 ALEMBERT/J CIVIL/LAW. PAGE 30 E0588
B23 / JURID LAW CONCPT GEN/LAWS

GODET M.,INDEX BIBLIOGRAPHICUS: INTERNATIONAL
CATALOGUE OF SOURCES OF CURRENT BIBLIOGRAPHIC
INFORMATION. EUR+WWI MOD/EUR SOCIETY SECT TAX
...JURID PHIL/SCI SOC MATH. PAGE 44 E0876
B25 / BIBLIOG/A DIPLOM EDU/PROP LAW

FORTESCUE J.,THE GOVERNANCE OF ENGLAND (1471-76).
UK LAW FINAN SECT LEGIS PROB/SOLV TAX DOMIN ADMIN
GP/REL COST ORD/FREE PWR 14/15. PAGE 39 E0776
B26 / CONSERVE CONSTN CHIEF NAT/G

FAIRLIE J.A.,COUNTY GOVERNMENT AND ADMINISTRATION.
UK USA-45 NAT/G SCHOOL FORCES BUDGET TAX CT/SYS
CHOOSE...JURID BIBLIOG 11/20. PAGE 36 E0713
B30 / ADMIN GOV/REL LOC/G MUNIC

US TARIFF COMMISSION,THE TARIFF; A BIBLIOGRAPHY: A
SELECT LIST OF REFERENCES. USA-45 LAW DIPLOM TAX
ADMIN...POLICY TREATY 20. PAGE 103 E2064
B34 / BIBLIOG/A TARIFFS ECO/TAC

GRAVES W.B.,AMERICAN STATE GOVERNMENT. CONSTN FINAN
EX/STRUC FORCES LEGIS BUDGET TAX CT/SYS REPRESENT
GOV/REL...BIBLIOG/A 19/20. PAGE 45 E0900
B36 / NAT/G PROVS ADMIN FEDERAL

HAMILTON W.H.,THE POWER TO GOVERN. ECO/DEV FINAN
INDUS ECO/TAC INT/TRADE TARIFFS TAX CONTROL CT/SYS
WAR COST PWR 18/20 SUPREME/CT. PAGE 50 E0991
B37 / LING CONSTN NAT/G POLICY

BALDWIN L.D.,WHISKEY REBELS; THE STORY OF A
FRONTIER UPRISING. USA-45 LAW ADJUD LEAD COERCE PWR
...BIBLIOG/A 18 PENNSYLVAN FEDERALIST. PAGE 8 E0145
B39 / REV POL/PAR TAX TIME/SEQ

JEFFERSON T.,"DEMOCRACY" (1816) IN BASIC WRITINGS."
USA-45 LOC/G NAT/G TAX CT/SYS CHOOSE ORD/FREE
...GEN/LAWS 18/19 JEFFERSN/T. PAGE 58 E1151
C44 / POPULISM MAJORIT REPRESENT CONSTN

GALLOWAY E.,ABSTRACTS OF POSTWAR LITERATURE (VOL.
IV) JAN.-JULY, 1945 NOS. 901-1074. POLAND USA+45
USSR WOR+45 INDUS LABOR PLAN ECO/TAC INT/TRADE TAX
EDU/PROP ADMIN COLONIAL INT/LAW. PAGE 42 E0829
B45 / BIBLIOG/A NUC/PWR NAT/G DIPLOM

US LIBRARY OF CONGRESS,CONSTITUTIONAL AND STATUTORY
PROVISIONS OF THE STATES (VOL. I). USA-45 CREATE
TAX CT/SYS CHOOSE SUFF INCOME PWR 20. PAGE 101
E2016
B45 / CONSTN FEDERAL PROVS JURID

KEIR D.L.,CASES IN CONSTITUTIONAL LAW. UK CHIEF
LEGIS DIPLOM TAX PARL/PROC CRIME GOV/REL...INT/LAW
JURID 17/20. PAGE 60 E1195
B48 / CONSTN LAW ADJUD CT/SYS

THOREAU H.D.,CIVIL DISOBEDIENCE (1849). USA-45 LAW
CONSTN TAX COERCE REPRESENT GP/REL SUPEGO...MAJORIT
CONCPT 19. PAGE 96 E1923
B49 / GEN/LAWS ORD/FREE POLICY

ANDERSON W.,STATE AND LOCAL GOVERNMENT IN THE
B51 / LOC/G

UNITED STATES. USA+45 CONSTN POL/PAR EX/STRUC LEGIS
BUDGET TAX ADJUD CT/SYS CHOOSE...CHARTS T 20.
PAGE 5 E0094
MUNIC PROVS GOV/REL

WOOD V.,DUE PROCESS OF LAW 1932-1949: SUPREME
COURT'S USE OF A CONSTITUTIONAL TOOL. USA+45 USA-45
SOCIETY TAX CRIME...POLICY CHARTS 20 SUPREME/CT.
PAGE 107 E2143
B51 / CONSTN TREND ADJUD GOV/REL

ANDREWS F.E.,CORPORATION GIVING. LAW TAX EDU/PROP
ADMIN...POLICY STAT CHARTS. PAGE 5 E0096
B52 / LG/CO GIVE SML/CO FINAN

JENNINGS W.I.,CONSTITUTIONAL LAWS OF THE
COMMONWEALTH. UK LAW CHIEF LEGIS TAX CT/SYS
PARL/PROC GOV/REL...INT/LAW 18/20 COMMONWLTH
ENGLSH/LAW COMMON/LAW. PAGE 58 E1165
B52 / CONSTN JURID ADJUD COLONIAL

LANCASTER L.W.,"GOVERNMENT IN RURAL AMERICA."
USA+45 ECO/DEV AGRI SCHOOL FORCES LEGIS JUDGE
BUDGET TAX CT/SYS...CHARTS BIBLIOG. PAGE 62 E1248
C52 / GOV/REL LOC/G MUNIC ADMIN

BATTEN T.R.,PROBLEMS OF AFRICAN DEVELOPMENT (2ND
ED.). AFR LAW SOCIETY SCHOOL ECO/TAC TAX...GEOG
HEAL SOC 20. PAGE 8 E0154
B54 / ECO/UNDEV AGRI LOC/G PROB/SOLV

SINCO,PHILIPPINE POLITICAL LAW: PRINCIPLES AND
CONCEPTS (10TH ED.). PHILIPPINE LOC/G EX/STRUC
BAL/PWR ECO/TAC TAX ADJUD ADMIN CONTROL CT/SYS SUFF
ORD/FREE...T 20. PAGE 91 E1831
B54 / LAW CONSTN LEGIS

CALDWELL L.K.,"THE GOVERNMENT AND ADMINISTRATION OF
NEW YORK." LOC/G MUNIC POL/PAR SCHOOL CHIEF LEGIS
PLAN TAX CT/SYS...MGT SOC/WK BIBLIOG 20 NEWYORK/C.
PAGE 19 E0365
C54 / PROVS ADMIN CONSTN EX/STRUC

CUSHMAN R.E.,LEADING CONSTITUTIONAL DECISIONS.
USA+45 USA-45 NAT/G EX/STRUC LEGIS JUDGE TAX
FEDERAL...DECISION 20 SUPREME/CT CASEBOOK. PAGE 28
E0559
B55 / CONSTN PROB/SOLV JURID CT/SYS

JAPAN MOMBUSHO DAIGAKU GAKIYUT,BIBLIOGRAPHY OF THE
STUDIES ON LAW AND POLITICS (PAMPHLET). CONSTN
INDUS LABOR DIPLOM TAX ADMIN...CRIMLGY INT/LAW 20
CHINJAP. PAGE 58 E1150
B55 / BIBLIOG LAW PHIL/SCI

SERRANO MOSCOSO E.,A STATEMENT OF THE LAWS OF
ECUADOR IN MATTERS AFFECTING BUSINESS (2ND ED.).
ECUADOR INDUS LABOR LG/CO NAT/G LEGIS TAX CONTROL
MARRIAGE 20. PAGE 90 E1805
B55 / FINAN ECO/UNDEV LAW CONSTN

ZABEL O.H.,GOD AND CAESAR IN NEBRASKA: A STUDY OF
LEGAL RELATIONSHIP OF CHURCH AND STATE, 1854-1954.
TAX GIVE ADMIN CONTROL GP/REL ROLE...GP/COMP 19/20
NEBRASKA. PAGE 108 E2168
B55 / SECT PROVS LAW EDU/PROP

ABELS J.,THE TRUMAN SCANDALS. USA+45 USA-45 POL/PAR
TAX LEGIT CT/SYS CHOOSE PRIVIL MORAL WEALTH 20
TRUMAN/HS PRESIDENT CONGRESS. PAGE 2 E0043
B56 / CRIME ADMIN CHIEF TRIBUTE

NOTZ R.L.,FEDERAL GRANTS-IN-AID TO STATES: ANALYSIS
OF LAWS IN FORCE ON SEPTEMBER 10, 1956. USA+45 LAW
SCHOOL PLAN ECO/TAC TAX RECEIVE...HEAL JURID 20.
PAGE 78 E1558
B56 / GIVE NAT/G PROVS GOV/REL

OGDEN F.D.,THE POLL TAX IN THE SOUTH. USA+45 USA-45
CONSTN ADJUD ADMIN PARTIC CRIME...TIME/SEQ GOV/COMP
METH/COMP 18/20 SOUTH/US. PAGE 78 E1572
B58 / TAX CHOOSE RACE/REL DISCRIM

COUNCIL OF STATE GOVERNMENTS,STATE GOVERNMENT: AN
ANNOTATED BIBLIOGRAPHY (PAMPHLET). USA+45 LAW AGRI
INDUS WORKER PLAN TAX ADJUST AGE/Y ORD/FREE...HEAL
MGT 20. PAGE 26 E0521
B59 / BIBLIOG/A PROVS LOC/G ADMIN

COWAN T.A.,"A SYMPOSIUM ON GROUP INTERESTS AND THE
L59 / ADJUD

LAW" USA+45 LAW MARKET LABOR PLAN INT/TRADE TAX RACE/REL RIGID/FLEX...JURID ANTHOL 20. PAGE 27 E0528
PWR INGP/REL CREATE

B60
BEEM H.D.,AN INTRODUCTION TO LEGAL BIBLIOGRAPHY FOT THE NON-PROFESSIONAL STUDENT. LOC/G NAT/G TAX 20. PAGE 9 E0177
BIBLIOG/A JURID METH ADJUD

B60
CARTER R.F.,COMMUNITIES AND THEIR SCHOOLS. USA+45 LAW FINAN PROVS BUDGET TAX LEAD PARTIC CHOOSE...SOC INT QU 20. PAGE 20 E0401
SCHOOL ACT/RES NEIGH INGP/REL

B60
DILEY A.V.,INTRODUCTION TO THE STUDY OF THE LAW OF THE CONSTITUTION. FRANCE UK USA+45 USA-45 CONSULT FORCES TAX ADMIN FEDERAL ORD/FREE SOVEREIGN ...IDEA/COMP 20 ENGLSH/LAW CON/INTERP PARLIAMENT. PAGE 32 E0627
CONSTN LAW LEGIS GEN/LAWS

B60
LASKIN B.,CANADIAN CONSTITUTIONAL LAW: TEXT AND NOTES ON DISTRIBUTION OF LEGISLATIVE POWER (2ND ED.). CANADA LOC/G ECO/TAC TAX CONTROL CT/SYS CRIME FEDERAL PWR...JURID 20 PARLIAMENT. PAGE 63 E1259
CONSTN NAT/G LAW LEGIS

B60
MUTHESIUS V.,DAS GESPENST DER WIRTSCHAFTLICHEN MACHT. GERMANY/W ECO/DEV FINAN MARKET TAX...JURID 20. PAGE 75 E1513
ECO/TAC NAT/G CONCPT LG/CO

B61
BEASLEY K.E.,STATE SUPERVISION OF MUNICIPAL DEBT IN KANSAS - A CASE STUDY. USA+45 USA-45 FINAN PROVS BUDGET TAX ADJUD ADMIN CONTROL SUPEGO. PAGE 9 E0167
MUNIC LOC/G LEGIS JURID

B61
NEW JERSEY LEGISLATURE-SENATE,PUBLIC HEARINGS BEFORE COMMITTEE ON REVISION AND AMENDMENT OF LAWS ON SENATE BILL NO. 8. USA+45 FINAN PROVS WORKER ACT/RES PLAN BUDGET TAX CRIME...IDEA/COMP 20 NEW/JERSEY URBAN/RNWL. PAGE 77 E1537
LEGIS MUNIC INDUS PROB/SOLV

B61
RUEDA B.,A STATEMENT OF THE LAWS OF COLOMBIA IN MATTERS AFFECTING BUSINESS (3RD ED.). INDUS FAM LABOR LG/CO NAT/G LEGIS TAX CONTROL MARRIAGE 20 COLOMB. PAGE 86 E1733
FINAN ECO/UNDEV LAW CONSTN

L61
GERWIG R.,"PUBLIC AUTHORITIES IN THE UNITED STATES." LAW CONSTN PROVS TAX ADMIN FEDERAL. PAGE 43 E0852
LOC/G MUNIC GOV/REL PWR

L61
KAUPER P.G.,"CHURCH AND STATE: COOPERATIVE SEPARATISM." NAT/G LEGIS OP/RES TAX EDU/PROP GP/REL TREND. PAGE 59 E1187
SECT CONSTN LAW POLICY

B62
DE LAVALLE H.,A STATEMENT OF THE LAWS OF PERU IN MATTERS AFFECTING BUSINESS (3RD ED.). PERU WORKER INT/TRADE INCOME ORD/FREE...INT/LAW 20. PAGE 30 E0586
CONSTN JURID FINAN TAX

B62
MCGRATH J.J.,CHURCH AND STATE IN AMERICAN LAW. LAW PROVS SCHOOL TAX GIVE CT/SYS GP/REL...POLICY ANTHOL 18/20 SUPREME/CT CHURCH/STA CASEBOOK. PAGE 71 E1414
SECT ADJUD CONSTN NAT/G

B62
SHAW C.,LEGAL PROBLEMS IN INTERNATIONAL TRADE AND INVESTMENT. WOR+45 ECO/DEV ECO/UNDEV MARKET DIPLOM TAX INCOME ROLE...ANTHOL BIBLIOG 20 TREATY UN IMF GATT. PAGE 91 E1816
INT/LAW INT/TRADE FINAN ECO/TAC

B63
CORLEY R.N.,THE LEGAL ENVIRONMENT OF BUSINESS. CONSTN LEGIS TAX ADMIN CT/SYS DISCRIM ATTIT PWR ...TREND 18/20. PAGE 26 E0509
NAT/G INDUS JURID DECISION

B63
DRINAN R.F.,RELIGION, THE COURTS, AND PUBLIC POLICY. USA+45 CONSTN BUDGET TAX GIVE ADJUD SANCTION GP/REL PRIVIL 20 CHURCH/STA. PAGE 33 E0649
SECT CT/SYS POLICY SCHOOL

B63
HORRELL M.,LEGISLATION AND RACE RELATIONS (PAMPHLET). SOUTH/AFR SCHOOL TAX DOMIN CONTROL 20. PAGE 55 E1098
LAW RACE/REL DISCRIM PARTIC

B63
LIVNEH E.,ISRAEL LEGAL BIBLIOGRAPHY IN EUROPEAN LANGUAGES. ISRAEL LOC/G JUDGE TAX...INT/LAW 20. PAGE 66 E1311
BIBLIOG LAW NAT/G CONSTN

B64
BOGEN J.I.,FINANCIAL HANDBOOK (4TH ED.). UNIV LAW PLAN TAX RISK 20. PAGE 13 E0257
FINAN DICTIONARY

B64
CURRIE D.P.,FEDERALISM AND THE NEW NATIONS OF AFRICA. CANADA USA+45 INT/TRADE TAX GP/REL ...NAT/COMP SOC/INTEG 20. PAGE 28 E0556
FEDERAL AFR ECO/UNDEV INT/LAW

B64
MASON A.T.,AMERICAN CONSTITUTIONAL LAW: INTRODUCTORY ESSAYS AND SELECTED CASES (3RD ED.). LAW LEGIS TAX ADJUD GOV/REL FEDERAL ORD/FREE PWR ...TIME/SEQ BIBLIOG T 19/20 SUPREME/CT. PAGE 69 E1379
CONSTN CT/SYS JURID

B64
MITAU G.T.,INSOLUBLE PROBLEMS: CASE PROBLEMS ON THE FUNCTIONS OF STATE AND LOCAL GOVERNMENT. USA+45 AIR FINAN LABOR POL/PAR PROB/SOLV TAX RECEIVE CONTROL GP/REL 20 CASEBOOK ZONING. PAGE 73 E1471
ADJUD LOC/G PROVS

B64
RICE C.E.,THE SUPREME COURT AND PUBLIC PRAYER. CONSTN SCHOOL SECT PROB/SOLV TAX ATTIT WORSHIP 18/20 SUPREME/CT CHURCH/STA. PAGE 84 E1692
JURID POLICY NAT/G

B64
TELLADO A.,A STATEMENT OF THE LAWS OF THE DOMINICAN REPUBLIC IN MATTERS AFFECTING BUSINESS (3RD ED.). DOMIN/REP AGRI DIST/IND EXTR/IND FINAN FAM WORKER ECO/TAC TAX CT/SYS MARRIAGE OWN...BIBLIOG 20 MIGRATION. PAGE 95 E1913
CONSTN LEGIS NAT/G INDUS

B65
ANTIEU C.J.,RELIGION UNDER THE STATE CONSTITUTIONS. USA+45 LAW SCHOOL TAX SANCTION PRIVIL ORD/FREE ...JURID 20 SUPREME/CT CHURCH/STA. PAGE 5 E0099
SECT CONSTN PROVS GP/REL

B65
CONGRESSIONAL QUARTERLY SERV,FEDERAL ROLE IN EDUCATION (PAMPHLET). LAW SCHOOL PLAN TAX ADJUD ...CHARTS SOC/INTEG 20 PRESIDENT. PAGE 25 E0487
ACADEM DISCRIM RECEIVE FEDERAL

B65
COOPER F.E.,STATE ADMINISTRATIVE LAW (2 VOLS.). LAW LEGIS PLAN TAX ADJUD CT/SYS FEDERAL PWR...CONCPT 20. PAGE 25 E0501
JURID CONSTN ADMIN PROVS

B65
LUGO-MARENCO J.J.,A STATEMENT OF THE LAWS OF NICARAGUA IN MATTERS AFFECTING BUSINESS. NICARAGUA AGRI DIST/IND EXTR/IND FINAN INDUS FAM WORKER INT/TRADE TAX MARRIAGE OWN BIO/SOC 20 TREATY RESOURCE/N MIGRATION. PAGE 67 E1332
CONSTN NAT/G LEGIS JURID

B65
NWOGUGU E.I.,THE LEGAL PROBLEMS OF FOREIGN INVESTMENT IN DEVELOPING COUNTRIES. WOR+45 INT/ORG DELIB/GP LEGIS PROB/SOLV INT/TRADE TAX ADJUD SANCTION...BIBLIOG 20 TREATY. PAGE 78 E1561
FOR/AID FINAN INT/LAW ECO/UNDEV

B65
PROEHL P.O.,FOREIGN ENTERPRISE IN NIGERIA. NIGERIA FINAN LABOR NAT/G TAX 20. PAGE 83 E1656
ECO/UNDEV ECO/TAC JURID CAP/ISM

B66
CAHN E.,CONFRONTING INJUSTICE. USA+45 PROB/SOLV TAX EDU/PROP PRESS CT/SYS GP/REL DISCRIM BIO/SOC ...IDEA/COMP BIBLIOG WORSHIP 20 BILL/RIGHT. PAGE 18 E0362
ORD/FREE CONSTN ADJUD

B66
CLARK G.,WORLD PEACE THROUGH WORLD LAW; TWO ALTERNATIVE PLANS. WOR+45 DELIB/GP FORCES TAX CONFER ADJUD SANCTION ARMS/CONT WAR CHOOSE PRIVIL 20 UN COLD/WAR. PAGE 23 E0450
INT/LAW PEACE PLAN INT/ORG

KING W.L.,MELVILLE WESTON FULLER: CHIEF JUSTICE OF
THE UNITED STATES, 1888-1910. USA-45 CONSTN FINAN
LABOR TAX GOV/REL PERS/REL ATTIT PERSON PWR...JURID
BIBLIOG 19/20 SUPREME/CT FULLER/MW HOLMES/OW.
PAGE 61 E1216
BIOG
CT/SYS
LAW
ADJUD
B67

LENT G.E.,"TAX INCENTIVES FOR INVESTMENT IN
DEVELOPING COUNTRIES" WOR+45 LAW INDUS PLAN BUDGET
TARIFFS ADMIN...METH/COMP 20. PAGE 64 E1285
ECO/UNDEV
TAX
FINAN
ECO/TAC
L67

ANDERSON W.,"THE PERILS OF 'SHARING'." USA+45
ECO/TAC RECEIVE LOBBY GOV/REL CENTRAL COST INCOME
...POLICY PLURIST CONGRESS. PAGE 5 E0095
BUDGET
TAX
FEDERAL
LAW
S67

BARTLETT J.L.,"AMERICAN BOND ISSUES IN THE EUROPEAN
ECONOMIC COMMUNITY." EUR+WWI LUXEMBOURG USA+45
DIPLOM CONTROL BAL/PAY EEC. PAGE 8 E0153
LAW
ECO/TAC
FINAN
TAX
S67

DOUTY H.M.,," REFERENCE TO DEVELOPING COUNTRIES."
JAMAICA MALAYSIA UK WOR+45 LAW FINAN ACT/RES BUDGET
CAP/ISM ECO/TAC TARIFFS RISK EFFICIENCY PROFIT
...CHARTS 20. PAGE 33 E0646
TAX
ECO/UNDEV
NAT/G
S67

BENTHAM J.,DEFENCE OF USURY (1787). UK LAW NAT/G
TEC/DEV ECO/TAC CONTROL ATTIT...CONCPT IDEA/COMP 18
SMITH/ADAM. PAGE 10 E0197
TAX
FINAN
ECO/DEV
POLICY
B88

SMITH A.,LECTURES ON JUSTICE, POLICE, REVENUE AND
ARMS (1763). UK LAW FAM FORCES TARIFFS AGREE COERCE
INCOME OWN WEALTH LAISSEZ...GEN/LAWS 17/18. PAGE 92
E1840
DIPLOM
JURID
OLD/LIB
TAX
B96

TAYLOR H. E1912

TAYLOR/AJP....A.J.P. TAYLOR

TAYLOR/Z....PRESIDENT ZACHARY TAYLOR

TEC/DEV....DEVELOPMENT OF TECHNIQUES

FOREIGN AFFAIRS. SPACE WOR+45 WOR-45 CULTURE
ECO/UNDEV FINAN NAT/G TEC/DEV INT/TRADE ARMS/CONT
NUC/PWR...POLICY 20 UN EURATOM ECSC EEC. PAGE 1
E0021
BIBLIOG
DIPLOM
INT/ORG
INT/LAW
N

LATIN AMERICA IN PERIODICAL LITERATURE. LAW TEC/DEV
DIPLOM RECEIVE EDU/PROP...GEOG HUM MGT 20. PAGE 2
E0024
BIBLIOG/A
L/A+17C
SOCIETY
ECO/UNDEV
N

CORNELL UNIVERSITY LIBRARY,SOUTHEAST ASIA
ACCESSIONS LIST. LAW SOCIETY STRUCT ECO/UNDEV
POL/PAR TEC/DEV DIPLOM LEAD REGION. PAGE 26 E0510
BIBLIOG
S/ASIA
NAT/G
CULTURE
N

MINISTRY OF OVERSEAS DEVELOPME,TECHNICAL CO-
OPERATION -- A BIBLIOGRAPHY. UK LAW SOCIETY DIPLOM
ECO/TAC FOR/AID...STAT 20 CMN/WLTH. PAGE 73 E1466
BIBLIOG
TEC/DEV
ECO/DEV
NAT/G
N

GRIFFIN A.P.C.,A LIST OF BOOKS RELATING TO
RAILROADS IN THEIR RELATION TO THE GOVERNMENT AND
THE PUBLIC (PAMPHLET). USA-45 LAW ECO/DEV NAT/G
TEC/DEV CAP/ISM LICENSE CENTRAL LAISSEZ...DECISION
19/20. PAGE 47 E0925
BIBLIOG/A
SERV/IND
ADJUD
ECO/TAC
B04

HARPER S.N.,THE GOVERNMENT OF THE SOVIET UNION. COM
USSR LAW CONSTN ECO/DEV PLAN TEC/DEV DIPLOM
INT/TRADE ADMIN REV NAT/LISM...POLICY 20. PAGE 50
E1001
MARXISM
NAT/G
LEAD
POL/PAR
B38

GRIFFITH E.S.,"THE CHANGING PATTERN OF PUBLIC
POLICY FORMATION." MOD/EUR WOR+45 FINAN CHIEF
CONFER ADMIN LEAD CONSERVE SOCISM TECHRACY...SOC
CHARTS CONGRESS. PAGE 47 E0938
LAW
POLICY
TEC/DEV
S44

REVES E.,THE ANATOMY OF PEACE. WOR+45 LAW CULTURE
NAT/G PLAN TEC/DEV EDU/PROP WAR NAT/LISM ATTIT
ALL/VALS SOVEREIGN...POLICY HUM TIME/SEQ 20.
PAGE 84 E1688
ACT/RES
CONCPT
NUC/PWR
PEACE
B45

AMERICAN DOCUMENTATION INST,CATALOGUE OF AUXILIARY
PUBLICATIONS IN MICROFILMS AND PHOTOPRINTS. USA-45
LAW AGRI CREATE TEC/DEV ADMIN...GEOG LING MATH 20.
PAGE 4 E0077
BIBLIOG
EDU/PROP
PSY
B46

MILLER B.S.,"A LAW IS PASSED: THE ATOMIC ENERGY ACT
OF 1946." POL/PAR CHIEF CONFER DEBATE CONTROL
PARL/PROC ATTIT KNOWL...POLICY CONGRESS. PAGE 73
E1457
TEC/DEV
LEGIS
DECISION
LAW
S48

WORMUTH F.D.,THE ORIGINS OF MODERN
CONSTITUTIONALISM. GREECE UK LEGIS CREATE TEC/DEV
BAL/PWR DOMIN ADJUD REV WAR PWR...JURID ROMAN/REP
CROMWELL/O. PAGE 107 E2146
NAT/G
CONSTN
LAW
B49

BURDETTE F.L.,LOBBYISTS IN ACTION (PAMPHLET).
CONSULT TEC/DEV INSPECT BARGAIN PARL/PROC SANCTION
20 CONGRESS. PAGE 17 E0329
LOBBY
ATTIT
POLICY
LAW
B50

COUNCIL BRITISH NATIONAL BIB,BRITISH NATIONAL
BIBLIOGRAPHY. UK AGRI CONSTRUC PERF/ART POL/PAR
SECT CREATE INT/TRADE LEAD...HUM JURID PHIL/SCI 20.
PAGE 26 E0519
BIBLIOG/A
NAT/G
TEC/DEV
DIPLOM
B50

DOROSH J.T.,GUIDE TO SOVIET BIBLIOGRAPHIES. USSR
LAW AGRI SCHOOL SECT FORCES TEC/DEV...ART/METH GEOG
HUM SOC 20. PAGE 32 E0639
BIBLIOG
METH
CON/ANAL
B50

CARTER P.G.,STATISTICAL BULLETINS: AN ANNOTATED
BIBLIOGRAPHY OF THE GENERAL STATISTICAL BULLETINS
AND MAJOR POL SUBDIV OF WORLD. CULTURE AGRI FINAN
INDUS LABOR TEC/DEV INT/TRADE CT/SYS WEALTH
...CRIMLGY SOC 20. PAGE 20 E0400
BIBLIOG/A
WOR+45
NAT/G
STAT
B54

WRIGHT Q.,PROBLEMS OF STABILITY AND PROGRESS IN
INTERNATIONAL RELATIONSHIPS. FUT WOR+45 WOR-45
SOCIETY LEGIS CREATE TEC/DEV ECO/TAC EDU/PROP ADJUD
WAR PEACE ORD/FREE PWR...KNO/TEST TREND GEN/LAWS
20. PAGE 108 E2155
INT/ORG
CONCPT
DIPLOM
B54

COMM. STUDY ORGAN. PEACE,REPORTS. WOR-45 ECO/DEV
ECO/UNDEV VOL/ASSN CONSULT FORCES PLAN TEC/DEV
DOMIN EDU/PROP NUC/PWR ATTIT PWR WEALTH...JURID
STERTYP FAO ILO 20 UN. PAGE 24 E0481
WOR+45
INT/ORG
ARMS/CONT
B55

ESTEP R.,AN AIR POWER BIBLIOGRAPHY. USA+45 TEC/DEV
BUDGET DIPLOM EDU/PROP DETER CIVMIL/REL...DECISION
INT/LAW 20. PAGE 35 E0698
BIBLIOG/A
FORCES
WEAPON
PLAN
B56

US COMMISSION GOVT SECURITY,RECOMMENDATIONS; AREA:
LEGISLATION. USA+45 USA-45 DELIB/GP PLAN TEC/DEV
CIVMIL/REL ORD/FREE...POLICY DECISION 20 PRIVACY.
PAGE 99 E1982
LEGIS
SANCTION
CRIME
CONTROL
B57

ATOMIC INDUSTRIAL FORUM,MANAGEMENT AND ATOMIC
ENERGY. WOR+45 SEA LAW MARKET NAT/G TEC/DEV INSPECT
INT/TRADE CONFER PEACE HEALTH...ANTHOL 20. PAGE 6
E0112
NUC/PWR
INDUS
MGT
ECO/TAC
B58

HUNT B.I.,BIPARTISANSHIP: A CASE STUDY OF THE
FOREIGN ASSISTANCE PROGRAM, 1947-56 (DOCTORAL
THESIS). USA+45 INT/ORG CONSULT LEGIS TEC/DEV
...BIBLIOG PRESIDENT TREATY NATO TRUMAN/HS
EISNHWR/DD CONGRESS. PAGE 56 E1114
FOR/AID
POL/PAR
GP/REL
DIPLOM
B58

MCDOUGAL M.S.,"PERSPECTIVES FOR A LAW OF OUTER
SPACE." FUT WOR+45 AIR CONSULT DELIB/GP TEC/DEV
CT/SYS ORD/FREE...POLICY JURID 20 UN. PAGE 70 E1404
INT/ORG
SPACE
INT/LAW
S58

DASH S.,THE EAVESDROPPERS. USA+45 DELIB/GP TEC/DEV
ORD/FREE...POLICY CRIMLGY JURID 20 PRIVACY. PAGE 29
E0569
CRIME
CONTROL
ACT/RES
LAW
B59

B59
MAYDA J.,ATOMIC ENERGY AND LAW. ECO/UNDEV FINAN
TEC/DEV FOR/AID EFFICIENCY PRODUC WEALTH...POLICY
TECHNIC 20. PAGE 70 E1391
NUC/PWR
L/A+17C
LAW
ADMIN

B59
REOCK E.C.,PROCEDURES AND STANDARDS FOR THE
APPORTIONMENT OF STATE LEGISLATURES (DOCTORAL
THESIS). USA+45 POL/PAR LEGIS TEC/DEV ADJUD
BIBLIOG. PAGE 84 E1686
PROVS
LOC/G
APPORT
REPRESENT

S59
CORY R.H. JR.,"INTERNATIONAL INSPECTION FROM
PROPOSALS TO REALIZATION." WOR+45 TEC/DEV ECO/TAC
ADJUD ORD/FREE PWR WEALTH...RECORD VAL/FREE 20.
PAGE 26 E0516
STRUCT
PSY
ARMS/CONT
NUC/PWR

S59
TIPTON J.B.,"PARTICIPATION OF THE UNITED STATES IN
THE INTERNATIONAL LABOR ORGANIZATION." USA+45 LAW
STRUCT ECO/DEV NAT/G INDUS TEC/DEV ECO/TAC
ADMIN PERCEPT ORD/FREE SKILL...STAT HIST/WRIT
GEN/METH ILO WORK 20. PAGE 96 E1928
LABOR
INT/ORG

B60
LENCZOWSKI G.,OIL AND STATE IN THE MIDDLE EAST. FUT
IRAN LAW ECO/UNDEV EXTR/IND NAT/G TOP/EX PLAN
TEC/DEV ECO/TAC LEGIT ADMIN COERCE ATTIT ALL/VALS
PWR...CHARTS 20. PAGE 64 E1283
ISLAM
INDUS
NAT/LISM

B60
STEIN E.,AMERICAN ENTERPRISE IN THE EUROPEAN COMMON
MARKET: A LEGAL PROFILE. EUR+WWI FUT USA+45 SOCIETY
STRUCT ECO/DEV NAT/G VOL/ASSN CONSULT PLAN TEC/DEV
ECO/TAC INT/TRADE ADMIN ATTIT RIGID/FLEX PWR...MGT
NEW/IDEA STAT TREND COMPUT/IR SIMUL EEC 20. PAGE 93
E1867
MARKET
ADJUD
INT/LAW

B60
WEBSTER J.A.,A GENERAL STUDY OF THE DEPARTMENT OF
DEFENSE INTERNAL SECURITY PROGRAM. USA+45 WORKER
TEC/DEV ADJUD CONTROL CT/SYS EXEC GOV/REL COST
...POLICY DECISION MGT 20 DEPT/DEFEN SUPREME/CT.
PAGE 105 E2105
ORD/FREE
PLAN
ADMIN
NAT/G

B60
WOETZEL R.K.,THE INTERNATIONAL CONTROL OF AIRSPACE
AND OUTERSPACE. FUT WOR+45 AIR CONSTN STRUCT
CONSULT PLAN TEC/DEV ADJUD RIGID/FLEX KNOWL
ORD/FREE PWR...TECHNIC GEOG MGT NEW/IDEA TREND
COMPUT/IR VAL/FREE 20 TREATY. PAGE 107 E2137
INT/ORG
JURID
SPACE
INT/LAW

S60
SANDERS R.,"NUCLEAR DYNAMITE: A NEW DIMENSION IN
FOREIGN POLICY." FUT WOR+45 ECO/DEV CONSULT TEC/DEV
PERCEPT...CONT/OBS TIME/SEQ TREND GEN/LAWS TOT/POP
20 TREATY. PAGE 87 E1745
INDUS
PWR
DIPLOM
NUC/PWR

S60
WRIGHT Q.,"LEGAL ASPECTS OF THE U-2 INCIDENT." COM
USA+45 USSR STRUCT NAT/G FORCES PLAN TEC/DEV ADJUD
RIGID/FLEX MORAL ORD/FREE...DECISION INT/LAW JURID
PSY TREND GEN/LAWS COLD/WAR VAL/FREE 20 U-2.
PAGE 108 E2157
PWR
POLICY
SPACE

B61
MURPHY E.F.,WATER PURITY: A STUDY IN LEGAL CONTROL
OF NATURAL RESOURCES. LOC/G ACT/RES PLAN TEC/DEV
LOBBY GP/REL COST ATTIT HEALTH ORD/FREE...HEAL
JURID 20 WISCONSIN WATER. PAGE 75 E1506
SEA
LAW
PROVS
CONTROL

B61
POOLEY B.J.,PLANNING AND ZONING IN THE UNITED
STATES. USA+45 MUNIC DELIB/GP ACT/RES PROB/SOLV
TEC/DEV ADJUD ADMIN REGION 20 ZONING. PAGE 81 E1628
PLAN
LOC/G
PROVS
LAW

B61
ROCHE J.P.,COURTS AND RIGHTS: THE AMERICAN
JUDICIARY IN ACTION (2ND ED.). UK USA+45 USA-45
STRUCT TEC/DEV SANCTION PERS/REL RACE/REL ORD/FREE
...METH/CNCPT GOV/COMP METH/COMP T 13/20. PAGE 85
E1710
JURID
CT/SYS
NAT/G
PROVS

S61
RICHSTEIN A.R.,"LEGAL RULES IN NUCLEAR WEAPONS
EMPLOYMENTS." FUT WOR+45 LAW SOCIETY FORCES PLAN
WEAPON RIGID/FLEX...HEAL CONCPT TREND VAL/FREE 20.
PAGE 85 E1696
NUC/PWR
TEC/DEV
MORAL
ARMS/CONT

B62
CURRY J.E.,RACE TENSIONS AND THE POLICE. LAW MUNIC
NEIGH TEC/DEV RUMOR CONTROL COERCE GP/REL ATTIT
...SOC 20 NEGRO. PAGE 28 E0558
FORCES
RACE/REL
CROWD

B62
DIESING P.,REASON IN SOCIETY; FIVE TYPES OF
DECISIONS AND THEIR SOCIAL CONDITIONS. SOCIETY
STRUCT LABOR CREATE TEC/DEV BARGAIN ADJUD ROLE
...JURID BIBLIOG 20. PAGE 31 E0625
RATIONAL
METH/COMP
DECISION
CONCPT

B62
DUPRE J.S.,SCIENCE AND THE NATION: POLICY AND
POLITICS. USA+45 LAW ACADEM FORCES ADMIN CIVMIL/REL
GOV/REL EFFICIENCY PEACE...TREND 20 SCI/ADVSRY.
PAGE 34 E0665
R+D
INDUS
TEC/DEV
NUC/PWR

B62
SCHWARTZ L.E.,INTERNATIONAL ORGANIZATIONS AND SPACE
COOPERATION. VOL/ASSN CONSULT CREATE TEC/DEV
SANCTION...POLICY INT/LAW PHIL/SCI 20 UN. PAGE 89
E1787
INT/ORG
DIPLOM
R+D
SPACE

B62
STERN A.C.,AIR POLLUTION (2 VOLS.). LAW INDUS
PROB/SOLV TEC/DEV INSPECT RISK BIO/SOC HABITAT
...OBS/ENVIR TESTS SAMP 20 POLLUTION. PAGE 93 E1871
AIR
OP/RES
CONTROL
HEALTH

B62
UNECA LIBRARY,NEW ACQUISITIONS IN THE UNECA
LIBRARY. LAW NAT/G PLAN PROB/SOLV TEC/DEV ADMIN
REGION...GEOG SOC 20 UN. PAGE 98 E1956
BIBLIOG
AFR
ECO/UNDEV
INT/ORG

B62
WADSWORTH J.J.,THE PRICE OF PEACE. WOR+45 TEC/DEV
CONTROL NUC/PWR PEACE ATTIT TREATY 20. PAGE 104
E2089
DIPLOM
INT/ORG
ARMS/CONT
POLICY

S62
GANDOLFI A.,"REFLEXIONS SUR L'IMPOT DE CAPITATION
EN AFRIQUE NOIRE." GHANA SENEGAL LAW FINAN ACT/RES
TEC/DEV ECO/TAC WEALTH...MGT TREND 20. PAGE 42
E0830
AFR
CHOOSE

S62
SCHACHTER O.,"DAG HAMMARSKJOLD AND THE RELATION OF
LAW TO POLITICS." FUT WOR+45 INT/ORG CONSULT PLAN
TEC/DEV BAL/PWR DIPLOM LEGIT ATTIT PERCEPT ORD/FREE
...POLICY JURID CONCPT OBS TESTS STERTYP GEN/LAWS
20 HAMMARSK/D. PAGE 87 E1751
ACT/RES
ADJUD

B63
GEERTZ C.,OLD SOCIETIES AND NEW STATES: THE QUEST
FOR MODERNITY IN ASIA AND AFRICA. AFR ASIA LAW
CULTURE SECT EDU/PROP REV...GOV/COMP NAT/COMP 20.
PAGE 42 E0842
ECO/UNDEV
TEC/DEV
NAT/LISM
SOVEREIGN

B63
HAUSMAN W.H.,MANAGING ECONOMIC DEVELOPMENT IN
AFRICA. AFR USA+45 LAW FINAN WORKER TEC/DEV WEALTH
...ANTHOL 20. PAGE 51 E1012
ECO/UNDEV
PLAN
FOR/AID
MGT

B63
HIGGINS R.,THE DEVELOPMENT OF INTERNATIONAL LAW
THROUGH THE POLITICAL ORGANS OF THE UNITED NATIONS.
WOR+45 FORCES DIPLOM AGREE COERCE ATTIT SOVEREIGN
...BIBLIOG 20 UN TREATY. PAGE 52 E1041
INT/ORG
INT/LAW
TEC/DEV
JURID

B63
MCDOUGAL M.S.,LAW AND PUBLIC ORDER IN SPACE. FUT
USA+45 ACT/RES TEC/DEV ADJUD...POLICY INT/LAW JURID
20. PAGE 70 E1410
SPACE
ORD/FREE
DIPLOM
DECISION

B63
VAN SLYCK P.,PEACE: THE CONTROL OF NATIONAL POWER.
CUBA WOR+45 FINAN NAT/G FORCES PROB/SOLV TEC/DEV
BAL/PWR ADMIN CONTROL ORD/FREE...POLICY INT/LAW UN
COLD/WAR TREATY. PAGE 103 E2069
ARMS/CONT
PEACE
INT/ORG
DIPLOM

L63
LOEVINGER L.,"JURIMETRICS* THE METHODOLOGY OF LEGAL
INQUIRY." COMPUTER CREATE PLAN TEC/DEV AUTOMAT
CT/SYS EFFICIENCY...DECISION PHIL/SCI NEW/IDEA
QUANT PREDICT. PAGE 66 E1318
COMPUT/IR
JURID
GEN/METH
ADJUD

L63
MCDOUGAL M.S.,"THE ENJOYMENT AND ACQUISITION OF
RESOURCES IN OUTER SPACE." CHRIST-17C FUT WOR+45
WOR-45 LAW EXTR/IND INT/ORG ACT/RES CREATE TEC/DEV
ECO/TAC LEGIT COERCE HEALTH KNOWL ORD/FREE PWR
WEALTH...JURID HIST/WRIT VAL/FREE. PAGE 70 E1408
PLAN
TREND

S63
BOHN L.,"WHOSE NUCLEAR TEST: NON-PHYSICAL
ADJUD

INSPECTION AND TEST BAN." WOR+45 R+D INT/ORG VOL/ASSN ORD/FREE...GEN/LAWS GEN/METH COLD/WAR 20. PAGE 13 E0262
ARMS/CONT
TEC/DEV
NUC/PWR

B64
BLOUSTEIN E.J., NUCLEAR ENERGY, PUBLIC POLICY, AND THE LAW. USA+45 NAT/G ADJUD ADMIN GP/REL OWN PEACE ATTIT HEALTH...ANTHOL 20. PAGE 13 E0251
TEC/DEV
LAW
POLICY
NUC/PWR

B64
HAAR C.M., LAW AND LAND: ANGLO-AMERICAN PLANNING PRACTICE. UK USA+45 NAT/G TEC/DEV BUDGET CT/SYS INGP/REL EFFICIENCY OWN...JURID 20. PAGE 49 E0967
LAW
PLAN
MUNIC
NAT/COMP

B64
HEKHUIS D.J., INTERNATIONAL STABILITY: MILITARY, ECONOMIC AND POLITICAL DIMENSIONS. FUT WOR+45 LAW ECO/UNDEV INT/ORG NAT/G VOL/ASSN FORCES ACT/RES BAL/PWR PWR WEALTH...STAT UN 20. PAGE 51 E1024
TEC/DEV
DETER
REGION

B64
NASA, PROCEEDINGS OF CONFERENCE ON THE LAW OF SPACE AND OF SATELLITE COMMUNICATIONS: CHICAGO 1963. FUT WOR+45 DELIB/GP PROB/SOLV TEC/DEV CONFER ADJUD NUC/PWR...POLICY IDEA/COMP 20 NASA. PAGE 76 E1522
SPACE
COM/IND
LAW
DIPLOM

B64
OSSENBECK F.J., OPEN SPACE AND PEACE. CHINA/COM FUT USA+45 USSR LAW PROB/SOLV TEC/DEV EDU/PROP NEUTRAL PEACE...AUD/VIS ANTHOL 20. PAGE 79 E1583
SPACE
ORD/FREE
DIPLOM
CREATE

B64
SCHWARTZ M.D., CONFERENCE ON SPACE SCIENCE AND SPACE LAW. FUT COM/IND NAT/G FORCES ACT/RES PLAN BUDGET DIPLOM NUC/PWR WEAPON...POLICY ANTHOL 20. PAGE 89 E1788
SPACE
LAW
PEACE
TEC/DEV

B64
STRONG C.F., HISTORY OF MODERN POLITICAL CONSTITUTIONS. STRUCT INT/ORG NAT/G LEGIS TEC/DEV DIPLOM INT/TRADE CT/SYS EXEC...METH/COMP T 12/20 UN. PAGE 94 E1888
CONSTN
CONCPT

B64
TAUBENFELD H.J., SPACE AND SOCIETY. USA+45 LAW FORCES CREATE TEC/DEV ADJUD CONTROL COST PEACE ...PREDICT ANTHOL 20. PAGE 95 E1911
SPACE
SOCIETY
ADJUST
DIPLOM

B64
THANT U., TOWARD WORLD PEACE. DELIB/GP TEC/DEV EDU/PROP WAR SOVEREIGN...INT/LAW 20 UN MID/EAST. PAGE 96 E1915
DIPLOM
BIOG
PEACE
COERCE

L64
MAYO L.H., "LEGAL-POLICY DECISION PROCESS: ALTERNATIVE THINKING AND THE PREDICTIVE FUNCTION." PROB/SOLV EFFICIENCY RATIONAL. PAGE 70 E1395
DECISION
SIMUL
JURID
TEC/DEV

S64
TRISKA J.F., "SOVIET TREATY LAW: A QUANTITATIVE ANALYSIS." WOR+45 LAW ECO/UNDEV AGRI COM/IND INDUS CREATE TEC/DEV DIPLOM ATTIT PWR WEALTH...JURID SAMP TIME/SEQ TREND CHARTS VAL/FREE 20 TREATY. PAGE 97 E1942
COM
ECO/TAC
INT/LAW
USSR

B65
CALIFORNIA LEGISLATURE, COMMITTEE ON ELECTIONS AND REAPPORTIONMENT, FINAL REPORT. USA+45 LAW COMPUTER TEC/DEV CHOOSE JURID. PAGE 19 E0366
DELIB/GP
APPORT
LEGIS
ADJUD

B65
UNESCO, HANDBOOK OF INTERNATIONAL EXCHANGES. COM/IND R+D ACADEM PROF/ORG VOL/ASSN CREATE TEC/DEV EDU/PROP AGREE 20 TREATY. PAGE 98 E1963
INDEX
INT/ORG
DIPLOM
PRESS

B65
WEIL G.L., A HANDBOOK ON THE EUROPEAN ECONOMIC COMMUNITY. BELGIUM EUR+WWI FRANCE GERMANY/W ITALY CONSTN ECO/DEV CREATE PARTIC GP/REL...DECISION MGT CHARTS 20 EEC. PAGE 105 E2107
INT/TRADE
INT/ORG
TEC/DEV
INT/LAW

S65
HIBBS A.R., "SPACE TECHNOLOGY* THE THREAT AND THE PROMISE." FUT VOL/ASSN TEC/DEV NUC/PWR COST EFFICIENCY UTIL UN TREATY. PAGE 52 E1038
SPACE
ARMS/CONT
PREDICT

S65
KHOURI F.J., "THE JORDON RIVER CONTROVERSY." LAW
ISLAM

SOCIETY ECO/UNDEV AGRI FINAN INDUS SECT FORCES ACT/RES PLAN TEC/DEV ECO/TAC EDU/PROP COERCE ATTIT DRIVE PERCEPT RIGID/FLEX ALL/VALS...GEOG SOC MYTH WORK. PAGE 61 E1212
INT/ORG
ISRAEL
JORDAN

B66
BEER U., FRUCHTBARKEITSREGELUNG ALS KONSEQUENZ VERANTWORTLICHER ELTERNSCHAFT. ASIA GERMANY/W INDIA LAW ECO/DEV ECO/UNDEV TEC/DEV ECO/TAC BIO/SOC SEX CATHISM...METH/COMP 20 CHINJAP BIRTH/CON. PAGE 9 E0178
CONTROL
GEOG
FAM
SECT

B66
DIZARD W.P., TELEVISION* A WORLD VIEW. WOR+45 ECO/UNDEV TEC/DEV LICENSE LITERACY...STAT OBS INT QU TREND AUD/VIS BIBLIOG. PAGE 32 E0632
COM/IND
ACT/RES
EDU/PROP
CREATE

B66
FRIEDMANN W.G., INTERNATIONAL FINANCIAL AID. USA+45 ECO/DEV ECO/UNDEV NAT/G VOL/ASSN EX/STRUC PLAN RENT GIVE BAL/PAY PWR...GEOG INT/LAW STAT TREND UN EEC COMECON. PAGE 41 E0806
INT/ORG
FOR/AID
TEC/DEV
ECO/TAC

B66
HOPKINS J.F.K., ARABIC PERIODICAL LITERATURE, 1961. ISLAM LAW CULTURE SECT...GEOG HEAL PHIL/SCI PSY SOC 20. PAGE 55 E1096
BIBLIOG/A
NAT/LISM
TEC/DEV
INDUS

B66
OSTERMANN R., A REPORT IN DEPTH ON CRIME IN AMERICA. FUT USA+45 MUNIC PUB/INST TEC/DEV MURDER EFFICIENCY ATTIT BIO/SOC...PSY 20. PAGE 79 E1584
CRIME
FORCES
CONTROL
LAW

B66
UNITED NATIONS, INTERNATIONAL SPACE BIBLIOGRAPHY. FUT INT/ORG TEC/DEV DIPLOM ARMS/CONT NUC/PWR ...JURID SOC UN. PAGE 98 E1969
BIBLIOG
SPACE
PEACE
R+D

B66
US DEPARTMENT OF STATE, RESEARCH ON THE USSR AND EASTERN EUROPE (EXTERNAL RESEARCH LIST NO 1-25). USSR LAW CULTURE SOCIETY NAT/G TEC/DEV EDU/PROP REGION...GEOG LING. PAGE 100 E1997
BIBLIOG/A
EUR+WWI
COM
MARXISM

S66
BROWNLIE I., "NUCLEAR PROLIFERATION* SOME PROBLEMS OF CONTROL." USA+45 USSR ECO/UNDEV INT/ORG FORCES TEC/DEV REGION CONSEN...RECORD TREATY. PAGE 16 E0318
NUC/PWR
ARMS/CONT
VOL/ASSN
ORD/FREE

B67
CHAPIN F.S. JR., SELECTED REFERENCES ON URBAN PLANNING METHODS AND TECHNIQUES. USA+45 LAW ECO/DEV LOC/G NAT/G SCHOOL CONSULT CREATE PROB/SOLV TEC/DEV SOC/WK. PAGE 21 E0420
BIBLIOG
NEIGH
MUNIC
PLAN

B67
MCBRIDE J.H., THE TEST BAN TREATY: MILITARY, TECHNOLOGICAL, AND POLITICAL IMPLICATIONS. USA+45 USSR DELIB/GP FORCES LEGIS TEC/DEV BAL/PWR TREATY. PAGE 70 E1399
ARMS/CONT
DIPLOM
NUC/PWR

B67
MCDOUGAL M.S., THE INTERPRETATION OF AGREEMENTS AND WORLD PUBLIC ORDER: PRINCIPLES OF CONTENT AND PROCEDURE. WOR+45 CONSTN PROB/SOLV TEC/DEV ...CON/ANAL TREATY. PAGE 71 E1412
INT/LAW
STRUCT
ECO/UNDEV
DIPLOM

B67
PADELFORD N.J., THE DYNAMICS OF INTERNATIONAL POLITICS (2ND ED.). WOR+45 LAW INT/ORG FORCES TEC/DEV REGION NAT/LISM PEACE ATTIT PWR ALL/IDEOS UN COLD/WAR NATO TREATY. PAGE 79 E1589
DIPLOM
NAT/G
POLICY
DECISION

B67
UNITED NATIONS, UNITED NATIONS PUBLICATIONS: 1945-1966. WOR+45 COM/IND DIST/IND FINAN TEC/DEV ADMIN...POLICY INT/LAW MGT CHARTS 20 UN UNESCO. PAGE 98 E1970
BIBLIOG/A
INT/ORG
DIPLOM
WRITING

B67
UNIVERSAL REFERENCE SYSTEM, PUBLIC POLICY AND THE MANAGEMENT OF SCIENCE (VOLUME IX). FUT SPACE WOR+45 LAW NAT/G TEC/DEV CONTROL NUC/PWR GOV/REL ...COMPUT/IR GEN/METH. PAGE 99 E1975
BIBLIOG/A
POLICY
MGT
PHIL/SCI

L67
BARRON J.A., "ACCESS TO THE PRESS." USA+45 TEC/DEV PRESS TV ADJUD AUD/VIS. PAGE 8 E0152
ORD/FREE
COM/IND
EDU/PROP
LAW

LAMBERT J.D.,"CORPORATE POLITICAL SPENDING AND   USA+45
CAMPAIGN FINANCE." LAW CONSTN FINAN LABOR LG/CO   POL/PAR
LOC/G NAT/G VOL/ASSN TEC/DEV ADJUD ADMIN PARTIC.   CHOOSE
PAGE 62 E1247   COST
                                                   L67

BLUMSTEIN A.,"POLICE TECHNOLOGY." USA+45 DELIB/GP   TEC/DEV
COMPUTER EDU/PROP CRIME COMPUT/IR. PAGE 13 E0253   FORCES
                                                       CRIMLGY
                                                       ADJUD
                                                   S67

DOYLE S.E.,"COMMUNICATION SATELLITES* INTERNAL   TEC/DEV
ORGANIZATION FOR DEVELOPMENT AND CONTROL." USA+45   SPACE
R+D ACT/RES DIPLOM NAT/LISM...POLICY INT/LAW   COM/IND
PREDICT UN. PAGE 33 E0647   INT/ORG
                                                   S67

EYRAUD M.,"LA FRANCE FACE A UN EVENTUEL TRAITE DE   NUC/PWR
NON DISSEMINATION DES ARMES NUCLEAIRES." FRANCE   ARMS/CONT
USA+45 EXTR/IND INDUS R+D INT/ORG ACT/RES TEC/DEV   POLICY
AGREE PRODUC ATTIT 20 TREATY AEC EURATOM. PAGE 36
E0708
                                                   S67

GIBSON G.H.,"LABOR PIRACY ON THE BRANDYWINE."   ECO/TAC
USA-45 INDUS R+D VOL/ASSN CAP/ISM ADJUD DRIVE...PSY   CREATE
19. PAGE 43 E0859   TEC/DEV
                                                       WORKER
                                                   S67

LAY S.H.,"EXCLUSIVE GOVERNMENTAL LIABILITY FOR   NAT/G
SPACE ACCIDENTS." USA+45 LAW FINAN SERV/IND TEC/DEV   SUPEGO
ADJUD. PAGE 64 E1272   SPACE
                                                       PROB/SOLV
                                                   B88

BENTHAM J.,DEFENCE OF USURY (1787). UK LAW NAT/G   TAX
TEC/DEV ECO/TAC CONTROL ATTIT...CONCPT IDEA/COMP 18   FINAN
SMITH/ADAM. PAGE 10 E0197   ECO/DEV
                                                       POLICY

TECHNIC....TECHNOCRATIC
                                                   B59

COMM. STUDY ORGAN. PEACE,ORGANIZING PEACE IN THE   INT/ORG
NUCLEAR AGE. FUT CONSULT DELIB/GP DOMIN ADJUD   ACT/RES
ROUTINE COERCE ORD/FREE...TECHNIC INT/LAW JURID   NUC/PWR
NEW/IDEA UN COLD/WAR 20. PAGE 24 E0483
                                                   B59

MAYDA J.,ATOMIC ENERGY AND LAW. ECO/UNDEV FINAN   NUC/PWR
TEC/DEV FOR/AID EFFICIENCY PRODUC WEALTH...POLICY   L/A+17C
TECHNIC 20. PAGE 70 E1391   LAW
                                                       ADMIN
                                                   B60

WOETZEL R.K.,THE INTERNATIONAL CONTROL OF AIRSPACE   INT/ORG
AND OUTERSPACE. FUT WOR+45 AIR CONSTN STRUCT   JURID
CONSULT PLAN TEC/DEV ADJUD RIGID/FLEX KNOWL   SPACE
ORD/FREE PWR...TECHNIC GEOG MGT NEW/IDEA TREND   INT/LAW
COMPUT/IR VAL/FREE 20 TREATY. PAGE 107 E2137
                                                   B61

KAPLAN M.A.,THE POLITICAL FOUNDATIONS OF   INT/ORG
INTERNATIONAL LAW. WOR+45 WOR-45 CULTURE SOCIETY   LAW
ECO/DEV DIPLOM PERCEPT...TECHNIC METH/CNCPT.
PAGE 59 E1184

TECHNIQUES....SEE TEC/DEV, METHODOLOGICAL INDEXES,
     PP. XIII-XIV

TECHNOCRACY....SEE TECHRACY, TECHNIC

TECHNOLOGY....SEE COMPUTER, TECHNIC, TEC/DEV

TECHRACY....SOCIO-POLITICAL ORDER DOMINATED BY TECHNICIANS
                                                   S44

GRIFFITH E.S.,"THE CHANGING PATTERN OF PUBLIC   LAW
POLICY FORMATION." MOD/EUR WOR+45 FINAN CHIEF   POLICY
CONFER ADMIN LEAD CONSERVE SOCISM TECHRACY...SOC   TEC/DEV
CHARTS CONGRESS. PAGE 47 E0938
                                                   B66

JACOBSON H.K.,DIPLOMATS, SCIENTISTS, AND   DIPLOM
POLITICIANS* THE UNITED STATES AND THE NUCLEAR TEST   ARMS/CONT
BAN NEGOTIATIONS. USA+45 USSR ACT/RES PLAN CONFER   TECHRACY
DETER NUC/PWR CONSEN ORD/FREE...INT TREATY. PAGE 57   INT/ORG
E1146

TEHERAN....TEHERAN CONFERENCE

TELLADO A. E1913

TEMPERANCE....TEMPERANCE MOVEMENTS

TENBROCK J. E1914

TENNESSEE VALLEY AUTHORITY....SEE TVA

TENNESSEE....TENNESSEE
                                                   B66

GREENE L.E.,GOVERNMENT IN TENNESSEE (2ND ED.).   PROVS
USA+45 DIST/IND INDUS POL/PAR EX/STRUC LEGIS PLAN   LOC/G
BUDGET GIVE CT/SYS...MGT T 20 TENNESSEE. PAGE 46   CONSTN
E0909   ADMIN
                                                   B67

GRAHAM H.D.,CRISIS IN PRINT: DESEGREGATION AND THE   PRESS
PRESS IN TENNESSEE. LAW SOCIETY MUNIC POL/PAR   PROVS
EDU/PROP LEAD REPRESENT DISCRIM ATTIT...IDEA/COMP   POLICY
BIBLIOG/A SOC/INTEG 20 TENNESSEE SUPREME/CT   RACE/REL
SOUTH/US. PAGE 45 E0896

TENNEY F. E0352

TERRELL/G....GLENN TERRELL

TERRY V. OHIO....SEE TERRY

TERRY....TERRY V. OHIO

TESTS....THEORY AND USES OF TESTS AND SCALES; SEE ALSO
     TESTS AND SCALES INDEX, P. XIV
                                                   B62

STERN A.C.,AIR POLLUTION (2 VOLS.). LAW INDUS   AIR
PROB/SOLV TEC/DEV INSPECT RISK BIO/SOC HABITAT   OP/RES
...OBS/ENVIR TESTS SAMP 20 POLLUTION. PAGE 93 E1871   CONTROL
                                                       HEALTH
                                                   S62

SCHACHTER O.,"DAG HAMMARSKJOLD AND THE RELATION OF   ACT/RES
LAW TO POLITICS." FUT WOR+45 INT/ORG CONSULT PLAN   ADJUD
TEC/DEV BAL/PWR DIPLOM LEGIT ATTIT PERCEPT ORD/FREE
...POLICY JURID CONCPT OBS TESTS STERTYP GEN/LAWS
20 HAMMARSK/D. PAGE 87 E1751

TEXAS....TEXAS
                                                   S67

SCOTT A.,"TWENTY-FIVE YEARS OF OPINION ON   ATTIT
INTEGRATION IN TEXAS." USA+45 USA-45 DISCRIM   ADJUST
...KNO/TEST TREND CHARTS 20 TEXAS. PAGE 89 E1794   RACE/REL
                                                       LAW

THAILAND....THAILAND; SEE ALSO S/ASIA
                                                   B50

EMBREE J.F.,BIBLIOGRAPHY OF THE PEOPLES AND   BIBLIOG/A
CULTURES OF MAINLAND SOUTHEAST ASIA. CAMBODIA LAOS   CULTURE
THAILAND VIETNAM LAW...GEOG HUM SOC MYTH LING   S/ASIA
CHARTS WORSHIP 20. PAGE 35 E0686

THANT U. E1915

THERAPY....SEE SPECIFICS, SUCH AS PROJ/TEST, DEEP/INT,
     SOC/EXP; ALSO SEE DIFFERENT VALUES (E.G., LOVE) AND
     TOPICAL TERMS (E.G., PRESS)

THING/STOR....ARTIFACTS AND MATERIAL EVIDENCE

THIRD/WRLD....THIRD WORLD - NONALIGNED NATIONS

THOM J.M. E1916

THOMAS A.J. E1917

THOMAS A.V. E1917

THOMAS/FA....F.A. THOMAS

THOMAS/N....NORMAN THOMAS

THOMAS/TK....TREVOR K. THOMAS
                                                   B63

US SENATE COMM ON JUDICIARY,PACIFICA FOUNDATION.   DELIB/GP
USA+45 LAW COM/IND 20 ODEGARD/P BINNS/JJ SCHINDLR/P   EDU/PROP
HEALEY/D THOMAS/TK. PAGE 102 E2051   ORD/FREE
                                                       ATTIT

THOMPSON D. E1918

THOMPSON E.B. E2142

THOMPSON J.M. E1919

THOMPSON J.W. E1920

THOMPSON K.W. E1921,E1922

THOREAU H.D. E1923

THOREAU/H....HENRY THOREAU

THORNTN/WT....WILLIAM T. THORNTON

THUCYDIDES....THUCYDIDES

THUILLIER G. E0407

THURSTON/L....LOUIS LEON THURSTONE

TIBET....TIBET; SEE ALSO ASIA, CHINA

TIEDT S.W. E1924

TILLICH/P....PAUL TILLICH

TIMASHEFF N.S. E1925,E1926

TIME (AS CONCEPT)....SEE CONCPT

TIME....TIMING, TIME FACTOR; SEE ALSO ANALYSIS OF TEMPORAL
     SEQUENCES INDEX, P. XIV

BELL J.,THE JOHNSON TREATMENT: HOW LYNDON JOHNSON   INGP/REL
TOOK OVER THE PRESIDENCY AND MADE IT HIS OWN.   TOP/EX
USA+45 DELIB/GP DIPLOM ADJUD MURDER CHOOSE PERSON   CONTROL
PWR...POLICY OBS INT TIME 20 JOHNSON/LB KENNEDY/JF   NAT/G
PRESIDENT CONGRESS. PAGE 10 E0183   **B65**

FLEMING R.W.,THE LABOR ARBITRATION PROCESS. USA+45   GP/REL
LAW BARGAIN ADJUD ROUTINE SANCTION COST...PREDICT   LABOR
CHARTS TIME 20. PAGE 38 E0763   CONSULT
                                                     DELIB/GP
                                                     B65

DETTER I.,"THE PROBLEM OF UNEQUAL TREATIES." CONSTN SOVEREIGN
NAT/G LEGIS COLONIAL COERCE PWR...GEOG UN TIME   DOMIN
TREATY. PAGE 31 E0610   INT/LAW
                                                     ECO/UNDEV
                                                     S66

TIME/SEQ....CHRONOLOGY AND GENETIC SERIES

DE TOCQUEVILLE A.,DEMOCRACY IN AMERICA (VOLUME   USA-45
ONE). LAW SOCIETY STRUCT NAT/G POL/PAR PROVS FORCES TREND
LEGIS TOP/EX DIPLOM LEGIT WAR PEACE ATTIT SOVEREIGN **B00**
...SELF/OBS TIME/SEQ CONGRESS 19. PAGE 30 E0594

MAINE H.S.,INTERNATIONAL LAW. MOD/EUR UNIV SOCIETY   INT/ORG
STRUCT ACT/RES EXEC WAR ATTIT PERSON ALL/VALS   LAW
...POLICY JURID CONCPT OBS TIME/SEQ TOT/POP.   PEACE
PAGE 68 E1349   INT/LAW
                                                     B00

HOLLAND T.E.,LETTERS UPON WAR AND NEUTRALITY.   LAW
WOR-45 NAT/G FORCES JUDGE ECO/TAC LEGIT CT/SYS   INT/LAW
NEUTRAL ROUTINE COERCE...JURID TIME/SEQ 20. PAGE 55 INT/ORG
E1085   WAR
                                                     B09

REINSCH P.,PUBLIC INTERNATIONAL UNION. WOR-45 LAW   FUT
LABOR INT/TRADE LEGIT PERSON ALL/VALS...SOCIALIST   INT/ORG
CONCPT TIME/SEQ TREND GEN/LAWS 19/20. PAGE 84 E1683 DIPLOM
                                                     B11

VECCHIO G.D.,THE FORMAL BASES OF LAW (TRANS. BY J.   LAW
LISLE). DOMIN LEGIT CONTROL COERCE UTIL MORAL PWR   JURID
...CONCPT TIME/SEQ 17/20 COMMON/LAW NATURL/LAW.   GEN/LAWS
PAGE 103 E2074   IDEA/COMP
                                                     B14

DICKINSON E.,THE EQUALITY OF STATES IN   LAW
INTERNATIONAL LAW. WOR-45 INT/ORG NAT/G DIPLOM   CONCPT
EDU/PROP LEGIT PEACE ATTIT ALL/VALS...JURID   SOVEREIGN
TIME/SEQ LEAGUE/NAT. PAGE 31 E0622   **B20**

MEYER H.H.B.,LIST OF REFERENCES ON THE TREATY-   BIBLIOG
MAKING POWER. USA-45 CONTROL PWR...INT/LAW TIME/SEQ DIPLOM
18/20 TREATY. PAGE 72 E1448   CONSTN
                                                     B20

OPPENHEIM L.,THE FUTURE OF INTERNATIONAL LAW.   INT/ORG
EUR+WWI MOD/EUR LAW LEGIS JUDGE LEGIT ORD/FREE   CT/SYS
...JURID TIME/SEQ GEN/LAWS 20. PAGE 79 E1578   INT/LAW
                                                     B21

BRYCE J.,INTERNATIONAL RELATIONS. CHRIST-17C   INT/ORG
EUR+WWI MOD/EUR CULTURE INTELL NAT/G DELIB/GP   POLICY
                                                     B22

CREATE BAL/PWR DIPLOM ATTIT DRIVE RIGID/FLEX
ALL/VALS...PLURIST JURID CONCPT TIME/SEQ GEN/LAWS
TOT/POP. PAGE 16 E0323

HOLMES O.W. JR.,THE COMMON LAW. FUT WOR-45 CULTURE   ADJUD
SOCIETY CREATE LEGIT ROUTINE ATTIT ALL/VALS...JURID CON/ANAL
METH/CNCPT TIME/SEQ GEN/LAWS TOT/POP VAL/FREE.   **B23**
PAGE 55 E1087

HUDSON M.,"THE PERMANENT COURT OF INTERNATIONAL   INT/ORG
JUSTICE AND THE QUESTION OF AMERICAN   ADJUD
PARTICIPATION." WOR-45 LEGIT CT/SYS ORD/FREE   DIPLOM
...JURID CONCPT TIME/SEQ GEN/LAWS VAL/FREE 20 ICJ.   INT/LAW
PAGE 56 E1108   **L25**

LAUTERPACHT H.,PRIVATE LAW SOURCES AND ANALOGIES OF INT/ORG
INTERNATIONAL LAW. WOR-45 NAT/G DELIB/GP LEGIT   ADJUD
COERCE ATTIT ORD/FREE PWR SOVEREIGN...JURID CONCPT   PEACE
HIST/WRIT TIME/SEQ GEN/METH LEAGUE/NAT 20. PAGE 63   INT/LAW
E1264   **B27**

CORBETT P.E.,CANADA AND WORLD POLITICS. LAW CULTURE NAT/G
SOCIETY STRUCT MARKET INT/ORG FORCES ACT/RES PLAN   CANADA
ECO/TAC LEGIT ORD/FREE PWR RESPECT...SOC CONCPT   **B28**
TIME/SEQ TREND CMN/WLTH 20 LEAGUE/NAT. PAGE 26
E0504

MAIR L.P.,THE PROTECTION OF MINORITIES. EUR+WWI   LAW
WOR-45 CONSTN INT/ORG NAT/G LEGIT CT/SYS GP/REL   SOVEREIGN
RACE/REL DISCRIM ORD/FREE RESPECT...JURID CONCPT   **B28**
TIME/SEQ 20. PAGE 68 E1352

COLUMBIA UNIVERSITY,A BIBLIOGRAPHY OF THE FACULTY   BIBLIOG
OF POLITICAL SCIENCE OF COLUMBIA UNIVERSITY,   ACADEM
1880-1930. USA-45 LAW NAT/G LEGIS DIPLOM LEAD WAR   PHIL/SCI
GOV/REL ATTIT...TIME/SEQ 19/20. PAGE 24 E0478   **B31**

FLEMMING D.,THE UNITED STATES AND THE LEAGUE OF   INT/ORG
NATIONS, 1918-1920. FUT USA-45 NAT/G LEGIS TOP/EX   EDU/PROP
DEBATE CHOOSE PEACE ATTIT SOVEREIGN...TIME/SEQ   **B32**
CON/ANAL CONGRESS LEAGUE/NAT 20 TREATY. PAGE 39
E0764

LUNT D.C.,THE ROAD TO THE LAW. UK USA-45 LEGIS   ADJUD
EDU/PROP OWN ORD/FREE...DECISION TIME/SEQ NAT/COMP   LAW
16/20 AUSTRAL ENGLSH/LAW COMMON/LAW. PAGE 67 E1333   JURID
                                                     CT/SYS
                                                     B32

MASTERS R.D.,INTERNATIONAL LAW IN INTERNATIONAL   INT/ORG
COURTS. BELGIUM EUR+WWI FRANCE GERMANY MOD/EUR   LAW
SWITZERLND WOR-45 SOCIETY STRATA STRUCT LEGIT EXEC   INT/LAW
ALL/VALS...JURID HIST/WRIT TIME/SEQ TREND GEN/LAWS   **B32**
20. PAGE 69 E1383

MORLEY F.,THE SOCIETY OF NATIONS. EUR+WWI UNIV   INT/ORG
WOR-45 LAW CONSTN ACT/RES PLAN EDU/PROP LEGIT   CONCPT
ROUTINE...POLICY TIME/SEQ LEAGUE/NAT TOT/POP 20.   **B32**
PAGE 75 E1496

DANGERFIELD R.,IN DEFENSE OF THE SENATE. USA-45   LEGIS
CONSTN NAT/G EX/STRUC TOP/EX ATTIT KNOWL   DELIB/GP
...METH/CNCPT STAT TIME/SEQ TREND CON/ANAL CHARTS   DIPLOM
CONGRESS 20 TREATY. PAGE 28 E0565   **B33**

LAUTERPACHT H.,THE FUNCTION OF LAW IN THE   INT/ORG
INTERNATIONAL COMMUNITY. WOR-45 NAT/G FORCES CREATE LAW
DOMIN LEGIT COERCE WAR PEACE ATTIT ORD/FREE PWR   INT/LAW
SOVEREIGN...JURID CONCPT METH/CNCPT TIME/SEQ   **B33**
GEN/LAWS GEN/METH LEAGUE/NAT TOT/POP VAL/FREE 20.
PAGE 63 E1265

HUDSON M.,BY PACIFIC MEANS. WOR-45 EDU/PROP   INT/ORG
ORD/FREE...CONCPT TIME/SEQ GEN/LAWS LEAGUE/NAT   CT/SYS
TOT/POP 20 TREATY. PAGE 56 E1110   PEACE
                                                     B35

RUTHERFORD M.L.,THE INFLUENCE OF THE AMERICAN BAR   ATTIT
ASSOCIATION ON PUBLIC OPINION AND LEGISLATION.   ADJUD
USA+45 LAW CONSTN LABOR LEGIS DOMIN EDU/PROP LEGIT   PROF/ORG
CT/SYS ROUTINE...TIME/SEQ 19/20 ABA. PAGE 87 E1739   JURID
                                                     B37

LEAGUE OF NATIONS-SECRETARIAT.,THE AIMS, METHODS   ADJUD
                                                     B38

AND ACTIVITY OF THE LEAGUE OF NATIONS. WOR+45   STRUCT
DIPLOM EDU/PROP LEGIT RIGID/FLEX ALL/VALS
...TIME/SEQ LEAGUE/NAT VAL/FREE 19/20. PAGE 64
E1273

  B39
BALDWIN L.D.,WHISKEY REBELS; THE STORY OF A   REV
FRONTIER UPRISING. USA-45 LAW ADJUD LEAD COERCE PWR   POL/PAR
...BIBLIOG/A 18 PENNSYLVAN FEDERALIST. PAGE 8 E0145   TAX
  TIME/SEQ

  B39
WILSON G.G.,HANDBOOK OF INTERNATIONAL LAW. FUT UNIV   INT/ORG
USA-45 WOR-45 SOCIETY LEGIT ATTIT DISPL DRIVE   LAW
ALL/VALS...INT/LAW TIME/SEQ TREND. PAGE 106 E2128   CONCPT
  WAR

  B40
CARR E.H.,THE TWENTY YEARS' CRISIS 1919-1939. FUT   INT/ORG
WOR-45 BAL/PWR ECO/TAC LEGIT TOTALISM ATTIT   DIPLOM
ALL/VALS...POLICY JURID CONCPT TIME/SEQ TREND   PEACE
GEN/LAWS TOT/POP 20. PAGE 20 E0393

  B40
MCILWAIN C.H.,CONSTITUTIONALISM, ANCIENT AND   CONSTN
MODERN. CHRIST-17C MOD/EUR NAT/G CHIEF PROB/SOLV   GEN/LAWS
INSPECT AUTHORIT ORD/FREE PWR...TIME/SEQ ROMAN/REP.   LAW
PAGE 71 E1418

  S40
FLORIN J.,"BOLSHEVIST AND NATIONAL SOCIALIST   LAW
DOCTRINES OF INTERNATIONAL LAW." EUR+WWI GERMANY   ATTIT
USSR R+D INT/ORG NAT/G DIPLOM DOMIN EDU/PROP SOCISM   TOTALISM
...CONCPT TIME/SEQ 20. PAGE 39 E0768   INT/LAW

  B41
MCCLURE W.,INTERNATIONAL EXECUTIVE AGREEMENTS.   TOP/EX
USA-45 WOR-45 INT/ORG NAT/G DELIB/GP ADJUD ROUTINE   DIPLOM
ORD/FREE PWR...TIME/SEQ TREND CON/ANAL. PAGE 70
E1401

  S41
WRIGHT Q.,"FUNDAMENTAL PROBLEMS OF INTERNATIONAL   INT/ORG
ORGANIZATION." UNIV WOR-45 STRUCT FORCES ACT/RES   ATTIT
CREATE DOMIN EDU/PROP LEGIT REGION NAT/LISM   PEACE
ORD/FREE PWR RESPECT SOVEREIGN...JURID SOC CONCPT
METH/CNCPT TIME/SEQ 20. PAGE 107 E2152

  B43
SERENI A.P.,THE ITALIAN CONCEPTION OF INTERNATIONAL LAW
LAW. EUR+WWI MOD/EUR INT/ORG NAT/G DOMIN COERCE   TIME/SEQ
ORD/FREE FASCISM...OBS/ENVIR TREND 20. PAGE 90   INT/LAW
E1804   ITALY

  B44
HUDSON M.,INTERNATIONAL TRIBUNALS PAST AND FUTURE.   INT/ORG
FUT WOR-45 LAW EDU/PROP ADJUD ORD/FREE...CONCPT   STRUCT
TIME/SEQ TREND GEN/LAWS TOT/POP VAL/FREE 18/20.   INT/LAW
PAGE 56 E1111

  B45
CONOVER H.F.,THE NAZI STATE: WAR CRIMES AND WAR   BIBLIOG
CRIMINALS. GERMANY CULTURE NAT/G SECT FORCES DIPLOM   WAR
INT/TRADE EDU/PROP...INT/LAW BIOG HIST/WRIT   CRIME
TIME/SEQ 20. PAGE 25 E0495

  B45
REVES E.,THE ANATOMY OF PEACE. WOR-45 LAW CULTURE   ACT/RES
NAT/G PLAN TEC/DEV EDU/PROP WAR NAT/LISM ATTIT   CONCPT
ALL/VALS SOVEREIGN...POLICY HUM TIME/SEQ 20.   NUC/PWR
PAGE 84 E1688   PEACE

  B47
HILL M.,IMMUNITIES AND PRIVILEGES OF INTERNATIONAL   INT/ORG
OFFICIALS. CANADA EUR+WWI NETHERLAND SWITZERLND LAW   ADMIN
LEGIS DIPLOM LEGIT RESPECT...TIME/SEQ LEAGUE/NAT UN
VAL/FREE 20. PAGE 52 E1046

  B47
MCILWAIN C.H.,CONSTITUTIONALISM: ANCIENT AND   CONSTN
MODERN. USA+45 ROMAN/EMP LAW CHIEF LEGIS CT/SYS   NAT/G
GP/REL ORD/FREE SOVEREIGN...POLICY TIME/SEQ   PARL/PROC
ROMAN/REP EUROPE. PAGE 71 E1419   GOV/COMP

  B47
TOWLE L.W.,INTERNATIONAL TRADE AND COMMERCIAL   MARKET
POLICY. WOR+45 LAW ECO/DEV FINAN INDUS NAT/G   INT/ORG
ECO/TAC WEALTH...TIME/SEQ ILO 20. PAGE 97 E1937   INT/TRADE

  B48
JESSUP P.C.,A MODERN LAW OF NATIONS. FUT WOR+45   INT/ORG
WOR-45 SOCIETY NAT/G DELIB/GP LEGIS BAL/PWR   ADJUD
EDU/PROP LEGIT PWR...INT/LAW JURID TIME/SEQ
LEAGUE/NAT 20. PAGE 58 E1166

  L49
COMM. STUDY ORGAN. PEACE,"A TEN YEAR RECORD,   INT/ORG
1939-1949." FUT WOR+45 LAW R+D CONSULT DELIB/GP   CONSTN
CREATE LEGIT ROUTINE ORD/FREE...TIME/SEQ UN 20.   PEACE
PAGE 24 E0480

  B50
BERMAN H.J.,JUSTICE IN RUSSIA; AN INTERPRETATION OF JURID
SOVIET LAW. USSR LAW STRUCT LABOR FORCES AGREE   ADJUD
GP/REL ORD/FREE SOCISM...TIME/SEQ 20. PAGE 11 E0207 MARXISM
  COERCE

  B50
JIMENEZ E.,VOTING AND HANDLING OF DISPUTES IN THE   DELIB/GP
SECURITY COUNCIL. WOR+45 CONSTN INT/ORG DIPLOM   ROUTINE
LEGIT DETER CHOOSE MORAL ORD/FREE PWR...JURID
TIME/SEQ COLD/WAR UN 20. PAGE 59 E1168

  L51
LISSITZYN O.J.,"THE INTERNATIONAL COURT OF   ADJUD
JUSTICE." WOR+45 INT/ORG LEGIT ORD/FREE...CONCPT   JURID
TIME/SEQ TREND GEN/LAWS VAL/FREE 20 ICJ. PAGE 65   INT/LAW
E1304

  B52
JACKSON E.,MEETING OF THE MINDS: A WAY TO PEACE   LABOR
THROUGH MEDIATION. WOR+45 INDUS INT/ORG NAT/G   JUDGE
DELIB/GP DIPLOM EDU/PROP LEGIT ORD/FREE...NEW/IDEA
SELF/OBS TIME/SEQ CHARTS GEN/LAWS TOT/POP 20 UN
TREATY. PAGE 57 E1139

  B52
VANDENBOSCH A.,THE UN: BACKGROUND, ORGANIZATION,   DELIB/GP
FUNCTIONS, ACTIVITIES. WOR+45 LAW CONSTN STRUCT   TIME/SEQ
INT/ORG CONSULT BAL/PWR EDU/PROP EXEC ALL/VALS   PEACE
...POLICY CONCPT UN 20. PAGE 103 E2071

  B54
MANGONE G.,A SHORT HISTORY OF INTERNATIONAL   INT/ORG
ORGANIZATION. MOD/EUR USA+45 USA-45 WOR+45 WOR-45   INT/LAW
LAW LEGIS CREATE LEGIT ROUTINE RIGID/FLEX PWR
...JURID CONCPT OBS TIME/SEQ STERTYP GEN/LAWS UN
TOT/POP VAL/FREE 18/20. PAGE 68 E1359

  B54
NUSSBAUM D.,A CONCISE HISTORY OF THE LAW OF   INT/ORG
NATIONS. ASIA CHRIST-17C EUR+WWI ISLAM MEDIT-7   LAW
MOD/EUR S/ASIA UNIV WOR+45 WOR-45 SOCIETY STRUCT   PEACE
EXEC ATTIT ALL/VALS...CONCPT HIST/WRIT TIME/SEQ.   INT/LAW
PAGE 78 E1560

  B55
BERNSTEIN M.H.,REGULATING BUSINESS BY INDEPENDENT   DELIB/GP
COMMISSION. USA+45 USA-45 LG/CO CHIEF LEGIS   CONTROL
PROB/SOLV ADJUD SANCTION GP/REL ATTIT...TIME/SEQ   CONSULT
19/20 MONOPOLY PRESIDENT CONGRESS. PAGE 11 E0214

  B55
CHOWDHURI R.N.,INTERNATIONAL MANDATES AND   DELIB/GP
TRUSTEESHIP SYSTEMS. WOR+45 STRUCT ECO/UNDEV   PLAN
INT/ORG LEGIS DOMIN EDU/PROP LEGIT ADJUD EXEC PWR   SOVEREIGN
...CONCPT TIME/SEQ UN 20. PAGE 22 E0434

  B55
KHADDURI M.,WAR AND PEACE IN THE LAW OF ISLAM.   ISLAM
CONSTN CULTURE SOCIETY STRATA NAT/G PROVS SECT   JURID
FORCES TOP/EX CREATE DOMIN EDU/PROP ADJUD COERCE   PEACE
ATTIT RIGID/FLEX ALL/VALS...CONCPT TIME/SEQ TOT/POP WAR
VAL/FREE. PAGE 61 E1209

  B57
DE VISSCHER C.,THEORY AND REALITY IN PUBLIC   INT/ORG
INTERNATIONAL LAW. WOR+45 WOR-45 SOCIETY NAT/G   LAW
CT/SYS ATTIT MORAL ORD/FREE PWR...JURID CONCPT   INT/LAW
METH/CNCPT TIME/SEQ GEN/LAWS LEAGUE/NAT TOT/POP
VAL/FREE COLD/WAR. PAGE 30 E0599

  B57
DUMBAULD E.,THE BILL OF RIGHTS AND WHAT IT MEANS   CONSTN
TODAY. USA+45 USA-45 CT/SYS...JURID STYLE TIME/SEQ   LAW
BIBLIOG 18/20 BILL/RIGHT. PAGE 33 E0656   ADJUD
  ORD/FREE

  B57
JENKS C.W.,THE INTERNATIONAL PROTECTION OF TRADE   LABOR
UNION FREEDOM. FUT WOR+45 WOR-45 VOL/ASSN DELIB/GP   INT/ORG
CT/SYS REGION ROUTINE...JURID METH/CNCPT RECORD
TIME/SEQ CHARTS ILO WORK OAS 20. PAGE 58 E1153

  B57
LEVONTIN A.V.,THE MYTH OF INTERNATIONAL SECURITY: A INT/ORG
JURIDICAL AND CRITICAL ANALYSIS. FUT WOR+45 WOR-45   INT/LAW
LAW NAT/G VOL/ASSN ACT/RES BAL/PWR ATTIT ORD/FREE   SOVEREIGN
...JURID METH/CNCPT TIME/SEQ TREND STERTYP 20.   MYTH
PAGE 64 E1289

ROSENNE S.,.THE INTERNATIONAL COURT OF JUSTICE. INT/ORG
WOR+45 LAW DOMIN LEGIT PEACE PWR SOVEREIGN...JURID CT/SYS
CONCPT RECORD TIME/SEQ CON/ANAL CHARTS UN TOT/POP INT/LAW
VAL/FREE LEAGUE/NAT 20 ICJ. PAGE 86 E1716
B57

WASSENBERGH H.A.,.POST-WAR INTERNATIONAL CIVIL COM/IND
AVIATION POLICY AND THE LAW OF THE AIR. WOR+45 AIR NAT/G
INT/ORG DOMIN LEGIT PEACE ORD/FREE...POLICY JURID INT/LAW
NEW/IDEA OBS TIME/SEQ TREND CHARTS 20 TREATY.
PAGE 105 E2101
B57

O'BRIEN F.W.,.JUSTICE REED AND THE FIRST AMENDMENT, ADJUD
THE RELIGION CLAUSES. USA+45 USA-45 NAT/G PROVS SECT
CONTROL FEDERAL...POLICY JURID TIME/SEQ 20 CT/SYS
SUPREME/CT CHRUCH/STA AMEND/I REED/STAN. PAGE 78
E1563
B58

OGDEN F.D.,.THE POLL TAX IN THE SOUTH. USA+45 USA-45 TAX
CONSTN ADJUD ADMIN PARTIC CRIME...TIME/SEQ GOV/COMP CHOOSE
METH/COMP 18/20 SOUTH/US. PAGE 78 E1572 RACE/REL
DISCRIM
B58

UNESCO,."TECHNIQUES OF MEDIATION AND CONCILIATION." INT/ORG
EUR+WWI USA+45 WOR+45 INDUS FACE/GP EX/STRUC CONSULT
EDU/PROP LEGIT PEACE ORD/FREE...INT/LAW TIME/SEQ DIPLOM
LEAGUE/NAT 20. PAGE 98 E1961
L58

ANDERSON J.N.D.,.ISLAMIC LAW IN THE MODERN WORLD. ISLAM
FAM KIN SECT LEGIT ADJUD ATTIT DRIVE...TIME/SEQ JURID
TREND GEN/LAWS 20 MUSLIM. PAGE 5 E0089
B59

SUTTON F.X.,."REPRESENTATION AND THE NATURE OF NAT/G
POLITICAL SYSTEMS." UNIV WOR-45 CULTURE SOCIETY CONCPT
STRATA INT/ORG FORCES JUDGE DOMIN LEGIT EXEC REGION
REPRESENT ATTIT ORD/FREE RESPECT...SOC HIST/WRIT
TIME/SEQ. PAGE 95 E1896
S59

ENGEL J.,.THE SECURITY OF THE FREE WORLD. USSR COM
WOR+45 STRATA STRUCT ECO/DEV ECO/UNDEV INT/ORG TREND
DELIB/GP FORCES DOMIN LEGIT ADJUD EXEC ARMS/CONT DIPLOM
COERCE...POLICY CONCPT NEW/IDEA TIME/SEQ GEN/LAWS
COLD/WAR WORK UN 20 NATO. PAGE 35 E0689
B60

JENNINGS R.,.PROGRESS OF INTERNATIONAL LAW. FUT INT/ORG
WOR+45 SOCIETY NAT/G VOL/ASSN DELIB/GP LAW
DIPLOM EDU/PROP LEGIT COERCE ATTIT DRIVE MORAL INT/LAW
ORD/FREE...JURID CONCPT OBS TIME/SEQ TREND
GEN/LAWS. PAGE 58 E1164
B60

KUNZ J.,."SANCTIONS IN INTERNATIONAL LAW." WOR+45 INT/ORG
WOR-45 LEGIT ARMS/CONT COERCE PEACE ATTIT ADJUD
...METH/CNCPT TIME/SEQ TREND 20. PAGE 62 E1234 INT/LAW
L60

NICHOLS J.P.,."HAZARDS OF AMERICAN PRIVATE FINAN
INVESTMENT IN UNDERDEVELOPED COUNTRIES." FUT ECO/UNDEV
L/A+17C USA+45 USA-45 EXTR/IND CONSULT BAL/PWR CAP/ISM
ECO/TAC DOMIN ADJUD ATTIT SOVEREIGN WEALTH NAT/LISM
...HIST/WRIT TIME/SEQ TREND VAL/FREE 20. PAGE 77
E1546
S60

SANDERS R.,."NUCLEAR DYNAMITE: A NEW DIMENSION IN INDUS
FOREIGN POLICY." FUT WOR+45 ECO/DEV CONSULT TEC/DEV PWR
PERCEPT...CONT/OBS TIME/SEQ TREND GEN/LAWS TOT/POP DIPLOM
20 TREATY. PAGE 87 E1745 NUC/PWR
S60

GUIZOT F.P.G.,.HISTORY OF THE ORIGIN OF LEGIS
REPRESENTATIVE GOVERNMENT IN EUROPE. CHRIST-17C REPRESENT
FRANCE MOD/EUR SPAIN UK LAW CHIEF FORCES POPULISM CONSTN
...MAJORIT TIME/SEQ GOV/COMP NAT/COMP 4/19 NAT/G
PARLIAMENT. PAGE 48 E0961
B61

ROBERTSON A.H.,.THE LAW OF INTERNATIONAL RIGID/FLEX
INSTITUTIONS IN EUROPE. EUR+WWI MOD/EUR INT/ORG ORD/FREE
NAT/G VOL/ASSN DELIB/GP...JURID TIME/SEQ TOT/POP 20
TREATY. PAGE 85 E1704
B61

WRIGHT Q.,.THE ROLE OF INTERNATIONAL LAW IN THE INT/ORG
ELIMINATION OF WAR. FUT WOR+45 WOR-45 NAT/G BAL/PWR ADJUD
DIPLOM DOMIN LEGIT PWR...POLICY INT/LAW JURID ARMS/CONT
CONCPT TIME/SEQ TREND GEN/LAWS COLD/WAR 20.
PAGE 108 E2158
B61

CASTANEDA J.,."THE UNDERDEVELOPED NATIONS AND THE INT/ORG
DEVELOPMENT OF INTERNATIONAL LAW." FUT UNIV LAW ECO/UNDEV
ACT/RES FOR/AID LEGIT PERCEPT SKILL...JURID PEACE
METH/CNCPT TIME/SEQ TOT/POP 20 UN. PAGE 21 E0405 INT/LAW
S61

COLOMBOS C.J.,.THE INTERNATIONAL LAW OF THE SEA. INT/LAW
WOR+45 EXTR/IND DIPLOM INT/TRADE TARIFFS AGREE WAR SEA
...TIME/SEQ 20 TREATY. PAGE 24 E0476 JURID
ADJUD
B62

HENDERSON W.O.,.THE GENESIS OF THE COMMON MARKET. ECO/DEV
EUR+WWI FRANCE MOD/EUR UK SEA COM/IND EXTR/IND INT/TRADE
COLONIAL DISCRIM...TIME/SEQ CHARTS BIBLIOG 18/20 DIPLOM
EEC TREATY. PAGE 52 E1030
B62

ROSENNE S.,.THE WORLD COURT: WHAT IT IS AND HOW IT INT/ORG
WORKS. WOR+45 WOR-45 LAW CONSTN JUDGE EDU/PROP ADJUD
LEGIT ROUTINE CHOOSE PEACE ORD/FREE...JURID OBS INT/LAW
TIME/SEQ CHARTS UN TOT/POP VAL/FREE 20. PAGE 86
E1717
B62

TRISKA J.F.,.THE THEORY, LAW, AND POLICY OF SOVIET COM
TREATIES. WOR+45 WOR-45 CONSTN INT/ORG NAT/G LAW
VOL/ASSN DOMIN LEGIT COERCE ATTIT PWR RESPECT INT/LAW
...POLICY JURID CONCPT OBS SAMP TIME/SEQ TREND USSR
GEN/LAWS 20. PAGE 97 E1941
B62

MANGIN G.,."L'ORGANIZATION JUDICIAIRE DES ETATS AFR
D'AFRIQUE ET DE MADAGASCAR." ISLAM WOR+45 STRATA LEGIS
STRUCT ECO/UNDEV NAT/G LEGIT EXEC...JURID TIME/SEQ COLONIAL
TOT/POP 20 SUPREME/CT. PAGE 68 E1357 MADAGASCAR
L62

NIZARD L.,."CUBAN QUESTION AND SECURITY COUNCIL." INT/ORG
L/A+17C USA+45 ECO/UNDEV NAT/G POL/PAR DELIB/GP JURID
ECO/TAC PWR...RELATIV OBS TIME/SEQ TREND GEN/LAWS DIPLOM
UN 20 UN. PAGE 77 E1551 CUBA
L62

BIERZANECK R.,."LA NON-RECONAISSANCE ET LE DROIT EDU/PROP
INTERNATIONAL CONTEMPORAIN." EUR+WWI FUT WOR+45 LAW JURID
ECO/DEV ATTIT RIGID/FLEX...CONCPT TIME/SEQ TOT/POP DIPLOM
20. PAGE 12 E0228 INT/LAW
S62

JOHNSON O.H.,."THE ENGLISH TRADITION IN LAW
INTERNATIONAL LAW." CHRIST-17C MOD/EUR EDU/PROP INT/LAW
LEGIT CT/SYS ORD/FREE...JURID CONCPT TIME/SEQ. UK
PAGE 59 E1170
S62

MANGIN G.,."LES ACCORDS DE COOPERATION EN MATIERE DE INT/ORG
JUSTICE ENTRE LA FRANCE ET LES ETATS AFRICAINS ET LAW
MALGACHE." AFR ISLAM WOR+45 STRUCT ECO/UNDEV NAT/G FRANCE
DELIB/GP PERCEPT ALL/VALS...JURID MGT TIME/SEQ 20.
PAGE 68 E1356
S62

VIGNES D.,."L'AUTORITE DES TRAITES INTERNATIONAUX EN STRUCT
DROIT INTERNE." EUR+WWI UNIV LAW CONSTN INTELL LEGIT
NAT/G POL/PAR DIPLOM ATTIT PERCEPT ALL/VALS FRANCE
...POLICY INT/LAW JURID CONCPT TIME/SEQ 20 TREATY.
PAGE 104 E2075
S62

CARTER G.M.,.FIVE AFRICAN STATES: RESPONSES TO AFR
DIVERSITY. CONSTN CULTURE STRATA LEGIS PLAN ECO/TAC SOCIETY
DOMIN EDU/PROP CT/SYS EXEC CHOOSE ATTIT HEALTH
ORD/FREE PWR...TIME/SEQ TOT/POP VAL/FREE. PAGE 20
E0398
B63

ROSNER G.,.THE UNITED NATIONS EMERGENCY FORCE. INT/ORG
FRANCE ISRAEL UAR UK WOR+45 CREATE WAR PEACE FORCES
ORD/FREE PWR...INT/LAW JURID HIST/WRIT TIME/SEQ UN.
PAGE 86 E1719
B63

VINES K.N.,.STUDIES IN JUDICIAL POLITICS: TULANE CT/SYS
STUDIES IN POLITICAL SCIENCE (VOL. 8). POL/PAR GOV/REL
JUDGE ADJUD SANCTION CRIME CHOOSE PWR...JURID STAT PROVS
TIME/SEQ CHARTS. PAGE 104 E2079
B63

CAHIER P.,."LE DROIT INTERNE DES ORGANISATIONS INT/ORG
INTERNATIONALES." UNIV CONSTN SOCIETY ECO/DEV R+D JURID
NAT/G TOP/EX LEGIT ATTIT PERCEPT...TIME/SEQ 19/20. DIPLOM
PAGE 18 E0357 INT/LAW
S63

S63

LEPAWSKY A.,"INTERNATIONAL DEVELOPMENT OF RIVER   INT/ORG
RESOURCES." CANADA EUR+WWI S/ASIA USA+45 SEA LEGIT   DELIB/GP
ADJUD ORD/FREE PWR WEALTH...MGT TIME/SEQ VAL/FREE
MEXIC/AMER 20. PAGE 64 E1287

B64

GARDNER L.C.,ECONOMIC ASPECTS OF NEW DEAL   ECO/TAC
DIPLOMACY. USA+45 WOR-45 LAW ECO/DEV INT/ORG NAT/G   DIPLOM
VOL/ASSN LEGIS TOP/EX EDU/PROP ORD/FREE PWR WEALTH
...POLICY TIME/SEQ VAL/FREE 20 ROOSEVLT/F. PAGE 42
E0836

B64

GRIFFITH W.E.,THE SINO-SOVIET RIFT. ASIA CHINA/COM   ATTIT
COM CUBA USSR YUGOSLAVIA NAT/G POL/PAR VOL/ASSN   TIME/SEQ
DELIB/GP FORCES TOP/EX DIPLOM EDU/PROP DRIVE PERSON   BAL/PWR
PWR...TREND 20 TREATY. PAGE 47 E0941   SOCISM

B64

IRION F.C.,APPORTIONMENT OF THE NEW MEXICO   APPORT
LEGISLATURE. NAT/G LEGIS PRESS CT/SYS ATTIT   REPRESENT
...POLICY TIME/SEQ 19/20 SUPREME/CT. PAGE 57 E1137   GOV/REL
                                                         PROVS

B64

MASON A.T.,AMERICAN CONSTITUTIONAL LAW: CONSTN
INTRODUCTORY ESSAYS AND SELECTED CASES (3RD ED.).   CT/SYS
LAW LEGIS TAX ADJUD GOV/REL FEDERAL ORD/FREE PWR   JURID
...TIME/SEQ BIBLIOG T 19/20 SUPREME/CT. PAGE 69
E1379

S64

BALDWIN G.B.,"THE DEPENDENCE OF SCIENCE ON LAW AND   NAT/G
GOVERNMENT--THE INTERNATIONAL GEOPHYSICAL YEAR--A   KNOWL
CASE STUDY." WOR+45 LAW INT/ORG PROF/ORG LEGIS PLAN
EDU/PROP...TIME/SEQ VAL/FREE 20. PAGE 8 E0144

S64

DERWINSKI E.J.,"THE COST OF THE INTERNATIONAL   MARKET
COFFEE AGREEMENT." L/A+17C USA+45 WOR+45 ECO/UNDEV   DELIB/GP
NAT/G VOL/ASSN LEGIS DIPLOM ECO/TAC FOR/AID LEGIT   INT/TRADE
ATTIT...TIME/SEQ CONGRESS 20 TREATY. PAGE 31 E0608

S64

GARDNER R.N.,"THE SOVIET UNION AND THE UNITED   COM
NATIONS." WOR+45 FINAN POL/PAR VOL/ASSN FORCES   INT/ORG
ECO/TAC DOMIN EDU/PROP LEGIT ADJUD ADMIN ARMS/CONT   USSR
COERCE ATTIT ALL/VALS...POLICY MAJORIT CONCPT OBS
TIME/SEQ TREND STERTYP UN. PAGE 42 E0838

S64

KUNZ J.,"THE CHANGING SCIENCE OF INTERNATIONAL   ADJUD
LAW." FUT WOR+45 WOR-45 INT/ORG LEGIT ORD/FREE   CONCPT
...JURID TIME/SEQ GEN/LAWS 20. PAGE 62 E1235   INT/LAW

S64

TRISKA J.F.,"SOVIET TREATY LAW: A QUANTITATIVE   COM
ANALYSIS." WOR+45 LAW ECO/UNDEV AGRI COM/IND INDUS   ECO/TAC
CREATE TEC/DEV DIPLOM ATTIT PWR WEALTH...JURID SAMP   INT/LAW
TIME/SEQ TREND CHARTS VAL/FREE 20 TREATY. PAGE 97   USSR
E1942

B65

FELLMAN D.,RELIGION IN AMERICAN PUBLIC LAW. USA+45   SECT
USA-45 NAT/G PROVS ADJUD SANCTION GP/REL PRIVIL   CONSTN
ORD/FREE...JURID TIME/SEQ 18/20 SUPREME/CT   LAW
CHURCH/STA. PAGE 37 E0733   POLICY

B65

VONGLAHN G.,LAW AMONG NATIONS: AN INTRODUCTION TO   CONSTN
PUBLIC INTERNATIONAL LAW. UNIV WOR+45 LAW INT/ORG   JURID
NAT/G LEGIT EXEC RIGID/FLEX...CONCPT TIME/SEQ   INT/LAW
GEN/LAWS UN TOT/POP 20. PAGE 104 E2084

B66

ANDERSON S.V.,CANADIAN OMBUDSMAN PROPOSALS. CANADA   NAT/G
LEGIS DEBATE PARL/PROC...MAJORIT JURID TIME/SEQ   CREATE
IDEA/COMP 20 OMBUDSMAN PARLIAMENT. PAGE 5 E0092   ADMIN
                                                         POL/PAR

B67

JONES C.O.,EVERY SECOND YEAR: CONGRESSIONAL   EFFICIENCY
BEHAVIOR AND THE TWO-YEAR TERM. LAW POL/PAR   LEGIS
PROB/SOLV DEBATE CHOOSE PERS/REL COST FEDERAL PWR   TIME/SEQ
...CHARTS 20 CONGRESS SENATE HOUSE/REP. PAGE 59   NAT/G
E1172

B67

US SENATE COMM ON FOREIGN REL,A SELECT CHRONOLOGY   ISLAM
AND BACKGROUND DOCUMENTS RELATING TO THE MIDDLE   TIME/SEQ
EAST. ISRAEL UAR LAW INT/ORG FORCES PROB/SOLV   DIPLOM
CONFER CONSEN PEACE ATTIT...POLICY 20 UN SENATE
TRUMAN/HS. PAGE 101 E2033

B98

POLLOCK F.,THE HISTORY OF ENGLISH LAW BEFORE THE   LAW
TIME OF EDWARD I (2 VOLS, 2ND ED.). UK CULTURE   ADJUD
LOC/G LEGIS LICENSE AGREE CONTROL CT/SYS SANCTION   JURID
CRIME...TIME/SEQ 13 COMMON/LAW CANON/LAW. PAGE 81
E1626

TIMING....SEE TIME

TINGSTERN H. E1927

TIPTON J.B. E1928

TITO/MARSH....JOSIP BROZ TITO

TIZARD/H....HENRY TIZARD

TOBAGO....SEE TRINIDAD

TOCQUEVILL....ALEXIS DE TOCQUEVILLE

TODD A. E1929

TOGO....SEE ALSO AFR

TOLEDO/O....TOLEDO, OHIO

TOMASEK R.D. E1930

TOMPKINS D.C. E1931,E1932,E1933

TONG T. E1934

TONGA....TONGA

TONNIES F. E1056

TOP/EX....TOP EXECUTIVES

B00

DE TOCQUEVILLE A.,DEMOCRACY IN AMERICA (VOLUME   USA+45
ONE). LAW SOCIETY STRUCT NAT/G POL/PAR PROVS FORCES   TREND
LEGIS TOP/EX DIPLOM LEGIT WAR PEACE ATTIT SOVEREIGN
...SELF/OBS TIME/SEQ CONGRESS 19. PAGE 30 E0594

B03

GRIFFIN A.P.C.,LIST OF BOOKS ON THE CONSTITUTION OF   BIBLIOG/A
THE UNITED STATES (PAMPHLET). USA+45 NAT/G EX/STRUC   CONSTN
JUDGE TOP/EX CT/SYS 18/20 CONGRESS PRESIDENT   LAW
SUPREME/CT. PAGE 46 E0920   JURID

B15

SAWYER R.A.,A LIST OF WORKS ON COUNTY GOVERNMENT.   BIBLIOG/A
LAW FINAN MUNIC TOP/EX ROUTINE CRIME...CLASSIF   LOC/G
RECORD 19/20. PAGE 87 E1748   GOV/REL
                                                         ADMIN

C20

BLACHLY F.F.,"THE GOVERNMENT AND ADMINISTRATION OF   NAT/G
GERMANY." GERMANY CONSTN LOC/G PROVS DELIB/GP   GOV/REL
EX/STRUC FORCES LEGIS TOP/EX CT/SYS...BIBLIOG/A   ADMIN
19/20. PAGE 12 E0235   PHIL/SCI

B29

BUELL R.,INTERNATIONAL RELATIONS. WOR+45 WOR-45   INT/ORG
CONSTN STRATA FORCES TOP/EX ADMIN ATTIT DRIVE   BAL/PWR
SUPEGO MORAL ORD/FREE PWR SOVEREIGN...JURID SOC   DIPLOM
CONCPT 20. PAGE 17 E0326

B30

BYNKERSHOEK C.,QUAESTIONUM JURIS PUBLICI LIBRI DUO.   INT/ORG
CHRIST-17C MOD/EUR CONSTN ELITES SOCIETY NAT/G   LAW
PROVS EX/STRUC FORCES TOP/EX BAL/PWR DIPLOM ATTIT   NAT/LISM
MORAL...TRADIT CONCPT. PAGE 18 E0352   INT/LAW

B30

WRIGHT Q.,MANDATES UNDER THE LEAGUE OF NATIONS.   INT/ORG
WOR-45 CONSTN ECO/DEV ECO/UNDEV NAT/G DELIB/GP   LAW
TOP/EX LEGIT ALL/VALS...JURID CONCPT LEAGUE/NAT 20.   INT/LAW
PAGE 107 E2151

B32

EAGLETON C.,INTERNATIONAL GOVERNMENT. BRAZIL FRANCE   INT/ORG
GERMANY ITALY UK USSR WOR-45 DELIB/GP TOP/EX PLAN   JURID
ECO/TAC EDU/PROP LEGIT ADJUD REGION ARMS/CONT   DIPLOM
COERCE ATTIT PWR...GEOG MGT VAL/FREE LEAGUE/NAT 20.   INT/LAW
PAGE 34 E0670

B32

FLEMMING D.,THE UNITED STATES AND THE LEAGUE OF   INT/ORG
NATIONS, 1918-1920. FUT USA+45 NAT/G LEGIS TOP/EX   EDU/PROP
DEBATE CHOOSE PEACE ATTIT SOVEREIGN...TIME/SEQ
CON/ANAL CONGRESS LEAGUE/NAT 20 TREATY. PAGE 39
E0764

DANGERFIELD R.,IN DEFENSE OF THE SENATE. USA-45
CONSTN NAT/G EX/STRUC TOP/EX ATTIT KNOWL
...METH/CNCPT STAT TIME/SEQ TREND CON/ANAL CHARTS
CONGRESS 20 TREATY. PAGE 28 E0565
B33
LEGIS
DELIB/GP
DIPLOM

HELLMAN F.S.,SELECTED LIST OF REFERENCES ON THE
CONSTITUTIONAL POWERS OF THE PRESIDENT INCLUDING
POWERS RECENTLY DELEGATED. USA-45 NAT/G EX/STRUC
TOP/EX CENTRAL FEDERAL PWR 20 PRESIDENT. PAGE 51
E1025
B33
BIBLIOG/A
JURID
LAW
CONSTN

BEMIS S.F.,GUIDE TO THE DIPLOMATIC HISTORY OF THE
UNITED STATES, 17751921. NAT/G LEGIS TOP/EX
PROB/SOLV CAP/ISM INT/TRADE TARIFFS ADJUD
...CON/ANAL 18/20. PAGE 10 E0184
B35
BIBLIOG/A
DIPLOM
USA-45

FIELD G.L.,THE SYNDICAL AND CORPORATIVE
INSTITUTIONS OF ITALIAN FASCISM. ITALY CONSTN
STRATA LABOR EX/STRUC TOP/EX ADJUD ADMIN LEAD
TOTALISM AUTHORIT...MGT 20 MUSSOLIN/B. PAGE 38
E0746
B38
FASCISM
INDUS
NAT/G
WORKER

LAVES W.H.C.,INTERNATIONAL SECURITY. EUR+WWI
GERMANY UK USA-45 LAW NAT/G DELIB/GP TOP/EX COERCE
PWR...POLICY FASCIST CONCPT HIST/WRIT GEN/LAWS
LEAGUE/NAT NAZI 20. PAGE 63 E1267
B39
ORD/FREE
LEGIT
ARMS/CONT
BAL/PWR

MCCLURE W.,INTERNATIONAL EXECUTIVE AGREEMENTS.
USA-45 WOR-45 INT/ORG NAT/G DELIB/GP ADJUD ROUTINE
ORD/FREE PWR...TIME/SEQ TREND CON/ANAL. PAGE 70
E1401
B41
TOP/EX
DIPLOM

BEARD C.A.,AMERICAN GOVERNMENT AND POLITICS (REV.
ED.). CONSTN MUNIC POL/PAR PROVS EX/STRUC LEGIS
TOP/EX CT/SYS GOV/REL...BIBLIOG T 18/20. PAGE 9
E0165
B44
LEAD
USA-45
NAT/G
LOC/G

WRIGHT Q.,"CONSTITUTIONAL PROCEDURES OF THE US FOR
CARRYING OUT OBLIGATIONS FOR MILITARY SANCTIONS."
EUR+WWI FUT USA-45 WOR-45 CONSTN INTELL NAT/G
CONSULT EX/STRUC LEGIS ROUTINE DRIVE...POLICY JURID
CONCPT OBS TREND TOT/POP 20. PAGE 108 E2153
S44
TOP/EX
FORCES
INT/LAW
WAR

TINGSTERN H.,PEACE AND SECURITY AFTER WW II. WOR-45
DELIB/GP TOP/EX LEGIT CT/SYS COERCE PEACE ATTIT
PERCEPT...CONCPT LEAGUE/NAT 20. PAGE 96 E1927
B45
INT/ORG
ORD/FREE
WAR
INT/LAW

BORGESE G.,COMMON CAUSE. LAW CONSTN SOCIETY STRATA
ECO/DEV INT/ORG POL/PAR FORCES LEGIS TOP/EX CAP/ISM
DIPLOM ADMIN EXEC ATTIT PWR 20. PAGE 14 E0269
B47
WOR+45
NAT/G
SOVEREIGN
REGION

PUSEY M.J.,CHARLES EVANS HUGHES (2 VOLS.). LAW
CONSTN NAT/G POL/PAR DIPLOM LEGIT WAR CHOOSE
PERS/REL DRIVE HEREDITY 19/20 DEPT/STATE LEAGUE/NAT
SUPREME/CT HUGHES/CE WWI. PAGE 83 E1663
B51
BIOG
TOP/EX
ADJUD
PERSON

ROSSITER C.,THE SUPREME COURT AND THE COMMANDER IN
CHIEF. LAW CONSTN DELIB/GP EX/STRUC LEGIS TOP/EX
ADJUD CONTROL...DECISION SOC/EXP PRESIDENT. PAGE 86
E1724
B51
CT/SYS
CHIEF
WAR
PWR

DE GRAZIA A.,POLITICAL ORGANIZATION. CONSTN LOC/G
MUNIC NAT/G CHIEF LEGIS TOP/EX ADJUD CT/SYS
PERS/REL...INT/LAW MYTH UN. PAGE 29 E0581
B52
FEDERAL
LAW
ADMIN

WRIGHT Q.,"CONGRESS AND THE TREATY-MAKING POWER."
USA+45 WOR+45 CONSTN INTELL NAT/G CHIEF CONSULT
EX/STRUC LEGIS TOP/EX CREATE GOV/REL DISPL DRIVE
RIGID/FLEX...TREND TOT/POP CONGRESS CONGRESS 20
TREATY. PAGE 108 E2154
L52
ROUTINE
DIPLOM
INT/LAW
DELIB/GP

KHADDURI M.,WAR AND PEACE IN THE LAW OF ISLAM.
CONSTN CULTURE SOCIETY STRATA NAT/G PROVS SECT
FORCES TOP/EX CREATE DOMIN EDU/PROP ADJUD COERCE
ATTIT RIGID/FLEX ALL/VALS...CONCPT TIME/SEQ TOT/POP
VAL/FREE. PAGE 61 E1209
B55
ISLAM
JURID
PEACE
WAR

PEASLEE A.J.,CONSTITUTIONS OF NATIONS. WOR+45 LAW
B56
CONSTN

NAT/G EX/STRUC LEGIS TOP/EX LEGIT CT/SYS ROUTINE
CHOOSE ORD/FREE PWR SOVEREIGN...CHARTS TOT/POP.
PAGE 80 E1605
CON/ANAL

JENNINGS I.,PARLIAMENT. UK FINAN INDUS POL/PAR
DELIB/GP EX/STRUC PLAN CONTROL...MAJORIT JURID
PARLIAMENT. PAGE 58 E1163
B57
PARL/PROC
TOP/EX
MGT
LEGIS

DAVIS K.C.,ADMINISTRATIVE LAW: CASES, TEXT,
PROBLEMS. LAW LOC/G NAT/G TOP/EX PAY CONTROL
GOV/REL INGP/REL FEDERAL 20 SUPREME/CT. PAGE 29
E0576
B58
ADJUD
JURID
CT/SYS
ADMIN

LAW COMMISSION OF INDIA,REFORM OF JUDICIAL
ADMINISTRATION. INDIA TOP/EX ADMIN DISCRIM
EFFICIENCY...METH/COMP 20. PAGE 63 E1269
B58
CT/SYS
ADJUD
GOV/REL
CONTROL

MACKENZIE W.J.M.,FREE ELECTIONS: AN ELEMENTARY
TEXTBOOK. WOR+45 NAT/G POL/PAR LEGIS TOP/EX
EDU/PROP LEGIT CT/SYS ATTIT PWR...OBS CHARTS
STERTYP T CONGRESS PARLIAMENT 20. PAGE 67 E1342
B58
EX/STRUC
CHOOSE

SPITZ D.,DEMOCRACY AND THE CHALLANGE OF POWER. FUT
USA+45 USA-45 LAW SOCIETY STRUCT LOC/G POL/PAR
PROVS DELIB/GP EX/STRUC LEGIS TOP/EX ACT/RES CREATE
DOMIN EDU/PROP LEGIT ADJUD ADMIN ATTIT DRIVE MORAL
ORD/FREE TOT/POP. PAGE 93 E1862
B58
NAT/G
PWR

SPIRO H.J.,GOVERNMENT BY CONSTITUTIONS: THE
POLITICAL SYSTEMS OF DEMOCRACY. CANADA EUR+WWI FUT
USA+45 WOR+45 WOR-45 LEGIS TOP/EX LEGIT ADMIN
CT/SYS ORD/FREE PWR...TREND TOT/POP VAL/FREE 20.
PAGE 93 E1861
B59
NAT/G
CONSTN

WILDNER H.,DIE TECHNIK DER DIPLOMATIE. TOP/EX ROLE
ORD/FREE...INT/LAW JURID IDEA/COMP NAT/COMP 20.
PAGE 106 E2122
B59
DIPLOM
POLICY
DELIB/GP
NAT/G

HECTOR L.J.,"GOVERNMENT BY ANONYMITY: WHO WRITES
OUR REGULATORY OPINIONS?" USA+45 NAT/G TOP/EX
CONTROL EXEC. PAGE 51 E1021
L59
ADJUD
REPRESENT
EX/STRUC
ADMIN

LENCZOWSKI G.,OIL AND STATE IN THE MIDDLE EAST. FUT
IRAN LAW ECO/UNDEV EXTR/IND NAT/G TOP/EX PLAN
TEC/DEV ECO/TAC LEGIT ADMIN COERCE ATTIT ALL/VALS
PWR...CHARTS 20. PAGE 64 E1283
B60
ISLAM
INDUS
NAT/LISM

PRICE D.,THE SECRETARY OF STATE. USA+45 CONSTN
ELITES INTELL CHIEF EX/STRUC TOP/EX LEGIT ATTIT PWR
SKILL...DECISION 20 CONGRESS. PAGE 82 E1650
B60
CONSULT
DIPLOM
INT/LAW

SCHMIDHAUSER J.R.,THE SUPREME COURT: ITS POLITICS,
PERSONALITIES, AND PROCEDURES. LAW DELIB/GP
EX/STRUC TOP/EX ADJUD CT/SYS CHOOSE RATIONAL PWR
SUPREME/CT. PAGE 88 E1760
B60
JUDGE
JURID
DECISION

ALGER C.F.,"NON-RESOLUTION CONSEQUENCES OF THE
UNITED NATIONS AND THEIR EFFECT ON INTERNATIONAL
CONFLICT." WOR+45 CONSTN ECO/DEV NAT/G CONSULT
DELIB/GP TOP/EX ACT/RES PLAN DIPLOM EDU/PROP
ROUTINE ATTIT ALL/VALS...INT/LAW TOT/POP UN 20.
PAGE 3 E0065
S61
INT/ORG
DRIVE
BAL/PWR

HARVEY W.B.,"THE RULE OF LAW IN HISTORICAL
PERSPECTIVE." USA+45 WOR+45 INTELL SOCIETY ECO/DEV
ECO/UNDEV NAT/G EX/STRUC LEGIS TOP/EX LEGIT SKILL
...CONCPT HIST/WRIT TOT/POP. PAGE 51 E1010
S61
ACT/RES
LAW

FROMAN L.A. JR.,PEOPLE AND POLITICS: AN ANALYSIS OF
THE AMERICAN POLITICAL SYSTEM. USA+45 CHIEF
DELIB/GP EX/STRUC LEGIS TOP/EX CT/SYS LOBBY
PERS/REL PWR...POLICY DECISION. PAGE 41 E0813
B62
POL/PAR
PROB/SOLV
GOV/REL

THOMPSON K.W.,AMERICAN DIPLOMACY AND EMERGENT
PATTERNS. USA+45 USA-45 WOR+45 WOR-45 LAW DELIB/GP
FORCES TOP/EX DIPLOM ATTIT DRIVE RIGID/FLEX
ORD/FREE PWR SOVEREIGN...POLICY 20. PAGE 96 E1922
B62
NAT/G
BAL/PWR

STEIN E.,"MR HAMMARSKJOLD, THE CHARTER LAW AND THE FUTURE ROLE OF THE UNITED NATIONS SECRETARY-GENERAL." WOR+45 CONSTN INT/ORG DELIB/GP FORCES TOP/EX BAL/PWR LEGIT ROUTINE RIGID/FLEX PWR ...POLICY JURID OBS STERTYP UN COLD/WAR 20 HAMMARSK/D. PAGE 93 E1869
L62
CONCPT
BIOG

FINKELSTEIN L.S.,"THE UNITED NATIONS AND ORGANIZATIONS FOR CONTROL OF ARMAMENT." FUT WOR+45 VOL/ASSN DELIB/GP TOP/EX CREATE EDU/PROP LEGIT ADJUD NUC/PWR ATTIT RIGID/FLEX ORD/FREE...POLICY DECISION CONCPT OBS TREND GEN/LAWS TOT/POP COLD/WAR. PAGE 38 E0752
S62
INT/ORG
PWR
ARMS/CONT

MCWHINNEY E.,"CO-EXISTENCE, THE CUBA CRISIS, AND COLD WAR-INTERNATIONAL WAR." CUBA USA+45 USSR WOR+45 NAT/G TOP/EX BAL/PWR DIPLOM DOMIN LEGIT PEACE RIGID/FLEX ORD/FREE...STERTYP COLD/WAR 20. PAGE 71 E1427
S62
CONCPT
INT/LAW

JACOBS P.,STATE OF UNIONS. USA+45 STRATA TOP/EX GP/REL RACE/REL DEMAND DISCRIM ATTIT PWR 20 CONGRESS NEGRO HOFFA/J. PAGE 57 E1145
B63
LABOR
ECO/TAC
BARGAIN
DECISION

NEWMAN E.S.,THE FREEDOM READER. USA+45 LEGIS TOP/EX PLAN ADJUD CONTROL CT/SYS DISCRIM...DECISION ANTHOL 20 SUPREME/CT CIV/RIGHTS. PAGE 77 E1541
B63
RACE/REL
LAW
POLICY
ORD/FREE

RICHARDS P.G.,PATRONAGE IN BRITISH GOVERNMENT. ELITES DELIB/GP TOP/EX PROB/SOLV CONTROL CT/SYS EXEC. PWR. PAGE 84 E1693
B63
EX/STRUC
REPRESENT
POL/PAR
ADMIN

CAHIER P.,"LE DROIT INTERNE DES ORGANISATIONS INTERNATIONALES." UNIV CONSTN SOCIETY ECO/DEV R+D NAT/G TOP/EX LEGIT ATTIT PERCEPT...TIME/SEQ 19/20. PAGE 18 E0357
S63
INT/ORG
JURID
DIPLOM
INT/LAW

HARNETTY P.,"CANADA, SOUTH AFRICA AND THE COMMONWEALTH." CANADA SOUTH/AFR LAW INT/ORG VOL/ASSN DELIB/GP LEGIS TOP/EX ECO/TAC LEGIT DRIVE MORAL...CONCPT CMN/WLTH 20. PAGE 50 E1000
S63
AFR
ATTIT

DORMAN M.,WE SHALL OVERCOME. USA+45 ELITES ACADEM FORCES TOP/EX MURDER...JURID 20 CIV/RIGHTS MISSISSIPP EVERS/MED CLEMSON. PAGE 32 E0638
B64
RACE/REL
LAW
DISCRIM

GARDNER L.C.,ECONOMIC ASPECTS OF NEW DEAL DIPLOMACY. USA-45 WOR-45 LAW ECO/DEV INT/ORG NAT/G VOL/ASSN LEGIS TOP/EX EDU/PROP ORD/FREE PWR WEALTH ...POLICY TIME/SEQ VAL/FREE 20 ROOSEVLT/F. PAGE 42 E0836
B64
ECO/TAC
DIPLOM

GRIFFITH W.E.,THE SINO-SOVIET RIFT. ASIA CHINA/COM COM CUBA USSR YUGOSLAVIA NAT/G POL/PAR VOL/ASSN DELIB/GP FORCES TOP/EX DIPLOM EDU/PROP DRIVE PERSON PWR...TREND 20 TREATY. PAGE 47 E0941
B64
ATTIT
TIME/SEQ
BAL/PWR
SOCISM

TODD A.,JUSTICE ON TRIAL: THE CASE OF LOUIS D. BRANDEIS. TOP/EX DISCRIM...JURID 20 WILSON/W CONGRESS SUPREME/CT BRANDEIS/L SENATE. PAGE 96 E1929
B64
PERSON
RACE/REL
PERS/REL
NAT/G

TOMPKINS D.C.,PRESIDENTIAL SUCCESSION. USA+45 CHIEF ADJUD 20 PRESIDENT CONGRESS. PAGE 96 E1933
B64
BIBLIOG/A
EX/STRUC
CONSTN
TOP/EX

POUNDS N.J.G.,"THE POLITICS OF PARTITION." AFR ASIA COM EUR+WWI FUT ISLAM S/ASIA USA-45 LAW ECO/DEV ECO/UNDEV AGRI INDUS INT/ORG POL/PAR PROVS SECT FORCES TOP/EX EDU/PROP LEGIT ATTIT MORAL ORD/FREE PWR RESPECT WEALTH. PAGE 82 E1640
L64
NAT/G
NAT/LISM

BELL J.,THE JOHNSON TREATMENT: HOW LYNDON JOHNSON TOOK OVER THE PRESIDENCY AND MADE IT HIS OWN. USA+45 DELIB/GP DIPLOM ADJUD MURDER CHOOSE PERSON PWR...POLICY OBS INT TIME 20 JOHNSON/LB KENNEDY/JF
B65
INGP/REL
TOP/EX
CONTROL
NAT/G

PRESIDENT CONGRESS. PAGE 10 E0183

IANNIELLO L.,MILESTONES ALONG THE MARCH: TWELVE HISTORIC CIVIL RIGHTS DOCUMENTS--FROM WORLD WAR II TO SELMA. USA+45 LAW FORCES TOP/EX PARTIC SUFF...T 20 NEGRO CIV/RIGHTS TRUMAN/HS SUPREME/CT KENNEDY/JF. PAGE 56 E1121
B65
RACE/REL
DISCRIM
CONSTN
NAT/G

NORDEN A.,WAR AND NAZI CRIMINALS IN WEST GERMANY: STATE, ECONOMY, ADMINISTRATION. ARMY, JUSTICE, SCIENCE. GERMANY GERMANY/W MOD/EUR ECO/DEV ACADEM EX/STRUC FORCES DOMIN ADMIN CT/SYS...POLICY MAJORIT PACIFIST 20. PAGE 77 E1554
B65
FASCIST
WAR
NAT/G
TOP/EX

PEASLEE A.J.,CONSTITUTIONS OF NATIONS* THIRD REVISED EDITION (VOLUME I* AFRICA). LAW EX/STRUC LEGIS TOP/EX LEGIT CT/SYS ROUTINE ORD/FREE PWR SOVEREIGN...CON/ANAL CHARTS. PAGE 80 E1606
B65
AFR
CHOOSE
CONSTN
NAT/G

FOX A.B.,"NATO AND CONGRESS." CONSTN DELIB/GP EX/STRUC FORCES TOP/EX BUDGET NUC/PWR GOV/REL ...GP/COMP CONGRESS NATO TREATY. PAGE 39 E0779
S65
CONTROL
DIPLOM

KEAY E.A.,THE NATIVE AND CUSTOMARY COURTS OF NIGERIA. NIGERIA CONSTN ELITES NAT/G TOP/EX PARTIC REGION...DECISION JURID 19/20. PAGE 60 E1190
B66
AFR
ADJUD
LAW

TORONTO....TORONTO, ONTARIO

TORY/PARTY....TORY PARTY

DICEY A.V.,LECTURES ON THE RELATION BETWEEN LAW AND PUBLIC OPINION IN ENGLAND DURING THE NINETEENTH CENTURY. UK LEGIS CT/SYS...JURID 19 TORY/PARTY BENTHAM/J ENGLSH/LAW. PAGE 31 E0621
B05
LAW
ADJUD
ATTIT
IDEA/COMP

HOLDSWORTH W.S.,A HISTORY OF ENGLISH LAW; THE CENTURIES OF DEVELOPMENT AND REFORM (VOL. XIV). UK CONSTN LOC/G NAT/G POL/PAR CHIEF EX/STRUC ADJUD COLONIAL ATTIT...INT/LAW JURID 18/19 TORY/PARTY COMMONWLTH WHIG/PARTY COMMON/LAW. PAGE 54 E1081
B64
LAW
LEGIS
LEAD
CT/SYS

TORZSAY-BIBER G. E1181

TOSCANO M. E1935

TOTALISM....TOTALITARIANISM

FIELD G.L.,THE SYNDICAL AND CORPORATIVE INSTITUTIONS OF ITALIAN FASCISM. ITALY CONSTN STRATA LABOR EX/STRUC TOP/EX ADJUD ADMIN LEAD TOTALISM AUTHORIT...MGT 20 MUSSOLIN/B. PAGE 38 E0746
B38
FASCISM
INDUS
NAT/G
WORKER

CARR E.H.,THE TWENTY YEARS' CRISIS 1919-1939. FUT WOR-45 BAL/PWR ECO/TAC LEGIT TOTALISM ATTIT ALL/VALS...POLICY JURID CONCPT TIME/SEQ TREND GEN/LAWS TOT/POP 20. PAGE 20 E0393
B40
INT/ORG
DIPLOM
PEACE

FLORIN J.,"BOLSHEVIST AND NATIONAL SOCIALIST DOCTRINES OF INTERNATIONAL LAW." EUR+WWI GERMANY USSR R+D INT/ORG NAT/G DIPLOM DOMIN EDU/PROP SOCISM ...CONCPT TIME/SEQ 20. PAGE 39 E0768
S40
LAW
ATTIT
TOTALISM
INT/LAW

GERTH H.,"THE NAZI PARTY: ITS LEADERSHIP AND COMPOSITION" (BMR)" GERMANY ELITES STRATA STRUCT EX/STRUC FORCES ECO/TAC CT/SYS CHOOSE TOTALISM AGE/Y AUTHORIT PWR 20. PAGE 43 E0851
S40
POL/PAR
DOMIN
LEAD
ADMIN

BENTHAM J.,"ON THE LIBERTY OF THE PRESS, AND PUBLIC DISCUSSION" IN J. BOWRING, ED., THE WORKS OF JEREMY BENTHAM." SPAIN UK LAW ELITES NAT/G LEGIS INSPECT LEGIT WRITING CONTROL PRIVIL TOTALISM AUTHORIT ...TRADIT 19 FREE/SPEE. PAGE 10 E0193
C43
ORD/FREE
PRESS
CONFER
CONSERVE

MASON J.B.,"THE JUDICIAL SYSTEM OF THE NAZI PARTY." GERMANY ELITES POL/PAR DOMIN CONTROL SANCTION TOTALISM...JURID 20 HITLER/A. PAGE 69 E1381
S44
FASCISM
CT/SYS
ADJUD
LAW

CONOVER H.F.,THE GOVERNMENTS OF THE MAJOR FOREIGN POWERS: A BIBLIOGRAPHY. FRANCE GERMANY ITALY UK
B45
BIBLIOG
NAT/G

USSR CONSTN LOC/G POL/PAR EX/STRUC FORCES ADMIN CT/SYS CIVMIL/REL TOTALISM...POLICY 19/20. PAGE 25 E0494 — DIPLOM

B46
CORRY J.A.,DEMOCRATIC GOVERNMENT AND POLITICS. WOR-45 EX/STRUC LOBBY TOTALISM...MAJORIT CONCPT METH/COMP NAT/COMP 20. PAGE 26 E0511 — NAT/G CONSTN POL/PAR JURID

B49
US LIBRARY OF CONGRESS,FREEDOM OF INFORMATION: SELECTIVE REPORT ON RECENT WRITINGS. USA+45 LAW CONSTN ELITES EDU/PROP PRESS LOBBY WAR TOTALISM ATTIT 20 UN UNESCO COLD/WAR. PAGE 101 E2018 — BIBLIOG/A ORD/FREE LICENSE COM/IND

B55
BENTON W.E.,NUREMBERG: GERMAN VIEWS OF THE WAR TRIALS. EUR+WWI GERMANY VOL/ASSN LEAD PARTIC COERCE INGP/REL RACE/REL TOTALISM SUPEGO ORD/FREE...ANTHOL NUREMBERG. PAGE 10 E0201 — CRIME WAR LAW JURID

B56
SIPKOV I.,LEGAL SOURCES AND BIBLIOGRAPHY OF BULGARIA. BULGARIA COM LEGIS WRITING ADJUD CT/SYS ...INT/LAW TREATY 20. PAGE 91 E1834 — BIBLIOG LAW TOTALISM MARXISM

B57
COSSIO C.,LA POLITICA COMO CONCIENCIA; MEDITACION SOBRE LA ARGENTINA DE 1955. WOR+45 LEGIS EDU/PROP PARL/PROC PARTIC ATTIT PWR CATHISM 20 ARGEN PERON/JUAN. PAGE 26 E0517 — POL/PAR REV TOTALISM JURID

S58
STAAR R.F.,"ELECTIONS IN COMMUNIST POLAND." EUR+WWI COM SOCIETY INT/ORG NAT/G POL/PAR LEGIS ACT/RES ECO/TAC EDU/PROP ADJUD ADMIN ROUTINE COERCE TOTALISM ATTIT ORD/FREE PWR 20. PAGE 93 E1864 — COM CHOOSE POLAND

B59
HOBSBAWM E.J.,PRIMITIVE REBELS; STUDIES IN ARCHAIC FORMS OF SOCIAL MOVEMENT IN THE 19TH AND 20TH CENTURIES. ITALY SPAIN CULTURE VOL/ASSN RISK CROWD GP/REL INGP/REL ISOLAT TOTALISM...PSY SOC 18/20. PAGE 53 E1058 — SOCIETY CRIME REV GUERRILLA

B59
HOOK S.,POLITICAL POWER AND PERSONAL FREEDOM: CRITICAL STUDIES IN DEMOCRACY, COMMUNISM AND CIVIL RIGHTS. UNIV LAW SOCIETY DIPLOM TOTALISM MARXISM SOCISM...PHIL/SCI IDEA/COMP 20 CIV/RIGHTS. PAGE 55 E1094 — ORD/FREE PWR WELF/ST CHOOSE

B59
KNIERIEM A.,THE NUREMBERG TRIALS. EUR+WWI GERMANY VOL/ASSN LEAD COERCE WAR INGP/REL TOTALISM SUPEGO ORD/FREE...CONCPT METH/COMP. PAGE 61 E1225 — INT/LAW CRIME PARTIC JURID

S60
GRACIA-MORA M.R.,"INTERNATIONAL RESPONSIBILITY FOR SUBVERSIVE ACTIVITIES AND HOSTILE PROPAGANDA BY PRIVATE PERSONS AGAINST." COM EUR+WWI L/A+17C UK USA+45 USSR WOR-45 CONSTN NAT/G LEGIT ADJUD REV PEACE TOTALISM ORD/FREE...INT/LAW 20. PAGE 45 E0895 — INT/ORG JURID SOVEREIGN

B61
COWEN D.V.,THE FOUNDATIONS OF FREEDOM. AFR SOUTH/AFR DOMIN LEGIT ADJUST DISCRIM TOTALISM ATTIT ORD/FREE...MAJORIT JURID SOC/INTEG WORSHIP 20 NEGRO. PAGE 27 E0529 — CONSTN ELITES RACE/REL

B61
MECHAM J.L.,THE UNITED STATES AND INTER-AMERICAN SECURITY, 1889-1960. L/A+17C USA+45 USA-45 CONSTN FORCES INT/TRADE PEACE TOTALISM ATTIT...JURID 19/20 UN OAS. PAGE 72 E1432 — DIPLOM WAR ORD/FREE INT/ORG

N61
DELEGACION NACIONAL DE PRENSA,FALANGE ESPANOL TRADICIONALISTA Y DE LAS JUNTAS OFENSIVAS NACIONALES SINDICALISTAS. IX CONSEJO NACIONAL (PAMPHLET). LAW VOL/ASSN TOTALISM AUTHORIT ORD/FREE FASCISM...ANTHOL 20 FRANCO/F FALANGIST. PAGE 31 E0605 — EDU/PROP FASCIST CONFER POL/PAR

B62
HEYDECKER J.J.,THE NUREMBERG TRIAL: HISTORY OF NAZI GERMANY AS REVEALED THROUGH THE TESTIMONY AT NUREMBERG. EUR+WWI GERMANY VOL/ASSN LEAD COERCE CROWD INGP/REL RACE/REL SUPEGO ORD/FREE...CONCPT 20 NAZI ANTI/SEMIT NUREMBERG JEWS. PAGE 52 E1036 — LAW CRIME PARTIC TOTALISM

B62
SOMMER T.,DEUTSCHLAND UND JAPAN ZWISCHEN DEN — DIPLOM

MACHTEN. GERMANY DELIB/GP BAL/PWR AGREE COERCE TOTALISM PWR 20 CHINJAP TREATY. PAGE 93 E1856 — WAR ATTIT

B63
PRYOR F.L.,THE COMMUNIST FOREIGN TRADE SYSTEM. COM CZECHOSLVK GERMANY YUGOSLAVIA LAW ECO/DEV DIST/IND POL/PAR PLAN DOMIN TOTALISM DRIVE RIGID/FLEX WEALTH ...STAT STAND/INT CHARTS 20. PAGE 83 E1657 — ATTIT ECO/TAC

S63
GIRAUD E.,"L'INTERDICTION DU RECOURS A LA FORCE, LA THEORIE ET LA PRATIQUE DES NATIONS UNIES." ALGERIA COM CUBA HUNGARY WOR+45 ADJUD TOTALISM ATTIT RIGID/FLEX PWR...POLICY JURID CONCPT UN 20 CONGO. PAGE 44 E0872 — INT/ORG FORCES DIPLOM

B64
DOOLIN D.J.,COMMUNIST CHINA: THE POLITICS OF STUDENT OPPOSITION. CHINA/COM ELITES STRATA ACADEM NAT/G WRITING CT/SYS LEAD PARTIC COERCE TOTALISM 20. PAGE 32 E0637 — MARXISM DEBATE AGE/Y PWR

B64
WAY H.F. JR.,LIBERTY IN THE BALANCE - CURRENT ISSUES IN CIVIL LIBERTIES. USA+45 USA-45 DELIB/GP RACE/REL DISCRIM TOTALISM MARXISM SOCISM...CONCPT 20 CONGRESS SUPREME/CT CIVIL/LIB. PAGE 105 E2104 — ORD/FREE EDU/PROP NAT/G JURID

B66
DALLIN A.,POLITICS IN THE SOVIET UNION: 7 CASES. COM USSR LAW POL/PAR CHIEF FORCES WRITING CONTROL PARL/PROC CIVMIL/REL TOTALISM...ANTHOL 20 KHRUSH/N STALIN/J CASEBOOK COM/PARTY. PAGE 28 E0563 — MARXISM DOMIN ORD/FREE GOV/REL

B66
LEHMANN L.,LEGAL UND OPPORTUN - POLITISCHE JUSTIZ IN DER BUNDESREPUBLIK. GERMANY/W EDU/PROP ADJUD CONTROL PARL/PROC COERCE TOTALISM ATTIT 20 COM/PARTY. PAGE 64 E1281 — ORD/FREE POL/PAR JURID LEGIS

TOTALITARIANISM....SEE TOTALISM

TOTOK W. E1936

TOURISM....SEE TRAVEL

TOUSSAIN/P....PIERRE DOMINIQUE TOUSSAINT L'OUVERTURE

TOWLE L.W. E1937

TOWNS....SEE MUNIC

TOWNSD/PLN....TOWNSEND PLAN

TOWNSEND PLAN....SEE TOWNSD/PLN

TOYNBEE/A....ARNOLD TOYNBEE

TRADE, INTERNATIONAL....SEE INT/TRADE

TRADIT....TRADITIONAL AND ARISTOCRATIC

B03
FAGUET E.,LE LIBERALISME. FRANCE PRESS ADJUD ADMIN DISCRIM CONSERVE SOCISM...TRADIT SOC LING WORSHIP PARLIAMENT. PAGE 36 E0711 — ORD/FREE EDU/PROP NAT/G LAW

C05
DUNNING W.A.,"HISTORY OF POLITICAL THEORIES FROM LUTHER TO MONTESQUIEU." LAW NAT/G SECT DIPLOM REV WAR ORD/FREE SOVEREIGN CONSERVE...TRADIT BIBLIOG 16/18. PAGE 33 E0663 — PHIL/SCI CONCPT GEN/LAWS

B30
BYNKERSHOEK C.,QUAESTIONUM JURIS PUBLICI LIBRI DUO. CHRIST-17C MOD/EUR CONSTN ELITES SOCIETY NAT/G PROVS EX/STRUC FORCES TOP/EX BAL/PWR DIPLOM ATTIT MORAL...TRADIT CONCPT. PAGE 18 E0352 — INT/ORG LAW NAT/LISM INT/LAW

C43
BENTHAM J.,"ON THE LIBERTY OF THE PRESS; AND PUBLIC DISCUSSION" IN J. BOWRING, ED., THE WORKS OF JEREMY BENTHAM." SPAIN UK LAW ELITES NAT/G LEGIS INSPECT LEGIT WRITING CONTROL PRIVIL TOTALISM AUTHORIT ...TRADIT 19 FREE/SPEE. PAGE 10 E0193 — ORD/FREE PRESS CONFER CONSERVE

B63
LIVELY E.,THE INVASION OF MISSISSIPPI. USA+45 LAW CONSTN NAT/G PROVS CT/SYS GOV/REL FEDERAL CONSERVE ...TRADIT 20 MISSISSIPP NEGRO NAACP WARRN/EARL KENNEDY/JF. PAGE 66 E1309 — RACE/REL CROWD COERCE MARXISM

B65
SCHUBERT G.,THE POLITICAL ROLE OF THE COURTS IN JUDICIAL POLICY MAKING. USA+45 CONSTN JUDGE — CT/SYS POLICY

FEEDBACK CHOOSE RACE/REL ORD/FREE...TRADIT PSY   DECISION
BIBLIOG/A 20 KENNEDY/JF SUPREME/CT. PAGE 89 E1776

TRADITIONAL....SEE CONSERVE, TRADIT

TRAINING....SEE SCHOOL, ACADEM, SKILL, EDU/PROP

TRANSFER....TRANSFER

TRANSITIVITY OF CHOICE....SEE DECISION

TRANSKEI....TRANSKEI

TRANSPORTATION....SEE DIST/IND

TRAVEL....TRAVEL AND TOURISM

TRAYNOR R.J. E1938

TREASURY DEPARTMENT....SEE DEPT/TREAS

TREATY....TREATIES; INTERNATIONAL AGREEMENTS

TOSCANO M.,THE HISTORY OF TREATIES AND   DIPLOM
INTERNATIONAL POLITICS (REV. ED.). WOR-45 AGREE WAR INT/ORG
...BIOG 19/20 TREATY WWI. PAGE 97 E1935   N

DE MARTENS G.F.,RECUEIL GENERALE DE TRAITES ET   BIBLIOG
AUTRES ACTES RELATIFS AUX RAPPORTS DE DROIT   INT/LAW
INTERNATIONAL (41 VOLS.). EUR+WWI MOD/EUR USA-45 DIPLOM
...INDEX TREATY 18/20. PAGE 30 E0587   N

SOCIETE DES NATIONS,TRAITES INTERNATIONAUX ET ACTES BIBLIOG
LEGISLATIFS. WOR-45 INT/ORG NAT/G...INT/LAW JURID DIPLOM
20 LEAGUE/NAT TREATY. PAGE 92 E1851   LEGIS
  ADJUD

BERNARD M.,FOUR LECTURES ON SUBJECTS CONNECTED WITH LAW
DIPLOMACY. WOR-45 NAT/G VOL/ASSN RIGID/FLEX MORAL ATTIT
PWR...JURID OBS GEN/LAWS GEN/METH 20 TREATY.   DIPLOM
PAGE 11 E0209   B00

HOLLAND T.E.,STUDIES IN INTERNATIONAL LAW. TURKEY INT/ORG
USSR WOR-45 CONSTN NAT/G DIPLOM DOMIN LEGIT COERCE LAW
WAR PEACE ORD/FREE PWR SOVEREIGN...JURID CHARTS 20 INT/LAW
PARLIAMENT SUEZ TREATY. PAGE 54 E1084   B00

CRANDALL S.B.,TREATIES: THEIR MAKING AND   LAW
ENFORCEMENT. MOD/EUR USA-45 CONSTN INT/ORG NAT/G B04
LEGIS EDU/PROP LEGIT EXEC PEACE KNOWL MORAL...JURID
CONGRESS 19/20 TREATY. PAGE 27 E0541

MEZERIK A.G.,ATOM TESTS AND RADIATION HAZARDS   NUC/PWR
(PAMPHLET). WOR+45 INT/ORG DIPLOM DETER 20 UN   ARMS/CONT
TREATY. PAGE 73 E1452   CONFER
  HEALTH

MEZERIK AG,OUTER SPACE: UN, US, USSR (PAMPHLET).   SPACE
USSR DELIB/GP FORCES DETER NUC/PWR SOVEREIGN   CONTROL
...POLICY 20 UN TREATY. PAGE 73 E1453   DIPLOM
  INT/ORG

TAYLOR H.,WHY THE PENDING TREATY WITH COLOMBIA   INT/LAW
SHOULD BE RATIFIED (PAMPHLET). PANAMA USA-45   DIPLOM
DELIB/GP INT/TRADE REV ORD/FREE...JURID TREATY
18/19 ROOSEVLT/T TAFT/WH COLOMB. PAGE 95 E1912

MEYER H.H.B.,LIST OF REFERENCES ON THE TREATY-   BIBLIOG
MAKING POWER. USA-45 CONTROL PWR...INT/LAW TIME/SEQ DIPLOM
18/20 TREATY. PAGE 72 E1448   CONSTN

HALL W.E.,A TREATISE ON INTERNATIONAL LAW. WOR-45   PWR
CONSTN INT/ORG NAT/G DIPLOM ORD/FREE LEAGUE/NAT 20 JURID
TREATY. PAGE 49 E0985   WAR
  INT/LAW

NAVILLE A.,LIBERTE, EGALITE, SOLIDARITE: ESSAIS   ORD/FREE
D'ANALYSE. STRATA FAM VOL/ASSN INT/TRADE GP/REL   SOC
MORAL MARXISM SOCISM...PSY TREATY. PAGE 76 E1529 IDEA/COMP
  DIPLOM

INSTITUT INTERMEDIAIRE INTL,REPERTOIRE GENERAL DES BIBLIOG
TRAITES ET AUTRES ACTES DIPLOMATIQUES CONCLUS   DIPLOM

DEPUIS 1895 JUSQU'EN 1920. MOD/EUR WOR-45 INT/ORG
VOL/ASSN DELIB/GP INT/TRADE WAR TREATY 19/20.
PAGE 56 E1125

FLEMMING D.,THE UNITED STATES AND THE LEAGUE OF   INT/ORG
NATIONS, 1918-1920. FUT USA-45 NAT/G LEGIS TOP/EX EDU/PROP
DEBATE CHOOSE PEACE ATTIT SOVEREIGN...TIME/SEQ
CON/ANAL CONGRESS LEAGUE/NAT 20 TREATY. PAGE 39
E0764

DANGERFIELD R.,IN DEFENSE OF THE SENATE. USA-45   LEGIS
CONSTN NAT/G EX/STRUC TOP/EX ATTIT KNOWL   DELIB/GP
...METH/CNCPT STAT TIME/SEQ TREND CON/ANAL CHARTS DIPLOM
CONGRESS 20 TREATY. PAGE 28 E0565

REID H.D.,RECUEIL DES COURS; TOME 45: LES   ORD/FREE
SERVITUDES INTERNATIONALES III. FRANCE CONSTN   DIPLOM
DELIB/GP PRESS CONTROL REV WAR CHOOSE PEACE MORAL LAW
MARITIME TREATY. PAGE 84 E1680

US TARIFF COMMISSION,THE TARIFF; A BIBLIOGRAPHY: A BIBLIOG/A
SELECT LIST OF REFERENCES. USA-45 LAW DIPLOM TAX   TARIFFS
ADMIN...POLICY TREATY 20. PAGE 103 E2064   ECO/TAC

HUDSON M.,BY PACIFIC MEANS. WOR-45 EDU/PROP   INT/ORG
ORD/FREE...CONCPT TIME/SEQ GEN/LAWS LEAGUE/NAT   CT/SYS
TOT/POP 20 TREATY. PAGE 56 E1110   PEACE

BRIERLY J.L.,THE LAW OF NATIONS (2ND ED.). WOR+45 DIPLOM
WOR-45 INT/ORG AGREE CONTROL COERCE WAR NAT/LISM INT/LAW
PEACE PWR 16/20 TREATY LEAGUE/NAT. PAGE 15 E0297 NAT/G

HUDSON M.O.,INTERNATIONAL LEGISLATION: 1929-1931. INT/LAW
WOR-45 SEA AIR AGRI FINAN LABOR DIPLOM ECO/TAC   PARL/PROC
REPAR CT/SYS ARMS/CONT WAR WEAPON...JURID 20 TREATY ADJUD
LEAGUE/NAT. PAGE 56 E1112   LAW

GRISWOLD A.W.,THE FAR EASTERN POLICY OF THE UNITED DIPLOM
STATES. ASIA S/ASIA USA-45 INT/ORG INT/TRADE WAR   POLICY
NAT/LISM...BIBLIOG 19/20 LEAGUE/NAT ROOSEVLT/T   CHIEF
ROOSEVLT/F WILSON/W TREATY. PAGE 47 E0943

MCNAIR A.D.,THE LAW OF TREATIES: BRITISH PRACTICE AGREE
AND OPINIONS. UK CREATE DIPLOM LEGIT WRITING ADJUD LAW
WAR...INT/LAW JURID TREATY. PAGE 71 E1424   CT/SYS
  NAT/G

BENES E.,INTERNATIONAL SECURITY. GERMANY UK NAT/G   EUR+WWI
DELIB/GP PLAN BAL/PWR ATTIT ORD/FREE PWR LEAGUE/NAT INT/ORG
20 TREATY. PAGE 10 E0186   WAR

WOLFERS A.,BRITAIN AND FRANCE BETWEEN TWO WORLD   DIPLOM
WARS. FRANCE UK INT/ORG NAT/G PLAN BARGAIN ECO/TAC WAR
AGREE ISOLAT ALL/IDEOS...DECISION GEOG 20 TREATY   POLICY
VERSAILLES INTERVENT. PAGE 107 E2139

BIRDSALL P.,VERSAILLES TWENTY YEARS AFTER. MOD/EUR DIPLOM
POL/PAR CHIEF CONSULT FORCES LEGIS REPAR PEACE   NAT/LISM
ORD/FREE...BIBLIOG 20 PRESIDENT TREATY. PAGE 12 WAR
E0231

MICAUD C.A.,THE FRENCH RIGHT AND NAZI GERMANY   DIPLOM
1933-1939: A STUDY OF PUBLIC OPINION. GERMANY UK AGREE
USSR POL/PAR ARMS/CONT COERCE DETER PEACE
RIGID/FLEX PWR MARXISM...FASCIST TREND 20
LEAGUE/NAT TREATY. PAGE 73 E1454

RUDIN H.R.,ARMISTICE 1918. FRANCE GERMANY MOD/EUR AGREE
UK USA-45 NAT/G CHIEF DELIB/GP FORCES BAL/PWR REPAR WAR
ARMS/CONT 20 WILSON/W TREATY. PAGE 86 E1732   PEACE
  DIPLOM

BEVERIDGE W.,THE PRICE OF PEACE. GERMANY UK WOR+45 INT/ORG
WOR-45 NAT/G FORCES CREATE LEGIT REGION WAR ATTIT TREND
KNOWL ORD/FREE PWR...POLICY NEW/IDEA GEN/LAWS   PEACE
LEAGUE/NAT 20 TREATY. PAGE 12 E0223

ENKE S.,INTERNATIONAL ECONOMICS. UK USA+45 USSR INT/TRADE
INT/ORG BAL/PWR BARGAIN CAP/ISM BAL/PAY...NAT/COMP FINAN
20 TREATY. PAGE 35 E0691   TARIFFS

ECO/TAC

...POLICY 16 MACHIAVELL TREATY. PAGE 14 E0272   CONTROL

B47
HYDE C.C.,INTERNATIONAL LAW, CHIEFLY AS INTERPRETED INT/LAW
AND APPLIED BY THE UNITED STATES (3 VOLS., 2ND REV.   DIPLOM
ED.). USA-45 WOR+45 WOR-45 INT/ORG CT/SYS WAR   NAT/G
NAT/LISM PEACE ORD/FREE...JURID 19/20 TREATY.   POLICY
PAGE 56 E1119

B56
SIPKOV I.,LEGAL SOURCES AND BIBLIOGRAPHY OF   BIBLIOG
BULGARIA. BULGARIA COM LEGIS WRITING ADJUD CT/SYS   LAW
...INT/LAW TREATY 20. PAGE 91 E1834   TOTALISM
                                                      MARXISM

N47
FOX W.T.R.,UNITED STATES POLICY IN A TWO POWER   DIPLOM
WORLD. COM USA+45 USSR FORCES DOMIN AGREE NEUTRAL   FOR/AID
NUC/PWR ORD/FREE SOVEREIGN 20 COLD/WAR TREATY   POLICY
EUROPE/W INTERVENT. PAGE 39 E0780

B57
FREUND G.,UNHOLY ALLIANCE. EUR+WWI GERMANY USSR   DIPLOM
FORCES ECO/TAC CONTROL WAR PWR...TREND TREATY.   PLAN
PAGE 40 E0796   POLICY

B48
HOLCOMBE A.N.,HUMAN RIGHTS IN THE MODERN WORLD.   ORD/FREE
WOR+45 LEGIS DIPLOM ADJUD PERSON...INT/LAW 20 UN   INT/ORG
TREATY CIVIL/LIB BILL/RIGHT. PAGE 54 E1071   CONSTN
                                                      LAW

B57
PALMER N.D.,INTERNATIONAL RELATIONS. WOR+45 INT/ORG   DIPLOM
NAT/G ECO/TAC EDU/PROP COLONIAL WAR PWR SOVEREIGN   BAL/PWR
...POLICY T 20 TREATY. PAGE 79 E1593   NAT/COMP

S48
GROSS L.,"THE PEACE OF WESTPHALIA, 1648-1948."   INT/LAW
WOR+45 WOR-45 CONSTN BAL/PWR FEDERAL 17/20 TREATY   AGREE
WESTPHALIA. PAGE 48 E0949   CONCPT
                                                      DIPLOM

B57
US SENATE COMM ON JUDICIARY,HEARING BEFORE   LEGIS
SUBCOMMITTEE ON COMMITTEE OF JUDICIARY, UNITED   CONSTN
STATES SENATE: S. J. RES. 3. USA+45 NAT/G CONSULT   CONFER
DELIB/GP DIPLOM ADJUD LOBBY REPRESENT 20 CONGRESS   AGREE
TREATY. PAGE 102 E2040

S48
MORGENTHAU H.J.,"THE TWILIGHT OF INTERNATIONAL   MORAL
MORALITY" (BMR) WOR+45 WOR-45 BAL/PWR WAR NAT/LISM   DIPLOM
PEACE...POLICY INT/LAW IDEA/COMP 15/20 TREATY   NAT/G
INTERVENT. PAGE 75 E1495

B57
WASSENBERGH H.A.,POST-WAR INTERNATIONAL CIVIL   COM/IND
AVIATION POLICY AND THE LAW OF THE AIR. WOR+45 AIR   NAT/G
INT/ORG DOMIN LEGIT PEACE ORD/FREE...POLICY JURID   INT/LAW
NEW/IDEA OBS TIME/SEQ TREND CHARTS 20 TREATY.
PAGE 105 E2101

B51
BISSAINTHE M.,DICTIONNAIRE DE BIBLIOGRAPHIE   BIBLIOG
HAITIENNE. HAITI ELITES AGRI DIPLOM INT/TRADE   L/A+17C
WRITING ORD/FREE CATHISM...ART/METH GEOG 19/20   SOCIETY
NEGRO TREATY. PAGE 12 E0234   NAT/G

B58
HUNT B.I.,BIPARTISANSHIP: A CASE STUDY OF THE   FOR/AID
FOREIGN ASSISTANCE PROGRAM, 1947-56 (DOCTORAL   POL/PAR
THESIS). USA+45 INT/ORG CONSULT LEGIS TEC/DEV   GP/REL
...BIBLIOG PRESIDENT TREATY NATO TRUMAN/HS   DIPLOM
EISNHWR/DD CONGRESS. PAGE 56 E1114

B51
CORBETT P.E.,LAW AND SOCIETY IN THE RELATIONS OF   INT/LAW
STATES. FUT WOR+45 WOR-45 CONTROL WAR PEACE PWR   DIPLOM
...POLICY JURID 16/20 TREATY. PAGE 26 E0505   INT/ORG

B58
MOSKOWITZ M.,HUMAN RIGHTS AND WORLD ORDER. INT/ORG   DIPLOM
PLAN GP/REL NAT/LISM SOVEREIGN...CONCPT 20 UN   INT/LAW
TREATY CIV/RIGHTS. PAGE 75 E1502   ORD/FREE

B51
INSTITUTE DES RELATIONS INTL,LES ASPECTS   WEAPON
ECONOMIQUES DU REARMEMENT (ETUDE DE L'INSTITUT DES   DEMAND
RELATIONS INTERNATIONALES A BRUXELLES). BELGIUM UK   ECO/TAC
USA+45 EXTR/IND FINAN FORCES WORKER PROB/SOLV   INT/TRADE
DIPLOM PRICE...POLICY 20 TREATY. PAGE 57 E1127

B58
SCHOEDER P.W.,THE AXIS ALLIANCE AND JAPANESE-   AGREE
AMERICAN RELATIONS 1941. ASIA GERMANY UK USA-45   DIPLOM
PEACE ATTIT...POLICY BIBLIOG 20 CHINJAP TREATY.   WAR
PAGE 88 E1763

B52
BRIGGS H.W.,THE LAW OF NATIONS (2ND ED.). WOR+45   INT/LAW
WOR-45 NAT/G LEGIS WAR...ANTHOL 20 TREATY. PAGE 15   DIPLOM
E0301   JURID

B58
SEYID MUHAMMAD V.A.,THE LEGAL FRAMEWORK OF WORLD   INT/LAW
TRADE. WOR+45 INT/ORG DIPLOM CONTROL...BIBLIOG 20   VOL/ASSN
TREATY UN IMF GATT. PAGE 90 E1807   INT/TRADE
                                                      TARIFFS

B52
DUNN F.S.,CURRENT RESEARCH IN INTERNATIONAL   BIBLIOG/A
AFFAIRS. UK USA+45...POLICY TREATY. PAGE 33 E0660   DIPLOM
                                                      INT/LAW

B58
SOC OF COMP LEGIS AND INT LAW,THE LAW OF THE SEA...   INT/LAW
(PAMPHLET). WOR+45 NAT/G INT/TRADE ADJUD CONTROL   INT/ORG
NUC/PWR WAR PEACE ATTIT ORD/FREE...JURID CHARTS 20   DIPLOM
UN TREATY RESOURCE/N. PAGE 92 E1850   SEA

B52
FERRELL R.H.,PEACE IN THEIR TIME. FRANCE UK USA-45   PEACE
INT/ORG NAT/G FORCES CREATE AGREE ARMS/CONT COERCE   DIPLOM
WAR TREATY 20 WILSON/W LEAGUE/NAT BRIAND/A. PAGE 37
E0741

B59
REIFF H.,THE UNITED STATES AND THE TREATY LAW OF   ADJUD
THE SEA. USA+45 USA-45 SEA SOCIETY INT/ORG CONSULT   INT/LAW
DELIB/GP LEGIS DIPLOM LEGIT ATTIT ORD/FREE PWR
WEALTH...GEOG JURID TOT/POP 20 TREATY. PAGE 84
E1681

B52
JACKSON E.,MEETING OF THE MINDS: A WAY TO PEACE   LABOR
THROUGH MEDIATION. WOR+45 INDUS INT/ORG NAT/G   JUDGE
DELIB/GP DIPLOM EDU/PROP LEGIT ORD/FREE...NEW/IDEA
SELF/OBS TIME/SEQ CHARTS GEN/LAWS TOT/POP 20 UN
TREATY. PAGE 57 E1139

B59
SCHNEIDER J.,TREATY-MAKING POWER OF INTERNATIONAL   INT/ORG
ORGANIZATIONS. FUT WOR+45 WOR-45 LAW NAT/G JUDGE   ROUTINE
DIPLOM LEGIT CT/SYS ORD/FREE PWR...INT/LAW JURID
GEN/LAWS TOT/POP UNESCO 20 TREATY. PAGE 88 E1762

B52
LIPPMANN W.,ISOLATION AND ALLIANCES: AN AMERICAN   DIPLOM
SPEAKS TO THE BRITISH. USA+45 USA-45 INT/ORG AGREE   SOVEREIGN
COERCE DETER WAR PEACE MORAL 20 TREATY INTERVENT.   COLONIAL
PAGE 65 E1301   ATTIT

B60
FISCHER L.,THE SOVIETS IN WORLD AFFAIRS. CHINA/COM   DIPLOM
COM EUR+WWI USSR INT/ORG CONFER LEAD ARMS/CONT REV   NAT/G
PWR...CHARTS 20 TREATY VERSAILLES. PAGE 38 E0755   POLICY
                                                      MARXISM

L52
WRIGHT Q.,"CONGRESS AND THE TREATY-MAKING POWER."   ROUTINE
USA+45 WOR+45 CONSTN INTELL NAT/G CHIEF CONSULT   DIPLOM
EX/STRUC LEGIS TOP/EX CREATE GOV/REL DISPL DRIVE   INT/LAW
RIGID/FLEX...TREND TOT/POP CONGRESS CONGRESS 20   DELIB/GP
TREATY. PAGE 108 E2154

B60
HEYSE T.,PROBLEMS FONCIERS ET REGIME DES TERRES   BIBLIOG
(ASPECTS ECONOMIQUES, JURIDIQUES ET SOCIAUX). AFR   AGRI
CONGO/BRAZ INT/ORG DIPLOM SOVEREIGN...GEOG TREATY   ECO/UNDEV
20. PAGE 52 E1037   LEGIS

B53
BRETTON H.L.,STRESEMANN AND THE REVISION OF   POLICY
VERSAILLES: A FIGHT FOR REASON. EUR+WWI GERMANY   DIPLOM
FORCES BUDGET ARMS/CONT WAR SUPEGO...BIBLIOG 20   BIOG
TREATY VERSAILLES STRESEMN/G. PAGE 15 E0294

B60
WOETZEL R.K.,THE INTERNATIONAL CONTROL OF AIRSPACE   INT/ORG
AND OUTERSPACE. FUT WOR+45 AIR CONSTN STRUCT   JURID
CONSULT PLAN TEC/DEV ADJUD RIGID/FLEX KNOWL   SPACE
ORD/FREE PWR...TECHNIC GEOG MGT NEW/IDEA TREND   INT/LAW
COMPUT/IR VAL/FREE 20 TREATY. PAGE 107 E2137

B56
BOTERO G.,THE REASON OF STATE AND THE GREATNESS OF   PHIL/SCI
CITIES. SECT CHIEF FORCES PLAN LEAD WAR MORAL   NEW/IDEA

L60
DEAN A.W.,"SECOND GENEVA CONFERENCE OF THE LAW OF   INT/ORG

THE SEA: THE FIGHT FOR FREEDOM OF THE SEAS." FUT JURID
USA+45 USSR WOR+45 WOR-45 SEA CONSTN STRUCT PLAN INT/LAW
INT/TRADE ADJUD ADMIN ORD/FREE...DECISION RECORD
TREND GEN/LAWS 20 TREATY. PAGE 30 E0600

S60
SANDERS R.,"NUCLEAR DYNAMITE: A NEW DIMENSION IN INDUS
FOREIGN POLICY." FUT WOR+45 ECO/DEV CONSULT TEC/DEV PWR
PERCEPT...CONT/OBS TIME/SEQ TREND GEN/LAWS TOT/POP DIPLOM
20 TREATY. PAGE 87 E1745 NUC/PWR

B61
ROBERTSON A.H.,THE LAW OF INTERNATIONAL RIGID/FLEX
INSTITUTIONS IN EUROPE. EUR+WWI MOD/EUR INT/ORG ORD/FREE
NAT/G VOL/ASSN DELIB/GP...JURID TIME/SEQ TOT/POP 20
TREATY. PAGE 85 E1704

L61
TAUBENFELD H.J.,"A TREATY FOR ANTARCTICA." FUT R+D
USA+45 INTELL INT/ORG LABOR 20 TREATY ANTARCTICA. ACT/RES
PAGE 95 E1909 DIPLOM

B62
AMERICAN LAW INSTITUTE,FOREIGN RELATIONS LAW OF THE PROF/ORG
UNITED STATES: RESTATEMENT, SECOND. USA+45 NAT/G LAW
LEGIS ADJUD EXEC ROUTINE GOV/REL...INT/LAW JURID DIPLOM
CONCPT 20 TREATY. PAGE 4 E0082 ORD/FREE

B62
BISHOP W.W. JR.,INTERNATIONAL LAW: CASES AND INT/LAW
MATERIALS. WOR+45 INT/ORG FORCES PROB/SOLV AGREE DIPLOM
WAR...JURID IDEA/COMP T 20 TREATY. PAGE 12 E0233 CONCPT
CT/SYS

B62
COLOMBOS C.J.,THE INTERNATIONAL LAW OF THE SEA. INT/LAW
WOR+45 EXTR/IND DIPLOM INT/TRADE TARIFFS AGREE WAR SEA
...TIME/SEQ 20 TREATY. PAGE 24 E0476 JURID
ADJUD

B62
DUROSELLE J.B.,HISTOIRE DIPLOMATIQUE DE 1919 A NOS DIPLOM
JOURS (3RD ED.). FRANCE INT/ORG CHIEF FORCES CONFER WOR+45
ARMS/CONT WAR PEACE ORD/FREE...T TREATY 20 WOR-45
COLD/WAR. PAGE 34 E0667

B62
FATOUROS A.A.,GOVERNMENT GUARANTEES TO FOREIGN NAT/G
INVESTORS. WOR+45 ECO/UNDEV INDUS WORKER ADJUD FINAN
...NAT/COMP BIBLIOG TREATY. PAGE 36 E0722 INT/TRADE
ECO/DEV

B62
GANJI M.,INTERNATIONAL PROTECTION OF HUMAN RIGHTS. ORD/FREE
WOR+45 CONSTN INT/TRADE CT/SYS SANCTION CRIME WAR DISCRIM
RACE/REL...CHARTS IDEA/COMP NAT/COMP BIBLIOG 20 LEGIS
TREATY NEGRO LEAGUE/NAT UN CIVIL/LIB. PAGE 42 E0831 DELIB/GP

B62
HENDERSON W.O.,THE GENESIS OF THE COMMON MARKET. ECO/DEV
EUR+WWI FRANCE MOD/EUR UK SEA COM/IND EXTR/IND INT/TRADE
COLONIAL DISCRIM...TIME/SEQ CHARTS BIBLIOG 18/20 DIPLOM
EEC TREATY. PAGE 52 E1030

B62
MCDOUGAL M.S.,THE PUBLIC ORDER OF THE OCEANS. ADJUD
WOR+45 WOR-45 SEA INT/ORG NAT/G CONSULT DELIB/GP ORD/FREE
DIPLOM LEGIT PEACE RIGID/FLEX...GEOG INT/LAW JURID
RECORD TOT/POP 20 TREATY. PAGE 70 E1407

B62
PERKINS D.,AMERICA'S QUEST FOR PEACE. USA+45 WOR+45 INT/LAW
DIPLOM CONFER NAT/LISM ATTIT 20 UN TREATY. PAGE 80 INT/ORG
E1610 ARMS/CONT
PEACE

B62
SHAW C.,LEGAL PROBLEMS IN INTERNATIONAL TRADE AND INT/LAW
INVESTMENT. WOR+45 ECO/DEV ECO/UNDEV MARKET DIPLOM INT/TRADE
TAX INCOME ROLE...ANTHOL BIBLIOG 20 TREATY UN IMF FINAN
GATT. PAGE 91 E1816 ECO/TAC

B62
SOMMER T.,DEUTSCHLAND UND JAPAN ZWISCHEN DEN DIPLOM
MACHTEN. GERMANY DELIB/GP BAL/PWR AGREE COERCE WAR
TOTALISM PWR 20 CHINJAP TREATY. PAGE 93 E1856 ATTIT

B62
WADSWORTH J.J.,THE PRICE OF PEACE. WOR+45 TEC/DEV DIPLOM
CONTROL NUC/PWR PEACE ATTIT TREATY 20. PAGE 104 INT/ORG
E2089 ARMS/CONT
POLICY

S62
CRANE R.D.,"LAW AND STRATEGY IN SPACE." FUT USA+45 CONCPT
WOR+45 AIR LAW INT/ORG NAT/G FORCES ACT/RES PLAN SPACE

BAL/PWR LEGIT ARMS/CONT COERCE ORD/FREE...POLICY
INT/LAW JURID SOC/EXP 20 TREATY. PAGE 27 E0542

S62
VIGNES D.,"L'AUTORITE DES TRAITES INTERNATIONAUX EN STRUCT
DROIT INTERNE." EUR+WWI UNIV LAW CONSTN INTELL LEGIT
NAT/G POL/PAR DIPLOM ATTIT PERCEPT ALL/VALS FRANCE
...POLICY INT/LAW JURID CONCPT TIME/SEQ 20 TREATY.
PAGE 104 E2075

C62
BACON F.,"OF THE TRUE GREATNESS OF KINGDOMS AND WAR
ESTATES" (1612) IN F. BACON, ESSAYS." ELITES FORCES PWR
DOMIN EDU/PROP LEGIT...POLICY GEN/LAWS 16/17 DIPLOM
TREATY. PAGE 7 E0129 CONSTN

B63
DEENER D.R.,CANADA - UNITED STATES TREATY DIPLOM
RELATIONS. CANADA USA+45 USA-45 NAT/G FORCES PLAN INT/LAW
PROB/SOLV AGREE NUC/PWR...TREND 18/20 TREATY. POLICY
PAGE 30 E0603

B63
DUNN F.S.,PEACE-MAKING AND THE SETTLEMENT WITH POLICY
JAPAN. ASIA USA+45 USA-45 FORCES BAL/PWR ECO/TAC PEACE
CONFER WAR PWR SOVEREIGN 20 CHINJAP COLD/WAR PLAN
TREATY. PAGE 33 E0661 DIPLOM

B63
FAWCETT J.E.S.,THE BRITISH COMMONWEALTH IN INT/LAW
INTERNATIONAL LAW. LAW INT/ORG NAT/G VOL/ASSN STRUCT
OP/RES DIPLOM ADJUD CENTRAL CONSEN...NET/THEORY COLONIAL
CMN/WLTH TREATY. PAGE 36 E0723

B63
HIGGINS R.,THE DEVELOPMENT OF INTERNATIONAL LAW INT/ORG
THROUGH THE POLITICAL ORGANS OF THE UNITED NATIONS. INT/LAW
WOR+45 FORCES DIPLOM AGREE COERCE ATTIT SOVEREIGN TEC/DEV
...BIBLIOG 20 UN TREATY. PAGE 52 E1041 JURID

B63
VAN SLYCK P.,PEACE: THE CONTROL OF NATIONAL POWER. ARMS/CONT
CUBA WOR+45 FINAN NAT/G FORCES PROB/SOLV TEC/DEV PEACE
BAL/PWR ADMIN CONTROL ORD/FREE...POLICY INT/LAW UN INT/ORG
COLD/WAR TREATY. PAGE 103 E2069 DIPLOM

S63
GARDNER R.N.,"COOPERATION IN OUTER SPACE." FUT USSR INT/ORG
WOR+45 AIR LAW COM/IND CONSULT DELIB/GP CREATE ACT/RES
KNOWL 20 TREATY. PAGE 42 E0837 PEACE
SPACE

S63
MODELSKI G.,"STUDY OF ALLIANCES." WOR+45 WOR-45 VOL/ASSN
INT/ORG NAT/G FORCES LEGIT ADMIN CHOOSE ALL/VALS CON/ANAL
PWR SKILL...INT/LAW CONCPT GEN/LAWS 20 TREATY. DIPLOM
PAGE 74 E1477

B64
DUBOIS J.,DANGER OVER PANAMA. FUT PANAMA SCHOOL DIPLOM
PROB/SOLV EDU/PROP MARXISM...POLICY 19/20 TREATY COERCE
INTERVENT CANAL/ZONE. PAGE 33 E0652

B64
FULBRIGHT J.W.,OLD MYTHS AND NEW REALITIES. USA+45 DIPLOM
USSR LEGIS INT/TRADE DETER ATTIT...POLICY 20 INT/ORG
COLD/WAR TREATY. PAGE 41 E0818 ORD/FREE

B64
GRIFFITH W.E.,THE SINO-SOVIET RIFT. ASIA CHINA/COM ATTIT
COM CUBA USSR YUGOSLAVIA NAT/G POL/PAR VOL/ASSN TIME/SEQ
DELIB/GP FORCES TOP/EX DIPLOM EDU/PROP DRIVE PERSON BAL/PWR
PWR...TREND 20 TREATY. PAGE 47 E0941 SOCISM

B64
JENKS C.W.,THE PROSPECTS OF INTERNATIONAL INT/LAW
ADJUDICATION. WOR+45 WOR-45 NAT/G DIPLOM CONTROL ADJUD
PWR...POLICY JURID CONCPT METH/COMP 19/20 ICJ CT/SYS
LEAGUE/NAT UN TREATY. PAGE 58 E1160 INT/ORG

B64
SCHWELB E.,HUMAN RIGHTS AND THE INTERNATIONAL INT/ORG
COMMUNITY. WOR+45 WOR-45 NAT/G SECT DELIB/GP DIPLOM ORD/FREE
PEACE RESPECT TREATY 20 UN. PAGE 89 E1792 INT/LAW

B64
TONG T.,UNITED STATES DIPLOMACY IN CHINA, DIPLOM
1844-1860. ASIA USA-45 ECO/UNDEV ECO/TAC COERCE INT/TRADE
GP/REL...INT/LAW 19 TREATY. PAGE 96 E1934 COLONIAL

S64
CARNEGIE ENDOWMENT INT. PEACE,"LEGAL QUESTIONS INT/ORG
(ISSUES BEFORE THE NINETEENTH GENERAL ASSEMBLY)." LAW
WOR+45 CONSTN NAT/G DELIB/GP ADJUD PEACE MORAL INT/LAW
ORD/FREE...RECORD UN 20 TREATY. PAGE 20 E0386

DERWINSKI E.J.,"THE COST OF THE INTERNATIONAL COFFEE AGREEMENT." L/A+17C USA+45 WOR+45 ECO/UNDEV NAT/G VOL/ASSN LEGIS DIPLOM ECO/TAC FOR/AID LEGIT ATTIT...TIME/SEQ CONGRESS 20 TREATY. PAGE 31 E0608

S64
MARKET
DELIB/GP
INT/TRADE

TRISKA J.F.,"SOVIET TREATY LAW: A QUANTITATIVE ANALYSIS." WOR+45 LAW ECO/UNDEV AGRI COM/IND INDUS CREATE TEC/DEV DIPLOM ATTIT PWR WEALTH...JURID SAMP TIME/SEQ TREND CHARTS VAL/FREE 20 TREATY. PAGE 97 E1942

S64
COM
ECO/TAC
INT/LAW
USSR

BAADE H.,THE SOVIET IMPACT ON INTERNATIONAL LAW. INT/ORG INT/TRADE LEGIT COLONIAL ARMS/CONT REV WAR ...CON/ANAL ANTHOL TREATY. PAGE 6 E0124

B65
INT/LAW
USSR
CREATE
ORD/FREE

CAVERS D.F.,THE CHOICE-OF-LAW PROCESS. PROB/SOLV ADJUD CT/SYS CHOOSE RATIONAL...IDEA/COMP 16/20 TREATY. PAGE 21 E0411

B65
JURID
DECISION
METH/COMP
ADMIN

COWEN Z.,THE BRITISH COMMONWEALTH OF NATIONS IN A CHANGING WORLD. UK ECO/UNDEV INT/ORG ECO/TAC INT/TRADE COLONIAL WAR GP/REL RACE/REL SOVEREIGN SOC/INTEG 20 TREATY EEC COMMONWLTH. PAGE 27 E0530

B65
JURID
DIPLOM
PARL/PROC
NAT/LISM

GOTLIEB A.,DISARMAMENT AND INTERNATIONAL LAW* A STUDY OF THE ROLE OF LAW IN THE DISARMAMENT PROCESS. USA+45 USSR PROB/SOLV CONFER ADMIN ROUTINE NUC/PWR ORD/FREE SOVEREIGN UN TREATY. PAGE 45 E0893

B65
INT/LAW
INT/ORG
ARMS/CONT
IDEA/COMP

HABERLER G.,A SURVEY OF INTERNATIONAL TRADE THEORY. CANADA FRANCE GERMANY ECO/TAC TARIFFS AGREE COST DEMAND WEALTH...ECOMETRIC 19/20 MONOPOLY TREATY. PAGE 49 E0968

B65
INT/TRADE
BAL/PAY
DIPLOM
POLICY

HAENSCH G.,PAN-AFRICANISM IN ACTION: AN ACCOUNT OF THE UAM TIC AND ALPHABETICAL IN GERMAN, ENGLISH, FRENCH AND SPANISH. WOR+45 INT/ORG NAT/G ARMS/CONT WAR...INT/LAW IDEA/COMP TREATY. PAGE 49 E0974

B65
DICTIONARY
DIPLOM
LING

JENKS C.W.,SPACE LAW. DIPLOM DEBATE CONTROL ORD/FREE TREATY 20 UN. PAGE 58 E1161

B65
SPACE
INT/LAW
JURID
INT/ORG

LUGO-MARENCO J.J.,A STATEMENT OF THE LAWS OF NICARAGUA IN MATTERS AFFECTING BUSINESS. NICARAGUA AGRI DIST/IND EXTR/IND FINAN INDUS FAM WORKER INT/TRADE TAX MARRIAGE OWN BIO/SOC 20 TREATY RESOURCE/N MIGRATION. PAGE 67 E1332

B65
CONSTN
NAT/G
LEGIS
JURID

MONCONDUIT F.,LA COMMISSION EUROPEENNE DES DROITS DE L'HOMME. DIPLOM AGREE GP/REL ORD/FREE PWR ...BIBLIOG 20 TREATY. PAGE 74 E1483

B65
INT/LAW
INT/ORG
ADJUD
JURID

MORRIS R.B.,THE PEACEMAKERS; THE GREAT POWERS AND AMERICAN INDEPENDENCE. BAL/PWR CONFER COLONIAL NEUTRAL PEACE ORD/FREE TREATY 18 PRE/US/AM. PAGE 75 E1499

B65
SOVEREIGN
REV
DIPLOM

NWOGUGU E.I.,THE LEGAL PROBLEMS OF FOREIGN INVESTMENT IN DEVELOPING COUNTRIES. WOR+45 INT/ORG DELIB/GP LEGIS PROB/SOLV INT/TRADE TAX ADJUD SANCTION...BIBLIOG 20 TREATY. PAGE 78 E1561

B65
FOR/AID
FINAN
INT/LAW
ECO/UNDEV

O'CONNELL D.P.,INTERNATIONAL LAW (2 VOLS.). WOR+45 WOR-45 ECO/DEV ECO/UNDEV INT/ORG NAT/G AGREE ...POLICY JURID CONCPT NAT/COMP 20 TREATY. PAGE 78 E1566

B65
INT/LAW
DIPLOM
CT/SYS

PARRY C.,THE SOURCES AND EVIDENCES OF INTERNATIONAL LAW. WOR+45 WOR-45 DIPLOM AGREE SOVEREIGN...METH 20 TREATY UN LEAGUE/NAT. PAGE 80 E1599

B65
INT/LAW
ADJUD
INT/ORG
CT/SYS

UNESCO,HANDBOOK OF INTERNATIONAL EXCHANGES. COM/IND R+D ACADEM PROF/ORG VOL/ASSN CREATE TEC/DEV EDU/PROP AGREE 20 TREATY. PAGE 98 E1963

B65
INDEX
INT/ORG
DIPLOM

US SENATE,US INTERNATIONAL SPACE PROGRAMS, 1959-65: STAFF REPORT FOR COMM ON AERONAUTICAL AND SPACE SCIENCES. WOR+45 VOL/ASSN CIVMIL/REL 20 CONGRESS NASA TREATY. PAGE 101 E2027

B65
SPACE
DIPLOM
PLAN
GOV/REL

BROWNLIE I.,"SOME LEGAL ASPECTS OF THE USE OF NUCLEAR WEAPONS." UK NEUTRAL DETER UN TREATY. PAGE 16 E0317

S65
LAW
NUC/PWR
WAR
INT/LAW

FOX A.B.,"NATO AND CONGRESS." CONSTN DELIB/GP EX/STRUC FORCES TOP/EX BUDGET NUC/PWR GOV/REL ...GP/COMP CONGRESS NATO TREATY. PAGE 39 E0779

S65
CONTROL
DIPLOM

HIBBS A.R.,"SPACE TECHNOLOGY* THE THREAT AND THE PROMISE." FUT VOL/ASSN TEC/DEV NUC/PWR COST EFFICIENCY UTIL UN TREATY. PAGE 52 E1038

S65
SPACE
ARMS/CONT
PREDICT

MARTIN A.,"PROLIFERATION." FUT WOR+45 PROB/SOLV REGION ADJUST...PREDICT NAT/COMP UN TREATY. PAGE 69 E1372

S65
RECORD
NUC/PWR
ARMS/CONT
VOL/ASSN

CANFIELD L.H.,THE PRESIDENCY OF WOODROW WILSON: PRELUDE TO A WORLD IN CRISIS. USA-45 ADJUD NEUTRAL WAR CHOOSE INGP/REL PEACE ORD/FREE 20 WILSON/W PRESIDENT TREATY LEAGUE/NAT. PAGE 19 E0373

B66
PERSON
POLICY
DIPLOM
GOV/REL

DYCK H.V.,WEIMAR GERMANY AND SOVIET RUSSIA 1926-1933. EUR+WWI GERMANY UK USSR ECO/TAC INT/TRADE NEUTRAL WAR ATTIT 20 WEIMAR/REP TREATY. PAGE 34 E0669

B66
DIPLOM
GOV/REL
POLICY

HAY P.,FEDERALISM AND SUPRANATIONAL ORGANIZATIONS: PATTERNS FOR NEW LEGAL STRUCTURES. EUR+WWI LAW NAT/G VOL/ASSN DIPLOM PWR...NAT/COMP TREATY EEC. PAGE 51 E1014

B66
SOVEREIGN
FEDERAL
INT/ORG
INT/LAW

HOYT E.C.,NATIONAL POLICY AND INTERNATIONAL LAW* CASE STUDIES FROM AMERICAN CANAL POLICY* MONOGRAPH NO. 1 -- 1966-1967. PANAMA UK ELITES BAL/PWR EFFICIENCY...CLASSIF NAT/COMP SOC/EXP COLOMB TREATY. PAGE 55 E1105

B66
INT/LAW
USA-45
DIPLOM
PWR

JACOBSON H.K.,DIPLOMATS, SCIENTISTS, AND POLITICIANS* THE UNITED STATES AND THE NUCLEAR TEST BAN NEGOTIATIONS. USA+45 USSR ACT/RES PLAN CONFER DETER NUC/PWR CONSEN ORD/FREE...INT TREATY. PAGE 57 E1146

B66
DIPLOM
ARMS/CONT
TECHRACY
INT/ORG

LEE L.T.,VIENNA CONVENTION ON CONSULAR RELATIONS. WOR+45 LAW INT/ORG CONFER GP/REL PRIVIL...INT/LAW 20 TREATY VIENNA/CNV. PAGE 64 E1277

B66
AGREE
DIPLOM
ADMIN

OBERMANN E.,VERTEIDIGUNG PER FREIHEIT. GERMANY/W WOR+45 INT/ORG COERCE NUC/PWR WEAPON MARXISM 20 UN NATO WARSAW/P TREATY. PAGE 78 E1571

B66
FORCES
ORD/FREE
WAR
PEACE

POLLACK R.S.,THE INDIVIDUAL'S RIGHTS AND INTERNATIONAL ORGANIZATION. LAW INT/ORG DELIB/GP SUPEGO...JURID SOC/INTEG 20 TREATY UN. PAGE 81 E1623

B66
INT/LAW
ORD/FREE
DIPLOM
PERSON

THOMPSON J.M.,RUSSIA, BOLSHEVISM, AND THE VERSAILLES PEACE. RUSSIA USSR INT/ORG NAT/G DELIB/GP AGREE REV WAR PWR 20 TREATY VERSAILLES BOLSHEVISM. PAGE 96 E1919

B66
DIPLOM
PEACE
MARXISM

WAINHOUSE D.W.,INTERNATIONAL PEACE OBSERVATION: A HISTORY AND FORECAST. INT/ORG PROB/SOLV BAL/PWR AGREE ARMS/CONT COERCE NUC/PWR...PREDICT METH/COMP 20 UN LEAGUE/NAT OAS TREATY. PAGE 104 E2092

B66
PEACE
DIPLOM

YOUNG W.,EXISTING MECHANISMS OF ARMS CONTROL. PROC/MFG OP/RES DIPLOM TASK CENTRAL...MGT TREATY. PAGE 108 E2165

B66
ARMS/CONT
ADMIN
NUC/PWR
ROUTINE

PRESS

GREIG D.W.,"THE ADVISORY JURISDICTION OF THE
INTERNATIONAL COURT AND THE SETTLEMENT OF DISPUTES
BETWEEN STATES." ISRAEL KOREA FORCES BUDGET DOMIN
LEGIT ADJUD COST...RECORD UN CONGO/LEOP TREATY.
PAGE 46 E0915
   L66
INT/LAW
CT/SYS

HIGGINS R.,"THE INTERNATIONAL COURT AND SOUTH WEST
AFRICA* SOME IMPLICATIONS OF THE JUDGMENT." AFR LAW
ECO/UNDEV JUDGE RACE/REL COST PWR...INT/LAW TREND
UN TREATY. PAGE 52 E1043
   L66
SOUTH/AFR
COLONIAL
CT/SYS
ADJUD

BROWNLIE I.,"NUCLEAR PROLIFERATION* SOME PROBLEMS
OF CONTROL." USA+45 USSR ECO/UNDEV INT/ORG FORCES
TEC/DEV REGION CONSEN...RECORD TREATY. PAGE 16
E0318
   S66
NUC/PWR
ARMS/CONT
VOL/ASSN
ORD/FREE

DETTER I.,"THE PROBLEM OF UNEQUAL TREATIES." CONSTN
NAT/G LEGIS COLONIAL COERCE PWR...GEOG UN TIME
TREATY. PAGE 31 E0610
   S66
SOVEREIGN
DOMIN
INT/LAW
ECO/UNDEV

GARCIA ROBLES A.,THE DENUCLEARIZATION OF LATIN
AMERICA (TRANS. BY MARJORIE URQUIDI). LAW PLAN
DIPLOM...ANTHOL 20 TREATY UN. PAGE 42 E0833
   B67
NUC/PWR
ARMS/CONT
L/A+17C
INT/ORG

LAWYERS COMM AMER POLICY VIET,VIETNAM AND
INTERNATIONAL LAW: AN ANALYSIS OF THE LEGALITY OF
THE US MILITARY INVOLVEMENT. VIETNAM LAW INT/ORG
COERCE WEAPON PEACE ORD/FREE 20 UN SEATO TREATY.
PAGE 64 E1271
   B67
INT/LAW
DIPLOM
ADJUD
WAR

MCBRIDE J.H.,THE TEST BAN TREATY: MILITARY,
TECHNOLOGICAL, AND POLITICAL IMPLICATIONS. USA+45
USSR DELIB/GP FORCES LEGIS TEC/DEV BAL/PWR TREATY.
PAGE 70 E1399
   B67
ARMS/CONT
DIPLOM
NUC/PWR

MCDOUGAL M.S.,THE INTERPRETATION OF AGREEMENTS AND
WORLD PUBLIC ORDER: PRINCIPLES OF CONTENT AND
PROCEDURE. WOR+45 CONSTN PROB/SOLV TEC/DEV
...CON/ANAL TREATY. PAGE 71 E1412
   B67
INT/LAW
STRUCT
ECO/UNDEV
DIPLOM

PADELFORD N.J.,THE DYNAMICS OF INTERNATIONAL
POLITICS (2ND ED.). WOR+45 LAW INT/ORG FORCES
TEC/DEV REGION NAT/LISM PEACE ATTIT PWR ALL/IDEOS
UN COLD/WAR NATO TREATY. PAGE 79 E1589
   B67
DIPLOM
NAT/G
POLICY
DECISION

POGANY A.H.,POLITICAL SCIENCE AND INTERNATIONAL
RELATIONS. BOOKS RECOMMENDED FOR AMERICAN CATHOLIC
COLLEGE LIBRARIES. INT/ORG LOC/G NAT/G FORCES
BAL/PWR ECO/TAC NUC/PWR...CATH INT/LAW TREATY 20.
PAGE 81 E1622
   B67
BIBLIOG
DIPLOM

US DEPARTMENT OF STATE,TREATIES IN FORCE. USA+45
WOR+45 AGREE WAR PEACE 20 TREATY. PAGE 100 E1999
   B67
BIBLIOG
DIPLOM
INT/ORG
DETER

US SENATE COMM ON FOREIGN REL,CONSULAR CONVENTION
WITH THE SOVIET UNION. USA+45 USSR DELIB/GP LEAD
REPRESENT ATTIT ORD/FREE CONGRESS TREATY. PAGE 101
E2031
   B67
LEGIS
LOBBY
DIPLOM

US SENATE COMM ON FOREIGN REL,TREATY ON OUTER
SPACE. WOR+45 AIR FORCES PROB/SOLV NUC/PWR SENATE
TREATY UN. PAGE 101 E2032
   B67
SPACE
DIPLOM
ARMS/CONT
LAW

US SENATE COMM ON FOREIGN REL,UNITED STATES
ARMAMENT AND DISARMAMENT PROBLEMS. USA+45 AIR
BAL/PWR DIPLOM FOR/AID NUC/PWR ORD/FREE SENATE
TREATY. PAGE 102 E2035
   B67
ARMS/CONT
WEAPON
FORCES
PROB/SOLV

WATT A.,THE EVOLUTION OF AUSTRALIAN FOREIGN POLICY
1938-65. ASIA S/ASIA USA+45 USA-45 INT/ORG NAT/G
FORCES FOR/AID TREATY 20 AUSTRAL. PAGE 105 E2103
   B67
DIPLOM
WAR

WAELBROECK M.,"THE APPLICATION OF EEC LAW BY
NATIONAL COURTS." EUR+WWI INT/ORG CT/SYS...JURID
   L67
INT/LAW
NAT/G

EEC TREATY. PAGE 104 E2090
LAW
PROB/SOLV

EYRAUD M.,"LA FRANCE FACE A UN EVENTUEL TRAITE DE
NON DISSEMINATION DES ARMES NUCLEAIRES." FRANCE
USA+45 EXTR/IND INDUS R+D INT/ORG ACT/RES TEC/DEV
AGREE PRODUC ATTIT 20 TREATY AEC EURATOM. PAGE 36
E0708
   S67
NUC/PWR
ARMS/CONT
POLICY

LARSEN P.B.,"THE UNITED STATES-ITALY AIR TRANSPORT
ARBITRATION: PROBLEMS OF TREATY INTERPRETATION AND
ENFORCEMENT." ITALY USA+45 AIR PROB/SOLV DIPLOM
DEBATE CONTROL CT/SYS...DECISION TREATY. PAGE 63
E1257
   S67
INT/LAW
ADJUD
INT/TRADE
DIST/IND

GREGG R.W.,INTERNATIONAL ORGANIZATION IN THE
WESTERN HEMISPHERE. L/A+17C USA+45 CULTURE PLAN
DOMIN AGREE CONTROL DETER PWR...GEOG 20 OAS TREATY.
PAGE 46 E0913
   B68
INT/ORG
DIPLOM
ECO/UNDEV

HULL R.H.,LAW AND VIETNAM. COM VIETNAM CONSTN
INT/ORG FORCES DIPLOM AGREE COERCE DETER WEAPON
PEACE ATTIT 20 UN TREATY. PAGE 56 E1113
   B68
POLICY
LAW
WAR
INT/LAW

TREND....PROJECTION OF HISTORICAL TRENDS

JOURNAL OF INTERNATIONAL AFFAIRS. WOR+45 ECO/UNDEV
POL/PAR ECO/TAC WAR PEACE PERSON ALL/IDEOS
...INT/LAW TREND. PAGE 1 E0010
   N
BIBLIOG
DIPLOM
INT/ORG
NAT/G

DE TOCQUEVILLE A.,DEMOCRACY IN AMERICA (VOLUME
ONE). LAW SOCIETY STRUCT NAT/G POL/PAR PROVS FORCES
LEGIS TOP/EX DIPLOM LEGIT WAR PEACE ATTIT SOVEREIGN
...SELF/OBS TIME/SEQ CONGRESS 19. PAGE 30 E0594
   B00
USA-45
TREND

LORIMER J.,THE INSTITUTES OF THE LAW OF NATIONS.
WOR-45 CULTURE SOCIETY NAT/G VOL/ASSN DIPLOM LEGIT
WAR PEACE DRIVE ORD/FREE SOVEREIGN...CONCPT RECORD
INT TREND HYPO/EXP GEN/METH TOT/POP VAL/FREE 20.
PAGE 66 E1327
   B00
INT/ORG
LAW
INT/LAW

PHILLIPS J.B.,"MODIFICATIONS OF THE JURY SYSTEM."
PARTIC EFFICIENCY ATTIT PERCEPT...TREND 19
SUPREME/CT JURY. PAGE 80 E1612
   S05
JURID
DELIB/GP
PERS/REL
POLICY

REINSCH P.,PUBLIC INTERNATIONAL UNION. WOR-45 LAW
LABOR INT/TRADE LEGIT PERSON ALL/VALS...SOCIALIST
CONCPT TIME/SEQ TREND GEN/LAWS 19/20. PAGE 84 E1683
   B11
FUT
INT/ORG
DIPLOM

BAILEY S.D.,VETO IN THE SECURITY COUNCIL
(PAMPHLET). COM USSR WOR+45 BAL/PWR PARL/PROC
ARMS/CONT PRIVIL PWR...INT/LAW TREND CHARTS 20 UN
SUEZ. PAGE 7 E0135
   N19
DELIB/GP
INT/ORG
DIPLOM

BUREAU OF NAT'L AFFAIRS INC.,A CURRENT LOOK AT:
(1) THE NEGRO AND TITLE VII, (2) SEX AND TITLE VII
(PAMPHLET). LAW LG/CO SML/CO RACE/REL...POLICY SOC
STAT DEEP/QU TREND CON/ANAL CHARTS 20 NEGRO
CIV/RIGHTS. PAGE 17 E0334
   N19
DISCRIM
SEX
WORKER
MGT

BRYCE J.,MODERN DEMOCRACIES. FUT NEW/ZEALND USA-45
LAW CONSTN POL/PAR PROVS VOL/ASSN EX/STRUC LEGIS
LEGIT CT/SYS EXEC KNOWL CONGRESS AUSTRAL 20.
PAGE 16 E0322
   B21
NAT/G
TREND

CORBETT P.E.,CANADA AND WORLD POLITICS. LAW CULTURE
SOCIETY STRUCT MARKET INT/ORG FORCES ACT/RES PLAN
ECO/TAC LEGIT ORD/FREE PWR RESPECT...SOC CONCPT
TIME/SEQ TREND CMN/WLTH 20 LEAGUE/NAT. PAGE 26
E0504
   B28
NAT/G
CANADA

HUDSON M.,"THE TEACHING OF INTERNATIONAL LAW IN
AMERICA." USA+45 LAW CONSULT ACT/RES CREATE
EDU/PROP ATTIT RIGID/FLEX...JURID CONCPT RECORD
HIST/WRIT TREND GEN/LAWS 18/20. PAGE 56 E1109
   L28
PERCEPT
KNOWL
INT/LAW

DARWIN L.,"WHAT IS EUGENICS." USA-45 LAW SOCIETY
FACE/GP FAM ACT/RES ECO/TAC HEALTH...HEAL TREND
   L29
PLAN
BIO/SOC

BUCK A.E.."PUBLIC BUDGETING." USA-45 FINAN LOC/G
NAT/G LEGIS BAL/PAY COST...JURID TREND BIBLIOG/A
20. PAGE 17 E0324
C29
BUDGET
ROUTINE
ADMIN

STOWELL E.C..INTERNATIONAL LAW. FUT UNIV WOR-45
SOCIETY CONSULT EX/STRUC FORCES ACT/RES PLAN DIPLOM
EDU/PROP LEGIT DISPL PWR SKILL...POLICY CONCPT OBS
TREND TOT/POP 20. PAGE 94 E1885
B31
INT/ORG
ROUTINE
INT/LAW

MASTERS R.D..INTERNATIONAL LAW IN INTERNATIONAL
COURTS. BELGIUM EUR+WWI FRANCE GERMANY MOD/EUR
SWITZERLND WOR-45 SOCIETY STRATA STRUCT LEGIT EXEC
ALL/VALS...JURID HIST/WRIT TIME/SEQ TREND GEN/LAWS
20. PAGE 69 E1383
B32
INT/ORG
LAW
INT/LAW

DANGERFIELD R..IN DEFENSE OF THE SENATE. USA-45
CONSTN NAT/G EX/STRUC TOP/EX ATTIT KNOWL
...METH/CNCPT STAT TIME/SEQ TREND CON/ANAL CHARTS
CONGRESS 20 TREATY. PAGE 28 E0565
B33
LEGIS
DELIB/GP
DIPLOM

HALL J..THEFT, LAW, AND SOCIETY. SOCIETY PROB/SOLV
...CRIMLGY SOC CONCPT TREND METH/COMP 18/20
LARCENCY. PAGE 49 E0982
B35
CRIME
LAW
ADJUD
ADJUST

LUCE R..LEGISLATIVE PROBLEMS. CONSTN CHIEF JUDGE
BUDGET CONFER ETIQUET CONTROL MORAL PWR NEW/LIB
CONGRESS. PAGE 67 E1331
B35
TREND
ADMIN
LEGIS

WILSON G.G..HANDBOOK OF INTERNATIONAL LAW. FUT UNIV
USA-45 WOR-45 SOCIETY LEGIT ATTIT DISPL DRIVE
ALL/VALS...INT/LAW TIME/SEQ TREND. PAGE 106 E2128
B39
INT/ORG
LAW
CONCPT
WAR

CARR E.H..THE TWENTY YEARS' CRISIS 1919-1939. FUT
WOR+45 BAL/PWR ECO/TAC LEGIT TOTALISM ATTIT
ALL/VALS...POLICY JURID CONCPT TIME/SEQ TREND
GEN/LAWS TOT/POP 20. PAGE 20 E0393
B40
INT/ORG
DIPLOM
PEACE

GILL N.N.."PERMANENT ADVISORY COMMISSIONS IN THE
FEDERAL GOVERNMENT." CLIENT FINAN OP/RES EDU/PROP
PARTIC ROUTINE INGP/REL KNOWL SKILL...CLASSIF
TREND. PAGE 43 E0860
S40
DELIB/GP
NAT/G
DECISION

MCCLURE W..INTERNATIONAL EXECUTIVE AGREEMENTS.
USA-45 WOR-45 INT/ORG NAT/G DELIB/GP ADJUD ROUTINE
ORD/FREE PWR...TIME/SEQ TREND CON/ANAL. PAGE 70
E1401
B41
TOP/EX
DIPLOM

HAMBRO C.J..HOW TO WIN THE PEACE. ECO/TAC EDU/PROP
ADJUD PERSON ALL/VALS...SOCIALIST TREND GEN/LAWS
20. PAGE 50 E0987
B42
FUT
INT/ORG
PEACE

KELSEN H..LAW AND PEACE IN INTERNATIONAL RELATIONS.
FUT WOR-45 NAT/G DELIB/GP DIPLOM LEGIT RIGID/FLEX
ORD/FREE SOVEREIGN...JURID CONCPT TREND STERTYP
GEN/LAWS LEAGUE/NAT 20. PAGE 60 E1197
B42
INT/ORG
ADJUD
PEACE
INT/LAW

MICAUD C.A..THE FRENCH RIGHT AND NAZI GERMANY
1933-1939: A STUDY OF PUBLIC OPINION. GERMANY UK
USSR POL/PAR ARMS/CONT COERCE DETER PEACE
RIGID/FLEX PWR MARXISM...FASCIST TREND 20
LEAGUE/NAT TREATY. PAGE 73 E1454
B43
DIPLOM
AGREE

SERENI A.P..THE ITALIAN CONCEPTION OF INTERNATIONAL
LAW. EUR+WWI MOD/EUR INT/ORG NAT/G DOMIN COERCE
ORD/FREE FASCISM...OBS/ENVIR TREND 20. PAGE 90
E1804
B43
LAW
TIME/SEQ
INT/LAW
ITALY

ADLER M.J..HOW TO THINK ABOUT WAR AND PEACE. WOR-45
LAW SOCIETY EX/STRUC DIPLOM KNOWL ORD/FREE...POLICY
TREND GEN/LAWS 20. PAGE 3 E0049
B44
INT/ORG
CREATE
ARMS/CONT
PEACE

HUDSON M..INTERNATIONAL TRIBUNALS PAST AND FUTURE.
FUT WOR+45 LAW EDU/PROP ADJUD ORD/FREE...CONCPT
TIME/SEQ TREND GEN/LAWS TOT/POP VAL/FREE 18/20.
PAGE 56 E1111
B44
INT/ORG
STRUCT
INT/LAW

WRIGHT Q.."CONSTITUTIONAL PROCEDURES OF THE US FOR
CARRYING OUT OBLIGATIONS FOR MILITARY SANCTIONS."
EUR+WWI FUT USA-45 WOR-45 CONSTN INTELL NAT/G
CONSULT EX/STRUC LEGIS ROUTINE DRIVE...POLICY JURID
CONCPT OBS TREND TOT/POP 20. PAGE 108 E2153
S44
TOP/EX
FORCES
INT/LAW
WAR

BEVERIDGE W..THE PRICE OF PEACE. GERMANY UK WOR+45
WOR-45 NAT/G FORCES CREATE LEGIT REGION WAR ATTIT
KNOWL ORD/FREE PWR...POLICY NEW/IDEA GEN/LAWS
LEAGUE/NAT 20 TREATY. PAGE 12 E0223
B45
INT/ORG
TREND
PEACE

ALEXANDER L.."WAR CRIMES, THEIR SOCIAL-
PSYCHOLOGICAL ASPECTS." EUR+WWI GERMANY LAW CULTURE
ELITES KIN POL/PAR PUB/INST FORCES DOMIN EDU/PROP
COERCE CRIME ATTIT SUPEGO HEALTH MORAL PWR FASCISM
...PSY OBS TREND GEN/LAWS NAZI 20. PAGE 3 E0061
S48
DRIVE
WAR

MARITAIN J..HUMAN RIGHTS: COMMENTS AND
INTERPRETATIONS. COM UNIV WOR+45 LAW CONSTN CULTURE
SOCIETY ECO/DEV ECO/UNDEV SCHOOL DELIB/GP EDU/PROP
ATTIT PERCEPT ALL/VALS...HUM SOC TREND UNESCO 20.
PAGE 68 E1365
B49
INT/ORG
CONCPT

US FEDERAL BUREAU INVESTIGAT.BIBLIOGRAPHY OF CRIME
AND KINDRED SUBJECTS (PAPER). USA+45 PROB/SOLV
TREND. PAGE 100 E2001
B50
BIBLIOG/A
CRIME
LAW
CRIMLGY

HOLCOMBE A.."OUR MORE PERFECT UNION." USA+45 USA-45
POL/PAR JUDGE CT/SYS EQUILIB FEDERAL PWR...MAJORIT
TREND BIBLIOG 18/20 CONGRESS PRESIDENT. PAGE 54
E1070
C50
CONSTN
NAT/G
ADMIN
PLAN

FRIEDMANN W..LAW AND SOCIAL CHANGE IN CONTEMPORARY
BRITAIN. UK LABOR LG/CO LEGIS JUDGE CT/SYS ORD/FREE
NEW/LIB...DECISION JURID TREND METH/COMP BIBLIOG 20
PARLIAMENT ENGLSH/LAW COMMON/LAW. PAGE 40 E0802
B51
LAW
ADJUD
SOCIETY
CONSTN

WHEARE K.C..MODERN CONSTITUTIONS (HOME UNIVERSITY
LIBRARY). UNIV LAW NAT/G LEGIS...CONCPT TREND
BIBLIOG. PAGE 106 E2115
B51
CONSTN
CLASSIF
PWR
CREATE

WOOD V..DUE PROCESS OF LAW 1932-1949: SUPREME
COURT'S USE OF A CONSTITUTIONAL TOOL. USA+45 USA-45
SOCIETY TAX CRIME...POLICY CHARTS 20 SUPREME/CT.
PAGE 107 E2143
B51
CONSTN
TREND
ADJUD
GOV/REL

LISSITZYN O.J.."THE INTERNATIONAL COURT OF
JUSTICE." WOR+45 INT/ORG LEGIT ORD/FREE...CONCPT
TIME/SEQ TREND GEN/LAWS VAL/FREE 20 ICJ. PAGE 65
E1304
L51
ADJUD
JURID
INT/LAW

LEEK J.H.."TREASON AND THE CONSTITUTION" (BMR)"
USA+45 USA-45 EDU/PROP COLONIAL CT/SYS REV WAR
ATTIT...TREND 18/20 SUPREME/CT CON/INTERP SMITH/ACT
COMMON/LAW. PAGE 64 E1278
S51
CONSTN
JURID
CRIME
NAT/G

BENTHAM A..HANDBOOK OF POLITICAL FALLACIES. FUT
MOD/EUR LAW INTELL LOC/G MUNIC NAT/G DELIB/GP LEGIS
CREATE EDU/PROP CT/SYS ATTIT RIGID/FLEX KNOWL PWR
...RELATIV PSY SOC CONCPT SELF/OBS TREND STERTYP
TOT/POP. PAGE 10 E0189
B52
POL/PAR

US DEPARTMENT OF STATE.RESEARCH ON EASTERN EUROPE
(EXCLUDING USSR). EUR+WWI LAW ECO/DEV NAT/G
PROB/SOLV DIPLOM ADMIN LEAD MARXISM...TREND 19/20.
PAGE 100 E1995
B52
BIBLIOG
R+D
ACT/RES
COM

WRIGHT Q.."CONGRESS AND THE TREATY-MAKING POWER."
USA+45 WOR+45 CONSTN INTELL NAT/G CHIEF CONSULT
EX/STRUC LEGIS TOP/EX CREATE GOV/REL DISPL DRIVE
RIGID/FLEX...TREND TOT/POP CONGRESS CONGRESS 20
TREATY. PAGE 108 E2154
L52
ROUTINE
DIPLOM
INT/LAW
DELIB/GP

WRIGHT Q..PROBLEMS OF STABILITY AND PROGRESS IN
INTERNATIONAL RELATIONSHIPS. FUT WOR+45 WOR-45
SOCIETY LEGIS CREATE TEC/DEV ECO/TAC EDU/PROP ADJUD
WAR PEACE ORD/FREE PWR...KNO/TEST TREND GEN/LAWS
20. PAGE 108 E2155
B54
INT/ORG
CONCPT
DIPLOM

B56
COHEN A.,THE SUTHERLAND PAPERS. USA+45 USA-45 LAW   CRIMLGY
CONTROL CRIME AGE/Y...TREND ANTHOL BIBLIOG 20.   PHIL/SCI
PAGE 23 E0461   ACT/RES
                                                           METH

B56
HOGAN J.D.,AMERICAN SOCIAL LEGISLATION. USA+45 FAM   STRUCT
AGE/Y ATTIT...JURID CONCPT TREND. PAGE 53 E1065   RECEIVE
                                                           LEGIS
                                                           LABOR

B57
BLOOMFIELD L.M.,EGYPT, ISRAEL AND THE GULF OF   ISLAM
AQABA: IN INTERNATIONAL LAW. LAW NAT/G CONSULT   INT/LAW
FORCES PLAN ECO/TAC ROUTINE COERCE ATTIT DRIVE   UAR
PERCEPT PERSON RIGID/FLEX LOVE PWR WEALTH...GEOG
CONCPT MYTH TREND. PAGE 13 E0250

B57
FREUND G.,UNHOLY ALLIANCE. EUR+WWI GERMANY USSR   DIPLOM
FORCES ECO/TAC CONTROL WAR PWR...TREND TREATY.   PLAN
PAGE 40 E0796   POLICY

B57
LEVONTIN A.V.,THE MYTH OF INTERNATIONAL SECURITY: A   INT/ORG
JURIDICAL AND CRITICAL ANALYSIS. FUT WOR+45 WOR-45   INT/LAW
LAW NAT/G VOL/ASSN ACT/RES BAL/PWR ATTIT ORD/FREE   SOVEREIGN
...JURID METH/CNCPT TIME/SEQ TREND STERTYP 20.   MYTH
PAGE 64 E1289

B57
WASSENBERGH H.A.,POST-WAR INTERNATIONAL CIVIL   COM/IND
AVIATION POLICY AND THE LAW OF THE AIR. WOR+45 AIR   NAT/G
INT/ORG DOMIN LEGIT PEACE ORD/FREE...POLICY JURID   INT/LAW
NEW/IDEA OBS TIME/SEQ TREND CHARTS 20 TREATY.
PAGE 105 E2101

B58
JENKS C.W.,THE COMMON LAW OF MANKIND. EUR+WWI   JURID
MOD/EUR SPACE WOR+45 INT/ORG BAL/PWR ARMS/CONT   SOVEREIGN
COERCE SUPEGO MORAL...TREND 20. PAGE 58 E1154

B59
ANDERSON J.N.D.,ISLAMIC LAW IN THE MODERN WORLD.   ISLAM
FAM KIN SECT LEGIT ADJUD ATTIT DRIVE...TIME/SEQ   JURID
TREND GEN/LAWS 20 MUSLIM. PAGE 5 E0089

B59
BROOKES E.H.,THE COMMONWEALTH TODAY. UK ROMAN/EMP   FEDERAL
INT/ORG RACE/REL NAT/LISM SOVEREIGN...TREND   DIPLOM
SOC/INTEG 20. PAGE 16 E0307   JURID
                                                           IDEA/COMP

B59
CHRISTMAN H.M.,THE PUBLIC PAPERS OF CHIEF JUSTICE   LAW
EARL WARREN. CONSTN POL/PAR EDU/PROP SANCTION   CT/SYS
HEALTH...TREND 20 SUPREME/CT WARRN/EARL. PAGE 22   PERSON
E0436   ADJUD

B59
MAYER A.J.,POLITICAL ORIGINS OF THE NEW DIPLOMACY,   TREND
1917-1918. EUR+WWI MOD/EUR USA-45 WAR PWR...POLICY   DIPLOM
INT/LAW BIBLIOG. PAGE 70 E1392

B59
PANHUYS H.F.,THE ROLE OF NATIONALITY IN   INT/LAW
INTERNATIONAL LAW. ADJUD CRIME WAR STRANGE...JURID   NAT/LISM
TREND. PAGE 80 E1596   INGP/REL

B59
SPIRO H.J.,GOVERNMENT BY CONSTITUTIONS: THE   NAT/G
POLITICAL SYSTEMS OF DEMOCRACY. CANADA EUR+WWI FUT   CONSTN
USA+45 WOR+45 WOR-45 LEGIS TOP/EX LEGIT ADMIN
CT/SYS ORD/FREE PWR...TREND TOT/POP VAL/FREE 20.
PAGE 93 E1861

B59
VAN CAENEGEM R.C.,ROYAL WRITS IN ENGLAND FROM THE   JURID
CONQUEST TO GLANVILL. UK JUDGE...TREND IDEA/COMP   CHIEF
11/12 COMMON/LAW. PAGE 103 E2067   ADJUD
                                                           CT/SYS

S59
CARLSTON K.S.,"NATIONALIZATION: AN ANALYTIC   INDUS
APPROACH." WOR+45 INT/ORG ECO/TAC DOMIN LEGIT ADJUD   NAT/G
COERCE ORD/FREE PWR WEALTH SOCISM...JURID CONCPT   NAT/LISM
TREND STERTYP TOT/POP VAL/FREE 20. PAGE 19 E0380   SOVEREIGN

B60
DUMON F.,LA COMMUNAUTE FRANCO-AFRO-MALGACHE: SES   JURID
ORIGINES, SES INSTITUTIONS, SON EVOLUTION. FRANCE   INT/ORG
MADAGASCAR POL/PAR DIPLOM ADMIN ATTIT...TREND T 20.   AFR
PAGE 33 E0657   CONSTN

B60
ENGEL J.,THE SECURITY OF THE FREE WORLD. USSR   COM
WOR+45 STRATA STRUCT ECO/DEV ECO/UNDEV INT/ORG   TREND
DELIB/GP FORCES DOMIN LEGIT ADJUD EXEC ARMS/CONT   DIPLOM
COERCE...POLICY CONCPT NEW/IDEA TIME/SEQ GEN/LAWS
COLD/WAR WORK UN 20 NATO. PAGE 35 E0689

B60
JENKS C.W.,HUMAN RIGHTS AND INTERNATIONAL LABOR   CONCPT
STANDARDS. WOR+45 CONSTN LABOR VOL/ASSN DELIB/GP
ACT/RES EDU/PROP MORAL RESPECT...JURID SOC TREND
GEN/LAWS WORK ILO 20. PAGE 58 E1156

B60
JENNINGS R.,PROGRESS OF INTERNATIONAL LAW. FUT   INT/ORG
WOR+45 WOR-45 SOCIETY NAT/G VOL/ASSN DELIB/GP   LAW
DIPLOM EDU/PROP LEGIT COERCE ATTIT DRIVE MORAL   INT/LAW
ORD/FREE...JURID CONCPT OBS TIME/SEQ TREND
GEN/LAWS. PAGE 58 E1164

B60
STEIN E.,AMERICAN ENTERPRISE IN THE EUROPEAN COMMON MARKET
MARKET: A LEGAL PROFILE. EUR+WWI FUT USA+45 SOCIETY   ADJUD
STRUCT ECO/DEV NAT/G VOL/ASSN CONSULT PLAN TEC/DEV   INT/LAW
ECO/TAC INT/TRADE ADMIN ATTIT RIGID/FLEX PWR...MGT
NEW/IDEA STAT TREND COMPUT/IR SIMUL EEC 20. PAGE 93
E1867

B60
WOETZEL R.K.,THE INTERNATIONAL CONTROL OF AIRSPACE   INT/ORG
AND OUTERSPACE. FUT WOR+45 AIR CONSTN STRUCT   JURID
CONSULT PLAN TEC/DEV ADJUD RIGID/FLEX KNOWL   SPACE
ORD/FREE PWR...TECHNIC GEOG MGT NEW/IDEA TREND   INT/LAW
COMPUT/IR VAL/FREE 20 TREATY. PAGE 107 E2137

L60
DEAN A.W.,"SECOND GENEVA CONFERENCE OF THE LAW OF   INT/ORG
THE SEA: THE FIGHT FOR FREEDOM OF THE SEAS." FUT   JURID
USA+45 USSR WOR+45 WOR-45 SEA CONSTN STRUCT PLAN   INT/LAW
INT/TRADE ADJUD ADMIN ORD/FREE...DECISION RECORD
TREND GEN/LAWS 20 TREATY. PAGE 30 E0600

L60
KUNZ J.,"SANCTIONS IN INTERNATIONAL LAW." WOR+45   INT/ORG
WOR-45 LEGIT ARMS/CONT COERCE PEACE ATTIT   ADJUD
...METH/CNCPT TIME/SEQ TREND 20. PAGE 62 E1234   INT/LAW

L60
MILLER A.S.,"THE MYTH OF NEUTRALITY IN   ADJUD
CONSTITUTIONAL ADJUDICATION." LAW...DECISION JURID   CONSTN
LING TREND IDEA/COMP. PAGE 73 E1456   MYTH
                                                           UTIL

L60
STEIN E.,"LEGAL REMEDIES OF ENTERPRISES IN THE   MARKET
EUROPEAN ECONOMIC COMMUNITY." EUR+WWI FUT ECO/DEV   ADJUD
INDUS PLAN ECO/TAC ADMIN PWR...MGT MATH STAT TREND
CON/ANAL EEC 20. PAGE 93 E1868

S60
NICHOLS J.P.,"HAZARDS OF AMERICAN PRIVATE   FINAN
INVESTMENT IN UNDERDEVELOPED COUNTRIES." FUT   ECO/UNDEV
L/A+17C USA+45 USA-45 EXTR/IND CONSULT BAL/PWR   CAP/ISM
ECO/TAC DOMIN ADJUD ATTIT SOVEREIGN WEALTH   NAT/LISM
...HIST/WRIT TIME/SEQ TREND VAL/FREE 20. PAGE 77
E1546

S60
O'BRIEN W.,"THE ROLE OF FORCE IN THE INTERNATIONAL   INT/ORG
JURIDICAL ORDER." WOR+45 NAT/G FORCES DOMIN ADJUD   COERCE
ARMS/CONT DETER NUC/PWR WAR ATTIT PWR...CATH
INT/LAW JURID CONCPT TREND STERTYP GEN/LAWS 20.
PAGE 78 E1564

S60
RHYNE C.S.,"LAW AS AN INSTRUMENT FOR PEACE." FUT   ADJUD
WOR+45 PLAN LEGIT ROUTINE ARMS/CONT NUC/PWR ATTIT   EDU/PROP
ORD/FREE...JURID METH/CNCPT TREND CON/ANAL HYPO/EXP   INT/LAW
COLD/WAR 20. PAGE 84 E1690   PEACE

S60
SANDERS R.,"NUCLEAR DYNAMITE: A NEW DIMENSION IN   INDUS
FOREIGN POLICY." FUT WOR+45 ECO/DEV CONSULT TEC/DEV   PWR
PERCEPT...CONT/OBS TIME/SEQ TREND GEN/LAWS TOT/POP   DIPLOM
20 TREATY. PAGE 87 E1745   NUC/PWR

S60
SCHACHTER O.,"THE ENFORCEMENT OF INTERNATIONAL   INT/ORG
JUDICIAL AND ARBITRAL DECISIONS." WOR+45 NAT/G   ADJUD
ECO/TAC DOMIN LEGIT ROUTINE COERCE ATTIT DRIVE   INT/LAW
ALL/VALS PWR...METH/CNCPT TREND TOT/POP 20 UN.
PAGE 87 E1750

S60
SCHWELB E.,"INTERNATIONAL CONVENTIONS ON HUMAN   INT/ORG
RIGHTS." FUT WOR+45 LAW CONSTN CULTURE SOCIETY   HUM

STRUCT VOL/ASSN DELIB/GP PLAN ADJUD SUPEGO LOVE
MORAL...SOC CONCPT STAT RECORD HIST/WRIT TREND 20
UN. PAGE 89 E1790

S60
THOMPSON K.W.,"MORAL PURPOSE IN FOREIGN POLICY: MORAL
REALITIES AND ILLUSIONS." WOR+45 WOR-45 LAW CULTURE   JURID
SOCIETY INT/ORG PLAN ADJUD ADMIN COERCE RIGID/FLEX   DIPLOM
SUPEGO KNOWL ORD/FREE PWR...SOC TREND SOC/EXP
TOT/POP 20. PAGE 96 E1921

S60
ULMER S.S.,"THE ANALYSIS OF BEHAVIOR PATTERNS ON   ATTIT
THE UNITED STATES SUPREME COURT" USA+45 LAW CT/SYS   ADJUD
PERS/REL RACE/REL PERSON...DECISION PSY SOC TREND   PROF/ORG
METH/COMP METH 20 SUPREME/CT CIVIL/LIB. PAGE 97   INGP/REL
E1951

S60
WRIGHT Q.,"LEGAL ASPECTS OF THE U-2 INCIDENT." COM   PWR
USA+45 USSR STRUCT NAT/G FORCES PLAN TEC/DEV ADJUD   POLICY
RIGID/FLEX MORAL ORD/FREE...DECISION INT/LAW JURID   SPACE
PSY TREND GEN/LAWS COLD/WAR VAL/FREE 20 U-2.
PAGE 108 E2157

B61
ANAND R.P.,COMPULSORY JURISDICTION OF INTERNATIONAL   INT/ORG
COURT OF JUSTICE. FUT WOR+45 SOCIETY PLAN LEGIT   COERCE
ADJUD ATTIT DRIVE PERSON ORD/FREE...JURID CONCPT   INT/LAW
TREND 20 ICJ. PAGE 5 E0086

B61
JENKS C.W.,INTERNATIONAL IMMUNITIES. PLAN EDU/PROP   INT/ORG
ADMIN PERCEPT...OLD/LIB JURID CONCPT TREND TOT/POP.   DIPLOM
PAGE 58 E1157

B61
MCDOUGAL M.S.,LAW AND MINIMUM WORLD PUBLIC ORDER.   INT/ORG
WOR+45 SOCIETY NAT/G DELIB/GP EDU/PROP LEGIT ADJUD   ORD/FREE
COERCE ATTIT PERSON...JURID CONCPT RECORD TREND   INT/LAW
TOT/POP 20. PAGE 70 E1406

B61
WRIGHT Q.,THE ROLE OF INTERNATIONAL LAW IN THE   INT/ORG
ELIMINATION OF WAR. FUT WOR+45 WOR-45 NAT/G BAL/PWR   ADJUD
DIPLOM DOMIN LEGIT PWR...POLICY INT/LAW JURID   ARMS/CONT
CONCPT TIME/SEQ TREND GEN/LAWS COLD/WAR 20.
PAGE 108 E2158

L61
KAUPER P.G.,"CHURCH AND STATE: COOPERATIVE   SECT
SEPARATISM." NAT/G LEGIS OP/RES TAX EDU/PROP GP/REL   CONSTN
TREND. PAGE 59 E1187   LAW
                                                       POLICY

L61
SAND P.T.,"AN HISTORICAL SURVEY OF INTERNATIONAL   INT/ORG
AIR LAW SINCE 1944." USA+45 USA-45 WOR+45 WOR-45   LAW
SOCIETY ECO/DEV NAT/G CONSULT EX/STRUC ACT/RES PLAN   INT/LAW
LEGIT ROUTINE...JURID CONCPT METH/CNCPT TREND 20.   SPACE
PAGE 87 E1744

L61
TAUBENFELD H.J.,"A REGIME FOR OUTER SPACE." FUT   INT/ORG
UNIV R+D ACT/RES PLAN BAL/PWR LEGIT ARMS/CONT   ADJUD
ORD/FREE...POLICY JURID TREND UN TOT/POP 20   SPACE
COLD/WAR. PAGE 95 E1910

S61
LIPSON L.,"AN ARGUMENT ON THE LEGALITY OF   INT/ORG
RECONNAISSANCE STATELLITES." COM USA+45 USSR WOR+45   LAW
AIR INTELL NAT/G CONSULT PLAN DIPLOM LEGIT ROUTINE   SPACE
ATTIT...INT/LAW JURID CONCPT METH/CNCPT TREND
COLD/WAR 20. PAGE 65 E1302

S61
MACHOWSKI K.,"SELECTED PROBLEMS OF NATIONAL   UNIV
SOVEREIGNTY WITH REFERENCE TO THE LAW OF OUTER   ACT/RES
SPACE." FUT WOR+45 AIR LAW INTELL SOCIETY ECO/DEV   NUC/PWR
PLAN EDU/PROP DETER DRIVE PERCEPT SOVEREIGN   SPACE
...POLICY INT/LAW OBS TREND TOT/POP 20. PAGE 67
E1339

S61
RICHSTEIN A.R.,"LEGAL RULES IN NUCLEAR WEAPONS   NUC/PWR
EMPLOYMENTS." FUT WOR+45 LAW SOCIETY FORCES PLAN   TEC/DEV
WEAPON RIGID/FLEX...HEAL CONCPT TREND VAL/FREE 20.   MORAL
PAGE 85 E1696   ARMS/CONT

B62
DUPRE J.S.,SCIENCE AND THE NATION: POLICY AND   R+D
POLITICS. USA+45 LAW ACADEM FORCES ADMIN CIVMIL/REL   INDUS
GOV/REL EFFICIENCY PEACE...TREND 20 SCI/ADVSRY.   TEC/DEV
PAGE 34 E0665   NUC/PWR

B62
TRISKA J.F.,THE THEORY, LAW, AND POLICY OF SOVIET   COM
TREATIES. WOR+45 WOR-45 CONSTN INT/ORG NAT/G   LAW
VOL/ASSN DOMIN LEGIT COERCE ATTIT PWR RESPECT   INT/LAW
...POLICY JURID CONCPT OBS SAMP TIME/SEQ TREND   USSR
GEN/LAWS 20. PAGE 97 E1941

L62
NIZARD L.,"CUBAN QUESTION AND SECURITY COUNCIL."   INT/ORG
L/A+17C USA+45 ECO/UNDEV NAT/G POL/PAR DELIB/GP   JURID
ECO/TAC PWR...RELATIV OBS TIME/SEQ TREND GEN/LAWS   DIPLOM
UN 20 UN. PAGE 77 E1551   CUBA

S62
CRANE R.D.,"SOVIET ATTITUDE TOWARD INTERNATIONAL   LAW
SPACE LAW." COM FUT USA+45 USSR AIR CONSTN DELIB/GP   ATTIT
DOMIN PWR...JURID TREND TOT/POP 20. PAGE 27 E0543   INT/LAW
                                                       SPACE

S62
FINKELSTEIN L.S.,"THE UNITED NATIONS AND   INT/ORG
ORGANIZATIONS FOR CONTROL OF ARMAMENT." FUT WOR+45   PWR
VOL/ASSN DELIB/GP TOP/EX CREATE EDU/PROP LEGIT   ARMS/CONT
ADJUD NUC/PWR ATTIT RIGID/FLEX ORD/FREE...POLICY
DECISION CONCPT OBS TREND GEN/LAWS TOT/POP
COLD/WAR. PAGE 38 E0752

S62
GANDOLFI A.,"REFLEXIONS SUR L'IMPOT DE CAPITATION   AFR
EN AFRIQUE NOIRE." GHANA SENEGAL LAW FINAN ACT/RES   CHOOSE
TEC/DEV ECO/TAC WEALTH...MGT TREND 20. PAGE 42
E0830

B63
CORLEY R.N.,THE LEGAL ENVIRONMENT OF BUSINESS.   NAT/G
CONSTN LEGIS TAX ADMIN CT/SYS DISCRIM ATTIT PWR   INDUS
...TREND 18/20. PAGE 26 E0509   JURID
                                                       DECISION

B63
DE GRAZIA A.,APPORTIONMENT AND REPRESENTATIVE   REPRESENT
GOVERNMENT. CONSTN POL/PAR LEGIS PLAN ADJUD DISCRIM   APPORT
RATIONAL...CONCPT STAT PREDICT TREND IDEA/COMP.   NAT/G
PAGE 29 E0583   MUNIC

B63
DEENER D.R.,CANADA - UNITED STATES TREATY   DIPLOM
RELATIONS. CANADA USA+45 USA-45 NAT/G FORCES PLAN   INT/LAW
PROB/SOLV AGREE NUC/PWR...TREND 18/20 TREATY.   POLICY
PAGE 30 E0603

B63
ELIAS T.O.,GOVERNMENT AND POLITICS IN AFRICA.   AFR
CONSTN CULTURE SOCIETY NAT/G POL/PAR DIPLOM   NAT/LISM
REPRESENT PERSON...SOC TREND BIBLIOG 4/20. PAGE 34   COLONIAL
E0681   LAW

B63
ROBERT J.,LA MONARCHIE MAROCAINE. MOROCCO LABOR   CHIEF
MUNIC POL/PAR EX/STRUC ORD/FREE PWR...JURID TREND T   CONSERVE
20. PAGE 85 E1702   ADMIN
                                                       CONSTN

B63
SCHMIDHAUSER J.R.,CONSTITUTIONAL LAW IN THE   LAW
POLITICAL PROCESS. SOCIETY LEGIS ADJUD CT/SYS   CONSTN
FEDERAL...SOC TREND IDEA/COMP ANTHOL T SUPREME/CT   JURID
SENATE CONGRESS HOUSE/REP. PAGE 88 E1761

B63
YOUNGER R.D.,THE PEOPLE'S PANEL: THE GRAND JURY IN   CT/SYS
THE UNITED STATES, 1634-1941. USA-45 LAW LEGIT   JURID
CONTROL TASK GP/REL ROLE...TREND 17/20 GRAND/JURY.   CONSTN
PAGE 108 E2166   LOC/G

L63
MCDOUGAL M.S.,"THE ENJOYMENT AND ACQUISITION OF   PLAN
RESOURCES IN OUTER SPACE." CHRIST-17C FUT WOR+45   TREND
WOR-45 LAW EXTR/IND INT/ORG ACT/RES CREATE TEC/DEV
ECO/TAC LEGIT COERCE HEALTH KNOWL ORD/FREE PWR
WEALTH...JURID HIST/WRIT VAL/FREE. PAGE 70 E1408

S63
GERHARD H.,"COMMODITY TRADE STABILIZATION THROUGH   PLAN
INTERNATIONAL AGREEMENTS." WOR+45 ECO/DEV ECO/UNDEV   ECO/TAC
NAT/G ROUTINE ORD/FREE...INT/LAW OBS TREND GEN/METH   INT/TRADE
TOT/POP 20. PAGE 43 E0850

S63
JOUGHIN L.,"ACADEMIC DUE PROCESS." DELIB/GP ADJUD   ACADEM
ROUTINE ORD/FREE...POLICY MAJORIT TREND. PAGE 59   LAW
E1175   PROF/ORG
                                                       CLIENT

B64
FRIEDMANN W.G.,THE CHANGING STRUCTURE OF   ADJUD

INTERNATIONAL LAW. WOR+45 INT/ORG NAT/G PROVS LEGIT TREND
ORD/FREE PWR...JURID CONCPT GEN/LAWS TOT/POP UN 20. INT/LAW
PAGE 41 E0805

B64

GRIFFITH W.E.,THE SINO-SOVIET RIFT. ASIA CHINA/COM   ATTIT
COM CUBA USSR YUGOSLAVIA NAT/G POL/PAR VOL/ASSN   TIME/SEQ
DELIB/GP FORCES TOP/EX DIPLOM EDU/PROP DRIVE PERSON   BAL/PWR
PWR...TREND 20 TREATY. PAGE 47 E0941   SOCISM

S64

CRANE R.D.,"BASIC PRINCIPLES IN SOVIET SPACE LAW."   COM
FUT WOR+45 AIR INT/ORG DIPLOM DOMIN ARMS/CONT   LAW
COERCE NUC/PWR PEACE ATTIT DRIVE PWR...INT/LAW   USSR
METH/CNCPT NEW/IDEA OBS TREND GEN/LAWS VAL/FREE   SPACE
MARX/KARL 20. PAGE 27 E0544

S64

GARDNER R.N.,"THE SOVIET UNION AND THE UNITED   COM
NATIONS." WOR+45 FINAN POL/PAR VOL/ASSN FORCES   INT/ORG
ECO/TAC DOMIN EDU/PROP LEGIT ADJUD ADMIN ARMS/CONT   USSR
COERCE ATTIT ALL/VALS...POLICY MAJORIT CONCPT OBS
TIME/SEQ TREND STERTYP UN. PAGE 42 E0838

S64

GINSBURGS G.,"WARS OF NATIONAL LIBERATION - THE   COERCE
SOVIET THESIS." COM USSR WOR+45 WOR-45 LAW CULTURE   CONCPT
INT/ORG DIPLOM LEGIT COLONIAL GUERRILLA WAR   INT/LAW
NAT/LISM ATTIT PERSON MORAL PWR...JURID OBS TREND   REV
MARX/KARL 20. PAGE 44 E0869

S64

KARPOV P.V.,"PEACEFUL COEXISTENCE AND INTERNATIONAL   COM
LAW." WOR+45 LAW SOCIETY INT/ORG VOL/ASSN FORCES   ATTIT
CREATE CAP/ISM DIPLOM ADJUD NUC/PWR PEACE MORAL   INT/LAW
ORD/FREE PWR MARXISM...MARXIST JURID CONCPT OBS   USSR
TREND COLD/WAR MARX/KARL 20. PAGE 59 E1186

S64

LIPSON L.,"PEACEFUL COEXISTENCE." COM USSR WOR+45   ATTIT
LAW INT/ORG DIPLOM LEGIT ADJUD ORD/FREE...CONCPT   JURID
OBS TREND GEN/LAWS VAL/FREE COLD/WAR 20. PAGE 65   INT/LAW
E1303   PEACE

S64

MAGGS P.B.,"SOVIET VIEWPOINT ON NUCLEAR WEAPONS IN   COM
INTERNATIONAL LAW." USSR WOR+45 INT/ORG FORCES   LAW
DIPLOM ARMS/CONT ATTIT ORD/FREE PWR...POLICY JURID   INT/LAW
CONCPT OBS TREND CON/ANAL GEN/LAWS VAL/FREE 20.   NUC/PWR
PAGE 67 E1347

S64

SKUBISZEWSKI K.,"FORMS OF PARTICIPATION OF   INT/ORG
INTERNATIONAL ORGANIZATION IN THE LAW MAKING   LAW
PROCESS." FUT WOR+45 NAT/G DELIB/GP DOMIN LEGIT   INT/LAW
KNOWL PWR...JURID TREND 20. PAGE 92 E1837

S64

TRISKA J.F.,"SOVIET TREATY LAW: A QUANTITATIVE   COM
ANALYSIS." WOR+45 LAW ECO/UNDEV AGRI COM/IND INDUS   ECO/TAC
CREATE TEC/DEV DIPLOM ATTIT PWR WEALTH...JURID SAMP   INT/LAW
TIME/SEQ TREND CHARTS VAL/FREE 20 TREATY. PAGE 97   USSR
E1942

B65

CONGRESSIONAL QUARTERLY SERV.,POLITICS IN AMERICA,   CHOOSE
1945-1964: THE POLITICS AND ISSUES OF THE POSTWAR   REPRESENT
YEARS. USA+45 LAW FINAN CHIEF DIPLOM APPORT SUFF   POL/PAR
...POLICY STAT TREND CHARTS 20 CONGRESS PRESIDENT.   LEGIS
PAGE 25 E0489

B65

KING D.B.,LEGAL ASPECTS OF THE CIVIL RIGHTS   LAW
MOVEMENT. SERV/IND VOL/ASSN LEGIS EDU/PROP ADJUD   DISCRIM
PARTIC CHOOSE...JURID SEGREGAT WORK. PAGE 61 E1215   TREND

B65

SCHUBERT G.,THE JUDICIAL MIND: THE ATTITUDES AND   CT/SYS
IDEOLOGIES OF SUPREME COURT JUSTICES 1946-1963.   JUDGE
USA+45 ELITES NAT/G CONTROL PERS/REL MAJORITY   ATTIT
CONSERVE...DECISION JURID MODAL STAT TREND GP/COMP   NEW/LIB
GAME. PAGE 88 E1774

B65

VON GLAHN G.,LAW AMONG NATIONS: AN INTRODUCTION TO   ACADEM
PUBLIC INTERNATIONAL LAW. WOR+45 WOR-45 INT/ORG   INT/LAW
NAT/G CREATE ADJUD WAR...GEOG CLASSIF TREND   GEN/LAWS
BIBLIOG. PAGE 104 E2082   LAW

S65

MCWHINNEY E.,"CHANGING INTERNATIONAL LAW METHOD AND   LAW
OBJECTIVES IN THE ERA OF THE SOVIET-WESTERN   TREND
DETENTE." COM USA+45 NAT/G BAL/PWR CT/SYS ATTIT
ORD/FREE...HUM JURID NEW/IDEA COLD/WAR VAL/FREE 20.
PAGE 71 E1430

S65

STEIN E.,"TOWARD SUPREMACY OF TREATY-CONSTITUTION   ADJUD
BY JUDICIAL FIAT: ON THE MARGIN OF THE COSTA CASE."   CONSTN
EUR+WWI ITALY WOR+45 INT/ORG NAT/G LEGIT REGION   SOVEREIGN
NAT/LISM PWR...JURID CONCPT TREND TOT/POP VAL/FREE   INT/LAW
20. PAGE 93 E1870

B66

DE TOCQUEVILLE A.,DEMOCRACY IN AMERICA (1834-1840)   POPULISM
(2 VOLS. IN I; TRANS. BY G. LAWRENCE). FRANCE   USA-45
CULTURE STRATA POL/PAR CT/SYS REPRESENT FEDERAL   CONSTN
ORD/FREE SOVEREIGN...MAJORIT TREND GEN/LAWS 18/19.   NAT/COMP
PAGE 30 E0596

B66

DIZARD W.P.,TELEVISION* A WORLD VIEW. WOR+45   COM/IND
ECO/UNDEV TEC/DEV LICENSE LITERACY...STAT OBS INT   ACT/RES
QU TREND AUD/VIS BIBLIOG. PAGE 32 E0632   EDU/PROP
                                                        CREATE

B66

FRIEDMANN W.G.,INTERNATIONAL FINANCIAL AID. USA+45   INT/ORG
ECO/DEV ECO/UNDEV NAT/G VOL/ASSN EX/STRUC PLAN RENT   FOR/AID
GIVE BAL/PAY PWR...GEOG INT/LAW STAT TREND UN EEC   TEC/DEV
COMECON. PAGE 41 E0806   ECO/TAC

L66

HIGGINS R.,"THE INTERNATIONAL COURT AND SOUTH WEST   SOUTH/AFR
AFRICA* SOME IMPLICATIONS OF THE JUDGMENT." AFR LAW   COLONIAL
ECO/UNDEV JUDGE RACE/REL COST PWR...INT/LAW TREND   CT/SYS
UN TREATY. PAGE 52 E1043   ADJUD

B67

BAILEY N.A.,LATIN AMERICA IN WORLD POLITICS. PWR   L/A+17C
CONSERVE MARXISM...INT/LAW TREND BIBLIOG/A T OAS   DIPLOM
COLD/WAR. PAGE 7 E0134   INT/ORG
                                                        ATTIT

B67

LAFAVE W.R.,INTERNATIONAL TRADE, INVESTMENT, AND   INT/TRADE
ORGANIZATION. INDUS PROB/SOLV TARIFFS CONTROL   INT/LAW
...TREND ANTHOL BIBLIOG 20 EEC. PAGE 62 E1245   INT/ORG

B67

SLATER J.,THE OAS AND UNITED STATES FOREIGN POLICY.   INT/ORG
KOREA L/A+17C USA+45 VOL/ASSN RISK COERCE PEACE   DIPLOM
ORD/FREE MARXISM...TREND 20 OAS. PAGE 92 E1838   ALL/IDEOS
                                                        ADJUD

S67

CARTER R.M.,"SOME FACTORS IN SENTENCING POLICY."   ADJUD
LAW PUB/INST CRIME PERS/REL...POLICY JURID SOC   CT/SYS
TREND CON/ANAL CHARTS SOC/EXP 20. PAGE 20 E0403   ADMIN

S67

SCOTT A.,"TWENTY-FIVE YEARS OF OPINION ON   ATTIT
INTEGRATION IN TEXAS." USA+45 USA-45 DISCRIM   ADJUST
...KNO/TEST TREND CHARTS 20 TEXAS. PAGE 89 E1794   RACE/REL
                                                        LAW

S67

SEIDLER G.L.,"MARXIST LEGAL THOUGHT IN POLAND."   MARXISM
POLAND SOCIETY R+D LOC/G NAT/G ACT/RES ADJUD CT/SYS   LAW
SUPEGO PWR...SOC TREND 20 MARX/KARL. PAGE 90 E1802   CONCPT
                                                        EFFICIENCY

L68

CHIU H.,"COMMUNIST CHINA'S ATTITUDE TOWARD THE   INT/ORG
UNITED NATIONS: A LEGAL ANALYSIS." CHINA/COM WOR+45   SOVEREIGN
LAW NAT/G DIPLOM CONFER ADJUD PARTIC ATTIT...POLICY   INT/ORG
TREND 20 UN. PAGE 22 E0432   REPRESENT

B89

FERNEUIL T.,LES PRINCIPES DE 1789 ET LA SCIENCE   CONSTN
SOCIALE. FRANCE NAT/G REV ATTIT...CONCPT TREND   POLICY
IDEA/COMP 18/19. PAGE 37 E0739   LAW

TRESOLINI R.J. E1939,E1940

TRIBAL....SEE KIN

TRIBUTE....FORMAL PAYMENTS TO DOMINANT POWER BY MINOR POWER
     GROUP; SEE ALSO SANCTION

B08

GRIFFIN A.P.C.,REFERENCES ON CORRUPT PRACTICES IN   BIBLIOG/A
ELECTIONS (PAMPHLET). USA-45 LAW CONSTN TRIBUTE   CHOOSE
CRIME REPRESENT...JURID 19/20. PAGE 47 E0934   SUFF
                                                        APPORT

N19

CARPER E.T.,LOBBYING AND THE NATURAL GAS BILL   LOBBY
(PAMPHLET). USA+45 SERV/IND BARGAIN PAY DRIVE ROLE   ADJUD
WEALTH 20 CONGRESS SENATE EISNHWR/DD. PAGE 20 E0389   TRIBUTE
                                                        NAT/G

KEFAUVER E.,CRIME IN AMERICA. USA+45 USA-45 MUNIC
NEIGH DELIB/GP TRIBUTE GAMBLE LOBBY SANCTION
...AUD/VIS 20 CAPONE/AL MAFIA MIAMI CHICAGO
DETROIT. PAGE 60 E1194
 B51
 ELITES
 CRIME
 PWR
 FORCES

LARROWE C.P.,SHAPE-UP AND HIRING HALL. TRIBUTE
ADJUD CONTROL SANCTION COERCE CRIME GP/REL PWR
...CHARTS 20 AFL/CIO NEWYORK/C SEATTLE. PAGE 63
E1256
 B55
 LABOR
 INDUS
 WORKER
 NAT/G

ABELS J.,THE TRUMAN SCANDALS. USA+45 USA-45 POL/PAR
TAX LEGIT CT/SYS CHOOSE PRIVIL MORAL WEALTH 20
TRUMAN/HS PRESIDENT CONGRESS. PAGE 2 E0043
 B56
 CRIME
 ADMIN
 CHIEF
 TRIBUTE

PINTO F.B.M.,ENRIQUECIMENTO ILICITO NO EXERCICIO DE
CARGOS PUBLICOS. BRAZIL L/A+17C USA+45 ELITES
TRIBUTE CONTROL INGP/REL ORD/FREE PWR...NAT/COMP
20. PAGE 81 E1617
 B60
 ADMIN
 NAT/G
 CRIME
 LAW

BORKIN J.,THE CORRUPT JUDGE. USA+45 CT/SYS ATTIT
SUPEGO MORAL RESPECT...BIBLIOG + SUPREME/CT
MANTON/M DAVIS/W JOHNSN/ALB. PAGE 14 E0271
 B62
 ADJUD
 TRIBUTE
 CRIME

SKOLNICK J.H.,JUSTICE WITHOUT TRIAL: LAW
ENFORCEMENT IN DEMOCRATIC SOCIETY. USA+45 LAW
TRIBUTE RACE/REL BIO/SOC PERSON...PSY SOC 20 NEGRO
BUREAUCRCY PROSTITUTN. PAGE 92 E1836
 B66
 FORCES
 CRIMLGY
 CRIME

TRIESTE....TRIESTE

TRINIDAD AND TOBAGO....SEE TRINIDAD

TRINIDAD....TRINIDAD AND TOBAGO; SEE ALSO L/A+17C

TRISKA J.F. E1941,E1942

TROBRIAND....TROBRIAND ISLANDS AND ISLANDERS

TROTIER A.H. E1943

TROTSKY/L....LEON TROTSKY

SHAPIRO J.P.,"SOVIET HISTORIOGRAPHY AND THE MOSCOW
TRIALS: AFTER THIRTY YEARS." USSR NAT/G LEGIT PRESS
CONTROL LEAD ATTIT MARXISM...NEW/IDEA METH 20
TROTSKY/L STALIN/J KHRUSH/N. PAGE 90 E1810
 S68
 HIST/WRIT
 EDU/PROP
 SANCTION
 ADJUD

TRUJILLO/R....RAFAEL TRUJILLO

TRUMAN DOCTRINE....SEE TRUMAN/DOC

TRUMAN/DOC....TRUMAN DOCTRINE

TRUMAN/HS....PRESIDENT HARRY S. TRUMAN

MCCONNELL G.,THE STEEL SEIZURE OF 1952 (PAMPHLET).
USA+45 FINAN INDUS PROC/MFG LG/CO EX/STRUC ADJUD
CONTROL GP/REL ORD/FREE PWR 20 TRUMAN/HS PRESIDENT
CONGRESS. PAGE 70 E1402
 N19
 DELIB/GP
 LABOR
 PROB/SOLV
 NAT/G

ABELS J.,THE TRUMAN SCANDALS. USA+45 USA-45 POL/PAR
TAX LEGIT CT/SYS CHOOSE PRIVIL MORAL WEALTH 20
TRUMAN/HS PRESIDENT CONGRESS. PAGE 2 E0043
 B56
 CRIME
 ADMIN
 CHIEF
 TRIBUTE

HUNT B.I.,BIPARTISANSHIP: A CASE STUDY OF THE
FOREIGN ASSISTANCE PROGRAM, 1947-56 (DOCTORAL
THESIS). USA+45 INT/ORG CONSULT LEGIS TEC/DEV
...BIBLIOG PRESIDENT TREATY NATO TRUMAN/HS
EISNHWR/DD CONGRESS. PAGE 56 E1114
 B58
 FOR/AID
 POL/PAR
 GP/REL
 DIPLOM

IANNIELLO L.,MILESTONES ALONG THE MARCH: TWELVE
HISTORIC CIVIL RIGHTS DOCUMENTS--FROM WORLD WAR II
TO SELMA. USA+45 LAW FORCES TOP/EX PARTIC SUFF...T
20 NEGRO CIV/RIGHTS TRUMAN/HS SUPREME/CT
KENNEDY/JF. PAGE 56 E1121
 B65
 RACE/REL
 DISCRIM
 CONSTN
 NAT/G

US SENATE COMM ON FOREIGN REL,A SELECT CHRONOLOGY
AND BACKGROUND DOCUMENTS RELATING TO THE MIDDLE
EAST. ISRAEL UAR LAW INT/ORG FORCES PROB/SOLV
CONFER CONSEN PEACE ATTIT...POLICY 20 UN SENATE
TRUMAN/HS. PAGE 101 E2033
 B67
 ISLAM
 TIME/SEQ
 DIPLOM

TRUST, PERSONAL....SEE RESPECT, SUPEGO

TRUST/TERR....TRUST TERRITORY

DUGARD J.,"THE REVOCATION OF THE MANDATE FOR SOUTH
WEST AFRICA." SOUTH/AFR WOR+45 STRATA NAT/G
DELIB/GP DIPLOM ADJUD SANCTION CHOOSE RACE/REL
...POLICY NAT/COMP 20 AFRICA/SW UN TRUST/TERR
LEAGUE/NAT. PAGE 33 E0654
 S68
 AFR
 INT/ORG
 DISCRIM
 COLONIAL

TSHOMBE/M....MOISE TSHOMBE

TULANE/U....TULANE UNIVERSITY

TUNIS....TUNIS, TUNISIA

CONWELL-EVANS T.P.,THE LEAGUE COUNCIL IN ACTION.
EUR+WWI TURKEY UK USSR WOR-45 INT/ORG FORCES JUDGE
ECO/TAC EDU/PROP LEGIT ROUTINE ARMS/CONT COERCE
ATTIT PWR...MAJORIT GEOG JURID CONCPT LEAGUE/NAT
TOT/POP VAL/FREE TUNIS 20. PAGE 25 E0498
 B29
 DELIB/GP
 INT/LAW

TUNISIA....SEE ALSO ISLAM, AFR

TURBERVILLE A.S. E0369

TURKESTAN....TURKESTAN

TURKEY....TURKEY; SEE ALSO ISLAM

HOLLAND T.E.,STUDIES IN INTERNATIONAL LAW. TURKEY
USSR WOR-45 CONSTN NAT/G DIPLOM DOMIN LEGIT COERCE
WAR PEACE ORD/FREE PWR SOVEREIGN...JURID CHARTS 20
PARLIAMENT SUEZ TREATY. PAGE 54 E1084
 B00
 INT/ORG
 LAW
 INT/LAW

CONWELL-EVANS T.P.,THE LEAGUE COUNCIL IN ACTION.
EUR+WWI TURKEY UK USSR WOR-45 INT/ORG FORCES JUDGE
ECO/TAC EDU/PROP LEGIT ROUTINE ARMS/CONT COERCE
ATTIT PWR...MAJORIT GEOG JURID CONCPT LEAGUE/NAT
TOT/POP VAL/FREE TUNIS 20. PAGE 25 E0498
 B29
 DELIB/GP
 INT/LAW

FULLER G.H.,TURKEY: A SELECTED LIST OF REFERENCES.
ISLAM TURKEY CULTURE ECO/UNDEV AGRI DIPLOM NAT/LISM
CONSERVE...GEOG HUM INT/LAW SOC 7/20 MAPS. PAGE 42
E0824
 B44
 BIBLIOG/A
 ALL/VALS

WORLD PEACE FOUNDATION,"INTERNATIONAL
ORGANIZATIONS: SUMMARY OF ACTIVITIES." INDIA
PAKISTAN TURKEY WOR+45 CONSTN CONSULT EX/STRUC
ECO/TAC EDU/PROP LEGIT ORD/FREE...JURID SOC UN 20
CYPRESS. PAGE 107 E2145
 L64
 INT/ORG
 ROUTINE

TURKIC....TURKIC PEOPLES

TURNER R.K. E1944

TUSKEGEE....TUSKEGEE, ALABAMA

TAPER B.,GOMILLION VERSUS LIGHTFOOT: THE TUSKEGEE
GERRYMANDER CASE. USA+45 LAW CONSTN LOC/G MUNIC
CT/SYS 20 NEGRO CIV/RIGHTS GOMILLN/CG LIGHTFT/PM
TUSKEGEE. PAGE 95 E1908
 B62
 APPORT
 REPRESENT
 RACE/REL
 ADJUD

TUSSMAN J. E1945,E1946

TV....TELEVISION; SEE ALSO PRESS, COM/IND

JANOWITZ M.,SOCIAL CONTROL OF ESCALATED RIOTS
(PAMPHLET). USA+45 USA-45 LAW SOCIETY MUNIC FORCES
PROB/SOLV EDU/PROP TV CRIME ATTIT...BIBLIOG 20
NEGRO CIV/RIGHTS. PAGE 58 E1148
 N19
 CROWD
 ORD/FREE
 CONTROL
 RACE/REL

MCWHINNEY E.,CONSTITUTIONALISM IN GERMANY AND THE
FEDERAL CONSTITUTINAL COURT. GERMANY/W POL/PAR TV
ADJUD CHOOSE EFFICIENCY ATTIT ORD/FREE MARXISM
...NEW/IDEA BIBLIOG 20. PAGE 71 E1428
 B62
 CONSTN
 CT/SYS
 CONTROL
 NAT/G

STREET H.,FREEDOM: THE INDIVIDUAL AND THE LAW. UK
COM/IND EDU/PROP PRESS RUMOR TV PWR 20 CIVIL/LIB
FILM. PAGE 94 E1886
 B63
 ORD/FREE
 NAT/G
 JURID
 PARL/PROC

BRENNAN J.T.,THE COST OF THE AMERICAN JUDICIAL
SYSTEM. USA+45 PROF/ORG TV ADMIN EFFICIENCY.
PAGE 15 E0292
 B66
 COST
 CT/SYS
 ADJUD

JURID
B67
FRIENDLY A.,CRIME AND PUBLICITY. TV CT/SYS SUPEGO   PRESS
20. PAGE 41 E0811   CRIME
                                                     ROLE
                                                     LAW

L67
BARRON J.A.,"ACCESS TO THE PRESS." USA+45 TEC/DEV   ORD/FREE
PRESS TV ADJUD AUD/VIS. PAGE 8 E0152   COM/IND
                                                     EDU/PROP
                                                     LAW

TVA....TENNESSEE VALLEY AUTHORITY

B61
ALFRED H.,PUBLIC OWNERSHIP IN THE USA: GOALS AND   CONTROL
PRIORITIES. LAW INDUS INT/TRADE ADJUD GOV/REL   OWN
EFFICIENCY PEACE SOCISM...POLICY ANTHOL 20 TVA.   ECO/DEV
PAGE 3 E0064   ECO/TAC

TWAIN/MARK....MARK TWAIN (SAMUEL CLEMENS)

TWENTIETH CENTURY FUND E1947

TYDINGS J.D. E1948

TYLER P. E1949

TYLER/JOHN....PRESIDENT JOHN TYLER

TYPOLOGY....SEE CLASSIF ────────U────────────────────────────

U.S. DEPARTMENT OF LABOR....SEE DEPT/LABOR

U OF MICHIGAN LAW SCHOOL E1950

U/THANT....U THANT

UA/PAR....UNITED AUSTRALIAN PARTY

UAM....UNION AFRICAINE ET MALGACHE; ALSO OCAM

UAR....UNITED ARAB REPUBLIC (EGYPT AND SYRIA 1958-1961,
    EGYPT AFTER 1958); SEE ALSO EGYPT, ISLAM

B12
FOUAD M.,LE REGIME DE LA PRESSE EN EGYPTE: THESE   ORD/FREE
POUR LE DOCTORAT. UAR LICENSE EDU/PROP ADMIN   LEGIS
SANCTION CRIME SUPEGO PWR...ART/METH JURID 19/20.   CONTROL
PAGE 39 E0778   PRESS

B29
PRATT I.A.,MODERN EGYPT: A LIST OF REFERENCES TO   BIBLIOG
MATERIAL IN THE NEW YORK PUBLIC LIBRARY. UAR   ISLAM
ECO/UNDEV...GEOG JURID SOC LING 20. PAGE 82 E1647   DIPLOM
                                                     NAT/G

B49
WALINE M.,LE CONTROLE JURIDICTIONNEL DE   JURID
L'ADMINISTRATION. BELGIUM FRANCE UAR JUDGE BAL/PWR   ADMIN
ADJUD CONTROL CT/SYS...GP/COMP 20. PAGE 104 E2093   PWR
                                                     ORD/FREE

B57
BLOOMFIELD L.M.,EGYPT, ISRAEL AND THE GULF OF   ISLAM
AQABA: IN INTERNATIONAL LAW. LAW NAT/G CONSULT   INT/LAW
FORCES PLAN ECO/TAC ROUTINE COERCE ATTIT DRIVE   UAR
PERCEPT PERSON RIGID/FLEX LOVE PWR WEALTH...GEOG
CONCPT MYTH TREND. PAGE 13 E0250

B57
CONOVER H.F.,NORTH AND NORTHEAST AFRICA; A SELECTED BIBLIOG/A
ANNOTATED LIST OF WRITINGS. ALGERIA MOROCCO SUDAN   DIPLOM
UAR CULTURE INT/ORG PROB/SOLV ADJUD NAT/LISM PWR   AFR
WEALTH...SOC 20 UN. PAGE 25 E0496   ECO/UNDEV

L60
LAUTERPACHT E.,"THE SUEZ CANAL SETTLEMENT." FRANCE   INT/ORG
ISLAM ISRAEL UAR UK BAL/PWR DIPLOM LEGIT...JURID   LAW
GEN/LAWS ANTHOL SUEZ VAL/FREE 20. PAGE 63 E1263

B63
ROSNER G.,THE UNITED NATIONS EMERGENCY FORCE.   INT/ORG
FRANCE ISRAEL UAR UK WOR+45 CREATE WAR PEACE   FORCES
ORD/FREE PWR...INT/LAW JURID HIST/WRIT TIME/SEQ UN.
PAGE 86 E1719

B65
AMERICAN UNIVERSITY IN CAIRO,GUIDE TO UAR   BIBLIOG
GOVERNMENT PUBLICATIONS AT THE AUC LIBRARY   NAT/G
(PAMPHLET). ISLAM UAR USA+45 ECO/UNDEV...SOC STAT   LEGIS
20. PAGE 4 E0084   LAW

B67
US SENATE COMM ON FOREIGN REL,A SELECT CHRONOLOGY   ISLAM
AND BACKGROUND DOCUMENTS RELATING TO THE MIDDLE   TIME/SEQ
EAST. ISRAEL UAR LAW INT/ORG FORCES PROB/SOLV   DIPLOM
CONFER CONSEN PEACE ATTIT...POLICY 20 UN SENATE
TRUMAN/HS. PAGE 101 E2033

S67
ALDRICH W.A.,"THE SUEZ CRISIS." UAR UK USA+45   DIPLOM
DELIB/GP FORCES BAL/PWR INT/TRADE CONFER CONTROL   INT/LAW
COERCE DETER 20. PAGE 3 E0058   COLONIAL

S67
MATTHEWS R.O.,"THE SUEZ CANAL DISPUTE* A CASE STUDY PEACE
IN PEACEFUL SETTLEMENT." FRANCE ISRAEL UAR UK NAT/G DIPLOM
CONTROL LEAD COERCE WAR NAT/LISM ROLE ORD/FREE PWR   ADJUD
...INT/LAW UN 20. PAGE 69 E1389

UAW....UNITED AUTO WORKERS

UDR....UNION POUR LA DEFENSE DE LA REPUBLIQUE (FRANCE)

UGANDA....SEE ALSO AFR

B64
FRANCK T.M.,EAST AFRICAN UNITY THROUGH LAW. MALAWI   AFR
TANZANIA UGANDA UK ZAMBIA CONSTN INT/ORG NAT/G   FEDERAL
ADMIN ROUTINE TASK NAT/LISM ATTIT SOVEREIGN   REGION
...RECORD IDEA/COMP NAT/COMP. PAGE 40 E0785   INT/LAW

S67
ADOKO A.,"THE CONSTITUTION OF UGANDA." AFR UGANDA   NAT/G
LOC/G CHIEF FORCES LEGIS ADJUD EXEC CHOOSE NAT/LISM CONSTN
...IDEA/COMP 20. PAGE 3 E0050   ORD/FREE
                                                     LAW

S67
BRADLEY A.W.,"CONSTITUTION-MAKING IN UGANDA."   NAT/G
UGANDA LAW CHIEF DELIB/GP LEGIS ADMIN EXEC   CREATE
PARL/PROC RACE/REL ORD/FREE...GOV/COMP 20. PAGE 15   CONSTN
E0284   FEDERAL

S67
MAYANJA A.,"THE GOVERNMENT'S PROPOSALS ON THE NEW   CONSTN
CONSTITUTION." AFR UGANDA LAW CHIEF LEGIS ADJUD   CONFER
REPRESENT FEDERAL PWR 20. PAGE 69 E1390   ORD/FREE
                                                     NAT/G

S67
READ J.S.,"CENSORED." UGANDA CONSTN INTELL SOCIETY   EDU/PROP
NAT/G DIPLOM PRESS WRITING ADJUD ADMIN COLONIAL   AFR
RISK...IDEA/COMP 20. PAGE 84 E1675   CREATE

U-2....RECONNAISSANCE AIRCRAFT

S60
WRIGHT Q.,"LEGAL ASPECTS OF THE U-2 INCIDENT." COM   PWR
USA+45 USSR STRUCT NAT/G FORCES PLAN TEC/DEV ADJUD   POLICY
RIGID/FLEX MORAL ORD/FREE...DECISION INT/LAW JURID   SPACE
PSY TREND GEN/LAWS COLD/WAR VAL/FREE 20 U-2.
PAGE 108 E2157

S62
LISSITZYN O.J.,"SOME LEGAL IMPLICATIONS OF THE U-2   LAW
AND RB-47 INCIDENTS." FUT USA+45 USSR WOR+45 AIR   CONCPT
NAT/G DIPLOM LEGIT MORAL ORD/FREE SOVEREIGN...JURID SPACE
GEN/LAWS GEN/METH COLD/WAR 20 U-2. PAGE 65 E1305   INT/LAW

UK....UNITED KINGDOM; SEE ALSO APPROPRIATE TIME/SPACE/
    CULTURE INDEX, COMMONWLTH

N
CONOVER H.F.,OFFICIAL PUBLICATIONS OF BRITISH EAST   BIBLIOG/A
AFRICA (PAMPHLET). UK LAW ECO/UNDEV AGRI EXTR/IND   AFR
SECT LEGIS BUDGET TAX...HEAL STAT 20. PAGE 25 E0491 ADMIN
                                                     COLONIAL

N
INDEX TO LEGAL PERIODICALS. CANADA NEW/ZEALND UK   BIBLIOG
USA+45 USA-45 CONSTN LEGIS JUDGE ADJUD ADMIN   INDEX
CONTROL CT/SYS FEDERAL...CRIMLGY INT/LAW 20   LAW
CMN/WLTH AUSTRAL. PAGE 1 E0006   JURID

N
PUBLISHERS' CIRCULAR, THE OFFICIAL ORGAN OF THE   BIBLIOG
PUBLISHERS' ASSOCIATION OF GREAT BRITAIN AND   NAT/G
IRELAND. EUR+WWI MOD/EUR UK LAW PROB/SOLV DIPLOM   WRITING
COLONIAL ATTIT...HUM 19/20 CMN/WLTH. PAGE 2 E0025   LEAD

N
MINISTRY OF OVERSEAS DEVELOPME,TECHNICAL CO-   BIBLIOG
OPERATION -- A BIBLIOGRAPHY. UK LAW SOCIETY DIPLOM   TEC/DEV
ECO/TAC FOR/AID...STAT 20 CMN/WLTH. PAGE 73 E1466   ECO/DEV
                                                     NAT/G

PUBLISHERS' CIRCULAR LIMITED,THE ENGLISH CATALOGUE   BIBLIOG   N
OF BOOKS. UK WOR+45 WOR-45 LAW CULTURE LOC/G NAT/G   ALL/VALS
ADMIN LEAD...MGT 19/20. PAGE 83 E1658   ALL/IDEOS
                                                         SOCIETY

MEYER C.S.,ELIZABETH I AND THE RELIGIOUS SETTLEMENT   GP/REL   NRE
OF 1559. UK ELITES CHIEF LEGIS DISCRIM CATHISM 16   SECT
CHURCH/STA ELIZABTH/I. PAGE 72 E1445   LAW
                                                         PARL/PROC

GRIFFIN A.P.C.,LIST OF BOOKS RELATING TO THE THEORY   BIBLIOG/A   B00
OF COLONIZATION, GOVERNMENT OF DEPENDENCIES,   COLONIAL
PROTECTORATES, AND RELATED TOPICS. FRANCE GERMANY   GOV/REL
ITALY SPAIN UK USA-45 WOR-45 ECO/TAC ADMIN CONTROL   DOMIN
REGION NAT/LISM ALL/VALS PWR...INT/LAW SOC 16/19.
PAGE 46 E0917

HISTORICUS,"LETTERS AND SOME QUESTIONS OF   WEALTH   L00
INTERNATIONAL LAW." FRANCE NETHERLAND UK USA-45   JURID
WOR-45 LAW NAT/G COERCE...SOC CONCPT GEN/LAWS   WAR
TOT/POP 19 CIVIL/WAR. PAGE 53 E1054   INT/LAW

BRYCE J.,STUDIES IN HISTORY AND JURISPRUDENCE (2   IDEA/COMP   B01
VOLS.). ICELAND SOUTH/AFR UK LAW PROB/SOLV   CONSTN
SOVEREIGN...PHIL/SCI NAT/COMP ROME/ANC ROMAN/LAW.   JURID
PAGE 16 E0321

GRIFFIN A.P.C.,LIST OF BOOKS ON SAMOA (PAMPHLET).   BIBLIOG/A   B01
GERMANY S/ASIA UK USA-45 WOR-45 ECO/UNDEV REGION   COLONIAL
ALL/VALS ORD/FREE ALL/IDEOS...GEOG INT/LAW 19 SAMOA   DIPLOM
GUAM. PAGE 46 E0918

GRIFFIN A.P.C.,A LIST OF BOOKS RELATING TO TRUSTS   BIBLIOG/A   B02
(2ND REV. ED.) (PAMPHLET). FRANCE GERMANY UK USA-45   JURID
WOR-45 LAW ECO/DEV INDUS LG/CO NAT/G CAP/ISM   ECO/TAC
CENTRAL DISCRIM PWR LAISSEZ 19/20. PAGE 46 E0919   VOL/ASSN

FORTESCUE G.K.,SUBJECT INDEX OF THE MODERN WORKS   BIBLIOG   B03
ADDED TO THE LIBRARY OF THE BRITISH MUSEUM IN THE   INDEX
YEARS 1881-1900 (3 VOLS.). UK LAW CONSTN FINAN   WRITING
NAT/G FORCES INT/TRADE COLONIAL 19. PAGE 39 E0775

GRIFFIN A.P.C.,LISTS PUBLISHED 1902-03: LABOR   BIBLIOG/A   B03
PARTICULARLY RELATING TO STRIKES (PAMPHLET). UK   LABOR
USA-45 FINAN WORKER PLAN BARGAIN CRIME GOV/REL   GP/REL
...POLICY 19/20 PARLIAMENT. PAGE 46 E0923   ECO/TAC

GRIFFIN A.P.C.,SELECT LIST OF BOOKS ON LABOR   BIBLIOG/A   B03
PARTICULARLY RELATING TO STRIKES. FRANCE GERMANY   GP/REL
MOD/EUR UK USA-45 LAW NAT/G DELIB/GP WORKER BARGAIN   MGT
LICENSE PAY ADJUD 19/20. PAGE 46 E0924   LABOR

MOREL E.D.,THE BRITISH CASE IN FRENCH CONGO.   DIPLOM   B03
CONGO/BRAZ FRANCE UK COERCE MORAL WEALTH...POLICY   INT/TRADE
INT/LAW 20 CONGO/LEOP. PAGE 74 E1490   COLONIAL
                                                         AFR

DICEY A.,LAW AND PUBLIC OPINION IN ENGLAND. LAW   ATTIT   B05
CULTURE INTELL SOCIETY NAT/G SECT JUDGE LEGIT   UK
CHOOSE RIGID/FLEX KNOWL...OLD/LIB CONCPT STERTYP
GEN/LAWS 20. PAGE 31 E0620

DICEY A.V.,LECTURES ON THE RELATION BETWEEN LAW AND   LAW   B05
PUBLIC OPINION IN ENGLAND DURING THE NINETEENTH   ADJUD
CENTURY. UK LEGIS CT/SYS...JURID 19 TORY/PARTY   ATTIT
BENTHAM/J ENGLSH/LAW. PAGE 31 E0621   IDEA/COMP

GRIFFIN A.P.C.,LIST OF BOOKS RELATING TO CHILD   BIBLIOG/A   B06
LABOR (PAMPHLET). BELGIUM FRANCE GERMANY MOD/EUR UK   LAW
USA-45 ECO/DEV INDUS WORKER CAP/ISM PAY ROUTINE   LABOR
ALL/IDEOS...MGT SOC 19/20. PAGE 47 E0929   AGE/C

GRIFFIN A.P.C.,LIST OF WORKS RELATING TO GOVERNMENT   BIBLIOG/A   B08
REGULATION OF INSURANCE UNITED STATES AND FOREIGN   FINAN
COUNTRIES (2ND. ED.) (PAMPHLET). FRANCE GERMANY UK   LAW
USA-45 WOR-45 LG/CO LOC/G NAT/G LEGIS LICENSE ADJUD   CONTROL
LOBBY CENTRAL ORD/FREE 19/20. PAGE 47 E0933

HARVARD UNIVERSITY LAW LIBRARY,CATALOGUE OF THE   BIBLIOG/A   B09
LIBRARY OF THE LAW SCHOOL OF HARVARD UNIVERSITY (3   LAW

VOLS.). UK USA-45 LEGIS JUDGE ADJUD CT/SYS...JURID   ADMIN
CHARTS 14/20. PAGE 51 E1008

LOBINGIER C.S.,THE PEOPLE'S LAW OR POPULAR   CONSTN   B09
PARTICIPATION IN LAW-MAKING. FRANCE SWITZERLND UK   LAW
LOC/G NAT/G PROVS LEGIS SUFF MAJORITY PWR POPULISM   PARTIC
...GOV/COMP BIBLIOG 19. PAGE 66 E1314

MCILWAIN C.H.,THE HIGH COURT OF PARLIAMENT AND ITS   LAW   B10
SUPREMACY B1910 1878 408. UK EX/STRUC PARL/PROC   LEGIS
GOV/REL INGP/REL PRIVIL 12/20 PARLIAMENT   CONSTN
ENGLSH/LAW. PAGE 71 E1416   NAT/G

POLLOCK F.,THE GENIUS OF THE COMMON LAW. CHRIST-17C   LAW   B12
UK FINAN CHIEF ACT/RES ADMIN GP/REL ATTIT SOCISM   CULTURE
...ANARCH JURID. PAGE 81 E1624   CREATE

BORCHARD E.M.,BIBLIOGRAPHY OF INTERNATIONAL LAW AND   BIBLIOG   B13
CONTINENTAL LAW. EUR+WWI MOD/EUR UK LAW INT/TRADE   INT/LAW
WAR PEACE...GOV/COMP NAT/COMP 19/20. PAGE 14 E0267   JURID
                                                         DIPLOM

CARLYLE A.J.,BIBLIOGRAPHY OF POLITICAL THEORY   BIBLIOG/A   B16
(PAMPHLET); FRANCE GERMANY UK USA-45...JURID 9/19.   CONCPT
PAGE 19 E0382   PHIL/SCI

SALMOND J.W.,JURISPRUDENCE. UK LOC/G NAT/G LEGIS   LAW   B16
PROB/SOLV LICENSE LEGIT CRIME PERS/REL OWN ORD/FREE   CT/SYS
...T 20. PAGE 87 E1742   JURID
                                                         ADJUD

WILSON W.,THE STATE: ELEMENTS OF HISTORICAL AND   NAT/G   B18
PRACTICAL POLITICS. FRANCE GERMANY ITALY UK USSR   JURID
CONSTN EX/STRUC LEGIS CT/SYS WAR PWR...POLICY   CONCPT
GOV/COMP 20. PAGE 106 E2131   NAT/COMP

GIBB A.D.,JUDICIAL CORRUPTION IN THE UNITED KINGDOM   MORAL   N19
(PAMPHLET). UK DELIB/GP CT/SYS CRIME PERSON SUPEGO   ATTIT
17/20 SCOTLAND. PAGE 43 E0856   ADJUD

POUND R.,ORGANIZATION OF THE COURTS (PAMPHLET).   CT/SYS   N19
MOD/EUR UK USA-45 ADJUD PWR...GOV/COMP 10/20   JURID
EUROPE. PAGE 82 E1635   STRUCT
                                                         ADMIN

HEADICAR B.M.,CATALOGUE OF THE BOOKS, PAMPHLETS,   BIBLIOG   B23
AND OTHER DOCUMENTS IN THE EDWARD FRY LIBRARY OF   INT/LAW
INTERNATIONAL LAW... UK INT/ORG 20. PAGE 51 E1019   DIPLOM

HOLDSWORTH W.S.,A HISTORY OF ENGLISH LAW; THE   LAW   B24
COMMON LAW AND ITS RIVALS (VOL. V). UK SEA EX/STRUC
LEGIS   ADJUD
WRITING ADMIN...INT/LAW JURID CONCPT IDEA/COMP   CT/SYS
WORSHIP 16/17 PARLIAMENT ENGLSH/LAW COMMON/LAW.
PAGE 54 E1073

HOLDSWORTH W.S.,A HISTORY OF ENGLISH LAW; THE   LAW   B24
COMMON LAW AND ITS RIVALS (VOL. VI). UK STRATA   CONSTN
EX/STRUC ADJUD ADMIN CONTROL CT/SYS...JURID CONCPT   LEGIS
GEN/LAWS 17 COMMONWLTH PARLIAMENT ENGLSH/LAW   CHIEF
COMMON/LAW. PAGE 54 E1074

HOLDSWORTH W.S.,A HISTORY OF ENGLISH LAW; THE   LAW   B24
COMMON LAW AND ITS RIVALS (VOL. IV). UK SEA AGRI   LEGIS
CHIEF ADJUD CONTROL CRIME GOV/REL...INT/LAW JURID   CT/SYS
NAT/COMP 16/17 PARLIAMENT COMMON/LAW CANON/LAW   CONSTN
ENGLSH/LAW. PAGE 54 E1075

WINFIELD P.H.,THE CHIEF SOURCES OF ENGLISH LEGAL   BIBLIOG/A   B25
HISTORY. UK CONSTN JUDGE ADJUD CT/SYS 13/18.   JURID
PAGE 107 E2133   LAW

BEALE J.H.,A BIBLIOGRAPHY OF EARLY ENGLISH LAW   BIBLIOG/A   B26
BOOKS. MOD/EUR UK PRESS ADJUD CT/SYS ATTIT...CHARTS   JURID
10/16. PAGE 8 E0161   LAW

FORTESCUE J.,THE GOVERNANCE OF ENGLAND (1471-76).   CONSERVE   B26
UK LAW FINAN SECT LEGIS PROB/SOLV TAX DOMIN ADMIN   CONSTN
GP/REL COST ORD/FREE PWR 14/15. PAGE 39 E0776   CHIEF
                                                         NAT/G

GOOCH G.P.,ENGLISH DEMOCRATIC IDEAS IN THE   B27   IDEA/COMP
SEVENTEENTH CENTURY (2ND ED.). UK LAW SECT FORCES   MAJORIT
DIPLOM LEAD PARL/PROC REV ATTIT AUTHORIT...ANARCH   EX/STRUC
CONCPT 17 PARLIAMENT CMN/WLTH REFORMERS. PAGE 45   CONSERVE
E0885

HOLDSWORTH W.S.,THE HISTORIANS OF ANGLO-AMERICAN   B28   HIST/WRIT
LAW. UK USA-45 INTELL LEGIS RESPECT...BIOG NAT/COMP   LAW
17/20 COMMON/LAW. PAGE 54 E1076   JURID

CAM H.M.,BIBLIOGRAPHY OF ENGLISH CONSTITUTIONAL   B29   BIBLIOG/A
HISTORY (PAMPHLET). UK LAW LOC/G NAT/G POL/PAR SECT   CONSTN
DELIB/GP ADJUD ORD/FREE 19/20 PARLIAMENT. PAGE 19   ADMIN
E0369   PARL/PROC

CONWELL-EVANS T.P.,THE LEAGUE COUNCIL IN ACTION.   B29   DELIB/GP
EUR+WWI TURKEY UK USSR WOR-45 INT/ORG FORCES JUDGE   INT/LAW
ECO/TAC EDU/PROP LEGIT ROUTINE ARMS/CONT COERCE
ATTIT PWR...MAJORIT GEOG JURID CONCPT LEAGUE/NAT
TOT/POP VAL/FREE TUNIS 20. PAGE 25 E0498

LEITZ F.,DIE PUBLIZITAT DER AKTIENGESELLSCHAFT.   B29   LG/CO
BELGIUM FRANCE GERMANY UK FINAN PRESS GP/REL PROFIT   JURID
KNOWL 20. PAGE 64 E1282   ECO/TAC
                                                                         NAT/COMP

BENTHAM J.,THE RATIONALE OF PUNISHMENT. UK LAW   B30   CRIME
LOC/G NAT/G LEGIS CONTROL...JURID GEN/LAWS   SANCTION
COURT/SYS 19. PAGE 10 E0192   COERCE
                                                                         ORD/FREE

FAIRLIE J.A.,COUNTY GOVERNMENT AND ADMINISTRATION.   B30   ADMIN
UK USA-45 NAT/G SCHOOL FORCES BUDGET TAX CT/SYS   GOV/REL
CHOOSE...JURID BIBLIOG 11/20. PAGE 36 E0713   LOC/G
                                                                         MUNIC

EAGLETON C.,INTERNATIONAL GOVERNMENT. BRAZIL FRANCE   B32   INT/ORG
GERMANY ITALY UK USSR WOR-45 DELIB/GP TOP/EX PLAN   JURID
ECO/TAC EDU/PROP LEGIT ADJUD REGION ARMS/CONT   DIPLOM
COERCE ATTIT PWR...GEOG MGT VAL/FREE LEAGUE/NAT 20.   INT/LAW
PAGE 34 E0670

GREAT BRIT COMM MINISTERS PWR,REPORT. UK LAW CONSTN   B32   EX/STRUC
CONSULT LEGIS PARL/PROC SANCTION SOVEREIGN   NAT/G
...DECISION JURID 20 PARLIAMENT. PAGE 45 E0902   PWR
                                                                         CONTROL

LUNT D.C.,THE ROAD TO THE LAW. UK USA-45 LEGIS   B32   ADJUD
EDU/PROP OWN ORD/FREE...DECISION TIME/SEQ NAT/COMP   LAW
16/20 AUSTRAL ENGLSH/LAW COMMON/LAW. PAGE 67 E1333   JURID
                                                                         CT/SYS

ENSOR R.C.K.,COURTS AND JUDGES IN FRANCE, GERMANY,   B33   CT/SYS
AND ENGLAND. FRANCE GERMANY UK LAW PROB/SOLV ADMIN   EX/STRUC
ROUTINE CRIME ROLE...METH/COMP 20 CIVIL/LAW.   ADJUD
PAGE 35 E0692   NAT/COMP

CLYDE W.M.,THE STRUGGLE FOR THE FREEDOM OF THE   B34   PRESS
PRESS FROM CAXTON TO CROMWELL. UK LAW LOC/G SECT   ORD/FREE
FORCES LICENSE WRITING SANCTION REV ATTIT PWR   CONTROL
...POLICY 15/17 PARLIAMENT CROMWELL/O MILTON/J.
PAGE 23 E0460

EVANS I.L.,NATIVE POLICY IN SOUTHERN AFRICA.   B34   AFR
RHODESIA SOUTH/AFR UK STRUCT PARTIC RACE/REL ATTIT   COLONIAL
WEALTH SOC/INTEG AFRICA/SW. PAGE 35 E0705   DOMIN
                                                                         LAW

CUMMING J.,A CONTRIBUTION TOWARD A BIBLIOGRAPHY   B35   BIBLIOG
DEALING WITH CRIME AND COGNATE SUBJECTS (3RD ED.).   CRIMLGY
UK LAW CULTURE PUB/INST ADJUD AGE BIO/SOC...PSY SOC   FORCES
SOC/WK STAT METH/COMP 20. PAGE 28 E0552   CT/SYS

RAM J.,THE SCIENCE OF LEGAL JUDGMENT: A TREATISE...   B35   LAW
UK CONSTN NAT/G LEGIS CREATE PROB/SOLV AGREE CT/SYS   JURID
...INT/LAW CONCPT 19 ENGLSH/LAW CANON/LAW CIVIL/LAW   EX/STRUC
CTS/WESTM. PAGE 83 E1672   ADJUD

HANSON L.,GOVERNMENT AND THE PRESS 1695-1763. UK   B36   LAW
LOC/G LEGIS LICENSE CONTROL SANCTION CRIME ATTIT   JURID

ORD/FREE 17/18 PARLIAMENT AMEND/I. PAGE 50 E0996   PRESS
                                                                         POLICY

HOLDSWORTH W.S.,A HISTORY OF ENGLISH LAW; THE   B38   LAW
CENTURIES OF SETTLEMENT AND REFORM (VOL. X). INDIA   LOC/G
UK CONSTN NAT/G CHIEF LEGIS ADMIN COLONIAL CT/SYS   EX/STRUC
CHOOSE ORD/FREE PWR...JURID 18 PARLIAMENT   ADJUD
COMMONWLTH COMMON/LAW. PAGE 54 E1077

HOLDSWORTH W.S.,A HISTORY OF ENGLISH LAW; THE   B38   LAW
CENTURIES OF SETTLEMENT AND REFORM (VOL. XII). UK   PROF/ORG
CONSTN STRATA LEGIS JUDGE ADJUD CT/SYS ATTIT   WRITING
...JURID CONCPT BIOG GEN/LAWS 18 ENGLSH/LAW   IDEA/COMP
BLACKSTN/W COMMON/LAW. PAGE 54 E1078

HOLDSWORTH W.S.,A HISTORY OF ENGLISH LAW; THE   B38   LAW
CENTURIES OF SETTLEMENT AND REFORM (VOL. XI). UK   COLONIAL
CONSTN NAT/G EX/STRUC DIPLOM ADJUD CT/SYS LEAD   LEGIS
CRIME ATTIT...INT/LAW JURID 18 CMN/WLTH PARLIAMENT   PARL/PROC
ENGLSH/LAW. PAGE 54 E1079

MCNAIR A.D.,THE LAW OF TREATIES: BRITISH PRACTICE   B38   AGREE
AND OPINIONS. UK CREATE DIPLOM LEGIT WRITING ADJUD   LAW
WAR...INT/LAW JURID TREATY. PAGE 71 E1424   CT/SYS
                                                                         NAT/G

BENES E.,INTERNATIONAL SECURITY. GERMANY UK NAT/G   B39   EUR+WWI
DELIB/GP PLAN BAL/PWR ATTIT ORD/FREE PWR LEAGUE/NAT   INT/ORG
20 TREATY. PAGE 10 E0186   WAR

LAVES W.H.C.,INTERNATIONAL SECURITY. EUR+WWI   B39   ORD/FREE
GERMANY UK USA-45 LAW NAT/G DELIB/GP TOP/EX COERCE   LEGIT
PWR...POLICY FASCIST CONCPT HIST/WRIT GEN/LAWS   ARMS/CONT
LEAGUE/NAT NAZI 20. PAGE 63 E1267   BAL/PWR

MCILWAIN C.H.,CONSTITUTIONALISM AND THE CHANGING   B39   CONSTN
WORLD. UK USA-45 LEGIS PRIVIL AUTHORIT SOVEREIGN   POLICY
...GOV/COMP 15/20 MAGNA/CART HOUSE/CMNS. PAGE 71   JURID
E1417

CONOVER H.F.,FOREIGN RELATIONS OF THE UNITED   B40   BIBLIOG/A
STATES: A LIST OF RECENT BOOKS (PAMPHLET). ASIA   USA-45
CANADA L/A+17C UK INT/ORG INT/TRADE TARIFFS NEUTRAL   DIPLOM
WAR PEACE...INT/LAW CON/ANAL 20 CHINJAP. PAGE 25
E0492

HOBBES T.,A DIALOGUE BETWEEN A PHILOSOPHER AND A   B40   CT/SYS
STUDENT OF THE COMMON LAWS OF ENGLAND (1667?). UK   CHIEF
SECT DOMIN ADJUD CRIME INCOME OWN UTIL ORD/FREE PWR   SANCTION
SOVEREIGN...JURID GEN/LAWS 17. PAGE 53 E1057

WOLFERS A.,BRITAIN AND FRANCE BETWEEN TWO WORLD   B40   DIPLOM
WARS. FRANCE UK INT/ORG NAT/G PLAN BARGAIN ECO/TAC   WAR
AGREE ISOLAT ALL/IDEOS...DECISION GEOG 20 TREATY   POLICY
VERSAILLES INTERVENT. PAGE 107 E2139

CRAIG A.,ABOVE ALL LIBERTIES. FRANCE UK USA-45 LAW   B42   ORD/FREE
CONSTN CULTURE INTELL NAT/G SECT JUDGE...IDEA/COMP   MORAL
BIBLIOG 18/20. PAGE 27 E0536   WRITING
                                                                         EDU/PROP

FORTESCU J.,IN PRAISE OF ENGLISH LAW (1464) (TRANS.   B42   LAW
BY S.B. CHRIMES). UK ELITES CHIEF FORCES CT/SYS   CONSTN
COERCE CRIME GOV/REL ILLEGIT...JURID GOV/COMP   LEGIS
GEN/LAWS 15. PAGE 39 E0774   ORD/FREE

FULLER G.H.,DEFENSE FINANCING: A SUPPLEMENTARY LIST   B42   BIBLIOG/A
OF REFERENCES (PAMPHLET). CANADA UK USA-45 ECO/DEV   FINAN
NAT/G DELIB/GP BUDGET ADJUD ARMS/CONT WEAPON COST   FORCES
PEACE PWR 20 AUSTRAL CHINJAP CONGRESS. PAGE 41   DIPLOM
E0821

CRAIG A.,"ABOVE ALL LIBERTIES." FRANCE UK LAW   C42   BIBLIOG/A
CULTURE INTELL SECT ORD/FREE 18/20. PAGE 27 E0537   EDU/PROP
                                                                         WRITING
                                                                         MORAL

ANDERSON R.B.,SUPPLEMENT TO BEALE'S BIBLIOGRAPHY OF   B43   BIBLIOG/A
EARLY ENGLISH LAW BOOKS. MOD/EUR UK CONSTN PRESS   JURID
ADJUD...CHARTS 10/15. PAGE 5 E0091   CT/SYS
                                                                         LAW

MICAUD C.A.,THE FRENCH RIGHT AND NAZI GERMANY
1933-1939: A STUDY OF PUBLIC OPINION. GERMANY UK
USSR POL/PAR ARMS/CONT COERCE DETER PEACE
RIGID/FLEX PWR MARXISM...FASCIST TREND 20
LEAGUE/NAT TREATY. PAGE 73 E1454
DIPLOM AGREE
B43

BENTHAM J.,"ON THE LIBERTY OF THE PRESS, AND PUBLIC
DISCUSSION" IN J. BOWRING, ED., THE WORKS OF JEREMY
BENTHAM." SPAIN UK LAW ELITES NAT/G LEGIS INSPECT
LEGIT WRITING CONTROL PRIVIL TOTALISM AUTHORIT
...TRADIT 19 FREE/SPEE. PAGE 10 E0193
ORD/FREE PRESS CONFER CONSERVE
C43

CHENEY F.,CARTELS, COMBINES, AND TRUSTS: A SELECTED
LIST OF REFERENCES. GERMANY UK USA-45 WOR-45
DELIB/GP OP/RES BARGAIN CAP/ISM ECO/TAC INT/TRADE
LICENSE LEGIT CONFER PRICE 20. PAGE 22 E0428
BIBLIOG/A LG/CO ECO/DEV INDUS
B44

FULLER G.H.,MILITARY GOVERNMENT: A LIST OF
REFERENCES (A PAMPHLET). ITALY UK USA-45 WOR-45 LAW
FORCES DOMIN ADMIN ARMS/CONT ORD/FREE PWR
...DECISION 20 CHINJAP. PAGE 41 E0822
BIBLIOG DIPLOM CIVMIL/REL SOVEREIGN
B44

RUDIN H.R.,ARMISTICE 1918. FRANCE GERMANY MOD/EUR
UK USA-45 NAT/G CHIEF DELIB/GP FORCES BAL/PWR REPAR
ARMS/CONT 20 WILSON/W TREATY. PAGE 86 E1732
AGREE WAR PEACE DIPLOM
B44

SUAREZ F.,A TREATISE ON LAWS AND GOD THE LAWGIVER
(1612) IN SELECTIONS FROM THREE WORKS, VOL. II.
FRANCE ITALY UK CULTURE NAT/G SECT CHIEF LEGIS
DOMIN LEGIT CT/SYS ORD/FREE PWR WORSHIP 16/17.
PAGE 94 E1892
LAW JURID GEN/LAWS CATH
B44

BEVERIDGE W.,THE PRICE OF PEACE. GERMANY UK WOR+45
WOR-45 NAT/G FORCES CREATE LEGIT REGION WAR ATTIT
KNOWL ORD/FREE PWR...POLICY NEW/IDEA GEN/LAWS
LEAGUE/NAT 20 TREATY. PAGE 12 E0223
INT/ORG TREND PEACE
B45

CONOVER H.F.,THE GOVERNMENTS OF THE MAJOR FOREIGN
POWERS: A BIBLIOGRAPHY. FRANCE GERMANY ITALY UK
USSR CONSTN LOC/G POL/PAR EX/STRUC FORCES ADMIN
CT/SYS CIVMIL/REL TOTALISM...POLICY 19/20. PAGE 25
E0494
BIBLIOG NAT/G DIPLOM
B45

GRIFFIN G.G.,A GUIDE TO MANUSCRIPTS RELATING TO
AMERICAN HISTORY IN BRITISH DEPOSITORIES. CANADA
IRELAND MOD/EUR UK USA-45 LAW DIPLOM ADMIN COLONIAL
WAR NAT/LISM SOVEREIGN...GEOG INT/LAW 15/19
CMN/WLTH. PAGE 47 E0936
BIBLIOG/A ALL/VALS NAT/G
B46

ENKE S.,INTERNATIONAL ECONOMICS. UK USA+45 USSR
INT/ORG BAL/PWR BARGAIN CAP/ISM BAL/PAY...NAT/COMP
20 TREATY. PAGE 35 E0691
INT/TRADE FINAN TARIFFS ECO/TAC
B47

LOCKE J.,TWO TREATISES OF GOVERNMENT (1690). UK LAW
SOCIETY LEGIS LEGIT AGREE REV OWN HEREDITY MORAL
CONSERVE...POLICY MAJORIT 17 WILLIAM/3 NATURL/LAW.
PAGE 66 E1316
CONCPT ORD/FREE NAT/G CONSEN
B47

CORWIN E.S.,LIBERTY AGAINST GOVERNMENT. UK USA-45
ROMAN/EMP LAW CONSTN PERS/REL OWN ATTIT 1/20
ROMAN/LAW ENGLSH/LAW AMEND/XIV. PAGE 26 E0513
JURID ORD/FREE CONCPT
B48

KEIR D.L.,CASES IN CONSTITUTIONAL LAW. UK CHIEF
LEGIS DIPLOM TAX PARL/PROC CRIME GOV/REL...INT/LAW
JURID 17/20. PAGE 60 E1195
CONSTN LAW ADJUD CT/SYS
B48

SLESSER H.,THE ADMINISTRATION OF THE LAW. UK CONSTN
EX/STRUC OP/RES PROB/SOLV CRIME ROLE...DECISION
METH/COMP 20 CIVIL/LAW ENGLSH/LAW CIVIL/LAW.
PAGE 92 E1839
LAW CT/SYS ADJUD
B48

DENNING A.,FREEDOM UNDER THE LAW. MOD/EUR UK LAW
SOCIETY CHIEF EX/STRUC LEGIS ADJUD CT/SYS PERS/REL
PERSON 17/20 ENGLSH/LAW. PAGE 31 E0606
ORD/FREE JURID NAT/G
B49

JACKSON R.H.,INTERNATIONAL CONFERENCE ON MILITARY
DIPLOM
B49

TRIALS. FRANCE GERMANY UK USA+45 USSR VOL/ASSN
DELIB/GP REPAR ADJUD CT/SYS CRIME WAR 20 WAR/TRIAL.
PAGE 57 E1141
INT/ORG INT/LAW CIVMIL/REL

WORMUTH F.D.,THE ORIGINS OF MODERN
CONSTITUTIONALISM. GREECE UK LEGIS CREATE TEC/DEV
BAL/PWR DOMIN ADJUD REV WAR PWR...JURID ROMAN/REP
CROMWELL/O. PAGE 107 E2146
NAT/G CONSTN LAW
B49

COUNCIL BRITISH NATIONAL BIB,BRITISH NATIONAL
BIBLIOGRAPHY. UK AGRI CONSTRUC PERF/ART POL/PAR
SECT CREATE INT/TRADE LEAD...HUM JURID PHIL/SCI 20.
PAGE 26 E0519
BIBLIOG/A NAT/G TEC/DEV DIPLOM
B50

MOCKFORD J.,SOUTH-WEST AFRICA AND THE INTERNATIONAL
COURT (PAMPHLET). AFR GERMANY SOUTH/AFR UK
ECO/UNDEV DIPLOM CONTROL DISCRIM...DECISION JURID
20 AFRICA/SW. PAGE 74 E1475
COLONIAL SOVEREIGN INT/LAW DOMIN
B50

WADE E.C.S.,CONSTITUTIONAL LAW; AN OUTLINE OF THE
LAW AND PRACTICE OF THE CONSTITUTION. UK LEGIS
DOMIN ADMIN GP/REL 16/20 CMN/WLTH PARLIAMENT
ENGLSH/LAW. PAGE 104 E2087
CONSTN NAT/G PARL/PROC LAW
B50

MONPIED E.,FEDERALIST BIBLIOGRAPHY: ARTICLES AND
DOCUMENTS PUBLISHED IN BRITISH PERIODICALS
1945-1951 (MIMEOGRAPHED). EUR+WWI UK WOR+45 DIPLOM
REGION ATTIT SOCISM...INT/LAW 20. PAGE 74 E1487
BIBLIOG/A INT/ORG FEDERAL CENTRAL
N51

COOKE C.A.,CORPORATION TRUST AND COMPANY: AN ESSAY
IN LEGAL HISTORY. UK STRUCT LEGIS CAP/ISM GP/REL
PROFIT 13/20 COMPNY/ACT. PAGE 25 E0499
LG/CO FINAN ECO/TAC JURID
B51

FRIEDMANN W.,LAW AND SOCIAL CHANGE IN CONTEMPORARY
BRITAIN. UK LABOR LG/CO LEGIS JUDGE CT/SYS ORD/FREE
NEW/LIB...DECISION JURID TREND METH/COMP BIBLIOG 20
PARLIAMENT ENGLSH/LAW COMMON/LAW. PAGE 40 E0802
LAW ADJUD SOCIETY CONSTN
B51

INSTITUTE DES RELATIONS INTL,LES ASPECTS
ECONOMIQUES DU REARMEMENT (ETUDE DE L'INSTITUT DES
RELATIONS INTERNATIONALES A BRUXELLES). BELGIUM UK
USA+45 EXTR/IND FINAN FORCES WORKER PROB/SOLV
DIPLOM PRICE...POLICY 20 TREATY. PAGE 57 E1127
WEAPON DEMAND ECO/TAC INT/TRADE
B51

BUCKLAND W.W.,ROMAN LAW AND COMMON LAW; A
COMPARISON IN OUTLINE (2ND REV. ED.). UK FAM LEGIT
AGREE CT/SYS OWN...JURID ROMAN/REP ROMAN/LAW
COMMON/LAW. PAGE 17 E0325
IDEA/COMP LAW ADJUD CONCPT
B52

DUNN F.S.,CURRENT RESEARCH IN INTERNATIONAL
AFFAIRS. UK USA+45...POLICY TREATY. PAGE 33 E0660
BIBLIOG/A DIPLOM INT/LAW
B52

FERRELL R.H.,PEACE IN THEIR TIME. FRANCE UK USA-45
INT/ORG NAT/G FORCES CREATE AGREE ARMS/CONT COERCE
WAR TREATY 20 WILSON/W LEAGUE/NAT BRIAND/A. PAGE 37
E0741
PEACE DIPLOM
B52

HOLDSWORTH W.S.,A HISTORY OF ENGLISH LAW; THE
CENTURIES OF SETTLEMENT AND REFORM, 1701-1875 (VOL.
XIII). UK POL/PAR PROF/ORG LEGIS JUDGE WRITING
ATTIT...JURID CONCPT BIOG GEN/LAWS 18/19 PARLIAMENT
REFORMERS ENGLSH/LAW COMMON/LAW. PAGE 54 E1080
LAW CONSTN IDEA/COMP CT/SYS
B52

JENNINGS W.I.,CONSTITUTIONAL LAWS OF THE
COMMONWEALTH. UK LAW CHIEF LEGIS TAX CT/SYS
PARL/PROC GOV/REL...INT/LAW 18/20 COMMONWLTH
ENGLSH/LAW COMMON/LAW. PAGE 58 E1165
CONSTN JURID ADJUD COLONIAL
B52

BUTLER D.E.,THE ELECTORAL SYSTEM IN BRITAIN,
1918-1951. UK LAW POL/PAR SUFF...STAT BIBLIOG 20
PARLIAMENT. PAGE 18 E0348
CHOOSE LEGIS REPRESENT PARTIC
B53

COKE E.,INSTITUTES OF THE LAWS OF ENGLAND
(1628-1658). UK LAW ADJUD PERS/REL ORD/FREE
...CRIMLGY 11/17. PAGE 24 E0471
JURID OWN CT/SYS CONSTN
B53

STOUT H.M.,BRITISH GOVERNMENT. UK FINAN LOC/G
POL/PAR DELIB/GP DIPLOM ADMIN COLONIAL CHOOSE
ORD/FREE...JURID BIBLIOG 20 COMMONWLTH. PAGE 94
E1883

B53
NAT/G
PARL/PROC
CONSTN
NEW/LIB

HAMSON C.J.,EXECUTIVE DISCRETION AND JUDICIAL
CONTROL; AN ASPECT OF THE FRENCH CONSEIL D'ETAT.
EUR+WWI FRANCE MOD/EUR UK NAT/G EX/STRUC PARTIC
CONSERVE...JURID BIBLIOG/A 18/20 SUPREME/CT.
PAGE 50 E0992

B54
ELITES
ADJUD
NAT/COMP

COOPER L.,"ADMINISTRATIVE JUSTICE." UK ADMIN
REPRESENT PWR...POLICY 20. PAGE 25 E0502

S54
LAW
ADJUD
CONTROL
EX/STRUC

BEANEY W.M.,THE RIGHT TO COUNSEL IN AMERICAN
COURTS. UK USA+45 USA-45 LAW NAT/G PROVS COLONIAL
PERCEPT 18/20 SUPREME/CT AMEND/VI AMEND/XIV
ENGLSH/LAW. PAGE 8 E0163

B55
ADJUD
CONSTN
CT/SYS

SMITH G.,A CONSTITUTIONAL AND LEGAL HISTORY OF
ENGLAND. UK ELITES NAT/G LEGIS ADJUD OWN HABITAT
POPULISM...JURID 20 ENGLSH/LAW. PAGE 92 E1844

B55
CONSTN
PARTIC
LAW
CT/SYS

SWEET AND MAXWELL,A LEGAL BIBLIOGRAPHY OF THE
BRITISH COMMONWEALTH OF NATIONS (2ND ED. 7 VOLS.).
UK LOC/G MUNIC JUDGE ADJUD CRIME OWN...JURID 14/20
CMN/WLTH. PAGE 95 E1900

B55
BIBLIOG/A
LAW
CONSTN
CT/SYS

WHEARE K.C.,GOVERNMENT BY COMMITTEE; AN ESSAY ON
THE BRITISH CONSTITUTION. UK NAT/G LEGIS INSPECT
CONFER ADJUD ADMIN CONTROL TASK EFFICIENCY ROLE
POPULISM 20. PAGE 106 E2116

B55
DELIB/GP
CONSTN
LEAD
GP/COMP

BROWNE D.G.,THE RISE OF SCOTLAND YARD: A HISTORY OF
THE METROPOLITAN POLICE. UK MUNIC CHIEF ADMIN CRIME
GP/REL 19/20. PAGE 16 E0316

B56
CRIMLGY
LEGIS
CONTROL
FORCES

DUNNILL F.,THE CIVIL SERVICE. UK LAW PLAN ADMIN
EFFICIENCY DRIVE NEW/LIB...STAT CHARTS 20
PARLIAMENT CIVIL/SERV. PAGE 33 E0662

B56
PERSON
WORKER
STRATA
SOC/WK

EMDEN C.S.,THE PEOPLE AND THE CONSTITUTION (2ND
ED.). UK LEGIS POPULISM 17/20 PARLIAMENT. PAGE 35
E0687

B56
CONSTN
PARL/PROC
NAT/G
LAW

WEIS P.,NATIONALITY AND STATELESSNESS IN
INTERNATIONAL LAW. UK WOR+45 WOR-45 LAW CONSTN
NAT/G DIPLOM EDU/PROP LEGIT ROUTINE RIGID/FLEX
...JURID RECORD CMN/WLTH 20. PAGE 105 E2109

B56
INT/ORG
SOVEREIGN
INT/LAW

JENNINGS I.,PARLIAMENT. UK FINAN INDUS POL/PAR
DELIB/GP EX/STRUC PLAN CONTROL...MAJORIT JURID
PARLIAMENT. PAGE 58 E1163

B57
PARL/PROC
TOP/EX
MGT
LEGIS

MEYER P.,ADMINISTRATIVE ORGANIZATION: A COMPARATIVE
STUDY OF THE ORGANIZATION OF PUBLIC ADMINISTRATION.
DENMARK FRANCE NORWAY SWEDEN UK USA+45 ELITES LOC/G
CONSULT LEGIS ADJUD CONTROL LEAD PWR SKILL
DECISION. PAGE 72 E1449

B57
ADMIN
METH/COMP
NAT/G
CENTRAL

POUND R.,THE DEVELOPMENT OF CONSTITUTIONAL
GUARANTEES OF LIBERTY. UK USA-45 CHIEF COLONIAL REV
...JURID CONCPT 15/20. PAGE 82 E1638

B57
LAW
CONSTN
ORD/FREE
ATTIT

ALLEN C.K.,ASPECTS OF JUSTICE. UK FAM COERCE CRIME
MARRIAGE AGE/Y LOVE 20 ENGLSH/LAW. PAGE 4 E0068

B58
JURID
MORAL
ORD/FREE

DEVLIN P.,THE CRIMINAL PROSECUTION IN ENGLAND. UK
NAT/G ADMIN ROUTINE EFFICIENCY...JURID SOC 20.
PAGE 31 E0617

B58
CRIME
LAW
METH
CT/SYS

EUSDEN J.D.,PURITANS, LAWYERS, AND POLITICS IN
EARLY SEVENTEENTH-CENTURY ENGLAND. UK CT/SYS
PARL/PROC RATIONAL PWR SOVEREIGN...IDEA/COMP
BIBLIOG 17 PURITAN COMMON/LAW. PAGE 35 E0702

B58
GP/REL
SECT
NAT/G
LAW

MANSERGH N.,COMMONWEALTH PERSPECTIVES. GHANA UK LAW
VOL/ASSN CONFER HEALTH SOVEREIGN...GEOG CHARTS
ANTHOL 20 CMN/WLTH AUSTRAL. PAGE 68 E1363

B58
DIPLOM
COLONIAL
INT/ORG
INGP/REL

MARTIN L.J.,INTERNATIONAL PROPAGANDA: ITS LEGAL AND
DIPLOMATIC CONTROL. UK USA+45 USSR CONSULT DELIB/GP
DOMIN CONTROL 20. PAGE 69 E1373

B58
EDU/PROP
DIPLOM
INT/LAW
ATTIT

MOEN N.W.,THE GOVERNMENT OF SCOTLAND 1603 - 1625.
UK JUDGE ADMIN GP/REL PWR 17 SCOTLAND COMMON/LAW.
PAGE 74 E1479

B58
CHIEF
JURID
CONTROL
PARL/PROC

SCHOEDER P.W.,THE AXIS ALLIANCE AND JAPANESE-
AMERICAN RELATIONS 1941. ASIA GERMANY UK USA-45
PEACE ATTIT...POLICY BIBLIOG 20 CHINJAP TREATY.
PAGE 88 E1763

B58
AGREE
DIPLOM
WAR

SHARMA M.P.,PUBLIC ADMINISTRATION IN THEORY AND
PRACTICE. INDIA UK USA+45 USA-45 EX/STRUC ADJUD
...POLICY CONCPT NAT/COMP 20. PAGE 90 E1813

B58
MGT
ADMIN
DELIB/GP
JURID

BRIGGS A.,CHARTIST STUDIES. UK LAW NAT/G WORKER
EDU/PROP COERCE SUFF GP/REL ATTIT...ANTHOL 19.
PAGE 15 E0300

B59
INDUS
STRATA
LABOR
POLICY

BROOKES E.H.,THE COMMONWEALTH TODAY. UK ROMAN/EMP
INT/ORG RACE/REL NAT/LISM SOVEREIGN...TREND
SOC/INTEG 20. PAGE 16 E0307

B59
FEDERAL
DIPLOM
JURID
IDEA/COMP

CORBETT P.E.,LAW IN DIPLOMACY. UK USA+45 USSR
CONSTN SOCIETY INT/ORG JUDGE LEGIT ATTIT ORD/FREE
TOT/POP LEAGUE/NAT 20. PAGE 26 E0507

B59
NAT/G
ADJUD
JURID
DIPLOM

DESMITH S.A.,JUDICIAL REVIEW OF ADMINISTRATIVE
ACTION. UK LOC/G CONSULT DELIB/GP ADMIN PWR
...DECISION JURID 20 ENGLSH/LAW. PAGE 31 E0609

B59
ADJUD
NAT/G
PROB/SOLV
CT/SYS

GINSBURG M.,LAW AND OPINION IN ENGLAND. UK CULTURE
KIN LABOR LEGIS EDU/PROP ADMIN CT/SYS CRIME OWN
HEALTH...ANTHOL 20 ENGLSH/LAW. PAGE 44 E0868

B59
JURID
POLICY
ECO/TAC

PAULSEN M.G.,LEGAL INSTITUTIONS TODAY AND TOMORROW.
UK USA+45 NAT/G PROF/ORG PROVS ADMIN PARL/PROC
ORD/FREE NAT/COMP. PAGE 80 E1604

B59
JURID
ADJUD
JUDGE
LEGIS

SISSON C.H.,THE SPIRIT OF BRITISH ADMINISTRATION
AND SOME EUROPEAN COMPARISONS. FRANCE GERMANY/W
SWEDEN UK LAW EX/STRUC INGP/REL EFFICIENCY ORD/FREE
...DECISION 20. PAGE 91 E1835

B59
GOV/COMP
ADMIN
ELITES
ATTIT

SQUIBB G.D.,THE HIGH COURT OF CHIVALRY. UK NAT/G
FORCES ADJUD WAR 14/20 PARLIAMENT ENGLSH/LAW.
PAGE 93 E1863

B59
CT/SYS
PARL/PROC
JURID

VAN CAENEGEM R.C.,ROYAL WRITS IN ENGLAND FROM THE
CONQUEST TO GLANVILL. UK JUDGE...TREND IDEA/COMP
11/12 COMMON/LAW. PAGE 103 E2067

B59
JURID
CHIEF
ADJUD
CT/SYS

VITTACHIT,EMERGENCY '58. CEYLON UK STRUCT NAT/G
FORCES ADJUD CRIME REV NAT/LISM 20. PAGE 104 E2081

B59
RACE/REL
DISCRIM
DIPLOM
SOVEREIGN

MENDELSON W.,"JUDICIAL REVIEW AND PARTY POLITICS" (BMR)" UK USA+45 USA-45 NAT/G LEGIS PROB/SOLV EDU/PROP ADJUD EFFICIENCY...POLICY NAT/COMP 19/20 AUSTRAL SUPREME/CT. PAGE 72 E1436 — S59 — CT/SYS POL/PAR BAL/PWR JURID

DILEY A.V.,INTRODUCTION TO THE STUDY OF THE LAW OF THE CONSTITUTION. FRANCE UK USA+45 USA-45 CONSULT FORCES TAX ADMIN FEDERAL ORD/FREE SOVEREIGN ...IDEA/COMP 20 ENGLSH/LAW CON/INTERP PARLIAMENT. PAGE 32 E0627 — B60 — CONSTN LAW LEGIS GEN/LAWS

HANBURY H.G.,ENGLISH COURTS OF LAW. UK EX/STRUC LEGIS CRIME ROLE 12/20 COMMON/LAW ENGLSH/LAW. PAGE 50 E0993 — B60 — JURID CT/SYS CONSTN GOV/REL

HEAP D.,AN OUTLINE OF PLANNING LAW (3RD ED.). UK LAW PROB/SOLV ADMIN CONTROL 20. PAGE 51 E1020 — B60 — MUNIC PLAN JURID LOC/G

LEWIS P.R.,LITERATURE OF THE SOCIAL SCIENCES: AN INTRODUCTORY SURVEY AND GUIDE. UK LAW INDUS DIPLOM INT/TRADE ADMIN...MGT 19/20. PAGE 65 E1294 — B60 — BIBLIOG/A SOC

PRASAD B.,THE ORIGINS OF PROVINCIAL AUTONOMY. INDIA UK FINAN LOC/G FORCES LEGIS CONTROL CT/SYS PWR ...JURID 19/20. PAGE 82 E1646 — B60 — CENTRAL PROVS COLONIAL NAT/G

RIENOW R.,INTRODUCTION TO GOVERNMENT (2ND ED.). UK USA+45 USSR POL/PAR ADMIN REV CHOOSE SUFF FEDERAL PWR...JURID GOV/COMP T 20. PAGE 85 E1697 — B60 — CONSTN PARL/PROC REPRESENT AUTHORIT

LAUTERPACHT E.,"THE SUEZ CANAL SETTLEMENT." FRANCE ISLAM ISRAEL UAR UK BAL/PWR DIPLOM LEGIT...JURID GEN/LAWS ANTHOL SUEZ VAL/FREE 20. PAGE 63 E1263 — L60 — INT/ORG LAW

GRACIA-MORA M.R.,"INTERNATIONAL RESPONSIBILITY FOR SUBVERSIVE ACTIVITIES AND HOSTILE PROPAGANDA BY PRIVATE PERSONS AGAINST." COM EUR+WWI L/A+17C UK USA+45 USSR WOR-45 CONSTN NAT/G LEGIT ADJUD REV PEACE TOTALISM ORD/FREE...INT/LAW 20. PAGE 45 E0895 — S60 — INT/ORG JURID SOVEREIGN

MARSHALL G.,"POLICE RESPONSIBILITY." UK LOC/G ADJUD ADMIN EXEC 20. PAGE 69 E1370 — S60 — CONTROL REPRESENT LAW FORCES

AYLMER G.,THE KING'S SERVANTS. UK ELITES CHIEF PAY CT/SYS WEALTH 17 CROMWELL/O CHARLES/I. PAGE 6 E0122 — B61 — ADMIN ROUTINE EX/STRUC NAT/G

BEDFORD S.,THE FACES OF JUSTICE: A TRAVELLER'S REPORT. AUSTRIA FRANCE GERMANY/W SWITZERLND UK UNIV WOR+45 WOR-45 CULTURE PARTIC GOV/REL MORAL...JURID OBS GOV/COMP 20. PAGE 9 E0174 — B61 — CT/SYS ORD/FREE PERSON LAW

FLINN M.W.,AN ECONOMIC AND SOCIAL HISTORY OF BRITAIN, 1066-1939. UK LAW STRATA STRUCT AGRI DIST/IND INDUS WORKER INT/TRADE WAR...CENSUS 11/20. PAGE 39 E0766 — B61 — SOCIETY SOC

GUIZOT F.P.G.,HISTORY OF THE ORIGIN OF REPRESENTATIVE GOVERNMENT IN EUROPE. CHRIST-17C FRANCE MOD/EUR SPAIN UK LAW CHIEF FORCES POPULISM ...MAJORIT TIME/SEQ GOV/COMP NAT/COMP 4/19 PARLIAMENT. PAGE 48 E0961 — B61 — LEGIS REPRESENT CONSTN NAT/G

JUSTICE,THE CITIZEN AND THE ADMINISTRATION: THE REDRESS OF GRIEVANCES (PAMPHLET). EUR+WWI UK LAW CONSTN STRATA NAT/G CT/SYS PARTIC COERCE...NEW/IDEA IDEA/COMP 20 OMBUDSMAN. PAGE 59 E1176 — B61 — INGP/REL LAW CONSULT ADJUD REPRESENT

ROCHE J.P.,COURTS AND RIGHTS: THE AMERICAN JUDICIARY IN ACTION (2ND ED.). UK USA+45 USA-45 STRUCT TEC/DEV SANCTION PERS/REL RACE/REL ORD/FREE ...METH/CNCPT GOV/COMP METH/COMP T 13/20. PAGE 85 — B61 — JURID CT/SYS NAT/G PROVS

E1710

UTLEY T.E.,OCCASION FOR OMBUDSMAN. UK CREATE CONTROL 20 OMBUDSMAN. PAGE 103 E2065 — B61 — PROB/SOLV INGP/REL REPRESENT ADJUD

BARLOW R.B.,CITIZENSHIP AND CONSCIENCE: STUDIES IN THEORY AND PRACTICE OF RELIGIOUS TOLERATION IN ENGLAND DURING EIGHTEENTH CENTURY. UK LAW VOL/ASSN EDU/PROP SANCTION REV GP/REL MAJORITY ATTIT ORD/FREE...BIBLIOG WORSHIP 18. PAGE 8 E0150 — B62 — SECT LEGIS DISCRIM

GROGAN V.,ADMINISTRATIVE TRIBUNALS IN THE PUBLIC SERVICE. IRELAND UK NAT/G CONTROL CT/SYS...JURID GOV/COMP 20. PAGE 48 E0945 — B62 — ADMIN LAW ADJUD DELIB/GP

HENDERSON W.O.,THE GENESIS OF THE COMMON MARKET. EUR+WWI FRANCE MOD/EUR UK SEA COM/IND EXTR/IND COLONIAL DISCRIM...TIME/SEQ CHARTS BIBLIOG 18/20 EEC TREATY. PAGE 52 E1030 — B62 — ECO/DEV INT/TRADE DIPLOM

PHILLIPS O.H.,CONSTITUTIONAL AND ADMINISTRATIVE LAW (3RD ED.). UK INT/ORG LOC/G CHIEF EX/STRUC LEGIS BAL/PWR ADJUD COLONIAL CT/SYS PWR...CHARTS 20. PAGE 80 E1613 — B62 — JURID ADMIN CONSTN NAT/G

JOHNSON O.H.,"THE ENGLISH TRADITION IN INTERNATIONAL LAW." CHRIST-17C MOD/EUR EDU/PROP LEGIT CT/SYS ORD/FREE...JURID CONCPT TIME/SEQ. PAGE 59 E1170 — S62 — LAW INT/LAW UK

EDDY J.P.,JUSTICE OF THE PEACE. UK LAW CONSTN CULTURE 14/20 COMMON/LAW. PAGE 34 E0674 — B63 — CRIME JURID CT/SYS ADJUD

GARNER J.F.,ADMINISTRATIVE LAW. UK LAW LOC/G NAT/G EX/STRUC LEGIS JUDGE BAL/PWR BUDGET ADJUD CONTROL CT/SYS...BIBLIOG 20. PAGE 42 E0840 — B63 — ADMIN JURID PWR GOV/REL

GRIFFITH J.A.G.,PRINCIPLES OF ADMINISTRATIVE LAW (3RD ED.). UK CONSTN EX/STRUC LEGIS ADJUD CONTROL CT/SYS PWR...CHARTS 20. PAGE 47 E0940 — B63 — JURID ADMIN NAT/G BAL/PWR

LEWIN J.,POLITICS AND LAW IN SOUTH AFRICA. SOUTH/AFR UK POL/PAR BAL/PWR ECO/TAC COLONIAL CONTROL GP/REL DISCRIM PWR 20 NEGRO. PAGE 65 E1293 — B63 — NAT/LISM POLICY LAW RACE/REL

LIVINGSTON W.S.,FEDERALISM IN THE COMMONWEALTH - A BIBLIOGRAPHICAL COMMENTARY. CANADA INDIA PAKISTAN UK STRUCT LOC/G NAT/G POL/PAR...NAT/COMP 20 AUSTRAL. PAGE 66 E1310 — B63 — BIBLIOG JURID FEDERAL CONSTN

PATRA A.C.,THE ADMINISTRATION OF JUSTICE UNDER THE EAST INDIA COMPANY IN BENGAL, BIHAR AND ORISSA. INDIA UK LG/CO CAP/ISM INT/TRADE ADJUD COLONIAL CONTROL CT/SYS...POLICY 20. PAGE 80 E1602 — B63 — ADMIN JURID CONCPT

ROSNER G.,THE UNITED NATIONS EMERGENCY FORCE. FRANCE ISRAEL UAR UK WOR+45 CREATE WAR PEACE ORD/FREE PWR...INT/LAW JURID HIST/WRIT TIME/SEQ UN. PAGE 86 E1719 — B63 — INT/ORG FORCES

ROYAL INSTITUTE PUBLIC ADMIN,BRITISH PUBLIC ADMINISTRATION. UK LAW FINAN INDUS LOC/G POL/PAR LEGIS LOBBY PARL/PROC CHOOSE JURID. PAGE 86 E1729 — B63 — BIBLIOG ADMIN MGT NAT/G

STREET H.,FREEDOM: THE INDIVIDUAL AND THE LAW. UK COM/IND EDU/PROP PRESS RUMOR TV PWR 20 CIVIL/LIB FILM. PAGE 94 E1886 — B63 — ORD/FREE NAT/G JURID PARL/PROC

WADE H.W.R.,TOWARDS ADMINISTRATIVE JUSTICE. UK USA+45 CONSTN CONSULT PROB/SOLV CT/SYS PARL/PROC — B63 — ADJUD IDEA/COMP

...POLICY JURID METH/COMP 20 ENGLSH/LAW. PAGE 104   ADMIN
E2088

B64

ENDACOTT G.B.,GOVERNMENT AND PEOPLE IN HONG KONG   CONSTN
1841-1962: A CONSTITUTIONAL HISTORY. UK LEGIS ADJUD   COLONIAL
REPRESENT ATTIT 19/20 HONG/KONG. PAGE 35 E0688   CONTROL
                                                       ADMIN

B64

FORBES A.H.,CURRENT RESEARCH IN BRITISH STUDIES. UK   BIBLIOG
CONSTN CULTURE POL/PAR SECT DIPLOM ADMIN...JURID   PERSON
BIOG WORSHIP 20. PAGE 39 E0769   NAT/G
                                                        PARL/PROC

B64

FRANCK T.M.,EAST AFRICAN UNITY THROUGH LAW. MALAWI   AFR
TANZANIA UGANDA UK ZAMBIA CONSTN INT/ORG NAT/G   FEDERAL
ADMIN ROUTINE TASK NAT/LISM ATTIT SOVEREIGN   REGION
...RECORD IDEA/COMP NAT/COMP. PAGE 40 E0785   INT/LAW

B64

HAAR C.M.,LAW AND LAND: ANGLO-AMERICAN PLANNING   LAW
PRACTICE. UK USA+45 NAT/G TEC/DEV BUDGET CT/SYS   PLAN
INGP/REL EFFICIENCY OWN...JURID 20. PAGE 49 E0967   MUNIC
                                                       NAT/COMP

B64

HEGEL G.W.,HEGEL'S POLITICAL WRITINGS (TRANS. BY   CONSTN
T.M. KNOX). GERMANY UK FINAN FORCES PARL/PROC   LEGIS
CHOOSE REPRESENT...BIOG 19. PAGE 51 E1022   JURID

B64

HOLDSWORTH W.S.,A HISTORY OF ENGLISH LAW; THE   LAW
CENTURIES OF DEVELOPMENT AND REFORM (VOL. XIV). UK   LEGIS
CONSTN LOC/G NAT/G POL/PAR CHIEF EX/STRUC ADJUD   LEAD
COLONIAL ATTIT...INT/LAW JURID 18/19 TORY/PARTY   CT/SYS
COMMONWLTH WHIG/PARTY COMMON/LAW. PAGE 54 E1081

B64

HOPKINSON T.,SOUTH AFRICA. SOUTH/AFR UK NAT/G   SOCIETY
POL/PAR LEGIS ECO/TAC PARL/PROC WAR...JURID AUD/VIS   RACE/REL
19/20. PAGE 55 E1097   DISCRIM

B64

JACKSON R.M.,THE MACHINERY OF JUSTICE IN ENGLAND.   CT/SYS
UK EDU/PROP CONTROL COST ORD/FREE...MGT 20   ADJUD
ENGLSH/LAW. PAGE 57 E1142   JUDGE
                                                        JURID

B64

LIGGETT E.,BRITISH POLITICAL ISSUES: VOLUME 1. UK   POL/PAR
LAW CONSTN LOC/G NAT/G ADJUD 20. PAGE 65 E1296   GOV/REL
                                                        CT/SYS
                                                        DIPLOM

B64

NATIONAL BOOK LEAGUE,THE COMMONWEALTH IN BOOKS: AN   BIBLIOG/A
ANNOTATED LIST. CANADA UK LOC/G SECT ADMIN...SOC   JURID
BIOG 20 CMN/WLTH. PAGE 76 E1526   NAT/G

B65

CARTER G.M.,POLITICS IN EUROPE. EUR+WWI FRANCE   GOV/COMP
GERMANY/W UK USSR LAW CONSTN POL/PAR VOL/ASSN PRESS   OP/RES
LOBBY PWR...ANTHOL SOC/INTEG EEC. PAGE 20 E0399   ECO/DEV

B65

CHARLTON K.,EDUCATION IN RENAISSANCE ENGLAND. ITALY   EDU/PROP
UK USA+45 WOR+45 LAW LOC/G NAT/G...IDEA/COMP 14/17   SCHOOL
HUMANISM. PAGE 21 E0423   ACADEM

B65

CHRIMES S.B.,ENGLISH CONSTITUTIONAL HISTORY (3RD   CONSTN
ED.). UK CHIEF CONSULT DELIB/GP LEGIS CT/SYS 15/20   BAL/PWR
COMMON/LAW PARLIAMENT. PAGE 22 E0435   NAT/G

B65

COWEN Z.,THE BRITISH COMMONWEALTH OF NATIONS IN A   JURID
CHANGING WORLD. UK ECO/UNDEV INT/ORG ECO/TAC   DIPLOM
INT/TRADE COLONIAL WAR GP/REL RACE/REL SOVEREIGN   PARL/PROC
SOC/INTEG 20 TREATY EEC COMMONWLTH. PAGE 27 E0530   NAT/LISM

B65

FORGAC A.A.,NEW DIPLOMACY AND THE UNITED NATIONS.   DIPLOM
FRANCE GERMANY UK USSR INT/ORG DELIB/GP EX/STRUC   ETIQUET
PEACE...INT/LAW CONCPT UN. PAGE 39 E0770   NAT/G

B65

HOLDSWORTH W.S.,A HISTORY OF ENGLISH LAW; THE   LAW
CENTURIES OF SETTLEMENT AND REFORM (VOL. XV). UK   INDUS
CONSTN SECT LEGIS JUDGE WRITING ADJUD CT/SYS CRIME   PROF/ORG
OWN...JURID IDEA/COMP 18 PARLIAMENT ENGLSH/LAW   ATTIT
COMMON/LAW. PAGE 54 E1082

B65

HOWE R.,THE STORY OF SCOTLAND YARD: A HISTORY OF   CRIMLGY

THE CID FROM THE EARLIEST TIMES TO THE PRESENT DAY.   CRIME
UK MUNIC EDU/PROP 6/20 SCOT/YARD. PAGE 55 E1104   FORCES
                                                        ADMIN

B65

MCWHINNEY E.,JUDICIAL REVIEW IN THE ENGLISH-   GOV/COMP
SPEAKING WORLD (3RD ED.). CANADA UK WOR+45 LEGIS   CT/SYS
CONTROL EXEC PARTIC...JURID 20 AUSTRAL. PAGE 71   ADJUD
E1431   CONSTN

B65

NEWBURY C.W.,BRITISH POLICY TOWARDS WEST AFRICA: DIPLOM
SELECT DOCUMENTS 1786-1874. AFR UK INT/TRADE DOMIN   POLICY
ADMIN COLONIAL CT/SYS COERCE ORD/FREE...BIBLIOG/A   NAT/G
18/19. PAGE 77 E1540   WRITING

B65

RADZINOWICZ L.,THE NEED FOR CRIMINOLOGY AND A   CRIMLGY
PROPOSAL FOR AN INSTITUTE OF CRIMINOLOGY. FUT UK   PROF/ORG
USA+45 SOCIETY ACT/RES PROB/SOLV CRIME...PSY SOC   ACADEM
BIBLIOG 20. PAGE 83 E1666   CONTROL

B65

SOPER T.,EVOLVING COMMONWEALTH. AFR CANADA INDIA   INT/ORG
IRELAND UK LAW CONSTN POL/PAR DOMIN CONTROL WAR PWR   COLONIAL
...AUD/VIS 18/20 COMMONWLTH OEEC. PAGE 93 E1857   VOL/ASSN

S65

BEVANS C.I.,"GHANA AND UNITED STATES - UNITED   NAT/G
KINGDOM AGREEMENTS." UK USA+45 LAW DELIB/GP   LEGIT
EX/STRUC ORD/FREE...JURID METH/CNCPT GEN/LAWS 20.   GHANA
PAGE 11 E0222   DIPLOM

S65

BROWNLIE I.,"SOME LEGAL ASPECTS OF THE USE OF   LAW
NUCLEAR WEAPONS." UK NEUTRAL DETER UN TREATY.   NUC/PWR
PAGE 16 E0317   WAR
                                                        INT/LAW

B66

ARCHER P.,FREEDOM AT STAKE. UK LAW NAT/G LEGIS   ORD/FREE
JUDGE CRIME MORAL...CONCPT 20 CIVIL/LIB. PAGE 5   NAT/COMP
E0103   POLICY

B66

BUTTERFIELD H.,DIPLOMATIC INVESTIGATIONS* ESSAYS IN   GEN/LAWS
THE THEORY OF INTERNATIONAL POLITICS. LAW INT/ORG   UK
FORCES BAL/PWR ARMS/CONT WAR ALL/VALS...HUM   DIPLOM
INT/LAW. PAGE 18 E0351

B66

CAMPBELL E.,PARLIAMENTARY PRIVILEGE IN AUSTRALIA.   LEGIS
UK LAW CONSTN COLONIAL ROLE ORD/FREE SOVEREIGN   PARL/PROC
18/20 COMMONWLTH AUSTRAL FREE/SPEE PARLIAMENT.   JURID
PAGE 19 E0370   PRIVIL

B66

DYCK H.V.,WEIMAR GERMANY AND SOVIET RUSSIA   DIPLOM
1926-1933. EUR+WWI GERMANY UK USSR ECO/TAC   GOV/REL
INT/TRADE NEUTRAL WAR ATTIT 20 WEIMAR/REP TREATY.   POLICY
PAGE 34 E0669

B66

FUCHS W.P.,STAAT UND KIRCHE IM WANDEL DER   SECT
JAHRHUNDERTE. EUR+WWI MOD/EUR UK REV...JURID CONCPT   NAT/G
4/20 EUROPE CHRISTIAN CHURCH/STA. PAGE 41 E0817   ORD/FREE
                                                        GP/REL

B66

GILLMOR D.M.,FREE PRESS AND FAIR TRIAL. UK USA+45   ORD/FREE
CONSTN PROB/SOLV PRESS CONTROL CRIME DISCRIM   ADJUD
RESPECT...AUD/VIS 20 CIVIL/LIB. PAGE 44 E0865   ATTIT
                                                        EDU/PROP

B66

HOGUE A.R.,ORIGINS OF THE COMMON LAW. UK STRUCT   LAW
AGRI CT/SYS SANCTION CONSERVE 12/14 ENGLSH/LAW   SOCIETY
COMMON/LAW. PAGE 54 E1068   CONSTN

B66

HOLDSWORTH W.S.,A HISTORY OF ENGLISH LAW; THE   BIOG
CENTURIES OF SETTLEMENT AND REFORM (VOL. XVI). UK   PERSON
LOC/G NAT/G EX/STRUC LEGIS CT/SYS LEAD ATTIT   PROF/ORG
...POLICY DECISION JURID IDEA/COMP 18 PARLIAMENT.   LAW
PAGE 54 E1083

B66

HOYT E.C.,NATIONAL POLICY AND INTERNATIONAL LAW*   INT/LAW
CASE STUDIES FROM AMERICAN CANAL POLICY* MONOGRAPH   USA-45
NO. 1 -- 1966-1967. PANAMA UK ELITES BAL/PWR   DIPLOM
EFFICIENCY...CLASSIF NAT/COMP SOC/EXP COLOMB   PWR
TREATY. PAGE 55 E1105

B66

MCNAIR A.D.,THE LEGAL EFFECTS OF WAR. UK FINAN   JURID
DIPLOM ORD/FREE 20 ENGLSH/LAW. PAGE 71 E1425   WAR

RUNCIMAN W.G.,RELATIVE DEPRIVATION AND SOCIAL JUSTICE: A STUDY OF ATTITUDES TO SOCIAL INEQUALITY IN TWENTIETH-CENTURY ENGLAND. UK LAW POL/PAR PWR ...CONCPT NEW/IDEA SAMP METH 19/20. PAGE 86 E1734
INT/TRADE
LABOR
B66
STRATA
STRUCT
DISCRIM
ATTIT

US DEPARTMENT OF STATE,RESEARCH ON WESTERN EUROPE, GREAT BRITAIN, AND CANADA (EXTERNAL RESEARCH LIST NO 3-25). CANADA GERMANY/W UK LAW CULTURE NAT/G POL/PAR FORCES EDU/PROP REGION MARXISM...GEOG SOC WORSHIP 20 CMN/WLTH. PAGE 100 E1998
B66
BIBLIOG/A
EUR+WWI
DIPLOM

WILSON G.,CASES AND MATERIALS ON CONSTITUTIONAL AND ADMINISTRATIVE LAW. UK LAW NAT/G EX/STRUC LEGIS BAL/PWR BUDGET DIPLOM ADJUD CONTROL CT/SYS GOV/REL ORD/FREE 20 PARLIAMENT ENGLSH/LAW. PAGE 106 E2126
B66
JURID
ADMIN
CONSTN
PWR

GREEN L.C.,"RHODESIAN OIL: BOOTLEGGERS OR PIRATES?" AFR RHODESIA UK WOR+45 INT/ORG NAT/G DIPLOM LEGIT COLONIAL SOVEREIGN 20 UN OAU. PAGE 46 E0907
S66
INT/TRADE
SANCTION
INT/LAW
POLICY

BOULTON D.,OBJECTION OVERRULED. UK LAW POL/PAR DIPLOM ADJUD SANCTION DEATH WAR CIVMIL/REL 20. PAGE 14 E0273
B67
FORCES
SOCISM
SECT

BROWN L.N.,FRENCH ADMINISTRATIVE LAW. FRANCE UK CONSTN NAT/G LEGIS DOMIN CONTROL EXEC PARL/PROC PWR ...JURID METH/COMP GEN/METH. PAGE 16 E0314
B67
EX/STRUC
LAW
IDEA/COMP
CT/SYS

COWLING M.,1867 DISRAELI, GLADSTONE, AND REVOLUTION; THE PASSING OF THE SECOND REFORM BILL. UK LEGIS LEAD LOBBY GP/REL INGP/REL...DECISION BIBLIOG 19 REFORMERS. PAGE 27 E0531
B67
PARL/PROC
POL/PAR
ATTIT
LAW

HODGKINSON R.G.,THE ORIGINS OF THE NATIONAL HEALTH SERVICE: THE MEDICAL SERVICES OF THE NEW POOR LAW, 1834-1871. UK INDUS MUNIC WORKER PROB/SOLV EFFICIENCY ATTIT HEALTH WEALTH SOCISM...JURID SOC/WK 19/20. PAGE 53 E1062
B67
HEAL
NAT/G
POLICY
LAW

RAE D.,THE POLITICAL CONSEQUENCES OF ELECTORAL LAWS. EUR+WWI ICELAND ISRAEL NEW/ZEALND UK USA+45 ADJUD APPORT GP/REL MAJORITY...MATH STAT CENSUS CHARTS BIBLIOG 20 AUSTRAL. PAGE 83 E1667
B67
POL/PAR
CHOOSE
NAT/COMP
REPRESENT

VILE M.J.C.,CONSTITUTIONALISM AND THE SEPARATION OF POWERS. FRANCE UK USA+45 USA-45 NAT/G ADJUD CONTROL GOV/REL...POLICY DECISION JURID GEN/LAWS 15/20 MONTESQ. PAGE 104 E2076
B67
CONSTN
BAL/PWR
CONCPT
LAW

ALDRICH W.A.,"THE SUEZ CRISIS." UAR UK USA+45 DELIB/GP FORCES BAL/PWR INT/TRADE CONFER CONTROL COERCE DETER 20. PAGE 3 E0058
S67
DIPLOM
INT/LAW
COLONIAL

ALEXANDER B.,"GIBRALTAR" SPAIN UK CONSTN WORKER PROB/SOLV FOR/AID RECEIVE CONTROL 20. PAGE 3 E0059
S67
DIPLOM
INT/ORG
ORD/FREE
ECO/TAC

CLOGGER T.J.,"THE BIG EAR." UK USA+45 USSR LAW LEGIS CRIME GP/REL INGP/REL ATTIT 20 FBI ESPIONAGE. PAGE 23 E0458
S67
DIPLOM
ORD/FREE
COM/IND
INSPECT

DOUTY H.M.," REFERENCE TO DEVELOPING COUNTRIES." JAMAICA MALAYSIA UK WOR+45 LAW FINAN ACT/RES BUDGET CAP/ISM ECO/TAC TARIFFS RISK EFFICIENCY PROFIT ...CHARTS 20. PAGE 33 E0646
S67
TAX
ECO/UNDEV
NAT/G

GANZ G.,"THE CONTROL OF INDUSTRY BY ADMINISTRATIVE PROCESS." UK DELIB/GP WORKER 20. PAGE 42 E0832
S67
INDUS
LAW
ADMIN
CONTROL

MACLEOD R.M.,"LAW, MEDICINE AND PUBLIC OPINION: THE RESISTANCE TO COMPULSORY HEALTH LEGISLATION
S67
LAW
HEALTH

1870-1907." UK CONSTN SECT DELIB/GP DEBATE PARL/PROC GP/REL MORAL 19. PAGE 67 E1344
ATTIT

MATTHEWS R.O.,"THE SUEZ CANAL DISPUTE* A CASE STUDY IN PEACEFUL SETTLEMENT." FRANCE ISRAEL UAR UK NAT/G CONTROL LEAD COERCE WAR NAT/LISM ROLE ORD/FREE PWR ...INT/LAW UN 20. PAGE 69 E1389
S67
PEACE
DIPLOM
ADJUD

MITCHELL J.D.B.,"THE CONSTITUTIONAL IMPLICATIONS OF JUDICIAL CONTROL OF THE ADMINISTRATION IN THE UNITED KINGDOM." UK LAW ADJUD ADMIN GOV/REL ROLE ...GP/COMP 20. PAGE 74 E1474
S67
CONSTN
CT/SYS
CONTROL
EX/STRUC

RICHARDSON J.J.,"THE MAKING OF THE RESTRICTIVE TRADE PRACTICES ACT 1956 A CASE STUDY OF THE POLICY PROCESS IN BRITAIN." UK FINAN MARKET LG/CO POL/PAR CONSULT PRESS ADJUD ADMIN AGREE LOBBY SANCTION ATTIT 20. PAGE 84 E1695
S67
LEGIS
ECO/TAC
POLICY
INDUS

BLACKSTONE W.,COMMENTARIES ON THE LAWS OF ENGLAND (4 VOLS.) (4TH ED.). UK CHIEF DELIB/GP LEGIS WORKER CT/SYS SANCTION CRIME OWN...CRIMLGY 18 ENGLSH/LAW. PAGE 12 E0238
B70
LAW
JURID
ADJUD
CONSTN

AUSTIN J.,LECTURES ON JURISPRUDENCE OR THE PHILOSOPHY OF POSITIVE LAW (VOL. II) (4TH ED., REV.). UK CONSTN STRUCT PROB/SOLV LEGIT CT/SYS SANCTION CRIME INGP/REL OWN SUPEGO ORD/FREE...T 19. PAGE 6 E0120
B73
LAW
ADJUD
JURID
METH/CNCPT

MAINE H.S.,LECTURES ON THE EARLY HISTORY OF INSTITUTIONS. IRELAND UK CONSTN ELITES STRUCT FAM KIN CHIEF LEGIS CT/SYS OWN SOVEREIGN...CONCPT 16 BENTHAM/J BREHON ROMAN/LAW. PAGE 68 E1351
B75
CULTURE
LAW
INGP/REL

BENTHAM J.,THE THEORY OF LEGISLATION. UK CREATE CRIME ATTIT ORD/FREE...CONCPT 18 REFORMERS. PAGE 10 E0196
B76
LEGIS
LAW
CRIMLGY
UTIL

GOODNOW F.J.,"AN EXECUTIVE AND THE COURTS: JUDICIAL REMEDIES AGAINST ADMINISTRATIVE ACTION" FRANCE UK USA-45 WOR-45 LAW CONSTN SANCTION ORD/FREE 19. PAGE 45 E0888
L86
CT/SYS
GOV/REL
ADMIN
ADJUD

BENTHAM J.,DEFENCE OF USURY (1787). UK LAW NAT/G TEC/DEV ECO/TAC CONTROL ATTIT...CONCPT IDEA/COMP 18 SMITH/ADAM. PAGE 10 E0197
B88
TAX
FINAN
ECO/DEV
POLICY

BURGESS J.W.,POLITICAL SCIENCE AND COMPARATIVE CONSTITUTIONAL LAW. FRANCE GERMANY UK USA+45 LEGIS DIPLOM ADJUD REPRESENT...CONCPT 19. PAGE 17 E0340
B90
CONSTN
LAW
LOC/G
NAT/G

GODWIN W.,POLITICAL JUSTICE. UK ELITES OWN KNOWL MORAL WEALTH...JURID 18/19. PAGE 44 E0877
B90
ORD/FREE
SOVEREIGN
STRUCT
CONCPT

LOWELL A.L.,ESSAYS ON GOVERNMENT. UK USA-45 LEGIS PARL/PROC...POLICY PREDICT 19. PAGE 66 E1328
B92
CONSTN
ADJUD
CT/SYS
NAT/G

ESMEIN A.,ELEMENTS DE DROIT CONSTITUTIONNEL. FRANCE UK CHIEF EX/STRUC LEGIS ADJUD CT/SYS PARL/PROC REV GOV/REL ORD/FREE...JURID METH/COMP 18/19. PAGE 35 E0697
B96
LAW
CONSTN
NAT/G
CONCPT

SMITH A.,LECTURES ON JUSTICE, POLICE, REVENUE AND ARMS (1763). UK LAW FAM FORCES TARIFFS AGREE COERCE INCOME OWN WEALTH LAISSEZ...GEN/LAWS 17/18. PAGE 92 E1840
B96
DIPLOM
JURID
OLD/LIB
TAX

POLLOCK F.,THE HISTORY OF ENGLISH LAW BEFORE THE TIME OF EDWARD I (2 VOLS, 2ND ED.). UK CULTURE LOC/G LEGIS LICENSE AGREE CONTROL CT/SYS SANCTION CRIME...TIME/SEQ 13 COMMON/LAW CANON/LAW. PAGE 81 E1626
B98
LAW
ADJUD
JURID

B99

BROOKS S.,BRITAIN AND THE BOERS. AFR SOUTH/AFR UK   WAR
CULTURE INSPECT LEGIT...INT/LAW 19/20 BOER/WAR.   DIPLOM
PAGE 16 E0309   NAT/G

ULMER S.S. E1951,E1952

UN....UNITED NATIONS; SEE ALSO INT/ORG, VOL/ASSN, INT/REL

N

AMERICAN POLITICAL SCIENCE REVIEW. USA+45 USA-45   BIBLIOG/A
WOR+45 WOR-45 INT/ORG ADMIN...INT/LAW PHIL/SCI   DIPLOM
CONCPT METH 20 UN. PAGE 1 E0002   NAT/G
  GOV/COMP

N

FOREIGN AFFAIRS. SPACE WOR+45 WOR-45 CULTURE   BIBLIOG
ECO/UNDEV FINAN NAT/G TEC/DEV INT/TRADE ARMS/CONT   DIPLOM
NUC/PWR...POLICY 20 UN EURATOM ECSC EEC. PAGE 1   INT/ORG
E0021   INT/LAW

N

ASIA FOUNDATION,LIBRARY NOTES. LAW CONSTN CULTURE   BIBLIOG/A
SOCIETY ECO/UNDEV INT/ORG NAT/G COLONIAL LEAD   ASIA
REGION NAT/LISM ATTIT 20 UN. PAGE 6 E0107   S/ASIA
  DIPLOM

N

UNITED NATIONS,OFFICIAL RECORDS OF THE UNITED   INT/ORG
NATIONS' GENERAL ASSEMBLY. WOR+45 BUDGET DIPLOM   DELIB/GP
ADMIN 20 UN. PAGE 98 E1964   INT/LAW
  WRITING

N

UNITED NATIONS,UNITED NATIONS PUBLICATIONS. WOR+45   BIBLIOG
ECO/UNDEV AGRI FINAN FORCES ADMIN LEAD WAR PEACE   INT/ORG
...POLICY INT/LAW 20 UN. PAGE 98 E1965   DIPLOM

N

UNITED NATIONS,YEARBOOK OF THE INTERNATIONAL LAW   BIBLIOG
COMMISSION....CON/ANAL 20 UN. PAGE 98 E1966   INT/ORG
  INT/LAW
  DELIB/GP

N19

AMERICAN CIVIL LIBERTIES UNION,"WE HOLD THESE   ORD/FREE
TRUTHS" FREEDOM, JUSTICE, EQUALITY: REPORT ON CIVIL   LAW
LIBERTIES (A PERIODICAL PAMPHLET COVERING 1951-53).   RACE/REL
USA+45 ACADEM NAT/G FORCES LEGIS COERCE CIVMIL/REL   CONSTN
GOV/REL DISCRIM PRIVIL MARXISM...OLD/LIB 20 ACLU UN
CIVIL/LIB. PAGE 4 E0076

N19

BAILEY S.D.,VETO IN THE SECURITY COUNCIL   DELIB/GP
(PAMPHLET). COM USSR WOR+45 BAL/PWR PARL/PROC   INT/ORG
ARMS/CONT PRIVIL PWR...INT/LAW TREND CHARTS 20 UN   DIPLOM
SUEZ. PAGE 7 E0135

N19

MEZERIK A.G.,ATOM TESTS AND RADIATION HAZARDS   NUC/PWR
(PAMPHLET). WOR+45 INT/ORG DIPLOM DETER 20 UN   ARMS/CONT
TREATY. PAGE 73 E1452   CONFER
  HEALTH

N19

MEZERIK AG,OUTER SPACE: UN, US, USSR (PAMPHLET).   SPACE
USSR DELIB/GP FORCES DETER NUC/PWR SOVEREIGN   CONTROL
...POLICY 20 UN TREATY. PAGE 73 E1453   DIPLOM
  INT/ORG

B45

UNCIO CONFERENCE LIBRARY,SHORT TITLE CLASSIFIED   BIBLIOG
CATALOG. WOR-45 DOMIN COLONIAL WAR...SOC/WK 20   DIPLOM
LEAGUE/NAT UN. PAGE 98 E1955   INT/ORG
  INT/LAW

C46

GOODRICH L.M.,"CHARTER OF THE UNITED NATIONS: CONSTN
COMMENTARY AND DOCUMENTS." EX/STRUC ADMIN...INT/LAW   INT/ORG
CON/ANAL BIBLIOG 20 UN. PAGE 45 E0890   DIPLOM

B47

HILL M.,IMMUNITIES AND PRIVILEGES OF INTERNATIONAL   INT/ORG
OFFICIALS. CANADA EUR+WWI NETHERLND SWITZERLND LAW   ADMIN
LEGIS DIPLOM LEGIT RESPECT...TIME/SEQ LEAGUE/NAT UN
VAL/FREE 20. PAGE 52 E1046

B47

INTERNATIONAL COURT OF JUSTICE,CHARTER OF THE   INT/LAW
UNITED NATIONS, STATUTE AND RULES OF COURT AND   INT/ORG
OTHER CONSTITUTIONAL DOCUMENTS. SWITZERLND LAW   CT/SYS
ADJUD INGP/REL...JURID 20 ICJ UN. PAGE 57 E1133   DIPLOM

B48

FENWICK C.G.,INTERNATIONAL LAW. WOR+45 WOR-45   INT/ORG
CONSTN NAT/G LEGIT CT/SYS REGION...CONCPT   JURID

LEAGUE/NAT UN 20. PAGE 37 E0737   INT/LAW

B48

HOLCOMBE A.N.,HUMAN RIGHTS IN THE MODERN WORLD.   ORD/FREE
WOR+45 LEGIS DIPLOM ADJUD PERSON...INT/LAW 20 UN   INT/ORG
TREATY CIVIL/LIB BILL/RIGHT. PAGE 54 E1071   CONSTN
  LAW

B49

US LIBRARY OF CONGRESS,FREEDOM OF INFORMATION: BIBLIOG/A
SELECTIVE REPORT ON RECENT WRITINGS. USA+45 LAW   ORD/FREE
CONSTN ELITES EDU/PROP PRESS LOBBY WAR TOTALISM   LICENSE
ATTIT 20 UN UNESCO COLD/WAR. PAGE 101 E2018   COM/IND

L49

COMM. STUDY ORGAN. PEACE,"A TEN YEAR RECORD,   INT/ORG
1939-1949." FUT WOR+45 LAW R+D CONSULT DELIB/GP   CONSTN
CREATE LEGIT ROUTINE ORD/FREE...TIME/SEQ UN 20.   PEACE
PAGE 24 E0480

B50

JIMENEZ E.,VOTING AND HANDLING OF DISPUTES IN THE   DELIB/GP
SECURITY COUNCIL. WOR+45 CONSTN INT/ORG DIPLOM   ROUTINE
LEGIT DETER CHOOSE MORAL ORD/FREE PWR...JURID
TIME/SEQ COLD/WAR UN 20. PAGE 59 E1168

B50

LAUTERPACHT H.,INTERNATIONAL LAW AND HUMAN RIGHTS.   DELIB/GP
USA+45 CONSTN STRUCT INT/ORG ACT/RES EDU/PROP PEACE   LAW
PERSON ALL/VALS...CONCPT CON/ANAL GEN/LAWS UN 20.   INT/LAW
PAGE 63 E1266

B50

ROSS A.,CONSTITUTION OF THE UNITED NATIONS. CONSTN   PEACE
CONSULT DELIB/GP ECO/TAC...INT/LAW JURID 20 UN   DIPLOM
LEAGUE/NAT. PAGE 86 E1721   ORD/FREE
  INT/ORG

B50

SOHN L.B.,CASES AND OTHER MATERIALS ON WORLD LAW.   CT/SYS
FUT WOR+45 LAW INT/ORG...INT/LAW JURID METH/CNCPT   CONSTN
20 UN. PAGE 92 E1852

B51

KELSEN H.,THE LAW OF THE UNITED NATIONS. WOR+45   INT/ORG
STRUCT RIGID/FLEX ORD/FREE...INT/LAW JURID CONCPT   ADJUD
CON/ANAL GEN/METH UN TOT/POP VAL/FREE 20. PAGE 60
E1198

L51

KELSEN H.,"RECENT TRENDS IN THE LAW OF THE UNITED   INT/ORG
NATIONS." KOREA WOR+45 CONSTN LEGIS DIPLOM LEGIT   LAW
DETER WAR RIGID/FLEX HEALTH ORD/FREE RESPECT   INT/LAW
...JURID CON/ANAL UN VAL/FREE 20 NATO. PAGE 60
E1199

B52

DE GRAZIA A.,POLITICAL ORGANIZATION. CONSTN LOC/G   FEDERAL
MUNIC NAT/G CHIEF LEGIS TOP/EX ADJUD CT/SYS   LAW
PERS/REL...INT/LAW MYTH UN. PAGE 29 E0581   ADMIN

B52

JACKSON E.,MEETING OF THE MINDS: A WAY TO PEACE   LABOR
THROUGH MEDIATION. WOR+45 INDUS INT/ORG NAT/G   JUDGE
DELIB/GP DIPLOM EDU/PROP LEGIT ORD/FREE...NEW/IDEA
SELF/OBS TIME/SEQ CHARTS GEN/LAWS TOT/POP 20 UN
TREATY. PAGE 57 E1139

B52

VANDENBOSCH A.,THE UN: BACKGROUND, ORGANIZATION,   DELIB/GP
FUNCTIONS, ACTIVITIES. WOR+45 LAW CONSTN STRUCT   TIME/SEQ
INT/ORG CONSULT BAL/PWR EDU/PROP EXEC ALL/VALS   PEACE
...POLICY CONCPT UN 20. PAGE 103 E2071

B53

OPPENHEIM L.,INTERNATIONAL LAW: A TREATISE (7TH   INT/LAW
ED., 2 VOLS.). LAW CONSTN PROB/SOLV INT/TRADE ADJUD   INT/ORG
AGREE NEUTRAL WAR ORD/FREE SOVEREIGN...BIBLIOG 20   DIPLOM
LEAGUE/NAT UN ILO. PAGE 79 E1579

B54

MANGONE G.,A SHORT HISTORY OF INTERNATIONAL   INT/ORG
ORGANIZATION. MOD/EUR USA+45 USA-45 WOR+45 WOR-45   INT/LAW
LAW LEGIS CREATE LEGIT ROUTINE RIGID/FLEX PWR
...JURID CONCPT OBS TIME/SEQ STERTYP GEN/LAWS UN
TOT/POP VAL/FREE 18/20. PAGE 68 E1359

B54

US SENATE COMM ON FOREIGN REL,REVIEW OF THE UNITED   BIBLIOG
NATIONS CHARTER: A COLLECTION OF DOCUMENTS. LEGIS   CONSTN
DIPLOM ADMIN ARMS/CONT WAR REPRESENT SOVEREIGN   INT/ORG
...INT/LAW 20 UN. PAGE 101 E2029   DEBATE

B55

CHOWDHURI R.N.,INTERNATIONAL MANDATES AND   DELIB/GP
TRUSTEESHIP SYSTEMS. WOR+45 STRUCT ECO/UNDEV   PLAN

INT/ORG LEGIS DOMIN EDU/PROP LEGIT ADJUD EXEC PWR ...CONCPT TIME/SEQ UN 20. PAGE 22 E0434 — SOVEREIGN

B55
COMM. STUDY ORGAN. PEACE,REPORTS. WOR-45 ECO/DEV ECO/UNDEV VOL/ASSN CONSULT FORCES PLAN TEC/DEV DOMIN EDU/PROP NUC/PWR ATTIT PWR WEALTH...JURID STERTYP FAO ILO 20 UN. PAGE 24 E0481 — WOR+45 INT/ORG ARMS/CONT

B55
HOGAN W.N.,INTERNATIONAL CONFLICT AND COLLECTIVE SECURITY: THE PRINCIPLE OF CONCERN IN INTERNATIONAL ORGANIZATION. CONSTN EX/STRUC BAL/PWR DIPLOM ADJUD CONTROL CENTRAL CONSEN PEACE...INT/LAW CONCPT METH/COMP 20 UN LEAGUE/NAT. PAGE 53 E1066 — INT/ORG WAR ORD/FREE FORCES

B55
UN HEADQUARTERS LIBRARY,BIBLIOGRAPHIE DE LA CHARTE DES NATIONS UNIES. CHINA/COM KOREA WOR+45 VOL/ASSN CONFER ADMIN COERCE PEACE ATTIT ORD/FREE SOVEREIGN ...INT/LAW 20 UNESCO UN. PAGE 97 E1953 — BIBLIOG/A INT/ORG DIPLOM

B56
SOHN L.B.,BASIC DOCUMENTS OF THE UNITED NATIONS. WOR+45 LAW INT/ORG LEGIT EXEC ROUTINE CHOOSE PWR ...JURID CONCPT GEN/LAWS ANTHOL UN TOT/POP OAS FAO ILO 20. PAGE 92 E1853 — DELIB/GP CONSTN

B56
SOHN L.B.,CASES ON UNITED NATIONS LAW. STRUCT DELIB/GP WAR PEACE ORD/FREE...DECISION ANTHOL 20 UN. PAGE 92 E1854 — INT/ORG INT/LAW ADMIN ADJUD

S56
POTTER P.B.,"NEUTRALITY, 1955." WOR+45 WOR-45 INT/ORG NAT/G WAR ATTIT...POLICY IDEA/COMP 17/20 LEAGUE/NAT UN COLD/WAR. PAGE 81 E1631 — NEUTRAL INT/LAW DIPLOM CONCPT

B57
COMM. STUDY ORGAN. PEACE,STRENGTHENING THE UNITED NATIONS. FUT USA+45 WOR+45 CONSTN NAT/G DELIB/GP FORCES LEGIS ECO/TAC LEGIT COERCE PEACE...JURID CONCPT UN COLD/WAR 20. PAGE 24 E0482 — INT/ORG ORD/FREE

B57
CONOVER H.F.,NORTH AND NORTHEAST AFRICA; A SELECTED ANNOTATED LIST OF WRITINGS. ALGERIA MOROCCO SUDAN UAR CULTURE INT/ORG PROB/SOLV ADJUD NAT/LISM PWR WEALTH...SOC 20 UN. PAGE 25 E0496 — BIBLIOG/A DIPLOM AFR ECO/UNDEV

B57
ROSENNE S.,THE INTERNATIONAL COURT OF JUSTICE. WOR+45 LAW DOMIN LEGIT PEACE PWR SOVEREIGN...JURID CONCPT RECORD TIME/SEQ CON/ANAL CHARTS UN TOT/POP VAL/FREE LEAGUE/NAT 20 ICJ. PAGE 86 E1716 — INT/ORG CT/SYS INT/LAW

B58
BOWETT D.W.,SELF-DEFENSE IN INTERNATIONAL LAW. EUR+WWI MOD/EUR WOR+45 WOR-45 SOCIETY INT/ORG CONSULT DIPLOM LEGIT COERCE ATTIT ORD/FREE...JURID 20 UN. PAGE 14 E0276 — ADJUD CONCPT WAR INT/LAW

B58
MOSKOWITZ M.,HUMAN RIGHTS AND WORLD ORDER. INT/ORG PLAN GP/REL NAT/LISM SOVEREIGN...CONCPT 20 UN TREATY CIV/RIGHTS. PAGE 75 E1502 — DIPLOM INT/LAW ORD/FREE

B58
RUSSELL R.B.,A HISTORY OF THE UNITED NATIONS CHARTER: THE ROLE OF THE UNITED STATES. SOCIETY NAT/G CONSULT DOMIN LEGIT ATTIT ORD/FREE PWR ...POLICY JURID CONCPT UN LEAGUE/NAT. PAGE 87 E1737 — USA-45 INT/ORG CONSTN

B58
SEYID MUHAMMAD V.A.,THE LEGAL FRAMEWORK OF WORLD TRADE. WOR+45 INT/ORG DIPLOM CONTROL...BIBLIOG 20 TREATY UN IMF GATT. PAGE 90 E1807 — INT/LAW VOL/ASSN INT/TRADE TARIFFS

B58
SOC OF COMP LEGIS AND INT LAW,THE LAW OF THE SEA... (PAMPHLET). WOR+45 NAT/G INT/TRADE ADJUD CONTROL NUC/PWR WAR PEACE ATTIT ORD/FREE...JURID CHARTS 20 UN TREATY RESOURCE/N. PAGE 92 E1850 — INT/LAW INT/ORG DIPLOM SEA

B58
STONE J.,AGGRESSION AND WORLD ORDER: A CRITIQUE OF UNITED NATIONS THEORIES OF AGGRESSION. LAW CONSTN DELIB/GP PROB/SOLV BAL/PWR DIPLOM DEBATE ADJUD CRIME PWR...POLICY IDEA/COMP 20 UN SUEZ LEAGUE/NAT. PAGE 94 E1879 — ORD/FREE INT/ORG WAR CONCPT

B58
STRONG C.F.,MODERN POLITICAL CONSTITUTIONS. LAW — CONSTN

CHIEF DELIB/GP EX/STRUC LEGIS ADJUD CHOOSE FEDERAL POPULISM...CONCPT BIBLIOG 20 UN. PAGE 94 E1887 — IDEA/COMP NAT/G

S58
MCDOUGAL M.S.,"PERSPECTIVES FOR A LAW OF OUTER SPACE." FUT WOR+45 AIR CONSULT DELIB/GP TEC/DEV CT/SYS ORD/FREE...POLICY JURID 20 UN. PAGE 70 E1404 — INT/ORG SPACE INT/LAW

C58
RAJAN M.S.,"UNITED NATIONS AND DOMESTIC JURISDICTION." WOR+45 WOR-45 PARL/PROC...IDEA/COMP BIBLIOG 20 UN. PAGE 83 E1670 — INT/LAW DIPLOM CONSTN INT/ORG

N58
US HOUSE COMM FOREIGN AFFAIRS,HEARINGS ON DRAFT LEGISLATION TO AMEND FURTHER THE MUTUAL SECURITY ACT OF 1954 (PAMPHLET). USA+45 CONSULT FORCES BUDGET DIPLOM DETER COST ORD/FREE...JURID 20 DEPT/DEFEN UN DEPT/STATE. PAGE 100 E2002 — LEGIS DELIB/GP CONFER WEAPON

B59
COMM. STUDY ORGAN. PEACE,ORGANIZING PEACE IN THE NUCLEAR AGE. FUT CONSULT DELIB/GP DOMIN ADJUD ROUTINE COERCE ORD/FREE...TECHNIC INT/LAW JURID NEW/IDEA UN COLD/WAR 20. PAGE 24 E0483 — INT/ORG ACT/RES NUC/PWR

B59
COLUMBIA U: BUREAU OF APPL SOC RES, ATTITUDES OF PROMINENT AMERICANS TOWARD "WORLD PEACE THROUGH WORLD LAW" (SUPRA-NATL ORGANIZATION FOR WAR PREVENTION). USA+45 USSR ELITES FORCES PLAN PROB/SOLV CONTROL WAR PWR...POLICY SOC QU IDEA/COMP 20 UN. PAGE 82 E1644 — ATTIT ACT/RES INT/LAW STAT

B60
CLARK G.,WORLD PEACE THROUGH WORLD LAW. FUT WOR+45 CONSULT FORCES ACT/RES CREATE PLAN ADMIN ROUTINE ARMS/CONT DETER ATTIT PWR...JURID VAL/FREE UNESCO 20 UN. PAGE 23 E0449 — INT/ORG LAW PEACE INT/LAW

B60
ENGEL J.,THE SECURITY OF THE FREE WORLD. USSR WOR+45 STRATA STRUCT ECO/DEV ECO/UNDEV INT/ORG DELIB/GP FORCES DOMIN LEGIT ADJUD EXEC ARMS/CONT COERCE...POLICY CONCPT NEW/IDEA TIME/SEQ GEN/LAWS COLD/WAR WORK UN 20 NATO. PAGE 35 E0689 — COM TREND DIPLOM

B60
UNITED WORLD FEDERALISTS,UNITED WORLD FEDERALISTS; PANORAMA OF RECENT BOOKS, FILMS, AND JOURNALS ON WORLD FEDERATION. THE UN, AND WORLD PEACE. CULTURE ECO/UNDEV PROB/SOLV FOR/AID ARMS/CONT NUC/PWR ...INT/LAW PHIL/SCI 20 UN. PAGE 98 E1971 — BIBLIOG/A DIPLOM INT/ORG PEACE

S60
SCHACHTER O.,"THE ENFORCEMENT OF INTERNATIONAL JUDICIAL AND ARBITRAL DECISIONS." WOR+45 NAT/G ECO/TAC DOMIN LEGIT ROUTINE COERCE ATTIT DRIVE ALL/VALS PWR...METH/CNCPT TREND TOT/POP 20 UN. PAGE 87 E1750 — INT/ORG ADJUD INT/LAW

S60
SCHWELB E.,"INTERNATIONAL CONVENTIONS ON HUMAN RIGHTS." FUT WOR+45 LAW CONSTN CULTURE SOCIETY STRUCT VOL/ASSN DELIB/GP PLAN ADJUD SUPEGO LOVE MORAL...SOC CONCPT STAT RECORD HIST/WRIT TREND 20 UN. PAGE 89 E1790 — INT/ORG HUM

B61
BAINS J.S.,STUDIES IN POLITICAL SCIENCE. INDIA WOR+45 WOR-45 CONSTN BAL/PWR ADJUD ADMIN PARL/PROC SOVEREIGN...SOC METH/COMP ANTHOL 17/20 UN. PAGE 7 E0137 — DIPLOM INT/LAW NAT/G

B61
MECHAM J.L.,THE UNITED STATES AND INTER-AMERICAN SECURITY, 1889-1960. L/A+17C USA+45 USA-45 CONSTN FORCES INT/TRADE PEACE TOTALISM ATTIT...JURID 19/20 UN OAS. PAGE 72 E1432 — DIPLOM WAR ORD/FREE INT/ORG

B61
RIENOW R.,CONTEMPORARY INTERNATIONAL POLITICS. WOR+45 INT/ORG BAL/PWR EDU/PROP COLONIAL NEUTRAL REGION WAR PEACE...INT/LAW 20 COLD/WAR UN. PAGE 85 E1698 — DIPLOM PWR POLICY NAT/G

L61
TAUBENFELD H.J.,"A REGIME FOR OUTER SPACE." FUT UNIV R+D ACT/RES PLAN BAL/PWR LEGIT ARMS/CONT ORD/FREE...POLICY JURID TREND UN TOT/POP 20 COLD/WAR. PAGE 95 E1910 — INT/ORG ADJUD SPACE

S61
ALGER C.F.,"NON-RESOLUTION CONSEQUENCES OF THE UNITED NATIONS AND THEIR EFFECT ON INTERNATIONAL — INT/ORG DRIVE

CONFLICT." WOR+45 CONSTN ECO/DEV NAT/G CONSULT BAL/PWR
DELIB/GP TOP/EX ACT/RES PLAN DIPLOM EDU/PROP
ROUTINE ATTIT ALL/VALS...INT/LAW TOT/POP UN 20.
PAGE 3 E0065

S61
CASTANEDA J.,"THE UNDERDEVELOPED NATIONS AND THE   INT/ORG
DEVELOPMENT OF INTERNATIONAL LAW." FUT UNIV LAW   ECO/UNDEV
ACT/RES FOR/AID LEGIT PERCEPT SKILL...JURID   PEACE
METH/CNCPT TIME/SEQ TOT/POP 20 UN. PAGE 21 E0405   INT/LAW

S61
JACKSON E.,"THE FUTURE DEVELOPMENT OF THE UNITED   INT/ORG
NATIONS: SOME SUGGESTIONS FOR RESEARCH." FUT LAW   PWR
CONSTN ECO/DEV FINAN PEACE WEALTH...WELF/ST CONCPT
UN 20. PAGE 57 E1140

S61
MILLER E.,"LEGAL ASPECTS OF UN ACTION IN THE   INT/ORG
CONGO." AFR CULTURE ADMIN PEACE DRIVE RIGID/FLEX   LEGIT
ORD/FREE...WELF/ST JURID OBS UN CONGO 20. PAGE 73
E1458

B62
ALEXANDROWICZ C.H.,WORLD ECONOMIC AGENCIES: LAW AND INT/LAW
PRACTICE. WOR+45 DIST/IND FINAN LABOR CONSULT   INT/ORG
INT/TRADE TARIFFS REPRESENT HEALTH...JURID 20 UN   DIPLOM
GATT EEC OAS ECSC. PAGE 3 E0063   ADJUD

B62
GANJI M.,INTERNATIONAL PROTECTION OF HUMAN RIGHTS.   ORD/FREE
WOR+45 CONSTN INT/TRADE CT/SYS SANCTION CRIME WAR   DISCRIM
RACE/REL...CHARTS IDEA/COMP NAT/COMP BIBLIOG 20   LEGIS
TREATY NEGRO LEAGUE/NAT UN CIVIL/LIB. PAGE 42 E0831 DELIB/GP

B62
GYORGY A.,PROBLEMS IN INTERNATIONAL RELATIONS. COM   DIPLOM
CT/SYS NUC/PWR ALL/IDEOS 20 UN EEC ECSC. PAGE 49   NEUTRAL
E0966   BAL/PWR
                                                     REV

B62
HADWEN J.G.,HOW UNITED NATIONS DECISIONS ARE MADE.   INT/ORG
WOR+45 LAW EDU/PROP LEGIT ADMIN PWR...DECISION   ROUTINE
SELF/OBS GEN/LAWS UN 20. PAGE 49 E0972

B62
JENKS C.W.,THE PROPER LAW OF INTERNATIONAL   LAW
ORGANISATIONS. DIPLOM LEGIT AGREE CT/SYS SANCTION   INT/ORG
REPRESENT SOVEREIGN...GEN/LAWS 20 UN UNESCO ILO   ADJUD
NATO OAS. PAGE 58 E1158   INT/LAW

B62
LAWSON R.,INTERNATIONAL REGIONAL ORGANIZATIONS.   INT/ORG
WOR+45 NAT/G VOL/ASSN CONSULT LEGIS EDU/PROP LEGIT   DELIB/GP
ADMIN EXEC ROUTINE HEALTH PWR WEALTH...JURID EEC   REGION
COLD/WAR 20 UN. PAGE 63 E1270

B62
LEVY H.V.,LIBERDADE E JUSTICA SOCIAL (2ND ED.).   ORD/FREE
BRAZIL COM L/A+17C USSR INT/ORG PARTIC GP/REL   MARXISM
WEALTH 20 UN COM/PARTY. PAGE 65 E1290   CAP/ISM
                                                     LAW

B62
NORGAARD C.A.,THE POSITION OF THE INDIVIDUAL IN   INT/LAW
INTERNATIONAL LAW. INT/ORG SUPEGO ORD/FREE   DIPLOM
SOVEREIGN...CONCPT 20 UN. PAGE 78 E1556   CRIME
                                                     JURID

B62
PERKINS D.,AMERICA'S QUEST FOR PEACE. USA+45 WOR+45 INT/LAW
DIPLOM CONFER NAT/LISM ATTIT 20 UN TREATY. PAGE 80   INT/ORG
E1610   ARMS/CONT
                                                     PEACE

B62
ROSENNE S.,THE WORLD COURT: WHAT IT IS AND HOW IT   INT/ORG
WORKS. WOR-45 LAW CONSTN JUDGE EDU/PROP   ADJUD
LEGIT ROUTINE CHOOSE PEACE ORD/FREE...JURID OBS   INT/LAW
TIME/SEQ CHARTS UN TOT/POP VAL/FREE 20. PAGE 86
E1717

B62
SCHWARTZ L.E.,INTERNATIONAL ORGANIZATIONS AND SPACE INT/ORG
COOPERATION. VOL/ASSN CONSULT CREATE TEC/DEV   DIPLOM
SANCTION...POLICY INT/LAW PHIL/SCI 20 UN. PAGE 89   R+D
E1787   SPACE

B62
SHAW C.,LEGAL PROBLEMS IN INTERNATIONAL TRADE AND   INT/LAW
INVESTMENT. WOR+45 ECO/DEV ECO/UNDEV MARKET DIPLOM   INT/TRADE
TAX INCOME ROLE...ANTHOL BIBLIOG 20 TREATY UN IMF   FINAN
GATT. PAGE 91 E1816   ECO/TAC

B62
UNECA LIBRARY,NEW ACQUISITIONS IN THE UNECA   BIBLIOG
LIBRARY. LAW NAT/G PLAN PROB/SOLV TEC/DEV ADMIN   AFR
REGION...GEOG SOC 20 UN. PAGE 98 E1956   ECO/UNDEV
                                                     INT/ORG

L62
"AMERICAN BEHAVIORAL SCIENTIST." USSR LAW NAT/G   BIBLIOG
...SOC 20 UN. PAGE 2 E0034   AFR
                                                     R+D

L62
CORET A.,"L'INDEPENDANCE DU SAMOA OCCIDENTAL."   NAT/G
S/ASIA LAW INT/ORG EXEC ALL/VALS SAMOA UN 20.   STRUCT
PAGE 26 E0508   SOVEREIGN

L62
GROSS L.,"IMMUNITIES AND PRIVILEGES OF DELIGATIONS   INT/ORG
TO THE UNITED NATIONS." USA+45 WOR+45 STRATA NAT/G   LAW
VOL/ASSN CONSULT DIPLOM EDU/PROP ROUTINE RESPECT   ELITES
...POLICY INT/LAW CONCPT UN 20. PAGE 48 E0950

L62
NIZARD L.,"CUBAN QUESTION AND SECURITY COUNCIL."   INT/ORG
L/A+17C USA+45 ECO/UNDEV NAT/G POL/PAR DELIB/GP   JURID
ECO/TAC PWR...RELATIV OBS TIME/SEQ TREND GEN/LAWS   DIPLOM
UN 20 UN. PAGE 77 E1551   CUBA

L62
NIZARD L.,"CUBAN QUESTION AND SECURITY COUNCIL."   INT/ORG
L/A+17C USA+45 ECO/UNDEV NAT/G POL/PAR DELIB/GP   JURID
ECO/TAC PWR...RELATIV OBS TIME/SEQ TREND GEN/LAWS   DIPLOM
UN 20 UN. PAGE 77 E1551   CUBA

L62
STEIN E.,"MR HAMMARSKJOLD, THE CHARTER LAW AND THE   CONCPT
FUTURE ROLE OF THE UNITED NATIONS SECRETARY-   BIOG
GENERAL." WOR+45 CONSTN INT/ORG DELIB/GP FORCES
TOP/EX BAL/PWR LEGIT ROUTINE RIGID/FLEX PWR
...POLICY JURID OBS STERTYP UN COLD/WAR 20
HAMMARSK/D. PAGE 93 E1869

B63
ATTIA G.E.D.,LES FORCES ARMEES DES NATIONS UNIES EN FORCES
COREE ET AU MOYENORIENT. KOREA CONSTN NAT/G   INT/LAW
DELIB/GP LEGIS PWR...IDEA/COMP NAT/COMP BIBLIOG UN
SUEZ. PAGE 6 E0114

B63
BOWETT D.W.,THE LAW OF INTERNATIONAL INSTITUTIONS.   INT/ORG
WOR+45 WOR-45 CONSTN DELIB/GP EX/STRUC JUDGE   ADJUD
EDU/PROP LEGIT CT/SYS EXEC ROUTINE RIGID/FLEX   DIPLOM
ORD/FREE PWR...JURID CONCPT ORG/CHARTS GEN/METH
LEAGUE/NAT OAS OEEC 20 UN. PAGE 14 E0277

B63
HIGGINS R.,THE DEVELOPMENT OF INTERNATIONAL LAW   INT/ORG
THROUGH THE POLITICAL ORGANS OF THE UNITED NATIONS. INT/LAW
WOR+45 FORCES DIPLOM AGREE COERCE ATTIT SOVEREIGN   TEC/DEV
...BIBLIOG 20 UN TREATY. PAGE 52 E1041   JURID

B63
ROBERTSON A.H.,HUMAN RIGHTS IN EUROPE. CONSTN   EUR+WWI
SOCIETY INT/ORG NAT/G VOL/ASSN DELIB/GP ACT/RES   PERSON
PLAN ADJUD REGION ROUTINE ATTIT LOVE ORD/FREE
RESPECT...JURID SOC CONCPT SOC/EXP UN 20. PAGE 85
E1705

B63
ROSNER G.,THE UNITED NATIONS EMERGENCY FORCE.   INT/ORG
FRANCE ISRAEL UAR UK WOR+45 CREATE WAR PEACE   FORCES
ORD/FREE PWR...INT/LAW JURID HIST/WRIT TIME/SEQ UN.
PAGE 86 E1719

B63
VAN SLYCK P.,PEACE: THE CONTROL OF NATIONAL POWER.   ARMS/CONT
CUBA WOR+45 FINAN NAT/G FORCES PROB/SOLV TEC/DEV   PEACE
BAL/PWR ADMIN CONTROL ORD/FREE...POLICY INT/LAW UN   INT/ORG
COLD/WAR TREATY. PAGE 103 E2069   DIPLOM

S63
BECHHOEFER B.G.,"UNITED NATIONS PROCEDURES IN CASE   INT/ORG
OF VIOLATIONS OF DISARMAMENT AGREEMENTS." COM   DELIB/GP
USA+45 USSR LAW CONSTN NAT/G EX/STRUC FORCES LEGIS
BAL/PWR EDU/PROP CT/SYS ARMS/CONT ORD/FREE PWR
...POLICY STERTYP UN VAL/FREE 20. PAGE 9 E0169

S63
GIRAUD E.,"L'INTERDICTION DU RECOURS A LA FORCE, LA INT/ORG
THEORIE ET LA PRATIQUE DES NATIONS UNIES." ALGERIA   FORCES
COM CUBA HUNGARY WOR+45 ADJUD TOTALISM ATTIT   DIPLOM
RIGID/FLEX PWR...POLICY JURID CONCPT UN 20 CONGO.
PAGE 44 E0872

C63
ATTIA G.E.O.,"LES FORCES ARMEES DES NATIONS UNIES   FORCES

EN COREE ET AU MOYENORIENT." KOREA CONSTN DELIB/GP   NAT/G
LEGIS PWR...IDEA/COMP NAT/COMP BIBLIOG UN SUEZ.   INT/LAW
PAGE 6 E0115

              B64
BOWETT D.W.,UNITED NATIONS FORCES* A LEGAL STUDY.   OP/RES
CYPRUS ISRAEL KOREA LAW CONSTN ACT/RES CREATE   FORCES
BUDGET CONTROL TASK PWR...INT/LAW IDEA/COMP UN   ARMS/CONT
CONGO/LEOP SUEZ. PAGE 14 E0278

              B64
DUBISSON M.,LA COUR INTERNATIONALE DE JUSTICE.   CT/SYS
FRANCE LAW CONSTN JUDGE DOMIN ADJUD...INT/LAW   INT/ORG
CLASSIF RECORD ORG/CHARTS UN. PAGE 33 E0651

              B64
FRIEDMANN W.G.,THE CHANGING STRUCTURE OF   ADJUD
INTERNATIONAL LAW. WOR+45 INT/ORG NAT/G PROVS LEGIT   TREND
ORD/FREE PWR...JURID CONCPT GEN/LAWS TOT/POP UN 20.   INT/LAW
PAGE 41 E0805

              B64
FRYDENSBERG P.,PEACE-KEEPING: EXPERIENCE AND   INT/ORG
EVALUATION: THE OSLO PAPERS. NORWAY FORCES PLAN   DIPLOM
CONTROL...INT/LAW 20 UN. PAGE 41 E0814   PEACE
                                  COERCE

              B64
GARDNER R.N.,IN PURSUIT OF WORLD ORDER* US FOREIGN   OBS
POLICY AND INTERNATIONAL ORGANIZATIONS. USA+45 USSR   INT/ORG
ECO/UNDEV FORCES LEGIS DIPLOM FOR/AID INT/TRADE   ALL/VALS
PEACE...INT/LAW PREDICT UN. PAGE 42 E0839

              B64
HEKHUIS D.J.,INTERNATIONAL STABILITY: MILITARY,   TEC/DEV
ECONOMIC AND POLITICAL DIMENSIONS. FUT WOR+45 LAW   DETER
ECO/UNDEV INT/ORG NAT/G VOL/ASSN FORCES ACT/RES   REGION
BAL/PWR PWR WEALTH...STAT UN 20. PAGE 51 E1024

              B64
JENKS C.W.,THE PROSPECTS OF INTERNATIONAL   INT/LAW
ADJUDICATION. WOR+45 WOR-45 NAT/G DIPLOM CONTROL   ADJUD
PWR...POLICY JURID CONCPT METH/COMP 19/20 ICJ   CT/SYS
LEAGUE/NAT UN TREATY. PAGE 58 E1160   INT/ORG

              B64
KAHNG T.J.,LAW, POLITICS, AND THE SECURITY COUNCIL*   DELIB/GP
AN INQUIRY INTO THE HANDLING OF LEGAL QUESTIONS.   ADJUD
LAW CONSTN NAT/G ACT/RES OP/RES CT/SYS TASK PWR   ROUTINE
...INT/LAW BIBLIOG UN. PAGE 59 E1180

              B64
MCDOUGAL M.S.,STUDIES IN WORLD PUBLIC ORDER. SPACE   INT/LAW
SEA INT/ORG CREATE AGREE NUC/PWR...POLICY PHIL/SCI   SOC
IDEA/COMP ANTHOL METH 20 UN. PAGE 71 E1411   DIPLOM

              B64
RUSSELL R.B.,UNITED NATIONS EXPERIENCE WITH   FORCES
MILITARY FORCES: POLITICAL AND LEGAL ASPECTS. AFR   DIPLOM
KOREA WOR+45 LEGIS PROB/SOLV ADMIN CONTROL   SANCTION
EFFICIENCY PEACE...POLICY INT/LAW BIBLIOG UN.   ORD/FREE
PAGE 87 E1738

              B64
SCHECHTER A.H.,INTERPRETATION OF AMBIGUOUS   INT/LAW
DOCUMENTS BY INTERNATIONAL ADMINISTRATIVE   DIPLOM
TRIBUNALS. WOR+45 EX/STRUC INT/TRADE CT/SYS   INT/ORG
SOVEREIGN 20 UN ILO EURCT/JUST. PAGE 87 E1752   ADJUD

              B64
SCHWELB E.,HUMAN RIGHTS AND THE INTERNATIONAL   INT/ORG
COMMUNITY. WOR+45 WOR-45 NAT/G SECT DELIB/GP DIPLOM   ORD/FREE
PEACE RESPECT TREATY 20 UN. PAGE 89 E1792   INT/LAW

              B64
SEGAL R.,SANCTIONS AGAINST SOUTH AFRICA. AFR   SANCTION
SOUTH/AFR NAT/G INT/TRADE RACE/REL PEACE PWR   DISCRIM
...INT/LAW ANTHOL 20 UN. PAGE 90 E1801   ECO/TAC
                                  POLICY

              B64
STANGER R.J.,ESSAYS ON INTERVENTION. PLAN PROB/SOLV   SOVEREIGN
BAL/PWR ADJUD COERCE WAR ROLE PWR...INT/LAW CONCPT   DIPLOM
20 UN INTERVENT. PAGE 93 E1865   POLICY
                                  LEGIT

              B64
STRONG C.F.,HISTORY OF MODERN POLITICAL   CONSTN
CONSTITUTIONS. STRUCT INT/ORG NAT/G LEGIS TEC/DEV   CONCPT
DIPLOM INT/TRADE CT/SYS EXEC...METH/COMP T 12/20
UN. PAGE 94 E1888

              B64
THANT U.,TOWARD WORLD PEACE. DELIB/GP TEC/DEV   DIPLOM
EDU/PROP WAR SOVEREIGN...INT/LAW 20 UN MID/EAST.   BIOG
PAGE 96 E1915   PEACE

              COERCE

              B64
UN PUB. INFORM. ORGAN.,EVERY MAN'S UNITED NATIONS.   INT/ORG
UNIV WOR+45 CONSTN CULTURE SOCIETY ECO/DEV   ROUTINE
ECO/UNDEV NAT/G ACT/RES PLAN ECO/TAC INT/TRADE
EDU/PROP LEGIT PEACE ATTIT ALL/VALS...POLICY HUM
INT/LAW CONCPT CHARTS UN TOT/POP 20. PAGE 97 E1954

              B64
WILLIAMS S.P.,TOWARD A GENUINE WORLD SECURITY   BIBLIOG/A
SYSTEM (PAMPHLET). WOR+45 INT/ORG FORCES PLAN   ARMS/CONT
NUC/PWR ORD/FREE...INT/LAW CONCPT UN PRESIDENT.   DIPLOM
PAGE 106 E2123   PEACE

              L64
WORLD PEACE FOUNDATION,"INTERNATIONAL   INT/ORG
ORGANIZATIONS: SUMMARY OF ACTIVITIES." INDIA   ROUTINE
PAKISTAN TURKEY WOR+45 CONSTN CONSULT EX/STRUC
ECO/TAC EDU/PROP LEGIT ORD/FREE...JURID SOC UN 20
CYPRESS. PAGE 107 E2145

              S64
CARNEGIE ENDOWMENT INT. PEACE,"HUMAN RIGHTS (ISSUES   INT/ORG
BEFORE THE NINETEENTH GENERAL ASSEMBLY)." AFR   PERSON
WOR+45 LAW CONSTN NAT/G EDU/PROP GP/REL DISCRIM   RACE/REL
PEACE ATTIT MORAL ORD/FREE...INT/LAW PSY CONCPT
RECORD UN 20. PAGE 20 E0385

              S64
CARNEGIE ENDOWMENT INT. PEACE,"LEGAL QUESTIONS   INT/ORG
(ISSUES BEFORE THE NINETEENTH GENERAL ASSEMBLY)."   LAW
WOR+45 CONSTN NAT/G DELIB/GP ADJUD PEACE MORAL   INT/LAW
ORD/FREE...RECORD UN 20 TREATY. PAGE 20 E0386

              S64
GARDNER R.N.,"THE SOVIET UNION AND THE UNITED   COM
NATIONS." WOR+45 FINAN POL/PAR VOL/ASSN FORCES   INT/ORG
ECO/TAC DOMIN EDU/PROP LEGIT ADJUD ADMIN ARMS/CONT   USSR
COERCE ATTIT ALL/VALS...POLICY MAJORIT CONCPT OBS
TIME/SEQ TREND STERTYP UN. PAGE 42 E0838

              S64
SCHWELB E.,"OPERATION OF THE EUROPEAN CONVENTION ON   INT/ORG
HUMAN RIGHTS." EUR+WWI LAW SOCIETY CREATE EDU/PROP   MORAL
ADJUD ADMIN PEACE ATTIT ORD/FREE PWR...POLICY
INT/LAW CONCPT OBS GEN/LAWS UN VAL/FREE ILO 20
ECHR. PAGE 89 E1791

              B65
BERKOWITZ M.,AMERICAN NATIONAL SECURITY: A READER   ORD/FREE
IN THEORY AND POLICY. USA+45 INT/ORG FORCES BAL/PWR   WAR
DIPLOM ECO/TAC DETER PWR...INT/LAW ANTHOL BIBLIOG   ARMS/CONT
20 UN. PAGE 11 E0203   POLICY

              B65
BRIGGS H.W.,THE INTERNATIONAL LAW COMMISSION. LAW   INT/LAW
CONSTN LEGIS CREATE ADJUD CT/SYS ROUTINE TASK   DELIB/GP
EFFICIENCY...CLASSIF OBS UN. PAGE 15 E0302

              B65
FORGAC A.A.,NEW DIPLOMACY AND THE UNITED NATIONS.   DIPLOM
FRANCE GERMANY UK USSR INT/ORG DELIB/GP EX/STRUC   ETIQUET
PEACE...INT/LAW CONCPT UN. PAGE 39 E0770   NAT/G

              B65
GOTLIEB A.,DISARMAMENT AND INTERNATIONAL LAW* A   INT/LAW
STUDY OF THE ROLE OF LAW IN THE DISARMAMENT   INT/ORG
PROCESS. USA+45 USSR PROB/SOLV CONFER ADMIN ROUTINE   ARMS/CONT
NUC/PWR ORD/FREE SOVEREIGN UN TREATY. PAGE 45 E0893   IDEA/COMP

              B65
JENKS C.W.,SPACE LAW. DIPLOM DEBATE CONTROL   SPACE
ORD/FREE TREATY 20 UN. PAGE 58 E1161   INT/LAW
                                JURID
                                INT/ORG

              B65
LASLEY J.,THE WAR SYSTEM AND YOU. LAW FORCES   MORAL
ARMS/CONT NUC/PWR NAT/LISM ATTIT...MAJORIT   PERSON
IDEA/COMP UN WORSHIP. PAGE 63 E1261   DIPLOM
                                WAR

              B65
PADELFORD N.,THE UNITED NATIONS IN THE BALANCE*   INT/ORG
ACCOMPLISHMENTS AND PROSPECTS. NAT/G VOL/ASSN   CONTROL
DIPLOM ADMIN COLONIAL CT/SYS REGION WAR ORD/FREE
...ANTHOL UN. PAGE 79 E1588

              B65
PARRY C.,THE SOURCES AND EVIDENCES OF INTERNATIONAL   INT/LAW
LAW. WOR+45 WOR-45 DIPLOM AGREE SOVEREIGN...METH 20   ADJUD
TREATY UN LEAGUE/NAT. PAGE 80 E1599   INT/ORG
                                CT/SYS

THOMAS A.V.,NONINTERVENTION: THE LAW AND ITS IMPORT   INT/LAW
IN THE AMERICAS. L/A+17C USA+45 USA-45 WOR+45   PWR
DIPLOM ADJUD...JURID IDEA/COMP 20 UN INTERVENT.   COERCE
PAGE 96 E1917
                                                     B65

VONGLAHN G.,LAW AMONG NATIONS: AN INTRODUCTION TO   CONSTN
PUBLIC INTERNATIONAL LAW. UNIV WOR+45 LAW INT/ORG   JURID
NAT/G LEGIT EXEC RIGID/FLEX...CONCPT TIME/SEQ   INT/LAW
GEN/LAWS UN TOT/POP 20. PAGE 104 E2084
                                                     S65

BROWNLIE I.,"SOME LEGAL ASPECTS OF THE USE OF   LAW
NUCLEAR WEAPONS." UK NEUTRAL DETER UN TREATY.   NUC/PWR
PAGE 16 E0317   WAR
                                                     INT/LAW
                                                     S65

FRIEDHEIM R.,"THE 'SATISFIED' AND 'DISSATISFIED'   INT/LAW
STATES NEGOTIATE INTERNATIONAL LAW* A CASE STUDY."   RECORD
DIPLOM CONFER ADJUD CONSEN PEACE ATTIT UN. PAGE 40
E0799
                                                     S65

HIBBS A.R.,"SPACE TECHNOLOGY* THE THREAT AND THE   SPACE
PROMISE." FUT VOL/ASSN TEC/DEV NUC/PWR COST   ARMS/CONT
EFFICIENCY UTIL UN TREATY. PAGE 52 E1038   PREDICT
                                                     S65

MARTIN A.,"PROLIFERATION." FUT WOR+45 PROB/SOLV   RECORD
REGION ADJUST...PREDICT NAT/COMP UN TREATY. PAGE 69 NUC/PWR
E1372   ARMS/CONT
                                                     VOL/ASSN
                                                     C65

SEARA M.V.,"COSMIC INTERNATIONAL LAW." LAW ACADEM   SPACE
ACT/RES DIPLOM COLONIAL CONTROL NUC/PWR SOVEREIGN   INT/LAW
...GEN/LAWS BIBLIOG UN. PAGE 90 E1799   IDEA/COMP
                                                     INT/ORG
                                                     B66

ASAMOAH O.Y.,THE LEGAL SIGNIFICANCE OF THE   INT/LAW
DECLARATIONS OF THE GENERAL ASSEMBLY OF THE UNITED   INT/ORG
NATIONS. WOR+45 CREATE CONTROL...BIBLIOG 20 UN.   DIPLOM
PAGE 5 E0105
                                                     B66

CLARK G.,WORLD PEACE THROUGH WORLD LAW: TWO   INT/LAW
ALTERNATIVE PLANS. WOR+45 DELIB/GP FORCES TAX   PEACE
CONFER ADJUD SANCTION ARMS/CONT WAR CHOOSE PRIVIL   PLAN
20 UN COLD/WAR. PAGE 23 E0450   INT/ORG
                                                     B66

DOUMA J.,BIBLIOGRAPHY ON THE INTERNATIONAL COURT   BIBLIOG/A
INCLUDING THE PERMANENT COURT, 1918-1964. WOR+45   INT/ORG
WOR-45 DELIB/GP WAR PRIVIL...JURID NAT/COMP 20 UN   CT/SYS
LEAGUE/NAT. PAGE 33 E0645   DIPLOM
                                                     B66

EPSTEIN F.T.,THE AMERICAN BIBLIOGRAPHY OF RUSSIAN   BIBLIOG
AND EAST EUROPEAN STUDIES FOR 1964. USSR LOC/G   COM
NAT/G POL/PAR FORCES ADMIN ARMS/CONT...JURID CONCPT MARXISM
20 UN. PAGE 35 E0694   DIPLOM
                                                     B66

FALK R.A.,THE STRATEGY OF WORLD ORDER* 4 VOLUMES.   ORD/FREE
WOR+45 ECO/UNDEV ACADEM INT/ORG ACT/RES DIPLOM   GEN/LAWS
ARMS/CONT WAR...NET/THEORY SIMUL BIBLIOG UN.   ANTHOL
PAGE 36 E0719   INT/LAW
                                                     B66

FRIEDMANN W.G.,INTERNATIONAL FINANCIAL AID. USA+45   INT/ORG
ECO/DEV ECO/UNDEV NAT/G VOL/ASSN EX/STRUC PLAN RENT FOR/AID
GIVE BAL/PAY PWR...GEOG INT/LAW STAT TREND UN EEC   TEC/DEV
COMECON. PAGE 41 E0806   ECO/TAC
                                                     B66

OBERMANN E.,VERTEIDIGUNG PER FREIHEIT. GERMANY/W   FORCES
WOR+45 INT/ORG COERCE NUC/PWR WEAPON MARXISM 20 UN   ORD/FREE
NATO WARSAW/P TREATY. PAGE 78 E1571   WAR
                                                     PEACE
                                                     B66

POLLACK R.S.,THE INDIVIDUAL'S RIGHTS AND   INT/LAW
INTERNATIONAL ORGANIZATION. LAW INT/ORG DELIB/GP   ORD/FREE
SUPEGO...JURID SOC/INTEG 20 TREATY UN. PAGE 81   DIPLOM
E1623   PERSON
                                                     B66

UNITED NATIONS,INTERNATIONAL SPACE BIBLIOGRAPHY.   BIBLIOG
FUT INT/ORG TEC/DEV DIPLOM ARMS/CONT NUC/PWR   SPACE
...JURID SOC UN. PAGE 98 E1969   PEACE
                                                     R+D

WAINHOUSE D.W.,INTERNATIONAL PEACE OBSERVATION: A   PEACE
HISTORY AND FORECAST. INT/ORG PROB/SOLV BAL/PWR   DIPLOM
AGREE ARMS/CONT COERCE NUC/PWR...PREDICT METH/COMP
20 UN LEAGUE/NAT OAS TREATY. PAGE 104 E2092
                                                     L66

GREIG D.W.,"THE ADVISORY JURISDICTION OF THE   INT/LAW
INTERNATIONAL COURT AND THE SETTLEMENT OF DISPUTES   CT/SYS
BETWEEN STATES." ISRAEL KOREA FORCES BUDGET DOMIN
LEGIT ADJUD COST...RECORD UN CONGO/LEOP TREATY.
PAGE 46 E0915
                                                     L66

HIGGINS R.,"THE INTERNATIONAL COURT AND SOUTH WEST   SOUTH/AFR
AFRICA* SOME IMPLICATIONS OF THE JUDGMENT." AFR LAW COLONIAL
ECO/UNDEV JUDGE RACE/REL COST PWR...INT/LAW TREND   CT/SYS
UN TREATY. PAGE 52 E1043   ADJUD
                                                     L66

KRENZ F.E.,"THE REFUGEE AS A SUBJECT OF   INT/LAWO
INTERNATIONAL LAW." FUT LAW NAT/G CREATE ADJUD   DISCRIM
ISOLAT STRANGE...RECORD UN. PAGE 62 E1230   NEW/IDEA
                                                     L66

YALEM R.J.,"THE STUDY OF INTERNATIONAL   VOL/ASSN
ORGANIZATION, 1920-1965* A SURVEY OF THE   INT/ORG
LITERATURE." WOR+45 WOR-45 REGION...INT/LAW CLASSIF BIBLIOG/A
RECORD HIST/WRIT CON/ANAL IDEA/COMP UN. PAGE 108
E2163
                                                     S66

ANAND R.P.,"ATTITUDE OF THE ASIAN-AFRICAN STATES   INT/LAW
TOWARD CERTAIN PROBLEMS OF INTERNATIONAL LAW."   ATTIT
L/A+17C S/ASIA ECO/UNDEV CREATE CONFER ADJUD   ASIA
COLONIAL...RECORD GP/COMP UN. PAGE 5 E0087   AFR
                                                     S66

DETTER I.,"THE PROBLEM OF UNEQUAL TREATIES." CONSTN SOVEREIGN
NAT/G LEGIS COLONIAL COERCE PWR...GEOG UN TIME   DOMIN
TREATY. PAGE 31 E0610   INT/LAW
                                                     ECO/UNDEV
                                                     S66

FINE R.I.,"PEACE-KEEPING COSTS AND ARTICLE 19 OF   FORCES
THE UN CHARTER* AN INVITATION TO RESPONSIBILITY."   COST
INT/ORG NAT/G ADJUD CT/SYS CHOOSE CONSEN...RECORD   CONSTN
IDEA/COMP UN. PAGE 38 E0750
                                                     S66

GREEN L.C.,"RHODESIAN OIL: BOOTLEGGERS OR PIRATES?" INT/TRADE
AFR RHODESIA UK WOR+45 INT/ORG NAT/G DIPLOM LEGIT   SANCTION
COLONIAL SOVEREIGN 20 UN OAU. PAGE 46 E0907   INT/LAW
                                                     POLICY
                                                     S66

LANDE G.R.,"THE EFFECT OF THE RESOLUTIONS OF THE   LEGIS
UNITED NATIONS GENERAL ASSEMBLY." WOR+45 LAW   EFFICIENCY
INT/ORG NAT/G CHOOSE ISOLAT ATTIT...CLASSIF   RESPECT
GEN/METH UN. PAGE 62 E1249
                                                     C66

BLAISDELL D.C.,"INTERNATIONAL ORGANIZATION." FUT   BIBLIOG
WOR+45 ECO/DEV DELIB/GP FORCES EFFICIENCY PEACE   INT/ORG
ORD/FREE...INT/LAW 20 UN LEAGUE/NAT NATO. PAGE 12   DIPLOM
E0239   ARMS/CONT
                                                     B67

GARCIA ROBLES A.,THE DENUCLEARIZATION OF LATIN   NUC/PWR
AMERICA (TRANS. BY MARJORIE URQUIDI). LAW PLAN   ARMS/CONT
DIPLOM...ANTHOL 20 TREATY UN. PAGE 42 E0833   L/A+17C
                                                     INT/ORG
                                                     B67

HOLCOMBE A.N.,A STRATEGY OF PEACE IN A CHANGING   PEACE
WORLD. USA+45 WOR+45 LAW NAT/G CREATE DIPLOM   PLAN
ARMS/CONT WAR...CHARTS 20 UN COLD/WAR. PAGE 54   INT/ORG
E1072   INT/LAW
                                                     B67

INTERNATIONAL CONCILIATION,ISSUES BEFORE THE 22ND   PROB/SOLV
GENERAL ASSEMBLY. WOR+45 ECO/UNDEV FINAN BAL/PWR   INT/ORG
BUDGET INT/TRADE STRANGE ORD/FREE...INT/LAW 20 UN   DIPLOM
COLD/WAR. PAGE 57 E1132   PEACE
                                                     B67

LAWYERS COMM AMER POLICY VIET,VIETNAM AND   INT/LAW
INTERNATIONAL LAW: AN ANALYSIS OF THE LEGALITY OF   DIPLOM
THE US MILITARY INVOLVEMENT. VIETNAM LAW INT/ORG   ADJUD
COERCE WEAPON PEACE ORD/FREE 20 UN SEATO TREATY.   WAR
PAGE 64 E1271
                                                     B67

PADELFORD N.J.,THE DYNAMICS OF INTERNATIONAL   DIPLOM
POLITICS (2ND ED.). WOR+45 LAW INT/ORG FORCES   NAT/G
TEC/DEV REGION NAT/LISM PEACE ATTIT PWR ALL/IDEOS   POLICY

UN COLD/WAR NATO TREATY. PAGE 79 E1589

DECISION

B67

PLANO J.C.,FORGING WORLD ORDER: THE POLITICS OF
INTERNATIONAL ORGANIZATION. PROB/SOLV DIPLOM
CONTROL CENTRAL RATIONAL ORD/FREE...INT/LAW CHARTS
BIBLIOG 20 UN LEAGUE/NAT. PAGE 81 E1618

INT/ORG
ADMIN
JURID

B67

UNITED NATIONS,UNITED NATIONS PUBLICATIONS:
1945-1966. WOR+45 COM/IND DIST/IND FINAN TEC/DEV
ADMIN...POLICY INT/LAW MGT CHARTS 20 UN UNESCO.
PAGE 98 E1970

BIBLIOG/A
INT/ORG
DIPLOM
WRITING

B67

US SENATE COMM ON FOREIGN REL,TREATY ON OUTER
SPACE. WOR+45 AIR FORCES PROB/SOLV NUC/PWR SENATE
TREATY UN. PAGE 101 E2032

SPACE
DIPLOM
ARMS/CONT
LAW

B67

US SENATE COMM ON FOREIGN REL,A SELECT CHRONOLOGY
AND BACKGROUND DOCUMENTS RELATING TO THE MIDDLE
EAST. ISRAEL UAR LAW INT/ORG FORCES PROB/SOLV
CONFER CONSEN PEACE ATTIT...POLICY 20 UN SENATE
TRUMAN/HS. PAGE 101 E2033

ISLAM
TIME/SEQ
DIPLOM

L67

"FOCUS ON WORLD LAW." WOR+45 NAT/G CT/SYS PEACE
...BIBLIOG 20 UN. PAGE 2 E0036

INT/LAW
INT/ORG
PROB/SOLV
CONCPT

L67

BAADE H.W.,"THE ACQUIRED RIGHTS OF INTERNATIONAL
PUBLIC SERVANTS; A CASE STUDY IN RECEPTION OF
PUBLIC LAW." WOR+45 DELIB/GP DIPLOM ORD/FREE
...INT/LAW JURID UN. PAGE 7 E0125

INT/ORG
WORKER
ADJUD
LAW

L67

LEGAULT A.,"ORGANISATION ET CONDUITE DES OPERATIONS
DE MAINTIEN DE LA PAIX." FORCES ACT/RES ADJUD AGREE
CONTROL NEUTRAL TASK PRIVIL ORD/FREE 20 UN. PAGE 64
E1279

INT/ORG
PEACE
WAR
INT/LAW

S67

COHN K.,"CRIMES AGAINST HUMANITY." GERMANY INT/ORG
SANCTION ATTIT ORD/FREE...MARXIST CRIMLGY 20 UN.
PAGE 24 E0469

WAR
INT/LAW
CRIME
ADJUD

S67

DALFEN C.M.,"THE WORLD COURT IN IDLE SPLENDOUR: THE
BASIS OF STATES' ATTITUDES." WOR+45 LAW ADJUD
COERCE...JURID 20 UN WORLD/CT. PAGE 28 E0562

CT/SYS
INT/ORG
INT/LAW
DIPLOM

S67

DOYLE S.E.,"COMMUNICATION SATELLITES* INTERNAL
ORGANIZATION FOR DEVELOPMENT AND CONTROL." USA+45
R+D ACT/RES DIPLOM NAT/LISM...POLICY INT/LAW
PREDICT UN. PAGE 33 E0647

TEC/DEV
SPACE
COM/IND
INT/ORG

S67

MATTHEWS R.O.,"THE SUEZ CANAL DISPUTE* A CASE STUDY
IN PEACEFUL SETTLEMENT." FRANCE ISRAEL UAR UK NAT/G
CONTROL LEAD COERCE WAR NAT/LISM ROLE ORD/FREE PWR
...INT/LAW UN 20. PAGE 69 E1389

PEACE
DIPLOM
ADJUD

S67

STEEL R.,"WHAT CAN THE UN DO?" RHODESIA ECO/UNDEV
DIPLOM ECO/TAC SANCTION...INT/LAW UN. PAGE 93 E1866

INT/ORG
BAL/PWR
PEACE
FOR/AID

N67

US SENATE COMM ON FOREIGN REL,SURVEY OF THE
ALLIANCE FOR PROGRESS: FOREIGN TRADE POLICIES
(PAMPHLET). L/A+17C LAW ECO/UNDEV ECO/TAC TARIFFS
20 GATT LAFTA UN. PAGE 102 E2037

INT/TRADE
REGION
AGREE
INT/ORG

B68

HULL R.H.,LAW AND VIETNAM. COM VIETNAM CONSTN
INT/ORG FORCES DIPLOM AGREE COERCE DETER WEAPON
PEACE ATTIT 20 UN TREATY. PAGE 56 E1113

POLICY
LAW
WAR
INT/LAW

L68

CHIU H.,"COMMUNIST CHINA'S ATTITUDE TOWARD THE
UNITED NATIONS: A LEGAL ANALYSIS." CHINA/COM WOR+45
LAW NAT/G DIPLOM CONFER ADJUD PARTIC ATTIT...POLICY
TREND 20 UN. PAGE 22 E0432

INT/LAW
SOVEREIGN
INT/ORG
REPRESENT

S68

DUGARD J.,"THE REVOCATION OF THE MANDATE FOR SOUTH
WEST AFRICA." SOUTH/AFR WOR+45 STRATA NAT/G

AFR
INT/ORG

DELIB/GP DIPLOM ADJUD SANCTION CHOOSE RACE/REL
...POLICY NAT/COMP 20 AFRICA/SW UN TRUST/TERR
LEAGUE/NAT. PAGE 33 E0654

DISCRIM
COLONIAL

UN HEADQUARTERS LIBRARY E1953

UN PUB. INFORM. ORGAN. E1954

UN/ILC....UNITED NATIONS INTERNATIONAL LAW COMMISSION

UN/SEC/GEN....UNITED NATIONS SECRETARY GENERAL

UNCIO CONFERENCE LIBRARY E1955

UNCSAT....UNITED NATIONS CONFERENCE ON THE APPLICATION OF
SCIENCE AND TECHNOLOGY FOR THE BENEFIT OF THE LESS
DEVELOPED AREAS

UNCTAD....UNITED NATIONS COMMISSION ON TRADE, AID, AND
DEVELOPMENT

UNDERDEVELOPED COUNTRIES....SEE ECO/UNDEV

UNDP....UNITED NATIONS DEVELOPMENT PROGRAM

UNECA LIBRARY E1956

UNEF....UNITED NATIONS EMERGENCY FORCE

UNESCO E1957,E1958,E1959,E1960,E1961,E1962,E1963

UNESCO....UNITED NATIONS EDUCATIONAL, SCIENTIFIC, AND
CULTURAL ORGANIZATION; SEE ALSO UN, INT/ORG

N

UNESCO,INTERNATIONAL BIBLIOGRAPHY OF POLITICAL
SCIENCE (VOLUMES 1-8). WOR+45 LAW NAT/G EX/STRUC
LEGIS PROB/SOLV DIPLOM ADMIN GOV/REL 20 UNESCO.
PAGE 98 E1957

BIBLIOG
CONCPT
IDEA/COMP

B49

MARITAIN J.,HUMAN RIGHTS: COMMENTS AND
INTERPRETATIONS. COM UNIV WOR+45 LAW CONSTN CULTURE
SOCIETY ECO/DEV ECO/UNDEV SCHOOL DELIB/GP EDU/PROP
ATTIT PERCEPT ALL/VALS...HUM SOC TREND UNESCO 20.
PAGE 68 E1365

INT/ORG
CONCPT

B49

US LIBRARY OF CONGRESS,FREEDOM OF INFORMATION:
SELECTIVE REPORT ON RECENT WRITINGS. USA+45 LAW
CONSTN ELITES EDU/PROP PRESS LOBBY WAR TOTALISM
ATTIT 20 UN UNESCO COLD/WAR. PAGE 101 E2018

BIBLIOG/A
ORD/FREE
LICENSE
COM/IND

B55

UN HEADQUARTERS LIBRARY,BIBLIOQRAPHIE DE LA CHARTE
DES NATIONS UNIES. CHINA/COM KOREA WOR+45 VOL/ASSN
CONFER ADMIN COERCE PEACE ATTIT ORD/FREE SOVEREIGN
...INT/LAW 20 UNESCO UN. PAGE 97 E1953

BIBLIOG/A
INT/ORG
DIPLOM

B59

SCHNEIDER J.,TREATY-MAKING POWER OF INTERNATIONAL
ORGANIZATIONS. FUT WOR+45 WOR-45 LAW NAT/G JUDGE
DIPLOM LEGIT CT/SYS ORD/FREE PWR...INT/LAW JURID
GEN/LAWS TOT/POP UNESCO 20 TREATY. PAGE 88 E1762

INT/ORG
ROUTINE

B60

CLARK G.,WORLD PEACE THROUGH WORLD LAW. FUT WOR+45
CONSULT FORCES ACT/RES CREATE PLAN ADMIN ROUTINE
ARMS/CONT DETER PWR...JURID VAL/FREE UNESCO
20 UN. PAGE 23 E0449

INT/ORG
LAW
PEACE
INT/LAW

B62

JENKS C.W.,THE PROPER LAW OF INTERNATIONAL
ORGANISATIONS. DIPLOM LEGIT AGREE CT/SYS SANCTION
REPRESENT SOVEREIGN...GEN/LAWS 20 UN UNESCO ILO
NATO OAS. PAGE 58 E1158

LAW
INT/ORG
ADJUD
INT/LAW

B65

UNESCO,INTERNATIONAL ORGANIZATIONS IN THE SOCIAL
SCIENCES(REV. ED.). LAW ADMIN ATTIT...CRIMLGY GEOG
INT/LAW PSY SOC STAT 20 UNESCO. PAGE 98 E1962

INT/ORG
R+D
PROF/ORG
ACT/RES

B67

UNITED NATIONS,UNITED NATIONS PUBLICATIONS:
1945-1966. WOR+45 COM/IND DIST/IND FINAN TEC/DEV
ADMIN...POLICY INT/LAW MGT CHARTS 20 UN UNESCO.
PAGE 98 E1970

BIBLIOG/A
INT/ORG
DIPLOM
WRITING

UNIDO....UNITED NATIONS INDUSTRIAL DEVELOPMENT ORGANIZATION

UNIFICA....UNIFICATION AND REUNIFICATION OF GEOGRAPHIC-
POLITICAL ENTITIES

UNIFORM NARCOTIC DRUG ACT....SEE NARCO/ACT

UNION AFRICAINE ET MALGACHE, ALSO OCAM....SEE UAM

UNION FOR THE NEW REPUBLIC....SEE UNR

UNION OF SOUTH AFRICA....SEE SOUTH/AFR

UNION OF SOVIET SOCIALIST REPUBLICS....SEE USSR

UNION POUR LA DEFENSE DE LA REPUBLIQUE (FRANCE)....SEE UDR

UNIONS....SEE LABOR

UNITED ARAB REPUBLIC....SEE UAR

UNITED AUTO WORKERS....SEE UAW

UNITED KINGDOM....SEE UK, COMMONWLTH

UNITED NATIONS....SEE UN

UNITED NATIONS INTERNATIONAL LAW COMMISSION....SEE UN/ILC

UNITED NATIONS SECURITY COUNCIL....SEE SECUR/COUN

UNITED NATIONS SPECIAL FUND....SEE UNSF

UNITED STATES ARMS CONTROL AND DISARMAMENT AGENCY....SEE
    ACD

UNITED STATES FEDERAL POWER COMMISSION....SEE FPC

UNITED STATES HOUSING CORPORATION....SEE US/HOUSING

UNITED STATES MILITARY ACADEMY....SEE WEST/POINT

UNITED STATES SENATE COMMITTEE ON FOREIGN RELATIONS....SEE
    FOREIGNREL

UNITED NATIONS E1964,E1965,E1966,E1967,E1969,E1970

UNITED WORLD FEDERALISTS E1971

UNIV....UNIVERSAL TO MAN

UNIVERSAL REFERENCE SYSTEM E1972,E1973,E1974,E1975,E1976

UNIVERSES....SEE UNIVERSES AND SAMPLING INDEX, P. XIV

UNIVERSITIES....SEE ACADEM

UNIVERSITIES RESEARCH ASSOCIATION, INC.....SEE UNIVS/RES

UNIVS/RES....UNIVERSITIES RESEARCH ASSOCIATION, INC.

UNLABR/PAR....UNION LABOR PARTY

UNPLAN/INT....IMPROMPTU INTERVIEW

UNR....UNION FOR THE NEW REPUBLIC

UNRRA....UNITED NATIONS RELIEF AND REHABILITATION AGENCY

UNRWA....UNITED NATIONS RELIEF AND WORKS AGENCY

UNSF....UNITED NATIONS SPECIAL FUND

UPPER VOLTA....SEE UPPER/VOLT

UPPER/VOLT....UPPER VOLTA; SEE ALSO AFR

URBAN/LEAG....URBAN LEAGUE

URBAN/RNWL....URBAN RENEWAL

                                                        B61
NEW JERSEY LEGISLATURE-SENATE,PUBLIC HEARINGS   LEGIS
BEFORE COMMITTEE ON REVISION AND AMENDMENT OF LAWS MUNIC
ON SENATE BILL NO. 8. USA+45 FINAN PROVS WORKER   INDUS
ACT/RES PLAN BUDGET TAX CRIME...IDEA/COMP 20   PROB/SOLV
NEW/JERSEY URBAN/RNWL. PAGE 77 E1537

                                                        B65
FRYE R.J.,HOUSING AND URBAN RENEWAL IN ALABAMA.   MUNIC
USA+45 NEIGH LEGIS BUDGET ADJUD ADMIN PARTIC...MGT PROB/SOLV
20 ALABAMA URBAN/RNWL. PAGE 41 E0815   PLAN
                                                   GOV/REL

URUGUAY....URUGUAY

                                                        N19
OPERATIONS AND POLICY RESEARCH,URUGUAY: ELECTION   POL/PAR
FACTBOOK: NOVEMBER 27, 1966 (PAMPHLET). URUGUAY LAW CHOOSE
NAT/G LEAD REPRESENT...STAT BIOG CHARTS 20. PAGE 79 PLAN
E1576   ATTIT

                                                        B33
AMERICAN FOREIGN LAW ASSN,BIOGRAPHICAL NOTES ON THE BIBLIOG/A
LAWS AND LEGAL LITERATURE OF URUGUAY AND CURACAO.   LAW
URUGUAY CONSTN FINAN SECT FORCES JUDGE DIPLOM   JURID
INT/TRADE ADJUD CT/SYS CRIME 20. PAGE 4 E0078   ADMIN

                                                        B47
CLAGETT H.L.,A GUIDE TO THE LAW AND LEGAL   BIBLIOG
LITERATURE OF URUGUAY. URUGUAY CONSTN COM/IND FINAN LAW
LABOR MUNIC JUDGE PRESS ADMIN CT/SYS...INT/LAW   JURID
PHIL/SCI 20. PAGE 23 E0445   L/A+17C

                                                        S67
FABREGA J.,"ANTECEDENTES EXTRANJEROS EN LA   CONSTN
CONSTITUCION PANAMENA." CUBA L/A+17C PANAMA URUGUAY JURID
EX/STRUC LEGIS DIPLOM ORD/FREE 19/20 COLOMB   NAT/G
MEXIC/AMER. PAGE 36 E0709   PARL/PROC

US AGENCY FOR INTERNATIONAL DEVELOPMENT....SEE US/AID

US ATOMIC ENERGY COMMISSION....SEE AEC

US ATTORNEY GENERAL....SEE ATTRNY/GEN

US BUREAU OF STANDARDS....SEE BUR/STNDRD

US BUREAU OF THE BUDGET....SEE BUR/BUDGET

US CENTRAL INTELLIGENCE AGENCY....SEE CIA

US CIVIL AERONAUTICS BOARD....SEE CAB

US CONGRESS RULES COMMITTEES....SEE RULES/COMM

US DEPARTMENT OF AGRICULTURE....SEE DEPT/AGRI

US DEPARTMENT OF COMMERCE....SEE DEPT/COM

US DEPARTMENT OF DEFENSE....SEE DEPT/DEFEN

US DEPARTMENT OF HEALTH, EDUCATION, AND WELFARE....SEE
    DEPT/HEW

US DEPARTMENT OF HOUSING AND URBAN DEVELOPMENT....SEE
    DEPT/HUD

US DEPARTMENT OF JUSTICE....SEE DEPT/JUST

US DEPARTMENT OF LABOR AND INDUSTRY....SEE DEPT/LABOR

US DEPARTMENT OF STATE....SEE DEPT/STATE

US DEPARTMENT OF THE INTERIOR....SEE DEPT/INTER

US DEPARTMENT OF THE TREASURY....SEE DEPT/TREAS

US FEDERAL AVIATION AGENCY....SEE FAA

US FEDERAL BUREAU OF INVESTIGATION....SEE FBI

US FEDERAL COMMUNICATIONS COMMISSION....SEE FCC

US FEDERAL COUNCIL FOR SCIENCE AND TECHNOLOGY....SEE
    FEDSCI/TEC

US FEDERAL HOUSING ADMINISTRATION....SEE FHA

US FEDERAL OPEN MARKET COMMITTEE....SEE FED/OPNMKT

US FEDERAL RESERVE SYSTEM....SEE FED/RESERV

US FEDERAL TRADE COMMISSION....SEE FTC

US HOUSE COMMITTEE ON SCIENCE AND ASTRONAUTICS....SEE
    HS/SCIASTR

US HOUSE COMMITTEE ON UNAMERICAN ACTIVITIES....SEE HUAC

US HOUSE OF REPRESENTATIVES....SEE HOUSE/REP

US INFORMATION AGENCY....SEE USIA

US INTERNAL REVENUE SERVICE....SEE IRS

US INTERNATIONAL COOPERATION ADMINISTRATION....SEE ICA

US INTERSTATE COMMERCE COMMISSION....SEE ICC

US MILITARY ACADEMY....SEE WEST/POINT

US NATIONAL AERONAUTICS AND SPACE ADMINISTRATION....SEE NASA

US OFFICE OF ECONOMIC OPPORTUNITY....SEE OEO

US OFFICE OF NAVAL RESEARCH....SEE NAVAL/RES

US OFFICE OF PRICE ADMINISTRATION....SEE OPA

US OFFICE OF WAR INFORMATION....SEE OWI

US PATENT OFFICE....SEE PATENT/OFF

US PEACE CORPS....SEE PEACE/CORP

US SECRETARY OF STATE....SEE SEC/STATE

US SECURITIES AND EXCHANGE COMMISSION....SEE SEC/EXCHNG

US SENATE COMMITTEE ON AERONAUTICS AND SPACE....SEE
    SEN/SPACE

US SENATE SCIENCE ADVISORY COMMISSION....SEE SCI/ADVSRY

US SENATE....SEE SENATE

US SMALL BUSINESS ADMINISTRATION....SEE SBA

US SOUTH....SEE SOUTH/US

US STEEL CORPORATION....SEE US/STEEL

US ADVISORY COMN INTERGOV REL E1977

US AIR FORCE E1978

US AIR FORCE ACADEMY ASSEMBLY E1979

US BUREAU OF THE CENSUS E1980

US COMMISSION GOVT SECURITY E1981,E1982

US COMMISSION ON CIVIL RIGHTS E1983,E1984,E1985,E1986

US COMMISSION ON CIVIL RIGHTS E1987

US SENATE COMM ON JUDICIARY E1988, 1989 1990

US CONGRESS JT ATOM ENRGY COMM E1991

US DEPARTMENT OF STATE E1993,E1994,E1995,E1996,E1997,E1998 ,
    E1999,E2000

US FEDERAL BUREAU INVESTIGAT E2001

US HOUSE COMM FOREIGN AFFAIRS E2002

US HOUSE COMM ON JUDICIARY E2003,E2004,E2005,E2006,E2007,E2008

US HOUSE RULES COMM E2009

US HOUSE UNAMER ACTIV COMM E2010

US HOUSE WAYS MEANS COMMITTEE E2011

US LIBRARY OF CONGRESS E2012,E2013,E2014,E2015,E2016,E2017 ,
    E2018,E2019,E2020

US OFFICE ECONOMIC OPPORTUNITY E2021

US PRES COMN CRIME IN DC E2022

US PRES COMN REGIS AND VOTING E2023

US PRES CONF ADMIN PROCEDURE E2024

US PRES TASK FORCE ADMIN JUS E2025

US SENATE COMM AERO SPACE SCI E2026,E2027

US SENATE COMM AERO SPACE SCI E2028

US SENATE COMM ON FOREIGN REL E2029,E2030,E2031,E2032,E2033 ,
    E2034,E2035,E2036,E2037,E2038

US SENATE COMM ON JUDICIARY E2039,E2040,E2041,E2042,E2043,E2044
    E2045,E2046,E2047,E2048,E2049,E2050,E2051,E2052,E2053 ,
    E2054,E2055,E2056,E2057,E2058,E1992

US SENATE COMM ON POST OFFICE E2059

US SENATE COMM POST OFFICE E2060

US SENATE SPEC COMM POLIT ACT E2061

US SUPERINTENDENT OF DOCUMENTS E2062,E2063

US TARIFF COMMISSION E2064

US/AID....UNITED STATES AGENCY FOR INTERNATIONAL DEVELOPMENT

US/HOUSING....UNITED STATES HOUSING CORPORATION

US/STEEL....UNITED STATES STEEL CORPORATION

US/WEST....WESTERN UNITED STATES

USA+45....UNITED STATES, 1945 TO PRESENT

USA-45....UNITED STATES, 1700 TO 1945

USIA....UNITED STATES INFORMATION AGENCY

US SENATE COMM ON FOREIGN REL,USIA FOREIGN SERVICE DIPLOM
PERSONNEL SYSTEM. USA+45 LAW CONSULT ADMIN 20 USIA. EDU/PROP
PAGE 102 E2038   PRIVIL
                                                           PROF/ORG
                                                              B67

USPNSKII/G....GLEB USPENSKII

USSR....UNION OF SOVIET SOCIALIST REPUBLICS; SEE ALSO
    RUSSIA, APPROPRIATE TIME/SPACE/CULTURE INDEX

LALL A.S.,NEGOTIATING DISARMAMENT* THE EIGHTEEN   OBS
NATION DISARMAMENT CONFERENCE* THE FIRST TWO YEARS, ARMS/CONT
1962-1964. ASIA FRANCE INDIA USA+45 USSR PROB/SOLV   DIPLOM
ADJUD NEUTRAL ATTIT...IDEA/COMP COLD/WAR. PAGE 62   OP/RES
E1246   B'

HOLLAND T.E.,STUDIES IN INTERNATIONAL LAW. TURKEY   INT/ORG
USSR WOR-45 CONSTN NAT/G DIPLOM DOMIN LEGIT COERCE   LAW
WAR PEACE ORD/FREE PWR SOVEREIGN...JURID CHARTS 20   INT/LAW
PARLIAMENT SUEZ TREATY. PAGE 54 E1084   B00

WILSON W.,THE STATE: ELEMENTS OF HISTORICAL AND   NAT/G
PRACTICAL POLITICS. FRANCE GERMANY ITALY UK USSR   JURID
CONSTN EX/STRUC LEGIS CT/SYS WAR PWR...POLICY   CONCPT
GOV/COMP 20. PAGE 106 E2131   NAT/COMP
                                                       B18

BAILEY S.D.,VETO IN THE SECURITY COUNCIL   DELIB/GP
(PAMPHLET). COM USSR WOR+45 BAL/PWR PARL/PROC   INT/ORG
ARMS/CONT PRIVIL PWR...INT/LAW TREND CHARTS 20 UN   DIPLOM
SUEZ. PAGE 7 E0135   N19

MEZERIK AG,OUTER SPACE: UN, US, USSR (PAMPHLET).   SPACE
USSR DELIB/GP FORCES DETER NUC/PWR SOVEREIGN   CONTROL
...POLICY 20 UN TREATY. PAGE 73 E1453   DIPLOM
                                                     INT/ORG
                                                       N19

CONWELL-EVANS T.P.,THE LEAGUE COUNCIL IN ACTION.   DELIB/GP
EUR+WWI TURKEY UK USSR WOR-45 INT/ORG FORCES JUDGE   INT/LAW
ECO/TAC EDU/PROP LEGIT COERCE ARMS/CONT ATTIT PWR...MAJORIT GEOG JURID CONCPT LEAGUE/NAT
TOT/POP VAL/FREE TUNIS 20. PAGE 25 E0498   B29

EAGLETON C.,INTERNATIONAL GOVERNMENT. BRAZIL FRANCE INT/ORG
GERMANY ITALY UK USSR WOR-45 DELIB/GP TOP/EX PLAN   JURID
ECO/TAC EDU/PROP LEGIT ADJUD REGION ARMS/CONT   DIPLOM
COERCE ATTIT PWR...GEOG MGT VAL/FREE LEAGUE/NAT 20. INT/LAW
PAGE 34 E0670   B32

HARPER S.N.,THE GOVERNMENT OF THE SOVIET UNION. COM MARXISM
USSR LAW CONSTN ECO/DEV PLAN TEC/DEV DIPLOM   NAT/G
INT/TRADE ADMIN REV NAT/LISM...POLICY 20. PAGE 50   LEAD
E1001   POL/PAR
                                                       B38

FLORIN J.,"BOLSHEVIST AND NATIONAL SOCIALIST   LAW
DOCTRINES OF INTERNATIONAL LAW." EUR+WWI GERMANY   ATTIT
USSR R+D INT/ORG NAT/G DIPLOM DOMIN EDU/PROP SOCISM TOTALISM
...CONCPT TIME/SEQ 20. PAGE 39 E0768   INT/LAW
                                                       S40

MICAUD C.A.,THE FRENCH RIGHT AND NAZI GERMANY   DIPLOM
1933-1939: A STUDY OF PUBLIC OPINION. GERMANY UK   AGREE
USSR POL/PAR ARMS/CONT COERCE DETER PEACE
RIGID/FLEX PWR MARXISM...FASCIST TREND 20
LEAGUE/NAT TREATY. PAGE 73 E1454   B43

US LIBRARY OF CONGRESS,RUSSIA: A CHECK LIST   BIBLIOG
PRELIMINARY TO A BASIC BIBLIOGRAPHY OF MATERIALS IN LAW
THE RUSSIAN LANGUAGE. COM USSR CULTURE EDU/PROP   SECT
MARXISM...ART/METH HUM LING 19/20. PAGE 101 E2015   B44

CONOVER H.F.,THE GOVERNMENTS OF THE MAJOR FOREIGN   BIBLIOG
POWERS: A BIBLIOGRAPHY. FRANCE GERMANY ITALY UK   NAT/G
                                                       B45

USSR CONSTN LOC/G POL/PAR EX/STRUC FORCES ADMIN   DIPLOM
CT/SYS CIVMIL/REL TOTALISM...POLICY 19/20. PAGE 25
E0494

B45

GALLOWAY E.,ABSTRACTS OF POSTWAR LITERATURE (VOL.   BIBLIOG/A
IV) JAN.-JULY, 1945 NOS. 901-1074. POLAND USA+45   NUC/PWR
USSR WOR+45 INDUS LABOR PLAN ECO/TAC INT/TRADE TAX NAT/G
EDU/PROP ADMIN COLONIAL INT/LAW. PAGE 42 E0829   DIPLOM

B47

ENKE S.,INTERNATIONAL ECONOMICS. UK USA+45 USSR   INT/TRADE
INT/ORG BAL/PWR BARGAIN CAP/ISM BAL/PAY...NAT/COMP FINAN
20 TREATY. PAGE 35 E0691   TARIFFS
                                                   ECO/TAC

N47

FOX W.T.R.,UNITED STATES POLICY IN A TWO POWER   DIPLOM
WORLD. COM USA+45 USSR FORCES DOMIN AGREE NEUTRAL FOR/AID
NUC/PWR ORD/FREE SOVEREIGN 20 COLD/WAR TREATY   POLICY
EUROPE/W INTERVENT. PAGE 39 E0780

B48

YAKOBSON S.,FIVE HUNDRED RUSSIAN WORKS FOR COLLEGE BIBLIOG
LIBRARIES (PAMPHLET). MOD/EUR USSR MARXISM SOCISM NAT/G
...ART/METH GEOG HUM JURID SOC 13/20. PAGE 108   CULTURE
E2162   COM

B49

JACKSON R.H.,INTERNATIONAL CONFERENCE ON MILITARY DIPLOM
TRIALS. FRANCE GERMANY UK USA+45 USSR VOL/ASSN   INT/ORG
DELIB/GP REPAR ADJUD CT/SYS CRIME WAR 20 WAR/TRIAL.INT/LAW
PAGE 57 E1141   CIVMIL/REL

B49

US DEPARTMENT OF STATE,SOVIET BIBLIOGRAPHY   BIBLIOG/A
(PAMPHLET). CHINA/COM COM USSR LAW AGRI INT/ORG   MARXISM
ECO/TAC EDU/PROP...POLICY GEOG 20. PAGE 99 E1994   CULTURE
                                                   DIPLOM

B50

BERMAN H.J.,JUSTICE IN RUSSIA; AN INTERPRETATION OF JURID
SOVIET LAW. USSR LAW STRUCT LABOR FORCES AGREE   ADJUD
GP/REL ORD/FREE SOCISM...TIME/SEQ 20. PAGE 11 E0207 MARXISM
                                                    COERCE

B50

DOROSH J.T.,GUIDE TO SOVIET BIBLIOGRAPHIES. USSR   BIBLIOG
LAW AGRI SCHOOL SECT FORCES TEC/DEV...ART/METH GEOG METH
HUM SOC 20. PAGE 32 E0639   CON/ANAL

B53

PIERCE R.A.,RUSSIAN CENTRAL ASIA, 1867-1917: A   BIBLIOG
SELECTED BIBLIOGRAPHY (PAMPHLET). USSR LAW CULTURE COLONIAL
NAT/G EDU/PROP WAR...GEOG SOC 19/20. PAGE 81 E1616 ADMIN
                                                   COM

C54

GUINS G.C.,"SOVIET LAW AND SOVIET SOCIETY." COM   LAW
USSR STRATA FAM NAT/G WORKER DOMIN RACE/REL   STRUCT
...BIBLIOG 20. PAGE 48 E0960   PLAN

B55

MID-EUROPEAN LAW PROJECT,CHURCH AND STATE BEHIND   LAW
THE IRON CURTAIN. COM CZECHOSLVK HUNGARY POLAND   MARXISM
USSR CULTURE SECT EDU/PROP GOV/REL CATHISM...CHARTS POLICY
ANTHOL BIBLIOG WORSHIP 20 CHURCH/STA. PAGE 73 E1455

B57

FREUND G.,UNHOLY ALLIANCE. EUR+WWI GERMANY USSR   DIPLOM
FORCES ECO/TAC CONTROL WAR PWR...TREND TREATY.   PLAN
PAGE 40 E0796   POLICY

B57

MILLS W.,INDIVIDUAL FREEDOM AND COMMON DEFENSE   ORD/FREE
(PAMPHLET). USA+45 USSR NAT/G EDU/PROP CRIME CHOOSE CONSTN
20 COLD/WAR. PAGE 73 E1463   INGP/REL
                                                   FORCES

B58

KURL S.,ESTONIA: A SELECTED BIBLIOGRAPHY. USSR   BIBLIOG
ESTONIA LAW INTELL SECT...ART/METH GEOG HUM SOC 20.CULTURE
PAGE 62 E1238   NAT/G

B58

MARTIN L.J.,INTERNATIONAL PROPAGANDA: ITS LEGAL AND EDU/PROP
DIPLOMATIC CONTROL. UK USA+45 USSR CONSULT DELIB/GP DIPLOM
DOMIN CONTROL 20. PAGE 69 E1373   INT/LAW
                                                    ATTIT

B58

MASON H.L.,TOYNBEE'S APPROACH TO WORLD POLITICS.   DIPLOM
AFR USA+45 USSR LAW WAR NAT/LISM ALL/IDEOS...HUM   CONCPT
BIBLIOG. PAGE 69 E1380   PHIL/SCI
                                                   SECT

B59

CORBETT P.E.,LAW IN DIPLOMACY. UK USA+45 USSR   NAT/G
CONSTN SOCIETY INT/ORG JUDGE LEGIT ATTIT ORD/FREE ADJUD
TOT/POP LEAGUE/NAT 20. PAGE 26 E0507   JURID
                                                   DIPLOM

B59

GSOVSKI V.,GOVERNMENT, LAW, AND COURTS IN THE   ADJUD
SOVIET UNION AND EASTERN EUROPE (2 VOLS.). COM USSR MARXISM
AGRI INDUS WORKER CT/SYS CRIME...BIBLIOG 20   CONTROL
EUROPE/E. PAGE 48 E0958   ORD/FREE

B59

OKINSHEVICH L.A.,LATIN AMERICA IN SOVIET WRITINGS, BIBLIOG
1945-1958: A BIBLIOGRAPHY. USSR LAW ECO/UNDEV LABOR WRITING
DIPLOM EDU/PROP REV...GEOG SOC 20. PAGE 78 E1573   COM
                                                    L/A+17C

B59

COLUMBIA U. BUREAU OF APPL SOC RES, ATTITUDES OF   ATTIT
PROMINENT AMERICANS TOWARD "WORLD PEACE THROUGH   ACT/RES
WORLD LAW" (SUPRA-NATL ORGANIZATION FOR WAR   INT/LAW
PREVENTION). USA+45 USSR ELITES FORCES PLAN   STAT
PROB/SOLV CONTROL WAR PWR...POLICY SOC QU IDEA/COMP
20 UN. PAGE 82 E1644

B60

ENGEL J.,THE SECURITY OF THE FREE WORLD. USSR   COM
WOR+45 STRATA STRUCT ECO/DEV ECO/UNDEV INT/ORG   TREND
DELIB/GP FORCES DOMIN LEGIT ADJUD EXEC ARMS/CONT   DIPLOM
COERCE...POLICY CONCPT NEW/IDEA TIME/SEQ GEN/LAWS
COLD/WAR WORK UN 20 NATO. PAGE 35 E0689

B60

FISCHER L.,THE SOVIETS IN WORLD AFFAIRS. CHINA/COM DIPLOM
COM EUR+WWI USSR INT/ORG CONFER LEAD ARMS/CONT REV NAT/G
PWR...CHARTS 20 TREATY VERSAILLES. PAGE 38 E0755   POLICY
                                                   MARXISM

B60

RIENOW R.,INTRODUCTION TO GOVERNMENT (2ND ED.). UK CONSTN
USA+45 USSR POL/PAR ADMIN REV CHOOSE SUFF FEDERAL PARL/PROC
PWR...JURID GOV/COMP T 20. PAGE 85 E1697   REPRESENT
                                                   AUTHORIT

L60

DEAN A.W.,"SECOND GENEVA CONFERENCE OF THE LAW OF INT/ORG
THE SEA: THE FIGHT FOR FREEDOM OF THE SEAS." FUT   JURID
USA+45 USSR WOR+45 WOR-45 SEA CONSTN STRUCT PLAN   INT/LAW
INT/TRADE ADJUD ADMIN ORD/FREE...DECISION RECORD
TREND GEN/LAWS 20 TREATY. PAGE 30 E0600

S60

GRACIA-MORA M.R.,"INTERNATIONAL RESPONSIBILITY FOR INT/ORG
SUBVERSIVE ACTIVITIES AND HOSTILE PROPAGANDA BY   JURID
PRIVATE PERSONS AGAINST." COM EUR+WWI L/A+17C UK   SOVEREIGN
USA+45 USSR WOR-45 CONSTN NAT/G LEGIT ADJUD REV
PEACE TOTALISM ORD/FREE...INT/LAW 20. PAGE 45 E0895

S60

WRIGHT Q.,"LEGAL ASPECTS OF THE U-2 INCIDENT." COM PWR
USA+45 USSR STRUCT NAT/G FORCES PLAN TEC/DEV ADJUD POLICY
RIGID/FLEX MORAL ORD/FREE...DECISION INT/LAW JURID SPACE
PSY TREND GEN/LAWS COLD/WAR VAL/FREE 20 U-2.
PAGE 108 E2157

C60

HAZARD J.N.,"SETTLING DISPUTES IN SOVIET SOCIETY: ADJUD
THE FORMATIVE YEARS OF LEGAL INSTITUTIONS." USSR   LAW
NAT/G PROF/ORG PROB/SOLV CONTROL CT/SYS ROUTINE REV COM
CENTRAL...JURID BIBLIOG 20. PAGE 51 E1017   POLICY

S61

LIPSON L.,"AN ARGUMENT ON THE LEGALITY OF   INT/ORG
RECONNAISSANCE STATELLITES." COM USA+45 USSR WOR+45 LAW
AIR INTELL NAT/G CONSULT PLAN DIPLOM LEGIT ROUTINE SPACE
ATTIT...INT/LAW JURID CONCPT METH/CNCPT TREND
COLD/WAR 20. PAGE 65 E1302

B62

BOCHENSKI J.M.,HANDBOOK ON COMMUNISM. USSR WOR+45 COM
LAW SOCIETY NAT/G POL/PAR SECT CRIME PERSON MARXISM DIPLOM
...SOC ANTHOL 20. PAGE 13 E0254   POLICY
                                                    CONCPT

B62

GRZYBOWSKI K.,SOVIET LEGAL INSTITUTIONS. USA+45   ADJUD
USSR ECO/DEV NAT/G EDU/PROP CONTROL CT/SYS CRIME   LAW
OWN ATTIT PWR SOCISM...NAT/COMP 20. PAGE 48 E0955 JURID

B62

LEVY H.V.,LIBERDADE E JUSTICA SOCIAL (2ND ED.).   ORD/FREE
BRAZIL COM L/A+17C USSR INT/ORG PARTIC GP/REL   MARXISM
WEALTH 20 UN COM/PARTY. PAGE 65 E1290   CAP/ISM
                                                   LAW

SWAYZE H.,POLITICAL CONTROL OF LITERATURE IN THE
USSR, 1946-1959. USSR NAT/G CREATE LICENSE...JURID
20. PAGE 95 E1898

MARXISM
WRITING
CONTROL
DOMIN
B62

TRISKA J.F.,THE THEORY, LAW, AND POLICY OF SOVIET
TREATIES. WOR+45 WOR-45 CONSTN INT/ORG NAT/G
VOL/ASSN DOMIN LEGIT COERCE ATTIT PWR RESPECT
...POLICY JURID CONCPT OBS SAMP TIME/SEQ TREND
GEN/LAWS 20. PAGE 97 E1941

COM
LAW
INT/LAW
USSR
B62

"AMERICAN BEHAVIORAL SCIENTIST." USSR LAW NAT/G
...SOC 20 UN. PAGE 2 E0034

BIBLIOG
AFR
R+D
L62

CRANE R.D.,"SOVIET ATTITUDE TOWARD INTERNATIONAL
SPACE LAW." COM FUT USA+45 USSR AIR CONSTN DELIB/GP
DOMIN PWR...JURID TREND TOT/POP 20. PAGE 27 E0543

LAW
ATTIT
INT/LAW
SPACE
S62

LISSITZYN O.J.,"SOME LEGAL IMPLICATIONS OF THE U-2
AND RB-47 INCIDENTS." FUT USA+45 USSR WOR+45 AIR
NAT/G DIPLOM LEGIT MORAL ORD/FREE SOVEREIGN...JURID
GEN/LAWS GEN/METH COLD/WAR 20 U-2. PAGE 65 E1305

LAW
CONCPT
SPACE
INT/LAW
S62

MCWHINNEY E.,"CO-EXISTENCE, THE CUBA CRISIS, AND
COLD WAR-INTERNATIONAL WAR." CUBA USA+45 USSR
WOR+45 NAT/G TOP/EX BAL/PWR DIPLOM DOMIN LEGIT
PEACE RIGID/FLEX ORD/FREE...STERTYP COLD/WAR 20.
PAGE 71 E1427

CONCPT
INT/LAW
S62

MORGAN G.G.,"SOVIET ADMINISTRATIVE LEGALITY: THE
ROLE OF THE ATTORNEY GENERAL'S OFFICE." COM USSR
CONTROL ROUTINE...CONCPT BIBLIOG 18/20. PAGE 74
E1493

LAW
CONSTN
LEGIS
ADMIN
C62

LAVROFF D.--G.,LES LIBERTES PUBLIQUES EN UNION
SOVIETIQUE (REV. ED.). USSR NAT/G WORKER SANCTION
CRIME MARXISM NEW/LIB...JURID BIBLIOG WORSHIP 20.
PAGE 63 E1268

ORD/FREE
LAW
ATTIT
COM
B63

US SENATE,DOCUMENTS ON INTERNATIONAL ASPECTS OF
EXPLORATION AND USE OF OUTER SPACE, 1954-62: STAFF
REPORT FOR COMM AERON SPACE SCI. USA+45 USSR LEGIS
LEAD CIVMIL/REL PEACE...POLICY INT/LAW ANTHOL 20
CONGRESS NASA KHRUSH/N. PAGE 101 E2026

SPACE
UTIL
GOV/REL
DIPLOM
B63

BECHHOEFER B.G.,"UNITED NATIONS PROCEDURES IN CASE
OF VIOLATIONS OF DISARMAMENT AGREEMENTS." COM
USA+45 USSR LAW CONSTN NAT/G EX/STRUC FORCES LEGIS
BAL/PWR EDU/PROP CT/SYS ARMS/CONT ORD/FREE PWR
...POLICY STERTYP UN VAL/FREE 20. PAGE 9 E0169

INT/ORG
DELIB/GP
S63

BERMAN H.J.,"THE DILEMMA OF SOVIET LAW REFORM."
NAT/G POL/PAR CT/SYS ALL/VALS ORD/FREE PWR...POLICY
JURID VAL/FREE 20. PAGE 11 E0208

COM
LAW
USSR
S63

GARDNER R.N.,"COOPERATION IN OUTER SPACE." FUT USSR
WOR+45 AIR LAW COM/IND CONSULT DELIB/GP CREATE
KNOWL 20 TREATY. PAGE 42 E0837

INT/ORG
ACT/RES
PEACE
SPACE
S63

MACWHINNEY E.,"LES CONCEPT SOVIETIQUE DE
'COEXISTENCE PACIFIQUE' ET LES RAPPORTS JURIDIQUES
ENTRE L'URSS ET LES ETATS OCIDENTAUX." COM FUT
WOR+45 LAW CULTURE INTELL POL/PAR ACT/RES BAL/PWR
...INT/LAW 20. PAGE 67 E1346

NAT/G
CONCPT
DIPLOM
USSR
S63

MCDOUGAL M.S.,"THE SOVIET-CUBAN QUARANTINE AND
SELF-DEFENSE." CUBA USA+45 USSR WOR+45 INT/ORG
NAT/G BAL/PWR NUC/PWR ATTIT...JURID CONCPT. PAGE 70
E1409

ORD/FREE
LEGIT
SOVEREIGN
S63

COHEN M.,LAW AND POLITICS IN SPACE: SPECIFIC AND
URGENT PROBLEMS IN THE LAW OF OUTER SPACE.
CHINA/COM COM USA+45 USSR WOR+45 COM/IND INT/ORG
NAT/G LEGIT NUC/PWR ATTIT BIO/SOC...JURID CONCPT
CONGRESS 20 STALIN/J. PAGE 24 E0464

DELIB/GP
LAW
INT/LAW
SPACE
B64

FEIFER G.,JUSTICE IN MOSCOW. USSR LAW CRIME

ADJUD
B64

...RECORD 20. PAGE 37 E0725

JURID
CT/SYS
MARXISM

FULBRIGHT J.W.,OLD MYTHS AND NEW REALITIES. USA+45
USSR LEGIS INT/TRADE DETER ATTIT...POLICY 20
COLD/WAR TREATY. PAGE 41 E0818

DIPLOM
INT/ORG
ORD/FREE
B64

GARDNER R.N.,IN PURSUIT OF WORLD ORDER* US FOREIGN
POLICY AND INTERNATIONAL ORGANIZATIONS. USA+45 USSR
ECO/UNDEV FORCES LEGIS DIPLOM FOR/AID INT/TRADE
PEACE...INT/LAW PREDICT UN. PAGE 42 E0839

OBS
INT/ORG
ALL/VALS
B64

GRIFFITH W.E.,THE SINO-SOVIET RIFT. ASIA CHINA/COM
COM CUBA USSR YUGOSLAVIA NAT/G POL/PAR VOL/ASSN
DELIB/GP FORCES TOP/EX DIPLOM EDU/PROP DRIVE PERSON
PWR...TREND 20 TREATY. PAGE 47 E0941

ATTIT
TIME/SEQ
BAL/PWR
SOCISM
B64

LAPENNA I.,STATE AND LAW: SOVIET AND YUGOSLAV
THEORY. USSR YUGOSLAVIA STRATA STRUCT NAT/G DOMIN
COERCE MARXISM...GOV/COMP IDEA/COMP 20. PAGE 63
E1253

JURID
COM
LAW
SOVEREIGN
B64

MCWHINNEY E.,"PEACEFUL COEXISTENCE" AND SOVIET-
WESTERN INTERNATIONAL LAW. USSR DIPLOM LEAD...JURID
20 COLD/WAR. PAGE 71 E1429

PEACE
IDEA/COMP
INT/LAW
ATTIT
B64

OSSENBECK F.J.,OPEN SPACE AND PEACE. CHINA/COM FUT
USA+45 USSR LAW PROB/SOLV TEC/DEV EDU/PROP NEUTRAL
PEACE...AUD/VIS ANTHOL 20. PAGE 79 E1583

SPACE
ORD/FREE
DIPLOM
CREATE
B64

CRANE R.D.,"BASIC PRINCIPLES IN SOVIET SPACE LAW."
FUT WOR+45 AIR INT/ORG DIPLOM DOMIN ARMS/CONT
COERCE NUC/PWR PEACE ATTIT DRIVE PWR...INT/LAW
METH/CNCPT NEW/IDEA OBS TREND GEN/LAWS VAL/FREE
MARX/KARL 20. PAGE 27 E0544

COM
LAW
USSR
SPACE
S64

GARDNER R.N.,"THE SOVIET UNION AND THE UNITED
NATIONS." WOR+45 FINAN POL/PAR VOL/ASSN FORCES
ECO/TAC DOMIN EDU/PROP LEGIT ADJUD ADMIN ARMS/CONT
COERCE ATTIT ALL/VALS...POLICY MAJORIT CONCPT OBS
TIME/SEQ TREND STERTYP UN. PAGE 42 E0838

COM
INT/ORG
USSR
S64

GINSBURGS G.,"WARS OF NATIONAL LIBERATION - THE
SOVIET THESIS." COM USSR WOR+45 WOR-45 LAW CULTURE
INT/ORG DIPLOM LEGIT COLONIAL GUERRILLA WAR
NAT/LISM ATTIT PERSON MORAL PWR...JURID OBS TREND
MARX/KARL 20. PAGE 44 E0869

COERCE
CONCPT
INT/LAW
REV
S64

KARPOV P.V.,"PEACEFUL COEXISTENCE AND INTERNATIONAL
LAW." WOR+45 LAW SOCIETY INT/ORG VOL/ASSN FORCES
CREATE CAP/ISM DIPLOM ADJUD NUC/PWR PEACE MORAL
ORD/FREE PWR MARXISM...MARXIST JURID CONCPT OBS
TREND COLD/WAR MARX/KARL 20. PAGE 59 E1186

COM
ATTIT
INT/LAW
USSR
S64

LIPSON L.,"PEACEFUL COEXISTENCE." COM USSR WOR+45
LAW INT/ORG DIPLOM LEGIT ADJUD ORD/FREE...CONCPT
OBS TREND GEN/LAWS VAL/FREE COLD/WAR 20. PAGE 65
E1303

ATTIT
JURID
INT/LAW
PEACE
S64

MAGGS P.B.,"SOVIET VIEWPOINT ON NUCLEAR WEAPONS IN
INTERNATIONAL LAW." USSR WOR+45 INT/ORG FORCES
DIPLOM ARMS/CONT ATTIT ORD/FREE PWR...POLICY JURID
CONCPT OBS TREND CON/ANAL GEN/LAWS VAL/FREE 20.
PAGE 67 E1347

COM
LAW
INT/LAW
NUC/PWR
S64

TRISKA J.F.,"SOVIET TREATY LAW: A QUANTITATIVE
ANALYSIS." WOR+45 LAW ECO/UNDEV AGRI COM/IND INDUS
CREATE TEC/DEV DIPLOM ATTIT PWR WEALTH...JURID SAMP
TIME/SEQ TREND CHARTS VAL/FREE 20 TREATY. PAGE 97
E1942

COM
ECO/TAC
INT/LAW
USSR
S64

BAADE H.,THE SOVIET IMPACT ON INTERNATIONAL LAW.
INT/ORG INT/TRADE LEGIT COLONIAL ARMS/CONT REV WAR
...CON/ANAL ANTHOL TREATY. PAGE 6 E0124

INT/LAW
USSR
CREATE
ORD/FREE
B65

CARTER G.M.,POLITICS IN EUROPE. EUR+WWI FRANCE
GERMANY/W UK USSR LAW CONSTN POL/PAR VOL/ASSN PRESS

GOV/COMP
OP/RES
B65

LOBBY PWR...ANTHOL SOC/INTEG EEC. PAGE 20 E0399   ECO/DEV

IDEA/COMP

B65
FORGAC A.A.,NEW DIPLOMACY AND THE UNITED NATIONS.   DIPLOM
FRANCE GERMANY UK USSR INT/ORG DELIB/GP EX/STRUC   ETIQUET
PEACE...INT/LAW CONCPT UN. PAGE 39 E0770   NAT/G

B65
GOTLIEB A.,DISARMAMENT AND INTERNATIONAL LAW* A   INT/LAW
STUDY OF THE ROLE OF LAW IN THE DISARMAMENT   INT/ORG
PROCESS. USA+45 USSR PROB/SOLV CONFER ADMIN ROUTINE   ARMS/CONT
NUC/PWR ORD/FREE SOVEREIGN UN TREATY. PAGE 45 E0893   IDEA/COMP

B65
HIGGINS R.,CONFLICT OF INTERESTS* INTERNATIONAL LAW   INT/LAW
IN A DIVIDED WORLD. ASIA USSR ECO/DEV ECO/UNDEV   IDEA/COMP
SECT INT/TRADE COLD/WAR WORSHIP. PAGE 52 E1042   ADJUST

B65
MOSTECKY V.,SOVIET LEGAL BIBLIOGRAPHY. USSR LEGIS   BIBLIOG/A
PRESS WRITING CONFER ADJUD CT/SYS REV MARXISM   LAW
...INT/LAW JURID DICTIONARY 20. PAGE 75 E1503   COM
                                                        CONSTN

S65
MAC CHESNEY B.,"SOME COMMENTS ON THE 'QUARANTINE'   INT/ORG
OF CUBA." USA+45 WOR+45 NAT/G BAL/PWR DIPLOM LEGIT   LAW
ROUTINE ATTIT ORD/FREE...JURID METH/CNCPT 20.   CUBA
PAGE 67 E1337   USSR

B66
BAHRO H.,DAS KINDSCHAFTSRECHT IN DER UNION DER   JURID
SOZIALISTITSCHEN SOWJETREPUBLIKEN. USSR SECT   AGE/C
EDU/PROP CONTROL PWR...SOC/WK 20. PAGE 7 E0133   PERS/REL
                                                        SUPEGO

B66
DALLIN A.,POLITICS IN THE SOVIET UNION: 7 CASES.   MARXISM
COM USSR LAW POL/PAR CHIEF FORCES WRITING CONTROL   DOMIN
PARL/PROC CIVMIL/REL TOTALISM...ANTHOL 20 KHRUSH/N   ORD/FREE
STALIN/J CASEBOOK COM/PARTY. PAGE 28 E0563   GOV/REL

B66
DYCK H.V.,WEIMAR GERMANY AND SOVIET RUSSIA   DIPLOM
1926-1933. EUR+WWI GERMANY UK USSR ECO/TAC   GOV/REL
INT/TRADE NEUTRAL WAR ATTIT 20 WEIMAR/REP TREATY.   POLICY
PAGE 34 E0669

B66
EPSTEIN F.T.,THE AMERICAN BIBLIOGRAPHY OF RUSSIAN   BIBLIOG
AND EAST EUROPEAN STUDIES FOR 1964. USSR LOC/G   COM
NAT/G POL/PAR FORCES ADMIN ARMS/CONT...JURID CONCPT   MARXISM
20 UN. PAGE 35 E0694   DIPLOM

B66
FRIED R.C.,COMPARATIVE POLITICAL INSTITUTIONS. USSR   NAT/G
EX/STRUC FORCES LEGIS JUDGE CONTROL REPRESENT   PWR
ALL/IDEOS 20 CONGRESS BUREAUCRCY. PAGE 40 E0798   EFFICIENCY
                                                        GOV/COMP

B66
JACOBSON H.K.,DIPLOMATS, SCIENTISTS, AND   DIPLOM
POLITICIANS* THE UNITED STATES AND THE NUCLEAR TEST   ARMS/CONT
BAN NEGOTIATIONS. USA+45 USSR ACT/RES PLAN CONFER   TECHRACY
DETER NUC/PWR CONSEN ORD/FREE...INT TREATY. PAGE 57   INT/ORG
E1146

B66
THOMPSON J.M.,RUSSIA, BOLSHEVISM, AND THE   DIPLOM
VERSAILLES PEACE. RUSSIA USSR INT/ORG NAT/G   PEACE
DELIB/GP AGREE REV WAR PWR 20 TREATY VERSAILLES   MARXISM
BOLSHEVISM. PAGE 96 E1919

B66
US DEPARTMENT OF STATE,RESEARCH ON THE USSR AND   BIBLIOG/A
EASTERN EUROPE (EXTERNAL RESEARCH LIST NO 1-25).   EUR+WWI
USSR LAW CULTURE SOCIETY NAT/G TEC/DEV DIPLOM   COM
EDU/PROP REGION...GEOG LING. PAGE 100 E1997   MARXISM

B66
US SENATE COMM AERO SPACE SCI,SOVIET SPACE   CONSULT
PROGRAMS, 1962-65: GOALS AND PURPOSES,   SPACE
ACHIEVEMENTS, PLANS, AND INTERNATIONAL   FUT
IMPLICATIONS. USA+45 USSR R+D FORCES PLAN EDU/PROP   DIPLOM
PRESS ADJUD ARMS/CONT ATTIT MARXISM. PAGE 101 E2028

S66
BROWNLIE I.,"NUCLEAR PROLIFERATION* SOME PROBLEMS   NUC/PWR
OF CONTROL." USA+45 USSR ECO/UNDEV INT/ORG FORCES   ARMS/CONT
TEC/DEV REGION CONSEN...RECORD TREATY. PAGE 16   VOL/ASSN
E0318   ORD/FREE

S66
CHIU H.,"COMMUNIST CHINA'S ATTITUDE TOWARD   INT/LAW
INTERNATIONAL LAW" CHINA/COM USSR LAW CONSTN DIPLOM   MARXISM
GP/REL 20 LENIN/VI. PAGE 22 E0431   CONCPT

B67
MCBRIDE J.H.,THE TEST BAN TREATY: MILITARY,   ARMS/CONT
TECHNOLOGICAL, AND POLITICAL IMPLICATIONS. USA+45   DIPLOM
USSR DELIB/GP FORCES LEGIS TEC/DEV BAL/PWR TREATY.   NUC/PWR
PAGE 70 E1399

B67
RAMUNDO B.A.,PEACEFUL COEXISTENCE: INTERNATIONAL   INT/LAW
LAW IN THE BUILDING OF COMMUNISM. USSR INT/ORG   PEACE
DIPLOM COLONIAL ARMS/CONT ROLE SOVEREIGN...POLICY   MARXISM
METH/COMP NAT/COMP BIBLIOG. PAGE 83 E1673   METH/CNCPT

B67
US SENATE COMM ON FOREIGN REL,CONSULAR CONVENTION   LEGIS
WITH THE SOVIET UNION. USA+45 USSR DELIB/GP LEAD   LOBBY
REPRESENT ATTIT ORD/FREE CONGRESS TREATY. PAGE 101   DIPLOM
E2031

S67
CLOGGER T.J.,"THE BIG EAR." UK USA+45 USSR LAW   DIPLOM
LEGIS CRIME GP/REL INGP/REL ATTIT 20 FBI ESPIONAGE.   ORD/FREE
PAGE 23 E0458   COM/IND
                                                       INSPECT

S67
MIRONENKO Y.,"A NEW EXTENSION OF CRIMINAL LIABILITY   ADJUD
IN THE USSR." COM USSR DOMIN EDU/PROP 20. PAGE 73   SANCTION
E1467   CRIME
                                                       MARXISM

S68
SHAPIRO J.P.,"SOVIET HISTORIOGRAPHY AND THE MOSCOW   HIST/WRIT
TRIALS: AFTER THIRTY YEARS." USSR NAT/G LEGIT PRESS   EDU/PROP
CONTROL LEAD ATTIT MARXISM...NEW/IDEA METH 20   SANCTION
TROTSKY/L STALIN/J KHRUSH/N. PAGE 90 E1810   ADJUD

UTAH....UTAH

UTIL....UTILITY, USEFULNESS

B14
VECCHIO G.D.,THE FORMAL BASES OF LAW (TRANS. BY J.   LAW
LISLE). DOMIN LEGIT CONTROL COERCE UTIL MORAL PWR   JURID
...CONCPT TIME/SEQ 17/20 COMMON/LAW NATURL/LAW.   GEN/LAWS
PAGE 103 E2074   IDEA/COMP

C20
DUNNING W.A.,"A HISTORY OF POLITICAL THINKERS FROM   IDEA/COMP
ROUSSEAU TO SPENCER." NAT/G REV NAT/LISM UTIL   PHIL/SCI
CONSERVE MARXISM POPULISM...JURID BIBLIOG 18/19.   CONCPT
PAGE 33 E0664   GEN/LAWS

S26
HALL A.B.,"DETERMINATION OF METHODS FOR   ADJUD
ASCERTAINING THE FACTORS THAT INFLUENCE JUDICIAL   DECISION
DECISIONS IN CASES INVOLVING DUE PROCESS" LAW JUDGE   CONSTN
DEBATE EFFICIENCY OPTIMAL UTIL...SOC CONCPT   JURID
PROBABIL STAT SAMP. PAGE 49 E0981

B38
CLARK J.P.,THE RISE OF A NEW FEDERALISM. LEGIS   FEDERAL
TARIFFS EFFICIENCY NAT/LISM UTIL...JURID SOC   PROVS
GEN/LAWS BIBLIOG 19/20. PAGE 23 E0451   NAT/G
                                                       GOV/REL

B40
HOBBES T.,A DIALOGUE BETWEEN A PHILOSOPHER AND A   CT/SYS
STUDENT OF THE COMMON LAWS OF ENGLAND (1667?). UK   CHIEF
SECT DOMIN ADJUD CRIME INCOME OWN UTIL ORD/FREE PWR   SANCTION
SOVEREIGN...JURID GEN/LAWS 17. PAGE 53 E1057

B60
ATOMIC INDUSTRIAL FORUM,ATOMS FOR INDUSTRY: WORLD   NUC/PWR
FORUM. WOR+45 FINAN COST UTIL...JURID ANTHOL 20.   INDUS
PAGE 6 E0113   PLAN
                                                       PROB/SOLV

L60
MILLER A.S.,"THE MYTH OF NEUTRALITY IN   ADJUD
CONSTITUTIONAL ADJUDICATION." LAW...DECISION JURID   CONSTN
LING TREND IDEA/COMP. PAGE 73 E1456   MYTH
                                                       UTIL

B62
FRIEDRICH C.J.,NOMOS V: THE PUBLIC INTEREST. UNIV   METH/CNCPT
ECO/TAC ADJUD UTIL ATTIT...POLICY LING LOG GEN/LAWS   CONCPT
20. PAGE 41 E0808   LAW
                                                       IDEA/COMP

B63
OTTOSON H.W.,LAND USE POLICY AND PROBLEMS IN THE   PROB/SOLV
UNITED STATES. USA+45 USA-45 LAW AGRI INDUS NAT/G   UTIL
GP/REL...CHARTS ANTHOL 19/20 HOMEST/ACT. PAGE 79   HABITAT
E1586   POLICY

US SENATE, DOCUMENTS ON INTERNATIONAL AS"ECTS OF EXPLORATION AND USE OF OUTER SPACE, 1954-62: STAFF REPORT FOR COMM AERON SPACE SCI. USA+45 USSR LEGIS LEAD CIVMIL/REL PEACE...POLICY INT/LAW ANTHOL 20 CONGRESS NASA KHRUSH/N. PAGE 101 E2026
SPACE UTIL GOV/REL DIPLOM B63

HIBBS A.R.,"SPACE TECHNOLOGY* THE THREAT . 'D THE PROMISE." FUT VOL/ASSN TEC/DEV NUC/PWR COST EFFICIENCY UTIL UN TREATY. PAGE 52 E1038
SPACE ARMS/CONT PREDICT S65

BENTHAM J.,THE THEORY OF LEGISLATION. UK CREATE CRIME ATTIT ORD/FREE...CONCPT 18 REFORMERS. PAGE 10 E0196
LEGIS LAW CRIMLGY UTIL B76

BENTHAM J.,A FRAGMENT ON GOVERNMENT (1776). CONSTN MUNIC NAT/G SECT AGREE HAPPINESS UTIL MORAL ORD/FREE...JURID CONCPT. PAGE 10 E0198
SOVEREIGN LAW DOMIN B91

TILITAR....UTILITARIANISM

TILITARIANISM....SEE UTILITAR

TILITY....SEE UTIL

UTLEY T.E. E2065

UTOPIA....ENVISIONED GENERAL SOCIAL CONDITIONS; SEE ALSO STERTYP

MORRIS C.,THE GREAT LEGAL PHILOSOPHERS: SELECTED READINGS IN JURISPRUDENCE. UNIV INTELL SOCIETY EDU/PROP MAJORITY UTOPIA PERSON KNOWL...ANTHOL. PAGE 75 E1497
JURID ADJUD PHIL/SCI IDEA/COMP B59

SCHUMAN S.I.,LEGAL POSITIVISM: ITS SCOPE AND LIMITATIONS. CONSTN NAT/G DIPLOM PARTIC UTOPIA ...POLICY DECISION PHIL/SCI CONCPT 20. PAGE 89 E1784
GEN/METH LAW METH/COMP B63

ANDRUS H.L.,LIBERALISM, CONSERVATISM, MORMONISM. USA+45 PLAN ADJUD CONTROL HAPPINESS ORD/FREE CONSERVE NEW/LIB WORSHIP 20. PAGE 5 E0097
SECT UTOPIA MORAL B65

NEGLEY G.,POLITICAL AUTHORITY AND MORAL JUDGMENT. INTELL SOCIETY LEGIS SANCTION UTOPIA SOVEREIGN MARXISM...INT/LAW LOG 20. PAGE 76 E1530
MORAL PWR CONTROL B65

LUSKY L.,"FOUR PROBLEMS IN LAWMAKING FOR PEACE." FORCES LEGIS CREATE ADJUD COERCE WAR MAJORITY PEACE PWR. PAGE 67 E1334
ORD/FREE INT/LAW UTOPIA RECORD S65

BERNSTEIN S.,ALTERNATIVES TO VIOLENCE: ALIENATED YOUTH AND RIOTS, RACE AND POVERTY. MUNIC PUB/INST SCHOOL INGP/REL RACE/REL UTOPIA DRIVE HABITAT ROLE WEALTH...INT 20. PAGE 11 E0215
AGE/Y SOC/WK NEIGH CRIME B67

UTTAR/PRAD....UTTAR PRADESH, INDIA

V

VALENZUELA G. E2066

VALIDITY (AS CONCEPT)....SEE METH/CNCPT

VALUE ADDED TAX....SEE VALUE/ADD

VALUE-FREE THOUGHT....SEE OBJECTIVE

VALUES....SEE VALUES INDEX, P. XIII

VAN CAENEGEM R.C. E2067

VAN DER SPRENKEL S. E2068

VAN ESSEN J.L.F. E1250,E1251

VAN SLYCK P. E2069

VANBUREN/M....PRESIDENT MARTIN VAN BUREN

VANCE H.L. E2070

VANDENBOSCH A. E2071

VANDERPOL A. E2072

VATICAN....VATICAN

VAUGHN W.P. E2073

VEBLEN/T....THORSTEIN VEBLEN

VECCHIO G.D. E2074

VENEZUELA....VENEZUELA; SEE ALSO L/A+17C

CLAGETT H.L.,A GUIDE TO THE LAW AND LEGAL LITERATURE OF VENEZUELA. VENEZUELA CONSTN LABOR LEGIS JUDGE ADJUD ADMIN CIVMIL/REL...CRIMLGY JURID CON/ANAL 20. PAGE 23 E0446
BIBLIOG L/A+17C INT/LAW LAW B47

NEUBURGER O.,GUIDE TO OFFICIAL PUBLICATIONS OF THE OTHER AMERICAN REPUBLICS: VENEZUELA (VOL. XIX). VENEZUELA FINAN LEGIS PLAN BUDGET DIPLOM CT/SYS PARL/PROC 19/20. PAGE 77 E1535
BIBLIOG/A NAT/G CONSTN LAW B48

VENICE....VENETIAN REPUBLIC

VERMONT....VERMONT

VERSAILLES....VERSAILLES, FRANCE

WOLFERS A.,BRITAIN AND FRANCE BETWEEN TWO WORLD WARS. FRANCE UK INT/ORG NAT/G PLAN BARGAIN ECO/TAC AGREE ISOLAT ALL/IDEOS...DECISION GEOG 20 TREATY VERSAILLES INTERVENT. PAGE 107 E2139
DIPLOM WAR POLICY B40

BRETTON H.L.,STRESEMANN AND THE REVISION OF VERSAILLES: A FIGHT FOR REASON. EUR+WWI GERMANY FORCES BUDGET ARMS/CONT WAR SUPEGO...BIBLIOG 20 TREATY VERSAILLES STRESEMN/G. PAGE 15 E0294
POLICY DIPLOM BIOG B53

FISCHER L.,THE SOVIETS IN WORLD AFFAIRS. CHINA/COM COM EUR+WWI USSR INT/ORG CONFER LEAD ARMS/CONT REV PWR...CHARTS 20 TREATY VERSAILLES. PAGE 38 E0755
DIPLOM NAT/G POLICY MARXISM B60

THOMPSON J.M.,RUSSIA, BOLSHEVISM, AND THE VERSAILLES PEACE. RUSSIA USSR INT/ORG NAT/G DELIB/GP AGREE REV WAR PWR 20 TREATY VERSAILLES BOLSHEVISM. PAGE 96 E1919
DIPLOM PEACE MARXISM B66

VERWOERD/H....HENDRIK VERWOERD

VETO....VETO AND VETOING

VICE/PRES....VICE-PRESIDENCY (ALL NATIONS)

FEERICK J.D.,FROM FAILING HANDS: THE STUDY OF PRESIDENTIAL SUCCESSION. CONSTN NAT/G PROB/SOLV LEAD PARL/PROC MURDER CHOOSE...NEW/IDEA BIBLIOG 20 KENNEDY/JF JOHNSON/LB PRESIDENT PRE/US/AM VICE/PRES. PAGE 36 E0724
EX/STRUC CHIEF LAW LEGIS B65

VICEREGAL....VICEROYALTY; VICEROY SYSTEM

VICHY....VICHY, FRANCE

VICTORIA/Q....QUEEN VICTORIA

VIENNA/CNV....VIENNA CONVENTION ON CONSULAR RELATIONS

LEE L.T.,VIENNA CONVENTION ON CONSULAR RELATIONS. WOR+45 LAW INT/ORG CONFER GP/REL PRIVIL...INT/LAW 20 TREATY VIENNA/CNV. PAGE 64 E1277
AGREE DIPLOM ADMIN B66

VIET MINH....SEE VIETNAM, GUERRILLA, COLONIAL

VIET/CONG....VIET CONG

VIETNAM....VIETNAM IN GENERAL; SEE ALSO S/ASIA, VIETNAM/N, VIETNAM/S

EMBREE J.F.,BIBLIOGRAPHY OF THE PEOPLES AND CULTURES OF MAINLAND SOUTHEAST ASIA. CAMBODIA LAOS THAILAND VIETNAM LAW...GEOG HUM SOC MYTH LING CHARTS WORSHIP 20. PAGE 35 E0686
BIBLIOG/A CULTURE S/ASIA B50

FALL B.B.,"THE VIET-MINH REGIME." VIETNAM LAW
ECO/UNDEV POL/PAR FORCES DOMIN WAR ATTIT MARXISM
...BIOG PREDICT BIBLIOG/A 20. PAGE 36 E0720
NAT/G
ADMIN
EX/STRUC
LEAD
C56

LAWYERS COMM AMER POLICY VIET,VIETNAM AND
INTERNATIONAL LAW: AN ANALYSIS OF THE LEGALITY OF
THE US MILITARY INVOLVEMENT. VIETNAM LAW INT/ORG
COERCE WEAPON PEACE ORD/FREE 20 UN SEATO TREATY.
PAGE 64 E1271
INT/LAW
DIPLOM
ADJUD
WAR
B67

RUSSELL B.,WAR CRIMES IN VIETNAM. USA+45 VIETNAM
FORCES DIPLOM WEAPON RACE/REL DISCRIM ISOLAT
BIO/SOC 20 COLD/WAR RUSSELL/B. PAGE 87 E1736
WAR
CRIME
ATTIT
POLICY
B67

US SENATE COMM ON FOREIGN REL,FOREIGN ASSISTANCE
ACT OF 1967. VIETNAM WOR+45 DELIB/GP CONFER CONTROL
WAR WEAPON BAL/PAY...CENSUS CHARTS SENATE. PAGE 102
E2036
FOR/AID
LAW
DIPLOM
POLICY
B67

HULL R.H.,LAW AND VIETNAM. COM VIETNAM CONSTN
INT/ORG FORCES DIPLOM AGREE COERCE DETER WEAPON
PEACE ATTIT 20 UN TREATY. PAGE 56 E1113
POLICY
LAW
WAR
INT/LAW
B68

VIETNAM/N....NORTH VIETNAM

US HOUSE UNAMER ACTIV COMM,HEARINGS ON BILLS TO
MAKE PUNISHABLE ASSISTANCE TO ENEMIES OF US IN TIME
OF UNDECLARED WAR. USA+45 VIETNAM/N EDU/PROP
CONTROL WAR MARXISM HOUSE/REP. PAGE 100 E2010
LAW
SANCTION
VOL/ASSN
GIVE
B66

VIETNAM/S....SOUTH VIETNAM

VIGNES D. E2075

VILE M.J.C. E2076

VILLA/P....PANCHO VILLA

VILLAGE....SEE MUNIC

VILLARD/OG....OSWALD GARRISON VILLARD

VINER J. E2077

VINER/J....JACOB VINER

VINES K.N. E2078,E2079

VINOGRADOFF P. E2080

VIOLENCE....SEE COERCE, ALSO PROCESSES AND PRACTICES INDEX,
    PART G, PAGE XIII

VIRGIN/ISL....VIRGIN ISLANDS

COUNCIL OF STATE GOVERNORS,AMERICAN LEGISLATURES:
STRUCTURE AND PROCEDURES. SUMMARY AND TABULATIONS
OF A 1959 SURVEY. PUERT/RICO USA+45 PAY ADJUD ADMIN
APPORT...IDEA/COMP 20 GUAM VIRGIN/ISL. PAGE 27
E0525
LEGIS
CHARTS
PROVS
REPRESENT
B59

VIRGINIA....VIRGINIA

GREEN F.M.,CONSTITUTIONAL DEVELOPMENT IN THE SOUTH
ATLANTIC STATES: 1776-1860: A STUDY IN THE
EVOLUTION OF DEMOCRACY. USA-45 ELITES SOCIETY
STRATA ECO/DEV AGRI POL/PAR EX/STRUC LEGIS CT/SYS
REGION...BIBLIOG 18/19 MARYLAND VIRGINIA GEORGIA
NORTH/CAR SOUTH/CAR. PAGE 46 E0905
CONSTN
PROVS
PLURISM
REPRESENT
B30

SMITH R.C.,THEY CLOSED THEIR SCHOOLS. USA+45 NEIGH
ADJUD CROWD CONSEN WEALTH...DECISION OBS INT 20
NEGRO VIRGINIA. PAGE 92 E1846
RACE/REL
DISCRIM
LOC/G
SCHOOL
B65

VISTA....VOLUNTEERS IN SERVICE TO AMERICA (VISTA)

VITTACHI T. E2081

VLASIC I.A. E1410

VOGEL J.H. E0372

VOL/ASSN....VOLUNTARY ASSOCIATION

BERNARD M.,FOUR LECTURES ON SUBJECTS CONNECTED WITH
DIPLOMACY. WOR-45 NAT/G VOL/ASSN RIGID/FLEX MORAL
PWR...JURID OBS GEN/LAWS GEN/METH 20 TREATY.
PAGE 11 E0209
LAW
ATTIT
DIPLOM
B00

LORIMER J.,THE INSTITUTES OF THE LAW OF NATIONS.
WOR-45 CULTURE SOCIETY NAT/G VOL/ASSN DIPLOM LEGIT
WAR PEACE DRIVE ORD/FREE SOVEREIGN...CONCPT RECORD
INT TREND HYPO/EXP GEN/METH TOT/POP VAL/FREE 20.
PAGE 66 E1327
INT/ORG
LAW
INT/LAW
B00

GRIFFIN A.P.C.,A LIST OF BOOKS RELATING TO TRUSTS
(2ND REV. ED.) (PAMPHLET). FRANCE GERMANY UK USA-45
WOR-45 LAW ECO/DEV INDUS LG/CO NAT/G CAP/ISM
CENTRAL DISCRIM PWR LAISSEZ 19/20. PAGE 46 E0919
BIBLIOG/A
JURID
ECO/TAC
VOL/ASSN
B02

GRIFFIN A.P.C.,LIST OF REFERENCES ON INDUSTRIAL
ARBITRATION (PAMPHLET). USA-45 STRATA VOL/ASSN
DELIB/GP WORKER ADJUD GP/REL...MGT 19/20. PAGE 46
E0921
BIBLIOG/A
INDUS
LABOR
BARGAIN
B03

BRYCE J.,MODERN DEMOCRACIES. FUT NEW/ZEALND USA-45
LAW CONSTN POL/PAR PROVS VOL/ASSN EX/STRUC LEGIS
LEGIT CT/SYS EXEC KNOWL CONGRESS AUSTRAL 20.
PAGE 16 E0322
NAT/G
TREND
B21

DEWEY J.,"ETHICS AND INTERNATIONAL RELATIONS." FUT
WOR-45 SOCIETY INT/ORG VOL/ASSN DIPLOM LEGIT
ORD/FREE...JURID CONCPT GEN/METH 20. PAGE 31 E0618
LAW
MORAL
S23

NAVILLE A.,LIBERTE, EGALITE, SOLIDARITE: ESSAIS
D'ANALYSE. STRATA FAM VOL/ASSN INT/TRADE GP/REL
MORAL MARXISM SOCISM...PSY TREATY. PAGE 76 E1529
ORD/FREE
SOC
IDEA/COMP
DIPLOM
B24

INSTITUT INTERMEDIAIRE INTL,REPERTOIRE GENERAL DES
TRAITES ET AUTRES ACTES DIPLOMATIQUES CONCLUS
DEPUIS 1895 JUSQU'EN 1920. MOD/EUR WOR-45 INT/ORG
VOL/ASSN DELIB/GP INT/TRADE WAR TREATY 19/20.
PAGE 56 E1125
BIBLIOG
DIPLOM
B26

WOLFF C.,JUS GENTIUM METHODO SCIENTIFICA
PERTRACTATUM. MOD/EUR INT/ORG VOL/ASSN LEGIT PEACE
ATTIT...JURID 20. PAGE 107 E2140
NAT/G
LAW
INT/LAW
WAR
B34

MCMAHON A.H.,"INTERNATIONAL BOUNDARIES." WOR-45
INT/ORG NAT/G LEGIT SKILL...CHARTS GEN/LAWS 20.
PAGE 71 E1423
GEOG
VOL/ASSN
INT/LAW
S35

BROWN A.D.,COMPULSORY MILITARY TRAINING: SELECT
LIST OF REFERENCES (PAMPHLET). USA-45 CONSTN
VOL/ASSN COERCE 20. PAGE 16 E0311
BIBLIOG/A
FORCES
JURID
ATTIT
B40

BRIERLY J.L.,THE OUTLOOK FOR INTERNATIONAL LAW. FUT
WOR-45 CONSTN NAT/G VOL/ASSN FORCES ECO/TAC DOMIN
LEGIT ADJUD ROUTINE PEACE ORD/FREE...INT/LAW JURID
METH LEAGUE/NAT 20. PAGE 15 E0298
INT/ORG
LAW
B44

JACKSON R.H.,INTERNATIONAL CONFERENCE ON MILITARY
TRIALS. FRANCE GERMANY UK USA+45 USSR VOL/ASSN
DELIB/GP REPAR ADJUD CT/SYS CRIME WAR 20 WAR/TRIAL.
PAGE 57 E1141
DIPLOM
INT/ORG
INT/LAW
CIVMIL/REL
B49

BIDDLE F.,THE FEAR OF FREEDOM. USA+45 LAW NAT/G
PUB/INST PROB/SOLV DOMIN CONTROL SANCTION REV
NAT/LISM 20. PAGE 12 E0227
ANOMIE
INGP/REL
VOL/ASSN
ORD/FREE
B51

FORSTER A.,THE TROUBLE MAKERS. USA+45 LAW CULTURE
SOCIETY STRUCT VOL/ASSN CROWD GP/REL MORAL...PSY
SOC CONCPT 20 NEGRO JEWS. PAGE 39 E0771
DISCRIM
SECT
RACE/REL
ATTIT
B52

BENTON W.E.,NUREMBERG: GERMAN VIEWS OF THE WAR
TRIALS. EUR+WWI GERMANY VOL/ASSN LEAD PARTIC COERCE
INGP/REL RACE/REL TOTALISM SUPEGO ORD/FREE...ANTHOL
CRIME
WAR
LAW
B55

NUREMBERG. PAGE 10 E0201   JURID

B55
COMM. STUDY ORGAN. PEACE.REPORTS. WOR-45 ECO/DEV WOR+45
ECO/UNDEV VOL/ASSN CONSULT FORCES PLAN TEC/DEV INT/ORG
DOMIN EDU/PROP NUC/PWR ATTIT PWR WEALTH...JURID ARMS/CONT
STERTYP FAO ILO 20 UN. PAGE 24 E0481

B55
MAZZINI J.,THE DUTIES OF MAN. MOD/EUR LAW SOCIETY SUPEGO
FAM NAT/G POL/PAR SECT VOL/ASSN EX/STRUC ACT/RES CONCPT
CREATE REV PEACE ATTIT ALL/VALS...GEN/LAWS WORK 19. NAT/LISM
PAGE 70 E1396

B55
UN HEADQUARTERS LIBRARY,BIBLIOGRAPHIE DE LA CHARTE BIBLIOG/A
DES NATIONS UNIES. CHINA/COM KOREA WOR+45 VOL/ASSN INT/ORG
CONFER ADMIN COERCE PEACE ATTIT ORD/FREE SOVEREIGN DIPLOM
...INT/LAW 20 UNESCO UN. PAGE 97 E1953

B56
CORBETT P.E.,MORALS LAW, AND POWER IN INTERNATIONAL SUPEGO
RELATIONS. WOR+45 WOR-45 INT/ORG VOL/ASSN DELIB/GP CONCPT
CREATE BAL/PWR DIPLOM LEGIT ARMS/CONT MORAL...JURID POLICY
GEN/LAWS TOT/POP LEAGUE/NAT 20. PAGE 26 E0506 INT/LAW

B56
KUPER L.,PASSIVE RESISTANCE IN SOUTH AFRICA. ORD/FREE
SOUTH/AFR LAW NAT/G POL/PAR VOL/ASSN DISCRIM RACE/REL
...POLICY SOC AUD/VIS 20. PAGE 62 E1237 ATTIT

B57
DIVINE R.A.,AMERICAN IMMIGRATION POLICY, 1924-52. GEOG
USA+45 USA-45 VOL/ASSN DELIB/GP ADJUD WAR ADJUST HABITAT
DISCRIM...POLICY JURID 20 DEPRESSION MIGRATION. LEGIS
PAGE 32 E0630 CONTROL

B57
JENKS C.W.,THE INTERNATIONAL PROTECTION OF TRADE LABOR
UNION FREEDOM. FUT WOR+45 WOR-45 VOL/ASSN DELIB/GP INT/ORG
CT/SYS REGION ROUTINE...JURID METH/CNCPT RECORD
TIME/SEQ CHARTS ILO WORK OAS 20. PAGE 58 E1153

B57
LEVONTIN A.V.,THE MYTH OF INTERNATIONAL SECURITY: A INT/ORG
JURIDICAL AND CRITICAL ANALYSIS. FUT WOR+45 WOR-45 INT/LAW
LAW NAT/G VOL/ASSN ACT/RES BAL/PWR ATTIT ORD/FREE SOVEREIGN
...JURID METH/CNCPT TIME/SEQ TREND STERTYP 20. MYTH
PAGE 64 E1289

B58
HOOD W.C.,FINANCING OF ECONOMIC ACTIVITY IN CANADA. BUDGET
CANADA FUT VOL/ASSN WORKER ECO/TAC ADJUD ADMIN FINAN
...CHARTS 20. PAGE 55 E1093 GP/REL
 ECO/DEV

B58
MANSERGH N.,COMMONWEALTH PERSPECTIVES. GHANA UK LAW DIPLOM
VOL/ASSN CONFER HEALTH SOVEREIGN...GEOG CHARTS COLONIAL
ANTHOL 20 CMN/WLTH AUSTRAL. PAGE 68 E1363 INT/ORG
 INGP/REL

B58
SEYID MUHAMMAD V.A.,THE LEGAL FRAMEWORK OF WORLD INT/LAW
TRADE. WOR+45 INT/ORG DIPLOM CONTROL...BIBLIOG 20 VOL/ASSN
TREATY UN IMF GATT. PAGE 90 E1807 INT/TRADE
 TARIFFS

B58
WOOD J.E.,CHURCH AND STATE IN SCRIPTURE HISTORY AND GP/REL
CONSTITUTIONAL LAW. LAW CONSTN SOCIETY PROVS SECT
VOL/ASSN BAL/PWR COLONIAL CT/SYS ATTIT...BIBLIOG 20 NAT/G
SUPREME/CT CHURCH/STA BIBLE. PAGE 107 E2142 ADJUD

L58
INT. SOC. SCI. BULL.,"TECHNIQUES OF MEDIATION AND VOL/ASSN
CONCILIATION." EUR+WWI USA+45 SOCIETY INDUS INT/ORG DELIB/GP
LABOR NAT/G LEGIS DIPLOM EDU/PROP CHOOSE ATTIT INT/LAW
RIGID/FLEX...JURID CONCPT GEN/LAWS 20. PAGE 57
E1129

S58
VOSE C.E.,"LITIGATION AS A FORM OF PRESSURE GROUP CONTROL
ACTIVITY" (BMR)" USA+45 ADJUD ORD/FREE NAACP. CT/SYS
PAGE 104 E2085 VOL/ASSN
 LOBBY

B59
HOBSBAWM E.J.,PRIMITIVE REBELS; STUDIES IN ARCHAIC SOCIETY
FORMS OF SOCIAL MOVEMENT IN THE 19TH AND 20TH CRIME
CENTURIES. ITALY SPAIN CULTURE VOL/ASSN RISK CROWD REV
GP/REL INGP/REL ISOLAT TOTALISM...PSY SOC 18/20. GUERRILLA
PAGE 53 E1058

B59
KNIERIEM A.,THE NUREMBERG TRIALS. EUR+WWI GERMANY INT/LAW

VOL/ASSN LEAD COERCE WAR INGP/REL TOTALISM SUPEGO CRIME
ORD/FREE...CONCPT METH/COMP. PAGE 61 E1225 PARTIC
 JURID

S59
POTTER P.B.,"OBSTACLES AND ALTERNATIVES TO INT/ORG
INTERNATIONAL LAW." WOR+45 NAT/G VOL/ASSN DELIB/GP LAW
BAL/PWR DOMIN ROUTINE...JURID VAL/FREE 20. PAGE 81 DIPLOM
E1632 INT/LAW

B60
BAKER G.E.,THE POLITICS OF REAPPORTIONMENT IN VOL/ASSN
WASHINGTON STATE. LAW POL/PAR CREATE EDU/PROP APPORT
PARL/PROC CHOOSE INGP/REL...CHARTS METH/COMP 20 PROVS
WASHINGT/G LEAGUE/WV. PAGE 7 E0139 LEGIS

B60
JENKS C.W.,HUMAN RIGHTS AND INTERNATIONAL LABOR CONCPT
STANDARDS. WOR+45 CONSTN LABOR VOL/ASSN DELIB/GP
ACT/RES EDU/PROP MORAL RESPECT...JURID SOC TREND
GEN/LAWS WORK ILO 20. PAGE 58 E1156

B60
JENNINGS R.,PROGRESS OF INTERNATIONAL LAW. FUT INT/ORG
WOR+45 WOR-45 SOCIETY NAT/G VOL/ASSN DELIB/GP LAW
DIPLOM EDU/PROP LEGIT COERCE ATTIT DRIVE MORAL INT/LAW
ORD/FREE...JURID CONCPT OBS TIME/SEQ TREND
GEN/LAWS. PAGE 58 E1164

B60
STEIN E.,AMERICAN ENTERPRISE IN THE EUROPEAN COMMON MARKET
MARKET: A LEGAL PROFILE. EUR+WWI FUT USA+45 SOCIETY ADJUD
STRUCT ECO/DEV NAT/G VOL/ASSN CONSULT PLAN TEC/DEV INT/LAW
ECO/TAC INT/TRADE ADMIN ATTIT RIGID/FLEX PWR...MGT
NEW/IDEA STAT TREND COMPUT/IR SIMUL EEC 20. PAGE 93
E1867

S60
SCHWELB E.,"INTERNATIONAL CONVENTIONS ON HUMAN INT/ORG
RIGHTS." FUT WOR+45 LAW CONSTN CULTURE SOCIETY HUM
STRUCT VOL/ASSN DELIB/GP PLAN ADJUD SUPEGO LOVE
MORAL...SOC CONCPT STAT RECORD HIST/WRIT TREND 20
UN. PAGE 89 E1790

B61
ROBERTSON A.H.,THE LAW OF INTERNATIONAL RIGID/FLEX
INSTITUTIONS IN EUROPE. EUR+WWI MOD/EUR INT/ORG ORD/FREE
NAT/G VOL/ASSN DELIB/GP...JURID TIME/SEQ TOT/POP 20
TREATY. PAGE 85 E1704

L61
FELLMAN D.,"ACADEMIC FREEDOM IN AMERICAN LAW." LAW ACADEM
CONSTN NAT/G VOL/ASSN PLAN PERSON KNOWL NEW/LIB. ORD/FREE
PAGE 37 E0732 LEGIS
 CULTURE

N61
DELEGACION NACIONAL DE PRENSA,FALANGE ESPANOL EDU/PROP
TRADICIONALISTA Y DE LAS JUNTAS OFENSIVAS FASCIST
NACIONALES SINDICALISTAS. IX CONSEJO NACIONAL CONFER
(PAMPHLET). LAW VOL/ASSN TOTALISM AUTHORIT ORD/FREE POL/PAR
FASCISM...ANTHOL 20 FRANCO/F FALANGIST. PAGE 31
E0605

B62
BARLOW R.B.,CITIZENSHIP AND CONSCIENCE: STUDIES IN SECT
THEORY AND PRACTICE OF RELIGIOUS TOLERATION IN LEGIS
ENGLAND DURING EIGHTEENTH CENTURY. UK LAW VOL/ASSN DISCRIM
EDU/PROP SANCTION REV GP/REL MAJORITY ATTIT
ORD/FREE...BIBLIOG WORSHIP 18. PAGE 8 E0150

B62
BEBR G.,JUDICIAL CONTROL OF THE EUROPEAN ADJUD
COMMUNITIES. EUR+WWI INT/ORG NAT/G DOMIN LEGIT PWR VOL/ASSN
...JURID CONCPT GEN/LAWS GEN/METH EEC 20. PAGE 9 INT/LAW
E0168

B62
HEYDECKER J.J.,THE NUREMBERG TRIAL: HISTORY OF NAZI LAW
GERMANY AS REVEALED THROUGH THE TESTIMONY AT CRIME
NUREMBERG. EUR+WWI GERMANY VOL/ASSN LEAD COERCE PARTIC
CROWD INGP/REL RACE/REL SUPEGO ORD/FREE...CONCPT 20 TOTALISM
NAZI ANTI/SEMIT NUREMBERG JEWS. PAGE 52 E1036

B62
LAWSON R.,INTERNATIONAL REGIONAL ORGANIZATIONS. INT/ORG
WOR+45 NAT/G VOL/ASSN CONSULT LEGIS EDU/PROP LEGIT DELIB/GP
ADMIN EXEC ROUTINE HEALTH PWR WEALTH...JURID EEC REGION
COLD/WAR 20 UN. PAGE 63 E1270

B62
SCHWARTZ L.E.,INTERNATIONAL ORGANIZATIONS AND SPACE INT/ORG
COOPERATION. VOL/ASSN CONSULT CREATE TEC/DEV DIPLOM
SANCTION...POLICY INT/LAW PHIL/SCI 20 UN. PAGE 89 R+D
E1787 SPACE

TRISKA J.F.,THE THEORY, LAW, AND POLICY OF SOVIET   COM   B62
TREATIES. WOR+45 WOR-45 CONSTN INT/ORG NAT/G   LAW
VOL/ASSN DOMIN LEGIT COERCE ATTIT PWR RESPECT   INT/LAW
...POLICY JURID CONCPT OBS SAMP TIME/SEQ TREND   USSR
GEN/LAWS 20. PAGE 97 E1941

US CONGRESS,COMMUNICATIONS SATELLITE LEGISLATION: SPACE   B62
HEARINGS BEFORE COMM ON AERON AND SPACE SCIENCES ON COM/IND
BILLS S2550 AND 2814. WOR+45 LAW VOL/ASSN PLAN   ADJUD
DIPLOM CONTROL OWN PEACE...NEW/IDEA CONGRESS NASA.   GOV/REL
PAGE 99 E1990

GROSS L.,"IMMUNITIES AND PRIVILEGES OF DELIGATIONS INT/ORG   L62
TO THE UNITED NATIONS." USA+45 WOR+45 STRATA NAT/G LAW
VOL/ASSN CONSULT DIPLOM EDU/PROP ROUTINE RESPECT   ELITES
...POLICY INT/LAW CONCPT UN 20. PAGE 48 E0950

FENWICK C.G.,"ISSUES AT PUNTA DEL ESTE: NON-   INT/ORG   S62
INTERVENTION VS COLLECTIVE SECURITY." L/A+17C   CUBA
USA+45 VOL/ASSN DELIB/GP ECO/TAC LEGIT ADJUD REGION
ORD/FREE OAS COLD/WAR 20. PAGE 37 E0738

FINKELSTEIN L.S.,"THE UNITED NATIONS AND   INT/ORG   S62
ORGANIZATIONS FOR CONTROL OF ARMAMENT." FUT WOR+45 PWR
VOL/ASSN DELIB/GP TOP/EX CREATE EDU/PROP LEGIT   ARMS/CONT
ADJUD NUC/PWR ATTIT RIGID/FLEX ORD/FREE...POLICY
DECISION CONCPT OBS TREND GEN/LAWS TOT/POP
COLD/WAR. PAGE 38 E0752

FAWCETT J.E.S.,THE BRITISH COMMONWEALTH IN   INT/LAW   B63
INTERNATIONAL LAW. LAW INT/ORG NAT/G VOL/ASSN   STRUCT
OP/RES DIPLOM ADJUD CENTRAL CONSEN...NET/THEORY   COLONIAL
CMN/WLTH TREATY. PAGE 36 E0723

LEAGUE WOMEN VOTERS NEW YORK,APPORTIONMENT WORKSHOP APPORT   B63
KIT. USA+45 VOL/ASSN DELIB/GP LEGIS ATTIT ORD/FREE REPRESENT
...METH/COMP 20 SUPREME/CT NEW/YORK. PAGE 64 E1275   PROVS
                          JURID

ROBERTSON A.H.,HUMAN RIGHTS IN EUROPE. CONSTN   EUR+WWI   B63
SOCIETY INT/ORG NAT/G VOL/ASSN DELIB/GP ACT/RES   PERSON
PLAN ADJUD REGION ROUTINE ATTIT LOVE ORD/FREE
RESPECT...JURID SOC CONCPT SOC/EXP UN 20. PAGE 85
E1705

US COMMISSION ON CIVIL RIGHTS,FREEDOM TO THE FREE. RACE/REL   B63
USA+45 USA-45 LAW VOL/ASSN CT/SYS ATTIT PWR...JURID DISCRIM
BIBLIOG 17/20 SUPREME/CT NEGRO CIV/RIGHTS. PAGE 99 NAT/G
E1986   POLICY

BOHN L.,"WHOSE NUCLEAR TEST: NON-PHYSICAL   ADJUD   S63
INSPECTION AND TEST BAN." WOR+45 R+D INT/ORG   ARMS/CONT
VOL/ASSN ORD/FREE...GEN/LAWS GEN/METH COLD/WAR 20. TEC/DEV
PAGE 13 E0262   NUC/PWR

HARNETTY P.,"CANADA, SOUTH AFRICA AND THE   AFR   S63
COMMONWEALTH." CANADA SOUTH/AFR LAW INT/ORG   ATTIT
VOL/ASSN DELIB/GP LEGIS TOP/EX ECO/TAC LEGIT DRIVE
MORAL...CONCPT CMN/WLTH 20. PAGE 50 E1000

MODELSKI G.,"STUDY OF ALLIANCES." WOR+45 WOR-45   VOL/ASSN   S63
INT/ORG NAT/G FORCES LEGIT ADMIN CHOOSE ALL/VALS   CON/ANAL
PWR SKILL...INT/LAW CONCPT GEN/LAWS 20 TREATY.   DIPLOM
PAGE 74 E1477

TALLON D.,"L'ETUDE DU DROIT COMPARE COMME MOYEN DE INT/ORG   S63
RECHERCHER LES MATIERES SUSCEPTIBLES D'UNIFICATION JURID
INTERNATIONALE." WOR+45 LAW SOCIETY VOL/ASSN   INT/LAW
CONSULT LEGIT CT/SYS RIGID/FLEX KNOWL 20. PAGE 95
E1906

WALKER H.,"THE INTERNATIONAL LAW OF COMMODITY   MARKET   S63
AGREEMENTS." FUT WOR+45 ECO/DEV ECO/UNDEV FINAN   VOL/ASSN
INT/ORG NAT/G CONSULT CREATE PLAN ECO/TAC ATTIT   INT/LAW
PERCEPT...CONCPT GEN/LAWS TOT/POP GATT 20. PAGE 105 INT/TRADE
E2095

DIAS R.W.M.,A BIBLIOGRAPHY OF JURISPRUDENCE (2ND   BIBLIOG/A   B64
ED.). VOL/ASSN LEGIS ADJUD CT/SYS OWN...INT/LAW   JURID
18/20. PAGE 31 E0619   LAW
                            CONCPT

GARDNER L.C.,ECONOMIC ASPECTS OF NEW DEAL   ECO/TAC   B64
DIPLOMACY. USA-45 WOR-45 LAW ECO/DEV INT/ORG NAT/G DIPLOM
VOL/ASSN LEGIS TOP/EX EDU/PROP ORD/FREE PWR WEALTH
...POLICY TIME/SEQ VAL/FREE 20 ROOSEVLT/F. PAGE 42
E0836

GRIFFITH W.E.,THE SINO-SOVIET RIFT. ASIA CHINA/COM ATTIT   B64
COM CUBA USSR YUGOSLAVIA NAT/G POL/PAR VOL/ASSN   TIME/SEQ
DELIB/GP FORCES TOP/EX DIPLOM EDU/PROP DRIVE PERSON BAL/PWR
PWR...TREND 20 TREATY. PAGE 47 E0941   SOCISM

HEKHUIS D.J.,INTERNATIONAL STABILITY: MILITARY,   TEC/DEV   B64
ECONOMIC AND POLITICAL DIMENSIONS. FUT WOR+45 LAW   DETER
ECO/UNDEV INT/ORG NAT/G VOL/ASSN FORCES ACT/RES   REGION
BAL/PWR PWR WEALTH...STAT UN 20. PAGE 51 E1024

IKLE F.C.,HOW NATIONS NEGOTIATE. COM EUR+WWI USA+45 NAT/G   B64
INTELL INT/ORG VOL/ASSN DELIB/GP ACT/RES CREATE   PWR
DOMIN EDU/PROP ADJUD ROUTINE ATTIT PERSON ORD/FREE POLICY
RESPECT SKILL...PSY SOC OBS VAL/FREE. PAGE 56 E1122

OPPENHEIMER M.,A MANUAL FOR DIRECT ACTION. USA+45   PLAN   B64
SCHOOL FORCES ADJUD CT/SYS SUFF RACE/REL DISCRIM   VOL/ASSN
...POLICY CHARTS 20. PAGE 79 E1580   JURID
                            LEAD

A CHECK LIST OF THE SPECIAL AND STANDING COMMITTEES BIBLIOG   B64
OF THE AMERICAN BAR ASSOCIATION (VOL. II). USA+45   LAW
LEGIS PRESS CONFER...JURID CON/ANAL. PAGE 80 E1607 VOL/ASSN

DERWINSKI E.J.,"THE COST OF THE INTERNATIONAL   MARKET   S64
COFFEE AGREEMENT." L/A+17C USA+45 WOR+45 ECO/UNDEV DELIB/GP
NAT/G VOL/ASSN LEGIS DIPLOM ECO/TAC FOR/AID LEGIT   INT/TRADE
ATTIT...TIME/SEQ CONGRESS 20 TREATY. PAGE 31 E0608

GARDNER R.N.,"THE SOVIET UNION AND THE UNITED   COM   S64
NATIONS." WOR+45 FINAN POL/PAR VOL/ASSN FORCES   INT/ORG
ECO/TAC DOMIN EDU/PROP LEGIT ADJUD ADMIN ARMS/CONT USSR
COERCE ATTIT ALL/VALS...POLICY MAJORIT CONCPT OBS
TIME/SEQ TREND STERTYP UN. PAGE 42 E0838

KARPOV P.V.,"PEACEFUL COEXISTENCE AND INTERNATIONAL COM   S64
LAW." WOR+45 LAW SOCIETY INT/ORG VOL/ASSN FORCES   ATTIT
CREATE CAP/ISM DIPLOM ADJUD NUC/PWR PEACE MORAL   INT/LAW
ORD/FREE PWR MARXISM...MARXIST JURID CONCPT OBS   USSR
TREND COLD/WAR MARX/KARL 20. PAGE 59 E1186

CARTER G.M.,POLITICS IN EUROPE. EUR+WWI FRANCE   GOV/COMP   B65
GERMANY/W UK USSR LAW CONSTN POL/PAR VOL/ASSN PRESS OP/RES
LOBBY PWR...ANTHOL SOC/INTEG EEC. PAGE 20 E0399   ECO/DEV

KING D.B.,LEGAL ASPECTS OF THE CIVIL RIGHTS   LAW   B65
MOVEMENT. SERV/IND VOL/ASSN LEGIS EDU/PROP ADJUD   DISCRIM
PARTIC CHOOSE...JURID SEGREGAT WORK. PAGE 61 E1215 TREND

NJ LEGIS REAPPORT PLAN COMM,PUBLIC HEARING ON   APPORT   B65
REDISTRICTING AND REAPPORTIONMENT. USA+45 CONSTN   REPRESENT
VOL/ASSN LEGIS DEBATE...POLICY GEOG CENSUS 20   PROVS
NEW/JERSEY. PAGE 77 E1552   JURID

PADELFORD N.,THE UNITED NATIONS IN THE BALANCE*   INT/ORG   B65
ACCOMPLISHMENTS AND PROSPECTS. NAT/G VOL/ASSN   CONTROL
DIPLOM ADMIN COLONIAL CT/SYS REGION WAR ORD/FREE
...ANTHOL UN. PAGE 79 E1588

SOPER T.,EVOLVING COMMONWEALTH. AFR CANADA INDIA   INT/ORG   B65
IRELAND UK LAW CONSTN POL/PAR DOMIN CONTROL WAR PWR COLONIAL
...AUD/VIS 18/20 COMMONWLTH OEEC. PAGE 93 E1857   VOL/ASSN

UNESCO,HANDBOOK OF INTERNATIONAL EXCHANGES. COM/IND INDEX   B65
R+D ACADEM PROF/ORG VOL/ASSN CREATE TEC/DEV   INT/ORG
EDU/PROP AGREE 20 TREATY. PAGE 98 E1963   DIPLOM
                             PRESS

US SENATE,US INTERNATIONAL SPACE PROGRAMS, 1959-65: SPACE   B65
STAFF REPORT FOR COMM ON AERONAUTICAL AND SPACE   DIPLOM
SCIENCES. WOR+45 VOL/ASSN CIVMIL/REL 20 CONGRESS   PLAN
NASA TREATY. PAGE 101 E2027   GOV/REL

AMRAM P.W.,"REPORT ON THE TENTH SESSION OF THE
HAGUE CONFERENCE ON PRIVATE INTERNATIONAL LAW."
USA+45 WOR+45 INT/ORG CREATE LEGIT ADJUD ALL/VALS
...JURID CONCPT METH/CNCPT OBS GEN/METH 20. PAGE 4
E0085

S65
VOL/ASSN
DELIB/GP
INT/LAW

HAZARD J.N.,"CO-EXISTENCE LAW BOWS OUT." WOR+45 R+D
INT/ORG VOL/ASSN CONSULT DELIB/GP ACT/RES CREATE
PEACE KNOWL...JURID CONCPT COLD/WAR VAL/FREE 20.
PAGE 51 E1018

S65
PROF/ORG
ADJUD

HIBBS A.R.,"SPACE TECHNOLOGY* THE THREAT AND THE
PROMISE." FUT VOL/ASSN TEC/DEV NUC/PWR COST
EFFICIENCY UTIL UN TREATY. PAGE 52 E1038

S65
SPACE
ARMS/CONT
PREDICT

MARTIN A.,"PROLIFERATION." FUT WOR+45 PROB/SOLV
REGION ADJUST...PREDICT NAT/COMP UN TREATY. PAGE 69
E1372

S65
RECORD
NUC/PWR
ARMS/CONT
VOL/ASSN

FRIEDMANN W.G.,INTERNATIONAL FINANCIAL AID. USA+45
ECO/DEV ECO/UNDEV NAT/G VOL/ASSN EX/STRUC PLAN RENT
GIVE BAL/PAY PWR...GEOG INT/LAW STAT TREND UN EEC
COMECON. PAGE 41 E0806

B66
INT/ORG
FOR/AID
TEC/DEV
ECO/TAC

GRUNEWALD D.,PUBLIC POLICY AND THE MODERN
COOPERATION: SELECTED READINGS. USA+45 LAW MARKET
VOL/ASSN CAP/ISM INT/TRADE CENTRAL OWN...SOC ANTHOL
20. PAGE 48 E0954

B66
LG/CO
POLICY
NAT/G
CONTROL

HAY P.,FEDERALISM AND SUPRANATIONAL ORGANIZATIONS:
PATTERNS FOR NEW LEGAL STRUCTURES. EUR+WWI LAW
NAT/G VOL/ASSN DIPLOM PWR...NAT/COMP TREATY EEC.
PAGE 51 E1014

B66
SOVEREIGN
FEDERAL
INT/ORG
INT/LAW

O'NEILL C.E.,CHURCH AND STATE IN FRENCH COLONIAL
LOUISIANA: POLICY AND POLITICS TO 1732. PROVS
VOL/ASSN DELIB/GP ADJUD ADMIN GP/REL ATTIT DRIVE
...POLICY BIBLIOG 17/18 LOUISIANA CHURCH/STA.
PAGE 78 E1568

B66
COLONIAL
NAT/G
SECT
PWR

US HOUSE UNAMER ACTIV COMM,HEARINGS ON BILLS TO
MAKE PUNISHABLE ASSISTANCE TO ENEMIES OF US IN TIME
OF UNDECLARED WAR. USA+45 VIETNAM/N EDU/PROP
CONTROL WAR MARXISM HOUSE/REP. PAGE 100 E2010

B66
LAW
SANCTION
VOL/ASSN
GIVE

YALEM R.J.,"THE STUDY OF INTERNATIONAL
ORGANIZATION, 1920-1965* A SURVEY OF THE
LITERATURE." WOR+45 WOR-45 REGION...INT/LAW CLASSIF
RECORD HIST/WRIT CON/ANAL IDEA/COMP UN. PAGE 108
E2163

L66
VOL/ASSN
INT/ORG
BIBLIOG/A

BROWNLIE I.,"NUCLEAR PROLIFERATION* SOME PROBLEMS
OF CONTROL." USA+45 USSR ECO/UNDEV INT/ORG FORCES
TEC/DEV REGION CONSEN...RECORD TREATY. PAGE 16
E0318

S66
NUC/PWR
ARMS/CONT
VOL/ASSN
ORD/FREE

SLATER J.,THE OAS AND UNITED STATES FOREIGN POLICY.
KOREA L/A+17C USA+45 VOL/ASSN RISK COERCE PEACE
ORD/FREE MARXISM...TREND 20 OAS. PAGE 92 E1838

B67
INT/ORG
DIPLOM
ALL/IDEOS
ADJUD

LAMBERT J.D.,"CORPORATE POLITICAL SPENDING AND
CAMPAIGN FINANCE." LAW CONSTN FINAN LABOR LG/CO
LOC/G NAT/G VOL/ASSN TEC/DEV ADJUD ADMIN PARTIC.
PAGE 62 E1247

L67
USA+45
POL/PAR
CHOOSE
COST

BLAKEY G.R.,"ORGANIZED CRIME IN THE UNITED STATES."
USA+45 USA-45 STRUCT LABOR NAT/G VOL/ASSN ADMIN
PERS/REL PWR...CRIMLGY INT 17/20. PAGE 12 E0240

S67
CRIME
ELITES
CONTROL

GIBSON G.H.,"LABOR PIRACY ON THE BRANDYWINE."
USA-45 INDUS R+D VOL/ASSN CAP/ISM ADJUD DRIVE...PSY
19. PAGE 43 E0859

S67
ECO/TAC
CREATE
TEC/DEV
WORKER

HILL D.G.,"HUMAN RIGHTS LEGISLATION IN ONTARIO."
CANADA R+D VOL/ASSN CONSULT INSPECT EDU/PROP ADJUD
AGREE TASK GP/REL INGP/REL DISCRIM 20 CIV/RIGHTS
ONTARIO CIVIL/LIB. PAGE 52 E1045

S67
DELIB/GP
ORD/FREE
LAW
POLICY

HUBERT C.J.,"PLANNED UNIT DEVELOPMENT" LAW VOL/ASSN
LEGIS EDU/PROP CT/SYS GOV/REL...NEW/IDEA 20
PLAN/UNIT. PAGE 56 E1107

S67
PLAN
MUNIC
HABITAT
ADJUD

VOLTAIRE.....VOLTAIRE (FRANCOIS MARIE AROUET)

VOLUNTARY ASSOCIATIONS....SEE VOL/ASSN

VON GLAHN G. E2082

VON RENESSE E.A. E2083

VON/TRESCK....VON TRESCKOW

VONGLAHN G. E2084

VOSE C.E. E2085,E2086

VOTING....SEE CHOOSE, SUFF

VTOL....VERTICAL TAKE-OFF AND LANDING AIRCRAFT

W

WADE E.C.S. E2087

WADE H.W.R. E2088

WADSWORTH J.J. E2089

WAELBROECK M. E2090

WAGES....SEE PRICE, WORKER, WEALTH

WAGNER J.B. E0773

WAGNER W.J. E2091

WAGNER/A....ADOLPH WAGNER

WAINHOUSE D.W. E2092

WALES....WALES

WALINE M. E2093

WALKER H. E2094,E2095

WALKER/E....EDWIN WALKER

WALL E.H. E2096

WALLACE E. E1795

WALLACE/G....GEORGE WALLACE

WALLACE/HA....HENRY A. WALLACE

WALTER P.A.F. E2097

WALTZ/KN....KENNETH N. WALTZ

WAR....SEE ALSO COERCE

LONDON INSTITUTE WORLD AFFAIRS,THE YEAR BOOK OF
WORLD AFFAIRS. FINAN BAL/PWR ARMS/CONT WAR
...INT/LAW BIBLIOG 20. PAGE 66 E1322

N
DIPLOM
FOR/AID
INT/ORG

TOSCANO M.,THE HISTORY OF TREATIES AND
INTERNATIONAL POLITICS (REV. ED.). WOR-45 AGREE WAR
...BIOG 19/20 TREATY WWI. PAGE 97 E1935

N
DIPLOM
INT/ORG

AMERICAN JOURNAL OF INTERNATIONAL LAW. WOR+45
WOR-45 CONSTN INT/ORG NAT/G CT/SYS ARMS/CONT WAR
...DECISION JURID NAT/COMP 20. PAGE 1 E0001

N
BIBLIOG/A
INT/LAW
DIPLOM
ADJUD

INTERNATIONAL AFFAIRS. WOR+45 WOR-45 ECO/UNDEV
INT/ORG NAT/G PROB/SOLV FOR/AID WAR...POLICY 20.
PAGE 1 E0007

N
BIBLIOG/A
DIPLOM
INT/LAW
INT/TRADE

JOURNAL OF INTERNATIONAL AFFAIRS. WOR+45 ECO/UNDEV
POL/PAR ECO/TAC WAR PEACE PERSON ALL/IDEOS
...INT/LAW TREND. PAGE 1 E0010

N
BIBLIOG
DIPLOM
INT/ORG
NAT/G

BIBLIOGRAPHIE DER SOZIALWISSENSCHAFTEN. WOR-45 CONSTN SOCIETY ECO/DEV ECO/UNDEV DIPLOM LEAD WAR PEACE...PHIL/SCI SOC 19/20. PAGE 1 E0019
N
BIBLIOG
LAW
CONCPT
NAT/G

AIR UNIVERSITY LIBRARY,INDEX TO MILITARY PERIODICALS. FUT SPACE WOR+45 REGION ARMS/CONT NUC/PWR WAR PEACE INT/LAW. PAGE 3 E0056
N
BIBLIOG/A
FORCES
NAT/G
DIPLOM

TURNER R.K.,BIBLIOGRAPHY ON WORLD ORGANIZATION. INT/TRADE CT/SYS ARMS/CONT WEALTH...INT/LAW 20. PAGE 97 E1944
N
BIBLIOG/A
INT/ORG
PEACE
WAR

UNITED NATIONS,UNITED NATIONS PUBLICATIONS. WOR+45 ECO/UNDEV AGRI FINAN FORCES ADMIN LEAD WAR PEACE ...POLICY INT/LAW 20 UN. PAGE 98 E1965
N
BIBLIOG
INT/ORG
DIPLOM

BATY T.,INTERNATIONAL LAW IN SOUTH AFRICA. AFR SOUTH/AFR LAW CONFER 19/20. PAGE 8 E0155
B00
JURID
WAR
SOVEREIGN
COLONIAL

DE TOCQUEVILLE A.,DEMOCRACY IN AMERICA (VOLUME ONE). LAW SOCIETY STRUCT NAT/G POL/PAR PROVS FORCES LEGIS TOP/EX DIPLOM LEGIT WAR PEACE ATTIT SOVEREIGN ...SELF/OBS TIME/SEQ CONGRESS 19. PAGE 30 E0594
B00
USA-45
TREND

GROTIUS H.,DE JURE BELLI AC PACIS. CHRIST-17C UNIV LAW SOCIETY PROVS LEGIT PEACE PERCEPT MORAL PWR ...CONCPT CON/ANAL GEN/LAWS. PAGE 48 E0952
B00
JURID
INT/LAW
WAR

HOLLAND T.E.,STUDIES IN INTERNATIONAL LAW. TURKEY USSR WOR-45 CONSTN NAT/G DIPLOM DOMIN LEGIT COERCE WAR PEACE ORD/FREE PWR SOVEREIGN...JURID CHARTS 20 PARLIAMENT SUEZ TREATY. PAGE 54 E1084
B00
INT/ORG
LAW
INT/LAW

LORIMER J.,THE INSTITUTES OF THE LAW OF NATIONS. WOR-45 CULTURE SOCIETY NAT/G VOL/ASSN DIPLOM LEGIT WAR PEACE DRIVE ORD/FREE SOVEREIGN...CONCPT RECORD INT TREND HYPO/EXP GEN/METH TOT/POP VAL/FREE 20. PAGE 66 E1327
B00
INT/ORG
LAW
INT/LAW

MAINE H.S.,INTERNATIONAL LAW. MOD/EUR UNIV SOCIETY STRUCT ACT/RES EXEC WAR ATTIT PERSON ALL/VALS ...POLICY JURID CONCPT OBS TIME/SEQ TOT/POP. PAGE 68 E1349
B00
INT/ORG
LAW
PEACE
INT/LAW

HISTORICUS,"LETTERS AND SOME QUESTIONS OF INTERNATIONAL LAW." FRANCE NETHERLAND UK USA-45 WOR-45 LAW NAT/G COERCE...SOC CONCPT GEN/LAWS TOT/POP 19 CIVIL/WAR. PAGE 53 E1054
L00
WEALTH
JURID
WAR
INT/LAW

CHANNING W.E.,DISCOURSES ON WAR (1820-1840). LAW SECT DIPLOM INT/TRADE ALL/VALS. PAGE 21 E0418
B03
WAR
PLAN
LOVE
ORD/FREE

DUNNING W.A.,"HISTORY OF POLITICAL THEORIES FROM LUTHER TO MONTESQUIEU." LAW NAT/G SECT DIPLOM REV WAR ORD/FREE SOVEREIGN CONSERVE...TRADIT BIBLIOG 16/18. PAGE 33 E0663
C05
PHIL/SCI
CONCPT
GEN/LAWS

HOLLAND T.E.,LETTERS UPON WAR AND NEUTRALITY. WOR-45 NAT/G FORCES JUDGE ECO/TAC LEGIT CT/SYS NEUTRAL ROUTINE COERCE...JURID TIME/SEQ 20. PAGE 55 E1085
B09
LAW
INT/LAW
INT/ORG
WAR

BORCHARD E.M.,BIBLIOGRAPHY OF INTERNATIONAL LAW AND CONTINENTAL LAW. EUR+WWI MOD/EUR UK LAW INT/TRADE WAR PEACE...GOV/COMP NAT/COMP 19/20. PAGE 14 E0267
B13
BIBLIOG
INT/LAW
JURID
DIPLOM

PUFENDORF S.,LAW OF NATURE AND OF NATIONS (ABRIDGED). UNIV LAW NAT/G DIPLOM AGREE WAR PERSON ALL/VALS PWR...POLICY 18 DEITY NATURL/LAW. PAGE 83 E1659
B16
CONCPT
INT/LAW
SECT
MORAL

SCHROEDER T.,FREE SPEECH FOR RADICALS (REV. ED.). USA-45 CONSTN INDUS LOC/G FORCES SANCTION WAR ATTIT SEX...JURID REFORMERS 20 FREE/SPEE. PAGE 88 E1767
B16
ORD/FREE
CONTROL
LAW
PRESS

WRIGHT Q.,"THE ENFORCEMENT OF INTERNATIONAL LAW THROUGH MUNICIPAL LAW IN THE US." USA-45 LOC/G NAT/G PUB/INST FORCES LEGIT CT/SYS PERCEPT ALL/VALS ...JURID 20. PAGE 107 E2149
L16
INT/ORG
LAW
INT/LAW
WAR

DE VICTORIA F.,DE INDIS ET DE JURE BELLI (1557) IN F. DE VICTORIA, DE INDIS ET DE JURE BELLI REFLECTIONES. UNIV NAT/G SECT CHIEF PARTIC COERCE PEACE MORAL...POLICY 16 INDIAN/AM CHRISTIAN CONSCN/OBJ. PAGE 30 E0598
B17
WAR
INT/LAW
OWN

PORTER K.H.,A HISTORY OF SUFFRAGE IN THE UNITED STATES. USA-45 LAW CONSTN LOC/G NAT/G POL/PAR WAR DISCRIM OWN ATTIT SEX 18/20 NEGRO FEMALE/SEX. PAGE 81 E1629
B18
SUFF
REPRESENT
CHOOSE
PARTIC

WILSON W.,THE STATE: ELEMENTS OF HISTORICAL AND PRACTICAL POLITICS. FRANCE GERMANY ITALY UK USSR CONSTN EX/STRUC LEGIS CT/SYS WAR PWR...POLICY GOV/COMP 20. PAGE 106 E2131
B18
NAT/G
JURID
CONCPT
NAT/COMP

LONDON SCHOOL ECONOMICS-POL,ANNUAL DIGEST OF PUBLIC INTERNATIONAL LAW CASES. INT/ORG MUNIC NAT/G PROVS ADMIN NEUTRAL WAR GOV/REL PRIVIL 20. PAGE 66 E1323
B19
BIBLIOG/A
INT/LAW
ADJUD
DIPLOM

VANDERPOL A.,LA DOCTRINE SCOLASTIQUE DU DROIT DE GUERRE. CHRIST-17C FORCES DIPLOM LEGIT SUPEGO MORAL ...BIOG AQUINAS/T SUAREZ/F CHRISTIAN. PAGE 103 E2072
B19
WAR
SECT
INT/LAW

STOWELL E.C.,INTERVENTION IN INTERNATIONAL LAW. UNIV LAW SOCIETY INT/ORG ACT/RES PLAN LEGIT ROUTINE WAR...JURID OBS GEN/LAWS 20. PAGE 94 E1884
B21
BAL/PWR
SOVEREIGN

HALL W.E.,A TREATISE ON INTERNATIONAL LAW. WOR-45 CONSTN INT/ORG NAT/G DIPLOM ORD/FREE LEAGUE/NAT 20 TREATY. PAGE 49 E0985
B24
PWR
JURID
WAR
INT/LAW

INSTITUT INTERMEDIAIRE INTL,REPERTOIRE GENERAL DES TRAITES ET AUTRES ACTES DIPLOMATIQUES CONCLUS DEPUIS 1895 JUSQU'EN 1920. MOD/EUR WOR-45 INT/ORG VOL/ASSN DELIB/GP INT/TRADE WAR TREATY 19/20. PAGE 56 E1125
B26
BIBLIOG
DIPLOM

STURZO L.,THE INTERNATIONAL COMMUNITY AND THE RIGHT OF WAR (TRANS. BY BARBARA BARCLAY CARTER). CULTURE CREATE PROB/SOLV DIPLOM ADJUD CONTROL PEACE PERSON ORD/FREE...INT/LAW IDEA/COMP PACIFIST 20 LEAGUE/NAT. PAGE 94 E1891
B29
INT/ORG
PLAN
WAR
CONCPT

COLUMBIA UNIVERSITY,A BIBLIOGRAPHY OF THE FACULTY OF POLITICAL SCIENCE OF COLUMBIA UNIVERSITY, 1880-1930. USA-45 LAW NAT/G LEGIS DIPLOM LEAD WAR GOV/REL ATTIT...TIME/SEQ 19/20. PAGE 24 E0478
B31
BIBLIOG
ACADEM
PHIL/SCI

GENTILI A.,DE JURE BELLI, LIBRI TRES (1612) (VOL. 2). FORCES DIPLOM AGREE PEACE SOVEREIGN. PAGE 43 E0849
B33
WAR
INT/LAW
MORAL
SUPEGO

LAUTERPACHT H.,THE FUNCTION OF LAW IN THE INTERNATIONAL COMMUNITY. WOR-45 NAT/G FORCES CREATE DOMIN LEGIT COERCE WAR PEACE ATTIT ORD/FREE PWR SOVEREIGN...JURID CONCPT METH/CNCPT TIME/SEQ GEN/LAWS GEN/METH LEAGUE/NAT TOT/POP VAL/FREE 20. PAGE 63 E1265
B33
INT/ORG
LAW
INT/LAW

REID H.D.,RECUEIL DES COURS; TOME 45: LES SERVITUDES INTERNATIONALES III. FRANCE CONSTN DELIB/GP PRESS CONTROL REV WAR CHOOSE PEACE MORAL MARITIME TREATY. PAGE 84 E1680
B33
ORD/FREE
DIPLOM
LAW

WOLFF C.,JUS GENTIUM METHODO SCIENTIFICA
B34
NAT/G

PERTRACTATUM. MOD/EUR INT/ORG VOL/ASSN LEGIT PEACE LAW
ATTIT...JURID 20. PAGE 107 E2140   INT/LAW
                                                         WAR

B35
FOREIGN AFFAIRS BIBLIOGRAPHY: A SELECTED AND   BIBLIOG/A
ANNOTATED LIST OF BOOKS ON INTERNATIONAL RELATIONS   DIPLOM
1919-1962 (4 VOLS.). CONSTN FORCES COLONIAL   INT/ORG
ARMS/CONT WAR NAT/LISM PEACE ATTIT DRIVE...POLICY
INT/LAW 20. PAGE 2 E0032

B36
BRIERLY J.L.,THE LAW OF NATIONS (2ND ED.). WOR+45   DIPLOM
WOR-45 INT/ORG AGREE CONTROL COERCE WAR NAT/LISM   INT/LAW
PEACE PWR 16/20 TREATY LEAGUE/NAT. PAGE 15 E0297   NAT/G

B36
HUDSON M.O.,INTERNATIONAL LEGISLATION: 1929-1931.   INT/LAW
WOR-45 SEA AIR AGRI FINAN LABOR DIPLOM ECO/TAC   PARL/PROC
REPAR CT/SYS ARMS/CONT WAR WEAPON...JURID 20 TREATY   ADJUD
LEAGUE/NAT. PAGE 56 E1112   LAW

B37
HAMILTON W.H.,THE POWER TO GOVERN. ECO/DEV FINAN   LING
INDUS ECO/TAC INT/TRADE TARIFFS TAX CONTROL CT/SYS   CONSTN
WAR COST PWR 18/20 SUPREME/CT. PAGE 50 E0991   NAT/G
                                                       POLICY

B37
KETCHAM E.H.,PRELIMINARY SELECT BIBLIOGRAPHY OF   BIBLIOG
INTERNATIONAL LAW (PAMPHLET). WOR-45 LAW INT/ORG   DIPLOM
NAT/G PROB/SOLV CT/SYS NEUTRAL WAR 19/20. PAGE 60   ADJUD
E1207   INT/LAW

B38
GRISWOLD A.W.,THE FAR EASTERN POLICY OF THE UNITED   DIPLOM
STATES. ASIA S/ASIA USA-45 INT/ORG INT/TRADE WAR   POLICY
NAT/LISM...BIBLIOG 19/20 LEAGUE/NAT ROOSEVLT/T   CHIEF
ROOSEVLT/F WILSON/W TREATY. PAGE 47 E0943

B38
HAGUE PERMANENT CT INTL JUSTIC,WORLD COURT REPORTS: INT/ORG
COLLECTION OF THE JUDGEMENTS ORDERS AND OPINIONS   CT/SYS
VOLUME 3 1932-35. WOR-45 LAW DELIB/GP CONFER WAR   DIPLOM
PEACE ATTIT...DECISION ANTHOL 20 WORLD/CT CASEBOOK.   ADJUD
PAGE 49 E0976

B38
MCNAIR A.D.,THE LAW OF TREATIES: BRITISH PRACTICE   AGREE
AND OPINIONS. UK CREATE DIPLOM LEGIT WRITING ADJUD   LAW
WAR...INT/LAW JURID TREATY. PAGE 71 E1424   CT/SYS
                                                       NAT/G

B38
SAINT-PIERRE C.I.,SCHEME FOR LASTING PEACE (TRANS.   INT/ORG
BY H. BELLOT). INDUS NAT/G CHIEF FORCES INT/TRADE   PEACE
CT/SYS WAR PWR SOVEREIGN WEALTH...POLICY 18.   AGREE
PAGE 87 E1741   INT/LAW

B39
BENES E.,INTERNATIONAL SECURITY. GERMANY UK NAT/G   EUR+WWI
DELIB/GP PLAN BAL/PWR ATTIT ORD/FREE PWR LEAGUE/NAT   INT/ORG
20 TREATY. PAGE 10 E0186   WAR

B39
WILSON G.G.,HANDBOOK OF INTERNATIONAL LAW. FUT UNIV   INT/ORG
USA-45 WOR-45 SOCIETY LEGIT ATTIT DISPL DRIVE   LAW
ALL/VALS...INT/LAW TIME/SEQ TREND. PAGE 106 E2128   CONCPT
                                                       WAR

C39
SCOTT J.B.,"LAW, THE STATE, AND THE INTERNATIONAL   LAW
COMMUNITY (2 VOLS.)" INTELL INT/ORG NAT/G SECT   PHIL/SCI
INT/TRADE WAR...INT/LAW GEN/LAWS BIBLIOG. PAGE 90   DIPLOM
E1798   CONCPT

B40
CONOVER H.F.,FOREIGN RELATIONS OF THE UNITED   BIBLIOG/A
STATES: A LIST OF RECENT BOOKS (PAMPHLET). ASIA   USA-45
CANADA L/A+17C UK INT/ORG INT/TRADE TARIFFS NEUTRAL   DIPLOM
WAR PEACE...INT/LAW CON/ANAL 20 CHINJAP. PAGE 25
E0492

B40
WOLFERS A.,BRITAIN AND FRANCE BETWEEN TWO WORLD   DIPLOM
WARS. FRANCE UK INT/ORG NAT/G PLAN BARGAIN ECO/TAC   WAR
AGREE ISOLAT ALL/IDEOS...DECISION GEOG 20 TREATY   POLICY
VERSAILLES INTERVENT. PAGE 107 E2139

B41
BIRDSALL P.,VERSAILLES TWENTY YEARS AFTER. MOD/EUR   DIPLOM
POL/PAR CHIEF CONSULT FORCES LEGIS REPAR PEACE   NAT/LISM
ORD/FREE...BIBLIOG 20 PRESIDENT TREATY. PAGE 12   WAR
E0231

B41
CHAFEE Z. JR.,FREE SPEECH IN THE UNITED STATES.   ORD/FREE
USA-45 ADJUD CONTROL CRIME WAR...BIBLIOG 20   CONSTN
FREE/SPEE AMEND/I SUPREME/CT. PAGE 21 E0413   ATTIT
                                                       JURID

B41
NIEMEYER G.,LAW WITHOUT FORCE: THE FUNCTION OF   COERCE
POLITICS IN INTERNATIONAL LAW. PLAN INSPECT DIPLOM   LAW
REPAR LEGIT ADJUD WAR ORD/FREE...IDEA/COMP   PWR
METH/COMP GEN/LAWS 20. PAGE 77 E1549   INT/LAW

B42
FEILCHENFELD E.H.,THE INTERNATIONAL ECONOMIC LAW OF   ECO/TAC
BELLIGERENT OCCUPATION. EUR+WWI MOD/EUR USA-45   INT/LAW
INT/ORG DIPLOM ADJUD ARMS/CONT LEAGUE/NAT 20.   WAR
PAGE 37 E0726

B42
HEGEL G.W.F.,PHILOSOPHY OF RIGHT. UNIV FAM SECT   NAT/G
CHIEF AGREE WAR MARRIAGE OWN ORD/FREE...POLICY   LAW
CONCPT. PAGE 51 E1023   RATIONAL

B42
US LIBRARY OF CONGRESS,SOCIAL AND CULTURAL PROBLEMS   BIBLIOG/A
IN WARTIME: APRIL 1941-MARCH 1942. WOR-45 CLIENT   WAR
SECT EDU/PROP CRIME LEISURE RACE/REL STRANGE ATTIT   SOC
DRIVE HEALTH...GEOG 20. PAGE 100 E2012   CULTURE

B43
BEMIS S.F.,THE LATIN AMERICAN POLICY OF THE UNITED   DIPLOM
STATES: AN HISTORICAL INTERPRETATION. INT/ORG AGREE   SOVEREIGN
COLONIAL WAR PEACE ATTIT ORD/FREE...POLICY INT/LAW   USA-45
CHARTS 18/20 MEXIC/AMER WILSON/W MONROE/DOC.   L/A+17C
PAGE 10 E0185

B43
CONOVER H.F.,THE BALKANS: A SELECTED LIST OF   BIBLIOG
REFERENCES. ALBANIA BULGARIA ROMANIA YUGOSLAVIA   EUR+WWI
INT/ORG PROB/SOLV DIPLOM LEGIT CONFER ADJUD WAR
NAT/LISM PEACE PWR 20 LEAGUE/NAT. PAGE 25 E0493

B43
US LIBRARY OF CONGRESS,SOCIAL AND CULTURAL PROBLEMS   BIBLIOG/A
IN WARTIME: APRIL-DECEMBER (SUPPLEMENT 1). WOR-45   WAR
SECT EDU/PROP CRIME LEISURE CIVMIL/REL RACE/REL   SOC
ATTIT DRIVE HEALTH...GEOG 20. PAGE 100 E2013   CULTURE

B43
US LIBRARY OF CONGRESS,SOCIAL AND CULTURAL PROBLEMS   BIBLIOG/A
IN WARTIME: JANUARY-MAY 1943 (SUPPLEMENT 2). WOR-45   WAR
FAM SECT PLAN EDU/PROP CRIME LEISURE RACE/REL DRIVE   SOC
HEALTH...GEOG 20 JEWS. PAGE 100 E2014   CULTURE

C43
BENTHAM J.,"PRINCIPLES OF INTERNATIONAL LAW" IN J.   INT/LAW
BOWRING, ED., THE WORKS OF JEREMY BENTHAM." UNIV   JURID
NAT/G NAT/G PROB/SOLV DIPLOM CONTROL SANCTION MORAL   WAR
ORD/FREE PWR SOVEREIGN 19. PAGE 10 E0194   PEACE

B44
DE HUSZAR G.B.,NEW PERSPECTIVES ON PEACE. UNIV   ATTIT
CULTURE SOCIETY ECO/DEV ECO/UNDEV NAT/G FORCES   MYTH
CREATE ECO/TAC DOMIN ADJUD COERCE DRIVE ORD/FREE   PEACE
...GEOG JURID PSY SOC CONCPT TOT/POP. PAGE 29 E0584   WAR

B44
FULLER G.H.,RENEGOTIATION OF WAR CONTRACTS: A   BIBLIOG
SELECTED LIST OF REFERENCES (PAMPHLET). USA-45   WAR
ECO/DEV LG/CO NAT/G OP/RES PLAN BAL/PWR LEGIT   LAW
CONTROL...MGT 20. PAGE 42 E0823   FINAN

B44
PUTTKAMMER E.W.,WAR AND THE LAW. UNIV USA-45 CONSTN   INT/ORG
CULTURE SOCIETY NAT/G POL/PAR ROUTINE ALL/VALS   LAW
...JURID CONCPT OBS WORK VAL/FREE 20. PAGE 83 E1664   WAR
                                                       INT/LAW

B44
RUDIN H.R.,ARMISTICE 1918. FRANCE GERMANY MOD/EUR   AGREE
UK USA-45 NAT/G CHIEF DELIB/GP FORCES BAL/PWR REPAR   WAR
ARMS/CONT 20 WILSON/W TREATY. PAGE 86 E1732   PEACE
                                                       DIPLOM

S44
WRIGHT Q.,"CONSTITUTIONAL PROCEDURES OF THE US FOR   TOP/EX
CARRYING OUT OBLIGATIONS FOR MILITARY SANCTIONS."   FORCES
EUR+WWI FUT USA-45 WOR-45 CONSTN INTELL NAT/G   INT/LAW
CONSULT EX/STRUC LEGIS ROUTINE DRIVE...POLICY JURID   WAR
CONCPT OBS TREND TOT/POP 20. PAGE 108 E2153

B45
BEVERIDGE W.,THE PRICE OF PEACE. GERMANY UK WOR+45   INT/ORG
WOR-45 NAT/G FORCES CREATE LEGIT REGION WAR ATTIT   TREND
KNOWL ORD/FREE PWR...POLICY NEW/IDEA GEN/LAWS   PEACE
LEAGUE/NAT 20 TREATY. PAGE 12 E0223

CONOVER H.F.,THE NAZI STATE: WAR CRIMES AND WAR BIBLIOG
CRIMINALS. GERMANY CULTURE NAT/G SECT FORCES DIPLOM WAR
INT/TRADE EDU/PROP...INT/LAW BIOG HIST/WRIT CRIME
TIME/SEQ 20. PAGE 25 E0495
B45

REVES E.,THE ANATOMY OF PEACE. WOR-45 LAW CULTURE ACT/RES
NAT/G PLAN TEC/DEV EDU/PROP WAR NAT/LISM ATTIT CONCPT
ALL/VALS SOVEREIGN...POLICY HUM TIME/SEQ 20. NUC/PWR
PAGE 84 E1688 PEACE
B45

TINGSTERN H.,PEACE AND SECURITY AFTER WW II. WOR-45 INT/ORG
DELIB/GP TOP/EX LEGIT CT/SYS COERCE PEACE ATTIT ORD/FREE
PERCEPT...CONCPT LEAGUE/NAT 20. PAGE 96 E1927 WAR
INT/LAW
B45

UNCIO CONFERENCE LIBRARY,SHORT TITLE CLASSIFIED BIBLIOG
CATALOG. WOR-45 DOMIN COLONIAL WAR...SOC/WK 20 DIPLOM
LEAGUE/NAT UN. PAGE 98 E1955 INT/ORG
INT/LAW
B45

WEST R.,CONSCIENCE AND SOCIETY: A STUDY OF THE COERCE
PSYCHOLOGICAL PREREQUISITES OF LAW AND ORDER. FUT INT/LAW
UNIV LAW SOCIETY STRUCT DIPLOM WAR PERS/REL SUPEGO ORD/FREE
...SOC 20. PAGE 105 E2112 PERSON
B45

WOOLBERT R.G.,FOREIGN AFFAIRS BIBLIOGRAPHY, BIBLIOG/A
1932-1942. INT/ORG SECT INT/TRADE COLONIAL RACE/REL DIPLOM
NAT/LISM...GEOG INT/LAW GOV/COMP IDEA/COMP 20. WAR
PAGE 107 E2144
B45

GRIFFIN G.G.,A GUIDE TO MANUSCRIPTS RELATING TO BIBLIOG/A
AMERICAN HISTORY IN BRITISH DEPOSITORIES. CANADA ALL/VALS
IRELAND MOD/EUR UK USA-45 LAW DIPLOM ADMIN COLONIAL NAT/G
WAR NAT/LISM SOVEREIGN...GEOG INT/LAW 15/19
CMN/WLTH. PAGE 47 E0936
B46

GORDON D.L.,THE HIDDEN WEAPON: THE STORY OF INT/ORG
ECONOMIC WARFARE. EUR+WWI USA+45 LAW FINAN INDUS ECO/TAC
NAT/G CONSULT FORCES PLAN DOMIN PWR WEALTH INT/TRADE
...INT/LAW CONCPT OBS TOT/POP NAZI 20. PAGE 45 WAR
E0891
B47

HYDE C.C.,INTERNATIONAL LAW, CHIEFLY AS INTERPRETED INT/LAW
AND APPLIED BY THE UNITED STATES (3 VOLS., 2ND REV. DIPLOM
ED.). USA-45 WOR+45 WOR-45 INT/ORG CT/SYS WAR NAT/G
NAT/LISM PEACE ORD/FREE...JURID 19/20 TREATY. POLICY
PAGE 56 E1119
B47

GRIFFITH E.S.,RESEARCH IN POLITICAL SCIENCE: THE BIBLIOG
WORK OF PANELS OF RESEARCH COMMITTEE, APSA. WOR+45 PHIL/SCI
WOR-45 COM/IND R+D FORCES ACT/RES WAR...GOV/COMP DIPLOM
ANTHOL 20. PAGE 47 E0939 JURID
B48

LOGAN R.W.,THE AFRICAN MANDATES IN WORLD POLITICS. WAR
EUR+WWI GERMANY ISLAM INT/ORG BARGAIN...POLICY COLONIAL
INT/LAW 20. PAGE 66 E1321 AFR
DIPLOM
B48

ALEXANDER L.,"WAR CRIMES, THEIR SOCIAL- DRIVE
PSYCHOLOGICAL ASPECTS." EUR+WWI GERMANY LAW CULTURE WAR
ELITES KIN POL/PAR PUB/INST FORCES DOMIN EDU/PROP
COERCE CRIME ATTIT SUPEGO HEALTH MORAL PWR FASCISM
...PSY OBS TREND GEN/LAWS NAZI 20. PAGE 3 E0061
S48

MORGENTHAU H.J.,"THE TWILIGHT OF INTERNATIONAL MORAL
MORALITY" (BMR)" WOR+45 WOR-45 BAL/PWR WAR NAT/LISM DIPLOM
PEACE...POLICY INT/LAW IDEA/COMP 15/20 TREATY NAT/G
INTERVENT. PAGE 75 E1495
S48

GROB F.,THE RELATIVITY OF WAR AND PEACE: A STUDY IN WAR
LAW, HISTORY, AND POLLTICS. WOR+45 WOR-45 LAW PEACE
DIPLOM DEBATE...CONCPT LING IDEA/COMP BIBLIOG INT/LAW
18/20. PAGE 48 E0944 STYLE
B49

JACKSON R.H.,INTERNATIONAL CONFERENCE ON MILITARY DIPLOM
TRIALS. FRANCE GERMANY UK USA+45 USSR VOL/ASSN INT/ORG
DELIB/GP REPAR ADJUD CT/SYS CRIME WAR 20 WAR/TRIAL. INT/LAW
PAGE 57 E1141 CIVMIL/REL
B49

KAFKA G.,FREIHEIT UND ANARCHIE. SECT COERCE DETER CONCPT
WAR ATTIT...IDEA/COMP 20 NATO. PAGE 59 E1179 ORD/FREE
JURID
INT/ORG
B49

US LIBRARY OF CONGRESS,FREEDOM OF INFORMATION: BIBLIOG/A
SELECTIVE REPORT ON RECENT WRITINGS. USA+45 LAW ORD/FREE
CONSTN ELITES EDU/PROP PRESS LOBBY WAR TOTALISM LICENSE
ATTIT 20 UN UNESCO COLD/WAR. PAGE 101 E2018 COM/IND
B49

WORMUTH F.D.,THE ORIGINS OF MODERN NAT/G
CONSTITUTIONALISM. GREECE UK LEGIS CREATE TEC/DEV CONSTN
BAL/PWR DOMIN ADJUD REV WAR PWR...JURID ROMAN/REP LAW
CROMWELL/O. PAGE 107 E2146
B49

BROWN D.M.,"RECENT JAPANESE POLITICAL AND WAR
HISTORICAL MATERIALS." ELITES CT/SYS CIVMIL/REL 20 FORCES
CHINJAP. PAGE 16 E0312
S49

NUMELIN R.,"THE BEGINNINGS OF DIPLOMACY." INT/TRADE DIPLOM
WAR GP/REL PEACE STRANGE ATTIT...INT/LAW CONCPT KIN
BIBLIOG. PAGE 78 E1559 CULTURE
LAW
C50

CORBETT P.E.,LAW AND SOCIETY IN THE RELATIONS OF INT/LAW
STATES. FUT WOR+45 WOR-45 CONTROL WAR PEACE PWR DIPLOM
...POLICY JURID 16/20 TREATY. PAGE 26 E0505 INT/ORG
B51

PUSEY M.J.,CHARLES EVANS HUGHES (2 VOLS.). LAW BIOG
CONSTN NAT/G POL/PAR DIPLOM LEGIT WAR CHOOSE TOP/EX
PERS/REL DRIVE HEREDITY 19/20 DEPT/STATE LEAGUE/NAT ADJUD
SUPREME/CT HUGHES/CE WWI. PAGE 83 E1663 PERSON
B51

ROSSITER C.,THE SUPREME COURT AND THE COMMANDER IN CT/SYS
CHIEF. LAW CONSTN DELIB/GP EX/STRUC LEGIS TOP/EX CHIEF
ADJUD CONTROL...DECISION SOC/EXP PRESIDENT. PAGE 86 WAR
E1724 PWR
B51

KELSEN H.,"RECENT TRENDS IN THE LAW OF THE UNITED INT/ORG
NATIONS." KOREA WOR+45 CONSTN LEGIS DIPLOM LEGIT LAW
DETER WAR RIGID/FLEX HEALTH ORD/FREE RESPECT INT/LAW
...JURID CON/ANAL UN VAL/FREE 20 NATO. PAGE 60
E1199
L51

LEEK J.H.,"TREASON AND THE CONSTITUTION" (BMR)" CONSTN
USA+45 USA-45 EDU/PROP COLONIAL CT/SYS REV WAR JURID
ATTIT...TREND 18/20 SUPREME/CT CON/INTERP SMITH/ACT CRIME
COMMON/LAW. PAGE 64 E1278 NAT/G
S51

BRIGGS H.W.,THE LAW OF NATIONS (2ND ED.). WOR+45 INT/LAW
WOR-45 NAT/G LEGIS WAR...ANTHOL 20 TREATY. PAGE 15 DIPLOM
E0301 JURID
B52

FERRELL R.H.,PEACE IN THEIR TIME. FRANCE UK USA-45 PEACE
INT/ORG NAT/G FORCES CREATE AGREE ARMS/CONT COERCE DIPLOM
WAR TREATY 20 WILSON/W LEAGUE/NAT BRIAND/A. PAGE 37
E0741
B52

LIPPMANN W.,ISOLATION AND ALLIANCES: AN AMERICAN DIPLOM
SPEAKS TO THE BRITISH. USA+45 USA-45 INT/ORG AGREE SOVEREIGN
COERCE DETER WAR PEACE MORAL 20 TREATY INTERVENT. COLONIAL
PAGE 65 E1301 ATTIT
B52

BRETTON H.L.,STRESEMANN AND THE REVISION OF POLICY
VERSAILLES: A FIGHT FOR REASON. EUR+WWI GERMANY DIPLOM
FORCES BUDGET ARMS/CONT WAR SUPEGO...BIBLIOG 20 BIOG
TREATY VERSAILLES STRESEMN/G. PAGE 15 E0294
B53

OPPENHEIM L.,INTERNATIONAL LAW: A TREATISE (7TH INT/LAW
ED., 2 VOLS.). LAW CONSTN PROB/SOLV INT/TRADE ADJUD INT/ORG
AGREE NEUTRAL WAR ORD/FREE SOVEREIGN...BIBLIOG 20 DIPLOM
LEAGUE/NAT UN ILO. PAGE 79 E1579
B53

PIERCE R.A.,RUSSIAN CENTRAL ASIA, 1867-1917: A BIBLIOG
SELECTED BIBLIOGRAPHY (PAMPHLET). USSR LAW CULTURE COLONIAL
NAT/G EDU/PROP WAR...GEOG SOC 19/20. PAGE 81 E1616 ADMIN
COM
B54

STONE J.,LEGAL CONTROLS OF INTERNATIONAL CONFLICT: INT/ORG

A TREATISE ON THE DYNAMICS OF DISPUTES AND WAR LAW. LAW
WOR+45 WOR-45 NAT/G DIPLOM CT/SYS SOVEREIGN...JURID WAR
CONCPT METH/CNCPT GEN/LAWS TOT/POP VAL/FREE INT/LAW
COLD/WAR LEAGUE/NAT 20. PAGE 94 E1878

B54
US SENATE COMM ON FOREIGN REL,REVIEW OF THE UNITED BIBLIOG
NATIONS CHARTER: A COLLECTION OF DOCUMENTS. LEGIS CONSTN
DIPLOM ADMIN ARMS/CONT WAR REPRESENT SOVEREIGN INT/ORG
...INT/LAW 20 UN. PAGE 101 E2029 DEBATE

B54
WRIGHT Q.,PROBLEMS OF STABILITY AND PROGRESS IN INT/ORG
INTERNATIONAL RELATIONSHIPS. FUT WOR+45 WOR-45 CONCPT
SOCIETY LEGIS CREATE TEC/DEV ECO/TAC EDU/PROP ADJUD DIPLOM
WAR PEACE ORD/FREE PWR...KNO/TEST TREND GEN/LAWS
20. PAGE 108 E2155

B55
BENTON W.E.,NUREMBERG: GERMAN VIEWS OF THE WAR CRIME
TRIALS. EUR+WWI GERMANY VOL/ASSN LEAD PARTIC COERCE WAR
INGP/REL RACE/REL TOTALISM SUPEGO ORD/FREE...ANTHOL LAW
NUREMBERG. PAGE 10 E0201 JURID

B55
CAVAN R.S.,CRIMINOLOGY (2ND ED.). USA+45 LAW FAM DRIVE
PUB/INST FORCES PLAN WAR AGE/Y PERSON ROLE SUPEGO CRIMLGY
...CHARTS 20 FBI. PAGE 21 E0409 CONTROL
METH/COMP

B55
HOGAN W.N.,INTERNATIONAL CONFLICT AND COLLECTIVE INT/ORG
SECURITY: THE PRINCIPLE OF CONCERN IN INTERNATIONAL WAR
ORGANIZATION. CONSTN EX/STRUC BAL/PWR DIPLOM ADJUD ORD/FREE
CONTROL CENTRAL CONSEN PEACE...INT/LAW CONCPT FORCES
METH/COMP 20 UN LEAGUE/NAT. PAGE 53 E1066

B55
KHADDURI M.,WAR AND PEACE IN THE LAW OF ISLAM. ISLAM
CONSTN CULTURE SOCIETY STRATA NAT/G PROVS SECT JURID
FORCES TOP/EX CREATE DOMIN EDU/PROP ADJUD COERCE PEACE
ATTIT RIGID/FLEX ALL/VALS...CONCPT TIME/SEQ TOT/POP WAR
VAL/FREE. PAGE 61 E1209

B55
SVARLIEN O.,AN INTRODUCTION TO THE LAW OF NATIONS. INT/LAW
SEA AIR INT/ORG NAT/G CHIEF ADMIN AGREE WAR PRIVIL DIPLOM
ORD/FREE SOVEREIGN...BIBLIOG 16/20. PAGE 95 E1897

B56
BOTERO G.,THE REASON OF STATE AND THE GREATNESS OF PHIL/SCI
CITIES. SECT CHIEF FORCES PLAN LEAD WAR MORAL NEW/IDEA
...POLICY 16 MACHIAVELL TREATY. PAGE 14 E0272 CONTROL

B56
SOHN L.B.,CASES ON UNITED NATIONS LAW. STRUCT INT/ORG
DELIB/GP WAR PEACE ORD/FREE...DECISION ANTHOL 20 INT/LAW
UN. PAGE 92 E1854 ADMIN
ADJUD

S56
POTTER P.B.,"NEUTRALITY, 1955." WOR+45 WOR-45 NEUTRAL
INT/ORG NAT/G WAR ATTIT...POLICY IDEA/COMP 17/20 INT/LAW
LEAGUE/NAT UN COLD/WAR. PAGE 81 E1631 DIPLOM
CONCPT

C56
FALL B.B.,"THE VIET-MINH REGIME." VIETNAM LAW NAT/G
ECO/UNDEV POL/PAR FORCES DOMIN WAR ATTIT MARXISM ADMIN
...BIOG PREDICT BIBLIOG/A 20. PAGE 36 E0720 EX/STRUC
LEAD

B57
ALIGHIERI D.,ON WORLD GOVERNMENT. ROMAN/EMP LAW POLICY
SOCIETY INT/ORG NAT/G POL/PAR ADJUD WAR GP/REL CONCPT
PEACE WORSHIP 15 WORLDUNITY DANTE. PAGE 4 E0067 DIPLOM
SECT

B57
DIVINE R.A.,AMERICAN IMMIGRATION POLICY, 1924-52. GEOG
USA+45 USA-45 VOL/ASSN DELIB/GP ADJUD WAR ADJUST HABITAT
DISCRIM...POLICY JURID 20 DEPRESSION MIGRATION. LEGIS
PAGE 32 E0630 CONTROL

B57
FREUND G.,UNHOLY ALLIANCE. EUR+WWI GERMANY USSR DIPLOM
FORCES ECO/TAC CONTROL WAR PWR...TREND TREATY. PLAN
PAGE 40 E0796 POLICY

B57
INSTITUT DE DROIT INTL,TABLEAU GENERAL DES INT/LAW
RESOLUTIONS (1873-1956). LAW NEUTRAL CRIME WAR DIPLOM
MARRIAGE PEACE...JURID 19/20. PAGE 56 E1124 ORD/FREE
ADJUD

B57
PALMER N.D.,INTERNATIONAL RELATIONS. WOR+45 INT/ORG DIPLOM
NAT/G ECO/TAC EDU/PROP COLONIAL WAR PWR SOVEREIGN BAL/PWR
...POLICY T 20 TREATY. PAGE 79 E1593 NAT/COMP

B57
SCHUBERT G.A.,THE PRESIDENCY IN THE COURTS. CONSTN PWR
FORCES DIPLOM TARIFFS ADJUD CONTROL WAR...DECISION CT/SYS
MGT CHARTS 18/20 PRESIDENT CONGRESS SUPREME/CT. LEGIT
PAGE 89 E1778 CHIEF

B57
SINEY M.C.,THE ALLIED BLOCKADE OF GERMANY: DETER
1914-1916. EUR+WWI GERMANY MOD/EUR USA-45 DIPLOM INT/TRADE
CONTROL NEUTRAL PWR 20. PAGE 91 E1832 INT/LAW
WAR

B58
BOWETT D.W.,SELF-DEFENSE IN INTERNATIONAL LAW. ADJUD
EUR+WWI MOD/EUR WOR+45 SOCIETY INT/ORG CONCPT
CONSULT DIPLOM LEGIT COERCE ATTIT ORD/FREE...JURID WAR
20 UN. PAGE 14 E0276 INT/LAW

B58
MASON H.L.,TOYNBEE'S APPROACH TO WORLD POLITICS. DIPLOM
AFR USA+45 USSR LAW WAR NAT/LISM ALL/IDEOS...HUM CONCPT
BIBLIOG. PAGE 69 E1380 PHIL/SCI
SECT

B58
SCHOEDER P.W.,THE AXIS ALLIANCE AND JAPANESE- AGREE
AMERICAN RELATIONS 1941. ASIA GERMANY UK USA-45 DIPLOM
PEACE ATTIT...POLICY BIBLIOG 20 CHINJAP TREATY. WAR
PAGE 88 E1763

B58
SOC OF COMP LEGIS AND INT LAW,THE LAW OF THE SEA... INT/LAW
(PAMPHLET). WOR+45 NAT/G INT/TRADE ADJUD CONTROL INT/ORG
NUC/PWR WAR PEACE ATTIT ORD/FREE...JURID CHARTS 20 DIPLOM
UN TREATY RESOURCE/N. PAGE 92 E1850 SEA

B58
STONE J.,AGGRESSION AND WORLD ORDER: A CRITIQUE OF ORD/FREE
UNITED NATIONS THEORIES OF AGGRESSION. LAW CONSTN INT/ORG
DELIB/GP PROB/SOLV BAL/PWR DIPLOM DEBATE ADJUD WAR
CRIME PWR...POLICY IDEA/COMP 20 UN SUEZ LEAGUE/NAT. CONCPT
PAGE 94 E1879

B59
GREENSPAN M.,THE MODERN LAW OF LAND WARFARE. WOR+45 ADJUD
INT/ORG NAT/G DELIB/GP FORCES ATTIT...POLICY PWR
HYPO/EXP STERTYP 20. PAGE 46 E0911 WAR

B59
KNIERIEM A.,THE NUREMBERG TRIALS. EUR+WWI GERMANY INT/LAW
VOL/ASSN LEAD COERCE WAR INGP/REL TOTALISM SUPEGO CRIME
ORD/FREE...CONCPT METH/COMP. PAGE 61 E1225 PARTIC
JURID

B59
MAYER A.J.,POLITICAL ORIGINS OF THE NEW DIPLOMACY, TREND
1917-1918. EUR+WWI MOD/EUR USA-45 WAR PWR...POLICY DIPLOM
INT/LAW BIBLIOG. PAGE 70 E1392

B59
PANHUYS H.F.,THE ROLE OF NATIONALITY IN INT/LAW
INTERNATIONAL LAW. ADJUD CRIME WAR STRANGE...JURID NAT/LISM
TREND. PAGE 80 E1596 INGP/REL

B59
COLUMBIA U. BUREAU OF APPL SOC RES, ATTITUDES OF ATTIT
PROMINENT AMERICANS TOWARD "WORLD PEACE THROUGH ACT/RES
WORLD LAW" (SUPRA-NATL ORGANIZATION FOR WAR INT/LAW
PREVENTION). USA+45 USSR ELITES FORCES PLAN STAT
PROB/SOLV CONTROL WAR PWR...POLICY SOC QU IDEA/COMP
20 UN. PAGE 82 E1644

B59
SQUIBB G.D.,THE HIGH COURT OF CHIVALRY. UK NAT/G CT/SYS
FORCES ADJUD WAR 14/20 PARLIAMENT ENGLSH/LAW. PARL/PROC
PAGE 93 E1863 JURID

S59
PUGWASH CONFERENCE,"ON BIOLOGICAL AND CHEMICAL ACT/RES
WARFARE." WOR+45 SOCIETY PROC/MFG INT/ORG FORCES BIO/SOC
EDU/PROP ADJUD RIGID/FLEX ORD/FREE PWR...DECISION WAR
PSY NEW/IDEA MATH VAL/FREE 20. PAGE 83 E1661 WEAPON

B60
SCHEIBER H.N.,THE WILSON ADMINISTRATION AND CIVIL ORD/FREE
LIBERTIES 1917-1921. LAW GOV/REL ATTIT 20 WILSON/W WAR
CIVIL/LIB. PAGE 87 E1754 NAT/G
CONTROL

S60
O'BRIEN W.,"THE ROLE OF FORCE IN THE INTERNATIONAL INT/ORG

JURIDICAL ORDER." WOR+45 NAT/G FORCES DOMIN ADJUD ARMS/CONT DETER NUC/PWR WAR ATTIT PWR...CATH INT/LAW JURID CONCPT TREND STERTYP GEN/LAWS 20. PAGE 78 E1564
COERCE

B61
BRENNAN D.G.,ARMS CONTROL, DISARMAMENT, AND NATIONAL SECURITY. WOR+45 NAT/G FORCES CREATE PROB/SOLV PARTIC WAR PEACE...DECISION INT/LAW ANTHOL BIBLIOG 20. PAGE 15 E0291
ARMS/CONT
ORD/FREE
DIPLOM
POLICY

B61
CONFERENCE ATLANTIC COMMUNITY,AN INTRODUCTORY BIBLIOGRAPHY. COM WOR+45 FORCES DIPLOM ECO/TAC WAR ...INT/LAW HIST/WRIT COLD/WAR NATO. PAGE 25 E0485
BIBLIOG/A
CON/ANAL
INT/ORG

B61
FLINN M.W.,AN ECONOMIC AND SOCIAL HISTORY OF BRITAIN, 1066-1939. UK LAW STRATA STRUCT AGRI DIST/IND INDUS WORKER INT/TRADE WAR...CENSUS 11/20. PAGE 39 E0766
SOCIETY
SOC

B61
LARSON A.,WHEN NATIONS DISAGREE. USA+45 WOR+45 INT/ORG ADJUD COERCE CRIME OWN SOVEREIGN...POLICY JURID 20. PAGE 63 E1258
INT/LAW
DIPLOM
WAR

B61
MECHAM J.L.,THE UNITED STATES AND INTER-AMERICAN SECURITY, 1889-1960. L/A+17C USA+45 USA-45 CONSTN FORCES INT/TRADE PEACE TOTALISM ATTIT...JURID 19/20 UN OAS. PAGE 72 E1432
DIPLOM
WAR
ORD/FREE
INT/ORG

B61
RIENOW R.,CONTEMPORARY INTERNATIONAL POLITICS. WOR+45 INT/ORG BAL/PWR EDU/PROP COLONIAL NEUTRAL REGION WAR PEACE...INT/LAW 20 COLD/WAR UN. PAGE 85 E1698
DIPLOM
PWR
POLICY
NAT/G

B61
SYATAUW J.J.G.,SOME NEWLY ESTABLISHED ASIAN STATES AND THE DEVELOPMENT OF INTERNATIONAL LAW. BURMA CEYLON INDIA INDONESIA ECO/UNDEV COLONIAL NEUTRAL WAR PEACE SOVEREIGN...CHARTS 19/20. PAGE 95 E1902
INT/LAW
ADJUST
SOCIETY
S/ASIA

B62
BIBLIOTHEQUE PALAIS DE LA PAIX,CATALOGUE OF THE PEACE PALACE LIBRARY, SUPPLEMENT 1937-1952 (7 VOLS.). WOR+45 WOR-45 INT/ORG NAT/G ADJUD WAR PEACE ...JURID 20. PAGE 12 E0225
BIBLIOG
INT/LAW
DIPLOM

B62
BISHOP W.W. JR.,INTERNATIONAL LAW: CASES AND MATERIALS. WOR+45 INT/ORG FORCES PROB/SOLV AGREE WAR...JURID IDEA/COMP T 20 TREATY. PAGE 12 E0233
INT/LAW
DIPLOM
CONCPT
CT/SYS

B62
COLOMBOS C.J.,THE INTERNATIONAL LAW OF THE SEA. WOR+45 EXTR/IND DIPLOM INT/TRADE TARIFFS AGREE WAR ...TIME/SEQ 20 TREATY. PAGE 24 E0476
INT/LAW
SEA
JURID
ADJUD

B62
DUROSELLE J.B.,HISTOIRE DIPLOMATIQUE DE 1919 A NOS JOURS (3RD ED.). FRANCE INT/ORG CHIEF FORCES CONFER ARMS/CONT WAR PEACE ORD/FREE...T TREATY 20 COLD/WAR. PAGE 34 E0667
DIPLOM
WOR+45
WOR-45

B62
GANJI M.,INTERNATIONAL PROTECTION OF HUMAN RIGHTS. WOR+45 CONSTN INT/TRADE CT/SYS SANCTION CRIME WAR RACE/REL...CHARTS IDEA/COMP NAT/COMP BIBLIOG 20 TREATY NEGRO LEAGUE/NAT UN CIVIL/LIB. PAGE 42 E0831
ORD/FREE
DISCRIM
LEGIS
DELIB/GP

B62
HIRSCHFIELD R.S.,THE CONSTITUTION AND THE COURT. SCHOOL WAR RACE/REL EQUILIB ORD/FREE...POLICY MAJORIT DECISION JURID 18/20 PRESIDENT COLD/WAR CIVIL/LIB SUPREME/CT CONGRESS. PAGE 53 E1051
ADJUD
PWR
CONSTN
LAW

B62
JACOBINI H.B.,INTERNATIONAL LAW: A TEXT. DIPLOM ADJUD NEUTRAL WAR PEACE T. PAGE 57 E1143
INT/LAW
CT/SYS
CONCPT

B62
SOMMER T.,DEUTSCHLAND UND JAPAN ZWISCHEN DEN MACHTEN. GERMANY DELIB/GP BAL/PWR AGREE COERCE TOTALISM PWR 20 CHINJAP TREATY. PAGE 93 E1856
DIPLOM
WAR
ATTIT

B62
US SENATE COMM ON JUDICIARY,CONSTITUTIONAL RIGHTS OF MILITARY PERSONNEL. USA+45 USA-45 FORCES DIPLOM WAR CONGRESS. PAGE 102 E2046
CONSTN
ORD/FREE
JURID
CT/SYS

B62
WOETZEL R.K.,THE NURENBERG TRIALS IN INTERNATIONAL LAW. CHRIST-17C MOD/EUR WOR+45 SOCIETY NAT/G DELIB/GP DOMIN LEGIT ROUTINE ATTIT DRIVE PERSON SUPEGO MORAL ORD/FREE...POLICY MAJORIT JURID PSY SOC SELF/OBS RECORD NAZI TOT/POP. PAGE 107 E2138
INT/ORG
ADJUD
WAR

S62
FALK R.A.,"THE REALITY OF INTERNATIONAL LAW." WOR+45 NAT/G LEGIT COERCE DETER WAR MORAL ORD/FREE PWR SOVEREIGN...JURID CONCPT VAL/FREE COLD/WAR 20. PAGE 36 E0714
INT/ORG
ADJUD
NUC/PWR
INT/LAW

S62
GREEN L.C.,"POLITICAL OFFENSES, WAR CRIMES AND EXTRADITION." WOR+45 YUGOSLAVIA INT/ORG LEGIT ROUTINE WAR ORD/FREE SOVEREIGN...JURID NAZI 20 INTERPOL. PAGE 46 E0906
LAW
CONCPT
INT/LAW

S62
GREENSPAN M.,"INTERNATIONAL LAW AND ITS PROTECTION FOR PARTICIPANTS IN UNCONVENTIONAL WARFARE." WOR+45 LAW INT/ORG NAT/G POL/PAR COERCE REV ORD/FREE ...INT/LAW TOT/POP 20. PAGE 46 E0912
FORCES
JURID
GUERRILLA
WAR

C62
BACON F.,"OF THE TRUE GREATNESS OF KINGDOMS AND ESTATES" (1612) IN F. BACON, ESSAYS." ELITES FORCES DOMIN EDU/PROP LEGIT...POLICY GEN/LAWS 16/17 TREATY. PAGE 7 E0129
WAR
PWR
DIPLOM
CONSTN

B63
BROWN R.M.,THE SOUTH CAROLINA REGULATORS. USA-45 LEGIS LEGIT ADJUD COLONIAL CONTROL WAR...BIBLIOG/A 18 CHARLESTON SOUTH/CAR. PAGE 16 E0315
ORD/FREE
JURID
PWR
PROVS

B63
DILLIARD I.,ONE MAN'S STAND FOR FREEDOM: MR. JUSTICE BLACK AND THE BILL OF RIGHTS. USA+45 POL/PAR SECT DELIB/GP FORCES ADJUD CONTROL WAR DISCRIM MORAL...BIBLIOG 20 NEGRO SUPREME/CT BILL/RIGHT BLACK/HL. PAGE 32 E0628
CONSTN
JURID
JUDGE
ORD/FREE

B63
DUNN F.S.,PEACE-MAKING AND THE SETTLEMENT WITH JAPAN. ASIA USA+45 USA-45 FORCES BAL/PWR ECO/TAC CONFER WAR PWR SOVEREIGN 20 CHINJAP COLD/WAR TREATY. PAGE 33 E0661
POLICY
PEACE
PLAN
DIPLOM

B63
JENKS C.W.,LAW, FREEDOM, AND WELFARE. WOR+45 GIVE ADJUD WAR PEACE HABITAT ORD/FREE. PAGE 58 E1159
INT/LAW
DIPLOM
SOVEREIGN
PROB/SOLV

B63
PACHTER H.M.,COLLISION COURSE: THE CUBAN MISSILE CRISIS AND COEXISTENCE. CUBA USA+45 DIPLOM ARMS/CONT PEACE MARXISM...DECISION INT/LAW 20 COLD/WAR KHRUSH/N KENNEDY/JF CASTRO/F. PAGE 79 E1587
WAR
BAL/PWR
NUC/PWR
DETER

B63
ROSNER G.,THE UNITED NATIONS EMERGENCY FORCE. FRANCE ISRAEL UAR UK WOR+45 CREATE WAR PEACE ORD/FREE PWR...INT/LAW JURID HIST/WRIT TIME/SEQ UN. PAGE 86 E1719
INT/ORG
FORCES

S63
MEYROWITZ H.,"LES JURISTES DEVANT L'ARME NUCLAIRE." FUT WOR+45 INTELL SOCIETY BAL/PWR DETER WAR...JURID CONCPT 20. PAGE 72 E1451
ACT/RES
ADJUD
INT/LAW
NUC/PWR

B64
FREUD A.,OF HUMAN SOVEREIGNTY. WOR+45 INDUS SECT ECO/TAC CRIME CHOOSE ATTIT MORAL MARXISM...POLICY BIBLIOG 20. PAGE 40 E0794
NAT/LISM
DIPLOM
WAR
PEACE

B64
GRZYBOWSKI K.,THE SOCIALIST COMMONWEALTH OF NATIONS: ORGANIZATIONS AND INSTITUTIONS. FORCES DIPLOM INT/TRADE ADJUD ADMIN LEAD WAR MARXISM SOCISM...BIBLIOG 20 COMECON WARSAW/P. PAGE 48 E0956
INT/LAW
COM
REGION
INT/ORG

B64
HOPKINSON T.,SOUTH AFRICA. SOUTH/AFR UK NAT/G POL/PAR LEGIS ECO/TAC PARL/PROC WAR...JURID AUD/VIS 19/20. PAGE 55 E1097
SOCIETY
RACE/REL
DISCRIM

B64
KISER S.L.,AMERICANISM IN ACTION. USA+45 LAW PROVS CAP/ISM DIPLOM RECEIVE CONTROL CT/SYS WAR FEDERAL
OLD/LIB
FOR/AID

ATTIT WEALTH 20 SUPREME/CT. PAGE 61 E1221 — MARXISM CONSTN

LOCKHART W.B.,CASES AND MATERIALS ON CONSTITUTIONAL RIGHTS AND LIBERTIES. USA+45 FORCES LEGIS DIPLOM PRESS CONTROL CRIME WAR PWR...AUD/VIS T WORSHIP 20 NEGRO. PAGE 66 E1317 — ORD/FREE CONSTN NAT/G
B64

REGALA R.,WORLD PEACE THROUGH DIPLOMACY AND LAW. S/ASIA WOR+45 ECO/UNDEV INT/ORG FORCES PLAN PROB/SOLV FOR/AID NUC/PWR WAR...POLICY INT/LAW 20. PAGE 84 E1679 — DIPLOM PEACE ADJUD
B64

ROBERTS HL,FOREIGN AFFAIRS BIBLIOGRAPHY, 1952-1962. ECO/DEV SECT PLAN FOR/AID INT/TRADE ARMS/CONT NAT/LISM ATTIT...INT/LAW GOV/COMP IDEA/COMP 20. PAGE 85 E1703 — BIBLIOG/A DIPLOM INT/ORG WAR
B64

STANGER R.J.,ESSAYS ON INTERVENTION. PLAN PROB/SOLV BAL/PWR ADJUD COERCE WAR ROLE PWR...INT/LAW CONCPT 20 UN INTERVENT. PAGE 93 E1865 — SOVEREIGN DIPLOM POLICY LEGIT
B64

THANT U.,TOWARD WORLD PEACE. DELIB/GP TEC/DEV EDU/PROP WAR SOVEREIGN...INT/LAW 20 UN MID/EAST. PAGE 96 E1915 — DIPLOM BIOG PEACE COERCE
B64

US AIR FORCE ACADEMY ASSEMBLY,OUTER SPACE: FINAL REPORT APRIL 1-4, 1964. FUT USA+45 WOR+45 LAW DELIB/GP CONFER ARMS/CONT WAR PEACE ATTIT MORAL ...ANTHOL 20 NASA. PAGE 99 E1979 — SPACE CIVMIL/REL NUC/PWR DIPLOM
B64

WRIGHT Q.,A STUDY OF WAR. LAW NAT/G PROB/SOLV BAL/PWR NAT/LISM PEACE ATTIT SOVEREIGN...CENSUS SOC/INTEG. PAGE 108 E2159 — WAR CONCPT DIPLOM CONTROL
B64

COHEN M.,"BASIC PRINCIPLES OF INTERNATIONAL LAW." UNIV WOR+45 WOR-45 BAL/PWR LEGIT ADJUD WAR ATTIT MORAL ORD/FREE PWR...JURID CONCPT MYTH TOT/POP 20. PAGE 23 E0463 — INT/ORG INT/LAW
S64

GINSBURGS G.,"WARS OF NATIONAL LIBERATION - THE SOVIET THESIS." COM USSR WOR+45 WOR-45 LAW CULTURE INT/ORG DIPLOM LEGIT COLONIAL GUERRILLA WAR NAT/LISM ATTIT PERSON MORAL PWR...JURID OBS TREND MARX/KARL 20. PAGE 44 E0869 — COERCE CONCPT INT/LAW REV
S64

BAADE H.,THE SOVIET IMPACT ON INTERNATIONAL LAW. INT/LAW INT/ORG INT/TRADE LEGIT COLONIAL ARMS/CONT REV WAR ...CON/ANAL ANTHOL TREATY. PAGE 6 E0124 — INT/LAW USSR CREATE ORD/FREE
B65

BERKOWITZ M.,AMERICAN NATIONAL SECURITY: A READER IN THEORY AND POLICY. USA+45 INT/ORG FORCES BAL/PWR DIPLOM ECO/TAC DETER PWR...INT/LAW ANTHOL BIBLIOG 20 UN. PAGE 11 E0203 — ORD/FREE WAR ARMS/CONT POLICY
B65

COWEN Z.,THE BRITISH COMMONWEALTH OF NATIONS IN A CHANGING WORLD. UK ECO/UNDEV INT/ORG ECO/TAC INT/TRADE COLONIAL WAR GP/REL RACE/REL SOVEREIGN SOC/INTEG 20 TREATY EEC COMMONWLTH. PAGE 27 E0530 — JURID DIPLOM PARL/PROC NAT/LISM
B65

HAENSCH G.,PAN-AFRICANISM IN ACTION: AN ACCOUNT OF THE UAM TIC AND ALPHABETICAL IN GERMAN, ENGLISH, FRENCH AND SPANISH. WOR+45 INT/ORG NAT/G ARMS/CONT WAR...INT/LAW IDEA/COMP TREATY. PAGE 49 E0974 — DICTIONARY DIPLOM LING
B65

LASLEY J.,THE WAR SYSTEM AND YOU. LAW FORCES ARMS/CONT NUC/PWR NAT/LISM ATTIT...MAJORIT IDEA/COMP UN WORSHIP. PAGE 63 E1261 — MORAL PERSON DIPLOM WAR
B65

MILLIS W.,AN END TO ARMS. LAW INT/ORG FORCES ACT/RES CREATE DIPLOM WAR...POLICY HUM NEW/IDEA HYPO/EXP. PAGE 73 E1462 — FUT PWR ARMS/CONT ORD/FREE
B65

NORDEN A.,WAR AND NAZI CRIMINALS IN WEST GERMANY: — FASCIST
B65

STATE, ECONOMY, ADMINISTRATION, ARMY, JUSTICE, SCIENCE. GERMANY GERMANY/W MOD/EUR ECO/DEV ACADEM EX/STRUC FORCES DOMIN ADMIN CT/SYS...POLICY MAJORIT PACIFIST 20. PAGE 77 E1554 — WAR NAT/G TOP/EX

PADELFORD N.,THE UNITED NATIONS IN THE BALANCE* ACCOMPLISHMENTS AND PROSPECTS. NAT/G VOL/ASSN DIPLOM ADMIN COLONIAL CT/SYS REGION WAR ORD/FREE ...ANTHOL UN. PAGE 79 E1588 — INT/ORG CONTROL
B65

RENNER K.,MENSCH UND GESELLSCHAFT - GRUNDRISS EINER SOZIOLOGIE (2ND ED.). STRATA FAM LABOR PROF/ORG WAR ...JURID CLASSIF 20. PAGE 84 E1685 — SOC STRUCT NAT/G SOCIETY
B65

SOPER T.,EVOLVING COMMONWEALTH. AFR CANADA INDIA IRELAND UK LAW CONSTN POL/PAR DOMIN CONTROL WAR PWR ...AUD/VIS 18/20 COMMONWLTH OEEC. PAGE 93 E1857 — INT/ORG COLONIAL VOL/ASSN
B65

VON GLAHN G.,LAW AMONG NATIONS: AN INTRODUCTION TO PUBLIC INTERNATIONAL LAW. WOR+45 WOR-45 INT/ORG NAT/G CREATE ADJUD WAR...GEOG CLASSIF TREND BIBLIOG. PAGE 104 E2082 — ACADEM INT/LAW GEN/LAWS LAW
B65

BROWNLIE I.,"SOME LEGAL ASPECTS OF THE USE OF NUCLEAR WEAPONS." UK NEUTRAL DETER UN TREATY. PAGE 16 E0317 — LAW NUC/PWR WAR INT/LAW
S65

LUSKY L.,"FOUR PROBLEMS IN LAWMAKING FOR PEACE." FORCES LEGIS CREATE ADJUD COERCE WAR MAJORITY PEACE PWR. PAGE 67 E1334 — ORD/FREE INT/LAW UTOPIA RECORD
S65

PRABHAKAR P.,"SURVEY OF RESEARCH AND SOURCE MATERIALS; THE SINO-INDIAN BORDER DISPUTE." CHINA/COM INDIA LAW NAT/G PLAN BAL/PWR WAR...POLICY 20 COLD/WAR. PAGE 82 E1645 — BIBLIOG ASIA S/ASIA DIPLOM
S65

WRIGHT Q.,"THE ESCALATION OF INTERNATIONAL CONFLICTS." WOR+45 WOR-45 FORCES DIPLOM RISK COST ATTIT ALL/VALS...INT/LAW QUANT STAT NAT/COMP. PAGE 108 E2160 — WAR PERCEPT PREDICT MATH
S65

BUTTERFIELD H.,DIPLOMATIC INVESTIGATIONS* ESSAYS IN THE THEORY OF INTERNATIONAL POLITICS. LAW INT/ORG FORCES BAL/PWR ARMS/CONT WAR ALL/VALS...HUM INT/LAW. PAGE 18 E0351 — GEN/LAWS UK DIPLOM
B66

CANFIELD L.H.,THE PRESIDENCY OF WOODROW WILSON: PRELUDE TO A WORLD IN CRISIS. USA-45 ADJUD NEUTRAL WAR CHOOSE INGP/REL PEACE ORD/FREE 20 WILSON/W PRESIDENT TREATY LEAGUE/NAT. PAGE 19 E0373 — PERSON POLICY DIPLOM GOV/REL
B66

CLARK G.,WORLD PEACE THROUGH WORLD LAW; TWO ALTERNATIVE PLANS. WOR+45 DELIB/GP FORCES TAX CONFER ADJUD SANCTION ARMS/CONT WAR CHOOSE PRIVIL 20 UN COLD/WAR. PAGE 23 E0450 — INT/LAW PEACE PLAN INT/ORG
B66

COPLIN W.D.,THE FUNCTIONS OF INTERNATIONAL LAW. WOR+45 ECO/DEV ECO/UNDEV ADJUD COLONIAL WAR OWN SOVEREIGN...POLICY GEN/LAWS 20. PAGE 25 E0503 — INT/LAW DIPLOM INT/ORG
B66

DOUMA J.,BIBLIOGRAPHY ON THE INTERNATIONAL COURT INCLUDING THE PERMANENT COURT, 1918-1964. WOR+45 WOR-45 DELIB/GP WAR PRIVIL...JURID NAT/COMP 20 UN LEAGUE/NAT. PAGE 33 E0645 — BIBLIOG/A INT/ORG CT/SYS DIPLOM
B66

DYCK H.V.,WEIMAR GERMANY AND SOVIET RUSSIA 1926-1933. EUR+WWI GERMANY UK USSR ECO/TAC INT/TRADE NEUTRAL WAR ATTIT 20 WEIMAR/REP TREATY. PAGE 34 E0669 — DIPLOM GOV/REL POLICY
B66

FALK R.A.,THE STRATEGY OF WORLD ORDER* 4 VOLUMES. WOR+45 ECO/UNDEV ACADEM INT/ORG ACT/RES DIPLOM ARMS/CONT WAR...NET/THEORY SIMUL BIBLIOG UN. PAGE 36 E0719 — ORD/FREE GEN/LAWS ANTHOL INT/LAW
B66

INTL ATOMIC ENERGY AGENCY,INTERNATIONAL CONVENTIONS ON CIVIL LIABILITY FOR NUCLEAR DAMAGE. FUT WOR+45 — DIPLOM INT/ORG
B66

ADJUD WAR COST PEACE SOVEREIGN...JURID 20. PAGE 57
E1135

DELIB/GP
NUC/PWR

B66

MCNAIR A.D.,THE LEGAL EFFECTS OF WAR. UK FINAN
DIPLOM ORD/FREE 20 ENGLSH/LAW. PAGE 71 E1425

JURID
WAR
INT/TRADE
LABOR

B66

OBERMANN E.,VERTEIDIGUNG PER FREIHEIT. GERMANY/W
WOR+45 INT/ORG COERCE NUC/PWR WEAPON MARXISM 20 UN
NATO WARSAW/P TREATY. PAGE 78 E1571

FORCES
ORD/FREE
WAR
PEACE

B66

SALTER L.M.,RESOLUTION OF INTERNATIONAL CONFLICT.
USA+45 INT/ORG SECT DIPLOM ECO/TAC FOR/AID DETER
NUC/PWR WAR 20. PAGE 87 E1743

PROB/SOLV
PEACE
INT/LAW
POLICY

B66

THOMPSON J.M.,RUSSIA, BOLSHEVISM, AND THE
VERSAILLES PEACE. RUSSIA USSR INT/ORG NAT/G
DELIB/GP AGREE REV WAR PWR 20 TREATY VERSAILLES
BOLSHEVISM. PAGE 96 E1919

DIPLOM
PEACE
MARXISM

B66

US HOUSE UNAMER ACTIV COMM,HEARINGS ON BILLS TO
MAKE PUNISHABLE ASSISTANCE TO ENEMIES OF US IN TIME
OF UNDECLARED WAR. USA+45 VIETNAM/N EDU/PROP
CONTROL WAR MARXISM HOUSE/REP. PAGE 100 E2010

LAW
SANCTION
VOL/ASSN
GIVE

L66

HOLSTI K.J.,"RESOLVING INTERNATIONAL CONFLICTS* A
TAXONOMY OF BEHAVIOR AND SOME FIGURES ON
PROCEDURES." WOR+45 WOR-45 INT/ORG ADJUD EFFICIENCY
...STAT IDEA/COMP. PAGE 55 E1089

DIPLOM
PROB/SOLV
WAR
CLASSIF

B67

BOHANNAN P.,LAW AND WARFARE. CULTURE CT/SYS COERCE
REV PEACE...JURID SOC CONCPT ANTHOL 20. PAGE 13
E0259

METH/COMP
ADJUD
WAR
LAW

B67

BOULTON D.,OBJECTION OVERRULED. UK LAW POL/PAR
DIPLOM ADJUD SANCTION DEATH WAR CIVMIL/REL 20.
PAGE 14 E0273

FORCES
SOCISM
SECT

B67

HOLCOMBE A.N.,A STRATEGY OF PEACE IN A CHANGING
WORLD. USA+45 WOR+45 LAW NAT/G CREATE DIPLOM
ARMS/CONT WAR...CHARTS 20 UN COLD/WAR. PAGE 54
E1072

PEACE
PLAN
INT/ORG
INT/LAW

B67

HOLSTI K.J.,INTERNATIONAL POLITICS* A FRAMEWORK FOR
ANALYSIS. WOR+45 WOR-45 NAT/G EDU/PROP DETER WAR
WEAPON PWR BIBLIOG. PAGE 55 E1090

DIPLOM
BARGAIN
POLICY
INT/LAW

B67

LAWYERS COMM AMER POLICY VIET,VIETNAM AND
INTERNATIONAL LAW: AN ANALYSIS OF THE LEGALITY OF
THE US MILITARY INVOLVEMENT. VIETNAM LAW INT/ORG
COERCE WEAPON PEACE ORD/FREE 20 UN SEATO TREATY.
PAGE 64 E1271

INT/LAW
DIPLOM
ADJUD
WAR

B67

MANVELL R.,THE INCOMPARABLE CRIME. GERMANY ACT/RES
DEATH...BIBLIOG 20 JEWS. PAGE 68 E1364

MURDER
CRIME
WAR
HIST/WRIT

B67

MARTIN L.W.,THE SEA IN MODERN STRATEGY. LAW ECO/TAC
WAR. PAGE 69 E1374

ROLE
PWR
NUC/PWR
DIPLOM

B67

MEYERS M.,SOURCES OF THE AMERICAN REPUBLIC: A
DOCUMENTARY HISTORY OF POLITICS, SOCIETY, AND
THOUGHT (VOL. I, REV. ED.). USA-45 CULTURE STRUCT
NAT/G LEGIS LEAD ATTIT...JURID SOC ANTHOL 17/19
PRESIDENT. PAGE 72 E1450

COLONIAL
REV
WAR

B67

RUSSELL B.,WAR CRIMES IN VIETNAM. USA+45 VIETNAM
FORCES DIPLOM WEAPON RACE/REL DISCRIM ISOLAT
BIO/SOC 20 COLD/WAR RUSSELL/B. PAGE 87 E1736

WAR
CRIME
ATTIT
POLICY

B67

US DEPARTMENT OF STATE,TREATIES IN FORCE. USA+45

BIBLIOG

WOR+45 AGREE WAR PEACE 20 TREATY. PAGE 100 E1999

DIPLOM
INT/ORG
DETER

B67

US SENATE COMM ON FOREIGN REL,FOREIGN ASSISTANCE
ACT OF 1967. VIETNAM WOR+45 DELIB/GP CONFER CONTROL
WAR WEAPON BAL/PAY...CENSUS CHARTS SENATE. PAGE 102
E2036

FOR/AID
LAW
DIPLOM
POLICY

B67

WATT A.,THE EVOLUTION OF AUSTRALIAN FOREIGN POLICY
1938-65. ASIA S/ASIA USA+45 USA-45 INT/ORG NAT/G
FORCES FOR/AID TREATY 20 AUSTRAL. PAGE 105 E2103

DIPLOM
WAR

L67

LEGAULT A.,"ORGANISATION ET CONDUITE DES OPERATIONS
DE MAINTIEN DE LA PAIX." FORCES ACT/RES ADJUD AGREE
CONTROL NEUTRAL TASK PRIVIL ORD/FREE 20 UN. PAGE 64
E1279

INT/ORG
PEACE
WAR
INT/LAW

S67

COHN K.,"CRIMES AGAINST HUMANITY." GERMANY INT/ORG
SANCTION ATTIT ORD/FREE...MARXIST CRIMLGY 20 UN.
PAGE 24 E0469

WAR
INT/LAW
CRIME
ADJUD

S67

MATTHEWS R.O.,"THE SUEZ CANAL DISPUTE* A CASE STUDY
IN PEACEFUL SETTLEMENT." FRANCE ISRAEL UAR UK NAT/G
CONTROL LEAD COERCE WAR NAT/LISM ROLE ORD/FREE PWR
...INT/LAW UN 20. PAGE 69 E1389

PEACE
DIPLOM
ADJUD

S67

MC REYNOLDS D.,"THE RESISTANCE." USA+45 LAW ADJUD
SANCTION INGP/REL PEACE 20. PAGE 70 E1398

ATTIT
WAR
LEGIT
FORCES

S67

TOMASEK R.D.,"THE CHILEAN-BOLIVIAN LAUCA RIVER
DISPUTE AND THE OAS." CHILE L/A+17C PROB/SOLV ADJUD
CONTROL PEACE 20 BOLIV OAS. PAGE 96 E1930

INT/ORG
DIPLOM
GEOG
WAR

B68

HULL R.H.,LAW AND VIETNAM. COM VIETNAM CONSTN
INT/ORG FORCES DIPLOM AGREE COERCE DETER WEAPON
PEACE ATTIT 20 UN TREATY. PAGE 56 E1113

POLICY
LAW
WAR
INT/LAW

C93

PLAYFAIR R.L.,"A BIBLIOGRAPHY OF MOROCCO." MOROCCO
CULTURE AGRI FORCES DIPLOM WAR HEALTH...GEOG JURID
SOC CHARTS. PAGE 81 E1620

BIBLIOG
ISLAM
MEDIT-7

B99

BROOKS S.,BRITAIN AND THE BOERS. AFR SOUTH/AFR UK
CULTURE INSPECT LEGIT...INT/LAW 19/20 BOER/WAR.
PAGE 16 E0309

WAR
DIPLOM
NAT/G

WAR/TRIAL....WAR TRIAL; SEE ALSO NUREMBERG

B49

JACKSON R.H.,INTERNATIONAL CONFERENCE ON MILITARY
TRIALS. FRANCE GERMANY UK USA+45 USSR VOL/ASSN
DELIB/GP REPAR ADJUD CT/SYS CRIME WAR 20 WAR/TRIAL.
PAGE 57 E1141

DIPLOM
INT/ORG
INT/LAW
CIVMIL/REL

L61

SILVING H.,"IN RE EICHMANN: A DILEMMA OF LAW AND
MORALITY" WOR+45 INSPECT ADJUST MORAL...JURID 20
WAR/TRIAL EICHMANN/A NATURL/LAW. PAGE 91 E1828

CT/SYS
INT/LAW
CONCPT

B66

HAUSNER G.,JUSTICE IN JERUSALEM. GERMANY ISRAEL
SOCIETY KIN DIPLOM LEGIT CT/SYS PARTIC MURDER
MAJORITY ATTIT FASCISM...INT/LAW JURID 20 JEWS
WAR/TRIAL. PAGE 51 E1013

ADJUD
CRIME
RACE/REL
COERCE

WAR/1812....WAR OF 1812

WARD R.E. E2098,E2099

WARD....SEE LOC/G, POL/PAR

WARD/LEST....LESTER WARD

WARRN/EARL....EARL WARREN

B56

DOUGLAS W.O.,WE THE JUDGES. INDIA USA+45 USA-45 LAW
NAT/G SECT LEGIS PRESS CRIME FEDERAL ORD/FREE
...POLICY GOV/COMP 19/20 WARRN/EARL MARSHALL/J
SUPREME/CT. PAGE 32 E0640

ADJUD
CT/SYS
CONSTN
GOV/REL

CHRISTMAN H.M.,THE PUBLIC PAPERS OF CHIEF JUSTICE EARL WARREN. CONSTN POL/PAR EDU/PROP SANCTION HEALTH...TREND 20 SUPREME/CT WARRN/EARL. PAGE 22 E0436
LAW
CT/SYS
PERSON
ADJUD
B59

MASON A.T.,"THE SUPREME COURT: TEMPLE AND FORUM" (BMR)" USA+45 USA-45 CONSTN DELIB/GP RACE/REL MAJORITY ORD/FREE...DECISION SOC/INTEG 19/20 SUPREME/CT WARRN/EARL CIV/RIGHTS. PAGE 69 E1377
CT/SYS
JURID
PWR
ATTIT
S59

MURPHY W.F.,CONGRESS AND THE COURT. USA+45 LAW LOBBY GP/REL RACE/REL ATTIT PWR...JURID INT BIBLIOG CONGRESS SUPREME/CT WARRN/EARL. PAGE 75 E1509
LEGIS
CT/SYS
GOV/REL
ADJUD
B62

CAHN E.,THE GREAT RIGHTS. USA+45 NAT/G PROVS CIVMIL/REL...IDEA/COMP ANTHOL BIBLIOG 18/20 MADISON/J BILL/RIGHT CIV/RIGHTS WARRN/EARL BLACK/HL. PAGE 18 E0361
CONSTN
LAW
ORD/FREE
INGP/REL
B63

LIVELY E.,THE INVASION OF MISSISSIPPI. USA+45 LAW CONSTN NAT/G PROVS CT/SYS GOV/REL FEDERAL CONSERVE ...TRADIT 20 MISSISSIPP NEGRO NAACP WARRN/EARL KENNEDY/JF. PAGE 66 E1309
RACE/REL
CROWD
COERCE
MARXISM
B63

WARSAW PACT....SEE WARSAW/PCT

WARSAW....WARSAW, POLAND

WARSAW/PCT....WARSAW PACT TREATY ORGANIZATION

GRZYBOWSKI K.,THE SOCIALIST COMMONWEALTH OF NATIONS: ORGANIZATIONS AND INSTITUTIONS. FORCES DIPLOM INT/TRADE ADJUD ADMIN LEAD WAR MARXISM SOCISM...BIBLIOG 20 COMECON WARSAW/P. PAGE 48 E0956
INT/LAW
COM
REGION
INT/ORG
B64

OBERMANN E.,VERTEIDIGUNG PER FREIHEIT. GERMANY/W WOR+45 INT/ORG COERCE NUC/PWR WEAPON MARXISM 20 UN NATO WARSAW/P TREATY. PAGE 78 E1571
FORCES
ORD/FREE
WAR
PEACE
B66

WASHING/BT....BOOKER T. WASHINGTON

WASHING/DC....WASHINGTON, D.C.

WASHINGT/G....PRESIDENT GEORGE WASHINGTON

CAMPBELL E.H.,UNITED STATES CITIZENSHIP AND QUALIFICATIONS FOR VOTING IN WASHINGTON. USA+45 NAT/G PROVS...CHARTS BIBLIOG 20 WASHINGT/G. PAGE 19 E0371
LAW
CONSTN
SUFF
CHOOSE
B51

BAKER G.E.,THE POLITICS OF REAPPORTIONMENT IN WASHINGTON STATE. LAW POL/PAR CREATE EDU/PROP PARL/PROC CHOOSE INGP/REL...CHARTS METH/COMP 20 WASHINGT/G LEAGUE/WV. PAGE 7 E0139
VOL/ASSN
APPORT
PROVS
LEGIS
B60

AVERY M.W.,GOVERNMENT OF WASHINGTON STATE. USA+45 MUNIC DELIB/GP EX/STRUC LEGIS GIVE CT/SYS PARTIC REGION EFFICIENCY 20 WASHINGT/G GOVERNOR. PAGE 6 E0121
PROVS
LOC/G
ADMIN
GOV/REL
B61

CAMPBELL E.H.,SURVEYS, SUBDIVISIONS AND PLATTING, AND BOUNDARIES: WASHINGTON STATE LAW AND JUDICIAL DECISIONS. USA+45 LAW LOC/G...DECISION JURID CON/ANAL BIBLIOG WASHINGT/G PARTITION WATER. PAGE 19 E0372
CONSTN
PLAN
GEOG
PROVS
B65

WASHINGTON S.H. E2100

WASHINGTON....WASHINGTON, STATE OF

WASP....WHITE-ANGLO-SAXON-PROTESTANT ESTABLISHMENT

WASSENBERGH H.A. E2101

WASSERSTROM R.A. E2102

WATANABE H. E2099

WATER POLLUTION....SEE POLLUTION

WATER....PERTAINING TO ALL NON-SALT WATER

MURPHY E.F.,WATER PURITY: A STUDY IN LEGAL CONTROL OF NATURAL RESOURCES. LOC/G ACT/RES PLAN TEC/DEV LOBBY GP/REL COST ATTIT HEALTH ORD/FREE...HEAL JURID 20 WISCONSIN WATER. PAGE 75 E1506
SEA
LAW
PROVS
CONTROL
B61

CAMPBELL E.H.,SURVEYS, SUBDIVISIONS AND PLATTING, AND BOUNDARIES: WASHINGTON STATE LAW AND JUDICIAL DECISIONS. USA+45 LAW LOC/G...DECISION JURID CON/ANAL BIBLIOG WASHINGT/G PARTITION WATER. PAGE 19 E0372
CONSTN
PLAN
GEOG
PROVS
B65

WATT A. E2103

WATTS....WATTS, LOS ANGELES

WAY H.F. E2104

WCC....WORLD COUNCIL CHURCHES

WCTU....WOMAN'S CHRISTIAN TEMPERANCE UNION

WEALTH....ACCESS TO GOODS AND SERVICES (ALSO POVERTY)

INTERNATIONAL STUDIES. ASIA S/ASIA WOR+45 ECO/UNDEV INT/ORG NAT/G LEAD ATTIT WEALTH...SOC 20. PAGE 1 E0009
BIBLIOG/A
DIPLOM
INT/LAW
INT/TRADE
N

PERSONNEL. USA+45 LAW LABOR LG/CO WORKER CREATE GOV/REL PERS/REL ATTIT WEALTH. PAGE 2 E0029
BIBLIOG/A
ADMIN
MGT
GP/REL
N

TURNER R.K.,BIBLIOGRAPHY ON WORLD ORGANIZATION. INT/TRADE CT/SYS ARMS/CONT WEALTH...INT/LAW 20. PAGE 97 E1944
BIBLIOG/A
INT/ORG
PEACE
WAR
N

HISTORICUS,"LETTERS AND SOME QUESTIONS OF INTERNATIONAL LAW." FRANCE NETHERLAND UK USA-45 WOR-45 LAW NAT/G COERCE...SOC CONCPT GEN/LAWS TOT/POP 19 CIVIL/WAR. PAGE 53 E1054
WEALTH
JURID
WAR
INT/LAW
L00

MOREL E.D.,THE BRITISH CASE IN FRENCH CONGO. CONGO/BRAZ FRANCE UK COERCE MORAL WEALTH...POLICY INT/LAW 20 CONGO/LEOP. PAGE 74 E1490
DIPLOM
INT/TRADE
COLONIAL
AFR
B03

GRIFFIN A.P.C.,LIST OF MORE RECENT WORKS ON FEDERAL CONTROL OF COMMERCE AND CORPORATIONS (PAMPHLET). USA-45 LAW ECO/DEV FINAN LG/CO TARIFFS TAX LICENSE CENTRAL ORD/FREE WEALTH LAISSEZ 19/20. PAGE 47 E0931
BIBLIOG/A
NAT/G
JURID
ECO/TAC
B07

CRAIG J.,ELEMENTS OF POLITICAL SCIENCE (3 VOLS.). CONSTN AGRI INDUS SCHOOL FORCES TAX CT/SYS SUFF MORAL WEALTH...CONCPT 19 CIVIL/LIB. PAGE 27 E0539
PHIL/SCI
NAT/G
ORD/FREE
B14

BREWER D.J.,THE MOVEMENT OF COERCION (PAMPHLET). CONSTN INDUS ADJUD COERCE OWN WEALTH...OLD/LIB JURID 19 SUPREME/CT. PAGE 15 E0296
GP/REL
LABOR
LG/CO
LAW
N18

SMITH R.H.,JUSTICE AND THE POOR. LAW RECEIVE ADJUD CRIME GOV/REL COST...JURID SOC/WK CONCPT STAT CHARTS GP/COMP 20. PAGE 92 E1847
CT/SYS
DISCRIM
WEALTH
B19

CARPER E.T.,LOBBYING AND THE NATURAL GAS BILL (PAMPHLET). USA+45 SERV/IND BARGAIN PAY DRIVE ROLE WEALTH 20 CONGRESS SENATE EISNHWR/DD. PAGE 20 E0389
LOBBY
ADJUD
TRIBUTE
NAT/G
N19

FEIS H.,"RESEARCH ACTIVITIES OF THE LEAGUE OF NATIONS." EUR+WWI WOR-45 R+D INT/ORG CT/SYS ARMS/CONT WEALTH...OBS RECORD LEAGUE/NAT ILO 20. PAGE 37 E0729
CONSULT
KNOWL
PEACE
L29

EVANS I.L.,NATIVE POLICY IN SOUTHERN AFRICA. RHODESIA SOUTH/AFR UK STRUCT PARTIC RACE/REL ATTIT WEALTH SOC/INTEG AFRICA/SW. PAGE 35 E0705
AFR
COLONIAL
DOMIN
LAW
B34

SAINT-PIERRE C.I.,SCHEME FOR LASTING PEACE (TRANS.
BY H. BELLOT). INDUS NAT/G CHIEF FORCES INT/TRADE
CT/SYS WAR PWR SOVEREIGN WEALTH...POLICY 18.
PAGE 87 E1741
INT/ORG
PEACE
AGREE
INT/LAW
B38

GILLETTE J.M.,PROBLEMS OF A CHANGING SOCIAL ORDER.
USA+45 STRATA FAM CONTROL CRIME RACE/REL HEALTH
WEALTH...GEOG GP/COMP. PAGE 43 E0862
BIO/SOC
ADJUST
ATTIT
SOC/WK
B42

BENTHAM J.,"THE RATIONALE OF REWARD" IN J. BOWRING,
ED., THE WORKS OF JEREMY BENTHAM (VOL. 2)" LAW
WORKER CREATE INSPECT PAY ROUTINE HAPPINESS PRODUC
SUPEGO WEALTH METH/CNCPT. PAGE 10 E0195
SANCTION
ECO/TAC
INCOME
PWR
C43

HILL N.,CLAIMS TO TERRITORY IN INTERNATIONAL LAW
AND RELATIONS. WOR-45 NAT/G DOMIN EDU/PROP LEGIT
REGION ROUTINE ORD/FREE PWR WEALTH...GEOG INT/LAW
JURID 20. PAGE 52 E1047
INT/ORG
ADJUD
SOVEREIGN
B45

GILLIN J.L.,SOCIAL PATHOLOGY. SOCIETY SECT CRIME
ANOMIE DISPL ORD/FREE WEALTH...CRIMLGY PSY WORSHIP.
PAGE 44 E0864
SOC
ADJUST
CULTURE
INGP/REL
B46

GORDON D.L.,THE HIDDEN WEAPON: THE STORY OF
ECONOMIC WARFARE. EUR+WWI USA-45 LAW FINAN INDUS
NAT/G CONSULT FORCES PLAN DOMIN PWR WEALTH
...INT/LAW CONCPT OBS TOT/POP NAZI 20. PAGE 45
E0891
INT/ORG
ECO/TAC
INT/TRADE
WAR
B47

TOWLE L.W.,INTERNATIONAL TRADE AND COMMERCIAL
POLICY. WOR+45 LAW ECO/DEV FINAN INDUS NAT/G
ECO/TAC WEALTH...TIME/SEQ ILO 20. PAGE 97 E1937
MARKET
INT/ORG
INT/TRADE
B47

ANGELL R.C.,"THE SOCIAL INTEGRATION OF AMERICAN
CITIES OF MORE THAN 1000,000 POPULATION" (BMR)"
USA+45 SOCIETY CRIME ADJUST WEALTH...GEOG SOC
CONCPT INDICATOR SAMP CHARTS SOC/INTEG 20. PAGE 5
E0098
MUNIC
CENSUS
GP/REL
S47

MANGONE G.,"THE IDEA AND PRACTICE OF WORLD
GOVERNMENT." FUT WOR+45 WOR-45 ECO/DEV LEGIS CREATE
LEGIT ROUTINE ATTIT MORAL PWR WEALTH...CONCPT
GEN/LAWS 20. PAGE 68 E1358
INT/ORG
SOCIETY
INT/LAW
L51

WALTER P.A.F.,RACE AND CULTURE RELATIONS. FAM
HEALTH WEALTH...POLICY CRIMLGY GEOG BIBLIOG T 20.
PAGE 105 E2097
RACE/REL
DISCRIM
GP/REL
CONCPT
B52

MAJUMDAR B.B.,PROBLEMS OF PUBLIC ADMINISTRATION IN
INDIA. INDIA INDUS PLAN BUDGET ADJUD CENTRAL DEMAND
WEALTH...WELF/ST ANTHOL 20 CIVIL/SERV. PAGE 68
E1353
ECO/UNDEV
GOV/REL
ADMIN
MUNIC
B53

CARTER P.G.,STATISTICAL BULLETINS: AN ANNOTATED
BIBLIOGRAPHY OF THE GENERAL STATISTICAL BULLETINS
AND MAJOR POL SUBDIV OF WORLD. CULTURE AGRI FINAN
INDUS LABOR TEC/DEV INT/TRADE CT/SYS WEALTH
...CRIMLGY SOC 20. PAGE 20 E0400
BIBLIOG/A
WOR+45
NAT/G
STAT
B54

COMM. STUDY ORGAN. PEACE,REPORTS. WOR-45 ECO/DEV
ECO/UNDEV VOL/ASSN CONSULT FORCES PLAN TEC/DEV
DOMIN EDU/PROP NUC/PWR ATTIT PWR WEALTH...JURID
STERTYP FAO ILO 20 UN. PAGE 24 E0481
WOR+45
INT/ORG
ARMS/CONT
B55

ABELS J.,THE TRUMAN SCANDALS. USA+45 USA-45 POL/PAR
TAX LEGIT CT/SYS CHOOSE PRIVIL MORAL WEALTH 20
TRUMAN/HS PRESIDENT CONGRESS. PAGE 2 E0043
CRIME
ADMIN
CHIEF
TRIBUTE
B56

SYKES G.M.,CRIME AND SOCIETY. LAW STRATA STRUCT
ACT/RES ROUTINE ANOMIE WEALTH...POLICY SOC/INTEG
20. PAGE 95 E1903
CRIMLGY
CRIME
CULTURE
INGP/REL
B56

BERLE A.A. JR.,ECONOMIC POWER AND FREE SOCIETY
(PAMPHLET). CLIENT CONSTN EX/STRUC ECO/TAC CONTROL
PARTIC PWR WEALTH MAJORIT. PAGE 11 E0205
LG/CO
CAP/ISM
INGP/REL
B57

BLOOMFIELD L.M.,EGYPT, ISRAEL AND THE GULF OF
AQABA: IN INTERNATIONAL LAW. LAW NAT/G CONSULT
FORCES PLAN ECO/TAC ROUTINE COERCE ATTIT DRIVE
PERCEPT PERSON RIGID/FLEX LOVE PWR WEALTH...GEOG
CONCPT MYTH TREND. PAGE 13 E0250
ISLAM
INT/LAW
UAR
B57

CONOVER H.F.,NORTH AND NORTHEAST AFRICA; A SELECTED
ANNOTATED LIST OF WRITINGS. ALGERIA MOROCCO SUDAN
UAR CULTURE INT/ORG PROB/SOLV ADJUD NAT/LISM PWR
WEALTH...SOC 20 UN. PAGE 25 E0496
BIBLIOG/A
DIPLOM
AFR
ECO/UNDEV
B57

CHAMBERLIN E.H.,LABOR UNIONS AND PUBLIC POLICY.
PLAN BARGAIN SANCTION INGP/REL JURID. PAGE 21 E0416
LABOR
WEALTH
PWR
NAT/G
B58

MAYDA J.,ATOMIC ENERGY AND LAW. ECO/UNDEV FINAN
TEC/DEV FOR/AID EFFICIENCY PRODUC WEALTH...POLICY
TECHNIC 20. PAGE 70 E1391
NUC/PWR
L/A+17C
LAW
ADMIN
B59

REIFF H.,THE UNITED STATES AND THE TREATY LAW OF
THE SEA. USA+45 USA-45 SEA SOCIETY INT/ORG CONSULT
DELIB/GP LEGIS DIPLOM LEGIT ATTIT ORD/FREE PWR
WEALTH...GEOG JURID TOT/POP 20 TREATY. PAGE 84
E1681
ADJUD
INT/LAW
B59

CARLSTON K.S.,"NATIONALIZATION: AN ANALYTIC
APPROACH." WOR+45 INT/ORG ECO/TAC DOMIN LEGIT ADJUD
COERCE ORD/FREE PWR WEALTH SOCISM...JURID CONCPT
TREND STERTYP TOT/POP VAL/FREE 20. PAGE 19 E0380
INDUS
NAT/G
NAT/LISM
SOVEREIGN
S59

CORY R.H. JR.,"INTERNATIONAL INSPECTION FROM
PROPOSALS TO REALIZATION." WOR+45 TEC/DEV ECO/TAC
ADJUD ORD/FREE PWR WEALTH...RECORD VAL/FREE 20.
PAGE 26 E0516
STRUCT
PSY
ARMS/CONT
NUC/PWR
S59

NICHOLS J.P.,"HAZARDS OF AMERICAN PRIVATE
INVESTMENT IN UNDERDEVELOPED COUNTRIES." FUT
L/A+17C USA+45 USA-45 EXTR/IND CONSULT BAL/PWR
ECO/TAC DOMIN ADJUD ATTIT SOVEREIGN WEALTH
...HIST/WRIT TIME/SEQ TREND VAL/FREE 20. PAGE 77
E1546
FINAN
ECO/UNDEV
CAP/ISM
NAT/LISM
S60

AYLMER G.,THE KING'S SERVANTS. UK ELITES CHIEF PAY
CT/SYS WEALTH 17 CROMWELL/O CHARLES/I. PAGE 6 E0122
ADMIN
ROUTINE
EX/STRUC
NAT/G
B61

JACKSON E.,"THE FUTURE DEVELOPMENT OF THE UNITED
NATIONS: SOME SUGGESTIONS FOR RESEARCH." FUT LAW
CONSTN ECO/DEV FINAN PEACE WEALTH...WELF/ST CONCPT
UN 20. PAGE 57 E1140
INT/ORG
PWR
S61

LASSWELL H.D.,"THE INTERPLAY OF ECONOMIC, POLITICAL
AND SOCIAL CRITERIA IN LEGAL POLICY." LAW LOVE
MORAL PWR RESPECT WEALTH...SOC IDEA/COMP. PAGE 63
E1262
JURID
POLICY
S61

BUREAU OF NATIONAL AFFAIRS,FEDERAL-STATE REGULATION
OF WELFARE FUNDS (REV. ED.). USA+45 LAW LEGIS
DEBATE AGE/O 20 CONGRESS. PAGE 17 E0337
WELF/ST
WEALTH
PLAN
SOC/WK
B62

CARLSTON K.S.,LAW AND ORGANIZATION IN WORLD
SOCIETY. WOR+45 FINAN ECO/TAC DOMIN LEGIT CT/SYS
ROUTINE COERCE ORD/FREE PWR WEALTH...PLURIST
DECISION JURID MGT METH/CNCPT GEN/LAWS 20. PAGE 19
E0381
INT/ORG
LAW
B62

LAWSON R.,INTERNATIONAL REGIONAL ORGANIZATIONS.
WOR+45 NAT/G VOL/ASSN CONSULT LEGIS EDU/PROP LEGIT
ADMIN EXEC ROUTINE HEALTH PWR WEALTH...JURID EEC
COLD/WAR 20 UN. PAGE 63 E1270
INT/ORG
DELIB/GP
REGION
B62

LEVY H.V.,LIBERDADE E JUSTICA SOCIAL (2ND ED.).
BRAZIL COM L/A+17C USSR INT/ORG PARTIC GP/REL
WEALTH 20 UN COM/PARTY. PAGE 65 E1290
ORD/FREE
MARXISM
CAP/ISM
LAW
B62

S62
GANDOLFI A.,"REFLEXIONS SUR L'IMPOT DE CAPITATION   AFR
EN AFRIQUE NOIRE." GHANA SENEGAL LAW FINAN ACT/RES   CHOOSE
TEC/DEV ECO/TAC WEALTH...MGT TREND 20. PAGE 42
E0830

B63
FISCHER-GALATI S.A.,RUMANIA; A BIBLIOGRAPHIC GUIDE   BIBLIOG/A
(PAMPHLET). ROMANIA INTELL ECO/DEV LABOR SECT   NAT/G
WEALTH...GEOG SOC/WK LING 20. PAGE 38 E0756   COM
                                                        LAW

B63
HAUSMAN W.H.,MANAGING ECONOMIC DEVELOPMENT IN   ECO/UNDEV
AFRICA. AFR USA+45 LAW FINAN WORKER TEC/DEV WEALTH   PLAN
...ANTHOL 20. PAGE 51 E1012   FOR/AID
                                                        MGT

B63
HOWARD W.S.,AMERICAN SLAVERS AND THE FEDERAL LAW: DIST/IND
1837-1862. USA-45 NAT/G LEGIT COERCE RACE/REL   CRIMLGY
WEALTH...POLICY BIBLIOG/A 19. PAGE 55 E1102   LAW
                                                        EXEC

B63
PRYOR F.L.,THE COMMUNIST FOREIGN TRADE SYSTEM. COM   ATTIT
CZECHOSLVK GERMANY YUGOSLAVIA LAW ECO/DEV DIST/IND   ECO/TAC
POL/PAR PLAN DOMIN TOTALSM DRIVE RIGID/FLEX WEALTH
...STAT STAND/INT CHARTS 20. PAGE 83 E1657

L63
LISSITZYN O.J.,"INTERNATIONAL LAW IN A DIVIDED   INT/ORG
WORLD." FUT WOR+45 CONSTN CULTURE ECO/DEV ECO/UNDEV   LAW
DIST/IND NAT/G FORCES ECO/TAC LEGIT ADJUD ADMIN
COERCE ATTIT HEALTH MORAL ORD/FREE PWR RESPECT
WEALTH VAL/FREE. PAGE 65 E1306

L63
MCDOUGAL M.S.,"THE ENJOYMENT AND ACQUISITION OF   PLAN
RESOURCES IN OUTER SPACE." CHRIST-17C FUT WOR+45   TREND
WOR-45 LAW EXTR/IND INT/ORG ACT/RES CREATE TEC/DEV
ECO/TAC LEGIT COERCE HEALTH KNOWL ORD/FREE PWR
WEALTH...JURID HIST/WRIT VAL/FREE. PAGE 70 E1408

L63
ROSE R.,"COMPARATIVE STUDIES IN POLITICAL FINANCE: FINAN
A SYMPOSIUM." ASIA EUR+WWI S/ASIA LAW CULTURE   POL/PAR
DELIB/GP LEGIS ACT/RES ECO/TAC EDU/PROP CHOOSE
ATTIT RIGID/FLEX SUPEGO PWR SKILL WEALTH...STAT
ANTHOL VAL/FREE. PAGE 85 E1714

S63
LEPAWSKY A.,"INTERNATIONAL DEVELOPMENT OF RIVER   INT/ORG
RESOURCES." CANADA EUR+WWI S/ASIA USA+45 SEA LEGIT   DELIB/GP
ADJUD ORD/FREE PWR WEALTH...MGT TIME/SEQ VAL/FREE
MEXIC/AMER 20. PAGE 64 E1287

B64
BUREAU OF NATIONAL AFFAIRS,STATE FAIR EMPLOYMENT   PROVS
LAWS AND THEIR ADMINISTRATION. INDUS ADJUD PERS/REL   DISCRIM
RACE/REL ATTIT ORD/FREE WEALTH 20. PAGE 17 E0338   WORKER
                                                        JURID

B64
FREISEN J.,STAAT UND KATHOLISCHE KIRCHE IN DEN   SECT
DEUTSCHEN BUNDESSTAATEN (2 VOLS.). GERMANY LAW FAM   CATHISM
NAT/G EDU/PROP GP/REL MARRIAGE WEALTH 19/20   JURID
CHURCH/STA. PAGE 40 E0793   PROVS

B64
GARDNER L.C.,ECONOMIC ASPECTS OF NEW DEAL   ECO/TAC
DIPLOMACY. USA-45 WOR-45 LAW ECO/DEV INT/ORG NAT/G   DIPLOM
VOL/ASSN LEGIS TOP/EX EDU/PROP ORD/FREE PWR WEALTH
...POLICY TIME/SEQ VAL/FREE 20 ROOSEVLT/F. PAGE 42
E0836

B64
HEKHUIS D.J.,INTERNATIONAL STABILITY: MILITARY,   TEC/DEV
ECONOMIC AND POLITICAL DIMENSIONS. FUT WOR+45 LAW   DETER
ECO/UNDEV INT/ORG NAT/G VOL/ASSN FORCES ACT/RES   REGION
BAL/PWR PWR WEALTH...STAT UN 20. PAGE 51 E1024

B64
KISER S.L.,AMERICANISM IN ACTION. USA+45 LAW PROVS   OLD/LIB
CAP/ISM DIPLOM RECEIVE CONTROL CT/SYS WAR FEDERAL   FOR/AID
ATTIT WEALTH 20 SUPREME/CT. PAGE 61 E1221   MARXISM
                                                        CONSTN

L64
POUNDS N.J.G.,"THE POLITICS OF PARTITION." AFR ASIA   NAT/G
COM EUR+WWI FUT ISLAM S/ASIA USA-45 LAW ECO/DEV   NAT/LISM
ECO/UNDEV AGRI INDUS INT/ORG POL/PAR PROVS SECT
FORCES TOP/EX EDU/PROP LEGIT ATTIT MORAL ORD/FREE
PWR RESPECT WEALTH. PAGE 82 E1640

S64
TRISKA J.F.,"SOVIET TREATY LAW: A QUANTITATIVE   COM
ANALYSIS." WOR+45 LAW ECO/UNDEV AGRI COM/IND INDUS   ECO/TAC
CREATE TEC/DEV DIPLOM ATTIT PWR WEALTH...JURID SAMP   INT/LAW
TIME/SEQ TREND CHARTS VAL/FREE 20 TREATY. PAGE 97   USSR
E1942

B65
HABERLER G.,A SURVEY OF INTERNATIONAL TRADE THEORY.   INT/TRADE
CANADA FRANCE GERMANY ECO/TAC TARIFFS AGREE COST   BAL/PAY
DEMAND WEALTH...ECOMETRIC 19/20 MONOPOLY TREATY.   DIPLOM
PAGE 49 E0968   POLICY

B65
SCHROEDER O.,DEFACTO SEGREGATION AND CIVIL RIGHTS.   ANTHOL
LAW PROVS SCHOOL WORKER ATTIT HABITAT HEALTH WEALTH   DISCRIM
...JURID CHARTS 19/20 NEGRO SUPREME/CT KKK. PAGE 88   RACE/REL
E1766   ORD/FREE

B65
SMITH R.C.,THEY CLOSED THEIR SCHOOLS. USA+45 NEIGH   RACE/REL
ADJUD CROWD CONSEN WEALTH...DECISION OBS INT 20   DISCRIM
NEGRO VIRGINIA. PAGE 92 E1846   LOC/G
                                                        SCHOOL

B65
US OFFICE ECONOMIC OPPORTUNITY,CATALOG OF FEDERAL   BIBLIOG
PROGRAMS FOR INDIVIDUAL AND COMMUNITY IMPROVEMENT.   CLIENT
USA+45 GIVE RECEIVE ADMIN HEALTH KNOWL SKILL WEALTH   ECO/TAC
CHARTS. PAGE 101 E2021   MUNIC

B65
US SENATE COMM ON JUDICIARY,ANTITRUST EXEMPTIONS   BAL/PAY
FOR AGREEMENTS RELATING TO BALANCE OF PAYMENTS.   ADJUD
FINAN ECO/TAC CONTROL WEALTH...POLICY 20 CONGRESS.   MARKET
PAGE 103 E2056   INT/TRADE

B66
AMERICAN JEWISH COMMITTEE,THE TYRANNY OF POVERTY   BIBLIOG/A
(PAMPHLET). USA+45 LAW ECO/DEV LOC/G MUNIC NAT/G   WEALTH
PUB/INST WORKER EDU/PROP CRIME...SOC/WK 20. PAGE 4   WELF/ST
E0080   PROB/SOLV

B66
PLATE H.,PARTEIFINANZIERUNG UND GRUNDESETZ. GERMANY   POL/PAR
NAT/G PLAN GIVE PAY INCOME WEALTH...JURID 20.   CONSTN
PAGE 81 E1619   FINAN

B66
TRESOLINI R.J.,CASES IN AMERICAN NATIONAL   NAT/G
GOVERNMENT AND POLITICS. LAW DIPLOM ADJUD LOBBY   LEGIS
FEDERAL ORD/FREE WEALTH...DECISION ANTHOL 20   CT/SYS
PRESIDENT. PAGE 97 E1940   POL/PAR

B67
BEAL E.F.,THE PRACTICE OF COLLECTIVE BARGAINING   BARGAIN
(3RD ED.). USA+45 WOR+45 ECO/DEV INDUS LG/CO   MGT
PROF/ORG WORKER ECO/TAC GP/REL WEALTH...JURID   LABOR
METH/CNCPT. PAGE 8 E0160   ADJUD

B67
BERNSTEIN S.,ALTERNATIVES TO VIOLENCE: ALIENATED   AGE/Y
YOUTH AND RIOTS. RACE AND POVERTY. MUNIC PUB/INST   SOC/WK
SCHOOL INGP/REL RACE/REL UTOPIA DRIVE HABITAT ROLE   NEIGH
WEALTH...INT 20. PAGE 11 E0215   CRIME

B67
BRAGER G.A.,COMMUNITY ACTION AGAINST POVERTY.   NEIGH
USA+45 LAW STRATA INGP/REL INCOME NEW/LIB...POLICY   WEALTH
WELF/ST ANTHOL. PAGE 15 E0285   SOC/WK
                                                        CREATE

B67
CAVES R.,AMERICAN INDUSTRY: STRUCTURE, CONDUCT,   ECO/DEV
PERFORMANCE (2ND ED.). USA+45 MARKET NAT/G ADJUD   INDUS
CONTROL GP/REL DEMAND WEALTH 20. PAGE 21 E0412   POLICY
                                                        ECO/TAC

B67
CLINARD M.B.,CRIMINAL BEHAVIOR SYSTEMS: A TYPOLOGY.   BIBLIOG
WOR+45 LAW SOCIETY STRUCT R+D AGE/Y ATTIT WEALTH   CRIME
...CLASSIF CHARTS METH/COMP METH. PAGE 23 E0457   CRIMLGY
                                                        PERSON

B67
COHEN M.R.,LAW AND THE SOCIAL ORDER: ESSAYS IN   JURID
LEGAL PHILOSOPHY. USA-45 CONSULT WORKER ECO/TAC   LABOR
ATTIT WEALTH...POLICY WELF/ST SOC 20 NEW/DEAL   IDEA/COMP
DEPRESSION. PAGE 24 E0467

B67
HODGKINSON R.G.,THE ORIGINS OF THE NATIONAL HEALTH   HEAL
SERVICE: THE MEDICAL SERVICES OF THE NEW POOR LAW,   NAT/G
1834-1871. UK INDUS MUNIC WORKER PROB/SOLV   POLICY
EFFICIENCY ATTIT HEALTH WEALTH SOCISM...JURID   LAW
SOC/WK 19/20. PAGE 53 E1062

B67
UNIVERSAL REFERENCE SYSTEM,CURRENT EVENTS AND   BIBLIOG/A
PROBLEMS OF MODERN SOCIETY (VOLUME V). WOR+45 LOC/G   SOCIETY
MUNIC NAT/G PLAN EDU/PROP CRIME RACE/REL WEALTH   PROB/SOLV
...COMPUT/IR GEN/METH. PAGE 98 E1974   ATTIT

S67
DANIEL C.,"FREEDOM, EQUITY, AND THE WAR ON   WEALTH
POVERTY." USA+45 WORKER ECO/TAC JURID. PAGE 29   INCOME
E0566   SOCIETY
                                                      ORD/FREE

S67
MAYER M.,"THE IDEA OF JUSTICE AND THE POOR." USA+45   INCOME
CLIENT CONSULT RENT ADJUD DISCRIM KNOWL 20. PAGE 70   WEALTH
E1393   LAW
                                                      ORD/FREE

B90
GODWIN W.,POLITICAL JUSTICE. UK ELITES OWN KNOWL   ORD/FREE
MORAL WEALTH...JURID 18/19. PAGE 44 E0877   SOVEREIGN
                                                      STRUCT
                                                      CONCPT

B96
SMITH A.,LECTURES ON JUSTICE, POLICE, REVENUE AND   DIPLOM
ARMS (1763). UK LAW FAM FORCES TARIFFS AGREE COERCE   JURID
INCOME OWN WEALTH LAISSEZ...GEN/LAWS 17/18. PAGE 92   OLD/LIB
E1840   TAX

WEAPON.....NON-NUCLEAR WEAPONS

B17
MEYER H.H.B.,LIST OF REFERENCES ON EMBARGOES   BIBLIOG
(PAMPHLET). USA-45 AGRI DIPLOM WRITING DEBATE   DIST/IND
WEAPON...INT/LAW 18/20 CONGRESS. PAGE 72 E1447   ECO/TAC
                                                      INT/TRADE

B36
HUDSON M.O.,INTERNATIONAL LEGISLATION: 1929-1931.   INT/LAW
WOR-45 SEA AIR AGRI FINAN LABOR DIPLOM ECO/TAC   PARL/PROC
REPAR CT/SYS ARMS/CONT WAR WEAPON...JURID 20 TREATY   ADJUD
LEAGUE/NAT. PAGE 56 E1112   LAW

B42
FULLER G.H.,DEFENSE FINANCING: A SUPPLEMENTARY LIST   BIBLIOG/A
OF REFERENCES (PAMPHLET). CANADA UK USA-45 ECO/DEV   FINAN
NAT/G DELIB/GP BUDGET ADJUD ARMS/CONT WEAPON COST   FORCES
PEACE PWR 20 AUSTRAL CHINJAP CONGRESS. PAGE 41   DIPLOM
E0821

B51
INSTITUTE DES RELATIONS INTL,LES ASPECTS   WEAPON
ECONOMIQUES DU REARMEMENT (ETUDE DE L'INSTITUT DES   DEMAND
RELATIONS INTERNATIONALES A BRUXELLES). BELGIUM UK   ECO/TAC
USA+45 EXTR/IND FINAN FORCES WORKER PROB/SOLV   INT/TRADE
DIPLOM PRICE...POLICY 20 TREATY. PAGE 57 E1127

B56
ESTEP R.,AN AIR POWER BIBLIOGRAPHY. USA+45 TEC/DEV   BIBLIOG/A
BUDGET DIPLOM EDU/PROP DETER CIVMIL/REL...DECISION   FORCES
INT/LAW 20. PAGE 35 E0698   WEAPON
                                                      PLAN

N58
US HOUSE COMM FOREIGN AFFAIRS,HEARINGS ON DRAFT   LEGIS
LEGISLATION TO AMEND FURTHER THE MUTUAL SECURITY   DELIB/GP
ACT OF 1954 (PAMPHLET). USA+45 CONSULT FORCES   CONFER
BUDGET DIPLOM DETER COST ORD/FREE...JURID 20   WEAPON
DEPT/DEFEN UN DEPT/STATE. PAGE 100 E2002

S59
PUGWASH CONFERENCE,"ON BIOLOGICAL AND CHEMICAL   ACT/RES
WARFARE." WOR+45 SOCIETY PROC/MFG INT/ORG FORCES   BIO/SOC
EDU/PROP ADJUD RIGID/FLEX ORD/FREE PWR...DECISION   WAR
PSY NEW/IDEA MATH VAL/FREE 20. PAGE 83 E1661   WEAPON

S61
RICHSTEIN A.R.,"LEGAL RULES IN NUCLEAR WEAPONS   NUC/PWR
EMPLOYMENTS." FUT WOR+45 LAW SOCIETY FORCES PLAN   TEC/DEV
WEAPON RIGID/FLEX...HEAL CONCPT TREND VAL/FREE 20.   MORAL
PAGE 85 E1696   ARMS/CONT

B64
SCHWARTZ M.D.,CONFERENCE ON SPACE SCIENCE AND SPACE   SPACE
LAW. FUT COM/IND NAT/G FORCES ACT/RES PLAN BUDGET   LAW
DIPLOM NUC/PWR WEAPON...POLICY ANTHOL 20. PAGE 89   PEACE
E1788   TEC/DEV

B66
OBERMANN E.,VERTEIDIGUNG PER FREIHEIT. GERMANY/W   FORCES
WOR+45 INT/ORG COERCE NUC/PWR WEAPON MARXISM 20 UN   ORD/FREE
NATO WARSAW/P TREATY. PAGE 78 E1571   WAR
                                                      PEACE

B67
HOLSTI K.J.,INTERNATIONAL POLITICS* A FRAMEWORK FOR   DIPLOM
ANALYSIS. WOR+45 WOR-45 NAT/G EDU/PROP DETER WAR   BARGAIN
WEAPON PWR BIBLIOG. PAGE 55 E1090   POLICY
                                                      INT/LAW

B67
LAWYERS COMM AMER POLICY VIET,VIETNAM AND   INT/LAW
INTERNATIONAL LAW: AN ANALYSIS OF THE LEGALITY OF   DIPLOM
THE US MILITARY INVOLVEMENT. VIETNAM LAW INT/ORG   ADJUD
COERCE WEAPON PEACE ORD/FREE 20 UN SEATO TREATY.   WAR
PAGE 64 E1271

B67
RUSSELL B.,WAR CRIMES IN VIETNAM. USA+45 VIETNAM   WAR
FORCES DIPLOM WEAPON RACE/REL DISCRIM ISOLAT   CRIME
BIO/SOC 20 COLD/WAR RUSSELL/B. PAGE 87 E1736   ATTIT
                                                      POLICY

B67
US SENATE COMM ON FOREIGN REL,UNITED STATES   ARMS/CONT
ARMAMENT AND DISARMAMENT PROBLEMS. USA+45 AIR   WEAPON
BAL/PWR DIPLOM FOR/AID NUC/PWR ORD/FREE SENATE   FORCES
TREATY. PAGE 102 E2035   PROB/SOLV

B67
US SENATE COMM ON FOREIGN REL,FOREIGN ASSISTANCE   FOR/AID
ACT OF 1967. VIETNAM WOR+45 DELIB/GP CONFER CONTROL   LAW
WAR WEAPON BAL/PAY...CENSUS CHARTS SENATE. PAGE 102   DIPLOM
E2036   POLICY

B68
HULL R.H.,LAW AND VIETNAM. COM VIETNAM CONSTN   POLICY
INT/ORG FORCES DIPLOM AGREE COERCE DETER WEAPON   LAW
PEACE ATTIT 20 UN TREATY. PAGE 56 E1113   WAR
                                                      INT/LAW

WEATHER....WEATHER

WEBER/MAX....MAX WEBER

WEBSTER J.A. E2105

WECHSLER H. E2106

WEIDNER E.W. E0094

WEIL G.L. E2107

WEIMAR/REP....WEIMAR REPUBLIC

B55
FLIESS P.J.,FREEDOM OF THE PRESS IN THE GERMAN   EDU/PROP
REPUBLIC, 1918-1933. GERMANY LAW CONSTN POL/PAR   ORD/FREE
LEGIS WRITING ADMIN COERCE MURDER MARXISM...POLICY   JURID
BIBLIOG 20 WEIMAR/REP. PAGE 39 E0765   PRESS

B66
DYCK H.V.,WEIMAR GERMANY AND SOVIET RUSSIA   DIPLOM
1926-1933. EUR+WWI GERMANY UK USSR ECO/TAC   GOV/REL
INT/TRADE NEUTRAL WAR ATTIT 20 WEIMAR/REP TREATY.   POLICY
PAGE 34 E0669

WEINSTEIN J.B. E2108

WEIS P. E2109

WEISSBERG G. E2110

WEITZEL R. E1936

WELF/ST....WELFARE STATE ADVOCATE

B53
MAJUMDAR B.B.,PROBLEMS OF PUBLIC ADMINISTRATION IN   ECO/UNDEV
INDIA. INDIA INDUS PLAN BUDGET ADJUD CENTRAL DEMAND   GOV/REL
WEALTH...WELF/ST ANTHOL 20 CIVIL/SERV. PAGE 68   ADMIN
E1353   MUNIC

B59
HOOK S.,POLITICAL POWER AND PERSONAL FREEDOM: ORD/FREE
CRITICAL STUDIES IN DEMOCRACY, COMMUNISM AND CIVIL   PWR
RIGHTS. UNIV LAW SOCIETY DIPLOM TOTALISM MARXISM   WELF/ST
SOCISM...PHIL/SCI IDEA/COMP 20 CIV/RIGHTS. PAGE 55   CHOOSE
E1094

S61
JACKSON E.,"THE FUTURE DEVELOPMENT OF THE UNITED   INT/ORG
NATIONS: SOME SUGGESTIONS FOR RESEARCH." FUT LAW   PWR
CONSTN ECO/DEV FINAN PEACE WEALTH...WELF/ST CONCPT
UN 20. PAGE 57 E1140

S61
MILLER E.,"LEGAL ASPECTS OF UN ACTION IN THE   INT/ORG
CONGO." AFR CULTURE ADMIN PEACE DRIVE RIGID/FLEX   LEGIT
ORD/FREE...WELF/ST JURID OBS UN CONGO 20. PAGE 73

E1458

                                                                    B62
BUREAU OF NATIONAL AFFAIRS,FEDERAL-STATE REGULATION   WELF/ST
OF WELFARE FUNDS (REV. ED.). USA+45 LAW LEGIS   WEALTH
DEBATE AGE/O 20 CONGRESS. PAGE 17 E0337   PLAN
                                                       SOC/WK

                                                                    B66
AMERICAN JEWISH COMMITTEE,GROUP RELATIONS IN THE   BIBLIOG/A
UNITED STATES: PROBLEMS AND PERSPECTIVES: A   USA+45
SELECTED, ANNOTATED BIBLIOGRAPHY (PAMPHLET). LAW   STRUCT
CONSTN STRATA SCHOOL SECT PROB/SOLV ATTIT...POLICY   GP/REL
WELF/ST SOC/WK 20. PAGE 4 E0079

                                                                    B66
AMERICAN JEWISH COMMITTEE,THE TYRANNY OF POVERTY   BIBLIOG/A
(PAMPHLET). USA+45 LAW ECO/DEV LOC/G MUNIC NAT/G   WEALTH
PUB/INST WORKER EDU/PROP CRIME...SOC/WK 20. PAGE 4   WELF/ST
E0080   PROB/SOLV

                                                                    B67
BRAGER G.A.,COMMUNITY ACTION AGAINST POVERTY.   NEIGH
USA+45 LAW STRATA INGP/REL INCOME NEW/LIB...POLICY   WEALTH
WELF/ST ANTHOL. PAGE 15 E0285   SOC/WK
                                                       CREATE

                                                                    B67
COHEN M.R.,LAW AND THE SOCIAL ORDER: ESSAYS IN   JURID
LEGAL PHILOSOPHY. USA-45 CONSULT WORKER ECO/TAC   LABOR
ATTIT WEALTH...POLICY WELF/ST SOC 20 NEW/DEAL   IDEA/COMP
DEPRESSION. PAGE 24 E0467

WELFARE....SEE RECEIVE, NEW/LIB, WELF/ST

WELFARE STATE....SEE NEW/LIB, WELF/ST

WELLFORD C.F. E0071

WENGLER W. E2111

WEST R. E2112

WEST GERMANY....SEE GERMANY/W

WEST/EDWRD....SIR EDWARD WEST

WEST/IND....WEST INDIES; SEE ALSO L/A+17C

                                                                    B42
BLANCHARD L.R.,MARTINIQUE: A SELECTED LIST OF   BIBLIOG/A
REFERENCES (PAMPHLET). WEST/IND AGRI LOC/G SCHOOL   SOCIETY
...ART/METH GEOG JURID CHARTS 20. PAGE 12 E0241   CULTURE
                                                       COLONIAL

WEST/POINT....UNITED STATES MILITARY ACADEMY

WEST/SAMOA....WESTERN SAMOA; SEE ALSO S/ASIA

WEST/VIRGN....WEST VIRGINIA

WESTERN EUROPE....SEE EUROPE/W

WESTERN SAMOA....SEE WEST/SAMOA

WESTIN A.F. E0399,E0563,E1654,E2113,E2114

WESTMINSTER HALL, COURTS OF....SEE CTS/WESTM

WESTPHALIA....PEACE OF WESTPHALIA

                                                                    S48
GROSS L.,"THE PEACE OF WESTPHALIA, 1648-1948."   INT/LAW
WOR+45 WOR-45 CONSTN BAL/PWR FEDERAL 17/20 TREATY   AGREE
WESTPHALIA. PAGE 48 E0949   CONCPT
                                                       DIPLOM

WHEARE K.C. E2115,E2116

WHIG/PARTY....WHIG PARTY (USE WITH SPECIFIC NATION)

                                                                    B64
HOLDSWORTH W.S.,A HISTORY OF ENGLISH LAW; THE   LAW
CENTURIES OF DEVELOPMENT AND REFORM (VOL. XIV). UK   LEGIS
CONSTN LOC/G NAT/G POL/PAR CHIEF EX/STRUC ADJUD   LEAD
COLONIAL ATTIT...INT/LAW JURID 18/19 TORY/PARTY   CT/SYS
COMMONWLTH WHIG/PARTY COMMON/LAW. PAGE 54 E1081

WHIP....SEE LEGIS, ROUTINE

WHITE G.M. E2117

WHITE/SUP....WHITE SUPREMACY - PERSONS, GROUPS, AND IDEAS

WHITE/T....THEODORE WHITE

WHITE/WA....WILLIAM ALLEN WHITE

WHITEHD/AN....ALFRED NORTH WHITEHEAD

WHITE-ANGLO-SAXON-PROTESTANT ESTABLISHMENT....SEE WASP

WHITEMAN M.M. E2118

WHITMAN/W....WALT WHITMAN

WHITNEY S.N. E2119

WHITRIDGE L.I. E2120

WHITTAKER C.H. E0694

WHO....WORLD HEALTH ORGANIZATION

WHYTE/WF....WILLIAM FOOTE WHYTE

WICKERSHAM E.D. E0160

WIGGINS J.R. E0533,E2121

WIGHT M. E0351

WILDNER H. E2122

WILHELM/I....WILHELM I (KAISER)

WILHELM/II....WILHELM II (KAISER)

WILKINS L.T. E0403

WILKINS/R....ROY WILKINS

WILLIAM/3....WILLIAM III (PRINCE OF ORANGE)

                                                                    B47
LOCKE J.,TWO TREATISES OF GOVERNMENT (1690). UK LAW   CONCPT
SOCIETY LEGIS LEGIT AGREE REV OWN HEREDITY MORAL   ORD/FREE
CONSERVE...POLICY MAJORIT 17 WILLIAM/3 NATURL/LAW.   NAT/G
PAGE 66 E1316   CONSEN

WILLIAMS O. E1648

WILLIAMS S.P. E2123

WILLIAMS/R....ROGER WILLIAMS

WILLIG S.H. E2124

WILLMORE J.N. E0330

WILLOUGHBY W.W. E2125

WILLOW/RUN....WILLOW RUN, MICHIGAN

WILLS....WILLS AND TESTAMENTS

WILSON G. E2126

WILSON G.D. E2127

WILSON G.G. E2128

WILSON J.F. E2129

WILSON R.R. E1363

WILSON W. E2130,E2131

WILSON/H....HAROLD WILSON

WILSON/J....JAMES WILSON

WILSON/W....PRESIDENT WOODROW WILSON

                                                                    B38
GRISWOLD A.W.,THE FAR EASTERN POLICY OF THE UNITED   DIPLOM
STATES. ASIA S/ASIA USA-45 INT/ORG INT/TRADE WAR   POLICY
NAT/LISM...BIBLIOG 19/20 LEAGUE/NAT ROOSEVLT/T   CHIEF
ROOSEVLT/F WILSON/W TREATY. PAGE 47 E0943

                                                                    B43
BEMIS S.F.,THE LATIN AMERICAN POLICY OF THE UNITED   DIPLOM
STATES: AN HISTORICAL INTERPRETATION. INT/ORG AGREE   SOVEREIGN
COLONIAL WAR PEACE ATTIT ORD/FREE...POLICY INT/LAW   USA-45
CHARTS 18/20 MEXIC/AMER WILSON/W MONROE/DOC.   L/A+17C
PAGE 10 E0185

RUDIN H.R..ARMISTICE 1918. FRANCE GERMANY MOD/EUR   AGREE   B44
UK USA-45 NAT/G CHIEF DELIB/GP FORCES BAL/PWR REPAR   WAR
ARMS/CONT 20 WILSON/W TREATY. PAGE 86 E1732   PEACE
                                                      DIPLOM

FERRELL R.H..PEACE IN THEIR TIME. FRANCE UK USA-45   PEACE   B52
INT/ORG NAT/G FORCES CREATE AGREE ARMS/CONT COERCE   DIPLOM
WAR TREATY 20 WILSON/W LEAGUE/NAT BRIAND/A. PAGE 37
E0741

SCHEIBER H.N..THE WILSON ADMINISTRATION AND CIVIL   ORD/FREE   B60
LIBERTIES 1917-1921. LAW GOV/REL ATTIT 20 WILSON/W   WAR
CIVIL/LIB. PAGE 87 E1754   NAT/G
                                                      CONTROL

TODD A..JUSTICE ON TRIAL: THE CASE OF LOUIS D.   PERSON   B64
BRANDEIS. TOP/EX DISCRIM...JURID 20 WILSON/W   RACE/REL
CONGRESS SUPREME/CT BRANDEIS/L SENATE. PAGE 96   PERS/REL
E1929   NAT/G

CANFIELD L.H..THE PRESIDENCY OF WOODROW WILSON: PERSON   B66
PRELUDE TO A WORLD IN CRISIS. USA-45 ADJUD NEUTRAL   POLICY
WAR CHOOSE INGP/REL PEACE ORD/FREE 20 WILSON/W   DIPLOM
PRESIDENT TREATY LEAGUE/NAT. PAGE 19 E0373   GOV/REL

GASS O.."THE LITERATURE OF AMERICAN GOVERNMENT."   NEW/LIB   S66
CONSTN DRIVE ORD/FREE...JURID CONCPT METH/CNCPT   CT/SYS
IDEA/COMP 20 WILSON/W BEARD/CA LINK/AS. PAGE 42   NAT/G
E0841

WINES R. E2132

WINFIELD P.H. E2133

WINTERS J.M. E2134,E2135

WIRETAPPING....SEE PRIVACY

WISCONSIN....WISCONSIN

MURPHY E.F..WATER PURITY: A STUDY IN LEGAL CONTROL   SEA   B61
OF NATURAL RESOURCES. LOC/G ACT/RES PLAN TEC/DEV   LAW
LOBBY GP/REL COST ATTIT HEALTH ORD/FREE...HEAL   PROVS
JURID 20 WISCONSIN WATER. PAGE 75 E1506   CONTROL

CARMICHAEL D.M.."FORTY YEARS OF WATER POLLUTION   HEALTH   L67
CONTROL IN WISCONSIN: A CASE STUDY." LAW EXTR/IND   CONTROL
INDUS MUNIC DELIB/GP PLAN PROB/SOLV SANCTION   ADMIN
...CENSUS CHARTS 20 WISCONSIN. PAGE 20 E0384   ADJUD

WISCONSN/U....WISCONSIN STATE UNIVERSITY

WITHERSPOON J.V. E0330

WITTGEN/L....LUDWIG WITTGENSTEIN

WOETZEL R.K. E2136,E2137,E2138

WOLFERS A. E2139

WOLFF C. E2140

WOLFF/C....CHRISTIAN WOLFF

DE VATTEL E..THE LAW OF NATIONS. AGRI FINAN CHIEF   LAW   B96
DIPLOM INT/TRADE AGREE OWN ALL/VALS MORAL ORD/FREE   CONCPT
SOVEREIGN...GEN/LAWS 18 NATURL/LAW WOLFF/C. PAGE 30   NAT/G
E0597   INT/LAW

WOLFF/RP....ROBERT PAUL WOLFF

WOLL P. E2141

WOMAN....SEE FEMALE/SEX

WOMEN....SEE FEMALE/SEX

WOOD B. E0624

WOOD J.E. E2142

WOOD V. E2143

WOOD/CHAS....SIR CHARLES WOOD

WOOLBERT R.G. E2144

WOR+45....WORLDWIDE, 1945 TO PRESENT

WOR-45....WORLDWIDE, TO 1945

WORK....SEE WORKER

WORK PROJECTS ADMINISTRATION....   WPA

YANG KUNG-SUN,THE BOOK OF LORD SHANG. LAW ECO/UNDEV   ASIA   B28
LOC/G NAT/G NEIGH PLAN ECO/TAC LEGIT ATTIT SKILL   JURID
...CONCPT CON/ANAL WORK TOT/POP. PAGE 108 E2164

PUTTKAMMER E.W..WAR AND THE LAW. UNIV USA-45 CONSTN   INT/ORG   B44
CULTURE SOCIETY NAT/G POL/PAR ROUTINE ALL/VALS   LAW
...JURID CONCPT OBS WORK VAL/FREE 20. PAGE 83 E1664   WAR
                                                      INT/LAW

MAZZINI J..THE DUTIES OF MAN. MOD/EUR LAW SOCIETY   SUPEGO   B55
FAM NAT/G POL/PAR SECT VOL/ASSN EX/STRUC ACT/RES   CONCPT
CREATE REV PEACE ATTIT ALL/VALS...GEN/LAWS WORK 19.   NAT/LISM
PAGE 70 E1396

JENKS C.W..THE INTERNATIONAL PROTECTION OF TRADE   LABOR   B57
UNION FREEDOM. FUT WOR+45 WOR-45 VOL/ASSN DELIB/GP   INT/ORG
CT/SYS REGION ROUTINE...JURID METH/CNCPT RECORD
TIME/SEQ CHARTS ILO WORK OAS 20. PAGE 58 E1153

TIPTON J.B.."PARTICIPATION OF THE UNITED STATES IN   LABOR   S59
THE INTERNATIONAL LABOR ORGANIZATION." USA+45 LAW   INT/ORG
STRUCT ECO/DEV ECO/UNDEV INDUS TEC/DEV ECO/TAC
ADMIN PERCEPT ORD/FREE SKILL...STAT HIST/WRIT
GEN/METH ILO WORK 20. PAGE 96 E1928

ENGEL J..THE SECURITY OF THE FREE WORLD. USSR   COM   B60
WOR+45 STRATA STRUCT ECO/DEV ECO/UNDEV INT/ORG   TREND
DELIB/GP FORCES DOMIN LEGIT ADJUD EXEC ARMS/CONT   DIPLOM
COERCE...POLICY CONCPT NEW/IDEA TIME/SEQ GEN/LAWS
COLD/WAR WORK UN 20 NATO. PAGE 35 E0689

JENKS C.W..HUMAN RIGHTS AND INTERNATIONAL LABOR   CONCPT   B60
STANDARDS. WOR+45 CONSTN LABOR VOL/ASSN DELIB/GP
ACT/RES EDU/PROP MORAL RESPECT...JURID SOC TREND
GEN/LAWS WORK ILO 20. PAGE 58 E1156

KING D.B..LEGAL ASPECTS OF THE CIVIL RIGHTS   LAW   B65
MOVEMENT. SERV/IND VOL/ASSN LEGIS EDU/PROP ADJUD   DISCRIM
PARTIC CHOOSE...JURID SEGREGAT WORK. PAGE 61 E1215   TREND

KHOURI F.J.."THE JORDON RIVER CONTROVERSY." LAW   ISLAM   S65
SOCIETY ECO/UNDEV AGRI FINAN INDUS SECT FORCES   INT/ORG
ACT/RES PLAN TEC/DEV ECO/TAC EDU/PROP COERCE ATTIT   ISRAEL
DRIVE PERCEPT RIGID/FLEX ALL/VALS...GEOG SOC MYTH   JORDAN
WORK. PAGE 61 E1212

WORKER....WORKER, LABORER

FULLER G.A..DEMOBILIZATION: A SELECTED LIST OF   N
REFERENCES. USA+45 LAW AGRI LABOR WORKER ECO/TAC   BIBLIOG/A
RATION RECEIVE EDU/PROP ROUTINE ARMS/CONT ALL/VALS   INDUS
20. PAGE 41 E0819   FORCES
                                                      NAT/G

ADVANCED MANAGEMENT. INDUS EX/STRUC WORKER OP/RES   N
...DECISION BIBLIOG/A 20. PAGE 1 E0015   MGT
                                                      ADMIN
                                                      LABOR
                                                      GP/REL

PERSONNEL. USA+45 LAW LABOR LG/CO WORKER CREATE   N
GOV/REL PERS/REL ATTIT WEALTH. PAGE 2 E0029   BIBLIOG/A
                                                      ADMIN
                                                      MGT
                                                      GP/REL

US SUPERINTENDENT OF DOCUMENTS,POLITICAL SCIENCE: N
GOVERNMENT, CRIME, DISTRICT OF COLUMBIA (PRICE LIST   BIBLIOG/A
54). USA+45 LAW CONSTN EX/STRUC WORKER ADJUD ADMIN   NAT/G
CT/SYS CHOOSE INGP/REL RACE/REL CONGRESS PRESIDENT.   CRIME
PAGE 103 E2063

GRIFFIN A.P.C..LIST OF REFERENCES ON INDUSTRIAL   N
ARBITRATION (PAMPHLET). USA-45 STRATA VOL/ASSN   B03
DELIB/GP WORKER ADJUD GP/REL...MGT 19/20. PAGE 46   BIBLIOG/A
                                                      INDUS
                                                      LABOR

E0921   BARGAIN

                                                           B03
GRIFFIN A.P.C.,LISTS PUBLISHED 1902-03: LABOR   BIBLIOG/A
PARTICULARLY RELATING TO STRIKES (PAMPHLET). UK   LABOR
USA-45 FINAN WORKER PLAN BARGAIN CRIME GOV/REL   GP/REL
...POLICY 19/20 PARLIAMENT. PAGE 46 E0923   ECO/TAC

                                                           B03
GRIFFIN A.P.C.,SELECT LIST OF BOOKS ON LABOR   BIBLIOG/A
PARTICULARLY RELATING TO STRIKES. FRANCE GERMANY   GP/REL
MOD/EUR UK USA-45 LAW NAT/G DELIB/GP WORKER BARGAIN   MGT
LICENSE PAY ADJUD 19/20. PAGE 46 E0924   LABOR

                                                           B06
GRIFFIN A.P.C.,LIST OF BOOKS RELATING TO CHILD   BIBLIOG/A
LABOR (PAMPHLET). BELGIUM FRANCE GERMANY MOD/EUR UK   LAW
USA-45 ECO/DEV INDUS WORKER CAP/ISM PAY ROUTINE   LABOR
ALL/IDEOS...MGT SOC 19/20. PAGE 47 E0929   AGE/C

                                                           B10
COLORADO CIVIL SERVICE COMN,SECOND BIENNIAL REPORT   PROVS
TO THE GOVERNOR, 1909-1910. USA+45 DELIB/GP LEGIS   LOC/G
LICENSE PAY 20 COLORADO CIVIL/SERV. PAGE 24 E0477   ADMIN
                                                        WORKER

                                                           N19
BUREAU OF NAT'L AFFAIRS INC.,A CURRENT LOOK AT: DISCRIM
(1) THE NEGRO AND TITLE VII, (2) SEX AND TITLE VII   SEX
(PAMPHLET). USA+45 LG/CO SML/CO RACE/REL...POLICY SOC   WORKER
STAT DEEP/QU TREND CON/ANAL CHARTS 20 NEGRO   MGT
CIV/RIGHTS. PAGE 17 E0334

                                                           N19
HOGARTY R.A.,NEW JERSEY FARMERS AND MIGRANT HOUSING   AGRI
RULES (PAMPHLET). USA+45 LAW ELITES FACE/GP LABOR   PROVS
PROF/ORG LOBBY PERS/REL RIGID/FLEX ROLE 20   WORKER
NEW/JERSEY. PAGE 53 E1067   HEALTH

                                                           B38
FIELD G.L.,THE SYNDICAL AND CORPORATIVE   FASCISM
INSTITUTIONS OF ITALIAN FASCISM. ITALY CONSTN   INDUS
STRATA LABOR EX/STRUC TOP/EX ADJUD ADMIN LEAD   NAT/G
TOTALISM AUTHORIT...MGT 20 MUSSOLIN/B. PAGE 38   WORKER
E0746

                                                           C43
BENTHAM J.,"THE RATIONALE OF REWARD" IN J. BOWRING,   SANCTION
ED., THE WORKS OF JEREMY BENTHAM (VOL. 2)" LAW   ECO/TAC
WORKER CREATE INSPECT PAY ROUTINE HAPPINESS PRODUC   INCOME
SUPEGO WEALTH METH/CNCPT. PAGE 10 E0195   PWR

                                                           B51
INSTITUTE DES RELATIONS INTL,LES ASPECTS   WEAPON
ECONOMIQUES DU REARMEMENT (ETUDE DE L'INSTITUT DES   DEMAND
RELATIONS INTERNATIONALES A BRUXELLES). BELGIUM UK   ECO/TAC
USA+45 EXTR/IND FINAN FORCES WORKER PROB/SOLV   INT/TRADE
DIPLOM PRICE...POLICY 20 TREATY. PAGE 57 E1127

                                                           B54
CAPLOW T.,THE SOCIOLOGY OF WORK. USA+45 USA-45   LABOR
STRATA MARKET FAM GP/REL INGP/REL ALL/VALS   WORKER
...DECISION STAT BIBLIOG SOC/INTEG 20. PAGE 19   INDUS
E0375   ROLE

                                                           C54
GUINS G.C.,"SOVIET LAW AND SOVIET SOCIETY." COM   LAW
USSR STRATA FAM NAT/G WORKER DOMIN RACE/REL   STRUCT
...BIBLIOG 20. PAGE 48 E0960   PLAN

                                                           B55
BLOOM G.F.,ECONOMICS OF LABOR RELATIONS. USA+45 LAW   ECO/DEV
CONSULT WORKER CAP/ISM PAY ADJUD CONTROL EFFICIENCY   ECO/TAC
ORD/FREE...CHARTS 19/20 AFL/CIO NLRB DEPT/LABOR.   LABOR
PAGE 13 E0249   GOV/REL

                                                           B55
LARROWE C.P.,SHAPE-UP AND HIRING HALL. TRIBUTE   LABOR
ADJUD CONTROL SANCTION COERCE CRIME GP/REL PWR   INDUS
...CHARTS 20 AFL/CIO NEWYORK/C SEATTLE. PAGE 63   WORKER
E1256   NAT/G

                                                           B55
WRONG D.H.,AMERICAN AND CANADIAN VIEWPOINTS. CANADA   DIPLOM
USA+45 CONSTN STRATA FAM SECT WORKER ECO/TAC   ATTIT
EDU/PROP ADJUD MARRIAGE...IDEA/COMP 20. PAGE 108   NAT/COMP
E2161   CULTURE

                                                           B56
DUNNILL F.,THE CIVIL SERVICE. UK LAW PLAN ADMIN   PERSON
EFFICIENCY DRIVE NEW/LIB...STAT CHARTS 20   WORKER
PARLIAMENT CIVIL/SERV. PAGE 33 E0662   STRATA
                                                        SOC/WK

                                                           B57
US COMMISSION GOVT SECURITY,RECOMMENDATIONS; AREA: POLICY

IMMIGRANT PROGRAM. USA+45 LAW WORKER DIPLOM   CONTROL
EDU/PROP WRITING ADMIN PEACE ATTIT...CONCPT ANTHOL   PLAN
20 MIGRATION SUBVERT. PAGE 99 E1981   NAT/G

                                                           B58
AMERICAN SOCIETY PUBLIC ADMIN,STRENGTHENING   ADMIN
MANAGEMENT FOR DEMOCRATIC GOVERNMENT. USA+45 ACADEM   NAT/G
EX/STRUC WORKER PLAN BUDGET CONFER CT/SYS   EXEC
EFFICIENCY ANTHOL. PAGE 4 E0083   MGT

                                                           B58
BUGEDA LANZAS J.,A STATEMENT OF THE LAWS OF CUBA IN   JURID
MATTERS AFFECTING BUSINESS (2ND ED. REV.,   NAT/G
ENLARGED). CUBA L/A+17C LAW FINAN FAM LEGIS ACT/RES   INDUS
ADMIN GP/REL...BIBLIOG 20 OAS. PAGE 17 E0327   WORKER

                                                           B58
HOOD W.C.,FINANCING OF ECONOMIC ACTIVITY IN CANADA.   BUDGET
CANADA FUT VOL/ASSN WORKER ECO/TAC ADJUD ADMIN   FINAN
...CHARTS 20. PAGE 55 E1093   GP/REL
                                                        ECO/DEV

                                                           B59
BRIGGS A.,CHARTIST STUDIES. UK LAW NAT/G WORKER   INDUS
EDU/PROP COERCE SUFF GP/REL ATTIT...ANTHOL 19.   STRATA
PAGE 15 E0300   LABOR
                                                        POLICY

                                                           B59
COUNCIL OF STATE GOVERNMENTS,STATE GOVERNMENT: AN   BIBLIOG/A
ANNOTATED BIBLIOGRAPHY (PAMPHLET). USA+45 LAW AGRI   PROVS
INDUS WORKER PLAN TAX ADJUST AGE/Y ORD/FREE...HEAL   LOC/G
MGT 20. PAGE 26 E0521   ADMIN

                                                           B59
GOMEZ ROBLES J.,A STATEMENT OF THE LAWS OF   JURID
GUATEMALA IN MATTERS AFFECTING BUSINESS (2ND ED.   NAT/G
REV., ENLARGED). GUATEMALA L/A+17C LAW FINAN FAM   INDUS
WORKER ACT/RES DIPLOM ADJUD ADMIN GP/REL 20 OAS.   LEGIT
PAGE 44 E0881

                                                           B59
GSOVSKI V.,GOVERNMENT, LAW, AND COURTS IN THE   ADJUD
SOVIET UNION AND EASTERN EUROPE (2 VOLS.). COM USSR   MARXISM
AGRI INDUS WORKER CT/SYS CRIME...BIBLIOG 20   CONTROL
EUROPE/E. PAGE 48 E0958   ORD/FREE

                                                           B59
U OF MICHIGAN LAW SCHOOL,ATOMS AND THE LAW. USA+45   NUC/PWR
PROVS WORKER PROB/SOLV DIPLOM ADMIN GOV/REL ANTHOL.   NAT/G
PAGE 97 E1950   CONTROL
                                                        LAW

                                                           S59
BELL D.,"THE RACKET RIDDEN LONGSHOREMEN" (BMR)"   CRIME
USA+45 SEA WORKER MURDER ROLE...SOC 20 NEWYORK/C.   LABOR
PAGE 9 E0182   DIST/IND
                                                        ELITES

                                                           B60
PAUL A.M.,CONSERVATIVE CRISIS AND THE RULE OF LAW.   CONSTN
USA-45 LABOR WORKER ATTIT ORD/FREE CONSERVE LAISSEZ   ADJUD
...DECISION JURID 19 SUPREME/CT. PAGE 80 E1603   STRUCT
                                                        PROF/ORG

                                                           B60
WEBSTER J.A.,A GENERAL STUDY OF THE DEPARTMENT OF   ORD/FREE
DEFENSE INTERNAL SECURITY PROGRAM. USA+45 WORKER   PLAN
TEC/DEV ADJUD CONTROL CT/SYS EXEC GOV/REL COST   ADMIN
...POLICY DECISION MGT 20 DEPT/DEFEN SUPREME/CT.   NAT/G
PAGE 105 E2105

                                                           B61
BARBASH J.,LABOR'S GRASS ROOTS. CONSTN NAT/G   LABOR
EX/STRUC LEGIS WORKER LEAD...MAJORIT BIBLIOG.   INGP/REL
PAGE 8 E0147   GP/REL
                                                        LAW

                                                           B61
CARROTHERS A.W.R.,LABOR ARBITRATION IN CANADA.   LABOR
CANADA LAW NAT/G CONSULT LEGIS WORKER ADJUD ADMIN   MGT
CT/SYS 20. PAGE 20 E0396   GP/REL
                                                        BARGAIN

                                                           B61
FLINN M.W.,AN ECONOMIC AND SOCIAL HISTORY OF   SOCIETY
BRITAIN, 1066-1939. UK LAW STRATA STRUCT AGRI   SOC
DIST/IND INDUS WORKER INT/TRADE WAR...CENSUS 11/20.
PAGE 39 E0766

                                                           B61
MERTON R.K.,CONTEMPORARY SOCIAL PROBLEMS: AN   CRIME
INTRODUCTION TO THE SOCIOLOGY OF DEVIANT BEHAVIOR   ANOMIE
AND SOCIAL DISORGANIZATION. FAM MUNIC FORCES WORKER   STRANGE
PROB/SOLV INGP/REL RACE/REL ISOLAT...CRIMLGY GEOG   SOC
PSY T 20 NEGRO. PAGE 72 E1444

NEW JERSEY LEGISLATURE-SENATE,PUBLIC HEARINGS BEFORE COMMITTEE ON REVISION AND AMENDMENT OF LAWS ON SENATE BILL NO. 8. USA+45 FINAN PROVS WORKER ACT/RES PLAN BUDGET TAX CRIME...IDEA/COMP 20 NEW/JERSEY URBAN/RNWL. PAGE 77 E1537
LEGIS MUNIC INDUS PROB/SOLV
B61

AGNEW P.C.,"INTRODUCING CHANGE IN A MENTAL HOSPITAL." CLIENT WORKER PROB/SOLV INGP/REL PERS/REL ADJUST. PAGE 3 E0054
ORD/FREE PUB/INST PSY ADMIN
S61

DE LAVALLE H.,A STATEMENT OF THE LAWS OF PERU IN MATTERS AFFECTING BUSINESS (3RD ED.). PERU WORKER INT/TRADE INCOME ORD/FREE...INT/LAW 20. PAGE 30 E0586
CONSTN JURID FINAN TAX
B62

FATOUROS A.A.,GOVERNMENT GUARANTEES TO FOREIGN INVESTORS. WOR+45 ECO/UNDEV INDUS WORKER ADJUD ...NAT/COMP BIBLIOG TREATY. PAGE 36 E0722
NAT/G FINAN INT/TRADE ECO/DEV
B62

MARS D.,SUGGESTED LIBRARY IN PUBLIC ADMINISTRATION. FINAN DELIB/GP EX/STRUC WORKER COMPUTER ADJUD ...DECISION PSY SOC METH/COMP 20. PAGE 68 E1368
BIBLIOG ADMIN METH MGT
B62

OTTENBERG M.,THE FEDERAL INVESTIGATORS. USA+45 LAW COM/IND DIST/IND WORKER DIPLOM INT/TRADE CONTROL FEDERAL HEALTH ORD/FREE FBI CIA FTC SEC FDA. PAGE 79 E1585
FORCES INSPECT NAT/G CRIME
B62

US COMMISSION ON CIVIL RIGHTS,EQUAL PROTECTION OF THE LAWS IN NORTH CAROLINA. USA+45 LOC/G NAT/G CONSULT LEGIS WORKER PROB/SOLV EDU/PROP ADJUD CHOOSE DISCRIM HEALTH 20 NEGRO NORTH/CAR CIV/RIGHTS. PAGE 99 E1984
ORD/FREE RESPECT LAW PROVS
B62

US COMMISSION ON CIVIL RIGHTS,HEARINGS BEFORE UNITED STATES COMMISSION ON CIVIL RIGHTS. USA+45 ECO/DEV NAT/G CONSULT WORKER EDU/PROP ADJUD DISCRIM ISOLAT HABITAT HEALTH RESPECT 20 NEGRO CIV/RIGHTS. PAGE 99 E1985
ORD/FREE LAW ADMIN LEGIS
B62

HAUSMAN W.H.,MANAGING ECONOMIC DEVELOPMENT IN AFRICA. AFR USA+45 LAW FINAN WORKER TEC/DEV WEALTH ...ANTHOL 20. PAGE 51 E1012
ECO/UNDEV PLAN FOR/AID MGT
B63

LAVROFF D.-.G.,LES LIBERTES PUBLIQUES EN UNION SOVIETIQUE (REV. ED.). USSR NAT/G WORKER SANCTION CRIME MARXISM NEW/LIB...JURID BIBLIOG WORSHIP 20. PAGE 63 E1268
ORD/FREE LAW ATTIT COM
B63

PALOTAI O.C.,PUBLICATIONS OF THE INSTITUTE OF GOVERNMENT, 1930-1962. LAW PROVS SCHOOL WORKER ACT/RES OP/RES CT/SYS GOV/REL...CRIMLGY SOC/WK. PAGE 79 E1594
BIBLIOG/A ADMIN LOC/G FINAN
B63

US SENATE COMM ON JUDICIARY,US PERSONNEL SECURITY PRACTICES. USA+45 DELIB/GP ADJUD ADMIN ORD/FREE ...CHARTS 20 CONGRESS CIVIL/SERV. PAGE 102 E2049
PLAN NAT/G CONTROL WORKER
B63

BROOKS T.R.,TOIL AND TROUBLE, A HISTORY OF AMERICAN LABOR. WORKER BARGAIN CAP/ISM ADJUD AUTOMAT EXEC GP/REL RACE/REL EFFICIENCY INCOME PROFIT MARXISM 17/20 KENNEDY/JF AFL/CIO NEGRO. PAGE 16 E0310
INDUS LABOR LEGIS
B64

BUREAU OF NATIONAL AFFAIRS,STATE FAIR EMPLOYMENT LAWS AND THEIR ADMINISTRATION. INDUS ADJUD PERS/REL RACE/REL ATTIT ORD/FREE WEALTH 20. PAGE 17 E0338
PROVS DISCRIM WORKER JURID
B64

TELLADO A.,A STATEMENT OF THE LAWS OF THE DOMINICAN REPUBLIC IN MATTERS AFFECTING BUSINESS (3RD ED.). DOMIN/REP AGRI DIST/IND EXTR/IND FINAN FAM WORKER ECO/TAC TAX CT/SYS MARRIAGE OWN...BIBLIOG 20 MIGRATION. PAGE 95 E1913
CONSTN LEGIS NAT/G INDUS
B64

KRISLOV S.,THE SUPREME COURT IN THE POLITICAL PROCESS. USA+45 LAW SOCIETY STRUCT WORKER ADMIN ROLE...JURID SOC 20 SUPREME/CT. PAGE 62 E1231
ADJUD DECISION CT/SYS CONSTN
B65

LUGO-MARENCO J.J.,A STATEMENT OF THE LAWS OF NICARAGUA IN MATTERS AFFECTING BUSINESS. NICARAGUA AGRI DIST/IND EXTR/IND FINAN INDUS FAM WORKER INT/TRADE TAX MARRIAGE OWN BIO/SOC 20 TREATY RESOURCE/N MIGRATION. PAGE 67 E1332
CONSTN NAT/G LEGIS JURID
B65

ROSE A.M.,MINORITY PROBLEMS: A TEXTBOOK OF READINGS IN INTERGROUP RELATIONS. UNIV USA+45 LAW SCHOOL WORKER PROB/SOLV GP/REL PERSON...PSY ANTHOL WORSHIP 20 NEGRO INDIAN/AM JEWS EUROPE. PAGE 85 E1713
RACE/REL DISCRIM ISOLAT ACT/RES
B65

SCHROEDER O.,DEFACTO SEGREGATION AND CIVIL RIGHTS. LAW PROVS SCHOOL WORKER ATTIT HABITAT HEALTH WEALTH ...JURID CHARTS 19/20 NEGRO SUPREME/CT KKK. PAGE 88 E1766
ANTHOL DISCRIM RACE/REL ORD/FREE
B65

AMERICAN JEWISH COMMITTEE,THE TYRANNY OF POVERTY (PAMPHLET). USA+45 LAW ECO/DEV LOC/G MUNIC NAT/G PUB/INST WORKER EDU/PROP CRIME...SOC/WK 20. PAGE 4 E0080
BIBLIOG/A WEALTH WELF/ST PROB/SOLV
B66

FLEISCHER B.M.,THE ECONOMICS OF DELINQUENCY. UNIV WORKER STRANGE ANOMIE...STAT CHARTS 20. PAGE 38 E0762
STRATA INCOME AGE/Y CRIME
B66

MC CONNELL J.P.,LAW AND BUSINESS: PATTERNS AND ISSUES IN COMMERCIAL LAW. USA+45 USA-45 LOC/G WORKER LICENSE CRIME REPRESENT GP/REL 20. PAGE 70 E1397
ECO/DEV JURID ADJUD MGT
B66

MOSKOW M.H.,TEACHERS AND UNIONS. SCHOOL WORKER ADJUD LOBBY ATTIT ORD/FREE 20. PAGE 75 E1501
EDU/PROP PROF/ORG LABOR BARGAIN
B66

US PRES COMN CRIME IN DC,REPORT OF THE US PRESIDENT'S COMMISSION ON CRIME IN THE DISTRICT OF COLUMBIA. LEGIS WORKER EDU/PROP ADJUD CONTROL CT/SYS GP/REL BIO/SOC HEALTH...CRIMLGY NEW/IDEA STAT 20. PAGE 101 E2022
CRIME FORCES AGE/Y SANCTION
B66

WASHINGTON S.H.,BIBLIOGRAPHY: LABOR-MANAGEMENT RELATIONS ACT, 1947 AS AMENDED BY LABOR-MANAGEMENT REPORTING AND DISCLOSURE ACT, 1959. USA+45 CONSTN INDUS DELIB/GP LEGIS WORKER BARGAIN ECO/TAC ADJUD GP/REL NEW/LIB...JURID CONGRESS. PAGE 105 E2100
BIBLIOG LAW LABOR MGT
B66

BAKKE E.W.,UNIONS, MANAGEMENT AND THE PUBLIC* READINGS AND TEXT. WORKER LOBBY...POLICY JURID ANTHOL T. PAGE 7 E0143
LABOR INDUS ADJUD GP/REL
B67

BEAL E.F.,THE PRACTICE OF COLLECTIVE BARGAINING (3RD ED.). USA+45 WOR+45 ECO/DEV INDUS LG/CO PROF/ORG WORKER ECO/TAC GP/REL WEALTH...JURID METH/CNCPT. PAGE 8 E0160
BARGAIN MGT LABOR ADJUD
B67

BONGER W.A.,CRIMINALITY AND ECONOMIC CONDITIONS. MOD/EUR STRUCT INDUS WORKER EDU/PROP CRIME HABITAT ALL/VALS...JURID SOC 20 REFORMERS. PAGE 14 E0265
PERSON CRIMLGY IDEA/COMP ANOMIE
B67

COHEN M.R.,LAW AND THE SOCIAL ORDER: ESSAYS IN LEGAL PHILOSOPHY. USA-45 CONSULT WORKER ECO/TAC ATTIT WEALTH...POLICY WELF/ST SOC 20 NEW/DEAL DEPRESSION. PAGE 24 E0467
JURID LABOR IDEA/COMP
B67

HODGKINSON R.G.,THE ORIGINS OF THE NATIONAL HEALTH SERVICE: THE MEDICAL SERVICES OF THE NEW POOR LAW, 1834-1871. UK INDUS MUNIC WORKER PROB/SOLV EFFICIENCY ATTIT HEALTH WEALTH SOCISM...JURID SOC/WK 19/20. PAGE 53 E1062
HEAL NAT/G POLICY LAW
B67

BAADE H.W.,"THE ACQUIRED RIGHTS OF INTERNATIONAL
INT/ORG
L67

PUBLIC SERVANTS; A CASE STUDY IN RECEPTION OF PUBLIC LAW." WOR+45 DELIB/GP DIPLOM ORD/FREE ...INT/LAW JURID UN. PAGE 7 E0125 — WORKER ADJUD LAW

S67

ALEXANDER B.,"GIBRALTAR" SPAIN UK CONSTN WORKER PROB/SOLV FOR/AID RECEIVE CONTROL 20. PAGE 3 E0059 — DIPLOM INT/ORG ORD/FREE ECO/TAC

S67

BERRODIN E.F.,"AT THE BARGAINING TABLE." LABOR DIPLOM ECO/TAC ADMIN...MGT 20 MICHIGAN. PAGE 11 E0216 — PROVS WORKER LAW BARGAIN

S67

DANIEL C.,"FREEDOM, EQUITY, AND THE WAR ON POVERTY." USA+45 WORKER ECO/TAC JURID. PAGE 29 E0566 — WEALTH INCOME SOCIETY ORD/FREE

S67

EDGEWORTH A.B. JR.,"CIVIL RIGHTS PLUS THREE YEARS: BANKS AND THE ANTI-DISCRIMINATION LAW" USA+45 SOCIETY DELIB/GP RACE/REL EFFICIENCY 20 NEGRO CIV/RIGHTS. PAGE 34 E0675 — WORKER DISCRIM FINAN LAW

S67

GANZ G.,"THE CONTROL OF INDUSTRY BY ADMINISTRATIVE PROCESS." UK DELIB/GP WORKER 20. PAGE 42 E0832 — INDUS LAW ADMIN CONTROL

S67

GIBSON G.H.,"LABOR PIRACY ON THE BRANDYWINE." USA-45 INDUS R+D VOL/ASSN CAP/ISM ADJUD DRIVE...PSY 19. PAGE 43 E0859 — ECO/TAC CREATE TEC/DEV WORKER

B70

BLACKSTONE W.,COMMENTARIES ON THE LAWS OF ENGLAND (4 VOLS.) (4TH ED.). UK CHIEF DELIB/GP LEGIS WORKER CT/SYS SANCTION CRIME OWN...CRIMLGY 18 ENGLSH/LAW. PAGE 12 E0238 — LAW JURID ADJUD CONSTN

B82

POLLOCK F.,ESSAYS IN JURISPRUDENCE AND ETHICS. UNIV LAW FINAN MARKET WORKER INGP/REL MORAL...POLICY GEN/LAWS. PAGE 81 E1625 — JURID CONCPT

WORKING....SEE ROUTINE

WORLD COUNCIL OF CHURCHES....SEE WCC

WORLD HEALTH ORGANIZATION....SEE WHO

WORLD WAR I....SEE WWI

WORLD WAR II....SEE WWII

WORLD PEACE FOUNDATION E2145

WORLD/BANK....WORLD BANK

WORLD/CONG....WORLD CONGRESS

WORLD/CT....WORLD COURT; SEE ALSO ICJ

B38

HAGUE PERMANENT CT INTL JUSTIC,WORLD COURT REPORTS: COLLECTION OF THE JUDGEMENTS ORDERS AND OPINIONS VOLUME 3 1932-35. WOR-45 LAW DELIB/GP CONFER WAR PEACE ATTIT...DECISION ANTHOL 20 WORLD/CT CASEBOOK. PAGE 49 E0976 — INT/ORG CT/SYS DIPLOM ADJUD

B43

HAGUE PERMANENT CT INTL JUSTIC,WORLD COURT REPORTS: COLLECTION OF THE JUDGEMENTS ORDERS AND OPINIONS VOLUME 4 1936-42. WOR-45 CONFER PEACE ATTIT ...DECISION JURID ANTHOL 20 WORLD/CT CASEBOOK. PAGE 49 E0977 — INT/ORG CT/SYS DIPLOM ADJUD

S67

DALFEN C.M.,"THE WORLD COURT IN IDLE SPLENDOUR: THE BASIS OF STATES' ATTITUDES." WOR+45 LAW ADJUD COERCE...JURID 20 UN WORLD/CT. PAGE 28 E0562 — CT/SYS INT/ORG INT/LAW DIPLOM

WORLDUNITY....WORLD UNITY, WORLD FEDERATION (EXCLUDING UN AND LEAGUE OF NATIONS)

B57

ALIGHIERI D.,ON WORLD GOVERNMENT. ROMAN/EMP LAW SOCIETY INT/ORG NAT/G POL/PAR ADJUD WAR GP/REL PEACE WORSHIP 15 WORLDUNITY DANTE. PAGE 4 E0067 — POLICY CONCPT DIPLOM

WORMUTH F.D. E2146

WORSHIP....SEE ALSO SECT

N

CANON LAW ABSTRACTS. LEGIT CONFER CT/SYS INGP/REL MARRIAGE ATTIT MORAL WORSHIP 20. PAGE 2 E0026 — BIBLIOG/A CATHISM SECT LAW

C01

BERKELEY G.,"DISCOURSE ON PASSIVE OBEDIENCE" (1712) THE WORKS... (VOL. IV)" UNIV DOMIN LEGIT CONTROL CRIME ADJUST CENTRAL MORAL ORD/FREE...POLICY WORSHIP. PAGE 10 E0202 — INGP/REL SANCTION RESPECT GEN/LAWS

B03

FAGUET E.,LE LIBERALISME. FRANCE PRESS ADJUD ADMIN DISCRIM CONSERVE SOCISM...TRADIT SOC LING WORSHIP PARLIAMENT. PAGE 36 E0711 — ORD/FREE EDU/PROP NAT/G LAW

B24

HOLDSWORTH W.S.,A HISTORY OF ENGLISH LAW; THE COMMON LAW AND ITS RIVALS (VOL. V). UK SEA EX/STRUC WRITING ADMIN...INT/LAW JURID CONCPT IDEA/COMP WORSHIP 16/17 PARLIAMENT ENGLSH/LAW COMMON/LAW. PAGE 54 E1073 — LAW LEGIS ADJUD CT/SYS

B35

ROBSON W.A.,CIVILISATION AND THE GROWTH OF LAW. UNIV CONSTN SOCIETY LEGIS ADJUD ATTIT PERCEPT MORAL ALL/IDEOS...CONCPT WORSHIP 20. PAGE 85 E1708 — LAW IDEA/COMP SOC

S40

GURVITCH G.,"MAJOR PROBLEMS OF THE SOCIOLOGY OF LAW." CULTURE SANCTION KNOWL MORAL...POLICY EPIST JURID WORSHIP. PAGE 48 E0963 — SOC LAW PHIL/SCI

B44

SUAREZ F.,A TREATISE ON LAWS AND GOD THE LAWGIVER (1612) IN SELECTIONS FROM THREE WORKS, VOL. II. FRANCE ITALY UK CULTURE NAT/G SECT CHIEF LEGIS DOMIN LEGIT CT/SYS ORD/FREE PWR WORSHIP 16/17. PAGE 94 E1892 — LAW JURID GEN/LAWS CATH

B46

GILLIN J.L.,SOCIAL PATHOLOGY. SOCIETY SECT CRIME ANOMIE DISPL ORD/FREE WEALTH...CRIMLGY PSY WORSHIP. PAGE 44 E0864 — SOC ADJUST CULTURE INGP/REL

B50

EMBREE J.F.,BIBLIOGRAPHY OF THE PEOPLES AND CULTURES OF MAINLAND SOUTHEAST ASIA. CAMBODIA LAOS THAILAND VIETNAM LAW...GEOG HUM SOC MYTH LING CHARTS WORSHIP 20. PAGE 35 E0686 — BIBLIOG/A CULTURE S/ASIA

B53

AYMARD A.,HISTOIRE GENERALE DES CIVILISATIONS (7 VOLS.). WOR+45 WOR-45 LAW SECT CREATE ATTIT ...ART/METH WORSHIP. PAGE 6 E0123 — BIBLIOG/A SOC

B55

MID-EUROPEAN LAW PROJECT,CHURCH AND STATE BEHIND THE IRON CURTAIN. COM CZECHOSLVK HUNGARY POLAND USSR CULTURE SECT EDU/PROP GOV/REL CATHISM...CHARTS ANTHOL BIBLIOG WORSHIP 20 CHURCH/STA. PAGE 73 E1455 — LAW MARXISM POLICY

B57

ALIGHIERI D.,ON WORLD GOVERNMENT. ROMAN/EMP LAW SOCIETY INT/ORG NAT/G POL/PAR ADJUD WAR GP/REL PEACE WORSHIP 15 WORLDUNITY DANTE. PAGE 4 E0067 — POLICY CONCPT DIPLOM SECT

B58

CABLE G.W.,THE NEGRO QUESTION: A SELECTION OF WRITINGS ON CIVIL RIGHTS IN THE SOUTH. USA+45 STRATA LOC/G POL/PAR GIVE EDU/PROP WRITING CT/SYS SANCTION CRIME CHOOSE WORSHIP 20 NEGRO CIV/RIGHTS CONV/LEASE SOUTH/US. PAGE 18 E0355 — RACE/REL CULTURE DISCRIM ORD/FREE

B59

FELLMANN D.,THE LIMITS OF FREEDOM. USA+45 USA-45 NAT/G SECT ROLE ORD/FREE WORSHIP 18/20 FREE/SPEE. PAGE 37 E0734 — CONCPT JURID CONSTN

B60

FELLMAN D.,THE SUPREME COURT AND EDUCATION. ACADEM NAT/G PROVS DELIB/GP ADJUD ORD/FREE...POLICY JURID WORSHIP 20 SUPREME/CT NEGRO CHURCH/STA. PAGE 37 E0731 — CT/SYS SECT RACE/REL SCHOOL

B60

POWELL T..THE SCHOOL BUS LAW: A CASE STUDY IN JURID
EDUCATION, RELIGION, AND POLITICS. USA+45 LAW NEIGH SCHOOL
SECT LEGIS EDU/PROP ADJUD CT/SYS LOBBY CATHISM
WORSHIP 20 CONNECTICT CHURCH/STA. PAGE 82 E1641

B61

COWEN D.V..THE FOUNDATIONS OF FREEDOM. AFR CONSTN
SOUTH/AFR DOMIN LEGIT ADJUST DISCRIM TOTALISM ATTIT ELITES
ORD/FREE...MAJORIT JURID SOC/INTEG WORSHIP 20 RACE/REL
NEGRO. PAGE 27 E0529

B61

JACOBS C.E..JUSTICE FRANKFURTER AND CIVIL BIOG
LIBERTIES. USA+45 USA-45 LAW NAT/G PROB/SOLV PRESS CONSTN
PERS/REL...JURID WORSHIP 20 SUPREME/CT FRANKFUR/F ADJUD
CIVIL/LIB. PAGE 57 E1144 ORD/FREE

B62

BARLOW R.B..CITIZENSHIP AND CONSCIENCE: STUDIES IN SECT
THEORY AND PRACTICE OF RELIGIOUS TOLERATION IN LEGIS
ENGLAND DURING EIGHTEENTH CENTURY. UK LAW VOL/ASSN DISCRIM
EDU/PROP SANCTION REV GP/REL MAJORITY ATTIT
ORD/FREE...BIBLIOG WORSHIP 18. PAGE 8 E0150

B63

LAVROFF D.-.G..LES LIBERTES PUBLIQUES EN UNION ORD/FREE
SOVIETIQUE (REV. ED.). USSR NAT/G WORKER SANCTION LAW
CRIME MARXISM NEW/LIB...JURID BIBLIOG WORSHIP 20. ATTIT
PAGE 63 E1268 COM

B63

LOWRY C.W..TO PRAY OR NOT TO PRAY. ADJUD SANCTION SECT
GP/REL ORD/FREE PWR CATHISM WORSHIP 20 SUPREME/CT CT/SYS
CHRISTIAN CHRUCH/STA. PAGE 67 E1330 CONSTN
PRIVIL

B64

FORBES A.H..CURRENT RESEARCH IN BRITISH STUDIES. UK BIBLIOG
CONSTN CULTURE POL/PAR SECT DIPLOM ADMIN...JURID PERSON
BIOG WORSHIP 20. PAGE 39 E0769 NAT/G
PARL/PROC

B64

KAUPER P.G..RELIGION AND THE CONSTITUTION. USA+45 CONSTN
USA-45 LAW NAT/G SCHOOL SECT GP/REL ATTIT...BIBLIOG JURID
WORSHIP 18/20 SUPREME/CT FREE/SPEE CHURCH/STA. ORD/FREE
PAGE 60 E1189

B64

LOCKHART W.B..CASES AND MATERIALS ON CONSTITUTIONAL ORD/FREE
RIGHTS AND LIBERTIES. USA+45 FORCES LEGIS DIPLOM CONSTN
PRESS CONTROL CRIME WAR PWR...AUD/VIS T WORSHIP 20 NAT/G
NEGRO. PAGE 66 E1317

B64

MARNELL W.H..THE FIRST AMENDMENT: THE HISTORY OF CONSTN
RELIGIOUS FREEDOM IN AMERICA. WOR+45 WOR-45 PROVS SECT
CREATE CT/SYS...POLICY BIBLIOG/A WORSHIP 16/20. ORD/FREE
PAGE 68 E1367 GOV/REL

B64

NEWMAN E.S..CIVIL LIBERTY AND CIVIL RIGHTS. USA+45 ORD/FREE
USA-45 CONSTN PROVS FORCES LEGIS CT/SYS RACE/REL LAW
ATTIT...MAJORIT JURID WORSHIP 20 SUPREME/CT NEGRO CONTROL
CIV/RIGHTS CHURCH/STA. PAGE 77 E1543 NAT/G

B64

RICE C.E..THE SUPREME COURT AND PUBLIC PRAYER. JURID
CONSTN SCHOOL SECT PROB/SOLV TAX ATTIT WORSHIP POLICY
18/20 SUPREME/CT CHURCH/STA. PAGE 84 E1692 NAT/G

B65

ANDRUS H.L..LIBERALISM, CONSERVATISM, MORMONISM. SECT
USA+45 PLAN ADJUD CONTROL HAPPINESS ORD/FREE UTOPIA
CONSERVE NEW/LIB WORSHIP 20. PAGE 5 E0097 MORAL

B65

BEGGS D.W..AMERICA'S SCHOOLS AND CHURCHES: PARTNERS SECT
IN CONFLICT. USA+45 PROVS EDU/PROP ADJUD DISCRIM GP/REL
ATTIT...IDEA/COMP ANTHOL BIBLIOG WORSHIP 20 SCHOOL
CHURCH/STA. PAGE 9 E0179 NAT/G

B65

HIGGINS R..CONFLICT OF INTERESTS* INTERNATIONAL LAW INT/LAW
IN A DIVIDED WORLD. ASIA USSR ECO/DEV ECO/UNDEV IDEA/COMP
SECT INT/TRADE COLD/WAR WORSHIP. PAGE 52 E1042 ADJUST

B65

LASLEY J..THE WAR SYSTEM AND YOU. LAW FORCES MORAL
ARMS/CONT NUC/PWR NAT/LISM ATTIT...MAJORIT PERSON
IDEA/COMP UN WORSHIP. PAGE 63 E1261 DIPLOM
WAR

B65

PARKER D..CIVIL LIBERTIES CASE STUDIES AND THE LAW. ORD/FREE

SECT ADJUD...CONCPT WORSHIP 20 SUPREME/CT JURID
CIV/RIGHTS FREE/SPEE. PAGE 80 E1598 CONSTN
JUDGE

B65

ROSE A.M..MINORITY PROBLEMS: A TEXTBOOK OF READINGS RACE/REL
IN INTERGROUP RELATIONS. UNIV USA+45 LAW SCHOOL DISCRIM
WORKER PROB/SOLV GP/REL PERSON...PSY ANTHOL WORSHIP ISOLAT
20 NEGRO INDIAN/AM JEWS EUROPE. PAGE 85 E1713 ACT/RES

B66

CAHN E..CONFRONTING INJUSTICE. USA+45 PROB/SOLV TAX ORD/FREE
EDU/PROP PRESS CT/SYS GP/REL DISCRIM BIO/SOC CONSTN
...IDEA/COMP BIBLIOG WORSHIP 20 BILL/RIGHT. PAGE 18 ADJUD
E0362

B66

DOUGLAS W.O..THE BIBLE AND THE SCHOOLS. USA+45 SECT
CULTURE ADJUD INGP/REL AGE/C AGE/Y ATTIT KNOWL NAT/G
WORSHIP 20 SUPREME/CT CHURCH/STA BIBLE CHRISTIAN. SCHOOL
PAGE 32 E0644 GP/REL

B66

KERR M.H..ISLAMIC REFORM: THE POLITICAL AND LEGAL LAW
THEORIES OF MUHAMMAD 'ABDUH AND RASHID RIDA. NAT/G CONCPT
SECT LEAD SOVEREIGN CONSERVE...JURID BIBLIOG ISLAM
WORSHIP 20. PAGE 60 E1204

B66

SWEET E.C..CIVIL LIBERTIES IN AMERICA. LAW CONSTN ADJUD
NAT/G PRESS CT/SYS DISCRIM ATTIT WORSHIP 20 ORD/FREE
CIVIL/LIB. PAGE 95 E1899 SUFF
COERCE

B66

US DEPARTMENT OF STATE,RESEARCH ON AFRICA (EXTERNAL BIBLIOG/A
RESEARCH LIST NO 5-25). LAW CULTURE ECO/UNDEV ASIA
POL/PAR DIPLOM EDU/PROP LEAD REGION MARXISM...GEOG S/ASIA
LING WORSHIP 20. PAGE 100 E1996 NAT/G

B66

US DEPARTMENT OF STATE,RESEARCH ON WESTERN EUROPE, BIBLIOG/A
GREAT BRITAIN, AND CANADA (EXTERNAL RESEARCH LIST EUR+WWI
NO 3-25). CANADA GERMANY/W UK LAW CULTURE NAT/G DIPLOM
POL/PAR FORCES EDU/PROP REGION MARXISM...GEOG SOC
WORSHIP 20 CMN/WLTH. PAGE 100 E1998

B66

US SENATE COMM ON JUDICIARY,SCHOOL PRAYER. USA+45 SCHOOL
LAW LOC/G SECT ADJUD WORSHIP 20 SENATE DEITY. JURID
PAGE 103 E2058 NAT/G

S66

SHEEHY E.P.,"SELECTED REFERENCE BOOKS OF BIBLIOG/A
1965-1966." AGRI PERF/ART PRESS...GEOG HUM JURID INDEX
SOC LING WORSHIP. PAGE 91 E1817 CLASSIF

B67

BOLES D.E..THE TWO SWORDS. USA+45 USA-45 LAW CONSTN SCHOOL
SOCIETY FINAN PRESS CT/SYS...HEAL JURID BIBLIOG EDU/PROP
WORSHIP 20 SUPREME/CT CHURCH/STA. PAGE 13 E0263 ADJUD

S67

KIM R.C.C.,"THE SUPREME COURT: ORALLE WITHOUT CT/SYS
TRUTH." USA+45 EDU/PROP RACE/REL ADJUST ALL/VALS PROB/SOLV
ORD/FREE...DECISION WORSHIP SUPREME/CT. PAGE 61 ADJUD
E1214 REPRESENT

WRAITH R.E. E2147

WRIGHT G. E2148

WRIGHT Q. E2149,E2150,E2151,E2152,E2153,E2154,E2155,E2156,E2157
E2158,E2159,E2160

WRITING....SEE ALSO HIST/WRIT

N

PUBLISHERS' CIRCULAR, THE OFFICIAL ORGAN OF THE BIBLIOG
PUBLISHERS' ASSOCIATION OF GREAT BRITAIN AND NAT/G
IRELAND. EUR+WWI MOD/EUR UK LAW PROB/SOLV DIPLOM WRITING
COLONIAL ATTIT...HUM 19/20 CMN/WLTH. PAGE 2 E0025 LEAD

N

DEUTSCHE BUCHEREI,JAHRESVERZEICHNIS DER DEUTSCHEN BIBLIOG
HOCHSCHULSCHRIFTEN. EUR+WWI GERMANY LAW ADMIN WRITING
PERSON...MGT SOC 19/20. PAGE 31 E0613 ACADEM
INTELL

N

DEUTSCHE BUCHEREI,JAHRESVERZEICHNIS DES DEUTSCHEN BIBLIOG
SCHRIFTUMS. AUSTRIA EUR+WWI GERMANY SWITZERLND LAW WRITING
LOC/G DIPLOM ADMIN...MGT SOC 19/20. PAGE 31 E0614 NAT/G

NEW YORK STATE LIBRARY,CHECKLIST OF OFFICIAL PUBLICATIONS OF THE STATE OF NEW YORK. USA+45 USA-45 LAW PROB/SOLV LEAD ATTIT 19/20. PAGE 77 E1539
BIBLIOG PROVS WRITING GOV/REL
N

SOUTH AFRICA STATE LIBRARY,SOUTH AFRICAN NATIONAL BIBLIOGRAPHY, SANB. SOUTH/AFR LAW NAT/G EDU/PROP ...MGT PSY SOC 20. PAGE 93 E1858
BIBLIOG PRESS WRITING
N

UNITED NATIONS,OFFICIAL RECORDS OF THE UNITED NATIONS' GENERAL ASSEMBLY. WOR+45 BUDGET DIPLOM ADMIN 20 UN. PAGE 98 E1964
INT/ORG DELIB/GP INT/LAW WRITING
N

FORTESCUE G.K.,SUBJECT INDEX OF THE MODERN WORKS ADDED TO THE LIBRARY OF THE BRITISH MUSEUM IN THE YEARS 1881-1900 (3 VOLS.). UK LAW CONSTN FINAN NAT/G FORCES INT/TRADE COLONIAL 19. PAGE 39 E0775
BIBLIOG INDEX WRITING
B03

MEYER H.H.B.,LIST OF REFERENCES ON EMBARGOES (PAMPHLET). USA-45 AGRI DIPLOM WRITING DEBATE WEAPON...INT/LAW 18/20 CONGRESS. PAGE 72 E1447
BIBLIOG DIST/IND ECO/TAC INT/TRADE
B17

MYERS D.P.,MANUAL OF COLLECTIONS OF TREATIES AND OF COLLECTIONS RELATING TO TREATIES. MOD/EUR INT/ORG LEGIS WRITING ADMIN SOVEREIGN...INT/LAW 19/20. PAGE 75 E1514
BIBLIOG/A DIPLOM CONFER
B22

SCHROEDER T.,FREE SPEECH BIBLIOGRAPHY. EUR+WWI WOR-45 NAT/G SECT ECO/TAC WRITING ADJUD ATTIT MARXISM SOCISM 16/20. PAGE 88 E1768
BIBLIOG/A ORD/FREE CONTROL LAW
B22

HOLDSWORTH W.S.,A HISTORY OF ENGLISH LAW; THE COMMON LAW AND ITS RIVALS (VOL. V). UK SEA EX/STRUC WRITING ADMIN...INT/LAW JURID CONCPT IDEA/COMP WORSHIP 16/17 PARLIAMENT ENGLSH/LAW COMMON/LAW. PAGE 54 E1073
LAW LEGIS ADJUD CT/SYS
B24

CLYDE W.M.,THE STRUGGLE FOR THE FREEDOM OF THE PRESS FROM CAXTON TO CROMWELL. UK LAW LOC/G SECT FORCES LICENSE WRITING SANCTION REV ATTIT PWR ...POLICY 15/17 PARLIAMENT CROMWELL/O MILTON/J. PAGE 23 E0460
PRESS ORD/FREE CONTROL
B34

THOMPSON J.W.,SECRET DIPLOMACY: A RECORD OF ESPIONAGE AND DOUBLE-DEALING: 1500-1815. CHRIST-17C MOD/EUR NAT/G WRITING RISK MORAL...ANTHOL BIBLIOG 16/19 ESPIONAGE. PAGE 96 E1920
DIPLOM CRIME
B37

HOLDSWORTH W.S.,A HISTORY OF ENGLISH LAW; THE CENTURIES OF SETTLEMENT AND REFORM (VOL. XII). UK CONSTN STRATA LEGIS JUDGE ADJUD CT/SYS ATTIT ...JURID CONCPT BIOG GEN/LAWS 18 ENGLSH/LAW BLACKSTN/W COMMON/LAW. PAGE 54 E1078
LAW PROF/ORG WRITING IDEA/COMP
B38

MCNAIR A.D.,THE LAW OF TREATIES: BRITISH PRACTICE AND OPINIONS. UK CREATE DIPLOM LEGIT WRITING ADJUD WAR...INT/LAW JURID TREATY. PAGE 71 E1424
AGREE LAW CT/SYS NAT/G
B38

CRAIG A.,ABOVE ALL LIBERTIES. FRANCE UK USA-45 LAW CONSTN CULTURE INTELL NAT/G SECT JUDGE...IDEA/COMP BIBLIOG 18/20. PAGE 27 E0536
ORD/FREE MORAL WRITING EDU/PROP
B42

CRAIG A.,"ABOVE ALL LIBERTIES." FRANCE UK LAW CULTURE INTELL SECT ORD/FREE 18/20. PAGE 27 E0537
BIBLIOG/A EDU/PROP WRITING MORAL
C42

BENTHAM J.,"ON THE LIBERTY OF THE PRESS, AND PUBLIC DISCUSSION" IN J. BOWRING, ED., THE WORKS OF JEREMY BENTHAM." SPAIN UK LAW ELITES NAT/G LEGIS INSPECT LEGIT WRITING CONTROL PRIVIL TOTALISM AUTHORIT ...TRADIT 19 FREE/SPEE. PAGE 10 E0193
ORD/FREE PRESS CONFER CONSERVE
C43

FRANKFURTER F.,"SOME REFLECTIONS ON THE READING OF STATUTES" USA+45 USA-45 PROB/SOLV CT/SYS TASK
JURID LAW
S47

EFFICIENCY...LING 20. PAGE 40 E0791
ADJUD WRITING

BOHATTA H.,INTERNATIONALE BIBLIOGRAPHIE. WOR+45 LAW CULTURE PRESS. PAGE 13 E0260
BIBLIOG DIPLOM NAT/G WRITING
B50

BISSAINTHE M.,DICTIONNAIRE DE BIBLIOGRAPHIE HAITIENNE. HAITI ELITES AGRI LEGIS DIPLOM INT/TRADE WRITING ORD/FREE CATHISM...ART/METH GEOG 19/20 NEGRO TREATY. PAGE 12 E0234
BIBLIOG L/A+17C SOCIETY NAT/G
B51

HOLDSWORTH W.S.,A HISTORY OF ENGLISH LAW; THE CENTURIES OF SETTLEMENT AND REFORM, 1701-1875 (VOL. XIII). UK POL/PAR PROF/ORG LEGIS JUDGE WRITING ATTIT...JURID CONCPT BIOG GEN/LAWS 18/19 PARLIAMENT REFORMERS ENGLSH/LAW COMMON/LAW. PAGE 54 E1080
LAW CONSTN IDEA/COMP CT/SYS
B52

UNESCO,THESES DE SCIENCES SOCIALES: CATALOGUE ANALYTIQUE INTERNATIONAL DE THESES INEDITES DE DOCTORAT, 1940-1950. INT/ORG DIPLOM EDU/PROP...GEOG INT/LAW MGT PSY SOC 20. PAGE 98 E1958
BIBLIOG ACADEM WRITING
B52

FLIESS P.J.,FREEDOM OF THE PRESS IN THE GERMAN REPUBLIC, 1918-1933. GERMANY LAW CONSTN POL/PAR LEGIS WRITING ADMIN COERCE MURDER MARXISM...POLICY BIBLIOG 20 WEIMAR/REP. PAGE 39 E0765
EDU/PROP ORD/FREE JURID PRESS
B55

PLISCHKE E.,AMERICAN FOREIGN RELATIONS: A BIBLIOGRAPHY OF OFFICIAL SOURCES. USA+45 USA-45 INT/ORG FORCES PRESS WRITING DEBATE EXEC...POLICY INT/LAW 18/20 CONGRESS. PAGE 81 E1621
BIBLIOG/A DIPLOM NAT/G
B55

PULLEN W.R.,A CHECK LIST OF LEGISLATIVE JOURNALS ISSUED SINCE 1937 BY THE STATES OF THE UNITED STATES OF AMERICA (PAMPHLET). USA+45 USA-45 LAW WRITING ADJUD ADMIN...JURID 20. PAGE 83 E1662
BIBLIOG PROVS EDU/PROP LEGIS
B55

TROTIER A.H.,DOCTORAL DISSERTATIONS ACCEPTED BY AMERICAN UNIVERSITIES 1954-55. SECT DIPLOM HEALTH ...ART/METH GEOG INT/LAW SOC LING CHARTS 20. PAGE 97 E1943
BIBLIOG ACADEM USA+45 WRITING
B55

SIPKOV I.,LEGAL SOURCES AND BIBLIOGRAPHY OF BULGARIA. BULGARIA COM LEGIS WRITING ADJUD CT/SYS ...INT/LAW TREATY 20. PAGE 91 E1834
BIBLIOG LAW TOTALISM MARXISM
B56

US COMMISSION GOVT SECURITY,RECOMMENDATIONS; AREA: IMMIGRANT PROGRAM. USA+45 LAW WORKER DIPLOM EDU/PROP WRITING ADMIN PEACE ATTIT...CONCPT ANTHOL 20 MIGRATION SUBVERT. PAGE 99 E1981
POLICY CONTROL PLAN NAT/G
B57

CABLE G.W.,THE NEGRO QUESTION: A SELECTION OF WRITINGS ON CIVIL RIGHTS IN THE SOUTH. USA+45 STRATA LOC/G POL/PAR GIVE EDU/PROP WRITING CT/SYS SANCTION CRIME CHOOSE WORSHIP 20 NEGRO CIV/RIGHTS CONV/LEASE SOUTH/US. PAGE 18 E0355
RACE/REL CULTURE DISCRIM ORD/FREE
B58

GARDINER H.C.,CATHOLIC VIEWPOINT ON CENSORSHIP. DEBATE COERCE GP/REL...JURID CONCPT 20. PAGE 42 E0835
WRITING LOBBY CATHISM EDU/PROP
B58

OKINSHEVICH L.A.,LATIN AMERICA IN SOVIET WRITINGS, 1945-1958: A BIBLIOGRAPHY. USSR LAW ECO/UNDEV LABOR DIPLOM EDU/PROP REV...GEOG SOC 20. PAGE 78 E1573
BIBLIOG WRITING COM L/A+17C
B59

KAUPER P.G.,CIVIL LIBERTIES AND THE CONSTITUTION. USA+45 SECT EDU/PROP WRITING ADJUD SEX ORD/FREE 20 SUPREME/CT CIVIL/LIB CHURCH/STA. PAGE 60 E1188
LAW CONSTN CT/SYS DECISION
B62

PRESS C.,STATE MANUALS, BLUE BOOKS AND ELECTION RESULTS. LAW LOC/G MUNIC LEGIS WRITING FEDERAL SOVEREIGN...DECISION STAT CHARTS 20. PAGE 82 E1648
BIBLIOG PROVS ADMIN CHOOSE
B62

SWAYZE H.,POLITICAL CONTROL OF LITERATURE IN THE
USSR, 1946-1959. USSR NAT/G CREATE LICENSE...JURID
20. PAGE 95 E1898

B62
MARXISM
WRITING
CONTROL
DOMIN

DOOLIN D.J.,COMMUNIST CHINA: THE POLITICS OF
STUDENT OPPOSITION. CHINA/COM ELITES STRATA ACADEM
NAT/G WRITING CT/SYS LEAD PARTIC COERCE TOTALISM
20. PAGE 32 E0637

B64
MARXISM
DEBATE
AGE/Y
PWR

HURST W.H.,JUSTICE HOLMES ON LEGAL HISTORY. USA-45
LAW SOCIETY NAT/G WRITING...POLICY PHIL/SCI SOC
CONCPT 20 HOLMES/OW SUPREME/CT ENGLSH/LAW. PAGE 56
E1117

B64
ADJUD
JURID
BIOG

NICE R.W.,TREASURY OF LAW. WOR+45 WOR-45 SECT ADJUD
MORAL ORD/FREE...INT/LAW JURID PHIL/SCI ANTHOL.
PAGE 77 E1545

B64
LAW
WRITING
PERS/REL
DIPLOM

HOLDSWORTH W.S.,A HISTORY OF ENGLISH LAW; THE
CENTURIES OF SETTLEMENT AND REFORM (VOL. XV). UK
CONSTN SECT LEGIS JUDGE WRITING ADJUD CT/SYS CRIME
OWN...JURID IDEA/COMP 18 PARLIAMENT ENGLSH/LAW
COMMON/LAW. PAGE 54 E1082

B65
LAW
INDUS
PROF/ORG
ATTIT

MOSTECKY V.,SOVIET LEGAL BIBLIOGRAPHY. USSR LEGIS
PRESS WRITING CONFER ADJUD CT/SYS REV MARXISM
...INT/LAW JURID DICTIONARY 20. PAGE 75 E1503

B65
BIBLIOG/A
LAW
COM
CONSTN

NEWBURY C.W.,BRITISH POLICY TOWARDS WEST AFRICA:
SELECT DOCUMENTS 1786-1874. AFR UK INT/TRADE DOMIN
ADMIN COLONIAL CT/SYS COERCE ORD/FREE...BIBLIOG/A
18/19. PAGE 77 E1540

B65
DIPLOM
POLICY
NAT/G
WRITING

DALLIN A.,POLITICS IN THE SOVIET UNION: 7 CASES.
COM USSR LAW POL/PAR CHIEF FORCES WRITING CONTROL
PARL/PROC CIVMIL/REL TOTALISM...ANTHOL 20 KHRUSH/N
STALIN/J CASEBOOK COM/PARTY. PAGE 28 E0563

B66
MARXISM
DOMIN
ORD/FREE
GOV/REL

NYC BAR ASSOCIATION RECORD,"PAPERBACKS FOR THE
BAR." USA+45 LEGIS ADJUD CT/SYS. PAGE 78 E1562

S66
BIBLIOG
JURID
LAW
WRITING

UNITED NATIONS,UNITED NATIONS PUBLICATIONS:
1945-1966. WOR+45 COM/IND DIST/IND FINAN TEC/DEV
ADMIN...POLICY INT/LAW MGT CHARTS 20 UN UNESCO.
PAGE 98 E1970

B67
BIBLIOG/A
INT/ORG
DIPLOM
WRITING

GOSSETT W.T.,"ELECTING THE PRESIDENT: NEW HOPE FOR
AN OLD IDEAL." FUT USA+45 USA-45 PROVS LEGIS
PROB/SOLV WRITING DEBATE ADJUD REPRESENT...MAJORIT
DECISION 20 HOUSE/REP PRESIDENT. PAGE 45 E0892

S67
CONSTN
CHIEF
CHOOSE
NAT/G

READ J.S.,"CENSORED." UGANDA CONSTN INTELL SOCIETY
NAT/G DIPLOM PRESS WRITING ADJUD ADMIN COLONIAL
RISK...IDEA/COMP 20. PAGE 84 E1675

S67
EDU/PROP
AFR
CREATE

WRONG D.H. E2161

WWI....WORLD WAR I

TOSCANO M.,THE HISTORY OF TREATIES AND
INTERNATIONAL POLITICS (REV. ED.). WOR-45 AGREE WAR
...BIOG 19/20 TREATY WWI. PAGE 97 E1935

N
DIPLOM
INT/ORG

PUSEY M.J.,CHARLES EVANS HUGHES (2 VOLS.). LAW
CONSTN NAT/G POL/PAR DIPLOM LEGIT WAR CHOOSE
PERS/REL DRIVE HEREDITY 19/20 DEPT/STATE LEAGUE/NAT
SUPREME/CT HUGHES/CE WWI. PAGE 83 E1663

B51
BIOG
TOP/EX
ADJUD
PERSON

WWII....WORLD WAR II

WYLIE M. E1315

WYOMING....WYOMING

XENOPHOBIA....SEE NAT/LISM

XENOPHON....XENOPHON

XHOSA....XHOSA TRIBE (SOUTH AFRICA)

YAKOBSON S. E2162

YALE/U....YALE UNIVERSITY

YALEM R.J. E2163

YALTA....YALTA CONFERENCE

YANG KUNG-SUN E2164

YANKEE/C....YANKEE CITY - LOCATION OF W.L. WARNEROS STUDY
OF SAME NAME

YARBROGH/R....RALPH YARBOROUGH

US SENATE COMM ON POST OFFICE,TO PROVIDE FOR AN
EFFECTIVE SYSTEM OF PERSONNEL ADMINISTRATION.
EFFICIENCY...MGT 20 CONGRESS CIVIL/SERV POSTAL/SYS
YARBROGH/R. PAGE 103 E2059

B59
ADMIN
NAT/G
EX/STRUC
LAW

YAZOO....YAZOO LAND SCANDAL

MAGRATH C.P.,YAZOO; LAW AND POLITICS IN THE NEW
REPUBLIC: THE CASE OF FLETCHER V. PECK. USA-45 LAW
...BIBLIOG 19 SUPREME/CT YAZOO. PAGE 67 E1348

B66
CT/SYS
DECISION
CONSTN
LOBBY

YEMEN....SEE ALSO ISLAM

YORUBA....YORUBA TRIBE

YOUNG C.M. E1165

YOUNG W. E1372,E2165

YOUNG/TURK....YOUNG TURK POLITICAL PARTY

YOUNGER R.D. E2166

YOUTH....SEE AGE/Y

YUDELMAN/M....MONTEGU YUDELMAN

YUGOSLAVIA....YUGOSLAVIA; SEE ALSO COM

CONOVER H.F.,THE BALKANS: A SELECTED LIST OF
REFERENCES. ALBANIA BULGARIA ROMANIA YUGOSLAVIA
INT/ORG PROB/SOLV DIPLOM LEGIT CONFER ADJUD WAR
NAT/LISM PEACE PWR 20 LEAGUE/NAT. PAGE 25 E0493

B43
BIBLIOG
EUR+WWI

GREEN L.C.,"POLITICAL OFFENSES, WAR CRIMES AND
EXTRADITION." WOR+45 YUGOSLAVIA INT/ORG LEGIT
ROUTINE WAR ORD/FREE SOVEREIGN...JURID NAZI 20
INTERPOL. PAGE 46 E0906

S62
LAW
CONCPT
INT/LAW

PRYOR F.L.,THE COMMUNIST FOREIGN TRADE SYSTEM. COM
CZECHOSLVK GERMANY YUGOSLAVIA LAW ECO/DEV DIST/IND
POL/PAR PLAN DOMIN TOTALISM DRIVE RIGID/FLEX WEALTH
...STAT STAND/INT CHARTS 20. PAGE 83 E1657

B63
ATTIT
ECO/TAC

GJUPANOVIC H.,LEGAL SOURCES AND BIBLIOGRAPHY OF
YUGOSLAVIA. COM YUGOSLAVIA LAW LEGIS DIPLOM ADMIN
PARL/PROC REGION CRIME CENTRAL 20. PAGE 44 E0873

B64
BIBLIOG/A
JURID
CONSTN
ADJUD

GRIFFITH W.E.,THE SINO-SOVIET RIFT. ASIA CHINA/COM
COM CUBA USSR YUGOSLAVIA NAT/G POL/PAR VOL/ASSN
DELIB/GP FORCES TOP/EX DIPLOM EDU/PROP DRIVE PERSON
PWR...TREND 20 TREATY. PAGE 47 E0941

B64
ATTIT
TIME/SEQ
BAL/PWR
SOCISM

LAPENNA I.,STATE AND LAW: SOVIET AND YUGOSLAV
THEORY. USSR YUGOSLAVIA STRATA STRUCT NAT/G DOMIN
COERCE MARXISM...GOV/COMP IDEA/COMP 20. PAGE 63
E1253

B64
JURID
COM
LAW
SOVEREIGN

YUKIO O. E2167

YUKON....YUKON, CANADA

ZABEL O.H. E2168

ZALESKI E. E1486,E1487

ZAMBIA....SEE ALSO AFR

                                                              B64
FRANCK T.M.,EAST AFRICAN UNITY THROUGH LAW. MALAWI   AFR
TANZANIA UGANDA UK ZAMBIA CONSTN INT/ORG NAT/G   FEDERAL
ADMIN ROUTINE TASK NAT/LISM ATTIT SOVEREIGN   REGION
...RECORD IDEA/COMP NAT/COMP. PAGE 40 E0785   INT/LAW

ZANDE....ZANDE, AFRICA

ZANZIBAR....SEE TANZANIA

ZAWODNY J.K. E2169

ZIEGLER B.M. E0965

ZIMMERN A. E2170

ZINN C.J. E2171

ZIONISM....SEE ISRAEL, NAT/LISM

ZLATOVRT/N....NIKOLAI ZLATOVRATSKII

ZONING....ZONING REGULATIONS

                                                              B61
POOLEY B.J.,PLANNING AND ZONING IN THE UNITED   PLAN
STATES. USA+45 MUNIC DELIB/GP ACT/RES PROB/SOLV   LOC/G
TEC/DEV ADJUD ADMIN REGION 20 ZONING. PAGE 81 E1628   PROVS
                                                       LAW

                                                              B64
MITAU G.T.,INSOLUBLE PROBLEMS: CASE PROBLEMS ON THE   ADJUD
FUNCTIONS OF STATE AND LOCAL GOVERNMENT. USA+45 AIR   LOC/G
FINAN LABOR POL/PAR PROB/SOLV TAX RECEIVE CONTROL   PROVS
GP/REL 20 CASEBOOK ZONING. PAGE 73 E1471

ZULU....ZULU - MEMBER OF BANTU NATION (SOUTHEAST AFRICA)

ZUNI....ZUNI - NEW MEXICAN INDIAN TRIBE

ZWINGLI/U....ULRICH ZWINGLI

Directory of Publishers

Abelard-Schuman Ltd., New York
Abeledo-Perrot, Buenos Aires
Abingdon Press, Nashville, Tenn.; New York
Academic Press, London; New York
Academy of the Rumanian People's Republic Scientific
    Documentation Center, Bucharest
Academy Publishers, New York
Accra Government Printer, Accra, Ghana
Acharya Book Depot, Baroda, India
Acorn Press, Phoenix, Ariz.
Action Housing, Inc., Pittsburgh, Pa.
Adams & Charles Black, London
Addison-Wesley Publishing Co., Inc., Reading, Mass.
Adelphi, Greenberg, New York
Adelphi Terrace, London
Advertising Research Foundation, New York
Advisory Committee on Intergovernmental Relations,
    Washington
Africa Bureau, London
Africa 1960 Committee, London
African Bibliographical Center, Inc., Washington
African Research Ltd., Exeter, England
Agarwal Press, Allahabad, India
Agathon Press, New York
Agency for International Development, Washington
Agrupacion Bibliotecalogica, Montevideo
Aguilar, S. A. de Ediciones, Madrid
Air University, Montgomery, Ala.
Akademiai Kiado, Budapest
Akademische Druck-und Verlagsanstalt, Graz, Austria
Akhil Bharat Sarva Seva Sangh, Rajghat, Varanasi, India;
    Rajghat, Kashi, India
Al Jadidah Press, Cairo
Alba House, New York
Eberhard Albert Verlag, Freiburg, Germany
Alcan, Paris
Aldine Publishing Co., Chicago
Aligarh Muslim University, Department of History,
    Aligarh, India
All-India Congress Committee, New Delhi
Allen and Unwin, Ltd., London
Howard Allen, Inc., Cleveland, Ohio
W. H. Allen & Co., Ltd., London
Alliance Inc., New York
Allied Publishers, Private, Ltd., Bombay; New Delhi
Allyn and Bacon, Inc., Boston
Almquist-Wiksell, Stockholm; Upsala
Ambassador Books, Ltd., Toronto, Ontario
American Academy of Arts and Sciences, Harvard University,
    Cambridge, Mass.
American Academy of Political and Social Science,
    Philadelphia
American Anthropological Association, Washington, D. C.
American Arbitration Association, New York
American-Asian Educational Exchange, New York
American Assembly, New York
American Association for the Advancement of Science,
    Washington, D. C.
American Association for the United Nations, New York
American Association of University Women, Washington, D. C.
American Bankers Association, New York
American Bar Association, Chicago
American Bar Foundation, Chicago
American Bibliographical Center-Clio Press, Santa Barbara,
    Calif.
American Bibliographic Service, Darien, Conn.
American Book Company, New York
American Civil Liberties Union, New York
American Council of Learned Societies, New York
American Council on Education, Washington
American Council on Public Affairs, Washington
American Data Processing, Inc., Detroit, Mich.
American Documentation Institute, Washington
American Economic Association, Evanston, Ill.
American Elsevier Publishing Co., Inc., New York
American Enterprise Institute for Public Policy Research,
    Washington, D. C.
American Features, New York
American Federation of Labor & Congress of Industrial
    Organizations, Washington, D. C.

American Foreign Law Association, Chicago
American Forest Products Industries, Washington, D. C.
American Friends of Vietnam, New York
American Friends Service Committee, New York
American Historical Association, Washington, D. C.
American Historical Society, New York
American Institute for Economic Research, Great Barrington,
    Mass.
American Institute of Consulting Engineers, New York
American Institute of Pacific Relations, New York
American International College, Springfield, Mass.
American Jewish Archives, Hebrew Union College—Jewish
    Institute of Religion, Cincinnati, Ohio
American Jewish Committee Institute of Human Relations,
    New York
American Judicature Society, Chicago
American Law Institute, Philadelphia
American Library Association, Chicago
American Management Association, New York
American Marketing Association, Inc., Chicago
American Municipal Association, Washington
American Museum of Natural History Press, New York
American Nepal Education Foundation, Eugene, Oregon
American Newspaper Publishers' Association, New York
American Opinion, Belmont, Mass.
American Philosophical Society, Philadelphia
American Political Science Association, Washington
American Psychiatric Association, New York
American Public Welfare Association, Chicago
American Research Council, Larchmont, N. Y.
American Society of African Culture, New York
American Society of International Law, Chicago
American Society for Public Administration, Chicago;
    Washington
American Textbook Publishers Council, New York
American Universities Field Staff, New York
American University, Washington, D. C.
American University of Beirut, Beirut
American University of Cairo, Cairo
American University Press, Washington
American University Press Services, Inc., New York
Ampersand Press, Inc., London, New York
Amsterdam Stock Exchange, Amsterdam
Anchor Books, New York
Anderson Kramer Association, Washington, D. C.
Anglo-Israel Association, London
Angus and Robertson, Sydney, Australia
Ann Arbor Publications, Ann Arbor, Mich.
Anthropological Publications, Oosterhout, Netherlands
Anti-Defamation League of B'nai B'rith, New York
Antioch Press, Yellow Springs, Ohio
Antwerp Institut Universitaire des Territoires d'Outre-Mer,
    Antwerp, Belgium
APEC Editora, Rio de Janeiro
Apollo Editions, New York
Ludwig Appel Verlag, Hamburg
Appleton-Century-Crofts, New York
Aqueduct Books, Rochester, N. Y.
Arbeitsgemeinschaft fur Forschung des Landes
    Nordrhein-Westfalen, Dusseldorf, Germany
Arcadia, New York
Architectural Press, London
Archon Books, Hamden, Conn.
Arco Publishing Company, New York
Arizona Department of Library and Archives, Tucson
Arizona State University, Bureau of Government Research,
    Tucson
Arlington House, New Rochelle, N. Y.
Arnold Foundation, Southern Methodist University, Dallas
Edward Arnold Publishers, Ltd., London
J. W. Arrowsmith, Ltd., London
Artes Graficas, Buenos Aires
Artes Graficas Industrias Reunidas SA, Rio de Janeiro
Asia Foundation, San Francisco
Asia Publishing House, Bombay; Calcutta; London; New York
Asia Society, New York
Asian Studies Center, Michigan State University, East Lan-
    sing, Mich.
Asian Studies Press, Bombay
Associated College Presses, New York

Associated Lawyers Publishing Co., Newark, N. J.
Association for Asian Studies, Ann Arbor
Association of National Advertisers, New York
Association of the Bar of the City of New York, New York
Association Press, New York
Associated University Bureaus of Business and Economic
  Research, Eugene, Ore.
M. L. Atallah, Rotterdam
Atheneum Publishers, New York
Atherton Press, New York
Athlone Press, London
Atlanta University Press, Atlanta, Ga.
The Atlantic Institute, Boulogne-sur-Seine
Atlantic Provinces Research Board, Fredericton,
  Newfoundland
Atma Ram & Sons, New Delhi
Atomic Industrial Forum, New York
Augustan Reprint Society, Los Angeles, Calif.
Augustana College Library, Rock Island, Ill.
Augustana Press, Rock Island, Ill.
J. J. Augustin, New York
Augustinus Verlag, Wurzburg
Australian National Research Council, Melbourne
Australian National University, Canberra
Australian Public Affairs Information Service, Sydney
Australian War Memorial, Canberra
Avi Publishing Co., Westport, Conn.
Avtoreferaty Dissertatsii, Moscow
N. W. Ayer and Sons, Inc., Philadelphia, Pa.
Aymon, Paris

La Baconniere, Neuchatel; Paris
Richard G. Badger, Boston
Baker Book House, Grand Rapids, Mich.
Baker, Vorhis, and Co., Boston
John Baker, London
A. A. Balkema, Capetown
Ballantine Books, Inc., New York
James Ballantine and Co., London
Baltimore Sun, Baltimore, Md.
Banco Central de Venezuela, Caracas
Bank for International Settlements, Basel
Bank of Finland Institute for Economic Research, Helsinki
Bank of Italy, Rome
Bankers Publishing Co., Boston
George Banta Publishing Co., Menasha, Wis.
Bantam Books, Inc., New York
A. S. Barnes and Co., Inc., Cranbury, N. J.
Barnes and Noble, Inc., New York
Barre Publishers, Barre, Mass.
Basic Books, Inc., New York
Batchworth Press Ltd., London
Bayerische Akademie der Wissenschaften, Munich
Bayerischer Schulbuch Verlag, Munich
Ebenezer Baylis and Son, Ltd., Worcester, England
Baylor University Press, Waco, Texas
Beacon Press, Boston
Bechte Verlag, Esslingen, Germany
H. Beck, Dresden
Bedminster Press, Inc., Totowa, N. J.
Beechhurst Press, New York
Behavioral Research Council, Great Barrington, Mass.
Belknap Press, Cambridge, Mass.
G. Bell & Sons, London
Bellman Publishing Co., Inc., Cambridge, Mass.
Matthew Bender and Co., Albany, New York
Bengal Publishers, Ltd., Calcutta
Marshall Benick, New York
Ernest Benn, Ltd., London
J. Bensheimer, Berlin; Leipzig; Mannheim
Benziger Brothers, New York
Berkley Publishing Corporation, New York
Bernard und Graefe Verlag fur Wehrwesen, Frankfurt
C. Bertelsmann Verlag, Gutersloh
Bharati Bhawan, Bankipore, India
Bharatiyi Vidya Bhavan, Bombay
G. R. Bhatkal for Popular Prakashan, Bombay
Bibliographical Society, London
Bibliographical Society of America, New York
Bibliographie des Staats, Dresden
Biblioteca de la II feria del libro exposicion nacional
  del periodismo, Panuco, Mexico
Biblioteca Nacional, Bogota

Biblioteka Imeni V. I. Lenina, Moscow
Bibliotheque des Temps Nouveaux, Paris
Bibliotheque Nationale, Paris
Adams & Charles Black, London
Basil Blackwell, Oxford
William Blackwood, Edinburgh
Blaisdell Publishing Co., Inc., Waltham, Mass.
Blanford Press, London
Blass, S. A., Madrid
Geoffrey Bles, London
BNA, Inc. (Bureau of National Affairs), Washington, D. C.
Board of Trade and Industry Estates Management Corp.,
  London
T. V. Boardman and Co., London
Bobbs-Merrill Company, Inc., Indianapolis, Ind.
The Bodley Head, London
Bogen-Verlag, Munich
Bohlau-Verlag, Cologne; Graz; Tubingen
H. G. Bohn, London
Boni and Gaer, New York
Bonn University, Bonn
The Book of the Month Club, Johannesburg
Bookcraft, Inc., Salt Lake City, Utah
Bookfield House, New York
Bookland Private, Ltd., Calcutta; London
Bookmailer, New York
Bookman Associates, Record Press, New York
Books for Libraries, Inc., Freeport, N. Y.
Books International, Jullundur City, India
Borsenverein der deutschen Buchhandler, Leipzig
Bossange, Paris
Boston Book Co., Boston
Boston College Library, Chestnut Hill, Boston
Boston University, African Research Program, Boston
Boston University Press, Boston
H. Bouvier Verlag, Bonn
Bowes and Bowes, Ltd., Cambridge, England
R. R. Bowker Co., New York
John Bradburn, New York
George Braziller, Inc., New York
Brentano's, New York
Brigham Young University, Provo, Utah
E. J. Brill, Leyden
British Borneo Research Project, London
British Broadcasting Corp., London
British Council, London
British Liberal Party Organization, London
British Museum, London
Broadman Press, Nashville, Tenn.
The Brookings Institution, Washington
Brown University Press, Providence, R. I.
A. Brown and Sons, Ltd., London
William C. Brown Co., Dubuque, Iowa
Brown-White-Lowell Press, Kansas City
Bruce Publishing Co., Milwaukee, Wis.
Buchdruckerei Meier, Bulach, Germany
Buchhandler-Vereinigung, Frankfurt
Buijten & Schipperheijn, Amsterdam
Building Contractors Council, Chicago
Bureau of Public Printing, Manila
Bureau of Social Science Research, Washington, D. C.
Business Economists Group, Oxford
Business Publications, Inc., Chicago
Business Service Corp., Detroit, Mich.
Buttenheim Publishing Corp., New York
Butterworth's, London; Washington, D. C.; Toronto

Anne Cabbott, Manchester, England
California, Assembly of the State of, Sacramento, Calif.
California State Library, Sacramento
Calman Levy, Paris
Camara Oficial del Libro, Madrid
Cambridge Book Co., Inc., Bronxville, N. Y.
Cambridge University Press, Cambridge; London; New York
Camelot Press Ltd., London
Campion Press, London
M. Campos, Rio de Janeiro
Canada, Civil Service Commission, Ottawa
Canada, Civil Service Commission, Organization
  Division, Ottawa
Canada, Ministry of National Health and Welfare, Ottawa
Canada, National Joint Council of the Public Service,
  Ottawa

Canadian Dept. of Mines and Technical Surveys, Ottawa
Canadian Institute of International Affairs, Toronto
Canadian Peace Research Institute, Clarkson, Ont.
Canadian Trade Committee, Montreal
Candour Publishing Co., London
Jonathan Cape, London
Cape and Smith, New York
Capricorn Books, New York
Caribbean Commission, Port-of-Spain, Trinidad
Carleton University Library, Ottawa
Erich Carlsohn, Leipzig
Carnegie Endowment for International Peace, New York
Carnegie Endowment for International Peace,
  Washington, D. C.
Carnegie Foundation for the Advancement of Teaching,
  New York
Carnegie Press, Pittsburgh, Pa.
Carswell Co., Ltd., Toronto, Canada
Casa de las Americas, Havana
Case Institute of Technology, Cleveland, Ohio
Frank Cass & Co., Ltd., London
Cassell & Co., Ltd., London
Castle Press, Pasadena, Calif.
Catholic Historical Society of Philadelphia, Philadelphia
Catholic Press, Beirut
Catholic Students Mission Crusade Press, Cincinnati, Ohio
Catholic University Press, Washington
The Caxton Printers, Ltd., Caldwell, Idaho
Cedesa, Brussels
Cellar Book Shop, Detroit, Mich.
Center for Applied Research in Education, New York
Center for Applied Research in Education, Washington, D. C.
Center for Research on Economic Development, Ann Arbor,
  Mich.
Center for the Study of Democratic Institutions,
  Santa Barbara, Calif.
Center of Foreign Policy Research, Washington, D. C.
Center of International Studies, Princeton
Center of Planning and Economic Research, Athens, Greece;
  Washington, D. C.
Central Asian Research Centre, London
Central Bank of Egypt, Cairo
Central Book Co., Inc., Brooklyn, N. Y.
Central Book Department, Allahabad, India
Central Law Book Supply, Inc., Manila
Central News Agency, Ltd., Capetown, S. Afr.
Central Publicity Commission, Indian National Congress,
  New Delhi
Centre de Documentation CNRS, Paris
Centre de Documentation Economique et Sociale Africaine,
  Brussels
Centre d'Etudes de Politique Etrangere, Paris
Centre de Recherches sur l'URSS et les pays de l'est,
  Strasbourg
Centro de Estudios Monetarios Latino-Americanos,
  Mexico City
Centro Editorial, Guatemala City
Centro Mexicano de Escritores, Mexico City
Centro Para el "Desarrollo Economico y Social de
  America Latina", Santiago, Chile
The Century Co., New York
Century House, Inc., Watkins Glen, N. Y.
Cercle de la Librairie, Paris
Leon Chaillez Editeur, Paris
Chaitanya Publishing House, Allahabad, India
Chamber of Commerce of the United States, Washington, D. C.
S. Chand and Co., New Delhi
Chandler Publishing Co., San Francisco
Chandler-Davis, Lexington, Mass.
Chandler-Davis Publishing Co., West Trenton, N. J.
Channel Press, Inc., Great Neck, N. Y.
Chapman and Hall, London
Geoffrey Chapman, London
Chatham College, Pittsburgh, Pa.
Chatto and Windus, Ltd., London
F. W. Cheshire, London
Chestnut Hill, Boston College Library, Boston
Chicago Joint Reference Library, Chicago
Chilean Development Corp., New York
Chilmark Press, New York
Chilton Books, New York
China Viewpoints, Hong Kong
Chinese-American Publishing Co., Shanghai

Chiswick Press, London
Christian Crusade, Tulsa, Okla.
Georg Christiansen, Itzehoe, Germany
Christopher Publishing House, Boston
Chulalongkorn University, Bangkok
Church League of America, Wheaton, Ill.
C. I. Associates, New York
Cincinnati Civil Service, Cincinnati, Ohio
Citadel Press, New York
City of Johannesburg Public Library, Johannesburg
Citizens Research Foundation, Paris
Citizens Research Foundation, Princeton, N. J.
Ciudad Universitaria, San Jose, Calif.
Ciudad y Espiritu, Buenos Aires
Claremont Colleges, Claremont, Calif.
Clarendon Press, London
Clark, Irwin and Co., Ltd., Toronto
Clark University Press, Worcester, Mass.
Classics Press, New York
Clay and Sons, London
Cleveland Civil Service Commission, Cleveland
Clio Press, Santa Barbara, Calif.
William Clowes and Sons, Ltd., London
Colin (Librairie Armand) Paris
College and University Press, New Haven
Collet's Holdings, Ltd., London
Colliers, New York
F. Collin, Brussels
Collins, London
Colloquium Verlag, Berlin
Colombo Plan Bureau, Colombo, Ceylon
Colonial Press Inc., Northport, Ala.; New York
Colorado Bibliographic Institute, Denver
Colorado Legislature Council, Denver
Colorado State Board of Library Commissioners, Denver
Columbia University, New York
Columbia University, Bureau of Applied Social Research,
  New York
Columbia University, Center for Urban Education, New York
Columbia University, East Asian Institute, New York
Columbia University, Graduate School of Business, New York
Columbia University, Institute of French Studies, New York
Columbia University, Institute of Public Administration,
  New York
Columbia University, Institute of Russian Studies, New York
Columbia University, Institute of War-Peace Studies,
  New York
Columbia University, Law Library, New York
Columbia University, Parker School, New York
Columbia University, School of International Affairs,
  New York
Columbia University, School of Library Service, New York
Columbia University Press, New York
Columbia University Teachers College, New York
Combat Forces Press, Washington, D. C.
Comet Press, New York
Comision Nacional Ejecutiva, Buenos Aires
Commerce Clearing House, Chicago; Washington; New York
Commercial Credit Co., Baltimore, Md.
Commissao do iv Centenario de Ciudade, Sao Paulo
Commission for Technical Cooperation, Lahore
Commission to Study the Organization of Peace, New York
Committee for Economic Development, New York
Committee on Africa, New York
Committee on Federal Tax Policy, New York
Committee on Near East Studies, Washington
Committee on Public Administration, Washington, D. C.
Committee to Frame World Constitution, New York
Common Council for American Unity, New York
Commonwealth Agricultural Bureau, London
Commonwealth Economic Commission, London
Community Publications, Manila
Community Renewal Program, San Francisco
Community Studies, Inc., Kansas City
Companhia Editora Forense, Rio de Janeiro
Companhia Editora Nacional, Sao Paulo
Compass Books, New York
Concordia Publishing House, St. Louis, Mo.
Confederate Publishing Co., Tuscaloosa, Ala.
Conference on Economic Progress, Washington, D. C.
Conference on State and Economic Enterprise in Modern
  Japan, Estes Park, Colo.
Congress for Cultural Freedom, Prabhakar

Congressional Quarterly Service, Washington
Connecticut Personnel Department, Hartford
Connecticut State Civil Service Commission, Hartford
Conseil d'Etat, Paris
Conservative Political Centre, London
Constable and Co., London
Archibald Constable and Co., Edinburgh
Cooper Square Publishers, New York
U. Cooper and Partners, Ltd., London
Corinth Books, New York
Cornell University, Dept. of Asian Studies, Ithaca
Cornell University, Graduate School of Business and Public
   Administration, Ithaca
Cornell University Press, Ithaca
Cornell University, School of Industry and Labor Planning,
   Ithaca
Council for Economic Education, Bombay
Council of Education, Johannesburg
Council of Europe, Strasbourg
Council of State Governments, Chicago, Ill.
Council of the British National Bibliography, Ltd., London
Council on Foreign Relations, New York
Council on Public Affairs, Washington, D. C.
Council on Religion and International Affairs, New York
Council on Social Work Education, Washington, D. C.
Covici, Friede, Inc., New York
Coward-McCann, Inc., New York
Cresset Press, London
Crestwood Books, Springfield, Va.
Criterion Books, Inc., New York
S. Crofts and Co., New York
Crosby, Lockwood, and Sons, Ltd., London
Crosscurrents Press, New York
Thomas Y. Crowell Co., New York
Crowell-Collier and MacMillan, New York
Crown Publishers, Inc., New York
C.S.I.C., Madrid
Cuadernos de la Facultad de Derecho Universidad
   Veracruzana, Mexico City
Cuerpo Facultativo de Archiveros, Bibliotecarios y
   Argueologos, Madrid
Cultural Center of the French Embassy, New York
Current Scene, Hong Kong
Current Thought, Inc., Durham, N. C.
Czechoslovak Foreign Institute in Exile, Chicago

Da Capo Press, New York
Daguin Freres, Editeurs, Paris
Daily Telegraph, London
Daily Worker Publishing Co., Chicago
Dalloz, Paris
Damascus Bar Association. Damascus
Dangary Publishing Co., Baltimore
David Davies Memorial Institute of Political Studies,
   London
David-Stewart, New York
John Day Co., Inc., New York
John de Graff, Inc., Tuckahoe, N. Y.
La Decima Conferencia Interamericana, Caracas
Delacorte Press, New York
Dell Publishing Co., New York
T. S. Denison & Co., Inc., Minneapolis, Minn.
J. M. Dent, London
Departamento de Imprensa Nacional, Rio de Janeiro
Deseret Book Co., Salt Lake City, Utah
Desert Research Institute Publications' Office, Reno, Nev.
Deus Books, Paulist Press, Glen Rock, N. J.
Andre Deutsch, Ltd., London
Deutsche Afrika Gesellschaft, Bonn
Deutsche Bibliographie, Frankfurt am Main
Deutsche Bucherei, Leipzig
Deutsche Gesellschaft fur Volkerrecht, Karlsruhe
Deutsche Gesellschaft fur Auswartige Politik, Bonn
Deutsche Verlagsanstalt, Stuttgart
Deutscher Taschenbuch Verlag, Munich
Deva Datta Shastri, Hoshiarpur
Development Loan Fund, Washington, D. C.
Devin-Adair, Co., New York
Diablo Press, Inc., Berkeley, Calif.
Dial Press, Inc., New York
Dibco Press, San Jose, Cal.
Dickenson Publishing Co., Inc., Belmont, Calif.
Didier Publishers, New York

Firmin Didot Freres, Paris
Dietz Verlag, Berlin
Difusao Europeia do Livro, Sao Paulo
Diplomatic Press, London
Direccion General de Accion Social, Lisbon
District of Columbia, Office of Urban Renewal,
   Washington, D. C.
Djambatan, Amsterdam
Dennis Dobson, London
Dobunken Co., Ltd., Tokyo
La Documentation Francaise, Paris
Documents Index, Arlington, Virginia
Dodd, Mead and Co., New York
Octave Doin et Fils, Paris
Dolphin Books, Inc., New York
Dominion Press, Chicago
Walter Doon Verlag, Bremen
George H. Doran Co., New York
Dorrance and Co., Inc., Philadelphia, Pa.
Dorsey Press, Homewood, Illinois
Doubleday and Co., Inc., Garden City, N. Y.
Dover Publications, New York
Dow Jones and Co., Inc., New York
Dragonfly Books, Hong Kong
Drei Masken Verlag, Munich
Droemersche Verlagsanstalt, Zurich
Droste Verlag, Dusseldorf
Druck und Verlag von Carl Gerolds Sohn, Vienna
Guy Drummond, Montreal
The Dryden Press, New York
Dryfus Conference on Public Affairs, Hanover, N. H.
Duckworth, London
Duell, Sloan & Pearce, New York
Dufour Editions, Inc., Chester Springs, Pa.
Carl Duisburg-Gesellschaft fur Nachwuchsforderung, Cologne
Duke University, School of Law, Durham, N. C.
Duke University Press, Durham, N. C.
Dulau and Co., London
Duncker und Humblot, Berlin
Duquesne University Press, Pittsburgh, Pa.
R. Dutt, London
E. P. Dutton and Co., Inc., Garden City, N. Y.

E. P. & Commercial Printing Co., Durban, S. Africa
East Africa Publishing House, Nairobi
East European Fund, Inc., New York
East-West Center Press, Honolulu
Eastern Kentucky Regional Development Commission,
   Frankfort, Ky.
Eastern World, Ltd., London
Emil Ebering, Berlin
Echter-Verlag, Wurzburg
Ecole Francaise d'Extreme Orient, Paris
Ecole Nationale d'Administration, Paris
Econ Verlag, Dusseldorf; Vienna
Economic Research Corp., Ltd., Montreal
Economic Society of South Africa, Johannesburg
The Economist, London
Edicao Saraiva, Sao Paulo
Ediciones Ariel, Barcelona
Ediciones Cultura Hispanica, Madrid
Ediciones del Movimiento, Borgos, Spain
Ediciones Nuestro Tiempo, Montevideo
Ediciones Rialp, Madrid
Ediciones Riaz, Lima
Ediciones Siglo Veinte, Buenos Aires
Ediciones Tercer Mundo, Bogota
Edicoes de Revista de Estudes Politos, Rio de Janeiro
Edicoes Do Val, Rio de Janeiro
Edicoes GRD, Rio de Janeiro
Edicoes o Cruzeiro, Rio de Janeiro
Edicoes Tempo Brasileiro, Ltda., Rio de Janeiro
Edinburgh House Press, Edinburgh
Editions Albin Michel, Paris
Editions Alsatia, Paris
Editions Berger-Levrault, Paris
Editions Cujas, Paris
Editions de l'Epargne, Paris
Editions de l'Institut de Sociologie de l'Universite Libre de
   Bruxelles, Brussels
Editions d'Organisation, Paris
Editions Denoel, Paris
Editions John Didier, Paris

Editions du Carrefour, Paris
Editions du Cerf, Paris
Editions du Livre, Monte Carlo
Editions du Monde, Paris
Editions du Rocher, Monaco
Editions du Seuil, Paris
Editions du Tiers-Monde, Algiers
Editions du Vieux Colombier, Paris
Editions Eyrolles, Paris
Editions Internationales, Paris
Editions Mont Chrestien, Paris
Editions Nauwelaerts, Louvain
Editions Ouvrieres, Paris
Editions A. Pedone, Paris
Editions Presence Africaine, Paris
Editions Rouff, Paris
Editions Sedif, Paris
Editions Sirey, Paris
Editions Sociales, Paris
Editions Techniques Nord Africaines, Rabat
Editions Universitaires, Paris
Editora Brasiliense, Sao Paulo
Editora Civilizacao Brasileira S. A., Rio de Janeiro
Editora Fulgor, Sao Paulo
Editora Saga, Rio de Janerio
Editores letras e artes, Rio de Janeiro
Editores Mexicanos, Mexico City
Editores Mexicanos Unidos, Mexico City
Editorial AIP, Miami
Editorial Amerinda, Buenos Aires
Editorial Columbia, Buenos Aires
Editorial Freeland, Buenos Aires
Editorial Gustavo Gili, Barcelona
Editorial Jus, Mexico City, Mexico
Editorial Lex, Havana
Editorial Losa da Buenos Aires, Buenos Aires
Editorial Marymar, Buenos Aires
Editorial Mentora, Barcelona
Editorial Nascimento, Santiago
Editorial Palestra, Buenos Aires
Editorial Patria, Mexico City
Editorial Pax, Bogota
Editorial Pax-Mexico, Mexico City
Editorial Platina, Buenos Aires
Editorial Porrua, Mexico City
Editorial Stylo Durangozgo, Mexico City
Editorial Universitaria de Buenos Aires, Buenos Aires
Editorial Universitaria de Puerto Rico, San Jose
Editorial Universitaria Santiago, Santiago
Le Edizioni de Favoro, Rome
Edizioni di Storia e Letteratura, Rome
Edizioni Scientifiche Italiane, Naples
Education and World Affairs, New York
Educational Heritage, Yonkers, N. Y.
Edwards Brothers, Ann Arbor
Effingham Wilson Publishers, London
Egyptian Library Press, Cairo
Egyptian Society of International Law, Cairo
Elex Books, London
Elsevier Publishing Co., Ltd., London
EMECE Editores, Buenos Aires
Emerson Books, New York
Empresa Editora Austral, Ltd., Santiago
Encyclopedia Britannica, Inc., Chicago
English Universities Press, London
Ferdinand Enke Verlag, Bonn; Erlangen; Stuttgart
Horst Erdmann Verlag, Schwarzwald
Paul Eriksson, Inc., New York
Escorpion, Buenos Aires
Escuela de Historia Moderna, Madrid
Escuela Nacional de Ciencias Politicas y Sociales,
  Mexico City
Escuela Superior de Administracion Publica America Central,
  San Jose, Costa Rica
Essener Verlagsanstalt, Essen
Essential Books, Ltd., London
Ethiopia, Ministry of Information, Addis Ababa
Etudes, Paris
Euroamerica, Madrid
Europa-Archiv, Frankfurt am Main
Europa Publications Ltd., London
Europa Verlag, Zurich; Vienna
Europaische Verlagsanstalt, Frankfurt

European Committee for Economic and Social Progress,
  Milan
European Free Trade Association, Geneva
Evangelischer Verlag, Zurich
Edward Evans and Sons, Shanghai
Everline Press, Princeton
Excerpta Criminologica Foundation, Leyden, Netherlands
Exchange Bibliographies, Eugene, Ore.
Export Press, Belgrade
Exposition Press, Inc., New York
Eyre and Spottiswoode, Ltd., London
Extending Horizon Books, Boston

F. and T. Publishers, Seattle, Washington
Faber and Faber, Ltd., London
Fabian Society, London
Facing Reality Publishing Corporation, Detroit, Mich.
Facts on File, Inc., New York
Fairchild Publishing, Inc., New York
Fairleigh Dickinson Press, Rutherford, N. J.
Falcon Press, London
Family Service Association of America, New York
Farrar and Rinehart, New York
Farrar, Strauss & Giroux, Inc., New York
Fawcett World Library, New York
F. W. Faxon Co., Inc., Boston
Fayard, Paris
Federal Legal Publications, Inc., New York
Federal Reserve Bank of New York, New York
Federal Trust for Education and Research, London
Fellowship Publications, New York
Feltrinelli Giangiacomo (Editore), Milan
Au Fil d'Ariadne, Paris
Filipiniana Book Guild, Manila
Financial Index Co., New York
Finnish Political Science Association, Helsinki
Fischer Bucherei, Frankfurt
Fischer Verlag, Stuttgart
Gustav Fischer Verlag, Jena
Flammarion, Paris
Fleet Publishing Co., New York
Fletcher School of Law and Diplomacy, Boston
R. Flint and Co., London
Florida State University, Tallahassee
Follett Publishing Co., Chicago
Fondation Nationale des Sciences Politiques, Paris
Fondo Historico y Bibliografico Jose Foribio, Medina,
  Santiago
Fondo de Cultura Economica, Mexico
B. C. Forbes and Sons, New York
Ford Foundation, New York
Fordham University Press, New York
Foreign Affairs Association of Japan, Tokyo
Foreign Affairs Bibliography, New York
Foreign Language Press, Peking
Foreign Language Publishing House, Moscow
Foreign Policy Association, New York
Foreign Policy Clearing House, Washington, D. C.
Foreign Policy Research Institute, University of
  Pennsylvania, Philadelphia, Pa.
Foreign Trade Library, Philadelphia
Arnold Forni Editore, Bologna
Forschungs-Berichte des Landes Nordrhein-Westfalen, Dussel-
  dorf, Germany
Fortress Press, Philadelphia, Pa.
Foundation for Economic Education, Irvington-on-Hudson,
  N. Y.
Foundation for Social Research, Los Angeles, Calif.
Foundation Press, Inc., Brooklyn, N. Y.; Mineola, N. Y.
Foundation Press, Inc., Chicago
Foundation for Research on Human Behavior, New York
France Editions Nouvelles, Paris
France, Ministere de l'Education Nationale, Paris
France, Ministere d'Etat aux Affaires Culturelles, Paris
France, Ministere des Finances et des Affaires Economiques,
  Paris
Francois Maspera, Paris
Francke Verlag, Munich
Ben Franklin Press, Pittsfield, Mass.
Burt Franklin, New York
Free Europe Committee, New York
Free Press, New York
Free Press of Glencoe, Glencoe, Ill.; New York

Free Speech League, New York
Freedom Books, New York
Freedom Press, London
Ira J. Friedman, Inc., Port Washington, N. Y.
Friends General Conference, Philadelphia, Pa.
Friendship Press, New York
M. L. Fuert, Los Angeles
Fund for the Republic, New York
Fundacao Getulio Vargas, Rio de Janeiro
Funk and Wagnalls Co., Inc., New York
Orell Fuessli Verlag, Zurich

Galaxy Books, Oxford
Gale Research Co., Detroit
Galton Publishing Co., New York
A. R. Geoghegan, Buenos Aires
George Washington University, Population Research Project, Washington, D. C.
Georgetown University Press, Washington, D. C.
Georgia State College, Atlanta, Ga.
Georgia State Library, Atlanta, Ga.
Germany (Territory under Allied Occupation, 1945—U. S. Zone) Office of Public Information, Information Control Division, Bonn
Germany, Bundesministerium fur Vertriebene, Fluechtlinge, und Kriegsbeschadigte (Federal Ministry for Expellees, Refugees, and War Victims), Bonn
Gerold & Co. Verlag, Vienna, Austria
Ghana University Press, Accra, Ghana
Gideon Press, Beirut
Gustavo Gili, Barcelona
Ginn and Co., Boston
Glanville Publishing Co., New York
Glasgow University Press, Glasgow
Gleditsch Brockhaus, Leipzig
Glencoe Free Press, London
Golden Bell Press, Denver, Colo.
Victor Gollancz, Ltd., London
Gordon and Breach Science Publications, New York
Gothic Printing Co., Capetown, S. Afr.
Gould Publications, Jamaica, N. Y.
Government Affairs Foundation, Albany, N. Y.
Government Data Publications, New York
Government of India National Library, Calcutta
Government Printing Office, Washington
Government Publications of Political Literature, Moscow
Government Research Institute, Cleveland
Grafica Americana, Caracas
Grafica Editorial Souza, Rio de Janeiro
Graficas Gonzales, Madrid
Graficas Uguina, Madrid
Graphic, New York
H. W. Gray, Inc., New York
Great Britain, Administrative Staff College, London
Great Britain, Committee on Ministers' Powers, London
Great Britain, Department of Technical Cooperation, London
Great Britain, Foreign Office, London
Great Britain, Ministry of Overseas Development, London
Great Britain, Treasury, London
Greater Bridgeport Region, Planning Agency, Trumbull
W. Green and Son, Edinburgh
Green Pagoda Press, Hong Kong
Greenwich Book Publications, New York
Greenwood Periodicals, New York
Griffin Press, Adelaide, Australia
Grolier, Inc., New York
J. Groning, Hamburg
Grosset and Dunlap, Inc., New York
Grossman Publishers, New York
G. Grote'sche Verlagsbuchhandlung, Rastalt, Germany
Group for the Advancement of Psychiatry, New York
Grove Press, Inc., New York
Grune and Stratton, New York
Gruyter and Co., Walter de, Berlin
E. Guilmato, Paris
Democratic Party of Guinea, Guinea
Gulf Publishing Co., Houston, Texas
J. Chr. Gunderson Boktrykkeri og Bokbinderi, Oslo
Hans E. Gunther Verlag, Stuttgart
Gutersloher Verlagshaus, Gutersloh

Hadar Publishing Co., Tel-Aviv
Hafner Publishing Co., Inc., New York

G. K. Hall, Boston
Robert Hall, London
Charles Hallberg and Co., Chicago
Hamburgisches Wirtschafts Archiv, Hamburg
Hamilton & Co., London
Hamilton County Research Foundation, Cincinnati
Hamish Hamilton, London
Hanover House, New York
Hansard Society, London
Harcourt, Brace and World, New York
Harlo Press, Detroit, Mich.
Harper and Row Publishers, New York; London
George Harrap and Co., London
Otto Harrassowitz, Wiesbaden
Harrison Co., Atlanta, Ga.
Rupert Hart-Davis, London
Hartford Printing Co., Hartford, Conn.
Harvard Center for International Affairs, Cambridge, Mass.
Harvard Law School, Cambridge, Mass.
Harvard Law Review Association, Cambridge, Mass.
Harvard University Center for East Asian Studies, Cambridge, Mass.
Harvard University, Center for Russian Research and Studies, Cambridge, Mass.
Harvard University, Graduate School of Business Administration, Cambridge, Mass.
Harvard University, Peabody Museum, Cambridge, Mass.
Harvard University, Widener Library, Cambridge
Harvard University Press, Cambridge
V. Hase und Kohler Verlag, Mainz
Hastings House, New York
Hauser Press, New Orleans, La.
Hawthorne Books, Inc., New York
Hayden Book Company, New York
The John Randolph Haynes and Dora Haynes Foundation, Los Angeles
The Edward D. Hazen Foundation, New Haven, Conn.
D. C. Heath and Co., Boston
Hebrew University Press, Jerusalem
Heffer and Sons Ltd., Cambridge, England
William S. Hein and Co., Buffalo
James H. Heineman, Inc., New York
Heinemann Ltd., London
Heirsemann, Leipzig
A. Hepple, Johannesburg
Helicon Press, Inc., Baltimore, Md.
Herald Press, Scottdale, Penna.
Herder and Herder, New York
Herder Book Co., New York, St. Louis
Johann Gottfried Herder, Marburg, Germany
Heritage Foundation, Chicago
The Heritage Press, New York
Hermitage Press, Inc., New York
Heron House Winslow, Washington, D. C.
Herzl Press, New York
Carl Heymanns Verlag, Berlin
Hill and Wang, Inc., New York
Hillary House Publishers, Ltd., New York
Hind Kitabs, Ltd., Bombay
Hinds, Noble, and Eldridge, New York
Ferdinand Hirt, Kiel, Germany
Historical Society of New Mexico, Albuquerque, N. M.
H. M. Stationery Office, London
Hobart and William Smith Colleges, Geneva, N. Y.
Hobbs, Dorman and Co., New York
Hodden and Staughton, London
William Hodge and Co., Ltd., London
Hodges Figgis and Co., Ltd., Dublin
J. G. Hodgson, Fort Collins, Colo.
Hogarth Press, London
The Hokuseido Press, Tokyo
Holborn Publishing House, London
Hollis and Carter, London
Hollywood A.S.P. Council, Hollywood, Calif.
Holt and Williams, New York
Holt, Rinehart and Winston, New York
Henry Holt and Co., New York
Holzner Verlag, Wurzburg
Home and Van Thal, London
Hong Kong Government Press, Hong Kong
Hong Kong University Press, Hong Kong
Hoover Institute on War, Revolution and Peace, Stanford, Calif.

Hope College, Holland, Mich.
Horizon Press, Inc., New York
Houghton, Mifflin Co., Boston
Houlgate House, Los Angeles
Howard University Press, Washington
Howell, Sosbin and Co., New York
Hudson Institute, Inc., Harmon-on-Hudson, New York
B. W. Huebsch, Inc., New York
H. Hugendubel Verlag, Munich
Human Relations Area Files Press (HRAF), New Haven
Human Rights Publications, Caulfield, Victoria, Australia
Human Sciences Research, Inc., Arlington, Va.
Humanities Press, New York
Humon and Rousseau, Capetown
Hungarian Academy of Science, Publishing House of, Budapest
Hunter College Library, New York
R. Hunter, London
Huntington Library, San Marino, Calif.
Hutchinson and Co., London
Hutchinson University Library, London

Ibadan University Press, Ibadan, Nigeria
Iberia Publishing Company, New York
Ibero-American Institute, Stockholm
Illini Union Bookstore, Champaign, Ill.
Illinois State Publications, Springfield
Ilmgau Verlag, Pfaffenhofen
Imago Publishing Co., Ltd., London
Imprenta Calderon, Honduras
Imprenta Mossen Alcover, Mallorca
Imprenta Nacional, Caracas
Imprimerie d'Extreme Orient, Hanoi
Imprimerie Nationale, Paris
Imprimerie Sefan, Tunis
Imprimerie Fr. Van Muysewinkel, Brussels
Incentivist Publications, Greenwich, Conn.
Index Society, New York
India and Pakistan: Combined Interservice Historical
  Section, New Delhi
India, Government of, Press, New Delhi
India, Ministry of Community Development, New Delhi
India, Ministry of Finance, New Delhi
India, Ministry of Health, New Delhi
India, Ministry of Home Affairs, New Delhi
India, Ministry of Information and Broadcasting, Faridabad;
  New Delhi
India, Ministry of Law, New Delhi
Indian Council on World Affairs, New Delhi
Indian Institute of Public Administration, New Delhi
Indian Ministry of Information and Broadcasting, New Delhi
Indian Press, Ltd., Allahabad
Indian School of International Studies, New Delhi
Indiana University, Bureau of Government Research,
  Bloomington
Indiana University, Institute of Training for Public
  Service, Department of Government, Bloomington
Indiana University Press, Bloomington
Indraprastha Estate, New Delhi
Industrial Areas Foundations, Chicago
Industrial Council for Social and Economic Studies, Upsala
Industrial Press, New York
Infantry Journal Press, Washington, D. C.
Information Bulletin Ltd., London
Insel Verlag, Frankfurt
Institut Afro-Asiatique d'Etudes Syndicales, Tel Aviv
Institut de Droit International, Paris
Institut des Hautes Etudes de l'Amerique Latine,
  Rio de Janeiro
Institut des Relations Internationales, Brussels
Institut fur Kulturwissenschaftliche Forschung, Freiburg
Institut fur Politische Wissenschaft, Frankfurt
Institut International de Collaboration Philosophique, Paris
Institute for Comparative Study of Political Systems,
  Washington, D. C.
Institute for Defense Analyses, Washington, D. C.
Institute for International Politics and Economics, Prague
Institute for International Social Research, Princeton, N. J.
Institute for Mediterranean Affairs, New York
Institute for Monetary Research, Washington, D. C.
Institute for Social Science Research, Washington, D. C.
Institute of Brazilian Studies, Rio de Janeiro
Institute of Early American History and Culture,
  Williamsburg, Va.

Institute of Economic Affairs, London
Institute of Ethiopian Studies, Addis Ababa
Institute of Human Relations Press, New York
Institute of Islamic Culture, Lahore
Institute of Labor and Industrial Relations, Urbana, Ill.
Institute of Judicial Administration, New York
Institute of National Planning, Cairo
Institute of Pacific Relations, New York
Institute of Professional Civil Servants, London
Institute of Public Administration, Dublin
Instituto de Antropologia e Etnologia de Para, Belem, Para,
  Brazil
Instituto Brasileiro de Estudos Afro-Asiaticos,
  Rio de Janeiro
Instituto Caro y Cuervo, Bogota
Instituto de Derecho Comparedo, Barcelona
Instituto de Estudios Africanos, Madrid
Instituto de Estudios Politicos, Madrid
Instituto de Investigaciones Historicas, Mexico City
Instituto Guatemalteco-Americano, Guatemala City
Instituto Internacional de Ciencias Administrativas,
  Rio de Janeiro
Instituto Nacional do Livro, Rio de Janeiro
Instituto Nazionale di Cultura Fascista, Firenze
Instituto Pan Americano de Geografia e Historia, Mexico City
Integrated Education Associates, Chicago
Inter-American Bibliographical and Library Association,
  Gainesville, Fla.
Inter-American Development Bank, Buenos Aires
Inter-American Statistical Institute, Washington
Intercollegiate Case Clearing House, Boston
International African Institute, London
International Association for Research in Income and Wealth,
  New Haven, Conn.
International Atomic Energy Commission, Vienna
International Bank for Reconstruction and Development,
  Washington, D. C.
International Center for African Economic and Social
  Documentation, Brussels
International Chamber of Commerce, New York
International City Managers' Association, Chicago
International Commission of Jurists, Geneva
International Committee for Peaceful Investment,
  Washington, D. C.
International Congress of History of Discoveries, Lisbon
International Congress of Jurists, Rio de Janeiro
International Cotton Advisory Committee, Washington, D. C.
International Court of Justice, The Hague
International Development Association, Washington, D. C.
International Economic Policy Association, Washington, D. C.
International Editions, New York
International Federation for Documentation, The Hague
International Federation for Housing and Planning, The Hague
International Finance, Princeton, N. J.
International Institute of Administrative Science, Brussels
International Institute of Differing Civilizations, Brussels
International Labour Office, Geneva
International Managers' Association, Chicago
International Monetary Fund, Washington
International Press Institute, Zurich
International Publications Service, New York
International Publishers Co., New York
International Publishing House, Meerat, India
International Review Service, New York
International Textbook Co., Scranton, Penna.
International Union for Scientific Study of Population,
  New York
International Universities Press, Inc., New York
Interstate Printers and Publishers, Danville, Ill.
Iowa State University, Center for Agricultural and Economic
  Development, Ames
Iowa State University Press, Ames
Irish Manuscripts Commission, Dublin
Richard D. Irwin, Inc., Homewood, Ill.
Isar Verlag, Munich
Isbister and Co., London
Italian Library of Information, New York; Rome
Italy, Council of Ministers, Rome

Jacaranda Press, Melbourne
Mouriel Jacobs, Inc., Philadelphia
Al Jadidah Press, Cairo
Jain General House, Jullundur, India
Japan, Ministry of Education, Tokyo

Japan, Ministry of Justice, Tokyo
Japanese National Commission for UNESCO, Tokyo
Jarrolds Publishers, Ltd., London
Jewish Publication Society of America, Philadelphia, Pa.
Johns Hopkins Press, Baltimore
Johns Hopkins School of Advanced International Studies, Baltimore
Johns Hopkins School of Hygiene, Baltimore
Johnson Publishing Co., Chicago
Christopher Johnson Publishers, Ltd., London
Johnstone and Hunter, London
Joint Center for Urban Studies, Cambridge, Mass.
Joint Committee on Slavic Studies, New York
Joint Council on Economic Education, New York
Joint Library of IMF and IBRD, Washington
Joint Reference Library, Chicago
Jonathan Cape, London
Jones and Evans Book Shop, Ltd., London
Marshall Jones, Boston
Jornal do Commercio, Rio de Janeiro
Michael Joseph, Ltd., London
Jowett, Leeds, England
Juilliard Publishers, Paris
Junker und Dunnhaupt Verlag, Berlin
Juta and Co., Ltd., Capetown, South Africa

Kallman Publishing Co., Gainesville, Fla.
Karl Karusa, Washington, D. C.
Katzman Verlag, Tubingen
Kay Publishing Co., Salt Lake City
Nicholas Kaye, London
Calvin K. Kazanjian Economics Foundation, Westport, Conn.
Kegan, Paul and Co., Ltd., London
P. G. Keller, Winterthur, Switz.
Augustus M. Kelley, Publishers, New York
Kelly and Walsh, Ltd., Baltimore, Md.
P. J. Kenedy, New York
Kennikat Press, Port Washington, N. Y.
Kent House, Port-of-Spain
Kent State University Bureau of Economic and Business Research, Kent, Ohio
Kentucky State Archives and Records Service, Frankfort
Kentucky State Planning Commission, Frankfort
Kenya Ministry of Economic Planning and Development, Nairobi
Charles H. Kerr and Co., Chicago
Khadiand Village Industries Commission, Bombay
Khayat's, Beirut
Khun Aroon, Bangkok
P. S. King and Son, Ltd., London
King's College, Cambridge
King's Crown Press, New York
Kino Kuniva Bookstore Co., Ltd., Tokyo
Kitab Mahal, Allahabad, India
Kitabistan, Allahabad
B. Klein and Co., New York
Ernst Klett Verlag, Stuttgart
V. Klostermann, Frankfurt
Fritz Knapp Verlag, Frankfurt
Alfred Knopf, New York
John Knox Press, Richmond, Va.
Kodansha International, Ltd., Tokyo
W. Kohlhammer Verlag, Stuttgart; Berlin; Cologne; Mainz
Korea Researcher and Publisher, Inc., Seoul
Korea, Ministry of Reconstruction, Seoul
Korea, Republic of, Seoul
Korea University, Asiatic Research Center, Seoul
Korean Conflict Research Foundation, Albany, N. Y.
Kosel Verlag, Munich
Kossuth Foundation, New York
Guillermo Kraft, Ltd., Buenos Aires
John F. Kraft, Inc., New York
Krasnzi Proletarii, Moscow
Kraus, Ltd., Dresden
Kraus Reprint Co., Vaduz, Liechtenstein
Kreuz-Verlag, Stuttgart
Kumasi College of Technology, The Library, Kumasi, Ghana
Kuwait, Arabia, Government Printing Press, Kuwait

Labor News Co., New York
Robert Laffont, Paris
Lambarde Press, Sidcup, Kent, England
Albert D. and Mary Lasker Foundation, Washington, D. C.

Harold Laski Institute of Political Science, Ahmedabad
Guiseppe Laterza e Figli, Bari, Italy
T. Werner Laurie, Ltd., London
Lawrence Brothers, Ltd., London
Lawrence and Wishart, London
Lawyers Co-operative Publishing Co., Rochester, N. Y.
League for Industrial Democracy, New York
League of Independent Voters, New Haven
League of Nations, Geneva
League of Women Voters, Cambridge
League of Women Voters of U. S., Washington, D. C.
Leeds University Press, Leeds, Engand
J. F. Lehmanns Verlag, Munich
Leicester University Press, London
F. Leitz, Frankfurt
Lemcke, Lemcke and Beuchner, New York
Michel Levy Freres, Paris
Lexington Publishing Co., New York
Liberal Arts Press, Inc., New York
Liberia Altiplano, La Paz
Liberia Anticuaria, Barcelona
Liberia Campos, San Juan
Liberia Panamericana, Buenos Aires
Liberty Bell Press, Jefferson City, Mo.
Librairie Academique Perrin, Paris
Librairie Artheme Fayard, Paris
Librairie Beauchemin, Montreal
Librairie Armand Colin, Paris
Librairie Firmin Didot et Cie., Paris
Librairie Droz, Geneva
Librairie de Medicis, Paris
Librairie de la Societe du Recueil Sirey, Paris
Librairie des Sciences Politiques et Sociales, Paris
Librairie Felix Alcan, Paris
Librairie Gallimard, Paris
Librairie Hachette et Cie., Paris
Librairie Julius Abel, Greiswald
Librairie La Rose, Paris
Librairie Letouzey, Paris
Librairie Payot, Paris
Librairie Philosophique J. Vrin, Paris
Librairie Plon, Paris
Librairie Marcel Riviere et Cie., Paris
Librairie Stock Delamain et Boutelleau, Paris
Library, Kumasi College of Technology, Kumasi
Library Association, London
Library of Congress, Washington
Library House, London
Library of International Relations, Chicago
Libyan Publishing, Tripoli
Light and Life Press, Winona Lake, Ind.
Lincoln University, Lincoln, Pa.
J. B. Lippincott Co., New York, Philadelphia
Little, Brown and Co., Boston
Liverpool University Press, Liverpool
Horace Liveright, New York
Living Books, New York
Livraria Agir Editora, Rio de Janeiro
Livraria Editora da Casa di Estudante do Brazil, Sao Paulo
Livraria Jose Olympio Editora, Rio de Janeiro
Livraria Martins Editora, Sao Paulo
Lok Sabha Secretariat, New Delhi
London Conservative Political Centre, London
London Historical Association, London
London Institute of World Affairs, London
London Library Association, London
London School of Economics, London
London Times, Inc., London
London University, School of Oriental and African Studies, London
Roy Long and Richard R. Smith, Inc., New York
Long House, New Canaan, Conn.
Longmans, Green and Co., New York, London
Los Angeles Board of Civil Service Commissioners, Los Angeles
Louisiana State Legislature, Baton Rouge
Louisiana State University Press, Baton Rouge
Loyola University Press, Chicago
Lucas Brothers, Columbia
Herman Luchterhand Verlag, Neuwied am Rhein
Lyle Stuart, Inc., New York

MIT Center of International Studies, Cambridge

974

MIT Press, Cambridge
MIT School of Industrial Management, Cambridge
Macfadden-Bartwell Corp., New York
MacGibbon and Kee, Ltd., London
Macmillan Co., New York; London
Macmillan Co., of Canada, Ltd., Toronto
Macrae Smith Co., Philadelphia, Pa.
Magistrats Druckerei, Berlin
Magnes Press, Jerusalem
S. P. Maisonneuve et La Rose, Paris
Malaysia Publications, Ltd., Singapore
Malhorta Brothers, New Delhi
Manager Government of India Press, Kosib
Manaktalas, Bombay
Manchester University Press, Manchester, England
Manhattan Publishing Co., New York
Manzsche Verlag, Vienna
Marathon Oil Co., Findlay, Ohio
Marisal, Madrid
Marquette University Press, Milwaukee
Marshall Benick, New York
Marzani and Munsell, New York
Marzun Kabushiki Kaisha, Tokyo
Mascat Publications, Ltd., Calcutta
Francois Maspera, Paris
Massachusetts Mass Transportation Commission, Boston
Masses and McInstream, New York
Maurice Falk Institute for Economic Research, Jerusalem
Maxwell Air Force Base, Montgomery, Ala.
Robert Maxwell and Co., Ltd., London
McBride, Nast and Co., New York
McClelland and Stewart, Ltd., London
McClure and Co., Chicago
McClure, Phillips and Co., New York
McCutchan Publishing Corp., Berkeley
McDonald and Evans, Ltd., London
McDowell, Obolensky, New York
McFadden Bartwell Corp., New York
McGill University Industrial Relations Section, Montreal
McGill University, Institute of Islamic Studies, Montreal
McGill University Press, Montreal
McGraw Hill Book Co., New York
David McKay Co., Inc., New York
McKinley Publishing Co., Philadelphia
George J. McLeod, Ltd., Toronto
McMullen Books, Inc., New York
Meador Publishing Co., Boston
Mediaeval Academy of Americana, Cambridge
Felix Meiner Verlag, Hamburg
Melbourne University Press, Melbourne, Victoria, Australia
Mendonca, Lisbon
Mental Health Materials Center, New York
Mentor Books, New York
Meredith Press, Des Moines
Meridian Books, New York
Merit Publishers, New York
The Merlin Press, Ltd., London
Charles E. Merrill Publishing Co., Inc., Columbus
Methuen and Co., Ltd., London
Metropolitan Book Co., Ltd., New Delhi
Metropolitan Housing and Planning Council, Chicago
Metropolitan Police District, Scotland Yard, London
Alfred Metzner Verlag, Frankfurt
Meyer London Memorial Library, London
Miami University Press, Oxford, Ohio
Michie Co., Charlottesville, Va.
Michigan Municipal League, Ann Arbor
Michigan State University, Agricultural Experiment Station, East Lansing
Michigan State University, Bureau of Business and Economic Research, East Lansing
Michigan State University, Bureau of Social and Political Research, East Lansing
Michigan State University, Governmental Research Bureau, East Lansing
Michigan State University, Institute for Community Development and Services, East Lansing
Michigan State University, Institute for Social Research, East Lansing
Michigan State University, Labor and Industrial Relations Center, East Lansing
Michigan State University Press, East Lansing

Michigan State University School of Business Administration, East Lansing
Michigan State University, Vietnam Advisory Group, East Lansing
Mid-European Studies Center, Free European Committee, New York
Middle East Institute, Washington
Middle East Research Associates, Arlington, Va.
Middlebury College, Middlebury, Vt.
Midwest Administration Center, Chicago
Midwest Beach Co., Sioux Falls
Milbank Memorial Fund, New York
M. S. Mill and Co., Inc., Division of William Morrow and Co., Inc., New York
Ministere de l'Education Nationale, Paris
Ministere d'Etat aux Affaires Culturelles, Paris
Ministerio de Educacao e Cultura, Rio de Janeiro
Ministerio de Relaciones Exteriores, Havana
Minnesota Efficiency in Government Commission, St. Paul
Minton, Balch and Co., New York
Missionary Research Library, New York
Ernst Siegfried Mittler und Sohn, Berlin
Modern Humanities Research Association, Chicago
T. C. B. Mohr, Tubingen
Moira Books, Detroit
Monarch Books, Inc., Derby, Conn.
Monthly Review, New York
Mont Pelerin Society, University of Chicago, Chicago
Hugh Moore Fund, New York
T. G. Moran's Sons, Inc., Baton Rouge
William Morrow and Co., Inc., New York
Morus Verlag, Berlin
Mosaik Verlag, Hamburg
Motilal Banarsidass, New Delhi
Mouton and Co., The Hague; Paris
C. F. Mueller Verlag, Karlsruhe, Germany
Muhammad Mosque of Islam #2, Chicago
Firma K. L. Mukhopadhyaz, Calcutta
F. A. W. Muldener, Gottingen, Germany
Frederick Muller, Ltd., London
Municipal Finance Officers Association of the United States and Canada, Chicago
Munksgaard International Booksellers and Publishers, Copenhagen
John Murray, London
Museum fur Volkerkunde, Vienna
Museum of Honolulu, Honolulu
Musterschmidt Verlag, Gottingen

NA Tipographia do Panorama, Lisbon
Nassau County Planning Committee, Long Island
Natal Witness, Ltd., Pietermaritzburg
The Nation Associates, New York
National Academy of Sciences-National Research Council, Washington, D. C.
National Archives of Rhodesia and Nyasaland, Salisbury
National Assembly on Teaching The Principles of the Bill of Rights, Washington
National Association of Counties Research Foundation, Washington, D. C.
National Association of County Officials, Chicago
National Association of Home Builders, Washington, D. C.
National Association of Local Government Officers, London
National Association of State Libraries, Boston
National Bank of Egypt, Cairo
National Bank of Libya, Tripoli
National Board of YMCA, New York
National Book League, London
National Bureau of Economic Research, New York
National Capitol Publishers, Manassas, Va.
National Central Library, London
National Citizens' Commission on International Cooperation, Washington, D. C.
National Council for the Social Sciences, New York
National Council for the Social Studies, New York
National Council of Applied Economic Research, New Delhi
National Council of Churches of Christ in USA, New York
National Council of National Front of Democratic Germany, Berlin
National Council on Aging, New York
National Council on Crime and Delinquency, New York
National Economic and Social Planning Agency, Washington

National Education Association, Washington
National Home Library Foundation, Washington, D. C.
National Industrial Conference Board, New York
National Institute for Personnel Research, Johannesburg
National Institute of Administration, Saigon
National Institute of Economic Research, Stockholm
National Labor Relations Board Library, Washington
National Labour Press, London
National Library of Canada, Ottawa
National Library Press, Ottawa
National Municipal League, New York
National Observer, Silver Springs, Md.
National Opinion Research Center, Chicago
National Peace Council, London
National Planning Association, Washington, D. C.
National Press, Palo Alto, Calif.
National Review, New York
National Science Foundation Scientific Information,
   Washington, D. C.
Natural History Press, Garden City, N. Y.
Nauka Publishing House, Moscow
Navahind, Hyderabad
Navajiran Publishing House, Ahmedabad
Thomas Nelson and Sons, London; New York
Neukirchener Verlag des Erziehungsvereins, Neukirchen
New American Library, New York
New Century Publishers, New York
New Jersey Department of Agriculture, Rural Advisory
   Council, Trenton
New Jersey Department of Civil Service, Trenton
New Jersey Department of Conservation and Economic
   Development, Trenton
New Jersey Division of State and Regional Planning,
   Trenton
New Jersey Housing and Renewal, Trenton
New Jersey State Department of Education, Trenton
New Jersey State Legislature, Trenton
New Republic, Washington, D. C.
New School of Social Research, New York
New World Press, New York
New York City College Institute for Pacific Relations,
   New York
New York City Department of Correction, New York
New York City Temporary Committee on City Finance,
   New York
New York Public Library, New York
New York State College of Agriculture, Ithaca
New York State Library, Albany
New York State School of Industrial and Labor Relations,
   Cornell University, Ithaca
New York, State University of, at Albany, Albany
New York, State University of, State Education Department,
   Albany
New York, State University of, State Education Department,
   Office of Foreign Area Studies, Albany
New York Times, New York
New York University School of Commerce, Accounts and
   Finance, New York
New York University, School of Law, New York
New York University Press, New York
Newark Public Library, Newark
Newman Press, Westminster, Md.
Martinus Nijhoff, The Hague; Geneva
James Nisbet and Co., Ltd., Welwyn, Herts, England
Noonday Press, New York
North American Review Publishing Co., New York
North Atlantic Treaty Organization, Brussels
North Holland Publishing Co., Amsterdam, Holland
Northern California Friends Committee on Legislation, San
   Francisco
Northern Michigan University Press, Marquette
Northwestern University, Evanston
Northwestern University, African Department, Evanston, Ill.
Northwestern University, International Relations
   Conference, Chicago
Northwestern University Press, Evanston, Ill.
W. W. Norton and Co., Inc., New York
Norwegian Institute of International Affairs, Oslo
Norwegian University Press, Oslo
Nouvelle Librairie Nationale, Paris
John Nuveen and Co., Chicago
Novelty and Co., Patna, India

Novostii Press Agency Publishing House, Moscow
Nymphenburger Verlagsbuchhandlung, Munich

Oak Publications, New York
Oak Ridge Associated Universities, Oak Ridge, Tenn.
Oceana Publishing Co., Dobbs Ferry, N. Y.
Octagon Publishing Co., New York
Odyssey Press, New York
Oesterreichische Ethnologische Gesellschaft, Vienna
Oficina Internacional de Investigaciones Sociales
   de Freres, Madrid
W.E.R. O'Gorman, Glendale, Calif.
O'Hare, Flanders, N. J.
Ohio State University, Columbus
Ohio State University, College of Commerce and
   Administration, Bureau of Business Research, Columbus
Ohio State University Press, Columbus
Ohio University Press, Athens
Old Lyme Press, Old Lyme, Conn.
R. Oldenbourg, Munich
Oliver and Boyd, London, Edinburgh
Guenter Olzog Verlag, Munich
Open Court Publishing Co., La Salle, Ill.
Operation America, Inc., Los Angeles
Operations and Policy Research, Inc., Washington, D. C.
Oregon Historical Society, Portland
Organization for European Economic Cooperation and Devel-
   opment (OEEC), Paris
Organization of African Unity, Addis Ababa
Organization of American States, Rio de Janeiro
Organization of Economic Aid, Washington, D. C.
Orient Longman's, Bombay
Oriole Press, Berkeley Heights, N. J.
P. O'Shey, New York
Osaka University of Commerce, Tokyo
James R. Osgood and Co., Boston
Oslo University Press, Oslo
Oswald-Wolff, London
John Ousley, Ltd., London
George Outram Co., Ltd., Glasgow
Overseas Development Institute, Ltd., London
R. E. Owen, Wellington, N. Z.
Oxford Book Co., New York
Oxford University Press, Capetown; London; Madras; Mel-
   bourne; New York

Pacific Books, Palo Alto, Calif.
Pacific Coast Publishing Co., Menlo Park, Calif.
Pacific Philosophy Institute, Stockton, Calif.
Pacific Press Publishing Association, Mountain View, Calif.
Pacifist Research Bureau, Philadelphia
Padma Publications, Ltd., Bombay
Hermann Paetel Verlag, Berlin
Pageant Press, New York
Paine-Whitman, New York
Pakistan Academy for Rural Development, Peshawar
Pakistan Association for Advancement of Science, Lahore
Pakistan Bibliographical Working Group, Karachi
Pakistan Educational Publishers, Ltd., Karachi
Pakistan Ministry of Finance, Rawalpindi
Pall Mall Press, London
Pan American Union, Washington
Pantheon Books, Inc., New York
John W. Parker, London
Patna University Press, Madras
B. G. Paul and Co., Madras
Paulist Press, Glen Rock, N. J.
Payne Fund, New York
Peabody Museum, Cambridge
Peace Publications, New York
Peace Society, London
P. Pearlman, Washington
Pegasus, New York
Peking Review, Peking
Pelican Books, Ltd., Hammonsworth, England
Pemberton Press, Austin
Penguin Books, Baltimore
Penn.-N.J.-Del. Metropolitan Project, Philadelphia, Pa.
Pennsylvania German Society, Lancaster, Pa.
Pennsylvania Historical and Museum Commission, Harrisburg
Pennsylvania State University, Department of Religious
   Studies, University Park, Pa.

Pennsylvania State University, Institute of Public Administration, University Park, Pa.
Pennsylvania State University Press, University Park, Pa.
People's Publishing House, Ltd., New Delhi
Pergamon Press, Inc., New York
Permanent Secretariat, AAPS Conference, Cairo
Perrine Book Co., Minneapolis
Personnel Administration, Washington
Personnel Research Association, New York
George A. Pflaum Publishers, Inc., Dayton, Ohio
Phelps-Stokes Fund, Capetown; New York
Philadelphia Bibliographical Center, Philadelphia
George Philip & Son, London
Philippine Historical Society, Manila
Philippine Islands Bureau of Science, Manila
Philosophical Library Inc., New York
Phoenix House, Ltd., London
Pichon et Durand-Auzias, Paris
B. M. Pickering, London
Oskar Piest, New York
Pilot Press, London
Pioneer Publishers, New York
R. Piper and Co. Verlag, Munich
Pitman Publishing Corp., New York
Plimpton Press, Norwood, Mass.
PLJ Publications, Manila
Pocket Books, Inc., New York
Polish Scientific Publishers, Warsaw
Polygraphischer Verlag, Zurich
The Polynesian Society, Inc., Wellington, N. Z.
Popular Book Depot, Bombay
Popular Prakashan, Bombay
Population Association of America, Washington
Population Council, New York
Post Printing Co., New York
Post Publishing Co., Bangkok
Potomac Books, Washington, D. C.
Clarkson N. Potter, Inc., New York
Prabhakar Sahityalok, Lucknow, India
Practicing Law Institute, New York
Frederick A. Praeger, Inc., New York
Prager, Berlin
Prensa Latino Americana, Santiago
Prentice Hall, Inc., Englewood Cliffs, N. J.
Prentice-Hall International, London
Presence Afrique, Paris
President's Press, New Delhi
Press & Information Division of the French Embassy, New York
The Press of Case Western Reserve University, Cleveland
Presses de l'Ecole des Hautes Etudes Commerciales, Montreal
Presses Universitaires de Bruxelles, Brussels
Presses Universitaires de France, Paris
Presseverband der Evangelischen Kirche im Rheinland, Dusseldorf
Princeton Research Publishing Co., Princeton
Princeton University, Princeton, N. J.
Princeton University, Center of International Studies, Woodrow Wilson School of Public and International Affairs, Princeton, N. J.
Princeton University, Department of Economics, Princeton, N. J.
Princeton University, Department of History, Princeton, N. J.
Princeton University, Department of Oriental Studies, Princeton, N. J.
Princeton University, Department of Philosophy, Princeton, N. J.
Princeton University, Department of Politics, Princeton, N. J.
Princeton University, Department of Psychology, Princeton
Princeton University, Department of Sociology, Princeton, N. J.
Princeton University, Econometric Research Program, Princeton, N. J.
Princeton University, Firestone Library, Princeton, N. J.
Princeton University, Industrial Relations Center, Princeton
Princeton University, International Finance Section, Princeton, N. J.
Princeton University, Princeton Public Opinion Research Project, Princeton, N. J.
Princeton University Press, Princeton
Edouard Privat, Toulouse

Arthur Probsthain, London
Professional Library Press, West Haven, Conn.
Programa Interamericano de Informacion Popular, San Jose
Progress Publishing Co., Indianapolis
Progressive Education Association, New York
Prolog Research and Publishing Association, New York
Prometheus Press, New York
Psycho-Sociological Press, New York
Public Administration Clearing House, Chicago
Public Administration Institute, Ankara
Public Administration Service, Chicago
Public Affairs Forum, Bombay
Public Affairs Press, Washington
Public Enterprises, Tequcigalpa
Public Personnel Association, Chicago
Publications Centre, University of British Columbia, Vancouver
Publications de l'Institut Pedagogique National, Paris
Publications de l'Institut Universitaire des Hautes Etudes Internationales, Paris
Publications du CNRS, Paris
Publisher's Circular, Ltd., London, England
Publisher's Weekly, Inc., New York
Publishing House Jugoslavia, Belgrade
Punjab University, Pakistan
Punjab University Extension Library, Ludhiana, Punjab
Purdue University Press, Lafayette, Ind.
Purnell and Sons, Capetown
G. P. Putnam and Sons, New York

Quadrangle Books, Inc., Chicago
Bernard Quaritch, London
Queen's Printer, Ottawa
Queen's University, Belfast
Quell Verlag, Stuttgart, Germany
Quelle und Meyer, Heidelberg
Queromon Editores, Mexico City

Atma Ram and Sons, New Delhi
Ramsey-Wallace Corporation, Ramsey, New Jersey
Rand Corporation, Publications of the Social Science Department, New York
Rand McNally and Co., Skokie, Ill.
Random House, Inc., New York
Regents Publishing House, Inc., New York
Regional Planning Association, New York
Regional Science Research Institute, Philadelphia
Henry Regnery Co., Chicago
D. Reidel Publishing Co., Dordrecht, Holland
E. Reinhardt Verlag, Munich
Reinhold Publishing Corp., New York; London
Remsen Press, New York
La Renaissance de Loire, Paris
Eugen Rentsch Verlag, Stuttgart
Republican National Committee, Washington, D. C.
Research Institute on Sino-Soviet Bloc, Washington, D. C.
Research Microfilm Publications, Inc., Annapolis
Resources for the Future, Inc., Washington, D. C.
Revista de Occidente, Madrid
Revue Administrative, Paris
Renyal and Co., Inc., New York
Reynal & Hitchcock, New York
Rheinische Friedrich Wilhelms Universitat, Bonn
Rice University, Fondren Library, Houston
Richards Rosen Press, New York
The Ridge Press, Inc., New York
Rinehart, New York
Ring-Verlag, Stuttgart
Riverside Editions, Cambridge
Robinson and Co., Durban, South Africa
J. A. Rogers, New York
Roques Roman, Trujillo
Rudolf M. Rohrer, Leipzig
Ludwig Rohrscheid Verlag, Bonn
Walter Roming and Co., Detroit
Ronald Press Co., New York
Roper Public Opinion Poll Research Center, New York
Ross and Haine, Inc., Minneapolis, Minn.
Fred B. Rothman and Co., S. Hackensack, N. J.
Rotterdam University Press, Rotterdam
Routledge and Kegan Paul, London
George Routledge and Sons, Ltd., London
Row-Peterson Publishing Co., Evanston, Ill.

Rowohlt, Hamburg
Roy Publishers, Inc., New York
Royal African Society, London
Royal Anthropological Institute, London
Royal Colonial Institute, London
Royal Commission of Canada's Economic Prospects, Ottawa
Royal Commonwealth Society, London
Royal Geographical Society, London
Royal Greek Embassy Information Service, Washington, D. C.
Royal Institute of International Affairs, London; New York
Royal Institute of Public Administration, London
Royal Netherlands Printing Office, Schiedam
Royal Statistical Society, London
Rubin Mass, Jerusalem
Rule of Law Press, Durham
Rupert Hart-Davis, London
Russell and Russell, Inc., New York
Russell Sage College, Institute for Advanced Study in Crisis, NDEA Institute, Troy, N. Y.
Russell Sage Foundation, New York
Rutgers University, New Brunswick, N. J.
Rutgers University Bureau of Government Research, New Brunswick, N. J.
Rutgers University, Institute of Management and Labor Relations, New Brunswick, N. J.
Rutgers University, Urban Studies Conference, New Brunswick, N. J.
Rutgers University Press, New Brunswick, N. J.
Rutten und Loening Verlag, Munich
Ryerson Press, Toronto

Sage Publications, Beverly Hills, Calif.
Sahitya Akademi, Bombay
St. Andrews College, Drygrange, Scotland
St. Clement's Press, London
St. George Press, Los Angeles
St. John's University Bookstore, Annapolis
St. John's University Press, Jamaica, N. Y.
St. Louis Post-Dispatch, St. Louis
St. Martin's Press, New York
St. Michael's College, Toronto
San Diego State College Library, San Diego
San Francisco State College, San Francisco
The Sapir Memorial Publication Fund, Menasha, Wis.
Sarah Lawrence College, New York
Sarah Lawrence College, Institute for Community Studies, New York
Porter Sargent, Publishers, Boston, Mass.
Sauerlaender and Co., Aarau, Switz.
Saunders and Ottey, London
W. B. Saunders Co., Philadelphia, Pa.
Scandinavian University Books, Copenhagen
Scarecrow Press, Metuchen, N. J.
L. N. Schaffrath, Geldern, Germany
Robert Schalkenbach Foundation, New York
Schenkman Publishing Co., Cambridge
P. Schippers, N. V., Amsterdam
Schocken Books, Inc., New York
Henry Schuman, Inc., New York
Carl Schunemann Verlag, Bremen
Curt E. Schwab, Stuttgart
Otto Schwartz und Co., Gottingen
Science and Behavior Books, Palo Alto, Calif.
Science Council of Japan, Tokyo
Science of Society Foundation, Baltimore, Md.
Science Press, New York
Science Research Associates, Inc., Chicago
Scientia Verlag, Aalen, Germany
SCM Press, London
Scott, Foresman and Co., Chicago
Scottish League for European Freedom, Edinburgh
Chas. Scribner's Sons, New York
Seabury Press, New York
Sears Publishing Co., Inc., New York
Secker and Warburg, Ltd., London
Secretaria del Consejo Nacional Economia, Tegucigalpa
Securities Study Project, Vancouver, Wash.
Seewald Verlag, Munich; Stuttgart
Selbstverlag Jakob Rosner, Vienna
Seldon Society, London
Robert C. Sellers and Associates, Washington, D. C.
Thomas Seltzer Inc., New York
Seminar, New Delhi

C. Serbinis Press, Athens
Service Bibliographique des Messageries Hachette, Paris
Service Center for Teaching of History, Washington, D. C.
Servicos de Imprensa e Informacao da Exbaixada, Lisbon
Sheed and Ward, New York
Shoestring Press, Hamden, Conn.
Shuter and Shooter, Pietermaritzburg
Siam Society, Bangkok
Sidgewick and Jackson, London
K. G. Siegler & Co., Bonn
Signet Books, New York
A. W. Sijthoff, Leyden, Netherlands
Silver Burdett, Morristown, N. J.
Simmons Boardman Publishing Co., New York
Simon and Schuster, Inc., New York
Simpkin, Marshall, et al., London
Sino-American Cultural Society, Washington
William Sloane Associates, New York
Small, Maynard and Co., Boston
Smith-Brook Printing Co., Denver
Smith College, Northampton, Mass.
Smith, Elder and Co., London
Smith, Keynes and Marshall, Buffalo, N. Y.
Allen Smith Co., Indianapolis, Ind.
Peter Smith, Gloucester, Mass.
Richard R. Smith Co. Inc., Peterborough, N. H.
Smithsonian Institute, Washington, D. C.
Social Science Research Center, Rio Piedras, Puerto Rico
Social Science Research Council, New York
Social Science Research Council, Committee on the Economy of China, Berkeley, Calif.
Social Science Research Council of Australia, Sydney
The Social Sciences, Mexico City
Societa Editrice del "Foro Italiano", Rome
Societas Bibliographica, Lausanne, Switzerland
Societe d'Edition d'Enseignement Superieur, Paris
Societe Francaise d'Imprimerie et Librairie, Paris
Society for Advancement of Management, New York
Society for Promoting Christian Knowledge, London
Society for the Study of Social Problems, Kalamazoo, Mich.
Society of Comparative Legislative and International Law, London
Sociological Abstracts, New York
Solidaridad Publishing House, Manila
Somerset Press, Inc., Somerville, N. J.
Soney and Sage Co., Newark, N. J.
South Africa Commission on Future Government, Capetown
South Africa State Library, Pretoria
South African Congress of Democrats, Johannesburg
South African Council for Scientific and Industrial Research, Pretoria
South African Institute of International Affairs, Johannesburg
South African Institute of Race Relations, Johannesburg
South African Public Library, Johannesburg
South Carolina Archives, State Library, Columbia
South Pacific Commission, Noumea, New Caledonia
South Western Publishing Co., Cincinnati, Ohio
Southern Illinois University Press, Carbondale, Ill.
Southern Methodist University Press, Dallas, Tex.
Southern Political Science Association, New York
Southworth Anthoensen Press, Portland, Maine
Sovetskaia Rossiia, Moscow
Soviet and East European Research and Translation Service, New York
Spartan Books, Washington, D. C.
Special Libraries Association, New York
Specialty Press of South Africa, Johannesburg
Robert Speller and Sons, New York
Lorenz Spindler Verlag, Nuremberg
Julius Springer, Berlin
Springer-Verlag, New York; Stuttgart; Gottingen; Vienna
Stackpole Co., New York
Gerhard Stalling, Oldenburg, Germany
Stanford Bookstore, Stanford
Stanford University Comparative Education Center, Stanford, Calif.
Stanford University Institute for Communications Research, Stanford
Stanford University, Institute of Hispanic-American and Luso-Brazilian Studies, Stanford, Calif.
Stanford University, Project on Engineering-Economic Planning, Stanford, Calif.

Stanford University Research Institute, Menlo Park, Calif.
Stanford University, School of Business Administration, Stanford, Calif.
Stanford University, School of Education, Stanford, Calif.
Stanford University Press, Stanford, Cal.
Staples Press, New York
State University of New York at Albany, Albany
Stein & Day Publishers, New York
Franz Steiner Verlag, Wiesbaden
Ulrich Steiner Verlag, Wurttemburg
H. E. Stenfert Kroese, Leyden
Sterling Printing and Publishing Co., Ltd., Karachi
Sterling Publishers, Ltd., London
Stevens and Hayes, London
Stevens and Sons, Ltd., London
George W. Stewart, Inc., New York
George Stilke Berlin
Frederick A. Stokes Publishing Co., New York
C. Struik, Capetown
Stuttgarter Verlags Kantor, Stuttgart
Summy-Birchard Co., Evanston, Ill.
Swann Sonnenschein and Co., London
Philip Swartzwelder, Pittsburgh, Pa.
Sweet and Maxwell, Ltd., London
Swiss Eastern Institute, Berne
Sydney University Press, Sydney, Australia
Syracuse University, Maxwell School of Citizenship and Public Affairs, Syracuse, N. Y.
Syracuse University Press, Syracuse
Szczesnez Verlag, Munich

Talleres Graficos de Manuel Casas, Mexico City
Talleres de Impresion de Estampillas y Valores, Mexico City
Taplinger Publishing Co., New York
Tavistock, London
Tax Foundation, New York
Teachers' College, Bureau of Publications, Columbia University, New York
Technical Assistance Information Clearing House, New York
Technology Press, Cambridge
de Tempel, Bruges, Belgium
B. G. Teubner, Berlin; Leipzig
Texas College of Arts and Industries, Kingsville
Texas Western Press, Dallas
Texian Press, Waco, Texas
Thacker's Press and Directories, Ltd., Calcutta
Thailand, National Office of Statistics, Bangkok
Thailand National Economic Development Board, Bangkok
Thames and Hudson, Ltd., London
Thammasat University Institute of Public Administration, Bangkok, Thailand
E. J. Theisen, East Orange, N. J.
Charles C. Thomas, Publisher, Springfield, Ill.
Tilden Press, New York
Time, Inc., New York
Time-Life Books, New York
Times Mirror Printing and Binding, New York
Tipografia de Archivos, Madrid
Tipografia Mendonca, Lisbon
Tipografia Nacional, Guatemala, Guatemala City
Tipographia Nacional Guatemala, Guatemala City
H. D. Tjeenk Willink, Haarlem, Netherlands
J. C. Topping, Cambridge, Mass.
Transatlantic Arts, Inc., New York
Trejos Hermanos, San Jose
Trenton State College, Trenton
Tri-Ocean Books, San Francisco
Trident Press, New York
Trowitzsch and Son, Berlin
Truebner and Co., London
Tufts University Press, Medford, Mass.
Tulane University, School of Business Administration, New Orleans, La.
Tulane University Press, New Orleans
Turnstile Press, London
Tuskegee Institute, Tuskegee, Ala.
Charles E. Tuttle Co., Tokyo
Twayne Publishers Inc., New York
The Twentieth Century Fund, New York
Twin Circle Publishing Co., New York
Typographische Anstalt, Vienna
Tyrolia Verlag, Innsbruck

UNESCO, Paris
N. V. Uitgeverij W. Van Hoeve, The Hague
Frederick Ungar Publishing Co., Inc., New York
Union Federaliste Inter-Universitaire, Paris
Union of American Hebrew Congregations, New York
Union of International Associations, Brussels
Union of Japanese Societies of Law and Politics, Tokyo
Union of South Africa, Capetown
Union of South Africa, Government Information Office, New York
Union Press, Hong Kong
Union Research Institute, Hong Kong
United Arab Republic, Information Department, Cairo
United Nations Economic Commission for Asia and the Far East, Secretariat of Bangkok, Bangkok
United Nations Educational, Scientific and Cultural Organization, Paris
United Nations Food and Agriculture Organization, Rome
United Nations International Conference on Peaceful Uses of Atomic Energy, Geneva
United Nations Publishing Service, New York
United States Air Force Academy, Colorado Springs, Colo.
United States Bureau of the Census, Washington, D. C.
United States Business and Defense Services Administration, Washington D.C.
United States Civil Rights Commission, Washington, D. C.
United States Civil Service Commission, Washington, D. C.
United States Consulate General, Hong Kong
United States Department of Agriculture, Washington, D. C.
United States Department of the Army, Washington
United States Department of the Army, Office of Chief of Military History, Washington, D. C.
United States Department of Correction, New York
United States Department of State, Washington
United States Department of State, Government Printing Office, Washington, D. C.
United States Government Printing Office, Washington
United States Housing and Home Financing Agency, Washington, D. C.
United States Mutual Security Agency, Washington, D. C.
United States National Archives General Services, Washington, D. C.
United States National Referral Center for Science and Technology, Washington, D. C.
United States National Resources Committee, Washington, D. C.
United States Naval Academy, Annapolis, Md.
United States Naval Institute, Annapolis, Md.
United States Naval Officers Training School, China Lake, Cal.
United States Operations Mission to Vietnam, Washington, D. C.
United States President's Committee to Study Military Assistance, Washington, D. C.
United States Small Business Administration, Washington, D. C.
United World Federalists, Boston
Universal Reference System; see Princeton Research Publishing Co., Princeton, N.J.
Universidad Central de Venezuela, Caracas
Universidad de Buenos Aires, Instituto Sociologia, Buenos Aires
Universidad de Chile, Santiago
Universidad de el Salvador, El Salvador
Universidad Nacional Autonomo de Mexico, Direccion General de Publicaciones, Mexico
Universidad Nacional de la Plata, Argentina
Universidad Nacional Instituto de Historia Antonoma de Mexico, Mexico City
Universidad Nacional Mayor de San Marcos, Lima
Universidad de Antioquia, Medellin, Colombia
Universite de Rabat, Rabat, Morocco
Universite Fouad I, Cairo
Universite Libre de Bruxelles, Brussels
Universite Mohammed V, Rabat, Morocco
University Books, Inc., Hyde Park, New York
University Bookstore, Hong Kong
University Microfilms, Inc., Ann Arbor
University of Alabama, Bureau of Public Administration, University, Ala.
University of Alabama Press, University, Ala.
University of Ankara, Ankara
University of Arizona Press, Tucson
University of Bombay, Bombay

University of Bonn, Bonn
University of British Columbia Press, Vancouver
University of California, Berkeley, Calif.
University of California at Los Angeles, Bureau of Government Research, Los Angeles
University of California at Los Angeles, Near Eastern Center, Los Angeles
University of California, Bureau of Business and Economic Research, Berkeley, Calif.
University of California, Bureau of Government Research, Los Angeles
University of California, Bureau of Public Administration, Berkeley
University of California, Department of Psychology, Los Angeles
University of California, Institute for International Studies, Berkeley, Calif.
University of California, Institute of East Asiatic Studies, Berkeley, Calif.
University of California, Institute of Governmental Affairs, Davis
University of California, Institute of Governmental Studies, Berkeley
University of California, Institute of Urban and Regional Development, Berkeley, Calif.
University of California, Latin American Center, Los Angeles
University of California Library, Berkeley, Calif.
University of California Press, Berkeley
University of California Survey Research Center, Berkeley, Calif.
University of Canterbury, Christchurch, New Zealand
University of Capetown, Capetown
University of Chicago, Chicago
University of Chicago, Center for Policy Study, Chicago
University of Chicago, Center for Program in Government Administration, Chicago
University of Chicago, Center of Race Relations, Chicago
University of Chicago, Graduate School of Business, Chicago
University of Chicago Law School, Chicago
University of Chicago, Politics Department, Chicago
University of Chicago Press, Chicago
University of Cincinnati, Cincinnati
University of Cincinnati, Center for Study of United States Foreign Policy, Cincinnati
University of Colorado Press, Boulder
University of Connecticut, Institute of Public Service, Storrs, Conn.
University of Dar es Salaam, Institute of Public Administration, Dar es Salaam
University of Denver, Denver
University of Detroit Press, Detroit
University of Edinburgh, Edinburgh, Scotland
University of Florida, Public Administration Clearing Service, Gainesville, Fla.
University of Florida, School of Inter-American Studies, Gainesville, Fla.
University of Florida Libraries, Gainesville
University of Florida Press, Gainesville
University of Georgia, Institute of Community and Area Development, Athens, Georgia
University of Georgia Press, Athens
University of Glasgow Press, Glasgow, Scotland
University of Glasgow Press, Fredericton, New Brunswick, Canada
University of Hawaii Press, Honolulu
University of Hong Kong Press, Hong Kong
University of Houston, Houston
University of Illinois, Champaign
University of Illinois, Graduate School of Library Science, Urbana
University of Illinois, Institute for Labor and Industrial Relations, Urbana
University of Illinois, Institute of Government and Public Affairs, Urbana, Ill.
University of Illinois Press, Urbana
University of Iowa, Center for Labor and Management, Iowa City
University of Iowa, School of Journalism, Iowa City
University of Iowa Press, Iowa City
University of Kansas, Bureau of Government Research, Lawrence, Kans.
University of Kansas Press, Lawrence
University of Karachi, Institute of Business and Public

Administration, Karachi
University of Karachi Press, Karachi
University of Kentucky, Bureau of Governmental Research, Lexington
University of Kentucky Press, Lexington
University of London, Institute of Advanced Legal Studies, London
University of London, Institute of Commonwealth Studies, London
University of London, Institute of Education, London
University of London, School of Oriental and African Studies, London
University of London Press, London
University of Lund, Lund, Sweden
University of Maine Studies, Augusta, Me.
University of Malaya, Kualalumpur
University of Manchester Press, Manchester, England
University of Maryland, Bureau of Governmental Research, College of Business and Public Administration, College Park, Md.
University of Maryland, Department of Agriculture and Extension Education, College Park, Md.
University of Massachusetts, Bureau of Government Research, Amherst, Mass.
University of Massachusetts Press, Amherst
University of Melbourne Press, Melbourne, Australia
University of Miami Law Library, Coral Gables
University of Miami Press, Coral Gables
University of Michigan, Center for Research on Conflict Resolution, Ann Arbor
University of Michigan, Department of History and Political Science, Ann Arbor
University of Michigan, Graduate School of Business Administration, Ann Arbor
University of Michigan, Institute for Social Research, Ann Arbor
University of Michigan, Institute of Public Administration, Ann Arbor
University of Michigan Law School, Ann Arbor
University of Michigan, Survey Research Center, Ann Arbor
University of Michigan Press, Ann Arbor
University of Minnesota, St. Paul; Duluth
University of Minnesota, Industrial Relations Center, Minneapolis
University of Minnesota Press, Minneapolis
University of Mississippi, Bureau of Public Administration, University, Miss.
University of Missouri, Research Center, School of Business and Public Administration, Columbia
University of Missouri Press, Columbia
University of Natal Press, Pietermaritzburg
University of Nebraska Press, Lincoln
University of New England, Grafton, Australia
University of New Mexico, Department of Government, Albuquerque, N. Mex.
University of New Mexico, School of Law, Albuquerque
University of New Mexico Press, Albuquerque
University of North Carolina, Department of City and Regional Planning, Chapel Hill
University of North Carolina, Institute for International Studies, Chapel Hill
University of North Carolina, Institute for Research in the Social Sciences, Center for Urban and Regional Studies, Chapel Hill
University of North Carolina, Institute of Government, Chapel Hill
University of North Carolina Library, Chapel Hill
University of North Carolina Press, Chapel Hill
University of Notre Dame, Notre Dame, Ind.
University of Notre Dame Press, Notre Dame, Ind.
University of Oklahoma Press, Norman
University of Oregon Press, Eugene
University of Panama, Panama City
University of Paris (Conferences du Palais de la Decouverte), Paris
University of Pennsylvania, Philadelphia, Pa.
University of Pennsylvania, Department of Translations, Philadelphia
University of Pennsylvania Law School, Philadelphia, Pa.
University of Pennsylvania Press, Philadelphia
University of Pittsburgh, Institute of Local Government, Pittsburgh, Pa.
University of Pittsburgh Book Centers, Pittsburgh
University of Pittsburgh Press, Pittsburgh

University of Puerto Rico, San Juan
University of Rochester, Rochester, N. Y.
University of Santo Tomas, Manila
University of South Africa, Pretoria
University of South Carolina Press, Columbia
University of Southern California, Middle East and North
Africa Program, Los Angeles
University of Southern California, School of International
Relations, Los Angeles
University of Southern California Press, Los Angeles
University of Southern California, School of Public
Administration, Los Angeles
University of State of New York, State Education
Department, Albany
University of Sussex, Sussex, England
University of Sydney, Department of Government and Public
Administration, Sydney
University of Tennessee, Knoxville
University of Tennessee, Bureau of Public Administration,
Knoxville
University of Tennessee, Municipal Technical Advisory
Service, Division of University Extension, Knoxville
University of Tennessee Press, Knoxville
University of Texas, Austin
University of Texas, Bureau of Business Research, Austin
University of Texas Press, Austin
University of the Philippines, Quezon City
University of the Punjab, Department of Public
Administration, Lahore, Pakistan
University of the Witwatersrand, Johannesburg
University of Toronto, Toronto
University of Toronto Press, Toronto; Buffalo, N. Y.
University of Utah Press, Salt Lake City
University of Vermont, Burlington
University of Virginia, Bureau of Public Administration,
Charlottesville
University of Wales Press, Cardiff
University of Washington, Bureau of Governmental Research
and Services, Seattle
University of Washington Press, Seattle
University of Wisconsin, Madison
University of Wisconsin Press, Madison
University Press, University of the South, Sewanee, Tenn.
University Press of Virginia, Charlottesville
University Publishers, Inc., New York
University Publishing Co., Lincoln, Nebr.
University Society, Inc., Ridgewood, N. J.
Unwin University Books, London
T. Fisher Unwin, Ltd., London
Upjohn Institute for Employment Research, Kalamazoo, Mich;
Los Angeles; Washington, D. C.
Urban America, New York
Urban Studies Center, New Brunswick, N. J.

VEB Verlag fur Buch-und Bibliothekwesen, Leipzig
Franz Vahlen, Berlin
Vallentine, Mitchell and Co., London
Van Nostrand Co., Inc., Princeton
Van Rees Press, New York
Vandenhoeck und Ruprecht, Gottingen
Vanderbilt University Press, Nashville, Tenn.
Vanguard Press, Inc., New York
E. C. Vann, Richmond, Va.
Vantage Press, New York
G. Velgaminov, New York
Verein fur Sozial Politik, Berlin
Vergara Editorial, Barcelona
Verlag Karl Alber, Freiburg
Verlag Georg D. W. Callwey, Munich
Verlag der Wiener Volksbuchhandlung, Vienna
Verlag der Wirtschaft, Berlin
Verlag Deutsche Polizei, Hamburg
Verlag Felix Dietrich, Osnabrueck
Verlag Kurt Dosch, Vienna
Verlag Gustav Fischer, Jena
Verlag Huber Frauenfeld, Stuttgart
Verlag fur Buch- und Bibliothekwesen, Leipzig
Verlag fur Literatur und Zeitgeschehen, Hannover, Germany
Verlag fur Recht und Gesellschaft, Basel
Verein fuer Sozialpolitik, Wirtschaft und Statistik, Berlin
Verlag Anton Hain, Meisenheim
Verlag Hans Krach, Mainz
Verlag Edward Krug, Wurttemburg

Verlag Helmut Kupper, Godesberg
Verlag August Lutzeyer, Baden-Baden
Verlag Mensch und Arbeit, Bruckmann, Munich
Verlag C. F. Muller, Karlsruhe
Verlag Anton Pustet, Munich
Verlag Rombach und Co., Freiburg
Verlag Heinrich Scheffler, Frankfurt
Verlag Hans Schellenberg, Winterthur, Switz.
Verlag P. Schippers, Amsterdam
Verlag Lambert Schneider, Heidelberg
Verlag K. W. Schutz, Gottingen
Verlag Styria, Graz, Austria
Lawrence Verry, Publishers, Mystic, Conn.
Viking Press, New York
Villanova Law School, Philadelphia
J. Villanueva, Buenos Aires
Vintage Books, New York
Virginia Commission on Constitutional Government,
Richmond
Virginia State Library, Richmond
Vishveshvaranand Vedic Research Institute, Hoshiarpur
Vista Books, London
F. & J. Voglrieder, Munich
Voigt und Gleibner, Frankfurt
Voltaire Verlag, Berlin
Von Engelhorn, Stuttgart
Vora and Co. Publishers, Bombay
J. Vrin, Paris

Karl Wachholtz Verlag, Neumunster
Wadsworth Publishing Co., Belmont, Cal.
Walker and Co., New York
Ives Washburn, Inc., New York
Washington State University Press, Pullman
Washington University Libraries, Washington
Franklin Watts, Inc., New York
Waverly Press, Inc., Baltimore, Md.
Wayne State University Press, Detroit, Mich.
Christian Wegner Verlag, Hamburg
Weidenfeld and Nicolson, London
R. Welch, Belmont, Mass.
Wellesley College, Wellesley, Mass.
Herbert Wendler & Co., Berlin
Wenner-Gren Foundation for Anthropological Research,
New York
Wesleyan University Press, Middletown, Conn.
West Publishing Co., St. Paul, Minn.
Westdeutscher Verlag, Cologne
Western Islands Publishing Co., Belmont, Mass.
Western Publishing Co., Inc., Racine, Wis.
Western Reserve University Press, Cleveland
Westminster Press, Philadelphia, Pa.
J. Whitaker and Sons, Ltd., London
Whitcombe and Tombs, Ltd., Christchurch
Whiteside, Inc., New York
Thomas Wilcox, Los Angeles
John Wiley and Sons, Inc., New York
William-Frederick Press, New York
Williams and Vorgate, Ltd., London
Williams and Wilkins Co., Baltimore, Md.
Wilshire Book Co., Hollywood, Calif.
H. W. Wilson Co., New York
Winburn Press, Lexington, Ky.
Allan Wingate, Ltd., London
Carl Winters Universitats-Buchhandlung, Heidelberg
Wisconsin State University Press, River Falls
Wisconsin State Historical Society, Madison
Witwatersrand University Press, Capetown
Woking Muslim Mission and Literary Trust, Surrey
Wolters, Groningen, Netherlands
Woodrow Wilson Foundation, New York
Woodrow Wilson Memorial Library, New York
World Law Fund, New York
World Peace Foundation, Boston
World Press, Ltd., Calcutta
World Publishing Co., Cleveland
World Trade Academy Press, New York
World University Library, New York

Yale University, New Haven, Conn.
Yale University, Department of Industrial Administration,
New Haven, Conn.

Yale University, Harvard Foundation, New Haven, Conn.
Yale University, Institute of Advanced Studies, New Haven, Conn.
Yale University Press, New Haven
Yale University, Southeast Asia Studies, New Haven
Yeshiva University Press, New York
Thomas Yoseloff, New York

T. L. Yuan, Tokyo

Zambia, Government Printer, Lusaka
Otto Zeller, Osnabruck, Germany
Zentral Verlag der NSDAP, Munich
Zwingli Verlag, Zurich

List of Periodicals Cited in this Volume

America
American Bar Association Journal
American Behavioral Scientist
American Journal of Comparative Law
American Journal of Economics and Sociology
American Journal of International Law
American Journal of Psychiatry
American Journal of Sociology
American Political Science Review
American Society of International Law, Proceedings
American Sociological Review
The Americas
Annals of the American Academy of Political and Social Science
Annuaire Francais de Droit International
Anti-Trust Bulletin
Assembly of Captive European Nations News
Background (now International Studies Quarterly)
The Bankers' Magazine
Boston University Law Review
Bulletin of the Atomic Scientists
California Law Review
Cambridge Law Journal
Canadian Bar Review
Canadian Public Administration
Catholic Lawyer
Centro
Civilisations
Co-Existence
Columbia Law Review
Commentary
Comparative Studies in Society and History
Conference of Teachers of International Law, Proceedings
Current History
Department of State Bulletin
Dissent
Ethics
Foreign Affairs
George Washington Law Review
German Foreign Policy
Harvard Law Review
Human Organization
Illinois University Studies in Social Science
Indiana Law Journal
Industrial and Labor Relations Review
Institut zur Erforschung der UdSSR, Bulletin
Instituto de Ciencias Sociales, Revista (Barcelona)
Inter-American Economic Affairs
Intercom
International Affairs
International and Comparative Law Quarterly
International Conciliation
International Journal
International Monetary Fund Staff Papers
International Organization
International Social Science Bulletin
International Studies

Journal of Administration Overseas
Journal of the American Judicature Society
Journal of Arms Control
Journal of Commonwealth Political Studies
Journal of Conflict Resolution
Journal of Criminal Law, Criminology, and Police Science
Journal of Farm Economics
Journal of Inter-American Studies
Journal of International Affairs
Journal of Modern History
Journal of Philosophy
Journal of Politics
Journal of Public Law
Journal of Social Issues
Journal of Social Philosophy
Labor History
Law and Contemporary Problems
Law and Society Review
McGill Law Journal
Michigan Law Review
Midwestern Journal of Political Science
Military Review
Minnesota Law Review
National Civic Review
New Politics
North Dakota Law Review
Notre Dame Lawyer
NYU Law Review
Orbis
Pacific Sociological Review
Parliamentary Affairs
Political Science Quarterly
Politique Etrangere
Psychoanalytic Quarterly
Public Administration
Public Interest
Public Law
Public Opinion Quarterly
Quarterly Review
Race
Revue Critical de Droit International Prive
Revue de Droit International
Revue de Droit Public et de la Science Politique
Revue Generale de Droit International Public
Revue Juridique et Politique d'Outre-mer
Royal Society of Arts, Journal
Russian Review
Rutgers Law Review
Science and Technology
Slavic Review
Social Problems
Social Research
Sociology and Social Research
Southwestern Social Science Quarterly
Stanford Law Review
Transition
Tri-Quarterly Review

University of Chicago Law Review
University of Colorado Studies
University of Illinois Law Forum
University of Pennsylvania Law Review
Vanderbilt Law Review
Virginia Law Review

Western Political Quarterly
Wisconsin Law Review
World Justice
World Politics
Yale Law Journal
Yale Review

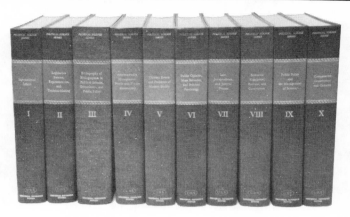
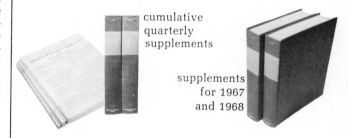